A Concordance to Byron's
DON JUAN

THE CORNELL CONCORDANCES

Supervisory Committee

M. H. Abrams

Ephim G. Fogel

S. M. Parrish, *General Editor*

POEMS OF MATTHEW ARNOLD

Edited by S. M. Parrish

POEMS OF W. B. YEATS

Edited by S. M. Parrish

POEMS OF EMILY DICKINSON

Edited by S. P. Rosenbaum

WRITINGS OF WILLIAM BLAKE

Edited by David V. Erdman

BYRON'S *DON JUAN*

Edited by Charles W. Hagelman, Jr.,
and Robert J. Barnes

A Concordance to Byron's
DON JUAN

Edited by

CHARLES W. HAGELMAN, JR.

and

ROBERT J. BARNES

Cornell University Press

ITHACA, NEW YORK

CORNELL UNIVERSITY PRESS

First published 1967

Ref
PR
4359
. H3

Library of Congress Catalog Card Number: 67–19472

PRINTED IN THE UNITED STATES OF AMERICA
BY VALLEY OFFSET, INC.
BOUND BY VAIL-BALLOU PRESS, INC.

PREFACE

"WHAT wondrous new machines have late been spinning?" Byron asks in Canto I of *Don Juan*. Whether he would have approved of computers manipulating his poetry we cannot say, but this computer-generated concordance to the poem supplies a reference tool long needed by Byron scholars. Based on the monumental variorum edition of *Don Juan* (Austin, Texas, 1956), with the permission of the University of Texas Press and of the editors, Truman Guy Steffan and Willis W. Pratt, the concordance indexes not only the complete poem but, in addition, the sixteen so-called "rejected stanzas" and 634 complete-line variant readings. As the users of the concordance will quickly discover, however, the concordance may be easily used with any edition of *Don Juan,* since each line is identified by canto, stanza, and line number as well as by the volume and page number in the variorum edition.

In the fall of 1965, a four-volume concordance to Byron's poems was privately published. This work, the result of much devoted labor by WPA workers in the nineteen-forties and Miss Ione Young in the fifties and sixties, was based on the widely used one-volume edition of Byron's poems edited by Paul Elmer More and originally published in 1905. Because this edition was based on the 1832–1833 edition (eight to nine years after Byron's death) rather than on manuscripts and editions published while Byron was alive, we rejected it as an adequate basis for a concordance. So far as the *Don Juan* is concerned, the More edition omits stanza 58 of Canto XI and contains a number of errors such as "weakest" for "meekest" (I, 29, 1), "mediation" for "meditation" (XII, 21, 4), "lightly" for "slightly" (XVII, 7, 6). The E. H. Coleridge edition of Byron's poetry, while monumental in many respects and still the Byron scholar's major research tool, is even older than the More text and is based primarily on the 1831 edition (seven years after Byron's death) of Byron's poems rather than on the first editions and the manuscripts. Only the variorum edition presents a complete and accurate text for the

study of Byron's use of language in *Don Juan*. This concordance provides the necessary index for such study.

One question which may occur to even the most casual user of the book is: Why, if this is a concordance to only one poem, was it necessary to list the title with each identification? Hopefully, later scholars will prepare a variorum edition to the rest of Byron's poems, a definitive edition that will contain all variant readings, which are frequently as interesting (and in the comic poems, as amusing) as the lines actually published. At that point, the concordance-maker will find about one-fourth of his job done. Since the *Don Juan* concordance is being preserved on magnetic tape, it can easily be merged with the data for the rest of Byron's poems. To this end, copies of complete input and output tapes have been deposited in computer-tape libraries at Lamar State College of Technology, the University of Toledo, and Texas A & M University. Cornell University and Rice University also have copies of the output tape. These tapes will be available to any scholars who may wish to manipulate the data for special studies.

Basic Text and Format

The technique of preparing the text for the computer was similar to that developed for the first volume in this series, *A Concordance to the Poems of Matthew Arnold* (Ithaca, 1959). Each line of Byron's *Don Juan* and the identification for the line was punched on an IBM card and "verified." The identification included the volume and page number in the variorum edition for the use of scholars who have access to it, and the canto, stanza, and line numbers for those using other editions. The embedded lyrics were designated by the symbol L before the stanza number. The rejected stanzas were designated by the symbol V before the stanza number. All variant lines selected for inclusion (see *Variants*, p. vii) were designated by the symbol V before the line number. A complete text of *Don Juan,* including the rejected stanzas and the selected variants, was printed from the punched cards and carefully proofread. The data on the cards were then transferred to magnetic tape. Before the computer generated the concordance, each line was assigned a sequence number by the computer so that the order of entries under each index word would be the same as the order of the lines in the edited text. As with the other Cornell concordances, the final IBM listings from the computer were reproduced for publication by an offset process so that the possibility of introducing errors during typesetting was eliminated.

Since the computers we used were not equipped with print chains containing a full set of punctuation marks, all punctuation marks have been omitted except for parentheses, dashes, and apostrophes. The first

two were included so that Byron's use of parenthetical statements could be studied; the apostrophe was needed to indicate possessive cases and contractions. Hyphenated entries are alphabetized as if they were written solid. Apostrophes are likewise ignored in alphabetizing with one exception: possessives which might otherwise be combined with other entries are printed after the base-word (*e.g.*, EYE's after EYE but before EYES, and EYES' after EYES).

Because the variorum edition of *Don Juan* does not regularize Byron's spellings, we have made a few changes to bring together or straighten out individual entries in the concordance. For example, Byron uses both SAINT and ST. in *Don Juan;* the concordance lists all these entries under SAINT. (Not to have done so would have separated SAINT from ST. by almost eighty pages.) All uses of GOD, and DAMN, and DAMNED have been spelled out, although Byron sometimes uses only the first and last letters (*e.g.*, I, 14, 8; XII, 65, 4). On the other hand, the three spellings of ANCLE(s), and the one of ANKLE, were preserved, since we could not justify changing the three to conform to the one nor the one to conform to the three. All Greek entries have been transliterated. The symbols in the prescription (X, 41) have been written out. The words HENCE/FORWARD (I, 120, 2–3) and WARB/LE (XII, 75, 5–6), the only examples in *Don Juan* of words broken from one line to the next, have been indexed only under HENCEFORWARD and WARBLE. Not to have done so would have added entries to both HENCE and FORWARD which do not belong there and would have created entries for WARB and LE which do not exist as meaningful words.

Variants

While the variant lines to *Don Juan* are an important feature of the concordance, they also provided the editors with the greatest problem. It was impossible to include all variant readings because of the sheer bulk of the material. (For a meticulous treatment of Byron's many revisions see Professor Steffan's discussion in volume I of the variorum.) Thus, certain principles were established at the outset which would show the Byronic vocabulary and word-play to the greatest advantage but at the same time would neither force the concordance to more than one volume nor do violence to the frequency count. First, we include only relatively complete alternate lines, eliminating fragments like false starts and pick-up revisions of a word or two. Second, we include only those complete lines which reflect a significant change of diction—two or more words. The only exception to the above editorial practices is the occasional inclusion of a variant where only one word was changed, but where the change was so interesting or so re-

vealing of Byron's process of composition that we felt the reader should be directed to that spot in the poem. The total number of variant lines included is 634, which added to the 16,064 published lines and the 127 lines in rejected stanzas makes a grand total of 16,825 lines in the edited input.

Omitted Words

The 173 omitted words on the list which follows are substantially the same as those omitted in previous Cornell concordances. For example, all forms of the first-person-singular personal pronoun were indexed because of the special value these references have to Byron scholars. However, contracted forms were also indexed to point the reader to Byron's wide and varied use of contractions in *Don Juan,* and all *-ing* forms of verbs were indexed so they would be readily available to persons interested in Byron's use of them as a rhyming device and as a means of enhancing the sense of action in *Don Juan.*

It is not yet practical to discriminate all homographs; the user, however, can make his own discriminations by checking the contexts printed in the concordance. DOES, TILL, and WILT were considered for listing. Because the first never appears as a noun, it was added to the list of omitted words. The second is used only as a preposition and conjunction; hence it was omitted along with the other prepositions and conjunctions. Since WILT was used only as a variant of the auxiliary WILL, it was also added to the list of omitted words. After careful study, four homographs, however, were selectively indexed.

PARTIALLY OMITTED WORDS

ART	(noun)	35	(7 occurrences of verb omitted)
MAY	(noun)	4	(307 occurrences of verb omitted)
MIGHT	(noun)	3	(184 occurrences of verb omitted)
WILL	(noun)	10	(234 occurrences of verb omitted)

OMITTED WORDS

A	ALSO	ANOTHER'S	BEHIND	CAN
ABOUT	ALTHOUGH	ARE	BELOW	CANNOT
ABOVE	AM	AT	BETWEEN	CANST
AFTER	AMONG		BETWIXT	COULD
AGAIN	AMONGST	BE	BEYOND	COULDST
AGAINST	AN	BECAUSE	BOTH	
AH	AND	BEEN	BUT	DID
ALL	ANOTHER	BEFORE	BY	DO

viii

DOES	HOWE'ER	O'ER	THEIR	WERE
DOST	HOWEVER	OF	THEIRS	WERT
DOTH		OFF	THEM	WHAT
DOWN	I'	OH	THEMSELVES	WHATE'ER
	IF	ON	THEN	WHATEVER
EACH	IN	ONLY	THERE	WHEN
E'ER	INDEED	OR	THEREFORE	WHENE'ER
EITHER	INTO	OTHER	THESE	WHENEVER
ERE	IS	OTHER'S	THEY	WHERE
EVER	IT	OTHERS	THINE	WHERE'ER
EVERY	ITS	OUT	THIS	WHETHER
	ITSELF	OVER	THOSE	WHICH
FOR			THOU	WHO
FROM	LESS	'S	THOUGH	WHOM
	LET	SAID	THRO	WHOSE
HAD	LETS	SAY	THROUGH	WHY
HADST		SAYS	THUS	WILT
HAS	MORE	SHALL	THY	WITH
HAST	MOST	SHALT	TILL	WITHIN
HATH	MUST	SHE	TO	WITHOUT
HAVE		SHOULD	TOO	WOULD
HE	NEITHER	SO	TOWARD	
HER	NEVER	SOME	TOWARDS	YE
HERE	NO	SUCH		YES
HERS	NOR		UP	YET
HERSELF	NOT	'T	UPON	YOU
HIM	NOW	T'		YOUR
HIMSELF		THAT	VERY	YOURS
HIS	O	THE		YOURSELF
HOW	O'	THEE	WAS	

Frequency Lists

The appendix contains two word-count tables, one which lists frequencies of occurrence of the 177 words omitted from the body of the concordance (see above), and a second which lists frequencies of occurrence of all 14,266 indexed entries. Since four words appear on both lists, the *Don Juan* vocabulary consists of 14,439 entries.

Those who use the frequency lists should be cautioned about their limitations. Both the number of words in the lists and the frequency count for individual words are padded because of the decision to include the rejected stanzas and selected variant readings. By checking the indexed entries, the user can readily count the number of times the word was used in rejected or variant lines and subtract that number from the total given in the frequency list.

The compilation of word-count tables is swiftly and efficiently carried out by the computer, but heretofore the lists had to be prepared for final publication by hand, because of the difficulties of columnar printing on the high-speed printers. A novel feature of our project is the achievement of completely machine-produced printed frequency lists.

Byron has often been called both the most "personal" and the most "colloquial" of the Romantic poets, and the frequency lists bear out these generalizations. There are 1,172 entries for I, and if the other forms of the first-person-singular personal pronoun and appropriate contractions are added (e.g., MY, ME, I'M), the number swells to almost 2,000. Contractions (a good indication of colloquialism) total over 1,000 without including those whose usage is recorded fewer than ten times. Other words in the higher range of frequencies show few surprises: Byron was fond of LOVE (219), TIME (160), EYES (151), and HEART (131). On the other hand, many words one might expect a Romantic poet to scatter in profusion (e.g., ENCHANTED, MAJESTIC, PAGAN, VILLAIN) occur only once in *Don Juan*.

Acknowledgments

The use of a computer on a project of this magnitude necessarily involves the help and cooperation of many others to provide the money, the computer time, and the technical skills required to make the editors' idea a reality. In no sense is this solely our handiwork; it is rather the result of much good will, infinite faith and patience, and long hours of hard work late at night, by a varied group of collaborators, some of whom will first become acquainted with the others in this section of the Preface. We may well have overlooked someone; we hope not.

We first acknowledge our gratitude to Lamar State College of Technology and to its President, Dr. F. L. McDonald, for support and encouragement during the time we have been at work on the project. We further acknowledge the financial support of the Lamar Research Council, without which this project could never have been started, much less completed. The Council has kept faith in the project and in us through the years; there is no adequate way to express our appreciation to it.

We record our gratitude to the representatives of corporate life who have donated so generously to this project, fully realizing that the results would in no way profit them nor provide information related to their businesses. We owe a considerable debt of gratitude to Gulf Oil Corporation, especially to the Port Arthur Refinery and to its General Manager, Mr. J. O. Timms. The IBM 7070 and its auxiliary equipment in the computer center of Gulf's Port Arthur Refinery was placed at our

disposal during the third shift (10:00 P.M. to 6:00 A.M.). We are grateful to Mr. J. B. Alexander and to the staff in the machine room for their guidance and assistance. We are further indebted to the Beaumont Office of Gulf States Utilities and to Mr. Bennie Lott for the hours we logged on the IBM 1410 in the computer center there, where all the final computer work was performed. Space does not permit us to record the names of all those who have contributed time, energy, and technical skills. We must begin by thanking Mr. Vernon Pike, who supervises IBM operations at Lamar State College and who saw to it that each line of the *Don Juan* (including specified variants) was accurately punched on an individual IBM card. For his painstaking labors and continued interest and cooperation we are duly grateful. The International Business Machines Corporation has been interested in our project from the beginning and has been most helpful in providing technical information and encouragement. We are especially indebted to Mr. Conley Todd of the Beaumont office.

The final print-out of the concordance was run at the Data Processing Center on the campus of Texas A & M University. We wish to thank its director, Dr. Robert L. Smith, and also the Director of the Center for Computer Research in the Humanities, Dr. Milton Huggett, for their many personal kindnesses to us, as well as for their help in preparing the manuscript for the publisher.

Our special thanks go to the two brilliant programmers whose devoted labors are responsible, in the long run, for the concordance. Mr. John K. Woodward, of Pittsford, New York, was responsible for the first version of the concordance—the first time, we believe, that a concordance was produced on an IBM 7070. Mr. Phil C. Nettleton, of Beaumont, Texas, was responsible for the concordance as published. We are very grateful for their hard work, their enthusiasm, and their patience with us as we learned to talk to those who talk to the machine.

We also wish to thank Professor Willis W. Pratt for his counsel and interest during the years; he has continued to help us with the poem just as he did when we sat together in his graduate seminar on *Don Juan*. We are appreciative of the interest that Professor Stephen Parrish, General Editor of the Cornell Concordances, has shown in our work; his help in the publication of the *Don Juan* concordance as one of this series has been invaluable. To Mrs. Audrey Wynn, secretary, Department of English, Lamar State College of Technology, we are especially grateful. Her unselfish and devoted service has helped to make it possible for us to complete this project. Thanks to her, we were spared many routine chores so that our time could be spent on the concordance.

Our wives, Elizabeth Hagelman and Evelyn Barnes, helped us in

xi

much of the drudgery that any large project necessarily entails. More important, they have suffered many long months as their ignorant husbands struggled to learn and finally to prevail.

CHARLES W. HAGELMAN, JR.

ROBERT J. BARNES

Toledo, Ohio, and Beaumont, Texas
November 1966

CONTENTS

Preface v

Concordance to Byron's *Don Juan* 1

Appendixes

Indexed Words in Frequency Order 939

Omitted Words in Frequency Order 981

A Concordance to Byron's
DON JUAN

```
                                                    PAGE VOL    CANTO  STANZA LN
A
   LORD H AMUNDEVILLE AND LADY A  . . . . . . . . .   382  3 DON JUAN 13    51   8
   PRESENT LORDS A B C--EARLS DUKES BY NAME . . . . .  383  3 DON JUAN 13    54   2
ABACK
   OR IF I'M WRONG I'LL NOT BE TA'EN ABACK--  . . . .  348  3 DON JUAN 12    71   6
ABASH'D
   AND THEN ABASH'D AT ITS OWN JOY WITHDREW . . . . .   81  2 DON JUAN  1   112   4
ABASHED
   AND ALL ABASHED TOO AT THE GENERAL STARE . . . . .   28  3 DON JUAN  6    45   6
ABATE
   AS DAY ADVANCED THE WEATHER SEEM'D TO ABATE . . .   172  2 DON JUAN  2    30   1
   WHOSE FORCE DESCRIPTION ONLY WOULD ABATE . . . . .  467  2 DON JUAN  5    97   3
   NOR BATE (ABATE) THEIR HEARERS OF AN INCH  . . . .  404  3 DON JUAN 13    98   4
   THAT AWFUL YAWN WHICH SLEEP CAN NOT ABATE  . . . .  405  3 DON JUAN 13   101   8
ABATED
   THEIR SPEED ABATED OR THEIR STRENGTH GREW DULL . .   59  3 DON JUAN  6   107   6
ABBEY
   UPON YOUR TOMB IN WESTMINSTER'S OLD ABBEY  . . . .  184  3 DON JUAN  9     2   4
   TO NORMAN ABBEY WHIRLED THE NOBLE PAIR-- . . . . .  384  3 DON JUAN 13    55   1
   THE NOBLE GUESTS ASSEMBLED AT THE ABBEY  . . . . .  396  3 DON JUAN 13    79   1
   WHO AFTER RUMMAGING THE ABBEY THROUGH THICK . . .   529  3 DON JUAN 16    58   5
ABBEY'S
   BUT THEN THE ABBEY'S WORTH THE WHOLE COLLECTION . .  280  3 DON JUAN 11    25   8
ABERNETHY
   WE TEASE MILD BAILLIE OR SOFT ABERNETHY  . . . . .  245  3 DON JUAN 10    42   8
ABERRATIONS
   SUCH ABERRATIONS THAN WE MEN OF RIGOUR  . . . . .   460  3 DON JUAN 15    11   4
ABETTORS
   AND THEN SHE HAD ALL SEVILLE FOR ABETTORS  . . . .   36  2 DON JUAN  1    28   4
ABEYANCE
   WHILE THINGS WERE IN ABEYANCE RIBAS SENT . . . . .   85  3 DON JUAN  7    38   1
   WHILE THIS HIGH POST OF HONOUR'S IN ABEYANCE . . .  248  3 DON JUAN 10    49   1
ABHOR
   ABHOR CONDEMN ABJURE THE MORTAL MADE . . . . . . .  268  2 DON JUAN  2   209   2
   SULTANS TOO MUCH ABHOR THIS SORT OF SIN  . . . . .   10  3 DON JUAN  6     7   5
   BY HABIT TO WHAT THEIR OWN HEARTS ABHOR--  . . . .  143  3 DON JUAN  8    62   6
ABHORR'D
   WAS NEITHER MUCH BELOVED NOR YET ABHORR'D  . . . .   57  2 DON JUAN  1    65   3
   TO PROVE HIMSELF THE THING HE MOST ABHORR'D  . . .   97  2 DON JUAN  1   139   8
ABHORRED
   AND OF A WIFE BY WHOM HE WAS ABHORRED . . . . . .    51  3 DON JUAN  6    90   4
   THEIR COUNTRY AND AS TRAITORS ARE ABHORRED . . . .   77  3 DON JUAN  7    22   6
   ADMIRING THOSE (BY DAINTY DAMES ABHORRED)  . . . .  209  3 DON JUAN  9    54   3
   HOW HER GREAT NAME IS NOW THROUGHOUT ABHORRED . .   258  3 DON JUAN 10    67   2
ABHORRENCE
   WITH GOD AND MAN'S ABHORRENCE FOR ITS GAINS . . . .  18  2 DON JUAN  D    14   8
ABIDE
   OR FOR THE SAKE OF DECENCY ABIDE  . . . . . . . .   106  2 DON JUAN  1   156   6
ABIDETH
   HE ABIDETH NIGHT AND DAY . . . . . . . . . . . . .  519  3 DON JUAN 16  L 3   4
ABILITY
   I DON'T KNOW THAT THERE MAY BE MUCH ABILITY . . . .  465  3 DON JUAN 15    20   1
ABJURE
   ABHOR CONDEMN ABJURE THE MORTAL MADE  . . . . . .   268  2 DON JUAN  2   209   2
ABLE
   AND HE WHO UNDERSTANDS IT WOULD BE ABLE . . . . . .   11  2 DON JUAN  D     4   7
   THAT EVEN THE ABLE SEAMAN DEEMING HIS  . . . . . .  173  2 DON JUAN  2    33   5
   AND SHOW THAT LATE HOURS WINE AND LOVE ARE ABLE . .  309  2 DON JUAN  3    66   7
   WHILE THE RIGHT HAND WHICH WROTE IT STILL IS ABLE .  398  2 DON JUAN  4    99   5
   AND RUNNING OUT AS FAST AS I WAS ABLE . . . . . .   428  2 DON JUAN  5    33   6
   STRETCHED IN THE STREET AND ABLE SCARCE TO PANT . .  428  2 DON JUAN  5    33   8
   MIGHT TEACH THEM THIS MUCH BETTER THAN I'M ABLE . .  444  2 DON JUAN  5    59   8
   THOSE NAVIGATORS MUST BE ABLE SEAMEN  . . . . . .     7  3 DON JUAN  6     2   3
   YOUNG PEOPLE AT HIS TIME OF LIFE SHOULD BE ABLE . .  235  3 DON JUAN 10    22   3
   HE NOW WAS GROWING UP LIKE A GREEN TREE ABLE  . . .  235  3 DON JUAN 10    22   5
   AN EXQUISITE SMALL CHAPEL HAD BEEN ABLE  . . . . .  389  3 DON JUAN 13    66   5
   FOR WEAPONS BUT WHAT MUSE SINCE HOMER'S ABLE . . .  482  3 DON JUAN 15    62   3
ABLUTIONS
   AND NOW HE ROSE AND AFTER DUE ABLUTIONS  . . . . .   52  3 DON JUAN  6    92   1
ABODE
   BESIDE HIS MISTRESS IN SOME SOFT ABODE  . . . . .    24  2 DON JUAN  1     6   6
   A TASTE SEEN IN THE CHOICE OF HIS ABODE  . . . . .  304  2 DON JUAN  3    56   4
   OF LIVING IN THEIR INSULAR ABODE  . . . . . . . .   317  2 DON JUAN  3    81   8
   WE MUST BE NEAR SOME PLACE OF MAN'S ABODE--  . . .  436  2 DON JUAN  5    45   1
ABODES
   HIS VERY CELLARS MIGHT BE KINGS' ABODES  . . . . .  320  3 DON JUAN 12     9   6
ABOLISHED
   TO HOLD SOME SINECURES HE WISHED ABOLISHED . . . .  535  3 DON JUAN 16    72   7
ABOLITION
   WHAT 'TWAS ERE ABOLITION AND THE THING  . . . . .   408  2 DON JUAN  4   115   4
ABOMINABLE
   AS THAT ABOMINABLE TITTLE TATTLE  . . . . . . . .   336  3 DON JUAN 12    43   7
ABORTIONS
   BEYOND THE DWARFING CITY'S PALE ABORTIONS  . . . .  145  3 DON JUAN  8    66   2
ABOUND
   OF THOSE PEDESTRIAN PAPHIANS WHO ABOUND  . . . . .  282  3 DON JUAN 11    30   4
   AND BEAUTEOUS EVEN WHERE BEAUTIES MOST ABOUND . . .  359  3 DON JUAN 13     2   6
   OF FOLLY'S FRUIT FOR THOUGH YOUR FOOLS ABOUND . . .  402  3 DON JUAN 13    95   5
ABOUNDED
   OF HIS WHOLE ARMY WHICH SO MUCH ABOUNDED . . . . .  125  3 DON JUAN  8    28   6
   'TIS ODD BUT TRUE--LAST WAR THE NEWS ABOUNDED . . .  383  3 DON JUAN 13    53   7
```

	PAGE	VOL	CANTO	STANZA	LN

ABOUNDS
A LADY WITH APOLOGIES ABOUNDS . . . . 118 2 DON JUAN 1 176 5
ABREAST
AS WERE SOME HUNDRED YOUNGSTERS ALL ABREAST . . . . . 140 3 DON JUAN 8 56 3
ABROAD
A SINGLE CRY WOULD BRING THEM ALL ABROAD . . . . . . 436 2 DON JUAN 5 45 5
THEY LIVED TILL SOME BASHAW WAS SENT ABROAD . . . . . 498 2 DON JUAN 5 152 4
LIKE AN IMPERIAL PEACOCK STALK ABROAD . . . . . . 104 3 DON JUAN 7 74 5
OUTWARD DISLIKE WHICH DON'T LOOK WELL ABROAD . . . . 240 3 DON JUAN 10 32 5
ABROAD SUCH THINGS DECIDE FEW WOMEN'S FATE-- . . . . 345 3 DON JUAN 12 64 5
ABROAD THOUGH DOUBTLESS THEY DO MUCH AMISS . . . . . 352 3 DON JUAN 12 79 5
SUNG OR REHEARSED THE LAST DANCE FROM ABROAD . . . . 406 3 DON JUAN 13 104 4
THAT FAITHFUL WERE THROUGH THICK AND THIN ABROAD . . . 452 3 DON JUAN 14 96 3
ABSENCE
UNTIL THE HOURS OF ABSENCE SHOULD RUN THROUGH . . . . 98 2 DON JUAN 1 141 6
HAS IN HIS ABSENCE WEDDED SOME RICH MISER . . . . . 288 2 DON JUAN 3 24 2
PERCEIVING IN HIS ABSENCE SUCH EXPENSES . . . . . 293 2 DON JUAN 3 35 6
MORE EASY BY THE ABSENCE OF ALL MEN . . . . . . 22 3 DON JUAN 6 32 2
OF ABSENCE LAY ONE'S OLD RESENTMENTS LEVEL . . . . 257 3 DON JUAN 10 66 7
THE ABSENCE OF THAT MORE SUBLIME CONSTRUCTION . . . . 262 3 DON JUAN 10 76 6
WHO FOUGHT AND FIGHT IN ABSENCE TOO MY BATTLES . . . . 452 3 DON JUAN 14 96 7
LIKE VIRTUE AND THE ABSENCE OF PRETENSION . . . . . 462 3 DON JUAN 15 14 7
OR MODESTY OR ABSENCE OR INANITY . . . . 490 3 DON JUAN 15 78 6
ABSENCES
WIVES IN THEIR HUSBANDS' ABSENCES GROW SUBTLER . . . . 287 2 DON JUAN 3 22 7
ABSENT
I'VE KNOWN THE ABSENT WRONG'D FOUR TIMES A DAY . . . . 288 2 DON JUAN 3 25 8
SHE HAD NO PULSE BUT DEATH SEEM'D ABSENT STILL . . . . 377 2 DON JUAN 4 60 3
FOR SOME HAD ABSENT LOVERS ALL HAD FRIENDS . . . . . 407 3 DON JUAN 13 105 1
TRUE HE WAS ABSENT AND 'TWAS RUMOUR'D TOOK . . . . . 430 3 DON JUAN 14 45 3
HOW SWEET THE TASK TO SHIELD AN ABSENT FRIEND . . . . 552 3 DON JUAN 16 104 7
BUT SELDOM PAY THE ABSENT NOR WOULD LOOK . . . . . 553 3 DON JUAN 16 106 4
ABSENTEES
THERE ALSO WERE SOME IRISH ABSENTEES . . . . . . 397 3 DON JUAN 13 83 8
ABSOLUTE
FOR ME I DEEM AN ABSOLUTE AUTOCRAT . . . . 194 3 DON JUAN 9 23 7
ABSOLUTION
THAT BEGG'D PEDRILLO FOR AN ABSOLUTION . . . . . . 179 2 DON JUAN 2 44 7
ABSORB
UPON SUCH THINGS WOULD VERY NEAR ABSORB . . . . . 160 2 DON JUAN 2 6 5
ABSTAIN'D
ALL EXCEPT JUAN WHO THROUGHOUT ABSTAIN'D . . . . . 200 2 DON JUAN 2 82 5
ABSTRACT
NOR EVER HAD FOR ABSTRACT FAME MUCH PASSION . . . . 189 3 DON JUAN 9 14 4
FIRED WITH AN ABSTRACT LOVE OF VIRTUE SHE . . . . . 430 3 DON JUAN 14 46 2
ABSTRACTION
FEEL SOME ABSTRACTION WHEN THEY GAZE ON HER . . . . 506 3 DON JUAN 16 14 3
WHO WONDERED AT THE ABSTRACTION OF HIS AIR . . . . . 544 3 DON JUAN 16 91 3
ABSTRUSE
THE SCIENCES AND MOST OF ALL THE ABSTRUSE . . . . . 44 2 DON JUAN 1 40 2
I THINK THAT DANTE'S MORE ABSTRUSE ECSTATICS . . . . 281 2 DON JUAN 3 11 7
FOR FEELINGS CAUSELESS OR AT LEAST ABSTRUSE . . . . 355 2 DON JUAN 4 22 8
ABSURD
SWEET PLAYFUL PHRASES WHICH WOULD SEEM ABSURD . . . . 351 2 DON JUAN 4 14 7
TO BRING THE OTHER THREE HERE WAS ABSURD . . . . . 97 3 DON JUAN 7 60 6
OR GOD BE WITH YOU--AND 'TIS NOT ABSURD . . . . . 274 3 DON JUAN 11 12 5
THEY WONDERED HOW A YOUNG MAN SO ABSURD . . . . . 543 3 DON JUAN 16 89 5
ABSURDITY
TO MEND THE PEOPLE'S AN ABSURDITY . . . . 266 3 DON JUAN 10 85 5
ABUNDANCE
FROM WHENCE SPRINGS UP ABUNDANCE OF ABUSES . . . . . 327 2 DON JUAN 3 88 V4
ABUSE
AS HELL--MERE MORTALS WHO THEIR POWER ABUSE-- . . . . 173 3 DON JUAN 8 123 7
THINK NOT FAIR CREATURES THAT I MEAN TO ABUSE YOU ALL-- . 329 3 DON JUAN 12 28 3
WHEN WE NO MORE CAN USE OR EVEN ABUSE THEE . . . . . 405 3 DON JUAN 13 100 8
OF COXCOMBRY OR CONQUEST NO ABUSE . . . . 461 3 DON JUAN 15 12 4
ABUSED
AND TURNING UP HER NOSE WITH LOOKS ABUSED . . . . . 109 2 DON JUAN 1 159 3
THE MERCY HE HAD GRANTED OFT ABUSED . . . . . . 303 2 DON JUAN 3 54 4
HE PRAISED THE PRESENT AND ABUSED THE PAST . . . . . 316 2 DON JUAN 3 79 1
EXCEPT NAPOLEON OR ABUSED IT MORE . . . . 187 3 DON JUAN 9 9 2
ABUSES
FROM WHENCE SPRINGS UP ABUNDANCE OF ABUSES . . . . . 327 2 DON JUAN 3 88 V4
OR ALL THE FIGURES CASTLEREAGH ABUSES . . . . . . 493 2 DON JUAN 5 143 5
ABYSS
CONTEMPT BUT FROM THE BATHOS' VAST ABYSS . . . . . 334 2 DON JUAN 3 100 4
AND SWIMMING LONG IN THE ABYSS OF THOUGHT . . . . . 191 3 DON JUAN 9 18 5
CLINGS TO ITS TEAT STICKS TO ME THROUGH THE ABYSS . . . 238 3 DON JUAN 10 28 4
SOME WALTZ SOME DRAW SOME FATHOM THE ABYSS . . . . . 340 3 DON JUAN 12 52 5
IF FROM GREAT NATURE'S OR OUR OWN ABYSS . . . . . 410 3 DON JUAN 14 1 1
ACADEMIC
TO QUIT HIS ACADEMIC OCCUPATION . . . . 175 2 DON JUAN 2 37 6
ACADEMICIANS
AS ALSO OF THE FIRST ACADEMICIANS . . . . 191 3 DON JUAN 9 17 2
ACCENT
WITH AN IONIAN ACCENT LOW AND SWEET . . . . . . 236 2 DON JUAN 2 150 7
SAID LOLAH WITH AN ACCENT RATHER ROUGH . . . . . 28 3 DON JUAN 6 44 6
IS MUSICAL--A DYING ACCENT DRIVEN . . . . 388 3 DON JUAN 13 63 4
ACCENTS
MUST BID YOU BOTH FAREWELL IN ACCENTS BLAND . . . . . 147 2 DON JUAN 1 221 V3

2

ACCENTS   (CONTINUED)
```
    WHOSE ACCENTS ARE THE STEPS OF MUSIC'S THRONE  . . . . .  237   2 DON JUAN  2    151  V8
    SUWARROW THOUGH ENGAGED WITH ACCENTS HIGH  . . . . .      100   3 DON JUAN  7     65   3
ACCEPT
    HOW TO ACCEPT A BETTER IN HIS TURN . . . . . . . . .      224   2 DON JUAN  2    128   8
    BE SUCH AS I CAN PROPERLY ACCEPT . . . . . . . . .       453   2 DON JUAN  5     72   6
    FOR SOMETIMES THEY ACCEPT SOME LONG PURSUER . . . . .     333   3 DON JUAN 12     37   1
    OF FRIENDSHIP WHICH YOU MAY ACCEPT OR PASS . . . . .      342   3 DON JUAN 12     57   3
    THE CIVIL LIST (HE DEIGNS TO ACCEPT OBLIGING ALL  . . .   528   3 DON JUAN 16     56   6
ACCEPTATION
    HIS SUBJECTS BY HIS GRACIOUS ACCEPTATION) . . . . . .     528   3 DON JUAN 16     56   7
ACCESSARIES
    THOSE TRUFFLES TOO ARE NO BAD ACCESSARIES  . . . . .      486   3 DON JUAN 15     68   1
ACCESSARY
    AN ACCESSARY AS I HAVE CAUSE TO GUESS . . . . . . .       443   3 DON JUAN 14     76   4
ACCIDENT
    SAW ONE WHOM SUCH AN ACCIDENT BEFELL  . . . . . .         430   2 DON JUAN  5     35   3
    WAS FAVOURED BY AN ACCIDENT OR BLUNDER  . . . . . .       136   3 DON JUAN  8     46   2
ACCLAMATION
    THESE ALSO WERE TWO WITS BY ACCLAMATION . . . . . .       401   3 DON JUAN 13     92   1
ACCOMPANIED
    ACCOMPANIED WITH A CONVULSIVE SPLASH . . . . . . .        184   2 DON JUAN  2     53   6
    AND AFTERWARDS ACCOMPANIED US THROUGH . . . . . . .       103   3 DON JUAN  7     72   3
    DULY ACCOMPANIED BY SHRIEKS AND GROANS  . . . . . .       179   3 DON JUAN  8    135   2
ACCOMPANY
    WILL PLEASE TO ACCOMPANY THOSE GENTLEMEN . . . . . .      458   2 DON JUAN  5     81   2
ACCOMPLISH
    AIR CAN ACCOMPLISH WITH HIS WIDE WINGS WAVING . . . .     263   3 DON JUAN 10     78   4
ACCOMPLISH'D
    WE HAVE NO ACCOMPLISH'D BLACKGUARDS LIKE TOM JONES  . .   409   3 DON JUAN 13    110   7
    SERENE ACCOMPLISH'D CHEERFUL BUT NOT LOUD  . . . . .      462   3 DON JUAN 15     15   1
ACCOMPLISHED
    YOUNG HANDSOME AND ACCOMPLISHED WHO WAS SAID  . . . .     283   3 DON JUAN 11     32   7
    TO SAVE HIS FAME WITH EACH ACCOMPLISHED BELLE  . . . .    295   3 DON JUAN 11     53   3
ACCOMPLISHMENT
    A FLOATING BALANCE OF ACCOMPLISHMENT  . . . . . . .       340   3 DON JUAN 12     52   2
    A CERTAIN QUANTUM OF ACCOMPLISHMENT  . . . . . . .        340   3 DON JUAN 12     52  V2
    AS IF SHE RATED SUCH ACCOMPLISHMENT  . . . . . . .        521   3 DON JUAN 16     42   2
ACCOMPLISHMENTS
    THEN FOR ACCOMPLISHMENTS OF CHIVALRY . . . . . . .         42   2 DON JUAN  1     38   5
    HAD LEFT ALL THE ACCOMPLISHMENTS SHE TAUGHT HER  . . .    339   3 DON JUAN 12     51   5
    WHOSE SOLE ACCOMPLISHMENTS WERE QUITE A BOOTY . . . .     471   3 DON JUAN 15     34   6
ACCOMPTS
    AT SIXTY YEARS AND DRAW THE ACCOMPTS OF EVIL  . . . .     113   2 DON JUAN  1    167   7
ACCORD
    SUFFERING EACH OTHER'S FOIBLES BY ACCORD . . . . . .       57   2 DON JUAN  1     65   5
    IT FELL DOWN OF ITS OWN ACCORD BEFORE . . . . . . .        44   3 DON JUAN  6     77   2
    POOR FREDERICK WHY DID SHE ACCORD PERUSALS . . . . .      332   3 DON JUAN 12     34   6
    WITH WHICH THE WINDS OF HEAVEN CAN CLAIM ACCORD . . .     402   3 DON JUAN 13     93   3
ACCORDED
    ACCORDED WITH HER MOORISH ORIGIN  . . . . . . . .          52   2 DON JUAN  1     56   2
ACCORDING
    ACCORDING TO ALL HINTS I COULD COLLECT  . . . . . .        38   2 DON JUAN  1     33   2
    ACCORDING TO SOME GOOD OLD WOMAN'S TALE . . . . . .        72   2 DON JUAN  1     95   8
    ACCORDING TO DIRECTION THEN RECEIVED . . . . . . .       161   2 DON JUAN  2      9   2
    ACCORDING TO THEIR SIZE AND AGE AND LENGTH . . . . .      283   2 DON JUAN  3     15  V7
    OR CA IRA ACCORDING TO THE FASHION ALL  . . . . . .      319   2 DON JUAN  3     85   4
    ONE OF THE TWO ACCORDING TO YOUR CHOICE  . . . . . .      357   2 DON JUAN  4     25   1
    FROM CROWNS TO KICKS ACCORDING TO THEIR VICES  . . . .    425   2 DON JUAN  5     27   8
    WITH ARGUMENTS ACCORDING TO THEIR FORTE . . . . . .       437   2 DON JUAN  5     48   7
    TO LODGE THERE WHEN A WAR BROKE OUT ACCORDING . . . .     498   2 DON JUAN  5    151   2
    ACCORDING TO THE ANCIENT EPIC LAWS . . . . . . .         503   2 DON JUAN  5    159   3
    SO STYLED ACCORDING TO THE USUAL FORMS  . . . . . .        12   3 DON JUAN  6     13   2
    WERE THEY ACCORDING TO THE BEST REPORT  . . . . . .        26   3 DON JUAN  6     40   5
    ACCORDING TO THE ARTILLERY'S HITS OR MISSES . . . . .     105   3 DON JUAN  7     76   3
    ACCORDING AS YOU TAKE THINGS WELL OR ILL--  . . . . .     264   3 DON JUAN 10     80   7
    IF IT BE CHANCE OR IF IT BE ACCORDING . . . . . . .      270   3 DON JUAN 11      4   1
    ACCORDING AS THEIR MINDS OR BACKS ARE BENT  . . . . .     340   3 DON JUAN 12     52   4
    ACCORDING AS THE SKIES THEIR SHADOWS THREW  . . . . .     385   3 DON JUAN 13     58   8
    IS POESY ACCORDING AS THE MIND GLOWS  . . . . . . .       414   3 DON JUAN 14      8   4
    ACCORDING TO THE BEST OF DICTIONARIES . . . . . . .       486   3 DON JUAN 15     68   5
    THE GUESTS WERE PLACED ACCORDING TO THEIR ROLL . . . .    488   3 DON JUAN 15     74   3
ACCORDS
    WAS SUCH AS FIRE ACCORDS TO A WET BLANKET  . . . . .      294   2 DON JUAN  3     36   8
ACCOUNT
    HAD OFTEN TURN'D THE ART TO SOME ACCOUNT . . . . . .      211   2 DON JUAN  2    105   4
    SHE NOW KEPT HOUSE UPON HER OWN ACCOUNT . . . . . .       295   2 DON JUAN  3     38   8
    THAT ADDING TO THE ACCOUNT HIS HIGHNESS' YEARS . . . .     10   3 DON JUAN  6      9   4
    ACCOUNT FOR EVERYTHING WHICH MAY LOOK BAD  . . . . .      127   3 DON JUAN  8     31   4
ACCOUNTS
    THE LAST IF LATE ACCOUNTS BE ACCURATE . . . . . . .      406   2 DON JUAN  4    112   2
    YOU'RE RIGHT ON BOTH ACCOUNTS TO HOLD YOUR TONGUE . . .   419   2 DON JUAN  5     16   7
ACCREDITED
    WHO MUST BE COURTEOUS TO THE ACCREDITED . . . . . .      287   3 DON JUAN 11     40   2
ACCURATE
    THE LAST IF LATE ACCOUNTS BE ACCURATE . . . . . . .      406   2 DON JUAN  4    112   2
    ALL VERY ACCURATE YOU MUST ALLOW  . . . . . . . .        181   3 DON JUAN  8    138   4
ACCURATELY
    UNTIL THE SUM WAS ACCURATELY SCANNED . . . . . . .       426   2 DON JUAN  5     29   6
```

		PAGE	VOL	CANTO	STANZA	LN
ACCURSED						
THROBB'D IN ACCURSED DREAMS WHICH SOMETIMES SPREAD	. . .	227	2 DON JUAN	2	134	6
ACCUSALS						
(FRIENDS OF THE PARTY) WHO BEGIN ACCUSALS	. . . . .	332	3 DON JUAN	12	34	4
ACCUSE						
JUST AS A FRIAR MAY ACCUSE HIS VOW . .	. . . . .	493	2 DON JUAN	5	142	6
THEY ACCUSE ME--ME--THE PRESENT WRITER OF	. . . .	67	3 DON JUAN	7	3	1
SINCE I'VE GROWN MORAL STILL I MUST ACCUSE YOU ALL	. .	329	3 DON JUAN	12	28	5
LET NONE ACCUSE OLD ENGLAND'S HOSPITALITY-- .	. .	381	3 DON JUAN	13	49	7
THE LAST IS APT THE FORMER TO ACCUSE . .	. . . .	564	3 DON JUAN	17	6	4
ACCUSED						
SOME HAVE ACCUSED ME OF A STRANGE DESIGN	. . . .	346	2 DON JUAN	4	5	1
HAS BEEN ACCUSED (I DOUBT NOT BY CONSPIRACY)	. . .	446	2 DON JUAN	5	61	2
AND NEXT HIS SAVAGE VIRTUE HE ACCUSED . .	. . .	493	2 DON JUAN	5	142	5
SOME PEOPLE HAVE ACCUSED ME OF MISANTHROPY	. . . .	192	3 DON JUAN	9	20	4
THE ACCUSED TO THINK THEIR LORDSHIPS WOULD DETERMINE	. .	391	3 DON JUAN	13	69	3
ACCUSTOM'D						
THE SIGHTS HE WAS ACCUSTOM'D TO BEHOLD	. . . .	303	2 DON JUAN	3	54	5
ACCUSTOMED						
WHO WERE ACCUSTOMED AS A SORT OF GOD .	. . . .	104	3 DON JUAN	7	74	3
ACHATES						
HE LIKE ACHATES FAITHFUL TO THE TOMB . .	. . .	109	2 DON JUAN	1	159	6
ACHE						
STRUCK NOT ON MEMORY THOUGH A HEAVY ACHE .	. . .	378	2 DON JUAN	4	62	5
ACHES						
(MY HEART OR HEAD ACHES WITH THE MEMORY YET)	. . .	408	3 DON JUAN	13	107	4
ACHIEVED						
GREAT THINGS WERE NOW TO BE ACHIEVED AT TABLE	. . .	482	3 DON JUAN	15	62	1
ACHILLES						
ACHILLES ORDER'D DINNER FOR NEW COMERS . .	. . .	221	2 DON JUAN	2	123	8
ENTOMB'D THE BRAVEST OF THE BRAVE ACHILLES	. . . .	385	2 DON JUAN	4	76	3
AND THOUGH HIS NAME THAN AJAX OR ACHILLES	. . . .	132	3 DON JUAN	8	39	2
NAMED AFTER THEE ACHILLES) AND QUITE THROUGH'T	. . .	153	3 DON JUAN	8	84	5
ACHILLES'						
SAVE CHANGE I'VE STOOD UPON ACHILLES' TOMB	. . . .	399	2 DON JUAN	4	101	7
ACHILLES' SELF WAS NOT MORE GRIM AND GORY	. . . .	73	3 DON JUAN	7	14	6
ACHITOPHEL						
CAN SNEER AT HIM WHO DREW ACHITOPHEL . .	. . .	334	2 DON JUAN	3	100	8
ACIDS						
AS ACIDS ROUSE A DORMANT ALKALI) . . .	. . . .	251	3 DON JUAN	10	54	4
SOME ACIDS WITH THE SWEETS--FOR SHE WAS HEADY	. . .	482	3 DON JUAN	15	61	4
ACKNOWLEDGE						
ACKNOWLEDGE AUGHT OF DREAD OF DEATH OR FOE	. . . .	155	3 DON JUAN	8	87	5
ACKNOWLEDGED						
AND OTHER MINDS ACKNOWLEDGED MY DOMINION .	. . .	345	2 DON JUAN	4	3	4
ACORN						
I RECK NOT IF AN ACORN GAVE IT BIRTH . .	. . .	436	3 DON JUAN	14	59	4
ACQUAINTANCE						
AMONGST HER NUMEROUS ACQUAINTANCE ALL . .	. . .	51	2 DON JUAN	1	55	1
AND MADE HIM A GOOD FRIEND BUT BAD ACQUAINTANCE	. .	303	2 DON JUAN	3	54	8
THE PURCHASER OF JUAN AND ACQUAINTANCE .	. . .	432	2 DON JUAN	5	40	1
HER SECOND TO CUT ONLY HIS--ACQUAINTANCE .	. . .	491	2 DON JUAN	5	139	2
OUR OLD ACQUAINTANCE AND AT LEAST I'LL TRY	. . .	266	3 DON JUAN	10	84	4
CAN FORM A SLIGHT ACQUAINTANCE WITH FRESH AIR	. . .	301	3 DON JUAN	11	66	8
AND THUS ACQUAINTANCE GREW AT NOBLE ROUTS	. . . .	369	3 DON JUAN	13	24	1
A LARGE ACQUAINTANCE LETS NOT VIRTUE SLUMBER	. . .	371	3 DON JUAN	13	30	3
ACQUAINTED						
SO LET US BE ACQUAINTED AS WE OUGHT . .	. . .	417	2 DON JUAN	5	13	6
ACQUIESCED						
BECAUSE THOUGH YOUNG HE ACQUIESCED WITH SUAVITY	. . .	368	3 DON JUAN	13	22	3
ACQUIRE						
ACQUIRE THE DEEP AND BITTER POWER TO GIVE	. . . .	402	2 DON JUAN	4	107	4
ACQUIRED						
BUT HOW FAITH IS ACQUIRED AND THEN INSURED	. . .	47	2 DON JUAN	1	47	5
THOUGH I ACQUIRED--BUT I PASS OVER THAT .	. . .	50	2 DON JUAN	1	53	2
WHICH IS ACQUIRED IN NATURE'S GOOD OLD COLLEGE	. . .	228	2 DON JUAN	2	136	8
MIGHT HAVE FROM TIME ACQUIRED SOME SLIGHT DEFECT	. .	529	3 DON JUAN	16	58	4
ACQUITTED						
HE ACQUITTED BOTH HIMSELF AND HORSE THE 'SQUIRES	. . .	425	3 DON JUAN	14	34	2
ACRES'						
AS THROUGH HIS PALMS BOB ACRES' VALOUR OOZED	. . .	493	2 DON JUAN	5	142	1
ACROPOLIS						
TO OUR THEME--THE MAN WHO HAS STOOD ON THE ACROPOLIS	. .	271	3 DON JUAN	11	7	1
ACROSS						
AND SWEPT AS 'TWERE ACROSS THEIR HEART'S DELIGHT	. . .	355	2 DON JUAN	4	21	3
ACT						
HE STOOD IN ACT TO SPEAK OR RATHER STAMMER	. . .	111	2 DON JUAN	1	163	1
WAS BUT A MOMENT'S ACT--AH WELL-A-DAY . .	. . .	121	2 DON JUAN	1	181	5
FOR THEY WHO WERE MOST RAVENOUS IN THE ACT	. . . .	198	2 DON JUAN	2	79	3
FOR THEY WHO HAD BEEN GAINERS BY THE ACT	. . . .	198	2 DON JUAN	2	79	V3
HIS BROW AS IF IN ACT TO BUTT AND THEN .	. . .	292	2 DON JUAN	3	32	7
OF MAGIC LADIES WHO BY ONE SOLE ACT . .	. . .	293	2 DON JUAN	3	34	7
PERHAPS YOU PROPHESY SOME SUDDEN ACT . .	. . .	296	2 DON JUAN	3	40	4
IN ARMS AT LEAST HE STOOD IN ACT TO SPRING	. . .	365	2 DON JUAN	4	39	7
WHICH WAS AN ODD ONE A TROOP GOING TO ACT	. . . .	388	2 DON JUAN	4	80	4
I THINK WITH ALEXANDER THAT THE ACT . .	. . .	428	2 DON JUAN	5	32	1
OF EATING WITH ANOTHER ACT OR TWO . . .	. . .	428	2 DON JUAN	5	32	2
BECAUSE A FOOLISH OR IMPRUDENT ACT . . .	. . .	58	3 DON JUAN	6	104	4
OF WHICH HOWE'ER THE MUSE DESCRIBES EACH ACT	. . .	107	3 DON JUAN	7	81	3

4

ACT   (CONTINUED)
WHICH YOUTH WOULD NOT ACT ILL TO KEEP IN MIND) . . . . . 224 3 DON JUAN 9   84   5
IT GROWS AN ACT OF PATRIOTIC CHARITY . . . . 357 3 DON JUAN 12   89   3
THOUGH APT TO ACT WITH FIRE UPON OCCASION . . . . . . 365 3 DON JUAN 13   14   5
STOOD LIKE CARACTACUS IN ACT TO RALLY . . . . 384 3 DON JUAN 13   56   3
AND ONLY THINK OR ACT OR FEEL WITH REFERENCE . . . . . 541 3 DON JUAN 16   85   6
HAS BEEN DECLARED AN ACT OF INURBANITY . . . . 565 3 DON JUAN 17   7   7
ACTED
BUT THE SEA ACTED AS A STRONG EMETIC . . . . 167 2 DON JUAN 2   21   8
ACTED UPON THE LIVING AS ON WIRE . . . . 133 3 DON JUAN 8   41   7
IF YOU HAVE ACTED ONCE A GENEROUS PART . . . . . . 184 3 DON JUAN 9   4   5
YOUR FACE--BUT YOU HAVE ACTED ON THE WHOLE . . . . . 232 3 DON JUAN 10   16   7
AS IF THEY ACTED WITH THE HEART INSTEAD . . . . . . 284 3 DON JUAN 11   34   4
BUT WHATSOE'ER SHE WISHED SHE ACTED RIGHT . . . . . 435 3 DON JUAN 14   57   6
SO WELL SHE ACTED ALL AND EVERY PART . . . . 547 3 DON JUAN 16   97   1
WHO ARE STRONGLY ACTED ON BY WHAT IS NEAREST . . . . 547 3 DON JUAN 16   97   8
ACTING
MIGHT END IN ACTING AS HIS OWN JACK KETCH . . . . . 63 3 DON JUAN 6   116   5
ACTION
HIS BRAIN ABOUT THE ACTION OF THE SKY . . . . . . 71 2 DON JUAN 1   93   6
SO THAT A SUIT OR ACTION WERE MADE GOOD . . . . . . 109 2 DON JUAN 1   160   5
WITH GRACEFUL ACTION SCIENCE NOT A JOT . . . . . . 392 2 DON JUAN 4   89   3
AS GOOD MEN WEAR WHO HAVE DONE A VIRTUOUS ACTION . . . 473 2 DON JUAN 5   107   8
AND ONE GOOD ACTION IN THE MIDST OF CRIMES . . . . . 156 3 DON JUAN 8   90   1
MAY BE THE HOARDER'S PRINCIPLE OF ACTION . . . . . . 321 3 DON JUAN 12   11   2
WHOSE LOSS IN THE LATE ACTION WE REGRET . . . . . . 383 3 DON JUAN 13   54   7
ACTIONS
BUT HERE ARE MEN WHO FOUGHT IN GALLANT ACTIONS . . . . 83 3 DON JUAN 7   34   1
TO TRACE ALL ACTIONS TO THEIR SECRET SPRINGS . . . . 436 3 DON JUAN 14   59   5
ACTIUM
BUT ACTIUM LOST FOR CLEOPATRA'S EYES . . . . 8 3 DON JUAN 6   4   7
ACTIVE
ACTIVE THOUGH NOT SO SPRIGHTLY AS A PAGE . . . . . . 51 2 DON JUAN 1   54   3
AN ACTIVE HERMIT EVEN IN AGE THE CHILD . . . . . . 144 3 DON JUAN 8   63   7
WHO LIKE DON JUAN TAKES AN ACTIVE SHARE . . . . . . 303 3 DON JUAN 11   70   2
ACTIVITY
WHERE LONDON STREETS FERMENT IN FULL ACTIVITY . . . . 272 3 DON JUAN 11   8   4
ACTOR
SO THAT IF ANY ACTOR MISS'D HIS PART . . . . 27 2 DON JUAN 1   11   3
ACTORS
THIS MAKES YOUR ACTORS ARTISTS AND ROMANCERS . . . . 547 3 DON JUAN 16   98   1
ACTS
TO PLAYS IN FIVE AND OPERAS IN THREE ACTS . . . . . 138 2 DON JUAN 1   203   4
OF PIOUS MEN HAVE PUBLISHED ON HIS ACTS . . . . . . 138 2 DON JUAN 1   203 V4
LIKE TITUS' YOUTH AND CAESAR'S EARLIEST ACTS . . . . 329 2 DON JUAN 3   92   3
LET RADICALS ITS OTHER ACTS ATTACK . . . . 378 3 DON JUAN 13   43   7
BUT MOSTLY SINGS OF HUMAN THINGS AND ACTS-- . . . . . 416 3 DON JUAN 14   13   4
ACTUAL
IT IS AN ACTUAL FACT THAT HE COMMANDER . . . . . . 93 3 DON JUAN 7   52   1
BY WAY OF LESSON AGAINST ACTUAL TURKS . . . . . . 93 3 DON JUAN 7   53   4
WHAT WERE THE ACTUAL AND OFFICIAL DUTIES . . . . . . 208 3 DON JUAN 9   51   2
ACTUALLY
WHEREAS THIS STORY'S ACTUALLY TRUE . . . . 137 2 DON JUAN 1   202   8
ACUTE
THE VERY TENDON WHICH IS MOST ACUTE-- . . . . . . 153 3 DON JUAN 8   84   3
BEFORE THE LORDS--WHOSE CHANCELLOR'S MORE ACUTE . . . 357 3 DON JUAN 12 V 18   3
ACUTEST
THAT SHE HAD PUZZLED ALL THE ACUTEST HINTERS . . . . 434 3 DON JUAN 14   56   3
ADAM
HE STOOD LIKE ADAM LINGERING NEAR HIS GARDEN . . . . 120 2 DON JUAN 1   180   5
AND HUGE TOMBS WORSE--MANKIND SINCE ADAM FELL . . . . 444 2 DON JUAN 5   59   6
THAT ONE WOULD THINK THE FIRST WHO BORE IT ADAM . . . 79 3 DON JUAN 7   25   8
SINCE ADAM WITH A FALL OR WITH AN APPLE . . . . . . 225 3 DON JUAN 10   1   8
THAT ADAM CALLED THE HAPPIEST OF MEN . . . . 434 3 DON JUAN 14   55   8
ADAM EXCHANGED HIS PARADISE FOR PLOUGHING . . . . . 444 3 DON JUAN 14   78   1
ADAMANT
OR ADAMANT TO FIND THE WORLD A SPIRIT . . . . . . 268 3 DON JUAN 11   1   7
ADAM'S
LIKE ADAM'S RECOLLECTION OF HIS FALL . . . . 90 2 DON JUAN 1   127   3
SOULS TO SAVE SINCE EVE'S SLIP AND ADAM'S FALL . . . 192 3 DON JUAN 9   19   3
WHO WOULD SUPPOSE FROM ADAM'S SIMPLE RATION . . . . . 486 3 DON JUAN 15   69   5
ADAMS
WAS MADE BY MRS ADAMS WHERE SHE CRIES . . . . . . 403 3 DON JUAN 13   96   7
ADAPTED
BUT NOT AT ALL ADAPTED TO MY RHYMES . . . . 22 2 DON JUAN 1   3   8
OF MONITORS ADAPTED TO RECALL . . . . 308 2 DON JUAN 3   65   3
LOOKED MORE ADAPTED TO BE PUT TO BED . . . . 26 3 DON JUAN 6   41   6
ADD
TO ADD A STORY TO THE TOWER OF BABEL . . . . 11 2 DON JUAN D   4   8
THEY ONLY ADD THEM ALL IN AN APPENDIX . . . . . . 46 2 DON JUAN 1   44   7
BESIDES I'VE NO MORE ON THIS HEAD TO ADD . . . . . 384 2 DON JUAN 4   74   5
AND STRIPPED AND LOOKED TO--BUT WHY SHOULD I ADD . . . 429 2 DON JUAN 5   34   5
THIS MUCH HOWEVER I MAY ADD--HER YEARS . . . . . . 468 2 DON JUAN 5   98   1
AND SCORN TO ADD A SYLLABLE UNTRUE . . . . 41 3 DON JUAN 6   70   3
A PATH TO ADD HIS OWN SLIGHT ARM AND FORCES . . . . 126 3 DON JUAN 8   30   7
AND WHEN YOU ADD TO THIS HER WOMANHOOD . . . . . . 218 3 DON JUAN 9   71   1
ADD WHAT MAY BE CALLED MARRIAGE IN DISGUISE . . . . . 220 3 DON JUAN 9   76   8
YOU'LL ADD TO MATRIMONY'S LIST OF CURES . . . . . . 343 3 DON JUAN 12   60   8
BUT I SHALL ADD THEM IN A BRIEF APPENDIX . . . . . 440 3 DON JUAN 14   68   7

```
                                           PAGE VOL      CANTO STANZA LN
ADD   (CONTINUED)
  WAS APT TO ADD A COLOURING FROM HER OWN  . . . . . .  463  3 DON JUAN 15    17    2
  BUT ADD THE WORDS CRIED HENRY WHICH YOU MADE  . . . . .  517  3 DON JUAN 16    39    1
ADDED
  ADDED TO THOSE HIS LADY WITH SUCH VIGOUR  . . . . . .  110  2 DON JUAN  1   161    6
  TO THESE WAS ADDED JUAN WHO BEFORE .  . . . . . . .  198  2 DON JUAN  2    78    3
  ADDED TO HIS CONNEXION WITH THE SEA  . . . . . . .  222  2 DON JUAN  2   125    4
  WITH ONE OR TWO SMALL SENSES ADDED JUST  . . . . . .  269  2 DON JUAN  2   212    7
  ESPECIALLY WHEN ADDED TO THE POWER .  . . . . . . .  395  2 DON JUAN  4    94    8
  AND THEN HE ADDED THAT HE NEEDS MUST SAY . . . . . .  451  2 DON JUAN  5    69    6
  SHE ADDED TO JUANNA THEIR NEW GUEST  . . . . . . .   29  3 DON JUAN  6    46    4
  (SHE ADDED IN A SOFT AND PITEOUS TONE)  . . . . . .   47  3 DON JUAN  6    82    6
  THE IMPERIAL BRIDE--AND ADDED LET THE BOAT  . . . . .   62  3 DON JUAN  6   113    2
  BUT WHEN I'VE ADDED THAT THE ELDER JACK SMITH  . . . .   76  3 DON JUAN  7    20    2
  AND ADDED GREATLY TO THE MISSING LIST .  . . . . . .   80  3 DON JUAN  7    27    8
  TO THIS WE HAVE ADDED SINCE THE LOVE OF MONEY  . . . .  405  3 DON JUAN 13   100    3
  THEY ADDED GRACEFUL NECKS WHITE HANDS AND ARMS . . . .  408  3 DON JUAN 13   107    8
  BUT ERE HE WENT HE ADDED A SLIGHT HINT  . . . . . .  440  3 DON JUAN 14    69    1
  WITH ALL THE ADDED CHARM OF FORM AND FEATURE . . . . .  478  3 DON JUAN 15    52    4
  ADDED HER SWEET VOICE TO THE LYRIC SOUND . . . . . .  518  3 DON JUAN 16    40    6
  HE ADDED MODESTLY WHEN REBELS RAILED)  . . . . . . .  535  3 DON JUAN 16    72    6
ADDING
  HIS FRIEND TOO ADDING A NEW SAVING CLAUSE  . . . . .  437  2 DON JUAN  5    47    6
  ADDING THAT THIS WAS COMMONEST AND BEST  . . . . . .  472  2 DON JUAN  5   105    6
  THAT ADDING TO THE ACCOUNT HIS HIGHNESS' YEARS . . . .   10  3 DON JUAN  6     9    4
  AND ADDING STILL A LITTLE THROUGH EACH CROSS . . . . .  317  3 DON JUAN 12     4    4
ADDIO'S
  THE LASCIAMI'S AND QUAVERING ADDIO'S . . . . . . .  523  3 DON JUAN 16    45    5
ADDISON'S
  LIKE ADDISON'S FAINT PRAISE SO WONT TO DAMN  . . . . .  552  3 DON JUAN 16   104    4
ADDITION
  AND THIS ADDITION WITH SUCH GEMS WAS BOUND . . . . .  457  2 DON JUAN  5    79    6
  THAT WITH THE ADDITION OF A SLIGHT PELISSE . . . . .  239  3 DON JUAN 10    30    7
ADDITIONAL
  AND HELP THEM WITH A LIE OR TWO ADDITIONAL . . . . .   37  2 DON JUAN  1    31    2
ADDITIONS
  NOT FINDING THAT THE ADDITIONS MUCH ENCUMBER . . . .  276  2 DON JUAN  3     3    8
ADDRESS
  HIMSELF A FAVOURITE VENTURED TO ADDRESS  . . . . . .  100  3 DON JUAN  7    65    2
  THAT CALM PATRICIAN POLISH IN THE ADDRESS  . . . . .  373  3 DON JUAN 13    34    2
  BY NATURE SOFT HIS WHOLE ADDRESS HELD OFF  . . . . .  462  3 DON JUAN 15    14    1
ADDRESS'D
  THE VINOUS GREEK TO WHOM HE HAD ADDRESS'D  . . . . .  297  2 DON JUAN  3    42    6
  THEY THUS ADDRESS'D--AND LAMBRO'S VISAGE FELL--  . . .  298  2 DON JUAN  3    44    2
ADDRESSED
  TO JUAN WHO WAS NEAREST HIM ADDRESSED  . . . . . .  140  3 DON JUAN  8    56    5
  'TIS NOT ADDRESSED TO YOU--THE MORE'S THE PITY . . . .  233  3 DON JUAN 10    17    2
  THEN HENRY TURNED TO JUAN AND ADDRESSED  . . . . . .  515  3 DON JUAN 16    35    1
ADDRESSES
  BUT THESE ARE MY ADDRESSES FROM THE THRONE . . . . .  331  2 DON JUAN  3    96    5
ADDRESSING
  ADDRESSING HIM IN TONES WHICH SEEMED TO THANK  . . . .  141  3 DON JUAN  8    57    7
  FOR ADELINE ADDRESSING FEW WORDS TO HIM  . . . . . .  489  3 DON JUAN 15    75    7
ADDS
  REPLETION RATHER ADDS TO WHAT HE FEELS . . . . . .  427  2 DON JUAN  5    31    4
  IT ADDS AN OUTWARD GRACE UNTO THEIR CARRIAGE--  . . . .  344  3 DON JUAN 12    62    6
  AND ADDS A THIRD TO WHAT WAS LATE A PAIR . . . . . .  481  3 DON JUAN 15    59   V8
ADELINE
  THE LADY ADELINE AMUNDEVILLE . . . . . . . . .  359  3 DON JUAN 13     2    1
  THE LADY ADELINE AMUNDEVILLE . . . . . . . . .  364  3 DON JUAN 13    12    2
  SWEET ADELINE AMIDST THE GAY WORLD'S HUM . . . . . .  365  3 DON JUAN 13    13    4
  BUT ADELINE HAD NOT THE LEAST OCCASION . . . . . .  372  3 DON JUAN 13    31    1
  THERE ALSO WAS OF COURSE IN ADELINE  . . . . . . .  373  3 DON JUAN 13    34    1
  BUT ADELINE WAS NOT INDIFFERENT FOR  . . . . . . .  374  3 DON JUAN 13    36    1
  LORD HENRY AND THE LADY ADELINE . . . . . . . .  381  3 DON JUAN 13    50    1
  MY DIAN OF THE EPHESIANS LADY ADELINE  . . . . . .  430  3 DON JUAN 14    46    3
  BUT ADELINE WAS FAR FROM THAT RIPE AGE . . . . . .  433  3 DON JUAN 14    54    1
  THE LADY ADELINE AS SOON'S SHE SAW . . . . . . .  436  3 DON JUAN 14    60    3
  THE LADY ADELINE RESOLVED TO TAKE  . . . . . . .  437  3 DON JUAN 14    61    1
  OUR GENTLE ADELINE HAD ONE DEFECT--  . . . . . . .  446  3 DON JUAN 14    85    1
  MY BUSINESS IS WITH LADY ADELINE . . . . . . . .  449  3 DON JUAN 14    90    7
  TO THUS MUCH ADELINE WOULD NOT ADVANCE . . . . . .  450  3 DON JUAN 14    92    6
  WHETHER DON JUAN AND CHASTE ADELINE  . . . . . . .  453  3 DON JUAN 14    97    1
  IT IS NOT CLEAR THAT ADELINE AND JUAN  . . . . . .  454  3 DON JUAN 14    99    7
  THE LADY ADELINE AMUNDEVILLE . . . . . . . . .  458  3 DON JUAN 15     5    2
  THE LADY ADELINE RIGHT HONOURABLE  . . . . . . .  458  3 DON JUAN 15     6    1
  BUT ADELINE WAS OF THE PUREST VINTAGE  . . . . . .  458  3 DON JUAN 15     7    1
  FAIR ADELINE THE MORE INGENUOUS .  . . . . . . .  460  3 DON JUAN 15    10    1
  ADELINE NO DEEP JUDGE OF CHARACTER .  . . . . . . .  463  3 DON JUAN 15    17    1
  WHEN ADELINE IN ALL HER GROWING SENSE  . . . . . .  468  3 DON JUAN 15    28    1
  HAD ADELINE READ MALTHUS  I CAN'T TELL . . . . . .  472  3 DON JUAN 15    38    1
  BUT ADELINE WHO PROBABLY PRESUMED  . . . . . . .  473  3 DON JUAN 15    39    1
  BUT ADELINE DETERMINED JUAN'S WEDDING  . . . . . .  473  3 DON JUAN 15    40    1
  OF ADELINE AURORA WAS OMITTED  . . . . . . . .  477  3 DON JUAN 15    48    2
  WHEN ADELINE REPLIED WITH SOME DISGUST  . . . . . .  477  3 DON JUAN 15    49    5
  IF--BUT HERE ADELINE WHO SEEM'D TO PIQUE . . . . . .  478  3 DON JUAN 15    50    5
  WHY ADELINE HAD THIS SLIGHT PREJUDICE--  . . . . . .  478  3 DON JUAN 15    52    1
  SINCE ADELINE WAS LIBERAL BY NATURE  . . . . . . .  478  3 DON JUAN 15    52    6
  IT WAS NOT ENVY--ADELINE HAD NONE  . . . . . . .  479  3 DON JUAN 15    54    1
```

		PAGE	VOL		CANTO	STANZA	LV

ADELINE (CONTINUED)
THE DASHING AND PROUD AIR OF ADELINE	480	3 DON JUAN 15	56	1
ADELINE AND DON JUAN RATHER BLENDED	482	3 DON JUAN 15	61	3
AURORA AND THE LADY ADELINE--	489	3 DON JUAN 15	75	2
FOR ADELINE ADDRESSING FEW WORDS TO HIM	489	3 DON JUAN 15	75	7
WITH HER WAS RARE AND ADELINE WHO AS YET	492	3 DON JUAN 15	81	2
THAN ADELINE (SUCH IS ADVICE) ADVISED	506	3 DON JUAN 16	12	4
THAT SOMETHING WAS THE MATTER--ADELINE	513	3 DON JUAN 16	30	7
FAIR ADELINE ENQUIRED IF HE WERE ILL	514	3 DON JUAN 16	32	3
THE LAST TIME WAS--I PRAY SAID ADELINE--	516	3 DON JUAN 16	37	1
JEST QUOTH MILOR WHY ADELINE YOU KNOW	517	3 DON JUAN 16	38	1
FOR ADELINE IS HALF A POETESS	517	3 DON JUAN 16	39	2
FAIR ADELINE WITH EYES FIXED ON THE GROUND	518	3 DON JUAN 16	40	4
FAIR ADELINE THOUGH IN A CARELESS WAY	521	3 DON JUAN 16	42	1
THUS ADELINE WOULD THROW INTO THE SHADE	522	3 DON JUAN 16	44	1
WAS ADELINE WELL VERSED AS COMPOSITIONS	523	3 DON JUAN 16	46	8
OF ADELINE IN BRINGING THIS SAME LAY	526	3 DON JUAN 16	51	2
BUT ADELINE WAS OCCUPIED BY FAME	546	3 DON JUAN 16	95	1
ON ADELINE WHILE PLAYING HER GRAND ROLE	546	3 DON JUAN 16	96	3
SOME DOUBT HOW MUCH OF ADELINE WAS REAL	546	3 DON JUAN 16	96	8
WHILE ADELINE DISPENSED HER AIRS AND GRACES	548	3 DON JUAN 16	100	1
BUT WITH THE LADY ADELINE THE MOST	549	3 DON JUAN 16	101	8
MEANWHILE SWEET ADELINE DESERVED THEIR PRAISES	550	3 DON JUAN 16	103	1

ADELINE'S
| THE LADY ADELINE'S SERENE SEVERITY | 432 | 3 DON JUAN 14 | 51 | 1 |
| HEAVEN KNOWS BUT ADELINE'S MALICIOUS EYES | 490 | 3 DON JUAN 15 | 78 | 7 |

ADEPT
| HER MAID ANTONIA WHO WAS AN ADEPT | 97 | 2 DON JUAN 1 | 140 | 4 |

ADIEU
| HERE IS THE GARDEN-KEY--FLY--FLY--ADIEU | 121 | 2 DON JUAN 1 | 182 | 6 |
| AND I MUST EVEN SURVIVE THIS LAST ADIEU | 134 | 2 DON JUAN 1 | 197 | 7 |

ADJUSTMENT
| AND HOTTENTOT ADJUSTMENT OF THEIR TRESSES | 550 | 3 DON JUAN 16 | 103 | V8 |

ADMIRABLE
| AND THIS WAS ADMIRABLE FOR SO HOT | 119 | 3 DON JUAN 8 | 16 | 1 |

ADMIRAL
| AND ADMIRAL RIBAS (KNOWN IN RUSSIAN STORY) | 83 | 3 DON JUAN 7 | 35 | 3 |

ADMIRARI
| GREAT HAPPINESS OF THE NIL ADMIRARI | 469 | 2 DON JUAN 5 | 100 | 8 |
| PERHAPS FROM HORACE HIS NIL ADMIRARI | 374 | 3 DON JUAN 13 | 35 | 1 |

ADMIRATION
THAN ADMIRATION DUE WHERE NATURE'S RICH	269	2 DON JUAN 2	211	3
THE PEOPLE'S AWE AND ADMIRATION RAISING	445	2 DON JUAN 5	60	6
AND MIEN EXCITED GENERAL ADMIRATION--	287	3 DON JUAN 11	39	2
SECURE OF ADMIRATION ITS IMPRESSION	372	3 DON JUAN 13	31	7
BUT ON THE WHOLE TO GENERAL ADMIRATION	425	3 DON JUAN 14	34	1

ADMIRATIONS
| THE ADMIRATIONS AND THE SPECULATIONS | 523 | 3 DON JUAN 16 | 45 | 2 |

ADMIRE
| NOT TO ADMIRE IS ALL THE ART I KNOW | 470 | 2 DON JUAN 5 | 101 | 1 |
| WHOSE DRAPERY HINTS WE MAY ADMIRE THEM FREELY | 390 | 3 DON JUAN 13 | 68 | 8 |

ADMIRED
THE SAME THINGS CANNOT ALWAYS BE ADMIRED	278	2 DON JUAN 3	7	4
THE ROSY FLOOD OF TWILIGHT'S SKY ADMIRED--	334	2 DON JUAN 3	101	6
FROM HIS TRANSLATION BUT HAD NONE ADMIRED	470	2 DON JUAN 5	101	7
THEY ALL ALIKE ADMIRED THEIR NEW CONNEXION	26	3 DON JUAN 6	40	8
JUAN ADMIRED THESE HIGHWAYS OF FREE MILLIONS	263	3 DON JUAN 10	77	4
I DON'T KNOW WHICH WAS MOST ADMIRED OR LESS	287	3 DON JUAN 11	39	3
DAUGHTERS ADMIRED HIS DRESS AND PIOUS MOTHERS	293	3 DON JUAN 11	48	7
OF CHARMS THAT SHOULD OR SHOULD NOT BE ADMIRED	408	3 DON JUAN 13	108	6
A FULL-GROWN CUPID VERY MUCH ADMIRED	428	3 DON JUAN 14	41	2
ADMIRED ADORED BUT ALSO SO CORRECT	434	3 DON JUAN 14	56	2
THE SUPPER TOO DISCUSSED THE DAMES ADMIRED	504	3 DON JUAN 16	8	2

ADMIRES
OR REGENT WHO ADMIRES SUCH KIND OF FOOD--	10	2 DON JUAN D	2	4
(NONE TRUSTS THE SEX MORE OR SO MUCH ADMIRES--	287	2 DON JUAN 3	22	5
AND THEN OF COURSE THE CIRCLE MUCH ADMIRES	521	3 DON JUAN 16	41	5

ADMIRING
BABA AND JUAN WHICH LAST STOOD ADMIRING	469	2 DON JUAN 5	100	3
ADMIRING THIS NEW NATIVE OF THE DEEP	36	3 DON JUAN 6	60	8
ADMIRING THOSE (BY DAINTY DAMES ABHORRED)	209	3 DON JUAN 9	54	3
ADMIRING MORE MINERVA THAN THE GRACES	494	3 DON JUAN 15	85	3

ADMIT
| ADMIT REJECT CONTEMN AND WHAT KNOW YOU | 411 | 3 DON JUAN 14 | 3 | 2 |

ADMITS
| WHO IS NO PAVIOUR NOR ADMITS A BARGE | 198 | 3 DON JUAN 9 | 31 | 6 |

ADMITTED
ADMITTED A SMALL PARTY AS NIGHT FELL--	282	3 DON JUAN 11	29	5
ADMITTED AS AN ASPIRANT TO ALL	295	3 DON JUAN 11	54	2
YET IF EXAMINED IT MIGHT BE ADMITTED	563	3 DON JUAN 17	3	7

ADMONITION
| WITHOUT A WORD OF PREVIOUS ADMONITION | 97 | 2 DON JUAN 1 | 139 | 5 |

ADOPTED
| A MODE ADOPTED SINCE BY MODERN YOUTH | 501 | 3 DON JUAN 16 | 1 | 4 |

ADORATION
| THIS SORT OF ADORATION OF THE REAL | 269 | 2 DON JUAN 2 | 211 | 7 |

ADORE
| WOULD HE ADORE A SULTAN HE OBEY | 15 | 2 DON JUAN D | 11 | 7 |
| A LOVELY STATUE WE ALMOST ADORE | 269 | 2 DON JUAN 2 | 211 | 6 |

ADORED
```
    SHE LOVED AND WAS BELOVED--SHE ADORED  . . . .  . . . .  257   2 DON JUAN  2    191    1
    OF SENTIMENT AND HE SHE MOST ADORED  . . . .  . . . .  209   3 DON JUAN  9     54    5
    THAT WORSE THAN WORST OF FOES THE ONCE ADORED  . . . .  258   3 DON JUAN 10     67    6
    MUCH I RESPECT AND MUCH I HAVE ADORED  . . .  . . . .  422   3 DON JUAN 14     27    1
    ADMIRED ADORED BUT ALSO SO CORRECT  .  . . . .  . . . .  434   3 DON JUAN 14     56    2
ADORES
    IN CATHERINE'S REIGN WHOM GLORY STILL ADORES  .  . . . .   52   3 DON JUAN  6     92    7
ADORN
    ROUND THE PATRICIAN LEFT-LEGS WHICH ADORN  . . .  . . . .  404   2 DON JUAN  4    110    7
ADORN'D
    THAT WHICH ADORN'D THE BRAIN OF DONNA INEZ  . . .  . . . .   27   2 DON JUAN  1     11    8
    THE LIMB WHICH IT ADORN'D ITS ONLY MOULD  .  . . . .  . . . .  312   2 DON JUAN  3     71    4
ADORNING
    SAD THOUGHT TO LOSE THE SPOUSE THAT WAS ADORNING  . . .  278   2 DON JUAN  3      7    7
ADORNS
    BUT THERE ARE FORMS WHICH TIME ADORNS NOT WEARS  . . .  468   2 DON JUAN  5     98   V3
ADRIAN
    ROOTED WHERE ONCE THE ADRIAN WAVE FLOW'D O'ER  . . .  337   2 DON JUAN  3    105    4
ADRIA'S
    THE SONG AND OAR OF ADRIA'S GONDOLIER  . . .  . . . .   87   2 DON JUAN  1    122    3
A-DRY
    AND FALL FOR LACK OF MOISTURE QUITE A-DRY BOB  . . .  .   10   2 DON JUAN  0      3    8
ADULATE
    IT IS NOT THAT I ADULATE THE PEOPLE  .  . . . .  . . . .  195   3 DON JUAN  9     25    1
ADULATIONS
    HE VARIED WITH SOME SKILL HIS ADULATIONS  . . .  . . . .  319   2 DON JUAN  3     84    6
ADULTERATION
    NOT QUITE ADULTERY BUT ADULTERATION  .  . . . .  . . . .  345   3 DON JUAN 12     63    8
    TILL OLD MAY UNDERGO ADULTERATION  . . . .  . . . .  458   3 DON JUAN 15      6    8
ADULTERER'S
    THE ADULTERER'S ADVOCATE WHEN DULY FEE'D  .  . . . .  151   2 DON JUAN  1   V  2    2
ADULTERY
    WHAT MEN CALL GALLANTRY AND GODS ADULTERY  . . . .  . .   56   2 DON JUAN  1     63    7
    COMMIT ADULTERY WITH THOMAS MOORE  . . . .  . . . .  139   2 DON JUAN  1    205   V8
    NOT QUITE ADULTERY BUT ADULTERATION  .  . . .  . . . .  345   3 DON JUAN 12     63    8
ADVANCE
    WHENEER IT SUITS HIS PURPOSE TO ADVANCE  .  . . . .  152   2 DON JUAN  1   V  3    3
    WITH BUT THE SINGLE OBJECT--TO ADVANCE  . . .  . . . .  152   2 DON JUAN  1   V  3  V3
    NOR WORK ADVANCE NOR COVERED WAY WAS THERE  . . . .  .   72   3 DON JUAN  7     11    7
    AS HATH BEEN DONE MERE CONQUEST TO ADVANCE  . . .  . .  113   3 DON JUAN  8      3    6
    BUT THOSE WHO SCALED FOUND OUT THAT THEIR ADVANCE  . .  136   3 DON JUAN  8     46    1
    ADVANCE BEYOND WHILE THEY COULD PASS FOR NEW  . . .  .  433   3 DON JUAN 14     53    4
    TO THUS MUCH ADELINE WOULD NOT ADVANCE  . . .  . . .  450   3 DON JUAN 14     92    6
ADVANCED
    THAN MANY PERSONS MORE ADVANCED IN LIFE  . . .  . . .  164   2 DON JUAN  2     15    4
    AS DAY ADVANCED THE WEATHER SEEM'D TO ABATE  .  . . .  172   2 DON JUAN  2     30    1
    AND HE ADVANCED THOUGH WITH BUT A BAD GRACE  .  . . .  472   2 DON JUAN  5    106    1
    ADVANCED IN ALL THEIR AZURE'S HIGHEST HUE  . . .  . .  294   3 DON JUAN 11     50    4
    AND HE AROSE ADVANCED--THE SHADE RETREATED  .  . . .  559   3 DON JUAN 16    119    2
ADVANCES
    ADVANCES OR REPULSES THEY BEHOLD  .  . . . .  . . . .  366   3 DON JUAN 13     17   V8
    ADVANCES WITH EXASPERATED RAP  .  . . . .  . . . .  459   3 DON JUAN 15      8    6
ADVANCING
    AND STILL MORE NEARLY TO THE PLACE ADVANCING  . . .  290   2 DON JUAN  3     29    1
    ADVANCING TO THE NEAREST DINNER TRAY  .  . . .  . . . .  297   2 DON JUAN  3     42    1
    'TWAS NINE WHEN STILL ADVANCING UNDISMAYED  .  . . .   81   3 DON JUAN  7     29    3
    BY THE ADVANCING MUSCOVITE--THE GROAN  . . .  . . . .  155   3 DON JUAN  8     87    7
ADVANTAGE
    AND HERE THE ADVANTAGE IS MY OWN I WEEN  . . .  . . .  137   2 DON JUAN  1    202    3
    AND MAY BECOME OF GREAT ADVANTAGE WHEN  . . .  . . .  205   2 DON JUAN  2     93    4
    HAD ALL THE ADVANTAGE TOO OF NOT BEING AIR  . . .  . .  232   2 DON JUAN  2    142    8
    LOSING THE ADVANTAGE OF A VIRTUOUS STATION  .  . . .  263   2 DON JUAN  2    201    4
    IN YEARS HE HAD THE ADVANTAGE OF TIME'S SEQUEL  . . .  367   3 DON JUAN 13     20    3
    THESE FORTY DAYS' ADVANTAGE OF HER YEARS--  .  . . .  432   3 DON JUAN 14     52    1
ADVANTAGES
    HINTED THE VAST ADVANTAGES WHICH THEY  . . . .  . . .  451   2 DON JUAN  5     69    2
    THESE WERE ADVANTAGES AND THEN HE THOUGHT--  .  . . .  368   3 DON JUAN 13     21    1
ADVENTURE
    WHEN CALLED NEXT DAY DECLINED THE ROUGH ADVENTURE  . .  425   3 DON JUAN 14     35   V8
ADVENTURES
    I SHALL PROCEED WITH HIS ADVENTURES IS  . . .  . . .  135   2 DON JUAN  1    199    2
    INTRIGUES ADVENTURES OF THE COMMON SCHOOL  . . .  . .  353   2 DON JUAN  4     17    5
    SEEMS FERTILE IN ADVENTURES STRANGE AND NEW  .  . . .  459   2 DON JUAN  5     83    6
    SOME RUMOUR ALSO OF SOME STRANGE ADVENTURES  .  . . .  284   3 DON JUAN 11     33    1
    BUT HIS ADVENTURES FORM A SORRY SIGHT--  .  . . .  363   3 DON JUAN 13      9    6
ADVENTUROUS
    PITY HE LOVED ADVENTUROUS LIFE'S VARIETY  . . . .  . .  296   2 DON JUAN  3     41    7
    AT ONCE ADVENTUROUS AND CONTEMPLATIVE  . . .  . . .  402   2 DON JUAN  4    107    2
ADVERSITY
    AND SHARP ADVERSITY WILL TEACH AT LAST  . . .  . . .  345   2 DON JUAN  4      2    2
    ADVERSITY IS THE FIRST PATH TO TRUTH  .  . . . .  . . . .  339   3 DON JUAN 12     50    5
ADVERTISE
    WHO ADVERTISE NEW POEMS BY YOUR LOOKS  . . .  . . . .  403   2 DON JUAN  4    108    3
ADVERTISEMENT
    THAN AN ADVERTISEMENT OR MUCH THE SAME  . . .  . . .  382   3 DON JUAN 13     51    4
ADVICE
    NONE CAN SAY THAT THIS WAS NOT GOOD ADVICE  . . .  . .  122   2 DON JUAN  1    183    1
    AND THEN BY THE ADVICE OF SOME OLD LADIES  . . .  . .  128   2 DON JUAN  1    190    7
```

ADVICE (CONTINUED)
   OF GOOD ADVICE--AND TWO OR THREE OF CREDIT . . . . . . 161 2 DON JUAN 2   9 8
   AND THAT'S ONE COMFORT FOR MY LOST ADVICE   . . . . . 200 3 DON JUAN 9   36 7
   WHICH SHOWS HOW VERY USEFUL GOOD ADVICE IS . . . . . . 333 3 DON JUAN 12   37 V8
   AH IF YOU HAD BUT FOLLOW'D MY ADVICE . . . . 430 3 DON JUAN 14   47 8
   THAT GOOD BUT RARELY CAME FROM GOOD ADVICE . . . . . . 439 3 DON JUAN 14   66 8
   SHE HAD A GOOD OPINION OF ADVICE . . . . 469 3 DON JUAN 15   29 1
   AND AFTER SO MUCH EXCELLENT ADVICE . . . . 490 3 DON JUAN 15   77 8
   THAN ADELINE (SUCH IS ADVICE) ADVISED . . . . 506 3 DON JUAN 16   12 4
ADVISE
   HIS DAUGHTER--HAD NOT SENT BEFORE TO ADVISE . . . . . 294 2 DON JUAN 3   37 4
ADVISED
   OF THE LAST AXIOM HE ADVISED HIS SPOUSE . . . . 439 3 DON JUAN 14   67 2
   SHE SERIOUSLY ADVISED HIM TO GET MARRIED . . . . . . 469 3 DON JUAN 15   29 8
   THAN ADELINE (SUCH IS ADVICE) ADVISED . . . . 506 3 DON JUAN 16   12 4
ADVOCATE
   THE ADULTERER'S ADVOCATE WHEN DULY FEE'D . . . . . . 151 2 DON JUAN 1 V 2 2
ADVOCATES
   THEN ADVOCATES INQUISITORS AND JUDGES . . . . 36 2 DON JUAN 1   28 7
AENEIDS
   AND FOR THEIR AENEIDS ILIADS AND ODYSSEYS   . . . . . 44 2 DON JUAN 1   41 6
AEOLIAN
   BUT LONGBOW WILD AS AN AEOLIAN HARP   . . . . 402 3 DON JUAN 13   93 2
AERIAL
   HER EYEBROW'S SHAPE WAS LIKE THE AERIAL BOW . . . . . 55 2 DON JUAN 1   61 3
AETNA
   SOME THOUGHT IT WAS MOUNT AETNA SOME THE HIGHLANDS   . . 209 2 DON JUAN 2   100 7
AFAR
   AFAR A DWARF BUFFOON STOOD TELLING TALES . . . . . . 293 2 DON JUAN 3   34 1
   OF TIME AND TIDE ROLLS ON AND BEARS AFAR . . . . . . 500 3 DON JUAN 15   99 5
AFFAIR
   I CAN'T TELL WHETHER JULIA SAW THE AFFAIR   . . . . . 59 2 DON JUAN 1   68 1
   IN MARINET'S AFFAIR--IN FACT 'TWAS SHABBY   . . . . . 184 3 DON JUAN 9   2 2
   RATHER THAN LIFE A MERE AFFAIR OF BREATH . . . . . . 190 3 DON JUAN 9   16 8
   THE EXACT AFFAIR ON WHICH HE WAS SENT O'ER . . . . . 283 3 DON JUAN 11   32 4
   I HAVE SEEN THAT SAD AFFAIR OF THE LATE QUEEN-- . . . 310 3 DON JUAN 11   84 4
   THAT'S YOUR AFFAIR NOT MINE A REAL SPIRIT   . . . . . 356 3 DON JUAN 12   87 7
   WHO ONE MIGHT THINK WAS SOMETHING IN THE AFFAIR . . . 430 3 DON JUAN 14   45 2
AFFAIRS
   'TIS IN ARRANGING ALL MY FRIENDS' AFFAIRS   . . . . . 33 2 DON JUAN 1   23 7
   FEW CHANGES E'ER CAN BETTER THEIR AFFAIRS   . . . . . 263 2 DON JUAN 2   201 5
   ALTHOUGH NO DOUBT HER FIRST OF LOVE AFFAIRS . . . . . 276 2 DON JUAN 3   4 5
   THEN HAVING SETTLED HIS MARINE AFFAIRS   . . . . . . 285 2 DON JUAN 3   19 1
   HE LEFT TO HIS VIZIER ALL STATE AFFAIRS   . . . . . . 496 2 DON JUAN 5   148 3
   THERE IS A TIDE IN THE AFFAIRS OF MEN . . . . 6 3 DON JUAN 6   1 1
   THERE IS A TIDE IN THE AFFAIRS OF WOMEN . . . . 7 3 DON JUAN 6   2 1
   THOUGHT (WHAT IN STATE AFFAIRS IS MOST ESSENTIAL) . . 285 3 DON JUAN 11   35 6
   WHERE NONE WERE DREAMT OF UNTO LOVE'S AFFAIRS   . . . 369 3 DON JUAN 13   25 5
   WHEN YOUR AFFAIRS COME ROUND ONE WAY OR T'OTHER   . . . 431 3 DON JUAN 14   48 7
   BUT WE'LL SAY NOTHING OF AFFAIRS OF STATE)   . . . . . 541 3 DON JUAN 16   84 4
AFFECT
   AFFECT NO MORE THAN LIGHTNING A CONDUCTOR   . . . . . 260 3 DON JUAN 10   71 8
AFFECTATION
   THE TENOR'S VOICE IS SPOILT BY AFFECTATION   . . . . . 391 2 DON JUAN 4   87 1
AFFECTED
   IS QUITE REFRESHING IN THE AFFECTED PHRASE   . . . . . 156 3 DON JUAN 8   90 2
   AND YET 'TIS NOT AFFECTED I OPINE . . . . 415 3 DON JUAN 14   12 6
   NOTHING AFFECTED STUDIED OR CONSTRUCTIVE . . . . . . 461 3 DON JUAN 15   12 3
AFFECTION
   SHE TOOK HIS LADY ALSO IN AFFECTION   . . . . 58 2 DON JUAN 1   67 3
   DANTE AND MILTON AND OF BOTH THE AFFECTION   . . . . . 281 2 DON JUAN 3   10 3
   A LONELY PURE AFFECTION UNOPPOSED   . . . . 304 2 DON JUAN 3   57 5
   OF THEIR EXCHANGING GLANCES OF AFFECTION . . . . . . 351 2 DON JUAN 4   13 8
   CALLED BROTHERLY AFFECTION COULD NOT MOVE   . . . . . 250 3 DON JUAN 10   53 6
AFFIDAVIT
   I DO DECLARE UPON AN AFFIDAVIT . . . . 444 3 DON JUAN 14   80 1
AFFLICTING
   AFFLICTING YOUNG FOLKS WITH A SORT OF DIZZINESS   . . . 108 3 DON JUAN 7   83 8
AFFORD
   AT LEAST TO THOSE OF INCOMES WHICH AFFORD   . . . . . 51 3 DON JUAN 6   90 6
   THE AWKWARD SQUAD AND COULD AFFORD TO SQUANDER . . . . 93 3 DON JUAN 7   52 3
   SAVE SUCH AS SOUTHEY CAN AFFORD TO GIVE . . . . 243 3 DON JUAN 10   37 4
AFFORDING
   THEY'RE RIGHT OUR DAYS ARE TOO BRIEF FOR AFFORDING   . . 270 3 DON JUAN 11   4 5
AFFORDS
   WHICH LAW AFFORDS TO MANY A DIRTY DEED . . . . 151 2 DON JUAN 1 V 2 4
   ALTHOUGH DEFIANCE OFT DECLINED AFFORDS   . . . . . . 153 2 DON JUAN 1 V 4 5
   AS BUT TO LOVERS A TRUE SENSE AFFORDS . . . . 351 2 DON JUAN 4   14 6
AFFRIGHT
   WHENCE HER FAIR HAIR ROSE TWINING WITH AFFRIGHT   . . . 158 3 DON JUAN 8   93 2
AFFRONT
   IT HAD BEEN AN AFFRONT ON THIS OCCASION . . . . 330 3 DON JUAN 12   30 5
AFFRONTING
   IN POLITESSE AND HAVE A SOUND AFFRONTING IN'T--   . . . 289 3 DON JUAN 11   43 6
AFLOAT
   AND KEEP THE SHIP AFLOAT THOUGH THREE FEET YET . . . . 172 2 DON JUAN 2   30 3
   THAT STILL COULD KEEP AFLOAT THE STRUGGLING TARS . . . 183 2 DON JUAN 2   51 3
   WERE COUNTED IN THEM WHEN THEY GOT AFLOAT   . . . . . 185 2 DON JUAN 2   54 8
   AND DRIVELS SEAS TO SET IT WELL AFLOAT   . . . . . . 333 2 DON JUAN 3   98 8
   FRAIL MARINERS AFLOAT WITHOUT A CHART . . . . 442 3 DON JUAN 14   74 5

```
                                                    PAGE VOL        CANTO STANZA LN
AFORESAID
  SO WELL NOT ONE OF THE AFORESAID PAINTS  . . . . . . .  47  2 DON JUAN  1     47   6
  (THE AFORESAID BABA) JUST THEN TO DO MORE  . . . . . .  57  3 DON JUAN  6    103   6
  THE ANIMALS AFORESAID OCCUPIED . . . . . . . . . . .   249  3 DON JUAN 10     51   1
AFRAID
  SOMETHING OF WHICH ITS MASTERS ARE AFRAID  . . . . . .  18  2 DON JUAN  D     14   3
  'TIS SURELY JUAN NOW--NO I'M AFRAID  . . . . . . . . .  63  2 DON JUAN  1     76   7
  OF GOBLINS BUT STILL MORE OF MEN AFRAID  . . . . . . .  98  2 DON JUAN  1    141   3
  YET HALF AFRAID TO VENTURE FOR THE DRAUGHT  . . . . .  155  2 DON JUAN  1  V   6   2
  HIS BERTH A LITTLE DAMP AND HIM AFRAID  . . . . . . .  169  2 DON JUAN  2     25   8
  BUT WAS USED SPARINGLY--SOME WERE AFRAID  . . . . . .  200  2 DON JUAN  2     82   2
  WHICH SHE MUST STILL PURSUE HOWE'ER AFRAID  . . . . .  361  2 DON JUAN  4     32   5
  HE WHISPERED JUAN NOT TO BE AFRAID . . . . . . . . .   473  2 DON JUAN  5    107   5
  OCCURRED WHAT OFTEN HAPPENS I'M AFRAID  . . . . . . .  355  3 DON JUAN 12     85   3
  BUT THEN THE ROLL-CALL DRAWS THEM BACK AFRAID  . . . . 417  3 DON JUAN 14     17   3
AFRIC
  AFRIC IS ALL THE SUN'S AND AS HER EARTH  . . . . . . . 374  2 DON JUAN  4     56   1
  FOR EUROPE PLOUGHS IN AFRIC LIKE BOS PIGER  . . . . .  348  2 DON JUAN 12     70   6
AFRICA
  SOME WENT TO AFRICA SOME STAID IN SPAIN  . . . . . . .  52  2 DON JUAN  1     56   7
  THOU MORAL WASHINGTON OF AFRICA . . . . . . . . . .   445  3 DON JUAN 14     82   4
AFRIC'S
  BORN OF THE SUN AS AFRIC'S CLIMATE IS . . . . . . . . 373  2 DON JUAN  4     54  V8
AFT
  AND TOSSED ALONG THE VESSEL FORE AND AFT . . . . . .  155  2 DON JUAN  1  V   6   4
  WHICH STRUCK HER AFT AND MADE AN AWKWARD RIFT  . . . . 170  2 DON JUAN  2     27   3
AFTERNOON
  AND THUS THEY WALK'D OUT IN THE AFTERNOON  . . . . . . 249  2 DON JUAN  2    176   7
  I CANTER BY THE SPOT EACH AFTERNOON  . . . . . . . . . 400  2 DON JUAN  4    103   1
AFTERNOONS
  HIS AFTERNOONS HE PASSED IN VISITS LUNCHEONS  . . . .  301  3 DON JUAN 11     66   1
AFTERWARDS
  ALTHOUGH THEIR PORTER AFTERWARDS CONFESS'D  . . . . .   34  2 DON JUAN  1     24   5
  AND AFTERWARDS ACCOMPANIED US THROUGH . . . . . . .   103  3 DON JUAN  7     72   3
  AND AFTERWARDS IF HE MUST NEEDS DESTROY  . . . . . .   123  3 DON JUAN  8     24   5
  KOUTOUSOW HE WHO AFTERWARDS BEAT BACK  . . . . . . .   147  3 DON JUAN  8     70   1
AGACERIE
  BEGAN TO TREAT HIM WITH SOME SMALL AGACERIE . . . . .  428  3 DON JUAN 14     41   8
AGAMEMMON
  BRAVE MEN WERE LIVING BEFORE AGAMEMMON  . . . . . . .   24  2 DON JUAN  1      5   1
AGE
  THE AGE DISCOVERS HE IS NOT THE TRUE ONE . . . . . .   21  2 DON JUAN  1      1   4
  BUT CAN'T FIND ANY IN THE PRESENT AGE . . . . . . .    24  2 DON JUAN  1      5   6
  YOUNG JUAN NOW WAS SIXTEEN YEARS OF AGE  . . . . . .   51  2 DON JUAN  1     54   1
  PREFER A SPOUSE WHOSE AGE IS SHORT OF THIRTY  . . . .  56  2 DON JUAN  1     62   8
  NOT ONLY OF THE AGE AND YEAR BUT MOON . . . . . . .    76  2 DON JUAN  1    103   3
  THIS IS THE AGE OF ODDITIES LET LOOSE . . . . . . .    91  2 DON JUAN  1    128   5
  THIS IS THE PATENT AGE OF NEW INVENTIONS . . . . . .   93  2 DON JUAN  1    132   1
  AT THAT AGE HE WOULD BE TOO OLD FOR SLAUGHTER  . . .  106  2 DON JUAN  1    155   2
  A YEAR OR TWO'S AN AGE WHEN RIGHTLY SPENT  . . . . .  228  2 DON JUAN  2    136   5
  ACCORDING TO THEIR SIZE AND AGE AND LENGTH  . . . . . 283  2 DON JUAN  3     15  V7
  A DAY OF GOLD FROM OUT AN AGE OF IRON . . . . . . .   294  2 DON JUAN  3     36   3
  JUST AS OLD AGE IS CREEPING ON APACE . . . . . . .    305  2 DON JUAN  3     59   5
  THIS IS A LIBERAL AGE AND THOUGHTS ARE FREE  . . . .  347  2 DON JUAN  4      7   6
  BY AGE IN EARTH HER DAYS AND PLEASURES WERE  . . . .  382  2 DON JUAN  4     71   5
  WAS JUAN WHO--AN AWKWARD THING AT HIS AGE  . . . . .  394  2 DON JUAN  4     92   7
  WHO SAY STRANGE THINGS FOR SO CORRECT AN AGE  . . . . 397  2 DON JUAN  4     98   4
  UNTIL THE MEMORY OF AN AGE IS FLED . . . . . . . .    399  2 DON JUAN  4    102   3
  AND AGE AND SEX WERE IN THE MARKET RANGED  . . . . .  414  2 DON JUAN  5      7   2
  AS MOST AT HIS AGE ARE OF HOPE AND HEALTH  . . . . .  415  2 DON JUAN  5      8   2
  THE CAPTIVES SEEMED TO MARK THEIR LOOKS AND AGE  . .  424  2 DON JUAN  5     26   3
  PERHAPS THE FAULT OF HER SOFT SEX AND AGE--  . . . .  490  2 DON JUAN  5    136   6
  OF WHOM ALL SUCH AS CAME OF AGE WERE STOWED  . . . .  498  2 DON JUAN  5    152   2
  THE AGE OF GOLD (WHEN GOLD WAS YET UNKNOWN  . . . . .  33  3 DON JUAN  6     55   2
  EXTREMELY COMMON IN THIS AGE WHOSE METAL . . . . . .   33  3 DON JUAN  6     55   7
  A LADY OF A CERTAIN AGE WHICH MEANS  . . . . . . .     41  3 DON JUAN  6     69   2
  HIMSELF IN AT THE AGE WHEN ALL GROW GOOD  . . . . .    43  3 DON JUAN  6     75   4
  I MEAN THAT EVERY AGE AND EVERY YEAR . . . . . . .   108  3 DON JUAN  7     83   2
  THINK WHAT IT IS TO BE IN YOUR OLD AGE . . . . . .   118  3 DON JUAN  8     14   2
  OF HIS OLD AGE IN WILDS OF DEEPEST MAZE  . . . . . . 143  3 DON JUAN  8     61   8
  AN ACTIVE HERMIT EVEN IN AGE THE CHILD . . . . . .   144  3 DON JUAN  8     63   7
  IN BATTLE TO OLD AGE AND UGLINESS  . . . . . . . .   167  3 DON JUAN  8    112  V4
  SPARED NEITHER SEX NOR AGE IN THEIR CAREER  . . . .  171  3 DON JUAN  8    119   2
  BESIDES HE WAS OF THAT DELIGHTED AGE . . . . . . .   217  3 DON JUAN  9     69   1
  THE TRUTH AND THOUGH GRIEF HER OLD AGE MIGHT SHORTEN  222  3 DON JUAN  9     81   5
  OF AGE AND LOOKING BACK TO YOUTH GIVE ONE TEAR--  . . 238  3 DON JUAN 10     27   8
  WHOSE AGE AND WHAT WAS BETTER STILL WHOSE NATION  . . 241  3 DON JUAN 10     33   3
  TALK NOT OF SEVENTY YEARS AS AGE IN SEVEN  . . . . . 309  3 DON JUAN 11     82   1
  WHICH IS THE MOST BARBAROUS IS THE MIDDLE AGE  . . .  315  3 DON JUAN 12      1   2
  FOR WHEN THEY HAPPEN AT A RIPER AGE  . . . . . . .   339  3 DON JUAN 12     50   2
  THOUGH THIS WE HOPE--HAS BEEN RESERVED FOR THIS AGE  376  3 DON JUAN 13     39  V5
  SLEEPS FROM THE CHIVALRY OF THIS BRIGHT AGE  . . . .  378  3 DON JUAN 13     44   6
  BUT WHAT WE CAN WE GLEAN IN THIS VILE AGE  . . . . .  403  3 DON JUAN 13     97   1
  AN AGE MAY COME FONT OF ETERNITY  . . . . . . . .    411  3 DON JUAN 14      3   5
  BUT ADELINE WAS FAR FROM THAT RIPE AGE . . . . . .   433  3 DON JUAN 14     54   1
  A PAGE WHERE TIME SHOULD HESITATE TO PRINT AGE  . . . 458  3 DON JUAN 15      7   5
  CAN'T LIKE RIPE AGE IN GOURMANDISE EXCEL . . . . .   487  3 DON JUAN 15     70   6
  HAS NOT THE NATURAL STAYS OF STRICT OLD AGE  . . . .  494  3 DON JUAN 15     85   6
  AN AGE--EXPECTANT POWERLESS WITH HIS EYES  . . . . .  511  3 DON JUAN 16     25   2
```

AGED
	PAGE	VOL	CANTO	STANZA	LN
CERTAINLY AGED--WHAT HER YEARS MIGHT BE	41	3 DON JUAN	6	69	3
CHILD OR AN AGED HELPLESS MAN OR TWO--	174	3 DON JUAN	8	124	4
THEY ERRED AS AGED MEN WILL DO BUT BY	285	3 DON JUAN	11	36	1
FOR LIKE AN AGED AUNT OR TIRESOME FRIEND	334	3 DON JUAN	12	39	4
LESS LIKE A YOUNG WIFE THAN AN AGED SISTER	440	3 DON JUAN	14	69	8
SINCE BURNING AGED WOMEN (SAVE A FEW--	565	3 DON JUAN	17	7	3

AGENT
A SUPERNATURAL AGENT--OR A MOUSE	509	3 DON JUAN	16	20	6

AGE'S
THEIR LUCKIER VOTARIES TILL OLD AGE'S TEDIUM	235	3 DON JUAN	10	22	7

AGES
WHO IN THE EARLIER AGES RAISED A BUSTLE	44	2 DON JUAN	1	41	3
TO MEET THE INGENUOUS YOUTH OF FUTURE AGES	46	2 DON JUAN	1	45	4
OF AGES TO WHAT STRAITS OLD TIME REDUCES	327	2 DON JUAN	3	88	6
OF AGES ON ITS WATER-FRETTED HALLS	362	2 DON JUAN	4	33	3
WHERE TWENTY AGES GATHER O'ER A NAME	398	2 DON JUAN	4	100	4
ALL EARS THOUGH LONG ALL AGES THOUGH SO SHORT	106	3 DON JUAN	7	79	2
WHICH MAKES ALL FEMALE AGES EQUAL--WHEN	217	3 DON JUAN	9	69	2
OF ALL THE BARBAROUS MIDDLE AGES THAT	315	3 DON JUAN	12	1	1
WHOSE TALE BELONGS TO HALLAM'S MIDDLE AGES	330	3 DON JUAN	12	30	8
COUNTRY WHERE A YOUNG COUPLE OF THE SAME AGES	346	3 DON JUAN	12	65	2
LOOK BACK O'ER AGES ERE UNTO THE STAKE FAST	411	3 DON JUAN	14	2	5
A DULL AND FAMILY LIKENESS THROUGH ALL AGES	416	3 DON JUAN	14	15	7
OLD SKELETON WITH AGES FOR YOUR BOOTY	459	3 DON JUAN	15	9	V5
LASH'D FROM THE FOAM OF AGES WHILE THE GRAVES	500	3 DON JUAN	15	99	7
ITS GLORY THROUGH ALL AGES SHINING SUNNY	529	3 DON JUAN	16	59	7
BECAUSE AS AGES UPON AGES PUSH ON	564	3 DON JUAN	17	6	3
BECAUSE AS AGES UPON AGES PUSH ON	564	3 DON JUAN	17	6	3
THE LOFTIEST MINDS OUTRUN THEIR TARDY AGES	566	3 DON JUAN	17	9	5

AGGRAVATE
BUT AGGRAVATE THE CRIME YOU HAVE NOT PREVENTED	353	3 DON JUAN	12	80	7

AGGREGATE
A DAILY PLAGUE WHICH IN THE AGGREGATE	420	3 DON JUAN	14	24	1

AGHAST
THE GOOD OLD GENTLEMAN WAS QUITE AGHAST	175	2 DON JUAN	2	37	1

AGITATED
FOR SHE SEEMED AGITATED FLUSHED AND FRIGHTENED	42	3 DON JUAN	6	72	7
SO AGITATED WAS SHE WITH HER ERROR	50	3 DON JUAN	6	89	7

AGO
HINT THAT SOME SIX OR SEVEN GOOD YEARS AGO	143	2 DON JUAN	1	212	4
THUS HORACE WROTE WE ALL KNOW LONG AGO	470	2 DON JUAN	5	101	5
SAW--WELL NO MATTER 'TWAS SO LONG AGO	517	3 DON JUAN	16	38	3

AGONIES
AND SAW HIS AGONIES WITH SUCH SUBLIMITY	36	2 DON JUAN	1	29	7
AND NATURAL AGONIES WITH A SLIGHT SHADE	102	3 DON JUAN	7	69	4
ARE PURCHASED BY ALL AGONIES AND CRIMES	174	3 DON JUAN	8	125	2

AGONIZED
STANDS ON HER TRIPOD AGONIZED AND FULL	59	3 DON JUAN	6	107	2

AGONIZING
OF HUMAN NATURE'S AGONIZING VOICE	142	3 DON JUAN	8	59	8

AGONY
OF SOME STRONG SWIMMER IN HIS AGONY	184	2 DON JUAN	2	53	8
OH DEAREST FATHER IN THIS AGONY	364	2 DON JUAN	4	38	4
GULBEYAZ PROVED IN THAT BRIEF AGONY	59	3 DON JUAN	6	106	7
BY THE INFINITIES OF AGONY	118	3 DON JUAN	8	13	3

AGRARIAN
WITH HIS AGRARIAN LAWS THE HIGH ESTATE	237	3 DON JUAN	10	25	3

AGREE
SO SAYS THE PROVERB--AND I QUITE AGREE	25	2 DON JUAN	1	8	4
AGREE TO A SHORT ARMISTICE WITH TRUTH	318	3 DON JUAN	3	83	8
AND DON'T AGREE AT ALL WITH THE WISE ROMAN	10	3 DON JUAN	6	7	6
IF I AGREE THAT WHAT IS IS THEN THIS I CALL	270	3 DON JUAN	11	5	3

AGREEABLE
THE FAVOUR OF THE EMPRESS WAS AGREEABLE	235	3 DON JUAN	10	22	1
A QUALITY AGREEABLE TO WOMAN	426	3 DON JUAN	14	36	5

AGREED
HIS PARENTS NE'ER AGREED EXCEPT IN DOTING	34	2 DON JUAN	1	25	3

AGREEING
UNTIL I SEE BOTH SIDES FOR ONCE AGREEING	190	3 DON JUAN	9	16	6

AGROUND
RUNNING AGROUND WAS TAKEN BY THE TURKS	81	3 DON JUAN	7	30	8

AGUE
AGUE IN ITS COLD FIT THEY FILL'D THEIR BOAT	189	2 DON JUAN	2	63	7
WHAT THEY SHOULD LAUGH AT--THE MERE AGUE STILL	366	3 DON JUAN	13	17	7

AGUISH
FOR WIT HATH NO GREAT FRIEND IN AGUISH FOLKS	540	3 DON JUAN	16	83	3
FOR LAUGHTER RARELY SHAKES THESE AGUISH FOLKS	540	3 DON JUAN	16	83	V3

AHEAD
THOUGH RIGHT AHEAD THE ROARING BREAKERS LAY	211	2 DON JUAN	2	104	4

AI
WHO WOULD NOT SIGH AI AI TAN KUTHEREIAN	554	3 DON JUAN	16	109	1
WHO WOULD NOT SIGH AI AI TAN KUTHEREIAN	554	3 DON JUAN	16	109	1

AID
BUT NOT A SERVANT STIRR'D TO AID THE FIGHT	122	2 DON JUAN	1	184	3
BUT SOON PHILOSOPHY CAME TO MY AID	268	2 DON JUAN	2	210	1
WITH SOME SMALL AID FROM SCISSORS PAINT AND TWEEZERS	458	2 DON JUAN	5	80	2
BY THIS OLD BLACK ENCHANTER'S UNSOUGHT AID	459	2 DON JUAN	5	83	8
EXCEPT HIS MAJESTY WHO WITH HER AID	22	3 DON JUAN	6	32	3

11

		PAGE	VOL		CANTO	STANZA	LN

AID (CONTINUED)
HER AID TO FAIR JUANNA WHOSE EXCESS . . . . 36 3 DON JUAN 6 61 3
WITHOUT THE AID OF PRINCE OR PLENIPO . . . . 53 3 DON JUAN 6 95 6
AND THEN HE CALLED HIS BRETHREN TO HIS AID . . . . . 64 3 DON JUAN 6 118 1
SEEING ARRIVE AN AID SO OPPORTUNE . . . . 140 3 DON JUAN 8 56 2
'TWERE NOT FOR WANT OF LAMPS TO AID HIS DODGING HIS . . . 281 3 DON JUAN 11 28 5
WITHOUT THE AID OF TOO SINCERE A POET . . . . 311 3 DON JUAN 11 87 8
TO AID THE DAMSEL AND DESTROY THE CAITIFF . . . . . 363 3 DON JUAN 13 10 2
AIDED
THE TURKISH FIRE AND AIDED BY THEIR OWN . . . . . . 81 3 DON JUAN 7 30 2
WITH THEIR ATTENDANT AIDED OUR ESCAPE . . . . 103 3 DON JUAN 7 72 2
AND THAT WHICH FURTHER AIDED THEM TO STRIVE . . . . 136 3 DON JUAN 8 47 6
AIDS
BESIDES THEIR RESURRECTION AIDS OUR GLORIES . . . . . 37 2 DON JUAN 1 31 5
AIGRETTE
AN EMERALD AIGRETTE WITH HAIDEE'S HAIR IN'T . . . . . 315 2 DON JUAN 3 77 6
AILS
OF CHARMS TO MAKE GOOD GOLD AND CURE BAD AILS . . . . 293 2 DON JUAN 3 34 5
AIM
MOST LIKELY TO ATTAIN HER AIM--HIS HEART . . . . . . 492 2 DON JUAN 5 140 8
WHERE EVERYBODY HAS SOME SEPARATE AIM . . . . 342 2 DON JUAN 12 58 5
AT WHICH ALL MODERN NATIONS VAINLY AIM . . . . 367 3 DON JUAN 13 20 5
IN RUSSET JACKET--LYNX-LIKE IS HIS AIM . . . . 394 3 DON JUAN 13 75 5
NOT STINGS AND FLITS THROUGH ETHER WITHOUT AIM . . . 400 3 DON JUAN 13 89 6
AS ALL MUST BLEND WHOSE PART IT IS TO AIM . . . . . 546 3 DON JUAN 16 95 5
AIR
POSSESS'D AN AIR AND GRACE BY NO MEANS COMMON . . . . 55 2 DON JUAN 1 61 7
SHE SEEM'D BY THE DISTRACTION OF HER AIR . . . . . . 80 2 DON JUAN 1 110 4
SOONER SHALL THIS BLUE OCEAN MELT TO AIR . . . . . . 166 2 DON JUAN 2 19 3
THE FOURTH DAY CAME BUT NOT A BREATH OF AIR . . . . 193 2 DON JUAN 2 70 1
THAT WAVED IN FOREST-TOPS AND SMOOTH'D THE AIR . . . 210 2 DON JUAN 2 103 4
THEY NEARLY REACH'D HER HEEL AND IN HER AIR . . . . 217 2 DON JUAN 2 116 6
WAS COARSER AND HER AIR THOUGH FIRM LESS FREE . . . 221 2 DON JUAN 2 122 6
BESIDES I HATE ALL MYSTERY AND THAT AIR . . . . . . 222 2 DON JUAN 2 124 3
HAD ALL THE ADVANTAGE TOO OF NOT BEING AIR . . . . . 232 2 DON JUAN 2 142 8
AND WRAPT HIM CLOSER LEST THE AIR TOO RAW . . . . . 232 2 DON JUAN 2 143 6
AS O'ER HIM LAY THE CALM AND STIRLESS AIR . . . . . 233 2 DON JUAN 2 144 4
STOP CRIED PHILOSOPHY WITH AIR SO GRECIAN . . . . . 268 2 DON JUAN 2 210 7
OVER HIS SHOULDER WITH A BACCHANT AIR . . . . 297 2 DON JUAN 3 43 2
THE VERY AIR SEEM'D LIGHTER FROM HER EYES . . . . . 313 2 DON JUAN 3 74 7
OF OCEAN--NO OF AIR AND THEN HE MAKES . . . . 333 2 DON JUAN 3 98 6
AND NOT A BREATH CREPT THROUGH THE ROSY AIR . . . . 335 2 DON JUAN 3 102 7
EARTH AIR STARS--ALL THAT SPRINGS FROM THE GREAT WHOLE . . 336 2 DON JUAN 3 104 7
THE HEAVENS AND EARTH AND AIR SEEM'D MADE FOR THEM . . 351 2 DON JUAN 4 13 2
STIRR'D WITH HER DREAM AS ROSE-LEAVES WITH THE AIR . . 359 2 DON JUAN 4 29 8
TERROR TO EARTH AND TEMPEST TO THE AIR . . . . . . 375 2 DON JUAN 4 57 4
AND EVER-DYING GLADIATOR'S AIR . . . . 377 2 DON JUAN 4 61 6
YET HAS A SENTIMENTAL KIND OF AIR . . . . 390 2 DON JUAN 4 85 6
YET HAS A KIND OF SOFT AND SILLY AIR . . . . 390 2 DON JUAN 4 85 V6
HAVE GOT A TRAVELL'D AIR WHICH SHOWS YOU ONE . . . . 392 2 DON JUAN 4 88 3
AND AIR--EARTH--WATER--FIRE LIVE--AND WE DEAD . . . 432 2 DON JUAN 5 39 6
THE LADY RISING UP WITH SUCH AN AIR . . . . 466 2 DON JUAN 5 96 1
BUT JUST REMARKED WITH AIR SEDATE AND WISE . . . . . 500 2 DON JUAN 5 155 5
AS DOTH A RAINBOW THE JUST CLEARING AIR . . . . . . 17 3 DON JUAN 6 23 8
BEATING FOR LOVE AS THE CAGED BIRDS FOR AIR . . . . 19 3 DON JUAN 6 26 8
HER SHAPE HER HAIR HER AIR HER EVERYTHING . . . . . 23 3 DON JUAN 6 35 2
THEN ONE VAST FIRE AIR EARTH AND STREAM EMBRACED . . 115 3 DON JUAN 8 7 5
HE RUSHED WHILE EARTH AND AIR WERE SADLY SHAKEN . . 129 3 DON JUAN 8 33 7
AIR 'MIDST THE REST WHO KEPT THEIR VALIANT FACES . . 130 3 DON JUAN 8 34 7
AIR MIDST THE REST WHOSE SHORT BREATH AND LONG FACES . . 130 3 DON JUAN 8 34 V7
WHEN THE STRIPT FOREST BOWS TO THE BLEAK AIR . . . . 155 3 DON JUAN 8 88 4
AND HUMAN BREATH IS POURED UPON THE AIR . . . . . . 155 3 DON JUAN 8 88 V2
THE LETTER OPEN WITH AN AIR WHICH POSED . . . . . . 211 3 DON JUAN 9 58 4
AS MY FRIEND JEFFREY WRITES WITH SUCH AN AIR . . . . 230 3 DON JUAN 10 11 6
FROM THE ENJOYMENT OF THE EARTH AND AIR . . . . . . 258 3 DON JUAN 10 68 7
BUT DOUBTLESS AS THE AIR THOUGH SELDOM SUNNY . . . . 259 3 DON JUAN 10 70 7
AIR CAN ACCOMPLISH WITH HIS WIDE WINGS WAVING . . . 263 3 DON JUAN 10 78 4
I DON'T KNOW WHAT THE REASON IS--THE AIR . . . . . . 270 3 DON JUAN 11 5 6
AN AIR AS SENTIMENTAL AS MOZART'S . . . . 292 3 DON JUAN 11 47 3
CAN FORM A SLIGHT ACQUAINTANCE WITH FRESH AIR . . . 301 3 DON JUAN 11 66 8
DISSOLVING IN THE WALTZ TO SOME SOFT AIR . . . . . . 303 3 DON JUAN 11 70 6
AND FRAILER SINCE WITHOUT A BREATH OF AIR . . . . . 306 3 DON JUAN 11 76 V5
BESIDES THE MARKED DISTINCTION OF HIS AIR . . . . . 355 3 DON JUAN 12 85 6
AND I SHALL TAKE A MUCH MORE SERIOUS AIR . . . . . . 454 3 DON JUAN 14 99 5
OR THAT HE HAD AN AIR OF INNOCENCE . . . . 468 3 DON JUAN 15 28 5
BUT STILL HER ASPECT HAD AN AIR SO LONELY . . . . . 475 3 DON JUAN 15 44 3
AND WITH AN AIR TO SAY THE LEAST IMPERIOUS . . . . . 477 3 DON JUAN 15 49 6
THE DASHING AND PROUD AIR OF ADELINE . . . . 480 3 DON JUAN 15 56 1
THE GRASS MY TABLE-CLOTH IN OPEN AIR . . . . 488 3 DON JUAN 15 73 6
ONCE TWICE THRICE PASSED REPASSED--THE THING OF AIR . . 510 3 DON JUAN 16 23 1
TO PUT THE QUESTION WITH AN AIR SEDATE . . . . . . 515 3 DON JUAN 16 35 6
THE AIR OF 'TWAS A FRIAR OF ORDERS GREY . . . . . . 517 3 DON JUAN 16 38 8
FOR HE MUTTERS HIS PRAYER IN THE MIDNIGHT AIR . . . 518 3 DON JUAN 16 L 1 3
THE LAWYERS IN THE STUDY AND IN AIR . . . . 533 3 DON JUAN 16 66 3
WHO WONDERED AT THE ABSTRACTION OF HIS AIR . . . . . 544 3 DON JUAN 16 91 3
HER GRACE TOO HAD A SORT OF AIR REBUKED-- . . . . . 568 3 DON JUAN 17 14 6
AIR-BALLOONS
OF AIR-BALLOONS AND OF THE MANY BARS . . . . 71 2 DON JUAN 1 92 6
AIRIEST
TOO SUBTLE FOR THE AIRIEST HUMAN HEAD . . . . 268 3 DON JUAN 11 1 4

AIRS
    WHILE ADELINE DISPENSED HER AIRS AND GRACES 548   3 DON JUAN 16   100   1
AIRY
    THE AIRY CHILD OF VAPOUR AND THE SUN 205   2 DON JUAN 2   92   2
    AND LOVE OF GLORY'S BUT AN AIRY LUST 399   2 DON JUAN 4   101   2
    AN AIRY INSTRUMENT WITH WHICH HE SOUGHT 406   2 DON JUAN 4   112   5
    OF THINGS DESTROYED AND LEFT IN AIRY DOUBT 201   3 DON JUAN 9   38   4
    UPON THEIR AIRY CONFINE HALF-SEAS-OVER   255   3 DON JUAN 10   61   8
    BUT A MERE AIRY AND FANTASTIC BASIS 413   3 DON JUAN 14   7   7
    BUT LIGHT AND AIRY STOOD ON THE ALERT 426   3 DON JUAN 14   37   1
AISLE
    IN A GRAND ARCH WHICH ONCE SCREENED MANY AN AISLE 386   3 DON JUAN 13   59   3
AJAR
    A KIND OF SHOCK THAT SETS ONE'S HEART AJAR 164   2 DON JUAN 2   14   6
AJAX
    PATROCLUS AJAX OR PROTESILAUS 385   2 DON JUAN 4   76   7
    THIS SIMILE ENOUGH FOR AJAX JUAN   126   3 DON JUAN 8   29   7
    AND THOUGH HIS NAME THAN AJAX OR ACHILLES 132   3 DON JUAN 8   39   2
ALABASTER
    WHITE WAXEN AND AS ALABASTER PALE 60   3 DON JUAN 6   109   4
    LIKE TO A LIGHTED ALABASTER VASE--   159   3 DON JUAN 8   96   8
ALACK
    'TIS NOT MY FAULT--I KEPT GOOD WATCH--ALACK 96   2 DON JUAN 1   137   4
ALACRITY
    I ONCE HAD A GREAT ALACRITY IN WIELDING 397   2 DON JUAN 4   98   5
    WAS MADE WITH ALL ALACRITY THE FIRST 91   3 DON JUAN 7   50   2
ALADDIN'S
    YES READY MONEY IS ALADDIN'S LAMP 321   3 DON JUAN 12   12   8
ALARM
    TO SCOLD A LITTLE AT THE FALSE ALARM 45   3 DON JUAN 6   79   3
ALARMED
    THE EMPRESS WAS ALARMED AND HER PHYSICIAN 244   3 DON JUAN 10   39   2
ALARMING
    THING QUITE IN COURSE AND NOT AT ALL ALARMING 68   2 DON JUAN 1   86   7
    AND MAKES MEN'S MISERIES OF ALARMING BREVITY   190   2 DON JUAN 2   64   8
ALAS
    BUT WHO ALAS CAN LOVE AND THEN BE WISE   84   2 DON JUAN 1   117   5
    ALAS 'TWAS NOT IN THEM BUT IN THY POWER 144   2 DON JUAN 1   214   7
    SAY VERY OFTEN TO MYSELF ALAS 147   2 DON JUAN 1   220   2
    THEIR VEIL AND PETTICOAT--ALAS TO DWELL 160   2 DON JUAN 2   6   4
    OR RATHER STOMACH WHICH ALAS ATTENDS 167   2 DON JUAN 2   21   2
    HAD LEFT THEIR BODIES AND WHAT'S WORSE ALAS 185   2 DON JUAN 2   55   2
    ALAS THEY WERE SO YOUNG SO BEAUTIFUL 258   2 DON JUAN 2   192   1
    ALAS FOR JUAN AND HAIDEE THEY WERE 258   2 DON JUAN 2   193   1
    ALAS THE LOVE OF WOMEN IT IS KNOWN 262   2 DON JUAN 2   199   1
    OER WHOSE SAD TALE LOVE ECHOS STILL ALAS-- 273   2 DON JUAN 2   V   2   3
    HE HEARS--ALAS NO MUSIC OF THE SPHERES   290   2 DON JUAN 3   28   3
    HE DID NOT KNOW (ALAS HOW MEN WILL LIE) 295   2 DON JUAN 3   38   1
    ALAS HIS COUNTRY SHOW'D NO PATH TO PRAISE 303   2 DON JUAN 3   55   6
    ALAS THERE IS NO INSTINCT LIKE THE HEART--   349   2 DON JUAN 4   10   8
    ALAS SAID JUAN 'TWERE A TALE DISTRESSING 419   2 DON JUAN 5   16   5
    ALAS MAN MAKES THAT GREAT WHICH MAKES HIM LITTLE . . . 444   2 DON JUAN 5   59   1
    WHERE ALL THE PASSIONS HAVE ALAS BUT ONE VENT 22   3 DON JUAN 6   32   8
    NEWTON (THAT PROVERB OF THE MIND) ALAS   69   3 DON JUAN 7   5   5
    ALAS WHAT TO THEIR MEMORY CAN LACK 73   3 DON JUAN 7   14   5
    WHOSE STATUES WARM (I FEAR ALAS TOO TRUE 'TIS) 208   3 DON JUAN 9   51   6
    UNEQUAL MATCHES SUCH AS ARE ALAS 236   3 DON JUAN 10   24   3
    ALAS THAT GLORY SHOULD BE CHILLED BY SNOW 254   3 DON JUAN 10   59   5
    ALAS COULD SHE BUT FULLY TRULY KNOW 258   3 DON JUAN 10   67   1
    ALAS HOW DEEPLY PAINFUL IS ALL PAYMENT   264   3 DON JUAN 10   79   1
    THE WORLD IN WHICH A MAN WAS BORN ALAS   306   3 DON JUAN 11   76   2
    BESIDES (ALAS HIS TASTE--FORGIVE AND PITY)   347   3 DON JUAN 12   68   7
    ALAS MUST NOBLEST VIEWS LIKE AN OLD SONG 363   3 DON JUAN 13   10   5
    ALAS TO THEM OF READY CASH BEREFT 379   3 DON JUAN 13   45   3
    THE DAYS OF COMEDY ARE GONE ALAS 402   3 DON JUAN 13   94   5
    ALAS POOR GHOST--WHAT UNEXPECTED WOES 403   3 DON JUAN 13   97   7
    ALAS WORLDS FALL--AND WOMAN SINCE SHE FELL'D   420   3 DON JUAN 14   23   1
    BUT TILL THAT POINT D'APPUI IS FOUND ALAS 446   3 DON JUAN 14   84   7
    ALAS BY ALL EXPERIENCE SELDOM YET 452   3 DON JUAN 14   95   1
    IN THEIR RESOLVES--ALAS THAT I SHOULD SAY SO   458   3 DON JUAN 15   6   4
    BY DEATH WHEN WE ARE LEFT ALAS BEHIND 475   3 DON JUAN 15   44   6
    IT WAS NOT--BUT 'TIS EASIER FAR ALAS 479   3 DON JUAN 15   54   7
    ALAS I MUST LEAVE UNDESCRIBED THE GIBIER 487   3 DON JUAN 15   71   1
    BUT I HAVE DINED AND MUST FOREGO ALAS 487   3 DON JUAN 15   71   7
    TREATING A TOPIC WHICH ALAS BUT BRINGS   500   3 DON JUAN 15   98   6
    THAT SCARLET CLOAK ALAS UNCLOSED WITH RIGOUR   530   3 DON JUAN 16   61   7
    THERE WERE SOME COUNTRY WAGS TOO--AND ALAS   539   3 DON JUAN 16   81   1
    ALAS HER STAR MUST WANE LIKE THAT OF DIAN 554   3 DON JUAN 16   109   3
    CAME OVER JUAN'S EAR WHICH THROBBED ALAS 556   3 DON JUAN 16   114   5
    AND THEY REVEALED--ALAS THAT ERE THEY SHOULD   561   3 DON JUAN 16   123   6
ALBANO'S
    HERE DANCED ALBANO'S BOYS AND HERE THE SEA SHONE 392   3 DON JUAN 13   71   5
ALBEIT
    AND JUAN AND HIS FRIEND ALBEIT THEY HEARD 439   2 DON JUAN 5   50   2
    UNCONSCIOUS ALBEIT TURNED OF QUICK SEVENTEEN   33   3 DON JUAN 6   54   6
    EVEN I--ALBEIT I'M SURE I DID NOT KNOW IT 296   3 DON JUAN 11   55   5
    ALBEIT MY YEARS WERE LESS DISCREET THAN FEW 334   3 DON JUAN 12   38   4
    ALBEIT ALL HUMAN HISTORY ATTESTS   404   3 DON JUAN 13   99   6
    AND EATS HER PARENTS ALBEIT THE DIGESTION 411   3 DON JUAN 14   2   2
    'TWIXT PLACE AND PATRIOTISM--ALBEIT COMPELLED 535   3 DON JUAN 16   72   4

13

			PAGE	VOL		CANTO	STANZA	LN
ALBION								
'TWAS A GREAT BANQUET SUCH AS ALBION OLD			538	3	DON JUAN	16	78	2
ALBION'S								
AT THE FIRST SIGHT OF ALBION'S CHALKY BELT--			257	3	DON JUAN	10	65	4
DON JUAN NOW SAW ALBION'S EARLIEST BEAUTIES--			259	3	DON JUAN	10	69	1
MAKE THIS A SACRED PART OF ALBION'S ISLE			279	3	DON JUAN	11	24	8
ALCHYMIC								
OF SOME ALCHYMIC FURNACE FROM WHENCE BROKE			266	3	DON JUAN	10	83	3
ALCHYMY								
JOY OF ITS ALCHYMY AND TO REPEAT			264	2	DON JUAN	2	203	5
ALCIBIADES								
BECAUSE HE HAD LIKE ALCIBIADES			460	3	DON JUAN	15	11	7
ALDERMAN								
A PRIEST A SHARK AN ALDERMAN OR PIKE			239	2	DON JUAN	2	157	8
BUT MOST AN ALDERMAN STRUCK APOPLECTIC			309	2	DON JUAN	3	66	5
WHO LOVED BLOOD AS AN ALDERMAN LOVES MARROW			70	3	DON JUAN	7	8	8
ALE								
SWEET IS OLD WINE IN BOTTLES ALE IN BARRELS			90	2	DON JUAN	1	126	5
A MIGHTY MUG OF MORAL DOUBLE ALE			533	3	DON JUAN	16	67	4
ALERT								
SUWARROW CHIEFLY WAS ON THE ALERT			95	3	DON JUAN	7	55	1
BUT LIGHT AND AIRY STOOD ON THE ALERT			426	3	DON JUAN	14	37	1
ALEXANDER								
I THINK WITH ALEXANDER THAT THE ACT			428	2	DON JUAN	5	32	1
BUT OH THOU GRAND LEGITIMATE ALEXANDER			52	3	DON JUAN	6	93	1
OH THOU HER LAWFUL GRANDSON ALEXANDER			52	3	DON JUAN	6	93	V1
I AM NEITHER ALEXANDER NOR HEPHAESTION			189	3	DON JUAN	9	14	3
SHUT UP THE BALD-COOT BULLY ALEXANDER			446	3	DON JUAN	14	83	1
ALFONSO								
ALFONSO WAS THE NAME OF JULIA'S LORD			57	2	DON JUAN	1	65	1
FOR DON ALFONSO AND SHE INLY SWORE			80	2	DON JUAN	1	109	2
BY THIS TIME DON ALFONSO WAS ARRIVED			96	2	DON JUAN	1	138	1
IN HEAVEN'S NAME DON ALFONSO WHAT D'YE MEAN			98	2	DON JUAN	1	142	2
SEARCH THEN THE ROOM ALFONSO SAID I WILL			98	2	DON JUAN	1	142	8
A HUSBAND LIKE ALFONSO AT MY SIDE			100	2	DON JUAN	1	145	6
YES DON ALFONSO HUSBAND NOW NO MORE			101	2	DON JUAN	1	146	1
UNGRATEFUL PERJURED BARBAROUS DON ALFONSO			101	2	DON JUAN	1	146	7
THE SENHOR DON ALFONSO STOOD CONFUSED			109	2	DON JUAN	1	159	1
BUT DON ALFONSO STOOD WITH DOWNCAST LOOKS			110	2	DON JUAN	1	161	1
ALFONSO SAW HIS WIFE AND THOUGHT OF JOB'S			110	2	DON JUAN	1	162	6
OR MADAM DIES--ALFONSO MUTTER'D DAMN HER			111	2	DON JUAN	1	163	5
WHAT'S TO BE DONE ALFONSO WILL BE BACK			114	2	DON JUAN	1	169	1
NOW DON ALFONSO ENTERING BUT ALONE			116	2	DON JUAN	1	173	1
ALFONSO PAUSED A MINUTE--THEN BEGUN			116	2	DON JUAN	1	174	1
ALFONSO NE'ER TO JUAN HAD ALLUDED			118	2	DON JUAN	1	177	2
ALFONSO CLOSED HIS SPEECH AND BEGG'D HER PARDON			120	2	DON JUAN	1	180	1
ALFONSO FIRST EXAMINED WELL THEIR FASHION			121	2	DON JUAN	1	181	7
BUT MET ALFONSO IN HIS DRESSING-GOWN			122	2	DON JUAN	1	183	7
ALFONSO POMMELL'D TO HIS HEART'S DESIRE			122	2	DON JUAN	1	184	4
ALFONSO GRAPPLED TO DETAIN THE FOE			124	2	DON JUAN	1	186	1
ALFONSO LEANING BREATHLESS BY THE DOOR			125	2	DON JUAN	1	187	4
AND HOW ALFONSO SUED FOR A DIVORCE			126	2	DON JUAN	1	188	7
ALFONSO'S								
THAT INEZ HAD ERE DON ALFONSO'S MARRIAGE			58	2	DON JUAN	1	66	7
AND COMPLIMENTED DON ALFONSO'S TASTE			58	2	DON JUAN	1	67	6
PERHAPS TO OPEN DON ALFONSO'S EYES			75	2	DON JUAN	1	101	7
AND THEN OF DON ALFONSO'S FIFTY YEARS			78	2	DON JUAN	1	107	4
COULD ENTER INTO DON ALFONSO'S HEAD			97	2	DON JUAN	1	139	2
IN DON ALFONSO'S FACTS WHICH JUST NOW WORE			111	2	DON JUAN	1	164	6
ALFONSO'S LOVES WITH INEZ WERE WELL KNOWN			118	2	DON JUAN	1	176	2
LIKE THROWING JUAN IN ALFONSO'S WAY			118	2	DON JUAN	1	177	8
HASTE--HASTE--I HEAR ALFONSO'S HURRYING FEET--			121	2	DON JUAN	1	182	7
ALFONSO'S SWORD HAD DROPP'D ERE HE COULD DRAW IT			123	2	DON JUAN	1	185	1
ALFONSO'S DAYS HAD NOT BEEN IN THE LAND			123	2	DON JUAN	1	185	6
ALGIERS								
WHO TOOK ALGIERS DECLARES I USED HIM VILELY			102	2	DON JUAN	1	148	8
ALICANT								
GUITARS AND CASTANETS FROM ALICANT			284	2	DON JUAN	3	17	6
ALIGHT								
AROUND US EVER RARELY TO ALIGHT			66	3	DON JUAN	7	1	2
ALIGHTING								
ALIGHTING RARELY--WERE SHE BUT A HORNET			400	3	DON JUAN	13	89	7
ALIIS								
DE REBUS CUNCTIS ET QUIBUSDAM ALIIS			502	3	DON JUAN	16	3	8
ALIKE								
HER DOWRY AND HER VEIL IN FORM ALIKE			221	2	DON JUAN	2	122	5
WERE LINK'D ALIKE AS FOR THE COMMON PEOPLE HE			284	2	DON JUAN	3	16	7
I SAID THEY WERE ALIKE THEIR FEATURES AND			368	2	DON JUAN	4	45	1
THE TIME MUST COME WHEN BOTH ALIKE DECAY'D			400	2	DON JUAN	4	104	5
AND WERE ALL CLAD ALIKE LIKE JUAN TOO			469	2	DON JUAN	5	99	3
THEY ALL ALIKE ADMIRED THEIR NEW CONNEXION			26	3	DON JUAN	6	40	8
ALIKE MIGHT PUZZLE EITHER WIT OR DUNCE			43	3	DON JUAN	6	74	4
HIS JEST ALIKE IN FACE OF FRIEND OR FOE			147	3	DON JUAN	8	70	6
WITH GOOD AND BAD AND WORSE ALIKE PROLIFIC			156	3	DON JUAN	8	89	4
SUCH WAS HIS TACT HE COULD ALIKE DELIGHT			428	3	DON JUAN	14	41	5
AT THE FULL BOARD AND SIT ALIKE DELIGHTED			534	3	DON JUAN	16	69	5
ALIQUANDO								
OMNIA VULT BELLE MATHO DICERE--DIC ALIQUANDO			465	3	DON JUAN	15	21	1
ET BENE DIC NEUTRUM DIC ALIQUANDO MALE			465	3	DON JUAN	15	21	2

14

ALIQUID
    (SURGIT AMARI ALIQUID)--THE TOLL 263   3 DON JUAN 10   78   8
ALIVE
    OR BE ALIVE AGAIN--AGAIN ALL HOAR 15   2 DON JUAN D   11   4
    THAT LURES TO FLAY ALIVE THE YOUNG BEGINNER 294   2 DON JUAN 3   36   6
    ALL HEROES WHEN ALIVE QUITE PROMPT TO SLAY US 385   2 DON JUAN 4   76   V8
    AT LEAST TO ALL THOSE WHO WERE LEFT ALIVE 136   3 DON JUAN 8   47   4
    I WONDER PEOPLE SHOULD BE LEFT ALIVE 316   3 DON JUAN 12   2   3
    BUT OH THAT I WERE DEAD--FOR WHILE ALIVE-- 569   3 DON JUAN 17 V 13   1
ALKALI
    AS ACIDS ROUSE A DORMANT ALKALI) 251   3 DON JUAN 10   54   4
ALLA
    AND ONLY SHOUTED ALLA AND BIS MILLAH 73   3 DON JUAN 7   13   8
ALLAH
    HURRA AND ALLAH AND ONE MOMENT MORE 111   3 DON JUAN 7   87   7
    AND ONE ENORMOUS SHOUT OF ALLAH ROSE 116   3 DON JUAN 8   8   1
    RESOUNDED ALLAH AND THE CLOUDS WHICH CLOSE 116   3 DON JUAN 8   8   5
    ALL SOUNDS IT PIERCETH ALLAH ALLAH HU 116   3 DON JUAN 8   8   8
    ALL SOUNDS IT PIERCETH ALLAH ALLAH HU 116   3 DON JUAN 8   8   8
    HE SHOUTED ALLAH AND SAW PARADISE 169   3 DON JUAN 8   115   3
ALLA'S
    OUR FRIENDS THE TURKS WHO WITH LOUD ALLA'S NOW 87   3 DON JUAN 7   42   1
ALLAY
    'TWAS SOMETHING CALCULATED TO ALLAY 200   3 DON JUAN 9   36   4
ALLAY'D
    INTO A RIVULET AND THUS ALLAY'D 385   3 DON JUAN 13   58   5
ALLAYED
    BLAZED AND THE CANNON'S ROAR WAS SCARCE ALLAYED . . . 178   3 DON JUAN 8   133   4
ALL-CLOUDLESS
    EXCEPT THE ALL-CLOUDLESS GLORY (WHICH FEW MEN'S IS) . . 186   3 DON JUAN 9   8   5
ALL-CONFESSED
    AND IN THIS SCENE OF ALL-CONFESSED INANITY 69   3 DON JUAN 7   6   5
ALLEGORY
    THE ALLEGORY) A MERE TYPE NO MORE 238   2 DON JUAN 2   155   6
ALLER
    BUT LAISSEZ ALLER--KNIGHTS AND DAMES I SING 467   3 DON JUAN 15   25   1
ALLEY
    SHOULD NOW BE BUTCHERED IN A CIVIC ALLEY 431   2 DON JUAN 5   37   8
ALLIANCE
    I THINK THAT WITH THIS HOLY NEW ALLIANCE 142   2 DON JUAN 1   211   1
    LA BELLE ALLIANCE OF DUNCES DOWN AT ZERO 296   3 DON JUAN 11   56   3
ALLIANCES
    AT SUCH ALLIANCES HIS SIRES WOULD FROWN 52   2 DON JUAN 1   57   4
ALLIED
    WERE SATE LIKE UGLY IMPS AS IF ALLIED 462   2 DON JUAN 5   87   4
    OUT BETWEEN FRIENDS AS WELL AS ALLIED NATIONS 136   3 DON JUAN 8   48   4
ALLIES
    EUROPE HAS SLAVES--ALLIES--KINGS--ARMIES STILL 19   2 DON JUAN D   16   7
    THE SIMPLE OLIVES BEST ALLIES OF WINE 488   3 DON JUAN 15   73   1
ALL-IN-ALL-SUFFICIENT
    AN ALL-IN-ALL-SUFFICIENT SELF-DIRECTOR 29   2 DON JUAN 1   15   3
ALLOTMENT
    IT SEEMS WHEN THIS ALLOTMENT WAS MADE OUT 394   2 DON JUAN 4   92   1
ALLOW
    THAT BEING ABOUT THE NUMBER I'LL ALLOW 271   2 DON JUAN 2   216   4
    NO QUOTH THE OTHER YET YOU WILL ALLOW 422   2 DON JUAN 5   23   4
    ALL WHO HAVE LOVED OR LOVE WILL STILL ALLOW   9   3 DON JUAN 6   6   4
    'TWAS FOOLISH NERVOUS AS SHE MUST ALLOW 47   3 DON JUAN 6   83   4
    THERE'S FORTUNE EVEN IN FAME WE MUST ALLOW 82   3 DON JUAN 7   33   6
    AND YET LIKE ALL MEN ELSE I MUST ALLOW 106   3 DON JUAN 7   80   5
    ALL VERY ACCURATE YOU MUST ALLOW 181   3 DON JUAN 8   138   4
    DEATH'S A REFORMER ALL MEN MUST ALLOW 237   3 DON JUAN 10   25   8
    BUT WHAT IS TO BE DONE I CAN'T ALLOW 275   3 DON JUAN 11   15   6
    MIXED GOTHIC SUCH AS ARTISTS ALL ALLOW 384   3 DON JUAN 13   55   4
    AS CLEAR AS SUCH A CLIMATE WILL ALLOW 506   3 DON JUAN 16   13   4
ALLOWANCE
    WHEN SHIPWRECK'S SHORT ALLOWANCE GROWS TOO SCANTY . . . 200   2 DON JUAN 2   83   7
ALLOWANCES
    AND ALL ALLOWANCES BESIDES OF PLUNDER 163   3 DON JUAN 8   103   1
ALLOW'D
    HER PERSON IF ALLOW'D AT LARGE TO RUN 313   2 DON JUAN 3   73   4
    AS FAR AS HER OWN GENTLE HEART ALLOW'D 476   3 DON JUAN 15   46   2
ALLOWED
    MY MODERN MUSE MAY BE ALLOWED TO SNORE 503   2 DON JUAN 5   159   V8
    CONTINUED YOUR OLD REGIMENT'S ALLOWED 99   3 DON JUAN 7   63   3
    MY DEBT IN BEING THUS ALLOWED TO DIE 100   3 DON JUAN 7   65   5
    THE NIGHT WAS DARK AND THE THICK MIST ALLOWED 115   3 DON JUAN 8   6   1
    AS SOON AS CROWNER'S QUEST ALLOWED PURSUED 277   3 DON JUAN 11   18   3
ALLOWS
    THE FIELD IS UNIVERSAL AND ALLOWS 13   2 DON JUAN D   7   5
    SHE WAS ALL WHICH PURE IGNORANCE ALLOWS 257   2 DON JUAN 2   190   5
    IS ALL THAT LIFE ALLOWS THE LUCKIEST SINNER 294   2 DON JUAN 3   36   4
    AT LEAST AS FAR AS BIENSEANCE ALLOWS 439   3 DON JUAN 14   67   4
ALLOY
    OF BEING WITHOUT ALLOY OF FOP OR BEAU 354   3 DON JUAN 12   84   7
    WHO LIKE TO MIX SOME SLIGHT ALLOY WITH FAME 414   3 DON JUAN 14   9   6
ALL'S
    THE TREE OF KNOWLEDGE HAS BEEN PLUCK'D--ALL'S KNOWN-- . . 90   2 DON JUAN 1   127   4
    (A RACE OF MERE IMPOSTORS WHEN ALL'S DONE-- 218   2 DON JUAN 2   118   6

			PAGE	VOL	CANTO	STANZA	LN

ALL'S   (CONTINUED)
(A SET OF HUMBUG RASCALS WHEN ALL'S DONE) . . . . . 219 2 DON JUAN 2 118 V6
THEN DRESSING NURSING PRAYING AND ALL'S OVER . . . . 263 2 DON JUAN 2 200 8
THAT ALL'S IDEAL--ALL OURSELVES I'LL STAKE THE . . . 269 3 DON JUAN 11   2 3
UPON MY FIDDLE--SEEING IF ALL'S SURE . . . . . . 341 3 DON JUAN 12 54 V7

ALL-SEEING
AND DEEM BECAUSE WE SEE WE ARE ALL-SEEING . . . . . 190 3 DON JUAN 9 16 4

ALL-SOFTENING
THAN THAT ALL-SOFTENING OVER-POWERING KNELL . . . . 439 2 DON JUAN 5 49 7

ALL-SUFFICIENT
A SOMETHING ALL-SUFFICIENT FOR THE HEART . . . . . 442 3 DON JUAN 14 74 1

ALLUDED
ALFONSO NE'ER TO JUAN HAD ALLUDED . . . . 118 2 DON JUAN 1 177 2

ALLURE
WHO TO IMMORAL COURSES WOULD ALLURE US . . . . . 267 2 DON JUAN 2 207 3
THESE ARE SOME SAD EXMAPLES TO ALLURE US . . . . 267 2 DON JUAN 2 207 V5
POSSESS'D THE ORE OF WHICH MERE HOPES ALLURE . . . 319 3 DON JUAN 12   8 3
SO ANIMATED THAT IT MIGHT ALLURE A . . . . . . 395 3 DON JUAN 13 78 3
FIRSTLY THEY MUST ALLURE THE CONVERSATION . . . . 404 3 DON JUAN 13 98 1

ALLURED
THEY HAD NOT SPOKEN BUT THEY FELT ALLURED . . . . 254 2 DON JUAN 2 187 5
WHEN HE ALLURED POOR DOLON--YOU HAD BETTER . . . . 407 3 DON JUAN 13 105 7

ALLURES
FORM NOT THE TRUE TEMPTATION WHICH ALLURES . . . . 332 2 DON JUAN 3 97 5
I KNOW ITS MIGHTY EMPIRE NOW ALLURES . . . . . . 194 3 DON JUAN 9 23 5

ALLUSIONS
WILL HINT ALLUSIONS NEVER MEANT NE'ER DOUBT . . . . 311 3 DON JUAN 11 88 7
REAPING ALLUSIONS PRIVATE AND INGLORIOUS . . . . . 369 3 DON JUAN 13 25 4

ALL-WHITE
THE GROAN THE ROLL IN DUST THE ALL-WHITE EYE . . . 118 3 DON JUAN 8 13 5

ALLY
SHE KEEPS IT FOR YOU LIKE A TRUE ALLY . . . . . . 350 3 DON JUAN 12 74 8

ALMA
STILL WE RESPECT THEE ALMA VENUS GENETRIX . . . . 554 3 DON JUAN 16 109 8

ALMANACK
ITS SESSIONS FORM OUR ONLY ALMANACK . . . . . . 378 3 DON JUAN 13 43 8

ALMIGHTY
THOSE DOWNCAST EYES BENEATH THE ALMIGHTY DOVE-- . . . 336 2 DON JUAN 3 103 6

ALMOST
WHOSE SUICIDE WAS ALMOST AN ANOMALY-- . . . . . . 29 2 DON JUAN 1 15 6
HIM ALMOST MAN BUT SHE FLEW IN A RAGE . . . . . . 51 2 DON JUAN 1 54 5
THEIR LOOKS CAST DOWN THEIR GREETINGS ALMOST DUMB . . 60 2 DON JUAN 1 70 3
AND ALMOST MIGHT HAVE MADE A TARQUIN QUAKE . . . . 62 2 DON JUAN 1 75 6
I'M ALMOST SORRY THAT I E'ER BEGUN . . . . 83 2 DON JUAN 1 115 8
AND SEEMS TO ME ALMOST A SORT OF BLUNDER . . . . . 100 2 DON JUAN 1 144 7
I FAVOUR'D NONE--NAY WAS ALMOST UNCIVIL . . . . . 102 2 DON JUAN 1 148 6
BUT ALMOST EVERY OTHER COUNTRY'S BLUE . . . . . . 163 2 DON JUAN 2 12 6
SEEM'D ALMOST PRYING INTO HIS FOR BREATH . . . . . 215 2 DON JUAN 2 113 2
DON JUAN ALMOST FAMISH'D AND HALF DROWN'D . . . . 224 2 DON JUAN 2 129 4
A MAST WAS ALMOST CRUMBLED TO A CRUTCH . . . . . 226 2 DON JUAN 2 132 6
A LOVELY STATUE WE ALMOST ADORE . . . . 269 2 DON JUAN 2 211 6
IS GOOD TO GOVERN--ALMOST AS A GUELF . . . . . . 299 2 DON JUAN 3 47 8
BUT ALMOST SANCTIFY THE SWEET EXCESS . . . . . . 357 2 DON JUAN 4 26 7
AND STUMBLED ALMOST EVERY STEP SHE MADE . . . . . 361 2 DON JUAN 4 32 3
OUR BARITONE I ALMOST HAD FORGOT . . . . 392 2 DON JUAN 4 89 1
THEY ALMOST LOST THEIR WAY AND HAD TO PICK IT-- . . . 433 2 DON JUAN 5 41 5
HE LOOKED IN ALMOST ALL RESPECTS A MAID . . . . . 458 2 DON JUAN 5 80 3
O'ER THEM IN ALMOST PYRAMIDIC PRIDE . . . . . . 462 2 DON JUAN 5 87 6
AN ALMOST TWELVEMONTH'S CONSTANCY ENDANGERS . . . . 472 2 DON JUAN 5 106 8
AND RAPTURE'S SELF WILL SEEM ALMOST A PAIN . . . . 474 2 DON JUAN 5 110 4
AND THEY HAD WASTED NOW ALMOST A QUARTER . . . . . 482 2 DON JUAN 5 122 8
ALMOST AS FAR AS PETERSBURGH AND LEND . . . . . . 52 3 DON JUAN 6 93 4
AND ALMOST EVERY DAY IN SAD REALITY . . . . . . 108 3 DON JUAN 7 83 3
I ALMOST LATELY HAVE BEGUN TO DOUBT . . . . . . 124 3 DON JUAN 8 26 1
GREW DUMB FOR YOU MIGHT ALMOST HEAR A LINNET . . . 142 3 DON JUAN 8 59 6
WERE ALMOST AS MUCH VIRGINS AS BEFORE . . . . . . 176 3 DON JUAN 8 129 8
ALMOST AS MUCH AS ON A NEW DISPATCH . . . . . . 213 3 DON JUAN 9 61 7
WITH POETS ALMOST CLERGYMEN OR WHOLLY . . . . . . 297 3 DON JUAN 11 57 4
HE ALMOST HONOURED HIM FOR HIS DOCILITY . . . . . 368 3 DON JUAN 13 22 2
AND RATED HIM ALMOST A WHIPPER-IN . . . . 425 3 DON JUAN 14 34 8
WAS ALMOST WORTHY TO BECOME HIS HENCHMAN . . . . . 425 3 DON JUAN 14 34 V8
I SOMETIMES ALMOST THINK THAT EYES HAVE EARS . . . 489 3 DON JUAN 15 76 1
STEAL FROM THE WALLS TILL YOU ALMOST DISCERN . . . 508 3 DON JUAN 16 18 V6
ALMOST AN HAIR'S BREADTH TOO MUCH ON ONE SIDE . . . 513 3 DON JUAN 16 29 8
SO THAT I ALMOST THINK THAT THE SAME SKIN . . . . 567 3 DON JUAN 17 11 7

ALOFT
OR THE FAINT DYING DAY-HYMN STOLE ALOFT . . . . . 335 2 DON JUAN 3 102 6

ALONE
THAT POESY HAS WREATHS FOR YOU ALONE . . . . . . 12 2 DON JUAN D 5 6
SINCE GOLD ALONE SHOULD NOT HAVE BEEN ITS PRICE . . 12 2 DON JUAN D 6 4
WITH VIRTUES EQUALL'D BY HER WIT ALONE . . . . . 26 2 DON JUAN 1 10 4
STANDING ALONE BESIDE HIS DESOLATE HEARTH . . . . 41 2 DON JUAN 1 36 5
HIM UP TO LEARN HIS CATECHISM ALONE . . . . . . 50 2 DON JUAN 1 52 6
WHO CANNOT LEAVE ALONE OUR HELPLESS CLAY . . . . . 56 2 DON JUAN 1 63 3
SHE SATE BUT NOT ALONE I KNOW NOT WELL . . . . . 77 2 DON JUAN 1 105 1
IS FIRST AND PASSIONATE LOVE--IT STANDS ALONE . . . 90 2 DON JUAN 1 127 2
NOW DON ALFONSO ENTERING BUT ALONE . . . . . . 116 2 DON JUAN 1 173 1
IT MIGHT BE THAT HER SILENCE SPRANG ALONE . . . . 118 2 DON JUAN 1 176 6
TO MOURN ALONE THE LOVE WHICH HAS UNDONE . . . . 131 2 DON JUAN 1 194 V8

ALONE   (CONTINUED)

	PAGE	VOL	CANTO		STANZA	LN
AND HOPELESS EYES WHICH ON THE DEEP ALONE	182	2	DON JUAN	2	49	V6
THEY WERE ALONE BUT NOT ALONE AS THEY	255	2	DON JUAN	2	188	1
THEY WERE ALONE BUT NOT ALONE AS THEY	255	2	DON JUAN	2	188	1
TO THEM BUT MOCKERIES OF THE PAST ALONE	262	2	DON JUAN	2	199	5
ONE MAN ALONE AT FIRST HER HEART CAN MOVE	276	2	DON JUAN	3	3	6
THEY KINDLY LEAVE US THOUGH NOT QUITE ALONE	305	2	DON JUAN	3	59	7
THEIR PLACE OF BIRTH ALONE IS MUTE	321	2	DON JUAN	3 L	2	4
AND MUSING THERE AN HOUR ALONE	321	2	DON JUAN	3 L	3	3
LEAVING MY PEOPLE TO PROCEED ALONE	331	2	DON JUAN	3	96	3
THAT TRASH OF SUCH SORT NOT ALONE EVADES	334	2	DON JUAN	3	100	3
THE LADY AND HER LOVER LEFT ALONE	334	2	DON JUAN	3	101	5
THEY WERE ALONE ONCE MORE FOR THEM TO BE	349	2	DON JUAN	4	10	1
THE EAGLE SOARS ALONE THE GULL AND CROW	358	2	DON JUAN	4	28	7
SHE DREAM'D OF BEING ALONE ON THE SEA-SHORE	361	2	DON JUAN	4	31	1
SHE DIED BUT NOT ALONE SHE HELD WITHIN	382	2	DON JUAN	4	70	1
THOSE SUFFERINGS DANTE SAW IN HELL ALONE	401	2	DON JUAN	4	105	8
THOSE SUFFERINGS ONCE RESERVED FOR HELL ALONE	401	2	DON JUAN	4	105	V8
A KIND OF DEATH COMES O'ER US ALL ALONE	443	2	DON JUAN	5	57	7
COULD YET BE KNOWN UNTO THE FATES ALONE	499	2	DON JUAN	5	153	4
BESIDES I HATE TO SLEEP ALONE QUOTH SHE	30	3	DON JUAN	6	48	1
ALONE FOR REASONS WHICH DON'T MATTER YOU	30	3	DON JUAN	6	49	2
THAT THE YOUNG STRANGER SHOULD NOT LIE ALONE	46	3	DON JUAN	6	81	4
HER NECK ALONE WAS SEEN BUT THAT WAS FOUND	48	3	DON JUAN	6	85	3
WOULD NOT ALONE HAVE MADE HIM INSECURE	58	3	DON JUAN	6	104	5
AT LENGTH THEY FOUND MERE CANNONADE ALONE	81	3	DON JUAN	7	30	4
IN SAFETY TO THE WAGGONS WHERE ALONE	102	3	DON JUAN	7	70	5
HE FOUND HIMSELF ALONE AND FRIENDS RETIRING	125	3	DON JUAN	8	27	8
ALONE CAN SAVE THE EARTH FROM HELL'S POLLUTION	138	3	DON JUAN	8	51	8
HE WAS NOT ALL ALONE AROUND HIM GREW	145	3	DON JUAN	8	65	1
AND FELT--THOUGH DONE WITH LIFE--HE WAS ALONE	170	3	DON JUAN	8	117	8
SO MUCH THE BETTER--I MAY STAND ALONE	312	3	DON JUAN	11	90	7
BUT IF LOVE DON'T CASH DOES AND CASH ALONE	322	3	DON JUAN	12	14	1
NOR BY MUSTACHIOS MOVED WERE LET ALONE	344	3	DON JUAN	12	61	6
FOR LETTING THAT PURE SANCTUARY ALONE	370	3	DON JUAN	13	27	4
WERE VANISHED TO BE WHAT THEY CALL ALONE--	381	3	DON JUAN	13	49	3
BUT IN A HIGHER NICHE ALONE BUT CROWN'D	387	3	DON JUAN	13	61	1
IN GUIDO'S FAMOUS FRESCO WHICH ALONE	428	3	DON JUAN	14	40	2
IN FACT HIS MANNER WAS HIS OWN ALONE	461	3	DON JUAN	15	13	4

ALONG

	PAGE	VOL	CANTO		STANZA	LN
OF MORTALS WHOM THY LURE HATH LED ALONG--	78	2	DON JUAN	1	106	6
AND TOSSED ALONG THE VESSEL FORE AND AFT	155	2	DON JUAN	1 V	6	4
GLIDED ALONG THE SMOOTH AND HARDEN'D SAND	253	2	DON JUAN	2	184	3
AND VESPER BELL'S THAT ROSE THE BOUGHS ALONG	337	2	DON JUAN	3	106	4
ALONG THIS HALL AND UP AND DOWN SOME SQUATTED	441	2	DON JUAN	5	53	1
AND NOW THEN YOU MUST COME ALONG WITH ME SIRS	458	2	DON JUAN	5	80	6
HAUGHTY AND HUGE ALONG THE DISTANCE LOWERS	460	2	DON JUAN	5	85	5
IN SUCH SORT THAT THE EYE ALONG IT CAST	465	2	DON JUAN	5	93	4
STILL HE FORGOT NOT HIS DISGUISE--ALONG	21	3	DON JUAN	6	30	1
ALONG THE REST CONTRIVED TO KEEP THIS DEN	22	3	DON JUAN	6	32	6
SPARKLED ALONG ITS ROOF AND MANY A VASE	54	3	DON JUAN	6	97	6
SLOWLY ALONG THE ROOM BUT SILENT STILL	61	3	DON JUAN	6	110	6
A BOROUGH IS COMPRISED ALONG THE HEIGHT	71	3	DON JUAN	7	10	2
OR LIKE A WISP ALONG THE MARSH SO DAMP	89	3	DON JUAN	7	46	5
ALONG THE LEAGUERED WALL AND BRISTLING BANK	110	3	DON JUAN	7	86	4
LIGHTENING ALONG HIS VEINS AND WHERE HE HEARD	129	3	DON JUAN	8	33	V3
AND AS HE RUSHED ALONG IT CAME TO PASS HE	130	3	DON JUAN	8	34	1
COMPASSION BREATHES ALONG THE SAVAGE MIND	164	3	DON JUAN	8	106	8
ALONG THE ASPECT WHETHER SMOOTH OR ROUGH	206	3	DON JUAN	9	48	6
ALONG HIS WASTED CHEEK AND SEEMED TO GRAVEL	245	3	DON JUAN	10	43	7
AT LENGTH THEY ROSE LIKE A WHITE WALL ALONG	257	3	DON JUAN	10	65	1
ALONG THE ROAD AS IF THEY WENT TO BURY	260	3	DON JUAN	10	71	5
BUT--I WON'T PREACH--COME POSTBOYS WHIRL ALONG	263	3	DON JUAN	10	77	V2
WHICH LOOKS ALONG THAT VALE OF GOOD AND ILL	272	3	DON JUAN	11	8	3
A ROW OF GENTLEMEN ALONG THE STREETS	281	3	DON JUAN	11	27	1
LIKE HARNESSED METEORS THEN ALONG THE FLOOR	302	3	DON JUAN	11	67	4
ALONG THE LAST FIELDS OF THAT GOTHIC GROUND)--	359	3	DON JUAN	13	2	4
BLUSHING WITH BACCHANT CORONALS ALONG	394	3	DON JUAN	13	76	2
ALONG THE CANVAS THEIR EYES GLANCE LIKE DREAMS	509	3	DON JUAN	16	19	4
MOST PEOPLE AS IT PLAYS ALONG THE ARRAS	509	3	DON JUAN	16	20	8
HE SWEEPS ALONG IN HIS DUSKY PALL	520	3	DON JUAN	16 L	6	3

ALOOF

	PAGE	VOL	CANTO		STANZA	LN
KEPT STILL ALOOF THE CREW WHO ERE THEY SUNK	174	2	DON JUAN	2	35	7
AND PATIENT SPIRIT HELD ALOOF HIS FATE	203	2	DON JUAN	2	88	4
HER OFFICE WAS TO KEEP ALOOF OR SMOTHER	21	3	DON JUAN	6	31	6
WAS SUCH AS RATHER SEEM'D TO KEEP ALOOF	462	3	DON JUAN	15	14	3

ALOUD

	PAGE	VOL	CANTO		STANZA	LN
HAVE VOICES--TONGUES TO CRY ALOUD FOR ME	19	2	DON JUAN	D	16	6
ALOUD BECAUSE HIS FEELINGS WERE TOO TENDER	50	3	DON JUAN	6	89	3

ALPHA

	PAGE	VOL	CANTO		STANZA	LN
THUS JUAN LEARN'D HIS ALPHA BETA BETTER	242	2	DON JUAN	2	163	7

ALPHABET

	PAGE	VOL	CANTO		STANZA	LN
AND GREEK--THE ALPHABET--I'M NEARLY SURE	28	2	DON JUAN	1	13	2
OF DIDO'S ALPHABET AND THIS IS RATIONAL	122	3	DON JUAN	8	23	7

ALPINE

	PAGE	VOL	CANTO		STANZA	LN
THAT OVERPOWERS SOME ALPINE RIVER'S RUSH	231	2	DON JUAN	2	141	6
FLOW'D LIKE AN ALPINE TORRENT WHICH THE SUN	313	2	DON JUAN	3	73	2
WITHIN AN ALPINE HOLLOW WHEN THE WIND	360	2	DON JUAN	4	30	2
OR THE SNOW MINARET ON AN ALPINE STEEP	40	3	DON JUAN	6	68	4

17

PAGE VOL CANTO STANZA LN

ALREADY
	PAGE	VOL	CANTO	STANZA	LN
AND OFFER POISON LONG ALREADY MIX'D	16	2 DON JUAN	D	12	8
HER YOUNG PHILOSOPHER WAS GROWN ALREADY	49	2 DON JUAN	1	50	8
WHO'VE MADE US YOUTH WAIT TOO--TOO LONG ALREADY	89	2 DON JUAN	1	125	4
WHO HAD ALREADY PERISH'D SUFFERING MADLY	199	2 DON JUAN	2	80	7
BUT I HAVE SPOKEN OF ALL THIS ALREADY--	246	2 DON JUAN	2	171	5
AND OH YE GENTLEMEN WHO HAVE ALREADY	288	2 DON JUAN	3	25	1
SUPPOSE BUT YOU ALREADY HAVE SUPPOSED	486	2 DON JUAN	5	131	1
ALREADY MANY A ONCE LOVE-BEATEN BREAST	63	3 DON JUAN	6	115	3
BUT ON THE THIRTEENTH WHEN ALREADY PART	85	3 DON JUAN	7	39	1
AFTER THE HARDSHIPS YOU'VE ALREADY BORNE	98	3 DON JUAN	7	62	4
THE TROOPS ALREADY DISEMBARKED PUSHED ON	119	3 DON JUAN	8	15	1
OUR KILLED ALREADY PILED UP TO THE CHIN	160	3 DON JUAN	8	98	6
ALREADY THEY BEHELD THE SILVER SHOWERS	222	3 DON JUAN	9	79	5
IF THAT THEY WERE NOT MARRIED ALL ALREADY	469	3 DON JUAN	15	30	8
OR WED ALREADY WHO OBJECT TO THIS	470	3 DON JUAN	15	32	3
BEYOND THE CHARMERS WE HAVE ALREADY CITED	477	3 DON JUAN	15	48	4
WAKING ALREADY AND RETURNED AT LENGTH	511	3 DON JUAN	16	25	7
MY TREMBLING LYRE ALREADY SEVERAL STRINGS	568	3 DON JUAN	17	13	5

ALTAR-PIECE
	PAGE	VOL	CANTO	STANZA	LN
LIKE CHERUBS ROUND AN ALTAR-PIECE THEY CLING	306	2 DON JUAN	3	60	5

ALTARS
	PAGE	VOL	CANTO	STANZA	LN
MY ALTARS ARE THE MOUNTAINS AND THE OCEAN	336	2 DON JUAN	3	104	6

ALTER
	PAGE	VOL	CANTO	STANZA	LN
I CANNOT STOP TO ALTER WORDS ONCE WRITTEN	221	3 DON JUAN	9	77	4

ALTERATIONS
	PAGE	VOL	CANTO	STANZA	LN
THESE FEW SHORT YEARS MAKE WOND'ROUS ALTERATIONS	59	2 DON JUAN	1	69	7
IN SHORT THE LIST OF ALTERATIONS BOTHERS	308	3 DON JUAN	11	81	6

ALTER'D
	PAGE	VOL	CANTO	STANZA	LN
FADED OR ALTER'D INTO SOMETHING NEW--	363	2 DON JUAN	4	35	2
BUT TIMES ARE ALTER'D SINCE A RHYMING LOVER	405	2 DON JUAN	4	111	2

ALTERING
	PAGE	VOL	CANTO	STANZA	LN
THAN CAN BE HID BY ALTERING HIS SHIRT HE	232	3 DON JUAN	10	15	4

ALTOGETHER
	PAGE	VOL	CANTO	STANZA	LN
INSTEAD OF STANDING STARING ALTOGETHER	46	2 DON JUAN	1	45	7
DEPENDENT ON THE PUBLIC ALTOGETHER	135	2 DON JUAN	1	199	3
HE CAGED IN ONE HUGE HAMPER ALTOGETHER	285	2 DON JUAN	3	18	8
COULD ALTOGETHER CALL THE PAST TO MIND	384	2 DON JUAN	4	75	3
OR GOT RID OF THE PARTIES ALTOGETHER	65	3 DON JUAN	6	119	4
A LITTLE SPOILED BUT NOT SO ALTOGETHER	338	3 DON JUAN	12	49	3
A LADY ALTOGETHER TO HIS MIND	353	3 DON JUAN	12	81	4

ALWAYS
	PAGE	VOL	CANTO	STANZA	LN
THE ENGLISH ALWAYS USE TO GOVERN DAMN	28	2 DON JUAN	1	14	8
WHICH ALWAYS SPOILS THE BREED IF IT INCREASES	52	2 DON JUAN	1	57	8
A REAL HUSBAND ALWAYS IS SUSPICIOUS	74	2 DON JUAN	1	99	1
SO MUCH HE ALWAYS DOUBTED I WAS MARRIED--	101	2 DON JUAN	1	147	7
PROLOGUE IS ALWAYS CERTAIN THROES AND THROBS	110	2 DON JUAN	1	162	4
A LADY ALWAYS DISTANT FROM THE FACT--	119	2 DON JUAN	1	178	6
HAVE ALWAYS DONE SO 'TIS OF NO GREAT USE	119	2 DON JUAN	1	179	2
FAMOUS FOR ALWAYS TALKING AND NEER FIGHTING	150	2 DON JUAN	1	V 1	3
AND DEEMS HE THAT WE ALWAYS WILL FORBEAR	153	2 DON JUAN	1	V 4	4
BUT THEN EXCEPTIONS ALWAYS PROVE ITS WORTH--	158	2 DON JUAN	2	2	6
(A VIRGIN ALWAYS ON HER MAID RELIES)	225	2 DON JUAN	2	131	2
AND FED BY SPOONFULS ELSE THEY ALWAYS BURST	239	2 DON JUAN	2	158	8
LOVE THOUGH GOOD ALWAYS IS NOT QUITE SO GOOD)	246	2 DON JUAN	2	170	2
CAME ALWAYS BACK TO COFFEE AND HAIDEE	246	2 DON JUAN	2	171	8
BUT ALWAYS DANGEROUS WHEN THE HIGH WINDS TORE	249	2 DON JUAN	2	177	V6
WAS THAT IN WHICH THE HEART IS ALWAYS FULL	258	2 DON JUAN	2	192	3
IS ALWAYS SO TO WOMEN ONE SOLE BOND	263	2 DON JUAN	2	200	2
FOR SURELY IF WE ALWAYS COULD PERCEIVE	270	2 DON JUAN	2	213	2
THE SAME THINGS CANNOT ALWAYS BE ADMIRED	278	2 DON JUAN	3	7	4
AND ALWAYS CHANGED AS TRUE AS ANY NEEDLE	317	2 DON JUAN	3	80	2
'TIS THAT OUR NATURE CANNOT ALWAYS BRING	346	2 DON JUAN	4	4	3
AND ALWAYS ENVY THOUGH WE DEEM IT FRANTIC	353	2 DON JUAN	4	18	8
NOT ALWAYS SIGNS WITH HIM OF CALMEST MOOD	365	2 DON JUAN	4	39	3
HE ALWAYS IS COMPLAINING OF HIS LOT	392	2 DON JUAN	4	89	5
(BECAUSE THE WORLD WON'T READ HIM ALWAYS SNARLING)	404	2 DON JUAN	4	109	6
IS ALWAYS MUCH MORE SPLENDID THAN A KING	408	2 DON JUAN	4	115	6
PROVIDED ALWAYS YOUR GREAT GOODNESS STILL	453	2 DON JUAN	5	72	7
'TWERE NOTHING--FOR HER EYES FLASHED ALWAYS FIRE	489	2 DON JUAN	5	134	2
HIS MAJESTY WAS ALWAYS SO POLITE	495	2 DON JUAN	5	146	4
WAS PRINCELY AS THE PROOFS HAVE ALWAYS SHOWN	499	2 DON JUAN	5	153	6
AND LOOKING AS HE ALWAYS LOOKED PERCEIVED	500	2 DON JUAN	5	155	2
BUT ALWAYS AT A MOST PROVOKING HEIGHT--	44	3 DON JUAN	6	76	8
OH FOOLISH MORTALS ALWAYS TAUGHT IN VAIN	101	3 DON JUAN	7	68	5
IN SUCH GOOD COMPANY AS ALWAYS THRONG	123	3 DON JUAN	8	24	6
BUT ALWAYS WITHOUT MALICE IF HE WARR'D	123	3 DON JUAN	8	25	1
KEPT ALWAYS PUSHING ONWARDS TO THE GLACIS	130	3 DON JUAN	8	34	V8
GREAT MEN HAVE ALWAYS SCORNED GREAT RECOMPENSES	186	3 DON JUAN	9	8	1
HAVE ALWAYS HAD A TENDENCY TO SPARE--	193	3 DON JUAN	9	21	6
AND ALWAYS USED HER FAVOURITES TOO WELL	214	3 DON JUAN	9	63	4
WITH RHYME BUT ALWAYS LEANT LESS TO IMPROVING	219	3 DON JUAN	9	74	6
BUT ALWAYS CHOOSING WITH DELIBERATION	248	3 DON JUAN	10	48	7
OH YE AMBROSIAL MOMENTS ALWAYS UPPER	304	3 DON JUAN	11	72	5
NOT WHAT YOU SEEM BUT ALWAYS WHAT YOU SEE	310	3 DON JUAN	11	86	8
I HAVE ALWAYS LIKED YOU BETTER THAN I STATE	329	3 DON JUAN	12	28	4
PERUSE 'TIS ALWAYS WITH A MORAL END	334	3 DON JUAN	12	39	2
AND IF MY THUNDERBOLT NOT ALWAYS RATTLES	356	3 DON JUAN	12	88	1
THE FAIR SEX SHOULD BE ALWAYS FAIR AND NO MAN	359	3 DON JUAN	13	3	7

		PAGE	VOL		CANTO	STANZA	LN

ALWAYS   (CONTINUED)
BE WARY WATCH THE TIME AND ALWAYS SERVE IT	366	3 DON JUAN	13	18	4
ALWAYS A PATRIOT AND SOMETIMES A PLACEMAN	368	3 DON JUAN	13	21	8
WHERE PEOPLE ALWAYS DID AS THEY WERE BID	368	3 DON JUAN	13	23	3
ON WHICH THE MUSE HAS ALWAYS SOUGHT TO ENTER--	375	3 DON JUAN	13	38	6
ALWAYS PREMISING THAT SAID SON AT COLLEGE	377	3 DON JUAN	13	42	7
BY HUMOURING ALWAYS WHAT THEY MIGHT ASSERT	426	3 DON JUAN	14	37	3
IS THAT FOR WHICH THE SEX ARE ALWAYS SEEKING	442	3 DON JUAN	14	74	2
'TIS STRANGE--BUT TRUE FOR TRUTH IS ALWAYS STRANGE	455	3 DON JUAN	14	101	1
DISSIMULATION ALWAYS SETS APART	457	3 DON JUAN	15	3	6
AND ALWAYS HAVE DONE SOMEHOW THESE GOOD LOOKS	493	3 DON JUAN	15	84	7
IN VIRGINS--ALWAYS IN A MODEST WAY	494	3 DON JUAN	15	86	7
TO KEEP OUR HOLY BEACONS ALWAYS BRIGHT	496	3 DON JUAN	15	90	4
I ALWAYS KNOCK MY HEAD AGAINST SOME ANGLE	496	3 DON JUAN	15	91	5
IS ALWAYS GREATEST AT A MIRACLE	503	3 DON JUAN	16	5	4
'TIS ALWAYS BEST TO TAKE THINGS UPON TRUST	503	3 DON JUAN	16	6	4
THOUGH SOMETIMES FAINTLY FLUSHED--AND ALWAYS CLEAR	545	3 DON JUAN	16	94	7

AMARI
| (SURGIT AMARI ALIQUID)--THE TOLL | 263 | 3 DON JUAN | 10 | 78 | 8 |

AMATEUR
| THE SUPPLICATOR BEING AN AMATEUR | 543 | 3 DON JUAN | 16 | 89 | 2 |

AMATORY
EGGS OYSTERS TOO ARE AMATORY FOOD	246	2 DON JUAN	2	170	6
HE MAY RESUME HIS AMATORY CARE	288	2 DON JUAN	3	24	5
WHEN AMATORY POETS SING THEIR LOVES	411	2 DON JUAN	5	1	1
SHE COULD REPAY EACH AMATORY LOOK YOU LENT	213	3 DON JUAN	9	62	5
MADE UP UPON AN AMATORY PATTERN	217	3 DON JUAN	9	70	5
WAS CHOSEN FROM OUT AN AMATORY SCORE	334	3 DON JUAN	12	38	3
OF AMATORY EGOTISM THE TUISM	506	3 DON JUAN	16	13	7
OR TIPTOE OF AN AMATORY MISS	556	3 DON JUAN	16	112	6

AMAZING
| A TOWN OF GARDENS WALLS AND WEALTH AMAZING | 445 | 2 DON JUAN | 5 | 60 | 2 |

AMAZON
| THIS MODERN AMAZON AND QUEEN OF QUEANS | 54 | 3 DON JUAN | 6 | 96 | 4 |

AMBASSADORS
| ALL THE AMBASSADORS OF ALL THE POWERS | 222 | 3 DON JUAN | 9 | 79 | 1 |
| AMBASSADORS BEGAN AS 'TWERE TO HUSTLE | 223 | 3 DON JUAN | 9 | 82 | 3 |

AMBER
THERE THE LARGE OLIVE RAINS ITS AMBER STORE	373	2 DON JUAN	4	55	1
WITH AMBER MOUTHS OF GREATER PRICE OR LESS	441	2 DON JUAN	5	53	6
THOUGHTS QUITE AS YELLOW BUT LESS CLEAR THAN AMBER	505	3 DON JUAN	16	11	4

AMBIGUOUS
| HER VILE AMBIGUOUS METHOD OF FLIRTATION | 222 | 3 DON JUAN | 9 | 81 | 7 |

AMBITION
PRIDE FAME AMBITION TO FILL UP HIS HEART	131	2 DON JUAN	1	194	5
AMBITION WAS MY IDOL WHICH WAS BROKEN	145	2 DON JUAN	1	217	1
HIS VAIN AMBITION IN ITS VAGUE CAREER	152	2 DON JUAN	1	V 3	4
ARE THESE THE DREAMS HIS YOUNG AMBITION SAW	155	2 DON JUAN	1	V 7	3
A LITTLE BREATH LOVE WINE AMBITION FAME	159	2 DON JUAN	2	4	7
AMBITION AVARICE VENGEANCE GLORY GLUE	422	3 DON JUAN	5	22	6
BY COMMONEST AMBITION THAT WHEN PASSION	8	3 DON JUAN	6	4	2
FOR LOVE WAR OR AMBITION WHICH REWARD	235	3 DON JUAN	10	22	6
AMBITION RENDS AND GAMING GAINS A LOSS	317	3 DON JUAN	12	4	2
HAD EVER BEEN HIS SOLE AND WHOLE AMBITION	536	3 DON JUAN	16	74	2
TO SOME SMALL PLAN OF INTEREST OR AMBITION--	541	3 DON JUAN	16	85	7

AMBITION'S
| THESE QUENCHED A MOMENT HER AMBITION'S THIRST-- | 212 | 3 DON JUAN | 9 | 59 | 5 |
| BLOOD ONLY SERVES TO WASH AMBITION'S HANDS | 212 | 3 DON JUAN | 9 | 59 | 8 |

AMBLE
| AND PEGASUS HATH A PSALMODIC AMBLE | 297 | 3 DON JUAN | 11 | 57 | 5 |

AMBO
| ARCADES AMBO ID EST--BLACKGUARDS BOTH | 394 | 2 DON JUAN | 4 | 93 | 8 |

AMBROSIAL
WORTHY OF THIS AMBROSIAL SIN SO SHOWN	90	2 DON JUAN	1	127	6
OF THESE AMBROSIAL PHARISAIC TIMES	156	3 DON JUAN	8	90	3
HIS BEARD HE PUFFED HIS PIPE'S AMBROSIAL GALES	172	3 DON JUAN	8	121	7
OH YE AMBROSIAL MOMENTS ALWAYS UPPER	304	3 DON JUAN	11	72	3
BUT OH AMBROSIAL CASH AH WHO WOULD LOSE THEE	405	3 DON JUAN	13	100	7

AMBUSH
| IN AMBUSH LAID WHO HAD PERCEIVED HIM LOITER | 273 | 3 DON JUAN | 11 | 11 | 2 |

AMEN
| WITH THE KIND WORLD'S AMEN--WHO WOULD HAVE THOUGHT IT | 328 | 3 DON JUAN | 12 | 26 | 8 |

AMEND
| THEY VOW TO AMEND THEIR LIVES AND YET THEY DON'T | 414 | 2 DON JUAN | 5 | 6 | 7 |

AMENDS
| MIGHT FOR LONG LYING MAKE HIMSELF AMENDS | 318 | 2 DON JUAN | 3 | 83 | 6 |
| AND I KNOW NOTHING WHICH COULD MAKE AMENDS | 231 | 3 DON JUAN | 10 | 12 | 3 |

AMERICA
| 'TIS SAID THE GREAT CAME FROM AMERICA | 92 | 2 DON JUAN | 1 | 131 | 1 |
| WHILE YET AMERICA WAS IN HER NON-AGE | 468 | 3 DON JUAN | 15 | 27 | 8 |

AMIABLE
THESE AMIABLE DESCRIPTIONS FROM THE SCRIBES	329	2 DON JUAN	3	92	6
THREE FIRESHIPS LOST THEIR AMIABLE EXISTENCE	80	3 DON JUAN	7	28	3
SHE MERELY WAS DEEMED AMIABLE AND WITTY	338	3 DON JUAN	12	47	4

AMIABLY
| 'TIS THUS THE GOOD WILL AMIABLY ERR | 463 | 3 DON JUAN | 15 | 17 | 3 |

AMIDST
| AMIDST THE SKELETONS OF THAT GAUNT CREW | 210 | 2 DON JUAN | 2 | 102 | 4 |
| AMIDST THE BARREN SAND AND ROCKS SO RUDE | 262 | 2 DON JUAN | 2 | 198 | 4 |

19

AMIDST   (CONTINUED)

	PAGE	VOL	CANTO		STANZA	LN
AMIDST THE SAVAGE DEEDS HE HAD DONE AND SEEN	304	2	DON JUAN	3	57	4
AMIDST THE ROAR OF LIBERATED ROME	339	2	DON JUAN	3	109	3
MY BOY --SAID HE AMIDST THIS MOTLEY CREW	417	2	DON JUAN	5	13	1
AMIDST SOME GROANING THOUSANDS DYING NEAR--	117	3	DON JUAN	8	11	3
SO ORDERED IT AMIDST THESE SULPHURY REVELS	135	3	DON JUAN	8	44	6
AMIDST SUCH SCENES--THOUGH THIS WAS QUITE A NEW ONE	138	3	DON JUAN	8	52	4
AMIDST THE BODIES LULLED IN BLOODY REST	157	3	DON JUAN	8	91	8
HER HIDDEN FACE WAS PLUNGED AMIDST THE DEAD	158	3	DON JUAN	8	93	3
FOR SAVING HER AMIDST THE WILD INSANITY	182	3	DON JUAN	8	140	6
IN SIGHT THEN LOST AMIDST THE FORESTRY	265	3	DON JUAN	10	82	4
OR SAT AMIDST THE BRICKS OF NINEVEH	271	3	DON JUAN	11	7	6
AND FOUND HIM NOT AMIDST THE VARIOUS PROGENIES	281	3	DON JUAN	11	28	3
TO SIT AMIDST THE RUINS OF THEIR GUILT	352	3	DON JUAN	12	78	7
SWEET ADELINE AMIDST THE GAY WORLD'S HUM	365	3	DON JUAN	13	13	4
ON THE MOST FAVOURED AND AMIDST THE BLAZE	373	3	DON JUAN	13	33	6
AMIDST THE COURT A GOTHIC FOUNTAIN PLAY'D	389	3	DON JUAN	13	65	1
AMIDST LIFE'S INFINITE VARIETY	464	3	DON JUAN	15	19	2
AMIDST THIS TUMULT OF FISH FLESH AND FOWL	488	3	DON JUAN	15	74	1

AMISS

	PAGE	VOL	CANTO		STANZA	LN
THE BARD I QUOTE FROM DOES NOT SING AMISS	69	2	DON JUAN	1	88	5
IN DEEP DESPAIR LEST HE HAD DONE AMISS	81	2	DON JJAN	1	112	5
A NAME THE LADIES MUST NOT TAKE AMISS	140	2	DON JUAN	1	206	V4
THAT PASSENGERS WOULD FIND IT MUCH AMISS	173	2	DON JUAN	2	33	3
SOME PEOPLE PREFER WINE--'TIS NOT AMISS	356	2	DON JUAN	4	24	6
EXPLAINS THE GARB WHICH JUAN TOOK AMISS	477	2	DON JUAN	5	114	8
BUT IT SUFFICES--LITTLE WAS AMISS	31	3	DON JUAN	6	51	5
THAT NOBODY CAN EVER TAKE AMISS	35	3	DON JUAN	6	59	3
COULD NOT AT FIRST EXPOUND WHAT WAS AMISS	43	3	DON JUAN	6	74	8
BUT I'M RESOLVED TO SAY NOUGHT THAT'S AMISS)--	326	3	DON JUAN	12	22	6
ABROAD THOUGH DOUBTLESS THEY DO MUCH AMISS	352	3	DON JUAN	12	79	5
OF PLATONISM WHICH LEADS SO OFT AMISS	450	3	DON JUAN	14	92	3
THOUGHT HER PREDICTIONS WENT NOT MUCH AMISS	492	3	DON JUAN	15	81	3
WHO HITHERTO HAD FOUND THINGS NOT AMISS	492	3	DON JUAN	15	81	V3
NOW THIS HE REALLY RATHER TOOK AMISS	544	3	DON JUAN	16	92	1

AMMON

	PAGE	VOL	CANTO		STANZA	LN
WINES TOO WHICH MIGHT AGAIN HAVE SLAIN YOUNG AMMON--	484	3	DON JUAN	15	65	3

AMMON'S

	PAGE	VOL	CANTO		STANZA	LN
AMMON'S (ILL PLEASED WITH ONE WORLD AND ONE FATHER)	427	2	DON JUAN	5	31	8
OR AMMON'S--FOR TWO FATHERS CLAIMED THIS ONE	427	2	DON JUAN	5	31	V8

A-MODE

	PAGE	VOL	CANTO		STANZA	LN
THEN BEING TAKEN BY THE TAIL--A-MODE	150	3	DON JUAN	8	76	V1

AMOR

	PAGE	VOL	CANTO		STANZA	LN
THE MAMMA MIA'S AND THE AMOR MIO'S	523	3	DON JUAN	16	45	3

AMOROUS

	PAGE	VOL	CANTO		STANZA	LN
I THEREFORE DO DENOUNCE ALL AMOROUS WRITING	412	2	DON JUAN	5	2	1
IN SHORT THE MAXIM FOR THE AMOROUS TRIBE IS	14	3	DON JUAN	6	17	7
AND SOMEWHAT MECHANTE IN HER AMOROUS SPHERE	438	3	DON JUAN	14	63	2

AMORT

	PAGE	VOL	CANTO		STANZA	LN
AND SOME OF US HAVE FELT THUS ALL AMORT	59	3	DON JUAN	6	106	5

AMOUNT

	PAGE	VOL	CANTO		STANZA	LN
YET COULD HIS CORPORAL PANGS AMOUNT TO HALF	373	2	DON JUAN	4	54	3
TO EXACT OF CUPID'S BILLS THE FULL AMOUNT	213	3	DON JUAN	9	62	7
TO GATHER TO A SOMEWHAT LARGE AMOUNT HE	535	3	DON JUAN	16	71	5

AMPHIBIOUS

	PAGE	VOL	CANTO		STANZA	LN
BUT TO DENOUNCE THE AMPHIBIOUS SORT OF HARLOT	344	3	DON JUAN	12	62	7

AMPHITHEATRE

	PAGE	VOL	CANTO		STANZA	LN
FORMED LIKE AN AMPHITHEATRE EACH DWELLING	78	3	DON JUAN	7	23	7

AMPLE

	PAGE	VOL	CANTO		STANZA	LN
WHERE THE SUBLIME SOARS FORTH ON WINGS MORE AMPLE	45	2	DON JUAN	1	42	6
BUT THERE WERE AMPLE REASONS FOR IT NONE	116	2	DON JUAN	1	174	5
LIKE BUBBLES ON AN OCEAN MUCH LESS AMPLE	189	3	DON JUAN	9	13	6

AMPLIFY

	PAGE	VOL	CANTO		STANZA	LN
AND AMPLIFY YOU LOSE MUCH BY CONCISION	478	3	DON JUAN	15	51	4

AMUNDEVILLE

	PAGE	VOL	CANTO		STANZA	LN
THE LADY ADELINE AMUNDEVILLE	359	3	DON JUAN	13	2	1
THE LADY ADELINE AMUNDEVILLE	364	3	DON JUAN	13	12	2
LORD H AMUNDEVILLE AND LADY A	382	3	DON JUAN	13	51	8
THE LADY ADELINE AMUNDEVILLE	458	3	DON JUAN	15	5	2
WHEN THE LORD OF THE HILL AMUNDEVILLE	518	3	DON JUAN	16	L 1	5
BUT STILL TO THE HOUSE OF AMUNDEVILLE	519	3	DON JUAN	16	L 3	3
AMUNDEVILLE IS LORD BY DAY	520	3	DON JUAN	16	L 5	5

AMUSE

	PAGE	VOL	CANTO		STANZA	LN
YOUNG MEN SHOULD TRAVEL IF BUT TO AMUSE	165	2	DON JUAN	2	16	5
WHOSE CHIEFLY HARMLESS TALENT WAS TO AMUSE	398	3	DON JUAN	13	86	5

AMUSED

	PAGE	VOL	CANTO		STANZA	LN
NOT ONE EXCEPT THE ATTORNEY WAS AMUSED	109	2	DON JUAN	1	159	5

AMUSEMENT

	PAGE	VOL	CANTO		STANZA	LN
SOME FOR AMUSEMENT OTHERS FOR OLD GRUDGES	36	2	DON JUAN	1	28	8
WHICH I WITH THEIR AMUSEMENT WILL CONNECT	141	2	DON JUAN	1	209	3
AS AN AMUSEMENT AFTER THE DIVAN	51	3	DON JUAN	6	91	6
IN HIS RESUMED AMUSEMENT I CONFESS	100	3	DON JUAN	7	65	4
HER NEXT AMUSEMENT WAS MORE FANCIFUL	212	3	DON JUAN	9	60	1

ANACREON

	PAGE	VOL	CANTO		STANZA	LN
DESCRIBED BY MAHOMET AND ANACREON MOORE	77	2	DON JUAN	1	104	5
ANACREON ONLY HAD THE SOUL TO TIE AN	554	3	DON JUAN	16	109	5

ANACREON'S

	PAGE	VOL	CANTO		STANZA	LN
ANACREON'S MORALS ARE A STILL WORSE SAMPLE	45	2	DON JUAN	1	42	2
IT MADE ANACREON'S SONG DIVINE	324	2	DON JUAN	3	L 11	3

```
                                                            PAGE VOL      CANTO    STANZA LN
ANALOGIES
   IS SHOWN THROUGH NATURE'S WHOLE ANALOGIES    . . . . . . 451  3 DON JUAN 14      94    4
ANALOGY
   AND SAID THERE WAS ANALOGY BETWEEN 'EM    . . . . . . .  28  2 DON JUAN  1      14    2
ANALYZE
   WELL WE WON'T ANALYZE--OUR STORY MUST . . . . . . . . . 221  3 DON JUAN  9      77    1
ANA-SEING
   TO THE SOFT OATH OF ANA-SEING SIKTUM . . . . . . . . . 409  2 DON JUAN  4     116   V8
ANATOMICAL
   ALTHOUGH HIS ANATOMICAL CONSTRUCTION . . . . . . . . . 191  2 DON JUAN  2      67    5
ANATOMY
   IN THIS ANATOMY I'VE FINISH'D NOW  . . . . . . . . . . 271  2 DON JUAN  2     216    2
ANCESTOR
   THAT IS IF SAME LORDSHIP HAS AN ANCESTOR . . . . . . . 314  3 DON JUAN 11     V 75   1
ANCESTORS
   BUT PEOPLE'S ANCESTORS ARE HISTORY'S GAME   . . . . . .  53  3 DON JUAN  6      94    5
   I CAN'T COMPLAIN WHOSE ANCESTORS ARE THERE  . . . . . . 242  3 DON JUAN 10      36    1
ANCHOR
   AT ANCHOR UNDER THE SERAGLIO WALL . . . . . . . . . . 407  2 DON JUAN  4     113    4
   TO SLACKEN SAIL AND ANCHOR WITH OUR RHYME   . . . . . . 503  2 DON JUAN  5     159    4
   HE HAD BROUGHT HIS SPENDING TO A HANDSOME ANCHOR--   . . 240  3 DON JUAN 10      31    4
ANCHORED
   EXTREMELY TRANQUIL ANCHORED AT ITS STATION  . . . . . .  78  3 DON JUAN  7      24    4
ANCHORITE
   BRONZED O'ER SOME LEAN AND STOIC ANCHORITE--  . . . . . 392  3 DON JUAN 13      72    4
ANCIENT
   I'LL THEREFORE TAKE OUR ANCIENT FRIEND DON JUAN  . . . .  21  2 DON JUAN  1       1    6
   WHICH ANCIENT MASS-BOOKS OFTEN ARE AND THIS ALL  . . . .  47  2 DON JUAN  1      46    3
   OF ANCIENT DAYS ERE TYRANNY GREW STRONG . . . . . . . 379  2 DON JUAN  4      65    8
   TO SO RESPECTABLE AN ANCIENT RITE . . . . . . . . . . 452  2 DON JUAN  5      71    2
   ACCORDING TO THE ANCIENT EPIC LAWS . . . . . . . . . . 503  2 DON JUAN  5     159    3
   (THAT WHICH SOME ANCIENT MUSE OR MODERN WIT . . . . . . 153  3 DON JUAN  8      84    4
   FROM OUR OLD CRASH SOME MYSTIC ANCIENT STRAIN . . . . . 201  3 DON JUAN  9      38    3
   THAT HE WAS NOT AN ANCIENT DEBAUCHEE . . . . . . . . . 251  3 DON JUAN 10      54    2
   A MODERN ANCIENT PISTOL--BY THE HILTS . . . . . . . . 297  3 DON JUAN 11      57    8
   SO WHEN HE SAW EACH ANCIENT DAME A SUITOR   . . . . . . 336  3 DON JUAN 12      42    5
   AND THE SKY SHOWS THAT VERY ANCIENT GRAY . . . . . . . 422  3 DON JUAN 14      28    5
   THAT ANCIENT LINE IN THE PALE MOONSHINE  . . . . . . . 519  3 DON JUAN 16    L  4    3
   HE REACHED THE ANCIENT WALL THEN STOOD STONE STILL  . . 559  3 DON JUAN 16     119    8
ANCLE
   BEFORE A PETTICOAT AND PEEPING ANCLE . . . . . . . . . 422  3 DON JUAN 14      27    8
ANCLES
   A CANTO--THEN THEIR FEET AND ANCLES--WELL   . . . . . . 160  2 DON JUAN  2       6    6
   AND BOSOMS ARMS AND ANCLES GLANCING BARE . . . . . . .  42  3 DON JUAN  6      72    4
ANCONA
   BUT BRED WITHIN THE MARCH OF OLD ANCONA   . . . . . . . 395  2 DON JUAN  4      94    2
ANDALUSIAN
   OR ANDALUSIAN GIRL FROM MASS RETURNING   . . . . . . . 350  3 DON JUAN 12      75    2
   AND JUAN LIKE A TRUE-BORN ANDALUSIAN  . . . . . . . . . 368  3 DON JUAN 13      23    7
ANECDOTE
   AND HERE I MUST AN ANECDOTE RELATE . . . . . . . . . . 207  3 DON JUAN  9      50    7
ANENT
   SPIRIT WOULD NAME AND THEREFORE EVEN I WON'T ANENT  . . 289  3 DON JUAN 11      43    4
ANGEL
   HER GUARDIAN ANGEL HAD GIVEN UP HIS GARRISON   . . . . .  30  2 DON JUAN  1      17    4
   AND THUS LIKE TO AN ANGEL O'ER THE DYING . . . . . . . 233  2 DON JUAN  2     144    1
   EACH WAS AN ANGEL AND EARTH PARADISE . . . . . . . . . 265  2 DON JUAN  2     204    8
ANGELS
   SUCH AS THE ANGELS THINK SO VERY FINE . . . . . . . .  64  2 DON JUAN  1      79    3
   WITH PROPHETS HOURIS ANGELS SAINTS DESCRIED . . . . . . 169  3 DON JUAN  8     115    7
ANGER
   COLDNESS OR ANGER EVEN DISDAIN OR HATE   . . . . . . .  61  2 DON JUAN  1      73    7
   NOT THAT HIS ANGER DID NOT SOMETIMES GLOW   . . . . . . 300  2 DON JUAN  3      48   V1
   HER ANGER PITCHED INTO A LOWER TUNE  . . . . . . . . . 490  2 DON JUAN  5     136    5
   HER ANGER AND BESEECH'D SHE'D HEAR HIM THROUGH--  . . .  57  3 DON JUAN  6     102    3
ANGLE
   TO SOME ODD ANGLE FOR WHICH ALL WERE STRAINING . . . . 121  3 DON JUAN  8      20    4
   ANGLE THE SOI-DISANT MATHEMATICIAN . . . . . . . . . . 399  3 DON JUAN 13      87    3
   I ALWAYS KNOCK MY HEAD AGAINST SOME ANGLE   . . . . . . 496  3 DON JUAN 15      91    5
ANGLES
   FEW ANGLES WERE THERE IN HER FORM 'TIS TRUE . . . . . .  27  3 DON JUAN  6      42    5
   WHICH SATAN ANGLES WITH FOR SOULS LIKE FLIES   . . . . 154  3 DON JUAN  8      86    8
   THE SERIOUS ANGLES IN THE ELOQUENCE  . . . . . . . . . 427  3 DON JUAN 14      38    2
ANGLICE
   BY SUVAROFF OR ANGLICE SUWARROW . . . . . . . . . . .  70  3 DON JUAN  7       8    7
ANGLING
   AND ANGLING TOO THAT SOLITARY VICE . . . . . . . . . . 407  3 DON JUAN 13     106    5
ANGRY
   HIS ANGRY WORD ONCE O'ER HE SHED NO BLOOD   . . . . . . 300  2 DON JUAN  3      48    6
   UPON THEIR PREY AS DARTS AN ANGRY ASP . . . . . . . . 370  2 DON JUAN  4      48    6
   YOU CAN'T SUPPOSE GULBEYAZ' ANGRY BROW  . . . . . . . . 486  2 DON JUAN  5     131    8
   LIKE OTHER ANGRY LADIES OF HER NATION--  . . . . . . .  65  3 DON JUAN  6     119    5
   UPON HIS ANGRY SULTANSHIP PELL-MELL  . . . . . . . . . 166  3 DON JUAN  8     109    4
   AND WILD DISMAY O'ER EVERY ANGRY COUSIN . . . . . . . 332  3 DON JUAN 12      34    3
   WERE ANGRY--AS THEY WELL MIGHT TO BE SURE   . . . . . . 543  3 DON JUAN 16      89    4
ANGUISH
   SO DEEP AN ANGUISH WRUNG GULBEYAZM BROW   . . . . . . .  58  3 DON JUAN  6     105    4
ANIMAL
   MAN'S A STRANGE ANIMAL AND MAKES STRANGE USE   . . . . .  91  2 DON JUAN  1     128    1
```

21

ANIMAL   (CONTINUED)
	PAGE	VOL	CANTO	STANZA	LN
WHO WERE NOT QUITE SO FOND OF ANIMAL FOOD	198	2 DON JUAN	2	78	2
WHO SHOES THE GLORIOUS ANIMAL WITH STILTS	297	3 DON JUAN	11	57	7

ANIMALS
	PAGE	VOL	CANTO	STANZA	LN
HE CHOSE FROM SEVERAL ANIMALS HE SAW--	285	2 DON JUAN	3	18	3
WILL WONDER WHERE SUCH ANIMALS COULD SUP	202	3 DON JUAN	9	39	3
LIVE ANIMALS AN OLD MAID OF THREESCORE	249	3 DON JUAN	10	50	6
THE ANIMALS AFORESAID OCCUPIED	249	3 DON JUAN	10	51	1

ANIMATED
	PAGE	VOL	CANTO	STANZA	LN
SO ANIMATED THAT IT MIGHT ALLURE A	395	3 DON JUAN	13	78	3

ANIMATION
	PAGE	VOL	CANTO	STANZA	LN
EACH PULSE TO ANIMATION TILL BENEATH	215	2 DON JUAN	2	113	6
WITHOUT THE ANIMATION OF THE WIND	504	3 DON JUAN	16	9	8
AT FIRST THEN KINDLING INTO ANIMATION	518	3 DON JUAN	16	40	5

ANIMOSITY
	PAGE	VOL	CANTO	STANZA	LN
NO PROCESS PROVED CONNUBIAL ANIMOSITY	496	2 DON JUAN	5	148	6

ANIMUS
	PAGE	VOL	CANTO	STANZA	LN
AND WHAT THE LAWYERS CALL A MALUS ANIMUS	37	2 DON JUAN	1	30	5

ANKLE
	PAGE	VOL	CANTO	STANZA	LN
ABOUT THE PRETTIEST ANKLE IN THE WORLD	312	2 DON JUAN	3	72	8

ANNALISTS
	PAGE	VOL	CANTO	STANZA	LN
AND 'GAINST THOSE FEW YOUR ANNALISTS HAVE THUNDERED	324	3 DON JUAN	12	19	6

ANNALS
	PAGE	VOL	CANTO	STANZA	LN
INTO THEIR ANNALS AND PERSUADE POOR FAME	74	3 DON JUAN	7	15	V7
UP ANNALS REVELATIONS POESY	286	3 DON JUAN	11	37	6
MOCK TYRANTS WHEN ROME'S ANNALS WAXED BUT DIRTY	299	3 DON JUAN	11	61	8
DIVORCED OR DOING THEREANENT YE ANNALS	308	3 DON JUAN	11	80	2
THE ANNALS OF FULL MANY A LINE UNDONE--	386	3 DON JUAN	13	60	6

ANNEX
	PAGE	VOL	CANTO	STANZA	LN
YOUR IMPRIMATUR WILL YE NOT ANNEX	403	2 DON JUAN	4	108	4
AN INNOCENT PREDOMINANCE ANNEX	451	3 DON JUAN	14	93	3

ANNIHILATED
	PAGE	VOL	CANTO	STANZA	LN
WHAT'S THIS IN ONE ANNIHILATED CITY	174	3 DON JUAN	8	124	5

ANNIHILATES
	PAGE	VOL	CANTO	STANZA	LN
OR OVER-COLD ANNIHILATES THE CHARM	13	3 DON JUAN	6	15	8

ANNOUNCE
	PAGE	VOL	CANTO	STANZA	LN
AS TO ANNOUNCE HIS VISITS A LONG WHILE	495	2 DON JUAN	5	146	5

ANNOUNCED
	PAGE	VOL	CANTO	STANZA	LN
ANNOUNCED HER RANK TWELVE RINGS WERE ON HER HAND	312	2 DON JUAN	3	72	3
RUSHED WHERE THE THICKEST FIRE ANNOUNCED MOST FOES	127	3 DON JUAN	8	32	8
A SLENDER STREAK OF BLOOD ANNOUNCED HOW NEAR	159	3 DON JUAN	8	95	2
ANNOUNCED WITH NO LESS POMP THAN VICTORY'S WINNER	383	3 DON JUAN	13	54	3
EACH CARRIAGE WAS ANNOUNCED AND LADIES ROSE	549	3 DON JUAN	16	101	3

ANNOUNCING
	PAGE	VOL	CANTO	STANZA	LN
ANNOUNCING THE APPOINTMENT OF THAT LOVER OF	85	3 DON JUAN	7	39	7

ANNOY
	PAGE	VOL	CANTO	STANZA	LN
WHICH NOW IS LEAGUED YOUNG FREEDOM TO ANNOY	106	3 DON JUAN	7	79	7
WITH MARTIAL STOICISM NOUGHT SEEMED TO ANNOY	172	3 DON JUAN	8	121	5

ANNOY'D
	PAGE	VOL	CANTO	STANZA	LN
A SOMETHING WHEREWITHAL TO BE ANNOY'D	444	3 DON JUAN	14	79	3

ANNUITIES
	PAGE	VOL	CANTO	STANZA	LN
'TIS SAID THAT PERSONS LIVING ON ANNUITIES	190	2 DON JUAN	2	65	1

ANNUL
	PAGE	VOL	CANTO	STANZA	LN
OF COUNSEL TO NONSUIT OR TO ANNUL	127	2 DON JUAN	1	189	4
PROMPTS DEEDS ETERNITY CAN NOT ANNUL	258	2 DON JUAN	2	192	5
HER THIRD WAS FEMININE ENOUGH TO ANNUL	212	3 DON JUAN	9	60	5

ANOMALY
	PAGE	VOL	CANTO	STANZA	LN
WHOSE SUICIDE WAS ALMOST AN ANOMALY--	29	2 DON JUAN	1	15	6

ANON
	PAGE	VOL	CANTO	STANZA	LN
WE'LL TALK OF THAT ANON--'TIS SWEET TO HEAR	87	2 DON JUAN	1	122	1
FOREVER AND ANON A SOMETHING SHOOK	359	2 DON JUAN	4	29	4
ANON--SHE WAS RELEASED AND THEN SHE STRAY'D	361	2 DON JUAN	4	32	1
ANON HER THIN WAN FINGERS BEAT THE WALL	380	2 DON JUAN	4	66	1
FOREVER AND ANON COMES INDIGESTION	269	3 DON JUAN	11	3	1
BUT EVER AND ANON TO SOOTHE YOUR VISION	392	3 DON JUAN	13	71	1

ANONYMOUS
	PAGE	VOL	CANTO	STANZA	LN
FOR MAKING SQUARES AND STREETS ANONYMOUS	370	3 DON JUAN	13	26	2

ANSWER
	PAGE	VOL	CANTO	STANZA	LN
A READY ANSWER WHICH AT ONCE ENABLES	117	2 DON JUAN	1	175	2
FOR I HAVE FOUND IT ANSWER--SO MAY YOU	163	2 DON JUAN	2	13	8
THE ANSWER ELOQUENT WHERE THE SOUL SHINES	241	2 DON JUAN	2	162	5
HE'LL ANSWER ALL FOR BETTER OR FOR WORSE	298	2 DON JUAN	3	45	7
AND ANSWER LET ONE LIVING HEAD	323	2 DON JUAN	3	L 8	4
WHERE MEN HAVE SOULS OR BODIES SHE MUST ANSWER	390	2 DON JUAN	4	84	8
TO ANSWER IN A VERY CLEAR ORATION	43	3 DON JUAN	6	74	5
FOR ANY FURTHER ANSWER THAT HE FOUND	58	3 DON JUAN	6	105	3
HE MADE NO ANSWER BUT HE TOOK THE CITY	93	3 DON JUAN	7	53	8
IN ANSWER MADE AN INCLINATION TO	141	3 DON JUAN	8	57	3
FOR ALL THE ANSWER TO HIS PROPOSITION	152	3 DON JUAN	8	81	1
TO ANSWER RIBAS' SUMMONS TO GIVE WAY	171	3 DON JUAN	8	120	8
'TIS SAID (FOR I'LL NOT ANSWER ABOVE GROUND	225	3 DON JUAN	10	1	3
JURY OF MATRONS SCARCE KNEW WHAT TO ANSWER	294	3 DON JUAN	11	51	4
PRAY DID YOU SEE HER ANSWER TO HIS LETTER	332	3 DON JUAN	12	35	8
AN END TO ANSWER OR A PLAN TO LAY--	342	3 DON JUAN	12	58	7

ANSWER'D
	PAGE	VOL	CANTO	STANZA	LN
AND ANSWER'D BUT TO NATURE'S JUST DEMANDS	42	2 DON JUAN	1	37	6
BUT HAS NOT ANSWER'D LIKE THE APPARATUS	92	2 DON JUAN	1	130	3
AND THAT THE MEDICINE ANSWER'D VERY WELL	113	2 DON JUAN	1	168	6
AND NO GREAT GOOD SEEM'D ANSWER'D IF SHE STAID	116	2 DON JUAN	1	173	6

PAGE VOL CANTO STANZA LN

ANSWER'D (CONTINUED)
TO STAY THERE HAD NOT ANSWER'D HER INTENT . . . . . . 161 2 DON JUAN 2 8 3
ALL ONE AN HOUR HENCE JUAN ANSWER'D NO . . . . . . 175 2 DON JUAN 2 36 2
AND ANSWER'D LIKE A STATESMAN OR A PROPHET . . . . . 438 3 DON JUAN 14 65 7
ANSWERED
AND BLEW ANOTHER ANSWERED TO THE CALL . . . . 369 2 DON JUAN 4 47 4
WHEN JUAN ANSWERED SPANISH HE REPLIED . . . . 418 2 DON JUAN 5 14 1
I HAVE ANSWERED ALL YOUR QUESTIONS WITHOUT PRESSING . . 419 2 DON JUAN 5 16 3
MORE EASILY THAN ANSWERED--THAT HE HAD TRIED . . . . 56 3 DON JUAN 6 100 3
WERE BRISKLY FIRED AND ANSWERED IN DUE ORDER . . . . 85 3 DON JUAN 7 38 8
THIS DIALOGUE FOR HE WHO ANSWERED KNEW . . . . . . 97 3 DON JUAN 7 59 7
THEN UP WITH ME--BUT JUAN ANSWERED LOOK . . . . . . 161 3 DON JUAN 8 99 1
FOR COUSINS ALSO ANSWERED THE SAME DAY . . . . . . 239 3 DON JUAN 10 30 4
HAD STIRRED HIM ANSWERED IN A WAY TO CLOUD IT . . . . 527 3 DON JUAN 16 54 8
ANSWERING
TWO BLANKETS STITCH'D TOGETHER ANSWERING ILL . . . . 188 2 DON JUAN 2 61 3
RECALL'D HIS ANSWERING SPIRITS BACK FROM DEATH . . . . 215 2 DON JUAN 2 113 4
ANSWERING THE CHRISTIAN THUNDERS WITH LIKE VOICES . . . 115 3 DON JUAN 8 7 4
FROM ANSWERING SHE BEGAN TO QUESTION THIS . . . . . 492 3 DON JUAN 15 81 1
ANSWERLESS
ARE QUESTIONS ANSWERLESS AND YET INCESSANT . . . . . 37 3 DON JUAN 6 63 8
ANSWERS
HOW ANSWERS EACH BOLD BACCHANAL . . . . 324 2 DON JUAN 3 L 9 6
A FEW BRIEF QUESTIONS AND THE ANSWERS GAVE . . . . . 387 2 DON JUAN 4 79 6
SHE LIKED QUICK ANSWERS IN ALL CONVERSATIONS . . . . 56 3 DON JUAN 6 101 3
HIS ANSWERS WITH A VERY GRACEFUL BOW . . . . 223 3 DON JUAN 9 83 3
QUITE WELL YES NO--THESE ANSWERS WERE MYSTERIOUS . . . 514 3 DON JUAN 16 33 1
HAD CAUSED HIS NERVES--MADE ANSWERS RATHER CLOUDED . . 527 3 DON JUAN 16 54 V8
ANTELOPE
BENT LIKE AN ANTELOPE A PAPHIAN PAIR . . . . 466 2 DON JUAN 5 96 3
ANTHEM
THE OWL HIS ANTHEM WHERE THE SILENCED QUIRE . . . . . 387 3 DON JUAN 13 62 7
ANTHONY
('TWAS SNOW THAT BROUGHT SAINT ANTHONY TO REASON) . . . 57 2 DON JUAN 1 64 4
IF ANTHONY BE WELL REMEMBERED YET . . . . 8 3 DON JUAN 6 4 5
ANTHONY'S
LIKE ANTHONY'S BY CAESAR BY THE FEW . . . . 479 3 DON JUAN 15 53 7
ANTHROPOPHAGI
WHAT ANTHROPOPHAGI IN NINE OF TEN . . . . 455 3 DON JUAN 14 102 5
ANTIC
SO CALLED THE ANTIC LONG HATH CEASED TO HEAR . . . . 188 3 DON JUAN 9 12 4
ANTI-CHAMBER
THE ANTI-CHAMBER--SEARCH THEM UNDER OVER . . . . . . 104 2 DON JUAN 1 153 2
ANTICIPATE
AND NONE LIKED TO ANTICIPATE THE BLOW . . . . 175 2 DON JUAN 2 36 6
AS EAGER TO ANTICIPATE THEIR GRAVE . . . . 184 2 DON JUAN 2 52 4
ANTICIPATE THE PROPHET'S PARADISE . . . . 458 2 DON JUAN 5 81 8
MAY SETTLE BUT FAR BE'T FROM ME TO ANTICIPATE . . . . 65 3 DON JUAN 6 119 7
ANTICIPATED
ABOUT THIS TIME AS MIGHT HAVE BEEN ANTICIPATED . . . . 236 3 DON JUAN 10 23 1
THEY ARE YOUNG BUT KNOW NOT YOUTH--IT IS ANTICIPATED . . 306 3 DON JUAN 11 75 1
ANTICIPATING
ANTICIPATING AUGHT ABOUT THE MATTER . . . . 454 3 DON JUAN 14 99 2
ANTI-CLIMAX
LET NOT THIS SEEM AN ANTI-CLIMAX--OH . . . . 254 3 DON JUAN 10 59 1
ANTIENT
THOSE ANTIENT GOOD INTENTIONS WHICH ONCE SHAVED . . . 124 3 DON JUAN 8 26 6
ANTIENTS
ANTIENTS AND MODERNS ALSO NOT A FEW . . . . 267 2 DON JUAN 2 207 V6
ANTIJACOBIN
AN EASTERN ANTIJACOBIN AT LAST . . . . 316 2 DON JUAN 3 79 3
ANTIPATHY
THERE'S SOMETHING OF ANTIPATHY AS 'TWERE . . . . . . 278 2 DON JUAN 3 6 1
ANTIPODES
THEIR MOTHERS AS THE ANTIPODES OF TIMON . . . . . . 53 3 DON JUAN 6 94 2
SIMPLE SERENE THE ANTIPODES OF SHAME . . . . 144 3 DON JUAN 8 63 5
WOULD SHOW MANKIND THEIR SOUL'S ANTIPODES . . . . . 455 3 DON JUAN 14 101 8
ANTIQUARIANS
(THE ANTIQUARIANS WHO CAN SETTLE TIME . . . . . . 122 3 DON JUAN 8 23 3
ANTIQUE
AND THUS THEY FORM A GROUP THAT'S QUITE ANTIQUE . . . 259 2 DON JUAN 2 194 7
THE ANTIQUE PERSIANS TAUGHT THREE USEFUL THINGS . . . 501 3 DON JUAN 16 1 1
OR STEP RAN SADLY THROUGH THAT ANTIQUE HOUSE . . . . 509 3 DON JUAN 16 20 4
ANTITHESIS
A KIND ANTITHESIS TO CONGREVE'S ROCKETS . . . . . . 91 2 DON JUAN 1 129 6
WHICH FORMS IN FACT TRUE LOVE'S ANTITHESIS . . . . . 279 2 DON JUAN 3 8 2
THE SOBER SAD ANTITHESIS TO GLOWING-- . . . . . . 422 3 DON JUAN 14 28 6
THE GRAND ANTITHESIS TO GREAT ENNUI . . . . 457 3 DON JUAN 15 2 3
ANTONIA
HER MAID ANTONIA WHO WAS AN ADEPT . . . . 97 2 DON JUAN 1 140 4
BUT JULIA MISTRESS AND ANTONIA MAID . . . . 98 2 DON JUAN 1 141 1
OH SOBB'D ANTONIA I COULD TEAR THEIR EYES OUT . . . . 104 2 DON JUAN 1 152 8
(ANTONIA LET ME HAVE A GLASS OF WATER) . . . . . . 106 2 DON JUAN 1 155 4
PERHAPS 'TIS OF ANTONIA YOU ARE JEALOUS . . . . . . 106 2 DON JUAN 1 156 1
ANTONIA WHERE'S MY POCKET-HANDKERCHIEF . . . . . . 107 2 DON JUAN 1 157 8
ANTONIA BUSTLED ROUND THE RANSACK'D ROOM . . . . . . 109 2 DON JUAN 1 159 2
BUT SAGE ANTONIA CUT HIM SHORT BEFORE . . . . 111 2 DON JUAN 1 163 2
ANTONIA LET HIM--NOT A LITTLE SORE . . . . 111 2 DON JUAN 1 164 4
ANTONIA PUZZLED JULIA DID NOT SPEAK . . . . 114 2 DON JUAN 1 169 7

23

```
                                                     PAGE VOL      CANTO STANZA LN
ANTONIA    (CONTINUED)
    ANTONIA CRIED OUT RAPE AND JULIA FIRE . . . . . . . . 122  2 DON JUAN  1   184   2
    ANTONIA IN HYSTERICS JULIA SWOON'D . . . . . . . . . 125  2 DON JUAN  1   187   3
ANTONIA'S
    FOLLOWING ANTONIA'S MOTIONS HERE AND THERE  . . . . . 109  2 DON JUAN  1   160   2
    ANTONIA'S SKILL WAS PUT UPON THE RACK . . . . . . . . 114  2 DON JUAN  1   169   3
    ANTONIA'S PATIENCE NOW WAS AT A STAND-- . . . . . . . 114  2 DON JUAN  1   170   5
ANTONY
    TITUS THE MASTER ANTONY THE SLAVE . . . . . . . . . . 266  2 DON JUAN  2   205   2
ANTRES
    WHAT ANTRES VAST AND DESARTS IDLE THEN  . . . . . . . 455  3 DON JUAN 14   102   1
ANVIL
    THE ANVIL OF HIS SPEECH RECEIVED THE HAMMER . . . . . 111  2 DON JUAN  1   163   3
ANXIETY
    HIS OWN ANXIETY HIS HEART TOO BLEEDING  . . . . . . . 299  2 DON JUAN  3    46   6
ANXIOUS
    BUT INEZ WAS SO ANXIOUS AND SO CLEAR  . . . . . . . .  75  2 DON JUAN  1   101   1
    WHICH MAKE ALL BODIES ANXIOUS TO GET OUT . . . . . . 220  3 DON JUAN  9    75   2
    BECAUSE HE NE'ER SEEM'D ANXIOUS TO SEDUCE . . . . . . 461  3 DON JUAN 15    12   2
ANY
    BUT CAN'T FIND ANY IN THE PRESENT AGE . . . . . . . .  24  2 DON JUAN  1     5   6
    SO THAT IF ANY ACTOR MISS'D HIS PART  . . . . . . . .  27  2 DON JUAN  1    11   3
    OF ANY MODERN FEMALE SAINT'S COMPARISON . . . . . . .  30  2 DON JUAN  1    17   2
    NOT ANY OF THE MANY COULD DIVINE   . . . . . . . . .  33  2 DON JUAN  1    23   2
    BUT IF THERE'S ANY THING IN WHICH I SHINE   . . . . .  33  2 DON JUAN  1    23   6
    ANY ONE ELSE--THEY WERE BECOME TRADITIONAL  . . . . .  37  2 DON JUAN  1    31   4
    BUT NOT A PAGE OF ANY THING THAT'S LOOSE . . . . . .  44  2 DON JUAN  1    40   6
    IF ANY SAID SO FOR TO BE PRECOCIOUS  . . . . . . . .  51  2 DON JUAN  1    54   7
    BETWEEN YOUNG PERSONS WITHOUT ANY DANGER . . . . . .  65  2 DON JUAN  1    80   2
    WITH ANY KIND OF TROUBLESOME CONTROL  . . . . . . . .  66  2 DON JUAN  1    82   6
    PEOPLE SHOULD HOLD THEIR TONGUES IN ANY CASE   . . .  77  2 DON JUAN  1   105   4
    WITH WAR OR PLAGUE OR FAMINE ANY WAY  . . . . . . . .  92  2 DON JUAN  1   131   5
    OF ANY WICKED WOMAN WHO CONTRIVED . . . . . . . . . .  96  2 DON JUAN  1   138   5
    AND DEAF THAT ANY OTHER IT WOULD VEX  . . . . . . . . 101  2 DON JUAN  1   147   4
    YOU NEVER YET TO ANY SAW ME CIVIL . . . . . . . . . . 102  2 DON JUAN  1   148  V6
    AND NOT FROM ANY LOVE TO YOU NOR ME . . . . . . . . . 103  2 DON JUAN  1   151   8
    IN ANY CASE ATTEMPTING A REPLY  . . . . . . . . . . . 119  2 DON JUAN  1   179   3
    IF ANY PERSON DOUBT IT I APPEAL . . . . . . . . . . . 138  2 DON JUAN  1   203   1
    IF ANY PERSON SHOULD PRESUME TO ASSERT  . . . . . . . 140  2 DON JUAN  1   207   1
    OR ANY OTHER THING THAT BRINGS REGRET . . . . . . . . 172  2 DON JUAN  2    31   5
    IF ANY LAUGHTER AT SUCH TIMES COULD BE   . . . . . . 183  2 DON JUAN  2    50   4
    THERE WAS SLIGHT CHANCE OF REACHING ANY SHORE . . . . 185  2 DON JUAN  2    54   5
    AND DEEMING THERE WERE REMEDIES FOR ANY ILL . . . . . 187  2 DON JUAN  2    59   7
    OF ANY CREDITORS THE WORST A JEW IT IS  . . . . . . . 190  2 DON JUAN  2    65   5
    LOVELY SEEM'D ANY OBJECT THAT SHOULD SWEEP  . . . . . 210  2 DON JUAN  2   103   7
    I CAN'T SAY THAT SHE GAVE THEM ANY TEA  . . . . . . . 233  2 DON JUAN  2   145   6
    FROM HAIDEE'S GLANCE THAN ANY GRAVEN LETTER . . . . . 242  2 DON JUAN  2   163   8
    NOR OFFER'D ANY SHE HAD NEVER HEARD  . . . . . . . . 257  2 DON JUAN  2   190   2
    FOR ANY LENGTH--CONTRIVED TO MAKE EACH OTHER CEASE  . 277  2 DON JUAN  3     5  V4
    CHASTE READER THEN IN ANY WAY TO PUT  . . . . . . . . 282  2 DON JUAN  3    12   3
    THAN ANY OF THE PARODIES OF PITT  . . . . . . . . . . 283  2 DON JUAN  3    14  V8
    OR THAT OF ANY OTHER STRONG EMOTION . . . . . . . . . 289  2 DON JUAN  3    26   6
    (NUPTIAL EXAMPLES ARE AS GOOD AS ANY) . . . . . . . . 301  2 DON JUAN  3    50   4
    AND ALWAYS CHANGED AS TRUE AS ANY NEEDLE  . . . . . . 317  2 DON JUAN  3    80   2
    THAT WITHOUT ANY DANGER OF A RIOT HE  . . . . . . . . 318  2 DON JUAN  3    83   5
    THAN ANY SINCE THE BIRTHDAY OF TYPOGRAPHY . . . . . . 330  2 DON JUAN  3    94   6
    IF I HAVE ANY FAULT IT IS DIGRESSION  . . . . . . . . 331  2 DON JUAN  3    96   2
    OR ANY SUCH LIKE SOVEREIGN BUFFOONS . . . . . . . . . 341  2 DON JUAN  3   110   2
    AND IF I LAUGH AT ANY MORTAL THING . . . . . . . . . 346  2 DON JUAN  4     4   1
    TOUCH'D HIS NOR THAT--NOR ANY HANDSOME LIMB . . . . . 396  2 DON JUAN  4    95   5
    THAN ANY OTHER SCRAPE A THING OF COURSE . . . . . . . 417  2 DON JUAN  5    12   8
    IF I COULD YIELD YOU ANY CONSOLATION  . . . . . . . . 417  2 DON JUAN  5    13   7
    FOR ANY LENGTH OF DAYS IN SUCH A PICKLE . . . . . . . 419  2 DON JUAN  5    17   4
    BUT THOSE WHO SATE NE'ER STIRRED IN ANY WISE  . . . . 441  2 DON JUAN  5    54   4
    OF ANY MUSSULMAN WHATE'ER HIS WORTH . . . . . . . . . 450  2 DON JUAN  5    67   4
    IF ANY TAKE ME FOR THAT WHICH I SEEM  . . . . . . . . 459  2 DON JUAN  5    82   6
    TO ANY SHOE UNLESS IT SHOD THE POPE . . . . . . . . . 470  2 DON JUAN  5   102   8
    IN ANY KIND OF MISCHIEF TO BE WROUGHT . . . . . . . . 477  2 DON JUAN  5   114   5
    TO GENTLEMEN IN ANY SUCH LIKE CASE  . . . . . . . . . 482  2 DON JUAN  5   123   2
    OR ANY INTERESTING BEAST OF PREY  . . . . . . . . . . 487  2 DON JUAN  5   132   2
    TO CUTTING SHORT THEIR HOPES OF HAVING ANY  . . . . . 487  2 DON JUAN  5   132   8
    AS ANY MENTIONED IN THE HISTORIES . . . . . . . . . . 495  2 DON JUAN  5   147   6
    AS ANY MAN'S CLAY MIXTURE UNDERGOES  . . . . . . . .  16  3 DON JUAN  6    20   5
    I DOUBT IF ANY NOW COULD MAKE IT WORSE  . . . . . . .  17  3 DON JUAN  6    23   4
    I KNOW NOT HOW BUT GOOD AS ANY OTHER  . . . . . . . .  21  3 DON JUAN  6    31   4
    WHICH MADE HIM WONDER MORE THAN ANY WONDER  . . . . .  34  3 DON JUAN  6    57  V7
    OF ANY SUPERNUMERARY BEAUTIES . . . . . . . . . . . .  35  3 DON JUAN  6    58   8
    AND BRIGHT AS ANY METEOR EVER BRED  . . . . . . . . .  42  3 DON JUAN  6    72   5
    INDEED ON ANY OTHER AS A MAN  . . . . . . . . . . . .  51  3 DON JUAN  6    91   2
    FOR ANY FURTHER ANSWER THAT HE FOUND  . . . . . . . .  58  3 DON JUAN  6   105   3
    FOR FEAR OF ANY ERROR LIKE THE LATE   . . . . . . . .  62  3 DON JUAN  6   112   8
    IN CASE OF ANY PREMATURE DISCLOSURE . . . . . . . . .  62  3 DON JUAN  6   114   8
    NAMES GREAT AS ANY THAT THE ROLL OF FAME HAS  . . . .  82  3 DON JUAN  7    32   8
    AS ANY OTHER NOTION AND NOT NATIONAL)--  . . . . . . 122  3 DON JUAN  8    23   8
    AS ANY OTHER BOON FOR WHICH MEN STICKLE . . . . . . . 134  3 DON JUAN  8    43   4
    MY CUE FOR ANY TIME TO BE TERRIFIC . . . . . . . . . 156  3 DON JUAN  8    89   2
    GLORY LIKE YOURS SHOULD ANY DARE GAINSAY  . . . . . . 183  3 DON JUAN  9     1   7
    AS ANY OF MORTALITY'S CONDITIONS  . . . . . . . . . . 191  3 DON JUAN  9    17   6
    MEN BECOME WOLVES ON ANY SLIGHT OCCASION . . . . . . 192  3 DON JUAN  9    20   8
```

ANY (CONTINUED)

	PAGE	VOL	CANTO	STANZA	LN
OR SCHERBATOFF OR ANY OTHER OFF	206	3 DON JUAN	9	48	2
MAKES US BELIEVE OURSELVES AS GOOD AS ANY	216	3 DON JUAN	9	68	8
ALL THESE OR ANY ONE OF THESE EXPLAIN	218	3 DON JUAN	9	72	7
FOR ANY SAGE'S CREED OR CALCULATION)--	225	3 DON JJAN	10	1	4
OF ANY SLIGHT TEMPTATION IN THEIR WAY	235	3 DON JUAN	10	21	4
KISS HANDS FEET ANY PART OF MAJESTY	286	3 DON JUAN	11	38	6
OR CHEERFUL WITHOUT ANY FLAWS OR STARTS	292	3 DON JUAN	11	47	5
AS EVER YET WAS ANY WORK SUBLIME	312	3 DON JUAN	11	90	5
BUT HAVE NOT LEARNED TO WISH IT ANY LESS	324	3 DON JUAN	12	17	8
TO LEAN ON FOR SUPPORT IN ANY WAY	324	3 DON JUAN	12	18	6
CHANGES IN YOUTH TO BE SURPRISED AT ANY	338	3 DON JUAN	12	49	8
AND TAKE MY WORD YOU WON'T HAVE ANY LESS	366	3 DON JUAN	13	18	3
AS MANY DOUBTS AS ANY OTHER DOCTRINE	377	3 DON JUAN	13	41	7
OF ANY WORSHIP WAKE SOME THOUGHTS DIVINE	387	3 DON JUAN	13	61	8
AFTER DUE SEARCH YOUR FAITH TO ANY QUESTION	411	3 DON JUAN	14	2	4
OF CHARACTER IN THOSE AT LEAST WHO HAVE GOT ANY	417	3 DON JUAN	14	16	8
IN ANY MANNER BY THE UNINITIATED	419	3 DON JUAN	14	22	8
THAT--BUT ASK ANY WOMAN IF SHE'D CHOOSE	421	3 DON JUAN	14	25	6
THE MARRIAGE STATE THE BEST OR WORST OF ANY)	452	3 DON JUAN	14	95	6
GREW FRIENDS IN THIS OR ANY OTHER SENSE	453	3 DON JUAN	14	97	2
PIOUS AND PURE BEYOND WHAT I CAN TERM ANY	472	3 DON JUAN	15	36	5
NOR EVEN SMILED ENOUGH FOR ANY VANITY	490	3 DON JUAN	15	78	4
SO MUCH AS I DO ANY KIND OF WRANGLE	496	3 DON JUAN	15	91	3
IF SHE HAD ANY WAS UPON HER FACE	525	3 DON JUAN	16	49	3
FOR ANY DEVIATION FROM THE GRACES	539	3 DON JUAN	16	79	7
OR HOPE OR LOVE WITH ANY OF THE WILES	544	3 DON JUAN	16	92	7
WHEN ANY DARE A NEW LIGHT TO PRESENT	564	3 DON JUAN	17	5	3

ANYBODY

	PAGE	VOL	CANTO	STANZA	LN
THAT ANYBODY SHOULD DISTURB YOU SO	29	3 DON JUAN	6	47	3
AS ANYBODY ON THE ELECTED ROLL	242	3 DON JUAN	10	35	3
WITH ANYBODY IN A RIDE OR WALK	464	3 DON JUAN	15	19	8

ANYBODY'S

	PAGE	VOL	CANTO	STANZA	LN
IN ANYBODY'S BUSINESS BUT THE KING'S	439	3 DON JUAN	14	66	2

ANYHOW

	PAGE	VOL	CANTO	STANZA	LN
(FOR WE MUST GET THEM ANYHOW OR GRIEVE)	270	2 DON JUAN	2	213	6

ANYONE

	PAGE	VOL	CANTO	STANZA	LN
WHEN THEY SUSPECT THAT ANYONE GOES SHARES	11	3 DON JUAN	6	10	7

ANYONE'S

	PAGE	VOL	CANTO	STANZA	LN
OF ANYONE'S ATTAINING TO HIS STATION	208	3 DON JUAN	9	52	6

ANYTHING

	PAGE	VOL	CANTO	STANZA	LN
HIS PEGASUS NOR ANYTHING THAT'S HIS	140	2 DON JUAN	1	206	2
HIS OX--HIS ASS--NOR ANYTHING THAT'S HIS	140	2 DON JUAN	1	206	V2
OR THINK OF ANYTHING EXCEPTING THEE	166	2 DON JUAN	2	19	6
HIS MUSE MADE INCREMENT OF ANYTHING	319	2 DON JUAN	3	85	5
COULD HARDLY CARRY ANYTHING AWAY	465	2 DON JUAN	5	93	5
I WON'T BE BAIL FOR ANYTHING BEYOND	469	2 DON JUAN	5	99	8
WOMAN'S THE HEART--OR ANYTHING INSTEAD	7	3 DON JUAN	6	2	V8
DONE ANYTHING EXCEEDINGLY UNKIND	193	3 DON JUAN	9	21	3
OF ANYTHING WHICH NATURE WOULD EXPRESS	373	3 DON JUAN	13	34	4
THAT ANYTHING HE VIEWS CAN GREATLY PLEASE	373	3 DON JUAN	13	34	7
'TIS PLEASANT IF THEN ANYTHING IS PLEASANT	422	3 DON JUAN	14	28	7
IN ANYTHING HOWEVER SHE MIGHT FLATTER	448	3 DON JUAN	14	88	2
FROM ANYTHING THIS EPIC WILL CONTAIN	502	3 DON JUAN	16	3	2

ANYWHERE

	PAGE	VOL	CANTO	STANZA	LN
IS IT FOR THIS I SCARCE WENT ANYWHERE	102	2 DON JUAN	1	148	3
A KINGDOM OR CONFUSION ANYWHERE	485	2 DON JUAN	5	129	3
NO SIGN THAT IT WAS CIRCULAR ANYWHERE	497	2 DON JUAN	5	150	4
WAVES AT SPRING-TIDE OR WOMEN ANYWHERE	23	3 DON JUAN	6	34	3
WAS HAPPIEST AMONGST MORTALS ANYWHERE	143	3 DON JUAN	8	61	5

APACE

	PAGE	VOL	CANTO	STANZA	LN
HE STUDIED STEADILY AND GREW APACE	48	2 DON JUAN	1	49	5
JUST AS OLD AGE IS CREEPING ON APACE	305	2 DON JUAN	3	59	5
RUSH BACK UPON HIS HEART WHICH FILLED APACE	478	2 DON JUAN	5	117	5
WITH THE FIRST DRAUGHT INTOXICATES APACE	216	3 DON JUAN	9	67	4
HIS TRAVELS TO THE CAPITAL APACE--	277	3 DON JUAN	11	18	4
WHEN HER SOFT LIQUID WORDS RUN ON APACE	426	3 DON JUAN	14	36	6

APART

	PAGE	VOL	CANTO	STANZA	LN
ITS SNOW THROUGH ALL--HER SOFT LIPS LIE APART	108	2 DON JUAN	1	158	7
MAN'S LOVE IS OF MAN'S LIFE A THING APART	131	2 DON JUAN	1	194	1
ONCE ALL IN ALL BUT NOW A THING APART	144	2 DON JUAN	1	215	3
FELT AS IF NEVER MORE TO BEAT APART	257	2 DON JUAN	2	191	8
WHEN THEY FROM THEIR SWEET FRIENDS ARE TORN APART	338	2 DON JUAN	3	108	3
WOULD WITHER LESS THAN THESE TWO TORN APART	349	2 DON JUAN	4	10	7
SHOULD AN HOUR COME TO BID THEM BREATHE APART	358	2 DON JUAN	4	27	3
AND LIPS APART WHICH SHOWED THE PEARLS BENEATH	38	3 DON JUAN	6	65	8
APART FROM ONE WHO HAD NO SIN TO SHOW	48	3 DON JUAN	6	84	7
WITH ALL ITS VEIL OF MYSTERY DRAWN APART	169	3 DON JUAN	8	115	4
IF THAT POLITENESS SET IT NOT APART	326	3 DON JUAN	12	22	5
(WHILE YET THE CHURCH WAS ROME'S) STOOD HALF APART	386	3 DON JUAN	13	59	2
THE POLITICIANS IN A NOOK APART	408	3 DON JUAN	13	109	1
FOR REASONS WHICH I CHOOSE TO KEEP APART	419	3 DON JUAN	14	21	6
SHE CALLED HER HUSBAND NOW AND THEN APART	438	3 DON JUAN	14	65	3
DISSIMULATION ALWAYS SETS APART	457	3 DON JUAN	15	3	6
APART FROM THE SURROUNDING WORLD AND STRONG	477	3 DON JUAN	15	47	7

APARTMENT

	PAGE	VOL	CANTO	STANZA	LN
YOU'VE MADE THE APARTMENT IN A FIT CONDITION--	104	2 DON JUAN	1	152	3
OF THE APARTMENT--AND APPEAR'D QUITE NEW	309	2 DON JUAN	3	67	4
JUAN FROM THE APARTMENT WITH A SIGN	371	2 DON JUAN	4	50	2

	PAGE	VOL		CANTO	STANZA	LN
APARTMENT (CONTINUED)						
WITH FURNITURE AN EXQUISITE APARTMENT	448	2 DON JUAN	5	64	7
THE APARTMENT ON A SUDDEN SHE SCREAMED OUT	41	3 DON JUAN	6	70	8
APARTMENT--FASHIONABLE BUT EXPENSIVE	313	3 DON JUAN	11	V 29	8
APARTMENTS						
BUT WHEN THEY REACHED THEIR OWN APARTMENTS THERE	23	3 DON JUAN	6	34	1
APATHY						
ITSELF TO APATHY FOR WE MUST STEEP	346	2 DON JUAN	4	4	4
APE						
IN ITALY HE'D APE THE TRECENTISTI	320	2 DON JUAN	3	86	7
IN ENGLAND HE WOULD APE THE TRECENTISTI	320	2 DON JUAN	3	86	V2
APES						
NO FASHION MADE THEM APES OF HER DISTORTIONS	145	3 DON JUAN	8	66	6
APICIUS						
WHEREON APICIUS WOULD BESTOW HIS BENISON	484	3 DON JUAN	15	65	6
APIECE						
THEY ALSO GAVE A PETTICOAT APIECE	226	2 DON JUAN	2	133	5
AND OTHERS OF TWELVE CONSONANTS A-PIECE	74	3 DON JUAN	7	15	5
APOLLO						
MEANTIME APOLLO PLUCKS ME BY THE EAR	347	2 DON JUAN	4	7	7
APOLLO'S						
CANTOS WOULD DO BUT AT APOLLO'S PLEADING	341	3 DON JUAN	12	55	6
APOLOGIES						
A LADY WITH APOLOGIES ABOUNDS	118	2 DON JUAN	1	176	5
APOLOGUE						
APOLOGUE FABLE POESY AND PARABLE	495	3 DON JUAN	15	89	1
APOLOGY						
WERE FORCED TO MAKE AN ODD SORT OF APOLOGY	44	2 DON JUAN	1	41	7
ALTHOUGH MY OPINION MAY REQUIRE APOLOGY	281	2 DON JUAN	3	11	3
SO MUCH LESS FIGHT AS MIGHT FORM AN APOLOGY	165	3 DON JUAN	8	108	4
APOPLECTIC						
BUT MOST AN ALDERMAN STRUCK APOPLECTIC	309	2 DON JUAN	3	66	5
APOSTASY'S						
APOSTASY'S SO FASHIONABLE TOO	20	2 DON JUAN	D	17	6
APOSTLE						
LIKE PETER THE APOSTLE--AND HE FISH'D	223	2 DON JUAN	2	126	2
APOSTLES						
THAT ALL THE APOSTLES WOULD HAVE DONE AS THEY DID	66	2 DON JUAN	1	83	8
APOSTROPHE						
TO HAIL HER WITH THE APOSTROPHE--OH THOU	506	3 DON JUAN	16	13	6
APOTHECARY'S						
BEYOND THE BEST APOTHECARY'S ART	167	2 DON JUAN	2	21	3
APPAL						
WHILE THE MERE VICTOR'S MAY APPAL OR STUN	114	3 DON JUAN	8	5	6
SHADOWS THE SOUL OF RICHARD MAY APPAL	499	3 DON JUAN	15	96	6
WHEN HE CAN'T TELL WHAT 'TIS THAT DOTH APPAL	559	3 DON JUAN	16	120	6
APPALS						
PERHAPS THERE'S NOTHING--I'LL NOT SAY APPALS	442	2 DON JUAN	5	56	5
APPARATUS						
BUT HAS NOT ANSWER'D LIKE THE APPARATUS	92	2 DON JUAN	1	130	3
APPAREL						
WITHOUT THE APPAREL OF BEING CIRCUMSPECT	434	3 DON JUAN	14	56	4
APPARENT						
LIKE SMALL STARS THROUGH THE MILKY WAY APPARENT	315	2 DON JUAN	3	77	4
SO THAT THE HEIR APPARENT STILL WAS FOUND	499	2 DON JUAN	5	153	7
APPEAL						
IF ANY PERSON DOUBT IT I APPEAL	138	2 DON JUAN	1	203	1
SOME TALK OF AN APPEAL UNTO SOME PASSION	437	2 DON JUAN	5	48	1
AND 'GAINST THE BODY MAKES A STRONG APPEAL	234	3 DON JUAN	10	20	5
IN AN APPEAL TO THE UNBORN WHOM THEY	324	3 DON JUAN	12	18	2
IN RIGHT GOOD EARNEST--ALSO AN APPEAL	357	3 DON JUAN	12	V 18	2
APPEAL'D						
MILTON APPEAL'D TO THE AVENGER TIME	15	2 DON JUAN	D	10	2
APPEALS						
THE POET MEANT NO DOUBT AND THUS APPEALS	69	2 DON JUAN	1	89	1
BUT I DIGRESS OF ALL APPEALS--ALTHOUGH	439	2 DON JUAN	5	49	1
APPEAR						
AND MAY APPEAR SO WHEN THE DOG-STAR RAGES--	11	2 DON JUAN	D	4	6
'TIS SWEET TO SEE THE EVENING STAR APPEAR	87	2 DON JUAN	1	122	5
THEY SHALL APPEAR BEFORE YOUR CURIOUS EYES	222	2 DON JUAN	2	124	6
AND AS THE SPOT WHERE THEY APPEAR HE NEARS	290	2 DON JUAN	3	28	1
THE SKIN RELIEVED APPEAR MORE FAIRLY FAIR	314	2 DON JUAN	3	76	2
THIS WAY OF WRITING WILL APPEAR EXOTIC	347	2 DON JUAN	4	6	4
AY QUOTH HIS FRIEND I THOUGHT IT WOULD APPEAR	420	2 DON JUAN	5	19	3
HER THOUGHTS AT LEAST TILL NOW APPEAR TO HAVE BEEN . . .	33	3 DON JUAN	6	54	4
WHICH MAKES THE SOUTHERN AUTUMN'S DAY APPEAR	395	3 DON JUAN	13	77	2
APPEARANCES APPEAR TO FORM THE JOINT	396	3 DON JUAN	13	81	3
'TIS TIME THAT SOME NEW PROPHET SHOULD APPEAR	496	3 DON JUAN	15	90	5
APPEAR TO WAKE AND SHADOWS WILD AND QUAINT	508	3 DON JUAN	16	18	5
APPEARANCE						
MAY NOT THINK MUCH OF LONDON'S FIRST APPEARANCE-- . . .	271	3 DON JUAN	11	7	7
APPEARANCES						
APPEARANCES APPEAR TO FORM THE JOINT	396	3 DON JUAN	13	81	3
APPEAR'D						
APPEAR'D LIKE TWO POOR HARMLESS WOMEN WHO	98	2 DON JUAN	1	141	2
WAS USED--NOR SAIL NOR SHORE APPEAR'D IN SIGHT	178	2 DON JUAN	2	41	7
WATER APPEAR'D YET THOUGH THE PEOPLE KNEW	178	2 DON JUAN	2	42	3
AND ALL WITHIN ITS ARCH APPEAR'D TO BE	204	2 DON JUAN	2	91	4
THE LAND APPEAR'D A HIGH AND ROCKY COAST	209	2 DON JUAN	2	100	1

26

```
APPEAR'D   (CONTINUED)
     BUT NONE OF THEM APPEAR'D TO SHARE HIS WOES . . . . . . . 213   2 DON JUAN   2    109   5
     SHE WAS APPEAR'D DISTINCT AND TALL AND FAIR . . . . . . . 216   2 DON JUAN   2    115   8
     OF THE APARTMENT--AND APPEAR'D QUITE NEW . . . . . . . . 309   2 DON JUAN   3     67   4
     MOST LOVE POSSESSION UNTO THEM APPEAR'D . . . . . . . . . 352   2 DON JUAN   4     16   7
     AND THAT BRIEF DREAM APPEAR'D A LIFE TOO LONG . . . . . . 362   2 DON JUAN   4     34   8
     HE SAW SOME FELLOW CAPTIVES WHO APPEAR'D . . . . . . . . 388   2 DON JUAN   4     80   1
     NEXT THAT HE NEVER JUDGED FROM WHAT APPEAR'D . . . . . . 439   3 DON JUAN  14     66   3
APPEARED
     APPEARED TO HIM BUT AS THE MAGIC VAPOUR . . . . . . . . . 266   3 DON JUAN  10     83   2
     IN COWL AND BEADS AND DUSKY GARB APPEARED . . . . . . . 510   3 DON JUAN  16     21   2
     AND YET HIS LOOKS APPEARED TO SANCTION BOTH . . . . . . 514   3 DON JUAN  16     33   2
     TO BEAR ON WHAT APPEARED TO HER THE SUBJECT . . . . . . 526   3 DON JUAN  16     51   3
APPEARING
     KNOWN BUT TO THEM AT LEAST APPEARING SUCH . . . . . . 351   2 DON JUAN   4     14   5
APPEARS
     WAVED AND O'ERSHADING HER WAN CHEEK APPEARS . . . . . . 108   2 DON JUAN   1    158   4
     OF HER DISHEVELLED TRESSES DARK APPEARS . . . . . . . . 108   2 DON JUAN   1    158  V4
     (THAT MODERN PHRASE APPEARS TO ME SAD STUFF . . . . . . 119   2 DON JUAN   1    178   3
     BE ON THIS SHEET 'TIS NOT WHAT IT APPEARS . . . . . . . 130   2 DON JUAN   1    192   7
     BUT THERE IS SOMETHING WHEN MAN'S EYE APPEARS . . . . . 479   2 DON JUAN   5    118   3
     BUT BY THE BOOKISH THEORIC IT APPEARS . . . . . . . . .  10   3 DON JUAN   6      9   2
     AND LO A FIFTH APPEARS--AND WHAT IS SHE . . . . . . . .  41   3 DON JUAN   6     69   1
     HE CLIMBED TO WHERE THE PARAPET APPEARS . . . . . . . . 147   3 DON JUAN   8     71   4
     TO ME APPEARS A STIFF YET GRAND ERECTION . . . . . . . 280   3 DON JUAN  11     25   7
     WHERE MINGLED AND YET SEPARATE APPEARS . . . . . . . . 447   3 DON JUAN  14     87   5
     FOR ME APPEARS A QUESTION FAR TOO NICE . . . . . . . . 478   3 DON JUAN  15     52   5
     A VISITANT AT INTERVALS APPEARS . . . . . . . . . . . 504   3 DON JUAN  16      7   4
APPELLANTS
     THE MAJOR PART OF SUCH APPELLANTS GO . . . . . . . . .  14   2 DON JUAN   0      9   7
     PERHAPS BECAUSE OUR APPELLANTS MADE OUT OF SEASON . . . 437   2 DON JUAN   5     48  V4
APPENDAGE
     A DULL AND DESOLATE APPENDAGE  GAZE . . . . . . . . . 373   3 DON JUAN  13     33   2
APPENDIX
     THEY ONLY ADD THEM ALL IN AN APPENDIX . . . . . . . .  46   2 DON JUAN   1     44   7
     BUT I SHALL ADD THEM IN A BRIEF APPENDIX . . . . . . . 440   3 DON JUAN  14     68   7
APPETITE
     FEEL NOW HIS APPETITE INCREASED MUCH MORE . . . . . . 198   2 DON JUAN   2     78   5
     A MOST PRODIGIOUS APPETITE THE STEAM . . . . . . . . . 237   2 DON JUAN   2    153   3
     SUCH APPETITE IN ONE SHE HAD DEEM'D DEAD . . . . . . . 239   2 DON JUAN   2    158   4
     I WONDER IF HIS APPETITE WAS GOOD . . . . . . . . . . 426   2 DON JUAN   5     30   1
     WITH THE PROPHETIC EYE OF APPETITE . . . . . . . . . . 439   2 DON JUAN   5     50   8
     OF CLARET SANDWICH AND AN APPETITE . . . . . . . . . . 444   2 DON JUAN   5     58   3
     FOR WHICH HE OWNED A PRESENT APPETITE . . . . . . . . 452   2 DON JUAN   5     71   4
     I WISH YOU A GOOD APPETITE--FAREWELL . . . . . . . . . 460   2 DON JUAN   5     84   2
     AND THAT OUTRAGEOUS APPETITE FOR LIES . . . . . . . . 154   3 DON JUAN   8     86   7
     HE SHOWS MORE APPETITE FOR WORDS THAN WAR . . . . . . 398   3 DON JUAN  13     84   4
APPETITES
     FOR HAVING USED THEIR APPETITES SO SADLY . . . . . . . 199   2 DON JUAN   2     80   8
     AND OTHERS STILL THEIR APPETITES CONSTRAIN'D . . . . . 200   2 DON JUAN   2     82   3
APPLAUDS
     NOR LESS APPLAUDS AS IN POLITENESS BOUND . . . . . . . 521   3 DON JUAN  16     41   6
APPLAUSE
     THE GLORIOUS MEED OF POPULAR APPLAUSE . . . . . . . . 318   2 DON JUAN   3     82   7
     LET THIS FIFTH CANTO MEET WITH DUE APPLAUSE . . . . . 503   2 DON JUAN   5    159   5
     WITH ITS PROUD BROW IT MERITS SLIGHT APPLAUSE . . . .  86   3 DON JUAN   7     40   6
     THERE WAS ENTHUSIASM AND MUCH APPLAUSE . . . . . . .  89   3 DON JUAN   7     47   2
     HIS LITTLE CAPTIVE GAINED HIM SOME APPLAUSE . . . . . 182   3 DON JUAN   8    140   5
     AND NOW IN THIS NEW FIELD WITH SOME APPLAUSE . . . . . 424   3 DON JUAN  14     33   1
     BUT THIS I MUST SAY IN MY OWN APPLAUSE . . . . . . . . 502   3 DON JUAN  16      2   4
APPLE
     AND IN THE MIDST A GOLDEN APPLE GREW-- . . . . . . . .  44   3 DON JUAN   6     76   1
     BUT VISIONS OF AN APPLE AND A BEE . . . . . . . . . .  46   3 DON JUAN   6     80   2
     WHEN NEWTON SAW AN APPLE FALL HE FOUND . . . . . . . 225   3 DON JUAN  10      1   1
     SINCE ADAM WITH A FALL OR WITH AN APPLE . . . . . . . 225   3 DON JUAN  10      1   8
APPLES
     MAN FELL WITH APPLES AND WITH APPLES ROSE . . . . . . 226   3 DON JUAN  10      2   1
     MAN FELL WITH APPLES AND WITH APPLES ROSE . . . . . . 226   3 DON JUAN  10      2   1
     SINCE EVE ATE APPLES MUCH DEPENDS ON DINNER . . . . . 404   3 DON JUAN  13     99   8
APPLICATION
     SHRINKS FROM THE APPLICATION OF HOT TOWELS . . . . . . 168   2 DON JUAN   2     23   4
     HIS STEADY APPLICATION AS A DANCER . . . . . . . . . . 294   3 DON JUAN  11     51   6
APPLIED
     PERHAPS 'TWAS IN A DIFFERENT WAY APPLIED . . . . . . . 113   2 DON JUAN   1    168   7
     HIS THOUGHTS HOW WELL APPLIED THE NAME OF GOD . . . . 154   2 DON JUAN   1    V  5  V2
     AND ALL LIPS WERE APPLIED UNTO ALL EARS . . . . . . . 221   3 DON JUAN   9     78   2
     TO FREEDOM HE APPLIED (A GRIEF AND A BORE) . . . . . . 288   3 DON JUAN  11     41   6
     UNLESS A MARRIAGE WAS APPLIED TO MEND . . . . . . . . 470   3 DON JUAN  15     33   6
APPLY
     OR THAT OF HER TO WHOM HE MIGHT APPLY . . . . . . . . 469   3 DON JUAN  15     30   6
APPOINTMENT
     ANNOUNCING THE APPOINTMENT OF THAT LOVER OF . . . . .  85   3 DON JUAN   7     39   7
APPRECIATED
     AND THERE IS MUCH WHICH COULD NOT BE APPRECIATED . . . 419   3 DON JUAN  14     22   7
APPREHENSION
     STINGS IN LIFE WITH APPREHENSION IN ITS SHEATH . . . . 188   3 DON JUAN   9     11  V7
APPREHENSIVE
     BUT APPREHENSIVE OF HIS SPECTRAL GUEST . . . . . . . 555   3 DON JUAN  16    111   5
APPRENSIONS
     OF IDLE APPRENSIONS WHICH LIKE WIND . . . . . . . . . 133   3 DON JUAN   8     40   4
```

27

PAGE VOL   CANTO STANZA LN

APPROACH
    THE APPROACH OF HOME TO HUSBANDS AND TO SIRES . . . . . 287 2 DON JUAN 3   22 1
    MOTIONED TO JUAN TO APPROACH AND THEN . . . . 470 2 DON JUAN 5   102 2
    GAUNT FAMINE NEVER SHALL APPROACH THE THRONE-- . . . . 175 3 DON JUAN 8   126 7
    THROUGH THIS AND MUCH AND MORE IS THE APPROACH . . . . 279 3 DON JUAN 11   23 1
APPROACHING
    TILL IN APPROACHING WERE AT LENGTH DESCRIED . . . . . . 87 3 DON JUAN 7   43 7
    BUT JUAN FELT THOUGH NOT APPROACHING HOME . . . . . . 265 3 DON JUAN 10   81 5
    LIKE A MEEK TRADESMAN WHEN APPROACHING PALELY . . . . 459 3 DON JUAN 15   8 3
APPROBATION
    AND IF THEIR APPROBATION WE EXPERIENCE . . . . 135 2 DON JUAN 1   199 7
    THE PUBLIC APPROBATION I EXPECT . . . . 141 2 DON JUAN 1   209 1
    SUFFICIENTLY (HE SAID) HIS APPROBATION . . . . 452 2 DON JUAN 5   70 7
    WITHOUT OUR KNOWLEDGE OR OUR APPROBATION . . . . . . 25 3 DON JUAN 6   38 4
    SHE COULD NOT TOO MUCH GIVE HER APPROBATION . . . . . 241 3 DON JUAN 10   33 1
APPROPRIATE
    THAT'S AN APPROPRIATE SIMILE THAT JACKALL-- . . . . . 196 3 DON JUAN 9   27 1
APPROPRIATELY
    THUS MOST APPROPRIATELY HAS BEEN SHOWN . . . . . . 33 3 DON JUAN 6   55 4
APPROVE
    AND THEREFORE DOUBTLESS TO APPROVE THE TRUTH . . . . 439 3 DON JUAN 14   67 1
APPROVED
    TIME HAS APPROVED ENNUI TO BE THE BEST . . . . . 343 2 DON JUAN 3 V 98 1
    (A THING APPROVED AS SAVING TIME AND TOIL)-- . . . . 351 3 DON JUAN 12   76 6
    SHE APPROVED HIS SILENCE SHE PERHAPS MISTOOK . . . . 553 3 DON JUAN 16   106 2
APPROVER
    OR AN APPROVER OR A MERE SPECTATOR . . . . 303 3 DON JUAN 11   69 7
APROPOS
    OH YE GREAT AUTHORS--APROPOS DES BOTTES-- . . . . 200 3 DON JUAN 9   36 1
    AS APROPOS OF HOPE OR RETROSPECTION . . . . 456 3 DON JUAN 15   1 3
APT
    ARE APT TO CARRY THINGS WITH A HIGH HAND . . . . . 11 3 DON JUAN 6   11 3
    AND APT TO BE TRANSFERRED TO THE FIRST BUYER . . . . 14 3 DON JUAN 6   16 6
    APT TO WEAR OUT ON TRIFLING PROVOCATIONS . . . . . 165 3 DON JUAN 8   107 8
    IS APT TO TIRE A CALM AND SHALLOW STATION . . . . 191 3 DON JUAN 9   18 6
    BUT I AM APT TO GROW TOO METAPHYSICAL . . . . . 203 3 DON JUAN 9   41 1
    WITH WHICH GREAT STATES SUCH THINGS ARE APT TO PUSH ON . 246 3 DON JUAN 10   45 5
    REQUIRES DECORUM AND IS APT TO DOUBLE . . . . . . 292 3 DON JUAN 11   46 7
    OF BEING APT TO TALK AT A GREAT RATE . . . . . . 329 3 DON JUAN 12   28 6
    PEOPLE ARE APT TO BLAME THE FATES FORSOOTH . . . . 339 3 DON JUAN 12   50 3
    ALTHOUGH WHEN LONG A LITTLE APT TO WEARY US . . . . 358 3 DON JUAN 13   1 6
    THOUGH APT TO ACT WITH FIRE UPON OCCASION . . . . 365 3 DON JUAN 13   14 5
    AND APT TO SOW AN AUTHOR'S WHEAT WITH TARES . . . . 369 3 DON JUAN 13   25 3
    YOUR MEN OF BUSINESS ARE NOT APT TO EXPRESS . . . . 443 3 DON JUAN 14   76 6
    ARE APT EXCEEDINGLY TO RUN TO SEED . . . . . . 445 3 DON JUAN 14   81 8
    BECAUSE SHE WAS NOT APT LIKE SOME OF US . . . . . 460 3 DON JUAN 15   10 3
    WAS APT TO ADD A COLOURING FROM HER OWN . . . . . 463 3 DON JUAN 15   17 2
    THE LAST IS APT THE FORMER TO ACCUSE . . . . . . 564 3 DON JUAN 17   6 4
    CHEERFUL--BUT SOMETIMES RATHER APT TO WHIMPER . . . . 567 3 DON JUAN 17   11 5
AQ
    AQ FERVENT OUNCE AND A HALF TWO DRAMS TINCT SENNAE . 244 3 DON JUAN 10   41 3
AQUA-VITA
    WAS LOST BY GETTING AT SOME AQUA-VITA . . . . . . 186 2 DON JUAN 2   56 8
ARAB
    AN ARAB HORSE A STATELY STAG A BARB . . . . . . 160 2 DON JUAN 2   6 1
    UNLIKE THE HONEST ARAB THIEVES SO BRAVE . . . . . 225 2 DON JUAN 2   130 6
    AN ARAB WITH A STRANGER FOR A GUEST . . . . . . 261 2 DON JUAN 2   196 4
    OF WONDERFUL REPLIES FROM ARAB JOKERS . . . . . . 293 2 DON JUAN 3   34 4
    THE ARAB LORE AND POET'S SONG WERE DONE . . . . . 334 2 DON JUAN 3   101 3
    SO ARAB DESERTS DRINK IN SUMMER'S RAIN . . . . . 212 3 DON JUAN 9   59 6
    SHE CANNOT STEP AS DOES AN ARAB BARB . . . . . . 350 3 DON JUAN 12   75 1
    THE WILDS AS DOTH AN ARAB TURN'D AVENGER . . . . . 424 3 DON JUAN 14   32 6
ARABIA
    AND MOCHA'S BERRY FROM ARABIA PURE . . . . 307 2 DON JUAN 3   63 3
ARABLE
    BY THOSE WHO SOW THEM IN A LAND THAT'S ARABLE . . . . 495 3 DON JUAN 15   89 3
ARABS
    HE HAD TRAVELL'D 'MONGST THE ARABS TURKS AND FRANKS . . 319 2 DON JUAN 3   84 1
ARAB-SPEARS
    THESE WORDS WENT THROUGH HIS SOUL LIKE ARAB-SPEARS . . 478 2 DON JUAN 5   117 7
ARAMINTA
    THAT PRODIGY MISS ARAMINTA SMITH . . . . 294 3 DON JUAN 11   52 5
ARCADES
    ARCADES AMBO ID EST--BLACKGUARDS BOTH . . . . . . 394 2 DON JUAN 4   93 8
ARCADIANS
    THEY AND THEIR BILLS ARCADIANS BOTH ARE LEFT . . . . 379 3 DON JUAN 13   45 1
ARCANUM'S
    THE GRAND ARCANUM'S NOT FOR MEN TO SEE ALL . . . . . 419 3 DON JUAN 14   22 5
ARCH
    AND ALL WITHIN ITS ARCH APPEAR'D TO BE . . . . . . 204 2 DON JUAN 2   91 4
    SO MUCH AS UNDER A TRIUMPHAL ARCH . . . . 121 3 DON JUAN 8   21 4
    IN A GRAND ARCH WHICH ONCE SCREENED MANY AN AISLE . . 386 3 DON JUAN 13   59 3
    IN GAZING ON THAT VENERABLE ARCH . . . . 386 3 DON JUAN 13   59 8
    THROUGH THE HUGE ARCH WHICH SOARS AND SINKS AGAIN . . 388 3 DON JUAN 13   63 5
    AND WHEN YOU MAY NOT BE SUBLIME BE ARCH . . . . . 468 3 DON JUAN 15   27 3
    TO THESE THEY ARE RAGS OR DUST WHERE IS THE ARCH . . 485 3 DON JUAN 15   67 2
ARCHDEACON
    UNTIL HIS LATE LIFE BY ARCHDEACON COXE . . . . . . 328 2 DON JUAN 3   90 8
ARCHED
    WHICH ARCHED THE HORIZON LIKE A FIERY CLOUD . . . . 115 3 DON JUAN 8   6 3

28

```
                                                          PAGE VOL      CANTO STANZA LN
ARCH-ENEMY
    TO EAT THE HEAD OF HIS ARCH-ENEMY  . . . . . . . . . 200  2 DON JUAN  2    83   3
ARCHER'S
    THE OLD ARCHER'S SHAFTS PERHAPS THE EARLY GRAVE  . . . . . 350  2 DON JUAN  4    12   7
ARCHES
    SHOUTS BRIDGES ARCHES PENSIONS FROM A NATION  . . . . . . 114  3 DON JUAN  8     4   3
ARCHIMEDES
    LIKE ARCHIMEDES I LEAVE EARTH AS 'TWAS  . . . . . . . 446  3 DON JUAN 14    84   8
ARCHITECT
    BRICKLAYER OF BABEL CALLED AN ARCHITECT  . . . . . . . 529  3 DON JUAN 16    58   2
    FROM TOWN VIZ ARCHITECT AND DEALER WERE  . . . . . . . 533  3 DON JUAN 16    66   5
ARCHITECTURE
    WHO GIVE THEMSELVES TO ARCHITECTURE WHOLLY  . . . . . . 448  2 DON JUAN  5    63   4
ARDENT
    'TIS TRUE HE HAD NO ARDENT LOVE FOR PEACE--  . . . . . 303  2 DON JUAN  3    55   5
ARDOUR
    DANGER AND SPOIL WITH ARDOUR MUCH ENCREASED  . . . . . . 90  3 DON JUAN  7    49   6
ARGO
    LIKE THE FIRST OLD GREEK PRIVATEER THE ARGO  . . . . . 191  2 DON JUAN  2    66   8
    MUCH PASSION SINCE THE MERCHANT-SHIP THE ARGO  . . . . . 443  3 DON JUAN 14    76   7
ARGUMENT
    I HATE IT AS I HATE AN ARGUMENT . . . . . . . . . 435  3 DON JUAN 14    58   7
    AND NOW I WILL GIVE UP ALL ARGUMENT  . . . . . . . . 498  3 DON JUAN 15    94   1
    THERE IS A COMMON-PLACE BOOK ARGUMENT . . . . . . . . 564  3 DON JUAN 17     5   1
ARGUMENTS
    WITH ARGUMENTS ACCORDING TO THEIR FORTE  . . . . . . . 437  2 DON JUAN  5    48   7
    AND PASSED FOR ARGUMENTS OF GOOD ENDURANCE  . . . . . . 294  3 DON JUAN 11    52   4
ARGUS
    AND THAT HIS ARGUS BITES HIM BY--THE BREECHES  . . . . . 287  2 DON JUAN  3    23   8
ARIEL
    (NOT THE MOST DAINTY ARIEL) AND PERPLEXES  . . . . . 269  3 DON JUAN 11     3   2
ARIOSTO
    THE WORLD NOT QUITE SO GREAT AS ARIOSTO  . . . . . . . 331  2 DON JUAN  3    96   8
    OF SMOLLET PRIOR ARIOSTO FIELDING  . . . . . . . . 397  2 DON JUAN  4    98   3
ARIS
    WOULD YOU DO LESS PRO FOCIS ET PRO ARIS  . . . . . . . 174  3 DON JUAN  8   124  V8
ARISE
    ARISE LIKE TITAN FROM THE SEA'S IMMERSION  . . . . . 14  2 DON JUAN  D     9   6
    THINK'ST THOU COULD HE--THE BLIND OLD MAN--ARISE  . . . . . 15  2 DON JUAN  D    11   1
    AND LOVE THAN EITHER AND THERE WOULD ARISE  . . . . . . 54  2 DON JUAN  1    60   5
    THE LONGINGS OF THE CANNIBAL ARISE  . . . . . . . . 194  2 DON JUAN  2    72   7
    BUT ONE ARISE--WE COME WE COME  . . . . . . . . . 323  2 DON JUAN  3  L  8   5
    NO DIRGE SAVE WHEN ARISE THE STORMY SEAS . . . . . . . 383  2 DON JUAN  4    72  V7
    THERE MIGHT ARISE SOME POUTING PETTY CARE  . . . . . . 480  2 DON JUAN  5   119   6
    ARISE WHEN WE SEE EMPERORS FALL WITH OATS  . . . . . . 198  3 DON JUAN  9    32   8
    AND HENCE ARISE THE WOES OF SENTIMENT . . . . . . . . 444  3 DON JUAN 14    79   6
ARISEN
    HER PASSIONS HAD ARISEN AND HER YOUTH'S FLOWER . . . . . 262  2 DON JUAN  2   198  V5
ARISING
    ARISING OUT OF BUSINESS OFTEN BROUGHT . . . . . . . . 365  3 DON JUAN 13    15   2
ARISTIPPUS
    AND ARISTIPPUS A MATERIAL CREW  . . . . . . . . . 267  2 DON JUAN  2   207   2
    DREST IN THE WAY THAT ARISTIPPUS WISHES  . . . . . . . 307  2 DON JUAN  3    62  V5
ARISTOCRACY
    LET TO THE MORNING POST ITS ARISTOCRACY  . . . . . . . 329  2 DON JUAN  3    93   6
    FLOURISHED ITS SOPHISTRY FOR ARISTOCRACY  . . . . . . 329  2 DON JUAN  3    93  V6
    AMONG THE PROUDEST OF OUR ARISTOCRACY . . . . . . . . 346  3 DON JUAN 12    66   6
ARISTOCRATIC
    ARISTOCRATIC AS WAS EVER SEEN  . . . . . . . . . 116  3 DON JUAN  8    10   4
    AND TURN ON THINGS WHICH NO ARISTOCRATIC . . . . . . . 289  3 DON JUAN 11    43   3
    BUT ALL WAS GENTLE AND ARISTOCRATIC  . . . . . . . 409  3 DON JUAN 13   110   1
    OF GOUT WHICH RUSTS ARISTOCRATIC HINGES . . . . . . . 515  3 DON JUAN 16    34   8
ARISTOTLE
    OF ARISTOTLE AND THE RULES 'TIS FIT  . . . . . . . 86  2 DON JUAN  1   120   7
    OR EVERY POET HIS OWN ARISTOTLE . . . . . . . . . 138  2 DON JUAN  1   204   8
    FROM ARISTOTLE PASSIM--SEE POIETIKES  . . . . . . . 342  2 DON JUAN  3   111   8
    AS THOSE OF ARISTOTLE THOUGH SOMETIMES  . . . . . . . 470  3 DON JUAN 15    32   7
ARISTOTLE'S
    WITH STRICT REGARD TO ARISTOTLE'S RULES  . . . . . . . 136  2 DON JUAN  1   201   2
ARITHMETIC
    OR TURNING MARRIAGE INTO ARITHMETIC  . . . . . . . 472  3 DON JUAN 15    38   8
    REQUIRES ARITHMETIC BEYOND MY FORCES  . . . . . . . 486  3 DON JUAN 15    69   4
    THE POETS OF ARITHMETIC ARE THEY  . . . . . . . . 548  3 DON JUAN 16    99   1
ARITHMETICIAN
    I AM NOT LIKE CASSIO AN ARITHMETICIAN . . . . . . . . 10  3 DON JUAN  6     9   1
ARK
    AS IF A SPANISH SHIP WERE NOAH'S ARK  . . . . . . . 161  2 DON JUAN  2     8   6
    SINCE NOAH'S ARK WENT CRUISING HERE AND THERE  . . . . . 191  2 DON JUAN  2    66   6
    AND HAD IT BEEN THE DOVE FROM NOAH'S ARK . . . . . . . 206  2 DON JUAN  2    95   5
ARM
    AND HALF RETIRING FROM THE GLOWING ARM  . . . . . . . 83  2 DON JUAN  1   115   2
    AROUND HIS SCARCE-CLAD LIMBS AND THE FAIR ARM  . . . . . 216  2 DON JUAN  2   114   2
    THEY TURN'D TO REST AND EACH CLASP'D BY AN ARM . . . . . 253  2 DON JUAN  2   184   7
    GLEAM IN THE MOONLIGHT AND HER WHITE ARM CLASPS  . . . . . 259  2 DON JUAN  2   194   2
    OF ARMS (IN THE EAST ALL ARM)--AND VARIOUS DYES  . . . . . 289  2 DON JUAN  3    27   7
    ONE LARGE GOLD BRACELET CLASP'D EACH LOVELY ARM  . . . . . 312  2 DON JUAN  3    71   1
    JUAN REPLIED NOT WHILE THIS ARM IS FREE  . . . . . . . 365  2 DON JUAN  4    40   2
    ONE ON THE ARM THE OTHER ON THE HEAD  . . . . . . . 370  2 DON JUAN  4    49   8
    ON HER SIRE'S ARM WHICH UNTIL NOW SCARCE HELD  . . . . . 375  2 DON JUAN  4    58   7
```

29

```
                                                          PAGE VOL     CANTO  STANZA LN
ARM    (CONTINUED)
    ONE ARM HAD ON A BANDAGE RATHER BLOODY   . . . . .  . 416   2 DON JUAN  5     11    6
    ELSE THEY SHALL FEEL THE WEIGHT OF THIS MY ARM . . . . . 459  2 DON JUAN  5     82    3
    AND RAISING UP AN ARM AS MOONLIGHT FAIR  . . . . . . . 466   2 DON JUAN  5     96    5
    WITH GREAT BLUE EYES A LOVELY HAND AND ARM . . . . . . 26    3 DON JUAN  6     41    3
    ONE WITH HER FLUSHED CHEEK LAID ON HER WHITE ARM . . . . 39  3 DON JUAN  6     66    1
    WHILE THEIR BELOVED FRIENDS BEGAN TO ARM . . . . . . . 105   3 DON JUAN  7     76    7
    BY MERELY WIELDING WITH POETIC ARM . . . . . . . . . 106     3 DON JUAN  7     79    3
    A PATH TO ADD HIS OWN SLIGHT ARM AND FORCES . . . . . 126    3 DON JUAN  8     30    7
    YOUR ARM AND I'LL BET MOSCOW TO A DOLLAR . . . . . . 160     3 DON JUAN  8     97    7
    RAISE BUT AN ARM 'TWILL BRUSH THEIR WEB AWAY  . . . . 196    3 DON JUAN  9     28    1
    A SINGLE LAUGH DEMOLISHED THE RIGHT ARM . . . . . . . 364    3 DON JUAN 13     11    2
    JUAN PUT FORTH ONE ARM--ETERNAL POWERS  . . . . . . . 559    3 DON JUAN 16    120    1
    HIS OTHER ARM FORTH--WONDER UPON WONDER . . . . . . . 560    3 DON JUAN 16    122    2
ARM-CHAIR
    THERE IS THE SOFA THERE THE GREAT ARM-CHAIR . . . . . 104    2 DON JUAN  1    153    3
ARM'D
    AND SUMMON LACKEYS ARM'D WITH FIRE AND SWORD . . . . . 97    2 DON JUAN  1    139    7
    AND ARM'D FROM BOOT TO TURBAN ONE AND ALL   . . . . . 369    2 DON JUAN  4     47    6
ARMED
    OF THE ARMED RIVER WHILE WITH STRAGGLING LIGHT . . . . 110   3 DON JUAN  7     86    5
ARMENIAN
    IN SEVERAL OATHS--ARMENIAN TURK AND GREEK-- . . . . . 229    2 DON JUAN  2    138    7
ARMIDA'S
    WROUGHT CHANGE WITH ALL ARMIDA'S FAIRY ART  . . . . . 60     2 DON JUAN  1     71    7
ARMIES
    EUROPE HAS SLAVES--ALLIES--KINGS--ARMIES STILL . . . . . 19  2 DON JUAN  0     16    7
    THE ARMIES OF THE CHRISTIAN EMPRESS CATHERINE . . . . . 99   3 DON JUAN  7     64    8
    THE HUM OF ARMIES GATHERING RANK ON RANK . . . . . . 110     3 DON JUAN  7     86    2
    WHICH OF THE ARMIES WOULD HAVE CAUSE TO MOURN . . . . . 150  3 DON JUAN  8     77    6
ARMISTICE
    AGREE TO A SHORT ARMISTICE WITH TRUTH . . . . . . . . 318    2 DON JUAN  3     83    8
ARMOUR
    GENERALS SOME ALL IN ARMOUR OF THE OLD  . . . . . . . 391    3 DON JUAN 13     70    1
    WITH MASSY PLATE FOR ARMOUR KNIVES AND FORKS  . . . . 482    3 DON JUAN 15     62    2
ARMS
    JUST AS HIS FEEBLE ARMS COULD STRIKE NO MORE  . . . . 212    2 DON JUAN  2    107    3
    AND JUAN SUNK TO SLEEP WITHIN HER ARMS  . . . . . . . 260    2 DON JUAN  2    195    2
    OF ARMS (IN THE EAST ALL ARM)--AND VARIOUS DYES . . . . 289  2 DON JUAN  3     27    7
    MIX'D IN EACH OTHER'S ARMS AND HEART IN HEART . . . . . 358  2 DON JUAN  4     27    1
    IN ARMS AT LEAST HE STOOD IN ACT TO SPRING  . . . . . 365    2 DON JUAN  4     39    7
    HIS ARMS WERE LIKE A SERPENT'S COIL THEN FLEW . . . . . 370  2 DON JUAN  4     48    5
    AND COOKS IN MOTION WITH THEIR CLEAN ARMS BARED . . . . 439  2 DON JUAN  5     50    6
    AND WRESTLING BOTH HIS ARMS INTO A GOWN . . . . . . . 456    2 DON JUAN  5     78    7
    WITH GENTLE FORCE HER WHITE ARMS HE UNWOUND . . . . . 484    2 DON JUAN  5    126    3
    THERE'S NOTHING WHETS THE BEAK OR ARMS THE CLAW . . . . 488  2 DON JUAN  5    133    3
    AND BOSOMS ARMS AND ANCLES GLANCING BARE . . . . . . 42      3 DON JUAN  6     72    4
    I DON'T KNOW WHETHER THEY HAD ARMS OR CREST . . . . . 76     3 DON JUAN  7     19    3
    NOW UNDER ARMS HO KATSKOFF TAKE HIM TO-- . . . . . . 100     3 DON JUAN  7     66    3
    THEIR ARMS AS HENS THEIR WINGS ABOUT THEIR YOUNG . . . . 101 3 DON JUAN  7     67    8
    ARMS TO WHICH MEN WILL NEVER MORE RESORT . . . . . . 106     3 DON JUAN  7     79    4
    OBSERVE YOUR LOVER WHEN HE LEAVES YOUR ARMS . . . . . 139    3 DON JUAN  8     53    7
    HER HUNDRED ARMS AND LEGS AND FAIN OUTRUN HER . . . . 231    3 DON JUAN 10     12    6
    IN ROYALTY'S VAST ARMS HE SIGHED FOR BEAUTY . . . . . 243    3 DON JUAN 10     37    8
    THEIR VIGOUR IN A THOUSAND ARMS IS DISSIPATED . . . . . 306  3 DON JUAN 11     75    3
    HIS HOST WITH BROAD ARMS 'GAINST THE THUNDER-STROKE . . 384  3 DON JUAN 13     56    4
    WITH HER SON IN HER BLESSED ARMS LOOK'D ROUND . . . . 387    3 DON JUAN 13     61    3
    THEY ADDED GRACEFUL NECKS WHITE HANDS AND ARMS . . . . 408   3 DON JUAN 13    107    8
ARMY
    MONTHS WITH THE RUSSIAN ARMY HERE AND THERE . . . . . 418    2 DON JUAN  5     15    6
    OR THAT THE RUSSIAN ARMY SHOULD REPENT ALL  . . . . . 105    3 DON JUAN  7     75    6
    THE ARMY LIKE A LION FROM HIS DEN  . . . . . . . . . 113     3 DON JUAN  8      2    3
    OF HIS WHOLE ARMY WHICH SO MUCH ABOUNDED  . . . . . . 125    3 DON JUAN  8     28    6
    THE RUSSIAN ARMY UPON THIS OCCASION  . . . . . . . . 176     3 DON JUAN  8    128    2
    MADE UP BY YOUTH FAME AND AN ARMY TAILOR-- . . . . . . 204   3 DON JUAN  9     44    2
    OF ALL THE STANDING ARMY WHO STOOD BY . . . . . . . 221      3 DON JUAN  9     78    8
ARMY'S
    BECAUSE THE ARMY'S GROWN MORE POPULAR . . . . . . . . 23     2 DON JUAN  1      4    5
    AND CARED AS LITTLE FOR HIS ARMY'S LOSS  . . . . . . 105     3 DON JUAN  7     77    5
ARNO
    LIKE ARNO IN THE SUMMER TO A SHALLOW  . . . . . . . . 228    3 DON JUAN 10      7    2
AROINT
    QUARTER IN CASE HE BADE THEM NOT AROINT . . . . . . . 170    3 DON JUAN  8    117    3
    AND SO THAT NO EXPLOSION CRY AROINT  . . . . . . . . 396     3 DON JUAN 13     81    5
AROSE
    AROSE A CLATTER MIGHT AWAKE THE DEAD  . . . . . . . . 95     2 DON JUAN  1    136    3
    THE PLEASANT SCANDAL WHICH AROSE NEXT DAY  . . . . . .*126   2 DON JUAN  1    188    5
    WITH SLOW AND STAGGERING EFFORT HE AROSE . . . . . . 213     2 DON JUAN  2    109    1
    AND THUS UPON HIS ELBOW HE AROSE  . . . . . . . . . 236      2 DON JUAN  2    150    1
    WHILE ONE NEW TEAR AROSE IN HAIDEE'S EYE . . . . . . 355     2 DON JUAN  4     21    8
    THEN SHRIEKING SHE AROSE AND SHRIEKING FELL . . . . . 363    2 DON JUAN  4     36    1
    AND WHIRL'D HER BRAIN TO MADNESS SHE AROSE . . . . . 380     2 DON JUAN  4     67    2
    SAD STRIFE AROSE FOR THEY WERE SO CROSS-GRAIN'D . . . . 394  2 DON JUAN  4     93    5
    AND WAFTED FAR AROSE A RICH PERFUME . . . . . . . . 460      2 DON JUAN  5     85    4
    ALSO AROSE ABOUT THE SELF-SAME TIME . . . . . . . . 51       3 DON JUAN  6     90    1
    AND HE AROSE ADVANCED--THE SHADE RETREATED . . . . . 559     3 DON JUAN 16    119    2
AROUND
    AND THE SEA YAWN'D AROUND HER LIKE A HELL  . . . . . 184     2 DON JUAN  2     52    5
    AND THEN THEY LOOK'D AROUND THEM AND DESPAIR'D . . . . 195   2 DON JUAN  2     74    3
```

AROUND   (CONTINUED)
    AROUND HIS SCARCE-CLAD LIMBS AND THE FAIR ARM . . . . . 216 2 DON JUAN 2   114   2
    AROUND THEM (WHAT I HOPE WILL NEVER VANISH) . . . . . . 220 2 DON JUAN 2   120   6
    AROUND THEM MADE THEM TO EACH OTHER PRESS . . . . . . 255 2 DON JUAN 2   188   6
    ROUND JUAN'S HEAD AND HIS AROUND HERS LIES . . . . . . 259 2 DON JUAN 2   194   3
    AROUND AS PRINCESS OF HER FATHER'S LAND . . . . 312 2 DON JUAN 3   72   1
    WITH HIS DEAR WAGGONERS AROUND HIS LAKES . . . . 333 2 DON JUAN 3   98   4
    AND HAIDEE CLUNG AROUND HIM JUAN 'TIS-- . . . . 364 2 DON JUAN 4   38   1
    AND RECK'D NOT WHO AROUND HER PILLOW SAT . . . . 378 2 DON JUAN 4   63   4
    AND GAZED AROUND THEM TO THE LEFT AND RIGHT . . . . . . 439 2 DON JUAN 5   50   7
    THE LAW OF ALL AROUND HER TO FULFIL . . . . 475 2 DON JUAN 5   112   2
    THEN RISING HAUGHTILY HE GLANCED AROUND . . . . 484 2 DON JUAN 5   126   5
    HEADS BOW KNEES BEND EYES WATCH AROUND A THRONE . . . . 484 2 DON JUAN 5   127   7
    HIS HIGHNESS CAST AROUND HIS GREAT BLACK EYES . . . . . 500 2 DON JUAN 5   155   1
    MANY AND BEAUTIFUL LAY THOSE AROUND . . . . 38 3 DON JUAN 6   65   1
    WHEN ALL AROUND RANG LIKE A TOCSIN BELL . . . . 48 3 DON JUAN 6   84   4
    AROUND US EVER RARELY TO ALIGHT . . . . 66 3 DON JUAN 7   1   2
    A GREEK HAD RAISED AROUND THIS ELEVATION . . . . 71 3 DON JUAN 7   10   5
    HE WAS NOT ALL ALONE AROUND HIM GREW . . . . 145 3 DON JUAN 8   65   1
    A GLANCE AROUND--AND SHRUGGED--AND TWITCHED HIS SLEEVE . 161 3 DON JUAN 8   99   6
    AND ALL AROUND WERE GROWN EXCEEDING WROTH . . . . . . 166 3 DON JUAN 8   109   5
    SAW NOTHING LIKE THE SCENE AROUND--YET LOOKING . . . . 172 3 DON JUAN 8   121   4
    WHILE EVERYTHING AROUND WAS CALM AND STILL . . . . . . 272 3 DON JUAN 11   8   5
    A TIDE OF WELL-CLAD WAITERS AND AROUND . . . . 282 3 DON JUAN 11   30   2
    AROUND THE WILD FOWL NESTLED IN THE BRAKE . . . . . . 385 3 DON JUAN 13   57   5
    FONDLY THE WHEELING FIRE-FLIES FLEW AROUND HER . . . . 435 3 DON JUAN 14   57   1
    RATTLES AROUND ME HER DISCORDANT HYMN . . . . 499 3 DON JUAN 15   97   4
    TWINE LIKE A KNOT OF SNAKES AROUND HIS FACE . . . . . 510 3 DON JUAN 16   23   6
    HE STARTED AND PERCEIVING SMILES AROUND . . . . . . 542 3 DON JUAN 16   88   2
    FROM ALL THE 'SQUIRES AND 'SQUIRESSES AROUND . . . . 544 3 DON JUAN 16   91   2
ARRAGON
    (HIS SIRE WAS OF CASTILE HIS DAM FROM ARRAGON) . . . . 42 2 DON JUAN 1   38   4
    HIS MOTHER'S FAMILY CAME OUT OF ARRAGON . . . . 43 2 DON JUAN 1   38 V4
ARRANGE
    THOUGH DOUBTS OF THEIR WELL DOING TO ARRANGE . . . . . 65 3 DON JUAN 6   120   2
ARRANGING
    'TIS IN ARRANGING ALL MY FRIENDS' AFFAIRS . . . . . . 33 2 DON JUAN 1   23   7
    ARRANGING THEM LIKE BOOKS ON THE SAME SHELF . . . . . . 470 3 DON JUAN 15   31   3
ARRAS
    ARRAS THEY PRICK'D AND CURTAINS WITH THEIR SWORDS . . . 99 2 DON JUAN 1   143   7
    MOST PEOPLE AS IT PLAYS ALONG THE ARRAS . . . . 509 3 DON JUAN 16   20   8
ARRAY
    OF HUMAN HEARTS THAN ALL THE LONG ARRAY . . . . 84 2 DON JUAN 1   116   5
    IN ALL THE FLASHING OF THEIR FULL ARRAY . . . . . . 442 2 DON JUAN 5   56   4
    ARRAY HER LIMBS BUT JUAN STANDING MUTE . . . . 19 3 DON JUAN 6   26   2
    WITH ALL THE DAMSELS IN THEIR LONG ARRAY . . . . 19 3 DON JUAN 6   26   2
    AT THE GIVEN SIGNAL JOINED TO THEIR ARRAY . . . . . . 20 3 DON JUAN 6   29   2
    TO WIELD THEM IN THEIR TERRIBLE ARRAY . . . . 113 3 DON JUAN 8   2   2
    THE WORLD GAVE GROUND BEFORE HER BRIGHT ARRAY . . . . 364 3 DON JUAN 13   11   5
    TO DRAW UP IN ARRAY A SINGLE DAY-BILL . . . . 482 3 DON JUAN 15   62   5
ARRAYED
    AND NOW BEING FEMININELY ALL 'ARRAYED . . . . 458 2 DON JUAN 5   80   1
    A CHILD OF NATURE CARELESSLY ARRAYED . . . . 36 3 DON JUAN 6   60   3
    ARRAYED HERSELF WITH MANTLE GEM AND VEIL . . . . 49 3 DON JUAN 6   87   4
    THAT THEY MUST INSTANTLY BE WELL ARRAYED . . . . 64 3 DON JUAN 6   118   3
    IT WAS NO MOUSE BUT LO A MONK ARRAYED . . . . 510 3 DON JUAN 16   21   1
ARRAYS
    AND IN WHATEVER ASPECT IT ARRAYS . . . . 61 2 DON JUAN 1   73   5
ARREST
    HE GAVE THE WORD ARREST OR SLAY THE FRANK . . . . . 369 2 DON JUAN 4   47   8
ARRIVAL
    OF HIS ARRIVAL SO THAT NO ONE STIRRED . . . . 294 2 DON JUAN 3   37   5
ARRIVALS
    AND LONG THE LATEST OF ARRIVALS HALTS . . . . 302 3 DON JUAN 11   68   6
ARRIVE
    SEEING ARRIVE AN AID SO OPPORTUNE . . . . 140 3 DON JUAN 8   56   2
ARRIVED
    BY THIS TIME DON ALFONSO WAS ARRIVED . . . . 96 2 DON JUAN 1   138   1
    SO NOBODY ARRIVED ON SHORE BUT HIM . . . . 212 2 DON JUAN 2   106   8
    NOR YET HAD HE ARRIVED BUT FOR THE OAR . . . . 212 2 DON JUAN 2   107   1
    BUT GREY WAS NOT ARRIVED AND CHATHAM GONE . . . . . 353 3 DON JUAN 12   82   8
    ARRIVED RETIRED TO HIS BUT TO DESPOND . . . . 555 3 DON JUAN 16   110   4
ARRIVES
    IS USED UNTIL THE TRUTH ARRIVES TOO LATE-- . . . . . 278 2 DON JUAN 3   6   4
    ARE SPURNED IN TURN UNTIL HER TURN ARRIVES . . . . . 333 3 DON JUAN 12   36   2
ARRIVING
    ARRIVING AT THE SUMMIT OF A HILL . . . . 286 2 DON JUAN 3   21   1
    HE KNEW NOT WHY ARRIVING AT THIS PASS . . . . 126 3 DON JUAN 8   29   3
    THE GREATER IS THE PLEASURE IN ARRIVING . . . . 260 3 DON JUAN 10   72   7
ARROGANCE
    WITH ALL THE ARROGANCE OF ENDLESS POWER . . . . 152 2 DON JUAN 1 V 3   7
ARROW
    NE'ER WITH SUCH FORCE THE SWIFTEST ARROW FLEW . . . . 218 2 DON JUAN 2   117   6
    AN ARROW FOR THE HEART LIKE A SWEET VOICE . . . . . 461 3 DON JUAN 15   13   8
ARROWS
    SHRUNK TO A SCABBARD WITH HIS ARROWS AT . . . . 205 3 DON JUAN 9   45   3
ARSENIEW
    MEKNOP SERGE LWOW ARSENIEW OF MODERN GREECE . . . . . 74 3 DON JUAN 7   15   3
    THOUGH LED BY ARSENIEW THAT GREAT SON OF SLAUGHTER . . 116 3 DON JUAN 8   9   4

31

```
                                                                    PAGE VOL      CANTO  STANZA LN
ART
      FOR HER FEINAGLE'S WERE AN USELESS ART    . . . . . . .    27   2 DON JUAN   1      11    5
      WROUGHT CHANGE WITH ALL ARMIDA'S FAIRY ART  . . . . . .    60   2 DON JUAN   1      71    7
      OH LOVE HOW PERFECT IS THY MYSTIC ART . . . . . . .        78   2 DON JUAN   1     106    3
      TO LOVE TOO MUCH HAS BEEN THE ONLY ART    . . . . . . .   130   2 DON JUAN   1     192    5
      ALL OTHER MAGAZINES OF ART OR SCIENCE . . . . . . . .     142   2 DON JUAN   1     211    3
      BEYOND THE BEST APOTHECARY'S ART  . . . . . . . . .       167   2 DON JUAN   2      21    3
      HAD OFTEN TURN'D THE ART TO SOME ACCOUNT  . . . . . .     211   2 DON JUAN   2     105    4
      THE POWER OF ART WAS TURN'D TO NOTHING FOR  . . . . .     314   2 DON JUAN   3      75    7
      THE WORLD WAS NOT FOR THEM NOR THE WORLD'S ART  . . .     358   2 DON JUAN   4      27    5
      TO FEEL FOR NONE IS THE TRUE SOCIAL ART   . . . . . .     423   2 DON JUAN   5      25    7
      WHICH PUZZLED NATURE MUCH TO KNOW WHAT ART MEANT  . .     448   2 DON JUAN   5      64    8
      NOT TO ADMIRE IS ALL THE ART I KNOW   . . . . . .        470   2 DON JUAN   5     101    1
      THE CUTTING OFF HIS HEAD WAS NOT THE ART  . . . . . .     492   2 DON JUAN   5     140    7
      SELF-LOVE IN MAN TOO BEATS ALL FEMALE ART   . . . . .     15   3 DON JUAN   6      19    5
      SO BEAUTIFUL THAT ART COULD LITTLE MEND HER   . . . .     50   3 DON JUAN   6      89    5
      AS WELL AS DILETTANTI IN WAR'S ART  . . . . . . . .       85   3 DON JUAN   7      39    5
      AND LECTURING ON THE NOBLE ART OF KILLING--   . . . .     96   3 DON JUAN   7      58    4
      HERE WAR FORGOT HIS OWN DESTRUCTIVE ART   . . . . . .    152   3 DON JUAN   8      82    5
      WHENE'ER HE CAN FOR THERE IS LITTLE ART   . . . . . .    154   3 DON JUAN   8      86    3
      WAR'S A BRAIN-SPATTERING WINDPIPE-SLITTING ART  . . .    184   3 DON JUAN   9       4    3
      HE WHO HAS NOUGHT TO GAIN CAN HAVE SMALL ART HE   . .    195   3 DON JUAN   9      26    5
      SEEING HOW ART CAN MAKE HER WORK MORE GRAND   . . . .    204   3 DON JUAN   9      44    5
      BENEATH HIS ART THE DAME PRESSED TO DISCLOSE THEM  . .   208   3 DON JUAN   9      51    7
      WAS WHAT HE CALLED THE ART OF HAPPINESS   . . . . .      374   3 DON JUAN  13      35    2
      AN ART ON WHICH THE ARTISTS GREATLY VARY  . . . . .      374   3 DON JUAN  13      35    3
      THESE LAST HAD DISAPPEAR'D--A LOSS TO ART   . . . . .    386   3 DON JUAN  13      59    4
      THE WITS WATCHED EVERY LOOP-HOLE FOR THEIR ART  . . .    408   3 DON JUAN  13     109    3
      PARS PARVA FUI BUT STILL ART AND PART . . . . . . .      419   3 DON JUAN  14      21    2
      LORD HENRY HEARD HER PLANS OF ARTLESS ART   . . . . .    438   3 DON JUAN  14      65    5
      AND TURNING HUMAN NATURE TO AN ART  . . . . . . . .      457   3 DON JUAN  15       3    4
      THE ART OF LIVING IN ALL CLIMES WITH EASE   . . . . .    460   3 DON JUAN  15      11    8
      PROFESSORS OF THAT GENIAL ART AND PATRONS   . . . . .    472   3 DON JUAN  15      37    3
      AND FRUITS AND ICE AND ALL THAT ART REFINES   . . . .    488   3 DON JUAN  15      72    1
      HE HAD THE ART OF DRAWING PEOPLE OUT   . . . . . .       492   3 DON JUAN  15      82    7
      A THING OF TEMPERAMENT AND NOT OF ART . . . . . . .      547   3 DON JUAN  16      97    5
ARTEM
      SECUNDUM ARTEM BUT ALTHOUGH WE SNEER  . . . . . . .      245   3 DON JUAN  10      42    2
ARTICLE
      I'M FOR A HANDSOME ARTICLE HIS CREDITOR   . . . . . .    142   2 DON JUAN   1     210    3
      SHOULD LET ITSELF BE SNUFFED OUT BY AN ARTICLE  . . .    298   3 DON JUAN  11      60    8
      EVEN WHERE THE ARTICLE AT HIGHEST RATE IS   . . . . .    469   3 DON JUAN  15      29    4
      HE READ AN ARTICLE THE KING ATTACKING   . . . . . .      512   3 DON JUAN  16      26    7
ARTICLES
      WITH OTHER ARTICLES OF LADIES FAIR  . . . . . . . .       99   2 DON JUAN   1     143    3
      LIGHT CLASSIC ARTICLES OF FEMALE WANT   . . . . . .      284   2 DON JUAN   3      17    4
      OF ARTICLES WHICH NOBODY REQUIRED   . . . . . . . .      448   2 DON JUAN   5      64    5
      THAN OTHER ARTICLES OF FEMALE DRESS   . . . . . . .       15   3 DON JUAN   6      19    4
      AND ONE BY ONE HER ARTICLES OF DRESS  . . . . . . .       36   3 DON JUAN   6      61    1
      (WHOSE ARTICLES ARE LIKE THE THIRTY NINE  . . . . .      383   3 DON JUAN  13      53    2
ARTIFICIAL
      STILL HE EXCELS THAT ARTIFICIAL HARD  . . . . . . .      297   3 DON JUAN  11      58    1
      WITH NATURE MANNERS WHICH ARE ARTIFICIAL  . . . . . .    467   3 DON JUAN  15      25    7
ARTILLERY
      OF OUR ARTILLERY AND HIS OWN 'TIS SAID  . . . . . .      160   3 DON JUAN   8      98    5
      SEEMS LOVE TURNED A LIEUTENANT OF ARTILLERY   . . . .    204   3 DON JUAN   9      44    8
ARTILLERY'S
      ACCORDING TO THE ARTILLERY'S HITS OR MISSES   . . . .    105   3 DON JUAN   7      76    3
      NOUGHT TO BE SEEN SAVE THE ARTILLERY'S FLAME  . . . .    115   3 DON JUAN   8       6    2
ARTISTS
      AN ART ON WHICH THE ARTISTS GREATLY VARY  . . . . .      374   3 DON JUAN  13      35    3
      MIXED GOTHIC SUCH AS ARTISTS ALL ALLOW  . . . . .        384   3 DON JUAN  13      55    4
      THE FRIEND OF ARTISTS IF NOT ARTS--THE OWNER  . . . .    528   3 DON JUAN  16      57    2
      THIS MAKES YOUR ACTORS ARTISTS AND ROMANCERS  . . . .    547   3 DON JUAN  16      98    1
ARTLESS
      LORD HENRY HEARD HER PLANS OF ARTLESS ART   . . . . .    438   3 DON JUAN  14      65    5
ARTLESSLY
      WOULD GIVE UP ARTLESSLY BOTH HEART AND HEAD   . . . .    460   3 DON JUAN  15      10    6
ARTS
      HE LEARN'D THE ARTS OF RIDING FENCING GUNNERY   . . .     42   2 DON JUAN   1      38    7
      ARTS SCIENCES NO BRANCH WAS MADE A MYSTERY  . . . .       43   2 DON JUAN   1      39    7
      THE ARTS AT LEAST ALL SUCH AS COULD BE SAID   . . . .     44   2 DON JUAN   1      40    3
      OF HIS OWN NATURE AND THE VARIOUS ARTS   . . . . .        91   2 DON JUAN   1     128    2
      WHERE GREW THE ARTS OF WAR AND PEACE--  . . . . .        320   2 DON JUAN   3  L   1    3
      THE ARTS OF WHICH THESE LANDS WERE ONCE THE FONT  . .    436   2 DON JUAN   5      46    6
      ALL ARTS TO TEACH THEIR SUBJECTS TO DESTROY   . . . .    157   3 DON JUAN   8      92    8
      TILL ALL THE ARTS AT LENGTH ARE BROUGHT ABOUT   . . .    202   3 DON JUAN   9      40    5
      BUT JUAN WAS A BACHELOR--OF ARTS  . . . . . . .          292   3 DON JUAN  11      47    1
      THEOLOGY FINE ARTS OR FINER STAYS   . . . . . .          340   3 DON JUAN  12      53    2
      BY NO QUITE LAWFUL MARRIAGE OF THE ARTS   . . . . .      390   3 DON JUAN  13      67    2
      THE FRIEND OF ARTISTS IF NOT ARTS--THE OWNER  . . . .    528   3 DON JUAN  16      57    2
      HAVE IN THEIR SEVERAL ARTS OR PARTS ASCENDENCE  . . .    537   3 DON JUAN  16      76    4
AS
      TO DEEM AS A MOST LOGICAL CONCLUSION  . . . . . .         12   2 DON JUAN   D       5    5
      SCOPE TO ALL SUCH AS FEEL THE INHERENT GLOW   . . . .     13   2 DON JUAN   D       7    6
      TO WORTH AS FREEDOM WISDOM AS TO WIT  . . . . . .         18   2 DON JUAN   D      15    6
      TO WORTH AS FREEDOM WISDOM AS TO WIT  . . . . . .         18   2 DON JUAN   D      15    6
      MY POLITICS AS YET ARE ALL TO EDUCATE   . . . . . .       20   2 DON JUAN   D      17    5
      OF SUCH AS THESE I SHOULD NOT CARE TO VAUNT   . . . .     21   2 DON JUAN   1       1    5
```

AS (CONTINUED)

	PAGE	VOL	CANTO	STANZA	LN
WERE FRENCH AND FAMOUS PEOPLE AS WE KNOW	22	2	DON JUAN	1	3	3
SO AS I SAID I'LL TAKE MY FRIEND DON JUAN	24	2	DON JUAN	1	5	8
FORBIDS ALL WANDERING AS THE WORST OF SINNING	25	2	DON JUAN	1	7	4
COULD NEVER MAKE A MEMORY SO FINE AS	27	2	DON JUAN	1	11	7
AS IF SHE DEEM'D THAT MYSTERY WOULD ENNOBLE 'EM	28	2	DON JUAN	1	13	8
EVEN HER MINUTEST MOTIONS WENT AS WELL	30	2	DON JUAN	1	17	5
AS THOSE OF THE BEST TIME-PIECE MADE BY HARRISON	30	2	DON JUAN	1	17	6
THE WORLD AS USUAL WICKEDLY INCLINED	31	2	DON JUAN	1	19	5
THEY LIVED RESPECTABLY AS MAN AND WIFE	35	2	DON JUAN	1	26	4
BUT AS HE HAD SOME LUCID INTERMISSIONS	35	2	DON JUAN	1	27	3
JUST AS THE SPARTAN LADIES DID OF YORE	36	2	DON JUAN	1	29	3
I'M NOT TO BLAME AS YOU WELL KNOW NO MORE IS	37	2	DON JUAN	1	31	3
AS NUMA'S (WHO WAS ALSO NAMED POMPILIUS)	40	2	DON JUAN	1	35	7
THE ARTS AT LEAST ALL SUCH AS COULD BE SAID	44	2	DON JUAN	1	40	3
OVID'S A RAKE AS HALF HIS VERSES SHOW HIM	45	2	DON JUAN	1	42	1
SO MUCH INDEED AS TO BE DOWNRIGHT RUDE	45	2	DON JUAN	1	43	6
AS SAINT AUGUSTINE IN HIS FINE CONFESSIONS	47	2	DON JUAN	1	47	7
I RECOMMEND AS MUCH TO EVERY WIFE	48	2	DON JUAN	1	48	8
WITH ALL THE PROMISE OF AS FINE A FACE	48	2	DON JUAN	1	49	3
AS E'ER TO MAN'S MATURER GROWTH WAS GIVEN	48	2	DON JUAN	1	49	4
TO SCHOOL (AS GOD BE PRAISED THAT I HAVE NONE)	50	2	DON JUAN	1	52	4
AS WELL AS ALL THE GREEK I SINCE HAVE LOST	50	2	DON JUAN	1	53	3
AS WELL AS ALL THE GREEK I SINCE HAVE LOST	50	2	DON JUAN	1	53	3
I THINK I PICK'D UP TOO AS WELL AS MOST	50	2	DON JUAN	1	53	5
I THINK I PICK'D UP TOO AS WELL AS MOST	50	2	DON JUAN	1	53	5
ACTIVE THOUGH NOT SO SPRIGHTLY AS A PAGE	51	2	DON JUAN	1	54	3
OF MANY CHARMS IN HER AS NATURAL	51	2	DON JUAN	1	55	5
AS SWEETNESS TO THE FLOWER OR SALT TO OCEAN	51	2	DON JUAN	1	55	6
THAT THEY BRED IN AND IN AS MIGHT BE SHOWN	52	2	DON JUAN	1	57	6
SPRUNG UP A BRANCH AS BEAUTIFUL AS FRESH	53	2	DON JUAN	1	58	4
SPRUNG UP A BRANCH AS BEAUTIFUL AS FRESH	53	2	DON JUAN	1	58	4
AS IF HER VEINS RAN LIGHTNING SHE IN SOOTH	55	2	DON JUAN	1	61	6
THEY LIVED TOGETHER AS MOST PEOPLE DO	57	2	DON JUAN	1	65	4
JUAN SHE SAW AND AS A PRETTY CHILD	59	2	DON JUAN	1	69	1
BUT AS FOR JUAN HE HAD NO MORE NOTION	60	2	DON JUAN	1	70	7
AS IF HER HEART HAD DEEPER THOUGHTS IN STORE	61	2	DON JUAN	1	72	3
EVEN BY ITS DARKNESS AS THE BLACKEST SKY	61	2	DON JUAN	1	73	2
AS BEING THE BEST JUDGE OF A LADY'S CASE	62	2	DON JUAN	1	75	8
AND THEN THERE ARE SUCH THINGS AS LOVE DIVINE	64	2	DON JUAN	1	79	1
SUCH AS THE ANGELS THINK SO VERY FINE	64	2	DON JUAN	1	79	3
PLATONIC PERFECT JUST SUCH LOVE AS MINE	64	2	DON JUAN	1	79	5
THAT ALL THE APOSTLES WOULD HAVE DONE AS THEY DID	66	2	DON JUAN	1	83	8
IN FEELINGS QUICK AS OVID'S MISS MEDEA	68	2	DON JUAN	1	86	4
BUT NOT AS YET IMAGINED IT COULD BE A	68	2	DON JUAN	1	86	6
OH LOVE IN SUCH A WILDERNESS AS THIS	69	2	DON JUAN	1	88	1
AS ALL HAVE FOUND ON TRIAL OR MAY FIND	69	2	DON JUAN	1	89	4
OR TRANSPORT AS WE KNEW ALL THAT BEFORE	69	2	DON JUAN	1	89	7
EVEN AS THE PAGE IS RUSTLED WHILE WE LOOK	72	2	DON JUAN	1	95	3
AS IF 'TWERE ONE WHEREON MAGICIANS BIND	72	2	DON JUAN	1	95	6
THOUGH WATCHFUL AS THE LYNX THEY NE'ER DISCOVER	75	2	DON JUAN	1	100	2
WHEN JULIA SATE WITHIN AS PRETTY A BOWER	77	2	DON JUAN	1	104	3
AS E'ER HELD HOURI IN THAT HEATHENISH HEAVEN	77	2	DON JUAN	1	104	4
BUT THEN NO DOUBT IT EQUALLY AS TRUE IS	79	2	DON JUAN	1	108	7
AS IF IT SAID DETAIN ME IF YOU PLEASE	81	2	DON JUAN	1	111	3
SHE WOULD HAVE SHRUNK AS FROM A TOAD OR ASP	81	2	DON JUAN	1	111	6
I'M SURE SHE WOULD HAVE SHRUNK AS FROM AN ASP	81	2	DON JUAN	1	111	V6
I CARE NOT FOR NEW PLEASURES AS THE OLD	85	2	DON JUAN	1	118	7
IN THE DESIGN AND AS I HAVE A HIGH SENSE	86	2	DON JUAN	1	120	6
'TIS SWEET TO LISTEN AS THE NIGHTWINDS CREEP	87	2	DON JUAN	1	122	6
BAY DEEP-MOUTH'D WELCOME AS WE DRAW NEAR HOME	88	2	DON JUAN	1	123	2
NO DOUBT IN FABLE AS THE UNFORGIVEN	90	2	DON JUAN	1	127	7
ARE WAYS TO BENEFIT MANKIND AS TRUE	93	2	DON JUAN	1	132	7
PERHAPS AS SHOOTING THEM AT WATERLOO	93	2	DON JUAN	1	132	8
'TWAS AS THE WATCHMEN SAY A CLOUDY NIGHT	94	2	DON JUAN	1	135	1
EVEN AS A SUMMER SKY'S WITHOUT A CLOUD	94	2	DON JUAN	1	135	6
POOR DONNA JULIA STARTING AS FROM SLEEP	97	2	DON JUAN	1	140	1
AS IF SHE HAD JUST NOW FROM OUT THEM CREPT	97	2	DON JUAN	1	140	6
OF LOOKING IN THE BED AS WELL AS UNDER	100	2	DON JUAN	1	144	8
OF LOOKING IN THE BED AS WELL AS UNDER	100	2	DON JUAN	1	144	8
I SHUNNED THEM AS I WOULD DO THE DEVIL	102	2	DON JUAN	1	148	V6
BUT AS MY MAID'S UNDREST PRAY TURN YOUR SPIES OUT	104	2	DON JUAN	1	152	7
I LEAVE YOU TO YOUR CONSCIENCE AS BEFORE	107	2	DON JUAN	1	157	5
LIKE SKIES THAT RAIN AND LIGHTEN AS A VEIL	108	2	DON JUAN	1	158	3
RELUCTANT PAST HER BRIGHT EYES ROLLED--AS A VEIL	108	2	DON JUAN	1	158	V3
QUICK THICK AND HEAVY--AS A THUNDER-SHOWER	110	2	DON JUAN	1	161	8
RELUCTANTLY STILL TARRYING THERE AS LATE AS	111	2	DON JUAN	1	164	3
RELUCTANTLY STILL TARRYING THERE AS LATE AS	111	2	DON JUAN	1	164	3
AN AWKWARD LOOK AS HE REVOLVED THE CASE	111	2	DON JUAN	1	164	7
NOTHING SO DEAR AS AN UNFILCH'D GOOD NAME	112	2	DON JUAN	1	165	5
SO MUCH AS WHEN WE CALL OUR OLD DEBTS IN	113	2	DON JUAN	1	167	6
BUT THAT CAN'T BE AS HAS BEEN OFTEN SHOWN	118	2	DON JUAN	1	176	4
ARE SUCH AS FIT WITH LADY'S FEET BUT THESE	121	2	DON JUAN	1	181	2
AT LAST AS THEY MORE FAINTLY WRESTLING LAY	124	2	DON JUAN	1	186	4
THE PASSION WHICH STILL RAGES AS BEFORE	132	2	DON JUAN	1	195	6
AS ROLL THE WAVES BEFORE THE SETTLED WIND	133	2	DON JUAN	1	196	4
AS VIBRATES MY FOND HEART TO MY FIX'D SOUL	133	2	DON JUAN	1	196	8
AS TURNS THE NEEDLE TREMBLING TO THE POLE	133-	2	DON JUAN	1	196	V7
AND YET I MAY AS WELL THE TASK FULFIL	134	2	DON JUAN	1	197	3

AS   (CONTINUED)

	PAGE	VOL	CANTO	STANZA	LN
IT TREMBLED AS MAGNETIC NEEDLES DO	134	2 DON JUAN	1	198	4
EXACTLY AS YOU PLEASE OR NOT THE ROD	140	2 DON JUAN	1	206	7
AND IF AS I BELIEVE THY VEIN BE GOOD	149	2 DON JUAN	1	222	3
AS WHEN HE SWORE BY GOD HE'D SELL HIS SHIRT	154	2 DON JUAN	1	V 5	3
BOTH BLACK AS IF YOU HAD TURNED HIM INSIDE OUT	154	2 DON JUAN	1	V 5	V7
PANTING FOR POWER AS HARTS FOR COOLING STREAMS	155	2 DON JUAN	1	V 6	1
PANTING FOR POWER AS TANTALUS FOR WATER	155	2 DON JUAN	1	V 6	V1
BUT THEN AS BARD MY DUTY TO MANKIND	155	2 DON JUAN	1	V 7	6
AS GEOGRAPHERS LAY DOWN A SHOAL IN MAPS	155	2 DON JUAN	1	V 7	8
AS I AM BLOOD--BONE--MARROW PASSION--FEELING--	156	2 DON JUAN	1	V 8	2
AND AS THE VEERING WIND SHIFTS SHIFT OUR SAILS	159	2 DON JUAN	2	4	4
AS IF A SPANISH SHIP WERE NOAH'S ARK	161	2 DON JUAN	2	8	6
(AS EVERY KIND OF PARTING HAS ITS STINGS)	161	2 DON JUAN	2	9	5
AS I WHO'VE CROSS'D IT OFT KNOW WELL ENOUGH	162	2 DON JUAN	2	11	4
SO JUAN WEPT AS WEPT THE CAPTIVE JEWS	165	2 DON JUAN	2	16	1
BUT DIE AS MANY AN EXILED HEART HATH DIED	166	2 DON JUAN	2	18	3
OF US DIES WITH THEM AS EACH FOND HOPE ENDS	167	2 DON JUAN	2	21	6
BUT THE SEA ACTED AS A STRONG EMETIC	167	2 DON JUAN	2	21	8
BUT THEY COULD NOT COME AT THE LEAK AS YET	171	2 DON JUAN	2	28	4
AS DAY ADVANCED THE WEATHER SEEM'D TO ABATE	172	2 DON JUAN	2	30	1
THE WIND BLEW FRESH AGAIN AS IT GREW LATE	172	2 DON JUAN	2	30	5
AS IF OLD OCEAN BAFFLED OUR INTENT	173	2 DON JUAN	2	32	V4
TO LOSE THEIR LIVES AS WELL AS SPOIL THEIR DIET	173	2 DON JUAN	2	33	4
TO LOSE THEIR LIVES AS WELL AS SPOIL THEIR DIET	173	2 DON JUAN	2	33	4
AS UPON SUCH OCCASIONS TARS WILL ASK	173	2 DON JUAN	2	33	7
AS RUM AND TRUE RELIGION THUS IT WAS	174	2 DON JUAN	2	34	2
THE HIGH WIND MADE THE TREBLE AND AS BASS	174	2 DON JUAN	2	34	4
AS IF DEATH WERE MORE DREADFUL BY HIS DOOR	174	2 DON JUAN	2	35	5
AND NEVER HAD AS YET A QUIET DAY	177	2 DON JUAN	2	40	4
THAT MADE HIS EYELIDS AS A WOMAN'S BE	179	2 DON JUAN	2	43	6
THEIR BEST CLOTHES AS IF GOING TO A FAIR	180	2 DON JUAN	2	45	2
AND OTHERS WENT ON AS THEY HAD BEGUN	180	2 DON JUAN	2	45	5
AS NOW MIGHT RENDER THEIR LONG SUFFERING LESS	180	2 DON JUAN	2	46	4
AS THERE WERE BUT TWO BLANKETS FOR A SAIL	181	2 DON JUAN	2	48	4
AS EAGER TO ANTICIPATE THEIR GRAVE	184	2 DON JUAN	2	52	4
THE BOATS AS STATED HAD GOT OFF BEFORE	185	2 DON JUAN	2	54	1
IT SEEM'D AS IF THEY HAD EXCHANGED THEIR CARE	186	2 DON JUAN	2	56	3
AS O'ER THE CUTTER'S EDGE HE TRIED TO CROSS	186	2 DON JUAN	2	57	4
HIS FATHER'S WHOM HE LOVED AS YE MAY THINK	187	2 DON JUAN	2	58	2
AS EVERY RISING WAVE HIS DREAD RENEW'D	187	2 DON JUAN	2	59	5
SO THAT THEMSELVES AS WELL AS HOPES WERE DAMP'D	188	2 DON JUAN	2	60	7
SO THAT THEMSELVES AS WELL AS HOPES WERE DAMP'D	188	2 DON JUAN	2	60	7
SHE HAD A CURIOUS CREW AS WELL AS CARGO	191	2 DON JUAN	2	66	7
SHE HAD A CURIOUS CREW AS WELL AS CARGO	191	2 DON JUAN	2	66	7
BUT AS THEY HAD BUT ONE OAR AND THAT BRITTLE	192	2 DON JUAN	2	69	7
AS A GREAT FAVOUR ONE OF THE FORE-PAWS	193	2 DON JUAN	2	71	6
HE DIED AS BORN A CATHOLIC IN FAITH	197	2 DON JUAN	2	76	5
THE SURGEON AS THERE WAS NO OTHER FEE	197	2 DON JUAN	2	77	1
AND SUCH THINGS AS THE ENTRAILS AND THE BRAINS	197	2 DON JUAN	2	77	6
AS IF NOT WARN'D SUFFICIENTLY BY THOSE	199	2 DON JUAN	2	80	6
AS FATTEST BUT HE SAVED HIMSELF BECAUSE	199	2 DON JUAN	2	81	2
WHICH SERVED THEM AS A SORT OF SPONGY PITCHER	201	2 DON JUAN	2	85	3
AS A FULL POT OF PORTER TO THEIR THINKING	201	2 DON JUAN	2	85	7
AS THE RICH MAN'S IN HELL WHO VAINLY SCREAM'D	202	2 DON JUAN	2	86	4
AS IF TO WIN A PART FROM OFF THE WEIGHT	203	2 DON JUAN	2	88	6
IT IS AS WELL TO THINK SO NOW AND THEN	205	2 DON JUAN	2	93	2
WAS NOT SO SAFE FOR ROOSTING AS A CHURCH	206	2 DON JUAN	2	95	4
AS MORNING BROKE THE LIGHT WIND DIED AWAY	207	2 DON JUAN	2	97	1
AND SEEM'D AS IF THEY HAD NO FURTHER CARE	208	2 DON JUAN	2	98	4
AND HIGHER GREW THE MOUNTAINS AS THEY DREW	209	2 DON JUAN	2	100	2
THE SPRAY INTO THEIR FACES AS THEY SPLASH'D	209	2 DON JUAN	2	101	8
AS THEY DREW NIGH THE LAND WHICH NOW WAS SEEN	210	2 DON JUAN	2	103	1
AS ONCE (A FEAT ON WHICH OURSELVES WE PRIDED)	211	2 DON JUAN	2	105	7
AS FOR THE OTHER TWO THEY COULD NOT SWIM	212	2 DON JUAN	2	106	7
JUST AS HIS FEEBLE ARMS COULD STRIKE NO MORE	212	2 DON JUAN	2	107	3
AND THE HARD WAVE O'ERWHELM'D HIM AS 'TWAS DASH'D	212	2 DON JUAN	2	107	4
AND AS HE GAZED HIS DIZZY BRAIN SPUN FAST	214	2 DON JUAN	2	110	1
AND DOWN HE SUNK AND AS HE SUNK THE SAND	214	2 DON JUAN	2	110	2
AS FAIR A THING AS E'ER WAS FORM'D OF CLAY	214	2 DON JUAN	2	110	8
AS FAIR A THING AS E'ER WAS FORM'D OF CLAY	214	2 DON JUAN	2	110	8
TO KINDLE FIRE AND AS THE NEW FLAMES GAVE	216	2 DON JUAN	2	115	5
AS ONE WHO WAS A LADY IN THE LAND	217	2 DON JUAN	2	116	8
WERE BLACK AS DEATH THEIR LASHES THE SAME HUE	218	2 DON JUAN	2	117	2
'TIS AS THE SNAKE LATE COIL'D WHO POURS HIS LENGTH	218	2 DON JUAN	2	117	7
FOR AS YOU KNOW THE SPANISH WOMEN BANISH	220	2 DON JUAN	2	120	4
AS BLACK BUT QUICKER AND OF SMALLER SIZE	221	2 DON JUAN	2	122	8
WHICH ARE (AS I MUST OWN) OF FEMALE GROWTH	221	2 DON JUAN	2	123	3
AND SOMETIMES CAUGHT AS MANY AS HE WISH'D	223	2 DON JUAN	2	126	4
AND SOMETIMES CAUGHT AS MANY AS HE WISH'D	223	2 DON JUAN	2	126	4
HER DOWRY WAS AS NOTHING TO HER SMILES	224	2 DON JUAN	2	128	4
AS FAR AS IN HER LAY TO TAKE HIM IN	224	2 DON JUAN	2	129	7
AS FAR AS IN HER LAY TO TAKE HIM IN	224	2 DON JUAN	2	129	7
THEY MADE A FIRE BUT SUCH A FIRE AS THEY	226	2 DON JUAN	2	132	1
MATERIALS AS WERE CAST UP ROUND THE BAY	226	2 DON JUAN	2	132	3
WHO SMOOTH'D HIS PILLOW AS SHE LEFT THE DEN	228	2 DON JUAN	2	135	2
(THE HEART WILL SLIP EVEN AS THE TONGUE AND PEN)	228	2 DON JUAN	2	135	6
AND ZOE SPENT HERS AS MOST WOMEN DO	228	2 DON JUAN	2	136	6
WHICH HASTENS AS PHYSICIANS SAY ONE'S FATE	230	2 DON JUAN	2	140	4

AS   (CONTINUED)

```
ALTHOUGH THE MORTAL QUITE AS FRESH AND FAIR . . . . .   . . 232   2 DON JUAN   2   142    7
AS AT THIS MOMENT I SHOULD LIKE TO DO . . . . . . .     . . 232   2 DON JUAN   2   142   V6
AND THEN SHE STOPP'D AND STOOD AS IF IN AWE . . . .     . . 232   2 DON JUAN   2   143    4
SHOULD REACH HIS BLOOD THEN O'ER HIM STILL AS DEATH .   . . 232   2 DON JUAN   2   143    7
AS O'ER HIM LAY THE CALM AND STIRLESS AIR . . . . .     . . 233   2 DON JUAN   2   144    4
THAT SLEEP WHICH SEEM'D AS IT WOULD NE'ER AWAKE . .     . . 234   2 DON JUAN   2   146    8
HUSH'D AS THE BABE UPON ITS MOTHER'S BREAST . . . .     . . 235   2 DON JUAN   2   148    2
DROOP'D AS THE WILLOW WHEN NO WINDS CAN BREATHE . .     . . 235   2 DON JUAN   2   148    3
FAIR AS THE CROWNING ROSE OF THE WHOLE WREATH . . .     . . 235   2 DON JUAN   2   148    5
SOFT AS THE CALLOW CYGNET IN ITS NEST . . . . . . .     . . 235   2 DON JUAN   2   148    6
FAIR AS THE ROSE JUST PLUCKED TO CROWN THE WREATH .     . . 235   2 DON JUAN   2   148   V5
AS WITH AN EFFORT SHE BEGAN TO SPEAK . . . . . . .      . . 236   2 DON JUAN   2   150    4
WHENCE MELODY DESCENDS AS FROM A THRONE . . . . . .     . . 236   2 DON JUAN   2   151    8
AND JUAN GAZED AS ONE WHO IS AWOKE . . . . . . . .      . . 237   2 DON JUAN   2   152    1
AS ALL HIS LATTER MEALS HAD BEEN QUITE RAW . . . .      . . 239   2 DON JUAN   2   157    4
AND AS HE INTERRUPTED NOT WENT EKING . . . . . . .      . . 241   2 DON JUAN   2   161    5
AS HE WHO STUDIES FERVENTLY THE SKIES . . . . . . .     . . 242   2 DON JUAN   2   163    5
AS WAS THE CASE AT LEAST WHERE I HAVE BEEN . . . .      . . 242   2 DON JUAN   2   164    4
AS FOR THE LADIES I HAVE NOUGHT TO SAY . . . . . .      . . 244   2 DON JUAN   2   166    1
SOME FEELINGS UNIVERSAL AS THE SUN . . . . . . . .      . . 244   2 DON JUAN   2   167    3
WERE SUCH AS COULD NOT IN HIS BREAST BE SHUT . . .      . . 244   2 DON JUAN   2   167    4
HE WAS IN LOVE--AS YOU WOULD BE NO DOUBT . . . . .      . . 244   2 DON JUAN   2   167    6
AS O'ER A BED OF ROSES THE SWEET SOUTH . . . . . .      . . 245   2 DON JUAN   2   168    8
WHILE VENUS FILLS THE HEART (WHICH QUITE AS WELL IS     . . 246   2 DON JUAN   2   170   V1
BESIDES HER MAID'S AS PRETTY FOR THEIR SIZE . . . .     . . 246   2 DON JUAN   2   171    4
TO HER AS 'TWERE THE KIND OF BEING SENT . . . . . .     . . 247   2 DON JUAN   2   172    3
NOT AS OF YORE TO CARRY OFF AN IO . . . . . . . .       . . 248   2 DON JUAN   2   174    7
FREE AS A MARRIED WOMAN OR SUCH OTHER . . . . . . .     . . 248   2 DON JUAN   2   175    3
FEMALE AS WHERE SHE LIKES MAY FREELY PASS . . . . .     . . 248   2 DON JUAN   2   175    4
SO MUCH AS TO PROPOSE TO TAKE A WALK-- . . . . . .      . . 249   2 DON JUAN   2   176    3
GUARDED BY SHOALS AND ROCKS AS BY AN HOST . . . . .     . . 249   2 DON JUAN   2   177    3
LAY AT THIS PERIOD QUIET AS THE SKY . . . . . . . .     . . 251   2 DON JUAN   2   181    3
AS I HAVE SAID UPON AN EXPEDITION . . . . . . . . .     . . 252   2 DON JUAN   2   182    2
WHICH THEN SEEMS AS IF THE WHOLE EARTH IT BOUNDED .     . . 252   2 DON JUAN   2   183    3
WORK'D BY THE STORMS YET WORK'D AS IT WERE PLANN'D      . . 253   2 DON JUAN   2   184    5
SUCH KISSES AS BELONG TO EARLY DAYS . . . . . . . .     . . 254   2 DON JUAN   2   186    4
AS IF THEIR SOULS AND LIPS EACH OTHER BECKON'D . .      . . 254   2 DON JUAN   2   187    6
THEY WERE ALONE BUT NOT ALONE AS THEY . . . . . . .     . . 255   2 DON JUAN   2   188    1
AS IF THERE WERE NO LIFE BENEATH THE SKY . . . . .      . . 255   2 DON JUAN   2   188    7
FELT AS IF NEVER MORE TO BEAT APART . . . . . . . .     . . 257   2 DON JUAN   2   191    8
AND HAIDEE BEING DEVOUT AS WELL AS FAIR . . . . . .     . . 258   2 DON JUAN   2   193    5
AND HAIDEE BEING DEVOUT AS WELL AS FAIR . . . . . .     . . 258   2 DON JUAN   2   193    5
AS THEY WHO WATCH O'ER WHAT THEY LOVE WHILE SLEEPING    . . 261   2 DON JUAN   2   196    8
AND THEIR REVENGE IS AS THE TIGER'S SPRING . . . .      . . 262   2 DON JUAN   2   199    6
DEADLY AND QUICK AND CRUSHING YET AS REAL . . . . .     . . 262   2 DON JUAN   2   199    7
IS IN ITS CAUSE AS ITS EFFECT SO SWEET . . . . . .      . . 264   2 DON JUAN   2   203    3
(THOUGH SHE WAS MASQUED THEN AS A FAIR VENETIAN) .      . . 268   2 DON JUAN   2   210    8
SOME FAVOUR'D OBJECT AND AS IN THE NICHE . . . . .      . . 269   2 DON JUAN   2   211    5
IN THE SAME OBJECT GRACES QUITE AS KILLING . . . .      . . 270   2 DON JUAN   2   213    3
AS WHEN SHE ROSE UPON US LIKE AN EVE . . . . . . .      . . 270   2 DON JUAN   2   213    4
HOW PLEASANT FOR THE HEART AS WELL AS LIVER . . . .     . . 270   2 DON JUAN   2   213    8
HOW PLEASANT FOR THE HEART AS WELL AS LIVER . . . .     . . 270   2 DON JUAN   2   213    8
AND DARKNESS AND DESTRUCTION AS ON HIGH . . . . . .     . . 270   2 DON JUAN   2   214    4
TWO HUNDRED AND ODD STANZAS AS BEFORE . . . . . . .     . . 271   2 DON JUAN   2   216    3
AS THOSE WHO DOTE ON ODOURS PLUCK THE FLOWERS . . .     . . 275   2 DON JUAN   3     2    5
AS YOU MAY FIND WHENE'ER YOU LIKE TO PROVE HER . .      . . 276   2 DON JUAN   3     3    5
YET LOVE MAY MAKE MARRIAGE AS GOOD WHITE WINE . . .     . . 277   2 DON JUAN   3     5   V5
THERE'S SOMETHING OF ANTIPATHY AS 'TWERE . . . . .      . . 278   2 DON JUAN   3     6    1
AND MERELY PRACTISED AS A SEA-ATTORNEY . . . . . .      . . 283   2 DON JUAN   3    14    8
WERE LINK'D ALIKE AS FOR THE COMMON PEOPLE HE . .       . . 284   2 DON JUAN   3    16    7
AS CAVALIER SERVENTE OR DESPISE HER . . . . . . . .     . . 288   2 DON JUAN   3    24    6
OF COLOUR'D GARBS AS BRIGHT AS BUTTERFLIES . . . .      . . 289   2 DON JUAN   3    27    8
OF COLOUR'D GARBS AS BRIGHT AS BUTTERFLIES . . . .      . . 289   2 DON JUAN   3    27    8
AND AS THE SPOT WHERE THEY APPEAR HE NEARS . . . .      . . 290   2 DON JUAN   3    28    1
LIKE DERVISES WHO TURN AS ON A PIVOT HE . . . . . .     . . 290   2 DON JUAN   3    29    6
WHILE PEACEFUL AS IF STILL AN UNWEAN'D LAMB . . . .     . . 292   2 DON JUAN   3    32    3
HIS BROW AS IF IN ACT TO BUTT AND THEN . . . . . .      . . 292   2 DON JUAN   3    32    7
CRIMSON AS CLEFT POMEGRANATES THEIR LONG TRESSES .      . . 292   2 DON JUAN   3    33    3
WAS SUCH AS FIRE ACCORDS TO A WET BLANKET . . . . .     . . 294   2 DON JUAN   3    36    8
WAS MUCH THE SAME AS FIRE GIVES A WET BLANKET . . .     . . 294   2 DON JUAN   3    36   V8
IS GOOD TO GOVERN--ALMOST AS A GUELF . . . . . . .      . . 299   2 DON JUAN   3    47    8
HE LAY DARK AS THE SCORPION IN YOUR PATH . . . . .      . . 300   2 DON JUAN   3    48   V4
(NUPTIAL EXAMPLES ARE AS GOOD AS ANY) . . . . . . .     . . 301   2 DON JUAN   3    50    4
(NUPTIAL EXAMPLES ARE AS GOOD AS ANY) . . . . . . .     . . 301   2 DON JUAN   3    50    4
WITH TEMPERANCE IN PLEASURE AS IN FOOD . . . . . .      . . 302   2 DON JUAN   3    53    4
SUCH AS LIT ONWARD TO THE GOLDEN FLEECE . . . . . .     . . 303   2 DON JUAN   3    55    3
JUST AS OLD AGE IS CREEPING ON APACE . . . . . . .      . . 305   2 DON JUAN   3    59    5
THEIR BREAD AS MINISTERS AND FAVOURITES--(THAT'S .      . . 310   2 DON JUAN   3    68    6
AS PLENTIFUL AS IN A COURT OR FAIR . . . . . . . .      . . 310   2 DON JUAN   3    68    8
AS PLENTIFUL AS IN A COURT OR FAIR . . . . . . . .      . . 310   2 DON JUAN   3    68    8
WITH BUTTONS FORM'D OF PEARLS AS LARGE AS PEAS . .      . . 311   2 DON JUAN   3    70    5
WITH BUTTONS FORM'D OF PEARLS AS LARGE AS PEAS . .      . . 311   2 DON JUAN   3    70    5
AND CLINGING AS IF LOTH TO LOSE ITS HOLD . . . . .      . . 312   2 DON JUAN   3    71    6
AROUND AS PRINCESS OF HER FATHER'S LAND . . . . . .     . . 312   2 DON JUAN   3    72    1
TO OFFER HIS YOUNG PINION AS HER FAN . . . . . . .      . . 313   2 DON JUAN   3    73    8
TO OFFER WILLING HOMAGE AS HER FAN . . . . . . . .      . . 313   2 DON JUAN   3    73   V8
AND PURE AS PSYCHE ERE SHE GREW A WIFE-- . . . . .      . . 313   2 DON JUAN   3    74    5
HER EYELASHES THOUGH DARK AS NIGHT WERE TINGED . .      . . 314   2 DON JUAN   3    75    1
```

AS   (CONTINUED)

	PAGE	VOL		CANTO	STANZA	LN
SURMOUNTED AS ITS CLASP--A GLOWING CRESCENT	315	2	DON JUAN	3	77	7
AS THE PSALM SAYS INDITING A GOOD MATTER	316	2	DON JUAN	3	78	8
AND ALWAYS CHANGED AS TRUE AS ANY NEEDLE	317	2	DON JUAN	3	80	2
AND ALWAYS CHANGED AS TRUE AS ANY NEEDLE	317	2	DON JUAN	3	80	2
AND SINGING AS HE SUNG IN HIS WARM YOUTH	318	2	DON JUAN	3	83	7
TO DO AT ROME AS ROMANS DO A PIECE	319	2	DON JUAN	3	84	7
HIMSELF FROM BEING AS PLIABLE AS PINDAR	319	2	DON JUAN	3	85	8
HIMSELF FROM BEING AS PLIABLE AS PINDAR	319	2	DON JUAN	3	85	8
EVEN AS I SING SUFFUSE MY FACE	323	2	DON JUAN	3	L 6	4
YOU HAVE THE PYRRHIC DANCE AS YET	324	2	DON JUAN	3	L 10	1
SUCH CHAINS AS HIS WERE SURE TO BIND	325	2	DON JUAN	3	L 12	6
SUCH AS THE DORIC MOTHERS BORE	325	2	DON JUAN	3	L 13	4
AS HERCULES MIGHT DEEM HIS OWN	325	2	DON JUAN	3	L 13	V6
MAY TURN HIS NAME UP AS A RARE DEPOSIT	327	2	DON JUAN	3	89	8
AS MOST ESSENTIAL TO THEIR HERO'S STORY	329	2	DON JUAN	3	92	7
THE WORLD NOT QUITE SO GREAT AS ARIOSTO	331	2	DON JUAN	3	96	8
AS THE FAR BELL OF VESPER MAKES HIM START	338	2	DON JUAN	3	108	5
AND THEN AS AN IMPROVEMENT 'TWILL BE SHOWN	342	2	DON JUAN	3	111	6
NOTHING SO DIFFICULT AS A BEGINNING	344	2	DON JUAN	4	1	1
OUR SIN THE SAME AND HARD AS HIS TO MEND	344	2	DON JUAN	4	1	6
MAN--AND AS WE WOULD HOPE--PERHAPS THE DEVIL	345	2	DON JUAN	4	2	3
BUT AS THE TORRENT WIDENS TOWARDS THE OCEAN	345	2	DON JUAN	4	2	7
AS BOY I THOUGHT MYSELF A CLEVER FELLOW	345	2	DON JUAN	4	3	1
I CHOSE A MODERN SUBJECT AS MORE MEET	347	2	DON JUAN	4	6	8
WHO HAVE IMPUTED SUCH DESIGNS AS SHOW	347	2	DON JUAN	4	7	3
AS BUT TO LOVERS A TRUE SENSE AFFORDS	351	2	DON JUAN	4	14	6
AS RARELY THEY BEHELD THROUGHOUT THEIR ROUND	352	2	DON JUAN	4	16	3
OH BEAUTIFUL AND RARE AS BEAUTIFUL	353	2	DON JUAN	4	17	1
THE PAST STILL WELCOME AS THE PRESENT THOUGHT	354	2	DON JUAN	4	20	8
EVEN AS THEY GAZED A SUDDEN TREMOR CAME	355	2	DON JUAN	4	21	2
AND SWEPT AS 'TWERE ACROSS THEIR HEART'S DELIGHT	355	2	DON JUAN	4	21	3
AS IF THEIR LAST DAY OF A HAPPY DATE	355	2	DON JUAN	4	22	3
JUAN GAZED ON HER AS TO ASK HIS FATE--	355	2	DON JUAN	4	22	5
FOR BEINGS PASSIONATE AS SAPPHO'S SONG	358	2	DON JUAN	4	27	6
UNSEEN AS SINGS THE NIGHTINGALE THEY WERE	358	2	DON JUAN	4	28	2
STIRR'D WITH HER DREAM AS ROSE-LEAVES WITH THE AIR	359	2	DON JUAN	4	29	8
OR AS THE STIRRING OF A DEEP CLEAR STREAM	360	2	DON JUAN	4	30	1
AND RAN BUT IT ESCAPED HER AS SHE CLASP'D	361	2	DON JUAN	4	32	8
WHICH FROZE TO MARBLE AS IT FELL SHE THOUGHT	362	2	DON JUAN	4	33	8
PALE AS THE FOAM THAT FROTH'D ON HIS DEAD BROW	362	2	DON JUAN	4	34	2
DEAR AS HER FATHER HAD BEEN TO HAIDEE	363	2	DON JUAN	4	36	6
DEAL WITH ME AS THOU WILT BUT SPARE THIS BOY	364	2	DON JUAN	4	38	8
OFT CAME AND WENT AS THERE RESOLVED TO DIE	365	2	DON JUAN	4	39	6
THEN LOOK'D CLOSE AT THE FLINT AS IF TO SEE	365	2	DON JUAN	4	40	6
STERN AS HER SIRE ON ME SHE CRIED LET DEATH	366	2	DON JUAN	4	42	4
SHE STOOD AS ONE WHO CHAMPION'D HUMAN FEARS--	367	2	DON JUAN	4	43	3
SHE DREW UP TO HER HEIGHT AS IF TO SHOW	367	2	DON JUAN	4	43	6
FOR SHE TOO WAS AS ONE WHO COULD AVENGE	367	2	DON JUAN	4	44	5
THERE WAS RESEMBLANCE SUCH AS TRUE BLOOD WEARS	368	2	DON JUAN	4	45	4
AND LOOKING ON HER AS TO LOOK HER THROUGH	368	2	DON JUAN	4	46	3
HE RAISED HIS WHISTLE AS THE WORD HE SAID	369	2	DON JUAN	4	47	3
UPON THEIR PREY AS DARTS AN ANGRY ASP	370	2	DON JUAN	4	48	6
BORN OF THE SUN AS AFRIC'S CLIMATE IS	373	2	DON JUAN	4	54	V8
AND AS THE SOIL IS SO THE HEART OF MAN	373	2	DON JUAN	4	55	8
AFRIC IS ALL THE SUN'S AND AS HER EARTH	374	2	DON JUAN	4	56	1
EVEN AS THE SIMOOM SWEEPS THE BLASTED PLAINS	375	2	DON JUAN	4	57	8
AND HER HEAD DROOP'D AS WHEN THE LILY LIES	376	2	DON JUAN	4	59	3
THE RULING PASSION SUCH AS MARBLE SHOWS	377	2	DON JUAN	4	61	1
BUT FIX'D AS MARBLE'S UNCHANGED ASPECT THROWS	377	2	DON JUAN	4	61	3
SHE WOKE AT LENGTH BUT NOT AS SLEEPERS WAKE	378	2	DON JUAN	4	62	1
THEN TO THE WALL SHE TURN'D AS IF TO WARP	379	2	DON JUAN	4	65	5
AS ONE WHO NE'ER HAD DWELT AMONG THE SICK	380	2	DON JUAN	4	67	3
AND FLEW AT ALL SHE MET AS ON HER FOES	380	2	DON JUAN	4	67	4
BRIEF BUT DELIGHTFUL--SUCH AS HAD NOT STAID	382	2	DON JUAN	4	71	6
AND AS MY MUSE IS A CAPRICIOUS ELF	384	2	DON JUAN	4	74	6
TO BE ITALIANS AS THEY WERE IN FACT	388	2	DON JUAN	4	80	2
AS FOR THE FIGURANTI THEY ARE LIKE	390	2	DON JUAN	4	85	1
AS FOR THE MEN THEY ARE A MIDDLING SET	391	2	DON JUAN	4	86	1
AND AS A SERVANT SOME PREFERMENT GET	391	2	DON JUAN	4	86	5
LADY TO LADY WELL AS MAN TO MAN	393	2	DON JUAN	4	91	6
THEY PLACED HIM O'ER THE WOMEN AS A SCOUT)	394	2	DON JUAN	4	92	8
THEY LEFT THIS BEING FREE AND NEUTRAL AS A SCOUT	394	2	DON JUAN	4	92	V5
BRIGHT--AND AS BLACK AND BURNING AS A COAL	395	2	DON JUAN	4	94	5
BRIGHT--AND AS BLACK AND BURNING AS A COAL	395	2	DON JUAN	4	94	5
AND THOUGH THUS CHAIN'D AS NATURAL HER HAND	396	2	DON JUAN	4	95	4
AS BOYS LOVE ROWS MY BOYHOOD LIKED A SQUABBLE	398	2	DON JUAN	4	99	1
THE GRASS UPON MY GRAVE WILL GROW AS LONG	398	2	DON JUAN	4	99	7
'TIS AS A SNOWBALL WHICH DERIVES ASSISTANCE	398	2	DON JUAN	4	100	5
WHO WOULD AS 'TWERE IDENTIFY THEIR DUST	399	2	DON JUAN	4	101	4
AS IF THE PEASANT'S COARSE CONTEMPT WERE VENTED	401	2	DON JUAN	4	105	3
AS IF THE PEASANT'S SCORN THIS MODE INVENTED	401	2	DON JUAN	4	105	V3
AS ON THE BEACH THE WAVES AT LAST ARE BROKE	402	2	DON JUAN	4	106	5
IF IN THE COURSE OF SUCH A LIFE AS WAS	402	2	DON JUAN	4	107	1
MEN WHO PARTAKE ALL PASSIONS AS THEY PASS	402	2	DON JUAN	4	107	3
THEIR IMAGES AGAIN AS IN A GLASS	402	2	DON JUAN	4	107	5
WHY THEN I'LL SWEAR AS POET WORDY SWORE	404	2	DON JUAN	4	109	5
I'LL SWEAR--AS MOTHER WORDSWORTH SWORE	404	2	DON JUAN	4	109	V5
AS SOMEONE SOMEWHERE SINGS ABOUT THE SKY	404	2	DON JUAN	4	110	2

AS   (CONTINUED)
BLUE AS THE GARTERS WHICH SERENELY LIE 404   2 DON JUAN   4   110   6
AS WELL AS THE SUBLIME DISCOVERY'S DATE 406   2 DON JUAN   4   112   4
AS WELL AS THE SUBLIME DISCOVERY'S DATE 406   2 DON JUAN   4   112   4
WHO HAD BID HIGH AS HUNDREDS SIX OR SEVEN 407   2 DON JUAN   4   114   V6
AS RENEGADOES WHILE IN HAPLESS GROUP 409   2 DON JUAN   4   115   5
THE FEMALES STOOD AS ONE BY ONE THEY PICK'D 'EM 409   2 DON JUAN   4   116   7
THE FEMALES STOOD TILL CHOSEN EACH AS VICTIM 409   2 DON JUAN   4   116   V7
AND PAIR THEIR RHYMES AS VENUS YOKES HER DOVES 411   2 DON JUAN   5   1   3
AS OVID'S VERSE MAY GIVE TO UNDERSTAND 411   2 DON JUAN   5   1   6
AS I WILL MAKE YOU QUICKLY UNDERSTAND 411   2 DON JUAN   5   1   V6
EXCEPT IN SUCH A WAY AS NOT TO ATTRACT 412   2 DON JUAN   5   2   2
BETWEEN THE BOSPHORUS AS THEY LASH AND LAVE 413   2 DON JUAN   5   5   5
USED TO IT NO DOUBT AS EELS ARE TO BE FLAY'D 414   2 DON JUAN   5   7   8
AS MOST AT HIS AGE ARE OF HOPE AND HEALTH 415   2 DON JUAN   5   8   2
SO LET US BE ACQUAINTED AS WE OUGHT 417   2 DON JUAN   5   13   6
SHE HAS SERVED ME ALSO MUCH THE SAME AS YOU 418   2 DON JUAN   5   14   7
WILL HARDLY LEAVE YOU (AS SHE'S NOT YOUR WIFE) 419   2 DON JUAN   5   17   3
AS IF THE CORN-SHEAF SHOULD OPPOSE THE SICKLE 419   2 DON JUAN   5   17   6
'TIS NOT MY PRESENT LOT AS I HAVE SAID 420   2 DON JUAN   5   18   6
SUCH AS I TOO WOULD SHED IF IN YOUR PLACE 420   2 DON JUAN   5   19   6
AND CAPABILITIES AS TO DISCOVER 424   2 DON JUAN   5   26   4
AS IS A SLAVE BY HIS INTENDED BIDDER 425   2 DON JUAN   5   27   1
SOME BY A PLACE--AS TEND THEIR YEARS OR NATURES . . . 425   2 DON JUAN   5   27   6
AS THOUGH THEY WERE IN A MERE CHRISTIAN FAIR 425   2 DON JUAN   5   28   5
JUST AS MY GREAT COAT WAS ABOUT ME CAST 428   2 DON JUAN   5   33   3
AND RUNNING OUT AS FAST AS I WAS ABLE 428   2 DON JUAN   5   33   6
AND RUNNING OUT AS FAST AS I WAS ABLE 428   2 DON JUAN   5   33   6
(AS HE BLED INWARDLY NO HIDEOUS RIVER 430   2 DON JUAN   5   35   6
SO AS I GAZED ON HIM I THOUGHT OR SAID-- 430   2 DON JUAN   5   35   8
IN AWE HE SAID AS THE CENTURION SAITH 430   2 DON JUAN   5   36   5
AND NOW AS SILENT AS AN UNSTRUNG DRUM 430   2 DON JUAN   5   36   V7
AND NOW AS SILENT AS AN UNSTRUNG DRUM 430   2 DON JUAN   5   36   V7
BUT LET ME QUIT THE THEME AS SUCH THINGS CLAIM . . . 431   2 DON JUAN   5   38   4
FROM ME I GAZED (AS OFT I HAVE GAZED THE SAME) . . . 431   2 DON JUAN   5   38   6
BUT LET US TO THE STORY AS BEFORE 432   2 DON JUAN   5   39   8
AS FAST AS OARS COULD PULL AND WATER FLOAT 432   2 DON JUAN   5   40   4
AS FAST AS OARS COULD PULL AND WATER FLOAT 432   2 DON JUAN   5   40   4
AS THEY WERE PLODDING ON THEIR WINDING WAY 434   2 DON JUAN   5   42   1
AS THEY WERE THREADING ON THEIR WAY THERE CAME . . . 434   2 DON JUAN   5   43   1
AND VARIOUS HUES AS IS THE TURKISH WONT-- 436   2 DON JUAN   5   46   4
AND NEARER AS THEY CAME A GENIAL SAVOUR 437   2 DON JUAN   5   47   1
MORE TENDER AS WE EVERY DAY BEHOLD 439   2 DON JUAN   5   49   6
AS THE BLACK EUNUCH ENTERED WITH HIS BRACE 441   2 DON JUAN   5   54   1
JUST AS ONE VIEWS A HORSE TO GUESS HIS PRICE . . . 441   2 DON JUAN   5   54   6
AS WONDERING WHAT THE DEVIL NOISE THAT IS 442   2 DON JUAN   5   55   8
BUT SADDENS MORE BY NIGHT AS WELL AS DAY 442   2 DON JUAN   5   56   5
BUT SADDENS MORE BY NIGHT AS WELL AS DAY 442   2 DON JUAN   5   56   6
AS IS A THEATRE LIT UP BY GAS 444   2 DON JUAN   5   58   6
WHERE ECHO WOKE AS IF FROM A LONG SLUMBER 448   2 DON JUAN   5   64   2
AS IF THE MILKY WAY THEIR FEET WAS UNDER 450   2 DON JUAN   5   66   4
BUT SUCH AS FIT AN ASIATIC BREECH 451   2 DON JUAN   5   68   5
BUT THEY AS SOON SHALL CIRCUMCISE MY HEAD 452   2 DON JUAN   5   71   8
SIR--AS I SAID AS SOON AS I HAVE SUPT 453   2 DON JUAN   5   72   4
SIR--AS I SAID AS SOON AS I HAVE SUPT 453   2 DON JUAN   5   72   4
SIR--AS I SAID AS SOON AS I HAVE SUPT 453   2 DON JUAN   5   72   4
BE SUCH AS I CAN PROPERLY ACCEPT 453   2 DON JUAN   5   72   6
AS DRESS YOURSELF-- AND POINTED OUT A SUIT . . . 453   2 DON JUAN   5   73   2
AS NOT BEING IN A MASQUERADING MOOD 453   2 DON JUAN   5   73   5
SAID BABA BUT PRAY DO AS I DESIRE 454   2 DON JUAN   5   74   2
WHICH GIRT A SLIGHT CHEMISE AS WHITE AS MILK . . . 456   2 DON JUAN   5   77   4
WHICH GIRT A SLIGHT CHEMISE AS WHITE AS MILK . . . 456   2 DON JUAN   5   77   4
WHICH--AS WE SAY--OR AS THE SCOTCH SAY WHILK . . . 456   2 DON JUAN   5   77   6
WHICH--AS WE SAY--OR AS THE SCOTCH SAY WHILK . . . 456   2 DON JUAN   5   77   6
AS SUITED THE ENSEMBLE OF HIS TOILET 457   2 DON JUAN   5   79   7
WHICH IS NOT QUITE SO LIGHT AS YOU MAY DEEM . . . 459   2 DON JUAN   5   82   4
IT SEEMED AS THOUGH THEY CAME UPON A SHRINE . . . 460   2 DON JUAN   5   85   7
WERE SATE LIKE UGLY IMPS AS IF ALLIED . . . 462   2 DON JUAN   5   87   4
THE HINGES BEING AS SMOOTH AS ROGERS' RHYMES . . . 463   2 DON JUAN   5   89   4
THE HINGES BEING AS SMOOTH AS ROGERS' RHYMES . . . 463   2 DON JUAN   5   89   4
AS IS THE CUSTOM OF THOSE EASTERN CLIMES . . . 463   2 DON JUAN   5   89   6
AS BABA WITH HIS FINGERS MADE THEM FALL . . . 463   2 DON JUAN   5   90   3
JUAN A MOMENT AS THIS PAIR SO SMALL . . . 463   2 DON JUAN   5   90   5
IT WAS AS IF THEIR LITTLE LOOKS COULD POISON . . . 463   2 DON JUAN   5   90   7
TO JUAN SOME SLIGHT LESSONS AS HIS GUIDE . . . 464   2 DON JUAN   5   91   2
'TWOULD BE AS WELL AND--(THOUGH THERE'S NOT MUCH IN'T) . 464   2 DON JUAN   5   91   5
AS VENUS ROSE WITH FROM THE WAVE ON THEM . . . 466   2 DON JUAN   5   96   2
AND RAISING UP AN ARM AS MOONLIGHT FAIR . . . 466   2 DON JUAN   5   96   5
HER PRESENCE WAS AS LOFTY AS HER STATE . . . 467   2 DON JUAN   5   97   1
HER PRESENCE WAS AS LOFTY AS HER STATE . . . 467   2 DON JUAN   5   97   1
SUCH AS WAS MARY'S QUEEN OF SCOTS TRUE--TEARS . . 468   2 DON JUAN   5   98   5
AS FAR AS OUTWARD SHOW MAY CORRESPOND . . . 469   2 DON JUAN   5   99   7
AS FAR AS OUTWARD SHOW MAY CORRESPOND . . . 469   2 DON JUAN   5   99   7
AS ALSO AT THE RACE AND COUNTY BALLS . . . 471   2 DON JUAN   5   103   8
ON SUCH AS THESE THE LIP TOO FONDLY LINGERS . . 472   2 DON JUAN   5   106   4
AS YOU WILL SEE IF SHE YOU LOVE SHALL BRING HERS . . 472   2 DON JUAN   5   106   6
AS IF WELL-USED TO THE RETREATING TRADE . . . 473   2 DON JUAN   5   107   3
AS GOOD MEN WEAR WHO HAVE DONE A VIRTUOUS ACTION . . 473   2 DON JUAN   5   107   8
BLOOD-RED AS SUNSET SUMMER CLOUDS WHICH RANGE . . 473   2 DON JUAN   5   108   5

AS   (CONTINUED)

	PAGE	VOL	CANTO	STANZA	LN
AS IF SHE RATHER ORDERED THAN WAS GRANTING--	474	2 DON JUAN	5	109	8
WAS THROWN AS 'TWERE ABOUT THE NECK OF YOU--	474	2 DON JUAN	5	110	3
AS THOUGH THEY WERE QUITE CONSCIOUS OF HER STATION--	475	2 DON JUAN	5	111	4
THEY TROD AS UPON NECKS AND TO COMPLETE	475	2 DON JUAN	5	111	5
A PONIARD DECKED HER GIRDLE AS THE SIGN	475	2 DON JUAN	5	111	7
HAD BEEN HER SLAVES' CHIEF PLEASURE AS HER WILL	475	2 DON JUAN	5	112	4
AS WE MAY ASCERTAIN WITH DUE PRECISION	477	2 DON JUAN	5	115	7
AND LEFT HIS CHEEKS AS PALE AS SNOWDROPS BLOWING	478	2 DON JUAN	5	117	6
AND LEFT HIS CHEEKS AS PALE AS SNOWDROPS BLOWING	478	2 DON JUAN	5	117	6
LIKE MOLTEN LEAD AS IF YOU THRUST A PIKE IN	479	2 DON JUAN	5	118	6
AND AS SHE ALSO RISKED HER LIFE TO GET	482	2 DON JUAN	5	122	4
GULBEYAZ WHO LOOKED ON HIM AS HER DEBTOR	483	2 DON JUAN	5	124	5
THIS WAS AN AWKWARD TEST AS JUAN FOUND	484	2 DON JUAN	5	126	1
BESIDES AS HAS BEEN SAID SHE WAS SO FAIR	485	2 DON JUAN	5	129	1
AS EVEN IN A MUCH HUMBLER LOT HAD MADE	485	2 DON JUAN	5	129	2
AND ALSO AS MAY BE PRESUMED SHE LAID	485	2 DON JUAN	5	129	4
AS WATER THROUGH AN UNEXPECTED LEAK	490	2 DON JUAN	5	137	6
TO BE IMPALED OR QUARTERED AS A DISH	492	2 DON JUAN	5	141	2
OR MINCED IN PIECES AS SMALL BAITS FOR FISH	492	2 DON JUAN	5	141	V4
AS THROUGH HIS PALMS BOB ACRES' VALOUR OOZED	493	2 DON JUAN	5	142	1
JUST AS A FRIAR MAY ACCUSE HIS VOW	493	2 DON JUAN	5	142	6
OR AS A DAME REPENTS HER OF HER OATH	493	2 DON JUAN	5	142	7
JUST AS A LANGUID SMILE BEGAN TO FLATTER	493	2 DON JUAN	5	143	6
IS IT EXCLAIMED GULBEYAZ AS YOU SAY	494	2 DON JUAN	5	145	1
AND CHRISTIAN MINGLE WITH THEM AS YOU MAY	494	2 DON JUAN	5	145	5
AND AS YOU'D HAVE ME PARDON YOUR PAST SCORNING--	494	2 DON JUAN	5	145	6
AS TO ANNOUNCE HIS VISITS A LONG WHILE	495	2 DON JUAN	5	146	5
HE WAS AS GOOD A SOVEREIGN OF THE SORT	495	2 DON JUAN	5	147	5
AS ANY MENTIONED IN THE HISTORIES	495	2 DON JUAN	5	147	6
WERE RULED AS CALMLY AS A CHRISTIAN QUEEN	496	2 DON JUAN	5	148	8
WERE RULED AS CALMLY AS A CHRISTIAN QUEEN	496	2 DON JUAN	5	148	8
OF WHOM ALL SUCH AS CAME OF AGE WERE STOWED	498	2 DON JUAN	5	152	2
WAS PRINCELY AS THE PROOFS HAVE ALWAYS SHOWN	499	2 DON JUAN	5	153	6
AS SUITS A MATRON WHO HAS PLAYED A PRANK	500	2 DON JUAN	5	154	4
AS THOSE WHOSE WIVES HAVE MADE THEM FIT FOR HEAVEN	500	2 DON JUAN	5	154	8
AND LOOKING AS HE ALWAYS LOOKED PERCEIVED	500	2 DON JUAN	5	155	2
SPOILT AS A PIPE OF CLARET IS WHEN PRICK'D	502	2 DON JUAN	5	158	5
MEANWHILE AS HOMER SOMETIMES SLEEPS PERHAPS	503	2 DON JUAN	5	159	7
MAN WITH HIS HEAD REFLECTS--(AS SPURZHEIM TELLS)	7	3 DON JUAN	6	2	V7
AS ARE THE BILLOWS WHEN THE BREEZE IS BRISK--	7	3 DON JUAN	6	3	6
GAVE WHAT I HAD--A HEART--AS THE WORLD WENT I	9	3 DON JUAN	6	5	6
AS THE TRIBUNALS SHOW THROUGH MANY A SESSION	11	3 DON JUAN	6	10	6
AND AS FOUR WIVES MUST HAVE QUADRUPLE CLAIMS	11	3 DON JUAN	6	11	7
GULBEYAZ WAS THE FOURTH AND (AS I SAID)	12	3 DON JUAN	6	12	1
NOT ONLY AS SIN BUT AS A BORE--	12	3 DON JUAN	6	12	4
NOT ONLY AS SIN BUT AS A BORE--	12	3 DON JUAN	6	12	4
THE GREATEST WISEST BRAVEST AS WAS BEST	12	3 DON JUAN	6	13	V2
WHO SAW HIS VIRTUES AS THEY SAW THE REST	12	3 DON JUAN	6	13	V4
THEY ARE PUT ON AS EASILY AS A HAT	13	3 DON JUAN	6	14	4
THEY ARE PUT ON AS EASILY AS A HAT	13	3 DON JUAN	6	14	4
AS A RULE BUT TRUTH MAY IF YOU TRANSLATE IT	15	3 DON JUAN	6	18	8
YET DISAPPOINTED JOYS ARE WOES AS DEEP	16	3 DON JUAN	6	20	4
AS ANY MAN'S CLAY MIXTURE UNDERGOES	16	3 DON JUAN	6	20	5
OUR LEAST OF SORROWS ARE SUCH AS WE WEEP	16	3 DON JUAN	6	20	6
A FAVOURITE HORSE FALLEN LAME JUST AS HE'S MOUNTED	16	3 DON JUAN	6	21	4
AS CERTAIN--THESE ARE PALTRY THINGS AND YET	16	3 DON JUAN	6	21	7
AS AFTER READING ATHANASIUS' CURSE	17	3 DON JUAN	6	23	2
AS DOTH A RAINBOW THE JUST CLEARING AIR	17	3 DON JUAN	6	23	8
UPON IN SHEETS WHITE AS WHAT BARDS CALL DRIVEN	18	3 DON JUAN	6	25	5
PERHAPS AS WRETCHED IF A PEASANT'S QUEAN	18	3 DON JUAN	6	25	8
BEATING FOR LOVE AS THE CAGED BIRDS FOR AIR	19	3 DON JUAN	6	26	8
MY WISH IS QUITE AS WIDE BUT NOT SO BAD	19	3 DON JUAN	6	27	4
I KNOW NOT HOW BUT GOOD AS ANY OTHER	21	3 DON JUAN	6	31	4
OF BEAUTIES COOL AS AN ITALIAN CONVENT	22	3 DON JUAN	6	32	7
CONTINUE AS I SAID THIS GOODLY ROW	22	3 DON JUAN	6	33	3
THEIR GUARDS BEING GONE AND AS IT WERE A TRUCE	23	3 DON JUAN	6	34	6
SO SILLY AS TO BUY SLAVES WHO MIGHT SHARE	24	3 DON JUAN	6	36	6
THEY ALL FOUND OUT AS FEW OR FEWER SPECKS	24	3 DON JUAN	6	37	4
WHETHER THERE ARE SUCH THINGS AS SYMPATHIES	25	3 DON JUAN	6	38	3
COMPANION SOMETHING NEWER STILL AS 'TWERE	25	3 DON JUAN	6	39	2
(TO SAVE DESCRIPTION) FAIR AS FAIR CAN BE	26	3 DON JUAN	6	40	4
LOLAH WAS DUSK AS INDIA AND AS WARM	26	3 DON JUAN	6	41	1
LOLAH WAS DUSK AS INDIA AND AS WARM	26	3 DON JUAN	6	41	1
AS IF SHE PITIED HER FOR BEING THERE	28	3 DON JUAN	6	45	4
WHAT SAY YOU CHILD--DUDU SAID NOTHING AS	30	3 DON JUAN	6	49	7
I MIGHT DESCRIBE AS I HAVE SEEN IT ALL	31	3 DON JUAN	6	51	4
DUDU AS HAS BEEN SAID WAS A SWEET CREATURE	32	3 DON JUAN	6	52	1
AND THEREFORE WAS SHE KIND AND GENTLE AS	33	3 DON JUAN	6	55	1
KISS RHYMES TO BLISS IN FACT AS WELL AS VERSE--	35	3 DON JUAN	6	59	7
KISS RHYMES TO BLISS IN FACT AS WELL AS VERSE--	35	3 DON JUAN	6	59	7
WHICH PAST WELL OFF--AS SHE COULD DO NO LESS	36	3 DON JUAN	6	61	5
OH YE WHOSE FATE IT IS AS ONCE 'TWAS MINE	37	3 DON JUAN	6	62	3
AND SHOWN THEMSELVES AS GHOSTS OF BETTER TASTE	38	3 DON JUAN	6	64	7
AND FAIR BROWS GENTLY DROOPING AS THE FRUIT	38	3 DON JUAN	6	65	6
AND SMILING THROUGH HER DREAM AS THROUGH A CLOUD	39	3 DON JUAN	6	66	4
AS SLIGHTLY STIRRING IN HER SNOWY SHROUD	39	3 DON JUAN	6	66	6
'TWAS NIGHT BUT THERE WERE LAMPS AS HATH BEEN SAID	40	3 DON JUAN	6	67	2
(AS NIGHT DEW ON A CYPRESS GLITTERING TINGES	40	3 DON JUAN	6	67	7

AS   (CONTINUED)

	PAGE	VOL		CANTO	STANZA	LN
A FOURTH AS MARBLE STATUE-LIKE AND STILL	40	3	DON JUAN	6	68	1
WHITE COLD AND PURE AS LOOKS A FROZEN RILL	40	3	DON JUAN	6	68	3
AS ERE THAT AWFUL PERIOD INTERVENES	41	3	DON JUAN	6	69	6
AND BRIGHT AS ANY METEOR EVER BRED	42	3	DON JUAN	6	72	5
AS FAST AS EVER HUSBAND BY HIS MATE	42	3	DON JUAN	6	73	3
AS FAST AS EVER HUSBAND BY HIS MATE	42	3	DON JUAN	6	73	3
WHICH AS ALL SPOKE AT ONCE AND MORE THAN ONCE	43	3	DON JUAN	6	74	2
BUT BEING NO ORATOR AS BRUTUS IS	43	3	DON JUAN	6	74	7
THAT JUST AS HER YOUNG LIP BEGAN TO OPE	44	3	DON JUAN	6	77	5
BEGAN AS IS THE CONSEQUENCE OF FEAR	45	3	DON JUAN	6	79	2
AND AS THE QUIETEST OF ALL SHE MIGHT	46	3	DON JUAN	6	81	5
AT LEAST TO DREAM SO LOUDLY AS JUST NOW	47	3	DON JUAN	6	83	2
'TWAS FOOLISH NERVOUS AS SHE MUST ALLOW	47	3	DON JUAN	6	83	4
WHERE SHE THEN WAS AS HER SOUND SLEEP DISCLOSED	48	3	DON JUAN	6	84	3
AS THUS JUANNA SPOKE DUDU TURNED ROUND	48	3	DON JUAN	6	85	1
ARE TRUE AS TRUTH HAS EVER BEEN OF LATE	48	3	DON JUAN	6	85	8
AT LEAST AS RED AS THE FLAMINGO'S CREST	48	3	DON JUAN	6	85	V4
AT LEAST AS RED AS THE FLAMINGO'S CREST	48	3	DON JUAN	6	85	V4
AS PASSION RISES WITH ITS BOSOM WORN	49	3	DON JUAN	6	87	3
INDEED ON ANY OTHER AS A MAN	51	3	DON JUAN	6	91	2
AT HAND AS ONE MAY LIKE TO HAVE A FAN	51	3	DON JUAN	6	91	4
AS AN AMUSEMENT AFTER THE DIVAN	51	3	DON JUAN	6	91	6
AS GREATEST OF ALL SOVEREIGNS AND WHORES	52	3	DON JUAN	6	92	8
ALMOST AS FAR AS PETERSBURGH AND LEND	52	3	DON JUAN	6	93	4
ALMOST AS FAR AS PETERSBURGH AND LEND	52	3	DON JUAN	6	93	4
THEIR MOTHERS AS THE ANTIPODES OF TIMON	53	3	DON JUAN	6	94	2
BUT AS IT WAS HIS HIGHNESS HAD TO HOLD	54	3	DON JUAN	6	96	1
IF MATTERS HAD BEEN MANAGED AS DESIRED	55	3	DON JUAN	6	99	5
AND AS HIS SPEECH GREW STILL MORE BROKEN-KNEED	56	3	DON JUAN	6	101	6
AND AS HE FLOUNDERED ON WITHOUT DUE SPEED	56	3	DON JUAN	6	101	V6
JUAN WAS GIVEN IN CHARGE AS HATH BEEN STATED	57	3	DON JUAN	6	102	6
AS SOON AS THEY RE-ENTERED THEIR OWN ROOM	57	3	DON JUAN	6	103	3
AS SOON AS THEY RE-ENTERED THEIR OWN ROOM	57	3	DON JUAN	6	103	3
WITHOUT EXCITING SUCH SUSPICION AS	57	3	DON JUAN	6	103	7
AS IF SHE HAD RECEIVED A SUDDEN BLOW	58	3	DON JUAN	6	105	6
SHE STOOD A MOMENT AS A PYTHONESS	59	3	DON JUAN	6	107	1
THE HEART ASUNDER--THEN AS MORE OR LESS	59	3	DON JUAN	6	107	5
WHITE WAXEN AND AS ALABASTER PALE	60	3	DON JUAN	6	109	4
MAY SERVE PERHAPS AS OUTLINES OR SLIGHT HINTS	60	3	DON JUAN	6	109	8
A FEELING IN EACH FOOTSTEP AS DISCLOSED	61	3	DON JUAN	6	111	5
MIGHT END IN ACTING AS HIS OWN JACK KETCH	63	3	DON JUAN	6	116	5
AND SCARCE SECURE AS SUCH DIGRESSIONS ARE FAIR	65	3	DON JUAN	6	120	7
AND SUCH AS THEY ARE SUCH MY PRESENT TALE IS	67	3	DON JUAN	7	2	1
AS LITTLE AS THE MOON STOPS FOR THE BAYING	70	3	DON JUAN	7	7	5
AS LITTLE AS THE MOON STOPS FOR THE BAYING	70	3	DON JUAN	7	7	5
WHO LOVED BLOOD AS AN ALDERMAN LOVES MARROW	70	3	DON JUAN	7	8	8
SO PLACED AS TO IMPEDE THE FIRE OF THOSE	71	3	DON JUAN	7	10	7
BUT THE TOWN DITCH BELOW WAS DEEP AS OCEAN	72	3	DON JUAN	7	11	3
AND WALLS AS THICK AS MOST SKULLS BORN AS YET	72	3	DON JUAN	7	12	2
AND WALLS AS THICK AS MOST SKULLS BORN AS YET	72	3	DON JUAN	7	12	2
AND WALLS AS THICK AS MOST SKULLS BORN AS YET	72	3	DON JUAN	7	12	2
TWO BATTERIES CAP-A-PIE AS OUR SAINT GEORGE	72	3	DON JUAN	7	12	3
BUT AS THE DANUBE COULD NOT WELL BE WADED	73	3	DON JUAN	7	13	6
IT SEEMS HAS GOT AN EAR AS WELL AS TRUMPET	74	3	DON JUAN	7	15	8
IT SEEMS HAS GOT AN EAR AS WELL AS TRUMPET	74	3	DON JUAN	7	15	8
AS ERE WAS VIRGIN OF A NUPTIAL CHIME	74	3	DON JUAN	7	16	4
ALL PROPER MEN OF WEAPONS AS E'ER SCOFFED HIGH	75	3	DON JUAN	7	17	3
BUT SUCH A GODFATHER'S AS GOOD A CARD	76	3	DON JUAN	7	19	4
THEIR COUNTRY AND AS TRAITORS ARE ABHORRED	77	3	DON JUAN	7	22	6
BUT A THIRD MOTIVE WAS AS PROBABLY	78	3	DON JUAN	7	24	5
UNLESS THEY ARE GAME AS BULL-DOGS AND FOX-TERRIERS	78	3	DON JUAN	7	24	8
AS THEY WHO PRINT THEM THINK IS NECESSARY	79	3	DON JUAN	7	26	6
WHILE THOUGH 'TWAS DAWN THE TURKS SLEPT FAST AS EVER	80	3	DON JUAN	7	28	8
AND THOUGH AS YET THE TURKS MADE NO RESISTANCE	80	3	DON JUAN	7	28	V5
NAMES GREAT AS ANY THAT THE ROLL OF FAME HAS	82	3	DON JUAN	7	32	8
AS GALLANTLY AS EVER HEROES FOUGHT	83	3	DON JUAN	7	34	2
AS GALLANTLY AS EVER HEROES FOUGHT	83	3	DON JUAN	7	34	2
HAD BEEN AS SHORT IN YOUTH AS INDIGESTION	84	3	DON JUAN	7	36	4
HAD BEEN AS SHORT IN YOUTH AS INDIGESTION	84	3	DON JUAN	7	36	4
HE DIED BENEATH A TREE AS MUCH UNBLEST ON	84	3	DON JUAN	7	36	6
AS E'ER WAS LOCUST ON THE LAND IT BLASTED	84	3	DON JUAN	7	36	8
WHO MEASURED MEN AS YOU WOULD DO A STEEPLE	84	3	DON JUAN	7	37	8
AS WELL AS DILETTANTI IN WAR'S ART	85	3	DON JUAN	7	39	5
AS WELL AS DILETTANTI IN WAR'S ART	85	3	DON JUAN	7	39	5
BUT AS IT WAS MERE LUST OF POWER TO O'ER-ARCH ALL	86	3	DON JUAN	7	40	5
LOVELY AS THOSE WHICH RIPENED EDEN'S FRUIT	86	3	DON JUAN	7	41	7
AS ROLL THE WATERS TO THE BREATHING WIND	90	3	DON JUAN	7	48	3
OR AS A LITTLE DOG WILL LEAD THE BLIND	90	3	DON JUAN	7	48	5
(THIS METAPHOR I THINK HOLDS GOOD AS AUGHT	90	3	DON JUAN	7	49	3
AS SOMETIMES HAPPENS IN A GREAT EXTREMITY	92	3	DON JUAN	7	51	4
JUST AS YOU'D BREAK A SUCKING SALAMANDER	93	3	DON JUAN	7	52	5
AND OTHERS OF THEMSELVES AS POET SAMUEL IS	94	3	DON JUAN	7	54	V8
IS TWICE AS STRONG AS THAT WHERE YOU WERE WOUNDED	98	3	DON JUAN	7	61	8
IS TWICE AS STRONG AS THAT WHERE YOU WERE WOUNDED	98	3	DON JUAN	7	61	8
LOW AS THE COMPLIMENT DESERVED SUWARROW	99	3	DON JUAN	7	63	2
FOR CASH AND CONQUEST AS IF FROM A CUSHION	99	3	DON JUAN	7	64	4
THEIR ARMS AS HENS THEIR WINGS ABOUT THEIR YOUNG	101	3	DON JUAN	7	67	8
AS LEAVING A SMALL FAMILY AT LARGE	103	3	DON JUAN	7	71	8

AS   (CONTINUED)

LOOKED ON AS IF IN DOUBT IF THEY COULD TRUST 104   3 DON JUAN   7   73   2
AS THEY COULD READ IN ALL EYES NOW TO THEM 104   3 DON JUAN   7   74   2
WHO WERE ACCUSTOMED AS A SORT OF GOD 104   3 DON JUAN   7   74   3
WHO CALCULATED LIFE AS SO MUCH DROSS 105   3 DON JUAN   7   77   3
AND AS THE WIND A WIDOWED NATION'S WAIL 105   3 DON JUAN   7   77   4
AND CARED AS LITTLE FOR HIS ARMY'S LOSS 105   3 DON JUAN   7   77   5
AS WIFE AND FRIENDS DID FOR THE BOILS OF JOB-- 105   3 DON JUAN   7   77   7
AS TERRIBLE AS THAT OF ILION 106   3 DON JUAN   7   78   3
AS TERRIBLE AS THAT OF ILION 106   3 DON JUAN   7   78   3
TO VIE WITH THEE WOULD BE ABOUT AS VAIN 106   3 DON JUAN   7   80   6
AS FOR A BROOK TO COPE WITH OCEAN'S FLOOD 106   3 DON JUAN   7   80   7
AS IN A GENERAL'S LETTER WHEN WELL WHACKED 107   3 DON JUAN   7   81   V5
WHEN MY POOR GREECE WAS ONCE AS NOW SURROUNDED 108   3 DON JUAN   7   82   4
AS PURPLE TO THE BABYLONIAN HARLOT 108   3 DON JUAN   7   84   3
HERE PAUSE WE FOR THE PRESENT--AS EVEN THEN 111   3 DON JUAN   7   87   1
THESE ARE BUT VULGAR OATHS AS YOU MAY DEEM 112   3 DON JUAN   8   1   2
UNRIDDLED AND AS MY TRUE MUSE EXPOUNDS 112   3 DON JJAN   8   1   5
AS HATH BEEN DONE MERE CONQUEST TO ADVANCE 113   3 DON JUAN   8   3   6
WHICH ROCKED AS 'TWERE BENEATH THE MIGHTY NOISES 115   3 DON JUAN   8   7   6
IN THE SAME MOMENT LOUD AS EVEN THE ROAR 116   3 DON JUAN   8   8   2
AS BRAVE AS EVER FACED BOTH BOMB AND BALL 116   3 DON JUAN   8   9   5
AS BRAVE AS EVER FACED BOTH BOMB AND BALL 116   3 DON JUAN   8   9   5
JUST NOW BEHAVED AS IN THE HOLY LAND 116   3 DON JUAN   8   9   8
ARISTOCRATIC AS WAS EVER SEEN 116   3 DON JUAN   8   10   4
HAD SET TO WORK AS BRISKLY AS THEIR BROTHERS 119   3 DON JUAN   8   15   4
HAD SET TO WORK AS BRISKLY AS THEIR BROTHERS 119   3 DON JUAN   8   15   4
CHEERFUL AS CHILDREN CLIMB THE BREASTS OF MOTHERS 119   3 DON JUAN   8   15   6
QUITE ORDERLY AS IF UPON PARADE 119   3 DON JUAN   8   15   8
WHICH REALLY POURED AS IF ALL HELL WERE RAINING 121   3 DON JUAN   8   20   6
SO MUCH AS UNDER A TRIUMPHAL ARCH 121   3 DON JUAN   8   21   4
A GLANCE ON THE DULL CLOUDS (AS THICK AS STARCH 121   3 DON JUAN   8   21   6
A GLANCE ON THE DULL CLOUDS (AS THICK AS STARCH 121   3 DON JUAN   8   21   6
WHICH STIFFENED HEAVEN) AS IF HE WISHED FOR DAY-- 121   3 DON JUAN   8   21   7
WITH SOMETHING NOT MUCH BETTER OR AS BAD 122   3 DON JUAN   8   22   3
AS ANY OTHER NOTION AND NOT NATIONAL)-- 122   3 DON JUAN   8   23   8
IN SUCH GOOD COMPANY AS ALWAYS THRONG 123   3 DON JUAN   8   24   6
STOPPED FOR A MINUTE AS PERHAPS HE OUGHT 126   3 DON JUAN   8   29   4
AS TRAVELLERS FOLLOW OVER BOG AND BRAKE 127   3 DON JUAN   8   32   4
AN IGNIS FATUUS OR AS SAILORS STRANDED 127   3 DON JUAN   8   32   5
FILLED AS WITH LIGHTNING--FOR HIS SPIRIT SHARED 129   3 DON JUAN   8   33   1
THE HOUR AS IS THE CASE WITH LIVELY BRAINS 129   3 DON JUAN   8   33   4
AND AS HE RUSHED ALONG IT CAME TO PASS HE 130   3 DON JUAN   8   34   1
BUT NOW REDUCED AS IS A BULKY VOLUME 130   3 DON JUAN   8   34   4
WHO HAD RETREATED AS THE PHRASE IS WHEN 130   3 DON JUAN   8   35   2
WHICH DID NOT COMBAT LIKE THE DEVIL AS YET-- 131   3 DON JUAN   8   37   6
MAN QUITE AS QUIETLY AS BLOWS THE MONSOON 132   3 DON JUAN   8   39   5
MAN QUITE AS QUIETLY AS BLOWS THE MONSOON 132   3 DON JUAN   8   39   5
WITH MANY OTHER WARRIORS AS WE SAID 133   3 DON JUAN   8   41   2
ACTED UPON THE LIVING AS ON WIRE 133   3 DON JUAN   8   41   7
THEY FELL AS THICK AS HARVESTS BENEATH HAIL 134   3 DON JUAN   8   43   1
THEY FELL AS THICK AS HARVESTS BENEATH HAIL 134   3 DON JUAN   8   43   1
PROVING THAT TRITE OLD TRUTH THAT LIFE'S AS FRAIL . . 134   3 DON JUAN   8   43   3
AS ANY OTHER BOON FOR WHICH MEN STICKLE 134   3 DON JUAN   8   43   4
AND SWEPT AS GALES SWEEP FOAM AWAY WHOLE RANKS . . . 134   3 DON JUAN   8   44   3
ALL NECK OR NOTHING AS LIKE PITCH OR ROSIN 135   3 DON JUAN   8   45   3
FLAME WAS SHOWERED FORTH ABOVE AS WELL'S BELOW . . . 135   3 DON JUAN   8   45   4
OR THOSE WHO THOUGHT IT BRAVE TO WAIT AS YET . . . 135   3 DON JUAN   8   45   8
OUT BETWEEN FRIENDS AS WELL AS ALLIED NATIONS . . . 136   3 DON JUAN   8   48   4
OUT BETWEEN FRIENDS AS WELL AS ALLIED NATIONS . . . 136   3 DON JUAN   8   48   4
AS SAY THAT WELLINGTON AT WATERLOO 136   3 DON JUAN   8   48   7
AS TIGERS COMBAT WITH AN EMPTY CRAW 137   3 DON JUAN   8   49   5
SO MUCH INTO THE RAW AS QUITE TO WRONG HER . . . 137   3 DON JUAN   8   50   6
AT LAST IT TAKES TO WEAPONS SUCH AS MEN 138   3 DON JUAN   8   51   3
WALKED O'ER THE WALLS OF ISMAIL AS IF NURST . . . 138   3 DON JUAN   8   52   3
AS WARM IN HEART AS FEMININE IN FEATURE . . . 138   3 DON JUAN   8   52   8
AS WARM IN HEART AS FEMININE IN FEATURE . . . 138   3 DON JUAN   8   52   8
AS IS THE HUNTER'S AT THE FIVE-BAR GATE . . . 140   3 DON JUAN   8   55   2
HE HATED CRUELTY AS ALL MEN HATE 140   3 DON JUAN   8   55   6
AS WERE SOME HUNDRED YOUNGSTERS ALL ABREAST . . . 140   3 DON JUAN   8   56   3
WHO CAME AS IF JUST DROPPED DOWN FROM THE MOON . . 140   3 DON JUAN   8   56   4
(AS PISTOL CALLS IT) BUT A YOUNG LIVONIAN . . . 140   3 DON JUAN   8   56   8
AS MUCH OF GERMAN AS OF SANSCRIT AND . . . 141   3 DON JUAN   8   57   2
AS MUCH OF GERMAN AS OF SANSCRIT AND . . . 141   3 DON JUAN   8   57   2
AS SOON AS THUNDER 'MIDST THE GENERAL NOISE . . 142   3 DON JUAN   8   59   7
AS SOON AS THUNDER 'MIDST THE GENERAL NOISE . . 142   3 DON JUAN   8   59   7
THEIR CHOICE THAN LIFE FORGIVE THEM AS BEGUILED . 143   3 DON JUAN   8   62   5
HE SHEWED HIMSELF AS KIND AS MORTAL CAN . . . 144   3 DON JUAN   8   64   8
HE SHEWED HIMSELF AS KIND AS MORTAL CAN . . . 144   3 DON JUAN   8   64   8
AND FRESH AS IS A TORRENT OR A TREE . . . 145   3 DON JUAN   8   65   8
AND WANDERED UP AND DOWN AS IN A DREAM . . . 148   3 DON JUAN   8   72   4
UNTIL THEY REACHED AS DAY-BREAK WAS EXPANDING . . 148   3 DON JUAN   8   72   5
JUST AS KOUTOUSOW'S MOST FORLORN OF HOPES . . 148   3 DON JUAN   8   73   3
BUT AS IT HAPPENS TO BRAVE MEN THEY BLUNDERED-- . 149   3 DON JUAN   8   75   5
FATAL TO BISHOPS AS TO SOLDIERS--THESE . . . 150   3 DON JUAN   8   76   2
COSSACQUES WERE ALL CUT OFF AS DAY WAS BREAKING . 150   3 DON JUAN   8   76   3
LEAVING AS LADDERS THEIR HEAPED CARCASES . . . 150   3 DON JUAN   8   76   6
FATAL TO WARRIORS AS TO WOMEN--THESE . . . 150   3 DON JUAN   8   76   V2
TROOPS AS ARE MEANT TO MARCH WITH GREATEST GLORY ON . . 151   3 DON JUAN   8   78   4

AS   (CONTINUED)

	PAGE	VOL	CANTO	STANZA	LN
SEIZED FAST AS IF 'TWERE BY THE SERPENT'S HEAD	153	3	DON JUAN	8	83	3
AND HOWLED FOR HELP AS WOLVES DO FOR A MEAL--	153	3	DON JUAN	8	83	6
AS DO THE SUBTLE SNAKES DESCRIBED OF OLD	153	3	DON JUAN	8	83	8
THE BLOOD MAY GUSH OUT AS THE DANUBE'S FLOW	155	3	DON JUAN	8	87	3
AS THE YEAR CLOSING WHIRLS THE SCARLET LEAVES	155	3	DON JUAN	8	88	3
AS OAKS BLOWN DOWN WITH ALL THEIR THOUSAND WINTERS	155	3	DON JUAN	8	88	8
AS AUTUMN WINDS DISPERSE THE YELLOW LEAVES	155	3	DON JUAN	8	88	V3
FOR CHECQUERED AS IS SEEN OUR HUMAN LOT	156	3	DON JUAN	8	89	3
I SKETCH YOUR WORLD EXACTLY AS IT GOES	156	3	DON JUAN	8	89	8
AND SHUDDER--WHILE AS BEAUTIFUL AS MAY	157	3	DON JUAN	8	91	5
AND SHUDDER--WHILE AS BEAUTIFUL AS MAY	157	3	DON JUAN	8	91	5
HAS FEELINGS PURE AND POLISHED AS A GEM--	157	3	DON JUAN	8	92	4
AS HE TURNED O'ER EACH PALE AND GORY CHEEK	158	3	DON JUAN	8	94	6
AND SHE WAS CHILL AS THEY AND ON HER FACE	159	3	DON JUAN	8	95	1
AS THE LAST LINK WITH ALL SHE HAD HELD DEAR	159	3	DON JUAN	8	95	6
WITH INFANT TERRORS GLARED AS FROM A TRANCE	159	3	DON JUAN	8	96	6
ON GREAT OCCASIONS SUCH AS AN ATTACK	160	3	DON JUAN	8	97	3
ON CITIES AS HATH BEEN THE PRESENT CASE)	160	3	DON JUAN	8	97	4
SUCH AS HE THOUGHT THE LEAST GIVEN UP TO PREY	162	3	DON JUAN	8	102	4
AS HUMAN BEINGS OR HIS WAYS ARE ODD	163	3	DON JUAN	8	104	4
OR SULTAN AS THE AUTHOR (TO WHOSE NOD	163	3	DON JUAN	8	104	6
ARE THEY--NOW FURIOUS AS THE SWEEPING WAVE	164	3	DON JUAN	8	106	5
NOW MOVED WITH PITY EVEN AS SOMETIMES NODS	164	3	DON JUAN	8	106	5
AS OBSTINATE AS SWEDISH CHARLES AT BENDER	165	3	DON JUAN	8	107	4
AS OBSTINATE AS SWEDISH CHARLES AT BENDER	165	3	DON JUAN	8	107	4
AS BEING A VIRTUE LIKE TERRESTRIAL PATIENCE	165	3	DON JUAN	8	107	7
SO MUCH LESS FIGHT AS MIGHT FORM AN APOLOGY	165	3	DON JUAN	8	108	4
STRUCK AT HIS FRIENDS AS BABIES BEAT THEIR NURSES	165	3	DON JUAN	8	108	8
AS GREAT A SCORNER OF THE NAZARENE	167	3	DON JUAN	8	111	2
AS EVER MAHOMET PICKED OUT FOR A MARTYR	167	3	DON JUAN	8	111	3
AS THOUGH THERE WERE ONE HEAVEN AND NONE BESIDES--	168	3	DON JUAN	8	114	6
STOPPED AS IF ONCE MORE WILLING TO CONCEDE	170	3	DON JUAN	8	117	2
AS HE BEFORE HAD DONE HE DID NOT HEED	170	3	DON JUAN	8	117	4
AS HE LOOKED DOWN UPON HIS CHILDREN GONE	170	3	DON JUAN	8	117	7
AS CARELESSLY AS HURLS THE MOTH HER WING	170	3	DON JUAN	8	118	3
AS CARELESSLY AS HURLS THE MOTH HER WING	170	3	DON JUAN	8	118	3
AS IF HE HAD THREE LIVES AS WELL AS TAILS	172	3	DON JUAN	8	121	8
AS IF HE HAD THREE LIVES AS WELL AS TAILS	172	3	DON JUAN	8	121	8
AS IF HE HAD THREE LIVES AS WELL AS TAILS	172	3	DON JUAN	8	121	8
MIRRORED THE CHRISTIAN FLAGS--AS MOONBEAMS ON THE WATER	173	3	DON JUAN	8	122	V8
ALL BY WHICH HELL IS PEOPLED OR AS SAD	173	3	DON JUAN	8	123	6
AS HELL--MERE MORTALS WHO THEIR POWER ABUSE--	173	3	DON JUAN	8	123	7
WAS HERE (AS HERETOFORE AND SINCE) LET LOOSE	173	3	DON JUAN	8	123	8
ARE HINTS AS GOOD AS SERMONS OR AS RHYMES	174	3	DON JUAN	8	125	6
ARE HINTS AS GOOD AS SERMONS OR AS RHYMES	174	3	DON JUAN	8	125	6
ARE HINTS AS GOOD AS SERMONS OR AS RHYMES	174	3	DON JUAN	8	125	6
AS WHEN THE FRENCH THAT DISSIPATED NATION	176	3	DON JUAN	8	129	4
WERE ALMOST AS MUCH VIRGINS AS BEFORE	176	3	DON JUAN	8	129	8
WERE ALMOST AS MUCH VIRGINS AS BEFORE	176	3	DON JUAN	8	129	8
AND AS IN THE GREAT JOY OF YOUR MILLENNIUM	180	3	DON JUAN	8	136	2
AS NOW OCCUR I THOUGHT THAT I WOULD PEN YOU 'EM	180	3	DON JUAN	8	136	4
AS WE NOW GAZE UPON THE MAMMOTH'S BONES	180	3	DON JUAN	8	137	3
AS THE REAL PURPOSE OF A PYRAMID	180	3	DON JUAN	8	137	8
AS THE FIRST CANTO PROMISED YOU HAVE NOW	181	3	DON JUAN	8	138	2
BUT THOUGH YOUR YEARS AS MAN TEND FAST TO ZERO	184	3	DON JUAN	9	2	7
A PROP NOT QUITE SO CERTAIN AS BEFORE	184	3	DON JUAN	9	3	4
THE SPANISH AND THE FRENCH AS WELL AS DUTCH	184	3	DON JUAN	9	3	5
THE SPANISH AND THE FRENCH AS WELL AS DUTCH	184	3	DON JUAN	9	3	5
I DON'T MEAN TO REFLECT--A MAN SO GREAT AS	186	3	DON JUAN	9	7	1
THOUGH AS AN IRISHMAN YOU LOVE POTATOES	186	3	DON JUAN	9	7	5
AND AS A HIGH-SOUL'D MINISTER OF STATE IS	186	3	DON JUAN	9	8	7
AS THESE NEW CANTOS TOUCH ON WARLIKE FEATS	187	3	DON JUAN	9	10	1
SUNS AS RAYS--WORLDS LIKE ATOMS--YEARS LIKE HOURS	189	3	DON JUAN	9	13	8
AS ALSO OF THE FIRST ACADEMICIANS	191	3	DON JUAN	9	17	2
THERE'S NO SUCH THING AS CERTAINTY THAT'S PLAIN	191	3	DON JUAN	9	17	5
AS ANY OF MORTALITY'S CONDITIONS	191	3	DON JUAN	9	17	6
BUT HEAVEN AS CASSIO SAYS IS ABOVE ALL--	192	3	DON JUAN	9	19	1
AS IS THE CHRISTIAN DOGMA RATHER ROUGH	195	3	DON JUAN	9	25	6
AS MUCH FROM MOBS AS KINGS--FROM YOU AS ME	195	3	DON JUAN	9	25	8
AS MUCH FROM MOBS AS KINGS--FROM YOU AS ME	195	3	DON JUAN	9	25	8
AS MUCH FROM MOBS AS KINGS--FROM YOU AS ME	195	3	DON JUAN	9	25	8
MAY STILL EXPATIATE FREELY AS WILL I	195	3	DON JUAN	9	26	7
BY NIGHT AS DO THAT MERCENARY PACK ALL	196	3	DON JUAN	9	27	3
(AS BEING THE BRAVE LIONS' KEEN PROVIDERS)	196	3	DON JUAN	9	27	7
AS YET ARE STRONGLY STINGING TO BE FREE	196	3	DON JUAN	9	28	8
WHERE BLOOD WAS TALKED OF AS WE WOULD OF WATER	197	3	DON JUAN	9	29	3
AND CARCASES THAT LAY AS THICK AS THATCH	197	3	DON JUAN	9	29	4
AND CARCASES THAT LAY AS THICK AS THATCH	197	3	DON JUAN	9	29	4
BETWEEN THESE NATIONS AS A MAIN OF COCKS	197	3	DON JUAN	9	29	7
BETWEEN YOUR TURK AND RUSSIAN AS A MAIN	197	3	DON JUAN	9	29	V7
AS IF HE WISHED THAT SHE SHOULD FARE LESS ILL	198	3	DON JUAN	9	31	3
AS SOMETIMES HAVE BEEN GREATER SAGES' LOTS--	200	3	DON JUAN	9	36	3
AND BRILLIANT BREECHES BRIGHT AS A CAIRN GORME	204	3	DON JUAN	9	43	5
WHITE STOCKINGS DRAWN UNCURDLED AS NEW MILK	204	3	DON JUAN	9	43	7
BEHOLD HIM PLACED AS IF UPON A PILLAR HE	204	3	DON JUAN	9	44	7
HIS SIDE AS A SMALL SWORD BUT SHARP AS EVER	205	3	DON JUAN	9	45	4
HIS SIDE AS A SMALL SWORD BUT SHARP AS EVER	205	3	DON JUAN	9	45	4
JUST THEN AS THEY ARE RATHER NUMEROUS FOUND	205	3	DON JUAN	9	46	4

AS   (CONTINUED)

	PAGE	VOL		CANTO	STANZA	LN
A LOVER AS HAD COST HER MANY A TEAR	209	3	DON JUAN	9	54	7
VICTORY AND PAUSING AS SHE SAW HIM KNEEL	211	3	DON JUAN	9	57	7
AS AN EAST INDIAN SUNRISE ON THE MAIN	212	3	DON JUAN	9	59	4
IN VAIN--AS FALL THE DEWS ON QUENCHLESS SANDS	212	3	DON JUAN	9	59	7
ALMOST AS MUCH AS ON A NEW DISPATCH	213	3	DON JUAN	9	61	7
ALMOST AS MUCH AS ON A NEW DISPATCH	213	3	DON JUAN	9	61	7
WHEN WROTH WHILE PLEASED SHE WAS AS FINE A FIGURE	213	3	DON JUAN	9	62	2
AS THOSE WHO LIKE THINGS ROSY RIPE AND SUCCULENT	213	3	DON JUAN	9	62	3
A MAN AS GILES SAYS FOR THOUGH SHE WOULD WIDOW ALL	214	3	DON JUAN	9	63	7
NATIONS SHE LIKED MAN AS AN INDIVIDUAL	214	3	DON JUAN	9	63	8
MAKES US BELIEVE OURSELVES AS GOOD AS ANY	216	3	DON JUAN	9	68	8
MAKES US BELIEVE OURSELVES AS GOOD AS ANY	216	3	DON JUAN	9	68	8
AS BOLD AS DANIEL IN THE LION'S DEN	217	3	DON JUAN	9	69	4
AS BOLD AS DANIEL IN THE LION'S DEN	217	3	DON JUAN	9	69	4
TO MAKE A TWILIGHT IN JUST AS SOLMS HEAT IS	217	3	DON JUAN	9	69	7
(THE LAST IF THEY HAVE SOUL ARE QUITE AS GOOD	218	3	DON JUAN	9	71	1
OR BETTER AS THE BEST EXAMPLES SAY	218	3	DON JUAN	9	71	4
SELFISH IN ITS BEGINNING AS ITS END	219	3	DON JUAN	9	73	2
AS FLOURISHING IN EVERY CHRISTIAN LAND	220	3	DON JUAN	9	76	6
AS THEY BEHELD THE YOUNGER CAST SOME LEERS	221	3	DON JUAN	9	78	4
SMILED AS SHE TALKED THE MATTER O'ER BUT TEARS	221	3	DON JUAN	9	78	6
OF RUBLES RAIN AS FAST AS SPECIE CAN	222	3	DON JUAN	9	79	6
OF RUBLES RAIN AS FAST AS SPECIE CAN	222	3	DON JUAN	9	79	6
AMBASSADORS BEGAN AS 'TWERE TO HUSTLE	223	3	DON JUAN	9	82	3
AS IF BORN FOR THE MINISTERIAL TRADE	223	3	DON JUAN	9	83	4
(AS IT WILL LOOK SOMETIMES WITH THE FIRST STARE	224	3	DON JUAN	9	84	4
AS ALSO DID MISS PROTASOFF THEN THERE	224	3	DON JUAN	9	84	6
WITH HER THEN AS IN HUMBLE DUTY BOUND	224	3	DON JUAN	9	85	1
AND THOUGH SO MUCH INFERIOR AS I KNOW	226	3	DON JUAN	10	3	5
I WISH TO DO AS MUCH BY POESY	226	3	DON JUAN	10	3	8
WHERE SHIPS HAVE FOUNDERED AS DOTH MANY A BOAT	227	3	DON JUAN	10	4	8
SO NARROW AS TO SHAME THEIR WINTRY BRINK	228	3	DON JUAN	10	7	3
HECTIC AND BRIEF AS SUMMER'S DAY NIGH DONE	229	3	DON JUAN	10	8	6
AS MAY BE WON BY FAVOUR OF THE MOON	229	3	DON JUAN	10	9	3
AS MY FRIEND JEFFREY WRITES WITH SUCH AN AIR	230	3	DON JUAN	10	11	6
AS CAESAR WORE HIS ROBE YOU WEAR YOUR GOWN	232	3	DON JUAN	10	15	8
(AS FAR AS RHYME AND CRITICISM COMBINE	232	3	DON JUAN	10	16	3
(AS FAR AS RHYME AND CRITICISM COMBINE	232	3	DON JUAN	10	16	3
AS AULD LANG SYNE BRINGS SCOTLAND ONE AND ALL	233	3	DON JUAN	10	18	1
AND THOUGH AS YOU REMEMBER IN A FIT	234	3	DON JUAN	10	19	1
BUT HIS JUST NOW WERE SPREAD AS IS A CUSHION	235	3	DON JUAN	10	21	5
ABOUT THIS TIME AS MIGHT HAVE BEEN ANTICIPATED	236	3	DON JUAN	10	23	1
ON OUR FRESH FEELINGS BUT--AS BEING PARTICIPATED	236	3	DON JUAN	10	23	5
UNEQUAL MATCHES SUCH AS ARE ALAS	236	3	DON JUAN	10	24	3
BUT ONE WHO IS NOT SO YOUTHFUL AS SHE WAS	236	3	DON JUAN	10	24	5
IF I CAN STAVE OFF THOUGHT WHICH AS A WHELP	238	3	DON JUAN	10	28	3
OF THIS ODD LABYRINTH OR AS THE KELP	238	3	DON JUAN	10	28	5
HOLDS BY THE ROCK OR AS A LOVER'S KISS	238	3	DON JUAN	10	28	6
DRAINS ITS FIRST DRAUGHT OF LIPS--BUT AS I SAID	238	3	DON JUAN	10	28	7
AS PURPLE CLOUDS BEFRINGE THE SUN BUT MOST	239	3	DON JUAN	10	29	7
AS THE SOLE SIGN OF MAN'S BEING IN HIS SENSES	240	3	DON JUAN	10	31	7
AND NO LESS TO GOD'S SON AS WELL AS MOTHER	240	3	DON JUAN	10	32	2
AND NO LESS TO GOD'S SON AS WELL AS MOTHER	240	3	DON JUAN	10	32	2
LOUD AS THE VIRTUES THOU DOST LOUDLY VAUNT	241	3	DON JUAN	10	34	2
BUT WENT TO HEAVEN IN AS SINCERE A WAY	242	3	DON JUAN	10	35	2
AS ANYBODY ON THE ELECTED ROLL	242	3	DON JUAN	10	35	3
SUCH AS THE CONQUEROR WILLIAM DID REPAY	242	3	DON JUAN	10	35	6
YET AS THEY FOUNDED CHURCHES WITH THE PRODUCE	242	3	DON JUAN	10	36	7
WHICH SHRINK FROM TOUCH AS MONARCHS DO FROM RHYMES	243	3	DON JUAN	10	37	3
SAVE SUCH AS SOUTHEY CAN AFFORD TO GIVE	243	3	DON JUAN	10	37	4
AS WELL AS FURTHER DRAIN THE WITHERED FORM	243	3	DON JUAN	10	38	4
AS WELL AS FURTHER DRAIN THE WITHERED FORM	243	3	DON JUAN	10	38	4
POOR LITTLE THING SHE WAS AS FAIR AS DOCILE	250	3	DON JUAN	10	52	1
POOR LITTLE THING SHE WAS AS FAIR AS DOCILE	250	3	DON JUAN	10	52	1
AS RARE IN LIVING BEINGS AS A FOSSILE	250	3	DON JUAN	10	52	3
AS RARE IN LIVING BEINGS AS A FOSSILE	250	3	DON JUAN	10	52	3
DON JUAN LOVED HER AND SHE LOVED HIM AS	250	3	DON JUAN	10	53	1
AS ACIDS ROUSE A DORMANT ALKALI)	251	3	DON JUAN	10	54	4
ALTHOUGH ('TWILL HAPPEN AS OUR PLANET GUIDES)	251	3	DON JUAN	10	54	5
AS PATRIOTS (NOW AND THEN) MAY LOVE A NATION	251	3	DON JUAN	10	55	3
OWING TO HIM--AS ALSO HER SALVATION	251	3	DON JUAN	10	55	5
BUT JUAN SEASONED AS WELL MIGHT BE	256	3	DON JUAN	10	64	6
UPON THE CAPTIVE FREEDOM HE'S AS FAR	258	3	DON JUAN	10	68	6
WHO WATCHES O'ER THE CHAIN AS THEY WHO WEAR	258	3	DON JUAN	10	68	8
BUT DOUBTLESS AS THE AIR THOUGH SELDOM SUNNY	259	3	DON JUAN	10	70	7
ALONG THE ROAD AS IF THEY WENT TO BURY	260	3	DON JUAN	10	71	5
LEAVENING HIS BLOOD AS CAYENNE DOTH A CURRY	260	3	DON JUAN	10	72	2
AS GOING AT FULL SPEED--NO MATTER WHERE ITS	260	3	DON JUAN	10	72	3
WERE POINTED OUT AS USUAL BY THE BEDRAL	261	3	DON JUAN	10	73	3
HE BREATHED A THOUSAND CRESSYS AS HE SAW	261	3	DON JUAN	10	74	2
'TWAS FIT THAT HERE AS IN THE HOLY LAND	262	3	DON JUAN	10	75	V2
AS THE SMART BOYS SPURRED FAST IN THEIR CAREER	263	3	DON JUAN	10	77	3
THE EARTH AS SCARCE THE EAGLE IN THE BROAD	263	3	DON JUAN	10	78	3
WITH THE YORK MAIL--BUT ONWARD AS WE ROLL	263	3	DON JUAN	10	78	7
AS MACHIAVEL SHOWS THOSE IN PURPLE RAIMENT	264	3	DON JUAN	10	79	3
JUST AS THE DAY BEGAN TO WANE AND DARKEN	264	3	DON JUAN	10	80	3
ACCORDING AS YOU TAKE THINGS WELL OR ILL--	264	3	DON JUAN	10	80	7
THE SUN WENT DOWN THE SMOKE ROSE UP AS FROM	265	3	DON JUAN	10	81	1

AS (CONTINUED)

	PAGE	VOL	CANTO	STANZA	LN
AS SOME HAVE QUALIFIED THAT WONDROUS PLACE	265	3 DON JUAN	10	81	4
AS ONE WHO THOUGH HE WERE NOT OF THE RACE	265	3 DON JUAN	10	81	6
DIRTY AND DUSKY BUT AS WIDE AS EYE	265	3 DON JUAN	10	82	2
DIRTY AND DUSKY BUT AS WIDE AS EYE	265	3 DON JUAN	10	82	2
APPEARED TO HIM BUT AS THE MAGIC VAPOUR	266	3 DON JUAN	10	83	2
THE GLOOMY CLOUDS WHICH O'ER IT AS A YOKE	266	3 DON JUAN	10	83	5
HE PAUSED--AND SO WILL I AS DOTH A CREW	266	3 DON JUAN	10	84	1
TO TELL YOU TRUTHS YOU WILL NOT TAKE AS TRUE	266	3 DON JUAN	10	84	5
AS SEVERAL PEOPLE THINK SUCH HAZARDS RUDE	270	3 DON JUAN	11	4	4
PERHAPS BUT AS I SUFFER FROM THE SHOCKS	270	3 DON JUAN	11	5	7
EXPOSED TO LOSE HIS LIFE AS WELL AS BREECHES	273	3 DON JUAN	11	11	8
EXPOSED TO LOSE HIS LIFE AS WELL AS BREECHES	273	3 DON JUAN	11	11	8
TO THINK SO FOR HALF ENGLISH AS I AM	274	3 DON JUAN	11	12	6
WHO FELL AS ROLLS AN OX O'ER IN HIS PASTURE	274	3 DON JUAN	11	13	5
AND ROARED OUT AS HE WRITHED HIS NATIVE MUD IN	274	3 DON JUAN	11	13	6
AND OFFERING AS USUAL LATE ASSISTANCE	275	3 DON JUAN	11	14	4
AS IF HIS VEINS WOULD POUR OUT HIS EXISTENCE	275	3 DON JUAN	11	14	6
LET ME DIE WHERE I AM AND AS THE FUEL	276	3 DON JUAN	11	16	4
AS SOON AS CROWNER'S QUEST ALLOWED PURSUED	277	3 DON JUAN	11	18	3
AS SOON AS CROWNER'S QUEST ALLOWED PURSUED	277	3 DON JUAN	11	18	3
THROUGH GROVES SO CALLED AS BEING VOID OF TREES	278	3 DON JUAN	11	21	1
MOUNT PLEASANT AS CONTAINING NOUGHT TO PLEASE	278	3 DON JUAN	11	21	3
OF TWILIGHT AS THE PARTY CROSSED THE BRIDGE	279	3 DON JUAN	11	23	8
LIKE GOLD AS IN COMPARISON TO DROSS	280	3 DON JUAN	11	26	3
AS ALSO BONFIRES MADE OF COUNTRY SEATS	281	3 DON JUAN	11	27	3
AS THUNDERED KNOCKERS BROKE THE LONG-SEALED SPELL	282	3 DON JUAN	11	29	3
ADMITTED A SMALL PARTY AS NIGHT FELL--	282	3 DON JUAN	11	29	5
THE MOB STOOD AND AS USUAL SEVERAL SCORE	282	3 DON JUAN	11	30	3
AND AS ROMANTIC HEADS ARE PRETTY PAINTERS	284	3 DON JUAN	11	33	3
YET AS THE CONSEQUENCES ARE AS BRIGHT	284	3 DON JUAN	11	34	3
YET AS THE CONSEQUENCES ARE AS BRIGHT	284	3 DON JUAN	11	34	3
AS IF THEY ACTED WITH THE HEART INSTEAD	284	3 DON JUAN	11	34	4
THAT THEY AS EASILY MIGHT DO THE YOUNGSTER	285	3 DON JUAN	11	35	7
AS HAWKS MAY POUNCE UPON A WOODLAND SONGSTER	285	3 DON JUAN	11	35	8
THEY ERRED AS AGED MEN WILL DO BUT BY	285	3 DON JUAN	11	36	1
BESTOWED UPON HIM AS THE PUBLIC LEARNED	287	3 DON JUAN	11	39	7
MORE THAN ON CONTINENTS--AS IF THE SEA	288	3 DON JUAN	11	42	7
THIS SUBJECT QUOTE AS IT WOULD BE SCHISMATIC	289	3 DON JUAN	11	43	5
JUAN AS AN INVETERATE PATRICIAN	290	3 DON JUAN	11	45	7
AN AIR AS SENTIMENTAL AS MOZART'S	292	3 DON JUAN	11	47	3
AN AIR AS SENTIMENTAL AS MOZART'S	292	3 DON JUAN	11	47	3
SUCH AS NO GENTLEMAN CAN QUITE REFUSE	293	3 DON JUAN	11	48	6
THOUGHT SUCH AN OPPORTUNITY AS THIS IS	293	3 DON JUAN	11	49	5
HIS STEADY APPLICATION AS A DANCER	294	3 DON JUAN	11	51	6
INTO AS FURIOUS ENGLISH) WITH HER BEST LOOK	294	3 DON JUAN	11	52	7
JUAN KNEW SEVERAL LANGUAGES--AS WELL	295	3 DON JUAN	11	53	1
ADMITTED AS AN ASPIRANT TO ALL	295	3 DON JUAN	11	54	2
THE COTERIES AND AS IN BANQUO'S GLASS	295	3 DON JUAN	11	54	3
AS EVERY PALTRY MAGAZINE CAN SHOW IT'S	295	3 DON JUAN	11	54	8
BUT I WILL FALL AT LEAST AS FELL MY HERO	296	3 DON JUAN	11	56	5
NOR REIGN AT ALL OR AS A MONARCH REIGN	296	3 DON JUAN	11	56	6
JUST AS HE REALLY PROMISED SOMETHING GREAT	298	3 DON JUAN	11	60	2
MUCH AS THEY MIGHT HAVE BEEN SUPPOSED TO SPEAK	298	3 DON JUAN	11	60	5
WITH THE SAME FEELINGS AS YOU'D COAX A VAMPIRE	299	3 DON JUAN	11	62	5
AS FROM MY GREAT GREAT HUMOUR YOU MAY LEARN	300	3 DON JUAN	11	63	V5
AND LET THE BABEL ROUND RUN AS IT MAY	303	3 DON JUAN	11	69	5
AND LOOK ON AS A MOURNER OR A SCORNER	303	3 DON JUAN	11	69	6
YAWNING A LITTLE AS THE NIGHT GROWS LATER	303	3 DON JUAN	11	69	8
OUR HERO AS A HERO YOUNG AND HANDSOME	305	3 DON JUAN	11	74	1
AS WILL ENVIRON A CONSPICUOUS MAN SOME	305	3 DON JUAN	11	74	5
AND UGLINESS DISEASE AS TOIL AND TROUBLE--	305	3 DON JUAN	11	74	7
WHERE ARE THE GRENVILLES TURNED AS USUAL WHERE	308	3 DON JUAN	11	79	7
TALK NOT OF SEVENTY YEARS AS AGE IN SEVEN	309	3 DON JUAN	11	82	1
TO-MORROW SEES ANOTHER RACE AS GAY	310	3 DON JUAN	11	86	2
WHICH 'TIS THE COMMON CRY AND LIE TO VAUNT AS	311	3 DON JUAN	11	87	3
BUT 'TIS AS WELL AT ONCE TO UNDERSTAND	311	3 DON JUAN	11	87	6
FOR BEING AS MUCH THE SUBJECT OF ATTACK	312	3 DON JUAN	11	90	4
AS EVER YET WAS ANY WORK SUBLIME	312	3 DON JUAN	11	90	5
STOOD AS THE UNPACKING GATHERED MORE SPECTATORS)	313	3 DON JUAN	11	V 29	6
JUAN AS A VOLUPTUARY WAS NEW	314	3 DON JUAN	11	V 75	V1
AND AS FOR OTHER LOVE THE ILLUSION'S O'ER	316	3 DON JUAN	12	2	6
AND SCORN HIS TEMPERATE BOARD AS NONE AT ALL	316	3 DON JUAN	12	3	6
WHY CALL THE MISER MISERABLE AS	319	3 DON JUAN	12	7	1
HIGH GROUND AS VIRGIN CYNTHIA SWAYS THE TIDES	322	3 DON JUAN	12	14	6
AND AS FOR HEAVEN BEING LOVE WHY NOT SAY HONEY	322	3 DON JUAN	12	14	7
MY JEFFREY HELD HIM UP AS AN EXAMPLE	323	3 DON JUAN	12	16	7
AS SERIOUS AS IF I HAD FOR INDITERS	325	3 DON JUAN	12	20	4
AS SERIOUS AS IF I HAD FOR INDITERS	325	3 DON JUAN	12	20	4
AND THEN MEN STARE AS IF A NEW ASS SPAKE	328	3 DON JUAN	12	26	5
TO BE PURSUED AS FOOD FOR INANITION)	328	3 DON JUAN	12	27	6
THE WOMEN MUCH DIVIDED--AS IS USUAL	329	3 DON JUAN	12	28	1
AS BEAUTIFUL AS HER OWN NATIVE LAND	329	3 DON JUAN	12	29	3
AS BEAUTIFUL AS HER OWN NATIVE LAND	329	3 DON JUAN	12	29	3
AS JUAN WAS A PERSON OF CONDITION	330	3 DON JUAN	12	30	4
AND ALL HER POINTS AS THOROUGH-BRED TO SHOW	330	3 DON JUAN	12	31	6
SUCH AS--UNLESS MISS (BLANK) MEANT TO HAVE CHOSEN	332	3 DON JUAN	12	34	5
AS I'LL TELL AUREA AT TO-MORROW'S ROUT	332	3 DON JUAN	12	35	6
I MEAN TO SHOW THINGS REALLY AS THEY ARE	335	3 DON JUAN	12	40	2

AS   (CONTINUED)

	PAGE	VOL	CANTO	STANZA	LN
NOT AS THEY OUGHT TO BE FOR I AVOW	335	3	DON JUAN 12	40	3
AS THAT ABOMINABLE TITTLE TATTLE	336	3	DON JUAN 12	43	7
AS BETTER KNOWING WHY THEY SHOULD BE SO	337	3	DON JUAN 12	46	2
THAT DAUGHTERS OF SUCH MOTHERS AS MAY KNOW	337	3	DON JUAN 12	46	4
AS WHO HAS NOT IF FEMALE YOUNG AND PRETTY	338	3	DON JUAN 12	47	2
TO THE NEXT COMER OR--AS IT WILL TELL	339	3	DON JUAN 12	51	7
ALL CARVED AND GILDED OR--AS IT WILL TELL	339	3	DON JUAN 12	51	V7
ACCORDING AS THEIR MINDS OR BACKS ARE BENT	340	3	DON JUAN 12	52	4
WITH MUSIC THE MOST MODERATE SHINE AS WITS	340	3	DON JUAN 12	52	7
ALTHOUGH THE HIGHEST BUT AS SWORDS HAVE HILTS	342	3	DON JUAN 12	56	3
THE ROYAL GAME OF GOOSE AS I MAY SAY	342	3	DON JUAN 12	58	4
I DON'T MEAN THIS AS GENERAL BUT PARTICULAR	343	3	DON JUAN 12	59	1
AND LIVED AS DID THE BROKEN-HEARTED FAIR	344	3	DON JUAN 12	61	7
AND ALL BY HAVING TACT AS WELL AS TASTE	346	3	DON JUAN 12	66	8
AND ALL BY HAVING TACT AS WELL AS TASTE	346	3	DON JUAN 12	66	8
WITH SUCH A CHART AS MAY BE SAFELY STUCK TO--	348	3	DON JUAN 12	70	5
AS A RESERVE A PLUNGE INTO REMORSE	349	3	DON JUAN 12	73	8
THAN STORMS IT AS A FOE WOULD TAKE A CITY	350	3	DON JUAN 12	74	6
SHE CANNOT STEP AS DOES AN ARAB BARB	350	3	DON JUAN 12	75	1
NOR WEAR AS GRACEFULLY AS GAULS HER GARB	350	3	DON JUAN 12	75	3
NOR WEAR AS GRACEFULLY AS GAULS HER GARB	350	3	DON JUAN 12	75	3
(A THING APPROVED AS SAVING TIME AND TOIL)--	351	3	DON JUAN 12	76	6
THEY LOSE THEIR CASTE AT ONCE AS DO THE PARIAS	352	3	DON JUAN 12	78	2
PERHAPS THIS IS AS IT SHOULD BE--IT IS	352	3	DON JUAN 12	79	1
FOR HER RETURN TO VIRTUE--AS THEY CALL	352	3	DON JUAN 12	79	7
AND AS FOR CHASTITY YOU'LL NEVER BIND IT	352	3	DON JUAN 12	80	5
WHICH FLASHED AS FAR AS WHERE THE MUSK-BULL BROWSES	353	3	DON JUAN 12	82	6
WHICH FLASHED AS FAR AS WHERE THE MUSK-BULL BROWSES	353	3	DON JUAN 12	82	6
OF SUCH A THRONE AS IS THE PROUDEST STATION	354	3	DON JUAN 12	83	4
AND FULL OF PROMISE AS THE SPRING OF PRIME	354	3	DON JUAN 12	84	4
AND JUAN WAS RECEIVED AS HATH BEEN SAID	355	3	DON JUAN 12	85	1
EXPOSED HIM AS WAS NATURAL TO TEMPTATION	355	3	DON JUAN 12	85	7
AND AS MY OBJECT IS MORALITY	355	3	DON JUAN 12	86	3
AS PHILIP'S SON PROPOSED TO DO WITH ATHOS	355	3	DON JUAN 12	86	8
IN LAW THAN EQUITY--AS I CAN FEEL--	357	3	DON JUAN 12	V 18	4
AND CRITICALLY HELD AS DELETERIOUS	358	3	DON JUAN 13	1	4
AS AN OLD TEMPLE DWINDLED TO A COLUMN	358	3	DON JUAN 13	1	8
THE KINDEST MAY BE TAKEN AS A TEST	359	3	DON JUAN 13	3	6
RELUCTANT AS ALL PLACEMEN TO RESIGN	360	3	DON JUAN 13	5	2
THAT ALL THEIR GLORY AS A COMPOSITION	364	3	DON JUAN 13	11	7
I TELL THE TALE AS IT IS TOLD NOR DARE	365	3	DON JUAN 13	13	1
AND THUS LORD HENRY WHO WAS CAUTIOUS AS	366	3	DON JUAN 13	16	1
AS MOST MEN DO THE LITTLE OR THE GREAT	367	3	DON JUAN 13	19	2
AND AS HE THOUGHT IN COUNTRY MUCH THE SAME--	367	3	DON JUAN 13	20	4
WHERE PEOPLE ALWAYS DID AS THEY WERE BID	368	3	DON JUAN 13	23	3
COULD BACK A HORSE AS DESPOTS RIDE A RUSSIAN	368	3	DON JUAN 13	23	8
AS IN FREEMASONRY A HIGHER BROTHER	369	3	DON JUAN 13	24	4
AS MANY OTHER NOBLE SCIONS WERE	370	3	DON JUAN 13	28	3
OF COUNSELLORS AS SOLOMON HAS SAID	371	3	DON JUAN 13	29	2
BUT AS THERE'S SAFETY GRAFTED IN THE NUMBER	371	3	DON JUAN 13	30	1
WAS FAINT AS OF AN EVERY-DAY POSSESSION	372	3	DON JUAN 13	31	8
IN SUCH A SORT AS CANNOT LEAVE BEHIND	372	3	DON JUAN 13	32	4
JUST AS A MANDARIN FINDS NOTHING FINE--	373	3	DON JUAN 13	34	5
AS A VOLCANO HOLDS THE LAVA MORE	374	3	DON JUAN 13	36	3
AND AS THE GOOD SHIPS SENT UPON THAT MESSAGE	376	3	DON JUAN 13	39	3
AND YOUNG BEGINNERS MAY AS WELL COMMENCE	376	3	DON JUAN 13	40	1
AS MANY DOUBTS AS ANY OTHER DOCTRINE	377	3	DON JUAN 13	41	7
AS MANY DOUBTS AS ANY OTHER DOCTRINE	377	3	DON JUAN 13	41	7
SIGH--AS THE POSTBOYS FASTEN ON THE TRACES	378	3	DON JUAN 13	44	8
OR GENEROUS DRAFT CONCEDED AS A GIFT	379	3	DON JUAN 13	45	5
AND CHANGED AS QUICKLY AS HEARTS AFTER MARRIAGE	379	3	DON JUAN 13	46	4
AND CHANGED AS QUICKLY AS HEARTS AFTER MARRIAGE	379	3	DON JUAN 13	46	4
AS MANY GUESTS OR MORE BEFORE WHOM GROAN	381	3	DON JUAN 13	49	5
AS MANY COVERS DULY DAILY LAID	381	3	DON JUAN 13	49	6
AND OAKS AS OLDEN AS THEIR PEDIGREE	381	3	DON JUAN 13	50	7
AND OAKS AS OLDEN AS THEIR PEDIGREE	381	3	DON JUAN 13	50	7
AS THUS ON THURSDAY THERE WAS A GRAND DINNER	383	3	DON JUAN 13	54	1
MIXED GOTHIC SUCH AS ARTISTS ALL ALLOW	384	3	DON JUAN 13	55	4
THE DAPPLED FORESTERS--AS DAY AWOKE	384	3	DON JUAN 13	56	6
BROAD AS TRANSPARENT DEEP AND FRESHLY FED	385	3	DON JUAN 13	57	7
ACCORDING AS THE SKIES THEIR SHADOWS THREW	385	3	DON JUAN 13	58	8
WHEN EACH HOUSE WAS A FORTALICE--AS TELL	386	3	DON JUAN 13	60	5
AS HINTING MORE (UNLESS OUR JUDGMENTS WARP US)	391	3	DON JUAN 13	69	7
OF MARTYRS AWED AS SPAGNOLETTO TAINTED	392	3	DON JUAN 13	71	7
AS IF 'TWOULD TO A SECOND SPRING RESIGN	395	3	DON JUAN 13	77	3
AS WHAT IS LOST IN GREEN IS GAINED IN YELLOW	395	3	DON JUAN 13	77	8
BUT TA'EN AT HAZARD AS THE RHYME MAY RUN	397	3	DON JUAN 13	83	6
COME OUT AND GLIMMER'D AS A SIX-WEEKS' STAR	398	3	DON JUAN 13	84	6
WHO DID NOT HATE SO MUCH THE SIN AS SINNER	399	3	DON JUAN 13	87	6
AS BEAUTIFUL AND BOUNDING AS A STEED	401	3	DON JUAN 13	92	6
AS BEAUTIFUL AND BOUNDING AS A STEED	401	3	DON JUAN 13	92	6
BUT LONGBOW WILD AS AN AEOLIAN HARP	402	3	DON JUAN 13	93	2
OR SOLITARY AS THEY CHOSE TO BEAR	406	3	DON JUAN 13	103	6
MET THE MORN AS THEY MIGHT IF FINE THEY RODE	406	3	DON JUAN 13	104	2
BUT FULL OF CUNNING AS ULYSSES' WHISTLE	407	3	DON JUAN 13	105	5
AS PHIDIAN FORMS CUT OUT OF MARBLE ATTIC	409	3	DON JUAN 13	110	3
THERE NOW ARE NO 'SQUIRE WESTERNS AS OF OLD	409	3	DON JUAN 13	110	4
BUT FAIR AS THEN OR FAIRER TO BEHOLD	409	3	DON JUAN 13	110	6

AS   (CONTINUED)

	PAGE	VOL	CANTO	STANZA	LN
BUT GENTLEMEN IN STAYS AS STIFF AS STONES	409	3	DON JUAN 13	110	8
BUT GENTLEMEN IN STAYS AS STIFF AS STONES	409	3	DON JUAN 13	110	8
MUCH AS OLD SATURN ATE HIS PROGENY	410	3	DON JUAN 14	1	6
IS POESY ACCORDING AS THE MIND GLOWS	414	3	DON JUAN 14	8	4
BUT JUST TO PLAY WITH AS AN INFANT PLAYS	414	3	DON JUAN 14	8	8
THE MONDE EXACTLY AS THEY OUGHT TO PAINT	418	3	DON JUAN 14	19	3
WHY DO THEIR SKETCHES FAIL THEM AS INDITERS	418	3	DON JUAN 14	20	5
AS CAPTAIN PARRY'S VOYAGE MAY DO TO JASON'S	419	3	DON JUAN 14	22	4
THE WORLD (AS SINCE THAT HISTORY LESS POLITE	420	3	DON JUAN 14	23	2
CONDEMN'D TO CHILD-BED AS MEN FOR THEIR SINS	420	3	DON JUAN 14	23	7
BUT AS TO WOMEN WHO CAN PENETRATE	420	3	DON JUAN 14	24	3
TO FLY FROM AS FROM HUNGRY PIKES A ROACH	421	3	DON JUAN 14	26	3
ARE THERE OFT DULL AND DREARY AS A DUN--	423	3	DON JUAN 14	29	7
BUT BE IT AS IT MAY A BARD MUST MEET	423	3	DON JUAN 14	30	4
THE WILDS AS DOTH AN ARAB TURN'D AVENGER	424	3	DON JUAN 14	32	6
SOME HOPED THINGS MIGHT NOT TURN OUT AS THEY FEAR'D	429	3	DON JUAN 14	44	3
AS THEY WILL DO LIKE LEAVES AT THE FIRST BREEZE	431	3	DON JUAN 14	48	6
BUT MIX'D WITH PITY PURE AS E'ER WAS PENN'D	432	3	DON JUAN 14	51	6
AND (AS HER JUNIOR BY SIX WEEKS) HIS YOUTH	432	3	DON JUAN 14	51	8
IF BUT TO KEEP THY CREDIT AS A MOWER	433	3	DON JUAN 14	53	8
AS I HAVE SAID IN--I FORGET WHAT PAGE	433	3	DON JUAN 14	54	5
MY MUSE DESPISES REFERENCE AS YOU HAVE GUESS'D	433	3	DON JUAN 14	54	6
I HATE IT AS I HATE A DROVE OF CATTLE	435	3	DON JUAN 14	58	5
WHO WHIRL THE DUST AS SIMOOMS WHIRL THE SAND	435	3	DON JUAN 14	58	6
I HATE IT AS I HATE AN ARGUMENT	435	3	DON JUAN 14	58	7
THE LADY ADELINE AS SOON'S SHE SAW	436	3	DON JUAN 14	60	3
SUCH MEASURES AS SHE THOUGHT MIGHT BEST IMPEDE	437	3	DON JUAN 14	61	2
AND NEXT A QUARREL (AS HE SEEMED TO FRET)	437	3	DON JUAN 14	62	7
BEWITCHING TORTURING AS THEY FREEZE OR GLOW	438	3	DON JUAN 14	63	7
AT LEAST AS FAR AS BIENSEANCE ALLOWS	439	3	DON JUAN 14	67	4
AT LEAST AS FAR AS BIENSEANCE ALLOWS	439	3	DON JUAN 14	67	4
SUCH AS ARE COINED IN CONVERSATION'S MINT	440	3	DON JUAN 14	69	3
RETIRED AND AS HE WENT OUT CALMLY KISSED HER	440	3	DON JUAN 14	69	7
PROPORTION'D AS A POPLAR OR A POLE	441	3	DON JUAN 14	71	5
STILL THERE WAS SOMETHING WANTING AS I'VE SAID--	441	3	DON JUAN 14	72	1
AN ACCESSARY AS I HAVE CAUSE TO GUESS	443	3	DON JUAN 14	76	4
CONVEY'D MEDEA AS HER SUPERCARGO	443	3	DON JUAN 14	76	8
AS FAR AS I KNOW THAT THE CHURCH RECEIVES	444	3	DON JUAN 14	78	4
AS FAR AS I KNOW THAT THE CHURCH RECEIVES	444	3	DON JUAN 14	78	4
MUCH AS A MONK MAY DO WITHIN HIS CELL	445	3	DON JUAN 14	81	4
AS NOW WITH THOSE OF SOI-DISANT SOUND MIND	446	3	DON JUAN 14	84	4
LIKE ARCHIMEDES I LEAVE EARTH AS 'TWAS	446	3	DON JUAN 14	84	8
AS SHE HAD SEEN NOUGHT CLAIMING ITS EXPANSION	446	3	DON JUAN 14	85	4
AND GATHER'D AS THEY RUN LIKE GROWING WATER	448	3	DON JUAN 14	88	6
UPON HER MIND THE MORE SO AS HER BREAST	448	3	DON JUAN 14	88	7
AS OBSTINACY BOTH IN MEN AND WOMEN	448	3	DON JUAN 14	89	5
BUT OF SUCH FRIENDSHIP AS MAN'S MAY TO MAN BE	450	3	DON JUAN 14	92	7
SHE WAS AS CAPABLE AS WOMAN CAN BE	450	3	DON JUAN 14	92	8
SHE WAS AS CAPABLE AS WOMAN CAN BE	450	3	DON JUAN 14	92	8
WILL THERE AS ALSO IN THE TIES OF BLOOD	451	3	DON JUAN 14	93	2
BUT TRUE--AS IF EXPEDIENT I COULD PROVE)	452	3	DON JUAN 14	96	2
TO LEAVE THEM HOVERING AS THE EFFECT IS FINE	453	3	DON JUAN 14	97	5
THAT IN OUR YOUTH AS DANGEROUS A PASSION	454	3	DON JUAN 14	100	2
AS E'ER BROUGHT MAN AND WOMAN TO THE BRINK	454	3	DON JUAN 14	100	3
AS FEW WOULD EVER DREAM COULD FORM THE LINK	454	3	DON JUAN 14	100	5
WITH SELF-LOVE IN THE CENTRE AS THEIR POLE	455	3	DON JUAN 14	102	4
AS APROPOS OF HOPE OR RETROSPECTION	456	3	DON JUAN 15	1	3
AS THOUGH THE LURKING THOUGHT HAD FOLLOW'D FREE	456	3	DON JUAN 15	1	4
OR MINIATURE AT LEAST AS IS MY NOTION	457	3	DON JUAN 15	2	6
AND AS FOR LOVE--OH LOVE--WE WILL PROCEED	458	3	DON JUAN 15	5	1
A PRETTY NAME AS ONE WOULD WISH TO READ	458	3	DON JUAN 15	5	3
THEY DIFFER AS WINE DIFFERS FROM ITS LABLE	458	3	DON JUAN 15	6	5
BRIGHT AS A NEW NAPOLEON FROM ITS MINTAGE	458	3	DON JUAN 15	7	3
OR GLORIOUS AS A DIAMOND RICHLY SET	458	3	DON JUAN 15	7	4
BUT OFT DENIED AS PATIENCE 'GINS TO FAIL HE	459	3	DON JUAN 15	8	5
AND TAKE AS MANY HEROES AS HEAVEN PLEASES	459	3	DON JUAN 15	9	8
AND TAKE AS MANY HEROES AS HEAVEN PLEASES	459	3	DON JUAN 15	9	8
WHERE SHE WAS INTERESTED (AS WAS SAID)	460	3	DON JUAN 15	10	2
UNTO SUCH FEELINGS AS SEEM'D INNOCENT	460	3	DON JUAN 15	10	7
AS IF THEY TOLD THE TRUTH COULD WELL BE SHOWN	461	3	DON JUAN 15	13	2
WAS SUCH AS RATHER SEEM'D TO KEEP ALOOF	462	3	DON JUAN 15	14	3
SO AS TO MAKE THEM FEEL HE KNEW HIS STATION	462	3	DON JUAN 15	15	6
AND EKE THE WISE AS HAS BEEN OFTEN SHOWN	463	3	DON JUAN 15	17	4
BUT SPECULATING AS I CAST MINE EYE	464	3	DON JUAN 15	19	4
I RATTLE ON EXACTLY AS I'D TALK	464	3	DON JUAN 15	19	7
JUST AS I FEEL THE IMPROVISATORE	465	3	DON JUAN 15	20	8
SUCH AS THE TIMES MAY FURNISH 'TIS A FLIGHT	467	3	DON JUAN 15	25	2
OR STARCH AS ARE THE EDICTS STATESMEN UTTER	468	3	DON JUAN 15	27	4
AS WOMEN HATE HALF MEASURES ON THE WHOLE	468	3	DON JUAN 15	28	7
SOME DIFFICULTIES AS IN HIS OWN PREFERENCE	469	3	DON JUAN 15	30	5
OBSERVED AS STRICTLY BOTH AT BOARD AND BED	470	3	DON JUAN 15	32	6
AS THOSE OF ARISTOTLE THOUGH SOMETIMES	470	3	DON JUAN 15	32	7
STRANGELY ENOUGH AS YET WITHOUT MISCARRIAGE	471	3	DON JUAN 15	35	3
THIS HE (AS FAR AS I CAN UNDERSTAND) MEANT	472	3	DON JUAN 15	38	4
THIS HE (AS FAR AS I CAN UNDERSTAND) MEANT	472	3	DON JUAN 15	38	4
AS ON THE WHOLE IT IS AN EVEN CHANCE	473	3	DON JUAN 15	39	4
THERE WAS MISS MILLPOND SMOOTH AS SUMMER'S SEA	474	3	DON JUAN 15	41	1
A RUSS OR TURK--THE ONE'S AS GOOD AS T'OTHER	474	3	DON JUAN 15	42	8

AS (CONTINUED)

	PAGE	VOL	CANTO		STANZA	LN
A RUSS OR TURK--THE ONE'S AS GOOD AS T'OTHER	474	3	DON JUAN	15	42	8
IN EYES WHICH SADLY SHONE AS SERAPHS' SHINE	476	3	DON JUAN	15	45	3
RADIANT AND GRAVE--AS PITYING MAN'S DECLINE	476	3	DON JUAN	15	45	5
SHE LOOK'D AS IF SHE SAT BY EDEN'S DOOR	476	3	DON JUAN	15	45	7
AS FAR AS HER OWN GENTLE HEART ALLOW'D	476	3	DON JUAN	15	46	2
AS FAR AS HER OWN GENTLE HEART ALLOW'D	476	3	DON JUAN	15	46	2
TO NOVEL POWER AND AS SHE WAS THE LAST	476	3	DON JUAN	15	46	7
AS SEEKING NOT TO KNOW IT SILENT LONE	476	3	DON JUAN	15	47	2
AS GROWS A FLOWER THUS QUIETLY SHE GREW	476	3	DON JUAN	15	47	3
HER SPIRIT SEEM'D AS SEATED ON A THRONE	477	3	DON JUAN	15	47	6
AGAINST HER BEING MENTION'D AS WELL FITTED	477	3	DON JUAN	15	48	6
MADE JUAN WONDER AS NO DOUBT HE MUST	477	3	DON JUAN	15	49	3
AS THAT PRIM SILENT COLD AURORA RABY	477	3	DON JUAN	15	49	8
AND THEREFORE FITTEST AS OF HIS PERSUASION	478	3	DON JUAN	15	50	2
AS USUAL--THE SAME REASON WHICH SHE LATE DID	478	3	DON JUAN	15	50	8
AS PURE AS SANCTITY ITSELF FROM VICE	478	3	DON JUAN	15	52	3
AS PURE AS SANCTITY ITSELF FROM VICE	478	3	DON JUAN	15	52	3
WHO LOOK UPON THEM AS THEY OUGHT TO DO	479	3	DON JUAN	15	53	8
MUCH AS SHE WOULD HAVE SEEN A GLOWWORM SHINE	480	3	DON JUAN	15	56	3
MORE WARM AS LOVELY AND NOT LESS SINCERE	481	3	DON JUAN	15	58	5
WAS SUCH AS LIES BETWEEN A FLOWER AND GEM	481	3	DON JUAN	15	58	8
AND AS MY FRIEND SCOTT SAYS I SOUND MY WARISON	481	3	DON JUAN	15	59	3
SERF LORD MAN WITH SUCH SKILL AS NONE WOULD SHARE IT IF	481	3	DON JUAN	15	59	6
AS CONGRESSES OF LATE DO) OF THE LADY	482	3	DON JUAN	15	61	2
AS WHITE AS CLEOPATRA'S MELTED PEARLS	484	3	DON JUAN	15	65	8
AS WHITE AS CLEOPATRA'S MELTED PEARLS	484	3	DON JUAN	15	65	8
AS FORM A SCIENCE AND A NOMENCLATURE	486	3	DON JUAN	15	69	7
TASTE OR THE GOUT--PRONOUNCE IT AS INCLINES	488	3	DON JUAN	15	72	3
BUT VARIOUS AS THE VARIOUS MEATS DISPLAY'D	488	3	DON JUAN	15	74	4
NO DAMSEL BUT A DISH AS HATH BEEN SAID	488	3	DON JUAN	15	74	6
WAS NOT SUCH AS TO ENCOURAGE HIM TO SHINE	489	3	DON JUAN	15	75	6
WHICH PIQUES A PREUX CHEVALIER--AS IT OUGHT	490	3	DON JUAN	15	77	2
OR SOMETHING WHICH WAS NOTHING AS URBANITY	490	3	DON JUAN	15	78	2
AND LOOK'D AS MUCH AS IF TO SAY I SAID IT--	491	3	DON JUAN	15	79	1
AND LOOK'D AS MUCH AS IF TO SAY I SAID IT--	491	3	DON JUAN	15	79	1
BECAUSE IT SOMETIMES AS I'VE SEEN OR READ IT	491	3	DON JUAN	15	79	3
AS ONCE OR TWICE TO SMILE IF NOT TO LISTEN	491	3	DON JUAN	15	80	8
WITH HER WAS RARE AND ADELINE WHO AS YET	492	3	DON JUAN	15	81	2
AS IF EACH CHARMING WORD WERE A DECREE	492	3	DON JUAN	15	82	4
BUT INNOCENTLY SO AS SOCRATES	494	3	DON JUAN	15	86	2
SO MUCH AS I DO ANY KIND OF WRANGLE	496	3	DON JUAN	15	91	3
AND ALSO MEEK AS A METAPHYSICIAN	497	3	DON JUAN	15	92	2
AS ELDON ON A LUNATIC COMMISSION--	497	3	DON JUAN	15	92	4
BUT AS SUBSERVIENT TO A MORAL USE	497	3	DON JUAN	15	93	4
WAS DANGEROUS--I THINK SHE IS AS HARMLESS	498	3	DON JUAN	15	94	7
AS SOME WHO LABOUR MORE AND YET MAY CHARM LESS	498	3	DON JUAN	15	94	8
OUR BUBBLES AS THE OLD BURST NEW EMERGE	500	3	DON JUAN	15	99	6
AND AS SHE TREATS ALL THINGS AND NE'ER RETREATS	502	3	DON JUAN	16	3	1
'TIS TIME TO STRIKE SUCH PUNY DOUBTERS DUMB AS	502	3	DON JUAN	16	4	7
RECEIVE AS GOSPEL AND WHICH GROW MORE ROOTED	503	3	DON JUAN	16	6	7
AS ALL TRUTHS MUST THE MORE THEY ARE DISPUTED	503	3	DON JUAN	16	6	8
THOUGHTS QUITE AS YELLOW BUT LESS CLEAR THAN AMBER	505	3	DON JUAN	16	11	4
AS CLEAR AS SUCH A CLIMATE WILL ALLOW	506	3	DON JUAN	16	13	4
AS CLEAR AS SUCH A CLIMATE WILL ALLOW	506	3	DON JUAN	16	13	4
THEN AS THE NIGHT WAS CLEAR THOUGH COLD HE THREW	508	3	DON JUAN	16	17	1
AS DOUBTLESS SHOULD BE PEOPLE OF HIGH BIRTH	508	3	DON JUAN	16	17	6
LOOK LIVING IN THE MOON AND AS YOU TURN	508	3	DON JUAN	16	18	2
AS IF TO ASK HOW YOU CAN DARE TO KEEP	508	3	DON JUAN	16	18	7
AS JUAN MUSED ON MUTABILITY	509	3	DON JUAN	16	20	1
MOST PEOPLE AS IT PLAYS ALONG THE ARRAS	509	3	DON JUAN	16	20	8
WITH STEPS THAT TROD AS HEAVY YET UNHEARD	510	3	DON JUAN	16	21	4
HE MOVED AS SHADOWY AS THE SISTERS WEIRD	510	3	DON JUAN	16	21	6
HE MOVED AS SHADOWY AS THE SISTERS WEIRD	510	3	DON JUAN	16	21	6
BUT SLOWLY AND AS HE PASSED JUAN BY	510	3	DON JUAN	16	21	7
AS STANDS A STATUE STOOD HE FELT HIS HAIR	510	3	DON JUAN	16	23	5
AND WOULD HAVE PASSED THE WHOLE OFF AS A DREAM	511	3	DON JUAN	16	25	5
ALL THERE WAS AS HE LEFT IT STILL HIS TAPER	512	3	DON JUAN	16	26	1
BURNT AND NOT BLUE AS MODEST TAPERS USE	512	3	DON JUAN	16	26	2
HE WOKE BETIMES AND AS MAY BE SUPPOSED	512	3	DON JUAN	16	28	1
SHE LOOKED AND SAW HIM PALE AND TURNED AS PALE	514	3	DON JUAN	16	31	1
BUT FOR THE REST AS HE HIMSELF SEEMED LOTH	514	3	DON JUAN	16	33	6
YOU LOOK QUOTH HE AS IF YOU HAD HAD YOUR REST	515	3	DON JUAN	16	35	3
GRACEFUL AS DIAN WHEN SHE DRAWS HER BOW	517	3	DON JUAN	16	38	5
AS TOUCHED AND PLAINTIVELY BEGAN TO PLAY	517	3	DON JUAN	16	38	7
WITH THAT SHE ROSE AS GRACEFUL AS A ROE	517	3	DON JUAN	16	38	V5
WITH THAT SHE ROSE AS GRACEFUL AS A ROE	517	3	DON JUAN	16	38	V5
WITH THAT SHE ROSE AND GLIDED OFF AS SNOW	517	3	DON JUAN	16	38	V5
AND 'TIS HELD AS FAITH TO THEIR BED OF DEATH	519	3	DON JUAN	16	L 3	7
SAY NOUGHT TO HIM AS HE WALKS THE HALL	520	3	DON JUAN	16	L 6	1
AS O'ER THE GRASS THE DEW	520	3	DON JUAN	16	L 6	4
NOR LESS APPLAUDS AS IN POLITENESS BOUND	521	3	DON JUAN	16	41	6
AS IF SHE RATED SUCH ACCOMPLISHMENT	521	3	DON JUAN	16	42	2
AS THE MERE PASTIME OF AN IDLE DAY	521	3	DON JUAN	16	42	3
WOULD NOW AND THEN AS 'TWERE WITHOUT DISPLAY	521	3	DON JUAN	16	42	5
AS DID THE CYNIC ON SOME LIKE OCCASION	522	3	DON JUAN	16	43	4
IN BABYLON'S BRAVURAS--AS THE HOME	523	3	DON JUAN	16	46	1
WAS ADELINE WELL VERSED AS COMPOSITIONS	523	3	DON JUAN	16	46	8
UPON HER FRIENDS AS EVERYBODY OUGHT	524	3	DON JUAN	16	47	4

AS   (CONTINUED)
```
    THOUGHTS BOUNDLESS DEEP BUT SILENT TOO AS SPACE      .  .  .  . 524  3 DON JUAN 16     48   8
    THEY PASSED AS SUCH THINGS DO FOR SUPERSTITION .  .  .  .  . 527  3 DON JUAN 16     54   2
    BUT AS LORD HENRY WAS A CONNOISSEUR-- .  .  .  .  .  .  .  . 528  3 DON JUAN 16     57   1
    BUT MERELY AS A CRITICAL REGALE .  .  .  .  .  .  .  .  .  . 528  3 DON JUAN 16     57   V8
    PALE AS IF PAINTED SO HER CHEEK BEING RED   .  .  .  .  .  . 532  3 DON JUAN 16     64   2
    BY NATURE AS IN HIGHER DAMES LESS HALE  .  .  .  .  .  .  . 532  3 DON JUAN 16     64   3
    BOTH BUSY (AS A GENERAL IN HIS TENT   .  .  .  .  .  .  .  . 533  3 DON JUAN 16     66   6
    BECAUSE AS SUITS THEIR RANK AND SITUATION   .  .  .  .  .  . 534  3 DON JUAN 16     68   5
    AND AS THE ISTHMUS OF THE GRAND CONNECTION  .  .  .  .  .  . 534  3 DON JUAN 16     69   7
    HIS WORD HAD THE SAME VALUE AS ANOTHER'S .  .  .  .  .  .  . 535  3 DON JUAN 16     71   8
    AS FOR HIS PLACE HE COULD BUT SAY THIS OF IT    .  .  .  .  . 536  3 DON JUAN 16     73   7
    HE WAS AS INDEPENDENT--AYE MUCH MORE--  .  .  .  .  .  .  . 537  3 DON JUAN 16     76   1
    AS COMMON SOLDIERS OR A COMMON--SHORE   .  .  .  .  .  .  . 537  3 DON JUAN 16     76   3
    THUS ON THE MOB ALL STATESMEN ARE AS EAGER  .  .  .  .  .  . 537  3 DON JUAN 16     76   7
    TO PROVE THEIR PRIDE AS FOOTMEN TO A BEGGAR .  .  .  .  .  . 537  3 DON JUAN 16     76   8
    JUST AS A REGULAR COMMON SOLDIER OR A WHORE .  .  .  .  .  . 537  3 DON JUAN 16     76   V3
    'TWAS A GREAT BANQUET SUCH AS ALBION OLD .  .  .  .  .  .  . 538  3 DON JUAN 16     78   2
    WAS WONT TO BOAST--AS IF A GLUTTON'S TRAY   .  .  .  .  .  . 538  3 DON JUAN 16     78   3
    AS BETWEEN ENGLISH BEEF AND SPARTAN BROTH--  .  .  .  .  .  . 541  3 DON JUAN 16     84   7
    BACCHUS AND CERES BEING AS WE KNOW .  .  .  .  .  .  .  .  . 542  3 DON JUAN 16     86   4
    AND SITTING AS IF NAILED UPON HIS CHAIR .  .  .  .  .  .  . 542  3 DON JUAN 16     87   4
    THOUGH KNIVES AND FORKS CLANGED ROUND AS IN A FRAY  .  .  . 542  3 DON JUAN 16     87   5
    AND HASTILY--AS NOTHING CAN CONFOUND    .  .  .  .  .  .  . 542  3 DON JUAN 16     88   4
    THIS WAS NO BAD MISTAKE AS IT OCCURRED  .  .  .  .  .  .  . 543  3 DON JUAN 16     89   1
    WERE ANGRY--AS THEY WELL MIGHT TO BE SURE   .  .  .  .  .  . 543  3 DON JUAN 16     89   4
    ESPECIALLY AS HE HAD BEEN RENOWNED .  .  .  .  .  .  .  .  . 544  3 DON JUAN 16     91   4
    AS JUAN SHOULD HAVE KNOWN HAD NOT HIS SENSES    .  .  .  .  . 545  3 DON JUAN 16     93   7
    HER ASPECT WAS AS USUAL STILL--NOT STERN--  .  .  .  .  .  . 545  3 DON JUAN 16     94   3
    AS DEEP SEAS IN A SUNNY ATMOSPHERE .  .  .  .  .  .  .  .  . 545  3 DON JUAN 16     94   8
    AS ALL MUST BLEND WHOSE PART IT IS TO AIM   .  .  .  .  .  . 546  3 DON JUAN 16     95   5
    (ESPECIALLY AS THE SIXTH YEAR IS ENDING) .  .  .  .  .  .  . 546  3 DON JUAN 16     95   6
    WHICH SHE WENT THROUGH AS THOUGH IT WERE A DANCE    .  .  . 546  3 DON JUAN 16     96   4
    FIVE AS THEY MIGHT DO IN A MODEST WAY   .  .  .  .  .  .  . 548  3 DON JUAN 16     99   3
    HOWEVER THE DAY CLOSED AS DAYS MUST CLOSE   .  .  .  .  .  . 549  3 DON JUAN 16    101   1
    AND CURTSEYING OFF AS CURTSIES COUNTRY DAME .  .  .  .  .  . 549  3 DON JUAN 16    101   4
    AS MUSIC CHIMES IN WITH A MELODRAME    .  .  .  .  .  .  .  . 552  3 DON JUAN 16    104   6
    'TIS TRUE HE SAW AURORA LOOK AS THOUGH  .  .  .  .  .  .  . 553  3 DON JUAN 16    106   1
    IN MAKING HIM AS SILENT AS A GHOST .  .  .  .  .  .  .  .  . 553  3 DON JUAN 16    107   2
    IN MAKING HIM AS SILENT AS A GHOST .  .  .  .  .  .  .  .  . 553  3 DON JUAN 16    107   2
    RAY FADES ON RAY AS YEARS ON YEARS DEPART   .  .  .  .  .  . 554  3 DON JUAN 16    109   4
    AND FULL OF SENTIMENTS SUBLIME AS BILLOWS   .  .  .  .  .  . 555  3 DON JUAN 16    110   1
    THE NIGHT WAS AS BEFORE HE WAS UNDREST  .  .  .  .  .  .  . 555  3 DON JUAN 16    111   1
    IT IS THE SABLE FRIAR AS BEFORE .  .  .  .  .  .  .  .  .  . 556  3 DON JUAN 16    113   2
    WITH AWFUL FOOTSTEPS REGULAR AS RHYME   .  .  .  .  .  .  . 556  3 DON JUAN 16    113   3
    OR (AS RHYMES MAY BE IN THESE DAYS) MUCH MORE   .  .  .  . 556  3 DON JUAN 16    113   4
    AS WIDE AS IF A LONG SPEECH WERE TO COME .  .  .  .  .  .  . 557  3 DON JUAN 16    115   4
    AS WIDE AS IF A LONG SPEECH WERE TO COME .  .  .  .  .  .  . 557  3 DON JUAN 16    115   4
    HIS EYES WERE OPEN AND (AS WAS BEFORE   .  .  .  .  .  .  . 557  3 DON JUAN 16    115   7
    DREADFUL AS DANTE'S RHIMA OR THIS STANZA .  .  .  .  .  .  . 557  3 DON JUAN 16    116   4
    THE DOOR FLEW WIDE NOT SWIFTLY--BUT AS FLY  .  .  .  .  .  . 558  3 DON JUAN 16    117   1
    DON JUAN SHOOK AS ERST HE HAD BEEN SHAKEN   .  .  .  .  .  . 558  3 DON JUAN 16    118   1
    HE SHUDDERED AS NO DOUBT THE BRAVEST COWERS .  .  .  .  .  . 559  3 DON JUAN 16    120   5
    GLEAMED FORTH AS THROUGH THE CASEMENT'S IVY SHROUD  .  .  . 560  3 DON JUAN 16    121   7
    WHICH BEAT AS IF THERE WAS A WARM HEART UNDER   .  .  .  . 560  3 DON JUAN 16    122   4
    HE FOUND AS PEOPLE ON MOST TRIALS MUST  .  .  .  .  .  .  . 560  3 DON JUAN 16    122   5
    AS EVER LURKED BENEATH A HOLY HOOD .  .  .  .  .  .  .  .  . 561  3 DON JUAN 16    123   2
    THE NEXT ARE SUCH AS ARE NOT DOOMED TO LOSE .  .  .  .  .  . 562  3 DON JUAN 17      1   5
    THE NEXT ARE ONLY CHILDREN AS THEY ARE STYLED   .  .  .  . 563  3 DON JUAN 17      2   1
    AS FAR AS WORDS MAKE RULES--OUR COMMON NOTION   .  .  .  . 563  3 DON JUAN 17      3   2
    AS FAR AS WORDS MAKE RULES--OUR COMMON NOTION   .  .  .  . 563  3 DON JUAN 17      3   2
    BECAUSE AS AGES UPON AGES PUSH ON  .  .  .  .  .  .  .  .  . 564  3 DON JUAN 17      6   3
    A SOMETHING LIKE IT--AS BEAR WITNESS LUTHER .  .  .  .  .  . 565  3 DON JUAN 17      6   8
    MISCHIEF IN FAMILIES AS SOME KNOW OR KNEW   .  .  .  .  .  . 565  3 DON JUAN 17      7   5
    MIGHT BE FILLED UP AS VAINLY AS BEFORE  .  .  .  .  .  .  . 566  3 DON JUAN 17      9   2
    MIGHT BE FILLED UP AS VAINLY AS BEFORE  .  .  .  .  .  .  . 566  3 DON JUAN 17      9   2
    AND SO FOR ONE WILL I--AS WELL I MAY--  .  .  .  .  .  .  . 566  3 DON JUAN 17     10   4
    JUST AS I MAKE MY MIND UP EVERY DAY .  .  .  .  .  .  .  .  . 566  3 DON JUAN 17     10   6
    SUCH AS ENABLES MAN TO SHOW HIS STRENGTH .  .  .  .  .  .  . 567  3 DON JUAN 17     12   3
    AS IF HE HAD COMBATED WITH MORE THAN ONE .  .  .  .  .  .  . 568  3 DON JUAN 17     14   3
    SEEMED PALE AND SHIVERED AS IF SHE HAD KEPT .  .  .  .  .  . 568  3 DON JUAN 17     14   7
ASCENDENCE
    HAVE IN THEIR SEVERAL ARTS OR PARTS ASCENDENCE  .  .  .  . 537  3 DON JUAN 16     76   4
ASCERTAIN
    TO ASCERTAIN THE ATMOSPHERIC STATE .  .  .  .  .  .  .  .  . 406  2 DON JUAN  4    112   6
    AS WE MAY ASCERTAIN WITH DUE PRECISION  .  .  .  .  .  .  . 477  2 DON JUAN  5    115   7
ASCERTAINED
    HAVE NOT EXACTLY ASCERTAINED THE POLE   .  .  .  .  .  .  . 376  3 DON JUAN 13     39   4
    OF THESE IS NOT EXACTLY ASCERTAINED--   .  .  .  .  .  .  . 507  3 DON JUAN 16     16   2
ASCETIC
    BUT CERTES IT CONDUCTS TO LIVES ASCETIC .  .  .  .  .  .  . 472  3 DON JUAN 15     38   7
ASHAMED
    SHE MADE THE CLEVEREST PEOPLE QUITE ASHAMED .  .  .  .  .  .  26  2 DON JUAN  1     10   5
    I'M VERY SORRY VERY MUCH ASHAMED   .  .  .  .  .  .  .  .  .  85  2 DON JUAN  1    119   7
    I AM ASHAMED OF HAVING SHED THESE TEARS .  .  .  .  .  .  . 106  2 DON JUAN  1    155   5
    MEN GROW ASHAMED OF BEING SO VERY FOND  .  .  .  .  .  .  . 278  2 DON JUAN  3      7   1
    CAESAR HIMSELF WOULD BE ASHAMED OF FAME .  .  .  .  .  .  . 455  3 DON JUAN 14    102   8
    AND WHAT WAS WORSE WAS NOT ASHAMED TO SHOW IT   .  .  .  . 524  3 DON JUAN 16     47   8
    PERHAPS SHE WAS ASHAMED OF SEEING FRAIL .  .  .  .  .  .  . 532  3 DON JUAN 16     64   5
    AND THEN TO BE ASHAMED OF SUCH MISTAKING .  .  .  .  .  .  . 558  3 DON JUAN 16    118   4
```

ASHES
   THE ASHES OF OUR HOPES IS A DEEP GRIEF . . . . 301 2 DON JUAN 3   51   7
   AND SHIVER THEM TO ASHES BUT TO TRAIL . . . . 348 2 DON JUAN 4   9   6
   HER CHEEK TURNED ASHES EARS RUNG BRAIN WHIRLED ROUND . . . 58 3 DON JUAN 6   105   5
   SPARE OR SMITE RARELY--MAN'S MAKE MILLIONS ASHES . . . 115 3 DON JUAN 8   6   8
   ASHES TO ASHES--WHY NOT LEAD TO LEAD . . . . 117 3 DON JUAN 8   10   8
   ASHES TO ASHES--WHY NOT LEAD TO LEAD . . . . 117 3 DON JUAN 8   10   8
   THOU RIDDLE WITHOUT WHOM EARTH'S ASHES END . . . . . 210 3 DON JUAN 9   56   V7
ASHORE
   AND THERE HE WENT ASHORE WITHOUT DELAY . . . . . . 286 2 DON JUAN 3   20   1
ASIA
   EUROPE AND ASIA YOU BEING QUITE AT EASE . . . . . . 413 2 DON JUAN 5   5   6
   ASIA WHERE KAFF LOOKS DOWN UPON THE KURDS . . . . . 49 3 DON JUAN 6   86   8
ASIAN
   THE EUROPEAN WITH THE ASIAN SHORE . . . . 412 2 DON JUAN 5   3   1
   THE ASIAN POMP OF OTTOMAN PARADE . . . . 440 2 DON JUAN 5   51   8
ASIATIC
   BUT SUCH AS FIT AN ASIATIC BREECH . . . . 451 2 DON JUAN 5   68   5
   BEGAN TO CLOTHE EACH ASIATIC HILL . . . . 49 3 DON JUAN 6   86   3
   AND TACITURN ASIATIC DISPOSITION . . . . 328 3 DON JUAN 12   27   2
   TO MAKE HIS LITTLE WILD ASIATIC TAME . . . . 336 3 DON JUAN 12   42   6
ASIDE
   THESE I COULD BEAR BUT CANNOT CAST ASIDE . . . . . 132 2 DON JUAN 1   195   5
   WHICH MAKES NOT OTHERS SMILE THEN TURN'D ASIDE . . . 356 2 DON JUAN 4   23   2
   WAS ON THE POINT OF BEING SET ASIDE . . . . 440 2 DON JUAN 5   51   4
   AND TURNS ASIDE HIS SCYTHE TO VULGAR THINGS . . . . 468 2 DON JUAN 5   98   4
   HE MUTTERED (BUT THE LAST WAS GIVEN ASIDE) . . . . 471 2 DON JUAN 5   103   3
   WERE LAID ASIDE BUT NOT BEFORE SHE OFFERED . . . . 36 3 DON JUAN 6   61   2
   SOME LAID ASIDE LIKE AN OLD OPERA HAT . . . . . . 308 3 DON JUAN 11   79   5
   REQUIRED AURORA SCARCELY LOOK'D ASIDE . . . . . . 490 3 DON JUAN 15   78   3
   ASIDE HIS VERY MIRROR SOON WAS PUT . . . . 513 3 DON JUAN 16   29   4
   NOW THIS (BUT WE WILL WHISPER IT ASIDE) . . . . . 522 3 DON JUAN 16   43   1
ASK
   AND IF THE MAN SHOULD ASK 'TIS BUT DENIAL . . . . 64 2 DON JUAN 1   78   7
   'TWILL ONE DAY ASK YOU WHY YOU USED ME SO . . . . 107 2 DON JUAN 1   157   6
   AS UPON SUCH OCCASIONS TARS WILL ASK . . . . . . 173 2 DON JUAN 2   33   7
   MUST BREAKFAST AND BETIMES--LEST THEY SHOULD ASK IT . . 233 2 DON JUAN 2   144   7
   (SUCH THINGS IN FACT IT DON'T ASK MUCH TO MAR) . . . 281 2 DON JUAN 3   10   6
   TO ASK HIM AWKWARD QUESTIONS ON THE WAY . . . . . 286 2 DON JUAN 3   20   3
   YOU'D BETTER ASK OUR MISTRESS WHO'S HIS HEIR . . . 297 2 DON JUAN 3   43   6
   COULD NOT THE BLOCKHEAD ASK FOR A BALLOON . . . . 333 2 DON JUAN 3   99   8
   JUAN GAZED ON HER AS TO ASK HIS FATE-- . . . . . 355 2 DON JUAN 4   22   5
   AND THESE ARE THINGS WHICH ASK A TENDER TEAR . . . 420 2 DON JUAN 5   19   5
   AND CONSCIENCE ASK A CURIOUS SORT OF QUESTION . . . 426 2 DON JUAN 5   30   4
   AND SHOULD YOU ASK HOW SHE A SULTAN'S BRIDE . . . . 477 2 DON JUAN 5   115   2
   OF ONE WHO DARED TO ASK IF HE HAD LOVED . . . . . 481 2 DON JUAN 5   121   4
   HER THIRD TO ASK HIM WHERE HE HAD BEEN BRED . . . . 491 2 DON JUAN 5   139   3
   COULD YOU ASK SUCH A QUESTION--BUT WE WILL . . . . 22 3 DON JUAN 6   33   2
   FROM SPAIN--BUT WHERE IS SPAIN--DON'T ASK SUCH STUFF . . 28 3 DON JUAN 6   44   4
   WHAT THAT IS--ASK THE PIG WHO SEES THE WIND . . . . 108 3 DON JUAN 7   84   8
   BUT ASK HIM WHAT HE THINKS OF IT A YEAR HENCE . . . 271 3 DON JUAN 11   7   8
   AND SHOULD YOU DOUBT PRAY ASK OF YOUR NEXT NEIGHBOUR . . 288 3 DON JUAN 11   41   4
   BUT SHOULD A LADY ASK ME TO OBLIGE HER . . . . . . 348 3 DON JUAN 12   70   V4
   ASK A BLIND MAN THE BEST JUDGE YOU'LL ATTACK . . . 348 3 DON JUAN 12   71   4
   I ASK IN TURN--WHY DO YOU PLAY AT CARDS . . . . . 415 3 DON JUAN 14   11   3
   THAT--BUT ASK ANY WOMAN IF SHE'D CHOOSE . . . . . 421 3 DON JUAN 14   25   6
   AND ASK THEM HOW THEY LIKE TO BE IN THRALL . . . . 446 3 DON JUAN 14   83   4
   AS IF TO ASK HOW YOU CAN DARE TO KEEP . . . . . . 508 3 DON JUAN 16   18   7
   TO ASK THE REVEREND PERSON WHAT HE WANTED . . . . 511 3 DON JUAN 16   23   8
   I ASK BUT THIS OF MINE TO--NOT DEFEND . . . . . . 552 3 DON JUAN 16   104   8
ASKANCE
   BY A LOOK SCARCE PERCEPTIBLY ASKANCE . . . . . . 546 3 DON JUAN 16   96   6
ASK'D
   YET WHEN THEY ASK'D HER FOR HER DEPOSITIONS . . . . 35 2 DON JUAN 1   27   5
   I ASK'D THE DOCTORS AFTER HIS DISEASE . . . . . : 39 2 DON JUAN 1   34   6
   HAIDEE SPOKE NOT OF SCRUPLES ASK'D NO VOWS . . . . 257 2 DON JUAN 2   190   1
   HE ASK'D NO FURTHER QUESTIONS AND PROCEEDED . . . . 300 2 DON JUAN 3   49   1
   THUS USUALLY WHEN HE WAS ASK'D TO SING . . . . . 319 2 DON JUAN 3   85   1
   ASK'D NEXT DAY IF MEN EVER HUNTED TWICE . . . . . 425 3 DON JUAN 14   35   8
ASKED
   HE ASKED THE MEANING OF THIS HOLIDAY . . . . . . 297 2 DON JUAN 3   42   5
   KATINKA ASKED HER ALSO WHENCE SHE CAME-- . . . . . 28 3 DON JUAN 6   44   3
   TO THIS LONG CATECHISM OF QUESTIONS ASKED . . . . 56 3 DON JUAN 6   100   4
   AN ENGLISH LADY ASKED OF AN ITALIAN . . . . . . 208 3 DON JUAN 9   51   1
   AND ASKED WHY SUCH A STRUCTURE HAD BEEN RAISED . . . 261 3 DON JUAN 10   74   8
   LATE AUTHORS ASKED HIM FOR A HINT OR TWO . . . . . 294 3 DON JUAN 11   50   6
   THEN ASKED HER GRACE WHAT NEWS WERE OF THE DUKE OF LATE . 515 3 DON JUAN 16   34   5
ASKING
   AND ASKING NOW AND THEN FOR CAST-OFF DRESSES . . . 252 2 DON JUAN 2   182   8
   SHE SAW THEM WATCH HER WITHOUT ASKING WHY . . . . 378 2 DON JUAN 4   63   3
   SHE TOOK THEIR MEDICINES WITHOUT ASKING WHY . . . . 378 2 DON JUAN 4   63   V3
   CONJECTURING WONDERING ASKING A NARRATION . . . . 43 3 DON JUAN 6   74   3
   ON WHICH AT THE THIRD ASKING OF THE BANNS . . . . 542 3 DON JUAN 16   88   1
ASK'ST
   THOU ASK'ST IF I CAN LOVE BE THIS THE PROOF . . . . 484 2 DON JUAN 5   127   1
ASLEEP
   WAS NOT ASLEEP--YES SEARCH AND SEARCH SHE CRIED . . . 100 2 DON JUAN 1   145   2
   ASLEEP THEY SHOOK THEM BY THE HAND AND HEAD . . . . 208 2 DON JUAN 2   98   7
   HE DID NOT FALL ASLEEP JUST AFTER DINNER . . . . . 426 3 DON JUAN 14   36   8

	PAGE	VOL		CANTO	STANZA	LN
ASP						
SHE WOULD HAVE SHRUNK AS FROM A TOAD OR ASP	81	2	DON JUAN	1	111	6
I'M SURE SHE WOULD HAVE SHRUNK AS FROM AN ASP	81	2	DON JUAN	1	111	V6
UPON THEIR PREY AS DARTS AN ANGRY ASP	370	2	DON JUAN	4	48	6
ASPECT						
AND IN WHATEVER ASPECT IT ARRAYS	61	2	DON JUAN	1	73	5
OF A SOFT CHEEK AND ASPECT DELICATE	203	2	DON JUAN	2	88	2
UNEQUAL IN ITS ASPECT HERE AND THERE	210	2	DON JUAN	2	103	2
HIS SLENDER FRAME AND PALLID ASPECT LAY	214	2	DON JUAN	2	110	7
WITH HERE AND THERE A CREEK WHOSE ASPECT WORE	249	2	DON JUAN	2	177	4
WHEN DAZZLED WITH HER ASPECT I MIGHT ERR	314	2	DON JUAN	3	76	V6
MORE LIKE AND LIKE TO LAMBRO'S ASPECT GREW--	363	2	DON JUAN	4	35	4
OH POWERS OF FORM--WHAT ASPECT SEES SHE THERE	363	2	DON JUAN	4	35	V7
BUT FIX'D AS MARBLE'S UNCHANGED ASPECT THROWS	377	2	DON JUAN	4	61	3
WHICH HAS AT TIMES AN ASPECT OF THE ODDEST	464	2	DON JUAN	5	91	7
A THIRD'S ALL PALLID ASPECT OFFERED MORE	40	3	DON JUAN	6	67	3
IN ASPECT PLAINLY CLAD BESMEARED WITH DUST	104	3	DON JUAN	7	73	6
ALONG THE ASPECT WHETHER SMOOTH OR ROUGH	206	3	DON JUAN	9	48	6
PARISIAN ASPECT WHICH UPSET OLD TROY	209	3	DON JUAN	9	53	5
GLORY AND TRIUMPH O'ER HER ASPECT BURST	212	3	DON JUAN	9	59	3
BUT STILL HER ASPECT HAD AN AIR SO LONELY	475	3	DON JUAN	15	44	3
ALL YOUTH--BUT WITH AN ASPECT BEYOND TIME	476	3	DON JUAN	15	45	4
HER ASPECT WAS AS USUAL STILL--NOT STERN--	545	3	DON JUAN	16	94	3
ASPECTS						
AND THUS THE CHILLIEST ASPECTS MAY CONCENTRE	375	3	DON JUAN	13	38	2
START FROM THE FRAMES WHICH FENCE THEIR ASPECTS STERN	508	3	DON JUAN	16	18	6
ASPIRANT						
ADMITTED AS AN ASPIRANT TO ALL	295	3	DON JUAN	11	54	2
PERHAPS SHE WISH'D AN ASPIRANT PROFOUNDER	435	3	DON JUAN	14	57	5
ASPIRANTS						
INTO ALL ASPIRANTS FOR MARTIAL PRAISE	85	3	DON JUAN	7	39	V4
ASPIRATIONS						
LONGINGS SUBLIME AND ASPIRATIONS HIGH	71	2	DON JUAN	1	93	2
ASS						
HIS OX--HIS ASS--NOR ANYTHING THAT'S HIS	140	2	DON JUAN	1	206	V2
A--NEVER MIND HIS TUTOR AN OLD ASS	158	2	DON JUAN	2	3	4
AN ASS WAS PRACTISING RECITATIVE	391	2	DON JUAN	4	87	8
CHEAPENING AN OX AN ASS A LAMB OR KID	425	2	DON JUAN	5	28	6
SCIENCE ENOUGH WHICH LEVELS TO AN ASS	69	3	DON JUAN	7	5	3
FOR A MUCH LONGER TIME THEN LIKE AN ASS--	126	3	DON JUAN	8	29	5
THEN LIKE AN ASS HE WENT UPON HIS WAY	126	3	DON JUAN	8	30	1
AND THEN MEN STARE AS IF A NEW ASS SPAKE	328	3	DON JUAN	12	26	5
ASSAIL						
OF ONE WHOSE HATE IS MASKED BUT TO ASSAIL	182	2	DON JUAN	2	49	4
THEY WERE ALL SUMMER LIGHTNING MIGHT ASSAIL	348	2	DON JUAN	4	9	5
HE JUDGED THEM PROPER TO ASSAIL THE WORKS	93	3	DON JUAN	7	53	6
ASSAILANT'S						
AND FIRED IT INTO ONE ASSAILANT'S PUDDING--	274	3	DON JUAN	11	13	4
ASSAULT						
MOST STRONGLY RECOMMENDED AN ASSAULT	83	3	DON JUAN	7	35	4
OF THE ASSAULT AND ALL THE CAMP WAS IN	94	3	DON JUAN	7	54	2
THE DAY BEFORE THE ASSAULT WHILE UPON DRILL	95	3	DON JUAN	7	56	1
IN WAR THAN LOVE HE HAD BETTER LEAD THE ASSAULT	98	3	DON JUAN	7	62	8
OR IT MAY BE TO-NIGHT THE ASSAULT I HAVE VOWED	99	3	DON JUAN	7	63	5
THE COLUMN ORDERED ON THE ASSAULT SCARCE PASSED	115	3	DON JUAN	8	7	1
TO GENTLEMEN ENGAGED IN THE ASSAULT	119	3	DON JUAN	8	16	7
HE WHOSE WHOLE LIFE HAS BEEN ASSAULT AND BATTERY	185	3	DON JUAN	9	5	3
ASSAULTS						
AND BAFFLED THE ASSAULTS OF ALL THEIR HOST	171	3	DON JUAN	8	120	4
ASSEMBLED						
AND HERE ASSEMBLED CROSS-LEGG'D ROUND THEIR TRAYS	291	2	DON JUAN	3	31	1
THE NOBLE GUESTS ASSEMBLED AT THE ABBEY	396	3	DON JUAN	13	79	1
TO BE ASSEMBLED AT A COUNTRY SEAT	402	3	DON JUAN	13	94	2
ASSEMBLED WITH OUR HOSTESS AND MINE HOST	568	3	DON JUAN	17	13	6
ASSEMBLIES						
AT GREAT ASSEMBLIES OR IN PARTIES SMALL	295	3	DON JUAN	11	54	4
ASSERT						
IF ANY PERSON SHOULD PRESUME TO ASSERT	140	2	DON JUAN	1	207	1
FOR THE MAN WAS WE SAFELY MAY ASSERT	95	3	DON JUAN	7	55	3
BY HUMOURING ALWAYS WHAT THEY MIGHT ASSERT	426	3	DON JUAN	14	37	3
ASSERTION						
'TIS POETRY--AT LEAST BY HIS ASSERTION	11	2	DON JUAN	D	4	5
BEING ONLY INJURED BY HIS OWN ASSERTION	14	2	DON JUAN	D	9	4
THE WORLD UPON THE WHOLE IS WORTH THE ASSERTION	377	3	DON JUAN	13	41	3
ASSES						
I HAVE SEEN SOME NATIONS LIKE O'ERLOADED ASSES	310	3	DON JUAN	11	84	7
ASSETS						
WHERE HIS ASSETS WERE WAXING RATHER FEW	240	3	DON JUAN	10	31	3
ASSIGN						
TILL FURTHER ORDERS SHOULD HIS DOOM ASSIGN	371	2	DON JUAN	4	50	V4
ASSIST						
WHO HELD THE PLACE AND TO ASSIST THE FOE'S	71	3	DON JUAN	7	10	8
ASSISTANCE						
'TIS AS A SNOWBALL WHICH DERIVES ASSISTANCE	398	2	DON JUAN	4	100	5
OF MODESTY DECLINED THE ASSISTANCE PROFFERED	36	3	DON JUAN	6	61	4
THE MATCH WAS LIT TOO SOON AND NO ASSISTANCE	80	3	DON JUAN	7	28	5
(WITH SOME ASSISTANCE FROM THE FROST AND SNOW)	147	3	DON JUAN	8	70	2
AND OFFERING AS USUAL LATE ASSISTANCE	275	3	DON JUAN	11	14	4
ASSISTED						
I CAN'T HELP THINKING PUBERTY ASSISTED	71	2	DON JUAN	1	93	8

PAGE VOL   CANTO STANZA LN

ASSUAGE
SO THAT WE CAN OUR NATIVE SUN ASSUAGE . . . . 217 3 DON JUAN 9   69   5
ASSUAGING
BUT VIOLENT THINGS WILL SOONER BEAR ASSUAGING . . . . . 305 2 DON JUAN 3   58   5
BUT THERE ARE HUMAN FEELINGS PAST ASSUAGING . . . . . . 305 2 DON JUAN 3   58   V5
BUT THEN THIS WRATH WILL PASS AND TIME ASSUAGING . . . . 305 2 DON JUAN 3   58   V5
ASSUME
ASSUME THEN LEAVE US ON OUR FREEZING WAY . . . . 66 3 DON JUAN 7   1   8
DAYS BETTER DRAWN BEFORE OR ELSE ASSUME . . . . 468 3 DON JUAN 15   26   7
ASSUMED
OR SAID HER CHEEKS ASSUMED THE DEEPEST DYES . . . . . 489 2 DON JUAN 5 134   3
STRICT AND HIS MIND ASSUMED A MANLIER VIGOUR . . . . . 460 3 DON JUAN 15   11   6
ASSURANCE
A MODEST CONFIDENCE AND CALM ASSURANCE . . . . 294 3 DON JUAN 11   52   2
MODEST I AM--YET WITH SOME SLIGHT ASSURANCE . . . . . 567 3 DON JUAN 17   11   2
ASSURE
YOU SNEER AND I ASSURE YOU THIS IS TRUE . . . . 163 2 DON JUAN 2   13   7
EXCUSE MY FREEDOM WHEN I HERE ASSURE YOU . . . . 63 3 DON JUAN 6 115   7
AND I ASSURE YOU THAT LIKE VIRGIN HONEY . . . . 330 3 DON JUAN 12   31   7
ASSURED
TELL ME--AND BE ASSURED THAT SINCE YOU STAIN . . . . . 105 2 DON JJAN 1 154   7
AND GLIDES AWAY ASSURED SHE NEVER HURTS YE . . . . . . 300 3 DON JJAN 11   63   8
PERHAPS 'TWAS HARDLY QUITE ASSURED ENOUGH . . . . . . 462 3 DON JUAN 15   14   5
ASTONISH'D
IN FACT MUCH MORE ASTONISH'D THAN DELIGHTED . . . . . 294 2 DON JUAN 3   37   7
ASTONISHED
HE DAZZLED BUT ASTONISHED NOT HER SENSE . . . . 480 3 DON JUAN 15   56   V7
ASTONISHMENT
WHATE'ER ASTONISHMENT THIS SEEMS TO CALL . . . . 333 3 DON JUAN 12   37   V6
ASTRAY
OF THE SAD CONSEQUENCE OF GOING ASTRAY . . . . 336 3 DON JUAN 12   44   6
ASTRINGENT
IS NOT A THING OF THAT ASTRINGENT QUALITY . . . . . . 501 2 DON JUAN 5 157   4
ASTRONOMER
BUT LOVER POET OR ASTRONOMER . . . . 506 3 DON JUAN 16   14   1
ASTRONOMY
BUT MY BEST CANTO SAVE ONE ON ASTRONOMY . . . . 356 3 DON JUAN 12   88   7
ASUNDER
THE HEART ASUNDER--THEN AS MORE OR LESS . . . . 59 3 DON JUAN 6 107   5
ASYOUR
CONSTRUCTION ASYOUR CURES FOR HECTIC PHTHISICS . . . . 349 3 DON JUAN 12   72   3
ATAGHAN
AND ATAGHAN OF GOLD AND SHOES OF YELLOW . . . . 451 2 DON JUAN 5   68   V7
ATALANTIS
FOR I DISDAIN TO WRITE AN ATALANTIS . . . . 311 3 DON JUAN 11   87   5
ATE
THEY ATE UP ALL THEY HAD AND DRANK THEIR WINE . . . . 192 2 DON JUAN 2   69   2
THE SAILORS ATE THE REST OF POOR PEDRILLO . . . . . . 197 2 DON JUAN 2   77   8
THE SAILORS ATE HIM ALL SAVE THREE OR FOUR . . . . . 198 2 DON JUAN 2   78   1
HE ATE AND HE WAS WELL SUPPLIED AND SHE . . . . . . 239 2 DON JUAN 2 158   1
WHO ATE LAST WAR MORE YANKEES THAN HE KILL'D . . . . 399 3 DON JUAN 13   88   4
SINCE EVE ATE APPLES MUCH DEPENDS ON DINNER . . . . . 404 3 DON JUAN 13   99   8
MUCH AS OLD SATURN ATE HIS PROGENY . . . . 410 3 DON JUAN 14   1   6
ATHANASIUS'
AS AFTER READING ATHANASIUS' CURSE . . . . 17 3 DON JUAN 6   23   2
ATHENS
IN SPAIN AND LUCCA ATHENS EVERYWHERE . . . . 488 3 DON JUAN 15   73   4
ATHOS
AS PHILIP'S SON PROPOSED TO DO WITH ATHOS . . . . . . 355 3 DON JUAN 12   86   8
ATHWART
NATIONS ATHWART THE DEEP THE GOLDEN RAYS . . . . . . 319 3 DON JUAN 12   8   4
ATLANTIC
O'ER FAR ATLANTIC CONTINENTS OR ISLANDS . . . . 523 3 DON JUAN 16   46   4
ATLAS
HE STOOD LIKE ATLAS WITH A WORLD OF WORDS . . . . . . 471 2 DON JUAN 5 104   1
ATMOSPHERE
ROUND HER SHE MADE AN ATMOSPHERE OF LIFE . . . . . . 313 2 DON JUAN 3   74   1
WERE NOTHING BUT THE NATURAL ATMOSPHERE . . . . 266 3 DON JUAN 10   83   7
AS DEEP SEAS IN A SUNNY ATMOSPHERE . . . . 545 3 DON JUAN 16   94   8
ATMOSPHERIC
TO ASCERTAIN THE ATMOSPHERIC STATE . . . . 406 2 DON JUAN 4 112   6
ATOMS
SUNS AS RAYS--WORLDS LIKE ATOMS--YEARS LIKE HOURS . . . 189 3 DON JUAN 9   13   8
ATROCIOUS
WAS IN HER EYES A THING THE MOST ATROCIOUS . . . . . . 51 2 DON JUAN 1   54   8
AND KEEPS THE ATROCIOUS READER IN SUSPENSE . . . . . 453 3 DON JUAN 14   97   6
ATROPOS
NOR SHEARS OF ATROPOS BEFORE THEIR VISIONS . . . . . 190 2 DON JUAN 2   64   6
ATTACHED
WHY--WHY--BESIDES FRED REALLY WAS ATTACHED . . . . . 332 3 DON JUAN 12   35   1
ATTACHES
THAT OPPOSITION ONLY MORE ATTACHES-- . . . . 439 3 DON JUAN 14   67   7
ATTACK
AND HOW TO PARRY THE RENEW'D ATTACK . . . . 114 2 DON JUAN 1 169   5
WITHOUT WHOM VENUS WILL NOT LONG ATTACK US . . . . . 245 2 DON JUAN 2 169   8
AH WHY THE LIVER WILT THOU THUS ATTACK . . . . 372 2 DON JUAN 4   53   3
THE RUSSIANS NOW WERE READY TO ATTACK . . . . 73 3 DON JUAN 7   14   1
TO ATTACK THE TURK'S FLOTILLA WHICH LAY NIGH . . . . . 78 3 DON JUAN 7   24   3
IN SHORT THIS LAST ATTACK THOUGH RICH IN GLORY . . . . 83 3 DON JUAN 7   35   1

50

		PAGE	VOL	CANTO	STANZA	LN

ATTACK   (CONTINUED)
```
  PRESAGING A MOST LUMINOUS ATTACK  . . . . . . . . . .  89  3 DON JUAN  7   46   4
  YOU SERVED AT WIDIN--YES--YOU LED THE ATTACK  . . . .  98  3 DON JUAN  7   61   1
  OFF EACH ATTACK WHEN PEOPLE ARE IN QUEST . . . . . . 123  3 DON JUAN  8   25   6
  ON GREAT OCCASIONS SUCH AS AN ATTACK . . . . . . . . 160  3 DON JUAN  8   97   3
  AND SCENT THE PREY THEIR MASTERS WOULD ATTACK ALL . . 196  3 DON JUAN  9   27   5
  THE FIRST ATTACK AT ONCE PROVED THE DIVINITY  . . . . 271  3 DON JUAN 11    6   1
  FOR BEING AS MUCH THE SUBJECT OF ATTACK . . . . . . . 312  3 DON JUAN 11   90   4
  ASK A BLIND MAN THE BEST JUDGE  YOU'LL ATTACK . . . . 348  3 DON JUAN 12   71   4
  LET RADICALS ITS OTHER ACTS ATTACK . . . . . . . . . 378  3 DON JUAN 13   43   7
```
ATTACK'D
```
  IN THEIR VOCATION HAD NOT BEEN ATTACK'D  . . . . . . 388  2 DON JUAN  4   80   6
```
ATTACKED
```
  AND WITH ALL PASSIONS IN THEIR TURN ATTACKED  . . . . 412  2 DON JUAN  5    2   6
  THE THIRD IN COLUMNS TWO ATTACKED BY WATER  . . . . .  91  3 DON JUAN  7   50   8
  BUT NOW THE TOWN IS GOING TO BE ATTACKED . . . . . . 107  3 DON JUAN  7   81   5
  BUT OF THE PORTION WHICH ATTACKED BY WATER  . . . . . 116  3 DON JUAN  8    9   2
```
ATTACKING
```
  HE READ AN ARTICLE THE KING ATTACKING . . . . . . . 512  3 DON JUAN 16   26   7
```
ATTAIN
```
  MOST LIKELY TO ATTAIN HER AIM--HIS HEART . . . . . . 492  2 DON JUAN  5  140   8
  THAT ALL IS DUBIOUS WHICH MAN MAY ATTAIN . . . . . . 191  3 DON JUAN  9   17   3
```
ATTAINED
```
  AND HAVE NOT YET ATTAINED TO MUCH SUCCESS  . . . . . 374  3 DON JUAN 13   35   4
```
ATTAINING
```
  WITH ALL ITS STARS AND WITH A STRETCH ATTAINING  . . 450  2 DON JUAN  5   66   5
  OF ANYONE'S ATTAINING TO HIS STATION . . . . . . . . 208  3 DON JUAN  9   52   6
```
ATTEMPT
```
  WHO DIED IN THE THEN GREAT ATTEMPT TO CLIMB . . . . . 261  3 DON JUAN 10   74   5
```
ATTEMPTING
```
  IN ANY CASE ATTEMPTING A REPLY . . . . . . . . . . . 119  2 DON JUAN  1  179   3
```
ATTEND
```
  AND SELF WOULD KNOW WHAT DUTY TO ATTEND . . . . . . . 100  3 DON JUAN  7   65   8
  IN HEALTH--WHEN ILL WE CALL THEM TO ATTEND US  . . . 245  3 DON JUAN 10   42   3
```
ATTENDANCE
```
  WHO DO NOT GIVE PROFESSIONAL ATTENDANCE  . . . . . . 537  3 DON JUAN 16   76   6
```
ATTENDANT
```
  THE GENTLE GIRL AND HER ATTENDANT--ONE  . . . . . . . 216  2 DON JUAN  2  115   2
  WITH THEIR ATTENDANT AIDED OUR ESCAPE . . . . . . . . 103  3 DON JUAN  7   72   2
```
ATTENDANTS
```
  SHE SPAKE SOME WORDS TO HER ATTENDANTS WHO . . . . . 469  2 DON JUAN  5   99   1
```
ATTENDS
```
  OR RATHER STOMACH WHICH ALAS ATTENDS . . . . . . . . 167  2 DON JUAN  2   21   2
```
ATTENTION
```
  PERHAPS EVEN MORE ATTENTION THAN IS DUE . . . . . . . 431  2 DON JUAN  5   38   5
  WHICH YOUR SUBLIME ATTENTION MAY BE WORTH  . . . . . 494  2 DON JUAN  5  144   6
  ALL THE ATTENTION POSSIBLE AND SEEN . . . . . . . . . 102  3 DON JUAN  7   70   4
  A GENERAL OBJECT OF ATTENTION MADE . . . . . . . . . 223  3 DON JUAN  9   83   2
  TO SOME SHE SHOWED ATTENTION OF THAT KIND  . . . . . 372  3 DON JUAN 13   32   2
```
ATTENTIONS
```
  WITH FOOD AND RAIMENT AND THOSE SOFT ATTENTIONS  . . 221  2 DON JUAN  2  123   2
  JUAN WAS DRAWN THUS INTO SOME ATTENTIONS . . . . . . 491  3 DON JUAN 15   80   1
  ITS KIND ATTENTIONS TO THEIR PROPER PALE . . . . . . 533  3 DON JUAN 16   67   6
```
ATTESTS
```
  ALBEIT ALL HUMAN HISTORY ATTESTS  . . . . . . . . . 404  3 DON JUAN 13   99   6
```
ATTIC
```
  HER WIT (SHE SOMETIMES TRIED AT WIT) WAS ATTIC ALL  . .  27  2 DON JUAN  1   12   3
  HER ATTIC FOREHEAD AND HER PHIDIAN NOSE  . . . . . .  27  3 DON JUAN  6   42   4
  NONE SAVE THE SPANISH FLY AND ATTIC BEE  . . . . . . 196  3 DON JUAN  9   28   7
  AND YET THE BRITISH DAMME'S RATHER ATTIC . . . . . . 289  3 DON JUAN 11   43   1
  AS PHIDIAN FORMS CUT OUT OF MARBLE ATTIC . . . . . . 409  3 DON JUAN 13  110   3
  AND REALLY IF THE SAGE SUBLIME AND ATTIC . . . . . . 494  3 DON JUAN 15   86   3
  FOR A SPOILT CARPET--BUT THE ATTIC BEE  . . . . . . . 522  3 DON JUAN 16   43   7
```
ATTICA
```
  AND LOOKED DOWN OVER ATTICA OR HE . . . . . . . . . 271  3 DON JUAN 11    7   2
```
ATTITUDE
```
  WITH MUCH SUSPICION IN HIS ATTITUDE  . . . . . . . . 109  2 DON JUAN  1  160   3
  AND TAKE WHAT KINGS CALL AN IMPOSING ATTITUDE  . . .  11  3 DON JUAN  6   11   4
  HERSELF IN HER SUBLIMEST ATTITUDE  . . . . . . . . . 193  3 DON JUAN  9   22   6
```
ATTORNEY
```
  WITH THAT SUBLIME OF RASCALS YOUR ATTORNEY . . . . . 103  2 DON JUAN  1  151   3
  NOT ONE EXCEPT THE ATTORNEY WAS AMUSED . . . . . . . 109  2 DON JUAN  1  159   5
  THE ATTORNEY LAST WHO LINGER'D NEAR THE DOOR  . . . . 111  2 DON JUAN  1  164   2
  BUT SEE THE WORLD IS ONLY ONE ATTORNEY . . . . . . . 281  3 DON JUAN 11   28   8
```
ATTORNIES-GENERAL
```
  ATTORNIES-GENERAL AWFUL TO THE SIGHT . . . . . . . . 391  3 DON JUAN 13   69   6
```
ATTRACT
```
  EXCEPT IN SUCH A WAY AS NOT TO ATTRACT  . . . . . . . 412  2 DON JUAN  5    2   2
  BY WHICH SIRENS CAN ATTRACT OUR GREAT  . . . . . . . 474  3 DON JUAN 15   42   6
  FAULTS WHICH ATTRACT BECAUSE THEY ARE NOT TAME . . . 480  3 DON JUAN 15   57   5
```
ATTRACTION
```
  DEEPEST ATTRACTION FOR WHEN TO THE VIEW . . . . . . . 218  2 DON JUAN  2  117   4
  NO LONGER NOW RESIST THE ATTRACTION OF GUNPOWDER . . 129  3 DON JUAN  8   33  V7
```
ATTRACTIONS
```
  HALF HER ATTRACTIONS--PROBABLY FROM PITY-- . . . . . 350  3 DON JUAN 12   74   4
  OF HIS ATTRACTIONS MARR'D THE FAIR PERSPECTIVE . . . 461  3 DON JUAN 15   12   5
```
ATTRACTIVE
```
  GREAT WISH TO PLEASE--A MOST ATTRACTIVE DOWER  . . . 395  2 DON JUAN  4   94   7
```
ATTRACTS
```
  FOR TOO MUCH TRUTH AT FIRST SIGHT NE'ER ATTRACTS . . 416  3 DON JUAN 14   13   6
```

51

	PAGE	VOL		CANTO	STANZA	LN

ATTRACTS   (CONTINUED)
    AND MORE ATTRACTS BY ALL IT DOTH CONCEAL-- . . . . . . 422 3 DON JUAN 14   27   4
    TO FEEL THAT FLATTERY WHICH ATTRACTS THE PROUD . . . . 493 3 DON JUAN 15   83   6
ATTUNED
    ATTUNED BY VOICES MORE OR LESS DIVINE . . . . 408 3 DON JUAN 13   107   3
AU
    AND GOD KNOWS WHO BESIDES IN AU AND OU . . . . . . 137 3 DON JUAN 8   49   2
AUBURN
    THAT SPARKLED O'ER THE AUBURN OF HER HAIR . . . . . . 217 2 DON JUAN 2   116   2
    HER HAIR I SAID WAS AUBURN BUT HER EYES . . . . 218 2 DON JUAN 2   117   1
    DOWN HER WHITE NECK LONG FLOATING AUBURN CURLS-- . . . 291 2 DON JUAN 3   30   5
    HER HAIR'S LONG AUBURN WAVES DOWN TO HER HEEL . . . . 313 2 DON JUAN 3   73   5
    ONE WITH HER AUBURN TRESSES LIGHTLY BOUND . . . . . . 38 3 DON JUAN 6   65   5
AUCTION
    TO BE PUT UP FOR AUCTION AMONGST TARTARS . . . . . . 415 2 DON JUAN 5   8   8
AUCTIONEER
    DAN PHOEBUS TAKES ME FOR AN AUCTIONEER . . . . 393 3 DON JUAN 13   74   4
AUCTIONS
    AT ALL SUCH AUCTIONS KNEW HOW TO PREVAIL . . . . . . 477 2 DON JUAN 5   114   6
AUDACIA
    AND THEN THERE WAS THE MISS AUDACIA SHOESTRING . . . . 474 3 DON JUAN 15   42   1
AUGHT
    THEY SAW NOT IN THEMSELVES AUGHT TO CONDEMN . . . . . 351 2 DON JUAN 4   13   4
    LAY JUAN NOR COULD AUGHT RENEW THE BEAT . . . . 362 2 DON JUAN 4   34   5
    TO TRY IF I COULD WRENCH AUGHT OUT OF DEATH . . . . . 431 2 DON JUAN 5   38   7
    THAN SHE FROM AUGHT AT WHICH THE EYE COULD CAVIL . . . 474 2 DON JUAN 5   109   6
    WITH AUGHT WHICH LOOKS LIKE DESPOTISM IN VIEW . . . . 474 2 DON JUAN 5   110   5
    AUGHT OF A SERIOUS SORROWING KIND ALTHOUGH . . . . . 480 2 DON JUAN 5   119   5
    AUGHT SAVE SOME LITTLE POUTING PETTY CARE . . . . . . 480 2 DON JUAN 5   119   V5
    IN ALL HER LIFE WITH AUGHT SAVE PRAYERS AND PRAISE . . 482 2 DON JUAN 5   122   3
    FOR AUGHT WE KNOW) RENOWN'S ALL FIT OR MISS . . . . . 82 3 DON JUAN 7   33   5
    (THIS METAPHOR I THINK HOLDS GOOD AS AUGHT . . . . . . 90 3 DON JUAN 7   49   3
    ACKNOWLEDGE AUGHT OF DREAD OF DEATH OR FOE . . . . . 155 3 DON JUAN 8   87   5
    HOURIS OR AUGHT EXCEPT HIS FLORID RACE . . . . 169 3 DON JUAN 8   116   3
    WITH YOU THAN AUGHT (SAVE SCOTT) IN YOUR PROUD CITY . . 233 3 DON JUAN 10   17   4
    TAKE LIVES TAKE WIVES TAKE AUGHT EXCEPT MEN'S PURSES . . 264 3 DON JUAN 10   79   2
    MY NATURAL TEMPER'S REALLY AUGHT BUT STERN . . . . . 300 3 DON JUAN 11   63   5
    BECAUSE THE SUN AND STARS AND AUGHT THAT SHINES . . . 423 3 DON JUAN 14   29   5
    ANTICIPATING AUGHT ABOUT THE MATTER . . . . 454 3 DON JUAN 14   99   2
    AND WHEN AUGHT IS TO BEFALL . . . . 519 3 DON JUAN 16 L 4   2
AUGUR
    FROM SIRE TO SON TO AUGUR GOOD OR ILL . . . . 49 2 DON JUAN 1   51   5
    IF I MIGHT AUGUR I SHOULD RATE BUT LOW . . . . 299 3 DON JUAN 11   61   6
AUGURED
    WHICH AUGURED OF THE DEAD HOWEVER QUICK . . . . . . 244 3 DON JUAN 10   39   5
AUGURY
    DEFYING AUGURY WITH THAT FOND KISS . . . . 356 2 DON JUAN 4   24   4
AUGUST
    'TIS NOT MERE SPLENDOUR MAKES THE SHOW AUGUST . . . . 354 3 DON JUAN 12   83   7
    TO RECOMMENCE IN AUGUST--NOW WAS DONE . . . . 377 3 DON JUAN 13   42   2
AUGUSTINE
    AS SAINT AUGUSTINE IN HIS FINE CONFESSIONS . . . . . . 47 3 DON JUAN 1   47   7
    BUT SAINT AUGUSTINE HAS THE GREAT PRIORITY . . . . . 503 3 DON JUAN 16   5   5
AUGUSTUS
    AND LORD AUGUSTUS FITZ-PLANTAGENET . . . . 399 3 DON JUAN 13   87   7
    AT LORD AUGUSTUS FITZ-PLANTAGENET . . . . 428 3 DON JUAN 14   42   8
    POOR LORD AUGUSTUS FITZ-PLANTAGENET . . . . 429 3 DON JUAN 14   44   8
    WITH LORD AUGUSTUS FITZ-PLANTAGENET . . . . 437 3 DON JUAN 14   62   8
AULD
    ARE OVER   HERE'S A HEALTH TO AULD LANG SYNE . . . . 232 3 DON JUAN 10   16   5
    AND WHEN I USE THE PHRASE OF AULD LANG SYNE . . . . . 233 3 DON JUAN 10   17   1
    AS AULD LANG SYNE BRINGS SCOTLAND ONE AND ALL . . . . 233 3 DON JUAN 10   18   1
    I CARE NOT--'TIS A GLIMPSE OF AULD LANG SYNE . . . . 233 3 DON JUAN 10   18   8
AUNT
    OR THE EAR-TRUMPET OF MY GOOD OLD AUNT . . . . 241 3 DON JUAN 10   34   5
    EACH AUNT EACH COUSIN HATH HER SPECULATION . . . . . 331 3 DON JUAN 12   33   1
    FOR LIKE AN AGED AUNT OR TIRESOME FRIEND . . . . . . 334 3 DON JUAN 12   39   4
AUNTS
    MARRYING THEIR COUSINS--NAY THEIR AUNTS AND NIECES . . . 52 2 DON JUAN 1   57   7
AUREA
    AS I'LL TELL AUREA AT TO-MORROW'S ROUT . . . . 332 3 DON JUAN 12   35   6
AURORA
    AND YOUNG AURORA KISS'D HER LIPS WITH DEW . . . . . . 232 2 DON JUAN 2   142   4
    A VERSIFIED AURORA BOREALIS . . . . 67 3 DON JUAN 7   2   3
    OR LIKE A FLYING HOUR BEFORE AURORA . . . . 428 3 DON JUAN 14   40   1
    AURORA RABY A YOUNG STAR WHO SHONE . . . . 475 3 DON JUAN 15   43   5
    OF ADELINE AURORA WAS OMITTED . . . . 477 3 DON JUAN 15   48   2
    AS THAT PRIM SILENT COLD AURORA RABY . . . . 477 3 DON JUAN 15   49   8
    WITH WHICH AURORA ON THOSE BAUBLES LOOK'D . . . . . . 479 3 DON JUAN 15   53   2
    LITTLE AURORA DEEM'D SHE WAS THE THEME . . . . 480 3 DON JUAN 15   55   1
    WAS NATURE'S ALL AURORA COULD NOT BE . . . . 481 3 DON JUAN 15   58   6
    AURORA AND THE LADY ADELINE-- . . . . 489 3 DON JUAN 15   75   2
    AURORA SAT WITH THAT INDIFFERENCE . . . . 490 3 DON JUAN 15   77   1
    REQUIRED   AURORA SCARCELY LOOK'D ASIDE . . . . 490 3 DON JUAN 15   78   3
    AURORA AT THE LAST (SO HISTORY MENTIONS . . . . 491 3 DON JUAN 15   80   5
    AURORA WHO IN HER INDIFFERENCE . . . . 493 3 DON JUAN 15   83   1
    AURORA WHO LOOK'D MORE ON BOOKS THAN FACES . . . . . 494 3 DON JUAN 15   85   1
    HE THOUGHT AURORA RABY'S EYES MORE BRIGHT . . . . . . 506 3 DON JUAN 16   12   3
    AURORA RABY WITH HER LARGE DARK EYES . . . . 514 3 DON JUAN 16   31   7

	PAGE	VOL	CANTO		STANZA	LN
AURORA (CONTINUED)						
AURORA--SINCE WE ARE TOUCHING UPON TASTE	524	3	DON JUAN	16	48	1
AURORA WITH HER PURE AND PLACID MIEN	552	3	DON JUAN	16	105	3
'TIS TRUE HE SAW AURORA LOOK AS THOUGH	553	3	DON JUAN	16	106	1
AND CERTAINLY AURORA HAD RENEWED	553	3	DON JUAN	16	107	5
AURORA'S						
AND THE VINE BLUSHES LIKE AURORA'S LIP	320	3	DON JUAN	12	9	5
AURORA'S SPIRIT WAS NOT OF THAT KIND	492	3	DON JUAN	15	81	8
WAS THAT HE CAUGHT AURORA'S EYE ON HIS	544	3	DON JUAN	16	92	1
SMILE OF AURORA'S THERE WAS NOUGHT TO PIQUE	544	3	DON JUAN	16	92	6
AUSONIA'S						
NOR IN HER EYE AUSONIA'S GLANCE IS BURNING	350	3	DON JUAN	12	75	4
AUSTERE						
SHE WAS A CATHOLIC TOO SINCERE AUSTERE	476	3	DON JUAN	15	46	1
AUSTERITIES						
AND WHEREFORE BLAME GAUNT WEALTH'S AUSTERITIES	319	3	DON JUAN	12	7	6
AUSTERITY						
BUT JUAN ALSO SHARED IN HER AUSTERITY	432	3	DON JUAN	14	51	5
AUTHOR						
TREAT A DISSENTING AUTHOR VERY MARTYRLY	142	2	DON JUAN	1	211	8
OR SULTAN AS THE AUTHOR (TO WHOSE NOD	163	3	DON JUAN	8	104	6
AUTHORITY						
I HAVE NO AUTHORITY TO TELL THE REASON	454	2	DON JUAN	5	74	8
SOME PEOPLE WOULD IMPOSE NOW WITH AUTHORITY	503	3	DON JUAN	16	5	1
AUTHOR'S						
THEIR FAVOUR IN AN AUTHOR'S CAP'S A FEATHER	135	2	DON JUAN	1	199	5
AND APT TO SOW AN AUTHOR'S WHEAT WITH TARES	369	3	DON JUAN	13	25	3
AUTHORS						
FOR AUTHORS FEAR DESCRIPTION MIGHT DISPARAGE	280	2	DON JUAN	3	9	4
OH YE GREAT AUTHORS LUMINOUS VOLUMINOUS	200	3	DON JUAN	9	35	1
OH YE GREAT AUTHORS--APROPOS DES BOTTES--	200	3	DON JUAN	9	36	1
LATE AUTHORS ASKED HIM FOR A HINT OR TWO	294	3	DON JUAN	11	50	6
HE SAW TEN THOUSAND LIVING AUTHORS PASS	295	3	DON JUAN	11	54	5
SOME SAY THAT AUTHORS ONLY SNATCH BY BRIBING	418	3	DON JUAN	14	19	4
AUTOCRAT						
FOR ME I DEEM AN ABSOLUTE AUTOCRAT	194	3	DON JUAN	9	23	7
AUTOCRATIC						
THE FAIR CZARINA'S AUTOCRATIC CREST	248	3	DON JUAN	10	49	6
AUTUMN						
AS AUTUMN WINDS DISPERSE THE YELLOW LEAVES	155	3	DON JUAN	8	88	V3
TO ENTERTAIN THIS AUTUMN A SELECT	382	3	DON JUAN	13	52	2
THE MELLOW AUTUMN CAME AND WITH IT CAME	394	3	DON JUAN	13	75	1
AN ENGLISH AUTUMN THOUGH IT HATH NO VINES	394	3	DON JUAN	13	76	1
AUTUMN'S						
'TWAS A RAW DAY OF AUTUMN'S BLEAK BEGINNING	414	2	DON JUAN	5	6	1
WHICH MAKES THE SOUTHERN AUTUMN'S DAY APPEAR	395	3	DON JUAN	13	77	2
AVAIL						
AND THREE DEAD WHOM THEIR STRENGTH COULD NOT AVAIL	209	2	DON JUAN	2	101	5
EAT DRINK AND LOVE WHAT CAN THE REST AVAIL US	267	2	DON JUAN	2	207	7
AVAILED						
AVAILED FOR EITHER NEITHER CHANGE OF PLACE	381	2	DON JUAN	4	68	6
AVANT						
BUT EN AVANT THE LIGHT LOVES LANGUISH O'ER	542	3	DON JUAN	16	86	1
AVARICE						
I THINK I MUST TAKE UP WITH AVARICE	144	2	DON JUAN	1	216	8
AMBITION AVARICE VENGEANCE GLORY GLUE	422	2	DON JUAN	5	22	6
WHOSE AVARICE ALL DISBURSEMENTS DID IMPORTUNE	222	3	DON JUAN	9	81	3
AND AVARICE--DISGUST A POLISHED NATION	223	3	DON JUAN	9	81	V8
AVE						
AVE MARIA O'ER THE EARTH AND SEA	334	2	DON JUAN	3	101	7
AVE MARIA BLESSED BE THE HOUR	335	2	DON JUAN	3	102	1
AVE MARIA 'TIS THE HOUR OF PRAYER	336	2	DON JUAN	3	103	1
AVE MARIA 'TIS THE HOUR OF LOVE	336	2	DON JUAN	3	103	2
AVE MARIA MAY OUR SPIRITS DARE	336	2	DON JUAN	3	103	3
AVE MARIA OH THAT FACE SO FAIR	336	2	DON JUAN	3	103	5
AVENGE						
FOR SHE TOO WAS AS ONE WHO COULD AVENGE	367	2	DON JUAN	4	44	5
AVENGED						
AND IN THEIR NATIVE BEAUTY STOOD AVENGED	314	2	DON JUAN	3	75	5
AVENGER						
MILTON APPEAL'D TO THE AVENGER TIME	15	2	DON JUAN	D	10	2
IF TIME THE AVENGER EXECRATES HIS WRONGS	15	2	DON JUAN	D	10	3
FOR SOON OR LATE LOVE IS HIS OWN AVENGER	383	2	DON JUAN	4	73	8
THE WILDS AS DOTH AN ARAB TURN'D AVENGER	424	3	DON JUAN	14	32	6
AVENGES						
SO VILE HE 'SCAPED THE DOOM WHICH OFT AVENGES	317	2	DON JUAN	3	80	5
AVER						
UPON MY SHOULDERS HERE I MUST AVER	378	3	DON JUAN	13	43	4
AVERAGE						
THAT BEING ABOUT THEIR AVERAGE NUMERAL	295	3	DON JUAN	11	54	6
MAY AVERAGE ON THE WHOLE WITH PARTURITION	420	3	DON JUAN	14	24	2
AVERAGED						
AND AVERAGED EACH FROM TEN TO A HUNDRED DOLLARS	283	2	DON JUAN	3	15	8
AVERSE						
BESIDES BEING MUCH AVERSE FROM SUCH A FATE	199	2	DON JUAN	2	81	3
AVERSION						
AND LEFT HIS WIDOW TO HER OWN AVERSION	39	2	DON JUAN	1	34	8
BUT SCANDAL'S MY AVERSION--I PROTEST	49	2	DON JUAN	1	51	7
BUT LAMBRO SAW ALL THESE THINGS WITH AVERSION	293	2	DON JUAN	3	35	5
WRIT IN A MANNER WHICH IS MY AVERSION	330	2	DON JUAN	3	94	8

	PAGE	VOL	CANTO	STANZA	LN

AVERSIONS
HIS FRIENDSHIPS THEREFORE AND NO LESS AVERSIONS . . . . 366 3 DON JUAN 13 17 1
AVOIDED
EVEN THOUGH HIMSELF AVOIDED THE OCCASION . . . . . . 355 3 DON JUAN 12 85 8
AVOUCH'D
AVOUCH'D HIS DEATH (SUCH PEOPLE NEVER DIE) . . . . . 295 2 DON JUAN 3 38 3
AVOW
NOT AS THEY OUGHT TO BE FOR I AVOW . . . . 335 3 DON JUAN 12 40 3
CONNECTIONS STRONGER THAN HE CHOSE TO AVOW . . . . . 516 3 DON JUAN 16 37 4
AVOWED
WHICH SOME SUPPOSED (THOUGH HE HAD NOT AVOWED IT) . . . 527 3 DON JUAN 16 54 7
AWAIT
A THOUSAND SCIMITARS AWAIT THE WORD . . . . . 364 3 DON JUAN 4 37 7
THEY PARTED FOR THE PRESENT THESE TO AWAIT . . . . 105 3 DON JUAN 7 76 2
TO ONE SMALL GRASS-GROWN PATCH (WHICH MUST AWAIT . . . 237 3 DON JUAN 10 25 5
WHICH CAN AWAIT WARM YOUTH IN ITS WILD RACE . . . . 326 3 DON JUAN 12 23 4
AWAIT THOSE WHO HAVE STUDIED THEIR BON MOTS . . . . 403 3 DON JUAN 13 97 8
AWAITS
'TIS TRUE THAT DEATH AWAITS BOTH YOU AND ME . . . . . 175 2 DON JUAN 2 36 3
AWAITS THEM TREACHERY IS ALL THEIR TRUST . . . . . . 263 2 DON JUAN 2 200 3
AWAITS AT LAST EVEN THOSE WHOM LONGEST MISS . . . . 350 2 DON JUAN 4 12 6
AWAITS IT EACH NEW MEETING OR ELECTION . . . . . 272 3 DON JUAN 11 9 8
AWAKE
AROSE A CLATTER MIGHT AWAKE THE DEAD . . . . . 95 2 DON JUAN 2 136 3
AND WARM IN CASE BY CHANCE HE SHOULD AWAKE . . . . 226 2 DON JUAN 2 133 4
THAT SLEEP WHICH SEEM'D AS IT WOULD NE'ER AWAKE . . . 234 2 DON JUAN 2 146 8
TO STIR HER VIANDS MADE HIM QUITE AWAKE . . . . . 237 2 DON JUAN 2 153 7
THE EYE MIGHT DOUBT IF IT WERE WELL AWAKE . . . . 314 2 DON JUAN 3 76 5
WHO SHALL AWAKE THE HEROIC LAY . . . . . . 322 2 DON JUAN 3 L 5 V3
BUT WIDE AWAKE SHE WAS AND ROUND HER BED . . . . 42 3 DON JUAN 6 72 1
AWAKEN
AND TRIED TO AWAKEN THEM BUT FOUND THEM DEAD . . . . 208 2 DON JUAN 2 98 8
HIS OWN INTERNAL GHOST BEGAN TO AWAKEN . . . . . 558 3 DON JUAN 16 118 5
AWAKEN'D
'TIS SWEET TO BE AWAKEN'D BY THE LARK . . . . . . 88 2 DON JUAN 1 123 5
AWAKES
WITH MIST AND EVERY BIRD WITH HIM AWAKES . . . . 230 2 DON JUAN 2 139 6
THEN DRESS THEN DINNER THEN AWAKES THE WORLD . . . . 302 3 DON JUAN 11 67 1
AWARD
HIS LAST AWARD WILL HAVE THE LONG GRASS GROW . . . . 299 3 DON JUAN 11 61 4
AT LEAST IN A COLD COUNTRY MAY AWARD . . . . . 322 3 DON JUAN 12 13 V6
AWARE
DISCOVERIES MADE BUT NONE COULD BE AWARE . . . . . 59 2 DON JUAN 1 68 3
GETTING THE BOATS OUT BEING WELL AWARE . . . . 180 2 DON JUAN 2 45 6
AWARE OF THEIR DUE ROYAL RIGHTS O'ER MEN . . . . 485 2 DON JUAN 5 128 8
AWARE THIS KIND OF BAGGAGE NEVER THRIVES . . . . 102 3 DON JUAN 7 70 7
AWAY
HIS HOUSE WAS SOLD HIS SERVANTS SENT AWAY . . . . 39 2 DON JUAN 1 34 3
THUS WOULD HE WHILE HIS LONELY HOURS AWAY . . . . 73 2 DON JUAN 1 96 1
THEN SPUR AWAY O'ER EMPIRES AND O'ER STATES . . . 76 2 DON JUAN 1 103 6
FOR WANT OF FACTS WOULD ALL BE THROWN AWAY) . . . . 86 2 DON JUAN 1 121 4
MY DEAR I WAS THE FIRST WHO CAME AWAY . . . . . 98 2 DON JUAN 1 141 8
THE MOMENT HE HAS SENT HIS FOOLS AWAY . . . . 114 2 DON JUAN 1 169 2
AND JUAN THROTTLED HIM TO GET AWAY . . . . . 124 2 DON JUAN 1 186 2
BECAUSE AT LEAST THE PAST WERE PAST AWAY-- . . . 156 2 DON JUAN 1 V 8 3
IN THE MEANTIME TO PASS HER HOURS AWAY . . . . 162 2 DON JUAN 2 10 1
FROM WHICH AWAY SO FAIR AND FAST THEY BORE . . . . 163 2 DON JUAN 2 13 4
AND CARRY AWAY PERHAPS A MAST OR SO . . . . . 170 2 DON JUAN 2 26 8
THE RUDDER TORE AWAY 'TWAS TIME TO SOUND . . . . 170 2 DON JUAN 2 27 7
IMMEDIATELY THE MASTS WERE CUT AWAY . . . . . 173 2 DON JUAN 2 32 1
WITHOUT THEIR WILL THEY CARRIED THEM AWAY . . . . 177 2 DON JUAN 2 40 2
HE WATCH'D IT WISTFULLY UNTIL AWAY . . . . . 204 2 DON JUAN 2 90 5
AS MORNING BROKE THE LIGHT WIND DIED AWAY . . . . 207 2 DON JUAN 2 97 1
THEY DIED AWAY TILL THUS REDUCED TO FEW . . . . 210 2 DON JUAN 2 102 V6
AWAY THE VAST SALT DREAD ETERNAL DEEP . . . . 210 2 DON JUAN 2 103 8
AND HOW THIS HEAVY FAINTNESS PASS'D AWAY . . . . 214 2 DON JUAN 2 111 5
BUT THAT LIKE OTHER THINGS HAS PASS'D AWAY . . . . 244 2 DON JUAN 2 166 5
SOME RUN AWAY AND BUT EXCHANGE THEIR CARES . . . . 263 2 DON JUAN 2 201 3
YET FOR ALL THAT KEEP NOT TOO LONG AWAY . . . . 288 2 DON JUAN 3 25 7
ARE THINGS THAT REALLY TAKE AWAY THE BREATH . . . . 309 2 DON JUAN 3 66 6
HER FATHER WATCH'D SHE TURN'D HER EYES AWAY . . . . 379 2 DON JUAN 4 64 2
ITS DWELLINGS DOWN ITS TENANTS PAST AWAY . . . . 383 2 DON JUAN 4 72 2
ARE SWEPT AWAY AND TOMB INHERITS TOMB . . . . 399 2 DON JUAN 4 102 2
HE STOPPED AGAIN AND TURNED AWAY HIS FACE . . . . 420 2 DON JUAN 5 19 2
AND ALSO WHEN MY SECOND RAN AWAY . . . . . 420 2 DON JUAN 5 19 8
SHE DID NOT RUN AWAY TOO DID SHE SIR . . . . 421 2 DON JUAN 5 20 7
NO FAITH--WHAT THEN--I RAN AWAY FROM HER . . . . 421 2 DON JUAN 5 20 8
AND MARCH AWAY--'TWERE EASIER DONE THAN SAID . . . 434 2 DON JUAN 5 43 8
COULD HARDLY CARRY ANYTHING AWAY . . . . . 465 2 DON JUAN 5 93 5
IN HOLY MATRIMONY SNORES AWAY . . . . . . 42 3 DON JUAN 6 73 4
AND TALKED AWAY AND MIGHT HAVE TALKED TILL NOW . . . 58 3 DON JUAN 6 105 2
AWAY HE WENT THEN UPON HIS COMMISSION . . . . 64 3 DON JUAN 6 117 1
AND DRILLED AWAY IN THE MOST CLASSIC RUSSIAN . . . 99 3 DON JUAN 7 64 2
AND FOUGHT AWAY WITH MIGHT AND MAIN NOT KNOWING . . . 120 3 DON JUAN 8 19 2
YET FOR ALL THIS HE DID NOT RUN AWAY . . . . 121 3 DON JUAN 8 21 8
MEN RUN AWAY MUCH RATHER THAN GO THROUGH . . . . 130 3 DON JUAN 8 35 3
AND NEVER RAN AWAY EXCEPT WHEN RUNNING . . . . 130 3 DON JUAN 8 35 7
AND THEREFORE WHEN HE RAN AWAY HE DID SO . . . . 133 3 DON JUAN 8 40 1
OF THE NEXT BASTION FIRED AWAY LIKE DEVILS . . . . 134 3 DON JUAN 8 44 2

AWAY   (CONTINUED)
    AND SWEPT AS GALES SWEEP FOAM AWAY WHOLE RANKS 134   3 DON JUAN 8   44   3
    HE HEWED AWAY LIKE DOCTORS OF THEOLOGY   165   3 DON JUAN 8   108   6
    RAISE BUT AN ARM 'TWILL BRUSH THEIR WEB AWAY 196   3 DON JUAN 9   28   1
    CERTES IT WOULD HAVE BEEN BUT THROWN AWAY 200   3 DON JUAN 9   36   6
    PINIONS TO FLEE AWAY AND BE AT REST   228   3 DON JUAN 10   6   3
    'TIS ONLY THAT THEY LOVE TO THROW AWAY   273   3 DON JUAN 11   10   3
    AND GLIDES AWAY ASSURED SHE NEVER HURTS YE 300   3 DON JUAN 11   63   8
    AND FAR AWAY THE LAST BUD OF HER RACE 329   3 DON JUAN 12   29   4
    CERVANTES SMILED SPAIN'S CHIVALRY AWAY 364   3 DON JUAN 13   11   1
    AWAY AWAY FRESH HORSES ARE THE WORD   379   3 DON JUAN 13   46   3
    AWAY AWAY FRESH HORSES ARE THE WORD 379   3 DON JUAN 13   46   3
    AND WORK AWAY LIKE SPIRIT UPON MATTER 423   3 DON JUAN 14   30   7
    THE SHADOW PASSED AWAY--BUT WHERE THE HALL 511   3 DON JUAN 16   24   2
    WOULD NOT BE DRIVEN AWAY 518   3 DON JUAN 16   L 1   8
    BUT BOTH WERE THROWN AWAY AMONGST THE FENS 540   3 DON JUAN 16   83   2
AWE
    THE DOUBLE BOBADIL TAKES SCORN FOR AWE 153   2 DON JUAN 1   V 4   8
    THE BRAGGADOCIO TAKES CONTEMPT FOR AWE 153   2 DON JUAN 1   V 4   V8
    AND THEN SHE STOPP'D AND STOOD AS IF IN AWE 232   2 DON JUAN 2   143   4
    IN AWE HE SAID AS THE CENTURION SAITH 430   2 DON JUAN 5   36   5
    THE PEOPLE'S AWE AND ADMIRATION RAISING 445   2 DON JUAN 5   60   6
    HAD NOT COME UP IN TIME TO CAST AN AWE 137   3 DON JUAN 8   49   3
    EVEN THE BOLD CHURCHMAN'S TOMB EXCITED AWE 261   3 DON JUAN 10   74   4
    THERE WAS AWE IN THE HOMAGE WHICH SHE DREW 477   3 DON JUAN 15   47   5
    TRANSGRESSES THE GREAT BOUNDS OF LOVE OR AWE 563   3 DON JUAN 17   2   6
AWED
    OF MARTYRS AWED AS SPAGNOLETTO TAINTED   392   3 DON JUAN 13   71   7
AWFUL
    THE CONSEQUENCE WAS AWFUL IN THE EXTREME 198   2 DON JUAN 2   79   2
    (FOR SLEEP IS AWFUL) AND ON TIPTOE CREPT 232   2 DON JUAN 2   143   5
    BEFORE THE CONSEQUENCES GROW TOO AWFUL 282   2 DON JUAN 3   12   7
    IS AWFUL TO THE VESSEL NEAR THE ROCK 305   2 DON JUAN 3   58   4
    IT WAS A MOMENT OF THAT AWFUL KIND-- 363   2 DON JUAN 4   36   7
    AS ERE THAT AWFUL PERIOD INTERVENES   41   3 DON JUAN 6   69   6
    THAT AWFUL PAUSE DIVIDING LIFE FROM DEATH 111   3 DON JUAN 7   87   2
    BUT STILL IT FALLS WITH VAST AND AWFUL SPLINTERS . . . 155   3 DON JUAN 8   88   7
    IT IS AN AWFUL TOPIC--BUT 'TIS NOT 156   3 DON JUAN 8   89   1
    BEFORE HIM SUMMED THE AWFUL SCROLL AND READ IT) . . . 259   3 DON JUAN 10   70   6
    OF WHICH YOUR LAWFUL AWFUL WEDLOCK FOUNT IS-- 312   3 DON JUAN 11   89   6
    ATTORNIES-GENERAL AWFUL TO THE SIGHT 391   3 DON JUAN 13   69   6
    THAT AWFUL YAWN WHICH SLEEP CAN NOT ABATE 405   3 DON JUAN 13   101   8
    WITHOUT AN AWFUL WISH TO PLUNGE WITHIN IT 412   3 DON JUAN 14   5   8
    WITH AWFUL FOOTSTEPS REGULAR AS RHYME 556   3 DON JUAN 16   113   3
    NIGH AND MORE NIGH THE AWFUL ECHOES DREW 557   3 DON JUAN 16   115   5
AWHILE
    WHATE'ER THOU TAKEST SPARE AWHILE POOR BEAUTY 459   3 DON JUAN 15   9   1
AWKWARD
    POOR JULIA'S HEART WAS IN AN AWKWARD STATE 62   2 DON JUAN 1   75   1
    AN AWKWARD LOOK AS HE REVOLVED THE CASE 111   2 DON JUAN 1   164   7
    JUAN CONTRIVED TO GIVE AN AWKWARD BLOW   124   2 DON JUAN 1   186   5
    AN AWKWARD SPECTACLE THEIR EYES BEFORE 125   2 DON JUAN 1   187   2
    I CAN'T BUT SAY IT IS AN AWKWARD SIGHT 163   2 DON JUAN 2   12   1
    WHICH STRUCK HER AFT AND MADE AN AWKWARD RIFT 170   2 DON JUAN 2   27   3
    TO ASK HIM AWKWARD QUESTIONS ON THE WAY 286   2 DON JUAN 3   20   3
    WAS JUAN WHO--AN AWKWARD THING AT HIS AGE 394   2 DON JUAN 4   92   7
    HIS GARMENT'S NOVELTY AND HIS BEING AWKWARD 456   2 DON JUAN 5   78   2
    THIS WAS AN AWKWARD TEST AS JUAN FOUND 484   2 DON JUAN 5   126   1
    THE DAGGER CLOSE AT HAND WHICH MADE IT AWKWARD 492   2 DON JUAN 5   140   2
    A KIND OF STATE MORE AWKWARD THAN UNCOMMON 10   3 DON JUAN 6   7   2
    THIS AWKWARD BUSINESS WITHOUT HARM TO OTHERS 63   3 DON JUAN 6   116   7
    THE AWKWARD SQUAD AND COULD AFFORD TO SQUANDER 93   3 DON JUAN 7   52   3
    TO THEM POOR THINGS IT IS AN AWKWARD STEP   103   3 DON JUAN 7   72   6
    AND HE COULD EVEN WITHSTAND THAT AWKWARD TEST 139   3 DON JUAN 8   53   5
    IT SOOTHES THE AWKWARD SQUAD OF THE REJECTED 333   3 DON JUAN 12   36   7
    AN AWKWARD INCLINATION TO GO WRONG 338   3 DON JUAN 12   48   4
    AND FORTUNE HAS AN AWKWARD PART TO PLAY 342   3 DON JUAN 12   58   2
    EPOCH THAT AWKWARD CORNER TURNED FOR DAYS 360   3 DON JUAN 13   4   2
    SOME PLEASANT JESTING AT THE AWKWARD STRANGER 424   3 DON JUAN 14   32   4
    THERE IS AN AWKWARD THING WHICH MUCH PERPLEXES 442   3 DON JUAN 14   73   1
    HE SATE WITH FEELINGS AWKWARD TO EXPRESS 555   3 DON JUAN 16   111   6
AWOKE
    IF THEY HAD NEVER BEEN AWOKE BEFORE   95   2 DON JUAN 1   136   4
    AND JUAN GAZED AS ONE WHO IS AWOKE 237   2 DON JUAN 2   152   1
    AND STARTING SHE AWOKE AND WHAT TO VIEW 363   2 DON JUAN 4   35   6
    THE DAPPLED FORESTERS--AS DAY AWOKE   384   3 DON JUAN 13   56   6
AWRY
    AND THEN SWUNG BACK NOR CLOSE--BUT STOOD AWRY 558   3 DON JUAN 16   117   3
AXIOM
    OF THE LAST AXIOM HE ADVISED HIS SPOUSE 439   3 DON JUAN 14   67   2
AXIS
    WELL--WELL THE WORLD MUST TURN UPON ITS AXIS   159   2 DON JUAN 2   4   1
AY
    AY QUOTH HIS FRIEND I THOUGHT IT WOULD APPEAR   420   2 DON JUAN 5   19   3
AYE
    AYE EVERY INCH A DUKE THERE WERE TWELVE PEERS 398   3 DON JUAN 13   85   2
    HE WAS AS INDEPENDENT--AYE MUCH MORE--   537   3 DON JUAN 16   76   1
AZURE
    RED SUN SINKS DOWN BEHIND THE AZURE HILL 252   2 DON JUAN 2   183   2

55

```
                                                         PAGE VOL      CANTO STANZA LN
AZURE   (CONTINUED)
    OF AZURE PINK AND WHITE WAS HER CHEMISE--     .  .  .  . 311  2 DON JUAN  3      70   3
    BUT STILL FROM THAT SUBLIMER AZURE HUE   .  .  .  .  .  . 524  3 DON JUAN 16      47   5
AZURE'S
    ADVANCED IN ALL THEIR AZURE'S HIGHEST HUE    .  .  .  .  . 294  3 DON JUAN 11      50   4
B
    PRESENT LORDS A B C--EARLS DUKES BY NAME .  .  .  .  .  . 383  3 DON JUAN 13      54   2
BABA
    WHILE HE WAS DRESSING BABA THEIR BLACK FRIEND  .  .  .  . 451  2 DON JUAN  5      69   1
    BABA EYED JUAN AND SAID BE SO GOOD  .  .  .  .  .  .  .  . 453  2 DON JUAN  5      73   1
    SAID BABA BUT PRAY DO AS I DESIRE   .  .  .  .  .  .  .  . 454  2 DON JUAN  5      74   2
    SAID BABA TO BE CURIOUS 'TWILL TRANSPIRE .  .  .  .  .  . 454  2 DON JUAN  5      74   6
    THAT I UNSEXED MY DRESS BUT BABA STROKING    .  .  .  .  . 454  2 DON JUAN  5      75   6
    THE NEGRO BABA HELPED A LITTLE TOO  .  .  .  .  .  .  .  . 456  2 DON JUAN  5      78   5
    WAS HARDLY LONG ENOUGH BUT BABA FOUND    .  .  .  .  .  . 457  2 DON JUAN  5      79   2
    WHILE BABA MADE HIM COMB HIS HEAD AND OIL IT   .  .  .  . 457  2 DON JUAN  5      79   8
    AND BABA SMILINGLY EXCLAIMED YOU SEE SIRS    .  .  .  .  . 458  2 DON JUAN  5      80   4
    YOU SIR SAID BABA NODDING TO THE ONE    .  .  .  .  .  .  . 458  2 DON JUAN  5      81   1
    BLOCKHEAD COME ON AND SEE QUOTH BABA WHILE   .  .  .  . 459  2 DON JUAN  5      83   1
    BABA LED JUAN ONWARD ROOM BY ROOM   .  .  .  .  .  .  .  . 460  2 DON JUAN  5      85   2
    AS BABA WITH HIS FINGERS MADE THEM FALL  .  .  .  .  .  . 463  2 DON JUAN  5      90   1
    BEFORE THEY ENTERED BABA PAUSED TO HINT  .  .  .  .  .  . 464  2 DON JUAN  5      91   1
    A LADY BABA STOPPED AND KNEELING SIGNED  .  .  .  .  .  . 466  2 DON JUAN  5      95   4
    WHAT ALL THIS MEANT WHILE BABA BOWED AND BENDED  .  .  . 466  2 DON JUAN  5      95   7
    SHE SIGNED TO BABA WHO FIRST KISSED THE HEM  .  .  .  .  . 466  2 DON JUAN  5      96   6
    WHO WORE THEIR UNIFORM BY BABA CHOSEN    .  .  .  .  .  . 469  2 DON JUAN  5      99   4
    BABA AND JUAN WHICH LAST STOOD ADMIRING  .  .  .  .  .  . 469  2 DON JUAN  5     100   3
    BABA WHEN ALL THE DAMSELS WERE WITHDRAWN .  .  .  .  .  . 470  2 DON JUAN  5     102   1
    BABA INDIGNANT AT THIS ILL-TIMED PRIDE   .  .  .  .  .  . 471  2 DON JUAN  5     103   1
    BABA PROPOSED THAT HE SHOULD KISS THE HAND   .  .  .  .  . 471  2 DON JUAN  5     104   8
    BABA RETIRE WHICH HE OBEYED IN STYLE .  .  .  .  .  .  .  . 473  2 DON JUAN  5     107   2
    AND BABA WHO HAD NE'ER BEEN KNOWN TO FAIL    .  .  .  .  . 477  2 DON JUAN  5     114   4
    THE LASH TO BABA--BUT HER GRAND RESOURCE .  .  .  .  .  . 491  2 DON JUAN  5     139   7
    FURTHER OLD BABA RATHER BRISKLY ENTERED  .  .  .  .  .  . 493  2 DON JUAN  5     143   8
    AND HERE SHE SUMMONED BABA AND REQUIRED  .  .  .  .  .  .  55  3 DON JUAN  6      99   1
    BABA WITH SOME EMBARRASSMENT REPLIED  .  .  .  .  .  .  .  56  3 DON JUAN  6     100   1
    WHEN BABA SAW THESE SYMPTOMS WHICH HE KNEW   .  .  .  .  .  57  3 DON JUAN  6     102   1
    (THE AFORESAID BABA) JUST THEN TO DO MORE    .  .  .  .  .  57  3 DON JUAN  6     103   4
    AND THROWN INTO THE SEA--THUS BABA SPOKE .  .  .  .  .  .  58  3 DON JUAN  6     104   7
    BABA THOUGHT SHE WOULD FAINT BUT THERE HE ERRED--   .  .  59  3 DON JUAN  6     106   2
    BABA WHO KNEW BY EXPERIENCE WHEN TO TALK .  .  .  .  .  .  61  3 DON JUAN  6     110   1
    GULBEYAZ STOPPED AND BECKONED BABA--SLAVE    .  .  .  .  .  62  3 DON JUAN  6     112   1
    BUT ONE WHICH BABA DID NOT LIKE TO BRAVE .  .  .  .  .  .  62  3 DON JUAN  6     112   3
    AND OF THIS BABA WILLINGLY TOOK NOTE .  .  .  .  .  .  .  .  62  3 DON JUAN  6     113   6
    MY BIDDING BABA VANISHED FOR TO STRETCH  .  .  .  .  .  .  63  3 DON JUAN  6     116   1
BABA'S
    BUT NOT BY BABA'S FAULT HE SAID AND SWORE ON .  .  .  .  .  57  3 DON JUAN  6     102   7
    FOR BABA'S FUNCTION STOPT SHORT AT THE DOOR  .  .  .  .  .  57  3 DON JUAN  6     103   4
BABE
    HUSH'D AS THE BABE UPON ITS MOTHER'S BREAST  .  .  .  .  . 235  2 DON JUAN  2     148   2
    CLASHED 'GAINST THE BABE AND MOTHER  .  .  .  .  .  .  . 146  3 DON JUAN  8      69   4
    A HALF-STARVED BABE A WRECK UPON LIFE'S OCEAN  .  .  .  . 563  3 DON JUAN 17       3   4
BABEL
    TO ADD A STORY TO THE TOWER OF BABEL .  .  .  .  .  .  .  .  11  2 DON JUAN  D       4   8
    METHINKS THE STORY OF THE TOWER OF BABEL .  .  .  .  .  . 444  2 DON JUAN  5      59   7
    BABEL WAS NIMROD'S HUNTING-BOX AND THEN  .  .  .  .  .  . 445  2 DON JUAN  5      60   1
    OF THAT SAME BABEL OR BECAUSE THEY WON'T .  .  .  .  .  . 447  2 DON JUAN  5      62   4
    AND LET THE BABEL ROUND RUN AS IT MAY .  .  .  .  .  .  . 303  3 DON JUAN 11      69   5
    THE GOTHIC BABEL OF A THOUSAND YEARS  .  .  .  .  .  .  . 381  3 DON JUAN 13      50   4
    BRICKLAYER OF BABEL CALLED AN ARCHITECT  .  .  .  .  .  . 529  3 DON JUAN 16      58   2
BABEL'S
    BY BABEL'S WATERS STILL REMEMBERING SION .  .  .  .  .  . 165  2 DON JUAN  2      16   2
BABES
    LIKE AN INVASION OF THEIR BABES AND SUCKLINGS  .  .  .  . 488  2 DON JUAN  5     133   4
BABIES
    STRUCK AT HIS FRIENDS AS BABIES BEAT THEIR NURSES  .  .  . 165  3 DON JUAN  8     108   8
BABY
    SHE MARVELL'D WHAT HE SAW IN SUCH A BABY .  .  .  .  .  . 477  3 DON JUAN 15      49   7
BABYLON
    ROME BABYLON TYRE CARTHAGE NINEVEH  .  .  .  .  .  .  .  . 142  3 DON JUAN  8      60   5
    OF TRAVELLERS TO MIGHTY BABYLON  .  .  .  .  .  .  .  .  . 279  3 DON JUAN 11      23   2
BABYLONIAN
    AS PURPLE TO THE BABYLONIAN HARLOT  .  .  .  .  .  .  .  . 108  3 DON JUAN  7      84   3
BABYLON'S
    FOR BABYLON'S THAN RUSSIA'S ROYAL HARLOT--   .  .  .  .  . 237  3 DON JUAN 10      26   7
    IN BABYLON'S BRAVURAS--AS THE HOME  .  .  .  .  .  .  .  . 523  3 DON JUAN 16      46   1
BACCHANAL
    IN BACCHANAL PROFUSION REEL TO EARTH .  .  .  .  .  .  .  .  88  2 DON JUAN  1     124   2
    HOW ANSWERS EACH BOLD BACCHANAL  .  .  .  .  .  .  .  .  . 324  2 DON JUAN  3  L   9   6
BACCHANT
    OVER HIS SHOULDER WITH A BACCHANT AIR    .  .  .  .  .  . 297  2 DON JUAN  3      43   2
    BLUSHING WITH BACCHANT CORONALS ALONG    .  .  .  .  .  . 394  3 DON JUAN 13      76   2
BACCHANTE
    PAIR'D OFF WITH A BACCHANTE BLOOMING VISAGE  .  .  .  .  . 394  2 DON JUAN  4      92   8
BACCHUS
    ARE ALSO LEARNT FROM CERES AND FROM BACCHUS  .  .  .  .  . 245  2 DON JUAN  2     169   7
    WHILE BACCHUS POURS OUT WINE OR HANDS A JELLY  .  .  .  . 246  2 DON JUAN  2     170   5
    WHILE BACCHUS WILL PURVEY WITH WINES AND JELLIES   .  .  . 246  2 DON JUAN  2     170  V5
    BACCHUS AND CERES BEING AS WE KNOW  .  .  .  .  .  .  .  . 542  3 DON JUAN 16      86   4
```

BACHELOR

		PAGE	VOL		CANTO	STANZA	LN
WHEN WICKED WIVES WHO LOVE SOME BACHELOR		18	3	DON JUAN	6	24	3
TO WISH HIM BACK A BACHELOR NOW AND THEN		168	3	DON JUAN	8	113	6
HE WAS A BACHELOR WHICH IS A MATTER		292	3	DON JUAN	11	46	1
BUT JUAN WAS A BACHELOR--OF ARTS		292	3	DON JUAN	11	47	1

BACK

		PAGE	VOL		CANTO	STANZA	LN
TO CALL THEM BACK INTO THEIR SEPARATE CAGES		46	2	DON JUAN	1	45	6
OF CALLING WHOLLY BACK ITS SELF-CONTROL		82	2	DON JUAN	1	114	4
WITH MORE THAN HALF THE CITY AT HIS BACK--		96	2	DON JUAN	1	137	2
WHAT'S TO BE DONE ALFONSO WILL BE BACK		114	2	DON JUAN	1	169	1
CALL'D BACK THE TANGLES OF HER WANDERING HAIR		114	2	DON JUAN	1	170	2
NOW SHRINKING BACK NOW MIDST THE FIRST HE SEEMS		155	2	DON JUAN	1	V 6	5
THROWN BACK UPON ITS HAUNCHES--A GAZELLE		160	2	DON JUAN	2	6	V2
THROWN BACK A MOMENT WITH THE GLANCING HAND		160	2	DON JUAN	2	7	2
TO BEG THE BEGGAR WHO COULD NOT RAIN BACK		202	2	DON JUAN	2	86	5
SHOULD SUCK HIM BACK TO HER INSATIATE GRAVE		213	2	DON JUAN	2	108	4
AND TINGLING VEIN SEEM'D THROBBING BACK TO LIFE		214	2	DON JUAN	2	111	7
AND THEN ONCE MORE HIS FEELINGS BACK WERE BROUGHT		215	2	DON JUAN	2	112	6
RECALL'D HIS ANSWERING SPIRITS BACK FROM DEATH		215	2	DON JUAN	2	113	4
LOOK'D BACK UPON HIM AND A MOMENT STAID		228	2	DON JUAN	2	135	3
CAME ALWAYS BACK TO COFFEE AND HAIDEE		246	2	DON JUAN	2	171	8
AND BRING OUR HEARTS BACK TO THEIR STARTING-POST		286	2	DON JUAN	3	21	8
YIELDING TO THEIR SMALL HANDS DRAWS BACK AGAIN		292	2	DON JUAN	3	32	8
EARTH RENDER BACK FROM OUT THY BREAST		323	2	DON JUAN	3	L 7	3
BROUGHT BACK THE SENSE OF PAIN WITHOUT THE CAUSE		378	2	DON JUAN	4	62	7
BACK TO OLD THOUGHTS WAX'D FULL OF FEARFUL MEANING		379	2	DON JUAN	4	64	8
WITH JUAN LEFT HALF-KILL'D SOME STANZAS BACK		384	2	DON JUAN	4	74	8
THE CAPTIVES BACK TO THEIR SAD BERTHS EACH THREW		393	2	DON JUAN	4	90	4
A QUANTITY OF CLOTHES FIT FOR THE BACK		450	2	DON JUAN	5	67	3
YOU STARTED BACK IN HORROR TO SURVEY		462	2	DON JUAN	5	88	2
TO HEAVING BACK THE PORTAL FOLDS IT SCARED		463	2	DON JUAN	5	90	4
RUSH BACK UPON HIS HEART WHICH FILLED APACE		478	2	DON JUAN	5	117	5
CALLED BACK THE STOIC TO HIS EYES WHICH SHONE		481	2	DON JUAN	5	121	5
GROW DEADLY PALE AND THEN BLUSH BACK AGAIN		483	2	DON JUAN	5	124	8
BACK TO THEIR CHAMBERS THOSE LONG GALLERIES		19	3	DON JUAN	6	26	5
SO LET US BACK TO LILLIPUT AND GUIDE		20	3	DON JUAN	6	28	6
COUNT DAMAS DROVE THEM BACK INTO THE WATER		82	3	DON JUAN	7	31	7
WHAT FOLLOWED--A SHOT LAID ME ON MY BACK		98	3	DON JUAN	7	61	5
TURNED BACK WITHIN ITS SOCKET--THESE REWARD		118	3	DON JUAN	8	13	6
AND RALLY BACK HIS ROMANS TO THE FIELD		125	3	DON JUAN	8	28	8
AND LED THEM BACK INTO THE HEAVIEST FIRE		133	3	DON JUAN	8	41	8
NOW BACK TO THY GREAT JOYS CIVILIZATION		146	3	DON JUAN	8	68	2
KOUTOUSOW HE WHO AFTERWARDS BEAT BACK		147	3	DON JUAN	8	70	1
IT HAPPENED WAS HIMSELF BEAT BACK JUST NOW		147	3	DON JUAN	8	70	4
UP JOHNSON CAME WITH HUNDREDS AT HIS BACK		160	3	DON JUAN	8	97	5
TO WISH HIM BACK A BACHELOR NOW AND THEN		168	3	DON JUAN	8	113	6
AND THROWING BACK A DIM LOOK ON HIS SONS		170	3	DON JUAN	8	118	7
WAS IMAGED BACK IN BLOOD THE SEA OF SLAUGHTER		172	3	DON JUAN	8	122	8
BUT PRAY GIVE BACK A LITTLE TO THE NATION		185	3	DON JUAN	9	6	8
FIRST OUT OF AND THEN BACK AGAIN TO CHAOS		201	3	DON JUAN	9	37	7
OF AGE AND LOOKING BACK TO YOUTH GIVE ONE TEAR--		238	3	DON JUAN	10	27	8
THUS FAR GO FORTH THOU LAY WHICH I WILL BACK		312	3	DON JUAN	11	90	2
FOR BOTH OUR PREJUDICES HE MUST BACK		349	3	DON JUAN	12	71	V6
COULD BACK A HORSE AS DESPOTS RIDE A RUSSIAN		368	3	DON JUAN	13	23	8
BACK TO THE NIGHT WIND BY THE WATERFALL		388	3	DON JUAN	13	63	7
HER WAY BACK TO THE WORLD BY DINT OF PLOTTERY		397	3	DON JUAN	13	82	6
MAY THE ROSE CALL BACK ITS TRUE COLOURS SOON		409	3	DON JUAN	13	111	6
LOOK BACK O'ER AGES ERE UNTO THE STAKE FAST		411	3	DON JUAN	14	2	5
HOW CLAY SHRINKS BACK FROM MORE QUIESCENT CLAY		412	3	DON JUAN	14	4	3
IT OCCUPIES ME TO TURN BACK REGARDS		415	3	DON JUAN	14	11	5
BUT THEN THE ROLL-CALL DRAWS THEM BACK AFRAID		417	3	DON JUAN	14	17	3
KNEW THAT HE HAD A RIDER ON HIS BACK		424	3	DON JUAN	14	32	8
UPON WHOSE BACK 'TIS BETTER NOT TO VENTURE		442	3	DON JUAN	14	73	8
BACK TO HIS CHAMBER SHORN OF HALF HIS STRENGTH		511	3	DON JUAN	16	25	8
THAT BRINGS LOCHABER BACK TO EYES THAT ROAM		523	3	DON JUAN	16	46	3
AND THEN SWUNG BACK NOR CLOSE--BUT STOOD AWRY		558	3	DON JUAN	16	117	3
BACK FELL THE SABLE FROCK AND DREARY COWL		561	3	DON JUAN	16	123	5

BACKED

		PAGE	VOL		CANTO	STANZA	LN
AND FISH AND SOUP BY SOME SIDE DISHES BACKED		428	2	DON JUAN	5	32	5

BACKGAMMON

		PAGE	VOL		CANTO	STANZA	LN
LIKE A BACKGAMMON BOARD THE PLACE WAS DOTTED		416	2	DON JUAN	5	10	1

BACKGROUND

		PAGE	VOL		CANTO	STANZA	LN
THIS HE DISCREETLY KEPT IN THE BACKGROUND		58	3	DON JUAN	6	105	1
OUR RIDICULES ARE KEPT IN THE BACK-GROUND--		402	3	DON JUAN	13	95	1

BACKS

		PAGE	VOL		CANTO	STANZA	LN
FROM OGLING ALL THEIR CHARMS FROM BREASTS TO BACKS		20	3	DON JUAN	6	29	8
SOMETIMES A LITTLE HEAVY ON THE BACKS		54	3	DON JUAN	6	96	7
THEY HAD BUT LITTLE BAGGAGE AT THEIR BACKS		87	3	DON JUAN	7	43	4
HAVING BEEN USED TO SERVE ON HORSES' BACKS		149	3	DON JUAN	8	74	5
BUT WHAT HE DID WAS TO LAY ON THEIR BACKS		158	3	DON JUAN	8	93	7
ACCORDING AS THEIR MINDS OR BACKS ARE BENT		340	3	DON JUAN	12	52	4

BACKWARD

		PAGE	VOL		CANTO	STANZA	LN
AND NIGHT IS BACKWARD LIKE A MANTLE ROLLED		230	2	DON JUAN	2	139	V8
HIS TOILET THOUGH NO DOUBT A LITTLE BACKWARD		456	2	DON JUAN	5	78	4
THOUGH HE DESERVED IT WELL FOR BEING SO BACKWARD		492	2	DON JUAN	5	140	6
BACKWARD AND FORWARD TO THE ECHOES FAINT		508	3	DON JUAN	16	18	3

BACKWARDS

		PAGE	VOL		CANTO	STANZA	LN
INSTEAD OF HEAVEN THEY STUMBLED BACKWARDS O'ER		121	3	DON JUAN	8	20	7

BACK-WOODSMAN

		PAGE	VOL		CANTO	STANZA	LN
THE GENERAL BOON BACK-WOODSMAN OF KENTUCKY		143	3	DON JUAN	8	61	4

```
BACON
    WHO HATING HOGS YET WISHED TO SAVE THEIR BACON . . . . .   87  3 DON JUAN  7    42   8
    BY THY HUMANE DISCOVERY FRIAR BACON . . . . . . . . . .  129  3 DON JUAN  8    33   8
    YOU KNOW OR DON'T KNOW THAT GREAT BACON SAITH . . . . .  414  3 DON JUAN 14     8   1
    WAS IT NOT SO GREAT LOCKE AND GREATER BACON . . . . . .  464  3 DON JUAN 15    18   1
BACON'S
    NOW LIKE FRIAR BACON'S BRAZEN HEAD I'VE SPOKEN . . . . .  145  2 DON JUAN  1   217   5
    LIKE SHAKSPEARE'S STEALING DEER LORD BACON'S BRIBES . .  329  2 DON JUAN  3    92   2
    OF FRIAR BACON'S BRIGHT INVENTION--SHARED . . . . . .  129  3 DON JUAN  8    33  V5
BAD
    SHE NEXT DECIDED HE WAS ONLY BAD . . . . . . . . . .   35  2 DON JUAN  1    27   4
    A BOOK--A DAMNED BAD PICTURE AND WORSE BUST . . . . .  146  2 DON JUAN  1   218  V8
    AND THE LONG-BOAT'S CONDITION WAS BUT BAD . . . . . .  181  2 DON JUAN  2    48   3
    OF CHARMS TO MAKE GOOD GOLD AND CURE BAD AILS . . . .  293  2 DON JUAN  3    34   5
    AND MADE HIM A GOOD FRIEND BUT BAD ACQUAINTANCE . . .  303  2 DON JUAN  3    54   8
    REJOINED THE OTHER WHEN OUR BAD LUCK MENDS HERE . . .  423  2 DON JUAN  5    24   6
    'TIS BAD AND MAY BE BETTER--ALL MEN'S LOT . . . . . .  423  2 DON JUAN  5    25   2
    POOR FELLOW FOR SOME REASON SURELY BAD . . . . . . .  429  2 DON JUAN  5    34   1
    GROUPS OF BAD STATUES TABLES CHAIRS AND PICTURES . .  465  2 DON JUAN  5    94   7
    AND HE ADVANCED THOUGH WITH BUT A BAD GRACE . . . . .  472  2 DON JUAN  5   106   1
    AND WORKS OF THE SAME POTTERY BAD OR GOOD . . . . . .  491  2 DON JUAN  5   138   5
    THAT IS WE CANNOT PARDON THEIR BAD TASTE . . . . . .   14  3 DON JUAN  6    17   1
    A BAD OLD WOMAN MAKING A WORSE WILL . . . . . . . .   16  3 DON JUAN  6    21   5
    MY WISH IS QUITE AS WIDE BUT NOT SO BAD . . . . . .   19  3 DON JUAN  6    27   4
    ALL BAD PROPENSITIES IN FIFTEEN HUNDRED . . . . . .   21  3 DON JUAN  6    31   7
    WITH SOMETHING NOT MUCH BETTER OR AS BAD . . . . . .  122  3 DON JUAN  8    22   3
    ACCOUNT FOR EVERYTHING WHICH MAY LOOK BAD . . . . .  127  3 DON JUAN  8    31   4
    WITH GOOD AND BAD AND WORSE ALIKE PROLIFIC . . . . .  156  3 DON JUAN  8    89   5
    ALL THAT THE BODY PERPETRATES OF BAD . . . . . . .  173  3 DON JUAN  8   123   2
    THEY TALKED BAD FRENCH OF SPANISH AND UPON ITS . . .  294  3 DON JUAN 11    50   5
    AND STILL PURSUES THE RIGHT--TO CURB THE BAD . . .  363  3 DON JUAN 13     9   3
    REGRETTING MUCH THAT SHE HAD CHOSEN SO BAD A LINE . .  430  3 DON JUAN 14    46   5
    THERE'S NOUGHT IN THIS BAD WORLD LIKE SYMPATHY . . .  430  3 DON JUAN 14    47   1
    THEY ARE BUT BAD PILOTS WHEN THE WEATHER'S ROUGH . .  431  3 DON JUAN 14    48   3
    IF BAD THE BEST WAY'S CERTAINLY TO TEAZE ON . . . .  478  3 DON JUAN 15    51   3
    THOSE TRUFFLES TOO ARE NO BAD ACCESSARIES . . . . .  486  3 DON JUAN 15    68   1
    THIS WAS NO BAD MISTAKE AS IT OCCURRED . . . . . .  543  3 DON JUAN 16    89   1
    BUT WHAT WAS BAD SHE DID NOT BLUSH IN TURN . . . .  545  3 DON JUAN 16    94   1
BADE
    DON JUAN BADE HIS VALET PACK HIS THINGS . . . . . .  161  2 DON JUAN  2     9   1
    THE UPHOLSTERER'S FIAT LUX HAD BADE TO ISSUE . . . .  309  2 DON JUAN  3    67  V8
    OLD LAMBRO BADE THEM TAKE HIM TO THE SHORE . . . .  371  2 DON JUAN  4    50   3
    WHO BADE ON TILL THE HUNDREDS REACH'D ELEVEN . . .  407  2 DON JUAN  4   114   6
    THE LADY EYED HIM O'ER AND O'ER AND BADE . . . . .  473  2 DON JUAN  5   107   1
    ALL EARTHLY GOODS SAVE TITHES) AND BADE THEM PUSH ON .   99  3 DON JUAN  7    64   6
    QUARTER IN CASE HE BADE THEM NOT AROINT . . . . .  170  3 DON JUAN  8   117   3
    AND BADE HIM COUNSEL JUAN  WITH A SMILE . . . . .  438  3 DON JUAN 14    65   4
BADLY
    BEFORE BEING BADLY SECONDED JUST THEN) . . . . . .  151  3 DON JUAN  8    79   3
    TO FIND HOW VERY BADLY SHE SELECTED . . . . . . .  333  3 DON JUAN 12    36   8
BAFFLED
    LIKE A MERE LOG AND BAFFLED OUR INTENT . . . . . .  173  2 DON JUAN  2    32   4
    AS IF OLD OCEAN BAFFLED OUR INTENT . . . . . . . .  173  2 DON JUAN  2    32  V4
    OF BAFFLED HEROES WHO STOOD SHYLY NEAR . . . . . .  148  3 DON JUAN  8    73   6
    THEIR BAFFLED RAGE AND PAIN WHILE WAXING COLDER . .  158  3 DON JUAN  8    94   5
    AND BAFFLED THE ASSAULTS OF ALL THEIR HOST . . . .  171  3 DON JUAN  8   120   4
BAG
    HIVED IN OUR BOSOMS LIKE THE BAG O' THE BEE . . . .  144  2 DON JUAN  1   214   5
    FULL GROWS HIS BAG AND WONDERFUL HIS FEATS . . . .  394  3 DON JUAN 13    75   6
BAGGAGE
    THEY HAD BUT LITTLE BAGGAGE AT THEIR BACKS . . . .   87  3 DON JUAN  7    43   4
    TO THE OTHER BAGGAGE OR TO THE SICK TENT . . . . .  100  3 DON JUAN  7    66   8
    AWARE THIS KIND OF BAGGAGE NEVER THRIVES . . . . .  102  3 DON JUAN  7    70   7
    COACH CHARIOT LUGGAGE BAGGAGE EQUIPAGE . . . . . .  378  3 DON JUAN 13    44   2
BAGGED
    SOME ARE SOON BAGGED BUT SOME REJECT THREE DOZEN . .  332  3 DON JUAN 12    34   1
    HAD BAGGED THIS POACHER UPON NATURE'S MANOR . . . .  531  3 DON JUAN 16    62   8
BAGS
    TO FAINT AND DAMAGED BREAD WET THROUGH THE BAGS . .  189  2 DON JUAN  2    62   7
    CONTAINING INGOTS BAGS OF DOLLARS COINS . . . . . .  321  3 DON JUAN 12    12   2
BAH
    OR A HA HA OR BAH--A YAWN OR POOH . . . . . . . .  456  3 DON JUAN 15     1   7
BAIL
    I WON'T BE BAIL FOR ANYTHING BEYOND . . . . . . .  469  2 DON JUAN  5    99   8
BAILLIE
    WE TEASE MILD BAILLIE OR SOFT ABERNETHY . . . . .  245  3 DON JUAN 10    42   8
BAIT
    HUT WHERE WE TRAVELLERS BAIT WITH DIM REFLECTION . .  238  3 DON JUAN 10    27  V6
    TO BAIT THEIR TENDER OR THEIR TENTER HOOKS . . . .  453  3 DON JUAN 14    97   8
BAITING
    I LEFT DON JUAN WITH HIS HORSES BAITING-- . . . .  203  3 DON JUAN  9    42   3
BAITS
    OR THROWN TO LIONS OR MADE BAITS FOR FISH . . . .  492  2 DON JUAN  5   141   4
    OR MINCED IN PIECES AS SMALL BAITS FOR FISH . . .  492  2 DON JUAN  5   141  V4
    MAY BE THE BAITS FOR GENTLEMEN OR LORDS . . . . .  340  3 DON JUAN 12    53   3
BAKED
    AND THEIR BAKED LIPS WITH MANY A BLOODY CRACK . . .  202  2 DON JUAN  2    86   1
    BAKED FRIED OR BURNT TURNED INSIDE-OUT OR DROWNED . .  201  3 DON JUAN  9    37   5
BAKING
    BUT WILL KEEP BAKING BROILING BURNING ON . . . . .   56  2 DON JUAN  1    63   4
```

```
                                                        PAGE VOL      CANTO STANZA LN
BALAAM
    TO BALAAM AND FROM TONGUE TO EAR O'ERFLOWS  . . . . . . . 328   3 DON JUAN 12    26   6
BALANCE
    AND FIND A DEUCED BALANCE WITH THE DEVIL . . . . . . . . 113   2 DON JUAN  1   167   8
    WHO HOLD THE BALANCE OF THE WORLD WHO REIGN . . . . . . . 318   3 DON JUAN 12     5   1
    A FLOATING BALANCE OF ACCOMPLISHMENT  . . . . . . . . . 340   3 DON JUAN 12    52   2
    I'VE SEEN THEM BALANCE EVEN THE SCALE WITH FIGHTERS  . . 418   3 DON JUAN 14    20   3
BALANCING
    IN BALANCING THE PROFIT AND THE LOSS  . . . . . . . . 113   3 DON JUAN  8     3   3
BALD-COOT
    SHUT UP THE BALD-COOT BULLY ALEXANDER . . . . . . . . 446   3 DON JUAN 14    83   1
BALDNESS
    YOUR BAYS MAY HIDE THE BALDNESS OF YOUR BROWS--  . . . .  13   2 DON JUAN  D     7   1
BALE
    A GLIMPSE OF SUNSHINE SET SOME HANDS TO BALE--  . . . . 176   2 DON JUAN  2    38   7
    AND MADE THEM BALE WITHOUT A MOMENT'S EASE  . . . . . . 188   2 DON JUAN  2    60   6
BALES
    WHILE THEY THRUST SHEETS SHIRTS JACKETS BALES OF MUSLIN . 171   2 DON JUAN  2    28   8
BALGOUNIE'S
    THE DEE THE DON BALGOUNIE'S BRIG'S BLACK WALL . . . . . 233   3 DON JUAN 10    18   3
BALK
    THIS PASSION MIGHT BLOW O'ER NOR DARED TO BALK . . . . .  61   3 DON JUAN  6   110   3
BALL
    HIS OWN SHALL ROLL BEFORE YOU LIKE A BALL  . . . . . . 369   2 DON JUAN  4    47   2
    AS BRAVE AS EVER FACED BOTH BOMB AND BALL  . . . . . . 116   3 DON JUAN  8     9   5
    COUNT CHAPEAU-BRAS TOO HAD A BALL BETWEEN  . . . . . . 116   3 DON JUAN  8    10   2
    MORE THAN THE CAP IN FACT THE BALL COULD MEAN  . . . . 117   3 DON JUAN  8    10   6
    THE DUKE OF RICHELIEU HAD A BALL BETWEEN . . . . . . . 117   3 DON JUAN  8    10  V2
    OF HOPES AND FEARS WHICH SHAKE A SINGLE BALL . . . . . 304   3 DON JUAN 11    72   8
    IF HE GOES AFTER DINNER TO A BALL . . . . . . . . . . 333   3 DON JUAN 12    37  V6
    IF HE CAN HICCUP NONSENSE AT A BALL . . . . . . . . . 333   3 DON JUAN 12    37  V6
    BUT NEXT TO DRESSING FOR A ROUT OR BALL . . . . . . . 505   3 DON JUAN 16    11   1
BALLAD
    IN SPAIN HE'D MAKE A BALLAD OR ROMANCE ON  . . . . . . 320   2 DON JUAN  3    86   3
BALLADS
    FORSOOTH SCARCE FIT FOR BALLADS IN THE STREET  . . . . 392   2 DON JUAN  4    89   6
BALLAST
    IN GETTING OUT GOODS BALLAST GUNS AND TREASURE . . . . 286   2 DON JUAN  3    20   8
BALLET-MASTER
    NOT LIKE A BALLET-MASTER IN THE VAN  . . . . . . . . 427   3 DON JUAN 14    38   7
BALLOON
    COULD NOT THE BLOCKHEAD ASK FOR A BALLOON  . . . . . . 333   2 DON JUAN  3    99   8
BALL-ROOM
    A BALL-ROOM BARD A FOOLSCAP HOT-PRESS DARLING  . . . . 404   2 DON JUAN  4   109   2
BALLS
    HER HAIR WAS DRIPPING AND THE VERY BALLS . . . . . . . 362   2 DON JUAN  4    33   5
    AS ALSO AT THE RACE AND COUNTY BALLS . . . . . . . . 471   2 DON JUAN  5   103   8
    AND WHAT WITH MASQUERADES AND FETES AND BALLS  . . . . 342   3 DON JUAN 12    57   7
    YOU MAY SEE SUCH AT ALL THE BALLS AND DINNERS  . . . . 346   3 DON JUAN 12    66   5
BALM
    AND LYING ON THEIR WEARINESS LIKE BALM  . . . . . . . 192   2 DON JUAN  2    68   4
BALTIC'S
    THEIR ROAR EVEN WITH THE BALTIC'S--SO YOU BE  . . . . .  52   3 DON JUAN  6    93   7
    SOMETHING ABOUT THE BALTIC'S NAVIGATION . . . . . . . 246   3 DON JUAN 10    45   6
BAMBOO
    CHEWING A PIECE OF BAMBOO AND SOME LEAD . . . . . . . 200   2 DON JUAN  2    82   6
BAN
    WHO QUEER A FLAT WHO (SPITE OF BOW-STREET'S BAN)  . . . 277   3 DON JUAN 11    19   5
BAND
    A BAND OF CHILDREN ROUND A SNOW-WHITE RAM  . . . . . . 292   2 DON JUAN  3    32   1
    BELOW HER BREAST WAS FASTEN'D WITH A BAND  . . . . . . 312   2 DON JUAN  3    72   5
BANDAGE
    ONE ARM HAD ON A BANDAGE RATHER BLOODY  . . . . . . . 416   2 DON JUAN  5    11   6
    HIS BANDAGE SLIPPED DOWN INTO A CRAVAT  . . . . . . . 205   3 DON JUAN  9    45   1
BANDAGES
    STOOD CALLING OUT FOR BANDAGES AND LINT . . . . . . . 275   3 DON JUAN 11    14   7
BANDS
    WHERE THE PRAETORIAN BANDS TAKE UP THE MATTER--  . . . 299   3 DON JUAN 11    62   2
BANISH
    FOR AS YOU KNOW THE SPANISH WOMEN BANISH . . . . . . . 220   2 DON JUAN  2   120   4
    (THE HYPOCRITE) WILL BANISH THEM LIKE MARIUS  . . . . 352   3 DON JUAN 12    78   6
    OR SERIOUS ARE THE TOPICS I MUST BANISH . . . . . . . 453   3 DON JUAN 14    98   5
    OF THOSE SWEET BITTER THOUGHTS WHICH BANISH SLEEP . . . 555   3 DON JUAN 16   110   7
BANISHMENT
    TO SHARE HER BEAUTY AND HER BANISHMENT  . . . . . . . 193   3 DON JUAN  9    22   8
BANK
    TO SAVE THE CREDIT OF THEIR BREAKING BANK  . . . . . . 500   2 DON JUAN  5   154   6
    UPON THE DANUBE'S LEFT BRANCH AND LEFT BANK . . . . . .  70   3 DON JUAN  7     9   2
    OF DANUBE'S BANK TOOK FORMIDABLE CHARGE . . . . . . .  72   3 DON JUAN  7    12   5
    ALONG THE LEAGUERED WALL AND BRISTLING BANK . . . . . 110   3 DON JUAN  7    86   4
    WHICH MAKES BANK CREDIT LIKE A BARK OF VAPOUR  . . . . 317   3 DON JUAN 12     4   8
    OR PAPER TURNED TO MONEY BY THE BANK  . . . . . . . . 396   3 DON JUAN 13    80   5
BANKER
    THAT IN THE LIEU OF DRAWING ON HIS BANKER  . . . . . . 240   3 DON JUAN 10    31   2
BANKER'S
    AND MRS RABBI THE RICH BANKER'S SQUAW . . . . . . . . 396   3 DON JUAN 13    79   6
BANKERS
    BANKERS--CONTRACTORS--BOROUGH MONGERS--BULLIES . . . . 314   3 DON JUAN 11  V 76   1
BANNER
    WAX'D BROAD AND WAVING LIKE A BANNER FREE  . . . . . . 204   2 DON JUAN  2    91   6
```

59

	PAGE	VOL	CANTO	STANZA	LN

BANNER   (CONTINUED)
   THEY FOUND THAT HE HAD FOUGHT BENEATH THEIR BANNER 95   3 DON JUAN 7   56   8
   FLUNG HOVERING GRACES O'ER HIM LIKE A BANNER 223   3 DON JUAN 9   83   8
   THE CONSTABLE BENEATH A WARRANT'S BANNER 531   3 DON JUAN 16   62   7
BANNERS
   WERE THEIR REWARD FOR FOLLOWING BILLY'S BANNERS 242   3 DON JUAN 10   36   4
BANNS
   BUT LOVE SANS BANNS IS BOTH A SIN AND SHAME 323   3 DON JUAN 12   15   7
   ON WHICH AT THE THIRD ASKING OF THE BANNS 542   3 DON JUAN 16   88   1
BANQUET
   LAMBRO'S RECEPTION AT HIS PEOPLE'S BANQUET 294   2 DON JUAN 3   36   7
   OF THIS OUR BANQUET WE MUST SOMETIMES CHANGE 65   2 DON JUAN 6   120   4
   WITH EVENING CAME THE BANQUET AND THE WINE 408   3 DON JUAN 13   107   1
   'TWAS A GREAT BANQUET SUCH AS ALBION OLD 538   3 DON JUAN 16   78   2
BANQUETEERS
   THE BANQUETEERS HAD DROPPED OFF ONE BY ONE-- 504   3 DON JUAN 16   8   3
BANQUETS
   LIKE SKULLS AT MEMPHIAN BANQUETS TO THE MIND 308   2 DON JUAN 3   65   4
   LONG BANQUETS AND TOO MANY GUESTS ALTHOUGH 542   3 DON JUAN 16   86   2
BANQUO'S
   EACH IN THEIR TURN LIKE BANQUO'S MONARCHS STALK 22   2 DON JUAN 1   2   5
   LIKE BANQUO'S OFFSPRING--FLOATING PAST ME SEEMS 233   3 DON JUAN 10   18   6
   THE COTERIES AND AS IN BANQUO'S GLASS 295   3 DON JUAN 11   54   3
BAPTIZE
   BAPTIZE POSTERITY OR FUTURE CLAY-- 324   3 DON JUAN 12   18   4
BAPTIZED
   BAPTIZED IN MOLTEN GOLD AND SWATHED IN DUN 205   2 DON JUAN 2   92   4
   THETIS BAPTIZED HER MORTAL SON IN STYX 346   2 DON JUAN 4   4   7
BAR
   WAS HAPLESS IN THEIR NUPTIALS FOR SOME BAR 281   2 DON JUAN 3   10   4
   A LIKE GOLD BAR ABOVE HER INSTEP ROLLED 312   2 DON JUAN 3   72   2
   AND EPIC IF PLAIN TRUTH SHOULD PROVE NO BAR 181   3 DON JUAN 8   138   5
   IT LAUGHS NOT--THERE IS NOW NO FLESHY BAR 188   3 DON JUAN 9   12   3
   HAVE SUCH A PRESCIENCE IT SHOULD BE NO BAR 194   3 DON JUAN 9   24   6
   NO LESS A VICTIM TO THE BOLT AND BAR 258   3 DON JUAN 10   68   4
   WHEN FOR A PASSPORT OR SOME OTHER BAR 288   3 DON JUAN 11   41   5
   WHO BOUND THE BAR OR SENATE IN THEIR SPELL 307   3 DON JUAN 11   77   4
   YET INEXPERIENCE COULD NOT BE HIS BAR 347   3 DON JUAN 12   69   6
   IN SENATES AT THE BAR IN WORDY FEUD 371   3 DON JUAN 13   29   5
   WHO LIMITS ALL HIS BATTLES TO THE BAR 398   3 DON JUAN 13   84   2
   IS THAT WHATEVER BAR THE REASON REARS 504   3 DON JUAN 16   7   6
BARACAN
   AND THE STRIPED WHITE GAUZE BARACAN THAT BOUND HER . . . 311   2 DON JUAN 3   70   7
   BUT A WHITE BARACAN AND SO TRANSPARENT 315   2 DON JUAN 3   77   2
BARB
   AN ARAB HORSE A STATELY STAG A BARB 160   2 DON JUAN 2   6   1
   SHE CANNOT STEP AS DOES AN ARAB BARB 350   2 DON JUAN 12   75   1
BARBADOES
   AND HONEST MEN FROM ICELAND TO BARBADOES 231   3 DON JUAN 10   13   5
BARBARIAN
   NOT A BARBARIAN BUT MUCH WORSE THAN THAT 194   3 DON JUAN 9   23   8
BARBARIC
   FULL OF BARBARIC CARVING PAINT AND GILDING 223   2 DON JUAN 2   127   8
BARBAROUS
   UNGRATEFUL PERJURED BARBAROUS DON ALFONSO 101   2 DON JUAN 1   146   7
   A JOINT UPON THEIR BARBAROUS SPITS THEY PUT ON 238   2 DON JUAN 2   154   4
   OF ALL THE BARBAROUS MIDDLE AGES THAT 315   3 DON JUAN 12   1   1
   WHICH IS THE MOST BARBAROUS IS THE MIDDLE AGE 315   3 DON JUAN 12   1   2
BARBER'S
   THERE BARBER'S BLOCKS WITH PERIWIGS IN CURL 278   3 DON JUAN 11   22   5
BARBETTE
   CASE-MATED ONE AND T'OTHER A BARBETTE 72   3 DON JUAN 7   12   4
BARD
   TOO MUCH THEIR MODEST BARD BY THIS OMISSION 46   2 DON JUAN 1   44   5
   THE BARD I QUOTE FROM DOES NOT SING AMISS 69   2 DON JUAN 1   88   5
   FOR MY PART I'M A MODERATE-MINDED BARD 85   2 DON JUAN 1   118   5
   STILL GENTLER PURCHASER THE BARD--THAT'S I-- 147   2 DON JUAN 1   221   2
   BUT THEN AS BARD MY DUTY TO MANKIND 155   2 DON JUAN 1 V 7   6
   THE TEIAN BARD OF SCIO'S ISLE 321   2 DON JUAN 3 L 2 V1
   A BALL-ROOM BARD A FOOLSCAP HOT-PRESS DARLING 404   2 DON JUAN 4   109   2
   HAD BEEN CALLED JEMMY AFTER THE GREAT BARD 76   3 DON JUAN 7   19   2
   FOR AFTER YEARS OF TRAVEL BY A BARD IN 262   3 DON JUAN 10   76   3
   THAT SWARTHY SPORUS NEITHER MAN NOR BARD 297   3 DON JUAN 11   58   5
   IS HEAVEN AND HEAVEN IS LOVE--SO SINGS THE BARD 322   3 DON JUAN 12   13   2
   THERE WAS THE YOUNG BARD RACKRHYME WHO HAD NEWLY . . . 398   3 DON JUAN 13   84   5
   BUT BE IT AS IT MAY A BARD MUST MEET 423   3 DON JUAN 14   30   4
   SO MUCH THE BARD HAD REALLY BEEN PROPHETIC 525   3 DON JUAN 16   50   5
BARD'S
   TO THE BARD'S TOMB AND NOT THE WARRIOR'S COLUMN 400   2 DON JUAN 4   104   4
BARDS
   AND BARDS BURN WHAT THEY CALL THEIR MIDNIGHT TAPER . . . 146   2 DON JUAN 1   218   6
   YET THERE WILL STILL BE BARDS THOUGH FAME IS SMOKE . . . 402   2 DON JUAN 4   106   1
   UPON IN SHEETS WHITE AS WHAT BARDS CALL DRIVEN 18   3 DON JUAN 6   25   5
   AND HEROES ARE BUT MADE FOR BARDS TO SING 118   3 DON JUAN 8   14   5
   (I WISH YOUR BARDS WOULD SING IT RATHER BETTER) 184   3 DON JUAN 9   3   8
   OF BARDS AND PROSERS WORDS ARE VOID OF COLOUR 428   3 DON JUAN 14   40   8
   BARDS MAY SING WHAT THEY PLEASE ABOUT CONTENT 444   3 DON JUAN 14   79   4
   BUT SPEAKERS BARDS DIPLOMATISTS AND DANCERS 547   3 DON JUAN 16   98   3
BARE
   FROM GLISTENING WAVES AND SKIES SO HOT AND BARE-- . . . 210   2 DON JUAN 2   103   6

BARE   (CONTINUED)
```
      BUT THAT PART OF THE COAST BEING SHOAL AND BARE    . . . . . 285   2 DON JUAN  3    19   6
      ARE GOOD MANURE FOR THEIR MORE BARE BIOGRAPHY  . . . . . 330   2 DON JUAN  3    94   4
      THAT ISLE IS NOW ALL DESOLATE AND BARE   . . . . . . 383   2 DON JUAN  4    72   1
      AND BOSOMS ARMS AND ANCLES GLANCING BARE . . . . . . .  42   3 DON JUAN  6    72   4
      SHORN OF ITS BEST AND LOVELIEST AND LEFT BARE  . . . . . 155   3 DON JUAN  8    88   6
      WHO PAINTED THEIR BARE LIMBS BUT NOT WITH GORE . . . . . 180   3 DON JUAN  8   136   8
      WHICH SHALL LAY BARE HER BOSOM TO THE SWORD  . . . . . . 258   3 DON JUAN 10    67   4
      IN LIEU OF A BARE BLADE AND BRAZEN FRONT . . . . . . . 275   3 DON JUAN 11    15   5
BARED
      AND COOKS IN MOTION WITH THEIR CLEAN ARMS BARED   . . . . 439   2 DON JUAN  5    50   6
BARGAIN
      SO THAT THEIR BARGAIN SOUNDED LIKE A BATTLE . . . . . . . 425   2 DON JUAN  5    28   7
      AND WHEN 'TWAS FOUND STRAIGHTWAY THE BARGAIN CLOSED  . . 476   2 DON JUAN  5   113   4
BARGAINS
      BORE OFF HIS BARGAINS TO A GILDED BOAT   . . . . . . . 432   2 DON JUAN  5    40   2
BARGE
      WHO IS NO PAVIOUR NOR ADMITS A BARGE . . . . . . . . 198   3 DON JUAN  9    31   6
      TO BE TRANSMITTED LIKE THE LORD MAYOR'S BARGE . . . . . 339   3 DON JUAN 12    51   6
BARING
      JEW ROTHSCHILD AND HIS FELLOW CHRISTIAN BARING . . . . . 318   3 DON JUAN 12     5   8
BARITONE
      OUR BARITONE I ALMOST HAD FORGOT   . . . . . . . . . 392   2 DON JUAN  4    89   1
BARK
      'TIS SWEET TO HEAR THE WATCHDOG'S HONEST BARK  . . . . .  88   2 DON JUAN  1   123   1
      BECAUSE THE TACKLE OF OUR SHATTER'D BARK . . . . . . . 206   2 DON JUAN  2    95   3
      LIKE CHARON'S BARK OF SPECTRES DULL AND PALE   . . . . . 209   2 DON JUAN  2   101   3
      ONE BARK BLEW UP A SECOND NEAR THE WORKS . . . . . . .  81   3 DON JUAN  7    30   7
      WHICH MAKES BANK CREDIT LIKE A BARK OF VAPOUR  . . . . . 317   3 DON JUAN 12     4   8
BARNAVE
      BARNAVE BRISSOT CONDORCET MIRABEAU . . . . . . . . . .  22   2 DON JUAN  1     3   1
BAROMETER
      FOR PARLIAMENT IS OUR BAROMETER . . . . . . . . . . 378   3 DON JUAN 13    43   6
BARON
      AND SPOKE MORE OF THE BARON THAN THE MONK  . . . . . . 389   3 DON JUAN 13    66   8
BARONS
      STEEL BARONS MOLTEN THE NEXT GENERATION . . . . . . . 390   3 DON JUAN 13    68   1
BAROUCHE
      BAROUCHE WHICH HAD THE GLORY TO DISPLAY ONCE   . . . . . 248   3 DON JUAN 10    49   5
BARRACK'S
      OR GRAVEN STONE FOUND IN A BARRACK'S STATION   . . . . . 327   2 DON JUAN  3    89   6
BARRACKS
      ALL WRATH IN BARRACKS PALACES OR COTS . . . . . . . . 200   3 DON JUAN  9    36   5
BARRELS
      SWEET IS OLD WINE IN BOTTLES ALE IN BARRELS . . . . . .  90   2 DON JUAN  1   126   5
BARREN
      AN UNKNOWN BARREN BEACH FOR BURIAL GROUND  . . . . . . 213   2 DON JUAN  2   109   8
      AMIDST THE BARREN SAND AND ROCKS SO RUDE . . . . . . . 262   2 DON JUAN  2   198   4
      THEY'RE BARREN AND NOT WORTH THE PAINS TO PULL . . . . . 402   3 DON JUAN 13    95   6
BARROW
      BARROW SOUTH TILLOTSON WHOM EVERY WEEK   . . . . . . . 243   2 DON JUAN  2   165   5
BARROWS
      HIGH BARROWS WITHOUT MARBLE OR A NAME . . . . . . . . 386   2 DON JUAN  4    77   1
BARS
      OF AIR-BALLOONS AND OF THE MANY BARS . . . . . . . . .  71   2 DON JUAN  1    92   6
BARTERS
      LURKED CHRISTIANITY WHICH SOMETIMES BARTERS . . . . . .  96   3 DON JUAN  7    57   6
BARTHOLOMEW
      FROM SAINT BARTHOLOMEW WE HAVE SAVED OUR SKIN  . . . . . 435   2 DON JUAN  5    44   4
BAS
      A LONDON BAS WILL BEAT THY SKY PERU  . . . . . . . . 406   2 DON JUAN  4   112   V8
BASE
      NOR COIN MY SELF-LOVE TO SO BASE A VICE  . . . . . . .  12   2 DON JUAN  D     6   2
      THAT FLIGHT WAS BASE AND DASTARDLY AND NO MAN  . . . . .  63   2 DON JUAN  1    77   3
      WITH BASE SUSPICION NOW NO LONGER HAUNTED   . . . . . . 120   2 DON JUAN  1   180   V6
      RESTING ITS BRIGHT BASE ON THE QUIVERING BLUE  . . . . . 204   2 DON JUAN  2    91   3
      LIKE TO A TORRENT WHICH A MOUNTAIN'S BASE  . . . . . . 231   2 DON JUAN  2   141   5
      WHILE WEEDS AND ORDURE RANKLE ROUND THE BASE   . . . . . 400   2 DON JUAN  4   103   8
      NOT RECKONING HIM TO BE A BASE BEZONIAN  . . . . . . . 140   3 DON JUAN  8    56   7
      POWER'S BASE PURVEYORS WHO FOR PICKINGS PROWL  . . . . . 196   3 DON JUAN  9    27   4
      WHICH MAKES ONE DRUNK AT ONCE WITHOUT THE BASE . . . . . 216   3 DON JUAN  9    67   6
      EVEN WITH THE VERY ORE WHICH MAKES THEM BASE   . . . . . 320   3 DON JUAN 12    10   6
      YET COULD NOT SPEAK OR MOVE BUT ON ITS BASE  . . . . . . 510   3 DON JUAN 16    23   4
BASED
      THE RAINBOW BASED ON OCEAN SPAN THE SKY  . . . . . . .  87   2 DON JUAN  1   122   8
BASELESS
      NO BASELESS FABRIC BUT A WRECK BEHIND . . . . . . . . 227   2 DON JUAN  2   134   V8
BASER
      THE BASER SIDES OF LITERATURE AND LIFE   . . . . . . . 232   3 DON JUAN 10    14   2
BASHAW
      THEY LIVED TILL SOME BASHAW WAS SENT ABROAD . . . . . . 498   2 DON JUAN  5   152   4
      'TIS TRUE THE REASON IS THAT THE BASHAW  . . . . . . . 498   2 DON JUAN  5   152   7
BASHFULLY
      ALL BASHFULLY TO STRUGGLE INTO LIGHT . . . . . . . . .  39   3 DON JUAN  6    66   8
BASIN
      THE MUSICO IS BUT A CRACK'D OLD BASIN . . . . . . . . 391   2 DON JUAN  4    86   2
BASINS
      AND SPARKLED INTO BASINS WHERE IT SPENT  . . . . . . . 389   3 DON JUAN 13    65   6
BASIS
      AND FORMED A BASIS OF ESTEEM WHICH ENDS  . . . . . . . 365   3 DON JUAN 13    15   7
      BUT A MERE AIRY AND FANTASTIC BASIS  . . . . . . . . 413   3 DON JUAN 14     7   7
```

		PAGE	VOL	CANTO	STANZA	LN
BASK	HAD MADE HIM LATELY BASK IN HIS BRIDE'S BEAUTY	51	3	DON JUAN	6	91	8
BASKET	SHE DREW OUT HER PROVISION FROM THE BASKET	233	2	DON JUAN	2	144	8
BASKING	WHO NOW ARE BASKING IN THEIR FULL-BLOWN PRIDE	466	3	DON JUAN	15	23	3
BASQUINA	THE BASQUINA AND THE MANTILLA THEY	220	2	DON JUAN	2	120	7
BASS	THE HIGH WIND MADE THE TREBLE AND AS BASS	174	2	DON JUAN	2	34	4
	AND FOR THE BASS THE BEAST CAN ONLY BELLOW	391	2	DON JUAN	4	87	2
BASTION	BUT A STONE BASTION WITH A NARROW GORGE	72	3	DON JUAN	7	12	1
	WHICH RAINED FROM BASTION BATTERY PARAPET	131	3	DON JUAN	8	37	2
	OF THE NEXT BASTION FIRED AWAY LIKE DEVILS	134	3	DON JUAN	8	44	2
	ONLY TO DRAW THEM 'TWIXT TWO BASTION CORNERS	149	3	DON JUAN	8	75	7
	THEY TOOK THE BASTION WHICH THE SERASKIER	151	3	DON JUAN	8	79	7
	UPON A TAKEN BASTION WHERE THERE LAY	157	3	DON JUAN	8	91	1
	BUT THE STONE BASTION STILL REMAINS WHEREIN	160	3	DON JUAN	8	98	7
	BUT THE STONE BASTION STILL KEPT UP ITS FIRE	171	3	DON JUAN	8	120	1
	HIMSELF OR BASTION LITTLE MATTERED NOW	172	3	DON JUAN	8	122	2
BASTIONS	BOMBS DRUMS GUNS BASTIONS BATTERIES BAYONETS BULLETS	106	3	DON JUAN	7	78	7
BATCHES	OF ELEGANT ET CETERA IN FRESH BATCHES--	340	3	DON JUAN	12	53	7
BATE	NOR BATE (ABATE) THEIR HEARERS OF AN INCH	404	3	DON JUAN	13	98	4
BATH	A BATH A BREAKFAST AND THE FINEST EYES	246	2	DON JUAN	2	171	2
	ESPOUSED TWO PARTNERS (MILLINERS OF BATH)	329	2	DON JUAN	3	93	8
	THOUGH ONCE SHE WAS SEEN READING THE BATH GUIDE	525	3	DON JUAN	16	50	2
BATHERS	SOME PRETTY SHELL IS BEST FOR MODERATE BATHERS	191	3	DON JUAN	9	18	8
BATHING	AND BATHING HIS CHILL TEMPLES TRIED TO SOOTHE	215	2	DON JUAN	2	113	5
	WELL--JUAN AFTER BATHING IN THE SEA	246	2	DON JUAN	2	171	7
	THAT BATHING PASS'D FOR NOTHING JUAN SEEM'D	247	2	DON JUAN	2	172	2
BATHOS'	CONTEMPT BUT FROM THE BATHOS' VAST ABYSS	334	2	DON JUAN	3	100	4
BATHS	LIKE RUSSIANS RUSHING FROM HOT BATHS TO SNOWS	349	3	DON JUAN	12	73	5
BATTALION	MARCHED WITH THE BRAVE BATTALION OF POLOUZKI--	150	3	DON JUAN	8	76	8
BATTER	I SING THEM BOTH AND AM ABOUT TO BATTER	70	3	DON JUAN	7	8	4
	TO GET AT THEE NOT BATTER DOWN A WALL	210	3	DON JUAN	9	56	4
	THEY SAY HIS SYSTEM 'TIS IN VAIN TO BATTER	268	3	DON JUAN	11	1	3
BATTERED	BY THE RESISTANCE OF THE CHASE THEY BATTERED	131	3	DON JUAN	8	37	8
BATTERIES	TWO BATTERIES CAP-A-PIE AS OUR SAINT GEORGE	72	3	DON JUAN	7	12	3
	THE RUSSIANS HAVING BUILT TWO BATTERIES ON	78	3	DON JUAN	7	23	1
	THE RUSSIAN BATTERIES WERE INCOMPLETE	79	3	DON JUAN	7	26	1
	IN THE NEW BATTERIES ERECTED THERE	80	3	DON JUAN	7	27	6
	LAND BATTERIES WORKED THEIR GUNS WITH GREAT PRECISION	81	3	DON JUAN	7	30	1
	IN THE MEANTIME THE BATTERIES PROCEEDED	85	3	DON JUAN	7	38	6
	NEW BATTERIES WERE ERECTED AND WAS HELD	92	3	DON JUAN	7	51	1
	BOMBS DRUMS GUNS BASTIONS BATTERIES BAYONETS BULLETS	106	3	DON JUAN	7	78	7
	BEYOND THE RUSSIAN BATTERIES A FEW TOISES	115	3	DON JUAN	8	7	2
	THE TURKISH BATTERIES THRASHED THEM LIKE A FLAIL	134	3	DON JUAN	8	43	5
	THEIR COLUMN THOUGH THE TURKISH BATTERIES THUNDERED	149	3	DON JUAN	8	75	1
BATTERING	TO SLAY THE PAGANS WHO RESISTED BATTERING	99	3	DON JUAN	7	64	7
	WORN OUT WITH BATTERING ISMAIL'S STUBBORN WALL	181	3	DON JUAN	8	139	6
BATTERS	LIE ROUND THE BATTERY BUT STILL IT BATTERS	160	3	DON JUAN	8	98	7
BATTERY	'TIS BUILT BEGIRT WITH BATTERY AND TRENCH	71	3	DON JUAN	7	9	V4
	TO TAKE A BATTERY ON THE RIGHT THE OTHERS	119	3	DON JUAN	8	15	2
	WHICH RAINED FROM BASTION BATTERY PARAPET	131	3	DON JUAN	8	37	2
	LIE ROUND THE BATTERY BUT STILL IT BATTERS	160	3	DON JUAN	8	98	7
	HE WHOSE WHOLE LIFE HAS BEEN ASSAULT AND BATTERY	185	3	DON JUAN	9	5	3
	BUZZ ROUND THE FORTUNE WITH THEIR BUSY BATTERY	331	3	DON JUAN	12	32	7
BATTISTA	PEDRO BATTISTA HELP ME DOWN BELOW)	167	2	DON JUAN	2	20	4
	BATTISTA THOUGH (A NAME CALL'D SHORTLY TITA)	186	2	DON JUAN	2	56	7
BATTLE	TO MAKE THE CRETANS BLOODIER IN BATTLE	238	2	DON JUAN	2	155	8
	SO THAT THEIR BARGAIN SOUNDED LIKE A BATTLE	425	2	DON JUAN	5	28	7
	PROVED DEATH IN BATTLE EQUAL TO A PENSION--	96	3	DON JUAN	7	58	8
	IN BATTLE TO OLD AGE AND UGLINESS	167	3	DON JUAN	8	112	V4
	LIKE ROLAND'S HORN IN RONCEVALLES' BATTLE	267	3	DON JUAN	10	87	8
	LIKE TO A ROMAN TRUMPET ERE A BATTLE	267	3	DON JUAN	10	87	V8
	WHEN MAN IN BATTLE OR IN QUARREL TILTS	342	3	DON JUAN	12	56	5
	A BATTLE WRECK OR HISTORY OF THE HEART	419	3	DON JUAN	14	21	4
BATTLED	SO LONG I'VE BATTLED EITHER MORE OR LESS	415	3	DON JUAN	14	12	3
BATTLE-FIELD	WHOSE EVERY BATTLE-FIELD IS HOLY GROUND	114	3	DON JUAN	8	5	3
	TO THE TRUE PORTRAIT OF ONE BATTLE-FIELD	117	3	DON JUAN	8	12	8

BATTLE'S
THE DEATH-CRY DROWNING IN THE BATTLE'S ROAR . . . . 111 3 DON JUAN 7 87 8
A FIELD OF BATTLE'S GHASTLY WILDERNESS . . . . . . 167 3 DON JUAN 8 112 6
BATTLES
FOR THEY REMEMBER BATTLES FIRES AND WRECKS . . . . . 172 2 DON JUAN 2 31 4
THAT BEEF AND BATTLES BOTH WERE OWING TO HER . . . . 238 2 DON JUAN 2 156 8
LEAVE BATTLES TO THE TURKISH HORDES . . . . . . 324 2 DON JUAN 3 L 9 3
OF ALL OUR MODERN BATTLES I WILL BET . . . . . 83 3 DON JUAN 7 34 7
BATTLES TO THE COMMAND FIELD MARSHAL SOUVAROFF . . . . 85 3 DON JUAN 7 39 8
YET IN THE END EXCEPT IN FREEDOM'S BATTLES . . . . . 114 3 DON JUAN 8 4 7
TO BATTLES SIEGES AND THAT KIND OF PLEASURE . . . . . 123 3 DON JUAN 8 24 7
THE WORST OF TEMPESTS AND THE BEST OF BATTLES . . . . 356 3 DON JUAN 12 88 3
WHO LIMITS ALL HIS BATTLES TO THE BAR . . . . . . 398 3 DON JUAN 13 84 2
WHO FOUGHT AND FIGHT IN ABSENCE TOO MY BATTLES . . . . 452 3 DON JUAN 14 96 7
BATTLING
AND THEY CONTINUED BATTLING HAND TO HAND . . . . . 123 2 DON JUAN 1 185 2
WARRIORS THEREON WERE BATTLING FURIOUSLY . . . . . . 461 2 DON JUAN 5 86 3
BAUBLES
WITH WHICH AURORA ON THOSE BAUBLES LOOK'D . . . . . 479 3 DON JUAN 15 53 2
BAWLERS
HER SALE SENT HOME SOME DISAPPOINTED BAWLERS . . . . 407 2 DON JUAN 4 114 5
BAY
BAY DEEP-MOUTH'D WELCOME AS WE DRAW NEAR HOME . . . . 88 2 DON JUAN 1 123 2
A DEVIL OF A SEA ROLLS IN THAT BAY . . . . 162 2 DON JUAN 2 11 3
AND THE REST RUBB'D THEIR EYES AND SAW A BAY . . . . 207 2 DON JUAN 2 97 5
MATERIALS AS WERE CAST UP ROUND THE BAY . . . . 226 2 DON JUAN 2 132 3
THE SILENT OCEAN AND THE STARLIGHT BAY . . . . . 255 2 DON JUAN 2 188 3
THE VERY BOTANY BAY IN MORAL GEOGRAPHY . . . . . 330 2 DON JUAN 3 94 2
BAYING
AS LITTLE AS THE MOON STOPS FOR THE BAYING . . . . . 70 3 DON JUAN 7 7 5
BAYONET
WAS TEACHING HIS RECRUITS TO USE THE BAYONET . . . . 92 3 DON JUAN 7 51 8
AND MADE THEM CHARGE WITH BAYONET THESE MACHINES . . . 93 3 DON JUAN 7 53 3
THE REEKING BAYONET AND THE FLASHING BLADE . . . . 146 3 DON JUAN 8 69 3
OF THE BRIGHT BAYONET AND THEY ALL SHOULD HURRY ON . . 151 3 DON JUAN 8 78 6
THE BAYONET PIERCES AND THE SABRE CLEAVES . . . . 155 3 DON JUAN 8 88 1
BAYONETS
BOMBS DRUMS GUNS BASTIONS BATTERIES BAYONETS BULLETS . . 106 3 DON JUAN 7 78 7
AND SIXTEEN BAYONETS PIERCED THE SERASKIER . . . . 152 3 DON JUAN 8 81 8
OF ALL THE FIVE ON BAYONETS MET HIS LOT . . . . . 166 3 DON JUAN 8 110 4
UNTO THE BAYONETS WHICH HAD PIERCED HIS YOUNG . . . . 170 3 DON JUAN 8 118 6
BAYS
YOUR BAYS MAY HIDE THE BALDNESS OF YOUR BROWS-- . . . 13 2 DON JUAN D 7 1
BEACH
THE BEACH WHICH LAY BEFORE HIM HIGH AND DRY . . . 212 2 DON JUAN 2 106 4
ROLL'D ON THE BEACH HALF SENSELESS FROM THE SEA . . . 212 2 DON JUAN 2 107 8
AN UNKNOWN BARREN BEACH FOR BURIAL GROUND . . . . 213 2 DON JUAN 2 109 8
AND WALKING OUT UPON THE BEACH BELOW . . . . . 224 2 DON JUAN 2 129 1
DROOPING AND DEWY ON THE BEACH HE LAY-- . . . . . 249 2 DON JUAN 2 176 6
AND THE SMALL RIPPLE SPLIT UPON THE BEACH . . . 250 2 DON JUAN 2 178 1
THEY FEAR'D NO EYES NOR EARS ON THAT LONE BEACH . . . 256 2 DON JUAN 2 189 1
AS ON THE BEACH THE WAVES AT LAST ARE BROKE . . . . 402 2 DON JUAN 4 106 5
BEACONS
TO KEEP OUR HOLY BEACONS ALWAYS BRIGHT . . . . . 496 3 DON JUAN 15 90 4
BEADS
A TURK WITH BEADS IN HAND AND PIPE IN MOUTH . . . . 387 2 DON JUAN 4 78 6
SAINT FROM HIS BEADS TO JOIN THE JOCUND RACE . . . . 395 3 DON JUAN 13 78 4
IN COWL AND BEADS AND DUSKY GARB APPEARED . . . . 510 3 DON JUAN 16 21 2
BEAK
THERE'S NOTHING WHETS THE BEAK OR ARMS THE CLAW . . . 488 2 DON JUAN 5 133 3
BEAKERS
MY MILD AND MIDNIGHT BEAKERS TO THE BRIM . . . . . 372 2 DON JUAN 4 53 7
BEAM
HER CHEEK ALL PURPLE WITH THE BEAM OF YOUTH . . . . 55 2 DON JUAN 1 61 4
LAID WITH ONE BLAST THE SHIP ON HER BEAM ENDS . . . 172 2 DON JUAN 2 30 8
UPON HIS SENSES AND THE KINDLING BEAM . . . . . 237 2 DON JUAN 2 153 5
A SPECTRAL RESIDENT--WHOSE PALLID BEAM . . . . . 279 3 DON JUAN 11 24 6
WHILE THE MILD EMERALD'S BEAM SHADES DOWN THE DYES . . 319 3 DON JUAN 12 8 7
WHICH FLOW'D ON FOR A MOMENT IN THE BEAM . . . . . 480 3 DON JUAN 15 55 5
BEAMS
AND THE YOUNG BEAMS OF THE EXCLUDED SUN . . . . . 229 2 DON JUAN 2 137 4
BUT DEATH IS IMAGED IN THEIR SHADOWY BEAMS . . . . 509 3 DON JUAN 16 19 6
BEAR
NEGLECT INDEED REQUIRES A SAINT TO BEAR IT . . . . 32 2 DON JUAN 1 20 3
BUT NOW I'LL BEAR NO MORE NOR HERE REMAIN . . . . 100 2 DON JUAN 1 145 7
THESE I COULD BEAR BUT CANNOT CAST ASIDE . . . . 132 2 DON JUAN 1 195 5
AND BEAR WITH LIFE TO LOVE AND PRAY FOR YOU . . . 134 2 DON JUAN 1 197 8
THOU SHALT NOT BEAR FALSE WITNESS LIKE THE BLUES . . 140 2 DON JUAN 1 206 3
THEY LIVE UPON THE LOVE OF LIFE AND BEAR . . . 191 2 DON JUAN 2 66 2
QUICK TO PERCEIVE AND STRONG TO BEAR AND MEANT . . . 302 2 DON JUAN 3 53 5
BUT VIOLENT THINGS WILL SOONER BEAR ASSUAGING . . . 305 2 DON JUAN 3 58 5
A MOMENT MORE WILL BRING THE SIGHT TO BEAR . . . . 366 2 DON JUAN 4 41 3
WOULD BEAR SUCH OUTRAGE AND FORBEAR TO KILL . . . . 368 2 DON JUAN 4 46 6
THROUGH YEARS OR MOONS THE INNER WEIGHT TO BEAR . . . 382 2 DON JUAN 4 71 3
WHOM TO THE SPOT THEIR SCHOOL-BOY FEELINGS BEAR . . . 387 2 DON JUAN 4 78 5
TO BEAR THE COMPLIMENTS OF MANY A BORE . . . . 404 2 DON JUAN 4 109 3
AND NEVER HAVING DREAMT WHAT 'TWAS TO BEAR . . . . 480 2 DON JUAN 5 119 4
YOU DON'T SLEEP SOUNDLY AND I CANNOT BEAR . . . . 29 3 DON JUAN 6 47 2
FOR KILLING NOTHING BUT A BEAR OR BUCK HE . . . . 143 3 DON JUAN 8 61 6

BEAR   (CONTINUED)
    THE BEAR IS CIVILIZED THE WOLF IS MILD . . . . .   157 3 DON JUAN 8   92   5
    BEAR IT YE MUSES ON YOUR BRIGHTEST WING . . . . . 175 3 DON JUAN 8   126   4
    TO BEAR THESE CROSSES) FOR EACH WANING PRUDE . . . 177 3 DON JUAN 8   131   6
    IN FACT THE ONLY CHRISTIAN SHE COULD BEAR . . . . 252 3 DON JUAN 10   57   1
    WOULD THIS DAMNED HEADACHE SUFFER ME TO BEAR IT . . 268 3 DON JUAN 11   1 V8
    HEAVEN'S BRANDY--THOUGH OUR BRAIN CAN HARDLY BEAR IT 269 3 DON JUAN 11   2   8
    SHOULD NEITHER COURT NEGLECT NOR DREAD TO BEAR IT . 356 3 DON JUAN 12   87   8
    BEAR A BOLD BROW AND FOR YOUR BOSOM NERVE IT . . . 367 3 DON JUAN 13   18 V4
    OR SOLITARY AS THEY CHOSE TO BEAR . . . . . .   406 3 DON JUAN 13   103   4
    THAT WHICH HUMANITY MAY BEAR OR BEAR NOT . . . .   431 3 DON JUAN 14   49   6
    THAT WHICH HUMANITY MAY BEAR OR BEAR NOT . . . .   431 3 DON JUAN 14   49   6
    TO BEAR A SON AND HEIR--AND ONE MISCARRIAGE . . .   434 3 DON JUAN 14   56   8
    IF ONCE THEIR PHANTASIES BE BROUGHT TO BEAR . . .   463 3 DON JUAN 15   16   6
    TO BEAR ON WHAT APPEARED TO HER THE SUBJECT . . .   526 3 DON JUAN 16   51   3
    A SOMETHING LIKE IT--AS BEAR WITNESS LUTHER . . .   565 3 DON JUAN 17   6   8
    THIS THEY MUST BEAR WITH AND PERHAPS MUCH MORE . .   566 3 DON JUAN 17   9   6
BEARABLE
    'TIS SAID IT MAKES REALITY MORE BEARABLE . . . .   495 3 DON JUAN 15   89   5
BEARD
    AND BEGGED BY EVERY HAIR OF MAHOMET'S BEARD . . .   62 3 DON JUAN 6   113   7
    HIS BEARD HE PUFFED HIS PIPE'S AMBROSIAL GALES . .   172 3 DON JUAN 8   121   7
    THIRDLY THAT JUAN HAD MORE BRAIN THAN BEARD . . .   439 3 DON JUAN 14   66   5
BEARDED
    SHAWLED TO THE NOSE AND BEARDED TO THE EYES . . .   495 2 DON JUAN 5   147   2
BEARDLESS
    HE WITH THE BEARDLESS CHIN AND GARMENTS TORN . .   98 3 DON JUAN 7   62   6
    BLUSHING AND BEARDLESS AND YET NE'ERTHELESS . . .   206 3 DON JUAN 9   47   2
BEARDS
    WITH BEARDS AND WHISKERS AND THE LIKE THE FOND . .   209 3 DON JUAN 9   53   4
BEARING
    INSTEAD OF BEARING UP WITHOUT DEBATE . . . . . .   394 2 DON JUAN 4   93   6
BEARS
    BEARS VEGETABLES IN A GRUMBLING WAY . . . . . .   191 3 DON JUAN 2   67   6
    WHICH BEARS THE GREATEST LIKENESS TO PALL MALL . .   124 3 DON JUAN 8   26   8
    WHICH BEARS THE SAME RELATION TO THE REAL . . . .   419 3 DON JUAN 14   22   3
    LOVE BEARS WITHIN ITS BREAST THE VERY GERM . . .   451 3 DON JUAN 14   94   1
    OF TIME AND TIDE ROLLS ON AND BEARS AFAR . . . .   500 3 DON JUAN 15   99   5
BEAR-SKINS
    IN THIS GAY CLIME OF BEAR-SKINS BLACK AND FURRY--   237 3 DON JUAN 10   26   3
BEAST
    AND FOR THE BASS THE BEAST CAN ONLY BELLOW . . .   391 2 DON JUAN 4   87   2
    OR ANY INTERESTING BEAST OF PREY . . . .   487 3 DON JUAN 5   132   2
    THAT SAD INEXPLICABLE BEAST OF PREY-- . . . . .   207 3 DON JUAN 9   50   2
BEASTS
    TRANSFORM'D THEIR LORDS TO BEASTS (BUT THAT'S A FACT) 293 2 DON JUAN 3   34   8
    BILLS BEASTS AND MEN AND--NO NOT WOMANKIND . . .   17 3 DON JUAN 6   22   2
    A MIXTURE OF WILD BEASTS AND DEMI-GODS . . . . .   164 3 DON JUAN 8   106   4
    BESIDES FISH BEASTS AND BIRDS THE SPARROW'S FALL .   192 3 DON JUAN 9   19   5
BEAT
    AND HEAR THE HEART BEAT WITH THE LOVE IT GRANTED .   73 2 DON JUAN 1   96   6
    I PRAISE YOUR VAST FORBEARANCE NOT TO BEAT . . .   103 2 DON JUAN 1   150   5
    THE WATERS BEAT WHILE HE THERETO WAS LASH'D . . .   212 2 DON JUAN 2   107   6
    FELT AS IF NEVER MORE TO BEAT APART . . . . . .   257 2 DON JUAN 2   191   8
    HOPE CARE NOR LOVE BEYOND HER HEART BEAT HERE . .   264 2 DON JUAN 2   202   8
    AND OH THAT QUICKENING OF THE HEART THAT BEAT . .   264 2 DON JUAN 2   203   1
    LAY JUAN NOR COULD AUGHT RENEW THE BEAT . . . .   362 2 DON JUAN 4   34   5
    LAY AT HER HEART WHOSE EARLIEST BEAT STILL TRUE .   378 2 DON JUAN 4   62   6
    ANON HER THIN WAN FINGERS BEAT THE WALL . . . .   380 2 DON JUAN 4   66   1
    A LONDON BAS WILL BEAT THY SKY PERU . . . . . .   406 2 DON JUAN 4   112 V8
    I'LL BET SOME PAIR OF STOCKINGS BEAT PERU . . . .   406 2 DON JUAN 4   112 V8
    IN THINKING THAT THEIR ENEMY IS BEAT . . . . . .   87 3 DON JUAN 7   42   4
    KOUTOUSOW HE WHO AFTERWARDS BEAT BACK . . . . .   147 3 DON JUAN 8   70   1
    IT HAPPENED WAS HIMSELF BEAT BACK JUST NOW . . .   147 3 DON JUAN 8   70   4
    FOR THOSE FOR WHOM IT SOON SHALL CEASE TO BEAT .   152 3 DON JUAN 8   82   4
    STRUCK AT HIS FRIENDS AS BABIES BEAT THEIR NURSES   165 3 DON JUAN 8   108   8
    CAMBYSES' ROARING ROMANS BEAT AT LEAST . . . . .   297 3 DON JUAN 11   58   7
    WHICH BEAT AS IF THERE WAS A WARM HEART UNDER . .   560 3 DON JUAN 16   122   4
BEATEN
    (OR BEATEN IF YOU INSIST ON GRAMMAR THOUGH . . .   87 3 DON JUAN 7   42   5
    WAS BEATEN--THOUGH THE PRUSSIANS SAY SO TOO-- . .   136 3 DON JUAN 8   48   8
    BEATING OR BEATEN SHE WILL LAUGH THE SAME)-- . .   183 3 DON JUAN 9   1   5
BEATING
    AND BEATING 'GAINST HIS BOSOM HAIDEE'S HEART . .   257 2 DON JUAN 2   191   7
    BEATING FOR LOVE AS THE CAGED BIRDS FOR AIR . . .   19 3 DON JUAN 6   26   8
    BEATING OR BEATEN SHE WILL LAUGH THE SAME)-- . .   183 3 DON JUAN 9   1   5
BEATRICE
    BUT DANTE'S BEATRICE AND MILTON'S EVE . . . . .   281 2 DON JUAN 3   10   7
    BY BEATRICE AND NOT A MISTRESS--I . . . . . .   281 2 DON JUAN 3   11   2
BEATS
    AND LOUDER THAN HER BREATHING BEATS HER HEART . .   108 2 DON JUAN 1   158   8
    THE HEROIC BOSOM BEATS NO MORE . . . .   322 2 DON JUAN 3 L 5   4
    SELF-LOVE IN MAN TOO BEATS ALL FEMALE ART . . .   15 3 DON JUAN 6   19   5
    (WHICH WILL COME OVER THINGS) BEATS LOVE OR LIQUOR   317 3 DON JUAN 12   4   5
    THE POINTER RANGES AND THE SPORTSMAN BEATS . . .   394 3 DON JUAN 13   75   4
BEATUS
    BEATUS ILLE PROCUL FROM NEGOTIIS . . . .   443 3 DON JUAN 14   7   1
BEAU
    IS BUT HEIGHTENING OF THE BEAU IDEAL . . . . . .   269 2 DON JUAN 2   211   8

PAGE VOL   CANTO STANZA LN

BEAU   (CONTINUED)
    OF BEING WITHOUT ALLOY OF FOP OR BEAU . . . . 354 3 DON JUAN 12   84   7
    ARE GROWN OF THE BEAU MONDE A PART POTENTIAL   . . . . . 418 3 DON JUAN 14   20   2
BEAUTEOUS
    THE STRANGEST THING WAS BEAUTEOUS SHE WAS WHOLLY   . . . . 33 3 DON JUAN 6   54   5
    JUAN I SAID WAS A MOST BEAUTEOUS BOY . . . . 209 3 DON JUAN 9   53   1
    HOW BEAUTEOUS ARE ROULEAUS HOW CHARMING CHESTS . . . . . 321 3 DON JUAN 12   12   1
    AND BEAUTEOUS EVEN WHERE BEAUTIES MOST ABOUND . . . . . 359 3 DON JUAN 13   2   6
    A BEAUTEOUS RIPPLE OF THE BRILLIANT STREAM . . . . . . 480 3 DON JUAN 15   55   3
BEAUTIES
    OF BEAUTIES COOL AS AN ITALIAN CONVENT   . . . . 22 3 DON JUAN 6   32   7
    OF ANY SUPERNUMERARY BEAUTIES . . . . 35 3 DON JUAN 6   58   8
    HER BEAUTIES SEIZED THE UNCONSCIOUS HOUR OF NIGHT . . . . 39 3 DON JUAN 6   66   7
    WHICH HOVERS OFT ABOUT SOME MARRIED BEAUTIES   . . . . . 208 3 DON JUAN 9   51   4
    DON JUAN NOW SAW ALBION'S EARLIEST BEAUTIES-- . . . . . 259 3 DON JUAN 10   69   1
    AND TO THE BEAUTIES OF A FOREIGN DAME . . . . 349 3 DON JUAN 12   72   6
    AND BEAUTEOUS EVEN WHERE BEAUTIES MOST ABOUND . . . . . 359 3 DON JUAN 13   2   6
    WHERE TIME THROUGH HEROES AND THROUGH BEAUTIES STEERS   . . 381 3 DON JUAN 13   50   6
    ALSO SOME BEAUTIES OF SIR PETER LELY . . . . 390 3 DON JUAN 13   68   7
    SEEN BEAUTIES BROUGHT TO MARKET BY THE SCORE   . . . . . 418 3 DON JUAN 14   18   4
    AND THE PALE SMILE OF BEAUTIES IN THE GRAVE . . . . . 509 3 DON JUAN 16   19   1
BEAUTIFUL
    SPRUNG UP A BRANCH AS BEAUTIFUL AS FRESH . . . . . . 53 2 DON JUAN 1   58   4
    HOW BEAUTIFUL SHE LOOK'D HER CONSCIOUS HEART   . . . . . 78 2 DON JUAN 1   106   1
    TO KEEP THEM BEAUTIFUL OR LEAVE THEM NEAT   . . . . . . 99 2 DON JUAN 1   143   6
    BUT BEAUTIFUL SHE LAY--HER EYES SHED TEARS . . . . . . 108 2 DON JUAN 1   158   V2
    EXTRACTS EMOTIONS BEAUTIFUL AND NEW . . . . 144 2 DON JUAN 1   214   4
    A MODE SO BEAUTIFUL AND SO UNHOLY . . . . 161 2 DON JUAN 2   7   V7
    ABOUT THIS TIME A BEAUTIFUL WHITE BIRD . . . . . . 206 2 DON JUAN 2   94   1
    BESIDES SO VERY BEAUTIFUL WAS SHE . . . . 224 2 DON JUAN 2   128   3
    ALAS THEY WERE SO YOUNG SO BEAUTIFUL . . . . 258 2 DON JUAN 2   192   1
    SO INNOCENT AND BEAUTIFUL A FAIR . . . . 258 2 DON JUAN 2   193   V3
    BEAUTY UPON THE BEAUTIFUL THEY LIGHTED . . . . . . 265 2 DON JUAN 2   204   3
    'TIS THE PERCEPTION OF THE BEAUTIFUL . . . . 269 2 DON JUAN 2   212   1
    'TIS BEAUTIFUL TO SEE A MATRON BRING . . . . . . 306 2 DON JUAN 3   60   3
    SO BEAUTIFUL--ITS VERY SHAPE WOULD CHARM . . . . . 312 2 DON JUAN 3   71   5
    THEY WERE SO SOFT AND BEAUTIFUL AND RIFE . . . . . 313 2 DON JUAN 3   74   3
    SINK O'ER THE EARTH SO BEAUTIFUL AND SOFT . . . . . 335 2 DON JUAN 3   102   4
    OH BEAUTIFUL AND RARE AS BEAUTIFUL . . . . 353 2 DON JUAN 4   17   1
    OH BEAUTIFUL AND RARE AS BEAUTIFUL . . . . 353 2 DON JUAN 4   17   1
    WHERE LATE HE TROD HER BEAUTIFUL HER OWN . . . . . 375 2 DON JUAN 4   58   4
    THOSE EYES SO BEAUTIFUL--BEHOLD NO MORE . . . . . 376 2 DON JUAN 4   59   V2
    GLAZED O'ER HER EYES--THE BEAUTIFUL THE BLACK-- . . . . 381 2 DON JUAN 4   69   7
    MADE HER A BEAUTIFUL EMBODIED STORM . . . . . . 489 2 DON JUAN 5   135   8
    YOUNG BEAUTIFUL AND DARING--WHO WOULD RISK . . . . . 7 3 DON JUAN 6   3   2
    AND FRESH AND BEAUTIFUL EXCEEDINGLY . . . . . . 24 3 DON JUAN 6   36   3
    MANY AND BEAUTIFUL LAY THOSE AROUND . . . . . . 38 3 DON JUAN 6   65   1
    SO BEAUTIFUL THAT ART COULD LITTLE MEND HER . . . . . 50 3 DON JUAN 6   89   5
    SO BEAUTIFUL SO FLEETING TO THE MUSE . . . . . . 108 3 DON JUAN 7   82   8
    AND SHUDDER--WHILE AS BEAUTIFUL AS MAY . . . . . 157 3 DON JUAN 8   91   5
    THOUGH BEAUTIFUL IN YOUTH HIS CARNAL SKIN-- . . . . . 188 3 DON JUAN 9   12   V7
    HOW BEAUTIFUL THAT MOMENT AND HOW ODD IS . . . . . 220 3 DON JUAN 9   75   5
    YE BEAUTIFUL ROULEAUS YE IRON CASKETS . . . . . . 321 3 DON JUAN 12   12   V1
    AS BEAUTIFUL AS HER OWN NATIVE LAND . . . . . . 329 3 DON JUAN 12   29   3
    AS BEAUTIFUL AND BOUNDING AS A STEED . . . . . . 401 3 DON JUAN 13   92   6
    AND THEN HER DRESS--WHAT BEAUTIFUL SIMPLICITY . . . . 550 3 DON JUAN 16   102   7
BEAUTIFULLY
    OH DARKLY DEEPLY BEAUTIFULLY BLUE . . . . 404 2 DON JUAN 4   110   1
BEAUTY
    SHEDS BEAUTY AND DEEP SOFTNESS O'ER THE WHOLE . . . . . 82 2 DON JUAN 1   114   6
    YOU WILL RETURN IN BEAUTY AND IN PRIDE   . . . . . . 132 2 DON JUAN 1   195   V1
    AND BEAUTY ALL CONCENTRATING LIKE RAYS   . . . . . . 254 2 DON JUAN 2   186   2
    BEAUTY UPON THE BEAUTIFUL THEY LIGHTED   . . . . . . 265 2 DON JUAN 2   204   3
    PROFUSION WITH YOUNG BEAUTY COVERS O'ER   . . . . . . 269 2 DON JUAN 2   211   4
    AT WASSAIL IN THEIR BEAUTY AND THEIR PRIDE   . . . . . 306 2 DON JUAN 3   61   4
    A BEAUTY AT THE SEASON'S CLOSE GROWN HECTIC   . . . . . 309 2 DON JUAN 3   66   1
    AND IN THEIR NATIVE BEAUTY STOOD AVENGED . . . . . 314 2 DON JUAN 3   75   5
    BEAUTY AND LOVE WERE HAIDEE'S MOTHER'S DOWER   . . . . . 374 2 DON JUAN 4   56   6
    MOURNS O'ER THE BEAUTY OF THE CYCLADES   . . . . . . 383 2 DON JUAN 4   72   8
    VALOUR WAS HIS AND BEAUTY DWELT WITH HER . . . . . 383 2 DON JUAN 4   73   4
    OF BEAUTY FLATTERY THREATS A SHILLING--NO   . . . . . 439 2 DON JUAN 5   49   3
    HER BEAUTY OF THAT OVERPOWERING KIND . . . . . . 467 2 DON JUAN 5   97   2
    AND TO WHICH BEAUTY OBSTINATELY CLINGS . . . . . 468 2 DON JUAN 5   98   V4
    HER BLOOD WAS HIGH HER BEAUTY SCARCE OF EARTH   . . . . 475 2 DON JUAN 5   112   5
    AND ALTHOUGH SENSITIVE TO BEAUTY HE . . . . . . 481 2 DON JUAN 5   121   7
    OF A YOUNG DOWNRIGHT BEAUTY IN THIS CASE . . . . . 486 2 DON JUAN 5   130   8
    ALTHOUGH HER BEAUTY WAS ENOUGH TO VEX . . . . . . 24 3 DON JUAN 6   37   2
    YET OF A BEAUTY THAT WOULD DRIVE YOU CRAZY . . . . . 26 3 DON JUAN 6   41   8
    HAD MADE HIM LATELY BASK IN HIS BRIDE'S BEAUTY   . . . . 51 3 DON JUAN 6   91   8
    TO SHARE HER BEAUTY AND HER BANISHMENT . . . . . 193 3 DON JUAN 9   22   8
    BEAUTY SPRINGS FORTH AND NATURE'S SELF TURNS PALER   . . 204 3 DON JUAN 9   44   4
    OF YOUTH AND VIGOUR BEAUTY AND THOSE THINGS . . . . . 227 3 DON JUAN 10   5   7
    WHICH SET THE BEAUTY OFF IN WHICH HE GLOWED   . . . . . 239 3 DON JUAN 10   29   6
    IN ROYALTY'S VAST ARMS HE SIGHED FOR BEAUTY   . . . . . 243 3 DON JUAN 10   37   8
    THEIR LOVE THEIR VIRTUE BEAUTY EDUCATION . . . . . 420 3 DON JUAN 14   24   7
    WHATE'ER THOU TAKEST SPARE AWHILE POOR BEAUTY   . . . . 459 3 DON JUAN 15   9   1
    FOR THIS AN HEIRESS AND FOR THAT A BEAUTY   . . . . . 471 3 DON JUAN 15   34   2
    HER BEAUTY ALSO SEEM'D TO FORM NO CLOG   . . . . . . 477 3 DON JUAN 15   48   5
    OWN'D TO A PENCHANT THOUGH DISCREET FOR BEAUTY . . . . . 494 3 DON JUAN 15   85   8

65

```
                                                          PAGE VOL       CANTO STANZA LN
BEAUTY   (CONTINUED)
   SOME PRAISED HER BEAUTY OTHERS HER GREAT GRACE . . . . .  550  3 DON JUAN 16   102    1
   UNLESS SOME BEAUTY WITH A KISS SHOULD BRIBE . . . . . .   567  3 DON JUAN 17    12    8
BEAUTY'S
   WARRANTED VIRGIN BEAUTY'S BRIGHTEST COLOURS . . . . . .   407  2 DON JUAN  4   114    3
   ITSELF WITH BEAUTY'S FRAIL INANITY . . . . . . . . .      219  3 DON JUAN  9    73    5
BEAUVEAU
   SOUPE A LA BEAUVEAU WHOSE RELIEF WAS DORY  . . . . . .    483  3 DON JUAN 15    63    7
BECALM'D
   THAT THE SAIL WAS BECALM'D BETWEEN THE SEAS . . . . . .   188  2 DON JUAN  2    60    2
BECAME
   THE HEARERS OF HER CASE BECAME REPEATERS . . . . . . .     36  2 DON JUAN  1    28    6
   INEZ BECAME SOLE GUARDIAN WHICH WAS FAIR . . . . . . .     42  2 DON JUAN  1    37    5
   IT WAS FOR THIS THAT I BECAME A BRIDE . . . . . . . .     100  2 DON JUAN  1   145    4
   BECAME DIVESTED OF HIS NATIVE MODESTY . . . . . . . .     157  2 DON JUAN  2     1    8
   AND THE SHIP CREAK'D THE TOWN BECAME A SPECK . . . . .    163  2 DON JUAN  2    13    3
   AND I BECAME A PRISONER TO THE FOE-- . . . . . . . .      98  3 DON JUAN  7    61    6
   THE EARTH WHICH HE BECAME LIKE A FELLED TREE . . . . .    169  3 DON JUAN  8   116    6
   BECAME A KIND OF FASHIONABLE MYSTERY . . . . . . . .      328  3 DON JUAN 12    27    8
   THOSE BECAME ONE WHO SOON WERE TO BE TWO . . . . . . .    334  3 DON JUAN 12    38    6
BECASSE
   THE CHASTE DESCRIPTION EVEN OF A BECASSE . . . . . .      487  3 DON JUAN 15    71    8
BECKET'S
   BLACK EDWARD'S HELM AND BECKET'S BLOODY STONE . . . . .   261  3 DON JUAN 10    73    2
BECKON'D
   AS IF THEIR SOULS AND LIPS EACH OTHER BECKON'D . . . .    254  2 DON JUAN  2   187    6
BECKONED
   GULBEYAZ STOPPED AND BECKONED BABA--SLAVE  . . . . . .     62  3 DON JUAN  6   112    1
BECOME
   ANY ONE ELSE--THEY WERE BECOME TRADITIONAL . . . . . .     37  2 DON JUAN  1    31    4
   WHATE'ER THE CAUSE MIGHT BE THEY HAD BECOME . . . . . .    60  2 DON JUAN  1    70    1
   WHAT WILL BECOME ON'T--I'M IN SUCH A FRIGHT . . . . . .   115  2 DON JUAN  1   171    3
   AND MAY BECOME OF GREAT ADVANTAGE WHEN  . . . . . . .     205  2 DON JUAN  2    93    4
   BECOME A THING OR NOTHING SAVE TO RANK . . . . . . .      327  2 DON JUAN  3    89    3
   I FEEL MY HEART BECOME SO SYMPATHETIC . . . . . . . .     372  2 DON JUAN  4    52    5
   'TWOULD NOT BECOME MYSELF TO DWELL UPON . . . . . . .     392  2 DON JUAN  4    88    1
   (BECAUSE THIS CANTO HAS BECOME TOO LONG) . . . . . .      410  2 DON JUAN  4   117    3
   THIS POEM WILL BECOME A MORAL MODEL . . . . . . . .       412  2 DON JUAN  5     2    8
   SOME THOUGHT HER DRESS DID NOT SO MUCH BECOME HER . . .    23  3 DON JUAN  6    35    3
   MEN BECOME WOLVES ON ANY SLIGHT OCCASION . . . . . .      192  3 DON JUAN  9    20    8
   OLD ENEMIES WHO HAVE BECOME NEW FRIENDS . . . . . . .     231  3 DON JUAN 10    12    1
   OLD FLAMES NEW WIVES BECOME OUR BITTEREST FOES-- . . .    231  3 DON JUAN 10    12    7
   WHEN NATURE WEARS THE GOWN THAT DOTH BECOME HER . . . .   380  3 DON JUAN 13    48    3
   WAS ALMOST WORTHY TO BECOME HIS HENCHMAN . . . . . . .    425  3 DON JUAN 14    34   V8
BECOMES
   THE EAR BECOMES MORE IRISH AND LESS NICE . . . . . .      366  2 DON JUAN  4    41    8
   WHAT WAS A PARADOX BECOMES A TRUTH OR . . . . . . .       565  3 DON JUAN 17     6    7
BECOMING
   THERE'S NOTHING SO BECOMING TO THE FACE  . . . . . . .    119  2 DON JUAN  1   178    8
   THOUGHT IT WOULD BE BECOMING TO DIE DRUNK  . . . . . .    174  2 DON JUAN  2    35    8
   BUT IN A STYLE BECOMING HIS CONDITION . . . . . . . .     246  3 DON JUAN 10    44    8
   'TIS SO BECOMING TO THE SOUL AND FACE . . . . . . . .     430  3 DON JUAN 14    47    2
   JUAN REPLIED WITH ALL BECOMING DEFERENCE . . . . . .      469  3 DON JUAN 15    30    1
BED
   'TWAS MIDNIGHT--DONNA JULIA WAS IN BED  . . . . . .        95  2 DON JUAN  1   136    1
   TO HOLD A LEVEE ROUND HIS LADY'S BED . . . . . . . .       97  2 DON JUAN  1   139    6
   UNDER THE BED THEY SEARCH'D AND THERE THEY FOUND-- . .    100  2 DON JUAN  1   144    1
   OF LOOKING IN THE BED AS WELL AS UNDER . . . . . . .      100  2 DON JUAN  1   144    6
   YOUNG JUAN SLIPP'D HALF-SMOTHER'D FROM THE BED . . . .    112  2 DON JUAN  1   165    8
   HE HAD A BED OF FURS AND A PELISSE . . . . . . . .        226  2 DON JUAN  2   133    1
   HAD MADE HER MISTRESS QUIT HER BED TO TRACE . . . . .     240  2 DON JUAN  2   159    4
   AS O'ER A BED OF ROSES THE SWEET SOUTH . . . . . . .      245  2 DON JUAN  2   168    8
   OCEAN THEIR WITNESS AND THE CAVE THEIR BED . . . . .      265  2 DON JUAN  2   204    4
   A SOFA LIKE A BED MAY COME BY WRONG . . . . . . . .       288  2 DON JUAN  3    25   V8
   WITH THEIR ROUGH FACES THRONGED ABOUT THE BED . . . .     431  2 DON JUAN  5    37    2
   HER FIFTH TO CALL HER MAIDS AND GO TO BED  . . . . . .    491  2 DON JUAN  5   139    5
   TO MAKE THE NUPTIAL COUCH A BED OF WARE . . . . . .        12  3 DON JUAN  6    12    8
   A BED IS NOT A THRONE AND THEY MAY SLEEP . . . . . .       16  3 DON JUAN  6    20    2
   LOOKED MORE ADAPTED TO BE PUT TO BED  . . . . . . .        26  3 DON JUAN  6    41    6
   SHE ALSO HAD COMPASSION AND A BED  . . . . . . . .         29  3 DON JUAN  6    47    8
   BUT WIDE AWAKE SHE WAS AND ROUND HER BED . . . . . .       42  3 DON JUAN  6    72    1
   BED FOR THE DREAM SHE HAD BEEN OBLIGED TO HEAR . . . .     45  3 DON JUAN  6    79    6
   ROSE THE SULTANA FROM A BED OF SPLENDOUR . . . . . .       50  3 DON JUAN  6    89    1
   BUT TO SIT UP WHILE OTHERS LIE IN BED . . . . . . .       290  3 DON JUAN 11    45    5
   AND SEDGES BROODING IN THEIR LIQUID BED . . . . . .       385  3 DON JUAN 13    57    6
   THE GREEK EVE HELEN FROM THE SPARTAN'S BED . . . . .      441  3 DON JUAN 14    72    5
   OBSERVED AS STRICTLY BOTH AT BOARD AND BED . . . . .      470  3 DON JUAN 15    32    6
   UNDREST AND RATHER SLOWLY WENT TO BED . . . . . . .       512  3 DON JUAN 16    27    4
   BY THE MARRIAGE BED OF THEIR LORDS 'TIS SAID . . . .      519  3 DON JUAN 16  L  3    5
   AND 'TIS HELD AS FAITH TO THEIR BED OF DEATH . . . .      519  3 DON JUAN 16  L  3    7
   'TIS WHITE AT LEAST WHEN THEY JUST RISE FROM BED . . .    532  3 DON JUAN 16    64    4
   OUTLINE OF AN HARANGUE--BUT I'LL TO BED . . . . . .       538  3 DON JUAN 16    77   V5
BED-CLOTHES
   CONTRIVED TO FLING THE BED-CLOTHES IN A HEAP  . . . . .    97  2 DON JUAN  1   140    5
BEDDING
   HOW MANY SONNETS HAD ENSUED THE BEDDING . . . . . .       279  2 DON JUAN  3     8   V8
   WITHOUT THE EXPENSE AND THE SUSPENSE OF BEDDING  . . .    177  3 DON JUAN  8   131    8
BEDEW
   AND MAY SERVE THEREFORE TO BEDEW THESE RHYMES . . . . .   156  3 DON JUAN  8    90    5
```

```
                                                           PAGE VOL     CANTO   STANZA LN
BEDEW'D
    BEDEW'D HIS SPIRIT IN HIS CALMER HOURS    .  .  .  .  .  .  . 304  2 DON JUAN  3     56    8
BED-FELLOW
    LEST THEIR TOO LAWFUL BED-FELLOW SHOULD WAKE   .  .  .  .  .  . 18  3 DON JUAN  6     24    8
BEDLAM
    BUT BEDLAM STILL EXISTS WITH ITS SAGE FETTER   .  .  .  .  .  . 280 3 DON JUAN 11     25    3
    SHUT UP THE WORLD AT LARGE LET BEDLAM OUT   .  .  .  .  .  .  . 446 3 DON JUAN 14     84    1
BEDLAMITES
    LIKE BIRDS OR BOYS OR BEDLAMITES BROKE LOOSE   .  .  .  .  .  . 23  3 DON JUAN  6     34    2
BEDRAL
    WERE POINTED OUT AS USUAL BY THE BEDRAL  .  .  .  .  .  .  . 261 3 DON JUAN 10     73    3
BEDS
    ALSO BENEATH THE CANOPY OF BEDS  .  .  .  .  .  .  .  .  .  .  . 18  3 DON JUAN  6     25    2
    THE WHOLE ODA FROM THEIR BEDS AT HALF-PAST THREE  .  .  .  .  . 46  3 DON JUAN  6     80    4
    WHO MAKE THE BEDS OF THOSE WHO WON'T TAKE QUARTER  .  .  .  . 167 3 DON JUAN  8    111    5
BEE
    HIVED IN OUR BOSOMS LIKE THE BAG O' THE BEE  .  .  .  .  .  . 144 2 DON JUAN  1    214    5
    A BEE FLEW OUT AND STUNG HER TO THE HEART   .  .  .  .  .  .  . 44  3 DON JUAN  6     77    7
    BUT VISIONS OF AN APPLE AND A BEE  .  .  .  .  .  .  . 46  3 DON JUAN  6     80    2
    NONE SAVE THE SPANISH FLY AND ATTIC BEE  .  .  .  .  .  .  . 196 3 DON JUAN  9     28    7
    FOR A SPOILT CARPET--BUT THE ATTIC BEE   .  .  .  .  .  . 522 3 DON JUAN 16     43    7
BEEF
    A PORTION OF THEIR BEEF UP FROM BELOW  .  .  .  .  .  .  . 181 2 DON JUAN  2     47    5
    BEEF VEAL AND MUTTON BETTER FOR DIGESTION   .  .  .  .  .  . 191 2 DON JUAN  2     67    8
    BUT BEEF IS RARE WITHIN THESE OXLESS ISLES   .  .  .  .  .  . 238 2 DON JUAN  2    154    1
    I SAY THAT BEEF IS RARE AND CAN'T HELP THINKING   .  .  .  . 238 2 DON JUAN  2    155    1
    FED UPON BEEF--I WON'T SAY MUCH OF BEER  .  .  .  .  . 238 2 DON JUAN  2    156    2
    THAT BEEF AND BATTLES BOTH WERE OWING TO HER   .  .  .  . 238 2 DON JUAN  2    156    8
    THAN COULD ROAST BEEF IN OUR ROUGH JOHN BULL WAY  .  .  . 487 3 DON JUAN 15     71    4
    AS BETWEEN ENGLISH BEEF AND SPARTAN BROTH--  .  .  .  . 541 3 DON JUAN 16     84    7
BEEF-STEAK
    THE BEST OF REMEDIES IS A BEEF-STEAK   .  .  .  .  .  . 163 2 DON JUAN  2     13    5
    AND LONG FOR FOOD BUT CHIEFLY A BEEF-STEAK   .  .  .  .  . 237 2 DON JUAN  2    153    8
    LIKE ESAU FOR MY BIRTHRIGHT A BEEF-STEAK .  .  .  .  .  . 435 2 DON JUAN  5     44    8
BEE-LIKE
    HEARD--AND THAT BEE-LIKE BUBBLING BUSY HUM   .  .  .  . 272 3 DON JUAN 11      8    7
BEER
    FED UPON BEEF--I WON'T SAY MUCH OF BEER  .  .  .  .  . 238 2 DON JUAN  2    156    2
    AND WHEN I THINK UPON A POT OF BEER--  .  .  .  .  .  . 263 3 DON JUAN 10     77    1
    DISCUSSED (HE HATED BEER YCLEPT THE SMALL)   .  .  .  . 533 3 DON JUAN 16     67    3
BEE'S
    ENOUGH TO GRATIFY A BEE'S SLIGHT MUNCHINGS   .  .  .  .  . 301 3 DON JUAN 11     66    5
BEES
    OF BEES THE VOICE OF GIRLS THE SONG OF BIRDS  .  .  .  .  . 88  2 DON JUAN  1    123    7
    WHICH BEING JOIN'D LIKE SWARMING BEES THEY CLUNG--  .  .  . 254 2 DON JUAN  2    187    7
    THAT HONEY OF YOUR FASHIONABLE BEES--  .  .  .  .  .  . 548 3 DON JUAN 16    100    6
BEFALL
    WHAT FURTHER HATH BEFALLEN OR MAY BEFALL .  .  .  .  .  . 181 3 DON JUAN  8    139    2
    AND WHEN AUGHT IS TO BEFALL  .  .  .  .  .  .  .  .  . 519 3 DON JUAN 16   L  4    2
BEFALLEN
    WHAT FURTHER HATH BEFALLEN OR MAY BEFALL .  .  .  .  .  . 181 3 DON JUAN  8    139    2
BEFELL
    NO MATTER HOW OR WHY THE THING BEFELL  .  .  .  .  .  .  . 77  2 DON JUAN  1    105    5
    SAW ONE WHOM SUCH AN ACCIDENT BEFELL   .  .  .  .  .  . 430 2 DON JUAN  5     35    3
    OF WHAT BEFELL OUR HERO IN THE LAND  .  .  .  .  .  . 311 3 DON JUAN 11     87    2
    WHAT THEN I ONLY KNOW IT SO BEFELL .  .  .  .  .  . 502 3 DON JUAN 16      4    4
BEFRINGE
    AS PURPLE CLOUDS BEFRINGE THE SUN BUT MOST   .  .  .  .  . 239 3 DON JUAN 10     29    7
BEG
    BUT THEN I BEG IT MAY BE UNDERSTOOD  .  .  .  .  .  .  . 68  2 DON JUAN  1     87    6
    BUT BEG SECURITY WILL BOLT THE DOOR  .  .  .  .  .  . 69  2 DON JUAN  1     89    8
    TO BEG HIS PARDON WHEN I ERR A BIT .  .  .  .  .  .  . 86  2 DON JUAN  1    120    8
    I WISH TO SLEEP AND BEG YOU WILL TAKE CARE   .  .  .  . 104 2 DON JUAN  1    153    5
    AND BEG THEY'LL TAKE MY WORD ABOUT THE MORAL   .  .  . 141 2 DON JUAN  1    209    2
    AND BEG THEY'LL WAIT WITH PATIENCE FOR THE MORAL  .  .  . 141 2 DON JUAN  1    209  V2
    TO BEG THE BEGGAR WHO COULD NOT RAIN BACK   .  .  .  . 202 2 DON JUAN  2     86    5
    COULD HE NOT BEG THE LOAN OF CHARLES WAIN   .  .  .  . 333 2 DON JUAN  3     99    3
    AND BEG HIS BRITISH GODSHIP'S HUMBLE PARDON  .  .  .  . 442 3 DON JUAN 14     75    4
    ABOVE ALL I BEG ALL MEN TO FORBEAR .  .  .  .  .  . 454 3 DON JUAN 14     99    1
BEGAN
    WHICH PYE BEING OPEN'D THEY BEGAN TO SING   .  .  .  .  . 10  2 DON JUAN  D      2    1
    WHO CALL'D HER CHASTE METHINKS BEGAN TOO SOON  .  .  .  . 82  2 DON JUAN  1    113    3
    BEGAN AT ONCE TO SCREAM AND YAWN AND WEEP   .  .  .  . 97  2 DON JUAN  1    140    3
    AND BLOOD ('TWAS FROM THE NOSE) BEGAN TO FLOW  .  .  .  . 124 2 DON JUAN  1    186    3
    AT SUNSET THEY BEGAN TO TAKE IN SAIL   .  .  .  .  .  . 170 2 DON JUAN  2     26    6
    A REEF BETWEEN THEM ALSO NOW BEGAN .  .  .  .  .  .  . 211 2 DON JUAN  2    104    5
    AS WITH AN EFFORT SHE BEGAN TO SPEAK   .  .  .  .  .  . 236 2 DON JUAN  2    150    4
    THEIR BONDS WHENE'ER SOME ZEPHYR CAUGHT BEGAN  .  .  . 313 2 DON JUAN  3     73    7
    O'ERTHROWN EVEN MEN HE SOON BEGAN TO SHOW   .  .  .  . 417 2 DON JUAN  5     12    4
    RECEIPTS IN FULL BEGAN TO THINK OF DINING   .  .  .  . 426 2 DON JUAN  5     29    8
    BEGAN TO BLUSH UP TO THE EYES AND THEN   .  .  .  .  . 483 2 DON JUAN  5    124    7
    SO HE BEGAN TO STAMMER SOME EXCUSES  .  .  .  .  .  . 493 2 DON JUAN  5    143    1
    JUST AS A LANGUID SMILE BEGAN TO FLATTER .  .  .  .  . 493 2 DON JUAN  5    143    6
    BEGAN TO SING DANCE CHATTER SMILE AND PLAY   .  .  .  . 23  3 DON JUAN  6     34    8
    THAT JUST AS HER YOUNG LIP BEGAN TO OPE  .  .  .  .  . 44  3 DON JUAN  6     77    5
    BEGAN AS IS THE CONSEQUENCE OF FEAR  .  .  .  .  .  . 45  3 DON JUAN  6     79    2
    BEGAN TO CLOTHE EACH ASIATIC HILL  .  .  .  .  .  . 49  3 DON JUAN  6     86    3
    HER CHEEK BEGAN TO FLUSH HER EYES TO SPARKLE   .  .  . 56  3 DON JUAN  6    101    7
    AT LENGTH SHE ROSE UP AND BEGAN TO WALK  .  .  .  .  . 61  3 DON JUAN  6    110    5
```

```
                                                          PAGE VOL        CANTO STANZA LN
BEGAN   (CONTINUED)
  BEGAN TO SIGNALIZE THE RUSS RETREAT  . . . . . . . .  87  3 DON JUAN  7   42   2
  GLORY BEGAN TO DAWN WITH DUE SUBLIMITY  . . . . . . .  92  3 DON JUAN  7   51   6
  BUT HERE A SORT OF SCENE BEGAN TO ENSUE  . . . . . . 101  3 DON JUAN  7   67   1
  WHILE THEIR BELOVED FRIENDS BEGAN TO ARM . . . . . . 105  3 DON JUAN  7   76   7
  THICKER THAN LEAVES THE LIVES BEGAN TO FALL . . . . . 116  3 DON JUAN  8    9   3
  STILL CLOSER SULPHURY CLOUDS BEGAN TO SMOTHER . . . . 146  3 DON JUAN  8   69   6
  BEGAN TO LAY ABOUT WITH STEEL AND LEAD-- . . . . . . 152  3 DON JUAN  8   81   4
  AMBASSADORS BEGAN AS 'TWERE TO HUSTLE . . . . . . . . 223  3 DON JUAN  9   82   3
  JUST AS THE DAY BEGAN TO WANE AND DARKEN . . . . . . 264  3 DON JUAN 10   80   3
  BEGAN TO TREAT HIM WITH SOME SMALL AGACERIE . . . . . 428  3 DON JUAN 14   41   8
  THIS NOBLE PERSONAGE BEGAN TO LOOK . . . . . . . . . 429  3 DON JUAN 14   43   1
  BEGAN TO THINK THE DUCHESS' CONDUCT FREE . . . . . . 430  3 DON JUAN 14   46   4
  MORE FOES BY THIS SAME SCROLL WHEN I BEGAN IT I . . . 482  3 DON JUAN 15   60   6
  FROM ANSWERING SHE BEGAN TO QUESTION THIS . . . . . . 492  3 DON JUAN 15   81   1
  BEGAN TO DREAD SHE'D THAW TO A COQUETTE-- . . . . . . 492  3 DON JUAN 15   81   4
  AND BEING PRESENT NOW BEGAN TO EXPRESS . . . . . . . 514  3 DON JUAN 16   32   6
  AS TOUCHED AND PLAINTIVELY BEGAN TO PLAY . . . . . . 517  3 DON JUAN 16   38   7
  AND THEREFORE JUAN NOW BEGAN TO RALLY . . . . . . . . 526  3 DON JUAN 16   53   1
  OF WEARINESS OR SCORN) BEGAN TO FEEL . . . . . . . . 546  3 DON JUAN 16   96   7
  HIS OWN INTERNAL GHOST BEGAN TO AWAKEN . . . . . . . 558  3 DON JUAN 16  118   5
BEGGAR
  TO BEG THE BEGGAR WHO COULD NOT RAIN BACK . . . . . . 202  2 DON JUAN  2   86   5
  TO PROVE THEIR PRIDE AS FOOTMEN TO A BEGGAR . . . . . 537  3 DON JUAN 16   76   8
  A BEGGAR AND A QUEEN OR WAS (OF LATE . . . . . . . . 541  3 DON JUAN 16   84   2
BEGG'D
  ALFONSO CLOSED HIS SPEECH AND BEGG'D HER PARDON . . . 120  2 DON JUAN  1  180   1
  THAT BEGG'D PEDRILLO FOR AN ABSOLUTION . . . . . . . 179  2 DON JUAN  2   44   7
BEGGED
  AND BEGGED THEY WOULD EXCUSE HER SHE'D GET OVER . . .  47  3 DON JUAN  6   83   7
  TO PROVE RELUCTANT AND BEGGED LEAVE TO CRAVE . . . .  62  3 DON JUAN  6  112   5
  AND BEGGED BY EVERY HAIR OF MAHOMET'S BEARD . . . . .  62  3 DON JUAN  6  113   7
  BEGGED TO BRING UP THE LITTLE GIRL AND OUT-- . . . . 330  3 DON JUAN 12   31   3
BEGGING
  IN BEGGING HIM FOR GOD'S SAKE JUST TO SHOW . . . . . 165  3 DON JUAN  8  108   3
BEGIN
  MY WAY IS TO BEGIN WITH THE BEGINNING . . . . . . . .  25  2 DON JUAN  1    7   2
  YOU'D BEST BEGIN WITH TRUTH AND WHEN YOU'VE LOST YOUR  91  2 DON JUAN  1  128   7
  AT LEAST 'TWAS RATHER EARLY TO BEGIN . . . . . . . . 113  2 DON JUAN  1  167   4
  MY TEETH BEGIN TO CHATTER MY VEINS FREEZE-- . . . . . 121  2 DON JUAN  1  181   6
  IN HEALTH AND PURSE BEGIN YOUR DAY TO DATE . . . . . 230  2 DON JUAN  2  140   6
  SO COWPER SAYS--AND I BEGIN TO BE . . . . . . . . . . 142  3 DON JUAN  8   60   3
  WHEREFORE THE RAVISHING DID NOT BEGIN . . . . . . . . 178  3 DON JUAN  8  132   4
  TO END OR TO BEGIN WITH THE NEXT GRAND . . . . . . . 220  3 DON JUAN  9   76   2
  PREACH TO POOR ROUGES AND WHEREFORE NOT BEGIN . . . . 266  3 DON JUAN 10   85   2
  BUT I AM SICK OF POLITICS BEGIN . . . . . . . . . . . 327  3 DON JUAN 12   25   1
  (FRIENDS OF THE PARTY) WHO BEGIN ACCUSALS . . . . . . 332  3 DON JUAN 12   34   4
  BUT NOW I WILL BEGIN MY POEM--'TIS . . . . . . . . . 341  3 DON JUAN 12   54   1
  FIRSTLY BEGIN WITH THE BEGINNING--(THOUGH . . . . . . 393  3 DON JUAN 13   73   5
  UNLESS HER HABITS SHOULD BEGIN TO MEND . . . . . . . 432  3 DON JUAN 14   51   4
  YES I'LL BEGIN A THOROUGH REFORMATION . . . . . . . . 498  3 DON JUAN 15   94   4
BEGINNER
  THAT LURES TO FLAY ALIVE THE YOUNG BEGINNER . . . . . 294  2 DON JUAN  3   36   6
BEGINNERS
  MOST YOUNG BEGINNERS MAY BE TAKEN SO . . . . . . . . 345  3 DON JUAN 12   63  V5
  BUT THEY WHO BLUNDER THUS ARE RAW BEGINNERS . . . . . 346  3 DON JUAN 12   66   1
  AND YOUNG BEGINNERS MAY AS WELL COMMENCE . . . . . . 376  3 DON JUAN 13   40   1
  WHILE THOSE WHO ARE NOT BEGINNERS SHOULD HAVE SENSE . 376  3 DON JUAN 13   40   3
BEGINNING
  MY WAY IS TO BEGIN WITH THE BEGINNING . . . . . . . .  25  2 DON JUAN  1    7   2
  BEGINNING WITH FORMOSUM PASTOR CORYDON . . . . . . .  45  2 DON JUAN  1   42   8
  OF THE HUMANE SOCIETY'S BEGINNING . . . . . . . . . .  92  2 DON JUAN  1  130   4
  BEEN STOVE IN THE BEGINNING OF THE GALE . . . . . . . 181  2 DON JUAN  2   48   2
  AT LEAST IN THE BEGINNING ERE ONE TIRES . . . . . . . 282  2 DON JUAN  3   13   6
  NOTHING SO DIFFICULT AS A BEGINNING . . . . . . . . . 344  2 DON JUAN  4    1   1
  'TWAS A RAW DAY OF AUTUMN'S BLEAK BEGINNING . . . . . 414  2 DON JUAN  5    6   1
  WHICH THEY HIT OFF AT ONCE IN THE BEGINNING . . . . .  32  3 DON JUAN  6   52   6
  SELFISH IN ITS BEGINNING AS ITS END . . . . . . . . 219  3 DON JUAN  9   73   2
  OF EPIC LOVE'S BEGINNING END AND MIDDLE . . . . . . . 337  3 DON JUAN 12   45   8
  FIRSTLY BEGIN WITH THE BEGINNING--(THOUGH . . . . . . 393  3 DON JUAN 13   73   5
  IN THIS SORT END AT LEAST WITH THE BEGINNING . . . . 393  3 DON JUAN 13   73   8
BEGINNINGS
  BEGINNINGS ARE FAIR FACES ENDS MERE FISHES-- . . . . 349  3 DON JUAN 12   73   2
BEGINS
  ON A LEE SHORE TILL IT BEGINS TO BLOW-- . . . . . . . 345  3 DON JUAN 12   63   3
  BECAUSE INDIFFERENCE BEGINS TO LULL . . . . . . . . . 360  3 DON JUAN 13    4   5
BEGIRT
  'TIS BUILT BEGIRT WITH BATTERY AND TRENCH . . . . . .  71  3 DON JUAN  7    9  V4
BEGONE
  BEGONE SHE CRIED WITH KINDLING EYES--AND DO . . . . .  63  3 DON JUAN  6  116   2
BEGOT
  THAN JOSE WHO BEGOT OUR HERO WHO . . . . . . . . . .  26  2 DON JUAN  1    9   7
  BEGOT--BUT THAT'S TO COME--WELL TO RENEW . . . . . .  26  2 DON JUAN  1    9   8
  TO SAVE A SIRE WHO BLUSHED THAT HE BEGOT HIM . . . . 166  3 DON JUAN  8  110   8
BEGOTTEN
  OR SWEARS THAT CERES HATH BEGOTTEN FAMINE . . . . . .  88  3 DON JUAN  7   45   8
BEGUILED
  THEIR CHOICE THAN LIFE FORGIVE THEM AS BEGUILED . . . 143  3 DON JUAN  8   62   5
BEGUN
  BUT CLOSED THE TYRANT-HATER HE BEGUN . . . . . . . .  15  2 DON JUAN  D   10   8
```

68

		PAGE	VOL		CANTO	STANZA	LN

BEGUN   (CONTINUED)

I'M ALMOST SORRY THAT I E'ER BEGUN	83	2	DON JUAN	1	115	8
ALFONSO PAUSED A MINUTE--THEN BEGUN	116	2	DON JUAN	1	174	1
AND OTHERS WENT ON AS THEY HAD BEGUN	180	2	DON JUAN	2	45	5
BUT E'ER TWAS WELL BEGUN--A HEAVY SEA	183	2	DON JUAN	2	50	V2
WAS SERVED OUT TO THE PEOPLE WHO BEGUN	189	2	DON JUAN	2	62	6
AND MORE ROBUST OF FIGURE--THEN BEGUN	216	2	DON JJAN	2	115	4
RETURN WE TO DON JUAN HE BEGUN	244	2	DON JUAN	2	167	1
SMALL SOCIAL PARTIES JUST BEGUN TO DINE	291	2	DON JUAN	3	31	2
AND HE BEGUN A LONG LOW ISLAND SONG	379	2	DON JUAN	4	65	7
TURN'D TO THE MERCHANT AND BEGUN TO BID	425	2	DON JUAN	5	28	2
THERE HAVE BEEN AND ARE HEROES WHO BEGUN	122	3	DON JUAN	8	22	2
I ALMOST LATELY HAVE BEGUN TO DOUBT	124	3	DON JUAN	8	26	1
I'VE NOT BEGUN WHAT WE HAVE TO GO THROUGH	341	3	DON JUAN	12	54	4
ENDS WHEN THE BODY OF THE BOOK'S BEGUN	356	3	DON JUAN	12	87	2
THE MAN WAS WELL-NIGH DEAD ERE MEN BEGUN	565	3	DON JUAN	17	8	5

BEHALF

| IN ITS BEHALF LET THOSE DENY WHO WILL | 504 | 3 | DON JUAN | 16 | 7 | 8 |

BEHAVE

| MAY TEACH US BETTER TO BEHAVE WHEN MASTERS | 422 | 2 | DON JUAN | 5 | 23 | 8 |

BEHAVED

JUST NOW BEHAVED AS IN THE HOLY LAND	116	3	DON JUAN	8	9	8
HE HAD BEHAVED WITH COURAGE AND HUMANITY--	182	3	DON JUAN	8	140	2
BEHAVED NO BETTER THAN A COMMON SEMPSTRESS	221	3	DON JUAN	9	77	8

BEHAVIOUR

| AND PUT HIMSELF UPON HIS GOOD BEHAVIOUR | 437 | 2 | DON JUAN | 5 | 47 | 5 |

BEHELD

BEHELD HIS NATIVE SPAIN RECEDING FAR	164	2	DON JUAN	2	14	2
AS RARELY THEY BEHELD THROUGHOUT THEIR ROUND	352	2	DON JUAN	4	16	3
WHERE I BEHELD WHAT NEVER WAS TO BE	413	2	DON JUAN	5	4	4
YET SMELT ROAST-MEAT BEHELD A HUGE FIRE SHINE	439	2	DON JUAN	5	50	5
WHEN HE BEHELD HIS LATEST HERO GRACE	169	3	DON JUAN	8	116	5
THE SOLDIERS WHO BEHELD HIM DROP HIS POINT	170	3	DON JUAN	8	117	1
AS THEY BEHELD THE YOUNGER CAST SOME LEERS	221	3	DON JUAN	9	78	4
ALREADY THEY BEHELD THE SILVER SHOWERS	222	3	DON JUAN	9	79	5
NO MORE TO BE BEHELD BUT IN SUCH VISIONS--	523	3	DON JUAN	16	46	7
BEHELD BETWEEN THE COUNTRY AND THE TOWN	541	3	DON JUAN	16	85	3

BEHMEN

| NOT ALL THE REVERIES OF JACOB BEHMEN | 7 | 3 | DON JUAN | 6 | 2 | 5 |

BEHOLD

IT WAS SUCH PLEASURE TO BEHOLD HIM SUCH	247	2	DON JUAN	2	173	1
THE SIGHTS HE WAS ACCUSTOM'D TO BEHOLD	303	2	DON JUAN	3	54	5
'TWAS TREASON TO BEHOLD HER AND NOT KNEEL	313	2	DON JUAN	3	74	V8
THE SPARKLING GEMS BENEATH YOU MIGHT BEHOLD	315	2	DON JUAN	3	77	3
ERE WHAT WE LEAST WISH TO BEHOLD WILL SLEEP	346	2	DON JUAN	4	4	6
SIGH'D TO BEHOLD THEM OF THEIR HOURS BEREFT	348	2	DON JUAN	4	8	5
BREAK WITH THE FIRST FALL THEY CAN NE'ER BEHOLD	350	2	DON JUAN	4	11	4
THOSE EYES SO BEAUTIFUL--BEHOLD NO MORE	376	2	DON JUAN	4	59	V2
WITH NO GREAT VOICE IS PLEASING TO BEHOLD	389	2	DON JUAN	4	83	5
MORE TENDER AS WE EVERY DAY BEHOLD	439	2	DON JUAN	5	49	6
WHEN THEY BEHOLD THE BRAVE OPPRESSED WITH ODDS	164	3	DON JUAN	8	106	2
BEHOLD THE WORLD AND CURSE YOUR VICTORIES	187	3	DON JUAN	9	9	8
BEHOLD HIM PLACED AS IF UPON A PILLAR HE	204	3	DON JUAN	9	44	7
BEHOLD HIM PLACED IN YOUTH AND GLORY'S PILLORY	204	3	DON JUAN	9	44	V7
THE LAWYER AND THE CRITIC BUT BEHOLD	232	3	DON JUAN	10	14	1
PLAIN SIMPLE FORNICATION--NOR BEHOLD	314	3	DON JUAN	11	V 76	2
ADVANCES OR REPULSES THEY BEHOLD	366	3	DON JUAN	13	17	V8
BUT FAIR AS THEN OR FAIRER TO BEHOLD	409	3	DON JUAN	13	110	6
THEIR UNION WAS A MODEL TO BEHOLD	447	3	DON JUAN	14	86	7
HOW DIFFERENTLY THE WORLD WOULD MEN BEHOLD	455	3	DON JUAN	14	101	4
SHEPHERD OR SWAIN WHOEVER MAY BEHOLD	506	3	DON JUAN	16	14	2
WERE SOMETHING VERY GLORIOUS TO BEHOLD	538	3	DON JUAN	16	78	4

BEHOLDER

| SO THAT THE PHILOSOPHICAL BEHOLDER | 292 | 2 | DON JUAN | 3 | 33 | 7 |

BEHOLDERS

| THEY PUT BEHOLDERS IN A TENDER TAKING | 27 | 3 | DON JUAN | 6 | 43 | 4 |
| WHICH LEADS BEHOLDERS ON A BOGGY WALK | 89 | 3 | DON JUAN | 7 | 46 | 6 |

BEHOLDING

| INTO EACH OTHER--AND BEHOLDING THIS | 253 | 2 | DON JUAN | 2 | 185 | 7 |

BEHOLDS

| THE WHILE THE WICKED WORLD BEHOLDS DELIGHTED | 75 | 2 | DON JUAN | 1 | 100 | 3 |
| BEHOLDS HER OWN SHY SHADOWY IMAGE PASS | 36 | 3 | DON JUAN | 6 | 60 | 6 |

BEING

WHICH PYE BEING OPEN'D THEY BEGAN TO SING	10	2	DON JUAN	D	2	1
AT BEING DISAPPOINTED IN YOUR WISH	10	2	DON JUAN	D	3	2
BEING ONLY INJURED BY HIS OWN ASSERTION	14	2	DON JUAN	D	9	4
OR BEING MOUNTED E'ER GOT DOWN AGAIN	26	2	DON JUAN	1	9	6
INSTEAD OF BEING SCATTER'D THROUGH THE PAGES	46	2	DON JUAN	1	45	2
AS BEING THE BEST JUDGE OF A LADY'S CASE	62	2	DON JUAN	1	75	8
JUAN BEING THEN GROWN UP TO MAN'S ESTATE	67	2	DON JUAN	1	85	2
HIS TEMPER NOT BEING UNDER GREAT COMMAND	123	2	DON JUAN	1	185	4
BUT I BEING FOND OF TRUE PHILOSOPHY	147	2	DON JUAN	1	220	1
AND SERVING HIM THE MORE BY BEING SO	151	2	DON JUAN	1	V 2	8
HIS HEADACHE BEING INCREASED BY EVERY BILLOW	169	2	DON JUAN	2	25	6
GETTING THE BOATS OUT BEING WELL AWARE	180	2	DON JUAN	2	45	6
BUT BEING THIRSTIEST AT THE MOMENT HE	197	2	DON JUAN	2	77	3
BESIDES BEING MUCH AVERSE FROM SUCH A FATE	199	2	DON JUAN	2	81	3
WITHOUT BEING MUCH MORE HORRIBLE THAN DANTE	200	2	DON JUAN	2	83	8
BUT BEING NAKED SHE WAS SHOCK'D YOU KNOW	224	2	DON JUAN	2	129	5

69

BEING   (CONTINUED)

	PAGE	VOL	CANTO		STANZA	LN
SHE BEING WISER BY A YEAR OR TWO	228	2 DON JUAN	2	136	4
HAD ALL THE ADVANTAGE TOO OF NOT BEING AIR	232	2 DON JUAN	2	142	8
BESIDES BEING LESS IN LOVE SHE YAWN'D A LITTLE	233	2 DON JUAN	2	145	3
BEING NO GRECIAN BUT HE HAD AN EAR	236	2 DON JUAN	2	151	2
BECAUSE 'TIS LIQUOR ONLY AND BEING FAR	238	2 DON JUAN	2	156	3
BUT ZOE BEING OLDER THAN HAIDEE	239	2 DON JUAN	2	158	5
NEXT THEY--HE BEING NAKED SAVE A TATTER'D	240	2 DON JUAN	2	160	1
IS PLEASANT BESIDES BEING TRUE LOVE'S ESSENCE	245	2 DON JUAN	2	169	4
TO HER AS 'TWERE THE KIND OF BEING SENT	247	2 DON JUAN	2	172	3
SO THAT HER FATHER BEING AT SEA SHE WAS	248	2 DON JUAN	2	175	2
MAN BEING REASONABLE MUST GET DRUNK	250	2 DON JUAN	2	179	1
AND FORTH THEY WANDER'D HER SIRE BEING GONE	252	2 DON JUAN	2	182	1
WHICH BEING JOIN'D LIKE SWARMING BEES THEY CLUNG--	254	2 DON JUAN	2	187	7
HAD RUN THE RISK OF BEING DAMN'D FOR EVER	258	2 DON JUAN	2	193	4
AND HAIDEE BEING DEVOUT AS WELL AS FAIR	258	2 DON JUAN	2	193	5
THEIRS BEING AN UNNATURAL SITUATION	263	2 DON JUAN	2	201	6
AND YET LAST NIGHT BEING AT A MASQUERADE	268	2 DON JUAN	2	209	6
THAT BEING ABOUT THE NUMBER I'LL ALLOW	271	2 DON JUAN	2	216	4
MEN GROW ASHAMED OF BEING SO VERY FOND	278	2 DON JUAN	3	7	1
TOSSED OVERBOARD UNSALEABLE (BEING OLD)	284	2 DON JUAN	3	16	4
BUT THAT PART OF THE COAST BEING SHOAL AND BARE	285	2 DON JUAN	3	19	6
OF THE TRUE REASON OF HIS NOT BEING SAD	289	2 DON JUAN	3	26	5
THE CAUSE BEING PAST HIS GUESSING OR UNRIDDLING	290	2 DON JUAN	3	28	6
HE--BEING A MAN WHO SELDOM USED A WORD	294	2 DON JUAN	3	37	1
HER TEARS TOO BEING RETURN'D INTO THEIR FOUNT	295	2 DON JUAN	3	38	7
THESE RASCALS BEING NEW COMERS KNEW NOT WHOM	298	2 DON JUAN	3	44	1
THEIR FURY BEING SPENT BY ITS OWN SHOCK	305	2 DON JUAN	3	58	6
HE BEING PAID TO SATIRISE OR FLATTER	316	2 DON JUAN	3	78	7
HIS POLAR STAR BEING ONE WHICH RATHER RANGES	317	2 DON JUAN	3	80	3
AND BEING FLUENT (SAVE INDEED WHEN FEE'D ILL)	317	2 DON JUAN	3	80	6
BUT NOW BEING LIFTED INTO HIGH SOCIETY	318	2 DON JUAN	3	83	1
HE DEEM'D BEING IN A LONE ISLE AMONG FRIENDS	318	2 DON JUAN	3	83	4
HIMSELF FROM BEING AS PLIABLE AS PINDAR	319	2 DON JUAN	3	85	8
AN INDEPENDENT BEING IN HIS DAY--	328	2 DON JUAN	3	91	3
'TIS BEING TOO EPIC AND I MUST CUT DOWN	342	2 DON JUAN	3	111	2
BEING PRIDE WHICH LEADS THE MIND TO SOAR TOO FAR	344	2 DON JUAN	4	1	7
BUT ALL THESE SAME THE LAST BEING OBSOLETE	347	2 DON JUAN	4	6	7
STRANGE STATE OF BEING (FOR 'TIS STILL TO BE)	360	2 DON JUAN	4	30	7
SHE DREAM'D OF BEING ALONE ON THE SEA-SHORE	361	2 DON JUAN	4	31	1
BUT AFTER BEING FIRED AT ONCE OR TWICE	366	2 DON JUAN	4	41	7
SHE RECOGNISED NO BEING AND NO SPOT	379	2 DON JUAN	4	64	3
TO BE SO BEING IN A GUSHING STREAM	380	2 DON JUAN	4	66	6
BUT CLOSED ITS LITTLE BEING WITHOUT LIGHT	382	2 DON JUAN	4	70	4
BUT BEING QUALIFIED IN ONE WAY YET	391	2 DON JUAN	4	86	3
BUT BEING THE PRIMA-DONNA'S NEAR RELATION	391	2 DON JUAN	4	87	5
THEY LEFT THIS BEING FREE AND NEUTRAL AS A SCOUT	394	2 DON JUAN	4	92	V5
HER CARGO FROM THE PLAGUE BEING SAFE AND SOUND	407	2 DON JUAN	4	113	5
BEING PIQUED BY CRITICS WHO HAVE DONE ME WRONG	410	2 DON JUAN	4	117	V5
EUROPE AND ASIA YOU BEING QUITE AT EASE	413	2 DON JUAN	5	5	6
THEY LOOKED LIKE PERSONS BEING LED TO SENTENCE	432	2 DON JUAN	5	40	5
THERE BEING NO SUCH PROFUSION IN THE NORTH	434	2 DON JUAN	5	42	4
BUT NO ONE EVER DREAMS OF BEING SHORT--	437	2 DON JUAN	5	48	8
WAS ON THE POINT OF BEING SET ASIDE	440	2 DON JUAN	5	51	4
AS NOT BEING IN A MASQUERADING MOOD	453	2 DON JUAN	5	73	5
HIS GARMENT'S NOVELTY AND HIS BEING AWKWARD	456	2 DON JUAN	5	78	2
AND NOW BEING FEMININELY ALL ARRAYED	458	2 DON JUAN	5	80	1
THE HINGES BEING AS SMOOTH AS ROGERS' RHYMES	463	2 DON JUAN	5	89	4
BEING A TRUE WOMAN IN A STATE OF NATURE	476	2 DON JUAN	5	113	V7
WHEN BEING MADE HER PROPERTY AT LAST	478	2 DON JUAN	5	116	4
FELT MOST INDIGNANT STILL AT NOT BEING FREE	481	2 DON JUAN	5	121	8
THAT BEING THE LAST THING A PROUD WOMAN TRIES	483	2 DON JUAN	5	125	6
EARTH BEING ONLY MADE FOR QUEENS AND KINGS	485	2 DON JUAN	5	128	4
THOUGH HE DESERVED IT WELL FOR BEING SO BACKWARD	492	2 DON JUAN	5	140	6
FOR BEING THE LAST WIFE OF THE EMPEROR	495	2 DON JUAN	5	146	7
HER REASON BEING WEAK HER PASSIONS STRONG	10	3 DON JUAN	6	8	5
IT BEING (NOT NOW BUT ONLY WHILE A LAD)	19	3 DON JUAN	6	27	6
THE GIANT THOUGHT OF BEING A TITAN'S BRIDE	20	3 DON JUAN	6	28	4
THEIR GUARDS BEING GONE AND AS IT WERE A TRUCE	23	3 DON JUAN	6	34	6
BEING SOMEWHAT LARGE AND LANGUISHING AND LAZY	26	3 DON JUAN	6	41	7
AS IF SHE PITIED HER FOR BEING THERE	28	3 DON JUAN	6	45	4
BUT BEING NO ORATOR AS BRUTUS IS	43	3 DON JUAN	6	74	7
BUT ENDED IN HIS BEING FOUND OUT AND SACKED	58	3 DON JUAN	6	104	6
NOW I SHOULD LIKE TO KNOW BEING RATHER CURIOUS	77	3 DON JUAN	7	21	V1
THIS BEING THE CASE MAY SHOW US WHAT FAME IS	82	3 DON JUAN	7	33	1
THIS FELLOW BEING SIX FOOT HIGH COULD RAISE	84	3 DON JUAN	7	37	5
AND EVERY DIFFICULTY BEING DISPELLED	92	3 DON JUAN	7	51	5
MY DEBT IN BEING THUS ALLOWED TO DIE	100	3 DON JUAN	7	65	5
BEING MUCH TOO GROSS TO SEE THEM IN DETAIL	105	3 DON JUAN	7	77	2
BEING GRENADIERS THEY MOUNTED ONE BY ONE	119	3 DON JUAN	8	15	5
THE LIGHTEST BEING THE SAFEST AT A DISTANCE	140	3 DON JUAN	8	55	7
THEY KNEW NOT WHERE BEING CARRIED BY THE STREAM	148	3 DON JUAN	8	72	2
THE CITY WITHOUT BEING FURTHER HAMPER'D	149	3 DON JUAN	8	75	4
THEN BEING TAKEN BY THE TAIL--A TAKING	150	3 DON JUAN	8	76	1
THEN BEING TAKEN BY THE TAIL--A-MODE	150	3 DON JUAN	8	76	V1
BUT COULD NOT EAT THEM BEING IN HIS TURN	150	3 DON JUAN	8	77	2
BEFORE BEING BADLY SECONDED JUST THEN)	151	3 DON JUAN	8	79	3
AS BEING A VIRTUE LIKE TERRESTRIAL PATIENCE	165	3 DON JUAN	8	107	7
AND BEING TOLD THE LATTER SENT A BEY	171	3 DON JUAN	8	120	7

	PAGE	VOL		CANTO	STANZA	LN
BEING (CONTINUED)						
SUCH TALES BEING FOR THE TEA HOURS OF SOME TABBY	184	3	DON JUAN	9	2	6
MAY LIKE BEING PRAISED FOR EVERY LUCKY BLUNDER	185	3	DON JUAN	9	5	6
YOU DID GREAT THINGS BUT NOT BEING GREAT IN MIND	187	3	DON JUAN	9	10	7
I SHOULD BE GLAD TO KNOW THAT WHICH IS BEING	190	3	DON JUAN	9	16	2
THE CONSEQUENCE IS BEING OF NO PARTY	195	3	DON JUAN	9	26	1
(AS BEING THE BRAVE LIONS' KEEN PROVIDERS)	196	3	DON JUAN	9	27	7
MILD CATHERINE OWED THE CHANCE OF BEING CROWN'D	205	3	DON JUAN	9	46	V4
WHICH BEING THE DAMN'DEST PART OF MATRIMONY	217	3	DON JUAN	9	70	7
ON OUR FRESH FEELINGS BUT--AS BEING PARTICIPATED	236	3	DON JUAN	10	23	5
AS THE SOLE SIGN OF MAN'S BEING IN HIS SENSES	240	3	DON JUAN	10	31	7
AND BEING TOLD IT WAS GOD'S HOUSE SHE SAID	262	3	DON JUAN	10	75	1
TO SET UP VAIN PRETENCES OF BEING GREAT	267	3	DON JUAN	10	87	3
OF BEING STARS AND THIS UNRIDDLED WONDER	269	3	DON JUAN	11	3	7
BEING QUITE PERSPICUOUS AND EXTREMELY FAIR	270	3	DON JUAN	11	5	4
AND BEING SOMEWHAT CHOLERIC AND SUDDEN	274	3	DON JUAN	11	13	2
THROUGH GROVES SO CALLED AS BEING VOID OF TREES	278	3	DON JUAN	11	21	1
IN THE GREAT WORLD--WHICH BEING INTERPRETED	290	3	DON JUAN	11	45	1
THAT BEING ABOUT THEIR AVERAGE NUMERAL	295	3	DON JUAN	11	54	6
SETS UP FOR BEING A SORT OF MORAL ME	298	3	DON JUAN	11	59	2
BEING TIRED IN TIME AND NEITHER LEAST NOR LAST	300	3	DON JUAN	11	64	4
CHANGE GROWS TOO CHANGEABLE WITHOUT BEING NEW	309	3	DON JUAN	11	82	6
FOR BEING TOO EXCURSIVE IN HIS HOMAGES--	312	3	DON JUAN	11	89	8
FOR BEING AS MUCH THE SUBJECT OF ATTACK	312	3	DON JUAN	11	90	4
AND AS FOR HEAVEN BEING LOVE WHY NOT SAY HONEY	322	3	DON JUAN	12	14	7
AMONGST THE PATHS OF BEING TAKEN IN	327	3	DON JUAN	12	25	3
OF BEING APT TO TALK AT A GREAT RATE	329	3	DON JUAN	12	28	6
WHO MIGHT NOT PROFIT MUCH BY BEING AT LARGE	335	3	DON JUAN	12	41	8
FOR BEING A MOST EXEMPLARY WIFE	338	3	DON JUAN	12	47	8
BEING LONG MARRIED AND THUS SET AT LARGE	339	3	DON JUAN	12	51	4
IT DOES NOR GOOD NOR HARM BEING MERELY MEANT	342	3	DON JUAN	12	57	4
OF BEING WITHOUT ALLOY OF FOP OR BEAU	354	3	DON JUAN	12	84	7
JUST TO CONSOLE SAD GLORY FOR BEING GLORIOUS	372	3	DON JUAN	13	32	8
BUT FROM BEING FARMERS WE TURN GLEANERS GLEANING	403	3	DON JUAN	13	96	1
WITHOUT THE APPAREL OF BEING CIRCUMSPECT	434	3	DON JUAN	14	56	4
WHOSE VIRTUE LIES IN NEVER BEING DETECTED	437	3	DON JUAN	14	61	8
HER GRACE TOO PASS'D FOR BEING AN INTRIGANTE	438	3	DON JUAN	14	63	1
AND BEING OF THE COUNCIL CALLED THE PRIVY	440	3	DON JUAN	14	68	1
AND BEING CONSUMPTIVE LIVE ON A MILK DIET	474	3	DON JUAN	15	41	8
A LOVELY BEING SCARCELY FORM'D OR MOULDED	475	3	DON JUAN	15	43	7
AGAINST HER BEING MENTION'D AS WELL FITTED	477	3	DON JUAN	15	48	6
BEING NO SIBYL IN THE NEW WORLD'S WAYS	480	3	DON JUAN	15	56	6
HALF VIRTUES AND WHOLE VICES BEING COMBINED	480	3	DON JUAN	15	57	4
AT RISK OF BEING QUIZZED FOR SUPERSTITION	512	3	DON JUAN	16	28	4
AND BEING PRESENT NOW BEGAN TO EXPRESS	514	3	DON JUAN	16	32	6
PALE AS IF PAINTED SO HER CHEEK BEING RED	532	3	DON JUAN	16	64	2
BACCHUS AND CERES BEING AS WE KNOW	542	3	DON JUAN	16	86	4
THE SUPPLICATOR BEING AN AMATEUR	543	3	DON JUAN	16	89	2
THE NIGHT BEFORE BUT BEING SICK OF SHAKING	558	3	DON JUAN	16	118	2
AT WHATSOEVER RISK OF BEING DEFEATED	559	3	DON JUAN	16	119	6
BEING WAN AND WORN WITH EYES THAT HARDLY BROOKED	568	3	DON JUAN	17	14	4
BEINGS						
LIKE HUMAN BEINGS DURING CIVIL WAR	178	2	DON JUAN	2	42	8
THUS THE FRAIL BEINGS WE WOULD FONDLY CHERISH	275	2	DON JUAN	3	2	7
BUT TIME WHICH BRINGS ALL BEINGS TO THEIR LEVEL	345	2	DON JUAN	4	2	1
BUT LIKE TWO BEINGS BORN FROM OUT A RILL	352	2	DON JUAN	4	15	5
FOR BEINGS PASSIONATE AS SAPPHO'S SONG	358	2	DON JUAN	4	27	6
AS HUMAN BEINGS OR HIS WAYS ARE ODD	163	3	DON JUAN	8	104	4
AS RARE IN LIVING BEINGS AS A FOSSILE	250	3	DON JUAN	10	52	3
BELEAGUER'D						
AND WAS BELEAGUER'D BOTH BY LAND AND WATER	70	3	DON JUAN	7	8	6
BELIE						
HE DEIGN'D NOT TO BELIE HIS SOUL IN SONGS	15	2	DON JUAN	0	10	5
BELIEF						
LIKE MOST IN THE BELIEF IN WHICH THEY'RE BRED	197	2	DON JUAN	2	76	6
BEYOND A SINGLE GENTLEMAN'S BELIEF	301	2	DON JUAN	3	51	8
FOR CERTAIN REASONS MY BELIEF IS SERIOUS	498	3	DON JUAN	15	95	8
'GAINST SUCH BELIEF THERE'S SOMETHING STRONGER STILL	504	3	DON JUAN	16	7	7
BELIEVE						
THEY BLUSH AND WE BELIEVE THEM AT LEAST I	119	2	DON JUAN	1	179	1
THOU SHALT BELIEVE IN MILTON DRYDEN POPE	139	2	DON JUAN	1	205	1
NOT TO BELIEVE MY VERSE AND THEIR OWN EYES	141	2	DON JUAN	1	208	4
AND IF AS I BELIEVE THY VEIN BE GOOD	149	2	DON JUAN	1	222	3
THEY HIRED HIM THOUGH TO HEAR HIM YOU'D BELIEVE	391	2	DON JUAN	4	87	7
I SCARCELY COULD BELIEVE THAT HE WAS DEAD	432	2	DON JUAN	5	39	V4
BELIEVE THE JEWS THOSE UNBELIEVERS WHO	447	2	DON JUAN	5	62	7
MUST BE BELIEVED THOUGH THEY BELIEVE NOT YOU	447	2	DON JUAN	5	62	8
ARE VERY SILENT WHEN THEY ONCE BELIEVE	94	3	DON JUAN	7	54	5
HE NEVER WOULD BELIEVE THE CITY WON	164	3	DON JUAN	8	105	4
YOU HARDLY WILL BELIEVE SUCH THINGS WERE TRUE	180	3	DON JUAN	8	136	3
MAKES US BELIEVE OURSELVES AS GOOD AS ANY	216	3	DON JUAN	9	68	8
BELIEVE THAT VIRTUE THAWED BEFORE THE RIVER	241	3	DON JUAN	10	33	8
AND YET WHO CAN BELIEVE IT I WOULD SHATTER	268	3	DON JUAN	11	1	5
ON PURPOSE TO BELIEVE SO MUCH THE MORE	271	3	DON JUAN	11	6	8
VIRTUOUS SHE WAS--AND HAD BEEN I BELIEVE	336	3	DON JUAN	12	43	2
WHICH THOSE MOST SWEAR TO WHO BELIEVE THEM MOST)--	383	3	DON JUAN	13	53	3
WOULD SOME BELIEVE THAT SUCH A TALE HAD BEEN	444	3	DON JUAN	14	80	4
SO THAT I VERILY BELIEVE IF THEY	466	3	DON JUAN	15	23	2
I SAY I DO BELIEVE A HAUNTED SPOT	499	3	DON JUAN	15	96	3

71

BELIEVE (CONTINUED)
    THE SCEPTICS WHO WOULD NOT BELIEVE COLUMBUS 502   3 DON JUAN 16   4   8
    WHO BIDS ALL MEN BELIEVE THE IMPOSSIBLE 503   3 DON JUAN 16   5   6
    BELIEVE--IF 'TIS IMPROBABLE YOU MUST 503   3 DON JUAN 16   6   2
BELIEVED
    AND NE'ER BELIEVED IN NEGATIVES TILL THESE 109   2 DON JUAN 1   160   7
    SHE HOPED HE WOULD IMPROVE--PERHAPS BELIEVED 161   2 DON JUAN 2   9   6
    MORE THAN CAN BE BELIEVED OR EVEN THOUGHT 191   2 DON JUAN 2   66   3
    BELIEVED LIKE SOUTHEY--AND PERUSED LIKE CRASHAW 316   2 DON JUAN 3   79   V8
    MUST BE BELIEVED THOUGH THEY BELIEVE NOT YOU 447   2 DON JUAN 5   62   8
    SOME NE'ER BELIEVED ONE HALF OF WHAT THEY HEARD 429   3 DON JUAN 14   44   5
    ALL NATIONS HAVE BELIEVED THAT FROM THE DEAD 504   3 DON JUAN 16   7   3
    FOR SUCH SIGHTS THOUGH THE TALE IS HALF BELIEVED 516   3 DON JUAN 16   36   7
BELIEVER
    WHICH DOTH YOUR TRUE BELIEVER SO MUCH PLEASE 17   3 DON JUAN 6   23   3
BELIEVERS
    TO SEE THEM TRUE BELIEVERS BUT NO LESS 452   2 DON JUAN 5   70   2
    THE TRUE BELIEVERS--AND HER INFANT BROW 262   3 DON JUAN 10   75   6
BELIEVING
    AND TURN'D BELIEVING THAT HE CALL'D AGAIN 228   2 DON JUAN 2   135   4
BELISARIUS
    CAESAR AND POMPEY MAHOMET BELISARIUS 266   2 DON JUAN 2   206   3
BELL
    THE CHIMNEY--WOULD IT PLEASE YOU RING THE BELL 104   2 DON JUAN 1   153   V4
    OR IN THE DESERT HEARD THE CAMEL'S BELL 201   2 DON JUAN 2   84   7
    THE LITTLE BOATMAN AND HIS PETER BELL 334   2 DON JUAN 3   100   7
    WHILE SWUNG THE DEEP BELL IN THE DISTANT TOWER 335   2 DON JUAN 3   102   5
    AS THE FAR BELL OF VESPER MAKES HIM START 338   2 DON JUAN 3   108   5
    THE TOCSIN OF THE SOUL--THE DINNER BELL 439   2 DON JUAN 5   49   8
    WHICH KNITS SOCIETY--THE DINNER BELL 439   2 DON JUAN 5   49   V8
    WHEN ALL AROUND RANG LIKE A TOCSIN BELL 48   3 DON JUAN 6   84   4
    THY WAITERS RUNNING MUCKS AT EVERY BELL 259   3 DON JUAN 10   69   4
    THE SILVERY BELL RUNG NOT FOR DINNER READY 482   3 DON JUAN 15   61   6
    NO MORE ON THIS--THE DINNER BELL HATH RUNG 538   3 DON JUAN 16   77   7
BELLA
    (AND OTHER CHIEF POINTS OF A BELLA DONNA) 395   2 DON JUAN 4   94   4
BELLE
    PRESCRIBED BY WAY OF BLISTER A YOUNG BELLE 113   2 DON JUAN 1   168   4
    TO SAVE HIS FAME WITH EACH ACCOMPLISHED BELLE 295   3 DON JUAN 11   53   5
    LA BELLE ALLIANCE OF DUNCES DOWN AT ZERO 296   3 DON JUAN 11   56   3
    OMNIA VULT BELLE MATHO DICERE--DIC ALIQUANDO 465   3 DON JUAN 15   21   1
BELLI
    OH THOU TETERRIMA CAUSA OF ALL BELLI-- 210   3 DON JUAN 9   55   1
BELLIES
    CERES IS COMMISSARY TO OUR BELLIES 246   2 DON JUAN 2   170   V3
BELL-MOUTHED
    HIS BELL-MOUTHED GOBLET MAKES ME FEEL QUITE DANISH . . . 392   3 DON JUAN 13   72   7
BELLONA
    BELLONA SHOOK HER SPEAR WITH SUCH SUBLIMITY 92   3 DON JUAN 7   51   V6
    BELLONA WHAT YOU WILL--THEY MEAN BUT WARS 112   3 DON JUAN 8   1   8
BELLOW
    YET STILL THEY DEIGN'D TO HICCUP OR TO BELLOW 318   2 DON JUAN 3   82   6
    AND FOR THE BASS THE BEAST CAN ONLY BELLOW 391   2 DON JUAN 4   87   2
BELL'S
    AND VESPER BELL'S THAT ROSE THE BOUGHS ALONG 337   2 DON JUAN 3   106   4
BELLS
    TURKEY CONTAINS NO BELLS AND YET MEN DINE 439   2 DON JUAN 5   50   1
    IN LIKE CHURCH BELLS WITH SIGH HOWL GROAN YELL PRAYER . . 141   3 DON JUAN 8   58   7
    A FOOL WHOSE BELLS HAVE CEASED TO RING AT ALL-- . . . 267   3 DON JUAN 10   86   8
BELL-WETHER
    OR A BELL-WETHER FORM THE FLOCK'S CONNECTION 90   3 DON JUAN 7   48   6
BELONG
    SUCH KISSES AS BELONG TO EARLY DAYS 254   2 DON JUAN 2   186   4
    TO THEE BOTH OH AND AH BELONG OF RIGHT 215   3 DON JUAN 9   65   2
BELONGS
    WHOSE TALE BELONGS TO HALLAM'S MIDDLE AGES 330   3 DON JUAN 12   30   8
BELOVED
    WAS NEITHER MUCH BELOVED NOR YET ABHORR'D 57   2 DON JUAN 1   65   3
    BELOVED AND LOVING MANY ALL IS O'ER 132   2 DON JUAN 1   195   2
    BELOVED JULIA HEAR ME STILL BESEECHING 167   2 DON JUAN 2   20   7
    SHE LOVED AND WAS BELOVED--SHE ADORED 257   2 DON JUAN 2   191   1
    FOR THERE IT LIES SO TRANQUIL SO BELOVED 261   2 DON JUAN 2   197   1
    ON THAT BELOVED DAUGHTER SHE HAD BEEN 304   2 DON JUAN 3   57   2
    HAIDEE AND HER BELOVED HID THEIR FEET 309   2 DON JUAN 3   67   V1
    A NYMPH AND HER BELOVED ALL UNSEEN 352   2 DON JUAN 4   15   4
    BELOVED IN HER OWN WAY AND RATHER WHISK 7   3 DON JUAN 6   3   4
    BELOVED AND DEPLORED WHILE SLOWLY STRAYED 40   3 DON JUAN 6   67   6
    WHILE THEIR BELOVED FRIENDS BEGAN TO ARM 105   3 DON JUAN 7   76   7
BELSHAZZAR
    THE WORDS WHICH SHOOK BELSHAZZAR IN HIS HALL 308   2 DON JUAN 3   65   5
BELT
    AND DRAWING FROM HIS BELT A PISTOL HE 365   2 DON JUAN 4   40   4
    THAT STRETCHES TO THE STONY BELT WHICH GIRDS 49   3 DON JUAN 6   86   7
    AT THE FIRST SIGHT OF ALBION'S CHALKY BELT-- 257   3 DON JUAN 10   65   4
BENCH
    THE BENCH TOO SEATS OR SUITS FULL MANY A DEBTOR . . . 280   3 DON JUAN 11   25   5
    THE LAW AT LEAST UNTIL THE BENCH REVERT TO TRUE . . . 314   3 DON JUAN 11   V 76   6
BENCHES
    ARE PUZZLES TO THE MOST PRECAUTIOUS BENCHES 531   3 DON JUAN 16   63   8

```
                                                        PAGE VOL      CANTO STANZA LN
BEND
    WOULD JUAN BEND THOUGH 'TWERE TO MAHOMET'S BRIDE  . . . . . 471  2 DON JUAN  5    103   5
    ABOUT HIS EARS AND NATHLESS WOULD NOT BEND  . .  . . . . . 471  2 DON JUAN  5    104   2
    HEADS BOW KNEES BEND EYES WATCH AROUND A THRONE  . . . . . 484  2 DON JUAN  5    127   7
    IN PROSE I BEND MY HUMBLE VERSE) DOTH CALL  . . . . . . . 163  3 DON JUAN  8    104   7
BENDED
    WHAT ALL THIS MEANT WHILE BABA BOWED AND BENDED  . . . . 466  2 DON JUAN  5     95   7
BENDER
    AS OBSTINATE AS SWEDISH CHARLES AT BENDER  . . . . . . . 165  3 DON JUAN  8    107   4
BENDING
    'TWAS BENDING CLOSE O'ER HIS AND THE SMALL MOUTH  . . . . 215  2 DON JUAN  2    113   1
    HER HAND ON HIS AND BENDING ON HIM EYES  . . . . . . . . 483  2 DON JUAN  5    125   2
    THEIR PLATES--WITHOUT IT MIGHT BE TOO MUCH BENDING  . . . 538  3 DON JUAN 16     79   4
BENE
    ET BENE DIC NEUTRUM DIC ALIQUANDO MALE  . . . . . . . . . 465  3 DON JUAN 15     21   2
BENEATH
    BENEATH THE LIE THIS STATE THING BREATHED O'ER THEE  . . .  19  2 DON JUAN  D     16   4
    UNLESS WITH BREAKERS CLOSE BENEATH HER LEE  . . . . . . . 180  2 DON JUAN  2     45   8
    EACH PULSE TO ANIMATION TILL BENEATH  . . . . . . . . . . 215  2 DON JUAN  2    113   6
    AND SHE BENT O'ER HIM AND HE LAY BENEATH  . . . . . . . . 235  2 DON JUAN  2    148   1
    NATURE WITH HIM TO THRILL BENEATH HIS TOUCH  . . . . . . 247  2 DON JUAN  2    173   3
    AS IF THERE WERE NO LIFE BENEATH THE SKY  . . . . . . . . 255  2 DON JUAN  2    188   7
    THE WORLDS TO COME OF BOTH OR FALL BENEATH  . . . . . . . 280  2 DON JUAN  3      9   5
    THAT HOLY STATE--BUT CERTAINLY BENEATH  . . . . . . . . . 280  2 DON JUAN  3      9  V5
    (FOR THAT'S THE NAME THEY LIKE TO PRAY BENEATH)--  . . . . 309  2 DON JUAN  3     66   4
    LIKE BRANCHES WHEN THE FRUIT BENEATH IS MELLOW  . . . . . 311  2 DON JUAN  3     70  V4
    THE SPARKLING GEMS BENEATH YOU MIGHT BEHOLD  . . . . . . 315  2 DON JUAN  3     77   3
    OUR VIRGINS DANCE BENEATH THE SHADE--  . . . . . . . . . 326  2 DON JUAN  3  L  15   2
    THOSE DOWNCAST EYES BENEATH THE ALMIGHTY DOVE--  . . . . 336  2 DON JUAN  3    103   6
    AND LIKE THE SOIL BENEATH IT WILL BRING FORTH  . . . . . 374  2 DON JUAN  4     56   5
    THE SHORES OF ILION LAY BENEATH THEIR LEE--  . . . . . . 384  2 DON JUAN  4     75   6
    AND BURIED SINKS BENEATH ITS OFFSPRING'S DOOM  . . . . . 399  2 DON JUAN  4    102   4
    WHICH ONCE-NAMED MYRIADS NAMELESS LIE BENEATH  . . . . . 399  2 DON JUAN  4    102   7
    THESE ARE BENEATH THE CANOPY OF HEAVEN  . . . . . . . . .  18  3 DON JUAN  6     25   1
    ALSO BENEATH THE CANOPY OF BEDS  . . . . . . . . . . . .  18  3 DON JUAN  6     25   2
    AND LIPS APART WHICH SHOWED THE PEARLS BENEATH  . . . . .  38  3 DON JUAN  6     65   8
    HE DIED BENEATH A TREE AS MUCH UNBLEST ON  . . . . . . .  84  3 DON JUAN  7     36   6
    OR ROAMS THE HERD BENEATH THE BULL'S PROTECTION  . . . .  90  3 DON JUAN  7     48   4
    THEY FOUND THAT HE HAD FOUGHT BENEATH THEIR BANNER  . . .  95  3 DON JUAN  7     56   8
    AND THAT BENEATH EACH TURKISH-FASHIONED VEST  . . . . . .  96  3 DON JUAN  7     57   5
    WHICH ROCKED AS 'TWERE BENEATH THE MIGHTY NOISES  . . . . 115  3 DON JUAN  8      7   6
    THEY FELL AS THICK AS HARVESTS BENEATH HAIL  . . . . . . 134  3 DON JUAN  8     43   1
    WHILE MOSQUES AND STREETS BENEATH HIS EYES LIKE THATCH  . 178  3 DON JUAN  8    133   3
    THERE LURKED A MAN BENEATH THE SPIRIT'S DRESS  . . . . . 206  3 DON JUAN  9     47   6
    BENEATH HIS ART THE DAME PRESSED TO DISCLOSE THEM  . . . 208  3 DON JUAN  9     51   7
    BENEATH HIS CEASELESS TOUCHES THE HESPERIAN  . . . . . . 208  3 DON JUAN  9     51  V7
    BENEATH THE VERY REVEREND ROWLEY POWLEY  . . . . . . . . 297  3 DON JUAN 11     57   6
    BENEATH HIS CARS OF CERES GROAN THE ROADS  . . . . . . . 320  3 DON JUAN 12      9   4
    WOULD BE MUCH BETTER TAUGHT BENEATH THE EYE  . . . . . . 329  3 DON JUAN 12     29   7
    BENEATH THE INFLUENCE OF THE EASTERN STAR  . . . . . . . 347  3 DON JUAN 12     69   4
    HAD SATE BENEATH THE GALLERY AT NIGHTS  . . . . . . . . . 353  3 DON JUAN 12     82   3
    (NOW FOR A COMMONPLACE) BENEATH THE SNOW  . . . . . . . . 374  3 DON JUAN 13     36   2
    AND FROM BENEATH HIS BOUGHS WERE SEEN TO SALLY  . . . . . 384  3 DON JUAN 13     56   5
    THEIR PEAKS BENEATH YOUR HUMAN FOOT AND THERE  . . . . . 412  3 DON JUAN 14      5   5
    BUT SINCE BENEATH IT UPON EARTH WE ARE BROUGHT  . . . . . 421  3 DON JUAN 14     26   4
    BENEATH THE SURFACE BUT WHAT DID IT MATTER  . . . . . . . 474  3 DON JUAN 15     41   6
    OR EARTH BENEATH OR HEAVEN OR T'OTHER PLACE  . . . . . . 510  3 DON JUAN 16     23   2
    THE CONSTABLE BENEATH A WARRANT'S BANNER  . . . . . . . . 531  3 DON JUAN 16     62   7
    A RED LIP WITH TWO ROWS OF PEARLS BENEATH  . . . . . . . 560  3 DON JUAN 16    121   6
    AS EVER LURKED BENEATH A HOLY HOOD  . . . . . . . . . . . 561  3 DON JUAN 16    123   2
BENEFACTRESS
    WITH A YOUNG BENEFACTRESS--SO WAS SHE  . . . . . . . . . 244  2 DON JUAN  2    167   7
BENEFIT
    ARE WAYS TO BENEFIT MANKIND AS TRUE  . . . . . . . . . .  93  2 DON JUAN  1    132   7
    FOR THE GREAT BENEFIT OF THOSE WHO KNOW  . . . . . . . . 190  3 DON JUAN  9     15   3
    OR DO THEY BENEFIT MANKIND LEAN MISER  . . . . . . . . . 321  3 DON JUAN 12     11   7
BENEVOLENCE
    BENEVOLENCE DESTROYS WHAT WE HAD GOT  . . . . . . . . . . 423  2 DON JUAN  5     25  V6
BENEVOLENT
    AND ALL KINDS OF BENEVOLENT MACHINES  . . . . . . . . . .  89  3 DON JUAN  7     47   8
BENIGN
    BENIGN CERULEANS OF THE SECOND SEX  . . . . . . . . . . . 403  2 DON JUAN  4    108   2
BENISON
    WHEREON APICIUS WOULD BESTOW HIS BENISON  . . . . . . . . 484  3 DON JUAN 15     65   6
BENT
    AND O'ER HIM BENT HIS SIRE AND NEVER RAISED  . . . . . . 203  2 DON JUAN  2     89   1
    THEN CHANGED LIKE TO A BOW THAT'S BENT AND THEN  . . . . 204  2 DON JUAN  2     91   7
    BENT WITH HUSH'D LIPS THAT DRANK HIS SCARCE-DRAWN BREATH  232  2 DON JUAN  2    143   8
    AND SHE BENT O'ER HIM AND HE LAY BENEATH  . . . . . . . . 235  2 DON JUAN  2    148   1
    ON HIM HER FLASHING EYES A MOMENT BENT  . . . . . . . . . 379  2 DON JUAN  4     65   4
    BENT LIKE AN ANTELOPE A PAPHIAN PAIR  . . . . . . . . . . 466  2 DON JUAN  5     96   3
    BENT AN ITALIAN SKY-BLUE PAPHIAN PAIR  . . . . . . . . . 467  2 DON JUAN  5     96  V3
    IN ORDERING MATTERS AFTER HIS OWN BENT  . . . . . . . . .  85  3 DON JUAN  7     38   3
    NOW MARS NOW MOMUS AND WHEN BENT TO STORM  . . . . . . .  95  3 DON JUAN  7     55   7
    MARCHED FORTH WITH NERVE AND SINEWS BENT TO SLAY--  . . . 113  3 DON JUAN  8      2   4
    FOLLOWING THE BENT OF BODY OR OF MIND)  . . . . . . . . . 193  3 DON JUAN  9     21   5
    WAS BENT WITH GRIEF THAT MAHOMET SHOULD RESIGN  . . . . . 262  3 DON JUAN 10     75   7
    ACCORDING AS THEIR MINDS OR BACKS ARE BENT  . . . . . . . 340  3 DON JUAN 12     52   4
    ALL MATCHLESS CREATURES AND YET BENT ON MATCHES  . . . . 340  3 DON JUAN 12     53   8
```

73

BENT   (CONTINUED)
　OF NATIONS AND HAD NEVER BENT OR BOW'D . . . . 476 3 DON JUAN 15   46 6
　SHALL FOOL ME TO THE TOP UP OF MY BENT-- . . . . . . 498 3 DON JUAN 15   94 3
BENUMB
　OF THESE THINGS OR BY RIDICULE BENUMB . . . . 498 3 DON JUAN 15   95 6
BEREFT
　OF WHICH YOUNG PASSION CANNOT BE BEREFT . . . . . . 62 2 DON JUAN 1   74 6
　SIGH'D TO BEHOLD THEM OF THEIR HOURS BEREFT . . . . 348 2 DON JUAN 4   8 5
　ALAS TO THEM OF READY CASH BEREFT . . . . 379 3 DON JUAN 13   45 3
BERKELEY
　WHEN BISHOP BERKELEY SAID THERE WAS NO MATTER . . . 268 3 DON JUAN 11   1 1
BERLIN
　AND THENCE THROUGH BERLIN DRESDEN AND THE LIKE . . . 255 3 DON JUAN 10   61 1
BERRY
　AND MOCHA'S BERRY FROM ARABIA PURE . . . . 307 2 DON JUAN 3   63 3
BERTH
　HIS BERTH A LITTLE DAMP AND HIM AFRAID . . . . . . 169 2 DON JUAN 2   25 8
BERTHS
　THE CAPTIVES BACK TO THEIR SAD BERTHS EACH THREW . . . 393 2 DON JUAN 4   90 4
BESEECH
　SAID--LADY I BESEECH YOU TO SUPPOSE THEM . . . . . . 208 3 DON JUAN 9   51 8
BESEECH'D
　HER ANGER AND BESEECH'D SHE'D HEAR HIM THROUGH-- . . . 57 3 DON JUAN 6 102 3
BESEECHING
　BESEECHING SHE NO FURTHER WOULD REFUSE . . . . . . 120 2 DON JUAN 1 180 7
　BELOVED JULIA HEAR ME STILL BESEECHING . . . . . . 167 2 DON JUAN 2   20 7
BESEEMED
　WHICH WELL BESEEMED THE DEVIL'S DRAWING-ROOM . . . . 265 3 DON JUAN 10   81 3
BESET
　IN THIS EXTENSIVE CITY SORE BESET . . . . 131 3 DON JUAN 8   37 4
　SO MANY TROUBLES FROM HER BIRTH BESET HER . . . . . 421 3 DON JUAN 14   25 3
BESIDE
　BESIDE HIS MISTRESS IN SOME SOFT ABODE . . . . . . 24 2 DON JUAN 1   6 6
　DON JUAN'S PARENTS LIVED BESIDE THE RIVER . . . . . 25 2 DON JUAN 1   8 7
　STANDING ALONE BESIDE HIS DESOLATE HEARTH . . . . . 41 2 DON JUAN 1   36 5
　HER THRONE AND POWER AND EVERYTHING BESIDE . . . . . 24 3 DON JUAN 6   36 8
　DUDU SAID NOTHING BUT SAT DOWN BESIDE . . . . 28 3 DON JUAN 6   45 1
　GEORGE WASHINGTON HAD THANKS AND NOUGHT BESIDE . . . 186 3 DON JUAN 9   8 4
　(WITH MORE BESIDE IF JUAN HAD NOT STOPPED'EM) . . . 244 3 DON JUAN 10   41 6
　NODDING BESIDE MY LADY IN HIS CARRIAGE . . . . . . 379 3 DON JUAN 13   46 2
　SPARED BY SOME CHANCE WHEN ALL BESIDE WAS SPOIL'D . . 387 3 DON JUAN 13   61 4
　AT LEAST NINE AND A NINTH BESIDE OF TEN . . . . . . 468 3 DON JUAN 15   26 4
BESIDES
　BESIDES THE PRINCE IS ALL FOR THE LAND-SERVICE . . . 23 2 DON JUAN 1   4 7
　BESIDES HER GOOD OLD GRANDMOTHER (WHO DOTED) . . . . 36 2 DON JUAN 1   28 5
　BESIDES THEIR RESURRECTION AIDS OUR GLORIES . . . . 37 2 DON JUAN 1   31 5
　LEAVING AT LAST NOT MUCH BESIDES CHRONOLOGY . . . . 76 2 DON JUAN 1 103 7
　AND WHILE SHE PONDER'D THIS BESIDES MUCH MORE . . . 80 2 DON JUAN 1 109 6
　BESIDES IT WANTED BUT FEW HOURS OF DAY . . . . . . 114 2 DON JUAN 1 169 6
　SILENCE IS BEST BESIDES THERE IS A TACT . . . . . . 119 2 DON JUAN 1 178 2
　BESIDES IN CANTO TWELFTH I MEAN TO SHOW . . . . . . 140 2 DON JUAN 1 207 7
　BESIDES BEING MUCH AVERSE FROM SUCH A FATE . . . . 199 2 DON JUAN 2   81 3
　BESIDES I HATE ALL MYSTERY AND THAT AIR . . . . . . 222 2 DON JUAN 2 124 3
　BESIDES SO VERY BEAUTIFUL WAS SHE . . . . 224 2 DON JUAN 2 128 3
　BESIDES BEING LESS IN LOVE SHE YAWN'D A LITTLE . . . 233 2 DON JUAN 2 145 3
　IS PLEASANT BESIDES BEING TRUE LOVE'S ESSENCE . . . 245 2 DON JUAN 2 169 4
　BESIDES HER MAID'S AS PRETTY FOR THEIR SIZE . . . . 246 2 DON JUAN 2 171 4
　BESIDES THAT WOULD A HAPPY LOT INSURE US . . . . . 267 2 DON JUAN 2 207 V3
　BESIDES THY PRICE IS SOMETHING DEARER STILL . . . . 372 2 DON JUAN 4   53 V4
　BESIDES I'VE NO MORE ON THIS HEAD TO ADD . . . . . 384 2 DON JUAN 4   74 5
　AND LONG BESIDES -- OH IF 'TIS REALLY SO . . . . . 419 2 DON JUAN 5   16 6
　BESIDES I'M HUNGRY AND JUST NOW WOULD TAKE . . . . 435 2 DON JUAN 5   44 7
　BESIDES FORBIDDEN FRUITS FOR SHE NE'ER PAUSED . . . 476 2 DON JUAN 5 113 V6
　BESIDES AS HAS BEEN SAID SHE WAS SO FAIR . . . . . 485 2 DON JUAN 5 129 1
　BESIDES I HATE TO SLEEP ALONE QUOTH SHE . . . . . . 30 3 DON JUAN 6   48 1
　THE HOLY CAMEL'S HUMP BESIDES THE KORAN . . . . . . 57 3 DON JUAN 6 102 8
　YOUR WARS ETERNALLY BESIDES ENJOYING . . . . 118 3 DON JUAN 8   14 7
　BESIDES ITS LAVA WITH ALL SORTS OF SHOT . . . . . . 119 3 DON JUAN 8   16 3
　WHICH FILLS A REGIMENT (BESIDES THEIR PAY . . . . . 134 3 DON JUAN 8   42 5
　AND GOD KNOWS WHO BESIDES IN AU AND OU . . . . . . 137 3 DON JUAN 8   49 2
　NO COMMON LANGUAGE AND BESIDES IN TIME . . . . . . 141 3 DON JUAN 8   58 2
　AND ALL ALLOWANCES BESIDES OF PLUNDER . . . . 163 3 DON JUAN 8 103 1
　AS THOUGH THERE WERE ONE HEAVEN AND NONE BESIDES-- . 168 3 DON JUAN 8 114 6
　THEIR FRIENDS FROM FOES--BESIDES SUCH THINGS FROM HASTE . 177 3 DON JUAN 8 130 4
　BESIDES FISH BEASTS AND BIRDS THE SPARROW'S FALL . . 192 3 DON JUAN 9   19 5
　BESIDES THE EMPRESS SOMETIMES LIKED A BOY . . . . . 206 3 DON JUAN 9   47 1
　BESIDES HE WAS OF THAT DELIGHTED AGE . . . . 217 3 DON JUAN 9   69 1
　BESIDES PLATONIC LOVE BESIDES THE LOVE . . . . . . 219 3 DON JUAN 9   74 1
　BESIDES PLATONIC LOVE BESIDES THE LOVE . . . . . . 219 3 DON JUAN 9   74 1
　THE SOUND THAN SENSE)--BESIDES ALL THESE PRETENCES . 219 3 DON JUAN 9   74 7
　UPON HIS CABINET BESIDES THE PRESENTS . . . . 222 3 DON JUAN 9   79 7
　BESIDES HE HAD SOME QUALITIES WHICH FIX . . . . . . 230 3 DON JUAN 10   10 1
　AND STILL LESS WAS IT SENSUAL FOR BESIDES . . . . . 251 3 DON JUAN 10   54 1
　BESIDES SOME VEINS OF IRON LEAD OR COPPER . . . . . 254 3 DON JUAN 10   60 3
　THEIR FARE AND ALSO PAUSE BESIDES TO FUDDLE . . . . 260 3 DON JUAN 10   71 6
　TO KNOW MYSELF AND ALL BESIDES MERE SPIRIT . . . . 268 3 DON JUAN 11   1 V7
　BESIDES THE MINISTERS AND UNDERLINGS . . . . 287 3 DON JUAN 11   40 1
　CASH RULES THE GROVE AND FELLS IT TOO BESIDES . . . 322 3 DON JUAN 12   14 2
　WHY--WHY--BESIDES FRED REALLY WAS ATTACHED . . . . . 332 3 DON JUAN 12   35 1

BESIDES   (CONTINUED)

	PAGE	VOL	CANTO	STANZA	LN
BESIDES HE HAD FOUND OUT THAT HE WAS NO TUTOR	336	3 DON JUAN	12	42	1
BESIDES THEIR KNOWLEDGE OF THE WORLD AND SENSE	336	3 DON JUAN	12	44	5
BESIDES THOSE SOOTHING SPEECHES OF THE PLEADERS	346	3 DON JUAN	12	65	7
BESIDES (ALAS HIS TASTE--FORGIVE AND PITY)	347	3 DON JUAN	12	68	7
BESIDES HE HAD NOT SEEN OF SEVERAL HUNDRED	353	3 DON JUAN	12	81	3
BESIDES THE MARKED DISTINCTION OF HIS AIR	355	3 DON JUAN	12	85	6
BESIDES THE MOST SUBLIME OF--HEAVEN KNOWS WHAT ELSE--	356	3 DON JUAN	12	88	5
BESIDES THE SAD'S A SOURCE OF THE SUBLIME	358	3 DON JUAN	13	1	5
BESIDES MY MUSE BY NO MEANS DEALS IN FICTION	416	3 DON JUAN	14	13	1
THAN THESE THINGS AND BESIDES I WISH TO SPARE 'EM	419	3 DON JUAN	14	21	5
BESIDES THERE MIGHT BE FALSEHOOD IN WHAT'S STATED	428	3 DON JUAN	14	42	6
BESIDES HIS CONDUCT SINCE IN ENGLAND GREW MORE	460	3 DON JUAN	15	11	5
THE PROSPECT AND THEIR MORALS AND BESIDES	471	3 DON JUAN	15	33	7
GREAT THOUGHTS WE CATCH FROM THENCE (BESIDES A COLD	506	3 DON JUAN	16	14	4
BESIEGE					
WITH SUITS AND PROSECUTIONS THEY BESIEGE US	11	3 DON JUAN	6	10	5
BESIEGING					
THOUGH PRINCES THE POSSESSOR WERE BESIEGING ALL	528	3 DON JUAN	16	56	4
BESMEARED					
IN ASPECT PLAINLY CLAD BESMEARED WITH DUST	104	3 DON JUAN	7	73	6
BESOM					
WITH A SOFT BESOM WILL I SWEEP YOUR HALLS	266	3 DON JUAN	10	84	7
BESPEAK					
IN THOSE WHO RARELY SMILE THEIR SMILES BESPEAK	544	3 DON JUAN	16	92	4
BESPOKE					
THERE WAS A SOMETHING WHICH BESPOKE COMMAND	217	2 DON JUAN	2	116	7
WAS WHAT HER DRESS BESPOKE A DAMSEL FAIR	24	3 DON JUAN	6	36	2
BESPRENT					
THERE SEEMED TO BE BESPRENT A DEAL OF GILDING	436	2 DON JUAN	5	46	3
BE'ST					
OH DOUBT--IF THOU BE'ST DOUBT FOR WHICH SOME TAKE THEE	269	3 DON JUAN	11	2	5
BEST					
AS THOSE OF THE BEST TIME-PIECE MADE BY HARRISON	30	2 DON JUAN	1	17	6
AND EVEN THE WISEST DO THE BEST THEY CAN	33	2 DON JUAN	1	21	3
AND SO I INTERFERED AND WITH THE BEST	34	2 DON JUAN	1	24	1
AND THEN THIS BEST AND MEEKEST WOMAN BORE	36	2 DON JUAN	1	29	1
TO WHOM IT MAY BE BEST TO HAVE RECOURSE--	38	2 DON JUAN	1	32	4
JUAN WAS TAUGHT FROM OUT THE BEST EDITION	46	2 DON JUAN	1	44	1
AND CERTAINLY THIS COURSE WAS MUCH THE BEST	58	2 DON JUAN	1	67	4
AS BEING THE BEST JUDGE OF A LADY'S CASE	62	2 DON JUAN	1	75	8
OF ITS DISEASE HE DID THE BEST HE COULD	70	2 DON JUAN	1	91	5
AT BEST NO BETTER THAN A GO-BETWEEN	84	2 DON JUAN	1	116	8
YOU'D BEST BEGIN WITH TRUTH AND WHEN YOU'VE LOST YOUR	91	2 DON JUAN	1	128	7
ALL PROPAGATED WITH THE BEST INTENTIONS	93	2 DON JUAN	1	132	3
TO SAY THE BEST IT WAS EXTREME ILL-BREEDING	116	2 DON JUAN	1	174	4
SILENCE IS BEST BESIDES THERE IS A TACT	119	2 DON JUAN	1	178	2
THE BEST IS THAT IN SHORTHAND TA'EN BY GURNEY	127	2 DON JUAN	1	189	7
THE BEST OF MOTHERS AND OF EDUCATIONS	157	2 DON JUAN	2	1	5
THE BEST OF REMEDIES IS A BEEF-STEAK	163	2 DON JUAN	2	13	5
BEYOND THE BEST APOTHECARY'S ART	167	2 DON JUAN	2	21	3
BUT STILL 'TIS BEST TO STRUGGLE TO THE LAST	176	2 DON JUAN	2	39	5
THEIR BEST CLOTHES AS IF GOING TO A FAIR	180	2 DON JUAN	2	45	2
THEY DID THEIR BEST TO MODIFY THEIR CASE	189	2 DON JUAN	2	63	3
BUT THE BEST DISH THAT E'ER WAS COOK'D SINCE HOMER'S	221	2 DON JUAN	2	123	7
WAS NOT EXACTLY THE BEST WAY TO SAVE	225	2 DON JUAN	2	130	2
AND THEREFORE WITH HER MAID SHE THOUGHT IT BEST	225	2 DON JUAN	2	131	1
SHE KNEW THAT THE BEST FEELINGS MUST HAVE VICTUAL	233	2 DON JUAN	2	145	1
THE BEST OF LIFE IS BUT INTOXICATION	250	2 DON JUAN	2	179	2
FOUND IN ONE SIGH THE BEST INTERPRETER	256	2 DON JUAN	2	189	6
THE BEST EXAMPLES WHICH I KNOW FOR LOVES	257	2 DON JUAN	2	191	V8
AND MADE THY BEST INTERPRETER A SIGH	275	2 DON JUAN	3	2	4
ROBBED FOR HIS DAUGHTER BY THE BEST OF FATHERS	284	2 DON JUAN	3	17	8
AND CERTAINLY HE SHOW'D THE BEST OF BREEDING	299	2 DON JUAN	3	46	2
SQUEEZED THROUGH THE RIND WHICH MAKES IT BEST FOR USE	307	2 DON JUAN	3	62	8
WAS FREEDOM'S BEST AND BRAVEST FRIEND	325	2 DON JUAN	3	L 12	2
TIME HAS APPROVED ENNUI TO BE THE BEST	343	2 DON JUAN	3	V 98	1
AND NO DOUBT OF ALL METHODS 'TIS THE BEST	356	2 DON JUAN	4	24	5
ALL THAT THE BEST CAN MINGLE AND EXPRESS	357	2 DON JUAN	4	26	4
THE LOVELIEST CHASTEST BEST BUT--QUITE A FOOL	405	2 DON JUAN	4	111	8
OF THE BEST FEELINGS OF MANKIND WHICH GROW	439	2 DON JUAN	5	49	5
WE KNOW WHERE THINGS AND MEN MUST END AT BEST	448	2 DON JUAN	5	63	5
ADDING THAT THIS WAS COMMONEST AND BEST	472	2 DON JUAN	5	105	6
BUT NO DOUBT EVERYTHING IS FOR THE BEST	6	3 DON JUAN	6	1	6
OF--BUT CHRONOLOGY BEST KNOWS THE YEARS	9	3 DON JUAN	6	6	8
THE GREATEST WISEST BRAVEST AS WAS BEST	12	3 DON JUAN	6	13	V2
ARE THE BEST TOKENS (TO A MODEST MIND)	13	3 DON JUAN	6	15	5
WERE THEY ACCORDING TO THE BEST REPORT	26	3 DON JUAN	6	40	5
AND EVERY COUCH IS OCCUPIED YOU HAD BEST	29	3 DON JUAN	6	46	6
I DID MY VERY BOYISH BEST TO SHINE	37	3 DON JUAN	6	62	5
WHAT PEDIGREE THE BEST WOULD HAVE TO SHOW	53	3 DON JUAN	6	94	8
BE TOO MINUTE AN OUTLINE IS THE BEST	55	3 DON JUAN	6	98	7
HIS BEST TO OBEY IN WHAT HE HAD BEEN TASKED	56	3 DON JUAN	6	100	4
BUT WHICH IS BEST YOU KNOW NO MORE THAN I	68	3 DON JUAN	7	4	8
THREE OF THE SMITHS WERE PETERS BUT THE BEST	76	3 DON JUAN	7	19	5
OR LOVED IT WAS WITH WHAT WE CALL THE BEST	123	3 DON JUAN	8	25	2
SO THAT YOU SCARCE COULD SAY WHO BEST HAD CHOSEN	135	3 DON JUAN	8	45	5
SHORN OF ITS BEST AND LOVELIEST AND LEFT BARE	155	3 DON JUAN	8	88	6
YOU ARE THE BEST OF CUT-THROATS--DO NOT START	184	3 DON JUAN	9	4	1

```
                                                        PAGE VOL    CANTO  STANZA LN
BEST   (CONTINUED)
      HE WHO SLEEPS BEST MAY BE THE MOST CONTENT  . . . . .  190  3 DON JUAN  9    15   8
      SOME PRETTY SHELL IS BEST FOR MODERATE BATHERS . . . .  191  3 DON JUAN  9    18   8
      AT LEAST HE PAYS NO RENT AND HAS BEST RIGHT . . . . .  198  3 DON JUAN  9    32   1
      MAINTAIN THOU ART THE BEST FOR AFTER ALL . . . . . .  210  3 DON JUAN  9    56   2
      OUR VEINS WHEN THINGS CALLED SOVEREIGNS THINK IT BEST . 212  3 DON JUAN  9    60   7
      OR BETTER AS THE BEST EXAMPLES SAY . . . . . . .  218  3 DON JUAN  9    71   4
      AND WAS NOT THE BEST WIFE UNLESS WE CALL . . . . .  222  3 DON JUAN  9    80   6
      WHICH WAFTED HIM FROM PETERSBURGH THE BEST . . . . .  248  3 DON JUAN  10   49   4
      WHERE JUNIPER EXPRESSES ITS BEST JUICE . . . . . .  256  3 DON JUAN  10   63   3
      DON JUAN HAVING DONE THE BEST HE COULD . . . . . .  277  3 DON JUAN  11   18   1
      BUT THE OLD WAY IS BEST FOR THE PURBLIND . . . . .  281  3 DON JUAN  11   27   4
      INTO AS FURIOUS ENGLISH) WITH HER BEST LOOK . . . .  294  3 DON JUAN  11   52   7
      BUT DON'T PRETEND TO SETTLE WHICH WAS BEST . . . .  309  3 DON JUAN  11   83   8
      THEIRS IS THE BEST BOWER-ANCHOR THE CHAIN CABLE . . .  316  3 DON JUAN  12    3   3
      AND SEVERAL OF HER BEST BON-MOTS WERE HAWKED ABOUT . .  338  3 DON JUAN  12   47   5
      AND THESE VICISSITUDES TELL BEST IN YOUTH . . . . .  339  3 DON JUAN  12   50   1
      ASK A BLIND MAN THE BEST JUDGE  YOU'LL ATTACK . . .  348  3 DON JUAN  12   71   4
      INTO THE BEST SOCIETY AND THERE . . . . . . . .  355  3 DON JUAN  12   85   2
      THE WORST OF TEMPESTS AND THE BEST OF BATTLES . . . .  356  3 DON JUAN  12   88   3
      BUT MY BEST CANTO SAVE ONE ON ASTRONOMY . . . . .  356  3 DON JUAN  12   88   7
      TO SHOW THE PEOPLE THE BEST WAY TO BREAK . . . . .  357  3 DON JUAN  12   89   4
      I LEAVE THEM TO THEIR TASTE NO DOUBT THE BEST . . . .  359  3 DON JUAN  13    3   2
      OR EVEN MERE FASHION WHICH INDEED'S THE BEST . . . .  370  3 DON JUAN  13   28   6
      TO LOSE THOSE BEST MONTHS IN A SWEATY CITY . . . .  380  3 DON JUAN  13   48   4
      THE VERY BEST OF VINEYARDS IS THE CELLAR . . . . .  394  3 DON JUAN  13   76   8
      THE BEST FIRST SPEECH THAT EVER YET WAS MADE . . . .  400  3 DON JUAN  13   90   8
      WHILE STRONGBOW'S BEST THINGS MIGHT HAVE COME FROM CATO . 401  3 DON JUAN  13   92   8
      BUT SEIZE THE LAST WORD WHICH NO DOUBT'S THE BEST . .  404  3 DON JUAN  13   98   8
      YOU BIND YOURSELF AND CALL SOME MODE THE BEST ONE . .  411  3 DON JUAN  14    2   6
      AND SHONE IN THE BEST PART OF DIALOGUE . . . . . .  426  3 DON JUAN  14   37   2
      THEIRS WAS THAT BEST OF UNIONS PAST ALL DOUBT . . . .  430  3 DON JUAN  14   45   7
      WHOSE RIPENESS IS BUT BITTER AT THE BEST . . . . .  433  3 DON JUAN  14   54   2
      SUCH MEASURES AS SHE THOUGHT MIGHT BEST IMPEDE . . .  437  3 DON JUAN  14   61   2
      'TIS BEST TO PAUSE AND THINK ERE YOU RUSH ON . . . .  438  3 DON JUAN  14   64   7
      HERSELF THAT HER INTENTIONS WERE THE BEST-- . . . .  448  3 DON JUAN  14   88   3
      THE MARRIAGE STATE THE BEST OR WORST OF ANY) . . . .  452  3 DON JUAN  14   95   6
      FEW MEN DARE SHOW THEIR THOUGHTS OF WORST OR BEST . .  457  3 DON JUAN  15    3   5
      WE'LL DO OUR BEST TO MAKE THE BEST ON'T--MARCH . . .  468  3 DON JUAN  15   27   1
      WE'LL DO OUR BEST TO MAKE THE BEST ON'T--MARCH . . .  468  3 DON JUAN  15   27   .1
      AND MORALLY DECIDED THE BEST STATE IS . . . . . .  469  3 DON JUAN  15   29   6
      OF THE BEST CLASS AND BETTER THAN HER CLASS-- . . .  475  3 DON JUAN  15   43   4
      IS WANTING AND OUR BEST TIES IN THE TOMB . . . . .  475  3 DON JUAN  15   44   8
      IF BAD THE BEST WAY'S CERTAINLY TO TEAZE ON . . . .  478  3 DON JUAN  15   51   3
      ACCORDING TO THE BEST OF DICTIONARIES . . . . . .  486  3 DON JUAN  15   68   5
      THE SIMPLE OLIVES BEST ALLIES OF WINE . . . . . .  488  3 DON JUAN  15   73   1
      MAKE MORE IMPRESSION THAN THE BEST OF BOOKS . . . .  493  3 DON JUAN  15   84   8
      TWIN OPPOSITES THE SECOND IS THE BEST . . . . . .  494  3 DON JUAN  15   87   4
      THIS WAS THE MODE OF CYRUS BEST OF KINGS-- . . . .  501  3 DON JUAN  16    1   3
      'TIS ALWAYS BEST TO TAKE THINGS UPON TRUST . . . .  503  3 DON JUAN  16    6   4
      WHAT FRIAR SAID JUAN AND HE DID HIS BEST . . . . .  515  3 DON JUAN  16   35   5
      WHICH BEST IS TO ENCOUNTER--GHOST OR NONE . . . . .  568  3 DON JUAN  17   14   1
BESTOW
      WHEREON APICIUS WOULD BESTOW HIS BENISON . . . . .  484  3 DON JUAN  15   65   6
BESTOWED
      BESTOWED UPON HIM AS THE PUBLIC LEARNED . . . . .  287  3 DON JUAN  11   39   7
BESTOWS
      THE ENDLESS SOOT BESTOWS A TINT FAR DEEPER . . . .  232  3 DON JUAN  10   15   3
BE'T
      MAY SETTLE BUT FAR BE'T FROM ME TO ANTICIPATE . . .   65  3 DON JUAN  6   119   7
      THE SUFFERERS--BE'T IN HEART OR INTELLECT-- . . . .  563  3 DON JUAN  17    2   7
BET
      STILL THEIR SALVATION WAS AN EVEN BET . . . . . .  171  2 DON JUAN  2    28   6
      I'LL BET SOME PAIR OF STOCKINGS BEAT PERU . . . . .  406  2 DON JUAN  4   112  V8
      OF ALL OUR MODERN BATTLES I WILL BET . . . . . .   83  3 DON JUAN  7    34   7
      THE WALLS WERE WON BUT 'TWAS AN EVEN BET . . . . .  150  3 DON JUAN  8    77   5
      YOUR ARM AND I'LL BET MOSCOW TO A DOLLAR . . . . .  160  3 DON JUAN  8    97   7
      GOOD AT ALL THINGS BUT BETTER AT A BET . . . . . .  399  3 DON JUAN  13   87   8
      YOU'LL NEVER GUESS I'LL BET YOU MILLIONS MILLIARDS-- .  454  3 DON JUAN  14  100   7
BETA
      THUS JUAN LEARN'D HIS ALPHA BETA BETTER . . . . .  242  2 DON JUAN  2   163   7
BETAKE
      UNTO THE NEAREST HUT THEMSELVES BETAKE  . . . . .  127  3 DON JUAN  8    32   6
BETE
      WHEN CONGREVE'S FOOL COULD VIE WITH MOLIERE'S BETE . .  402  3 DON JUAN  13   94   6
BETHOUGHT
      AND THEN A SLAVE BETHOUGHT HER OF A HARP . . . . .  379  2 DON JUAN  4    65   1
BETIDE
      BUT JUST SUPPOSE THAT MOMENT SHOULD BETIDE . . . .   67  2 DON JUAN  1    84   5
      WHAT MAY THIS MIDNIGHT VIOLENCE BETIDE  . . . . .   98  2 DON JUAN  1   142   5
BETIMES
      NO--NO--I'D SEND HIM OUT BETIMES TO COLLEGE . . . .   50  2 DON JUAN  1    52   7
      IS GLITTERING YOUTH WHICH I HAVE SPENT BETIMES-- . .  145  2 DON JUAN  1   217   7
      IS THAT SAME TIME WHICH I HAVE SPENT BETIMES  . . .  145  2 DON JUAN  1   217  V7
      MUST BREAKFAST AND BETIMES--LEST THEY SHOULD ASK IT .  233  2 DON JUAN  2   144   7
      THE GENTLEMEN GOT UP BETIMES TO SHOOT . . . . . .  405  3 DON JUAN  13  101   1
      HE WOKE BETIMES AND AS MAY BE SUPPOSED  . . . . .  512  3 DON JUAN  16   28   1
BETOKEN
      OF HIS FIERCE PULSE BETOKEN A CONDITION . . . . .  244  3 DON JUAN  10   39   4
```

76

BETRAY
   OF TRUTH--SUCH TRUTHS ARE TREASON THEY BETRAY 77   3 DON JUAN 7   22   5
   BUT THUS IT IS SOME WOMEN WILL BETRAY US . . . . 441 3 DON JUAN 14   72   8
BETRAY'D
   YET SHE BETRAY'D AT TIMES A GLEAM OF SENSE . . . . 381 2 DON JUAN 4   68   1
BETRAYED
   I'VE SEEN A FRIEND BETRAYED FOUR TIMES A DAY . . . . . . 288 3 DON JUAN 3   25 V8
   THE TRAITS OF SLEEPING SORROW AND BETRAYED 40   3 DON JUAN 6   67   4
   WHICH HESITATION MORE BETRAYED THAN MASQUED-- 56   3 DON JUAN 6   100   6
   JUAN HAD NOT BETRAYED HIMSELF IN FACT 58   3 DON JUAN 6   104   2
BETRAYING
   YET NE'ER BETRAYING THIS IN CONVERSATION . . . . 462 3 DON JUAN 15   15   4
   (BETRAYING ONLY NOW AND THEN HER SOUL . . . . 546 3 DON JUAN 16   96   5
BETRAYS
   BUT PASSION MOST DISSEMBLES YET BETRAYS 61   2 DON JUAN 1   73   1
BETS
   AFTER MALE LOSS OF TIME AND HEARTS AND BETS . . . . . . 333 3 DON JUAN 12   36   3
BETTER
   FROM BETTER COMPANY HAVE KEPT YOUR OWN 12   2 DON JUAN D   5   2
   A BETTER CAVALIER NE'ER MOUNTED HORSE 26   2 DON JUAN 1   9   5
   'TWERE BETTER TO HAVE TWO OF FIVE AND TWENTY 56   2 DON JUAN 1   62   4
   SUCH THOUGHTS AND BE THE BETTER WHEN THEY'RE OVER 64   2 DON JUAN 1   78   6
   AT BEST NO BETTER THAN A GO-BETWEEN 84   2 DON JUAN 1   116   8
   'TWERE BETTER SURE TO DIE SO THAN BE SHUT . . . . 112 2 DON JUAN 1   166   7
   GRIEVED BUT PERHAPS HER FEELINGS MAY BE BETTER . . . . . 129 2 DON JUAN 1   191   7
   POOR FELLOW HE HAD BETTER FAR BEEN BLIND . . . . 155 2 DON JUAN 1 V 7   4
   SO THAT HE HAD MUCH BETTER CAUSE TO GRIEVE . . . . . . 164 2 DON JUAN 2   15   3
   BETTER PERHAPS FOR MAN THAT AN EMBARGO . . . . 191 2 DON JUAN 2   66 V7
   BEEF VEAL AND MUTTON BETTER FOR DIGESTION . . . . 191 2 DON JUAN 2   67   8
   HAVING NO PAPER FOR THE WANT OF BETTER . . . . 195 2 DON JUAN 2   74   7
   'TWAS BETTER THAT HE DID NOT FOR IN FACT . . . . 198 2 DON JUAN 2   79   1
   NIGHT FELL--THIS SEEM'D A BETTER OMEN STILL . . . . . . 206 2 DON JUAN 2   94   8
   BUT FINDING NO PLACE FOR THEIR LANDING BETTER . . . . . 211 2 DON JUAN 2   104   7
   A BETTER SWIMMER YOU COULD SCARCE SEE EVER . . . . . . 211 2 DON JUAN 2   105   5
   HOW TO ACCEPT A BETTER IN HIS TURN . . . . 224 2 DON JUAN 2   128   8
   BETTER THAN HER KNEW WHAT IN FACT SHE MEANT . . . . . . 228 2 DON JUAN 2   136   3
   SHOWS STARS AND WOMEN IN A BETTER LIGHT . . . . 237 2 DON JUAN 2   152   8
   THUS JUAN LEARN'D HIS ALPHA BETA BETTER . . . . 242 2 DON JUAN 2   163   7
   A BETTER WELCOME TO THE TEMPEST-TOST . . . . 249 2 DON JUAN 2   177   5
   FEW CHANGES E'ER CAN BETTER THEIR AFFAIRS . . . . 263 2 DON JUAN 2   201   5
   BUT ALL THE BETTER FOR THE HAPPY PAIR . . . . 288 2 DON JUAN 3   24   3
   YOU'D BETTER ASK OUR MISTRESS WHO'S HIS HEIR . . . . . 297 2 DON JUAN 3   43   6
   AND THAT GOOD WINE NE'ER WASH'D DOWN BETTER FARE . . . . 298 2 DON JUAN 3   45   4
   HE'LL ANSWER ALL FOR BETTER OR FOR WORSE . . . . 298 2 DON JUAN 3   45   7
   FOR SOMETHING BETTER IF NOT WHOLLY GOOD . . . . 302 2 DON JUAN 3   53   6
   PERHAPS NO BETTER THAN THEY HAVE TREATED ME . . . . . . 347 2 DON JUAN 4   7   2
   THE LEAST GLANCE BETTER UNDERSTOOD THAN WORDS . . . . . 351 2 DON JUAN 4   14   2
   IT WERE MUCH BETTER TO HAVE BOTH THAN NEITHER . . . . . 357 2 DON JUAN 4   25   8
   MAY TEACH US BETTER TO BEHAVE WHEN MASTERS . . . . . . 422 2 DON JUAN 5   23   8
   'TIS BAD AND MAY BE BETTER--ALL MEN'S LOT . . . . 423 2 DON JUAN 5   25   2
   'TIS THEREFORE BETTER LOOKING BEFORE LEAPING-- . . . . . 436 2 DON JUAN 5   45   6
   MIGHT TEACH THEM THIS MUCH BETTER THAN I'M ABLE . . . . 444 2 DON JUAN 5   59   8
   'TWOULD GREATLY TEND TO BETTER THEIR CONDITION . . . . . 451 2 DON JUAN 5   69   7
   SO MUCH THE BETTER JUAN SAID FOR THEM . . . . 459 2 DON JUAN 5   82   2
   JUAN'S WAS GOOD AND MIGHT HAVE BEEN STILL BETTER . . . . 483 2 DON JUAN 5   124   1
   AND WHAT'S STILL BETTER--TEACHES THEM THAT OTHERS . . . 491 2 DON JUAN 5   138 V2
   MORALS WERE BETTER AND THE FISH NO WORSE . . . . 496 2 DON JUAN 5   149   8
   THAT THEY HAVE NOTHING BETTER NEAR OR NEWER 35   3 DON JUAN 6   59   6
   AND SHOWN THEMSELVES AS GHOSTS OF BETTER TASTE 38   3 DON JUAN 6   64   7
   THE TRUE EFFECT AND SO WE HAD BETTER NOT 55   3 DON JUAN 6   98   6
   CONCEALED HER FEATURES BETTER THAN A VEIL 60   3 DON JUAN 6   109   2
   IN WAR THAN LOVE HE HAD BETTER LEAD THE ASSAULT 98   3 DON JUAN 7   62   8
   WHICH IS STILL BETTER THUS IN VERSE TO WAGE . . . . . . 118 3 DON JUAN 8   14   6
   WITH SOMETHING NOT MUCH BETTER OR AS BAD . . . . 122 3 DON JUAN 8   22   3
   PERHAPS MAY FIND IT BETTER THAN A NEW ONE)-- . . . . . 126 3 DON JUAN 8   29   8
   IN SHORT HOWE'ER OUR BETTER FAITH DERIDES . . . . 168 3 DON JUAN 8   114   4
   (I WISH YOUR BARDS WOULD SING IT RATHER BETTER) . . . . 184 3 DON JUAN 9   3   8
   OR BETTER AS THE BEST EXAMPLES SAY . . . . 218 3 DON JUAN 9   71   4
   BEHAVED NO BETTER THAN A COMMON SEMPSTRESS . . . . . . 221 3 DON JUAN 9   77   8
   SUCH CLYTEMNESTRA THOUGH PERHAPS 'TIS BETTER . . . . . 222 3 DON JUAN 9   80   7
   WHOSE AGE AND WHAT WAS BETTER STILL WHOSE NATION . . . . 241 3 DON JUAN 10   33   3
   UNLESS YOU MAKE THEIR BETTERS BETTER--FIE . . . . 267 3 DON JUAN 10   85   7
   TO THE OLD TEXT STILL BETTER--LEST IT SHOULD . . . . . 270 3 DON JUAN 11   4   2
   THE DRUID'S GROVES ARE GONE--SO MUCH THE BETTER . . . . 280 3 DON JUAN 11   25   1
   WHICH GROWS NO BETTER THOUGH 'TIS TIME IT SHOULD . . . . 301 3 DON JUAN 11   65   8
   SO MUCH THE BETTER--I MAY STAND ALONE . . . . 312 3 DON JUAN 11   90   7
   I HAVE ALWAYS LIKED YOU BETTER THAN I STATE . . . . . . 329 3 DON JUAN 12   28   4
   WOULD BE MUCH BETTER TAUGHT BENEATH THE EYE . . . . . . 329 3 DON JUAN 12   29   7
   AND AFTER ALL POOR FREDERICK MAY DO BETTER-- . . . . . 332 3 DON JUAN 12   35   7
   AS BETTER KNOWING WHY THEY SHOULD BE SO . . . . 337 3 DON JUAN 12   46   2
   TURN OUT MUCH BETTER FOR THE SMITHFIELD SHOW . . . . . 337 3 DON JUAN 12   46   6
   I'VE GOT A BETTER SIMILIE THAN THAT . . . . 375 3 DON JUAN 13   37 V1
   GOOD AT ALL THINGS BUT BETTER AT A BET . . . . 399 3 DON JUAN 13   87   8
   IS BETTER THAN AN HUMDRUM TETE-A-TETE . . . . 402 3 DON JUAN 13   94   4
   WHEN HE ALLURED POOR DOLON--YOU HAD BETTER . . . . . . 407 3 DON JUAN 13   105   7
   TRADE WILL BE ALL THE BETTER FOR THESE CANTOS . . . . . 416 3 DON JUAN 14   14   8
   ALL THIS WERE VERY WELL AND CAN'T BE BETTER . . . . . . 421 3 DON JUAN 14   25   1
   IN SHORT THERE NEVER WAS A BETTER HEARER . . . . 426 3 DON JUAN 14   37   8
   'TIS BETTER ON THE WHOLE TO HAVE FELT AND SEEN . . . . 431 3 DON JUAN 14   49   5

```
                                                             PAGE VOL    CANTO    STANZA LN

BETTER   (CONTINUED)
     IT WERE MUCH BETTER TO BE WED OR DEAD . . . . . . .  438  3 DON JUAN 14     64    5
     AND PASS FOR WANT OF BETTER THOUGH NOT NEW . . . . . 440  3 DON JUAN 14     69    4
     UPON WHOSE BACK 'TIS BETTER NOT TO VENTURE . . . . . 442  3 DON JUAN 14     73    8
     SOME TRUTHS ARE BETTER KEPT BEHIND A SCREEN . . . .  444  3 DON JUAN 14     80    6
     BUT ALL ARE BETTER THAN THE SIGH SUPPREST . . . . .  457  3 DON JUAN 15      3    1
     DAYS BETTER DRAWN BEFORE OR ELSE ASSUME . . . . . .  468  3 DON JUAN 15     26    7
     OF THE BEST CLASS AND BETTER THAN HER CLASS-- . . .  475  3 DON JUAN 15     43    4
     BUT DRAW THE LONG BOW BETTER NOW THAN EVER . . . . . 501  3 DON JUAN 16      1    8
     AND KNEW NO BETTER IN HER IMMORALITY . . . . . . .   532  3 DON JUAN 16     64    7
     THE LOVE OF HIGHER THINGS AND BETTER DAYS . . . . .  554  3 DON JUAN 16    108    1
BETTERS
     FROM POETS OR THE MORALISTS THEIR BETTERS . . . . .  308  2 DON JUAN  3     64    8
     IT BETTERS PRESENT TIMES WITH ME OR YOU . . . . . .  422  2 DON JUAN  5     23    3
     THAT YE ARE DOGS--YOUR BETTERS FAR) YE MAY . . . . .  70  3 DON JUAN  7      7    2
     UNLESS YOU MAKE THEIR BETTERS BETTER--FIE . . . . .  267  3 DON JUAN 10     85    7
BEVERAGE
     A SAD SOUR SOBER BEVERAGE--BY TIME . . . . . . . .   277  2 DON JUAN  3      5    6
     THE BEVERAGE WAS VARIOUS SHERBETS . . . . . . . . .  307  2 DON JUAN  3     62    6
BEVY
     EACH BEVY WITH THE MERCHANT IN HIS STATION . . . .   414  2 DON JUAN  5      7    3
BEWAIL
     WHEN WE KNOW WHAT ALL ARE WE MUST BEWAIL US . . . .   67  3 DON JUAN  7      2    5
BEWARE
     BEWARE BEWARE OF THE BLACK FRIAR . . . . . . . . .   518  3 DON JUAN 16  L   1    1
     BEWARE BEWARE OF THE BLACK FRIAR . . . . . . . . .   518  3 DON JUAN 16  L   1    1
     BUT BEWARE BEWARE OF THE BLACK FRIAR . . . . . . .   520  3 DON JUAN 16  L   5    1
     BUT BEWARE BEWARE OF THE BLACK FRIAR . . . . . . .   520  3 DON JUAN 16  L   5    1
BEWILDER'D
     SO JUAN STOOD BEWILDER'D ON THE DECK . . . . . . .   163  2 DON JUAN  2     13    1
BEWILDERING
     TWO THINGS FOR DYING PEOPLE QUITE BEWILDERING . . .  179  2 DON JUAN  2     43    8
BEWITCH'D
     OF ROCKS BEWITCH'D THAT OPEN TO THE KNOCKERS . . .   293  2 DON JUAN  3     34    6
BEWITCHING
     BEWITCHING TORTURING AS THEY FREEZE OR GLOW . . . .  438  3 DON JUAN 14     63    7
BEY
     AND BEING TOLD THE LATTER SENT A BEY . . . . . . .   171  3 DON JUAN  8    120    7
BEZONIAN
     NOT RECKONING HIM TO BE A BASE BEZONIAN . . . . . .  140  3 DON JUAN  8     56    7
BIAS
     THE LURKING BIAS BE IT TRUTH OR ERROR . . . . . .   413  3 DON JUAN 14      6    5
BIBLE
     AND READ YOUR BIBLE SIR AND MIND YOUR PURSE . . . .  147  2 DON JUAN  1    220    8
BICKERINGS
     NO BICKERINGS NO CONNUBIAL TURMOIL . . . . . . . .   447  3 DON JUAN 14     86    6
BID
     HE KNEW NOT WHEREFORE THAT WHICH HE WAS BID . . . .  111  2 DON JUAN  1    163    8
     MUST BID YOU BOTH FAREWELL IN ACCENTS BLAND . . . .  147  2 DON JUAN  1    221   V3
     RING FOR YOUR VALET--BID HIM QUICKLY BRING . . . .   251  2 DON JUAN  2    180    1
     TO BID MEN COME AND GO AND COME AGAIN-- . . . . . .  299  2 DON JUAN  3     47    2
     SHOULD AN HOUR COME TO BID THEM BREATHE APART . . .  358  2 DON JUAN  4     27    3
     WHO HAD BID HIGH AS HUNDREDS SIX OR SEVEN . . . . .  407  2 DON JUAN  4    114   V6
     TURN'D TO THE MERCHANT AND BEGUN TO BID . . . . . .  425  2 DON JUAN  5     28    2
     BUT BID MY WOMEN FORM THE MILKY WAY . . . . . . . .  494  2 DON JUAN  5    145    3
     BID IRELAND'S LONDONDERRY'S MARQUESS SHOW . . . . .  207  3 DON JUAN  9     49    3
     WHERE PEOPLE ALWAYS DID AS THEY WERE BID . . . . .   368  3 DON JUAN 13     23    3
     UPON MY HEAD HAVE BID THEIR THUNDERS BREAK . . . .   414  3 DON JUAN 14     10    3
BIDDER
     AS IS A SLAVE BY HIS INTENDED BIDDER . . . . . . .   425  2 DON JUAN  5     27    1
BIDDING
     AND TAKING LATELY BY SUWARROW'S BIDDING . . . . . .  418  2 DON JUAN  5     15    7
     MY BIDDING BABA VANISHED FOR TO STRETCH . . . . . .   63  3 DON JUAN  6    116    3
     BY BIDDING OTHERS CARRY WHILE THEY RIDE . . . . . .  367  3 DON JUAN 13     19    8
BIDET
     FRENCH STUFFS LACE TWEEZERS TOOTHPICKS A BIDET . .   284  2 DON JUAN  3     17   V5
BIDS
     WHO BIDS ALL MEN BELIEVE THE IMPOSSIBLE . . . . . .  503  3 DON JUAN 16      5    6
BIENSEANCE
     AT LEAST AS FAR AS BIENSEANCE ALLOWS . . . . . . .   439  3 DON JUAN 14     67    4
BIGAMY
     ARE PROSECUTED FOR THAT FALSE CRIME BIGAMY) . . . .  164  3 DON JUAN  8    105    3
BIGGER
     WORDSWORTH'S LAST QUARTO BY THE WAY IS BIGGER . . .  330  2 DON JUAN  3     94    5
     HER PREFERENCE OF A BOY TO MEN MUCH BIGGER . . . .   218  3 DON JUAN  9     72    3
BIGOTS
     REDEEMING WORLDS TO BE BY BIGOTS SHAKEN . . . . . .  464  3 DON JUAN 15     18    5
BILE
     THE LIVER IS THE LAZARET OF BILE . . . . . . . . .  271  2 DON JUAN  2    215    1
     NOUGHT'S MORE SUBLIME THAN ENERGETIC BILE . . . . .  489  2 DON JUAN  5    135    4
     INDEED I'VE NOT THE NECESSARY BILE . . . . . . . .  300  3 DON JUAN 11     63    4
BILIOUS
     HE HAD BEEN ILL BROUGHT UP AND WAS BORN BILIOUS . .  40  2 DON JUAN  1     35    8
     WOULD THAT I WERE LESS BILIOUS--BUT OH FIE ON'T . .  566  3 DON JUAN 17     10    5
BILL
     A SCOLDING WIFE A SULLEN SON A BILL . . . . . . . .  16  3 DON JUAN  6     21    1
     JACK THOMSON AND BILL THOMSON--ALL THE REST . . . .  76  3 DON JUAN  7     19    1
     MUST I PASS OVER IN MY BILL OF FARE . . . . . . . . 488  3 DON JUAN 15     73    2
BILLETS
     TO HIS BILLETS WHY WALTZ WITH HIM WHY I PRAY . . .  332  3 DON JUAN 12     34    7
```

BILLIARDS
THEN THERE WERE BILLIARDS CARDS TOO BUT NO DICE-- . . . . . 407 3 DON JUAN 13   106   1
IT ALL SPRUNG FROM A HARMLESS GAME AT BILLIARDS . . . . 454 3 DON JUAN 14   100   8
BILLINGSGATE
(SEE BILLINGSGATE) MADE EVEN THE TONGUE MORE FREE . . . . 288 3 DON JUAN 11   42   8
BILLOW
HIS HEADACHE BEING INCREASED BY EVERY BILLOW . . . . . . 169 2 DON JUAN 2   25   6
REGALED TWO SHARKS WHO FOLLOW'D O'ER THE BILLOW-- . . . . 197 2 DON JUAN 2   77   7
AND DOLPHIN'S LEAP AND LITTLE BILLOW CROST . . . . 251 2 DON JUAN 2   181   6
NEATH WHICH HER BREAST HEAVED LIKE A LITTLE BILLOW . . . 311 2 DON JUAN 3   70   4
STIRRED UP AND DOWN HER BOSOM LIKE A BILLOW . . . . 60 3 DON JUAN 6   108   6
OR LIKE A BILLOW LEFT BY STORMS BEHIND . . . . 504 3 DON JUAN 16   9   7
LET IN THE RIPPLING SOUND OF THE LAKE'S BILLOW . . . . . 507 3 DON JUAN 16   15   4
BILLOW'S
AND RARELY CEASED THE HAUGHTY BILLOW'S ROAR . . . . 249 2 DON JUAN 2   177   6
BILLOWS
COULD JUAN'S PASSION WHILE THE BILLOWS ROAR . . . . 168 2 DON JUAN 2   23   7
OF BILLOWS BUT AT INTERVALS THERE GUSH'D . . . . 184 2 DON JUAN 2   53   5
AS ARE THE BILLOWS WHEN THE BREEZE IS BRISK-- . . . . 7 3 DON JUAN 6   3   6
AND MADE THE VERY BILLOWS PAY THEM TOLL . . . . 257 3 DON JUAN 10   65   8
AND FULL OF SENTIMENTS SUBLIME AS BILLOWS . . . . 555 3 DON JUAN 16   110   1
BILL'S
AND CANNOT FIND A BILL'S SMALL ITEMS COSTLY . . . . 283 3 DON JUAN 11   31   4
BILLS
THE INFLAMMATION OF HIS WEEKLY BILLS . . . . 293 3 DON JUAN 3   35   8
BILLS BEASTS AND MEN AND--NO NOT WOMANKIND . . . . 17 3 DON JUAN 6   22   2
BILLS--WOMEN--WIVES DOGS HORSES--AND MANKIND . . . . . . 17 3 DON JUAN 6   22   V2
THE REST WERE JACKS AND GILLS AND WILLS AND BILLS . . . . 76 3 DON JUAN 7   20   1
MORTALITY THOU HAST THY MONTHLY BILLS . . . . 117 3 DON JUAN 8   12   4
TO EXACT OF CUPID'S BILLS THE FULL AMOUNT . . . . 213 3 DON JUAN 9   62   7
HIS BILLS IN AND HOWEVER WE MAY STORM . . . . 243 3 DON JUAN 10   38   6
THY LONG LONG BILLS WHENCE NOTHING IS DEDUCTED . . . . 259 3 DON JUAN 10   69   8
WHO DID NOT LIMIT MUCH HIS BILLS PER WEEK . . . . . 259 3 DON JUAN 10   70   3
AND TRADESMEN WITH LONG BILLS AND LONGER FACES . . . . 378 3 DON JUAN 13   44   7
THEY AND THEIR BILLS ARCADIANS BOTH ARE LEFT . . . . . 379 3 DON JUAN 13   45   1
BILLY'S
WERE THEIR REWARD FOR FOLLOWING BILLY'S BANNERS . . . . 242 3 DON JUAN 10   36   4
BIN
ALSO THERE BIN ANOTHER PIOUS REASON . . . . 370 3 DON JUAN 13   26   1
BIND
HATH BUT TWO OBJECTS HOW TO SERVE AND BIND . . . . . . 18 2 DON JUAN D   15   3
AS IF 'TWERE ONE WHEREON MAGICIANS BIND . . . . 72 2 DON JUAN 1   95   6
SUCH CHAINS AS HIS WERE SURE TO BIND . . . . 325 2 DON JUAN 3 L 12   6
GOOD TO THE SOUL WHICH WE NO MORE CAN BIND . . . . . . 360 2 DON JUAN 4   30   6
BUT HERE HE WAS--WHERE EACH TIE THAT CAN BIND . . . . . 139 3 DON JUAN 8   54   3
WHO NEITHER WISHES TO BE BOUND NOR BIND . . . . . . 195 3 DON JUAN 9   26   6
AND AS FOR CHASTITY YOU'LL NEVER BIND IT . . . . . . 352 3 DON JUAN 12   80   5
YOU BIND YOURSELF AND CALL SOME MODE THE BEST ONE . . . 411 3 DON JUAN 14   2   6
BIOGRAPHY
ARE GOOD MANURE FOR THEIR MORE BARE BIOGRAPHY . . . . . 330 2 DON JUAN 3   94   4
BIRD
ABOUT THIS TIME A BEAUTIFUL WHITE BIRD . . . . . . 206 2 DON JUAN 2   94   1
'TWAS WELL THIS BIRD OF PROMISE DID NOT PERCH . . . . 206 2 DON JUAN 2   95   2
WITH MIST AND EVERY BIRD WITH HIM AWAKES . . . . . . 230 2 DON JUAN 2   139   6
AND HER VOICE WAS THE WARBLE OF A BIRD . . . . . . 236 2 DON JUAN 2   151   3
TO SEE HER BIRD REPOSING IN HIS NEST . . . . 245 2 DON JUAN 2   168   4
AND FLEW TO HER YOUNG MATE LIKE A YOUNG BIRD . . . . . 257 2 DON JUAN 2   190   6
TO THE YOUNG BIRD THE PARENT'S BROODING WINGS . . . . . 338 2 DON JUAN 3   107   3
(THAT ROYAL BIRD WHOSE TAIL'S A DIADEM) . . . . . . 104 3 DON JUAN 7   74   6
I THINK I HEAR A LITTLE BIRD WHO SINGS . . . . . . 137 3 DON JUAN 8   50   3
AND WHERE IS FUM THE FOURTH OUR ROYAL BIRD . . . . . 307 3 DON JUAN 11   78   4
TO QUAFF A BROOK WHICH MURMURED LIKE A BIRD . . . . . 384 3 DON JUAN 13   56   8
BIRDS
OF BEES THE VOICE OF GIRLS THE SONG OF BIRDS . . . . 88 2 DON JUAN 1   123   7
A LANGUAGE TOO BUT LIKE TO THAT OF BIRDS . . . . . 351 2 DON JUAN 4   14   4
BEATING FOR LOVE AS THE CAGED BIRDS FOR AIR . . . . . 19 3 DON JUAN 6   26   8
LIKE BIRDS OR BOYS OR BEDLAMITES BROKE LOOSE . . . . 23 3 DON JUAN 6   34   2
AND SINGING BIRDS WITHOUT WERE HEARD TO WARBLE . . . 55 3 DON JUAN 6   98   3
(WIDOWS OF FORTY WERE THESE BIRDS LONG CAGED) . . . . 178 3 DON JUAN 9   132   3
BESIDES FISH BEASTS AND BIRDS THE SPARROW'S FALL . . . 192 3 DON JUAN 9   19   5
FOR CATS AND BIRDS MORE PENCHANT NE'ER DISPLAYED . . . 249 3 DON JUAN 10   50   7
BIRD'S-EYE
A BIRD'S-EYE VIEW TOO OF THAT WILD SOCIETY . . . . . 416 3 DON JUAN 14   14   3
BIRON
WHICH GAVE HER DUKES THE GRACELESS NAME OF BIRON . . . 253 3 DON JUAN 10   58   4
BIRTH
AND MISCHIEF-MAKING MONKEY FROM HIS BIRTH . . . . . 34 2 DON JUAN 1   25   2
AND HOW THE DEUCE THEY EVER COULD HAVE BIRTH . . . . 71 2 DON JUAN 1   92   3
SWEET TO THE FATHER IS HIS FIRST-BORN'S BIRTH . . . 88 2 DON JUAN 1   124   6
OR WITH A FAMISH'D BOAT'S-CREW HAD YOUR BIRTH . . . . 201 2 DON JUAN 2   84   6
THEIR PLACE OF BIRTH ALONE IS MUTE . . . . 321 2 DON JUAN 3 L 2   4
FOR GOOD OR EVIL BURNING FROM ITS BIRTH . . . . . 374 2 DON JUAN 4   56   3
BEFORE PELIDES' DEATH OR HOMER'S BIRTH . . . . . 400 2 DON JUAN 4   104   8
THAT HE A MAN OF RANK AND BIRTH HAD BEEN . . . . . 415 2 DON JUAN 5   9   V6
TO HEAR AND TO OBEY HAD BEEN FROM BIRTH . . . . . 475 2 DON JUAN 5   112   1
THOUGH WHAT IS SOUL OR MIND THEIR BIRTH OR GROWTH . . . 17 3 DON JUAN 6   22   7
HER VERY PLACE OF BIRTH WAS BUT A SPECTRE . . . . 182 3 DON JUAN 9   141   5
BUT I AM HALF A SCOT BY BIRTH AND BRED . . . . . 233 3 DON JUAN 10   17   7
BUT THOUGH I OWE IT LITTLE BUT MY BIRTH . . . . . 257 3 DON JUAN 10   66   3

79

	PAGE	VOL		CANTO	STANZA	LN

BIRTH   (CONTINUED)
```
        DUKES--FOOLS BY BIRTH WHILE CLOGHER'S BISHOP SULLIES . . .   314   3 DON JUAN 11   V 76   5
        IN BIRTH IN RANK IN FORTUNE LIKEWISE EQUAL   . . . .   367   3 DON JUAN 13     20   1
        SO MANY TROUBLES FROM HER BIRTH BESET HER   . . . .   421   3 DON JUAN 14     25   3
        I RECK NOT IF AN ACORN GAVE IT BIRTH . . . . . .   436   3 DON JUAN 14     59   4
        PROUD OF HIS BIRTH AND PROUD OF EVERYTHING   . . . .   440   3 DON JUAN 14     70   2
        ALTHOUGH HER BIRTH AND WEALTH HAD GIVEN HER VOGUE . . .   477   3 DON JUAN 15     48   3
        AS DOUBTLESS SHOULD BE PEOPLE OF HIGH BIRTH . . . .   508   3 DON JUAN 16     17   6
        THE COMPANY WHOSE BIRTH WEALTH WORTH HAVE COST . . . .   568   3 DON JUAN 17     13   4
BIRTHDAY
        THAN ANY SINCE THE BIRTHDAY OF TYPOGRAPHY   . . . . .   330   2 DON JUAN  3     94   6
BIRTH-DAYS
        ON BIRTH-DAYS GLORIOUS WITH A STAR AND STRING . . . .   440   3 DON JUAN 14     70   6
BIRTHRIGHT
        LIKE ESAU FOR MY BIRTHRIGHT A BEEF-STEAK . . . . . .   435   2 DON JUAN  5     44   8
BIRTHS
        AND THE NEW BIRTHS OF BOTH THEIR STALE VIRGINITIES . . .   330   2 DON JUAN  3     95   7
        AND NOBLE BIRTHS NOR DREAD THE ENUMERATION--   . . . .   432   3 DON JUAN 14     52   4
BIS
        AND ONLY SHOUTED ALLA AND BIS MILLAH . . . . . . .    73   3 DON JUAN  7     13   8
BISCUIT
        TWO CASKS OF BISCUIT AND A KEG OF BUTTER . . . . .   180   2 DON JUAN  2     46   7
        AND ALSO FOR THE BISCUIT CASKS AND BUTTER   . . . .   188   2 DON JUAN  2     61   8
BISHOP
        WHEN BISHOP BERKELEY SAID THERE WAS NO MATTER . . . .   268   3 DON JUAN 11      1   1
        DUKES--FOOLS BY BIRTH WHILE CLOGHER'S BISHOP SULLIES . .   314   3 DON JUAN 11   V 76   5
        A DIFFERENCE 'TWIXT A BISHOP AND A DEAN . . . . .   541   3 DON JUAN 16     84   5
BISHOPS
        HAVE I NOT HAD TWO BISHOPS AT MY FEET . . . . . .   103   2 DON JUAN  1    150   1
        FATAL TO BISHOPS AS TO SOLDIERS--THESE . . . . . .   150   3 DON JUAN  8     76   2
        BUT THOUGH THREE BISHOPS TOLD HER THE TRANSGRESSION . .   252   3 DON JUAN 10     56   3
        BISHOPS WHO HAD NOT LEFT A SINGLE SERMON . . . . .   391   3 DON JUAN 13     69   5
        QUEENS BISHOPS KNIGHTS ROOKS PAWNS THE WORLD'S A GAME . .   400   3 DON JUAN 13     89   2
BIT
        AND BIT HER LIPS (FOR ELSE SHE MIGHT HAVE SCREAM'D) . .    51   2 DON JUAN  1     54   6
        TO BEG HIS PARDON WHEN I ERR A BIT . . . . . . .    86   2 DON JUAN  1    120   8
        THEY BIT THEIR LIPS AND WHISPERED WITH A WRIGGLE . . .   501   3 DON JUAN  5    156   V7
        OF FOE O'ER HIM SNATCHED AT IT AND BIT   . . . . .   153   3 DON JUAN  8     84   2
        SOME HEIRESSES HAVE BIT AT SHARPERS' HOOKS . . . . .   308   3 DON JUAN 11     81   3
        REPUBLICS ALSO GET INVOLVED A BIT . . . . . . . .   318   3 DON JUAN 12      6   5
BITCHES
        LIKE LAP-DOGS THE LEAST CIVIL SONS OF BITCHES . . . .   288   3 DON JUAN 11     41   8
        THAN WITCHES BITCHES OR PHYSICIANS BREW . . . . . .   482   3 DON JUAN 15     62   8
        NOT WITCHES ONLY BITCHES--WHO CREATE . . . . . . .   565   3 DON JUAN 17      7   4
BITE
        AND PICK IT UP AND BITE IT TO THE CORE   . . . . .    44   3 DON JUAN  6     77   4
        THAT MADMEN MAY NOT BITE YOU ON A VISIT . . . . . .   280   3 DON JUAN 11     25   4
BITES
        AND THAT HIS ARGUS BITES HIM BY--THE BREECHES . . . .   287   2 DON JUAN  3     23   8
BITS
        AND THERE WE GO--BUT WHERE FIVE BITS OF LEAD . . . .   432   2 DON JUAN  5     39   2
BITTER
        UP JUAN SPRUNG TO HAIDEE'S BITTER SHRIEK . . . . .   364   2 DON JUAN  4     37   1
        ACQUIRE THE DEEP AND BITTER POWER TO GIVE   . . . .   402   2 DON JUAN  4    107   4
        WHICH (THOUGH I HATE TO SAY A THING THAT'S BITTER) . .   237   3 DON JUAN 10     26   4
        PERHAPS HE LONGED IN BITTER FROSTS FOR CLIMES . . . .   243   3 DON JUAN 10     37   5
        WHICH FORM THAT BITTER DRAUGHT THE HUMAN SPECIES . . .   261   3 DON JUAN 10     73   8
        WHOSE RIPENESS IS BUT BITTER AT THE BEST . . . . .   433   3 DON JUAN 14     54   2
        OF THOSE SWEET BITTER THOUGHTS WHICH BANISH SLEEP . . .   555   3 DON JUAN 16    110   7
BITTEREST
        GOD GRANT YOU FEEL NOT THEN THE BITTEREST GRIEF . . .   107   2 DON JUAN  1    157   7
        OLD FLAMES NEW WIVES BECOME OUR BITTEREST FOES-- . . .   231   3 DON JUAN 10     12   7
BITTERS
        'TIS TRUE THERE BE SOME BITTERS WITH THE SWEETS . . .   502   3 DON JUAN 16      3   5
BLACK
        HER STREAMING HAIR THE BLACK CURLS STRIVE BUT FAIL . .   108   2 DON JUAN  1    158   5
        SO BLACK THE LONG WORN LION'S HIDE IN HUE   . . . .   154   2 DON JUAN  1   V  5   7
        BOTH BLACK AS IF YOU HAD TURNED HIM INSIDE OUT . . . .   154   2 DON JUAN  1   V  5   V7
        THEIR THROATS WERE OVENS THEIR SWOLN TONGUES WERE BLACK .   202   2 DON JUAN  2     86   3
        JUST LIKE A BLACK EYE IN A RECENT SCUFFLE   . . . .   205   2 DON JUAN  2     92   7
        WERE BLACK AS DEATH THEIR LASHES THE SAME HUE . . . .   218   2 DON JUAN  2    117   2
        AS BLACK BUT QUICKER AND OF SMALLER SIZE . . . . .   221   2 DON JUAN  2    122   8
        AND WHEN AT LAST HE OPEN'D HIS BLACK EYES   . . . .   225   2 DON JUAN  2    131   4
        AND HIS BLACK CURLS WERE DEWY WITH THE SPRAY . . . .   234   2 DON JUAN  2    147   6
        THEIR LARGE BLACK EYES AND SOFT SERAPHIC CHEEKS . . .   292   2 DON JUAN  3     33   2
        FOR THOSE LARGE BLACK EYES WERE SO BLACKLY FRINGED . .   314   2 DON JUAN  3     75   3
        JUAN HAD ON A SHAWL OF BLACK AND GOLD . . . . . .   315   2 DON JUAN  3     77   1
        DWARFS DANCING GIRLS BLACK EUNUCHS AND A POET . . . .   316   2 DON JUAN  3     78   2
        I SEE THEIR GLORIOUS BLACK EYES SHINE . . . . . .   326   2 DON JUAN  3   L 15   3
        THAT LARGE BLACK PROPHET EYE SEEM'D TO DILATE . . . .   355   2 DON JUAN  4     22   1
        OF HER BLACK EYES SEEM'D TURN'D TO TEARS AND MURK . . .   362   2 DON JUAN  4     33   6
        THAT I MUST HAVE RECOURSE TO BLACK BOHEA . . . . .   372   2 DON JUAN  4     52   6
        GLAZED O'ER HER EYES--THE BEAUTIFUL THE BLACK-- . . .   381   2 DON JUAN  4     69   7
        BRIGHT--AND AS BLACK AND BURNING AS A COAL   . . . .   395   2 DON JUAN  4     94   5
        MEANTIME (YON OLD BLACK EUNUCH SEEMS TO EYE US) . . .   423   2 DON JUAN  5     24   7
        JUST NOW A BLACK OLD NEUTRAL PERSONAGE   . . . . .   424   2 DON JUAN  5     26   1
        LET'S KNOCK THAT OLD BLACK FELLOW ON THE HEAD . . . .   434   2 DON JUAN  5     43   7
        AS THE BLACK EUNUCH ENTERED WITH HIS BRACE   . . . .   441   2 DON JUAN  5     54   1
        TO THRUST ITS BLACK EYES THROUGH THE DOOR OR LATTICE . .   442   2 DON JUAN  5     55   7
```

BLACK   (CONTINUED)

	PAGE	VOL	CANTO	STANZA	LN
THE BLACK HOWEVER WITHOUT HARDLY DEIGNING	450	2 DON JUAN	5	66	1
I WISH TO BE PERSPICUOUS AND THE BLACK	450	2 DON JUAN	5	67	1
WHILE HE WAS DRESSING BABA THEIR BLACK FRIEND	451	2 DON JUAN	5	69	1
BY THIS OLD BLACK ENCHANTER'S UNSOUGHT AID	459	2 DON JUAN	5	83	8
WHOSE COLOUR WAS NOT BLACK NOR WHITE NOR GRAY	462	2 DON JUAN	5	88	4
HER BROW GREW BLACK BUT SHE WOULD NOT UPBRAID	483	2 DON JUAN	5	125	5
AND THEN HIS HIGHNESS' EUNUCHS BLACK AND WHITE	495	2 DON JUAN	5	146	2
HIS HIGHNESS CAST AROUND HIS GREAT BLACK EYES	500	2 DON JUAN	5	155	1
THE BLACK BOUGH) TEAR-DROPS THROUGH HER EYES' DARK FRINGES	40	3 DON JUAN	6	67	8
A LOW SOFT OTTOMAN) AND BLACK DESPAIR	60	3 DON JUAN	6	108	5
FOR SEEING ONE WITH RIBBONS BLACK AND BLUE	141	3 DON JUAN	8	57	5
AND BLACK SILK NECKCLOTH--AND REPLIED YOU'RE RIGHT	161	3 DON JUAN	8	99	7
WHITE BLACK OR COPPER--THE DEAD BONES WILL GRIN	188	3 DON JUAN	9	12	8
A SCARLET COAT BLACK FACINGS A LONG PLUME	204	3 DON JUAN	9	43	2
A QUINTESSENTIAL LAUDANUM OR BLACK DROP	216	3 DON JUAN	9	67	5
TOO WISE TO LOOK THROUGH OPTICS BLACK OR BLUE)--	218	3 DON JUAN	9	71	8
THE DEE THE DON BALGOUNIE'S BRIG'S BLACK WALL	233	3 DON JUAN	10	18	3
IN THIS GAY CLIME OF BEAR-SKINS BLACK AND FURRY--	237	3 DON JUAN	10	26	3
BLACK EDWARD'S HELM AND BECKET'S BLOODY STONE	261	3 DON JUAN	10	73	2
BY THOSE WHO LOVE TO SAY THAT WHITE IS BLACK	312	3 DON JUAN	11	90	6
BLACK LETTER UPON FOOLSCAP WHILE OUR HAIR	315	3 DON JUAN	12	1	7
UPON THE BLACK LOAM LONG MANURED BY VICE	335	3 DON JUAN	12	40	7
NO DOUBT I SHOULD BE TOLD THAT BLACK IS FAIR	348	3 DON JUAN	12	70	8
IT IS I WILL NOT SWEAR THAT BLACK IS WHITE	348	3 DON JUAN	12	71	1
BUT I SUSPECT IN FACT THAT WHITE IS BLACK	348	3 DON JUAN	12	71	2
BUT BY THE GODS I SWEAR THAT WHITE IS BLACK	348	3 DON JUAN	12	71	V2
AN EYE'S AN EYE AND WHETHER BLACK OR BLUE	359	3 DON JUAN	13	3	3
WHO LOOK'D A WHITE LAMB YET WAS A BLACK SHEEP	396	3 DON JUAN	13	79	8
A LITTLE BLACK UPON THIS NEW FLIRTATION	429	3 DON JUAN	14	43	2
OH WILBERFORCE THOU MAN OF BLACK RENOWN	445	3 DON JUAN	14	82	1
BROKE IN UPON BY THE BLACK FRIAR OF LATE	515	3 DON JUAN	16	35	4
OH HAVE YOU NEVER HEARD OF THE BLACK FRIAR	516	3 DON JUAN	16	36	1
BEWARE BEWARE OF THE BLACK FRIAR	518	3 DON JUAN	16	L 1	1
BUT BEWARE BEWARE OF THE BLACK FRIAR	520	3 DON JUAN	16	L 5	1
THEN GRAMMERCY FOR THE BLACK FRIAR	520	3 DON JUAN	16	L 6	5
HER BLACK BRIGHT DOWNCAST YET ESPIEGLE EYE	532	3 DON JUAN	16	65	1

BLACKBIRD

	PAGE	VOL	CANTO	STANZA	LN
AND BE THE ONLY BLACKBIRD IN THE DISH	10	2 DON JUAN	D	3	4

BLACKBIRDS

| LIKE FOUR AND TWENTY BLACKBIRDS IN A PYE | 9 | 2 DON JUAN | D | 1 | 8 |

BLACKENED

| CHILLED BY THE NIGHT--AND BLACKENED BY THE SUN | 210 | 2 DON JUAN | 2 | 102 | V5 |

BLACKEST

| EVEN BY ITS DARKNESS AS THE BLACKEST SKY | 61 | 2 DON JUAN | 1 | 73 | 2 |

BLACK-EYED

WHO ONLY SAW THE BLACK-EYED GIRLS IN GREEN	167	3 DON JUAN	8	111	4
THESE BLACK-EYED VIRGINS MAKE THE MOSLEMS FIGHT	168	3 DON JUAN	8	114	5
WHO ON A LARK WITH BLACK-EYED SAL (HIS BLOWING)	277	3 DON JUAN	11	19	7

BLACKGUARDS

| ARCADES AMBO ID EST--BLACKGUARDS BOTH | 394 | 2 DON JUAN | 4 | 93 | 8 |
| WE HAVE NO ACCOMPLISH'D BLACKGUARDS LIKE TOM JONES | 409 | 3 DON JUAN | 13 | 110 | 7 |

BLACKING

| AND A LONG EULOGY OF PATENT BLACKING | 512 | 3 DON JUAN | 16 | 26 | 8 |

BLACKLEG

| HORSE BY A BLACKLEG BROADCLOTH BY A TAILOR | 424 | 2 DON JUAN | 5 | 26 | 7 |

BLACKLY

| FOR THOSE LARGE BLACK EYES WERE SO BLACKLY FRINGED | 314 | 2 DON JUAN | 3 | 75 | 3 |

BLACKS

AND DWARFS AND BLACKS AND SUCH LIKE THINGS THAT GAIN	310	2 DON JUAN	3	68	5
ALL SAVE THE BLACKS SEEM'D JADED WITH VEXATION	414	2 DON JUAN	5	7	5
WITH WHITES AND BLACKS IN GROUPS ON SHOW FOR SALE	416	2 DON JUAN	5	10	2
FOUR BLACKS WERE AT HIS ELBOW IN A TRICE	458	2 DON JUAN	5	80	8
YOU HAVE FREED THE BLACKS--NOW PRAY SHUT UP THE WHITES	445	3 DON JUAN	14	82	8

BLACKSMITH

| AND THAT HIS FATHER WAS AN HONEST BLACKSMITH | 76 | 3 DON JUAN | 7 | 20 | 4 |

BLADE

| THE REEKING BAYONET AND THE FLASHING BLADE | 146 | 3 DON JUAN | 8 | 69 | 3 |
| IN LIEU OF A BARE BLADE AND BRAZEN FRONT | 275 | 3 DON JUAN | 11 | 15 | 5 |

BLADES

| WHICH SCARCELY ROSE MUCH HIGHER THAN GRASS BLADES | 136 | 3 DON JUAN | 8 | 47 | 8 |

BLAIR

| I STUDY ALSO BLAIR THE HIGHEST REACHERS | 243 | 2 DON JUAN | 2 | 165 | 6 |

BLAME

I'M NOT TO BLAME AS YOU WELL KNOW NO MORE IS	37	2 DON JUAN	1	31	3
THE BLAME ON ME UNLESS YOU WISH THEY WERE	282	2 DON JUAN	3	12	4
BUT THEN THEIR OWN POLYGAMY'S TO BLAME	502	2 DON JUAN	5	158	6
AND SO MUST TELL THE TRUTH HOWE'ER YOU BLAME IT	10	3 DON JUAN	6	8	4
AND WHEREFORE BLAME GAUNT WEALTH'S AUSTERITIES	319	3 DON JUAN	12	7	6
FOR SILLY WARDS WILL BRING THEIR GUARDIANS BLAME	336	3 DON JUAN	12	42	4
PEOPLE ARE APT TO BLAME THE FATES FORSOOTH	339	3 DON JUAN	12	50	3
OF PASSIONS TOO I HAVE PROVED ENOUGH TO BLAME	414	3 DON JUAN	14	9	4
A HETEROGENEOUS MASS OF GLORIOUS BLAME	480	3 DON JUAN	15	57	3

BLAMEABLE

| A HABIT RATHER BLAMEABLE WHICH IS | 79 | 3 DON JUAN | 7 | 25 | 1 |

BLAMED

| HIS PATIENT AND PERHAPS WAS TO BE BLAMED | 154 | 3 DON JUAN | 8 | 85 | 6 |
| THAT IS WHEN THEY SUCCEED BUT GREATLY BLAMED | 448 | 3 DON JUAN | 14 | 89 | 4 |

BLAND

| A LITTLE PRESSURE THRILLING AND SO BLAND | 60 | 2 DON JUAN | 1 | 71 | 4 |

81

BLAND   (CONTINUED)
    MUST BID YOU BOTH FAREWELL IN ACCENTS BLAND . . . . . . 147 2 DON JUAN 1   221 V3
    IT MAY SEEM STRANGE TO FIND HIS MANNERS BLAND . . . . . 299 2 DON JUAN 3   47   5
    IN LIQUID LINES MELLIFLUOUSLY BLAND . . . . 411 2 DON JUAN 5   1   2
BLANK
    SOME PEOPLE LIKE BLANK VERSE I'M FOND OF RHYME . . . . . 136 2 DON JUAN 1   201 V5
    ALL FURTHER IS A BLANK--I WON'T DISPARAGE   . . . . . . 280 2 DON JUAN 3   9 V4
    AND WHEN HIS BONES ARE DUST HIS GRAVE A BLANK . . . . . 327 2 DON JUAN 3   89   1
    THE BLANK GREY WAS NOT MADE TO BLAST THEIR HAIR . . . . 348 2 DON JUAN 4   9   3
    SUCH AS--UNLESS MISS (BLANK) MEANT TO HAVE CHOSEN . . . 332 3 DON JUAN 12   34   5
    WITH OTHER COUNTESSES OF BLANK--BUT RANK . . . . . . 396 3 DON JUAN 13   80   1
BLANK-BLANK
    AT BLANK-BLANK SQUARE--FOR WE WILL BREAK NO SQUARES . . . 369 3 DON JUAN 13   25   1
    LORD HENRY'S MANSION WAS IN BLANK-BLANK SQUARE . . . . . 369 3 DON JUAN 13   25   8
    AT HENRY'S MANSION THEN IN BLANK-BLANK SQUARE . . . . . 370 3 DON JUAN 13   28   1
BLANKET
    WAS SUCH AS FIRE ACCORDS TO A WET BLANKET . . . . . 294 2 DON JUAN 3   36   8
    WAS MUCH THE SAME AS FIRE GIVES A WET BLANKET . . . . . 294 2 DON JUAN 3   36 V8
BLANKETS
    AS THERE WERE BUT TWO BLANKETS FOR A SAIL . . . . . 181 2 DON JUAN 2   48   4
    TWO BLANKETS STITCH'D TOGETHER ANSWERING ILL . . . . . 188 2 DON JUAN 2   61   3
BLANK-VERSE
    PROSE POETS LIKE BLANK-VERSE I'M FOND OF RHYME . . . . . 136 2 DON JUAN 1   201   5
BLASE
    A LITTLE BLASE--'TIS NOT TO BE WONDERED . . . . . . 353 3 DON JUAN 12   81   5
BLASPHEME
    WENT RAGING MAD--LORD HOW THEY DID BLASPHEME . . . . . 198 2 DON JUAN 2   79   4
BLASPHEMED
    AND JUAN TOO BLASPHEMED AN OCTAVE HIGHER . . . . . . 122 2 DON JUAN 1   184   6
BLASPHEMIES
    THAT SCRIPTURES OUT OF CHURCH ARE BLASPHEMIES . . . . . 403 3 DON JUAN 13   96   8
BLASPHEMY
    STRANGE SOUNDS OF WAILING BLASPHEMY DEVOTION . . . . . 174 2 DON JUAN 2   34   7
    PLATONIC BLASPHEMY THE SOUL OF SWEARING . . . . . . 289 3 DON JUAN 11   43   8
BLAST
    LAID WITH ONE BLAST THE SHIP ON HER BEAM ENDS . . . . . 172 2 DON JUAN 2   30   8
    THE BLANK GREY WAS NOT MADE TO BLAST THEIR HAIR . . . . 348 2 DON JUAN 4   9   3
    SADDER THAN OWL-SONGS OR THE MIDNIGHT BLAST . . . . . 432 3 DON JUAN 14   50   2
BLASTED
    EVEN AS THE SIMOOM SWEEPS THE BLASTED PLAINS . . . . 375 2 DON JUAN 4   57   8
    THE BLEEDING FLOWER AND BLASTED FRUIT OF LOVE . . . . 382 2 DON JUAN 4   70   8
    AS E'ER WAS LOCUST ON THE LAND IT BLASTED . . . . . 84 3 DON JUAN 7   36   8
BLAZE
    NOT EVEN A SPRIGHTLY BLUNDER'S SPARK CAN BLAZE . . . . . 17 2 DON JUAN D   13   5
    AND THE BLOOD'S LAVA AND THE PULSE A BLAZE . . . . . 254 2 DON JUAN 2   186   6
    A LITTLE SCORCHED AT PRESENT WITH THE BLAZE . . . . 156 3 DON JUAN 8   90   6
    IN ONE VOLUPTUOUS BLAZE--AND THEN HE DIED . . . . . 169 3 DON JUAN 8   115   8
    THOUSANDS BLAZE LOVE HOPE DIE--HOW HAPPY THEY-- . . . . 229 3 DON JUAN 10   8   8
    ON HIM THE DIAMOND POURS ITS BRILLIANT BLAZE . . . . . 319 3 DON JUAN 12   8   6
    ON THE MOST FAVOURED AND AMIDST THE BLAZE . . . . . 373 3 DON JUAN 13   33   6
    IMPOSED NOT UPON HER SHE SAW HER BLAZE . . . . . 480 3 DON JUAN 15   56   2
BLAZED
    WHILE THE WHOLE RAMPART BLAZED LIKE ETNA WHEN . . . . 115 3 DON JUAN 8   7   7
    BLAZED AND THE CANNON'S ROAR WAS SCARCE ALLAYED . . . . 178 3 DON JUAN 8   133   4
BLAZON
    AND BLAZON O'ER THE DOOR THEIR NAMES IN BRASS . . . . . 283 3 DON JUAN 11   31   8
BLEAK
    'TWAS A RAW DAY OF AUTUMN'S BLEAK BEGINNING . . . . 414 2 DON JUAN 5   6   1
    WHEN THE STRIPT FOREST BOWS TO THE BLEAK AIR . . . . . 155 3 DON JUAN 8   88   4
BLEAKNESS
    IF BRITAIN MOURN HER BLEAKNESS WE CAN TELL HER . . . . . 394 3 DON JUAN 13   76   7
BLED
    HE BUT REQUESTED TO BE BLED TO DEATH . . . . . . 197 2 DON JUAN 2   76   1
    THE SURGEON HAD HIS INSTRUMENTS AND BLED . . . . . . 197 2 DON JUAN 2   76   2
    AND PERSIAN CARPETS WHICH THE HEART BLED TO STAIN . . . 310 2 DON JUAN 3   68   3
    MUST WE BUT BLUSH--OUR FATHERS BLED . . . . . . 323 2 DON JUAN 3 L 7   2
    (AS HE BLED INWARDLY NO HIDEOUS RIVER . . . . . . 430 2 DON JUAN 5   35   6
    WHICH FOR THE LAST THOUGH NOT THE FIRST TIME BLED . . . 431 2 DON JUAN 5   37   4
    IN VAIN HE KICKED AND SWORE AND WRITHED AND BLED . . . 153 3 DON JUAN 8   83   5
BLEED
    JUAN WHO SAW THE MOON'S LATE MINION BLEED . . . . . 275 3 DON JUAN 11   14   5
    OR WISH TO MAKE A RIVAL'S BOSOM BLEED . . . . . . 351 3 DON JUAN 12   77   6
BLEEDING
    BUT SUNK AGAIN UPON HIS BLEEDING KNEE . . . . . . 213 2 DON JUAN 2   109   2
    HIS OWN ANXIETY HIS HEART TOO BLEEDING . . . . . 299 2 DON JUAN 3   46   6
    NO NOVELS E'ER HAD SET THEIR YOUNG HEARTS BLEEDING . . . 354 2 DON JUAN 4   19   4
    O'ER THE SHARP SHINGLES WITH HER BLEEDING FEET . . . . . 361 2 DON JUAN 4   32   2
    HIS MAN WAS PROSTRATE BLEEDING AT HIS FOOT . . . . . 370 2 DON JUAN 4   49 V5
    THE BLEEDING FLOWER AND BLASTED FRUIT OF LOVE . . . . . 382 2 DON JUAN 4   70   8
BLEND
    OF MURMURING LIBERTY'S WIDE WAVES WHICH BLEND . . . . 52 3 DON JUAN 6   93   6
    A MADDENING SPIRIT WHICH WOULD STRIVE TO BLEND . . . . . 219 3 DON JUAN 9   73   4
    AS ALL MUST BLEND WHOSE PART IT IS TO AIM . . . . . 546 3 DON JUAN 16   95   5
BLENDED
    ADELINE AND DON JUAN RATHER BLENDED . . . . . . 482 3 DON JUAN 15   61   3
BLENDING
    AND BLENDING EVERY COLOUR INTO ONE . . . . . . 205 2 DON JUAN 2   92   6
    WITHOUT MORE PREFACE IN HER BLUE EYES BLENDING . . . . . 478 2 DON JUAN 5   116   5
    AND DIGNITY WITH COURTESY SO BLENDING . . . . . . 546 3 DON JUAN 16   95   4

82

BLESS
```
BY THE IMMORTAL WISH AND POWER TO BLESS . . . . . . . 357   2 DON JUAN   4     26    8
WHICH MADE HIM DAILY BLESS HIS OWN NEUTRALITY . . . .  64    3 DON JUAN   6    117    8
```
BLESSED
```
AVE MARIA BLESSED BE THE HOUR . . . . . . . . . . . .  335   2 DON JUAN   3    102    1
WITH HER SON IN HER BLESSED ARMS LOOK'D ROUND . . . .  387   3 DON JUAN  13     61    3
```
BLESSEDNESS
```
OF SINGLE BLESSEDNESS AND THOUGHT IT GOOD  . . . . .   177   3 DON JUAN   8    131    4
```
BLESSES
```
THE INNOCENCE WHICH HAPPY CHILDHOOD BLESSES . . . . .  292   2 DON JJAN   3     33    5
```
BLESSING
```
THOU CANST NOT BE MY BLESSING OR MY CURSE  . . . . .   144   2 DON JUAN   1    215    4
HAVE YOU NO FRIENDS -- I HAD--BUT BY GOD'S BLESSING .  419   2 DON JUAN   5     16    1
A BLESSING IS SOUND SLEEP--JUANNA LAY . . . . . . . .  42    3 DON JUAN   6     73    2
SMOOTHED EVEN THE SIMPLON'S STEEP AND BY GOD'S BLESSING . 215 3 DON JUAN  9     66    7
MAKES MOUNTAINS PASSABLE AND BY HEAVEN'S BLESSING . .  215   3 DON JUAN   9     66   V7
HEROES MUST DIE AND BY GOD'S BLESSING 'TIS . . . . .   277   3 DON JUAN  11     20    2
```
BLEST
```
FOR NOT THE BLEST SHERBET SUBLIMED WITH SNOW  . . . .  251   2 DON JUAN   2    180    4
AND LOVED BY A YOUNG HEART TOO DEEPLY BLEST . . . . .  274   2 DON JUAN   3      1    4
THAN YOUR SIRES' ISLANDS OF THE BLEST . . . . . . . .  321   2 DON JUAN   3  L   2    6
MUST WE BUT WEEP O'ER DAYS MORE BLEST . . . . . . . .  323   2 DON JUAN   3  L   7    1
MY BRAIN WITH BLEST FUMES TILL MY EYES GROW DIM . . .  372   2 DON JUAN   4     53   V7
OF TYRANTS AND BEEN BLEST FROM SHORE TO SHORE . . . .  187   3 DON JUAN   9      9    4
A BLEST HOUR FOR POSTILLIONS--CHARIOTS FLY . . . . .   377   3 DON JUAN  13     42   V3
```
BLEW
```
INCREASED AT NIGHT UNTIL IT BLEW A GALE . . . . . . .  170   2 DON JUAN   2     26    2
THE WIND BLEW FRESH AGAIN AS IT GREW LATE . . . . . .  172   2 DON JUAN   2     30    5
AGAIN THE WEATHER THREATEN'D--AGAIN BLEW . . . . . .   178   2 DON JUAN   2     42    1
THAN WHAT IT HAD BEEN FOR SO STRONG IT BLEW . . . . .  185   2 DON JUAN   2     54    4
'TWAS A ROUGH NIGHT AND BLEW SO STIFFLY YET . . . . .  188   2 DON JUAN   2     60    1
SO CHANGEABLE HAD BEEN THE WINDS THAT BLEW . . . . .   209   2 DON JUAN   2    100    6
AND BLEW ANOTHER ANSWERED TO THE CALL . . . . . . . .  369   2 DON JUAN   4     47    4
THEY BLEW UP IN THE MIDDLE OF THE RIVER . . . . . . .  80    3 DON JUAN   7     28    7
ONE BARK BLEW UP A SECOND NEAR THE WORKS . . . . . .   81    3 DON JUAN   7     30    7
TOWARDS WHICH THE IMPATIENT WIND BLEW HALF A GALE . .  256   3 DON JUAN  10     64    3
```
BLIGHT
```
BLOSSOM AND BOUGH LIE WITHER'D WITH ONE BLIGHT . . .   382   2 DON JJAN   4     70    6
```
BLIGHTED
```
TILL SOME CONFOUNDED ESCAPADE HAS BLIGHTED . . . . .   75    2 DON JUAN   1    100    5
TO PART WITH ALL TILL EVERY HOPE WAS BLIGHTED) . . .   173   2 DON JUAN   2     32    7
```
BLIND
```
THINK'ST THOU COULD HE--THE BLIND OLD MAN--ARISE . .   15    2 DON JJAN   D     11    1
EUTROPIUS OF ITS MANY MASTERS--BLIND . . . . . . . .   18    2 DON JUAN   D     15    5
UNLESS THIS WORLD AND T'OTHER TOO BE BLIND . . . . .   112   2 DON JUAN   1    165    4
UNLESS THE WORLD AND HEAVEN ITSELF BE BLIND . . . . .  112   2 DON JUAN   1    165   V4
TO ALL EXCEPT ONE IMAGE MADLY BLIND  . . . . . . . .   133   2 DON JUAN   1    196    6
IF AFTER ALL THERE SHOULD BE SOME SO BLIND . . . . .   141   2 DON JUAN   1    208    1
POOR FELLOW HE HAD BETTER FAR BEEN BLIND . . . . . .   155   2 DON JUAN   1  V  7    4
NOR INFLAMMATIONS REDDEN HIS BLIND EYE . . . . . . .   168   2 DON JUAN   2     22    8
THE LESBIAN SAPPHO AND THE BLIND OLD MAN . . . . . .   320   2 DON JUAN   3  L  1   V2
THE PRESENT CENTURY WAS GROWING BLIND . . . . . . . .  328   2 DON JUAN   3     90    6
OF FORMS AND FEATURES IT WOULD STRIKE YOU BLIND . . .  467   2 DON JUAN   5     97    6
BY ALL HIS EDICTS EVEN TO THE BLIND  . . . . . . . .   12    3 DON JUAN   6     13   V3
OR AS A LITTLE DOG WILL LEAD THE BLIND . . . . . . .   90    3 DON JUAV   7     48    5
OVER THE HILLS A FIRE ENOUGH TO BLIND . . . . . . . .  126   3 DON JUAN   8     30    4
OFT ARE SOON CLOSED ALL HEROES ARE NOT BLIND . . . .   133   3 DON JUAN   8     40    6
ASK A BLIND MAN THE BEST JUDGE  YOU'LL ATTACK . . . .  348   3 DON JUAN  12     71    4
NOT EVEN IN FOOLS--WHO--HOWSOEVER BLIND . . . . . . .  372   3 DON JUAN  13     32   V6
FOLLIES TRICK'D OUT SO BRIGHTLY THAT THEY BLIND-- . .  480   3 DON JUAN  15     57    6
```
BLINDLY
```
OR PANDERING BLINDLY TO HIS OWN DISGRACE . . . . . .   74    2 DON JUAV   1     99    4
```
BLINDNESS
```
AND TURN HIM LIKE THE CYCLOPS MAD WITH BLINDNESS . .   304   2 DON JUAN   3     57    8
AND SEND HIM FORTH LIKE SAMSON--STRONG IN BLINDNESS .  304   2 DON JUAN   3     57   V8
AND MAKE HIM SAMSONLIKE--MORE FIERCE WITH BLINDNESS .  304   2 DON JUAV   3     57   V8
```
BLISS
```
WHERE ALL WAS PEACE AND INNOCENCE AND BLISS . . . . .  30    2 DON JUAN   1     18    5
HERE IS THE EMPIRE OF THY PERFECT BLISS . . . . . . .  69    2 DON JUAN   1     88    3
KISS RHYMES TO BLISS IN FACT AS WELL AS VERSE-- . . .  35    3 DON JUAV   6     59    7
```
BLISSES
```
UNCERTAINTY IS ONE OF MANY BLISSES . . . . . . . . .   105   3 DON JUAN   7     76    5
```
BLISTER
```
PRESCRIBED BY WAY OF BLISTER A YOUNG BELLE . . . . .   113   2 DON JUAN   1    168    4
```
BLISTER'D
```
BLISTER'D AND SCORCH'D AND STAGNANT ON THE SEA . . .   194   2 DON JUAN   2     72    2
```
BLOATED
```
ON LIFE'S WORN CONFINE JADED BLOATED SATED . . . . .   267   3 DON JUAN  10     87    2
```
BLOCKHEAD
```
COULD NOT THE BLOCKHEAD ASK FOR A BALLOON  . . . . .   333   2 DON JUAN   3     99    8
BLOCKHEAD COME ON AND SEE QUOTH BABA WHILE . . . . .   459   2 DON JUAN   5     83    1
```
BLOCKS
```
THERE BARBER'S BLOCKS WITH PERIWIGS IN CURL . . . . .  278   3 DON JUAN  11     22    5
```
BLONDE
```
SHE WAS A FINE AND SOMEWHAT FULL-BLOWN BLONDE . . . .  428   3 DON JUAN  14     42    1
```
BLOOD
```
THE BLOOD OF MONARCHS WITH HIS PROPHECIES  . . . . .   15    2 DON JUAN   D     11    3
OF MOOR OR HEBREW BLOOD HE TRACED HIS SOURCE . . . .   26    2 DON JUAN   1      9    3
(HER BLOOD WAS NOT ALL SPANISH BY THE BY . . . . . .   52    2 DON JUAN   1     56    3
```

BLOOD   (CONTINUED)

	PAGE	VOL		CANTO	STANZA	LN
HIS BLOOD LESS NOBLE THAN SUCH BLOOD SHOULD BE	52	2 DON JUAN	1	57	3
HIS BLOOD LESS NOBLE THAN SUCH BLOOD SHOULD BE	52	2 DON JUAN	1	57	3
RUIN'D ITS BLOOD BUT MUCH IMPROVED ITS FLESH	53	2 DON JUAN	1	58	2
BY BLOOD OR INK 'TIS SWEET TO PUT AN END	90	2 DON JUAN	1	126	2
WHEN OLD KING DAVID'S BLOOD GREW DULL IN MOTION	113	2 DON JUAN	1	168	5
WHY DON'T YOU KNOW THAT IT MAY END IN BLOOD	115	2 DON JUAN	1	171	6
HIS BLOOD WAS UP THOUGH YOUNG HE WAS A TARTAR	122	2 DON JUAN	1	184	7
AND BLOOD ('TWAS FROM THE NOSE) BEGAN TO FLOW	124	2 DON JUAN	1	186	3
SOME BLOOD AND SEVERAL FOOTSTEPS BUT NO MORE	125	2 DON JUAN	1	187	6
MY BLOOD STILL RUSHES WHERE MY SPIRIT'S SET	133	2 DON JUAN	1	196	3
AS I AM BLOOD--BONE--MARROW PASSION--FEELING--	156	2 DON JUAN	1 V	8	7
AND OUT THEY SPOKE OF LOTS FOR FLESH AND BLOOD	194	2 DON JUAN	2	73	7
FOR HIS CONGEALING BLOOD AND SENSES DIM	214	2 DON JUAN	2	111	4
HEAVEN KNOWS WHAT CASH HE GOT OR BLOOD HE SPILT	223	2 DON JUAN	2	127	5
HAD DYED IT WITH THE HEADLONG BLOOD WHOSE RACE	231	2 DON JUAN	2	141	3
SHOULD REACH HIS BLOOD THEN O'ER HIM STILL AS DEATH	232	2 DON JUAN	2	143	7
FOR LOVE MUST BE SUSTAIN'D LIKE FLESH AND BLOOD--	246	2 DON JUAN	2	170	4
AND TURN'D HER PURE HEART'S PUREST BLOOD TO TEARS	274	2 DON JUAN	3	1	8
HIS ANGRY WORD ONCE O'ER HE SHED NO BLOOD	300	2 DON JUAN	3	48	6
AND SHED THE BLOOD OF SCIO'S VINE	324	2 DON JUAN	3 L	9	4
THE HERACLEIDAN BLOOD MIGHT OWN	325	2 DON JUAN	3 L	13	6
WE KNOW NOT THIS--THE BLOOD FLOWS ON TOO FAST	345	2 DON JUAN	4	2	6
PURE BLOOD TO STAGNATE THEIR GREAT HEARTS TO FAIL	348	2 DON JUAN	4	9	2
THEN TURN'D TO JUAN IN WHOSE CHEEK THE BLOOD	365	2 DON JUAN	4	39	5
REPLIED YOUR BLOOD BE THEN ON YOUR OWN HEAD	365	2 DON JUAN	4	40	5
HER FATHER'S BLOOD BEFORE HER FATHER'S FACE	367	2 DON JUAN	4	44	7
THERE WAS RESEMBLANCE SUCH AS TRUE BLOOD WEARS	368	2 DON JUAN	4	45	4
WITH THE BLOOD RUNNING LIKE A LITTLE BROOK	370	2 DON JUAN	4	49	6
THE MOORISH BLOOD PARTAKES THE PLANET'S HOUR	374	2 DON JUAN	4	56	4
HIS BLOOD WAS RUNNING ON THE VERY FLOOR	375	2 DON JUAN	4	58	3
WERE DABBLED WITH THE DEEP BLOOD WHICH RAN O'ER	376	2 DON JUAN	4	59	2
THE BLOOD GUSHED FROM HER LIPS AND EARS AND EYES	376	2 DON JUAN	4	59	V1
THE SPOUTING BLOOD GUSHED THROUGH HER MOUTH HER EYES	376	2 DON JUAN	4	59	V1
WEAK STILL WITH LOSS OF BLOOD HE SCARCE COULD URGE	387	2 DON JUAN	4	79	5
WITH HUMAN BLOOD THAT COLUMN WAS CEMENTED	401	2 DON JUAN	4	105	1
PERHAPS HIS RECENT LOSS OF BLOOD MIGHT PULL	415	2 DON JUAN	5	8	5
SELL FLESH AND BLOOD WHEN DINNER HAS OPPREST ONE	426	2 DON JUAN	5	30	6
AND IS THIS BLOOD THEN FORMED BUT TO BE SHED	432	2 DON JUAN	5	39	4
THE BLOOD OF ALL HIS LINE'S CASTILIAN LORDS	471	2 DON JUAN	5	104	3
AND INTO HER CLEAR CHEEK THE BLOOD WAS BROUGHT	473	2 DON JUAN	5	108	4
HER BLOOD WAS HIGH HER BEAUTY SCARCE OF EARTH	475	2 DON JUAN	5	112	5
FELT THE WARM BLOOD WHICH IN HIS FACE WAS GLOWING	478	2 DON JUAN	5	117	4
AND THEN HER THIRST OF BLOOD WAS QUENCHED IN TEARS	490	2 DON JUAN	5	136	8
IT TEACHES THEM THAT THEY ARE FLESH AND BLOOD	491	2 DON JUAN	5	138	1
WHO LOVED BLOOD AS AN ALDERMAN LOVES MARROW	70	3 DON JUAN	7	8	8
LET THERE BE BLOOD SAYS MAN AND THERE'S A SEA	86	3 DON JUAN	7	41	2
OF BLOOD AND TEARS MUST FLOW THE UNEBBING SEA	101	3 DON JUAN	7	68	8
AND NOT MUCH SYMPATHY FOR BLOOD SURVEYED	102	3 DON JUAN	7	69	2
BUT STILL WE MODERNS EQUAL YOU IN BLOOD	106	3 DON JUAN	7	80	8
OH BLOOD AND THUNDER AND OH BLOOD AND WOUNDS	112	3 DON JUAN	8	1	1
OH BLOOD AND THUNDER AND OH BLOOD AND WOUNDS	112	3 DON JUAN	8	1	1
SO WAS HIS BLOOD STIRRED WHILE HE FOUND RESISTANCE	140	3 DON JUAN	8	55	1
BLOOD UNTIL HEATED--AND EVEN THERE HIS OWN	140	3 DON JUAN	8	55	7
WHOSE BLOOD THE PUDDLE GREATLY DID ENRICH	147	3 DON JUAN	8	71	3
NOW THAWED INTO A MARSH OF HUMAN BLOOD	148	3 DON JUAN	8	73	8
THE BLOOD MAY GUSH OUT AS THE DANUBE'S FLOW	155	3 DON JUAN	8	87	3
A SLENDER STREAK OF BLOOD ANNOUNCED HOW NEAR	159	3 DON JUAN	8	95	2
WAS IMAGED BACK IN BLOOD THE SEA OF SLAUGHTER	172	3 DON JUAN	8	122	8
WHERE BLOOD WAS TALKED OF AS WE WOULD OF WATER	197	3 DON JUAN	9	29	3
OF BLOOD AND WATER LEADEN CASTLEREAGH	207	3 DON JUAN	9	50	6
BLOOD ONLY SERVES TO WASH AMBITION'S HANDS	212	3 DON JUAN	9	59	4
I SCOTCHED NOT KILLED THE SCOTCHMAN IN MY BLOOD	234	3 DON JUAN	10	19	7
VALOUR MUCH ALSO TO THE BLOOD HE SHOWED	239	3 DON JUAN	10	29	4
WHICH WITH THE BLOOD TOO READILY WILL CLAIM KIN	244	3 DON JUAN	10	40	6
IN NEITHER CLIME TIME BLOOD WITH HER DEFENDER	252	3 DON JUAN	10	57	7
LEAVENING HIS BLOOD AS CAYENNE DOTH A CURRY	260	3 DON JUAN	10	72	2
TO FIND RETORTS FOR INNOCENT BLOOD SHED	314	3 DON JUAN	11 V	75	4
HIS BRUSH WITH ALL THE BLOOD OF ALL THE SAINTED	392	3 DON JUAN	13	71	8
WILL THERE AS ALSO IN THE TIES OF BLOOD	451	3 DON JUAN	14	93	2
BLOOD IS NOT WATER AND WHERE SHALL WE FIND	475	3 DON JUAN	15	44	4
IT MAKES MY BLOOD BOIL LIKE THE SPRINGS OF HECLA	497	3 DON JUAN	15	92	7
SPANGLED WITH GEMS--THE MONK MADE HIS BLOOD CURDLE	556	3 DON JUAN	16	113	6
FORTH INTO SOMETHING MUCH LIKE FLESH AND BLOOD	561	3 DON JUAN	16	123	4

BLOOD-HORSE
| DASHED ON LIKE A SPURRED BLOOD-HORSE IN A RACE | 139 | 3 DON JUAN | 8 | 54 | 8 |

BLOOD-HOUNDS
| SHOULD EVER BE THOSE BLOOD-HOUNDS FROM WHOSE WILD | 401 | 2 DON JUAN | 4 | 105 | 6 |

BLOODIER
| TO MAKE THE CRETANS BLOODIER IN BATTLE | 238 | 2 DON JUAN | 2 | 155 | 8 |

BLOODLESS
| BUT PRESS'D HER BLOODLESS LIP TO JUAN'S CHEEK | 114 | 2 DON JUAN | 1 | 169 | 8 |

BLOOD-RED
| BLOOD-RED AS SUNSET SUMMER CLOUDS WHICH RANGE | 473 | 2 DON JUAN | 5 | 108 | 5 |

BLOOD'S
| AND THE BLOOD'S LAVA AND THE PULSE A BLAZE | 254 | 2 DON JUAN | 2 | 186 | 6 |

BLOOD-SHOT
| FLOWED FROM THEIR BLOOD-SHOT EYES ALL RED WITH STRIFE | 171 | 3 DON JUAN | 8 | 119 | 7 |

BLOODY
| AND THEIR BAKED LIPS WITH MANY A BLOODY CRACK | 202 | 2 DON JUAN | 2 | 86 | 1 |

		PAGE	VOL		CANTO	STANZA	LV

BLOODY   (CONTINUED)

ONE ARM HAD ON A BANDAGE RATHER BLOODY	416	2 DON JUAN	5	11	6
LIKE HAIL TO MAKE A BLOODY DIURETIC	117	3 DON JUAN	8	12	3
THUS ON THEY WALLOWED IN THE BLOODY MIRE	121	3 DON JUAN	8	20	1
STARS MEDALS AND A BLOODY SWORD IN HAND	141	3 DON JUAN	8	57	6
NAPOLEON ON HIS BOLD AND BLOODY TRACK	147	3 DON JUAN	8	70	3
AMIDST THE BODIES LULLED IN BLOODY REST	157	3 DON JUAN	8	91	8
YOU'LL FIND TEN THOUSAND HANDSOME COXCOMBS BLOODY	167	3 DON JUAN	8	112	8
ITS BLOODY BOND AND SAVED PERHAPS SOME PRETTY	174	3 DON JUAN	8	124	3
WITH BLOODY HANDS HE WROTE HIS FIRST DISPATCH	178	3 DON JUAN	8	133	5
THOUGH BOLD AND BLOODY WAS THE LORD OF THING	217	3 DON JUAN	9	70	2
BLACK EDWARD'S HELM AND BECKET'S BLOODY STONE	261	3 DON JUAN	10	73	2
OH JACK I'M FLOORED BY THAT 'ERE BLOODY FRENCHMAN	274	3 DON JUAN	11	13	8
THE CRAVAT STAINED WITH BLOODY DROPS FELL DOWN	276	3 DON JUAN	11	17	1

BLOOM

THE BLOOM TOO HAD RETURN'D TO HAIDEE'S CHEEKS	295	2 DON JUAN	3	38	6
WE LEFT OUR HERO JUAN IN THE BLOOM	227	3 DON JUAN	10	5	1
MERIDIAN-BORN TO BLOOM IN THIS OPINION	246	3 DON JUAN	10	44	2
A FRUIT TO BLOOM UPON THEIR WITHERING BOUGH	330	3 DON JUAN	12	31	2

BLOOMED

| BLOOMED ALSO IN LESS TRANSITORY HUES | 293 | 3 DON JUAN | 11 | 48 | 2 |

BLOOMING

PAIR'D OFF WITH A BACCHANTE BLOOMING VISAGE	394	2 DON JUAN	4	92	8
AND LADY MARYS BLOOMING INTO GIRLS	390	3 DON JUAN	13	68	4
FOR WHICH SEE SHAKSPEARE'S EVER BLOOMING GARDEN--	442	3 DON JUAN	14	75	2
THEY HAVE AT HAND A BLOOMING GLUT OF BRIDES	471	3 DON JUAN	15	33	8

BLOSSOM

| BLOSSOM AND BOUGH LIE WITHER'D WITH ONE BLIGHT | 382 | 2 DON JUAN | 4 | 70 | 6 |

BLOSSOMS

| OF THESE BRIEF BLOSSOMS THE IMMEDIATE FRUITS | 168 | 3 DON JUAN | 8 | 113 | 8 |

BLOTTED

| A BLOTTED SHIELD NO SHIRE'S TRUE KNIGHT WOULD WEAR | 153 | 2 DON JUAN | 1 | V 4 | 6 |
| A SORT OF BLOTTED SHIELD FEW KNIGHTS WOULD WEAR | 153 | 2 DON JUAN | 1 | V 4 | V6 |

BLOW

JUAN CONTRIVED TO GIVE AN AWKWARD BLOW	124	2 DON JUAN	1	186	5
DEATH SHUNS THE WRETCH WHO FAIN THE BLOW WOULD MEET	134	2 DON JUAN	1	197	6
I WAS MOST READY TO RETURN A BLOW	143	2 DON JUAN	1	212	6
FOR THE SKY SHOW'D IT WOULD COME ON TO BLOW	170	2 DON JUAN	2	26	7
AND NONE LIKED TO ANTICIPATE THE BLOW	175	2 DON JUAN	2	36	6
WITH TWILIGHT IT AGAIN CAME ON TO BLOW	207	2 DON JUAN	2	96	1
WITH HIM IT NEVER WAS A WORD AND BLOW	300	2 DON JUAN	3	48	5
AND HIS ONE BLOW LEFT LITTLE WORK FOR TWO	300	2 DON JUAN	3	48	8
AND HIS BLOW DID WHAT WORDS COULD NOT UNDO	300	2 DON JUAN	3	48	V8
PALE STATUE-LIKE AND STERN SHE WOO'D THE BLOW	367	2 DON JUAN	4	43	4
ON THE ROUGH DEEP BUT THIS LAST BLOW--AND HERE	420	2 DON JUAN	5	19	1
AS IF SHE HAD RECEIVED A SUDDEN BLOW	58	3 DON JUAN	6	105	6
THIS PASSION MIGHT BLOW O'ER NOR DARED TO BALK	61	3 DON JUAN	6	110	3
WITH DEADLIER ENGINES AND A SPEEDIER BLOW	106	3 DON JUAN	7	80	3
'TWAS BLOW FOR BLOW DISPUTING INCH BY INCH	150	3 DON JUAN	8	77	7
'TWAS BLOW FOR BLOW DISPUTING INCH BY INCH	150	3 DON JUAN	8	77	7
FOR THE SAME BLOW WHICH LAID HER MOTHER HERE	159	3 DON JUAN	8	95	4
HOW EAGER ALL THE EARTH IS FOR THE BLOW	258	3 DON JUAN	10	67	3
ON A LEE SHORE TILL IT BEGINS TO BLOW--	345	3 DON JUAN	12	63	3

BLOWING

THESE TO SECURE IN THIS STRONG BLOWING WEATHER	285	2 DON JUAN	3	18	7
AND LEFT HIS CHEEKS AS PALE AS SNOWDROPS BLOWING	478	2 DON JUAN	5	117	6
WHO ON A LARK WITH BLACK-EYED SAL (HIS BLOWING)	277	3 DON JUAN	11	19	7
WITH A SIROCCO FOR EXAMPLE BLOWING	422	3 DON JUAN	14	28	2

BLOWN

| AS OAKS BLOWN DOWN WITH ALL THEIR THOUSAND WINTERS | 155 | 3 DON JUAN | 8 | 88 | 8 |
| AND MINE'S A BUBBLE NOT BLOWN UP FOR PRAISE | 414 | 3 DON JUAN | 14 | 8 | 7 |

BLOWS

THE BLOWS UPON HIS CUTLASS AND THEN PUT	370	2 DON JUAN	4	49	3
AMONGST THEM ALL HARD BLOWS TO INFLICT OR WARD	76	3 DON JUAN	7	19	6
MAN QUITE AS QUIETLY AS BLOWS THE MONSOON	132	3 DON JUAN	8	39	5
FLING UP A STRAW 'TWILL SHOW THE WAY THE WIND BLOWS	414	3 DON JUAN	14	8	2

BLUCHER

| AND THAT IF BLUCHER BULOW GNEISENAU | 137 | 3 DON JUAN | 8 | 49 | 1 |

BLUE

'TIS THAT I STILL RETAIN MY BUFF AND BLUE	20	2 DON JUAN	D	17	4
AT MIDNIGHT ON THE BLUE AND MOONLIT DEEP	87	2 DON JUAN	1	122	2
AND CLAP A WHITE CAPE ON THEIR MANTLES BLUE	94	2 DON JUAN	1	134	5
AND LOSE IN SHINING SNOW THEIR SUMMITS BLUE	94	2 DON JUAN	1	134	V5
BUT ALMOST EVERY OTHER COUNTRY'S BLUE	163	2 DON JUAN	2	12	6
SOONER SHALL THIS BLUE OCEAN MELT TO AIR	166	2 DON JUAN	2	19	3
LULL'D THEM LIKE TURTLES SLEEPING ON THE BLUE	192	2 DON JUAN	2	68	5
THE SEA AND SKY WERE BLUE AND CLEAR AND MILD--	193	2 DON JUAN	2	70	4
RESTING ITS BRIGHT BASE ON THE QUIVERING BLUE	204	2 DON JUAN	2	91	3
WHERE THE BLUE VEINS LOOK'D SHADOWY SHRUNK AND WEAK	234	2 DON JUAN	2	147	5
THE SANDS UNTUMBLED THE BLUE WAVES UNTOST	251	2 DON JUAN	2	181	4
AND ALL THE STARS THAT CROWDED THE BLUE SPACE	262	2 DON JUAN	2	198	7
EMBROIDER'D DELICATELY O'ER WITH BLUE	308	2 DON JUAN	3	64	6
ON CRIMSON SATIN BORDER'D WITH PALE BLUE	309	2 DON JUAN	3	67	2
FORLORN AND GAZING ON THE DEEP BLUE SURGE	387	2 DON JUAN	4	79	3
FROM THE BLUE SKIES DERIVED A DOUBLE BLUE	393	2 DON JUAN	4	90	6
FROM THE BLUE SKIES DERIVED A DOUBLE BLUE	393	2 DON JUAN	4	90	6
OH DARKLY DEEPLY BEAUTIFULLY BLUE	404	2 DON JUAN	4	110	1
BLUE AS THE GARTERS WHICH SERENELY LIE	404	2 DON JUAN	4	110	6
BY MEASURING THE INTENSITY OF BLUE	406	2 DON JUAN	4	112	7

85

BLUE (CONTINUED)
```
     BROKE FOAMING O'ER THE BLUE SYMPLEGADES . . . . .   413  2 DON JUAN  5      5   2
     WITHOUT MORE PREFACE IN HER BLUE EYES BLENDING . . . . .  478  2 DON JUAN  5    116   5
     WITH GREAT BLUE EYES A LOVELY HAND AND ARM . . .    26  3 DON JUAN  6     41   3
     JUST WHEN THE FADING LAMPS WANED DIM AND BLUE . . . . .   41  3 DON JUAN  6     70   5
     AND HER PROUD BROW'S BLUE VEINS TO SWELL AND DARKLE . . .   56  3 DON JUAN  6    101   8
     FOR SEEING ONE WITH RIBBONS BLACK AND BLUE . . . . .  141  3 DON JUAN  8     57   5
     IN ITS MERIDIAN HER BLUE EYES OR GREY-- . . . . .  218  3 DON JUAN  9     71   2
     TOO WISE TO LOOK THROUGH OPTICS BLACK OR BLUE)-- . . . . .  218  3 DON JUAN  9     71   8
     SCOTCH PLAIDS SCOTCH SNOODS THE BLUE HILLS AND CLEAR STREAMS 233  3 DON JUAN 10     18   2
     THE SEVENTH WILL BRING BLUE DEVILS OR A DUN . . . . . .  243  3 DON JUAN 10     38   8
     THE BLUE SEA'S BORDER AND DON JUAN FELT-- . . . . .  257  3 DON JUAN 10     65   2
     NOW) YOU MAY CROSS THE BLUE DEEP AND WHITE FOAM-- . . . .  290  3 DON JUAN 11     44   3
     WHICH NOW HE FOUND WAS BLUE INSTEAD OF GREEN . . . .  294  3 DON JUAN 11     51   8
     AMONGST LIVE POETS AND BLUE LADIES PAST . . . . .  300  3 DON JUAN 11     64   2
     BUT IT IS TIME THAT I SHOULD HOIST MY BLUE PETER . . . .  309  3 DON JUAN 11     83   5
     SCOTCH WITH BLUE GREEN RIBBONS--IRISH WITH A BLUE . . .  314  3 DON JUAN 11   V 76   2
     SCOTCH WITH BLUE GREEN RIBBONS--IRISH WITH A BLUE . . .  314  3 DON JUAN 11   V 76   2
     OF WHITE CLIFFS WHITE NECKS BLUE EYES BLUER STOCKINGS . . .  346  3 DON JUAN 12     67   7
     AN EYE'S AN EYE AND WHETHER BLACK OR BLUE . . . .  359  3 DON JUAN 13      3   3
     ITS WINDINGS THROUGH THE WOODS NOW CLEAR NOW BLUE . . .  385  3 DON JUAN 13     58   7
     BLUE DEVILS AND BLUE-STOCKINGS AND ROMANCES . . . . .  444  3 DON JUAN 14     79   7
     HATH GOT BLUE DEVILS FOR HIS MORNING MIRRORS . . . .  457  3 DON JUAN 15      4   4
     WITH A SLIGHT SHADE OF BLUE TOO IT MIGHT BE . . . . .  474  3 DON JUAN 15     41   5
     BURNT AND NOT BLUE AS MODEST TAPERS USE . . . . .  512  3 DON JUAN 16     26   2
     SHE ALSO HAD A TWILIGHT TINGE OF BLUE . . . . . .  524  3 DON JUAN 16     47   1
     HER LAUGHING BLUE EYES WITH A GLANCE COULD SEIZE . . .  548  3 DON JUAN 16    100   4
     BUT STILL THE SHADE REMAINED THE BLUE EYES GLARED . . .  560  3 DON JUAN 16    121   1
BLUE-COAT
     DRAWN BY THE BLUE-COAT MISSES OF A COTERIE . . . . . .  404  2 DON JUAN  4    109   8
BLUELY
     THE RIVER FROM THE LAKE ALL BLUELY DASH'D . . . .  447  3 DON JUAN 14     87   6
BLUER
     OF WHITE CLIFFS WHITE NECKS BLUE EYES BLUER STOCKINGS . .  346  3 DON JUAN 12     67   7
BLUES
     THOU SHALT NOT BEAR FALSE WITNESS LIKE THE BLUES . .  140  2 DON JUAN  1    206   3
     OR ALL THE STUFF WHICH UTTERED BY THE BLUES IS . . . .  493  2 DON JUAN  5    143  V5
     THE BLUES THAT TENDER TRIBE WHO SIGH O'ER SONNETS . . .  294  3 DON JUAN 11     50   1
BLUE-STOCKING
     SAPPHO THE SAGE BLUE-STOCKING IN WHOSE GRAVE . . .  266  2 DON JUAN  2    205   4
BLUE-STOCKINGS
     BLUE DEVILS AND BLUE-STOCKINGS AND ROMANCES . . . . .  444  3 DON JUAN 14     79   7
BLUESTRING
     WHOSE HEART WAS FIX'D UPON A STAR OR BLUESTRING . . . .  474  3 DON JUAN 15     42   3
BLUNDER
     THEY MAKE SOME BLUNDER WHICH THEIR LADIES TELL US . . . .   74  2 DON JUAN  1     98   8
     AND SEEMS TO ME ALMOST A SORT OF BLUNDER . . . . .  100  2 DON JUAN  1    144   7
     I HAVE BUT ONE SIMILE AND THAT'S A BLUNDER . . . .   34  3 DON JUAN  6     57   7
     WAS FAVOURED BY AN ACCIDENT OR BLUNDER . . . . .  136  3 DON JUAN  8     46   2
     MAY LIKE BEING PRAISED FOR EVERY LUCKY BLUNDER . . .  185  3 DON JUAN  9      5   6
     THE WORLD WHICH AT THE WORST'S A GLORIOUS BLUNDER-- . . .  269  3 DON JUAN 11      3   8
     BUT THEY WHO BLUNDER THUS ARE RAW BEGINNERS . . . .  346  3 DON JUAN 12     66   1
     THAT HE HAD MADE AT FIRST A SILLY BLUNDER . . . .  560  3 DON JUAN 16    122   6
BLUNDERED
     YOUNG WOMEN AND CORRECT THEM WHEN THEY BLUNDERED . . . .   21  3 DON JUAN  6     31   8
     BUT AS IT HAPPENS TO BRAVE MEN THEY BLUNDERED-- . . .  149  3 DON JUAN  8     75   5
     THE TENTH OR TWENTIETH NAME WOULD BE BUT BLUNDERED . . .  324  3 DON JUAN 12     19   4
BLUNDERING
     A GO-BETWEEN YET BLUNDERING IN EXTREMES . . . . . .  155  2 DON JUAN  1   V  6   3
     HIS HASTE IMPATIENCE IS A BLUNDERING GUIDE . . . . .  304  3 DON JUAN 11     71   6
BLUNDER'S
     NOT EVEN A SPRIGHTLY BLUNDER'S SPARK CAN BLAZE . . . . .   17  2 DON JUAN  D     13   5
BLUNDERS
     THAN SOME WIVES (WHO MAKE BLUNDERS NO LESS STUPID) . .  205  3 DON JUAN  9     45   7
     IN THIS WHATEVER OTHER BLUNDERS LIE . . . . . .  378  3 DON JUAN 13     43   3
BLUNT
     A KIND OF BLUNT COMPASSION FOR THE SAD . . . . . .  417  2 DON JUAN  5     12   5
BLUSH
     THEY BLUSH AND WE BELIEVE THEM AT LEAST I . . . . .  119  2 DON JUAN  1    179   1
     FROM HEART TO CHEEK IS CURB'D INTO A BLUSH . . . .  231  2 DON JUAN  2    141   4
     FOR GREEKS AND FREEDOM--FOR GREECE A TEAR . . . . .  323  2 DON JUAN  3  L  6   6
     MUST WE BUT BLUSH--OUR FATHERS BLED . . . . .  323  2 DON JUAN  3  L  7   2
     BEGAN TO BLUSH UP TO THE EYES AND THEN . . . . .  483  2 DON JUAN  5    124   7
     GROW DEADLY PALE AND THEN BLUSH BACK AGAIN . . . .  483  2 DON JUAN  5    124   8
     THE NEW-BOUGHT VIRGIN MADE HER BLUSH AND SHAKE . . . .  501  2 DON JUAN  5    156   2
     A SLIGHT BLUSH A SOFT TREMOR A CALM KIND . . . . .   13  3 DON JUAN  6     15   1
     OF FAVOURITISM BUT NOT YET IN THE BLUSH-- . . . .  227  3 DON JUAN 10      5   2
     MEANING A VIRGIN'S FIRST BLUSH AT A ROUT . . . . .  330  3 DON JUAN 12     31   5
     AT THE FIRST BLUSH FOR A FAIR BRITON HIDES . . . .  350  3 DON JUAN 12     74   3
     BUT WHAT WAS BAD SHE DID NOT BLUSH IN TURN . . . .  545  3 DON JUAN 16     94   1
BLUSH'D
     SHE BLUSH'D AND FROWN'D NOT BUT SHE STROVE TO SPEAK . . .   81  2 DON JUAN  1    112   7
BLUSHED
     I CAN'T TELL WHY SHE BLUSHED NOR CAN EXPOUND . . . .   48  3 DON JUAN  6     85   5
     TO SAVE A SIRE WHO BLUSHED THAT HE BEGOT HIM . . . .  166  3 DON JUAN  8    110   8
     FAIR VIRGINS BLUSHED UPON HIM WEDDED DAMES . . . .  293  3 DON JUAN 11     48   1
     BLUSHED TOO BUT IT WAS HIDDEN BY THEIR ROUGE . . . . .  293  3 DON JUAN 11     48  V2
BLUSHES
     PERHAPS SOME VIRTUOUS BLUSHES--LET THEM GO-- . . . . .   13  2 DON JUAN  D      7   2
```

BLUSHES   (CONTINUED)
   AND BURNING BLUSHES THOUGH FOR NO TRANSGRESSION . . . . . 62 2 DON JUAN 1   74   3
   BLUSHES FOR THOSE WHO WILL NOT--BUT TO SIGH . . . . . . 286 3 DON JUAN 11   38   4
   AND THE VINE BLUSHES LIKE AURORA'S LIP . . . . 320 3 DON JUAN 12   9   5
   TO PATRIOT SYMPATHY A BRITON'S BLUSHES-- . . . . 425 3 DON JUAN 14   35   4
   THAN TO WAX WHITE--FOR BLUSHES ARE FOR QUALITY . . . . 532 3 DON JUAN 16   64   8
BLUSHING
   AND REDLY RAN HIS BLUSHING WATERS DOWN . . . . 175 3 DON JUAN 8   127   4
   BLUSHING AND BEARDLESS AND YET NE'ERTHELESS . . . . . . 206 3 DON JUAN 9   47   2
   BLUSHING WITH BACCHANT CORONALS ALONG . . . . 394 3 DON JUAN 13   76   2
BLUSTERING
   FOR BLUSTERING BUNGLING TRIMMING WRANGLING WRITING . . . 150 2 DON JUAN 1 V 1   5
BOA
   HE LAY COILED LIKE THE BOA IN THE WOOD . . . . 300 2 DON JUAN 3   48   4
BOABDIL
   BOABDIL WEPT OF DONNA JULIA'S KIN . . . . 52 2 DON JUAN 1   56   6
BOARD
   TO SAVE ONE HALF THE PEOPLE THEN ON BOARD . . . . 181 2 DON JUAN 2   48   8
   ON BOARD OF ONE OF THESE AND UNDER HATCHES . . . . . . 371 2 DON JUAN 4   50   7
   WE WERE TRANSFER'D ON BOARD HER IN A HURRY . . . . . . 389 2 DON JUAN 4   82   5
   LIKE A BACKGAMMON BOARD THE PLACE WAS DOTTED . . . . . 416 2 DON JUAN 5   10   1
   THE EUNUCH MADE A SIGN TO THOSE ON BOARD . . . . 433 2 DON JUAN 5   41   7
   AND SCORN HIS TEMPERATE BOARD AS NONE AT ALL . . . . . 316 3 DON JUAN 12   3   6
   THEIR TABLE WAS A BOARD TO TEMPT EVEN GHOSTS . . . . . 404 3 DON JUAN 13   99   3
   OBSERVED AS STRICTLY BOTH AT BOARD AND BED . . . . . . 470 3 DON JUAN 15   32   6
   AT THE FULL BOARD AND SIT ALIKE DELIGHTED . . . . 534 3 DON JUAN 16   69   5
BOARDS
   AND WOUNDED SEVERAL SHUTTERS AND SOME BOARDS . . . . . 99 2 DON JUAN 1   143   8
BOARS
   IF SHE HATH NO WILD BOARS SHE HATH A TAME . . . . 395 3 DON JUAN 13   78   7
BOAST
   FOR THERE ONE LEARNS--'TIS NOT FOR ME TO BOAST . . . . . 50 2 DON JUAN 1   53   1
   YET IF I NAME MY GUILT 'TIS NOT TO BOAST . . . . 130 2 DON JUAN 1   193   5
   WOULD SHE BE PROUD OR BOAST HERSELF THE FREE . . . . . 258 3 DON JUAN 10   68   1
   NONE THAN THEMSELVES COULD BOAST A LONGER LINE . . . . 381 3 DON JUAN 13   50   5
   WAS WONT TO BOAST--AS IF A GLUTTON'S TRAY . . . . 538 3 DON JUAN 16   78   3
BOASTS
   THE SENTIMENTAL BOASTS TO BE UNMOVED . . . . 442 3 DON JUAN 14   73   6
BOAT
   THAT A TIGHT BOAT WILL LIVE IN A ROUGH SEA . . . . . . 180 2 DON JUAN 2   45   7
   NINE IN THE CUTTER THIRTY IN THE BOAT . . . . 185 2 DON JUAN 2   54   7
   AND FOR THE BOAT--THE CREW KEPT CROWDING IN IT . . . . 186 2 DON JUAN 2   57   8
   AGUE IN ITS COLD FIT THEY FILL'D THEIR BOAT . . . . . . 189 2 DON JUAN 2   63   7
   'TIS THUS WITH PEOPLE IN AN OPEN BOAT . . . . 191 2 DON JUAN 2   66   1
   THE FIFTH DAY AND THEIR BOAT LAY FLOATING THERE . . . . 193 2 DON JUAN 2   70   3
   THE MEN WITHIN THE BOAT AND IN THIS GUISE . . . . 206 2 DON JUAN 2   94   6
   THE BOAT MADE WAY YET NOW THEY WERE SO LOW . . . . . . 207 2 DON JUAN 2   96   3
   AND AT THE BOTTOM OF THE BOAT THREE WERE . . . . 208 2 DON JUAN 2   98   6
   THEY RAN THE BOAT FOR SHORE AND OVERSET HER . . . . . . 211 2 DON JUAN 2   104   8
   HE STILL WAS IN THE BOAT AND HAD BUT DOZED . . . . . . 215 2 DON JUAN 2   112   3
   HE WISHES FOR A BOAT TO SAIL THE DEEPS-- . . . . 333 2 DON JUAN 3   98   5
   ANOTHER OUTCRY FOR A LITTLE BOAT . . . . 333 2 DON JUAN 3   98   7
   THEY LAID HIM IN A BOAT AND PLIED THE OAR . . . . 371 2 DON JUAN 4   50   5
   BORE OFF HIS BARGAINS TO A GILDED BOAT . . . . 432 2 DON JUAN 5   40   2
   THE IMPERIAL BRIDE--AND ADDED LET THE BOAT . . . . 62 3 DON JUAN 6   113   2
   BUT WHAT IF CARRYING SAIL CAPSIZE THE BOAT . . . . . . 191 3 DON JUAN 9   18   3
   WHERE SHIPS HAVE FOUNDERED AS DOTH MANY A BOAT . . . . 227 3 DON JUAN 10   4   8
BOATMAN
   THE LITTLE BOATMAN AND HIS PETER BELL . . . . 334 2 DON JUAN 3   100   7
BOATS
   SOME HOISTED OUT THE BOATS AND THERE WAS ONE . . . . . 179 2 DON JUAN 2   44   6
   GETTING THE BOATS OUT BEING WELL AWARE . . . . 180 2 DON JUAN 2   45   6
   THE OTHER BOATS THE YAWL AND PINNACE HAD . . . . 181 2 DON JUAN 2   48   1
   AND TWO BOATS COULD NOT HOLD FAR LESS BE STORED . . . . 181 2 DON JUAN 2   48   7
   THE BOATS PUT OFF O'ERCROWDED WITH THEIR CREWS . . . . 183 2 DON JUAN 2   51   6
   THE BOATS PULLED OFF WITH THEIR HALF NAKED CREWS . . . 183 2 DON JUAN 2   51 V6
   THE BOATS AS STATED HAD GOT OFF BEFORE . . . . 185 2 DON JUAN 2   54   1
   PEDLARS AND BOATS AND WAGGONS OH YE SHADES . . . . . . 334 2 DON JUAN 3   100   1
   TO FIND OUR WAY TO MARMORA WITHOUT BOATS . . . . 464 2 DON JUAN 5   92   6
   THEIR DELHIS MANNED SOME BOATS AND SAILED AGAIN . . . . 82 3 DON JUAN 7   31   3
   BOATS WHEN 'TWAS WATER SKAITING WHEN 'TWAS ICE . . . . 407 3 DON JUAN 13   106   3
BOAT'S-CREW
   OR WITH A FAMISH'D BOAT'S-CREW HAD YOUR BIRTH . . . . . 201 2 DON JUAN 2   84   6
BOAZ
   YOU MAY BE BOAZ AND I--MODEST RUTH . . . . 403 3 DON JUAN 13   96   4
BOB
   BOB SOUTHEY YOU'RE A POET--POET-LAUREATE . . . .   9 2 DON JUAN D   1   1
   YOU BOB ARE RATHER INSOLENT YOU KNOW . . . . 10 2 DON JUAN D   3   1
   GASPING ON DECK BECAUSE YOU SOAR TOO HIGH BOB . . . . . 10 2 DON JUAN D   3   7
   AND FALL FOR LACK OF MOISTURE QUITE A-DRY BOB . . . . . 10 2 DON JUAN D   3   8
   AN EPIC FROM BOB SOUTHEY EVERY SPRING--) . . . . 332 2 DON JUAN 3   97   4
   AS THROUGH HIS PALMS BOB ACRES' VALOUR OOZED . . . . . 493 2 DON JUAN 5   142   1
BOBADIL
   THE DOUBLE BOBADIL TAKES SCORN FOR AWE . . . . 153 2 DON JUAN 1 V 4   8
BOB-MAJOR
   LIKE A BOB-MAJOR FROM A VILLAGE STEEPLE . . . . 109 3 DON JUAN 7   85   8
BOCCACIO'S
   EVERGREEN FOREST WHICH BOCCACIO'S LORE . . . . 337 2 DON JUAN 3   105   6
BODDICES
   BUT NEVER PUT ON PANTALOONS OR BODDICES . . . . 44 2 DON JUAN 1   41   4

```
                                                PAGE VOL      CANTO STANZA LN
BODE
    TO BODE HIM NO GREAT GOOD HE DEPRECATED  . . . . . .    57   3 DON JUAN  6    102    2
BODED
    BODED NO GOOD WHATEVER IT EXPRESS'D  . . . . . . .     297   2 DON JUAN  3     42    4
    A THING WHICH VICTORY BY NO MEANS BODED  . . . . . .   119   3 DON JUAN  8     16    6
BODIES
    FOR KILLING BODIES AND FOR SAVING SOULS  . . . . . .    93   2 DON JUAN  1    132    2
    HAD LEFT THEIR BODIES AND WHAT'S WORSE ALAS . . . . .  185   2 DON JUAN  2     55    2
    WHERE MEN HAVE SOULS OR BODIES SHE MUST ANSWER . . . . 390   2 DON JUAN  4     84    8
    BUT ON THEY MARCHED DEAD BODIES TRAMPLING O'ER . . . . 120   3 DON JUAN  8     19    5
    OVER A HEAP OF BODIES FELT HIS HEEL  . . . . . . .     153   3 DON JUAN  8     83    2
    AMIDST THE BODIES LULLED IN BLOODY REST  . . . . . .   157   3 DON JUAN  8     91    8
    THOSE MOVEMENTS THOSE IMPROVEMENTS IN OUR BODIES . . . 220   3 DON JUAN  9     75    1
    WHICH MAKE ALL BODIES ANXIOUS TO GET OUT . . . . . .   220   3 DON JUAN  9     75    2
    OF PHYSICS BODIES WHETHER SHORT OR TALL  . . . . . .   511   3 DON JUAN 16     24    6
    SUCH BODIES COULD HAVE SOULS OR SOULS SUCH BODIES . . . 543  3 DON JUAN 16     90    8
    SUCH BODIES COULD HAVE SOULS OR SOULS SUCH BODIES . . . 543  3 DON JUAN 16     90    8
BODING
    AND THUS SOME BODING FLASH'D THROUGH EITHER FRAME . . . 355  2 DON JUAN  4     21    6
BODY
    AND THEN THEY LEFT OFF EATING THE DEAD BODY  . . . . . 200  2 DON JUAN  2     82    8
    MAY MAKE UP FOR A BULLET IN HIS BODY  . . . . . .       77  2 DON JUAN  7     21    3
    AND HE WHOSE VERY BODY WAS ALL MIND  . . . . . . .     139   3 DON JUAN  8     54    5
    FOR ONE ROUGH WEATHER-BEATEN VETERAN BODY  . . . . .   167   3 DON JUAN  8    112    7
    ALL THAT THE BODY PERPETRATES OF BAD . . . . . . .     173   3 DON JUAN  8    123    2
    FOLLOWING THE BENT OF BODY OR OF MIND)  . . . . . .    193   3 DON JUAN  9     21    5
    NOT ONLY IN THE BODY BUT THE PROEM . . . . . . . .     193   3 DON JUAN  9     22    3
    AND 'GAINST THE BODY MAKES A STRONG APPEAL . . . . .   234   3 DON JUAN 10     20    5
    OF WORLDS AND SPECIES--MATTERS--SOULS AND BODY . . . . 269  3 DON JUAN 11      3   V7
    HIS POCKETS FIRST AND THEN HIS BODY RIDDLED  . . . .   276   3 DON JUAN 11     17    8
    ENDS WHEN THE BODY OF THE BOOK'S BEGUN . . . . . .     356   3 DON JUAN 12     87    2
    THE GOODLIEST SOIL OF BODY AND OF MIND . . . . . .     359   3 DON JUAN 13      2    8
    CERTES IT WAS NOT BODY HE WAS WELL . . . . . . .       441   3 DON JUAN 14     71    4
    HINTING THAT SOUL AND BODY ON THE WHOLE  . . . . . .   558   3 DON JUAN 16    118    7
    IT TOUCHED NO SOUL NOR BODY BUT THE WALL . . . . . .   559   3 DON JUAN 16    120    2
    OF THOSE IN WHICH THE BODY SEEMED TO DRIVE . . . . .   569   3 DON JUAN 17   V 13    5
BOEOTIAN
    AND THAT DEEP-MOUTHED BOEOTIAN SAVAGE LANDOR . . . . . 298  3 DON JUAN 11     59    7
BOG
    AS TRAVELLERS FOLLOW OVER BOG AND BRAKE  . . . . . .   127   3 DON JUAN  8     32    4
BOGGY
    WHICH LEADS BEHOLDERS ON A BOGGY WALK  . . . . . . .    89   3 DON JUAN  7     46    6
BOGLE
    IN MIND A SORT OF SENTIMENTAL BOGLE  . . . . . .      304   3 DON JUAN 11     72    4
BOHEA
    THAT I MUST HAVE RECOURSE TO BLACK BOHEA . . . . . .   372   2 DON JUAN  4     52    6
BOIL
    FOR GENTLEMEN WHOSE PASSIONS MAY BOIL OER  . . . . .   313   3 DON JUAN 11   V 29    5
    IT MAKES MY BLOOD BOIL LIKE THE SPRINGS OF HECLA . . . 497  3 DON JUAN 15     92    7
BOIL'D
    CLOVES CINNAMON AND SAFFRON TOO WERE BOIL'D  . . . .   307   2 DON JUAN  3     63    7
    BOIL'D UP AND PROVED HER TRULY OF HIS RACE . . . . .   367   2 DON JUAN  4     44    8
BOILED
    BOILED IN HIS VEINS AND RATHER THAN DESCEND  . . . .   471   2 DON JUAN  5    104    4
BOILING
    TO SHOW ITS BOILING SURF AND BOUNDING SPRAY  . . . .   211   2 DON JUAN  2    104    6
BOILS
    AND THE LOUD BREAKER BOILS AGAINST THE ROCK  . . . .    94   2 DON JUAN  1    134    7
    AS WIFE AND FRIENDS DID FOR THE BOILS OF JOB-- . . . . 105  3 DON JUAN  7     77    7
    OF CITIES THAT BOILS OVER WITH THEIR SCUM-- . . . . .  272   3 DON JUAN 11      8    8
BOLD
    AGAINST ALL NOBLE MALADIES HE'S BOLD . . . . . . .     168   2 DON JUAN  2     22    5
    ALL THIS THE MOST WERE PATIENT AND SOME BOLD . . . .   178   2 DON JUAN  2     42    4
    HOW ANSWERS EACH BOLD BACCHANAL  . . . . . . . .      324   2 DON JUAN  3   L  9    6
    THIS SPIRIT'S WELL BUT IT MAY WAX TOO BOLD . . . . .   454   2 DON JUAN  5     75    3
    THE BRITON MUST BE BOLD WHO REALLY DURST . . . . . .   136   3 DON JUAN  8     48    5
    NAPOLEON ON HIS BOLD AND BLOODY TRACK  . . . . . .    147   3 DON JUAN  8     70    3
    AS BOLD AS DANIEL IN THE LION'S DEN  . . . . . . .    217   3 DON JUAN  9     69    4
    THOUGH BOLD AND BLOODY WAS THE KIND OF THING . . . .   217   3 DON JUAN  9     70    2
    EVEN THE BOLD CHURCHMAN'S TOMB EXCITED AWE . . . . .   261   3 DON JUAN 10     74    4
    BOLD BRITONS WE ARE NOW ON SHOOTER'S HILL  . . . . .   264   3 DON JUAN 10     80    8
    BEAR A BOLD BROW AND FOR YOUR BOSOM NERVE IT . . . .   367   3 DON JUAN 13     18   V4
    BECAUSE BOLD BRITONS HAVE A TONGUE AND FREE QUILL . . . 367  3 DON JUAN 13     20    5
    BUT INNOCENCE IS BOLD EVEN AT THE STAKE  . . . . .    437   3 DON JUAN 14     61    5
    THERE WERE SOME HUNTERS BOLD AND COURSERS KEEN . . . . 539  3 DON JUAN 16     80    1
BOLDLY
    WHO LIVE BY LIES YET DARE NOT BOLDLY LIE . . . . . .   285   3 DON JUAN 11     36    5
    ALSO A SO-SO MATRON BOLDLY FIGHT . . . . . . . .      397   3 DON JUAN 13     82    5
    BOLDLY REFERRING TO THE LIST OF PEERS  . . . . . .    432   3 DON JUAN 14     52    3
BOLERO
    HE GLANCED LIKE A PERSONIFIED BOLERO . . . . . . .    427   3 DON JUAN 14     39    8
BOLOGNA
    FROM AN OLD ROMAN PRINCESS AT BOLOGNA  . . . . . .    389   2 DON JUAN  4     83    8
BOLT
    BUT BEG SECURITY WILL BOLT THE DOOR  . . . . . . .     69   2 DON JUAN  1     89    8
    DO PRAY UNDO THE BOLT A LITTLE FASTER--  . . . . . .    96   2 DON JUAN  1    137    5
    NO LESS A VICTIM TO THE BOLT AND BAR . . . . . . .    258   3 DON JUAN 10     68    4
BOLTED
    NO SOONER WAS IT BOLTED THAN--OH SHAME . . . . . .    112   2 DON JUAN  1    165    1
```

```
                                                          PAGE VOL        CANTO STANZA LN
BOLTS
     AND GUARDS AND BOLTS AND WALLS AND NOW AND THEN    . . . .  22   3 DON JUAN  6     32   4
BOLUS
     BOLUS POTASSAE SULPHURET SUMENDUS . . . . . . . . . 244   3 DON JUAN 10     41   7
BOMB
     AS BRAVE AS EVER FACED BOTH BOMB AND BALL    . . . . . 116   3 DON JUAN  8      9   5
     AT SHRINKING FROM A BULLET OR A BOMB  . . . . . . . 132   3 DON JUAN  8     38   6
BOMBARD
     THE FIRST WAS TO BOMBARD IT AND KNOCK DOWN  . . . . .  78   3 DON JUAN  7     23   3
BOMBAZEEN
     MISS BOMBAZEEN MISS MACKSTAY MISS O'TABBEY  . . . . . 396   3 DON JUAN 13     79   5
BOMBS
     BOMBS DRUMS GUNS BASTIONS BATTERIES BAYONETS BULLETS . . 106   3 DON JUAN  7     78   7
BON
     AWAIT THOSE WHO HAVE STUDIED THEIR BON MOTS . . . . . 403   3 DON JUAN 13     97   8
     TO INTRODUCE A BON MOT HEAD AND EARS . . . . . . . 408   3 DON JUAN 13    109   4
     IMBIBED THE GAY BON MOT OR HAPPY HOAX . . . . . . . 540   3 DON JUAN 16     83   5
BONAPARTE
     OH YE GREAT BULLETINS OF BONAPARTE . . . . . . . . 108   3 DON JUAN  7     82   1
     HAD BONAPARTE WON AT WATERLOO  . . . . . . . . . 449   3 DON JUAN 14     90   1
BONAPARTE'S
     THE SHADE OF BONAPARTE'S NOBLE DARING-- . . . . . . 318   3 DON JUAN 12      5   7
BOND
     IS ALWAYS SO TO WOMEN ONE SOLE BOND  . . . . . . . 263   2 DON JUAN  2    200   2
     YET 'TIS SO NOMINATED IN THE BOND  . . . . . . . . 278   2 DON JUAN  3      7   5
     WHICH IS BUT A PRECARIOUS BOND IN SOOTH . . . . . .  14   3 DON JUAN  6     16   5
     ITS BLOODY BOND AND SAVED PERHAPS SOME PRETTY . . . . 174   3 DON JUAN  8    124   3
     AND GREECE AND BOUND FAIR HELEN IN A BOND  . . . . . 209   3 DON JUAN  9     53  V6
BONDAGE
     ESTABLISHED BETWEEN THEM AND BONDAGE THEY  . . . . .  23   3 DON JUAN  6     34   7
BONDS
     WHERE SHALL I TURN ME NOT TO VIEW ITS BONDS . . . . .  19   2 DON JUAN  D     16   1
     THEIR BONDS WHENE'ER SOME ZEPHYR CAUGHT BEGAN  . . . . 313   2 DON JUAN  3     73   7
     WHEN FREED FROM BONDS (WHICH ARE OF NO GREAT USE . . .  23   3 DON JUAN  6     34   4
BONE
     AS I AM BLOOD--BONE--MARROW PASSION--FEELING-- . . . 156   2 DON JUAN  1   V  8   2
     WHICH ON ROUGH ROADS LEAVES SCARCELY A WHOLE BONE)  . . 197   3 DON JUAN  9     30   3
     ELEVEN THOUSAND MAIDENHEADS OF BONE  . . . . . . . 255   3 DON JUAN 10     62   7
     ENDS IN A RUSTY CASQUE AND DUBIOUS BONE  . . . . . . 261   3 DON JUAN 10     73   6
BONES
     ONE BREAKS YOUR BONES ONE SETS THEM IN THEIR SOCKETS .  91   2 DON JUAN  1    129   4
     AND WHEN HIS BONES ARE DUST HIS GRAVE A BLANK . . . . 327   2 DON JUAN  3     89   1
     I PASS EACH DAY WHERE DANTE'S BONES ARE LAID  . . . . 400   2 DON JUAN  4    104   1
     AS WE NOW GAZE UPON THE MAMMOTH'S BONES  . . . . . . 180   3 DON JUAN  8    137   3
     WHITE BLACK OR COPPER--THE DEAD BONES WILL GRIN . . . 188   3 DON JUAN  9     12   8
     IN LIEU OF SONS OF THESE HE MADE NO BONES  . . . . . 410   3 DON JUAN 14      1   8
BONFIRES
     AS ALSO BONFIRES MADE OF COUNTRY SEATS  . . . . . . 281   3 DON JUAN 11     27   3
BON-MOTS
     AND SEVERAL OF HER BEST BON-MOTS WERE HAWKED ABOUT  . . 338   3 DON JUAN 12     47   5
BONN
     BUT JUAN POSTED ON THROUGH MANHEIM BONN  . . . . . . 255   3 DON JUAN 10     62   1
BONNE
     IF THAT A BONNE FORTUNE BE REALLY BONNE  . . . . . . 438   3 DON JUAN 14     64   8
     IF THAT A BONNE FORTUNE BE REALLY BONNE  . . . . . . 438   3 DON JUAN 14     64   8
     THERE WAS A GOODLY SOUPE A LA BONNE FEMME  . . . . . 483   3 DON JUAN 15     63   1
     BUT THOUGH A BONNE VIVANTE I MUST CONFESS  . . . . . 483   3 DON JUAN 15     64   5
BONNET
     OR RATHER BONNET WHICH THE FAIR SEX WEAR . . . . . .  13   3 DON JUAN  6     14   5
BONNETS
     LINE THE INTERIOR OF THEIR HEADS OR BONNETS . . . . . 294   3 DON JUAN 11     50   3
     AND SETTLED BONNETS BY THE NEWEST CODE   . . . . . . 406   3 DON JUAN 13    104   6
BONOS
     AND SOLACE YOUR SLIGHT LAPSE 'GAINST BONOS MORES . . . 432   3 DON JUAN 14     50   7
BONY
     AND FAMINE WITH HER GAUNT AND BONY GROWTH   . . . . .  88   3 DON JUAN  7     45   6
BOOBIES
     AT LENGTH THEY CAUGHT TWO BOOBIES AND A NODDY . . . . 200   2 DON JUAN  2     82   7
BOOBY
     THE SPOUSE OF POTIPHAR THE LADY BOOBY . . . . . . . 486   2 DON JUAN  5    131   2
BOOK
     THIS TOO WAS A SEAL'D BOOK TO LITTLE JUAN-- . . . . .  48   2 DON JUAN  1     48   1
     SOMETIMES HE TURN'D TO GAZE UPON HIS BOOK   . . . . .  72   2 DON JUAN  1     95   1
     DIVIDED IN TWELVE BOOKS EACH BOOK CONTAINING  . . . . 135   2 DON JUAN  1    200   2
     A BOOK--A DAMNED BAD PICTURE AND WORSE BUST . . . . . 146   2 DON JUAN  1    218  V8
     GO LITTLE BOOK FROM THIS MY SOLITUDE  . . . . . . . 149   2 DON JUAN  1    222   1
     AND READ (THE ONLY BOOK SHE COULD) THE LINES . . . . 241   2 DON JUAN  2    162   3
     TURNS OFTENER TO THE STARS THAN TO HIS BOOK . . . . . 242   2 DON JUAN  2    163   6
     THE BOOK WHICH TREATS OF THIS ERRONEOUS PAIR . . . . 282   2 DON JUAN  3     12   6
     A BOOK FRIEND SINGLE LADY OR A GLASS  . . . . . . . 444   2 DON JUAN  5     58   2
     AND DECORATES THE BOOK OF COMMON PRAYER   . . . . . .  17   3 DON JUAN  6     23   7
     SET DOWN HIS SAYINGS IN HER COMMON-PLACE BOOK . . . . 294   3 DON JUAN 11     52   8
     WHO IN HIS COMMON-PLACE BOOK HAD A PAGE   . . . . . . 403   3 DON JUAN 13     97   5
     THERE IS A COMMON-PLACE BOOK ARGUMENT . . . . . . . 564   3 DON JUAN 17      5   1
BOOKISH
     BUT BY THE BOOKISH THEORIC IT APPEARS . . . . . . .  10   3 DON JUAN  6      9   2
BOOK'S
     ENDS WHEN THE BODY OF THE BOOK'S BEGUN   . . . . . . 356   3 DON JUAN 12     87   2
     I WISH SHE HAD HIS BOOK'S THE ELEVENTH COMMANDMENT   . . 472   3 DON JUAN 15     38   2
```

		PAGE	VOL	CANTO	STANZA	LN
BOOKS						
OR MRS TRIMMER'S BOOKS ON EDUCATION		29	2	DON JUAN 1	16	3
AND OPEN'D CERTAIN TRUNKS OF BOOKS AND LETTERS		36	2	DON JUAN 1	28	2
THERE POETS FIND MATERIALS FOR THEIR BOOKS		70	2	DON JUAN 1	90	5
DIVIDED IN TWELVE BOOKS EACH BOOK CONTAINING		135	2	DON JUAN 1	200	2
AT THE FIRST TWO BOOKS HAVING TOO MUCH TRUTH		397	2	DON JUAN 4	97	4
OH YE WHO MAKE THE FORTUNES OF ALL BOOKS		403	2	DON JUAN 4	108	1
WHEN THE SALE OF NEW BOOKS IS NOT SO FLEET		79	3	DON JUAN 7	26	5
THESE FIRST TWELVE BOOKS ARE MERELY FLOURISHES		341	3	DON JUAN 12	54	5
AND TUMBLED BOOKS OR CRITICISED THE PICTURES		406	3	DON JUAN 13	102	2
HAD MUSIC--WALKING--RIDING--BOOKS--AND TALK		407	3	DON JUAN 13	104	V2
AND THAT THEIR BOOKS HAVE BUT ONE STYLE IN COMMON--		418	3	DON JUAN 14	19	7
THE SUREST WAY FOR LADIES AND FOR BOOKS		453	3	DON JUAN 14	97	7
ARRANGING THEM LIKE BOOKS ON THE SAME SHELF		470	3	DON JUAN 15	31	3
MAKE MORE IMPRESSION THAN THE BEST OF BOOKS		493	3	DON JUAN 15	84	8
AURORA WHO LOOK'D MORE ON BOOKS THAN FACES		494	3	DON JUAN 15	85	1
BOOMING						
LONG BOOMING OF EACH PEAL ON PEAL O'ERCAME		115	3	DON JUAN 8	6	6
BOOMS						
AT HALF-PAST EIGHT O'CLOCK BOOMS HENCOOPS SPARS		183	2	DON JUAN 2	51	1
BOON						
STRONG PALPITATION RISES 'TIS HER BOON		267	2	DON JUAN 2	208	6
AS ANY OTHER BOON FOR WHICH MEN STICKLE		134	3	DON JUAN 8	43	4
THE GENERAL BOON BACK-WOODSMAN OF KENTUCKY		143	3	DON JUAN 8	61	4
CITE IS THAT BOON LIVED HUNTING UP TO NINETY		143	3	DON JUAN 8	62	8
BOORS						
OF THE IMMORTAL PETER'S POLISHED BOORS		194	3	DON JUAN 9	23	3
THE BOORS CRIED DANG IT WHO'D HAVE THOUGHT IT--SIRES		425	3	DON JUAN 14	34	4
BOOT						
AND ARM'D FROM BOOT TO TURBAN ONE AND ALL		369	2	DON JUAN 4	47	6
BOOTIES						
THY PACKETS ALL WHOSE PASSENGERS ARE BOOTIES		259	3	DON JUAN 10	69	5
BOOTY						
OH FOR A GLASS OF MAX WE'VE MISS'D OUR BOOTY--		276	3	DON JUAN 11	16	3
GOD DAMN YOU LADS I'VE MISSED A HANDSOME BOOTY		276	3	DON JUAN 11	16	V3
GAUNT GOURMAND WITH WHOLE NATIONS FOR YOUR BOOTY		459	3	DON JUAN 15	9	5
OLD SKELETON WITH AGES FOR YOUR BOOTY		459	3	DON JUAN 15	9	V5
WHOSE SOLE ACCOMPLISHMENTS WERE QUITE A BOOTY		471	3	DON JUAN 15	34	6
BOOZE						
BOOZE IN THE KEN OR AT THE SPELLKEN HUSTLE		277	3	DON JUAN 11	19	4
BORDER						
AND ROUND THEM RAN A YELLOW BORDER TOO		308	2	DON JUAN 3	64	4
THE UPPER BORDER RICHLY WROUGHT DISPLAY'D		308	2	DON JUAN 3	64	5
AND FOURSCORE CANNON ON THE DANUBE'S BORDER		85	3	DON JUAN 7	38	7
THE BLUE SEA'S BORDER AND DON JUAN FELT--		257	3	DON JUAN 10	65	2
BORDER'D						
ON CRIMSON SATIN BORDER'D WITH PALE BLUE		309	2	DON JUAN 3	67	2
BORE						
AND THEN THIS BEST AND MEEKEST WOMAN BORE		36	2	DON JUAN 1	29	1
OF POETS AND ROMANCERS--YOU'RE A BORE		84	2	DON JUAN 1	116	6
THEY SO EMBELLISH THAT 'TIS QUITE A BORE		137	2	DON JUAN 1	202	6
FROM WHICH AWAY SO FAIR AND FAST THEY BORE		163	2	DON JUAN 2	13	4
BUT THE BOY BORE UP LONG AND WITH A MILD		203	2	DON JUAN 2	88	3
HE BORE THESE SNEERS AGAINST HIS NEAR RELATIONS		299	2	DON JUAN 3	46	5
SUCH AS THE DORIC MOTHERS BORE		325	2	DON JUAN 3	L 13	4
AND THEN THEY BOUND HIM WHERE HE FELL AND BORE		371	2	DON JUAN 4	50	1
O'ERCHARGED WITH RAIN HER SUMMON'D HANDMAIDS BORE		376	2	DON JUAN 4	59	4
AND BORE HIM WITH SOME GAIETY AND GRACE		388	2	DON JUAN 4	81	6
TO BEAR THE COMPLIMENTS OF MANY A BORE		404	2	DON JUAN 4	109	3
BORE OFF HIS BARGAINS TO A GILDED BOAT		432	2	DON JUAN 5	40	2
WHATEER THE GARDEN BORE OR MART DISCLOSED		476	2	DON JUAN 5	113	V4
NOT ONLY AS SIN BUT AS A BORE--		12	3	DON JUAN 6	12	4
UPON THE GOLDEN FRUIT THE VISION BORE		44	3	DON JUAN 6	77	6
THE DISCIPLINE OF THE WHOLE HAREM BORE		57	3	DON JUAN 6	103	2
THAT ONE WOULD THINK THE FIRST WHO BORE IT ADAM		79	3	DON JUAN 7	25	8
FOR SIX HOURS BORE THEY WITHOUT INTERMISSION		81	3	DON JUAN 7	30	1
HIS YOUTH AND CONSTITUTION BORE HIM THROUGH		245	3	DON JUAN 10	43	3
WAS GIVEN TO HER FAVOURITE AND NOW BORE HIS		248	3	DON JUAN 10	49	8
TELL THEM SIR WILLIAM CURTIS IS A BORE		267	3	DON JUAN 10	86	5
PRIVATE THOUGH PUBLICLY IMPORTANT BORE		283	3	DON JUAN 11	32	2
TO FREEDOM HE APPLIED (A GRIEF AND A BORE)		288	3	DON JUAN 11	41	6
BUT SINCE THEY ARE THAT EPOCH IS A BORE		316	3	DON JUAN 12	2	4
AND THEN EVEN THEN SOME BORE MAY MAKE THEM LOSE IT		408	3	DON JUAN 13	109	6
THERE'S LITTLE LEFT BUT TO BE BORED OR BORE		418	3	DON JUAN 14	18	6
WHO IN HIS LIFE-TIME EACH WAS DEEMED A BORE		566	3	DON JUAN 17	9	4
BOREALIS						
A VERSIFIED AURORA BOREALIS		67	3	DON JUAN 7	2	3
BORED						
FORM'D OF TWO MIGHTY TRIBES THE BORES AND BORED		402	3	DON JUAN 13	95	8
THERE'S LITTLE LEFT BUT TO BE BORED OR BORE		418	3	DON JUAN 14	18	6
BORES						
PRESERVE OF BORES WHO OUGHT TO BE MADE GAME		395	3	DON JUAN 13	78	8
FORM'D OF TWO MIGHTY TRIBES THE BORES AND BORED		402	3	DON JUAN 13	95	8
BORN						
IN SEVILLE WAS HE BORN A PLEASANT CITY		25	2	DON JUAN 1	8	1
HE HAD BEEN ILL BROUGHT UP AND WAS BORN BILIOUS		40	2	DON JUAN 1	35	8
WHICH SOME ARE BORN WITH BUT THE MOST PART LEARN		71	2	DON JUAN 1	93	3
ALL THINGS THAT HAVE BEEN BORN WERE BORN TO DIE		147	2	DON JUAN 1	220	3
ALL THINGS THAT HAVE BEEN BORN WERE BORN TO DIE		147	2	DON JUAN 1	220	3

BORN   (CONTINUED)
    WERE SETTLED LONG ERE JUAN'S SIRE WAS BORN . . . . 169 2 DON JUAN 2   24   4
    HE DIED AS BORN A CATHOLIC IN FAITH . . . . 197 2 DON JUAN 2   76   5
    MUST SHARE IT--HAPPINESS WAS BORN A TWIN . . . . 247 2 DON JUAN 2   172   8
    HAIDEE WAS PASSION'S CHILD BORN WHERE THE SUN . . . . . 264 2 DON JUAN 2   202   2
    ALTHOUGH THEY BOTH ARE BORN IN THE SAME CLIME . . . . . 277 2 DON JUAN 3   5   4
    BORN TO SOME FRIEND WHO HOLDS HIS WIFE AND RICHES . . . 287 2 DON JUAN 3   23   7
    BUT LIKE TWO BEINGS BORN FROM OUT A RILL . . . . 352 2 DON JUAN 4   15   5
    LOVE WAS BORN WITH THEM IN THEM SO INTENSE . . . . . . 358 2 DON JUAN 4   27   7
    BORN OF THE SUN AS AFRIC'S CLIMATE IS . . . . 373 2 DON JUAN 4   54 V8
    LEGITIMACY ITS BORN VOTARIES WHEN . . . . 485 2 DON JUAN 5   128   7
    THOUGH NOT ALL BORN OF THE SAME SIRES AND MOTHERS . . . 491 2 DON JUAN 5   138   6
    AND WALLS AS THICK AS MOST SKULLS BORN AS YET . . . . . 72 3 DON JUAN 7   12   2
    WAS BORN IN CUMBERLAND AMONG THE HILLS . . . . 76 3 DON JUAN 7   20   3
    AS IF BORN FOR THE MINISTERIAL TRADE . . . . 223 3 DON JUAN 9   83   4
    BORN IN A SECOND WEDLOCK AND ABOVE . . . . 240 3 DON JUAN 10   32   7
    THE WORLD IN WHICH A MAN WAS BORN ALAS . . . . 306 3 DON JUAN 11   76   2
    BOTH WITS--ONE BORN SO AND THE OTHER BRED . . . . 402 3 DON JUAN 13   93   7
    EXCEPT PERHAPS THAT YOU WERE BORN TO DIE . . . . 411 3 DON JUAN 14   3   3
    BORN WITH THAT HAPPY SOUL WHICH SELDOM FAINTS . . . . . 424 3 DON JUAN 14   31   5
    WERE MORE--BUT I WAS BORN FOR OPPOSITION . . . . 466 3 DON JUAN 15   22   8
    WHEN AN HEIR IS BORN HE IS HEARD TO MOURN . . . . 519 3 DON JUAN 16   L 4   1
    POOR SOUL FOR SHE WAS COUNTRY BORN AND BRED . . . . . . 532 3 DON JUAN 16   64   6
BORNE
    'TWAS BORNE BY THE RUDE WAVE WHEREIN 'TWAS CAST . . . . 204 2 DON JUAN 2   90   6
    AND ALL WHICH MUST BE BORNE AND NEVER TOLD . . . . . . 350 2 DON JUAN 4   11   6
    OF SILENCE WOULD NOT LONG BE BORNE BY THOUGHT . . . . . 402 2 DON JUAN 4   106 V4
    WHICH I DEPLORE SO MUCH FOR I HAVE BORNE . . . . 420 2 DON JUAN 5   18   7
    HIM BORNE INTO THE HOUSE AND UP THE STAIR . . . . 429 2 DON JUAN 5   34   4
    AFTER THE HARDSHIPS YOU'VE ALREADY BORNE . . . . 98 3 DON JUAN 7   62   4
    WHATE'ER IS TO BE BORNE--BUT NOT RESIGN . . . . 161 3 DON JUAN 8   100   7
    TO YOUR INSTRUCTOR   JUAN NOW WAS BORNE . . . . 264 3 DON JUAN 10   80   2
    AND SUCH A STRAW BORNE ON BY HUMAN BREATH . . . . 414 3 DON JUAN 14   8   3
BOROUGH
    A BOROUGH IS COMPRISED ALONG THE HEIGHT . . . . 71 3 DON JUAN 7   10   2
    BANKERS--CONTRACTORS--BOROUGH MONGERS--BULLIES . . . . 314 3 DON JUAN 11   V 76   1
BOROUGHS
    BURROWING FOR BOROUGHS LIKE A RAT OR RABBIT . . . . . . 534 3 DON JUAN 16   70   2
BORROW
    THESE PHRASES OF REFINEMENT I MUST BORROW . . . . 288 3 DON JUAN 11   42   2
BORROWED
    ALTHOUGH YOU BORROWED ALL THAT E'ER THE MUSES . . . . . 493 2 DON JUAN 5   143   3
    PERHAPS WE HAVE BORROWED THIS FROM THE CHINESE-- . . . 373 3 DON JUAN 13   34   8
BORROWING
    BY BORROWING A NEW ONE FROM AN OX . . . . 91 2 DON JUAN 1   129   8
BOS
    FOR EUROPE PLOUGHS IN AFRIC LIKE BOS PIGER . . . . . . 348 3 DON JUAN 12   70   6
BOSCAN
    BOSCAN OR GARCILASSO--BY THE WIND . . . . 72 2 DON JUAN 1   95   2
BOSOM
    A BOSOM WHEREON HE HIS HEAD MIGHT LAY . . . . 73 2 DON JUAN 1   96   5
    WHICH TREMBLED LIKE THE BOSOM WHERE 'TWAS PLACED . . . 83 2 DON JUAN 1   115   3
    THEIR VERY WALK WOULD MAKE YOUR BOSOM SWELL . . . . . 159 2 DON JUAN 2   5   6
    A SIGH FROM HIS HEAVED BOSOM--AND HERS TOO . . . . . . 216 2 DON JUAN 2   114   8
    MORE THAN WITHIN THE BOSOM OF A NUN . . . . 244 2 DON JUAN 2   167   5
    AND BEATING 'GAINST HIS BOSOM HAIDEE'S HEART . . . . . 257 2 DON JUAN 2   191   7
    IF LOVE PATERNAL IN HIS BOSOM PLEADED . . . . 300 2 DON JUAN 3   49   5
    THERE HIS WORN BOSOM AND KEEN EYE WOULD MELT . . . . . 302 2 DON JUAN 3   52   6
    THE HEROIC BOSOM BEATS NO MORE . . . . 322 2 DON JUAN 3   L 5   4
    HER BOSOM WAS THE WEAPON--AND EVEN SO . . . . 367 2 DON JUAN 4   43 V6
    OF THOSE WITH WHICH HIS HAIDEE'S BOSOM BOUNDED . . . . 373 2 DON JUAN 4   54   4
    HER FEELINGS SUDDEN THROUGH HER BOSOM SENT . . . . . . 379 2 DON JUAN 4   65 V6
    AS PASSION RISES WITH ITS BOSOM WORN . . . . 49 3 DON JUAN 6   87   3
    STIRRED UP AND DOWN HER BOSOM LIKE A BILLOW . . . . . 60 3 DON JUAN 6   108   6
    UNTIL EACH HIGH HEROIC BOSOM BURNED . . . . 99 3 DON JUAN 7   64   3
    WITHIN HER BOSOM (WHICH WAS NOT TOO TOUGH) . . . . . . 206 3 DON JUAN 9   48   4
    MY BOSOM UNDERWENT A GLORIOUS GLOW . . . . 226 3 DON JUAN 10   3   3
    HIS BOSOM--FOR HE NEVER HAD A SISTER . . . . 250 3 DON JUAN 10   53   7
    WHICH SHALL LAY BARE HER BOSOM TO THE SWORD . . . . . 258 3 DON JUAN 10   67   4
    OR WISH TO MAKE A RIVAL'S BOSOM BLEED . . . . 351 3 DON JUAN 12   77   6
    BEAR A BOLD BROW AND FOR YOUR BOSOM NERVE IT . . . . . 367 3 DON JUAN 13   18 V4
    OF WHICH ANOTHER'S BOSOM IS THE ZONE . . . . 554 3 DON JUAN 16   108   8
BOSOM'S
    SUSTAIN'D HIS HEAD UPON HER BOSOM'S CHARMS . . . . . . 260 2 DON JUAN 2   195   4
BOSOMS
    HIVED IN OUR BOSOMS LIKE THE BAG O' THE BEE . . . . . 144 2 DON JUAN 1   214   5
    ARE LAID WITHIN OUR BOSOMS BUT TO PERISH . . . . 275 2 DON JUAN 3   2   8
    THEIR BOSOMS WHO HAVE BEEN INDUCED TO ROAM . . . . . . 286 2 DON JUAN 3   21   4
    WITH HIS RUDE SCYTHE SUCH GENTLE BOSOMS HE . . . . . . 348 2 DON JUAN 4   8   4
    THEIR DELICATE LIMBS A THOUSAND BOSOMS THERE . . . . . 19 3 DON JUAN 6   26   7
    AND BOSOMS ARMS AND ANCLES GLANCING BARE . . . . 42 3 DON JUAN 6   72   4
BOSPHORUS
    BETWEEN THE BOSPHORUS AS THEY LASH AND LAVE . . . . . 413 2 DON JUAN 5   5   5
    EACH VILLA ON THE BOSPHORUS LOOKS A SCREEN . . . . . . 436 2 DON JUAN 5   46   7
    YOU KNOW HOW NEAR US THE DEEP BOSPHORUS FLOATS . . . . 464 2 DON JUAN 5   92   4
BOTANY
    THE VERY BOTANY BAY IN MORAL GEOGRAPHY . . . . 330 2 DON JUAN 3   94   2
BOTCHING
    AND BOTCHING PATCHING LEAVING STILL BEHIND . . . . . . 18 2 DON JUAN D   14   2

	PAGE	VOL	CANTO	STANZA	LN
BOTHERS					
INTO A CAMP I KNOW THAT NOUGHT SO BOTHERS	103	3 DON JUAN	7	71	6
IN SHORT THE LIST OF ALTERATIONS BOTHERS	308	3 DON JUAN	11	81	6
BOTTES					
OH YE GREAT AUTHORS--APROPOS DES BOTTES--	200	3 DON JUAN	9	36	1
BOTTLE					
I'LL CALL THE WORK LONGINUS O'ER A BOTTLE	138	2 DON JUAN	1	204	7
WHAT SAY YOU TO A BOTTLE OF CHAMPAGNE	375	3 DON JUAN	13	37	2
I HATE A MOTIVE LIKE A LINGERING BOTTLE	435	3 DON JUAN	14	58	1
OR LIKE A SODA BOTTLE WHEN ITS SPRAY	504	3 DON JUAN	16	9	5
A REEL WITHIN A BOTTLE IS A MYSTERY	531	3 DON JUAN	16	62	1
BOTTLE-CONJURER					
WHICH TO THAT BOTTLE-CONJURER JOHN BULL	88	3 DON JUAN	7	44	3
BOTTLES					
SWEET IS OLD WINE IN BOTTLES ALE IN BARRELS	90	2 DON JUAN	1	126	5
BOTTOM					
AND AT THE BOTTOM OF THE BOAT THREE WERE	208	2 DON JUAN	2	98	6
BECAUSE DEFORMED YET DIED ALL GAME AND BOTTOM	166	3 DON JUAN	8	110	7
THERE WAS THE PUREST PLATONISM AT BOTTOM	251	3 DON JUAN	10	54	7
BECAUSE SHE THOUGHT HIM A GOOD HEART AT BOTTOM	338	3 DON JUAN	12	49	2
ARE THEY AT BOTTOM VIRTUOUS EVEN WHEN VICIOUS	349	3 DON JUAN	12	73	6
BOUDOIR					
RETIRED INTO HER BOUDOIR A SWEET PLACE	54	3 DON JUAN	6	97	2
THE SCENES LIKE CATHERINE'S BOUDOIR AT THREE-SCORE	146	3 DON JUAN	8	68	7
A DOOR THAT'S IN OR BOUDOIR OUT OF THE WAY	303	3 DON JUAN	11	69	3
BOUDOIR'S					
IF ONCE BEYOND HER BOUDOIR'S PRECINCTS IN YE WENT	214	3 DON JUAN	9	63	5
BOUGH					
BLOSSOM AND BOUGH LIE WITHER'D WITH ONE BLIGHT	382	2 DON JUAN	4	70	6
THE BLACK BOUGH) TEAR-DROPS THROUGH HER EYES' DARK FRINGES	40	3 DON JUAN	6	67	8
TO ITS OWN BOUGH AND DANGLED YET IN SIGHT	44	3 DON JUAN	6	76	7
A FRUIT TO BLOOM UPON THEIR WITHERING BOUGH	330	3 DON JUAN	12	31	2
BOUGHS					
TO YOU I ENVY NEITHER FRUIT NOR BOUGHS--	13	2 DON JUAN	D	7	3
AND VESPER BELL'S THAT ROSE THE BOUGHS ALONG	337	2 DON JUAN	3	106	4
AND FROM BENEATH HIS BOUGHS WERE SEEN TO SALLY	384	3 DON JUAN	13	56	5
BOUGHT					
A GOOD DEAL MAY BE BOUGHT FOR FIFTY LOUIS	79	2 DON JUAN	1	108	8
BOUGHT UP FOR DIFFERENT PURPOSES AND PASSIONS	407	2 DON JUAN	4	113	8
HOW SOME WERE BOUGHT BY PACHAS SOME BY JEWS	409	2 DON JUAN	4	116	2
SOME BOUGHT THE JET WHILE OTHERS CHOSE THE PALE	416	2 DON JUAN	5	10	4
ARE BOUGHT UP OTHERS BY A WARLIKE LEADER	425	2 DON JUAN	5	27	5
MOST PROPER FOR THE CHRISTIANS HE HAD BOUGHT	450	2 DON JUAN	5	67	8
THERE WAS NO END UNTO THE THINGS SHE BOUGHT	476	2 DON JUAN	5	113	5
FOR HER MUST BE UPROOTED--OR BE BOUGHT	476	2 DON JUAN	5	113	V5
SHE ORDERED HIM DIRECTLY TO BE BOUGHT	477	2 DON JUAN	5	114	3
I SEE YOU'VE BOUGHT ANOTHER GIRL 'TIS PITY	500	2 DON JUAN	5	155	7
SO PRECIOUS THAT IT WAS NOT TO BE BOUGHT	528	3 DON JUAN	16	56	3
BOUND					
HER HAIR HAD SILVER ONLY BOUND TO BE	221	2 DON JUAN	2	122	4
YET DEEM'D HERSELF IN COMMON PITY BOUND	224	2 DON JUAN	2	129	6
BUT THREE RAGUSAN VESSELS BOUND FOR SCIO	248	2 DON JUAN	2	174	8
AND THE STRIPED WHITE GAUZE BARACAN THAT BOUND HER	311	2 DON JUAN	3	70	7
FOR THEIRS WERE BUOYANT SPIRITS NEVER BOUND	352	2 DON JUAN	4	16	5
AND THEN THEY BOUND HIM WHERE HE FELL AND BORE	371	2 DON JUAN	4	50	1
BUT TO THE NARRATIVE THE VESSEL BOUND	407	2 DON JUAN	4	113	1
ONE PERSON THRICE IN HOLY WEDLOCK BOUND	421	2 DON JUAN	5	20	5
AND THIS ADDITION WITH SUCH GEMS WAS BOUND	457	2 DON JUAN	5	79	6
HIS EMPIRE ALSO WAS WITHOUT A BOUND	497	2 DON JUAN	5	150	5
ONE WITH HER AUBURN TRESSES LIGHTLY BOUND	38	3 DON JUAN	6	65	5
WHO NEITHER WISHES TO BE BOUND NOR BIND	195	3 DON JUAN	9	26	6
AND GREECE AND BOUND FAIR HELEN IN A BOND	209	3 DON JUAN	9	53	V6
WITH HER THEN AS IN HUMBLE DUTY BOUND	224	3 DON JUAN	9	85	1
WHO BOUND THE BAR OR SENATE IN THEIR SPELL	307	3 DON JUAN	11	77	4
CHASTE WERE HIS STEPS EACH KEPT WITHIN DUE BOUND	427	3 DON JUAN	14	39	1
THE CHARMING OF THESE CHARMERS WHO SEEM BOUND	518	3 DON JUAN	16	40	2
NOR LESS APPLAUDS AS IN POLITENESS BOUND	521	3 DON JUAN	16	41	6
EVEN IN THE COUNTRY CIRCLE'S NARROW BOUND--	544	3 DON JUAN	16	91	6
BOUNDARY					
AGAINST THE BOUNDARY IT SCARCELY WET	251	2 DON JUAN	2	181	8
BOUNDED					
WHICH THEN SEEMS AS IF THE WHOLE EARTH IT BOUNDED	252	2 DON JUAN	2	183	3
THEIR LEADER SANG--AND BOUNDED TO HER SONG	291	2 DON JUAN	3	30	7
OF THOSE WITH WHICH HIS HAIDEE'S BOSOM BOUNDED	373	2 DON JUAN	4	54	4
BOUNDING					
TO SHOW ITS BOILING SURF AND BOUNDING SPRAY	211	2 DON JUAN	2	104	6
WENT BOUNDING FOR THE ISLAND OF THE FREE	256	3 DON JUAN	10	64	2
AS BEAUTIFUL AND BOUNDING AS A STEED	401	3 DON JUAN	13	92	6
BOUNDLESS					
TO PERFECT KNOWLEDGE OF THE BOUNDLESS SKIES	71	2 DON JUAN	1	92	7
THOUGHTS BOUNDLESS DEEP BUT SILENT TOO AS SPACE	524	3 DON JUAN	16	48	8
BOUNDS					
HIM PAST ALL BOUNDS BECAUSE SHE SMILED TO SEE	239	2 DON JUAN	2	158	3
WHICH BOUNDS RAVENNA'S IMMEMORIAL WOOD	337	2 DON JUAN	3	105	3
TO FIX THE DUE BOUNDS OF THIS DANGEROUS QUALITY	448	3 DON JUAN	14	89	8
TRANSGRESSES THE GREAT BOUNDS OF LOVE OR AWE	563	3 DON JUAN	17	2	6
BOUNTIES					
(I MEAN IN FORTUNE'S MATRIMONIAL BOUNTIES)	312	3 DON JUAN	11	89	4
BOUNTY					
TO SOME CIVILITY TO OTHERS BOUNTY	535	3 DON JUAN	16	71	3

BOURN
    UNTO THAT RATHER SOMEWHAT MISTY BOURN . . . . 133 3 DON JUAN 8   41   3
BOUT
    WARM BOUT ARE BROKEN INTO THEIR NEW TRICKS . . . . 122 3 DON JUAN 8   22   7
BOUTS
    WERE SONNETS TO HERSELF OR BOUTS RIMES   . . . . 525 3 DON JUAN 16   50   8
BOW
    HER ZONE TO VENUS OR HIS BOW TO CUPID . . . . 51 2 DON JUAN 1   55   7
    HER EYEBROW'S SHAPE WAS LIKE THE AERIAL BOW . . . . 55 2 DON JUAN 1   61   3
    TO PAY THEM WITH AND SOME LOOK'D O'ER THE BOW . . . . . . 179 2 DON JUAN 2   44   5
    THEN CHANGED LIKE TO A BOW THAT'S BENT AND THEN . . . . . 204 2 DON JUAN 2   91   7
    AND LAYING DOWN MY PEN I MAKE MY BOW . . . . 271 2 DON JUAN 2 216   6
    AND NOW AND THEN WITH TOUGH STRINGS OF THE BOW . . . . . 463 2 DON JUAN 5   89   5
    HEADS BOW KNEES BEND EYES WATCH AROUND A THRONE . . . . . 484 2 DON JUAN 5 127   7
    KATINKA TOO AND WITH A GENTLE BOW . . . . 31 3 DON JUAN 6   50   3
    ISMAIL'S NO MORE   THE CRESCENT'S SILVER BOW . . . . . . 172 3 DON JUAN 8 122   4
    FOR I HAVE DRAWN MUCH LESS WITH A LONG BOW . . . . 181 3 DON JUAN 8 138   6
    HIS BOW CONVERTED INTO A COCKED HAT . . . . 205 3 DON JUAN 9   45   5
    HIS ANSWERS WITH A VERY GRACEFUL BOW . . . . 223 3 DON JUAN 9   83   3
    DIFFER EXCEPT IN ROBBING WITH A BOW . . . . 275 3 DON JUAN 11   15   4
    IS IDLE LET US LIKE MOST OTHERS BOW . . . . 286 3 DON JUAN 11   38   5
    WITH FASCINATION IN HIS VERY BOW   . . . . 354 3 DON JUAN 12   84   3
    TO DRAW THE BOW TO RIDE AND SPEAK THE TRUTH . . . . . 501 3 DON JUAN 16   1   2
    BUT DRAW THE LONG BOW BETTER NOW THAN EVER . . . . . 501 3 DON JUAN 16   1   8
    GRACEFUL AS DIAN WHEN SHE DRAWS HER BOW . . . . . 517 3 DON JUAN 16   38   5
BOW'D
    OF NATIONS AND HAD NEVER BENT OR BOW'D . . . . 476 3 DON JUAN 15   46   6
BOWED
    WHAT ALL THIS MEANT WHILE BABA BOWED AND BENDED . . . 466 2 DON JUAN 5   95   7
    THEY BOWED OBEISANCE AND WITHDREW RETIRING . . . . 469 2 DON JUAN 5 100   1
    HAD BOWED THEMSELVES BEFORE THE IMPERIAL EYES . . . 19 3 DON JUAN 6   26   3
    AND BOWED HER THROBBING HEAD O'ER TREMBLING KNEES . . 59 3 DON JUAN 6 107   8
    HE SHALL IF THAT HE DARE HERE JUAN BOWED . . . . . 99 3 DON JUAN 7   63   1
    ARE BOWED AND PUT THE SUN OUT LIKE A TAPER . . . . . 266 3 DON JUAN 10   83   6
BOWELS
    ABOUT THE LOWER REGION OF THE BOWELS . . . . 168 2 DON JUAN 2   23   2
BOWER
    WHEN JULIA SATE WITHIN AS PRETTY A BOWER . . . . . 77 2 DON JUAN 1 104   3
    SHE AND HER WAVE-WORN LOVE HAD MADE THEIR BOWER . . . 262 2 DON JUAN 2 198   5
    BUT AFTER ALL IT IS THE ONLY BOWER . . . . 301 2 DON JUAN 11   66   6
    BUT IN THE COUNTRY LADIES SEEK THEIR BOWER . . . . . 409 3 DON JUAN 13 111   3
BOWER-ANCHOR
    THEIRS IS THE BEST BOWER-ANCHOR THE CHAIN CABLE . . . 316 3 DON JUAN 12   3   3
BOWERS
    TILL THEY WERE EXILED FROM THEIR EARLIER BOWERS . . . 30 2 DON JUAN 1   18   4
    HE THOUGHT OF WOOD NYMPHS AND IMMORTAL BOWERS . . . . 72 2 DON JUAN 1   94   3
    WITH CYPRESS BRANCHES HAST THOU WREATHED THY BOWERS . 275 2 DON JUAN 3   2   3
    THROUGH ORANGE BOWERS AND JASMINE AND SO FORTH . . . 434 2 DON JUAN 5   42   2
BOWL
    FILL HIGH THE BOWL WITH SAMIAN WINE   . . . . . . 324 2 DON JUAN 3 L 11   1
    FILL HIGH THE BOWL WITH SAMIAN WINE   . . . . . . 325 2 DON JUAN 3 L 13   1
    FILL HIGH THE BOWL WITH SAMIAN WINE   . . . . . . 326 2 DON JUAN 3 L 15   1
BOWS
    WHEN THE STRIPT FOREST BOWS TO THE BLEAK AIR . . . . 155 3 DON JUAN 8   88   4
    HIGH DASHED THE SPRAY THE BOWS DIPPED IN THE SEA . . 256 3 DON JUAN 10   64   4
    BOWS HAVE THEY GENERALLY WITH TWO STRINGS . . . . . 501 3 DON JUAN 16   1   5
    RETIRED WITH MOST UNFASHIONABLE BOWS . . . . 549 3 DON JUAN 16 101   5
BOWSPRIT
    FOREMAST AND BOWSPRIT WERE CUT DOWN AND THEY . . . . 173 2 DON JUAN 2   32   5
BOW-STREET'S
    WHO QUEER A FLAT WHO (SPITE OF BOW-STREET'S BAN) . . 277 3 DON JUAN 11   19   5
BOW-STRING
    ABOUT A BOW-STRING--QUITE IN VAIN NOT YET   . . . . 471 2 DON JUAN 5 103   4
    OF YEARS TO FILL A BOWSTRING OR THE THRONE . . . . 499 2 DON JUAN 5 153   2
BOWSTRUNG
    HIS LATELY BOWSTRUNG BROTHER CAUSED HIS RISE . . . . 495 2 DON JUAN 5 147   4
BOX
    (FOR SOMETIMES WE MUST BOX WITHOUT THE MUFFLE) . . . 205 2 DON JUAN 2   92   8
BOXER
    OR A GOOD BOXER INTO A SAD PICKLE . . . . 134 3 DON JUAN 8   43   6
    FOR LIKE A RACER OR A BOXER TRAINING . . . . 366 3 DON JUAN 13   18   7
BOXES
    NOR MUCH TO CLIMB THROUGH LITTLE BOXES FRAMED . . . 278 3 DON JUAN 11   21   4
BOXING
    LOUNGING AND BOXING AND THE TWILIGHT HOUR . . . . . 301 3 DON JUAN 11   66   2
BOY
    AT TWELVE HE WAS A FINE BUT QUIET BOY . . . . 49 2 DON JUAN 1   50   2
    BUT THE BOY BORE UP LONG AND WITH A MILD . . . . . 203 2 DON JUAN 2   88   3
    THE BOY EXPIRED--THE FATHER HELD THE CLAY . . . . . 204 2 DON JUAN 2   90   1
    ALL TRANQUILLY THE SHIPWRECK'D BOY WAS LYING . . . . 233 2 DON JUAN 2 144   3
    PAID DAILY VISITS TO HER BOY AND TOOK . . . . 248 2 DON JUAN 2 174   2
    AS BOY I THOUGHT MYSELF A CLEVER FELLOW . . . . . . 345 2 DON JUAN 4   3   1
    AND JUAN WAS A BOY OF SAINTLY BREEDING . . . . . . 354 2 DON JUAN 4   19   6
    DEAL WITH ME AS THOU WILT BUT SPARE THIS BOY . . . . 364 2 DON JUAN 4   38   8
    WHEN HAIDEE THREW HERSELF HER BOY BEFORE . . . . . 366 2 DON JUAN 4   42   3
    MY BOY --SAID HE AMIDST THIS MOTLEY CREW . . . . . 417 2 DON JUAN 5   13   1
    THERE WAS NOT NOW A LUGGAGE BOY BUT SOUGHT . . . . . 90 3 DON JUAN 7   49   5
    HE'S A FINE BOY THE WOMEN MAY BE SENT . . . . 100 3 DON JUAN 7   66   7
    BUT JUAN WAS QUITE A BROTH OF A BOY . . . . 123 3 DON JUAN 8   24   1

```
                                                           PAGE VOL      CANTO STANZA LN
BOY    (CONTINUED)
     EXCLAIMING--JUAN JUAN ON BOY BRACE . . . . . . .  . 160  3 DON JUAN  8     97   6
     BESIDES THE EMPRESS SOMETIMES LIKED A BOY    . . . . . 206  3 DON JUAN  9     47   7
     JUAN I SAID WAS A MOST BEAUTEOUS BOY . .  . . . . . 209  3 DON JUAN  9     53   1
     HER PREFERENCE OF A BOY TO MEN MUCH BIGGER . . . . . 218  3 DON JUAN  9     72   3
     ALL MY BOY FEELINGS ALL MY GENTLER DREAMS  . . . . . 233  3 DON JUAN 10     18   4
     THOUGH ON THE WHOLE NO DOUBT THE DARDAN BOY . . . . . 441  3 DON JUAN 14     72   6
BOYHOOD
     AS BOYS LOVE ROWS MY BOYHOOD LIKED A SQUABBLE . . . . 398  2 DON JUAN  4     99   1
BOYISH
     HE BUOY'D HIS BOYISH LIMBS AND STROVE TO PLY  . . . . 212  2 DON JUAN  2    106   2
     I DID MY VERY BOYISH BEST TO SHINE . . . . . . . .  37  3 DON JUAN  6     62   5
     YOU LOVE THIS BOYISH NEW SERAGLIO GUEST  . . . . . .  63  3 DON JUAN  6    115   5
     AND HAD RETAINED HIS BOYISH LOOK BEYOND  . . . . . . 209  3 DON JUAN  9     53   2
BOY'S
     AND THE BOY'S EYES WHICH THE DULL FILM HALF GLAZED . . 203  2 DON JUAN  2     89   5
     'TWAS THE BOY'S MITE AND LIKE THE WIDOW'S MAY  . . . .  9  3 DON JUAN  6      6   1
BOYS
     AS BOYS LOVE ROWS MY BOYHOOD LIKED A SQUABBLE . . . . 398  2 DON JUAN  4     99   1
     LIKE BIRDS OR BOYS OR BEDLAMITES BROKE LOOSE . . . .  23  3 DON JUAN  6     34   2
     AN UNIFORM TO BOYS IS LIKE A FAN . . . . . . . . . 108  3 DON JUAN  7     84   4
     HIS FIVE BRAVE BOYS NO LESS THE FOE DEFIED . . . . . 165  3 DON JUAN  8    107   5
     NO MORE IT DOTH--ITS PLOUGHS BUT CHANGE THEIR BOYS  . . 228  3 DON JUAN 10      7   7
     AS THE SMART BOYS SPURRED FAST IN THEIR CAREER . . . . 263  3 DON JUAN 10     77   3
     AT LENGTH THE BOYS DREW UP BEFORE A DOOR . . . . . . 313  3 DON JUAN 11   V 29   1
     TO HERD WITH BOYS OR HOARD WITH GOOD THREESCORE-- . . . 316  3 DON JUAN 12      2   2
     HERE DANCED ALBANO'S BOYS AND HERE THE SEA SHONE . . . 392  3 DON JUAN 13     71   5
     THE FIRST THING BOYS LIKE AFTER PLAY AND FRUIT . . . . 405  3 DON JUAN 13    101   3
BRACE
     AS THE BLACK EUNUCH ENTERED WITH HIS BRACE . . . . . 441  2 DON JUAN  5     54   1
     AND FOR ONE KISS WOULD FAIN IMPRINT A BRACE  . . . . 472  2 DON JUAN  5    106   5
     EXCLAIMING--JUAN JUAN ON BOY BRACE . . . . . . . . 160  3 DON JUAN  8     97   6
BRACELET
     ONE LARGE GOLD BRACELET CLASP'D EACH LOVELY ARM  . . . 312  2 DON JUAN  3     71   1
BRAGGADOCIO
     THE BRAGGADOCIO TAKES CONTEMPT FOR AWE   . . . . . . 153  2 DON JUAN  1   V  4   V8
BRAHMINS
     OF HIGHEST CASTE--THE BRAHMINS OF THE TON  . . . . . 397  3 DON JUAN 13     83   4
BRAIDS
     IN BRAIDS BEHIND AND THOUGH HER STATURE WERE . . . . 217  2 DON JUAN  2    116   4
BRAIN
     THAT WHICH ADORN'D THE BRAIN OF DONNA INEZ . . . . .  27  2 DON JUAN  1     11   8
     THAT YOU MIGHT BRAIN THEM WITH THEIR LADY'S FAN  . . .  33  2 DON JUAN  1     21   5
     HER BRAIN THOUGH IN A DREAM (AND THEN SHE SIGH'D)  . .  67  2 DON JUAN  1     84   3
     HIS BRAIN ABOUT THE ACTION OF THE SKY  . . . . . . .  71  2 DON JUAN  1     93   6
     AND AS HE GAZED HIS DIZZY BRAIN SPUN FAST  . . . . . 214  2 DON JUAN  2    110   1
     OR IF TOO CLASSIC FOR HIS VULGAR BRAIN . . . . . . . 333  2 DON JUAN  3     99   5
     WHICH SHAKE SO MUCH THE HUMAN BRAIN AND BREAST-- . . . 343  2 DON JUAN  3   V 98   3
     MY BRAIN WITH BLEST FUMES TILL MY EYES GROW DIM  . . . 372  2 DON JUAN  4     53   V7
     THE TEARS RUSH'D FORTH FROM HER O'ERCLOUDED BRAIN  . . 380  2 DON JUAN  4     66   7
     AND WHIRL'D HER BRAIN TO MADNESS SHE AROSE . . . . . 380  2 DON JUAN  4     67   2
     HER CHEEK TURNED ASHES EARS RUNG BRAIN WHIRLED ROUND . .  58  3 DON JUAN  6    105   5
     SO LOFTY THAT I FEEL MY BRAIN TURN ROUND . . . . . . 224  3 DON JUAN  9     85   5
     WHICH IS A SIGNAL TO MY NERVES AND BRAIN . . . . . . 224  3 DON JUAN  9     85   7
     HEAVEN'S BRANDY--THOUGH OUR BRAIN CAN HARDLY BEAR IT . . 269  3 DON JUAN 11      2   8
     ABOVE HIS BURNT-OUT BRAIN AND SAPLESS CINDERS  . . . . 299  3 DON JUAN 11     61   5
     THIRDLY THAT JUAN HAD MORE BRAIN THAN BEARD  . . . . 439  3 DON JUAN 14     66   5
BRAIN'S
     FROM HIS OWN BRAIN'S OPPRESSION WHILE IT REELS . . . . 427  2 DON JUAN  5     31   6
BRAINS
     AND SUCH THINGS AS THE ENTRAILS AND THE BRAINS . . . . 197  2 DON JUAN  2     77   6
     THE HOUR AS IS THE CASE WITH LIVELY BRAINS . . . . . 129  3 DON JUAN  8     33   4
     THE OCEAN'S TIDES AND MORTAL'S BRAINS SHE SWAYS  . . . 506  3 DON JUAN 16     14   7
BRAIN-SPATTERING
     WAR'S A BRAIN-SPATTERING WINDPIPE-SLITTING ART . . . . 184  3 DON JUAN  9      4   3
BRAKE
     AS TRAVELLERS FOLLOW OVER BOG AND BRAKE  . . . . . . 127  3 DON JUAN  8     32   4
     AROUND THE WILD FOWL NESTLED IN THE BRAKE  . . . . . 385  3 DON JUAN 13     57   5
BRANCH
     FOR EVERY BRANCH OF EVERY SCIENCE KNOWN--  . . . . .  26  2 DON JUAN  1     10   2
     ARTS SCIENCES NO BRANCH WAS MADE A MYSTERY . . . . .  43  2 DON JUAN  1     39   7
     SPRUNG UP A BRANCH AS BEAUTIFUL AS FRESH . . . . . .  53  2 DON JUAN  1     58   4
     WHERE THE WILD BRANCH OF THE CORK FOREST GREW  . . . .  70  2 DON JUAN  1     90   4
     UPON THE DANUBE'S LEFT BRANCH AND LEFT BANK  . . . . .  70  3 DON JUAN  7      9   2
     FOR WAR CUTS UP NOT ONLY BRANCH BUT ROOT . . . . . .  86  3 DON JUAN  7     41   8
     SO THAT THE BRANCH A GOODLY VERDURE FLINGS . . . . . 436  3 DON JUAN 14     59   3
BRANCHES
     WITH CYPRESS BRANCHES HAST THOU WREATHED THY BOWERS  . . 275  2 DON JUAN  3      2   3
     THROUGH THE WAVED BRANCHES O'ER THE GREENSWARD GLANCING . 290  2 DON JUAN  3     29   3
     LIKE BRANCHES WHEN THE FRUIT BENEATH IS MELLOW . . . . 311  2 DON JUAN  3     70   V4
     KNOW NOT SINCE KNOWLEDGE SAW HER BRANCHES STRIPT . . . 210  3 DON JUAN  9     55   6
BRANCHING
     THE BRANCHING STAG SWEPT DOWN WITH ALL HIS HERD  . . . 384  3 DON JUAN 13     56   7
BRANCHLESS
     WITHOUT THEIR SAP HOW BRANCHLESS WERE THE TRUNK  . . . 250  2 DON JUAN  2    179   5
BRANDS
     WHERE HYMEN'S TORCH BUT BRANDS ONE STRUMPET MORE . . . 353  2 DON JUAN  4     17   7
BRANDY
     I FIND THAT WINE OR BRANDY IS FORBID TOO . . . . . . 145  2 DON JUAN  1    216   V6
     HEAVEN'S BRANDY--THOUGH OUR BRAIN CAN HARDLY BEAR IT . . 269  3 DON JUAN 11      2   8
```

```
                                                              PAGE VOL      CANTO STANZA LN
BRANDY'S
     (IN LOVE OR BRANDY'S FERVENT FERMENTATION)  .  .  .  .  .  . 287  3 DON JUAN 11      39   6
BRASS
     I THINK IT MAY BE OF CORINTHIAN BRASS .  .  .  .  .  .  .  .  34  3 DON JUAN  6      56   1
     AND BLAZON O'ER THE DOOR THEIR NAMES IN BRASS  .  .  .  .  . 283  3 DON JUAN 11      31   8
     ON A BRASS PLATE WAS GIVEN TO KNOCKS AND FAME  .  .  .  .  . 283  3 DON JUAN 11      31  V8
BRATS
     OF FEEDING BRATS THE MOMENT HIS WIFE WEANS  .  .  .  .  .  . 325  3 DON JUAN 12      21   8
BRAVE
     BRAVE MEN WERE LIVING BEFORE AGAMEMMON  .  .  .  .  .  .  .   24  2 DON JUAN  1       5   1
     A ROD TO WEAKNESS TO THE BRAVE A REED .  .  .  .  .  .  .  . 151  2 DON JUAN  1  V   2   6
     BRAVE INEZ NOW SET UP A SUNDAY SCHOOL .  .  .  .  .  .  .  . 162  2 DON JUAN  2      10   2
     THEN SHRIEK'D THE TIMID AND STOOD STILL THE BRAVE  .  .  .  . 184  2 DON JUAN  2      52   2
     UNLIKE THE HONEST ARAB THIEVES SO BRAVE .  .  .  .  .  .  . 225  2 DON JUAN  2     130   6
     ENTOMB'D THE BRAVEST OF THE BRAVE ACHILLES  .  .  .  .  .  . 385  2 DON JUAN  4      76   3
     BUT ONE WHICH .BABA DID NOT LIKE TO BRAVE .  .  .  .  .  .   62  3 DON JUAN  6     112   3
     O'ER THE PROMOTED COUPLE OF BRAVE MEN .  .  .  .  .  .  .  . 101  3 DON JUAN  7      68   1
     AS BRAVE AS EVER FACED BOTH BOMB AND BALL  .  .  .  .  .  . 116  3 DON JUAN  8       9   5
     OR THOSE WHO THOUGHT IT BRAVE TO WAIT AS YET  .  .  .  .  . 135  3 DON JUAN  8      45   8
     BUT AS IT HAPPENS TO BRAVE MEN THEY BLUNDERED--  .  .  .  . 149  3 DON JUAN  8      75   5
     MARCHED WITH THE BRAVE BATTALION OF POLOUZKI--  .  .  .  . 150  3 DON JUAN  8      76   8
     BUT TO OUR SUBJECT A BRAVE TARTAR KHAN--  .  .  .  .  .  .  . 163  3 DON JUAN  8     104   5
     BUT FLANKED BY FIVE BRAVE SONS (SUCH IS POLYGAMY  .  .  .  . 164  3 DON JUAN  8     105   1
     TO TAKE HIM WAS THE POINT THE TRULY BRAVE  .  .  .  .  .  . 164  3 DON JUAN  8     106   1
     WHEN THEY BEHOLD THE BRAVE OPPRESSED WITH ODDS  .  .  .  . 164  3 DON JUAN  8     106   2
     HIS FIVE BRAVE BOYS NO LESS THE FOE DEFIED .  .  .  .  .  . 165  3 DON JUAN  8     107   5
     FOR SIX AND THIRTY THOUSAND BRAVE DEFENDERS .  .  .  .  .  . 175  3 DON JJAN  8     127  V7
     WHO STILL HAVE SHOWN THEMSELVES MORE BRAVE THAN WITTY  .  . 194  3 DON JUAN  9      23   4
     (AS BEING THE BRAVE LIONS' KEEN PROVIDERS)  .  .  .  .  .  . 196  3 DON JUAN  9      27   7
BRAVELY
     BUT BRAVELY RUSHED ON HIS FIRST HEAVENLY NIGHT  .  .  .  .  . 168  3 DON JUAN  8     114   3
BRAVEST
     WAS FREEDOM'S BEST AND BRAVEST FRIEND .  .  .  .  .  .  .  . 325  2 DON JUAN  3  L  12   2
     ENTOMB'D THE BRAVEST OF THE BRAVE ACHILLES  .  .  .  .  .  . 385  2 DON JUAN  4      76   3
     THE GREATEST WISEST BRAVEST AS WAS BEST .  .  .  .  .  .  .  12  3 DON JUAN  6      13  V2
     PUTTING THE VERY BRAVEST WHO WERE KNOCKED  .  .  .  .  .  . 134  3 DON JUAN  8      43   7
     HE SHUDDERED AS NO DOUBT THE BRAVEST COWERS .  .  .  .  .  . 559  3 DON JUAN 16     120   5
BRAVURAS
     THOSE BRAVURAS (WHICH I STILL AM LEARNING  .  .  .  .  .  . 350  3 DON JUAN 12      75   6
     IN BABYLON'S BRAVURAS--AS THE HOME .  .  .  .  .  .  .  .  . 523  3 DON JUAN 16      46   1
BRAZEN
     NOW LIKE FRIAR BACON'S BRAZEN HEAD I'VE SPOKEN  .  .  .  .  . 145  3 DON JUAN  1     217   5
     THE BRAZEN UPPERMOST) KIND READER PASS .  .  .  .  .  .  .   34  3 DON JUAN  6      56   3
     IN LIEU OF A BARE BLADE AND BRAZEN FRONT .  .  .  .  .  .  . 275  3 DON JUAN 11      15   5
     THEN ROLL THE BRAZEN THUNDERS OF THE DOOR  .  .  .  .  .  . 302  3 DON JUAN 11      67   6
BRAZILS
     PRESENTED BY THE PRINCE OF THE BRAZILS .  .  .  .  .  .  .  . 185  3 DON JUAN  9       6   2
BREACH
     WHICH MOSTLY ENDS IN SOME SMALL BREACH OF BOTH .  .  .  .  . 493  2 DON JUAN  5     142   8
     I DOUBT FEW READERS E'ER WOULD MOUNT THE BREACH  .  .  .  .  83  3 DON JUAN  7      35   8
     YOU WERE THE FIRST I' THE BREACH  I WAS NOT SLACK .  .  .   98  3 DON JUAN  7      61   3
BREAD
     BREAD HAS BEEN MADE (INDIFFERENT) FROM POTATOES  .  .  .  .   92  2 DON JUAN  1     130   1
     SOME POUNDS OF BREAD THOUGH INJURED BY THE WET .  .  .  .  . 181  2 DON JUAN  2      47   2
     TO FAINT AND DAMAGED BREAD WET THROUGH THE BAGS  .  .  .  . 189  2 DON JUAN  2      62   7
     FOR BREAKFAST OF EGGS COFFEE BREAD AND FISH .  .  .  .  .  . 226  2 DON JUAN  2     133   8
     BUT THERE WERE EGGS FRUIT COFFEE BREAD FISH HONEY .  .  .  . 233  2 DON JUAN  2     145   7
     THEIR BREAD AS MINISTERS AND FAVOURITES--(THAT'S  .  .  .  . 310  2 DON JUAN  3      68   6
     LET THIS ONE TOIL FOR BREAD--THAT RACK FOR RENT  .  .  .  . 190  3 DON JUAN  9      15   7
     ON THEM AND BREAD 'TWAS OFT MY LUCK TO DINE .  .  .  .  .  . 488  3 DON JUAN 15      73   5
BREADTH
     THE BREADTH OF PAVEMENT AND YON SHRINE WHERE FAME IS  .  .  . 279  3 DON JUAN 11      24   5
     ALMOST AN HAIR'S BREADTH TOO MUCH ON ONE SIDE .  .  .  .  . 513  3 DON JUAN 16      29   8
BREAK
     AND BREAK THE--WHICH COMMANDMENT IS'T THEY BREAK  .  .  .  .  74  2 DON JUAN  1      98   4
     AND BREAK THE--WHICH COMMANDMENT IS'T THEY BREAK  .  .  .  .  74  2 DON JUAN  1      98   4
     AND BREAK A PROMISE AFTER HAVING MADE IT HER  .  .  .  .  . 142  2 DON JUAN  1     210   5
     BECAUSE HER MISTRESS WOULD NOT LET HER BREAK  .  .  .  .  . 234  2 DON JUAN  2     146   7
     SHE HAD NO NEED OF THIS DAY NE'ER WILL BREAK  .  .  .  .  . 314  2 DON JUAN  3      76   3
     HE COUNTED THEM AT BREAK OF DAY--  .  .  .  .  .  .  .  .  . 322  2 DON JUAN  3  L   4   7
     WOULD BREAK YOUR SHIELD HOWEVER BROAD .  .  .  .  .  .  .  . 325  2 DON JUAN  3  L  14   6
     BREAK WITH THE FIRST FALL THEY CAN NE'ER BEHOLD  .  .  .  . 350  2 DON JUAN  4      11   4
     TO BREAK THE LIFELESS SPLENDOR OF THE WHOLE .  .  .  .  .  . 442  2 DON JUAN  5      56   8
     I YIELD THUS FAR BUT SOON WILL BREAK THE CHARM .  .  .  .  . 459  2 DON JUAN  5      82   5
     JUST AS YOU'D BREAK A SUCKING SALAMANDER .  .  .  .  .  .  .  93  3 DON JUAN  7      52   5
     TO BREAK THE RULES BY BRINGING ONE'S OWN BRIDE .  .  .  .  . 103  3 DON JUAN  7      71   5
     IS PERPETRATED ERE A WORD CAN BREAK  .  .  .  .  .  .  .  . 141  3 DON JUAN  8      58   5
     BUT NOW I CHOOSE TO BREAK OFF IN THE MIDDLE .  .  .  .  .  . 181  3 DON JUAN  8     139   5
     WITH HIS DISPATCH FORGOT TO BREAK THE SEAL  .  .  .  .  .  . 211  3 DON JUAN  9      57   8
     TO SHOW THE PEOPLE THE BEST WAY TO BREAK .  .  .  .  .  .  . 357  3 DON JUAN 12      89   4
     AT BLANK-BLANK SQUARE--FOR WE WILL BREAK NO SQUARES  .  .  . 369  3 DON JUAN 13      25   1
     UPON MY HEAD HAVE BID THEIR THUNDERS BREAK  .  .  .  .  .  . 414  3 DON JUAN 14      10   3
     THEY BREAK THEIR RANKS AND GLADLY LEAVE THE DRILL  .  .  .  . 417  3 DON JUAN 14      17   2
     WHEREWITH WE BREAK OUR BUBBLES ON THE OCEAN  .  .  .  .  . 457  3 DON JUAN 15       2   4
     TO SEE MEN LET THESE SCOUNDREL SOVEREIGNS BREAK LAW  .  .  . 497  3 DON JUAN 15      92   8
BREAKER
     AND THE LOUD BREAKER BOILS AGAINST THE ROCK .  .  .  .  .  .  94  2 DON JUAN  1     134   7
BREAKER-BEATEN
     IT WAS A WILD AND BREAKER-BEATEN COAST  .  .  .  .  .  .  . 249  2 DON JUAN  2     177   1
```

95

		PAGE	VOL		CANTO	STANZA	LN

BREAKERS
UNLESS WITH BREAKERS CLOSE BENEATH HER LEE	. . . .	180	2 DON JUAN	2	45	8
SOME SWORE THAT THEY HEARD BREAKERS OTHERS GUNS	. . .	207	2 DON JUAN	2	96	7
THOUGH RIGHT AHEAD THE ROARING BREAKERS LAY .	. . .	211	2 DON JUAN	2	104	4
TURNS UP MORE DANGEROUS BREAKERS THAN THE EUXINE	. .	413	2 DON JUAN	5	5	8
OF BREAKERS HAS NOT DAUNTED MY SLIGHT TRIM .	. . .	227	3 DON JUAN	10	4	6

BREAKFAST
FOR BREAKFAST OF EGGS COFFEE BREAD AND FISH . .	. .	226	2 DON JUAN	2	133	8
MUST BREAKFAST AND BETIMES--LEST THEY SHOULD ASK IT	.	233	2 DON JUAN	2	144	7
AND SO SHE COOK'D THEIR BREAKFAST TO A TITTLE	. .	233	2 DON JUAN	2	145	5
AND THE FIRST BREAKFAST SPOILT PREPARED A NEW ONE .	.	234	2 DON JUAN	2	146	6
A BATH A BREAKFAST AND THE FINEST EYES	. . . .	246	2 DON JUAN	2	171	2
FOR LOVE OR BREAKFAST PRIVATE PLEASING LONE .	. . .	54	3 DON JUAN	6	97	3
BUT SYSTEM DOTH REVERSE THE TITAN'S BREAKFAST	. . .	411	3 DON JUAN	14	2	1
THE MORNING CAME--AND BREAKFAST TEA AND TOAST	. . .	568	3 DON JUAN	17	13	2

BREAKING
STILL BREAKING BUT WITH STAMINA SO STEADY	. . . .	89	2 DON JUAN	1	125	6
TO SAVE THE CREDIT OF THEIR BREAKING BANK	. . . .	500	2 DON JUAN	5	154	6
STOLE ON YOUR SPIRIT LIKE A MAY-DAY BREAKING	. . .	27	3 DON JUAN	6	43	2
COSSACQUES WERE ALL CUT OFF AS DAY WAS BREAKING	. .	150	3 DON JUAN	8	76	3
INTO THE EXCURSIVE BREAKING THE INDENTURES	. . . .	284	3 DON JUAN	11	33	5
THEY RUN BEFORE THE WIND THROUGH HIGH SEAS BREAKING	.	442	3 DON JUAN	14	74	6
BUT WHAT WITH KEEPING SOME AND BREAKING OTHERS .	.	535	3 DON JUAN	16	71	7

BREAKS
ONE BREAKS YOUR BONES ONE SETS THEM IN THEIR SOCKETS	.	91	2 DON JUAN	1	129	4
OR BREAKS THEIR HOPES OR HEARTS OR HEADS OR NECKS .	.	172	2 DON JUAN	2	31	6
AND 'TIS NO DOUBT A SIGHT TO SEE WHEN BREAKS	. . .	230	2 DON JUAN	2	139	4
THE MOON BREAKS HALF UNVEILED EACH FURTHER CHARM	. .	39	3 DON JUAN	6	66	5
WHICH RISES FOAMS AND BREAKS BUT NOT IN VAIN	. . .	60	3 DON JUAN	6	108	V7

BREAST
NOTHING BUT WHAT WAS GOOD HER BREAST WAS PEACEABLE--	. .	66	2 DON JUAN	1	83	5
MY BREAST HAS BEEN ALL WEAKNESS IS SO YET	. . . .	133	2 DON JUAN	1	196	1
HUSH'D AS THE BABE UPON ITS MOTHER'S BREAST .	. . .	235	2 DON JUAN	2	148	2
WERE SUCH AS COULD NOT IN HIS BREAST BE SHUT	. . .	244	2 DON JUAN	2	167	4
AND THEN ON THE PALE CHEEK HER BREAST NOW WARMS	. .	260	2 DON JUAN	2	195	6
A CHILD THE MOMENT WHEN IT DRAINS THE BREAST	. . .	261	2 DON JUAN	2	196	2
A CHILD THE FIRST TIME THAT IT SUCKS THE BREAST	. .	261	2 DON JUAN	2	196	V2
OF SUCH QUICKSILVER CLAY THAT IN HIS BREAST .	. . .	268	2 DON JUAN	2	209	3
PILLOW'D UPON A FAIR AND HAPPY BREAST	. . . .	274	2 DON JUAN	3	1	2
AND PLACE THEM ON THEIR BREAST--BUT PLACE TO DIE--	.	275	2 DON JUAN	3	2	6
NEATH WHICH HER BREAST HEAVED LIKE A LITTLE BILLOW	.	311	2 DON JUAN	3	70	4
BELOW HER BREAST WAS FASTEN'D WITH A BAND	. . .	312	2 DON JUAN	3	72	5
EARTH RENDER BACK FROM OUT THY BREAST	. . . .	323	2 DON JUAN	3	L 7	3
THOU BRING'ST THE CHILD TOO TO THE MOTHER'S BREAST	.	338	2 DON JUAN	3	107	8
WHICH SHAKE SO MUCH THE HUMAN BRAIN AND BREAST--	. .	343	2 DON JUAN	3	V 98	3
AND BREAST MATERNAL WEAN'D AT ONCE FOREVER	. . .	349	2 DON JUAN	4	10	6
AND CALLED FROM JUAN'S BREAST A FAINT LOW SIGH .	. .	355	2 DON JUAN	4	21	7
AND THEN DISMISS'D THE OMEN FROM HER BREAST .	. .	356	2 DON JUAN	4	24	3
HERSELF UPON HIS BREAST AND THERE SHE GREW	. . .	483	2 DON JUAN	5	125	8
A SINCERE WOMAN'S BREAST--FOR OVER-WARM	. . . .	13	3 DON JUAN	6	15	7
THROUGH THE HEAVED BREAST THE DREAM OF SOME FAR SHORE	.	40	3 DON JUAN	6	67	5
AND HID HER FACE WITHIN JUANNA'S BREAST	. . . .	48	3 DON JUAN	6	85	2
WHICH FABLE PLACES IN HER BREAST OF WAIL	. . . .	49	3 DON JUAN	6	87	6
ALREADY MANY A ONCE LOVE-BEATEN BREAST	. . . .	63	3 DON JUAN	6	115	3
MAY WIN PERHAPS A RIBBON AT THE BREAST	. . . .	118	3 DON JUAN	8	13	8
AND HERE HE WAS--WHO UPON WOMAN'S BREAST .	. . .	139	3 DON JUAN	8	53	1
AND HIDE HER LITTLE PALPITATING BREAST	. . . .	157	3 DON JUAN	8	91	7
BECAUSE A HUNCHBACK--MADE HIS BREAST THE SHIELD	. .	166	3 DON JUAN	8	110	V7
UPON THE RUSSIAN STEEL HIS BREAST HE FLUNG	. . .	170	3 DON JUAN	8	118	2
THOUGH HOARY NOW AND WITH A WITHERING BREAST	. . .	228	3 DON JUAN	10	6	5
UPON HER MIND THE MORE SO AS HER BREAST	. . . .	448	3 DON JUAN	14	88	7
LOVE BEARS WITHIN ITS BREAST THE VERY GERM	. . .	451	3 DON JUAN	14	94	1
EXCEPT ITSELF--SUCH IS THE HUMAN BREAST	. . . .	505	3 DON JUAN	16	10	3

BREASTS
TO THINK SUCH BREASTS MUST SUCKLE SLAVES .	. . .	326	2 DON JUAN	3	L 15	6
FROM OGLING ALL THEIR CHARMS FROM BREASTS TO BACKS	. .	20	3 DON JUAN	6	29	8
CHEERFUL AS CHILDREN CLIMB THE BREASTS OF MOTHERS .	.	119	3 DON JUAN	8	15	6

BREATH
AND WHEN AT LENGTH THEY'RE OUT OF BREATH THEY SIGH	. .	119	2 DON JUAN	1	179	5
A LITTLE BREATH LOVE WINE AMBITION FAME	. . . .	159	2 DON JUAN	2	4	7
THE FOURTH DAY CAME BUT NOT A BREATH OF AIR .	. . .	193	2 DON JUAN	2	70	1
PEDRILLO AND SO GENTLY EBB'D HIS BREATH	. . . .	197	2 DON JUAN	2	76	3
SEEM'D ALMOST PRYING INTO HIS FOR BREATH .	. . .	215	2 DON JUAN	2	113	2
BENT WITH HUSH'D LIPS THAT DRANK HIS SCARCE-DRAWN BREATH	.	232	2 DON JUAN	2	143	8
TILL PAUSING AT THE LAST HER BREATH TO TAKE .	. . .	241	2 DON JUAN	2	161	7
THESE TWO FORM THE LAST GASP OF PASSION'S BREATH	. .	280	2 DON JUAN	3	9	V3
THESE TWO ARE LEVELLERS AND HUMAN BREATH .	. . .	280	2 DON JUAN	3	9	V3
SO THESE POINT THE EPIGRAM OF HUMAN BREATH .	. . .	280	2 DON JUAN	3	9	V3
ARE THINGS THAT REALLY TAKE AWAY THE BREATH .	. . .	309	2 DON JUAN	3	66	6
AND NOT A BREATH CREPT THROUGH THE ROSY AIR .	. . .	335	2 DON JUAN	3	102	7
EXCEPT MERE BREATH AND SINCE THE SILENT SHORE	. . .	350	2 DON JUAN	4	12	5
UNTIL SHE SOBB'D FOR BREATH AND SOON THEY WERE	. . .	361	2 DON JUAN	4	31	6
HAD STOPP'D THIS CANTO AND DON JUAN'S BREATH	. . .	366	2 DON JUAN	4	42	2
NO SIGN SAVE BREATH OF HAVING LEFT THE GRAVE	. . .	378	2 DON JUAN	4	63	8
BUT YESTERDAY AND WHO HAD MIGHTIER BREATH	. . .	430	2 DON JUAN	5	36	3
NODS FROM THE TREE WAS SLUMBERING WITH SOFT BREATH	. .	38	3 DON JUAN	6	65	7
THOUSANDS OF WHOM WERE DRAWING THEIR LAST BREATH .	.	111	3 DON JUAN	7	87	4
AIR MIDST THE REST WHOSE SHORT BREATH AND LONG FACES	.	130	3 DON JUAN	8	34	V7
HER STEADY BREATH (WHICH SOME MONTHS THE SAME STILL IS)	.	132	3 DON JUAN	8	39	6

96

BREATH   (CONTINUED)
  RETIRE A LITTLE MERELY TO TAKE BREATH 133   3 DON JUAN   8   40   8
  THE BREATH OF MORN AND MAN WHERE FOOT BY FOOT   146   3 DON JUAN   8   69   7
  AND HUMAN BREATH IS POURED UPON THE AIR   155   3 DON JUAN   8   88   V2
  MARK HOW ITS LIPLESS MOUTH GRINS WITHOUT BREATH   . . . 188   3 DON JUAN   9   11   8
  RATHER THAN LIFE A MERE AFFAIR OF BREATH 190   3 DON JUAN   9   16   8
  BECAUSE DECEMBER WITH HIS BREATH SO HOARY   229   3 DON JUAN 10   9   6
  SHOULD NOT VEER ROUND WITH EVERY BREATH NOR SEIZE . . . 231   3 DON JUAN 10   13   7
  HIS BREATH--HE FROM HIS SWELLING THROAT UNTIED 276   3 DON JUAN 11   16   7
  AND FRAILER SINCE WITHOUT A BREATH OF AIR   306   3 DON JUAN 11   76   V5
  LETS OUT IMPATIENTLY HIS RUSHING BREATH   412   3 DON JUAN 14   4   7
  AND SUCH A STRAW BORNE ON BY HUMAN BREATH   414   3 DON JUAN 14   8   3
  THE GHOST HAD A REMARKABLY SWEET BREATH 560   3 DON JUAN 16   121   4
BREATHE
  DROOP'D AS THE WILLOW WHEN NO WINDS CAN BREATHE   . . . 235   2 DON JUAN   2   148   3
  SHOULD AN HOUR COME TO BID THEM BREATHE APART 358   2 DON JUAN   4   27   3
  IN LOVERS' PARTS HIS PASSION MORE TO BREATHE   392   2 DON JUAN   4   89   7
  TO BREATHE DESTRUCTION ON ITS WINDING WAY   113   3 DON JUAN   8   2   6
BREATHED
  BENEATH THE LIE THIS STATE THING BREATHED O'ER THEE . . . 19   2 DON JUAN   0   16   4
  SOME HUNDREDS BREATHED--THE REST WERE SILENT ALL . . . 175   3 DON JUAN   8   127   8
  HE BREATHED A THOUSAND CRESSYS AS HE SAW 261   3 DON JUAN 10   74   2
BREATHES
  BREATHES ALSO TO THE HEART AND O'ER IT THROWS   82   2 DON JUAN   1   114   7
  LOVE WHO HEROICALLY BREATHES A VEIN   168   2 DON JUAN   2   23   3
  WHICH BREATHES OF NATIONS SAVED NOT WORLDS UNDONE . . . 114   3 DON JUAN   8   5   4
  COMPASSION BREATHES ALONG THE SAVAGE MIND   164   3 DON JUAN   8   106   8
BREATHING
  AND LOUDER THAN HER BREATHING BEATS HER HEART   108   2 DON JUAN   1   158   8
  BREATHING ALL GENTLY O'ER HIS CHEEK AND MOUTH 245   2 DON JUAN   2   168   7
  IN A NEW FACE THE UGLIEST CREATURE BREATHING   24   2 DON JUAN   6   37   8
  AS ROLL THE WATERS TO THE BREATHING WIND 90   3 DON JUAN   7   48   3
BREATHLESS
  ALFONSO LEANING BREATHLESS BY THE DOOR   125   2 DON JUAN   1   187   4
  THERE BREATHLESS WITH HIS DIGGING NAILS HE CLUNG . . . 213   2 DON JUAN   2   108   1
  LAY IN A BREATHLESS HUSHED AND STONY SLEEP 40   3 DON JUAN   6   68   2
BRED
  OR GENTLEMEN WHO THOUGH WELL-BORN AND BRED 33   2 DON JUAN   1   22   3
  THAT THEY BRED IN AND IN AS MIGHT BE SHOWN 52   2 DON JUAN   1   57   6
  LIKE MOST IN THE BELIEF IN WHICH THEY'RE BRED 197   2 DON JUAN   2   76   6
  ALL HOPE TO LOOK UPON HER SWEET FACE BRED   377   2 DON JUAN   4   60   6
  BUT BRED WITHIN THE MARCH OF OLD ANCONA 395   2 DON JUAN   4   94   2
  HER THIRD TO ASK HIM WHERE HE HAD BEEN BRED 491   2 DON JUAN   5   139   3
  AND BRIGHT AS ANY METEOR EVER BRED 42   3 DON JUAN   6   72   5
  THE LADIES--WHO BY NO MEANS HAD BEEN BRED   101   3 DON JUAN   7   67   2
  BUT I AM HALF A SCOT BY BIRTH AND BRED   233   3 DON JUAN 10   17   7
  HIS HOLY TEMPLES IN THE LANDS WHICH BRED   262   3 DON JUAN 10   75   5
  AND ABOUT TWICE TWO THOUSAND PEOPLE BRED 290   3 DON JUAN 11   45   3
  PROUDEST OF PARIAN PATRICIAN (BRED 314   3 DON JUAN 11   V 75   6
  THAN THOSE BRED UP BY PRUDES WITHOUT A HEART   337   3 DON JUAN 12   46   8
  BOTH WITS--ONE BORN SO AND THE OTHER BRED   402   3 DON JUAN 13   93   7
  TO LIKE TOO READILY OR TOO HIGH BRED 460   3 DON JUAN 15   10   4
  THE ISLAND GIRL BRED UP BY THE LONE SEA 481   3 DON JUAN 15   58   4
  MY MUSE HATH BRED AND STILL PERHAPS MAY BREED 482   3 DON JUAN 15   60   5
  FOR I WAS BRED A MODERATE PRESBYTERIAN   496   3 DON JUAN 15   91   8
  POOR SOUL FOR SHE WAS COUNTRY BORN AND BRED 532   3 DON JUAN 16   64   6
  AND YET GREAT HEROES HAVE BEEN BRED BY BOTH 541   3 DON JUAN 16   84   8
  THOUGH TOO WELL BRED TO QUIZ MEN TO THEIR FACES   . . . 548   3 DON JUAN 16   100   3
BREECH
  BUT SUCH AS FIT AN ASIATIC BREECH 451   2 DON JUAN   5   68   5
BREECHES
  WITH A CLEAN SHIRT AND VERY SPACIOUS BREECHES 240   2 DON JUAN   2   160   8
  AND THAT HIS ARGUS BITES HIM BY--THE BREECHES 287   2 DON JUAN   3   23   8
  AND BRILLIANT BREECHES BRIGHT AS A CAIRN GORME 204   3 DON JUAN   9   43   5
  EXPOSED TO LOSE HIS LIFE AS WELL AS BREECHES   273   3 DON JUAN 11   11   8
  WOULD RISK TO PLEASE IT MY LAST RAG OF BREECHES   . . . 421   3 DON JUAN 14   26   V8
BREECHES'
  BUT KEEP YOUR HANDS OUT OF HIS BREECHES' POCKET   . . . 264   3 DON JUAN 10   79   8
BREED
  WHICH ALWAYS SPOILS THE BREED IF IT INCREASES 52   2 DON JUAN   1   57   8
  THIS HEATHENISH CROSS RESTORED THE BREED AGAIN 53   2 DON JUAN   1   58   1
  WHERE WAVES MIGHT WASH AND SEALS MIGHT BREED AND LURK . . 362   2 DON JUAN   4   33   4
  HUGER THAN TWELVE OF OUR DEGENERATE BREED   391   3 DON JUAN 13   70   4
  PROUDER OF SUCH A TOY THAN OF THEIR BREED   391   3 DON JUAN 13   70   V6
  BUT STRONGBOW'S WIT WAS OF MORE POLISH'D BREED 401   3 DON JUAN 13   92   4
  BUT FORM GOOD HOUSEKEEPERS TO BREED A NATION   420   3 DON JUAN 14   24   8
  MY MUSE HATH BRED AND STILL PERHAPS MAY BREED 482   3 DON JUAN 15   60   5
BREEDING
  WAS THAT HIS BREEDING SHOULD BE STRICTLY MORAL 43   2 DON JUAN   1   39   4
  THAT PASIPHAE PROMOTED BREEDING CATTLE   238   2 DON JUAN   2   155   7
  WITH SUCH TRUE BREEDING OF A GENTLEMAN   296   2 DON JUAN   3   41   3
  AND CERTAINLY HE SHOW'D THE BEST OF BREEDING   299   2 DON JUAN   3   46   2
  AND JUAN WAS A BOY OF SAINTLY BREEDING   354   2 DON JUAN   4   19   6
  TO HIM WHOSE BREEDING MARCHES WITH HIS QUALITY 369   3 DON JUAN 13   24   8
BREEDS
  BECAUSE IT BREEDS NO MORE MOUTHS THAN IT NOURISHES   . . 471   3 DON JUAN 15   35   4
BREEZE
  THEY DARED NOT TAKE IT IN FOR ALL THE BREEZE   188   2 DON JUAN   2   60   4
  SAVE IN THE BREEZE THAT CAME NOT SAVAGELY   194   2 DON JUAN   2   72   4

BREEZE   (CONTINUED)
```
    AS ARE THE BILLOWS WHEN THE BREEZE IS BRISK--  . . . .     7   3 DON JUAN  6     3    6
    AS THEY WILL DO LIKE LEAVES AT THE FIRST BREEZE   . . .  431   3 DON JUAN 14    48    6
BRENTA
    (LONG ERE I DREAMT OF DATING FROM THE BRENTA) . . . . .  143   2 DON JUAN  1   212    5
BRETHREN
    IN GIVING TO HIS BRETHREN THEIR FULL MEED   . . . . . .   14   2 DON JUAN  D     8    6
    ME AND MY EPIC BRETHREN GONE BEFORE  . . . . . . . . .   137   2 DON JUAN  1   202    2
    AND THEN HE CALLED HIS BRETHREN TO HIS AID . . . . . .    64   3 DON JUAN  6   118    1
BREVITY
    AND MAKES MEN'S MISERIES OF ALARMING BREVITY  . . . . .  190   2 DON JUAN  2    64    8
BREW
    WITH WHICH I COULD NOT BREW A PASTORAL   . . . . . . .   423   3 DON JUAN 14    30    3
    THAN WITCHES BITCHES OR PHYSICIANS BREW . . . . . . .    482   3 DON JUAN 15    62    8
BREWED
    THAT E'ER WERE BREWED FROM ELEMENTS OR GORE . . . . . .  356   3 DON JUAN 12    88    4
BREWING
    WHERE EVERY KIND OF MISCHIEF'S DAILY BREWING  . . . . .  326   3 DON JUAN 12    23    3
BRIAREUS
    OH ENVIABLE BRIAREUS WITH THY HANDS  . . . . . . . .     20   3 DON JUAN  6    28    1
BRIBE
    MUST BE RECITED AND--WITHOUT A BRIBE . . . . . . . .    187   3 DON JUAN  9    10    6
    UNLESS SOME BEAUTY WITH A KISS SHOULD BRIBE  . . . . .   567   3 DON JUAN 17    12    8
BRIBED
    I'VE BRIBED MY GRANDMOTHER'S REVIEW--THE BRITISH . . .   141   2 DON JUAN  1   209    8
BRIBES
    LIKE SHAKSPEARE'S STEALING DEER LORD BACON'S BRIBES  . .  329   2 DON JUAN  3    92    2
    WHETHER YOU'RE PAID BY GOVERNMENT IN BRIBES . . . . .    200   3 DON JUAN  9    35    4
BRIBING
    SOME SAY THAT AUTHORS ONLY SNATCH BY BRIBING  . . . .    418   3 DON JUAN 14    19    4
BRICK
    A MIGHTY MASS OF BRICK AND SMOKE AND SHIPPING . . . . .  265   3 DON JUAN 10    82    1
BRICKLAYER
    BRICKLAYER OF BABEL CALLED AN ARCHITECT  . . . . . . .   529   3 DON JUAN 16    58    2
BRICKS
    (THOUGH CLAUDIUS RICH ESQUIRE SOME BRICKS HAS GOT . . .  447   2 DON JUAN  5    62    5
    OR SAT AMIDST THE BRICKS OF NINEVEH  . . . . . . .      271   3 DON JUAN 11     7    6
    OF BRICKS TO LET THE DUST IN AT YOUR EASE . . . . . .    278   3 DON JUAN 11    21    5
BRIDAL
    JUST AT THE CLOSE OF THE FIRST BRIDAL YEAR  . . . . .    125   3 DON JUAN  8    27    4
    BEFORE THE BRIDAL HOURS HAVE DANCED THEIR MEASURE . . .  168   3 DON JUAN  8   113    3
    HE FLITS ON THE BRIDAL EVE  . . . . . . . . .           519   3 DON JUAN 16   L 3    6
BRIDE
    IT WAS FOR THIS THAT I BECAME A BRIDE . . . . . .       100   2 DON JUAN  1   145    4
    HAIDEE WAS NATURE'S BRIDE AND KNEW NOT THIS . . . .      264   2 DON JUAN  2   202    1
    WOULD JUAN BEND THOUGH 'TWERE TO MAHOMET'S BRIDE  . . .  471   2 DON JUAN  5   103    5
    SHE WAS A SULTAN'S BRIDE (THANK HEAVEN NOT MINE) . . .   475   2 DON JUAN  5   111    8
    AND SHOULD YOU ASK HOW SHE A SULTAN'S BRIDE  . . . . .   477   2 DON JUAN  5   115    2
    BRIDE OF THE SUN AND SISTER OF THE MOON  . . . . . .     494   2 DON JUAN  5   144    1
    THE GIANT THOUGHT OF BEING A TITAN'S BRIDE  . . . . .     20   3 DON JUAN  6    28    4
    (IF THAT HIS HIGHNESS WEARIED OF HIS BRIDE) . . . . .     24   3 DON JUAN  6    36    7
    THE IMPERIAL BRIDE--AND ADDED LET THE BOAT  . . . . .     62   3 DON JUAN  6   113    2
    TO BREAK THE RULES BY BRINGING ONE'S OWN BRIDE  . . . .  103   3 DON JUAN  7    71    5
    OR HAWK OR BRIDE MOST MORTALS AFTER ONE  . . . . . .     122   3 DON JUAN  8    22    6
    OF IMPORT BOTH TO VIRGIN AND TO BRIDE . . . . . . .     292   3 DON JUAN 11    46    2
    UPON AN HEIRESS OR HIS NEIGHBOUR'S BRIDE . . . . . .     304   3 DON JUAN 11    71    2
    BUT IN OLD ENGLAND WHEN A YOUNG BRIDE ERRS  . . . .      345   3 DON JUAN 12    64    7
    OF WHAT SHE HAD GONE THROUGH WITH--SINCE A BRIDE . . .   525   3 DON JUAN 16    50    6
BRIDEGROOMS
    THAT FUTURE BRIDEGROOMS SWORE AND SIGHED AND PAID IT . .  293   3 DON JUAN 11    49    8
    THAT BRIDEGROOMS AFTER THEY ARE FAIRLY GROOM'D  . . . .  473   3 DON JUAN 15    39    5
BRIDE'S
    HAD MADE HIM LATELY BASK IN HIS BRIDE'S BEAUTY  . . . .   51   3 DON JUAN  6    91    8
BRIDES
    FOR RICH MEN AND THEIR BRIDES TO LAY THEIR HEADS  . . .   18   3 DON JUAN  6    25    4
    THOUGHT NOT UPON THE CHARMS OF FOUR YOUNG BRIDES . . .   168   3 DON JUAN  8   114    2
    WITHOUT CASH MALTHUS TELLS YOU TAKE NO BRIDES  . . . .   322   3 DON JUAN 12    14    4
    THEY HAVE AT HAND A BLOOMING GLUT OF BRIDES  . . . . .   471   3 DON JUAN 15    33    8
BRIDGE
    OF TWILIGHT AS THE PARTY CROSSED THE BRIDGE . . . . .    279   3 DON JUAN 11    23    8
BRIDGES
    SHOUTS BRIDGES ARCHES PENSIONS FROM A NATION  . . . .    114   3 DON JUAN  8     4    3
BRIDLED
    THE MISSES BRIDLED AND THE MATRONS FROWN'D  . . . . .    429   3 DON JUAN 14    44    2
BRIEF
    AND THAT BRIEF DREAM APPEAR'D A LIFE TOO LONG  . . . .   362   2 DON JUAN  4    34    8
    BRIEF BUT DELIGHTFUL--SUCH AS HAD NOT STAID . . . . .    382   2 DON JUAN  4    71    6
    A FEW BRIEF QUESTIONS AND THE ANSWERS GAVE  . . . . .    387   2 DON JUAN  4    79    6
    GULBEYAZ PROVED IN THAT BRIEF AGONY  . . . . . . .       59   3 DON JUAN  6   106    7
    OF THESE BRIEF BLOSSOMS THE IMMEDIATE FRUITS  . . . .    168   3 DON JUAN  8   113    8
    HECTIC AND BRIEF AS SUMMER'S DAY NIGH DONE  . . . . .    229   3 DON JUAN 10     8    6
    THE LAWYER'S BRIEF IS LIKE THE SURGEON'S KNIFE . . . .   232   3 DON JUAN 10    14    6
    THEY'RE RIGHT OUR DAYS ARE TOO BRIEF FOR AFFORDING . .   270   3 DON JUAN 11     4    5
    AND THEN SHE DROPS A BRIEF AND MODERN CURTSY  . . . .    300   3 DON JUAN 11    63    7
    IN BRIEF THE LITTLE ORPHAN OF THE EAST   . . . . . .     338   3 DON JUAN 12    48    7
    BUT I SHALL ADD THEM IN A BRIEF APPENDIX  . . . . . .    440   3 DON JUAN 14    68    7
BRIEFLY
    WHAT ARE YE--WHAT YOU SEE US BRIEFLY PAST   . . . . .     97   3 DON JUAN  7    59    6
BRIG
    HAIL'D A STRANGE BRIG CORPO DI CAIO MARIO   . . . . .    389   2 DON JUAN  4    82    4
    SAY THAT HE SCUDS BEFORE IT LIKE A BRIG  . . . . . .     109   3 DON JUAN  7    85    4
```

```
                                                               PAGE VOL    CANTO STANZA LN
BRIGADIER
    ALSO THE GENERAL MARKOW BRIGADIER  . . . . . . . . . . 117  3 DON JUAN  8    11    1
BRIGADIERS
    BUT WISHING TO BE ONE DAY BRIGADIERS  . . . . . . . .  75  3 DON JUAN  7    18    4
BRIGANTINE
    OR BRIGANTINE OR PINK OF NO GREAT TONNAGE  . . . . . . 468  3 DON JUAN 15    27    7
BRIGHT
    (WHO DOES NOT OFTEN CLAIM THE BRIGHT REVERSION)  . . .  14  2 DON JUAN  0     9    2
    BRIGHT WITH INTELLIGENCE AND FAIR AND SMOOTH  . . . .  55  2 DON JUAN  1    61    2
    BRIGHT AND IMMACULATE UNMIX'D AND PURE  . . . . . . .  64  2 DON JUAN  1    79    2
    BY GUSTS AND MANY A SPARKLING HEARTH WAS BRIGHT  . . .  94  2 DON JUAN  1   135    3
    RELUCTANT PAST HER BRIGHT EYES ROLLED--AS A VEIL  . . 108  2 DON JUAN  1   158   V3
    RESTING ITS BRIGHT BASE ON THE QUIVERING BLUE  . . . . 204  2 DON JUAN  2    91    3
    BRIGHT HUES WHEN OUT OF DOORS AND YET WHILE WAVE  . . 220  2 DON JUAN  2   120    5
    BRIGHT PHOEBUS WHILE THE MOUNTAINS STILL ARE WET  . . 230  2 DON JUAN  2   139    5
    SPREAD LIKE A ROSY OCEAN VAST AND BRIGHT . . . . . . . 253  2 DON JUAN  2   185    2
    OF COLOUR'D GARBS AS BRIGHT AS BUTTERFLIES  . . . . . 289  2 DON JUAN  3    27    8
    FINISHED WITH BRIGHT GOLD LACE HER JACKET'S FELLOW  . 311  2 DON JUAN  3    70   V4
    THOSE THEIR BRIGHT RISE HAD LIGHTED TO SUCH JOYS  . . 352  2 DON JUAN  4    16    2
    WITH HIS BROAD BRIGHT AND DROPPING ORB WERE GONE  . . 355  2 DON JUAN  4    22    4
    A RUEFUL GLANCE UPON THE WAVES (WHICH BRIGHT ALL  . . 393  2 DON JUAN  4    90    5
    BRIGHT--AND AS BLACK AND BURNING AS A COAL  . . . . . 395  2 DON JUAN  4    94    5
    CASTS OFF ITS BRIGHT SKIN YEARLY LIKE THE SNAKE  . . . 421  2 DON JUAN  5    21    8
    'TIS TRUE IT GETS ANOTHER BRIGHT AND FRESH  . . . . . 422  2 DON JUAN  5    22    1
    BUT EVERY FOOL DESCRIBES IN THESE BRIGHT DAYS  . . . . 440  2 DON JUAN  5    52    2
    THE GIANT DOOR WAS BROAD AND BRIGHT AND HIGH  . . . . 461  2 DON JUAN  5    86    1
    OBJECT ON OBJECT FLASHED SO BRIGHT AND FAST . . . . . 465  2 DON JUAN  5    93    6
    BUT O'ER HER BRIGHT BROW FLASHED A TUMULT STRANGE  . . 473  2 DON JUAN  5   108    3
    BRIGHT WITH THE VERY WEAKNESS HE REPROVED  . . . . . . 481  2 DON JUAN  5   121    6
    AND BRIGHT AS ANY METEOR EVER BRED . . . . . . . . . .  42  3 DON JUAN  6    72    5
    OF WOLVES WILL THE BRIGHT MUSE WITHDRAW ONE RAY  . . .  70  3 DON JUAN  7     7    6
    MORE EVIL IN AN HOUR THAN THIRTY BRIGHT  . . . . . . .  86  3 DON JUAN  7    41    5
    TO THEIR TWO SELVES ONE WHOLE BRIGHT BULLETIN  . . . . 121  3 DON JUAN  8    19    8
    OF FRIAR BACON'S BRIGHT INVENTION--SHARED  . . . . . . 129  3 DON JUAN  8    33   V5
    OF THE BRIGHT BAYONET AND THEY ALL SHOULD HURRY ON  . 151  3 DON JUAN  8    78    6
    AND BRIGHT ETERNITY WITHOUT DISGUISE  . . . . . . . . 169  3 DON JUAN  8   115    5
    AND BRILLIANT BREECHES BRIGHT AS A CAIRN GORME . . . . 204  3 DON JUAN  9    43    5
    YET AS THE CONSEQUENCES ARE AS BRIGHT . . . . . . . . 284  3 DON JUAN 11    34    3
    THOSE BRIGHT MOTHS FLUTTERING ROUND A DYING FLAME  . . 349  3 DON JUAN 12    72    4
    THE WORLD GAVE GROUND BEFORE HER BRIGHT ARRAY  . . . . 364  3 DON JUAN 13    11    5
    SLEEPS FROM THE CHIVALRY OF THIS BRIGHT AGE . . . . . 378  3 DON JUAN 13    44    6
    BRIGHT AS A NEW NAPOLEON FROM ITS MINTAGE  . . . . . . 458  3 DON JUAN 15     7    3
    TO KEEP OUR HOLY BEACONS ALWAYS BRIGHT  . . . . . . . 496  3 DON JUAN 15    90    4
    HE THOUGHT AURORA RABY'S EYES MORE BRIGHT  . . . . . . 506  3 DON JUAN 16    12    3
    GLANCED WITHOUT PAUSING ON HIM A BRIGHT EYE . . . . . 510  3 DON JUAN 16    21    8
    HER BLACK BRIGHT DOWNCAST YET ESPIEGLE EYE  . . . . . 532  3 DON JUAN 16    65    1
    FOR HE HAD TWO BOTH TOLERABLY BRIGHT . . . . . . . . . 558  3 DON JUAN 16   117    6
BRIGHTEN'D
    BRIGHTEN'D AND FOR A MOMENT SEEM'D TO ROAM  . . . . . 203  2 DON JUAN  2    89    6
BRIGHTER
    OUR COMING AND LOOK BRIGHTER WHEN WE COME  . . . . . .  88  2 DON JUAN  1   123    4
    AND THINKS HEAVEN BRIGHTER EVEN THAN NEWTON'S PAGE  . 242  2 DON JUAN  2   163   V7
    OR FRESHER BRIGHTER BUT THE YEAR GONE THROUGH  . . . . 422  2 DON JUAN  5    22    V
    WHICH STILL ELSEWHERE MAY ROUSE A BRIGHTER SPRING--  . 188  3 DON JUAN  9    11    4
    THEY CAN TRANSFIGURE BRIGHTER THAN A RAPHAEL  . . . . 463  3 DON JUAN 15    16    8
    AND NOTHING BRIGHTER GLEAMED THROUGH THE SALOON  . . . 504  3 DON JUAN 16     8    7
BRIGHTEST
    IN WHOM OUR BRIGHTEST DAYS WE WOULD RETRACE . . . . . 305  2 DON JUAN  3    59    3
    WARRANTED VIRGIN BEAUTY'S BRIGHTEST COLOURS . . . . . 407  2 DON JUAN  4   114    3
    WHO WITH THE BRIGHTEST GEORGIANS MIGHT COMPARE . . . .  24  3 DON JUAN  6    36    4
    BEAR IT YE MUSES ON YOUR BRIGHTEST WING . . . . . . . 175  3 DON JUAN  8   126    4
BRIGHTLY
    FOLLIES TRICK'D OUT SO BRIGHTLY THAT THEY BLIND--  . . 480  3 DON JUAN 15    57    6
BRIGHTNESS
    AND KNEW SUCH BRIGHTNESS WAS BUT THE REFLECTION  . . . 351  2 DON JUAN  4    13    7
BRIG'S
    THE DEE THE DON BALGOUNIE'S BRIG'S BLACK WALL . . . . 233  3 DON JUAN 10    18    3
BRILLIANT
    AND BRILLIANT BREECHES BRIGHT AS A CAIRN GORME . . . . 204  3 DON JUAN  9    43    5
    SO BRILLIANT WHERE THE LIST OF ROUTS AND DANCES IS--  . 308  3 DON JUAN 11    80    3
    ON HIM THE DIAMOND POURS ITS BRILLIANT BLAZE . . . . . 319  3 DON JUAN 12     8    6
    AH NUTBROWN PARTRIDGES  AH BRILLIANT PHEASANTS . . . . 394  3 DON JUAN 13    75    7
    DOUBTLESS IT IS A BRILLIANT MASQUERADE  . . . . . . . 417  3 DON JUAN 14    17    5
    WITH THE NEW VENUS OF THEIR BRILLIANT OCEAN . . . . . 434  3 DON JUAN 14    55    4
    A BEAUTEOUS RIPPLE OF THE BRILLIANT STREAM . . . . . . 480  3 DON JUAN 15    55    3
    EXULTING IN THEIR BRILLIANT LUCUBRATIONS . . . . . . . 533  3 DON JUAN 16    66    8
    A BRILLIANT DINER OUT THOUGH BUT A CURATE . . . . . . 540  3 DON JUAN 16    82    2
BRIM
    WHEN O'ER THE BRIM THE SPARKLING BUMPERS REACH . . . . 250  2 DON JUAN  2   178    3
    MY MILD AND MIDNIGHT BEAKERS TO THE BRIM . . . . . . . 372  2 DON JUAN  4    53    7
BRIMSTONE
    AND SMOOTHED THE BRIMSTONE OF THAT STREET OF HELL . . 124  3 DON JUAN  8    26    7
BRING
    RING FOR YOUR VALET--BID HIM QUICKLY BRING . . . . . . 251  2 DON JUAN  2   180    1
    A PLEASURE NAUGHT BUT DRUNKENNESS CAN BRING . . . . . 251  2 DON JUAN  2   180   V3
    AND IF 'TIS LOST LIFE HATH NO MORE TO BRING . . . . . 262  2 DON JUAN  2   199    4
    AND BRING OUR HEARTS BACK TO THEIR STARTING-POST  . . 286  2 DON JUAN  3    21    8
    'TIS BEAUTIFUL TO SEE A MATRON BRING . . . . . . . . . 306  2 DON JUAN  3    60    3
    THE READER BUT 'TWOULD NOT BE HARD TO BRING . . . . . 332  2 DON JUAN  3    97    6
```

99

```
                                                        PAGE VOL      CANTO STANZA LN
BRING   (CONTINUED)
      THE READER--BUT THE RULE IS --AND I'LL BRING     . . .   332  2 DON JUAN  3    97  V6
      'TIS THAT OUR NATURE CANNOT ALWAYS BRING . . .   . . .   346  2 DON JUAN  4     4   3
      YEARS COULD BUT BRING THEM CRUEL THINGS OR WRONG . . .   358  2 DON JUAN  4    27   4
      ON THE FIRST FOE WHOM LAMBRO'S CALL MIGHT BRING  . . .   365  2 DON JUAN  4    39   8
      A MOMENT MORE WILL BRING THE SIGHT TO BEAR . . . . . .   366  2 DON JUAN  4    41   3
      AND LIKE THE SOIL BENEATH IT WILL BRING FORTH    . . .   374  2 DON JUAN  4    56   5
      WHICH THE WEST INDIAN MARKET SCARCE WOULD BRING  . . .   408  2 DON JUAN  4   115   2
      A SINGLE CRY WOULD BRING THEM ALL ABROAD . . .   . . .   436  2 DON JUAN  5    45   5
      AS YOU WILL SEE IF SHE YOU LOVE SHALL BRING HERS . . .   472  2 DON JUAN  5   106   5
      I SHOULD BUT BRING DISGRACE UPON THE DYER . . .  . . .   489  2 DON JUAN  5   134   4
      BRING DOWN THE FRUIT WHICH STILL PERVERSELY CLUNG . . .   44  3 DON JUAN  6    76   5
      BRING THE TWO SLAVES SHE SAID IN A LOW TONE . .  . . .    62  3 DON JUAN  6   112   2
      TO BRING THE OTHER THREE HERE WAS ABSURD . . .   . . .    97  3 DON JUAN  7    60   6
      WILL BRING THE OTHER ERE THE LAKE-LIKE BROW . .  . . .   229  3 DON JUAN 10     8   3
      THE SEVENTH WILL BRING BLUE DEVILS OR A DUN . .  . . .   243  3 DON JUAN 10    38   8
      WARS REVELS LOVES--DO THESE BRING MEN MORE EASE  . . .   321  3 DON JUAN 12    11   5
      BEGGED TO BRING UP THE LITTLE GIRL AND OUT-- . . . . .   330  3 DON JUAN 12    31   3
      FOR SILLY WARDS WILL BRING THEIR GUARDIANS BLAME . . .   336  3 DON JUAN 12    42   4
      TO BRING WHAT WAS A JEST TO A SERIOUS END . . .  . . .   491  3 DON JUAN 15    79   6
BRINGEST
      OH HESPERUS THOU BRINGEST ALL GOOD THINGS--  . . . . .   338  2 DON JUAN  3   107   1
BRINGING
      BRINGING WARM WATER WREATHING HER LONG TRESSES   . . .   252  2 DON JUAN  2   182   7
      BY BRINGING WOMEN HERE THEY SHALL BE SHOWN . .   . . .   102  3 DON JUAN  7    70   3
      TO BREAK THE RULES BY BRINGING ONE'S OWN BRIDE   . . .   103  3 DON JUAN  7    71   5
      OF ADELINE IN BRINGING THIS SAME LAY . . . . .   . . .   526  3 DON JUAN 16    51   2
BRINGS
      OR ANY OTHER THING THAT BRINGS REGRET . . . .    . . .   172  2 DON JUAN  2    31   5
      BUT TIME WHICH BRINGS ALL BEINGS TO THEIR LEVEL  . . .   345  2 DON JUAN  4     2   1
      SHE HARDLY KNEW TO SUCH PERFECTION BRINGS . . .  . . .   485  2 DON JUAN  5   128   6
      YOUR SLAVE BRINGS TIDINGS--HE HOPES NOT TOO SOON-- . .   494  2 DON JUAN  5   144   5
      AND WHY BECAUSE IT BRINGS SELF-APPROBATION . .   . . .   114  3 DON JUAN  8     4   1
      AS AULD LANG SYNE BRINGS SCOTLAND ONE AND ALL .  . . .   233  3 DON JUAN 10    18   1
      CARE LIKE A HOUSE-KEEPER BRINGS EVERY WEEK . .   . . .   243  3 DON JUAN 10    38   5
      AND THIS REFLECTION BRINGS ME TO PLAIN PHYSICS   . . .   349  3 DON JUAN 12    72   5
      TREATING A TOPIC WHICH ALAS BUT BRINGS . . . .   . . .   500  3 DON JUAN 15    98   6
      OR LIKE AN OPIATE WHICH BRINGS TROUBLED REST .   . . .   505  3 DON JUAN 16    10   1
      THAT BRINGS LOCHABER BACK TO EYES THAT ROAM . .  . . .   523  3 DON JUAN 16    46   3
BRING'ST
      THOU BRING'ST THE CHILD TOO TO THE MOTHER'S BREAST . .   338  2 DON JUAN  3   107   8
BRINK
      WITH TENDERNESS--STOOD HOWLING ON THE BRINK . .  . . .   187  2 DON JUAN  2    58   4
      SO NARROW AS TO SHAME THEIR WINTRY BRINK . . .   . . .   228  3 DON JUAN 10     7   3
      AND YET 'TIS VERY PUZZLING ON THE BRINK . . . .  . . .   234  3 DON JUAN 10    20   6
      HAD KEPT HIM FROM THE BRINK OF HIPPOCRENE . . .  . . .   294  3 DON JUAN 11    51   7
      SALOON ROOM HALL O'ERFLOW BEYOND THEIR BRINK .   . . .   302  3 DON JUAN 11    68   5
      THE WOODS SLOPED DOWNWARDS TO ITS BRINK AND STOOD . .   385  3 DON JUAN 13    57   7
      AS E'ER BROUGHT MAN AND WOMAN TO THE BRINK . .   . . .   454  3 DON JUAN 14   100   3
BRISK
      AS ARE THE BILLOWS WHEN THE BREEZE IS BRISK--    . . . .   7  3 DON JUAN  6     3   6
BRISKLY
      FURTHER OLD BABA RATHER BRISKLY ENTERED . . .    . . .   493  2 DON JUAN  5   143   8
      WERE BRISKLY FIRED AND ANSWERED IN DUE ORDER .   . . .    85  3 DON JUAN  7    38   8
      HAD SET TO WORK AS BRISKLY AS THEIR BROTHERS .   . . .   119  3 DON JUAN  8    15   4
BRISSOT
      BARNAVE BRISSOT CONDORCET MIRABEAU . . . . . .   . . .    22  2 DON JUAN  1     3   1
BRISTLING
      ROSE OVER THE TOWN'S RIGHT SIDE IN BRISTLING TIER . . .   72  3 DON JUAN  7    12   7
      ALONG THE LEAGUERED WALL AND BRISTLING BANK .    . . .   110  3 DON JUAN  7    86   4
      WHEN UP THE BRISTLING MOSLEM ROSE AT LAST . .    . . .   115  3 DON JUAN  8     7   3
BRITAIN
      THOUGH BRITAIN OWES (AND PAYS YOU TOO) SO MUCH   . . .   184  3 DON JUAN  9     3   1
      RENOWNED FOR RUINING GREAT BRITAIN GRATIS . .    . . .   186  3 DON JUAN  9     8   8
      GREAT BRITAIN WHICH THE MUSE MAY PENETRATE .     . . .   327  3 DON JUAN 12    24   6
      IN BRITAIN--WHICH OF COURSE TRUE PATRIOTS FIND   . . .   359  3 DON JUAN 13     2   7
      IF BRITAIN MOURN HER BLEAKNESS WE CAN TELL HER   . . .   394  3 DON JUAN 13    76   7
BRITAIN'S
      I RECOLLECT GREAT BRITAIN'S COAST LOOKS WHITE    . . .   163  2 DON JUAN  2    12   5
      OF BRITAIN'S YOUTH DEPENDS UPON THEIR WEIGHT .   . . .   140  3 DON JUAN  8    55   4
      OF BRITAIN'S PRESENT WEALTH AND HAPPINESS--  .   . . .   371  3 DON JUAN 13    29   8
BRITANNIA'S
      NELSON WAS ONCE BRITANNIA'S GOD OF WAR  . . .    . . .    23  2 DON JUAN  1     4   1
BRITISH
      I'VE BRIBED MY GRANDMOTHER'S REVIEW--THE BRITISH . . .   141  2 DON JUAN  1   209   8
      A WANDERER FROM THE BRITISH WORLD OF FASHION .   . . .   244  2 DON JUAN  2   166   2
      OUR BRITISH FRIEND THESE ARE THE WIVES OF OTHERS . . .   103  3 DON JUAN  7    71   2
      BETWEEN THE BRITISH CABINET AND RUSSIAN . . .    . . .   246  3 DON JUAN 10    45   3
      AND YET THE BRITISH DAMME'S RATHER ATTIC . .     . . .   289  3 DON JUAN 11    43   1
      AND BEG HIS BRITISH GODSHIP'S HUMBLE PARDON .    . . .   442  3 DON JUAN 14    75   4
BRITON
      THE BRITON MUST BE BOLD WHO REALLY DURST . .     . . .   136  3 DON JUAN  8    48   5
      AT THE FIRST BLUSH FOR A FAIR BRITON HIDES .     . . .   350  3 DON JUAN 12    74   3
BRITON'S
      A TERRIER TOO WHICH ONCE HAD BEEN A BRITON'S     . . .   285  2 DON JUAN  3    18   4
      TO PATRIOT SYMPATHY A BRITON'S BLUSHES--  . .    . . .   425  3 DON JUAN 14    35   4
BRITONS
      WHICH BRITONS DEEM THEIR UTI POSSIDETIS . . .    . . .   246  3 DON JUAN 10    45   8
      BOLD BRITONS WE ARE NOW ON SHOOTER'S HILL . .    . . .   264  3 DON JUAN 10    80   8
      BECAUSE BOLD BRITONS HAVE A TONGUE AND FREE QUILL . .   367  3 DON JUAN 13    20   5
```

```
                                                        PAGE VOL      CANTO STANZA LN
BRITTLE
    BUT AS THEY HAD BUT ONE OAR AND THAT BRITTLE  . .  . . . 192  2 DON JUAN  2     69    7
    COULD STIR HIS PULSE OR MAKE HIS FAITH FEEL BRITTLE  . . 396  2 DON JUAN  4     95    7
    WHAT SPEAKS OF HEAVEN SHOULD BY NO MEANS BE BRITTLE  . . 444  2 DON JUAN  5     59    3
BROAD
    WAX'D BROAD AND WAVING LIKE A BANNER FREE   . . . . . . 204  2 DON JUAN  2     91    6
    WITH CLIFFS ABOVE AND A BROAD SANDY SHORE   . . . . - . 249  2 DON JUAN  2    177    2
    WHENCE THE BROAD MOON ROSE CIRCLING INTO SIGHT . . . . 253  2 DON JUAN  2    185    4
    WOULD BREAK YOUR SHIELD HOWEVER BROAD . . . . . . . 325  2 DON JUAN  3  L 14    6
    WITH HIS BROAD BRIGHT AND DROPPING ORB WERE GONE  . . . 355  2 DON JUAN  4     22    4
    THE GIANT DOOR WAS BROAD AND BRIGHT AND HIGH  . . . . 461  2 DON JUAN  5     86    1
    IF RATHER BROAD MADE STOCKS RISE AND THEIR HOLDERS  . . 208  3 DON JUAN  9     52    8
    THE EARTH AS SCARCE THE EAGLE IN THE BROAD  . . . . . 263  3 DON JUAN 10     78    3
    HIS HOST WITH BROAD ARMS 'GAINST THE THUNDER-STROKE  . 384  3 DON JUAN 13     56    4
    BROAD AS TRANSPARENT DEEP AND FRESHLY FED  . . . . . 385  3 DON JUAN 13     57    2
BROADCLOTH
    HORSE BY A BLACKLEG BROADCLOTH BY A TAILOR  . . . . . 424  2 DON JUAN  5     26    7
BROADENING
    BROADENING TO GRINS HE COLOURED MORE THAN ONCE . . . . 542  3 DON JUAN 16     88    3
BROADLY
    OF OURS ALTHOUGH THEY PROPAGATE MORE BROADLY  . . . . 472  3 DON JUAN 15     36    6
BROADSIDE
    BEFORE THEY GIVE THEIR BROADSIDE BY-AND-BY  . . . . . 266  3 DON JUAN 10     84    2
BROILING
    BUT WILL KEEP BAKING BROILING BURNING ON .  . . . . .  56  2 DON JUAN  1     63    4
BROKE
    UNTIL AT LENGTH THE SMOTHER'D FIRE BROKE OUT  . . . .  35  2 DON JUAN  1     26    7
    WHEN YOU BROKE IN UPON US WITH YOUR FELLOWS . . . . . 106  2 DON JUAN  1    156    3
    DAY HAS NOT BROKE--THERE'S NO ONE IN THE STREET  . . . 121  2 DON JUAN  1    182    8
    BURGLARIOUSLY BROKE HIS COFFIN'S LID  . . . . . . . 146  2 DON JUAN  1    219    6
    NEW BROKE A CAMELOPARD A GAZELLE   . . . . . . . 160  2 DON JUAN  2      6    2
    A SQUALL CAME ON AND WHILE SOME GUNS BROKE LOOSE  . . . 172  2 DON JUAN  2     30    6
    DAY BROKE AND THE WIND LULL'D THE MASTS WERE GONE .  . . 176  2 DON JUAN  2     38    2
    AS MORNING BROKE THE LIGHT WIND DIED AWAY  . . . . . 207  2 DON JUAN  2     97    1
    THE MORN BROKE AND FOUND JUAN SLUMBERING STILL .  . . 229  2 DON JUAN  2    137    1
    NOT YET A DREAMER TILL THE SPELL IS BROKE  . . . . . 237  2 DON JUAN  2    152    3
    EACH BROKE TO DROWN HER YET SHE COULD NOT DIE  . . . . 361  2 DON JUAN  4     31    8
    AS ON THE BEACH THE WAVES AT LAST ARE BROKE .  . . . . 402  2 DON JUAN  4    106    5
    BROKE FOAMING O'ER THE BLUE SYMPLEGADES  . . . . . . 413  2 DON JUAN  5      5    2
    AND THEN HER SEX'S SHAME BROKE IN AT LAST   . . . . . 490  2 DON JUAN  5    137    3
    TO LODGE THERE WHEN A WAR BROKE OUT ACCORDING  . . . . 498  2 DON JUAN  5    151    2
    LIKE BIRDS OR BOYS OR BEDLAMITES BROKE LOOSE  . . . .  23  3 DON JUAN  6     34    2
    NOT ALL THE CLAMOUR BROKE HER HAPPY STATE   . . . . .  42  3 DON JUAN  6     73    5
    THAT BROKE FOR NOTHING ON THEIR SLEEPING EAR  . . . .  45  3 DON JUAN  6     79    4
    WITHIN THESE WALLS TO BE BROKE IN UPON   . . . . .  46  3 DON JUAN  6     81    2
    WAS SHOWN AND SOME MORE NOBLE HEART BROKE THROUGH .  . . 174  3 DON JUAN  8    124    2
    OF SOME ALCHYMIC FURNACE FROM WHENCE BROKE  . . . . . 266  3 DON JUAN 10     83    3
    AS THUNDERED KNOCKERS BROKE THE LONG-SEALED SPELL .  . . 282  3 DON JUAN 11     29    3
    WHAT TIME HE CHOSE FOR DRESS AND BROKE HIS FAST  . . . 406  3 DON JUAN 13    103    7
    HE BROKE 'TIS TRUE SOME STATUTES OF THE LAWS  . . . . 424  3 DON JUAN 14     33    5
    THEN BROKE HIS PACKET TO SEE WHAT WAS IN'T   . . . . . 440  3 DON JUAN 14     69    5
    TO INDICATE A CUPIDON BROKE LOOSE  . . . . . . . . 461  3 DON JUAN 15     12    6
    BROKE IN UPON BY THE BLACK FRIAR OF LATE . . . . . 515  3 DON JUAN 16     35    4
    TRUE SHE SAID LITTLE--'TWAS THE REST THAT BROKE  . . . 552  3 DON JUAN 16    104    1
BROKEN
    AMBITION WAS MY IDOL WHICH WAS BROKEN .  . . . . . . 145  2 DON JUAN  1    217    1
    SOME BROKEN PLANKS AND OARS THAT TO THE TOUCH  . . . . 226  2 DON JUAN  2    132    4
    WAS BROKEN WORDS THEY THOUGHT A LANGUAGE THERE--  . . . 256  2 DON JUAN  2    189    4
    HE HERS UNTIL THEY END IN BROKEN GASPS   . . . . . . 259  2 DON JUAN  2    194    6
    THE HEART--WHICH MAY BE BROKEN HAPPY THEY   . . . . . 350  2 DON JUAN  4     11    1
    A BROKEN PILLAR NOT UNCOUTHLY HEWN . . . . . . . . 400  2 DON JUAN  4    103    5
    TO TEACH HIM GREATER HAD HIS OWN LEG BROKEN .  . . . . 117  3 DON JUAN  8     11    8
    WARM BOUT ARE BROKEN INTO THEIR NEW TRICKS  . . . . . 122  3 DON JUAN  8     22    7
    BROKEN IN CARRIAGES AND ALL THE PHANTASIES  . . . . . 308  3 DON JUAN 11     80    5
    WHEN ONCE YOU HAVE BROKEN THEIR CONFOUNDED ICE . . . . 375  3 DON JUAN 13     38    8
    NOR BROKEN MY OWN HEAD NOR THAT OF PRISCIAN .  . . . . 467  3 DON JUAN 15     24    6
BROKEN-HEARTED
    AND LIVED AS DID THE BROKEN-HEARTED FAIR . . . . . . 344  3 DON JUAN 12     61    7
BROKEN-KNEED
    AND AS HIS SPEECH GREW STILL MORE BROKEN-KNEED .  . .  56  3 DON JUAN  6    101    6
BRONZE
    OF GILDED BRONZE AND CARVED IN CURIOUS GUISE   . . . . 461  2 DON JUAN  5     86    2
BRONZED
    BRONZED O'ER SOME LEAN AND STOIC ANCHORITE--   . . . . 392  3 DON JUAN 13     72    4
BROODED
    HIS MIND THE MORE O'ER THIS ITS MYSTERY BROODED  . . . 118  2 DON JUAN  1    177    6
BROODING
    TO THE YOUNG BIRD THE PARENT'S BROODING WINGS  . . . . 338  2 DON JUAN  3    107    3
    AND SEDGES BROODING IN THEIR LIQUID BED .  . . . . . 385  3 DON JUAN 13     57    6
BROODS
    HOW LONELY EVERY FREEBORN CREATURE BROODS   . . . . . 358  2 DON JUAN  4     28    5
    JUST AT THE VERY TIME WHEN HE LEAST BROODS  . . . . . 371  2 DON JUAN  4     51    5
BROOK
    AND WOULD NOT BROOK AT ALL THIS SORT OF THING  . . . . 143  2 DON JUAN  1    212    7
    AND HAIDEE'S SWEET LIPS MURMUR'D LIKE A BROOK  . . . . 359  2 DON JUAN  4     29    6
    WITH THE BLOOD RUNNING LIKE A LITTLE BROOK  . . . . . 370  2 DON JUAN  4     49    6
    TO BROOK A RUFFLED ROSE-LEAF BY HIS SIDE .  . . . . .  50  3 DON JUAN  6     89    4
    AS FOR A BROOK TO COPE WITH OCEAN'S FLOOD   . . . . . 106  3 DON JUAN  7     80    7
    KILL A MAN'S FAMILY AND HE MAY BROOK IT . . . . . . 264  3 DON JUAN 10     79    7
```

101

```
                                                              PAGE VOL      CANTO STANZA LN
BROOK   (CONTINUED)
      TO QUAFF A BROOK WHICH MURMURED LIKE A BIRD . . . . . .  384  3 DON JUAN 13       56   8
      BUT SUCH SMALL LICENCES MUST LOVERS BROOK    . . . . .   429  3 DON JUAN 14       43   3
      OR WHAT HIS CONSORT DID IF HE COULD BROOK    . . . . .   430  3 DON JUAN 14       45  -5
BROOK'D
      HE NEITHER BROOK'D NOR CLAIM'D SUPERIORITY . . . . .     462  3 DON JUAN 15       15   8
      FOR THERE ARE FEW THINGS BY MANKIND LESS BROOK'D . . .   479  3 DON JUAN 15       53   4
BROOKED
      AND THOUGH HER DIGNITY BROOKED NO COMPLAINING . . . .    247  3 DON JUAN 10       47   6
      WAS GREAT BECAUSE HIS MASTER BROOKED NO LESS   . . . .   512  3 DON JUAN 16       28   7
      BEING WAN AND WORN WITH EYES THAT HARDLY BROOKED . . .   568  3 DON JUAN 17       14   4
BROOKS
      YOUNG JUAN WANDER'D BY THE GLASSY BROOKS . . . . . .      70  2 DON JUAN  1       90   1
BROOM'S
      A LEGAL BROOM'S A MORAL CHIMNEY-SWEEPER . . . . . .      232  3 DON JUAN 10       15   1
BROTH
      THEY MADE A MOST SUPERIOR MESS OF BROTH . . . . . .      221  2 DON JUAN  2      123   5
      BUT JUAN WAS QUITE A BROTH OF A BOY . . . . . . .        123  3 DON JUAN  8       24   1
      AS BETWEEN ENGLISH BEEF AND SPARTAN BROTH-- . . . .      541  3 DON JUAN 16       84   7
BROTHER
      TO ALL THE BROTHER TARS WHO MAY HAVE NEED HENCE . .      171  2 DON JUAN  2       29   5
      WITHOUT EVEN THE INCUMBRANCE OF A BROTHER   . . . .      248  2 DON JUAN  2      175   5
      AND MOTHER BROTHER GUARDIAN SHE HAD NONE . . . . .       252  2 DON JUAN  2      182   3
      WHICH MIX'D ALL FEELINGS FRIEND CHILD LOVER BROTHER .    357  2 DON JUAN  4       26   3
      HIS LATELY BOWSTRUNG BROTHER CAUSED HIS RISE . . . .     495  2 DON JUAN  5      147   4
      WHO WISHED THEY HAD A BROTHER JUST LIKE HER . . . .       25  3 DON JUAN  6       39   6
      INFORMED HIM THAT HE HAD A LITTLE BROTHER . . . . .      240  3 DON JUAN 10       32   6
      NOR BROTHER FATHER SISTER DAUGHTER LOVE . . . . . .      250  3 DON JUAN 10       53   2
      PERHAPS YOU'LL HAVE A VISIT FROM THE BROTHER . . . .     343  3 DON JUAN 12       60   3
      AS IN FREEMASONRY A HIGHER BROTHER . . . . . . .         369  3 DON JUAN 13       24   4
      SHE TOOK UP WITH SOME FOREIGN YOUNGER BROTHER . . . .    474  3 DON JUAN 15       42   7
BROTHERLY
      CALLED BROTHERLY AFFECTION COULD NOT MOVE    . . . . .   250  3 DON JUAN 10       53   6
BROTHERS
      BUT THEN THEY ONLY SEEM SO MANY BROTHERS . . . . . .      63  2 DON JUAN  1       77   8
      THAT URNS AND PIPKINS ARE BUT FRAGILE BROTHERS . . .     491  2 DON JUAN  5      138   4
      BY SERVICE WITH MY MILITARY BROTHERS . . . . . . .      103  3 DON JUAN  7       71   4
      HAD SET TO WORK AS BRISKLY AS THEIR BROTHERS . . . .     119  3 DON JUAN  8       15   4
      ENQUIRED HIS INCOME AND IF HE HAD BROTHERS . . . . .     293  3 DON JUAN 11       48   8
      HAVE TAKEN UP AT LENGTH WITH YOUNGER BROTHERS . . . .    308  3 DON JUAN 11       81   2
      AND DAUGHTERS BROTHERS SISTERS KITH OR KIN . . . . .     470  3 DON JUAN 15       31   2
BROUGHAM
      TIS PITY THAT THEY HAD NO BROUGHAM IN SPAIN-- . . . .    150  2 DON JUAN  1    V  1   2
BROUGHT
      FOR ALL THE GLORY YOUR CONVERSION BROUGHT    . . . .     12   2 DON JUAN  D        6   3
      (THE JURY BROUGHT THEIR VERDICT IN INSANITY) . . . .      29  2 DON JUAN  1       15   8
      HE HAD BEEN ILL BROUGHT UP AND WAS BORN BILIOUS . .      40  2 DON JUAN  1       35   8
      IS BROUGHT UP MUCH MORE WISELY THAN ANOTHER . . . .      42  2 DON JUAN  1       37   8
      ('TWAS SNOW THAT BROUGHT SAINT ANTHONY TO REASON) . .    57  2 DON JUAN  1       64   4
      BUT NO DEVICE COULD BE BROUGHT INTO PLAY-- . . . . .     114  2 DON JUAN  1      169   4
      THE NINE DAYS' WONDER WHICH WAS BROUGHT TO LIGHT . .     126  2 DON JUAN  1      188   6
      THE QUEEN OF DENMARK FOR OPHELIA BROUGHT . . . . . .     165  2 DON JUAN  2       17   5
      BROUGHT FORTH IN PURPLE CRADLED IN VERMILLION . . . .    205  2 DON JUAN  2       92   3
      AND THEN ONCE MORE HIS FEELINGS BACK WERE BROUGHT . .    215  2 DON JUAN  2      112   6
      CHARM'D WITH EACH OTHER ALL THINGS CHARM'D THAT BROUGHT . 354 2 DON JUAN  4       20   7
      BROUGHT BACK THE SENSE OF PAIN WITHOUT THE CAUSE . . .   378  2 DON JUAN  4       62   7
      THUS TO THEIR EXTREME VERGE THE PASSIONS BROUGHT . .     402  2 DON JUAN  4      106   6
      THUS TO THEIR LAST SANDS ARE THE PASSIONS BROUGHT . .    402  2 DON JUAN  4      106 V6
      TWELVE NEGRESSES FROM NUBIA BROUGHT A PRICE . . . .      408  2 DON JUAN  4      115   1
      WHAT BROUGHT YOU HERE--OH NOTHING VERY RARE-- . . .      418  2 DON JUAN  5       15   2
      THOSE HONOURABLE SCARS WHICH BROUGHT HIM FAME . . .      431  2 DON JUAN  5       38   2
      WONDERING WHAT NEXT TILL THE CAIQUE WAS BROUGHT . .      432  2 DON JUAN  5       40   6
      AND THERE YOU SEE THIS TURN HAS BROUGHT US THROUGH . .   436  2 DON JUAN  5       45   7
      AND INTO HER CLEAR CHEEK THE BLOOD WAS BROUGHT . . .     473  2 DON JUAN  5      108   4
      WHATE'ER SHE SAW AND COVETED WAS BROUGHT . . . . .       476  2 DON JUAN  5      113   1
      AND BROUGHT BEFORE THE EMPRESS WHO HAD MADE . . . .      64   3 DON JUAN  6      118   5
      THEY BROUGHT HIM AND HIS COMRADES TO HEAD-QUARTERS .      96  3 DON JUAN  7       57   2
      A YARD OR TWO OF GROUND WHICH BROUGHT THEM NIGHER .      121  3 DON JUAN  8       20   3
      TO BE PRODUCED WHEN BROUGHT UP TO THE TEST   . . . .     123  3 DON JUAN  8       25   4
      TILL ALL THE ARTS AT LENGTH ARE BROUGHT ABOUT . . .      202  3 DON JUAN  9       40   5
      AND THIRDLY HE WHO BROUGHT YOU THE DISPATCH . . . .      215  3 DON JUAN  9       65   8
      HE HAD BROUGHT HIS SPENDING TO A HANDSOME ANCHOR-- .     240  3 DON JUAN 10       31   4
      HE MIGHT--AND BROUGHT THEM UP WITH SKILL IN TIME . .     295  3 DON JUAN 11       53   2
      OF VESTALS BROUGHT INTO THE MARRIAGE MART . . . . .      337  3 DON JUAN 12       46   7
      ARISING OUT OF BUSINESS OFTEN BROUGHT . . . . . .        365  3 DON JUAN 13       15   2
      'TIS THE WHOLE SPIRIT BROUGHT TO A QUINTESSENCE . . .    375  3 DON JUAN 13       38   1
      I HAVE BROUGHT THIS WORLD ABOUT MY EARS AND EKE . .      414  3 DON JUAN 14       10   1
      SEEN BEAUTIES BROUGHT TO MARKET BY THE SCORE   . . .     418  3 DON JUAN 14       18   4
      BUT SINCE BENEATH IT UPON EARTH WE ARE BROUGHT . . .     421  3 DON JUAN 14       26   4
      BUT HERE A MESSENGER BROUGHT IN DISPATCHES . . . . .     439  3 DON JUAN 14       67   8
      AS E'ER BROUGHT MAN AND WOMAN TO THE BRINK . . . .       454  3 DON JUAN 14      100   3
      IF ONCE THEIR PHANTASIES BE BROUGHT TO BEAR . . . .      463  3 DON JUAN 15       16   6
      THERE WAS A PICTURE DEALER WHO HAD BROUGHT . . . .       528  3 DON JUAN 16       56   1
      HAD BROUGHT THE CAPO D'OPERA NOT FOR SALE . . . . .      528  3 DON JUAN 16       57   7
      BROUGHT TO SURVEY THESE GREY WALLS WHICH THOUGH SO THICK . 529 3 DON JUAN 16      58   3
BROW
      EACH EYE A SERMON AND HER BROW A HOMILY . . . . .        29   2 DON JUAN  1       15   2
      HER GLOSSY HAIR WAS CLUSTER'D O'ER A BROW    . . . .     55   2 DON JUAN  1       61   1
      YOUNG YET HER ELDER AND OF BROW LESS GRAVE . . . .       216  2 DON JUAN  2      115   3
```

102

BROW   (CONTINUED)
    HER BROW WAS OVERHUNG WITH COINS OF GOLD 217   2 DON JUAN 2   116   1
    HER BROW WAS WHITE AND LOW HER CHEEK'S PURE DYE   218   2 DON JUAN 2   118   1
    HIS BROW AS IF IN ACT TO BUTT AND THEN   292   2 DON JUAN 3   32   7
    A KING SATE ON THE ROCKY BROW   322   2 DON JUAN 3   L 4   1
    PALE AS THE FOAM THAT FROTH'D ON HIS DEAD BROW   . . . 362   2 DON JUAN 4   34   2
    AN OPEN BROW A LITTLE MARKED WITH CARE   416   2 DON JUAN 5   11   5
    BUT O'ER HER BRIGHT BROW FLASHED A TUMULT STRANGE   . . 473   2 DON JUAN 5   108   3
    TO CROSS HER BROW SHE WONDERED HOW SO NEAR 480   2 DON JUAN 5   119   7
    HER BROW GREW BLACK BUT SHE WOULD NOT UPBRAID   . . . 483   2 DON JUAN 5   125   5
    YOU CAN'T SUPPOSE GULBEYAZ' ANGRY BROW   486   2 DON JUAN 5   131   8
    AND LOVE'S A GOD OR WAS BEFORE THE BROW   9   3 DON JUAN 6   6   6
    BUT SHE ROSE UP AND KISSED THE MATRON'S BROW   31   3 DON JUAN 6   50   1
    ABOVE HER BROW LAY DREAMING SOFT AND WARM   39   3 DON JUAN 6   66   3
    SO DEEP AN ANGUISH WRUNG GULBEYAZM BROW   58   3 DON JUAN 6   105   4
    AND HER BROW CLEARED BUT NOT HER TROUBLED EYE   . . . 61   3 DON JUAN 6   110   7
    WITH ITS PROUD BROW IT MERITS SLIGHT APPLAUSE   86   3 DON JUAN 7   40   6
    UPON THEM HIS SLOW BROW AND PIERCING EYE-- 97   3 DON JUAN 7   59   3
    ON HER UNWRINKLED BROW NOR COULD YOU VIEW   145   3 DON JUAN 8   65   5
    HAD SCARRED HER BROW AND LEFT ITS CRIMSON TRACE   . . . 159   3 DON JUAN 8   95   5
    THOUGH MODEST ON HIS UNEMBARRASSED BROW   223   3 DON JUAN 9   83   5
    WILL BRING THE OTHER ERE THE LAKE-LIKE BROW   229   3 DON JUAN 10   8   3
    THE TRUE BELIEVERS--AND HER INFANT BROW   262   3 DON JUAN 10   75   6
    SHE RINGS THE WORLD'S TE DEUM AND HER BROW   286   3 DON JUAN 11   38   3
    THOUGH ROYALTY WAS WRITTEN ON HIS BROW   354   3 DON JUAN 12   84   5
    BEAR A BOLD BROW AND FOR YOUR BOSOM NERVE IT   367   3 DON JUAN 13   18   V4
    WHAT ARE THE FILLETS ON THE VICTOR'S BROW   485   3 DON JUAN 15   67   1
    (WHO WATCHED THE CHANGES OF DON JUAN'S BROW   516   3 DON JUAN 16   37   2
BROWN
    GOOD TEETH WITH CURLING RATHER DARK BROWN HAIR 416   2 DON JUAN 5   11   3
BROW'S
    AND HER PROUD BROW'S BLUE VEINS TO SWELL AND DARKLE   . . . 56   3 DON JUAN 6   101   8
BROWS
    YOUR BAYS MAY HIDE THE BALDNESS OF YOUR BROWS--   13   2 DON JUAN D   7   1
    AND JESTEST WITH THE BROWS OF MIGHTIEST MEN   266   2 DON JUAN 2   206   2
    WHO CLEARED HER SPARKLING EYES AND SMOOTHED HER BROWS   . 500   2 DON JUAN 5   154   3
    AND FAIR BROWS GENTLY DROOPING AS THE FRUIT   38   3 DON JUAN 6   65   6
    WERE THERE WITH BROWS THAT DID NOT MUCH INVITE 391   3 DON JUAN 13   69   2
    'GAINST RHYME I NEVER SHOULD HAVE KNOCK'D MY BROWS   . . 467   3 DON JUAN 15   24   5
BROWSES
    WHICH FLASHED AS FAR AS WHERE THE MUSK-BULL BROWSES   . . . 353   3 DON JUAN 12   82   6
BRUMMELL
    WHERE'S BRUMMELL DISHED WHERE'S LONG POLE WELLESLEY DIDDLED 307   3 DON JUAN 11   78   1
BRUNETTE
    AND THROUGH HER CLEAR BRUNETTE COMPLEXION SHONE A 395   2 DON JUAN 4   94   6
BRUSH
    RAISE BUT AN ARM 'TWILL BRUSH THEIR WEB AWAY   196   3 DON JUAN 9   28   1
    AND BRUSH A WEB OR TWO FROM OFF THE WALLS   266   3 DON JUAN 10   84   8
    HIS BRUSH WITH ALL THE BLOOD OF ALL THE SAINTED   . . . 392   3 DON JUAN 13   71   8
BRUSHES
    OF STOCKINGS SLIPPERS BRUSHES COMBS COMPLETE   99   2 DON JUAN 1   143   4
    BUT LEAPS AND BURSTS AND SOMETIMES FOX'S BRUSHES   . . . 425   3 DON JUAN 14   35   2
BRUSSELS
    AND ROBES SWEET FRIENDSHIP IN A BRUSSELS LACE   430   3 DON JUAN 14   47   4
BRUTAL
    AND DROVE THEM WITH THEIR BRUTAL YELLS TO SEEK 158   3 DON JUAN 8   94   2
BRUTE
    WORN FOR A HUSBAND OR SOME OTHER BRUTE   230   2 DON JUAN 2   139   8
    THE RUDEST BRUTE THAT ROAMS SIBERIA'S WILD   157   2 DON JUAN 8   92   3
BRUTES
    LIKE BRUTES--AND THUS HIS DANGEROUS POST KEPT HE   . . . 175   2 DON JUAN 2   36   5
BRUTUS
    BUT BEING NO ORATOR AS BRUTUS IS   43   3 DON JUAN 6   74   7
    OF BRUTUS AT THE PAGEANT OF TIBERIUS   477   3 DON JUAN 15   49   2
BRYANT
    THEY SAY SO--(BRYANT SAYS THE CONTRARY)   385   2 DON JUAN 4   76   4
BUBBLE
    AND MINE'S A BUBBLE NOT BLOWN UP FOR PRAISE 414   3 DON JUAN 14   8   7
    BUBBLE AND SQUEAK WOULD SPOIL MY LIQUID LAY   487   3 DON JUAN 15   71   6
BUBBLES
    LIKE BUBBLES ON AN OCEAN MUCH LESS AMPLE   189   3 DON JUAN 9   13   6
    ITS LITTLE TORRENT IN A THOUSAND BUBBLES   389   3 DON JUAN 13   65   7
    WHEREWITH WE BREAK OUR BUBBLES ON THE OCEAN   457   3 DON JUAN 15   2   4
    OUR BUBBLES AS THE OLD BURST NEW EMERGE   500   3 DON JUAN 15   99   6
BUBBLING
    A SOLITARY SHRIEK THE BUBBLING CRY   184   2 DON JUAN 2   53   7
    HE HEARD HIS RIVULET'S LIGHT BUBBLING RUN   289   2 DON JUAN 3   27   3
    HEARD--AND THAT BEE-LIKE BUBBLING BUSY HUM   272   3 DON JUAN 11   8   7
BUCK
    FOR KILLING NOTHING BUT A BEAR OR BUCK HE   143   3 DON JUAN 8   61   6
BUD
    AND FAR AWAY THE LAST BUD OF HER RACE 329   3 DON JUAN 12   29   4
BUDDING
    LUXURIANT BUDDING CHEERFUL WITHOUT MIRTH 32   3 DON JUAN 6   53   3
    THE COLOUR OF A BUDDING ROSE'S CREST   48   3 DON JUAN 6   85   4
    THEIR TENDER PARENTS IN THEIR BUDDING DAYS   562   3 DON JUAN 17   1   6
BUFF
    'TIS THAT I STILL RETAIN MY BUFF AND BLUE   20   2 DON JUAN D   17   4
BUFFO
    BY ONE OF THESE THE BUFFO OF THE PARTY   388   2 DON JUAN 4   81   1

103

```
                                                 PAGE VOL    CANTO STANZA LN
BUFFOON
    AFAR A DWARF BUFFOON STOOD TELLING TALES . . . . . . .  293  2 DON JUAN  3    34   1
    HERO BUFFOON HALF-DEMON AND HALF-DIRT . . . . . . . .    95  3 DON JUAN  7    55   5
BUFFOONS
    OR ANY SUCH LIKE SOVEREIGN BUFFOONS   . . . . . . .     341  2 DON JUAN  3   110   2
    AND WORDSWORTH--BOTH POETICAL BUFFOONS  . . . . . . .   341  2 DON JUAN  3   110  V2
BUGLE
    THE TRUMP AND BUGLE TILL HE SPAKE WERE DUMB--  . . . .  430  2 DON JUAN  5    36   7
BUILD
    SHOWS THAT WE BUILD WHEN WE SHOULD BUT ENTOMB US   . .  448  2 DON JUAN  5    63   8
    OH YE WHO BUILD UP MONUMENTS DEFILED . . . . . . .     199  3 DON JUAN  9    33   3
    TO BUILD A COLLEGE OR TO FOUND A RACE . . . . . .      320  3 DON JUAN 12    10   2
    TO BUILD UP COMMON THINGS WITH COMMON PLACES  . . . .  413  3 DON JUAN 14     7   8
BUILDING
    BUT THIS I KNOW IT WAS A SPACIOUS BUILDING  . . . . .  223  2 DON JUAN  2   127   7
    IT WAS INDEED A WIDE EXTENSIVE BUILDING  . . . . . .   436  2 DON JUAN  5    46   1
BUILDINGS
    MORE MODERN BUILDINGS AND THOSE BUILT OF YORE  . . .   443  2 DON JUAN  5    57   6
    WITH BUILDINGS IN THE ORIENTAL TASTE . . . . . . .      70  3 DON JUAN  7     9   3
    THE PUBLIC BUILDINGS AND THE PRIVATE TOO . . . . .      78  3 DON JUAN  7    23   4
    NEW BUILDINGS OF CORRECTEST CONFORMATION . . . . . .   529  3 DON JUAN 16    58   7
BUILDS
    HE THERE BUILDS UP A FORMIDABLE DYKE  . . . . . . .    330  2 DON JUAN  3    95   1
BUILT
    HE WAS A GREEK AND ON HIS ISLE HAD BUILT . . . . .     223  2 DON JUAN  2   127   1
    MORE MODERN BUILDINGS AND THOSE BUILT OF YORE  . . . . 443  2 DON JUAN  5    57   6
    'TIS BUILT BEGIRT WITH BATTERY AND TRENCH  . . . .      71  3 DON JUAN  7     9  V4
    THE RUSSIANS HAVING BUILT TWO BATTERIES ON . . . .      78  3 DON JUAN  7    23   1
    WHEN THEY BUILT UP UNTO HIS DARLING TREES--  . . . .   144  3 DON JUAN  8    64   2
    HAVE BUILT AND LAID OUT GROUND AT SUCH A RATE  . . .   393  3 DON JUAN 13    74   3
BULK
    IN FULL VOLUPTUOUS BUT NOT O'ERGROWN BULK   . . . .    561  3 DON JUAN 16   123   7
BULKY
    BUT NOW REDUCED AS IS A BULKY VOLUME  . . . . . .      130  3 DON JUAN  8    34   4
BULL
    THIS IS NO BULL ALTHOUGH IT SOUNDS SO FOR  . . . .      40  3 DON JUAN  6    67   1
    I'VE HEARD OF STORIES OF A COCK AND BULL . . . . .      46  3 DON JUAN  6    80   1
    HOW PEACE SHOULD MAKE JOHN BULL THE FRENCHMAN'S FOE  .  77  3 DON JUAN  7    22   8
    WHICH TO THAT BOTTLE-CONJURER JOHN BULL  . . . . .      88  3 DON JUAN  7    44   3
    A SECRETARY--LAP DOG AND A BULL DOG--AND . . . . .     249  3 DON JUAN 10    50  V1
    EXCHANGED FOR THIN POTATIONS BY JOHN BULL--  . . . .   310  3 DON JUAN 11    85   7
    THAN COULD ROAST BEEF IN OUR ROUGH JOHN BULL WAY  . .  487  3 DON JUAN 15    71   4
    BULL SOMETHING OF THE LOWER WORLD'S CONDITION  . . .   497  3 DON JUAN 15    92   6
BULL-DOG
    A BULL-DOG AND A BULL-FINCH AND AN ERMINE  . . . . .   249  3 DON JUAN 10    50   1
BULL-DOGS
    UNLESS THEY ARE GAME AS BULL-DOGS AND FOX-TERRIERS  . . 78  3 DON JUAN  7    24   8
BULLET
    MAY MAKE UP FOR A BULLET IN HIS BODY  . . . . . .       77  3 DON JUAN  7    21   3
    AT SHRINKING FROM A BULLET OR A BOMB  . . . . . .      132  3 DON JUAN  8    38   6
BULLETIN
    HE FELL IMMORTAL IN A BULLETIN . . . . . . . .          76  3 DON JUAN  7    20   8
    PRAISE) IF A MAN'S NAME IN A BULLETIN . . . . . .       77  3 DON JUAN  7    21   2
    TO THEIR TWO SELVES ONE WHOLE BRIGHT BULLETIN  . . .   121  3 DON JUAN  8    19   8
BULLETINS
    OH YE GREAT BULLETINS OF BONAPARTE  . . . . . . .      108  3 DON JUAN  7    82   1
BULLETS
    KILLED BY FIVE BULLETS FROM AN OLD GUN-BARREL  . . .   429  2 DON JUAN  5    34   8
    BOMBS DRUMS GUNS BASTIONS BATTERIES BAYONETS BULLETS  . 106  3 DON JUAN  7    78   7
BULL-FIGHTS
    EXCEPT TO BULL-FIGHTS MASS PLAY ROUT AND REVEL . . .   102  2 DON JUAN  1   148   4
BULL-FINCH
    A BULL-DOG AND A BULL-FINCH AND AN ERMINE  . . . .     249  3 DON JUAN 10    50   1
BULLIED
    I'LL NOT BE BULLIED DECENT OR INDECENT   . . . . .     410  2 DON JUAN  4   117  V6
    WHO BUTCHERED HALF THE EARTH AND BULLIED T'OTHER . . . 265  3 DON JUAN 10    81   8
BULLIES
    BANKERS--CONTRACTORS--BOROUGH MONGERS--BULLIES  . . .  314  3 DON JUAN 11  V 76   1
BULL'S
    OR ROAMS THE HERD BENEATH THE BULL'S PROTECTION  . .    90  3 DON JUAN  7    48   4
    PUT TO SUCH TRIAL JOHN BULL'S PARTIAL PATIENCE . . .   136  3 DON JUAN  8    48   6
BULLY
    BULLY IN SENATES SKULKER IN THE FIELD . . . . . .      151  2 DON JUAN  1  V  2   1
    THERE WAS PAROLLES TOO THE LEGAL BULLY  . . . . .      398  3 DON JUAN 13    84   1
    SHUT UP THE BALD-COOT BULLY ALEXANDER . . . . . .      446  3 DON JUAN 14    83   1
BULOW
    AND THAT IF BLUCHER BULOW GNEISENAU  . . . . . . .     137  3 DON JUAN  8    49   1
BUMPER
    THE FOAM WHICH MADE ITS VIRGIN BUMPER GAY   . . . .    504  3 DON JUAN 16     9   3
BUMPERS
    WHEN O'ER THE BRIM THE SPARKLING BUMPERS REACH . . .   250  2 DON JUAN  2   178   3
    FULL OF DEEP RAPTURES AND OF BUMPERS THEY--  . . . .   343  2 DON JUAN  3  V 98   7
    EXPEDIENT OF FULL BUMPERS FOR THE EYE . . . . . .      216  3 DON JUAN  9    67   7
BUNGLER
    A BUNGLER EVEN IN ITS DISGUSTING TRADE  . . . . .       18  2 DON JUAN  D    14   1
BUNGLING
    FOR BLUSTERING BUNGLING TRIMMING WRANGLING WRITING  . . 150  2 DON JUAN  1  V  1   5
BUON
    STRANGE TOO IN MY BUON CAMERADO SCOTT . . . . . . .    323  3 DON JUAN 12    16   5
```

BUONAPARTE
    FRANCE TOO HAD BUONAPARTE AND DEMOURIER . . . . . . 22 2 DON JUAN 1 2 7
    SHE FELL WITH BUONAPARTE--WHAT STRANGE THOUGHTS . . . . 198 3 DON JUAN 9 32 7
BUONAPARTE'S
    THAN BUONAPARTE'S CANCER--COULD I DASH ON . . . . . 189 3 DON JUAN 9 14 6
BUOYANT
    FOR THEIRS WERE BUOYANT SPIRITS NEVER BOUND . . . . . . 352 2 DON JUAN 4 16 5
BUOY'D
    HE BUOY'D HIS BOYISH LIMBS AND STROVE TO PLY . . . . . 212 2 DON JUAN 2 106 2
BURDENS
    HOW SOME TO BURDENS WERE OBLIGED TO STOOP . . . . . . 409 2 DON JUAN 4 116 3
BURGAGE
    ALSO A LAWSUIT UPON TENURES BURGAGE . . . . 530 3 DON JUAN 16 60 3
BURGLARIOUSLY
    BURGLARIOUSLY BROKE HIS COFFIN'S LID . . . . 146 2 DON JUAN 1 219 6
BURGOYNE
    PRINCE FERDINAND GRANBY BURGOYNE KEPPEL HOWE . . . . . 22 2 DON JUAN 1 2 2
BURGUNDY
    NOR BURGUNDY IN ALL ITS SUNSET GLOW . . . . 251 2 DON JUAN 2 180 6
BURIAL
    AN UNKNOWN BARREN BEACH FOR BURIAL GROUND . . . . . 213 2 DON JUAN 2 109 8
    MEN ARE BUT MAGGOTS OF SOME HUGE EARTH'S BURIAL) . . . . 202 3 DON JUAN 9 39 8
BURIED
    BUT AH HE DIED AND BURIED WITH HIM LAY . . . . . . 39 2 DON JUAN 1 34 1
    'TIS STRANGE OLD PEOPLE DONT LIKE TO BE BURIED . . . . . 89 2 DON JUAN 1 125 V8
    HALF BURIED IN THE TRESSES WHICH IT GRASPS . . . . . 259 2 DON JUAN 2 194 4
    AND BURIED SINKS BENEATH ITS OFFSPRING'S DOOM . . . . . 399 2 DON JUAN 4 102 4
    BUT BURIED IN THE HEAP OF SUCH TRANSACTIONS . . . . . 83 3 DON JUAN 7 34 3
    AND HAD JUST BURIED THE FAIR FACED LANSKOI . . . . . 206 3 DON JUAN 9 47 8
    GLIMMER ON HIGH THEIR BURIED LOCKS STILL WAVE . . . . 509 3 DON JUAN 16 19 3
BURKE
    CAST BY CANOVA OR DESCRIBED BY BURKE . . . . 315 2 DON JUAN 3 76 V8
    CANOVA'S MARBLE OR THE WORDS OF BURKE . . . . 315 2 DON JUAN 3 76 V8
BURLESQUE
    TURNS WHAT WAS ONCE ROMANTIC TO BURLESQUE . . . . . 345 2 DON JUAN 4 3 8
    RESTORES ALL HUMAN FEELINGS TO BURLESQUE . . . . . . 345 2 DON JUAN 4 3 V8
BURN
    MY EYEBALLS BURN AND THROB BUT HAVE NO TEARS . . . . 130 2 DON JUAN 1 192 8
    AND BARDS BURN WHAT THEY CALL THEIR MIDNIGHT TAPER . . . 146 2 DON JUAN 1 218 6
    SHE ONLY WISHED TO SINK BURN AND DESTROY . . . . . . 490 2 DON JUAN 5 136 V7
    TO BURN A TOWN WHICH NEVER DID THEM HARM . . . . . . 105 3 DON JUAN 7 76 8
    WITHOUT RESISTANCE SEE THEIR CITY BURN . . . . . . 150 3 DON JUAN 8 77 4
    MUST BURN MORE MILDLY ERE IT CAN ENLIGHTEN . . . . . 281 3 DON JUAN 11 27 8
BURNED
    AND DISTANT FROM EACH OTHER BURNED THE LIGHTS . . . . . 38 3 DON JUAN 6 64 2
    UNTIL EACH HIGH HEROIC BOSOM BURNED . . . . 99 3 DON JUAN 7 64 3
    A LAMP BURNED HIGH WHILE HE LEANT FROM A NICHE . . . . 507 3 DON JUAN 16 16 5
    WHICH STILL IN JUAN'S CANDLESTICKS BURNED HIGH . . . . 558 3 DON JUAN 16 117 5
BURNING
    BUT WILL KEEP BAKING BROILING BURNING ON . . . . . . 56 2 DON JUAN 1 63 4
    FOR THAT COMPRESSION IN ITS BURNING CORE . . . . . . 61 2 DON JUAN 1 72 5
    AND BURNING BLUSHES THOUGH FOR NO TRANSGRESSION . . . . 62 2 DON JUAN 1 74 3
    THE SEVENTH DAY AND NO WIND--THE BURNING SUN . . . . . 194 2 DON JUAN 2 72 1
    AND ALL THE BURNING TONGUES THE PASSION TEACH . . . . . 256 2 DON JUAN 2 189 5
    AND WHEN THOSE DEEP AND BURNING MOMENTS PASS'D . . . . . 260 2 DON JUAN 2 195 1
    THE HAND FROM BURNING UNDERNEATH THEM PLACED . . . . . 307 2 DON JUAN 3 63 6
    WHERE BURNING SAPPHO LOVED AND SUNG . . . . 320 2 DON JUAN 3 L 1 2
    MY OWN THE BURNING TEAR-DROP LAVES . . . . 326 2 DON JUAN 3 L 15 5
    FOR GOOD OR EVIL BURNING FROM ITS BIRTH . . . . . . 374 2 DON JUAN 4 56 3
    BRIGHT--AND AS BLACK AND BURNING AS A COAL . . . . . 395 2 DON JUAN 4 94 5
    AT LEAST THE SHARP POINTS OF THAT BURNING MARLE . . . . 124 3 DON JUAN 8 26 V7
    OF BURNING STREETS LIKE MOONLIGHT ON THE WATER . . . . 172 3 DON JUAN 8 122 7
    OF BURNING CITIES THOSE FULL MOONS OF SLAUGHTER . . . . 173 3 DON JUAN 8 122 V7
    FAR FLASHED HER BURNING TOWERS O'ER DANUBE'S STREAM . . . 175 3 DON JUAN 8 127 3
    COULD RHYME LIKE NERO O'ER A BURNING CITY . . . . . 179 3 DON JUAN 8 134 8
    NOR IN HER EYE AUSONIA'S GLANCE IS BURNING . . . . . 350 3 DON JUAN 12 75 4
    SINCE BURNING AGED WOMEN (SAVE A FEW-- . . . . . . 565 3 DON JUAN 17 7 3
BURNS
    LIKE BURNS (WHOM DOCTOR CURRIE WELL DESCRIBES) . . . . 329 2 DON JUAN 3 92 4
BURNT
    CHRISTIANS HAVE BURNT EACH OTHER QUITE PERSUADED . . . . 66 2 DON JUAN 1 83 7
    BAKED FRIED OR BURNT TURNED INSIDE-OUT OR DROWNED . . . . 201 3 DON JUAN 9 37 5
    BURNT AND NOT BLUE AS MODEST TAPERS USE . . . . . . 512 3 DON JUAN 16 26 2
BURNT-OUT
    ABOVE HIS BURNT-OUT BRAIN AND SAPLESS CINDERS . . . . . 299 3 DON JUAN 11 61 5
BURROWING
    BURROWING FOR BOROUGHS LIKE A RAT OR RABBIT . . . . . 534 3 DON JUAN 16 70 2
BURST
    AND THEN OF THESE SOME PART BURST INTO TEARS . . . . . 208 2 DON JUAN 2 98 1
    AND FED BY SPOONFULS ELSE THEY ALWAYS BURST . . . . . 239 2 DON JUAN 2 158 8
    THE FIRE BURST FORTH FROM HER NUMIDIAN VEINS . . . . . 375 2 DON JUAN 4 57 7
    A VEIN HAD BURST AND HER SWEET LIPS' PURE DYES . . . . . 376 2 DON JUAN 4 59 1
    AND TROWSERS NOT SO TIGHT THAT THEY WOULD BURST . . . . 451 2 DON JUAN 5 68 4
    SO THAT HE SPOKE NOT BUT BURST INTO TEARS . . . . . 478 2 DON JUAN 5 117 8
    AND WAITED BUT THE SIGNAL'S VOICE TO BURST . . . . . 91 3 DON JUAN 7 50 4
    WILL OFTENTIMES MAKE DEADLY QUARRELS BURST . . . . . 136 3 DON JUAN 8 48 3
    GLORY AND TRIUMPH O'ER HER ASPECT BURST . . . . . . 212 3 DON JUAN 9 59 3
    AND WAS NOT LIKELY ALL AT ONCE TO BURST . . . . . . 437 3 DON JUAN 14 62 3
    OUR BUBBLES AS THE OLD BURST NEW EMERGE . . . . . . 500 3 DON JUAN 15 99 6

                                                              PAGE VOL   CANTO STANZA LN

BURSTING
NOW OVERHEAD A RAINBOW BURSTING THROUGH . . .   . . . 204 2 DON JUAN 2   91   1
TAUGHT TO CONCEAL THEIR BURSTING HEARTS DESPOND   . . . 263 2 DON JUAN 2   200   4
A PRETTY LAD BUT BURSTING WITH CONCEIT   . . . . 392 2 DON JUAN 4   89   2
BURSTS
BUT LEAPS AND BURSTS AND SOMETIMES FOX'S BRUSHES . . . 425 3 DON JUAN 14   35   2
BURTHEN
DEATH LEFT NO DOUBT AND THE DEAD BURTHEN LAY . . . . . 204 2 DON JUAN 2   90   3
SET TO SOME THOUSANDS ('TIS THE USUAL BURTHEN . . . . 529 3 DON JUAN 16   59   2
BURTHENS
KICK OFF THEIR BURTHENS--MEANING THE HIGH CLASSES . . . 310 3 DON JUAN 11   84   8
BURY
ALONG THE ROAD AS IF THEY WENT TO BURY . . . . . . 260 3 DON JUAN 10   71   5
BUSEY
THE LADIES SCILLY BUSEY--MISS ECLAT . . . . 396 3 DON JUAN 13   79   4
BUSHES
WHO AFTER A LONG CHASE O'ER HILLS DALES BUSHES . . . 425 3 DON JUAN 14   35   6
BUSINESS
AND PUT THE BUSINESS PAST ALL KIND OF DOUBT . .   . . . 35 2 DON JUAN 1   26   8
SEES HALF THE BUSINESS IN A WICKED WAY . . . . . . 82 2 DON JUAN 1   113   6
UNDER PRETENCE OF BUSINESS INDISPENSIBLE . . . . . . 103 2 DON JUAN 1   151   2
HE HAD NO BUSINESS TO COMMIT A SIN . .   . . 113 2 DON JUAN 1   167   2
FROM THIS MY SUBJECT HAS NO BUSINESS HERE   . . . . . 238 2 DON JUAN 2   156   4
WHICH PUT OFF BUSINESS TO THE ENSUING SESSION . . . . 331 2 DON JUAN 3   96   6
WOULD RECONCILE HIM TO THE BUSINESS QUITE . . . . . 452 2 DON JUAN 5   71   6
THIS AWKWARD BUSINESS WITHOUT HARM TO OTHERS . . . . 63 3 DON JUAN 6   116   7
TURNS OUT TO BE A BUTCHER IN GREAT BUSINESS . . . . 108 3 DON JUAN 7   83   7
HIS MORNS HE PASSED IN BUSINESS--WHICH DISSECTED . . 301 3 DON JUAN 11   65   1
WAS LIKE ALL BUSINESS A LABORIOUS NOTHING . . . . . 301 3 DON JUAN 11   65   2
AND NOW TO BUSINESS OH MY GENTLE JUAN . . . . . . 326 3 DON JUAN 12   23   1
ARISING OUT OF BUSINESS OFTEN BROUGHT . . . . . . 365 3 DON JUAN 13   15   2
IN ANYBODY'S BUSINESS BUT THE KING'S . . . . . . 439 3 DON JUAN 14   66   2
YOUR MEN OF BUSINESS ARE NOT APT TO EXPRESS   . . . . 443 3 DON JUAN 14   76   6
MY BUSINESS IS WITH LADY ADELINE . . . . 449 3 DON JUAN 14   90   7
BECAUSE MY BUSINESS IS TO DRESS SOCIETY . . . . . 497 3 DON JUAN 15   93   5
BUST
A NAME A WRETCHED PICTURE AND WORSE BUST . . . . . 146 2 DON JUAN 1   218   8
A BOOK--A DAMNED BAD PICTURE AND WORSE BUST . . . . 146 2 DON JUAN 1   218   V8
THERE WAS AN IRISH LADY TO WHOSE BUST . . . . . . 219 2 DON JUAN 2   119   3
BUT ONLY GIVE A BUST OF MARRIAGES . . . . 279 2 DON JUAN 3   8   4
AND THIS OMISSION LIKE THAT OF THE BUST . . . . . 477 3 DON JUAN 15   49   1
IT PRESSED UPON A HARD BUT GLOWING BUST . . . . . 560 3 DON JUAN 16   122   3
BUSTLE
WHO IN THE EARLIER AGES RAISED A BUSTLE . . . . . 44 2 DON JUAN 1   41   3
AND COULD BE VERY BUSY WITHOUT BUSTLE . . . . . . 132 3 DON JUAN 8   39   8
BUT WHEN THE LEVEE ROSE AND ALL WAS BUSTLE . . . . 223 3 DON JUAN 9   82   1
WHO IN HIS TIME HAD MADE HEROIC BUSTLE . . . . . 277 3 DON JUAN 11   19   2
THERE WAS MUCH BUSTLE TOO AND PREPARATION . . . . 534 3 DON JUAN 16   68   3
BUSTLED
ANTONIA BUSTLED ROUND THE RANSACK'D ROOM . . . . . 109 2 DON JUAN 1   159   2
BUSY
SO THAT ALL HANDS WERE BUSY BEYOND MEASURE . . . . 286 2 DON JUAN 3   20   7
A BUSY CHARACTER IN THE DULL SCENE . . . . 352 2 DON JUAN 4   15   4
RIGHT I WAS BUSY AND FORGOT WHY YOU . . . . . . 100 3 DON JUAN 7   66   1
FOR HE WAS DIZZY BUSY AND HIS VEINS . . . . . . 129 3 DON JUAN 8   33   2
AND COULD BE VERY BUSY WITHOUT BUSTLE . . . . . . 132 3 DON JUAN 8   39   8
HEARD--AND THAT BEE-LIKE BUBBLING BUSY HUM   . . . . 272 3 DON JUAN 11   8   7
BUZZ ROUND THE FORTUNE WITH THEIR BUSY BATTERY . . . 331 3 DON JUAN 12   32   7
HE ALSO HAD BEEN BUSY SEEING SIGHTS-- . . . . . 353 3 DON JUAN 12   82   1
THERE WERE TWO LAWYERS BUSY ON A MORTGAGE   . . . . 530 3 DON JUAN 16   60   1
BOTH BUSY (AS A GENERAL IN HIS TENT . . . . . . 533 3 DON JUAN 16   66   6
BUTCHER
VERNON THE BUTCHER CUMBERLAND WOLFE HAWKE . . . . 22 2 DON JUAN 1   2   1
TURNS OUT TO BE A BUTCHER IN GREAT BUSINESS . . . . 108 3 DON JUAN 7   83   7
BEFORE THEY BUTCHER LITTLE LEILA GAZED   . . . . . 261 3 DON JUAN 10   74   7
BUTCHERED
SHOULD NOW BE BUTCHERED IN A CIVIC ALLEY . . . . . 431 2 DON JUAN 5   37   8
WHO BUTCHERED HALF THE EARTH AND BULLIED T'OTHER . . 265 3 DON JUAN 10   81   8
BUTCHER'S
WHEN DEMAGOGUES WOULD WITH A BUTCHER'S KNIFE . . . 536 3 DON JUAN 16   74   5
BUTCHERS
BY BUTCHERS IN HER STREETS THAN FOR THE STAUNCHEST OR . . 314 3 DON JUAN 11 V 75   5
BUTCHERY
IS BUTCHERY SOMETIMES A SINGLE SORROW . . . . . . 102 3 DON JUAN 7   69   7
BUTLER
AND DAUGHTERS SOMETIMES RUN OFF WITH THE BUTLER . . 287 2 DON JUAN 3   22   8
BUTT
WITH MAUDLIN CLARENCE IN HIS MALMSEY BUTT . . . . 112 2 DON JUAN 1   166   8
IN PREFERENCE SURE TO CLARENCE' MALMSEY BUTT . . . 112 2 DON JUAN 1   166   V8
HIS BROW AS IF IN ACT TO BUTT AND THEN   . . . . . 292 2 DON JUAN 3   32   7
BUTTER
TWO CASKS OF BISCUIT AND A KEG OF BUTTER . . . . . 180 2 DON JUAN 2   46   7
AND ALSO FOR THE BISCUIT CASKS AND BUTTER . . . . 188 2 DON JUAN 2   61   8
BUTTERED
LORD HENRY SAID HIS MUFFIN WAS ILL BUTTERED . . . 514 3 DON JUAN 16   31   4
BUTTERFLIES
OF COLOUR'D GARBS AS BRIGHT AS BUTTERFLIES   . . . . 289 2 DON JUAN 3   27   8
WHO THINK THAT NOVELTIES ARE BUTTERFLIES . . . . . 328 3 DON JUAN 12   27   5
BUTTERFLY
MY MUSE THE BUTTERFLY HATH BUT HER WINGS . . . . . 400 3 DON JUAN 13   89   5

```
                                                         PAGE VOL      CANTO STANZA LN
BUTTONS
     WITH BUTTONS FORM'D OF PEARLS AS LARGE AS PEAS . . . . . 311   2 DON JUAN  3      70   5
BUXOM
     SOME VOICES OF THE BUXOM MIDDLE-AGED  . . . . . . . . 178   3 DON JUAN  8     132   1
BUY
     TO HEAD THE POLL I WONDER WHO WOULD BUY IT . . . . . . 154   2 DON JUAN  1    V  5   4
     NEXT JUAN STOOD TILL SOME MIGHT CHOOSE TO BUY . . . . . 416   2 DON JUAN  5      10   8
     I WISH TO GOD THAT SOMEBODY WOULD BUY US . . . . . . . 423   2 DON JUAN  5      24   8
     SO SILLY AS TO BUY SLAVES WHO MIGHT SHARE  . . . . . .  24   3 DON JUAN  6      36   6
BUYER
     AND APT TO BE TRANSFERRED TO THE FIRST BUYER  . . . . .  14   3 DON JUAN  6      16   6
BUYS
     BUYS THEM IN MARRIAGE--AND WHAT RESTS BEYOND  . . . . . 263   2 DON JUAN  2     200   6
     THEY HAVE A KING WHO BUYS AND SELLS  . . . . . . . 325   2 DON JUAN  3    L 14   2
BUZZ
     BUZZ ROUND THE FORTUNE WITH THEIR BUSY BATTERY . . . . . 331   2 DON JUAN 12      32   7
BY-AND-BY
     THE SAME KATINKA UNTIL BY-AND-BY  . . . . . . . . .  30   3 DON JUAN  6      49   3
     THE PEOPLE BY-AND-BY WILL BE THE STRONGER  . . . . . . 137   3 DON JUAN  8      50   4
     I BY-AND-BY MAY TELL YOU IF AT ALL . . . . . . . . . 181   3 DON JUAN  8     139   4
     BEFORE THEY GIVE THEIR BROADSIDE BY-AND-BY  . . . . . . 266   3 DON JUAN 10      84   2
     JUST NOW ENOUGH BUT BY-AND-BY I'LL PRATTLE  . . . . . . 267   3 DON JUAN 10      87   7
BYE
     AND SO YOUR HUMBLE SERVANT AND GOOD BYE  . . . . . . . 147   2 DON JUAN  1     221   4
     TELLS AN ODD STORY OF WHICH BY THE BYE  . . . . . . . 516   3 DON JUAN 16      36   4
C
     PRESENT LORDS A B C--EARLS DUKES BY NAME . . . . . . . 383   3 DON JUAN 13      54   2
CA
     OR CA IRA ACCORDING TO THE FASHION ALL  . . . . . . . 319   2 DON JUAN  3      85   4
CABIN
     FROM HIS DULL CABIN FOUND HIMSELF A SLAVE  . . . . . . 387   2 DON JUAN  4      79   2
CABIN'D
     WOUNDED AND FETTER'D CABIN'D CRIBB'D CONFINED  . . . . . 384   2 DON JUAN  4      75   1
CABINET
     UPON HIS CABINET BESIDES THE PRESENTS . . . . . . . . 222   3 DON JUAN  9      79   7
     BETWEEN THE BRITISH CABINET AND RUSSIAN . . . . . . . 246   3 DON JUAN 10      45   3
     LORD HENRY WALK'D INTO HIS CABINET . . . . . . . . . 440   3 DON JUAN 14      68   2
CABLE
     THEIRS IS THE BEST BOWER-ANCHOR THE CHAIN CABLE  . . . . 316   3 DON JUAN 12       3   3
CABLE'S
     WITHIN A CABLE'S LENGTH THEIR VESSELS LAY  . . . . . .  81   3 DON JUAN  7      29   4
CADES
     FLOATS SCUMLIKE UPPERMOST AND THESE JACK CADES  . . . . 334   2 DON JUAN  3     100   5
CADIZ
     CADIZ PERHAPS--BUT THAT YOU SOON MAY SEE-- .  . . . . .  25   2 DON JUAN  1       8   6
     SHE SENT HER SON TO BE SHIPP'D OFF FROM CADIZ  . . . . . 128   2 DON JUAN  1     190   8
     I SAID THAT JUAN HAD BEEN SENT TO CADIZ-- . . . . . . 159   2 DON JUAN  2       5   1
     HER SON TO CADIZ ONLY TO EMBARK . . . . . . . . . . 161   2 DON JUAN  2       8   2
     WAS A SMALL PRESENT MADE TO HIM AT CADIZ . . . . . . . 199   2 DON JUAN  2      81   7
     WAS THE DISEASE PRESENTED HIM AT CADIZ . . . . . . . . 199   2 DON JUAN  2      81  V7
CADMUS
     YOU HAVE THE LETTERS CADMUS GAVE-- . . . . . . . . . 324   2 DON JUAN  3    L 10   5
CAESAR
     OH LOVE OF WHOM GREAT CAESAR WAS THE SUITOR . . . . . . 266   2 DON JUAN  2     205   1
     CAESAR AND POMPEY MAHOMET BELISARIUS . . . . . . . . 266   2 DON JUAN  2     206   3
     CAESAR HIMSELF WHO IN THE VERY SIGHT  . . . . . . . . 125   3 DON JUAN  8      28   5
     NO CAESAR BUT A FINE YOUNG LAD WHO FOUGHT  . . . . . . 126   3 DON JUAN  8      29   2
     AS CAESAR WORE HIS ROBE YOU WEAR YOUR GOWN  . . . . . . 232   3 DON JUAN 10      15   8
     CAESAR HIMSELF WOULD BE ASHAMED OF FAME  . . . . . . . 455   3 DON JUAN 14     102   8
     LIKE ANTHONY'S BY CAESAR BY THE FEW  . . . . . . . . 479   3 DON JUAN 15      53   7
CAESAR'S
     LIKE TITUS' YOUTH AND CAESAR'S EARLIEST ACTS  . . . . . 329   2 DON JUAN  3      92   3
     OUTBALANCE ALL THE CAESAR'S VICTORIES . . . . . . . .   8   3 DON JUAN  6       4   8
     OH CAESAR'S COMMENTARIES NOW IMPART YE  . . . . . . . 108   3 DON JUAN  7      82   5
CAETERA
     WITHIN--ET CAETERA  SHALL I GO ON--NO . . . . . . . . 374   3 DON JUAN 13      36   4
CAGE
     IF THEY WERE FITTED FOR THE PURPOSED CAGE  . . . . . . 424   2 DON JUAN  5      26   5
CAGED
     HE CAGED IN ONE HUGE HAMPER ALTOGETHER  . . . . . . . 285   2 DON JUAN  3      18   8
     BEATING FOR LOVE AS THE CAGED BIRDS FOR AIR . . . . . .  19   3 DON JUAN  6      26   8
     IN CITIES CAGED THE PRESENT CASE IN POINT I . . . . . . 143   3 DON JUAN  8      62   7
     (WIDOWS OF FORTY WERE THESE BIRDS LONG CAGED) . . . . . 178   3 DON JUAN  8     132   3
CAGES
     TO CALL THEM BACK INTO THEIR SEPARATE CAGES . . . . . .  46   2 DON JUAN  1      45   6
CAIN
     MY LEIPSIC AND MY MONT SAINT JEAN SEEMS CAIN . . . . . 296   3 DON JUAN 11      56   2
CAIO
     HAIL'D A STRANGE BRIG CORPO DI CAIO MARIO  . . . . . . 389   2 DON JUAN  4      82   4
CAIQUE
     WONDERING WHAT NEXT TILL THE CAIQUE WAS BROUGHT  . . . . 432   2 DON JUAN  5      40   6
CAIRN
     AND BRILLIANT BREECHES BRIGHT AS A CAIRN GORME . . . . . 204   3 DON JUAN  9      43   5
CAITIFF
     TO AID THE DAMSEL AND DESTROY THE CAITIFF  . . . . . . 363   3 DON JUAN 13      10   2
CALCULATE
     UNLESS A MAN CAN CALCULATE HIS MEANS . . . . . . . . 325   3 DON JUAN 12      21   7
CALCULATED
     AND THEN--THEY CALCULATED ON HIS RANSOM . . . . . . . 415   2 DON JUAN  5       9   8
```

107

	PAGE	VOL			CANTO	STANZA	LN

CALCULATED (CONTINUED)
WHO CALCULATED LIFE AS SO MUCH DROSS 105   3 DON JUAN 7   77 3
'TWAS SOMETHING CALCULATED TO ALLAY 200   3 DON JUAN 9   36 4
CALCULATING
NOT CALCULATING HOW MUCH THEY CONDENSED 535   3 DON JUAN 16   71 6
CALCULATION
IN SHORT SHE WAS A WALKING CALCULATION 29   2 DON JUAN 1   16 1
FOR ANY SAGE'S CREED OR CALCULATION)-- 225   3 DON JUAN 10   1 4
OR REVEL IN THE JOYS OF CALCULATION 320   3 DON JUAN 12   10 8
AND HER'S WERE THOSE WHICH CAN FACE CALCULATION . . . 432   3 DON JUAN 14   52 2
CALCULATORS
TO CALCULATORS WHEN THEY COUNT ON WOMAN 429   3 DON JUAN 14   43 8
CALDERON
ALL CALDERON AND GREATER PART OF LOPE 27   2 DON JUAN 1   11 2
CALEDON
WHETHER IN CALEDON OR ITALY 231   3 DON JUAN 10   13 6
CALENTURES
THE CALENTURES OF MUSIC WHICH O'ERCOME 523   3 DON JUAN 16   46 5
CALIDA
NON EGO HOC FERREM CALIDA JUVENTA 143   2 DON JUAN 1   212 1
CALL
IN SHORT IN ALL THINGS SHE WAS FAIRLY WHAT I CALL . . . 27   2 DON JUAN 1   12 5
AND WHAT THE LAWYERS CALL A MALUS ANIMUS 37   2 DON JUAN 1   30 5
TO CALL THEM BACK INTO THEIR SEPARATE CAGES 46   2 DON JUAN 1   45 6
THERE WAS THE DONNA JULIA WHOM TO CALL 51   2 DON JUAN 1   55 3
WHAT MEN CALL GALLANTRY AND GODS ADULTERY 56   2 DON JUAN 1   63 7
FOND OF A LITTLE LOVE (WHICH I CALL LEISURE) 85   2 DON JUAN 1   118 6
CALL ME THE ONLY VIRTUOUS WIFE IN SPAIN 102   2 DON JUAN 1   149 4
WHO IS THE MAN YOU SEARCH FOR HOW D'YE CALL 105   2 DON JUAN 1   154 4
SO MUCH AS WHEN WE CALL OUR OLD DEBTS IN 113   2 DON JUAN 1   167 6
OF RHETORIC WHICH THE LEARN'D CALL RIGMAROLE 116   2 DON JUAN 1   174 8
I'LL CALL THE WORK LONGINUS O'ER A BOTTLE 138   2 DON JUAN 1   204 7
AND BARDS BURN WHAT THEY CALL THEIR MIDNIGHT TAPER . . 146   2 DON JUAN 1   218 6
FOR AFTER ALL WE CANNOT CALL THEE DEVIL 266   2 DON JUAN 2   205 8
MEN CALL INCONSTANCY IS NOTHING MORE 269   2 DON JUAN 2   211 2
HARK RISING TO THE IGNOBLE CALL-- 324   2 DON JUAN 3 L 9 5
I KNOW THAT WHAT OUR NEIGHBOURS CALL LONGUEURS 332   2 DON JUAN 3   97 1
INHERENT WHAT WE MORTALS CALL ROMANTIC 353   2 DON JUAN 4   18 7
I HAVE SEEN SUCH--BUT MUST NOT CALL TO MIND 363   2 DON JUAN 4   36 8
SMILED SCORNFULLY AND SAID WITHIN MY CALL 364   2 DON JUAN 4   37 6
ON THE FIRST FOE WHOM LAMBRO'S CALL MIGHT BRING . . . 365   2 DON JUAN 4   39 8
AND BLEW ANOTHER ANSWERED TO THE CALL 369   2 DON JUAN 4   47 4
OF WHAT SHE WAS AND IS IF YE COULD CALL 380   2 DON JUAN 4   66 5
COULD ALTOGETHER CALL THE PAST TO MIND 384   2 DON JUAN 4   75 3
THE THINGS DOWN SAID--INCENSE ME AND I CALL 454   2 DON JUAN 5   75 7
HER FIFTH TO CALL HER MAIDS AND GO TO BED 491   2 DON JUAN 5   139 5
AND TAKE WHAT KINGS CALL AN IMPOSING ATTITUDE 11   3 DON JUAN 6   11 4
WHICH IT CAN EITHER PAIN OR EVIL CALL 17   3 DON JUAN 6   22 5
UPON IN SHEETS WHITE AS WHAT BARDS CALL DRIVEN 18   3 DON JUAN 6   25 5
WHICH SOME CALL THE SUBLIME I WISH THEY'D TRY IT . . . 32   3 DON JUAN 6   53 6
MATRONS AND MAIDS AND THOSE WHOM YOU MAY CALL 42   3 DON JUAN 6   71 3
TO CALL MEN LOVE-BEGOTTEN OR PROCLAIM 53   3 DON JUAN 6   94 1
TO CALL A MAN A WHORESON--OR TO SAY 53   3 DON JUAN 6   94 V1
WHAT SAGES CALL CHANCE PROVIDENCE OR FATE-- 105   3 DON JUAN 7   76 4
WHEN I CALL FADING MARTIAL IMMORTALITY 108   3 DON JUAN 7   83 1
SO BE THEY THEIR INSPIRERS CALL THEM MARS 112   3 DON JUAN 8   1 7
OR LOVED IT WAS WITH WHAT WE CALL THE BEST 123   3 DON JUAN 8   25 2
UNTO HIS CALL UNLIKE THE SPIRITS FROM 132   3 DON JUAN 8   38 2
AT LEAST NINE-TENTHS OF WHAT WE CALL SO--GOD 163   3 DON JUAN 8   104 2
IN PROSE I BEND MY HUMBLE VERSE) DOTH CALL 163   3 DON JUAN 8   104 7
OF WHAT IT HAD BEEN THERE THE MUEZZIN'S CALL 182   3 DON JUAN 8   141 6
WHY DO THEY CALL ME MISANTHROPE BECAUSE 193   3 DON JUAN 9   21 7
TO BE THE FIRST OF WHAT WE USED TO CALL 198   3 DON JUAN 9   32 2
I NE'ER DECIDE WHAT I SHALL SAY AND THIS I CALL . . . 203   3 DON JUAN 9   41 5
SOME CALL THEE THE WORST CAUSE OF WAR BUT I 210   3 DON JUAN 9   56 1
AND WAS NOT THE BEST WIFE UNLESS WE CALL 222   3 DON JUAN 9   80 6
IN HEALTH--WHEN ILL WE CALL THEM TO ATTEND US 245   3 DON JUAN 10   42 3
IF I AGREE THAT WHAT IS IS THEN THIS I CALL 270   3 DON JUAN 11   5 3
OH GOLD WHY CALL WE MISERS MISERABLE 316   3 DON JUAN 12   3 1
WHY CALL THE MISER MISERABLE AS 319   3 DON JUAN 12   7 1
WHILE HE DESPISING EVERY SENSUAL CALL 320   3 DON JUAN 12   9 7
THE FOOL WILL CALL SUCH MANIA A DISEASE-- 321   3 DON JUAN 12   11 3
WHATE'ER ASTONISHMENT THIS SEEMS TO CALL 333   3 DON JUAN 12   37 V6
I CALL SUCH THINGS TRANSMISSION FOR THERE IS 340   3 DON JUAN 12   52 1
FOR HER RETURN TO VIRTUE--AS THEY CALL 352   3 DON JUAN 12   79 7
WERE VANISHED TO BE WHAT THEY CALL ALONE-- 381   3 DON JUAN 13   49 3
MAY THE ROSE CALL BACK ITS TRUE COLOURS SOON 409   3 DON JUAN 13   111 6
YOU BIND YOURSELF AND CALL SOME MODE THE BEST ONE . . 411   3 DON JUAN 14   2 6
WHICH PRETTY WOMEN--THE SWEET SOULS--CALL SOUL . . . 441   3 DON JUAN 14   71 3
BEFORE YOU LEARN TO CALL THIS SUPERSTITION 500   3 DON JUAN 15   98 8
CALL'D
A NOBLE STREAM AND CALL'D THE GUADALQUIVIR 25   2 DON JUAN 1   8 8
FOR INEZ CALL'D SOME DRUGGISTS AND PHYSICIANS 35   2 DON JUAN 1   27 1
HE DIED OF THE SLOW FEVER CALL'D THE TERTIAN 39   2 DON JUAN 1   34 7
WHO CALL'D HER CHASTE METHINKS BEGAN TOO SOON 82   2 DON JUAN 1   113 3
CALL'D BACK THE TANGLES OF HER WANDERING HAIR 114   2 DON JUAN 1   170 2
THE SHIP CALL'D THE MOST HOLY TRINIDADA 169   2 DON JUAN 2   24 1
BATTISTA THOUGH (A NAME CALL'D SHORTLY TITA) 186   2 DON JUAN 2   56 7
HE HAD AN ONLY DAUGHTER CALL'D HAIDÉE 224   2 DON JUAN 2   128 1

CALL'D   (CONTINUED)
	PAGE	VOL		CANTO	STANZA	LN
AND TURN'D BELIEVING THAT HE CALL'D AGAIN	228	2	DON JUAN	2	135	4
AND CALL'D HER FATHER'S OLD SLAVES UP WHO SWORE	229	2	DON JUAN	2	138	6
LIKE EARTHQUAKES FROM THE HIDDEN FIRE CALL'D CENTRAL	271	2	DON JUAN	2	215	8
A DROWSY FROWZY POEM CALL'D THE EXCURSION	330	2	DON JUAN	3	94	7
CALL'D SOCIAL HAUNTS OF HATE AND VICE AND CARE	358	2	DON JUAN	4	28	4
TILL WHAT IS CALL'D IN OSSIAN THE FIFTH DUAN	410	2	DON JUAN	4	117	8
DEATH SO CALL'D IS A THING WHICH MAKES MEN WEEP	411	3	DON JUAN	14	3	7
AND WERE HER OBJECT ONLY WHAT'S CALL'D GLORY	416	3	DON JUAN	14	13	7
WHETHER THEIR TALK WAS OF THE KIND CALL'D SMALL	453	3	DON JUAN	14	98	4
WERE THINGS BUT ONLY CALL'D BY THEIR RIGHT NAME	455	3	DON JUAN	14	102	7
WHY CALL'D HE HARMONY A STATE SANS WEDLOCK	471	3	DON JUAN	15	35	7
THAT COOKERY COULD HAVE CALL'D FORTH SUCH RESOURCES	486	3	DON JUAN	15	69	6

CALLED
AND CALLED FROM JUAN'S BREAST A FAINT LOW SIGH	355	2	DON JUAN	4	21	7
WHICH MIGHT HAVE CALLED DIANA'S CHORUS COUSIN	469	2	DON JUAN	5	99	6
CALLED BACK THE STOIC TO HIS EYES WHICH SHONE	481	2	DON JUAN	5	121	5
OR WHETHER THEY WERE MAIDS WHO CALLED HER MOTHER	21	3	DON JUAN	6	31	2
AND THEN HE CALLED HIS BRETHREN TO HIS AID	64	3	DON JUAN	6	118	1
THE FORTRESS IS CALLED ISMAIL AND IS PLACED	70	3	DON JUAN	7	9	1
SIXTEEN CALLED THOMSON AND NINETEEN NAMED SMITH	75	3	DON JUAN	7	18	8
HAD BEEN CALLED JEMMY AFTER THE GREAT BARD	76	3	DON JUAN	7	19	2
NOT THAT HIS MANHOOD COULD BE CALLED IN QUESTION	84	3	DON JUAN	7	36	2
(HERE HE CALLED UP A POLISH ORDERLY)	100	3	DON JUAN	7	66	4
AND THESE HE CALLED ON AND WHAT'S STRANGE THEY CAME	132	3	DON JUAN	8	38	1
OPENED THE GATE CALLED KILIA TO THE GROUPS	148	3	DON JUAN	8	73	5
FOR WHAT IS SOMETIMES CALLED POETIC DICTION	154	3	DON JUAN	8	86	6
CALLED SAVIOUR OF THE NATIONS--NOT YET SAVED	185	3	DON JUAN	9	5	7
SO CALLED THE ANTIC LONG HATH CEASED TO HEAR	188	3	DON JUAN	9	12	4
CALLED CAVALIER SERVENTE--A PYGMALION	208	3	DON JUAN	9	51	5
OUR VEINS WHEN THINGS CALLED SOVEREIGNS THINK IT BEST	212	3	DON JUAN	9	60	7
ADD WHAT MAY BE CALLED MARRIAGE IN DISGUISE	220	3	DON JUAN	9	76	8
IN A MOST NATURAL WHIRL CALLED GRAVITATION	225	3	DON JUAN	10	1	6
OF WHAT IS CALLED ETERNITY TO STARE	234	3	DON JUAN	10	20	7
HE FELT LIKE OTHER PLANTS CALLED SENSITIVE	243	3	DON JUAN	10	37	2
CALLED BROTHERLY AFFECTION COULD NOT MOVE	250	3	DON JUAN	10	53	6
THROUGH GROVES SO CALLED AS BEING VOID OF TREES	278	3	DON JUAN	11	21	1
THROUGH ROWS MOST MODESTLY CALLED PARADISE	278	3	DON JUAN	11	21	7
IS CALLED ON TO SUPPORT HIS CLAIM OR SHOW IT	296	3	DON JUAN	11	55	3
CALLED PARKS WHERE THERE IS NEITHER FRUIT NOR FLOWER	301	3	DON JUAN	11	66	4
ABOUT WHAT'S CALLED SUCCESS OR NOT SUCCEEDING	341	3	DON JUAN	12	55	2
A JEST AT VICE BY VIRTUE'S CALLED A CRIME	358	3	DON JUAN	13	1	3
PEACE WAR THE TAXES AND WHAT'S CALLED THE NATION	360	3	DON JUAN	13	6	2
WAS WHAT HE CALLED THE ART OF HAPPINESS	374	3	DON JUAN	13	35	2
WHEN CALLED NEXT DAY DECLINED THE ROUGH ADVENTURE	425	3	DON JUAN	14	35	V8
THAT ADAM CALLED THE HAPPIEST OF MEN	434	3	DON JUAN	14	55	8
SHE CALLED HER HUSBAND NOW AND THEN APART	438	3	DON JUAN	14	65	3
AND BEING OF THE COUNCIL CALLED THE PRIVY	440	3	DON JUAN	14	68	1
THERE IS A FLOWER CALLED LOVE IN IDLENESS	442	3	DON JUAN	14	75	1
BUT FOR THAT HOUR CALLED HALF-HOUR GIVEN TO DRESS	482	3	DON JUAN	15	61	7
BRICKLAYER OF BABEL CALLED AN ARCHITECT	529	3	DON JUAN	16	58	2
AND THROW DOWN OLD WHICH HE CALLED RESTORATION	529	3	DON JUAN	16	58	8
TO BE CALLED UP FOR HER EXAMINATION	532	3	DON JUAN	16	65	8
THOUGH NOT EXACTLY WHAT'S CALLED OPEN HOUSE	534	3	DON JUAN	16	68	8
THEY ERR--'TIS MERELY WHAT IS CALLED MOBILITY	547	3	DON JUAN	16	97	4
OF WHAT IS CALLED THE WORLD AND THE WORLD'S WAYS	554	3	DON JUAN	16	108	3

CALLING
OF CALLING WHOLLY BACK ITS SELF-CONTROL	82	2	DON JUAN	1	114	4
FOR CALLING NAMES AND TAKING THEM AGAIN	150	2	DON JUAN	1	V 1	4
STOOD CALLING OUT FOR BANDAGES AND LINT	275	3	DON JUAN	11	14	7

CALLOUS
INDIFFERENT FROM THE FIRST OR CALLOUS GROWN	59	2	DON JUAN	1	68	6

CALLOW
SOFT AS THE CALLOW CYGNET IN ITS NEST	235	2	DON JUAN	2	148	6

CALLS
AND STILL IT HALF CALLS UP THE REALMS OF FAIRY	413	2	DON JUAN	5	4	3
SOMETIMES CALLS MURDER AND AT OTHERS GLORY	79	3	DON JUAN	7	26	8
DEBT HE CALLS WEALTH AND TAXES PARADISE	88	3	DON JUAN	7	45	5
HE WAS WHAT ERIN CALLS IN HER SUBLIME	122	3	DON JUAN	8	23	1
(AS PISTOL CALLS IT) BUT A YOUNG LIVONIAN	140	3	DON JUAN	8	56	8
CALLS ILION'S THE FIRST DAMAGES ON RECORD	209	3	DON JUAN	9	53	8
BECAUSE YOU'LL SAY NOUGHT CALLS FOR SUCH A TRIAL--	319	3	DON JUAN	12	7	7
IN MAKING MEN WHAT COURTESY CALLS FRIENDS	365	3	DON JUAN	13	15	8

CALM
FOR ON THE THIRD DAY THERE CAME ON A CALM	192	2	DON JUAN	2	68	2
AS O'ER HIM LAY THE CALM AND STIRLESS AIR	233	2	DON JUAN	2	144	4
ON ONE SIDE AND THE DEEP SEA CALM AND CHILL	252	2	DON JUAN	2	183	6
CAN CALM--FOR WHAT IT MADE ME ON THAT SAME	272	2	DON JUAN	2	V 1	7
THEN CALM CONCENTRATED AND STILL AND SLOW	300	2	DON JUAN	3	48	3
CALM IN HIS VOICE AND CALM WITHIN HIS EYE--	365	2	DON JUAN	4	39	2
CALM IN HIS VOICE AND CALM WITHIN HIS EYE--	365	2	DON JUAN	4	39	2
SO CALM THOUGH PIERCED THROUGH STOMACH HEART AND LIVER	430	2	DON JUAN	5	35	4
A SLIGHT BLUSH A SOFT TREMOR A CALM KIND	13	3	DON JUAN	6	15	1
WHERE ALL WAS HARMONY AND CALM AND QUIET	32	3	DON JUAN	6	53	2
THE CALM DUDU SO TURBULENTLY WAKE	42	3	DON JUAN	6	71	8
IS APT TO TIRE A CALM AND SHALLOW STATION	191	3	DON JUAN	9	18	6
WHILE EVERYTHING AROUND WAS CALM AND STILL	272	3	DON JUAN	11	8	5
A MODEST CONFIDENCE AND CALM ASSURANCE	294	3	DON JUAN	11	52	2
THE KINDER VETERAN WITH CALM WORDS WILL COURT YOU	337	3	DON JUAN	12	45	5

109

CALM   (CONTINUED)
    THAT CALM PATRICIAN POLISH IN THE ADDRESS . . . . . . 373 3 DON JUAN 13   34   2
    SURVEYED HIM WITH A KIND OF CALM SURPRISE . . . . . . 514 3 DON JUAN 16   31   8
CALMER
    BEDEW'D HIS SPIRIT IN HIS CALMER HOURS . . . . 304 2 DON JUAN 3   56   8
    IN CURRENTS THROUGH THE CALMER WATER SPREAD . . . . . 385 3 DON JUAN 13   57   4
CALMEST
    NOT ALWAYS SIGNS WITH HIM OF CALMEST MOOD . . . . . . 365 2 DON JUAN 4   39   3
CALMLY
    CALMLY SHE HEARD EACH CALUMNY THAT ROSE . . . . 36 2 DON JUAN 1   29   6
    WERE RULED AS CALMLY AS A CHRISTIAN QUEEN . . . . . . 496 2 DON JUAN 5   148   8
    SMOKING HIS PIPE QUITE CALMLY 'MIDST THE DIN . . . . 160 3 DON JUAN 8   98   4
    WHERE THE CHIEF PACHA CALMLY HELD HIS POST . . . . . 171 3 DON JUAN 8   120   2
    AND RATHER CALMLY INTO THE HEART GLIDES . . . . 350 3 DON JUAN 12   74   5
    RETIRED AND AS HE WENT OUT CALMLY KISSED HER . . . . 440 3 DON JUAN 14   69   7
    HAD SHE KNOWN THIS SHE WOULD HAVE CALMLY SMILED-- . . 480 3 DON JUAN 15   55   7
CALMS
    THERE'S NOUGHT NO DOUBT SO MUCH THE SPIRIT CALMS . . . 174 2 DON JUAN 2   34   1
CALMUCK
    HE SAID--AND IN THE KINDEST CALMUCK TONE-- . . . . . 102 3 DON JUAN 7   70   1
CALMUCKS
    BEFORE A COMPANY OF CALMUCKS DRILLING . . . . 96 3 DON JUAN 7   58   2
CALUMNIATED
    AND THE CALUMNIATED QUEEN SEMIRAMIS-- . . . . 445 2 DON JUAN 5   60   8
CALUMNY
    CALMLY SHE HEARD EACH CALUMNY THAT ROSE . . . . 36 2 DON JUAN 1   29   6
CALVIN
    BY FENELON BY CALVIN AND OF CHRIST . . . . 68 3 DON JUAN 7   4   V2
CAMBYSES'
    CAMBYSES' ROARING ROMANS BEAT AT LEAST . . . . 297 3 DON JUAN 11   58   7
CAME
    HIS MOTHER'S FAMILY CAME OUT OF ARRAGON . . . . 43 2 DON JUAN 1   38   V4
    AND HOW THE GODDESSES CAME DOWN TO MEN . . . . 72 2 DON JUAN 1   94   4
    'TIS SAID THE GREAT CAME FROM AMERICA . . . . 92 2 DON JUAN 1   131   1
    MY DEAR I WAS THE FIRST WHO CAME AWAY . . . . 98 2 DON JUAN 1   141   8
    THE ONLY MISCHIEF WAS IT CAME TOO LATE . . . . 122 2 DON JUAN 1   183   2
    LIGHTS CAME AT LENGTH AND MEN AND MAIDS WHO FOUND . . 125 2 DON JUAN 1   187   1
    A SQUALL CAME ON AND WHILE SOME GUNS BROKE LOOSE . . . 172 2 DON JUAN 2   30   6
    BUT NOW THERE CAME A FLASH OF HOPE ONCE MORE . . . . 176 2 DON JUAN 2   38   1
    THEN CAME THE CARPENTER AT LAST WITH TEARS . . . . . 179 2 DON JUAN 2   43   1
    FOR ON THE THIRD DAY THERE CAME ON A CALM . . . . . . 192 2 DON JUAN 2   68   2
    THE FOURTH DAY CAME BUT NOT A BREATH OF AIR . . . . . 193 2 DON JUAN 2   70   1
    SAVE IN THE BREEZE THAT CAME NOT SAVAGELY . . . . . . 194 2 DON JUAN 2   72   4
    BUT ERE THEY CAME TO THIS THEY THAT DAY SHARED . . . 195 2 DON JUAN 2   74   1
    IT CAME AND WENT AND FLUTTER'D ROUND THEM TILL . . . 206 2 DON JUAN 2   94   7
    WITH TWILIGHT IT AGAIN CAME ON TO BLOW . . . . 207 2 DON JUAN 2   96   1
    AND DOWN THE CLIFF THE ISLAND VIRGIN CAME . . . . . . 232 2 DON JUAN 2   142   1
    SHE CAME INTO THE CAVE BUT IT WAS MERELY . . . . . . 245 2 DON JUAN 2   168   3
    AND EVERY MORN HIS COLOUR FRESHLIER CAME . . . . . . 245 2 DON JUAN 2   169   1
    CAME ALWAYS BACK TO COFFEE AND HAIDEE . . . . 246 2 DON JUAN 2   171   8
    THEN CAME HER FREEDOM FOR SHE HAD NO MOTHER . . . . . 248 2 DON JUAN 2   175   1
    BUT SOON PHILOSOPHY CAME TO MY AID . . . . 268 2 DON JUAN 2   210   1
    THUS SHE CAME OFTEN NOT A MOMENT LOSING . . . . 282 2 DON JUAN 3   13   7
    HE IS NOR WHENCE HE CAME--AND LITTLE CARE . . . . . . 298 2 DON JUAN 3   45   2
    IN SMALL FINE CHINA CUPS CAME IN AT LAST . . . . . . 307 2 DON JUAN 3   63   4
    EVEN AS THEY GAZED A SUDDEN TREMOR CAME . . . . 355 2 DON JUAN 4   21   2
    OFT CAME AND WENT AS THERE RESOLVED TO DIE . . . . . 365 2 DON JUAN 4   39   6
    SOME TWENTY OF HIS TRAIN CAME RANK ON RANK . . . . . 369 2 DON JUAN 4   47   7
    CORRUPTION CAME NOT IN EACH MIND TO KILL . . . . . . 377 2 DON JUAN 4   60   5
    THE HARPER CAME AND TUNED HIS INSTRUMENT . . . . . . 379 2 DON JUAN 4   65   2
    SHORT SOLACE VAIN RELIEF--THOUGHT CAME TOO QUICK . . 380 2 DON JUAN 4   67   1
    WHO CAME AT STATED MOMENTS TO INVITE ALL . . . . . . 393 2 DON JUAN 4   90   3
    FOR NIGHT WAS CLOSING ERE THEY CAME TO LAND . . . . . 433 2 DON JUAN 5   41   6
    AS THEY WERE THREADING ON THEIR WAY THERE CAME . . . 434 2 DON JUAN 5   43   1
    AND NEARER AS THEY CAME A GENIAL SAVOUR . . . . 437 2 DON JUAN 5   47   1
    IT SEEMED AS THOUGH THEY CAME UPON A SHRINE . . . . . 460 2 DON JUAN 5   85   7
    BUT NOT BY THE SAME DOOR THROUGH WHICH CAME IN . . . 469 2 DON JUAN 5   100   2
    FIRST CAME HER DAMSELS A DECOROUS FILE . . . . 495 2 DON JUAN 5   146   1
    BEFORE HE CAME ESPECIALLY AT NIGHT . . . . 495 2 DON JUAN 5   146   6
    BUT THEN THEY NEVER CAME TO THE SEVEN TOWERS . . . . 497 2 DON JUAN 5   150   8
    OF WHOM ALL SUCH AS CAME OF AGE WERE STOWED . . . . . 498 2 DON JUAN 5   152   2
    KATINKA ASKED HER ALSO WHENCE SHE CAME-- . . . . . . 28 3 DON JUAN 6   44   3
    BY WHICH ITS NOMENCLATURE CAME TO PASS . . . . 33 3 DON JUAN 6   55   3
    WHAT ARE WE AND WHENCE CAME WE WHAT SHALL BE . . . . 37 3 DON JUAN 6   63   6
    NEITHER CAME CROWDING LIKE THE WAVES OF OCEAN . . . . 42 3 DON JUAN 6   71   4
    THEN OUT IT CAME AT LENGTH THAT TO DUDU . . . . 57 3 DON JUAN 6   102   5
    FOR SOME TIME TILL THEY CAME IN NEARER VIEW . . . . . 87 3 DON JUAN 7   43   3
    AND AS HE RUSHED ALONG IT CAME TO PASS HE . . . . . . 130 3 DON JUAN 8   34   1
    JUST AT THIS CRISIS UP CAME JOHNSON TOO . . . . 130 3 DON JUAN 8   35   1
    AND THESE HE CALLED ON AND WHAT'S STRANGE THEY CAME . 132 3 DON JUAN 8   38   1
    CAME MOUNTING QUICKLY UP FOR IT WAS NOW . . . . 135 3 DON JUAN 8   45   2
    WHO CAME AS IF JUST DROPPED DOWN FROM THE MOON . . . 140 3 DON JUAN 8   56   4
    CRIME CAME NOT NEAR HIM--SHE IS NOT THE CHILD . . . . 143 3 DON JUAN 8   62   1
    UP CAME JOHN JOHNSON (I WILL NOT SAY JACK . . . . . . 160 3 DON JUAN 8   97   1
    UP JOHNSON CAME WITH HUNDREDS AT HIS BACK . . . . . . 160 3 DON JUAN 8   97   5
    AND SWEARING IF THE INFANT CAME TO ILL . . . . 162 3 DON JUAN 8   102   5
    HAUSTUS (AND HERE THE SURGEON CAME AND CUPPED HIM) . 244 3 DON JUAN 10   41   4
    FROM POLAND THEY CAME ON THROUGH PRUSSIA PROPER . . . 254 3 DON JUAN 10   60   1
    CAME UP ALL MARVELLING AT SUCH A DEED . . . . 275 3 DON JUAN 11   14   3

	PAGE	VOL	CANTO	STANZA	LN

CAME   (CONTINUED)
THE MELLOW AUTUMN CAME AND WITH IT CAME . . . . 394 3 DON JUAN 13 75 1
THE MELLOW AUTUMN CAME AND WITH IT CAME . . . . 394 3 DON JUAN 13 75 1
THAT WHEN A CULPRIT CAME FOR CONDEMNATION . . . . 399 3 DON JUAN 13 88 7
HIS COUNTRY'S PRIDE HE CAME DOWN TO THE COUNTRY . . . . 401 3 DON JUAN 13 91 8
WITH EVENING CAME THE BANQUET AND THE WINE . . . . . . 408 3 DON JUAN 13 107 1
AT SIXTEEN SHE CAME OUT PRESENTED VAUNTED . . . . . . 434 3 DON JUAN 14 55 1
THAT GOOD BUT RARELY CAME FROM GOOD ADVICE . . . . . . 439 3 DON JUAN 14 66 8
THOUGH GOD KNOWS WHENCE IT CAME FROM THERE WAS TOO . . . 483 3 DON JUAN 15 63 2
THOUGH HE CAME IN HIS MIGHT WITH KING HENRY'S RIGHT . . . 518 3 DON JUAN 16 L 2 1
AND LO UPON THAT DAY IT CAME TO PASS . . . . 539 3 DON JUAN 16 81 5
THE EVENING ALSO WANED--AND COFFEE CAME . . . . . . 549 3 DON JUAN 16 101 2
CAME OVER JUAN'S EAR WHICH THROBBED ALAS . . . . . . 556 3 DON JUAN 16 114 5
THE MORNING CAME--AND BREAKFAST TEA AND TOAST . . . . . 568 3 DON JUAN 17 13 2
CAMEL
THROUGH NEEDLES' EYES IT EASIER FOR THE CAMEL IS . . . . 397 2 DON JUAN 4 97 7
CAMELEON
IT CHANGED OF COURSE A HEAVENLY CAMELEON . . . . 205 2 DON JUAN 2 92 1
CAMELIONS
TOOK LIKE CAMELIONS SOME SLIGHT TINGE OF FEAR . . . . . 148 3 DON JUAN 8 73 4
CAMELOPARD
NEW BROKE A CAMELOPARD A GAZELLE . . . . 160 2 DON JUAN 2 6 2
CAMEL'S
OR IN THE DESERT HEARD THE CAMEL'S BELL . . . . 201 2 DON JUAN 2 84 7
AND LONG LONG DESERTS SCORCH THE CAMEL'S FOOT . . . . . 373 2 DON JUAN 4 55 6
THE HOLY CAMEL'S HUMP BESIDES THE KORAN . . . . 57 3 DON JUAN 6 102 8
CAMERADO
STRANGE TOO IN MY BUON CAMERADO SCOTT . . . . 323 3 DON JUAN 12 16 5
CAMILLA
LIKE SWIFT CAMILLA HE SCARCE SKIMM'D THE GROUND . . . . 427 3 DON JUAN 14 39 3
CAMP
THE COURT CAMP CHURCH THE VESSEL AND THE MART . . . . . 131 2 DON JUAN 1 194 3
BUT TO THE TALE--GREAT JOY UNTO THE CAMP . . . . . . 89 3 DON JUAN 7 46 1
THE FLEET AND CAMP SALUTED WITH GREAT GRACE . . . . . 89 3 DON JUAN 7 47 3
THE WHOLE CAMP RUNG WITH JOY YOU WOULD HAVE THOUGHT . . . 90 3 DON JUAN 7 49 1
OF THE ASSAULT AND ALL THE CAMP WAS IN . . . . 94 3 DON JUAN 7 54 2
INTO A CAMP I KNOW THAT NOUGHT SO BOTHERS . . . . . 103 3 DON JUAN 7 71 6
LOVE RULES THE CAMP THE COURT THE GROVE--FOR LOVE . . . 322 3 DON JUAN 12 13 1
NOW IF THE COURT AND CAMP AND GROVE BE NOT . . . . . 323 3 DON JUAN 12 16 1
CAMPAIGN
THAN IN THY GREEK GAZETTE OF THAT CAMPAIGN . . . . . . 106 3 DON JUAN 7 80 4
'TWAS ONLY THE FATIGUE OF LAST CAMPAIGN . . . . 244 3 DON JUAN 10 40 8
CAMPBELL
SCOTT ROGERS CAMPBELL MOORE AND CRABBE WILL TRY . . . . 13 2 DON JUAN D 7 7
SIR WALTER REIGNED BEFORE ME MOORE AND CAMPBELL . . . . 297 3 DON JUAN 11 57 1
CAMPBELL'S
AND CAMPBELL'S HIPPOCRENE IS SOMEWHAT DROUTHY . . . . . 139 2 DON JUAN 1 205 6
AND CAMPBELL'S SPRING SEEMS SOMEWHAT DRY AND DROUTHY . . . 139 2 DON JUAN 1 205 V6
CAMPS
IF COURTS AND CAMPS BE QUITE SO SENTIMENTAL . . . . . 322 3 DON JUAN 12 13 8
WITHOUT CASH CAMPS WERE THIN AND COURTS WERE NONE . . . . 322 3 DON JUAN 12 14 3
IN CAMPS IN SHIPS IN COTTAGES OR COURTS-- . . . . . 424 3 DON JUAN 14 31 4
CANALS
ON HER CANALS WHERE GOD TAKES SEA AND LAND . . . . . . 198 3 DON JUAN 9 31 7
AND CUT THROUGH SUCH CANALS OF CONTRADICTION . . . . . 495 3 DON JUAN 15 88 7
CANCER
THAN BUONAPARTE'S CANCER--COULD I DASH ON . . . . . . 189 3 DON JUAN 9 14 6
CANDIA
OF CANDIA CYPRUS RHODES OR OTHER ISLANDS . . . . 209 2 DON JUAN 2 100 8
CANDIDATE
OF THE OFFICIAL CANDIDATE I'LL TOUCH . . . . 538 3 DON JUAN 16 77 6
CANDIDATES
OF CANDIDATES REQUESTING TO BE PLACED . . . . 248 3 DON JUAN 10 48 3
CANDIDE
VOLTAIRE SAYS NO HE TELLS YOU THAT CANDIDE . . . . . . 427 2 DON JUAN 5 31 1
CANDIOTE
A CANDIOTE CLOAK WHICH TO THE KNEE MIGHT REACH . . . . . 451 2 DON JUAN 5 68 3
CANDLE
SHE SNUFF'D THE CANDLE CURTSIED AND WITHDREW . . . . . 116 2 DON JUAN 1 173 8
THEIR MOON THEIR SUN THEIR GAS THEIR FARTHING CANDLE . . . 342 3 DON JUAN 12 56 8
CANDLES
TO VIRGIN MARY SEVERAL POUNDS OF CANDLES . . . . 128 2 DON JUAN 1 190 6
OF CANDLES TO THEIR SAINTS--BUT THERE WERE NONE . . . . 179 2 DON JUAN 2 44 4
CANDLESTICKS
WHICH STILL IN JUAN'S CANDLESTICKS BURNED HIGH . . . . . 558 3 DON JUAN 16 117 5
CANDY
THAN THEIR HE RELATIVES) LIKE FLIES O'ER CANDY . . . . . 331 3 DON JUAN 12 32 6
CANKER-WORM
FOR CAUSES YOUNG OR OLD THE CANKER-WORM . . . . 243 3 DON JUAN 10 38 2
CANNIBAL
THE LONGINGS OF THE CANNIBAL ARISE . . . . 194 2 DON JUAN 2 72 7
CANNON
WHILE TWO AND TWENTY CANNON DULY SET . . . . 72 3 DON JUAN 7 12 6
AND FOURSCORE CANNON ON THE DANUBE'S BORDER . . . . . . 85 3 DON JUAN 7 38 7
THREE HUNDRED CANNON THREW UP THEIR EMETIC . . . . . 117 3 DON JUAN 8 12 1
AND THE LOUD CANNON PEALED HIS HOARSEST STRAINS . . . . 129 3 DON JUAN 8 33 6
THE VERY CANNON DEAFENED BY THE DIN . . . . 142 3 DON JUAN 8 59 5
CANNONADE
OFF ISMAIL AND COMMENCED A CANNONADE . . . . 81 3 DON JUAN 7 29 5

111

	PAGE	VOL		CANTO	STANZA	LN
CANNONADE (CONTINUED)						
AT LENGTH THEY FOUND MERE CANNONADE ALONE	81	3	DON JUAN	7	30	4
IN PREPARATIONS FOR A CANNONADE	106	3	DON JUAN	7	78	2
CANNON'S						
BLAZED AND THE CANNON'S ROAR WAS SCARCE ALLAYED	178	3	DON JUAN	8	133	4
CANNON-SHOT						
WITHIN A CANNON-SHOT LENGTH OF THE PLACE	89	3	DON JUAN	7	47	5
CANONICAL						
IS THAT WHICH MAY BE CHRISTENED LOVE CANONICAL	220	3	DON JUAN	9	76	3
CANONIZATION						
CANONIZATION FOR THE SELF-SAME CAUSE	319	3	DON JUAN	12	7	5
CANOPY						
UNDER A CANOPY AND THERE RECLINED	466	2	DON JUAN	5	95	2
THESE ARE BENEATH THE CANOPY OF HEAVEN	18	3	DON JUAN	6	25	1
ALSO BENEATH THE CANOPY OF BEDS	18	3	DON JUAN	6	25	2
WITH THICK'NING CANOPY THE CONFLICT O'ER	116	3	DON JUAN	8	8	6
ON TIPTOE THROUGH THEIR SEA-COAL CANOPY	265	3	DON JUAN	10	82	6
CANOVA						
CAST BY CANOVA OR DESCRIBED BY BURKE	315	2	DON JUAN	3	76	V8
CANOVA'S						
CANOVA'S MARBLE OR THE WORDS OF BURKE	315	2	DON JUAN	3	76	V8
CAN'T						
BUT CAN'T FIND ANY IN THE PRESENT AGE	24	2	DON JUAN	1	5	6
BUT THIS I HEARD HER SAY AND CAN'T BE WRONG	28	2	DON JUAN	1	14	5
I CAN'T SAY MUCH FOR FRIEND OR YET RELATION)	38	2	DON JUAN	1	32	5
I CAN'T HELP THINKING JUVENAL WAS WRONG	45	2	DON JUAN	1	43	3
I CAN'T BUT SAY THAT HIS MAMMA WAS RIGHT	48	2	DON JUAN	1	48	2
I CAN'T TELL WHETHER JULIA SAW THE AFFAIR	59	2	DON JUAN	1	68	1
I CAN'T HELP THINKING PUBERTY ASSISTED	71	2	DON JUAN	1	93	8
AND THEN--GOD KNOWS WHAT NEXT--I CAN'T GO ON	83	2	DON JUAN	1	115	7
I CAN'T TELL HOW OR WHY OR WHAT SUSPICION	97	2	DON JUAN	1	139	1
I CAN'T TELL WHY SHE SHOULD TAKE ALL THIS TROUBLE	97	2	DON JUAN	1	140	7
BUT THAT CAN'T BE AS HAS BEEN OFTEN SHOWN	118	2	DON JUAN	1	176	4
I CAN'T HELP PUTTING IN MY CLAIM TO PRAISE--	149	2	DON JUAN	1	222	6
I CAN'T SAY THAT IT PUZZLES ME AT ALL	158	2	DON JUAN	2	3	1
I CAN'T DESCRIBE IT THOUGH SO MUCH IT STRIKE	159	2	DON JUAN	2	5	7
I CAN'T BUT SAY IT IS AN AWKWARD SIGHT	163	2	DON JUAN	2	12	1
I CAN'T SAY THAT SHE GAVE THEM ANY TEA	233	2	DON JUAN	2	145	6
I SAY THAT BEEF IS RARE AND CAN'T HELP THINKING	238	2	DON JUAN	2	155	1
I CAN'T BUT SAY IT SEEMS TO ME MOST TRULY A	267	2	DON JUAN	2	208	3
I CAN'T HELP THINKING THAT ALL FORMER STRIFE	301	2	DON JUAN	3	50	V5
AND SIGH I CAN'T GET OUT LIKE YORICK'S STARLING	404	2	DON JUAN	4	109	4
BECAUSE IF DROWN'D THEY CAN'T--IF SPARED THEY WON'T	414	2	DON JUAN	5	6	8
BECAUSE THEY CAN'T FIND OUT THE VERY SPOT	447	2	DON JUAN	5	62	3
WHERE I CAN'T SAY OR GOLD OR DIAMOND FLINGS	465	2	DON JUAN	5	94	5
YOU CAN'T SUPPOSE GULBEYAZ' ANGRY BROW	486	2	DON JUAN	5	131	8
I CAN'T TELL WHY SHE BLUSHED NOR CAN EXPOUND	48	3	DON JUAN	6	85	5
YOU CAN'T REPEAT NINE NAMES FROM EACH GAZETTE	83	3	DON JUAN	7	34	8
QUITE DISAPPEARED--THE GODS KNOW HOW (I CAN'T	127	3	DON JUAN	8	31	3
AND FARMERS CAN'T RAISE CERES FROM HER FALL	198	3	DON JUAN	9	32	6
I CAN'T COMPLAIN WHOSE ANCESTORS ARE THERE	242	3	DON JUAN	10	36	1
AND THOUGH I CAN'T HELP THINKING 'TWAS SCARCE FAIR	242	3	DON JUAN	10	36	5
BUT WHAT IS TO BE DONE I CAN'T ALLOW	275	3	DON JUAN	11	15	6
IN THUNDER HOLDS THE WAY IT CAN'T WELL MISS	277	3	DON JUAN	11	20	6
OR CAN'T DO OTHERWISE THAN LIE BUT DO IT	285	3	DON JUAN	11	36	7
SUCH IS YOUR COLD COQUETTE WHO CAN'T SAY NO	345	3	DON JUAN	12	63	1
CAN'T FORM A FRIENDSHIP BUT THE WORLD O'ERAWES IT	346	3	DON JUAN	12	65	3
I CAN'T OBLIGE YOU READER TO READ ON	356	3	DON JUAN	12	87	6
I CAN'T EXACTLY TRACE THEIR RULE OF RIGHT	397	3	DON JUAN	13	82	1
THE GULF OF ROCK YAWNS--YOU CAN'T GAZE A MINUTE	412	3	DON JUAN	14	5	7
AND YET I CAN'T HELP SCRIBBLING ONCE A WEEK	414	3	DON JUAN	14	10	5
BUT THIS CAN'T WELL BE TRUE JUST NOW FOR WRITERS	418	3	DON JUAN	14	20	1
ALL THIS WERE VERY WELL AND CAN'T BE BETTER	421	3	DON JUAN	14	25	1
WHICH NEVER MEETS AND THEREFORE CAN'T FALL OUT	430	3	DON JUAN	14	45	8
THAT LIKE TO MAKE A QUARREL WHEN THEY CAN'T	438	3	DON JUAN	14	63	5
BUT NOW I CAN'T TELL WHERE IT MAY NOT RUN	466	3	DON JUAN	15	22	4
HAD ADELINE READ MALTHUS I CAN'T TELL	472	3	DON JUAN	15	38	1
WITH THINGS I CAN'T WITHSTAND OR UNDERSTAND	484	3	DON JUAN	15	66	3
CAN'T LIKE RIPE AGE IN GOURMANDISE EXCEL	487	3	DON JUAN	15	70	6
OF WHICH I CAN'T TELL WHENCE THEIR KNOWLEDGE SPRINGS	489	3	DON JUAN	15	76	4
YET MIXED SO SLIGHTLY THAT YOU CAN'T COMPLAIN	502	3	DON JUAN	16	3	6
I CAN'T TELL WHY TO THIS DISSIMULATION--	518	3	DON JUAN	16	40	3
ONE CAN'T TELL HOW IT E'ER GOT IN OR OUT	531	3	DON JUAN	16	62	2
WHEN HE CAN'T TELL WHAT 'TIS THAT DOTH APPAL	559	3	DON JUAN	16	120	6
CANT						
TILL AFTER CLOYING THE GAZETTES WITH CANT	21	2	DON JUAN	1	1	3
AND RECOLLECT THE TIME WHEN ALL THIS CANT	397	2	DON JUAN	4	98	7
CANTABS						
OF VERSE (THE NAME WITH WHICH WE CANTABS PLEASE	341	2	DON JUAN	3	110	7
CANTEMIR						
OF CANTEMIR OR KNOLLES WHERE FEW SHINE	495	2	DON JUAN	5	147	7
SO CANTEMIR CAN TELL YOU OR DETOTT	21	3	DON JUAN	6	31	5
CANTER						
I CANTER BY THE SPOT EACH AFTERNOON	400	2	DON JUAN	4	103	1
I THINK TO CANTER GENTLY THROUGH A HUNDRED	341	3	DON JUAN	12	55	8
CANTERBURY						
ON WITH THE HORSES OFF TO CANTERBURY	260	3	DON JUAN	10	71	1
THEY SAW AT CANTERBURY THE CATHEDRAL	261	3	DON JUAN	10	73	1
CANTO						
HERE ENDS THIS CANTO--NEED I SING OR SAY	126	2	DON JUAN	1	188	1

		PAGE	VOL	CANTO	STANZA	LN
CANTO	(CONTINUED)					
BESIDES IN CANTO TWELFTH I MEAN TO SHOW		140	2 DON JUAN	1	207	7
A CANTO--THEN THEIR FEET AND ANCLES--WELL		160	2 DON JUAN	2	6	6
PERHAPS IT MAY BE LINED WITH THIS MY CANTO		165	2 DON JUAN	2	16	9
EACH CANTO OF THE TWELVE OR TWENTY-FOUR		271	2 DON JUAN	2	216	5
OH--THE THIRD CANTO--AND THE PRETTY PAIR--		317	2 DON JUAN	3	81	6
IN ENGLAND A SIX CANTO QUARTO TALE		320	2 DON JUAN	3	86	2
(IN COPYING) THIS LONG CANTO INTO TWO		342	2 DON JUAN	3	111	3
HAD STOPP'D THIS CANTO AND DON JUAN'S BREATH		366	2 DON JUAN	4	42	2
(BECAUSE THIS CANTO HAS BECOME TOO LONG)		410	2 DON JUAN	4	117	3
LET THIS FIFTH CANTO MEET WITH DUE APPLAUSE		503	2 DON JUAN	5	159	5
THIS CANTO ERE MY MUSE PERCEIVES FATIGUE		109	3 DON JUAN	7	85	6
AS THE FIRST CANTO PROMISED YOU HAVE NOW		181	3 DON JUAN	8	138	2
IN THIS TWELFTH CANTO 'TIS MY WISH TO BE		325	3 DON JUAN	12	20	3
HERE THE TWELFTH CANTO OF OUR INTRODUCTION		356	3 DON JUAN	12	87	1
BUT MY BEST CANTO SAVE ONE ON ASTRONOMY		356	3 DON JUAN	12	88	7
TO THE NEXT CANTO WHERE PERHAPS I SHALL		453	3 DON JUAN	14	98	6
OUR HERO WAS IN CANTO THE SIXTEENTH		567	3 DON JUAN	17	12	1
CANTOS						
TO PASS THAN THOSE TWO CANTOS INTO FAMILIES		397	2 DON JUAN	4	97	8
AS THESE NEW CANTOS TOUCH ON WARLIKE FEATS		187	3 DON JUAN	9	10	1
BUT HOW SHALL I RELATE IN OTHER CANTOS		311	3 DON JUAN	11	87	1
THAT FROM THE FIRST OF CANTOS UP TO THIS		341	3 DON JUAN	12	54	3
CANTOS WOULD DO BUT AT APOLLO'S PLEADING		341	3 DON JUAN	12	55	6
TRADE WILL BE ALL THE BETTER FOR THESE CANTOS		416	3 DON JUAN	14	14	8
CANVAS						
NOR RAG OF CANVAS WHAT COULD THEY EXPECT		176	2 DON JUAN	2	39	4
NIMRODS WHOSE CANVAS SCARCE CONTAIN'D THE STEED		391	3 DON JUAN	13	70	6
ALONG THE CANVAS THEIR EYES GLANCE LIKE DREAMS		509	3 DON JUAN	16	19	4
CANVASS						
THEY FILL THE CANVASS UP--AND VERBUM SAT		463	3 DON JUAN	15	16	5
NOR CANVASS WHAT SO EMINENT A HAND MEANT		472	3 DON JUAN	15	38	6
CAP						
HIS CAP AND HEAD WHICH PROVES THE HEAD TO BE		116	3 DON JUAN	8	10	3
MORE THAN THE CAP IN FACT THE BALL COULD MEAN		117	3 DON JUAN	8	10	6
I HAVE SEEN CROWNS WORN INSTEAD OF A FOOL'S CAP--		310	3 DON JUAN	11	84	5
THERE WAS A COUNTRY GIRL IN A CLOSE CAP		530	3 DON JUAN	16	61	3
CAPABILITIES						
AND CAPABILITIES AS TO DISCOVER		424	2 DON JUAN	5	26	4
CAPABLE						
SHE WAS AS CAPABLE AS WOMAN CAN BE		450	3 DON JUAN	14	92	8
CAPACITY						
IF SUCH CAN E'ER BE DRAWN BY MAN'S CAPACITY		449	3 DON JUAN	14	90	6
CAP-A-PIE						
TWO BATTERIES CAP-A-PIE AS OUR SAINT GEORGE		72	3 DON JUAN	7	12	3
CAPE						
AND CLAP A WHITE CAPE ON THEIR MANTLES BLUE		94	2 DON JUAN	1	134	5
SOME HE DISPOSED OF OFF CAPE MATAPAN		284	2 DON JUAN	3	16	1
BUT NOW WAS NOT MUCH PLEASED WITH CAPE SIGAEUM		384	2 DON JUAN	4	75	8
CAPER						
AND MY INTERNAL SPIRIT CUT A CAPER		226	3 DON JUAN	10	3	4
CAPIENDUS						
ET HAUSTUS TER IN DIE CAPIENDUS		244	3 DON JUAN	10	41	8
CAPITAL						
WITH SLAVES TO SELL OFF IN THE CAPITAL		407	2 DON JUAN	4	113	2
THAT PLEASANT CAPITAL OF PAINTED SNOWS		203	3 DON JUAN	9	42	8
AND KONINGSBERG THE CAPITAL WHOSE VAUNT		254	3 DON JUAN	10	60	2
HIS TRAVELS TO THE CAPITAL APACE--		277	3 DON JUAN	11	18	4
CAPITULATION						
TO FRIGHTEN THEM INTO CAPITULATION		78	3 DON JUAN	7	24	6
CAPO						
HAD BROUGHT THE CAPO D'OPERA NOT FOR SALE		528	3 DON JUAN	16	57	7
CAPON'S						
BUT THIS I KNOW THAT THIS ROAST CAPON'S FAT		298	2 DON JUAN	3	45	3
CAPRICE						
AND NO GREAT MISCHIEF'S DONE BY THEIR CAPRICE		135	2 DON JUAN	1	199	6
IN WHAT WAY FEMININE CAPRICE MAY DISSIPATE		65	3 DON JUAN	6	119	8
NINE TIMES IN TEN 'TIS BUT CAPRICE OR FASHION		351	3 DON JUAN	12	77	3
CAPRICES						
JUDGE THEN IF HER CAPRICES E'ER STOOD STILL		475	2 DON JUAN	5	112	6
A LOVER WITH CAPRICES SOFT AND DEAR		438	3 DON JUAN	14	63	4
BUT NATURE'S NATURE AND HAS MORE CAPRICES		478	3 DON JUAN	15	52	7
AND MORALS OF THE COUNTRY FROM CAPRICES		531	3 DON JUAN	16	63	3
CAPRICIOUS						
LOVE'S A CAPRICIOUS POWER I'VE KNOWN IT HOLD		168	2 DON JUAN	2	22	1
AND AS MY MUSE IS A CAPRICIOUS ELF		384	2 DON JUAN	4	74	6
INTO GAZETTES BUT FAME (CAPRICIOUS STRUMPET)		74	3 DON JUAN	7	15	7
CAP'S						
THEIR FAVOUR IN AN AUTHOR'S CAP'S A FEATHER		135	2 DON JUAN	1	199	5
CAPS						
SOME LEATHERN CAPS AND WHAT REMAIN'D OF SHOES		195	2 DON JUAN	2	74	2
SOME WHO ONCE SET THEIR CAPS AT CAUTIOUS DUKES		308	3 DON JUAN	11	81	1
CAPSIZE						
BUT WHAT IF CARRYING SAIL CAPSIZE THE BOAT		191	3 DON JUAN	9	18	3
CAPTAIN						
IN HIS ROUGH EYES AND TOLD THE CAPTAIN HE		179	2 DON JUAN	2	43	2
AS CAPTAIN PARRY'S VOYAGE MAY DO TO JASON'S		419	3 DON JUAN	14	22	4
CAPTAINS						
A LIST OF SHIPS AND CAPTAINS AND KINGS REIGNING		135	2 DON JUAN	1	200	4
SHOULD CAPTAINS THE REMARK OR CRITICS MAKE		141	2 DON JUAN	1	208	7

	PAGE	VOL		CANTO	STANZA	LN
CAPTIVE						
SO JUAN WEPT AS WEPT THE CAPTIVE JEWS	165	2	DON JUAN	2	16	1
THOSE CAPTIVE SOOTHERS OF A CAPTIVE'S HOURS	54	3	DON JUAN	6	97	8
DON JUAN RAISED HIS LITTLE CAPTIVE FROM	158	3	DON JUAN	8	94	7
HIS LITTLE CAPTIVE GAINED HIM SOME APPLAUSE	182	3	DON JUAN	8	140	5
UPON THE CAPTIVE FREEDOM HE'S AS FAR	258	3	DON JUAN	10	68	6
CAPTIVE'S						
THOSE CAPTIVE SOOTHERS OF A CAPTIVE'S HOURS	54	3	DON JUAN	6	97	8
CAPTIVES						
HE SAW SOME FELLOW CAPTIVES WHO APPEAR'D	388	2	DON JUAN	4	80	1
THE CAPTIVES BACK TO THEIR SAD BERTHS EACH THREW	393	2	DON JUAN	4	90	4
THE CAPTIVES SEEMED TO MARK THEIR LOOKS AND AGE	424	2	DON JUAN	5	26	3
WITH HIS TWO CAPTIVES BY SO QUEER A ROAD	436	2	DON JUAN	5	45	3
ONE OR TWO STARED THE CAPTIVES IN THE FACE	441	2	DON JUAN	5	54	5
THERE CAPTIVES LED IN TRIUMPH DROOP THE EYE	461	2	DON JUAN	5	86	5
CAPTIVES JUST NOW ESCAPED WAS THE REPLY	97	3	DON JUAN	7	59	5
CAPTURE						
FIRST ISMAIL'S CAPTURE CAUGHT YOUR FANCY QUITE	215	3	DON JUAN	9	65	6
CAPTURES						
BY WINDS AND WAVES AND SOME IMPORTANT CAPTURES	283	2	DON JUAN	3	15	2
CARACTACUS						
STOOD LIKE CARACTACUS IN ACT TO RALLY	384	3	DON JUAN	13	56	3
CARAVAGGIO'S						
OR GLOOMY CARAVAGGIO'S GLOOMIER STAIN	392	3	DON JUAN	13	72	3
CARAVAN						
OR HEAVING WHELM THE HELPLESS CARAVAN	373	2	DON JUAN	4	55	7
OF THE LONG CARAVAN WHICH IN THE CHILL	49	3	DON JUAN	6	86	5
CARCASES						
LEAVING AS LADDERS THEIR HEAPED CARCASES	150	3	DON JUAN	8	76	6
AND CARCASES THAT LAY AS THICK AS THATCH	197	3	DON JUAN	9	29	4
CARCASSES						
THEY LAY LIKE CARCASSES AND HOPE WAS NONE	194	2	DON JUAN	2	72	3
CARD						
BUT SUCH A GODFATHER'S AS GOOD A CARD	76	3	DON JUAN	7	19	4
INTENTIONS WHICH FORM ALL MANKIND'S TRUMP CARD	123	3	DON JUAN	8	25	3
RECEIVED INSTRUCTIONS HOW TO PLAY HIS CARD	247	3	DON JUAN	10	46	6
CARDS						
THEN THERE WERE BILLIARDS CARDS TOO BUT NO DICE--	407	3	DON JUAN	13	106	1
I ASK IN TURN--WHY DO YOU PLAY AT CARDS	415	3	DON JUAN	14	11	3
MAY DROP IN WITHOUT CARDS AND TAKE THEIR STATION	534	3	DON JUAN	16	69	4
CARE						
OF SUCH AS THESE I SHOULD NOT CARE TO VAUNT	21	2	DON JUAN	1	1	5
FOR NATIVE SPANISH SHE HAD NO GREAT CARE	28	2	DON JUAN	1	13	5
WHICH WITH A LONG MINORITY AND CARE	42	2	DON JUAN	1	37	3
PERHAPS SHE DID NOT KNOW OR DID NOT CARE	59	2	DON JUAN	1	68	5
I CARE NOT FOR NEW PLEASURES AS THE OLD	85	2	DON JUAN	1	118	7
I WISH TO SLEEP AND BEG YOU WILL TAKE CARE	104	2	DON JUAN	1	153	5
FOR REPUTATIONS HE HAD LITTLE CARE	109	2	DON JUAN	1	160	4
IT SEEM'D AS IF THEY HAD EXCHANGED THEIR CARE	186	2	DON JUAN	2	56	3
AND SEEM'D AS IF THEY HAD NO FURTHER CARE	208	2	DON JUAN	2	98	4
ITS GENTLE TOUCH AND TREMBLING CARE A SIGH	215	2	DON JUAN	2	113	7
AND LIFTING HIM WITH CARE INTO THE CAVE	216	2	DON JUAN	2	115	1
THEY HAD NO FURTHER FEELING HOPE NOR CARE--	256	2	DON JUAN	2	189	V6
HOPE CARE NOR LOVE BEYOND HER HEART BEAT HERE	264	2	DON JUAN	2	202	8
HE MAY RESUME HIS AMATORY CARE	288	2	DON JUAN	3	24	5
HE IS NOR WHENCE HE CAME--AND LITTLE CARE	298	2	DON JUAN	3	45	2
THE VATES IRRITABILIS TAKES CARE	317	2	DON JUAN	3	81	2
AND WHEN A SCOUNDREL HAS IT--HE TAKES CARE	317	2	DON JUAN	3	81	V2
WHAT WAS IT MADE THEM THUS EXEMPT FROM CARE	353	2	DON JUAN	4	18	4
CALL'D SOCIAL HAUNTS OF HATE AND VICE AND CARE	358	2	DON JUAN	4	28	4
PROTECTS HIS TOMB BUT GREATER CARE IS PAID	400	2	DON JUAN	4	104	V3
AN OPEN BROW A LITTLE MARKED WITH CARE	416	2	DON JUAN	5	11	5
THE EUNUCH HAVING EYED THEM O'ER WITH CARE	425	2	DON JUAN	5	28	1
MORE CIRCUMSTANCES VAIN WAS EVERY CARE	429	2	DON JUAN	5	34	6
WHAT YOU MAY BE I NEITHER KNOW NOR CARE	454	2	DON JUAN	5	74	1
THERE MIGHT ARISE SOME POUTING PETTY CARE	480	2	DON JUAN	5	119	6
AUGHT SAVE SOME LITTLE POUTING PETTY CARE	480	2	DON JUAN	5	119	V5
AND I OF YOUR YOUNG CHARGE WILL TAKE DUE CARE	29	3	DON JUAN	6	47	6
WITH COST AND CARE AND WARMTH INDUCED TO SHOOT	38	3	DON JUAN	6	65	4
BY THE NORTH POLE--THEY SOUGHT HER CAUSE OF CARE	42	3	DON JUAN	6	72	6
ENQUIRIES AFTER THEM WITH KINDEST CARE	64	3	DON JUAN	6	118	6
THEIR HASTE OR WASTE I NEITHER KNOW NOR CARE	80	3	DON JUAN	7	27	2
NOR CARE A PINCH OF SNUFF ABOUT HIS CORPS)--	127	3	DON JUAN	8	31	8
NOR CARE A SINGLE DAMN ABOUT HIS CORPS	127	3	DON JUAN	8	31	V8
OF CARE OR GAIN THE GREEN WOODS WERE THEIR PORTIONS	145	3	DON JUAN	8	66	4
WE DON'T MUCH CARE WITH WHOM WE MAY ENGAGE	217	3	DON JUAN	9	69	3
OUR YOUNG LIEUTENANT TO THE GENIAL CARE	224	3	DON JUAN	9	84	2
I CARE NOT--'TIS A GLIMPSE OF AULD LANG SYNE	233	3	DON JUAN	10	18	8
CARE LIKE A HOUSE-KEEPER BRINGS EVERY WEEK	243	3	DON JUAN	10	38	5
MUST STEER WITH CARE THROUGH ALL THAT GLITTERING SEA	303	3	DON JUAN	11	70	3
LET HIM TAKE CARE THAT THAT WHICH HE PURSUES	304	3	DON JUAN	11	71	3
MY MUSES DO NOT CARE A PINCH OF ROSIN	341	3	DON JUAN	12	55	1
AND CARE BUT FOR DISCOVERIES AND NOT DEEDS	352	3	DON JUAN	12	80	4
TAKE CARE WHAT YOU REPLY TO SUCH A LETTER	407	3	DON JUAN	13	105	8
SOME HEART-ACHES HAD BEEN SPARED ME YET I CARE NOT--	431	3	DON JUAN	14	49	2
WITH NO GREAT CARE FOR WHAT IS NICKNAMED GLORY	464	3	DON JUAN	15	19	3
CHILD TO THE CARE OF GUARDIANS GOOD AND KIND	475	3	DON JUAN	15	44	2
I WRITE THE WORLD NOR CARE IF THE WORLD READ	482	3	DON JUAN	15	60	3
CARED						
SO THERE WERE QUARRELS CARED NOT FOR THE CAUSE	109	2	DON JUAN	1	159	7

CARED   (CONTINUED)
    LITTLE CARED THEY FOR MAHOMET OR MUFTI 75   3 DON JUAN 7   17   5
    AND CARED AS LITTLE FOR HIS ARMY'S LOSS 105   3 DON JUAN 7   77   5
    HE KNEW NOT WHERE HE WAS NOR GREATLY CARED 129   3 DON JUAN 8   33   1
    JUAN WHO CARED NOT A TOBACCO-STOPPER 254   3 DON JUAN 10   60   5
    CARED MOST ABOUT IT NEED NOT NOW BE PLEADED-- 324   3 DON JUAN 12   17   5
    PROFIT HE CARED NOT FOR LET OTHERS REAP IT 536   3 DON JUAN 16   75   4
CAREEN
    WITH ORDERS TO THE PEOPLE TO CAREEN 286   2 DON JUAN 3   20   6
CAREER
    HIS VAIN AMBITION IN ITS VAGUE CAREER 152   2 DON JUAN 1 V 3   4
    WARRIOR FROM WARRIOR IN THEIR GRIM CAREER 125   3 DON JUAN 8   27   2
    SPARED NEITHER SEX NOR AGE IN THEIR CAREER 171   3 DON JUAN 8   119   2
    AS THE SMART BOYS SPURRED FAST IN THEIR CAREER . . . 263   3 DON JUAN 10   77   3
    'TIS TRUE THAT THY CAREER IS NOT A NEW ONE 326   3 DON JUAN 12   23   5
    GOD HELP US SINCE WE HAVE NEED ON OUR CAREER 496   3 DON JUAN 15   90   3
CAREFUL
    THE WATCHFUL MOTHERS AND THE CAREFUL SISTERS 331   3 DON JUAN 12   32   3
    FROM THESE THEY WILL BE CAREFUL TO SELECT 471   3 DON JUAN 15   34   1
CARELESS
    HE WAS A MORTAL OF THE CARELESS KIND   31   2 DON JUAN 1   19   1
    ON ITS OWN STRENGTH WITH CARELESS NERVES AND THEWS-- . 131   3 DON JUAN 8   36   6
    JUAN THOUGH CARELESS YOUNG AND MAGNIFIQUE 259   3 DON JUAN 10   70   1
    OR CARELESS BUT THE EFFORT WAS NOT VALID 515   3 DON JUAN 16   35   7
    FAIR ADELINE THOUGH IN A CARELESS WAY 521   3 DON JUAN 16   42   1
CARELESSLY
    A CHILD OF NATURE CARELESSLY ARRAYED   36   3 DON JUAN 6   60   3
    AS CARELESSLY AS HURLS THE MOTH HER WING 170   3 DON JUAN 8   118   3
    THAN MY FORERUNNERS CARELESSLY I SING 181   3 DON JUAN 8   138   7
CARES
    NOT HAVING OF MY OWN DOMESTIC CARES 33   2 DON JUAN 1   23   8
    SOME RUN AWAY AND BUT EXCHANGE THEIR CARES 263   2 DON JUAN 2   201   3
    FOR NO ONE CARES FOR MATRIMONIAL CODINGS 279   2 DON JUAN 3   8   5
    CONTINUED STILL HER HOSPITABLE CARES 285   2 DON JUAN 3   19   5
    WERE ONCE HER CARES HOW IDLE SEEM'D THEY NOW) 362   2 DON JUAN 4   34   4
    I KNOW NOT IF HE HAD DOMESTIC CARES-- 496   2 DON JUAN 5   148   5
    THE SOUL OUT (LIKE THE STONE) WITH PETTY CARES . . . 16   3 DON JUAN 6   20   8
    WHILE THE POOR RICH WRETCH OBJECT OF THESE CARES . . 331   3 DON JUAN 12   33   7
CARESS'D
    CARESS'D HIM OFTEN SUCH A THING MIGHT BE 59   2 DON JUAN 1   69   2
CARESSES
    OF HEADS THAN THEIR CARESSES OF THE HEART 13   3 DON JUAN 6   14   8
CAREST
    TO SEE IT--THE KING HISSED AND THEN CAREST 309   3 DON JUAN 11   83   7
CARGO
    TO GET UP PART OF THE CARGO AND WHAT NOT 171   2 DON JUAN 2   28   3
    SHE HAD A CURIOUS CREW AS WELL AS CARGO 191   2 DON JUAN 2   66   7
    HER CARGO FROM THE PLAGUE BEING SAFE AND SOUND . . . 407   2 DON JUAN 4   113   5
    THE FILLING UP THEIR WHOLE CONNUBIAL CARGO-- 51   3 DON JUAN 6   90   7
CARGOES
    THE CARGOES HE CONFISCATED AND GAIN 223   2 DON JUAN 2   126   5
CARLESSLY
    ONE HAND ON JUAN'S CARLESSLY WAS THROWN 80   2 DON JUAN 1   109   7
CARLO
    THERE ROSE A CARLO DOLCE OR A TITIAN 392   3 DON JUAN 13   71   3
CARLTON
    WITH CARLTON OR WITH OTHER HOUSES TRY 266   3 DON JUAN 10   85   3
    WHEELS WHIRL FROM CARLTON PALACE TO SOHO 378   3 DON JUAN 13   44   3
CARNAGE
    AND THUS FOR WIDER CARNAGE TAUGHT TO PANT 16   2 DON JUAN D   12   3
    RECORDS RAVENNA'S CARNAGE ON ITS FACE 400   2 DON JUAN 4   103   7
    CARNAGE (SO WORDSWORTH TELLS YOU) IS GOD'S DAUGHTER 116   3 DON JUAN 8   9   6
    OF CARNAGE LIKE THE NILE'S SUN-SODDEN SLIME 152   3 DON JUAN 8   82   7
    OF CARNAGE WHEN THIS OLD MAN WAS PIERCED THROUGH . . 171   3 DON JUAN 8   119   3
    OF CARNAGE--AND I THINK HE WAS MORE GLAD IN HER . . 182   3 DON JUAN 8   140   7
    OF CARNAGE--AND HER FAIR AND INFANT GRACE 182   3 DON JUAN 8   140 V7
CARNAL
    THOUGH BEAUTIFUL IN YOUTH HIS CARNAL SKIN-- 188   3 DON JUAN 9   12 V7
CARNATION
    AND JUAN GREW CARNATION WITH VEXATION 545   3 DON JUAN 16   93   3
CARNIVAL
    LAST CARNIVAL SHE MADE A DEAL OF STRIFE 389   2 DON JUAN 4   83   6
    SHE TOO WAS FORTUNATE LAST CARNIVAL 390   2 DON JUAN 4   84   4
CARNIVOROUS
    BUT MAN IS A CARNIVOROUS PRODUCTION 191   2 DON JUAN 2   67   1
CAROLINES
    WHERE ARE THE LADY CAROLINES AND FRANCESES 308   3 DON JUAN 11   80   1
CAROTID-ARTERY-CUTTING
    CAROTID-ARTERY-CUTTING CASTLEREAGH-- 254   3 DON JUAN 10   59   4
CAROUSE
    HAVE PUBLIC DAYS WHEN ALL MEN MAY CAROUSE 534   3 DON JUAN 16   68   7
CARP
    WITH WHICH I STILL CAN HARP AND CARP AND FIDDLE . . 181   3 DON JUAN 8   139   1
    AT LONGBOW'S PHRASES YOU MIGHT SOMETIMES CARP . . . 402   3 DON JUAN 13   93   6
CARPE
    BUT CARPE DIEM JUAN CARPE CARPE 310   3 DON JUAN 11   86   1
    BUT CARPE DIEM JUAN CARPE CARPE 310   3 DON JUAN 11   86   1
    BUT CARPE DIEM JUAN CARPE CARPE 310   3 DON JUAN 11   86   1
CARPENTER
    THEN CAME THE CARPENTER AT LAST WITH TEARS 179   2 DON JUAN 2   43   1

115

CARPET
 TOBACCO ON A LITTLE CARPET--TROY . . . . 172 3 DON JUAN 8 121 3
 FOR A SPOILT CARPET--BUT THE ATTIC BEE . . . . . . 522 3 DON JUAN 16 43 7
CARPETED
 HAIDEE AND JUAN CARPETED THEIR FEET . . . . 309 2 DON JUAN 3 67 1
CARPETS
 AND PERSIAN CARPETS WHICH THE HEART BLED TO STAIN . . . 310 2 DON JUAN 3 68 3
 SO COSTLY WERE THEY CARPETS EVERY STITCH . . . . . . 449 2 DON JUAN 5 65 6
CARRIAGE
 FORGOT WITH HIM HER VERY PRUDENT CARRIAGE . . . . . 58 2 DON JUAN 1 66 8
 UPON THE WHOLE HIS CARRIAGE WAS SERENE . . . . . . 415 2 DON JUAN 5 9 2
 (A CURSED SORT OF CARRIAGE WITHOUT SPRINGS . . . . . 197 3 DON JUAN 9 30 2
 WALKED ON BEHIND HIS CARRIAGE O'ER THE SUMMIT . . . . 272 3 DON JUAN 11 9 2
 BEHIND HIS CARRIAGE AND LIKE HANDY LADS . . . . . . 273 3 DON JUAN 11 11 3
 BUT JUAN NOW IS STEPPING FROM HIS CARRIAGE . . . . . 282 3 DON JUAN 11 30 8
 IT ADDS AN OUTWARD GRACE UNTO THEIR CARRIAGE-- . . . 344 3 DON JUAN 12 62 6
 NODDING BESIDE MY LADY IN HIS CARRIAGE . . . . . . 379 3 DON JUAN 13 46 2
 EACH CARRIAGE WAS ANNOUNCED AND LADIES ROSE . . . . . 549 3 DON JUAN 16 101 3
CARRIAGES
 BEHIND THEIR CARRIAGES THEIR NEW PORTMANTEAU . . . . 165 2 DON JUAN 2 16 7
 THROUGH CROWDS AND CARRIAGES BUT WAXING THINNER . . . 282 3 DON JUAN 11 29 2
 BROKEN IN CARRIAGES AND ALL THE PHANTASIES . . . . . 308 3 DON JUAN 11 80 5
CARRIED
 WITHOUT THEIR WILL THEY CARRIED THEM AWAY . . . . . 177 2 DON JUAN 2 40 2
 THAT CARRIED OFF HIS NEIGHBOUR BY THE THIGH . . . . . 212 2 DON JUAN 2 106 4
 THEY KNEW NOT WHERE BEING CARRIED BY THE STREAM . . . 148 3 DON JUAN 8 72 2
 WHEN MATTERS MUST BE CARRIED BY THE TOUCH . . . . . 151 3 DON JUAN 8 78 5
 FOR MORALS MARRIAGE AND THIS QUESTION CARRIED . . . . 469 3 DON JUAN 15 29 7
 AND THEN HE HAD GOOD LOOKS--THAT POINT WAS CARRIED . . 493 3 DON JUAN 15 84 1
CARRION
 FLOCK O'ER THEIR CARRION JUST LIKE MEN BELOW . . . . 358 2 DON JUAN 4 28 8
CARRY
 AND CARRY PRECEPT TO THE HIGHEST PITCH . . . . . . 138 2 DON JUAN 1 204 6
 AND CARRY AWAY PERHAPS A MAST OR SO . . . . 170 2 DON JUAN 2 26 8
 AND CARRY THEM TO SHORE THESE HOPES WERE FINE . . . . 192 2 DON JUAN 2 69 6
 NOT AS OF YORE TO CARRY OFF AN IO . . . . 248 2 DON JUAN 2 174 7
 MIGHT CARRY OUT TO COLCHIS IN OLD DAYS . . . . . . 303 2 DON JUAN 3 55 V4
 NAY QUOTH THE MAID THE SULTAN'S SELF SHAN'T CARRY ME . 460 2 DON JUAN 5 84 7
 COULD HARDLY CARRY ANYTHING AWAY . . . . 465 2 DON JUAN 5 93 5
 ARE APT TO CARRY THINGS WITH A HIGH HAND . . . . . . 11 3 DON JUAN 6 11 3
 BY BIDDING OTHERS CARRY WHILE THEY RIDE . . . . . . 367 3 DON JUAN 13 19 8
CARRYING
 BY CARRYING OFF COUNT CESARE CICOGNA . . . . 389 2 DON JUAN 4 83 7
 BUT WHAT IF CARRYING SAIL CAPSIZE THE BOAT . . . . . 191 3 DON JUAN 9 18 3
CARS
 BENEATH HIS CARS OF CERES GROAN THE ROADS . . . . . 320 3 DON JUAN 12 9 4
CARTE
 RESOLVED TO THRUST THE MYSTERY CARTE AND TIERCE . . . 559 3 DON JUAN 16 119 5
CARTHAGE
 ROME BABYLON TYRE CARTHAGE NINEVEH . . . . 142 3 DON JUAN 8 60 5
 FOR FAME'S A CARTHAGE NOT SO SOON REBUILT . . . . . 352 3 DON JUAN 12 78 8
CARTRIDGES
 YOU SHOULD BUT GIVE FEW CARTRIDGES TO SUCH . . . . . 151 3 DON JUAN 8 78 3
 BUT OH YE MODERN HEROES WITH YOUR CARTRIDGES . . . . 485 3 DON JUAN 15 67 7
CARVED
 OF GILDED BRONZE AND CARVED IN CURIOUS GUISE . . . . 461 2 DON JUAN 5 86 2
 WITH A CARVED LADY ON A MONUMENT . . . . 40 3 DON JUAN 6 68 8
 ALL CARVED AND GILDED OR--AS IT WILL TELL . . . . . 339 3 DON JUAN 12 51 V7
CARVING
 FULL OF BARBARIC CARVING PAINT AND GILDING . . . . . 223 2 DON JUAN 2 127 8
CARVINGS
 SYMMETRICAL BUT DECK'D WITH CARVINGS QUAINT-- . . . . 389 3 DON JUAN 13 65 2
CASCADE
 ITS OUTLET DASH'D INTO A STEEP CASCADE . . . . . . 385 3 DON JUAN 13 58 1
 AND HE STOOD GAZING OUT ON THE CASCADE . . . . . . 507 3 DON JUAN 16 15 7
CASE
 LAST--YOURS HAS LATELY BEEN A COMMON CASE-- . . . . 9 2 DON JUAN D 1 4
 THE HEARERS OF HER CASE BECAME REPEATERS . . . . . . 36 2 DON JUAN 1 28 6
 IN CASE OUR LORD THE KING SHOULD GO TO WAR AGAIN . . . 42 2 DON JUAN 1 38 6
 AND PITYING SORE HIS MUTILATED CASE . . . . 46 2 DON JUAN 1 44 6
 AS BEING THE BEST JUDGE OF A LADY'S CASE . . . . . . 62 2 DON JUAN 1 75 8
 THINKING GOD MIGHT NOT UNDERSTAND HER CASE . . . . . 62 2 DON JUAN 1 75 V8
 OF HIS OWN CASE AND NEVER HIT THE TRUE ONE . . . . . 68 2 DON JUAN 1 86 3
 THE LAST INDEED'S INFALLIBLY THE CASE . . . . 74 2 DON JUAN 1 99 6
 IN CASE HE THOUGHT HIS WIFE TOO GREAT A PRIZE . . . . 75 2 DON JUAN 1 101 8
 PEOPLE SHOULD HOLD THEIR TONGUES IN ANY CASE . . . . 77 2 DON JUAN 1 105 4
 AN AWKWARD LOOK AS HE REVOLVED THE CASE . . . . . . 111 2 DON JUAN 1 164 7
 IN ANY CASE ATTEMPTING A REPLY . . . . 119 2 DON JUAN 1 179 3
 IN JUAN'S CASE WERE BUT EMPLOY'D IN VAIN . . . . . . 157 2 DON JUAN 2 1 6
 OF EYES WERE CRYING FOR THEIR OWNER'S CASE . . . . . 186 2 DON JUAN 2 56 6
 THEY DID THEIR BEST TO MODIFY THEIR CASE . . . . . . 189 2 DON JUAN 2 63 3
 BUT IN THIS CASE I ALSO MUST REMARK . . . . 206 2 DON JUAN 2 95 1
 BUT WITH OUR DAMSEL THIS WAS NOT THE CASE . . . . . 220 2 DON JUAN 2 121 1
 AND WARM IN CASE BY CHANCE HE SHOULD AWAKE . . . . . 226 2 DON JUAN 2 133 4
 RATHER BY DEEDS THAN WORDS BECAUSE THE CASE . . . . . 240 2 DON JUAN 2 159 2
 AS WAS THE CASE AT LEAST WHERE I HAVE BEEN . . . . . 242 2 DON JUAN 2 164 4
 IT IS A HARD ALTHOUGH A COMMON CASE . . . . 305 2 DON JUAN 3 59 1
 JUAN WAS TOLD ABOUT THEIR CURIOUS CASE . . . . . . 388 2 DON JUAN 4 81 4
 THAT THERE HAD BEEN A LADY IN THE CASE . . . . . . 420 2 DON JUAN 5 19 4

PAGE VOL   CANTO STANZA LN

CASE   (CONTINUED)
I WISH THE CASE COULD COME BEFORE A JURY HERE 446   2 DON JUAN   5   61   8
TO GENTLEMEN IN ANY SUCH LIKE CASE 482   2 DON JUAN   5   123   2
OF A YOUNG DOWNRIGHT BEAUTY IN THIS CASE 486   2 DON JUAN   5   130   8
IN CASE OF ANY PREMATURE DISCLOSURE 62   3 DON JUAN   6   114   8
THIS BEING THE CASE MAY SHOW US WHAT FAME IS 82   3 DON JUAN   7   33   1
THE HOUR AS IS THE CASE WITH LIVELY BRAINS 129   3 DON JUAN   8   33   4
IN CITIES CAGED THE PRESENT CASE IN POINT I 143   3 DON JUAN   8   62   7
ON CITIES AS HATH BEEN THE PRESENT CASE) 160   3 DON JUAN   8   97   4
QUARTER IN CASE HE BADE THEM NOT AROINT 170   3 DON JUAN   8   117   3
IN ALL THE CIRCUMSTANCES OF THE CASE 277   3 DON JUAN 11   18   2
THEY KNOW NOT HOW) THE ONE HALF THE PRESENT CASE . . . 314   3 DON JUAN 11 V 75   7
FIRST SAVE IN CASE OF PIGEONS--HOW THE GROVE 322   3 DON JUAN 12   13 V5
AND BETWEEN PITY FOR HER CASE AND YOURS 343   3 DON JUAN 12   60   7
POOR THING EVE'S WAS A TRIFLING CASE TO HER'S 345   3 DON JUAN 12   64   8
OR SEPARATE MAINTENANCE IN CASE 'TWAS DOOM'D-- 473   3 DON JUAN 15   39   3
BOTH IN THE CASE OF LOVER AND OF FRIEND 491   3 DON JUAN 15   79   4
A CASE WHICH TO THE JURIES WE MAY LEAVE 493   3 DON JUAN 15   84   4
TO STATE THE CASE IT MIGHT BE TA'EN FOR GRANTED . . . 514   3 DON JUAN 16   33   7
CASE-MATED
CASE-MATED ONE AND T'OTHER A BARBETTE 72   3 DON JUAN   7   12   4
CASEMENT
RAMPART WALL CASEMENT HOUSE--FOR THERE WAS NOT 131   3 DON JUAN   8   37   3
CASEMENT'S
GLEAMED FORTH AS THROUGH THE CASEMENT'S IVY SHROUD . . . 560   3 DON JUAN 16   121   7
CASES
A HINT IN TENDER CASES IS ENOUGH 119   2 DON JUAN   1   178   1
COMMON IN MANY CASES WAS IN THIS 79   3 DON JUAN   7   25   3
BECAUSE MY CASES PUT HIS LORDSHIP TO'T-- 357   3 DON JUAN 12 V 18   5
CASH
FOR AN ESTATE OR CASH OR COUNTRY-SEAT 89   2 DON JUAN   1   125   5
IN MY YOUNG DAYS THEY LENT ME CASH THAT WAY 190   2 DON JUAN   2   65   7
HEAVEN KNOWS WHAT CASH HE GOT OR BLOOD HE SPILT . . . 223   2 DON JUAN   2   127   5
LET NOT HIS MODE OF RAISING CASH SEEM STRANGE 283   2 DON JUAN   3   14   1
THE MOST BY READY CASH--BUT ALL HAVE PRICES 425   2 DON JUAN   5   27   7
WHICH LEAVES YOU MINUS OF THE CASH YOU COUNTED 16   3 DON JUAN   6   21   6
FOR CASH AND CONQUEST AS IF FROM A CUSHION 99   3 DON JUAN   7   64   4
AND RICH IN RUBLES DIAMONDS CASH AND CREDIT 259   3 DON JUAN 10   70   2
THEIR CASH TO SHOW HOW MUCH THEY HAVE A YEAR 273   3 DON JUAN 11   10   4
THEIR CASH COMES FROM THEIR WEALTH GOES TO A JEW . . . 306   3 DON JUAN 11   75   4
BUT IF LOVE DON'T CASH DOES AND CASH ALONE 322   3 DON JUAN 12   14   1
BUT IF LOVE DON'T CASH DOES AND CASH ALONE 322   3 DON JUAN 12   14   1
CASH RULES THE GROVE AND FELLS IT TOO BESIDES 322   3 DON JUAN 12   14   2
WITHOUT CASH CAMPS WERE THIN AND COURTS WERE NONE . . . 322   3 DON JUAN 12   14   3
WITHOUT CASH MALTHUS TELLS YOU TAKE NO BRIDES 322   3 DON JUAN 12   14   4
SO CASH RULES LOVE THE RULER ON HIS OWN 322   3 DON JUAN 12   14   5
ALAS TO THEM OF READY CASH BEREFT 379   3 DON JUAN 13   45   3
BUT OH AMBROSIAL CASH AH WHO WOULD LOSE THEE 405   3 DON JUAN 13   100   7
CASHMIRE
A SHAWL WHOSE FOLDS IN CASHMIRE HAD BEEN NURST 451   2 DON JUAN   5   68   6
CASK
FOR GROG AND SOMETIMES DRINK RUM FROM THE CASK 173   2 DON JUAN   2   33   8
WATER A TWENTY GALLON CASK OR SO 181   2 DON JUAN   2   47   3
CASKETS
YE BEAUTIFUL ROULEAUS YE IRON CASKETS 321   3 DON JUAN 12   12 V1
CASKS
TWO CASKS OF BISCUIT AND A KEG OF BUTTER 180   2 DON JUAN   2   46   7
AND ALSO FOR THE BISCUIT CASKS AND BUTTER 188   2 DON JUAN   2   61   8
CASQUE
ENDS IN A RUSTY CASQUE AND DUBIOUS BONE 261   3 DON JUAN 10   73   6
THE CASQUE WHICH NEVER STOOPED EXCEPT TO TIME 261   3 DON JUAN 10   74   3
CASSANDRA
THAN WHOM CASSANDRA WAS NOT MORE PROPHETIC 372   2 DON JUAN   4   52   3
CASSIMERE
OF YELLOW CASSIMERE WE MAY PRESUME 204   3 DON JUAN   9   43   6
CASSIO
I AM NOT LIKE CASSIO AN ARITHMETICIAN 10   3 DON JUAN   6   9   1
BUT HEAVEN AS CASSIO SAYS IS ABOVE ALL-- 192   3 DON JUAN   9   19   1
CAST
WHERE JURIES CAST UP WHAT A WIFE IS WORTH 57   2 DON JUAN   1   64   5
THEIR LOOKS CAST DOWN THEIR GREETINGS ALMOST DUMB . . . 60   2 DON JUAN   1   70   3
HE CAST A RUEFUL LOOK OR TWO AND DID 111   2 DON JUAN   1   163   7
AND CAST THEIR LANGUID EYES DOWN AND LET LOOSE 119   2 DON JUAN   1   179   6
THESE I COULD BEAR BUT CANNOT CAST ASIDE 132   2 DON JUAN   1   195   5
I CAST THEE ON THE WATERS GO THY WAYS 149   2 DON JUAN   1   222   2
AND ALL THINGS FOR A CHANCE HAD BEEN CAST LOOSE . . . 183   2 DON JUAN   2   51   2
'TWAS BORNE BY THE RUDE WAVE WHEREIN 'TWAS CAST . . . 204   2 DON JUAN   2   90   6
MATERIALS AS WERE CAST UP ROUND THE BAY 226   2 DON JUAN   2   132   3
HE WAS HER OWN HER OCEAN-TREASURE CAST 247   2 DON JUAN   2   173   7
AND NOW AND THEN HER EYE TO HEAVEN IS CAST 260   2 DON JUAN   2   195   5
CAST BY CANOVA OR DESCRIBED BY BURKE 315   2 DON JUAN   3   76 V8
THE VERY INSTANT TILL THE CHANGE THAT CAST 381   2 DON JUAN   4   69   5
WITH WHOM IT IS OUR LUCK TO CAST OUR LOT 417   2 DON JUAN   5   13   4
JUST AS MY GREAT COAT WAS ABOUT ME CAST 428   2 DON JUAN   5   33   3
IN SUCH SORT THAT THE EYE ALONG IT CAST 465   2 DON JUAN   5   93   4
PASSION AND POWER A GLANCE ON HIM SHE CAST 478   2 DON JUAN   5   116   6
HIS HIGHNESS CAST AROUND HIS GREAT BLACK EYES 500   2 DON JUAN   5   155   1
A SLIGHT EXAMPLE JUST TO CAST A SHADE 22   3 DON JUAN   6   32   5
OF COSSACQUES AND THEIR PREY TURNED ROUND AND CAST . . 97   3 DON JUAN   7   59   2

PAGE VOL CANTO STANZA LN

CAST   (CONTINUED)
    HAD NOT COME UP IN TIME TO CAST AN AWE . . . . 137 3 DON JUAN 8   49   3
    OF HIS OPINION WHEN I SEE CAST DOWN . . . . 142 3 DON JUAN 8   60   4
    PAUSED FOR A MOMENT FROM THE FIGHT AND CAST . . . . . 169 3 DON JUAN 8   116   7
    FOR A NEW FLAME A THOUGHT TO CAST OF GLOOM ENOUGH . . . . 206 3 DON JUAN 9   48   5
    AS THEY BEHELD THE YOUNGER CAST SOME LEERS . . . . . 221 3 DON JUAN 9   78   4
    THAN THE MORE GLOWING DAMES WHOSE LOT IS CAST . . . . 347 3 DON JUAN 12   69   3
    AND WHAT I WRITE I CAST UPON THE STREAM . . . . . . 415 3 DON JUAN 14   11   7
    BUT SPECULATING AS I CAST MINE EYE . . . . 464 3 DON JUAN 15   19   4
    AND SHE WITHDREW BUT CAST NOT DOWN HER EYE . . . . . 545 3 DON JUAN 16   94   4
    AND USUAL--JUAN WHEN HE CAST A GLANCE . . . . 546 3 DON JUAN 16   96   2
CASTALIAN
    PROSCRIBED FROM TASTING YOUR CASTALIAN TEA . . . . . 403 2 DON JUAN 4   108   8
CASTANETS
    GUITARS AND CASTANETS FROM ALICANT . . . . 284 2 DON JUAN 3   17   6
CASTE
    THEY LOSE THEIR CASTE AT ONCE AS DO THE PARIAS . . . . 352 3 DON JUAN 12   78   2
    OF HIGHEST CASTE--THE BRAHMINS OF THE TON . . . . . 397 3 DON JUAN 13   83   4
CASTELLATED
    UNTIL HE REACHED THE CASTELLATED RHINE-- . . . . . . 255 3 DON JUAN 10   61   2
CASTILE
    (HIS SIRE WAS OF CASTILE HIS DAM FROM ARRAGON) . . . . 42 2 DON JUAN 1   38   4
CASTILIAN
    THE BLOOD OF ALL HIS LINE'S CASTILIAN LORDS . . . . . 471 2 DON JUAN 5   104   3
    AND WHICH WAS SOFTEST RUSSIAN OR CASTILIAN . . . . . 294 3 DON JUAN 11   50   7
CASTING
    AND IF I HAD TO GIVE A CASTING VOICE . . . . 357 2 DON JUAN 4   25   5
CASTLEREAGH
    THE INTELLECTUAL EUNUCH CASTLEREAGH . . . . 15 2 DON JUAN D   11   8
    SO GOOD--I WONDER CASTLEREAGH DON'T TAX 'EM . . . . . 264 2 DON JUAN 2   203   8
    OR ALL THE FIGURES CASTLEREAGH ABUSES . . . . 493 2 DON JUAN 5   143   5
    MEANTIME THE TAXES CASTLEREAGH AND DEBT . . . . . . 174 3 DON JUAN 8   125   5
    OF BLOOD AND WATER LEADEN CASTLEREAGH . . . . 207 3 DON JUAN 9   50   6
    CAROTID-ARTERY-CUTTING CASTLEREAGH-- . . . . 254 3 DON JUAN 10   59   4
    THE LAST EXPIRED IN CUT THROAT CASTLEREAGH . . . . . 254 3 DON JUAN 10   59 V4
    WHERE LITTLE CASTLEREAGH THE DEVIL CAN TELL . . . . . 307 3 DON JUAN 11   77   2
CAST-OFF
    AND ASKING NOW AND THEN FOR CAST-OFF DRESSES . . . . 252 2 DON JUAN 2   182   8
CASTS
    CASTS OFF ITS BRIGHT SKIN YEARLY LIKE THE SNAKE . . . 421 2 DON JUAN 5   21   8
CASUALLY
    AND HAVING CASUALLY GLANCED IT THROUGH . . . . . . 440 3 DON JUAN 14   69   6
CASUIST
    BUT JUAN WAS NO CASUIST NOR HAD PONDERED . . . . . . 353 3 DON JUAN 12   81   1
CASUISTS
    SOME KINDER CASUISTS ARE PLEASED TO SAY . . . . . . 336 2 DON JUAN 3   104   1
    AND 'TWILL PERPLEX THE CASUISTS IN MORALITY . . . . . 448 3 DON JUAN 14   89   7
CAT
    BUT LIKE CONVEYING TO THE CAT THE MOUSE . . . . . . 225 2 DON JUAN 2   130   3
    TWO PARROTS WITH A PERSIAN CAT AND KITTENS . . . . . 285 2 DON JUAN 3   18   2
    YE POWERS IT IS THE--THE--THE--POOH THE CAT . . . . . 556 3 DON JUAN 16   112   3
CATALOGUE
    BY HOMER'S CATALOGUE OF SHIPS IS CLEAR . . . . . . 393 3 DON JUAN 13   74   6
    NOW IT SO HAPPEN'D IN THE CATALOGUE . . . . 477 3 DON JUAN 15   48   1
CATCH
    WHICH PAINTERS CANNOT CATCH LIKE FACES SINNING . . . . 32 3 DON JUAN 6   52   4
    THOSE WHO CATCH COLD IN SHADOWS OF DEATH'S VALLEY . . . 131 3 DON JUAN 8   36   8
    WHICH PASSED OR CATCH THE FIRST GLIMPSE OF THE CLIFFS . . 256 3 DON JUAN 10   64   8
    AND CAUGHT THEM--WHAT DO THEY NOT CATCH METHINKS . . . 364 3 DON JUAN 13   12   7
    TO CATCH A GLIMPSE EVEN OF A PRETTY PEASANT . . . . . 422 3 DON JUAN 14   28   8
    GREAT THOUGHTS WE CATCH FROM THENCE (BESIDES A COLD . . 506 3 DON JUAN 16   14   4
CATCHES
    AND SEVERAL WHO SUNG FEWER PSALMS THAN CATCHES . . . . 539 3 DON JUAN 16   80   8
CATECHISM
    HIM UP TO LEARN HIS CATECHISM ALONE . . . . 50 2 DON JUAN 1   52   6
    TO THIS LONG CATECHISM OF QUESTIONS ASKED . . . . . 56 3 DON JUAN 6   100   2
CATERING
    THAN HUMAN INSECTS CATERING FOR SPIDERS . . . . . . 196 3 DON JUAN 9   27   8
CATERS
    WITH WHICH THIS MORALEST OF CITIES CATERS . . . . . 313 3 DON JUAN 11 V 29   4
CATHAY
    FROM CEYLON INDE OR FAR CATHAY UNLOADS . . . . . . 320 3 DON JUAN 12   9   2
CATHEDRAL
    THEY SAW AT CANTERBURY THE CATHEDRAL . . . . 261 3 DON JUAN 10   73   1
CATHERINE
    HAD CATHERINE AND THE SULTAN UNDERSTOOD . . . . . . 53 3 DON JUAN 6   95   1
    THE ARMIES OF THE CHRISTIAN EMPRESS CATHERINE . . . . 99 3 DON JUAN 7   64   8
    MILD CATHERINE OWED THE CHANCE OF BEING CROWN'D . . . . 205 3 DON JUAN 9   46 V4
    AND CATHERINE WHO LOVED ALL THINGS (SAVE HER LORD . . . 209 3 DON JUAN 9   54   1
    CATHERINE WHO WAS THE GRAND EPITOME . . . . 211 3 DON JUAN 9   57   1
    CATHERINE I SAY WAS VERY GLAD TO SEE . . . . 211 3 DON JUAN 9   57   5
    OH CATHERINE (FOR OF ALL INTERJECTIONS . . . . . . 215 3 DON JUAN 9   65   1
    AND CATHERINE (WE MUST SAY THUS MUCH FOR CATHERINE) . . 217 3 DON JUAN 9   70   1
    AND CATHERINE (WE MUST SAY THUS MUCH FOR CATHERINE) . . 217 3 DON JUAN 9   70   1
    CATHERINE WAS GENEROUS--ALL SUCH LADIES ARE . . . . . 222 3 DON JUAN 9   80   1
    LOVE HAD MADE CATHERINE MAKE EACH LOVER'S FORTUNE . . . 222 3 DON JUAN 9   81   1
    MADE THE CHASTE CATHERINE LOOK A LITTLE GRIM . . . . . 246 3 DON JUAN 10   44   3
    SO CATHERINE WHO HAD A HANDSOME WAY . . . . 247 3 DON JUAN 10   46   1
    MADE CATHERINE TASTE NEXT NIGHT A QUIET SLUMBER-- . . . 248 3 DON JUAN 10   48   4
    WHICH CATHERINE IN A MOMENT OF IVRESSE . . . . . . 287 3 DON JUAN 11   39   5

118

CATHERINE'S
    IN CATHERINE'S REIGN WHOM GLORY STILL ADORES . . . . . . 52 3 DON JUAN 6   92   7
    THE SCENES LIKE CATHERINE'S BOUDOIR AT THREE-SCORE . . . 146 3 DON JUAN 8   68   7
    FAIR CATHERINE'S PASTIME--WHO LOOKED ON THE MATCH . . . . 197 3 DON JUAN 9   29   6
CATHOLIC
    HE DIED AS BORN A CATHOLIC IN FAITH . . . . 197 2 DON JUAN 2   76   5
    'TIS STRANGE THAT POETS OF THE CATHOLIC FAITH . . . . 280 2 DON JUAN 3   9 V5
    IN CATHOLIC EYES BUT TOLD HIM TOO TO SMOTHER . . . . . 240 3 DON JUAN 10   32   4
    THOSE VEGETABLES OF THE CATHOLIC CREED . . . . 445 3 DON JUAN 14   81   7
    SHE WAS A CATHOLIC TOO SINCERE AUSTERE . . . . 476 3 DON JUAN 15   46   1
    JUAN REJOINED--SHE WAS A CATHOLIC . . . . 478 3 DON JUAN 15   50   1
CATHOLICS
    WHEN OVER CATHOLICS THE OCEAN ROLLS . . . . 185 2 DON JUAN 2   55   3
CATILINE
    BY SALLUST IN HIS CATILINE WHO CHASED . . . . 61 3 DON JUAN 6 111   6
CATO
    HEROIC STOIC CATO THE SENTENTIOUS . . . . 10 3 DON JUAN 6   7   7
    FOR MY PART I PRETEND NOT TO BE CATO . . . . 68 3 DON JUAN 7   4   6
    WHILE STRONGBOW'S BEST THINGS MIGHT HAVE COME FROM CATO . 401 3 DON JUAN 13   92   8
CATOS
    TWO WEEDS WHICH POSE OUR ECONOMIC CATOS . . . . 472 3 DON JUAN 15   37   8
CATS
    OVER THE FLOORS WERE SPREAD GAZELLES AND CATS . . . . . 310 2 DON JUAN 3   68   4
    FOR CATS AND BIRDS MORE PENCHANT NE'ER DISPLAYED . . . . 249 3 DON JUAN 10   50   7
CATTLE
    THAT PASIPHAE PROMOTED BREEDING CATTLE . . . . 238 2 DON JUAN 2 155   7
    FOR THIS SUPERIOR YOKE OF HUMAN CATTLE . . . . 425 2 DON JUAN 5   28   8
    MAKES MEN LIKE CATTLE FOLLOW HIM WHO LEADS . . . . . . 132 3 DON JUAN 8   38   8
    WHICH IS THE CUD ESCHEWED BY HUMAN CATTLE . . . . . . 336 3 DON JUAN 12   43   8
    I HATE IT AS I HATE A DROVE OF CATTLE . . . . 435 3 DON JUAN 14   58   5
CATULLUS
    CATULLUS SCARCELY HAS A DECENT POEM . . . . 45 2 DON JUAN 1   42   3
    HORACE CATULLUS SCHOLARS OVID TUTOR . . . . 266 2 DON JUAN 2 205   3
CAUCASUS
    BY THOUGHT OF FROSTY CAUCASUS BUT FEW . . . . 396 2 DON JUAN 4   96   6
CAUGHT
    AND JUAN CAUGHT HIM UP AND ERE HE STEPP'D . . . . . . 187 2 DON JUAN 2   58   7
    AT LENGTH THEY CAUGHT TWO BOOBIES AND A NODDY . . . . 200 2 DON JUAN 2   82   7
    AND BY GOOD FORTUNE GLIDING SOFTLY CAUGHT HER . . . . 208 2 DON JUAN 2   99   3
    AND SOMETIMES CAUGHT AS MANY AS HE WISH'D . . . . . . 223 2 DON JUAN 2 126   4
    THEIR BONDS WHENE'ER SOME ZEPHYR CAUGHT BEGAN . . . . 313 2 DON JUAN 3   73   7
    THE SHARP ROCKS LOOK'D BELOW EACH DROP THEY CAUGHT . . . 362 2 DON JUAN 4   33   7
    AND CAUGHT HER FALLING AND FROM OFF THE WALL . . . . . 364 2 DON JUAN 4   37   2
    JUAN THE LATEST OF HER WHIMS HAD CAUGHT . . . . 477 2 DON JUAN 5 114   1
    WHEN JUAN CAUGHT A GLIMPSE OF THIS SAD SIGHT . . . . . 158 3 DON JUAN 8   93   4
    FIRST ISMAIL'S CAPTURE CAUGHT YOUR FANCY QUITE . . . . 215 3 DON JUAN 9   65   6
    AND CAUGHT THEM--WHAT DO THEY NOT CATCH METHINKS . . . 364 3 DON JUAN 13   12   7
    INTO CLOSE CONTACT THOUGH RESERVED NOR CAUGHT . . . . 365 3 DON JUAN 13   15   4
    THAT FEW OR NONE MORE THAN HIMSELF HAD CAUGHT . . . . . 368 3 DON JUAN 13   21   3
    WAS NOT EXACTLY PLEASED TO BE SO CAUGHT . . . . . . 490 3 DON JUAN 15   77   6
    THERE WERE TWO POACHERS CAUGHT IN A STEEL TRAP . . . . 530 3 DON JUAN 16   61   1
    WAS THAT HE CAUGHT AURORA'S EYE ON HIS . . . . 544 3 DON JUAN 16   92   1
    AND THAT IN HIS CONFUSION HE HAD CAUGHT . . . . . . 560 3 DON JUAN 16 122   7
CAULKING
    TO THINK HIS SKULL HAD NOT SOME NEED OF CAULKING . . . . 565 3 DON JUAN 17   8   6
CAUSA
    OH THOU TETERRIMA CAUSA OF ALL BELLI-- . . . . 210 3 DON JUAN 9   55   1
CAUSE
    HIS DEATH CONTRIVED TO SPOIL A CHARMING CAUSE . . . . . 38 2 DON JUAN 1   33   5
    WHATE'ER THE CAUSE MIGHT BE THEY HAD BECOME . . . . . . 60 2 DON JUAN 1   70   1
    BUT WHATSOE'ER THE CAUSE IS ONE MAY SAY . . . . 76 2 DON JUAN 1 102   5
    AND THERE IS NO GREAT CAUSE TO QUAKE . . . . 86 2 DON JUAN 1 120   3
    AND NEVER ONCE HE HAS HAD CAUSE TO SCOLD . . . . 101 2 DON JUAN 1 147   5
    I SHUNNED THEM TO LEAVE NO CAUSE FOR CAVIL . . . . . . 102 2 DON JUAN 1 148 V6
    SO THERE WERE QUARRELS CARED NOT FOR THE CAUSE . . . . 109 2 DON JUAN 1 159   7
    THE DEPOSITIONS AND THE CAUSE AT FULL . . . . 127 2 DON JUAN 1 189   2
    'TWAS A FINE CAUSE FOR THOSE IN LAW DELIGHTING . . . . 150 2 DON JUAN 1 V 1   1
    SO THAT HE HAD MUCH BETTER CAUSE TO GRIEVE . . . . . . 164 2 DON JUAN 2   15   3
    BUT THE SAME CAUSE CONDUCIVE TO HIS LOSS . . . . 186 2 DON JUAN 2   57   2
    THE FREQUENT FOG-BANKS GAVE THEM CAUSE TO DOUBT-- . . . 207 2 DON JUAN 2   96   6
    ONE SHOULD NOT RAIL WITHOUT A DECENT CAUSE . . . . . . 219 2 DON JUAN 2 119   2
    IS IN ITS CAUSE AS ITS EFFECT SO SWEET . . . . 264 2 DON JUAN 2 203   3
    BUT KNEW THE CAUSE NO MORE THAN A PHILOSOPHER . . . . 289 2 DON JUAN 3   26   8
    THE CAUSE BEING PAST HIS GUESSING OR UNRIDDLING . . . 290 2 DON JUAN 3   28   6
    OF WHICH THE FIRST NE'ER KNOWS THE SECOND CAUSE . . . 318 2 DON JUAN 3   82   8
    HE FELT A GRIEF BUT KNOWING CAUSE FOR NONE . . . . . 355 2 DON JUAN 4   22   6
    VENGEANCE ON HIM WHO WAS THE CAUSE OF ALL . . . . . . 364 2 DON JUAN 4   37   4
    IF CAUSE SHOULD BE--A LIONESS THOUGH TAME . . . . . . 367 2 DON JUAN 4   44   6
    BROUGHT BACK THE SENSE OF PAIN WITHOUT THE CAUSE . . . 378 2 DON JUAN 4   62   7
    OF GORE DIVULGED THE CAUSE) THAT HE WAS DEAD . . . . . 430 2 DON JUAN 5   35   7
    THE CAUSE OF THIS ODD TRAVESTY--FORBEAR . . . . . . 454 2 DON JUAN 5   74   5
    A WOMAN'S TRUE BUT THEN THERE IS A CAUSE . . . . 455 2 DON JUAN 5   76   2
    YOUR PATIENCE) SHOWS THE CAUSE MUST STILL BE STRONGER . 488 2 DON JUAN 5 133   8
    AND THIS STRONG SECOND CAUSE (TO TIRE NO LONGER . . . 488 2 DON JUAN 5 133 V7
    BY THE NORTH POLE--THEY SOUGHT HER CAUSE OF CARE . . . 42 3 DON JUAN 6   72   6
    THE CAUSE OF KILLING TCHITCHITZKOFF AND SMITH . . . . 79 3 DON JUAN 7   25   4
    THUS THE SAME CAUSE WHICH MAKES A VERSE WANT FEET . . . 79 3 DON JUAN 7   26   3
    BUT SHORTLY HE HAD CAUSE TO BE CONTENT . . . . 85 3 DON JUAN 7   38   5
    WAS WORTHY OF A SPARTAN HAD THE CAUSE . . . . 86 3 DON JUAN 7   40   2

```
                                                              PAGE VOL      CANTO  STANZA  LN
CAUSE   (CONTINUED)
        AND ALL PRESAGED GOOD FORTUNE TO THEIR CAUSE    . . . . .   89   3 DON JUAN   7      47    4
        WHICH OF THE ARMIES WOULD HAVE CAUSE TO MOURN   . . . . .  150   3 DON JUAN   8      77    6
        AND THAT'S THE CAUSE NO DOUBT WHY IF WE SCAN    . . . . .  167   3 DON JUAN   8     112    5
        UNLESS HER CAUSE BY RIGHT BE SANCTIFIED  . . . . . .       184   3 DON JUAN   9       4    4
        INCREASES TILL YOU SHALL MAKE COMMON CAUSE  . . . . .      196   3 DON JUAN   9      28    6
        SOME CALL THEE THE WORST CAUSE OF WAR BUT I  . . . . .     210   3 DON JUAN   9      56    1
        OF THAT GREAT CAUSE OF WAR OR PEACE OR WHAT  . . . . .     211   3 DON JUAN   9      57    2
        (LET DEEPER SAGES THE TRUE CAUSE DETERMINE)  . . . . .     249   3 DON JUAN  10      50    3
        WHATE'ER THE CAUSE THE CHURCH MADE LITTLE OF IT--  . . .   252   3 DON JUAN  10      56    7
        I HAVE NO GREAT CAUSE TO LOVE THAT SPOT OF EARTH  . . .    257   3 DON JUAN  10      66    1
        FOR THE LESS CAUSE THERE IS FOR ALL THIS FLURRY  . . . .   260   3 DON JUAN  10      72    6
        CANONIZATION FOR THE SELF-SAME CAUSE  .  . . . . . .       319   3 DON JUAN  12       7    5
        HAS CAUSE TO WISH HER SIRE HAD HAD MALE HEIRS  . . . .     331   3 DON JUAN  12      33    8
        A VERDICT--GRIEVOUS FOE TO THOSE WHO CAUSE IT--  . . . .   346   3 DON JUAN  12      65    5
        WHICH IS THE ONLY CAUSE THAT WE CAN GUESS  .  . . . .      371   3 DON JUAN  13      29    7
        THE CAUSE I KNOW NOT NOR CAN SOLVE BUT SUCH . . . . .      388   3 DON JUAN  13      64    7
        HIS CAUSE BY LEANING MUCH FROM MIGHT TO RIGHT  . . . .     391   3 DON JUAN  13      69    4
        AND THAT'S ONE CAUSE SHE MEETS WITH CONTRADICTION  . . .   416   3 DON JUAN  14      13    5
        AN ACCESSARY AS I HAVE CAUSE TO GUESS .  . . . . . .       443   3 DON JUAN  14      76    4
        THE CAUSE OF THIS EFFECT OR THIS DEFECT--  . . . . .       502   3 DON JUAN  16       2    1
        FOR THIS EFFECT DEFECTIVE COMES BY CAUSE .  . . . . .      502   3 DON JUAN  16       2    2
        WAS LONG AND THUS FAR THERE WAS NO GREAT CAUSE .  . . .    511   3 DON JUAN  16      24    3
        THE CAUSE BUT JUAN SAID HE WAS QUITE WELL  .  . . . .      514   3 DON JUAN  16      32    8
        THE COUNTRY WOULD HAVE FAR MORE CAUSE TO WEEP IT  . . .    537   3 DON JUAN  16      75    6
        SHOULD CAUSE MORE FEAR THAN A WHOLE HOST'S IDENTITY  . .   559   3 DON JUAN  16     120    8
CAUSED
        OUT THROUGH A FEVER CAUSED BY ITS OWN HEAT  . . . . .      168   2 DON JUAN   2      22    2
        NOR TO THE TROUBLE WHICH HER FANCIES CAUSED .  . . . .     476   2 DON JUAN   5     113    6
        HIS LATELY BOWSTRUNG BROTHER CAUSED HIS RISE  . . . .      495   2 DON JUAN   5     147    4
        THEN SLACKENED IT WHICH IS THE MARCH MOST CAUSED .  . .     61   3 DON JUAN   6     111    3
        WITH ALL THE MYSTERY BY MIDNIGHT CAUSED  .  . . . . .      507   3 DON JUAN  16      15    5
        HAD CAUSED HIS NERVES--MADE ANSWERS RATHER CLOUDED  . .    527   3 DON JUAN  16      54   V8
CAUSELESS
        IS'T WISE OR FITTING CAUSELESS TO EXPLORE  . . . . .       101   2 DON JUAN   1     146    5
        FOR FEELINGS CAUSELESS OR AT LEAST ABSTRUSE .  . . . .     355   2 DON JUAN   4      22    8
CAUSES
        TAKE TOWNS BY STORM NO CAUSES CAN I GUESS  .  . . . .      176   3 DON JUAN   8     129    5
        YOU PLEASE (IT CAUSES ALL THE THINGS WHICH BE  . . . .     211   3 DON JUAN   9      57    3
        FOR CAUSES YOUNG OR OLD THE CANKER-WORM .  . . . . .       243   3 DON JUAN  10      38    2
CAUSING
        A LAD OF SIXTEEN CAUSING A DIVORCE .  . . . . . .          158   2 DON JUAN   2       2    7
CAUTION
        BUT SHE WAS A PHILOSOPHER WHOSE CAUTION  .  . . . . .      246   3 DON JUAN  10      44   V4
CAUTIOUS
        SOME WHO ONCE SET THEIR CAPS AT CAUTIOUS DUKES  . . . .    308   3 DON JUAN  11      81    1
        BE HYPOCRITICAL BE CAUTIOUS BE  .  . . . . . . .          310   3 DON JUAN  11      86    7
        AND THUS LORD HENRY WHO WAS CAUTIOUS AS . . . .  .        366   3 DON JUAN  13      16    1
        (I STATE THIS FOR I AM CAUTIOUS TO A PITCH .  . . . .      507   3 DON JUAN  16      16    3
        COURTEOUS AND CAUTIOUS THEREFORE IN HIS COUNTY .  . . .    535   3 DON JUAN  16      71    1
CAVALIER
        A BETTER CAVALIER NE'ER MOUNTED HORSE  . . . . . .         26   2 DON JUAN   1       9    5
        BUT FOR A CAVALIER OF HIS CONDITION  . . . . . .           97   2 DON JUAN   1     139    3
        HAD IT BUT BEEN FOR A STOUT CAVALIER  . . . . . .         115   2 DON JUAN   1     172    1
        AS CAVALIER SERVENTE OR DESPISE HER  .  . . . . . .        288   2 DON JUAN   3      24    6
        AFTER THE TAKING OF THE CAVALIER  .  . . . . . .          148   3 DON JUAN   8      73    2
        CALLED CAVALIER SERVENTE--A PYGMALION .  . . . . . .       208   3 DON JUAN   9      51    5
CAVALIERE
        FORTY FEET HIGH UPON A CAVALIERE   . . . . . . .           72   3 DON JUAN   7      12    8
CAVALIERS
        THE GALLANT CAVALIERS WHO FOUGHT IN VAIN . . . . . .       386   3 DON JUAN  13      60    7
CAVE
        BEFORE THE ENTRANCE OF A CLIFF-WORN CAVE .  . . . .        213   2 DON JUAN   2     108    6
        AND LIFTING HIM WITH CARE INTO THE CAVE  .  . . . .        216   2 DON JUAN   2     115    1
        AND SUCH WAS SHE THE LADY OF THE CAVE .  . . . . .         220   2 DON JUAN   2     120    1
        TO PLACE HIM IN THE CAVE FOR PRESENT REST  .  . . . .      225   2 DON JUAN   2     131    3
        FAST IN HIS CAVE AND NOTHING CLASH'D UPON .  . . . .       229   2 DON JUAN   2     137    2
        AND NEAR THE CAVE HER QUICK LIGHT FOOTSTEPS DREW  . . .    232   2 DON JUAN   2     142    2
        SHE CAME INTO THE CAVE BUT IT WAS MERELY .  . . . .        245   2 DON JUAN   2     168    3
        OCEAN THEIR WITNESS AND THE CAVE THEIR BED  . . . . .      265   2 DON JUAN   2     204    4
        THE DREAM CHANGED IN A CAVE SHE STOOD ITS WALLS  . . .     362   2 DON JUAN   4      33    1
        ON OURS OR SPARS WITHIN SOME DUSKY CAVE  .  . . . . .      509   3 DON JUAN  16      19    5
CAVERN
        PALACE OR GARDEN PARADISE OR CAVERN  .  . . . . . .         24   2 DON JUAN   1       6    7
        THE SECRET CAVERN OF THIS LURKING TREASURE--  . . . .      104   2 DON JUAN   1     153    7
        AND WHEN INTO THE CAVERN HAIDEE STEPP'D  .  . . . . .      232   2 DON JUAN   2     143    1
        CORRODING IN THE CAVERN OF THE HEART  .  . . . . . .       457   3 DON JUAN  15       3    2
CAVERNS
        DEEP IN THE CAVERNS OF THE DEADLY TIDE-- . . . . . .        63   3 DON JUAN   6     115    4
CAVES
        THE VOICELESS SANDS AND DROPPING CAVES THAT LAY  . . .     255   2 DON JUAN   2     188    5
CAVIL
        I SHUNNED THEM TO LEAVE NO CAUSE FOR CAVIL  .  . . . .     102   2 DON JUAN   1     148   V6
        THAN SHE FROM AUGHT AT WHICH THE EYE COULD CAVIL  . . .    474   2 DON JUAN   5     109    6
        UNLESS IT TEACHES ONE TO QUOTE AND CAVIL)  .  . . . .      380   3 DON JUAN  13      47    8
        AND THEREFORE MORTALS CAVIL NOT AT ALL  .  . . . . .       503   3 DON JUAN  16       6    1
CAW
        CAW ME CAW THEE--FOR SIX MONTHS HATH BEEN HATCHING  . .    307   3 DON JUAN  11      78    7
        CAW ME CAW THEE--FOR SIX MONTHS H'ATH BEEN HATCHING  . .   307   3 DON JUAN  11      78    7
```

120

CAYENNE
LEAVENING HIS BLOOD AS CAYENNE DOTH A CURRY . . . . . . 260 3 DON JUAN 10   72   2
CAZZANI
DID NOT THE ITALIAN MUSICO CAZZANI . . . . 102 2 DON JUAN 1   149   1
CEASE
FOR ANY LENGTH--CONTRIVED TO MAKE EACH OTHER CEASE . . 277 2 DON JUAN 3   5 V4
WHETHER MY VERSE'S FAME BE DOOM'D TO CEASE . . . . . 398 2 DON JUAN 4   99   4
FOR THOSE FOR WHOM IT SOON SHALL CEASE TO BEAT . . . . 152 3 DON JUAN 8   82   4
AND THEN BEFORE SIGHS CEASE FOR OFT THE ONE . . . . . 229 3 DON JUAN 10   8   2
TO PAIN THE MOMENT WHEN YOU CEASE TO PLEASE . . . . . 231 3 DON JUAN 10   13   8
IN WHICH THE NEVA'S ICE WOULD CEASE TO LIVE . . . . . 243 3 DON JUAN 10   37   6
WITH SCHNAPPS--DEMOCRITUS WOULD CEASE TO SMILE . . . . 260 3 DON JUAN 10   71 V7
WITH RUST SHOULD SURELY CEASE TO HACK AND HEW . . . . 433 3 DON JUAN 14   53   6
CEASED
SHE CEASED AND TURN'D UPON HER PILLOW PALE . . . . . 108 2 DON JUAN 1   158   1
AND RARELY CEASED THE HAUGHTY BILLOW'S ROAR . . . . . 249 2 DON JUAN 2   177   6
TO THOSE WHO HAVE CEASED TO HEAR SUCH OR NE'ER HEARD . 351 2 DON JUAN 4   14   8
HER STRUGGLES CEASED WITH ONE CONVULSIVE GROAN . . . . 375 2 DON JUAN 4   58   6
THE DUKE OF WELLINGTON HAD CEASED TO SHOW . . . . . 137 3 DON JUAN 8   49   6
BUT HERE IT SEEMED HIS JOKES HAD CEASED TO TAKE . . . 147 3 DON JUAN 8   70   8
THE GOOD OLD KHAN WHO LONG HAD CEASED TO SEE . . . . 169 3 DON JUAN 8   116   2
SO CALLED THE ANTIC LONG HATH CEASED TO HEAR . . . . 188 3 DON JUAN 9   12   4
A FOOL WHOSE BELLS HAVE CEASED TO RING AT ALL-- . . . 267 3 DON JUAN 10   86   8
BE GILT WHO SATE HATH CEASED TO BE THE SAME . . . . . 509 3 DON JUAN 16   19   8
THE LADY'S VOICE CEASED AND THE THRILLING WIRES . . . 521 3 DON JUAN 16   41   1
BUT SHOULD THE DAY COME WHEN PLACE CEASED TO EXIST . . 537 3 DON JUAN 16   75   5
CEASELESS
FROM THAT IXION GRINDSTONE'S CEASELESS TOIL . . . . . 17 2 DON JUAN D   13   6
MAKING THEIR SUMMER LIVES ONE CEASELESS SONG . . . . 337 2 DON JUAN 3   106   2
ON HIS SOUL LIKE A CEASELESS SUNRISE DART-- . . . . . 169 3 DON JUAN 8   115   6
BENEATH HIS CEASELESS TOUCHES THE HESPERIAN . . . . . 208 3 DON JUAN 9   51 V7
CEDAR
HER WRITHING FELL SHE LIKE A CEDAR FELL'D . . . . . 375 2 DON JUAN 4   58   8
CEDARS
WHO GREW LIKE CEDARS ROUND HIM GLORIOUSLY-- . . . . . 169 3 DON JUAN 8   116   4
CEILING
SO THAT I SEEM TO STAND UPON THE CEILING) . . . . . 156 2 DON JUAN 1 V 8   6
CELEBRATED
NOBLE RICH CELEBRATED AND A STRANGER . . . . 305 3 DON JUAN 11   74   2
SO CELEBRATED FOR HIS MORALS WHEN . . . . 323 3 DON JUAN 12   16   6
DESIRABLE DISTINGUISH'D CELEBRATED . . . . 428 3 DON JUAN 14   42   2
CELEBRITY
THE DINERS OF CELEBRITY DINED WELL . . . . 487 3 DON JUAN 15   70   2
CELESTIAL
ON WHOM HER REVERIES CELESTIAL RAN . . . . 64 2 DON JUAN 1   79   8
QUITE A CELESTIAL KALEIDOSCOPE . . . . 205 2 DON JUAN 2   93   8
IS SHARPEN'D FROM ITS HIGH CELESTIAL FLAVOUR . . . . 277 2 DON JUAN 3   5   7
CELL
MUCH AS A MONK MAY DO WITHIN HIS CELL . . . . 445 3 DON JUAN 14   81   4
CELLAR
THE VERY BEST OF VINEYARDS IS THE CELLAR . . . . . . 394 3 DON JUAN 13   76   8
CELLARS
HIS VERY CELLARS MIGHT BE KINGS' ABODES . . . . . . 320 3 DON JUAN 12   9   6
CELLS
IN HOLLOW HALLS WITH SPARRY ROOFS AND CELLS . . . . . 253 2 DON JUAN 2   184   6
MORE TO SECURE THEM IN THEIR NAVAL CELLS . . . . . . 393 2 DON JUAN 4   91   5
THE CELLS TOO AND REFECTORY I WEEN . . . . 389 3 DON JUAN 13   66   4
CEMENTED
WITH HUMAN BLOOD THAT COLUMN WAS CEMENTED . . . . . 401 2 DON JUAN 4   105   1
CENSORIOUS
BY NAMING STREETS SINCE MEN ARE SO CENSORIOUS . . . . 369 3 DON JUAN 13   25   2
CENTAUR
INTO THAT MORAL CENTAUR MAN AND WIFE . . . . 502 2 DON JUAN 5   158   8
AND WHATNOT--THOUGH HE HAD RIDDEN LIKE A CENTAUR . . . 425 3 DON JUAN 14   35 V7
BUT BOTH TOGETHER FORM A KIND OF CENTAUR . . . . . . 442 3 DON JUAN 14   73   7
CENTAUR-NESSUS
AND CENTAUR-NESSUS GARB OF MORTAL CLOTHING . . . . . 301 3 DON JUAN 11   65   4
CENTER
WERE SCARLET FROM WHOSE GLOWING CENTER GREW . . . . . 309 2 DON JUAN 3   67   6
CENTER'D
UNTIL IT CENTER'D IN AN ONLY SON . . . . 54 2 DON JUAN 1   59   3
CENTRAL
LIKE EARTHQUAKES FROM THE HIDDEN FIRE CALL'D CENTRAL . . 271 2 DON JUAN 2   215   8
CENTRE
YET IN THE VERY CENTRE PAST ALL PRICE . . . . 375 3 DON JUAN 13   37   5
A MIGHTY WINDOW HOLLOW IN THE CENTRE . . . . 387 3 DON JUAN 13   62   1
WITH SELF-LOVE IN THE CENTRE AS THEIR POLE . . . . . 455 3 DON JUAN 14   102   4
CENTS
WHERE ARE THOSE MARTYRED SAINTS THE FIVE PER CENTS . . . 307 3 DON JUAN 11   77   7
CENTURIES
THAT HAD FOR CENTURIES BEEN KNOWN IN SPAIN . . . . . 128 2 DON JUAN 1   190   3
OR OF SOME CENTURIES TO TAKE A LEASE . . . . 398 2 DON JUAN 4   99   6
CENTURION
IN AWE HE SAID AS THE CENTURION SAITH . . . . 430 2 DON JUAN 5   36   5
CENTURY
THE PRESENT CENTURY WAS GROWING BLIND . . . . 328 2 DON JUAN 3   90   6
ARE THINGS WHICH IN THIS CENTURY DON'T STRIKE . . . . 330 2 DON JUAN 3   95   5
THAN MIGHT SUFFICE A MODERATE CENTURY THROUGH . . . . 309 3 DON JUAN 11   82   4
AND MITFORD IN THE NINETEENTH CENTURY . . . . 325 3 DON JUAN 12   19   7
HAD MADE MORE PROGRESS THAN FOR THE LAST CENTURY . . . 536 3 DON JUAN 16   73   4

	PAGE	VOL	CANTO	STANZA	LN
CEREMONIES					
WITH ALL THE CEREMONIES OF HIS RANK	500	2 DON JUAN	5	154	2
CEREMONY					
HIS HEAD UNTIL THE CEREMONY ENDED	466	2 DON JUAN	5	95	8
CERERIS					
VETABO CERERIS SACRUM QUI VULGARET--	419	3 DON JUAN	14	21	7
CERES					
ARE ALSO LEARNT FROM CERES AND FROM BACCHUS	245	2 DON JUAN	2	169	7
CERES PRESENTS A PLATE OF VERMICELLI--	246	2 DON JUAN	2	170	3
CERES IS COMMISSARY TO OUR BELLIES	246	2 DON JUAN	2	170	V3
OR SWEARS THAT CERES HATH BEGOTTEN FAMINE	88	3 DON JUAN	7	45	8
AND FARMERS CAN'T RAISE CERES FROM HER FALL	198	3 DON JUAN	9	32	6
BENEATH HIS CARS OF CERES GROAN THE ROADS	320	3 DON JUAN	12	9	4
BACCHUS AND CERES BEING AS WE KNOW	542	3 DON JUAN	16	86	4
CERTAIN					
IS NOT THE CERTAIN PATH TO FUTURE PRAISE	14	2 DON JUAN	D	8	8
AND OPEN'D CERTAIN TRUNKS OF BOOKS AND LETTERS	36	2 DON JUAN	1	28	2
I'M VERY CERTAIN MINE WOULD NOT HAVE DONE SO	80	2 DON JUAN	1	110	8
PROLOGUE IS ALWAYS CERTAIN THROES AND THROBS	110	2 DON JUAN	1	162	4
A CERTAIN PORTION OF UNCERTAIN PAPER	146	2 DON JUAN	1	218	2
'TIS VERY CERTAIN THE DESIRE OF LIFE	190	2 DON JUAN	2	64	1
FOR CERTAIN MERCHANTMEN UPON THE LOOK	248	2 DON JUAN	2	174	6
EXCEPT SOME CERTAIN PORTIONS OF THE PREY	284	2 DON JUAN	3	17	3
THESE AT SOME CERTAIN PORTIONED HOURS WERE SPREAD	310	2 DON JUAN	3	69	V6
OF CERTAIN STEWS AND ROAST-MEATS AND PILAUS	437	2 DON JUAN	5	47	2
A CERTAIN PRESS OR CUPBOARD NICHED IN YONDER	450	2 DON JUAN	5	66	6
WAS ALSO CERTAIN THAT THE EARTH WAS SQUARE	497	2 DON JUAN	5	150	2
AS CERTAIN--THESE ARE PALTRY THINGS AND YET	16	3 DON JUAN	6	21	7
BUT CERTAIN 'TIS THEY ALL FELT FOR THEIR NEW	25	3 DON JUAN	6	39	1
A LADY OF A CERTAIN AGE WHICH MEANS	41	3 DON JUAN	6	69	2
'TWAS CERTAIN THAT HIS CONDUCT HAD BEEN PURE	58	3 DON JUAN	6	104	3
JUAN AND JOHNSON JOINED A CERTAIN CORPS	120	3 DON JUAN	8	19	1
A PROP NOT QUITE SO CERTAIN AS BEFORE	184	3 DON JUAN	9	3	4
OTHERS TALKED LEARNEDLY OF CERTAIN TUMOURS	244	3 DON JUAN	10	40	3
WHICH THOUGH 'TIS CERTAIN TO PERPLEX AND FRIGHTEN	281	3 DON JUAN	11	27	7
A CERTAIN QUANTUM OF ACCOMPLISHMENT	340	3 DON JUAN	12	52	V2
THAT IS UP TO A CERTAIN POINT WHICH POINT	396	3 DON JUAN	13	81	1
I THINK THAT WERE I CERTAIN OF SUCCESS	415	3 DON JUAN	14	12	1
WITHOUT THE COXCOMBRY OF CERTAIN SHE MEN	424	3 DON JUAN	14	31	8
WHOSE VERDICT FOR SUCH SIN A CERTAIN CURE IS)--	436	3 DON JUAN	14	60	8
INDEED A CERTAIN FAIR AND FAIRY ONE	475	3 DON JUAN	15	43	3
BUT AFTER THERE ARE SOMETIMES CERTAIN SIGNS	488	3 DON JUAN	15	72	5
FOR CERTAIN REASONS MY BELIEF IS SERIOUS	498	3 DON JUAN	15	95	8
CERTAINLY					
REVENGE IN PERSON'S CERTAINLY NO VIRTUE	37	2 DON JUAN	1	30	7
AND CERTAINLY THIS COURSE WAS MUCH THE BEST	58	2 DON JUAN	1	67	4
BUT VACCINATION CERTAINLY HAS BEEN	91	2 DON JUAN	1	129	5
THAT HOLY STATE--BUT CERTAINLY BENEATH	280	2 DON JUAN	3	9	V5
AND CERTAINLY HE SHOW'D THE BEST OF BREEDING	299	2 DON JUAN	3	46	2
BUT CERTAINLY TO ONE DEEM'D DEAD RETURNING	300	2 DON JUAN	3	49	7
AND THOUGH HE CERTAINLY RAN MANY RISKS	20	3 DON JUAN	6	29	3
CERTAINLY AGED--WHAT HER YEARS MIGHT BE	41	3 DON JUAN	6	69	3
THOUGH CERTAINLY MORE DIFFICULT TO RHYME AT	423	3 DON JUAN	14	29	4
IF BAD THE BEST WAY'S CERTAINLY TO TEAZE ON	478	3 DON JUAN	15	51	3
AND CERTAINLY AURORA HAD RENEWED	553	3 DON JUAN	16	107	5
CERTAINTY					
THERE'S NO SUCH THING AS CERTAINTY THAT'S PLAIN	191	3 DON JUAN	9	17	5
OF THOUGHT WE COULD BUT SNATCH A CERTAINTY	410	3 DON JUAN	14	1	2
CERTES					
ALL THESE ARE CERTES ENTERTAINING FACTS	329	2 DON JUAN	3	92	1
THOUGH CERTES BY NO MEANS SO GRAND A SIGHT	444	2 DON JUAN	5	58	5
BUT CERTES MATTERS TOOK A DIFFERENT FACE	89	3 DON JUAN	7	47	1
CERTES IT WOULD HAVE BEEN BUT THROWN AWAY	200	3 DON JUAN	9	36	6
INDIFFERENCE CERTES DON'T PRODUCE DISTRESS	374	3 DON JUAN	13	35	6
CERTES IT WAS NOT BODY HE WAS WELL	441	3 DON JUAN	14	71	4
CERTES BUT A PREVENTATIVE AND THEREFORE	470	3 DON JUAN	15	31	7
BUT CERTES IT CONDUCTS TO LIVES ASCETIC	472	3 DON JUAN	15	38	7
CERULEANS					
BENIGN CERULEANS OF THE SECOND SEX	403	2 DON JUAN	4	108	2
CERUSE					
THE PAINTING AND THE PAINTED YOUTH CERUSE	293	3 DON JUAN	11	48	4
CERVANTES					
VERSE AND BY SOLOMON AND BY CERVANTES	67	3 DON JUAN	7	3	8
HAD NOT CERVANTES IN THAT TOO TRUE TALE	361	3 DON JUAN	13	8	7
CERVANTES SMILED SPAIN'S CHIVALRY AWAY	364	3 DON JUAN	13	11	1
CESARE					
BY CARRYING OFF COUNT CESARE CICOGNA	389	2 DON JUAN	4	83	7
CESAREAN					
TO WHERE THE LAST CESAREAN FORTRESS STOOD	337	2 DON JUAN	3	105	5
CETERA					
HAIL MUSE ET CETERA--WE LEFT JUAN SLEEPING	274	2 DON JUAN	3	1	1
OF ORIENTAL PLANTS ET CETERA	434	2 DON JUAN	5	42	5
THRONES WORLDS ET CETERA ARE SO OFT UPSET	8	3 DON JUAN	6	4	1
OF ELEGANT ET CETERA IN FRESH BATCHES--	340	3 DON JUAN	12	53	7
CEYLON					
FROM CEYLON INDE OR FAR CATHAY UNLOADS	320	3 DON JUAN	12	9	2
CHACE					
A SYLVAN TRIBE OF CHILDREN OF THE CHACE	145	3 DON JUAN	8	65	2
CHAFE					
SHE WAS NOT ONE TO WEEP AND RAVE AND CHAFE	373	2 DON JUAN	4	54	5

122

CHAFED
   AND CHAFED AT POOR DUDU WHO ONLY SIGHED . . . . 45 3 DON JUAN 6 79 7
CHAFF
   OF CHAFF ALTHOUGH OUR GLEANINGS BE NOT GRIST . . . . . 403 3 DON JUAN 13 97 2
CHAFING
   AND CHAFING HIM THE SOFT WARM HAND OF YOUTH . . . . . . 215 2 DON JUAN 2 113 3
CHAIN
   DEEMING THE CHAIN IT WEARS EVEN MEN MAY FIT . . . . . . 18 2 DON JUAN D 15 4
   THY CLANKING CHAIN AND ERIN'S YET GREEN WOUNDS . . . . . 19 2 DON JUAN D 16 5
   WHETHER THE WORD WAS DEATH OR BUT THE CHAIN-- . . . . . 299 2 DON JUAN 3 47 4
   A CHAIN O'ER ALL SHE DID THAT IS A CHAIN . . . . . . 474 2 DON JUAN 5 110 2
   A CHAIN O'ER ALL SHE DID THAT IS A CHAIN . . . . . . 474 2 DON JUAN 5 110 2
   AND NOW WOULD CHAIN THEM TO THE VERY MIND-- . . . . . 258 3 DON JUAN 10 67 8
   WHO WATCHES O'ER THE CHAIN AS THEY WHO WEAR . . . . . 258 3 DON JUAN 10 68 8
   THEIRS IS THE BEST BOWER-ANCHOR THE CHAIN CABLE . . . . 316 3 DON JUAN 12 3 3
CHAIN'D
   BY SWAMPING ONE OF THE PRIZES HE HAD CHAIN'D . . . . . 283 2 DON JUAN 3 15 5
   CHAIN'D TO A ROCK SHE KNEW NOT HOW BUT STIR . . . . . 361 2 DON JUAN 4 31 2
   WOUNDED AND CHAIN'D SO THAT HE CANNOT MOVE . . . . . 371 2 DON JUAN 4 51 7
   WERE TO BE CHAIN'D AND LOTTED OUT PER COUPLE . . . . . 393 2 DON JUAN 4 91 7
   WITH RAUCOCANTI LUCKLESSLY WAS CHAIN'D . . . . . 394 2 DON JUAN 4 93 1
   AND THOUGH THUS CHAIN'D AS NATURAL HER HAND . . . . . 396 2 DON JUAN 4 95 4
CHAINED
   CHILL AND CHAINED TO COLD EARTH WE LIFT ON HIGH . . . . 66 3 DON JUAN 7 1 5
CHAIN-PUMP
   KEPT TWO HAND AND ONE CHAIN-PUMP STILL IN USE . . . . 172 2 DON JUAN 2 30 4
CHAINS
   A TINKERING SLAVE-MAKER WHO MENDS OLD CHAINS . . . . 18 2 DON JUAN D 14 7
   UNTIL THE CHAINS AND LEATHERS WERE WORN THROUGH . . . . 178 2 DON JUAN 2 42 5
   SUCH CHAINS AS HIS WERE SURE TO BIND . . . . 325 2 DON JUAN 3 L 12 6
CHAIR
   SWEEPING THE MARBLE UNDERNEATH HER CHAIR . . . . 60 3 DON JUAN 6 108 3
   AND SITTING AS IF NAILED UPON HIS CHAIR . . . . . 542 3 DON JUAN 16 87 4
CHAIRS
   GROUPS OF BAD STATUES TABLES CHAIRS AND PICTURES . . . . 465 2 DON JUAN 5 94 7
CHAISE
   WHETHER THEY COME BY HORSE OR CHAISE OR COACH . . . . 279 3 DON JUAN 11 23 3
CHAISES
   OF PEGASUS--OR AT THE LEAST POST CHAISES . . . . . 197 3 DON JUAN 9 30 7
CHALK
   CHALK MIMICS PAINTING THEN FESTOONS ARE TWIRLED . . . . 302 3 DON JUAN 11 67 5
CHALKY
   AT THE FIRST SIGHT OF ALBION'S CHALKY BELT-- . . . . 257 3 DON JUAN 10 65 4
CHAMAS'S
   WITH TU MI CHAMAS'S FROM PORTINGALE . . . . . 523 3 DON JUAN 16 45 7
CHAMBER
   OF NIGHT WHICH ROBE THE CHAMBER OR WHERE POPPING . . . . 442 2 DON JUAN 5 55 5
   IT WAS A SPACIOUS CHAMBER (ODA IS . . . . 31 3 DON JUAN 6 51 1
   THERE WAS DEEP SILENCE IN THE CHAMBER DIM . . . . 38 3 DON JUAN 6 64 1
   OF THE STAR CHAMBER THAN OF HABEAS CORPUS . . . . 391 3 DON JUAN 13 69 8
   THE GOTHIC CHAMBER WHERE HE WAS ENCLOSED . . . . . 507 3 DON JUAN 16 15 3
   HIS CHAMBER DOOR WIDE OPEN--AND WENT FORTH . . . . 508 3 DON JUAN 16 17 2
   BACK TO HIS CHAMBER SHORN OF HALF HIS STRENGTH . . . . 511 3 DON JUAN 16 25 8
CHAMBERLAIN
   THE VERY MODEL OF A CHAMBERLAIN-- . . . . 440 3 DON JUAN 14 70 7
CHAMBERS
   WHO SHUT IN CHAMBERS THINK IT LONELINESS . . . . . 255 2 DON JUAN 2 188 2
   A RANGE OR SUITE OF FURTHER CHAMBERS WHICH . . . . 449 2 DON JUAN 5 65 2
   IN KINGLY CHAMBERS OR IMPERIAL HALLS . . . . . 471 2 DON JUAN 5 103 7
   BACK TO THEIR CHAMBERS THOSE LONG GALLERIES . . . . 19 3 DON JUAN 6 26 5
   HUGE HALLS LONG GALLERIES SPACIOUS CHAMBERS JOIN'D . . . 390 3 DON JUAN 13 67 1
CHAMBRE
   UNDRESSING IS A WOE OUR ROBE DE CHAMBRE . . . . . 505 3 DON JUAN 16 11 2
CHAMPAGNE
   WHAT SAY YOU TO A BOTTLE OF CHAMPAGNE . . . . . 375 3 DON JUAN 13 37 2
   AND THEN THERE WAS CHAMPAGNE WITH FOAMING WHIRLS . . . 484 3 DON JUAN 15 65 7
   IS LIKE THE LAST GLASS OF CHAMPAGNE WITHOUT . . . 504 3 DON JUAN 16 9 2
   TO THESE THE INVENTION OF CHAMPAGNE AND TRUFFLES . . . 542 3 DON JUAN 16 86 7
CHAMPAIGNE
   A LOBSTER SALAD AND CHAMPAIGNE AND CHAT . . . . 94 2 DON JUAN 1 135 8
   SCARCELY O'ERPASS'D THE CREAM OF YOUR CHAMPAIGNE . . . 250 2 DON JUAN 2 178 2
CHAMPION
   LIKE TO THE CHAMPION IN THE FISTY RING . . . . 296 3 DON JUAN 11 55 2
   AND CHAMPION HIM TO THE UTMOST--HE WOULD KEEP IT . . . 536 3 DON JUAN 16 75 2
CHAMPION'D
   SHE STOOD AS ONE WHO CHAMPION'D HUMAN FEARS-- . . . . 367 2 DON JUAN 4 43 3
CHANCE
   AND EVEN IF BY CHANCE--AND WHO CAN TELL . . . . . 64 2 DON JUAN 1 78 1
   LAWYER BY TRADE--AND ORATOR BY CHANCE . . . . . 152 2 DON JUAN 1 V 3 V5
   AND SWIMMERS WHO MAY CHANCE TO BE SURVIVORS . . . . 172 2 DON JUAN 2 31 8
   AND ALL THINGS FOR A CHANCE HAD BEEN CAST LOOSE . . . 183 2 DON JUAN 2 51 2
   THERE WAS SLIGHT CHANCE OF REACHING ANY SHORE . . . 185 2 DON JUAN 2 54 5
   THEY THOUGHT THAT IN SUCH PERILS MORE THAN CHANCE . . . 208 2 DON JUAN 2 99 7
   AND WARM IN CASE BY CHANCE HE SHOULD AWAKE . . . 226 2 DON JUAN 2 133 4
   EVEN TILL AN ICEBERG IT MAY CHANCE TO GROW . . . 398 2 DON JUAN 4 100 7
   AND YOU AND I MAY CHANCE ERE MORNING RISE . . . 464 2 DON JUAN 5 92 5
   IF FOND OF A CHANCE OGLE AT HER GLASS . . . . . 36 3 DON JUAN 6 60 4
   WHAT SAGES CALL CHANCE PROVIDENCE OR FATE-- . . . 105 3 DON JUAN 7 76 4
   JUAN BY SOME STRANGE CHANCE WHICH OFT DIVIDES . . . 125 3 DON JUAN 8 27 1

123

CHANCE (CONTINUED)
    HER LIFE TO CHANCE BUT POINT ME OUT SOME NOOK . . . . . 161 3 DON JUAN 8   99   3
    MY CHANCE SO HAPPEN--DEEDS) WITH ALL WHO WAR . . . . . 194 3 DON JUAN 9   24   2
    MILD CATHERINE OWED THE CHANCE OF BEING CROWN'D . . . . 205 3 DON JUAN 9   46 V4
    IF IT BE CHANCE OR IF IT BE ACCORDING . . . . 270 3 DON JUAN 11   4   1
    (A CHANCE STILL) 'TIS A VOYAGE OR VESSEL LOST . . . . . 376 3 DON JUAN 13   39   8
    SPARED BY SOME CHANCE WHEN ALL BESIDE WAS SPOIL'D . . . 387 3 DON JUAN 13   61   4
    AS ON THE WHOLE IT IS AN EVEN CHANCE . . . . 473 3 DON JUAN 15   39   4
    BY SOME ODD CHANCE TOO HE WAS PLACED BETWEEN . . . . . 489 3 DON JUAN 15   75   1
CHANCED
    IF AT THAT MOMENT HE HAD CHANCED TO CLAW IT . . . . . 123 2 DON JUAN 1 185   5
    WHICH IN THEIR WAY THAT MOMENT CHANCED TO FALL . . . . 206 2 DON JUAN 2   95   7
    THERE CHANCED TO BE AN ODD MALE AND ODD FEMALE . . . . 394 2 DON JUAN 4   92   2
    IT CHANCED AMONGST THE OTHER PEOPLE LOTTED . . . . . . 416 2 DON JUAN 5   10   5
    IT CHANCED SOME DIPLOMATICAL RELATIONS . . . . 365 3 DON JUAN 13   15   1
CHANCELLOR'S
    BEFORE THE LORDS--WHOSE CHANCELLOR'S MORE ACUTE . . . . 357 3 DON JUAN 12 V 18   3
CHANCELLORS
    THOUGH ALL EXCHEQUER CHANCELLORS ENDEAVOUR . . . . . . 547 3 DON JUAN 16   98   6
CHANCERY
    TO A CHANCERY SUIT AND MESSUAGES AND LANDS . . . . . . 42 2 DON JUAN 1   37   2
    THAT SUIT IN CHANCERY--WHICH SOME PERSONS PLEAD . . . . 324 3 DON JUAN 12   18   1
    THAT SUIT IN CHANCERY--(I HAVE A CHANCERY SUIT . . . . 357 3 DON JUAN 12 V 18   1
    THAT SUIT IN CHANCERY--(I HAVE A CHANCERY SUIT . . . . 357 3 DON JUAN 12 V 18   1
    A CHILD OF CHANCERY THAT STAR-CHAMBER WARD . . . . . . 564 3 DON JUAN 17   4   4
CHANCES
    THEIR CHANCES--THEY'RE TOO NUMEROUS LIKE THE THIRTY . . . 299 3 DON JUAN 11   61   7
'CHANGE
    ON 'CHANGE AND EVEN THY SILVER SOIL PERU . . . . 318 3 DON JUAN 12   6   7
CHANGE
    WHICH MAKES ME WISH YOU'D CHANGE YOUR LAKES FOR OCEAN . . 12 2 DON JUAN D   5   8
    WROUGHT CHANGE WITH ALL ARMIDA'S FAIRY ART . . . . . . 60 2 DON JUAN 1   71   7
    CHANGE HORSES MAKING HISTORY CHANGE ITS TUNE . . . . . 76 2 DON JUAN 1 103   5
    CHANGE HORSES MAKING HISTORY CHANGE ITS TUNE . . . . . 76 2 DON JUAN 1 103   5
    THE SAME THINGS CHANGE THEIR NAMES AT SUCH A RATE . . . 278 2 DON JUAN 3   6   6
    FOR INTO A PRIME MINISTER BUT CHANGE . . . . 283 2 DON JUAN 3   14   3
    SERENELY SAVAGE WITH A LITTLE CHANGE . . . . 367 2 DON JUAN 4   44   3
    AVAILED FOR EITHER NEITHER CHANGE OF PLACE . . . . . . 381 2 DON JUAN 4   68   6
    THE VERY INSTANT TILL THE CHANGE THAT CAST . . . . . . 381 2 DON JUAN 4   69   5
    BUT LET ME CHANGE THIS THEME WHICH GROWS TOO SAD . . . 384 2 DON JUAN 4   74   1
    SAVE CHANGE I'VE STOOD UPON ACHILLES' TOMB . . . . . . 399 2 DON JUAN 4 101   7
    AND THEN THE MERCHANT GIVING CHANGE AND SIGNING . . . . 426 2 DON JUAN 5   29   7
    WHEN HE WAS GONE THERE WAS A SUDDEN CHANGE . . . . . . 473 2 DON JUAN 5 108   1
    BY WAY OF CHANGE FROM THEIR SEPULCHRAL SITES . . . . . 38 3 DON JUAN 6   64   6
    OF THIS OUR BANQUET WE MUST SOMETIMES CHANGE . . . . . 65 3 DON JUAN 6 120   4
    OR WIDOW MAID OR MOTHER SHE CAN CHANGE HER . . . . . . 214 3 DON JUAN 9   64   5
    NO MORE IT DOTH--ITS PLOUGHS BUT CHANGE THEIR BOYS . . . 228 3 DON JUAN 10   7   7
    THRO' SUCH A SCENE OF CHANGE AND DREAD AND SLAUGHTER . . 252 3 DON JUAN 10   56   2
    A SILENT CHANGE DISSOLVES THE GLITTERING MASS . . . . . 306 3 DON JUAN 11   76   6
    CHANGE GROWS TOO CHANGEABLE WITHOUT BEING NEW . . . . . 309 3 DON JUAN 11   82   6
    BUT WOULD NOT CHANGE MY FREE THOUGHTS FOR A THRONE . . . 312 3 DON JUAN 11   90   8
    THE OBSEQUIOUS LANDLORD HATH THE CHANGE RESTORED . . . . 379 3 DON JUAN 13   46   5
    OF STRONGBOW'S TALK YOU WOULD NOT CHANGE A WORD . . . . 402 3 DON JUAN 13   93   5
    OF CHANGE AND HOW SHOULD THIS BE OTHERWISE . . . . . . 451 3 DON JUAN 14   94   2
    HOW OFT WOULD VICE AND VIRTUE PLACES CHANGE . . . . . . 455 3 DON JUAN 14 101   5
CHANGEABLE
    SO CHANGEABLE HAD BEEN THE WINDS THAT BLEW . . . . . . 209 2 DON JUAN 2 100   6
    AND WHY BECAUSE SHE'S CHANGEABLE AND CHASTE . . . . . . 230 3 DON JUAN 10   11   1
    CHANGE GROWS TOO CHANGEABLE WITHOUT BEING NEW . . . . . 309 3 DON JUAN 11   82   6
    CHANGEABLE TOO--YET SOMEHOW IDEM SEMPER . . . . 567 3 DON JUAN 17   11   3
CHANGED
    CHANGED FOR THE DAME GREW DISTANT THE YOUTH SHY . . . . 60 2 DON JUAN 1   70   2
    THEN CHANGED LIKE TO A BOW THAT'S BENT AND THEN . . . . 204 2 DON JUAN 2   91   7
    IT CHANGED OF COURSE A HEAVENLY CAMELEON . . . . 205 2 DON JUAN 2   92   1
    I'VE CHANGED FOR SOME FEW YEARS THE DAY TO NIGHT . . . . 230 2 DON JUAN 2 140 V3
    AND ALWAYS CHANGED AS TRUE AS ANY NEEDLE . . . . 317 2 DON JUAN 3   80   2
    THE DREAM CHANGED IN A CAVE SHE STOOD ITS WALLS . . . . 362 2 DON JUAN 4   33   1
    THEY CHANGED FROM ROOM TO ROOM BUT ALL FORGOT . . . . . 379 2 DON JUAN 4   64   5
    IN TIME TO HIS OLD TUNE HE CHANGED THE THEME . . . . . 380 2 DON JUAN 4   66   2
    ALL FEELINGS CHANGED BUT THIS WAS LAST TO VARY . . . . 413 2 DON JUAN 5   4   5
    POOR CREATURES THEIR GOOD LOOKS WERE SADLY CHANGED . . . 414 2 DON JUAN 5   7   4
    AND CHANGED AS QUICKLY AS HEARTS AFTER MARRIAGE . . . . 379 3 DON JUAN 13   46   4
CHANGELESS
    MOONS CHANGING HAD ROLL'D ON AND CHANGELESS FOUND . . . 352 2 DON JUAN 4   16   1
CHANGES
    FEW CHANGES E'ER CAN BETTER THEIR AFFAIRS . . . . 263 2 DON JUAN 2 201   5
    BUT CHANGES NIGHT AND DAY TOO LIKE THE SKY . . . . . . 270 2 DON JUAN 2 214   2
    HE WAS A MAN WHO HAD SEEN MANY CHANGES . . . . 317 2 DON JUAN 3   80   1
    THE UNUSUAL QUICKNESS OF THESE COMMON CHANGES . . . . . 309 3 DON JUAN 11   81   8
    I HAVE SEEN MORE CHANGES DOWN FROM MONARCHS TO . . . . 309 3 DON JUAN 11   82   2
    CHANGES IN YOUTH TO BE SURPRISED AT ANY . . . . 338 3 DON JUAN 12   49   8
    (WHO WATCHED THE CHANGES OF DON JUAN'S BROW . . . . . . 516 3 DON JUAN 16   37   2
CHANGING
    MOONS CHANGING HAD ROLL'D ON AND CHANGELESS FOUND . . . 352 2 DON JUAN 4   16   1
CHANNELS
    OF FASHION--SAY WHAT STREAMS NOW FILL THOSE CHANNELS . . 308 3 DON JUAN 11   80   6
CHANSON
    IN FRANCE FOR INSTANCE HE WOULD WRITE A CHANSON . . . . 320 2 DON JUAN 3   86   1
CHAOS
    FIRST OUT OF AND THEN BACK AGAIN TO CHAOS . . . . 201 3 DON JUAN 9   37   7

CHAPEAU-BRAS
  COUNT CHAPEAU-BRAS TOO HAD A BALL BETWEEN . . . . 116 3 DON JUAN 8   10   2
CHAPEL
  AN EXQUISITE SMALL CHAPEL HAD BEEN ABLE . . . . 389 3 DON JUAN 13   66   5
CHAPTERS
  HIS PRISONERS DIVIDING THEM LIKE CHAPTERS . . . . . . 283 2 DON JUAN 3   15   6
CHARACTER
  IN CHARACTER--BUT IT WOULD NOT BE FAIR . . . . 49 2 DON JUAN 1   51   4
  LOSING ELECTIONS CHARACTER AND TEMPER . . . . 150 2 DON JUAN 1 V 1   7
  A BUSY CHARACTER IN THE DULL SCENE . . . . 352 2 DON JUAN 4   15   4
  AND WITH THAT GENTLE SERIOUS CHARACTER . . . . 250 3 DON JUAN 10   52   2
  OF CHARACTER IN THOSE AT LEAST WHO HAVE GOT ANY . . . 417 3 DON JUAN 14   16   8
  ADELINE NO DEEP JUDGE OF CHARACTER . . . . 463 3 DON JUAN 15   17   1
  JUAN KNEW NOUGHT OF SUCH A CHARACTER-- . . . . 481 3 DON JUAN 15   58   1
CHARACTERS
  NEW CHARACTERS THE EPISODES ARE THREE . . . . 135 2 DON JUAN 1   200   5
  BY WHOSE DEGREES ALL CHARACTERS ARE CLASSED-- . . . . 524 3 DON JUAN 16   48   3
CHARGE
  THE FOREMOST IN THE CHARGE OR IN THE SALLY . . . . . 431 2 DON JUAN 5   37   7
  AND I OF YOUR YOUNG CHARGE WILL TAKE DUE CARE . . . . 29 3 DON JUAN 6   47   6
  BUT NOW I MUST TRANSFER HER TO THE CHARGE . . . . . . 46 3 DON JUAN 6   81   7
  JUAN WAS GIVEN IN CHARGE AS HATH BEEN STATED . . . . 57 3 DON JUAN 6   102   6
  OF DANUBE'S BANK TOOK FORMIDABLE CHARGE . . . . 72 3 DON JUAN 7   12   5
  AND MADE THEM CHARGE WITH BAYONET THESE MACHINES . . . 93 3 DON JUAN 7   53   3
  THE HEARTS OF THE HEROIC ON A CHARGE . . . . 103 3 DON JUAN 7   71   7
  THE MARCH THE CHARGE THE SHOUTS OF EITHER FAITH . . . 111 3 DON JUAN 7   87   6
  HE TURNED HIS EYES UPON HIS LITTLE CHARGE . . . . . . 198 3 DON JUAN 9   31   2
  THIS SECRET CHARGE ON JUAN TO DISPLAY . . . . 247 3 DON JUAN 10   46   3
  A GOODLY GUARDIAN FOR HIS INFANT CHARGE . . . . 335 3 DON JUAN 12   41   7
  OUR HERO GLADLY SAW HIS LITTLE CHARGE . . . . 339 3 DON JUAN 12   51   2
CHARGED
  TILL SLOWLY CHARGED WITH THUNDER THEY DISPLAY . . . . 375 2 DON JUAN 4   57   3
CHARGER
  SO THAT HIS HORSE OR CHARGER HUNTER HACK . . . . . . 424 3 DON JUAN 14   32   7
CHARING
  THE LINE OF LIGHTS TOO UP TO CHARING CROSS . . . . . 280 3 DON JUAN 11   26   1
CHARIOT
  THAT JUAN'S CHARIOT ROLLING LIKE A DRUM . . . . 277 3 DON JUAN 11   20   5
  COACH CHARIOT LUGGAGE BAGGAGE EQUIPAGE . . . . 378 3 DON JUAN 13   44   2
CHARIOTS
  THROUGH STREET AND SQUARE FAST FLASHING CHARIOTS HURLED . 302 3 DON JUAN 11   67   3
  A BLEST HOUR FOR POSTILLIONS--CHARIOTS FLY . . . . . 377 3 DON JUAN 13   42 V3
CHARIOTS'
  WHERE THE TRIUMPHAL CHARIOTS' HAUGHTY MARCH . . . . . 485 3 DON JUAN 15   67   4
CHARITABLE
  SO GENTLE CHARMING CHARITABLE CHASTE-- . . . . 346 3 DON JUAN 12   66   7
CHARITY
  THEIR CHARITY INCREASED ABOUT THEIR GUEST . . . . . . 225 2 DON JUAN 2   131   5
  THE VIRTUES EVEN THE MOST EXALTED CHARITY . . . . . . 408 2 DON JUAN 4   115   7
  THEN SHE WAS GIVEN TO CHARITY AND PITY . . . . 338 3 DON JUAN 12   47   6
  IT GROWS AN ACT OF PATRIOTIC CHARITY . . . . 357 3 DON JUAN 12   89   3
  ITS MOTIVE FOR THAT CHARITY WE OWE . . . . 553 3 DON JUAN 16   106   3
CHARLATAN
  A CHARLATAN A COXCOMB--AND HAVE BEEN . . . . 84 2 DON JUAN 1   116   7
CHARLEMAGNE'S
  LIKE CHARLEMAGNE'S--AND ALL SUCH PEERS IN LOOK . . . 398 3 DON JUAN 13   85   3
CHARLES
  COULD HE NOT BEG THE LOAN OF CHARLES WAIN . . . . . . 333 2 DON JUAN 3   99   3
  AS OBSTINATE AS SWEDISH CHARLES AT BENDER . . . . . . 165 3 DON JUAN 8   107   4
  BUT IN THE WAR WHICH STRUCK CHARLES FROM HIS THRONE . . 386 3 DON JUAN 13   60   4
CHARLOTTE
  WHERE'S CHARLOTTE (THAT'S NOT EASILY OWN'D) . . . . . 307 3 DON JUAN 11   78 V3
CHARM
  BUT THEN THE SITUATION HAD ITS CHARM . . . . 83 2 DON JUAN 1   115   6
  YIELDED TO THE DEEP TWILIGHT'S PURPLE CHARM . . . . . 253 2 DON JUAN 2   184   8
  AND ALL ITS CHARM LIKE DEATH WITHOUT ITS TERRORS . . . 261 2 DON JUAN 2   197   8
  HAVE SUCH A CHARM FOR US POOR HUMAN CREATURES . . . . 267 2 DON JUAN 2   208   8
  SO BEAUTIFUL--ITS VERY SHAPE WOULD CHARM . . . . . . 312 3 DON JUAN 3   71   5
  BEFORE ONE CHARM OR HOPE HAD TAKEN WING . . . . 348 2 DON JUAN 4   8   8
  I YIELD THUS FAR BUT SOON WILL BREAK THE CHARM . . . . 459 2 DON JUAN 5   82   5
  OR OVER-COLD ANNIHILATES THE CHARM . . . . 13 3 DON JUAN 6   15   8
  IT WOULD NOT SPOIL SOME SEPARATE CHARM TO PARE . . . . 27 3 DON JUAN 6   42   8
  THE MOON BREAKS HALF UNVEILED EACH FURTHER CHARM . . . 39 3 DON JUAN 6   66   5
  OH THOU ETERNAL HOMER WHO COULDST CHARM . . . . 106 3 DON JUAN 7   79   1
  HAS SPAIN HAD HEROES WHILE ROMANCE COULD CHARM . . . 364 3 DON JUAN 13   11   4
  TO THIS GREY RUIN WITH A VOICE TO CHARM . . . . 388 3 DON JUAN 13   64   5
  WITH ALL THE ADDED CHARM OF FORM AND FEATURE . . . . 478 3 DON JUAN 15   52   4
  WHICH CHARM MOST PEOPLE IN THEIR EARLIER DAY . . . . 479 3 DON JUAN 15   53   3
  AS SOME WHO LABOUR MORE AND YET MAY CHARM LESS . . . . 498 3 DON JUAN 15   94   8
CHARM'D
  CHARM'D WITH EACH OTHER ALL THINGS CHARM'D THAT BROUGHT . 354 2 DON JUAN 4   20   7
  CHARM'D WITH EACH OTHER ALL THINGS CHARM'D THAT BROUGHT . 354 2 DON JUAN 4   20   7
  THE DICE SEEM'D CHARM'D TOO WITH HIS REPARTEES . . . . 399 3 DON JUAN 13   86   8
CHARMED
  WHICH CHARMED THE CHARMING MARY MONTAGU . . . . 412 2 DON JUAN 5   3   8
CHARMER
  CHARMS FROM THE CHARMER YET SOME NEVER GROW . . . . . 468 2 DON JUAN 5   98   7
CHARMERS
  BEYOND THE CHARMERS WE HAVE ALREADY CITED . . . . . . 477 3 DON JUAN 15   48   4
  THE CHARMING OF THESE CHARMERS WHO SEEM BOUND . . . . 518 3 DON JUAN 16   40   2

125

PAGE VOL   CANTO STANZA LN

CHARMING
HIS DEATH CONTRIVED TO SPOIL A CHARMING CAUSE . . . . . . 38 2 DON JUAN 1 33 5
AT SIX A CHARMING CHILD AND AT ELEVEN . . . . 48 2 DON JUAN 1 49 2
AT SIX I SAID HE WAS A CHARMING CHILD . . . . 49 2 DON JUAN 1 50 1
WAS MARRIED CHARMING CHASTE AND TWENTY-THREE . . . . . . 54 2 DON JUAN 1 59 8
WHICH WITH A LITTLE PATIENCE MIGHT GROW CHARMING . . . . 68 2 DON JUAN 1 86 8
THE CHARMING CREATURES LIE WITH SUCH A GRACE . . . . . . 119 2 DON JUAN 1 178 7
WHICH CHARMED THE CHARMING MARY MONTAGU . . . . 412 2 DON JUAN 5 3 8
HOW BEAUTEOUS ARE ROULEAUS HOW CHARMING CHESTS . . . . . 321 3 DON JUAN 12 12 1
HER CHARMING FIGURE AND ROMANTIC HISTORY . . . . 328 3 DON JUAN 12 27 7
SO GENTLE CHARMING CHARITABLE CHASTE-- . . . . 346 3 DON JUAN 12 66 7
AS IF EACH CHARMING WORD WERE A DECREE . . . . 492 3 DON JUAN 15 82 4
THE CHARMING OF THESE CHARMERS WHO SEEM BOUND . . . . 518 3 DON JUAN 16 40 2
CHARMS
OF MANY CHARMS IN HER AS NATURAL . . . . 51 2 DON JUAN 1 55 5
THE CHARMS OF MAID WIFE AND STILL LESS OF WIDOW . . . . 144 2 DON JUAN 1 216 2
SUSTAIN'D HIS HEAD UPON HER BOSOM'S CHARMS . . . . . 260 2 DON JUAN 2 195 4
OF CHARMS TO MAKE GOOD GOLD AND CURE BAD AILS . . . . 293 2 DON JUAN 3 34 5
CHARMS FROM THE CHARMER YET SOME NEVER GROW . . . . . 468 2 DON JUAN 5 98 7
SOME STRESS ON CHARMS WHICH SELDOM ARE IF E'ER . . . . 485 2 DON JUAN 5 129 5
HIS HIGHNESS GAZED UPON GULBEYAZ' CHARMS . . . . . 12 3 DON JUAN 6 13 6
FROM OGLING ALL THEIR CHARMS FROM BREASTS TO BACKS . . 20 3 DON JUAN 6 29 8
WITH THE MOST REGULATED CHARMS OF FEATURE . . . . . 32 3 DON JUAN 6 52 3
BUT JUAN NEVER LEFT THEM WHILE THEY HAD CHARMS . . . 139 3 DON JUAN 8 53 8
THOUGHT NOT UPON THE CHARMS OF FOUR YOUNG BRIDES . . . 168 3 DON JUAN 8 114 2
WHOSE CHARMS MADE ALL MEN SPEAK AND WOMEN DUMB . . . 365 3 DON JUAN 13 13 6
DOWN TO THE HARP--BECAUSE TO MUSIC'S CHARMS . . . . 408 3 DON JUAN 13 107 7
OF CHARMS THAT SHOULD OR SHOULD NOT BE ADMIRED . . . 408 3 DON JUAN 13 108 6
THE CHARMS OF OTHER DAYS IN STARLIGHT GLEAMS . . . . 509 3 DON JUAN 16 19 2
CHARON'S
LIKE CHARON'S BARK OF SPECTRES DULL AND PALE . . . . 209 2 DON JUAN 2 101 3
CHART
WITH SUCH A CHART AS MAY BE SAFELY STUCK TO-- . . . . 348 3 DON JUAN 12 70 5
SUCH ARE--BUT I HAVE LOST THE LONDON CHART . . . . . 370 3 DON JUAN 13 27 8
FRAIL MARINERS AFLOAT WITHOUT A CHART . . . . 442 3 DON JUAN 14 74 5
CHARTS
WHOSE CHARTS LAY DOWN ITS CURRENTS TO A HAIR . . . . 7 3 DON JUAN 6 2 4
CHASE
HIS HELL-DOGS AND THEIR CHASE AND THE FAIR THRONG . . . 337 2 DON JUAN 3 106 6
WITH US THERE IS MORE LAW GIVEN TO THE CHASE . . . . 482 2 DON JUAN 5 123 4
BY THE RESISTANCE OF THE CHASE THEY BATTERED . . . . 131 3 DON JUAN 8 37 8
THOU ARE NO NOVICE IN THE HEADLONG CHASE . . . . . 326 3 DON JUAN 12 23 6
RIFE WITH MORE HORNS THAN HOUNDS--SHE HATH THE CHASE . . 395 3 DON JUAN 13 78 2
WHO AFTER A LONG CHASE O'ER HILLS DALES BUSHES . . . 425 3 DON JUAN 14 35 6
TO EARLY RISERS AFTER A LONG CHASE . . . . 426 3 DON JUAN 14 36 2
CHASED
BY SALLUST IN HIS CATILINE WHO CHASED . . . . 61 3 DON JUAN 6 111 6
CHASSEURS
HE FOUND A NUMBER OF CHASSEURS ALL SCATTERED . . . . 131 3 DON JUAN 8 37 7
CHASTE
WAS MARRIED CHARMING CHASTE AND TWENTY-THREE . . . . 54 2 DON JUAN 1 59 8
WHICH TIME HAD LATELY RENDER'D MUCH MORE CHASTE . . . 58 2 DON JUAN 1 67 2
WHO CALL'D HER CHASTE METHINKS BEGAN TOO SOON . . . 82 2 DON JUAN 1 113 3
HERE MY CHASTE MUSE A LIBERTY MUST TAKE-- . . . . . 86 2 DON JUAN 1 120 1
CHASTE MUSE--(WELL IF YOU MUST YOU MUST)--THE VEIL . . 160 2 DON JUAN 2 7 1
PRESSURE OF HANDS PERHAPS EVEN A CHASTE KISS-- . . . 242 2 DON JUAN 2 164 7
THOU MAK'ST THE CHASTE CONNUBIAL STATE PRECARIOUS . . 266 2 DON JUAN 2 206 1
CHASTE READER THEN IN ANY WAY TO PUT . . . . . . 282 2 DON JUAN 3 12 3
SOME CHASTE LIAISON OF THE KIND--I MEAN . . . . . 288 2 DON JUAN 3 25 2
TRUE KNIGHTS CHASTE DAMES HUGE GIANTS KINGS DESPOTIC . . 347 2 DON JUAN 4 6 6
HERE I MIGHT ENTER ON A CHASTE DESCRIPTION . . . . 397 2 DON JUAN 4 97 1
SHE ROSE AND PAUSING ONE CHASTE MOMENT THREW . . . 483 2 DON JUAN 5 125 7
WITH ALL THEIR CHASTE INTEGRITY OF LAWS . . . . . 35 3 DON JUAN 6 58 5
AND THEN SHE GAVE JUANNA A CHASTE KISS . . . . . . 35 3 DON JUAN 6 59 1
HAD MADE THEM CHASTE--THEY RAVISHED VERY LITTLE . . . 176 3 DON JUAN 8 128 8
OF LIGHT TO SAVE THE VENERABLY CHASTE-- . . . . . 177 3 DON JUAN 8 130 6
IS WHEN CHASTE MATRONS TO THEIR OTHER TIES . . . . 220 3 DON JUAN 9 76 7
AND WHY BECAUSE SHE'S CHANGEABLE AND CHASTE . . . . 230 3 DON JUAN 10 11 1
MADE THE CHASTE CATHERINE LOOK A LITTLE GRIM . . . . 246 3 DON JUAN 10 44 3
HERE ARE CHASTE WIVES PURE LIVES HERE PEOPLE PAY . . 273 3 DON JUAN 11 10 1
SO GENTLE CHARMING CHARITABLE CHASTE-- . . . . . 346 3 DON JUAN 12 66 7
CHASTE WAS SHE TO DETRACTION'S DESPERATION . . . . 365 3 DON JUAN 13 14 1
IN MY YOUNG DAYS THAT CHASTE AND GOODLY VEIL . . . 422 3 DON JUAN 14 27 4
CHASTE WERE HIS STEPS EACH KEPT WITHIN DUE BOUND . . 427 3 DON JUAN 14 39 1
THE CHASTE AND THOSE WHO ARE NOT SO MUCH INSPIRED . . 428 3 DON JUAN 14 41 6
THIS SORT OF CHASTE LIAISON FOR A FRIEND . . . . . 438 3 DON JUAN 14 64 4
WHETHER DON JUAN AND CHASTE ADELINE . . . . 453 3 DON JUAN 14 97 1
WAS THERE CHASTE DAME WHO HAD NOT IN HER HEAD . . . 470 3 DON JUAN 15 32 4
THE CHASTE DESCRIPTION EVEN OF A BECASSE . . . . . 487 3 DON JUAN 15 71 8
IT HAPPENED LUCKILY THE CHASTE ORB SHONE . . . . . 506 3 DON JUAN 16 13 3
OF KNIGHTS AND DAMES HEROIC AND CHASTE TOO . . . . 508 3 DON JUAN 16 17 5
AND DREADING THE CHASTE ECHOES OF HER SHOE . . . . 556 3 DON JUAN 16 112 8
CHASTELY
SAD RAKES TO SADDER HUSBANDS CHASTELY TAMING . . . . 418 3 DON JUAN 14 18 5
CHASTEN'D
WHICH STRUGGLED THROUGH AND CHASTEN'D DOWN THE WHOLE . . 54 2 DON JUAN 1 60 8
CHASTENED
IN THE MORE CHASTENED DOMES OF WESTERN KINGS . . . . 465 2 DON JUAN 5 94 3
CHASTER
START NOT STILL CHASTER READER--SHE'LL BE NICE HENCEFORWARD 86 2 DON JUAN 1 120 2
THAT--BUT MY CHASTER EAR WILL NOT RECEIVE . . . . . 336 3 DON JUAN 12 43 4

	PAGE	VOL		CANTO	STANZA	LN
CHASTEST						
THE LOVELIEST CHASTEST BEST BUT--QUITE A FOOL	405	2	DON JUAN	4	111	8
LIKE CHASTEST WIVES FROM CONSTANT HUSBANDS' SIDES	125	3	DON JUAN	8	27	3
HIS YOUTH WAS NOT THE CHASTEST THAT MIGHT BE	251	3	DON JUAN	10	54	6
UNLESS I KNEW THE VERY CHASTEST SQUARES	370	3	DON JUAN	13	26	8
CHASTITIES						
AND STOCKINGS VIRTUES LOVES AND CHASTITIES	347	3	DON JUAN	12	67	V8
CHASTITY						
YE WHO HAVE KEPT YOUR CHASTITY WHEN YOUNG	486	2	DON JUAN	5	130	2
THEIR CHASTITY IN THESE UNHAPPY CLIMES	501	2	DON JUAN	5	157	3
AND AS FOR CHASTITY YOU'LL NEVER BIND IT	352	3	DON JUAN	12	80	5
CHAT						
A LOBSTER SALAD AND CHAMPAIGNE AND CHAT	94	2	DON JUAN	1	135	8
RELIEVED HER THOUGHTS DULL SILENCE AND QUICK CHAT	378	2	DON JUAN	4	63	6
TO MEET HOWEVER 'TIS NO TIME TO CHAT	290	3	DON JUAN	11	44	6
CHATHAM						
BUT GREY WAS NOT ARRIVED AND CHATHAM GONE	353	3	DON JUAN	12	82	8
CHATTED						
OTHERS IN MONOSYLLABLE TALK CHATTED	441	2	DON JUAN	5	53	3
CHATTER						
MY TEETH BEGIN TO CHATTER MY VEINS FREEZE--	121	2	DON JUAN	1	181	6
HAVE SUNG OR EVEN A DANDY'S DANDIEST CHATTER	493	2	DON JUAN	5	143	4
BEGAN TO SING DANCE CHATTER SMILE AND PLAY	23	3	DON JUAN	6	34	8
AND WILL NOT TOSS AND CHATTER THE NIGHT THROUGH	30	3	DON JUAN	6	49	6
CHATTERING						
WHILE I AM CHATTERING BEYOND ALL EXPRESSION	331	2	DON JUAN	3	96	V4
CHAUNT						
OH FOR A FORTY-PARSON-POWER TO CHAUNT	241	3	DON JUAN	10	34	1
CHE						
VOI CHE ENTRATE THE HINGE SEEMED TO SPEAK	557	3	DON JUAN	16	116	3
CHEAPENED						
THE KING HIMSELF HAD CHEAPENED IT BUT THOUGHT	528	3	DON JUAN	16	56	5
CHEAPENING						
CHEAPENING AN OX AN ASS A LAMB OR KID	425	2	DON JUAN	5	28	6
CHEATED						
TILL THE EYE CHEATED OPENS THICK WITH TEARS	227	2	DON JUAN	2	134	8
CHEATING						
SAVING HIS SOUL BY CHEATING IN THE WARE	80	3	DON JUAN	7	27	4
CHECK						
WHICH RUSHES TO SOME SHORE WHOSE SHINGLES CHECK	60	3	DON JUAN	6	108	7
MEN'S WRONGS AND RATHER CHECK THAN PUNISH CRIMES	361	3	DON JUAN	13	8	6
CHECKED						
FOR NE'ER TILL NOW SHE KNEW A CHECKED DESIRE	489	2	DON JUAN	5	134	6
EVEN YE WHO KNOW WHAT A CHECKED WOMAN IS	489	2	DON JUAN	5	134	7
CHECKS						
CHECKS TO A LAKE WHOSE WAVES IN CIRCLES SPREAD	231	2	DON JUAN	2	141	7
IF FREE FROM PASSION WHICH ALL FRIENDSHIP CHECKS	451	3	DON JUAN	14	93	5
I HAVE SEARCHED THE WORLD AND MIDST SUCCESS OR CHECKS	451	3	DON JUAN	14	93	V5
'TIS RARELY FOUND BUT WOULD REPAY ALL CHECKS	451	3	DON JUAN	14	93	V5
CHECQUERED						
FOR CHECQUERED AS IS SEEN OUR HUMAN LOT	156	3	DON JUAN	8	89	3
CHECQUERED WITH ALL THE TRACERY OF THE HALL	559	3	DON JUAN	16	120	4
CHEEK						
HER CHEEK ALL PURPLE WITH THE BEAM OF YOUTH	55	2	DON JUAN	1	61	4
GLOW'D IN HER CHEEK AND YET SHE FELT NO WRONG	78	2	DON JUAN	1	106	2
WAVED AND O'ERSHADING HER WAN CHEEK APPEARS	108	2	DON JUAN	1	158	4
BUT PRESS'D HER BLOODLESS LIP TO JUAN'S CHEEK	114	2	DON JUAN	1	169	8
OF A SOFT CHEEK AND ASPECT DELICATE	203	2	DON JUAN	2	88	2
AND HER TRANSPARENT CHEEK ALL PURE AND WARM	216	2	DON JUAN	2	114	4
FROM HEART TO CHEEK IS CURB'D INTO A BLUSH	231	2	DON JUAN	2	141	4
FOR STILL HE LAY AND ON HIS THIN WORN CHEEK	234	2	DON JUAN	2	147	1
AND LOOK'D UPON THE LADY IN WHOSE CHEEK	236	2	DON JUAN	2	150	2
BREATHING ALL GENTLY O'ER HIS CHEEK AND MOUTH	245	2	DON JUAN	2	168	7
AND THEN ON THE PALE CHEEK HER BREAST NOW WARMS	260	2	DON JUAN	2	195	6
NOW PILLOW'D CHEEK TO CHEEK IN LOVING SLEEP	359	2	DON JUAN	4	29	1
NOW PILLOW'D CHEEK TO CHEEK IN LOVING SLEEP	359	2	DON JUAN	4	29	1
THEN TURN'D TO JUAN IN WHOSE CHEEK THE BLOOD	365	2	DON JUAN	4	39	5
THE OLD MAN'S CHEEK GREW PALE BUT NOT WITH DREAD	365	2	DON JUAN	4	40	3
THE SECOND HAD HIS CHEEK LAID OPEN BUT	370	2	DON JUAN	4	49	1
AND INTO HER CLEAR CHEEK THE BLOOD WAS BROUGHT	473	2	DON JUAN	5	108	4
ONE WITH HER FLUSHED CHEEK LAID ON HER WHITE ARM	39	3	DON JUAN	6	66	1
HER CHEEK BEGAN TO FLUSH HER EYES TO SPARKLE	56	3	DON JUAN	6	101	7
HER CHEEK TURNED ASHES EARS RUNG BRAIN WHIRLED ROUND	58	3	DON JUAN	6	105	5
AS HE TURNED O'ER EACH PALE AND GORY CHEEK	158	3	DON JUAN	8	94	6
O'ERSPREADS THE CHEEK WHICH SEEMS TOO PURE FOR CLAY	229	3	DON JUAN	10	8	7
WILL FEED UPON THE FAIREST FRESHEST CHEEK	243	3	DON JUAN	10	38	3
ALONG HIS WASTED CHEEK AND SEEMED TO GRAVEL	245	3	DON JUAN	10	43	7
PALE AS IF PAINTED SO HER CHEEK BEING RED	532	3	DON JUAN	16	64	2
AND SOMETHING LIKE A SMILE UPON HER CHEEK	544	3	DON JUAN	16	92	2
CHEEK'S						
HER BROW WAS WHITE AND LOW HER CHEEK'S PURE DYE	218	2	DON JUAN	2	118	1
WHO GAZED UPON HER CHEEK'S TRANSCENDANT HUE	27	3	DON JUAN	6	42	3
CHEEKS						
THEIR LARGE BLACK EYES AND SOFT SERAPHIC CHEEKS	292	2	DON JUAN	3	33	2
THE BLOOM TOO HAD RETURN'D TO HAIDEE'S CHEEKS	295	2	DON JUAN	3	38	6
AND LEFT HIS CHEEKS AS PALE AS SNOWDROPS BLOWING	478	2	DON JUAN	5	117	6
OR SAID HER CHEEKS ASSUMED THE DEEPEST DYES	489	2	DON JUAN	5	134	3
BETWEEN THE EYES AND LOLAH ON BOTH CHEEKS	31	3	DON JUAN	6	50	2
GOOD HOURS OF FAIR CHEEKS ARE THE FAIREST TINTERS	409	3	DON JUAN	13	111	7

127

PAGE VOL CANTO STANZA LN

CHEER
    HOME TO THE WEARY TO THE HUNGRY CHEER . . . . 338 2 DON JUAN 3   107 2
    GREAT PLENTY MUCH FORMALITY SMALL CHEER . . . . 538 3 DON JUAN 16   78 7
CHEER'D
    AND THESE TWO TENDED HIM AND CHEER'D HIM BOTH . . . . 221 2 DON JUAN 2   123 1
CHEERFUL
    THERE'S SOMETHING CHEERFUL IN THAT SORT OF LIGHT . . . . 94 2 DON JUAN 1   135 5
    LUXURIANT BUDDING CHEERFUL WITHOUT MIRTH . . . . 32 3 DON JUAN 6   53 3
    CHEERFUL AS CHILDREN CLIMB THE BREASTS OF MOTHERS . . . 119 3 DON JUAN 8   15 6
    OR CHEERFUL WITHOUT ANY FLAWS OR STARTS . . . . . . 292 3 DON JUAN 11   47 5
    SERENE ACCOMPLISH'D CHEERFUL BUT NOT LOUD . . . . . 462 3 DON JUAN 15   15 1
    CHEERFUL--BUT SOMETIMES RATHER APT TO WHIMPER . . . . 567 3 DON JUAN 17   11 5
CHEERFULNESS
    AND CHEERFULNESS THE HANDMAID OF THEIR TOIL . . . . . . 145 3 DON JUAN 8   67 2
CHEERY
    ON WHAT I'VE SEEN OR PONDER'D SAD OR CHEERY . . . . . 415 3 DON JUAN 14   11 6
CHEESE-PARING
    KNOW NOT WHAT VISIONS SPRING FROM EACH CHEESE-PARING . . 316 3 DON JUAN 12   3 8
CHEMISE
    OF AZURE PINK AND WHITE WAS HER CHEMISE-- . . . . . 311 2 DON JUAN 3   70 3
    WHICH GIRT A SLIGHT CHEMISE AS WHITE AS MILK . . . . . 456 2 DON JUAN 5   77 4
CHEOPS
    CHEOPS ERECTED THE FIRST PYRAMID . . . . 146 2 DON JUAN 1   219 2
    SINCE NOT A PINCH OF DUST REMAINS OF CHEOPS . . . . . 146 2 DON JUAN 1   219 8
CHEQUERED
    THE HISTORY OF DIVORCES WHICH THOUGH CHEQUERED . . . . 209 3 DON JUAN 9   53 7
CHERISH
    THUS THE FRAIL BEINGS WE WOULD FONDLY CHERISH . . . . 275 2 DON JUAN 3   2 7
CHERISH'D
    SHE MUST NOT OWN BUT CHERISH'D MORE THE WHILE . . . . 61 2 DON JUAN 1   72 4
    HOWEVER DEAR OR CHERISH'D IN THEIR DAY . . . . . . 379 2 DON JUAN 4   64 4
CHERISHED
    HIS THIRD WAS SABRED AND THE FOURTH MOST CHERISHED . . . 166 3 DON JUAN 8   110 3
CHERSONESE
    THE TYRANT OF THE CHERSONESE . . . . 325 2 DON JUAN 3 L 12 1
CHERUB
    WHEN HE PUT ON THE CHERUB TO PERPLEX . . . . . . 474 2 DON JUAN 5   109 3
CHERUBIM
    NOT PRACTISE OH FOR TRUMPS OF CHERUBIM . . . . . . 241 3 DON JUAN 10   34 4
CHERUBS
    LIKE CHERUBS ROUND AN ALTAR-PIECE THEY CLING . . . . 306 2 DON JUAN 3   60 5
CHESS
    UPON THEIR HAMS WERE OCCUPIED AT CHESS . . . . . . 441 2 DON JUAN 5   53 2
CHESS-BOARD
    GOOD COMPANY'S A CHESS-BOARD--THERE ARE KINGS . . . . 400 3 DON JUAN 13   89 1
CHESSMAN
    FROM OUR NEXT NEIGHBOUR'S LAND WHERE LIKE A CHESSMAN . . 288 3 DON JUAN 11   42 3
CHEST
    CLOSET AND CLOTHES'-PRESS CHEST AND WINDOW-SEAT . . . . 99 2 DON JUAN 1   143 2
    A MISER FILLING HIS MOST HOARDED CHEST . . . . . . 261 2 DON JUAN 2   196 6
CHESTERFIELD
    HE THOUGHT AT HEART LIKE COURTLY CHESTERFIELD . . . . 425 3 DON JUAN 14   35 5
CHESTS
    HOW BEAUTEOUS ARE ROULEAUS HOW CHARMING CHESTS . . . . 321 3 DON JUAN 12   12 1
CHEVALIER
    THERE WAS THE PREUX CHEVALIER DE LA RUSE . . . . . 398 3 DON JUAN 13   86 3
    WHICH PIQUES A PREUX CHEVALIER--AS IT OUGHT . . . . . 490 3 DON JUAN 15   77 2
CHEVALIERS
    FOR OUT OF THESE THREE PREUX CHEVALIERS HOW . . . . . 82 3 DON JUAN 7   33 2
CHEWING
    CHEWING A PIECE OF BAMBOO AND SOME LEAD . . . . . 200 2 DON JUAN 2   82 6
CHIAN
    AND FLASKS OF SAMIAN AND OF CHIAN WINE . . . . . . 291 2 DON JUAN 3   31 4
CHICKS
    THE FORMER KNOW WHAT'S WHAT WHILE NEW-FLEDGED CHICKS . . 230 3 DON JUAN 10   10 3
CHIEF
    THE POLISHED CHIEF WHO DEIGNED TO SMILE . . . . . 321 2 DON JUAN 3 L 2 V1
    (AND OTHER CHIEF POINTS OF A BELLA DONNA) . . . . . 395 2 DON JUAN 4   94 4
    HAD BEEN HER SLAVES' CHIEF PLEASURE AS HER WILL . . . 475 2 DON JUAN 5   112 4
    THE CHIEF DAME OF THE ODA UPON WHOM . . . . . . 57 3 DON JUAN 6   103 1
    IN CHIEF IN PROPER PERSON DEIGNED TO DRILL . . . . . 93 3 DON JUAN 7   52 2
    IS NEITHER MAN NOR WOMAN THE CHIEF THREW ON . . . . 97 3 DON JUAN 7   60 3
    WHO WERE THUS HONOURED BY THE GREATEST CHIEF . . . . 101 3 DON JUAN 7   68 2
    WHERE THE CHIEF PACHA CALMLY HELD HIS POST . . . . . 171 3 DON JUAN 8   120 2
    WAS LEFT UPON HIS WAY TO THE CHIEF CITY . . . . . 194 3 DON JUAN 9   23 2
    CHIEF IMPULSE WITH A FEW FRAIL PAPER PELLETS . . . . 298 3 DON JUAN 11   60 V8
    NOT THAT I DEEM OUR CHIEF JUDGE IS A HOLLOW MAN--) . . 357 3 DON JUAN 12 V 18 8
    HER CHIEF RESOURCE WAS IN HER OWN HIGH SPIRIT . . . . 372 3 DON JUAN 13   31 4
    EXPERIENCE IS THE CHIEF PHILOSOPHER . . . . . . 463 3 DON JUAN 15   17 5
CHIEFLY
    BUT THAT WHICH CHIEFLY MAY AND MUST SURPRISE . . . . 73 2 DON JUAN 1   97 4
    AND THAT WHICH CHIEFLY PROVED HIS SAVING CLAUSE . . . . 199 2 DON JUAN 2   81 6
    BUT CHIEFLY BY A SPECIES OF SELF-SLAUGHTER . . . . . 210 2 DON JUAN 2   102 7
    AND LONG FOR FOOD BUT CHIEFLY A BEEF-STEAK . . . . . 237 2 DON JUAN 2   153 4
    LEARNING THAT LANGUAGE CHIEFLY FROM ITS PREACHERS . . . 243 2 DON JUAN 2   165 4
    SUWARROW CHIEFLY WAS ON THE ALERT . . . . 95 3 DON JUAN 7   55 1
    WHOSE CHIEFLY HARMLESS TALENT WAS TO AMUSE . . . . . 398 3 DON JUAN 13   86 5
CHIEFS
    THEIR CHIEFS TO ORDER--WERE ALL CUT TO PIECES . . . . 149 3 DON JUAN 8   74 8
    STATESMEN CHIEFS ORATORS QUEENS PATRIOTS KINGS . . . . 306 3 DON JUAN 11   76 7

CHIEFTAIN
     THIS CHIEFTAIN--SOMEHOW WOULD NOT YIELD AT ALL 163   3 DON JUAN 8   104   8
CHIEFTAIN'S
     THE CHIEFTAIN'S TROPHY AND THE POET'S VOLUME   400   2 DON JUAN 4   104   6
CHILD
     AT SIX A CHARMING CHILD AND AT ELEVEN 48   2 DON JUAN 1   49   2
     AT SIX I SAID HE WAS A CHARMING CHILD 49   2 DON JUAN 1   50   1
     JUAN SHE SAW AND AS A PRETTY CHILD 59   2 DON JUAN 1   69   1
     BUT FOR A CHILD WHAT PIECE OF WORK IS HERE 115   2 DON JUAN 1   172   3
     AND OCEAN SLUMBER'D LIKE AN UNWEAN'D CHILD 193   2 DON JUAN 2   70   2
     THE OTHER FATHER HAD A WEAKLIER CHILD 203   2 DON JUAN 2   88   1
     THE AIRY CHILD OF VAPOUR AND THE SUN 205   2 DON JUAN 2   92   2
     A CHILD THE MOMENT WHEN IT DRAINS THE BREAST 261   2 DON JUAN 2   196   2
     A CHILD THE FIRST TIME THAT IT SUCKS THE BREAST 261   2 DON JUAN 2   196   V2
     HAIDEE WAS PASSION'S CHILD BORN WHERE THE SUN 264   2 DON JUAN 2   202   2
     HE LOVED HIS CHILD AND WOULD HAVE WEPT THE LOSS OF HER . 289   2 DON JUAN 3   26   7
     OVER THE INNOCENCE OF THAT SWEET CHILD 302   2 DON JUAN 3   52   7
     THOU BRING'ST THE CHILD TOO TO THE MOTHER'S BREAST . . 338   2 DON JUAN 3   107   8
     DAMM'D FROM ITS FOUNTAIN--THE CHILD FROM THE KNEE . . . 349   2 DON JUAN 4   10   5
     THE CHILD DIVIDED IT WERE LESS TO SEE 349   2 DON JUAN 4   10   V5
     WHICH MIX'D ALL FEELINGS FRIEND CHILD LOVER BROTHER . . 357   2 DON JUAN 4   26   3
     HAVE DAWN'D A FAIR AND SINLESS CHILD OF SIN 382   2 DON JUAN 4   70   3
     AT A PER-CENTAGE A CHILD CROSS DOG ILL 16   3 DON JUAN 6   21   3
     WHAT SAY YOU CHILD--DUDU SAID NOTHING AS 30   3 DON JUAN 6   49   7
     A CHILD OF NATURE CARELESSLY ARRAYED 36   3 DON JUAN 6   60   3
     YOU SURELY ARE UNWELL CHILD WE MUST SEE 46   3 DON JUAN 6   80   6
     THE FIAT OF THIS SPOILED CHILD OF THE NIGHT 86   3 DON JUAN 7   41   3
     ARE NOTHING BUT A CHILD OF MURDER'S RATTLES 114   3 DON JUAN 8   4   8
     A THING OF IMPULSE AND A CHILD OF SONG 123   3 DON JUAN 8   24   2
     EVEN FROM A CHILD FELT LIKE A CHILD HOWE'ER 139   3 DON JUAN 8   53   2
     EVEN FROM A CHILD FELT LIKE A CHILD HOWE'ER 139   3 DON JUAN 8   53   2
     CRIME CAME NOT NEAR HIM--SHE IS NOT THE CHILD 143   3 DON JUAN 8   62   1
     AN ACTIVE HERMIT EVEN IN AGE THE CHILD 144   3 DON JUAN 8   63   7
     A FEMALE CHILD OF TEN YEARS TRIED TO STOOP 157   3 DON JUAN 8   91   6
     TWO VILLAINOUS COSSACQUES PURSUED THE CHILD 157   3 DON JUAN 8   92   1
     UPON THIS CHILD--I SAVED HER--MUST NOT LEAVE 161   3 DON JUAN 8   99   2
     THIS CHILD WHO IS PARENTLESS AND THEREFORE MINE 161   3 DON JUAN 8   100   8
     THE CHILD'S A PRETTY CHILD--A VERY PRETTY-- 162   3 DON JUAN 8   101   2
     CHILD OR AN AGED HELPLESS MAN OR TWO-- 174   3 DON JUAN 8   124   4
     BUT JUAN TURNED HIS EYES ON THE SWEET CHILD 199   3 DON JUAN 9   33   1
     YOU HAD REASON--'TWAS THAT A YOUNG CHILD OF GRACE . . . 329   3 DON JUAN 12   29   2
     THE PRIDE OF A MERE CHILD WITH A NEW SASH ON 351   3 DON JUAN 12   77   5
     THE VIRGIN MOTHER OF THE GOD-BORN CHILD 387   3 DON JUAN 13   61   2
     CHILD TO THE CARE OF GUARDIANS GOOD AND KIND 475   3 DON JUAN 15   44   2
     SHE HAD SO MUCH OR LITTLE OF THE CHILD 480   3 DON JUAN 15   55   8
     PRONOUNCES THAT AN ONLY 'S A SPOILT CHILD-- 563   3 DON JUAN 17   2   3
     A CHILD OF CHANCERY THAT STAR-CHAMBER WARD 564   3 DON JUAN 17   4   4
CHILD-BED
     CONDEMN'D TO CHILD-BED AS MEN FOR THEIR SINS 420   3 DON JUAN 14   23   7
CHILDHOOD
     THE INNOCENCE WHICH HAPPY CHILDHOOD BLESSES 292   2 DON JUAN 3   33   5
     MY CHILDHOOD IN THIS CHILDISHNESS OF MINE 233   3 DON JUAN 10   18   7
CHILDISHNESS
     MY CHILDHOOD IN THIS CHILDISHNESS OF MINE 233   3 DON JUAN 10   18   7
CHILDREN
     THE LISP OF CHILDREN AND THEIR EARLIEST WORDS 88   2 DON JUAN 1   123   8
     (SO CHILDREN CUTTING TEETH RECEIVE A CORAL) 141   2 DON JUAN 1   209   4
     FOR NAUGHTY CHILDREN WHO WOULD RATHER PLAY 162   2 DON JUAN 2   10   3
     BUT HE POOR FELLOW HAD A WIFE AND CHILDREN 179   2 DON JUAN 2   43   7
     A BAND OF CHILDREN ROUND A SNOW-WHITE RAM 292   2 DON JUAN 3   32   1
     TO FIND OUR CHILDREN RUNNING RESTIVE--THEY 305   2 DON JUAN 3   59   2
     HER CHILDREN UP (IF NURSING THEM DON'T THIN HER) 306   2 DON JUAN 3   60   4
     ALL THESE WERE THEIRS FOR THEY WERE CHILDREN STILL . . 352   2 DON JUAN 4   15   1
     AND CHILDREN STILL THEY SHOULD HAVE EVER BEEN 352   2 DON JUAN 4   15   3
     CHEERFUL AS CHILDREN CLIMB THE BREASTS OF MOTHERS . . . 119   3 DON JUAN 8   15   6
     A SYLVAN TRIBE OF CHILDREN OF THE CHACE 145   3 DON JUAN 8   65   2
     WHO FOUGHT WITH HIS FIVE CHILDREN IN THE VAN 164   3 DON JUAN 8   105   8
     AS HE LOOKED DOWN UPON HIS CHILDREN GONE 170   3 DON JUAN 8   117   7
     AND LAY BEFORE THEM WITH HIS CHILDREN NEAR 171   3 DON JUAN 8   119   4
     BUT YE--OUR CHILDREN'S CHILDREN THINK HOW WE 179   3 DON JUAN 8   135   7
     THE NEXT ARE ONLY CHILDREN AS THEY ARE STYLED 563   3 DON JUAN 17   2   1
     WHO GROW UP CHILDREN ONLY SINCE THE OLD SAW 563   3 DON JUAN 17   2   2
CHILDREN'S
     HOW MOTHERS LOVE THEIR CHILDREN'S SQUALLS AND CHUCKLINGS 488   2 DON JUAN 5   133   6
     BUT YE--OUR CHILDREN'S CHILDREN THINK HOW WE 179   3 DON JUAN 8   135   7
CHILD'S
     INTO HIS DYING CHILD'S MOUTH--BUT IN VAIN 203   2 DON JUAN 2   89   8
     AND POOR JUANNA TOO THE CHILD'S FIRST NIGHT 46   3 DON JUAN 6   81   1
     THE CHILD'S A PRETTY CHILD--A VERY PRETTY-- 162   3 DON JUAN 8   101   2
     PERPLEXING FOR MOST VIRGINS--A CHILD'S FATHER 533   3 DON JUAN 16   47   8
CHILL
     AND BATHING HIS CHILL TEMPLES TRIED TO SOOTHE 215   2 DON JUAN 2   113   5
     ON ONE SIDE AND THE DEEP SEA CALM AND CHILL 252   2 DON JUAN 2   183   6
     DAYS LAY SHE IN THAT STATE UNCHANGED THOUGH CHILL . . . 377   2 DON JUAN 4   60   1
     OF THE LONG CARAVAN WHICH IN THE CHILL 49   3 DON JUAN 6   86   5
     CHILL AND CHAINED TO COLD EARTH WE LIFT ON HIGH 66   3 DON JUAN 7   1   5
     IN THE CHILL DARK WHEN COURAGE DOES NOT GLOW 121   3 DON JUAN 8   21   3
     AND SHE WAS CHILL AS THEY AND ON HER FACE 159   3 DON JUAN 8   95   1
     PERHAPS THE SEASON'S CHILL AND THEIR LONG STATION . . . 176   3 DON JUAN 8   128   6
     OF MEN'S REGARD THE FEVER OR THE CHILL 366   3 DON JUAN 13   17   8

```
                                                               PAGE VOL        CANTO STANZA LN

CHILL'D
    BY NIGHT CHILL'D BY DAY SCORCH'D THUS ONE BY ONE    . . . . 210  2 DON JUAN  2   102   5
    AND FELT HER VEINS CHILL'D BY THE NEIGHBOURING SEA  . . . 233  2 DON JUAN  2   145   4
CHILLED
    CHILLED BY THE NIGHT--AND BLACKENED BY THE SUN . . . . . 210  2 DON JUAN  2   102  V5
    ALAS THAT GLORY SHOULD BE CHILLED BY SNOW  . . . . .   254  3 DON JUAN 10    59   5
CHILLER
    AND WAXING CHILLER IN HER COURTESY . . . . . . . .     430  3 DON JUAN 14    46   6
CHILLIEST
    AND THUS THE CHILLIEST ASPECTS MAY CONCENTRE  . . . . . 375  3 DON JUAN 13    38   2
CHILLING
    HE FELT THAT CHILLING HEAVINESS OF HEART . . . . . .   167  2 DON JUAN  2    21   1
    OF THIS DELUSION STILL THE CHILLING YOKE . . . . . .   402  2 DON JUAN  4   106  V3
CHILLY
    AND THE HEART'S DEW OF PAIN SPRANG FAST AND CHILLY  . . .  58  3 DON JUAN  6   105   7
    I FEEL SOME CHILLY MIDNIGHT SHUDDERINGS . . . . .     500  3 DON JUAN 15    98   4
CHIME
    AND WAS THRUST IN TO CLOSE THE OCTAVE'S CHIME . . . .   14  3 DON JUAN  6    18   6
    AS ERE WAS VIRGIN OF A NUPTIAL CHIME . . . . . .      74  3 DON JUAN  7    16   4
    UPON THE EAR AND SOUNDS OF HORROR CHIME  . . . . .    141  3 DON JUAN  8    58   6
    IN MINE IRREGULARITY OF CHIME  . . . . . . . .        465  3 DON JUAN 15    20   6
CHIMERA
    THEIR POST BUT THEIR'S IS MERELY A CHIMERA  . . . .    360  3 DON JUAN 13     5   3
CHIMES
    AS MUSIC CHIMES IN WITH A MELODRAME  . . . . . .      552  3 DON JUAN 16   104   6
CHIMNEY
    THE CHIMNEY--WHICH WOULD REALLY HOLD A LOVER . . . .   104  2 DON JUAN  1   153   4
    THE CHIMNEY--WOULD IT PLEASE YOU RING THE BELL . . . . 104  2 DON JUAN  1   153  V4
CHIMNEY-SMOKE
    ON SEEING HIS OWN CHIMNEY-SMOKE FELT GLAD  . . . . .   289  2 DON JUAN  3    26   3
CHIMNEY-SWEEPER
    A LEGAL BROOM'S A MORAL CHIMNEY-SWEEPER  . . . . .    232  3 DON JUAN 10    15   1
CHIN
    HE WITH THE BEARDLESS CHIN AND GARMENTS TORN . . .     98  3 DON JUAN  7    62   6
    OUR KILLED ALREADY PILED UP TO THE CHIN  . . . . .   160  3 DON JUAN  8    98   6
    A DIMPLED CHIN A NECK OF IVORY STOLE . . . . . .     561  3 DON JUAN 16   123   3
CHINA
    IN SMALL FINE CHINA CUPS CAME IN AT LAST . . . . .    307  2 DON JUAN  3    63   4
    SOCIETY THAT CHINA WITHOUT FLAW . . . . . . . .       352  3 DON JUAN 12    78   5
CHINA'S
    IN SMALL-EYED CHINA'S CROCKERY-WARE METROPOLIS . . . . 271  3 DON JUAN 11     7   5
CHINESE
    MOVED BY THE CHINESE NYMPH OF TEARS GREEN TEA  . . .   372  2 DON JUAN  4    52   2
    PERHAPS WE HAVE BORROWED THIS FROM THE CHINESE-- . . . 373  3 DON JUAN 13    34   8
CHINS
    HAVE SHAVING TOO ENTAILED UPON THEIR CHINS--  . . . .  420  3 DON JUAN 14    23   8
CHIRURGEONS
    IF THERE MIGHT BE CHIRURGEONS WHO COULD SOLDER . . . . 158  3 DON JUAN  8    94   3
CHISEL
    NE'ER COMPASS'D NOR LESS MORTAL CHISEL WROUGHT . . . . 219  2 DON JUAN  2   119   8
CHISELL'D
    WHEN EXQUISITELY CHISELL'D STILL LAY THERE . . . . .   377  2 DON JUAN  4    61   2
CHISELLED
    IN CHISELLED STONE AND PAINTED GLASS AND ALL . . . .   507  3 DON JUAN 16    16   7
CHIVALRIC
    DAMSELS AND RUBLES AND CHIVALRIC ORDERS  . . . . .    235  3 DON JUAN 10    21  V7
CHIVALRY
    THEN FOR ACCOMPLISHMENTS OF CHIVALRY . . . . . .      42  2 DON JUAN  1    38   5
    WHO SANG WHEN CHIVALRY WAS MORE QUIXOTIC . . . . .    347  3 DON JUAN  4     6   4
    PONDERING ON GLORY CHIVALRY AND KINGS  . . . . . .    197  3 DON JUAN  9    30   4
    CERVANTES SMILED SPAIN'S CHIVALRY AWAY . . . . . .    364  3 DON JUAN 13    11   1
    SLEEPS FROM THE CHIVALRY OF THIS BRIGHT AGE  . . . .   378  3 DON JUAN 13    44   6
CHOCOLATE
    LORD HENRY WHO HAD NOW DISCUSSED HIS CHOCOLATE . . . . 515  3 DON JUAN 16    34   1
CHOICE
    NO CHOICE WAS LEFT HIS FEELINGS OR HIS PRIDE . . . .   41  2 DON JUAN  1    36   7
    HAD HIS FIRST CHOICE OF MORSELS FOR HIS PAINS  . . . . 197  2 DON JUAN  2    77   2
    A TASTE SEEN IN THE CHOICE OF HIS ABODE  . . . . .   304  2 DON JUAN  3    56   4
    ONE OF THE TWO ACCORDING TO YOUR CHOICE  . . . . .   357  2 DON JUAN  4    25   1
    WOULD LEAVE HIS PROPOSITION TO THEIR CHOICE  . . . .   452  2 DON JUAN  5    70   3
    THEIR CHOICE THAN LIFE FORGIVE THEM AS BEGUILED  . . . 143  3 DON JUAN  8    62   5
    SO YOU MAY TAKE YOUR CHOICE OF THIS OR THAT)-- . . .   211  3 DON JUAN  9    57   4
    THAT THE YOUNG LADY MADE A MONSTROUS CHOICE  . . . .   334  3 DON JUAN 12    38   8
    SUPPRESSION LADY PINCHBECK WAS HIS CHOICE  . . . . .   336  3 DON JUAN 12    42   8
    OR SHOULD IT SHAKE THE CHOICE WILL MORE PERPLEX-- . . . 371  3 DON JUAN 13    30   4
    HATH YET A PURCHASED CHOICE OF CHOICEST WINES  . . . . 394  3 DON JUAN 13    76   5
    THE DEVIL HATH NOT IN ALL HIS QUIVER'S CHOICE  . . . . 461  3 DON JUAN 15    13   7
CHOICEST
    HATH YET A PURCHASED CHOICE OF CHOICEST WINES  . . . . 394  3 DON JUAN 13    76   5
CHOIR
    COMPOSED A CHOIR OF GIRLS TEN OR A DOZEN . . . . .    469  2 DON JUAN  5    99   2
CHOKED
    THROUGH COACHES DRAYS CHOKED TURNPIKES AND A WHIRL . . . 278  3 DON JUAN 11    22   1
CHOKENOFF
    AND TSCHITSSHAKOFF AND ROGUENOFF AND CHOKENOFF . . . .  74  3 DON JUAN  7    15   4
CHOLERIC
    AND BEING SOMEWHAT CHOLERIC AND SUDDEN  . . . . . .   274  3 DON JUAN 11    13   2
CHOOSE
    I DON'T CHOOSE TO SAY MUCH UPON THIS HEAD  . . . . .   33  2 DON JUAN  1    22   5
```

CHOOSE   (CONTINUED)
```
   'TIS A SAD THING I CANNOT CHOOSE BUT SAY . . . . . . . . .    56  2 DON JUAN  1    63   1
   GASPS AND WHATEVER ELSE THE OWNERS CHOOSE-- . . . . . . . .   110  2 DON JUAN  1   162   5
   THOU SHALT NOT WRITE IN SHORT BUT WHAT I CHOOSE   . . . . .   140  2 DON JUAN  1   206   5
   AND NONE TO BE THE SACRIFICE WOULD CHOOSE   . . . . . . .    195  2 DON JUAN  2    74   4
   MAY CHOOSE BETWEEN THE HEADACHE AND THE HEARTACHE . . . . .   356  2 DON JUAN  4    24   8
   BUT WHICH TO CHOOSE I REALLY HARDLY KNOW . . . . . . . .    357  2 DON JUAN  4    25   4
   HOPING NO VERY OLD VIZIER MIGHT CHOOSE   . . . . . . . .    409  2 DON JUAN  4   116   6
   NEXT JUAN STOOD TILL SOME MIGHT CHOOSE TO BUY  . . . . .    416  2 DON JUAN  5    10   8
   I NEVER SAW SUCH EYES--BUT HARK NOW CHOOSE   . . . . . .    162  3 DON JUAN  8   101   3
   BUT NOW I CHOOSE TO BREAK OFF IN THE MIDDLE . . . . . .    181  3 DON JUAN  8   139   5
   MAY CHOOSE TO TAX ME WITH WHICH IS NOT FAIR . . . . . .    230  3 DON JUAN 10    11   4
   I COULD SAY MORE BUT DO NOT CHOOSE TO ENCROACH . . . . .    279  3 DON JUAN 11    23   5
   FOR REASONS WHICH I CHOOSE TO KEEP APART . . . . . . .    419  3 DON JUAN 14    21   6
   THAT--BUT ASK ANY WOMAN IF SHE'D CHOOSE . . . . . . .    421  3 DON JUAN 14    25   6
   TO JEST YOU'LL CHOOSE SOME OTHER THEME JUST NOW   . . . .    516  3 DON JUAN 16    37   6
CHOOSES
   I WISH YOUR FATE MAY YIELD YE WHEN SHE CHOOSES . . . . .     14  2 DON JUAN  0     8   3
CHOOSING
   BUT ALWAYS CHOOSING WITH DELIBERATION . . . . . . . . .    248  3 DON JUAN 10    48   7
   IN PLAY THERE ARE TWO PLEASURES FOR YOUR CHOOSING--  . . .    415  3 DON JUAN 14    12   7
CHORAL
   WITH CHORAL STEP AND VOICE THE VIRGIN THRONG   . . . . .    291  2 DON JUAN  3    30   8
   AND HARMONIZED BY THE OLD CHORAL WALL . . . . . . . .    388  3 DON JUAN 13    63   8
CHORDS
   IN VAIN--IN VAIN STRIKE OTHER CHORDS  . . . . . . . .    324  2 DON JUAN  3  L  9   1
CHORUS
   CLAMOUR'D IN CHORUS TO THE ROARING OCEAN . . . . . . .    174  2 DON JUAN  2    34   8
   WHICH MIGHT HAVE CALLED DIANA'S CHORUS COUSIN . . . . .    469  2 DON JUAN  5    99   6
   YOUR HEART JOINS CHORUS FAME IS BUT A DIN  . . . . . .    199  3 DON JUAN  9    34   8
CHOSE
   WHO CHOSE TO GO WHERE'ER HE HAD A MIND  . . . . . . .     31  2 DON JUAN  1    19   3
   THOUGH SEVERAL THOUSAND PEOPLE CHOSE TO TRY . . . . . .     33  2 DON JUAN  1    23   3
   WHO SAW THEIR SPOUSES KILL'D AND NOBLY CHOSE  . . . . .     36  2 DON JUAN  1    29   4
   HER GREAT GREAT GRANDMAMMA CHOSE TO REMAIN . . . . . .     52  2 DON JUAN  1    56   8
   HE CHOSE FROM SEVERAL ANIMALS HE SAW--   . . . . . . .    285  2 DON JUAN  3    18   3
   I CHOSE A MODERN SUBJECT AS MORE MEET  . . . . . . .    347  2 DON JUAN  4     6   8
   SOME BOUGHT THE JET WHILE OTHERS CHOSE THE PALE  . . . .    416  2 DON JUAN  5    10   4
   HE CHOSE HIMSELF TO POINT OUT WHAT HE THOUGHT  . . . . .    450  2 DON JUAN  5    67   7
   OR SOLITARY AS THEY CHOSE TO BEAR  . . . . . . . .    406  3 DON JUAN 13   103   4
   WHAT TIME HE CHOSE FOR DRESS AND BROKE HIS FAST  . . . .    406  3 DON JUAN 13   103   7
   WHEN WHERE AND HOW HE CHOSE FOR THAT REPAST . . . . . .    406  3 DON JUAN 13   103   8
   CONNECTIONS STRONGER THAN HE CHOSE TO AVOW  . . . . . .    516  3 DON JUAN 16    37   4
   (BY DOING EASILY WHENE'ER SHE CHOSE  . . . . . . . .    522  3 DON JUAN 16    44   2
CHOSEN
   THAT I HAVE CHOSEN A CONFESSOR SO OLD  . . . . . . .    101  2 DON JUAN  1   147   3
   I YET HAVE CHOSEN FROM OUT THE YOUTH OF SEVILLE  . . . .    102  2 DON JUAN  1   148   2
   WHO WAS HER CHOSEN WHAT WAS SAID OR DONE . . . . . . .    264  2 DON JUAN  2   202   6
   THE FEMALES STOOD TILL CHOSEN EACH AS VICTIM  . . . . .    409  2 DON JUAN  4   116  V7
   WHO WORE THEIR UNIFORM BY BABA CHOSEN  . . . . . . .    469  2 DON JUAN  5    99   4
   SO THAT YOU SCARCE COULD SAY WHO BEST HAD CHOSEN  . . . .    135  3 DON JUAN  8    45   5
   AND HERE HE CRIED IS FREEDOM'S CHOSEN STATION  . . . . .    272  3 DON JUAN 11     9   5
   SUCH AS--UNLESS MISS (BLANK) MEANT TO HAVE CHOSEN  . . .    332  3 DON JUAN 12    34   5
   WAS CHOSEN FROM OUT AN AMATORY SCORE  . . . . . . .    334  3 DON JUAN 12    38   3
   SUCH THOUGHTS ARE QUITE BELOW THE STRAIN THEY HAVE CHOSEN .   341  3 DON JUAN 12    55   3
   'TIS TRUE I MIGHT HAVE CHOSEN PICCADILLY  . . . . . .    370  3 DON JUAN 13    27   1
   REGRETTING MUCH THAT SHE HAD CHOSEN SO BAD A LINE . . . .    430  3 DON JUAN 14    46   5
CHREMATOFF
   SCHEREMATOFF AND CHREMATOFF KOKLOPHTI  . . . . . . .     75  3 DON JUAN  7    17   1
CHRIST
   BY FENELON BY CALVIN AND OF CHRIST . . . . . . . .     68  3 DON JUAN  7     4  V2
CHRISTENED
   IS THAT WHICH MAY BE CHRISTENED LOVE CANONICAL . . . . .    220  3 DON JUAN  9    76   3
CHRISTIAN
   IN EVERY CHRISTIAN LANGUAGE EVER NAMED   . . . . . .     26  2 DON JUAN  1    10   3
   I SPEAK OF CHRISTIAN LANDS IN THIS COMPARISON  . . . . .    248  2 DON JUAN  2   175   7
   AS THOUGH THEY WERE IN A MERE CHRISTIAN FAIR . . . . .    425  2 DON JUAN  5    28   5
   NO CHRISTIAN KNOLL TO TABLE SAW NO LINE . . . . . . .    439  2 DON JUAN  5    50   3
   GAVE IT A SLIGHT KICK WITH HIS CHRISTIAN FOOT  . . . . .    453  2 DON JUAN  5    73   6
   TO SUPPER BUT YOU WORTHY CHRISTIAN NUN   . . . . . .    458  2 DON JUAN  5    81   3
   HAD SHE BUT BEEN A CHRISTIAN I'VE A NOTION  . . . . .    475  2 DON JUAN  5   112   7
   AND MERELY SAYING CHRISTIAN CANST THOU LOVE . . . . . .    478  2 DON JUAN  5   116   7
   AND CHRISTIAN MINGLE WITH THEM AS YOU MAY  . . . . . .    494  2 DON JUAN  5   145   5
   WERE RULED AS CALMLY AS A CHRISTIAN QUEEN  . . . . . .    496  2 DON JUAN  5   148   8
   THAT A MERE CHRISTIAN SHOULD BE HALF SO PRETTY . . . . .    500  2 DON JUAN  5   155   8
   NOW IF THIS HOLDS GOOD IN A CHRISTIAN LAND . . . . . .     11  3 DON JUAN  6    11   1
   WHEN THEY SURVEY WITH CHRISTIAN EYES OR HEATHEN  . . . .     24  3 DON JUAN  6    37   7
   THE ARMIES OF THE CHRISTIAN EMPRESS CATHERINE  . . . .     99  3 DON JUAN  7    64   8
   ANSWERING THE CHRISTIAN THUNDERS WITH LIKE VOICES . . . .    115  3 DON JUAN  8     7   4
   BY TURK AND CHRISTIAN EQUALLY HE COULD   . . . . . .    129  3 DON JUAN  8    33  V6
   BY CHRISTIAN SOLDIERY A SINGLE SPOT  . . . . . . .    131  3 DON JUAN  8    37   5
   FROM WHENCE THEY SALLIED ON THOSE CHRISTIAN SCORNERS . . .    149  3 DON JUAN  8    75   8
   THE FIFTH WHO BY A CHRISTIAN MOTHER NOURISHED  . . . . .    166  3 DON JUAN  8   110   5
   MIRRORED THE CHRISTIAN FLAGS--AS MOONBEAMS ON THE WATER . .    173  3 DON JUAN  8   122  V8
   AS IS THE CHRISTIAN DOGMA RATHER ROUGH   . . . . . .    195  3 DON JUAN  9    25   6
   AS FLOURISHING IN EVERY CHRISTIAN LAND   . . . . . .    220  3 DON JUAN  9    76   6
   IN FACT THE ONLY CHRISTIAN SHE COULD BEAR  . . . . . .    252  3 DON JUAN 10    57   1
   JEW ROTHSCHILD AND HIS FELLOW CHRISTIAN BARING . . . . .    318  3 DON JUAN 12     5   8
   SCOTT WHO CAN PAINT YOUR CHRISTIAN KNIGHT OR SARACEN . . .    481  3 DON JUAN 15    59   5
```

	PAGE	VOL	CANTO	STANZA	LN
CHRISTIANITY					
BY THEIR EXAMPLES OF TRUE CHRISTIANITY	69	3 DON JUAN	7	6	3
LURKED CHRISTIANITY WHICH SOMETIMES BARTERS	96	3 DON JUAN	7	57	6
CHRISTIANS					
CHRISTIANS HAVE BURNT EACH OTHER QUITE PERSUADED	66	2 DON JUAN	1	83	7
SOME CHRISTIANS HAVE A COMFORTABLE CREED	202	2 DON JUAN	2	86	8
MOST PROPER FOR THE CHRISTIANS HE HAD BOUGHT	450	2 DON JUAN	5	67	8
BY MOWING CHRISTIANS DOWN ON EVERY SIDE	165	3 DON JUAN	8	107	3
GOOD CHRISTIANS THAT TO WHICH THEY ALL ARE GOING	278	3 DON JUAN	11	21	V8
CHRIST'S					
IF HE SPEAK TRUTH SHE IS CHRIST'S SISTER AND	116	3 DON JUAN	8	9	7
CHRONICLE					
'TIS WRITTEN IN THE HEBREW CHRONICLE	113	2 DON JUAN	1	168	3
THUS FAR OUR CHRONICLE AND NOW WE PAUSE	503	2 DON JUAN	5	159	1
THE THIRD SORT TO BE NOTED IN OUR CHRONICLE	220	3 DON JUAN	9	76	5
TURPIN'S OR MONMOUTH GEOFFRY'S CHRONICLE	503	3 DON JUAN	16	5	2
CHRONICLERS					
THAT INJURED QUEEN BY CHRONICLERS SO COARSE	446	2 DON JUAN	5	61	1
CHRONOLOGICAL					
IN CHRONOLOGICAL COMMEMORATION	327	2 DON JUAN	3	89	4
CHRONOLOGY					
LEAVING AT LAST NOT MUCH BESIDES CHRONOLOGY	76	2 DON JUAN	1	103	7
OF--BUT CHRONOLOGY BEST KNOWS THE YEARS	9	3 DON JUAN	6	6	8
THE STRICTEST IN CHRONOLOGY AND VIRTUE	433	3 DON JUAN	14	53	3
CHRYSOSTOM					
TO JEROME AND TO CHRYSOSTOM INURED	47	2 DON JUAN	1	47	3
CHUCKLINGS					
HOW MOTHERS LOVE THEIR CHILDREN'S SQUALLS AND CHUCKLINGS	488	2 DON JUAN	5	133	6
CHURCH					
FOR HALF HIS DAYS WERE PASS'D AT CHURCH THE OTHER	48	2 DON JUAN	1	49	7
THE COURT CAMP CHURCH THE VESSEL AND THE MART	131	2 DON JUAN	1	194	3
WAS NOT SO SAFE FOR ROOSTING AS A CHURCH	206	2 DON JUAN	2	95	4
I GRANT YOU IN A CHURCH 'TIS VERY WELL	444	2 DON JUAN	5	59	2
IN LIKE CHURCH BELLS WITH SIGH HOWL GROAN YELL PRAYER	141	3 DON JUAN	8	58	7
WHATE'ER THE CAUSE THE CHURCH MADE LITTLE OF IT--	252	3 DON JUAN	10	56	7
A HOSPITAL A CHURCH--AND LEAVE BEHIND	320	3 DON JUAN	12	10	3
IS WHEN WITHOUT REGARD TO CHURCH OR STATE	345	3 DON JUAN	12	64	3
(WHILE YET THE CHURCH WAS ROME'S) STOOD HALF APART	386	3 DON JUAN	13	59	2
THAT SCRIPTURES OUT OF CHURCH ARE BLASPHEMIES	403	3 DON JUAN	13	96	8
AS FAR AS I KNOW THAT THE CHURCH RECEIVES	444	3 DON JUAN	14	78	4
MADE NORMAN CHURCH HIS PREY	518	3 DON JUAN	16	L 1	6
TO TURN CHURCH LANDS TO LAY	518	3 DON JUAN	16	L 2	2
FOR HE'S SEEN IN THE PORCH AND HE'S SEEN IN THE CHURCH	518	3 DON JUAN	16	L 2	7
THERE WERE SOME MASSY MEMBERS OF THE CHURCH	539	3 DON JUAN	16	80	6
CHURCHES					
YET AS THEY FOUNDED CHURCHES WITH THE PRODUCE	242	3 DON JUAN	10	36	7
UNTYING SQUIRES TO FIGHT AGAINST THE CHURCHES	530	3 DON JUAN	16	60	6
CHURCHMAN'S					
EVEN THE BOLD CHURCHMAN'S TOMB EXCITED AWE	261	3 DON JUAN	10	74	4
CHURCH'S					
THROUGH HIS MEANS AND THE CHURCH'S MIGHT BE PAVED	251	3 DON JUAN	10	55	6
FOR HE IS YET THE CHURCH'S HEIR	520	3 DON JUAN	16	L 5	3
CHUSE					
SO PICK AND CHUSE--PERHAPS YOU'LL BE CONTENT	40	3 DON JUAN	6	68	7
CHYMIC					
TIME IS TIME WAS TIME'S PAST A CHYMIC TREASURE	145	2 DON JUAN	1	217	6
CICALAS					
THE SHRILL CICALAS PEOPLE OF THE PINE	337	2 DON JUAN	3	106	1
CICERONIAN					
HE REVEL'D IN HIS CICERONIAN GLORY	401	3 DON JUAN	13	91	4
CICOGNA					
BY CARRYING OFF COUNT CESARE CICOGNA	389	2 DON JUAN	4	83	7
CI-DEVANT					
WITNESS THOSE CI-DEVANT JEUNES HOMMES WHO STEM	418	3 DON JUAN	14	18	7
CINCINNATUS					
THE HIGH ROMAN FASHION TOO OF CINCINNATUS	186	3 DON JUAN	9	7	3
CINDERS					
ABOVE HIS BURNT-OUT BRAIN AND SAPLESS CINDERS	299	3 DON JUAN	11	61	5
CINNAMON					
CLOVES CINNAMON AND SAFFRON TOO WERE BOIL'D	307	2 DON JUAN	3	63	7
CIRCASSIA					
WHOM IF THEY WERE AT HOME IN SWEET CIRCASSIA	25	3 DON JUAN	6	39	7
CIRCASSIAN					
FOR ONE CIRCASSIAN A SWEET GIRL WERE GIVEN	407	2 DON JUAN	4	114	2
CIRCASSIANS					
AND THERE WITH GEORGIANS RUSSIANS AND CIRCASSIANS	407	2 DON JUAN	4	113	7
AND THEREFORE OF CIRCASSIANS HAD GOOD STORE	51	3 DON JUAN	6	91	5
CIRCLE					
TO A SEDATE GREY CIRCLE OF OLD SMOKERS	293	2 DON JUAN	3	34	2
IN THE DISSOLVING CIRCLE ALL THE NATIONS'	223	3 DON JUAN	9	82	2
THE CIRCLE SMIL'D THEN WHISPER'D AND THEN SNEER'D	429	3 DON JUAN	14	44	1
AND THEN OF COURSE THE CIRCLE MUCH ADMIRES	521	3 DON JUAN	16	41	5
CIRCLE'S					
EVEN IN THE COUNTRY CIRCLE'S NARROW BOUND--	544	3 DON JUAN	16	91	6
CIRCLES					
CHECKS TO A LAKE WHOSE WAVES IN CIRCLES SPREAD	231	2 DON JUAN	2	141	7
HIGH IN HIGH CIRCLES GENTLE IN HER OWN	338	3 DON JUAN	12	48	1
CIRCLING					
CIRCLING ALL NATURE HUSH'D AND DIM AND STILL	252	2 DON JUAN	2	183	4
WHENCE THE BROAD MOON ROSE CIRCLING INTO SIGHT	253	2 DON JUAN	2	185	4

132

```
                                                              PAGE VOL      CANTO STANZA LN
CIRCULAR
    NO SIGN THAT IT WAS CIRCULAR ANYWHERE . . . . . . . . 497  2 DON JUAN  5    150   4
CIRCULATING
    OF ONE OF THE MOST CIRCULATING SCANDALS . . . . . . . 128  2 DON JUAN  1    190   2
    MAKE SOME PREFER THE CIRCULATING MEDIUM . . . . . . . 235  3 DON JUAN 10     22   8
CIRCULATION
    WITH CLOWNISH HEEL YOUR POPULAR CIRCULATION . . . . . 200  3 DON JUAN  9     35   7
CIRCUMCISE
    BUT THEY AS SOON SHALL CIRCUMCISE MY HEAD . . . . . . 452  2 DON JUAN  5     71   8
CIRCUMCISION
    IF THEY WOULD CONDESCEND TO CIRCUMCISION . . . . . . . 451  2 DON JUAN  5     69   8
CIRCUMSPECT
    (ALTHOUGH THEIR TALK'S OBSCURE AND CIRCUMSPECT) . . . .  38  2 DON JUAN  1     33   4
    WITHOUT THE APPAREL OF BEING CIRCUMSPECT . . . . . . . 434  3 DON JUAN 14     56   4
    IN WHICH YOU CANNOT BE TOO CIRCUMSPECT . . . . . . . . 526  3 DON JUAN 16     52   5
CIRCUMSPECTION
    HUT WHENCE WISE TRAVELLERS DRIVE WITH CIRCUMSPECTION . . . 238  3 DON JUAN 10     27   6
    WHO LIKE TO PLAY THE FOOL WITH CIRCUMSPECTION . . . . . 304  3 DON JUAN 11     71   8
CIRCUMSTANCE
    TORY BY NURTURE WHIG BY CIRCUMSTANCE . . . . . . . . 152  2 DON JJAN  1  V  3   1
    THIS CIRCUMSTANCE MAY SERVE TO GIVE A NOTION . . . . .  72  3 DON JUAN  7     11   1
    ABOUT A CIRCUMSTANCE WHICH HAS CONFOUNDED . . . . . . 125  3 DON JUAN  8     28   4
    FLUNG HERE BY FATE OR CIRCUMSTANCE WHICH TAME . . . . 139  3 DON JUAN  8     54   6
    AND IN EACH CIRCUMSTANCE OF LOVE OR WAR . . . . . . . 441  3 DON JUAN 14     71   7
CIRCUMSTANCES
    MEN ARE THE SPORT OF CIRCUMSTANCES WHEN . . . . . . . 419  2 DON JUAN  5     17   7
    THE CIRCUMSTANCES SEEM THE SPORT OF MEN . . . . . . . 419  2 DON JUAN  5     17   8
    MORE CIRCUMSTANCES VAIN WAS EVERY CARE . . . . . . . 429  2 DON JUAN  5     34   6
    IN ALL THE CIRCUMSTANCES OF THE CASE . . . . . . . . 277  3 DON JUAN 11     18   2
    TO HIS OWN CIRCUMSTANCES THERE MIGHT LIE . . . . . . 469  3 DON JUAN 15     30   4
    IF IN THE CIRCUMSTANCES WHICH ENSUED . . . . . . . . 553  3 DON JUAN 16    107   3
CIRQUE
    SOME LIKENESS WHICH THE GLITTERING CIRQUE CONFINES . . . 321  3 DON JUAN 12     12   6
CITE
    CITE IS THAT BOON LIVED HUNTING UP TO NINETY . . . . . 143  3 DON JUAN  8     62   8
CITED
    BEYOND THE CHARMERS WE HAVE ALREADY CITED . . . . . . 477  3 DON JUAN 15     48   4
CITIES
    LOST FOR HIS REPARTEE WAS TAKING CITIES . . . . . . .  93  3 DON JUAN  7     53  V8
    IN CITIES CAGED THE PRESENT CASE IN POINT I . . . . . 143  3 DON JUAN  8     62   7
    ON CITIES AS HATH BEEN THE PRESENT CASE) . . . . . . 160  3 DON JUAN  8     97   4
    OF BURNING CITIES THOSE FULL MOONS OF SLAUGHTER . . . 173  3 DON JUAN  8    122  V7
    O'ER SILENCED CITIES MERELY SERVED TO FLATTER . . . . 197  3 DON JUAN  9     29   5
    OF CITIES THAT BOILS OVER WITH THEIR SCUM-- . . . . . 272  3 DON JUAN 11      8   8
    WHOSE CITIES NIGHT BY NO MEANS DEIGNS TO GLOSS . . . . 280  3 DON JUAN 11     26   5
    WITH WHICH THIS MORALEST OF CITIES CATERS . . . . . . 313  3 DON JUAN 11  V 29   4
CITY
    IN SEVILLE WAS HE BORN A PLEASANT CITY . . . . . . .  25  2 DON JUAN  1      8   1
    WITH MORE THAN HALF THE CITY AT HIS BACK-- . . . . .  96  2 DON JUAN  1    137   2
    COMMANDS THE CITY AND UPON ITS SITE . . . . . . . .  71  3 DON JUAN  7     10   4
    HE MADE NO ANSWER BUT HE TOOK THE CITY . . . . . . .  93  3 DON JUAN  7     53   8
    HURLING DEFIANCE CITY STREAM AND SHORE . . . . . . . 116  3 DON JUAN  8      8   4
    IN THIS EXTENSIVE CITY SORE BESET . . . . . . . . . 131  3 DON JUAN  8     37   4
    HIS THANKS AND HOPES TO TAKE THE CITY SOON . . . . . 140  3 DON JUAN  8     56   6
    THE MADDENED TURKS THEIR CITY STILL DISPUTE . . . . . 146  3 DON JUAN  8     69   8
    THE CITY WITHOUT BEING FURTHER HAMPER'D . . . . . . . 149  3 DON JUAN  8     75   4
    WITHOUT RESISTANCE SEE THEIR CITY BURN . . . . . . . 150  3 DON JUAN  8     77   4
    ROLLS BY THE CITY WALL BUT DEED NOR WORD . . . . . . 155  3 DON JUAN  8     87   4
    AND GROANS AND THUS THE PEOPLED CITY GRIEVES . . . . 155  3 DON JUAN  8     88   5
    WILL SERVE WHEN THERE IS PLUNDER IN A CITY-- . . . . 162  3 DON JUAN  8    101   6
    HE NEVER WOULD BELIEVE THE CITY WON . . . . . . . . 164  3 DON JUAN  8    105   4
    WHAT'S THIS IN ONE ANNIHILATED CITY . . . . . . . . 174  3 DON JUAN  8    124   5
    COULD RHYME LIKE NERO O'ER A BURNING CITY . . . . . . 179  3 DON JUAN  8    134   8
    WAS LEFT UPON HIS WAY TO THE CHIEF CITY . . . . . . . 194  3 DON JUAN  9     23   2
    WAS A TA'EN CITY--THIRTY THOUSAND SLAIN . . . . . . . 212  3 DON JUAN  9     59   2
    WITH YOU THAN AUGHT (SAVE SCOTT) IN YOUR PROUD CITY . . . 233  3 DON JUAN 10     17   4
    A CITY WHICH PRESENTS TO THE INSPECTOR . . . . . . . 255  3 DON JUAN 10     62   6
    TOWARD THE GREAT CITY--YE WHO HAVE A SPARK IN . . . . 264  3 DON JUAN 10     80   5
    MEANETH THE WEST OR WORST END OF A CITY . . . . . . . 290  3 DON JUAN 11     45   2
    THAN STORMS IT AS A FOE WOULD TAKE A CITY . . . . . . 350  3 DON JUAN 12     74   6
    TO LOSE THOSE BEST MONTHS IN A SWEATY CITY . . . . . 380  3 DON JUAN 13     48   4
    A MOST IMPORTANT OUTWORK OF THE CITY-- . . . . . . . 545  3 DON JUAN 16     93   6
CITY'S
    THE CITY'S SHAPE SUGGESTED THIS 'TIS TRUE . . . . . .  78  3 DON JUAN  7     23   6
    BEYOND THE DWARFING CITY'S PALE ABORTIONS . . . . . . 145  3 DON JUAN  8     66   2
    THE CITY'S TAKEN--ONLY PART BY PART-- . . . . . . . . 152  3 DOV JUAN  8     82   1
    THE CITY'S TAKEN BUT NOT RENDERED--NO . . . . . . . . 155  3 DON JUAN  8     87   1
    IF YET THE CITY'S REST WERE WON OR LOST . . . . . . . 171  3 DON JUAN  8    120   6
    OF THIS ENORMOUS CITY'S SPREADING SPAWN . . . . . . . 281  3 DON JUAN 11     28   4
CIVIC
    FROM CIVIC REVELRY TO RURAL MIRTH . . . . . . . . .  88  2 DON JUAN  1    124   4
    SHOULD NOW BE BUTCHERED IN A CIVIC ALLEY . . . . . . 431  2 DON JUAN  5     37   8
CIVIL
    YOU NEVER YET TO ANY SAW ME CIVIL . . . . . . . . . 102  2 DON JUAN  1    148  V6
    LIKE HUMAN BEINGS DURING CIVIL WAR . . . . . . . . . 178  2 DON JUAN  2     42   8
    LIKE LAP-DOGS THE LEAST CIVIL SONS OF BITCHES . . . . 288  3 DON JUAN 11     41   8
    YOU SHOULD BE CIVIL IN A MODEST WAY . . . . . . . . 459  3 DON JUAN 15      9   6
    THE CIVIL LIST (HE DEIGNS TO ACCEPT OBLIGING ALL . . . 528  3 DON JUAN 16     56   6
    SOONER COME PLACE INTO THE CIVIL LIST . . . . . . . . 536  3 DON JUAN 16     75   1
```

```
                                                     PAGE VOL      CANTO STANZA LN
CIVILISATION
   SO THAT CIVILISATION THEY MAY LEARN    . . . . . .   92  2 DON JUAN  1   131    6
CIVILITY
   TO SOME CIVILITY TO OTHERS BOUNTY . . . . . . . . .  535  3 DON JUAN 16    71    3
CIVILIZATION
   THE INCONVENIENCE OF CIVILIZATION . . . . . . . .    144  3 DON JUAN  8    64    5
   NOW BACK TO THY GREAT JOYS CIVILIZATION . . . . . .  146  3 DON JUAN  8    68    2
CIVILIZED
   THE BEAR IS CIVILIZED THE WOLF IS MILD  . . . . . .  157  3 DON JUAN  8    92    5
CLAD
   AND WERE ALL CLAD ALIKE LIKE JUAN TOO . . . . . .    469  2 DON JUAN  5    99    3
   IN ASPECT PLAINLY CLAD BESMEARED WITH DUST  . . . .  104  3 DON JUAN  7    73    6
CLAIM
   (WHO DOES NOT OFTEN CLAIM THE BRIGHT REVERSION)  . .   14  2 DON JUAN  0     9    2
   I HAVE NO FURTHER CLAIM ON YOUR YOUNG HEART . . . .  130  2 DON JUAN  1   192    3
   I CAN'T HELP PUTTING IN MY CLAIM TO PRAISE--  . . .  149  2 DON JUAN  1   222    6
   SHE HAD SO MUCH EARTH COULD NOT CLAIM THE WHOLE  . .  377  2 DON JUAN  4    60    8
   BUT LET ME QUIT THE THEME AS SUCH THINGS CLAIM .  .  431  2 DON JUAN  5    38    4
   SHE THOUGHT THAT HER LORD'S HEART (EVEN COULD SHE CLAIM IT)  10  3 DON JUAN  6     8    6
   SHE COULD BUT CLAIM THE FIFTEENTH HUNDRED PART .  .   10  3 DON JUAN  6     9    7
   A COUPLET OR AN ELEGY TO CLAIM . . . . . . . .      120  3 DON JUAN  8    17    6
   WHICH WITH THE BLOOD TOO READILY WILL CLAIM KIN . .  244  3 DON JUAN 10    40    6
   IS CALLED ON TO SUPPORT HIS CLAIM OR SHOW IT  . . .  296  3 DON JUAN 11    55    3
   NEW VESTALS CLAIM MEN'S EYES WITH THE SAME PRAISE .  340  3 DON JUAN 12    53    6
   O'ER JUAN HE COULD NO DISTINCTION CLAIM  . . . .    367  3 DON JUAN 13    20    2
   WITH WHICH THE WINDS OF HEAVEN CAN CLAIM ACCORD . .  402  3 DON JUAN 13    93    3
CLAIMANT
   THEY HATE A MURDERER MUCH LESS THAN A CLAIMANT . .   264  3 DON JUAN 10    79    5
CLAIM'D
   HE NEITHER BROOK'D NOR CLAIM'D SUPERIORITY  . . . .  462  3 DON JUAN 15    15    8
CLAIMED
   OR AMMON'S--FOR TWO FATHERS CLAIMED THIS ONE . . .   427  2 DON JUAN  5    31   V8
CLAIMING
   AS SHE HAD SEEN NOUGHT CLAIMING ITS EXPANSION  . .   446  3 DON JUAN 14    85    4
CLAIMS
   AND AS FOUR WIVES MUST HAVE QUADRUPLE CLAIMS . .  .   11  3 DON JUAN  6    11    7
   AGAINST HIS HEART PREFERRED THEIR USUAL CLAIMS . .   293  3 DON JUAN 11    48    5
CLAMOUR
   NOT ALL THE CLAMOUR BROKE HER HAPPY STATE  . . . .   42  3 DON JUAN  6    73    5
   WITH SUCH A CLAMOUR--I HAD THOUGHT IT RIGHT . . . .   46  3 DON JUAN  6    81    3
CLAMOUR'D
   CLAMOUR'D IN CHORUS TO THE ROARING OCEAN . . . . .  174  2 DON JUAN  2    34    8
CLAN
   INTO A SCENE AND SWELL THE CLIENTS' CLAN . . . . .  437  3 DON JUAN 14    62    4
CLANGED
   THOUGH KNIVES AND FORKS CLANGED ROUND AS IN A FRAY . 542  3 DON JUAN 16    87    5
CLANKING
   THY CLANKING CHAIN AND ERIN'S YET GREEN WOUNDS . .   19  2 DON JUAN  0    16    5
CLAP
   AND CLAP A WHITE CAPE ON THEIR MANTLES BLUE . . . .   94  2 DON JUAN  1   134    5
CLAPPING
   THAT IS--THE LADY CLAPPING HIS HANDS TWICE . . . .  458  2 DON JUAN  5    80    7
CLAP-TRAP
   OF CLAP-TRAP WHICH YOUR RECENT POETS PRIZE . . . .  222  2 DON JUAN  2   124    4
CLARENCE
   WITH MAUDLIN CLARENCE IN HIS MALMSEY BUTT  . . . .  112  2 DON JUAN  1   166    8
CLARENCE'
   IN PREFERENCE SURE TO CLARENCE' MALMSEY BUTT . . .  112  2 DON JUAN  1   166   V8
CLARET
   THE COPIOUS USE OF CLARET IS FORBID TOO . . . . .   144  2 DON JUAN  1   216    6
   OF CLARET SANDWICH AND AN APPETITE . . . . . . .    444  2 DON JUAN  5    58    3
   SPOILT AS A PIPE OF CLARET IS WHEN PRICK'D . . . .  502  2 DON JUAN  5   158    5
   BUT THEN THEY HAVE THEIR CLARET AND MADEIRA . . . .  360  3 DON JUAN 13     5    5
   THE CLARET LIGHT AND THE MADEIRA STRONG . . . . .   394  3 DON JUAN 13    76    6
CLARETLESS
   LEAVING ALL CLARETLESS THE UNMOISTENED THROTTLE  . .  435  3 DON JUAN 14    58    3
CLASH'D
   FAST IN HIS CAVE AND NOTHING CLASH'D UPON  . . . .  229  2 DON JUAN  2   137    2
   THOUGH MUCH IN TEMPER BUT THEY NEVER CLASH'D . . .  447  3 DON JUAN 14    87    2
CLASHED
   CLASHED 'GAINST THE SCYMITAR AND BABE AND MOTHER . . 146  3 DON JUAN  8    69    4
CLASP
   YET THERE'S NO DOUBT SHE ONLY MEANT TO CLASP . . .   81  2 DON JUAN  1   111    4
   SURMOUNTED AS ITS CLASP--A GLOWING CRESCENT . . . .  315  2 DON JUAN  3    77    7
   HIS DAUGHTER WHILE COMPRESS'D WITHIN HIS CLASP . .   370  2 DON JUAN  4    48    2
CLASP'D
   THEY TURN'D TO REST AND EACH CLASP'D BY AN ARM . .   253  2 DON JUAN  2   184    7
   ONE LARGE GOLD BRACELET CLASP'D EACH LOVELY ARM . .  312  2 DON JUAN  3    71    1
   AND RAN BUT IT ESCAPED HER AS SHE CLASP'D  . . . .  361  2 DON JUAN  4    32    8
CLASPS
   GLEAM IN THE MOONLIGHT AND HER WHITE ARM CLASPS . .  259  2 DON JUAN  2   194    2
CLASS
   HER TALENTS WERE OF THE MORE SILENT CLASS  . . . .   30  3 DON JUAN  6    49    8
   IT SOONER FOR THE SOUL OF ME AND CLASS . . . . .     34  3 DON JUAN  6    56    5
   PARENTAL FEELINGS AND THE OTHER CLASS . . . . . .   250  3 DON JUAN 10    53    5
   TO KEEP THE WHEELS GOING OF THE HIGHER CLASS . . .  342  3 DON JUAN 12    57    5
   YET THINK A SPECIMEN OF EVERY CLASS  . . . .  .     402  3 DON JUAN 13    94    3
   OF THE BEST CLASS AND BETTER THAN HER CLASS-- . . .  475  3 DON JUAN 15    43    4
   OF THE BEST CLASS AND BETTER THAN HER CLASS-- . . .  475  3 DON JUAN 15    43    4
```

CLASSED
	PAGE	VOL		CANTO	STANZA	LN
AND HENCEFORTH·FOUND HIMSELF MORE GAILY CLASSED	300	3	DON JUAN	11	64	6
BY WHOSE DEGREES ALL CHARACTERS ARE CLASSED--	524	3	DON JUAN	16	48	3

CLASSES
	PAGE	VOL		CANTO	STANZA	LN
KICK OFF THEIR BURTHENS--MEANING THE HIGH CLASSES	310	3	DON JUAN	11	84	8
PROFESSIONAL--ALL CLASSES MOSTLY PULL	403	3	DON JUAN	13	95	V4

CLASSIC
	PAGE	VOL		CANTO	STANZA	LN
HIS CLASSIC STUDIES MADE A LITTLE PUZZLE	44	2	DON JUAN	1	41	1
IN CLOISTERS OF THE CLASSIC SALAMANCA	175	2	DON JUAN	2	37	7
LIGHT CLASSIC ARTICLES OF FEMALE WANT	284	2	DON JUAN	3	17	4
OR IF TOO CLASSIC FOR HIS VULGAR BRAIN	333	2	DON JUAN	3	99	5
AND DRILLED AWAY IN THE MOST CLASSIC RUSSIAN	99	3	DON JUAN	7	64	2
SUCH CLASSIC PAS--SANS FLAWS--SET OFF OUR HERO	427	3	DON JUAN	14	39	7

CLASSICAL
	PAGE	VOL		CANTO	STANZA	LN
THEIR CLASSICAL PROFILES AND GLITTERING DRESSES	292	2	DON JUAN	3	33	1
WITH MOTIVES THE MOST CLASSICAL AND PURE	528	3	DON JUAN	16	57	3

CLATTER
	PAGE	VOL		CANTO	STANZA	LN
AROSE A CLATTER MIGHT AWAKE THE DEAD	95	2	DON JUAN	1	136	3
WHICH SETS THE TEETH ON EDGE AND A SLIGHT CLATTER	556	3	DON JUAN	16	114	2

CLAUDIUS
	PAGE	VOL		CANTO	STANZA	LN
(THOUGH CLAUDIUS RICH ESQUIRE SOME BRICKS HAS GOT	447	3	DON JUAN	5	62	5

CLAUSE
	PAGE	VOL		CANTO	STANZA	LN
AND THAT WHICH CHIEFLY PROVED HIS SAVING CLAUSE	199	2	DON JUAN	2	81	6
HIS FRIEND TOO ADDING A NEW SAVING CLAUSE	437	2	DON JUAN	5	47	6
IN OUTWARD SHOW WHICH IS A SAVING CLAUSE)	35	2	DON JUAN	6	58	3
THAT CLAUSE IS HARD) AND SECONDLY PROCEED	393	3	DON JUAN	13	73	6

CLAW
	PAGE	VOL		CANTO	STANZA	LN
IF AT THAT MOMENT HE HAD CHANCED TO CLAW IT	123	2	DON JUAN	1	185	5
THERE'S NOTHING WHETS THE BEAK OR ARMS THE CLAW	488	2	DON JUAN	5	133	3

CLAWS
	PAGE	VOL		CANTO	STANZA	LN
AND WITHOUT THAT THEIR POISON AND THEIR CLAWS	196	3	DON JUAN	9	28	2

CLAY
	PAGE	VOL		CANTO	STANZA	LN
WHO CANNOT LEAVE ALONE OUR HELPLESS CLAY	56	2	DON JUAN	1	63	3
I WOULD TO HEAVEN THAT I WERE SO MUCH CLAY--	156	2	DON JUAN	1	V 8	1
THE BOY EXPIRED--THE FATHER HELD THE CLAY	204	2	DON JUAN	2	90	1
AS FAIR A THING AS E'ER WAS FORM'D OF CLAY	214	2	DON JUAN	2	110	8
OF SUCH QUICKSILVER CLAY THAT IN HIS BREAST	268	2	DON JUAN	2	209	3
OUR LITTLE SELVES RE-FORM'D IN FINER CLAY	305	2	DON JUAN	3	59	4
WAS NOT FOR THEM--THEY HAD TOO LITTLE CLAY	348	2	DON JUAN	4	9	8
THE PRECIOUS PORCELAIN OF HUMAN CLAY	350	2	DON JUAN	4	11	3
HER HUMAN CLAY IS KINDLED FULL OF POWER	374	2	DON JUAN	4	56	2
AND NOTHING OUTWARD TELLS OF HUMAN CLAY	383	2	DON JUAN	4	72	4
TO GAZE ONCE MORE ON THE COMMANDING CLAY	431	2	DON JUAN	5	37	3
ALTHOUGH OF CLAY ARE YET NOT QUITE OF MUD	491	2	DON JUAN	5	138	3
AS ANY MAN'S CLAY MIXTURE UNDERGOES	16	3	DON JUAN	6	20	5
FOR DEEMING HUMAN CLAY BUT COMMON DIRT	96	3	DON JUAN	7	58	5
THEIR CLAY FOR THE LAST TIME THEIR SOULS ENCUMBER--	120	3	DON JUAN	8	18	5
FROM THE MANURE OF HUMAN CLAY THOUGH DECKED	199	3	DON JUAN	9	34	5
THE WHOLE THING IS OF CLOTHING SOULS IN CLAY	220	3	DON JUAN	9	75	8
O'ERSPREADS THE CHEEK WHICH SEEMS TOO PURE FOR CLAY	229	3	DON JUAN	10	8	7
MY GUARD MY OLD GUARD EXCLAIMED THAT GOD OF CLAY--	254	3	DON JUAN	10	59	2
BAPTIZE POSTERITY OR FUTURE CLAY--	324	3	DON JUAN	12	18	4
HOW CLAY SHRINKS BACK FROM MORE QUIESCENT CLAY	412	3	DON JUAN	14	4	3
HOW CLAY SHRINKS BACK FROM MORE QUIESCENT CLAY	412	3	DON JUAN	14	4	3
AND HE DID NOT SEEM FORMED OF CLAY	518	3	DON JUAN	16	L 2	6

CLEAN
	PAGE	VOL		CANTO	STANZA	LN
WITH A CLEAN SHIRT AND VERY SPACIOUS BREECHES	240	2	DON JUAN	2	160	8
AND COOKS IN MOTION WITH THEIR CLEAN ARMS BARED	439	2	DON JUAN	5	50	6
STRIPT TO HIS WAISTCOAT AND THAT NOT TOO CLEAN	104	3	DON JUAN	7	73	7

CLEAR
	PAGE	VOL		CANTO	STANZA	LN
BUT INEZ WAS SO ANXIOUS AND SO CLEAR	75	2	DON JUAN	1	101	1
THE SEA AND SKY WERE BLUE AND CLEAR AND MILD--	193	2	DON JUAN	2	70	4
SO SOFT SO SWEET SO DELICATELY CLEAR	236	2	DON JUAN	2	151	4
OR AS THE STIRRING OF A DEEP CLEAR STREAM	360	2	DON JUAN	4	30	1
WHICH SHE ESSAY'D IN VAIN TO CLEAR (HOW SWEET	362	2	DON JUAN	4	34	3
AND THROUGH HER CLEAR BRUNETTE COMPLEXION SHONE A	395	2	DON JUAN	4	94	6
AND INTO HER CLEAR CHEEK THE BLOOD WAS BROUGHT	473	2	DON JUAN	5	108	4
TO ANSWER IN A VERY CLEAR ORATION	43	3	DON JUAN	6	74	5
SCOTCH PLAIDS SCOTCH SNOODS THE BLUE HILLS AND CLEAR STREAMS	233	3	DON JUAN	10	18	2
EXTREMELY WHOLESOME THOUGH BUT RARELY CLEAR	266	3	DON JUAN	10	83	8
TRAPS FOR THE TRAVELLER EVERY HIGHWAY'S CLEAR	273	3	DON JUAN	11	10	6
ITS WINDINGS THROUGH THE WOODS NOW CLEAR NOW BLUE	385	3	DON JUAN	13	58	7
BY HOMER'S CATALOGUE OF SHIPS IS CLEAR	393	3	DON JUAN	13	74	6
IT IS NOT CLEAR THAT ADELINE AND JUAN	454	3	DON JUAN	14	99	7
TRUTH'S FOUNTAINS MAY BE CLEAR--HER STREAMS ARE MUDDY	495	3	DON JUAN	15	88	6
SOME MILLIONS MUST BE WRONG THAT'S PRETTY CLEAR	496	3	DON JUAN	15	90	1
THOUGHTS QUITE AS YELLOW BUT LESS CLEAR THAN AMBER	505	3	DON JUAN	16	11	4
AS CLEAR AS SUCH A CLIMATE WILL ALLOW	506	3	DON JUAN	16	13	4
THEN AS THE NIGHT WAS CLEAR THOUGH COLD HE THREW	508	3	DON JUAN	16	17	1
THOUGH SOMETIMES FAINTLY FLUSHED--AND ALWAYS CLEAR	545	3	DON JUAN	16	94	7

CLEAR'D
	PAGE	VOL		CANTO	STANZA	LN
HE CLEAR'D HEDGE DITCH AND DOUBLE POST AND RAIL	424	3	DON JUAN	14	33	2

CLEARED
	PAGE	VOL		CANTO	STANZA	LN
WHO CLEARED HER SPARKLING EYES AND SMOOTHED HER BROWS	500	2	DON JUAN	5	154	3
AND HER BROW CLEARED BUT NOT HER TROUBLED EYE	61	3	DON JUAN	6	110	7

CLEARER
	PAGE	VOL		CANTO	STANZA	LN
CLEARER THAN THAT WITHOUT AND ITS WIDE HUE	204	2	DON JUAN	2	91	5
HE NE'ER PRESUMED TO MAKE AN ERROR CLEARER--	426	3	DON JUAN	14	37	7

CLEARING
	PAGE	VOL		CANTO	STANZA	LN
AS DOTH A RAINBOW THE JUST CLEARING AIR	17	3	DON JUAN	6	23	8

```
                                                        PAGE VOL    CANTO STANZA LN
CLEARLY
    KNOW VERY CLEARLY--OR AT LEAST LIE STILL . . . . . . . 270   3 DON JUAN 11      4    8
CLEAVES
    THE BAYONET PIERCES AND THE SABRE CLEAVES  . . . . . . 155   3 DON JUAN  8     88    1
CLEFT
    CRIMSON AS CLEFT POMEGRANATES THEIR LONG TRESSES . . . 292   2 DON JUAN  3     33    3
    EVEN TIME THE PITILESS IN SORROW CLEFT  . . . . . . . 348   2 DON JUAN  4      8    3
CLEOPATRA'S
    BUT ACTIUM LOST FOR CLEOPATRA'S EYES . . . . . . . . .   8   3 DON JUAN  6      4    7
    AS WHITE AS CLEOPATRA'S MELTED PEARLS . . . . . . . . 484   3 DON JUAN 15     65    8
CLERGY
    BECAUSE THE CLERGY TAKE THE THING IN HAND  . . . . . . 220   3 DON JUAN  9     76    4
    THE OTHER THAT'S TO SAY THE CLERGY--WHO  . . . . . . . 414   3 DON JUAN 14     10    2
CLERGYMAN
    I TELL HIM IF A CLERGYMAN HE LIES . . . . . . . . . . 141   2 DON JUAN  1    208    6
CLERGYMEN
    WITH POETS ALMOST CLERGYMEN OR WHOLLY . . . . . . . . 297   3 DON JUAN 11     57    4
CLERKS
    THE VERY CLERKS--THOSE SOMEWHAT DIRTY SPRINGS . . . . 287   3 DON JUAN 11     40    5
CLEVER
    OR LIKE ALL VERY CLEVER PEOPLE COULD NOT . . . . . . .  73   2 DON JUAN  1     97    8
    A FOOLISH CLEVER FELLOW IDEM SEMPER . . . . . . . . . 150   2 DON JUAN  1   V 1    8
    AS BOY I THOUGHT MYSELF A CLEVER FELLOW  . . . . . . . 345   2 DON JUAN  4      3    1
    BUT JOHNSON WAS A CLEVER FELLOW WHO . . . . . . . . . 130   3 DON JUAN  8     35    5
    BUT STILL SO LIKE THAT PSYCHE WERE MORE CLEVER . . . . 205   3 DON JUAN  9     45    6
    (WHO BY THE BY WHEN CLEVER ARE MORE HANDY  . . . . . . 331   3 DON JUAN 12     32    4
    BY MANY WINDINGS TO THEIR CLEVER CLINCH  . . . . . . . 404   3 DON JUAN 13     98    2
    AT SPEAKING TRUTH PERHAPS THEY ARE LESS CLEVER . . . . 501   3 DON JUAN 16      1    7
    LITTLE THAT'S GREAT BUT MUCH OF WHAT IS CLEVER . . . . 547   3 DON JUAN 16     98    4
CLEVEREST
    SHE MADE THE CLEVEREST PEOPLE QUITE ASHAMED . . . . .  26   2 DON JUAN  1     10    5
CLIENTS
    HAVE NOT ESSAY'D TO MULTIPLY THEIR CLIENTS . . . . . . 142   2 DON JUAN  1    211    5
CLIENTS'
    INTO A SCENE AND SWELL THE CLIENTS' CLAN . . . . . . . 437   3 DON JUAN 14     62    4
CLIFF
    THE CLIFF TOWARDS SUNSET ON THAT DAY SHE FOUND . . . . 224   2 DON JUAN  2    129    2
    AND DOWN THE CLIFF THE ISLAND VIRGIN CAME  . . . . . . 232   2 DON JUAN  2    142    1
CLIFFS
    WITH CLIFFS ABOVE AND A BROAD SANDY SHORE  . . . . . . 249   2 DON JUAN  2    177    2
    WHICH PASSED OR CATCH THE FIRST GLIMPSE OF THE CLIFFS  . 256   3 DON JUAN 10     64    8
    THY CLIFFS DEAR DOVER HARBOUR AND HOTEL  . . . . . . . 259   3 DON JUAN 10     69    2
    OF WHITE CLIFFS WHITE NECKS BLUE EYES BLUER STOCKINGS . 346   3 DON JUAN 12     67    7
CLIFF-WORN
    BEFORE THE ENTRANCE OF A CLIFF-WORN CAVE . . . . . . . 213   2 DON JUAN  2    108    6
CLIMACTERIC
    HER CLIMACTERIC TEASED HER LIKE HER TEENS  . . . . . . 247   3 DON JUAN 10     47    5
CLIMATE
    WHICH MAKE THE ENGLISH CLIMATE OF OUR YEARS  . . . . . 270   2 DON JUAN  2    214    8
    BORN OF THE SUN AS AFRIC'S CLIMATE IS  . . . . . . . . 373   2 DON JUAN  4     54   V8
    AND CLIMATE STOPPED ALL SCANDAL (NOW AND THEN)-- . . . 241   3 DON JUAN 10     33    4
    AND CLIMATE--STOPPED THE LION SCANDAL'S DEN  . . . . . 241   3 DON JUAN 10     33   V4
    THE CLIMATE WAS TOO COLD THEY SAID FOR HIM . . . . . . 246   3 DON JUAN 10     44    1
    WHAT WITH A SMALL DIVERSITY OF CLIMATE . . . . . . . . 327   3 DON JUAN 12     24    1
    IN THAT FAIR CLIME WHICH DON'T DEPEND ON CLIMATE . . . 423   3 DON JUAN 14     29    2
    AS CLEAR AS SUCH A CLIMATE WILL ALLOW . . . . . . . . 506   3 DON JUAN 16     13    4
CLIMATE'S
    IS MUCH MORE COMMON WHERE THE CLIMATE'S SULTRY . . . .  56   2 DON JUAN  1     63    8
CLIMAX
    DREADING THAT CLIMAX OF ALL HUMAN ILLS  . . . . . . . 293   2 DON JUAN  3     35    7
    FORMS A SAD CLIMAX TO ROMANTIC HOMAGES . . . . . . . . 346   3 DON JUAN 12     65    6
CLIMB
    CHEERFUL AS CHILDREN CLIMB THE BREASTS OF MOTHERS . . . 119   3 DON JUAN  8     15    6
    WAS MADE AT LENGTH WITH THOSE WHO DARED TO CLIMB . . . 151   3 DON JUAN  8     79    4
    FOR A LIEUTENANT TO CLIMB UP BUT SKILL . . . . . . . . 215   3 DON JUAN  9     66    6
    WHO DIED IN THE THEN GREAT ATTEMPT TO CLIMB  . . . . . 261   3 DON JUAN 10     74    5
    NOR MUCH TO CLIMB THROUGH LITTLE BOXES FRAMED  . . . . 278   3 DON JUAN 11     21    4
    'MIDST ROYAL DUKES AND DAMES CONDEMNED TO CLIMB  . . . 302   3 DON JUAN 11     68    7
CLIMBED
    HE CLIMBED TO WHERE THE PARAPET APPEARS  . . . . . . . 147   3 DON JUAN  8     71    4
CLIMBING
    SOME LIKEN IT TO CLIMBING UP A HILL  . . . . . . . . . 146   2 DON JUAN  1    218    3
CLIME
    ALTHOUGH THEY BOTH ARE BORN IN THE SAME CLIME  . . . . 277   2 DON JUAN  3      5    4
    BUT SEEM THE GROWTH OF A MOST DIFFERENT CLIME  . . . . 277   2 DON JUAN  3      5   V4
    STILL O'ER HIS MIND THE INFLUENCE OF THE CLIME . . . . 304   2 DON JUAN  3     56    1
    THE TIME THE CLIME THE SPOT WHERE I SO OFT . . . . . . 335   2 DON JUAN  3    102    2
    TO THE KIND READER OF OUR SOBER CLIME  . . . . . . . . 347   2 DON JUAN  4      6    1
    THAT IS TO SAY--IN A MERIDIAN CLIME . . . . . . . . . 482   2 DON JUAN  5    123    3
    AND CLIME AND TIME AND COUNTRY AND COMPLEXION  . . . .  26   3 DON JUAN  6     40    7
    LIKE FLOWERS OF DIFFERENT HUE AND CLIME AND ROOT . . .  38   3 DON JUAN  6     65    2
    A THING OF MUCH LESS IMPORT IN THAT CLIME--  . . . . .  51   3 DON JUAN  6     90    5
    WHICH FLASHES O'ER A WASTE AND ICY CLIME . . . . . . .  67   3 DON JUAN  7      2    4
    SWEAR THAT PAT'S LANGUAGE SPRUNG FROM THE SAME CLIME  . 122   3 DON JUAN  8     23    5
    IN THIS GAY CLIME OF BEAR-SKINS BLACK AND FURRY-- . . . 237   3 DON JUAN 10     26    3
    IN NEITHER CLIME TIME BLOOD WITH HER DEFENDER  . . . . 252   3 DON JUAN 10     57    7
    HE HAD THEN THE GRACE TOO RARE IN EVERY CLIME  . . . . 354   3 DON JUAN 12     84    6
    IN THAT FAIR CLIME WHICH DON'T DEPEND ON CLIMATE . . . 423   3 DON JUAN 14     29    2
CLIMES
    AND THROUGH ALL CLIMES THE SNOWY AND THE SUNNY . . . .  78   2 DON JUAN  1    107    7
```

	PAGE	VOL		CANTO	STANZA	LN

CLIMES   (CONTINUED)
ALL EUROPEAN CLIMES BY LAND OR SEA . . . . 129 2 DON JUAN 1   191   2
BUT LIKE THE CLIMES THAT KNOW NOR SNOW NOR HAIL . . . . 348 2 DON JUAN 4   9   4
AS IS THE CUSTOM OF THOSE EASTERN CLIMES . . . . 463 2 DON JUAN 5   89   6
THEIR CHASTITY IN THESE UNHAPPY CLIMES . . . . 501 2 DON JUAN 5   157   3
MADRID'S AND MOSCOW'S CLIMES WERE OF A PIECE . . . . . 239 3 DON JUAN 10   30   8
PERHAPS HE LONGED IN BITTER FROSTS FOR CLIMES . . . . . 243 3 DON JUAN 10   37   5
THE ART OF LIVING IN ALL CLIMES WITH EASE . . . . . . 460 3 DON JUAN 15   11   8
CLINCH
BY MANY WINDINGS TO THEIR CLEVER CLINCH . . . . 404 3 DON JUAN 13   98   2
CLING
LIKE CHERUBS ROUND AN ALTAR-PIECE THEY CLING . . . . . 306 2 DON JUAN 3   60   5
STRIP YOUR GREEN FIELDS AND TO YOUR HARVESTS CLING . . . 175 3 DON JUAN 8   126   6
CLINGING
AND CLINGING AS IF LOTH TO LOSE ITS HOLD . . . . 312 2 DON JUAN 3   71   6
CLINGS
WHATE'ER OF PEACE ABOUT OUR HEARTHSTONE CLINGS . . . . . 338 2 DON JUAN 3   107   5
AND TO WHICH BEAUTY OBSTINATELY CLINGS . . . . 468 2 DON JUAN 5   98   V4
CLINGS TO ITS TEAT STICKS TO ME THROUGH THE ABYSS . . . 238 3 DON JUAN 10   28   4
CLIP
WHICH FOR AN INSTANT CLIP ENJOYMENT'S WINGS . . . . . . 227 3 DON JUAN 10   5   8
CLIPT
AND DROOPING LIKE AN EAGLE'S WITH CLIPT PINION . . . . . 246 3 DON JUAN 10   44   6
CLOAK
A CANDIOTE CLOAK WHICH TO THE KNEE MIGHT REACH . . . . . 451 2 DON JUAN 5   68   3
OF HELL SHALL PALL THEM IN A DEEPER CLOAK . . . . . . 110 3 DON JUAN 7   86   8
AND SCARLET CLOAK (I HATE THE SIGHT TO SEE SINCE-- . . . 530 3 DON JUAN 16   61   4
THAT SCARLET CLOAK ALAS UNCLOSED WITH RIGOUR . . . . . 530 3 DON JUAN 16   61   7
THAT SCARLET CLOAK--GOD HELP US--WHEN CLOSE WRAPPED . . 530 3 DON JUAN 16   61   V7
CLOG
AND CLOG THE FOUNTAIN OF ETERNAL TEARS . . . . 275 2 DON JUAN 3   1   V8
HER BEAUTY ALSO SEEM'D TO FORM NO CLOG . . . . 477 3 DON JUAN 15   48   5
CLOGHER'S
DUKES--FOOLS BY BIRTH WHILE CLOGHER'S BISHOP SULLIES . . . 314 3 DON JUAN 11 V 76   5
CLOISTERS
IN CLOISTERS OF THE CLASSIC SALAMANCA . . . . 175 3 DON JUAN 2   37   7
ELSEWHERE PRESERVED THE CLOISTERS STILL WERE STABLE . . . 389 3 DON JUAN 13   66   3
CLOOTZ
PETION CLOOTZ DANTON MARAT LAFAYETTE . . . . 22 2 DON JUAN 1   3   2
CLOSE
SHE KEPT HER COUNSEL IN SO CLOSE A WAY . . . . 59 2 DON JUAN 1   68   8
UNLESS WITH BREAKERS CLOSE BENEATH HER LEE . . . . . . 180 2 DON JUAN 2   45   8
THEY COULD NOT RESCUE HIM ALTHOUGH SO CLOSE . . . . . . 186 2 DON JUAN 2   57   6
'TWAS BENDING CLOSE O'ER HIS AND THE SMALL MOUTH . . . 215 2 DON JUAN 2   113   1
THOSE EYES TO CLOSE THOUGH WEARINESS AND PAIN . . . . . 235 2 DON JUAN 2   149   3
SO DRAMAS CLOSE WITH DEATH OR SETTLEMENT FOR LIFE . . . 280 2 DON JUAN 3   9   V7
A BEAUTY AT THE SEASON'S CLOSE GROWN HECTIC . . . . . . 309 2 DON JUAN 3   66   1
THEN LOOK'D CLOSE AT THE FLINT AS IF TO SEE . . . . . . 365 2 DON JUAN 4   40   6
ALTHOUGH HER PAROXYSM DREW TOWARDS ITS CLOSE . . . . . 380 2 DON JUAN 4   67   6
THEY FOLLOWED CLOSE BEHIND THEIR SABLE GUIDE . . . . . 440 2 DON JUAN 5   51   2
THIS MASSY PORTAL STOOD AT THE WIDE CLOSE . . . . . . 462 2 DON JUAN 5   87   1
THE DAGGER CLOSE AT HAND WHICH MADE IT AWKWARD . . . . . 492 2 DON JUAN 5   140   2
AND WAS THRUST IN TO CLOSE THE OCTAVE'S CHIME . . . . . 14 3 DON JUAN 6   18   6
RESOUNDED ALLAH AND THE CLOUDS WHICH CLOSE . . . . . . 116 3 DON JUAN 8   8   5
AT OTHER TIMES REPULSED BY THE CLOSE FIRE . . . . 121 3 DON JUAN 8   20   5
JUST AT THE CLOSE OF THE FIRST BRIDAL YEAR . . . . . . 125 3 DON JUAN 8   27   4
INTO CLOSE CONTACT THOUGH RESERVED NOR CAUGHT . . . . . 365 3 DON JUAN 13   15   4
THERE WAS A COUNTRY GIRL IN A CLOSE CAP . . . . 530 3 DON JUAN 16   61   3
THAT SCARLET CLOAK--GOD HELP US--WHEN CLOSE WRAPPED . . 530 3 DON JUAN 16   61   V7
HOWEVER THE DAY CLOSED AS DAYS MUST CLOSE . . . . . . 549 3 DON JUAN 16   101   1
AND THEN SWUNG BACK NOR CLOSE--BUT STOOD AWRY . . . . . 558 3 DON JUAN 16   117   3
CLOSED
BUT CLOSED THE TYRANT-HATER HE BEGUN . . . . 15 2 DON JUAN D   10   8
CLOSED THE ORATION OF THE TRUSTY MAID . . . . 116 2 DON JUAN 1   173   4
ALFONSO CLOSED HIS SPEECH AND BEGG'D HER PARDON . . . . 120 2 DON JUAN 1   180   1
AND FRUITS AND DATE-BREAD LOAVES CLOSED THE REPAST . . 307 2 DON JUAN 3   63   2
BUT CLOSED ITS LITTLE BEING WITHOUT LIGHT . . . . . . 382 2 DON JUAN 4   70   4
AND WHEN 'TWAS FOUND STRAIGHTWAY THE BARGAIN CLOSED . . 476 2 DON JUAN 5   113   4
OFT ARE SOON CLOSED ALL HEROES ARE NOT BLIND . . . . . 133 3 DON JUAN 8   40   6
HOWEVER THE DAY CLOSED AS DAYS MUST CLOSE . . . . . . 549 3 DON JUAN 16   101   1
CLOSER
AND WRAPT HIM CLOSER LEST THE AIR TOO RAW . . . . . . 232 2 DON JUAN 2   143   6
STILL CLOSER SULPHURY CLOUDS BEGAN TO SMOTHER . . . . . 146 3 DON JUAN 8   69   6
CLOSER THAT ALL THE DEADLIER THEY MIGHT WRING . . . . . 170 3 DON JUAN 8   118   5
CLOSET
CLOSET AND CLOTHES'-PRESS CHEST AND WINDOW-SEAT . . . . 99 2 DON JUAN 1   143   2
THERE IS THE CLOSET THERE THE TOILET THERE . . . . . . 104 2 DON JUAN 1   153   1
THIS PRETTY GENTLEMAN WITHIN THE CLOSET . . . . 114 2 DON JUAN 1   170   8
AND JULIA INSTANT TO THE CLOSET FLEW . . . . 121 2 DON JUAN 1   182   2
IN DIGGING THE FOUNDATION OF A CLOSET . . . . 327 2 DON JUAN 3   89   7
IN DIGGING DRAINS FOR A NEW WATER CLOSET . . . . 327 2 DON JUAN 3   89   V7
BECAUSE HE KEPT THEM QUIET IN HIS CLOSET HE . . . . . . 496 2 DON JUAN 5   148   V6
CLOSING
FOR NIGHT WAS CLOSING ERE THEY CAME TO LAND . . . . . . 433 2 DON JUAN 5   41   6
OF CLOSING 'GAINST THE LIGHT THEIR ORBS OF VISION . . . . 50 3 DON JUAN 6   88   5
AS THE YEAR CLOSING WHIRLS THE SCARLET LEAVES . . . . 155 3 DON JUAN 8   88   3
HE SAW HOWEVER AT THE CLOSING SESSION . . . . 354 3 DON JUAN 12   83   1
CLOTHE
BEGAN TO CLOTHE EACH ASIATIC HILL . . . . 49 3 DON JUAN 6   86   3

137

```
                                                      PAGE VOL      CANTO STANZA LN
CLOTHED
     OF WHAT I THEN DREAMT CLOTHED IN THEIR OWN PALL     . . . . 233  3 DON JUAN 10     18    5
     IN SHORT HE HARDLY COULD BE CLOTHED WITH LESS   . . . . . 555  3 DON JUAN 16    111    4
CLOTHES
     THEIR BEST CLOTHES AS IF GOING TO A FAIR . . . . . . . 180  2 DON JUAN  2     45    2
     AND MOST OF THEM HAD LITTLE CLOTHES BUT RAGS   . . . . . 189  2 DON JUAN  2     62    8
     A QUANTITY OF CLOTHES FIT FOR THE BACK   . . . . . . . 450  2 DON JUAN  5     67    3
     I OFFER YOU A HANDSOME SUIT OF CLOTHES   . . . . . . . 455  2 DON JUAN  5     76    1
     HIS CLOTHES WERE NOT CURBED TO THEIR USUAL CUT . . . . 513  3 DON JUAN 16     29    6
CLOTHES'-PRESS
     CLOSET AND CLOTHES'-PRESS CHEST AND WINDOW-SEAT  . . . .  99  2 DON JUAN  1    143    6
CLOTHING
     THE WHOLE THING IS OF CLOTHING SOULS IN CLAY   . . . . . 220  3 DON JUAN  9     75    8
     TOO OFTEN ALL THE CLOTHING MEAT OR FUEL   . . . . . . . 256  3 DON JUAN 10     63    7
     AND CENTAUR-NESSUS GARB OF MORTAL CLOTHING . . . . . . 301  3 DON JUAN 11     65    4
CLOUD
     EVEN AS A SUMMER SKY'S WITHOUT A CLOUD   . . . . . . .  94  2 DON JUAN  1    135    6
     AND SMILING THROUGH HER DREAM AS THROUGH A CLOUD  . . .  39  3 DON JUAN  6     66    4
     AND THROWS A CLOUD O'ER LONGMAN AND JOHN MURRAY  . . .  79  3 DON JUAN  7     26    4
     WHICH ARCHED THE HORIZON LIKE A FIERY CLOUD . . . . . 115  3 DON JUAN  8      6    3
     WHAT CAN YE RECOGNIZE--A GILDED CLOUD . . . . . . . . 373  3 DON JUAN 13     33    8
     HAD STIRRED HIM ANSWERED IN A WAY TO CLOUD IT  . . . . 527  3 DON JUAN 16     54    8
     THE MOON PEEPED JUST ESCAPED FROM A GREY CLOUD . . . . 560  3 DON JUAN 16    121    8
CLOUDED
     OF RIVALSHIP ROSE IN EACH CLOUDED EYE . . . . . . . . 221  3 DON JUAN  9     78    7
     HAD CAUSED HIS NERVES--MADE ANSWERS RATHER CLOUDED . . 527  3 DON JUAN 16     54   V8
CLOUDS
     THE SCATTERING CLOUDS SHONE SPANNING THE DARK SEA . . . 204  2 DON JUAN  2     91    2
     NOW O'ER IT CLOUDS AND THUNDER MUST BE DRIVEN   . . . . 270  2 DON JUAN  2    214    3
     AND CLOUDS COME O'ER THE SUNSET OF OUR DAY  . . . . . . 305  2 DON JUAN  3     59    6
     LIKE FLEECY CLOUDS ABOUT THE MOON FLOW'D ROUND HER . . 311  2 DON JUAN  3     70    8
     LIKE SUMMER CLOUDS ALL SILVERY SMOOTH AND FAIR . . . . 375  2 DON JUAN  4     57    2
     BLOOD-RED AS SUNSET SUMMER CLOUDS WHICH RANGE  . . . . 473  2 DON JUAN  5    108    5
     RESOUNDED ALLAH AND THE CLOUDS WHICH CLOSE . . . . . . 116  3 DON JUAN  8      8    5
     A GLANCE ON THE DULL CLOUDS (AS THICK AS STARCH  . . . 121  3 DON JUAN  8     21    6
     STILL CLOSER SULPHURY CLOUDS BEGAN TO SMOTHER  . . . . 146  3 DON JUAN  8     69    6
     AS PURPLE CLOUDS BEFRINGE THE SUN BUT MOST . . . . . . 239  3 DON JUAN 10     29    7
     THE GLOOMY CLOUDS WHICH O'ER IT AS A YOKE  . . . . . . 266  3 DON JUAN 10     83    5
     ALL PURGED AND PIOUS FROM THEIR NATIVE CLOUDS  . . . . 396  3 DON JUAN 13     80    4
     LIKE FLEECY CLOUDS INTO THE SKY RETIRED  . . . . . . . 504  3 DON JUAN 16      8    6
CLOUDY
     'TWAS AS THE WATCHMEN SAY A CLOUDY NIGHT . . . . . . .  94  2 DON JUAN  1    135    1
CLOVE
     RECEIVED A CUT WHICH CLOVE HIS TURBAN THROUGH  . . . . 370  2 DON JUAN  4     48   V8
CLOVES
     CLOVES CINNAMON AND SAFFRON TOO WERE BOIL'D . . . . . 307  2 DON JUAN  3     63    7
CLOWNISH
     WITH CLOWNISH HEEL YOUR POPULAR CIRCULATION . . . . . 200  3 DON JUAN  9     35    7
CLOYED
     CONTENTED WHEN TRANSLATED MEANS BUT CLOYED  . . . . . 444  3 DON JUAN 14     79    5
CLOYING
     TILL AFTER CLOYING THE GAZETTES WITH CANT  . . . . . .  21  2 DON JUAN  1      1    3
CLOYS
     AND THESE WERE NOT OF THE VAIN KIND WHICH CLOYS  . . . 352  2 DON JUAN  4     16    4
CLUBS
     BUT THE CLUBS FOUND IT RATHER SERIOUS LAUGHTER . . . . 398  3 DON JUAN 13     86    6
     SAVE IN THE CLUBS NO MAN OF HONOUR PLAYS-- . . . . . . 407  3 DON JUAN 13    106    2
CLUE
     THAT LABYRINTH WHOSE CLUE IS OF THE SAME . . . . . . . 349  3 DON JUAN 12     72    2
     BUT WHAT'S REALITY  WHO HAS ITS CLUE . . . . . . . . . 495  3 DON JUAN 15     89    6
CLUNG
     WITHIN HIS GRASP HE CLUNG TO IT AND SORE . . . . . . . 212  2 DON JUAN  2    107    5
     THERE BREATHLESS WITH HIS DIGGING NAILS HE CLUNG  . . . 213  2 DON JUAN  2    108    1
     THEIR LIPS DREW NEAR AND CLUNG INTO A KISS . . . . . . 253  2 DON JUAN  2    185    8
     WHICH BEING JOIN'D LIKE SWARMING BEES THEY CLUNG-- . . 254  2 DON JUAN  2    187    7
     AND HAIDEE CLUNG AROUND HIM JUAN 'TIS-- . . . . . . . 364  2 DON JUAN  4     38    1
     BRING DOWN THE FRUIT WHICH STILL PERVERSELY CLUNG  . .  44  3 DON JUAN  6     76    6
     TO THE LIVE LEG STILL CLUNG THE SEVERED HEAD  . . . . 153  3 DON JUAN  8     84    8
     WHILE COURAGE CLUNG BUT TO A SINGLE TWIG--AM I . . . . 164  3 DON JUAN  8    105    5
     AGAINST THE LIGHT WHEREIN SHE DIES HE CLUNG  . . . . . 170  3 DON JUAN  8    118    4
CLUSTER'D
     HER GLOSSY HAIR WAS CLUSTER'D O'ER A BROW  . . . . . .  55  2 DON JUAN  1     61    1
CLUSTERING
     HER CLUSTERING HAIR WHOSE LONGER LOCKS WERE ROLL'D  . . 217  2 DON JUAN  2    116    3
CLYTEMNESTRA
     SUCH CLYTEMNESTRA THOUGH PERHAPS 'TIS BETTER  . . . . 222  3 DON JUAN  9     80    7
COACH
     WHETHER THEY COME BY HORSE OR CHAISE OR COACH  . . . . 279  3 DON JUAN 11     23    3
     COACH CHARIOT LUGGAGE BAGGAGE EQUIPAGE   . . . . . . . 378  3 DON JUAN 13     44    2
     BY VARIOUS JOLTINGS OF LIFE'S HACKNEY COACH . . . . . 421  3 DON JUAN 14     26    5
COACHES
     THROUGH COACHES DRAYS CHOKED TURNPIKES AND A WHIRL  . . 278  3 DON JUAN 11     22    1
COAL
     BRIGHT--AND AS BLACK AND BURNING AS A COAL . . . . . . 395  2 DON JUAN  4     94    5
COALS
     SIR HUMPHREY DAVY'S LANTERN BY WHICH COALS . . . . . .  93  2 DON JUAN  1    132    4
     TAKES OFF ONE PECK OF PURGATORIAL COALS . . . . . . . 185  2 DON JUAN  2     55    5
COARSE
     AS IF THE PEASANT'S COARSE CONTEMPT WERE VENTED  . . . 401  2 DON JUAN  4    105    3
```

138

PAGE VOL   CANTO STANZA LN

COARSE   (CONTINUED)
   THAT INJURED QUEEN BY CHRONICLERS SO COARSE 446   2 DON JUAN 5   61   1
   OR TO COARSE EFFORTS VERY LOUD AND LONG 540   3 DON JUAN 16   83   7
COARSER
   WAS COARSER AND HER AIR THOUGH FIRM LESS FREE 221   2 DON JUAN 2   122   6
COAST
   I RECOLLECT GREAT BRITAIN'S COAST LOOKS WHITE 163   2 DON JUAN 2   12   5
   THE LAND APPEAR'D A HIGH AND ROCKY COAST 209   2 DON JUAN 2   100   1
   IT WAS A WILD AND BREAKER-BEATEN COAST 249   2 DON JUAN 2   177   1
   THE COAST--I THINK IT WAS THE COAST THAT I 251   2 DON JUAN 2   181   1
   THE COAST--I THINK IT WAS THE COAST THAT I 251   2 DON JUAN 2   181   1
   WAS JUST DESCRIBING--YES IT WAS THE COAST-- 251   2 DON JUAN 2   181   2
   WHO DYING ON THE COAST OF ITHACA 285   2 DON JUAN 3   18   5
   BUT THAT PART OF THE COAST BEING SHOAL AND BARE 285   2 DON JUAN 3   19   6
   HAVE YOU EXPLORED THE LIMITS OF THE COAST 502   3 DON JUAN 16   4   5
COAT
   WITH NOTHING BUT THE SKY FOR A GREAT COAT 189   2 DON JUAN 2   63   8
   JUST AS MY GREAT COAT WAS ABOUT ME CAST 428   2 DON JUAN 5   33   3
   A SCARLET COAT BLACK FACINGS A LONG PLUME 204   3 DON JUAN 9   43   2
COAX
   WITH THE SAME FEELINGS AS YOU'D COAX A VAMPIRE 299   3 DON JUAN 11   62   5
COBBETT
   LIKE MOSES OR LIKE COBBETT WHO HAVE NE'ER 193   3 DON JUAN 9   21   V2
COBBLING
   COBBLING AT MANACLES FOR ALL MANKIND-- 18   2 DON JUAN D   14   6
COCHINEAL
   IF FROM A SHELL-FISH OR FROM COCHINEAL 505   3 DON JUAN 16   10   7
COCK
   AND NEXT PROCEEDED QUIETLY TO COCK 365   2 DON JUAN 4   40   8
   I'VE HEARD OF STORIES OF A COCK AND BULL 46   3 DON JUAN 6   80   1
   GOOD MORROW--FOR THE COCK HAD CROWN AND LIGHT 49   3 DON JUAN 6   86   2
   WHO WAKE IN WINTER ERE THE COCK CAN SUMMON 426   3 DON JUAN 14   36   3
COCK'D
   OH VALIANT MAN WITH SWORD DRAWN AND COCK'D TRIGGER . . . 103   2 DON JUAN 1   150   7
COCKED
   UPON THE HEAD BEFORE THEIR GUNS WERE COCKED 134   3 DON JUAN 8   43   8
   OVER A COCKED HAT IN A CROWDED ROOM 204   3 DON JUAN 9   43   4
   HIS BOW CONVERTED INTO A COCKED HAT 205   3 DON JUAN 9   45   5
COCKER'S
   OF LATE YEARS TO DISPENSE WITH COCKER'S RIGOURS 547   3 DON JUAN 16   98   7
COCKING
   THAT COCKING OF A PISTOL WHEN YOU KNOW 366   2 DON JUAN 4   41   2
COCKNEY
   YOUR VEINS OF COCKNEY SPIRIT SMILE OR MOURN 264   3 DON JUAN 10   80   6
COCKNEYS
   COCKNEYS OF LONDON MUSCADINS OF PARIS 174   3 DON JUAN 8   124   7
COCKS
   BETWEEN THESE NATIONS AS A MAIN OF COCKS 197   3 DON JUAN 9   29   7
CODE
   AND SETTLED BONNETS BY THE NEWEST CODE 406   3 DON JUAN 13   104   6
COELEBS'
   OR COELEBS' WIFE SET OUT IN QUEST OF LOVERS 29   2 DON JUAN 1   16   4
COERC'D
   POOR THING OF USAGES COERC'D COMPELL'D 420   3 DON JUAN 14   23   5
COFFEE
   FOR BREAKFAST OF EGGS COFFEE BREAD AND FISH 226   2 DON JUAN 2   133   8
   BUT THERE WERE EGGS FRUIT COFFEE BREAD FISH HONEY . . . 233   2 DON JUAN 2   145   7
   THE COFFEE MADE WOULD FAIN HAVE WAKEN'D JUAN 234   2 DON JUAN 2   146   2
   CAME ALWAYS BACK TO COFFEE AND HAIDEE 246   2 DON JUAN 2   171   8
   UP WITH THE COFFEE WHICH (I THINK) THEY SPOIL'D 307   2 DON JUAN 3   63   8
   FOR TEA AND COFFEE LEAVE US MUCH MORE SERIOUS 372   2 DON JUAN 4   52   8
   HE DRANK SIX CUPS OF COFFEE AT THE LEAST 52   3 DON JUAN 6   92   4
   AND SCARCE TO THE MOGUL A CUP OF COFFEE 199   3 DON JUAN 9   33   6
   THE EVENING ALSO WANED--AND COFFEE CAME 549   3 DON JUAN 16   101   2
COFFEEHOUSE
   AND LORD MOUNT COFFEEHOUSE THE IRISH PEER 102   2 DON JUAN 1   149   7
   GO TO THE COFFEE-HOUSE AND TAKE ANOTHER 431   3 DON JUAN 14   48   8
COFFIN
   AND SENDS NEW WERTERS YEARLY TO THEIR COFFIN 345   3 DON JUAN 12   63   6
COFFIN'D
   FROM DAY-BREAK AND WHEN COFFIN'D AT FOURSCORE 230   2 DON JUAN 2   140   7
COFFIN'S
   BURGLARIOUSLY BROKE HIS COFFIN'S LID 146   2 DON JUAN 1   219   6
COGNIAC
   UNLESS WHEN QUALIFIED WITH THEE COGNIAC 372   2 DON JUAN 4   53   1
CO-HEIRESSES
   AND THE TWO FAIR CO-HEIRESSES GILTBEDDING 473   3 DON JUAN 15   40   5
COHORN'S
   THE GREEK OR TURKISH COHORN'S IGNORANCE 136   3 DON JUAN 8   46   3
COIL
   HIS ARMS WERE LIKE A SERPENT'S COIL THEN FLEW 370   2 DON JUAN 4   48   5
COIL'D
   'TIS AS THE SNAKE LATE COIL'D WHO POURS HIS LENGTH . . . 218   2 DON JUAN 2   117   7
COILED
   HE LAY COILED LIKE THE BOA IN THE WOOD 300   2 DON JUAN 3   48   4
COIN
   NOR COIN MY SELF-LOVE TO SO BASE A VICE 12   2 DON JUAN D   6   2
COINCIDENCE
   A STRANGE COINCIDENCE TO USE A PHRASE 45   3 DON JUAN 6   78   7

139

		PAGE	VOL	CANTO	STANZA	LN

COINED
SUCH AS ARE COINED IN CONVERSATION'S MINT . . . . . . 440 3 DON JUAN 14 69 3
COINED FROM SURVIVING SUPERSTITION'S MINT . . . . . 510 3 DON JUAN 16 22 5
COINS
HER BROW WAS OVERHUNG WITH COINS OF GOLD . . . . . 217 2 DON JUAN 2 116 1
CONTAINING INGOTS BAGS OF DOLLARS COINS . . . . . . 321 3 DON JUAN 12 12 2
COKE
ALSO OBSERVE THAT LIKE THE GREAT LORD COKE . . . . . 494 3 DON JUAN 15 87 1
COLCHIAN
HIS PREDECESSORS IN THE COLCHIAN DAYS . . . . 303 2 DON JUAN 3 55 4
COLCHIS
MIGHT CARRY OUT TO COLCHIS IN OLD DAYS . . . . . . 303 2 DON JUAN 3 55 V4
COLD
BUT BE MUCH PUZZLED BY A COUGH AND COLD . . . . . . 168 2 DON JUAN 2 22 3
AGUE IN ITS COLD FIT THEY FILL'D THEIR BOAT . . . . 189 2 DON JUAN 2 63 7
FAMINE DESPAIR COLD THIRST AND HEAT HAD DONE . . . . 210 2 DON JUAN 2 102 1
AND WET AND COLD AND LIFELESS AT HER FEET . . . . . 362 2 DON JUAN 4 34 1
AND SUBJECT WHEN THE HOUSE IS THIN TO COLD . . . . 389 2 DON JUAN 4 83 3
BUT AFTER ALL 'TIS NOTHING BUT COLD SNOW . . . . . 398 2 DON JUAN 4 100 8
BUT I GROW SAD--AND LET A TALE GROW COLD . . . . . 413 2 DON JUAN 5 4 7
WHITE COLD AND PURE AS LOOKS A FROZEN RILL . . . . 40 3 DON JUAN 6 68 3
CHILL AND CHAINED TO COLD EARTH WE LIFT ON HIGH . . 66 3 DON JUAN 7 1 5
HARK THROUGH THE SILENCE OF THE COLD DULL NIGHT . . 110 3 DON JUAN 7 86 1
THOSE WHO CATCH COLD IN SHADOWS OF DEATH'S VALLEY . 131 3 DON JUAN 8 36 8
FOR THAT WERE VULGAR COLD AND COMMONPLACE . . . . 160 3 DON JUAN 8 97 2
EXCEPT COLD WEATHER AND COMMISERATION . . . . . . 176 3 DON JUAN 8 129 6
THE CLIMATE WAS TOO COLD THEY SAID FOR HIM . . . . 246 3 DON JUAN 10 44 1
AT LEAST IN A COLD COUNTRY MAY AWARD . . . . . . 322 3 DON JUAN 12 13 V6
OF HOT OR COLD MERCURIAL OR SEDATE . . . . 327 3 DON JUAN 12 24 2
SUCH IS YOUR COLD COQUETTE WHO CAN'T SAY NO . . . 345 3 DON JUAN 12 63 1
WHAT THEY SHOULD LAUGH AT--THE NOW HOT OR COLD . . 366 3 DON JUAN 13 17 V7
A HIDDEN NECTAR UNDER A COLD PRESENCE . . . . . . 375 3 DON JUAN 13 38 3
AND YOUR COLD PEOPLE ARE BEYOND ALL PRICE . . . . 375 3 DON JUAN 13 38 7
WHEN ERE THE INK BE DRY THE SOUND GROWS COLD . . . 382 3 DON JUAN 13 51 5
IN THIS OUR PARTY POLISH'D SMOOTH AND COLD . . . . 409 3 DON JUAN 13 110 2
HE WAS A COLD GOOD HONOURABLE MAN . . . . 440 3 DON JUAN 14 70 1
SERENE AND NOBLE--CONJUGAL BUT COLD . . . . . . 447 3 DON JUAN 14 86 8
NOW THIS AT ALL EVENTS MUST RENDER COLD . . . . . 468 3 DON JUAN 15 26 5
AS THAT PRIM SILENT COLD AURORA RABY . . . . . . 477 3 DON JUAN 15 49 8
GREAT THOUGHTS WE CATCH FROM THENCE (BESIDES A COLD 506 3 DON JUAN 16 14 4
THEN AS THE NIGHT WAS CLEAR THOUGH COLD HE THREW . 508 3 DON JUAN 16 17 1
BUT SEEING HIM ALL COLD AND SILENT STILL . . . . 514 3 DON JUAN 16 32 1
QUITE FULL RIGHT DULL GUESTS HOT AND DISHES COLD . 538 3 DON JUAN 16 78 6
FOLLOWED HIS VEINS NO LONGER COLD BUT HEATED . . . 559 3 DON JUAN 16 119 4
COLD-BLOODED
COLD-BLOODED SMOOTH-FACED PLACID MISCREANT . . . . 16 2 DON JUAN D 12 1
COLDER
WHICH COLDER HEARTS ENDURE TILL THEY ARE LAID . . . 382 2 DON JUAN 4 71 4
THEIR BAFFLED RAGE AND PAIN WHILE WAXING COLDER . . 158 3 DON JUAN 8 94 5
COLDLY
AND LOOKING COLDLY IN HER FACE HE CRIED . . . . . 484 2 DON JUAN 5 126 6
COLDNESS
YET JULIA'S VERY COLDNESS STILL WAS KIND . . . . . 60 2 DON JUAN 1 71 1
COLDNESS OR ANGER EVEN DISDAIN OR HATE . . . . . 61 2 DON JUAN 1 73 7
AND WHETHER COLDNESS PRIDE OR VIRTUE DIGNIFY . . . 435 3 DON JUAN 14 57 7
SUCH WAS HER COLDNESS OR HER SELF-POSSESSION . . . 480 3 DON JUAN 15 57 8
COLERIDGE
AND COLERIDGE TOO HAS LATELY TAKEN WING . . . . . 10 2 DON JUAN D 2 5
LIKE COLERIDGE INTO A METAPHYSICIAN . . . . . . 70 2 DON JUAN 1 91 8
THOU SHALT NOT SET UP WORDSWORTH COLERIDGE SOUTHEY 139 2 DON JUAN 1 205 2
OR COLERIDGE LONG BEFORE HIS FLIGHTY PEN . . . . 329 2 DON JUAN 3 93 5
SOME PERSONS THINK THAT COLERIDGE HATH THE SWAY . 298 3 DON JUAN 11 59 5
COLLAR
THAT YOU AND I WILL WIN SAINT GEORGE'S COLLAR . . . 160 3 DON JUAN 8 97 8
COLLARS
IN NUMBER'D LOTS THEY ALL HAD CUFFS AND COLLARS . . 283 2 DON JUAN 3 15 7
COLLECT
ACCORDING TO ALL HINTS I COULD COLLECT . . . . . 38 2 DON JUAN 1 33 2
BUT STILL I THINK I CAN COLLECT MY MIND . . . . . 133 2 DON JUAN 1 196 5
I STRUGGLE BUT CAN NOT COLLECT MY MIND . . . . . 133 2 DON JUAN 1 196 V2
COLLECTION
BUT THEN THE ABBEY'S WORTH THE WHOLE COLLECTION . . 280 3 DON JUAN 11 25 8
COLLECTIVE
WHERE'ER COLLECTIVE WISDOM CAN PARADE . . . . . . 371 3 DON JUAN 13 29 6
COLLEGE
NO--NO--I'D SEND HIM OUT BETIMES TO COLLEGE . . . . 50 2 DON JUAN 1 52 7
WHICH IS ACQUIRED IN NATURE'S GOOD OLD COLLEGE . . 228 2 DON JUAN 2 136 8
WAS WHIPT AT COLLEGE--A HARSH SIRE--ODD SPOUSE . . 328 2 DON JUAN 3 91 7
HE WAS YOUR MASTER OF YOUR STUPID COLLEGE . . . . 264 3 DON JUAN 10 80 V2
TO BUILD A COLLEGE OR TO FOUND A RACE . . . . . 320 3 DON JUAN 12 10 2
ALWAYS PREMISING THAT SAID SON AT COLLEGE . . . . 377 3 DON JUAN 13 42 7
COLLOQUY
JOHNSON WHO KNEW BY THIS LONG COLLOQUY . . . . . . 100 3 DON JUAN 7 65 1
COLOGNE
FROM THENCE HE WAS DRAWN ONWARDS TO COLOGNE . . . . 255 3 DON JUAN 10 62 5
COLONEL
O'ER WHICH LIEUTENANT COLONEL YESOUSKOI . . . . . 150 3 DON JUAN 8 76 7
COLONIAL
'TIS THERE THE MART OF THE COLONIAL TRADE IS . . . 159 2 DON JUAN 2 5 3

COLOSSUS
   THOU HAST STRUCK ONE IMMENSE COLOSSUS DOWN 445   3 DON JUAN 14   82   3
COLOUR
   AND BLENDING EVERY COLOUR INTO ONE 205   2 DON JUAN 2   92   6
   AND EVERY MORN HIS COLOUR FRESHLIER CAME 245   2 DON JUAN 2   169   1
   WHOSE COLOUR WAS NOT BLACK NOR WHITE NOR GRAY 462   2 DON JUAN 5   88   4
   HER EYE DILATED AND HER COLOUR HEIGHTENED   42   3 DON JUAN 6   72   8
   THE COLOUR OF A BUDDING ROSE'S CREST   48   3 DON JUAN 6   85   4
   TO COLOUR UP HIS RAYS FROM YOUR DESPATCHES 107   3 DON JUAN 7   81   8
   LEND TO THAT COLOUR A TRANSCENDANT RAY 218   3 DON JUAN 9   71   6
   OF BARDS AND PROSERS WORDS ARE VOID OF COLOUR 428   3 DON JUAN 14   40   8
   I KNOW NOT BUT HER COLOUR NE'ER WAS HIGH-- 545   3 DON JUAN 16   94   6
COLOUR'D
   OF COLOUR'D GARBS AS BRIGHT AS BUTTERFLIES 289   2 DON JUAN 3   27   8
COLOURED
   SO THAT THE STREETS OF COLOURED LAMPS ARE FULL 88   3 DON JUAN 7   44   5
   BROADENING TO GRINS HE COLOURED MORE THAN ONCE 542   3 DON JUAN 16   88   3
COLOURING
   WAS APT TO ADD A COLOURING FROM HER OWN 463   3 DON JUAN 15   17   2
   THE DIFFICULTY LIES IN COLOURING 467   3 DON JUAN 15   25   5
COLOURINGS
   SHORN OF ITS GLASS OF THOUSAND COLOURINGS 387   3 DON JUAN 13   62   2
COLOURS
   SIMPLER AND YET OF COLOURS NOT SO GRAVE 220   2 DON JUAN 2   120   3
   AND TAKE ALL COLOURS--LIKE THE HANDS OF DYERS 326   2 DON JUAN 3   87   8
   AND IN SUCH COLOURS THAT THEY SEEM TO LIVE 402   2 DON JUAN 4   107   6
   WARRANTED VIRGIN BEAUTY'S BRIGHTEST COLOURS 407   2 DON JUAN 4   114   3
   OH THAT MY WORDS WERE COLOURS BUT THEIR TINTS 60   3 DON JUAN 6   109   7
   A THOUSAND AND A THOUSAND COLOURS THEY   66   3 DON JUAN 7   1   7
   MAY THE ROSE CALL BACK ITS TRUE COLOURS SOON 409   3 DON JUAN 13   111   6
COLUMBIA'S
   COLUMBIA'S STOCK HATH HOLDERS NOT UNKNOWN 318   3 DON JUAN 12   6   6
COLUMBUS
   IF SOME COLUMBUS OF THE MORAL SEAS 455   3 DON JUAN 14   101   7
   COLUMBUS FOUND A NEW WORLD IN A CUTTER 468   3 DON JUAN 15   27   6
   THE SCEPTICS WHO WOULD NOT BELIEVE COLUMBUS 502   3 DON JUAN 16   4   8
COLUMN
   TO THE BARD'S TOMB AND NOT THE WARRIOR'S COLUMN 400   2 DON JUAN 4   104   4
   WITH HUMAN BLOOD THAT COLUMN WAS CEMENTED 401   2 DON JUAN 4   105   1
   WITH HUMAN FILTH THAT COLUMN IS DEFILED 401   2 DON JUAN 4   105   2
   THE COLUMN ORDERED ON THE ASSAULT SCARCE PASSED 115   3 DON JUAN 8   7   1
   FELL IN WITH WHAT WAS LATE THE SECOND COLUMN 130   3 DON JUAN 8   34   2
   THE TOWN WAS ENTERED FIRST ONE COLUMN MADE 146   3 DON JUAN 8   69   1
   WHERE THREE PARTS OF HIS COLUMN YET REMAIN 148   3 DON JUAN 8   72   6
   THEIR COLUMN THOUGH THE TURKISH BATTERIES THUNDERED . . . 149   3 DON JUAN 8   75   1
   ANOTHER COLUMN ALSO SUFFERED MUCH-- 151   3 DON JUAN 8   78   1
   AS AN OLD TEMPLE DWINDLED TO A COLUMN 358   3 DON JUAN 13   1   8
   COLUMN DATE FALMOUTH THERE HAS LATELY BEEN HERE 383   3 DON JUAN 13   54   5
COLUMNS
   DETACHMENT OF THREE COLUMNS TOOK ITS STATION   91   3 DON JUAN 7   50   3
   WAS ALSO IN THREE COLUMNS WITH A THIRST   91   3 DON JUAN 7   50   6
   THE THIRD IN COLUMNS TWO ATTACKED BY WATER   91   3 DON JUAN 7   50   8
   THE COLUMNS WERE IN MOVEMENT ONE AND ALL 116   3 DON JUAN 8   9   1
COM
   R PULV COM THREE GRAINS IPECACUANHAE 244   3 DON JUAN 10   41   5
COMB
   WHILE BABA MADE HIM COMB HIS HEAD AND OIL IT 457   2 DON JUAN 5   79   8
COMBAT
   THAT OF DESPISING THOSE WE COMBAT WITH   79   3 DON JUAN 7   25   2
   WHICH DID NOT COMBAT LIKE THE DEVIL AS YET-- 131   3 DON JUAN 8   37   6
   AS TIGERS COMBAT WITH AN EMPTY CRAW 137   3 DON JUAN 8   49   5
   HE WHO WILL COMBAT EVIL LONG IN USE 363   3 DON JUAN 13   10   V1
COMBATED
   AS IF HE HAD COMBATED WITH MORE THAN ONE 568   3 DON JUAN 17   14   3
COMBED
   AND ABOVE ALL BE COMBED EVEN TO A HAIR   64   3 DON JUAN 6   118   4
COMBINATION
   BY THE MERE COMBINATION OF A COTERIE 397   3 DON JUAN 13   82   4
COMBINE
   THAT LOVE AND MARRIAGE RARELY CAN COMBINE 277   2 DON JUAN 3   5   3
   (AS FAR AS RHYME AND CRITICISM COMBINE 232   3 DON JUAN 10   16   3
COMBINED
   MIGHT SHOCK A CONNOISSEUR BUT WHEN COMBINED 390   3 DON JUAN 13   67   3
   HALF VIRTUES AND WHOLE VICES BEING COMBINED 480   3 DON JUAN 15   57   4
COMBS
   OF STOCKINGS SLIPPERS BRUSHES COMBS COMPLETE   99   2 DON JUAN 1   143   4
COME
   BEGOT--BUT THAT'S TO COME--WELL TO RENEW   26   2 DON JUAN 1   9   8
   TO TEACH HIM MANNERS FOR THE TIME TO COME   34   2 DON JUAN 1   25   8
   OUR COMING AND LOOK BRIGHTER WHEN WE COME   88   2 DON JUAN 1   123   4
   COME COME 'TIS NO TIME NOW FOR FOOLING THERE 114   2 DON JUAN 1   170   6
   COME COME 'TIS NO TIME NOW FOR FOOLING THERE 114   2 DON JUAN 1   170   6
   OF TWENTY-FIVE OR THIRTY--(COME MAKE HASTE) 115   2 DON JUAN 1   172   2
   COME SIR GET IN)--MY MASTER MUST BE NEAR 115   2 DON JUAN 1   172   5
   OR ELSE THE THING HAD HARDLY COME TO PASS) 158   2 DON JUAN 2   3   6
   (AND SO MY SOBER MUSE--COME LET'S BE STEADY-- 160   2 DON JUAN 2   6   8
   FOR THE SKY SHOW'D IT WOULD COME ON TO BLOW 170   2 DON JUAN 2   26   7
   BUT THEY COULD NOT COME AT THE LEAK AS YET 171   2 DON JUAN 2   28   4
   BECAUSE TILL PEOPLE KNOW WHAT'S COME TO PASS 185   2 DON JUAN 2   55   6

COME   (CONTINUED)
AND WHEN THE WISH'D-FOR SHOWER AT LENGTH WAS COME 203   2 DON JUAN   2   89   4
THE WORLDS TO COME OF BOTH OR FALL BENEATH 280   2 DON JUAN   3   9   5
A SOFA LIKE A BED MAY COME BY WRONG 288   2 DON JUAN   3   25   V8
TO BID MEN COME AND GO AND COME AGAIN-- 299   2 DON JUAN   3   47   2
TO BID MEN COME AND GO AND COME AGAIN-- 299   2 DON JUAN   3   47   2
AND CLOUDS COME O'ER THE SUNSET OF OUR DAY 305   2 DON JUAN   3   59   6
(PROVIDED THEY DON'T COME IN AFTER DINNER) 306   2 DON JUAN   3   60   2
BUT ONE ARISE--WE COME WE COME 323   2 DON JUAN   3 L 8   5
BUT ONE ARISE--WE COME WE COME 323   2 DON JUAN   3 L 8   5
OF POPE AND DRYDEN ARE WE COME TO THIS 334   2 DON JUAN   3   100   5
SHOULD AN HOUR COME TO BID THEM BREATHE APART 358   2 DON JUAN   4   27   3
THE TIME MAY COME WHEN YOU MAY HEAR ME TOO 392   2 DON JUAN   4   88   6
OF POETS WHO COME DOWN TO US THROUGH DISTANCE 398   2 DON JUAN   4   100   1
THE TIME MUST COME WHEN BOTH ALIKE DECAY'D 400   2 DON JUAN   4   104   5
GO AND HE GOETH COME AND FORTH HE STEPP'D 430   2 DON JUAN   5   36   6
I WISH THE CASE COULD COME BEFORE A JURY HERE 446   2 DON JUAN   5   61   8
AND NOW THEN YOU MUST COME ALONG WITH ME SIRS 458   2 DON JUAN   5   80   6
BLOCKHEAD COME ON AND SEE QUOTH BABA WHILE 459   2 DON JUAN   5   83   1
THE MOMENT TILL TOO LATE TO COME AGAIN   6   3 DON JUAN   6   1   5
STRIPT TO HIS SHIRT WAS COME TO LEAD THE VAN 90   3 DON JUAN   7   49   8
WHENCE COME YE--FROM CONSTANTINOPLE LAST 97   3 DON JUAN   7   59   4
WHO WHEN WE COME TO SUM UP THE TOTALITY 108   3 DON JUAN   7   83   5
PAST PRESENT AND TO COME--BUT ALL MAY YIELD 117   3 DON JUAN   8   12   7
KNEW WHEN AND HOW TO CUT AND COME AGAIN 130   3 DON JUAN   8   35   6
WHICH MADE SOME THINK AND OTHERS KNOW A HELL COME . . . 134   3 DON JUAN   8   42   8
HAD NOT COME UP IN TIME TO CAST AN AWE 137   3 DON JUAN   8   49   3
THEN COMES THE TUG OF WAR--'TWILL COME AGAIN 138   3 DON JUAN   8   51   5
SO CUVIER SAYS--AND THEN SHALL COME AGAIN 201   3 DON JUAN   9   38   1
I NEVER KNOW THE WORD WHICH WILL COME NEXT 203   3 DON JUAN   9   41   8
FROM THEE WE COME TO THEE WE GO AND WHY 210   3 DON JUAN   9   56   3
BUT COUGHS WILL COME WHEN SIGHS DEPART--AND NOW 229   3 DON JUAN 10   8   1
MUST COME MUCH RATHER SHOULD HE COURT THE RAY 229   3 DON JUAN 10   9   7
TO COME OFF HANDSOMELY IN THAT REGARD 235   3 DON JUAN 10   22   4
BUT TIME THE COMFORTER WILL COME AT LAST 248   3 DON JUAN 10   48   1
BUT--I WON'T WEEP--COME POSTBOYS WHIRL ALONG 263   3 DON JUAN 10   77   V2
WHETHER THEY COME BY HORSE OR CHAISE OR COACH 279   3 DON JUAN 11   23   3
YOU LEAVE BEHIND--THE NEXT OF MUCH YOU COME 290   3 DON JUAN 11   44   5
(WHICH WILL COME OVER THINGS) BEATS LOVE OR LIQUOR . . 317   3 DON JUAN 12   4   5
THE TIME WILL COME SHE'LL WISH THAT SHE HAD SNATCHED . 332   3 DON JUAN 12   35   3
COME OUT AND GLIMMER'D AS A SIX-WEEKS' STAR 398   3 DON JUAN 13   84   6
WHILE STRONGBOW'S BEST THINGS MIGHT HAVE COME FROM CATO 401   3 DON JUAN 13   92   8
AN AGE MAY COME FONT OF ETERNITY 411   3 DON JUAN 14   3   5
WHEN YOUR AFFAIRS COME ROUND ONE WAY OR T'OTHER 431   3 DON JUAN 14   48   7
TO COME BETWEEN MINE EPIC AND ITS INDEX 440   3 DON JUAN 14   68   8
AND HATE THOSE WHO WON'T LET THEM COME TO PASS 491   3 DON JUAN 15   79   8
FOR YOU HAVE GOT THAT PLEASURE STILL TO COME 498   3 DON JUAN 15   95   4
MIGHT COME OR GO BUT JUAN COULD NOT STATE 511   3 DON JUAN 16   24   7
BUT COME I'LL SET YOUR STORY TO A TUNE 517   3 DON JUAN 16   38   4
SOONER COME PLACE INTO THE CIVIL LIST 536   3 DON JUAN 16   75   1
BUT SHOULD THE DAY COME WHEN PLACE CEASED TO EXIST . . 537   3 DON JUAN 16   75   5
AS WIDE AS IF A LONG SPEECH WERE TO COME 557   3 DON JUAN 16   115   4
OR HOW IS'T MATTER TREMBLES TO COME NEAR IT 557   3 DON JUAN 16   116   8
(I'LL TAKE THE LIKENESS I CAN FIRST COME AT) 564   3 DON JUAN 17   4   5
COMEDIES
ALL COMEDIES ARE ENDED BY A MARRIAGE 280   2 DON JUAN   3   9   2
COMEDY
THE DAYS OF COMEDY ARE GONE ALAS 402   3 DON JUAN 13   94   5
COMER
THEIR TALK OF COURSE RAN MOST ON THE NEW COMER 23   3 DON JUAN   6   35   1
TO THE NEXT COMER OR--AS IT WILL TELL 339   3 DON JUAN 12   51   7
COMERS
ACHILLES ORDER'D DINNER FOR NEW COMERS 221   2 DON JUAN   2   123   8
THESE RASCALS BEING NEW COMERS KNEW NOT WHOM 298   2 DON JUAN   3   44   1
KEPT FOR ALL COMERS AT ALL HOURS TO DINE 310   2 DON JUAN   3   69   8
COMES
IF HE COMES HERE TO TAKE A DEPOSITION 104   2 DON JUAN   1   152   1
THE PEOPLE'S SYCOPHANT--TILL DANGER COMES 151   2 DON JUAN   1 V 2   V7
A KIND OF DEATH COMES O'ER US ALL ALONE 443   2 DON JUAN   5   57   7
THEN COMES THE TUG OF WAR--'TWILL COME AGAIN 138   3 DON JUAN   8   51   5
FOREVER AND ANON COMES INDIGESTION 269   3 DON JUAN 11   3   1
THEIR CASH COMES FROM THEIR WEALTH GOES TO A JEW . . . 306   3 DON JUAN 11   75   4
FOR THIS EFFECT DEFECTIVE COMES BY CAUSE 502   3 DON JUAN 16   2   2
HE COMES--BUT NOT TO GRIEVE 519   3 DON JUAN 16 L 3   8
HE WAS FREE TO CONFESS--(WHENCE COMES THIS PHRASE . . 536   3 DON JUAN 16   73   1
COMET
HENCE MY OLD COMET GIVE THE STARS DUE WARNING-- . . . 494   2 DON JUAN   5   145   4
COMFORT
SUGGESTED SOME SLIGHT COMFORT IN HIS WAY 105   3 DON JUAN   7   75   3
AND THAT'S ONE COMFORT FOR MY LOST ADVICE 200   3 DON JUAN   9   36   7
(IF BUT FOR COMFORT) THAT ALL THINGS ARE KIND 377   3 DON JUAN 13   41   4
COMFORTABLE
SOME CHRISTIANS HAVE A COMFORTABLE CREED 202   2 DON JUAN   2   86   8
A MISTRESS AND SUCH COMFORTABLE QUARTERS 415   2 DON JUAN   5   8   7
INTO A COMFORTABLE TETE-A-TETE 482   2 DON JUAN   5   122   6
COMFORTER
BUT TIME THE COMFORTER WILL COME AT LAST 248   3 DON JUAN 10   48   1
COMFORTS
OF IN-DOOR COMFORTS STILL SHE HATH A MINE-- 395   3 DON JUAN 13   77   5

		PAGE	VOL	CANTO	STANZA	LN

COMING
OUR COMING AND LOOK BRIGHTER WHEN WE COME · · · · · · 88 2 DON JUAN 1 123 4
NOUGHT BUT THE HEAVY SEA AND COMING NIGHT · · · · · 178 2 DON JUAN 2 41 8
LEAVES NOTHING TILL THE COMING OF THE JUST-- · · · · 399 2 DON JUAN 4 101 6
TO HINT THAT HE IS COMING UP THIS WAY · · · · · · 494 2 DON JUAN 5 144 8
SOUND AND THEN BY A CRY THE SULTAN'S COMING · · · · · 494 2 DON JUAN 5 145 8
YOUR COMING HAS BEEN UNEXPECTED HERE · · · · · · 29 3 DON JUAN 6 46 5
BUT COMING YOUNG FROM LANDS AND SCENES ROMANTIC · · · 347 3 DON JUAN 12 68 1
UNTIL PREFERMENT COMING AT A SURE RATE · · · · · · 540 3 DON JUAN 16 82 4
COMITATUS
WITH HIM RETIRED HIS POSSE COMITATUS · · · · · · · 111 2 DON JUAN 1 164 1
COMMAND
EVEN THEN THEIR LOVE THEY COULD NOT ALL COMMAND · · · 114 2 DON JUAN 1 170 3
HIS TEMPER NOT BEING UNDER GREAT COMMAND · · · · · 123 2 DON JUAN 1 185 4
THERE WAS A SOMETHING WHICH BESPOKE COMMAND · · · · 217 2 DON JUAN 2 116 7
NOW IN A PERSON USED TO MUCH COMMAND-- · · · · · 299 2 DON JUAN 3 47 1
THOUGH DOUBTLESS HE WHO CAN COMMAND HIMSELF · · · · 299 2 DON JUAN 3 47 7
FRETTED WITH GOLD OR SILVER--BY COMMAND · · · · · 310 2 DON JUAN 3 69 5
FOR SORROW O'ER EACH SENSE HELD STERN COMMAND · · · 396 2 DON JUAN 4 95 2
AND OTHERS ROSE TO THE COMMAND OF CREWS · · · · · 409 2 DON JUAN 4 116 4
OF HALF-VOLUPTUOUSNESS AND HALF COMMAND · · · · · 473 2 DON JUAN 5 108 8
SHE DEEMED HER LEAST COMMAND MUST YIELD DELIGHT · · · 485 2 DON JUAN 5 128 3
BATTLES TO THE COMMAND FIELD MARSHAL SOUVAROFF · · · 85 3 DON JUAN 7 39 8
THE GENERAL WHO HELD HIM IN COMMAND · · · · · · 141 3 DON JUAN 8 57 4
THAT GREAT ENCHANTER AT WHOSE ROD'S COMMAND · · · · 204 3 DON JUAN 9 44 3
WHO TOOK BY TURNS THAT DIFFICULT COMMAND · · · · · 205 3 DON JUAN 9 46 5
HOWE'ER OUR FRIEND DON JUAN MIGHT COMMAND · · · · · 329 3 DON JUAN 12 29 5
'TIS NOT IN MORTALS TO COMMAND SUCCESS · · · · · 366 3 DON JUAN 13 18 1
COMMANDANT
I FOUND THE MILITARY COMMANDANT · · · · · · · 428 2 DON JUAN 5 33 7
PERCEIVING THEN NO MORE THE COMMANDANT · · · · · · 127 3 DON JUAN 8 31 1
COMMANDED
PERCEIVING NOR COMMANDER NOR COMMANDED · · · · · · 127 3 DON JUAN 8 32 1
COMMANDER
IT IS AN ACTUAL FACT THAT HE COMMANDER · · · · · 93 3 DON JUAN 7 52 1
PERCEIVING NOR COMMANDER NOR COMMANDED · · · · · · 127 3 DON JUAN 8 32 1
COMMANDING
TO GAZE ONCE MORE ON THE COMMANDING CLAY · · · · · 431 2 DON JUAN 5 37 3
COMMANDMENT
AND BREAK THE--WHICH COMMANDMENT IS'T THEY BREAK · · · 74 2 DON JUAN 1 98 4
I WISH SHE HAD HIS BOOK'S THE ELEVENTH COMMANDMENT · · 472 3 DON JUAN 15 38 2
COMMANDMENTS
I'LL WRITE POETICAL COMMANDMENTS WHICH · · · · · 138 2 DON JUAN 1 204 2
COMMANDS
THE KING COMMANDS US AND THE DOCTOR QUACKS US · · · 159 2 DON JUAN 2 4 5
FOR THROUGH THE SOUTH THE CUSTOM STILL COMMANDS · · · 472 2 DON JUAN 5 105 7
COMMANDS THE CITY AND UPON ITS SITE · · · · · 71 3 DON JUAN 7 10 4
COMMANDS--THE INTELLECTUAL LORD OF ALL · · · · · 320 3 DON JUAN 12 9 8
COMMEMORATION
IN CHRONOLOGICAL COMMEMORATION · · · · · · · 327 3 DON JUAN 3 89 4
YET THERE WERE SEVERAL WORTH COMMEMORATION · · · · 74 3 DON JUAN 7 16 3
AND THEREFORE WORTHY OF COMMEMORATION · · · · · · 176 3 DON JUAN 8 128 4
COMMENCE
ON WHICH THEY MIGHT REPOSE OR EVEN COMMENCE · · · · 177 2 DON JUAN 2 40 5
COMMENCE WITH FEELINGS WARM AND PROSPECTS HIGH · · · 421 2 DON JUAN 5 21 5
AND YOUNG BEGINNERS MAY AS WELL COMMENCE · · · · · 376 3 DON JUAN 13 40 1
THIRDLY COMMENCE NOT WITH THE END--OR SINNING · · · 393 3 DON JUAN 13 73 7
COMMENCED (FROM SUCH SLIGHT THINGS WILL GREAT COMMENCE) · 493 3 DON JUAN 15 83 5
COMMENCED
AND NOW COMMENCED A STRICT INVESTIGATION · · · · · 43 3 DON JUAN 6 74 1
OFF ISMAIL AND COMMENCED A CANNONADE · · · · · · 81 3 DON JUAN 7 29 5
COMMENCED (FROM SUCH SLIGHT THINGS WILL GREAT COMMENCE) · 493 3 DON JUAN 15 83 5
AND PROMISES TO ALL--WHICH LAST COMMENCED · · · · 535 3 DON JUAN 16 71 4
COMMENT
A COMMENT ON THE GOSPEL'S SIN NO MORE · · · · · 352 3 DON JUAN 12 79 2
COMMENTARIES
OH CAESAR'S COMMENTARIES NOW IMPART YE · · · · · 108 3 DON JUAN 7 82 5
COMMENTATOR'S
DEEM THIS A COMMENTATOR'S PHANTASY · · · · · · 281 2 DON JUAN 3 11 4
COMMENTS
HAVE FILLED THEIR PAPERS WITH THEIR COMMENTS VARIOUS · · 352 3 DON JUAN 12 78 4
COMMERCIAL
SEEMED TO HIM HALF COMMERCIAL HALF PEDANTIC · · · · 347 3 DON JUAN 12 68 5
COMMISERATION
GULBEYAZ SHEWED THEM BOTH COMMISERATION · · · · · 65 3 DON JUAN 6 119 3
EXCEPT COLD WEATHER AND COMMISERATION · · · · · · 176 3 DON JUAN 8 129 6
COMMISSARY
CERES IS COMMISSARY TO OUR BELLIES · · · · · · 246 2 DON JUAN 2 170 V3
COMMISSION
AWAY HE WENT THEN UPON HIS COMMISSION · · · · · · 64 3 DON JUAN 6 117 1
JUAN WHOSE WAS A DELICATE COMMISSION · · · · · · 283 3 DON JUAN 11 32 1
AS ELDON ON A LUNATIC COMMISSION-- · · · · · · 497 3 DON JUAN 15 92 4
COMMIT
IN GANGS OF FIFTY THIEVES COMMIT THEIR CRIMES · · · 79 2 DON JUAN 1 108 5
HE HAD NO BUSINESS TO COMMIT A SIN · · · · · · 113 2 DON JUAN 1 167 2
COMMIT--FLIRTATION WITH THE MUSE OF MOORE · · · · 139 2 DON JUAN 1 205 8
COMMIT ADULTERY WITH THOMAS MOORE · · · · · · 139 2 DON JUAN 1 205 V8
COMMODIOUS
COMMODIOUS BUT IMMORAL THEY ARE FOUND · · · · · · 282 3 DON JUAN 11 30 6

143

	PAGE	VOL		CANTO	STANZA	LN
COMMODITIES						
FOR BOTH COMMODITIES DWELL BY THE THAMES	293	3	DON JUAN	11	48	3
COMMON						
LAST--YOURS HAS LATELY BEEN A COMMON CASE--	9	2	DON JUAN	D	1	4
TO BE THE MOST REMOTE FROM COMMON USE	44	2	DON JUAN	1	40	4
POSSESS'D AN AIR AND GRACE BY NO MEANS COMMON	55	2	DON JUAN	1	61	7
IS MUCH MORE COMMON WHERE THE CLIMATE'S SULTRY	56	2	DON JUAN	1	63	8
THAT IS TO SAY A THOUGHT BEYOND THE COMMON	63	2	DON JUAN	1	77	5
NEVER COULD SHE SURVIVE THAT COMMON LOSS	67	2	DON JUAN	1	84	4
THIS MAY SEEM STRANGE BUT YET 'TIS VERY COMMON	74	2	DON JUAN	1	98	1
THE COMMON PRIVILEGES OF MY SEX	101	2	DON JUAN	1	147	2
IS THAT SAME TIME SO COMMON YET SO PRECIOUS	145	2	DON JUAN	1	217	V7
YET DEEM'D HERSELF IN COMMON PITY BOUND	224	2	DON JUAN	2	129	6
WERE LINK'D ALIKE AS FOR THE COMMON PEOPLE HE	284	2	DON JUAN	3	16	7
IT IS A HARD ALTHOUGH A COMMON CASE	305	2	DON JUAN	3	59	1
QUITE COMMON IN THOSE COUNTIES ARE A KIND	308	2	DON JUAN	3	65	2
INTRIGUES ADVENTURES OF THE COMMON SCHOOL	353	2	DON JUAN	4	17	5
TO MATCH A COMMON FURY WITH HER RAGE	490	2	DON JUAN	5	136	2
AND DECORATES THE BOOK OF COMMON PRAYER	17	3	DON JUAN	6	23	7
EXTREMELY COMMON IN THIS AGE WHOSE METAL	33	3	DON JUAN	6	55	7
WHEN THINGS BEYOND THE COMMON HAVE OCCURRED--	59	3	DON JUAN	6	106	6
WHICH WITH YOUR CONQUERORS IS A COMMON PRANK	71	3	DON JUAN	7	9	6
COMMON IN MANY CASES WAS IN THIS	79	3	DON JUAN	7	25	3
MANY OF COMMON READERS GIVE A GUESS	82	3	DON JUAN	7	33	3
FOR DEEMING HUMAN CLAY BUT COMMON DIRT	96	3	DON JUAN	7	58	5
ALL COMMON FELLOWS WHO MIGHT WRITHE AND WINCE	117	3	DON JUAN	8	11	4
NO COMMON LANGUAGE AND BESIDES IN TIME	141	3	DON JUAN	8	58	2
INCREASES TILL YOU SHALL MAKE COMMON CAUSE	196	3	DON JUAN	9	28	6
BEHAVED NO BETTER THAN A COMMON SEMPSTRESS	221	3	DON JUAN	9	77	8
BUT AT THE LEAST I HAVE SHUNNED THE COMMON SHORE	227	3	DON JUAN	10	4	7
WHILE COMMON MEN GROW IGNORANTLY OLD	232	3	DON JUAN	10	14	5
ONLY THE COMMON RUN WHO MUST PURSUE	305	3	DON JUAN	11	73	2
THE UNUSUAL QUICKNESS OF THESE COMMON CHANGES	309	3	DON JUAN	11	81	8
WHICH 'TIS THE COMMON CRY AND LIE TO VAUNT AS	311	3	DON JUAN	11	87	3
OF COMMON LIKINGS WHICH MAKE SOME DEPLORE	366	3	DON JUAN	13	17	6
TO BUILD UP COMMON THINGS WITH COMMON PLACES	413	3	DON JUAN	14	7	8
TO BUILD UP COMMON THINGS WITH COMMON PLACES	413	3	DON JUAN	14	7	8
AND THAT THEIR BOOKS HAVE BUT ONE STYLE IN COMMON--	418	3	DON JUAN	14	19	7
EXTREMELY DISAGREEABLE BUT COMMON	429	3	DON JUAN	14	43	7
SHE MERELY FELT A COMMON SYMPATHY	449	3	DON JUAN	14	91	5
SHE DEEMED HIS MERITS SOMETHING MORE THAN COMMON	473	3	DON JUAN	15	40	6
CONFOUNDED HIM IN COMMON WITH THE CROWD	493	3	DON JUAN	15	83	2
AS COMMON SOLDIERS OR A COMMON--SHORE	537	3	DON JUAN	16	76	3
AS COMMON SOLDIERS OR A COMMON--SHORE	537	3	DON JUAN	16	76	3
JUST AS A REGULAR COMMON SOLDIER OR A WHORE	537	3	DON JUAN	16	76	V3
THE POOR PRIEST WAS REDUCED TO COMMON SENSE	540	3	DON JUAN	16	83	6
AS FAR AS WORDS MAKE RULES--OUR COMMON NOTION	563	3	DON JUAN	17	3	2
TO PAINT A SOLE SENSATION--THOUGH QUITE COMMON--	569	3	DON JUAN	17	V 13	4
COMMONERS						
FOR COMMONERS HAD EVER THEM MISTOOK	398	3	DON JUAN	13	85	5
COMMONEST						
ADDING THAT THIS WAS COMMONEST AND BEST	472	2	DON JUAN	5	105	6
BY COMMONEST AMBITION THAT WHEN PASSION	8	3	DON JUAN	6	4	2
FROM OUT THE COMMONEST DEMANDS OF NATURE	486	3	DON JUAN	15	69	8
COMMONPLACE						
FOR THAT WERE VULGAR COLD AND COMMONPLACE	160	2	DON JUAN	8	97	2
SET DOWN HIS SAYINGS IN HER COMMON-PLACE BOOK	294	3	DON JUAN	11	52	8
(NOW FOR A COMMONPLACE) BENEATH THE SNOW	374	3	DON JUAN	13	36	2
WHO IN HIS COMMON-PLACE BOOK HAD A PAGE	403	3	DON JUAN	13	97	5
A KIND OF COMMON-PLACE EVEN IN THEIR CRIMES	417	3	DON JUAN	14	16	4
ANOTHER GENTLE COMMON-PLACE OR TWO	440	3	DON JUAN	14	69	2
THE PRESENT WITH THEIR COMMON-PLACE COSTUME	468	3	DON JUAN	15	26	8
THERE IS A COMMON-PLACE BOOK ARGUMENT	564	3	DON JUAN	17	5	1
COMMONS						
SAVE DEATH OR DOCTORS' COMMONS--SO HE DIED	41	2	DON JUAN	1	36	8
THE HOUSE OF COMMONS DAMOCLES OF WORDS	153	2	DON JUAN	1	V 4	1
AND FOUNDED DOCTORS' COMMONS--I HAVE CONNED	209	3	DON JUAN	9	53	6
THE HOUSE OF COMMONS TURNED TO A TAX-TRAP--	310	3	DON JUAN	11	84	3
OF DOCTORS' COMMONS BUT SHE DREADED FIRST	437	3	DON JUAN	14	62	5
HAVE TIED TOGETHER COMMONS LORDS AND KINGS	536	3	DON JUAN	16	74	8
COMMOTION						
THE ODA IN A GENERAL COMMOTION	42	3	DON JUAN	6	71	2
SHE PUT ALL CORONETS INTO COMMOTION	434	3	DON JUAN	14	55	2
COMMUNION						
MASTERS OF THEIR OWN TIME--OR IN COMMUNION	406	3	DON JUAN	13	103	3
COMPACT						
BUT IT WILL SERVE TO KEEP MY VERSE COMPACT)	119	2	DON JUAN	1	178	4
COMPANION						
AT LENGTH ONE WHISPER'D HIS COMPANION WHO	194	2	DON JUAN	2	73	1
JUAN'S COMPANION WAS A ROMAGNOLE	395	2	DON JUAN	4	94	1
WHISPERED TO HIS COMPANION--'TWAS THE SAME	434	2	DON JUAN	5	43	3
IN THE FAIR FORM OF THEIR COMPANION NEW	24	3	DON JUAN	6	37	5
WHICH MADE THEM LIKE THEIR NEW COMPANION	25	3	DON JUAN	6	38	V7
COMPANION SOMETHING NEWER STILL AS 'TWERE	25	3	DON JUAN	6	39	2
COMPANY						
FROM BETTER COMPANY HAVE KEPT YOUR OWN	12	2	DON JUAN	D	5	2
DREST TO RECEIVE SO MUCH GOOD COMPANY	106	2	DON JUAN	1	156	8
TO FIND SO MUCH GOOD COMPANY INVITED	294	2	DON JUAN	3	37	8
BUT IN GOOD COMPANY--THE GOUT OR STONE	305	2	DON JUAN	3	59	8

144

COMPANY   (CONTINUED)
IN COMPANY A VERY PLEASANT FELLOW 318   2 DON JUAN 3   82   2
TO THOSE WHO LIKE THEIR COMPANY ABOUT 41   3 DON JUAN 6   70   7
BEFORE A COMPANY OF CALMUCKS DRILLING 96   3 DON JUAN 7   58   2
SUWARROW WHEN HE SAW THIS COMPANY 97   3 DON JUAN 7   59   1
IN SUCH GOOD COMPANY AS ALWAYS THRONG 123   3 DON JUAN 8   24   6
OF THE GOOD COMPANY CAN WIN A CORNER 303   3 DON JUAN 11   69   2
A SCOUNDREL AND YOU'LL HAVE GOOD COMPANY 310   3 DON JUAN 11   86   V8
UNLESS GOOD COMPANY HE KEPT TOO LONG 443   3 DON JUAN 14   77   6
SHOW OFF--TO PLEASE THEIR COMPANY OR MOTHER 522   3 DON JUAN 16   44   8
THE COMPANY PREPARED TO SEPARATE 527   3 DON JUAN 16   55   2
WITH THE SUBSTANTIAL COMPANY ENGROSSED 543   3 DON JUAN 16   90   4
THE COMPANY WHOSE BIRTH WEALTH WORTH HAVE COST . . 568   3 DON JUAN 17   13   4
COMPANY'S
GOOD COMPANY'S A CHESS-BOARD--THERE ARE KINGS 400   3 DON JUAN 13   89   1
COMPARATIVE
HAD SUFFER'D MORE--HIS HARDSHIPS WERE COMPARATIVE . . . 229   2 DON JUAN 2   137   7
SCOTT THE SUPERLATIVE OF MY COMPARATIVE-- 481   3 DON JUAN 15   59   4
COMPARE
WITH ITS STRANGE WHIRLS AND EDDIES CAN COMPARE--   7   3 DON JUAN 6   2   6
WHO WITH THE BRIGHTEST GEORGIANS MIGHT COMPARE 24   3 DON JUAN 6   36   4
FEW SPECIMENS YET LEFT US CAN COMPARE 384   3 DON JUAN 13   55   5
COMPARED
COMPARED WITH WHAT HAIDEE DID WITH HIS TREASURE . . . 295   2 DON JUAN 3   39   6
COMPARED WITH THOSE OF OUR PURE PEARLS OF PRICE . . . 349   3 DON JUAN 12   72   7
BUT RARELY SEEN LIKE GOLD COMPARED WITH PAPER 510   3 DON JUAN 16   22   7
ARE TUTORS GUARDIANS AND SO FORTH COMPARED 564   3 DON JUAN 17   4   2
COMPARISON
OF ANY MODERN FEMALE SAINT'S COMPARISON 30   2 DON JUAN 1   17   2
I SPEAK OF CHRISTIAN LANDS IN THIS COMPARISON 248   2 DON JUAN 2   175   7
LIKE GOLD AS IN COMPARISON TO DROSS 280   3 DON JUAN 11   26   3
OR LIKE THE OLD COMPARISON OF SNOWS 335   3 DON JUAN 12   41   3
HAVING WOUND UP WITH THIS SUBLIME COMPARISON 481   3 DON JUAN 15   59   1
COMPASS
NO DOUBT IN LITTLE COMPASS ROUND OR SQUARE 112   2 DON JUAN 1   166   4
A VOICE OF NO GREAT COMPASS AND NOT SWEET 392   2 DON JUAN 4   89   4
COULD RISK OR COMPASS SUCH STRANGE PHANTASIES 477   2 DON JUAN 5   115   3
COMPASS'D
NE'ER COMPASS'D NOR LESS MORTAL CHISEL WROUGHT . . . 219   2 DON JUAN 2   119   8
COMPASSION
AND THEIR COMPASSION GREW TO SUCH A SIZE 225   2 DON JUAN 2   131   6
A KIND OF BLUNT COMPASSION FOR THE SAD 417   2 DON JUAN 5   12   5
SHE ALSO HAD COMPASSION AND A BED 29   3 DON JUAN 6   47   8
COMPASSION BREATHES ALONG THE SAVAGE MIND 164   3 DON JUAN 8   106   8
COMPEERS
AND TALL BEYOND HER SEX AND THEIR COMPEERS 367   2 DON JUAN 4   43   5
DEPARTED LIKE THE REST OF THEIR COMPEERS 381   3 DON JUAN 13   50   2
COMPELL'D
POOR THING OF USAGES COERC'D COMPELL'D 420   3 DON JUAN 14   23   5
COMPELLED
SOME SUCKING HERO IS COMPELLED TO REAR 108   3 DON JUAN 7   83   4
UNLESS COMPELLED BY FATE OR WAVE OR WIND 139   3 DON JUAN 8   54   1
'TWIXT PLACE AND PATRIOTISM--ALBEIT COMPELLED . . . 535   3 DON JUAN 16   72   4
COMPELS
FOR WARNING TO THE REST COMPELS THESE RAPS 155   2 DON JUAN 1   V 7   7
COMPETE
WITHOUT DOORS TOO SHE MAY COMPETE IN MELLOW 395   3 DON JUAN 13   77   7
COMPETENT
WERE PROVED BY COMPETENT FALSE WITNESSES 109   2 DON JUAN 1   160   8
JUST KILLED AND SCARCELY COMPETENT TO PANT 429   2 DON JUAN 5   33   V8
COMPETITION
AND THEN THERE WAS A GENERAL COMPETITION 330   3 DON JUAN 12   30   2
COMPLACENCY
TO SHOW WITH WHAT COMPLACENCY HE CREEPS 333   2 DON JUAN 3   98   3
COMPLAIN
I CAN'T COMPLAIN WHOSE ANCESTORS ARE THERE 242   3 DON JUAN 10   36   1
SHE HAD NOTHING TO COMPLAIN OF OR REPROVE 447   3 DON JUAN 14   86   5
YET MIXED SO SLIGHTLY THAT YOU CAN'T COMPLAIN . . . 502   3 DON JUAN 16   3   6
COMPLAINED
ALSO THE MUFFIN WHEREOF HE COMPLAINED 515   3 DON JUAN 16   34   2
COMPLAINING
HE ALWAYS IS COMPLAINING OF HIS LOT 392   2 DON JUAN 4   89   5
AND THOUGH HER DIGNITY BROOKED NO COMPLAINING . . . 247   3 DON JUAN 10   47   6
COMPLAINT
OF MERIT AND COMPLAINT OF PRESENT DAYS 14   2 DON JUAN D   8   7
'TIS SAID--INDEED A GENERAL COMPLAINT-- 418   3 DON JUAN 14   19   1
COMPLAINTS
AND LIVED CONTENTEDLY WITHOUT COMPLAINTS 424   3 DON JUAN 14   31   3
COMPLETE
OR GENTLEMAN OF SEVENTY YEARS COMPLETE 89   2 DON JUAN 1   125   3
OF STOCKINGS SLIPPERS BRUSHES COMBS COMPLETE 99   2 DON JUAN 1   143   4
MY MISERY CAN SCARCE BE MORE COMPLETE 134   2 DON JUAN 1   197   4
OF ALL OUR PUMPS--A WRECK COMPLETE SHE ROLL'D . . . 178   2 DON JUAN 2   42   6
AND WHEN THEY DEEM'D ITS MOISTURE WAS COMPLETE . . . 201   2 DON JUAN 2   85   4
THEIR SOFA OCCUPIED THREE PARTS COMPLETE 309   2 DON JUAN 3   67   3
WHICH MADE THEIR NEW ESTABLISHMENT COMPLETE 316   2 DON JUAN 3   78   3
IN THAT COMPLETE PERFECTION WHICH ENSURES 332   2 DON JUAN 3   97   3
THEY TROD AS UPON NECKS AND TO COMPLETE 475   2 DON JUAN 5   111   5
THE TWO FIRST FEELINGS RAN THEIR COURSE COMPLETE . . . 213   3 DON JUAN 9   61   1

145

```
                                                       PAGE VOL     CANTO  STANZA LN
COMPLETE   (CONTINUED)
      OF FREEDOM SHALL COMPLETE THEIR EDUCATION    . . . . . .   354  3 DON JUAN 12     83   6
      TO SPOIL HIS UNDERTAKING OR COMPLETE   . . . . . . .      423  3 DON JUAN 14     30   6
COMPLETELY
      BUT THAT WHICH MORE COMPLETELY FAITH EXACTS  . . . . .     138  2 DON JUAN  1    203   6
      THAT SOON HIS HEAD WAS MOST COMPLETELY CROWNED . . . .     457  2 DON JUAN  5     79   4
      IN HIS GRAVE OFFICE SO COMPLETELY SKILL'D  . . . . .      399  3 DON JUAN 13     88   6
      COMPLETELY SANS CULOTTE AND WITHOUT VEST  . . . . .       555  3 DON JUAN 16    111   3
COMPLEXION
      AND THROUGH HER CLEAR BRUNETTE COMPLEXION SHONE A  . . .   395  2 DON JUAN  4     94   6
      IN MAKE OF A COMPLEXION WHITE AND RUDDY  . . . . . .      416  2 DON JUAN  5     11   2
      AND CLIME AND TIME AND COUNTRY AND COMPLEXION  . . . .      26  3 DON JUAN  6     40   7
COMPLIMENT
      THIS COMPLIMENT WHICH DREW ALL EYES UPON . . . . . .      501  2 DON JUAN  5    156   1
      LOW AS THE COMPLIMENT DESERVED SUWARROW  . . . . . .       99  3 DON JUAN  7     63   2
      RATHER BY DEFERENCE THAN COMPLIMENT   . . . . . . .       493  3 DON JUAN 15     83   7
COMPLIMENTED
      AND COMPLIMENTED DON ALFONSO'S TASTE  . . . . . . .        58  2 DON JUAN  1     67   6
COMPLIMENTS
      TO BEAR THE COMPLIMENTS OF MANY A BORE   . . . . . .      404  2 DON JUAN  4    109   3
COMPOSE
      I HARDLY COULD COMPOSE ANOTHER LINE   . . . . . . .       415  3 DON JUAN 14     12   2
      COULD WRITE RHYMES AND COMPOSE MORE THAN SHE WROTE  . .    524  3 DON JUAN 16     47   2
COMPOSED
      COMPOSED A CHOIR OF GIRLS TEN OR A DOZEN . . . . . .      469  2 DON JUAN  5     99   2
      FORGETTING QUITE THE WOMAN (WHICH COMPOSED  . . . . .     211  3 DON JUAN  9     58   2
COMPOSITION
      AND THAT'S THE MORAL OF THIS COMPOSITION . . . . . .       50  3 DON JUAN  6     88   1
      THAT ALL THEIR GLORY AS A COMPOSITION . . . . . . .      364  3 DON JUAN 13     11   7
COMPOSITIONS
      WAS ADELINE WELL VERSED AS COMPOSITIONS  . . . . . .      523  3 DON JUAN 16     46   8
COMPREHEND
      BUT NOT A WORD COULD JUAN COMPREHEND  . . . . . . .       241  2 DON JUAN  2    161   2
      WE WHOSE MINDS COMPREHEND ALL THINGS NO MORE  . . . .     432  2 DON JUAN  5     39   7
      I COMPREHEND FOR WITHOUT TRANSFORMATION  . . . . . .      192  3 DON JUAN  9     20   7
COMPREHENDS
      CONDUCT LIKE THIS BY NO MEANS COMPREHENDS   . . . . .      37  2 DON JUAN  1     30   6
COMPREHENSION
      LESS FOR THE COMPREHENSION THAN THE EAR  . . . . . .      152  2 DON JUAN  1  V  3   6
      HIS MAXIMS WHICH TO MARTIAL COMPREHENSION   . . . . .      96  3 DON JUAN  7     58   7
COMPREHENSIONS
      TO FEMALES OF PERSPICUOUS COMPREHENSIONS . . . . . .      491  3 DON JUAN 15     80   3
COMPRESS'D
      HIS DAUGHTER WHILE COMPRESS'D WITHIN HIS CLASP  . . .     370  2 DON JUAN  4     48   2
COMPRESSION
      FOR THAT COMPRESSION IN ITS BURNING CORE . . . . . .       61  2 DON JUAN  1     72   5
COMPRISE
      EVEN IF IT SHOULD COMPRISE A PACK OF FABLES  . . . .      117  2 DON JUAN  1    175   6
COMPRISED
      A BOROUGH IS COMPRISED ALONG THE HEIGHT  . . . . . .       71  3 DON JUAN  7     10   2
      CONTRIVED TO GET ITSELF COMPRISED WITHIN IT  . . . .     142  3 DON JUAN  8     59   4
COMPROMISE
      HERE WAS AN HONOURABLE COMPROMISE   . . . . . . .        472  2 DON JUAN  5    105   1
COMPROMISED
      FELT RESTLESS AND PERPLEXED AND COMPROMISED  . . . .     506  3 DON JUAN 16     12   2
COMPUNCTION
      RAGE FEAR HATE JEALOUSY REVENGE COMPUNCTION  . . . .     271  2 DON JUAN  2    215   6
COMRADE
      DON JUAN TURNING TO HIS COMRADE WHO   . . . . . . .      459  2 DON JUAN  5     83   2
      A WOUNDED COMRADE SPRAWLING IN HIS GORE  . . . . . .     121  3 DON JUAN  8     20   8
COMRADE'S
      AND WHEN HIS COMRADE'S THOUGHT EACH SUFFERER KNEW  . .    194  2 DON JUAN  2     73   5
      YOUR NAMES--MINE'S JOHNSON AND MY COMRADE'S JUAN . . .     97  3 DON JUAN  7     60   1
COMRADES
      HER COMRADES ALSO THOUGHT THEMSELVES UNDONE  . . . .     501  2 DON JUAN  5    156   3
      THEY BROUGHT HIM AND HIS COMRADES TO HEAD-QUARTERS  .      96  3 DON JUAN  7     57   2
      IN FAIR PROPORTION WITH THEIR COMRADES--THEN  . . . .    163  3 DON JUAN  8    103   2
CON
      NEM CON AMONGST THE WOMEN WHICH I GRIEVE . . . . . .      493  3 DON JUAN 15     84   2
      TO SAY LEADS OFT TO CRIM CON WITH THE MARRIED--  . .     493  3 DON JUAN 15     84   3
CONCATENATION
      ALL FELT A SOFT KIND OF CONCATENATION . . . . . . .       25  3 DON JUAN  6     38   6
CONCEAL
      TAUGHT TO CONCEAL THEIR BURSTING HEARTS DESPOND  . . .    263  2 DON JUAN  2    200   4
      DYES WITH HIS MORNING LIGHT--AND WOULD CONCEAL  . . .     313  2 DON JUAN  3     73   3
      AND MORE ATTRACTS BY ALL IT DOTH CONCEAL--  . . . .      422  3 DON JUAN 14     27   4
CONCEAL'D
      CONCEAL'D AMONGST HIS PREMISES 'TIS TRUE . . . . . .      118  2 DON JUAN  1    177   5
CONCEALED
      CONCEALED HER FEATURES BETTER THAN A VEIL   . . . . .      60  3 DON JUAN  6    109   2
      WHICH DID NOT SHOW BUT YET CONCEALED A STORM  . . . .     474  3 DON JUAN 15     41  V2
CONCEDE
      STOPPED AS IF ONCE MORE WILLING TO CONCEDE  . . . . .     170  3 DON JUAN  8    117   2
CONCEDED
      OR GENEROUS DRAFT CONCEDED AS A GIFT  . . . . . . .      379  3 DON JUAN 13     45   5
CONCEIT
      A PRETTY LAD BUT BURSTING WITH CONCEIT   . . . . . .     392  2 DON JUAN  4     89   2
CONCEITS
      A WILDERNESS OF THE MOST RARE CONCEITS   . . . . . .     502  3 DON JUAN 16      3   3
```

146

CONCEIVE
    WERE NOT DRAWN FROM THEIR SPOUSES YOU CONCEIVE 281   2 DON JUAN 3   10   8
    A STERN REPOSE WHICH YOU WOULD SCARCE CONCEIVE 94   3 DON JUAN 7   54   3
CONCEIVED
    SHE NOW CONCEIVED ALL DIFFICULTIES PAST 478   2 DON JUAN 5   116   2
    CONCEIVED THAT PHRASE WAS QUITE ENOUGH TO MOVE 478   2 DON JUAN 5   116   8
CONCENTRATED
    THEN CALM CONCENTRATED AND STILL AND SLOW 300   2 DON JUAN 3   48   3
CONCENTRATING
    AND BEAUTY ALL CONCENTRATING LIKE RAYS 254   2 DON JUAN 2   186   2
CONCENTRE
    AND THUS THE CHILLIEST ASPECTS MAY CONCENTRE 375   3 DON JUAN 13   38   2
CONCERN
    'TWAS SURELY NO CONCERN OF THEIRS NOR MINE 33   2 DON JUAN 1   23   4
    'TWAS STRANGE THAT ONE SO YOUNG SHOULD THUS CONCERN . . . 71   2 DON JUAN 1   93   5
    THERE IS A SORT OF UNEXPREST CONCERN 164   2 DON JUAN 2   14   5
    BUT HERE I LEAVE THE GENERAL CONCERN 120   3 DON JUAN 8   17   1
    TO JACK HOWE'ER THIS GAVE BUT SLIGHT CONCERN 133   3 DON JUAN 8   41   5
    WITH SUCH SMALL GEAR TO GIVE MYSELF CONCERN 300   3 DON JUAN 11   63   3
    BUT SMALL CONCERN ABOUT THE WHEN OR WHERE 430   3 DON JUAN 14   45   4
    BUT THIS IS NOT AT PRESENT MY CONCERN 436   3 DON JUAN 14   59   7
    YET GREW A LITTLE PALE--WITH WHAT CONCERN 545   3 DON JUAN 16   94   5
CONCERN'D
    AT WHICH THE NAVAL PEOPLE ARE CONCERN'D 23   2 DON JUAN 1   4   6
    AND NEVER DREAM'D HIS LADY WAS CONCERN'D 31   2 DON JUAN 1   19   4
CONCERT
    WHERE HEART AND SOUL AND SENSE IN CONCERT MOVE 254   2 DON JUAN 2   186   5
CONCISION
    OF TYRANNY OF ALL KINDS MY CONCISION 466   3 DON JUAN 15   22   7
    AND AMPLIFY YOU LOSE MUCH BY CONCISION 478   3 DON JUAN 15   51   4
CONCLUDED
    HAD BEEN THE HAPPY LOVER HE CONCLUDED 118   2 DON JUAN 1   177   4
CONCLUSION
    TO DEEM AS A MOST LOGICAL CONCLUSION 12   2 DON JUAN D   5   5
CONCLUSIONS
    I'D TRY CONCLUSIONS WITH THOSE JANIZARIES 299   3 DON JUAN 11   62   7
CONCOCTION
    SOME SAID 'TWAS A CONCOCTION OF THE HUMOURS 244   3 DON JUAN 10   40   5
    THE PLAN AT PRESENT'S SIMPLY IN CONCOCTION 356   3 DON JUAN 12   87   5
CONCORD
    AND TUNE THE CONCORD TO A FINER MOOD 451   3 DON JUAN 14   93   4
CONCUBINE
    YEARS AND A FIFTEEN-HUNDREDTH CONCUBINE 10   3 DON JUAN 6   8   8
    IN HIS MONASTIC CONCUBINE OF SNOW-- 14   3 DON JUAN 6   17   6
CONCUR
    EXTREMELY PURE WHICH MADE THEM ALL CONCUR 25   3 DON JUAN 6   39   4
CONCUSSION
    FEW YOUTHFUL MINDS CAN STAND THE STRONG CONCUSSION . . . 235   3 DON JUAN 10   21   3
CONDE
    FOWLS A LA CONDE SLICES EKE OF SALMON 484   3 DON JUAN 15   65   1
CONDEMN
    AND SO HAVE BEEN FORGOTTEN--I CONDEMN NONE 24   2 DON JUAN 1   5   5
    CONDEMN THE ROYAL LADY'S TASTE WHO WORE 238   2 DON JUAN 2   155   4
    ABHOR CONDEMN ABJURE THE MORTAL MADE 268   2 DON JUAN 2   209   2
    THEY SAW NOT IN THEMSELVES AUGHT TO CONDEMN 351   2 DON JUAN 4   13   4
    I OWN IT I DEPLORE IT I CONDEMN IT 10   3 DON JUAN 6   8   2
    AND WHOM FOR THIS AT LAST MUST WE CONDEMN 157   3 DON JUAN 8   92   6
CONDEMNATION
    THAT WHEN A CULPRIT CAME FOR CONDEMNATION 399   3 DON JUAN 13   88   7
CONDEMN'D
    CONDEMN'D TO CHILD-BED AS MEN FOR THEIR SINS 420   3 DON JUAN 14   23   7
CONDEMNED
    SENATES AND SAGES HAVE CONDEMNED ITS USE-- 256   3 DON JUAN 10   63   5
    'MIDST ROYAL DUKES AND DAMES CONDEMNED TO CLIMB 302   3 DON JUAN 11   68   7
CONDENSED
    ITS QUANTITY IS BUT CONDENSED TO QUALITY 381   3 DON JUAN 13   49   8
    NOT CALCULATING HOW MUCH THEY CONDENSED 535   3 DON JUAN 16   71   6
CONDESCEND
    NOR FOES--ALL NATIONS--CONDESCEND TO SMILE-- 17   2 DON JUAN D   13   4
    IF EVER I SHOULD CONDESCEND TO PROSE 138   2 DON JUAN 1   204   1
    IF THEY WOULD CONDESCEND TO CIRCUMCISION 451   2 DON JUAN 5   69   8
    HOW POWER COULD CONDESCEND TO DO WITHOUT 104   3 DON JUAN 7   74   8
CONDESCENDED
    AT LENGTH HE CONDESCENDED TO ENQUIRE 171   3 DON JUAN 8   120   5
CONDESCENDING
    SHE MEANT TO BE EXTREMELY CONDESCENDING 475   2 DON JUAN 5   112   V1
    AND DEEMED HERSELF EXTREMELY CONDESCENDING 478   2 DON JUAN 5   116   3
    MY LORDS AND LADIES PROUDLY CONDESCENDING 538   3 DON JUAN 16   79   2
    THIS DAY AND WATCHING WITCHING CONDESCENDING 546   3 DON JUAN 16   95   2
CONDESCENDS
    REMEMBER UGOLINO CONDESCENDS 200   2 DON JUAN 2   83   2
    GOES WHEN SOME PERSON CONDESCENDS TO PRAISE 156   3 DON JUAN 8   90   V4
CONDESCENSION
    HER PLUMPNESS HER IMPERIAL CONDESCENSION 218   3 DON JUAN 9   72   2
CONDITION
    WOULD FULLY SUIT A WIDOW OF CONDITION 67   2 DON JUAN 1   85   3
    AND TURN'D WITHOUT PERCEIVING HIS CONDITION 70   2 DON JUAN 1   91   7
    BUT FOR A CAVALIER OF HIS CONDITION 97   2 DON JUAN 1   139   3
    YOU'VE MADE THE APARTMENT IN A FIT CONDITION-- 104   2 DON JUAN 1   152   3

147

CONDITION   (CONTINUED)
    THE WORST OF ALL WAS THAT IN THEIR CONDITION 180   2 DON JUAN   2   46   1
    AND THE LONG-BOAT'S CONDITION WAS BUT BAD 181   2 DON JUAN   2   48   3
    'TWOULD GREATLY TEND TO BETTER THEIR CONDITION 451   2 DON JUAN   5   69   7
    FOR THIS FIRST FAULT AND THAT ON NO CONDITION 47   3 DON JUAN   6   82   5
    AGAINST ALL WOMEN OF WHATE'ER CONDITION 64   3 DON JUAN   6   117   3
    OF THE IMPERIAL FAVOURITE'S CONDITION 208   3 DON JUAN   9   52   3
    OF HIS FIERCE PULSE BETOKEN A CONDITION 244   3 DON JUAN 10   39   4
    BUT IN A STYLE BECOMING HIS CONDITION 246   3 DON JUAN 10   44   8
    WAS WELL RECEIVED BY PERSONS OF CONDITION 290   3 DON JUAN 11   45   8
    TO THE SURPRISE OF PEOPLE OF CONDITION 328   3 DON JUAN 12   27   4
    AS JUAN WAS A PERSON OF CONDITION 330   3 DON JUAN 12   30   4
    ALSO A FOREIGNER OF HIGH CONDITION 382   3 DON JUAN 13   52   7
    THE REAL SUFFERINGS OF THEIR SHE CONDITION 420   3 DON JUAN 14   24   4
    IF I HAD NEVER PROVED THE SOFT CONDITION 467   3 DON JUAN 15   24   2
    BULL SOMETHING OF THE LOWER WORLD'S CONDITION 497   3 DON JUAN 15   92   6
    SHADOWS--BUT YOU MUST BE IN MY CONDITION 500   3 DON JUAN 15   98   7
    BOTH WHICH ARE LIMITED TO NO CONDITION 541   3 DON JUAN 16   85   8
CONDITIONS
    AND LAID CONDITIONS HE THOUGHT VERY HARD ON 120   2 DON JUAN   1   180   3
    SURVIVE THROUGH VERY DESPERATE CONDITIONS 190   2 DON JUAN   2   64   4
    AS ANY OF MORTALITY'S CONDITIONS 191   3 DON JUAN   9   17   6
CONDOLENCE
    A FEW WORDS OF CONDOLENCE ON HIS STATE 515   3 DON JUAN 16   35   2
CONDORCET
    BARNAVE BRISSOT CONDORCET MIRABEAU 22   2 DON JUAN   1   3   1
CONDUCIVE
    BUT THE SAME CAUSE CONDUCIVE TO HIS LOSS 186   2 DON JUAN   2   57   2
CONDUCT
    THEIR CONDUCT WAS EXCEEDINGLY WELL-BRED 35   2 DON JUAN   1   26   5
    REQUIRED THIS CONDUCT--WHICH SEEM'D VERY ODD 35   2 DON JUAN   1   27   8
    CONDUCT LIKE THIS BY NO MEANS COMPREHENDS 37   2 DON JUAN   1   30   6
    IMMORAL CONDUCT BY THE FANCIED SWAY 84   2 DON JUAN   1   116   3
    OF CONDUCT WAS WHICH HE OBSERVED IN GREECE 319   2 DON JUAN   3   84   8
    'TWAS CERTAIN THAT HIS CONDUCT HAD BEEN PURE . . . 58   3 DON JUAN   6   104   3
    STEAM-ENGINES WILL CONDUCT HIM TO THE MOON 226   3 DON JUAN 10   2   8
    BEGAN TO THINK THE DUCHESS' CONDUCT FREE 430   3 DON JUAN 14   46   4
    HER CONDUCT HAD BEEN PERFECTLY CORRECT 446   3 DON JUAN 14   85   3
    BESIDES HIS CONDUCT SINCE IN ENGLAND GREW MORE . . 460   3 DON JUAN 15   11   5
    SAFE CONDUCT THROUGH THE ROCKS OF RE-ELECTIONS . . 546   3 DON JUAN 16   95   8
CONDUCTED
    BUT WHAT CONDUCTED IF THE QUESTION'S FAIR 418   2 DON JUAN   5   15   4
CONDUCTOR
    HERE THEIR CONDUCTOR TAPPING AT THE WICKET 433   2 DON JUAN   5   41   1
    AFFECT NO MORE THAN LIGHTNING A CONDUCTOR 260   3 DON JUAN 10   71   8
CONDUCT'S
    DESERVES THE WORST HIS CONDUCT'S LESS DEFENSIBLE . 103   2 DON JUAN   1   151   6
CONDUCTS
    BUT CERTES IT CONDUCTS TO LIVES ASCETIC 472   3 DON JUAN 15   38   7
CONFERENCE
    THE CONFERENCE OR CONGRESS (FOR IT ENDED 482   3 DON JUAN 15   61   1
    ALSO THE CONFERENCE WHICH WE HAVE SEEN 489   3 DON JUAN 15   75   5
CONFERRED
    THIS SPECIAL HONOUR WAS CONFERRED BECAUSE 182   3 DON JUAN   8   140   1
    OF FITTING OUT HER FAVOURITES CONFERRED 247   3 DON JUAN 10   46   2
CONFESS
    IN HIS RESUMED AMUSEMENT I CONFESS 100   3 DON JUAN   7   65   4
    PERHAPS SHE HAD NOTHING TO CONFESS--NO MATTER . . 252   3 DON JUAN 10   56   6
    TO TASTE--THE TRUTH IS IF MEN WOULD CONFESS . . . 347   3 DON JUAN 12   69   7
    BUT THOUGH A BONNE VIVANTE I MUST CONFESS 483   3 DON JUAN 15   64   5
    HE WAS FREE TO CONFESS--(WHENCE COMES THIS PHRASE 536   3 DON JUAN 16   73   1
CONFESS'D
    ALTHOUGH THEIR PORTER AFTERWARDS CONFESS'D 34   2 DON JUAN   1   24   5
CONFESSION
    SHE ALSO HAD NO PASSION FOR CONFESSION 252   3 DON JUAN 10   56   5
    OF YOUR OWN THOUGHTS IN ALL THEIR SELF CONFESSION 413   3 DON JUAN 14   6   4
CONFESSIONS
    AS SAINT AUGUSTINE IN HIS FINE CONFESSIONS 47   2 DON JUAN   1   47   7
CONFESSOR
    BETWEEN HIS TUTORS CONFESSOR AND MOTHER 48   2 DON JUAN   1   49   8
    THAT I HAVE CHOSEN A CONFESSOR SO OLD 101   2 DON JUAN   1   147   3
CONFEST
    WHO FAIN WOULD HAVE A MUTUAL FLAME CONFEST 14   3 DON JUAN   6   17   3
    THE MAN IN ALL THE REST MIGHT BE CONFEST 139   3 DON JUAN   8   53   3
    THE ONLY TRUTH THAT YET HAS BEEN CONFEST 361   3 DON JUAN 13   7   3
CONFIDENCE
    FOR THE OLD NEGRO'S CONFIDENCE IN CREEPING . . . 436   2 DON JUAN   5   45   2
    A MODEST CONFIDENCE AND CALM ASSURANCE 294   3 DON JUAN 11   52   2
CONFIDENTIAL
    QUITE IN A CONFIDENTIAL QUEENLY WAY 466   2 DON JUAN   5   95   3
CONFINE
    UPON THEIR AIRY CONFINE HALF-SEAS-OVER 255   3 DON JUAN 10   61   8
    ON LIFE'S WORN CONFINE JADED BLOATED SATED . . . 267   3 DON JUAN 10   87   2
    ON GENERAL TOPICS POEMS MUST CONFINE 290   3 DON JUAN 11   44   7
CONFINED
    STATES TO BE CURB'D AND THOUGHTS TO BE CONFINED . . 18   2 DON JUAN   D   14   4
    WOUNDED AND FETTER'D CABIN'D CRIBB'D CONFINED . . 384   2 DON JUAN   4   75   1
    WAS NOT CONFINED TO FEELING FOR HER FRIEND . . . 432   3 DON JUAN 14   51   2
CONFINES
    SOME LIKENESS WHICH THE GLITTERING CIRQUE CONFINES . . 321   3 DON JUAN 12   12   6

CONFIRM
	PAGE	VOL	CANTO		STANZA	LN
ALL THESE CONFIRM MY STATEMENT A GOOD DEAL	138	2	DON JUAN	1	203	5
WHICH SHOULD CONFIRM OR SHAKE OR MAKE A FAITH	431	2	DON JUAN	5	38	8
PERHAPS SHE MIGHT WISH TO CONFIRM HIM IN IT	526	3	DON JUAN	16	51	7

CONFIRM'D
GENTLY BUT PALPABLY CONFIRM'D ITS GRASP	81	2	DON JUAN	1	111	2

CONFIRMED
THOUGH OFT WELL FOUNDED WHICH CONFIRMED BUT MORE	366	3	DON JUAN	13	17	2

CONFISCATED
THE CARGOES HE CONFISCATED AND GAIN	223	2	DON JUAN	2	126	5

CONFITURES
BUT EVEN SANS CONFITURES IT NO LESS TRUE IS	486	3	DON JUAN	15	68	7

CONFLICT
WITH THICK'NING CANOPY THE CONFLICT O'ER	116	3	DON JUAN	8	8	6

CONFLICTS
THOUGH PALE WITH CONFLICTS BETWEEN LOVE AND PRIDE--	50	3	DON JUAN	6	89	6

CONFORMATION
NEW BUILDINGS OF CORRECTEST CONFORMATION	529	3	DON JUAN	16	58	7

CONFOUND
I'M A PHILOSOPHER CONFOUND THEM ALL	17	3	DON JUAN	6	22	1
AND HASTILY--AS NOTHING CAN CONFOUND	542	3	DON JUAN	16	88	4

CONFOUNDED
TILL SOME CONFOUNDED ESCAPADE HAS BLIGHTED	75	2	DON JUAN	1	100	5
WITH YOUR CONFOUNDED FANTASIES TO MORE	84	2	DON JUAN	1	116	2
SHADOWS OF GLORY (LEST I BE CONFOUNDED)	108	3	DON JUAN	7	82	6
ABOUT A CIRCUMSTANCE WHICH HAS CONFOUNDED	125	3	DON JUAN	8	28	4
WHEN ONCE YOU HAVE BROKEN THEIR CONFOUNDED ICE	375	3	DON JUAN	13	38	8
CONFOUNDED HIM IN COMMON WITH THE CROWD	493	3	DON JUAN	15	83	2

CONFOUNDS
BUT WHETHER 'TWAS THAT ONE'S OWN GUILT CONFOUNDS	118	2	DON JUAN	1	176	3

CONFUSED
THE SENHOR DON ALFONSO STOOD CONFUSED	109	2	DON JUAN	1	159	1
CONFUSED IN THE CONFUSION AND DISTRAIT	542	3	DON JUAN	16	87	3
BUT WHAT CONFUSED HIM MORE THAN SMILE OR STARE	544	3	DON JUAN	16	91	1

CONFUSION
DOUBT UPON ME CONFUSION OVER ALL	105	2	DON JUAN	1	154	2
WHO TOLD HIM TO BE DAMN'D--IN HIS CONFUSION	179	2	DON JUAN	2	44	8
A RICH CONFUSION FORMED A DISARRAY	465	2	DON JUAN	5	93	3
A KINGDOM OR CONFUSION ANYWHERE	485	2	DON JUAN	5	129	3
ALL THIS SHE TOLD WITH SOME CONFUSION AND	45	3	DON JUAN	6	78	1
WITHOUT CONFUSION OF THE SORTS AND SE"ES	269	3	DON JUAN	11	3	6
OF WHEELS AND ROAR OF VOICES AND CONFUSION	278	3	DON JUAN	11	22	2
TO THE PERFORMER'S DIFFIDENT CONFUSION	521	3	DON JUAN	16	41	8
WHICH TIED IN ONE FIRM KNOT WITHOUT CONFUSION	536	3	DON JUAN	16	74	V7
CONFUSED IN THE CONFUSION AND DISTRAIT	542	3	DON JUAN	16	87	3
AND THAT IN HIS CONFUSION HE HAD CAUGHT	560	3	DON JUAN	16	122	7

CONGEAL
THAT IS TILL DEEPER GRIEFS CONGEAL OUR TEARS	164	2	DON JUAN	2	15	8

CONGEALING
FOR HIS CONGEALING BLOOD AND SENSES DIM	214	2	DON JUAN	2	111	4

CONGRATULATIONS
ROUND THE YOUNG MAN WITH THEIR CONGRATULATIONS	223	3	DON JUAN	9	82	4

CONGRESS
CONSPIRACY OR CONGRESS TO BE MADE--	18	2	DON JUAN	D	14	5
I HAVE SEEN A CONGRESS DOING ALL THAT'S MEAN--	310	3	DON JUAN	11	84	6
O'ER CONGRESS WHETHER ROYALIST OR LIBERAL	318	3	DON JUAN	12	5	2
THE CONFERENCE OR CONGRESS (FOR IT ENDED	482	3	DON JUAN	15	61	1

CONGRESSES
AS CONGRESSES OF LATE DO) OF THE LADY	482	3	DON JUAN	15	61	2

CONGREVE'S
A KIND ANTITHESIS TO CONGREVE'S ROCKETS	91	2	DON JUAN	1	129	6
WHEN CONGREVE'S FOOL COULD VIE WITH MOLIERE'S BETE	402	3	DON JUAN	13	94	6

CONJECTURES
IN VARIOUS CONJECTURES FOR NONE KNEW	209	2	DON JUAN	2	100	4

CONJECTURING
CONJECTURING WONDERING ASKING A NARRATION	43	3	DON JUAN	6	74	3

CONJUGAL
SERENE AND NOBLE--CONJUGAL BUT COLD	447	3	DON JUAN	14	86	8

CONNECT
WHICH I WITH THEIR AMUSEMENT WILL CONNECT	141	2	DON JUAN	1	209	3

CONNECTED
A GUARDIAN GREEN IN YEARS A WARD CONNECTED	252	3	DON JUAN	10	57	6

CONNECTION
OR A BELL-WETHER FORM THE FLOCK'S CONNECTION	90	3	DON JUAN	7	48	6
WITH MODERN HISTORY HAS BUT SMALL CONNECTION	186	3	DON JUAN	9	7	4
AND AS THE ISTHMUS OF THE GRAND CONNECTION	534	3	DON JUAN	16	69	7

CONNECTION'S
AT THEIR LORD'S SON'S OR SIMILAR CONNECTION'S	546	3	DON JUAN	16	95	7

CONNECTIONS
IN LOVE AND WAR) HOW ODD ARE THE CONNECTIONS	215	3	DON JUAN	9	65	3
CONNECTIONS STRONGER THAN HE CHOSE TO AVOW	516	3	DON JUAN	16	37	4

CONNECTS
THE SENSUAL FOR A SHORT TIME BUT CONNECTS US--	442	3	DON JUAN	14	73	5

CONNED
AND FOUNDED DOCTORS' COMMONS--I HAVE CONNED	209	3	DON JUAN	9	53	6

CONNEXION
AND THAT STILL KEEPING UP THE OLD CONNEXION	58	2	DON JUAN	1	67	1
ADDED TO HIS CONNEXION WITH THE SEA	222	2	DON JUAN	2	125	4
OF FAULT OR TEMPER RUIN'D THE CONNEXION	281	2	DON JUAN	3	10	5

	PAGE	VOL		CANTO	STANZA	LN

CONNEXION   (CONTINUED)
   TEARS SHED INTO THE GRAVE OF THE CONNEXION . . . . . 301 2 DON JUAN 3   50 7
   THEY ALL ALIKE ADMIRED THEIR NEW CONNEXION . . . . . 26 3 DON JUAN 6   40 .8
CONNEXIONS
   TO LAST--OF ALL CONNEXIONS THE MOST STEADY . . . . . 288 2 DON JUAN 3   25 5
   A SECOND FOR HER EXCELLENT CONNEXIONS . . . . 471 3 DON JUAN 15   34 7
CONNOISSEUR
   MIGHT SHOCK A CONNOISSEUR BUT WHEN COMBINED . . . . . 390 3 DON JUAN 13   67 3
   BUT AS LORD HENRY WAS A CONNOISSEUR-- . . . . 528 3 DON JUAN 16   57 1
CONNUBIAL
   THOU MAK'ST THE CHASTE CONNUBIAL STATE PRECARIOUS . . 266 2 DON JUAN 2 206 1
   THERE'S NOTHING WRONG IN A CONNUBIAL KISS . . . . . 279 2 DON JUAN 3   8 6
   NO PROCESS PROVED CONNUBIAL ANIMOSITY . . . . 496 2 DON JUAN 5 148 6
   AND FOR THEIR RIGHTS CONNUBIAL MAKE A STAND . . . . . 11 3 DON JUAN 6   11 5
   THE FILLING UP THEIR WHOLE CONNUBIAL CARGO-- . . . . 51 3 DON JUAN 6   90 7
   MAY BE THE TRAPS FOR THEIR CONNUBIAL LORDS . . . . . 340 3 DON JUAN 12   53 V3
   NO BICKERINGS NO CONNUBIAL TURMOIL . . . . 447 3 DON JUAN 14   86 6
CONNUBIALLY
   HIS HIGHNESS QUITE CONNUBIALLY INCLINED . . . . . . 12 3 DON JUAN 6   13 V5
CONQUER
   FRANCE COULD NOT EVEN CONQUER YOUR GREAT NAME . . . . 183 3 DON JUAN 9   1 3
   I KNOW NOT WHO MAY CONQUER IF I COULD . . . . 194 3 DON JUAN 9   24 5
CONQUEROR
   FOR THIS GREAT CONQUEROR PLAYED THE CORPORAL . . . . 95 3 DON JUAN 7   56 2
   SUWARROW NOW WAS CONQUEROR--A MATCH . . . . 178 3 DON JUAN 8 133 1
   SUCH AS THE CONQUEROR WILLIAM DID REPAY . . . . . . 242 3 DON JUAN 10   35 6
   THE CONQUEROR AT LEAST WHO ERE TIME RENDERS . . . . . 299 3 DON JUAN 11   61 3
CONQUERORS
   THEY ALL WERE HEROES CONQUERORS AND CUCKOLDS . . . . 266 2 DON JUAN 2 206 8
   WHICH WITH YOUR CONQUERORS IS A COMMON PRANK . . . . 71 3 DON JUAN 7   9 6
CONQUEST
   FOR CASH AND CONQUEST AS IF FROM A CUSHION . . . . . 99 3 DON JUAN 7   64 4
   AS HATH BEEN DONE MERE CONQUEST TO ADVANCE . . . . . 113 3 DON JUAN 8   3 6
   OF CONQUEST AND ITS CONSEQUENCES WHICH . . . . 156 3 DON JUAN 8   90 7
   OF CONQUEST AND HIS GUARD OF GRENADIERS . . . . . . 253 3 DON JUAN 10   58 8
   OF COXCOMBRY OR CONQUEST NO ABUSE . . . . 461 3 DON JUAN 15   12 4
CONQUESTS
   'TIS NOT HIS CONQUESTS KEEP HIS NAME IN FASHION . . .   8 3 DON JUAN 6   4 6
CONSCIENCE
   A QUIET CONSCIENCE MAKES ONE SO SERENE . . . . 66 2 DON JUAN 1   83 6
   I LEAVE YOU TO YOUR CONSCIENCE AS BEFORE . . . . . . 107 2 DON JUAN 1 157 5
   BUT AT SIXTEEN THE CONSCIENCE RARELY GNAWS . . . . . 113 2 DON JUAN 1 167 5
   FINE TRUTHS EVEN CONSCIENCE TOO HAS A TOUGH JOB . . . 264 2 DON JUAN 2 203 6
   AND CONSCIENCE ASK A CURIOUS SORT OF QUESTION . . . . 426 2 DON JUAN 5   30 4
   AND FOR YOUR CONSCIENCE ONLY LEARN TO NERVE IT-- . . 366 3 DON JUAN 13   18 6
   BUT LEAVE THEM TO THE CONSCIENCE OF THE NATIONS . . . 464 3 DON JUAN 15   18 8
CONSCIOUS
   HOW BEAUTIFUL SHE LOOK'D HER CONSCIOUS HEART . . . . 78 2 DON JUAN 1 106 1
   AS THOUGH THEY WERE QUITE CONSCIOUS OF HER STATION-- . 475 2 DON JUAN 5 111 4
CONSENT
   AND WHISPERING I WILL NE'ER CONSENT--CONSENTED . . . . 84 2 DON JUAN 1 117 8
CONSENTED
   AND WHISPERING I WILL NE'ER CONSENT--CONSENTED . . . . 84 2 DON JUAN 1 117 8
   JUAN CONSENTED TO MARCH ON THROUGH THUNDER . . . . . 163 3 DON JUAN 8 103 3
   SHE HAD CONSENTED TO CREATE AGAIN . . . . 434 3 DON JUAN 14   55 7
CONSEQUENCE
   SINCE AFTER ALL THE CONSEQUENCE IS VAPOUR . . . . . 146 2 DON JUAN 1 218 V4
   THE CONSEQUENCE WAS EASILY FORESEEN-- . . . . 192 2 DON JUAN 2   69 1
   THE CONSEQUENCE WAS AWFUL IN THE EXTREME . . . . . . 198 2 DON JUAN 2   79 2
   DISMAY THE USUAL CONSEQUENCE OF DREAMS . . . . 45 3 DON JUAN 6   78 2
   BEGAN AS IS THE CONSEQUENCE OF FEAR . . . . 45 3 DON JUAN 6   79 2
   SULTANA THINK UPON THE CONSEQUENCE . . . . 62 3 DON JUAN 6 114 2
   AND THE SWEET CONSEQUENCE OF LARGE SOCIETY . . . . . 146 3 DON JUAN 8   68 3
   THE CONSEQUENCE IS BEING OF NO PARTY . . . . 195 3 DON JUAN 9   26 1
   OF THE SAD CONSEQUENCE OF GOING ASTRAY . . . . 336 3 DON JUAN 12   44 6
CONSEQUENCES
   BEFORE THE CONSEQUENCES GROW TOO AWFUL . . . . 282 2 DON JUAN 3   12 7
   (ALTHOUGH THE CONSEQUENCES OF SUCH FRISKS . . . . . . 20 3 DON JUAN 6   29 5
   OF CONQUEST AND ITS CONSEQUENCES WHICH . . . . 156 3 DON JUAN 8   90 7
   YET AS THE CONSEQUENCES ARE AS BRIGHT . . . . 284 3 DON JUAN 11   34 3
CONSEQUENTIAL
   OF WHAT THEY DEEM THEMSELVES MOST CONSEQUENTIAL-- . . 418 3 DON JUAN 14   20 6
CONSIDER
   AND ALL ARE TO BE SOLD IF YOU CONSIDER . . . . 425 2 DON JUAN 5   27 3
CONSIDERABLE
   WAS RECKONED A CONSIDERABLE TIME . . . . 296 3 DON JUAN 11   55 7
   CONSIDERABLE TALENT IN MY WAY . . . . 453 3 DON JUAN 14   98 8
CONSIDERATION
   AND HIS DISGUISE WITH DUE CONSIDERATION . . . . 55 3 DON JUAN 6   99 6
CONSIDER'D
   IF ALL THINGS BE CONSIDER'D FIRST THERE WAS . . . . . 158 2 DON JUAN 2   3 2
CONSIGNED
   OF EVERY MONARCH TILL THEY ARE CONSIGNED . . . . . . 12 3 DON JUAN 6   13 3
   AN ORDER FROM HER MAJESTY CONSIGNED . . . . 224 3 DON JUAN 9   84 1
CONSIST
   THE PARTY MIGHT CONSIST OF THIRTY-THREE . . . . . . 397 3 DON JUAN 13   83 3
CONSISTED
   HIS SUITE CONSISTED OF THREE SERVANTS AND . . . . . 169 2 DON JUAN 2   25 1
   CONSISTED OF--WE GIVE THE SEX THE PAS-- . . . . . . 396 3 DON JUAN 13   79 2

150

	PAGE	VOL			CANTO	STANZA	LN
CONSISTENT							
BUT IF A WRITER SHOULD BE QUITE CONSISTENT	494	3	DON	JUAN	15	87	7
CONSISTORY							
AND MERELY STATE THOUGH NOT FOR THE CONSISTORY	531	3	DON	JUAN	16	62	5
CONSOLATION							
IF I COULD YIELD YOU ANY CONSOLATION	417	2	DON	JUAN	5	13	7
AND STRANGE TO SAY THEY FOUND SOME CONSOLATION	105	3	DON	JUAN	7	75	7
DREW QUIET CONSOLATION THROUGH ITS HINT	241	3	DON	JUAN	10	34	7
HE HAD HIS JUDGE'S JOKE FOR CONSOLATION	399	3	DON	JUAN	13	88	8
NO DOUBT A CONSOLATION TO HIS DUST	565	3	DON	JUAN	17	8	8
CONSOLE							
JUST TO CONSOLE SAD GLORY FOR BEING GLORIOUS	372	3	DON	JUAN	13	32	8
CONSOLED							
AND SHE WOULD HAVE CONSOLED BUT KNEW NOT HOW	480	2	DON	JUAN	5	119	1
WAS MUCH CONSOLED BY HIS OWN REPARTEE	522	3	DON	JUAN	16	43	8
CONSOLING							
CONSOLING US WITH--WOULD YOU HAD THOUGHT TWICE	430	3	DON	JUAN	14	47	7
CONSOMME							
THE SALMI THE CONSOMME THE PUREE	487	3	DON	JUAN	15	71	2
CONSONANTS							
AND OTHERS OF TWELVE CONSONANTS A-PIECE	74	3	DON	JUAN	7	15	5
CONSORT							
FOR WHEN HIS PIOUS CONSORT GAVE HIM STONES	410	3	DON	JUAN	14	1	7
OR WHAT HIS CONSORT DID IF HE COULD BROOK	430	3	DON	JUAN	14	45	5
CONSORTS							
AND KINGS AND CONSORTS OFT ARE MYSTIFIED	477	2	DON	JUAN	5	115	6
CONSPICUOUS							
UNTIL TO SOME CONSPICUOUS SQUARE THEY PASS	283	3	DON	JUAN	11	31	7
AS WILL ENVIRON A CONSPICUOUS MAN SOME	305	3	DON	JUAN	11	74	5
CONSPIRACY							
CONSPIRACY OR CONGRESS TO BE MADE--	18	2	DON	JUAN	D	14	5
HAS BEEN ACCUSED (I DOUBT NOT BY CONSPIRACY)	446	2	DON	JUAN	5	61	2
CONSTABLE							
THE CONSTABLE BENEATH A WARRANT'S BANNER	531	3	DON	JUAN	16	62	7
CONSTANCY							
HAD NOT ONE WORD TO SAY OF CONSTANCY	257	2	DON	JUAN	2	190	8
AN ALMOST TWELVEMONTH'S CONSTANCY ENDANGERS	472	2	DON	JUAN	5	106	8
CONSTANT							
LOVE CONSTANT LOVE HAS BEEN MY CONSTANT GUEST	268	2	DON	JUAN	2	209	5
LOVE CONSTANT LOVE HAS BEEN MY CONSTANT GUEST	268	2	DON	JUAN	2	209	5
LIKE CHASTEST WIVES FROM CONSTANT HUSBANDS' SIDES	125	3	DON	JUAN	8	27	3
RECRUITED ALL WITH CONSTANT MARRIED MEN	323	3	DON	JUAN	12	16	2
CONSTANTINE							
OF ROME TRANSPLANTED FELL WITH CONSTANTINE	461	2	DON	JUAN	5	86	8
CONSTANTINOPLE							
FOR THE SLAVE MARKET OF CONSTANTINOPLE	393	2	DON	JUAN	4	91	8
WHENCE COME YE--FROM CONSTANTINOPLE LAST	97	3	DON	JUAN	7	59	4
WHO HAS SAILED WHERE PICTURESQUE CONSTANTINOPLE IS . . .	271	3	DON	JUAN	11	7	3
CONSTANTINOPLE AND SUCH DISTANT PLACES	368	3	DON	JUAN	13	23	2
CONSTERNATION							
THE MOMENT OF THE GENERAL CONSTERNATION	78	3	DON	JUAN	7	24	2
CONSTITUTE							
TO CONSTITUTE A READER THERE MUST GO	393	3	DON	JUAN	13	73	3
CONSTITUTION							
HIS YOUTH AND CONSTITUTION BORE HIM THROUGH	245	3	DON	JUAN	10	43	3
THE GLORIOUS--FREE--AND HAPPY CONSTITUTION	536	3	DON	JUAN	16	74	V8
THE THREE STRINGS OF OUR HAPPY CONSTITUTION	536	3	DON	JUAN	16	74	V8
SAY CONSTITUTION STEAD OF PROSTITUTION	537	3	DON	JUAN	16	76	V7
CONSTITUTIONAL							
A KING IN CONSTITUTIONAL POSSESSION	354	3	DON	JUAN	12	83	3
CONSTITUTIONS							
ON CONSTITUTIONS AND STEAM-BOATS OF VAPOUR	325	3	DON	JUAN	12	21	5
CONSTRAIN'D							
AND OTHERS STILL THEIR APPETITES CONSTRAIN'D	200	2	DON	JUAN	2	82	3
CONSTRUCTED							
BECAUSE THEY WERE CONSTRUCTED IN A HURRY	79	3	DON	JUAN	7	26	2
THEY DREW CONSTRUCTED LADDERS REPAIRED FLAWS	89	3	DON	JUAN	7	47	6
CONSTRUCTION							
ALTHOUGH HIS ANATOMICAL CONSTRUCTION	191	2	DON	JUAN	2	67	5
A KIND CONSTRUCTION UPON THEM AND ME	34	3	DON	JUAN	6	56	7
THE ABSENCE OF THAT MORE SUBLIME CONSTRUCTION	262	3	DON	JUAN	10	76	6
CONSTRUCTION ASYOUR CURES FOR HECTIC PHTHISICS	349	3	DON	JUAN	12	72	3
YOU'LL FIND IT OF A DIFFERENT CONSTRUCTION	356	3	DON	JUAN	12	87	3
CONSTRUCTIVE							
NOTHING AFFECTED STUDIED OR CONSTRUCTIVE	461	3	DON	JUAN	15	12	3
CONSULE							
CONSULE PLANCO HORACE SAID AND SO	143	2	DON	JUAN	1	212	2
CONSULTING							
CONSULTING THE SOCIETY FOR VICE	336	3	DON	JUAN	12	42	7
CONSUMERS							
TO THE CONSUMERS OF FISH FOWL AND GAME	546	3	DON	JUAN	16	95	3
CONSUMING							
TO PROVE THE PUBLIC DEBT IS NOT CONSUMING US--	200	3	DON	JUAN	9	35	5
CONSUMPTIVE							
AND BEING CONSUMPTIVE LIVE ON A MILK DIET	474	3	DON	JUAN	15	41	8
CONTACT							
IN CONTACT AND SOMETIMES EVEN A FAIR STRANGER'S . . .	472	2	DON	JUAN	5	106	7
INTO CLOSE CONTACT THOUGH RESERVED NOR CAUGHT . . .	365	3	DON	JUAN	13	15	4
CONTAGIOUS							
EXAMPLES OF THIS KIND ARE SO CONTAGIOUS	96	2	DON	JUAN	1	138	7

```
                                                       PAGE VOL      CANTO   STANZA  LN
CONTAIN
  FROM ANYTHING THIS EPIC WILL CONTAIN . . . . . . . .  502  3 DON JUAN 16       3   2
CONTAIN'D
  NIMRODS WHOSE CANVAS SCARCE CONTAIN'D THE STEED   . . . 391  3 DON JUAN 13      70   6
CONTAINED
  SUPERBLY AND CONTAINED A WORLD OF ZEST  . . . . . . .  488  3 DON JUAN 15      74   8
CONTAINING
  DIVIDED IN TWELVE BOOKS EACH BOOK CONTAINING   . . . .  135  2 DON JUAN  1     200   2
  MOUNT PLEASANT AS CONTAINING NOUGHT TO PLEASE  . . . .  278  3 DON JUAN 11      21   3
  CONTAINING INGOTS BAGS OF DOLLARS COINS  . . . . . .   321  3 DON JUAN 12      12   2
CONTAINS
  TURKEY CONTAINS NO BELLS AND YET MEN DINE  . . . . .   439  2 DON JUAN  5      50   1
CONTEMN
  ADMIT REJECT CONTEMN AND WHAT KNOW YOU  . . . . . .    411  3 DON JUAN 14       3   2
CONTEMPLATION
  IN THAT SLIGHT STARTLE FROM HIS CONTEMPLATION--   . . . 225  3 DON JUAN 10       1   2
  I SAY DON JUAN WRAPT IN CONTEMPLATION . . . . . . .    272  3 DON JUAN 11       9   1
  THE MIND IS LOST IN MIGHTY CONTEMPLATION . . . . . .   486  3 DON JUAN 15      69   1
  FOR CONTEMPLATION RATHER THAN HIS PILLOW . . . . . .   507  3 DON JUAN 16      15   2
  'TWAS A MERE QUIET SMILE OF CONTEMPLATION  . . . . .   545  3 DON JUAN 16      93   1
CONTEMPLATIVE
  AT ONCE ADVENTUROUS AND CONTEMPLATIVE . . . . . . .    402  2 DON JUAN  4     107   2
CONTEMPT
  THE BRAGGADOCIO TAKES CONTEMPT FOR AWE  . . . . . .    153  2 DON JUAN  1   V  4  V8
  CONTEMPT BUT FROM THE BATHOS' VAST ABYSS . . . . . .   334  2 DON JUAN  3     100   4
  AS IF THE PEASANT'S COARSE CONTEMPT WERE VENTED  . . .  401  2 DON JUAN  4     105   3
CONTEND
  CONTEND NOT WITH YOU ON THE WINGED STEED . . . . . .    14  2 DON JUAN  D       8   2
  AND TO CONTEND WITH THOUGHTS SHE COULD NOT SMOTHER  . . 80  2 DON JUAN  1     110   3
CONTENDED
  THE PALE CONTENDED WITH THE PURPLE ROSE  . . . . . .   236  2 DON JUAN  2     150   3
  OTHERS CONTENDED THEY WERE BUT IN SPRING . . . . . .    23  3 DON JUAN  6      35   6
CONTENT
  MODERATE IN ALL HIS HABITS AND CONTENT  . . . . . .    302  2 DON JUAN  3      53   3
  SO PICK AND CHUSE--PERHAPS YOU'LL BE CONTENT   . . . .  40  3 DON JUAN  6      68   7
  BUT SHORTLY HE HAD CAUSE TO BE CONTENT  . . . . . .     85  3 DON JUAN  7      38   5
  WHY SHOULD NOT LIFE BE EQUALLY CONTENT  . . . . . .    189  3 DON JUAN  9      13   3
  HE WHO SLEEPS BEST MAY BE THE MOST CONTENT   . . . .   190  3 DON JUAN  9      15   8
  AND TILL SHE DOTH I FAIN MUST BE CONTENT . . . . . .   193  3 DON JUAN  9      22   7
  OF METAPHYSICS OTHERS ARE CONTENT . . . . . . . .     340  3 DON JUAN 12      52   6
  A LAUREATE'S ODE OR SERVILE PEER'S CONTENT   . . . .   435  3 DON JUAN 14      58   8
  BARDS MAY SING WHAT THEY PLEASE ABOUT CONTENT  . . . . 444  3 DON JUAN 14      79   4
  PURSUED AN INSTANT FOR HER OWN CONTENT  . . . . . .    521  3 DON JUAN 16      42   4
CONTENTED
  CONTENTED WHEN TRANSLATED MEANS BUT CLOYED   . . . .   444  3 DON JUAN 14      79   5
CONTENTEDLY
  AND LIVED CONTENTEDLY WITHOUT COMPLAINTS . . . . . .   424  3 DON JUAN 14      31   3
CONTENTS
  AND IF THEIR FULL CONTENTS I DO NOT GIVE YE . . . . .  440  3 DON JUAN 14      68   5
CONTESTS
  BUT COUNTRY CONTESTS COST HIM RATHER DEARER . . . . .  534  3 DON JUAN 16      70   3
CONTEXT
  AND FROM ITS CONTEXT THOUGHT SHE COULD DIVINE   . . .  516  3 DON JUAN 16      37   3
CONTINENCE
  BUT ON THE WHOLE THEIR CONTINENCE WAS GREAT  . . . .   177  3 DON JUAN  8     131   1
CONTINENT
  SOME DIE SOME FLY SOME LANGUISH ON THE CONTINENT  . . . 308  3 DON JUAN 11      80   7
CONTINENTAL
  YOUR CONTINENTAL OATHS ARE BUT INCONTINENT   . . . .   289  3 DON JUAN 11      43   2
CONTINENT'S
  MATCHED WITH THE CONTINENT'S ILLUMINATION  . . . . .   280  3 DON JUAN 11      26   4
CONTINENTS
  MORE THAN ON CONTINENTS--AS IF THE SEA  . . . . . .    288  3 DON JUAN 11      42   7
  O'ER FAR ATLANTIC CONTINENTS OR ISLANDS  . . . . . .   523  3 DON JUAN 16      46   4
CONTINUANCE
  OF THE CONTINUANCE OF THE GALE TO RUN . . . . . . .    189  2 DON JUAN  2      62   2
CONTINUATION
  OR HINTS CONTINUATION OF THE SPECIES  . . . . . . .     44  2 DON JUAN  1      40   7
CONTINUE
  BUT MORE OR LESS CONTINUE STILL TO TEASE ON  . . . .   437  2 DON JUAN  5      48   6
  CONTINUE AS I SAID THIS GOODLY ROW  . . . . . . .      22  3 DON JUAN  6      33   3
  YOU LOLAH MUST CONTINUE STILL TO LIE  . . . . . . .    30  3 DON JUAN  6      49   1
  BUT TO CONTINUE--I SAY NOT THE FIRST  . . . . . . .   138  3 DON JUAN  8      52   1
  SHOULD SO CONTINUE--'TIS A POINT OF HONOUR   . . . .   231  3 DON JUAN 10      12   2
  BUT TO CONTINUE THOUGH HER YEARS WERE WANING   . . .   247  3 DON JUAN 10      47   4
CONTINUED
  AT KESWICK AND THROUGH STILL CONTINUED FUSION  . . . . 12  2 DON JUAN  D       5   3
  AND THEY CONTINUED BATTLING HAND TO HAND . . . . . .   123  2 DON JUAN  1     185   2
  CONTINUED STILL HER HOSPITABLE CARES  . . . . . . .   285  2 DON JUAN  3      19   5
  CONTINUED YOUR OLD REGIMENT'S ALLOWED  . . . . . . .    99  3 DON JUAN  7      63   3
CONTRACTED
  HAS NOT CONTRACTED MUCH MORE DEBT THAN KNOWLEDGE   . . 377  3 DON JUAN 13      42   8
CONTRACTIONS
  THUS EVEN GOOD FAME MAY SUFFER SAD CONTRACTIONS  . . .  83  3 DON JUAN  7      34   5
CONTRACTOR'S
  OR SOME CONTRACTOR'S PERSONAL CUPIDITY  . . . . . .     80  3 DON JUAN  7      27   3
CONTRACTORS
  BANKERS--CONTRACTORS--BOROUGH MONGERS--BULLIES . . . .  314  3 DON JUAN 11   V 76   1
CONTRADICT
  IF PEOPLE CONTRADICT THEMSELVES CAN I . . . . . . .    495  3 DON JUAN 15      88   1
```

152

CONTRADICTED
   OR CONTRADICTED BUT WITH PROUD HUMILITY . . . . 368 3 DON JUAN 13   22   4
CONTRADICTING
   HELP CONTRADICTING THEM AND EVERYBODY . . . . 495 3 DON JUAN 15   88   2
CONTRADICTION
   AND THAT'S ONE CAUSE SHE MEETS WITH CONTRADICTION . . . . 416 3 DON JUAN 14   13   5
   IS THAT WHICH PASSES WITH LEAST CONTRADICTION . . . . . . 457 3 DON JUAN 15   3   8
   AND CUT THROUGH SUCH CANALS OF CONTRADICTION . . . . . . 495 3 DON JUAN 15   88   7
   IN SOME THINGS MINE'S BEYOND ALL CONTRADICTION . . . . . 502 3 DON JUAN 16   2   7
CONTRARY
   THEY SAY SO--(BRYANT SAYS THE CONTRARY) . . . . 385 2 DON JUAN 4   76   4
   HAS QUITE THE CONTRARY EFFECT ON VICE . . . . 501 2 DON JUAN 5   157   8
   THE CONTRARY BUT THEN 'TIS IN THE HEAD . . . . 284 3 DON JUAN 11   34   2
   NOR SEEM EMBARRASSED--QUITE THE CONTRARY . . . . 545 3 DON JUAN 16   94   2
CONTRAST
   BY CONTRAST WHICH IS WHAT WE JUST WERE WISHING ALL . . . 37 2 DON JUAN 1   31   6
   AND HORRID WAS THE CONTRAST TO THE VIEW-- . . . . 431 2 DON JUAN 5   38   3
CONTRIBUTE
   THEY DO NOT MUCH CONTRIBUTE TO HIS GLORY . . . . 329 2 DON JUAN 3   92   8
CONTRIVANCES
   AND RICH WITH ALL CONTRIVANCES WHICH GRACE . . . . . . 54 3 DON JUAN 6   97   4
CONTRIVE
   UPON THE MOMENT COULD CONTRIVE WITH SUCH . . . . 226 2 DON JUAN 2   132   2
   IF YOU COULD JUST CONTRIVE HE SAID TO STINT . . . . . . 464 2 DON JUAN 5   91   3
   PACES WERE LEFT WHEREON YOU COULD CONTRIVE . . . . . . 136 3 DON JUAN 8   47   2
   BUT IF YOU CAN CONTRIVE GET NEXT AT SUPPER . . . . . . 304 3 DON JUAN 11   72   1
CONTRIVED
   HIS DEATH CONTRIVED TO SPOIL A CHARMING CAUSE . . . . . 38 2 DON JUAN 1   33   5
   OF ANY WICKED WOMAN WHO CONTRIVED . . . . 96 2 DON JUAN 1   138   5
   CONTRIVED TO FLING THE BED-CLOTHES IN A HEAP . . . . . 97 2 DON JUAN 1   140   5
   JUAN CONTRIVED TO GIVE AN AWKWARD BLOW . . . . 124 2 DON JUAN 1   186   5
   BUT IN THE LONG-BOAT THEY CONTRIVED TO STOW . . . . . . 181 2 DON JUAN 2   47   1
   SIX FLASKS OF WINE AND THEY CONTRIVED TO GET . . . . . 181 2 DON JUAN 2   47   4
   CONTRIVED TO HELP PEDRILLO TO A PLACE . . . . 186 2 DON JUAN 2   56   2
   FOR ANY LENGTH--CONTRIVED TO MAKE EACH OTHER CEASE . . 277 2 DON JUAN 3   5   V4
   ALONG THE REST CONTRIVED TO KEEP THIS DEN . . . . . . 22 3 DON JUAN 6   32   6
   CONTRIVED TO GET ITSELF COMPRISED WITHIN IT . . . . . 142 3 DON JUAN 8   59   4
   CONTRIVED TO TALK ABOUT THE GODS OF LATE . . . . . . 298 3 DON JUAN 11   60   4
CONTROL
   WITH ANY KIND OF TROUBLESOME CONTROL . . . . 66 2 DON JUAN 1   82   6
   WITH THINGS NOT VERY SUBJECT TO CONTROL . . . . 70 2 DON JUAN 1   91   6
CONTROLLESS
   YOUR SYSTEM FEIGNS O'ER THE CONTROLLESS CORE . . . . . 84 2 DON JUAN 1   116   4
CONTROUL
   OF THOSE WHO HOLD THE KINGDOMS IN CONTROUL . . . . . . 455 3 DON JUAN 14   102   6
CONUNDRUM
   TO SERVE IN THIS CONUNDRUM OF A DISH . . . . 465 3 DON JUAN 15   21   8
CONVALESCENCE
   AND EVERY DAY HELP'D ON HIS CONVALESCENCE . . . . . . 245 2 DON JUAN 2   169   2
   READY FOR JAIL THEIR PLACE OF CONVALESCENCE . . . . . 530 3 DON JUAN 16   61   2
CONVENIENCE
   TO MARCH A GREAT CONVENIENCE TO OUR MEN . . . . 136 3 DON JUAN 8   47   3
CONVENIENT
   'TWOULD BE CONVENIENT FOR THESE MUTES HAVE EYES . . . . 464 2 DON JUAN 5   92   1
   WITH HER THE LATTER THOUGH AT TIMES CONVENIENT . . . . 214 3 DON JUAN 9   63   1
CONVENT
   JULIA WAS SENT INTO A CONVENT SHE . . . . 129 2 DON JUAN 1   191   6
   OF BEAUTIES COOL AS AN ITALIAN CONVENT . . . . 22 3 DON JUAN 6   32   7
   LESS ON A CONVENT THAN A CORONET . . . . 398 3 DON JUAN 13   85   8
CONVERSATION
   AT LEAST HER CONVERSATION WAS OBSCURE . . . . 28 2 DON JUAN 1   13   6
   GROW TIRED OF SCIENTIFIC CONVERSATION . . . . 33 2 DON JUAN 1   22   4
   UNTIL TOO LATE FOR USEFUL CONVERSATION . . . . 84 2 DON JUAN 1   117   2
   BUT NO ONE TROUBLED HIM WITH CONVERSATION . . . . . 441 2 DON JUAN 5   54   8
   THERE CANNOT BE MUCH CONVERSATION THERE . . . . . . 141 3 DON JUAN 8   58   8
   FIRSTLY THEY MUST ALLURE THE CONVERSATION . . . . . 404 3 DON JUAN 13   98   1
   YET NE'ER BETRAYING THIS IN CONVERSATION . . . . . 462 3 DON JUAN 15   15   4
   BY DEEMING THAT MY MUSE'S CONVERSATION . . . . . . 498 3 DON JUAN 15   94   6
   WITH FASHIONABLE WINES AND CONVERSATION . . . . . . 534 3 DON JUAN 16   69   6
   IN A MOST EDIFYING CONVERSATION . . . . 550 3 DON JUAN 16   103   4
CONVERSATIONAL
   BUT THERE'S A CONVERSATIONAL FACILITY . . . . 465 3 DON JUAN 15   20   3
CONVERSATIONIST
   KIT-CAT THE FAMOUS CONVERSATIONIST . . . . 403 3 DON JUAN 13   97   4
CONVERSATION'S
   SUCH AS ARE COINED IN CONVERSATION'S MINT . . . . . 440 3 DON JUAN 14   69   3
CONVERSATIONS
   SHE LIKED QUICK ANSWERS IN ALL CONVERSATIONS . . . . 56 3 DON JUAN 6   101   3
CONVERSAZIONE
   THE CONVERSAZIONE THE DUET . . . . 408 3 DON JUAN 13   107   2
CONVERSE
   FOR NONE LIKES MORE TO HEAR HIMSELF CONVERSE . . . . 298 2 DON JUAN 3   45   8
   SUPPOSE THE CONVERSE OF THIS PRECEDENT . . . . . . 564 3 DON JUAN 17   5   5
CONVERSION
   FOR ALL THE GLORY YOUR CONVERSION BROUGHT . . . . . 12 2 DON JUAN D   6   3
CONVERTED
   HIS BOW CONVERTED INTO A COCKED HAT . . . . 205 3 DON JUAN 9   45   5
   CONVERTED FOES SHOULD SCORN TO JOIN WITH THOSE . . . 231 3 DON JUAN 10   12   8
   THE LITTLE TURK REFUSED TO BE CONVERTED . . . . . 251 3 DON JUAN 10   55   8
   SOME FOR HAVING TURNED CONVERTED CULLIES . . . . . 314 3 DON JUAN 11   V 76   3

		PAGE	VOL	CANTO	STANZA	LN

CONVEYANCE
YOU'LL MOUNT WITH OUR YOUNG HERO THE CONVEYANCE . . . . 248 3 DON JUAN 10 49 3
CONVEY'D
CONVEY'D MEDEA AS HER SUPERCARGO . . . . 443 3 DON JUAN 14 76 8
CONVEYED
WHICH FLATTERS BUT IS FLATTERY CONVEYED . . . . . . 372 3 DON JUAN 13 32 3
CONVEYING
BUT LIKE CONVEYING TO THE CAT THE MOUSE . . . . . . 225 2 DON JUAN 2 130 3
CONVICT
SUCH NAMES AT PRESENT CUT A CONVICT FIGURE . . . . . 330 2 DON JUAN 3 94 1
CONVICTED
AND STAND CONVICTED OF MORE TRUTH THAN TREASON . . . . 76 2 DON JUAN 1 102 6
CONVINCED
SHE FOR THE FUTURE OF HER STRENGTH CONVINCED . . . . 66 2 DON JUAN 1 82 3
CONVINCES
CONVINCES ALL MEN EVEN A POLITICIAN . . . . 478 3 DON JUAN 15 51 6
CONVULSION
IT WAS BUT A CONVULSION WHICH THOUGH SHORT . . . . . 59 3 DON JUAN 6 106 3
CONVULSIONS
AND FOAM AND ROLL WITH STRANGE CONVULSIONS RACK'D . . . 198 2 DON JUAN 2 79 5
CONVULSIVE
ACCOMPANIED WITH A CONVULSIVE SPLASH . . . . 184 2 DON JUAN 2 53 6
HER STRUGGLES CEASED WITH ONE CONVULSIVE GROAN . . . . 375 2 DON JUAN 4 58 6
COOINGS
FOR NO ONE CARES FOR MATRIMONIAL COOINGS . . . . . . 279 2 DON JUAN 3 8 5
COOK'D
BUT THE BEST DISH THAT E'ER WAS COOK'D SINCE HOMER'S . . 221 2 DON JUAN 2 123 7
AND SO SHE COOK'D THEIR BREAKFAST TO A TITTLE . . . . 233 2 DON JUAN 2 145 5
COOKERY
OF ZOE'S COOKERY NO DOUBT WAS STEALING . . . . . . 237 2 DON JUAN 2 153 4
OF WHICH PERHAPS THE COOKERY RATHER VARIES . . . . . 486 3 DON JUAN 15 68 3
THAT COOKERY COULD HAVE CALL'D FORTH SUCH RESOURCES . . 486 3 DON JUAN 15 69 6
COOKS
WHAT MUST I GO TO THE OBLIVIOUS COOKS . . . . 403 2 DON JUAN 4 108 5
AND COOKS IN MOTION WITH THEIR CLEAN ARMS BARED . . . 439 2 DON JUAN 5 50 6
COOL
HIS DAILY TASK HAD KEPT HIS FANCY COOL . . . . . . 158 2 DON JUAN 2 2 3
THE UMBRAGE OF THE WOOD SO COOL AND DUN . . . . . . 289 2 DON JUAN 3 27 5
THE THIRD A WARY COOL OLD SWORDER TOOK . . . . . . 370 2 DON JUAN 4 49 2
OF BEAUTIES COOL AS AN ITALIAN CONVENT . . . . . . 22 3 DON JUAN 6 32 7
COOL AND QUITE ENGLISH IMPERTURBABLE . . . . 365 3 DON JUAN 13 14 4
COOLING
PANTING FOR POWER AS HARTS FOR COOLING STREAMS . . . . 155 2 DON JUAN 2 V 6 1
IT WAS THE COOLING HOUR JUST WHEN THE ROUNDED . . . . 252 2 DON JUAN 2 183 1
AND SHERBET COOLING IN THE POROUS VASE . . . . . . 291 2 DON JUAN 3 31 5
COOLLY
YOU TAKE THINGS COOLLY SIR SAID JUAN WHY . . . . . . 421 2 DON JUAN 5 21 1
COPE
WITH CRABBE IT MAY BE DIFFICULT TO COPE . . . . . . 139 2 DON JUAN 1 205 5
WAS ALSO GREAT WITH WHICH THEY HAD TO COPE . . . . . 178 2 DON JUAN 2 41 4
AS FOR A BROOK TO COPE WITH OCEAN'S FLOOD . . . . . 106 3 DON JUAN 7 80 7
COPIOUS
THE COPIOUS USE OF CLARET IS FORBID TOO . . . . . . 144 2 DON JUAN 1 216 6
COPPER
WHITE BLACK OR COPPER--THE DEAD BONES WILL GRIN . . . 188 3 DON JUAN 9 12 8
BESIDES SOME VEINS OF IRON LEAD OR COPPER . . . . . 254 3 DON JUAN 10 60 3
COPY
SHE COULD HAVE SERVED HIM FOR THE PROMPTER'S COPY . . . 27 2 DON JUAN 1 11 4
SHOWN IN THE FOLLOWING COPY OF HER LETTER . . . . . 129 2 DON JUAN 1 191 8
COPYING
(IN COPYING) THIS LONG CANTO INTO TWO . . . . 342 2 DON JUAN 3 111 3
COQUETRY
COQUETRY OR A WISH TO TAKE THE LEAD . . . . 351 3 DON JUAN 12 77 4
AND FOR COQUETRY SHE DISDAINED TO WEAR IT . . . . . 372 3 DON JUAN 13 31 6
COQUETTE
SUCH IS YOUR COLD COQUETTE WHO CAN'T SAY NO . . . . . 345 3 DON JUAN 12 63 1
BEGAN TO DREAD SHE'D THAW TO A COQUETTE-- . . . . . 492 3 DON JUAN 15 81 4
CORAL
(SO CHILDREN CUTTING TEETH RECEIVE A CORAL) . . . . . 141 2 DON JUAN 1 209 4
MOTHER OF PEARL AND CORAL THE LESS COSTLY . . . . . 306 2 DON JUAN 3 61 8
CORDAGE
THE WIND SUNG CORDAGE STRAIN'D AND SAILORS SWORE . . . 163 2 DON JUAN 2 13 2
CORDIAL
THEN WAS THE CORDIAL POUR'D AND MANTLE FLUNG . . . . 216 2 DON JUAN 2 114 1
TO NO MEN ARE SUCH CORDIAL GREETINGS GIVEN . . . . . 500 2 DON JUAN 5 154 7
BUT TO DENY THE MOB A CORDIAL WHICH IS . . . . . . 256 3 DON JUAN 10 63 6
CORDIALS
OF HERBS AND CORDIALS THEY PRODUCED THEIR STORE . . . 376 2 DON JUAN 4 59 6
CORE
FOR THAT COMPRESSION IN ITS BURNING CORE . . . . . . 61 2 DON JUAN 1 72 5
YOUR SYSTEM FEIGNS O'ER THE CONTROLLESS CORE . . . . 84 2 DON JUAN 1 116 4
MY SHAME AND SORROW DEEP IN MY HEART'S CORE . . . . . 132 2 DON JUAN 1 195 4
AND PICK IT UP AND BITE IT TO THE CORE . . . . . . 44 3 DON JUAN 6 77 4
CORINTHIAN
I THINK IT MAY BE OF CORINTHIAN BRASS . . . . 34 3 DON JUAN 6 56 1
CORK
WHERE THE WILD BRANCH OF THE CORK FOREST GREW . . . . 70 2 DON JUAN 1 90 4
CORN
GRASS BEFORE SCYTHES OR CORN BELOW THE SICKLE . . . . 134 3 DON JUAN 8 43 2

154

```
                                                      PAGE VOL     CANTO STANZA LN
CORN    (CONTINUED)
    ONLY TO KEEP ITS CORN AT THE OLD PRICE     . . . . . .  335  3 DON JUAN 12      40    8
    THE CORN IS CUT THE MANOR FULL OF GAME     . . . . . .  394  3 DON JUAN 13      75    3
CORNELIAN
    THE MOTTO CUT UPON A WHITE CORNELIAN    . . . . . . .   134  2 DON JUAN  1     198    7
CORNER
    OF THE GOOD COMPANY CAN WIN A CORNER    . . . . . . .   303  3 DON JUAN 11      69    2
    EPOCH THAT AWKWARD CORNER TURNED FOR DAYS     . . . .   360  3 DON JUAN 13       4    2
    A CORNER FOR HERSELF AND THEREFORE FICTION    . . . .   457  3 DON JUAN 15       3    7
    HAD GATHERED A LARGE TEAR INTO ITS CORNER     . . . .   532  3 DON JUAN 16      65    2
CORNERS
    ONLY TO DRAW THEM 'TWIXT TWO BASTION CORNERS    . . .   149  3 DON JUAN  8      75    7
CORNIANI
    DID NOT HIS COUNTRYMAN COUNT CORNIANI . . . . . . . .   102  2 DON JUAN  1     149    3
CORNISH
    THOSE CORNISH PLUNDERERS OF PARNASSIAN WRECKS    . . .  403  2 DON JUAN  4     108    6
CORN-SHEAF
    AS IF THE CORN-SHEAF SHOULD OPPOSE THE SICKLE    . . .  419  2 DON JUAN  5      17    6
CORONALS
    BLUSHING WITH BACCHANT CORONALS ALONG . . . . . . . .   394  3 DON JUAN 13      76    2
CORONET
    LESS ON A CONVENT THAN A CORONET    . . . . . . . . .   398  3 DON JUAN 13      85    8
CORONETS
    SMART UNIFORMS AND SPARKLING CORONETS . . . . . . . .   333  3 DON JUAN 12      36    1
    SHE PUT ALL CORONETS INTO COMMOTION   . . . . . . . .   434  3 DON JUAN 14      55    2
CORPO
    HAIL'D A STRANGE BRIG CORPO DI CAIO MARIO     . . . .   389  2 DON JUAN  4      82    4
CORPORAL
    YET COULD HIS CORPORAL PANGS AMOUNT TO HALF     . . .   373  2 DON JUAN  4      54    3
    FOR THIS GREAT CONQUEROR PLAYED THE CORPORAL    . . .    95  3 DON JUAN  7      56    2
    WITHIN HIM AND TO QUELL HIS CORPORAL QUAKING--  . . .   558  3 DON JUAN 16     118    6
CORPORAL'S
    HIS TIME A CORPORAL'S DUTY TO FULFIL    . . . . . . .    93  3 DON JUAN  7      52    4
CORPORATION
    MERE FREEDOMS OF THE FEMALE CORPORATION   . . . . . .   429  3 DON JUAN 14      43    4
CORPS
    JUAN AND JOHNSON JOINED A CERTAIN CORPS   . . . . . .   120  3 DON JUAN  8      19    1
    TO CORPS THE GREATER PART OF WHICH WERE CURSES    . .   126  3 DON JUAN  8      30    8
    OF HIS OWN CORPS NOR EVEN THE CORPS WHICH HAD   . . .   127  3 DON JUAN  8      31    2
    OF HIS OWN CORPS NOR EVEN THE CORPS WHICH HAD   . . .   127  3 DON JUAN  8      31    2
    NOR CARE A PINCH OF SNUFF ABOUT HIS CORPS)--  . . . .   127  3 DON JUAN  8      31    8
    NOR CARE A SINGLE DAMN ABOUT HIS CORPS    . . . . . .   127  3 DON JUAN  8      31   V8
    AND SO WHEN ALL HIS CORPS WERE DEAD OR DYING    . . .   131  3 DON JUAN  8      36    1
CORPSE
    SAVE ONE A CORPSE FROM OUT THE FAMISH'D THREE   . . .   213  2 DON JUAN  2     109    6
CORPSES
    AND GALVANISM HAS SET SOME CORPSES GRINNING     . . .    92  2 DON JUAN  1     130    2
    AND HANDSOME CORPSES STREW'D UPON THE SHORE     . . .   229  2 DON JUAN  2     138    4
    AND THOUGH I HAVE SEEN MANY CORPSES NEVER     . . . .   430  2 DON JUAN  5      35    2
CORPUS
    OF THE STAR CHAMBER THAN OF HABEAS CORPUS     . . . .   391  3 DON JUAN 13      69    8
CORRECT
    WHO SAY STRANGE THINGS FOR SO CORRECT AN AGE    . . .   397  2 DON JUAN  4      98    4
    YOUNG WOMEN AND CORRECT THEM WHEN THEY BLUNDERED    .    21  2 DON JUAN  6      31    8
    MIDST WHOM WE HAVE HEARD FROM SOURCES QUITE CORRECT    382  3 DON JUAN 13      52    4
    ADMIRED ADORED BUT ALSO SO CORRECT  . . . . . . . .    434  3 DON JUAN 14      56    2
    HER CONDUCT HAD BEEN PERFECTLY CORRECT    . . . . . .   446  3 DON JUAN 14      85    3
CORRECTEST
    NEW BUILDINGS OF CORRECTEST CONFORMATION  . . . . . .   529  3 DON JUAN 16      58    7
CORRECTOR
    THE LAW'S EXPOUNDER AND THE STATE'S CORRECTOR   . . .    29  2 DON JUAN  1      15    5
CORRESPOND
    AS FAR AS OUTWARD SHOW MAY CORRESPOND . . . . . . . .   469  2 DON JUAN  5      99    7
CORRESPONDENT
    TO MAKE EACH CORRESPONDENT A NEW DEBTOR   . . . . . .   406  3 DON JUAN 13     104    8
CORRESPONDENTS
    TO HIS TUNIS CORRESPONDENTS SAVE ONE MAN  . . . . . .   284  2 DON JUAN  3      16    3
CORRODING
    CORRODING IN THE CAVERN OF THE HEART    . . . . . . .   457  3 DON JUAN 15       3    2
CORRUPTION
    CORRUPTION CAME NOT IN EACH MIND TO KILL  . . . . . .   377  2 DON JUAN  4      60    5
    THOUGH THEY MAY MAKE CORRUPTION GAPE OR STARE   . . .   114  3 DON JUAN  8       4    6
    CORRUPTION COULD NOT MAKE THEIR HEARTS HER SOIL    . .  145  3 DON JUAN  8      67    4
    CORRUPTION FOR ITS CROP) WITH THE POOR DEVILS   . . .   237  3 DON JUAN 10      25    6
    BY FOUL CORRUPTION INTO STREAMS--EVEN THEY    . . . .   287  3 DON JUAN 11      40    7
CORSES
    TO CORPS THE GREATER PART OF WHICH WERE CORSES    . .   126  3 DON JUAN  8      30    8
CORTEJO
    WAS IT FOR THIS THAT NO CORTEJO ERE   . . . . . . . .   102  2 DON JUAN  1     148    1
CORUSCATION
    PALL MALL AND SO FORTH HAVE A CORUSCATION     . . . .   280  3 DON JUAN 11      26    2
    HAVE WANED INTO A CRESCENT'S CORUSCATION  . . . . . .   293  3 DON JUAN 11      49    4
CORYDON
    BEGINNING WITH FORMOSUM PASTOR CORYDON    . . . . . .    45  2 DON JUAN  1      42    8
COSI
    CAN PAINT COSI VIAGGINO I RICCHI    . . . . . . . .    380  3 DON JUAN 13      47    5
COSMOGONY
    OH WORLD WHICH WAS AND IS WHAT IS COSMOGONY     . . .   192  3 DON JUAN  9      20    3
COSSACQUE
    HOW SHALL I SPELL THE NAME OF EACH COSSACQUE    . . .    73  3 DON JUAN  7      14    3
    TO RUSSIAN TARTAR ENGLISH FRENCH COSSACQUE    . . . .    89  3 DON JUAN  7      46    2
```

		PAGE	VOL	CANTO	STANZA	LN
COSSACQUES						
IN SIGHT TWO HORSEMEN WHO WERE DEEMED COSSACQUES		87	3 DON JUAN	7	43	2
SOME COSSACQUES HOVERING LIKE HAWKS ROUND A HILL		95	3 DON JUAN	7	56	3
OF COSSACQUES AND THEIR PREY TURNED ROUND AND CAST		97	3 DON JUAN	7	59	2
THE KOZAKS OR IF SO YOU PLEASE COSSACQUES--		149	3 DON JUAN	8	74	1
COSSACQUES WERE ALL CUT OFF AS DAY WAS BREAKING		150	3 DON JUAN	8	76	3
TWO VILLAINOUS COSSACQUES PURSUED THE CHILD		157	3 DON JUAN	8	92	1
THE READIEST WAY OF REASONING WITH COSSACQUES		158	3 DON JUAN	8	93	8
COSSAQUE						
HE MADE 'GAINST COSSAQUE SABRES IN THE WIDE		249	3 DON JUAN	10	51	5
COST						
(ALTHOUGH IT COST ME HALF AN HOUR IN SPINNING)		25	2 DON JUAN	1	7	6
AND MUST HAVE COST HIS MAJESTY A TREASURE		85	2 DON JUAN	1	118	4
AND YET CAN NOT REGRET WHAT IT HATH COST		130	2 DON JUAN	1	193	3
DENYING THE RECEIPT OF WHAT IT COST		142	2 DON JUAN	1	210	6
HAD COST HIS ENEMIES A LONG REPENTANCE		303	2 DON JUAN	3	54	7
MONSTERS WHO COST A NO LESS MONSTROUS SUM		462	2 DON JUAN	5	88	8
HER TOILET WHICH COST LITTLE FOR SHE WAS		36	3 DON JUAN	6	60	2
WITH COST AND CARE AND WARMTH INDUCED TO SHOOT		38	3 DON JUAN	6	65	4
A LOVER AS HAD COST HER MANY A TEAR		209	3 DON JUAN	9	54	7
A MOMENT'S GOOD THING MAY HAVE COST THEM YEARS		408	3 DON JUAN	13	109	6
AND SINCE THAT TIME IT NEED NOT COST MUCH SHOWING		444	3 DON JUAN	14	78	5
OR ELSE 'TWILL COST US ALL ANOTHER MILLION		446	3 DON JUAN	14	83	8
COST HER AN EFFORT WHICH IS A SAD TOIL		447	3 DON JUAN	14	86	2
THE COST WOULD BE A TRIFLE--AN OLD SONG		529	3 DON JUAN	16	59	1
BUT COUNTRY CONTESTS COST HIM RATHER DEARER		534	3 DON JUAN	16	70	3
MIGHT COST BOTH MEN AND MASTER TOO--THEIR PLACES		539	3 DON JUAN	16	79	8
HAD FALLEN LAST MARKET COST HIS HOST THREE VOTES		543	3 DON JUAN	16	89	8
THE COMPANY WHOSE BIRTH WEALTH WORTH HAVE COST		568	3 DON JUAN	17	13	4
COSTIVE						
WITH GORE LIKE NADIR SHAH THAT COSTIVE SOPHY		199	3 DON JUAN	9	33	4
COSTLY						
MOTHER OF PEARL AND CORAL THE LESS COSTLY		306	2 DON JUAN	3	61	8
SO COSTLY WERE THEY CARPETS EVERY STITCH		449	2 DON JUAN	5	65	6
VIED WITH EACH OTHER ON THIS COSTLY SPOT		55	3 DON JUAN	6	98	2
AND CANNOT FIND A BILL'S SMALL ITEMS COSTLY		283	3 DON JUAN	11	31	4
COSTS						
IT COSTS THREE FRANCS FOR EVERY MASS THAT'S SAID		185	2 DON JUAN	2	55	8
HOW MUCH IT COSTS US YET EACH RISING THROB		264	2 DON JUAN	2	203	2
COSTUME						
THE PRESENT WITH THEIR COMMON-PLACE COSTUME		468	3 DON JUAN	15	26	8
COTERIE						
DRAWN BY THE BLUE-COAT MISSES OF A COTERIE		404	2 DON JUAN	4	109	8
BY THE MERE COMBINATION OF A COTERIE		397	3 DON JUAN	13	82	4
COTERIES						
THE COTERIES AND AS IN BANQUO'S GLASS		295	3 DON JUAN	11	54	3
COTS						
ALL WRATH IN BARRACKS PALACES OR COTS		200	3 DON JUAN	9	36	5
COTTAGES						
IN CAMPS IN SHIPS IN COTTAGES OR COURTS--		424	3 DON JUAN	14	31	4
COUCH						
HIS COUCH AND THAT HE MIGHT BE MORE AT EASE		226	2 DON JUAN	2	133	3
THEIR LADY TO HER COUCH WITH GUSHING EYES		376	2 DON JUAN	4	59	5
TO MAKE THE NUPTIAL COUCH A BED OF WARE		12	3 DON JUAN	6	12	8
AND EVERY COUCH IS OCCUPIED YOU HAD BEST		29	3 DON JUAN	6	46	4
OF LOLAH--THOUGH HER COUCH IS NOT SO LARGE		46	3 DON JUAN	6	81	8
WAVED O'ER HIS COUCH HE MEDITATED FOND		555	3 DON JUAN	16	110	6
COUCHED						
BY HIS DISPATCHES COUCHED IN PITHY PHRASE		85	3 DON JUAN	7	39	6
THERE COUCHED ALL SNUGLY ON HIS PILLOW'S NOOK		512	3 DON JUAN	16	27	5
COUCHES						
WERE COUCHES TOILETS--AND MUCH MORE THAN THIS		31	3 DON JUAN	6	51	3
COUGH						
BUT BE MUCH PUZZLED BY A COUGH AND COLD		168	2 DON JUAN	2	22	3
SIGH LIKE HIS SON THAN COUGH LIKE HIS GRANDFATHER		228	3 DON JUAN	10	6	8
COUGHING						
TO SIGH INSTEAD OF COUGHING--AND CRYING-- PISH		228	3 DON JUAN	10	6	V8
COUGHS						
BUT COUGHS WILL COME WHEN SIGHS DEPART--AND NOW		229	3 DON JUAN	10	8	1
COULEUR						
COULEUR DE ROSE WHO'S NEITHER WHITE NOR SCARLET		344	3 DON JUAN	12	62	8
COUNCIL						
HIS DAILY COUNCIL UPON WAYS AND MEANS		54	3 DON JUAN	6	96	2
A GENERAL COUNCIL IN WHICH UNANIMITY		92	3 DON JUAN	7	51	2
AND BEING OF THE COUNCIL CALLED THE PRIVY		440	3 DON JUAN	14	68	1
COUNCILS						
THAT STRANGER TO MOST COUNCILS HERE PREVAILED		92	3 DON JUAN	7	51	3
A MAN KNOWN IN THE COUNCILS OF THE NATION		365	3 DON JUAN	13	14	3
COUNSEL						
FROM COUNSEL LEARNED IN THOSE KINDS OF LAWS		38	2 DON JUAN	1	33	3
SHE KEPT HER COUNSEL IN SO CLOSE A WAY		59	2 DON JUAN	1	68	8
OUR COUNSEL--(JUAN MIND YOU MUST NOT SLEEP)		115	2 DON JUAN	1	172	4
OF COUNSEL TO NONSUIT OR TO ANNUL		127	2 DON JUAN	1	189	4
THE LIBELLER'S GRATIS COUNSEL DIRTY SHIELD		151	2 DON JUAN	1	V 2	3
FEE BY A COUNSEL FELON BY A JAILOR		424	2 DON JUAN	5	26	8
AND BADE HIM COUNSEL JUAN WITH A SMILE		438	3 DON JUAN	14	65	4
COUNSELLORS						
OF COUNSELLORS AS SOLOMON HAS SAID		371	3 DON JUAN	13	29	2
OF COUNSELLORS FOR MEN--THUS FOR THE SEX		371	3 DON JUAN	13	30	2

```
                                                    PAGE VOL    CANTO  STANZA LN
COUNT
    IS IT FOR THIS THAT GENERAL COUNT O'REILLY  . . . . . . . 102  2 DON JUAN   1     148    7
    DID NOT HIS COUNTRYMAN COUNT CORNIANI . .  . . . . . . .  102  2 DON JUAN   1     149    3
    THE COUNT STRONGSTROGANOFF I PUT IN PAIN .  . . . . . . . 102  2 DON JUAN   1     149    6
    BY CARRYING OFF COUNT CESARE CICOGNA . .  . . . . . . . . 389  2 DON JUAN   4      83    7
    COUNT DAMAS DROVE THEM BACK INTO THE WATER  . . . . . . .  82  3 DON JUAN   7      31    7
    COUNT CHAPEAU-BRAS TOO HAD A BALL BETWEEN  . . . . . . .  116  3 DON JUAN   8      10    2
    TO CALCULATORS WHEN THEY COUNT ON WOMAN .  . . . . . . .  429  3 DON JUAN  14      43    8
COUNTED
    WERE COUNTED IN THEM WHEN THEY GOT AFLOAT  . . . . . . .  185  2 DON JUAN   2      54    8
    THEY COUNTED THIRTY CROWDED IN A SPACE  . . . . . . . .   189  2 DON JUAN   2      63    1
    HE COUNTED THEM AT BREAK OF DAY--  . . . . . . . . . .    322  2 DON JUAN   3  L   4    5
    WHICH LEAVES YOU MINUS OF THE CASH YOU COUNTED . . . . .   16  3 DON JUAN   6      21    6
COUNTENANCE
    MAKING THE COUNTENANCE A MASQUE OF REST  . . . . . . .    457  3 DON JUAN  15       3    3
COUNTER
    THE GAMESTER'S COUNTER OR THE STATESMAN'S DROSS  . . . .  317  3 DON JUAN  12       4    6
COUNTERBALANCE
    A THING TO COUNTERBALANCE HUMAN WOES . . . . . . . .      226  3 DON JUAN  10       2    5
COUNTESS
    OFFSPRING OF SOME SAGE HUSBAND--HUNTING COUNTESS  . . .   312  3 DON JUAN  11      89    2
    THE DUCHESS OF FITZ-FULKE THE COUNTESS CRABBEY . . . .    396  3 DON JUAN  13      79    3
COUNTESSES
    AND COUNTESSES MATURE IN ROBES AND PEARLS  . . . . . .    390  3 DON JUAN  13      68    6
    WITH OTHER COUNTESSES OF BLANK--BUT RANK . . . . . . .    396  3 DON JUAN  13      80    1
COUNTIES
    QUITE COMMON IN THOSE COUNTIES ARE A KIND  . . . . . .    308  2 DON JUAN   3      65    2
    FIRING THE COUNTIES TILL THEY IMPIOUS WAR WAGE . . . . .  530  3 DON JUAN  16      60   V5
    THOSE WHO IN COUNTIES HAVE GREAT LAND RESOURCES  . . . .  534  3 DON JUAN  16      68    6
COUNTING
    I KNOW NOT NEVER COUNTING PAST THEIR TEENS  . . . . . .    41  3 DON JUAN   6      69    4
COUNTRIES
    ESPECIALLY IN COUNTRIES NEAR THE SUN . . . . . . .        56  3 DON JUAN   1      62    5
    OF LADIES OF ALL COUNTRIES AT THE WILL  . . . . . . .     22  3 DON JUAN   6      33    4
    COUNTRIES OF GREATER HEAT BUT LESSER SUCTION  . . . . .   262  3 DON JUAN  10      76    4
    ALL COUNTRIES HAVE THEIR LIONS BUT IN THEE  . . . . . .   327  3 DON JUAN  12      24    7
COUNTRY
    ALAS HIS COUNTRY SHOW'D NO PATH TO PRAISE  . . . . . .    303  2 DON JUAN   3      55    6
    MY COUNTRY ON THY VOICELESS SHORE . .  . . . . . . . .    322  2 DON JUAN   3  L   5    2
    AND CLIME AND TIME AND COUNTRY AND COMPLEXION  . . . .     26  3 DON JUAN   6      40    7
    NOT FIGHTING FOR THEIR COUNTRY OR ITS CROWN  . . . . .     75  3 DON JUAN   7      18    3
    WAS HE SINCE SO RENOWNED IN COUNTRY QUARTERS  . . . . .    76  3 DON JUAN   7      19    7
    THEIR COUNTRY AND AS TRAITORS ARE ABHORRED  . . . . . .    77  3 DON JUAN   7      22    6
    DEFENCE OF FREEDOM COUNTRY OR OF LAWS . . . . . . . .      86  3 DON JUAN   7      40    4
    GOD MADE THE COUNTRY AND MAN MADE THE TOWN  . . . . . .   142  3 DON JUAN   8      60    2
    WHICH LOVES SO WELL ITS COUNTRY AND ITS KING  . . . . .   175  3 DON JUAN   8     126    2
    TO FREE HIS COUNTRY PITT TOO HAD HIS PRIDE  . . . . . .   186  3 DON JUAN   9       8    6
    A COUNTRY IN ALL SENSES THE MOST DEAR . . . . . . . .     263  3 DON JUAN  10      77    5
    AS ALSO BONFIRES MADE OF COUNTRY SEATS  . . . . . . .     281  3 DON JUAN  11      27    3
    I'VE SEEN THE COUNTRY GENTLEMEN TURN SQUEAKERS--  . . .   310  3 DON JUAN  11      85    4
    A MORAL COUNTRY BUT I HOLD MY HAND--  . . . . . . . .     311  3 DON JUAN  11      87    4
    AT LEAST IN A COLD COUNTRY MAY AWARD  . . . . . . . .     322  3 DON JUAN  12      13   V6
    COUNTRY WHERE A YOUNG COUPLE OF THE SAME AGES  . . . .    346  3 DON JUAN  12      65    2
    INTO A COUNTRY WHERE 'TIS HALF A FASHION . . . . . . .    347  3 DON JUAN  12      68    4
    OF HIS OWN COUNTRY--SELDOM SINCE THAT DAY  . . . . . .    364  3 DON JUAN  13      11    3
    AND AS HE THOUGHT IN COUNTRY MUCH THE SAME--  . . . . .   367  3 DON JUAN  13      20    4
    THE LONDON WINTER AND THE COUNTRY SUMMER . . . . . . .    380  3 DON JUAN  13      48    1
    ERE PATRIOTS THEIR TRUE COUNTRY CAN REMEMBER--  . . . .   380  3 DON JUAN  13      48    7
    DEPARTURE FOR HIS COUNTRY SEAT TO-DAY . . . . . . . .     382  3 DON JUAN  13      51    7
    HIS COUNTRY'S PRIDE HE CAME DOWN TO THE COUNTRY  . . .    401  3 DON JUAN  13      91    8
    TO BE ASSEMBLED AT A COUNTRY SEAT . . . . . . . . .       402  3 DON JUAN  13      94    2
    BUT IN THE COUNTRY LADIES SEEK THEIR BOWER  . . . . . .   409  3 DON JUAN  13     111    3
    AND ONCE O'ER SEVERAL COUNTRY GENTLEMEN  . . . . . . .    424  3 DON JUAN  14      33    8
    THERE WAS A COUNTRY GIRL IN A CLOSE CAP  . . . . . . .    530  3 DON JUAN  16      61    3
    AND MORALS OF THE COUNTRY FROM CAPRICES . . . . . . .     531  3 DON JUAN  16      63    3
    POOR SOUL FOR SHE WAS COUNTRY BORN AND BRED  . . . . .    532  3 DON JUAN  16      64    6
    ALL COUNTRY GENTLEMEN ESQUIRED OR KNIGHTED  . . . . . .   534  3 DON JUAN  16      69    3
    BUT COUNTRY CONTESTS COST HIM RATHER DEARER  . . . . .    534  3 DON JUAN  16      70    3
    WHICH THREATENED THE WHOLE COUNTRY WITH PERDITION  . . .  536  3 DON JUAN  16      74    4
    THE COUNTRY WOULD HAVE FAR MORE CAUSE TO WEEP IT  . . .   537  3 DON JUAN  16      75    6
    THERE WERE SOME COUNTRY WAGS TOO--AND ALAS  . . . . .     539  3 DON JUAN  16      81    1
    BEHELD BETWEEN THE COUNTRY AND THE TOWN . . . . . . .     541  3 DON JUAN  16      85    3
    EVEN IN THE COUNTRY CIRCLE'S NARROW BOUND--  . . . . .    544  3 DON JUAN  16      91    6
    AND CURTSEYING OFF AS CURTSIES COUNTRY DAME  . . . . .    549  3 DON JUAN  16     101    4
COUNTRYMAN
    DID NOT HIS COUNTRYMAN COUNT CORNIANI . . . . . . . .     102  2 DON JUAN   1     149    3
COUNTRYMEN
    WERE STILL AT LEAST OUR COUNTRYMEN . . . . . . . . .      324  2 DON JUAN   3  L  11    6
    MY GENTLE COUNTRYMEN WE WILL RENEW . . . . . . . . .      266  3 DON JUAN  10      84    3
COUNTRY'S
    BUT ALMOST EVERY OTHER COUNTRY'S BLUE . . . . . . . .     163  2 DON JUAN   2      12    6
    HIS COUNTRY'S WRONGS AND HIS DESPAIR TO SAVE HER  . . .   302  2 DON JUAN   3      53    7
    (IT IS THE COUNTRY'S CUSTOM) BUT IN VAIN .  . . . . . .   314  2 DON JUAN   3      75    2
    HE DIED DESERVING WELL HIS COUNTRY'S TEARS  . . . . . .   152  3 DON JUAN   8      80    5
    GO HEAR IT IN YOUR FAMISHED COUNTRY'S CRIES  . . . . .    187  3 DON JUAN   9       9    7
    WHO FATTEN ON THEIR COUNTRY'S GORE AND DEBTS  . . . . .   187  3 DON JUAN   9      10    5
    WHEN A MAN'S COUNTRY'S GOING TO THE DEVIL  . . . . . .    257  3 DON JUAN  10      66    8
    PERHAPS THOUGHT HE IT IS THE COUNTRY'S WONT .  . . . .    275  3 DON JUAN  11      15    1
    ALL KINDS OF TOIL SAVE FOR OUR COUNTRY'S GOOD--  . . .    301  3 DON JUAN  11      65    7
    HIS COUNTRY'S PRIDE HE CAME DOWN TO THE COUNTRY  . . .    401  3 DON JUAN  13      91    8
```

157

COUNTRY-SEAT
    FOR AN ESTATE OR CASH OR COUNTRY-SEAT . . . .   89 2 DON JUAN 1   125   5
COUNTY
    AS ALSO AT THE RACE AND COUNTY BALLS . . . . 471 2 DON JUAN 5   103   8
    AND COUNTY MEETINGS AND THE PARLIAMENT . . . . 360 3 DON JUAN 13   5   7
    THOSE WHO IN COUNTY INTEREST TRY THEIR FORCES . . . . . 534 3 DON JUAN 16   68 V6
    COURTEOUS AND CAUTIOUS THEREFORE IN HIS COUNTY . . . . . 535 3 DON JUAN 16   71   1
COUPLE
    WHICH SERVES THE HAPPY COUPLE FOR A TAVERN . . . . . .   24 2 DON JUAN 1   6   8
    WERE TO BE CHAIN'D AND LOTTED OUT PER COUPLE . . . . . 393 2 DON JUAN 4   91   7
    WE LEAVE THIS ROYAL COUPLE TO REPOSE . . . .   16 3 DON JUAN 6   20   1
    O'ER THE PROMOTED COUPLE OF BRAVE MEN . . . . 101 3 DON JUAN 7   68   1
    COUNTRY WHERE A YOUNG COUPLE OF THE SAME AGES . . . . . 346 3 DON JUAN 12   65   2
COUPLED
    OR LIKE A SYSTEM COUPLED WITH A DOUBT . . . . 504 3 DON JUAN 16   9   4
COUPLET
    A COUPLET OR AN ELEGY TO CLAIM . . . . 120 3 DON JUAN 8   17   6
    INTO A RUSSIAN COUPLET RATHER DULL . . . . 212 3 DON JUAN 9   60   3
COURAGE
    ITS VERY COURAGE STAGNATES TO A VICE . . . . . .   18 2 DON JUAN D   15   8
    WHICH COURAGE GIVES WHILE POOR PEDRILLO'S PAIR . . . . . 186 2 DON JUAN 2   56   5
    THE ONLY HOPE OF COURAGE DWELLS . . . . 325 2 DON JUAN 3 L 14   4
    JUAN WAS YOUNG--HAD COURAGE--AND WAS FULL . . . . . . 415 2 DON JUAN 5   8 V1
    IN THE CHILL DARK WHEN COURAGE DOES NOT GLOW . . . . . 121 3 DON JUAN 8   21   3
    IN COURAGE WAS OBLIGED TO SNATCH A SHIELD . . . . . . 125 3 DON JUAN 8   28   7
    WHILE COURAGE CLUNG BUT TO A SINGLE TWIG--AM I . . . . . 164 3 DON JUAN 8   105   5
    HE HAD BEHAVED WITH COURAGE AND HUMANITY-- . . . . . 182 3 DON JUAN 8   140   2
    AND THERE'S A COURAGE WHICH GROWS OUT OF FEAR . . . . . 412 3 DON JUAN 14   5   2
COURIER
    RECORDED IN THE MONITEUR AND COURIER . . . .   22 2 DON JUAN 1   2   8
    IN WRITING COURSER BY MISTAKE FOR COURIER . . . . . . 446 2 DON JUAN 5   61   7
    IN AN ERRATUM OF HER HORSE FOR COURIER . . . . 446 2 DON JUAN 5   61 V7
    A COURIER TO THE PRINCE AND HE SUCCEEDED . . . . . .   85 3 DON JUAN 7   38   2
    A COURIER ON THE SPUR INSPIRED NEW HEART . . . . . .   85 3 DON JUAN 7   39   3
COURLAND
    THROUGH COURLAND ALSO WHICH THAT FAMOUS FARCE SAW . . . . 253 3 DON JUAN 10   58   3
COURSE
    HIS FATHER'S NAME WAS JOSE--DON OF COURSE . . . . . .   26 2 DON JUAN 1   9   1
    AND CERTAINLY THIS COURSE WAS MUCH THE BEST . . . . .   58 2 DON JUAN 1   67   4
    THING QUITE IN COURSE AND NOT AT ALL ALARMING . . . . .   68 2 DON JUAN 1   86   7
    WERE IN THE ENGLISH NEWSPAPERS OF COURSE . . . . . . 126 2 DON JUAN 1   188   8
    PUZZLED HIS TUTORS VERY MUCH OF COURSE . . . . 158 2 DON JUAN 2   2   8
    IT CHANGED OF COURSE A HEAVENLY CAMELEON . . . . . . 205 2 DON JUAN 2   92   1
    UPON ITS COURSE) PASS'D OFT BEFORE THEIR EYES . . . . . 206 2 DON JUAN 2   94   4
    OR THOUGHT THEY SAW AND SHAPED THEIR COURSE FOR SHORE . . . 207 2 DON JUAN 2   97   6
    WERE MAD FOR LAND AND THUS THEIR COURSE THEY RAN . . . . 211 2 DON JUAN 2   104   3
    (BUT THAT OF COURSE IS RARE) AND THEN DESPOND . . . . 278 2 DON JUAN 3   7   3
    HE SHAPED HIS COURSE TO WHERE HIS DAUGHTER FAIR . . . . 285 2 DON JUAN 3   19   4
    IF IN THE COURSE OF SUCH A LIFE AS WAS . . . . . . 402 2 DON JUAN 4   107   1
    THAN ANY OTHER SCRAPE A THING OF COURSE . . . . . . 417 2 DON JUAN 5   12   8
    WAS TO SIT DOWN AGAIN AND CRY OF COURSE . . . . . . 491 2 DON JUAN 5   139   8
    SHE WAS OF COURSE THE FAVOURITE OF THE FOUR . . . . . 495 2 DON JUAN 5   146   8
    THEIR TALK OF COURSE RAN MOST ON THE NEW COMER . . . .   23 3 DON JUAN 6   35   1
    ITS FARTHER COURSE BUT MUST RECEIVE ITS WRECK . . . .   60 3 DON JUAN 6   108   8
    THE TWO FIRST FEELINGS RAN THEIR COURSE COMPLETE . . . . 213 3 DON JUAN 9   61   1
    THE EFFECT ON JUAN WAS OF COURSE SUBLIME . . . . . . 261 3 DON JUAN 10   74   1
    LIKE OTHER SLAVES OF COURSE MUST PAY HIS RANSOM . . . . 305 3 DON JUAN 11   74   3
    MY TOPIC WITH OF COURSE THE DUE RESTRICTION . . . . . 311 3 DON JUAN 11   88   2
    THEY WARM INTO A SCRAPE BUT KEEP OF COURSE . . . . . 349 3 DON JUAN 12   73   7
    IN BRITAIN--WHICH OF COURSE TRUE PATRIOTS FIND . . . . 359 3 DON JUAN 13   2   7
    THERE ALSO WAS OF COURSE IN ADELINE . . . . 373 3 DON JUAN 13   34   1
    PURSUED ITS COURSE NOW GLEAMING AND NOW HIDING . . . . 385 3 DON JUAN 13   58   6
    OF COURSE WITH SOME RESERVE AND SLIGHT RESTRICTION . . . . 416 3 DON JUAN 14   13   3
    BUT NEVER YET (EXCEPT OF COURSE A MISS . . . . . . 470 3 DON JUAN 15   32   1
    THAT IN THE COURSE OF SOME SIX THOUSAND YEARS . . . . 504 3 DON JUAN 16   7   2
    BELOW HIS WINDOW WAVED (OF COURSE) A WILLOW . . . . . 507 3 DON JUAN 16   15   6
    OF COURSE THE OTHERS COULD NOT BUT EXPRESS . . . . . 517 3 DON JUAN 16   39   4
    AND THEN OF COURSE THE CIRCLE MUCH ADMIRES . . . . . 521 3 DON JUAN 16   41   5
    OF COURSE THESE GROUPS WERE SCATTERED HERE AND THERE . . . 533 3 DON JUAN 16   66   1
COURSER
    IN WRITING COURSER BY MISTAKE FOR COURIER . . . . . 446 2 DON JUAN 5   61   7
COURSERS
    OF COURSERS ALSO SPAKE THEY HENRY RID . . . . . . 368 3 DON JUAN 13   23   5
    THERE WERE SOME HUNTERS BOLD AND COURSERS KEEN . . . . 539 3 DON JUAN 16   80   1
COURSES
    WHO TO IMMORAL COURSES WOULD ALLURE US . . . . . . 267 2 DON JUAN 2   207   3
    OF INTELLECT EXPENDED ON TWO COURSES . . . . . . 486 2 DON JUAN 15   69   2
    BELOW STAIRS ON THE SCORE OF SECOND COURSES . . . . . 534 3 DON JUAN 16   68   4
COURT
    THE COURT CAMP CHURCH THE VESSEL AND THE MART . . . . 131 2 DON JUAN 1   194   3
    AS PLENTIFUL AS IN A COURT OR FAIR . . . . 310 2 DON JUAN 3   68   8
    HIS WOND'ROUS JOURNEY TO SOME FOREIGN COURT . . . . . 440 2 DON JUAN 5   52   3
    SNATCHED FROM A PRISON TO PRESIDE AT COURT . . . . . 495 2 DON JUAN 5   147   3
    OF WORLDS TO LOSE YET STILL TO PAY MY COURT I . . . .   9 3 DON JUAN 6   5   5
    AND SO HE SAYS NO MORE--BUT PAYS HIS COURT . . . .   82 3 DON JUAN 7   32   5
    MUCH LESS THAN IS THE HOPE OF EVERY COURT . . . . . 106 3 DON JUAN 7   79   6
    THE COURT THAT WATCHED EACH LOOK HER VISAGE WORE . . . . 211 3 DON JUAN 9   58   5
    THE WHOLE COURT LOOKED IMMEDIATELY MOST SWEET . . . . 213 3 DON JUAN 9   61   3
    THE WHOLE COURT MELTED INTO ONE WIDE WHISPER . . . . 221 3 DON JUAN 9   78   1

COURT   (CONTINUED)
    MUST COME MUCH RATHER SHOULD HE COURT THE RAY . . . . 229 3 DON JUAN 10   9   7
    AT WHICH THE WHOLE COURT WAS EXTREMELY TROUBLED . . . 244 3 DON JJAN 10   39   7
    LOVE RULES THE CAMP THE COURT THE GROVE--FOR LOVE . . . 322 3 DON JJAN 12   13   1
    NOW IF THE COURT AND CAMP AND GROVE BE NOT . . . . . 323 3 DON JUAN 12   16   1
    I'VE KNOWN THEM COURT AN HEIRESS FOR THEIR LOVER . . . 331 3 DON JUAN 12   33   4
    THE KINDER VETERAN WITH CALM WORDS WILL COURT YOU . . . 337 3 DON JJAN 12   45   5
    SHOULD NEITHER COURT NEGLECT NOR DREAD TO BEAR IT . . . 356 3 DON JUAN 12   87   8
    COURT MYSTERIES HAVING BEEN HIMSELF A MINISTER . . . . 368 3 DON JUAN 13   21   4
    AMIDST THE COURT A GOTHIC FOUNTAIN PLAY'D . . . . . . 389 3 DON JUAN 13   65   1
    NO DOUBT IF I HAD WISH'D TO PAY MY COURT . . . . . . 466 3 DON JUAN 15   22   5
COURTED
    JUAN INSTEAD OF COURTING COURTS WAS COURTED . . . . . 239 3 DON JUAN 10   29   1
COURTEOUS
    WHO MUST BE COURTEOUS TO THE ACCREDITED . . . . . . 287 3 DON JUAN 11   40   2
    COURTEOUS AND CAUTIOUS THEREFORE IN HIS COUNTY . . . . 535 3 DON JUAN 16   71   1
COURTEOUSLY
    PASS'D BUT HE STROVE QUITE COURTEOUSLY TO QUELL . . . 298 2 DON JUAN 3   44   4
    PROUD WITH THE PROUD YET COURTEOUSLY PROUD . . . . . 462 3 DON JUAN 15   15   5
COURTESIES
    TO USE ALL FIT AND PROPER COURTESIES . . . . 472 2 DON JUAN 5   105   5
COURTESY
    PRAY HAVE THE COURTESY TO MAKE IT KNOWN . . . . . . 105 2 DON JUAN 1   154   3
    AND YOU AN EQUAL COURTESY SHOULD SHOW-- . . . . . . 419 2 DON JUAN 5   16   4
    WHICH IS REQUIRED BY PROPER COURTESY . . . . 311 3 DON JUAN 11   88   3
    IN MAKING MEN WHAT COURTESY CALLS FRIENDS . . . . . 365 3 DON JUAN 13   15   8
    A GENTLE GENIAL COURTESY OF MIND . . . . 372 3 DON JUAN 13   32   6
    AND WAXING CHILLER IN HER COURTESY . . . . 430 3 DON JUAN 14   46   6
    IN COURTESY THEIR WISH TO SEE DISPLAYED . . . . . . 517 3 DON JUAN 16   39   5
    AND DIGNITY WITH COURTESY SO BLENDING . . . . 546 3 DON JUAN 16   95   4
COURTIER
    NO COURTIER COULD AND SCARCELY WOMAN CAN . . . . . . 296 2 DON JUAN 3   41   5
COURTIER'S
    OR ROUGHLY TREADING ON THE COURTIER'S KIBES . . . . . 200 3 DON JUAN 9   35   6
COURTIERS
    THE COURTIERS STARED THE LADIES WHISPERED AND . . . . 205 3 DON JUAN 9   46   1
COURTING
    JUAN INSTEAD OF COURTING COURTS WAS COURTED . . . . . 239 3 DON JUAN 10   29   1
COURTISAN
    PATRIOT BY FORCE AND COURTISAN BY CRAFT . . . . . . 155 2 DON JUAN 1 V 6   6
COURTLY
    HE THOUGHT AT HEART LIKE COURTLY CHESTERFIELD . . . . 425 3 DON JUAN 14   35   5
    TALL STATELY FORM'D TO LEAD THE COURTLY VAN . . . . . 440 3 DON JUAN 14   70   5
COURTS
    JUAN INSTEAD OF COURTING COURTS WAS COURTED . . . . . 239 3 DON JUAN 10   29   1
    IF COURTS AND CAMPS BE QUITE SO SENTIMENTAL . . . . . 322 3 DON JUAN 12   13   8
    WITHOUT CASH CAMPS WERE THIN AND COURTS WERE NONE . . . 322 3 DON JUAN 12   14   3
    IN CAMPS IN SHIPS IN COTTAGES OR COURTS-- . . . . . 424 3 DON JUAN 14   31   4
COUSIN
    WHICH MIGHT HAVE CALLED DIANA'S CHORUS COUSIN . . . . 469 2 DON JUAN 5   99   6
    EACH AUNT EACH COUSIN HATH HER SPECULATION . . . . . 331 3 DON JUAN 12   33   1
    AND WILD DISMAY O'ER EVERY ANGRY COUSIN . . . . . . 332 3 DON JUAN 12   34   3
COUSINS
    MARRYING THEIR COUSINS--NAY THEIR AUNTS AND NIECES . . . 52 2 DON JUAN 1   57   7
    FOR COUSINS ALSO ANSWERED THE SAME DAY . . . . . . 239 3 DON JUAN 10   30   4
COVER
    FOR SOMETIMES SUCH A WORLD OF VIRTUES COVER . . . . . 405 2 DON JUAN 4   111   6
COVERED
    NOR WORK ADVANCE NOR COVERED WAY WAS THERE . . . . . 72 3 DON JUAN 7   11   7
COVERS
    MISS EDGEWORTH'S NOVELS STEPPING FROM THEIR COVERS . . . 29 2 DON JUAN 1   16   2
    PROFUSION WITH YOUNG BEAUTY COVERS O'ER . . . . . . 269 2 DON JUAN 2   211   4
    AS MANY COVERS DULY DAILY LAID . . . . 381 3 DON JUAN 13   49   6
COVET
    THOU SHALT NOT COVET MR SOTHEBY'S MUSE . . . . . . 140 2 DON JUAN 1   206   1
    OF TOIL IS WHAT WE COVET MOST AND YET . . . . 412 3 DON JUAN 14   4   2
COVETED
    WHATE'ER SHE SAW AND COVETED WAS BROUGHT . . . . . . 476 2 DON JUAN 5   113   1
    WHO NEVER COVETED THEIR NEIGHBOUR'S LOT . . . . . . 323 3 DON JUAN 12   16   3
COWERS
    THE PATRIARCH OF THE FLOCK ALL GENTLY COWERS . . . . 292 2 DON JUAN 3   32   4
    HE SHUDDERED AS NO DOUBT THE BRAVEST COWERS . . . . . 559 3 DON JUAN 16   120   5
COWL
    IN COWL AND BEADS AND DUSKY GARB APPEARED . . . . . 510 3 DON JUAN 16   21   2
    'TIS SHADOWED BY HIS COWL . . . . 519 3 DON JUAN 16 L 4   6
    BACK FELL THE SABLE FROCK AND DREARY COWL . . . . . 561 3 DON JUAN 16   123   5
COWPER
    SO COWPER SAYS--AND I BEGIN TO BE . . . . 142 3 DON JUAN 8   60   3
COW'S
    A COW'S SHAPE FOR A MASK--WAS ONLY (SINKING . . . . . 238 2 DON JUAN 2   155   5
COXCOMB
    A CHARLATAN A COXCOMB--AND HAVE BEEN . . . . 84 2 DON JUAN 1   116   7
    THE QUAINT OLD CRUEL COXCOMB IN HIS GULLET . . . . . 407 3 DON JUAN 13   106   7
    NOW JUAN THOUGH NO COXCOMB IN PRETENCE . . . . . . 490 3 DON JUAN 15   77   5
COXCOMBRY
    WITHOUT THE COXCOMBRY OF CERTAIN SHE MEN . . . . . . 424 3 DON JUAN 14   31   8
    OF COXCOMBRY OR CONQUEST NO ABUSE . . . . 461 3 DON JUAN 15   12   4
COXCOMB'S
    SHE WAS A PITCH BEYOND A COXCOMB'S FLIGHT . . . . . 435 3 DON JUAN 14   57   4

159

```
                                                              PAGE VOL      CANTO STANZA LN
COXCOMBS
    YOU'LL FIND TEN THOUSAND HANDSOME COXCOMBS BLOODY . . .    167  3 DON JUAN  8   112   8
    SELF-LOVE THERE'S SAFETY IN A CROWD OF COXCOMBS   . . .    371  3 DON JUAN 13    30   8
COXE
    UNTIL HIS LATE LIFE BY ARCHDEACON COXE   . . . . . .       328  2 DON JUAN  3    90   8
CRABBE
    SCOTT ROGERS CAMPBELL MOORE AND CRABBE WILL TRY  . . .      13  2 DON JUAN  D     7   7
    WITH CRABBE IT MAY BE DIFFICULT TO COPE . . . . .         139  2 DON JUAN  1   205   5
CRABBEY
    THE DUCHESS OF FITZ-FULKE THE COUNTESS CRABBEY . . . .    396  3 DON JUAN 13    79   3
CRACK
    THEY'RE ON THE STAIR JUST NOW AND IN A CRACK . . . .       96  2 DON JUAN  1   137   6
    AND THEIR BAKED LIPS WITH MANY A BLOODY CRACK . . . .     202  2 DON JUAN  2    86   1
    HE WAS A JOLLY FELLOW AND COULD CRACK . . . . . .         147  3 DON JUAN  8    70   5
CRACK'D
    THE MUSICO IS BUT A CRACK'D OLD BASIN  . . . . . .        391  2 DON JUAN  4    86   2
CRACKED
    WHO LITTLE THOUGHT THAT HIS OWN CRACKED EXISTENCE . . .   440  2 DON JUAN  5    51   3
    CRACKED SHIVERED VANISHED SCARCELY GAZED ON ERE  . . .    306  3 DON JUAN 11    76   5
CRACKS
    FOR WHICH THEIR MOUTHS GAPED LIKE THE CRACKS OF EARTH  .  201  2 DON JUAN  2    84   2
CRADLED
    BROUGHT FORTH IN PURPLE CRADLED IN VERMILLION . . . .     205  2 DON JUAN  2    92   3
CRAFT
    PATRIOT BY FORCE AND COURTISAN BY CRAFT . . . . . .       155  2 DON JUAN  1  V 6   6
CRAGGY
    REMAIN'D UNKNOWN WITHIN HIS CRAGGY NOOK . . . . . .       248  2 DON JUAN  2   174   4
CRAM
    A TURBOT FOR RELIEF OF THOSE WHO CRAM . . . . . .         483  3 DON JUAN 15    63   3
CRAMM'D
    OR CRAMM'D TWELVE SHEETS INTO ONE LITTLE LETTER  . . .    406  3 DON JUAN 13   104   7
CRANED
    AND NEVER CRANED AND MADE BUT FEW FAUX PAS . . . . .      424  3 DON JUAN 14    33   3
CRASH
    LOUDER THAN THE LOUD OCEAN LIKE A CRASH . . . . . .       184  2 DON JUAN  2    53   2
    FROM OUR OLD CRASH SOME MYSTIC ANCIENT STRAIN . . . .     201  2 DON JUAN  9    38   3
    ITS INNER CRASH IS LIKE AN EARTHQUAKE'S RUIN . . . .      446  3 DON JUAN 14    85   8
CRASHAW
    WITH TRUTH LIKE SOUTHEY AND WITH VERSE LIKE CRASHAW  . .  316  2 DON JUAN  3    79   8
    BELIEVED LIKE SOUTHEY--AND PERUSED LIKE CRASHAW  . . .    316  2 DON JUAN  3    79  V8
CRAVAT
    TO GIVE SOME REBEL PACHA A CRAVAT . . . . . . .           463  2 DON JUAN  5    89   7
    HIS BANDAGE SLIPPED DOWN INTO A CRAVAT  . . . . .         205  3 DON JUAN  9    45   1
    THE CRAVAT STAINED WITH BLOODY DROPS FELL DOWN . . . .    276  3 DON JUAN 11    17   1
CRAVE
    TO PROVE RELUCTANT AND BEGGED LEAVE TO CRAVE  . . . .      62  3 DON JUAN  6   112   5
CRAVING
    HAD TOLD HIS SON TO SATISFY HIS CRAVING . . . . . .       263  3 DON JUAN 10    78   6
CRAW
    AS TIGERS COMBAT WITH AN EMPTY CRAW . . . . . .           137  3 DON JUAN  8    49   5
CRAWLS
    THE QUIET SHEEP FEEDS AND THE TORTOISE CRAWLS . . . .     386  2 DON JUAN  4    77   8
CRAZED
    BECAUSE THE FIRST IS CRAZED BEYOND ALL HOPE . . . . .     139  2 DON JUAN  1   205   3
CRAZY
    YET OF A BEAUTY THAT WOULD DRIVE YOU CRAZY . . . . .       26  3 DON JUAN  6    41   8
CREAK
    EXCEPT THE CREAK OF WHEELS WHICH ON THEIR PIVOT HE . .    272  3 DON JUAN 11     8   6
    IT OPENED WITH A MOST INFERNAL CREAK . . . . . .         557  3 DON JUAN 16   116   1
CREAK'D
    AND THE SHIP CREAK'D THE TOWN BECAME A SPECK . . . .      163  2 DON JUAN  2    13   3
CREAM
    SCARCELY O'ERPASS'D THE CREAM OF YOUR CHAMPAIGNE . . .    250  2 DON JUAN  2   178   2
    WHO SEEM'D THE CREAM OF EQUANIMITY . . . . . . .         474  3 DON JUAN 15    41   3
CREATE
    SOCIETY ITSELF WHICH SHOULD CREATE . . . . . .           423  2 DON JUAN  5    25   5
    SHE HAD CONSENTED TO CREATE AGAIN . . . . . . .          434  3 DON JUAN 14    55   7
    NOT WITCHES ONLY BITCHES--WHO CREATE  . . . . . .        565  3 DON JUAN 17     7   4
CREATION
    UNTO THE NEW CREATION RISING OUT  . . . . . .            201  3 DON JUAN  9    38   2
    AND EVERY NEW CREATION HATH DECREASED . . . . . .        202  3 DON JUAN  9    39   6
    GLEAMS ONLY THROUGH THE DAWN OF ITS CREATION . . . .     316  3 DON JUAN 12     2   8
CREATIVE
    BE FOR MERE FANCY'S SPORT A THEME CREATIVE . . . . .     363  3 DON JUAN 13    10   6
CREATURE
    DEAR IS THE HELPLESS CREATURE WE DEFEND . . . . . .       90  2 DON JUAN  1   126   6
    THE CREATURE WAS HIS FATHER'S DOG THAT DIED . . . . .    193  2 DON JUAN  2    71   3
    A SOMETHING TO BE LOVED A CREATURE MEANT . . . . .       247  2 DON JUAN  2   172   5
    I SAW THE PRETTIEST CREATURE FRESH FROM MILAN . . . .    268  2 DON JUAN  2   209   7
    HOW LONELY EVERY FREEBORN CREATURE BROODS  . . . .       358  2 DON JUAN  4    28   5
    IN A NEW FACE THE UGLIEST CREATURE BREATHING . . . .      24  3 DON JUAN  6    37   8
    DUDU AS HAS BEEN SAID WAS A SWEET CREATURE . . . . .      32  3 DON JUAN  6    52   1
    PERVADED HIM--ALTHOUGH A GENEROUS CREATURE . . . .       138  3 DON JUAN  8    52   7
    AND WHEN AT LAST THE PRETTY CREATURE GETS  . . . .       333  3 DON JUAN 12    36   5
    FOR PREJUDICE IT WAS--AGAINST A CREATURE . . . . .       478  3 DON JUAN 15    52   2
CREATURES
    THE CHARMING CREATURES LIE WITH SUCH A GRACE . . . .     119  2 DON JUAN  1   178   7
    HAVE SUCH A CHARM FOR US POOR HUMAN CREATURES . . . .    267  2 DON JUAN  2   208   8
    YET SOME OF YOU ARE MOST SERAPHIC CREATURES-- . . . .    405  2 DON JUAN  4   111   1
```

160

		PAGE	VOL	CANTO	STANZA	LN
CREATURES	(CONTINUED)					
POOR CREATURES THEIR GOOD LOOKS WERE SADLY CHANGED	. .	414	2 DON JUAN	5	7	4
'TIS PLEASANT PURCHASING OUR FELLOW CREATURES	. . . .	425	2 DON JUAN	5	27	2
AFTER DISPOSING OF TWO FELLOW CREATURES	.	426	2 DON JUAN	5	30	V2
YOU NEVER THOUGHT ABOUT THOSE LITTLE CREATURES .	. .	462	2 DON JUAN	5	87	8
THOSE HOURIS LIKE ALL OTHER PRETTY CREATURES	. . . .	167	3 DON JUAN	8	111	7
WITH SOME OF THOSE FAIR CREATURES WHO HAVE PRIDED	. .	327	3 DON JUAN	12	25	6
THINK NOT FAIR CREATURES THAT I MEAN TO ABUSE YOU ALL--	.	329	3 DON JUAN	12	28	3
ALL MATCHLESS CREATURES AND YET BENT ON MATCHES	. . .	340	3 DON JUAN	12	53	8
CREDENTIAL						
TO PROPER PLACEMEN EVERY RUSS CREDENTIAL	.	285	3 DON JUAN	11	35	2
CREDIT						
OF GOOD ADVICE--AND TWO OR THREE OF CREDIT	. . . .	161	2 DON JUAN	2	9	8
TO SAVE THE CREDIT OF THEIR BREAKING BANK	. . . .	500	2 DON JUAN	5	154	6
AND RICH IN RUBLES DIAMONDS CASH AND CREDIT .	. . .	259	3 DON JUAN	10	70	2
NOT TO BE OVERLOOKED--AND GAVE SUCH CREDIT	. . . .	293	3 DON JUAN	11	49	7
WHICH MAKES BANK CREDIT LIKE A BARK OF VAPOUR	. . .	317	3 DON JUAN	12	4	8
IF BUT TO KEEP THY CREDIT AS A MOWER	.	433	3 DON JUAN	14	53	8
WILL PIQUE A GENTLEMAN FOR HIS OWN CREDIT	. . . .	491	3 DON JUAN	15	79	5
CREDITED						
THE THEME HALF CREDITED THE STRANGE TRADITION	. . .	527	3 DON JUAN	16	54	4
CREDITOR						
I'M FOR A HANDSOME ARTICLE HIS CREDITOR . .	. .	142	2 DON JUAN	1	210	3
SOLE CREDITOR WHOSE PROCESS DOTH INVOLVE IN'T	. . .	458	3 DON JUAN	15	7	7
CREDITORS						
OF ANY CREDITORS THE WORST A JEW IT IS	.	190	2 DON JUAN	2	65	5
OF PAYING DEBTS WHICH CREDITORS REGRET)	.	412	3 DON JUAN	14	4	6
CREDULOUS						
THE CREDULOUS HOPE OF MUTUAL MINDS IS O'ER	. . . .	144	2 DON JUAN	1	216	5
CREECH						
(SO TAKE IT IN THE VERY WORDS OF CREECH)	.	470	2 DON JUAN	5	101	4
CREED						
SO WAS HER CREED IN HER OWN INNOCENCE	.	78	2 DON JUAN	1	106	8
SOME CHRISTIANS HAVE A COMFORTABLE CREED	.	202	2 DON JUAN	2	86	8
AGAINST THE CREED AND MORALS OF THE LAND	.	346	2 DON JUAN	4	5	2
AND SUCH THEIR CREED WAS TILL THEY WERE INVADED	. . .	73	3 DON JUAN	7	13	4
FOR ANY SAGE'S CREED OR CALCULATION)--	.	225	3 DON JUAN	10	1	4
IN THE FAITH OF THEIR PROCREATIVE CREED	.	324	3 DON JUAN	12	18	3
WHICH LIKE A CREED NE'ER SAYS ALL IT INTENDS	. . .	407	3 DON JUAN	13	105	5
THAN TRUE HATH BEEN A CREED SO STRICTLY HELD)	. . .	420	3 DON JUAN	14	23	3
THOSE VEGETABLES OF THE CATHOLIC CREED	.	445	3 DON JUAN	14	81	7
AND THY PURE CREED MADE SANCTION OF ALL ILL .	. . .	464	3 DON JUAN	15	18	4
CREED'S						
TO KEEP ONE CREED'S A TASK GROWN QUITE HERCULEAN	. . .	20	2 DON JUAN	D	17	7
CREEDS						
AND THAT ODD IMPULSE WHICH IN WARS OR CREEDS	. . . .	132	3 DON JUAN	8	38	7
CREEK						
WITH HERE AND THERE A CREEK WHOSE ASPECT WORE	. . .	249	2 DON JUAN	2	177	4
UP IN A LITTLE CREEK BELOW A WALL	.	432	2 DON JUAN	5	40	7
CREEP						
'TIS SWEET TO LISTEN AS THE NIGHTWINDS CREEP	. . .	87	2 DON JUAN	1	122	6
THAT ALL THE REST CREEP IN AND FORM A JUNCTION	. . .	271	2 DON JUAN	2	215	4
JUAN AND SHUDDERING O'ER HIS FRAME WOULD CREEP .	. .	359	2 DON JUAN	4	29	5
CREEPER						
RETAINS THE SABLE STAINS OF THE DARK CREEPER	. . . .	232	3 DON JUAN	10	15	5
CREEPING						
TO FEEL THE POISON THROUGH HER SPIRIT CREEPING	. . .	274	2 DON JUAN	3	1	5
JUST AS OLD AGE IS CREEPING ON APACE	.	305	2 DON JUAN	3	59	5
FOR THE OLD NEGRO'S CONFIDENCE IN CREEPING	. . . .	436	2 DON JUAN	5	45	2
CREEPS						
TO SHOW WITH WHAT COMPLACENCY HE CREEPS	.	333	2 DON JUAN	3	98	3
CREPT						
AS IF SHE HAD JUST NOW FROM OUT THEM CREPT	. . . .	97	2 DON JUAN	1	140	6
(FOR SLEEP IS AWFUL) AND ON TIPTOE CREPT .	. . . .	232	2 DON JUAN	2	143	5
AND NOT A BREATH CREPT THROUGH THE ROSY AIR .	. . .	335	2 DON JUAN	3	102	7
AND THOUGH IT WAS NO OPIATE SLUMBER CREPT .	. . . .	512	3 DON JUAN	16	27	7
CRESCENT						
SURMOUNTED AS ITS CLASP--A GLOWING CRESCENT .	. . .	315	2 DON JUAN	3	77	7
AND THE MOSQUE CRESCENT STRUGGLED INTO SIGHT	. . . .	49	3 DON JUAN	6	86	4
CRESCENT'S						
ISMAIL'S NO MORE THE CRESCENT'S SILVER BOW .	. . .	172	3 DON JUAN	8	122	4
HAVE WANED INTO A CRESCENT'S CORUSCATION	.	293	3 DON JUAN	11	49	4
CRESCENTS						
GLITTERING LIKE CRESCENTS O'ER A TURK'S PAVILION	. . .	205	2 DON JUAN	2	92	5
CRESSYS						
HE BREATHED A THOUSAND CRESSYS AS HE SAW	.	261	3 DON JUAN	10	74	2
CREST						
THE COLOUR OF A BUDDING ROSE'S CREST	.	48	3 DON JUAN	6	85	4
AT LEAST AS RED AS THE FLAMINGO'S CREST	.	48	3 DON JUAN	6	85	V4
I DON'T KNOW WHETHER THEY HAD ARMS OR CREST . .	. .	76	3 DON JUAN	7	19	3
THE FAIR CZARINA'S AUTOCRATIC CREST	.	248	3 DON JUAN	10	49	6
AND SOME WHO HAD BUT TALENT FOR THEIR CREST .	. . .	370	3 DON JUAN	13	28	4
TIME SHEDS A MOMENT O'ER EACH SPARKLING CREST	. . . .	480	3 DON JUAN	15	55	6
CRESTS						
(NOT OF OLD VICTORS ALL WHOSE HEADS AND CRESTS	. . . .	321	3 DON JUAN	12	12	3
CRETANS						
TO MAKE THE CRETANS BLOODIER IN BATTLE	. . . .	238	2 DON JUAN	2	155	8
SO WERE THE CRETANS--FROM WHICH I INFER . . .	. .	238	2 DON JUAN	2	156	7
CREW						
KEPT STILL ALOOF THE CREW WHO ERE THEY SUNK . .	. .	174	2 DON JUAN	2	35	7

161

```
                                                                PAGE VOL        CANTO STANZA LN
CREW   (CONTINUED)
     AND IN THEM CROWDED SEVERAL OF THE CREW  . . .   . . .  . 185  2 DON JUAN  2    54   2
     AND FOR THE BOAT--THE CREW KEPT CROWDING IN IT .  . . .  . 186  2 DON JUAN  2    57   8
     SHE HAD A CURIOUS CREW AS WELL AS CARGO  . .   . . . .   . 191  2 DON JUAN  2    66   7
     AND THUS IT WAS WITH THIS OUR HAPLESS CREW  . .   . . .  . 192  2 DON JUAN  2    68   1
     THERE WERE TWO FATHERS IN THIS GHASTLY CREW .  . . . .   . 202  2 DON JUAN  2    87   1
     AMIDST THE SKELETONS OF THAT GAUNT CREW  . . .  . . . .  . 210  2 DON JUAN  2   102   4
     AND ARISTIPPUS A MATERIAL CREW . . . .    . . . .       . 267  2 DON JUAN  2   207   2
     'TWIXT HER AND JUAN INTERPOSED THE CREW  . . .   . . .   . 370  2 DON JUAN  4    48   3
     WAS INTERRUPTED BY THE PIRATE CREW . .  .   . . . .      . 393  2 DON JUAN  4    90   2
     MY BOY --SAID HE AMIDST THIS MOTLEY CREW .  . . . .      . 417  2 DON JUAN  5    13   1
     THEY FORMED A VERY NYMPH-LIKE LOOKING CREW  . .   . . .  . 469  2 DON JUAN  5    99   5
     BUT WHAT WAS STRANGEST IN THIS VIRGIN CREW  . .   . . .  .  24  3 DON JUAN  6    37   1
     HE PAUSED--AND SO WILL I AS DOTH A CREW  . . .   . . .   . 266  3 DON JUAN 10    84   1
     BETWEEN THE TYRANT'S AND THE TRIBUNES' CREW .  . . . .   . 306  3 DON JUAN 11    75   6
CREWS
     THE BOATS PUT OFF O'ERCROWDED WITH THEIR CREWS  . .   . . . 183  2 DON JUAN  2    51   6
     THE BOATS PULLED OFF WITH THEIR HALF NAKED CREWS  . .  ·. . 183  2 DON JUAN  2    51  V6
     AND OTHERS ROSE TO THE COMMAND OF CREWS  . . .   . . .   . 409  2 DON JUAN  4   116   4
CRIBB'D
     WOUNDED AND FETTER'D CABIN'D CRIBB'D CONFINED  .    . . . . 384  2 DON JUAN  4    75   1
CRICKETS
     I'M FOND OF FIRE AND CRICKETS AND ALL THAT  . .   . . .  .  94  2 DON JUAN  1   135   7
CRIED
     NOW JULIA FOUND AT LENGTH A VOICE AND CRIED . .   . . .  .  98  2 DON JUAN  1   142   1
     WAS NOT ASLEEP--YES SEARCH AND SEARCH SHE CRIED   . . .  . 100  2 DON JUAN  1   145   2
     ANTONIA CRIED OUT RAPE AND JULIA FIRE . . .  .   . . .   . 122  2 DON JUAN  1   184   2
     FAREWELL MY SPAIN A LONG FAREWELL HE CRIED  . .   . . .  . 166  2 DON JUAN  2    18   1
     GIVE US MORE GROG THEY CRIED FOR IT WILL BE .  . . . .   . 175  2 DON JUAN  2    36   1
     STOP CRIED PHILOSOPHY WITH AIR SO GRECIAN  . . .  . . .  . 268  2 DON JUAN  2   210   7
     STERN AS HER SIRE ON ME SHE CRIED LET DEATH .  . . . .   . 366  2 DON JUAN  4    42   4
     I CRIED UPON MY FIRST WIFE'S DYING DAY  . . .  .   . . . . 420  2 DON JUAN  5    19   7
     AND LOOKING COLDLY IN HER FACE HE CRIED  . . .   . . .   . 484  2 DON JUAN  5   126   6
     AND SAID THAT SHE WAS SORRY SHE HAD CRIED  . . .  . . .  .  45  3 DON JUAN  6    79   8
     SOFTER THAN THE SOFT SYBARITE'S WHO CRIED  . . .  . . .  .  50  3 DON JUAN  6    89   2
     BEGONE SHE CRIED WITH KINDLING EYES--AND DO .  . . . .   .  63  3 DON JUAN  6   116   2
     AND HERE HE CRIED IS FREEDOM'S CHOSEN STATION  .   . . . . 272  3 DON JUAN 11     9   5
     THE DYING MAN CRIED HOLD I'VE GOT MY GRUEL  . .   . . .  . 276  3 DON JUAN 11    16   2
     THE BOORS CRIED DANG IT WHO'D HAVE THOUGHT IT--SIRES . . . 425  3 DON JUAN 14    34   4
     BUT ADD THE WORDS CRIED HENRY WHICH YOU MADE  . .  . . .  . 517 3 DON JUAN 16    39   1
CRIES
     AND THEN THE MOTHER CRIES THE FATHER SWEARS  . . .   . . .  75 2 DON JUAN  1   100   7
     'TIS BUT MY CURIOSITY THAT CRIES  . . .  .   . . . .    . 268  2 DON JUAN  2   210  V6
     GO HEAR IT IN YOUR FAMISHED COUNTRY'S CRIES  . . .   . . . 187  3 DON JUAN  9     9   7
     WHERE IS THE WORLD CRIES YOUNG AT EIGHTY  WHERE  . .   . . 306  3 DON JUAN 11    76   1
     WAS MADE BY MRS ADAMS WHERE SHE CRIES  . . .  .   . . .  . 403  3 DON JUAN 13    96   7
CRIM
     TO SAY LEADS OFT TO CRIM CON WITH THE MARRIED--   . . .  . 493  3 DON JUAN 15    84   3
CRIME
     NOR TURN HIS VERY TALENT TO A CRIME  . . .  .    . . .   .  15  2 DON JUAN  D    10   6
     IF PEOPLE GO BEYOND 'TIS QUITE A CRIME  . . .  .   . . . .  65  2 DON JUAN  1    80   7
     OF HUMAN FRAILTY FOLLY ALSO CRIME . . .  .   . . . .     . 277  2 DON JUAN  3     5   2
     BUT HERE A SMALL DELAY FORMS A GREAT CRIME  . .   . . .  . 482  2 DON JUAN  5   123   5
     LITTLE WAS HEARD OF CRIMINAL OR CRIME . . .  .   . . .   . 496  2 DON JUAN  5   149   2
     AND IF ONE LADY'S SLIP COULD LEAVE A CRIME ON  .   . . . .  53  3 DON JUAN  6    94   6
     BUT NE'ER THE LESS I HOPE IT IS NO CRIME . .  .   . . .  .  67  3 DON JUAN  7     2   6
     RINGS O'ER THE DIALOGUE AND MANY A CRIME . .  .   . . .  . 141  3 DON JUAN  8    58   4
     CRIME CAME NOT NEAR HIM--SHE IS NOT THE CHILD  .   . . . . 143  3 DON JUAN  8    62   1
     ENGENDERED MONSTROUS SHAPES OF EVERY CRIME  . .   . . .  . 152  3 DON JUAN  8    82   8
     ARE PROSECUTED FOR THAT FALSE CRIME BIGAMY) .  . . . .   . 164  3 DON JUAN  8   105   3
     BUT AGGRAVATE THE CRIME YOU HAVE NOT PREVENTED  .  . . . . 353  3 DON JUAN 12    80   7
     A JEST AT VICE BY VIRTUE'S CALLED A CRIME  . . .  . . .  . 358  3 DON JUAN 13     1   3
     MOURNFUL--BUT MOURNFUL OF ANOTHER'S CRIME  . . .  . . .  . 476  3 DON JUAN 15    45   6
CRIMES
     IN GANGS OF FIFTY THIEVES COMMIT THEIR CRIMES  .   . . .  .  79 2 DON JUAN  1   108   5
     WHICH IN THE NORTH PREVENTS PRECOCIOUS CRIMES  .   . . .  . 501 2 DON JUAN  5   157   5
     AND ONE GOOD ACTION IN THE MIDST OF CRIMES  . .   . . .  . 156  3 DON JUAN  8    90   1
     ARE PURCHASED BY ALL AGONIES AND CRIMES  . . .   . . .   . 174  3 DON JUAN  8   125   2
     MEN'S WRONGS AND RATHER CHECK THAN PUNISH CRIMES  . .  . . 361  3 DON JUAN 13     8   6
     A KIND OF COMMON-PLACE EVEN IN THEIR CRIMES  . . .   . . . 417  3 DON JUAN 14    16   4
CRIMINAL
     LITTLE WAS HEARD OF CRIMINAL OR CRIME . . . .  .   . . . . 496  2 DON JUAN  5   149   2
CRIMSON
     CRIMSON AS CLEFT POMEGRANATES THEIR LONG TRESSES  . .  . . 292  2 DON JUAN  3    33   3
     ON CRIMSON SATIN BORDER'D WITH PALE BLUE . .  .   . . .  . 309  2 DON JUAN  3    67   2
     ALL GOLD AND CRIMSON SHONE HER JELICK'S FELLOW  .  . . .  . 311 2 DON JUAN  3    70   6
     A PAIR OF DRAWERS--OF FINE CRIMSON SATIN . .  .   . . .  . 456  2 DON JUAN  5    77  V2
     TO WOMEN THERE IS SCARCE A CRIMSON VARLET  . . .  . . .  . 108  3 DON JUAN  7    84   5
     HAD SCARRED HER BROW AND LEFT ITS CRIMSON TRACE  . .  . . 159  3 DON JUAN  8    95   5
     SUNK AND THE CRIMSON CROSS GLARED O'ER THE FIELD  . .  . . 172  3 DON JUAN  8   122   5
CRISIS
     JUST IN THE VERY CRISIS SHE SHOULD NOT  . . .   . . .   . 258  2 DON JUAN  2   193   8
     JUST AT THIS CRISIS UP CAME JOHNSON TOO . .  .   . . .   . 130  3 DON JUAN  8    35   1
CRISPED
     THROWN TOPSY-TURVY TWISTED CRISPED AND CURLED  . .   . . . 201  3 DON JUAN  9    37   4
CRISPER
     THE ELDER LADIES' WRINKLES CURLED MUCH CRISPER .   . . . . 221  3 DON JUAN  9    78   3
CRITIC
     I'LL PROVE THAT SUCH THE OPINION OF THE CRITIC IS . . . . 342  2 DON JUAN  3   111   7
     THE LAWYER AND THE CRITIC BUT BEHOLD  . . . .  .   . . . . 232  3 DON JUAN 10    14   1
```

```
                                                     PAGE VOL      CANTO STANZA LN
CRITICAL
    BUT MERELY AS A CRITICAL REGALE . . . . . . . . . . . 528  3 DON JUAN 16     57 V8
CRITICALLY
    AND CRITICALLY HELD AS DELETERIOUS . . . . . . . . . 358  3 DON JUAN 13      1   4
CRITICISE
    WE MAY PRESUME TO CRITICISE OR PRAISE . . . . . . . . 360  3 DON JUAN 13      4   4
CRITICISED
    AND TUMBLED BOOKS OR CRITICISED THE PICTURES . . . . . 406  3 DON JUAN 13    102   2
CRITICISM
    THIS IS TRUE CRITICISM AND YOU MAY KISS-- . . . . . . 140  2 DON JUAN  1    206   6
    (AS FAR AS RHYME AND CRITICISM COMBINE . . . . . . . 232  3 DON JUAN 10     16   3
CRITIC'S
    WHICH MIGHT DEFY A CROTCHET CRITIC'S RIGOUR . . . . . 427  3 DON JUAN 14     39   6
CRITICS
    SHOULD CAPTAINS THE REMARK OR CRITICS MAKE . . . . . 141  2 DON JUAN  1    208   7
    BEING PIQUED BY CRITICS WHO HAVE DONE ME WRONG . . . . 410  2 DON JUAN  4    117 V5
    TO CRITICS OR' TO HAIL THE SETTING SUN . . . . . . . 466  3 DON JUAN 15     22   6
CRITIQUE
    JOHN KEATS WHO WAS KILLED OFF BY ONE CRITIQUE . . . . 298  3 DON JUAN 11     60   1
CROCKERY
    A DIFFERENCE BETWEEN CROCKERY WARE AND PLATE . . . . 541  3 DON JUAN 16     84   6
CROCKERY-WARE
    IN SMALL-EYED CHINA'S CROCKERY-WARE METROPOLIS . . . . 271  3 DON JUAN 11      7   5
CROCODILES
    AND MAMMOTHS AND YOUR WINGED CROCODILES . . . . . . . 201  3 DON JUAN  9     38   8
CROMWELL'S
    LIKE CROMWELL'S PRANKS--BUT ALTHOUGH TRUTH EXACTS . . . 329  2 DON JUAN  3     92   5
CROP
    HAS GENERALLY NO GREAT CROP TO SPARE IT HE . . . . . .  14  2 DON JUAN  D      9   3
    CORRUPTION FOR ITS CROP) WITH THE POOR DEVILS . . . . 237  3 DON JUAN 10     25   6
    IF THAT THE WEEDS O'ERLIVE NOT THE FIRST CROP-- . . . 368  3 DON JUAN 13     22   7
CROSS
    THIS HEATHENISH CROSS RESTORED THE BREED AGAIN . . . .  53  2 DON JUAN  1     58   1
    BUT HEAVEN FORBID THAT SUCH A THOUGHT SHOULD CROSS . . .  67  2 DON JUAN  1     84   2
    AS O'ER THE CUTTER'S EDGE HE TRIED TO CROSS . . . . . 186  2 DON JUAN  2     57   4
    TO CROSS HER BROW SHE WONDERED HOW SO NEAR . . . . . 480  2 DON JUAN  5    119   7
    AT A PER-CENTAGE A CHILD CROSS DOG ILL . . . . . . .  16  3 DON JUAN  6     21   3
    WAS NOT LIKE JACOB'S) OR TO CROSS A DITCH . . . . . .  93  3 DON JUAN  7     52   8
    SUNK AND THE CRIMSON CROSS GLARED O'ER THE FIELD . . . 172  3 DON JUAN  8    122   5
    THE LINE OF LIGHTS TOO UP TO CHARING CROSS . . . . . 280  3 DON JUAN 11     26   1
    NOW) YOU MAY CROSS THE BLUE DEEP AND WHITE FOAM-- . . 290  3 DON JUAN 11     44   3
    AND ADDING STILL A LITTLE THROUGH EACH CROSS . . . . 317  3 DON JUAN 12      4   4
CROSS'D
    AS I WHO'VE CROSS'D IT OFT KNOW WELL ENOUGH . . . . . 162  2 DON JUAN  2     11   4
    AN OYSTER MAY BE CROSS'D IN LOVE--AND WHY . . . . . . 445  3 DON JUAN 14     81   1
CROSSED
    AND SOME SUCH VISIONS CROSSED HER MAJESTY . . . . . . 215  3 DON JUAN  9     66   3
    OF TWILIGHT AS THE PARTY CROSSED THE BRIDGE . . . . . 279  3 DON JUAN 11     23   8
CROSSES
    TO BEAR THESE CROSSES) FOR EACH WANING PRUDE . . . . 177  3 DON JUAN  8    131   6
CROSS-GRAIN'D
    SAD STRIFE AROSE FOR THEY WERE SO CROSS-GRAIN'D . . . 394  2 DON JUAN  4     93   5
CROSS-LEGG'D
    AND HERE ASSEMBLED CROSS-LEGG'D ROUND THEIR TRAYS . . 291  2 DON JUAN  3     31   1
CROSS-LEGGED
    IN THE MEANTIME CROSS-LEGGED WITH GREAT SANG FROID . . 172  3 DON JUAN  8    121   1
CROSS-QUESTIONED
    BUT JUAN WHEN CROSS-QUESTIONED ON THE VISION . . . . 527  3 DON JUAN 16     54   6
CROST
    AND DOLPHIN'S LEAP AND LITTLE BILLOW CROST . . . . . 251  2 DON JUAN  2    181   6
CROTCHET
    WHICH MIGHT DEFY A CROTCHET CRITIC'S RIGOUR . . . . . 427  3 DON JUAN 14     39   6
CROW
    THE EAGLE SOARS ALONE THE GULL AND CROW . . . . . . 358  2 DON JUAN  4     28   7
CROWD
    WITH THE PILED WOOD ROUND WHICH THE FAMILY CROWD . . .  94  2 DON JUAN  1    135   4
    A CROWD OF SHIVERING SLAVES OF EVERY NATION . . . . . 414  2 DON JUAN  5      7   1
    AND RAVEN RINGLETS GATHERED IN DARK CROWD . . . . . .  39  3 DON JUAN  6     66   2
    SELF-LOVE THERE'S SAFETY IN A CROWD OF COXCOMBS . . . 371  3 DON JUAN 13     30   8
    OBSERVANT OF THE FOIBLES OF THE CROWD . . . . . . . 462  3 DON JUAN 15     15   3
    BUT I MUST CROWD ALL INTO ONE GRAND MESS . . . . . . 483  3 DON JUAN 15     64   1
    CONFOUNDED HIM IN COMMON WITH THE CROWD . . . . . . 493  3 DON JUAN 15     83   2
CROWDED
    AND IN THEM CROWDED SEVERAL OF THE CREW . . . . . . 185  2 DON JUAN  2     54   2
    THEY COUNTED THIRTY CROWDED IN A SPACE . . . . . . . 189  2 DON JUAN  2     63   1
    AND ALL THE STARS THAT CROWDED THE BLUE SPACE . . . . 262  2 DON JUAN  2    198   7
    OVER A COCKED HAT IN A CROWDED ROOM . . . . . . . . 204  3 DON JUAN  9     43   4
    THAN OTHERS CROWDED IN THE FOREST'S MAZE-- . . . . . 562  3 DON JUAN 17      1   4
CROWDING
    AND FOR THE BOAT--THE CREW KEPT CROWDING IN IT . . . . 186  2 DON JUAN  2     57   8
    NEITHER CAME CROWDING LIKE THE WAVES OF OCEAN . . . .  42  3 DON JUAN  6     71   4
CROWDS
    IN DESERTS FORESTS CROWDS OR BY THE SHORE . . . . . 443  2 DON JUAN  5     57   2
    THROUGH CROWDS AND CARRIAGES BUT WAXING THINNER . . . 282  3 DON JUAN 11     29   2
    AT ONCE THE LIE AND THE ELITE OF CROWDS . . . . . . 396  3 DON JUAN 13     80   2
CROWN
    FAIR AS THE ROSE JUST PLUCKED TO CROWN THE WREATH . . . 235  2 DON JUAN  2    148 V5
    GOOD MORROW--FOR THE COCK HAD CROWN AND LIGHT . . . .  49  3 DON JUAN  6     86   2
    NOT FIGHTING FOR THEIR COUNTRY OR ITS CROWN . . . . .  75  3 DON JUAN  7     18   3
```

```
                                                           PAGE VOL      CANTO STANZA LN
CROWN   (CONTINUED)
    O'ER WHOM AN EMPRESS HER CROWN JEWELS SCATTERING  . . .  217  3 DON JUAN  9      70   V5
    A HUGE DUN CUPOLA LIKE A FOOLSCAP CROWN . . . . .  . . .  265  3 DON JUAN 10      82    7
CROWN'D
    MILD CATHERINE OWED THE CHANCE OF BEING CROWN'D   . . .  205  3 DON JUAN  9      46   V4
    CROWN'D BY HIGH WOODLANDS WHERE THE DRUID OAK . . . . .  384  3 DON JUAN 13      56    2
    BUT IN A HIGHER NICHE ALONE BUT CROWN'D . . . .  . . .  387  3 DON JUAN 13      61    1
CROWNED
    THAT SOON HIS HEAD WAS MOST COMPLETELY CROWNED . .  . .  457  2 DON JUAN  5      79    4
    NO LESS DESERVING TO BE HANGED THAN CROWNED . . . . . .  499  2 DON JUAN  5     153    8
    LIFE'S HALF-WAY HOUSE WHERE DAMES WITH VIRTUE CROWNED .   43  3 DON JUAN  6      75    5
    SINCE FIRST HER MAJESTY WAS SINGLY CROWNED . . . .  . .  205  3 DON JUAN  9      46    6
CROWNER'S
    AS SOON AS CROWNER'S QUEST ALLOWED PURSUED . . . . . .  277  3 DON JUAN 11      18    3
CROWNING
    FAIR AS THE CROWNING ROSE OF THE WHOLE WREATH . . . . .  235  2 DON JUAN  2     148    5
CROWNS
    FROM CROWNS TO KICKS ACCORDING TO THEIR VICES . . . . .  425  2 DON JUAN  5      27    8
    I HAVE SEEN CROWNS WORN INSTEAD OF A FOOL'S CAP-- . . .  310  3 DON JUAN 11      84    5
CROW-QUILL
    WITH A NEAT LITTLE CROW-QUILL SLIGHT AND NEW . . . . .  134  2 DON JUAN  1     198    2
CRUCIFIX
    AND FIRST A LITTLE CRUCIFIX HE KISS'D . . . . . . .  . .  197  2 DON JUAN  2      76    7
CRUEL
    YEARS COULD BUT BRING THEM CRUEL THINGS OR WRONG . . .  358  2 DON JUAN  4      27    4
    GOOD GOVERNMENT HAS LEFT THEM SEEMS BUT CRUEL . . . . .  256  3 DON JUAN 10      63    8
    THE CRUEL NAZARENES WHO HAD LAID LOW . . . . . . .  . .  262  3 DON JUAN 10      75    4
    THE QUAINT OLD CRUEL COXCOMB IN HIS GULLET . . . . . .  407  3 DON JUAN 13     106    7
CRUELTY
    HE HATED CRUELTY AS ALL MEN HATE . . . . . . .  . . . .  140  3 DON JUAN  8      55    6
CRUISED
    THE WILD SEAS AND WILD MEN WITH WHOM HE CRUISED . . . .  303  2 DON JUAN  3      54    6
CRUISERS
    DESPATCHING SINGLE CRUISERS HERE AND THERE . . . . . .  285  2 DON JUAN  3      19    2
CRUISING
    SINCE NOAH'S ARK WENT CRUISING HERE AND THERE . . . . .  191  2 DON JUAN  2      66    6
    WHILST HER PIRATICAL PAPA WAS CRUISING . . . . . .  . .  282  2 DON JUAN  3      13    8
CRUIZING
    WITH QUIET CRUIZING O'ER THE OCEAN WOMAN . . . . . . .  376  3 DON JUAN 13      40    2
CRUMBLED
    A MAST WAS ALMOST CRUMBLED TO A CRUTCH . . . . . .  . .  226  2 DON JUAN  2     132    6
CRUPPER
    WHICH SITS FOREVER UPON MEMORY'S CRUPPER . . . . . . .  304  3 DON JUAN 11      72    5
CRUSHING
    DEADLY AND QUICK AND CRUSHING YET AS REAL . . . . . . .  262  2 DON JUAN  2     199    7
CRUTCH
    A MAST WAS ALMOST CRUMBLED TO A CRUTCH . . . . . .  . .  226  2 DON JUAN  2     132    6
    YOU HAVE REPAIRED LEGITIMACY'S CRUTCH-- . . . . . .  . .  184  3 DON JUAN  9       3    3
CRY
    HAVE VOICES--TONGUES TO CRY ALOUD FOR ME . . . . . . .   19  2 DON JUAN  D      16    6
    THAT THEY WILL NOT CRY OUT BEFORE THEY'RE HURT . . . .  140  2 DON JUAN  1     207    3
    AND CRY THAT THEY THE MORAL CANNOT FIND . . . . . . . .  141  2 DON JUAN  1     208    5
    A SOLITARY SHRIEK THE BUBBLING CRY . . . . . . . .  . .  184  2 DON JUAN  2      53    7
    AND ALL WAS STILLNESS SAVE THE SEA-BIRD'S CRY . . . . .  251  2 DON JUAN  2     181    5
    A SINGLE CRY WOULD BRING THEM ALL ABROAD . . . . . . .  436  2 DON JUAN  5      45    5
    WAS TO SIT DOWN AGAIN AND CRY OF COURSE . . . . . . . .  491  2 DON JUAN  5     139    8
    SOUND AND THEN BY A CRY THE SULTAN'S COMING . . . . . .  494  2 DON JUAN  5     145    8
    NOR GIVE MY VOICE TO SLAVERY'S JACKALL CRY . . . . . .  195  3 DON JUAN  9      26    8
    THOUGH PRIESTS AND SLAVES MAY JOIN IN THE SERVILE CRY   195  3 DON JUAN  9      26   V8
    WHICH 'TIS THE COMMON CRY AND LIE TO VAUNT AS . . . .  311  3 DON JUAN 11      87    3
    AND SO THAT NO EXPLOSION CRY AROINT . . . . . . .  . .  396  3 DON JUAN 13      81    5
    OR SWISS ROUSSEAU CRY VOILA LA PERVENCHE . . . . .  . .  442  3 DON JUAN 14      75    8
CRYING
    OF EYES WERE CRYING FOR THEIR OWNER'S CASE . . . . . .  186  2 DON JUAN  2      56    6
    DISSOLVED LIKE SNOW BEFORE A WOMAN CRYING . . . . . . .  492  2 DON JUAN  5     141    8
    TO SIGH INSTEAD OF COUGHING--AND CRYING-- PISH . . . .  228  3 DON JUAN 10       6   V8
    A KERCHIEF CRYING GIVE SAL THAT--AND DIED . . . . . . .  276  3 DON JUAN 11      16    8
CRYSTAL
    PAST HIM IN CRYSTAL AND A JOY IN FLOWERS . . . . . . .  304  2 DON JUAN  3      56    7
    THESE WERE RANGED ROUND EACH IN ITS CRYSTAL EWER . . .  307  2 DON JUAN  3      63    1
    CRYSTAL AND MARBLE PLATE AND PORCELAIN . . . . . .  . .  310  2 DON JUAN  3      68    1
CUBLESS
    THE CUBLESS TIGRESS IN HER JUNGLE RAGING . . . . . . .  305  2 DON JUAN  3      58    1
CUBS
    FROM TIGRESSES AND CUBS TO DUCKS AND DUCKLINGS . . . .  488  2 DON JUAN  5     133    2
CUCKOLDS
    THEY ALL WERE HEROES CONQUERORS AND CUCKOLDS . . . . .  266  2 DON JUAN  2     206    8
CUD
    WHICH IS THE CUD ESCHEWED BY HUMAN CATTLE . . . . . . .  336  3 DON JUAN 12      43    8
CUE
    MY CUE FOR ANY TIME TO BE TERRIFIC . . . . . . . .  . .  156  3 DON JUAN  8      89    2
    I'LL NOT GAINSAY THEM IT IS NOT MY CUE . . . . . .  . .  359  3 DON JUAN 13       3    1
CUFFED
    HAD CUFFED EACH OTHER--ONLY FOR THEIR CUFFS . . . . . .  395  2 DON JUAN  4      93   V8
CUFFS
    IN NUMBER'D LOTS THEY ALL HAD CUFFS AND COLLARS . . .  283  2 DON JUAN  3      15    7
    HAD CUFFED EACH OTHER--ONLY FOR THEIR CUFFS . . . . . .  395  2 DON JUAN  4      93   V8
CULL
    PROFESSIONAL AND THERE IS NOUGHT TO CULL . . . . . . .  402  3 DON JUAN 13      95    4
```

	PAGE	VOL	CANTO	STANZA	LN

CULLIES
    SOME FOR HAVING TURNED CONVERTED CULLIES . . . . 314 3 DON JUAN 11 V 76 3
CULOTTE
    COMPLETELY SANS CULOTTE AND WITHOUT VEST . . . . 555 3 DON JUAN 16 111 3
CULPRIT
    THAT WHEN A CULPRIT CAME FOR CONDEMNATION . . . . . . 399 3 DON JUAN 13 88 7
    THE PRESENT CULPRIT WAS EXTREMELY PALE . . . . 532 3 DON JUAN 16 64 1
CULTIVATED
    WELL CULTIVATED IT WILL RENDER DOUBLE . . . . 351 3 DON JUAN 12 76 8
CULVIER
    MAN 'MIDST THY MOULDY MAMMOTHS GRAND CULVIER . . . . . 250 3 DON JUAN 10 52 4
CUMBERLAND
    VERNON THE BUTCHER CUMBERLAND WOLFE HAWKE . . . . . . 22 2 DON JUAN 1 2 1
    WAS BORN IN CUMBERLAND AMONG THE HILLS . . . . 76 3 DON JUAN 7 20 3
CUNCTIS
    DE REBUS CUNCTIS ET QUIBUSDAM ALIIS . . . . 502 3 DON JUAN 16 3 8
CUNNING
    SO FAR ABOVE THE CUNNING POWERS OF HELL . . . . . . 30 2 DON JUAN 1 17 3
    WAS NOTHING BUT A VALOUROUS KIND OF CUNNING . . . . . 130 3 DON JUAN 8 35 8
    BUT FULL OF CUNNING AS ULYSSES' WHISTLE . . . . . . 407 3 DON JUAN 13 105 6
    AND SMILING BUT IN SECRET--CUNNING ROGUE . . . . . . 426 3 DON JUAN 14 37 6
CUP
    PRESENTED THE O'ERFLOWING CUP AND SAID . . . . . . 297 2 DON JUAN 3 43 3
    FILL HIGH THE CUP WITH SAMIAN WINE . . . . 324 2 DON JUAN 3 L 9 2
    DASH DOWN YON CUP OF SAMIAN WINE . . . . . . 326 2 DON JUAN 3 L 16 6
    AND SCARCE TO THE MOGUL A CUP OF COFFEE . . . . . . 199 3 DON JUAN 9 33 6
    HIS GRACE HIS GOD-KNOWS-WHAT FOR CUPID'S CUP . . . . 216 3 DON JUAN 9 67 3
CUPBOARD
    A CERTAIN PRESS OR CUPBOARD NICHED IN YONDER . . . . . 450 2 DON JUAN 5 66 6
CUPID
    HER ZONE TO VENUS OR HIS BOW TO CUPID . . . . 51 2 DON JUAN 1 55 7
    IF SHE HAD NOT MISTAKEN HIM FOR CUPID . . . . 205 3 DON JUAN 9 45 8
    A FULL-GROWN CUPID VERY MUCH ADMIRED . . . . 428 3 DON JUAN 14 41 2
CUPIDITY
    OR SOME CONTRACTOR'S PERSONAL CUPIDITY . . . . . . 80 3 DON JUAN 7 27 3
CUPIDON
    TO INDICATE A CUPIDON BROKE LOOSE . . . . 461 3 DON JUAN 15 12 6
CUPID'S
    SELF-LOVE THAT WHETSTONE OF DAN CUPID'S DART . . . . 15 3 DON JUAN 6 19 V5
    TO EXACT OF CUPID'S BILLS THE FULL AMOUNT . . . . . 213 3 DON JUAN 9 62 7
    HIS GRACE HIS GOD-KNOWS-WHAT FOR CUPID'S CUP . . . . 216 3 DON JUAN 9 67 3
CUPOLA
    A LITTLE CUPOLA MORE NEAT THAN SOLEMN . . . . . . 400 2 DON JUAN 4 104 2
    SOPHIA'S CUPOLA WITH GOLDEN GLEAM . . . . 412 2 DON JUAN 5 3 4
    A HUGE DUN CUPOLA LIKE A FOOLSCAP CROWN . . . . . . 265 3 DON JUAN 10 82 7
CUPPED
    HAUSTUS (AND HERE THE SURGEON CAME AND CUPPED HIM) . . . 244 3 DON JUAN 10 41 4
CUPS
    IN SMALL FINE CHINA CUPS CAME IN AT LAST . . . . . . 307 2 DON JUAN 3 63 4
    GOLD CUPS OF FILIGREE MADE TO SECURE . . . . 307 2 DON JUAN 3 63 5
    HE DRANK SIX CUPS OF COFFEE AT THE LEAST . . . . . . 52 3 DON JUAN 6 92 4
CURATE
    A BRILLIANT DINER OUT THOUGH BUT A CURATE . . . . . 540 3 DON JUAN 16 82 2
CURB
    THE SILKEN FILLET'S CURB AND SOUGHT TO SHUN . . . . . 313 2 DON JUAN 3 73 6
    AND STILL PURSUES THE RIGHT--TO CURB THE BAD . . . . 363 3 DON JUAN 13 9 3
    AND WITH SUCH HURRY THAT ERE HE COULD CURB IT . . . . 543 3 DON JUAN 16 88 7
CURB'D
    STATES TO BE CURB'D AND THOUGHTS TO BE CONFINED . . . . 18 2 DON JUAN D 14 4
    FROM HEART TO CHEEK IS CURB'D INTO A BLUSH . . . . 231 2 DON JUAN 2 141 4
CURBED
    HIS CLOTHES WERE NOT CURBED TO THEIR USUAL CUT . . . . 513 3 DON JUAN 16 29 6
CURDLE
    AT TIMES WOULD CURDLE O'ER SOME HEAVY GROAN . . . . . 140 3 DON JUAN 8 55 8
    SPANGLED WITH GEMS--THE MONK MADE HIS BLOOD CURDLE . . 556 3 DON JUAN 16 113 8
CURE
    OF CHARMS TO MAKE GOOD GOLD AND CURE BAD AILS . . . . 293 2 DON JUAN 3 34 5
    THAT KILLING HIM IS NOT THE WAY TO CURE YOU . . . . . 63 3 DON JUAN 6 115 8
    THE REGIMENTAL SURGEON COULD NOT CURE . . . . . . 154 3 DON JUAN 8 85 5
    CURE THEM OF TOURS HUSSAR AND HIGHLAND DRESSES . . . . 267 3 DON JUAN 10 86 2
    A CURE FOR GRIEF--FOR WHAT CAN EVER RANKLE . . . . . 422 3 DON JUAN 14 27 7
    WHOSE VERDICT FOR SUCH SIN A CERTAIN CURE IS)-- . . . . 436 3 DON JUAN 14 60 8
CURED
    THE HOARSE HARSH WAVES KEPT TIME FRIGHT CURED THE QUALMS . 174 2 DON JUAN 2 34 5
    HE WOULD HAVE HOSPITABLY CURED THE STRANGER . . . . . 225 2 DON JUAN 2 130 7
CURES
    YOU'LL ADD TO MATRIMONY'S LIST OF CURES . . . . . 343 3 DON JUAN 12 60 8
    CONSTRUCTION ASYOUR CURES FOR HECTIC PHTHISICS . . . . 349 3 DON JUAN 12 72 3
    DOCTORS LESS FAMOUS FOR THEIR CURES THAN FEES . . . . 431 3 DON JUAN 14 48 4
CURING
    THEIR MANNERS MENDING AND THEIR MORALS CURING . . . . . 162 2 DON JUAN 2 10 V7
CURIOSITY
    I LOATHE THAT LOW VICE CURIOSITY . . . . . . 33 2 DON JUAN 1 23 5
    OR NEITHER--OUT OF CURIOSITY . . . . 268 2 DON JUAN 2 210 6
    'TIS BUT MY CURIOSITY THAT CRIES . . . . . . 268 2 DON JUAN 2 210 V6
    AND SHOWED BUT LITTLE ROYAL CURIOSITY . . . . . . 496 2 DON JUAN 5 148 4
CURIOUS
    SHE HAD A CURIOUS CREW AS WELL AS CARGO . . . . . . 191 2 DON JUAN 2 66 7
    THEY SHALL APPEAR BEFORE YOUR CURIOUS EYES . . . . . 222 2 DON JUAN 2 124 6

	PAGE	VOL	CANTO	STANZA	LN
CURIOUS (CONTINUED)					
THIS REVEL SEEM'D A CURIOUS MODE OF MOURNING	300	2 DON JUAN	3	49	8
JUAN WAS TOLD ABOUT THEIR CURIOUS CASE	388	2 DON JUAN	4	81	2
AND CONSCIENCE ASK A CURIOUS SORT OF QUESTION	426	2 DON JUAN	5	30	4
SAID BABA TO BE CURIOUS 'TWILL TRANSPIRE	454	2 DON JUAN	5	74	6
OF GILDED BRONZE AND CARVED IN CURIOUS GUISE	461	2 DON JUAN	5	86	2
NOW I SHOULD LIKE TO KNOW BEING RATHER CURIOUS	77	3 DON JUAN	7	21	V1
WHICH CURL IN CURIOUS WREATHS--HOW SOON THE SMOKE	110	3 DON JUAN	7	86	7
OF OUR SENSATIONS WHAT A CURIOUS WAY	220	3 DON JUAN	9	75	7
HAD SEEN THE WORLD--WHICH IS A CURIOUS SIGHT	292	3 DON JUAN	11	47	7
OF THIS SAME MYSTIC FRIAR'S CURIOUS DOINGS	527	3 DON JUAN	16	53	7
DRAPERIED HER FORM WITH CURIOUS FELICITY	550	3 DON JUAN	16	102	8
AND JUAN PUZZLED BUT STILL CURIOUS THRUST	560	3 DON JUAN	16	122	1
CURIOUSLY					
SOME FEMALE HEAD MOST CURIOUSLY PRESUMES	442	2 DON JUAN	5	55	6
CURL					
WHICH CURL IN CURIOUS WREATHS--HOW SOON THE SMOKE	110	3 DON JUAN	7	86	7
THERE BARBER'S BLOCKS WITH PERIWIGS IN CURL	278	3 DON JUAN	11	22	5
A STRAGGLING CURL SHOWED HE HAD BEEN FAIR-HAIRED	560	3 DON JUAN	16	121	5
CURL'D					
EACH SEA CURL'D O'ER THE STERN AND KEPT THEM WET	188	2 DON JUAN	2	60	5
HER LOCKS CURL'D NEGLIGENTLY ROUND HER FACE	220	2 DON JUAN	2	121	3
CURLED					
THROWN TOPSY-TURVY TWISTED CRISPED AND CURLED	201	3 DON JUAN	9	37	4
THE ELDER LADIES' WRINKLES CURLED MUCH CRISPER	221	3 DON JUAN	9	78	3
CURLING					
GOOD TEETH WITH CURLING RATHER DARK BROWN HAIR	416	2 DON JUAN	5	11	3
CURLS					
HER STREAMING HAIR THE BLACK CURLS STRIVE BUT FAIL	108	2 DON JUAN	1	158	5
HIS DEWY CURLS LONG DRENCH'D BY EVERY STORM	216	2 DON JUAN	2	114	6
AND HIS BLACK CURLS WERE DEWY WITH THE SPRAY	234	2 DON JUAN	2	147	6
DOWN HER WHITE NECK LONG FLOATING AUBURN CURLS--	291	2 DON JUAN	3	30	5
HIS CURLS FELL NEGLIGENTLY O'ER HIS FRONT	513	3 DON JUAN	16	29	5
CURLY					
AND SHE WOULD SOFTLY STIR HIS LOCKS SO CURLY	245	2 DON JUAN	2	168	5
OF WRATH AND RHYME WHEN JUVENILE AND CURLY	234	3 DON JUAN	10	19	2
CURLY-HEADED					
A LITTLE CURLY-HEADED GOOD-FOR-NOTHING	34	2 DON JUAN	1	25	1
CUROUS					
AND THUS THEY FORMED A RATHER CUROUS PAIR	252	3 DON JUAN	10	57	5
CURRAN					
WHERE GRATTAN CURRAN SHERIDAN ALL THOSE	307	3 DON JUAN	11	77	3
CURRENCY					
WHICH PASSES GHOSTS IN CURRENCY LIKE GOLD	510	3 DON JUAN	16	22	6
CURRENT					
WITH GOOD DISCRETION AND IN CURRENT RHYME	135	2 DON JUAN	1	200	V8
SET BY A CURRENT TOWARD IT THEY WERE LOST	209	2 DON JUAN	2	100	3
MEANTIME THE CURRENT WITH A RISING GALE	209	2 DON JUAN	2	101	1
HAD SOIL'D THE CURRENT OF HER SINLESS YEARS	274	2 DON JUAN	3	1	7
CURRENTS					
WHOSE CHARTS LAY DOWN ITS CURRENTS TO A HAIR	7	3 DON JUAN	6	2	4
IN CURRENTS THROUGH THE CALMER WATER SPREAD	385	3 DON JUAN	13	57	4
CURRIE					
LIKE BURNS (WHOM DOCTOR CURRIE WELL DESCRIBES)	329	3 DON JUAN	3	92	4
CURRY					
LEAVENING HIS BLOOD AS CAYENNE DOTH A CURRY	260	3 DON JUAN	10	72	2
CURSE					
THOU CANST NOT BE MY BLESSING OR MY CURSE	144	2 DON JUAN	1	215	4
NO SCANDALS MADE THE DAILY PRESS A CURSE--	496	2 DON JUAN	5	149	7
IN THE DAMNED LINE ('TIS WORTH AT LEAST A CURSE)	15	3 DON JUAN	6	18	V5
WITH ONE GOOD HEARTY CURSE I VENT MY GALL	17	3 DON JUAN	6	22	3
AS AFTER READING ATHANASIUS' CURSE	17	3 DON JUAN	6	23	2
BEHOLD THE WORLD AND CURSE YOUR VICTORIES	187	3 DON JUAN	9	9	8
CURSED					
SOME CURSED THE DAY ON WHICH THEY SAW THE SUN	180	2 DON JUAN	2	45	3
OR BY ONE'S EARLY VALET'S CURSED KNOCK	237	2 DON JUAN	2	152	5
PRICKING HER FINGERS WITH THOSE CURSED PINS	36	3 DON JUAN	6	61	7
(A CURSED SORT OF CARRIAGE WITHOUT SPRINGS	197	3 DON JUAN	9	30	2
LOVE--(THOUGH SHE HAD A CURSED TASTE FOR WAR	222	3 DON JUAN	9	80	5
CURSES					
WHEN THEY DISPUTE WITH SCEPTICS AND WITH CURSES	165	3 DON JUAN	8	108	7
SUCH IS THE SHORTEST WAY TO GENERAL CURSES	264	3 DON JUAN	10	79	4
CURST					
WAS EVER HEARD OF SUCH A CURST DISASTER	96	2 DON JUAN	1	137	3
OH JULIA--(THIS CURST VESSEL PITCHES SO)--	167	2 DON JUAN	2	20	6
OF EVERY KING THAT EVER CURST A NATION	194	3 DON JUAN	9	24	V8
CURTAINED					
FOUR-POSTED AND SILK CURTAINED WHICH ARE GIVEN	18	3 DON JUAN	6	25	3
CURTAINS					
ARRAS THEY PRICK'D AND CURTAINS WITH THEIR SWORDS	99	2 DON JUAN	1	143	7
CURTIS					
TELL THEM SIR WILLIAM CURTIS IS A BORE	267	3 DON JUAN	10	86	5
CURTSEY					
WITH THE THREE-THOUSANDTH CURTSEY THERE THE WALTZ	302	3 DON JUAN	11	68	2
CURTSEYING					
AND CURTSEYING OFF AS CURTSIES COUNTRY DAME	549	3 DON JUAN	16	101	4
CURTSIED					
SHE SNUFF'D THE CANDLE CURTSIED AND WITHDREW	116	2 DON JUAN	1	173	8
AND CURTSIED OFF THE STAGE--THEIR LORDS THE SAME	549	3 DON JUAN	16	101	V4

166

CURTSIES
    (CURTSIES ARE NEITHER USED BY TURKS NOR GREEKS) . . . . . 31 3 DON JUAN 6 50 4
    AND CURTSEYING OFF AS CURTSIES COUNTRY DAME . . . . . . 549 3 DON JUAN 16 101 4
CURTSY
    AND THEN SHE DROPS A BRIEF AND MODERN CURTSY . . . . . 300 3 DON JUAN 11 63 7
CUSHION
    FOR CASH AND CONQUEST AS IF FROM A CUSHION . . . . . . 99 3 DON JUAN 7 64 4
    BUT HIS JUST NOW WERE SPREAD AS IS A CUSHION . . . . . 235 3 DON JUAN 10 21 5
CUSHIONS
    THE VELVET CUSHIONS--(FOR A THRONE MORE MEET)-- . . . . 309 2 DON JUAN 3 67 5
CUSTOM
    'TWAS AN OLD CUSTOM OF THE GREEK AND ROMAN . . . . . . 205 2 DON JUAN 2 93 3
    (IT IS THE COUNTRY'S CUSTOM) BUT IN VAIN . . . . 314 2 DON JUAN 3 75 2
    REVERSING THE GOOD CUSTOM OF OLD DAYS . . . . 316 2 DON JUAN 3 79 2
    AS IS THE CUSTOM OF THOSE EASTERN CLIMES . . . . 463 2 DON JUAN 5 89 6
    FOR THROUGH THE SOUTH THE CUSTOM STILL COMMANDS . . . 472 2 DON JUAN 5 105 7
    HER STATE (IT IS THE CUSTOM OF HER NATION) . . . . . . 475 2 DON JUAN 5 111 6
    THAN IS THE CUSTOM OF THE GENTLE SEX . . . . 24 3 DON JUAN 6 37 6
CUSTOM-HOUSE
    HAVING NO CUSTOM-HOUSE NOR QUARANTINE . . . . 286 2 DON JUAN 3 20 2
    THY CUSTOM-HOUSE WITH ALL ITS DELICATE DUTIES . . . . 259 3 DON JUAN 10 69 3
CUSTOMS
    OF ALL THE CUSTOMS OF THIS POLISHED NATION . . . . . . 452 2 DON JUAN 5 70 8
    AN OUTLINE OF THE CUSTOMS OF THE EAST . . . . 35 3 DON JUAN 6 58 4
    EXACTED BY THE CUSTOMS OF THE EAST . . . . 52 3 DON JUAN 6 92 2
CUT
    NOW TELL ME DON'T YOU CUT A PRETTY FIGURE . . . . . . 103 2 DON JUAN 1 150 8
    BUT SAGE ANTONIA CUT HIM SHORT BEFORE . . . . 111 2 DON JUAN 1 163 2
    THE MOTTO CUT UPON A WHITE CORNELIAN . . . . 134 2 DON JUAN 1 198 7
    IMMEDIATELY THE MASTS WERE CUT AWAY . . . . 173 2 DON JUAN 2 32 1
    FOREMAST AND BOWSPRIT WERE CUT DOWN AND THEY . . . . . 173 2 DON JUAN 2 32 5
    THAT EVER SCUTTLED SHIP OR CUT A THROAT . . . . 296 2 DON JUAN 3 41 2
    SUCH NAMES AT PRESENT CUT A CONVICT FIGURE . . . . . . 330 2 DON JUAN 3 94 1
    'TIS BEING TOO EPIC AND I MUST CUT DOWN . . . . 342 2 DON JUAN 3 111 2
    CUT FROM ITS FOREST ROOT OF YEARS--THE RIVER . . . . . 349 2 DON JUAN 4 10 4
    HAD FALLEN WITH HIS RIGHT SHOULDER HALF CUT THROUGH . . 370 2 DON JUAN 4 48 8
    RECEIVED A CUT WHICH CLOVE HIS TURBAN THROUGH . . . . 370 2 DON JUAN 4 48 V8
    AND HE HIMSELF O'ERMASTER'D AND CUT DOWN . . . . 375 2 DON JUAN 4 58 2
    THE PARCAE THEN CUT SHORT THE FURTHER SPINNING . . . . 414 2 DON JUAN 5 6 3
    CUT OFF A THOUSAND HEADS BEFORE-- --NOW PRAY . . . . . 453 2 DON JUAN 5 72 1
    SHE WOULD HAVE CUT THE TREE OF KNOWLEDGE DOWN . . . . 476 2 DON JUAN 5 113 V7
    HER FIRST THOUGHT WAS TO CUT OFF JUAN'S HEAD . . . . . 491 2 DON JUAN 5 139 1
    HER SECOND TO CUT ONLY HIS--ACQUAINTANCE . . . . 491 2 DON JUAN 5 139 2
    SHE LOOKED (THIS SIMILE'S QUITE NEW) JUST CUT . . . . 27 3 DON JUAN 6 43 5
    WHOSE HEADS WERE HEROES WHICH CUT OFF IN VAIN . . . . 113 3 DON JUAN 8 2 7
    KNEW WHEN AND HOW TO CUT AND COME AGAIN . . . . 130 3 DON JUAN 8 35 6
    THEIR CHIEFS TO ORDER--WERE ALL CUT TO PIECES . . . . 149 3 DON JUAN 8 74 8
    COSSACQUES WERE ALL CUT OFF AS DAY WAS BREAKING . . . 150 3 DON JUAN 8 76 3
    WHICH WAS CUT OFF AND SCARCE EVEN THEN LET GO . . . . 154 3 DON JUAN 8 85 8
    BY GOD WE'LL BE TOO LATE FOR THE FIRST CUT . . . . . . 162 3 DON JUAN 8 101 8
    JUST NOW YOUR'S WERE CUT OUT IN DIFFERENT SECTIONS . . 215 3 DON JUAN 9 65 5
    AND MY INTERNAL SPIRIT CUT A CAPER . . . . 226 3 DON JUAN 10 3 4
    THE LAST EXPIRED IN CUT THROAT CASTLEREAGH . . . . . . 254 3 DON JUAN 10 59 V4
    HAD SUCH BEEN CUT IN PHAETON'S TIME THE GOD . . . . . 263 3 DON JUAN 10 78 5
    HE FROM THE WORLD HAD CUT OFF A GREAT MAN . . . . . . 277 3 DON JUAN 11 19 1
    THE CORN IS CUT THE MANOR FULL OF GAME . . . . 394 3 DON JUAN 13 75 3
    AS PHIDIAN FORMS CUT OUT OF MARBLE ATTIC . . . . 409 3 DON JUAN 13 110 3
    AND CUT THROUGH SUCH CANALS OF CONTRADICTION . . . . 495 3 DON JUAN 15 88 7
    HIS CLOTHES WERE NOT CURBED TO THEIR USUAL CUT . . . . 513 3 DON JUAN 16 29 6
    CUT THROUGH AND THROUGH (OH DAMNABLE INCISION) . . . . 536 3 DON JUAN 16 74 6
    AND NOT A JOKE HE CUT BUT EARNED ITS PRAISE . . . . . 540 3 DON JUAN 16 82 3
CUTLASS
    THE BLOWS UPON HIS CUTLASS AND THEN PUT . . . . 370 2 DON JUAN 4 49 3
CUTS
    FOR WAR CUTS UP NOT ONLY BRANCH BUT ROOT . . . . 86 3 DON JUAN 7 41 8
CUTTER
    WERE ALL THAT COULD BE THROWN INTO THE CUTTER . . . . 180 2 DON JUAN 2 46 8
    NINE IN THE CUTTER THIRTY IN THE BOAT . . . . 185 2 DON JUAN 2 54 7
    AND THE POOR LITTLE CUTTER QUICKLY SWAMP'D . . . . . . 188 2 DON JUAN 2 60 8
    THEY GRIEVED FOR THOSE WHO PERISH'D WITH THE CUTTER . . 188 2 DON JUAN 2 61 7
    COLUMBUS FOUND A NEW WORLD IN A CUTTER . . . . 468 3 DON JUAN 15 27 6
CUTTER'S
    AS O'ER THE CUTTER'S EDGE HE TRIED TO CROSS . . . . . 186 2 DON JUAN 2 57 4
CUT-THROATS
    YOU ARE THE BEST OF CUT-THROATS--DO NOT START . . . . 184 3 DON JUAN 9 4 1
CUTTING
    (SO CHILDREN CUTTING TEETH RECEIVE A CORAL) . . . . . 141 2 DON JUAN 1 209 4
    TO CUTTING SHORT THEIR HOPES OF HAVING ANY . . . . . . 487 2 DON JUAN 5 132 8
    THE CUTTING OFF HIS HEAD WAS NOT THE ART . . . . 492 2 DON JUAN 5 140 7
CUVIER
    SO CUVIER SAYS--AND THEN SHALL COME AGAIN . . . . . . 201 3 DON JUAN 9 38 1
CYBELE'S
    THE HOWLING HEBREWS OF CYBELE'S PRIEST-- . . . . 297 3 DON JUAN 11 58 8
CYCLADES
    (ONE OF THE WILD AND SMALLER CYCLADES) . . . . 223 2 DON JUAN 2 127 2
    MOURNS O'ER THE BEAUTY OF THE CYCLADES . . . . 383 2 DON JUAN 4 72 8
CYCLOPS
    AND TURN HIM LIKE THE CYCLOPS MAD WITH BLINDNESS . . . 304 2 DON JUAN 3 57 8
CYGNET
    SOFT AS THE CALLOW CYGNET IN ITS NEST . . . . 235 2 DON JUAN 2 148 6

```
                                                        PAGE VOL      CANTO STANZA LN
CYNIC
     WHICH IN A SAINT OR CYNIC EVER WAS . . . . . . .  . 319  3 DON JUAN 12      7    3
     AS DID THE CYNIC ON SOME LIKE OCCASION  . . . . . . 522  3 DON JUAN 16     43    4
CYNTHIA
     HIGH GROUND AS VIRGIN CYNTHIA SWAYS THE TIDES . .  . 322  3 DON JUAN 12     14    6
CYPRESS
     WITH CYPRESS BRANCHES HAST THOU WREATHED THY BOWERS  . . 275  2 DON JUAN  3      2    3
     THE CYPRESS GROVES OLYMPUS HIGH AND HOAR . . . .  . 412  2 DON JUAN  5      3    5
     (AS NIGHT DEW ON A CYPRESS GLITTERING TINGES . . . .  40  3 DON JUAN  6     67    7
CYPRESSES
     O'ERTOPPED WITH CYPRESSES DARK-GREEN AND TALL . . . . 432  2 DON JUAN  5     40    8
CYPRUS
     OF CANDIA CYPRUS RHODES OR OTHER ISLANDS . . . . . . 209  2 DON JUAN  2    100    8
CYRUS
     THIS WAS THE MODE OF CYRUS BEST OF KINGS-- . . . . . 501  3 DON JUAN 16      1    3
CYTHEREA'S
     MORE MUSE-LIKE--SAY LIKE CYTHEREA'S SHELL  . . . . . 339  3 DON JUAN 12     51    8
CZARINA'S
     THE FAIR CZARINA'S AUTOCRATIC CREST  . . . . . . . . 248  3 DON JUAN 10     49    6
D
     THE DUKE OF D-- THE SHOOTING SEASON SPENDS . . . . . 382  3 DON JUAN 13     52    5
DABBLE
     THERE'S NOTHING WOMEN LOVE TO DABBLE IN . . . . . . 470  3 DON JUAN 15     31    4
DABBLED
     WERE DABBLED WITH THE DEEP BLOOD WHICH RAN O'ER . . . 376  2 DON JUAN  4     59    2
DABBLING
     DABBLING ITS SLEEK YOUNG HANDS IN ERIN'S GORE . . . .  16  2 DON JUAN  D     12    2
DAGGER
     SLIPPERS OF SAFFRON DAGGER RICH AND HANDY  . . . . . 451  2 DON JUAN  5     68    7
     THE DAGGER CLOSE AT HAND WHICH MADE IT AWKWARD . . . . 492  2 DON JUAN  5    140    2
DAILY
     DAILY OR MONTHLY OR THREE MONTHLY I  . . . . . . . . 142  2 DON JUAN  1    211    4
     HIS DAILY TASK HAD KEPT HIS FANCY COOL  . . . . . . 158  2 DON JUAN  2      2    3
     PAID DAILY VISITS TO HER BOY AND TOOK . . . . . . . 248  2 DON JUAN  2    174    2
     THOUGHT DAILY SERVICE WAS HER ONLY MISSION . . . . . 252  2 DON JUAN  2    182    6
     NO SCANDALS MADE THE DAILY PRESS A CURSE-- . . . . . 496  2 DON JUAN  5    149    7
     'TIS THE VILE DAILY DROP ON DROP WHICH WEARS . . . .  16  3 DON JUAN  6     20    7
     HIS DAILY COUNCIL UPON WAYS AND MEANS . . . . . . .  54  3 DON JUAN  6     96    2
     WHICH MADE HIM DAILY BLESS HIS OWN NEUTRALITY . . .  64  3 DON JUAN  6    117    8
     THAT DAILY SHILLING WHICH MAKES WARRIORS TOUGH)-- . . 134  3 DON JUAN  8     42    6
     UPON THE NOTHINGS WHICH ARE DAILY SPENT . . . . . . 189  3 DON JUAN  9     13    5
     YE TWICE TEN HUNDRED THOUSAND DAILY SCRIBES . . . . 200  3 DON JUAN  9     35    2
     EMPLOYED FOR SINCE IT IS THEIR DAILY LABOUR . . . . 288  3 DON JUAN 11     41    2
     WHERE EVERY KIND OF MISCHIEF'S DAILY BREWING . . . . 326  3 DON JUAN 12     23    3
     INDEED WE SEE THE DAILY PROOF DISPLAYED . . . . . . 371  3 DON JUAN 13     29    4
     AS MANY COVERS DULY DAILY LAID . . . . . . . . . . 381  3 DON JUAN 13     49    6
     A DAILY PLAGUE WHICH IN THE AGGREGATE . . . . . . . 420  3 DON JUAN 14     24    1
     OH DEATH THOU DUNNEST OF ALL DUNS THOU DAILY . . . . 459  3 DON JUAN 15      8    1
     THE FOURTH WE HEAR AND SEE AND SAY TOO DAILY . . . . 465  3 DON JUAN 15     21    6
DAINTY
     A DAINTY DISH TO SET BEFORE THE KING . . . . . . .  10  2 DON JUAN  D      2    3
     ADMIRING THOSE (BY DAINTY DAMES ABHORRED) . . . . . 209  3 DON JUAN  9     54    3
     (NOT THE MOST DAINTY ARIEL) AND PERPLEXES . . . . . 269  3 DON JUAN 11      3    2
DALES
     WHO AFTER A LONG CHASE O'ER HILLS DALES BUSHES . . . 425  3 DON JUAN 14     35    6
DAM
     (HIS SIRE WAS OF CASTILE HIS DAM FROM ARRAGON) . . .  42  2 DON JUAN  1     38    4
DAMAGE
     TO DO NOT MUCH LESS DAMAGE THAN THE TABLE  . . . . . 309  2 DON JUAN  3     66    8
DAMAGED
     THEIR STOCK WAS DAMAGED BY THE WEATHER'S STRESS . . 180  2 DON JUAN  2     46    6
     TO FAINT AND DAMAGED BREAD WET THROUGH THE BAGS . . 189  2 DON JUAN  2     62    7
DAMAGES
     ARE WORSE THAN THE WORST DAMAGES MEN PAY . . . . . .  20  3 DON JUAN  6     29    6
     CALLS ILION'S THE FIRST DAMAGES ON RECORD  . . . . . 209  3 DON JUAN  9     53    8
     OR WHETHER HE WAS TAKEN IN FOR DAMAGES  . . . . . . 312  3 DON JUAN 11     89    7
     THEN THERE'S THE VULGAR TRICK OF THOSE DAMNED DAMAGES . 346  3 DON JUAN 12     65    4
DAMAS
     COUNT DAMAS DROVE THEM BACK INTO THE WATER . . . . .  82  3 DON JUAN  7     31    7
     THE PRINCE DELIGNE AND LANGERON AND DAMAS . . . . .  82  3 DON JUAN  7     32    7
DAMASK
     AND THICK WITH DAMASK FLOWERS OF SILK INLAID  . . . . 308  2 DON JUAN  3     64    3
DAMASQUE
     A GOLDEN SCABBARD ON A DAMASQUE SWORD . . . . . . . . 422  3 DON JUAN 14     27    5
DAME
     CHANGED FOR THE DAME GREW DISTANT THE YOUTH SHY . . .  60  2 DON JUAN  1     70    2
     OR AS A DAME REPENTS HER OF HER OATH . . . . . . . . 493  2 DON JUAN  5    142    7
     A DAME WHO KEPT UP DISCIPLINE AMONG  . . . . . . . .  21  3 DON JUAN  6     30    5
     THE DAME REPLIED BETWEEN YOUR DREAMS AND YOU . . . .  30  3 DON JUAN  6     48    7
     THE CHIEF DAME OF THE ODA UPON WHOM  . . . . . . . .  57  3 DON JUAN  6    103    1
     BENEATH HIS ART THE DAME PRESSED TO DISCLOSE THEM . . 208  3 DON JUAN  9     51    7
     SO WHEN HE SAW EACH ANCIENT DAME A SUITOR . . . . . 336  3 DON JUAN 12     42    5
     AND TO THE BEAUTIES OF A FOREIGN DAME . . . . . . . 349  3 DON JUAN 12     72    6
     WAS THERE CHASTE DAME WHO HAD NOT IN HER HEAD . . . 470  3 DON JUAN 15     32    4
     AND CURTSEYING OFF AS CURTSIES COUNTRY DAME . . . . 549  3 DON JUAN 16    101    4
     IS LIKE--A DUCKLING BY DAME PARTLETT REARED . . . . 564  3 DON JUAN 17      4    6
DAMES
     TRUE KNIGHTS CHASTE DAMES HUGE GIANTS KINGS DESPOTIC . 347  2 DON JUAN  4      6    6
     LIFE'S HALF-WAY HOUSE WHERE DAMES WITH VIRTUE CROWNED . 43  3 DON JUAN  6     75    5

                                 168
```

```
                                                                 PAGE VOL    CANTO STANZA LN
DAMES   (CONTINUED)
      ADMIRING THOSE (BY DAINTY DAMES ABHORRED)    . . . . .  . 209  3 DON JUAN  9     54   3
      OF GENTLE DAMES AMONG WHOSE RECREATIONS .  . . . . . . . 223  3 DON JUAN  9     82   6
      FAIR VIRGINS BLUSHED UPON HIM WEDDED DAMES .  . . . . .  293  3 DON JUAN 11     48   1
      'MIDST ROYAL DUKES AND DAMES CONDEMNED TO CLIMB  . . . . 302  3 DON JUAN 11     68   7
      NAY MARRIED DAMES WILL NOW AND THEN DISCOVER  . . . . .  331  3 DON JUAN 12     33   2
      THAN THE MORE GLOWING DAMES WHOSE LOT IS CAST  . . . . . 347  3 DON JUAN 12     69   3
      NOR USE THOSE PALISADES BY DAMES ERECTED . . . . . . . . 437  3 DON JUAN 14     61   7
      BUT LAISSEZ ALLER--KNIGHTS AND DAMES I SING . . . . . .  467  3 DON JUAN 15     25   1
      THE SUPPER TOO DISCUSSED THE DAMES ADMIRED  . . . . . .  504  3 DON JUAN 16      8   2
      OF KNIGHTS AND DAMES HEROIC AND CHASTE TOO  . . . . . .  508  3 DON JUAN 16     17   5
      BY NATURE AS IN HIGHER DAMES LESS HALE  . . . . .  . . . 532  3 DON JUAN 16     64   3
DAMM'D
      DAMM'D FROM ITS FOUNTAIN--THE CHILD FROM THE KNEE . . .  349  2 DON JUAN  4     10   5
DAMME'S
      THOUGH HARDLY HEARD THROUGH MULTIFARIOUS DAMME'S  . . .  279  3 DON JUAN 11     24   3
      AND YET THE BRITISH DAMME'S RATHER ATTIC . .  . . . . .  289  3 DON JUAN 11     43   1
      BUT DAMME'S QUITE ETHEREAL THOUGH TOO DARING  . . . . .  289  3 DON JUAN 11     43   7
DAMN
      THE ENGLISH ALWAYS USE TO GOVERN DAMN . . . . . . . . .   28  2 DON JUAN  1     14   8
      OR MADAM DIES--ALFONSO MUTTER'D DAMN HER . . . . . . .   111  2 DON JUAN  1    163   5
      BUT DAMN ME--IF I EVER SAW THE LIKE  . . . . . . . . .   159  2 DON JUAN  2      5  V8
      I'M A PHILOSOPHER GOD DAMN THEM ALL  . . . . . . . . .    17  3 DON JUAN  6     22  V1
      IS MORE THAN I KNOW AND SO DAMN THEM BOTH  . . . . . .    17  3 DON JUAN  6     22  V8
      'TIS STRANGE THAT HE SHOULD FURTHER DAMN HIS EYES  . .    88  3 DON JUAN  7     45   1
      NOR CARE A SINGLE DAMN ABOUT HIS CORPS . . . . . . .     127  3 DON JUAN  8     31  V8
      WITH DAMN YOUR EYES YOUR MONEY OR YOUR LIFE . . . . .    273  3 DON JUAN 11     10   8
      OF ENGLISH SAVE THEIR SHIBBOLETH GOD DAMN . . . . . .    274  3 DON JUAN 11     12   2
      GOD DAMN YOU LADS I'VE MISSED A HANDSOME BOOTY . . . .   276  3 DON JUAN 11     16  V3
      LIKE ADDISON'S FAINT PRAISE SO WONT TO DAMN . . . . .    552  3 DON JUAN 16    104   4
DAMNABLE
      CUT THROUGH AND THROUGH (OH DAMNABLE INCISION) . . . .   536  3 DON JUAN 16     74   6
DAMNABLY
      WERE DAMNABLY MISTAKEN FEW ARE SLOW . . . . . . . . .     87  3 DON JUAN  7     42   3
DAMNATION
      AND CANNOT TUNE THOSE DISCORDS OF DAMNATION . . . . .     74  3 DON JUAN  7     16  V1
DAMN'D
      ALTHOUGH ONE MUST BE DAMN'D FOR YOU NO DOUBT  . . . .     85  2 DON JUAN  1    119   2
      WHO TOLD HIM TO BE DAMN'D--IN HIS CONFUSION . . . . .    179  2 DON JUAN  2     44   8
      HAD RUN THE RISK OF BEING DAMN'D FOR EVER  . . . . . .   258  2 DON JUAN  2    193   4
      SO NOW ALL THINGS ARE DAMN'D ONE FEELS AT EASE  . . .     17  3 DON JUAN  6     23   1
DAMN'DEST
      WHICH BEING THE DAMN'DEST PART OF MATRIMONY . . . . .    217  3 DON JUAN  9     70   7
DAMNED
      WISHING THEM--NOT EXACTLY DAMNED BUT DEAD HE  . . . .     89  2 DON JUAN  1    125  V6
      A BOOK--A DAMNED BAD PICTURE AND WORSE BUST . . . . .    146  2 DON JUAN  1    218  V8
      THEIR POET--A DAMNED RASCAL--BUT NO LESS . . . . . .     318  2 DON JUAN  3     82  V1
      IN THE DAMNED LINE ('TIS WORTH AT LEAST A CURSE) . . .    15  3 DON JUAN  6     18  V5
      FOR THEY ARE DAMNED THAT ONCE ALL FAMOUS OATH  . . . .    88  3 DON JUAN  7     45   2
      AND WRINKLES (THE DAMNED DEMOCRATS) WON'T FLATTER . .    236  3 DON JUAN 10     24   8
      WOULD THIS DAMNED HEADACHE SUFFER ME TO BEAR IT  . . .   268  3 DON JUAN 11      1  V8
      THEN THERE'S THE VULGAR TRICK OF THOSE DAMNED DAMAGES .  346  3 DON JUAN 12     65   4
DAMNING
      NO DOUBT THIS PATIENCE WHEN THE WORLD IS DAMNING US . .   37  2 DON JUAN  1     30   1
DAMOCLES
      THE HOUSE OF COMMONS DAMOCLES OF WORDS  . . . . . . .    153  2 DON JUAN  1  V  4   1
D'AMOUR
      FOLLOW'D BY PETITS PUITS D'AMOUR--A DISH . . . . . . .   486  3 DON JUAN 15     68   2
DAMP
      HIS BERTH A LITTLE DAMP AND HIM AFRAID  . . . . . . .    169  2 DON JUAN  2     25   8
      HOW LONG IN HIS DAMP TRANCE YOUNG JUAN LAY  . . . . .    214  2 DON JUAN  2    111   1
      WHICH WEIGH'D UPON THEM YET ALL DAMP AND SALT  . . . .   234  2 DON JUAN  2    147   7
      OR LIKE A WISP ALONG THE MARSH SO DAMP  . . . . . . .     89  3 DON JUAN  7     46   5
DAMP'D
      SO THAT THEMSELVES AS WELL AS HOPES WERE DAMP'D  . . .   188  2 DON JUAN  2     60   7
      ALTHOUGH A SQUALL OR TWO HAD DAMP'D HIS RAPTURES . . .   283  2 DON JUAN  3     15   4
DAMSEL
      BUT WITH OUR DAMSEL THIS WAS NOT THE CASE  . . . . . .   220  2 DON JUAN  2    121   1
      WAS WHAT HER DRESS BESPOKE A DAMSEL FAIR . . . . . . .    24  3 DON JUAN  6     36   2
      TO AID THE DAMSEL AND DESTROY THE CAITIFF  . . . . . .   363  3 DON JUAN 13     10   2
      NO DAMSEL BUT A DISH AS HATH BEEN SAID  . . . . . . .    488  3 DON JUAN 15     74   6
DAMSEL'S
      LOLAH DEMANDED THE NEW DAMSEL'S NAME--  . . . . . . .     28  3 DON JUAN  6     44   1
DAMSELS
      BABA WHEN ALL THE DAMSELS WERE WITHDRAWN . . . . . . .   470  2 DON JUAN  5    102   1
      FIRST CAME HER DAMSELS A DECOROUS FILE  . . . . . . .    495  2 DON JUAN  5    146   1
      JUAN AMONGST THE DAMSELS IN DISGUISE . . . . . . . . .   500  2 DON JUAN  5    155   3
      WITH ALL THE DAMSELS IN THEIR LONG ARRAY . . . . . . .    19  3 DON JUAN  6     26   2
      THE DAMSELS WHO HAD THOUGHTS OF SOME GREAT HARM  . . .    45  3 DON JUAN  6     79   1
      BUT SIX OLD DAMSELS EACH OF SEVENTY YEARS  . . . . . .   177  3 DON JUAN  8    130   7
      DAMSELS AND DANCES REVELS READY MONEY . . . . . . . .    235  3 DON JUAN 10     21   7
      DAMSELS GREAT WEALTH AND ILLUSTRIOUS ORDERS . . . . .    235  3 DON JUAN 10     21  V7
      DAMSELS AND RUBLES AND CHIVALRIC ORDERS  . . . . . . .   235  3 DON JUAN 10     21  V7
DAN
      SELF-LOVE THAT WHETSTONE OF DAN CUPID'S DART . . . . .    15  3 DON JUAN  6     19  V5
      DAN PHOEBUS TAKES ME FOR AN AUCTIONEER  . . . . . . .    393  3 DON JUAN 13     74   4
DANCE
      PERCEIVED IT WAS THE PYRRHIC DANCE SO MARTIAL  . . . .   290  2 DON JUAN  3     29   7
      SONG DANCE WINE MUSIC STORIES FROM THE PERSIAN . . . .   293  2 DON JUAN  3     35   3
```

		PAGE	VOL		CANTO	STANZA	LN

DANCE   (CONTINUED)

YOU HAVE THE PYRRHIC DANCE AS YET	324	2 DON JUAN	3	L 10	1
OUR VIRGINS DANCE BENEATH THE SHADE--	326	2 DON JUAN	3	L 15	2
WHICH MIGHT GO FAR BUT SHE DON'T DANCE WITH VIGOUR	390	2 DON JUAN	4	85	7
WHOSE SMILE MAKES ALL THE PLANETS DANCE WITH MIRTH	494	2 DON JUAN	5	144	4
BEGAN TO SING DANCE CHATTER SMILE AND PLAY	23	3 DON JUAN	6	34	8
THE ONLY DANCE WHICH TEACHES GIRLS TO THINK	302	3 DON JUAN	11	68	3
OR IF HE DANCE NOT BUT HATH HIGHER VIEWS	304	3 DON JUAN	11	71	1
SUNG OR REHEARSED THE LAST DANCE FROM ABROAD	406	3 DON JUAN	13	104	4
SOMETIMES A DANCE (THOUGH RARELY ON FIELD DAYS	408	3 DON JUAN	13	108	1
MAY RETROGRADE A LITTLE IN THE DANCE	473	3 DON JUAN	15	39	6
LIKE HOLBEIN'S DANCE OF DEATH--BUT 'TIS THE SAME)--	473	3 DON JUAN	15	39	8
THE SONG WAS SILENT AND THE DANCE EXPIRED	504	3 DON JUAN	16	8	4
WHICH SHE WENT THROUGH AS THOUGH IT WERE A DANCE	546	3 DON JUAN	16	96	4

DANCED

BEFORE THE BRIDAL HOURS HAVE DANCED THEIR MEASURE	168	3 DON JUAN	8	113	3
AND PARTS AND HEARTS HE DANCED AND SUNG AND HAD	292	3 DON JUAN	11	47	2
HERE DANCED ALBANO'S BOYS AND HERE THE SEA SHONE	392	3 DON JUAN	13	71	5
AND THEN HE DANCED--ALL FOREIGNERS EXCEL	427	3 DON JUAN	14	38	1
OF PANTOMIME--HE DANCED I SAY RIGHT WELL	427	3 DON JUAN	14	38	3
HE DANCED WITHOUT THEATRICAL PRETENCE	427	3 DON JUAN	14	38	6

DANCER

AND THEN THERE'S THE GROTESCA--SUCH A DANCER	390	2 DON JUAN	4	84	7
OURSELVES A SINGER DANCER MUCH IN FASHION	216	3 DON JUAN	9	68	4
HIS STEADY APPLICATION AS A DANCER	294	3 DON JUAN	11	51	6

DANCERS

| AND THEN THERE ARE THE DANCERS THERE'S THE NINI | 390 | 2 DON JUAN | 4 | 84 | 1 |
| BUT SPEAKERS BARDS DIPLOMATISTS AND DANCERS | 547 | 3 DON JUAN | 16 | 98 | 3 |

DANCES

DAMSELS AND DANCES REVELS READY MONEY	235	3 DON JUAN	10	21	7
SO BRILLIANT WHERE THE LIST OF ROUTS AND DANCES IS--	308	3 DON JUAN	11	80	3
REDUCED TO PRACTICE AND PERFORM'D LIKE DANCES	444	3 DON JUAN	14	79	8

DANCING

SEEING A TROOP OF HIS DOMESTICS DANCING	290	2 DON JUAN	3	29	5
LINK'D HAND IN HAND AND DANCING EACH TOO HAVING	291	2 DON JUAN	3	30	4
HENCE ALL THIS RICE MEAT DANCING WINE AND FIDDLING	295	2 DON JUAN	3	39	1
DWARFS DANCING GIRLS BLACK EUNUCHS AND A POET	316	2 DON JUAN	3	78	2
THE DWARFS AND DANCING GIRLS HAD ALL RETIRED	334	2 DON JUAN	3	101	2
DANCING ALL FREE AND HAPPY IN THE SUN)	393	2 DON JUAN	4	90	7
HE FLITTED TO AND FRO A DANCING LIGHT	89	3 DON JUAN	7	46	7

DANDIES

| AND DANDIES ALL ARE GONE ON THE WIND'S WINGS | 306 | 3 DON JUAN | 11 | 76 | 8 |
| WITH DANDIES DINED HEARD SENATORS DECLAIMING | 418 | 3 DON JUAN | 14 | 18 | 3 |

DANDIEST

| HAVE SUNG OR EVEN A DANDY'S DANDIEST CHATTER | 493 | 2 DON JUAN | 5 | 143 | 4 |

DANDY

IN SHORT ALL THINGS WHICH FORM A TURKISH DANDY	451	2 DON JUAN	5	68	8
EACH OUT-AT-ELBOW PEER OR DESPERATE DANDY	331	3 DON JUAN	12	32	2
WHICH MAKES A DANDY WHILE IT SPOILS A MAN	461	3 DON JUAN	15	12	8

DANDY'S

| HAVE SUNG OR EVEN A DANDY'S DANDIEST CHATTER | 493 | 2 DON JUAN | 5 | 143 | 4 |

DANG

| THE BOORS CRIED DANG IT WHO'D HAVE THOUGHT IT--SIRES | 425 | 3 DON JUAN | 14 | 34 | 4 |

DANGER

BETWEEN YOUNG PERSONS WITHOUT ANY DANGER	65	2 DON JUAN	1	80	2
AND HALF FORGOT THEIR DANGER AND DESPAIR	114	2 DON JUAN	1	170	4
THE PEOPLE'S SYCOPHANT--TILL DANGER COMES	151	2 DON JUAN	1	V 2	V7
THE GREATEST DANGER HERE WAS FROM A SHARK	212	2 DON JUAN	2	106	5
AND SOLD HIM INSTANTLY WHEN OUT OF DANGER	225	2 DON JUAN	2	130	8
THAT WITHOUT ANY DANGER OF A RIOT HE	318	2 DON JUAN	3	83	5
IN SOME SHAPE LET NONE THINK TO FLY THE DANGER	383	2 DON JUAN	4	73	7
DANGER AND SPOIL WITH ARDOUR MUCH ENCREASED	90	3 DON JUAN	7	49	6
FROM IGNORANCE OF DANGER WHICH INDUES	131	3 DON JUAN	8	36	4
AND WHAT A WHIRLPOOL FULL OF DEPTH AND DANGER	214	3 DON JUAN	9	64	3
BEFORE HE CAN ESCAPE FROM SO MUCH DANGER	305	3 DON JUAN	11	74	4
'TIS ALSO SUBJECT TO THE DOUBLE DANGER	424	3 DON JUAN	14	32	2
IN HIM BECAUSE SHE THOUGHT HE WAS IN DANGER--	449	3 DON JUAN	14	91	7

DANGEROUS

SUMMER'S INDEED A VERY DANGEROUS SEASON	76	2 DON JUAN	1	102	2
A FEELING DANGEROUS TO A PRUDENT SPOUSE	81	2 DON JUAN	1	111	8
THERE IS A DANGEROUS SILENCE IN THAT HOUR	82	2 DON JUAN	1	114	1
AND PURGATIVES ARE DANGEROUS TO HIS REIGN	168	2 DON JUAN	2	23	5
LIKE BRUTES--AND THUS HIS DANGEROUS POST KEPT HE	175	2 DON JUAN	2	36	5
BUT ALWAYS DANGEROUS WHEN THE HIGH WINDS TORE	249	2 DON JUAN	2	177	V6
'TIS DANGEROUS TO READ OF LOVES UNLAWFUL	282	2 DON JUAN	3	12	8
THE DANGEROUS LIFE IN WHICH HE HAD GROWN OLD	303	2 DON JUAN	3	54	3
TURNS UP MORE DANGEROUS BREAKERS THAN THE EUXINE	413	2 DON JUAN	5	5	8
SEDUCED BY YOUTH AND DANGEROUS EXAMPLES	236	3 DON JUAN	10	23	2
INTENSE INTENTIONS ARE A DANGEROUS MATTER	448	3 DON JUAN	14	88	4
TO FIX THE DUE BOUNDS OF THIS DANGEROUS QUALITY	448	3 DON JUAN	14	89	8
THAT IN OUR YOUTH AS DANGEROUS A PASSION	454	3 DON JUAN	14	100	2
WAS DANGEROUS--I THINK SHE IS AS HARMLESS	498	3 DON JUAN	15	94	7

DANGERS

| HAD EER ESCAPED MORE DANGERS ON THE DEEP | 229 | 2 DON JUAN | 2 | 137 | V7 |

DANGLED

| TO ITS OWN BOUGH AND DANGLED YET IN SIGHT | 44 | 3 DON JUAN | 6 | 76 | 7 |

DANIEL

AND DANIEL TAMED THE LIONS IN THEIR DEN	445	2 DON JUAN	5	60	5
WHAT DANIEL READ WAS SHORT-HAND OF THE LORD'S	179	3 DON JUAN	8	134	5
AS BOLD AS DANIEL IN THE LION'S DEN	217	3 DON JUAN	9	69	4

```
                                                       PAGE VOL    CANTO  STANZA LN
DANISH
    HIS BELL-MOUTHED GOBLET MAKES ME FEEL QUITE DANISH   . . . 392  3 DON JUAN 13   72    7
DANK
    THE STARS PEEP THROUGH THE VAPOURS DIM AND DANK   . . . . 110  3 DON JUAN  7   86    6
DANTE
    WITHOUT BEING MUCH MORE HORRIBLE THAN DANTE . . . . . . 200  2 DON JUAN  2   83    8
    DANTE AND MILTON AND OF BOTH THE AFFECTION  . . . . . . 281  2 DON JUAN  3   10    3
    SOME PERSONS SAY THAT DANTE MEANT THEOLOGY  . . . . . . 281  2 DON JUAN  3   11    1
    THOSE SUFFERINGS DANTE SAW IN HELL ALONE .  . . . . . . 401  2 DON JUAN  4  105    8
    A WOOD OBSCURE LIKE THAT WHERE DANTE FOUND  . . . . . .  43  3 DON JUAN  6   75    3
DANTE'S
    BUT DANTE'S BEATRICE AND MILTON'S EVE . . . . . . . . 281  2 DON JUAN  3   10    7
    I THINK THAT DANTE'S MORE ABSTRUSE ECSTATICS  . . . . . 281  2 DON JUAN  3   11    7
    I PASS EACH DAY WHERE DANTE'S BONES ARE LAID  . . . . . 400  2 DON JUAN  4  104    1
    I SAY NO MORE THAN HAS BEEN SAID IN DANTE'S . . . . . .  67  3 DON JUAN  7    3    7
    BUT GETTING NIGH GRIM DANTE'S OBSCURE WOOD  . . . . . . 238  3 DON JUAN 10   27    3
    DREADFUL AS DANTE'S RHIMA OR THIS STANZA .  . . . . . . 557  3 DON JUAN 16  116    4
DANTON
    PETION CLOOTZ DANTON MARAT LAFAYETTE  . . . . . . . .  22  2 DON JUAN  1    3    2
DANUBE
    OF DANUBE--WITH SOME STRENGTH BUT LITTLE TASTE  . . . .  71  3 DON JUAN  7    9   V3
    BUT AS THE DANUBE COULD NOT WELL BE WADED  . . . . . .  73  3 DON JUAN  7   13    6
DANUBE'S
    UPON THE DANUBE'S LEFT BRANCH AND LEFT BANK . . . . . .  70  3 DON JUAN  7    9    2
    OF DANUBE'S BANK TOOK FORMIDABLE CHARGE .  . . . . . .  72  3 DON JUAN  7   12    5
    AND FOURSCORE CANNON ON THE DANUBE'S BORDER . . . . . .  85  3 DON JUAN  7   38    7
    AND IN THE DANUBE'S WATERS SHONE THE SAME-- . . . . . . 115  3 DON JUAN  8    6    4
    THE BLOOD MAY GUSH OUT AS THE DANUBE'S FLOW  . . . . . 155  3 DON JUAN  8   87    3
    FAR FLASHED HER BURNING TOWERS O'ER DANUBE'S STREAM  . . 175  3 DON JUAN  8  127    3
DAPHNE
    OH LADY DAPHNE LET ME MEASURE YOU . . . . . . . . . 406  2 DON JUAN  4  112    8
DAPPLED
    THE DAPPLED FORESTERS--AS DAY AWOKE   . . . . . . . . 384  3 DON JUAN 13   56    6
D'APPUI
    BUT TILL THAT POINT D'APPUI IS FOUND ALAS  . . . . . . 446  3 DON JUAN 14   84    7
DARDAN
    THOUGH ON THE WHOLE NO DOUBT THE DARDAN BOY . . . . . . 441  3 DON JUAN 14   72    6
DARDANELLES
    THEY HEARD NEXT DAY--THAT IN THE DARDANELLES   . . . . 393  2 DON JUAN  4   91    1
DARE
    THAT EVEN ITS GROSSEST FLATTERERS DARE NOT PRAISE  . . .  17  2 DON JUAN  D   13    3
    AND WILL NOT DARE TO TRUST ITSELF WITH TRUTH  . . . . .  61  2 DON JUAN  1   72    7
    DARE YOU SUSPECT ME WHOM THE THOUGHT WOULD KILL  . . . .  98  2 DON JUAN  1  142    7
    HOW DARE YOU THINK YOUR LADY WOULD GO ON SO . . . . . . 101  2 DON JUAN  1  146    8
    AND DARE NOT SET MY SEAL UPON THIS SHEET .  . . . . . . 134  2 DON JUAN  1  197    2
    AVE MARIA MAY OUR SPIRITS DARE . . . . . . . . . . 336  2 DON JUAN  3  103    3
    HE SHALL IF THE DARE HERE JUAN BOWED . . . . . . . .  99  3 DON JUAN  7   63    1
    GLORY LIKE YOURS SHOULD ANY DARE GAINSAY .  . . . . . . 183  3 DON JUAN  9    1    7
    WHO LIVE BY LIES YET DARE NOT BOLDLY LIE  .  . . . . . 285  3 DON JUAN 11   36    5
    I TELL THE TALE AS IT IS TOLD NOR DARE  . . . . . . . 365  3 DON JUAN 13   13    1
    PERHAPS OF ALL MOST DESPERATE WHICH WILL DARE . . . . . 412  3 DON JUAN 14    5    3
    FEW MEN DARE SHOW THEIR THOUGHTS OF WORST OR BEST  . . . 457  3 DON JUAN 15    3    5
    AS IF TO ASK HOW YOU CAN DARE TO KEEP  . . . . . . . 508  3 DON JUAN 16   18    7
    WHEN ANY DARE A NEW LIGHT TO PRESENT  . . . . . . . . 564  3 DON JUAN 17    5    3
DARED
    THEY DARED NOT TAKE IT IN FOR ALL THE BREEZE   . . . . 188  2 DON JUAN  2   60    4
    OF ONE WHO DARED TO ASK IF HE HAD LOVED  .  . . . . . 481  2 DON JUAN  5  121    4
    THIS PASSION MIGHT BLOW O'ER NOR DARED TO BALK  . . . .  61  3 DON JUAN  6  110    3
    WAS MADE AT LENGTH WITH THOSE WHO DARED TO CLIMB  . . . 151  3 DON JUAN  8   79    4
DARING
    YOUNG BEAUTIFUL AND DARING--WHO WOULD RISK  . . . . . .   7  3 DON JUAN  6    3    2
    BUT DAMME'S QUITE ETHEREAL THOUGH TOO DARING   . . . . 289  3 DON JUAN 11   43    7
    THE SHADE OF BONAPARTE'S NOBLE DARING--  .  . . . . . 318  3 DON JUAN 12    5    7
    WITH THOSE WHO POPE SAYS GREATLY DARING DINE  . . . . . 383  3 DON JUAN 13   53    6
    FOR GOTHIC DARING SHOWN IN ENGLISH MONEY .  . . . . . . 529  3 DON JUAN 16   59    8
DARK
    WAS LARGE AND DARK SUPPRESSING HALF ITS FIRE   . . . .  54  2 DON JUAN  1   60    2
    'TWAS MIDNIGHT--DARK AND SOMBRE WAS THE NIGHT  . . . .  94  2 DON JUAN  1  135   V1
    SHE LAY HER DARK EYES FLASHING THROUGH THEIR TEARS  . . 108  2 DON JUAN  1  158    2
    OF HER DISHEVELLED TRESSES DARK APPEARS  .  . . . . . 108  2 DON JUAN  1  158   V4
    BUT WHY--WE LEAVE THE READER IN THE DARK--  . . . . . 161  2 DON JUAN  2    8    4
    THE SCATTERING CLOUDS SHONE SPANNING THE DARK SEA  . . . 204  2 DON JUAN  2   91    2
    WITH THE QUICK WAVE AND GAIN ERE IT WAS DARK  . . . . . 212  2 DON JUAN  2  106    3
    AND SAW EACH OTHER'S DARK EYES DARTING LIGHT  . . . . . 253  2 DON JUAN  2  185    6
    HE LAY DARK AS THE SCORPION IN YOUR PATH .  . . . . . 300  2 DON JUAN  3   48   V4
    HER EYELASHES THOUGH DARK AS NIGHT WERE TINGED  . . . . 314  2 DON JUAN  3   75    1
    JOY SPARKLING IN THEIR DARK EYES LIKE A GEM   . . . . 351  2 DON JUAN  4   13    6
    OH POWERS OF HEAVEN WHAT DARK EYE MEETS SHE THERE  . . . 363  2 DON JUAN  4   35    7
    IN THE LARGE DARK EYE'S MUTUAL-DARTED FLAME   . . . . 367  2 DON JUAN  4   44    4
    BUT HER LARGE DARK EYE SHOW'D DEEP PASSION'S FORCE  . . 374  2 DON JUAN  4   56    7
    WITH RESOLUTION IN HIS DARK GRAY EYE  . . . . . . . 416  2 DON JUAN  5   10    7
    GOOD TEETH WITH CURLING RATHER DARK BROWN HAIR  . . . . 416  2 DON JUAN  5   11    3
    HE PAUSED AND HIS DARK EYE GREW FULL OF GLOOM  . . . . 420  2 DON JUAN  5   18    3
    THAT SHE WAS FAIR OR DARK OR SHORT OR TALL  . . . . . .  33  3 DON JUAN  6   54    7
    AND RAVEN RINGLETS GATHERED IN DARK CROWD  . . . . . .  39  3 DON JUAN  6   66    2
    THE BLACK BOUGH) TEAR-DROPS THROUGH HER EYES' DARK FRINGES  40  3 DON JUAN  6   67    8
    THE NIGHT WAS DARK AND THE THICK MIST ALLOWED  . . . . 115  3 DON JUAN  8    6    1
    IN THE CHILL DARK WHEN COURAGE DOES NOT GLOW  . . . . . 121  3 DON JUAN  8   21    3
    SOME ODD MISTAKES TOO HAPPENED IN THE DARK  . . . . . . 177  3 DON JUAN  8  130    1
```

		PAGE	VOL		CANTO	STANZA	LN
DARK	(CONTINUED)						
	DARK RIDDLE OF ALL LIFE EARTH'S LIFELESS END	210	3	DON JUAN	9	56	V7
	RETAINS THE SABLE STAINS OF THE DARK CREEPER	232	3	DON JUAN	10	15	5
	HE HATH NO MORN NOR NIGHT BUT ALL IS DARK	348	3	DON JUAN	12	71	7
	AURORA RABY WITH HER LARGE DARK EYES	514	3	DON JUAN	16	31	7
DARKEN							
	JUST AS THE DAY BEGAN TO WANE AND DARKEN	264	2	DON JUAN	10	80	3
DARKEN'D							
	HER SERIOUS SAYINGS DARKEN'D TO SUBLIMITY	27	2	DON JUAN	1	12	4
DARKENED							
	THAT FLASHED AND AFTER DARKENED IN THE SHADE	507	3	DON JUAN	16	15	8
DARKENING							
	AND IN THE DOOR-WAY DARKENING DARKNESS STOOD	558	3	DON JUAN	16	117	7
DARK-GREEN							
	O'ERTOPPED WITH CYPRESSES DARK-GREEN AND TALL	432	2	DON JUAN	5	40	8
DARKLE							
	AND HER PROUD BROW'S BLUE VEINS TO SWELL AND DARKLE	56	3	DON JUAN	6	101	8
DARKLED							
	AND GRIMLY DARKLED O'ER THEIR FACES PALE	182	2	DON JUAN	2	49	6
DARKLY							
	OH DARKLY DEEPLY BEAUTIFULLY BLUE	404	2	DON JUAN	4	110	1
DARKNESS							
	THE DARKNESS OF HER ORIENTAL EYE	52	2	DON JUAN	1	56	1
	EVEN BY ITS DARKNESS AS THE BLACKEST SKY	61	2	DON JUAN	1	73	2
	AND DARKNESS AND DESTRUCTION AS ON HIGH	270	2	DON JUAN	2	214	4
	IN DARKNESS--I CAN ONLY HOPE THEY DID	178	3	DON JUAN	8	132	8
	THERE REMBRANDT MADE HIS DARKNESS EQUAL LIGHT	392	3	DON JUAN	13	72	2
	THE STARRY DARKNESS ROUND HER LIKE A GIRDLE	556	3	DON JUAN	16	113	7
	AND IN THE DOOR-WAY DARKENING DARKNESS STOOD	558	3	DON JUAN	16	117	7
DARLING							
	A BALL-ROOM BARD A FOOLSCAP HOT-PRESS DARLING	404	2	DON JUAN	4	109	2
	WHEN THEY BUILT UP UNTO HIS DARLING TREES--	144	3	DON JJAN	8	64	2
DART							
	SELF-LOVE THAT WHETSTONE OF DAN CUPID'S DART	15	3	DON JUAN	6	19	V5
	ON HIS SOUL LIKE A CEASELESS SUNRISE DART--	169	3	DON JUAN	8	115	6
	UNWITHERING MYRTLE ROUND THE UNBLUNTED DART	554	3	DON JUAN	16	109	6
DARTING							
	AND SAW EACH OTHER'S DARK EYES DARTING LIGHT	253	2	DON JUAN	2	185	6
DARTS							
	AND DARTS IN ONE QUICK GLANCE A LONG REPLY	241	2	DON JUAN	2	162	6
	UPON THEIR PREY AS DARTS AN ANGRY ASP	370	2	DON JUAN	4	48	6
DASH							
	SAVE THE WILD WIND AND THE REMORSELESS DASH	184	2	DON JUAN	2	53	4
	AGAIN TO BE O'ERCOME AGAIN TO DASH ON	257	2	DON JUAN	2	191	6
	DASH DOWN YON CUP OF SAMIAN WINE	326	2	DON JUAN	3	L 16	6
	DASH INTO POETRY WHICH IS BUT PASSION	402	2	DON JUAN	4	106	7
	YET MEN RESOLVED TO DASH THROUGH THICK AND THIN	94	3	DON JUAN	7	54	4
	THAN BUONAPARTE'S CANCER--COULD I DASH ON	189	3	DON JUAN	9	14	6
	ENTREATING YOU TO PAUSE BEFORE YOU DASH ON	337	3	DON JUAN	12	45	6
	THERE WAS THE DUKE OF DASH WHO WAS A--DUKE	398	3	DON JUAN	13	85	1
DASH'D							
	THOUGH THE TWO SHARKS STILL FOLLOW'D THEM AND DASH'D	209	2	DON JUAN	2	101	7
	AND THE HARD WAVE O'ERWHELM'D HIM AS 'TWAS DASH'D	212	2	DON JUAN	2	107	4
	ITS OUTLET DASH'D INTO A STEEP CASCADE	385	3	DON JUAN	13	58	1
	THE RIVER FROM THE LAKE ALL BLUELY DASH'D	447	3	DON JUAN	14	87	6
DASHED							
	DASHED ON LIKE A SPURRED BLOOD-HORSE IN A RACE	139	3	DON JUAN	8	54	8
	HE DASHED HIMSELF UPON HIS FOES AND FLUNG	170	3	DON JUAN	8	118	V2
	HIGH DASHED THE SPRAY THE BOWS DIPPED IN THE SEA	256	3	DON JUAN	10	64	4
DASHES							
	AND THE SEA DASHES ROUND THE PROMONTORY	94	2	DON JUAN	1	134	6
DASHING							
	AND STANDING UPON DECK THE DASHING SPRAY	162	2	DON JUAN	2	11	5
	NOT VERY DASHING BUT EXTREMELY WINNING	32	3	DON JUAN	6	52	2
	OTHERS IN THAT OFF-HAND AND DASHING STYLE	351	3	DON JUAN	12	76	2
	A DASHING DEMOISELLE OF GOOD ESTATE	474	3	DON JUAN	15	42	2
	THE DASHING AND PROUD AIR OF ADELINE	480	3	DON JUAN	15	56	1
DASTARDLY							
	THAT FLIGHT WAS BASE AND DASTARDLY AND NO MAN	63	2	DON JUAN	1	77	3
DATE							
	IN HEALTH AND PURSE BEGIN YOUR DAY TO DATE	230	2	DON JUAN	2	140	6
	AS IF THEIR LAST DAY OF A HAPPY DATE	355	2	DON JUAN	4	22	3
	AS WELL AS THE SUBLIME DISCOVERY'S DATE	406	2	DON JUAN	4	112	4
	I RATHER THINK THE MOON SHOULD DATE THE DEARS	230	3	DON JUAN	10	10	8
	AT A LONG DATE--TILL THEY CAN GET A FRESH ONE--	379	3	DON JUAN	13	45	6
	COLUMN DATE FALMOUTH THERE HAS LATELY BEEN HERE	383	3	DON JUAN	13	54	5
	THAT POETS WERE SO FROM THEIR EARLIEST DATE	393	3	DON JUAN	13	74	5
DATE-BREAD							
	AND FRUITS AND DATE-BREAD LOAVES CLOSED THE REPAST	307	2	DON JUAN	3	63	2
DATED							
	AND PROPHECY--EXCEPT IT SHOULD BE DATED	286	3	DON JUAN	11	37	7
DATES							
	I LIKE TO BE PARTICULAR IN DATES	76	2	DON JUAN	1	103	2
	IN FEMALE DATES STRIKES TIME ALL OF A HEAP	433	3	DON JUAN	14	52	8
DATING							
	(LONG ERE I DREAMT OF DATING FROM THE BRENTA)	143	2	DON JUAN	1	212	5
DAUGHTER							
	WHO LEFT AN ONLY DAUGHTER MY NARRATION	54	2	DON JUAN	1	59	4
	THEY ARE UNWORTHY OF MY FATHER'S DAUGHTER	106	2	DON JUAN	1	155	6

172

DAUGHTER   (CONTINUED)
    MISTRESS AND MAID THE FIRST WAS ONLY DAUGHTER 222   2 DON JUAN   2   124   7
    HE HAD AN ONLY DAUGHTER CALL'D HAIDEE 224   2 DON JUAN   2   128   1
    ROBBED FOR HIS DAUGHTER BY THE BEST OF FATHERS 284   2 DON JUAN   3   17   8
    HE SHAPED HIS COURSE TO WHERE HIS DAUGHTER FAIR 285   2 DON JUAN   3   19   4
    HIS DAUGHTER--HAD NOT SENT BEFORE TO ADVISE 294   2 DON JUAN   3   37   4
    ON THAT BELOVED DAUGHTER SHE HAD BEEN 304   2 DON JUAN   3   57   2
    HIS DAUGHTER WHILE COMPRESS'D WITHIN HIS CLASP 370   2 DON JUAN   4   48   2
    HER DAUGHTER TEMPER'D WITH A MILDER RAY 375   2 DON JUAN   4   57   1
    CARNAGE (SO WORDSWORTH TELLS YOU) IS GOD'S DAUGHTER . . 116   3 DON JUAN   8   9   6
    NOR BROTHER FATHER SISTER DAUGHTER LOVE 250   3 DON JUAN 10   53   2
    AND WHERE THE DAUGHTER WHOM THE ISLES LOVED WELL . . . 307   3 DON JUAN 11   77   6
    SAFE WITH A LADY WHOSE LAST GROWN-UP DAUGHTER 339   3 DON JUAN 12   51   3
    THAT USUAL PARAGON AN ONLY DAUGHTER 474   3 DON JUAN 15   41   2
    AND FRIGHTS--ESPECIALLY IF 'TIS A DAUGHTER 564   3 DON JUAN 17   4   7
DAUGHTER'S
    YOUR NATURE'S FIRMNESS--KNOW YOUR DAUGHTER'S TOO . . . 366   2 DON JUAN   4   42   8
    TO SAY HER DAUGHTER'S FEELINGS ARE TREPANNED 343   3 DON JUAN 12   60   2
DAUGHTERS
    AND HEARTLESS DAUGHTERS--WORN--AND PALE--AND POOR . . . 15   2 DON JUAN   D   11   6
    THE SONS NO MORE WERE SHORT THE DAUGHTERS PLAIN 53   2 DON JUAN   1   58   5
    WHICH EVE HAS LEFT HER DAUGHTERS SINCE HER FALL 256   2 DON JUAN   2   189   8
    OF HIS GAZELLE-EYED DAUGHTERS SHE WAS ONE 264   2 DON JUAN   2   202   4
    AND DAUGHTERS SOMETIMES RUN OFF WITH THE BUTLER 287   2 DON JUAN   3   22   8
    A LADY WITH HER DAUGHTERS OR HER NIECES 306   2 DON JUAN   3   60   7
    HE HAD FIFTY DAUGHTERS AND FOUR DOZEN SONS 498   2 DON JUAN   5   152   1
    DAUGHTERS ADMIRED HIS DRESS AND PIOUS MOTHERS 293   3 DON JUAN 11   48   7
    THAT DAUGHTERS OF SUCH MOTHERS AS MAY KNOW 337   3 DON JUAN 12   46   4
    AND DAUGHTERS BROTHERS SISTERS KITH OR KIN 470   3 DON JUAN 15   31   2
DAUNTED
    OF BREAKERS HAS NOT DAUNTED MY SLIGHT TRIM 227   3 DON JUAN 10   4   6
DAVID
    FOR DAVID LIVED BUT JUAN NEARLY DIED 113   2 DON JUAN   1   168   8
    LIKE DAVID FLINGS SMOOTH PEBBLES 'GAINST A GIANT . . . 138   3 DON JUAN   8   51   2
DAVID'S
    WHEN OLD KING DAVID'S BLOOD GREW DULL IN MOTION . . . 113   2 DON JUAN   1   168   5
DAVUS
    TO VENTURE A SOLUTION DAVUS SUM 365   3 DON JUAN 13   13   2
DAVY'S
    SIR HUMPHREY DAVY'S LANTERN BY WHICH COALS 93   2 DON JUAN   1   132   4
DAWN
    OF DEWY DAWN WOUND SLOWLY ROUND EACH HEIGHT 49   3 DON JUAN   6   86   6
    WHILE THOUGH 'TWAS DAWN THE TURKS SLEPT FAST AS EVER . . 80   3 DON JUAN   7   28   8
    GLORY BEGAN TO DAWN WITH DUE SUBLIMITY 92   3 DON JUAN   7   51   6
    SWORE THEY SHOULD SEE HIM BY THE DAWN OF DAY 105   3 DON JUAN   7   75   5
    GLEAMS ONLY THROUGH THE DAWN OF ITS CREATION 316   3 DON JUAN 12   2   8
DAWN'D
    HAVE DAWN'D A FAIR AND SINLESS CHILD OF SIN 382   2 DON JUAN   4   70   3
DAY
    AND SAW INTO HERSELF EACH DAY BEFORE ALL 43   2 DON JUAN   1   39   2
    AND NEXT DAY PAID A VISIT TO HIS MOTHER 63   2 DON JUAN   1   76   2
    IT WAS UPON A DAY A SUMMER'S DAY-- 76   2 DON JUAN   1   102   1
    IT WAS UPON A DAY A SUMMER'S DAY-- 76   2 DON JUAN   1   102   1
    'TWAS ON A SUMMER'S DAY--THE SIXTH OF JUNE-- 76   2 DON JUAN   1   103   1
    THEIR NOMENCLATURE THERE IS NOT A DAY 82   2 DON JUAN   1   113   4
    SUPPOSE FROM JUNE THE SIXTH (THE FATAL DAY 86   2 DON JUAN   1   121   2
    ABOUT THE DAY--THE ERA'S MORE OBSCURE 86   2 DON JUAN   1   121   8
    'TWILL ONE DAY ASK YOU WHY YOU USED ME SO 107   2 DON JUAN   1   157   6
    BESIDES IT WANTED BUT FEW HOURS OF DAY 114   2 DON JUAN   1   169   6
    DAY HAS NOT BROKE--THERE'S NO ONE IN THE STREET . . . 121   2 DON JUAN   1   182   8
    THE PLEASANT SCANDAL WHICH AROSE NEXT DAY 126   2 DON JUAN   1   188   5
    I THOUGHT OF A PERUKE THE OTHER DAY) 143   2 DON JUAN   1   213   3
    I THOUGHT OF DYEING IT THE OTHER DAY) 143   2 DON JUAN   1   213   V3
    INFANTS OF THREE YEARS OLD WERE TAUGHT THAT DAY . . . 162   2 DON JUAN   2   10   5
    AS DAY ADVANCED THE WEATHER SEEM'D TO ABATE 172   2 DON JUAN   2   30   1
    DAY BROKE AND THE WIND LULL'D THE MASTS WERE GONE . . 176   2 DON JUAN   2   38   2
    AND NEVER HAD AS YET A QUIET DAY 177   2 DON JUAN   2   40   4
    SOME CURSED THE DAY ON WHICH THEY SAW THE SUN 180   2 DON JUAN   2   45   3
    'TWAS TWILIGHT AND THE SUNLESS DAY WENT DOWN 182   2 DON JUAN   2   49   1
    AND MUST HAVE MEALS AT LEAST ONE MEAL A DAY 191   2 DON JUAN   2   67   2
    FOR ON THE THIRD DAY THERE CAME ON A CALM 192   2 DON JUAN   2   68   2
    ON WHAT IN FACT NEXT DAY WERE THEY TO DINE 192   2 DON JUAN   2   69   4
    THE FOURTH DAY CAME BUT NOT A BREATH OF AIR 193   2 DON JUAN   2   70   1
    THE FIFTH DAY AND THEIR BOAT LAY FLOATING THERE . . . 193   2 DON JUAN   2   70   3
    ON THE SIXTH DAY THEY FED UPON HIS HIDE 193   2 DON JUAN   2   71   1
    THE SEVENTH DAY AND NO WIND--THE BURNING SUN 194   2 DON JUAN   2   72   1
    BUT ERE THEY CAME TO THIS THEY THAT DAY SHARED . . . 195   2 DON JUAN   2   74   1
    THE DAY BEFORE FAST SLEEPING ON THE WATER 208   2 DON JUAN   2   99   1
    BY NIGHT CHILL'D BY DAY SCORCH'D THUS ONE BY ONE . . . 210   2 DON JUAN   2   102   5
    AND TIME HAD NOTHING MORE OF NIGHT NOR DAY 214   2 DON JUAN   2   111   3
    THE CLIFF TOWARDS SUNSET ON THAT DAY SHE FOUND . . . 224   2 DON JUAN   2   129   2
    IN HEALTH AND PURSE BEGIN YOUR DAY TO DATE 230   2 DON JUAN   2   140   6
    I'VE CHANGED FOR SOME FEW YEARS THE DAY TO NIGHT . . . 230   2 DON JUAN   2   140   V3
    A PURPLE HECTIC PLAY'D LIKE DYING DAY 234   2 DON JUAN   2   147   2
    WHERE I LIKE OTHER DOGS HAVE HAD MY DAY 244   2 DON JUAN   2   166   3
    AND EVERY DAY BY DAY-BREAK--RATHER EARLY 245   2 DON JUAN   2   168   1
    AND EVERY DAY HELP'D ON HIS CONVALESCENCE 245   2 DON JUAN   2   169   1
    FOR LITTLE HAD HE WANDER'D SINCE THE DAY 249   2 DON JUAN   2   176   4
    SERMONS AND SODA WATER THE DAY AFTER 250   2 DON JUAN   2   178   8

	PAGE	VOL		CANTO	STANZA	LN

DAY   (CONTINUED)

	PAGE	VOL		CANTO	STANZA	LN
BUT CHANGES NIGHT AND DAY TOO LIKE THE SKY	270	2 DON JUAN	2	214	2
HE LEFT HIS SHIP TO BE HOVE DOWN NEXT DAY	286	2 DON JUAN	3	20	5
I'VE KNOWN THE ABSENT WRONG'D FOUR TIMES A DAY	288	2 DON JUAN	3	25	8
I'VE SEEN A FRIEND BETRAYED FOUR TIMES A DAY	288	2 DON JUAN	3	25	V8
A DAY OF GOLD FROM OUT AN AGE OF IRON	294	2 DON JUAN	3	36	3
SO LITTLE THEY EXPECTED HIM THAT DAY	300	2 DON JUAN	3	49	4
AND CLOUDS COME O'ER THE SUNSET OF OUR DAY	305	2 DON JUAN	3	59	6
SHE HAD NO NEED OF THIS DAY NE'ER WILL BREAK	314	2 DON JUAN	3	76	3
HE COUNTED THEM AT BREAK OF DAY--	322	2 DON JUAN	3	L 4	5
AN INDEPENDENT BEING IN HIS DAY--	328	2 DON JUAN	3	91	3
OF THOSE WHO SAIL THE SEAS ON THE FIRST DAY	338	2 DON JUAN	3	108	2
ARE SOMEWHAT SICK AND SORRY THE NEXT DAY	343	2 DON JUAN	3	V 98	8
THE LONG YEAR LINK'D WITH HEAVY DAY ON DAY	350	2 DON JUAN	4	11	5
THE LONG YEAR LINK'D WITH HEAVY DAY ON DAY	350	2 DON JUAN	4	11	5
AS IF THEIR LAST DAY OF A HAPPY DATE	355	2 DON JUAN	4	22	3
HOWEVER DEAR OR CHERISH'D IN THEIR DAY	379	2 DON JUAN	4	64	4
THEY HEARD NEXT DAY--THAT IN THE DARDANELLES	393	2 DON JUAN	4	91	1
I PASS EACH DAY WHERE DANTE'S BONES ARE LAID	400	2 DON JUAN	4	104	1
'TWAS A RAW DAY OF AUTUMN'S BLEAK BEGINNING	414	2 DON JUAN	5	6	1
I CRIED UPON MY FIRST WIFE'S DYING DAY	420	2 DON JUAN	5	19	7
PERHAPS WE SHALL BE ONE DAY BY AND BY	423	2 DON JUAN	5	24	5
AND SUCH AN END THAT HE WHO MANY A DAY	431	2 DON JUAN	5	37	5
MORE TENDER AS WE EVERY DAY BEHOLD	439	2 DON JUAN	5	49	6
BUT SADDENS MORE BY NIGHT AS WELL AS DAY	442	2 DON JUAN	5	56	6
REIGN'D TILL ONE SUMMER'S DAY HE TOOK TO GRAZING	445	2 DON JUAN	5	60	4
BUT WISHING TO BE ONE DAY BRIGADIERS	75	3 DON JUAN	7	18	4
THEIR GALLIC NAMES UPON A GLORIOUS DAY	77	3 DON JUAN	7	22	3
ALL THAT THE RUSSIANS DID UPON THIS DAY	82	3 DON JUAN	7	32	2
(FOR DAY NE'ER SAW HIS MERITS) COULD DECREE	86	3 DON JUAN	7	41	4
THE DAY BEFORE THE ASSAULT WHILE UPON DRILL	95	3 DON JUAN	7	56	1
SWORE THEY SHOULD SEE HIM BY THE DAWN OF DAY	105	3 DON JUAN	7	75	5
AND ALMOST EVERY DAY IN SAD REALITY	108	3 DON JUAN	7	83	3
WHICH STIFFENED HEAVEN) AS IF HE WISHED FOR DAY--	121	3 DON JUAN	8	21	7
BUT SEEING FLASHING FORWARD LIKE THE DAY	126	3 DON JUAN	8	30	3
COSSACQUES WERE ALL CUT OFF AS DAY WAS BREAKING	150	3 DON JUAN	8	76	3
THAT THEY SHOULD ALL BE SHOT ON THE NEXT DAY	162	3 DON JUAN	8	102	6
A THING WHICH HAPPENS EVERYWHERE EACH DAY--	163	3 DON JUAN	8	103	7
THE WEB OF THESE TARANTULAS EACH DAY	196	3 DON JUAN	9	28	5
BUT LET IT GO--IT WILL ONE DAY BE FOUND	201	3 DON JUAN	9	37	1
DID NOT HIS DEEDS UNRIDDLE THEM EACH DAY--	207	3 DON JUAN	9	50	4
FAIR WEATHER FOR THE DAY THOUGH RATHER SPACIOUS	211	3 DON JUAN	9	58	7
HECTIC AND BRIEF AS SUMMER'S DAY NIGH DONE	229	3 DON JUAN	10	8	6
TO HOARD UP WARMTH AGAINST A WINTRY DAY	229	3 DON JUAN	10	9	8
FOR COUSINS ALSO ANSWERED THE SAME DAY	239	3 DON JUAN	10	30	4
WHICH PORTIONS OUT UPON THE JUDGMENT DAY	242	3 DON JUAN	10	35	4
HIS SERVICES HE KISSED HANDS THE NEXT DAY	247	3 DON JUAN	10	46	5
JUST AS THE DAY BEGAN TO WANE AND DARKEN	264	3 DON JUAN	10	80	3
DECIDE AND EVERYBODY ONE DAY WILL	270	3 DON JUAN	11	4	7
HE'LL FIND IT RATHER DIFFICULT SOME DAY	298	3 DON JUAN	11	59	3
AMONGST THE HIGHER SPIRITS OF THE DAY	300	3 DON JUAN	11	64	7
WHENEVER--WHICH MEANS EVERY DAY--THEY'D SHOWN	338	3 DON JUAN	12	48	3
OF HIS OWN COUNTRY--SELDOM SINCE THAT DAY	364	3 DON JUAN	13	11	3
THE DAPPLED FORESTERS--AS DAY AWOKE	384	3 DON JUAN	13	56	6
WHICH MAKES THE SOUTHERN AUTUMN'S DAY APPEAR	395	3 DON JUAN	13	77	2
AND RANK'D WITH WHAT IS EVERY DAY DISPLAY'D--	400	3 DON JUAN	13	90	7
THE MIDDLE-AGED TO MAKE THE DAY MORE SHORT	405	3 DON JUAN	13	101	4
A SLEEP WITHOUT DREAMS AFTER A ROUGH DAY	412	3 DON JUAN	14	4	1
AND WHEN UPON A SILENT SULLEN DAY	422	3 DON JUAN	14	28	1
ASK'D NEXT DAY IF MEN EVER HUNTED TWICE	425	3 DON JUAN	14	35	8
WHEN CALLED NEXT DAY DECLINED THE ROUGH ADVENTURE	425	3 DON JUAN	14	35	V8
DECEMBER'S DROWSY DAY TO HIS DULL RACE--	426	3 DON JUAN	14	36	4
FIND ONE EACH DAY OF THE DELIGHTFUL YEAR	438	3 DON JUAN	14	63	6
WHICH YOU SHOULD PERPETRATE SOME SUMMER'S DAY	445	3 DON JUAN	14	82	6
WERE SHAKEN DOWN AND DOGS HAD HAD THEIR DAY	466	3 DON JUAN	15	23	4
WHICH CHARM MOST PEOPLE IN THEIR EARLIER DAY	479	3 DON JUAN	15	53	3
THE EVAPORATION OF A JOYOUS DAY	504	3 DON JUAN	16	9	1
TITUS EXCLAIMED I'VE LOST A DAY OF ALL	505	3 DON JUAN	16	11	5
THOUGH HE IS NOT SEEN BY DAY	518	3 DON JUAN	16	L 2	8
HE ABIDETH NIGHT AND DAY	519	3 DON JUAN	16	L 3	4
AMUNDEVILLE IS LORD BY DAY	520	3 DON JUAN	16	L 5	5
AS THE MERE PASTIME OF AN IDLE DAY	521	3 DON JUAN	16	42	3
OF JUAN'S NERVOUS FEELINGS ON THAT DAY	526	3 DON JUAN	16	51	4
BUT SHOULD THE DAY COME WHEN PLACE CEASED TO EXIST	537	3 DON JUAN	16	75	5
BUT 'TWAS A PUBLIC FEAST AND PUBLIC DAY--	538	3 DON JUAN	16	78	5
AND LO UPON THAT DAY IT CAME TO PASS	539	3 DON JUAN	16	81	5
DULLY PAST O'ER THE DINNER OF THE DAY	542	3 DON JUAN	16	87	1
THIS DAY AND WATCHING WITCHING CONDESCENDING	546	3 DON JUAN	16	95	2
HOWEVER THE DAY CLOSED AS DAYS MUST CLOSE	549	3 DON JUAN	16	101	1
JUST AS I MAKE MY MIND UP EVERY DAY	566	3 DON JUAN	17	10	6

DAY-BILL

	PAGE	VOL		CANTO	STANZA	LN
TO DRAW UP IN ARRAY A SINGLE DAY-BILL	482	3 DON JUAN	15	62	5

DAY-BREAK

	PAGE	VOL		CANTO	STANZA	LN
SHE AND HER MAID AND PROMISED BY DAY-BREAK	226	2 DON JUAN	2	133	6
FROM DAY-BREAK AND WHEN COFFIN'D AT FOURSCORE	230	2 DON JUAN	2	140	7
AND EVERY DAY BY DAY-BREAK--RATHER EARLY	245	2 DON JUAN	2	168	1
UNTIL THEY REACHED AS DAY-BREAK WAS EXPANDING	148	3 DON JUAN	8	72	5

DAY-DAWN

	PAGE	VOL		CANTO	STANZA	LN
FOR LIKE A DAY-DAWN SHE WAS YOUNG AND PURE	335	3 DON JUAN	12	41	2

174

		PAGE	VOL	CANTO	STANZA	LN
DAY-HYMN						
OR THE FAINT DYING DAY-HYMN STOLE ALOFT		335	2 DON JUAN	3	102	6
DAYLIGHT'S						
IN DECENT LONDON WHEN THE DAYLIGHT'S O'ER		282	3 DON JUAN	11	30	5
DAY'S						
WHICH YIELDED A DAY'S LIFE AND TO THEIR MIND		208	2 DON JUAN	2	99	4
SEEMING TO WEEP THE DYING DAY'S DECAY		338	2 DON JUAN	3	108	6
DAYS						
OF MERIT AND COMPLAINT OF PRESENT DAYS		14	2 DON JUAN	D	8	7
IF FALLEN IN EVIL DAYS ON EVIL TONGUES		15	2 DON JUAN	D	10	1
HAVE MOMENTS HOURS AND DAYS SO UNPREPARED		33	2 DON JUAN	1	21	4
FOR HALF HIS DAYS WERE PASS'D AT CHURCH THE OTHER		48	2 DON JUAN	1	49	7
'TWAS IN NOVEMBER WHEN FINE DAYS ARE FEW		94	2 DON JUAN	1	134	3
ALFONSO'S DAYS HAD NOT BEEN IN THE LAND		123	2 DON JUAN	1	185	6
MY DAYS OF LOVE ARE OVER ME NO MORE		144	2 DON JUAN	1	216	1
THE WORLD WILL FIND THEE AFTER MANY DAYS		149	2 DON JUAN	1	222	4
DAYS NEARLY O'ER MIGHT BE DISPOSED TO RIOT		173	2 DON JUAN	2	33	6
HAVING BEEN SEVERAL DAYS IN GREAT DISTRESS		180	2 DON JUAN	2	46	2
AND THE DIM DESOLATE DEEP TWELVE DAYS HAD FEAR		182	2 DON JUAN	2	49	7
GAZED DIM AND DESOLATE--TWELVE DAYS HAD FEAR		182	2 DON JUAN	2	49	V7
IN MY YOUNG DAYS THEY LENT ME CASH THAT WAY		190	2 DON JUAN	2	65	7
WHO DIED TWO DAYS BEFORE AND NOW HAD FOUND		213	2 DON JUAN	2	109	7
SAVE ON THE DEAD LONG SUMMER DAYS WHICH MAKE		249	2 DON JUAN	2	177	7
SUCH KISSES AS BELONG TO EARLY DAYS		254	2 DON JUAN	2	186	4
OUR DAYS AND PUT ONE'S SERVANTS INTO MOURNING		278	2 DON JUAN	3	7	8
THERE HIS FEW PEACEFUL DAYS TIME HAD SWEPT O'ER		302	2 DON JUAN	3	52	5
HIS PREDECESSORS IN THE COLCHIAN DAYS		303	2 DON JUAN	3	55	4
MIGHT CARRY OUT TO COLCHIS IN OLD DAYS		303	2 DON JUAN	3	55	V4
IN WHOM OUR BRIGHTEST DAYS WE WOULD RETRACE		305	2 DON JUAN	3	59	3
REVERSING THE GOOD CUSTOM OF OLD DAYS		316	2 DON JUAN	3	79	2
MUST WE BUT WEEP O'ER DAYS MORE BLEST		323	2 DON JUAN	3 L	7	1
THEY TOOK IT UP WHEN MY DAYS GREW MORE MELLOW		345	2 DON JUAN	4	3	3
DAYS LAY SHE IN THAT STATE UNCHANGED THOUGH CHILL		377	2 DON JUAN	4	60	1
OF ANCIENT DAYS ERE TYRANNY GREW STRONG		379	2 DON JUAN	4	65	8
TWELVE DAYS AND NIGHTS SHE WITHER'D THUS AT LAST		381	2 DON JUAN	4	69	1
BY AGE IN EARTH HER DAYS AND PLEASURES WERE		382	2 DON JUAN	4	71	5
SOME DAYS AND NIGHTS ELAPSED BEFORE THAT HE		384	2 DON JUAN	4	75	2
WHEN NIGHTS ARE EQUAL BUT NOT SO THE DAYS		414	2 DON JUAN	5	6	2
FOR ANY LENGTH OF DAYS IN SUCH A PICKLE		419	2 DON JUAN	5	17	4
THE GLITTERING LIME-TWIGS OF OUR LATTER DAYS		422	2 DON JUAN	5	22	7
BUT EVERY FOOL DESCRIBES IN THESE BRIGHT DAYS		440	2 DON JUAN	5	52	2
BE IN THESE DAYS) SOME INFIDELS WHO DON'T		447	2 DON JUAN	5	62	2
GULBEYAZ FOR THE FIRST TIME IN HER DAYS		482	2 DON JUAN	5	122	1
THEIR NEVER KNOWING THEIR OWN MIND TWO DAYS		64	3 DON JUAN	6	117	6
THIS WAS POTEMKIN--A GREAT THING IN DAYS		84	3 DON JUAN	7	37	1
ENJOYED THE LONELY VIGOROUS HARMLESS DAYS		143	3 DON JUAN	8	61	7
MOTION WAS IN THEIR DAYS REST IN THEIR SLUMBERS		145	3 DON JUAN	8	67	1
THEY MUST BE PAID THOUGH SIX DAYS SMOOTHLY RUN		243	3 DON JUAN	10	38	7
FOR ONE OR TWO DAYS READER WE REQUEST		248	3 DON JUAN	10	49	2
THEY'RE RIGHT OUR DAYS ARE TOO BRIEF FOR AFFORDING		270	3 DON JUAN	11	4	5
(FOR IN THOSE DAYS WE HAD NOT GOT TO GAS) --		278	3 DON JUAN	11	22	8
WITH REGULAR DESCENT IN THESE OUR DAYS		340	3 DON JUAN	12	53	4
EPOCH THAT AWKWARD CORNER TURNED FOR DAYS		360	3 DON JUAN	13	4	2
THE DAYS OF COMEDY ARE GONE ALAS		402	3 DON JUAN	13	94	5
YOUTH FADES AND LEAVES OUR DAYS NO LONGER SUNNY		405	3 DON JUAN	13	100	5
AND THE HARD FROST DESTROY'D THE SCENTING DAYS		407	3 DON JUAN	13	106	4
SOMETIMES A DANCE (THOUGH RARELY ON FIELD DAYS		408	3 DON JUAN	13	108	1
IN MY YOUNG DAYS THAT CHASTE AND GOODLY VEIL		422	3 DON JUAN	14	27	2
THE DIFFERENCE IS THAT IN THE DAYS OF OLD		468	3 DON JUAN	15	26	1
DAYS BETTER DRAWN BEFORE OR ELSE ASSUME		468	3 DON JUAN	15	26	7
OF DEEDS AND DAYS WHEN THEY HAD FILL'D THE EAR		476	3 DON JUAN	15	46	5
THE NIGHTS AND DAYS MOST PEOPLE CAN REMEMBER		505	3 DON JUAN	16	11	6
THE CHARMS OF OTHER DAYS IN STARLIGHT GLEAMS		509	3 DON JUAN	16	19	2
AND HIS MASS OF THE DAYS THAT ARE GONE		518	3 DON JUAN	16 L	1	4
HAVE PUBLIC DAYS WHEN ALL MEN MAY CAROUSE		534	3 DON JUAN	16	68	7
I KNEW HIM IN HIS LIVELIER LONDON DAYS		540	3 DON JUAN	16	82	1
HOWEVER THE DAY CLOSED AS DAYS MUST CLOSE		549	3 DON JUAN	16	101	1
THE LOVE OF HIGHER THINGS AND BETTER DAYS		554	3 DON JUAN	16	108	1
OR (AS RHYMES MAY BE IN THESE DAYS) MUCH MORE		556	3 DON JUAN	16	113	4
THEIR TENDER PARENTS IN THEIR BUDDING DAYS		562	3 DON JUAN	17	1	6
DAYS'						
THE NINE DAYS' WONDER WHICH WAS BROUGHT TO LIGHT		126	2 DON JUAN	1	188	6
THESE FORTY DAYS' ADVANTAGE OF HER YEARS--		432	3 DON JUAN	14	52	1
DAZZLED						
WHEN DAZZLED WITH HER ASPECT I MIGHT ERR		314	2 DON JUAN	3	76	V6
I AM NOT DAZZLED BY THIS SPLENDID ROOF		484	2 DON JUAN	5	127	5
AND NOT BE DAZZLED BY ITS EARLY GLARE		224	3 DON JUAN	9	84	V6
YET SHE WAS NOTHING DAZZLED BY THE METEOR		480	3 DON JUAN	15	56	7
HE DAZZLED BUT ASTONISHED NOT HER SENSE		480	3 DON JUAN	15	56	V7
DAZZLING						
A DAZZLING MASS OF GEMS AND GOLD AND GLITTER		465	2 DON JUAN	5	93	7
BUT WHEN SHE SAW HIS DAZZLING EYE WAX DIM		246	3 DON JUAN	10	44	5
DE						
COULEUR DE ROSE WHO'S NEITHER WHITE NOR SCARLET		344	3 DON JUAN	12	62	8
THERE WAS THE PREUX CHEVALIER DE LA RUSE		398	3 DON JUAN	13	86	3
DE REBUS CUNCTIS ET QUIBUSDAM ALIIS		502	3 DON JUAN	16	3	8
UNDRESSING IS A WOE OUR ROBE DE CHAMBRE		505	3 DON JUAN	16	11	2
DEAD						
WISHING EACH OTHER NOT DIVORCED BUT DEAD		35	2 DON JUAN	1	26	3

DEAD (CONTINUED)

	PAGE	VOL	CANTO		STANZA	LN
DEAD SCANDALS FORM GOOD SUBJECTS FOR DISSECTION	37	2	DON JUAN	1	31	8
THE LANGUAGES ESPECIALLY THE DEAD	44	2	DON JUAN	1	40	1
WISHING THEM--NOT EXACTLY DAMNED BUT DEAD HE	89	2	DON JUAN	1	125	V6
AROSE A CLATTER MIGHT AWAKE THE DEAD	95	2	DON JUAN	1	136	3
IF DEAD HIS MODE OF DYING MIGHT BE PUT	112	2	DON JUAN	1	166	V7
THEY WON'T LAY OUT THEIR MONEY ON THE DEAD--	185	2	DON JUAN	2	55	7
YOU HARDLY COULD PERCEIVE WHEN HE WAS DEAD	197	2	DON JUAN	2	76	4
AND THEN THEY LEFT OFF EATING THE DEAD BODY	200	2	DON JUAN	2	82	8
DEATH LEFT NO DOUBT AND THE DEAD BURTHEN LAY	204	2	DON JUAN	2	90	3
AND TRIED TO AWAKEN THEM BUT FOUND THEM DEAD	208	2	DON JUAN	2	98	8
AND THREE DEAD WHOM THEIR STRENGTH COULD NOT AVAIL	209	2	DON JUAN	2	101	5
INSENSIBLE--NOT DEAD BUT NEARLY SO--	224	2	DON JUAN	2	129	3
JUAN SLEPT LIKE A TOP OR LIKE THE DEAD	227	2	DON JUAN	2	134	2
SUCH APPETITE IN ONE SHE HAD DEEM'D DEAD	239	2	DON JUAN	2	158	4
SAVE ON THE DEAD LONG SUMMER DAYS WHICH MAKE	249	2	DON JUAN	2	177	7
A SECOND HICCUP'D OUR OLD MASTER'S DEAD	297	2	DON JUAN	3	43	5
BUT CERTAINLY TO ONE DEEM'D DEAD RETURNING	300	2	DON JUAN	3	49	7
IF ALL THE DEAD COULD NOW RETURN TO LIFE	301	2	DON JUAN	3	50	1
A REMNANT OF OUR SPARTAN DEAD	323	2	DON JUAN	3	L 7	4
AH NO--THE VOICES OF THE DEAD	323	2	DON JUAN	3	L 8	2
HAIDEE AND JUAN THOUGHT NOT OF THE DEAD	351	2	DON JUAN	4	13	1
PALE AS THE FOAM THAT FROTH'D ON HIS DEAD BROW	362	2	DON JUAN	4	34	2
AND GAZING ON THE DEAD SHE THOUGHT HIS FACE	363	2	DON JUAN	4	35	1
NO HIDEOUS SIGN PROCLAIM'D HER SURELY DEAD	377	2	DON JUAN	4	60	4
RATHER THE DEAD FOR LIFE SEEM'D SOMETHING NEW	378	2	DON JUAN	4	62	2
THE VERY GENERATIONS OF THE DEAD	399	2	DON JUAN	4	102	1
OF GORE DIVULGED THE CAUSE) THAT HE WAS DEAD	430	2	DON JUAN	5	35	7
AND AIR--EARTH--WATER--FIRE LIVE--AND WE DEAD	432	2	DON JUAN	5	39	6
I SCARCELY COULD BELIEVE THAT HE WAS DEAD	432	2	DON JUAN	5	39	V4
WILL IT SAID JUAN SHARPLY STRIKE ME DEAD	452	2	DON JUAN	5	71	7
BUT ON THEY MARCHED DEAD BODIES TRAMPLING O'ER	120	3	DON JUAN	8	19	5
OF DEAD AND DYING THOUSANDS--SOMETIMES GAINING	121	3	DON JUAN	8	20	2
AND SO WHEN ALL HIS CORPS WERE DEAD OR DYING	131	3	DON JUAN	8	36	1
HIS SOUL (LIKE GALVANISM UPON THE DEAD)	133	3	DON JUAN	8	41	6
WAS FROM A PISTOL SHOT THAT LAID HIM DEAD	152	3	DON JUAN	8	81	2
HER HIDDEN FACE WAS PLUNGED AMIDST THE DEAD	158	3	DON JUAN	8	93	3
THE OLD PACHA SITS AMONG SOME HUNDREDS DEAD	160	3	DON JUAN	8	98	3
WHITE BLACK OR COPPER--THE DEAD BONES WILL GRIN	188	3	DON JUAN	9	12	8
WHICH AUGURED OF THE DEAD HOWEVER QUICK	244	3	DON JUAN	10	39	5
WHO NOW THAT HE IS DEAD HAS NOT A FOE	254	3	DON JUAN	10	59	V3
THE LIST GROWS LONG OF LIVE AND DEAD PRETENDERS	299	3	DON JUAN	11	61	1
HER LATE PERFORMANCE HAD BEEN A DEAD SET	428	3	DON JUAN	14	42	7
IT WERE MUCH BETTER TO BE WED OR DEAD	438	3	DON JUAN	14	64	5
NOW HERE I HAVE GOT THE PREACHER AT A DEAD LOCK	471	3	DON JUAN	15	35	8
ALL NATIONS HAVE BELIEVED THAT FROM THE DEAD	504	3	DON JUAN	16	7	3
BUT BY DIM LIGHTS THE PORTRAITS OF THE DEAD	508	3	DON JUAN	16	17	7
THE MAN WAS WELL-NIGH DEAD ERE MEN BEGUN	565	3	DON JUAN	17	8	5
BUT OH THAT I WERE DEAD--FOR WHILE ALIVE--	569	3	DON JUAN	17	V 13	1

DEADLIER

	PAGE	VOL	CANTO		STANZA	LN
WITH DEADLIER ENGINES AND A SPEEDIER BLOW	106	3	DON JUAN	7	80	3
CLOSER THAT ALL THE DEADLIER THEY MIGHT WRING	170	3	DON JUAN	8	118	5

DEADLY

	PAGE	VOL	CANTO		STANZA	LN
WITH THE DEEP DEADLY THOUGHT THAT THEY MUST PART	203	2	DON JUAN	2	88	8
DEADLY AND QUICK AND CRUSHING YET AS REAL	262	2	DON JUAN	2	199	7
LOVE'S THE FIRST NET WHICH SPREADS ITS DEADLY MESH	422	2	DON JUAN	5	22	5
GROW DEADLY PALE AND THEN BLUSH BACK AGAIN	483	2	DON JUAN	5	124	6
DEEP IN THE CAVERNS OF THE DEADLY TIDE--	63	3	DON JUAN	6	115	4
WILL OFTENTIMES MAKE DEADLY QUARRELS BURST	136	3	DON JUAN	8	48	3
MY JUAN WHOM I LEFT IN DEADLY PERIL	300	3	DON JUAN	11	64	1
SOME DEADLY SHOTS TOO SEPTEMBRIZERS SEEN	539	3	DON JUAN	16	80	3
INFLICTED ON THE DISH A DEADLY WOUND	542	3	DON JUAN	16	88	6

DEAF

	PAGE	VOL	CANTO		STANZA	LN
AND DEAF THAT ANY OTHER IT WOULD VEX	101	2	DON JUAN	1	147	4
THEY WERE MISSHAPEN PIGMIES DEAF AND DUMB--	462	2	DON JUAN	5	88	7
AND SHRIEK FOR WATER INTO A DEAF EAR--	117	3	DON JUAN	8	11	5

DEAFENED

	PAGE	VOL	CANTO		STANZA	LN
THE VERY CANNON DEAFENED BY THE DIN	142	3	DON JUAN	8	59	5
THE LOUDEST WIT I E'ER WAS DEAFENED WITH	539	3	DON JUAN	16	81	8

DEAL

	PAGE	VOL	CANTO		STANZA	LN
A GOOD DEAL LIKE HIM TOO THOUGH QUITE THE SAME NONE	24	2	DON JUAN	1	5	3
A GOOD DEAL MAY BE BOUGHT FOR FIFTY LOUIS	79	2	DON JUAN	1	108	8
ALL THESE CONFIRM MY STATEMENT A GOOD DEAL	138	2	DON JUAN	1	203	5
AND IN THY STEAD I'VE GOT A DEAL OF JUDGMENT	144	2	DON JUAN	1	215	7
THE SKIN HAS PASSED THROUGH SUCH A DEAL OF DIRT	154	2	DON JUAN	1	V 5	5
BY WHICH NO DOUBT A GOOD DEAL MAY BE MADE	223	2	DON JUAN	2	126	8
DEAL WITH ME AS THOU WILT BUT SPARE THIS BOY	364	2	DON JUAN	4	38	8
LAST CARNIVAL SHE MADE A DEAL OF STRIFE	389	2	DON JUAN	4	83	6
(OF WHICH I MIGHT HAVE A GOOD DEAL TO SAY	434	2	DON JUAN	5	42	3
THERE SEEMED TO BE BESPRENT A DEAL OF GILDING	436	2	DON JUAN	5	46	3
A GOOD DEAL PRACTISED HERE UPON OCCASION	464	2	DON JUAN	5	92	8
HAD HIS INSTRUCTIONS WHERE AND HOW TO DEAL	477	2	DON JUAN	5	114	V6
SHE WAS A GOOD DEAL SHOCKED NOT SHOCKED AT TEARS	479	2	DON JUAN	5	118	1
AND YAWNED A GOOD DEAL WITH DISCREET SURPRIZE	42	3	DON JUAN	6	73	4
WHEN AFTER A GOOD DEAL OF HEAVY FIRING	125	3	DON JUAN	8	27	7
OF PRESENT LIFE A GOOD DEAL MORE THAN WE--	161	3	DON JUAN	8	100	3
THOUGH THERE'S A SHORTER A GOOD DEAL THAN THIS	326	3	DON JUAN	12	22	4
I THEREFORE DEAL IN GENERALITIES	444	3	DON JUAN	14	80	8

DEALER

	PAGE	VOL	CANTO		STANZA	LN
THERE WAS A PICTURE DEALER WHO HAD BROUGHT	528	3	DON JUAN	16	56	1
FROM TOWN VIZ ARCHITECT AND DEALER WERE	533	3	DON JUAN	16	66	5

DEALS
```
  GOES WHEN SOME PERT PRETENDER DEALS HIS PRAISE  .  .  .  .  .  156   3 DON JUAN  8    90  V4
  BESIDES MY MUSE BY NO MEANS DEALS IN FICTION    .  .  .  .  .  416   3 DON JUAN 14    13   1
DEALT
  TO THE GAZETTE--WHICH DOUBTLESS FAIRLY DEALT   .  .  .  .  .  120   3 DON JUAN  8    18   2
  THOSE HAUGHTY SHOP-KEEPERS WHO STERNLY DEALT   .  .  .  .  .  257   3 DON JUAN 10    65   6
  THE MOST SINCERE THAT EVER DEALT IN FICTION .  .  .  .  .  .  502   3 DON JUAN 16     2   8
DEAN
  A DIFFERENCE 'TWIXT A BISHOP AND A DEAN  .  .  .  .  .  .  .  541   3 DON JUAN 16    84   5
DEAR
  BY HARBOURING SOME DEAR FRIEND EXTREMELY VICIOUS  .  .  .  .   74   2 DON JUAN  1    99   5
  DEAR IS THE HELPLESS CREATURE WE DEFEND  .  .  .  .  .  .  .   90   2 DON JUAN  1   126   6
  AGAINST THE WORLD AND DEAR THE SCHOOLBOY SPOT  .  .  .  .  .   90   2 DON JUAN  1   126   7
  MY DEAR I WAS THE FIRST WHO CAME AWAY .  .  .  .  .  .  .  .   98   2 DON JUAN  1   141   8
  NOTHING SO DEAR AS AN UNFILCH'D GOOD NAME  .  .  .  .  .  .  112   2 DON JUAN  1   165   5
  TO WHOM SHE KNEW HIS MOTHER'S FAME WAS DEAR .  .  .  .  .  .  118   2 DON JUAN  1   176   8
  SO DEAR IS STILL THE MEMORY OF THAT DREAM  .  .  .  .  .  .  130   2 DON JUAN  1   193   4
  A PLEASURE--LIKE ALL PLEASURES--RATHER DEAR  .  .  .  .  .  238   2 DON JUAN  2   156   6
  I WILL MY DEAR PHILOSOPHY I SAID  .  .  .  .  .  .  .  .  .  268   2 DON JUAN  2   210   3
  WITH HIS DEAR WAGGONERS AROUND HIS LAKES .  .  .  .  .  .  .  333   2 DON JUAN  3    98   4
  WHATE'ER OUR HOUSEHOLD GODS PROTECT OF DEAR  .  .  .  .  .  338   2 DON JUAN  3   107   6
  DEAR UNTO ALL BUT DEAREST TO THEIR EYES  .  .  .  .  .  .  .  354   2 DON JUAN  4    20   2
  DEAR AS HER FATHER HAD BEEN TO HAIDEE .  .  .  .  .  .  .  .  363   2 DON JUAN  4    36   6
  HOWEVER DEAR OR CHERISH'D IN THEIR DAY  .  .  .  .  .  .  .  379   2 DON JUAN  4    64   4
  (PLAIN TRUTH DEAR MURRAY NEEDS FEW FLOWERS OF SPEECH)  .  .  470   2 DON JUAN  5   101   2
  I'M PUZZLED WHAT TO DO WITH YOU MY DEAR  .  .  .  .  .  .  .   29   3 DON JUAN  6    46   3
  OUT OF THEIR HIDES IF PARCHMENT HAD GROWN DEAR .  .  .  .  .   75   3 DON JUAN  7    17   7
  OF DEEDS TO HUMAN HAPPINESS MOST DEAR .  .  .  .  .  .  .  .  108   3 DON JUAN  7    83   6
  DEFENDED AT A PRICE EXTREMELY DEAR .  .  .  .  .  .  .  .  .  151   3 DON JUAN  8    79   8
  AS THE LAST LINK WITH ALL SHE HAD HELD DEAR .  .  .  .  .  .  159   3 DON JUAN  8    95   6
  IS RATHER DEAR--I'M SURE I MEAN NO HARM  .  .  .  .  .  .  .  186   3 DON JUAN  9     7   8
  HE STRIPS FROM MAN THAT MANTLE (FAR MORE DEAR  .  .  .  .  .  188   3 DON JUAN  9    12   6
  DEAR JEFFREY ONCE MY MOST REDOUBTED FOE  .  .  .  .  .  .  .  232   3 DON JUAN 10    16   2
  THY CLIFFS DEAR DOVER HARBOUR AND HOTEL  .  .  .  .  .  .  .  259   3 DON JUAN 10    69   2
  A COUNTRY IN ALL SENSES THE MOST DEAR .  .  .  .  .  .  .  .  263   3 DON JUAN 10    77   5
  BUT WHAT THEY PLEASE AND IF THAT THINGS BE DEAR  .  .  .  .  273   3 DON JUAN 11    10   2
  IN THE DEAR OFFICES OF PEACE OR WAR .  .  .  .  .  .  .  .  .  288   3 DON JUAN 11    41   3
  A LOVER WITH CAPRICES SOFT AND DEAR  .  .  .  .  .  .  .  .  438   3 DON JUAN 14    63   4
  AND DEEM'D THAT FALLEN WORSHIP FAR MORE DEAR .  .  .  .  .  476   3 DON JUAN 15    46   3
DEARER
  BESIDES THY PRICE IS SOMETHING DEARER STILL .  .  .  .  .  .  372   2 DON JUAN  4    53  V4
  BUT COUNTRY CONTESTS COST HIM RATHER DEARER .  .  .  .  .  .  534   3 DON JUAN 16    70   3
DEAREST
  FAREWELL TOO DEAREST JULIA--(HERE HE DREW  .  .  .  .  .  .  166   2 DON JUAN  2    18   7
  DEAR UNTO ALL BUT DEAREST TO THEIR EYES  .  .  .  .  .  .  .  354   2 DON JUAN  4    20   2
  OH DEAREST FATHER IN THIS AGONY  .  .  .  .  .  .  .  .  .  .  364   2 DON JUAN  4    38   4
DEARLY
  SOME WENT OFF DEARLY FIFTEEN HUNDRED DOLLARS   .  .  .  .  .  407   2 DON JUAN  4   114   1
  WAS DEARLY PURCHASED BY HIS LAND'S PERDITION   .  .  .  .  .  364   3 DON JUAN 13    11   8
DEARS
  FOR WERE THE SULTAN JUST TO ALL HIS DEARS  .  .  .  .  .  .   10   3 DON JUAN  6     9   6
  I RATHER THINK THE MOON SHOULD DATE THE DEARS  .  .  .  .  .  230   3 DON JUAN 10    10   8
  THERE WERE THE SIX MISS RAWBOLDS--PRETTY DEARS .  .  .  .  .  398   3 DON JUAN 13    85   6
  ARE SOMEHOW ECHOED TO THE PRETTY DEARS   .  .  .  .  .  .  .  489   3 DON JUAN 15    76   3
DEARTH
  'TIS SOMETHING IN THE DEARTH OF FAME  .  .  .  .  .  .  .  .  323   2 DON JUAN  3 L  6   1
  AND YET THOUGH I HAVE SAID THERE WAS NO DEARTH .  .  .  .  .  450   2 DON JUAN  5    67   6
DEATH
  HIS DEATH CONTRIVED TO SPOIL A CHARMING CAUSE  .  .  .  .  .   38   2 DON JUAN  1    33   5
  SAVE DEATH OR DOCTORS' COMMONS--SO HE DIED .  .  .  .  .  .   41   2 DON JUAN  1    36   8
  THE UNEXPECTED DEATH OF SOME OLD LADY .  .  .  .  .  .  .  .   89   2 DON JUAN  1   125   2
  WHO THREATEN'D DEATH--SO JUAN KNOCK'D HIM DOWN .  .  .  .  .  122   2 DON JUAN  1   183   8
  DEATH SHUNS THE WRETCH WHO FAIN THE BLOW WOULD MEET  .  .  .  134   2 DON JUAN  1   197   6
  AND FLESH (WHICH DEATH MOWS DOWN TO HAY) IS GRASS  .  .  .  147   2 DON JUAN  1   220   4
  OR DEATH OF THOSE WE DOTE ON WHEN A PART .  .  .  .  .  .  .  167   2 DON JUAN  2    21   5
  SEA-SICKNESS DEATH HIS LOVE WAS PERFECT HOW ELSE  .  .  .  .  168   2 DON JUAN  2    23   6
  AS IF DEATH WERE MORE DREADFUL BY HIS DOOR .  .  .  .  .  .  174   2 DON JUAN  2    35   5
  'TIS TRUE THAT DEATH AWAITS BOTH YOU AND ME  .  .  .  .  .  175   2 DON JUAN  2    36   3
  BEEN THEIR FAMILIAR AND NOW DEATH WAS HERE .  .  .  .  .  .  182   2 DON JUAN  2    49   8
  HE BUT REQUESTED TO BE BLED TO DEATH  .  .  .  .  .  .  .  .  197   2 DON JUAN  2    76   1
  DEATH LEFT NO DOUBT AND THE DEAD BURTHEN LAY   .  .  .  .  .  204   2 DON JUAN  2    90   3
  FOR DEATH THOUGH VANQUISH'D STILL RETIRED WITH STRIFE   .  .  214   2 DON JUAN  2   111   8
  AND WISH'D IT DEATH IN WHICH HE HAD REPOSED  .  .  .  .  .  215   2 DON JUAN  2   112   5
  RECALL'D HIS ANSWERING SPIRITS BACK FROM DEATH .  .  .  .  .  215   2 DON JUAN  2   113   4
  WERE BLACK AS DEATH THEIR LASHES THE SAME HUE  .  .  .  .  .  218   2 DON JUAN  2   117   2
  SHOULD REACH HIS BLOOD THEN O'ER HIM STILL AS DEATH  .  .  .  232   2 DON JUAN  2   143   7
  AND ALL ITS CHARM LIKE DEATH WITHOUT ITS TERRORS   .  .  .  261   2 DON JUAN  2   197   8
  BUT THIS IS NOT THE DEATH THAT IT SHOULD DIE--  .  .  .  .  272   2 DON JUAN  2 V 1   3
  ALL TRAGEDIES ARE FINISH'D BY A DEATH .  .  .  .  .  .  .  .  280   2 DON JUAN  3     9   1
  THEY SAY NO MORE OF DEATH OR OF THE LADY .  .  .  .  .  .  .  280   2 DON JUAN  3     9   8
  SO DRAMAS CLOSE WITH DEATH OR SETTLEMENT FOR LIFE  .  .  .  280   2 DON JUAN  3     9  V7
  AVOUCH'D HIS DEATH (SUCH PEOPLE NEVER DIE)  .  .  .  .  .  .  295   2 DON JUAN  3    38   3
  WHETHER THE WORD WAS DEATH OR BUT THE CHAIN--  .  .  .  .  .  299   2 DON JUAN  3    47   4
  A GENIUS WHO HAS DRUNK HIMSELF TO DEATH  .  .  .  .  .  .  .  309   2 DON JUAN  3    66   2
  THE DEATH OF FRIENDS AND THAT WHICH SLAYS EVEN MORE--  .  .  350   2 DON JUAN  4    12   3
  THE DEATH OF FRIENDSHIP LOVE YOUTH ALL THAT IS  .  .  .  .  350   2 DON JUAN  4    12   4
  THE OCEAN-BURIED RISEN FROM DEATH TO BE  .  .  .  .  .  .  .  363   2 DON JUAN  4    36   4
  PERCHANCE THE DEATH OF ONE SHE LOVED TOO WELL  .  .  .  .  .  363   2 DON JUAN  4    36   5
  STERN AS HER SIRE ON ME SHE CRIED LET DEATH .  .  .  .  .  366   2 DON JUAN  4    42   4
```

DEATH   (CONTINUED)

	PAGE	VOL	CANTO	STANZA	LN
LIKE ONE LIFE COULD NOT HOLD NOR DEATH DESTROY	376	2 DON JUAN	4	59	8
SHE HAD NO PULSE BUT DEATH SEEM'D ABSENT STILL	377	2 DON JUAN	4	60	3
AND LOSE THEIR OWN IN UNIVERSAL DEATH	399	2 DON JUAN	4	102	8
BEFORE PELIDES' DEATH OR HOMER'S BIRTH	400	2 DON JUAN	4	104	8
CAN THIS BE DEATH THEN WHAT IS LIFE OR DEATH	430	2 DON JUAN	5	36	1
CAN THIS BE DEATH THEN WHAT IS LIFE OR DEATH	430	2 DON JUAN	5	36	1
TO TRY IF I COULD WRENCH AUGHT OUT OF DEATH	431	2 DON JUAN	5	38	7
DEATH TO HIS PUBLISHER TO HIM 'TIS SPORT	440	2 DON JUAN	5	52	5
A KIND OF DEATH COMES O'ER US ALL ALONE	443	2 DON JUAN	5	57	7
O'ER THEM LIKE DEATH UPON A MONARCH'S PRIDE	462	2 DON JUAN	5	87	V6
PROVED DEATH IN BATTLE EQUAL TO A PENSION--	96	3 DON JUAN	7	58	8
THAT AWFUL PAUSE DIVIDING LIFE FROM DEATH	111	3 DON JUAN	7	87	2
BUT WHEN THEY LIGHT UPON IMMEDIATE DEATH	133	3 DON JUAN	8	40	7
WHO PASSES FOR IN LIFE AND DEATH MOST LUCKY	143	3 DON JUAN	8	61	2
WHERE IF MEN SEEK HER NOT AND DEATH BE MORE	143	3 DON JUAN	8	62	4
THOUGH LIFE AND DEATH AND VICTORY WERE AT STAKE	147	3 DON JUAN	8	70	7
AND DEATH IS DRUNK WITH GORE THERE'S NOT A STREET	152	3 DON JUAN	8	82	2
ACKNOWLEDGE AUGHT OF DREAD OF DEATH OR FOE	155	3 DON JUAN	8	87	5
DEATH LAUGHS--GO PONDER O'ER THE SKELETON	188	3 DON JUAN	9	11	1
DEATH LAUGHS AT ALL YOU WEEP FOR--LOOK UPON	188	3 DON JUAN	9	11	5
AND THUS DEATH LAUGHS--IT IS SAD MERRIMENT	189	3 DON JUAN	9	13	1
FOR ME I SOMETIMES THINK THAT LIFE IS DEATH	190	3 DON JUAN	9	16	7
THOU GATE OF LIFE AND DEATH--THOU NONDESCRIPT	210	3 DON JUAN	9	55	2
BECAUSE SHE PUT A FAVOURITE TO DEATH	222	3 DON JUAN	9	81	6
AND DEATH THE SOVEREIGN'S SOVEREIGN THOUGH THE GREAT	237	3 DON JUAN	10	25	1
HE LIVED (NOT DEATH BUT JUAN) IN A HURRY	237	3 DON JUAN	10	26	1
QUIT AND THOUGH DEATH HAD THREATENED AN EJECTION	245	3 DON JUAN	10	43	2
DEATH SO CALL'D IS A THING WHICH MAKES MEN WEEP	411	3 DON JUAN	14	3	7
LESS FROM DISGUST OF LIFE THAN DREAD OF DEATH	412	3 DON JUAN	14	4	1
A PAPER KITE WHICH FLIES 'TWIXT LIFE AND DEATH	414	3 DON JUAN	14	8	5
OH DEATH THOU DUNNEST OF ALL DUNS THOU DAILY	459	3 DON JUAN	15	8	1
LIKE HOLBEIN'S DANCE OF DEATH--BUT 'TIS THE SAME)--	473	3 DON JUAN	15	39	8
BY DEATH WHEN WE ARE LEFT ALAS BEHIND	475	3 DON JUAN	15	44	6
A VIGIL THERE WHERE ALL BUT DEATH SHOULD SLEEP	508	3 DON JUAN	16	18	8
BUT DEATH IS IMAGED IN THEIR SHADOWY BEAMS	509	3 DON JUAN	16	19	6
AND 'TIS HELD AS FAITH TO THEIR BED OF DEATH	519	3 DON JUAN	16	L 3	7
AND RATHER VARIABLY FOR STONY DEATH	560	3 DON JUAN	16	121	2

DEATH-CRY
THE DEATH-CRY DROWNING IN THE BATTLE'S ROAR	111	3 DON JUAN	7	87	8

DEATH-DISGORGING
THE DEATH-DISGORGING RAMPART ONCE AGAIN	151	3 DON JUAN	8	79	5

DEATHLESS
OF THINE IMAGINARY DEATHLESS TREE	101	3 DON JUAN	7	68	7

DEATH-LIKE
PILLOW'D HIS DEATH-LIKE FOREHEAD THEN SHE WRUNG	216	2 DON JUAN	2	114	5

DEATH'S
THOSE WHO CATCH COLD IN SHADOWS OF DEATH'S VALLEY	131	3 DON JUAN	8	36	8
DEATH'S A REFORMER ALL MEN MUST ALLOW	237	3 DON JUAN	10	25	8

DEATHS
AND MANY DEATHS DO THEY ESCAPE BY THIS	350	2 DON JUAN	4	12	2
('MONGST OTHER DEATHS THE GENERAL RIBAUPIERRE'S	147	3 DON JUAN	8	71	6
ABOUT THE PRESENT FAMILY'S DEATHS AND WOOINGS	527	3 DON JUAN	16	53	8

DEATH-WATCH
LIKE THE DEATH-WATCH WITHIN OUR EARS THE ILLS	117	3 DON JUAN	8	12	6

DEATH-WOUND
THE DROPS FELL FROM HIS DEATH-WOUND AND HE DREW ILL	276	3 DON JUAN	11	16	6

DEBARRED
GREAT GALILEO WAS DEBARRED THE SUN	565	3 DON JUAN	17	8	1

DEBATE
INSTEAD OF BEARING UP WITHOUT DEBATE	394	2 DON JUAN	4	93	6
WHICH MADE A LONG DEBATE BUT I MUST HALT	83	3 DON JUAN	7	35	6
UPON DEBATE THE PAPERS ECHOED YET	400	3 DON JUAN	13	90	5

DEBATER
AND THE LORD HENRY WAS A GREAT DEBATER	367	3 DON JUAN	13	20	7

DEBATES
TO HEAR DEBATES WHOSE THUNDER ROUSED (NOT ROUSES)	353	3 DON JUAN	12	82	4
LISTENING DEBATES NOT VERY WISE OR WITTY	380	3 DON JUAN	13	48	6

DEBAUCHEE
THAT HE WAS NOT AN ANCIENT DEBAUCHEE	251	3 DON JUAN	10	54	2

DEBONNAIRE
HOWEVER DISCIPLINED AND DEBONNAIRE--	355	3 DON JUAN	12	85	4

DEBT
DEBT HE CALLS WEALTH AND TAXES PARADISE	88	3 DON JUAN	7	45	5
MY DEBT IN BEING THUS ALLOWED TO DIE	100	3 DON JUAN	7	65	5
MEANTIME THE TAXES CASTLEREAGH AND DEBT	174	3 DON JUAN	8	125	5
TO PROVE THE PUBLIC DEBT IS NOT CONSUMING US--	200	3 DON JUAN	9	35	5
MEANTIME READ ALL THE NATIONAL DEBT SINKERS	357	3 DON JUAN	12	89	7
AND DEBT AND WHATNOT FOR THEIR SOLACE SENT	360	3 DON JUAN	13	5	8
HAS NOT CONTRACTED MUCH MORE DEBT THAN KNOWLEDGE	377	3 DON JUAN	13	42	8
THE VERY SUICIDE THAT PAYS HIS DEBT	412	3 DON JUAN	14	4	4
TO TELL HOW HE REDUCED THE NATION'S DEBT	440	3 DON JUAN	14	68	4
AND FOR WHICH NATURE MIGHT FOREGO HER DEBT--	458	3 DON JUAN	15	7	6
THE DEBT UNSUNK YET SINKS ALL IT RECEIVES	548	3 DON JUAN	16	99	2

DEBTOR
GULBEYAZ WHO LOOKED ON HIM AS HER DEBTOR	483	2 DON JUAN	5	124	5
AND WATERLOO HAS MADE THE WORLD YOUR DEBTOR--	184	3 DON JUAN	9	3	7
THE BENCH TOO SEATS OR SUITS FULL MANY A DEBTOR	280	3 DON JUAN	11	25	5
TO MAKE EACH CORRESPONDENT A NEW DEBTOR	406	3 DON JUAN	13	104	8
SOME SPLENDID DEBTOR HE WOULD TAKE BY SAP	459	3 DON JUAN	15	8	4

		PAGE	VOL		CANTO	STANZA	LN

DEBTS
  SO MUCH AS WHEN WE CALL OUR OLD DEBTS IN 113   2 DON JUAN   1   167   6
  WHO FATTEN ON THEIR COUNTRY'S GORE AND DEBTS 187   3 DON JUAN   9   10   5
  OF PAYING DEBTS WHICH CREDITORS REGRET) 412   3 DON JUAN 14   4   6
DEBUT
  WITH THIS DEBUT WHICH MADE A STRONG IMPRESSION 400   3 DON JUAN 13   90   6
DECANTED
  WHEN ONCE DECANTED--I PRESUME TO GUESS SO 458   3 DON JUAN 15   6   6
DECAY
  SEEMING TO WEEP THE DYING DAY'S DECAY 338   2 DON JUAN   3   108   6
  A LONG AND SNAKE-LIKE LIFE OF DULL DECAY 348   2 DON JUAN   4   9   7
  SHAPED BY DECAY PERCHANCE HATH GIVEN THE POWER 388   3 DON JUAN 13   64   2
DECAY'D
  THE TIME MUST COME WHEN BOTH ALIKE DECAY'D 400   2 DON JUAN   4   104   5
DECAYING
  FOR ITS DECAYING FAME AND FORMER WORTH 257   3 DON JUAN 10   66   5
DECEASED
  BY THE DECEASED WHO LIE IN FAMOUS SLUMBER 120   3 DON JUAN   8   18   3
DECEIT
  GIRD MORE DECEIT WITHIN A PETTICOAT 296   2 DON JUAN   3   41   6
DECEIVE
  NOW THOUGH WE KNOW OF OLD THAT LOOKS DECEIVE 493   3 DON JUAN 15   84   6
DECEMBER
  BECAUSE DECEMBER WITH HIS BREATH SO HOARY 229   3 DON JUAN 10   9   6
DECEMBER'S
  DECEMBER'S DROWSY DAY TO HIS DULL RACE-- 426   3 DON JUAN 14   36   4
DECENCIES
  TEACH THEM THE DECENCIES OF GOOD THREESCORE 267   3 DON JUAN 10   86   1
DECENCY
  OR FOR THE SAKE OF DECENCY ABIDE 106   2 DON JUAN   1   156   6
DECENT
  CATULLUS SCARCELY HAS A DECENT POEM 45   2 DON JUAN   1   42   3
  LIKE GARDEN GODS--AND NOT SO DECENT EITHER 46   2 DON JUAN   1   45   8
  ONE SHOULD NOT RAIL WITHOUT A DECENT CAUSE 219   2 DON JUAN   2   119   2
  PAIR OF SCARCE DECENT TROWSERS--WENT TO WORK 240   2 DON JUAN   2   160   2
  AFTER A DECENT TIME MUST BE GALLANTED 276   2 DON JUAN   3   4   4
  I'LL NOT BE BULLIED DECENT OR INDECENT 410   2 DON JUAN   4   117 V6
  IN DECENT LONDON WHEN THE DAYLIGHT'S O'ER 282   3 DON JUAN 11   30   5
  I THINK I SHOULD HAVE MADE A DECENT SPOUSE 467   3 DON JUAN 15   24   1
DECIDE
  AND THEN DECIDE WITHOUT GREAT WRONG TO EITHER 357   2 DON JUAN   4   25   7
  THIS I MUST LEAVE SULTANAS TO DECIDE 477   2 DON JUAN   5   115   4
  THE WORLD NOT THE WORLD'S MASTERS WILL DECIDE 184   3 DON JUAN   9   4   6
  TO BE OR NOT TO BE--ERE I DECIDE 190   3 DON JUAN   9   16   1
  I NE'ER DECIDE WHAT I SHALL SAY AND THIS I CALL . . . 203   3 DON JUAN   9   41   5
  DECIDE AND EVERYBODY ONE DAY WILL 270   3 DON JUAN 11   4   7
  ABROAD SUCH THINGS DECIDE FEW WOMEN'S FATE-- 345   3 DON JUAN 12   64   5
  MUST THE EVENT DECIDE BETWEEN THE TWO 449   3 DON JUAN 14   90   3
DECIDED
  SHE NEXT DECIDED HE WAS ONLY BAD 35   2 DON JUAN   1   27   4
  THEY TELL ME 'TIS DECIDED YOU DEPART 130   2 DON JUAN   1   192   1
  DECIDED THUS AND SHOW'D GOOD REASON WHY 281   2 DON JUAN   3   11   6
  BECAUSE ITS OWN GOOD PLEASURE HATH DECIDED 366   3 DON JUAN 13   16   8
  AND MORALLY DECIDED THE BEST STATE IS 469   3 DON JUAN 15   29   6
DECIMATE
  FOR WHICH MEN VAINLY DECIMATE THE THRONG 144   3 DON JUAN   8   63   2
DECK
  GASPING ON DECK BECAUSE YOU SOAR TOO HIGH BOB 10   2 DON JUAN   D   3   7
  AND STANDING UPON DECK THE DASHING SPRAY 162   2 DON JUAN   2   11   5
  SO JUAN STOOD BEWILDER'D ON THE DECK 163   2 DON JUAN   2   13   1
DECK'D
  HAD DECK'D HER OUT IN ALL THE HUES OF HEAVEN 407   2 DON JUAN   4   114   4
  SYMMETRICAL BUT DECK'D WITH CARVINGS QUAINT-- 389   3 DON JUAN 13   65   2
  (THERE'S FAME) YOUNG PARTRIDGE' FILLETS DECK'D WITH TRUFFLES 484   3 DON JUAN 15   66   8
DECKED
  A PONIARD DECKED HER GIRDLE AS THE SIGN 475   2 DON JUAN   5   111   7
  FROM THE MANURE OF HUMAN CLAY THOUGH DECKED 199   3 DON JUAN   9   34   5
  WITH MANY MORE BY RANK AND FASHION DECKED 382   3 DON JUAN 13   52   6
  DECKED BY THE RAYS REFLECTED FROM HIS HOST 383   3 DON JUAN 13   53   5
DECKS
  THE WATER LEFT THE HOLD AND WASH'D THE DECKS 172   2 DON JUAN   2   31   2
DECLAIMING
  WITH DANDIES DINED HEARD SENATORS DECLAIMING 418   3 DON JUAN 14   18   3
DECLARATION
  IS JUST TWO MINUTES FOR YOUR DECLARATION-- 482   2 DON JUAN   5   123   7
DECLARE
  WAS TO DECLARE HOW SAGE AND STILL AND STEADY 49   2 DON JUAN   1   50   7
  THAT THEREFORE DO I PREVIOUSLY DECLARE 369   3 DON JUAN 13   25   7
  I DO DECLARE UPON AN AFFIDAVIT 444   3 DON JUAN 14   80   1
DECLARED
  DECLARED WITH ALL HIS GRAND DISCOVERIES RECENT 69   3 DON JUAN   7   5   6
  HAS BEEN DECLARED AN ACT OF INURBANITY 565   3 DON JUAN 17   7   7
DECLARES
  WHO TOOK ALGIERS DECLARES I USED HIM VILELY 102   2 DON JUAN   1   148   8
  BECAUSE THE PUBLISHER DECLARES IN SOOTH 397   2 DON JUAN   4   97   6
DECLINE
  TO IRRIGATE THE DRYNESS OF DECLINE 360   3 DON JUAN 13   5   6
  TO GENTLY SMOOTHE THE PROGRESS OF DECLINE 360   3 DON JUAN 13   5 V6
  THEN IF SHE HATH NOT THAT SERENE DECLINE 395   3 DON JUAN 13   77   1
  RADIANT AND GRAVE--AS PITYING MAN'S DECLINE 476   3 DON JUAN 15   45   5

179

```
                                                       PAGE VOL       CANTO STANZA LN
DECLINED
    ALTHOUGH DEFIANCE OFT DECLINED AFFORDS  . . . . . . 153  2 DON JUAN  1   V  4   5
    OF MODESTY DECLINED THE ASSISTANCE PROFFERED  . . . .  36  3 DON JUAN  6      61  4
    HER FACE DECLINED AND WAS UNSEEN HER HAIR  . . . . .  60  3 DON JUAN  6     108  1
    MUST BE DECLINED WHILE LIFE'S THIN THREAD'S SPUN OUT  . . . 376  3 DON JUAN 13      40  7
    WHEN CALLED NEXT DAY DECLINED THE ROUGH ADVENTURE . . . 425  3 DON JUAN 14      35  V8
DECLIVITY
    DESCENDING RATHER QUICKLY THE DECLIVITY  . . . . . . 290  2 DON JUAN  3      29  2
    SUNSET THE TIME THE PLACE THE SAME DECLIVITY  . . . . 272  3 DON JUAN 11       8  2
DECOMPOSE
    THE DEVIL MAY DECOMPOSE BUT NEVER SETTLE . . . . . . .  33  3 DON JUAN  6      55  8
DECORATE
    TRIMMED EITHER HEADS OR HEARTS TO DECORATE  . . . . .  13  3 DON JUAN  6      14  6
    STILL UNIMPAIR'D TO DECORATE THE SCENE  . . . . . . 389  3 DON JUAN 13      66  6
DECORATED
    AND DIVERS SMOKED SUPERB PIPES DECORATED . . . . . . 441  2 DON JUAN  5      53  5
DECORATES
    AND DECORATES THE BOOK OF COMMON PRAYER  . . . . . .  17  3 DON JUAN  6      23  7
DECOROUS
    FIRST CAME HER DAMSELS A DECOROUS FILE  . . . . . . 495  2 DON JUAN  5     146  1
    FLIRTATION--BUT DECOROUS THE MERE PRAISE  . . . . . 408  3 DON JUAN 13     108  5
DECORUM
    REQUIRES DECORUM AND IS APT TO DOUBLE . . . . . . . 292  3 DON JUAN 11      46  7
DECREASED
    AND EVERY NEW CREATION HATH DECREASED . . . . . . . 202  3 DON JUAN  9      39  6
DECREE
    (FOR DAY NE'ER SAW HIS MERITS) COULD DECREE . . . . .  86  3 DON JUAN  7      41  4
    AS IF EACH CHARMING WORD WERE A DECREE  . . . . . . 492  3 DON JUAN 15      82  4
DEDICATE
    MEANTIME--SIR LAUREATE--I PROCEED TO DEDICATE . . . .  20  2 DON JUAN  D      17  1
DEDUCE
    FROM WHOM I NOW DEDUCE THESE MORAL LESSONS  . . . . 375  3 DON JUAN 13      38  5
DEDUCTED
    THY LONG LONG BILLS WHENCE NOTHING IS DEDUCTED . . . 259  3 DON JUAN 10      69  8
DEE
    THE DEE THE DON BALGOUNIE'S BRIG'S BLACK WALL  . . . 233  3 DON JUAN 10      18  3
DEED
    WHICH LAW AFFORDS TO MANY A DIRTY DEED  . . . . . . 151  2 DON JUAN  1   V  2   4
    NOR MUCH DISPOSED TO WAIT IN WORD OR DEED  . . . . .  56  3 DON JUAN  6     101  2
    WHATEVER DEED BE DONE I WILL RELATE 'EM  . . . . . . 107  3 DON JUAN  7      81  V6
    ROLLS BY THE CITY WALL BUT DEED NOR WORD . . . . . . 155  3 DON JUAN  8      87  4
    CAME UP ALL MARVELLING AT SUCH A DEED . . . . . . . 275  3 DON JUAN 11      14  3
DEEDS
    RATHER BY DEEDS THAN WORDS BECAUSE THE CASE  . . . . 240  2 DON JUAN  2     159  2
    PROMPTS DEEDS ETERNITY CAN NOT ANNUL  . . . . . . . 258  2 DON JUAN  2     192  5
    WAS MINGLED WITH HIS EVIL DEEDS AND WAYS . . . . . . 303  2 DON JUAN  3      55  V2
    AMIDST THE SAVAGE DEEDS HE HAD DONE AND SEEN  . . . . 304  2 DON JUAN  3      57  4
    GREAT DEEDS ARE DOING--HOW SHALL I RELATE 'EM  . . . 107  3 DON JUAN  7      81  6
    OF DEEDS TO HUMAN HAPPINESS MOST DEAR . . . . . . . 108  3 DON JUAN  7      83  6
    MY CHANCE SO HAPPEN--DEEDS) WITH ALL WHO WAR  . . . . 194  3 DON JUAN  9      24  2
    DID NOT HIS DEEDS UNRIDDLE THEM EACH DAY-- . . . . . 207  3 DON JUAN  9      50  4
    AND CARE BUT FOR DISCOVERIES AND NOT DEEDS . . . . . 352  3 DON JUAN 12      80  4
    OF DEEDS AND DAYS WHEN THEY HAD FILL'D THE EAR  . . . 476  3 DON JUAN 15      46  5
DEEM
    TO DEEM AS A MOST LOGICAL CONCLUSION  . . . . . . .  12  2 DON JUAN  D       5  5
    NONE CAN DEEM HARSHLIER OF ME THAN I DEEM  . . . . . 130  2 DON JUAN  1     193  6
    NONE CAN DEEM HARSHLIER OF ME THAN I DEEM  . . . . . 130  2 DON JUAN  1     193  6
    AND DEEM NOT WHAT I DEEM'D MY SOUL INVINCIBLE  . . . 143  2 DON JUAN  1     213  8
    AND DEEM THAT IT WAS SAVED PERHAPS IN VAIN  . . . . 213  2 DON JUAN  2     108  8
    DEEM THIS A COMMENTATOR'S PHANTASY  . . . . . . . . 281  2 DON JUAN  3      11  4
    I COULD NOT DEEM MYSELF A SLAVE . . . . . . . . . . 321  2 DON JUAN  3   L  3   6
    AS HERCULES MIGHT DEEM HIS OWN  . . . . . . . . . . 325  2 DON JUAN  3   L 13  V6
    AND ALWAYS ENVY THOUGH WE DEEM IT FRANTIC  . . . . . 353  2 DON JUAN  4      18  8
    WHICH FOR HIMSELF HE SEEM'D TO DEEM NO WORSE  . . . . 417  2 DON JUAN  5      12  7
    WHICH IS NOT QUITE SO LIGHT AS YOU MAY DEEM  . . . . 459  2 DON JUAN  5      82  4
    THESE ARE BUT VULGAR OATHS AS YOU MAY DEEM  . . . . 112  3 DON JUAN  8       1  2
    TO DEEM THE WOODS SHALL BE OUR HOME AT LAST--  . . . 142  3 DON JUAN  8      60  8
    AND DEEM BECAUSE WE SEE WE ARE ALL-SEEING  . . . . . 190  3 DON JUAN  9      16  4
    FOR ME I DEEM AN ABSOLUTE AUTOCRAT  . . . . . . . . 194  3 DON JUAN  9      23  7
    IF THIS BE TRUE FOR WE MUST DEEM THE MODE  . . . . . 226  3 DON JUAN 10       2  2
    YOU'LL DEEM NO DOUBT THEY PUT IT TO A GOOD USE . . . 242  3 DON JUAN 10      36  8
    WHICH BRITONS DEEM THEIR UTI POSSIDETIS  . . . . . . 246  3 DON JUAN 10      45  8
    WEAKNESS FOR WHAT MOST PEOPLE DEEM MERE VERMIN--  . . 249  3 DON JUAN 10      50  5
    HOW ALL THE NATIONS DEEM HER THEIR WORST FOE  . . . . 258  3 DON JUAN 10      67  5
    NOT THAT I DEEM OUR CHIEF JUDGE IS A HOLLOW MAN--)  . 357  3 DON JUAN 12   V 18  8
    SOME DEEM IT BUT THE DISTANT ECHO GIVEN  . . . . . . 388  3 DON JUAN 13      63  6
    OF WHAT THEY DEEM THEMSELVES MOST CONSEQUENTIAL--  . 418  3 DON JUAN 14      20  6
    SOME WOULD NOT DEEM SUCH WOMEN COULD BE FOUND  . . . 429  3 DON JUAN 14      44  4
    THAN WHEN SOME SQUEAMISH PEOPLE DEEM HER FRAIL  . . . 483  3 DON JUAN 15      64  4
    WAS WEAK ENOUGH TO DEEM POPE A GREAT POET  . . . . . 524  3 DON JUAN 16      47  7
    ARE SO DIVINE THAT I MUST DEEM THEM REAL--  . . . . 553  3 DON JUAN 16      07  8
DEEM'D
    AS IF SHE DEEM'D THAT MYSTERY WOULD ENNOBLE 'EM  . .  28  2 DON JUAN  1      13  8
    'TIS ALSO PLEASANT TO BE DEEM'D MAGNANIMOUS  . . . .  37  2 DON JUAN  1      30  3
    AND EVERYBODY BUT HIS MOTHER DEEM'D  . . . . . . . .  51  2 DON JUAN  1      54  4
    HER PLAN SHE DEEM'D BOTH INNOCENT AND FEASIBLE . . .  66  2 DON JUAN  1      83  1
    AND DEEM NOT WHAT I DEEM'D MY SOUL INVINCIBLE  . . . 143  2 DON JUAN  1     213  8
    AND WHEN THEY DEEM'D ITS MOISTURE WAS COMPLETE . . . 201  2 DON JUAN  2      85  4
    YET DEEM'D HERSELF IN COMMON PITY BOUND  . . . . . . 224  2 DON JUAN  2     129  6
```

DEEM'D   (CONTINUED)
SUCH APPETITE IN ONE SHE HAD DEEM'D DEAD . . . . 239 2 DON JUAN 2   158   4
TO BE HER HAPPINESS AND WHOM SHE DEEM'D . . . . 247 2 DON JUAN 2   172   6
BUT CERTAINLY TO ONE DEEM'D DEAD RETURNING . . . . . . 300 2 DON JUAN 3   49   7
HE DEEM'D BEING IN A LONE ISLE AMONG FRIENDS . . . . . 318 2 DON JUAN 3   83   4
HIM WHOM SHE DEEM'D A HABITANT WHERE DWELL . . . . . . 363 2 DON JUAN 4   36   3
IF THE SOPRANO MIGHT BE DEEM'D TO BE MALE . . . . . . 394 2 DON JUAN 4   92   4
AND DEEM'D THAT FALLEN WORSHIP FAR MORE DEAR . . . . . 476 3 DON JUAN 15   46   3
LITTLE AURORA DEEM'D SHE WAS THE THEME . . . . 480 3 DON JUAN 15   55   1
OF FLUTTERERS THOUGH SHE DEEM'D HE HAD MORE SENSE . . . 493 3 DON JUAN 15   83   3
DEEMED
AND DEEMED HERSELF EXTREMELY CONDESCENDING . . . . . 478 2 DON JUAN 5   116   3
SHE DEEMED HER LEAST COMMAND MUST YIELD DELIGHT . . . . 485 2 DON JUAN 5   128   3
BUT A MAN'S GRANDMOTHER IS DEEMED FAIR GAME . . . . . . 53 3 DON JUAN 6   94 V5
IN SIGHT TWO HORSEMEN WHO WERE DEEMED COSSACQUES . . . . 87 3 DON JUAN 7   43   2
SHE MERELY WAS DEEMED AMIABLE AND WITTY . . . . 338 3 DON JUAN 12   47   4
HATH WON THE EXPERIENCE WHICH IS DEEMED SO WEIGHTY . . . 339 3 DON JUAN 12   50   8
SINCE LAUGHTER NOW-A-DAYS IS DEEMED TOO SERIOUS . . . . 358 3 DON JUAN 13   1   2
SHE DEEMED HIS MERITS SOMETHING MORE THAN COMMON . . . . 473 3 DON JUAN 15   40   6
SHE NEITHER DEEMED HIS FEELINGS WERE INTENSE . . . . . 493 3 DON JUAN 15   83 V5
AND HAYLEY'S TRIUMPHS WHICH SHE DEEMED PATHETIC . . . . 525 3 DON JUAN 16   50   3
SO MUCH HE DEEMED HIS PATRONAGE AN HONOUR . . . . . . 528 3 DON JUAN 16   57   6
WHO IN HIS LIFE-TIME EACH WAS DEEMED A BORE . . . . . . 566 3 DON JUAN 17   9   4
DEEMING
DEEMING THE CHAIN IT WEARS EVEN MEN MAY FIT . . . . . . 18 2 DON JUAN D   15   4
THAT EVEN THE ABLE SEAMAN DEEMING HIS . . . . 173 2 DON JUAN 2   33   5
AND DEEMING THERE WERE REMEDIES FOR ANY ILL . . . . . 187 2 DON JUAN 2   59   7
FOR DEEMING HUMAN CLAY BUT COMMON DIRT . . . . 96 2 DON JUAN 7   58   5
BY DEEMING THAT MY MUSE'S CONVERSATION . . . . 498 3 DON JUAN 15   94   6
DEEMING THE SAGE WOULD BE MUCH MORTIFIED . . . . 522 3 DON JUAN 16   43   5
DEEMS
AND DEEMS HE THAT WE ALWAYS WILL FORBEAR . . . . 153 2 DON JUAN 1   V 4   4
PROPHETICALLY OR THAT WHICH ONE DEEMS . . . . 45 3 DON JUAN 6   78   6
BUT DEEMS HIMSELF THE FIRST IN GLORY'S VAN . . . . . . 108 3 DON JUAN 7   84   6
HE DEEMS IT IS HIS PROPER PLACE TO BE . . . . 303 3 DON JUAN 11   70   5
DEEP
HIS LIKE ALL DEEP GRIEF PLUNGED IN SOLITUDE . . . . . . 68 2 DON JUAN 1   87   4
IN DEEP DESPAIR LEST HE HAD DONE AMISS . . . . 81 2 DON JUAN 1   112   5
SHEDS BEAUTY AND DEEP SOFTNESS O'ER THE WHOLE . . . . . 82 2 DON JUAN 1   114   6
AT MIDNIGHT ON THE BLUE AND MOONLIT DEEP . . . . 87 2 DON JUAN 1   122   2
MY SHAME AND SORROW DEEP IN MY HEART'S CORE . . . . . . 132 2 DON JUAN 1   195   4
AND THE DIM DESOLATE DEEP TWELVE DAYS HAD FEAR . . . . 182 2 DON JUAN 2   49   7
AND HOPELESS EYES WHICH ON THE DEEP ALONE . . . . . . 182 2 DON JUAN 2   49 V6
INTO THE DEEP WITHOUT A TEAR OR GROAN . . . . 202 2 DON JUAN 2   87   8
WITH THE DEEP DEADLY THOUGHT THAT THEY MUST PART . . . 203 2 DON JUAN 2   88   8
TO HEAVE INTO THE DEEP WITH THOSE BEFORE . . . . 209 2 DON JUAN 2   101   6
AWAY THE VAST SALT DREAD ETERNAL DEEP . . . . 210 2 DON JUAN 2   103   8
HAD EER ESCAPED MORE DANGERS ON THE DEEP . . . . 229 2 DON JUAN 2   137 V7
ON ONE SIDE AND THE DEEP SEA CALM AND CHILL . . . . . 252 2 DON JUAN 2   183   6
YIELDED TO THE DEEP TWILIGHT'S PURPLE CHARM . . . . . 253 2 DON JUAN 2   184   8
AND WHEN THOSE DEEP AND BURNING MOMENTS PASS'D . . . . 260 2 DON JUAN 2   195   1
THE ASHES OF OUR HOPES IS A DEEP GRIEF . . . . 301 2 DON JUAN 3   51   7
THAN THE STERN SINGLE DEEP AND WORDLESS IRE . . . . . 305 2 DON JUAN 3   58   7
WHILE SWUNG THE DEEP BELL IN THE DISTANT TOWER . . . . 335 2 DON JUAN 3   102   5
FULL OF DEEP RAPTURES AND OF BUMPERS THEY-- . . . . . 343 2 DON JUAN 3 V 98   7
THEY SHOULD HAVE LIVED TOGETHER DEEP IN WOODS . . . . . 358 2 DON JUAN 4   28   1
A GENTLE SLUMBER BUT IT WAS NOT DEEP . . . . 359 2 DON JUAN 4   29   3
OR AS THE STIRRING OF A DEEP CLEAR STREAM . . . . . . 360 2 DON JUAN 4   30   1
FROM TWO SMART SABRE GASHES DEEP AND RED-- . . . . . . 370 2 DON JUAN 4   49   7
BUT HER LARGE DARK EYE SHOW'D DEEP PASSION'S FORCE . . . 374 2 DON JUAN 4   56   7
WERE DABBLED WITH THE DEEP BLOOD WHICH RAN O'ER . . . . 376 2 DON JUAN 4   59   2
FORLORN AND GAZING ON THE DEEP BLUE SURGE . . . . . . 387 2 DON JUAN 4   79   3
ACQUIRE THE DEEP AND BITTER POWER TO GIVE . . . . . . 402 2 DON JUAN 4   107   4
IN ALL WHO O'ER THE GREAT DEEP TAKE THEIR WAYS . . . . 414 2 DON JUAN 5   6   6
ON THE ROUGH DEEP BUT THIS LAST BLOW--AND HERE . . . . 420 2 DON JUAN 5   19   1
YOU KNOW HOW NEAR US THE DEEP BOSPHORUS FLOATS . . . . 464 2 DON JUAN 5   92   4
AND THE DEEP PASSIONS FLASHING THROUGH HER FORM . . . . 489 2 DON JUAN 5   135   7
YET DISAPPOINTED JOYS ARE WOES AS DEEP . . . . 16 3 DON JUAN 6   20   4
ADMIRING THIS NEW NATIVE OF THE DEEP . . . . 36 3 DON JUAN 6   60   8
THERE WAS DEEP SILENCE IN THE CHAMBER DIM . . . . . . 38 3 DON JUAN 6   64   1
THE NIGHTINGLE THAT SINGS WITH THE DEEP THORN . . . . . 49 3 DON JUAN 6   87   5
SO DEEP AN ANGUISH WRUNG GULBEYAZM BROW . . . . 58 3 DON JUAN 6   105   4
BY DEEP EMOTION--YOU MAY SOMETIMES TRACE . . . . 61 3 DON JUAN 6   111   4
DEEP IN THE CAVERNS OF THE DEADLY TIDE-- . . . . 63 3 DON JUAN 6   115   4
BUT THE TOWN DITCH BELOW WAS DEEP AS OCEAN . . . . . . 72 3 DON JUAN 7   11   3
THE VASTY DEEP TO WHOM YOU MAY EXCLAIM . . . . 132 3 DON JUAN 8   38   3
HAD FEATHERS WHEN A TRAVELLER ON DEEP WAYS IS . . . . . 197 3 DON JUAN 9   30   8
WHICH THREATENS INUNDATIONS DEEP AND YELLOW . . . . . 228 3 DON JUAN 10   7   4
NOW) YOU MAY CROSS THE BLUE DEEP AND WHITE FOAM-- . . . 290 3 DON JUAN 11   44   3
NATIONS ATHWART THE DEEP THE GOLDEN RAYS . . . . 319 3 DON JUAN 12   8   4
BROAD AS TRANSPARENT DEEP AND FRESHLY FED . . . . . . 385 3 DON JUAN 13   57   2
THROUGH THE SERENE AND PLACID GLASSY DEEP . . . . . . 447 3 DON JUAN 14   87   7
ADELINE NO DEEP JUDGE OF CHARACTER . . . . 463 3 DON JUAN 15   17   1
DEEP SECRETS TO HER ROLLING LIGHT ARE TOLD . . . . . . 506 3 DON JUAN 16   14   6
THOUGHTS BOUNDLESS DEEP BUT SILENT TOO AS SPACE . . . . 524 3 DON JUAN 16   48   8
AS DEEP SEAS IN A SUNNY ATMOSPHERE . . . . 545 3 DON JUAN 16   94   8
WHEN DEEP SLEEP FELL ON MEN AND THE WORLD WORE . . . . 556 3 DON JUAN 16   113   6
DEEPEN'D
THROUGH WHICH THE DEEPEN'D GLORIES ONCE COULD ENTER . . . 387 3 DON JUAN 13   62   3

		PAGE	VOL	CANTO	STANZA	LN

DEEPER
AS IF HER HEART HAD DEEPER THOUGHTS IN STORE . . . . . . 61 2 DON JUAN 1 72 3
THEN THERE WERE SIGHS THE DEEPER FOR SUPPRESSION . . . . 62 2 DON JUAN 1 74 1
THAT IS TILL DEEPER GRIEFS CONGEAL OUR TEARS . . . . . 164 2 DON JUAN 2 15 8
OF HELL SHALL PALL THEM IN A DEEPER CLOAK . . . . . . 110 3 DON JUAN 7 86 8
THE ENDLESS SOOT BESTOWS A TINT FAR DEEPER . . . . . . 232 3 DON JUAN 10 15 3
(LET DEEPER SAGES THE TRUE CAUSE DETERMINE) . . . . . 249 3 DON JUAN 10 50 3
DEEPEST
DEEPEST ATTRACTION FOR WHEN TO THE VIEW . . . . . . 218 2 DON JUAN 2 117 4
DEEPEST IN THOSE WHO LONG THE MOST TO DIE . . . . . 350 2 DON JUAN 4 11 8
OR SAID HER CHEEKS ASSUMED THE DEEPEST DYES . . . . . 489 2 DON JUAN 5 134 3
OF HIS OLD AGE IN WILDS OF DEEPEST MAZE . . . . . . 143 3 DON JUAN 8 61 8
DEEPLY
IN ALL THESE HE WAS MUCH AND DEEPLY READ . . . . . . 44 2 DON JUAN 1 40 5
AND LOVED BY A YOUNG HEART TOO DEEPLY BLEST . . . . . 274 2 DON JUAN 3 1 4
THE HENNA SHOULD BE DEEPLY DYED TO MAKE . . . . . . 314 2 DON JUAN 3 76 1
WE PONDER DEEPLY ON EACH PAST EMOTION . . . . . . 345 2 DON JUAN 4 2 8
OH DARKLY DEEPLY BEAUTIFULLY BLUE . . . . . . 404 2 DON JUAN 4 110 1
ALAS HOW DEEPLY PAINFUL IS ALL PAYMENT . . . . . . 264 3 DON JUAN 10 79 1
DEEP-MOUTH'D
BAY DEEP-MOUTH'D WELCOME AS WE DRAW NEAR HOME . . . . 88 2 DON JUAN 1 123 2
DEEP-MOUTHED
AND THAT DEEP-MOUTHED BOEOTIAN SAVAGE LANDOR . . . . . 298 3 DON JUAN 11 59 7
DEEP-PURPLE
OF HER DEEP-PURPLE ROBE AND SPEAKING LOW . . . . . 466 2 DON JUAN 5 96 7
DEEPS
HE WISHES FOR A BOAT TO SAIL THE DEEPS-- . . . . . . 333 2 DON JUAN 3 98 5
DEER
LIKE SHAKSPEARE'S STEALING DEER LORD BACON'S BRIBES . . . 329 2 DON JUAN 3 92 2
DEFACE
THE GROSSER PARTS BUT FEARFUL TO DEFACE . . . . . . 46 2 DON JUAN 1 44 4
DEFACED
OR WAS AT LEAST UNLESS 'TIS SINCE DEFACED . . . . . 71 3 DON JUAN 7 9 5
DEFEAT
THAT NO DEFEAT CAN DRIVE ME FROM THE NINE . . . . . 415 3 DON JUAN 14 12 4
DEFEATED
AT WHATSOEVER RISK OF BEING DEFEATED . . . . 559 3 DON JUAN 16 119 6
DEFECT
COULD REMEDY THIS LUBBERLY DEFECT . . . . . . 80 3 DON JUAN 7 28 6
FROM OFF THE MARBLE WHICH HAD NO DEFECT . . . . . . 434 3 DON JUAN 14 56 6
OUR GENTLE ADELINE HAD ONE DEFECT-- . . . . . . 446 3 DON JUAN 14 85 1
FOR ONE A SONGSTRESS WHO HATH NO DEFECT . . . . . 471 3 DON JUAN 15 34 3
THE CAUSE OF THIS EFFECT OR THIS DEFECT-- . . . . . 502 3 DON JUAN 16 2 1
MIGHT HAVE FROM TIME ACQUIRED SOME SLIGHT DEFECT . . . 529 3 DON JUAN 16 58 4
DEFECTIVE
FOR THIS EFFECT DEFECTIVE COMES BY CAUSE . . . . . . 502 3 DON JUAN 16 2 2
DEFENCE
DEFENCE OF FREEDOM COUNTRY OR OF LAWS . . . . 86 3 DON JUAN 7 40 4
DEFENCES
BY LAST NIGHT'S GHOST BEEN DRIVEN FROM THEIR DEFENCES . . 545 3 DON JUAN 16 93 8
DEFEND
DEAR IS THE HELPLESS CREATURE WE DEFEND . . . . . . 90 2 DON JUAN 1 126 6
I ASK BUT THIS OF MINE TO--NOT DEFEND . . . . . . 552 3 DON JUAN 16 104 8
DEFENDED
DEFENDED AT A PRICE EXTREMELY DEAR . . . . 151 3 DON JUAN 8 79 8
DEFENDER
IN NEITHER CLIME TIME BLOOD WITH HER DEFENDER . . . . 252 3 DON JUAN 10 57 7
DEFENDERS
FOR SIX AND THIRTY THOUSAND BRAVE DEFENDERS . . . . . 175 3 DON JUAN 8 127 V7
DEFENSIBLE
DESERVES THE WORST HIS CONDUCT'S LESS DEFENSIBLE . . . . 103 2 DON JUAN 1 151 6
DEFERENCE
OF DUDU THOUGH THEY HELD THEIR TONGUES FROM DEFERENCE . . 31 3 DON JUAN 6 50 8
JUAN REPLIED WITH ALL BECOMING DEFERENCE . . . . . 469 3 DON JUAN 15 30 1
WHICH SHOW'D SUCH DEFERENCE TO WHAT FEMALES SAY . . . 492 3 DON JUAN 15 82 3
RATHER BY DEFERENCE THAN COMPLIMENT . . . . . 493 3 DON JUAN 15 83 7
DEFIANCE
ALTHOUGH DEFIANCE OFT DECLINED AFFORDS . . . . . . 153 2 DON JUAN 1 V 4 5
HURLING DEFIANCE CITY STREAM AND SHORE . . . . . . 116 3 DON JUAN 8 8 4
DEFIED
BUT SHE DEFIED ALL MEANS THEY COULD EMPLOY . . . . . 376 2 DON JUAN 4 59 7
HIS FIVE BRAVE BOYS NO LESS THE FOE DEFIED . . . . . 165 3 DON JUAN 8 107 5
DEFIES
ALL THAT DEFIES THE WORST WHICH PEN EXPRESSES . . . . 173 3 DON JUAN 8 123 5
DEFILED
WITH HUMAN FILTH THAT COLUMN IS DEFILED . . . . . 401 2 DON JUAN 4 105 2
OH YE WHO BUILD UP MONUMENTS DEFILED . . . . . . 199 3 DON JUAN 9 33 3
DEFLENDUS
WHILE THAT HIATUS MAXIME DEFLENDUS . . . . 245 3 DON JUAN 10 42 5
DEFLOWERED
WERE ALL DEFLOWERED BY DIFFERENT GRENADIERS . . . . . 177 3 DON JUAN 8 130 8
DEFOIX
FOR HUMAN VANITY THE YOUNG DEFOIX . . . . . . 400 2 DON JUAN 4 103 4
DEFORMED
BECAUSE DEFORMED YET DIED ALL GAME AND BOTTOM . . . . 166 3 DON JUAN 8 110 7
DEFY
I MAY ENSURE THE PUBLIC AND DEFY . . . . . . 142 2 DON JUAN 1 211 2
THE TRUTH IN MASQUERADE AND I DEFY . . . . . . 286 3 DON JUAN 11 37 2
WHICH MIGHT DEFY A CROTCHET CRITIC'S RIGOUR . . . . . 427 3 DON JUAN 14 39 6

		PAGE	VOL	CANTO	STANZA	LN

DEFYING
DEFYING AUGURY WITH THAT FOND KISS 356   2 DON JUAN   4   24   4
DEGENERATE
DEGENERATE INTO HANDS LIKE MINE 322   2 DON JUAN   3 L 5   6
HUGER THAN TWELVE OF OUR DEGENERATE BREED 391   3 DON JUAN 13   70   4
DEGRADATION
HE WAGED IN VENGEANCE OF HER DEGRADATION 303   2 DON JUAN   3   55   8
TO SAY BY DEGRADATION)-- MINGLED THERE 310   2 DON JUAN   3   68   7
DEGREE
IN THAT POINT SO PRECISE IN EACH DEGREE 52   2 DON JUAN   1   57   5
THOUGH DIFFERING IN STATURE AND DEGREE 26   3 DON JUAN   6   40   6
GOOD PEOPLE ALL OF EVERY DEGREE 325   3 DON JUAN 12   20   1
I HAVE NAMED A FEW NOT FOREMOST IN DEGREE 397   3 DON JUAN 13   83   5
DEGREES
THE HAND WHICH STILL HELD JUAN'S BY DEGREES 81   2 DON JUAN   1   111   1
BUT BY DEGREES THEIR SENSES WERE RESTORED 257   2 DON JUAN   2   191   5
TO DUB THE LAST OF HONOURS IN DEGREES) 341   2 DON JUAN   3   110   8
SHE SUNK DOWN ON HER SEAT BY SLOW DEGREES 59   3 DON JUAN   6   107   7
BUT BY DEGREES THAT THEY WERE FAIRER FAR 347   3 DON JUAN 12   69   2
THEN BY DEGREES RECALLED HIS ENERGIES 511   3 DON JUAN 16   25   4
UPON HIM BY DEGREES AND SO HE SLEPT 512   3 DON JUAN 16   27   8
BY WHOSE DEGREES ALL CHARACTERS ARE CLASSED-- 524   3 DON JUAN 16   48   3
DEIGN
FOR THEM AND THEIRS WITH ALL WHO DEIGN TO READ 271   2 DON JUAN   2   216   8
DEIGN'D
HE DEIGN'D NOT TO BELIE HIS SOUL IN SONGS 15   2 DON JUAN   0   10   5
YET STILL THEY DEIGN'D TO HICCUP OR TO BELLOW 318   2 DON JUAN   3   82   6
WHOM FRANCE AND FORTUNE LATELY DEIGN'D TO WAFT HERE . . . 398   3 DON JUAN 13   86   4
DEIGNED
THE POLISHED CHIEF WHO DEIGNED TO SMILE 321   2 DON JUAN   3 L 2   V1
HAD DEIGNED THAT NIGHT TO BE GULBEYAZ' GUEST 12   3 DON JUAN   6   13   V6
IN CHIEF IN PROPER PERSON DEIGNED TO DRILL 93   3 DON JUAN   7   52   2
FREDERICK THE GREAT FROM MOLWITZ DEIGNED TO RUN 122   3 DON JUAN   8   22   4
WHOSE HOUNDS NE'ER ERRED NOR GREYHOUNDS DEIGNED TO LURCH . 539   3 DON JUAN 16   80   2
DEIGNING
THE BLACK HOWEVER WITHOUT HARDLY DEIGNING 450   2 DON JUAN   5   66   1
DEIGNS
TO YOU THE UNFLATTERING MUSE DEIGNS TO INSCRIBE . . . 187   3 DON JUAN   9   10   2
OR DUTCHESS PRINCESS EMPRESS DEIGNS TO PROVE 216   3 DON JUAN   9   68   5
WHOSE CITIES NIGHT BY NO MEANS DEIGNS TO GLOSS 280   3 DON JUAN 11   26   5
THE CIVIL LIST (HE DEIGNS TO ACCEPT OBLIGING ALL . . . 528   3 DON JUAN 16   56   6
DEJECTED
AND ON OUR SOPHAS MAKES US LIE DEJECTED 301   3 DON JUAN 11   65   5
DEJECTION
JUST TO RELIEVE HER SPIRITS FROM DEJECTION 483   3 DON JUAN 15   64   8
DELAY
AND THERE HE WENT ASHORE WITHOUT DELAY 286   2 DON JUAN   3   20   1
AND NOW DELAY THE PROGRESS OF DON JUAN 410   2 DON JUAN   4   117   7
BUT HERE A SMALL DELAY FORMS A GREAT CRIME 482   2 DON JUAN   5   123   5
I WRITE WHAT'S UPPERMOST WITHOUT DELAY 413   3 DON JUAN 14   7   5
DEL'ENCLOS
UGLY FOR INSTANCE--NINON DEL'ENCLOS 468   2 DON JUAN   5   98   8
DELETERIOUS
'TIS PITY WINE SHOULD BE SO DELETERIOUS 372   2 DON JUAN   4   52   7
AND CRITICALLY HELD AS DELETERIOUS 358   3 DON JUAN 13   1   4
DELHIS
THEIR DELHIS MANNED SOME BOATS AND SAILED AGAIN . . . 82   3 DON JUAN   7   31   3
DELIBERATION
BUT ALWAYS CHOOSING WITH DELIBERATION 248   3 DON JUAN 10   48   7
DELICACIES
AND WHEN THE DELICACIES OF THE LAW 352   3 DON JUAN 12   78   3
DELICACY
FROM DELICACY TO DON JUAN'S EAR 118   2 DON JUAN   1   176   7
EVEN TO THE DELICACY OF THEIR HAND 368   2 DON JUAN   4   45   3
DELICATE
OF A SOFT CHEEK AND ASPECT DELICATE 203   2 DON JUAN   2   88   2
AND HAVE TEN THOUSAND DELICATE INVENTIONS 221   2 DON JUAN   2   123   4
THEIR DELICATE LIMBS A THOUSAND BOSOMS THERE 19   3 DON JUAN   6   26   7
BUT STILL HIS STATE WAS DELICATE THE HUE 245   3 DON JUAN 10   43   5
THY CUSTOM-HOUSE WITH ALL ITS DELICATE DUTIES 259   3 DON JUAN 10   69   3
JUAN WHOSE WAS A DELICATE COMMISSION 283   3 DON JUAN 11   32   1
AND WINS EVEN BY A DELICATE DISSENT 493   3 DON JUAN 15   83   8
DELICATELY
SO SOFT SO SWEET SO DELICATELY CLEAR 236   2 DON JUAN   2   151   4
EMBROIDER'D DELICATELY O'ER WITH BLUE 308   2 DON JUAN   3   64   6
DELIGHT
AND SWEPT AS 'TWERE ACROSS THEIR HEART'S DELIGHT . . . 355   2 DON JUAN   4   21   3
SHE DEEMED HER LEAST COMMAND MUST YIELD DELIGHT . . . 485   2 DON JUAN   5   128   3
OF GENTLE FEMININE DELIGHT AND SHOWN 13   3 DON JUAN   6   15   2
A TOPIC SCANDAL DOTH DELIGHT TO ROUSE 370   3 DON JUAN 13   26   6
SUCH WAS HIS TACT HE COULD ALIKE DELIGHT 428   3 DON JUAN 14   41   5
WHICH MINISTERS UNTO THE SOUL'S DELIGHT 457   3 DON JUAN 15   2   7
DELIGHTED
THE WHILE THE WICKED WORLD BEHOLDS DELIGHTED 75   2 DON JUAN   1   100   3
IN FACT MUCH MORE ASTONISH'D THAN DELIGHTED 294   2 DON JUAN   3   37   7
NO LESS DELIGHTED TO EMPLOY HIS LEISURE 123   3 DON JUAN   8   24   8
AND I SHALL BE DELIGHTED TO LEARN WHO 184   3 DON JUAN   9   4   7
BESIDES HE WAS OF THAT DELIGHTED AGE 217   3 DON JUAN   9   69   1
DON JUAN WAS DELIGHTED TO SECURE 335   3 DON JUAN 12   41   6

183

DELIGHTED   (CONTINUED)
        AT THE FULL BOARD AND SIT ALIKE DELIGHTED   534   3 DON JUAN 16   69   5
        DELIGHTED WITH THE DINNER AND THEIR HOST 549   3 DON JUAN 16   101   7
DELIGHTFUL
        BRIEF BUT DELIGHTFUL--SUCH AS HAD NOT STAID 382   2 DON JUAN 4   71   6
        WHAT A DELIGHTFUL THING'S A TURNPIKE ROAD   263   3 DON JUAN 10   78   1
        FIND ONE EACH DAY OF THE DELIGHTFUL YEAR 438   3 DON JUAN 14   63   6
DELIGHTING
        'TWAS A FINE CAUSE FOR THOSE IN LAW DELIGHTING 150   2 DON JUAN 1   V 1   1
        FORMED RATHER FOR INSTRUCTING THAN DELIGHTING 412   2 DON JUAN 5   2   5
DELIGHTS
        BUT THEIRS WAS LOVE IN WHICH THE MIND DELIGHTS 353   2 DON JUAN 4   17   2
        TEMPERANCE DELIGHTS HER BUT LONG FASTING RUFFLES . . . 542   3 DON JUAN 16   86   8
DELIGNE
        THE PRINCE DELIGNE AND LANGERON AND DAMAS   82   3 DON JUAN 7   32   7
        'TIS TRUE THE MEMOIRS OF THE PRINCE DELIGNE 82   3 DON JUAN 7   33   7
        THE PRINCE DELIGNE WAS WOUNDED IN THE KNEE 116   3 DON JUAN 8   10   1
DELIRIOUS
        HOWEVER THEY MIGHT SAVOUR OF DELIRIOUS   514   3 DON JUAN 16   33   3
DELIVERANCE
        HAD SENT THEM THIS FOR THEIR DELIVERANCE 208   2 DON JUAN 2   99   8
DELIVER'D
        WHO HAD DELIVER'D WELL A VERY SET 400   3 DON JUAN 13   90   3
DELIVERED
        BUT IF SHE WERE DELIVERED SAFE AND SOUND 162   3 DON JUAN 8   102   7
DELOS
        WHERE DELOS ROSE AND PHOEBUS SPRUNG   320   2 DON JUAN 3   L 1   4
DELPHIAN
        TO MARSHALL ONWARDS TO THE DELPHIAN HEIGHT 467   3 DON JUAN 15   25   V5
DELUGE
        THAN THE ETERNAL DELUGE WHICH DEVOURS 189   3 DON JUAN 9   13   7
DELUSION
        OF THIS DELUSION STILL THE CHILLING YOKE 402   2 DON JUAN 4   106   V3
        THERE MAILS FAST FLYING OFF LIKE A DELUSION 278   3 DON JUAN 11   22   4
DEMAGOGUES
        WITHOUT ME THERE ARE DEMAGOGUES ENOUGH 195   3 DON JUAN 9   25   2
        WHEN DEMAGOGUES WOULD WITH A BUTCHER'S KNIFE 536   3 DON JUAN 16   74   5
DEMAND
        ALL STRUT AND STAYS AND WHISKERS TO DEMAND 343   3 DON JUAN 12   60   4
DEMANDED
        LULL'D EVEN THE SAVAGE HUNGER WHICH DEMANDED 195   2 DON JUAN 2   75   3
        LOLAH DEMANDED THE NEW DAMSEL'S NAME-- 28   3 DON JUAN 6   44   1
DEMANDS
        AND ANSWER'D BUT TO NATURE'S JUST DEMANDS   42   2 DON JUAN 1   37   6
        AND SPAWNS HIS QUARTO AND DEMANDS YOUR PRAISE-- 440   3 DON JUAN 5   52   4
        FROM OUT THE COMMONEST DEMANDS OF NATURE 486   3 DON JUAN 15   69   8
DEMEANOUR
        OF MILD DEMEANOUR THOUGH OF SAVAGE MOOD 302   2 DON JUAN 3   53   2
        SHOWING A MUCH MORE RECONCIL'D DEMEANOUR 388   2 DON JUAN 4   81   7
DEMI-GODS
        A MIXTURE OF WILD BEASTS AND DEMI-GODS   164   3 DON JUAN 8   106   4
DEMOCRACY
        SEASON'D HIS PEDLAR POEMS WITH DEMOCRACY 329   2 DON JUAN 3   93   4
DEMOCRAT
        A DEMOCRAT SOME ONCE OR TWICE A YEAR   152   2 DON JUAN 1   V 3   2
DEMOCRATIC
        BECAUSE I HATE EVEN DEMOCRATIC ROYALTY   466   3 DON JUAN 15   23   8
DEMOCRATS
        AND WRINKLES (THE DAMNED DEMOCRATS) WON'T FLATTER . . . 236   3 DON JUAN 10   24   8
DEMOCRITUS
        WITH SCHNAPPS--DEMOCRITUS WOULD CEASE TO SMILE 260   3 DON JUAN 10   71   V7
DEMOISELLE
        A DASHING DEMOISELLE OF GOOD ESTATE   474   3 DON JUAN 15   42   2
DEMOLISHED
        A SINGLE LAUGH DEMOLISHED THE RIGHT ARM 364   3 DON JUAN 13   11   2
        BUT THAT WITH THEM ALL LAW WOULD BE DEMOLISHED 535   3 DON JUAN 16   72   8
DEMON
        BUT WHEN IT WAS SHE HAD THAT LURKING DEMON 448   3 DON JUAN 14   89   1
DEMONS
        BY ALL THE DEMONS OF ALL PASSIONS SHOWED 61   3 DON JUAN 6   111   7
DEMOURIER
        FRANCE TOO HAD BUONAPARTE AND DEMOURIER 22   2 DON JUAN 1   2   7
DEMUR
        AT EIGHTEEN SHE WITH DUE DEMUR HAD GRANTED 434   3 DON JUAN 14   55   V5
DEMURRED
        JUAN DEMURRED AT THIS FIRST NOTICE TO 245   3 DON JUAN 10   43   1
DEN
        WHO SMOOTH'D HIS PILLOW AS SHE LEFT THE DEN 228   2 DON JUAN 2   135   2
        TO-MORROW'D SEE US IN SOME OTHER DEN 435   2 DON JUAN 5   44   5
        AND DANIEL TAMED THE LIONS IN THEIR DEN 445   2 DON JUAN 5   60   5
        WHAT FEAR YOU THINK YOU THIS A LION'S DEN   458   2 DON JUAN 5   81   6
        ALONG THE REST CONTRIVED TO KEEP THIS DEN   22   3 DON JUAN 6   32   6
        THE ARMY LIKE A LION FROM HIS DEN 113   3 DON JUAN 8   2   3
        THE RESTLESS TITAN HICCUPS IN HIS DEN 115   3 DON JUAN 8   7   8
        DESTRUCTION'S JAWS INTO THE DEVIL'S DEN 130   3 DON JUAN 8   35   4
        AS BOLD AS DANIEL IN THE LION'S DEN   217   3 DON JUAN 9   69   4
        AND CLIMATE--STOPPED THE LION SCANDAL'S DEN 241   3 DON JUAN 10   33   V4
        (THE DEN OF MANY A DIPLOMATIC LOST LIE) 283   3 DON JUAN 11   31   6
DENIAL
        AND IF THE MAN SHOULD ASK 'TIS BUT DENIAL 64   2 DON JUAN 1   78   7

184

```
                                                       PAGE VOL    CANTO STANZA LN
DENIED
    WITH SOME REMORSE RECEIVED (THOUGH FIRST DENIED) . . . . . 193  2 DON JUAN  2     71   5
    BUT OFT DENIED AS PATIENCE 'GINS TO FAIL HE . . . . . . . 459  3 DON JUAN 15      8   5
    A GREAT RESOURCE TO ALL AND NE'ER DENIED . . . . . . . . 506  3 DON JUAN 16     12   7
DENMARK
    THE QUEEN OF DENMARK FOR OPHELIA BROUGHT . . . . . . . . 165  2 DON JUAN  2     17   5
DENOUNCE
    I THEREFORE DO DENOUNCE ALL AMOROUS WRITING . . . . . . . 412  2 DON JUAN  5      2   1
    BUT TO DENOUNCE THE AMPHIBIOUS SORT OF HARLOT . . . . . . 344  3 DON JUAN 12     62   7
DENY
    OR WASTE A WORLD SINCE NO ONE CAN DENY . . . . . . . . . 210  3 DON JUAN  9     56   5
    BUT TO DENY THE MOB A CORDIAL WHICH IS . . . . . . . . . 256  3 DON JUAN 10     63   6
    FOR ME I KNOW NOUGHT NOTHING I DENY . . . . . . . . . . 411  3 DON JUAN 14      3   1
    HIS TALENT I WILL NOT DENY NOR DWELL . . . . . . . . . . 473  3 DON JUAN 15     38   V5
    HE WHO DOUBTS ALL THINGS NOTHING CAN DENY . . . . . . . . 495  3 DON JUAN 15     88   5
    IN ITS BEHALF LET THOSE DENY WHO WILL . . . . . . . . . 504  3 DON JUAN 16      7   8
DENYING
    DENYING SEVERAL LITTLE THINGS HE WANTED . . . . . . . . . 120  2 DON JUAN  1    180   4
    DENYING THE RECEIPT OF WHAT IT COST . . . . . . . . . . 142  2 DON JUAN  1    210   6
    AND WEAR MY HEAD DENYING THAT I WEAR IT . . . . . . . . 268  3 DON JUAN 11      1   8
DEPART
    THEY TELL ME 'TIS DECIDED YOU DEPART . . . . . . . . . . 130  2 DON JUAN  1    192   1
    BUT COUGHS WILL COME WHEN SIGHS DEPART--AND NOW . . . . . 229  3 DON JUAN 10      8   1
    RAY FADES ON RAY AS YEARS ON YEARS DEPART . . . . . . . . 554  3 DON JUAN 16    109   4
DEPARTED
    DEPARTED LIKE THE REST OF THEIR COMPEERS . . . . . . . . 381  3 DON JUAN 13     50   2
    SKIRMISH OF WITS O'ER THE DEPARTED ONE . . . . . . . . . 552  3 DON JUAN 16    105   2
DEPARTURE
    OF HIS DEPARTURE HAD BEEN SENT HIM BY . . . . . . . . . 169  2 DON JUAN  2     24   7
    OF THEIR DEPARTURE SUCH IS MODERN FAME . . . . . . . . . 382  3 DON JUAN 13     51   2
    DEPARTURE FOR HIS COUNTRY SEAT TO-DAY . . . . . . . . . . 382  3 DON JUAN 13     51   7
DEPEND
    ON WHICH THE PASSION'S SELF SEEMS TO DEPEND . . . . . . . 219  3 DON JUAN  9     73   6
    IN THAT FAIR CLIME WHICH DON'T DEPEND ON CLIMATE . . . . 423  3 DON JUAN 14     29   2
DEPENDENT
    DEPENDENT ON THE PUBLIC ALTOGETHER . . . . . . . . . . . 135  2 DON JUAN  1    199   3
DEPENDING
    DEPENDING MORE UPON THE HISTORIAN'S STYLE . . . . . . . . 328  2 DON JUAN  3     90   3
DEPENDS
    ON EACH HARANGUE DEPENDS SOME HOSTILE SWORDS . . . . . . 153  2 DON JUAN  1   V  4  3
    AND LOVE WHICH ALSO MUCH DEPENDS ON FOOD . . . . . . . . 246  2 DON JUAN  2    170   V4
    DEPENDS SO MUCH UPON THE GASTRIC JUICE . . . . . . . . . 428  2 DON JUAN  5     32   8
    OF BRITAIN'S YOUTH DEPENDS UPON THEIR WEIGHT . . . . . . 140  3 DON JUAN  8     55   4
    SINCE EVE ATE APPLES MUCH DEPENDS ON DINNER . . . . . . . 404  3 DON JUAN 13     99   8
DEPLORE
    WHICH I DEPLORE SO MUCH FOR I HAVE BORNE . . . . . . . . 420  2 DON JUAN  5     18   7
    I OWN IT I DEPLORE IT I CONDEMN IT . . . . . . . . . . .  10  3 DON JUAN  6      8   2
    OF COMMON LIKINGS WHICH MAKE SOME DEPLORE . . . . . . . . 366  3 DON JUAN 13     17   6
DEPLORED
    BELOVED AND DEPLORED WHILE SLOWLY STRAYED . . . . . . . .  40  3 DON JUAN  6     67   6
DEPOSIT
    SHE WHISPER'D IN GREAT WRATH--I MUST DEPOSIT . . . . . . 114  2 DON JUAN  1    170   7
    MAY TURN HIS NAME UP AS A RARE DEPOSIT . . . . . . . . . 327  2 DON JUAN  3     89   8
DEPOSITED
    WHERE ALL SIGHS ARE DEPOSITED AND NOW . . . . . . . . . 506  3 DON JUAN 16     13   2
DEPOSITION
    IF HE COMES HERE TO TAKE A DEPOSITION . . . . . . . . . 104  2 DON JUAN  1    152   1
DEPOSITIONS
    YET WHEN THEY ASK'D HER FOR HER DEPOSITIONS . . . . . . .  35  2 DON JUAN  1     27   5
    THE DEPOSITIONS AND THE CAUSE AT FULL . . . . . . . . . 127  2 DON JUAN  1    189   2
DEPRAVITY
    HE KNEW THE WORLD AND WOULD NOT SEE DEPRAVITY . . . . . . 368  3 DON JUAN 13     22   5
DEPRECATED
    TO BODE HIM NO GREAT GOOD HE DEPRECATED . . . . . . . . .  57  3 DON JUAN  6    102   2
DEPRECIATED
    BUT NOT THE LESS FOR THIS TO BE DEPRECIATED . . . . . . . 344  3 DON JUAN 12     62   3
DEPTH
    LULL'D LIKE THE DEPTH OF OCEAN WHEN AT REST . . . . . . . 235  2 DON JUAN  2    148   4
    IN WINTER'S DEPTH OR WANT OF REST AND VICTUAL . . . . . . 176  3 DON JUAN  8    128   7
    AND WHAT A WHIRLPOOL FULL OF DEPTH AND DANGER . . . . . . 214  3 DON JUAN  9     64   3
    THERE WAS A DEPTH OF FEELING TO EMBRACE . . . . . . . . 524  3 DON JUAN 16     48   7
DEPTHS
    HUSH'D INTO DEPTHS BEYOND THE WATCHER'S DIVING . . . . . 261  2 DON JUAN  2    197   6
    OUR HEARTS FIRST IN THE DEPTHS OF LETHE'S SPRING . . . . 346  2 DON JUAN  4      4   5
DERIDE
    THOUGH AT THE FIRST I MIGHT PERCHANCE DERIDE . . . . . . 466  3 DON JUAN 15     23   5
DERIDES
    IN SHORT HOWE'ER OUR BETTER FAITH DERIDES . . . . . . . 168  3 DON JUAN  8    114   4
DERIVED
    FROM THE BLUE SKIES DERIVED A DOUBLE BLUE . . . . . . . . 393  2 DON JUAN  4     90   6
DERIVES
    'TIS AS A SNOWBALL WHICH DERIVES ASSISTANCE . . . . . . . 398  2 DON JUAN  4    100   5
DERVISES
    LIKE DERVISES WHO TURN AS ON A PIVOT HE . . . . . . . . 290  2 DON JUAN  3     29   6
DES
    OH YE GREAT AUTHORS--APROPOS DES BOTTES-- . . . . . . . . 200  3 DON JUAN  9     36   1
DESARTS
    WHAT ANTRES VAST AND DESARTS IDLE THEN . . . . . . . . . 455  3 DON JUAN 14    102   1
DESCEND
    DESCEND--THE FAULT IS MINE THIS FATAL SHORE . . . . . . . 366  2 DON JUAN  4     42   5
```

185

```
                                                          PAGE VOL      CANTO STANZA LN
DESCEND  (CONTINUED)
    IN VAIN THE DEWS OF HEAVEN DESCEND ABOVE . . . . . . . 382  2 DON JUAN  4   70    7
    BOILED IN HIS VEINS AND RATHER THAN DESCEND . . . . . . 471  2 DON JUAN  5   104   4
DESCENDING
    DESCENDING RATHER QUICKLY THE DECLIVITY . . . . . . . . 290  2 DON JUAN  3   29    2
DESCENDS
    WHENCE MELODY DESCENDS AS FROM A THRONE . . . . . . . . 236  2 DON JUAN  2   151   8
DESCENT
    WITH REGULAR DESCENT IN THESE OUR DAYS . . . . . . . . 340  3 DON JUAN 12   53    4
DESCRIBE
    HOW NOR CAN I INDEED DESCRIBE THE WHERE-- . . . . . . . 112  2 DON JUAN  1   166   2
    I CAN'T DESCRIBE IT THOUGH SO MUCH IT STRIKE . . . . . 159  2 DON JUAN  2   5     7
    FAR LESS DESCRIBE PRESENT THE VERY VIEW . . . . . . . . 412  2 DON JUAN  5   3     7
    I WON'T DESCRIBE DESCRIPTION IS MY FORTE . . . . . . . 440  2 DON JUAN  5   52    1
    I MIGHT DESCRIBE AS I HAVE SEEN IT ALL . . . . . . . . 31   2 DON JUAN  6   51    4
    AND THIS SAME STATE WE WON'T DESCRIBE WE COULD . . . . 238  3 DON JUAN 10   27    1
    I WON'T DESCRIBE--THAT IS IF I CAN HELP . . . . . . . . 238  3 DON JUAN 10   28    1
    'TIS THAT IN FACT THERE'S LITTLE TO DESCRIBE . . . . . 418  3 DON JUAN 14   20    8
    IS MORE THAN I SHALL VENTURE TO DESCRIBE-- . . . . . . 567  3 DON JUAN 17   12    7
DESCRIBED
    DESCRIBED BY MAHOMET AND ANACREON MOORE . . . . . . . . 77   2 DON JUAN  1   104   5
    CAST BY CANOVA OR DESCRIBED BY BURKE . . . . . . . . . 315  2 DON JUAN  3   76    V8
    DESCRIBED--WHAT'S STRANGE--IN WORDS EXTREMELY FEW . . . 34   3 DON JUAN  6   57    6
    CAN NEVER BE DESCRIBED WE ALL HAVE HEARD . . . . . . . 59   3 DON JUAN  6   106   4
    AS DO THE SUBTLE SNAKES DESCRIBED OF OLD . . . . . . . 153  3 DON JUAN  8   83    8
    AND NE'ER TO BE DESCRIBED FOR TO THE DOLOUR . . . . . . 428  3 DON JUAN 14   40    7
DESCRIBES
    LIKE BURNS (WHOM DOCTOR CURRIE WELL DESCRIBES) . . . . 329  2 DON JUAN  3   92    4
    BUT EVERY FOOL DESCRIBES IN THESE BRIGHT DAYS . . . . . 440  2 DON JUAN  5   52    2
    OF WHICH HOWE'ER THE MUSE DESCRIBES EACH ACT . . . . . 107  3 DON JUAN  7   81    3
DESCRIBING
    WAS JUST DESCRIBING--YES IT WAS THE COAST-- . . . . . . 251  2 DON JUAN  2   181   2
    I DON'T MUCH LIKE DESCRIBING PEOPLE MAD . . . . . . . . 384  2 DON JUAN  4   74    3
    DESCRIBING PRIAM'S PELEUS' OR JOVE'S SON . . . . . . . 164  3 DON JUAN  8   105   6
    THAT NO ONE HAS SUCCEEDED IN DESCRIBING . . . . . . . . 418  3 DON JUAN 14   19    2
DESCRIED
    TILL IN APPROACHING WERE AT LENGTH DESCRIED . . . . . . 87   3 DON JUAN  7   43    7
    WITH PROPHETS HOURIS ANGELS SAINTS DESCRIED . . . . . . 169  3 DON JUAN  8   115   7
    IS NOT AT ONCE TOO PALPABLY DESCRIED . . . . . . . . . 304  3 DON JUAN 11   71    4
DESCRIPTION
    FOR AUTHORS FEAR DESCRIPTION MIGHT DISPARAGE . . . . . 280  2 DON JUAN  3   9     4
    HERE I MIGHT ENTER ON A CHASTE DESCRIPTION . . . . . . 397  2 DON JUAN  4   97    1
    I WON'T DESCRIBE DESCRIPTION IS MY FORTE . . . . . . . 440  2 DON JUAN  5   52    1
    WHOSE FORCE DESCRIPTION ONLY WOULD ABATE . . . . . . . 467  2 DON JUAN  5   97    3
    (TO SAVE DESCRIPTION) FAIR AS FAIR CAN BE . . . . . . . 26   3 DON JUAN  6   40    4
    DESCRIPTION AND I WON'T REFLECT--THAT IS . . . . . . . 238  3 DON JUAN 10   28    2
    IS ONE OF WHICH THERE'S NO DESCRIPTION RECENT . . . . . 416  3 DON JUAN 14   15    3
    I WILL NOT MAKE HIS GREAT DESCRIPTION LESS . . . . . . 442  3 DON JUAN 14   75    3
    THE CHASTE DESCRIPTION EVEN OF A BECASSE . . . . . . . 487  3 DON JUAN 15   71    8
DESCRIPTIONS
    THESE AMIABLE DESCRIPTIONS FROM THE SCRIBES . . . . . . 329  2 DON JUAN  3   92    6
    VARIED EACH RAY--BUT ALL DESCRIPTIONS GARBLE . . . . . 55   3 DON JUAN  6   98    5
DESCRIPTIVE
    A GUST--WHICH ALL DESCRIPTIVE POWER TRANSCENDS-- . . . 172  2 DON JUAN  2   30    7
DESERT
    OR IN THE DESERT HEARD THE CAMEL'S BELL . . . . . . . . 201  2 DON JUAN  2   84    7
DESERTED
    HIS HOME DESERTED FOR THE LONELY WOOD . . . . . . . . . 68   2 DON JUAN  1   87    2
DESERTION
    THIS WERE THE WORST DESERTION--RENEGADOES . . . . . . . 231  3 DON JUAN 10   13    1
DESERTS
    AND LONG LONG DESERTS SCORCH THE CAMEL'S FOOT . . . . . 373  2 DON JUAN  4   55    6
    IN DESERTS FORESTS CROWDS OR BY THE SHORE . . . . . . . 443  2 DON JUAN  5   57    2
    SO ARAB DESERTS DRINK IN SUMMER'S RAIN . . . . . . . . 212  3 DON JUAN  9   59    6
DESERT-SPRING
    NOR THE FIRST SPARKLE OF THE DESERT-SPRING . . . . . . 251  2 DON JUAN  2   180   5
DESERVE
    THERE IS NO DOUBT THAT YOU DESERVE YOUR RATION . . . . 185  3 DON JUAN  9   6     7
    BUT DO YOU MORE SEMPRONIUS--DON'T DESERVE IT . . . . . 366  3 DON JUAN 13   18    2
DESERVED
    IF EVER YOU INDEED DESERVED THE NAME . . . . . . . . . 101  2 DON JUAN  1   146   2
    THOUGH HE DESERVED IT WELL FOR BEING SO BACKWARD . . . 492  2 DON JUAN  5   140   6
    LOW AS THE COMPLIMENT DESERVED SUWARROW . . . . . . . . 99   3 DON JUAN  7   63    2
    NO ONE COULD ENVY HER DESERVED PROSPERITY . . . . . . . 550  3 DON JUAN 16   102   6
    MEANWHILE SWEET ADELINE DESERVED THEIR PRAISES . . . . 550  3 DON JUAN 16   103   1
DESERVES
    DESERVES THE WORST HIS CONDUCT'S LESS DEFENSIBLE . . . 103  2 DON JUAN  1   151   6
DESERVING
    NO LESS DESERVING TO BE HANGED THAN CROWNED . . . . . . 499  2 DON JUAN  5   153   8
    THOUGH ALL DESERVING EQUALLY TO TURN . . . . . . . . . 120  3 DON JUAN  8   17    5
    HE DIED DESERVING WELL HIS COUNTRY'S TEARS . . . . . . 152  3 DON JUAN  8   80    5
DESIDERATUM
    AND FACT IS TRUTH THE GRAND DESIDERATUM . . . . . . . . 107  3 DON JUAN  7   81    2
DESIGN
    THE REGULARITY OF MY DESIGN . . . . . . . . . . . . . . 25   2 DON JUAN  1   7     3
    IN THE DESIGN AND AS I HAVE A HIGH SENSE . . . . . . . 86   2 DON JUAN  1   120   6
    SOME HAVE ACCUSED ME OF A STRANGE DESIGN . . . . . . . 346  2 DON JUAN  4   5     1
    WITH THIS SAME LEGEND)--IF YOU BUT DESIGN . . . . . . . 516  3 DON JUAN 16   37    5
DESIGNS
    WHO HAVE IMPUTED SUCH DESIGNS AS SHOW . . . . . . . . . 347  2 DON JUAN  4   7     3
    OF THEIR DESIGNS BY SAYING THEY MEANT WELL . . . . . . 123  3 DON JUAN  8   25    7
```

DESIRABLE
DESIRABLE DISTINGUISH'D CELEBRATED 428   3 DON JUAN 14   42   2
DESIRE
A SOMETHING IN THEM WHICH WAS NOT DESIRE 54   2 DON JUAN 1   60   6
ALFONSO POMMELL'D TO HIS HEART'S DESIRE 122   2 DON JUAN 1   184   4
'TIS VERY CERTAIN THE DESIRE OF LIFE 190   2 DON JUAN 2   64   1
AND FIRMER FAITH NO LADYE-LOVE DESIRE 396   2 DON JUAN 4   96   3
SAID BABA BUT PRAY DO AS I DESIRE 454   2 DON JUAN 5   74   2
FOR NE'ER TILL NOW SHE KNEW A CHECKED DESIRE 489   2 DON JUAN 5   134   6
WOULD LIKE (I THINK) TO TRUST ALL TO DESIRE 14   3 DON JUAN 6   16   4
BUT HERE THE EFFECT FELL SHORT OF THEIR DESIRE 82   3 DON JUAN 7   31   6
ARE TOUCHED WITH A DESIRE TO SHIELD AND SAVE-- 164   3 DON JUAN 8   106   3
DESIRED
BUT THAT WHICH DONNA INEZ MOST DESIRED 43   2 DON JUAN 1   39   1
THOUGH FULL OF ALL THINGS WHICH COULD BE DESIRED 448   2 DON JUAN 5   64   3
A SECOND TIME DESIRED HIM TO KNEEL DOWN 470   2 DON JUAN 5   102   3
IF MATTERS HAD BEEN MANAGED AS DESIRED 55   3 DON JUAN 6   99   5
DESIRES
INDULGENCE OF THEIR INNOCENT DESIRES 282   2 DON JUAN 3   13   2
DESK
AND THE SAD TRUTH WHICH HOVERS O'ER MY DESK 345   2 DON JUAN 4   3   7
THAT FORMS THIS DESK OF WHAT THEY MEAN--LYKANTHROPY . . . 192   3 DON JUAN 9   20   6
DESOLATE
STANDING ALONE BESIDE HIS DESOLATE HEARTH 41   2 DON JUAN 1   36   5
AND THE DIM DESOLATE DEEP TWELVE DAYS HAD FEAR 182   2 DON JUAN 2   49   7
GAZED DIM AND DESOLATE--TWELVE DAYS HAD FEAR 182   2 DON JUAN 2   49 V7
THAT ISLE IS NOW ALL DESOLATE AND BARE 383   2 DON JUAN 4   72   1
A DULL AND DESOLATE APPENDAGE   GAZE 373   3 DON JUAN 13   33   2
NOW YAWNS ALL DESOLATE NOW LOUD NOW FAINTER 387   3 DON JUAN 13   62   5
HAVE SOMETHING GHASTLY DESOLATE AND DREAD 508   3 DON JUAN 16   17   8
DESOLATING
PRAYING INSTRUCTING DESOLATING PLUNDERING 95   3 DON JUAN 7   55   6
DESOLATION
NOT I HAVE MADE THIS DESOLATION FEW 368   2 DON JUAN 4   46   5
WAR PESTILENCE THE DESPOT'S DESOLATION 146   3 DON JUAN 8   68   4
HOWE'ER THE MIGHTY LOCUST DESOLATION 175   3 DON JUAN 8   126   5
DESPAIR
IN DEEP DESPAIR LEST HE HAD DONE AMISS 81   2 DON JUAN 1   112   5
AND HALF FORGOT THEIR DANGER AND DESPAIR 114   2 DON JUAN 1   170   4
A PASSION WHICH PURSUES THOUGH IN DESPAIR 114   2 DON JUAN 1   170 V4
DESPAIR OF ALL RECOVERY SPOILS LONGEVITY 190   2 DON JUAN 2   64   7
FAMINE DESPAIR COLD THIRST AND HEAT HAD DONE 210   2 DON JUAN 2   102   1
AND FELT AGAIN WITH HIS DESPAIR O'ERWROUGHT 215   2 DON JUAN 2   112   4
YET WHAT CAN PEOPLE DO EXCEPT DESPAIR 278   2 DON JUAN 3   6   5
HIS COUNTRY'S WRONGS AND HIS DESPAIR TO SAVE HER 302   2 DON JUAN 3   53   7
BUT OVERWROUGHT WITH PASSION AND DESPAIR 375   2 DON JUAN 4   57   6
A LOW SOFT OTTOMAN) AND BLACK DESPAIR 60   3 DON JUAN 6   108   5
SNATCH WHEN DESPAIR MAKES HUMAN HEARTS LESS PLIANT . . . 138   3 DON JUAN 8   51   4
DESPAIR'D
AND THEN THEY LOOK'D AROUND THEM AND DESPAIR'D 195   2 DON JUAN 2   74   3
DESPAIRING
AND WITH HYAENA LAUGHTER DIED DESPAIRING 198   2 DON JUAN 2   79   8
DESPATCH
IN THE DESPATCH I KNEW A MAN WHOSE LOSS 120   3 DON JUAN 8   18   7
DESPATCHES
THEIR LIES YCLEPED DESPATCHES WITHOUT RISK OR 498   2 DON JUAN 5   151   7
TO COLOUR UP HIS RAYS FROM YOUR DESPATCHES 107   3 DON JUAN 7   81   8
DESPATCHING
DESPATCHING SINGLE CRUISERS HERE AND THERE 285   2 DON JUAN 3   19   2
DESPERATE
THEIR DESPERATE EFFORTS SEEM'D ALL USELESS GROWN 176   2 DON JUAN 2   38   6
SURVIVE THROUGH VERY DESPERATE CONDITIONS 190   2 DON JUAN 2   64   4
AN OMINOUS AND WILD AND DESPERATE SOUND 194   2 DON JUAN 2   73   4
WHILE SOME MORE DESPERATE DOWAGER HAS BEEN WAGING 486   2 DON JUAN 5   130   3
WHERE FIGHTS NOT TO THE LAST SOME DESPERATE HEART 152   3 DON JUAN 8   82   3
FOR THEM IN SAVING SUCH A DESPERATE FOE-- 165   3 DON JUAN 8   108   5
EACH OUT-AT-ELBOW PEER OR DESPERATE DANDY 331   3 DON JUAN 12   32   2
BY RENDERING DESPERATE THOSE WHO HAD ELSE REPENTED . . . 353   3 DON JUAN 12   80   8
PERHAPS OF ALL MOST DESPERATE WHICH WILL DARE 412   3 DON JUAN 14   5   3
HAD NOTHING LEFT IT BUT A DESPERATE LOYALTY 466   3 DON JUAN 15   23 V8
WHICH AFTER ALL AT SUCH A DESPERATE RATE RUNS 472   3 DON JUAN 15   37   5
DESPERATION
CHASTE WAS SHE TO DETRACTION'S DESPERATION 365   3 DON JUAN 13   14   1
DESPISE
TO THEIR OWN GOOD THIS WARNING TO DESPISE 141   2 DON JUAN 1   208   2
AS CAVALIER SERVENTE OR DESPISE HER 288   2 DON JUAN 3   24   6
DESPISES
MY MUSE DESPISES REFERENCE AS YOU HAVE GUESS'D 433   3 DON JUAN 14   54   6
DESPISING
THAT OF DESPISING THOSE WE COMBAT WITH 79   3 DON JUAN 7   25   2
WHILE HE DESPISING EVERY SENSUAL CALL 320   3 DON JUAN 12   9   7
DESPITE
DESPITE OF ALL THEIR EFFORTS AND EXPEDIENTS 171   2 DON JUAN 2   29   3
DESPITE HER INJURED LOVE AND FIERY PRIDE 62   3 DON JUAN 6   113   5
BEFORE MAY-DAY PERHAPS DESPITE HIS DUTY 243   3 DON JUAN 10   37   7
DESPITE THE SNAKE SOCIETY'S LOUD RATTLES 452   3 DON JUAN 14   96   8
DESPOND
TAUGHT TO CONCEAL THEIR BURSTING HEARTS DESPOND 263   2 DON JUAN 2   200   4
(BUT THAT OF COURSE IS RARE) AND THEN DESPOND 278   2 DON JUAN 3   7   3
ARRIVED RETIRED TO HIS BUT TO DESPOND 555   3 DON JUAN 16   110   4

		PAGE	VOL	CANTO	STANZA	LN

DESPONDS
THY LATE REVIVING ROMAN SOUL DESPONDS . . . . 19 2 DON JUAN D 16 3
DESPOT
ANOTHER DESPOT OF THE KIND . . . . 325 2 DON JUAN 3 L 12 5
DESPOTIC
TRUE KNIGHTS CHASTE DAMES HUGE GIANTS KINGS DESPOTIC . . . 347 2 DON JUAN 4 6 6
DESPOTISM
WITH AUGHT WHICH LOOKS LIKE DESPOTISM IN VIEW . . . . . 474 2 DON JUAN 5 110 5
OF EVERY DESPOTISM IN EVERY NATION . . . . 194 3 DON JUAN 9 24 8
DESPOT'S
WAR PESTILENCE THE DESPOT'S DESOLATION . . . . . . 146 3 DON JUAN 8 68 4
DESPOTS
WHEN STARS AND WHORES AND DESPOTS COULD MAKE GREAT . . . 84 3 DON JUAN 7 37 V2
THOUGH DESPOTS KNOW IT NOT--TILL THE PROGRESSION . . . 354 3 DON JUAN 12 83 5
COULD BACK A HORSE AS DESPOTS RIDE A RUSSIAN . . . . 368 3 DON JUAN 13 23 8
DESSAIX
JOUBERT HOCHE MARCEAU LANNES DESSAIX MOREAU . . . . . 22 2 DON JUAN 1 3 5
DESSERT
ABOVE THEM THEIR DESSERT GREW ON ITS VINE . . . . . 291 2 DON JUAN 3 31 6
DESTAEL
WOULD BE OLD GOETHE'S--(SEE WHAT SAYS DESTAEL) . . . 320 2 DON JUAN 3 86 6
DESTINED
BY NAME--WAS DESTINED FOR THE PORT LEGHORN . . . . . 169 2 DON JUAN 2 24 V2
FOR ALTHOUGH DESTINED TO THE TURKISH MART HE . . . . 388 2 DON JUAN 4 81 3
DESTINY
LONG WITH HER DESTINY BUT SHE SLEEPS WELL . . . . . 382 2 DON JUAN 4 71 7
FROM THEM AT LEAST THEIR DESTINY HE HEARD . . . . . 388 2 DON JUAN 4 80 3
BUT FOR THE DESTINY OF THIS YOUNG TROOP . . . . . . 409 2 DON JUAN 4 116 1
BUT DESTINY AND PASSION SPREAD THE NET . . . . . 364 3 DON JUAN 13 12 5
DESTROY
THEY TAMED HIM DOWN AMONGST THEM TO DESTROY . . . . . 49 2 DON JUAN 1 50 4
THEY WILL DESTROY A FACE WHICH MORTAL THOUGHT . . . . 219 2 DON JUAN 2 119 7
LIKE ONE LIFE COULD NOT HOLD NOR DEATH DESTROY . . . . 376 2 DON JUAN 4 59 8
BUT WHICH NEGLECT IS HASTENING TO DESTROY . . . . . 400 2 DON JUAN 4 103 6
AND LOVE DESTROY AND SAPPING SORROW WRINGS . . . . . 468 2 DON JUAN 5 98 6
SHE ONLY WISHED TO SINK BURN AND DESTROY . . . . . 490 2 DON JUAN 5 136 V7
AND AFTERWARDS IF HE MUST NEEDS DESTROY . . . . . 123 3 DON JUAN 8 24 5
ALL ARTS TO TEACH THEIR SUBJECTS TO DESTROY . . . . . 157 3 DON JUAN 8 92 8
THE USUAL HIRSUTE SEASONS WHICH DESTROY . . . . . 209 3 DON JUAN 9 53 3
TO AID THE DAMSEL AND DESTROY THE CAITIFF . . . . . 363 3 DON JUAN 13 10 2
DESTROY'D
WHICH EVER THE DESTROYER YET DESTROY'D . . . . . . 339 2 DON JUAN 3 109 2
AND THE HARD FROST DESTROY'D THE SCENTING DAYS . . . . 407 3 DON JUAN 13 106 4
DESTROYED
OF THINGS DESTROYED AND LEFT IN AIRY DOUBT . . . . . 201 3 DON JUAN 9 38 4
DESTROYER
WHICH EVER THE DESTROYER YET DESTROY'D . . . . . . 339 2 DON JUAN 3 109 2
DESTROYING
HALF-PAY FOR LIFE MAKE MANKIND WORTH DESTROYING . . . 118 3 DON JUAN 8 14 8
IN MORE DESTROYING NATURE AND THE HEAT . . . . . 152 3 DON JUAN 8 82 6
DESTROYS
BY THE MERE SENSES AND THAT WHICH DESTROYS . . . . . 352 2 DON JUAN 4 16 6
KINDNESS DESTROYS WHAT LITTLE WE HAD GOT . . . . . 423 2 DON JUAN 5 25 6
BENEVOLENCE DESTROYS WHAT WE HAD GOT . . . . . . 423 2 DON JUAN 5 25 V6
DESTRUCTION
AND DARKNESS AND DESTRUCTION AS ON HIGH . . . . 270 2 DON JUAN 2 214 4
FROM OUT THE WIDE DESTRUCTION WHICH ENTOMBING ALL . . . 399 3 DON JUAN 4 101 5
I DO NOT MEAN DESTRUCTION AND EXPOSURE . . . . . 62 3 DON JUAN 6 114 7
TO BREATHE DESTRUCTION ON ITS WINDING WAY . . . . . 113 3 DON JUAN 8 2 6
DESTRUCTION'S
DESTRUCTION'S JAWS INTO THE DEVIL'S DEN . . . . . . 130 3 DON JUAN 8 35 4
DESTRUCTIVE
HERE WAR FORGOT HIS OWN DESTRUCTIVE ART . . . . . 152 3 DON JUAN 8 82 5
DESULTORY
SHOWN IN THIS SORT OF DESULTORY RHYME . . . . . 465 3 DON JUAN 15 20 2
DETACHMENT
DETACHMENT OF THREE COLUMNS TOOK ITS STATION . . . 91 3 DON JUAN 7 50 3
DETAIL
COULD I DO JUSTICE TO THE FULL DETAIL . . . . . 467 2 DON JUAN 5 97 7
ALL THAT A POET DRAGS INTO DETAIL . . . . . 60 3 DON JUAN 6 109 6
BEING MUCH TOO GROSS TO SEE THEM IN DETAIL . . . 105 3 DON JUAN 7 77 2
BUT COULD WE KNOW THEM IN DETAIL PERCHANCE . . . . 113 3 DON JUAN 8 3 2
OR MASS FOR SHOULD I STRETCH INTO DETAIL . . . . . 483 3 DON JUAN 15 64 2
DETAILED
BUT WISHED FOR A STILL MORE DETAILED NARRATION . . . . 526 3 DON JUAN 16 53 6
DETAIN
AS IF IT SAID DETAIN ME IF YOU PLEASE . . . . . 81 2 DON JUAN 1 111 3
ALFONSO GRAPPLED TO DETAIN THE FOE . . . . . 124 2 DON JUAN 1 186 1
DETAIN'D
THE GOOD OLD GENTLEMAN HAD BEEN DETAIN'D . . . . . 283 2 DON JUAN 3 15 1
DETECT
I HAVE SEEN JOHN HALF DETECT HIMSELF A FOOL-- . . . . 310 3 DON JUAN 11 85 8
DETECTED
WHOSE VIRTUE LIES IN NEVER BEING DETECTED . . . . . 437 3 DON JUAN 14 61 8
DETERMINATION
WAS JULIA'S INNOCENT DETERMINATION . . . . . . 65 2 DON JUAN 1 81 2
DETERMINE
(LET DEEPER SAGES THE TRUE CAUSE DETERMINE) . . . . 249 3 DON JUAN 10 50 3
THE ACCUSED TO THINK THEIR LORDSHIPS WOULD DETERMINE . . 391 3 DON JUAN 13 69 3
THE REASON WHY IS EASY TO DETERMINE . . . . . . 416 3 DON JUAN 14 15 4

		PAGE	VOL	CANTO	STANZA	LN
DETERMINED						
	SHE NOW DETERMINED THAT A VIRTUOUS WOMAN	63	2 DON JUAN	1	77	1
	WHILE SOUVAROFF DETERMINED TO OBTAIN IT	92	3 DON JUAN	7	51	7
	THEY HONOURED SUCH DETERMINED SCORN OF LIFE	171	3 DON JUAN	8	119	8
	DETERMINED RIGHT OR WRONG ON FRIEND OR FOE	366	3 DON JUAN	13	16	4
	BUT ADELINE DETERMINED JUAN'S WEDDING	473	3 DON JUAN	15	40	1
DETERR'D						
	HAD THOUGHT ONE MAN MIGHT BE DETERR'D BY TWO	98	2 DON JUAN	1	141	4
DETEST						
	I HATE INCONSTANCY--I LOATHE DETEST	268	2 DON JUAN	2	209	1
	BUT I DETEST ALL FICTION EVEN IN SONG	10	3 DON JUAN	6	8	3
	MEN LOVE IN HASTE BUT THEY DETEST AT LEISURE	361	3 DON JUAN	13	6	8
DETESTATION						
	TO THIS MY PLAIN SWORN DOWNRIGHT DETESTATION	194	3 DON JUAN	9	24	7
DETOTT						
	SO CANTEMIR CAN TELL YOU OR DETOTT	21	3 DON JUAN	6	31	5
DETRACTION'S						
	CHASTE WAS SHE TO DETRACTION'S DESPERATION	365	3 DON JUAN	13	14	1
DEUCE						
	AND HOW THE DEUCE THEY EVER COULD HAVE BIRTH	71	2 DON JUAN	1	92	3
	IS MORE THAN I KNOW--THE DEUCE TAKE THEM BOTH	17	3 DON JUAN	6	22	8
	WHICH SOMETIMES PLAYS THE DEUCE WITH WOMANKIND	480	3 DON JUAN	15	57	2
DEUCED						
	AND FIND A DEUCED BALANCE WITH THE DEVIL	113	2 DON JUAN	1	167	8
DEUM						
	SHE RINGS THE WORLD'S TE DEUM AND HER BROW	286	3 DON JUAN	11	38	3
DEVIATE						
	AND DEVIATE INTO MATTERS RATHER DRY	203	3 DON JUAN	9	41	4
DEVIATION						
	FOR ANY DEVIATION FROM THE GRACES	539	3 DON JUAN	16	79	7
DEVICE						
	BUT NO DEVICE COULD BE BROUGHT INTO PLAY--	114	2 DON JUAN	1	169	4
DEVIL						
	SENT TO THE DEVIL SOMEWHAT ERE HIS TIME	21	2 DON JUAN	1	1	8
	BUT THEN SHE HAD A DEVIL OF A SPIRIT	32	2 DON JUAN	1	20	5
	AND WONDERS WHY THE DEVIL HE GOT HEIRS	75	2 DON JUAN	1	100	8
	I SHUNNED THEM AS I WOULD DO THE DEVIL	102	2 DON JUAN	1	148	V6
	AND FIND A DEUCED BALANCE WITH THE DEVIL	113	2 DON JUAN	1	167	8
	SAW JUAN'S LAST ELOPEMENT WITH THE DEVIL	138	2 DON JUAN	1	203	8
	(LIKE TRUANT ROGUES) THE DEVIL OR THE FOOL	162	2 DON JUAN	2	10	4
	A DEVIL OF A SEA ROLLS IN THAT BAY	162	2 DON JUAN	2	11	3
	SOME PLAY THE DEVIL AND THEN WRITE A NOVEL	263	2 DON JUAN	2	201	8
	FOR AFTER ALL WE CANNOT CALL THEE DEVIL	266	2 DON JUAN	2	205	8
	IF ONLY FROM THE DEVIL THEY WOULD INSURE US	267	2 DON JUAN	2	207	5
	ELSE HOW THE DEVIL IS IT THAT FRESH FEATURES	267	2 DON JUAN	2	208	7
	MAN--AND AS WE WOULD HOPE--PERHAPS THE DEVIL	345	2 DON JUAN	4	2	3
	ARE WHAT I FOUND THERE--BUT THE DEVIL A PHRYGIAN	387	2 DON JUAN	4	78	8
	HOW GET OUT HOW THE DEVIL GOT WE IN	435	2 DON JUAN	5	44	2
	AS WONDERING WHAT THE DEVIL NOISE THAT IS	442	2 DON JUAN	5	55	8
	WHAT THE DEVIL SHALL I DO WITH ALL THIS GAUZE	455	2 DON JUAN	5	76	6
	HER FEATURES ALL THE SWEETNESS OF THE DEVIL	474	2 DON JUAN	5	109	2
	THOUGH SUCH A SHE'S A DEVIL (IF THAT THERE BE ONE)	7	3 DON JUAN	6	3	7
	THE DEVIL MAY DECOMPOSE BUT NEVER SETTLE	33	3 DON JUAN	6	55	8
	IS TO THE DEVIL NOW NO FURTHER PRIZE	88	3 DON JUAN	7	45	3
	WHY JOHNSON WHAT THE DEVIL DO YOU MEAN	102	3 DON JUAN	7	70	2
	WHICH DID NOT COMBAT LIKE THE DEVIL AS YET--	131	3 DON JUAN	8	37	6
	ALL THAT THE DEVIL WOULD DO IF RUN STARK MAD	173	3 DON JUAN	8	123	4
	WHEN A MAN'S COUNTRY'S GOING TO THE DEVIL	257	3 DON JUAN	10	66	8
	(BUT THAT I NEVER DOUBTED NOR THE DEVIL)	271	3 DON JUAN	11	6	2
	STONE-HENGE IS NOT--BUT WHAT THE DEVIL IS IT--	280	3 DON JUAN	11	25	2
	WHERE LITTLE CASTLEREAGH THE DEVIL CAN TELL	307	3 DON JUAN	11	77	2
	AND WHERE--OH WHERE THE DEVIL ARE THE RENTS	307	3 DON JUAN	11	77	8
	WHICH TAKES SO MUCH--TO GIVE THE DEVIL HIS DUE--	351	3 DON JUAN	12	76	3
	THE DEVIL HATH NOT IN ALL HIS QUIVER'S CHOICE	461	3 DON JUAN	15	13	7
	THE DEVIL WAS IN THE GIRL COULD IT BE PRIDE	490	3 DON JUAN	15	78	5
	GAVE HIM TO LAY THE DEVIL WHO LOOKS O'ER LINCOLN	540	3 DON JUAN	16	82	7
	THE DEVIL MAY TAKE THAT STEALTHY PACE OF HIS	556	3 DON JUAN	16	112	4
DEVILISH						
	SOME DEVILISH ESCAPADE OR STIR WHICH SHOWS	328	3 DON JUAN	12	26	2
	AND THAT SAME DEVILISH DOCTRINE OF THE PERSIAN	377	3 DON JUAN	13	41	5
DEVILISM						
	LIKE MAGNETISM OR DEVILISM OR WHAT	25	3 DON JUAN	6	38	7
DEVIL'S						
	THE DEVIL'S SO VERY SLY--SHE SHOULD DISCOVER	64	2 DON JUAN	1	78	2
	THE DEVIL'S IN THE MOON FOR MISCHIEF THEY	82	2 DON JUAN	1	113	2
	THE DEVIL'S IN THE URCHIN AND NO GOOD--	115	2 DON JUAN	1	171	4
	DESTRUCTION'S JAWS INTO THE DEVIL'S DEN	130	3 DON JUAN	8	35	4
	WHICH WELL BESEEMED THE DEVIL'S DRAWING-ROOM	265	3 DON JUAN	10	81	3
DEVILS						
	AND DEVILS FOR MY SUPERNATURAL SCENERY	136	2 DON JUAN	1	201	V8
	OF THE NEXT BASTION FIRED AWAY LIKE DEVILS	134	3 DON JUAN	8	44	2
	CORRUPTION FOR ITS CROP) WITH THE POOR DEVILS	237	3 DON JUAN	10	25	6
	THE SEVENTH WILL BRING BLUE DEVILS OR A DUN	243	3 DON JUAN	10	38	8
	BLUE DEVILS AND BLUE-STOCKINGS AND ROMANCES	444	3 DON JUAN	14	79	7
	HATH GOT BLUE DEVILS FOR HIS MORNING MIRRORS	457	3 DON JUAN	15	4	4
DEVOTEE						
	A DEVOTEE WHEN SOARS THE HOST IN SIGHT	261	2 DON JUAN	2	196	3
DEVOTION						
	SELECTED FOR DISCRETION AND DEVOTION	51	2 DON JUAN	1	55	2

189

	PAGE	VOL		CANTO	STANZA	LN

DEVOTION   (CONTINUED)
FIGHTING DEVOTION DUST--PERHAPS A NAME . . . . 159 2 DON JUAN 2   4   8
STRANGE SOUNDS OF WAILING BLASPHEMY DEVOTION . . . . . 174 2 DON JUAN 2   34   7
IN NAMELESS PRINT--THAT I HAVE NO DEVOTION . . . . . . 336 2 DON JUAN 3   104   2
AND WHAT IS THAT DEVOTION DOUBTLESS--HOW . . . . . .   22 3 DON JUAN 6   33   1
TO SHELTER THEIR DEVOTION FROM THE WIND . . . . 384 3 DON JUAN 13   55   8
A HECATOMB OF SUITORS WITH DEVOTION . . . . 434 3 DON JUAN 14   55   6
DEVOUR'D
DEVOUR'D IT LONGING FOR THE OTHER TOO . . . . 193 2 DON JUAN 2   71   8
DEVOURED
AND TRANSIENT AND DEVOURED BY THE SAME HARPY . . . . . 310 3 DON JUAN 11   86   3
DEVOURS
THAN THE ETERNAL DELUGE WHICH DEVOURS . . . . 189 3 DON JUAN 9   13   7
DEVOUT
AND HAIDEE BEING DEVOUT AS WELL AS FAIR . . . . 258 2 DON JUAN 2   193   5
DEVOUTLY
THAT I DEVOUTLY WISHED THE THREE WERE FOUR . . . . . . 271 3 DON JUAN 11   6   7
DEW
THE FRESHNESS OF THE HEART CAN FALL LIKE DEW . . . . . 144 2 DON JUAN 1   214   2
A DROP OF DEW WHEN EVERY DROP HAD SEEM'D . . . . . . 202 2 DON JUAN 2   86   6
AND YOUNG AURORA KISS'D HER LIPS WITH DEW . . . . . . 232 2 DON JUAN 2   142   4
FALLING LIKE DEW UPON A THOUGHT PRODUCES . . . . . . 327 2 DON JUAN 3   88   2
(AS NIGHT DEW ON A CYPRESS GLITTERING TINGES . . . . .   40 3 DON JUAN 6   67   7
AND THE HEART'S DEW OF PAIN SPRANG FAST AND CHILLY . . .   58 3 DON JUAN 6   105   7
AS O'ER THE GRASS THE DEW . . . . 520 3 DON JUAN 16 L   6   4
DEWS
IN VAIN THE DEWS OF HEAVEN DESCEND ABOVE . . . . . . 382 3 DON JUAN 4   70   7
IN VAIN--AS FALL THE DEWS ON QUENCHLESS SANDS . . . . . 212 3 DON JUAN 9   59   7
DEWY
HIS DEWY CURLS LONG DRENCH'D BY EVERY STORM . . . . . 216 2 DON JUAN 2   114   6
AND HIS BLACK CURLS WERE DEWY WITH THE SPRAY . . . . . 234 2 DON JUAN 2   147   6
DROOPING AND DEWY ON THE BEACH HE LAY-- . . . . . . 249 2 DON JUAN 2   176   6
OF DEWY DAWN WOUND SLOWLY ROUND EACH HEIGHT . . . . .   49 3 DON JUAN 6   86   6
DEXT'ROUS
THEIR PASSIONS AND ARE DEXT'ROUS SOME BY FEATURES . . . 425 2 DON JUAN 5   27   4
DEY
HAD A LARGE ORDER FROM THE DEY OF TRIPOLI . . . . . . 284 2 DON JUAN 3   16   8
DI
HAIL'D A STRANGE BRIG CORPO DI CAIO MARIO . . . . . . 389 2 DON JUAN 4   82   4
DIADEM
(THAT ROYAL BIRD WHOSE TAIL'S A DIADEM) . . . . 104 3 DON JUAN 7   74   6
DIALOGUE
THIS DIALOGUE FOR HE WHO ANSWERED KNEW . . . .   97 3 DON JUAN 7   59   7
RINGS O'ER THE DIALOGUE AND MANY A CRIME . . . . . . 141 3 DON JUAN 8   58   4
AND SHONE IN THE BEST PART OF DIALOGUE . . . . 426 3 DON JUAN 14   37   2
DIALOGUES
LONG DIALOGUES WHICH PASS'D WITHOUT A WORD . . . . . . 489 3 DON JUAN 15   76   8
WHICH PLATO IN HIS DIALOGUES DRAMATIC . . . . 494 3 DON JUAN 15   86   5
DIAMOND
WHERE I CAN'T SAY OR GOLD OR DIAMOND FLINGS . . . . . 465 2 DON JUAN 5   94   5
ONE MONSTROUS DIAMOND DREW MUCH OBSERVATION . . . . . 287 3 DON JUAN 11   39   4
ON HIM THE DIAMOND POURS ITS BRILLIANT BLAZE . . . . . 319 3 DON JUAN 12   8   6
OR GLORIOUS AS A DIAMOND RICHLY SET . . . . 458 3 DON JUAN 15   7   4
DIAMONDS
AND RICH IN RUBLES DIAMONDS CASH AND CREDIT . . . . . 259 3 DON JUAN 10   70   2
DIAN
MY DIAN OF THE EPHESIANS LADY ADELINE . . . . 430 3 DON JUAN 14   46   3
GRACEFUL AS DIAN WHEN SHE DRAWS HER BOW . . . . 517 3 DON JUAN 16   38   5
ALAS HER STAR MUST WANE LIKE THAT OF DIAN . . . . . . 554 3 DON JUAN 16   109   3
DIANA'S
WHICH MIGHT HAVE CALLED DIANA'S CHORUS COUSIN . . . . . 469 2 DON JUAN 5   99   6
DIAPASONS
MY MUSIC HAS SOME MYSTIC DIAPASONS . . . . 419 3 DON JUAN 14   22   6
DIC
OMNIA VULT BELLE MATHO DICERE--DIC ALIQUANDO . . . . . 465 3 DON JUAN 15   21   1
ET BENE DIC NEUTRUM DIC ALIQUANDO MALE . . . . 465 3 DON JUAN 15   21   2
ET BENE DIC NEUTRUM DIC ALIQUANDO MALE . . . . 465 3 DON JUAN 15   21   2
DICE
THE DICE SEEM'D CHARM'D TOO WITH HIS REPARTEES . . . . 399 3 DON JUAN 13   86   8
THEN THERE WERE BILLIARDS CARDS TOO BUT NO DICE-- . . . 407 3 DON JUAN 13   106   1
DICEDRABBIT
HIS SON THE HONOURABLE DICK DICEDRABBIT . . . . 534 3 DON JUAN 16   70   6
DICERE
OMNIA VULT BELLE MATHO DICERE--DIC ALIQUANDO . . . . . 465 3 DON JUAN 15   21   1
DICK
THERE WAS DICK DUBIOUS THE METAPHYSICIAN . . . . . . 399 3 DON JUAN 13   87   1
HIS SON THE HONOURABLE DICK DICEDRABBIT . . . . 534 3 DON JUAN 16   70   6
DICKEY
'TIS GRANTED AND THE VALET MOUNTS THE DICKEY-- . . . . 380 3 DON JUAN 13   47   1
DICTION
FOR WHAT IS SOMETIMES CALLED POETIC DICTION . . . . . 154 3 DON JUAN 8   86   6
THOUGH EVERY SCRIBE IN SOME SLIGHT TURN OF DICTION . . . 311 3 DON JUAN 11   88   6
DICTIONARIES
ACCORDING TO THE BEST OF DICTIONARIES . . . . 486 3 DON JUAN 15   68   5
DIDDLED
FULL FLASH ALL FANCY UNTIL FAIRLY DIDDLED . . . . . . 276 3 DON JUAN 11   17   7
WHERE'S BRUMMELL DISHED WHERE'S LONG POLE WELLESLEY DIDDLED 307 3 DON JUAN 11   78   1
DIDO'S
OF DIDO'S ALPHABET AND THIS IS RATIONAL . . . . 122 3 DON JUAN 8   23   7

190

	PAGE	VOL	CANTO	STANZA	LN
DID'S					
THE QUANTITY OF GOOD SHE DID'S UNKNOWN	338	3	DON JUAN 12	48	5
DIE					
THE GOAL IS GAIN'D WE DIE YOU KNOW--AND THEN--	93	2	DON JUAN 1	133	8
'TWERE BETTER SURE TO DIE SO THAN BE SHUT	112	2	DON JUAN 1	166	7
ALL THINGS THAT HAVE BEEN BORN WERE BORN TO DIE	147	2	DON JUAN 1	220	3
AND LIVE AND DIE MAKE LOVE AND PAY OUR TAXES	159	2	DON JUAN 2	4	3
AND SUCH LIGHT GRIEFS ARE NOT A THING TO DIE ON	165	2	DON JUAN 2	16	4
BUT DIE AS MANY AN EXILED HEART HATH DIED	166	2	DON JUAN 2	18	3
THOUGHT IT WOULD BE BECOMING TO DIE DRUNK	174	2	DON JUAN 2	35	8
BUT LET US DIE LIKE MEN NOT SINK BELOW	175	2	DON JUAN 2	36	4
AND THOUGH 'TIS TRUE THAT MAN CAN ONLY DIE ONCE	176	2	DON JUAN 2	39	7
AND STRIVES TO STRANGLE HIM BEFORE HE DIE	184	2	DON JUAN 2	52	8
THAT SOME I REALLY THINK DO NEVER DIE	190	2	DON JUAN 2	65	4
AND WHO SHOULD DIE TO BE HIS FELLOW'S FOOD	194	2	DON JUAN 2	73	8
WHO DIE IN RIGHTEOUSNESS SHE LEAN'D AND THERE	233	2	DON JUAN 2	144	2
UNLESS HE WISH'D TO DIE UPON THE PLACE--	240	2	DON JUAN 2	159	6
SAVE THEIRS AND THAT THEIR LIFE COULD NEVER DIE	255	2	DON JUAN 2	188	8
IF SOULS COULD DIE HAD PERISH'D IN THAT PASSION	257	2	DON JUAN 2	191	4
FOR ALL OF THEIRS UPON THAT DIE IS THROWN	262	2	DON JUAN 2	199	3
BUT THIS IS NOT THE DEATH THAT IT SHOULD DIE--	272	2	DON JUAN 2	V 1	3
AND PLACE THEM ON THEIR BREAST--BUT PLACE TO DIE--	275	2	DON JUAN 3	2	6
AVOUCH'D HIS DEATH (SUCH PEOPLE NEVER DIE)	295	2	DON JUAN 3	38	3
THERE SWAN-LIKE LET ME SING AND DIE	326	2	DON JUAN 3	L 16	4
MEANT TO GROW OLD BUT DIE IN HAPPY SPRING	348	2	DON JUAN 4	8	7
DEEPEST IN THOSE WHO LONG THE MOST TO DIE	350	2	DON JUAN 4	11	8
WHOM THE GODS LOVE DIE YOUNG WAS SAID OF YORE	350	2	DON JUAN 4	12	1
WHY DID THEY NOT THEN DIE--THEY HAD LIVED TOO LONG	358	2	DON JUAN 4	27	2
EACH BROKE TO DROWN HER YET SHE COULD NOT DIE	361	2	DON JUAN 4	31	8
OFT CAME AND WENT AS THERE RESOLVED TO DIE	365	2	DON JUAN 4	39	6
I LOVE HIM--I WILL DIE WITH HIM I KNEW	366	2	DON JUAN 4	42	7
NOR EVEN DIOGENES--WE LIVE AND DIE	68	3	DON JUAN 7	4	7
MY DEBT IN BEING THUS ALLOWED TO DIE	100	3	DON JUAN 7	65	5
BUT AT THE LEAST YOU MAY DIE GLORIOUSLY--	161	3	DON JUAN 8	100	5
THAT ONE SHOULD DIE THAN TWO DRAG ON THE FETTER)	222	3	DON JUAN 9	80	8
THOUSANDS BLAZE LOVE HOPE DIE--HOW HAPPY THEY--	229	3	DON JUAN 10	8	8
BUT JUAN WAS NOT MEANT TO DIE SO SOON	229	3	DON JUAN 10	9	1
ET HAUSTUS TER IN DIE CAPIENDUS	244	3	DON JUAN 10	41	8
LET ME DIE WHERE I AM AND AS THE FUEL	276	3	DON JUAN 11	16	4
HEROES MUST DIE AND BY GOD'S BLESSING 'TIS	277	3	DON JUAN 11	20	2
SOME DIE SOME FLY SOME LANGUISH ON THE CONTINENT	308	3	DON JUAN 11	80	7
EXCEPT PERHAPS THAT YOU WERE BORN TO DIE	411	3	DON JUAN 14	3	3
DIED					
BEFORE UNLUCKILY DON JOSE DIED	38	2	DON JUAN 1	32	8
HE DIED AND MOST UNLUCKILY BECAUSE	38	2	DON JUAN 1	33	1
BUT AH HE DIED AND BURIED WITH HIM LAY	39	2	DON JUAN 1	34	1
HE DIED OF THE SLOW FEVER CALL'D THE TERTIAN	39	2	DON JUAN 1	34	7
SAVE DEATH OR DOCTORS' COMMONS--SO HE DIED	41	2	DON JUAN 1	36	8
AND IF IN THE MEANTIME HER HUSBAND DIED	67	2	DON JUAN 1	84	1
HAS MADNESS SEIZED YOU WOULD THAT I HAD DIED	98	2	DON JUAN 1	142	3
FOR DAVID LIVED BUT JUAN NEARLY DIED	113	2	DON JUAN 1	168	8
BUT DIE AS MANY AN EXILED HEART HATH DIED	166	2	DON JUAN 2	18	3
THE CREATURE WAS HIS FATHER'S DOG THAT DIED	193	2	DON JUAN 2	71	3
HE DIED AS BORN A CATHOLIC IN FAITH	197	2	DON JUAN 2	76	5
AND WITH HYAENA LAUGHTER DIED DESPAIRING	198	2	DON JUAN 2	79	8
BUT HE DIED EARLY AND WHEN HE WAS GONE	202	2	DON JUAN 2	87	4
AS MORNING BROKE THE LIGHT WIND DIED AWAY	207	2	DON JUAN 2	97	1
THEY DIED AWAY TILL THUS REDUCED TO FEW	210	2	DON JUAN 2	102	V6
WHO DIED TWO DAYS BEFORE AND NOW HAD FOUND	213	2	DON JUAN 2	109	7
SHE DIED BUT NOT ALONE SHE HELD WITHIN	382	2	DON JUAN 4	70	1
THUS LIVED--THUS DIED SHE NEVER MORE ON HER	382	2	DON JUAN 4	71	1
WHO LIVED TOO LONG FOR MEN BUT DIED TOO SOON	400	2	DON JUAN 4	103	3
HE DIED AT FIFTY FOR A QUEEN OF FORTY	9	3	DON JUAN 6	5	1
HE DIED BENEATH A TREE AS MUCH UNBLEST ON	84	3	DON JUAN 7	36	6
HE DIED DESERVING WELL HIS COUNTRY'S TEARS	152	3	DON JUAN 8	80	5
BECAUSE DEFORMED YET DIED ALL GAME AND BOTTOM	166	3	DON JUAN 8	110	7
IN ONE VOLUPTUOUS BLAZE--AND THEN HE DIED	169	3	DON JUAN 8	115	8
EPAMINONDAS SAVED HIS THEBES AND DIED	186	3	DON JUAN 9	8	2
WHO DIED IN THE THEN GREAT ATTEMPT TO CLIMB	261	3	DON JUAN 10	74	5
A KERCHIEF CRYING GIVE SAL THAT--AND DIED	276	3	DON JUAN 11	16	8
DIED FROM THE TOUCH THAT KINDLED THEM TO SOUND	521	3	DON JUAN 16	41	2
DIEM					
BUT CARPE DIEM JUAN CARPE CARPE	310	3	DON JUAN 11	86	1
DIES					
OR MADAM DIES--ALFONSO MUTTER'D DAMN HER	111	2	DON JUAN 1	163	5
OF US DIES WITH THEM AS EACH FOND HOPE ENDS	167	2	DON JUAN 2	21	6
AH SURELY NOTHING DIES BUT SOMETHING MOURNS	338	2	DON JUAN 3	108	8
AGAINST THE LIGHT WHEREIN SHE DIES HE CLUNG	170	3	DON JUAN 8	118	4
DIET					
TO LOSE THEIR LIVES AS WELL AS SPOIL THEIR DIET	173	2	DON JUAN 2	33	4
AND BEING CONSUMPTIVE LIVE ON A MILK DIET	474	3	DON JUAN 15	41	8
DIFFER					
DIFFER EXCEPT IN ROBBING WITH A BOW	275	3	DON JUAN 11	15	4
THAT MANNERS HARDLY DIFFER MORE THAN DRESS	402	3	DON JUAN 13	94	8
THEY DIFFER AS WINE DIFFERS FROM ITS LABLE	458	3	DON JUAN 15	6	5
DIFFERENCE					
THERE'S ONLY ONE SLIGHT DIFFERENCE BETWEEN	137	2	DON JUAN 1	202	1
SUCH DIFFERENCE DOTH A FEW MONTHS MAKE YOU'D THINK	228	3	DON JUAN 10	7	5
BY TURNS THE DIFFERENCE OF THE SEVERAL SEXES	442	3	DON JUAN 14	73	3

DIFFERENCE   (CONTINUED)
    THE DIFFERENCE IS THAT IN THE DAYS OF OLD 468   3 DON JUAN 15   26   1
    NOR WOULD BE THUS--THE DIFFERENCE IN THEM 481   3 DON JUAN 15   58   7
    THERE IS A DIFFERENCE SAYS THE SONG BETWEEN 541   3 DON JUAN 16   84   1
    A DIFFERENCE 'TWIXT A BISHOP AND A DEAN 541   3 DON JUAN 16   84   5
    A DIFFERENCE BETWEEN CROCKERY WARE AND PLATE 541   3 DON JUAN 16   84   6
    UPON THE WHOLE IS GREATER THAN THE DIFFERENCE 541   3 DON JUAN 16   85   2
DIFFERENT
    WHERE DIFFERENT TALENTS FIND THEIR DIFFERENT MARTS . . . 91   2 DON JUAN 1   128   6
    WHERE DIFFERENT TALENTS FIND THEIR DIFFERENT MARTS . . . 91   2 DON JUAN 1   128   6
    PERHAPS 'TWAS IN A DIFFERENT WAY APPLIED 113   2 DON JUAN 1   168   7
    FOR SAILORS ARE IN FACT A DIFFERENT KIND 170   2 DON JUAN 2   26   5
    HER DRESS WAS VERY DIFFERENT FROM THE SPANISH 220   2 DON JUAN 2   120   2
    BUT SEEM THE GROWTH OF A MOST DIFFERENT CLIME 277   2 DON JUAN 3   5   V4
    PIECED OUT FOR DIFFERENT MARTS IN THE LEVANT 284   2 DON JUAN 3   17   2
    OF VELVET PANNELS EACH OF DIFFERENT HUE 308   2 DON JUAN 3   64   2
    AND KNEW THE SELF-LOVES OF THE DIFFERENT NATIONS . . . 319   2 DON JUAN 3   84   2
    HE GAVE THE DIFFERENT NATIONS SOMETHING NATIONAL . . . 319   2 DON JUAN 3   85   2
    THAT EACH PULL'D DIFFERENT WAYS WITH MANY AN OATH . . . 394   2 DON JUAN 4   93   7
    THAT EACH PULLED DIFFERENT WAYS--AND WAXING ROUGH . . . 395   2 DON JUAN 4   93   V7
    BOUGHT UP FOR DIFFERENT PURPOSES AND PASSIONS 407   2 DON JUAN 4   113   8
    LIKE FLOWERS OF DIFFERENT HUE AND CLIME AND ROOT . . . 38   3 DON JUAN 6   65   2
    BUT CERTES MATTERS TOOK A DIFFERENT FACE 89   3 DON JUAN 7   47   1
    WERE ALL DEFLOWERED BY DIFFERENT GRENADIERS 177   3 DON JUAN 8   130   8
    JUST NOW YOUR'S WERE CUT OUT IN DIFFERENT SECTIONS . . 215   3 DON JUAN 9   65   5
    YOU'LL FIND IT OF A DIFFERENT CONSTRUCTION 356   3 DON JUAN 12   87   3
    WITH MORE EASE TOO SHE'D TELL A DIFFERENT STORY . . . 416   3 DON JUAN 14   13   8
    IN ENGLAND RANKS QUITE ON A DIFFERENT LIST 436   3 DON JUAN 14   60   6
    BUT THOUGH THE FLOWER IS DIFFERENT WITH THE FRENCH . . 442   3 DON JUAN 14   75   7
    THE SAME SELF-INTEREST WITH A DIFFERENT LEANING) . . . 535   3 DON JUAN 16   70   8
DIFFERENTLY
    HOW DIFFERENTLY THE WORLD WOULD MEN BEHOLD 455   3 DON JUAN 14   101   4
DIFFERING
    THEIR STATURE DIFFERING BUT IN SEX AND YEARS 368   2 DON JUAN 4   45   2
    ALL RAGAMUFFINS DIFFERING BUT IN HUE 417   2 DON JUAN 5   13   3
    THOUGH DIFFERING IN STATURE AND DEGREE 26   3 DON JUAN 6   40   6
DIFFERS
    THEY DIFFER AS WINE DIFFERS FROM ITS LABLE 458   3 DON JUAN 15   6   5
DIFFICULT
    BUT VERY DIFFICULT TO SHUT THEIR EYES 77   2 DON JUAN 1   105   8
    WITH CRABBE IT MAY BE DIFFICULT TO COPE 139   2 DON JUAN 1   205   5
    'TWAS DIFFICULT TO GET OUT SUCH PROVISION 180   2 DON JUAN 2   46   3
    NOTHING SO DIFFICULT AS A BEGINNING 344   2 DON JUAN 4   1   1
    IT DIFFICULT TO SHUN SOME STRANGE MISTAKES 96   3 DON JUAN 7   57   8
    WHO TOOK BY TURNS THAT DIFFICULT COMMAND 205   3 DON JUAN 9   46   5
    HE'LL FIND IT RATHER DIFFICULT SOME DAY 298   3 DON JUAN 11   59   3
    WHICH IT WERE RATHER DIFFICULT TO PROVE 322   3 DON JUAN 12   13   3
    BUT THOU ART THE MOST DIFFICULT TO RHYME AT 327   3 DON JUAN 12   24   5
    FOR THEN THEY ARE VERY DIFFICULT TO STOP 368   3 DON JUAN 13   22   8
    FORMS THE MOST DIFFICULT IN PUNCTUATION 396   3 DON JUAN 13   81   2
    IS DIFFICULT PRAY TELL ME CAN YOU MAKE FAST 411   3 DON JUAN 14   2   3
    BUT EVEN THIS IS DIFFICULT HEAVEN KNOWS 421   3 DON JUAN 14   25   2
    THOUGH CERTAINLY MORE DIFFICULT TO RHYME AT 423   3 DON JUAN 14   29   4
    WITH SLOTH HATH FOUND IT DIFFICULT TO DWELL 445   3 DON JUAN 14   81   6
    THE THIRD IS STILL MORE DIFFICULT TO STAND TO . . . 465   3 DON JUAN 15   21   7
    A SITUATION DIFFICULT I WEEN 489   3 DON JUAN 15   75   3
    SO VERY DIFFICULT THEY SAY IT IS 492   3 DON JUAN 15   81   8
    'TWERE DIFFICULT TO SAY WHAT WAS THE OBJECT 526   3 DON JUAN 16   51   1
    PERHAPS THESE ARE MOST DIFFICULT TO TAME 531   3 DON JUAN 16   63   6
    'TWERE DIFFICULT TO SAY--BUT JUAN LOOKED 568   3 DON JUAN 17   14   2
DIFFICULTIES
    SHE NOW CONCEIVED ALL DIFFICULTIES PAST 478   2 DON JUAN 5   116   2
    ALL DIFFICULTIES WHETHER GREAT OR SMALL 423   3 DON JUAN 14   30   5
    SOME DIFFICULTIES AS IN HIS OWN PREFERENCE 469   3 DON JUAN 15   30   5
DIFFICULTY
    ONE DIFFICULTY STILL REMAINED--HIS HAIR 457   2 DON JUAN 5   79   1
    AND EVERY DIFFICULTY BEING DISPELLED 92   3 DON JUAN 7   51   5
    THE DIFFICULTY LIES IN COLOURING 467   3 DON JUAN 15   25   5
DIFFIDENT
    TO THE PERFORMER'S DIFFIDENT CONFUSION 521   3 DON JUAN 16   41   8
DIG
    AND DIG AND SWEAT AND TURN THEMSELVES ABOUT 202   3 DON JUAN 9   40   3
DIGEST
    BECAUSE HE COULD NO MORE DIGEST HIS DINNER-- 199   3 DON JUAN 9   33   8
DIGESTION
    BEEF VEAL AND MUTTON BETTER FOR DIGESTION 191   2 DON JUAN 2   67   8
    OR IF IT WERE IF ALSO HIS DIGESTION 426   2 DON JUAN 5   30   2
    BUT WOULD MUCH RATHER HAVE A SOUND DIGESTION 189   3 DON JUAN 9   14   5
    AND WITH IT ALL THE PROCESS OF DIGESTION 232   3 DON JUAN 10   14   8
    AND EATS HER PARENTS ALBEIT THE DIGESTION 411   3 DON JUAN 14   2   2
DIGGING
    THERE BREATHLESS WITH HIS DIGGING NAILS HE CLUNG . . . 213   2 DON JUAN 2   108   1
    IN DIGGING THE FOUNDATION OF A CLOSET 327   2 DON JUAN 3   89   7
    IN DIGGING DRAINS FOR A NEW WATER CLOSET 327   2 DON JUAN 3   89   V7
DIGNIFY
    AND WHETHER COLDNESS PRIDE OR VIRTUE DIGNIFY 435   3 DON JUAN 14   57   7
DIGNITY
    AND THOUGH HER DIGNITY BROOKED NO COMPLAINING 247   3 DON JUAN 10   47   6
    AND DIGNITY WITH COURTESY SO BLENDING 546   3 DON JUAN 16   95   4

DIGRESS
    BUT I DIGRESS OF ALL APPEALS--ALTHOUGH . . . . 439 2 DON JUAN 5   49   1
DIGRESSING
    BUT I'M DIGRESSING WHAT ON EARTH HAD NERO . . . . . . 341 2 DON JUAN 3   110   1
DIGRESSION
    IF I HAVE ANY FAULT IT IS DIGRESSION . . . . 331 2 DON JUAN 3   96   2
    OH PARDON ME DIGRESSION--OR AT LEAST . . . . 334 3 DON JUAN 12   39   1
    I'M AT MY OLD LUNES--DIGRESSION AND FORGET . . . . . 364 3 DON JUAN 13   12   1
DIGRESSIONS
    AND SCARCE SECURE AS SUCH DIGRESSIONS ARE FAIR . . . . 65 3 DON JUAN 6   120   7
    SINCE WITH DIGRESSIONS WE TOO LONG HAVE TARRIED . . . . 493 3 DON JUAN 15   84   5
DILATE
    THAT LARGE BLACK PROPHET EYE SEEM'D TO DILATE . . . . . 355 2 DON JUAN 4   22   1
DILATED
    HER EYE DILATED AND HER COLOUR HEIGHTENED . . . . . . 42 3 DON JUAN 6   72   8
    UPON EACH OTHER WITH DILATED GLANCE . . . . 159 3 DON JUAN 8   96   2
DILETTANTI
    AS WELL AS DILETTANTI IN WAR'S ART . . . . 85 3 DON JUAN 7   39   5
    AND NO GREAT DILETTANTI IN TOPOGRAPHY . . . . 149 3 DON JUAN 8   74   6
    WHAT DILETTANTI DO WITH VAST PARADE) . . . . 522 3 DON JUAN 16   44   3
DILIGENCE
    IT MIGHT BE SEEN WITH DILIGENCE WAS SOUGHT . . . . . 476 2 DON JUAN 5   113   3
DIM
    AND LIGHTED AT TOO PURE A SHRINE TO DIM ITS . . . . . 65 2 DON JUAN 1   81   5
    AND THE DIM DESOLATE DEEP TWELVE DAYS HAD FEAR . . . . 182 2 DON JUAN 2   49   7
    GAZED DIM AND DESOLATE--TWELVE DAYS HAD FEAR . . . . . 182 2 DON JUAN 2   49 V7
    FORSOOK THE DIM EYES OF THESE SHIPWRECK'D MEN . . . . 204 2 DON JUAN 2   91   8
    FOR HIS CONGEALING BLOOD AND SENSES DIM . . . . . . 214 2 DON JUAN 2   111   4
    CIRCLING ALL NATURE HUSH'D AND DIM AND STILL . . . . . 252 2 DON JUAN 2   183   4
    MY BRAIN WITH BLEST FUMES TILL MY EYES GROW DIM . . . . 372 2 DON JUAN 4   53 V7
    HER EYE MIGHT FLASH ON HIS BUT FOUND IT DIM . . . . . 396 2 DON JUAN 4   95   3
    THERE WAS DEEP SILENCE IN THE CHAMBER DIM . . . . . . 38 3 DON JUAN 6   64   1
    JUST WHEN THE FADING LAMPS WANED DIM AND BLUE . . . . . 41 3 DON JUAN 6   70   5
    THE STARS PEEP THROUGH THE VAPOURS DIM AND DANK . . . . 110 3 DON JUAN 7   86   6
    AND THE SAD SECOND MOON GROWS DIM AGAIN . . . . . . 168 3 DON JUAN 8   113   4
    AND THROWING BACK A DIM LOOK ON HIS SONS . . . . . . 170 3 DON JUAN 8   118   7
    THE STARS I OWN MY TELESCOPE IS DIM . . . . 227 3 DON JUAN 10   4   2
    HUT WHERE WE TRAVELLERS BAIT WITH DIM REFLECTION . . . 238 3 DON JUAN 10   27 V6
    WHO THOUGH HER SPECTACLES AT LAST GREW DIM . . . . . 241 3 DON JUAN 10   34   6
    BUT WHEN SHE SAW HIS DAZZLING EYE WAX DIM . . . . . . 246 3 DON JUAN 10   44   5
    WHEN EVEN THE SEA LOOKS DIM WITH ALL ITS SPRAY . . . . 422 3 DON JUAN 14   28   3
    AND NOW AND THEN A NIGHTINGALE)--IS DIM . . . . . . 499 3 DON JUAN 15   97   2
    BUT BY DIM LIGHTS THE PORTRAITS OF THE DEAD . . . . . 508 3 DON JUAN 16   17   7
DIMITY
    A PRODIGY--HER MORNING DRESS WAS DIMITY . . . . . . 27 2 DON JUAN 1   12   6
    NO MATTER WHETHER RUSSET SILK OR DIMITY . . . . . . 421 3 DON JUAN 14   26   8
DIMMED
    BEYOND ITS DIMMED EYE'S SPHERE--BUT WOULD MUCH RATHER . 228 3 DON JUAN 10   6   7
DIMPLED
    A DIMPLED CHIN A NECK OF IVORY STOLE . . . . 561 3 DON JUAN 16   123   3
DIN
    THAT ALL IS SETTLED--THERE WAS LITTLE DIN . . . . . . 94 3 DON JUAN 7   54   6
    THE VERY CANNON DEAFENED BY THE DIN . . . . 142 3 DON JUAN 8   59   5
    SMOKING HIS PIPE QUITE CALMLY 'MIDST THE DIN . . . . . 160 3 DON JUAN 8   98   4
    WERE ALSO HEARD TO WONDER IN THE DIN . . . . 178 3 DON JUAN 8   132   2
    YOUR HEART JOINS CHORUS FAME IS BUT A DIN . . . . . . 199 3 DON JUAN 9   34   8
    A JARGON A MERE PHILANTHROPIC DIN . . . . 266 3 DON JUAN 10   85   6
DINDON
    RELIEVED WITH DINDON A LA PERIGUEUX . . . . 483 3 DON JUAN 15   63   4
DINE
    ON WHAT IN FACT NEXT DAY WERE THEY TO DINE . . . . . 192 2 DON JUAN 2   69   4
    DINE WITH THEM ON HIS PASTOR AND HIS MASTER . . . . . 198 2 DON JUAN 2   78   8
    'TIS SURELY FAIR TO DINE UPON OUR FRIENDS . . . . . . 200 2 DON JUAN 2   83   6
    SMALL SOCIAL PARTIES JUST BEGUN TO DINE . . . . . . 291 2 DON JUAN 3   31   2
    KEPT FOR ALL COMERS AT ALL HOURS TO DINE . . . . . . 310 2 DON JUAN 3   69   8
    TURKEY CONTAINS NO BELLS AND YET MEN DINE . . . . . . 439 2 DON JUAN 5   50   1
    I'VE DONE NOW GO AND DINE FROM OFF THE PLATE . . . . . 185 3 DON JUAN 9   6   1
    WITH THOSE WHO POPE SAYS GREATLY DARING DINE . . . . . 383 3 DON JUAN 13   53   6
    YOUR STOMACH ERE YOU DINE THE FRENCH WILL DO . . . . . 488 3 DON JUAN 15   72   4
    ON THEM AND BREAD 'TWAS OFT MY LUCK TO DINE . . . . . 488 3 DON JUAN 15   73   5
    FOR MAN THEREIN WITH EYES AND HEART TO DINE . . . . . 489 3 DON JUAN 15   75   4
DINED
    WHO ON THE VERY LOFTIEST KINGS HAVE DINED-- . . . . . 12 3 DON JUAN 6   13   5
    AND HAVING VOTED DINED DRANK GAMED AND WHORED . . . . 306 3 DON JUAN 11   75   7
    WITH DANDIES DINED HEARD SENATORS DECLAIMING . . . . . 418 3 DON JUAN 14   18   3
    THE DINERS OF CELEBRITY DINED WELL . . . . 487 3 DON JUAN 15   70   2
    BUT I HAVE DINED AND MUST FOREGO ALAS . . . . 487 3 DON JUAN 15   71   7
DINER
    A BRILLIANT DINER OUT THOUGH BUT A CURATE . . . . . . 540 3 DON JUAN 16   82   2
DINERS
    THE DINERS OF CELEBRITY DINED WELL . . . . 487 3 DON JUAN 15   70   2
DINING
    RECEIPTS IN FULL BEGAN TO THINK OF DINING . . . . . . 426 2 DON JUAN 5   29   8
DINNER
    WHILE SEATED AFTER DINNER AT HIS EASE . . . . 24 2 DON JUAN 1   6   5
    HE ALSO FOUND THAT HE HAD LOST HIS DINNER . . . . . . 72 2 DON JUAN 1   94   8
    ACHILLES ORDER'D DINNER FOR NEW COMERS . . . . . . 221 2 DON JUAN 2   123   8
    THE HAPPIEST MORTALS EVEN AFTER DINNER-- . . . . . . 294 2 DON JUAN 3   36   2
    ADVANCING TO THE NEAREST DINNER TRAY . . . . 297 2 DON JUAN 3   42   1

	PAGE	VOL	CANTO	STANZA	LN

DINNER   (CONTINUED)
    (PROVIDED THEY DON'T COME IN AFTER DINNER) . . . . . . 306 2 DON JUAN 3   60   2
    THE DINNER MADE ABOUT A HUNDRED DISHES . . . . . . 307 2 DON JUAN 3   62   1
    SELL FLESH AND BLOOD WHEN DINNER HAS OPPREST ONE . . 426 2 DON JUAN 5   30   6
    THE TOCSIN OF THE SOUL--THE DINNER BELL . . . . . . 439 2 DON JUAN 5   49   8
    WHICH KNITS SOCIETY--THE DINNER BELL . . . . . . 439 2 DON JUAN 5   49   V8
    BECAUSE HE COULD NO MORE DIGEST HIS DINNER-- . . . . 199 3 DON JUAN 9   33   8
    OF DOORS 'GAINST DUNS AND TO AN EARLY DINNER . . . . 282 3 DON JUAN 11   29   4
    THEN DRESS THEN DINNER THEN AWAKES THE WORLD . . . . 302 3 DON JUAN 11   67   1
    IF HE GOES AFTER DINNER TO A BALL . . . . . . 333 3 DON JUAN 12   37   V6
    AS THUS ON THURSDAY THERE WAS A GRAND DINNER . . . . 383 3 DON JUAN 13   54   1
    WHO LOVED PHILOSOPHY AND A GOOD DINNER . . . . . . 399 3 DON JUAN 13   87   2
    SINCE EVE ATE APPLES MUCH DEPENDS ON DINNER . . . . 404 3 DON JUAN 13   99   8
    HE DID NOT FALL ASLEEP JUST AFTER DINNER . . . . . . 426 3 DON JUAN 14   36   8
    THE SILVERY BELL RUNG NOT FOR DINNER READY . . . . 482 3 DON JUAN 15   61   6
    THE DINNER AND THE SOIREE TOO WERE DONE . . . . . . 504 3 DON JUAN 16   8   1
    NO MORE ON THIS--THE DINNER BELL HATH RUNG . . . . 538 3 DON JUAN 16   77   7
    DULLY PAST O'ER THE DINNER OF THE DAY . . . . . . 542 3 DON JUAN 16   87   1
    DELIGHTED WITH THE DINNER AND THEIR HOST . . . . . . 549 3 DON JUAN 16   101   7
DINNER'S
    WAS RUNG BY DINNER'S KNELL TILL THEN ALL WERE . . . 406 3 DON JUAN 13   103   2
DINNERS
    YOU MAY SEE SUCH AT ALL THE BALLS AND DINNERS . . . 346 3 DON JUAN 12   66   5
    AND DIPLOMATIC DINNERS OR AT OTHER-- . . . . . . 369 3 DON JUAN 13   24   2
    MORE WITH THESE DINNERS THAN THE KILLED OR WOUNDED-- . 383 3 DON JUAN 13   53   8
    OF MODERN DINNERS WHERE MORE MYSTERY LURKS . . . . 482 3 DON JUAN 15   62   6
    GONE TO WHERE VICTORIES MUST LIKE DINNERS GO . . . . 485 3 DON JUAN 15   67   5
DINT
    YOU--GENTLEMEN BY DINT OF LONG SECLUSION . . . . . . 12 2 DON JUAN D   5   1
    AND NOW BY DINT OF FINGERS AND OF EYES . . . . . . 242 3 DON JUAN 2   163   1
    DO JUST WHATE'ER THEY PLEASE BY DINT OF FEATURES . . 167 3 DON JUAN 8   111   8
    TO THOSE WHO BY THE DINT OF GLASS AND VAPOUR . . . . 226 3 DON JUAN 10   3   6
    HER WAY BACK TO THE WORLD BY DINT OF PLOTTERY . . . 397 3 DON JUAN 13   82   6
DIOGENES
    NOR EVEN DIOGENES--WE LIVE AND DIE . . . . . . 68 3 DON JUAN 7   4   7
    BUT LONDON'S SO WELL LIT THAT IF DIOGENES . . . . 281 3 DON JUAN 11   28   1
    ON SUNIUM OR HYMETTUS LIKE DIOGENES . . . . . . 488 3 DON JUAN 15   73   7
DIPLOMATIC
    A HALF-WAY HOUSE OF DIPLOMATIC REST . . . . . . 472 2 DON JUAN 5   105   2
    THEIR DIRTY DIPLOMATIC HANDS TO VENT . . . . . . 498 2 DON JUAN 5   151   5
    THE IMPORT OF THIS DIPLOMATIC PHRASE . . . . . . 207 3 DON JUAN 9   49   2
    DON JUAN OUR YOUNG DIPLOMATIC SINNER . . . . . . 282 3 DON JUAN 11   29   6
    (THE DEN OF MANY A DIPLOMATIC LOST LIE) . . . . 283 3 DON JUAN 11   31   6
    AND DIPLOMATIC DINNERS OR AT OTHER-- . . . . . . 369 3 DON JUAN 13   24   2
DIPLOMATICAL
    IT CHANCED SOME DIPLOMATICAL RELATIONS . . . . . . 365 3 DON JUAN 13   15   1
DIPLOMATIST
    BOTH TO THE DUCHESS AND DIPLOMATIST . . . . . . 436 3 DON JUAN 14   60   2
DIPLOMATISTS
    DIPLOMATISTS OF RATHER WAVERING KINGS . . . . . . 287 3 DON JUAN 11   40   3
    BUT SPEAKERS BARDS DIPLOMATISTS AND DANCERS . . . . 547 3 DON JUAN 16   98   3
DIPPED
    HIGH DASHED THE SPRAY THE BOWS DIPPED IN THE SEA . . 256 3 DON JUAN 10   64   4
DIPT
    MAY PAUSE IN PONDERING HOW ALL SOULS ARE DIPT . . . 210 3 DON JUAN 9   55   4
DIRE
    DIRE WAS THE SCUFFLE AND OUT WENT THE LIGHT . . . . 122 2 DON JUAN 1   184   1
DIRECT
    DIRECT YOUR QUESTIONS TO MY NEIGHBOUR THERE . . . . 298 2 DON JUAN 3   45   6
DIRECTION
    ACCORDING TO DIRECTION THEN RECEIVED . . . . . . 161 2 DON JUAN 2   9   2
    MAKES THAT OF MULTITUDES TAKE ONE DIRECTION . . . . 90 3 DON JUAN 7   48   2
    YOU NEED NOT TAKE THEM UNDER YOUR DIRECTION . . . . 186 3 DON JUAN 9   7   6
    AND SENT THE DOCTORS IN A NEW DIRECTION . . . . . . 245 3 DON JUAN 10   43   4
    DIRECTION BE SO 'TIS BUT IN A HURRY . . . . . . 260 3 DON JUAN 10   72   4
DIRECTLY
    SHE ORDERED HIM DIRECTLY TO BE BOUGHT . . . . . . 477 2 DON JUAN 5   114   3
DIRGE
    WHAT WAS NO DIRGE EXCEPT THE HOLLOW SEA'S . . . . 383 2 DON JUAN 4   72   7
    NO DIRGE SAVE WHEN ARISE THE STORMY SEAS . . . . . . 383 2 DON JUAN 4   72   V7
DIRGES
    OF HIS QUENCH'D HEART AND THE SEA DIRGES LOW . . . . 362 2 DON JUAN 4   34   6
DIRK
    OMITTING TURBAN SLIPPERS PISTOLS DIRK-- . . . . 240 2 DON JUAN 2   160   6
DIRKS
    LIKE MEN WITH TURBANS SCYMITARS AND DIRKS . . . . 93 3 DON JUAN 7   53   2
DIRT
    THE SKIN HAS PASSED THROUGH SUCH A DEAL OF DIRT . . 154 2 DON JUAN 1 V 5   5
    FOR DEEMING HUMAN CLAY BUT COMMON DIRT . . . . . . 96 3 DON JUAN 7   58   5
DIRTY
    BECAUSE NO DOUBT 'TWAS FOR HIS DIRTY FEE . . . . 103 2 DON JUAN 1   151   7
    THE LIBELLER'S GRATIS COUNSEL DIRTY SHIELD . . . . 151 2 DON JUAN 1 V 2   3
    WHICH LAW AFFORDS TO MANY A DIRTY DEED . . . . 151 2 DON JUAN 1 V 2   4
    FROM THE DULL PALACE TO THE DIRTY HOVEL . . . . 263 2 DON JUAN 2   201   7
    THEIR DIRTY DIPLOMATIC HANDS TO VENT . . . . . . 498 2 DON JUAN 5   151   5
    AND THAT'S THE REASON HE HIMSELF'S SO DIRTY . . . . 232 3 DON JUAN 10   15   2
    DIRTY AND DUSKY BUT AS WIDE AS EYE . . . . . . 265 3 DON JUAN 10   82   2
    THE VERY CLERKS--THOSE SOMEWHAT DIRTY SPRINGS . . . 287 3 DON JUAN 11   40   5
    MOCK TYRANTS WHEN ROME'S ANNALS WAXED BUT DIRTY . . 299 3 DON JUAN 11   61   8

	PAGE	VOL	CANTO	STANZA	LN

DIRTY (CONTINUED)
OTHERS FOR OTHER DIRTY WORK GONE THROUGH . . . . 314 3 DON JUAN 11 V 76 4
OH TIME WHY DOST NOT PAUSE THY SCYTHE SO DIRTY . . . . 433 3 DON JUAN 14 53 5
DISAGREEABLE
WET STILL MORE DISAGREEABLE AND STRIKING . . . . . . 479 2 DON JUAN 5 118 4
EXTREMELY DISAGREEABLE BUT COMMON . . . . 429 3 DON JUAN 14 43 7
DISAPPEAR'D
THESE LAST HAD DISAPPEAR'D--A LOSS TO ART . . . . . 386 3 DON JUAN 13 59 4
DISAPPEARED
QUITE DISAPPEARED--THE GODS KNOW HOW (I CAN'T . . . . . 127 3 DON JUAN 8 31 3
DISAPPEARING
AND FOLLOW FAR THE DISAPPEARING SUN . . . . 355 2 DON JUAN 4 22 2
DISAPPOINTED
AT BEING DISAPPOINTED IN YOUR WISH . . . . 10 2 DON JUAN D 3 2
A DISAPPOINTED LAWYER AT FULL LENGTH . . . . 155 2 DON JUAN 1 V 6 8
WAS FOR SOME RUM A DISAPPOINTED SUITOR . . . . 175 2 DON JUAN 2 36 8
HER SALE SENT HOME SOME DISAPPOINTED BAWLERS . . . . 407 2 DON JUAN 4 114 5
YET DISAPPOINTED JOYS ARE WOES AS DEEP . . . . . . 16 3 DON JUAN 6 20 4
TILL DULY DISAPPOINTED OR DISMISSED . . . . 536 3 DON JUAN 16 75 3
DISAPPOINTMENT
SO THAT SOME DISAPPOINTMENT THERE ENSUED . . . . . . 177 3 DON JUAN 8 131 2
DISARM
LET HIM DISARM OR BY MY FATHER'S HEAD . . . . 369 2 DON JUAN 4 47 1
DISARRAY
A RICH CONFUSION FORMED A DISARRAY . . . . 465 2 DON JUAN 5 93 3
DISASTER
WAS EVER HEARD OF SUCH A CURST DISASTER . . . . . . 96 2 DON JUAN 1 137 3
EVEN IN EXTREMITY OF THEIR DISASTER . . . . . . 198 2 DON JUAN 2 78 7
DISASTERS
WE KNOW WHAT SLAVERY IS AND OUR DISASTERS . . . . . 422 2 DON JUAN 5 23 7
DISBURSEMENTS
WHOSE AVARICE ALL DISBURSEMENTS DID IMPORTUNE . . . . 222 3 DON JUAN 9 81 3
DISCERN
IN THOUGHTS LIKE THESE TRUE WISDOM MAY DISCERN . . . 71 2 DON JUAN 1 93 1
STEAL FROM THE WALLS TILL YOU ALMOST DISCERN . . . . 508 3 DON JUAN 16 18 V6
DISCERNMENT
WHICH SHOWED WHAT GREAT DISCERNMENT WAS THE DONOR'S . . 247 3 DON JUAN 10 46 8
'TWILL TEACH DISCERNMENT TO THE SENSITIVE . . . . . 431 3 DON JUAN 14 49 7
DISCIPLINE
A DAME WHO KEPT UP DISCIPLINE AMONG . . . . 21 3 DON JUAN 6 30 5
THE DISCIPLINE OF THE WHOLE HAREM BORE . . . . . . 57 3 DON JUAN 6 103 2
DISCIPLINED
HOWEVER DISCIPLINED AND DEBONNAIRE-- . . . . 355 3 DON JUAN 12 85 4
DISCLOSE
WHICH IF WITHDRAWN WOULD BUT DISCLOSE THE FROWN . . . 182 2 DON JUAN 2 49 3
BENEATH HIS ART THE DAME PRESSED TO DISCLOSE THEM . . . 208 3 DON JUAN 9 51 7
IN WHICH SIR ISAAC NEWTON COULD DISCLOSE . . . . . . 226 3 DON JUAN 10 2 3
DISCLOSED
WHATEER THE GARDEN BORE OR MART DISCLOSED . . . . . 476 2 DON JUAN 5 113 V4
PHEDRA AND ALL WHICH STORY HAS DISCLOSED . . . . . 486 2 DON JUAN 5 131 3
WHERE SHE THEN WAS AS HER SOUND SLEEP DISCLOSED . . . 48 3 DON JUAN 6 84 3
A FEELING IN EACH FOOTSTEP AS DISCLOSED . . . . . . 61 3 DON JUAN 6 111 5
UNTIL A ROYAL SMILE AT LENGTH DISCLOSED . . . . . . 211 3 DON JUAN 9 58 6
AND WHETHER IT OUGHT NOT TO BE DISCLOSED . . . . . 512 3 DON JUAN 16 28 3
DISCLOSURE
IN CASE OF ANY PREMATURE DISCLOSURE . . . . 62 3 DON JUAN 6 114 8
DISCORD
SINCE THERE IS DISCORD AFTER BOTH AT LEAST) . . . . . 90 3 DON JUAN 7 49 4
DISCORDANT
RATTLES AROUND ME HER DISCORDANT HYMN . . . . 499 3 DON JUAN 15 97 4
DISCORD'S
AND ONE ON TITHES WHICH SURE ARE DISCORD'S TORCHES . . 530 3 DON JUAN 16 60 4
DISCORDS
AND CANNOT TUNE THOSE DISCORDS OF NARRATION . . . . . 74 3 DON JUAN 7 16 1
AND CANNOT TUNE THOSE DISCORDS OF DAMNATION . . . . . 74 3 DON JUAN 7 16 V1
DISCOUNT
AT A SAD DISCOUNT WHILE YOUR OVER-CHILLY . . . . . 14 3 DON JUAN 6 16 7
AT SIGHT NOR WOULD PERMIT YOU TO DISCOUNT . . . . . 213 3 DON JUAN 9 62 8
HAWKED ABOUT AT A DISCOUNT SMALL OR LARGE-- . . . . 379 3 DON JUAN 13 45 7
DISCOUNTED
TO PAY UNPAID PROTESTED OR DISCOUNTED . . . . 16 3 DON JUAN 6 21 2
MUST GET ITSELF DISCOUNTED BY A JEW . . . . 318 3 DON JUAN 12 6 8
DISCOURAGED
FOLKS ARE DISCOURAGED AND MOST SURELY NO MEN . . . . 205 2 DON JUAN 2 93 5
DISCOVER
THE DEVIL'S SO VERY SLY--SHE SHOULD DISCOVER . . . . 64 2 DON JUAN 1 78 2
THOUGH WATCHFUL AS THE LYNX THEY NE'ER DISCOVER . . . 75 2 DON JUAN 1 100 2
AND MAKE NO FURTHER NOISE TILL YOU DISCOVER . . . . 104 2 DON JUAN 1 153 6
AND CAPABILITIES AS TO DISCOVER . . . . 424 2 DON JUAN 5 26 4
AND IF THEY SHOULD DISCOVER YOUR DISGUISE . . . . . 464 2 DON JUAN 5 92 3
WITH STRICT ENQUIRY I COULD N'ER DISCOVER . . . . . 41 3 DON JUAN 6 70 2
DISCOVER STARS AND SAIL IN THE WIND'S EYE . . . . . 226 3 DON JUAN 10 3 7
NAY MARRIED DAMES WILL NOW AND THEN DISCOVER . . . . 331 3 DON JUAN 12 33 2
DISCOVER'D
WOULD BE DISCOVER'D IN THE HUMAN SOUL . . . . 455 3 DON JUAN 14 102 2
DISCOVERED
WHICH HE PERHAPS HAD NOT DISCOVERED SOON . . . . . . 513 3 DON JUAN 16 30 3
DISCOVERIES
DISCOVERIES MADE BUT NONE COULD BE AWARE . . . . . . 59 2 DON JUAN 1 68 3

195

		PAGE	VOL	CANTO	STANZA	LN
DISCOVERIES	**(CONTINUED)**					
WHAT OPPOSITE DISCOVERIES WE HAVE SEEN		91	2 DON JUAN	1	129	1
DECLARED WITH ALL HIS GRAND DISCOVERIES RECENT		69	3 DON JUAN	7	5	6
AND CARE BUT FOR DISCOVERIES AND NOT DEEDS		352	3 DON JUAN	12	80	4
DISCOVERING						
TIRING OLD READERS NOR DISCOVERING NEW		414	3 DON JUAN	14	10	6
DISCOVERS						
THE AGE DISCOVERS HE IS NOT THE TRUE ONE		21	2 DON JUAN	1	1	4
IN WHICH NOT ENVY'S SELF A FLAW DISCOVERS		29	2 DON JUAN	1	16	6
NO FRIEND LIKE TO A WOMAN EARTH DISCOVERS		451	3 DON JUAN	14	93	7
DISCOVERY						
BY THY HUMANE DISCOVERY FRIAR BACON		129	3 DON JUAN	8	33	8
WHAT A SUBLIME DISCOVERY 'TWAS TO MAKE THE		269	3 DON JUAN	11	2	1
DISCOVERY'S						
AS WELL AS THE SUBLIME DISCOVERY'S DATE		406	2 DON JUAN	4	112	4
DISCREET						
AND YAWNED A GOOD DEAL WITH DISCREET SURPRIZE		42	3 DON JUAN	6	73	8
ALBEIT MY YEARS WERE LESS DISCREET THAN FEW		334	3 DON JUAN	12	38	4
OWN'D TO A PENCHANT THOUGH DISCREET FOR BEAUTY		494	3 DON JUAN	15	85	8
DISCREETLY						
MUST BE POSTPONED DISCREETLY FOR THE PRESENT		410	2 DON JUAN	4	117	4
THIS HE DISCREETLY KEPT IN THE BACKGROUND		58	3 DON JUAN	6	105	1
DISCREPANCIES						
BUT OF ALL NATURE'S DISCREPANCIES NONE		541	3 DON JUAN	16	85	1
DISCRETION						
DISCRETION AND WERE NOT SO PEACEABLE		40	2 DON JUAN	1	35	6
SELECTED FOR DISCRETION AND DEVOTION		51	2 DON JUAN	1	55	2
WITH GOOD DISCRETION AND IN CURRENT RHYME		135	2 DON JUAN	1	200	V8
THAT SAGE (SAID JOHN) SURRENDERS AT DISCRETION		88	3 DON JUAN	7	44	6
DISCUSS						
YOUNG MEN WHO--THOUGH THEY HATED TO DISCUSS		344	3 DON JUAN	12	61	3
TO SHOW IT--(POINTS WE NEED NOT NOW DISCUSS)--		460	3 DON JUAN	15	10	5
DISCUSS'D						
DISCUSS'D THE WORLD AND SETTLED ALL THE SPHERES		408	3 DON JUAN	13	109	2
WILL BE DISCUSS'D HEREAFTER I OPINE		453	3 DON JUAN	14	97	3
DISCUSSED						
DISCUSSED THE FASHION WHICH MIGHT NEXT PREVAIL		406	3 DON JUAN	13	104	5
DISCUSSED THE PAST AND FUTURE PARLIAMENT		409	3 DON JUAN	13	109	V2
THE SUPPER TOO DISCUSSED THE DAMES ADMIRED		504	3 DON JUAN	16	8	2
LORD HENRY WHO HAD NOW DISCUSSED HIS CHOCOLATE		515	3 DON JUAN	16	34	1
DISCUSSED (HE HATED BEER YCLEPT THE SMALL)		533	3 DON JUAN	16	67	3
DISCUSSION						
WHO (AFTER SOME DISCUSSION AND SOME DOUBT		394	3 DON JUAN	4	92	3
THERE WAS JUST THEN A KIND OF A DISCUSSION		246	3 DON JUAN	10	45	1
DISCUSSION WHICH IS NEITHER HERE NOR THERE		270	3 DON JUAN	11	5	2
OF SUCH DISCUSSION SHE WAS THERE A GUEST		480	3 DON JUAN	15	55	2
THEREFORE I WOULD SOLICIT FREE DISCUSSION		564	3 DON JUAN	17	6	1
DISDAIN						
COLDNESS OR ANGER EVEN DISDAIN OR HATE		61	2 DON JUAN	1	73	7
YET IF PERCHANCE REMEMBERED STILL DISDAIN YOU 'EM		180	3 DON JUAN	8	136	6
FOR I DISDAIN TO WRITE AN ATALANTIS		311	3 DON JUAN	11	87	5
DISDAIN'D						
IS IT FOR THIS I HAVE DISDAIN'D TO HOLD		101	2 DON JUAN	1	147	1
HERS WAS A PHRENSY WHICH DISDAIN'D TO RAVE		380	2 DON JUAN	4	67	7
DISDAINED						
AND FOR COQUETRY SHE DISDAINED TO WEAR IT		372	3 DON JUAN	13	31	6
(I HAVE HAD OF BOTH SOME NOT TO BE DISDAINED)		505	3 DON JUAN	16	11	7
DISDAINING						
AND LOVES OR HATES DISDAINING TO BE GUIDED		366	3 DON JUAN	13	16	7
DISEASE						
I ASK'D THE DOCTORS AFTER HIS DISEASE		39	2 DON JUAN	1	34	6
OF ITS DISEASE HE DID THE BEST HE COULD		70	2 DON JUAN	1	91	5
WAS THE DISEASE PRESENTED HIM AT CADIZ		199	2 DON JUAN	2	81	V7
AND UGLINESS DISEASE AS TOIL AND TROUBLE--		305	3 DON JUAN	11	74	7
THE FOOL WILL CALL SUCH MANIA A DISEASE--		321	3 DON JUAN	12	11	3
DISEASED						
A MIND DISEASED NO REMEDY CAN PHYSIC--		166	2 DON JUAN	2	19	7
DISEASES						
SUPPRESS THEN SOME SLIGHT FEMININE DISEASES		459	3 DON JUAN	15	9	7
DISEMBARKED						
THE TROOPS ALREADY DISEMBARKED PUSHED ON		119	3 DON JUAN	8	15	1
DISEMBODIED						
WERE ODDS AGAINST A DISEMBODIED SOUL		558	3 DON JUAN	16	118	8
DISFIGURE						
THAT LIVE GAZETTE HAD SCATTER'D TO DISFIGURE		460	3 DON JUAN	15	11	2
DISGRACE						
OR PANDERING BLINDLY TO HIS OWN DISGRACE		74	2 DON JUAN	1	99	4
SHE NEVER WOULD DISGRACE THE RING SHE WORE		80	2 DON JUAN	1	109	4
I SHOULD BUT BRING DISGRACE UPON THE DYER		489	2 DON JUAN	5	134	4
AND STINGINESS DISGRACE HER SEX AND STATION		222	3 DON JUAN	9	81	4
OF PEERS TO PROVE THEIR TITLE NO DISGRACE		314	3 DON JUAN	11	V 75	8
DISGUISE						
UNTIL SHE SPOKE THEN THROUGH ITS SOFT DISGUISE		54	2 DON JUAN	1	60	3
LEST THEY SHOULD SEEM PRINCESSES IN DISGUISE		222	2 DON JUAN	2	124	2
THAT THIS DISGUISE MAY LEAD TO NO MISTAKE		459	2 DON JUAN	5	82	8
AND IF THEY SHOULD DISCOVER YOUR DISGUISE		464	2 DON JUAN	5	92	3
HIS YOUTH AND FEATURES FAVOURED THE DISGUISE		477	2 DON JUAN	5	115	1
JUAN AMONGST THE DAMSELS IN DISGUISE		500	2 DON JUAN	5	155	3
DON JUAN IN HIS FEMININE DISGUISE		19	3 DON JUAN	6	26	1

196

PAGE VOL   CANTO STANZA LN

DISGUISE (CONTINUED)
	PAGE	VOL	CANTO	STANZA	LN
STILL HE FORGOT NOT HIS DISGUISE--ALONG	21	3 DON JUAN	6	30	1
ALTHOUGH THEY COULD NOT SEE THROUGH HIS DISGUISE	25	3 DON JUAN	6	38	5
AND HIS DISGUISE WITH DUE CONSIDERATION	55	3 DON JUAN	6	99	6
AND BRIGHT ETERNITY WITHOUT DISGUISE	169	3 DON JUAN	8	115	5
ADD WHAT MAY BE CALLED MARRIAGE IN DISGUISE	220	3 DON JUAN	9	76	8

DISGUST
	PAGE	VOL	CANTO	STANZA	LN
AND AVARICE--DISGUST A POLISHED NATION	223	3 DON JUAN	9	81	V8
LESS FROM DISGUST OF LIFE THAN DREAD OF DEATH	412	3 DON JUAN	14	4	8
WHEN ADELINE REPLIED WITH SOME DISGUST	477	3 DON JUAN	15	49	5

DISGUSTING
	PAGE	VOL	CANTO	STANZA	LN
A BUNGLER EVEN IN ITS DISGUSTING TRADE	18	2 DON JUAN	D	14	1

DISH
	PAGE	VOL	CANTO	STANZA	LN
A DAINTY DISH TO SET BEFORE THE KING	10	2 DON JUAN	D	2	3
AND BE THE ONLY BLACKBIRD IN THE DISH	10	2 DON JUAN	D	3	4
BUT THE BEST DISH THAT E'ER WAS COOK'D SINCE HOMER'S	221	2 DON JUAN	2	123	7
TO PAY HIM A FRESH VISIT WITH A DISH	226	2 DON JUAN	2	133	7
TO BE IMPALED OR QUARTERED AS A DISH	492	2 DON JUAN	5	141	2
TO SERVE IN THIS CONUNDRUM OF A DISH	465	3 DON JUAN	15	21	8
FOLLOW'D BY PETITS PUITS D'AMOUR--A DISH	486	3 DON JUAN	15	68	2
NO DAMSEL BUT A DISH AS HATH BEEN SAID	488	3 DON JUAN	15	74	6
HE SATE HIM PENSIVE O'ER A DISH OF TEA	513	3 DON JUAN	16	30	2
INFLICTED ON THE DISH A DEADLY WOUND	542	3 DON JUAN	16	88	6

DISH'D
	PAGE	VOL	CANTO	STANZA	LN
HE SOUGHT IN THE SLAVE-MARKET TOO AND DISH'D	223	2 DON JUAN	2	126	6

DISHED
	PAGE	VOL	CANTO	STANZA	LN
TO MAKE HIM PRISONER WAS ALSO DISHED	152	3 DON JUAN	8	80	8
WHERE'S BRUMMELL DISHED WHERE'S LONG POLE WELLESLEY DIDDLED	307	3 DON JUAN	11	78	1

DISHES
	PAGE	VOL	CANTO	STANZA	LN
THE DINNER MADE ABOUT A HUNDRED DISHES	307	2 DON JUAN	3	62	1
AND FISH AND SOUP BY SOME SIDE DISHES BACKED	428	2 DON JUAN	5	32	5
ANOTHER PART OF HISTORY FOR THE DISHES	65	3 DON JUAN	6	120	3
QUITE FULL RIGHT DULL GUESTS HOT AND DISHES COLD	538	3 DON JUAN	16	78	6

DISHEVELLED
	PAGE	VOL	CANTO	STANZA	LN
OF HER DISHEVELLED TRESSES DARK APPEARS	108	2 DON JUAN	1	158	V4

DISINTERESTEDNESS
	PAGE	VOL	CANTO	STANZA	LN
SUCH PURE DISINTERESTEDNESS OF PASSION	331	3 DON JUAN	12	33	3

DISLIKE
	PAGE	VOL	CANTO	STANZA	LN
MEN EVEN WHEN DYING DISLIKE INANITION	180	2 DON JUAN	2	46	5
OR SHOW THE SAME DISLIKE TO SUITORS' KISSES	287	2 DON JUAN	3	23	4
STILL I HAVE NO DISLIKE TO LEARNED NATURES	405	2 DON JUAN	4	111	5
THOSE WHO DISLIKE TO LOOK UPON A FRAY	126	3 DON JUAN	8	30	5
OUTWARD DISLIKE WHICH DON'T LOOK WELL ABROAD	240	3 DON JUAN	10	32	5
SHE SHOWED A GREAT DISLIKE TO HOLY WATER	252	3 DON JUAN	10	56	4

DISLIKES
	PAGE	VOL	CANTO	STANZA	LN
FOR JEALOUSY DISLIKES THE WORLD TO KNOW IT	57	2 DON JUAN	1	65	8

DISMAY
	PAGE	VOL	CANTO	STANZA	LN
DISMAY THE USUAL CONSEQUENCE OF DREAMS	45	3 DON JUAN	6	78	2
JOHN JOHNSON SEEING THEIR EXTREME DISMAY	105	3 DON JUAN	7	75	1
AND WILD DISMAY O'ER EVERY ANGRY COUSIN	332	3 DON JUAN	12	34	3
TO LAUGH HIM OUT OF HIS SUPPOSED DISMAY	526	3 DON JUAN	16	51	6

DISMISS
	PAGE	VOL	CANTO	STANZA	LN
SHE TO DISMISS HER GUARDS AND HE HIS HAREM	53	3 DON JUAN	6	95	7

DISMISS'D
	PAGE	VOL	CANTO	STANZA	LN
AND THEN DISMISS'D THE OMEN FROM HER BREAST	356	2 DON JUAN	4	24	3

DISMISSED
	PAGE	VOL	CANTO	STANZA	LN
TILL DULY DISAPPOINTED OR DISMISSED	536	3 DON JUAN	16	75	3

DISORDERLY
	PAGE	VOL	CANTO	STANZA	LN
AND RUSHING IN DISORDERLY THOUGH LED	369	2 DON JUAN	4	47	5

DISORDERS
	PAGE	VOL	CANTO	STANZA	LN
EXHAUSTION OR DISORDERS OF THE SAME KIN	244	3 DON JUAN	10	40	4

DISPARAGE
	PAGE	VOL	CANTO	STANZA	LN
FOR AUTHORS FEAR DESCRIPTION MIGHT DISPARAGE	280	2 DON JUAN	3	9	4
ALL FURTHER IS A BLANK--I WON'T DISPARAGE	280	2 DON JUAN	3	9	V4
THOUGH LIFE AND LOVE I LIKE NOT TO DISPARAGE	280	2 DON JUAN	3	9	V4
IT IS--I MEANT AND MEAN NOT TO DISPARAGE	344	3 DON JUAN	12	62	4
THE POSTBOYS HAVE NO REASON TO DISPARAGE	379	3 DON JUAN	13	46	6

DISPARGE
	PAGE	VOL	CANTO	STANZA	LN
WITHOUT THOSE SAD EXPENSES WHICH DISPARGE	471	3 DON JUAN	15	35	5

DISPARITY
	PAGE	VOL	CANTO	STANZA	LN
THERE WAS NO GREAT DISPARITY OF YEARS	447	3 DON JUAN	14	87	1

DISPATCH
	PAGE	VOL	CANTO	STANZA	LN
THREE LINES OF THE DISPATCH IN TAKING SCHMACKSMITH	76	3 DON JUAN	7	20	6
WITH BLOODY HANDS HE WROTE HIS FIRST DISPATCH	178	3 DON JUAN	8	133	5
WHILE JUAN IS SENT OFF WITH THE DISPATCH	181	3 DON JUAN	8	139	7
WAS LEFT UPON HIS WAY WITH THE DISPATCH	197	3 DON JUAN	9	29	2
WITH HIS DISPATCH FORGOT TO BREAK THE SEAL	211	3 DON JUAN	9	57	8
ALMOST AS MUCH AS ON A NEW DISPATCH	213	3 DON JUAN	9	61	7
AND THIRDLY HE WHO BROUGHT YOU THE DISPATCH	215	3 DON JUAN	9	65	8

DISPATCHES
	PAGE	VOL	CANTO	STANZA	LN
BY HIS DISPATCHES COUCHED IN PITHY PHRASE	85	3 DON JUAN	7	39	6
BUT HERE A MESSENGER BROUGHT IN DISPATCHES	439	3 DON JUAN	14	67	8
WRITING DISPATCHES) IN THEIR SEVERAL STATIONS	533	3 DON JUAN	16	66	7

DISPELLED
	PAGE	VOL	CANTO	STANZA	LN
AND EVERY DIFFICULTY BEING DISPELLED	92	3 DON JUAN	7	51	5

DISPENSE
	PAGE	VOL	CANTO	STANZA	LN
FOR THEY WERE FORCED WITH STEERING TO DISPENSE	177	2 DON JUAN	2	40	3
OF LATE YEARS TO DISPENSE WITH COCKER'S RIGOURS	547	3 DON JUAN	16	98	7

DISPENSED
	PAGE	VOL	CANTO	STANZA	LN
EXCEEDING SAGELY FROM THAT HOUR DISPENSED	66	2 DON JUAN	1	82	5

197

DISPENSED   (CONTINUED)
	PAGE	VOL	CANTO	STANZA	LN
HE WAS ALL THINGS TO ALL MEN AND DISPENSED	535	3 DON JUAN	16	71	2
WHILE ADELINE DISPENSED HER AIRS AND GRACES	548	3 DON JUAN	16	100	1

DISPERSE
AS AUTUMN WINDS DISPERSE THE YELLOW LEAVES	155	3 DON JUAN	8	88	V3

DISPLAY
TILL SLOWLY CHARGED WITH THUNDER THEY DISPLAY	375	2 DON JUAN	4	57	3
THIS SECRET CHARGE ON JUAN TO DISPLAY	247	3 DON JUAN	10	46	3
BAROUCHE WHICH HAD THE GLORY TO DISPLAY ONCE	248	3 DON JUAN	10	49	5
SAY SOMETHING TO THE PURPOSE AND DISPLAY	453	3 DON JUAN	14	98	7
WOULD NOW AND THEN AS 'TWERE WITHOUT DISPLAY	521	3 DON JUAN	16	42	5
YET WITH DISPLAY IN FACT AT TIMES RELENT	521	3 DON JUAN	16	42	6
IF WE MAY JUDGE FROM EACH NEW YEAR'S DISPLAY	548	3 DON JUAN	16	99	V5

DISPLAY'D
THE UPPER BORDER RICHLY WROUGHT DISPLAY'D	308	2 DON JUAN	3	64	5
HIS STRAIN DISPLAY'D SOME FEELING--RIGHT OR WRONG	326	2 DON JUAN	3	87	5
THE NEGROES MORE PHILOSOPHY DISPLAY'D--	414	2 DON JUAN	5	7	7
AND RANK'D WITH WHAT IS EVERY DAY DISPLAY'D--	400	3 DON JUAN	13	90	7
DISPLAY'D SOME SYLPH-LIKE FIGURES IN ITS MAZE	408	3 DON JUAN	13	108	3
BUT VARIOUS AS THE VARIOUS MEATS DISPLAY'D	488	3 DON JUAN	15	74	4

DISPLAYED
DISPLAYED MUCH MORE OF NERVE PERHAPS OF WIT	283	2 DON JUAN	3	14	V7
AND A MAGNIFICIENT LARGE HALL DISPLAYED	440	2 DON JUAN	5	51	7
A PERFECT TRANSFORMATION HERE DISPLAYED	458	2 DON JUAN	5	80	5
'TWAS LIKE THE FAWN WHICH IN THE LAKE DISPLAYED	36	3 DON JUAN	6	60	5
FOR CATS AND BIRDS MORE PENCHANT NE'ER DISPLAYED	249	3 DON JUAN	10	50	7
THE TALENT AND GOOD HUMOUR HE DISPLAYED	355	3 DON JUAN	12	85	5
INDEED WE SEE THE DAILY PROOF DISPLAYED	371	3 DON JUAN	13	29	4
IN COURTESY THEIR WISH TO SEE DISPLAYED	517	3 DON JUAN	16	39	5
TO SOMETHING LIKE THIS WHEN TOO OFT DISPLAYED	522	3 DON JUAN	16	44	5

DISPLAYS
FORETELLS THE HEAVIEST TEMPEST IT DISPLAYS	61	2 DON JUAN	1	73	3
HIS PARTS OF SPEECH AND IN THE STRANGE DISPLAYS	207	3 DON JUAN	9	49	4
AND SPARKLING ON FROM HEAP TO HEAP DISPLAYS	319	3 DON JUAN	12	8	2

DISPLEASE
OR IF THAT SIMPLE SENTENCE SHOULD DISPLEASE	109	3 DON JUAN	7	85	3
HAS SHOWN I KNOW NOT WHY THEY SHOULD DISPLEASE	494	3 DON JUAN	15	86	6

DISPLEASING
ON PAIN OF MUCH DISPLEASING THE GYNOCRASY	526	3 DON JUAN	16	52	8

DISPOSE
BUT FIRST OF LITTLE LEILA WE'LL DISPOSE	335	3 DON JUAN	12	41	1

DISPOSED
AND NOT AT ALL DISPOSED TO PROVE A MARTYR	122	2 DON JUAN	1	184	8
DAYS NEARLY O'ER MIGHT BE DISPOSED TO RIOT	173	2 DON JUAN	2	33	6
SOME HE DISPOSED OF OFF CAPE MATAPAN	284	2 DON JUAN	3	16	1
SHE DID NOT FIND HERSELF THE LEAST DISPOSED	48	3 DON JUAN	6	84	5
NOR MUCH DISPOSED TO WAIT IN WORD OR DEED	56	3 DON JUAN	6	101	2
TO BE DISPOSED OF IN A WAY SO NEW	101	3 DON JUAN	7	67	3
JUAN FELT SOMEWHAT PENSIVE AND DISPOSED	507	3 DON JUAN	16	15	1
THOUGH FOR THE PUBLIC WEAL DISPOSED TO VENTURE HIGH	536	3 DON JUAN	16	73	6

DISPOSING
AFTER DISPOSING OF TWO FELLOW CREATURES	426	2 DON JUAN	5	30	V2

DISPOSITION
ITSELF AND SHOWED A FEVERISH DISPOSITION	244	3 DON JUAN	10	39	6
AND TACITURN ASIATIC DISPOSITION	328	3 DON JUAN	12	27	2

DISPUTE
THE MADDENED TURKS THEIR CITY STILL DISPUTE	146	3 DON JUAN	8	69	8
WHEN THEY DISPUTE WITH SCEPTICS AND WITH CURSES	165	3 DON JUAN	8	108	7
SPACE TO DISPUTE WHAT NO ONE EVER COULD	270	3 DON JUAN	11	4	6
'TIS NONSENSE TO DISPUTE ABOUT A HUE--	359	3 DON JUAN	13	3	5

DISPUTED
AS ALL TRUTHS MUST THE MORE THEY ARE DISPUTED	503	3 DON JUAN	16	6	8

DISPUTES
AND THUS YOUR HOURI (IT MAY BE) DISPUTES	168	3 DON JUAN	8	113	7

DISPUTING
'TWAS BLOW FOR BLOW DISPUTING INCH BY INCH	150	3 DON JUAN	8	77	7

DISSATISFIED
DISSATISFIED NOR KNOWING WHAT HE WANTED	73	2 DON JUAN	1	96	2

DISSECTED
HIS MORNS HE PASSED IN BUSINESS--WHICH DISSECTED	301	3 DON JUAN	11	65	1

DISSECTING
DISSECTING THE WHOLE INSIDE OF A QUESTION	232	3 DON JUAN	10	14	7

DISSECTION
DEAD SCANDALS FORM GOOD SUBJECTS FOR DISSECTION	37	2 DON JUAN	1	31	8
BUT OTHERS PONDER'D ON A NEW DISSECTION	199	2 DON JUAN	2	80	5

DISSEMBLES
BUT PASSION MOST DISSEMBLES YET BETRAYS	61	2 DON JUAN	1	73	1

DISSENT
AND WINS EVEN BY A DELICATE DISSENT	493	3 DON JUAN	15	83	8

DISSENTING
TREAT A DISSENTING AUTHOR VERY MARTYRLY	142	2 DON JUAN	1	211	8

DISSENTIONS
AND THESE DISSENTIONS MAKE A SORRY SIGHT	496	3 DON JUAN	15	90	V4

DISSERT
THAT I DISSERT LIKE GRACE BEFORE A FEAST	334	3 DON JUAN	12	39	3

DISSIMULATION
DISSIMULATION ALWAYS SETS APART	457	3 DON JUAN	15	3	6
I CAN'T TELL WHY TO THIS DISSIMULATION--	518	3 DON JUAN	16	40	3

DISSIPATE
IN WHAT WAY FEMININE CAPRICE MAY DISSIPATE	65	3 DON JUAN	6	119	8

```
                                                          PAGE VOL   CANTO STANZA LN
DISSIPATED
      AND HAGGARD WITH A DISSIPATED LIFE . . . . . . .   . 389  2 DON JUAN  4    83    2
      AS WHEN THE FRENCH THAT DISSIPATED NATION  . . . . . 176  3 DON JUAN  8   129    4
      DON JUAN GREW I FEAR A LITTLE DISSIPATED . . . . . . 236  3 DON JUAN 10    23    3
      THEIR VIGOUR IN A THOUSAND ARMS IS DISSIPATED  . . . 306  3 DON JUAN 11    75    3
DISSIPATION
      SOME MIND THEIR HOUSEHOLD OTHERS DISSIPATION  . . . . 263 2 DON JUAN  2   201    2
DISSOLVED
      LIKE MOUNTAIN MISTS AT LENGTH DISSOLVED IN RAIN  . . 380  2 DON JUAN  4    66    8
      DISSOLVED LIKE SNOW BEFORE A WOMAN CRYING  . . . . . 492  2 DON JUAN  5   141    8
DISSOLVES
      A SILENT CHANGE DISSOLVES THE GLITTERING MASS  . . . 306  3 DON JUAN 11    76    6
DISSOLVING
      IN THE DISSOLVING CIRCLE ALL THE NATIONS'  . . . . . 223  3 DON JUAN  9    82    2
      DISSOLVING IN THE WALTZ TO SOME SOFT AIR . . . . . . 303  3 DON JUAN 11    70    6
DISTAFF
      IN THIS VILE GARB THE DISTAFF WEB AND WOOF . . . . . 484  2 DON JUAN  5   127    3
DISTANCE
      BY DISTANCE MELLOW'D O'ER THE WATERS SWEEP  . . . . . 87 2 DON JUAN  1   122    4
      WHEN GAZING ON THEM MYSTIFIED BY DISTANCE  . . . . . 163 2 DON JUAN  2    12    7
      A GENTLEMANLY DISTANCE NOT TOO NEAR  . . . . . . . . 366 2 DON JUAN  4    41    5
      AND IDA IN THE DISTANCE STILL THE SAME  . . . . . . . 386 2 DON JUAN  4    77    3
      OF POETS WHO COME DOWN TO US THROUGH DISTANCE . . . . 398 2 DON JUAN  4   100    1
      HE MOTIONED THEM TO STOP AT SOME SMALL DISTANCE  . . 440  2 DON JUAN  5    51    5
      HAUGHTY AND HUGE ALONG THE DISTANCE LOWERS  . . . . . 460 2 DON JUAN  5    85    5
      IN THIS IMPERIAL HALL AT DISTANCE LAY . . . . . . . . 466 2 DON JUAN  5    95    1
      AT SOME SMALL DISTANCE ALL HE SAW WITHIN . . . . . . 469  2 DON JUAN  5   100    4
      A SAD MISCALCULATION ABOUT DISTANCE  . . . . . . . .  80  3 DON JUAN  7    28    1
      THE LIGHTEST BEING THE SAFEST AT A DISTANCE  . . . . 140  3 DON JUAN  8    55    5
      KEEP MERELY FIRING AT A FOOLISH DISTANCE . . . . . . 151  3 DON JUAN  8    78    8
      AND JUAN'S SUITE LATE SCATTERED AT A DISTANCE  . . . 275  3 DON JUAN 11    14    2
DISTANT
      CHANGED FOR THE DAME GREW DISTANT THE YOUTH SHY  . .   60  2 DON JUAN  1    70    2
      A LADY ALWAYS DISTANT FROM THE FACT--  . . . . . . . 119  2 DON JUAN  1   178    6
      ON THE SNOW-TOPS OF DISTANT HILLS THE STREAK  . . . . 234 2 DON JUAN  2   147    3
      BY A DISTANT ORGAN DOUBTING IF HE BE . . . . . . . . 237  2 DON JUAN  2   152    2
      THE DISTANT DOG-BARK AND PERCEIVED BETWEEN  . . . . . 289 2 DON JUAN  3    27    4
      SOUND LIKE A DISTANT TORRENT'S FALL  . . . . . . . . 323  2 DON JUAN  3  L  8    3
      WHILE SWUNG THE DEEP BELL IN THE DISTANT TOWER . . . 335  2 DON JUAN  3   102    5
      AND DISTANT FROM EACH OTHER BURNED THE LIGHTS  . . .  38  3 DON JUAN  6    64    2
      RATHER TOO HIGH AND DISTANT THAT SHE THREW . . . . .  44  3 DON JUAN  6    76    3
      WITH DISTANT SHRIEKS WERE HEARD HEAVEN TO UPBRAID--  146  3 DON JUAN  8    69    5
      CONSTANTINOPLE AND SUCH DISTANT PLACES  . . . . . . . 368 3 DON JUAN 13    23    2
      SOME DEEM IT BUT THE DISTANT ECHO GIVEN  . . . . . . 388  3 DON JUAN 13    63    6
DISTILLED
      SLOWLY DISTILLED INTO THE GLIMMERING GLASS  . . . . . 278 3 DON JUAN 11    22    7
DISTINCT
      DISTINCT AND HIGH AND PALPABLE TO VIEW  . . . . . . . 207 2 DON JUAN  2    97    8
      SHE WAS APPEAR'D DISTINCT AND TALL AND FAIR . . . . . 216 2 DON JUAN  2   115    8
DISTINCTION
      FAST BY THE HEAD AND ALL DISTINCTION GONE  . . . . . 179  2 DON JUAN  2    44    2
      BESIDES THE MARKED DISTINCTION OF HIS AIR  . . . . . 355  3 DON JUAN 12    85    6
      O'ER JUAN HE COULD NO DISTINCTION CLAIM  . . . . . . 367  3 DON JUAN 13    20    2
      SUCH SMALL DISTINCTION BETWEEN FRIENDS AND FOES  . . 421  3 DON JUAN 14    25    4
DISTINGUISH
      NOW HERE WE SHOULD DISTINGUISH FOR HOWE'ER . . . . .  13  3 DON JUAN  6    14    1
DISTINGUISH'D
      DESIRABLE DISTINGUISH'D CELEBRATED . . . . . . . . . 428  3 DON JUAN 14    42    2
DISTINGUISHED
      TO SOME DISTINGUISHED STRANGERS IN THAT FRAY  . . . . 82 3 DON JUAN  7    32    6
      UPON THE SHADES OF THOSE DISTINGUISHED MEN . . . . . 373  3 DON JUAN 13    33    3
DISTORTION
      AND TRUCULENT DISTORTION OF THEIR TRESSES  . . . . . 550  3 DON JUAN 16   103    8
DISTORTIONS
      NO FASHION MADE THEM APES OF HER DISTORTIONS  . . . . 145 3 DON JUAN  8    66    6
DISTRACTION
      SHE SEEM'D BY THE DISTRACTION OF HER AIR . . . . . .  80  2 DON JUAN  1   110    4
DISTRAIT
      SO MUCH DISTRAIT HE WAS THAT ALL COULD SEE  . . . . . 513 3 DON JUAN 16    30    6
      CONFUSED IN THE CONFUSION AND DISTRAIT  . . . . . . . 542 3 DON JUAN 16    87    3
DISTRESS
      TO WEATHER OUT MUCH LONGER THE DISTRESS  . . . . . . 178  2 DON JUAN  2    41    3
      HAVING BEEN SEVERAL DAYS IN GREAT DISTRESS  . . . . . 180 2 DON JUAN  2    46    2
      ARE SIMILES AT HAND FOR THE DISTRESS . . . . . . . . 487  2 DON JUAN  5   132    3
      OF INSPIRATION GATHERED FROM DISTRESS. . . . . . . .  59  3 DON JUAN  6   107    3
      SO MUCH DID JUAN'S SETTING OFF DISTRESS HER  . . . . 247  3 DON JUAN 10    47    7
      INDIFFERENCE CERTES DON'T PRODUCE DISTRESS  . . . . . 374 3 DON JUAN 13    35    6
      IF IN MY EXTREMITY OF RHYME'S DISTRESS  . . . . . . . 442 3 DON JUAN 14    75    5
DISTRESSES
      ALL THAT WE READ HEAR DREAM OF MAN'S DISTRESSES  . . 173  3 DON JUAN  8   123    3
      THAT HIRED HUZZAS REDEEM NO LAND'S DISTRESSES  . . . 267  3 DON JUAN 10    86    4
DISTRESSING
      ALAS SAID JUAN 'TWERE A TALE DISTRESSING . . . . . . 419  2 DON JUAN  5    16    5
DISTRIBUTION
      IN SILENT HORROR AND THEIR DISTRIBUTION  . . . . . . 195  2 DON JUAN  2    75    2
DISTURB
      AND THEREFORE PAUSED NOT TO DISTURB THE SLUMBER  . .  96  2 DON JUAN  1   138    4
      THAT ANYBODY SHOULD DISTURB YOU SO . . . . . . . . .  29  3 DON JUAN  6    47    3
DISTURB'D
      THAT NO ONE LIKES TO BE DISTURB'D AT MEALS . . . . .  69  2 DON JUAN  1    89    5
```

```
                                                        PAGE VOL      CANTO STANZA LN
DISTURBING
    WITHOUT DISTURBING HER YET SLUMBERING GUEST . . . . .  245  2 DON JUAN  2    168    6
DITCH
    BUT THE TOWN DITCH BELOW WAS DEEP AS OCEAN . . . . .    72  3 DON JUAN  7     11    3
    WAS NOT LIKE JACOB'S) OR TO CROSS A DITCH . . . . . .   93  3 DON JUAN  7     52    8
    FOR HAVING THROWN HIMSELF INTO A DITCH . . . . . .    147  3 DON JUAN  8     71    1
    THREW THEM ALL DOWN INTO THE DITCH AGAIN . . . . . .  147  3 DON JUAN  8     71    8
    HE CLEAR'D HEDGE DITCH AND DOUBLE POST AND RAIL . . . 424  3 DON JUAN 14     33    2
DITCHER
    THEY WRUNG IT OUT AND THOUGH A THIRSTY DITCHER . . . . 201  2 DON JUAN  2     85    5
DITCHES
    IN DITCHES FIELDS OR WHERESOE'ER THEY FELT . . . . .  120  3 DON JUAN  8     18    4
    THAT WATER LAND OF DUTCHMEN AND OF DITCHES . . . . .  256  3 DON JUAN 10     63    2
DIURETIC
    LIKE HAIL TO MAKE A BLOODY DIURETIC . . . . . . .     117  3 DON JUAN  8     12    3
DIVAN
    AS AN AMUSEMENT AFTER THE DIVAN . . . . . . . .        51  3 DON JUAN  6     91    6
    A GOODLY SPIRIT FOR A STATE DIVAN . . . . . . . .     440  3 DON JUAN 14     70    3
DIVERS
    THUS DROWNINGS ARE MUCH TALK'D OF BY THE DIVERS . . . 172  2 DON JUAN  2     31    7
    TO HURL THESE FLEET-DITCH DIVERS DOWN THEIR LAKES . . 334  2 DON JUAN  3    100   V8
    AND DIVERS SMOKED SUPERB PIPES DECORATED . . . . . .  441  2 DON JUAN  5     53    5
DIVERSION
    HERE WAS NO LACK OF INNOCENT DIVERSION . . . . . .    293  2 DON JUAN  3     35    1
    BUT HEAVEN MUST BE DIVERTED ITS DIVERSION . . . . .   377  3 DON JUAN 13     41    1
DIVERSITY
    WHAT WITH A SMALL DIVERSITY OF CLIMATE . . . . . .    327  3 DON JUAN 12     24    1
DIVERT
    BUT DONNA INEZ TO DIVERT THE TRAIN . . . . . . .      128  2 DON JUAN  1    190    1
DIVERTED
    AND NOW THEY WERE DIVERTED BY THEIR SUITE . . . . .   316  2 DON JUAN  3     78    1
    BUT HEAVEN MUST BE DIVERTED ITS DIVERSION . . . . .   377  3 DON JUAN 13     41    1
DIVESTED
    BECAME DIVESTED OF HIS NATIVE MODESTY . . . . . .     157  2 DON JUAN  2      1    8
DIVIDE
    WITH THE FREE FORESTERS DIVIDE NO SPOIL . . . . .     145  3 DON JUAN  8     67    6
    WHICH MORTALS GENEROUSLY WOULD DIVIDE . . . . . .     367  3 DON JUAN 13     19    7
DIVIDED
    DIVIDED IN TWELVE BOOKS EACH BOOK CONTAINING . . . .  135  2 DON JUAN  1    200    2
    WHICH HE DIVIDED WITH PEDRILLO WHO . . . . . . .      193  2 DON JUAN  2     71    7
    PART WAS DIVIDED PART THROWN IN THE SEA . . . . . .   197  2 DON JUAN  2     77    5
    THE CHILD DIVIDED IT WERE LESS TO SEE . . . . . .     349  2 DON JUAN  4     10   V5
    AND NOW TO SEE THEM THUS DIVIDED STAND . . . . . .    368  2 DON JUAN  4     45    5
    THE WOMEN MUCH DIVIDED--AS IS USUAL . . . . . .       329  3 DON JUAN 12     28    1
DIVIDES
    JUAN BY SOME STRANGE CHANCE WHICH OFT DIVIDES . . . . 125  3 DON JUAN  8     27    1
DIVIDING
    HIS PRISONERS DIVIDING THEM LIKE CHAPTERS . . . . .   283  2 DON JUAN  3     15    6
    THAT AWFUL PAUSE DIVIDING LIFE FROM DEATH . . . . .   111  3 DON JUAN  7     87    2
DIVINE
    NOT ANY OF THE MANY COULD DIVINE . . . . . . .        33  2 DON JUAN  1     23    2
    AND THEN THERE ARE SUCH THINGS AS LOVE DIVINE . . .   64  2 DON JUAN  1     79    1
    AND HERE THOU ART A GOD INDEED DIVINE . . . . . .     69  2 DON JUAN  1     88    4
    YOU NEVER COULD DIVINE HIS REAL THOUGHT . . . . .    296  2 DON JUAN  3     41    4
    HIS QUESTION MUCH TOO MERRY TO DIVINE . . . . . .    297  2 DON JUAN  3     42    7
    AND MUST THY LYRE SO LONG DIVINE . . . . . . .       322  2 DON JUAN  3   L  5    5
    IT MADE ANACREON'S SONG DIVINE . . . . . . .         324  2 DON JUAN  3   L 11    3
    A LITTLE HEAVY BUT NO LESS DIVINE . . . . . . .      328  2 DON JUAN  3     91    2
    MUST SINK AT LAST INTO A SWOON DIVINE-- . . . . .    343  2 DON JUAN  3   V 98    6
    ABOUT THE RIGHT DIVINE HOW FAR WE SHOULD . . . . .   426  2 DON JUAN  5     30    5
    FOR ALL WAS VAST STILL FRAGRANT AND DIVINE . . . .   460  2 DON JUAN  5     85    8
    SHE THOUGHT HERS GAVE A DOUBLE RIGHT DIVINE . . . .  485  2 DON JUAN  5    129    7
    WHICH NONE DIVINE AND EVERYONE OBEYS . . . . . .     207  3 DON JUAN  9     49    6
    OF ANY WORSHIP WAKE SOME THOUGHTS DIVINE . . . . .   387  3 DON JUAN 13     61    8
    ATTUNED BY VOICES MORE OR LESS DIVINE . . . . . .    408  3 DON JUAN 13    107    3
    JUAN WAS SOMETHING SHE COULD NOT DIVINE . . . . .    480  3 DON JUAN 15     56    5
    THE FIRST--BUT WHAT SHE COULD NOT WELL DIVINE . . .  513  3 DON JUAN 16     30    8
    AND FROM ITS CONTEXT THOUGHT SHE COULD DIVINE . . .  516  3 DON JUAN 16     37    3
    ARE SO DIVINE THAT I MUST DEEM THEM REAL-- . . . .   553  3 DON JUAN 16    107    8
DIVINER
    GREAT SOCRATES AND THOU DIVINER STILL . . . . . .    464  3 DON JUAN 15     18    2
DIVING
    HUSH'D INTO DEPTHS BEYOND THE WATCHER'S DIVING . . . 261  2 DON JUAN  2    197    6
DIVINITIES
    HAVE PROVED BUT DROPSIES TAKEN FOR DIVINITIES . . .  330  2 DON JUAN  3     95    8
DIVINITY
    THE FIRST ATTACK AT ONCE PROVED THE DIVINITY . . .   271  3 DON JUAN 11      6    1
DIVORCE
    THE LAWYERS DID THEIR UTMOST FOR DIVORCE . . . . .    38  2 DON JUAN  1     32    6
    AND HOW ALFONSO SUED FOR A DIVORCE . . . . . . .     126  2 DON JUAN  1    188    7
    A LAD OF SIXTEEN CAUSING A DIVORCE . . . . . . .     158  2 DON JUAN  2      2    7
DIVORCED
    WISHING EACH OTHER NOT DIVORCED BUT DEAD . . . . .    35  2 DON JUAN  1     26    3
    DIVORCED OR DOING THEREANENT YE ANNALS . . . . .     308  3 DON JUAN 11     80    2
DIVORCES
    THE HISTORY OF DIVORCES WHICH THOUGH CHEQUERED . . . 209  3 DON JUAN  9     53    7
DIVORCING
    OR MARRIAGE BY DIVORCING THEM THUS ODDLY . . . . .   472  3 DON JUAN 15     36    2
DIVULGED
    OF GORE DIVULGED THE CAUSE) THAT HE WAS DEAD . . . . 430  2 DON JUAN  5     35    7
```

```
                                                                 PAGE VOL      CANTO STANZA LN
DIZZINESS
    FOR ALL WAS DOUBT AND DIZZINESS HE THOUGHT  . . . . . .  215  2 DON JUAN  2   112   2
    AFFLICTING YOUNG FOLKS WITH A SORT OF DIZZINESS  . . . .  108  3 DON JUAN  7    83   8
DIZZY
    AND AS HE GAZED HIS DIZZY BRAIN SPUN FAST  . . . . . .   214  2 DON JUAN  2   110   1
    FOR HE WAS DIZZY BUSY AND HIS VEINS  . . . . . . . . .   129  3 DON JUAN  8    33   2
DOATING
    THE MOUTH OF SOME ONE IN HIS PLAYS SO DOATING  . . . . .   77  3 DON JUAN  7    21   7
DOCILE
    POOR LITTLE THING  SHE WAS AS FAIR AS DOCILE  . . . . .  250  3 DON JUAN 10    52   1
    THEIR DOCILE ESQUIRES ALSO DID THE SAME  . . . . . . .   549  3 DON JUAN 16   101   6
DOCILITY
    HE ALMOST HONOURED HIM FOR HIS DOCILITY  . . . . . . .   368  3 DON JUAN 13    22   2
DOCTOR
    WITH WHICH THE DOCTOR PAID OFF AN OLD POX  . . . . . .    91  2 DON JUAN  1   129   7
    THE KING COMMANDS US AND THE DOCTOR QUACKS US  . . . .   159  2 DON JUAN  2     4   5
    LIKE BURNS (WHOM DOCTOR CURRIE WELL DESCRIBES)  . . . .  329  2 DON JUAN  3    92   4
DOCTORS
    I ASK'D THE DOCTORS AFTER HIS DISEASE . . . . . . . .     39  2 DON JUAN  1    34   6
    HE HEWED AWAY LIKE DOCTORS OF THEOLOGY  . . . . . . .   165  3 DON JUAN  8   108   6
    AND SENT THE DOCTORS IN A NEW DIRECTION . . . . . . .   245  3 DON JUAN 10    43   4
    DOCTORS LESS FAMOUS FOR THEIR CURES THAN FEES  . . . .   431  3 DON JUAN 14    48   4
DOCTORS'
    SAVE DEATH OR DOCTORS' COMMONS--SO HE DIED  . . . . .     41  2 DON JUAN  1    36   8
    AND FOUNDED DOCTORS' COMMONS--I HAVE CONNED . . . . .    209  3 DON JUAN  9    53   6
    OF DOCTORS' COMMONS BUT SHE DREADED FIRST  . . . . .    437  3 DON JUAN 14    62   5
DOCTRINE
    AND THAT SAME DEVILISH DOCTRINE OF THE PERSIAN  . . . .  377  3 DON JUAN 13    41   5
    AS MANY DOUBTS AS ANY OTHER DOCTRINE  . . . . . . . .   377  3 DON JUAN 13    41   7
DOCTRINES
    DOUBTLESS TO THAT OF DOCTRINES THE MOST TRUE  . . . . .  101  3 DON JUAN  7    67   5
DODGING
    'TWERE NOT FOR WANT OF LAMPS TO AID HIS DODGING HIS  . . . 281  3 DON JUAN 11    28   5
DOG
    THE CREATURE WAS HIS FATHER'S DOG THAT DIED . . . . . .  193  2 DON JUAN  2    71   3
    AT A PER-CENTAGE A CHILD CROSS DOG ILL  . . . . . . .    16  3 DON JUAN  6    21   3
    OR AS A LITTLE DOG WILL LEAD THE BLIND  . . . . . . .    90  3 DON JUAN  7    48   5
    A SECRETARY--LAP DOG AND A BULL DOG--AND . . . . . . .  249  3 DON JUAN 10    50   V1
    A SECRETARY--LAP DOG AND A BULL DOG--AND . . . . . . .  249  3 DON JUAN 10    50   V1
DOG-BARK
    THE DISTANT DOG-BARK AND PERCEIVED BETWEEN  . . . . . .  289  2 DON JUAN  3    27   4
DOG-DAYS
    LOVE WITH YOU AND BEEN IN THE DOG-DAYS STUNG  . . . . .  486  2 DON JUAN  5   130   4
DOGMA
    AS IS THE CHRISTIAN DOGMA RATHER ROUGH  . . . . . . .   195  3 DON JUAN  9    25   6
DOGS
    KNOWING (DOGS HAVE SUCH INTELLECTUAL NOSES) . . . . . .  187  2 DON JUAN  2    58   5
    WHERE I LIKE OTHER DOGS HAVE HAD MY DAY . . . . . . .   244  2 DON JUAN  2   166   3
    THOSE SERVILE DOGS ARE NOT SO PROUDLY EYED  . . . . .   418  2 DON JUAN  5    14   3
    FOR DOGS OR TO BE SLAIN WITH PANGS REFINED  . . . . .   492  2 DON JUAN  5   141   3
    BILLS--WOMEN--WIVES DOGS HORSES--AND MANKIND  . . . . .   17  3 DON JUAN  6    22   V2
    DOGS OR MEN (FOR I FLATTER YOU IN SAYING . . . . . . .   70  3 DON JUAN  7     7   1
    THAT YE ARE DOGS--YOUR BETTERS FAR) YE MAY  . . . . .    70  3 DON JUAN  7     7   2
    WITH SCHNAPPS--SAD DOGS WHOM HUNDSFOT OR FERFLUCTER  . .  260  3 DON JUAN 10    71   7
    WERE SHAKEN DOWN AND DOGS HAD HAD THEIR DAY . . . . .   466  3 DON JUAN 15    23   4
    FOR THE LORD HENRY LINKED WITH DOGS AND HORSES  . . . .  534  3 DON JUAN 16    68   2
DOG-STAR
    AND MAY APPEAR SO WHEN THE DOG-STAR RAGES--  . . . . .    11  2 DON JUAN  0     4   6
DOING
    THOUGH DOUBTS OF THEIR WELL DOING TO ARRANGE  . . . . .   65  3 DON JUAN  6   120   2
    GREAT DEEDS ARE DOING--HOW SHALL I RELATE 'EM  . . . .   107  3 DON JUAN  7    81   6
    DIVORCED OR DOING THEREANENT YE ANNALS  . . . . . . .   308  3 DON JUAN 11    80   2
    I HAVE SEEN A CONGRESS DOING ALL THAT'S MEAN--  . . . .  310  3 DON JUAN 11    84   6
    (BY DOING EASILY WHENE'ER SHE CHOSE  . . . . . . . .    522  3 DON JUAN 16    44   2
DOINGS
    FOR MY PART TO SUCH DOINGS I'M A STRANGER  . . . . . .    65  2 DON JUAN  1    80   4
    THERE'S DOUBTLESS SOMETHING IN DOMESTIC DOINGS . . . .   279  2 DON JUAN  3     8   1
    OF THIS SAME MYSTIC FRIAR'S CURIOUS DOINGS  . . . . .   527  3 DON JUAN 16    53   7
DOLCE
    THERE ROSE A CARLO DOLCE OR A TITIAN . . . . . . . .    392  3 DON JUAN 13    71   3
DOLLAR
    YOUR ARM AND I'LL BET MOSCOW TO A DOLLAR . . . . . . .   160  3 DON JUAN  8    97   7
DOLLARS
    AND AVERAGED EACH FROM TEN TO A HUNDRED DOLLARS  . . . .  283  2 DON JUAN  3    15   8
    SOME WENT OFF DEARLY FIFTEEN HUNDRED DOLLARS  . . . .   407  2 DON JUAN  4   114   1
    CONTAINING INGOTS BAGS OF DOLLARS COINS  . . . . . .   321  3 DON JUAN 12    12   2
DOLON
    WHEN HE ALLURED POOR DOLON--YOU HAD BETTER  . . . . . .  407  3 DON JUAN 13   105   7
DOLOUR
    AND NE'ER TO BE DESCRIBED FOR TO THE DOLOUR  . . . . .  428  3 DON JUAN 14    40   7
DOLPHIN'S
    AND DOLPHIN'S LEAP AND LITTLE BILLOW CROST  . . . . .   251  2 DON JUAN  2   181   6
DOME
    SOME DOME SURMOUNTED BY HIS MEAGRE FACE  . . . . . . .  320  3 DON JUAN 12    10   4
DOMES
    IN THE MORE CHASTENED DOMES OF WESTERN KINGS  . . . . .  465  2 DON JUAN  5    94   3
DOMESTIC
    BUT FOR DOMESTIC QUARRELS ONE WILL DO . . . . . . . .    31  2 DON JUAN  1    19   8
    NOT HAVING OF MY OWN DOMESTIC CARES  . . . . . . . .     33  2 DON JUAN  1    23   8
```

201

		PAGE	VOL	CANTO	STANZA	LV

DOMESTIC   (CONTINUED)
VICTORIOUS VIRTUE AND DOMESTIC TRUTH . . . . 78 2 DON JUAN 1 107 3
THERE'S DOUBTLESS SOMETHING IN DOMESTIC DOINGS . . . . 279 2 DON JUAN 3 8 1
I KNOW NOT IF HE HAD DOMESTIC CARES-- . . . . 496 2 DON JUAN 5 148 5
WITH SOME SLIGHT HEART-QUAKE OF DOMESTIC TREASON-- . . 370 3 DON JUAN 13 26 5
DOMESTICS
SEEING A TROOP OF HIS DOMESTICS DANCING . . . . . . 290 2 DON JUAN 3 29 5
DOMINION
AND OTHER MINDS ACKNOWLEDGED MY DOMINION . . . . . . 345 2 DON JUAN 4 3 4
DOMOS
AND ET SEPULCHRI IMMEMOR STRUIS DOMOS . . . . 448 2 DON JUAN 5 63 7
DON
I'LL THEREFORE TAKE OUR ANCIENT FRIEND DON JUAN . . . 21 2 DON JUAN 1 1 6
SO AS I SAID I'LL TAKE MY FRIEND DON JUAN . . . . . 24 2 DON JUAN 1 5 8
NARRATING SOMEWHAT OF DON JUAN'S FATHER . . . . . . 25 2 DON JUAN 1 7 7
DON JUAN'S PARENTS LIVED BESIDE THE RIVER . . . . . 25 2 DON JUAN 1 8 7
HIS FATHER'S NAME WAS JOSE--DON OF COURSE . . . . . 26 2 DON JUAN 1 9 1
DON JOSE LIKE A LINEAL SON OF EVE . . . . . . 30 2 DON JUAN 1 18 7
DON JOSE AND HIS LADY QUARREL'D--WHY . . . . . 33 2 DON JUAN 1 23 1
DON JOSE AND THE DONNA INEZ LED . . . . . . 35 2 DON JUAN 1 26 1
BEFORE UNLUCKILY DON JOSE DIED . . . . 38 2 DON JUAN 1 32 8
IS MORE THAN I KNOW--BUT DON JUAN'S MOTHER . . . . 47 2 DON JUAN 1 46 7
PRODUCED HER DON MORE HEIRS AT LOVE THAN LAW . . . 53 2 DON JUAN 1 58 8
THAT INEZ HAD ERE DON ALFONSO'S MARRIAGE . . . . . 58 2 DON JUAN 1 66 7
AND COMPLIMENTED DON ALFONSO'S TASTE . . . . . . 58 2 DON JUAN 1 67 6
IN YOUNG DON JUAN'S FAVOUR AND TO HIM ITS . . . . 65 2 DON JUAN 1 81 3
PERHAPS TO OPEN DON ALFONSO'S EYES . . . . . . 75 2 DON JUAN 1 101 7
AND THEN OF DON ALFONSO'S FIFTY YEARS . . . . . 78 2 DON JUAN 1 107 4
FOR DON ALFONSO AND SHE INLY SWORE . . . . . . 80 2 DON JUAN 1 109 2
BUT KEEPING JULIA AND DON JUAN STILL . . . . . 86 2 DON JUAN 1 121 5
BY THIS TIME DON ALFONSO WAS ARRIVED . . . . . 96 2 DON JUAN 1 138 1
COULD ENTER INTO DON ALFONSO'S HEAD . . . . . . 97 2 DON JUAN 1 139 2
IN HEAVEN'S NAME DON ALFONSO WHAT D'YE MEAN . . . 98 2 DON JUAN 1 142 1
YES DON ALFONSO HUSBAND NOW NO MORE . . . . . 101 2 DON JUAN 1 146 1
UNGRATEFUL PERJURED BARBAROUS DON ALFONSO . . . . 101 2 DON JUAN 1 146 7
THE DUKE OF ICHAR AND DON FERNAN NUNEZ . . . . 103 2 DON JUAN 1 150 2
THE SENHOR DON ALFONSO STOOD CONFUSED . . . . . 109 2 DON JUAN 1 159 1
BUT DON ALFONSO STOOD WITH DOWNCAST LOOKS . . . . 110 2 DON JUAN 1 161 1
IN DON ALFONSO'S FACTS WHICH JUST NOW WORE . . . 111 2 DON JUAN 1 164 6
NOW DON ALFONSO ENTERING BUT ALONE . . . . . . 116 2 DON JUAN 1 173 1
FROM DELICACY TO DON JUAN'S EAR . . . . . . 118 2 DON JUAN 1 176 7
THIS WAS DON JUAN'S EARLIEST SCRAPE BUT WHETHER . . 135 2 DON JUAN 1 199 1
DON JUAN BADE HIS VALET PACK HIS THINGS . . . . 161 2 DON JUAN 2 9 1
DON JUAN STOOD AND GAZING FROM THE STERN . . . . 164 2 DON JUAN 2 14 1
A SMALL OLD SPANIEL--WHICH HAD BEEN DON JOSE'S . . 187 2 DON JUAN 2 58 1
DON JUAN ALMOST FAMISH'D AND HALF DROWN'D . . . . 224 2 DON JUAN 2 129 4
RETURN WE TO DON JUAN HE BEGUN . . . . 244 2 DON JUAN 2 167 1
LEAVING DON JUAN AND HAIDEE TO PLEAD . . . . . 271 2 DON JUAN 2 216 7
HAD STOPP'D THIS CANTO AND DON JUAN'S BREATH . . . 366 2 DON JUAN 4 42 2
I LEAVE DON JUAN FOR THE PRESENT SAFE-- . . . . 373 2 DON JUAN 4 54 1
DON JUAN HERE PERMITTED TO EMERGE . . . . . . 387 2 DON JUAN 4 79 1
THEREFORE I'LL MAKE DON JUAN LEAVE THE SHIP SOON . 397 2 DON JUAN 4 97 5
AND NOW DELAY THE PROGRESS OF DON JUAN . . . . 410 2 DON JUAN 4 117 1
INTO DON JUAN'S HEAD A THOUGHT WHICH HE . . . . 434 2 DON JUAN 5 43 2
DON JUAN TURNING TO HIS COMRADE WHO . . . . . 459 2 DON JUAN 5 83 2
DON JUAN IN HIS FEMININE DISGUISE . . . . . . 19 3 DON JUAN 6 26 1
DON JUAN AT HIS HANDS AND INFORMATION . . . . . 55 3 DON JUAN 6 99 2
DON JUAN WHO WAS MUCH MORE SENTIMENTAL . . . . 105 3 DON JUAN 7 75 4
THOUGH 'TWAS DON JUAN'S FIRST OF FIELDS AND THOUGH . 121 3 DON JUAN 8 21 1
EXCEPT DON JUAN--A MERE NOVICE WHOSE . . . . . 131 3 DON JUAN 8 36 2
BUT OF THE FIRST OUR LITTLE FRIEND DON JUAN . . . 138 3 DON JUAN 8 52 2
DON JUAN RAISED HIS LITTLE CAPTIVE FROM . . . . 158 3 DON JUAN 8 94 7
DON JUAN WHO HAD SHONE IN THE LATE SLAUGHTER . . 197 3 DON JUAN 9 29 1
I LEFT DON JUAN WITH HIS HORSES BAITING-- . . . 203 3 DON JUAN 9 42 3
THE DEE THE DON BALGOUNIE'S BRIG'S BLACK WALL . . 233 3 DON JUAN 10 18 3
DON JUAN WHO WAS REAL OR IDEAL-- . . . . . . 234 3 DON JUAN 10 20 1
DON JUAN GREW A VERY POLISHED RUSSIAN-- . . . . 235 3 DON JUAN 10 21 1
DON JUAN GREW I FEAR A LITTLE DISSIPATED . . . . 236 3 DON JUAN 10 23 3
ALL PRIVATE FAVOURITES OF DON JUAN FOR . . . . 249 3 DON JUAN 10 50 2
DON JUAN LOVED HER AND SHE LOVED HIM AS . . . . 250 3 DON JUAN 10 53 1
THE BLUE SEA'S BORDER AND DON JUAN FELT-- . . . 257 3 DON JUAN 10 65 5
DON JUAN NOW SAW ALBION'S EARLIEST BEAUTIES-- . . 259 3 DON JUAN 10 69 1
DON JUAN HAD GOT OUT ON SHOOTER'S HILL . . . . 272 3 DON JUAN 11 8 1
I SAY DON JUAN WRAPT IN CONTEMPLATION . . . . . 272 3 DON JUAN 11 9 1
BEFORE DON JUAN'S FEET HE COULD NOT TELL . . . . 276 3 DON JUAN 11 17 1
DON JUAN HAVING DONE THE BEST HE COULD . . . . 277 3 DON JUAN 11 18 1
DON JUAN OUR YOUNG DIPLOMATIC SINNER . . . . . 282 3 DON JUAN 11 29 6
DON JUAN WAS PRESENTED AND HIS DRESS . . . . . 287 3 DON JUAN 11 39 1
WHO LIKE DON JUAN TAKES AN ACTIVE SHARE . . . . 303 3 DON JUAN 11 70 2
HOWE'ER OUR FRIEND DON JUAN MIGHT COMMAND . . . 329 3 DON JUAN 12 29 5
DON JUAN WAS DELIGHTED TO SECURE . . . . . . 335 3 DON JUAN 12 41 6
DON JUAN SAW THAT MICROCOSM ON STILTS . . . . . 342 3 DON JUAN 12 56 1
TO WEAN DON JUAN FROM THE SIREN'S WILE . . . . 438 3 DON JUAN 14 65 6
WHETHER DON JUAN AND CHASTE ADELINE . . . . . 453 3 DON JUAN 14 97 1
TO READ DON QUIXOTE IN THE ORIGINAL . . . . . 453 3 DON JUAN 14 98 2
BUT RIGHT OR WRONG DON JUAN WAS WITHOUT IT . . . 461 3 DON JUAN 15 13 3
ADELINE AND DON JUAN RATHER BLENDED . . . . . 482 3 DON JUAN 15 61 3
DON JUAN SAT NEXT AN A L'ESPAGNOLE-- . . . . . 488 3 DON JUAN 15 74 5
(WHO WATCHED THE CHANGES OF DON JUAN'S BROW . . . 516 3 DON JUAN 16 37 2

DON   (CONTINUED)
     DON JUAN WHEN THE MIDNIGHT HOUR OF PILLOWS . . . . . 555 3 DON JUAN 16   110   3
     DON JUAN SHOOK AS ERST HE HAD BEEN SHAKEN . . . . .   558 3 DON JUAN 16   118   1
DONE
     QUITE INNOCENTLY DONE AND HARMLESS STYLED . . . . .   59 2 DON JUAN 1   69   3
     THAT ALL THE APOSTLES WOULD HAVE DONE AS THEY DID . . .   66 2 DON JUAN 1   83   8
     I'M VERY CERTAIN MINE WOULD NOT HAVE DONE SO . . . .   80 2 DON JUAN 1   110   8
     IN DEEP DESPAIR LEST HE HAD DONE AMISS . . . . . .   81 2 DON JUAN 1   112   5
     AND NOW SIR I HAVE DONE AND SAY NO MORE . . . . . .   107 2 DON JUAN 1   157   1
     WHAT'S TO BE DONE ALFONSO WILL BE BACK . . . . . .   114 2 DON JUAN 1   169   1
     HE WOULD NOT JUSTIFY WHAT HE HAD DONE . . . . . .   116 2 DON JUAN 1   174   3
     HAVE ALWAYS DONE SO 'TIS OF NO GREAT USE . . . . . . 119 2 DON JUAN 1   179   2
     AND MIGHT HAVE DONE SO BY THE GARDEN-GATE . . . . .   122 2 DON JUAN 1   183   6
     AND NO GREAT MISCHIEF'S DONE BY THEIR CAPRICE . . . . 135 2 DON JUAN 1   199   6
     PERHAPS MORE MISCHIEF HAD BEEN DONE BUT FOR . . . .   174 2 DON JUAN 2   35   1
     WAS ALL THAT FOR THE PRESENT COULD BE DONE . . . . . 189 2 DON JUAN 2   62   4
     THEY GLARED UPON EACH OTHER--ALL WAS DONE . . . . .   194 2 DON JUAN 2   72   5
     ONE GLANCE ON HIM AND SAID HEAVEN'S WILL BE DONE . . 202 2 DON JUAN 2   87   6
     FAMINE DESPAIR COLD THIRST AND HEAT HAD DONE . . . . 210 2 DON JUAN 2   102   1
     (A RACE OF MERE IMPOSTORS WHEN ALL'S DONE-- . . . .   218 2 DON JUAN 2   118   6
     (A SET OF HUMBUG RASCALS WHEN ALL'S DONE) . . . . .   219 2 DON JUAN 2   118 V6
     I NE'ER SAW JUSTICE DONE AND YET SHE WAS . . . . . . 219 2 DON JUAN 2   119   4
     BUT I HAVE DONE WITH KISSES--HAVING KISSED . . . . . 232 2 DON JUAN 2   142 V7
     WHO WAS HER CHOSEN WHAT WAS SAID OR DONE . . . . . . 264 2 DON JUAN 2   202   6
     AND NOW 'TWAS DONE--ON THE LONE SHORE WERE PLIGHTED . 265 2 DON JUAN 2   204   1
     TO SEE HIS ORDERS DONE TOO OUT OF HAND-- . . . . .   299 2 DON JUAN 3   47   3
     AMIDST THE SAVAGE DEEDS HE HAD DONE AND SEEN . . . . 304 2 DON JUAN 3   57   4
     HAD DONE THEIR WORK OF SPLENDOUR INDIAN MATS . . . . 310 2 DON JUAN 3   68   2
     YET IN THESE TIMES HE MIGHT HAVE DONE MUCH WORSE . . 326 2 DON JUAN 3   87   4
     THE ARAB LORE AND POET'S SONG WERE DONE . . . . . . 334 2 DON JUAN 3   101   3
     OF FEELING FOR SOME KINDNESS DONE WHEN POWER . . . . 339 2 DON JUAN 3   109   7
     DONE THINE THE PRESENT VOUCHES FOR THE PAST . . . . . 368 2 DON JUAN 4   46   8
     BEING PIQUED BY CRITICS WHO HAVE DONE ME WRONG . . . 410 2 DON JUAN 4   117 V5
     AND MARCH AWAY--'TWERE EASIER DONE THAN SAID . . . . 434 2 DON JUAN 5   43   8
     YES SAID THE OTHER AND WHEN DONE WHAT THEN . . . . . 435 2 DON JUAN 5   44   1
     HERE WEALTH HAD DONE ITS UTMOST TO ENCUMBER . . . .   448 2 DON JUAN 5   64   6
     I SAY A THING IT MUST AT ONCE BE DONE . . . . . .   458 2 DON JUAN 5   81   5
     WEALTH HAD DONE WONDERS--TASTE NOT MUCH SUCH THINGS . 465 2 DON JUAN 5   94   1
     AS GOOD MEN WEAR WHO HAVE DONE A VIRTUOUS ACTION . . 473 2 DON JUAN 5   107   8
     OR LOT'S WIFE DONE IN SALT--OR WHAT YOU WILL . . . .   40 3 DON JUAN 6   68   5
     WHATEVER DEED BE DONE I WILL RELATE 'EM . . . . . .   107 3 DON JUAN 7   81 V6
     AS HATH BEEN DONE MERE CONQUEST TO ADVANCE . . . . . 113 3 DON JUAN 8   3   6
     WHO LANDED LOWER DOWN THEIR LANDING DONE . . . . . . 119 3 DON JUAN 8   15   3
     POOR THING WHAT'S TO BE DONE I'M PUZZLED QUITE . .   161 3 DON JUAN 8   99   8
     DONE I'LL NOT QUIT HER TILL SHE SEEMS SECURE . . . . 161 3 DON JUAN 8   100   2
     AS HE BEFORE HAD DONE HE DID NOT HEED . . . . . .   170 3 DON JUAN 8   117   4
     AND FELT--THOUGHT DONE WITH LIFE--HE WAS ALONE . . . 170 3 DON JUAN 8   117   8
     I'VE DONE NOW GO AND DINE FROM OFF THE PLATE . . . . 185 3 DON JUAN 9   6   1
     DONE ANYTHING EXCEEDINGLY UNKIND . . . .   193 3 DON JUAN 9   21   3
     AND ORDERS AND ON ALL THAT HE HAD DONE-- . . . . .   197 3 DON JUAN 9   30   5
     OR DONE IS LIGHT TO WHAT SHE'LL SAY OR DO-- . . . .   214 3 DON JUAN 9   64   7
     HECTIC AND BRIEF AS SUMMER'S DAY NIGH DONE . . . . . 229 3 DON JUAN 10   8   6
     BUT WHAT IS TO BE DONE I CAN'T ALLOW . . . . . .   275 3 DON JUAN 11   15   6
     DON JUAN HAVING DONE THE BEST HE COULD . . . . . .   277 3 DON JUAN 11   18   1
     I'VE DONE TO FIND THE SAME THROUGHOUT LIFE'S JOURNEY . 281 3 DON JUAN 11   28   7
     FROM WHAT SOME PEOPLE SAY 'TWILL BE WHEN DONE . . .   356 3 DON JUAN 12   87   4
     AND THEREFORE HAVE HIS VOLUMES DONE SUCH HARM . . .   364 3 DON JUAN 13   11   6
     TO RECOMMENCE IN AUGUST--NOW WAS DONE . . . .   377 3 DON JUAN 13   42   2
     I'VE DONE WITH MY TIRADE THE WORLD WAS GONE . . . . 381 3 DON JUAN 13   49   1
     THAN I HAVE YET DONE IN THIS EPIC SATIRE . . . . . .   454 3 DON JUAN 14   99   6
     THE SECOND MAY BE SADLY DONE OR GAILY . . . .   465 3 DON JUAN 15   21   4
     AND ALWAYS HAVE DONE SOMEHOW THESE GOOD LOOKS . . .   493 3 DON JUAN 15   84   7
     THE DINNER AND THE SOIREE TOO WERE DONE . . . . . .   504 3 DON JUAN 16   8   1
     THE GHOST AT LEAST HAD DONE HIM THIS MUCH GOOD . . . 553 3 DON JUAN 16   107   1
DONNA
     THAT WHICH ADORN'D THE BRAIN OF DONNA INEZ . . . . .   27 2 DON JUAN 1   11   8
     NOW DONNA INEZ HAD WITH ALL HER MERIT . . . . . .   32 2 DON JUAN 1   20   1
     DON JOSE AND THE DONNA INEZ LED . . . .   35 2 DON JUAN 1   26   1
     BUT THAT WHICH DONNA INEZ MOST DESIRED . . . . . .   43 2 DON JUAN 1   39   1
     FOR DONNA INEZ DREADED THE MYTHOLOGY . . . .   44 2 DON JUAN 1   41   8
     'TIS NOT WITH DONNA INEZ I WOULD SHUT . . . . . .   50 2 DON JUAN 1   52   5
     THERE WAS THE DONNA JULIA WHOM TO CALL . . . . . .   51 2 DON JUAN 1   55   3
     BOABDIL WEPT OF DONNA JULIA'S KIN . . . .   52 2 DON JUAN 1   56   6
     'TIS SAID THAT DONNA JULIA'S GRANDMAMMA . . . . . .   53 2 DON JUAN 1   58   7
     WITH DONNA INEZ QUITE A FAVOURITE FRIEND . . . . .   58 2 DON JUAN 1   66   2
     THAT DONNA JULIA KNEW THE REASON WHY . . . . . .   60 2 DON JUAN 1   70   6
     AND THEN HE THOUGHT OF DONNA JULIA'S EYES . . . . .   71 2 DON JUAN 1   92   8
     IS THAT THE DONNA INEZ DID NOT TEASE . . . . . .   73 2 DON JUAN 1   97   5
     'TWAS MIDNIGHT--DONNA JULIA WAS IN BED . . . . . .   95 2 DON JUAN 1   136   1
     POOR DONNA JULIA STARTING AS FROM SLEEP . . . . . .   97 2 DON JUAN 1   140   1
     BUT DONNA INEZ TO DIVERT THE TRAIN . . . .   128 2 DON JUAN 1   190   1
     BUT TO OUR TALE THE DONNA INEZ SENT . . . .   161 2 DON JUAN 2   8   1
     (AND OTHER CHIEF POINTS OF A BELLA DONNA) . . . . .   395 2 DON JUAN 4   94   4
     HIS MOTHER DONNA INEZ FINDING TOO . . . .   240 3 DON JUAN 10   31   1
DONOR
     SO THAT HE WOULD HAVE BEEN THE VERY DONOR . . . . .   528 3 DON JUAN 16   57   4
DONOR'S
     WHICH SHOWED WHAT GREAT DISCERNMENT WAS THE DONOR'S . . . 247 3 DON JUAN 10   46   8
DON'T
     I DON'T CHOOSE TO SAY MUCH UPON THIS HEAD . . . . .   33 2 DON JUAN 1   22   5

DON'T   (CONTINUED)

	PAGE	VOL		CANTO	STANZA	LN
I DON'T THINK SAPPHO'S ODE A GOOD EXAMPLE	45	2 DON JUAN	1	42	4
I REALLY DON'T KNOW WHAT NOR JULIA EITHER	65	2 DON JUAN	1	81	8
NOW TELL ME DON'T YOU CUT A PRETTY FIGURE	103	2 DON JUAN	1	150	8
HE HAD BEEN HID--I DON'T PRETEND TO SAY	112	2 DON JUAN	1	166	1
WHY DON'T YOU KNOW THAT IT MAY END IN BLOOD	115	2 DON JUAN	1	171	6
BUT IF YOU DON'T I'LL LAY IT ON BY GOD	140	2 DON JUAN	1	206	8
BUT VULGAR ILLNESSES DON'T LIKE TO MEET	168	2 DON JUAN	2	22	6
SO GOOD--I WONDER CASTLEREAGH DON'T TAX 'EM	264	2 DON JUAN	2	203	8
AND DON'T SAY MUCH OF PARADISE OR WIFE	280	2 DON JUAN	3	9	V8
(SUCH THINGS IN FACT IT DON'T ASK MUCH TO MAR)	281	2 DON JUAN	3	10	6
(PROVIDED THEY DON'T COME IN AFTER DINNER)	306	2 DON JUAN	3	60	2
HER CHILDREN UP (IF NURSING THEM DON'T THIN HER)	306	2 DON JUAN	3	60	4
ARE THINGS WHICH IN THIS CENTURY DON'T STRIKE	330	2 DON JUAN	3	95	5
I DON'T PRETEND THAT I QUITE UNDERSTAND	346	2 DON JUAN	4	5	4
I DON'T MUCH LIKE DESCRIBING PEOPLE MAD	384	2 DON JUAN	4	74	3
WHICH MIGHT GO FAR BUT SHE DON'T DANCE WITH VIGOUR	390	2 DON JUAN	4	85	7
THEY VOW TO AMEND THEIR LIVES AND YET THEY DON'T	414	2 DON JUAN	5	6	7
SAID JUAN BUT I REALLY DON'T SEE HOW	422	2 DON JUAN	5	23	2
BE IN THESE DAYS) SOME INFIDELS WHO DON'T	447	2 DON JUAN	5	62	2
OR IF YOU DON'T THE FAULT IS NOT IN ME	450	2 DON JUAN	5	66	8
THESE DON'T EXPRESS ONE HALF WHAT I SHOULD SAY	487	2 DON JUAN	5	132	6
WHY DON'T THEY KNEAD TWO VIRTUOUS SOULS FOR LIFE	502	2 DON JUAN	5	158	7
AND DON'T AGREE AT ALL WITH THE WISE ROMAN	10	3 DON JUAN	6	7	5
FROM SPAIN--BUT WHERE IS SPAIN--DON'T ASK SUCH STUFF	28	3 DON JUAN	6	44	4
YOU DON'T SLEEP SOUNDLY AND I CANNOT BEAR	29	3 DON JUAN	6	47	2
THAN YOU WOULD MAKE THE HALF OF--DON'T SAY NO	29	3 DON JUAN	6	47	5
ALONE FOR REASONS WHICH DON'T MATTER YOU	30	3 DON JUAN	6	49	2
BUT THAT YOU WON'T--THEN DON'T--I AM NOT LESS FREE	34	3 DON JUAN	6	56	8
I DON'T KNOW WHETHER THEY HAD ARMS OR CREST	76	3 DON JUAN	7	19	3
I DON'T KNOW HOW THE THING OCCURRED--IT MIGHT	125	3 DON JUAN	8	28	1
FOR IF HE DON'T I DOUBT IF MEN WILL LONGER--	137	3 DON JUAN	8	50	2
(I DON'T MUCH PIQUE MYSELF UPON ORTHOGRAPHY	149	3 DON JUAN	8	74	2
OR IF THESE DO NOT MOVE YOU DON'T FORGET	174	3 DON JUAN	8	125	3
I DON'T THINK THAT YOU USED KINNAIRD QUITE WELL	184	3 DON JUAN	9	2	1
I DON'T MEAN TO REFLECT--A MAN SO GREAT AS	186	3 DON JUAN	9	7	1
YOUR WISE MEN DON'T KNOW MUCH OF NAVIGATION	191	3 DON JUAN	9	18	4
(WHEN SHE DON'T PIN MEN'S LIMBS IN LIKE A JAILOR)--	204	3 DON JUAN	9	44	6
WE DON'T MUCH CARE WITH WHOM WE MAY ENGAGE	217	3 DON JUAN	9	69	2
OUTWARD DISLIKE WHICH DON'T LOOK WELL ABROAD	240	3 DON JUAN	10	32	5
I DON'T KNOW HOW HE GREW SICK	244	3 DON JUAN	10	39	1
HER NOTE SHE DON'T FORGET THE INFANT GIRL	249	3 DON JUAN	10	51	7
I DON'T KNOW WHAT THE REASON IS--THE AIR	270	3 DON JUAN	11	5	6
I RECOLLECT SOME INNKEEPERS WHO DON'T	275	3 DON JUAN	11	15	3
I DON'T MEAN THAT THEY ARE PASSIONLESS BUT QUITE	284	3 DON JUAN	11	34	1
AND BY WE'LL TALK OF THAT AND IF WE DON'T	285	3 DON JUAN	11	36	2
I DON'T KNOW WHICH WAS MOST ADMIRED OR LESS	287	3 DON JUAN	11	39	3
BUT DON'T PRETEND TO SETTLE WHICH WAS BEST	309	3 DON JUAN	11	83	8
THIS--WHEN I SPEAK I DON'T HINT BUT SPEAK OUT	311	3 DON JUAN	11	88	8
AND DON'T KNOW JUSTLY WHAT WE WOULD BE AT--	315	3 DON JUAN	12	1	5
BUT IF LOVE DON'T CASH DOES AND CASH ALONE	322	3 DON JUAN	12	14	1
WELL IF I DON'T SUCCEED I HAVE SUCCEEDED	324	3 DON JUAN	12	17	1
I DON'T MEAN THIS AS GENERAL BUT PARTICULAR	343	3 DON JUAN	12	59	1
(WHATEVER PEOPLE SAY) I DON'T KNOW WHETHER	355	3 DON JUAN	12	86	4
BUT DO YOU MORE SEMPRONIUS--DON'T DESERVE IT	366	3 DON JUAN	13	18	2
INDIFFERENCE CERTES DON'T PRODUCE DISTRESS	374	3 DON JUAN	13	35	6
SOMETIMES A LITTLE LATER I DON'T ERR	378	3 DON JUAN	13	43	2
'TIS TRUE YOU DON'T--BUT PALE AND STRUCK WITH TERROR	413	3 DON JUAN	14	6	1
YOU KNOW OR DON'T KNOW THAT GREAT BACON SAITH	414	3 DON JUAN	14	8	1
IN THAT FAIR CLIME WHICH DON'T DEPEND ON CLIMATE	423	3 DON JUAN	14	29	2
(FOR FOREIGNERS DON'T KNOW THAT A FAUX PAS	436	3 DON JUAN	14	60	5
I DON'T KNOW WHAT AND THEREFORE CANNOT TELL--	441	3 DON JUAN	14	71	2
I DON'T KNOW THAT THERE MAY BE MUCH ABILITY	465	3 DON JUAN	15	20	1
AND DON'T REGRET THE TIME YOU MAY HAVE LOST	498	3 DON JUAN	15	95	3

DONT

	PAGE	VOL		CANTO	STANZA	LN
'TIS STRANGE OLD PEOPLE DONT LIKE TO BE BURIED	89	2 DON JUAN	1	125	V8

DOOM

	PAGE	VOL		CANTO	STANZA	LN
SO VILE HE 'SCAPED THE DOOM WHICH OFT AVENGES	317	2 DON JUAN	3	80	5
WHEN NERO PERISH'D BY THE JUSTEST DOOM	339	2 DON JUAN	3	109	1
TILL FURTHER ORDERS SHOULD HIS DOOM ASSIGN	371	2 DON JUAN	4	50	V4
AND BURIED SINKS BENEATH ITS OFFSPRING'S DOOM	399	2 DON JUAN	4	102	4
AT PRESENT WEIGHED DOWN BY A DOOM WHICH HAD	417	2 DON JUAN	5	12	3
SIX TARTARS AND A DRAG-CHAIN-- --TO THIS DOOM	418	2 DON JUAN	5	15	3
'TIS NOT SAID JUAN FOR MY PRESENT DOOM	420	2 DON JUAN	5	18	1
SUCH DOOM MAY BE YOUR OWN IN AFTER TIMES	174	3 DON JUAN	8	125	4
IF SUCH DOOM WAITS EACH INTELLECTUAL GIANT	566	3 DON JUAN	17	10	1

DOOM'D

	PAGE	VOL		CANTO	STANZA	LN
WHETHER MY VERSE'S FAME BE DOOM'D TO CEASE	398	2 DON JUAN	4	99	4
OR SEPARATE MAINTENANCE IN CASE 'TWAS DOOM'D--	473	3 DON JUAN	15	39	3

DOOMED

	PAGE	VOL		CANTO	STANZA	LN
THE NEXT ARE SUCH AS ARE NOT DOOMED TO LOSE	562	3 DON JUAN	17	1	5

DOOMSDAY

	PAGE	VOL		CANTO	STANZA	LN
HEAVEN'S FREEHOLDS IN A SORT OF DOOMSDAY SCROLL	242	3 DON JUAN	10	35	5

DOOR

	PAGE	VOL		CANTO	STANZA	LN
AND LOOK'D EXTREMELY AT THE OPENING DOOR	63	2 DON JUAN	1	76	3
BUT BEG SECURITY WILL BOLT THE DOOR	69	2 DON JUAN	1	89	8
SLEEPING MOST PROBABLY--WHEN AT HER DOOR	95	2 DON JUAN	1	136	2
THE DOOR WAS FASTEN'D BUT WITH VOICE AND FIST	95	2 DON JUAN	1	136	7
A MOMENT AT THE DOOR THAT WE MAY BE	106	2 DON JUAN	1	156	7

```
                                                              PAGE VOL      CANTO STANZA LV
DOOR    (CONTINUED)
    THE ATTORNEY LAST WHO LINGER'D NEAR THE DOOR      . . . . . 111  2 DON JUAN   1    164    2
    THE DOOR WAS FASTEN'D IN HIS LEGAL FACE  . . . . . . . 111  2 DON JUAN   1    164    8
    THE DOOR IS OPEN--YOU MAY YET SLIP THROUGH   . . . . . 121  2 DON JUAN   1    182    4
    ALFONSO LEANING BREATHLESS BY THE DOOR   . . . . . . 125  2 DON JUAN   1    187    4
    AS IF DEATH WERE MORE DREADFUL BY HIS DOOR   . . . . 174  2 DON JUAN   2     35    5
    THE SOLITUDE OF PASSING HIS OWN DOOR  . . . . . . . 302  2 DON JUAN   3     52    3
    OF A SMALL IRON DOOR 'TWAS OPENED AND . . . . . . . 433  2 DON JUAN   5     41    2
    TO THRUST ITS BLACK EYES THROUGH THE DOOR OR LATTICE . . 442  2 DON JUAN   5     55    7
    THE GIANT DOOR WAS BROAD AND BRIGHT AND HIGH   . . . . 461  2 DON JUAN   5     86    1
    TO OPE THIS DOOR WHICH THEY COULD REALLY DO . . . . . 463  2 DON JUAN   5     89    3
    BUT NOT BY THE SAME DOOR THROUGH WHICH CAME IN . . . . 469  2 DON JUAN   5    100    2
    FOR BABA'S FUNCTION STOPT SHORT AT THE DOOR . . . . . 57  3 DON JUAN   6    103    4
    THEY REACHED THE HOTEL FORTH STREAMED FROM THE FRONT DOOR . 282  3 DON JUAN  11     30    1
    AND BLAZON O'ER THE DOOR THEIR NAMES IN BRASS   . . . . 283  3 DON JUAN  11     31    8
    THEN ROLL THE BRAZEN THUNDERS OF THE DOOR   . . . . . 302  3 DON JUAN  11     67    6
    A DOOR THAT'S IN OR BOUDOIR OUT OF THE WAY   . . . . . 303  3 DON JUAN  11     69    3
    AT LENGTH THE BOYS DREW UP BEFORE A DOOR . . . . . . 313  3 DON JUAN  11   V 29    1
    AN ERRING WOMAN FINDS AN OPENER DOOR . . . . . . . 352  3 DON JUAN  12     79    6
    AND OUT OF DOOR HATH SHOWERS AND MISTS AND SLEET   . . . 423  3 DON JUAN  14     30    2
    SHE LOOK'D AS IF SHE SAT BY EDEN'S DOOR  . . . . . . 476  3 DON JUAN  15     45    7
    HIS CHAMBER DOOR WIDE OPEN--AND WENT FORTH   . . . . . 508  3 DON JUAN  16     17    2
    HE SHUT HIS DOOR AND AFTER HAVING READ   . . . . . . 512  3 DON JUAN  16     27    2
    STATED) HIS MOUTH WHAT OPENED NEXT--THE DOOR   . . . . 557  3 DON JUAN  16    115    8
    THE DOOR FLEW WIDE NOT SWIFTLY--BUT AS FLY   . . . . . 558  3 DON JUAN  16    117    1
DOORS
    BRIGHT HUES WHEN OUT OF DOORS AND YET WHILE WAVE   . . . 220  2 DON JUAN   2    120    5
    AND THUS THEY PARTED EACH BY SEPARATE DOORS . . . . . 460  2 DON JUAN   5     85    1
    WITH TO BE LET UPON THEIR DOORS PROCLAIMED   . . . . . 278  3 DON JUAN  11     21    6
    OF DOORS 'GAINST DUNS AND TO AN EARLY DINNER   . . . . 282  3 DON JUAN  11     29    4
    TITHES TAXES DUNS AND DOORS WITH DOUBLE KNOCKINGS  . . . 346  3 DON JUAN  12     67    8
    WITHOUT DOORS TOO SHE MAY COMPETE IN MELLOW   . . . . . 395  3 DON JUAN  13     77    7
    KNOCKEST AT DOORS AT FIRST WITH MODEST TAP   . . . . . 459  3 DON JUAN  15      8    2
    DOORS THERE WERE MANY THROUGH WHICH BY THE LAWS   . . . 511  3 DON JUAN  16     24    5
DOOR-WAY
    AND IN THE DOOR-WAY DARKENING DARKNESS STOOD   . . . . 558  3 DON JUAN  16    117    7
D'OPERA
    HAD BROUGHT THE CAPO D'OPERA NOT FOR SALE   . . . . . 528  3 DON JUAN  16     57    7
DORIC
    SUCH AS THE DORIC MOTHERS BORE . . . . . . . . . 325  2 DON JUAN   3   L 13    4
DORMANT
    AS ACIDS ROUSE A DORMANT ALKALI)   . . . . . . . . 251  3 DON JUAN  10     54    4
DORUS
    THAT NEUTRALISED DULL DORUS OF THE NINE  . . . . . . 297  3 DON JUAN  11     58    4
DORY
    SOUPE A LA BEAUVEAU WHOSE RELIEF WAS DORY   . . . . . 483  3 DON JUAN  15     63    7
DOTE
    OR DEATH OF THOSE WE DOTE ON WHEN A PART . . . . . . 167  2 DON JUAN   2     21    5
    AS THOSE WHO DOTE ON ODOURS PLUCK THE FLOWERS  . . . . 275  2 DON JUAN   3      2    5
DOTED
    BESIDES HER GOOD OLD GRANDMOTHER (WHO DOTED)   . . . . 36  2 DON JUAN   1     28    5
DOTING
    HIS PARENTS NE'ER AGREED EXCEPT IN DOTING   . . . . . 34  2 DON JUAN   1     25    3
DOTTED
    LIKE A BACKGAMMON BOARD THE PLACE WAS DOTTED   . . . . 416  2 DON JUAN   5     10    1
DOUBLE
    TO PROVE HER MISTRESS HAD BEEN SLEEPING DOUBLE . . . . 97  2 DON JUAN   1    140    8
    TO DOUBLE EVEN THE SWEETNESS OF A FLOWER . . . . . . 144  2 DON JUAN   1    214    8
    THE DOUBLE BOBADIL TAKES SCORN FOR AWE   . . . . . . 153  2 DON JUAN   1   V  4    8
    FROM THE BLUE SKIES DERIVED A DOUBLE BLUE   . . . . . 393  2 DON JUAN   4     90    6
    SHE THOUGHT HERS GAVE A DOUBLE RIGHT DIVINE   . . . . . 485  2 DON JUAN   5    129    7
    OR DOUBLE POST AND RAIL WHERE THE EXISTENCE . . . . . 140  3 DON JUAN   8     55    3
    BY THOSE WHO SCOUR THOSE DOUBLE VALES OF STRIFE   . . . 232  3 DON JUAN  10     14    4
    OF POLITICIANS AND THEIR DOUBLE FRONT . . . . . . . 285  3 DON JUAN  11     36    4
    REQUIRES DECORUM AND IS APT TO DOUBLE . . . . . . . 292  3 DON JUAN  11     46    7
    THE SINGLE LADIES WISHING TO BE DOUBLE   . . . . . . 342  3 DON JUAN  12     58    7
    TITHES TAXES DUNS AND DOORS WITH DOUBLE KNOCKINGS  . . . 346  3 DON JUAN  12     67    8
    WELL CULTIVATED IT WILL RENDER DOUBLE . . . . . . . 351  3 DON JUAN  12     76    8
    'TIS ALSO SUBJECT TO THE DOUBLE DANGER   . . . . . . 424  3 DON JUAN  14     32    2
    HE CLEAR'D HEDGE DITCH AND DOUBLE POST AND RAIL   . . . 424  3 DON JUAN  14     33    2
    OF DOUBLE NATURE AND THUS DOUBLY NAMED--   . . . . . . 448  3 DON JUAN  14     89    2
    OF SINGLE GENTLEMEN WHO WOULD BE DOUBLE  . . . . . . 477  3 DON JUAN  15     48    8
    PRESENTS THE PROBLEM OF A DOUBLE FIGURE  . . . . . . 530  3 DON JUAN  16     61    8
    A MIGHTY MUG OF MORAL DOUBLE ALE   . . . . . . . . 533  3 DON JUAN  16     67    4
DOUBLED
    THE SOVEREIGN SHOCKED AND ALL HIS MEDICINES DOUBLED   . . 244  3 DON JUAN  10     39    8
DOUBLE-DAMN'D
    NEXT OWNER FOR THEIR DOUBLE-DAMN'D POST-OBITS   . . . . 89  2 DON JUAN   1    125    8
DOUBLES
    WHICH DOUBLES WHAT THEY THINK OF THE TRANSGRESSION . . . 11  3 DON JUAN   6     10    4
DOUBLY
    AND HOW YE MAY BE DOUBLY WIDOWS--WIVES   . . . . . . 123  2 DON JUAN   1    185    8
    A SAD TALE SADDENS DOUBLY WHEN 'TIS LONG . . . . . . 419  2 DON JUAN   5     16    8
    A DULL STORY'S DOUBLY GRIEVOUS WHEN 'TIS LONG  . . . . 419  2 DON JUAN   5     16   V8
    THESE MUST SEEM DOUBLY MINDFUL OF THEIR VOWS   . . . . 500  2 DON JUAN   5    154    5
    OF DOUBLE NATURE AND THUS DOUBLY NAMED--  . . . . . . 448  3 DON JUAN  14     89    2
DOUBT
    AND PUT THE BUSINESS PAST ALL KIND OF DOUBT . . . . . 35  2 DON JUAN   1     26    8
    NO DOUBT THIS PATIENCE WHEN THE WORLD IS DAMNING US . . . 37  2 DON JUAN   1     30    1
```

DOUBT (CONTINUED)

	PAGE	VOL	CANTO		STANZA	LN
ALTHOUGH NO DOUBT HIS REAL INTENT WAS GOOD	45	2	DON JUAN	1	43	4
SOME PEOPLE WHISPER (BUT NO DOUBT THEY LIE	58	2	DON JUAN	1	66	5
THERE SURELY WILL BE LITTLE DOUBT WITH SOME	60	2	DON JUAN	1	70	5
'TWAS BUT A DOUBT BUT NE'ER MAGICIAN'S WAND	60	2	DON JUAN	1	71	6
THE POET MEANT NO DOUBT AND THUS APPEALS	69	2	DON JUAN	1	89	1
THE SUN NO DOUBT IS THE PREVAILING REASON	76	2	DON JUAN	1	102	4
BUT THEN NO DOUBT IT EQUALLY AS TRUE IS	79	2	DON JUAN	1	108	7
YET THERE'S NO DOUBT SHE ONLY MEANT TO CLASP	81	2	DON JUAN	1	111	4
ALTHOUGH ONE MUST BE DAMN'D FOR YOU NO DOUBT	85	2	DON JUAN	1	119	2
NO DOUBT IN FABLE AS THE UNFORGIVEN	90	2	DON JUAN	1	127	7
BECAUSE NO DOUBT 'TWAS FOR HIS DIRTY FEE	103	2	DON JUAN	1	151	7
DOUBT UPON ME CONFUSION OVER ALL	105	2	DON JUAN	1	154	2
NO DOUBT IN LITTLE COMPASS ROUND OR SQUARE	112	2	DON JUAN	1	166	4
I DOUBT ALL LIKENESS ENDS BETWEEN THE PAIR	124	2	DON JUAN	1	186	8
IF ANY PERSON DOUBT IT I APPEAL	138	2	DON JUAN	1	203	1
SHALL SUPERSEDE BEYOND ALL DOUBT ALL THOSE	138	2	DON JUAN	1	204	3
NO DOUBT WE WEEP FOR THOSE THE HEART ENDEARS--	164	2	DON JUAN	2	15	7
NO DOUBT HE WOULD HAVE BEEN MUCH MORE PATHETIC	167	2	DON JUAN	2	21	7
THERE'S NOUGHT NO DOUBT SO MUCH THE SPIRIT CALMS	174	2	DON JUAN	2	34	1
NO DOUBT THE VESSEL WAS ABOUT TO SINK	187	2	DON JUAN	2	58	6
DEATH LEFT NO DOUBT AND THE DEAD BURTHEN LAY	204	2	DON JUAN	2	90	3
THE FREQUENT FOG-BANKS GAVE THEM CAUSE TO DOUBT--	207	2	DON JUAN	2	96	6
FOR ALL WAS DOUBT AND DIZZINESS HE THOUGHT	215	2	DON JUAN	2	112	2
BY WHICH NO DOUBT A GOOD DEAL MAY BE MADE	223	2	DON JUAN	2	126	8
AND 'TIS NO DOUBT A SIGHT TO SEE WHEN BREAKS	230	2	DON JUAN	2	139	4
SINCE AFTER ALL NO DOUBT THE YOUTHFUL PAIR	233	2	DON JUAN	2	144	6
OF ZOE'S COOKERY NO DOUBT WAS STEALING	237	2	DON JUAN	2	153	4
GOAT'S FLESH THERE IS NO DOUBT AND KID AND MUTTON	238	2	DON JUAN	2	154	2
NO DOUBT LESS OF HER LANGUAGE THAN HER LOOK	242	2	DON JUAN	2	163	4
HE WAS IN LOVE--AS YOU WOULD BE NO DOUBT	244	2	DON JUAN	2	167	6
HEAVEN KNOWS HOW LONG--NO DOUBT THEY NEVER RECKON'D	254	2	DON JUAN	2	187	2
PERPLEXING QUESTION BUT NO DOUBT THE MOON	267	2	DON JUAN	2	208	4
NO DOUBT CAN SOOTHE THEM WITH A LULLABY--	272	2	DON JUAN	2 V	1	5
ALTHOUGH NO DOUBT HER FIRST OF LOVE AFFAIRS	276	2	DON JUAN	3	4	5
MOST NATURALLY SOME SMALL DOUBT INSPIRES--	287	2	DON JUAN	3	22	3
A MELODY WHICH MADE HIM DOUBT HIS EARS	290	2	DON JUAN	3	28	5
NO DOUBT WHATE'ER MIGHT BE THEIR FORMER STRIFE	301	2	DON JUAN	3	50	5
THE EYE MIGHT DOUBT IF IT WERE WELL AWAKE	314	2	DON JUAN	3	76	5
THERE WAS NO DOUBT HE EARN'D HIS LAUREATE PENSION	317	2	DON JUAN	3	80	7
AND NO DOUBT OF ALL METHODS 'TIS THE BEST	356	2	DON JUAN	4	24	5
THAT DOUBT SHOULD MINGLE WITH MY FILIAL JOY	364	2	DON JUAN	4	38	7
WHO (AFTER SOME DISCUSSION AND SOME DOUBT	394	2	DON JUAN	4	92	3
AND HEARD TROY DOUBTED TIME WILL DOUBT OF ROME	399	2	DON JUAN	4	101	8
USED TO IT NO DOUBT AS EELS ARE TO BE FLAY'D	414	2	DON JUAN	5	7	8
UNLESS HE'S DRUNK AND THEN NO DOUBT HE'S FREED	427	2	DON JUAN	5	31	5
HAS BEEN ACCUSED (I DOUBT NOT BY CONSPIRACY)	446	2	DON JUAN	5	61	2
NO DOUBT IN PROPER PLACE AND TIME AND SEASON	454	2	DON JUAN	5	74	7
HIS TOILET THOUGH NO DOUBT A LITTLE BACKWARD	456	2	DON JUAN	5	78	4
BUT NO DOUBT EVERYTHING IS FOR THE BEST	6	3	DON JUAN	6	1	6
I DOUBT IF ANY NOW COULD MAKE IT WORSE	17	3	DON JUAN	6	23	4
A GOODLY SINECURE NO DOUBT BUT MADE	22	3	DON JUAN	6	32	1
I DOUBT FEW READERS E'ER WOULD MOUNT THE BREACH	83	3	DON JUAN	7	35	8
LOOKED ON AS IF IN DOUBT IF THEY COULD TRUST	104	3	DON JUAN	7	73	2
WITH ALL THE POMP OF POWER IT WAS A DOUBT	104	3	DON JUAN	7	74	7
I ALMOST LATELY HAVE BEGUN TO DOUBT	124	3	DON JUAN	8	26	1
FOR IF HE DON'T I DOUBT IF MEN WILL LONGER--	137	3	DON JUAN	8	50	2
I RATHER DOUBT AND I WOULD FAIN SAY FIE ON'T	138	3	DON JUAN	8	51	6
AND THAT'S THE CAUSE NO DOUBT WHY IF WE SCAN	167	3	DON JUAN	8	112	5
THERE IS NO DOUBT THAT YOU DESERVE YOUR RATION	185	3	DON JUAN	9	6	7
THIS WORLD I DOUBT IF DOUBT ITSELF BE DOUBTING	191	3	DON JUAN	9	17	8
THIS WORLD I DOUBT IF DOUBT ITSELF BE DOUBTING	191	3	DON JUAN	9	17	8
ALTHOUGH NO DOUBT IT WAS BEYOND ALL PRICE	200	3	DON JUAN	9	36	8
OF THINGS DESTROYED AND LEFT IN AIRY DOUBT	201	3	DON JUAN	9	38	4
THAT SPHINX WHOSE WORDS WOULD EVER BE A DOUBT	207	3	DON JUAN	9	50	3
NO DOUBT GAVE PAIN WHERE EACH NEW PAIR OF SHOULDERS	208	3	DON JUAN	9	52	7
FOR SUCH ALL WOMEN ARE AT FIRST NO DOUBT	220	3	DON JUAN	9	75	4
YOU'LL DEEM NO DOUBT THEY PUT IT TO A GOOD USE	242	3	DON JUAN	10	36	8
OH DOUBT--IF THOU BE'ST DOUBT FOR WHICH SOME TAKE THEE	269	3	DON JUAN	11	2	5
OH DOUBT--IF THOU BE'ST DOUBT FOR WHICH SOME TAKE THEE	269	3	DON JUAN	11	2	5
BUT WHICH I DOUBT EXTREMELY--THOU SOLE PRISM	269	3	DON JUAN	11	2	6
AND INSOLENCE NO DOUBT IS WHAT THEY ARE	288	3	DON JUAN	11	41	1
AND SHOULD YOU DOUBT PRAY ASK OF YOUR NEXT NEIGHBOUR	288	3	DON JUAN	11	41	4
WILL HINT ALLUSIONS NEVER MEANT NE'ER DOUBT	311	3	DON JUAN	11	88	7
TO DOUBT (NO LESS THAN LANDLORDS OF THEIR RENTAL)	322	3	DON JUAN	12	13	7
EXCEPTING MARRIAGE WHICH IS LOVE NO DOUBT	323	3	DON JUAN	12	15	2
SO GOOD AN OPPORTUNITY NO DOUBT--	332	3	DON JUAN	12	35	4
NO DOUBT I SHOULD BE TOLD THAT BLACK IS FAIR	348	3	DON JUAN	12	70	8
BUT ONCE THERE (IF YOU DOUBT THIS PRITHEE TRY)	350	3	DON JUAN	12	74	7
NO DOUBT HIS SENSIBILITIES WERE LESS	353	3	DON JUAN	12	81	8
AND--THOUGH NO DOUBT 'TIS FOR THE PUBLIC WEAL	357	3	DON JUAN	12 V	18	4
I LEAVE THEM TO THEIR TASTE NO DOUBT THE BEST	359	3	DON JUAN	13	3	2
THEIRS WAS THAT BEST OF UNIONS PAST ALL DOUBT	430	3	DON JUAN	14	45	7
THOUGH ON THE WHOLE NO DOUBT THE DARDAN BOY	441	3	DON JUAN	14	72	6
THIS I COULD PROVE BEYOND A SINGLE DOUBT	446	3	DON JUAN	14	84	5
NO DOUBT THE SECRET INFLUENCE OF THE SEX	451	3	DON JUAN	14	93	1
SINCERE HE WAS--AT LEAST YOU COULD NOT DOUBT IT	461	3	DON JUAN	15	13	5
NO DOUBT IF I HAD WISH'D TO PAY MY COURT	466	3	DON JUAN	15	22	5
THAT IS NO DOUBT THE ONLY REASON WHEREFORE	470	3	DON JUAN	15	31	8

	PAGE	VOL	CANTO	STANZA	LN

DOUBT   (CONTINUED)
MADE JUAN WONDER AS NO DOUBT HE MUST	477	3 DON JUAN	15	49	3
OR LIKE A SYSTEM COUPLED WITH A DOUBT	504	3 DON JUAN	16	9	4
I LEAVE TO THOSE WHO ARE FOND OF SOLVING DOUBT	531	3 DON JUAN	16	62	4
SOME DOUBT HOW MUCH OF ADELINE WAS REAL	546	3 DON JUAN	16	95	8
HE SHUDDERED AS NO DOUBT THE BRAVEST COWERS	559	3 DON JUAN	16	120	5
NO DOUBT A CONSOLATION TO HIS DUST	565	3 DON JUAN	17	8	8

DOUBTED
SO MUCH HE ALWAYS DOUBTED I WAS MARRIED--	101	2 DON JUAN	1	147	7
AND HEARD TROY DOUBTED TIME WILL DOUBT OF ROME	399	2 DON JUAN	4	101	8
HE DOUBTED NOT A FEW HOURS OF REFLECTION	452	2 DON JUAN	5	71	5
BUT NO ONE DOUBTED ON THE WHOLE THAT SHE	24	3 DON JUAN	6	36	1
(BUT THAT I NEVER DOUBTED NOR THE DEVIL)	271	3 DON JUAN	11	6	2
WHOSE FAME SHE RATHER DOUBTED WITH POSTERITY	432	3 DON JUAN	14	51	3

DOUBTERS
| 'TIS TIME TO STRIKE SUCH PUNY DOUBTERS DUMB AS | 502 | 3 DON JUAN | 16 | 4 | 7 |

DOUBTING
| BY A DISTANT ORGAN DOUBTING IF HE BE | 237 | 2 DON JUAN | 2 | 152 | 2 |
| THIS WORLD I DOUBT IF DOUBT ITSELF BE DOUBTING | 191 | 3 DON JUAN | 9 | 17 | 8 |

DOUBTLESS
(BUT DOUBTLESS NOBODY WILL BE SO PERT)	140	2 DON JUAN	1	207	5
MEANTIME THEY'LL DOUBTLESS PLEASE TO RECOLLECT	141	2 DON JUAN	1	209	5
HAD DOUBTLESS HEARD ABOUT THE STYGIAN RIVER	258	2 DON JUAN	2	193	6
THERE'S DOUBTLESS SOMETHING IN DOMESTIC DOINGS	279	2 DON JUAN	3	8	1
THOUGH DOUBTLESS HE WHO CAN COMMAND HIMSELF	299	2 DON JUAN	3	47	7
AND WHAT IS THAT DEVOTION DOUBTLESS--HOW	22	3 DON JUAN	6	33	1
THE STRICTER DOUBTLESS GROW THE VESTAL DUTIES	35	3 DON JUAN	6	58	7
AND DOUBTLESS WOULD BE FOREMOST ON THE FOE	98	3 DON JUAN	7	62	3
DOUBTLESS TO THAT OF DOCTRINES THE MOST TRUE	101	3 DON JUAN	7	57	5
TO THE GAZETTE--WHICH DOUBTLESS FAIRLY DEALT	120	3 DON JUAN	8	18	2
BUT DOUBTLESS THEY PREFER A FINE YOUNG MAN	167	3 DON JUAN	8	112	3
YET EUROPE DOUBTLESS OWES YOU GREATLY MORE	184	3 DON JUAN	9	3	2
BUT DOUBTLESS AS THE AIR THOUGH SELDOM SUNNY	259	3 DON JUAN	10	70	7
ABROAD THOUGH DOUBTLESS THEY DO MUCH AMISS	352	3 DON JUAN	12	79	5
DOUBTLESS IT IS A BRILLIANT MASQUERADE	417	3 DON JUAN	14	17	5
AND THEREFORE DOUBTLESS TO APPROVE THE TRUTH	439	3 DON JUAN	14	67	1
BECAUSE 'TIS FRAILER DOUBTLESS THAN A STANCH ONE	446	3 DON JUAN	14	85	6
AS DOUBTLESS SHOULD BE PEOPLE OF HIGH BIRTH	508	3 DON JUAN	16	17	6

DOUBT'S
| I WONDER (ALTHOUGH MARS NO DOUBT'S A GOD I | 77 | 3 DON JUAN | 7 | 21 | 1 |
| BUT SEIZE THE LAST WORD WHICH NO DOUBT'S THE BEST | 404 | 3 DON JUAN | 13 | 98 | 8 |

DOUBTS
I HAD MY DOUBTS PERHAPS I HAVE THEM STILL	49	2 DON JUAN	1	51	1
WITH FLUTTERING DOUBTS IF ALL BE WELL OR ILL--	286	2 DON JUAN	3	21	5
THOUGH DOUBTS OF THEIR WELL DOING TO ARRANGE	65	3 DON JUAN	6	120	2
UPON HIS TALENT HENRY HAD NO DOUBTS	369	3 DON JUAN	13	24	5
AS MANY DOUBTS AS ANY OTHER DOCTRINE	377	3 DON JUAN	13	41	7
AND THUS WE SEE--WHO DOUBTS THE MORNING POST	383	3 DON JUAN	13	53	1
HE WHO DOUBTS ALL THINGS NOTHING CAN DENY	495	3 DON JUAN	15	88	5

DOVE
AND SEND HIM LIKE A DOVE OF PROMISE FORTH	161	2 DON JUAN	2	8	8
WEBFOOTED NOT UNLIKE A DOVE IN SIZE	206	2 DON JUAN	2	94	2
AND HAD IT BEEN THE DOVE FROM NOAH'S ARK	206	2 DON JUAN	2	95	5
THOSE DOWNCAST EYES BENEATH THE ALMIGHTY DOVE--	336	2 DON JUAN	3	103	6
OF FAITHFUL PAIRS--(I NEEDS MUST RHYME WITH DOVE	219	3 DON JUAN	9	74	3

DOVER
| THY CLIFFS DEAR DOVER HARBOUR AND HOTEL | 259 | 3 DON JUAN | 10 | 69 | 2 |
| EVEN IN THE HOPEFUL ISLE WHOSE OUTLET'S DOVER | 331 | 3 DON JUAN | 12 | 33 | 6 |

DOVE'S
| OH SAITH THE PSALMIST THAT I HAD A DOVE'S | 228 | 3 DON JUAN | 10 | 6 | 2 |

DOVES
THEY TWINED LIKE SERPENTS AND THEY KISSED LIKE DOVES	257	2 DON JUAN	2	191	V7
MORE THAN FOR THOSE OF NIGHTINGALES OR DOVES	354	2 DON JUAN	4	19	8
AND PAIR THEIR RHYMES AS VENUS YOKES HER DOVES	411	2 DON JUAN	5	1	3

DOWAGER
| WHILE SOME MORE DESPERATE DOWAGER HAS BEEN WAGING | 486 | 2 DON JUAN | 5 | 130 | 3 |

DOWAGERS
| BUT SIXTEEN DOWAGERS TEN UNWED SHE SAGES | 330 | 3 DON JUAN | 12 | 30 | 7 |

DOWER
WHEN HAPPINESS HAD BEEN THEIR ONLY DOWER	354	2 DON JUAN	4	20	5
BEAUTY AND LOVE WERE HAIDEE'S MOTHER'S DOWER	374	2 DON JUAN	4	56	6
GREAT WISH TO PLEASE--A MOST ATTRACTIVE DOWER	395	2 DON JUAN	4	94	7

DOWNCAST
BUT DON ALFONSO STOOD WITH DOWNCAST LOOKS	110	2 DON JUAN	1	161	1
OF DOWNCAST LENGTH IN WHOSE SILK SHADOW LIES	218	2 DON JUAN	2	117	3
THOSE DOWNCAST EYES BENEATH THE ALMIGHTY DOVE--	336	2 DON JUAN	3	103	6
HER BLACK BRIGHT DOWNCAST YET ESPIEGLE EYE	532	3 DON JUAN	16	65	1

DOWNRIGHT
SO MUCH INDEED AS TO BE DOWNRIGHT RUDE	45	2 DON JUAN	1	43	6
OF A YOUNG DOWNRIGHT BEAUTY IN THIS CASE	486	2 DON JUAN	5	130	8
AND YET A HEADLONG HEADSTRONG DOWNRIGHT SHE	7	3 DON JUAN	6	3	1
TO THIS MY PLAIN SWORN DOWNRIGHT DETESTATION	194	3 DON JUAN	9	24	7
IN ISLANDS IS IT SEEMS DOWNRIGHT AND THOROUGH	288	3 DON JUAN	11	42	6
FOR DOWNRIGHT RUDENESS YE MAY STAY AT HOME	290	3 DON JUAN	11	44	1

DOWNWARD
AND TUMBLE DOWNWARD LIKE THE FLYING FISH	10	2 DON JUAN	D	3	6
AND FURTHER DOWNWARD TALL AND TOWERING STILL IS	385	2 DON JUAN	4	76	5
BUT THESE ARE TRIFLES DOWNWARD FLIES MY LORD	379	3 DON JUAN	13	46	1

DOWNWARDS
| THE WOODS SLOPED DOWNWARDS TO ITS BRINK AND STOOD | 385 | 3 DON JUAN | 13 | 57 | 7 |

207

		PAGE	VOL		CANTO	STANZA	LN

DOWRY
HER DOWRY AND HER VEIL IN FORM ALIKE . . . . 221 2 DON JUAN 2 122 5
HER DOWRY WAS AS NOTHING TO HER SMILES . . . . . . 224 2 DON JUAN 2 128 4

DOZE
TO TOSS TO TUMBLE DOZE REVIVE AND QUAKE . . . . . . 18 3 DON JUAN 6 24 7

DOZED
HE STILL WAS IN THE BOAT AND HAD BUT DOZED . . . . . 215 2 DON JUAN 2 112 3

DOZEN
COMPOSED A CHOIR OF GIRLS TEN OR A DOZEN . . . . . 469 2 DON JUAN 5 99 2
HE HAD FIFTY DAUGHTERS AND FOUR DOZEN SONS . . . . 498 2 DON JUAN 5 152 1
FIRST ONE OR TWO THEN FIVE SIX AND A DOZEN . . . . 135 3 DON JUAN 8 45 1
SOME ARE SOON BAGGED BUT SOME REJECT THREE DOZEN . . . 332 3 DON JUAN 12 34 1
I THOUGHT AT SETTING OFF ABOUT TWO DOZEN . . . . 341 3 DON JUAN 12 55 5
I'VE KNOWN A DOZEN WEDDINGS MADE EVEN THUS . . . . 344 3 DON JUAN 12 61 1

DRACHENFELS
WHICH DRACHENFELS FROWNS OVER LIKE A SPECTRE . . . . 255 3 DON JUAN 10 62 2

DRAFT
OR GENEROUS DRAFT CONCEDED AS A GIFT . . . . 379 3 DON JUAN 13 45 5
ON READY MONEY OR A DRAFT ON RANSOM . . . . 459 3 DON JUAN 15 8 8

DRAG
THAT ONE SHOULD DIE THAN TWO DRAG ON THE FETTER) . . . 222 3 DON JUAN 9 80 8

DRAG-CHAIN
SIX TARTARS AND A DRAG-CHAIN-- --TO THIS DOOM . . . . 418 2 DON JUAN 5 15 3

DRAGON
OR PRAY MEDEA FOR A SINGLE DRAGON . . . . 333 2 DON JUAN 3 99 4

DRAGS
ALL THAT A POET DRAGS INTO DETAIL . . . . 60 3 DON JUAN 6 109 6

DRAIN
AS WELL AS FURTHER DRAIN THE WITHERED FORM . . . . 243 3 DON JUAN 10 38 4

DRAINED
WHEN IT'S LAST WEANING DRAUGHT IS DRAINED FOREVER . . . 349 2 DON JUAN 4 10 V6

DRAINER
THE DRAINER OF OBLIVION EVEN THE SOT . . . . 457 3 DON JUAN 15 4 3

DRAINS
A CHILD THE MOMENT WHEN IT DRAINS THE BREAST . . . . 261 2 DON JUAN 2 196 2
IN DIGGING DRAINS FOR A NEW WATER CLOSET . . . . . 327 2 DON JUAN 3 89 V7
DRAINS ITS FIRST DRAUGHT OF LIPS--BUT AS I SAID . . . 238 3 DON JUAN 10 28 7

DRAM
SODAE-SULPHAT SIX DRAMS HALF DRAM MANNAE OPTIM . . . 244 3 DON JUAN 10 41 2

DRAMA
SOME DRAMA OF THE MARRIAGE UNITIES . . . . 470 3 DON JUAN 15 32 5

DRAMAS
SO DRAMAS CLOSE WITH DEATH OR SETTLEMENT FOR LIFE . . . 280 2 DON JUAN 3 9 V7

DRAMATIC
WHICH PLATO IN HIS DIALOGUES DRAMATIC . . . . . . 494 3 DON JUAN 15 86 5

DRAMS
SOME TAKE A LOVER SOME TAKE DRAMS OR PRAYERS . . . . 263 2 DON JUAN 2 201 1
SODAE-SULPHAT SIX DRAMS HALF DRAM MANNAE OPTIM . . . 244 3 DON JUAN 10 41 2
AQ FERVENT OUNCE AND A HALF TWO DRAMS TINCT SENNAE . . 244 3 DON JUAN 10 41 3

DRANK
SOME PLUNDER'D SOME DRANK SPIRITS SOME SUNG PSALMS . . . 174 2 DON JUAN 2 34 3
THEY ATE UP ALL THEY HAD AND DRANK THEIR WINE . . . 192 2 DON JUAN 2 69 2
BENT WITH HUSH'D LIPS THAT DRANK HIS SCARCE-DRAWN BREATH . 232 2 DON JUAN 2 143 8
HE DRANK SIX CUPS OF COFFEE AT THE LEAST . . . . 52 3 DON JUAN 6 92 4
AND HAVING VOTED DINED DRANK GAMED AND WHORED . . . 306 3 DON JUAN 11 75 7

DRAPERIED
DRAPERIED HER FORM WITH CURIOUS FELICITY . . . . . 550 3 DON JUAN 16 102 8

DRAPERIES
WITH FLOATING DRAPERIES AND WITH FLYING HAIR . . . . 42 3 DON JUAN 6 72 2

DRAPERY
SOME HALF-TORN DRAPERY SCATTER'D ON THE GROUND . . . 125 2 DON JUAN 1 187 5
THE MILLINERS WHO FURNISH DRAPERY MISSES . . . . . 293 3 DON JUAN 11 49 1
WHOSE DRAPERY HINTS WE MAY ADMIRE THEM FREELY . . . 390 3 DON JUAN 13 68 8

DRAUGHT
YET HALF AFRAID TO VENTURE FOR THE DRAUGHT . . . . 155 2 DON JUAN 1 V 6 2
PREFERR'D A DRAUGHT FROM THE FAST-FLOWING VEINS . . . 197 2 DON JUAN 2 77 4
MIGHT NOT HAVE THOUGHT THE SCANTY DRAUGHT SO SWEET . . 201 2 DON JUAN 2 85 6
VIE WITH THAT DRAUGHT OF HOCK AND SODA-WATER . . . 251 2 DON JUAN 2 180 8
WHEN IT'S LAST WEANING DRAUGHT IS DRAINED FOREVER . . . 349 2 DON JUAN 4 10 V6
WITH THE FIRST DRAUGHT INTOXICATES APACE . . . . . 216 3 DON JUAN 9 67 4
DRAINS ITS FIRST DRAUGHT OF LIPS--BUT AS I SAID . . . 238 3 DON JUAN 10 28 7
WHICH FORM THAT BITTER DRAUGHT THE HUMAN SPECIES . . . 261 3 DON JUAN 10 73 8
OF THE TRUTH'S RAYS SPOIL NOT MY DRAUGHT OF SPIRIT . . 269 3 DON JUAN 11 2 7

DRAUGHTS
OF FRIENDS--AND OPIATE DRAUGHTS--THERE'S LOVE AND WINE . . 343 2 DON JUAN 3 V 98 2

DRAW
BAY DEEP-MOUTH'D WELCOME AS WE DRAW NEAR HOME . . . . 88 2 DON JUAN 1 123 2
AT SIXTY YEARS AND DRAW THE ACCOMPTS OF EVIL . . . 113 2 DON JUAN 1 167 7
ALFONSO'S SWORD HAD DROPP'D ERE HE COULD DRAW IT . . . 123 2 DON JUAN 1 185 1
ONLY TO DRAW THEM 'TWIXT TWO BASTION CORNERS . . . 149 3 DON JUAN 8 75 7
TO DRAW A HIGH PRIZE NOW HOWE'ER HE GOT HER I . . . 333 3 DON JUAN 12 37 7
SOME WALTZ SOME DRAW SOME FATHOM THE ABYSS . . . . 340 3 DON JUAN 12 52 7
AND DRAW THEM NIGHTLY WHEN A TICKET'S SENT . . . . 342 3 DON JUAN 12 57 6
TO DRAW THE LINE BETWEEN THE FALSE AND TRUE . . . . 449 3 DON JUAN 14 90 7
YOUR WRITERS WHO MUST EITHER DRAW AGAIN . . . . . 468 3 DON JUAN 15 26 6
TO DRAW UP IN ARRAY A SINGLE DAY-BILL . . . . . . 482 3 DON JUAN 15 62 5
TO DRAW THE BOW TO RIDE AND SPEAK THE TRUTH . . . . 501 3 DON JUAN 16 1 2
BUT DRAW THE LONG BOW BETTER NOW THAN EVER . . . . 501 3 DON JUAN 16 1 8

DRAWCANSIR
AND NOT IN LITERATURE A GREAT DRAWCANSIR . . . . . 294 3 DON JUAN 11 51 2

208

DRAWERS
   A PAIR OF DRAWERS--OF FINE CRIMSON SATIN . . . . 456 2 DON JUAN 5   77 V2
DRAWING
   AND DRAWING FROM HIS BELT A PISTOL HE . . . . 365 2 DON JUAN 4   40   4
   THOUSANDS OF WHOM WERE DRAWING THEIR LAST BREATH . . . 111 3 DON JUAN 7   87   4
   THAT IN THE LIEU OF DRAWING ON HIS BANKER . . . . . . 240 3 DON JUAN 10   31   2
   HE HAD THE ART OF DRAWING PEOPLE OUT . . . . 492 3 DON JJAN 15   82   7
DRAWING-ROOM
   TO FOLLOW HIM BEYOND THE DRAWING-ROOM . . . . 227 3 DON JUAN 10   5   5
   WHICH WELL BESEEMED THE DEVIL'S DRAWING-ROOM . . . . . 265 3 DON JUAN 10   81   3
DRAWLING
   OF LONDONDERRY DRAWLING AGAINST TIME . . . . 74 3 DON JUAN 7   16   6
DRAWN
   OH VALIANT MAN WITH SWORD DRAWN AND COCK'D TRIGGER . . 103 2 DON JUAN 1   150   7
   DRAWN FROM THE STARS AND FILTER'D THROUGH THE SKIES . . 269 2 DON JUAN 2   212   4
   WERE NOT DRAWN FROM THEIR SPOUSES YOU CONCEIVE . . . . 281 2 DON JUAN 3   10   8
   DRAWN BY THE BLUE-COAT MISSES OF A COTERIE . . . . . . 404 2 DON JUAN 4   109   8
   WITH ALL ITS VEIL OF MYSTERY DRAWN APART . . . . . . 169 3 DON JJAN 8   115   4
   FOR I HAVE DRAWN MUCH LESS WITH A LONG BOW . . . . . . 181 3 DON JUAN 8   138   6
   WHITE STOCKINGS DRAWN UNCURDLED AS NEW MILK . . . . . 204 3 DON JUAN 9   43   7
   FROM THENCE HE WAS DRAWN ONWARDS TO COLOGNE . . . . . 255 3 DON JUAN 10   62   5
   IF SUCH CAN E'ER BE DRAWN BY MAN'S CAPACITY . . . . . 449 3 DON JUAN 14   90   6
   DAYS BETTER DRAWN BEFORE OR ELSE ASSUME . . . . 468 3 DON JUAN 15   26   7
   JUAN WAS DRAWN THUS INTO SOME ATTENTIONS . . . . . . 491 3 DON JUAN 15   80   1
   A NOISE LIKE TO WET FINGERS DRAWN ON GLASS . . . . . 556 3 DON JUAN 16   114   1
DRAWS
   YIELDING TO THEIR SMALL HANDS DRAWS BACK AGAIN . . . . 292 2 DON JUAN 3   32   8
   BUT THEN THE ROLL-CALL DRAWS THEM BACK AFRAID . . . . 417 3 DON JUAN 14   17   3
   GRACEFUL AS DIAN WHEN SHE DRAWS HER BOW . . . . 517 3 DON JUAN 16   38   5
DRAYS
   THROUGH COACHES DRAYS CHOKED TURNPIKES AND A WHIRL . . 278 3 DON JUAN 11   22   1
DREAD
   THEY MAKE YOU DREAD THAT THEY'LL RECITE THEM TOO . . . 79 2 DON JUAN 1   108   4
   AS EVERY RISING WAVE HIS DREAD RENEW'D . . . . 187 2 DON JUAN 2   59   5
   AWAY THE VAST SALT DREAD ETERNAL DEEP . . . . 210 2 DON JUAN 2   103   8
   THE OLD MAN'S CHEEK GREW PALE BUT NOT WITH DREAD . . . 365 2 DON JUAN 4   40   3
   POLYGAMY MAY WELL BE HELD IN DREAD . . . . 12 3 DON JUAN 6   12   3
   NOT TO BE RASHLY TOUCHED BUT STILL MORE DREAD . . . . 37 3 DON JUAN 6   62   2
   FROM FOOLS WHO DREAD TO KNOW THE TRUTH OF LIFE . . . . 69 3 DON JUAN 7   6 V8
   WHICH HAMLET TELLS US IS A PASS OF DREAD . . . . . . 133 3 DON JUAN 8   41   4
   ACKNOWLEDGE AUGHT OF DREAD OF DEATH OR FOE . . . . . . 155 3 DON JUAN 8   87   5
   WITH JOY TO SAVE AND DREAD OF SOME MISCHANCE . . . . . 159 3 DON JUAN 8   96   4
   THIS HOURLY DREAD OF ALL WHOSE THREATENED STING . . . 188 3 DON JUAN 9   11   6
   OR ON MIGHT DREAD HER MAJESTY HAD NOT ROOM ENOUGH . . . 206 3 DON JUAN 9   48   3
   THRO' SUCH A SCENE OF CHANGE AND DREAD AND SLAUGHTER . . 252 3 DON JUAN 10   56   2
   SHOULD NEITHER COURT NEGLECT NOR DREAD TO BEAR IT . . . 356 3 DON JUAN 12   87   8
   LESS FROM DISGUST OF LIFE THAN DREAD OF DEATH . . . . 412 3 DON JUAN 14   4   8
   AND NOBLE BIRTHS NOR DREAD THE ENUMERATION-- . . . . . 432 3 DON JUAN 14   52   4
   NO WONDER THEN A PURER SOUL SHOULD DREAD . . . . . . 438 3 DON JUAN 14   64   3
   BUT I MAY HAVE AND YOU TOO READER DREAD IT . . . . . . 488 3 DON JUAN 15   72   8
   BEGAN TO DREAD SHE'D THAW TO A COQUETTE-- . . . . . . 492 3 DON JUAN 15   81   4
   HAVE SOMETHING GHASTLY DESOLATE AND DREAD . . . . . . 508 3 DON JUAN 16   17   8
   WITH SOME WHILE OTHERS WHO HAD MORE IN DREAD . . . . . 527 3 DON JUAN 16   54   3
   AND THEN HIS DREAD GREW WRATH AND HIS WRATH FIERCE . . 559 3 DON JUAN 16   119   1
DREADED
   FOR DONNA INEZ DREADED THE MYTHOLOGY . . . . 44 2 DON JUAN 1   41   8
   OF DOCTORS' COMMONS BUT SHE DREADED FIRST . . . . . . 437 3 DON JUAN 14   62   5
DREADFUL
   AS IF DEATH WERE MORE DREADFUL BY HIS DOOR . . . . . . 174 2 DON JUAN 2   35   5
   THEN SOME LEAP'D OVERBOARD WITH DREADFUL YELL . . . . 184 2 DON JUAN 2   52   3
   IS DREADFUL TO THE SHEPHERD AND THE FLOCK . . . . . . 305 2 DON JUAN 3   58   2
   A DREADFUL IMPULSE TO EACH LOUD MEANDER . . . . 52 3 DON JUAN 6   93   5
   A DREADFUL TRADE LIKE HIS WHO GATHERS SAMPHIRE . . . . 299 3 DON JUAN 11   62   3
   DREADFUL AS DANTE'S RHIMA OR THIS STANZA . . . . . . 557 3 DON JUAN 16   116   4
DREADING
   DREADING THAT CLIMAX OF ALL HUMAN ILLS . . . . 293 2 DON JUAN 3   35   7
   AND DREADING THE CHASTE ECHOES OF HER SHOE . . . . . . 556 3 DON JUAN 16   112   8
DREAM
   HER BRAIN THOUGH IN A DREAM (AND THEN SHE SIGH'D) . . . 67 2 DON JUAN 1   84   3
   SO DEAR IS STILL THE MEMORY OF THAT DREAM . . . . . . 130 2 DON JUAN 1   193   4
   AND JUAN TOO WAS HELP'D OUT FROM HIS DREAM . . . . . . 237 2 DON JUAN 2   153   1
   AN OPIUM DREAM OF TOO MUCH YOUTH AND READING . . . . . 354 2 DON JUAN 4   19   2
   STIRR'D WITH HER DREAM AS ROSE-LEAVES WITH THE AIR . . 359 2 DON JUAN 4   29   8
   WALKS O'ER IT WAS SHE SHAKEN BY THE DREAM . . . . . . 360 2 DON JUAN 4   30   3
   THE DREAM CHANGED IN A CAVE SHE STOOD ITS WALLS . . . 362 2 DON JUAN 4   33   1
   AND THAT BRIEF DREAM APPEAR'D A LIFE TOO LONG . . . . 362 2 DON JUAN 4   34   8
   HER RECOLLECTION ON HER FLASH'D THE DREAM . . . . . . 380 2 DON JUAN 4   66   4
   THE TWELVE ISLES AND THE MORE THAN I COULD DREAM . . . 412 2 DON JUAN 5   3   6
   AND SMILING THROUGH HER DREAM AS THROUGH A CLOUD . . . 39 3 DON JUAN 6   66   4
   THROUGH THE HEAVED BREAST THE DREAM OF SOME FAR SHORE . . 40 3 DON JUAN 6   67   5
   SHE DREAMED A DREAM OF WALKING IN A WOOD-- . . . . . . 43 3 DON JUAN 6   75   2
   BED FOR THE DREAM SHE HAD BEEN OBLIGED TO HEAR . . . . 45 3 DON JUAN 6   79   6
   SHE PROMISED NEVER MORE TO HAVE A DREAM . . . . 47 3 DON JUAN 6   83   1
   AT LEAST TO DREAM SO LOUDLY AS JUST NOW . . . . 47 3 DON JUAN 6   83   2
   OF ALL SAVE DUDU'S DREAM WHICH WAS NO JOKE . . . . . . 58 3 DON JUAN 6   104   8
   AND SO THEY ARE YET THUS IS GLORY'S DREAM . . . . . . 112 3 DON JUAN 8   1   4
   AND WANDERED UP AND DOWN AS IN A DREAM . . . . 148 3 DON JUAN 8   72   4
   ALL THAT WE READ HEAR DREAM OF MAN'S DISTRESSES . . . 173 3 DON JUAN 8   123   3
   TO SWIM OR SINK--I HAVE HAD AT LEAST MY DREAM . . . . 415 3 DON JUAN 14   11   8

<pre>
                                                          PAGE VOL   CANTO STANZA LN
DREAM   (CONTINUED)
     AS FEW WOULD EVER DREAM COULD FORM THE LINK 454   3 DON JUAN 14   100   5
     AND WOULD HAVE PASSED THE WHOLE OFF AS A DREAM 511   3 DON JUAN 16   25   5
DREAM'D
     AND NEVER DREAM'D HIS LADY WAS CONCERN'D   31   2 DON JUAN 1   19   4
     MY MOTHER DREAM'D NOT IN MY NATAL HOUR   106   2 DON JUAN 1   155   7
     DREAM'D OF A THOUSAND WRECKS O'ER WHICH SHE STUMBLED . . 229   2 DON JUAN 2   138   3
     OF WHOM THESE TWO YEARS SHE HAD NIGHTLY DREAM'D 247   2 DON JUAN 2   172   4
     I DREAM'D THAT GREECE MIGHT STILL BE FREE   321   2 DON JUAN 3   L 3   1
     SHE DREAM'D OF BEING ALONE ON THE SEA-SHORE   361   2 DON JUAN 4   31   1
DREAMED
     WHO IN THEIR TRANSPORT NEVER DREAMED OF WOE   353   2 DON JUAN 4   18   V3
     BUT ALL THIS TIME HOW SLEPT OR DREAMED DUDU   41   3 DON JUAN 6   70   1
     SHE DREAMED A DREAM OF WALKING IN A WOOD--   43   3 DON JUAN 6   75   2
     PRETENSIONS WHICH THEY NEVER DREAMED TO HAVE SHOWN-- . . 344   3 DON JUAN 12   61   4
DREAMER
     NOT YET A DREAMER TILL THE SPELL IS BROKE   237   2 DON JUAN 2   152   3
DREAMING
     ABOVE HER BROW LAY DREAMING SOFT AND WARM   39   3 DON JUAN 6   66   3
     SAVE THAT OF DREAMING ONCE MAL-A-PROPOS   48   3 DON JUAN 6   84   8
DREAMLESS
     YOUNG JUAN SLEPT ALL DREAMLESS--BUT THE MAID   228   2 DON JUAN 2   135   1
DREAMS
     ARE THESE THE DREAMS HIS YOUNG AMBITION SAW   155   2 DON JUAN 1   V 7   3
     THROBB'D IN ACCURSED DREAMS WHICH SOMETIMES SPREAD . .   227   2 DON JUAN 2   134   6
     BUT DREAMS OF WHAT HAS BEEN NO MORE TO BE   244   2 DON JUAN 2   166   8
     BUT NO ONE EVER DREAMS OF BEING SHORT--   437   2 DON JUAN 5   48   8
     WHATE'ER THEIR DREAMS BE IF OF JOYS OR WOES   16   3 DON JUAN 6   20   3
     AND THEN I HAVE THE WORST DREAMS THAT CAN BE   30   3 DON JUAN 6   48   5
     THE DAME REPLIED BETWEEN YOUR DREAMS AND YOU   30   3 DON JUAN 6   48   7
     I FEAR JUANNA'S DREAMS WOULD BE BUT FEW   30   3 DON JUAN 6   48   8
     DISMAY THE USUAL CONSEQUENCE OF DREAMS   45   3 DON JUAN 6   78   2
     HER FUTURE DREAMS SHOULD ALL BE KEPT IN HAND   47   3 DON JUAN 6   82   8
     IS OF ALL DREAMS THE FIRST HALLUCINATION   88   3 DON JUAN 7   44   4
     ALL MY BOY FEELINGS ALL MY GENTLER DREAMS   233   3 DON JUAN 10   18   4
     A SLEEP WITHOUT DREAMS AFTER A ROUGH DAY   412   3 DON JUAN 14   4   1
     ALONG THE CANVAS THEIR EYES GLANCE LIKE DREAMS   509   3 DON JUAN 16   19   4
     ALL MOUNTAINEERS WITH DREAMS THAT THEY ARE NIGH LANDS . 523   3 DON JUAN 16   46   6
DREAMT
     (LONG ERE I DREAMT OF DATING FROM THE BRENTA)   143   2 DON JUAN 1   212   5
     AND NEVER HAVING DREAMT OF FALSEHOOD SHE   257   2 DON JUAN 2   190   7
     AND NEVER HAVING DREAMT WHAT 'TWAS TO BEAR   480   2 DON JUAN 5   119   4
     MORE VIRGIN VALOUR NEVER DREAMT OF FLYING   131   3 DON JUAN 8   36   3
     IN RHYMES OR DREAMT (FOR FANCY WILL PLAY TRICKS) . . .   230   3 DON JUAN 10   10   5
     OF WHAT I THEN DREAMT CLOTHED IN THEIR OWN PALL 233   3 DON JUAN 10   18   5
     WHERE NONE WERE DREAMT OF UNTO LOVE'S AFFAIRS   369   3 DON JUAN 13   25   5
     A VIGIL OR DREAMT RATHER MORE THAN SLEPT   568   3 DON JUAN 17   14   8
DREAR
     OF SUCH SENSATIONS IN THE DROWSY DREAR   220   3 DON JUAN 9   75   V7
     THE SEASON RATHER THAN TO WINTER DREAR--   395   3 DON JUAN 13   77   4
     YOU LOOK DOWN O'ER THE PRECIPICE AND DREAR   412   3 DON JUAN 14   5   6
DREARY
     OR DULL REPENTANCE HATH HAD DREARY LEISURE   168   3 DON JUAN 8   113   5
     LIFE'S SAD POST-HORSES O'ER THE DREARY FRONTIER . . .   238   3 DON JUAN 10   27   7
     THE DREARY FUIMUS OF ALL THINGS HUMAN   376   3 DON JUAN 13   40   6
     WHY DRINK WHY READ--TO MAKE SOME HOUR LESS DREARY . . . 415   3 DON JUAN 14   11   4
     ARE THERE OFT DULL AND DREARY AS A DUN--   423   3 DON JUAN 14   29   7
     AND HENCE HIGH LIFE IS OFT A DREARY VOID   444   3 DON JUAN 14   79   1
     BACK FELL THE SABLE FROCK AND DREARY COWL   561   3 DON JUAN 16   123   5
DRENCH'D
     HIS DEWY CURLS LONG DRENCH'D BY EVERY STORM   216   2 DON JUAN 2   114   6
DRESDEN
     AND THENCE THROUGH BERLIN DRESDEN AND THE LIKE   255   3 DON JUAN 10   61   1
DRESS
     A PRODIGY--HER MORNING DRESS WAS DIMITY   27   2 DON JUAN 1   12   6
     A DRESS THROUGH WHICH THE EYES GIVE SUCH A VOLLEY . . .   160   2 DON JUAN 2   7   7
     HER DRESS WAS VERY DIFFERENT FROM THE SPANISH   220   2 DON JUAN 2   120   2
     HER DRESS WAS MANY-COLOUR'D FINELY SPUN   220   2 DON JUAN 2   121   7
     THE OTHER FEMALE'S DRESS WAS NOT UNLIKE   221   2 DON JUAN 2   122   1
     THEIR LOVES AND FEASTS AND HOUSE AND DRESS AND MODE . . 317   2 DON JUAN 3   81   7
     TO HELP THE LADIES IN THEIR DRESS AND LACING   391   2 DON JUAN 4   86   V6
     HIS FIGURE AND THE SPLENDOUR OF HIS DRESS   415   2 DON JUAN 5   9   3
     AND SOME SEEMED MUCH IN LOVE WITH THEIR OWN DRESS . .   441   2 DON JUAN 5   53   4
     AS DRESS YOURSELF-- AND POINTED OUT A SUIT   453   2 DON JUAN 5   73   2
     THAT I UNSEXED MY DRESS BUT BABA STROKING   454   2 DON JUAN 5   75   4
     THAN OTHER ARTICLES OF FEMALE DRESS   15   3 DON JUAN 6   19   4
     SOME THOUGHT HER DRESS DID NOT SO MUCH BECOME HER . .   23   3 DON JUAN 6   35   3
     WAS WHAT HER DRESS BESPOKE A DAMSEL FAIR   24   3 DON JUAN 6   36   2
     AND ONE BY ONE HER ARTICLES OF DRESS   36   3 DON JUAN 6   61   1
     THEIR DRESS WAS MOSLEM BUT YOU MIGHT HAVE GUESSED . .   96   3 DON JUAN 7   57   3
     THERE LURKED A MAN BENEATH THE SPIRIT'S DRESS   206   3 DON JUAN 9   47   6
     LIKE A RACE-HORSE MUCH TO EACH DRESS HE SPORTED . . .   239   3 DON JUAN 10   29   5
     DON JUAN WAS PRESENTED AND HIS DRESS   287   3 DON JUAN 11   39   1
     DAUGHTERS ADMIRED HIS DRESS AND PIOUS MOTHERS   293   3 DON JUAN 11   48   7
     THEN DRESS THEN DINNER THEN AWAKES THE WORLD   302   3 DON JUAN 11   67   1
     THAT MANNERS HARDLY DIFFER MORE THAN DRESS   402   3 DON JUAN 13   94   8
     WHAT TIME HE CHOSE FOR DRESS AND BROKE HIS FAST . . .   406   3 DON JUAN 13   103   7
     BUT FOR THAT HOUR CALLED HALF-HOUR GIVEN TO DRESS . .   482   3 DON JUAN 15   61   7
     I WISH TO GOD YOU'DE DRESS US SOME SUCH PARTRIDGES . .   485   3 DON JUAN 15   67   V8
</pre>

210

		PAGE	VOL	CANTO	STANZA	LN

DRESS   (CONTINUED)
```
    SO EVERYONE MAY DRESS IT TO HIS WISH  . . . . . . .  486   3 DON JUAN 15      68    4
    BECAUSE MY BUSINESS IS TO DRESS SOCIETY . . . . . .  497   3 DON JUAN 15      93    5
    KNOCKED TO INFORM HIM IT WAS TIME TO DRESS  . . . .  512   3 DON JUAN 16      28    8
    AND THEN HER DRESS--WHAT BEAUTIFUL SIMPLICITY . . .  550   3 DON JUAN 16     102    7
DRESS'D
    AND DRESS'D HIM FOR THE PRESENT LIKE A TURK . . . .  240   2 DON JUAN  2     160    4
DRESSED
    ALSO HE DRESSED UP FOR THE NONCE FASCINES  . . . .   93   3 DON JUAN  7      53    1
    HE DRESSED AND LIKE YOUNG PEOPLE HE WAS WONT  . . .  513   3 DON JUAN 16      29    1
DRESSES
    AND ASKING NOW AND THEN FOR CAST-OFF DRESSES . . .  252   2 DON JUAN  2     182    8
    THEIR CLASSICAL PROFILES AND GLITTERING DRESSES  . .  292   2 DON JUAN  3      33    1
    OF ALL THE DRESSES I SELECT HAIDEE'S . . . . . . .  311   2 DON JUAN  3      70    1
    CURE THEM OF TOURS HUSSAR AND HIGHLAND DRESSES . . .  267   3 DON JUAN 10      86    2
    AND YOU MAY GET THE WEDDING DRESSES READY  . . . .  343   3 DON JUAN 12      59    8
    THEIR HIDEOUS WIVES THEIR HORRID SELVES AND DRESSES .  550   3 DON JUAN 16     103    7
DRESSING
    THEN DRESSING NURSING PRAYING AND ALL'S OVER . . .  263   2 DON JUAN  2     200    8
    WHILE HE WAS DRESSING BABA THEIR BLACK FRIEND  . . .  451   2 DON JUAN  5      69    1
    AND STITCHED ITS LEAVES INTO A DRESSING GOWN  . . .  476   2 DON JUAN  5     113   V8
    BUT NEXT TO DRESSING FOR A ROUT OR BALL . . . . .  505   3 DON JUAN 16      11    1
DRESSING-GOWN
    BUT MET ALFONSO IN HIS DRESSING-GOWN . . . . . . .  122   2 DON JUAN  1     183    7
DREST
    DREST TO RECEIVE SO MUCH GOOD COMPANY . . . . . .  106   2 DON JUAN  1     156    8
    DREST TO A SYBARITE'S MOST PAMPER'D WISHES  . . . .  307   2 DON JUAN  3      62    5
    DREST IN THE WAY THAT ARISTIPPUS WISHES . . . . .  307   2 DON JUAN  3      62   V5
    RECOMMENDATION--AND TO BE WELL DREST . . . . . . .  371   3 DON JUAN 13      28    7
    DREST VOTED SHONE AND MAYBE SOMETHING MORE . . . .  418   3 DON JUAN 14      18    2
    BUT SO FAR LIKE A LADY THAT 'TWAS DREST . . . . .  488   3 DON JUAN 15      74    7
DREW
    FAREWELL TOO DEAREST JULIA--(HERE HE DREW  . . . .  166   2 DON JUAN  2      18    7
    AND HIGHER GREW THE MOUNTAINS AS THEY DREW . . . .  209   2 DON JUAN  2     100    2
    AS THEY DREW NIGH THE LAND WHICH NOW WAS SEEN  . .  210   2 DON JUAN  2     103    1
    AND WATCH'D WITH EAGERNESS EACH THROB THAT DREW  . .  216   2 DON JUAN  2     114    7
    AND NEAR THE CAVE HER QUICK LIGHT FOOTSTEPS DREW . .  232   2 DON JUAN  2     142    2
    SHE DREW OUT HER PROVISION FROM THE BASKET . . . .  233   2 DON JUAN  2     144    8
    AND WITHOUT WORD A SIGN HER FINGER DREW ON . . . .  234   2 DON JUAN  2     146    4
    THEIR LIPS DREW NEAR AND CLUNG INTO A KISS . . . .  253   2 DON JUAN  2     185    8
    CAN SNEER AT HIM WHO DREW ACHITOPHEL . . . . . .  334   2 DON JUAN  3     100    8
    SHE DREW UP TO HER HEIGHT AS IF TO SHOW  . . . . .  367   2 DON JUAN  4      43    6
    ALTHOUGH HER PAROXYSM DREW TOWARDS ITS CLOSE . . .  380   2 DON JUAN  4      67    6
    DREW ALL EYES ON HIM GIVING THEM TO GUESS  . . . .  415   2 DON JUAN  5       9    5
    AND THEN HE SWORE AGAIN BUT SWEARING DREW  . . . .  455   2 DON JUAN  5      76   V7
    DREW HIMSELF UP TO HIS FULL HEIGHT AGAIN . . . . .  470   2 DON JUAN  5     102    6
    THIS COMPLIMENT WHICH DREW ALL EYES UPON . . . . .  501   2 DON JUAN  5     156    1
    BUT HERE THE MOTHER OF THE MAIDS DREW NEAR . . . .   29   3 DON JUAN  6      46    1
    FOR ON THE SIXTEENTH AT FULL GALLOP DREW . . . . .   87   3 DON JUAN  7      43    1
    THEY DREW CONSTRUCTED LADDERS REPAIRED FLAWS . . .   89   3 DON JUAN  7      47    6
    DREW QUIET CONSOLATION THROUGH ITS HINT  . . . . .  241   3 DON JUAN 10      34    7
    DREW FORTH A POCKET-PISTOL FROM HIS VESTURE  . . . .  274   3 DON JUAN 11      13    3
    THE DROPS FELL FROM HIS DEATH-WOUND AND HE DREW ILL  276   3 DON JUAN 11      16    6
    ONE MONSTROUS DIAMOND DREW MUCH OBSERVATION . . . .  287   3 DON JUAN 11      39    4
    AT LENGTH THE BOYS DREW UP BEFORE A DOOR . . . . .  313   3 DON JUAN 11   V 29    1
    TO HOMER'S ILIAD SINCE IT DREW TO TROY . . . . .  441   3 DON JUAN 14      72    4
    THERE WAS AWE IN THE HOMAGE WHICH SHE DREW . . . .  477   3 DON JUAN 15      47    5
    NIGH AND MORE NIGH THE AWFUL ECHOES DREW . . . . .  557   3 DON JUAN 16     115    5
DRIED
    WHEN DRIED TO SUMMER DUST TILL TAUGHT BY PAIN  . .  201   2 DON JUAN  2      84    3
DRIFT
    IF PEOPLE WOULD BUT SEE ITS REAL DRIFT-- . . . . .   50   3 DON JUAN  6      88    2
DRILL
    IN CHIEF IN PROPER PERSON DEIGNED TO DRILL . . . .   93   3 DON JUAN  7      52    2
    THE DAY BEFORE THE ASSAULT WHILE UPON DRILL  . . . .   95   3 DON JUAN  7      56    1
    THEY BREAK THEIR RANKS AND GLADLY LEAVE THE DRILL .  417   3 DON JUAN 14      17    2
DRILL'D
    OF HIS DRILL'D NYMPHS BUT LIKE A GENTLEMAN . . . .  427   3 DON JUAN 14      38    8
DRILLED
    AND DRILLED AWAY IN THE MOST CLASSIC RUSSIAN . . .   99   3 DON JUAN  7      64    2
DRILLING
    SURVEYING DRILLING ORDERING JESTING PONDERING  . . .   95   3 DON JUAN  7      55    2
    BEFORE A COMPANY OF CALMUCKS DRILLING  . . . . . .   96   3 DON JUAN  7      58    2
DRINK
    FOR GROG AND SOMETIMES DRINK RUM FROM THE CASK . .  173   2 DON JUAN  2      33    8
    EAT DRINK AND LOVE WHAT CAN THE REST AVAIL US  . .  267   2 DON JUAN  2     207    7
    SO ARAB DESERTS DRINK IN SUMMER'S RAIN . . . . .  212   3 DON JUAN  9      59    6
    WHY DRINK WHY READ--TO MAKE SOME HOUR LESS DREARY .  415   3 DON JUAN 14      11    4
DRINKER
    AND SIR JOHN POTTLEDEEP THE MIGHTY DRINKER . . . .  398   3 DON JUAN 13      84    8
DRINKING
    DRINKING SALT-WATER LIKE A MOUNTAIN-STREAM . . . .  198   2 DON JUAN  2      79    6
    THEY NE'ER TILL NOW HAD KNOWN THE JOYS OF DRINKING  . .  201   2 DON JUAN  2      85    8
DRINKS
    SHE SITS UPON HIS KNEE AND DRINKS HIS SIGHS  . . . .  259   2 DON JUAN  2     194    5
    THAT DRINKS AND STILL IS DRY  AT LAST THEY PERISHED--  166   3 DON JUAN  8     110    1
    IN LOVE DRINKS ALL LIFE'S FOUNTAINS (SAVE TEARS) DRY .  216   3 DON JUAN  9      67    8
DRIPPING
    DROOP'D DRIPPING ON THE OAR (THEIR JURY-MAST)  . . .  214   2 DON JUAN  2     110    5
    HER HAIR WAS DRIPPING AND THE VERY BALLS . . . . .  362   2 DON JUAN  4      33    5
```

```
                                                        PAGE VOL      CANTO STANZA LN
DRIVE
    YET OF A BEAUTY THAT WOULD DRIVE YOU CRAZY  . . . . .  . .  26  3 DON JUAN  6    41    8
    HUT WHENCE WISE TRAVELLERS DRIVE WITH CIRCUMSPECTION .  . . 238  3 DON JUAN 10    27    6
    BUT I WON'T WEEP--AND SO DRIVE ON POSTILLIONS  . . . .  . . 263  3 DON JUAN 10    77    2
    THAT NO DEFEAT CAN DRIVE ME FROM THE NINE  . . . . .  . . . 415  3 DON JUAN 14    12    4
    OF THOSE IN WHICH THE BODY SEEMED TO DRIVE  . . . . .  . . 569  3 DON JUAN 17  V 13    5
DRIVELS
    AND DRIVELS SEAS TO SET IT WELL AFLOAT  . . . . . .  . . . 333  2 DON JUAN  3    98    8
DRIVEN
    NOW O'ER IT CLOUDS AND THUNDER MUST BE DRIVEN  . . . .  . . 270  2 DON JUAN  2   214    3
    UPON IN SHEETS WHITE AS WHAT BARDS CALL DRIVEN . . . .  . .  18  3 DON JUAN  6    25    5
    BY GERMAN POSTBOYS DRIVEN A GERMAN MILE  . . . . . .  . . . 260  3 DON JUAN 10    71   V8
    IS MUSICAL--A DYING ACCENT DRIVEN  . . . . . . . .  . . . . 388  3 DON JUAN 13    63    4
    WOULD NOT BE DRIVEN AWAY  . . . . . . . . . .  . . . . . . 518  3 DON JUAN 16  L  1    8
    SOME EXILES FROM THE TOWN WHO HAD BEEN DRIVEN  . . . .  . . 539  3 DON JUAN 16    81    2
    BY LAST NIGHT'S GHOST BEEN DRIVEN FROM THEIR DEFENCES  . . 545  3 DON JUAN 16    93    8
DRIVES
    SOME GENTLEMAN WHO FIGHTS OR WRITES OR DRIVES  . . . .  . . 333  3 DON JUAN 12    36    6
DRIVING
    AT THE GREAT END OF TRAVEL--WHICH IS DRIVING  . . . .  . . 260  3 DON JUAN 10    72    8
    BY DRIVING THE YORK MAIL--BUT AH MY SINKING SOUL  . . . .  263  3 DON JUAN 10    78   V7
DROOP
    BUT DROOP NOT FORTUNE AT YOUR TIME OF LIFE  . . . . .  . . 419  2 DON JUAN  5    17    1
    THERE CAPTIVES LED IN TRIUMPH DROOP THE EYE . . . .  . . . 461  2 DON JUAN  5    86    5
    TO THIS VAIN REFUGE MADE THE GOOD HEART DROOP  . . . .  . . 157  3 DON JUAN  8    91    4
DROOP'D
    DROOP'D DRIPPING ON THE OAR (THEIR JURY-MAST)  . . . .  . . 214  2 DON JUAN  2   110    5
    DROOP'D AS THE WILLOW WHEN NO WINDS CAN BREATHE  . . .  . . 235  2 DON JUAN  2   148    3
    AND HER HEAD DROOP'D AS WHEN THE LILY LIES  . . . . .  . . 376  2 DON JUAN  4    59    3
DROOPING
    LAY DROOPING OER THE OAR WHICH SERVED FOR MAST . . . .  . . 214  2 DON JUAN  2   110   V5
    DROOPING AND DEWY ON THE BEACH HE LAY--  . . . . . .  . . . 249  2 DON JUAN  2   176    6
    AND SEATED HER ALL DROOPING BY HIS SIDE  . . . . . .  . . . 484  2 DON JUAN  5   126    4
    AND FAIR BROWS GENTLY DROOPING AS THE FRUIT . . . .  . . .  38  3 DON JUAN  6    65    6
    AND ONE HAND O'ER THE OTTOMAN LAY DROOPING  . . . . .  . .  60  3 DON JUAN  6   109    3
    AND DROOPING LIKE AN EAGLE'S WITH CLIPT PINION . . . .  . . 246  3 DON JUAN 10    44    6
DROOPS
    LEAF AND IMAGINATION DROOPS HER PINION  . . . . . .  . . . 345  2 DON JUAN  4     3    6
DROP
    A DROP OF DEW WHEN EVERY DROP HAD SEEM'D  . . . . . .  . . 202  2 DON JUAN  2    86    6
    A DROP OF DEW WHEN EVERY DROP HAD SEEM'D  . . . . . .  . . 202  2 DON JUAN  2    86    6
    BUT WORDS ARE THINGS AND A SMALL DROP OF INK  . . . .  . . 327  2 DON JUAN  3    88    1
    THE SHARP ROCKS LOOK'D BELOW EACH DROP THEY CAUGHT  . . .  362  2 DON JUAN  4    33    7
    'TIS THE VILE DAILY DROP ON DROP WHICH WEARS  . . . .  . .  16  3 DON JUAN  6    20    7
    'TIS THE VILE DAILY DROP ON DROP WHICH WEARS  . . . .  . .  16  3 DON JUAN  6    20    7
    THE SOLDIERS WHO BEHELD HIM DROP HIS POINT  . . . . .  . . 170  3 DON JUAN  8   117    1
    A QUINTESSENTIAL LAUDANUM OR BLACK DROP  . . . . . .  . . . 216  3 DON JUAN  9    67    5
    MAY DROP IN WITHOUT CARDS AND TAKE THEIR STATION  . . . .  534  3 DON JUAN 16    69    4
DROPP'D
    ALFONSO'S SWORD HAD DROPP'D ERE HE COULD DRAW IT  . . .  . 123  2 DON JUAN  1   185    1
    WHILE HIS SALT TEARS DROPP'D INTO THE SALT SEA . . .  . . . 165  2 DON JUAN  2    17    2
    DROPP'D IN THEIR LAPS SCARCE PLUCK'D THEIR MELLOW STORE .  291  2 DON JUAN  3    31    8
DROPPED
    A MOMENT AND THEN DROPPED BUT TO RESUME  . . . . . .  . . . 420  2 DON JUAN  5    18    5
    WHO CAME AS IF JUST DROPPED DOWN FROM THE MOON  . . . .  . 140  3 DON JUAN  8    56    4
    THE BANQUETEERS HAD DROPPED OFF ONE BY ONE--  . . . .  . . 504  3 DON JUAN 16     8    3
    THE GUESTS DROPPED IN--THE LAST BUT ONE HER GRACE . . .  . 568  3 DON JUAN 17    13    7
DROPPING
    THE VOICELESS SANDS AND DROPPING CAVES THAT LAY  . . .  . . 255  2 DON JUAN  2   188    5
    WITH HIS BROAD BRIGHT AND DROPPING ORB WERE GONE  . . .  . 355  2 DON JUAN  4    22    4
    SPLENDID BUT SILENT SAVE IN ONE WHERE DROPPING . . .  . . . 442  2 DON JUAN  5    55    3
DROPS
    HE SQUEEZED FROM OUT A RAG SOME DROPS OF RAIN . . . .  . . 203  2 DON JUAN  2    89    7
    BUT POOR DUDU WITH LARGE DROPS IN HER OWN  . . . . .  . . .  47  3 DON JUAN  6    82    2
    THE DROPS FELL FROM HIS DEATH-WOUND AND HE DREW ILL . .  . 276  3 DON JUAN 11    16    6
    THE CRAVAT STAINED WITH BLOODY DROPS FELL DOWN . . .  . . . 276  3 DON JUAN 11    17    1
    AND THEN SHE DROPS A BRIEF AND MODERN CURTSY  . . . .  . . 300  3 DON JUAN 11    63    7
    WHICH LEAVES FEW DROPS OF THAT IMMORTAL RAIN  . . . .  . . 375  3 DON JUAN 13    37    4
DROPSIES
    HAVE PROVED BUT DROPSIES TAKEN FOR DIVINITIES  . . . .  . . 330  2 DON JUAN  3    95    8
DROSS
    WHO CALCULATED LIFE AS SO MUCH DROSS  . . . . . . .  . . . 105  3 DON JUAN  7    77    3
    TO WASTE SO MUCH GOLD FOR A LITTLE DROSS  . . . . . .  . . 113  3 DON JUAN  8     3    5
    LIKE GOLD AS IN COMPARISON TO DROSS  . . . . . . .  . . . 280  3 DON JUAN 11    26    3
    THE GAMESTER'S COUNTER OR THE STATESMAN'S DROSS . . .  . . 317  3 DON JUAN 12     4    6
    FOR FAME IS DROSS OR WORSE--AND AT THE LAST . . . .  . . . 317  3 DON JUAN 12     4   V7
DROUTH
    LIKE FLOWERS WELL WATERED AFTER A LONG DROUTH--  . . .  . . 213  3 DON JUAN  9    61    4
DROUTHY
    AND CAMPBELL'S HIPPOCRENE IS SOMEWHAT DROUTHY  . . . .  . . 139  2 DON JUAN  1   205    6
    AND CAMPBELL'S SPRING SEEMS SOMEWHAT DRY AND DROUTHY .  . . 139  2 DON JUAN  1   205   V6
DROVE
    COUNT DAMAS DROVE THEM BACK INTO THE WATER  . . . . .  . .  82  3 DON JUAN  7    31    7
    AND DROVE THEM WITH THEIR BRUTAL YELLS TO SEEK  . . . .  . 158  3 DON JUAN  8    94    2
    PURSUED HIS PATH AND DROVE PAST SOME HOTELS  . . . .  . . . 282  3 DON JUAN 11    29    7
    I HATE IT AS I HATE A DROVE OF CATTLE  . . . . . . .  . . . 435  3 DON JUAN 14    58    5
DROWN
    EACH BROKE TO DROWN HER YET SHE COULD NOT DIE  . . . .  . . 361  2 DON JUAN  4    31    8
DROWN'D
    DON JUAN ALMOST FAMISH'D AND HALF DROWN'D  . . . . .  . . . 224  2 DON JUAN  2   129    4
    BECAUSE IF DROWN'D THEY CAN'T--IF SPARED THEY WON'T  . .  . 414  2 DON JUAN  5     6    8
```

212

```
                                                          PAGE VOL    CANTO STANZA LN
DROWNED
    AND THOSE WHO ARE NOT DROWNED AT LEAST MAY SLEEP  . . . .  229  2 DON JUAN   2    137   V8
    BAKED FRIED OR BURNT TURNED INSIDE-OUT OR DROWNED . . . .  201  3 DON JUAN   9     37    5
DROWNING
    THE DEATH-CRY DROWNING IN THE BATTLE'S ROAR . . . . . .    111  3 DON JUAN   7     87    8
DROWNINGS
    THUS DROWNINGS ARE MUCH TALK'D OF BY THE DIVERS   . . . .  172  2 DON JUAN   2     31    7
DROWSY
    A DROWSY FROWZY POEM CALL'D THE EXCURSION   . . . . . .    330  2 DON JUAN   3     94    7
    OF SUCH SENSATIONS IN THE DROWSY DREAR   . . . . . . .     220  3 DON JUAN   9     75   V7
    DECEMBER'S DROWSY DAY TO HIS DULL RACE-- . . . . . . .     426  3 DON JUAN  14     36    4
DRUGGISTS
    FOR INEZ CALL'D SOME DRUGGISTS AND PHYSICIANS . . . . .     35  2 DON JUAN   1     27    1
DRUID
    CROWN'D BY HIGH WOODLANDS WHERE THE DRUID OAK . . . . .    384  3 DON JUAN  13     56    2
DRUID'S
    THE DRUID'S GROVES ARE GONE--SO MUCH THE BETTER   . . . .  280  3 DON JUAN  11     25    1
DRUM
    A PIPE TOO AND A DRUM AND SHORTLY AFTER   . . . . . .      290  2 DON JUAN   3     28    7
    AND NOW NOUGHT LEFT HIM BUT THE MUFFLED DRUM   . . . .     430  2 DON JUAN   5     36    8
    AND NOW AS SILENT AS AN UNSTRUNG DRUM . . . . . . .        430  2 DON JUAN   5     36   V7
    THAT JUAN'S CHARIOT ROLLING LIKE A DRUM . . . . . . .      277  3 DON JUAN  11     20    5
DRUMS
    THE PRINCE'S TYRANT--TILL HE HEARS THE DRUMS   . . . .     151  2 DON JUAN   1   V 2   V8
    UNLESS TO MAKE THEIR KETTLE DRUMS A NEW SKIN   . . . .      75  3 DON JUAN   7     17    6
    BOMBS DRUMS GUNS BASTIONS BATTERIES BAYONETS BULLETS . .   106  3 DON JUAN   7     78    7
DRUNK
    THE SECOND DRUNK THE THIRD SO QUAINT AND MOUTHEY   . . .   139  2 DON JUAN   1    205    4
    HAVING GOT DRUNK EXCEEDINGLY TODAY . . . . . . .           156  2 DON JUAN   1   V 8    5
    THOUGHT IT WOULD BE BECOMING TO DIE DRUNK   . . . . .      174  2 DON JUAN   2     35    8
    LEFT HIM SO DRUNK HE JUMP'D INTO THE WAVE   . . . . .      186  2 DON JUAN   2     57    3
    MAN BEING REASONABLE MUST GET DRUNK   . . . . . .          250  2 DON JUAN   2    179    1
    BUT TO RETURN--GET VERY DRUNK AND WHEN   . . . . .         250  2 DON JUAN   2    179    7
    THE SERVANTS ALL WERE GETTING DRUNK OR IDLING   . . .      295  2 DON JUAN   3     39    3
    A GENIUS WHO HAS DRUNK HIMSELF TO DEATH   . . . . .        309  2 DON JUAN   3     66    2
    UNLESS HE'S DRUNK AND THEN NO DOUBT HE'S FREED . . . .     427  2 DON JUAN   5     31    5
    AND DEATH IS DRUNK WITH GORE THERE'S NOT A STREET . . .    152  3 DON JUAN   8     82    2
    WHICH MAKES ONE DRUNK AT ONCE WITHOUT THE BASE . . . .     216  3 DON JUAN   9     67    6
DRUNKEN
    A DRUNKEN GENTLEMAN OF FORTY'S SURE   . . . . . . .        333  3 DON JUAN  12     37   V5
DRUNKENNESS
    A SUDDEN FIT OF DRUNKENNESS OR SPLEEN . . . . . . .         98  2 DON JUAN   1    142    6
    A PLEASURE NAUGHT BUT DRUNKENNESS CAN BRING . . . .        251  2 DON JUAN   2    180   V3
DRY
    AND CAMPBELL'S SPRING SEEMS SOMEWHAT DRY AND DROUTHY . .   139  2 DON JUAN   1    205   V6
    THE BEACH WHICH LAY BEFORE HIM HIGH AND DRY . . . . .      212  2 DON JUAN   2    106    4
    MUCH LESS EXPERIENCE OF DRY LAND THAN OCEAN . . . . .      289  2 DON JUAN   3     26    2
    BUT NOW THEIR EYES AND ALSO LIPS WERE DRY   . . . . .      295  2 DON JUAN   3     38    5
    TALKING'S DRY WORK I HAVE NO TIME TO SPARE  . . . . .      297  2 DON JUAN   3     43    4
    THAT DRINKS AND STILL IS DRY   AT LAST THEY PERISHED--     166  3 DON JUAN   8    110    1
    AND DEVIATE INTO MATTERS RATHER DRY   . . . . . . .        203  3 DON JUAN   9     41    4
    ARE OR WOULD BE THOU SEA OF LIFE'S DRY LAND . . . . .      210  3 DON JUAN   9     56    8
    IN LOVE DRINKS ALL LIFE'S FOUNTAINS (SAVE TEARS) DRY . .   216  3 DON JUAN   9     67    8
    OF PEERESSES WHOSE FOLLIES HAD RUN DRY   . . . . . .       329  3 DON JUAN  12     29    8
    I'LL LEAVE A SINGLE READER'S EYELID DRY   . . . . .        355  3 DON JUAN  12     86    5
    WHEN ERE THE INK BE DRY THE SOUND GROWS COLD  . . . .      382  3 DON JUAN  13     51    5
    WHICH THE POOR THING AT TIMES ESSAYED TO DRY  . . . .      532  3 DON JUAN  16     65    3
DRYDEN
    THOU SHALT BELIEVE IN MILTON DRYDEN POPE  . . . . . .      139  2 DON JUAN   1    205    1
    OF POPE AND DRYDEN ARE WE COME TO THIS   . . . . . .       334  2 DON JUAN   3    100    2
DRYDEN'S
    AND DRYDEN'S LAY MADE HAUNTED GROUND TO ME  . . . . .      337  2 DON JUAN   3    105    7
DRYING
    THE DRYING UP A SINGLE TEAR HAS MORE   . . . . . .         113  3 DON JUAN   8      3    7
DRYNESS
    TO IRRIGATE THE DRYNESS OF DECLINE . . . . . . .           360  3 DON JUAN  13      5    6
DUAN
    TILL WHAT IS CALL'D IN OSSIAN THE FIFTH DUAN  . . . .      410  2 DON JUAN   4    117    8
DUB
    TO DUB THE LAST OF HONOURS IN DEGREES)   . . . . . .       341  2 DON JUAN   3    110    8
DUBIOUS
    A THOUSAND PERILS IN THIS DUBIOUS SHAPE   . . . . .        103  3 DON JUAN   7     72    4
    LO DUSKY MASSES STEAL IN DUBIOUS SIGHT   . . . . .         110  3 DON JUAN   7     86    3
    WHICH ROUSSEAU POINTS OUT TO THE DUBIOUS FAIR . . . .      139  3 DON JUAN   8     53    6
    THAT ALL IS DUBIOUS WHICH MAN MAY ATTAIN  . . . . .        191  3 DON JUAN   9     17    3
    ENDS IN A RUSTY CASQUE AND DUBIOUS BONE   . . . . .        261  3 DON JUAN  10     73    6
    TO ME SEEMS BUT A DUBIOUS KIND OF REED   . . . . .         324  3 DON JUAN  12     18    5
    WITHIN AND WHAT SEES'T THOU   A DUBIOUS SPARK  . . . .     348  3 DON JUAN  12     71    8
    THERE WAS DICK DUBIOUS THE METAPHYSICIAN . . . . . .       399  3 DON JUAN  13     87    1
DUBLIN
    WHERE ARE THE DUBLIN SHOUTS--AND LONDON HISSES  . . . .    308  3 DON JUAN  11     79    6
DUCHESS
    THE DUCHESS OF FITZ-FULKE THE COUNTESS CRABBEY  . . .      396  3 DON JUAN  13     79    3
    THE DUCHESS OF FITZ-FULKE WHO LOVED TRACASSERIE   . . .    428  3 DON JUAN  14     41    7
    BOTH TO THE DUCHESS AND DIPLOMATIST   . . . . . .          436  3 DON JUAN  14     60    2
    THE DUCHESS OF FITZ-FULKE PLAYED WITH HER VEIL . . . .     514  3 DON JUAN  16     31    5
DUCHESS'
    BEGAN TO THINK THE DUCHESS' CONDUCT FREE  . . . . .        430  3 DON JUAN  14     46    4
DUCK
    STILL SWAM--THOUGH NOT EXACTLY LIKE A DUCK  . . . . .      177  2 DON JUAN   2     40    8
```

		PAGE	VOL	CANTO	STANZA	LN

DUCKLING
   IS LIKE--A DUCKLING BY DAME PARTLETT REARED . . . . . . 564 3 DON JUAN 17 4 6
DUCKLINGS
   FROM TIGRESSES AND CUBS TO DUCKS AND DUCKLINGS . . . . . 488 2 DON JUAN 5 133 2
DUCKS
   FROM TIGRESSES AND CUBS TO DUCKS AND DUCKLINGS . . . . . 488 2 DON JUAN 5 133 2
DUDGEON
   LIE DOWN IN DUDGEON TO SIGH FOR THE LIGHT . . . . 18 3 DON JUAN 6 24 4
DUDU
   LOLAH KATINKA AND DUDU IN SHORT . . . . 26 3 DON JUAN 6 40 3
   A KIND OF SLEEPY VENUS SEEMED DUDU . . . . 27 3 DON JUAN 6 42 1
   DUDU SAID NOTHING BUT SAT DOWN BESIDE . . . . 28 3 DON JUAN 6 45 1
   AND I SHALL PLACE JUANNA WITH DUDU . . . . 30 3 DON JUAN 6 49 4
   WHAT SAY YOU CHILD--DUDU SAID NOTHING AS . . . . 30 3 DON JUAN 6 49 7
   OF DUDU THOUGH THEY HELD THEIR TONGUES FROM DEFERENCE . . 31 3 DON JUAN 6 50 8
   DUDU AS HAS BEEN SAID WAS A SWEET CREATURE . . . . . . 32 3 DON JUAN 6 52 1
   AND THUS MY NARRATIVE PROCEEDS--DUDU . . . . 34 3 DON JUAN 6 57 2
   DUDU WAS FOND OF KISSING--WHICH I'M SURE . . . . 35 3 DON JUAN 6 59 2
   BUT ALL THIS TIME HOW SLEPT OR DREAMED DUDU . . . . . . 41 3 DON JUAN 6 70 1
   THE CALM DUDU SO TURBULENTLY WAKE . . . . 42 3 DON JUAN 6 71 8
   DUDU HAD NEVER PASSED FOR WANTING SENSE . . . . 43 3 DON JUAN 6 74 6
   AND CHAFED AT POOR DUDU WHO ONLY SIGHED . . . . 45 3 DON JUAN 6 79 7
   WITH YOU DUDU A GOOD NIGHT'S REST HAVE KNOWN . . . . . 46 3 DON JUAN 6 81 6
   BUT POOR DUDU WITH LARGE DROPS IN HER OWN . . . . . . 47 3 DON JUAN 6 82 2
   AS THUS JUANNA SPOKE DUDU TURNED ROUND . . . . 48 3 DON JUAN 6 85 1
   THEN OUT IT CAME AT LENGTH THAT TO DUDU . . . . 57 3 DON JUAN 6 102 5
   AT WHICH DUDU LOOKED STRANGE AND JUAN SILLY . . . . . . 64 3 DON JUAN 6 118 7
DUDU'S
   BUT RATHER SKIM THE EARTH WHILE DUDU'S FORM . . . . . . 26 3 DON JUAN 6 41 5
   OF ALL SAVE DUDU'S DREAM WHICH WAS NO JOKE . . . . . . 58 3 DON JUAN 6 104 8
DUE
   INSTEAD OF HOARDING IT WITH DUE PRECISION . . . . 192 2 DON JUAN 2 68 8
   SAVE ZOE WHO ALTHOUGH WITH DUE PRECISION . . . . 252 2 DON JUAN 2 182 4
   THAN ADMIRATION DUE WHERE NATURE'S RICH . . . . 269 2 DON JUAN 2 211 3
   HIS VERSES RARELY WANTED THEIR DUE FEET-- . . . . 316 2 DON JUAN 3 78 5
   EVEN PETRARCH'S SELF IF JUDGED WITH DUE SEVERITY . . . . 411 2 DON JUAN 5 1 7
   PERHAPS EVEN MORE ATTENTION THAN IS DUE . . . . 431 2 DON JUAN 5 38 5
   AS WE MAY ASCERTAIN WITH DUE PRECISION . . . . 477 2 DON JUAN 5 115 7
   AWARE OF THEIR DUE ROYAL RIGHTS O'ER MEN . . . . 485 2 DON JUAN 5 128 8
   HENCE MY OLD COMET GIVE THE STARS DUE WARNING-- . . . . 494 2 DON JUAN 5 145 4
   LET THIS FIFTH CANTO MEET WITH DUE APPLAUSE . . . . . . 503 2 DON JUAN 5 159 5
   AND I OF YOUR YOUNG CHARGE WILL TAKE DUE CARE . . . . . 29 3 DON JUAN 6 47 6
   AND NOW HE ROSE AND AFTER DUE ABLUTIONS . . . . 52 3 DON JUAN 6 92 1
   AND HIS DISGUISE WITH DUE CONSIDERATION . . . . 55 3 DON JUAN 6 99 6
   AND AS HE FLOUNDERED ON WITHOUT DUE SPEED . . . . . . 56 3 DON JUAN 6 101 V6
   WERE BRISKLY FIRED AND ANSWERED IN DUE ORDER . . . . . 85 3 DON JUAN 7 38 8
   GLORY BEGAN TO DAWN WITH DUE SUBLIMITY . . . . 92 3 DON JUAN 7 51 6
   MAINTAINED WITH ALL THE DUE PREVARICATION . . . . . . 246 3 DON JUAN 10 45 4
   NO TITLE TO POINT OUT WITH DUE PRECISION . . . . 283 3 DON JUAN 11 32 3
   AND WAS RECEIVED WITH ALL THE DUE GRIMACE . . . . . . 285 3 DON JUAN 11 35 3
   MY TOPIC WITH OF COURSE THE DUE RESTRICTION . . . . . . 311 3 DON JUAN 11 88 2
   WHO HAVE A DUE RESPECT FOR THEIR OWN WISHES . . . . . 349 3 DON JUAN 12 73 4
   WHICH TAKES SO MUCH--TO GIVE THE DEVIL HIS DUE-- . . . . 351 3 DON JUAN 12 76 3
   WHICH JUDGED MANKIND AT THEIR DUE ESTIMATION . . . . . 372 3 DON JUAN 13 31 5
   AFTER DUE SEARCH YOUR FAITH TO ANY QUESTION . . . . . 411 3 DON JUAN 14 2 4
   CHASTE WERE HIS STEPS EACH KEPT WITHIN DUE BOUND . . . . 427 3 DON JUAN 14 39 1
   AT EIGHTEEN SHE WITH DUE DEMUR HAD GRANTED . . . . . . 434 3 DON JUAN 14 55 V5
   TO FIX THE DUE BOUNDS OF THIS DANGEROUS QUALITY . . . . 448 3 DON JUAN 14 89 8
   (KEEPING THE DUE PROPORTIONS STILL IN SIGHT) . . . . . 467 3 DON JUAN 15 25 6
DUET
   THE CONVERSAZIONE THE DUET . . . . 408 3 DON JUAN 13 107 2
DUETS
   OH THE LONG EVENINGS OF DUETS AND TRIOS . . . . 523 3 DON JUAN 16 45 1
DUG
   THINK IF THEN GEORGE THE FOURTH SHOULD BE DUG UP . . . 202 3 DON JUAN 9 39 1
DUKE
   THE DUKE OF ICHAR AND DON FERNAN NUNEZ . . . . 103 2 DON JUAN 1 150 2
   THE DUKE OF RICHELIEU HAD A BALL BETWEEN . . . . 117 3 DON JUAN 8 10 V2
   THE DUKE OF WELLINGTON HAD CEASED TO SHOW . . . . . . 137 3 DON JUAN 8 49 6
   YOU MY LORD DUKE IS FAR ABOVE REFLECTION . . . . 186 3 DON JUAN 9 7 2
   SHRINK TO A SATURN I HAVE SEEN A DUKE . . . . 309 3 DON JUAN 11 83 2
   THE DUKE OF D-- THE SHOOTING SEASON SPENDS . . . . . . 382 3 DON JUAN 13 52 5
   THERE WAS THE DUKE OF DASH WHO WAS A--DUKE . . . . . 398 3 DON JUAN 13 85 1
   THERE WAS THE DUKE OF DASH WHO WAS A--DUKE . . . . . 398 3 DON JUAN 13 85 1
   AYE EVERY INCH A DUKE THERE WERE TWELVE PEERS . . . . . 398 3 DON JUAN 13 85 2
   BUT WHAT IS ODD NONE EVER NAMED THE DUKE . . . . . . 430 3 DON JUAN 14 45 1
   THEN ASKED HER GRACE WHAT NEWS WERE OF THE DUKE OF LATE . 515 3 DON JUAN 16 34 5
DUKES
   WHICH GAVE HER DUKES THE GRACELESS NAME OF BIRON . . . 253 3 DON JUAN 10 58 4
   'MIDST ROYAL DUKES AND DAMES CONDEMNED TO CLIMB . . . 302 3 DON JUAN 11 68 7
   SOME WHO ONCE SET THEIR CAPS AT CAUTIOUS DUKES . . . . 308 3 DON JUAN 11 81 1
   DUKES--FOOLS BY BIRTH WHILE CLOGHER'S BISHOP SULLIES . . 314 3 DON JUAN 11 V 76 5
   PRESENT LORDS A B C--EARLS DUKES BY NAME . . . . . . 383 3 DON JUAN 13 54 2
   BUT WHETHER ENGLISH DUKES GREW RARE OF LATE . . . . . 474 3 DON JUAN 15 42 4
DULCI
   OMNE TULIT PUNCTUM QUAE MISCUIT UTILE DULCI . . . . . 396 3 DON JUAN 13 81 8
DULL
   WHEN OLD KING DAVID'S BLOOD GREW DULL IN MOTION . . . 113 2 DON JUAN 1 168 5
   ARE VARIOUS BUT THEY NONE OF THEM ARE DULL . . . . . 127 2 DON JUAN 1 189 6

214

DULL   (CONTINUED)

		PAGE	VOL	CANTO		STANZA	LN
AND THE BOY'S EYES WHICH THE DULL FILM HALF GLAZED		203	2	DON JUAN	2	89	5
LIKE CHARON'S BARK OF SPECTRES DULL AND PALE		209	2	DON JUAN	2	101	3
FROM THE DULL PALACE TO THE DIRTY HOVEL		263	2	DON JUAN	2	201	7
WITHOUT WHICH LIFE WOULD BE EXTREMELY DULL		269	2	DON JUAN	2	212	5
SOME DULL MS OBLIVION LONG HAS SANK		327	2	DON JUAN	3	89	5
A LONG AND SNAKE-LIKE LIFE OF DULL DECAY		348	2	DON JUAN	4	9	7
A BUSY CHARACTER IN THE DULL SCENE		352	2	DON JUAN	4	15	4
TO LOSE ITSELF WHEN THE OLD WORLD GROWS DULL		353	2	DON JUAN	4	17	3
RELIEVED HER THOUGHTS DULL SILENCE AND QUICK CHAT		378	2	DON JUAN	4	63	6
HER SWEET FACE INTO SHADOW DULL AND SLOW		381	2	DON JUAN	4	69	6
FROM HIS DULL CABIN FOUND HIMSELF A SLAVE		387	2	DON JUAN	4	79	2
THEY TOOK HER WORD THAT HIS DULL ROAR WAS MELLOW		391	2	DON JUAN	4	87	V6
YET I MUST OWN HE LOOKED A LITTLE DULL		415	2	DON JUAN	5	8	3
A DULL STORY'S DOUBLY GRIEVOUS WHEN 'TIS LONG		419	2	DON JUAN	5	16	V8
THEIR SPEED ABATED OR THEIR STRENGTH GREW DULL		59	3	DON JUAN	6	107	6
HARK THROUGH THE SILENCE OF THE COLD DULL NIGHT		110	3	DON JUAN	7	86	1
A GLANCE ON THE DULL CLOUDS (AS THICK AS STARCH		121	3	DON JUAN	8	21	6
OR DULL REPENTANCE HATH HAD DREARY LEISURE		168	3	DON JUAN	8	113	5
INTO A RUSSIAN COUPLET RATHER DULL		212	3	DON JUAN	9	60	3
TOO DULL EVEN FOR THE DULLEST OF EXCESSES--		267	3	DON JUAN	10	86	6
THAT NEUTRALISED DULL DORUS OF THE NINE		297	3	DON JUAN	11	58	4
AND AFTER THAT SERENE AND SOMEWHAT DULL		360	3	DON JUAN	13	4	1
A DULL AND DESOLATE APPENDAGE GAZE		373	3	DON JUAN	13	33	2
RIDICULOUS ENOUGH BUT ALSO DULL		402	3	DON JUAN	13	95	2
AND NOW BECAUSE I FEEL IT GROWING DULL		415	3	DON JUAN	14	10	8
A DULL AND FAMILY LIKENESS THROUGH ALL AGES		416	3	DON JUAN	14	15	7
ARE THERE OFT DULL AND DREARY AS A DUN--		423	3	DON JUAN	14	29	7
DECEMBER'S DROWSY DAY TO HIS DULL RACE--		426	3	DON JUAN	14	36	4
NOW GRAVE NOW GAY BUT NEVER DULL OR PERT		426	3	DON JUAN	14	37	5
QUITE FULL RIGHT DULL GUESTS HOT AND DISHES COLD		538	3	DON JUAN	16	78	6

DULLEST

		PAGE	VOL	CANTO		STANZA	LN
TOO DULL EVEN FOR THE DULLEST OF EXCESSES--		267	3	DON JUAN	10	86	6

DULLY

		PAGE	VOL	CANTO		STANZA	LN
BUT) OF FINE UNCLIPT GOLD WHERE DULLY RESTS		321	3	DON JUAN	12	12	5
DULLY PAST O'ER THE DINNER OF THE DAY		542	3	DON JUAN	16	87	1

DULY

		PAGE	VOL	CANTO		STANZA	LN
AND DULY SEATED ON THE IMMORTAL HILL		12	2	DON JUAN	D	6	8
WHO THANK'D ME DULY BY RETURN OF POST--		142	2	DON JUAN	1	210	2
THE ADULTERER'S ADVOCATE WHEN DULY FEE'D		151	2	DON JUAN	1	V 2	2
WAS STEERING DULY FOR THE PORT LEGHORN		169	2	DON JUAN	2	24	2
IN SICILY--ALL SINGERS DULY REAR'D		388	2	DON JUAN	4	80	5
WHILE TWO AND TWENTY CANNON DULY SET		72	3	DON JUAN	7	12	6
DULY ACCOMPANIED BY SHRIEKS AND GROANS		179	3	DON JUAN	8	135	2
AS MANY COVERS DULY DAILY LAID		381	3	DON JUAN	13	49	6
TILL DULY DISAPPOINTED OR DISMISSED		536	3	DON JUAN	16	75	3

DUMB

		PAGE	VOL	CANTO		STANZA	LN
THEIR LOOKS CAST DOWN THEIR GREETINGS ALMOST DUMB		60	2	DON JUAN	1	70	3
THEN HE HIMSELF SUNK DOWN ALL DUMB AND SHIVERING		204	2	DON JUAN	2	90	7
THE PEASANTS GAVE THE POOR DUMB THING A PITTANCE		285	2	DON JUAN	3	18	6
AND THAT HIS SORROW MAY NOT BE A DUMB ONE		288	2	DON JUAN	3	24	7
'TIS BUT THE LIVING WHO ARE DUMB		323	2	DON JUAN	3	L 8	6
THE TRUMP AND BUGLE TILL HE SPAKE WERE DUMB--		430	2	DON JUAN	5	36	7
THEY WERE MISSHAPEN PIGMIES DEAF AND DUMB--		462	2	DON JUAN	5	88	7
GREW DUMB FOR YOU MIGHT ALMOST HEAR A LINNET		142	3	DON JUAN	8	59	6
WHOSE CHARMS MADE ALL MEN SPEAK AND WOMEN DUMB		365	3	DON JUAN	13	13	6
NO BUT YOU HAVE HEARD--I UNDERSTAND--BE DUMB		498	3	DON JUAN	15	95	2
'TIS TIME TO STRIKE SUCH PUNY DOUBTERS DUMB AS		502	3	DON JUAN	16	4	7
SURPRISE HAS THIS EFFECT--TO MAKE ONE DUMB		557	3	DON JUAN	16	115	2

DUMBER

		PAGE	VOL	CANTO		STANZA	LN
AND WAIT UNTIL THE NIGHTINGALE GROWS DUMBER		380	3	DON JUAN	13	48	5

DUMPY

		PAGE	VOL	CANTO		STANZA	LN
HER STATURE TALL--I HATE A DUMPY WOMAN		55	2	DON JUAN	1	61	8

DUN

		PAGE	VOL	CANTO		STANZA	LN
BAPTIZED IN MOLTEN GOLD AND SWATHED IN DUN		205	2	DON JUAN	2	92	4
THE UMBRAGE OF THE WOOD SO COOL AND DUN		289	2	DON JUAN	3	27	5
THE SEVENTH WILL BRING BLUE DEVILS OR A DUN		243	3	DON JUAN	10	38	8
A HUGE DUN CUPOLA LIKE A FOOLSCAP CROWN		265	3	DON JUAN	10	82	7
ARE THERE OFT DULL AND DREARY AS A DUN--		423	3	DON JUAN	14	29	7

DUNCAN

		PAGE	VOL	CANTO		STANZA	LN
FORGETTING DUNCAN NELSON HOWE AND JERVIS		23	2	DON JUAN	1	4	8

DUNCE

		PAGE	VOL	CANTO		STANZA	LN
ALIKE MIGHT PUZZLE EITHER WIT OR DUNCE		43	3	DON JUAN	6	74	4
AND SO MAY EVERYONE EXCEPT A DUNCE		336	3	DON JUAN	12	44	3
COULD HARDLY BE UNITED BY A DUNCE		517	3	DON JUAN	16	39	8
A WISE MAN MORE THAN LAUGHTER FROM A DUNCE--		542	3	DON JUAN	16	88	5

DUNCES

		PAGE	VOL	CANTO		STANZA	LN
DUNCES WERE WHIPT OR SET UPON A STOOL		162	2	DON JUAN	2	10	6
LA BELLE ALLIANCE OF DUNCES DOWN AT ZERO		296	3	DON JUAN	11	56	3

DUNGEON

		PAGE	VOL	CANTO		STANZA	LN
THE WHIP THE RACK OR DUNGEON AT THE LEAST		296	2	DON JUAN	3	40	5

DUNGHILL'S

		PAGE	VOL	CANTO		STANZA	LN
LIKE KNOTS OF VIPERS ON A DUNGHILL'S SOIL		271	2	DON JUAN	2	215	5

DUNNEST

		PAGE	VOL	CANTO		STANZA	LN
OH DEATH THOU DUNNEST OF ALL DUNS THOU DAILY		459	3	DON JUAN	15	8	1

DUNS

		PAGE	VOL	CANTO		STANZA	LN
OF DOORS 'GAINST DUNS AND TO AN EARLY DINNER		282	3	DON JUAN	11	29	4
TITHES TAXES DUNS AND DOORS WITH DOUBLE KNOCKINGS		346	3	DON JUAN	12	67	8
OH DEATH THOU DUNNEST OF ALL DUNS THOU DAILY		459	3	DON JUAN	15	8	1

```
                                                      PAGE VOL     CANTO  STANZA LN
DUOMO
     (HIS MAGGIOR DUOMO A SMART SUBTLE GREEK . . . . . . .  259  3 DON JUAN 10     70   5
DURA
     OH DURA ILIA MESSORUM--OH . . . . . . . . . . . . .    190  3 DON JUAN  9     15   1
     EVEN NIMROD'S SELF MIGHT LEAVE THE PLAINS OF DURA .  . . . 395  3 DON JUAN 13   78   5
DURATION
     BY LENGTH I MEAN DURATION THEIRS ENDURED . . . . . .    254  2 DON JUAN  2    187   1
DURING
     SHE DID THIS DURING EVEN HER HUSBAND'S LIFE-- . . . . .   48  2 DON JUAN  1     48   7
     DURING THIS INQUISITION JULIA'S TONGUE . . . . . . .    100  2 DON JUAN  1    145   1
     LIKE HUMAN BEINGS DURING CIVIL WAR . . . . . . . .     178  2 DON JUAN  2     42   8
DURST
     THE BRITON MUST BE BOLD WHO REALLY DURST . . . . . .    136  3 DON JUAN  8     48   5
DUSK
     LOLAH WAS DUSK AS INDIA AND AS WARM . . . . . . .       26  3 DON JUAN  6     41   1
DUSKY
     ITS TWINKLE THROUGH THE LATTICE DUSKY QUITE . . . . .    18  3 DON JUAN  6     24   6
     LO DUSKY MASSES STEAL IN DUBIOUS SIGHT . . . . . .     110  3 DON JUAN  7     86   3
     DIRTY AND DUSKY BUT AS WIDE AS EYE . . . . . . .       265  3 DON JUAN 10     82   2
     ON OURS OR SPARS WITHIN SOME DUSKY CAVE . . . . . .    509  3 DON JUAN 16     19   5
     IN COWL AND BEADS AND DUSKY GARB APPEARED . . . . .    510  3 DON JUAN 16     21   2
     HE SWEEPS ALONG IN HIS DUSKY PALL . . . . . . .        520  3 DON JUAN 16   L  6   3
DUST
     TO HAVE WHEN THE ORIGINAL IS DUST . . . . . . .        146  2 DON JUAN  1    218   7
     SINCE NOT A PINCH OF DUST REMAINS OF CHEOPS . . . .    146  2 DON JUAN  1    219   8
     FIGHTING DEVOTION DUST--PERHAPS A NAME . . . . . .     159  2 DON JUAN  2      4   8
     WHEN DRIED TO SUMMER DUST TILL TAUGHT BY PAIN . . . .   201  2 DON JUAN  2     84   3
     TO HINT THAT FLESH IS FORM'D OF FIERY DUST . . . . .   269  2 DON JUAN  2    212   8
     WHICH RAIN DOWN ON THE DUST OF OUR YEARS . . . . .     270  2 DON JUAN  2    214  V8
     AND WHEN HIS BONES ARE DUST HIS GRAVE A BLANK . . . .   327  2 DON JUAN  3     89   1
     WHO WOULD AS 'TWERE IDENTIFY THEIR DUST . . . . .      399  2 DON JUAN  4    101   4
     PROTECTS HIS DUST BUT REVERENCE HERE IS PAID . . . .   400  2 DON JUAN  4    104   3
     IN ASPECT PLAINLY CLAD BESMEARED WITH DUST . . . .     104  3 DON JUAN  7     73   6
     THE GROAN THE ROLL IN DUST THE ALL-WHITE EYE . . . .   118  3 DON JUAN  8     13   5
     AND THE TWO ARE SO MIXED WITH HUMAN DUST . . . . .     221  3 DON JUAN  9     77   5
     OF BRICKS TO LET THE DUST IN AT YOUR EASE . . . . .    278  3 DON JUAN 11     21   5
     THE TURNPIKES GLOW WITH DUST AND ROTTEN ROW . . . .    378  3 DON JUAN 13     44   5
     WHO WHIRL THE DUST AS SIMOOMS WHIRL THE SAND . . . .   435  3 DON JUAN 14     58   6
     TO THESE  THEY ARE RAGS OR DUST  WHERE IS THE ARCH . . 485  3 DON JUAN 15     67   2
     NO DOUBT A CONSOLATION TO HIS DUST . . . . . . .       565  3 DON JUAN 17      8   8
DUTCH
     A MONKEY A DUTCH MASTIFF A MACKAW . . . . . . .        285  2 DON JUAN  3     18   1
     THE SPANISH AND THE FRENCH AS WELL AS DUTCH . . . .    184  3 DON JUAN  9      3   5
     OR DUTCH WITH THIRST--WHAT HO A FLASK OF RHENISH . .   392  3 DON JUAN 13     72   8
DUTCHESS
     OR DUTCHESS PRINCESS EMPRESS DEIGNS TO PROVE . . . .   216  3 DON JUAN  9     68   5
DUTCHMEN
     THAT WATER LAND OF DUTCHMEN AND OF DITCHES . . . . .   256  3 DON JUAN 10     63   2
DUTEOUS
     BETWEEN OUR DUTEOUS OFFSPRING--AND THE GOUT . . . .    376  3 DON JUAN 13     40  V8
DUTIES
     THE STRICTER DOUBTLESS GROW THE VESTAL DUTIES . . . .   35  3 DON JUAN  6     58   7
     WHERE THOUSAND LOVES AND TIES AND DUTIES GROW . . .    174  3 DON JUAN  8    124   6
     WHAT WERE THE ACTUAL AND OFFICIAL DUTIES . . . . .     208  3 DON JUAN  9     51   2
     THY CUSTOM-HOUSE WITH ALL ITS DELICATE DUTIES . . .    259  3 DON JUAN 10     69   3
     HIS DUTIES WARLIKE LOVING OR OFFICIAL . . . . . .      294  3 DON JUAN 11     51   5
DUTY
     SAVE THAT HER DUTY BOTH TO MAN AND GOD . . . . .        35  2 DON JUAN  1     27   7
     BUT THEN AS BARD MY DUTY TO MANKIND . . . . . .        155  2 DON JUAN  1   V  7   6
     BUT I MUST DO MY DUTY--HOW THOU HAST . . . . . .       368  2 DON JUAN  4     46   7
     THEIR DUTY WAS--FOR THEY WERE STRONG AND THOUGH . .    463  2 DON JUAN  5     89   1
     THOUGH AN UNUSUAL FIT OF LOVE OR DUTY . . . . . .       51  3 DON JUAN  6     91   7
     HIS TIME A CORPORAL'S DUTY TO FULFIL . . . . . .        93  3 DON JUAN  7     52   4
     AND SELF WOULD KNOW WHAT DUTY TO ATTEND . . . . .      100  3 DON JUAN  7     65   8
     WITH HER THEN AS IN HUMBLE DUTY BOUND . . . . . .      224  3 DON JUAN  9     85   1
     AND THOUGH THE DUTY WAXED A LITTLE HARD . . . . .      235  3 DON JUAN 10     22   2
     BEFORE MAY-DAY PERHAPS DESPITE HIS DUTY . . . . .      243  3 DON JUAN 10     37   7
     BUT ERE THEY COULD PERFORM THIS PIOUS DUTY . . . .     276  3 DON JUAN 11     16   1
     WHAT THOUGH SHE NOW AND THEN MAY SLIP FROM DUTY . .    459  3 DON JUAN 15      9   3
     FOR T'OTHER ONE WHO PROMISES MUCH DUTY . . . . .       471  3 DON JUAN 15     34   4
     AND SOCRATES THAT MODEL OF ALL DUTY . . . . . .        494  3 DON JUAN 15     85   7
     IN POLITICS MY DUTY IS TO SHOW JOHN . . . . . .        497  3 DON JUAN 15     92   5
DWARF
     AFAR A DWARF BUFFOON STOOD TELLING TALES . . . . .     293  2 DON JUAN  3     34   1
DWARFING
     BEYOND THE DWARFING CITY'S PALE ABORTIONS . . . . .    145  3 DON JUAN  8     66   2
DWARFS
     AND DWARFS AND BLACKS AND SUCH LIKE THINGS THAT GAIN . 310  2 DON JUAN  3     68   5
     DWARFS DANCING GIRLS BLACK EUNUCHS AND A POET . . . .  316  2 DON JUAN  3     78   2
     THE DWARFS AND DANCING GIRLS HAD ALL RETIRED . . . .   334  2 DON JUAN  3    101   2
     TWO LITTLE DWARFS THE LEAST YOU COULD SUPPOSE . . .    462  2 DON JUAN  5     87   3
DWELL
     THEIR VEIL AND PETTICOAT--ALAS TO DWELL . . . . .      160  2 DON JUAN  2      6   4
     HIM WHOM SHE DEEM'D A HABITANT WHERE DWELL . . . .     363  2 DON JUAN  4     36   3
     BY THE SEA SHORE WHEREON SHE LOVED TO DWELL . . . .    382  2 DON JUAN  4     71   8
     'TWOULD NOT BECOME MYSELF TO DWELL UPON . . . . .      392  2 DON JUAN  4     88   1
     TO QUIT HER GENTLE PARTNER AND TO DWELL . . . . .       48  3 DON JUAN  6     84   6
     UPON THE REST 'TIS NOT WORTH WHILE TO DWELL . . . .    184  3 DON JUAN  9      2   5
     TO THOSE WHO UPON LAND OR WATER DWELL . . . . . .      259  3 DON JUAN 10     69   6
```

216

	PAGE	VOL	CANTO	STANZA	LN
DWELL (CONTINUED)					
FOR BOTH COMMODITIES DWELL BY THE THAMES	293	3 DON JUAN	11	48	3
I WILL NOT DWELL UPON RAGOUTS OR ROASTS	404	3 DON JUAN	13	99	5
WITH SLOTH HATH FOUND IT DIFFICULT TO DWELL	445	3 DON JUAN	14	81	6
'TIS NOT MY PURPOSE ON HIS VIEWS TO DWELL	472	3 DON JUAN	15	38	5
HIS TALENT I WILL NOT DENY NOR DWELL	473	3 DON JUAN	15	38	V5
WHERE ALL THE DWELLERS OF THE EARTH MUST DWELL	502	3 DON JUAN	16	4	6
DWELLERS					
WHERE ALL THE DWELLERS OF THE EARTH MUST DWELL	502	3 DON JUAN	16	4	6
DWELLING					
FORMED LIKE AN AMPHITHEATRE EACH DWELLING	78	3 DON JUAN	7	23	7
DWELLINGS					
ITS DWELLINGS DOWN ITS TENANTS PAST AWAY	383	2 DON JUAN	4	72	2
DWELLS					
FEARLESS--BECAUSE NO FEELING DWELLS IN ICE	18	2 DON JUAN	D	15	7
THE ONLY HOPE OF COURAGE DWELLS	325	2 DON JUAN	3	L 14	4
THERE MANY AN ENVOY EITHER DWELT OR DWELLS	283	3 DON JUAN	11	31	5
DWELT					
WITHOUT A WELCOME THERE HE LONG HAD DWELT	302	2 DON JUAN	3	52	4
AS ONE WHO NE'ER HAD DWELT AMONG THE SICK	380	2 DON JUAN	4	67	3
VALOUR WAS HIS AND BEAUTY DWELT WITH HER	383	2 DON JUAN	4	73	4
THERE MANY AN ENVOY EITHER DWELT OR DWELLS	283	3 DON JUAN	11	31	5
DWINDLE					
THE DYING EMBERS DWINDLE IN THE GRATE--	499	3 DON JUAN	15	97	7
DWINDLED					
AS AN OLD TEMPLE DWINDLED TO A COLUMN	358	3 DON JUAN	13	1	8
D'YE					
IN HEAVEN'S NAME DON ALFONSO WHAT D'YE MEAN	98	2 DON JUAN	1	142	2
WHO IS THE MAN YOU SEARCH FOR HOW D'YE CALL	105	2 DON JUAN	1	154	4
DYE					
IN GROVELING ON TO POWER SUCH STAINS NOW DYE IT	154	2 DON JUAN	1	V 5	6
HER BROW WAS WHITE AND LOW HER CHEEK'S PURE DYE	218	2 DON JUAN	2	118	1
SO MUCH THE PRESENT DYE SHE WAS REMOTE	524	3 DON JUAN	16	47	6
DYED					
HAD DYED IT WITH THE HEADLONG BLOOD WHOSE RACE	231	2 DON JUAN	2	141	3
THE HENNA SHOULD BE DEEPLY DYED TO MAKE	314	2 DON JUAN	3	76	1
DYED PURPLE NONE AT PRESENT CAN TELL HOW	505	3 DON JUAN	16	10	6
DYEING					
I THOUGHT OF DYEING IT THE OTHER DAY	143	2 DON JUAN	1	213	V3
DYER					
I SHOULD BUT BRING DISGRACE UPON THE DYER	489	2 DON JUAN	5	134	4
DYERS					
AND TAKE ALL COLOURS--LIKE THE HANDS OF DYERS	326	2 DON JUAN	3	87	8
DYES					
OF ARMS (IN THE EAST ALL ARM)--AND VARIOUS DYES	289	2 DON JUAN	3	27	7
DYES WITH HIS MORNING LIGHT--AND WOULD CONCEAL	313	2 DON JUAN	3	73	3
A VEIN HAD BURST AND HER SWEET LIPS' PURE DYES	376	2 DON JUAN	4	59	1
OR SAID HER CHEEKS ASSUMED THE DEEPEST DYES	489	2 DON JUAN	5	134	3
WHILE THE MILD EMERALD'S BEAM SHADES DOWN THE DYES	319	3 DON JUAN	12	8	7
DYING					
DYING INTESTATE JUAN WAS SOLE HEIR	42	2 DON JUAN	1	37	1
IF DEAD HIS MODE OF DYING MIGHT BE PUT	112	2 DON JUAN	1	166	V7
TWO THINGS FOR DYING PEOPLE QUITE BEWILDERING	179	2 DON JUAN	2	43	8
MEN EVEN WHEN DYING DISLIKE INANITION	180	2 DON JUAN	2	46	5
INTO HIS DYING CHILD'S MOUTH--BUT IN VAIN	203	2 DON JUAN	2	89	8
A STRANGER DYING WITH SO WHITE A SKIN	224	2 DON JUAN	2	129	8
AND THUS LIKE TO AN ANGEL O'ER THE DYING	233	2 DON JUAN	2	144	1
A PURPLE HECTIC PLAY'D LIKE DYING DAY	234	2 DON JUAN	2	147	2
WHO DYING ON THE COAST OF ITHACA	285	2 DON JUAN	3	18	5
PERHAPS THAN EVEN THE MENTAL PANGS OF DYING	301	2 DON JUAN	3	51	4
OR THE FAINT DYING DAY-HYMN STOLE ALOFT	335	2 DON JUAN	3	102	6
SEEMING TO WEEP THE DYING DAY'S DECAY	338	2 DON JUAN	3	108	6
I CRIED UPON MY FIRST WIFE'S DYING DAY	420	2 DON JUAN	5	19	7
BUT ALL HIS GREAT PREPARATIVES FOR DYING	492	2 DON JUAN	5	141	7
AMIDST SOME GROANING THOUSANDS DYING NEAR--	117	3 DON JUAN	8	11	3
OF DEAD AND DYING THOUSANDS--SOMETIMES GAINING	121	3 DON JUAN	8	20	2
AND SO WHEN ALL HIS CORPS WERE DEAD OR DYING	131	3 DON JUAN	8	36	1
A DYING MOSLEM WHO HAD FELT THE FOOT	153	3 DON JUAN	8	84	1
THE DYING MAN CRIED HOLD I'VE GOT MY GRUEL	276	3 DON JUAN	11	16	2
THOSE BRIGHT MOTHS FLUTTERING ROUND A DYING FLAME	349	3 DON JUAN	12	72	4
IS MUSICAL--A DYING ACCENT DRIVEN	388	3 DON JUAN	13	63	4
THE DYING EMBERS DWINDLE IN THE GRATE--	499	3 DON JUAN	15	97	7
THAN DYING TAPERS--AND THE PEEPING MOON	504	3 DON JUAN	16	8	8
DYKE					
HE THERE BUILDS UP A FORMIDABLE DYKE	330	2 DON JUAN	3	95	1
EAGER					
AS EAGER TO ANTICIPATE THEIR GRAVE	184	2 DON JUAN	2	52	4
WITH EAGER EYES AND LIGHT BUT HURRIED TREAD	42	3 DON JUAN	6	72	3
HOW EAGER ALL THE EARTH IS FOR THE BLOW	258	3 DON JUAN	10	67	3
FULL MANY AN EAGER GENTLEMAN OFT RUES	304	3 DON JUAN	11	71	5
THUS ON THE MOB ALL STATESMEN ARE AS EAGER	537	3 DON JUAN	16	76	7
BUT JUAN EAGER NOW THE TRUTH TO PIERCE	559	3 DON JUAN	16	119	3
EAGERLY					
AND YET THE REST RUSHED EAGERLY--NO WONDER	163	3 DON JUAN	8	103	5
EAGERNESS					
AND WATCH'D WITH EAGERNESS EACH THROB THAT DREW	216	2 DON JUAN	2	114	7
EAGLE					
THE EAGLE SOARS ALONE THE GULL AND CROW	358	2 DON JUAN	4	28	7
THE PRISONED EAGLE WILL NOT PAIR NOR I	484	2 DON JUAN	5	126	7
THE EARTH AS SCARCE THE EAGLE IN THE BROAD	263	3 DON JUAN	10	78	3

217

		PAGE	VOL	CANTO	STANZA	LN

EAGLE'S
AND DROOPING LIKE AN EAGLE'S WITH CLIPT PINION . . . . . 246 3 DON JUAN 10 44 6
EAR
FROM DELICACY TO DON JUAN'S EAR . . . . 118 2 DON JUAN 1 176 7
LESS FOR THE COMPREHENSION THAN THE EAR . . . . . . 152 2 DON JUAN 1 V 3 6
BEING NO GRECIAN BUT HE HAD AN EAR . . . . 236 2 DON JUAN 2 151 2
MEANTIME APOLLO PLUCKS ME BY THE EAR . . . . 347 2 DON JUAN 4 7 7
IT HAS A STRANGE QUICK JAR UPON THE EAR . . . . . . 366 2 DON JUAN 4 41 1
THE EAR BECOMES MORE IRISH AND LESS NICE . . . . . 366 2 DON JUAN 4 41 8
THAT BROKE FOR NOTHING ON THEIR SLEEPING EAR . . . . 45 3 DON JUAN 6 79 4
THINE EAR IF IT SHOULD REACH--AND NOW RHYMES WANDER . . 52 3 DON JUAN 6 93 3
THINE EAR IMPERIAL AND JUST NOW RHYMES WANDER . . . . 52 3 DON JUAN 6 93 V3
HE SCRATCHED HIS EAR THE INFALLIBLE RESOURCE . . . . 56 3 DON JUAN 6 100 7
IT SEEMS HAS GOT AN EAR AS WELL AS TRUMPET . . . . . 74 3 DON JUAN 7 15 8
HOW SWEETLY ON THE EAR SUCH ECHOES SOUND . . . . . 114 3 DON JUAN 8 5 5
THE EAR FAR MORE THAN THUNDER FOR HEAVEN'S FLASHES . . 115 3 DON JUAN 8 6 7
AND SHRIEK FOR WATER INTO A DEAF EAR-- . . . . . . 117 3 DON JUAN 8 11 5
UPON THE EAR AND SOUNDS OF HORROR CHIME . . . . . . 141 3 DON JUAN 8 58 6
AND YET WAS WHAT YOU ARE FROM EAR TO EAR . . . . . . 188 3 DON JUAN 9 12 2
AND YET WAS WHAT YOU ARE FROM EAR TO EAR . . . . . . 188 3 DON JUAN 9 12 2
TO BALAAM AND FROM TONGUE TO EAR O'ERFLOWS . . . . . 328 3 DON JUAN 12 26 6
THAT--BUT MY CHASTER EAR WILL NOT RECEIVE . . . . . 336 3 DON JUAN 12 43 4
AND HAVE OR HAD AN EAR THAT SERVED ME PRETTILY)-- . . 350 3 DON JUAN 12 75 8
AND THEN HE HAD AN EAR FOR MUSIC'S SOUND . . . . . . 427 3 DON JUAN 14 39 5
OF DEEDS AND DAYS WHEN THEY HAD FILL'D THE EAR . . . 476 3 DON JUAN 15 46 5
CAME OVER JUAN'S EAR WHICH THROBBED ALAS . . . . . 556 3 DON JUAN 16 114 5
EARL
BECAUSE THE NEIGHBOURING SCOTCH EARL OF GIFTGABBIT . . 534 3 DON JUAN 16 70 4
EARLIER
TILL THEY WERE EXILED FROM THEIR EARLIER BOWERS . . . 30 2 DON JUAN 1 18 4
WHO IN THE EARLIER AGES RAISED A BUSTLE . . . . . . 44 2 DON JUAN 1 41 3
A LITTLE EARLIER THAN THE WANING MOON . . . . 409 3 DON JUAN 13 111 4
WHICH CHARM MOST PEOPLE IN THEIR EARLIER DAY . . . . 479 3 DON JUAN 15 53 3
EARLIEST
THE LISP OF CHILDREN AND THEIR EARLIEST WORDS . . . . 88 2 DON JUAN 1 123 8
THIS WAS DON JUAN'S EARLIEST SCRAPE BUT WHETHER . . . 135 2 DON JUAN 1 199 1
LIKE TITUS' YOUTH AND CAESAR'S EARLIEST ACTS . . . . 329 2 DON JUAN 3 92 3
LAY AT HER HEART WHOSE EARLIEST BEAT STILL TRUE . . . 378 2 DON JUAN 4 62 6
DON JUAN NOW SAW ALBION'S EARLIEST BEAUTIES-- . . . . 259 3 DON JUAN 10 69 1
THAT POETS WERE SO FROM THEIR EARLIEST DATE . . . . 393 3 DON JUAN 13 74 5
THE SEA-COAL FIRES THE EARLIEST OF THE YEAR . . . . 395 3 DON JUAN 13 77 6
THE EARLIEST KNOWLEDGE FROM THE TREE SO KNOWING . . . 444 3 DON JUAN 14 78 3
EARLIEST TO RISE AND LAST TO QUIT THE SEARCH . . . . 539 3 DON JUAN 16 80 4
EARLS
PRESENT LORDS A B C--EARLS DUKES BY NAME . . . . . 383 3 DON JUAN 13 54 2
TO SILKEN ROWS OF GAY AND GARTER'D EARLS . . . . . 390 3 DON JUAN 13 68 2
EARLY
FOR EARLY STOMACHS TO PROVE WHOLESOME FOOD . . . . . 45 2 DON JUAN 1 43 2
AT LEAST 'TWAS RATHER EARLY TO BEGIN . . . . 113 2 DON JUAN 1 167 4
BUT HE DIED EARLY AND WHEN HE WAS GONE . . . . . . 202 2 DON JUAN 2 87 4
AND WOKE HER MAID SO EARLY THAT SHE GRUMBLED . . . . 229 2 DON JUAN 2 138 5
OR BY ONE'S EARLY VALET'S CURSED KNOCK . . . . . . 237 2 DON JUAN 2 152 5
AND EVERY DAY BY DAY-BREAK--RATHER EARLY . . . . . 245 2 DON JUAN 2 168 1
SUCH KISSES AS BELONG TO EARLY DAYS . . . . 254 2 DON JUAN 2 186 4
THE OLD ARCHER'S SHAFTS PERHAPS THE EARLY GRAVE . . . 350 2 DON JUAN 4 12 7
FOR NO ONE SAVE IN VERY EARLY YOUTH . . . . 14 3 DON JUAN 6 16 3
PARTAKE OF MINE BUT BY TO-MORROW EARLY . . . . . . 29 3 DON JUAN 6 46 7
IN EARLY YOUTH TO TURN A LADY'S MAID-- . . . . . . 37 3 DON JUAN 6 62 4
AND NOT BE DAZZLED BY ITS EARLY GLARE . . . . . . 224 3 DON JUAN 9 84 V6
THEY CANNOT QUENCH YOUNG FEELINGS FRESH AND EARLY . . 234 3 DON JUAN 10 19 6
OF DOORS 'GAINST DUNS AND TO AN EARLY DINNER . . . . 282 3 DON JUAN 11 29 4
OF EARLY LIFE BUT THIS IS A NEW LAND . . . . 326 3 DON JUAN 12 23 7
(SUCH EARLY TRAVELLER IS THE TRUTH THOU LEARNEST)-- . . 345 3 DON JUAN 12 64 6
THEY SEPARATED AT AN EARLY HOUR . . . . 409 3 DON JUAN 13 111 1
BUT JUAN HAD BEEN EARLY TAUGHT TO RANGE . . . . . . 424 3 DON JUAN 14 32 5
TO EARLY RISERS AFTER A LONG CHASE . . . . 426 3 DON JUAN 14 36 2
EARLY IN YEARS AND YET MORE INFANTINE . . . . . . 476 3 DON JUAN 15 45 1
SOME WONDERING 'TWAS SO EARLY SOME SO LATE . . . . . 527 3 DON JUAN 16 55 4
EARN
HE MUST HIS LAURELS SEPARATELY EARN . . . . 120 3 DON JUAN 8 17 3
WERE HARDLY RUDE ENOUGH TO EARN THEIR PAY . . . . . 287 3 DON JUAN 11 40 8
EARN'D
THERE WAS NO DOUBT HE EARN'D HIS LAUREATE PENSION . . 317 2 DON JUAN 3 80 8
EARNED
AND TO SAY TRUTH IT HAD BEEN FAIRLY EARNED . . . . 287 3 DON JUAN 11 39 8
AND NOT A JOKE HE CUT BUT EARNED ITS PRAISE . . . . 540 3 DON JUAN 16 82 3
EARNEST
WILL KISS NOT IN SAD METAPHOR--BUT EARNEST-- . . . . 286 3 DON JUAN 11 38 V7
A WIFE MAKES OR TAKES LOVE IN UPRIGHT EARNEST . . . 345 3 DON JUAN 12 64 4
IN RIGHT GOOD EARNEST--ALSO AN APPEAL . . . . . . 357 3 DON JUAN 12 V 18 7
EARNESTNESS
HER EARNESTNESS WOULD NE'ER HAVE MADE AN END . . . . 241 2 DON JUAN 2 161 4
EARS
THEY FEAR'D NO EYES NOR EARS ON THAT LONE BEACH . . . 256 2 DON JUAN 2 189 1
A MELODY WHICH MADE HIM DOUBT HIS EARS . . . . . . 290 2 DON JUAN 3 28 5
RANG IN HER SAD EARS LIKE A MERMAID'S SONG . . . . 362 2 DON JUAN 4 34 7
THE BLOOD GUSHED FROM HER LIPS AND EARS AND EYES . . 376 2 DON JUAN 4 59 V1
ABOUT HIS EARS AND NATHLESS WOULD NOT BEND . . . . 471 2 DON JUAN 5 104 2
OR WONDERED AT HER EARS WITHOUT A RING . . . . . . 23 3 DON JUAN 6 35 4

EARS   (CONTINUED)

	PAGE	VOL		CANTO	STANZA	LN
HER CHEEK TURNED ASHES EARS RUNG BRAIN WHIRLED ROUND	58	3	DON JUAN	6	105	5
THE WOMEN WITH THEIR HAIR ABOUT THEIR EARS	102	3	DON JUAN	7	69	3
ALL EARS THOUGH LONG ALL AGES THOUGH SO SHORT	106	3	DON JUAN	7	79	2
LIKE THE DEATH-WATCH WITHIN OUR EARS THE ILLS	117	3	DON JUAN	8	12	6
BECAUSE IT MIGHT NOT SOLACE EARS POLITE	158	3	DON JUAN	8	93	6
AND ALL LIPS WERE APPLIED UNTO ALL EARS	221	3	DON JUAN	9	78	2
AND INTELLECT THAT NEITHER EYES NOR EARS	398	3	DON JUAN	13	85	4
THE SCANTY BUT RIGHT-WELL THRASHED EARS OF TRUTH	403	3	DON JUAN	13	96	2
TO INTRODUCE A BON MOT HEAD AND EARS	408	3	DON JUAN	13	109	4
I HAVE BROUGHT THIS WORLD ABOUT MY EARS AND EKE	414	3	DON JUAN	14	10	1
THERE'S MUSIC IN ALL THINGS IF MEN HAD EARS	458	3	DON JUAN	15	5	7
I SOMETIMES ALMOST THINK THAT EYES HAVE EARS	489	3	DON JUAN	15	76	1
TO SOOTHE OUR EARS LEST ITALY SHOULD FAIL	523	3	DON JUAN	16	45	8
NO LONGER READY EARS AND SHORT-HAND PENS	540	3	DON JUAN	16	83	4

EARSHOT

	PAGE	VOL		CANTO	STANZA	LN
THIS MUCH IS SURE THAT OUT OF EARSHOT THINGS	489	3	DON JUAN	15	76	2

EARTH

	PAGE	VOL		CANTO	STANZA	LN
UPON THE MOST UNQUIET IMP ON EARTH	34	2	DON JUAN	1	25	4
LET'S OWN SINCE IT CAN DO NO GOOD ON EARTH	41	2	DON JUAN	1	36	3
HE THOUGHT ABOUT HIMSELF AND THE WHOLE EARTH	71	2	DON JUAN	1	92	1
IN BACCHANAL PROFUSION REEL TO EARTH	88	2	DON JUAN	1	124	2
HAD SIGNS OR FOOTMARKS BUT THE EARTH SAID NOUGHT	100	2	DON JUAN	1	144	4
FOR ME ON EARTH EXCEPT SOME YEARS TO HIDE	132	2	DON JUAN	1	195	3
TO WEAN HIM FROM THE WICKEDNESS OF EARTH	161	2	DON JUAN	2	8	7
SOONER SHALL EARTH RESOLVE ITSELF TO SEA	166	2	DON JUAN	2	19	4
SOONER SHALL HEAVEN KISS EARTH--(HERE HE FELL SICKER)	167	2	DON JUAN	2	20	1
FOR WHICH THEIR MOUTHS GAPED LIKE THE CRACKS OF EARTH	201	2	DON JUAN	2	84	2
TO WHAT PART OF THE EARTH THEY HAD BEEN TOST	209	2	DON JUAN	2	100	5
HE KNEW NOT FOR THE EARTH WAS GONE FOR HIM	214	2	DON JUAN	2	111	2
WHICH THEN SEEMS AS IF THE WHOLE EARTH IT BOUNDED	252	2	DON JUAN	2	183	3
EACH WAS AN ANGEL AND EARTH PARADISE	265	2	DON JUAN	2	204	8
EARTH RENDER BACK FROM OUT THY BREAST	323	2	DON JUAN	3	L 7	3
AVE MARIA O'ER THE EARTH AND SEA	334	2	DON JUAN	3	101	7
SINK O'ER THE EARTH SO BEAUTIFUL AND SOFT	335	2	DON JUAN	3	102	4
EARTH AIR STARS--ALL THAT SPRINGS FROM THE GREAT WHOLE	336	2	DON JUAN	3	104	7
BUT I'M DIGRESSING WHAT ON EARTH HAD NERO	341	2	DON JUAN	3	110	1
THE HEAVENS AND EARTH AND AIR SEEM'D MADE FOR THEM	351	2	DON JUAN	4	13	2
GUSH FROM THE EARTH UNTIL THE LAND RUNS O'ER	373	2	DON JUAN	4	55	3
AFRIC IS ALL THE SUN'S AND AS HER EARTH	374	2	DON JUAN	4	56	1
TERROR TO EARTH AND TEMPEST TO THE AIR	375	2	DON JUAN	4	57	4
SHE HAD SO MUCH EARTH COULD NOT CLAIM THE WHOLE	377	2	DON JUAN	4	60	8
BY AGE IN EARTH HER DAYS AND PLEASURES WERE	382	2	DON JUAN	4	71	5
WILL SINK WHERE LIE THE SONGS AND WARS OF EARTH	400	2	DON JUAN	4	104	7
INSTINCT OF GORE AND GLORY EARTH HAS KNOWN	401	2	DON JUAN	4	105	7
AND AIR--EARTH--WATER--FIRE LIVE--AND WE DEAD	432	2	DON JUAN	5	39	6
HER BLOOD WAS HIGH HER BEAUTY SCARCE OF EARTH	475	2	DON JUAN	5	112	5
EARTH BEING ONLY MADE FOR QUEENS AND KINGS	485	2	DON JUAN	5	128	4
('TWAS THUS HE SPAKE) AND EMPRESS OF THE EARTH	494	2	DON JUAN	5	144	2
WAS ALSO CERTAIN THAT THE EARTH WAS SQUARE	497	2	DON JUAN	5	150	2
OF EARTH WAS WRINKLED BY THE SINS AND TEARS	9	3	DON JUAN	6	6	7
BUT RATHER SKIM THE EARTH WHILE DUDU'S FORM	26	3	DON JUAN	6	41	5
BUT SHE WAS A SOFT LANDSCAPE OF MILD EARTH	32	3	DON JUAN	6	53	1
CHILL AND CHAINED TO COLD EARTH WE LIFT ON HIGH	66	3	DON JUAN	7	1	5
THEN ONE VAST FIRE AIR EARTH AND STREAM EMBRACED	115	3	DON JUAN	8	7	5
HE RUSHED WHILE EARTH AND AIR WERE SADLY SHAKEN	129	3	DON JUAN	8	33	7
ALONE CAN SAVE THE EARTH FROM HELL'S POLLUTION	138	3	DON JUAN	8	51	8
ON EARTH IN PARADISE AND WHEN ONCE SEEN	167	3	DON JUAN	8	111	6
THE EARTH WHICH HE BECAME LIKE A FELLED TREE	169	3	DON JUAN	8	116	6
A MODE OF PROVING THAT THE EARTH TURNED ROUND	225	3	DON JUAN	10	1	5
US LAND ON EARTH WILL DO NO LESS IN HEAVEN	242	3	DON JUAN	10	36	V8
I HAVE NO GREAT CAUSE TO LOVE THAT SPOT OF EARTH	257	3	DON JUAN	10	66	1
HOW EAGER ALL THE EARTH IS FOR THE BLOW	258	3	DON JUAN	10	67	3
FROM THE ENJOYMENT OF THE EARTH AND AIR	258	3	DON JUAN	10	68	7
THE EARTH AS SCARCE THE EAGLE IN THE BROAD	263	3	DON JUAN	10	78	3
WHO BUTCHERED HALF THE EARTH AND BULLIED T'OTHER	265	3	DON JUAN	10	81	8
HE TOOK TO REGULARLY PEOPLING EARTH	312	3	DON JUAN	11	89	5
THE TWICE TWO THOUSAND FOR WHOM EARTH WAS MADE	381	3	DON JUAN	13	49	2
SHE MADE THE EARTH BELOW SEEM HOLY GROUND	387	3	DON JUAN	13	61	5
THE EARTH HAS NOTHING LIKE A SHE EPISTLE	407	3	DON JUAN	13	105	2
BUT SINCE BENEATH IT UPON EARTH WE ARE BROUGHT	421	3	DON JUAN	14	26	4
THEY ARE SO MUCH INTERTWISTED WITH THE EARTH	436	3	DON JUAN	14	59	2
AND SET THE OTHER HALF OF EARTH TO RIGHTS	445	3	DON JUAN	14	82	7
LIKE ARCHIMEDES I LEAVE EARTH AS 'TWAS	446	3	DON JUAN	14	84	8
NO FRIEND LIKE TO A WOMAN EARTH DISCOVERS	451	3	DON JUAN	14	93	7
THEIR EARTH IS BUT AN ECHO OF THE SPHERES	458	3	DON JUAN	15	5	8
WHERE ALL THE DWELLERS OF THE EARTH MUST DWELL	502	3	DON JUAN	16	4	6
OR EARTH BENEATH OR HEAVEN OR T'OTHER PLACE	510	3	DON JUAN	16	23	2
HOW EARTH COULD ROUND THE SOLAR ORBIT RUN	565	3	DON JUAN	17	8	3

EARTHLY

	PAGE	VOL		CANTO	STANZA	LN
IN VIRTUES NOTHING EARTHLY COULD SURPASS HER	30	2	DON JUAN	1	17	7
BUT AN UNHALLOW'D EARTHLY SOUND OF FIDDLING	290	2	DON JUAN	3	28	4
ALL EARTHLY GOODS SAVE TITHES) AND BADE THEM PUSH ON	99	3	DON JUAN	7	64	6
AN EARTHLY PARADISE OF OR MOLU	302	3	DON JUAN	11	67	8

EARTHQUAKE'S

	PAGE	VOL		CANTO	STANZA	LN
ITS INNER CRASH IS LIKE AN EARTHQUAKE'S RUIN	446	3	DON JUAN	14	85	8

EARTHQUAKES

	PAGE	VOL		CANTO	STANZA	LN
AND THEN HE THOUGHT OF EARTHQUAKES AND OF WARS	71	2	DON JUAN	1	92	4
LIKE EARTHQUAKES FROM THE HIDDEN FIRE CALL'D CENTRAL	271	2	DON JUAN	2	215	8

EARTH'S
         PRESERVE YOUR STATE--THOUGH EVE EARTH'S MOTHER FELL . . . 460 2 DON JUAN 5   84   V6
         TO RISE AGAINST EARTH'S TYRANTS   NEVER LET IT . . . . 179 3 DON JUAN 8   135   5
         MEN ARE BUT MAGGOTS OF SOME HUGE EARTH'S BURIAL) . . . 202 3 DON JUAN 9   39   8
         THOU RIDDLE WITHOUT WHOM EARTH'S ASHES END . . . . . 210 3 DON JUAN 9   56   V7
         DARK RIDDLE OF ALL LIFE EARTH'S LIFELESS END . . . . 210 3 DON JUAN 9   56   V7
EAR-TRUMPET
         OR THE EAR-TRUMPET OF MY GOOD OLD AUNT . . . . . . 241 3 DON JUAN 10   34   5
EASE
         WHILE SEATED AFTER DINNER AT HIS EASE . . . . 24 2 DON JUAN 1   6   5
         SHE SAW THAT JUAN WAS NOT AT HIS EASE . . . . 73 2 DON JUAN 1   97   3
         AND MADE THEM BALE WITHOUT A MOMENT'S EASE . . . . . 188 2 DON JUAN 2   60   6
         AND THERE HE LIVED EXCEEDINGLY AT EASE . . . . . . 223 2 DON JUAN 2   127   4
         HIS COUCH AND THAT HE MIGHT BE MORE AT EASE . . . . . 226 2 DON JUAN 2   133   3
         HER TALE IS TOLD WITH SO MUCH SIMPLE EASE-- . . . . . 273 2 DON JUAN 2 V 2   6
         WITH EASE BUT WHERE I SOUGHT FOR ILION'S WALLS . . . . 386 2 DON JUAN 4   77   7
         EUROPE AND ASIA YOU BEING QUITE AT EASE . . . . . . 413 2 DON JUAN 5   5   6
         SO NOW ALL THINGS ARE DAMN'D ONE FEELS AT EASE . . . . 17 3 DON JUAN 6   23   1
         A SCHOONER OR--BUT IT IS TIME TO EASE . . . . 109 3 DON JUAN 7   85   5
         WHERE THERE WERE FEWER HOUSES AND MORE EASE . . . . . 144 3 DON JUAN 8   64   4
         OF BRICKS TO LET THE DUST IN AT YOUR EASE . . . . . 278 3 DON JUAN 11   21   5
         WARS REVELS LOVES--DO THESE BRING MEN MORE EASE . . . . 321 3 DON JUAN 12   11   5
         AND SUCH IS EUROPE'S FASHIONABLE EASE . . . . 373 3 DON JUAN 13   34   V8
         WITH MORE EASE TOO SHE'D TELL A DIFFERENT STORY . . . . 416 3 DON JUAN 14   13   8
         ESPECIALLY WHEN WE ARE ILL AT EASE . . . . 431 3 DON JUAN 14   48   2
         THE ART OF LIVING IN ALL CLIMES WITH EASE . . . . . 460 3 DON JUAN 15   11   8
         THE FAIR FITZ-FULKE SEEMED VERY MUCH AT EASE . . . . 548 3 DON JUAN 16   100   2
EASED
         EASED HER AT LAST (ALTHOUGH WE NEVER MEANT . . . . . 173 2 DON JUAN 2   32   6
EASIER
         THROUGH NEEDLES' EYES IT EASIER FOR THE CAMEL IS . . . 397 2 DON JUAN 4   97   7
         AND MARCH AWAY--'TWERE EASIER DONE THAN SAID . . . . 434 2 DON JUAN 5   43   8
         FAR EASIER THOUGH FOR THE GOOD TOWN OF MANCHESTER . . . 314 3 DON JUAN 11 V 75   3
         A WAVERING SPIRIT MAY BE EASIER WRECK'D . . . . . . 446 3 DON JUAN 14   85   5
         IT WAS NOT--BUT 'TIS EASIER FAR ALAS . . . . 479 3 DON JUAN 15   54   7
EASILY
         YOUNG SLENDER AND PACK'D EASILY HE LAY . . . . . . 112 2 DON JUAN 1   166   3
         IT MAY BE EASILY SUPPOSED WHILE THIS . . . . 173 2 DON JUAN 2   33   1
         THE CONSEQUENCE WAS EASILY FORESEEN-- . . . . 192 2 DON JUAN 2   69   1
         MY PEN AND EASILY FLEW IN A RAGE . . . . 397 2 DON JUAN 4   98   V6
         THEY ARE PUT ON AS EASILY AS A HAT . . . . 13 3 DON JUAN 6   14   4
         MORE EASILY THAN ANSWERED--THAT HE HAD TRIED . . . . . 56 3 DON JUAN 6   100   3
         THAT THEY AS EASILY MIGHT DO THE YOUNGSTER . . . . . 285 3 DON JUAN 11   35   7
         WHERE'S CHARLOTTE (THAT'S NOT EASILY OWN'D) . . . . . 307 3 DON JUAN 11   78   V3
         NOW I COULD MUCH MORE EASILY SKETCH A HAREM . . . . . 419 3 DON JUAN 14   21   3
         (BY DOING EASILY WHENE'ER SHE CHOSE . . . . 522 3 DON JUAN 16   44   2
EAST
         OF ARMS (IN THE EAST ALL ARM)--AND VARIOUS DYES . . . 289 2 DON JUAN 3   27   7
         THUS IN THE EAST THEY ARE EXTREMELY STRICT . . . . . 502 2 DON JUAN 5   158   1
         AN OUTLINE OF THE CUSTOMS OF THE EAST . . . . 35 3 DON JUAN 6   58   4
         EXACTED BY THE CUSTOMS OF THE EAST . . . . 52 3 DON JUAN 6   92   2
         HOW THE NEW WORLDINGS OF THE THEN NEW EAST . . . . . 202 3 DON JUAN 9   39   2
         AS AN EAST INDIAN SUNRISE ON THE MAIN . . . . 212 3 DON JUAN 9   59   4
         IN BRIEF THE LITTLE ORPHAN OF THE EAST . . . . . . 338 3 DON JUAN 12   48   7
         THUS THE LOW WORLD NORTH SOUTH OR WEST OR EAST . . . . 342 3 DON JUAN 12   56   6
         ON ROADS EAST SOUTH NORTH WEST THERE IS A RUN . . . . 377 3 DON JUAN 13   42   4
EASTERN
         THE GREATEST HEIRESS OF THE EASTERN ISLES . . . . . 224 2 DON JUAN 2   128   2
         AN EASTERN ANTIJACOBIN AT LAST . . . . 316 2 DON JUAN 3   79   3
         AS IS THE CUSTOM OF THOSE EASTERN CLIMES . . . . . . 463 2 DON JUAN 5   89   6
         FOR EASTERN STAYS ARE LITTLE MADE TO PAD . . . . . . 492 2 DON JUAN 5   140   3
         EXPENDED ALL THEIR EASTERN PHRASEOLOGY . . . . . . 165 3 DON JUAN 8   108   2
         BENEATH THE INFLUENCE OF THE EASTERN STAR . . . . . 347 3 DON JUAN 12   69   4
EASY
         THIS WAS AN EASY MATTER WITH A MAN . . . . 33 2 DON JUAN 1   21   1
         OR ELSE 'TWERE EASY TO WITHDRAW HER WAIST . . . . . . 83 2 DON JUAN 1   115   5
         AND FITS HER LOOSELY--LIKE AN EASY GLOVE . . . . . . 276 2 DON JUAN 3   3   4
         (AND SHE HAD SOME NOT EASY TO WITHSTAND) . . . . . . 396 2 DON JUAN 4   95   6
         MORE EASY BY THE ABSENCE OF ALL MEN . . . . 22 3 DON JUAN 6   32   2
         THIS FEELING 'TIS NOT EASY TO EXPRESS . . . . 415 3 DON JUAN 14   12   5
         THE REASON WHY IS EASY TO DETERMINE . . . . 416 3 DON JUAN 14   15   4
         THE PAPER WAS RIGHT EASY TO PERUSE . . . . 512 3 DON JUAN 16   26   6
EAT
         TO EAT THE HEAD OF HIS ARCH-ENEMY . . . . 200 2 DON JUAN 2   83   3
         THEY WOULD HAVE EAT HER OLIVE-BRANCH AND ALL . . . . 206 2 DON JUAN 2   95   8
         THAT HE WAS FAINT AND MUST NOT TALK BUT EAT . . . . . 236 2 DON JUAN 2   150   8
         EAT DRINK AND LOVE WHAT CAN THE REST AVAIL US . . . . 267 2 DON JUAN 2   207   7
         BUT COULD NOT EAT THEM BEING IN HIS TURN . . . . . . 150 3 DON JUAN 8   77   2
EATING
         WAS KILL'D AND PORTION'D OUT FOR PRESENT EATING . . . 193 2 DON JUAN 2   70   8
         AND THEN THEY LEFT OFF EATING THE DEAD BODY . . . . . 200 2 DON JUAN 2   82   8
         WHO ALL THE TIME WERE EATING UP HIS MUTTON . . . . . 299 2 DON JUAN 3   46   8
         OF EATING WITH ANOTHER ACT OR TWO . . . . 428 2 DON JUAN 5   32   2
         AND EATING ICES WERE O'ERHEARD TO SAY . . . . 239 3 DON JUAN 10   30   6
         BUT THINKS LESS OF GOOD EATING THAN THE WHISPER . . . 487 3 DON JUAN 15   70   7
EATS
         OR EATS FROM OUT THE PALM OR PLAYFUL LOWERS . . . . . 292 2 DON JUAN 3   32   6
         ONE SYSTEM EATS ANOTHER UP AND THIS . . . . 410 3 DON JUAN 14   1   5
         AND EATS HER PARENTS ALBEIT THE DIGESTION . . . . . 411 3 DON JUAN 14   2   5
         WHO EATS FIRE GRATIS (SINCE THE PAY'S BUT SMALL) . . . 446 3 DON JUAN 14   83   6

                                                    PAGE VOL   CANTO STANZA LN

EBB
    WHICH KNOWS NO EBB TO ITS IMPERIOUS FLOW . . . . 366 3 DON JUAN 13   16   6
EBB'D
    PEDRILLO AND SO GENTLY EBB'D HIS BREATH . . . . 197 2 DON JUAN 2   76   3
EBBED
    SO JUAN'S VIRTUE EBBED I KNOW NOT HOW . . . . 493 2 DON JUAN 5   142   2
EBONY
    THE TABLES MOST OF EBONY INLAID . . . . 310 2 DON JUAN 3   69   2
ECCLESIASTES
    ECCLESIASTES SAID THAT ALL IS VANITY-- . . . . 69 3 DON JUAN 7   6   1
ECHO
    THE SORT OF SOUND WE ECHO WITH A TEAR . . . . 236 2 DON JUAN 2   151   6
    TO SOUNDS WHICH ECHO FURTHER WEST . . . . 321 2 DON JUAN 3 L 2   5
    WHERE ECHO WOKE AS IF FROM A LONG SLUMBER . . . . . . 448 2 DON JUAN 5   64   2
    AN ECHO OF A SYLLABLE THAT'S WRONG . . . . 336 3 DON JUAN 12   43   5
    SOME DEEM IT BUT THE DISTANT ECHO GIVEN . . . . 388 3 DON JUAN 13   63   6
    THEIR EARTH IS BUT AN ECHO OF THE SPHERES . . . . . . 458 3 DON JUAN 15   5   8
    NO SOUND EXCEPT THE ECHO OF HIS SIGH . . . . 509 3 DON JUAN 16   20   3
ECHOED
    OF THE LAST FOE IS ECHOED BY HIS OWN . . . . 155 3 DON JJAN 8   87   8
    UPON DEBATE THE PAPERS ECHOED YET . . . . 400 3 DON JUAN 13   90   5
    ARE SOMEHOW ECHOED TO THE PRETTY DEARS . . . . 489 3 DON JUAN 15   76   3
ECHOES
    A MARBLE FOUNTAIN ECHOES THROUGH THE GLOOMS . . . . . 442 2 DON JUAN 5   55   4
    HOW SWEETLY ON THE EAR SUCH ECHOES SOUND . . . . . . 114 3 DON JUAN 8   5   5
    ITS SHRILLER ECHOES--LIKE AN INFANT MADE . . . . . . 385 3 DON JUAN 13   58   3
    BACKWARD AND FORWARD TO THE ECHOES FAINT . . . . . . 508 3 DON JUAN 16   18   3
    AND DREADING THE CHASTE ECHOES OF HER SHOE . . . . . 556 3 DON JUAN 16   112   8
    NIGH AND MORE NIGH THE AWFUL ECHOES DREW . . . . . . 557 3 DON JUAN 16   115   5
ECHOING
    OF ECHOING THUNDER AND THEN ALL WAS HUSH'D . . . . . 184 2 DON JUAN 2   53   3
ECHOS
    OER WHOSE SAD TALE LOVE ECHOS STILL ALAS-- . . . . . 273 2 DON JUAN 2 V 2   3
    WERE THE SOLE ECHOS SAVE MY STEED'S AND MINE . . . . 337 2 DON JUAN 3   106   3
ECLAT
    THE REASON'S OBVIOUS IF THERE'S AN ECLAT . . . . . . 352 3 DON JUAN 12   78   1
    THE LADIES SCILLY BUSEY--MISS ECLAT . . . . 396 3 DON JUAN 13   79   4
    WITH THE KIND VIEW OF SAVING AN ECLAT . . . . 436 3 DON JUAN 14   60   1
ECLECTIC
    A RAKE TURN'D METHODISTIC OR ECLECTIC-- . . . . . . 309 2 DON JUAN 3   66   3
ECONOMIC
    TWO WEEDS WHICH POSE OUR ECONOMIC CATOS . . . . . . 472 3 DON JUAN 15   37   8
ECONOMY
    WILL TURN UPON POLITICAL ECONOMY . . . . 356 3 DON JUAN 12   88   8
ECSTATICS
    I THINK THAT DANTE'S MORE ABSTRUSE ECSTATICS . . . . 281 2 DON JUAN 3   11   7
EDDIES
    WITH ITS STRANGE WHIRLS AND EDDIES CAN COMPARE-- . . .   7 3 DON JUAN 6   2   6
EDEN
    THUS WAS ANOTHER EDEN THEY WERE NEVER . . . . 349 2 DON JUAN 4   10   2
    WHERE ALL IS EDEN OR A WILDERNESS . . . . 373 2 DON JUAN 4   54   8
EDEN'S
    LOVELY AS THOSE WHICH RIPENED EDEN'S FRUIT . . . . . 86 3 DON JUAN 7   41   7
    SHE LOOK'D AS IF SHE SAT BY EDEN'S DOOR . . . . . . 476 3 DON JUAN 15   45   7
EDGE
    AS O'ER THE CUTTER'S EDGE HE TRIED TO CROSS . . . . 186 2 DON JUAN 2   57   4
    IF BUT TO SET ITS EDGE TO A FRESH POLISH . . . . . 433 3 DON JUAN 14   53   V7
    WHICH SETS THE TEETH ON EDGE AND A SLIGHT CLATTER . . 556 3 DON JUAN 16   114   2
EDGEWORTH'S
    MISS EDGEWORTH'S NOVELS STEPPING FROM THEIR COVERS . . 29 2 DON JUAN 1   16   2
EDICTS
    BY ALL HIS EDICTS EVEN TO THE BLIND . . . . 12 3 DON JUAN 6   13   V3
    THEIR GOODS AND EDICTS OUT FROM POLE TO POLE . . . . 257 3 DON JUAN 10   65   7
    OR STARCH AS ARE THE EDICTS STATESMEN UTTER . . . . 468 3 DON JUAN 15   27   4
EDIFICE
    AN EDIFICE NO LESS SUBLIME THAN STRONG . . . . . . 529 3 DON JUAN 16   59   5
EDIFYING
    A VIRGIN-LIKE AND EDIFYING THRONG . . . . 21 3 DON JUAN 6   30   3
    IN A MOST EDIFYING CONVERSATION . . . . 550 3 DON JUAN 16   103   4
EDINBURGH
    AND THAT THE EDINBURGH REVIEW AND QUARTERLY . . . . 142 2 DON JUAN 1   211   7
EDITION
    JUAN WAS TAUGHT FROM OUT THE BEST EDITION . . . . . 46 2 DON JUAN 1   44   1
    THERE'S MORE THAN ONE EDITION AND THE READINGS . . . 127 2 DON JUAN 1   189   5
EDITOR
    TILL SOME LESS RIGID EDITOR SHALL STOOP . . . . . . 46 2 DON JUAN 1   45   5
    I SENT IT IN A LETTER TO THE EDITOR . . . . 142 2 DON JUAN 1   210   1
EDUCATE
    MY POLITICS AS YET ARE ALL TO EDUCATE . . . . 20 2 DON JUAN D   17   5
    TO EDUCATE--YE YOUTH OF EUROPE--YOU BY . . . . . . 486 2 DON JUAN 5   131   6
EDUCATED
    THAT SONS SHOULD NOT BE EDUCATED SO . . . . 50 2 DON JUAN 1   53   8
EDUCATION
    OR MRS TRIMMER'S BOOKS ON EDUCATION . . . . 29 2 DON JUAN 1   16   3
    WITH PERSONS OF NO SORT OF EDUCATION . . . . 33 2 DON JUAN 1   22   2
    IF SUCH AN EDUCATION WAS THE TRUE ONE . . . . 48 2 DON JUAN 1   48   3
    PERHAPS TO FINISH JUAN'S EDUCATION . . . . 75 2 DON JUAN 1   101   6
    THE GREAT SUCCESS OF JUAN'S EDUCATION . . . . 162 2 DON JUAN 2   10   7
    IN FACT HE HAD NO SINGING EDUCATION . . . . 391 2 DON JUAN 4   87   3

221

	PAGE	VOL	CANTO	STANZA	LN
EDUCATION (CONTINUED)					
MEANTIME THE EDUCATION THEY WENT THROUGH	499	2	DON JUAN 5	153	5
ALTHOUGH THEIR HARAM EDUCATION LED	101	3	DON JUAN 7	67	4
AMONGST YOU ABOUT LEILA'S EDUCATION	329	3	DON JUAN 12	28	8
TO UNDERTAKE THE ORPHAN'S EDUCATION	330	3	DON JUAN 12	30	3
OF FREEDOM SHALL COMPLETE THEIR EDUCATION	354	3	DON JUAN 12	83	6
OF MAN'S OPINIONS FORMS THEIR EDUCATION	354	3	DON JUAN 12	83	V6
TO VIRTUE PROPER OR GOOD EDUCATION	372	3	DON JUAN 13	31	3
BOTH LAWYERS AND BOTH MEN OF EDUCATION	401	3	DON JUAN 13	92	3
THEIR LOVE THEIR VIRTUE BEAUTY EDUCATION	420	3	DON JUAN 14	24	7
FOR A YOUNG GENTLEMAN'S FIT EDUCATION	432	3	DON JUAN 14	52	6
THAT WHERE THEIR EDUCATION HARSH OR MILD	563	3	DON JUAN 17	2	5
EDUCATIONS					
THE BEST OF MOTHERS AND OF EDUCATIONS	157	2	DON JUAN 2	1	5
EDWARD'S					
BLACK EDWARD'S HELM AND BECKET'S BLOODY STONE	261	3	DON JUAN 10	73	2
EELS					
USED TO IT NO DOUBT AS EELS ARE TO BE FLAY'D	414	2	DON JUAN 5	7	8
EER					
HAD EER ESCAPED MORE DANGERS ON THE DEEP	229	2	DON JUAN 2	137	V7
EFFECT					
AND FOR THE MOMENT IT HAD SOME EFFECT	176	2	DON JUAN 2	39	2
IS IN ITS CAUSE AS ITS EFFECT SO SWEET	264	2	DON JUAN 2	203	3
AND THIS EXTREME EFFECT (TO TIRE NO LONGER	488	2	DON JUAN 5	133	7
HAS QUITE THE CONTRARY EFFECT ON VICE	501	2	DON JUAN 5	157	8
THE TRUE EFFECT AND SO WE HAD BETTER NOT	55	3	DON JUAN 6	98	6
BEFORE THEY REACHED A SPOT TO TAKE EFFECT	80	3	DON JUAN 7	28	4
BUT HERE THE EFFECT FELL SHORT OF THEIR DESIRE	82	3	DON JUAN 7	31	6
THE EFFECT ON JUAN WAS OF COURSE SUBLIME	261	3	DON JUAN 10	74	1
TO LEAVE THEM HOVERING AS THE EFFECT IS FINE	453	3	DON JUAN 14	97	5
THE CAUSE OF THIS EFFECT OR THIS DEFECT--	502	3	DON JUAN 16	2	1
FOR THIS EFFECT DEFECTIVE COMES BY CAUSE	502	3	DON JUAN 16	2	2
BUT SO FAR THE IMMEDIATE EFFECT	526	3	DON JUAN 16	52	1
SURPRISE HAS THIS EFFECT--TO MAKE ONE DUMB	557	3	DON JUAN 16	115	2
EFFEMINATE					
THE EFFEMINATE GARB--THUS AFTER A SHORT PAUSE	455	2	DON JUAN 5	76	4
AND FOR THE EFFEMINATE VILLEGGIATURA--	395	3	DON JUAN 13	78	1
EFFORT					
WITH SLOW AND STAGGERING EFFORT HE AROSE	213	2	DON JUAN 2	109	1
AS WITH AN EFFORT SHE BEGAN TO SPEAK	236	2	DON JUAN 2	150	4
COST HER AN EFFORT WHICH IS A SAD TOIL	447	3	DON JUAN 14	86	2
OR CARELESS BUT THE EFFORT WAS NOT VALID	515	3	DON JUAN 16	35	7
EFFORTS					
THE NOBLEST EFFORTS FOR HERSELF AND MATE	62	2	DON JUAN 1	75	3
DESPITE OF ALL THEIR EFFORTS AND EXPEDIENTS	171	2	DON JUAN 2	29	3
THEIR DESPERATE EFFORTS SEEM'D ALL USELESS GROWN	176	2	DON JUAN 2	38	6
TO THESE KIND EFFORTS MADE A LOW REPLY	215	2	DON JUAN 2	113	8
(SO THAT THEIR EFFORTS SHOULD AT LENGTH PREVAIL)	105	3	DON JUAN 7	77	6
OF QUIXOTE SHOWN HOW ALL SUCH EFFORTS FAIL	361	3	DON JUAN 13	8	8
'TWILL MAKE IF PROVED VAST EFFORTS WITHOUT PAINING	366	3	DON JUAN 13	18	8
(THOUGH PARRY'S EFFORTS LOOK A LUCKY PRESAGE)	376	3	DON JUAN 13	39	5
OR TO COARSE EFFORTS VERY LOUD AND LONG	540	3	DON JUAN 16	83	7
EFFRONTERY					
GRACED WITH SOME MERIT AND WITH MORE EFFRONTERY	401	3	DON JUAN 13	91	7
EGAD					
EGAD THEY FOUND THE SECOND TIME WHAT THEY	134	3	DON JUAN 8	42	1
EGGS					
FOR BREAKFAST OF EGGS COFFEE BREAD AND FISH	226	2	DON JUAN 2	133	8
BUT ZOE THE MEANTIME SOME EGGS WAS FRYING	233	2	DON JUAN 2	144	5
BUT THERE WERE EGGS FRUIT COFFEE BREAD FISH HONEY	233	2	DON JUAN 2	145	7
AND ZOE WHEN THE EGGS WERE READY AND	234	2	DON JUAN 2	146	1
EGGS OYSTERS TOO ARE AMATORY FOOD	246	2	DON JUAN 2	170	6
OYSTERS AND EGGS ARE ALSO LOVING FOOD	246	2	DON JUAN 2	170	V6
EGO					
NON EGO HOC FERREM CALIDA JUVENTA	143	2	DON JUAN 1	212	1
EGOTISM					
UNIVERSE UNIVERSAL EGOTISM	269	3	DON JUAN 11	2	2
OF AMATORY EGOTISM THE TUISM	506	3	DON JUAN 16	13	7
EGYPT					
MOROCCO BETWIXT EGYPT AND TANGIER	28	3	DON JUAN 6	44	8
EGYPTIAN					
OR HIEROGLYPHICS ON EGYPTIAN STONES	180	3	DON JUAN 8	137	5
EGYPT'S					
WHAT ARE THE HOPES OF MAN OLD EGYPT'S KING	146	2	DON JUAN 1	219	1
IN EGYPT'S RAYS TO HARP AT A FIXED HOUR)	388	3	DON JUAN 13	64	4
EIGHT					
THEN THERE WAS RUM EIGHT GALLONS IN A PUNCHEON	181	2	DON JUAN 2	47	8
AT HALF-PAST EIGHT O'CLOCK BOOMS HENCOOPS SPARS	183	2	DON JUAN 2	51	1
I HEARD A SHOT--'TWAS EIGHT O'CLOCK SCARCE PAST--	428	2	DON JUAN 5	33	5
WHERE IS THE WORLD OF EIGHT YEARS PAST 'TWAS THERE--	306	3	DON JUAN 11	76	3
EIGHT-AND-FORTY					
ERNEIS RADULPHUS--EIGHT-AND-FORTY MANORS	242	3	DON JUAN 10	36	2
EIGHTEEN					
SOME THIRTY YEARS BEFORE AT FAIR EIGHTEEN	236	3	DON JUAN 10	24	V6
WHETHER HIS WINTERS BE EIGHTEEN OR EIGHTY	339	3	DON JUAN 12	50	7
AT EIGHTEEN THOUGH BELOW HER FEET STILL PANTED	434	3	DON JUAN 14	55	4
AT EIGHTEEN SHE WITH DUE DEMUR HAD GRANTED	434	3	DON JUAN 14	55	V5
EIGHTY					
IT STANDS SOME EIGHTY VERSTS FROM THE HIGH SEA	71	3	DON JUAN 7	9	7

222

```
                                                                    PAGE VOL    CANTO   STANZA LN
EIGHTY  (CONTINUED)
   ALSO THE EIGHTY GREATEST LIVING POETS . . . . . . .    . 295  3 DON JUAN 11       54    7
   WHERE IS THE WORLD CRIES YOUNG AT EIGHTY  WHERE     . . . . 306  3 DON JUAN 11       76    1
   WHETHER HIS WINTERS BE EIGHTEEN OR EIGHTY  . . . . .    . 339  3 DON JUAN 12       50    7
EJECTION
   QUIT AND THOUGH DEATH HAD THREATENED AN EJECTION  . . . . 245  3 DON JUAN 10       43    2
EKE
   I HAVE BROUGHT THIS WORLD ABOUT MY EARS AND EKE    . . . . 414  3 DON JUAN 14       10    1
   AND EKE THE WISE AS HAS BEEN OFTEN SHOWN . . . . . .    . 463  3 DON JUAN 15       17    4
   LIKE ALL WHO GIVE AND EKE RECEIVE IT GRATIS  . . . .    . 469  3 DON JUAN 15       29    2
   FOWLS A LA CONDE SLICES EKE OF SALMON . . . . . . .    . 484  3 DON JUAN 15       65    1
EKENHEAD
   LEANDER MR EKENHEAD AND I DID  . . . . . . . . . .    . 211  2 DON JUAN  2      105    8
EKING
   AND AS HE INTERRUPTED NOT WENT EKING . . . . . . .    . 241  2 DON JUAN  2      161    5
ELAPSED
   SOME DAYS AND NIGHTS ELAPSED BEFORE THAT HE . . . . .    . 384  2 DON JUAN  4       75    2
ELATE
   SAID JUAN HAD NOT GOT HIS USUAL LOOK ELATE  . . . .    . 515  3 DON JUAN 16       34    3
ELBOW
   AND THUS UPON HIS ELBOW HE AROSE  . . . . . . . .    . 236  2 DON JUAN  2      150    1
   HIS HEAD UPON HIS ELBOW AND HE SAW . . . . . . . .    . 239  2 DON JUAN  2      157    2
   BUT SEEING AT HIS ELBOW A MERE LAD . . . . . . . .    . 417  2 DON JUAN  5       12    1
   FOUR BLACKS WERE AT HIS ELBOW IN A TRICE . . . . . .    . 458  2 DON JUAN  5       80    8
ELDER
   YOUNG YET HER ELDER AND OF BROW LESS GRAVE . . . . .    . 216  2 DON JUAN  2      115    3
   WAS FOR THE ELDER AND THE STOUTER FIRST . . . . . .    . 451  2 DON JUAN  5       68    2
   BUT WHEN I'VE ADDED THAT THE ELDER JACK SMITH  . . . .    . 76   3 DON JUAN  7       20    2
   THE ELDER LADIES' WRINKLES CURLED MUCH CRISPER . . . .    . 221  3 DON JUAN  9       78    3
ELDERLY
   THE ELDERLY WALKED THROUGH THE LIBRARY  . . . . . .    . 406  3 DON JUAN 13      102    1
ELDEST
   THE ELDEST WAS A TRUE AND TAMELESS TARTAR  . . . . .    . 167  3 DON JUAN  8      111    1
ELDON
   AS ELDON ON A LUNATIC COMMISSION-- . . . . . . . .    . 497  3 DON JUAN 15       92    4
ELECT
   THE PUBLIC MIND SO FEW ARE THE ELECT . . . . . . .    . 330  2 DON JUAN  3       95    6
   A THING QUITE NECESSARY TO THE ELECT . . . . . . .    . 526  3 DON JUAN 16       52    3
ELECTED
   AS ANYBODY ON THE ELECTED ROLL . . . . . . . . .    . 242  3 DON JUAN 10       35    3
ELECTION
   AWAITS IT EACH NEW MEETING OR ELECTION . . . . . .    . 272  3 DON JUAN 11        9    8
   TALK O'ER THEMSELVES THE PAST AND NEXT ELECTION  . . . . 534  3 DON JUAN 16       69    8
ELECTIONEERER
   LORD HENRY WAS A GREAT ELECTIONEERER  . . . . . . .    . 534  3 DON JUAN 16       70    1
ELECTIONS
   LOSING ELECTIONS CHARACTER AND TEMPER . . . . . . .    . 150  2 DON JUAN  1   V  1    7
ELEGANCE
   SHED ITS IONIAN ELEGANCE WHICH SHOW'D . . . . . .    . 304  2 DON JUAN  3       56    2
   AND ELEGANCE WAS SPRINKLED O'ER HIS FIGURE  . . . .    . 427  3 DON JUAN 14       39    2
ELEGANT
   INTO AN ELEGANT EXTRACT (MUCH LESS MASSY)  . . . . .    . 130  3 DON JUAN  8       34    5
   OF ELEGANT ET CETERA IN FRESH BATCHES-- . . . . . .    . 340  3 DON JUAN 12       53    7
ELEGY
   A COUPLET OR AN ELEGY TO CLAIM . . . . . . . . .    . 120  3 DON JUAN  8       17    6
ELEMENT
   CAN EVERY ELEMENT OUR ELEMENTS MAR . . . . . . . .    . 432  2 DON JUAN  5       39    5
ELEMENTS
   CAN EVERY ELEMENT OUR ELEMENTS MAR . . . . . . . .    . 432  2 DON JUAN  5       39    5
   OF ALL THE ELEMENTS WHICH PEOPLE SAY . . . . . . .    . 32   3 DON JUAN  6       53   V5
   THAT E'ER WERE BREWED FROM ELEMENTS OR GORE . . . . .    . 356  3 DON JUAN 12       88    4
ELEVATION
   A GREEK HAD RAISED AROUND THIS ELEVATION  . . . . .    . 71   3 DON JUAN  7       10    5
ELEVEN
   AT SIX A CHARMING CHILD AND AT ELEVEN . . . . . .    . 48   2 DON JUAN  1       49    2
   WHO BADE ON TILL THE HUNDREDS REACH'D ELEVEN  . . . .    . 407  2 DON JUAN  4      114    6
   ELEVEN THOUSAND MAIDENHEADS OF BONE  . . . . . . .    . 255  3 DON JUAN 10       62    7
   AND RISE AT NINE IN LIEU OF LONG ELEVEN . . . . . .    . 539  3 DON JUAN 16       81    4
ELEVENTH
   I WISH SHE HAD HIS BOOK'S THE ELEVENTH COMMANDMENT  . . . 472  3 DON JUAN 15       38    2
ELF
   AND AS MY MUSE IS A CAPRICIOUS ELF . . . . . . . .    . 384  2 DON JUAN  4       74    6
ELIGIBLE
   SO THAT THEIR PLAN AND PROSODY ARE ELIGIBLE . . . . .    . 70   2 DON JUAN  1       90    7
ELITE
   AT ONCE THE LIE AND THE ELITE OF CROWDS  . . . . .    . 396  3 DON JUAN 13       80    2
ELIZABETH
   UNLIKE OUR OWN HALF-CHASTE ELIZABETH . . . . . . .    . 222  3 DON JUAN  9       81    2
ELL
   BUT TAKE AN ELL--AND MAKE A GREAT SENSATION . . . . .    . 404  3 DON JUAN 13       98    5
ELLE
   THE SEAL A SUNFLOWER ELLE VOUS SUIT PARTOUT . . . . .    . 134  2 DON JUAN  1      198    6
ELOPEMENT
   SAW JUAN'S LAST ELOPEMENT WITH THE DEVIL . . . . . .    . 138  2 DON JUAN  1      203    8
ELOQUENCE
   FOR THEN THEIR ELOQUENCE GROWS QUITE PROFUSE  . . . .    . 119  2 DON JUAN  1      179    4
   OF ELOQUENCE IN PIETY AND PROSE-- . . . . . . . .    . 243  2 DON JUAN  2      165    7
   THE SERIOUS ANGLES IN THE ELOQUENCE  . . . . . . .    . 427  3 DON JUAN 14       38    2
   YET LEAVE THE GATE WHICH ELOQUENCE SLIPS THROUGH . . . . 557  3 DON JUAN 16      115    3
```

223

```
                                                        PAGE VOL      CANTO STANZA LN
ELOQUENT
    HER EYES WERE ELOQUENT HER WORDS WOULD POSE . . . . .  236  2 DON JUAN  2    150   5
    THE ANSWER ELOQUENT WHERE THE SOUL SHINES   . . . . .  241  2 DON JUAN  2    162   5
    HERE RAUCOCANTI'S ELOQUENT RECITAL . . . . . . . . .   393  2 DON JUAN  4     90   1
ELSE
    TO--GOD KNOWS WHERE--FOR NO ONE ELSE CAN KNOW  . . . .   14  2 DON JUAN  D      9   8
    ANY ONE ELSE--THEY WERE BECOME TRADITIONAL   . . . . .   37  2 DON JUAN  1     31   4
    AND BIT HER LIPS (FOR ELSE SHE MIGHT HAVE SCREAM'D)  . .  51  2 DON JUAN  1     54   6
    OR ELSE 'TWERE EASY TO WITHDRAW HER WAIST  . . . . . .   83  2 DON JUAN  1    115   5
    GASPS AND WHATEVER ELSE THE OWNERS CHOOSE--  . . . . .  110  2 DON JUAN  1    162   5
    BUT NOTHING ELSE THE TIME OF WORDS WAS O'ER  . . . . .  111  2 DON JUAN  1    163   6
    OR ELSE THE THING HAD HARDLY COME TO PASS)   . . . . .  158  2 DON JUAN  2      3   6
    SEA-SICKNESS DEATH HIS LOVE WAS PERFECT HOW ELSE  . . . 168  2 DON JUAN  2     23   6
    AND FED BY SPOONFULS ELSE THEY ALWAYS BURST  . . . . .  239  2 DON JUAN  2    158   8
    ELSE HOW THE DEVIL IS IT THAT FRESH FEATURES   . . . .  267  2 DON JUAN  2    208   7
    ELSE THEY SHALL FEEL THE WEIGHT OF THIS MY ARM . . . .  459  2 DON JUAN  5     82   3
    BUT TEARS MUST STOP LIKE ALL THINGS ELSE AND SOON  . .  481  2 DON JUAN  5    121   1
    BUT WOMAN WITH THE HEART--OR SOMETHING ELSE  . . . . .    7  2 DON JUAN  6      2  V8
    AND YET LIKE ALL MEN ELSE I MUST ALLOW   . . . . . .   106  3 DON JUAN  7     80   5
    BUT ELSE UNHURT SHE OPENED HER LARGE EYES  . . . . . .  159  3 DON JUAN  8     95   7
    BY RENDERING DESPERATE THOSE WHO HAD ELSE REPENTED  . . 353  3 DON JUAN 12     80   8
    BESIDES THE MOST SUBLIME OF--HEAVEN KNOWS WHAT ELSE--   356  3 DON JUAN 12     88   5
    IF YOU HAVE NOUGHT ELSE HERE'S AT LEAST SATIETY  . . .  416  3 DON JUAN 14     14   5
    OR ELSE 'TWILL COST US ALL ANOTHER MILLION   . . . . .  446  3 DON JUAN 14     83   8
    DAYS BETTER DRAWN BEFORE OR ELSE ASSUME  . . . . . . .  468  3 DON JUAN 15     26   7
ELSEWHERE
    ELSEWHERE WAS NOTHING--SHE HAD NOUGHT TO FEAR  . . . .  264  2 DON JUAN  2    202   7
    WHICH STILL ELSEWHERE MAY ROUSE A BRIGHTER SPRING--  .  188  3 DON JUAN  9     11   4
    ELSEWHERE PRESERVED THE CLOISTERS STILL WERE STABLE  .  389  3 DON JUAN 13     66   3
    AND SENATE WHEN INVITED ELSEWHERE TRULY  . . . . . . .  398  3 DON JUAN 13     84   3
    WHICH YOU MIGHT ELSEWHERE HOPE TO FIND IN VAIN . . . .  502  3 DON JUAN 16      3   4
ELYSIUM
    TO HIM IT WAS ELYSIUM TO BE THERE  . . . . . . . . .   139  3 DON JUAN  8     53   4
'EM
    AS IF SHE DEEM'D THAT MYSTERY WOULD ENNOBLE 'EM  . . .   28  2 DON JUAN  1     13   8
    AND SAID THERE WAS ANALOGY BETWEEN 'EM   . . . . . . .   28  2 DON JUAN  1     14   2
    BUT I MUST LEAVE THE PROOFS TO THOSE WHO'VE SEEN 'EM .   28  2 DON JUAN  1     14   4
    AND ALL MAY THINK WHICH WAY THEIR JUDGMENTS LEAN 'EM .   28  2 DON JUAN  1     14   6
    SO GOOD--I WONDER CASTLEREAGH DON'T TAX 'EM  . . . . .  264  2 DON JUAN  2    203   8
    ANOTHER TIME HE MIGHT HAVE LIKED TO SEE 'EM  . . . . .  384  2 DON JUAN  4     75   7
    YOU MAY DO RIGHT FORBIDDING THEM TO SHOW 'EM  . . . . . 403  2 DON JUAN  4    107   7
    THE FEMALES STOOD AS ONE BY ONE THEY PICK'D 'EM  . . .  409  2 DON JUAN  4    116   7
    AND FOR THEIR OTHER MATTERS MEET AND SHARE 'EM  . . . .  53  3 DON JUAN  6     95   8
    GREAT DEEDS ARE DOING--HOW SHALL I RELATE 'EM  . . . .  107  3 DON JUAN  7     81   6
    WHATEVER DEED BE DONE I WILL RELATE 'EM  .  . . . . . . 107  3 DON JUAN  7     81  V6
    AS NOW OCCUR I THOUGHT THAT I WOULD PEN YOU 'EM  . . .  180  3 DON JUAN  8    136   4
    YET IF PERCHANCE REMEMBERED STILL DISDAIN YOU 'EM  . .  180  3 DON JUAN  8    136   6
    JUST NOW--BUT BY AND BY THE TRUTH WILL SHOW 'EM  . . .  193  3 DON JUAN  9     22   5
    I SAY WILL THESE GREAT RELICS WHEN THEY SEE 'EM  . . .  202  3 DON JUAN  9     40   7
    OF ALL HIS FEELINGS--ONLY HE FORGOT 'EM  . . . . . . .  251  3 DON JUAN 10     54   8
    THAN THESE THINGS AND BESIDES I WISH TO SPARE 'EM  . .  419  3 DON JUAN 14     21   5
EMACIATED
    SO HERE THOUGH FAINT EMACIATED AND STARK . . . . . .   212  2 DON JUAN  2    106   1
EMASCULATED
    EMASCULATED TO THE MARROW IT . . . . . . . . . . . .    18  2 DON JUAN  D     15   2
EMBARGO
    BETTER PERHAPS FOR MAN THAT AN EMBARGO   . . . . . . .  191  2 DON JUAN  2     66  V7
    THAN WHERE TWO WIVES ARE UNDER AN EMBARGO  . . . . . .   51  3 DON JUAN  6     90   8
EMBARGOED
    WHEN RAPP THE HARMONIST EMBARGOED MARRIAGE   . . . . .  471  3 DON JUAN 15     35   1
    FOUND HIS OWN LEGS EMBARGOED FROM MERE WALKING . . . .  565  3 DON JUAN 17      8   4
EMBARK
    HER SON TO CADIZ ONLY TO EMBARK  . . . . . . . . . .   161  2 DON JUAN  2      8   2
EMBARK'D
    JUAN EMBARK'D--THE SHIP GOT UNDER WAY  . . . . . . . .  162  2 DON JUAN  2     11   1
EMBARKED
    EMBARKED HIMSELF AND THEM AND OFF THEY WENT THENCE  . . 432  2 DON JUAN  5     40   3
    OF THE TROOPS WERE EMBARKED THE SIEGE TO RAISE . . . .   85  3 DON JUAN  7     39   2
    HERE HE EMBARKED AND WITH A FLOWING SAIL . . . . . . .  256  3 DON JUAN 10     64   1
EMBARRASS
    WHOSE LITTLE NIBBLING RUSTLE WILL EMBARRASS . . . . .   509  3 DON JUAN 16     20   7
EMBARRASS'D
    EMBARRASS'D AT FIRST STARTING WITH A NOVICE  . . . . .   62  2 DON JUAN  1     74   8
    EMBARRASS'D SOMEWHAT BOTH WITH FIRE AND WATER  . . . .  423  3 DON JUAN 14     30   8
EMBARRASSED
    WAS MUCH EMBARRASSED NEVER HAVING MET  . . . . . . . .  482  2 DON JUAN  5    122   4
    TO WHICH EMBARRASSED PEOPLE HAVE RECOURSE  . . . . . .   56  3 DON JUAN  6    100   8
    NOR SEEM EMBARRASSED--QUITE THE CONTRARY . . . . . . .  545  3 DON JUAN 16     94   2
EMBARRASSMENT
    AND MUCH EMBARRASSMENT IN EITHER EYE   . . . . . . . .   60  2 DON JUAN  1     70   4
    BABA WITH SOME EMBARRASSMENT REPLIED . . . . . . . .    56  3 DON JUAN  6    100   1
EMBELLISH
    THEY SO EMBELLISH THAT 'TIS QUITE A BORE . . . . . .   137  2 DON JUAN  1    202   6
EMBERS
    THE DYING EMBERS DWINDLE IN THE GRATE--  . . . . . .   499  3 DON JUAN 15     97   7
EMBLEM
    THE FIRST THE EMBLEM (RARELY THOUGH) OF WHAT   . . . .  290  3 DON JUAN 11     44   4
EMBLEMS
    OR A SINGULTUS--EMBLEMS OF EMOTION . . . . . . . . .   457  3 DON JUAN 15      2   2
```

	PAGE	VOL	CANTO	STANZA	LN
EMBODIED					
MADE HER A BEAUTIFUL EMBODIED STORM	489	2 DON JUAN	5	135	8
EMBOSOM'D					
IT STOOD EMBOSOM'D IN A HAPPY VALLEY	384	3 DON JUAN	13	56	1
EMBOSS'D					
A SUN EMBOSS'D IN GOLD WHOSE RAYS OF TISSUE	309	2 DON JUAN	3	67	7
EMBRACE					
THERE WAS A DEPTH OF FEELING TO EMBRACE	524	3 DON JUAN	16	48	7
EMBRACED					
AND JULIA SATE WITH JUAN HALF EMBRACED	83	2 DON JUAN	1	115	1
THEN ONE VAST FIRE AIR EARTH AND STREAM EMBRACED	115	3 DON JUAN	8	7	5
EMBRACES					
KISSES SWEET WORDS EMBRACES AND ALL THAT	13	3 DON JUAN	6	14	2
EMBROIDER'D					
EMBROIDER'D DELICATELY O'ER WITH BLUE	308	2 DON JUAN	3	64	6
EMBROIDERY					
MEDALS RANKS RIBBONS LACE EMBROIDERY SCARLET	108	3 DON JUAN	7	84	1
EMERALD					
AN EMERALD AIGRETTE WITH HAIDEE'S HAIR IN'T	315	2 DON JUAN	3	77	6
EMERALD'S					
WHILE THE MILD EMERALD'S BEAM SHADES DOWN THE DYES	319	3 DON JUAN	12	8	7
EMERGE					
DON JUAN HERE PERMITTED TO EMERGE	387	2 DON JUAN	4	79	1
OUR BUBBLES AS THE OLD BURST NEW EMERGE	500	3 DON JUAN	15	99	6
EMETIC					
BUT THE SEA ACTED AS A STRONG EMETIC	167	2 DON JUAN	2	21	8
THREE HUNDRED CANNON THREW UP THEIR EMETIC	117	3 DON JUAN	8	12	1
EMIGRATION					
THAT HALF ITS PRODUCE TENDS TO EMIGRATION	472	3 DON JUAN	15	37	6
EMIGRATIONS					
SEVERAL PREPARED THEMSELVES FOR EMIGRATIONS	239	3 DON JUAN	10	30	5
EMINENT					
NOR CANVASS WHAT SO EMINENT A HAND MEANT	472	3 DON JUAN	15	38	6
EMOTION					
OR THAT OF ANY OTHER STRONG EMOTION	289	2 DON JUAN	3	26	6
WE PONDER DEEPLY ON EACH PAST EMOTION	345	2 DON JUAN	4	2	8
BY DEEP EMOTION--YOU MAY SOMETIMES TRACE	61	3 DON JUAN	6	111	4
OR A SINGULTUS--EMBLEMS OF EMOTION	457	3 DON JUAN	15	2	2
A THEME FOR PITY OR SOME WORSE EMOTION	563	3 DON JUAN	17	3	6
EMOTIONS					
EXTRACTS EMOTIONS BEAUTIFUL AND NEW	144	2 DON JUAN	1	214	4
HE STOPP'D--WHAT SINGULAR EMOTIONS FILL	286	2 DON JUAN	3	21	3
EMPEROR					
FOR BEING THE LAST WIFE OF THE EMPEROR	495	2 DON JUAN	5	146	7
EMPERORS					
EMPERORS ARE ONLY HUSBANDS IN WIVES' EYES	477	2 DON JUAN	5	115	5
ARISE WHEN WE SEE EMPERORS FALL WITH OATS	198	3 DON JUAN	9	32	8
EMPHASIS					
WITH EMPHASIS AND ALSO WITH GOOD SENSE--	427	3 DON JUAN	14	38	4
EMPHATIC					
AND OUR SOPHIAS ARE NOT SO EMPHATIC	409	3 DON JUAN	13	110	5
EMPIRE					
HERE IS THE EMPIRE OF THY PERFECT BLISS	69	2 DON JUAN	1	88	3
WHICH NEEDED NOT AN EMPIRE TO PERSUADE	483	2 DON JUAN	5	125	3
HIS EMPIRE ALSO WAS WITHOUT A BOUND	497	2 DON JUAN	5	150	5
I KNOW ITS MIGHTY EMPIRE NOW ALLURES	194	3 DON JUAN	9	23	5
THIS IS THE LITERARY LOWER EMPIRE	299	3 DON JUAN	11	62	1
EMPIRES					
THEN SPUR AWAY O'ER EMPIRES AND O'ER STATES	76	2 DON JUAN	1	103	6
OF EMPIRES HEAVE BUT LIKE SOME PASSING WAVES	500	3 DON JUAN	15	99	8
EMPLOY					
BUT SHE DEFIED ALL MEANS THEY COULD EMPLOY	376	2 DON JUAN	4	59	7
NO LESS DELIGHTED TO EMPLOY HIS LEISURE	123	3 DON JUAN	8	24	8
THEIR NATURES OR THEIR SOVEREIGNS WHO EMPLOY	157	3 DON JUAN	8	92	7
EMPLOY'D					
IN JUAN'S CASE WERE BUT EMPLOY'D IN VAIN	157	2 DON JUAN	2	1	6
HAVE MUCH EMPLOY'D THE MUSE OF HISTORY'S PEN	266	2 DON JUAN	2	206	4
EMPLOYED					
EMPLOYED FOR SINCE IT IS THEIR DAILY LABOUR	288	3 DON JUAN	11	41	2
EMPLOYING					
AND STILL MORE WOMEN SPRING FROM NOT EMPLOYING	444	3 DON JUAN	14	78	7
EMPLOYMENT					
AND THIS AT PRESENT WAS HER KIND EMPLOYMENT	548	3 DON JUAN	16	100	8
EMPRESS					
('TWAS THUS HE SPAKE) AND EMPRESS OF THE EARTH	494	2 DON JUAN	5	144	2
GULBEYAZ WAS AN EMPRESS BUT HAD BEEN	18	3 DON JUAN	6	25	7
AND BROUGHT BEFORE THE EMPRESS WHO HAD MADE	64	3 DON JUAN	6	118	5
THE ARMIES OF THE CHRISTIAN EMPRESS CATHERINE	99	3 DON JUAN	7	64	8
GLORY TO GOD AND TO THE EMPRESS (POWERS	178	3 DON JUAN	8	133	7
THE EMPRESS SMILED THE REIGNING FAVOURITE FROWNED--	205	3 DON JUAN	9	46	2
BESIDES THE EMPRESS SOMETIMES LIKED A BOY	206	3 DON JUAN	9	47	7
THEN RECOLLECTING THE WHOLE EMPRESS NOR	211	3 DON JUAN	9	58	1
OR DUTCHESS PRINCESS EMPRESS DEIGNS TO PROVE	216	3 DON JUAN	9	68	5
O'ER WHOM AN EMPRESS HER CROWN JEWELS SCATTERING	217	3 DON JUAN	9	70	V5
BUT IN SUCH MATTERS RUSSIA'S MIGHTY EMPRESS	221	3 DON JUAN	9	77	7
THE FAVOUR OF THE EMPRESS WAS AGREEABLE	235	3 DON JUAN	10	22	1
UNTO AN EMPRESS WHO PREFERRED YOUNG MEN	241	3 DON JUAN	10	33	2
THE EMPRESS WAS ALARMED AND HER PHYSICIAN	244	3 DON JUAN	10	39	2
EMPRESSEMENT					
BUT JUAN WAS RECEIVED WITH MUCH EMPRESSEMENT --	288	3 DON JUAN	11	42	1

225

```
                                                        PAGE VOL     CANTO  STANZA  LN
EMPRESS'S
   ALL PRAISED THE EMPRESS'S MATERNAL LOVE  . . . . . .  240  3 DON JUAN 10      32    8
EMPTY
   (SIGNS OF TRUE GENIUS AND OF EMPTY POCKETS) . . . . .   91  2 DON JUAN  1     129    2
   AS TIGERS COMBAT WITH AN EMPTY CRAW  . . . . . . . .   137  3 DON JUAN  8      49    5
EMULATION
   KEPT THE PLACE OPEN FOR THEIR EMULATION  . . . . . .   248  3 DON JUAN 10      48    8
   SO FIRST THERE WAS A GENEROUS EMULATION  . . . . . .   330  3 DON JUAN 12      30    1
EN
   BUT EN AVANT THE  LIGHT LOVES LANGUISH O'ER  . . . .   542  3 DON JUAN 16      86    1
ENABLES
   A READY ANSWER WHICH AT ONCE ENABLES  . . . . . . .   117  2 DON JUAN  1     175    2
   SUCH AS ENABLES MAN TO SHOW HIS STRENGTH . . . . . .   567  3 DON JUAN 17      12    3
ENAMOURED
   PATIENT--BUT NOT ENAMOURED OF ENDURANCE  . . . . . .   567  3 DON JUAN 17      11    4
ENCHANTED
   AT SEVENTEEN TOO THE WORLD WAS STILL ENCHANTED  . . .  434  3 DON JUAN 14      55    3
ENCHANTER
   THAT GREAT ENCHANTER AT WHOSE ROD'S COMMAND  . . . .   204  3 DON JUAN  9      44    3
ENCHANTER'S
   BY THIS OLD BLACK ENCHANTER'S UNSOUGHT AID  . . . . .  459  2 DON JUAN  5      83    8
ENCHANTS
   THE GESTURE WHICH ENCHANTS THE EYE THAT SPEAKS . . .   292  2 DON JUAN  3      33    4
ENCLOSED
   THE GOTHIC CHAMBER WHERE HE WAS ENCLOSED  . . . . . .  507  3 DON JUAN 16      15    3
ENCOUNTER
   HOW TO ENCOUNTER WITH THIS MARTIAL SCOLD . . . . . .    54  3 DON JUAN  6      96    3
   WHICH BEST IS TO ENCOUNTER--GHOST OR NONE  . . . . .   568  3 DON JUAN 17      14    1
ENCOURAGE
   AND NOT TO ENCOURAGE WHISPERING IN THE HOUSE  . . . .  439  3 DON JUAN 14      67   V4
   WAS NOT SUCH AS TO ENCOURAGE HIM TO SHINE  . . . . .   489  3 DON JUAN 15      75    6
ENCOURAGEMENT
   BECAUSE IT LEFT ENCOURAGEMENT BEHIND  . . . . . . .   208  2 DON JUAN  2      99    6
   WITH THIS ENCOURAGEMENT HE LED THE WAY  . . . . . .   465  2 DON JUAN  5      93    1
ENCOURAGES
   WHAT NATURE NATURALLY MOST ENCOURAGES)--  . . . . . .  471  3 DON JUAN 15      35    6
ENCREASE
   STILL I'LL RECORD A FEW IF BUT TO ENCREASE  . . . . .   74  3 DON JUAN  7      15    1
ENCREASED
   BY WHICH THE MORE A HAREM IS ENCREASED  . . . . . .    35  3 DON JUAN  6      58    6
   DANGER AND SPOIL WITH ARDOUR MUCH ENCREASED . . . . .   90  3 DON JUAN  7      49    6
   HAD RAISED AN INTEREST IN HER WHICH ENCREASED  . . .   338  3 DON JUAN 12      48    8
   BY WHICH THEIR POWER OF MISCHIEF IS ENCREASED  . . .   342  3 DON JUAN 12      56    4
ENCROACH
   I COULD SAY MORE BUT DO NOT CHOOSE TO ENCROACH . . .   279  3 DON JUAN 11      23    5
ENCROACHING
   BY REBEL PACHAS AND ENCROACHING GIAOURS  . . . . . .   497  2 DON JUAN  5     150    7
ENCUMBER
   BY STEALTH HER HUSBAND'S TEMPLES TO ENCUMBER  . . . .   96  2 DON JUAN  1     138    6
   NOT FINDING THAT THE ADDITIONS MUCH ENCUMBER  . . . .  276  2 DON JUAN  3       3    8
   HERE WEALTH HAD DONE ITS UTMOST TO ENCUMBER . . . . .  448  2 DON JUAN  5      64    6
   THEIR CLAY FOR THE LAST TIME THEIR SOULS ENCUMBER--  .  120  3 DON JUAN  8      18    5
   NOR DID SHE FIND THE QUANTITY ENCUMBER  . . . . . .   248  3 DON JUAN 10      48    6
   VARIETY ITSELF WILL MORE ENCUMBER  . . . . . . . .   371  3 DON JUAN 13      30    5
   THE SLIGHTEST OBSTACLE WHICH MAY ENCUMBER  . . . . .   371  3 DON JUAN 13      30   V5
ENCUMBER'D
   BUT LIKE A HAWK ENCUMBER'D WITH HIS HOOD--  . . . . .   10  2 DON JUAN  D       2    6
ENCUMBERS
   THE LUST WHICH STINGS THE SPLENDOUR WHICH ENCUMBERS  .  145  3 DON JUAN  8      67    5
ENCYCLOPEDIZE
   WHICH ENCYCLOPEDIZE BOTH FLESH AND FISH  . . . . . .   486  3 DON JUAN 15      68    6
END
   FOR MALICE STILL IMPUTES SOME PRIVATE END)  . . . . .   58  2 DON JUAN  1      66    6
   AND SO IS SPRING ABOUT THE END OF MAY . . . . . . .    76  2 DON JUAN  1     102    3
   BY BLOOD OR INK 'TIS SWEET TO PUT AN END . . . . . .    90  2 DON JUAN  1     126    2
   FEW MORTALS KNOW WHAT END THEY WOULD BE AT . . . . .    93  2 DON JUAN  1     133    5
   WHY DON'T YOU KNOW THAT IT MAY END IN BLOOD . . . . .   115  2 DON JUAN  1     171    6
   WHAT IS THE END OF FAME 'TIS BUT TO FILL . . . . . .   146  2 DON JUAN  1     218    1
   HER EARNESTNESS WOULD NE'ER HAVE MADE AN END  . . . .  241  2 DON JUAN  2     161    4
   HE HERS UNTIL THEY END IN BROKEN GASPS  . . . . . .   259  2 DON JUAN  2     194    6
   BUT THOSE WHO HAVE NE'ER END WITH ONLY ONE  . . . . .  276  2 DON JUAN  3       4    8
   MUST END IN LANGUOR--MEN WON'T SLEEP LIKE SWINE--  . .  343  2 DON JUAN  3    V 98    4
   IN POESY UNLESS PERHAPS THE END  . . . . . . . . .   344  2 DON JUAN  4       1    2
   AND SUCH AN END THAT HE WHO MANY A DAY  . . . . . .   431  2 DON JUAN  5      37    5
   WE KNOW WHERE THINGS AND MEN MUST END AT BEST  . . .   448  2 DON JUAN  5      63    5
   MIGHT PROBABLY OBTAIN BOTH IN THE END  . . . . . . .  451  2 DON JUAN  5      69    3
   A THOUSAND TIMES OF HIM HAD MADE AN END  . . . . . .  471  2 DON JUAN  5     104    6
   THE SPIRIT IN THE END WILL HAVE ITS WAY . . . . . .   474  2 DON JUAN  5     110    8
   THERE WAS NO END UNTO THE THINGS SHE BOUGHT . . . . .  476  2 DON JUAN  5     113    5
   OF WHICH THE SUREST SIGN IS IN THE END  . . . . . .     6  3 DON JUAN  6       1    7
   THERE WAS A WAY TO END THEIR STRIFE ALTHOUGH  . . . .   53  3 DON JUAN  6      95    4
   BUT SUCH PRECIPITATION MAY END ILL  . . . . . . . .    62  3 DON JUAN  6     114    5
   MIGHT END IN ACTING AS HIS OWN JACK KETCH  . . .  •  .   63  3 DON JUAN  6     116    5
   YET IN THE END EXCEPT IN FREEDOM'S BATTLES  . . . . .  114  3 DON JUAN  8       4    7
   BUT LET ME PUT AN END UNTO MY THEME  . . . . . . .   175  3 DON JUAN  8     127    1
   THERE WAS AN END OF ISMAIL--HAPLESS TOWN  . . . . . .  175  3 DON JUAN  8     127    4
   THEY WRITE AND FOR WHAT END BUT NOTE OR TEXT  . . . .  203  3 DON JUAN  9      41    7
   THOU RIDDLE WITHOUT WHOM EARTH'S ASHES END  . . . . .  210  3 DON JUAN  9      56   V7
   DARK RIDDLE OF ALL LIFE EARTH'S LIFELESS END . . . . .  210  3 DON JUAN  9      56   V7
```

```
                                                          PAGE VOL    CANTO STANZA LN
END   (CONTINUED)
    SELFISH IN ITS BEGINNING AS ITS END      . . . . .    219  3 DON JUAN  9    73   2
    TO END OR TO BEGIN WITH THE NEXT GRAND   . . . . .    220  3 DON JUAN  9    76   2
    THIS IS THE WAY PHYSICIANS MEND OR END US  . . . .    245  3 DON JUAN 10    42   1
    AT THE GREAT END OF TRAVEL--WHICH IS DRIVING . . .    260  3 DON JUAN 10    72   8
    MEANETH THE WEST OR WORST END OF A CITY  . . . . .    290  3 DON JUAN 11    45   2
    BUT THESE ARE FEW AND IN THE END THEY MAKE  . . . .   328  3 DON JUAN 12    26   1
    PERUSE 'TIS ALWAYS WITH A MORAL END  . . . . . .      334  3 DON JUAN 12    39   2
    OF EPIC LOVE'S BEGINNING END AND MIDDLE  . . . . .    337  3 DON JUAN 12    45   8
    AN END TO ANSWER OR A PLAN TO LAY--  . . . . . .      342  3 DON JUAN 12    58   6
    KNOW HOW TO END THIS HALF AND HALF FLIRTATION . . .   345  3 DON JUAN 12    63  V7
    THIRDLY COMMENCE NOT WITH THE END--OR SINNING . . .   393  3 DON JUAN 13    73   7
    IN THIS SORT END AT LEAST WITH THE BEGINNING . . .    393  3 DON JUAN 13    73   8
    OR MAKE A WERTER OF HIM IN THE END . . . . . .        438  3 DON JUAN 14    64   2
    OR GRAVE LORD GEORGE WITH WHOM PERHAPS MIGHT END .    470  3 DON JUAN 15    33   4
    TO BRING WHAT WAS A JEST TO A SERIOUS END  . . . .    491  3 DON JUAN 15    79   6
ENDANGERS
    AN ALMOST TWELVEMONTH'S CONSTANCY ENDANGERS . . . .    472  2 DON JUAN  5   106   8
ENDEAR'D
    A THING WHICH EACH ENDEARMENT MORE ENDEAR'D . . . .    352  2 DON JUAN  4    16   8
ENDEARMENT
    A THING WHICH EACH ENDEARMENT MORE ENDEAR'D . . . .    352  2 DON JUAN  4    16   8
ENDEARS
    BECAUSE THAT NUMBER RARELY MUCH ENDEARS  . . . . .     78  2 DON JUAN  1   107   6
    NO DOUBT WE WEEP FOR THOSE THE HEART ENDEARS-- . . .   164  2 DON JUAN  2    15   7
ENDEAVOUR
    THOUGH ALL EXCHEQUER CHANCELLORS ENDEAVOUR  . . . .    547  3 DON JUAN 16    98   6
ENDEAVOURING
    THE EXPRESSION AND ENDEAVOURING TO RESUME   . . . .    298  2 DON JUAN  3    44   5
ENDED
    ALL COMEDIES ARE ENDED BY A MARRIAGE  . . . . .       280  2 DON JUAN  3     9   2
    HIS HEAD UNTIL THE CEREMONY ENDED . . . . . .         466  2 DON JUAN  5    95   8
    THUS ENDED MANY A FAIR SULTANA'S TRIP . . . . .       496  2 DON JUAN  5   149  V5
    BUT ENDED IN HIS BEING FOUND OUT AND SACKED . . . .    58  3 DON JUAN  6   104   6
    THE LONDON WINTER'S ENDED IN JULY--  . . . . .        378  3 DON JUAN 13    43   1
    THE CONFERENCE OR CONGRESS (FOR IT ENDED . . . . .    482  3 DON JUAN 15    61   1
ENDING
    ENDING IN ISCHSKIN OUSCKIN IFFSKCHY OUSKI   . . . .     74  3 DON JUAN  7    16   7
    QUICK SILVER SMALL TALK ENDING (IF YOU NOTE IT) . . .  328  3 DON JUAN 12    26   7
    THE ENGLISH WINTER--ENDING IN JULY . . . . . .        377  3 DON JUAN 13    42   1
    (ESPECIALLY AS THE SIXTH YEAR IS ENDING) . . . . .    546  3 DON JUAN 16    95   6
ENDLESS
    OF ENDLESS TORMENTS AND PERPETUAL MOTION  . . . . .     17  2 DON JUAN  D    13   8
    WITH ALL THE ARROGANCE OF ENDLESS POWER  . . . . .    152  2 DON JUAN  1  V  3   7
    BUT PAYS OFF MOMENTS IN AN ENDLESS SHOWER  . . . .    258  2 DON JUAN  2   192   6
    THE ENDLESS SOOT BESTOWS A TINT FAR DEEPER  . . . .    232  3 DON JUAN 10    15   3
    WOULD YOU HAVE ENDLESS LIGHTNING IN THE SKIES . . .    451  3 DON JUAN 14    94   6
END'S
    SO THE END'S GAIN'D WHAT SIGNIFIES THE ROUTE  . . .    478  3 DON JUAN 15    51   8
ENDS
    THE MORE SO IN OBTAINING OUR OWN ENDS. . . . . .       37  2 DON JUAN  1    30   4
    I DOUBT ALL LIKENESS ENDS BETWEEN THE PAIR . . . .    124  2 DON JUAN  1   186   8
    HERE ENDS THIS CANTO--NEED I SING OR SAY . . . . .    126  2 DON JUAN  1   188   1
    OF US DIES WITH THEM AS EACH FOND HOPE ENDS . . . .   167  2 DON JUAN  2    21   6
    LAID WITH ONE BLAST THE SHIP ON HER BEAM ENDS . . .    172  2 DON JUAN  2    30   8
    THE MOMENT AFTER HE POLITELY ENDS . . . . . .         200  2 DON JUAN  2    83   4
    AND HAVING PICKED UP SEVERAL ODDS AND ENDS  . . . .    318  2 DON JUAN  3    83   2
    WHICH MOSTLY ENDS IN SOME SMALL BREACH OF BOTH . . .   493  2 DON JUAN  5   142   8
    AN ISLE NEAR ISMAIL HAD TWO ENDS IN VIEW . . . . .     78  3 DON JUAN  7    23   2
    AND OTHERS OF THEMSELVES AND LATTER ENDS . . . . .     94  3 DON JUAN  7    54   8
    ENDS IN A RUSTY CASQUE AND DUBIOUS BONE  . . . . .    261  3 DON JUAN 10    73   6
    BEGINNINGS ARE FAIR FACES ENDS MERE FISHES-- . . .    349  3 DON JUAN 12    73   2
    ENDS WHEN THE BODY OF THE BOOK'S BEGUN   . . . . .    356  3 DON JUAN 12    87   2
    AND FORMED A BASIS OF ESTEEM WHICH ENDS  . . . . .    365  3 DON JUAN 13    15   7
    AND HARDLY HEAVEN--BECAUSE IT NEVER ENDS . . . . .    407  3 DON JUAN 13   105   3
ENDURANCE
    AND PASSED FOR ARGUMENTS OF GOOD ENDURANCE  . . . .    294  3 DON JUAN 11    52   4
    PATIENT--BUT NOT ENAMOURED OF ENDURANCE  . . . . .    567  3 DON JUAN 17    11   4
ENDURE
    WHICH COLDER HEARTS ENDURE TILL THEY ARE LAID . . .    382  2 DON JUAN  4    71   4
    A TOWN WHICH DID A FAMOUS SIEGE ENDURE   . . . . .     70  3 DON JUAN  7     8   5
    JUAN REPLIED--AT LEAST I WILL ENDURE . . . . .        161  3 DON JUAN  8   100   6
    LORD HENRY AT HIS TABLE SHOULD ENDURE . . . . .       543  3 DON JUAN 16    89   6
ENDURED
    SERMONS HE READ AND LECTURES HE ENDURED  . . . . .     47  2 DON JUAN  1    47   1
    BY LENGTH I MEAN DURATION THEIRS ENDURED . . . . .    254  2 DON JUAN  2   187   1
ENDURING
    HIS GRACE WAS AN ENDURING MARRIED MAN . . . . .       437  3 DON JUAN 14    62   2
ENEMIES
    HAD COST HIS ENEMIES A LONG REPENTANCE   . . . . .    303  2 DON JUAN  3    54   7
    OLD ENEMIES WHO HAVE BECOME NEW FRIENDS  . . . . .    231  3 DON JUAN 10    12   1
ENEMY
    LIKE ONE WHO GRAPPLES WITH HIS ENEMY  . . . . .       184  2 DON JUAN  2    52   7
    O'ER HIS WORST ENEMY WHEN AT HIS KNEES   . . . . .     17  3 DON JUAN  6    23   5
    BUT WHEN THEY SAW THE ENEMY RETIRE . . . . .           82  3 DON JUAN  7    31   2
    IN THINKING THAT THEIR ENEMY IS BEAT . . . . .         87  3 DON JUAN  7    42   4
ENERGETIC
    NOUGHT'S MORE SUBLIME THAN ENERGETIC BILE   . . . .    489  2 DON JUAN  5   135   4
ENERGIES
    THEN BY DEGREES RECALLED HIS ENERGIES. . . . . .      511  3 DON JUAN 16    25   4
```

ENERGY
    THEIR ENERGY LIKE LIFE FORMS ALL THEIR FAME . . . . . . 377 2 DON JUAN 4   61   7
ENGAGE
    WE DON'T MUCH CARE WITH WHOM WE MAY ENGAGE . . . . . . 217 3 DON JUAN 9   69   3
    AND HAPPIEST THEY WHO HORSES CAN ENGAGE . . . . 378 3 DON JUAN 13   44   4
ENGAGED
    BUT NEXT WHEN I'M ENGAGED TO SING THERE--DO GO . . . . 392 2 DON JUAN 4   88   8
    SUWARROW THOUGH ENGAGED WITH ACCENTS HIGH . . . . . . 100 3 DON JUAN 7   65   3
    TO GENTLEMEN ENGAGED IN THE ASSAULT . . . . 119 3 DON JUAN 8   16   7
ENGENDERED
    ENGENDERED MONSTROUS SHAPES OF EVERY CRIME . . . . . . 152 3 DON JUAN 8   82   8
ENGINEERING
    (PRITHEE EXCUSE THIS ENGINEERING SLANG) . . . . 72 3 DON JUAN 7   11   6
ENGINEER'S
    WHETHER IT WAS THEIR ENGINEER'S STUPIDITY . . . . . . 80 3 DON JUAN 7   27   1
ENGINES
    WITH DEADLIER ENGINES AND A SPEEDIER BLOW . . . . . . 106 3 DON JUAN 7   80   3
    OF WAR'S MOST MORTAL ENGINES TO THEIR FOES . . . . . . 116 3 DON JUAN 8   8   3
    BUT SINCE STEAM ENGINES PRAISE AND HONOUR VAPOUR . . . 317 3 DON JUAN 12   4 V8
ENGLAND
    HOLLAND FRANCE ENGLAND GERMANY OR SPAIN . . . . 157 2 DON JUAN 2   1   2
    IN ENGLAND A SIX CANTO QUARTO TALE . . . . 320 2 DON JUAN 3   86   2
    IN ENGLAND HE WOULD APE THE TRECENTISTI . . . . 320 2 DON JUAN 3   86 V2
    IN MORAL ENGLAND WHERE THE THING'S A TAX) . . . . . . 20 3 DON JUAN 6   29   7
    BUT IN OLD ENGLAND WHEN A YOUNG BRIDE ERRS . . . . . . 345 3 DON JUAN 12   64   7
    IN ENGLAND RANKS QUITE ON A DIFFERENT LIST . . . . . . 436 3 DON JUAN 14   60   6
    BESIDES HIS CONDUCT SINCE IN ENGLAND GREW MORE . . . . 460 3 DON JUAN 15   11   5
ENGLAND'S
    LET NONE ACCUSE OLD ENGLAND'S HOSPITALITY-- . . . . . 381 3 DON JUAN 13   49   7
ENGLISH
    SHE LIKED THE ENGLISH AND THE HEBREW TONGUE . . . . . . 28 2 DON JUAN 1   14   1
    THE ENGLISH ALWAYS USE TO GOVERN DAMN . . . . 28 2 DON JUAN 1   14   8
    WERE THERE NOT ALSO RUSSIANS ENGLISH MANY . . . . . . 102 2 DON JUAN 1   149   5
    WERE IN THE ENGLISH NEWSPAPERS OF COURSE . . . . . . 126 2 DON JUAN 1   188   8
    FOR WE ALL KNOW THAT ENGLISH PEOPLE ARE . . . . . . 238 2 DON JUAN 2   156   1
    MUCH ENGLISH I CANNOT PRETEND TO SPEAK . . . . . . 243 2 DON JUAN 2   165   3
    WHICH MAKE THE ENGLISH CLIMATE OF OUR YEARS . . . . . 270 2 DON JUAN 2   214   8
    HE HAD AN ENGLISH LOOK THAT IS WAS SQUARE . . . . . . 416 2 DON JUAN 5   11   1
    ARE THINGS WHICH MAKE AN ENGLISH EVENING PASS . . . . 444 2 DON JUAN 5   58   4
    REQUIRES IT THAT'S TO SAY THE ENGLISH RHYME . . . . . 14 3 DON JUAN 6   18   2
    WHO NAME THE FRENCH IN ENGLISH SAVE TO SHEW . . . . . 77 3 DON JUAN 7   22   7
    TO RUSSIAN TARTAR ENGLISH FRENCH COSSACQUE . . . . . 89 3 DON JUAN 7   46   2
    AN ENGLISH NAVAL OFFICER WHO WISHED . . . . 152 3 DON JUAN 8   80   7
    AN ENGLISH LADY ASKED OF AN ITALIAN . . . . 208 3 DON JUAN 9   51   1
    OF ENGLISH SAVE THEIR SHIBBOLETH GOD DAMN . . . . . 274 3 DON JUAN 11   12   2
    TO THINK SO FOR HALF ENGLISH AS I AM . . . . 274 3 DON JUAN 11   12   6
    INTO AS FURIOUS ENGLISH) WITH HER BEST LOOK . . . . . 294 3 DON JUAN 11   52   7
    COOL AND QUITE ENGLISH IMPERTURBABLE . . . . 365 3 DON JUAN 13   14   4
    THE ENGLISH WINTER--ENDING IN JULY . . . . 377 3 DON JUAN 13   42   1
    AN ENGLISH AUTUMN THOUGH IT HATH NO VINES . . . . . 394 3 DON JUAN 13   76   1
    FOR ENNUI IS A GROWTH OF ENGLISH ROOT . . . . 405 3 DON JUAN 13   101   5
    BUT WHETHER ENGLISH DUKES GREW RARE OF LATE . . . . . 474 3 DON JUAN 15   42   4
    WHICH PROVE PLAIN ENGLISH TRUER OF THE TWO . . . . . 488 3 DON JUAN 15   72   6
    FOR GOTHIC DARING SHOWN IN ENGLISH MONEY . . . . . . 529 3 DON JUAN 16   59   8
    HAD ENGLISH INFLUENCE IN THE SELF-SAME SPHERE HERE . . 534 3 DON JUAN 16   70   5
    IS'T ENGLISH NO--'TIS ONLY PARLIAMENTARY) . . . . . 536 3 DON JUAN 16   73   2
    AS BETWEEN ENGLISH BEEF AND SPARTAN BROTH-- . . . . . 541 3 DON JUAN 16   84   7
ENGLISHMAN
    HE GLORIED IN THE NAME OF ENGLISHMAN . . . . 537 3 DON JUAN 16   75   8
ENGLISHMEN
    'MONGST THEM WERE SEVERAL ENGLISHMEN OF PITH . . . . . 75 3 DON JUAN 7   18   7
    WELL LIKE MOST ENGLISHMEN AND LOVED THE RACES . . . . 368 3 DON JUAN 13   23   6
ENGLISHWOMAN'S
    AND ABOVE ALL AN ENGLISHWOMAN'S ROVES . . . . 284 3 DON JUAN 11   33   4
ENGRAVE
    ENGRAVE UPON THE PLATE YOU ROSE AT FOUR . . . . . . 230 2 DON JUAN 2   140   8
ENGRAVED
    AND SEE HIS STATUE RAISED--AND PRINT ENGRAVED . . . . 185 3 DON JUAN 9   5 V8
ENGROSS
    AND FOR THE FAME YOU WOULD ENGROSS BELOW . . . . . . 13 2 DON JUAN D   7   4
ENGROSSED
    WITH THE SUBSTANTIAL COMPANY ENGROSSED . . . . . . 543 3 DON JUAN 16   90   4
ENHANCE
    WAR'S MERIT IT BY NO MEANS MIGHT ENHANCE . . . . . . 113 3 DON JUAN 8   3   4
ENJOINING
    ENJOINING SILENCE STRICT TO ZOE WHO . . . . 228 2 DON JUAN 2   136   2
ENJOY
    THE PROMISED PARTY TO ENJOY ITS SWEETS . . . . . . 394 3 DON JUAN 13   75   2
ENJOYED
    ENJOYED THE LONELY VIGOROUS HARMLESS DAYS . . . . . 143 3 DON JUAN 8   61   7
ENJOYING
    HANDSOME AND YOUNG ENJOYING ALL THE PRESENT . . . . . 371 2 DON JUAN 4   51   4
    YOUR WARS ETERNALLY BESIDES ENJOYING . . . . 118 3 DON JUAN 8   14   7
    SOME HOURS TO MAKE THE REMNANT WORTH ENJOYING . . . . 444 3 DON JUAN 14   78   8
ENJOYMENT
    FROM THE ENJOYMENT OF THE EARTH AND AIR . . . . . . 258 3 DON JUAN 10   68   7
    AND STORE IT UP FOR MISCHIEVOUS ENJOYMENT . . . . . 548 3 DON JUAN 16   100   7
ENJOYMENT'S
    WHICH FOR AN INSTANT CLIP ENJOYMENT'S WINGS . . . . . 227 3 DON JUAN 10   5   8

ENLARGEMENT
   ENLARGEMENT OF EXISTENCE TO PARTAKE . . . . 247 2 DON JUAN 2 173 2
ENLIGHTEN
   MUST BURN MORE MILDLY ERE IT CAN ENLIGHTEN . . . . . 281 3 DON JUAN 11 27 8
ENLIST
   FOR MY PART I'LL ENLIST ON NEITHER SIDE . . . . 190 3 DON JUAN 9 16 5
ENNOBLE
   AS IF SHE DEEM'D THAT MYSTERY WOULD ENNOBLE 'EM . . . . 28 2 DON JUAN 1 13 8
ENNUI
   AFTER LONG TRAVEL ENNUI LOVE OR SLAUGHTER . . . . . . 251 2 DON JUAN 2 180 7
   TO PROVE ITS GRAND INGREDIENT IS ENNUI . . . . 332 2 DON JUAN 3 97 8
   TO HELP THE TASTE OF MORTALS FOR ENNUI . . . . 332 2 DON JUAN 3 97 V8
   TO SHOW HOW ESSENTIAL TO IT IS ENNUI . . . . 332 2 DON JUAN 3 97 V8
   TIME HAS APPROVED ENNUI TO BE THE BEST . . . . 343 2 DON JUAN 3 V 98 1
   FOR ENNUI IS A GROWTH OF ENGLISH ROOT . . . . 405 3 DON JUAN 13 101 5
   THIS PARADISE OF PLEASURE AND ENNUI . . . . 417 3 DON JUAN 14 17 8
   THE GRAND ANTITHESIS TO GREAT ENNUI . . . . 457 3 DON JUAN 15 2 3
ENORMOUS
   THAN AN ENORMOUS ROOM WITHOUT A SOUL . . . . 442 2 DON JUAN 5 56 7
   IN MOCKERY TO THE ENORMOUS GATE WHICH ROSE . . . . . 462 2 DON JUAN 5 87 5
   AND ONE ENORMOUS SHOUT OF ALLAH ROSE . . . . 116 3 DON JUAN 8 8 1
   OF THIS ENORMOUS CITY'S SPREADING SPAWN . . . . 281 3 DON JUAN 11 28 4
ENOUGH
   WITH JUST ENOUGH OF TALENT AND NO MORE . . . . 16 2 DON JUAN D 12 6
   ARE QUITE ENOUGH FOR ME SO THEY BUT HOLD . . . . 85 2 DON JUAN 1 118 8
   A HINT IN TENDER CASES IS ENOUGH . . . . 119 2 DON JUAN 1 178 1
   AS I WHO'VE CROSS'D IT OFT KNOW WELL ENOUGH . . . . . 162 2 DON JUAN 2 11 4
   WAS SCANT ENOUGH IN VAIN THE TELESCOPE . . . . 178 2 DON JUAN 2 41 6
   BUT SCARCE ENOUGH TO SERVE THEM FOR A LUNCHEON-- . . . 181 2 DON JUAN 2 47 7
   AND ALL THE REST WERE THIN ENOUGH HEAVEN KNOWS . . . . 199 2 DON JUAN 2 80 2
   WITH JUST ENOUGH OF LIFE TO FEEL ITS PAIN . . . . . . 213 2 DON JUAN 2 108 7
   SAYING HE HAD GORGED ENOUGH TO MAKE A HORSE ILL . . . 240 2 DON JUAN 2 159 8
   ENOUGH--THE FAITHFUL AND THE FAIRY PAIR . . . . 353 2 DON JUAN 4 18 2
   GAVE LIGHT ENOUGH TO HINT THEIR FARTHER WAY . . . . . 442 2 DON JUAN 5 56 2
   BUT NOT ENOUGH TO SHOW THE IMPERIAL HALLS . . . . . . 442 2 DON JUAN 5 56 3
   WAS HARDLY LONG ENOUGH BUT BABA FOUND . . . . 457 2 DON JUAN 5 79 2
   CONCEIVED THAT PHRASE WAS QUITE ENOUGH TO MOVE . . . . 478 2 DON JUAN 5 116 8
   (ENOUGH GOD KNOWS) WOULD MUCH FALL SHORT OF THIS . . . 489 2 DON JUAN 5 134 8
   BUT WORDS ARE NOT ENOUGH IN SUCH A MATTER . . . . . . 493 2 DON JUAN 5 143 2
   WAS SCARCE ENOUGH FOR HE HAD FIFTY-NINE . . . . 10 3 DON JUAN 6 8 7
   ALTHOUGH HER BEAUTY WAS ENOUGH TO VEX . . . . 24 3 DON JUAN 6 37 2
   JUANNA--WELL A PRETTY NAME ENOUGH . . . . 28 3 DON JUAN 6 44 2
   YOUR FATHER'S SON 'TIS QUITE ENOUGH FOR ME . . . . . . 52 3 DON JUAN 6 93 8
   SCIENCE ENOUGH WHICH LEVELS TO AN ASS . . . . 69 3 DON JUAN 7 5 3
   AND MORE MIGHT BE FOUND OUT IF I COULD POKE ENOUGH . . 74 3 DON JUAN 7 15 6
   BUT FIGHTING THOUGHTLESSLY ENOUGH TO WIN . . . . . . 121 3 DON JUAN 8 19 7
   THIS SIMILE ENOUGH FOR AJAX JUAN . . . . 126 3 DON JUAN 8 29 7
   OVER THE HILLS A FIRE ENOUGH TO BLIND . . . . 126 3 DON JUAN 8 30 4
   THE FIRST TIME THOUGHT QUITE TERRIBLE ENOUGH . . . . . 134 3 DON JUAN 8 42 2
   'TIS STRANGE ENOUGH--THE ROUGH TOUGH SOLDIERS WHO . . 171 3 DON JUAN 8 119 1
   WITHOUT ME THERE ARE DEMAGOGUES ENOUGH . . . . 195 3 DON JUAN 9 25 2
   OR ON MIGHT DREAD HER MAJESTY HAD NOT ROOM ENOUGH . . 206 3 DON JUAN 9 48 3
   FOR A NEW FLAME A THOUGHT TO CAST OF GLOOM ENOUGH . . 206 3 DON JUAN 9 48 5
   HER THIRD WAS FEMININE ENOUGH TO ANNUL . . . . 212 3 DON JUAN 9 60 5
   ENOUGH TO MAKE A STRIPLING VERY VAIN . . . . 218 3 DON JUAN 9 72 8
   AND THAT'S ENOUGH FOR LOVE IS VANITY . . . . 219 3 DON JUAN 9 73 1
   IT IS ENOUGH THAT FORTUNE FOUND HIM FLUSH . . . . . . 227 3 DON JUAN 10 5 6
   HE WAS NOT YET QUITE OLD ENOUGH TO PROVE . . . . . . 250 3 DON JUAN 10 53 4
   'TWAS STRANGE ENOUGH SHE SHOULD RETAIN THE IMPRESSION 252 3 DON JUAN 10 56 1
   JUST NOW ENOUGH BUT BY-AND-BY I'LL PRATTLE . . . . . 267 3 DON JUAN 10 87 7
   WERE HARDLY RUDE ENOUGH TO EARN THEIR PAY . . . . . . 287 3 DON JUAN 11 40 8
   ENOUGH TO GRATIFY A BEE'S SLIGHT MUNCHINGS . . . . . 301 3 DON JUAN 11 66 5
   OF RANK ENOUGH TO SET IN STONE OR LEAD . . . . 314 3 DON JUAN 11 V 75 2
   AND THAT'S ENOUGH SUCCEEDED IN MY YOUTH . . . . 324 3 DON JUAN 12 17 2
   'TWAS NOT HER FORTUNE--HE HAS ENOUGH WITHOUT . . . . . 332 3 DON JUAN 12 35 2
   ENOUGH TO MAKE FOR PORT ERE TIME SHALL SUMMON . . . . 376 3 DON JUAN 13 40 4
   'TIS NOT ENOUGH TO SPELL OR EVEN TO READ . . . . . . 393 3 DON JUAN 13 73 4
   PROUD OF HIS LEARNING (JUST ENOUGH TO QUOTE) . . . . . 401 3 DON JUAN 13 91 3
   RIDICULOUS ENOUGH BUT ALSO DULL . . . . 402 3 DON JUAN 13 95 2
   AND QUITE ENOUGH FOR ME TO KEEP IN MIND-- . . . . . . 414 3 DON JUAN 14 9 3
   OF PASSIONS TOO I HAVE PROVED ENOUGH TO BLAME . . . . 414 3 DON JUAN 14 9 4
   OH JOB YOU HAD TWO FRIENDS ONE'S QUITE ENOUGH . . . . 431 3 DON JUAN 14 48 1
   WHOSE MERIT NONE ENOUGH CAN SING OR SAY . . . . 445 3 DON JUAN 14 82 2
   METHINKS LOVE'S VERY TITLE SAYS ENOUGH . . . . 451 3 DON JUAN 14 94 7
   PERHAPS 'TWAS HARDLY QUITE ASSURED ENOUGH . . . . . . 462 3 DON JUAN 15 14 5
   IMAGINATION'S QUITE ENOUGH FOR THAT . . . . 463 3 DON JUAN 15 16 3
   STRANGELY ENOUGH AS YET WITHOUT MISCARRIAGE . . . . . 471 3 DON JUAN 15 35 3
   THAT JUAN HAD ENOUGH OF MAINTENANCE . . . . 473 3 DON JUAN 15 39 2
   IN HER OWN MIND AND THAT'S ENOUGH FOR WOMAN . . . . . 473 3 DON JUAN 15 40 2
   THOUGH LADIES' ROBES SEEM SCANT ENOUGH FOR LESS . . . 482 3 DON JUAN 15 61 8
   NOR EVEN SMILED ENOUGH FOR ANY VANITY . . . . 490 3 DON JUAN 15 78 4
   SLIGHT BUT SELECT AND JUST ENOUGH TO EXPRESS . . . . 491 3 DON JUAN 15 80 2
   NOR THOUGHT HE HAD PRIDE ENOUGH--FOR SHE WAS PROUD . . 493 3 DON JUAN 15 83 V6
   WAS WEAK ENOUGH TO DEEM POPE A GREAT POET . . . . . . 524 3 DON JUAN 16 47 7
   NOR INSOLENT ENOUGH TO SCORN THE SCORNER . . . . . . 532 3 DON JUAN 16 65 6
   YOU SEE HERE WAS ENOUGH OF OCCUPATION . . . . 534 3 DON JUAN 16 68 1
ENQUIRE
   AT LENGTH HE CONDESCENDED TO ENQUIRE . . . . 171 3 DON JUAN 8 120 5
   LET SPENDTHRIFTS' HEIRS ENQUIRE OF YOURS--WHO'S WISER . 321 3 DON JUAN 12 11 8

		PAGE	VOL	CANTO	STANZA	LV
ENQUIRED						
	ENQUIRED HIS INCOME AND IF HE HAD BROTHERS	293	3 DON JUAN 11	48	8
	FAIR ADELINE ENQUIRED IF HE WERE ILL	514	3 DON JUAN 16	32	3
ENQUIRIES						
	ENQUIRIES AFTER THEM WITH KINDEST CARE	64	3 DON JUAN 6	118	6
ENQUIRY						
	WITH STRICT ENQUIRY I COULD N'ER DISCOVER	41	3 DON JUAN 6	70	2
ENRICH						
	THAT WENT BEFORE IN THESE I SHALL ENRICH	138	2 DON JUAN 1	204	4
	WHOSE BLOOD THE PUDDLE GREATLY DID ENRICH	147	3 DON JUAN 8	71	3
ENSEMBLE						
	AS SUITED THE ENSEMBLE OF HIS TOILET	457	2 DON JUAN 5	79	7
	THE TOUT ENSEMBLE OF HIS MOVEMENTS WORE A	428	3 DON JUAN 14	40	5
ENSLAVED						
	AND EUROPE'S LIBERATOR--STILL ENSLAVED	185	3 DON JUAN 9	5	8
	HIS PRIDE TOO FELT THAT SHE WAS NOT ENSLAVED	251	3 DON JUAN 10	55	4
	WHILE WELLINGTON HAS BUT ENSLAVED THE WHITES	325	3 DON JUAN 12	20	7
ENSLAVER						
	HAD STUNG HIM FROM A SLAVE TO AN ENSLAVER	302	2 DON JUAN 3	53	8
ENSUE						
	BUT HERE A SORT OF SCENE BEGAN TO ENSUE	101	3 DON JUAN 7	67	1
ENSUED						
	HOW MANY SONNETS HAD ENSUED THE BEDDING	279	2 DON JUAN 3	8	V8
	SO THAT SOME DISAPPOINTMENT THERE ENSUED	177	3 DON JUAN 8	131	2
	IF IN THE CIRCUMSTANCES WHICH ENSUED	553	3 DON JUAN 16	107	3
ENSUING						
	WHICH PUT OFF BUSINESS TO THE ENSUING SESSION	331	2 DON JUAN 3	96	6
ENSURE						
	I MAY ENSURE THE PUBLIC AND DEFY	142	2 DON JUAN 1	211	2
	QUOTH JOHNSON--NEITHER WILL I QUITE ENSURE	161	3 DON JUAN 8	100	4
ENSURED						
	WE FROM IMPALEMENT HAD ENSURED OUR SKIN	435	2 DON JUAN 5	44	V4
ENSURES						
	IN THAT COMPLETE PERFECTION WHICH ENSURES	332	2 DON JUAN 3	97	3
ENTAIL						
	IF STARS AND TITLES COULD ENTAIL LONG PRAISE	84	3 DON JUAN 7	37	3
ENTAILED						
	HAVE SHAVING TOO ENTAILED UPON THEIR CHINS--	420	3 DON JUAN 14	23	8
ENTANGLE						
	BUT HERE AGAIN WHY WILL I THUS ENTANGLE	496	3 DON JUAN 15	91	1
ENTANGLED						
	LIKE A GOOD SHIP ENTANGLED AMONG ICE	490	3 DON JUAN 15	77	7
ENTER						
	COULD ENTER INTO DON ALFONSO'S HEAD	97	2 DON JUAN 1	139	2
	WE ENTER ON OUR NAUTICAL EXISTENCE	163	2 DON JUAN 2	12	8
	HERE I MIGHT ENTER ON A CHASTE DESCRIPTION	397	2 DON JUAN 4	97	1
	ON WHICH THE MUSE HAS ALWAYS SOUGHT TO ENTER-- . . .	375	3 DON JUAN 13	38	6
	THROUGH WHICH THE DEEPEN'D GLORIES ONCE COULD ENTER .	387	3 DON JUAN 13	62	3
ENTER'D						
	HE ENTER'D IN THE HOUSE NO MORE HIS HOME	301	2 DON JUAN 3	51	1
	HE ENTER'D IN THE HOUSE--HIS HOME NO MORE	302	2 DON JUAN 3	52	1
ENTERED						
	AS THE BLACK EUNUCH ENTERED WITH HIS BRACE	441	2 DON JUAN 5	54	1
	BEFORE THEY ENTERED BABA PAUSED TO HINT	464	2 DON JUAN 5	91	1
	FURTHER OLD BABA RATHER BRISKLY ENTERED	493	2 DON JUAN 5	143	8
	THE TOWN WAS ENTERED OH ETERNITY--	142	3 DON JUAN 8	60	1
	THE TOWN WAS ENTERED FIRST ONE COLUMN MADE	146	3 DON JUAN 8	69	1
ENTERING						
	NOW DON ALFONSO ENTERING BUT ALONE	116	2 DON JUAN 1	173	1
ENTERTAIN						
	LIKE TO THE NOTIONS WE NOW ENTERTAIN	201	3 DON JUAN 9	38	5
	TO ENTERTAIN THIS AUTUMN A SELECT	382	3 DON JUAN 13	52	2
ENTERTAINING						
	ALL THESE ARE CERTES ENTERTAINING FACTS	329	2 DON JUAN 3	92	1
ENTHUSIASM						
	THERE WAS ENTHUSIASM AND MUCH APPLAUSE	89	3 DON JUAN 7	47	2
	AND RASH ENTHUSIASM IN GOOD SOCIETY	374	3 DON JUAN 13	35	7
ENTIRE						
	THEY FURNISH'D HIM ENTIRE EXCEPT SOME STITCHES	240	2 DON JUAN 2	160	7
ENTIRELY						
	AT LEAST ENTIRELY FOR HE HAD SEEN TOO MANY	338	3 DON JUAN 12	49	7
ENTOMB						
	SHOWS THAT WE BUILD WHEN WE SHOULD BUT ENTOMB US . . .	448	2 DON JUAN 5	63	8
	HERE PEALS THE PEOPLE'S VOICE NOR CAN ENTOMB IT . . .	272	3 DON JUAN 11	9	6
ENTOMB'D						
	ENTOMB'D THE BRAVEST OF THE BRAVE ACHILLES	385	2 DON JUAN 4	76	3
ENTOMBING						
	FROM OUT THE WIDE DESTRUCTION WHICH ENTOMBING ALL . . .	399	2 DON JUAN 4	101	5
ENTRAIL						
	SO THAT ALL MISCHIEFS SPRING UP FROM THIS ENTRAIL . . .	271	2 DON JUAN 2	215	7
ENTRAILS						
	AND SUCH THINGS AS THE ENTRAILS AND THE BRAINS	197	2 DON JUAN 2	77	6
ENTRANCE						
	BEFORE THE ENTRANCE OF A CLIFF-WORN CAVE	213	2 DON JUAN 2	108	6
	WHENCE IS OUR EXIT AND OUR ENTRANCE--WELL I	210	3 DON JUAN 9	55	3
	WHICH KINDLE MANHOOD BUT CAN NE'ER ENTRANCE	554	3 DON JUAN 16	108	6
	A SINGLE SHADE'S SUFFICIENT TO ENTRANCE A	557	3 DON JUAN 16	116	6
ENTRATE						
	VOI CHE ENTRATE THE HINGE SEEMED TO SPEAK	557	3 DON JUAN 16	116	3

```
                                                       PAGE VOL      CANTO STANZA LN
ENTRE
      (THIS SHOULD BE ENTRE NOUS FOR JULIA THOUGHT  . . . . .  67  2 DON JUAN  1      84    7
ENTREATING
      SO JUAN'S SPANIEL SPITE OF HIS ENTREATING  . . . . . .  193  2 DON JUAN  2      70    7
      ENTREATING YOU TO PAUSE BEFORE YOU DASH ON . . . . . .  337  3 DON JUAN 12      45    6
ENTREMETS
      AND ENTREMETS TO PIDDLE WITH AT HAND . . . . . . . .  484  3 DON JUAN 15      66    5
ENTRENCHMENT
      O'ER THE ENTRENCHMENT AND THE PALISADE  . . . . . .  119  3 DON JUAN  8      15    7
ENTWINE
      WHERE TRANSPORT AND SECURITY ENTWINE . . . . . . . .   69  2 DON JUAN  1      88    2
ENTWINED
      OR LOVE--I WON'T SAY MORE ABOUT ENTWINED . . . . . .   69  2 DON JUAN  1      89    6
ENTWINES
      THE PATHS O'ER WHICH THE FAR FESTOON ENTWINES . . . .  394  3 DON JUAN 13      76    3
ENTWINING
      A SORT OF ROSE ENTWINING WITH A THISTLE . . . . . .  407  3 DON JUAN 13     105   V6
ENUMERATION
      AND NOBLE BIRTHS NOR DREAD THE ENUMERATION--  . . . .  432  3 DON JUAN 14      52    4
ENVIABLE
      OH ENVIABLE BRIAREUS WITH THY HANDS  . . . . . . .   20  3 DON JUAN  6      28    1
ENVIED
      BY RAILING AT THE UNKNOWN AND ENVIED PASSION . . . .  337  3 DON JUAN 12      45    2
ENVIRON
      AH WHAT IS MAN WHAT PERILS STILL ENVIRON . . . . . .  294  2 DON JUAN  3      36    1
      AS WILL ENVIRON A CONSPICUOUS MAN  SOME  . . . . . .  305  3 DON JUAN 11      74    5
ENVOY
      THERE MANY AN ENVOY EITHER DWELT OR DWELLS . . . . .  283  3 DON JUAN 11      31    5
      THE ENVOY OF THE SECRET RUSSIAN MISSION . . . . . .  382  3 DON JUAN 13      52    8
ENVOYS
      EXCEPT IN SHAPE OF ENVOYS WHO WERE SENT . . . . . .  498  2 DON JUAN  5     151    1
ENVY
      TO YOU I ENVY NEITHER FRUIT NOR BOUGHS-- . . . . . .   13  2 DON JUAN  D       7    3
      THE FAME YOU ENVY AND THE SKILL YOU NEED . . . . . .   14  2 DON JUAN  D       8    4
      AND EVEN THE GOOD WITH INWARD ENVY GROAN . . . . . .   26  2 DON JUAN  1      10    6
      WHICH MAKE THE READER ENVY HIS TRANSGRESSIONS . . . .   47  2 DON JUAN  1      47    8
      AND ALWAYS ENVY THOUGH WE DEEM IT FRANTIC  . . . . .  353  2 DON JUAN  4      18    8
      WHICH HATE NOR ENVY E'ER COULD TINGE WITH WRONG . . .  144  3 DON JUAN  8      63    6
      IT WAS NOT ENVY--ADELINE HAD NONE  . . . . . . . .  479  3 DON JUAN 15      54    1
      NO ONE COULD ENVY HER DESERVED PROSPERITY  . . . . .  550  3 DON JUAN 16     102    6
ENVYING
      RAILING AT POWER--BUT ENVYING ALL IT'S TOOLS  . . . .  152  2 DON JUAN  1  V   3   V7
ENVY'S
      IN WHICH NOT ENVY'S SELF A FLAW DISCOVERS  . . . . .   29  2 DON JUAN  1      16    6
EPAMINONDAS
      EPAMINONDAS SAVED HIS THEBES AND DIED . . . . . . .  186  3 DON JUAN  9       8    2
EPAULETTES
      HIS WINGS SUBDUED TO EPAULETTES HIS QUIVER . . . . .  205  3 DON JUAN  9      45    2
EPHESIAN
      I'VE HEARD THEM IN THE EPHESIAN RUINS HOWL  . . . . .  196  3 DON JUAN  9      27    2
EPHESIANS
      MY DIAN OF THE EPHESIANS LADY ADELINE . . . . . . .  430  3 DON JUAN 14      46    3
EPIC
      AND NOW MY EPIC RENEGADE WHAT ARE YE AT  . . . . . .    9  2 DON JUAN  D       1    5
      MOST EPIC POETS PLUNGE IN MEDIAS RES  . . . . . . .   24  2 DON JUAN  1       6    1
      MY POEM'S EPIC AND IS MEANT TO BE  . . . . . . . .  135  2 DON JUAN  1     200    1
      ME AND MY EPIC BRETHREN GONE BEFORE  . . . . . . .  137  2 DON JUAN  1     202    2
      THE EPIC HARP--THE LYRIC LUTE--  . . . . . . . . .  321  2 DON JUAN  3  L   2   V2
      AN EPIC FROM BOB SOUTHEY EVERY SPRING--)  . . . . . .  332  2 DON JUAN  3      97    4
      'TIS BEING TOO EPIC AND I MUST CUT DOWN . . . . . .  342  2 DON JUAN  3     111    2
      ACCORDING TO THE ANCIENT EPIC LAWS . . . . . . . .  503  2 DON JUAN  5     159    3
      MAKE EPIC POESY SO RARE AND RICH  . . . . . . . .  156  3 DON JUAN  8      90    8
      AND EPIC IF PLAIN TRUTH SHOULD PROVE NO BAR . . . .  181  3 DON JUAN  8     138    5
      OF EPIC LOVE'S BEGINNING END AND MIDDLE  . . . . . .  337  3 DON JUAN 12      45    8
      BY THAT REAL EPIC UNTO ALL WHO HAVE THOUGHT . . . . .  363  3 DON JUAN 13       9    8
      TO COME BETWEEN MINE EPIC AND ITS INDEX  . . . . . .  440  3 DON JUAN 14      68    8
      THAN I HAVE YET DONE IN THIS EPIC SATIRE . . . . . .  454  3 DON JUAN 14      99    6
      FROM ANYTHING THIS EPIC WILL CONTAIN  . . . . . . .  502  3 DON JUAN 16       3    2
EPICAL
      MY EPICAL PRETENSIONS TO THE LAUREL  . . . . . . .  141  2 DON JUAN  1     209    6
EPICENE
      THE GENDER STILL WAS EPICENE AT LEAST . . . . . . .   35  3 DON JUAN  6      58    2
EPIC'S
      SO THAT MY NAME OF EPIC'S NO MISNOMER . . . . . . .  135  2 DON JUAN  1     200    8
EPICURUS
      THOU MAK'ST PHILOSOPHERS THERE'S EPICURUS  . . . . .  267  2 DON JUAN  2     207    1
EPIGRAM
      SO THESE POINT THE EPIGRAM OF HUMAN BREATH  . . . . .  280  2 DON JUAN  3       9   V3
      FORTH INTO UNIVERSAL EPIGRAM . . . . . . . . . .  552  3 DON JUAN 16     104    2
EPIGRAMS
      TO ALL THOSE NAUSEOUS EPIGRAMS OF MARTIAL  . . . . .   45  2 DON JUAN  1      43    8
      MADE EPIGRAMS OCCASIONALLY TOO . . . . . . . . .  524  3 DON JUAN 16      47    3
EPILEPTICAL
      HALF EPILEPTICAL AND HALF HYSTERICAL--  . . . . . .  183  2 DON JUAN  2      50    7
EPISODE
      WHAT WENT BEFORE--BY WAY OF EPISODE  . . . . . . .   24  2 DON JUAN  1       6    4
EPISODES
      NEW CHARACTERS THE EPISODES ARE THREE . . . . . . .  135  2 DON JUAN  1     200    5
EPISTLE
      THE EARTH HAS NOTHING LIKE A SHE EPISTLE . . . . . .  407  3 DON JUAN 13     105    2
```

	PAGE	VOL	CANTO	STANZA	LN
EPITAPHS					
WHERE ARE THE EPITAPHS OUR FATHERS READ	399	2 DON JUAN	4	102	5
EPITOME					
CATHERINE WHO WAS THE GRAND EPITOME	211	3 DON JUAN	9	57	1
EPOCH					
WITHOUT WHOSE EPOCH MY POETIC SKILL	86	2 DON JUAN	1	121	3
BUT SINCE THEY ARE THAT EPOCH IS A BORE	316	3 DON JUAN	12	2	4
EPOCH THAT AWKWARD CORNER TURNED FOR DAYS	360	3 DON JUAN	13	4	2
EPOPEE					
SOME FINE EXAMPLES OF THE EPOPEE	332	2 DON JUAN	3	97	7
EQUAL					
BUT WHETHER JULIA TO THE TASK WAS EQUAL	66	2 DON JUAN	1	82	7
WHEN NIGHTS ARE EQUAL BUT NOT SO THE DAYS	414	2 DON JUAN	5	6	2
AND YOU AN EQUAL COURTESY SHOULD SHOW--	419	2 DON JUAN	5	16	4
HIS GLORY MIGHT HALF EQUAL HIS ESTATE--	84	3 DON JUAN	7	37	4
PROVED DEATH IN BATTLE EQUAL TO A PENSION--	96	3 DON JUAN	7	58	8
BUT STILL WE MODERNS EQUAL YOU IN BLOOD	106	3 DON JUAN	7	80	8
WHICH MAKES ALL FEMALE AGES EQUAL--WHEN	217	3 DON JUAN	9	69	2
IN BIRTH IN RANK IN FORTUNE LIKEWISE EQUAL	367	3 DON JUAN	13	20	1
THERE REMBRANDT MADE HIS DARKNESS EQUAL LIGHT	392	3 DON JUAN	13	72	2
EQUALL'D					
WITH VIRTUES EQUALL'D BY HER WIT ALONE	26	2 DON JUAN	1	10	4
EQUALLY					
BUT THEN NO DOUBT IT EQUALLY AS TRUE IS	79	2 DON JUAN	1	108	7
THOUGH ALL DESERVING EQUALLY TO TURN	120	3 DON JUAN	8	17	5
BY TURK AND CHRISTIAN EQUALLY HE COULD	129	3 DON JUAN	8	33	V6
WHY SHOULD NOT LIFE BE EQUALLY CONTENT	189	3 DON JUAN	9	13	3
EQUALS					
HAVING NO EQUALS NOTHING WHICH HAD E'ER	480	2 DON JUAN	5	119	2
EQUANIMITY					
WHO SEEM'D THE CREAM OF EQUANIMITY	474	3 DON JUAN	15	41	3
EQUINOCTIAL					
MAKE MY SOUL PASS THE EQUINOCTIAL LINE	255	3 DON JUAN	10	61	6
FOR THEY HAVE PASSED LIFE'S EQUINOCTIAL LINE	360	3 DON JUAN	13	5	4
WHICH NE'ER CAN PASS THE EQUINOCTIAL LINE	373	3 DON JUAN	13	34	3
EQUINOX					
THAT HORRID EQUINOX THAT HATEFUL SECTION	238	3 DON JUAN	10	27	4
EQUIPAGE					
COACH CHARIOT LUGGAGE BAGGAGE EQUIPAGE	378	3 DON JUAN	13	44	2
EQUIPPED					
NEXT WITH A VIRGIN ZONE HE WAS EQUIPPED	456	2 DON JUAN	5	77	3
EQUITY					
IN LAW THAN EQUITY--AS I CAN FEEL--	357	3 DON JUAN	12	V 18	4
ERA					
I KNOW THAT SOME WOULD FAIN POSTPONE THIS ERA	360	3 DON JUAN	13	5	1
ERA'S					
ABOUT THE DAY--THE ERA'S MORE OBSCURE	86	2 DON JUAN	1	121	8
'ERE					
OH JACK I'M FLOORED BY THAT 'ERE BLOODY FRENCHMAN	274	3 DON JUAN	11	13	8
ERECT					
AND THIN PRODUCED A PLAN WHEREBY TO ERECT	529	3 DON JUAN	16	58	6
ERECTED					
CHEOPS ERECTED THE FIRST PYRAMID	146	2 DON JUAN	1	219	2
IN THE NEW BATTERIES ERECTED THERE	80	3 DON JUAN	7	27	6
NEW BATTERIES WERE ERECTED AND WAS HELD	92	3 DON JUAN	7	51	1
NOR USE THOSE PALISADES BY DAMES ERECTED	437	3 DON JUAN	14	61	7
ERECTION					
TO ME APPEARS A STIFF YET GRAND ERECTION	280	3 DON JUAN	11	25	7
ERIN					
HE WAS WHAT ERIN CALLS IN HER SUBLIME	122	3 DON JUAN	8	23	1
AFTER THE GOOD EXAMPLE OF GREEN ERIN	286	3 DON JUAN	11	38	7
HEART-BALLADS OF GREEN ERIN OR GREY HIGHLANDS	523	3 DON JUAN	16	46	2
ERIN'S					
DABBLING ITS SLEEK YOUNG HANDS IN ERIN'S GORE	16	2 DON JUAN	D	12	2
THY CLANKING CHAIN AND ERIN'S YET GREEN WOUNDS	19	2 DON JUAN	D	16	5
ERMINE					
A BULL-DOG AND A BULL-FINCH AND AN ERMINE	249	3 DON JUAN	10	50	1
JUDGES IN VERY FORMIDABLE ERMINE	391	3 DON JUAN	13	69	1
THERE IS A SAMENESS IN ITS GEMS AND ERMINE	416	3 DON JUAN	14	15	6
ERNEIS					
ERNEIS RADULPHUS--EIGHT-AND-FORTY MANORS	242	3 DON JUAN	10	36	2
EROS					
OF EROS BUT THOUGH THOU HAST PLAYED US MANY TRICKS	554	3 DON JUAN	16	109	7
ERR					
TO BEG HIS PARDON WHEN I ERR A BIT	86	2 DON JUAN	1	120	8
SHE WAS SO LIKE A VISION I MIGHT ERR	314	2 DON JUAN	3	76	6
WHEN DAZZLED WITH HER ASPECT I MIGHT ERR	314	2 DON JUAN	3	76	V6
A HEAVY PRICE MUST ALL PAY WHO THUS ERR	383	2 DON JUAN	4	73	6
SO THAT I DO NOT GROSSLY ERR IN FACTS	149	3 DON JUAN	8	74	3
(IF THAT MY MEMORY DOTH NOT GREATLY ERR)	242	3 DON JUAN	10	36	3
WITH THIS O'ERWHELMING WORLD WHERE ALL MUST ERR	250	3 DON JUAN	10	52	6
SOMETIMES A LITTLE LATER I DON'T ERR	378	3 DON JUAN	13	43	2
'TIS THUS THE GOOD WILL AMIABLY ERR	463	3 DON JUAN	15	17	3
SOMETIMES UNLESS MY FEELINGS RATHER ERR)	506	3 DON JUAN	16	14	5
WAS MORE SHAKESPEARIAN IF I DO NOT ERR	524	3 DON JUAN	16	48	4
THEY ERR--'TIS MERELY WHAT IS CALLED MOBILITY	547	3 DON JUAN	16	97	4
ERRATUM					
IN AN ERRATUM OF HER HORSE FOR COURIER	446	2 DON JUAN	5	61	V7
ERR'D					
AND PLUMAGE (PROBABLY IT MIGHT HAVE ERR'D	206	2 DON JUAN	2	94	3

ERRED
    THE FAIR SULTANA ERRED FROM INANITION 10   3 DON JUAN 6   9   5
    BABA THOUGHT SHE WOULD FAINT BUT THERE HE ERRED-- 59   3 DON JUAN 6 106   2
    THEY ERRED AS AGED MEN WILL DO BUT BY 285   3 DON JUAN 11   36   1
    WHOSE HOUNDS NE'ER ERRED NOR GREYHOUNDS DEIGNED TO LURCH . 539   3 DON JUAN 16   80   2
ERRING
    AN ERRING WOMAN FINDS AN OPENER DOOR 352   3 DON JUAN 12   79   6
ERRONEOUS
    THE BOOK WHICH TREATS OF THIS ERRONEOUS PAIR 282   2 DON JUAN 3   12   6
ERROR
    BUT WITH A MORAL TO EACH ERROR TACKED 412   2 DON JUAN 5   2   4
    SO AGITATED WAS SHE WITH HER ERROR 50   3 DON JUAN 6   89   7
    FOR FEAR OF ANY ERROR LIKE THE LATE 62   3 DON JUAN 6 112   8
    THE LURKING BIAS BE IT TRUTH OR ERROR 413   3 DON JUAN 14   6   5
    HE NE'ER PRESUMED TO MAKE AN ERROR CLEARER-- 426   3 DON JUAN 14   37   7
ERRORS
    TO OTHERS' SHARE LET FEMALE ERRORS FALL 29   2 DON JUAN 1   16   7
    THERE LIES THE THING WE LOVE WITH ALL ITS ERRORS . . . 261   2 DON JUAN 2 197   7
    TO HUNT OUR ERRORS UP WITH A GOOD GRACE 430   3 DON JUAN 14   47   6
    REMEMBER WITHOUT TELLING PASSION'S ERRORS 457   3 DON JUAN 15   4   2
ERRS
    BUT IN OLD ENGLAND WHEN A YOUNG BRIDE ERRS 345   3 DON JUAN 12   64   7
ERSE
    OLD ERSE OR IRISH OR IT MAY BE PUNIC-- 122   3 DON JUAN 8   23   2
ERST
    DON JUAN SHOOK AS ERST HE HAD BEEN SHAKEN 558   3 DON JUAN 16 118   1
ESAU
    LIKE ESAU FOR MY BIRTHRIGHT A BEEF-STEAK 435   2 DON JUAN 5   44   8
ESCALADE
    WE ONLY CAN BUT TALK OF ESCALADE 106   3 DON JUAN 7   78   6
ESCAPADE
    TILL SOME CONFOUNDED ESCAPADE HAS BLIGHTED 75   2 DON JUAN 1 100   5
    SOME DEVILISH ESCAPADE OR STIR WHICH SHOWS 328   3 DON JUAN 12   26   2
ESCAPE
    AND LET FEW OPPORTUNITIES ESCAPE 32   2 DON JUAN 1   20   7
    COULD NOT ESCAPE THE GENTLE JULIA'S EYES 73   2 DON JUAN 1   97   2
    AND YET SHE DID NOT LET ONE TEAR ESCAPE HER 134   2 DON JUAN 1 198   5
    AND MANY DEATHS DO THEY ESCAPE BY THIS 350   2 DON JUAN 4   12   2
    AND TRUSTING JUAN MAY ESCAPE THE FISHES 65   3 DON JUAN 6 120   5
    WITH THEIR ATTENDANT AIDED OUR ESCAPE 103   3 DON JUAN 7   72   2
    OF A TRUE POET TO ESCAPE FROM FICTION 154   3 DON JUAN 8   86   2
    BEFORE HE CAN ESCAPE FROM SO MUCH DANGER 305   3 DON JUAN 11   74   4
ESCAPED
    HAD EER ESCAPED MORE DANGERS ON THE DEEP 229   2 DON JUAN 2 137   V7
    AND RAN BUT IT ESCAPED HER AS SHE CLASP'D 361   3 DON JUAN 4   32   8
    CAPTIVES JUST NOW ESCAPED WAS THE REPLY 97   3 DON JUAN 7   59   5
    BUT WHETHER THEY ESCAPED OR NO LIES HID 178   3 DON JUAN 8 132   7
    THE MOON PEEPED JUST ESCAPED FROM A GREY CLOUD . . 560   3 DON JUAN 16 121   8
ESCAPES
    PURPLE AND GUSHING SWEET ARE OUR ESCAPES 88   2 DON JUAN 1 124   3
ESCAPING
    ESCAPING WITH A FEW SLIGHT SCARLESS SNEERS 397   3 DON JUAN 13   82   8
ESCHEWED
    WHICH IS THE CUD ESCHEWED BY HUMAN CATTLE 336   3 DON JUAN 12   43   8
ESPECIAL
    FOR ONE ESPECIAL PERSON OUT OF MANY 216   3 DON JUAN 9   68   7
    EXAMINED BY THIS LEARNED AND ESPECIAL 294   3 DON JUAN 11   51   3
    AND REND'RING GENERAL THAT WHICH IS ESPECIAL . . . 467   3 DON JUAN 15   25   8
ESPECIALLY
    THE LANGUAGES ESPECIALLY THE DEAD 44   2 DON JUAN 1   40   1
    ESPECIALLY IN COUNTRIES NEAR THE SUN 56   2 DON JUAN 1   62   5
    SWEET IS REVENGE--ESPECIALLY TO WOMEN 88   2 DON JUAN 1 124   7
    ESPECIALLY IN FRANCE AND ITALY 129   2 DON JUAN 1 191   4
    ESPECIALLY WHEN LIFE IS RATHER NEW 163   2 DON JUAN 2   12   4
    THAT A REPORT (ESPECIALLY THE GREEKS) 295   2 DON JUAN 3   38   2
    ESPECIALLY WHEN ADDED TO THE POWER 395   2 DON JUAN 4   94   8
    BEFORE HE CAME ESPECIALLY AT NIGHT 495   2 DON JUAN 5 146   6
    ESPECIALLY SULTANAS AND THEIR WAYS 64   3 DON JUAN 6 117   4
    THAT ONE LIFE SAVED ESPECIALLY IF YOUNG 199   3 DON JUAN 9   34   2
    ESPECIALLY OF WAR AND TAXING--HOW 202   3 DON JUAN 9   40   6
    ESPECIALLY WHEN SUCH LEAD TO HIGH PLACES 223   3 DON JUAN 9   82   8
    ESPECIALLY FOR FOREIGNERS--AND MOSTLY 283   3 DON JUAN 11   31   2
    WHOM A GOOD MIEN ESPECIALLY IF NEW 305   3 DON JUAN 11   73   6
    ESPECIALLY WHEN YOUNG FOR THAT'S ESSENTIAL 418   3 DON JUAN 14   20   4
    ESPECIALLY WHEN WE ARE ILL AT EASE 431   3 DON JUAN 14   48   2
    ESPECIALLY WITH POLITICS ON HAND 435   3 DON JUAN 14   58   4
    ESPECIALLY WHEN THEY WOULD LOOK LIKE LIES 444   3 DON JUAN 14   80   7
    AND JUAN TOO ESPECIALLY THE LATTER 454   3 DON JUAN 14   99   4
    ESPECIALLY UPON A PRINTED PAGE 494   3 DON JUAN 15   85   4
    ESPECIALLY AS HE HAD BEEN RENOWNED 544   3 DON JUAN 16   91   4
    (ESPECIALLY AS THE SIXTH YEAR IS ENDING) 546   3 DON JUAN 16   95   6
    AND FRIGHTS--ESPECIALLY IF 'TIS A DAUGHTER . . . 564   3 DON JUAN 17   4   7
ESPIEGLE
    HER BLACK BRIGHT DOWNCAST YET ESPIEGLE EYE . . . 532   3 DON JUAN 16   65   1
ESPOUSED
    ESPOUSED TWO PARTNERS (MILLINERS OF BATH) 329   2 DON JUAN 3   93   8
ESQUIRE
    (THOUGH CLAUDIUS RICH ESQUIRE SOME BRICKS HAS GOT . . . 447   2 DON JUAN 5   62   5
ESQUIRED
    ALL COUNTRY GENTLEMEN ESQUIRED OR KNIGHTED 534   3 DON JUAN 16   69   3

		PAGE	VOL		CANTO	STANZA	LN

ESQUIRES
  THEIR DOCILE ESQUIRES ALSO DID THE SAME 549   3 DON JUAN 16   101   6

ESSAY'D
  HAVE NOT ESSAY'D TO MULTIPLY THEIR CLIENTS 142   2 DON JUAN 1   211   5
  WHICH SHE ESSAY'D IN VAIN TO CLEAR (HOW SWEET 362   2 DON JUAN 4   34   3

ESSAYED
  WHICH THE POOR THING AT TIMES ESSAYED TO DRY 532   3 DON JUAN 16   65   3

ESSAYING
  READ OR READ NOT WHAT I AM NOW ESSAYING 70   3 DON JUAN 7   7   3

ESSENCE
  IS PLEASANT BESIDES BEING TRUE LOVE'S ESSENCE 245   2 DON JUAN 2   169   4
  THE UNMINGLED ESSENCE OF THE GRAPE AND YET 458   3 DON JUAN 15   7   2

ESSENTIAL
  AS MOST ESSENTIAL TO THEIR HERO'S STORY 329   2 DON JUAN 3   92   7
  TO SHOW HOW ESSENTIAL TO IT IS ENNUI 332   2 DON JUAN 3   97   V8
  THOUGHT (WHAT IN STATE AFFAIRS IS MOST ESSENTIAL) . . . 285   3 DON JUAN 11   35   6
  ESPECIALLY WHEN YOUNG FOR THAT'S ESSENTIAL 418   3 DON JUAN 14   20   4

EST
  ARCADES AMBO ID EST--BLACKGUARDS BOTH 394   2 DON JUAN 4   93   8

ESTABLISHED
  ESTABLISHED BETWEEN THEM AND BONDAGE THEY 23   3 DON JUAN 6   34   7
  THE FOURTH AT ONCE ESTABLISHED THE WHOLE TRINITY . . . 271   3 DON JUAN 11   6   5

ESTABLISHMENT
  WHICH MADE THEIR NEW ESTABLISHMENT COMPLETE 316   2 DON JUAN 3   78   3

ESTATE
  JUAN BEING THEN GROWN UP TO MAN'S ESTATE 67   2 DON JUAN 1   85   2
  FOR AN ESTATE OR CASH OR COUNTRY-SEAT 89   2 DON JUAN 1   125   5
  HIS GLORY MIGHT HALF EQUAL HIS ESTATE 84   3 DON JUAN 7   37   4
  A MORTGAGE ON HUMANITY'S ESTATE-- 105   3 DON JUAN 7   76   6
  A PEASANT'S SWEAT IS WORTH HIS LORD'S ESTATE 190   3 DON JUAN 9   15   6
  WITH HIS AGRARIAN LAWS THE HIGH ESTATE 237   3 DON JUAN 10   25   3
  MAN'S VERY SYMPATHY WITH THEIR ESTATE 420   3 DON JUAN 14   24   5
  A DASHING DEMOISELLE OF GOOD ESTATE 474   3 DON JUAN 15   42   2
  BETWEEN SOME GREYHOUNDS ON MY LORD'S ESTATE 527   3 DON JUAN 16   55   6
  (FOR LITTLE THINGS UPON MY LORD'S ESTATE 544   3 DON JUAN 16   91   7

ESTEEM
  STATE STATION HEAVEN MANKIND'S MY OWN ESTEEM 130   2 DON JUAN 1   193   2
  A GREEK OF GREAT ESTEEM AMONGST HIS NATION 71   3 DON JUAN 7   10   V5
  HOWE'ER HE MIGHT ESTEEM THIS MORAL NATION 347   3 DON JUAN 12   68   6
  AND FORMED A BASIS OF ESTEEM WHICH ENDS 365   3 DON JUAN 13   15   7
  HE GAINED ESTEEM WHERE IT WAS WORTH THE MOST 553   3 DON JUAN 16   107   4

ESTEEMING
  ESTEEMING IT A LITTLE HARD HE SHOULD 277   3 DON JUAN 11   18   5

ESTIMATION
  WHICH JUDGED MANKIND AT THEIR DUE ESTIMATION 372   3 DON JUAN 13   31   5

ESTRANGE
  AND FEW THERE ARE WHOM THESE CAN NOT ESTRANGE 131   2 DON JUAN 1   194   6

ESTRANGED
  FROM FRIENDS AND HOME AND FREEDOM FAR ESTRANGED 414   2 DON JUAN 5   7   6

ET
  HAIL MUSE ET CETERA--WE LEFT JUAN SLEEPING 274   2 DON JUAN 3   1   1
  OF ORIENTAL PLANTS ET CETERA 434   2 DON JUAN 5   42   5
  AND ET SEPULCHRI IMMEMOR STRUIS DOMOS 448   2 DON JUAN 5   63   7
  THRONES WORLDS ET CETERA ARE SO OFT UPSET 8   3 DON JUAN 6   4   1
  WOULD YOU DO LESS PRO FOCIS ET PRO ARIS 174   3 DON JUAN 8   124   V8
  ET HAUSTUS TER IN DIE CAPIENDUS 244   3 DON JUAN 10   41   8
  OF ELEGANT ET CETERA IN FRESH BATCHES-- 340   3 DON JUAN 12   53   7
  WITHIN--ET CAETERA   SHALL I GO ON--NO 374   3 DON JUAN 13   36   4
  ET BENE DIC NEUTRUM DIC ALIQUANDO MALE 465   3 DON JUAN 15   21   2
  DE REBUS CUNCTIS ET QUIBUSDAM ALIIS 502   3 DON JUAN 16   3   8

ETERNAL
  AWAY THE VAST SALT DREAD ETERNAL DEEP 210   2 DON JUAN 2   103   8
  AND CLOG THE FOUNTAIN OF ETERNAL TEARS 275   2 DON JUAN 3   1   V8
  ETERNAL SUMMER GILDS THEM YET   320   2 DON JUAN 3   L 1   5
  O'ER THE LAOCOON'S ALL ETERNAL THROES 377   2 DON JUAN 4   61   5
  OH THOU ETERNAL HOMER WHO COULDST CHARM 106   3 DON JUAN 7   79   1
  OH THOU ETERNAL HOMER I HAVE NOW   106   3 DON JUAN 7   80   1
  VIBRATE TO THE ETERNAL NAME   HARK THROUGH 116   3 DON JUAN 8   8   7
  ETERNAL SUCH NAMES MINGLED) ISMAIL'S OUR'S 178   3 DON JUAN 8   133   8
  THAN THE ETERNAL DELUGE WHICH DEVOURS 189   3 DON JUAN 9   13   7
  INTERMINABLE--NOT ETERNAL--SPEAKERS-- 310   3 DON JUAN 11   85   2
  HOW LESS WHAT WE MAY BE THE ETERNAL SURGE 500   3 DON JUAN 15   99   4
  JUAN PUT FORTH ONE ARM--ETERNAL POWERS 559   3 DON JUAN 16   120   1

ETERNALLY
  YOUR WARS ETERNALLY BESIDES ENJOYING 118   3 DON JUAN 8   14   7

ETERNITY
  PROMPTS DEEDS ETERNITY CAN NOT ANNUL 258   2 DON JUAN 2   192   5
  THE TOWN WAS ENTERED OH ETERNITY-- 142   3 DON JUAN 8   60   1
  AND BRIGHT ETERNITY WITHOUT DISGUISE 169   3 DON JUAN 8   115   5
  THE OCEAN OF ETERNITY THE ROAR 227   3 DON JUAN 10   4   5
  OF WHAT IS CALLED ETERNITY TO STARE 234   3 DON JUAN 10   20   7
  AN AGE MAY COME FONT OF ETERNITY 411   3 DON JUAN 14   3   5
  THAT WATERY OUTLINE OF ETERNITY 457   3 DON JUAN 15   2   5

ETHER
  NOT STINGS AND FLITS THROUGH ETHER WITHOUT AIM 400   3 DON JUAN 13   89   6

ETHEREAL
  BUT DAMME'S QUITE ETHEREAL THOUGH TOO DARING 289   3 DON JUAN 11   43   7

ETHERIAL
  ETHERIAL LUSTRE WITH WHAT SWEET PERSUASION 65   2 DON JUAN 1   81   6
  IF HE MUST FAIN SWEEP O'ER THE ETHERIAL PLAIN 333   2 DON JUAN 3   99   1

		PAGE	VOL		CANTO	STANZA	LN
ETIQUETTE							
THERE'S NOTHING IN THE WORLD LIKE ETIQUETTE		471	2	DON JUAN	5	103	6
BUT ETIQUETTE FORBADE THEM ALL TO GIGGLE		501	2	DON JUAN	5	156	8
ETNA							
WHILE THE WHOLE RAMPART BLAZED LIKE ETNA WHEN		115	3	DON JUAN	8	7	7
EULOGY							
AND SWALLOWING EULOGY MUCH MORE THAN SATIRE HE		185	3	DON JUAN	9	5	5
AND A LONG EULOGY OF PATENT BLACKING		512	3	DON JUAN	16	26	8
EUNUCH							
THE INTELLECTUAL EUNUCH CASTLEREAGH		15	2	DON JUAN	D	11	8
MEANTIME (YON OLD BLACK EUNUCH SEEMS TO EYE US)		423	2	DON JUAN	5	24	7
THE EUNUCH HAVING EYED THEM O'ER WITH CARE		425	2	DON JUAN	5	28	1
THE EUNUCH MADE A SIGN TO THOSE ON BOARD		433	2	DON JUAN	5	41	7
AS THE BLACK EUNUCH ENTERED WITH HIS BRACE		441	2	DON JUAN	5	54	1
EUNUCHS							
DWARFS DANCING GIRLS BLACK EUNUCHS AND A POET		316	2	DON JUAN	3	78	2
AND THEN HIS HIGHNESS' EUNUCHS BLACK AND WHITE		495	2	DON JUAN	5	146	2
BY EUNUCHS FLANKED WHILE AT THEIR HEAD THERE STALKED		21	3	DON JUAN	6	30	4
EUPHONY							
OUR EUPHONY--THERE WAS STRONGENOFF AND STROKONOFF		74	3	DON JUAN	7	15	2
EUPHUES							
THEN THERE'S MY GENTLE EUPHUES WHO THEY SAY		298	3	DON JUAN	11	59	1
EUREKA							
EUREKA I HAVE FOUND IT WHAT I MEAN		443	3	DON JUAN	14	76	1
EUROPE							
EUROPE HAS SLAVES--ALLIES--KINGS--ARMIES STILL		19	2	DON JUAN	D	16	7
EUROPE AND ASIA YOU BEING QUITE AT EASE		413	2	DON JUAN	5	5	6
TO EDUCATE--YE YOUTH OF EUROPE--YOU BY		486	2	DON JUAN	5	131	6
YET EUROPE DOUBTLESS OWES YOU GREATLY MORE		184	3	DON JUAN	9	3	2
YOU MIGHT HAVE FREED FALL'N EUROPE FROM THE UNITY		187	3	DON JUAN	9	9	3
ARE THE TRUE LORDS OF EUROPE EVERY LOAN		318	3	DON JUAN	12	6	2
FOR EUROPE PLOUGHS IN AFRIC LIKE BOS PIGER		348	3	DON JUAN	12	70	6
EUROPEAN							
ALL EUROPEAN CLIMES BY LAND OR SEA		129	2	DON JUAN	1	191	2
A MOMENT AT THE EUROPEAN YOUTH		387	2	DON JUAN	4	78	4
THE EUROPEAN WITH THE ASIAN SHORE		412	2	DON JUAN	5	3	1
EUROPE'S							
AND EUROPE'S LIBERATOR--STILL ENSLAVED		185	3	DON JUAN	9	5	8
(THAT MAKE OLD EUROPE'S JOURNALS SQUEAK AND GIBBER ALL)		318	3	DON JUAN	12	5	4
UPON THE REST OF EUROPE'S SOCIAL STATE		327	3	DON JUAN	12	24	4
AND SUCH IS EUROPE'S FASHIONABLE EASE		373	3	DON JUAN	13	34	V8
EUTROPIUS							
EUTROPIUS OF ITS MANY MASTERS--BLIND		18	2	DON JUAN	D	15	5
EUXINE							
THE WIND SWEPT DOWN THE EUXINE AND THE WAVE		413	2	DON JUAN	5	5	1
TURNS UP MORE DANGEROUS BREAKERS THAN THE EUXINE		413	2	DON JUAN	5	5	8
EVADES							
THAT TRASH OF SUCH SORT NOT ALONE EVADES		334	2	DON JUAN	3	100	3
EVAPORATE							
THROUGH WHICH THE SPECTRE SEEMED TO EVAPORATE		511	3	DON JUAN	16	24	8
EVAPORATION							
THE EVAPORATION OF A JOYOUS DAY		504	3	DON JUAN	16	9	1
EVE							
DON JOSE LIKE A LINEAL SON OF EVE		30	2	DON JUAN	1	18	7
HIS EVE WITH ALL THE INNOCENCE SHE VAUNTED		120	2	DON JUAN	1	180	V6
WHICH EVE HAS LEFT HER DAUGHTERS SINCE HER FALL		256	2	DON JUAN	2	189	8
AS WHEN SHE ROSE UPON US LIKE AN EVE		270	2	DON JUAN	2	213	4
BUT DANTE'S BEATRICE AND MILTON'S EVE		281	2	DON JUAN	3	10	7
KEEP YOUR GOOD NAME THOUGH EVE HERSELF ONCE FELL		460	2	DON JUAN	5	84	6
PRESERVE YOUR STATE--THOUGH EVE EARTH'S MOTHER FELL		460	2	DON JUAN	5	84	V6
EVE AND PAVED (GOD KNOWS HOW) THE ROAD TO EVIL		474	2	DON JUAN	5	109	4
MOST THINGS WERE IN THIS POSTURE ON THE EVE		94	3	DON JUAN	7	54	1
WHOSE FANGS EVE TAUGHT HER HUMAN SEED TO FEEL		153	3	DON JUAN	8	83	4
UPON THE TREE WHICH EVE SO FONDLY SEARCHED		192	3	DON JUAN	9	19	8
WHICH EVE MIGHT QUIT WITHOUT MUCH SACRIFICE--		278	3	DON JUAN	11	21	8
SINCE EVE ATE APPLES MUCH DEPENDS ON DINNER		404	3	DON JUAN	13	99	8
THE GREEK EVE HELEN FROM THE SPARTAN'S BED		441	3	DON JUAN	14	72	5
EVE MADE UP MILLINERY WITH FIG LEAVES--		444	3	DON JUAN	14	78	2
HE FLITS ON THE BRIDAL EVE		519	3	DON JUAN	16	L 3	6
EVEN							
THAT EVEN ITS GROSSEST FLATTERERS DARE NOT PRAISE		17	2	DON JUAN	D	13	3
NOT EVEN A SPRIGHTLY BLUNDER'S SPARK CAN BLAZE		17	2	DON JUAN	D	13	5
A BUNGLER EVEN IN ITS DISGUSTING TRADE		18	2	DON JUAN	D	14	1
DEEMING THE CHAIN IT WEARS EVEN MEN MAY FIT		18	2	DON JUAN	D	15	4
AND EVEN THE GOOD WITH INWARD ENVY GROAN		26	2	DON JUAN	1	10	6
FOR SHE HAD NOT EVEN ONE--THE WORST OF ALL		29	2	DON JUAN	1	16	8
EVEN HER MINUTEST MOTIONS WENT AS WELL		30	2	DON JUAN	1	17	5
AND EVEN THE WISEST DO THE BEST THEY CAN		33	2	DON JUAN	1	21	3
SAGEST OF WOMEN EVEN OF WIDOWS SHE		42	2	DON JUAN	1	38	1
SHE DID THIS DURING EVEN HER HUSBAND'S LIFE--		48	2	DON JUAN	1	48	7
AGAINST ALL EVIL SPEAKING EVEN IN JEST		49	2	DON JUAN	1	51	8
LADIES EVEN OF THE MOST UNEASY VIRTUE		56	2	DON JUAN	1	62	7
EVEN INNOCENCE ITSELF HAS MANY A WILE		61	2	DON JUAN	1	72	6
EVEN BY ITS DARKNESS AS THE BLACKEST SKY		61	2	DON JUAN	1	73	2
COLDNESS OR ANGER EVEN DISDAIN OR HATE		61	2	DON JUAN	1	73	7
AND EVEN IF BY CHANCE--AND WHO CAN TELL		64	2	DON JUAN	1	78	1
EVEN SEVEN YEARS HENCE IT WOULD NOT BE TOO LATE		67	2	DON JUAN	1	85	4
EVEN AS THE PAGE IS RUSTLED WHILE WE LOOK		72	2	DON JUAN	1	95	3
AND EVEN IF I KNEW I SHOULD NOT TELL--		77	2	DON JUAN	1	105	3

235

EVEN   (CONTINUED)

EVEN AS A SUMMER SKY'S WITHOUT A CLOUD . . . . . . 94 2 DON JUAN 1   135   6
EVEN THEN THEIR LOVE THEY COULD NOT ALL COMMAND . . . . 114 2 DON JUAN 1   170   3
EVEN IF IT SHOULD COMPRISE A PACK OF FABLES . . . . . 117 2 DON JUAN 1   175   6
AND I MUST EVEN SURVIVE THIS LAST ADIEU . . . . . . 134 2 DON JUAN 1   197   7
TO DOUBLE EVEN THE SWEETNESS OF A FLOWER . . . . . . 144 2 DON JUAN 1   214   8
IN THE THIRD FORM OR EVEN IN THE FOURTH . . . . . . 158 2 DON JUAN 2   2   2
EVEN NATIONS FEEL THIS WHEN THEY GO TO WAR . . . . . 164 2 DON JUAN 2   14   4
AT LEAVING EVEN THE MOST UNPLEASANT PEOPLE . . . . . 164 2 DON JUAN 2   14   7
AT QUITTING EVEN THOSE WE QUIT IN STRIFE . . . . . 164 2 DON JUAN 2   15   6
STILL THEIR SALVATION WAS AN EVEN BET . . . . 171 2 DON JUAN 2   28   6
THAT EVEN THE ABLE SEAMAN DEEMING HIS . . . . 173 2 DON JUAN 2   33   5
AND EVEN PEDRILLO HIS MOST REVEREND TUTOR . . . . . 175 2 DON JUAN 2   36   7
ON WHICH THEY MIGHT REPOSE OR EVEN COMMENCE . . . . . 177 2 DON JUAN 2   40   5
MEN EVEN WHEN DYING DISLIKE INANITION . . . . 180 2 DON JUAN 2   46   5
MEN WILL PROVE HUNGRY EVEN WHEN NEXT PERDITION . . . . 180 2 DON JUAN 2   46 V5
MORE THAN CAN BE BELIEVED OR EVEN THOUGHT . . . . . 191 2 DON JUAN 2   66   3
LULL'D EVEN THE SAVAGE HUNGER WHICH DEMANDED . . . . 195 2 DON JUAN 2   75   3
EVEN IN EXTREMITY OF THEIR DISASTER . . . . 198 2 DON JUAN 2   78   7
PROVED EVEN STILL A MORE NUTRITIOUS MATTER . . . . . 208 2 DON JUAN 2   99   5
EVEN OF THE HIGHEST FOR A FEMALE MOULD . . . . . . 217 2 DON JUAN 2   116   5
NOT EVEN A VISION OF HIS FORMER WOES . . . . 227 2 DON JUAN 2   134   5
(THE HEART WILL SLIP EVEN AS THE TONGUE AND PEN) . . . 228 2 DON JUAN 2   135   6
FOR JUAN SO THAT EVEN WHEN HE PRAY'D . . . . 235 2 DON JUAN 2   149   6
AND THINKS HEAVEN BRIGHTER EVEN THAN NEWTON'S PAGE . . 242 2 DON JUAN 2   163 V7
PRESSURE OF HANDS PERHAPS EVEN A CHASTE KISS-- . . . . 242 2 DON JUAN 2   164   7
WITHOUT EVEN THE INCUMBRANCE OF A BROTHER . . . . . 248 2 DON JUAN 2   175   5
SHOWERS TRIPLE LIGHT AND SCORCHES EVEN THE KISS . . . . 264 2 DON JUAN 2   202   3
FINE TRUTHS EVEN CONSCIENCE TOO HAS A TOUGH JOB . . . . 264 2 DON JUAN 2   203   6
THE HAPPIEST MORTALS EVEN AFTER DINNER-- . . . . . . 294 2 DON JUAN 3   36   2
WHICH SCARCE EVEN FRANCE THE PARAGON OF NATIONS . . . . 299 2 DON JUAN 3   46   3
PERHAPS THAN EVEN THE MENTAL PANGS OF DYING . . . . . 301 2 DON JUAN 3   51   4
TOO PURE EVEN FOR THE PUREST HUMAN TIES . . . . . . 313 2 DON JUAN 3   74   6
EVEN GOOD MEN LIKE TO MAKE THE PUBLIC STARE-- . . . . 317 2 DON JUAN 3   81   4
EVEN AS I SING SUFFUSE MY FACE . . . . 323 2 DON JUAN 3 L   6   4
FRAIL MAN WHEN PAPER--EVEN A RAG LIKE THIS . . . . . 327 2 DON JUAN 3   88   7
HIS STATION GENERATION EVEN HIS NATION . . . . . . 327 2 DON JUAN 3   89   2
EVEN TIME THE PITILESS IN SORROW CLEFT . . . . . . 348 2 DON JUAN 4   8   3
THE DEATH OF FRIENDS AND THAT WHICH SLAYS EVEN MORE-- . 350 2 DON JUAN 4   12   3
AWAITS AT LAST EVEN THOSE WHOM LONGEST MISS . . . . . 350 2 DON JUAN 4   12   6
EVEN AS THEY GAZED A SUDDEN TREMOR CAME . . . . . . 355 2 DON JUAN 4   21   2
OF PLEASURE AND OF PAIN--EVEN WHILE I KISS . . . . . 364 2 DON JUAN 4   38   5
MAKING HER STATURE TALL EVEN TALLER--NEAR . . . . . 367 2 DON JUAN 4   43 V5
HER BOSOM WAS THE WEAPON--AND EVEN SO . . . . 367 2 DON JUAN 4   43 V6
EVEN TO THE DELICACY OF THEIR HAND . . . . 368 2 DON JUAN 4   45   3
EVEN AS THE SIMOOM SWEEPS THE BLASTED PLAINS . . . . 375 2 DON JUAN 4   57   8
EVEN WHEN THEY SMOTE HER IN THE HOPE TO SAVE . . . . 380 2 DON JUAN 4   67   8
EVEN TILL AN ICEBERG IT MAY CHANCE TO GROW . . . . . 398 2 DON JUAN 4   100   7
THE VIRTUES EVEN THE MOST EXALTED CHARITY . . . . . 408 2 DON JUAN 4   115   7
EVEN PETRARCH'S SELF IF JUDGED WITH DUE SEVERITY . . . 411 2 DON JUAN 5   1   7
A SPELL FROM WHICH EVEN YET I AM NOT QUITE FREE . . . . 413 2 DON JUAN 5   4   6
COULD SCARCE BE SHOWN EVEN BY A MERE SPECTATOR . . . . 416 2 DON JUAN 5   11   8
O'ERTHROWN EVEN MEN HE SOON BEGAN TO SHOW . . . . . 417 2 DON JUAN 5   12   4
PERHAPS EVEN MORE ATTENTION THAN IS DUE . . . . . . 431 2 DON JUAN 5   38   5
OCCUR IN ORIENT PALACES AND EVEN . . . . 465 2 DON JUAN 5   94   2
IN CONTACT AND SOMETIMES EVEN A FAIR STRANGER'S . . . . 472 2 DON JUAN 5   106   7
THERE WAS A SELF-WILL EVEN IN HER SMALL FEET . . . . 475 2 DON JUAN 5   111   3
YET EVEN HER TYRANNY HAD SUCH A GRACE . . . . 476 2 DON JUAN 5   113   7
AS EVEN IN A MUCH HUMBLER LOT HAD MADE . . . . . . 485 2 DON JUAN 5   129   2
EVEN YE WHO KNOW WHAT A CHECKED WOMAN IS . . . . . 489 2 DON JUAN 5   134   7
HAVE SUNG OR EVEN A DANDY'S DANDIEST CHATTER . . . . 493 2 DON JUAN 5   143   4
BUT I DETEST ALL FICTION EVEN IN SONG . . . . 10 3 DON JUAN 6   8   3
SHE THOUGHT THAT HER LORD'S HEART (EVEN COULD SHE CLAIM IT) 10 3 DON JUAN 6   8   6
BY ALL HIS EDICTS EVEN TO THE BLIND . . . . 12 3 DON JUAN 6   13 V3
EVEN WERE SAINT FRANCIS' PARAMOUR THEIR GUEST . . . . 14 3 DON JUAN 6   17   5
AND EVEN THOSE WERE NEARER THAN THEY KNEW . . . . . 31 3 DON JUAN 6   51   8
MY FAULTS EVEN WITH YOUR OWN WHICH MEANETH PUT . . . . 34 3 DON JUAN 6   56   6
SHE DID NOT EVEN LOOK INTO THE MIRROR . . . . 50 3 DON JUAN 6   89   8
THEIR ROAR EVEN WITH THE BALTIC'S--SO YOU BE . . . . 52 3 DON JUAN 6   93   7
THEIR WORK EVEN BY THE WAY IN WHICH HE TRODE . . . . 61 3 DON JUAN 6   111   8
YOUR ORDERS EVEN IN THEIR SEVEREST SENSE . . . . . 62 3 DON JUAN 6   114   4
EVEN AT YOUR OWN IMPERATIVE EXPENSE . . . . 62 3 DON JUAN 6   114   6
BUT YOUR OWN FEELINGS EVEN SHOULD ALL THE REST . . . . 63 3 DON JUAN 6   115   1
AND ABOVE ALL BE COMBED EVEN TO A HAIR . . . . . . 64 3 DON JUAN 6   118   4
NOR EVEN DIOGENES--WE LIVE AND DIE . . . . 68 3 DON JUAN 7   4   7
THERE'S FORTUNE EVEN IN FAME WE MUST ALLOW . . . . 82 3 DON JUAN 7   33   6
THUS EVEN GOOD FAME MAY SUFFER SAD CONTRACTIONS . . . . 83 3 DON JUAN 7   34   5
HIS PURSE HIS SOUL HIS SENSE AND EVEN HIS NONSENSE . . 88 3 DON JUAN 7   44   7
WILL TOUCH EVEN HEROES AND SUCH WAS SUWARROW . . . . 102 3 DON JUAN 7   69   8
HERE PAUSE WE FOR THE PRESENT--AS EVEN THEN . . . . . 111 3 DON JUAN 7   87   1
IN THE SAME MOMENT LOUD AS EVEN THE ROAR . . . . . 116 3 DON JUAN 8   8   2
OF HIS OWN CORPS NOR EVEN THE CORPS WHICH HAD . . . . 127 3 DON JUAN 8   31   2
EVEN FROM A CHILD FELT LIKE A CHILD HOWE'ER . . . . . 139 3 DON JUAN 8   53   2
AND HE COULD EVEN WITHSTAND THAT AWKWARD TEST . . . . 139 3 DON JUAN 8   53   5
BLOOD UNTIL HEATED--AND EVEN THERE HIS OWN . . . . . 140 3 DON JUAN 8   55   7
AN ACTIVE HERMIT EVEN IN AGE THE CHILD . . . . . . 144 3 DON JUAN 8   63   7
'TIS TRUE HE SHRANK FROM MEN EVEN OF HIS NATION . . . . 144 3 DON JUAN 8   64   1
THE WALLS WERE WON BUT 'TWAS AN EVEN BET . . . . . 150 3 DON JUAN 8   77   5
EVEN WITH HIS LIFE--FOR (BUT THEY LIE) 'TIS SAID . . . 153 3 DON JUAN 8   84   7

EVEN   (CONTINUED)
    WHICH WAS CUT OFF AND SCARCE EVEN THEN LET GO 154   3 DON JUAN 8   85   8
    NOW MOVED WITH PITY EVEN AS SOMETIMES NODS 164   3 DON JUAN 8   106   6
    FRANCE COULD NOT EVEN CONQUER YOUR GREAT NAME 183   3 DON JUAN 9   1   3
    NOT LEAVING EVEN HIS FUNERAL EXPENSES 186   3 DON JUAN 9   8   3
    TURNS LIFE TO TERROR EVEN THOUGH IN ITS SHEATH 188   3 DON JUAN 9   11   7
    THAN EVEN THE TAILOR'S) HIS INCARNATE SKIN 188   3 DON JUAN 9   12   7
    MUCH FLATTERY--EVEN VOLTAIRE'S AND THAT'S A PITY . . . 194   3 DON JUAN 9   23   6
    EVEN WORLDS MISCARRY WHEN TOO OFT THEY PUP 202   3 DON JUAN 9   39   5
    SMOOTHED EVEN THE SIMPLON'S STEEP AND BY GOD'S BLESSING . 215   3 DON JUAN 9   66   7
    BUT SIGHS SUBSIDE AND TEARS (EVEN WIDOWS') SHRINK . . . 228   3 DON JUAN 10   7   1
    MIDDLE-AGED LADIES EVEN MORE THAN YOUNG 230   3 DON JUAN 10   10   2
    EVEN SHUFFLING SOUTHEY THAT INCARNATE LIE 231   3 DON JUAN 10   13   2
    ALTHOUGH HE WAS NOT OLD NOR EVEN A MAID-- 249   3 DON JUAN 10   50   9
    ALL PHANTASIES NOT EVEN EXCEPTING MINE 255   3 DON JUAN 10   61   4
    WHAT EVEN YOUNG STRANGERS FEEL A LITTLE STRONG 257   3 DON JUAN 10   65   3
    EVEN THE BOLD CHURCHMAN'S TOMB EXCITED AWE 261   3 DON JUAN 10   74   4
    TOO DULL EVEN FOR THE DULLEST OF EXCESSES-- 267   3 DON JUAN 10   86   6
    AND EVEN THAT HE HAD SO RARELY HEARD 274   3 DON JUAN 11   12   3
    BY FOUL CORRUPTION INTO STREAMS--EVEN THEY 287   3 DON JUAN 11   40   7
    (SEE BILLINGSGATE) MADE EVEN THE TONGUE MORE FREE . . . 288   3 DON JUAN 11   42   8
    SPIRIT WOULD NAME AND THEREFORE EVEN I WON'T ANENT . . 289   3 DON JUAN 11   43   4
    EVEN I--ALBEIT I'M SURE I DID NOT KNOW IT 296   3 DON JUAN 11   55   5
    AND EVEN MY MUSE'S WORST REPROOF'S A SMILE 300   3 DON JUAN 11   63   6
    MAKES ONE IN LOVE EVEN WITH ITS VERY FAULTS 302   3 DON JUAN 11   68   4
    I KNEW THAT NOUGHT WAS LASTING BUT NOW EVEN 309   3 DON JUAN 11   82   5
    ON 'CHANGE AND EVEN THY SILVER SOIL PERU 318   3 DON JUAN 12   6   7
    EVEN WITH THE VERY ORE WHICH MAKES THEM BASE 320   3 DON JUAN 12   10   6
    EVEN PLUTARCH'S LIVES HAVE BUT PICKED OUT A FEW . . . 324   3 DON JUAN 12   19   5
    THAT EVEN THE PUREST PEOPLE MAY MISTAKE 328   3 DON JUAN 12   26   3
    EVEN IN THE HOPEFUL ISLE WHOSE OUTLET'S DOVER 331   3 DON JUAN 12   33   6
    I'VE KNOWN A DOZEN WEDDINGS MADE EVEN THUS 344   3 DON JUAN 12   61   1
    THE SHOW OF VIRTUE EVEN IN THE VITIATED-- 344   3 DON JUAN 12   62   5
    ARE THEY AT BOTTOM VIRTUOUS EVEN WHEN VICIOUS 349   3 DON JUAN 12   73   6
    EVEN THOUGH HIMSELF AVOIDED THE OCCASION 355   3 DON JUAN 12   85   8
    AND BEAUTEOUS EVEN WHERE BEAUTIES MOST ABOUND 359   3 DON JUAN 13   2   6
    OR EVEN MERE FASHION WHICH INDEED'S THE BEST 370   3 DON JUAN 13   28   6
    NOT EVEN IN FOOLS--WHO--HOWSOEVER BLIND 372   3 DON JUAN 13   32   V6
    BUT EVEN THE FAINTEST RELICS OF A SHRINE 387   3 DON JUAN 13   61   7
    'TIS NOT ENOUGH TO SPELL OR EVEN TO READ 393   3 DON JUAN 13   73   2
    EVEN NIMROD'S SELF MIGHT LEAVE THE PLAINS OF DURA . . 395   3 DON JUAN 13   78   5
    THEIR TABLE WAS A BOARD TO TEMPT EVEN GHOSTS 404   3 DON JUAN 13   99   3
    WHEN WE NO MORE CAN USE OR EVEN ABUSE THEE 405   3 DON JUAN 13   100   8
    AND THEN EVEN THEN SOME BORE MAY MAKE THEM LOSE IT . . 408   3 DON JUAN 13   109   8
    A KIND OF COMMON-PLACE EVEN IN THEIR CRIMES 417   3 DON JUAN 14   16   4
    I'VE SEEN THEM BALANCE EVEN THE SCALE WITH FIGHTERS . . 418   3 DON JUAN 14   20   3
    BUT EVEN THIS IS DIFFICULT HEAVEN KNOWS 421   3 DON JUAN 14   25   2
    WHICH EVEN THOSE WHO OBEY WOULD FAIN BE THOUGHT . . . 421   3 DON JUAN 14   26   2
    WHEN EVEN THE SEA LOOKS DIM WITH ALL ITS SPRAY 422   3 DON JUAN 14   28   3
    TO CATCH A GLIMPSE EVEN OF A PRETTY PEASANT 422   3 DON JUAN 14   28   8
    THEY COULD NOT EVEN GLEAN THE SLIGHTEST SPLINTERS . . . 434   3 DON JUAN 14   56   5
    BUT INNOCENCE IS BOLD EVEN AT THE STAKE 437   3 DON JUAN 14   61   5
    THOUGH EVEN THAT WERE SOMETIMES TOO FEROCIOUS 443   3 DON JUAN 14   77   5
    THE DRAINER OF OBLIVION EVEN THE SOT 457   3 DON JUAN 15   4   3
    BECAUSE I HATE EVEN DEMOCRATIC ROYALTY 466   3 DON JUAN 15   23   8
    EVEN WHERE THE ARTICLE AT HIGHEST RATE IS 469   3 DON JUAN 15   29   4
    AS ON THE WHOLE IT IS AN EVEN CHANCE 473   3 DON JUAN 15   39   4
    CONVINCES ALL MEN EVEN A POLITICIAN 478   3 DON JUAN 15   51   6
    WHEN WILL YOUR NAMES LEND LUSTRE EVEN TO PARTRIDGES . . 485   3 DON JUAN 15   67   8
    BUT EVEN SANS CONFITURES IT NO LESS TRUE IS 486   3 DON JUAN 15   68   7
    I MUST NOT INTRODUCE EVEN A SPARE RIB HERE 487   3 DON JUAN 15   71   5
    THE CHASTE DESCRIPTION EVEN OF A BECASSE 487   3 DON JUAN 15   71   8
    NOR EVEN SMILED ENOUGH FOR ANY VANITY 490   3 DON JUAN 15   78   4
    AND WINS EVEN BY A DELICATE DISSENT 493   3 DON JUAN 15   83   8
    EVEN MY VERACIOUS SELF--BUT THAT'S A LIE 495   3 DON JUAN 15   88   3
    A PICTURE IS THE PAST EVEN ERE ITS FRAME 509   3 DON JUAN 16   19   7
    EVEN FROM OUR GRAMMAR UPWARDS FRIENDS OF YORE 542   3 DON JUAN 16   86   5
    EVEN IN THE COUNTRY CIRCLE'S NARROW BOUND-- 544   3 DON JUAN 16   91   6
    AND FAMILIES EVEN TO THE LAST RELATION 550   3 DON JUAN 16   103   6
    SO THAT EVEN THOSE WHOSE FAITH IS THE MOST GREAT . . . 556   3 DON JUAN 16   114   7
EVENING
    HER EVENING SILK OR IN THE SUMMER MUSLIN 27   2 DON JUAN 1   12   7
    'TIS SWEET TO SEE THE EVENING STAR APPEAR 87   2 DON JUAN 1   122   5
    THE OTHER EVENING ('TWAS ON FRIDAY LAST)-- 428   2 DON JUAN 5   33   1
    ARE THINGS WHICH MAKE AN ENGLISH EVENING PASS 444   2 DON JUAN 5   58   4
    WITH EVENING CAME THE BANQUET AND THE WINE 408   3 DON JUAN 13   107   1
    THE EVENING ALSO WANED--AND COFFEE CAME 549   3 DON JUAN 16   101   2
EVENINGS
    I PASS MY EVENINGS IN LONG GALLERIES SOLELY 444   2 DON JUAN 5   58   7
    PREPARED EACH MORN FOR EVENINGS LIST OH LIST-- 403   3 DON JUAN 13   97   6
    OH THE LONG EVENINGS OF DUETS AND TRIOS 523   3 DON JUAN 16   45   1
EVENT
    MUST THE EVENT DECIDE BETWEEN THE TWO 449   3 DON JUAN 14   90   3
EVENTIDE
    AND STOOD WITHIN HIS HALL AT EVENTIDE 306   2 DON JUAN 3   61   2
EVENTS
    IS YET WITHIN THE UNREAD EVENTS OF TIME 312   3 DON JUAN 11   90   1
    NOW THIS AT ALL EVENTS MUST RENDER COLD 468   3 DON JUAN 15   26   5
EVER-DYING
    AND EVER-DYING GLADIATOR'S AIR 377   2 DON JUAN 4   61   6

	PAGE	VOL	CANTO	STANZA	LN
EVERGREEN					
EVERGREEN FOREST WHICH BOCCACIO'S LORE	337	2 DON JUAN	3	105	6
EVERMORE					
THE SPOTS WHICH WERE HER REALMS FOR EVERMORE	443	2 DON JUAN	5	57	4
EVERYBODY					
AND EVERYBODY BUT HIS MOTHER DEEM'D	51	2 DON JUAN	1	54	4
THE VERY THING WHICH EVERYBODY FEELS	69	2 DON JUAN	1	89	3
WHICH EVERYBODY DOES WITHOUT WHO CAN	393	2 DON JUAN	4	91	4
ON THAT SWEET ORE WHICH EVERYBODY NURSES	264	3 DON JUAN	10	79	6
DECIDE AND EVERYBODY ONE DAY WILL	270	3 DON JUAN	11	4	7
LIKE MANY PEOPLE EVERYBODY KNOWS	335	3 DON JUAN	12	41	5
WHERE EVERYBODY HAS SOME SEPARATE AIM	342	3 DON JUAN	12	58	5
AND EVERYBODY SEES THAT WHAT THEY LACK	348	3 DON JUAN	12	71	V4
THE LUCK OF FINDING EVERYBODY SOLVENT	458	3 DON JUAN	15	7	8
HELP CONTRADICTING THEM AND EVERYBODY	495	3 DON JUAN	15	88	2
AND EVERYBODY WONDERING MORE OR LESS	514	3 DON JUAN	16	32	2
AND THAT IT IS SO EVERYBODY KNOWS	522	3 DON JUAN	16	44	6
UPON HER FRIENDS AS EVERYBODY OUGHT	524	3 DON JUAN	16	47	4
AND EVERYBODY OUT OF THEIR OWN SPHERE	538	3 DON JUAN	16	78	8
WAS EVER EVERYBODY YET SO QUITE	564	3 DON JUAN	17	5	8
EVERYBODY'S					
SO THAT I TRUST FOR EVERYBODY'S SAKE	459	2 DON JUAN	5	82	7
IF YOU ARE RIGHT THEN EVERYBODY'S WRONG	564	3 DON JUAN	17	5	4
IF YOU ARE WRONG THEN EVERYBODY'S RIGHT	564	3 DON JUAN	17	5	7
EVERY-DAY					
WAS FAINT AS OF AN EVERY-DAY POSSESSION	372	3 DON JUAN	13	31	8
EVERYONE					
WHICH NONE DIVINE AND EVERYONE OBEYS	207	3 DON JUAN	9	49	6
AND SO MAY EVERYONE EXCEPT A DUNCE	336	3 DON JUAN	12	44	3
SO EVERYONE MAY DRESS IT TO HIS WISH	486	3 DON JUAN	15	68	4
EVERYTHING					
LET EVERYTHING BE NOTED WITH PRECISION	104	2 DON JUAN	1	152	5
BUT NO DOUBT EVERYTHING IS FOR THE BEST	6	3 DON JUAN	6	1	6
HER SHAPE HER HAIR HER AIR HER EVERYTHING	23	3 DON JUAN	6	35	2
HER THRONE AND POWER AND EVERYTHING BESIDE	24	3 DON JUAN	6	36	8
FOR EVERYTHING SEEMED RESTING ON HIS NOD	104	3 DON JUAN	7	74	1
ACCOUNT FOR EVERYTHING WHICH MAY LOOK BAD	127	3 DON JUAN	8	31	4
WHILE EVERYTHING AROUND WAS CALM AND STILL	272	3 DON JUAN	11	8	5
PROUD OF HIS BIRTH AND PROUD OF EVERYTHING	440	3 DON JUAN	14	70	2
EVERYWHERE					
HE SEARCH'D THEY SEARCH'D AND RUMMAGED EVERYWHERE	99	2 DON JUAN	1	143	1
AND HUMAN LIVES ARE LAVISHED EVERYWHERE	155	3 DON JUAN	8	88	2
A THING WHICH HAPPENS EVERYWHERE EACH DAY--	163	3 DON JUAN	8	103	7
OR WEALTH WHICH IS A PASSPORT EVERYWHERE	370	3 DON JUAN	13	28	5
'TIS ROUND HIM NEAR HIM HERE THERE EVERYWHERE	412	3 DON JUAN	14	5	1
IN SPAIN AND LUCCA ATHENS EVERYWHERE	488	3 DON JUAN	15	73	4
EVE'S					
SOULS TO SAVE SINCE EVE'S SLIP AND ADAM'S FALL	192	3 DON JUAN	9	19	3
POOR THING EVE'S WAS A TRIFLING CASE TO HER'S	345	3 DON JUAN	12	64	8
EVIDENCES					
AND EVIDENCES WHICH REGALE ALL READERS	346	3 DON JUAN	12	65	8
AND YET WHAT ARE YOUR OTHER EVIDENCES	411	3 DON JUAN	14	2	8
EVIDENTLY					
THE SHIP WAS EVIDENTLY SETTLING NOW	179	2 DON JUAN	2	44	1
OF A HIGH SPIRIT EVIDENTLY THOUGH	417	2 DON JUAN	5	12	2
EVIL					
IF FALLEN IN EVIL DAYS ON EVIL TONGUES	15	2 DON JUAN	D	10	1
IF FALLEN IN EVIL DAYS ON EVIL TONGUES	15	2 DON JUAN	D	10	1
EVIL AND GOOD HAVE HAD THEIR TITHE OF TALK	22	2 DON JUAN	1	2	3
AGAINST ALL EVIL SPEAKING EVEN IN JEST	49	2 DON JUAN	1	51	8
AND WHICH IN RAVAGE THE MORE LOATHSOME EVIL IS--	92	2 DON JUAN	1	131	7
THAT FOR SO LONG OPPOSED THIS GAMING EVIL	102	2 DON JUAN	1	148	V4
AT SIXTY YEARS AND DRAW THE ACCOMPTS OF EVIL	113	2 DON JUAN	1	167	7
OH LOVE THOU ART THE VERY GOD OF EVIL	266	2 DON JUAN	2	205	7
WAS MINGLED WITH HIS EVIL DEEDS AND WAYS	303	2 DON JUAN	3	55	V2
FOR GOOD OR EVIL BURNING FROM ITS BIRTH	374	2 DON JUAN	4	56	3
EVE AND PAVED (GOD KNOWS HOW) THE ROAD TO EVIL	474	2 DON JUAN	5	109	4
WHICH IT CAN EITHER PAIN OR EVIL CALL	17	3 DON JUAN	6	22	5
MORE EVIL IN AN HOUR THAN THIRTY BRIGHT	86	3 DON JUAN	7	41	5
THE THIRD THE USUAL ORIGIN OF EVIL	271	3 DON JUAN	11	6	4
ALTHOUGH THE WORLD HAS SUCH AN EVIL TONGUE	336	3 DON JUAN	12	43	3
HE WHO WILL COMBAT EVIL LONG IN USE	363	3 DON JUAN	13	10	V1
ALTHOUGH SHE WAS NOT EVIL NOR MEANT ILL	364	3 DON JUAN	13	12	4
EVINCE					
THE GENERAL MARKOW WHO COULD THUS EVINCE	117	3 DON JUAN	8	11	6
EVOLUTION					
AN EVOLUTION OFT PERFORMED OF LATE)	308	3 DON JUAN	11	79	5
EVOLUTIONS					
AND PRAYERS AND OTHER PIOUS EVOLUTIONS	52	3 DON JUAN	6	92	3
EV'RY					
AND WHEN THEY HAVE MADE THE SHORE THROUGH EV'RY SHOCK	442	3 DON JUAN	14	74	7
EWER					
THESE WERE RANGED ROUND EACH IN ITS CRYSTAL EWER	307	2 DON JUAN	3	63	1
EXACT					
TO TEACH HIS PEOPLE TO BE MORE EXACT	296	2 DON JUAN	3	40	6
TO EXACT OF CUPID'S BILLS THE FULL AMOUNT	213	3 DON JUAN	9	62	7
THE EXACT AFFAIR ON WHICH HE WAS SENT O'ER	283	3 DON JUAN	11	32	4
EXACTED					
EXACTED BY THE CUSTOMS OF THE EAST	52	3 DON JUAN	6	92	2

238

EXACTLY
    AND NOT EXACTLY EITHER ONE OR TWO 57   2 DON JUAN 1   65   6
    WISHING THEM--NOT EXACTLY DAMNED BUT DEAD HE 89   2 DON JUAN 1   125 V6
    EXACTLY AS YOU PLEASE OR NOT THE ROD 140   2 DON JUAN 1   206   7
    STILL SWAM--THOUGH NOT EXACTLY LIKE A DUCK 177   2 DON JUAN 2   40   8
    WAS NOT EXACTLY THE BEST WAY TO SAVE 225   2 DON JUAN 2   130   2
    STUCK ALL EXACTLY IN THE PROPER SPOT 37   3 DON JUAN 6   62   8
    I SKETCH YOUR WORLD EXACTLY AS IT GOES 156   3 DON JUAN 8   89   8
    I SHALL NOT SAY EXACTLY WHAT HE SAID 158   3 DON JUAN 8   93   5
    AND HERE EXACTLY FOLLOWS WHAT HE SAID-- 178   3 DON JUAN 8   133   6
    I CANNOT TELL EXACTLY WHAT IT WAS 250   3 DON JUAN 10   53   3
    EXACTLY WHY IT WAS BEFORE HIM THROWN 276   3 DON JUAN 11   17   3
    MY FRIENDS THE WHIGS EXACTLY WHERE THEY WERE 308   3 DON JUAN 11   79   8
    HAVE NOT EXACTLY ASCERTAINED THE POLE 376   3 DON JUAN 13   39   4
    I CAN'T EXACTLY TRACE THEIR RULE OF RIGHT 397   3 DON JUAN 13   82   1
    THE MONDE EXACTLY AS THEY OUGHT TO PAINT 418   3 DON JUAN 14   19   3
    ALL THINGS PURSUE EXACTLY THE SAME ROUTE 446   3 DON JUAN 14   84   3
    I RATTLE ON EXACTLY AS I'D TALK 464   3 DON JUAN 15   19   7
    WAS NOT EXACTLY PLEASED TO BE SO CAUGHT 490   3 DON JUAN 15   77   6
    IF HE HAD KNOWN EXACTLY HIS OWN PLIGHT 506   3 DON JUAN 16   12   5
    OF THESE IS NOT EXACTLY ASCERTAINED-- 507   3 DON JUAN 16   16   2
    THOUGH NOT EXACTLY WHAT'S CALLED OPEN HOUSE 534   3 DON JUAN 16   68   8
    THAT HE EXACTLY THE JUST MEDIUM HIT 535   3 DON JUAN 16   72   3
EXACTS
    BUT THAT WHICH MORE COMPLETELY FAITH EXACTS 138   2 DON JUAN 1   203   6
    LIKE CROMWELL'S PRANKS--BUT ALTHOUGH TRUTH EXACTS 329   2 DON JUAN 3   92   5
EXAGGERATION
    IN THIS FOR FEMALES LIKE EXAGGERATION 105   3 DON JUAN 7   75   8
EXAGGERATIONS
    (FOR SUCH EXAGGERATIONS HERE AND THERE I SEE) 446   2 DON JUAN 5   61   6
EXALT
    WITH MUCH TO EXCITE THERE'S LITTLE TO EXALT 417   3 DON JUAN 14   16   1
EXALTED
    THE VIRTUES EVEN THE MOST EXALTED CHARITY 408   2 DON JUAN 4   115   7
EXAMINATION
    TO BE CALLED UP FOR HER EXAMINATION 532   3 DON JUAN 16   65   8
EXAMINE
    WHICH STARE HIM IN THE FACE HE WON'T EXAMINE 88   3 DON JUAN 7   45   7
EXAMINED
    ALFONSO FIRST EXAMINED WELL THEIR FASHION 121   2 DON JUAN 1   181   7
    I HAVE EXAMINED FEW PAIR OF THAT HUE) 404   2 DON JUAN 4   110   5
    EXAMINED BY THIS LEARNED AND ESPECIAL 294   3 DON JUAN 11   51   3
    YET IF EXAMINED IT MIGHT BE ADMITTED 563   3 DON JUAN 17   3   7
EXAMPLE
    ONE SAD EXAMPLE MORE THAT ALL IS VANITY 29   2 DON JUAN 1   15   7
    I DON'T THINK SAPPHO'S ODE A GOOD EXAMPLE 45   2 DON JUAN 1   42   4
    'TWERE WELL IF OTHERS FOLLOW'D MY EXAMPLE 147   2 DON JUAN 1   221   8
    A STRANGE EXAMPLE OF THE FORCE OF LAW 155   2 DON JUAN 1 V 7   1
    WHICH LEARN'D FROM THIS EXAMPLE NOT TO FLY 337   2 DON JUAN 3   106   7
    A SLIGHT EXAMPLE JUST TO CAST A SHADE 22   3 DON JUAN 6   32   5
    BUT STILL IT IS SO AND WITH SUCH EXAMPLE 189   3 DON JUAN 9   13   2
    AFTER THE GOOD EXAMPLE OF GREEN ERIN 286   3 DON JUAN 11   38   7
    MY JEFFREY HELD HIM UP AS AN EXAMPLE 323   3 DON JUAN 12   16   7
    WITH A SIROCCO FOR EXAMPLE BLOWING 422   3 DON JUAN 14   28   2
EXAMPLES
    EXAMPLES OF THIS KIND ARE SO CONTAGIOUS 96   2 DON JUAN 1   138   7
    THE BEST EXAMPLES WHICH I KNOW FOR LOVES 257   2 DON JUAN 2   191 V8
    (NUPTIAL EXAMPLES ARE AS GOOD AS ANY) 301   2 DON JUAN 3   50   4
    SOME FINE EXAMPLES OF THE EPOPEE 332   2 DON JUAN 3   97   7
    OF GOOD EXAMPLES PITY THAT SO FEW BY 486   2 DON JUAN 5   131   4
    BY THEIR EXAMPLES OF TRUE CHRISTIANITY 69   3 DON JUAN 7   6   3
    OR BETTER AS THE BEST EXAMPLES SAY 218   3 DON JUAN 9   71   4
    SEDUCED BY YOUTH AND DANGEROUS EXAMPLES 236   3 DON JUAN 10   23   2
    (IF 'TIS NOT VAIN EXAMPLES TO RECALL) 333   3 DON JUAN 12   37   6
    EXAMPLES MAY BE FOUND OF SUCH PURSUITS 343   3 DON JUAN 12   59   2
EXASPERATED
    ADVANCES WITH EXASPERATED RAP 459   3 DON JUAN 15   8   6
EXCEED
    FOR IF MY PURE LIBATIONS EXCEED THREE 372   2 DON JUAN 4   52   4
EXCEEDED
    FINDING THEMSELVES SO VERY MUCH EXCEEDED 26   2 DON JUAN 1   10   7
EXCEEDING
    AND SINCE EXCEEDING VALOROUS AND SAGE 24   2 DON JUAN 1   5   2
    AND SOMETIMES LADIES HIT EXCEEDING HARD 33   2 DON JUAN 1   21   6
    EXCEEDING SAGELY FROM THAT HOUR DISPENSED 66   2 DON JUAN 1   82   5
    E'ER SAW HER MOST POLITE OF SONS EXCEEDING 299   2 DON JUAN 3   46   4
    AND ALL AROUND WERE GROWN EXCEEDING WROTH 166   3 DON JUAN 8   109   5
EXCEEDINGLY
    EXCEEDINGLY REMARKABLE AT TIMES 22   2 DON JUAN 1   3   7
    THEIR CONDUCT WAS EXCEEDINGLY WELL-BRED 35   2 DON JUAN 1   26   5
    IT SURELY WAS EXCEEDINGLY ILL-BRED 97   2 DON JUAN 1   139   4
    HAVING GOT DRUNK EXCEEDINGLY TODAY 156   2 DON JUAN 1 V 8   5
    AND THERE HE LIVED EXCEEDINGLY AT EASE 223   2 DON JUAN 2   127   4
    AND HERE WAS ONE EXCEEDINGLY UNPLEASANT 371   2 DON JUAN 4   51   2
    WHICH MADE HIM SEEM EXCEEDINGLY ILL-BRED 483   2 DON JUAN 5   124   4
    AND FRESH AND BEAUTIFUL EXCEEDINGLY 24   3 DON JUAN 6   36   3
    DONE ANYTHING EXCEEDINGLY UNKIND 193   3 DON JUAN 9   21   3
    ARE APT EXCEEDINGLY TO RUN TO SEED 445   3 DON JUAN 14   81   8
EXCEL
    AND THEN HE DANCED--ALL FOREIGNERS EXCEL 427   3 DON JUAN 14   38   1
    CAN'T LIKE RIPE AGE IN GOURMANDISE EXCEL 487   3 DON JUAN 15   70   6

239

EXCELLENCY
    MAY IT PLEASE YOUR EXCELLENCY THUS REPLIED 103   3 DON JUAN 7   71   1
EXCELLENT
    WITH MEMORY EXCELLENT TO GET BY ROTE 401   3 DON JUAN 13   91   5
    A SECOND FOR HER EXCELLENT CONNEXIONS 471   3 DON JUAN 15   34   7
    AND AFTER SO MUCH EXCELLENT ADVICE 490   3 DON JUAN 15   77   8
EXCELS
    STILL HE EXCELS THAT ARTIFICIAL HARD 297   3 DON JUAN 11   58   1
EXCEPT
    HIS PARENTS NE'ER AGREED EXCEPT IN DOTING 34   2 DON JUAN 1   25   3
    BUT VIRGIL'S SONGS ARE PURE EXCEPT THAT HORRID ONE . . . 45   2 DON JUAN 1   42   7
    AND JULIA'S VOICE WAS LOST EXCEPT IN SIGHS 84   2 DON JUAN 1   117   1
    EXCEPT TO BULL-FIGHTS MASS PLAY ROUT AND REVEL 102   2 DON JUAN 1   148   4
    NOT ONE EXCEPT THE ATTORNEY WAS AMUSED 109   2 DON JUAN 1   159   5
    HE GAIN'D NO POINT EXCEPT SOME SELF-REBUKES 110   2 DON JUAN 1   161   5
    FOR ME ON EARTH EXCEPT SOME YEARS TO HIDE 132   2 DON JUAN 1   195   3
    TO ALL EXCEPT ONE IMAGE MADLY BLIND 133   2 DON JUAN 1   196   6
    ALL EXCEPT JUAN WHO THROUGHOUT ABSTAIN'D 200   2 DON JUAN 2   82   5
    THEY FURNISH'D HIM ENTIRE EXCEPT SOME STITCHES 240   2 DON JUAN 2   160   7
    YET WHAT CAN PEOPLE DO EXCEPT DESPAIR 278   2 DON JUAN 3   6   5
    EXCEPT SOME CERTAIN PORTIONS OF THE PREY 284   2 DON JUAN 3   17   3
    BUT ALL EXCEPT THEIR SUN IS SET 320   2 DON JUAN 3 L   1   6
    EXCEPT MERE BREATH AND SINCE THE SILENT SHORE 350   2 DON JUAN 4   12   5
    WHAT WAS NO DIRGE EXCEPT THE HOLLOW SEA'S 383   2 DON JUAN 4   72   7
    EXCEPT IN SUCH A WAY AS NOT TO ATTRACT 412   2 DON JUAN 5   2   2
    EXCEPT THAT I HAVE FOUND IT NOTHING NEW 418   2 DON JUAN 5   14   8
    THE WOMEN PARDONED ALL EXCEPT HER FACE 476   2 DON JUAN 5   113   8
    RATHER THAN SIN--EXCEPT TO HIS OWN WISH 492   2 DON JUAN 5   141   6
    EXCEPT IN SHAPE OF ENVOYS WHO WERE SENT 498   2 DON JUAN 5   151   1
    AND ALL (EXCEPT MAHOMETANS) FORBEAR 12   3 DON JUAN 6   12   7
    AND NO ONE VIRTUE YET EXCEPT STARVATION 15   3 DON JUAN 6   19   7
    EXCEPT HIS MAJESTY WHO WITH HER AID 22   3 DON JUAN 6   32   3
    YET IN THE END EXCEPT IN FREEDOM'S BATTLES 114   3 DON JUAN 8   4   7
    AND NEVER RAN AWAY EXCEPT WHEN RUNNING 130   3 DON JUAN 8   35   7
    EXCEPT DON JUAN--A MERE NOVICE WHOSE 131   3 DON JUAN 8   36   2
    HOURIS OR AUGHT EXCEPT HIS FLORID RACE 169   3 DON JUAN 8   116   3
    EXCEPT COLD WEATHER AND COMMISERATION 176   3 DON JUAN 8   129   6
    EXCEPT THE ALL-CLOUDLESS GLORY (WHICH FEW MEN'S IS) . . 186   3 DON JUAN 9   8   5
    EXCEPT NAPOLEON OR ABUSED IT MORE 187   3 DON JUAN 9   9   2
    EXCEPT WHERE 'TIS A MERE INSANITY 219   3 DON JUAN 9   73   3
    THE CASQUE WHICH NEVER STOOPED EXCEPT TO TIME 261   3 DON JUAN 10   74   3
    TAKE LIVES TAKE WIVES TAKE AUGHT EXCEPT MEN'S PURSES . . 264   3 DON JUAN 10   79   2
    EXCEPT THE CREAK OF WHEELS WHICH ON THEIR PIVOT HE . . 272   3 DON JUAN 11   8   6
    DIFFER EXCEPT IN ROBBING WITH A BOW 275   3 DON JUAN 11   15   4
    AND PROPHECY--EXCEPT IT SHOULD BE DATED 286   3 DON JUAN 11   37   7
    EXCEPT THE WHIGS NOT GETTING INTO PLACE 309   3 DON JUAN 11   82   8
    AND HATE ALL VICE EXCEPT ITS REPUTATION 327   3 DON JUAN 12   25   8
    AND SO MAY EVERYONE EXCEPT A DUNCE 336   3 DON JUAN 12   44   3
    EXCEPT PERHAPS THAT YOU WERE BORN TO DIE 411   3 DON JUAN 14   3   3
    BUT NEVER YET (EXCEPT OF COURSE A MISS 470   3 DON JUAN 15   32   1
    EXCEPT ITSELF--SUCH IS THE HUMAN BREAST 505   3 DON JUAN 16   10   3
    NO SOUND EXCEPT THE ECHO OF HIS SIGH 509   3 DON JUAN 16   20   3
EXCEPTING
    TO JUAN'S EYES EXCEPTING NATURAL HISTORY 43   2 DON JUAN 1   39   8
    EXCEPTING THE POST-OBITS OF THEOLOGY 76   2 DON JUAN 1   103   8
    EXCEPTING THE VENETIAN FAZZIOLI 160   2 DON JUAN 2   7   8
    OR THINK OF ANYTHING EXCEPTING THEE 166   2 DON JUAN 2   19   6
    EXCEPTING OUR FIRST PARENTS SUCH A PAIR 258   2 DON JUAN 2   193   3
    THE FACT EXCEPTING SOME EXPERIENCED FEW 342   2 DON JUAN 3   111   5
    EXCEPTING ONLY WHEN THE FORMER'S PICK'D 502   2 DON JUAN 5   158   3
    ALL PHANTASIES NOT EVEN EXCEPTING MINE 255   3 DON JUAN 10   61   4
    EXCEPTING MARRIAGE WHICH IS LOVE NO DOUBT 323   3 DON JUAN 12   15   2
    AND OF ALL THINGS EXCEPTING TITHES AND LEASES 531   3 DON JUAN 16   63   5
EXCEPTION
    WITH THE EXCEPTION OF THE SECOND LINE 69   2 DON JUAN 1   88   6
    SPAIN MAY PROVE AN EXCEPTION TO THE RULE 158   2 DON JUAN 2   2   5
    BUT HEAR THAT SEVERAL PEOPLE TAKE EXCEPTION 397   2 DON JUAN 4   97   3
EXCEPTIONS
    BUT THEN EXCEPTIONS ALWAYS PROVE ITS WORTH-- 158   2 DON JUAN 2   2   6
    WITH SLIGHT EXCEPTIONS ALL THE WAYS SEEM ONE 279   3 DON JUAN 11   23   4
    THERE WERE BUT TWO EXCEPTIONS TO THIS KEEN 552   3 DON JUAN 16   105   1
EXCESS
    BUT ALMOST SANCTIFY THE SWEET EXCESS 357   2 DON JUAN 4   26   7
    THE OTHER THANKING HIM FOR THIS EXCESS 452   2 DON JUAN 5   70   4
    HER AID TO FAIR JUANNA WHOSE EXCESS 36   3 DON JUAN 6   61   3
    IN THE OTHER LINE--BUT NOT TO SUCH EXCESS 176   3 DON JUAN 8   129   3
    ALTHOUGH HE HAD KNOWN PLEASURE IN EXCESS 314   3 DON JUAN 11 V 75 V2
    BUT NEITHER LOVE NOR HATE IN MUCH EXCESS 361   3 DON JUAN 13   8   1
    SOCIETY IS SMOOTH'D TO THAT EXCESS 402   3 DON JUAN 13   94   7
    MY MUSE WOULD RUN MUCH MORE INTO EXCESS 483   3 DON JUAN 15   64   3
EXCESSES
    ALL THAT THE MIND WOULD SHRINK FROM OF EXCESSES . . . 173   3 DON JUAN 8   123   1
    TOO DULL EVEN FOR THE DULLEST OF EXCESSES-- 267   3 DON JUAN 10   86   6
EXCHANGE
    SWORD GOWN GAIN GLORY OFFER IN EXCHANGE 131   2 DON JUAN 1   194   4
    SOME RUN AWAY AND BUT EXCHANGE THEIR CARES 263   2 DON JUAN 2   201   3
    OF TUMBLING FIRST AND HAVING IN EXCHANGE 424   3 DON JUAN 14   32   3
    HOW MUCH WOULD NOVELS GAIN BY THE EXCHANGE 455   3 DON JUAN 14   101   3
EXCHANGED
    IT SEEM'D AS IF THEY HAD EXCHANGED THEIR CARE 186   2 DON JUAN 2   56   3

```
                                                                PAGE VOL      CANTO STANZA LN
EXCHANGED   (CONTINUED)
    EXCHANGED FOR THIN POTATIONS BY JOHN BULL-- . . . . . . . 310  3 DON JUAN 11       85   7
    ADAM EXCHANGED HIS PARADISE FOR PLOUGHING   . . . . . . . 444  3 DON JUAN 14       78   1
EXCHANGING
    OF THEIR EXCHANGING GLANCES OF AFFECTION . . . . . . . . 351  2 DON JUAN  4       13   8
EXCHEQUER
    THOUGH ALL EXCHEQUER CHANCELLORS ENDEAVOUR . . . . . . . 547  3 DON JUAN 16       98   6
EXCISE
    AND WORDSWORTH HAS HIS PLACE IN THE EXCISE . . . . . .  12  2 DON JUAN  D        6   6
EXCITE
    WITH MUCH TO EXCITE THERE'S LITTLE TO EXALT . . . . . . 417  3 DON JUAN 14       16   1
EXCITED
    EVEN THE BOLD CHURCHMAN'S TOMB EXCITED AWE . . . . . . . 261  3 DON JUAN 10       74   4
    AND MIEN EXCITED GENERAL ADMIRATION-- . . . . . . . . . 287  3 DON JUAN 11       39   2
EXCITING
    WITHOUT EXCITING SUCH SUSPICION AS . . . . .  /  . . . .  57  3 DON JUAN  6      103   7
EXCLAIM
    THE VASTY DEEP TO WHOM YOU MAY EXCLAIM   . . . . . . . . 132  3 DON JUAN  8       38   3
EXCLAIM'D
    THAT ALL THE WORLD EXCLAIM'D WHAT MAGNANIMITY . . . . .  36  2 DON JUAN  1       29   8
EXCLAIMED
    AND BABA SMILINGLY EXCLAIMED YOU SEE SIRS   . . . . . . 458  2 DON JUAN  5       80   4
    FAREWELL THEY MUTUALLY EXCLAIMED THIS SOIL . . . . . . . 459  2 DON JUAN  5       83   5
    IS IT EXCLAIMED GULBEYAZ AS YOU SAY   . . . . . . . . . 494  2 DON JUAN  5      145   1
    MY GUARD MY OLD GUARD EXCLAIMED THAT GOD OF CLAY--  . . 254  3 DON JUAN 10       59   2
    TITUS EXCLAIMED I'VE LOST A DAY OF ALL  . . . . . . . . 505  3 DON JUAN 16       11   5
EXCLAIMING
    EXCLAIMING FOOLING SWEARING AT THE INERT  . . . . . . .  96  3 DON JUAN  7       58   3
    EXCLAIMING--JUAN JUAN ON BOY BRACE . . . . . . . . . . 160  3 DON JUAN  8       97   6
EXCLAIMS
    SHAKESPEARE EXCLAIMS--HANG UP PHILOSOPHY . . . . . . . . 272  2 DON JUAN  2    V  1   1
EXCLUDED
    AND THE YOUNG BEAMS OF THE EXCLUDED SUN  . . . . . . . . 229  2 DON JUAN  2      137   4
EXCOMMUNICATION
    AND THE POPE THUNDER EXCOMMUNICATION  . . . : . . . . . 478  3 DON JUAN 15       50   4
EXCURSION
    AND WORDSWORTH IN A RATHER LONG EXCURSION   . . . . . .  11  2 DON JUAN  D        4   1
    A DROWSY FROWZY POEM CALL'D THE EXCURSION  . . . . . . 330  2 DON JUAN  3       94   7
EXCURSIVE
    INTO THE EXCURSIVE BREAKING THE INDENTURES  . . . . . . 284  3 DON JUAN 11       33   5
    FOR BEING TOO EXCURSIVE IN HIS HOMAGES-- . . . . . . . 312  3 DON JUAN 11       89   8
EXCUSE
    AT FIRST HE TRIED TO HAMMER AN EXCUSE . . . . . . . . . 110  2 DON JUAN  1      162   1
    YOU MUST EXCUSE THIS EXTRACT 'TIS WHERE SHE . . . . . . 165  2 DON JUAN  2       17   4
    HIS GLANCE INQUIRED OF HERS FOR SOME EXCUSE . . . . . . 355  2 DON JUAN  4       22   7
    AND BEGGED THEY WOULD EXCUSE HER SHE'D GET OVER  . . .  47  3 DON JUAN  6       83   7
    EXCUSE MY FREEDOM WHEN I HERE ASSURE YOU . . . . . . .  63  3 DON JUAN  6      115   7
    (PRITHEE EXCUSE THIS ENGINEERING SLANG) . . . . . . .  72  3 DON JUAN  7       11   6
    HARK HOW THE ROAR INCREASES--NO EXCUSE  . . . . . . . 162  3 DON JUAN  8      101   5
    (FATE IS A GOOD EXCUSE FOR OUR OWN WILL) . . . . . . . 364  3 DON JUAN 13       12   6
    (EXCUSE A FOREIGN SLIPSLOP NOW AND THEN  . . . . . . . 380  3 DON JUAN 13       47   6
    FOR WHICH MY SOLE EXCUSE IS--'TIS MY WAY . . . . . . . 413  3 DON JUAN 14        7   3
EXCUSES
    SOME STRANGE EXCUSES FOR HIS LATE PROCEEDING  . . . . . 116  2 DON JUAN  1      174   2
    SO HE BEGAN TO STAMMER SOME EXCUSES   . . . . . . . . . 493  2 DON JUAN  5      143   1
EXECRATES
    IF TIME THE AVENGER EXECRATES HIS WRONGS . . . . . . .  15  2 DON JUAN  D       10   3
EXECUTES
    BUT VERY RARELY EXECUTES ITS FUNCTION . . . . . . . . . 271  2 DON JUAN  2      215   2
EXECUTION
    THE TONES THE FEELING AND THE EXECUTION  . . . . . . . 521  3 DON JUAN 16       41   7
EXEMPLARY
    RESIGNS HERSELF WITH EXEMPLARY PATIENCE . . . . . . . . 440  2 DON JUAN  5       52   7
    FOR BEING A MOST EXEMPLARY WIFE . . . . . . . . . . . 338  3 DON JUAN 12       47   8
EXEMPT
    WHAT WAS IT MADE THEM THUS EXEMPT FROM CARE . . . . . . 353  2 DON JUAN  4       18   4
EXERT
    AT LEAST THEY THINK SO TO EXERT THEIR STATE . . . . . . 367  3 DON JUAN 13       19   4
EXERTION
    EXERTION MIGHT BE USEFUL ON OCCASION  . . . . . . . .  65  2 DON JUAN  1       81   4
    WHICH LEFT SCARCE ROOM FOR MOTION OR EXERTION . . . . . 189  2 DON JUAN  2       63   2
    FOR ALL HER PAST EXERTION AND SOFT PHRASES . . . . . . 550  3 DON JUAN 16      103   3
EXHALES
    THE PRIEST INSTRUCTS AND SO OUR LIFE EXHALES  . . . . . 159  2 DON JUAN  2        4   6
EXHAUSTION
    EXHAUSTION OR DISORDERS OF THE SAME KIN . . . . . . . . 244  3 DON JUAN 10       40   4
EXHORTATION
    MY MUSE BY EXHORTATION MEANS TO MEND  . . . . . . . . 334  3 DON JUAN 12       39   6
EXILED
    TILL THEY WERE EXILED FROM THEIR EARLIER BOWERS  . . .  30  2 DON JUAN  1       18   4
    BUT DIE AS MANY AN EXILED HEART HATH DIED   . . . . . 166  2 DON JUAN  2       18   3
EXILES
    SOME EXILES FROM THE TOWN WHO HAD BEEN DRIVEN  . . . . 539  3 DON JUAN 16       81   2
EXIST
    SUCH LOVE IS INNOCENT AND MAY EXIST   . . . . . . . .  65  2 DON JUAN  1       80   1
    LOVE MAY EXIST WITH MARRIAGE AND SHOULD EVER  . . . . 323  3 DON JUAN 12       15   5
    AND MARRIAGE ALSO MAY EXIST WITHOUT   . . . . . . . . 323  3 DON JUAN 12       15   6
    BUT SHOULD THE DAY COME WHEN PLACE CEASED TO EXIST  . . 537  3 DON JUAN 16       75   5
EXISTED
    THAT SUCH EXISTED (AND THEY MAY LIVE NOW . . . . . . .  82  3 DON JUAN  7       33   4
```

241

		PAGE	VOL	CANTO	STANZA	LN
EXISTENCE						
	'TIS WOMAN'S WHOLE EXISTENCE MAN MAY RANGE	131	2 DON JUAN	1	194	2
	WE ENTER ON OUR NAUTICAL EXISTENCE	163	2 DON JUAN	2	12	8
	ENLARGEMENT OF EXISTENCE TO PARTAKE	247	2 DON JUAN	2	173	2
	LIFE SEEMS THE SMALLEST PORTION OF EXISTENCE	398	2 DON JUAN	4	100	3
	WHO LITTLE THOUGHT THAT HIS OWN CRACKED EXISTENCE	440	2 DON JUAN	5	51	3
	OUR ULTIMATE EXISTENCE WHAT'S OUR PRESENT	37	3 DON JUAN	6	63	7
	THREE FIRESHIPS LOST THEIR AMIABLE EXISTENCE	80	3 DON JUAN	7	28	3
	OR DOUBLE POST AND RAIL WHERE THE EXISTENCE	140	3 DON JUAN	8	55	3
	THEY SOMETIMES WITH A HANKERING FOR EXISTENCE	151	3 DON JUAN	8	78	7
	AS IF HIS VEINS WOULD POUR OUT HIS EXISTENCE	275	3 DON JUAN	11	14	6
	HAD MORE OF HER EXISTENCE FOR IN HER	524	3 DON JUAN	16	48	6
	THE HEART IN AN EXISTENCE OF ITS OWN	554	3 DON JUAN	16	108	7
EXISTENT						
	HOW COULD HE POSSIBLY SHOW THINGS EXISTENT	494	3 DON JUAN	15	87	8
EXISTS						
	EXISTS THE REMNANT OF A LINE	325	2 DON JUAN	3	L 13	3
	EXISTS WHEN THE ONCE THINKERS ARE LESS REAL	234	3 DON JUAN	10	20	3
	BUT BEDLAM STILL EXISTS WITH ITS SAGE FETTER	280	3 DON JUAN	11	25	3
	EXISTS--AND WHERE THAT SHALL I NOT RECALL	499	3 DON JUAN	15	96	4
EXIT						
	WHENCE IS OUR EXIT AND OUR ENTRANCE--WELL I	210	3 DON JUAN	9	55	3
EXMAPLES						
	THESE ARE SOME SAD EXMAPLES TO ALLURE US	267	2 DON JUAN	2	207	V5
EXORDIUM						
	AND WHEREFORE THIS EXORDIUM--WHY JUST NOW	226	3 DON JUAN	10	3	1
EXOTIC						
	THIS WAY OF WRITING WILL APPEAR EXOTIC	347	2 DON JUAN	4	6	2
	IN SOME EXOTIC GARDEN SOMETIMES FOUND	38	3 DON JUAN	6	65	3
EXPANDED						
	COULD E'ER EXPRESS IN ITS EXPANDED SHAPE	375	3 DON JUAN	13	37	8
EXPANDING						
	AND TIMIDLY EXPANDING INTO LIFE	27	3 DON JUAN	6	43	8
	UNTIL THEY REACHED AS DAY-BREAK WAS EXPANDING	148	3 DON JUAN	8	72	5
EXPANSION						
	AS SHE HAD SEEN NOUGHT CLAIMING ITS EXPANSION	446	3 DON JUAN	14	85	4
EXPATIATE						
	MAY STILL EXPATIATE FREELY AS WILL I	195	3 DON JUAN	9	26	7
EXPECT						
	THE PUBLIC APPROBATION I EXPECT	141	2 DON JUAN	1	209	1
	NOR RAG OF CANVAS WHAT COULD THEY EXPECT	176	2 DON JUAN	2	39	4
	AN USURER COULD SCARCE EXPECT MUCH MORE--	356	3 DON JUAN	12	88	6
EXPECTANT						
	AN AGE--EXPECTANT POWERLESS WITH HIS EYES	511	3 DON JUAN	16	25	2
	EXPECTANT OF THE GHOST'S FRESH OPERATIONS	555	3 DON JUAN	16	111	8
EXPECTED						
	'TWAS NOT TO BE EXPECTED THAT HE SHOULD	198	2 DON JUAN	2	78	6
	SO LITTLE THEY EXPECTED HIM THAT DAY	300	2 DON JUAN	3	49	4
EXPECTING						
	EXPECTING ALL THE WELCOME OF A LOVER	12	3 DON JUAN	6	13	7
EXPECTS						
	IT SEEMS THE VIRGIN'S HEART EXPECTS YOUR HAND	343	3 DON JUAN	12	60	6
EXPEDIENT						
	EXPEDIENT OF FULL BUMPERS FOR THE EYE	216	3 DON JUAN	9	67	7
	HOWEVER 'TIS EXPEDIENT TO BE WARY	374	3 DON JUAN	13	35	5
	BUT TRUE--AS IF EXPEDIENT I COULD PROVE)	452	3 DON JUAN	14	96	2
	THOUGH THIS WAS MOST EXPEDIENT ON THE WHOLE	546	3 DON JUAN	16	96	1
EXPEDIENTS						
	DESPITE OF ALL THEIR EFFORTS AND EXPEDIENTS	171	2 DON JUAN	2	29	3
EXPEDITION						
	AS I HAVE SAID UPON AN EXPEDITION	252	2 DON JUAN	2	182	2
EXPELLED						
	AND EXPELLED THE FRIARS ONE FRIAR STILL	518	3 DON JUAN	16	L 1	7
EXPENCE						
	BUT NOT AT THE EXPENCE OF A WHOLE NATION	185	3 DON JUAN	9	6	V8
EXPENDED						
	EXPENDED ALL THEIR EASTERN PHRASEOLOGY	165	3 DON JUAN	8	108	2
	OF INTELLECT EXPENDED ON TWO COURSES	486	3 DON JUAN	15	69	2
EXPENSE						
	EVEN AT YOUR OWN IMPERATIVE EXPENSE	62	3 DON JUAN	6	114	6
	MAINTAINED AT THE EXPENSE OF YOUR GOOD KING	118	3 DON JUAN	8	14	3
	WITHOUT THE EXPENSE AND THE SUSPENSE OF BEDDING	177	3 DON JUAN	8	131	8
EXPENSES						
	PERCEIVING IN HIS ABSENCE SUCH EXPENSES	293	2 DON JUAN	3	35	6
	NOT LEAVING EVEN HIS FUNERAL EXPENSES	186	3 DON JUAN	9	8	3
	IS LEARNING TO REDUCE HIS PAST EXPENSES	240	3 DON JUAN	10	31	8
	WITHOUT THOSE SAD EXPENSES WHICH DISPARGE	471	3 DON JUAN	15	35	5
EXPENSIVE						
	APARTMENT--FASHIONABLE BUT EXPENSIVE	313	3 DON JUAN	11	V 29	8
EXPERIENCE						
	OF ALL EXPERIENCE 'TIS THE USUAL PRICE	122	2 DON JUAN	1	183	3
	AND IF THEIR APPROBATION WE EXPERIENCE	135	2 DON JUAN	1	199	7
	MUCH LESS EXPERIENCE OF DRY LAND THAN OCEAN	289	2 DON JUAN	3	26	2
	SOME BY EXPERIENCE OTHERS BY TRADITION	477	2 DON JUAN	5	115	8
	BABA WHO KNEW BY EXPERIENCE WHEN TO TALK	61	3 DON JUAN	6	110	1
	THE WORLD BY EXPERIENCE RATHER THAN BY LECTURE	337	3 DON JUAN	12	46	5
	HATH WON THE EXPERIENCE WHICH IS DEEMED SO WEIGHTY	339	3 DON JUAN	12	50	8
	'TWAS RATHER HER EXPERIENCE MADE HER SAGE	433	3 DON JUAN	14	54	3
	ALAS BY ALL EXPERIENCE SELDOM YET	452	3 DON JUAN	14	95	1
	EXPERIENCE IS THE CHIEF PHILOSOPHER	463	3 DON JUAN	15	17	5

242

EXPERIENCED
  THE FACT EXCEPTING SOME EXPERIENCED FEW . . . . 342 2 DON JUAN 3   111   5
EXPERIMENT
  SOME NEW EXPERIMENT TO SHOW HIS PARTS . . . . 91 2 DON JUAN 1   128   4
EXPIRE
  ITS STORMS EXPIRE IN WATER-DROPS THE EYE . . . . 270 2 DON JUAN 2   214   6
EXPIRED
  THE BOY EXPIRED--THE FATHER HELD THE CLAY . . . . . . 204 2 DON JUAN 2   90   1
  THAT BOTH ARE TIED TILL ONE SHALL HAVE EXPIRED . . . . 278 2 DON JUAN 3   7   6
  AND EVERY SOUND OF REVELRY EXPIRED . . . . 334 2 DON JUAN 3   101   4
  THE LAST EXPIRED IN CUT THROAT CASTLEREAGH . . . . . 254 3 DON JUAN 10   59 V4
  THE SONG WAS SILENT AND THE DANCE EXPIRED . . . . . . 504 3 DON JUAN 16   8   4
EXPIRES
  AND THE PAUSE FOLLOWED WHICH WHEN SONG EXPIRES . . . . . 521 3 DON JUAN 16   41   3
EXPIRING
  EXPIRING IN THE HOPE OF SENSATION-- . . . . 569 3 DON JUAN 17 V 13   7
EXPLAIN
  I WISH HE WOULD EXPLAIN HIS EXPLANATION . . . . 10 2 DON JUAN D   2   8
  YET SUCH THINGS ARE WHICH I CAN NOT EXPLAIN . . . . . 299 2 DON JUAN 3   47   6
  I THINK I CAN EXPLAIN MYSELF WITHOUT . . . . 207 3 DON JUAN 9   50   1
  ALL THESE OR ANY ONE OF THESE EXPLAIN . . . . 218 3 DON JUAN 9   72   7
  WHICH FURTHER TO EXPLAIN WOULD BE A TRUISM . . . . . 506 3 DON JUAN 16   13   8
  FOR HOW COULD IT GO ON EXPLAIN WHO CAN . . . . . . 537 3 DON JUAN 16   75   7
EXPLAINING
  EXPLAINING METAPHYSICS TO THE NATION-- . . . . 10 2 DON JUAN D   2   7
EXPLAINS
  EXPLAINS THE GARB WHICH JUAN TOOK AMISS . . . . 477 2 DON JUAN 5   114   8
EXPLANATION
  I WISH HE WOULD EXPLAIN HIS EXPLANATION . . . . 10 2 DON JUAN D   2   8
  NO SORT OF EXPLANATION COULD BE HAD . . . . 35 2 DON JUAN 1   27   6
  HIS SPIRITS AND WITHOUT MORE EXPLANATION . . . . . . 526 3 DON JUAN 16   53   2
EXPLICITLY
  EXPLICITLY OUR SEVERAL POSTS MY FRIEND . . . . 100 3 DON JUAN 7   65   7
EXPLOITS
  OF HER EXPLOITS FOR THIS WERE TICKLISH GROUND . . . . . 428 3 DON JUAN 14   42   5
EXPLORE
  IS'T WISE OR FITTING CAUSELESS TO EXPLORE . . . . . . 101 2 DON JUAN 1   146   5
EXPLORED
  THE PASSAGE YOU SO OFTEN HAVE EXPLORED-- . . . . . . 121 2 DON JUAN 1   182   5
  HAVE YOU EXPLORED THE LIMITS OF THE COAST . . . . . . 502 3 DON JUAN 16   4   5
EXPLOSION
  AND SO THAT NO EXPLOSION CRY AROINT . . . . 396 3 DON JUAN 13   81   5
EXPOSED
  POETS AND PRIVATE TUTORS ARE EXPOSED . . . . 486 2 DON JUAN 5   131   5
  EXPOSED TO LOSE HIS LIFE AS WELL AS BREECHES . . . . . 273 3 DON JUAN 11   11   8
  EXPOSED HIM AS WAS NATURAL TO TEMPTATION . . . . . . 355 3 DON JUAN 12   85   7
EXPOSURE
  THE WRONGS TO WHOSE EXPOSURE IT IS SLOW-- . . . . . . 107 2 DON JUAN 1   157   4
  I DO NOT MEAN DESTRUCTION AND EXPOSURE . . . . 62 3 DON JUAN 6   114   7
EXPOUND
  COULD NOT AT FIRST EXPOUND WHAT WAS AMISS . . . . . . 43 3 DON JUAN 6   74   8
  TO EXPOUND THEIR VAIN AND VISIONARY GLEAMS . . . . . . 45 3 DON JUAN 6   78   4
  I CAN'T TELL WHY SHE BLUSHED NOR CAN EXPOUND . . . . . 48 3 DON JUAN 6   85   5
EXPOUNDER
  THE LAW'S EXPOUNDER AND THE STATE'S CORRECTOR . . . . . 29 2 DON JUAN 1   15   5
EXPOUNDING
  EXPOUNDING AND ILLUSTRATING THE RIDDLE . . . . 337 3 DON JUAN 12   45   7
EXPOUNDS
  UNRIDDLED AND AS MY TRUE MUSE EXPOUNDS . . . . 112 3 DON JUAN 8   1   5
EXPRESS
  ALL THAT THE BEST CAN MINGLE AND EXPRESS . . . . . . 357 2 DON JUAN 4   26   4
  IN SUCH A TRIFLE SCARCELY COULD EXPRESS . . . . . . 452 2 DON JUAN 5   70   6
  THESE DON'T EXPRESS ONE HALF WHAT I SHOULD SAY . . . . 487 2 DON JUAN 5   132   6
  WHAT SHE COULD NE'ER EXPRESS--THEN HOW SHOULD I . . . . 59 3 DON JUAN 6   106   8
  AMONG THE FOREMOST BUT IF YOU'D EXPRESS . . . . . . 100 3 DON JUAN 7   65   6
  AND STILL MORE IN HIS EYE WHICH SEEMED TO EXPRESS . . . 206 3 DON JUAN 9   47   4
  OF ANYTHING WHICH NATURE WOULD EXPRESS . . . . 373 3 DON JUAN 13   34   4
  COULD E'ER EXPRESS IN ITS EXPANDED SHAPE . . . . . . 375 3 DON JUAN 13   37   8
  THIS FEELING 'TIS NOT EASY TO EXPRESS . . . . 415 3 DON JUAN 14   12   5
  YOUR MEN OF BUSINESS ARE NOT APT TO EXPRESS . . . . . 443 3 DON JUAN 14   76   6
  SLIGHT BUT SELECT AND JUST ENOUGH TO EXPRESS . . . . . 491 3 DON JUAN 15   80   2
  AND BEING PRESENT NOW BEGAN TO EXPRESS . . . . 514 3 DON JUAN 16   32   6
  OF COURSE THE OTHERS COULD NOT BUT EXPRESS . . . . . 517 3 DON JUAN 16   39   4
  HE SATE WITH FEELINGS AWKWARD TO EXPRESS . . . . . . 555 3 DON JUAN 16   111   6
EXPRESS'D
  BODED NO GOOD WHATEVER IT EXPRESS'D . . . . 297 2 DON JUAN 3   42   4
  THIS HE EXPRESS'D HALF SMILING AND HALF SERIOUS . . . 477 3 DON JUAN 15   49   4
EXPRESSED
  (SEE LITTLETON) WHENE'ER I HAVE EXPRESSED . . . . . . 494 3 DON JUAN 15   87   2
EXPRESSES
  ALL THAT DEFIES THE WORST WHICH PEN EXPRESSES . . . . 173 3 DON JUAN 8   123   5
  WHERE JUNIPER EXPRESSES ITS BEST JUICE . . . . 256 3 DON JUAN 10   63   3
EXPRESSION
  FLASH'D AN EXPRESSION MORE OF PRIDE THAN IRE . . . . . 54 2 DON JUAN 1   60   4
  THE EXPRESSION AND ENDEAVOURING TO RESUME . . . . . . 298 2 DON JUAN 3   44   5
  WHILE I SOLILOQUIZE BEYOND EXPRESSION . . . . 331 2 DON JUAN 3   96   4
  WHILE I AM CHATTERING BEYOND ALL EXPRESSION . . . . . 331 2 DON JUAN 3   96 V4
  HOW LIKE THEY LOOKED THE EXPRESSION WAS THE SAME . . . 367 2 DON JUAN 4   44   2
  FULL OF EXPRESSION RIGHT OR WRONG THAT STRIKE . . . . 32 3 DON JUAN 6   52   7

	PAGE	VOL	CANTO	STANZA	LN

EXPREST
AND THUS IN EVERY LOOK SHE SAW EXPREST . . . . . . 241 2 DON JUAN 2 162 7
YET LET THEM THINK THAT HORACE HAS EXPREST . . . . . 448 2 DON JUAN 5 63 1
AND JUAN NOW HIS WILLINGNESS EXPREST . . . . . . 472 2 DON JUAN 5 105 4
TILL SOMEONE WITH A GROAN EXPREST A WISH . . . . . . 542 3 DON JUAN 16 87 7
EXPURGATED
EXPURGATED BY LEARNED MEN WHO PLACE . . . . 46 2 DON JUAN 1 44 2
EXQUISITE
WITH FURNITURE AN EXQUISITE APARTMENT . . . . . . 448 2 DON JUAN 5 64 7
AN EXQUISITE SMALL CHAPEL HAD BEEN ABLE . . . . . 389 3 DON JUAN 13 66 5
EXQUISITELY
WHEN EXQUISITELY CHISELL'D STILL LAY THERE . . . . . 377 2 DON JUAN 4 61 2
EXTENDS
LIKE GARLIC HOWSOEVER SHE EXTENDS . . . . 231 3 DON JUAN 10 12 5
EXTENSION
A FINE EXTENSION OF THE FACULTIES . . . . 269 2 DON JUAN 2 212 2
EXTENSIVE
IT WAS INDEED A WIDE EXTENSIVE BUILDING . . . . . 436 2 DON JUAN 5 46 1
IN THIS EXTENSIVE CITY SORE BESET . . . . 131 3 DON JUAN 8 37 4
AND JUAN FOUND HIMSELF IN AN EXTENSIVE . . . . . 313 3 DON JUAN 11 V 29 7
EXTENT
WITHIN THE EXTENT OF THIS FORTIFICATION . . . . . . 71 3 DON JUAN 7 10 1
WELL LOOKED UPON BY BOTH TO THAT EXTENT . . . . . 342 3 DON JUAN 12 57 2
EXTERNAL
A STRONG EXTERNAL MOTIVE AND IN THIS . . . . . . 544 3 DON JUAN 16 92 5
EXTINGUISHED
AND IS EXTINGUISHED SOONER THAN SHE OUGHT . . . . 83 3 DON JUAN 7 34 6
EXTRACT
YOU MUST EXCUSE THIS EXTRACT 'TIS WHERE SHE . . . . 165 2 DON JUAN 2 17 4
INTO AN ELEGANT EXTRACT (MUCH LESS MASSY) . . . . 130 3 DON JUAN 8 34 5
EXTRACTS
EXTRACTS EMOTIONS BEAUTIFUL AND NEW . . . . . . 144 2 DON JUAN 1 214 4
EXTRANEOUS
BUT AN EXTRANEOUS MIXTURE WHICH NO PEN . . . . . 462 2 DON JUAN 5 88 5
EXTRAS
WITH OTHER EXTRAS WHICH WE NEED NOT MENTION-- . . . 218 3 DON JUAN 9 72 6
EXTREME
TO SAY THE BEST IT WAS EXTREME ILL-BREEDING . . . . 116 2 DON JUAN 1 174 4
THE CONSEQUENCE WAS AWFUL IN THE EXTREME . . . . 198 2 DON JUAN 2 79 2
THUS TO THEIR EXTREME VERGE THE PASSIONS BROUGHT . . 402 2 DON JUAN 4 106 6
AND THIS EXTREME EFFECT (TO TIRE NO LONGER . . . . 488 2 DON JUAN 5 133 7
JOHN JOHNSON SEEING THEIR EXTREME DISMAY . . . . 105 3 DON JUAN 7 75 1
EXTREMELY
AND LOOK'D EXTREMELY AT THE OPENING DOOR . . . . 63 2 DON JUAN 1 76 3
BY HARBOURING SOME DEAR FRIEND EXTREMELY VICIOUS . . 74 2 DON JUAN 1 99 5
THEIR LIVES AND FORTUNES WERE EXTREMELY VARIOUS . . 266 2 DON JUAN 2 206 5
WITHOUT WHICH LIFE WOULD BE EXTREMELY DULL . . . . 269 2 DON JUAN 2 212 5
EXTREMELY TAKEN WITH HIS OWN RELIGION . . . . . 387 2 DON JUAN 4 78 7
SHE MEANT TO BE EXTREMELY CONDESCENDING . . . . 475 2 DON JUAN 5 112 V1
AND DEEMED HERSELF EXTREMELY CONDESCENDING . . . 478 2 DON JUAN 5 116 3
THIS WAS A TRUTH TO US EXTREMELY TRITE . . . . . 485 2 DON JUAN 5 128 1
THUS IN THE EAST THEY ARE EXTREMELY STRICT . . . . 502 2 DON JUAN 5 158 1
I KNOW GULBEYAZ WAS EXTREMELY WRONG . . . . . 10 3 DON JUAN 6 8 1
EXTREMELY PURE WHICH MADE THEM ALL CONCUR . . . 25 3 DON JUAN 6 39 4
NOT VERY DASHING BUT EXTREMELY WINNING . . . . . 32 3 DON JUAN 6 52 2
EXTREMELY COMMON IN THIS AGE WHOSE METAL . . . . 33 3 DON JUAN 6 55 7
DESCRIBED--WHAT'S STRANGE--IN WORDS EXTREMELY FEW . 34 3 DON JUAN 6 57 6
AND SAID SHE FELT HERSELF EXTREMELY WELL . . . . 48 3 DON JUAN 6 84 2
AND THOUGH HE WISHED EXTREMELY TO GET THROUGH . . 63 3 DON JUAN 6 116 6
EXTREMELY TRANQUIL ANCHORED AT ITS STATION . . . . 78 3 DON JUAN 7 24 4
DEFENDED AT A PRICE EXTREMELY DEAR . . . . . . 151 3 DON JUAN 8 79 8
AT WHICH THE WHOLE COURT WAS EXTREMELY TROUBLED . . 244 3 DON JUAN 10 39 7
EXTREMELY WHOLESOME THOUGH BUT RARELY CLEAR . . . 266 3 DON JUAN 10 83 8
BUT WHICH I DOUBT EXTREMELY--THOU SOLE PRISM . . . 269 3 DON JUAN 11 2 6
BEING QUITE PERSPICUOUS AND EXTREMELY FAIR . . . . 270 3 DON JUAN 11 5 4
HE FOUND HIMSELF EXTREMELY IN THE FASHION . . . . 284 3 DON JUAN 11 33 7
BOTH LONGED EXTREMELY TO BE SUNG IN SPANISH . . . 295 3 DON JUAN 11 53 8
EXTREMELY DISAGREEABLE BUT COMMON . . . . . . 429 3 DON JUAN 14 43 7
HERSELF EXTREMELY ON THE INOCULATION . . . . . 478 3 DON JUAN 15 50 6
THE PRESENT CULPRIT WAS EXTREMELY PALE . . . . . 532 3 DON JUAN 16 64 1
EXTREMES
A GO-BETWEEN YET BLUNDERING IN EXTREMES . . . . 155 2 DON JUAN 1 V 6 3
TO KEEP EXTREMES FROM MEETING WHEN ONCE SET . . . 492 3 DON JUAN 15 81 6
EXTREMEST
SO RECOLLECT THAT THE EXTREMEST GRACE . . . . . 482 2 DON JUAN 5 123 6
EXTREMITY
EVEN IN EXTREMITY OF THEIR DISASTER . . . . . . 198 2 DON JUAN 2 78 7
AS SOMETIMES HAPPENS IN A GREAT EXTREMITY . . . . 92 3 DON JUAN 7 51 4
THINGS SPEEDILY WERE WAXING TO EXTREMITY . . . . 92 3 DON JUAN 7 51 V6
IF IN MY EXTREMITY OF RHYME'S DISTRESS . . . . . 442 3 DON JUAN 14 75 5
EXUBERANT
THOUGH SOMEWHAT LARGE EXUBERANT AND TRUCULENT . . . 213 3 DON JUAN 9 62 1
EXULTATION
A SUBJECT OF SUBLIMEST EXULTATION-- . . . . . . 175 3 DON JUAN 8 126 3
EXULTING
EXULTING IN THEIR BRILLIANT LUCUBRATIONS . . . . . 533 3 DON JUAN 16 66 8
EYE
A NEST OF TUNEFUL PERSONS TO MY EYE . . . . . . 9 2 DON JUAN D 1 7
EACH EYE A SERMON AND HER BROW A HOMILY . . . . . 29 2 DON JUAN 1 15 2

                                                              PAGE VOL   CANTO STANZA LN
EYE   (CONTINUED)
    THE DARKNESS OF HER ORIENTAL EYE   52   2 DON JUAN   1   56   1
    HER EYE (I'M VERY FOND OF HANDSOME EYES)   54   2 DON JUAN   1   60   1
    AND MUCH EMBARRASSMENT IN EITHER EYE   60   2 DON JUAN   1   70   4
    ITS WORKINGS THROUGH THE VAINLY GUARDED EYE   61   2 DON JUAN   1   73   4
    'TIS SWEET TO KNOW THERE IS AN EYE WILL MARK   88   2 DON JUAN   1   123   3
    WHILE THE O'ERPOWERING EYE THAT TURNS YOU PALE . . .   160   2 DON JUAN   2   7   3
    NOR INFLAMMATIONS REDDEN HIS BLIND EYE   168   2 DON JUAN   2   22   8
    JUST LIKE A BLACK EYE IN A RECENT SCUFFLE   205   2 DON JUAN   2   92   7
    TILL THE EYE CHEATED OPENS THICK WITH TEARS   227   2 DON JUAN   2   134   8
    AND SMILES AND SPARKLES OF THE SPEAKING EYE   241   2 DON JUAN   2   162   2
    WITH ONE STAR SPARKLING THROUGH IT LIKE AN EYE . . .   252   2 DON JUAN   2   183   8
    AND NOW AND THEN HER EYE TO HEAVEN IS CAST   260   2 DON JUAN   2   195   5
    ITS STORMS EXPIRE IN WATER-DROPS THE EYE   270   2 DON JUAN   2   214   6
    THE GESTURE WHICH ENCHANTS THE EYE THAT SPEAKS . . .   292   2 DON JUAN   3   33   4
    AND O'ER HIS EYE A MOMENTARY GLOOM   298   2 DON JUAN   3   44   3
    THERE HIS WORN BOSOM AND KEEN EYE WOULD MELT . . .   302   2 DON JUAN   3   52   6
    THE EYE MIGHT DOUBT IF IT WERE WELL AWAKE   314   2 DON JUAN   3   76   5
    FROM A TRUE LOVER SHADOW'D MY MIND'S EYE   337   2 DON JUAN   3   106   8
    WHILE ONE NEW TEAR AROSE IN HAIDEE'S EYE   355   2 DON JUAN   4   21   8
    THAT LARGE BLACK PROPHET EYE SEEM'D TO DILATE . . .   355   2 DON JUAN   4   22   1
    OH POWERS OF HEAVEN WHAT DARK EYE MEETS SHE THERE . . 363   2 DON JUAN   4   35   7
    CALM IN HIS VOICE AND CALM WITHIN HIS EYE--   365   2 DON JUAN   4   39   2
    A FAIRER MARK AND WITH A FIX'D EYE SCANN'D   367   2 DON JUAN   4   43   7
    BUT HER LARGE DARK EYE SHOW'D DEEP PASSION'S FORCE .   374   2 DON JUAN   4   56   7
    SHE LOOK'D ON MANY A FACE WITH VACANT EYE   378   2 DON JUAN   4   63   1
    HER EYE MIGHT FLASH ON HIS BUT FOUND IT DIM   396   2 DON JUAN   4   95   3
    WITH RESOLUTION IN HIS DARK GRAY EYE   416   2 DON JUAN   5   10   7
    HE PAUSED AND HIS DARK EYE GREW FULL OF GLOOM . . .   420   2 DON JUAN   5   18   3
    MEANTIME (YON OLD BLACK EUNUCH SEEMS TO EYE US) . .   423   2 DON JUAN   5   24   7
    WITH THE PROPHETIC EYE OF APPETITE   439   2 DON JUAN   5   50   8
    THERE CAPTIVES LED IN TRIUMPH DROOP THE EYE   461   2 DON JUAN   5   86   5
    IN SUCH SORT THAT THE EYE ALONG IT CAST   465   2 DON JUAN   5   93   4
    THAN SHE FROM AUGHT AT WHICH THE EYE COULD CAVIL . .   474   2 DON JUAN   5   109   6
    HER EYE IN PASSING ON HIS WAY TO SALE   477   2 DON JUAN   5   114   2
    BUT THERE IS SOMETHING WHEN MAN'S EYE APPEARS . . .   479   2 DON JUAN   5   118   3
    HER EYES ANOTHER'S EYE COULD SHED A TEAR   480   2 DON JUAN   5   119   8
    FELT AN ODD GLISTENING MOISTURE IN HER EYE   480   2 DON JUAN   5   120   8
    HER EYE DILATED AND HER COLOUR HEIGHTENED   42   3 DON JUAN   6   72   8
    AND HER BROW CLEARED BUT NOT HER TROUBLED EYE . . .   61   3 DON JUAN   6   110   7
    UPON THEM HIS SLOW BROW AND PIERCING EYE--   97   3 DON JUAN   7   59   3
    THE GROAN THE ROLL IN DUST THE ALL-WHITE EYE . . .   118   3 DON JUAN   8   13   5
    AND STILL MORE IN HIS EYE WHICH SEEMED TO EXPRESS .   206   3 DON JUAN   9   47   4
    AND LIGHTED FIRST HER EYE AND THEN HER MOUTH . . .   213   3 DON JUAN   9   61   2
    EXPEDIENT OF FULL BUMPERS FOR THE EYE   216   3 DON JUAN   9   67   7
    OF RIVALSHIP ROSE IN EACH CLOUDED EYE   221   3 DON JUAN   9   78   7
    DISCOVER STARS AND SAIL IN THE WIND'S EYE   226   3 DON JUAN   10   3   7
    IN THE WIND'S EYE I HAVE SAILED AND SAIL BUT FOR . .   227   3 DON JUAN   10   4   1
    BUT WHEN SHE SAW HIS DAZZLING EYE WAX DIM   246   3 DON JUAN   10   44   5
    DIRTY AND DUSKY BUT AS WIDE AS EYE   265   3 DON JUAN   10   82   2
    IS THAT I FIND NO SPOT WHERE MAN CAN REST EYE ON .   269   3 DON JUAN   11   3   5
    YE VILLAINS AND ABOVE ALL KEEP A SHARP EYE   310   3 DON JUAN   11   86   5
    WOULD BE MUCH BETTER TAUGHT BENEATH THE EYE   329   3 DON JUAN   12   29   7
    NOR IN HER EYE AUSONIA'S GLANCE IS BURNING   350   3 DON JUAN   12   75   4
    TO EYE OR HEART--IT IS THE PEOPLE'S TRUST   354   3 DON JUAN   12   83   8
    AN EYE'S AN EYE AND WHETHER BLACK OR BLUE   359   3 DON JUAN   13   3   3
    BUT SPECULATING AS I CAST MINE EYE   464   3 DON JUAN   15   19   4
    GLANCED WITHOUT PAUSING ON HIM A BRIGHT EYE   510   3 DON JUAN   16   21   8
    OR THAT OUR SIRES HAD A MORE GIFTED EYE   516   3 DON JUAN   16   36   6
    HER BLACK BRIGHT DOWNCAST YET ESPIEGLE EYE   532   3 DON JUAN   16   65   1
    WAS THAT HE CAUGHT AURORA'S EYE ON HIS   544   3 DON JUAN   16   92   1
    AND SHE WITHDREW BUT CAST NOT DOWN HER EYE   545   3 DON JUAN   16   94   4
EYEBALLS
    MY EYEBALLS BURN AND THROB BUT HAVE NO TEARS . . .   130   2 DON JUAN   1   192   8
EYEBROW'S
    HER EYEBROW'S SHAPE WAS LIKE THE AERIAL BOW   55   2 DON JUAN   1   61   3
EYED
    THOSE SERVILE DOGS ARE NOT SO PROUDLY EYED   418   2 DON JUAN   5   14   3
    THE EUNUCH HAVING EYED THEM O'ER WITH CARE   425   2 DON JUAN   5   28   1
    BABA EYED JUAN AND SAID BE SO GOOD   453   2 DON JUAN   5   73   1
    THE LADY EYED HIM O'ER AND O'ER AND BADE   473   2 DON JUAN   5   107   1
EYELASH
    A SINGLE TEAR UPON HIS EYELASH STAID   420   2 DON JUAN   5   18   4
EYELASHES
    HER EYELASHES THOUGH DARK AS NIGHT WERE TINGED . . .   314   2 DON JUAN   3   75   1
EYELID
    I'LL LEAVE A SINGLE READER'S EYELID DRY   355   3 DON JUAN   12   86   5
EYELIDS
    THAT MADE HIS EYELIDS AS A WOMAN'S BE   179   2 DON JUAN   2   43   6
    MORE IN THE EYELIDS THAN THE EYES RESIGNED   13   3 DON JUAN   6   15   3
EYELIDS'
    THEIR WAY THROUGH HER SEALED EYELIDS' GLOSSY FRINGES . 40   3 DON JUAN   6   67   V7
EYE'S
    IN THE LARGE DARK EYE'S MUTUAL-DARTED FLAME   367   2 DON JUAN   4   44   4
    BEYOND ITS DIMMED EYE'S SPHERE--BUT WOULD MUCH RATHER 228   3 DON JUAN   10   6   7
    AN EYE'S AN EYE AND WHETHER BLACK OR BLUE   359   3 DON JUAN   13   3   3
EYES
    WITH TIME AND TRIALS AND THOSE HELPLESS EYES . . .   15   2 DON JUAN   D   11   5
    TO JUAN'S EYES EXCEPTING NATURAL HISTORY   43   2 DON JUAN   1   39   8

EYES   (CONTINUED)

		PAGE	VOL	CANTO	STANZA	LN
WAS IN HER EYES A THING THE MOST ATROCIOUS		51	2 DON JUAN	1	54	8
HER EYE (I'M VERY FOND OF HANDSOME EYES)		54	2 DON JUAN	1	60	1
WITH OTHER PEOPLE'S EYES OR IF HER OWN		59	2 DON JUAN	1	68	2
AND THEN HE THOUGHT OF DONNA JULIA'S EYES		71	2 DON JUAN	1	92	8
COULD NOT ESCAPE THE GENTLE JULIA'S EYES		73	2 DON JUAN	1	97	2
PERHAPS TO OPEN DON ALFONSO'S EYES		75	2 DON JUAN	1	101	7
BUT VERY DIFFICULT TO SHUT THEIR EYES		77	2 DON JUAN	1	105	8
THE TEARS WERE GUSHING FROM HER GENTLE EYES		84	2 DON JUAN	1	117	3
OH SOBB'D ANTONIA I COULD TEAR THEIR EYES OUT		104	2 DON JUAN	1	152	8
SHE LAY HER DARK EYES FLASHING THROUGH THEIR TEARS		108	2 DON JUAN	1	158	2
BUT BEAUTIFUL SHE LAY--HER EYES SHED TEARS		108	2 DON JUAN	1	158	V2
RELUCTANT PAST HER BRIGHT EYES ROLLED--AS A VEIL		108	2 DON JUAN	1	158	V3
WITH PRYING SNUB-NOSE AND SMALL EYES HE STOOD		109	2 DON JUAN	1	160	1
AND CAST THEIR LANGUID EYES DOWN AND LET LOOSE		119	2 DON JUAN	1	179	6
AN AWKWARD SPECTACLE THEIR EYES BEFORE		125	2 DON JUAN	1	187	2
NOT TO BELIEVE MY VERSE AND THEIR OWN EYES		141	2 DON JUAN	1	208	4
A DRESS THROUGH WHICH THE EYES GIVE SUCH A VOLLEY		160	2 DON JUAN	2	7	7
IN HIS ROUGH EYES AND TOLD THE CAPTAIN HE		179	2 DON JUAN	2	43	2
THUS TO THEIR HOPELESS EYES THE NIGHT WAS SHOWN		182	2 DON JUAN	2	49	5
AND HOPELESS EYES WHICH ON THE DEEP ALONE		182	2 DON JUAN	2	49	V6
OF EYES WERE CRYING FOR THEIR OWNER'S CASE		186	2 DON JUAN	2	56	6
(ALTHOUGH THEY SPOKE NOT) IN THEIR WOLFISH EYES		194	2 DON JUAN	2	72	8
HIS EYES FROM OFF HIS FACE BUT WIPED THE FOAM		203	2 DON JUAN	2	89	2
AND THE BOY'S EYES WHICH THE DULL FILM HALF GLAZED		203	2 DON JUAN	2	89	5
FORSOOK THE DIM EYES OF THESE SHIPWRECK'D MEN		204	2 DON JUAN	2	91	8
UPON ITS COURSE) PASS'D OFT BEFORE THEIR EYES		206	2 DON JUAN	2	94	4
AND THE REST RUBB'D THEIR EYES AND SAW A BAY		207	2 DON JUAN	2	97	5
AND FELL UPON THEIR GLAZED EYES LIKE A SCREEN		210	2 DON JUAN	2	103	5
HIS EYES HE OPEN'D SHUT AGAIN UNCLOSED		215	2 DON JUAN	2	112	1
AND SLOWLY BY HIS SWIMMING EYES WAS SEEN		215	2 DON JUAN	2	112	7
AND BY HIS EYES--THOUGH SLOWLY--THERE WAS SEEN		215	2 DON JUAN	2	112	V7
HER HAIR I SAID WAS AUBURN BUT HER EYES		218	2 DON JUAN	2	117	1
HER HAIR WAS THICKER BUT LESS LONG HER EYES		221	2 DON JUAN	2	122	7
THEY SHALL APPEAR BEFORE YOUR CURIOUS EYES		222	2 DON JUAN	2	124	6
AND WHEN AT LAST HE OPEN'D HIS BLACK EYES		225	2 DON JUAN	2	131	4
BUT THE FAIR FACE WHICH MET HIS EYES FORBADE		235	2 DON JUAN	2	149	2
THOSE EYES TO CLOSE THOUGH WEARINESS AND PAIN		235	2 DON JUAN	2	149	3
HER EYES WERE ELOQUENT HER WORDS WOULD POSE		236	2 DON JUAN	2	150	5
AND NOW BY DINT OF FINGERS AND OF EYES		242	2 DON JUAN	2	163	1
BY FEMALE LIPS AND EYES--THAT IS I MEAN		242	2 DON JUAN	2	164	2
A BATH A BREAKFAST AND THE FINEST EYES		246	2 DON JUAN	2	171	2
AND SAW EACH OTHER'S DARK EYES DARTING LIGHT		253	2 DON JUAN	2	185	6
THEY FEAR'D NO EYES NOR EARS ON THAT LONE BEACH		256	2 DON JUAN	2	189	1
THEY LOOK UPON EACH OTHER AND THEIR EYES		259	2 DON JUAN	2	194	1
AND THEY WERE HAPPY FOR TO THEIR YOUNG EYES		265	2 DON JUAN	2	204	7
BUT THEN HER TEETH AND THEN OH HEAVEN HER EYES		268	2 DON JUAN	2	210	4
IN SHORT IT IS THE USE OF OUR OWN EYES		269	2 DON JUAN	2	212	6
AND WATCH'D BY EYES THAT NEVER YET KNEW WEEPING		274	2 DON JUAN	3	1	3
THEIR LARGE BLACK EYES AND SOFT SERAPHIC CHEEKS		292	2 DON JUAN	3	33	2
AND LONG HE PAUSED TO RE-ASSURE HIS EYES		294	2 DON JUAN	3	37	6
BUT NOW THEIR EYES AND ALSO LIPS WERE DRY		295	2 DON JUAN	3	38	5
THE VERY AIR SEEM'D LIGHTER FROM HER EYES		313	2 DON JUAN	3	74	2
FOR THOSE LARGE BLACK EYES WERE SO BLACKLY FRINGED		314	2 DON JUAN	3	75	3
I SEE THEIR GLORIOUS BLACK EYES SHINE		326	2 DON JUAN	3	L 15	3
THOSE DOWNCAST EYES BENEATH THE ALMIGHTY DOVE--		336	2 DON JUAN	3	103	6
JOY SPARKLING IN THEIR DARK EYES LIKE A GEM		351	2 DON JUAN	4	13	6
DEAR UNTO ALL BUT DEAREST TO THEIR EYES		354	2 DON JUAN	4	20	2
SENSELESS TO FEEL AND WITH SEAL'D EYES TO SEE		360	2 DON JUAN	4	30	8
OF HER BLACK EYES SEEM'D TURN'D TO TEARS AND MURK		362	2 DON JUAN	4	33	6
MY BRAIN WITH BLEST FUMES TILL MY EYES GROW DIM		372	2 DON JUAN	4	53	V7
THEIR LADY TO HER COUCH WITH GUSHING EYES		376	2 DON JUAN	4	59	5
THE BLOOD GUSHED FROM HER LIPS AND EARS AND EYES		376	2 DON JUAN	4	59	V1
THE SPOUTING BLOOD GUSHED THROUGH HER MOUTH HER EYES		376	2 DON JUAN	4	59	V1
THOSE EYES SO BEAUTIFUL--BEHOLD NO MORE		376	2 DON JUAN	4	59	V2
HER FATHER WATCH'D SHE TURN'D HER EYES AWAY		379	2 DON JUAN	4	64	2
AT LENGTH THOSE EYES WHICH THEY WOULD FAIN BE WEANING		379	2 DON JUAN	4	64	7
ON HIM HER FLASHING EYES A MOMENT BENT		379	2 DON JUAN	4	65	4
GLAZED O'ER HER EYES--THE BEAUTIFUL THE BLACK--		381	2 DON JUAN	4	69	7
WITH EYES THAT LOOK'D INTO THE VERY SOUL		395	2 DON JUAN	4	94	3
THROUGH NEEDLES' EYES IT EASIER FOR THE CAMEL IS		397	2 DON JUAN	4	97	7
DREW ALL EYES ON HIM GIVING THEM TO GUESS		415	2 DON JUAN	5	9	5
THINGS WHICH IN HUNGRY MORTALS' EYES FIND FAVOUR		437	2 DON JUAN	5	47	3
OF PURCHASED INFIDELS SOME RAISED THEIR EYES		441	2 DON JUAN	5	54	2
TO THRUST ITS BLACK EYES THROUGH THE DOOR OR LATTICE		442	2 DON JUAN	5	55	7
OR FASCINATE WHOME'ER THEY FIXED THEIR EYES ON		463	2 DON JUAN	5	90	8
'TWOULD BE CONVENIENT FOR THESE MUTES HAVE EYES		464	2 DON JUAN	5	92	1
OF EYES WHICH PUT OUT EACH SURROUNDING GEM		466	2 DON JUAN	5	96	4
THE VERGE OF HEAVEN AND IN HER LARGE EYES WROUGHT		473	2 DON JUAN	5	108	6
EMPERORS ARE ONLY HUSBANDS IN WIVES' EYES		477	2 DON JUAN	5	115	5
WITHOUT MORE PREFACE IN HER BLUE EYES BLENDING		478	2 DON JUAN	5	116	5
HER EYES ANOTHER'S EYE COULD SHED A TEAR		480	2 DON JUAN	5	119	8
CALLED BACK THE STOIC TO HIS EYES WHICH SHONE		481	2 DON JUAN	5	121	5
BEGAN TO BLUSH UP TO THE EYES AND THEN		483	2 DON JUAN	5	124	7
HER HAND ON HIS AND BENDING ON HIM EYES		483	2 DON JUAN	5	125	2
HEADS BOW KNEES BEND EYES WATCH AROUND A THRONE		484	2 DON JUAN	5	127	7
IF I SAID FIRE FLASHED FROM GULBEYAZ' EYES		489	2 DON JUAN	5	134	1
'TWERE NOTHING--FOR HER EYES FLASHED ALWAYS FIRE		489	2 DON JUAN	5	134	5
SHAWLED TO THE NOSE AND BEARDED TO THE EYES		495	2 DON JUAN	5	147	2

EYES   (CONTINUED)
HE SAW WITH HIS OWN EYES THE MOON WAS ROUND . . . . .   497 2 DON JUAN 5   150   1
WHO CLEARED HER SPARKLING EYES AND SMOOTHED HER BROWS . . 500 2 DON JUAN 5   154   3
HIS HIGHNESS CAST AROUND HIS GREAT BLACK EYES . . . . . 500 2 DON JUAN 5   155   1
THIS COMPLIMENT WHICH DREW ALL EYES UPON . . . .   501 2 DON JUAN 5   156   1
BUT ACTIUM LOST FOR CLEOPATRA'S EYES . . . .   8 3 DON JUAN 6   4   7
MORE IN THE EYELIDS THAN THE EYES RESIGNED . . . . . .   13 3 DON JUAN 6   15   3
HAD BOWED THEMSELVES BEFORE THE IMPERIAL EYES . . . . .   19 3 DON JUAN 6   26   3
WHEN THEY SURVEY WITH CHRISTIAN EYES OR HEATHEN . . . .   24 3 DON JUAN 6   37   7
WITH GREAT BLUE EYES A LOVELY HAND AND ARM . . . . . .   26 3 DON JUAN 6   41   3
HER EYES WERE NOT TOO SPARKLING YET HALF-SHUT . . . . .   27 3 DON JUAN 6   43   3
BETWEEN THE EYES AND LOLAH ON BOTH CHEEKS . . . . . .   31 3 DON JUAN 6   50   2
WITH EAGER EYES AND LIGHT BUT HURRIED TREAD . . . . . .   42 3 DON JUAN 6   72   3
AT LEAST--AND THEN SHE TOO UNCLOSED HER EYES . . . . .   42 3 DON JUAN 6   73   7
LOLAH'S EYES SPARKLED AT THE PROPOSITION . . . .   47 3 DON JUAN 6   82   1
HER CHEEK BEGAN TO FLUSH HER EYES TO SPARKLE . . . . .   56 3 DON JUAN 6   101   7
BEGONE SHE CRIED WITH KINDLING EYES--AND DO . . . . . .   63 3 DON JUAN 6   116   2
OUR EYES IN SEARCH OF EITHER LOVELY LIGHT . . . . . .   66 3 DON JUAN 7   1   6
'TIS STRANGE THAT HE SHOULD FURTHER DAMN HIS EYES . . .   88 3 DON JUAN 7   45   1
WITH FLASHING EYES AND STARTING TEARS AND FLUNG . . . .   101 3 DON JUAN 7   67   7
MEANTIME THESE TWO POOR GIRLS WITH SWIMMING EYES . . . .   104 3 DON JUAN 7   73   1
AS THEY COULD READ IN ALL EYES NOW TO THEM . . . . . .   104 3 DON JUAN 7   74   2
THAT WHICH A PORTAL TO THEIR EYES DID SEEM-- . . . . .   148 3 DON JUAN 8   72   6
WITH FLASHING EYES AND WEAPONS MATCHED WITH THEM . . . .   157 3 DON JUAN 8   92   2
BUT ELSE UNHURT SHE OPENED HER LARGE EYES . . . . . .   159 3 DON JUAN 8   95   7
JUST AT THIS INSTANT WHILE THEIR EYES WERE FIXED . . . .   159 3 DON JUAN 8   96   1
I NEVER SAW SUCH EYES--BUT HARK NOW CHOOSE . . . . . .   162 3 DON JUAN 8   101   3
SO FULLY FLASHED THE PHANTOM ON HIS EYES . . . .   169 3 DON JUAN 8   115   1
FLOWED FROM THEIR BLOOD-SHOT EYES ALL RED WITH STRIFE .   171 3 DON JUAN 8   119   7
WHILE MOSQUES AND STREETS BENEATH HIS EYES LIKE THATCH .   178 3 DON JUAN 8   133   3
HE TURNED HIS EYES UPON HIS LITTLE CHARGE . . . . . .   198 3 DON JUAN 9   31   2
BUT JUAN TURNED HIS EYES ON THE SWEET CHILD . . . . . .   199 3 DON JUAN 9   33   1
HER FACE WAS NOBLE HER EYES FINE MOUTH GRACIOUS . . . .   211 3 DON JUAN 9   58   8
IN ITS MERIDIAN HER BLUE EYES OR GREY-- . . . .   218 3 DON JUAN 9   71   2
IN CATHOLIC EYES BUT TOLD HIM TOO TO SMOTHER . . . . .   240 3 DON JUAN 10   32   4
WITH DAMN YOUR EYES YOUR MONEY OR YOUR LIFE . . . . . .   273 3 DON JUAN 11   10   8
OF OTHER STONES TO SOOTHE THE MISER'S EYES . . . . . .   319 3 DON JUAN 12   8   8
THE LITTLE LEILA WITH HER ORIENT EYES . . . .   328 3 DON JUAN 12   27   1
NEW VESTALS CLAIM MEN'S EYES WITH THE SAME PRAISE . . .   340 3 DON JUAN 12   53   6
OF WHITE CLIFFS WHITE NECKS BLUE EYES BLUER STOCKINGS .   346 3 DON JUAN 12   67   7
AT LEAST OF THOSE WHOSE EYES ARE IN THEIR HEARTS . . . .   390 3 DON JUAN 13   67   6
YOUR EYES TO REVEL IN A LIVELIER SIGHT . . . .   392 3 DON JUAN 13   72   6
AND INTELLECT THAT NEITHER EYES NOR EARS . . . .   398 3 DON JUAN 13   85   4
OR ON THE WATCH THEIR LONGING EYES WOULD FIX . . . . .   406 3 DON JUAN 13   102   7
IN EYES WHICH SADLY SHONE AS SERAPHS' SHINE . . . . .   476 3 DON JUAN 15   45   3
FOR MAN THEREIN WITH EYES AND HEART TO DINE . . . . .   489 3 DON JUAN 15   75   4
WITH TWO TRANSCENDANT EYES SEEMED TO LOOK THROUGH HIM .   489 3 DON JUAN 15   75   8
I SOMETIMES ALMOST THINK THAT EYES HAVE EARS . . . . .   489 3 DON JUAN 15   76   1
HEAVEN KNOWS BUT ADELINE'S MALICIOUS EYES . . . . . .   490 3 DON JUAN 15   78   7
HE THOUGHT AURORA RABY'S EYES MORE BRIGHT . . . . . .   506 3 DON JUAN 16   12   3
ALONG THE CANVAS THEIR EYES GLANCE LIKE DREAMS . . . .   509 3 DON JUAN 16   19   4
AN AGE--EXPECTANT POWERLESS WITH HIS EYES . . . . . .   511 3 DON JUAN 16   25   2
HE RUBBED HIS EYES AND THEY DID NOT REFUSE . . . . . .   512 3 DON JUAN 16   26   4
AURORA RABY WITH HER LARGE DARK EYES . . . .   514 3 DON JUAN 16   31   7
FAIR ADELINE WITH EYES FIXED ON THE GROUND . . . . . .   518 3 DON JUAN 16   40   4
BUT HIS EYES MAY BE SEEN FROM THE FOLDS BETWEEN . . . .   519 3 DON JUAN 16 L 4   7
THAT BRINGS LOCHABER BACK TO EYES THAT ROAM . . . . .   523 3 DON JUAN 16   46   3
HER LAUGHING BLUE EYES WITH A GLANCE COULD SEIZE . . . .   548 3 DON JUAN 16   100   4
WERE HIS EYES OPEN--YES AND HIS MOUTH TOO . . . . . .   557 3 DON JUAN 16   115   1
HIS EYES WERE OPEN AND (AS WAS BEFORE . . . .   557 3 DON JUAN 16   115   7
BUT STILL THE SHADE REMAINED THE BLUE EYES GLARED . . .   560 3 DON JUAN 16   121   1
BEING WAN AND WORN WITH EYES THAT HARDLY BROOKED . . . .   568 3 DON JUAN 17   14   4
EYES'
THE BLACK BOUGH) TEAR-DROPS THROUGH HER EYES' DARK FRINGES . 40 3 DON JUAN 6   67   8
EYE-SIGHT
AND THE WHOLE MATTER RESTS UPON EYE-SIGHT . . . . . .   348 3 DON JUAN 12   71   3
FABLE
NO DOUBT IN FABLE AS THE UNFORGIVEN . . . .   90 2 DON JUAN 1   127   7
THAT THE OLD FABLE OF THE MINOTAUR-- . . . .   238 2 DON JUAN 1   155   2
THIS IS A FACT AND NO POETIC FABLE-- . . . .   428 2 DON JUAN 5   33   2
WHICH FABLE PLACES IN HER BREAST OF WAIL . . . .   49 3 DON JUAN 6   87   6
APOLOGUE FABLE POESY AND PARABLE . . . .   495 3 DON JUAN 15   89   1
'TIS WONDERFUL WHAT FABLE WILL NOT DO . . . .   495 3 DON JUAN 15   89   4
FABLES
EVEN IF IT SHOULD COMPRISE A PACK OF FABLES . . . . .   117 2 DON JUAN 1   175   6
THEIR LABYRINTH OF FABLES TO THREAD THROUGH . . . . .   137 2 DON JUAN 1   202   7
FABRIC
NO BASELESS FABRIC BUT A WRECK BEHIND . . . .   227 2 DON JUAN 2   134   V8
FACE
WITH ALL THE PROMISE OF AS FINE A FACE . . . .   48 2 DON JUAN 1   49   3
SHOULD RATHER FACE AND OVERCOME TEMPTATION . . . . . .   63 2 DON JUAN 1   77   2
BUT THERE WERE SHE AND JUAN FACE TO FACE-- . . . . .   77 2 DON JUAN 1   105   6
BUT THERE WERE SHE AND JUAN FACE TO FACE-- . . . . .   77 2 DON JUAN 1   105   6
THE DOOR WAS FASTEN'D IN HIS LEGAL FACE . . . . . .   111 2 DON JUAN 1   164   8
MY MISTRESS ALL FOR THAT HALF-GIRLISH FACE . . . . . .   115 2 DON JUAN 1   171   8
THERE'S NOTHING SO BECOMING TO THE FACE . . . . . .   119 2 DON JUAN 1   178   8
FLIES IN ONE'S FACE AND MAKES IT WEATHER-TOUGH . . . .   162 2 DON JUAN 2   11   6
FOR JUAN WORE THE MAGISTERIAL FACE . . . .   186 2 DON JUAN 2   56   4
HIS EYES FROM OFF HIS FACE BUT WIPED THE FOAM . . . .   203 2 DON JUAN 2   89   2

FACE   (CONTINUED)
```
A LOVELY FEMALE FACE OF SEVENTEEN . . . . . . . .   215   2 DON JUAN   2   112    8
THEY WILL DESTROY A FACE WHICH MORTAL THOUGHT  . . . . .   219   2 DON JUAN   2   119    7
HER LOCKS CURL'D NEGLIGENTLY ROUND HER FACE  . . . . .   220   2 DON JUAN   2   121    3
AND HAIDEE MET THE MORNING FACE TO FACE  . . . . . .   231   2 DON JUAN   2   141    1
AND HAIDEE MET THE MORNING FACE TO FACE  . . . . . .   231   2 DON JUAN   2   141    1
BUT THE FAIR FACE WHICH MET HIS EYES FORBADE  . . . . .   235   2 DON JUAN   2   149    2
FOR WOMAN'S FACE WAS NEVER FORM'D IN VAIN  . . . . . .   235   2 DON JUAN   2   149    5
OF HIS FAIR FACE AND FOUND BY SYMPATHY  . . . . . . .   241   2 DON JUAN   2   162    4
SAW NOTHING HAPPIER THAN HER GLOWING FACE  . . . . .   262   2 DON JUAN   2   198    8
EVEN AS I SING SUFFUSE MY FACE . . . . . . . .   323   2 DON JUAN   3   L  6    4
AVE MARIA OH THAT FACE SO FAIR . . . . . . .   336   2 DON JUAN   3   103    5
A WORDLESS MUSIC AND HER FACE SO FAIR . . . . . .   359   2 DON JUAN   4    29    7
AND GAZING ON THE DEAD SHE THOUGHT HIS FACE  . . . . .   363   2 DON JUAN   4    35    1
HER FATHER'S FACE--BUT NEVER STOPP'D HIS HAND  . . . . .   367   2 DON JUAN   4    43    8
HER FATHER'S BLOOD BEFORE HER FATHER'S FACE  . . . . .   367   2 DON JUAN   4    44    7
ALL HOPE TO LOOK UPON HER SWEET FACE BRED  . . . . .   377   2 DON JUAN   4    60    6
SHE LOOK'D ON MANY A FACE WITH VACANT EYE  . . . . . .   378   2 DON JUAN   4    63    1
NOTHING COULD MAKE HER MEET HER FATHER'S FACE  . . . . .   381   2 DON JUAN   4    68    2
HER SWEET FACE INTO SHADOW DULL AND SLOW . . . . . .   381   2 DON JUAN   4    69    6
STILL KEPT HIS SPIRITS UP--AT LEAST HIS FACE  . . . . .   388   2 DON JUAN   4    81    4
THE MORE'S THE PITY WITH HER FACE AND FIGURE  . . . . .   390   2 DON JUAN   4    85    8
MAY THE SERAGLIO DO TO SET HIS FACE IN  . . . . . .   391   2 DON JUAN   4    86    4
RECORDS RAVENNA'S CARNAGE ON ITS FACE . . . . . .   400   2 DON JUAN   4   103    7
HE STOPPED AGAIN AND TURNED AWAY HIS FACE  . . . . .   420   2 DON JUAN   5    19    2
ONE OR TWO STARED THE CAPTIVES IN THE FACE  . . . . .   441   2 DON JUAN   5    54    5
WHICH E'ER SET OFF A MARRIAGE-MORNING FACE  . . . . .   455   2 DON JUAN   5    76    8
TOOK LEAVE WITH SUCH A FACE OF SATISFACTION  . . . . .   473   2 DON JUAN   5   107    7
THE WOMEN PARDONED ALL EXCEPT HER FACE . . . . . .   476   2 DON JUAN   5   113    8
THE VERY WOMEN HALF-FORGAVE HER FACE  . . . . . . .   476   2 DON JUAN   5   113  V8
WITH HAIDEE'S ISLE AND SOFT IONIAN FACE  . . . . .   478   2 DON JUAN   5   117    3
FELT THE WARM BLOOD WHICH IN HIS FACE WAS GLOWING . . . .   478   2 DON JUAN   5   117    4
AND LOOKING COLDLY IN HER FACE HE CRIED  . . . . . .   484   2 DON JUAN   5   126    6
ON SUCH A SUBJECT THEN SUPPOSE THE FACE  . . . . . .   486   2 DON JUAN   5   130    7
IN A NEW FACE THE UGLIEST CREATURE BREATHING  . . . . .    24   3 DON JUAN   6    37    8
AND HID HER FACE WITHIN JUANNA'S BREAST . . . . . .    48   3 DON JUAN   6    85    2
HER FACE DECLINED AND WAS UNSEEN HER HAIR  . . . . .    60   3 DON JUAN   6   108    1
WHICH STARE HIM IN THE FACE HE WON'T EXAMINE  . . . . .    88   3 DON JUAN   7    45    7
BUT CERTES MATTERS TOOK A DIFFERENT FACE  . . . . . .    89   3 DON JUAN   7    47    1
A FROWN ON NATURE'S OR ON HUMAN FACE--  . . . . . .   145   3 DON JUAN   8    65    6
HIS JEST ALIKE IN FACE OF FRIEND OR FOE  . . . . . .   147   3 DON JUAN   8    70    6
HER HIDDEN FACE WAS PLUNGED AMIDST THE DEAD  . . . . .   158   3 DON JUAN   8    93    3
AND SHE WAS CHILL AS THEY AND ON HER FACE  . . . . .   159   3 DON JUAN   8    95    1
A PURE TRANSPARENT PALE YET RADIANT FACE . . . . . .   159   3 DON JUAN   8    96    7
BUT WITH A HEAVENLY RAPTURE ON HIS FACE . . . . . .   169   3 DON JUAN   8   116    1
HER FACE WAS NOBLE HER EYES FINE MOUTH GRACIOUS . . . .   211   3 DON JUAN   9    58    8
AND SO THEY FELL IN LOVE--SHE WITH HIS FACE  . . . . .   216   3 DON JUAN   9    67    2
YOUR FACE--BUT YOU HAVE ACTED ON THE WHOLE  . . . . .   232   3 DON JUAN  10    16    7
WHO SEEING A HANDSOME STRIPLING WITH SMOOTH FACE  . . . .   285   3 DON JUAN  11    35    5
SOME DOME SURMOUNTED BY HIS MEAGRE FACE  . . . . .   320   3 DON JUAN  12    10    4
ALSO BECAUSE THE FIGURE AND THE FACE . . . . . .   360   3 DON JUAN  13     4    7
'TIS SO BECOMING TO THE SOUL AND FACE . . . . . .   430   3 DON JUAN  14    47    2
AND HER'S WERE THOSE WHICH CAN FACE CALCULATION . . . .   432   3 DON JUAN  14    52    2
TWINE LIKE A KNOT OF SNAKES AROUND HIS FACE  . . . . .   510   3 DON JUAN  16    23    6
HIS FORM YOU MAY TRACE BUT NOT HIS FACE  . . . . .   519   3 DON JUAN  16   L  4    5
IF SHE HAD ANY WAS UPON HER FACE  . . . . . . .   525   3 DON JUAN  16    49    3
WAS OBVIOUS IN EACH FEATURE OF HER FACE  . . . . . .   550   3 DON JUAN  16   102    3
THE LATEST FACE WITH HIS VIRGIN FACE . . . . . .   568   3 DON JUAN  17    13    8
```
FACED
```
HAD FACED NAPOLEON'S FOES UNTIL THEY FLED--  . . . . .   431   2 DON JUAN   5    37    6
AS BRAVE AS EVER FACED BOTH BOMB AND BALL  . . . . .   116   3 DON JUAN   8     9    5
AND THAT THE REST HAD FACED UNTO THE RIGHT  . . . . .   125   3 DON JUAN   8    28    3
AND HAD JUST BURIED THE FAIR FACED LANSKOI  . . . . .   206   3 DON JUAN   9    47    8
```
FACES
```
WHEN TWO SUCH FACES ARE SO 'TWOULD BE WISE  . . . . .    77   2 DON JUAN   1   105    7
AND THEN THEY STARED EACH OTHERS' FACES ROUND  . . . .   100   2 DON JUAN   1   144    5
AND GRIMLY DARKLED O'ER THEIR FACES PALE . . . . .   182   2 DON JUAN   2    49    6
THE SPRAY INTO THEIR FACES AS THEY SPLASH'D  . . . . .   209   2 DON JUAN   2   101    8
THEIR FACES WERE NOT MADE FOR WRINKLES THEIR  . . . . .   348   2 DON JUAN   4     9    1
WITH THEIR ROUGH FACES THRONGED ABOUT THE BED  . . . .   431   2 DON JUAN   5    37    2
WITH KIND REMARKS UPON THEIR MIEN AND FACES  . . . . .    28   3 DON JUAN   6    45    8
WHICH PAINTERS CANNOT CATCH LIKE FACES SINNING  . . . .    32   3 DON JUAN   6    52    4
AIR 'MIDST THE REST WHO KEPT THEIR VALIANT FACES  . . .   130   3 DON JUAN   8    34    7
AIR MIDST THE REST WHOSE SHORT BREATH AND LONG FACES . .   130   3 DON JUAN   8    34   V7
THEIR MARTIAL FACES ON THE PARAPET . . . . . .   135   3 DON JUAN   8    45    7
OF THE GREAT NAMES WHICH IN OUR FACES STARE  . . . . .   143   3 DON JUAN   8    61    3
IT IS TO SPECULATE ON HANDSOME FACES . . . . .   223   3 DON JUAN   9    82    7
BEGINNINGS ARE FAIR FACES ENDS MERE FISHES--  . . . . .   349   3 DON JUAN  12    73    2
AND TRADESMEN WITH LONG BILLS AND LONGER FACES  . . . .   378   3 DON JUAN  13    44    7
WITH THEIR GREEN FACES FIX'D UPON THE FLOOD  . . . . .   385   3 DON JUAN  13    57    8
STRANGE FACES LIKE TO MEN IN MASQUERADE  . . . . .   389   3 DON JUAN  13    65    3
AURORA WHO LOOK'D MORE ON BOOKS THAN FACES  . . . . .   494   3 DON JUAN  15    85    1
THOUGH TOO WELL BRED TO QUIZ MEN TO THEIR FACES  . . . .   548   3 DON JUAN  16   100    3
WHICH TURNED UPON THEIR LATE GUESTS' MIENS AND FACES . .   550   3 DON JUAN  16   103    5
```
FACETIOUS
```
AND WITHOUT TURNING HIS FACETIOUS HEAD  . . . . . .   297   2 DON JUAN   3    43    1
BUT PUNNED IT DOWN TO THIS FACETIOUS PHRASE--  . . . .   183   3 DON JUAN   9     1    4
```
FACILITY
```
BUT THERE'S A CONVERSATIONAL FACILITY . . . . .   465   3 DON JUAN  15    20    3
THOUGH SEEMING SO FROM ITS SUPPOSED FACILITY  . . . . .   547   3 DON JUAN  16    97    6
```

FACINGS
      A SCARLET COAT BLACK FACINGS A LONG PLUME   204   3 DON JUAN 9   43   2
FACT
      WHICH SAVES IN FACT THE TROUBLE OF AN INDEX 46   2 DON JUAN 1   44   8
      JULIA IN FACT HAD TOLERABLE GROUNDS   118   2 DON JUAN 1   176   1
      A LADY ALWAYS DISTANT FROM THE FACT--   119   2 DON JUAN 1   178   6
      FOR SAILORS ARE IN FACT A DIFFERENT KIND   170   2 DON JUAN 2   26   5
      THE WIND IN FACT PERHAPS WAS RATHER LESS   178   2 DON JUAN 2   41   1
      WHO LET HIM DO IN FACT WHATE'ER HE WOULD   187   2 DON JUAN 2   59   3
      ON WHAT IN FACT NEXT DAY WERE THEY TO DINE   192   2 DON JUAN 2   69   4
      'TWAS BETTER THAT HE DID NOT FOR IN FACT   198   2 DON JUAN 2   79   1
      BETTER THAN HER KNEW WHAT IN FACT SHE MEANT   228   2 DON JUAN 2   136   3
      WHICH FORMS IN FACT TRUE LOVE'S ANTITHESIS   279   2 DON JUAN 3   8   2
      (SUCH THINGS IN FACT IT DON'T ASK MUCH TO MAR) 281   2 DON JUAN 3   10   6
      TRANSFORM'D THEIR LORDS TO BEASTS (BUT THAT'S A FACT)   293   2 DON JUAN 3   34   8
      IN FACT MUCH MORE ASTONISH'D THAN DELIGHTED   294   2 DON JUAN 3   37   7
      HE FLEW INTO A PASSION AND IN FACT   296   2 DON JUAN 3   40   2
      THE FACT EXCEPTING SOME EXPERIENCED FEW   342   2 DON JUAN 3   111   5
      BUT THE FACT IS THAT I HAVE NOTHING PLANN'D   346   2 DON JUAN 4   5   6
      TO BE ITALIANS AS THEY WERE IN FACT   388   2 DON JUAN 4   80   2
      IN FACT HE HAD NO SINGING EDUCATION   391   2 DON JUAN 4   87   3
      I THOUGHT IN FACT YOU COULD NOT BE A GREEK   418   2 DON JUAN 5   14   2
      MAKES US FEEL OUR MORTALITY IN FACT   428   2 DON JUAN 5   32   3
      THIS IS A FACT AND NO POETIC FABLE--   428   2 DON JUAN 5   33   2
      PASSED WITHOUT WORDS--IN FACT SHE COULD NOT SPEAK . . 490   2 DON JUAN 5   137   2
      KISS RHYMES TO BLISS IN FACT AS WELL AS VERSE-- . . . 35   3 DON JUAN 6   59   7
      JUAN HAD NOT BETRAYED HIMSELF IN FACT   58   3 DON JUAN 6   104   2
      IT IS AN ACTUAL FACT THAT HE COMMANDER   93   3 DON JUAN 7   52   1
      IN FACT THEY CAN BE SAFE YOU SHOULD HAVE BEEN 102   3 DON JUAN 7   70   6
      IF NOT IN POETRY AT LEAST IN FACT   107   3 DON JUAN 7   81   1
      AND FACT IS TRUTH THE GRAND DESIDERATUM   107   3 DON JUAN 7   81   2
      MORE THAN THE CAP IN FACT THE BALL COULD MEAN 117   3 DON JUAN 8   10   6
      BUT THEN THE FACT'S A FACT--AND 'TIS THE PART   154   3 DON JUAN 8   86   1
      IN MARINET'S AFFAIR--IN FACT 'TWAS SHABBY   184   3 DON JUAN 9   2   2
      IN FACT YOUR GRACE IS STILL BUT A YOUNG HERO   184   3 DON JUAN 9   2   8
      IN FACT IF NOT IN RANK AND THE SUSPICION   208   3 DON JUAN 9   52   5
      IN FACT THE ONLY CHRISTIAN SHE COULD BEAR   252   3 DON JUAN 10   57   1
      A FACT WITHOUT SOME LEAVEN OF A LIE   286   3 DON JUAN 11   37   4
      THAT TILL WE SEE WHAT'S WHAT IN FACT WE'RE FAR 335   3 DON JUAN 12   40   4
      IN FACT THERE'S NOTHING MAKES ME SO MUCH GRIEVE . . .   336   3 DON JUAN 12   43   6
      BUT I SUSPECT IN FACT THAT WHITE IS BLACK   348   3 DON JUAN 12   71   2
      AND IF IN FACT SHE TAKES TO A GRANDE PASSION   351   3 DON JUAN 12   77   1
      PEOPLE SOME TEN TIMES LESS IN FACT TO MIND IT   352   3 DON JUAN 12   80   3
      THE FACT--I'VE HEARD IT--ONCE PERHAPS TOO MUCH . . .   388   3 DON JUAN 13   64   8
      THE FACT FOR WORDS AND LET THE FRENCH TRANSLATE . . .   405   3 DON JUAN 13   101   7
      'TIS THAT IN FACT THERE'S LITTLE TO DESCRIBE   418   3 DON JUAN 14   20   8
      IN FACT HIS MANNER WAS HIS OWN ALONE   461   3 DON JUAN 15   13   4
      THOUGH PROBABLY MUCH LESS A FACT THAN GUESS)   491   3 DON JUAN 15   80   6
      OF NICETY WHERE A FACT IS TO BE GAINED)   507   3 DON JUAN 16   16   4
      YET WITH DISPLAY IN FACT AT TIMES RELENT   521   3 DON JUAN 16   42   6
FACTIOUS
      HE WOULD NOT TREAD A FACTIOUS PATH TO PRAISE   536   3 DON JUAN 16   73   5
FACTITIOUS
      THIS IS IN OTHERS A FACTITIOUS STATE   354   2 DON JUAN 4   19   1
      FACTITIOUS PASSIONS WIT WITHOUT MUCH SALT   417   3 DON JUAN 14   16   5
FACT'S
      THE FACT'S ABOUT THE SAME I AM SECURE   70   3 DON JUAN 7   8   3
      BUT THEN THE FACT'S A FACT--AND 'TIS THE PART   154   3 DON JUAN 8   86   1
FACTS
      FOR WANT OF FACTS WOULD ALL BE THROWN AWAY) 86   2 DON JUAN 1   121   4
      FOR FACTS AGAINST A VIRTUOUS WOMAN'S FAME   101   2 DON JUAN 1   146   6
      IN DON ALFONSO'S FACTS WHICH JUST NOW WORE   111   2 DON JUAN 1   164   6
      TO HISTORY TRADITION AND TO FACTS   138   2 DON JUAN 1   203   2
      ALL THESE ARE CERTES ENTERTAINING FACTS   329   2 DON JUAN 3   92   1
      BUT FACTS ARE FACTS NO KNIGHT COULD BE MORE TRUE . . . 396   2 DON JUAN 4   96   2
      BUT FACTS ARE FACTS NO KNIGHT COULD BE MORE TRUE . . . 396   2 DON JUAN 4   96   2
      ALL THAT I KNOW IS THAT THE FACTS I STATE   48   3 DON JUAN 6   85   7
      SO THAT I DO NOT GROSSLY ERR IN FACTS   149   3 DON JUAN 8   74   3
      SHE GATHERS A REPERTORY OF FACTS   416   3 DON JUAN 14   13   2
FACULTIES
      A FINE EXTENSION OF THE FACULTIES   269   2 DON JUAN 2   212   2
FACULTY
      THE FACULTY--WHO SAID THAT HE MUST TRAVEL   245   3 DON JUAN 10   43   8
FADED
      FADED OR ALTER'D INTO SOMETHING NEW--   363   2 DON JUAN 4   35   2
FADES
      YOUTH FADES AND LEAVES OUR DAYS NO LONGER SUNNY . . . 405   3 DON JUAN 13   100   5
      RAY FADES ON RAY AS YEARS ON YEARS DEPART   554   3 DON JUAN 16   109   4
FADING
      JUST WHEN THE FADING LAMPS WANED DIM AND BLUE   41   3 DON JUAN 6   70   5
      A PORTION OF YOUR FADING TWILIGHT HUES   108   3 DON JUAN 7   82   7
      WHEN I CALL FADING MARTIAL IMMORTALITY   108   3 DON JUAN 7   83   1
FAIL
      HER STREAMING HAIR THE BLACK CURLS STRIVE BUT FAIL . . 108   2 DON JUAN 1   158   5
      OF LOVE WHEN I FORGET YOU MAY I FAIL   160   2 DON JUAN 2   7   5
      PURE BLOOD TO STAGNATE THEIR GREAT HEARTS TO FAIL . . 348   2 DON JUAN 4   9   2
      SO LUCKILY FOR BOTH MY PHRASES FAIL   467   2 DON JUAN 5   97   8
      AND BABA WHO HAD NE'ER BEEN KNOWN TO FAIL   477   2 DON JUAN 5   114   4
      OF QUIXOTE SHOWN HOW ALL SUCH EFFORTS FAIL   361   3 DON JUAN 13   8   8

                                     249

FAIL   (CONTINUED)
   WHY DO THEIR SKETCHES FAIL THEM AS INDITERS . . . . 418 3 DON JUAN 14   20   5
   AND ONLY FRETTED WHEN THE SCENT 'GAN FAIL . . . . 424 3 DON JUAN 14   33   4
   BUT OFT DENIED AS PATIENCE 'GINS TO FAIL HE . . . . 459 3 DON JUAN 15   8   5
   TO SOOTHE OUR EARS LEST ITALY SHOULD FAIL . . . . 523 3 DON JUAN 16   45   8
   BUT FOR HIS JUDGMENT--NEVER KNOWN TO FAIL . . . . 528 3 DON JUAN 16   57   8
FAIN
   BUT THERE'S A RUMOUR WHICH I FAIN WOULD HUSH . . . . 53 2 DON JUAN 1   58   6
   DEATH SHUNS THE WRETCH WHO FAIN THE BLOW WOULD MEET . . . 134 2 DON JUAN 1   197   6
   THE COFFEE MADE WOULD FAIN HAVE WAKEN'D JUAN . . . . . . 234 2 DON JUAN 2   146   2
   IF HE MUST FAIN SWEEP O'ER THE ETHERIAL PLAIN . . . . . 333 2 DON JUAN 3   99   1
   AT LENGTH THOSE EYES WHICH THEY WOULD FAIN BE WEANING . . 379 2 DON JUAN 4   64   7
   AND FOR ONE KISS WOULD FAIN IMPRINT A BRACE . . . . . . 472 2 DON JUAN 5   106   5
   WHO FAIN WOULD HAVE A MUTUAL FLAME CONFEST . . . . 14 3 DON JUAN 6   17   3
   HE WOULD FIND OTHERS WHO WOULD FAIN BE RID SO . . . . . 133 3 DON JUAN 8   40   3
   I RATHER DOUBT AND I WOULD FAIN SAY FIE ON'T . . . . . . 138 3 DON JUAN 8   51   6
   AND TILL SHE DOTH I FAIN MUST BE CONTENT . . . . 193 3 DON JUAN 9   22   7
   HER HUNDRED ARMS AND LEGS AND FAIN OUTRUN HER . . . . . 231 3 DON JUAN 10   12   6
   PERHAPS HE FAIN WOULD LIBERATE MANKIND . . . . 320 3 DON JUAN 12   10   5
   I KNOW THAT SOME WOULD FAIN POSTPONE THIS ERA . . . . . 360 3 DON JUAN 13   5   1
   WHICH EVEN THOSE WHO OBEY WOULD FAIN BE THOUGHT . . . . 421 3 DON JUAN 14   26   2
   WHICH FAIN WOULD LULL ITS RIVER-CHILD TO SLEEP . . . . . 447 3 DON JUAN 14   87   8
FAINT
   TO FAINT AND DAMAGED BREAD WET THROUGH THE BAGS . . . . 189 2 DON JUAN 2   62   7
   SO HERE THOUGH FAINT EMACIATED AND STARK . . . . 212 2 DON JUAN 2   106   1
   RAISED HIGHER THE FAINT HEAD WHICH O'ER IT HUNG . . . . 216 2 DON JUAN 2   114   3
   THAT HE WAS FAINT AND MUST NOT TALK BUT EAT . . . . . . 236 2 DON JUAN 2   150   8
   OR THE FAINT DYING DAY-HYMN STOLE ALOFT . . . . 335 2 DON JUAN 3   102   6
   AND CALLED FROM JUAN'S BREAST A FAINT LOW SIGH . . . . . 355 2 DON JUAN 4   21   7
   SOME FAINT LAMPS GLEAMING FROM THE LOFTY WALLS . . . . . 442 2 DON JUAN 5   56   1
   BABA THOUGHT SHE WOULD FAINT BUT THERE HE ERRED-- . . . 59 3 DON JUAN 6   106   2
   OF HEALTH BUT FLICKERED WITH A FAINT REFLECTION . . . . 245 3 DON JUAN 10   43   6
   WAS FAINT AS OF AN EVERY-DAY POSSESSION . . . . 372 3 DON JUAN 13   31   8
   BACKWARD AND FORWARD TO THE ECHOES FAINT . . . . 508 3 DON JUAN 16   18   3
   LIKE ADDISON'S FAINT PRAISE SO WONT TO DAMN . . . . . . 552 3 DON JUAN 16   104   4
FAINTER
   ROSE STILL BUT FAINTER WERE THE THUNDERS GROWN . . . . . 175 3 DON JUAN 8   127   6
   NOW YAWNS ALL DESOLATE NOW LOUD NOW FAINTER . . . . . . 387 3 DON JUAN 13   62   5
FAINTEST
   BUT EVEN THE FAINTEST RELICS OF A SHRINE . . . . 387 3 DON JUAN 13   61   7
FAINTING
   ALTHOUGH SHE WAS NOT OF THE FAINTING SORT . . . . 59 3 DON JUAN 6   106   1
FAINTLY
   AT LAST AS THEY MORE FAINTLY WRESTLING LAY . . . . 124 2 DON JUAN 1   186   4
   THOUGH SOMETIMES FAINTLY FLUSHED--AND ALWAYS CLEAR . . . 545 3 DON JUAN 16   94   7
FAINTNESS
   AND HOW THIS HEAVY FAINTNESS PASS'D AWAY . . . . 214 2 DON JUAN 2   111   5
FAINTS
   BORN WITH THAT HAPPY SOUL WHICH SELDOM FAINTS . . . . . 424 3 DON JUAN 14   31   5
FAIR
   AND FANS TURN INTO FALCHIONS IN FAIR HANDS . . . . 33 2 DON JUAN 1   21   7
   INEZ BECAME SOLE GUARDIAN WHICH WAS FAIR . . . . 42 2 DON JUAN 1   37   5
   IN CHARACTER--BUT IT WOULD NOT BE FAIR . . . . 49 2 DON JUAN 1   51   4
   BRIGHT WITH INTELLIGENCE AND FAIR AND SMOOTH . . . . . . 55 2 DON JUAN 1   61   2
   WITH OTHER ARTICLES OF LADIES FAIR . . . . 99 2 DON JUAN 1   143   5
   SMALL PITY HAD HE FOR THE YOUNG AND FAIR . . . . 109 2 DON JUAN 1   160   6
   THE WIND WAS FAIR THE WATER PASSING ROUGH . . . . 162 2 DON JUAN 2   11   2
   FROM WHICH AWAY SO FAIR AND FAST THEY BORE . . . . 163 2 DON JUAN 2   13   4
   THAN I RESIGN THINE IMAGE OH MY FAIR . . . . 166 2 DON JUAN 2   19   5
   THEIR BEST CLOTHES AS IF GOING TO A FAIR . . . . 180 2 DON JUAN 2   45   2
   'TIS SURELY FAIR TO DINE UPON OUR FRIENDS . . . . 200 2 DON JUAN 2   83   6
   AS FAIR A THING AS E'ER WAS FORM'D OF CLAY . . . . 214 2 DON JUAN 2   110   8
   AROUND HIS SCARCE-CLAD LIMBS AND THE FAIR ARM . . . . . 216 2 DON JUAN 2   114   2
   SHE WAS APPEAR'D DISTINCT AND TALL AND FAIR . . . . . . 216 2 DON JUAN 2   115   8
   ALTHOUGH THE MORTAL QUITE AS FRESH AND FAIR . . . . . . 232 2 DON JUAN 2   142   7
   FAIR AS THE CROWNING ROSE OF THE WHOLE WREATH . . . . . 235 2 DON JUAN 2   148   5
   FAIR AS THE ROSE JUST PLUCKED TO CROWN THE WREATH . . . 235 2 DON JUAN 2   148 V5
   BUT THE FAIR FACE WHICH MET HIS EYES FORBADE . . . . . . 235 2 DON JUAN 2   149   2
   OTHERS ARE FAIR AND FERTILE AMONG WHICH . . . . 238 2 DON JUAN 2   154   7
   AND THEN FAIR HAIDEE TRIED HER TONGUE AT SPEAKING . . . 241 2 DON JUAN 2   161   1
   OF HIS FAIR FACE AND FOUND BY SYMPATHY . . . . 241 2 DON JUAN 2   162   4
   AND THUS A MOON ROLL'D ON AND FAIR HAIDEE . . . . 248 2 DON JUAN 2   174   1
   AND HAIDEE BEING DEVOUT AS WELL AS FAIR . . . . 258 2 DON JUAN 2   193   5
   (THOUGH SHE WAS MASQUED THEN AS A FAIR VENETIAN) . . . . 268 2 DON JUAN 2   210   8
   THE REAL NAME OF THE FAIR VERONESE-- . . . . 273 2 DON JUAN 2   V 2   2
   PILLOW'D UPON A FAIR AND HAPPY BREAST . . . . 274 2 DON JUAN 3   1   2
   HAD SOWN THE RUIN OF HER FEW FAIR YEARS . . . . 275 2 DON JUAN 3   1 V7
   A KIND OF FLATTERY THAT'S HARDLY FAIR . . . . 278 2 DON JUAN 3   6   3
   THE FAULT WAS THEIRS NOT MINE IT IS NOT FAIR . . . . . . 282 2 DON JUAN 3   12   2
   HE SHAPED HIS COURSE TO WHERE HIS DAUGHTER FAIR . . . . 285 2 DON JUAN 3   19   4
   IF SINGLE PROBABLY HIS PLIGHTED FAIR . . . . 288 2 DON JUAN 3   24   1
   BEFORE THEM AND FAIR SLAVES ON EVERY SIDE . . . . 306 2 DON JUAN 3   61   6
   AS PLENTIFUL AS IN A COURT OR FAIR . . . . 310 2 DON JUAN 3   68   8
   THE SKIN RELIEVED APPEAR MORE FAIRLY FAIR . . . . 314 2 DON JUAN 3   76   2
   AVE MARIA OH THAT FACE SO FAIR . . . . 336 2 DON JUAN 3   103   5
   HIS HELL-DOGS AND THEIR CHASE AND THE FAIR THRONG . . . 337 2 DON JUAN 3   106   6
   A WORDLESS MUSIC AND HER FACE SO FAIR . . . . 359 2 DON JUAN 4   29   7
   LIKE SUMMER CLOUDS ALL SILVERY SMOOTH AND FAIR . . . . . 375 2 DON JUAN 4   57   2
   O'ER THE FAIR VENUS BUT FOREVER FAIR . . . . 377 2 DON JUAN 4   61   4

250

FAIR   (CONTINUED)
    O'ER THE FAIR VENUS BUT FOREVER FAIR . . . . 377 2 DON JUAN 4   61   4
    HAVE DAWN'D A FAIR AND SINLESS CHILD OF SIN . . . . . 382 2 DON JUAN 4   70   3
    YE COULD NOT KNOW WHERE LIES A THING SO FAIR . . . . 383 2 DON JUAN 4   72   5
    THE REST ARE HARDLY FITTED FOR A FAIR . . . . 390 2 DON JUAN 4   85   4
    YOU WAS NOT LAST YEAR AT THE FAIR OF LUGO . . . . . . 392 2 DON JUAN 4   88   7
    BUT WHAT CONDUCTED IF THE QUESTION'S FAIR . . . . . . 418 2 DON JUAN 5   15   4
    AS THOUGH THEY WERE IN A MERE CHRISTIAN FAIR . . . . 425 2 DON JUAN 5   28   5
    AND RAISING UP AN ARM AS MOONLIGHT FAIR . . . . 466 2 DON JUAN 5   96   5
    IN CONTACT AND SOMETIMES EVEN A FAIR STRANGER'S . . . 472 2 DON JUAN 5   106   7
    BESIDES AS HAS BEEN SAID SHE WAS SO FAIR . . . . . . 485 2 DON JUAN 5   129   1
    THUS ENDED MANY A FAIR SULTANA'S TRIP . . . . 496 2 DON JUAN 5   149 V5
    THE FAIR SULTANA ERRED FROM INANITION . . . . 10 3 DON JUAN 6   9   5
    OR RATHER BONNET WHICH THE FAIR SEX WEAR . . . . 13 3 DON JUAN 6   14   5
    IF FAIR GULBEYAZ OVERDID HER PART . . . . 15 3 DON JUAN 6   19   1
    AFTER ALL) OR LIKE IRISH AT A FAIR . . . . 23 3 DON JUAN 6   34   5
    WAS WHAT HER DRESS BESPOKE A DAMSEL FAIR . . . . 24 3 DON JUAN 6   36   2
    IN THE FAIR FORM OF THEIR COMPANION NEW . . . . 24 3 DON JUAN 6   37   5
    (TO SAVE DESCRIPTION) FAIR AS FAIR CAN BE . . . . . . 26 3 DON JUAN 6   40   4
    (TO SAVE DESCRIPTION) FAIR AS FAIR CAN BE . . . . . . 26 3 DON JUAN 6   40   4
    THAT SHE WAS FAIR OR DARK OR SHORT OR TALL . . . . . . 33 3 DON JUAN 6   54   7
    HER AID TO FAIR JUANNA WHOSE EXCESS . . . . 36 3 DON JUAN 6   61   3
    OF THE FAIR OCCUPANTS IF THERE BE SPRITES . . . . . . 38 3 DON JUAN 6   64   4
    AND FAIR BROWS GENTLY DROOPING AS THE FRUIT . . . . . 38 3 DON JUAN 6   65   6
    BUT THERE SHE SLEPT NOT QUITE SO FAIR TO SEE . . . . . 41 3 DON JUAN 6   69   5
    BUT A MAN'S GRANDMOTHER IS DEEMED FAIR GAME . . . . . 53 3 DON JUAN 6   94 V5
    AND THE STAINED GLASS WHICH LIGHTED THIS FAIR GROT . . 55 3 DON JUAN 6   98   4
    O'ER HER FAIR FRONT LIKE MORNING'S ON A LILY . . . . . 58 3 DON JUAN 6   105   8
    AND SCARCE SECURE AS SUCH DIGRESSIONS ARE FAIR . . . . 65 3 DON JUAN 6   120   7
    WHICH ROUSSEAU POINTS OUT TO THE DUBIOUS FAIR . . . . 139 3 DON JUAN 8   53   6
    WHENCE HER FAIR HAIR ROSE TWINING WITH AFFRIGHT . . . 158 3 DON JUAN 8   93   2
    IN FAIR PROPORTION WITH THEIR COMRADES--THEN . . . . 163 3 DON JUAN 8   103   2
    OF CARNAGE--AND HER FAIR AND INFANT GRACE . . . . . 182 3 DON JUAN 8   140 V7
    FAIR CATHERINE'S PASTIME--WHO LOOKED ON THE MATCH . . 197 3 DON JUAN 9   29   6
    AND HAD JUST BURIED THE FAIR FACED LANSKOI . . . . . 206 3 DON JUAN 9   47   8
    AND GREECE AND BOUND FAIR HELEN IN A BOND . . . . . . 209 3 DON JUAN 9   53 V6
    FAIR WEATHER FOR THE DAY THOUGH RATHER SPACIOUS . . . 211 3 DON JUAN 9   58   7
    YOUR FORTUNE WAS IN A FAIR WAY TO SWELL . . . . 214 3 DON JUAN 9   63   6
    MAY CHOOSE TO TAX ME WITH WHICH IS NOT FAIR . . . . . 230 3 DON JUAN 10   11   4
    SOME THIRTY YEARS BEFORE AT FAIR EIGHTEEN . . . . . 236 3 DON JUAN 10   24 V6
    AND THOUGH I CAN'T HELP THINKING 'TWAS SCARCE FAIR . 242 3 DON JUAN 10   36   5
    THE FAIR CZARINA'S AUTOCRATIC CREST . . . . 248 3 DON JUAN 10   49   6
    POOR LITTLE THING SHE WAS AS FAIR AS DOCILE . . . . 250 3 DON JUAN 10   52   1
    BEING QUITE PERSPICUOUS AND EXTREMELY FAIR . . . . . 270 3 DON JUAN 11   5   4
    OF FAIR PHILOSOPHY OR WHERE 'TIS THEY TREAD . . . . . 284 3 DON JUAN 11   34 V6
    FAIR VIRGINS BLUSHED UPON HIM WEDDED DAMES . . . . . 293 3 DON JUAN 11   48   1
    (IN MOORE'S PHRASE) WHERE THE FASHIONABLE FAIR . . . 301 3 DON JUAN 11   66   7
    WITH SOME OF THOSE FAIR CREATURES WHO HAVE PRIDED . . 327 3 DON JUAN 12   25   6
    THINK NOT FAIR CREATURES THAT I MEAN TO ABUSE YOU ALL-- . 329 3 DON JUAN 12   28   3
    AND LIVED AS DID THE BROKEN-HEARTED FAIR . . . . . . 344 3 DON JUAN 12   61   7
    NO DOUBT I SHOULD BE TOLD THAT BLACK IS FAIR . . . . 348 3 DON JUAN 12   70   8
    BEGINNINGS ARE FAIR FACES ENDS MERE FISHES-- . . . . 349 3 DON JUAN 12   73   2
    AT THE FIRST BLUSH FOR A FAIR BRITON HIDES . . . . . 350 3 DON JUAN 12   74   3
    THE FAIR SEX SHOULD BE ALWAYS FAIR AND NO MAN . . . . 359 3 DON JUAN 13   3   7
    THE FAIR SEX SHOULD BE ALWAYS FAIR AND NO MAN . . . . 359 3 DON JUAN 13   3   7
    THE FAIR MOST FATAL JUAN EVER MET . . . . 364 3 DON JUAN 13   12   3
    WAS THE QUEEN-BEE THE GLASS OF ALL THAT'S FAIR . . . 365 3 DON JUAN 13   13   5
    WITH FAIR LONG LOCKS HAD ALSO KEPT THEIR STATION . . 390 3 DON JUAN 13   68   5
    BUT FAIR AS THEN OR FAIRER TO BEHOLD . . . . 409 3 DON JUAN 13   110   6
    GOOD HOURS OF FAIR CHEEKS ARE THE FAIREST TINTERS . . 409 3 DON JUAN 13   111   7
    IN THAT FAIR CLIME WHICH DON'T DEPEND ON CLIMATE . . 423 3 DON JUAN 14   29   2
    THEY'LL ONLY MAKE MISTAKES ABOUT THE FAIR . . . . . 454 3 DON JUAN 14   99   3
    FAIR ADELINE THE MORE INGENUOUS . . . . 460 3 DON JUAN 15   10   1
    OF HIS ATTRACTIONS MARR'D THE FAIR PERSPECTIVE . . . 461 3 DON JUAN 15   12   5
    SO THAT THE OUTLINE'S TOLERABLY FAIR . . . . 463 3 DON JUAN 15   16   4
    AND THE TWO FAIR CO-HEIRESSES GILTBEDDING . . . . . . 473 3 DON JUAN 15   40   5
    INDEED A CERTAIN FAIR AND FAIRY ONE . . . . 475 3 DON JUAN 15   43   3
    FAIR ADELINE ENQUIRED IF HE WERE ILL . . . . 514 3 DON JUAN 16   32   3
    FAIR ADELINE WITH EYES FIXED ON THE GROUND . . . . . 518 3 DON JUAN 16   40   4
    HEAVEN SAIN HIM FAIR OR FOUL . . . . 520 3 DON JUAN 16 L 6   9
    FAIR ADELINE THOUGH IN A CARELESS WAY . . . . 521 3 DON JUAN 16   42   1
    FOR SOME VIVACITY AMONG THE FAIR . . . . 544 3 DON JUAN 16   91   5
    THE FAIR FITZ-FULKE SEEMED VERY MUCH AT EASE . . . . 548 3 DON JUAN 16   100   2
FAIRER
    A FAIRER MARK AND WITH A FIX'D EYE SCANN'D . . . . . 367 2 DON JUAN 4   43   7
    THOUGH ON MORE THOROUGH-BRED OR FAIRER FINGERS . . . 472 2 DON JUAN 5   106   2
    ALTHOUGH NO FAIRER--SMALLER--SOFTER HAND . . . . . . 472 2 DON JUAN 5   106 V2
    BUT BY DEGREES THAT THEY WERE FAIRER FAR . . . . . . 347 3 DON JUAN 12   69   2
    BUT FAIR AS THEN OR FAIRER TO BEHOLD . . . . 409 3 DON JUAN 13   110   6
FAIREST
    WILL FEED UPON THE FAIREST FRESHEST CHEEK . . . . . . 243 3 DON JUAN 10   38   3
    GOOD HOURS OF FAIR CHEEKS ARE THE FAIREST TINTERS . . 409 3 DON JUAN 13   111   7
FAIR-HAIRED
    A STRAGGLING CURL SHOWED HE HAD BEEN FAIR-HAIRED . . 560 3 DON JUAN 16   121   5
FAIRLY
    IN SHORT IN ALL THINGS SHE WAS FAIRLY WHAT I CALL . . 27 2 DON JUAN 1   12   5
    THE SKIN RELIEVED APPEAR MORE FAIRLY FAIR . . . . . 314 2 DON JUAN 3   76   2
    AND WHEN WE ONCE WERE FAIRLY OUT AND WHEN . . . . . . 435 2 DON JUAN 5   44   3
    WE WILL HAVE ALL THINGS SETTLED FOR YOU FAIRLY . . . 29 3 DON JUAN 6   46   8

		PAGE	VOL	CANTO	STANZA	LN

FAIRLY (CONTINUED)
TO THE GAZETTE--WHICH DOUBTLESS FAIRLY DEALT	120	3 DON JUAN	8	18	2
FULL FLASH ALL FANCY UNTIL FAIRLY DIDDLED	276	3 DON JUAN	11	17	7
AND TO SAY TRUTH IT HAD BEEN FAIRLY EARNED	287	3 DON JUAN	11	39	8
UNTIL I FAIRLY KNOCK'D IT UP WITH RHYME	414	3 DON JUAN	14	9	8
THAT BRIDEGROOMS AFTER THEY ARE FAIRLY GROOM'D	473	3 DON JUAN	15	39	5

FAIRY
WROUGHT CHANGE WITH ALL ARMIDA'S FAIRY ART	60	2 DON JUAN	1	71	7
ENOUGH--THE FAITHFUL AND THE FAIRY PAIR	353	2 DON JUAN	4	18	2
AND STILL IT HALF CALLS UP THE REALMS OF FAIRY	413	2 DON JUAN	5	4	3
OTHERS HAVE LOST THEIR FRESH AND FAIRY LOOKS	308	3 DON JUAN	11	81	5
INDEED A CERTAIN FAIR AND FAIRY ONE	475	3 DON JUAN	15	43	3

FAITH
BUT HOW FAITH IS ACQUIRED AND THEN INSURED	47	2 DON JUAN	1	47	5
BUT THAT WHICH MORE COMPLETELY FAITH EXACTS	138	2 DON JUAN	1	203	6
HE DIED AS BORN A CATHOLIC IN FAITH	197	2 DON JUAN	2	76	5
THE FUTURE STATES OF BOTH ARE LEFT TO FAITH	280	2 DON JUAN	3	9	3
'TIS STRANGE THAT POETS OF THE CATHOLIC FAITH	280	2 DON JUAN	3	9	V5
HE FOUND--BUT SOUGHT NOT I HAVE PLEDGED MY FAITH	366	2 DON JUAN	4	42	6
COULD STIR HIS PULSE OR MAKE HIS FAITH FEEL BRITTLE	396	2 DON JUAN	4	95	7
AND FIRMER FAITH NO LADYE-LOVE DESIRE	396	2 DON JUAN	4	96	3
NO FAITH--WHAT THEN--I RAN AWAY FROM HER	421	2 DON JUAN	5	20	8
WHICH SHOULD CONFIRM OR SHAKE OR MAKE A FAITH	431	2 DON JUAN	5	38	8
THE MARCH THE CHARGE THE SHOUTS OF EITHER FAITH	111	3 DON JUAN	7	87	6
IN SHORT HOWE'ER OUR BETTER FAITH DERIDES	168	3 DON JUAN	8	114	4
IN THE FAITH OF THEIR PROCREATIVE CREED	324	3 DON JUAN	12	18	3
HAS EVER PUZZLED FAITH WITHAL OR YOKED HER IN	377	3 DON JUAN	13	41	8
AFTER DUE SEARCH YOUR FAITH TO ANY QUESTION	411	3 DON JUAN	14	2	1
SHE HELD THEIR OLD FAITH AND OLD FEELINGS FAST	476	3 DON JUAN	15	46	8
BECAUSE SHE DID NOT PIN HER FAITH ON FEATURE	480	3 DON JUAN	15	56	8
AND 'TIS HELD AS FAITH TO THEIR BED OF DEATH	519	3 DON JUAN	16	L 3	7
SO THAT EVEN THOSE WHOSE FAITH IS THE MOST GREAT	556	3 DON JUAN	16	114	7

FAITHFUL
AND IS IT THUS A FAITHFUL WIFE YOU TREAT	103	2 DON JUAN	1	150	3
HE LIKE ACHATES FAITHFUL TO THE TOMB	109	2 DON JUAN	1	159	6
ENOUGH--THE FAITHFUL AND THE FAIRY PAIR	353	2 DON JUAN	4	18	2
OF FAITHFUL PAIRS--(I NEEDS MUST RHYME WITH DOVE	219	3 DON JUAN	9	74	3
THAT FAITHFUL WERE THROUGH THICK AND THIN ABROAD	452	3 DON JUAN	14	96	3

FAITHLESS
| A THANKLESS HUSBAND NEXT A FAITHLESS LOVER | 263 | 2 DON JUAN | 2 | 200 | 7 |
| FIERCE LOVES AND FAITHLESS WARS--I AM NOT SURE | 70 | 3 DON JUAN | 7 | 8 | 1 |

FALCHIONS
| AND FANS TURN INTO FALCHIONS IN FAIR HANDS | 33 | 2 DON JUAN | 1 | 21 | 7 |

FALIERO
| BUT JUAN WAS MY MOSCOW AND FALIERO | 296 | 3 DON JUAN | 11 | 56 | 1 |

FALL
AND FALL FOR LACK OF MOISTURE QUITE A-DRY BOB	10	2 DON JUAN	D	3	8
TO OTHERS' SHARE LET FEMALE ERRORS FALL	29	2 DON JUAN	1	16	7
LIKE ADAM'S RECOLLECTION OF HIS FALL	90	2 DON JUAN	1	127	3
THAT I SHOULD FALL INTO A MONSTER'S POWER	106	2 DON JUAN	1	155	8
THE FRESHNESS OF THE HEART CAN FALL LIKE DEW	144	2 DON JUAN	1	214	2
WHICH IN THEIR WAY THAT MOMENT CHANCED TO FALL	206	2 DON JUAN	2	95	7
WHICH EVE HAS LEFT HER DAUGHTERS SINCE HER FALL	256	2 DON JUAN	2	189	8
THE WORLDS TO COME OF BOTH OR FALL BENEATH	280	2 DON JUAN	3	9	5
SOUND LIKE A DISTANT TORRENT'S FALL	323	2 DON JUAN	3	L 8	3
BREAK WITH THE FIRST FALL THEY CAN NE'ER BEHOLD	350	2 DON JUAN	4	11	4
AS BABA WITH HIS FINGERS MADE THEM FALL	463	2 DON JUAN	5	90	3
(ENOUGH GOD KNOWS) WOULD MUCH FALL SHORT OF THIS	489	2 DON JUAN	5	134	8
I THINK THAT SEVERAL VOLUMES WOULD FALL SHORT	82	3 DON JUAN	7	32	3
HAD MET A PARTY TOWARDS THE TWILIGHT'S FALL	95	3 DON JUAN	7	56	4
THICKER THAN LEAVES THE LIVES BEGAN TO FALL	116	3 DON JUAN	8	9	3
AT LAST FALL SICK OF IMITATING JOB	137	3 DON JUAN	8	50	8
SOULS TO SAVE SINCE EVE'S SLIP AND ADAM'S FALL	192	3 DON JUAN	9	19	3
BESIDES FISH BEASTS AND BIRDS THE SPARROW'S FALL	192	3 DON JUAN	9	19	5
AND FARMERS CAN'T RAISE CERES FROM HER FALL	198	3 DON JUAN	9	32	6
ARISE WHEN WE SEE EMPERORS FALL WITH OATS	198	3 DON JUAN	9	32	8
IN VAIN--AS FALL THE DEWS ON QUENCHLESS SANDS	212	3 DON JUAN	9	59	7
WHEN NEWTON SAW AN APPLE FALL HE FOUND	225	3 DON JUAN	10	1	1
SINCE ADAM WITH A FALL OR WITH AN APPLE	225	3 DON JUAN	10	1	8
BUT I WILL FALL AT LEAST AS FELL MY HERO	296	3 DON JUAN	11	56	5
CAN TENDER SOULS RELATE THE RISE AND FALL	304	3 DON JUAN	11	72	7
WORN OUT WITH IMPORTUNITY OR FALL	333	3 DON JUAN	12	37	2
ALAS WORLDS FALL--AND WOMAN SINCE SHE FELL'D	420	3 DON JUAN	14	23	1
HE DID NOT FALL ASLEEP JUST AFTER DINNER	426	3 DON JUAN	14	36	8
WHICH NEVER MEETS AND THEREFORE CAN'T FALL OUT	430	3 DON JUAN	14	45	8
LET NO MAN GRUMBLE WHEN HIS FRIENDS FALL OFF	431	3 DON JUAN	14	48	5
OWN THEY FORESAW THAT YOU WOULD FALL AT LAST	432	3 DON JUAN	14	50	6
WILL FALL BUT IF THEY DO 'TWILL BE THEIR RUIN	454	3 DON JUAN	14	99	8
SINCE HE WAS SURE HIS MOTHER WOULD FALL SICK	478	3 DON JUAN	15	50	3

FALLEN
IF FALLEN IN EVIL DAYS ON EVIL TONGUES	15	2 DON JUAN	D	10	1
HAD FALLEN WITH HIS RIGHT SHOULDER HALF CUT THROUGH	370	2 DON JUAN	4	48	8
A FAVOURITE HORSE FALLEN LAME JUST AS HE'S MOUNTED	16	2 DON JUAN	6	21	4
(WITHOUT THE GENERAL WHO HAD FALLEN SOME TIME	151	3 DON JUAN	8	79	8
BUT THESE HAD FALLEN NOT WHEN THE FRIARS FELL	386	3 DON JUAN	13	60	3
AND DEEM'D THAT FALLEN WORSHIP FAR MORE DEAR	476	3 DON JUAN	15	46	3
PERHAPS BECAUSE 'TWAS FALLEN HER SIRES WERE PROUD	476	3 DON JUAN	15	46	4
HAD FALLEN LAST MARKET COST HIS HOST THREE VOTES	543	3 DON JUAN	16	89	8

FALLING
| OR LULL'D BY FALLING WATERS SWEET THE HUM | 88 | 2 DON JUAN | 1 | 123 | 6 |

252

```
                                                              PAGE VOL      CANTO STANZA LN

FALLING   (CONTINUED)
    FALLING LIKE DEW UPON A THOUGHT PRODUCES  . . . . .   . . 327   2 DON JUAN   3      88    2
    BUT HIS LIFE FALLING INTO JOHNSON'S WAY  . . . . . .   . . 328   2 DON JUAN   3      91    5
    AND CAUGHT HER FALLING AND FROM OFF THE WALL  . . . .  . . 364   2 DON JUAN   4      37    2
    THINK OF THE THUNDERER'S FALLING DOWN BELOW . . . . . . . . 254   3 DON JUAN  10     59    3
FALL'N
    YOU MIGHT HAVE FREED FALL'N EUROPE FROM THE UNITY  . . . . 187   3 DON JUAN   9       9    3
    NOW THAT THE LION'S FALL'N MAY RISE AGAIN  . . . . . . . . 296   3 DON JUAN  11     56    4
FALLOW
    GRIEF A RICH FIELD WHICH NEVER WOULD LIE FALLOW  . . . . . 228   3 DON JUAN  10      7    6
FALLS
    NOW MY SERE FANCY FALLS INTO THE YELLOW . . . . . . . . . 345   2 DON JUAN   4       3    5
    BUT STILL IT FALLS WITH VAST AND AWFUL SPLINTERS  . . . . 155   3 DON JUAN   8      88    7
    OF HER FIRST FRUIT BUT HOW HE FALLS AND RISES . . . . . . 210   3 DON JUAN   9      55    7
FALMOUTH
    COLUMN DATE FALMOUTH  THERE HAS LATELY BEEN HERE  . . . . 383   3 DON JUAN  13     54    5
FALSE
    WERE PROVED BY COMPETENT FALSE WITNESSES . . . . . . . . . 109   2 DON JUAN   1     160    8
    THOU SHALT NOT BEAR FALSE WITNESS LIKE THE BLUES  . . . . 140   2 DON JUAN   1     206    3
    AND WHO CAN KNOW ALL FALSE WHAT THEN WE SEE . . . . . . . 360   2 DON JUAN   4      30   V8
    SO MANY FALSE LONG TRESSES ALL TO SPARE . . . . . . . . . 457   2 DON JUAN   5      79    3
    FOR OVER-WARMTH IF FALSE IS WORSE THAN TRUTH  . . . . . .  14   3 DON JUAN   6      16    1
    TO SCOLD A LITTLE AT THE FALSE ALARM . . . . . . . . . .  45   3 DON JUAN   6      79    3
    ARE PROSECUTED FOR THAT FALSE CRIME BIGAMY)  . . . . . . . 164   3 DON JUAN   8     105    3
    FALSE FRIEND WHO HELD OUT FREEDOM TO MANKIND  . . . . . . 258   3 DON JUAN  10     67    7
    FOR TRUE OR FALSE POLITENESS (AND SCARCE THAT . . . . . . 290   3 DON JUAN  11     44    2
    TO DRAW THE LINE BETWEEN THE FALSE AND TRUE . . . . . . . 449   3 DON JUAN  14     90    5
    (I WILL NOT SAY IT WAS A FALSE OR TRUE ONE) . . . . . . . 449   3 DON JUAN  14     91    6
    ARE FALSE BUT MAY BE RENDER'D ALSO TRUE . . . . . . . . . 495   3 DON JUAN  15     89    2
    AND FALSE--THOUGH TRUE FOR SURELY THEY'RE SINCEREST  . . . 547   3 DON JUAN  16     97    7
FALSEHOOD
    AND NEVER HAVING DREAMT OF FALSEHOOD SHE . . . . . . . . . 257   2 DON JUAN   2     190    7
    SO WELL THE VERY TRUTH SEEMS FALSEHOOD TO IT  . . . . . . 285   3 DON JUAN  11     36    8
    BESIDES THERE MIGHT BE FALSEHOOD IN WHAT'S STATED . . . . 428   3 DON JUAN  14     42    6
FALSTAFF
    THE WITLESS FALSTAFF OF A HOARY HAL  . . . . . . . . . . 267   3 DON JUAN  10     86    7
FAME
    AND FOR THE FAME YOU WOULD ENGROSS BELOW. . . . . . . . .  13   2 DON JUAN   D       7    4
    THE FAME YOU ENVY AND THE SKILL YOU NEED. . . . . . . . .  14   2 DON JUAN   D       8    4
    FOLLOWERS OF FAME NINE FARROW OF THAT SOW . . . . . . . .  22   2 DON JUAN   1       2    6
    FOR FACTS AGAINST A VIRTUOUS WOMAN'S FAME . . . . . . . . 101   2 DON JUAN   1     146    6
    HOW CAN YOU DO SUCH THINGS AND KEEP YOUR FAME . . . . . . 112   2 DON JUAN   1     165    3
    TO WHOM SHE KNEW HIS MOTHER'S FAME WAS DEAR . . . . . . . 118   2 DON JUAN   1     176    8
    PRIDE FAME AMBITION TO FILL UP HIS HEART  . . . . . . . . 131   2 DON JUAN   1     194    5
    WHAT IS THE END OF FAME 'TIS BUT TO FILL  . . . . . . . . 146   2 DON JUAN   1     218    1
    A LITTLE BREATH LOVE WINE AMBITION FAME . . . . . . . . . 159   2 DON JUAN   2       4    7
    THE LAST WAS OF GREAT FAME AND LIKED TO SHOW IT . . . . . 316   2 DON JUAN   3      78    4
    HAVE FOUND THE FAME YOUR SHORES REFUSE  . . . . . . . . . 321   2 DON JUAN   3   L   2    3
    'TIS SOMETHING IN THE DEARTH OF FAME  . . . . . . . . . . 323   2 DON JUAN   3   L   6    1
    THEIR ENERGY LIKE LIFE FORMS ALL THEIR FAME . . . . . . . 377   2 DON JUAN   4      61    7
    THE SITUATION SEEMS STILL FORM'D FOR FAME-- . . . . . . . 386   2 DON JUAN   4      77    5
    WHETHER MY VERSE'S FAME BE DOOM'D TO CEASE  . . . . . . . 398   2 DON JUAN   4      99    4
    OF TIME AND TONGUES THE FOSTER-BABES OF FAME  . . . . . . 398   2 DON JUAN   4     100    2
    WHERE PERISH'D IN HIS FAME THE HERO-BOY . . . . . . . . . 400   2 DON JUAN   4     103    2
    YET THERE WILL STILL BE BARDS THOUGH FAME IS SMOKE  . . . 402   2 DON JUAN   4     106    1
    THAT TASTE IS GONE THAT FAME IS BUT A LOTTERY . . . . . . 404   2 DON JUAN   4     109    7
    THOSE HONOURABLE SCARS WHICH BROUGHT HIM FAME . . . . . . 431   2 DON JUAN   5      38    2
    INTO GAZETTES BUT FAME (CAPRICIOUS STRUMPET) . . . . . . .  74   3 DON JUAN   7      15    7
    INTO THEIR ANNALS AND PERSUADE POOR FAME. . . . . . . . .  74   3 DON JUAN   7      15   V7
    NAMES GREAT AS ANY THAT THE ROLL OF FAME HAS. . . . . . .  82   3 DON JUAN   7      32    8
    THIS BEING THE CASE MAY SHOW US WHAT FAME IS. . . . . . .  82   3 DON JUAN   7      33    1
    THERE'S FORTUNE EVEN IN FAME WE MUST ALLOW. . . . . . . .  82   3 DON JUAN   7      33    6
    THUS EVEN GOOD FAME MAY SUFFER SAD CONTRACTIONS . . . . .  83   3 DON JUAN   7      34    5
    OF HONEST FAME THAN SHEDDING SEAS OF GORE . . . . . . . . 113   3 DON JUAN   8       3    8
    TO TRACK OUR HERO ON HIS PATH OF FAME . . . . . . . . . . 120   3 DON JUAN   8      17    2
    NOT ONLY FAMOUS BUT OF THAT GOOD FAME . . . . . . . . . . 144   3 DON JUAN   8      63    3
    BETWEEN YOUR FAME AND FEELINGS PRIDE AND PITY-- . . . . . 162   3 DON JUAN   8     101    4
    OH WELLINGTON (OR VILAINTON--FOR FAME . . . . . . . . . . 183   3 DON JUAN   9       1    1
    AND NOW--WHAT IS YOUR FAME SHALL THE MUSE TUNE IT YE . . . 187   3 DON JUAN   9       9    5
    NOR EVER HAD FOR ABSTRACT FAME MUCH PASSION . . . . . . . 189   3 DON JUAN   9      14    4
    THROUGH FIFTY VICTORIES TO SHAME OR FAME . . . . . . . . . 189   3 DON JUAN   9      14    7
    THROUGH PLEASURES THICK AND THIN TO FAME OR SHAME . . . . 189   3 DON JUAN   9      14   V7
    YOUR HEART JOINS CHORUS FAME IS BUT A DIN . . . . . . . . 199   3 DON JUAN   9      34    8
    MADE UP BY YOUTH FAME AND AN ARMY TAILOR-- . . . . . . . . 204   3 DON JUAN   9      44    2
    WHO MARCHED TO MOSCOW LED BY FAME THE SYREN . . . . . . . 253   3 DON JUAN  10     58    6
    FOR ITS DECAYING FAME AND FORMER WORTH . . . . . . . . . . 257   3 DON JUAN  10     66    5
    THE BREADTH OF PAVEMENT AND YON SHRINE WHERE FAME IS  . . 279   3 DON JUAN  11     24    5
    ON A BRASS PLATE WAS GIVEN TO KNOCKS AND FAME . . . . . . 283   3 DON JUAN  11     31   V8
    TO SAVE HIS FAME WITH EACH ACCOMPLISHED BELLE . . . . . . 295   3 DON JUAN  11     53    3
    OR FAME OR NAME FOR WIT WAR SENSE OR NONSENSE . . . . . . 305   3 DON JUAN  11     73    7
    FOR FAME IS DROSS OR WORSE--AND AT THE LAST . . . . . . . 317   3 DON JUAN  12      4   V7
    HAS SAVED THE FAME OF THOUSAND SPLENDID SINNERS . . . . . 346   3 DON JUAN  12     66    3
    A JEST A RIDDLE FAME THROUGH THIN AND THICK SOUGHT . . . . 363   3 DON JUAN  13     10    7
    OF THEIR DEPARTURE SUCH IS MODERN FAME  . . . . . . . . . 382   3 DON JUAN  13     51    2
    THE SLAP-DASH REGIMENT SO WELL KNOWN TO FAME  . . . . . . 383   3 DON JUAN  13     54    6
    WHO LIKE TO MIX SOME SLIGHT ALLOY WITH FAME . . . . . . . 414   3 DON JUAN  14      9    6
    OF FAME OR PROFIT WHEN THE WORLD GROWS WEARY . . . . . . . 415   3 DON JUAN  14     11    2
    WHOSE FAME SHE RATHER DOUBTED WITH POSTERITY  . . . . . . 432   3 DON JUAN  14     51    3
    CAESAR HIMSELF WOULD BE ASHAMED OF FAME . . . . . . . . . 455   3 DON JUAN  14    102    8
```

                                     253

FAME   (CONTINUED)
```
    OF MARRIAGE--(WHICH MIGHT FORM A PAINTER'S FAME    . . . .  473  3 DON JUAN 15    39   7
    HIS FAME TOO--FOR HE HAD THAT KIND OF FAME  . . . . . .    480  3 DON JUAN 15    57   1
    HIS FAME TOO--FOR HE HAD THAT KIND OF FAME  . . . . . .    480  3 DON JUAN 15    57   1
    (THERE'S FAME) YOUNG PARTRIDGE' FILLETS DECK'D WITH TRUFFLES 484  3 DON JUAN 15    66   8
    WHY FAME--BUT FAME YOU KNOW'S SOMETIMES A LIAR--     . .    516  3 DON JUAN 16    36   3
    WHY FAME--BUT FAME YOU KNOW'S SOMETIMES A LIAR--     . .    516  3 DON JUAN 16    36   3
    BUT ADELINE WAS OCCUPIED BY FAME  . . . . . . .           546  3 DON JUAN 16    95   1
FAMED
    HIS MOTHER WAS A LEARNED LADY FAMED  . . . . . .          26   2 DON JUAN  1    10   1
    IS NO LESS FAMED FOR TOLERANCE THAN PIETY  . . . . .      396  3 DON JUAN 13    80   8
FAME'S
    FOR FAME'S A CARTHAGE NOT SO SOON REBUILT  . . . . .      352  3 DON JUAN 12    78   8
FAMILIAR
    BEEN THEIR FAMILIAR AND NOW DEATH WAS HERE  . . . . .     182  2 DON JUAN  2    49   8
FAMILIARLY
    THE SQUIRES FAMILIARLY FORMAL AND  . . . . . .           538  3 DON JUAN 16    79   1
FAMILIES
    TO PASS THAN THOSE TWO CANTOS INTO FAMILIES . . . .      397  2 DON JUAN  4    97   8
    FOR SOME WERE THINKING OF THEIR WIVES AND FAMILIES  . .   94   3 DON JUAN  7    54  V7
    AND FAMILIES EVEN TO THE LAST RELATION  . . . . .        550  3 DON JUAN 16   103   6
    MISCHIEF IN FAMILIES AS SOME KNOW OR KNEW  . . . .       565  3 DON JUAN 17     7   5
FAMILY
    HIS MOTHER'S FAMILY CAME OUT OF ARRAGON  . . . . .       43   2 DON JUAN  1    38  V4
    THE MISSAL TOO (IT WAS THE FAMILY MISSAL)  . . . . .     47   2 DON JUAN  1    46   1
    WITH THE PILED WOOD ROUND WHICH THE FAMILY CROWD  . .    94   2 DON JUAN  1   135   4
    FOR THERE THE SPANISH FAMILY MONCADA  . . . . . .        169  2 DON JUAN  2    24   3
    YET A FINE FAMILY IS A FINE THING  . . . . . . .         306  2 DON JUAN  3    60   1
    AS LEAVING A SMALL FAMILY AT LARGE  . . . . . .          103  3 DON JUAN  7    71   8
    HER FRIENDS LIKE THE SAD FAMILY OF HECTOR  . . . . .     182  3 DON JUAN  8   141   3
    A NERVOUS FAMILY TO WHOSE HEART OR HAND  . . . . .       205  3 DON JUAN  9    46  V3
    KILL A MAN'S FAMILY AND HE MAY BROOK IT  . . . . .       264  3 DON JUAN 10    79   7
    THE FAMILY VAULT RECEIVES ANOTHER LORD  . . . . .        306  3 DON JUAN 11    75   8
    I THINK YOU'LL FIND FROM MANY A FAMILY PICTURE  . . .    337  3 DON JUAN 12    46   3
    A DULL AND FAMILY LIKENESS THROUGH ALL AGES  . . . .     416  3 DON JUAN 14    15   7
    OF AN OLD FAMILY SOME GAY SIR JOHN  . . . . . .          470  3 DON JUAN 15    33   3
    THE FAMILY PHYSICIAN HAD GREAT SKILL  . . . . .          514  3 DON JUAN 16    32   5
FAMILY'S
    A FEMALE FAMILY'S A SERIOUS MATTER  . . . . . .          287  2 DON JUAN  3    22   4
    ABOUT THE PRESENT FAMILY'S DEATHS AND WOOINGS  . . .     527  3 DON JUAN 16    53   8
FAMINE
    WITH WAR OR PLAGUE OR FAMINE ANY WAY  . . . . .          92   2 DON JUAN  1   131   5
    FAMINE DESPAIR COLD THIRST AND HEAT HAD DONE  . . . .    210  2 DON JUAN  2   102   1
    AND FAMINE WITH HER GAUNT AND BONY GROWTH  . . . .       88   3 DON JUAN  7    45   6
    OR SWEARS THAT CERES HATH BEGOTTEN FAMINE  . . . .       88   3 DON JUAN  7    45   8
    THEN FEED HER FAMINE FAT WITH WELLESLEY'S GLORY  . .     174  3 DON JUAN  8   125   8
    GAUNT FAMINE NEVER SHALL APPROACH THE THRONE--  . .      175  3 DON JUAN  8   126   7
FAMINES
    THY PLAGUES THY FAMINES THY PHYSICIANS YET TICK  . . .   117  3 DON JUAN  8    12   5
FAMISH'D
    OR WITH A FAMISH'D BOAT'S-CREW HAD YOUR BIRTH  . . .     201  2 DON JUAN  2    84   6
    SAVE ONE A CORPSE FROM OUT THE FAMISH'D THREE  . . .     213  2 DON JUAN  2   109   6
    DON JUAN ALMOST FAMISH'D AND HALF DROWN'D  . . . .       224  2 DON JUAN  2   129   4
    AND FEELING STILL THE FAMISH'D VULTURE GNAW  . . .       239  2 DON JUAN  2   157   6
    THAT FAMISH'D PEOPLE MUST BE SLOWLY NURST  . . . .       239  2 DON JUAN  2   158   7
FAMISHED
    GO HEAR IT IN YOUR FAMISHED COUNTRY'S CRIES  . . . .     187  3 DON JUAN  9     9   7
FAMOUS
    WERE FRENCH AND FAMOUS PEOPLE AS WE KNOW  . . . .        22   2 DON JUAN  1     3   3
    FAMOUS FOR ORANGES AND WOMEN--HE  . . . . . .            25   2 DON JUAN  1     8   2
    FAMOUS FOR ALWAYS TALKING AND NEER FIGHTING  . . .       150  2 DON JUAN  1     1  V3
    'TWAS FAMOUS TOO FOR THISBE AND FOR PYRAMUS  . . . .     445  2 DON JUAN  5    60   7
    A TOWN WHICH DID A FAMOUS SIEGE ENDURE  . . . .          70   3 DON JUAN  7     8   5
    FOR THEY ARE DAMNED THAT ONCE ALL FAMOUS OATH  . .       88   3 DON JUAN  7    45   2
    BY THE DECEASED WHO LIE IN FAMOUS SLUMBER  . . .         120  3 DON JUAN  8    18   3
    NOT ONLY FAMOUS BUT OF THAT GOOD FAME  . . . . .         144  3 DON JUAN  8    63   3
    FAMOUS FOR MINES OF SALT AND YOKES OF IRON  . . . .      253  3 DON JUAN 10    58   2
    THROUGH COURLAND ALSO WHICH THAT FAMOUS FARCE SAW  .     253  3 DON JUAN 10    58   3
    AMONGST A PEOPLE FAMOUS FOR REFLECTION  . . . . .        304  3 DON JUAN 11    71   7
    AND GENERAL FIREFACE FAMOUS IN THE FIELD  . . . .        399  3 DON JUAN 13    88   2
    KIT-CAT THE FAMOUS CONVERSATIONIST  . . . . . .          403  3 DON JUAN 13    97   4
    FOR I WAS RATHER FAMOUS IN MY TIME  . . . . . .          414  3 DON JUAN 14     9   7
    IN GUIDO'S FAMOUS FRESCO WHICH ALONE  . . . . .          428  3 DON JUAN 14    40   2
    DOCTORS LESS FAMOUS FOR THEIR CURES THAN FEES  . . .     431  3 DON JUAN 14    48   4
FAN
    THAT YOU MIGHT BRAIN THEM WITH THEIR LADY'S FAN  . .     33   2 DON JUAN  1    21   5
    TO OFFER HIS YOUNG PINION AS HER FAN  . . . . .          313  2 DON JUAN  3    73   8
    TO OFFER WILLING HOMAGE AS HER FAN  . . . . . .          313  2 DON JUAN  3    73  V8
    AT HAND AS ONE MAY LIKE TO HAVE A FAN  . . . . .         51   3 DON JUAN  6    91   4
    AN UNIFORM TO BOYS IS LIKE A FAN  . . . . .              108  3 DON JUAN  7    84   4
FANCIED
    IMMORAL CONDUCT BY THE FANCIED SWAY  . . . . .           84   2 DON JUAN  1   116   3
    SOME FANCIED THEY SAW LAND AND SOME SAID NO  . . .       207  2 DON JUAN  2    96   5
FANCIES
    AND SOMETIMES MIX'D UP FANCIES WITH REALITIES  . . .     32   2 DON JUAN  1    20   6
    AND REVELL'D IN THE FANCIES OF THE TIME  . . . .         347  2 DON JUAN  4     6   5
    NOR TO THE TROUBLE WHICH HER FANCIES CAUSED  . . .       476  2 DON JUAN  5   113   6
    AND ALL MY FANCIES WHIRLING LIKE A MILL  . . . .         224  3 DON JUAN  9    85   6
    OR LADIES' FANCIES--RATHER TRANSITORY  . . . . .         229  3 DON JUAN 10     9   4
```

	PAGE	VOL	CANTO		STANZA	LV
FANCIFUL						
HER NEXT AMUSEMENT WAS MORE FANCIFUL	212	3	DON JJAN	9	60	1
FANCY						
HIS DAILY TASK HAD KEPT HIS FANCY COOL	158	2	DON JUAN	2	2	3
IS THIS A FANCY WHICH OUR REASON SCORNS	338	2	DON JUAN	3	108	7
NOW MY SERE FANCY FALLS INTO THE YELLOW	345	2	DON JUAN	4	3	5
A LIVELY READER'S FANCY DOES THE REST	55	3	DON JUAN	6	98	8
FIRST ISMAIL'S CAPTURE CAUGHT YOUR FANCY QUITE . . .	215	3	DON JUAN	9	65	6
AND PALSIED FANCY WHICH NO LONGER ROVES	228	3	DON JUAN	10	6	6
IN RHYMES OR DREAMT (FOR FANCY WILL PLAY TRICKS) . .	230	3	DON JUAN	10	10	5
FULL FLASH ALL FANCY UNTIL FAIRLY DIDDLED	276	3	DON JUAN	11	17	7
FANCY'S						
BE FOR MERE FANCY'S SPORT A THEME CREATIVE	363	3	DON JUAN	13	10	6
FANGS						
NOT SCANDAL'S FANGS COULD FIX ON MUCH THAT'S SEIZABLE . .	66	2	DON JJAN	1	83	3
WHOSE FANGS EWE TAUGHT HER HUMAN SEED TO FEEL . . .	153	3	DON JUAN	8	83	4
FANNY'S						
YOUNG HOPEFUL'S MISTRESS OR MISS FANNY'S LOVER . . .	75	2	DON JUAN	1	100	4
FANS						
AND FANS TURN INTO FALCHIONS IN FAIR HANDS	33	2	DON JUAN	1	21	7
FANTASIES						
WITH YOUR CONFOUNDED FANTASIES TO MORE	84	2	DON JUAN	1	116	2
FANTASTIC						
BUT A MERE AIRY AND FANTASTIC BASIS	413	3	DON JUAN	14	7	7
FAR						
SO FAR ABOVE THE CUNNING POWERS OF HELL	30	2	DON JUAN	1	17	3
AND THE FAR MOUNTAINS WAX A LITTLE HOARY	94	2	DON JJAN	1	134	4
POOR FELLOW HE HAD BETTER FAR BEEN BLIND	155	2	DON JUAN	1 V	7	4
BEHELD HIS NATIVE SPAIN RECEDING FAR	164	2	DON JUAN	2	14	2
AND TWO BOATS COULD NOT HOLD FAR LESS BE STORED . .	181	2	DON JUAN	2	48	7
AS FAR AS IN HER LAY TO TAKE HIM IN	224	2	DON JUAN	2	129	7
BECAUSE 'TIS LIQUOR ONLY AND BEING FAR	238	2	DON JUAN	2	156	3
WITH THE FAR MOUNTAIN-CRESCENT HALF SURROUNDED . .	252	2	DON JUAN	2	183	5
AS THE FAR BELL OF VESPER MAKES HIM START . . .	338	2	DON JUAN	3	108	5
BEING PRIDE WHICH LEADS THE MIND TO SOAR TOO FAR .	344	2	DON JUAN	4	1	7
AND FOLLOW FAR THE DISAPPEARING SUN	355	2	DON JUAN	4	22	2
WHICH MIGHT GO FAR BUT SHE DON'T DANCE WITH VIGOUR .	390	2	DON JUAN	4	85	7
FAR LESS DESCRIBE PRESENT THE VERY VIEW . . .	412	2	DON JUAN	5	3	7
FROM FRIENDS AND HOME AND FREEDOM FAR ESTRANGED .	414	2	DON JUAN	5	7	6
ABOUT THE RIGHT DIVINE HOW FAR WE SHOULD . . .	426	2	DON JUAN	5	30	5
OR THREE OR TWO OR ONE SEND VERY FAR . . .	432	2	DON JUAN	5	39	3
I YIELD THUS FAR BUT SOON WILL BREAK THE CHARM . .	459	2	DON JUAN	5	82	5
AND WAFTED FAR AROSE A RICH PERFUME . . .	460	2	DON JUAN	5	85	6
WITH A FAR REACHING GLANCE--A PAPHIAN PAIR . .	466	2	DON JUAN	5	96	V3
AS FAR AS OUTWARD SHOW MAY CORRESPOND . . .	469	2	DON JUAN	5	99	7
THUS FAR OUR CHRONICLE AND NOW WE PAUSE . . .	503	2	DON JUAN	5	159	1
THROUGH THE HEAVED BREAST THE DREAM OF SOME FAR SHORE .	40	3	DON JUAN	6	67	5
IS LIGHTER FAR OF HEART AND VOICE THAN THOSE . .	49	3	DON JUAN	6	87	7
ALMOST AS FAR AS PETERSBURGH AND LEND . . .	52	3	DON JJAN	6	93	4
MAY SETTLE BUT FAR BE'T FROM ME TO ANTICIPATE . .	65	3	DON JUAN	6	119	7
THAT YE ARE DOGS--YOUR BETTERS FAR) YE MAY . .	70	3	DON JUAN	7	7	2
THE EAR FAR MORE THAN THUNDER FOR HEAVEN'S FLASHES .	115	3	DON JUAN	8	6	7
FAR FLASHED HER BURNING TOWERS O'ER DANUBE'S STREAM .	175	3	DON JUAN	8	127	3
READER I HAVE KEPT MY WORD--AT LEAST SO FAR . .	181	3	DON JUAN	8	138	1
YOU MY LORD DUKE IS FAR ABOVE REFLECTION . .	186	3	DON JUAN	9	7	2
BUT STILL HE SMILES AND WHETHER NEAR OR FAR . .	188	3	DON JUAN	9	12	5
HE STRIPS FROM MAN THAT MANTLE (FAR MORE DEAR .	188	3	DON JUAN	9	12	6
'TIS TRUE WE SPECULATE BOTH FAR AND WIDE . .	190	3	DON JUAN	9	16	3
WITH THOUGHT--AND OF THOUGHT'S FOES BY FAR MOST RUDE .	194	3	DON JUAN	9	24	3
FAR SWEETER THAN THE GREENEST LAURELS SPRUNG . .	199	3	DON JUAN	9	34	4
THE WAYS THAT LEAD THERE BE THEY NEAR OR FAR . .	222	3	DON JUAN	9	80	3
AND LEAVING LAND FAR OUT OF SIGHT WOULD SKIM . .	227	3	DON JUAN	10	4	4
AND FAR BE IT FROM MY MUSES TO PRESUME . . .	227	3	DON JUAN	10	5	3
THE ENDLESS SOOT BESTOWS A TINT FAR DEEPER . .	232	3	DON JUAN	10	15	7
(AS FAR AS RHYME AND CRITICISM COMBINE . .	232	3	DON JUAN	10	16	3
UPON THE CAPTIVE FREEDOM HE'S AS FAR . .	258	3	DON JUAN	10	68	6
THUS FAR GO FORTH THOU LAY WHICH I WILL BACK . .	312	3	DON JUAN	11	90	2
FAR EASIER THOUGH FOR THE GOOD TOWN OF MANCHESTER .	314	3	DON JUAN	11 V	75	3
FROM CEYLON INDE OR FAR CATHAY UNLOADS . .	320	3	DON JUAN	12	9	2
AND FAR AWAY THE LAST BUD OF HER RACE . .	329	3	DON JUAN	12	29	4
THAT TILL WE SEE WHAT'S WHAT IN FACT WE'RE FAR . .	335	3	DON JUAN	12	40	4
SEEKING FAR LESS TO SAVE YOU THAN TO HURT YOU . .	337	3	DON JUAN	12	45	3
HOW FAR IT PROFITS IS ANOTHER MATTER-- . . .	339	3	DON JUAN	12	51	1
BUT BY DEGREES THAT THEY WERE FAIRER FAR . .	347	3	DON JUAN	12	69	2
WHICH FLASHED AS FAR AS WHERE THE MUSK-BULL BROWSES .	353	3	DON JUAN	12	82	6
NOW HATRED IS BY FAR THE LONGEST PLEASURE . .	361	3	DON JUAN	13	6	7
THE PATHS O'ER WHICH THE FAR FESTOON ENTWINES . .	394	3	DON JUAN	13	76	3
THOUGH SHE WAS FAR FROM THAT LEAP YEAR WHOSE LEAP .	433	3	DON JUAN	14	52	7
BUT ADELINE WAS FAR FROM THAT RIPE AGE . .	433	3	DON JUAN	14	54	1
AT LEAST AS FAR AS BIENSEANCE ALLOWS . .	439	3	DON JUAN	14	67	4
AS FAR AS I KNOW THAT THE CHURCH RECEIVES . .	444	3	DON JUAN	14	78	4
AT HOME FAR MORE THAN EVER YET WAS LOVE-- . .	452	3	DON JUAN	14	96	4
THIS HE (AS FAR AS I CAN UNDERSTAND) MEANT . .	472	3	DON JUAN	15	38	4
AS FAR AS HER OWN GENTLE HEART ALLOW'D . .	476	3	DON JUAN	15	46	2
AND DEEM'D THAT FALLEN WORSHIP FAR MORE DEAR . .	476	3	DON JUAN	15	46	3
FOR ME APPEARS A QUESTION FAR TOO NICE . .	478	3	DON JUAN	15	52	5
HER PLACE WAS FAR BEYOND IT AND HER MIND . .	479	3	DON JUAN	15	54	2
IT WAS NOT--BUT 'TIS EASIER FAR ALAS . . .	479	3	DON JUAN	15	54	7
BUT SO FAR LIKE A LADY THAT 'TWAS DREST . .	488	3	DON JUAN	15	74	7

FAR   (CONTINUED)
```
  SO FAR RELAX'D HER THOUGHTS FROM THEIR SWEET PRISON  . . . 491  3 DON JUAN 15     80    7
  AND GIRLS OF SIXTEEN ARE THUS FAR SOCRATIC  . . . . .  494  3 DON JUAN 15     86    1
  WAS LONG AND THUS FAR THERE WAS NO GREAT CAUSE . . . . 511  3 DON JUAN 16     24    3
  O'ER FAR ATLANTIC CONTINENTS OR ISLANDS  . . . . . .  523  3 DON JUAN 16     46    4
  BUT SO FAR THE IMMEDIATE EFFECT . . . . . . . . .  526  3 DON JUAN 16     52    1
  THE COUNTRY WOULD HAVE FAR MORE CAUSE TO WEEP IT  . . . 537  3 DON JUAN 16     75    6
  BUT NOT TO GO TOO FAR I HOLD IT LAW  . . . . . . .  563  3 DON JUAN 17      2    4
  AS FAR AS WORDS MAKE RULES--OUR COMMON NOTION  . . . .  563  3 DON JUAN 17      3    2
FARCE
  SEVERE SUBLIME THE PROPHET WROTE NO FARCE ON  . . . .  179  3 DON JUAN  8    134    6
  THROUGH COURLAND ALSO WHICH THAT FAMOUS FARCE SAW . . . 253  3 DON JUAN 10     58    3
  WITHOUT THE FARCE OF FRIENDSHIP OR ROMANCE  . . . . .  450  3 DON JUAN 14     92    2
FARE
  AND THAT GOOD WINE NE'ER WASH'D DOWN BETTER FARE  . . . 298  2 DON JUAN  3     45    4
  AS IF HE WISHED THAT SHE SHOULD FARE LESS ILL . . . .  198  3 DON JUAN  9     31    3
  THEIR FARE AND ALSO PAUSE BESIDES TO FUDDLE . . . . .  260  3 DON JUAN 10     71    6
  MUST I PASS OVER IN MY BILL OF FARE  . . . . . . .  488  3 DON JUAN 15     73    2
FAREWELL
  AND SO FAREWELL--FORGIVE ME LOVE ME--NO  . . . . . .  132  2 DON JUAN  1    195    7
  MUST BID YOU BOTH FAREWELL IN ACCENTS BLAND . . . . .  147  2 DON JUAN  1    221   V3
  HIS FIRST--PERHAPS HIS LAST--FAREWELL OF SPAIN  . . . .  162  2 DON JUAN  2     11    8
  FAREWELL MY SPAIN A LONG FAREWELL HE CRIED  . . . . .  166  2 DON JUAN  2     18    1
  FAREWELL MY SPAIN A LONG FAREWELL HE CRIED  . . . . .  166  2 DON JUAN  2     18    1
  FAREWELL WHERE GUADALQUIVIR'S WATERS GLIDE  . . . . .  166  2 DON JUAN  2     18    5
  FAREWELL MY MOTHER AND SINCE ALL IS O'ER  . . . . . .  166  2 DON JUAN  2     18    5
  FAREWELL TOO DEAREST JULIA--(HERE HE DREW  . . . . .  166  2 DON JUAN  2     18    7
  THEN ROSE FROM SEA TO SKY THE WILD FAREWELL . . . . .  184  2 DON JUAN  2     52    1
  FAREWELL THEY MUTUALLY EXCLAIMED THIS SOIL  . . . . .  459  2 DON JUAN  5     83    5
  FAREWELL SAID JUAN SHOULD WE MEET NO MORE . . . . . .  460  2 DON JUAN  5     84    1
  I WISH YOU A GOOD APPETITE--FAREWELL  . . . . . . .  460  2 DON JUAN  5     84    2
  NOR WHAT THE MEANING OF THE MAN'S FAREWELL  . . . . .  276  3 DON JUAN 11     17    4
FARM
  AND HALF A MILLION FOR YOUR SABINE FARM . . . . . .  186  3 DON JUAN  9      7    7
  FISHERY AND FARM BOTH INTO HIS OWN HAND . . . . . .  198  3 DON JUAN  9     31    8
FARMERS
  GENTLEMEN FARMERS--A RACE WORN OUT QUITE  . . . . . .  198  3 DON JUAN  9     32    3
  AND FARMERS CAN'T RAISE CERES FROM HER FALL . . . . .  198  3 DON JUAN  9     32    6
  BUT FROM BEING FARMERS WE TURN GLEANERS GLEANING  . . .  403  3 DON JUAN 13     96    1
FARROW
  FOLLOWERS OF FAME NINE FARROW OF THAT SOW . . . . . .   22  2 DON JUAN  1      2    6
FARTHER
  ON THROUGH A FARTHER RANGE OF GOODLY ROOMS  . . . . .  442  2 DON JUAN  5     55    2
  GAVE LIGHT ENOUGH TO HINT THEIR FARTHER WAY . . . . .  442  2 DON JUAN  5     56    2
  ITS FARTHER COURSE BUT MUST RECEIVE ITS WRECK . . . .   60  3 DON JUAN  6    108    8
FARTHING
  THEIR MOON THEIR SUN THEIR GAS THEIR FARTHING CANDLE . .  342  3 DON JUAN 12     56    8
FASCINATE
  OR FASCINATE WHOME'ER THEY FIXED THEIR EYES ON  . . . .  463  2 DON JUAN  5     90    8
FASCINATING
  AFTER SOME FASCINATING HESITATION--  . . . . . . .  518  3 DON JUAN 16     40    1
  AND THAT WAS OF A FASCINATING KIND . . . . . . . .  525  3 DON JUAN 16     49    4
FASCINATION
  WITH FASCINATION IN HIS VERY BOW  . . . . . . . .  354  3 DON JUAN 12     84    3
FASCINES
  IN FORMER WORKS MADE NEW PREPARED FASCINES  . . . . .   89  3 DON JUAN  7     47    7
  ALSO HE DRESSED UP FOR THE NONCE FASCINES . . . . . .   93  3 DON JUAN  7     53    1
FASHION
  ALFONSO FIRST EXAMINED WELL THEIR FASHION . . . . . .  121  2 DON JUAN  1    181    7
  A WANDERER FROM THE BRITISH WORLD OF FASHION  . . . . .  244  2 DON JUAN  2    166    2
  AND SHE WAS WORSHIPP'D AFTER NATURE'S FASHION . . . . .  257  2 DON JUAN  2    191    2
  OR CA IRA ACCORDING TO THE FASHION ALL  . . . . . .  319  2 DON JUAN  3     85    4
  OR AT LEAST WAS SO ERE IT GREW A FASHION  . . . . . .  402  2 DON JUAN  4    106    8
  THE LAST OF THESE WAS NEVER MUCH THE FASHION  . . . . .  437  2 DON JUAN  5     48    3
  AFTER THE MANNER THEN IN FASHION THERE  . . . . . .  457  2 DON JUAN  5     79    5
  'TIS NOT HIS CONQUESTS KEEP HIS NAME IN FASHION . . . .    8  3 DON JUAN  6      4    6
  NO FASHION MADE THEM APES OF HER DISTORTIONS  . . . . .  145  3 DON JUAN  8     66    6
  A VIRTUE MUCH IN FASHION NOW-A-DAYS . . . . . . . .  176  3 DON JUAN  8    128    3
  THE HIGH ROMAN FASHION TOO OF CINCINNATUS . . . . . .  186  3 DON JUAN  9      7    3
  SAYS SHAKESPEARE WHO JUST NOW IS MUCH IN FASHION  . . .  189  3 DON JUAN  9     14    2
  OURSELVES A SINGER DANCER MUCH IN FASHION . . . . . .  216  3 DON JUAN  9     68    4
  HE FOUND HIMSELF EXTREMELY IN THE FASHION . . . . . .  284  3 DON JUAN 11     33    7
  OF FASHION--SAY WHAT STREAMS NOW FILL THOSE CHANNELS . .  308  3 DON JUAN 11     80    6
  OR WHAT'S STILL WORSE TO PUT YOU OUT OF FASHION--  . . .  337  3 DON JUAN 12     45    4
  INTO A COUNTRY WHERE 'TIS HALF A FASHION  . . . . . .  347  3 DON JUAN 12     68    4
  NINE TIMES IN TEN 'TIS BUT CAPRICE OR FASHION . . . .  351  3 DON JUAN 12     77    3
  OR EVEN MERE FASHION WHICH INDEED'S THE BEST  . . . . .  370  3 DON JUAN 13     28    6
  WITH MANY MORE BY RANK AND FASHION DECKED . . . . . .  382  3 DON JUAN 13     52    6
  DISCUSSED THE FASHION WHICH MIGHT NEXT PREVAIL . . . .  406  3 DON JUAN 13    104    5
FASHIONABLE
  APOSTASY'S SO FASHIONABLE TOO  . . . . . . . . .   20  2 DON JUAN  D     17    6
  (IN MOORE'S PHRASE) WHERE THE FASHIONABLE FAIR  . . . .  301  3 DON JUAN 11     66    7
  APARTMENT--FASHIONABLE BUT EXPENSIVE  . . . . . . .  313  3 DON JUAN 11   V 29    8
  BECAME A KIND OF FASHIONABLE MYSTERY  . . . . . . .  328  3 DON JUAN 12     27    8
  AND SUCH IS EUROPE'S FASHIONABLE EASE . . . . . . .  373  3 DON JUAN 13     34   V8
  WITH FASHIONABLE WINES AND CONVERSATION . . . . . .  534  3 DON JUAN 16     69    6
  THAT HONEY OF YOUR FASHIONABLE BEES--  . . . . . . .  548  3 DON JUAN 16    100    6
FAST
  THAT HOWSOEVER PEOPLE FAST AND PRAY . . . . . . . .   56  2 DON JUAN  1     63    5
```

FAST   (CONTINUED)
INDENT THERE FOR THE PRESENT AT THE LEAST HE'S FAST   115   2 DON JJAN   1   172   6
FROM WHICH AWAY SO FAIR AND FAST THEY BORE   163   2 DON JUAN   2   13   4
FAST BY THE HEAD AND ALL DISTINCTION GONE   179   2 DON JUAN   2   44   2
INSTEAD OF SAIL WERE TO THE OAR MADE FAST   188   2 DON JUAN   2   61   4
THE DAY BEFORE FAST SLEEPING ON THE WATER   208   2 DON JUAN   2   99   1
FAST TO THE SAND LEST THE RETURNING WAVE 213   2 DON JUAN   2   108   2
AND AS HE GAZED HIS DIZZY BRAIN SPUN FAST   214   2 DON JUAN   2   110   1
FAST IN HIS CAVE AND NOTHING CLASH'D UPON   229   2 DON JUAN   2   137   2
SHE SLEPT NOT BUT ALL TENDERLY THOUGH FAST   260   2 DON JUAN   2   195   3
WE KNOW NOT THIS--THE BLOOD FLOWS ON TOO FAST   .   .   . 345   2 DON JUAN   4   2   6
BUT SPENDS SO FAST SHE HAS NOT NOW A PAUL   390   2 DON JUAN   4   84   6
AND RUNNING OUT AS FAST AS I WAS ABLE 428   2 DON JUAN   5   33   6
AS FAST AS OARS COULD PULL AND WATER FLOAT   432   2 DON JUAN   5   40   4
OBJECT ON OBJECT FLASHED SO BRIGHT AND FAST   465   2 DON JUAN   5   93   6
BUT NOW IT FLOWED IN NATURAL AND FAST 490   2 DON JUAN   5   137   5
AS FAST AS EVER HUSBAND BY HIS MATE   42   3 DON JUAN   6   73   3
AND THE HEART'S DEW OF PAIN SPRANG FAST AND CHILLY   .   .   . 58   3 DON JUAN   6   105   7
WHILE THOUGH 'TWAS DAWN THE TURKS SLEPT FAST AS EVER .   .   . 80   3 DON JJAN   7   28   8
SEIZED FAST AS IF 'TWERE BY THE SERPENT'S HEAD 153   3 DON JUAN   8   83   3
BUT THOUGH YOUR YEARS AS MAN TEND FAST TO ZERO 184   3 DJN JUAN   9   2   7
OF RUBLES RAIN AS FAST AS SPECIE CAN 222   3 DON JUAN   9   79   6
AS THE SMART BOYS SPURRED FAST IN THEIR CAREER 263   3 DON JUAN   10   77   3
THERE MAILS FAST FLYING OFF LIKE A DELUSION 278   3 DON JUAN   11   22   4
AND (SHOULD SHE NOT HOLD FAST BY LOVE OR PRIDE)   .   .   . 292   3 DON JUAN   11   46   4
THROUGH STREET AND SQUARE FAST FLASHING CHARIOTS HURLED .   . 302   3 DON JUAN   11   67   3
WHICH HOLD FAST OTHER PLEASURES GREAT AND SMALL   .   .   . 316   3 DON JUAN   12   3   4
WHAT TIME HE CHOSE FOR DRESS AND BROKE HIS FAST   .   .   . 406   3 DON JUAN   13   103   7
IS DIFFICULT PRAY TELL ME CAN YOU MAKE FAST 411   3 DON JUAN   14   2   3
LOOK BACK O'ER AGES ERE UNTO THE STAKE FAST 411   3 DON JUAN   14   2   5
SHE HELD THEIR OLD FAITH AND OLD FEELINGS FAST 476   3 DON JUAN   15   46   8
FASTEN
INDENT SIGH--AS THE POSTBOYS FASTEN ON THE TRACES   378   3 DON JUAN   13   44   8
FASTEN'D
INDENT THE DOOR WAS FASTEN'D BUT WITH VOICE AND FIST   95   2 DON JUAN   1   136   7
THE DOOR WAS FASTEN'D IN HIS LEGAL FACE 111   2 DON JUAN   1   164   8
BELOW HER BREAST WAS FASTEN'D WITH A BAND   312   2 DON JUAN   3   72   5
FASTER
INDENT DO PRAY UNDO THE BOLT A LITTLE FASTER--   96   2 DON JUAN   1   137   5
FOR THE TURK'S TEETH STUCK FASTER THAN A SKEWER .   .   . 154   3 DON JUAN   8   85   3
FAST-FLOWING
INDENT PREFERR'D A DRAUGHT FROM THE FAST-FLOWING VEINS   .   .   . 197   2 DON JUAN   2   77   4
FASTING
INDENT TEMPERANCE DELIGHTS HER BUT LONG FASTING RUFFLES   .   .   . 542   3 DON JUAN   16   86   8
FAT
INDENT BUT THIS I KNOW THAT THIS ROAST CAPON'S FAT 298   2 DON JUAN   3   45   3
THEN FEED HER FAMINE FAT WITH WELLESLEY'S GLORY .   .   . 174   3 DON JUAN   8   125   8
A FAT FEN VICARAGE AND NOUGHT TO THINK ON   540   3 DON JUAN   16   82   8
FATAL
INDENT SUPPOSE FROM JUNE THE SIXTH (THE FATAL DAY 86   2 DON JUAN   1   121   2
TO LIFT OUR FATAL LOVE TO GOD FROM MAN 131   2 DON JUAN   1   194   V8
WHICH MAKES IT FATAL TO BE LOVED AH WHY 275   2 DON JUAN   3   2   2
DESCEND--THE FAULT IS MINE THIS FATAL SHORE 366   2 DON JUAN   4   42   5
FATAL TO BISHOPS AS TO SOLDIERS--THESE 150   3 DON JUAN   8   76   2
FATAL TO WARRIORS AS TO WOMEN--THESE   150   3 DON JUAN   8   76   V2
THE FAIR MOST FATAL JUAN EVER MET   364   3 DON JUAN   13   12   3
FATE
INDENT I WISH YOUR FATE MAY YIELD YE WHEN SHE CHOOSES 14   2 DON JUAN   D   8   3
A SORT OF INCOME-TAX LAID ON BY FATE 122   2 DON JUAN   1   183   4
BESIDES BEING MUCH AVERSE FROM SUCH A FATE   199   2 DON JUAN   2   81   3
AND IF PEDRILLO'S FATE SHOULD SHOCKING BE   200   2 DON JUAN   2   83   1
AND PATIENT SPIRIT HELD ALOOF HIS FATE 203   2 DON JUAN   2   88   4
WHICH HASTENS AS PHYSICIANS SAY ONE'S FATE   230   2 DON JUAN   2   140   4
WAS URGENT THAT THE GENTLEMAN WHOSE FATE 240   2 DON JUAN   2   159   3
BUT WAS IN THEM THEIR NATURE OR THEIR FATE   354   2 DON JUAN   4   19   3
JUAN GAZED ON HER AS TO ASK HIS FATE-- 355   2 DON JUAN   4   22   5
WITH THIS HIS TUNEFUL NEIGHBOUR THAN HIS FATE 394   2 DON JUAN   4   93   4
TO STRIVE TOO WITH OUR FATE WERE SUCH A STRIFE 419   2 DON JUAN   5   17   5
WE NEEDS MUST FOLLOW WHEN FATE PUTS FROM SHORE .   .   . 460   2 DON JUAN   5   84   5
OH YE WHOSE FATE IT IS AS ONCE 'TWAS MINE   37   3 DON JUAN   6   62   3
WHAT SAGES CALL CHANCE PROVIDENCE OR FATE-- 105   3 DON JUAN   7   76   4
HOWEVER HEAVEN KNOWS HOW THE FATE WHO LEVELS .   .   . 134   3 DON JUAN   8   44   4
UNLESS COMPELLED BY FATE OR WAVE OR WIND 139   3 DON JUAN   8   54   1
FLUNG HERE BY FATE OR CIRCUMSTANCE WHICH TAME .   .   . 139   3 DON JUAN   8   54   6
HER FATE HAD BEEN TO THAT OF ALL HER RACE   159   3 DON JUAN   8   95   3
(SINCE IT WAS NOT THEIR FAULT BUT ONLY FATE 177   3 DON JUAN   8   131   5
THE FATE OF NATIONS--BUT THIS RUSS SO WITTY 179   3 DON JUAN   8   134   7
WHAT INDIGESTION IS--THAT INWARD FATE 190   3 DON JUAN   9   15   4
POOR FELLOW HIS WAS AN UNTOWARD FATE-- 298   3 DON JUAN   11   60   6
ABROAD SUCH THINGS DECIDE FEW WOMEN'S FATE-- .   .   . 345   3 DON JUAN   12   64   5
(FATE IS A GOOD EXCUSE FOR OUR OWN WILL) 364   3 DON JUAN   13   12   6
AND YET SUCH IS MY FOLLY OR MY FATE   496   3 DON JUAN   15   91   4
FATES
INDENT THEY ARE A SORT OF POST-HOUSE WHERE THE FATES   76   2 DON JUAN   1   103   4
OF SEAMEN'S FATES AND THE LOUD TEMPESTS RAISE .   .   . 414   2 DON JUAN   5   6   4
COULD YET BE KNOWN UNTO THE FATES ALONE 499   2 DON JUAN   5   153   4
PEOPLE ARE APT TO BLAME THE FATES FORSOOTH   339   3 DON JUAN   12   50   3
FATHER
INDENT NARRATING SOMEWHAT OF DON JUAN'S FATHER 25   2 DON JUAN   1   7   7

257

```
                                                              PAGE VOL        CANTO STANZA LN
FATHER   (CONTINUED)
      I KNEW HIS FATHER WELL AND HAVE SOME SKILL  . . . . . .  49  2 DON JUAN  1    51    3
      AND THEN THE MOTHER CRIES THE FATHER SWEARS . . . . . .  75  2 DON JUAN  1   100    7
      SWEET TO THE FATHER IS HIS FIRST-BORN'S BIRTH . . . . .  88  2 DON JUAN  1   124    6
      THE OTHER FATHER HAD A WEAKLIER CHILD  . . . . . . . . 203  2 DON JUAN  2    88    1
      THE BOY EXPIRED--THE FATHER HELD THE CLAY  . . . . . . 204  2 DON JUAN  2    90    1
      AT LAST HER FATHER TOOK A VOYAGE TO SEA  . . . . . . . 248  2 DON JUAN  2   174   V5
      SO THAT HER FATHER BEING AT SEA SHE WAS  . . . . . . . 248  2 DON JUAN  2   175    2
      DEAR AS HER FATHER HAD BEEN TO HAIDEE . . . . . . . . 363  2 DON JUAN  4    36    6
      'TIS LAMBRO--'TIS MY FATHER KNEEL WITH ME-- . . . . . 364  2 DON JUAN  4    38    2
      OH DEAREST FATHER IN THIS AGONY . . . . . . . . . . . 364  2 DON JUAN  4    38    4
      THE FATHER PAUSED A MOMENT THEN WITHDREW . . . . . . . 368  2 DON JUAN  4    46    1
      HER FATHER WATCH'D SHE TURN'D HER EYES AWAY . . . . . 379  2 DON JUAN  4    64    2
      AMMON'S (ILL PLEASED WITH ONE WORLD AND ONE FATHER) . 427  2 DON JUAN  5    31    8
      AND THAT HIS FATHER WAS AN HONEST BLACKSMITH . . . . .  76  3 DON JUAN  7    20    4
      NOR BROTHER FATHER SISTER DAUGHTER LOVE . . . . . . . 250  3 DON JUAN 10    53    2
      PERPLEXING FOR MOST VIRGINS--A CHILD'S FATHER . . . . 533  3 DON JUAN 16    67    8
FATHER'S
      HIS FATHER'S NAME WAS JOSE--DON OF COURSE  . . . . . .  26  2 DON JUAN  1     9    1
      THEY ARE UNWORTHY OF MY FATHER'S DAUGHTER . . . . . . 106  2 DON JUAN  1   155    6
      HIS FATHER'S WHOM HE LOVED AS YE MAY THINK . . . . . . 187  2 DON JUAN  2    58    2
      THE CREATURE WAS HIS FATHER'S DOG THAT DIED . . . . . 193  2 DON JUAN  2    71    3
      HE SAW INCREASING ON HIS FATHER'S HEART . . . . . . . 203  2 DON JUAN  2    88    7
      BUT TAKING HIM INTO HER FATHER'S HOUSE  . . . . . . . 225  2 DON JUAN  2   130    1
      AND PENSIVE TO HER FATHER'S HOUSE SHE WENT . . . . . . 228  2 DON JUAN  2   136    1
      AND CALL'D HER FATHER'S OLD SLAVES UP WHO SWORE . . . 229  2 DON JUAN  2   138    6
      AT LAST HER FATHER'S PROWS PUT OUT TO SEA . . . . . . 248  2 DON JUAN  2   174    5
      HER FATHER'S HOSPITALITY SEEM'D MIDDLING . . . . . . . 295  2 DON JUAN  3    39    5
      AROUND AS PRINCESS OF HER FATHER'S LAND . . . . . . . 312  2 DON JUAN  3    72    1
      LIKE TO HER FATHER'S FEATURES TILL EACH TRACE . . . . 363  2 DON JUAN  4    35    3
      'TIS--'TIS HER FATHER'S--FIX'D UPON THE PAIR . . . . . 363  2 DON JUAN  4    35    8
      HER FATHER'S FACE--BUT NEVER STOPP'D HIS HAND . . . . 367  2 DON JUAN  4    43    8
      HER FATHER'S BLOOD BEFORE HER FATHER'S FACE . . . . . 367  2 DON JUAN  4    44    7
      HER FATHER'S BLOOD BEFORE HER FATHER'S FACE . . . . . 367  2 DON JUAN  4    44    7
      LET HIM DISARM OR BY MY FATHER'S HEAD . . . . . . . . 369  2 DON JUAN  4    47    1
      IN VAIN SHE STRUGGLED IN HER FATHER'S GRASP-- . . . . 370  2 DON JUAN  4    48    4
      NOTHING COULD MAKE HER MEET HER FATHER'S FACE . . . . 381  2 DON JUAN  4    68    2
      NONE BUT HER OWN AND FATHER'S GRAVE IS THERE . . . . . 383  2 DON JUAN  4    72    3
      YOUR FATHER'S SON 'TIS QUITE ENOUGH FOR ME . . . . . .  52  3 DON JUAN  6    93    8
      WAS HIGH-BORN WEALTHY BY HER FATHER'S WILL . . . . . . 359  3 DON JUAN 13     2    5
FATHERS
      THERE WERE TWO FATHERS IN THIS GHASTLY CREW . . . . . 202  2 DON JUAN  2    87    1
      ROBBED FOR HIS DAUGHTER BY THE BEST OF FATHERS . . . . 284  2 DON JUAN  3    17    8
      MUST WE BUT BLUSH--OUR FATHERS BLED  . . . . . . . . . 323  2 DON JUAN  3  L  7    2
      WHERE ARE THE EPITAPHS OUR FATHERS READ . . . . . . . 399  2 DON JUAN  4   102    5
      OR AMMON'S--FOR TWO FATHERS CLAIMED THIS ONE . . . . . 427  2 DON JUAN  5    31   V8
      THAT TIME HAS LEFT OUR FATHERS OF THEIR HALL . . . . . 507  3 DON JUAN 16    16    8
FATHOM
      SOME WALTZ SOME DRAW SOME FATHOM THE ABYSS . . . . . . 340  3 DON JUAN 12    52    5
FATIGUE
      THIS CANTO ERE MY MUSE PERCEIVES FATIGUE . . . . . . . 109  3 DON JUAN  7    85    6
      'TWAS ONLY THE FATIGUE OF LAST CAMPAIGN . . . . . . . 244  3 DON JUAN 10    40    8
      THAT THE FATIGUE WAS GREATER THAN THE PROFIT . . . . . 536  3 DON JUAN 16    73    8
FATIGUED
      FATIGUED WITH THESE HEREDITARY GLORIES  . . . . . . . 392  3 DON JUAN 13    71    2
FATTEN
      WHO FATTEN ON THEIR COUNTRY'S GORE AND DEBTS . . . . . 187  3 DON JUAN  9    10    5
FATTEST
      AS FATTEST BUT HE SAVED HIMSELF BECAUSE . . . . . . . 199  2 DON JUAN  2    81    2
FATUI
      FOLLOWING THE IGNES FATUI OF MANKIND . . . . . . . . . 479  3 DON JUAN 15    54    6
FATUUS
      AN IGNIS FATUUS OR AS SAILORS STRANDED  . . . . . . . 127  3 DON JUAN  8    32    5
FAULT
      BUT THEN 'TIS NOT MY FAULT IF OTHERS HURT YOU . . . . .  37  2 DON JUAN  1    30    8
      AND ALL THE FAULT OF THAT INDECENT SUN  . . . . . . . .  56  2 DON JUAN  1    63    2
      BUT NOT MY FAULT--I TELL THEM ALL IN TIME . . . . . . .  65  2 DON JUAN  1    80    8
      'TIS NOT MY FAULT--I KEPT GOOD WATCH--ALACK . . . . . .  96  2 DON JUAN  1   137    4
      I KNOW NOT IF THE FAULT BE MEN'S OR THEIRS . . . . . . 276  2 DON JUAN  3     4    1
      OF FAULT OR TEMPER RUIN'D THE CONNEXION . . . . . . . 281  2 DON JUAN  3    10    5
      THE FAULT WAS THEIRS NOT MINE IT IS NOT FAIR . . . . . 282  2 DON JUAN  3    12    2
      IF I HAVE ANY FAULT IT IS DIGRESSION . . . . . . . . . 331  2 DON JUAN  3    96    2
      THEY FOUND NO FAULT WITH TIME SAVE THAT HE FLED . . . 351  2 DON JUAN  4    13    3
      DESCEND--THE FAULT IS MINE THIS FATAL SHORE . . . . . 366  2 DON JUAN  4    42    5
      OR IF YOU DON'T THE FAULT IS NOT IN ME . . . . . . . . 450  2 DON JUAN  5    66    8
      PERHAPS THE FAULT OF HER SOFT SEX AND AGE-- . . . . . 490  2 DON JUAN  5   136    6
      FOR THIS FIRST FAULT AND THAT ON NO CONDITION . . . . .  47  3 DON JUAN  6    82    5
      BUT NOT BY BABA'S FAULT HE SAID AND SWORE ON . . . . .  57  3 DON JUAN  6   102    7
      'TIS NOT THEIR FAULT NOR MINE IF THIS BE SO-- . . . . .  68  3 DON JUAN  7     4    5
      SHEWED THAT SOMEWHERE SOMEHOW THERE WAS A FAULT . . . .  83  3 DON JUAN  7    35    2
      WHY GENERAL IF HE HATH NO GREATER FAULT . . . . . . . .  98  3 DON JUAN  7    62    7
      HOUNDS WHEN THE HUNTSMAN TUMBLES ARE AT FAULT . . . . 119  3 DON JUAN  8    16    8
      (SINCE IT WAS NOT THEIR FAULT BUT ONLY FATE . . . . . 177  3 DON JUAN  8   131    5
      SUSPICIOUS PEOPLE WHO FIND FAULT IN HASTE . . . . . . 230  3 DON JUAN 10    11    3
      A SORT OF VARNISH OVER EVERY FAULT . . . . . . . . . . 417  3 DON JUAN 14    16    3
      WHOSE GREATEST FAULT WAS LEAVING FEW TO FIND . . . . . 479  3 DON JUAN 15    54    4
FAULTS
      SHE KEPT A JOURNAL WHERE HIS FAULTS WERE NOTED . . . . .  36  2 DON JUAN  1    28    1
      MY FAULTS EVEN WITH YOUR OWN WHICH MEANETH PUT . . . . .  34  3 DON JUAN  6    56    6
```

FAULTS   (CONTINUED)
     MAKES ONE IN LOVE EVEN WITH ITS VERY FAULTS 302   3 DON JUAN 11   68   4
     IN FAULTS WHICH SOMETIMES SHOW THE SOIL'S FERTILITY . . 368   3 DON JUAN 13   22   6
     THAT TIME WOULD TEMPER JUAN'S FAULTS OF YOUTH 439   3 DON JUAN 14   67   5
     FAULTS WHICH ATTRACT BECAUSE THEY ARE NOT TAME 480   3 DON JUAN 15   57   5
FAUX
     AND NEVER CRANED AND MADE BUT FEW FAUX PAS 424   3 DON JUAN 14   33   3
     (FOR FOREIGNERS DON'T KNOW THAT A FAUX PAS 436   3 DON JUAN 14   60   5
FAVOUR
     IN YOUNG DON JUAN'S FAVOUR AND TO HIM ITS 65   2 DON JUAN 1   81   3
     THEIR FAVOUR IN AN AUTHOR'S CAP'S A FEATHER 135   2 DON JUAN 1   199   5
     AS A GREAT FAVOUR ONE OF THE FORE-PAWS 193   2 DON JUAN 2   71   6
     THINGS WHICH IN HUNGRY MORTALS' EYES FIND FAVOUR . . . 437   2 DON JUAN 5   47   3
     THE FAVOURITE BUT WHAT'S FAVOUR AMONGST FOUR 12   2 DON JUAN 6   12   2
     AS MAY BE WON BY FAVOUR OF THE MOON 229   3 DON JUAN 10   9   3
     THE FAVOUR OF THE EMPRESS WAS AGREEABLE 235   3 DON JUAN 10   22   1
     FOR THOSE WHOM FAVOUR OR WHOM FORTUNE SWELLS 283   3 DON JUAN 11   31   3
     WHO FAVOUR MALGRE MALTHUS GENERATION-- 472   3 DON JUAN 15   37   2
FAVOUR'D
     I FAVOUR'D NONE--NAY WAS ALMOST UNCIVIL 102   2 DON JUAN 1   148   6
     HOW JUAN NAKED FAVOUR'D BY THE NIGHT 126   2 DON JUAN 1   188   2
     SOME FAVOUR'D OBJECT AND AS IN THE NICHE 269   2 DON JUAN 2   211   5
FAVOURED
     HIS YOUTH AND FEATURES FAVOURED THE DISGUISE 477   2 DON JUAN 5   115   1
     WAS FAVOURED BY AN ACCIDENT OR BLUNDER 136   2 DON JUAN 8   46   2
     ON THE MOST FAVOURED AND AMIDST THE BLAZE 373   3 DON JUAN 13   33   6
FAVOURITE
     HER FAVOURITE SCIENCE WAS THE MATHEMATICAL 27   2 DON JUAN 1   12   1
     WITH DONNA INEZ QUITE A FAVOURITE FRIEND 58   2 DON JUAN 1   66   2
     HAD BEEN THE FAVOURITE OF FULL MANY A MESS 318   2 DON JUAN 3   82   3
     SHE WAS OF COURSE THE FAVOURITE OF THE FOUR 495   2 DON JUAN 5   146   8
     THE FAVOURITE BUT WHAT'S FAVOUR AMONGST FOUR 12   3 DON JUAN 6   12   2
     A FAVOURITE HORSE FALLEN LAME JUST AS HE'S MOUNTED . . 16   3 DON JUAN 6   21   4
     HIMSELF A FAVOURITE VENTURED TO ADDRESS 100   3 DON JUAN 7   65   2
     WAS ONE OF THEIR MOST FAVOURITE POSITIONS 191   3 DON JUAN 9   17   4
     THE EMPRESS SMILED THE REIGNING FAVOURITE FROWNED-- . 205   3 DON JUAN 9   46   2
     BECAUSE SHE PUT A FAVOURITE TO DEATH 222   3 DON JUAN 9   81   6
     WAS GIVEN TO HER FAVOURITE AND NOW BORE HIS 248   3 DON JUAN 10   49   8
     JUAN TOO WAS A SORT OF FAVOURITE WITH HER 338   3 DON JUAN 12   49   1
     NO MARVEL THEN HE WAS A FAVOURITE 428   3 DON JUAN 14   41   1
     I MUST ALTHOUGH A FAVOURITE PLAT OF MINE 488   3 DON JUAN 15   73   3
FAVOURITE'S
     OF THE IMPERIAL FAVOURITE'S CONDITION 208   3 DON JUAN 9   52   3
FAVOURITES
     THEIR BREAD AS MINISTERS AND FAVOURITES--(THAT'S . . 310   2 DON JUAN 3   68   6
     AND ALWAYS USED HER FAVOURITES TOO WELL 214   3 DON JUAN 9   63   4
     OF FITTING OUT HER FAVOURITES CONFERRED 247   3 DON JUAN 10   46   2
     ALL PRIVATE FAVOURITES OF DON JUAN FOR 249   3 DON JUAN 10   50   2
FAVOURITISM
     OF FAVOURITISM BUT NOT YET IN THE BLUSH-- 227   3 DON JUAN 10   5   2
FAVOURS
     WHO FAVOURS WHAT SHE SHOULD NOT FOUND HIS WAY . . . 126   2 DON JUAN 1   188   3
FAWN
     'TWAS LIKE THE FAWN WHICH IN THE LAKE DISPLAYED . . . 36   3 DON JUAN 6   60   5
FAZZIOLI
     EXCEPTING THE VENETIAN FAZZIOLI 160   2 DON JUAN 2   7   8
FEAR
     SHOULD RASHLY QUOTE FOR FEAR OF A MISTAKE) 74   2 DON JUAN 1   98   6
     FOR FEAR SOME PRUDISH READERS SHOULD GROW SKITTISH . 141   2 DON JUAN 1   209   7
     AND THE DIM DESOLATE DEEP TWELVE DAYS HAD FEAR . . . 182   2 DON JUAN 2   49   7
     GAZED DIM AND DESOLATE--TWELVE DAYS HAD FEAR 182   2 DON JUAN 2   49   V7
     ELSEWHERE WAS NOTHING--SHE HAD NOUGHT TO FEAR . . . 264   2 DON JUAN 2   202   7
     RAGE FEAR HATE JEALOUSY REVENGE COMPUNCTION 271   2 DON JUAN 2   215   6
     FOR AUTHORS FEAR DESCRIPTION MIGHT DISPARAGE 280   2 DON JUAN 3   9   4
     WITH JOY AND SORROW HOPE AND FEAR TO SEE 363   2 DON JUAN 4   36   2
     FOR FEAR OF SEEMING RATHER TOUCH'D MYSELF-- 384   2 DON JUAN 4   74   4
     TRAMPLED WHAT THEY SCARCE TROD FOR FEAR OF STAINING . 450   2 DON JUAN 5   66   3
     WHAT FEAR YOU THINK YOU THIS A LION'S DEN 458   2 DON JUAN 5   81   6
     THE MATRON FROWNED WHY SO--FOR FEAR OF GHOSTS 30   3 DON JUAN 6   48   2
     I FEAR JUANNA'S DREAMS WOULD BE BUT FEW 30   3 DON JUAN 6   48   8
     BEGAN AS IS THE CONSEQUENCE OF FEAR 45   3 DON JUAN 6   79   2
     FOR FEAR OF ANY ERROR LIKE THE LATE 62   3 DON JUAN 6   112   8
     MUST I RESTRAIN ME THROUGH THE FEAR OF STRIFE 69   3 DON JUAN 7   6   7
     TOOK LIKE CAMELIONS SOME SLIGHT TINGE OF FEAR . . . 148   3 DON JUAN 8   73   4
     IN JUAN'S LOOK PAIN PLEASURE HOPE FEAR MIXED 159   3 DON JUAN 8   96   3
     WHOSE STATUES WARM (I FEAR ALAS TOO TRUE 'TIS) . . . 208   3 DON JUAN 9   51   6
     DON JUAN GREW I FEAR A LITTLE DISSIPATED 236   3 DON JUAN 10   23   3
     WHILE I WITHOUT REMORSE OF RHYME OR FEAR 393   3 DON JUAN 13   74   2
     AND THERE'S A COURAGE WHICH GROWS OUT OF FEAR . . . 412   3 DON JUAN 14   5   2
     FOR FEAR WE SHOULD SUPPOSE US QUITE IN HEAVEN . . . 525   3 DON JUAN 16   49   8
     SHOULD CAUSE MORE FEAR THAN A WHOLE HOST'S IDENTITY . 559   3 DON JUAN 16   120   8
FEAR'D
     THEY FEAR'D NO EYES NOR EARS ON THAT LONE BEACH . . . 256   2 DON JUAN 2   189   1
     HE FEAR'D HIS NECK TO VENTURE SUCH A NAG ON 333   2 DON JUAN 3   99   6
     SOME HOPED THINGS MIGHT NOT TURN OUT AS THEY FEAR'D . 429   3 DON JUAN 14   44   3
     IT WAS NOT THAT SHE FEAR'D THE VERY WORST 437   3 DON JUAN 14   62   1
FEARED
     MORE FEARED THAN ALL THE SULTANS EVER SEEN 104   3 DON JUAN 7   73   8
FEARFUL
     THE GROSSER PARTS BUT FEARFUL TO DEFACE 46   2 DON JUAN 1   44   4

259

FEARFUL   (CONTINUED)
    TO BE A LOVELY AND A FEARFUL THING   262   2 DON JUAN 2   199   2
    'TIS MELANCHOLY AND A FEARFUL SIGN   277   2 DON JUAN 3   5   1
    BACK TO OLD THOUGHTS WAX'D FULL OF FEARFUL MEANING . .   379   2 DON JUAN 4   64   8
    YET LIKE THEIR MASTERS FEARFUL OF OFFENDING   539   3 DON JUAN 16   79   6
FEARLESS
    FEARLESS--BECAUSE NO FEELING DWELLS IN ICE   18   2 DON JUAN D   15   7
FEARS
    AND OF THE FOLLY OF ALL PRUDISH FEARS   78   2 DON JUAN 1   107   2
    OR FOR SO YOUNG A HUSBAND'S JEALOUS FEARS--   106   2 DON JUAN 1   155   3
    IT WITH A PAIR OF PISTOLS AND THEIR FEARS   174   2 DON JUAN 2   35   4
    AND IF HE WEPT AT LENGTH THEY WERE NOT FEARS   179   2 DON JUAN 2   43   5
    COULD NOT YET SEPARATE THEIR HOPES FROM FEARS   208   2 DON JUAN 2   98   3
    WITH LOVE FOR MANY AND WITH FEARS FOR SOME   286   2 DON JUAN 3   21   6
    SHE STOOD AS ONE WHO CHAMPION'D HUMAN FEARS-- . . .   367   2 DON JUAN 4   43   3
    OF HOPES AND FEARS WHICH SHAKE A SINGLE BALL . . .   304   3 DON JUAN 11   72   8
    TO PLUNGE WITH ALL YOUR FEARS--BUT WHERE YOU KNOW NOT   413   3 DON JUAN 14   6   7
    GAVE HER A RIGHT TO HAVE MATERNAL FEARS   432   3 DON JUAN 14   52   5
FEASIBLE
    HER PLAN SHE DEEM'D BOTH INNOCENT AND FEASIBLE   66   2 DON JUAN 1   83   1
FEAST
    PERHAPS YOU THINK IN STUMBLING ON THIS FEAST   296   2 DON JUAN 3   40   1
    T' OUR TALE--THE FEAST WAS OVER THE SLAVES GONE . .   334   2 DON JUAN 3   101   1
    OF LACQUEYS USHER TO THE FEAST PREPARED   439   2 DON JUAN 5   50   4
    THAT THEY WERE GOING TO A MARRIAGE FEAST   90   3 DON JUAN 7   49   2
    THAT I DISSERT LIKE GRACE BEFORE A FEAST   334   3 DON JUAN 12   39   3
    IN THE FEAST PECKING LESS THAN I CAN TELL   487   3 DON JUAN 15   70   4
    BUT 'TWAS A PUBLIC FEAST AND PUBLIC DAY--   538   3 DON JUAN 16   78   5
FEASTS
    THEIR LOVES AND FEASTS AND HOUSE AND DRESS AND MODE . .   317   2 DON JUAN 3   81   7
    OF HIM WHO FEASTS AND FIGHTS AND ROARS AND REVELS . . .   237   3 DON JUAN 10   25   4
    TO PASS THE STYX FOR MORE SUBSTANTIAL FEASTS   404   3 DON JUAN 13   99   4
    (HIS FEASTS ARE NOT THE WORST PART OF HIS WORKS) . .   482   3 DON JUAN 15   62   4
FEAT
    AS ONCE (A FEAT ON WHICH OURSELVES WE PRIDED)   211   2 DON JUAN 2   105   7
FEATHER
    THEIR FAVOUR IN AN AUTHOR'S CAP'S A FEATHER   135   2 DON JUAN 1   199   5
    ARE THINGS THE TURNING OF A HAIR OR FEATHER   65   3 DON JUAN 6   119   6
FEATHERS
    HAD FEATHERS WHEN A TRAVELLER ON DEEP WAYS IS   197   3 DON JUAN 9   30   8
FEATS
    AS THESE NEW CANTOS TOUCH ON WARLIKE FEATS   187   3 DON JUAN 9   10   1
    FULL GROWS HIS BAG AND WONDERFUL HIS FEATS   394   3 DON JUAN 13   75   6
FEATURE
    WITH THE MOST REGULATED CHARMS OF FEATURE   32   3 DON JUAN 6   52   3
    SELDOM HE VARIED FEATURE HUE OR MUSCLE   132   3 DON JUAN 8   39   7
    AS WARM IN HEART AS FEMININE IN FEATURE   138   3 DON JUAN 8   52   8
    WITH ALL THE ADDED CHARM OF FORM AND FEATURE   478   3 DON JUAN 15   52   4
    BECAUSE SHE DID NOT PIN HER FAITH ON FEATURE   480   3 DON JUAN 15   56   8
    WAS OBVIOUS IN EACH FEATURE OF HER FACE   550   3 DON JUAN 16   102   3
FEATURES
    ELSE HOW THE DEVIL IS IT THAT FRESH FEATURES   267   2 DON JUAN 2   208   7
    LIKE TO HER FATHER'S FEATURES TILL EACH TRACE   363   2 DON JUAN 4   35   3
    I SAID THEY WERE ALIKE THEIR FEATURES AND   368   2 DON JUAN 4   45   1
    YOU READ MY STANZAS AND I READ YOUR FEATURES   405   2 DON JUAN 4   111   3
    THEIR PASSIONS AND ARE DEXT'ROUS SOME BY FEATURES . .   425   2 DON JUAN 5   27   4
    THE GATE SO SPLENDID WAS IN ALL ITS FEATURES . . .   462   2 DON JUAN 5   87   7
    OF FORMS AND FEATURES IT WOULD STRIKE YOU BLIND . . .   467   2 DON JUAN 5   97   6
    HER FEATURES ALL THE SWEETNESS OF THE DEVIL   474   2 DON JUAN 5   109   2
    HIS YOUTH AND FEATURES FAVOURED THE DISGUISE   477   2 DON JUAN 5   115   1
    CONCEALED HER FEATURES BETTER THAN A VEIL   60   3 DON JUAN 6   109   2
    DO JUST WHATE'ER THEY PLEASE BY DINT OF FEATURES . .   167   3 DON JUAN 8   111   8
FED
    ON THE SIXTH DAY THEY FED UPON HIS HIDE   193   2 DON JUAN 2   71   1
    FED UPON BEEF--I WON'T SAY MUCH OF BEER   238   2 DON JUAN 2   156   2
    WHO WATCH'D HIM LIKE A MOTHER WOULD HAVE FED   239   2 DON JUAN 2   158   2
    AND FED BY SPOONFULS ELSE THEY ALWAYS BURST   239   2 DON JUAN 2   158   2
    HE FOUGHT BUT HAS NOT FED SO WELL OF LATE   185   3 DON JUAN 9   6   5
    OF OFFICE OR THE HOUSE OF OFFICE FED   287   3 DON JUAN 11   40   6
    BROAD AS TRANSPARENT DEEP AND FRESHLY FED   385   3 DON JUAN 13   57   2
    WITH WHAT HE HAD SEEN HIS PHANTASY HE FED   512   3 DON JUAN 16   27   6
FEE
    BUT SCARCE A FEE WAS PAID ON EITHER SIDE   38   2 DON JUAN 1   32   7
    BECAUSE NO DOUBT 'TWAS FOR HIS DIRTY FEE   103   2 DON JUAN 1   151   7
    THE SURGEON AS THERE WAS NO OTHER FEE   197   2 DON JUAN 2   77   1
    FEE BY A COUNSEL FELON BY A JAILOR   424   2 DON JUAN 5   26   8
    THEIR FEE BUT ERE THE WATERED WHEELS MAY HISS HENCE . .   379   3 DON JUAN 13   46   7
FEEBLE
    PRETTY WERE BUT TO GIVE A FEEBLE NOTION   51   2 DON JUAN 1   55   4
    JUST AS HIS FEEBLE ARMS COULD STRIKE NO MORE . . .   212   2 DON JUAN 2   107   3
    AND PRIDE MY FEEBLE--LET US RAMBLE ON   466   3 DON JUAN 15   22   2
FEE'D
    I WOULD NOT YOU FOR NOTHING SHOULD BE FEE'D-- . . .   104   2 DON JUAN 1   152   6
    THE ADULTERER'S ADVOCATE WHEN DULY FEE'D   151   2 DON JUAN 1 V 2   2
    AND BEING FLUENT (SAVE INDEED WHEN FEE'D ILL)   317   2 DON JUAN 3   80   6
FEED
    THEN FEED HER FAMINE FAT WITH WELLESLEY'S GLORY . . .   174   3 DON JUAN 8   125   8
    WILL FEED UPON THE FAIREST FRESHEST CHEEK   243   3 DON JUAN 10   38   3
FEEDING
    OF FEEDING BRATS THE MOMENT HIS WIFE WEANS   325   3 DON JUAN 12   21   8

```
                                                          PAGE VOL    CANTO  STANZA LN
FEEDS
    THE QUIET SHEEP FEEDS AND THE TORTOISE CRAWLS  . . . . .  386  2 DON JUAN   4     77   8
    FEEDS YOU BY PRINTING HALF THE REALM'S STARVATION--  . . .  200  3 DON JUAN   9     35   8
FEEL
    SCOPE TO ALL SUCH AS FEEL THE INHERENT GLOW  . . . . . .   13  2 DON JUAN   D      7   6
    FOR I WILL NEVER FEEL THEM--ITALY  . . . . . . . . .   19  2 DON JUAN   D     16   2
    PREFERENCE THAT WE MUST FEEL UPON OCCASION  . . . . .   63  2 DON JUAN   1     77   6
    GOD GRANT YOU FEEL NOT THEN THE BITTEREST GRIEF  . . . .  107  2 DON JUAN   1    157   7
    TO NEWSPAPERS WHOSE TRUTH ALL KNOW AND FEEL . . . . .  138  2 DON JUAN   1    203   3
    AND FEEL NO MORE THE SPIRIT TO RETORT I  . . . . . .  143  2 DON JUAN   1    213   6
    EVEN NATIONS FEEL THIS WHEN THEY GO TO WAR  . . . . .  164  2 DON JUAN   2     14   4
    FEEL NOW HIS APPETITE INCREASED MUCH MORE  . . . . .  198  2 DON JUAN   2     78   5
    WITH JUST ENOUGH OF LIFE TO FEEL ITS PAIN  . . . . .  213  2 DON JUAN   2    108   7
    FEEL RAPTURE BUT NOT SUCH TRUE JOY ARE REAPING . . . .  261  2 DON JUAN   2    196   7
    TORTURE IS THEIRS WHAT THEY INFLICT THEY FEEL  . . . .  262  2 DON JUAN   2    199   8
    MADE BUT TO LOVE TO FEEL THAT SHE WAS HIS  . . . . .  264  2 DON JUAN   2    202   5
    TO FEEL THE POISON THROUGH HER SPIRIT CREEPING . . . .  274  2 DON JUAN   3      1   5
    AND STILL THEY SEEM RESENTFULLY TO FEEL  . . . . . .  313  2 DON JUAN   3     73   5
    HER OVERPOWERING PRESENCE MADE YOU FEEL  . . . . . .  313  2 DON JUAN   3     74   7
    I KNOW NOT HOW--HER PRESENCE MADE YE FEEL  . . . . .  313  2 DON JUAN   3     74  V7
    TO FEEL AT LEAST A PATRIOT'S SHAME . . . . . . . .  323  2 DON JUAN   3  L  6   3
    WE FEEL WITHOUT HIM WORDSWORTH SOMETIMES WAKES . . . .  333  2 DON JUAN   3     98   2
    I FEEL THIS TEDIOUSNESS WILL NEVER DO--  . . . . . .  342  2 DON JUAN   3    111   1
    SENSELESS TO FEEL AND WITH SEAL'D EYES TO SEE  . . . .  360  2 DON JUAN   4     30   8
    I FEEL MY HEART BECOME SO SYMPATHETIC . . . . . . .  372  2 DON JUAN   4     52   5
    COULD STIR HIS PULSE OR MAKE HIS FAITH FEEL BRITTLE  . . .  396  2 DON JUAN   4     95   7
    TO FEEL FOR NONE IS THE TRUE SOCIAL ART  . . . . . .  423  2 DON JUAN   5     25   7
    MAKES US FEEL OUR MORTALITY IN FACT  . . . . . . .  428  2 DON JUAN   5     32   3
    ELSE THEY SHALL FEEL THE WEIGHT OF THIS MY ARM . . . .  459  2 DON JUAN   5     82   3
    WHOSE FANGS EVE TAUGHT HER HUMAN SEED TO FEEL  . . . .  153  3 DON JUAN   8     83   4
    SO LOFTY THAT I FEEL MY BRAIN TURN ROUND . . . . . .  224  3 DON JUAN   9     85   5
    WHAT EVEN YOUNG STRANGERS FEEL A LITTLE STRONG . . . .  257  3 DON JUAN  10     65   3
    I FEEL A MIXED REGRET AND VENERATION  . . . . . . .  257  3 DON JUAN  10     66   4
    IN LAW THAN EQUITY--AS I CAN FEEL--  . . . . . . .  357  3 DON JUAN  12  V 18   4
    HIS BELL-MOUTHED GOBLET MAKES ME FEEL QUITE DANISH  . . .  392  3 DON JUAN  13     72   7
    AND NOW BECAUSE I FEEL IT GROWING DULL  . . . . . .  415  3 DON JUAN  14     10   8
    SO AS TO MAKE THEM FEEL HE KNEW HIS STATION  . . . .  462  3 DON JUAN  15     15   6
    JUST AS I FEEL THE IMPROVVISATORE  . . . . . . . .  465  3 DON JUAN  15     20   8
    TO FEEL IN FRIENDLESS PALACES A HOME . . . . . . .  475  3 DON JUAN  15     44   7
    TO FEEL THAT FLATTERY WHICH ATTRACTS THE PROUD . . . .  493  3 DON JUAN  15     83   6
    I FEEL SOME CHILLY MIDNIGHT SHUDDERINGS  . . . . . .  500  3 DON JUAN  15     98   4
    FEEL SOME ABSTRACTION WHEN THEY GAZE ON HER  . . . .  506  3 DON JUAN  16     14   3
    HIS READINESS TO FEEL HIS PULSE AND TELL . . . . . .  514  3 DON JUAN  16     32   7
    AND ONLY THINK OR ACT OR FEEL WITH REFERENCE . . . .  541  3 DON JUAN  16     85   6
    OF WEARINESS OR SCORN) BEGAN TO FEEL  . . . . . . .  546  3 DON JUAN  16     96   7
FEELING
    FEARLESS--BECAUSE NO FEELING DWELLS IN ICE . . . . .   18  2 DON JUAN   D     15   7
    TO PUBLIC FEELING WHICH ON THIS OCCASION . . . . . .   38  2 DON JUAN   1     33   7
    THE PUBLIC FEELING AND THE LAWYERS' FEES . . . . . .   39  2 DON JUAN   1     34   2
    A FEELING DANGEROUS TO A PRUDENT SPOUSE  . . . . . .   81  2 DON JUAN   1    111   8
    AS I AM BLOOD--BONE--MARROW PASSION--FEELING--  . . . .  156  2 DON JUAN   1  V 8   2
    NOW FEELING ALL THE VULTURE IN HIS JAWS  . . . . . .  193  2 DON JUAN   2     71   4
    OR SLEEP OR WHATSOE'ER IT WAS BY FEELING . . . . . .  237  2 DON JUAN   2    153   2
    AND FEELING STILL THE FAMISH'D VULTURE GNAW  . . . .  239  2 DON JUAN   2    157   6
    THEY HAD NO FURTHER FEELING HOPE NOR CARE--  . . . .  256  2 DON JUAN   2    189  V6
    YET 'TIS A PAINFUL FEELING AND UNWILLING . . . . . .  270  2 DON JUAN   2    213   1
    HIS STRAIN DISPLAY'D SOME FEELING--RIGHT OR WRONG  . . .  326  2 DON JUAN   3     87   5
    AND FEELING IN A POET IS THE SOURCE  . . . . . . .  326  2 DON JUAN   3     87   6
    OF OTHERS' FEELING BUT THEY ARE SUCH LIARS . . . . .  326  2 DON JUAN   3     87   7
    OF FEELING FOR SOME KINDNESS DONE WHEN POWER . . . .  339  2 DON JUAN   3    109   7
    WHATEVER FEELING SHOOK HER IT SEEM'D SHORT . . . . .  356  2 DON JUAN   4     23   3
    OF THIS THEIR MUTUAL FEELING SHE REPLIED--  . . . . .  356  2 DON JUAN   4     23   6
    A FEELING IN EACH FOOTSTEP AS DISCLOSED  . . . . . .   61  3 DON JUAN   6    111   5
    WHAT DOST THOU KNOW OF LOVE OR FEELING--WRETCH . . . .   63  3 DON JUAN   6    116   1
    OF FEELING FOR HOWEVER HABIT SEARS . . . . . . . .  102  3 DON JUAN   7     69   5
    THIS FEELING 'TIS NOT EASY TO EXPRESS  . . . . . . .  415  3 DON JUAN  14     12   5
    WAS NOT CONFINED TO FEELING FOR HER FRIEND . . . . .  432  3 DON JUAN  14     51   2
    THE TONES THE FEELING AND THE EXECUTION  . . . . . .  521  3 DON JUAN  16     41   7
    THERE WAS A DEPTH OF FEELING TO EMBRACE  . . . . . .  524  3 DON JUAN  16     48   7
FEELINGS
    NO CHOICE WAS LEFT HIS FEELINGS OR HIS PRIDE . . . .   41  2 DON JUAN   1     36   7
    IN FEELINGS QUICK AS OVID'S MISS MEDEA . . . . . .   68  2 DON JUAN   1     86   4
    GRIEVED BUT PERHAPS HER FEELINGS MAY BE BETTER . . . .  129  2 DON JUAN   1    191   7
    AND THEN ONCE MORE HIS FEELINGS BACK WERE BROUGHT  . . .  215  2 DON JUAN   2    112   6
    SHE KNEW THAT THE BEST FEELINGS MUST HAVE VICTUAL  . . .  233  2 DON JUAN   2    145   1
    SOME FEELINGS UNIVERSAL AS THE SUN . . . . . . . .  244  2 DON JUAN   2    167   3
    BY THEIR OWN FEELINGS HALLOW'D AND UNITED  . . . . .  265  2 DON JUAN   2    204   5
    ALL FEELINGS WHICH O'ERLEAP THE YEARS LONG LOST  . . .  286  2 DON JUAN   3     21   7
    A THING TO HUMAN FEELINGS THE MOST TRYING  . . . . .  301  2 DON JUAN   3     51   2
    HIS ONLY SHRINE OF FEELINGS UNDEFILED  . . . . . . .  302  2 DON JUAN   3     52   8
    HIS FEELINGS FROM ALL MILK OF HUMAN KINDNESS . . . .  304  2 DON JUAN   3     57   7
    BUT THERE ARE HUMAN FEELINGS PAST ASSUAGING  . . . .  305  2 DON JUAN   3     58  V5
    RESTORES ALL HUMAN FEELINGS TO BURLESQUE . . . . . .  345  2 DON JUAN   4      3  V8
    YOUNG INNATE FEELINGS ALL HAVE FELT BELOW  . . . . .  353  2 DON JUAN   4     18   5
    FOR FEELINGS CAUSELESS OR AT LEAST ABSTRUSE  . . . .  355  2 DON JUAN   4     22   8
    WHICH MIX'D ALL FEELINGS FRIEND CHILD LOVER BROTHER  . . .  357  2 DON JUAN   4     26   3
    HER FEELINGS SUDDEN THROUGH HER BOSOM SENT . . . . .  379  2 DON JUAN   4     65  V6
    WHOM TO THE SPOT THEIR SCHOOL-BOY FEELINGS BEAR  . . . .  387  2 DON JUAN   4     78   5
    AND THE UNQUIET FEELINGS WHICH FIRST WOKE  . . . . .  402  2 DON JUAN   4    106   3
```

261

FEELINGS   (CONTINUED)

	PAGE	VOL		CANTO	STANZA	LN
ALL FEELINGS CHANGED BUT THIS WAS LAST TO VARY	413	2 DON JUAN	5	4	5
COMMENCE WITH FEELINGS WARM AND PROSPECTS HIGH	421	2 DON JUAN	5	21	5
SOME TO MEN'S FEELINGS OTHERS TO THEIR REASON	437	2 DON JUAN	5	48	2
OF THE BEST FEELINGS OF MANKIND WHICH GROW	439	2 DON JUAN	5	49	5
FOR KINDER FEELINGS WHATSOE'ER THEIR NATION	480	2 DON JUAN	5	120	4
RESTORE ME THOSE PURE FEELINGS GONE FOREVER	9	3 DON JUAN	6	5	8
ALOUD BECAUSE HIS FEELINGS WERE TOO TENDER	50	3 DON JUAN	6	89	3
BUT YOUR OWN FEELINGS EVEN SHOULD ALL THE REST	63	3 DON JUAN	6	115	1
THOUGH LITTLE VERSED IN FEELINGS ORIENTAL	105	3 DON JUAN	7	75	2
HAS FEELINGS PURE AND POLISHED AS A GEM--	157	3 DON JUAN	8	92	4
BETWEEN YOUR FAME AND FEELINGS PRIDE AND PITY--	162	3 DON JUAN	8	101	4
THE TWO FIRST FEELINGS RAN THEIR COURSE COMPLETE	213	3 DON JUAN	9	61	1
ALL MY BOY FEELINGS ALL MY GENTLER DREAMS	233	3 DON JUAN	10	18	4
THEY CANNOT QUENCH YOUNG FEELINGS FRESH AND EARLY	234	3 DON JUAN	10	19	6
ON OUR FRESH FEELINGS BUT--AS BEING PARTICIPATED	236	3 DON JUAN	10	23	5
PARENTAL FEELINGS AND THE OTHER CLASS	250	3 DON JUAN	10	53	5
OF ALL HIS FEELINGS--ONLY HE FORGOT 'EM	251	3 DON JUAN	10	54	8
WITH THE SAME FEELINGS AS YOU'D COAX A VAMPIRE	299	3 DON JUAN	11	62	5
TO SAY HER DAUGHTER'S FEELINGS ARE TREPANNED	343	3 DON JUAN	12	60	2
BUT HARROW UP HIS FEELINGS TILL THEY WITHER	355	3 DON JUAN	12	86	6
HIS FEELINGS HAD NOT THOSE STRANGE FITS LIKE TERTIANS	366	3 DON JUAN	13	17	5
AND KINDLED FEELINGS IN THE ROUGHEST HEART	386	3 DON JUAN	13	59	6
OUR FEELINGS 'GAINST THE NATURE OF THE SOIL	447	3 DON JUAN	14	86	4
AND YOUR TRUE FEELINGS FULLY UNDERSTOOD	451	3 DON JUAN	14	93	6
UNTO SUCH FEELINGS AS SEEM'D INNOCENT	460	3 DON JUAN	15	10	7
FEELINGS OF YOUTH LIKE THOSE WHICH OVERTHROWN LIE	475	3 DON JUAN	15	44	5
SHE HELD THEIR OLD FAITH AND OLD FEELINGS FAST	476	3 DON JUAN	15	46	8
SHE NEITHER DEEMED HIS FEELINGS WERE INTENSE	493	3 DON JUAN	15	83	V5
SOMETIMES UNLESS MY FEELINGS RATHER ERR)	506	3 DON JUAN	16	14	5
OF JUAN'S NERVOUS FEELINGS ON THAT DAY	526	3 DON JUAN	16	51	4
IN HIM SOME FEELINGS HE HAD LATELY LOST	553	3 DON JUAN	16	107	6
OR HARDENED FEELINGS WHICH PERHAPS IDEAL	553	3 DON JUAN	16	107	7
HE SATE WITH FEELINGS AWKWARD TO EXPRESS	555	3 DON JUAN	16	111	6

FEELS

	PAGE	VOL		CANTO	STANZA	LN
THE VERY THING WHICH EVERYBODY FEELS	69	2 DON JUAN	1	89	3
REPLETION RATHER ADDS TO WHAT HE FEELS	427	2 DON JUAN	5	31	4
SO NOW ALL THINGS AS DAMN'D ONE FEELS AT EASE	17	3 DON JUAN	6	23	1
AT LEAST HE FEELS IT AND SOME SAY HE SEES	109	3 DON JUAN	7	85	1
SOME HUNGER TOO THEY SAY THE PEOPLE FEELS--	185	3 DON JUAN	9	6	6

FEES

	PAGE	VOL		CANTO	STANZA	LN
THE PUBLIC FEELING AND THE LAWYERS' FEES	39	2 DON JUAN	1	34	2
INTO SOME SIXTY THOUSAND NEW KNIGHTS' FEES	242	3 DON JUAN	10	35	8
DOCTORS LESS FAMOUS FOR THEIR CURES THAN FEES	431	3 DON JUAN	14	48	4
BUT LUCKILY I HAVE PAID FEW PARISH FEES SINCE)	530	3 DON JUAN	16	61	6

FEET

	PAGE	VOL		CANTO	STANZA	LN
HAVE I NOT HAD TWO BISHOPS AT MY FEET	103	2 DON JUAN	1	150	1
ARE SUCH AS FIT WITH LADY'S FEET BUT THESE	121	2 DON JUAN	1	181	2
HASTE--HASTE--I HEAR ALFONSO'S HURRYING FEET--	121	2 DON JUAN	1	182	7
A CANTO--THEN THEIR FEET AND ANCLES--WELL	160	2 DON JUAN	2	6	6
THE PUMPS AND THERE WERE FOUR FEET WATER FOUND	170	2 DON JUAN	2	27	8
AND KEEP THE SHIP AFLOAT THOUGH THREE FEET YET	172	2 DON JUAN	2	30	3
HER SMALL SNOW FEET HAD SLIPPERS BUT NO STOCKING	220	2 DON JUAN	2	121	8
HAIDEE AND JUAN CARPETED THEIR FEET	309	2 DON JUAN	3	67	1
HAIDEE AND HER BELOVED HID THEIR FEET	309	2 DON JUAN	3	67	V1
HIS VERSES RARELY WANTED THEIR DUE FEET--	316	2 DON JUAN	3	78	5
O'ER THE SHARP SHINGLES WITH HER BLEEDING FEET	361	2 DON JUAN	4	32	2
AND WET AND COLD AND LIFELESS AT HER FEET	362	2 DON JUAN	4	34	1
AS IF THE MILKY WAY THEIR FEET WAS UNDER	450	2 DON JUAN	5	66	4
THERE WAS A SELF-WILL EVEN IN HER SMALL FEET	475	2 DON JUAN	5	111	3
AND FEET SO SMALL THEY SCARCE SEEMED MADE TO TREAD	26	3 DON JUAN	6	41	4
HER FEET THAT HER FIRST MOVEMENT WAS TO STOOP	44	3 DON JUAN	6	77	3
FORTY FEET HIGH UPON A CAVALIERE	72	3 DON JUAN	7	12	8
THUS THE SAME CAUSE WHICH MAKES A VERSE WANT FEET	79	3 DON JUAN	7	26	3
SOME HUNDRED FEET IN HEIGHT NOT TO SAY MILES	201	3 DON JUAN	9	38	7
BUT WHEN ON THE LIEUTENANT AT HER FEET	213	3 DON JUAN	9	61	5
BEFORE DON JUAN'S FEET HE COULD NOT TELL	276	3 DON JUAN	11	17	2
KISS HANDS FEET ANY PART OF MAJESTY	286	3 DON JUAN	11	38	6
AT EIGHTEEN THOUGH BELOW HER FEET STILL PANTED	434	3 DON JUAN	14	55	5

FEIGNS

	PAGE	VOL		CANTO	STANZA	LN
YOUR SYSTEM FEIGNS O'ER THE CONTROLLESS CORE	84	2 DON JUAN	1	116	4

FEINAGLE'S

	PAGE	VOL		CANTO	STANZA	LN
FOR HER FEINAGLE'S WERE AN USELESS ART	27	2 DON JUAN	1	11	5

FELICITY

	PAGE	VOL		CANTO	STANZA	LN
DRAPERIED HER FORM WITH CURIOUS FELICITY	550	3 DON JUAN	16	102	8

FELL

	PAGE	VOL		CANTO	STANZA	LN
FOR THERE WE HAVE THEM ALL AT ONE FELL SWOOP	46	2 DON JUAN	1	45	1
WHEN PROUD GRENADA FELL AND FORCED TO FLY	52	2 DON JUAN	1	56	5
SOONER SHALL HEAVEN KISS EARTH--(HERE HE FELL SICKER)	167	2 DON JUAN	2	20	1
AND FELL ALL RAVENOUSLY ON THEIR PROVISION	192	2 DON JUAN	2	68	7
AND THE LOT FELL ON JUAN'S LUCKLESS TUTOR	195	2 DON JUAN	2	75	8
AND THE SAME NIGHT THERE FELL A SHOWER OF RAIN	201	2 DON JUAN	2	84	1
NIGHT FELL--THIS SEEM'D A BETTER OMEN STILL	206	2 DON JUAN	2	94	8
AND FELL UPON THEIR GLAZED EYES LIKE A SCREEN	210	2 DON JUAN	2	103	5
HE FELL UPON HIS SIDE AND HIS STRETCH'D HAND	214	2 DON JUAN	2	110	4
HE FELL UPON WHATE'ER WAS OFFER'D LIKE	239	2 DON JUAN	2	157	7
THEY THUS ADDRESS'D--AND LAMBRO'S VISAGE FELL--	298	2 DON JUAN	3	44	2
WHICH FROZE TO MARBLE AS IT FELL SHE THOUGHT	362	2 DON JUAN	4	33	8
THEN SHRIEKING SHE AROSE AND SHRIEKING FELL	363	2 DON JUAN	4	36	1

FELL   (CONTINUED)

	PAGE	VOL	CANTO		STANZA	LN
AND THEN THEY BOUND HIM ,WHERE HE FELL AND BORE	371	2	DON JUAN	4	50	1
AND ALL BECAUSE A LADY FELL IN LOVE	371	2	DON JUAN	4	51	8
HER WRITHING FELL SHE LIKE A CEDAR FELL'D	375	2	DON JUAN	4	58	8
AND HUGE TOMBS WORSE--MANKIND SINCE ADAM FELL	444	2	DON JUAN	5	59	6
KEEP YOUR GOOD NAME THOUGH EVE HERSELF ONCE FELL	460	2	DON JUAN	5	84	6
PRESERVE YOUR STATE--THOUGH EVE EARTH'S MOTHER FELL	460	2	DON JUAN	5	84	V6
OF ROME TRANSPLANTED FELL WITH CONSTANTINE	461	2	DON JUAN	5	86	8
ONE NECK WHICH HE WITH ONE FELL STROKE MIGHT PIERCE	19	3	DON JUAN	6	27	3
IT FELL DOWN OF ITS OWN ACCORD BEFORE	44	3	DON JUAN	6	77	2
FELL IN LONG TRESSES LIKE THE WEEPING WILLOW	60	3	DON JUAN	6	108	2
HE FELL IMMORTAL IN A BULLETIN	76	3	DON JUAN	7	20	8
BUT HERE THE EFFECT FELL SHORT OF THEIR DESIRE	82	3	DON JUAN	7	31	6
OF OFFICERS A THIRD FELL ON THE SPOT	119	3	DON JUAN	8	16	5
FELL IN WITH WHAT WAS LATE THE SECOND COLUMN	130	3	DON JUAN	8	34	2
THEY FELL AS THICK AS HARVESTS BENEATH HAIL	134	3	DON JUAN	8	43	1
JUAN AND JOHNSON WHEREUPON THEY FELL	166	3	DON JUAN	8	109	2
SHE FELL WITH BUONAPARTE--WHAT STRANGE THOUGHTS	198	3	DON JUAN	9	32	7
IN THY PERENNIAL FOUNTAIN--HOW MAN FELL I	210	3	DON JUAN	9	55	5
AND SO THEY FELL IN LOVE--SHE WITH HIS FACE	216	3	DON JUAN	9	67	2
FELL INTO THAT NO LESS IMPERIOUS PASSION	216	3	DON JUAN	9	68	2
MAN FELL WITH APPLES AND WITH APPLES ROSE	226	3	DON JUAN	10	2	1
WHO FELL AS ROLLS AN OX O'ER IN HIS PASTURE	274	3	DON JUAN	11	13	5
THE DROPS FELL FROM HIS DEATH-WOUND AND HE DREW ILL	276	3	DON JUAN	11	16	6
THE CRAVAT STAINED WITH BLOODY DROPS FELL DOWN	276	3	DON JUAN	11	17	1
ADMITTED A SMALL PARTY AS NIGHT FELL--	282	3	DON JUAN	11	29	5
BUT I WILL FALL AT LEAST AS FELL MY HERO	296	3	DON JUAN	11	56	5
BUT THESE HAD FALLEN NOT WHEN THE FRIARS FELL	386	3	DON JUAN	13	60	3
HIS CURLS FELL NEGLIGENTLY O'ER HIS FRONT	513	3	DON JUAN	16	29	5
WHEN DEEP SLEEP FELL ON MEN AND THE WORLD WORE	556	3	DON JUAN	16	113	6
ON WHICH THE MOONBEAMS FELL IN SILVERY SHOWERS	559	3	DON JUAN	16	120	3
BACK FELL THE SABLE FROCK AND DREARY COWL	561	3	DON JUAN	16	123	5

FELL'D

	PAGE	VOL	CANTO		STANZA	LN
HER WRITHING FELL SHE LIKE A CEDAR FELL'D	375	2	DON JUAN	4	58	8
ALAS WORLDS FALL--AND WOMAN SINCE SHE FELL'D	420	3	DON JUAN	14	23	1

FELLED

	PAGE	VOL	CANTO		STANZA	LN
THE EARTH WHICH HE BECAME LIKE A FELLED TREE	169	3	DON JUAN	8	116	6

FELLOW

	PAGE	VOL	CANTO		STANZA	LN
POOR FELLOW HE HAD MANY THINGS TO WOUND HIM	41	2	DON JUAN	1	36	2
POOR LITTLE FELLOW HE HAD NO IDEA	68	2	DON JUAN	1	86	2
A FOOLISH CLEVER FELLOW IDEM SEMPER	150	2	DON JUAN	1	V 1	8
POOR FELLOW HE HAD BETTER FAR BEEN BLIND	155	2	DON JUAN	1	V 7	4
BUT HE POOR FELLOW HAD A WIFE AND CHILDREN	179	2	DON JUAN	2	43	7
A SAD OLD FELLOW WAS HE IF YOU PLEASE	223	2	DON JUAN	2	127	6
IN SHORT HE WAS A VERY PRETTY FELLOW	235	2	DON JUAN	2	148	7
I KNOW NOT QUOTH THE FELLOW WHO OR WHAT	298	2	DON JUAN	3	45	1
ALL GOLD AND CRIMSON SHONE HER JELICK'S FELLOW	311	2	DON JUAN	3	70	6
FINISHED WITH BRIGHT GOLD LACE HER JACKET'S FELLOW	311	2	DON JUAN	3	70	V4
IN COMPANY A VERY PLEASANT FELLOW	318	2	DON JUAN	3	82	2
MORE THAN SUCH MADMEN'S FELLOW MAN--THE MOON'S	341	2	DON JUAN	3	110	4
AS BOY I THOUGHT MYSELF A CLEVER FELLOW	345	2	DON JUAN	4	3	1
NOT SOUND POOR FELLOW BUT SEVERELY WOUNDED	373	2	DON JUAN	4	54	2
HE SAW SOME FELLOW CAPTIVES WHO APPEAR'D	388	2	DON JUAN	4	80	1
THE LITTLE FELLOW REALLY LOOK'D QUITE HEARTY	388	2	DON JUAN	4	81	5
AN IGNORANT NOTELESS TIMELESS TUNELESS FELLOW	391	2	DON JUAN	4	87	4
'TIS PLEASANT PURCHASING OUR FELLOW CREATURES	425	2	DON JUAN	5	27	2
AFTER DISPOSING OF TWO FELLOW CREATURES	426	2	DON JUAN	5	30	V2
POOR FELLOW FOR SOME REASON SURELY BAD	429	2	DON JUAN	5	34	1
LET'S KNOCK THAT OLD BLACK FELLOW ON THE HEAD	434	2	DON JUAN	5	43	7
THIS FELLOW BEING SIX FOOT HIGH COULD RAISE	84	3	DON JUAN	7	37	5
AND THIS YOUNG FELLOW SAY WHAT CAN HE DO	98	3	DON JUAN	7	62	5
BUT JOHNSON WAS A CLEVER FELLOW WHO	130	3	DON JUAN	8	35	5
BY JOVE HE WAS A NOBLE FELLOW JOHNSON	132	3	DON JUAN	8	39	1
HE WAS A JOLLY FELLOW AND COULD CRACK	147	3	DON JUAN	8	70	5
YET YOU'RE A NOBLE FELLOW AND BUT WAIT	185	3	DON JUAN	9	6	V1
THE FELLOW TO LIE GROANING ON THE ROAD	275	3	DON JUAN	11	15	7
POOR FELLOW HIS WAS AN UNTOWARD FATE--	298	3	DON JUAN	11	60	6
JEW ROTHSCHILD AND HIS FELLOW CHRISTIAN BARING	318	3	DON JUAN	12	5	8
PERHAPS THE FINE OLD FELLOW SPOKE IN JEST--	361	3	DON JUAN	13	7	5

FELLOW'S

	PAGE	VOL	CANTO		STANZA	LN
AND WHO SHOULD DIE TO BE HIS FELLOW'S FOOD	194	2	DON JUAN	2	73	8

FELLOWS

	PAGE	VOL	CANTO		STANZA	LN
YOU'RE SHABBY FELLOWS--TRUE--BUT POETS STILL	12	2	DON JUAN	D	6	7
WHEN YOU BROKE IN UPON US WITH YOUR FELLOWS	106	2	DON JUAN	1	156	3
AND WITH HIS FELLOWS OF THE THIRD SEX GET	391	2	DON JUAN	4	86	V5
ALL COMMON FELLOWS WHO MIGHT WRITHE AND WINCE	117	3	DON JUAN	8	11	4
OF TITANS GIANTS FELLOWS OF ABOUT	201	3	DON JUAN	9	38	6
BUT THEY WERE MOSTLY NERVOUS SIX-FOOT FELLOWS	205	3	DON JUAN	9	46	7
(FELLOWS WHOM MESSALINA'S SELF WOULD PENSION)	218	3	DON JUAN	9	72	4

FELLS

	PAGE	VOL	CANTO		STANZA	LN
CASH RULES THE GROVE AND FELLS IT TOO BESIDES	322	3	DON JUAN	12	14	2

FELON

	PAGE	VOL	CANTO		STANZA	LN
FEE BY A COUNSEL FELON BY A JAILOR	424	2	DON JUAN	5	26	8

FELT

	PAGE	VOL	CANTO		STANZA	LN
SHE FELT IT GOING AND RESOLVED TO MAKE	62	2	DON JUAN	1	75	2
GLOW'D IN HER CHEEK AND YET SHE FELT NO WRONG	78	2	DON JUAN	1	106	2
HE FELT THAT CHILLING HEAVINESS OF HEART	167	2	DON JUAN	2	21	1
OF OCEAN WHEN THEY WOKE THEY FELT A QUALM	192	2	DON JUAN	2	68	6
THEY FELT THE FRESHNESS OF ITS GROWING GREEN	210	2	DON JUAN	2	103	3

<pre>
                                                      PAGE VOL   CANTO STANZA LN
FELT   (CONTINUED)
    AND FELT AGAIN WITH HIS DESPAIR O'ERWROUGHT . . . . 215 2 DON JUAN 2   112   4
    AND FELT HER VEINS CHILL'D BY THE NEIGHBOURING SEA . . . 233 2 DON JUAN 2   145   4
    THEY HAD NOT SPOKEN BUT THEY FELT ALLURED . . . . 254 2 DON JUAN 2   187   5
    THEY FELT NO TERRORS FROM THE NIGHT THEY WERE . . . . . 256 2 DON JUAN 2   189   2
    FELT AS IF NEVER MORE TO BEAT APART . . . . 257 2 DON JUAN 2   191   8
    ALL IT HATH FELT INFLICTED PASS'D AND PROVED . . . . . 261 2 DON JUAN 2   197   5
    ON SEEING HIS OWN CHIMNEY-SMOKE FELT GLAD . . . . . . 289 2 DON JUAN 3   26   3
    FOR WITHOUT HEARTS THERE IS NO HOME--AND FELT . . . . 302 2 DON JUAN 3   52   2
    HAVE FELT THAT MOMENT IN ITS FULLEST POWER . . . . . 335 2 DON JUAN 3   102   3
    YOUNG INNATE FEELINGS ALL HAVE FELT BELOW . . . . . . 353 2 DON JUAN 4   18   5
    HE FELT A GRIEF BUT KNOWING CAUSE FOR NONE . . . . . 355 2 DON JUAN 4   22   6
    FELT THE WARM BLOOD WHICH IN HIS FACE WAS GLOWING . . 478 2 DON JUAN 5   117   4
    FELT AN ODD GLISTENING MOISTURE IN HER EYE . . . . . 480 2 DON JUAN 5   120   8
    FELT MOST INDIGNANT STILL AT NOT BEING FREE . . . . . 481 2 DON JUAN 5   121   8
    FOR SHE FELT HUMBLED--AND HUMILIATION . . . . 490 2 DON JUAN 5   137   7
    ALL FELT A SOFT KIND OF CONCATENATION . . . . 25 3 DON JUAN 6   38   6
    BUT CERTAIN 'TIS THEY ALL FELT FOR THEIR NEW . . . . . 25 3 DON JUAN 6   39   1
    FOR LAUGHTER--BUT SHE FELT HER SPIRITS LOW . . . . . 47 3 DON JUAN 6   83   6
    AND SAID SHE FELT HERSELF EXTREMELY WELL . . . . . . 48 3 DON JUAN 6   84   2
    AND SOME OF US HAVE FELT THUS ALL AMORT . . . . . . 59 3 DON JUAN 6   106   5
    THAT HE HIMSELF FELT ONLY LIKE A YOUTH . . . . 69 3 DON JUAN 7   5   7
    IN DITCHES FIELDS OR WHERESOE'ER THEY FELT . . . . . 120 3 DON JUAN 8   18   4
    EVEN FROM A CHILD FELT LIKE A CHILD HOWE'ER . . . . . 139 3 DON JUAN 8   53   2
    OVER A HEAP OF BODIES FELT HIS HEEL . . . . 153 3 DON JUAN 8   83   2
    A DYING MOSLEM WHO HAD FELT THE FOOT . . . . 153 3 DON JUAN 8   84   1
    AND FELT--THOUGH DONE WITH LIFE--HE WAS ALONE . . . 170 3 DON JUAN 8   117   8
    TO THOSE WHO HAD FELT THE INCONVENIENT STATE . . . 177 3 DON JUAN 8   131   3
    HAVE SEEN AND FELT HOW STRONGLY YOU RESTORE . . . . 184 3 DON JUAN 9   3   6
    HE FELT LIKE OTHER PLANTS CALLED SENSITIVE . . . . . 243 3 DON JUAN 10   37   2
    HIS PRIDE TOO FELT THAT SHE WAS NOT ENSLAVED . . . . 251 3 DON JUAN 10   55   4
    THE BLUE SEA'S BORDER AND DON JUAN FELT-- . . . . . 257 3 DON JUAN 10   65   2
    BUT JUAN FELT THOUGH NOT APPROACHING HOME . . . . . 265 3 DON JUAN 10   81   5
    'TIS BETTER ON THE WHOLE TO HAVE FELT AND SEEN . . 431 3 DON JUAN 14   49   5
    SHE MERELY FELT A COMMON SYMPATHY . . . . 449 3 DON JUAN 14   91   5
    FELT ON THE WHOLE AN INTEREST INTENSE-- . . . . . 468 3 DON JUAN 15   28   3
    FELT RESTLESS AND PERPLEXED AND COMPROMISED . . . 506 3 DON JUAN 16   12   2
    JUAN FELT SOMEWHAT PENSIVE AND DISPOSED . . . . . 507 3 DON JUAN 16   15   1
    AS STANDS A STATUE STOOD HE FELT HIS HAIR . . . . 510 3 DON JUAN 16   23   5
FEMALE
    TO OTHERS' SHARE LET FEMALE ERRORS FALL . . . . . . 29 2 DON JUAN 1   16   7
    OF ANY MODERN FEMALE SAINT'S COMPARISON . . . . . . 30 2 DON JUAN 1   17   2
    A LOVELY FEMALE FACE OF SEVENTEEN . . . . 215 2 DON JUAN 2   112   8
    EVEN OF THE HIGHEST FOR A FEMALE MOULD . . . . . . 217 2 DON JUAN 2   116   5
    WHICH ARE (AS I MUST OWN) OF FEMALE GROWTH . . . . 221 2 DON JUAN 2   123   3
    I'LL TELL YOU WHO THEY WERE THIS FEMALE PAIR . . . 222 2 DON JUAN 2   124   1
    BY FEMALE LIPS AND EYES--THAT IS I MEAN . . . . . 242 2 DON JUAN 2   164   2
    FEMALE AS WHERE SHE LIKES MAY FREELY PASS . . . . 248 2 DON JUAN 2   175   4
    LIGHT CLASSIC ARTICLES OF FEMALE WANT . . . . . . 284 2 DON JUAN 3   17   4
    A FEMALE FAMILY'S A SERIOUS MATTER . . . . 287 2 DON JUAN 3   22   4
    THERE CHANCED TO BE AN ODD MALE AND ODD FEMALE . . 394 2 DON JUAN 4   92   2
    ALTHOUGH A FEMALE MODERATELY FICKLE . . . . . . 419 2 DON JUAN 5   17   2
    SOME FEMALE HEAD MOST CURIOUSLY PRESUMES . . . . 442 2 DON JUAN 5   55   6
    MOVES--FEMALE HEARTS ARE SUCH A GENIAL SOIL . . . 480 2 DON JUAN 5   120   3
    THAN OTHER ARTICLES OF FEMALE DRESS . . . . 15 3 DON JUAN 6   19   4
    SELF-LOVE IN MAN TOO BEATS ALL FEMALE ART . . . . 15 3 DON JUAN 6   19   5
    THE FEMALE RANKS SO THAT NONE STIRRED OR TALKED . . 21 3 DON JUAN 6   30   1
    A FEMALE CHILD OF TEN YEARS TRIED TO STOOP . . . 157 3 DON JUAN 8   91   6
    WHICH MAKES ALL FEMALE AGES EQUAL--WHEN . . . . 217 3 DON JUAN 9   69   2
    AS WHO HAS NOT IF FEMALE YOUNG AND PRETTY . . . . 338 3 DON JUAN 12   47   1
    YET NEITHER FRIGHTENED BY A FEMALE FUSS . . . . 344 3 DON JUAN 12   61   5
    I LOVE THE MYSTERY OF A FEMALE MISSAL . . . . . 407 3 DON JUAN 13   105   4
    FEMALE OR MALE A SCHOOL-BOY OR A QUEEN . . . . . 421 3 DON JUAN 14   25   8
    MERE FREEDOMS OF THE FEMALE CORPORATION . . . . 429 3 DON JUAN 14   43   4
    IN FEMALE DATES STRIKES TIME ALL OF A HEAP . . . 433 3 DON JUAN 14   52   8
    I'VE ALSO SEEN SOME FEMALE FRIENDS ('TIS ODD . . 452 3 DON JUAN 14   96   1
FEMALE'S
    THE OTHER FEMALE'S DRESS WAS NOT UNLIKE . . . . 221 2 DON JUAN 2   122   1
FEMALES
    THE FEMALES STOOD AS ONE BY ONE THEY PICK'D 'EM . . 409 2 DON JUAN 4   116   7
    THE FEMALES STOOD TILL CHOSEN EACH AS VICTIM . . . 409 2 DON JUAN 4   116 V7
    THIS LABYRINTH OF FEMALES AND EACH STATION . . . . 34 3 DON JUAN 6   57   5
    AND BETWEEN FEMALES MEANS NO MORE THAN THIS-- . . . 35 3 DON JUAN 6   59   5
    IN THIS FOR FEMALES LIKE EXAGGERATION . . . . . . 105 3 DON JUAN 7   75   8
    TO FEMALES OF PERSPICUOUS COMPREHENSIONS . . . . 491 3 DON JUAN 15   80   1
    WHICH SHOW'D SUCH DEFERENCE TO WHAT FEMALES SAY . . 492 3 DON JUAN 15   82   3
    FEW FEMALES WITHOUT SOME SUCH GENTLE LEAVEN . . . 525 3 DON JUAN 16   49   7
FEMININE
    MY HEART IS FEMININE NOR CAN FORGET-- . . . . . 133 2 DON JUAN 1   196   5
    IF 'TIS SUMMED UP WITH FEMININE PRECISION . . . . 10 3 DON JUAN 6   9   3
    OF GENTLE FEMININE DELIGHT AND SHOWN . . . . . . 13 3 DON JUAN 6   15   2
    DON JUAN IN HIS FEMININE DISGUISE . . . . 19 3 DON JUAN 6   26   1
    IN WHAT WAY FEMININE CAPRICE MAY DISSIPATE . . . . 65 3 DON JUAN 6   119   8
    AS WARM IN HEART AS FEMININE IN FEATURE . . . . 138 3 DON JUAN 8   52   4
    HER THIRD WAS FEMININE ENOUGH TO ANNUL . . . . 212 3 DON JUAN 9   60   5
    SUPPRESS THEN SOME SLIGHT FEMININE DISEASES . . . 459 3 DON JUAN 15   9   7
FEMININELY
    AND NOW BEING FEMININELY ALL ARRAYED . . . . . 458 2 DON JUAN 5   80   1
FEMME
    THERE WAS A GOODLY SOUPE A LA BONNE FEMME . . . . 483 3 DON JUAN 15   63   1
</pre>

	PAGE	VOL		CANTO	STANZA	LN
FEN						
A HUMAN HYDRA ISSUING FROM ITS FEN	113	3 DON	JUAN	8	2	5
A FAT FEN VICARAGE AND NOUGHT TO THINK ON	540	3 DON	JUAN	16	82	8
FENCE						
START FROM THE FRAMES WHICH FENCE THEIR ASPECTS STERN	508	3 DON	JUAN	16	18	6
FENCED						
FRAUGHT WITH THIS FINE INTENTION AND WELL FENCED	66	2 DON	JUAN	1	82	1
FENCING						
HE LEARN'D THE ARTS OF RIDING FENCING GUNNERY	42	2 DON	JUAN	1	38	7
FENELON						
BY FENELON BY LUTHER AND BY PLATO	68	3 DON	JUAN	7	4	2
BY FENELON BY CALVIN AND OF CHRIST	68	3 DON	JUAN	7	4	V2
FENS						
BUT BOTH WERE THROWN AWAY AMONGST THE FENS	540	3 DON	JUAN	16	83	2
FERDINAND						
PRINCE FERDINAND GRANBY BURGOYNE KEPPEL HOWE	22	2 DON	JUAN	1	2	2
FERFLUCTER						
WITH SCHNAPPS--SAD DOGS WHOM HUNDSFOT OR FERFLUCTER	260	3 DON	JUAN	10	71	7
FERMENT						
WHERE LONDON STREETS FERMENT IN FULL ACTIVITY	272	3 DON	JUAN	11	8	4
FERMENTATION						
(IN LOVE OR BRANDY'S FERVENT FERMENTATION)	287	3 DON	JUAN	11	39	6
FERNAN						
THE DUKE OF ICHAR AND DON FERNAN NUNEZ	103	2 DON	JUAN	1	150	2
FEROCIOUS						
THOUGH EVEN THAT WERE SOMETIMES TOO FEROCIOUS	443	3 DON	JUAN	14	77	5
FEROCITIES						
FROM THEIR FEROCITIES PRODUCED BY VANITY	182	3 DON	JUAN	8	140	4
FEROCITY						
IN FIX'D FEROCITY WHEN JOYOUS TEARS	368	2 DON	JUAN	4	45	6
FERREM						
NON EGO HOC FERREM CALIDA JUVENTA	143	2 DON	JUAN	1	212	1
FERTILE						
OTHERS ARE FAIR AND FERTILE AMONG WHICH	238	2 DON	JUAN	2	154	7
SEEMS FERTILE IN ADVENTURES STRANGE AND NEW	459	2 DON	JUAN	5	83	6
FERTILITY						
IN FAULTS WHICH SOMETIMES SHOW THE SOIL'S FERTILITY	368	3 DON	JUAN	13	22	6
FERVENT						
AQ FERVENT OUNCE AND A HALF TWO DRAMS TINCT SENNAE	244	3 DON	JUAN	10	41	3
(IN LOVE OR BRANDY'S FERVENT FERMENTATION)	287	3 DON	JUAN	11	39	6
FERVENTLY						
AS HE WHO STUDIES FERVENTLY THE SKIES	242	2 DON	JUAN	2	163	5
FERVOUR						
HE LIED WITH SUCH A FERVOUR OF INTENTION--	317	2 DON	JUAN	3	80	7
FESTAL						
THE FESTAL MIDNIGHT AND THE LEVEE MORN	404	2 DON	JUAN	4	110	8
FESTIVITY						
'MIDST OTHER INDICATIONS OF FESTIVITY	290	2 DON	JUAN	3	29	4
FESTOON						
THE PATHS O'ER WHICH THE FAR FESTOON ENTWINES	394	3 DON	JUAN	13	76	3
FESTOONS						
CHALK MIMICS PAINTING THEN FESTOONS ARE TWIRLED	302	3 DON	JUAN	11	67	5
FETES						
AND WHAT WITH MASQUERADES AND FETES AND BALLS	342	3 DON	JUAN	12	57	7
FETTER						
THAT ONE SHOULD DIE THAN TWO DRAG ON THE FETTER)	222	3 DON	JUAN	9	80	8
BUT BEDLAM STILL EXISTS WITH ITS SAGE FETTER	280	3 DON	JUAN	11	25	3
THE GILDING WEARS SO SOON FROM OFF HER FETTER	421	3 DON	JUAN	14	25	5
FETTER'D						
THOUGH LINK'D AMONG A FETTER'D RACE	323	2 DON	JUAN	3	L 6	2
WOUNDED AND FETTER'D CABIN'D CRIBB'D CONFINED	384	2 DON	JUAN	4	75	1
FETTERED						
OF PORCELAIN HELD IN THE FETTERED FLOWERS	54	3 DON	JUAN	6	97	7
FETTERS						
TO LENGTHEN FETTERS BY ANOTHER FIX'D	16	2 DON	JUAN	D	12	7
OR SHOULD BE LEFT WITH FETTERS OR WITHOUT	394	2 DON	JUAN	4	92	V5
FEUD						
IN SENATES AT THE BAR IN WORDY FEUD	371	3 DON	JUAN	13	29	5
FEUDAL						
OF THE GOOD FEUDAL TIMES FOREVER GONE	255	3 DON	JUAN	10	62	3
FEUDS						
AND ALL OUR LITTLE FEUDS AT LEAST ALL MINE	232	3 DON	JUAN	10	16	1
FEVER						
HE DIED OF THE SLOW FEVER CALL'D THE TERTIAN	39	2 DON	JUAN	1	34	7
OUT THROUGH A FEVER CAUSED BY ITS OWN HEAT	168	2 DON	JUAN	2	22	2
THAT FEVER WHICH PRECEDES THE LANGUID ROUT	220	3 DON	JUAN	9	75	6
OF MEN'S REGARD THE FEVER OR THE CHILL	366	3 DON	JUAN	13	17	8
FEVERISH						
HER OWN WAS FRESHEST THOUGH A FEVERISH FLUSH	231	2 DON	JUAN	2	141	2
ITSELF AND SHOWED A FEVERISH DISPOSITION	244	3 DON	JUAN	10	39	6
FEW						
AND LET FEW OPPORTUNITIES ESCAPE	32	2 DON	JUAN	1	20	7
THESE FEW SHORT YEARS MAKE WOND'ROUS ALTERATIONS	59	2 DON	JUAN	1	69	7
FEW MORTALS KNOW WHAT END THEY WOULD BE AT	93	2 DON	JUAN	1	133	5
'TWAS IN NOVEMBER WHEN FINE DAYS ARE FEW	94	2 DON	JUAN	1	134	3
BESIDES IT WANTED BUT FEW HOURS OF DAY	114	2 DON	JUAN	1	169	6
BY A FEW TIMELY WORDS TO TURN THE TABLES	117	2 DON	JUAN	1	175	4
AND FEW THERE ARE WHOM THESE CAN NOT ESTRANGE	131	2 DON	JUAN	1	194	6
A SORT OF BLOTTED SHIELD FEW KNIGHTS WOULD WEAR	153	2 DON	JUAN	1	V 4	V6

FEW   (CONTINUED)

	PAGE	VOL		CANTO	STANZA	LN
THERE WAS NO LIGHT IN HEAVEN BUT A FEW STARS	183	2	DON JUAN	2	51	5
AND THEN THEY WERE TOO MANY THOUGH SO FEW--	185	2	DON JUAN	2	54	6
A FEW TEA-SPOONFULS OF THEIR RUM AND WINE	189	2	DON JUAN	2	62	5
WHILE A FEW PRAY'D--(THE FIRST TIME FOR SOME YEARS)--	208	2	DON JUAN	2	98	5
THEY PERISH'D UNTIL WITHER'D TO THESE FEW	210	2	DON JUAN	2	102	6
THEY DIED AWAY TILL THUS REDUCED TO FEW	210	2	DON JUAN	2	102	V6
I'VE CHANGED FOR SOME FEW YEARS THE DAY TO NIGHT	230	2	DON JUAN	2	140	V3
FEW THINGS SURPASS OLD WINE AND THEY MAY PREACH	250	2	DON JUAN	2	178	5
FEW CHANGES E'ER CAN BETTER THEIR AFFAIRS	263	2	DON JUAN	2	201	5
ANTIENTS AND MODERNS ALSO NOT A FEW	267	2	DON JUAN	2	207	V6
HAD SOWN THE RUIN OF HER FEW FAIR YEARS	275	2	DON JUAN	3	1	V7
SO THAT THE FEW WHO MET HIM HARDLY HEEDED	300	2	DON JUAN	3	49	3
THERE HIS FEW PEACEFUL DAYS TIME HAD SWEPT O'ER	302	2	DON JUAN	3	52	5
FLASH'D O'ER HIS SOUL A FEW HEROIC RAYS	303	2	DON JUAN	3	55	2
FOR SOME FEW YEARS HIS LOT HAD BEEN O'ERCAST	316	2	DON JUAN	3	79	5
THAT WITHOUT NOTICE FEW FULL MOONS SHALL PASS IT	317	2	DON JUAN	3	81	3
WHICH GOT HIM A FEW PRESENTS AND SOME THANKS	319	2	DON JUAN	3	84	5
THE PUBLIC MIND SO FEW ARE THE ELECT	330	2	DON JUAN	3	95	6
THE FACT EXCEPTING SOME EXPERIENCED FEW	342	2	DON JUAN	3	111	5
NOT I HAVE MADE THIS DESOLATION FEW	368	2	DON JUAN	4	46	5
A FEW BRIEF QUESTIONS AND THE ANSWERS GAVE	387	2	DON JUAN	4	79	6
IN A FEW WORDS HE TOLD THEIR HAPLESS STORY	389	2	DON JUAN	4	82	1
BY THOUGHT OF FROSTY CAUCASUS BUT FEW	396	2	DON JUAN	4	96	6
SAVE A FEW GLEAN'D FROM THE SEPULCHRAL GLOOM	399	2	DON JUAN	4	102	6
I HAVE EXAMINED FEW PAIR OF THAT HUE)	404	2	DON JUAN	4	110	5
HE DOUBTED NOT A FEW HOURS OF REFLECTION	452	2	DON JUAN	5	71	5
(PLAIN TRUTH DEAR MURRAY NEEDS FEW FLOWERS OF SPEECH)	470	2	DON JUAN	5	101	2
OF GOOD EXAMPLES PITY THAT SO FEW BY	486	2	DON JUAN	5	131	4
BUT WHEN YOU HAVE SUPPOSED THE FEW WE KNOW	486	2	DON JUAN	5	131	7
FOR WHAT IS STEALING YOUNG ONES FEW OR MANY	487	2	DON JUAN	5	132	7
OF CANTEMIR OR KNOLLES WHERE FEW SHINE	495	2	DON JUAN	5	147	7
YOU'LL PARDON TO MY MUSE A FEW SHORT NAPS	503	2	DON JUAN	5	159	8
AT LEAST WE THINK SO THOUGH BUT FEW HAVE GUESS'D	6	3	DON JUAN	6	1	4
THEY ALL FOUND OUT AS FEW OR FEWER SPECKS	24	3	DON JUAN	6	37	4
IN WISHING HER THEIR SISTER SAVE A FEW	25	3	DON JUAN	6	39	5
FEW ANGLES WERE THERE IN HER FORM 'TIS TRUE	27	3	DON JUAN	6	42	5
I FEAR JUANNA'S DREAMS WOULD BE BUT FEW	30	3	DON JUAN	6	48	8
DESCRIBED--WHAT'S STRANGE--IN WORDS EXTREMELY FEW	34	3	DON JUAN	6	57	6
THIS WEAKNESS IN A FEW HOURS AND RECOVER	47	3	DON JUAN	6	83	8
STILL I'LL RECORD A FEW IF BUT TO ENCREASE	74	3	DON JUAN	7	15	1
I DOUBT FEW READERS E'ER WOULD MOUNT THE BREACH	83	3	DON JUAN	7	35	8
WERE DAMNABLY MISTAKEN FEW ARE SLOW	87	3	DON JUAN	7	42	3
TO WHOM HE SPOKE AND MADE HIS WORDS BUT FEW	97	3	DON JUAN	7	59	8
BEYOND THE RUSSIAN BATTERIES A FEW TOISES	115	3	DON JUAN	8	7	2
THAT JOHNSON AND SOME FEW WHO HAD NOT SCAMPERED	135	3	DON JUAN	8	44	7
NOR YET TOO MANY NOR TOO FEW THEIR NUMBERS	145	3	DON JUAN	8	67	3
YOU SHOULD BUT GIVE FEW CARTRIDGES TO SUCH	151	3	DON JUAN	8	78	3
WHICH FEW WILL SING I TRUST BUT NONE FORGET IT--	179	3	DON JUAN	8	135	3
EXCEPT THE ALL-CLOUDLESS GLORY (WHICH FEW MEN'S IS)	186	3	DON JUAN	9	8	5
WHO PROMISED TO BE GREAT IN SOME FEW HOURS	222	3	DON JUAN	9	79	3
SUCH DIFFERENCE DOTH A FEW MONTHS MAKE YOU'D THINK	228	3	DON JUAN	10	7	5
FEW YOUTHFUL MINDS CAN STAND THE STRONG CONCUSSION	235	3	DON JUAN	10	21	3
WHERE HIS ASSETS WERE WAXING RATHER FEW	240	3	DON JUAN	10	31	3
CHIEF IMPULSE WITH A FEW FRAIL PAPER PELLETS	298	3	DON JUAN	11	60	V8
WHICH OPENS TO THE THOUSAND HAPPY FEW	302	3	DON JUAN	11	67	7
OR LITTLE OVERTURNS AND NOT THE FEW	305	3	DON JUAN	11	73	4
EVEN PLUTARCH'S LIVES HAVE BUT PICKED OUT A FEW	324	3	DON JUAN	12	19	5
AND 'GAINST THOSE FEW YOUR ANNALISTS HAVE THUNDERED	324	3	DON JUAN	12	19	6
BUT THESE ARE FEW AND IN THE END THEY MAKE	328	3	DON JUAN	12	26	1
ALBEIT MY YEARS WERE LESS DISCREET THAN FEW	334	3	DON JUAN	12	38	4
ABROAD SUCH THINGS DECIDE FEW WOMEN'S FATE--	345	3	DON JUAN	12	64	5
UPON FOR THERE ARE VERY FEW THINGS WEARIER	367	3	DON JUAN	13	19	5
SO THAT FEW MEMBERS KEPT THE HOUSE UP LATER	367	3	DON JUAN	13	20	8
THAT FEW OR NONE MORE THAN HIMSELF HAD CAUGHT	368	3	DON JUAN	13	21	3
WHICH LEAVES FEW DROPS OF THAT IMMORTAL RAIN	375	3	DON JUAN	13	37	4
FEW SPECIMENS YET LEFT US CAN COMPARE	384	3	DON JUAN	13	55	5
ESCAPING WITH A FEW SLIGHT SCARLESS SNEERS	397	3	DON JUAN	13	82	8
I HAVE NAMED A FEW NOT FOREMOST IN DEGREE	397	3	DON JUAN	13	83	5
THE HOURS WHICH HOW TO PASS IS BUT TO FEW KNOWN	406	3	DON JUAN	13	103	5
IN PIOUS LIBELS BY NO MEANS A FEW	414	3	DON JUAN	14	10	4
AND NEVER CRANED AND MADE BUT FEW FAUX PAS	424	3	DON JUAN	14	33	3
AS FEW WOULD EVER DREAM COULD FORM THE LINK	454	3	DON JUAN	14	100	5
FEW MEN DARE SHOW THEIR THOUGHTS OF WORST OR BEST	457	3	DON JUAN	15	3	5
FOR FEW OF THE SOFT SEX ARE VERY STABLE	458	3	DON JUAN	15	6	3
FOR THERE ARE FEW THINGS BY MANKIND LESS BROOK'D	479	3	DON JUAN	15	53	4
LIKE ANTHONY'S BY CAESAR BY THE FEW	479	3	DON JUAN	15	53	7
WHOSE GREATEST FAULT WAS LEAVING FEW TO FIND	479	3	DON JUAN	15	54	4
FOR ADELINE ADDRESSING FEW WORDS TO HIM	489	3	DON JUAN	15	75	7
BUT WONDER THEY SO FEW ARE SINCE MY TALE IS	502	3	DON JUAN	16	3	7
A FEW WORDS OF CONDOLENCE ON HIS STATE	515	3	DON JUAN	16	35	2
FEW FEMALES WITHOUT SOME SUCH GENTLE LEAVEN	525	3	DON JUAN	16	49	7
OF THESE FEW COULD SAY MORE THAN HAS BEEN SAID	527	3	DON JUAN	16	54	1
BUT LUCKILY I HAVE PAID FEW PARISH FEES SINCE)	530	3	DON JUAN	16	61	6
FROM THOSE WHO HAVE FEW RESOURCES OF THEIR OWN	541	3	DON JUAN	16	85	5
MOST ORATORS BUT VERY FEW FINANCIERS	547	3	DON JUAN	16	98	5
SINCE BURNING AGED WOMEN (SAVE A FEW--	565	3	DON JUAN	17	7	3

FEWER

	PAGE	VOL		CANTO	STANZA	LN
THEY ALL FOUND OUT AS FEW OR FEWER SPECKS	24	3	DON JUAN	6	37	4

FEWER   (CONTINUED)
    WHERE THERE WERE FEWER HOUSES AND MORE EASE . . . . . . 144 3 DON JUAN 8   64   4
    (BUT HERE PERHAPS THE INSTANCES ARE FEWER) . . . . . . 333 3 DON JUAN 12   37   3
    RATHER THAN SELLER HAD HIS WANTS BEEN FEWER . . . . . . 528 3 DON JUAN 16   57   5
    AND SEVERAL WHO SUNG FEWER PSALMS THAN CATCHES . . . . . 539 3 DON JUAN 16   80   8
FEZ
    HER MOTHER WAS A MOORISH MAID FROM FEZ . . . . 373 2 DON JUAN 4   54   7
FIAT
    THE UPHOLSTERER'S FIAT LUX HAD BADE TO ISSUE . . . . . 309 2 DON JUAN 3   67 V8
    THE FIAT OF THIS SPOILED CHILD OF THE NIGHT . . . . . . 86 3 DON JUAN 7   41   3
FICKLE
    ALTHOUGH A FEMALE MODERATELY FICKLE . . . . 419 3 DON JUAN 5   17   2
FICTION
    BUT I DETEST ALL FICTION EVEN IN SONG . . . . 10 3 DON JUAN 6   8   3
    OF A TRUE POET TO ESCAPE FROM FICTION . . . . 154 3 DON JUAN 8   86   2
    AND RECOLLECT THE WORK IS ONLY FICTION . . . . 311 3 DON JUAN 11   88   4
    BESIDES MY MUSE BY NO MEANS DEALS IN FICTION . . . . . 416 3 DON JUAN 14   13   1
    STRANGER THAN FICTION IF IT COULD BE TOLD . . . . . . 455 3 DON JUAN 14   101   2
    A CORNER FOR HERSELF AND THEREFORE FICTION . . . . . . 457 3 DON JUAN 15   3   7
    THAT SHE MUST OFTEN NAVIGATE O'ER FICTION . . . . . . 495 3 DON JUAN 15   88   8
    THE MOST SINCERE THAT EVER DEALT IN FICTION . . . . . 502 3 DON JUAN 16   2   8
FIDDLE
    WITH WHICH I STILL CAN HARP AND CARP AND FIDDLE . . . . 181 3 DON JUAN 8   139   1
    UPON MY FIDDLE--SEEING IF ALL'S SURE . . . . 341 3 DON JUAN 12   54 V7
FIDDLED
    GONE DOWN IT SEEMS TO SCOTLAND TO BE FIDDLED . . . . . 307 3 DON JUAN 11   78   5
FIDDLING
    BUT AN UNHALLOW'D EARTHLY SOUND OF FIDDLING . . . . . 290 2 DON JUAN 3   28   4
    HENCE ALL THIS RICE MEAT DANCING WINE AND FIDDLING . . . 295 2 DON JUAN 3   39   1
FIE
    I RATHER DOUBT AND I WOULD FAIN SAY FIE ON'T . . . . . 138 3 DON JUAN 8   51   6
    UNLESS YOU MAKE THEIR BETTERS BETTER--FIE . . . . . . 267 3 DON JUAN 10   85   7
    WOULD THAT I WERE LESS BILIOUS--BUT OH FIE ON'T . . . . 566 3 DON JUAN 17   10   5
FIELD
    THE FIELD IS UNIVERSAL AND ALLOWS . . . . 13 2 DON JUAN D   7   5
    BULLY IN SENATES SKULKER IN THE FIELD . . . . 151 2 DON JUAN 1 V 2   1
    BATTLES TO THE COMMAND FIELD MARSHAL SOUVAROFF . . . . 85 3 DON JUAN 7   39   8
    AND RALLY BACK HIS ROMANS TO THE FIELD . . . . 125 3 DON JUAN 8   28   8
    A FIELD OF BATTLE'S GHASTLY WILDERNESS . . . . 167 3 DON JUAN 8   112   6
    SUNK AND THE CRIMSON CROSS GLARED O'ER THE FIELD . . . 172 3 DON JUAN 8   122   5
    HAD PERISHED IN THE FIELD OR BY THE WALL . . . . . . 182 3 DON JUAN 8   141   4
    GRIEF A RICH FIELD WHICH NEVER WOULD LIE FALLOW . . . . 228 3 DON JUAN 10   7   6
    A GREEN FIELD IS A SIGHT WHICH MAKES HIM PARDON . . . . 262 3 DON JUAN 10   76   5
    WITH SOME SMALL PROFIT THROUGH THAT FIELD SO STERILE . . 300 3 DON JUAN 11   64   3
    AND GENERAL FIREFACE FAMOUS IN THE FIELD . . . . . . 399 3 DON JUAN 13   88   2
    SOMETIMES A DANCE (THOUGH RARELY ON FIELD DAYS . . . . 408 3 DON JUAN 13   108   1
    AND NOW IN THIS NEW FIELD WITH SOME APPLAUSE . . . . . 424 3 DON JUAN 14   33   1
FIELDING
    OF SMOLLET PRIOR ARIOSTO FIELDING . . . . 397 2 DON JUAN 4   98   3
FIELDS
    IN DITCHES FIELDS OR WHERESOE'ER THEY FELT . . . . . . 120 3 DON JUAN 8   18   4
    THOUGH 'TWAS DON JUAN'S FIRST OF FIELDS AND THOUGH . . . 121 3 DON JUAN 8   21   1
    STRIP YOUR GREEN FIELDS AND TO YOUR HARVESTS CLING . . . 175 3 DON JUAN 8   126   6
    ALONG THE LAST FIELDS OF THAT GOTHIC GROUND)-- . . . . 359 3 DON JUAN 13   2   4
FIENDS
    AND FIGHT LIKE FIENDS FOR PAY OR POLITICS . . . . . . 122 3 DON JUAN 8   22   8
FIERCE
    AND MAKE HIM SAMSONLIKE--MORE FIERCE WITH BLINDNESS . . 304 2 DON JUAN 3   57 V8
    FOAMING O'ER HER LONE HEAD SO FIERCE AND HIGH . . . . 361 2 DON JUAN 4   31   7
    AND SUNG OF LOVE THE FIERCE NAME STRUCK THROUGH ALL . . 380 2 DON JUAN 4   66   3
    MADE FIERCE REMONSTRANCES AND THEN A THREAT . . . . . 471 2 DON JUAN 5   103   2
    AND MUCH MORE TENDER ON THE WHOLE THAN FIERCE . . . . 19 3 DON JUAN 6   27   5
    FIERCE LOVES AND FAITHLESS WARS--I AM NOT SURE . . . . 70 3 DON JUAN 7   8   1
    THAT SHE WAS HANDSOME AND THOUGH FIERCE LOOKED LENIENT . 214 3 DON JUAN 9   63   3
    OF HIS FIERCE PULSE BETOKEN A CONDITION . . . . . . 244 3 DON JUAN 10   39   4
    AND HOW SHOULD THE MOST FIERCE OF ALL BE FIRM . . . . 451 3 DON JUAN 14   94   5
    AND THEN HIS DREAD GREW WRATH AND HIS WRATH FIERCE . . 559 3 DON JUAN 16   119   1
FIERCEST
    THE LIVELIEST FIRE AND SAW THE FIERCEST FLOOD . . . . 129 3 DON JUAN 8   33 V4
FIERY
    THE SUN ROSE RED AND FIERY A SURE SIGN . . . . 189 2 DON JUAN 2   62   1
    TO HINT THAT FLESH IS FORM'D OF FIERY DUST . . . . . 269 2 DON JUAN 2   212   8
    BUT THOU--OH SWEET FURY OF THE FIERY RILL . . . . . . 372 2 DON JUAN 4   53 V2
    DESPITE HER INJURED LOVE AND FIERY PRIDE . . . . . . 62 3 DON JUAN 6   113   5
    WHICH ARCHED THE HORIZON LIKE A FIERY CLOUD . . . . . 115 3 DON JUAN 8   6   3
    'TIS STRANGE THE MIND THAT VERY FIERY PARTICLE . . . . 298 3 DON JUAN 11   60   7
FIFTEEN
    SOME WENT OFF DEARLY FIFTEEN HUNDRED DOLLARS . . . . . 407 2 DON JUAN 4   114   1
    I WISH THEIR YEARS HAD BEEN FIFTEEN AND TWENTY . . . .   9 3 DON JUAN 6   5   2
    ALL BAD PROPENSITIES IN FIFTEEN HUNDRED . . . . 21 3 DON JUAN 6   31   7
FIFTEEN-HUNDREDTH
    YEARS AND A FIFTEEN-HUNDREDTH CONCUBINE . . . . 10 3 DON JUAN 6   8   8
FIFTEENTH
    SHE COULD BUT CLAIM THE FIFTEENTH HUNDRED PART . . . . 10 3 DON JUAN 6   9   7
FIFTH
    THE FIFTH DAY AND THEIR BOAT LAY FLOATING THERE . . . 193 2 DON JUAN 2   70   3
    TILL WHAT IS CALL'D IN OSSIAN THE FIFTH DUAN . . . . 410 2 DON JUAN 4   117   8
    HER FIFTH TO CALL HER MAIDS AND GO TO BED . . . . . 491 2 DON JUAN 5   139   1
    LET THIS FIFTH CANTO MEET WITH DUE APPLAUSE . . . . . 503 2 DON JUAN 5   159   5

		PAGE	VOL		CANTO	STANZA	LN

FIFTH   (CONTINUED)
   AND LO A FIFTH APPEARS--AND WHAT IS SHE 41   3 DON JUAN   6   69   1
   THE FIFTH WHO BY A CHRISTIAN MOTHER NOURISHED 166   3 DON JUAN   8   110   5
FIFTY
   OF FIFTY AND SUCH HUSBANDS ARE IN PLENTY 56   2 DON JUAN   1   62   2
   AND THEN OF DON ALFONSO'S FIFTY YEARS 78   2 DON JUAN   1   107   4
   WHEN PEOPLE SAY I'VE TOLD YOU FIFTY TIMES 79   2 DON JUAN   1   108   1
   WHEN POETS SAY I'VE WRITTEN FIFTY RHYMES 79   2 DON JUAN   1   108   3
   IN GANGS OF FIFTY THIEVES COMMIT THEIR CRIMES 79   2 DON JUAN   1   108   5
   AT FIFTY LOVE FOR LOVE IS RARE 'TIS TRUE 79   2 DON JUAN   1   108   6
   A GOOD DEAL MAY BE BOUGHT FOR FIFTY LOUIS 79   2 DON JUAN   1   108   8
   FIFTY OR SIXTY--IT IS ALL THE SAME-- 101   2 DON JUAN   1   146   4
   FOR FIFTY TONS OF WATER WERE UPTHROWN 171   2 DON JUAN   2   29   6
   BECAUSE HE HAD JOURNEYED FIFTY MILES AND FOUND 497   2 DON JUAN   5   150   3
   HE HAD FIFTY DAUGHTERS AND FOUR DOZEN SONS 498   2 DON JUAN   5   152   1
   HE DIED AT FIFTY FOR A QUEEN OF FORTY 9   3 DON JUAN   6   5   1
   FOR FIFTY THOUSAND HEROES NAME BY NAME 120   3 DON JUAN   8   17   4
   THEY SHOULD AT LEAST HAVE FIFTY ROUBLES ROUND 162   3 DON JUAN   8   102   8
   THROUGH FIFTY VICTORIES TO SHAME OR FAME 189   3 DON JUAN   9   14   7
FIFTY-NINE
   WAS SCARCE ENOUGH FOR HE HAD FIFTY-NINE 10   3 DON JUAN   6   8   7
FIG
   EVE MADE UP MILLINERY WITH FIG LEAVES-- 444   3 DON JUAN 14   78   2
FIGHT
   BUT NOT A SERVANT STIRR'D TO AID THE FIGHT 122   2 DON JUAN   1   184   3
   A SAILOR WHEN THE PRIZE HAS STRUCK IN FIGHT 261   2 DON JUAN   2   196   5
   A HUNDRED THOUSAND MEN MIGHT FIGHT AGAIN 386   2 DON JUAN   4   77   6
   I THEREFORE IF YOU WISH ME TO FIGHT FREELY 103   3 DON JUAN   7   72   7
   AND FIGHT LIKE FIENDS FOR PAY OR POLITICS 122   3 DON JUAN   8   22   8
   WHO THUS COULD FORM A LINE AND FIGHT AGAIN 136   3 DON JUAN   8   47   5
   SO MUCH LESS FIGHT AS MIGHT FORM AN APOLOGY 165   3 DON JUAN   8   108   4
   THESE BLACK-EYED VIRGINS MAKE THE MOSLEMS FIGHT 168   3 DON JUAN   8   114   5
   PAUSED FOR A MOMENT FROM THE FIGHT AND CAST 169   3 DON JUAN   8   116   7
   HIS ONLY OBJECT AND 'GAINST ODDS TO FIGHT 363   3 DON JUAN 13   9   4
   ALSO A SO-SO MATRON BOLDLY FIGHT 397   3 DON JUAN 13   82   5
   WHO FOUGHT AND FIGHT IN ABSENCE TOO MY BATTLES 452   3 DON JUAN 14   96   7
   UNTYING SQUIRES TO FIGHT AGAINST THE CHURCHES 530   3 DON JUAN 16   60   6
FIGHTER
   UPON THE ROAD UNLESS HE PROVE A FIGHTER 273   3 DON JUAN 11   11   6
FIGHTERS
   THE NEGROES AND IS WORTH A MILLION FIGHTERS 325   3 DON JUAN 12   20   6
   I'VE SEEN THEM BALANCE EVEN THE SCALE WITH FIGHTERS . . 418   3 DON JUAN 14   20   3
FIGHTING
   FAMOUS FOR ALWAYS TALKING AND NEER FIGHTING 150   2 DON JUAN   1 V 1   3
   FIGHTING DEVOTION DUST--PERHAPS A NAME 159   2 DON JUAN   2   4   8
   NOT FIGHTING FOR THEIR COUNTRY OR ITS CROWN 75   3 DON JUAN   7   18   3
   BUT FIGHTING THOUGHTLESSLY ENOUGH TO WIN 121   3 DON JUAN   8   19   7
   OF FORTRESSES BUT FIGHTING WHERE IT PLEASES 149   3 DON JUAN   8   74   7
FIGHTS
   WHERE FIGHTS NOT TO THE LAST SOME DESPERATE HEART . . . 152   3 DON JUAN   8   82   3
   OF HIM WHO FEASTS AND FIGHTS AND ROARS AND REVELS . . . 237   3 DON JUAN 10   25   4
   SOME GENTLEMAN WHO FIGHTS OR WRITES OR DRIVES 333   3 DON JUAN 12   36   6
FIGURANTI
   AS FOR THE FIGURANTI THEY ARE LIKE 390   2 DON JUAN   4   85   1
FIGURATIVE
   AND GROW QUITE FIGURATIVE WITH THEIR FIGURES 547   3 DON JUAN 16   98   8
FIGURE
   NOW TELL ME DON'T YOU CUT A PRETTY FIGURE 103   2 DON JUAN   1   150   8
   AND TRUTH TO SAY HE MADE A FOOLISH FIGURE 110   2 DON JUAN   1   161   2
   AND MORE ROBUST OF FIGURE--THEN BEGUN 216   2 DON JUAN   2   115   4
   SUCH NAMES AT PRESENT CUT A CONVICT FIGURE 330   2 DON JUAN   3   94   1
   THE MORE'S THE PITY WITH HER FACE AND FIGURE 390   2 DON JUAN   4   85   8
   HIS FIGURE AND THE SPLENDOUR OF HIS DRESS 415   2 DON JUAN   5   9   3
   WHEN WROTH WHILE PLEASED SHE WAS AS FINE A FIGURE . . . 213   3 DON JUAN   9   62   2
   HER SWEET SMILE AND HER THEN MAJESTIC FIGURE 218   3 DON JUAN   9   72   1
   HER CHARMING FIGURE AND ROMANTIC HISTORY 328   3 DON JUAN 12   27   7
   ALSO BECAUSE THE FIGURE AND THE FACE 360   3 DON JUAN 13   4   7
   I'LL HAVE ANOTHER FIGURE IN A TRICE-- 375   3 DON JUAN 13   37   1
   AND ELEGANCE WAS SPRINKLED O'ER HIS FIGURE 427   3 DON JUAN 14   39   2
   A FIGURE FIT TO WALK BEFORE A KING 440   3 DON JUAN 14   70   4
   IN FIGURE SHE HAD SOMETHING OF SUBLIME 476   3 DON JUAN 15   45   2
   STRAINED ON THE SPOT WHERE FIRST THE FIGURE GLEAMED . . 511   3 DON JUAN 16   25   3
   PRESENTS THE PROBLEM OF A DOUBLE FIGURE 530   3 DON JUAN 16   61   8
FIGURES
   WHO SAW THOSE FIGURES ON THE MARGIN KISS ALL 47   2 DON JUAN   1   46   5
   THE MOVING FIGURES AND THE SPARKLING SHEEN 289   2 DON JUAN   3   27   6
   OR ALL THE FIGURES CASTLEREAGH ABUSES 493   2 DON JUAN   5   143   5
   DISPLAY'D SOME SYLPH-LIKE FIGURES IN ITS MAZE 408   3 DON JUAN 13   108   3
   AND GROW QUITE FIGURATIVE WITH THEIR FIGURES 547   3 DON JUAN 16   98   8
FILCH'D
   FIRE WHICH PROMETHEUS FILCH'D FOR US FROM HEAVEN . . . 90   2 DON JUAN   1   127   8
FILE
   THE FILE OF PIRATES SAVE THE FOREMOST WHO 370   2 DON JUAN   4   48   7
   FIRST CAME HER DAMSELS A DECOROUS FILE 495   2 DON JUAN   5   146   1
   YOUR RANK AND FILE BY THOUSANDS WHILE THE REST 118   3 DON JUAN   8   13   7
FILIAL
   THAT DOUBT SHOULD MINGLE WITH MY FILIAL JOY 364   2 DON JUAN   4   38   7
FILIGREE
   GOLD CUPS OF FILIGREE MADE TO SECURE 307   2 DON JUAN   3   63   5

```
                                                          PAGE VOL      CANTO  STANZA LN
FILL
   PRIDE FAME AMBITION TO FILL UP HIS HEART  . . . . .  .  .  131  2 DON JUAN   1    194   5
   WHAT IS THE END OF FAME 'TIS BUT TO FILL  . . .  .  .  .   146  2 DON JUAN   1    218   1
   THOUGH EVERY WAVE ROLL'D MENACING TO FILL  . . .  . .     188  2 DON JUAN   2     61   5
   TROUBLED HIM NOT AND HE MIGHT SLEEP HIS FILL  .  .  .  .  229  2 DON JUAN   2    137   5
   HE STOPP'D--WHAT SINGULAR EMOTIONS FILL  . . . . .  .  .  286  2 DON JUAN   3     21   3
   FILL HIGH THE CUP WITH SAMIAN WINE . . .  .  .  .  .  .   324  2 DON JUAN   3  L  9   2
   FILL HIGH THE BOWL WITH SAMIAN WINE   . . . .  .  .  .    324  2 DON JUAN   3  L 11   1
   FILL HIGH THE BOWL WITH SAMIAN WINE   . . . .  .  .  .    325  2 DON JUAN   3  L 13   1
   FILL HIGH THE BOWL WITH SAMIAN WINE   . . . .  .  .  .    326  2 DON JUAN   3  L 15   1
   THEY WERE NOT MADE IN THE REAL WORLD TO FILL  .  .  .  .  352  2 DON JUAN   4     15   3
   (IN EACH SENSE OF THE WORD) WHENE'ER I FILL  . . .  .  .  372  2 DON JUAN   4     53   6
   OF YEARS TO FILL A BOWSTRING OR THE THRONE  . . .  . .    499  2 DON JUAN   5    153   2
   WHOM HE FORSOOK TO FILL THE LAUREATE'S STY  . . .  .  .   231  3 DON JUAN  10     13   4
   OF FASHION--SAY WHAT STREAMS NOW FILL THOSE CHANNELS  .  . 308  3 DON JUAN  11     80   6
   HAVE TAKEN UP TO FILL THE FOLLOWING SERMON  . . .  .  .   416  3 DON JUAN  14     15   2
   BUT WHEN OF THE FIRST SIGHT YOU HAVE HAD YOUR FILL  .  .  417  3 DON JUAN  14     17   6
   BUT HOW TO FILL UP THAT SAME VACANT PART . . . .  .  .    442  3 DON JUAN  14     74   3
   THEY FILL THE CANVASS UP--AND VERBUM SAT . . . .  .  .    463  3 DON JUAN  15     16   5
   HOW WAS THY TOIL REWARDED  WE MIGHT FILL . . .  .  .  .   464  3 DON JUAN  15     18   6
FILL'D
   AND FILL'D THEIR SIGN-POSTS THEN LIKE WELLESLEY NOW . .  .  22  2 DON JUAN   1      2   4
   AGUE IN ITS COLD FIT THEY FILL'D THEIR BOAT . . .  .  .   189  2 DON JUAN   2     63   7
   THE QUESTIONER FILL'D UP A GLASS OF WINE  . . .  .  .  .  297  2 DON JUAN   3     42   8
   OF DEEDS AND DAYS WHEN THEY HAD FILL'D THE EAR . . .  .   476  3 DON JUAN  15     46   5
FILLED
   RUSH BACK UPON HIS HEART WHICH FILLED APACE  . . .  .  .  478  2 DON JUAN   5    117   5
   FILLED AS WITH LIGHTNING--FOR HIS SPIRIT SHARED  . . .  . 129  3 DON JUAN   8     33   3
   TO BE FILLED UP BY SPADE OR MATTOCK'S NEAR  . . .  .  .   245  3 DON JUAN  10     42   6
   HAVE FILLED THEIR PAPERS WITH THEIR COMMENTS VARIOUS  . . 352  3 DON JUAN  12     78   4
   THE VACANCIES ARE FILLED UP--SEE GAZETTE  . . .  .  .  .  383  3 DON JUAN  13     54   8
   MIGHT BE FILLED UP AS VAINLY AS BEFORE  . . . .  .  .  .  566  3 DON JUAN  17      9   2
FILLET'S
   THE SILKEN FILLET'S CURB AND SOUGHT TO SHUN  . . .  .  .  313  2 DON JUAN   3     73   6
   THE SILKEN FILLET'S SLIGHT RESTRAINT AND SHUN  . . .  .   313  2 DON JUAN   3     73  V6
FILLETS
   (THERE'S FAME) YOUNG PARTRIDGE' FILLETS DECK'D WITH TRUFFLES 484 3 DON JUAN 15  66   8
   WHAT ARE THE FILLETS ON THE VICTOR'S BROW  . . . .  .  .  485  3 DON JUAN  15     67   1
FILLING
   A MISER FILLING HIS MOST HOARDED CHEST  . . . .  .  .  .  261  2 DON JUAN   2    196   6
   THE FILLING UP THEIR WHOLE CONNUBIAL CARGO--  . . . .  .   51  3 DON JUAN   6     90   7
FILLS
   WHILE VENUS FILLS THE HEART (WITHOUT HEART REALLY  .  .  . 246  2 DON JUAN   2    170   1
   WHILE VENUS FILLS THE HEART (WHICH QUITE AS WELL IS  . .  246  2 DON JUAN   2    170  V1
   OR FILLS WITH LOVE THE PILGRIM ON HIS WAY  . . .  .  .  . 338  2 DON JUAN   3    108   4
   I'VE SAID ALL I KNOW OF A NAME THAT FILLS  . . . .  .  .   76  3 DON JUAN   7     20   5
   WHICH FILLS A REGIMENT (BESIDES THEIR PAY  . . . .  .  .  134  3 DON JUAN   8     42   5
FILM
   AND THE BOY'S EYES WHICH THE DULL FILM HALF GLAZED  . .  203  2 DON JUAN   2     89   5
FILTER'D
   DRAWN FROM THE STARS AND FILTER'D THROUGH THE SKIES  . .  269  2 DON JUAN   2    212   4
   MY LADY'S PRATTLE FILTER'D THROUGH HER WOMAN  . . .  .    418  3 DON JUAN  14     19   8
FILTERED
   WHO PASS LIKE WATER FILTERED IN A TANK  . . . .  .  .  .  396  3 DON JUAN  13     80   3
FILTH
   WITH HUMAN FILTH THAT COLUMN IS DEFILED  . . . .  .  .  .  401  2 DON JUAN   4    105   2
FILTHY
   BECAUSE OF FILTHY LOVES OF GODS AND GODDESSES  . . .  .   44  2 DON JUAN   1     41   2
FIN
   (UNHEEDED TWICE) TO HAVE A FIN OF FISH  . . . .  .  .  .  542  3 DON JUAN  16     87   8
FINANCIERS
   MOST ORATORS BUT VERY FEW FINANCIERS . . . . .  .  .  .   547  3 DON JUAN  16     98   5
FIND
   BUT CAN'T FIND ANY IN THE PRESENT AGE  . . . .  .  .  .    24  2 DON JUAN   1      5   6
   FOR NEITHER OF THEM COULD I EVER FIND  . . . .  .  .  .    34  2 DON JUAN   1     24   4
   AS ALL HAVE FOUND ON TRIAL OR MAY FIND  . . . .  .  .  .   69  2 DON JUAN   1     89   4
   THERE POETS FIND MATERIALS FOR THEIR BOOKS  . . .  .  .   70  2 DON JUAN   1     90   5
   WHERE DIFFERENT TALENTS FIND THEIR DIFFERENT MARTS  . .   91  2 DON JUAN   1    128   6
   AND FIND A DEUCED BALANCE WITH THE DEVIL  . . .  .  .  .  113  2 DON JUAN   1    167   8
   AND CRY THAT THEY THE MORAL CANNOT FIND  . . . .  .  .  .  141  2 DON JUAN   1    208   5
   I FIND THAT WINE OR BRANDY IS FORBID TOO . . . .  .  .    145  2 DON JUAN   1    216  V6
   THE WORLD WILL FIND THEE AFTER MANY DAYS . . . .  .  .    149  2 DON JUAN   1    222   4
   AND FIND A QUINSY VERY HARD TO TREAT . . . . .  .  .  .   168  2 DON JUAN   2     22   4
   THAT PASSENGERS WOULD FIND IT MUCH AMISS . . . .  .  .    173  2 DON JUAN   2     33   3
   AS YOU MAY FIND WHENE'ER YOU LIKE TO PROVE HER . . .  .   276  2 DON JUAN   3      3   5
   TO FIND SO MUCH GOOD COMPANY INVITED  . . . .  .  .  .    294  2 DON JUAN   3     37   8
   IT MAY SEEM STRANGE TO FIND HIS MANNERS BLAND  . . .  .   299  2 DON JUAN   3     47   5
   TO FIND OUR HEARTHSTONE TURN'D INTO A TOMB  . . .  .  .   301  2 DON JUAN   3     51   5
   TO FIND OUR CHILDREN RUNNING RESTIVE--THEY  . . .  .  .   305  2 DON JUAN   3     59   2
   AND TOOK HIS KINGDOM FROM HIM YOU WILL FIND  . . .  .  .  308  2 DON JUAN   3     65   6
   THEY'LL NEVER FIND IT OUT UNLESS I OWN  . . . .  .  .  .  342  2 DON JUAN   3    111   4
   TO FIND THREE PERFECT PIPES OF THE THIRD SEX . . .  .  .  391  2 DON JUAN   4     86   8
   THINGS WHICH IN HUNGRY MORTALS' EYES FIND FAVOUR . . .  . 437  2 DON JUAN   5     47   3
   BECAUSE THEY CAN'T FIND OUT THE VERY SPOT  . . . .  .  .  447  2 DON JUAN   5     62   3
   AND YOU WILL FIND US NOT TOO FOND OF JOKING  . . .  .  .  454  2 DON JUAN   5     75   4
   TO FIND OUR WAY TO MARMORA WITHOUT BOATS . . . .  .  .    464  2 DON JUAN   5     92   6
   WILL SCARCELY FIND PHILOSOPHY FOR MORE  . . . .  .  .  .   12  3 DON JUAN   6     12   6
   SHE DID NOT FIND HERSELF THE LEAST DISPOSED  . . .  .  .   48  3 DON JUAN   6     84   5
   BUT THEY WILL NOT FIND LIBERTY A TROY--  . . . .  .  .    106  3 DON JUAN   7     79   8
```

	PAGE	VOL	CANTO	STANZA	LN

FIND   (CONTINUED)

	PAGE	VOL	CANTO	STANZA	LN
BUT GLORY'S GLORY AND IF YOU WOULD FIND	108	3 DON JUAN	7	84	7
PERHAPS MAY FIND IT BETTER THAN A NEW ONE)--	126	3 DON JUAN	8	29	8
HE STUMBLED ON TO TRY IF HE COULD FIND	126	3 DON JUAN	8	30	6
HE WOULD FIND OTHERS WHO WOULD FAIN BE RID SO	133	3 DON JUAN	8	40	3
YOU'LL FIND TEN THOUSAND HANDSOME COXCOMBS BLOODY	167	3 DON JUAN	8	112	8
SUSPICIOUS PEOPLE WHO FIND FAULT IN HASTE	230	3 DON JUAN	10	11	3
SHE COULD NOT FIND AT FIRST A FIT SUCCESSOR	247	3 DON JUAN	10	47	8
NOR DID SHE FIND THE QUANTITY ENCUMBER	248	3 DON JUAN	10	48	6
OR ADAMANT TO FIND THE WORLD A SPIRIT	268	3 DON JUAN	11	1	7
IS THAT I FIND NO SPOT WHERE MAN CAN REST EYE ON	269	3 DON JUAN	11	3	5
MAY FIND HIMSELF WITHIN THAT ISLE OF RICHES	273	3 DON JUAN	11	11	7
I'VE DONE TO FIND THE SAME THROUGHOUT LIFE'S JOURNEY	281	3 DON JUAN	11	28	7
AND CANNOT FIND A BILL'S SMALL ITEMS COSTLY	283	3 DON JUAN	11	31	4
HE'LL FIND IT RATHER DIFFICULT SOME DAY	298	3 DON JUAN	11	59	3
TO FIND RETORTS FOR INNOCENT BLOOD SHED	314	3 DON JUAN	11	V 75	4
TO FIND HOW VERY BADLY SHE SELECTED	333	3 DON JUAN	12	36	8
(I WISH THAT OTHERS WOULD FIND OUT THE SAME)	336	3 DON JUAN	12	42	2
I THINK YOU'LL FIND FROM MANY A FAMILY PICTURE	337	3 DON JUAN	12	46	3
FOR ME I LEAVE THE MATTER WHERE I FIND IT	352	3 DON JUAN	12	80	1
YOU'LL FIND IT OF A DIFFERENT CONSTRUCTION	356	3 DON JUAN	12	87	3
IN BRITAIN--WHICH OF COURSE TRUE PATRIOTS FIND	359	3 DON JUAN	13	2	7
THE VERY LOWEST FIND OUT AN INFERIOR	367	3 DON JUAN	13	19	3
FIND ONE WHERE NOTHING NAUGHTY CAN BE SHOWN	370	3 DON JUAN	13	27	6
BEFORE THEY FIND AN HOUR TO INTRODUCE IT	408	3 DON JUAN	13	109	7
PERHAPS MANKIND MIGHT FIND THE PATH THEY MISS--	410	3 DON JUAN	14	1	3
AND YOU WILL FIND THOUGH SHUDDERING AT THE MIRROR	413	3 DON JUAN	14	6	3
AND YOU WILL FIND HER SUM OF YEARS IN PLENTY	433	3 DON JUAN	14	54	8
FIND ONE EACH DAY OF THE DELIGHTFUL YEAR	438	3 DON JUAN	14	63	6
AND YOU WILL BE PERHAPS SURPRISED TO FIND	446	3 DON JUAN	14	84	2
THAT VIOLENT THINGS MORE QUICKLY FIND A TERM	451	3 DON JUAN	14	94	3
WE SURELY SHALL FIND SOMETHING WORTH RESEARCH	468	3 DON JUAN	15	27	5
BLOOD IS NOT WATER AND WHERE SHALL WE FIND	475	3 DON JUAN	15	44	4
WHOSE GREATEST FAULT WAS LEAVING FEW TO FIND	479	3 DON JUAN	15	54	4
WHICH YOU MIGHT ELSEWHERE HOPE TO FIND IN VAIN	502	3 DON JUAN	16	3	4
ALSO THEREON--BUT THAT'S NOT MUCH WE FIND	525	3 DON JUAN	16	49	6

FINDING

	PAGE	VOL	CANTO	STANZA	LN
FINDING THEMSELVES SO VERY MUCH EXCEEDED	26	2 DON JUAN	1	10	7
BUT FINDING NO PLACE FOR THEIR LANDING BETTER	211	2 DON JUAN	2	104	3
NOT FINDING THAT THE ADDITIONS MUCH ENCUMBER	276	2 DON JUAN	3	3	8
OF GETTING ON HIMSELF AND FINDING STATIONS	239	3 DON JUAN	10	30	3
HIS MOTHER DONNA INEZ FINDING TOO	240	3 DON JUAN	10	31	1
THE LUCK OF FINDING EVERYBODY SOLVENT	458	3 DON JUAN	15	7	8
THAN FINDING THUS THEIR GENIUS STAND REBUKED	479	3 DON JUAN	15	53	6

FINDS

	PAGE	VOL	CANTO	STANZA	LN
THE ODDS ARE THAT HE FINDS A HANDSOME URN	287	2 DON JUAN	3	23	5
WHERE GEOGRAPHY FINDS NO ONE TO OBLIGE HER	348	3 DON JUAN	12	70	4
AN ERRING WOMAN FINDS AN OPENER DOOR	352	3 DON JUAN	12	79	6
JUST AS A MANDARIN FINDS NOTHING FINE--	373	3 DON JUAN	13	34	5
BUT FOR POST HORSES WHO FINDS SYMPATHY	377	3 DON JUAN	13	42	5

FINE

	PAGE	VOL	CANTO	STANZA	LN
COULD NEVER MAKE A MEMORY SO FINE AS	27	2 DON JUAN	1	11	7
AS SAINT AUGUSTINE IN HIS FINE CONFESSIONS	47	2 DON JUAN	1	47	7
WITH ALL THE PROMISE OF AS FINE A FACE	48	2 DON JUAN	1	49	3
AT TWELVE HE WAS A FINE BUT QUIET BOY	49	2 DON JUAN	1	50	2
SUCH AS THE ANGELS THINK SO VERY FINE	64	2 DON JUAN	1	79	3
FRAUGHT WITH THIS FINE INTENTION AND WELL FENCED	66	2 DON JUAN	1	82	7
'TWAS IN NOVEMBER WHEN FINE DAYS ARE FEW	94	2 DON JUAN	1	134	3
HIS SPEECH WAS A FINE SAMPLE ON THE WHOLE	116	2 DON JUAN	1	174	7
'TWAS A FINE CAUSE FOR THOSE IN LAW DELIGHTING	150	2 DON JUAN	1	V 1	1
BEFORE THE SEA UNTIL IT SHOULD GROW FINE	189	2 DON JUAN	2	62	3
AND CARRY THEM TO SHORE THESE HOPES WERE FINE	192	2 DON JUAN	2	69	6
FINE TRUTHS EVEN CONSCIENCE TOO HAS A TOUGH JOB	264	2 DON JUAN	2	203	6
A FINE EXTENSION OF THE FACULTIES	269	2 DON JUAN	2	212	2
YET A FINE FAMILY IS A FINE THING	306	2 DON JUAN	3	60	1
YET A FINE FAMILY IS A FINE THING	306	2 DON JUAN	3	60	1
IN SMALL FINE CHINA CUPS CAME IN AT LAST	307	2 DON JUAN	3	63	4
HER HAIR WAS STARR'D WITH GEMS HER VEIL'S FINE FOLD	312	2 DON JUAN	3	72	4
SOME FINE EXAMPLES OF THE EPOPEE	332	2 DON JUAN	3	97	7
MY OWN MEANING WHEN I WOULD BE VERY FINE	346	2 DON JUAN	4	5	5
ALL THIS IS VERY FINE AND MAY BE TRUE	422	2 DON JUAN	5	23	1
A PAIR OF DRAWERS--OF FINE CRIMSON SATIN	456	2 DON JUAN	5	77	V2
PRESENTED A FINE MARK TO THROW A SHELL IN	78	3 DON JUAN	7	23	8
HE'S A FINE BOY THE WOMEN MAY BE SENT	100	3 DON JUAN	7	66	7
NO CAESAR BUT A FINE YOUNG LAD WHO FOUGHT	126	3 DON JUAN	8	29	4
BUT DOUBTLESS THEY PREFER A FINE YOUNG MAN	167	3 DON JUAN	8	112	3
HER FACE WAS NOBLE HER EYES FINE MOUTH GRACIOUS	211	3 DON JUAN	9	58	8
WHEN WROTH WHILE PLEASED SHE WAS AS FINE A FIGURE	213	3 DON JUAN	9	62	2
THROUGH ALL THE PURPLE AND FINE LINEN FITTER	237	3 DON JUAN	10	26	6
THAT'S RATHER FINE THE GENTLE SOUND OF THAMIS--	279	3 DON JUAN	11	24	1
BUT) OF FINE UNCLIPT GOLD WHERE DULLY RESTS	321	3 DON JUAN	12	12	5
'TIS FINE TO SEE THEM SCATTERING REFUSALS	332	3 DON JUAN	12	34	7
THEOLOGY FINE ARTS OR FINER STAYS	340	3 DON JUAN	12	53	2
PERHAPS THE FINE OLD FELLOW SPOKE IN JEST--	361	3 DON JUAN	13	7	5
JUST AS A MANDARIN FINDS NOTHING FINE--	373	3 DON JUAN	13	34	5
THE PEERAGE TO A MANSION VERY FINE	381	3 DON JUAN	13	50	4
MET THE MORN AS THEY MIGHT IF FINE THEY RODE	406	3 DON JUAN	13	104	2
SHE WAS A FINE AND SOMEWHAT FULL-BLOWN BLONDE	428	3 DON JUAN	14	42	1
TO LEAVE THEM HOVERING AS THE EFFECT IS FINE	453	3 DON JUAN	14	97	5

```
                                                             PAGE VOL      CANTO  STANZA  LN
FINED
   FORBID BY HEAVENLY FINED BY HUMAN LAWS    . . . . . . . .  113  2 DON JUAN   1     167    3
FINELY
   HER DRESS WAS MANY-COLOUR'D FINELY SPUN   . . . . . . . .  220  2 DON JUAN   2     121    2
FINER
   I'VE SEEN MUCH FINER WOMEN RIPE AND REAL . . . . . . . .   218  2 DON JUAN   2     118    7
   THAT FINER SIMPLER MUSIC NE'ER WAS HEARD .  . . . . . . .  236  2 DON JUAN   2     151    5
   OUR LITTLE SELVES RE-FORM'D IN FINER CLAY   . . . . . . .  305  2 DON JUAN   3      59    4
   THEOLOGY FINE ARTS OR FINER STAYS . . . . . . . . . . .    340  3 DON JUAN  12      53    2
   AND TUNE THE CONCORD TO A FINER MOOD . . . . . . . . .     451  3 DON JUAN  14      93    4
FINEST
   A BATH A BREAKFAST AND THE FINEST EYES  . . . . . . . .    246  2 DON JUAN   2     171    2
   WERE OF THE FINEST THAT E'ER FLOUNCED IN NETS . . . . .    307  2 DON JUAN   3      62    4
   THUS HE PROFANELY TERMED THE FINEST LACE . . . . . . .     455  2 DON JUAN   5      76    7
FINGER
   AND WITHOUT WORD A SIGN HER FINGER DREW ON  . . . . . .    234  2 DON JUAN   2     146    4
FINGERS
   HIS FINGERS WITH A PURE PLATONIC SQUEEZE . . . . . . .      81  2 DON JUAN   1     111    5
   HER SMALL WHITE FINGERS SCARCE COULD REACH THE TAPER . .   134  2 DON JUAN   1     198   V3
   AND NOW BY DINT OF FINGERS AND OF EYES . . . . . . . .     242  2 DON JUAN   2     163    1
   ANON HER THIN WAN FINGERS BEAT THE WALL . . . . . . . .    380  2 DON JUAN   4      66    1
   AS BABA WITH HIS FINGERS MADE THEM FALL  . . . . . . .     463  2 DON JUAN   5      90    3
   THOUGH ON MORE THOROUGH-BRED OR FAIRER FINGERS . . . . .   472  2 DON JUAN   5     106    2
   PRICKING HER FINGERS WITH THOSE CURSED PINS . . . . . .     36  3 DON JUAN   6      61    7
   A NOISE LIKE TO WET FINGERS DRAWN ON GLASS . . . . . .     556  3 DON JUAN  16     114    1
FINISH
   PERHAPS TO FINISH JUAN'S EDUCATION . . . . . . . . .        75  2 DON JUAN   1     101    6
FINISH'D
   IN THIS ANATOMY I'VE FINISH'D NOW . . . . . . . . . .      271  2 DON JUAN   2     216    2
   ALL TRAGEDIES ARE FINISH'D BY A DEATH . . . . . . . .      280  2 DON JUAN   3       9    1
FINISHED
   FINISHED WITH BRIGHT GOLD LACE HER JACKET'S FELLOW   . .   311  2 DON JUAN   3      70   V4
   A FINISHED GENTLEMAN FROM TOP TO TOE . . . . . . .         354  3 DON JUAN  12      84    8
FIRE
   UNTIL AT LENGTH THE SMOTHER'D FIRE BROKE OUT   . . . .      35  2 DON JUAN   1      26    7
   WAS LARGE AND DARK SUPPRESSING HALF ITS FIRE   . . . .      54  2 DON JUAN   1      60    2
   FIRE WHICH PROMETHEUS FILCH'D FOR US FROM HEAVEN . . .      90  2 DON JUAN   1     127    8
   I'M FOND OF FIRE AND CRICKETS AND ALL THAT . . . . .        94  2 DON JUAN   1     135    7
   AND SUMMON LACKEYS ARM'D WITH FIRE AND SWORD   . . . .      97  2 DON JUAN   1     139    7
   ANTONIA CRIED OUT RAPE AND JULIA FIRE . . . . . . .        122  2 DON JUAN   1     184    2
   OF FIRE THAN WATER SPITE OF OATHS AND TEARS . . . . .      174  2 DON JUAN   2      35    6
   TO KINDLE FIRE AND AS THE NEW FLAMES GAVE  . . . . .       216  2 DON JUAN   2     115    5
   THEY MADE A FIRE BUT SUCH A FIRE AS THEY . . . . . .       226  2 DON JUAN   2     132    1
   THEY MADE A FIRE BUT SUCH A FIRE AS THEY . . . . . .       226  2 DON JUAN   2     132    1
   OF THE NEW FIRE WHICH ZOE KEPT UP KNEELING  . . . . .      237  2 DON JUAN   2     153    6
   AND IN THE FIRE HIS RECENT RAGS THEY SCATTER'D . . . .     240  2 DON JUAN   2     160    3
   LIKE EARTHQUAKES FROM THE HIDDEN FIRE CALL'D CENTRAL . .   271  2 DON JUAN   2     215    8
   WAS SUCH AS FIRE ACCORDS TO A WET BLANKET  . . . . . .     294  2 DON JUAN   3      36    8
   WAS MUCH THE SAME AS FIRE GIVES A WET BLANKET  . . . .     294  2 DON JUAN   3      36   V8
   THUS SUNG HE AND SUCH IS THE INHERENT FIRE  . . . . .      319  2 DON JUAN   3      84   V1
   THE FIRE BURST FORTH FROM HER NUMIDIAN VEINS   . . . .     375  2 DON JUAN   4      57    7
   'TIS SAID NO ONE IN HAND CAN HOLD A FIRE . . . . . .       396  2 DON JUAN   4      96    5
   AND AIR--EARTH--WATER--FIRE LIVE--AND WE DEAD  . . . .     432  2 DON JUAN   5      39    6
   YET SMELT ROAST-MEAT BEHELD A HUGE FIRE SHINE  . . . .     439  2 DON JUAN   5      50    5
   IF I SAID FIRE FLASHED FROM GULBEYAZ' EYES . . . . .       489  2 DON JUAN   5     134    1
   'TWERE NOTHING--FOR HER EYES FLASHED ALWAYS FIRE  . . .    489  2 DON JUAN   5     134    2
   IF TRUE 'TIS NO GREAT LEASE OF ITS OWN FIRE . . . . .       14  3 DON JUAN   6      16    2
   SO PLACED AS TO IMPEDE THE FIRE OF THOSE . . . . . .        71  3 DON JUAN   7      10    7
   AND BY A FIRE OF MUSQUETRY AND GRAPE  . . . . . . .         81  3 DON JUAN   7      29    7
   THE TURKISH FIRE AND AIDED BY THEIR OWN  . . . . . .        81  3 DON JUAN   7      30    2
   AND GALLED THE RUSSIANS WITH A HEAVY FIRE  . . . . .        82  3 DON JUAN   7      31    4
   ALL WAS PREPARED--THE FIRE THE SWORD THE MEN   . . . .     113  3 DON JUAN   8       2    1
   THEN ONE VAST FIRE AIR EARTH AND STREAM EMBRACED  . . .    115  3 DON JUAN   8       7    5
   THE FIRE WAS THAT WERE RED VESUVIUS LOADED . . . . .       119  3 DON JUAN   8      16    2
   AT OTHER TIMES REPULSED BY THE CLOSE FIRE  . . . . .       121  3 DON JUAN   8      20    5
   OVER THE HILLS A FIRE ENOUGH TO BLIND . . . . . . .        126  3 DON JUAN   8      30    4
   RUSHED WHERE THE THICKEST FIRE ANNOUNCED MOST FOES   . . ·127  3 DON JUAN   8      32    8
   AND WHERE THE HOTTEST FIRE WAS SEEN AND HEARD  . . . .     129  3 DON JUAN   8      33    5
   THE LIVELIEST FIRE AND SAW THE FIERCEST FLOOD  . . . .     129  3 DON JUAN   8      33   V4
   AND LED THEM BACK INTO THE HEAVIEST FIRE . . . . . .       133  3 DON JUAN   8      41    8
   BUT THE STONE BASTION STILL KEPT UP ITS FIRE   . . . .     171  3 DON JUAN   8     120    1
   MIGHT SCATTER FIRE THROUGH ICE LIKE HECLA'S FLAME . . .    254  3 DON JUAN  10      59    8
   THOUGH APT TO ACT WITH FIRE UPON OCCASION  . . . . .       365  3 DON JUAN  13      14    5
   LIE WITH THEIR HALLELUJAHS QUENCH'D LIKE FIRE  . . . .     387  3 DON JUAN  13      62    8
   EMBARRASS'D SOMEWHAT BOTH WITH FIRE AND WATER  . . . .     423  3 DON JUAN  14      30    8
   WHO EATS FIRE GRATIS (SINCE THE PAY'S BUT SMALL) . . .     446  3 DON JUAN  14      83    6
FIRED
   THE ROSY SKY WITH THE LAST SUNLIGHT FIRED  . . . . .       335  2 DON JUAN   3     101   V6
   BUT AFTER BEING FIRED AT ONCE OR TWICE . . . . . .         366  2 DON JUAN   4      41    7
   WERE BRISKLY FIRED AND ANSWERED IN DUE ORDER   . . . .      85  3 DON JUAN   7      38    8
   OF THE NEXT BASTION FIRED AWAY LIKE DEVILS . ·. . . .      134  3 DON JUAN   8      44    2
   AND FIRED IT INTO ONE ASSAILANT'S PUDDING--  . . . .       274  3 DON JUAN  11      13    4
   FIRED WITH AN ABSTRACT LOVE OF VIRTUE SHE  . . . . .       430  3 DON JUAN  14      46    2
FIREFACE
   AND GENERAL FIREFACE FAMOUS IN THE FIELD . . . . . ·. . .  399  3 DON JUAN  13      88    2
FIRE-FLIES
   FONDLY THE WHEELING FIRE-FLIES FLEW AROUND HER . . . . .   435  3 DON JUAN  14      57    1
FIRES
   FOR THEY REMEMBER BATTLES FIRES AND WRECKS . . . . .       172  2 DON JUAN   2      31    4

                                          271
```

	PAGE	VOL	CANTO	STANZA	LV

FIRES (CONTINUED)
THE SEA-COAL FIRES THE EARLIEST OF THE YEAR . . . . . . 395 3 DON JUAN 13   77   6
SWORE PRAISES AND RECALL'D THEIR FORMER FIRES . . . . . 425 3 DON JUAN 14   34   6
FIRESHIPS
THREE FIRESHIPS LOST THEIR AMIABLE EXISTENCE . . . . . 80 3 DON JUAN 7   28   3
FIRE-SIDE
TO THE FIRE-SIDE (A SIGHT TO TOUCH A SINNER) . . . . . 306 2 DON JUAN 3   60   6
FIRING
FIRING AND THRUSTING SLASHING SWEATING GLOWING . . . . . 120 3 DON JUAN 8   19   6
WHEN AFTER A GOOD DEAL OF HEAVY FIRING . . . . 125 3 DON JUAN 8   27   7
KEEP MERELY FIRING AT A FOOLISH DISTANCE . . . . . . 151 3 DON JUAN 8   78   8
FIRING THE COUNTIES TILL THEY IMPIOUS WAR WAGE . . . . . 530 3 DON JUAN 16   60   V5
FIRM
WAS COARSER AND HER AIR THOUGH FIRM LESS FREE . . . . . 221 2 DON JUAN 2 122   6
AND HOW SHOULD THE MOST FIERCE OF ALL BE FIRM . . . . . 451 3 DON JUAN 14   94   5
WHICH TIED IN ONE FIRM KNOT WITHOUT CONFUSION . . . . . 536 3 DON JUAN 16   74   V7
WILL HAVE A FIRM POST OBIT ON POSTERITY . . . . . . 566 3 DON JUAN 17   9   8
FIRMAN
WAITING FOR HIS SUBLIMITY'S FIRMAN . . . . 393 2 DON JUAN 4   91   2
FIRMER
AND FIRMER FAITH NO LADYE-LOVE DESIRE . . . . 396 2 DON JUAN 4   96   3
FIRMNESS
'TIS TO RETORT WITH FIRMNESS AND WHEN HE . . . . . . 117 2 DON JUAN 1 175   7
YOUR NATURE'S FIRMNESS--KNOW YOUR DAUGHTER'S TOO . . . . 366 2 DON JUAN 4   42   8
FIRMNESS YCLEPT IN HEROES KINGS AND SEAMEN . . . . . 448 3 DON JUAN 14   89   3
IT HAD BEEN FIRMNESS NOW 'TIS PERTINACITY . . . . . . 449 3 DON JUAN 14   90   2
FIRST
WHERE OUR FIRST PARENTS NEVER LEARN'D TO KISS . . . . . 30 2 DON JUAN 1   18   3
AND SO THEY WERE SUBMITTED FIRST TO HER ALL . . . . . 43 2 DON JUAN 1   39   6
INDIFFERENT FROM THE FIRST OR CALLOUS GROWN . . . . . 59 2 DON JUAN 1   68   6
EMBARRASS'D AT FIRST STARTING WITH A NOVICE . . . . . 62 2 DON JUAN 1   74   8
A HAND MAY FIRST AND THEN A LIP BE KIST . . . . . . 65 2 DON JUAN 1   80   3
IS FIRST AND PASSIONATE LOVE--IT STANDS ALONE . . . . . 90 2 DON JUAN 1 127   2
FIRST KNOCKS WERE HEARD THEN MADAM--MADAM--HIST . . . . 95 2 DON JUAN 1 136   8
MY DEAR I WAS THE FIRST WHO CAME AWAY . . . . 98 2 DON JUAN 1 141   8
AT FIRST HE TRIED TO HAMMER AN EXCUSE . . . . 110 2 DON JUAN 1 162   1
ALFONSO FIRST EXAMINED WELL THEIR FASHION . . . . . . 121 2 DON JUAN 1 181   7
FIRST VOW'D (AND NEVER HAD SHE VOW'D IN VAIN) . . . . . 128 2 DON JUAN 1 190   5
BECAUSE THE FIRST IS CRAZED BEYOND ALL HOPE . . . . . 139 2 DON JUAN 1 205   3
THIS STORY IS NOT MORAL FIRST I PRAY . . . . 140 2 DON JUAN 1 207   2
OF WHICH WE ARE LAVISH FIRST AND THEN RAPACIOUS . . . . 145 2 DON JUAN 1 217   V8
CHEOPS ERECTED THE FIRST PYRAMID . . . . 146 2 DON JUAN 1 219   2
THE FOUR FIRST RHYMES ARE SOUTHEY'S EVERY LINE . . . . . 149 2 DON JUAN 1 222   7
NOW SHRINKING BACK NOW MIDST THE FIRST HE SEEMS . . . . 155 2 DON JUAN 1 V 6   1
IF ALL THINGS BE CONSIDER'D FIRST THERE WAS . . . . . 158 2 DON JUAN 2   3   2
HIS FIRST--PERHAPS HIS LAST--FAREWELL OF SPAIN . . . . . 162 2 DON JUAN 2   11   8
FIRST PARTINGS FORM A LESSON HARD TO LEARN . . . . . 164 2 DON JUAN 2   14   3
BOTH MAIN AND MIZEN FIRST THE MIZEN WENT . . . . . . 173 2 DON JUAN 2   32   2
AND FIRST ONE UNIVERSAL SHRIEK THERE RUSH'D . . . . . 184 2 DON JUAN 2   53   1
LIKE THE FIRST OLD GREEK PRIVATEER THE ARGO . . . . . 191 2 DON JUAN 2   66   8
AND THOUGH AT FIRST THEIR STRENGTH IT MIGHT RENEW . . . 192 2 DON JUAN 2   68   3
WITH SOME REMORSE RECEIVED (THOUGH FIRST DENIED) . . . . 193 2 DON JUAN 2   71   5
AND FIRST A LITTLE CRUCIFIX HE KISS'D . . . . 197 2 DON JUAN 2   76   7
HAD HIS FIRST CHOICE OF MORSELS FOR HIS PAINS . . . . . 197 2 DON JUAN 2   77   2
THERE WERE SOME OTHER REASONS THE FIRST WAS . . . . . 199 2 DON JUAN 2   81   4
WHILE A FEW PRAY'D--(THE FIRST TIME FOR SOME YEARS)-- . . 208 2 DON JUAN 2   98   5
MISTRESS AND MAID THE FIRST WAS ONLY DAUGHTER . . . . . 222 2 DON JUAN 2 124   7
WHILE THE SUN SMILED ON HER WITH HIS FIRST FLAME . . . . 232 2 DON JUAN 2 142   3
AND THE FIRST BREAKFAST SPOILT PREPARED A NEW ONE . . . 234 2 DON JUAN 2 146   6
LIKE A RICH WRECK--HER FIRST LOVE AND HER LAST . . . . . 247 2 DON JUAN 2 173   8
TO BE HER SOUL'S FIRST IDOL AND ITS LAST . . . . . . 247 2 DON JUAN 2 173   V8
NOR THE FIRST SPARKLE OF THE DESERT-SPRING . . . . . 251 2 DON JUAN 2 180   5
OF NATURE'S ORACLE--FIRST LOVE--THAT ALL . . . . . . 256 2 DON JUAN 2 189   7
EXCEPTING OUR FIRST PARENTS SUCH A PAIR . . . . . . 258 2 DON JUAN 2 193   3
A CHILD THE FIRST TIME THAT IT SUCKS THE BREAST . . . . 261 2 DON JUAN 2 196   V2
FOR THE FIRST PASSION STAYS THERE SUCH A WHILE . . . . . 271 2 DON JUAN 2 215   3
IN HER FIRST PASSION WOMAN LOVES HER LOVER . . . . . 276 2 DON JUAN 3   3   1
ONE MAN ALONE AT FIRST HER HEART CAN MOVE . . . . . . 276 2 DON JUAN 3   3   6
ALTHOUGH NO DOUBT HER FIRST OF LOVE AFFAIRS . . . . . 276 2 DON JUAN 3   4   5
THE FIRST AND TALLEST HER WHITE KERCHIEF WAVING . . . . 291 2 DON JUAN 3   30   2
OF WHICH THE FIRST NE'ER KNOWS THE SECOND CAUSE . . . . 318 2 DON JUAN 3   82   8
FOR THE FIRST MRS MILTON LEFT HIS HOUSE . . . . . . 328 2 DON JUAN 3   91   8
OF THOSE WHO SAIL THE SEAS ON THE FIRST DAY . . . . . 338 2 DON JUAN 3 108   2
OUR HEARTS FIRST IN THE DEPTHS OF LETHE'S SPRING . . . . 346 2 DON JUAN 4   4   5
BREAK WITH THE FIRST FALL THEY CAN NE'ER BEHOLD . . . . 350 2 DON JUAN 4   11   4
OF LOVE HAD FIRST O'ERWHELM'D THEM FROM SUCH SKIES . . . 354 2 DON JUAN 4   20   4
ON THE FIRST FOE WHOM LAMBRO'S CALL MIGHT BRING . . . . 365 2 DON JUAN 4   39   8
AT THE FIRST NOTES IRREGULAR AND SHARP . . . . . . 379 2 DON JUAN 4   65   3
AT THE FIRST TWO BOOKS HAVING TOO MUCH TRUTH . . . . . 397 2 DON JUAN 4   97   4
AND THE UNQUIET FEELINGS WHICH FIRST WOKE . . . . . . 402 2 DON JUAN 4 106   3
HUMBOLDT THE FIRST OF TRAVELLERS BUT NOT . . . . . . 406 2 DON JUAN 4 112   1
I CRIED UPON MY FIRST WIFE'S DYING DAY . . . . 420 2 DON JUAN 5   19   7
LOVE'S THE FIRST NET WHICH SPREADS ITS DEADLY MESH . . . 422 2 DON JUAN 5   22   5
FIRST BUT FOR ONE AND AFTER FOR THE PAIR . . . . . . 425 2 DON JUAN 5   28   3
WHICH FOR THE LAST THOUGH NOT THE FIRST TIME BLED . . . 431 2 DON JUAN 5   37   4
HE LED THEM ONWARD FIRST THROUGH A LOW THICKET . . . . . 433 2 DON JUAN 5   41   3
WAS FOR THE ELDER AND THE STOUTER FIRST . . . . . . 451 2 DON JUAN 5   68   2
SHE SIGNED TO BABA WHO FIRST KISSED THE HEM . . . . . 466 2 DON JUAN 5   96   6
GULBEYAZ FOR THE FIRST TIME IN HER DAYS . . . . . . 482 2 DON JUAN 5 122   1

FIRST   (CONTINUED)

	PAGE	VOL	CANTO		STANZA	LN
HER FIRST THOUGHT WAS TO CUT OFF JUAN'S HEAD	491	2	DON JUAN	5	139	1
AND FIRST HE WONDERED WHY HE HAD REFUSED	493	2	DON JUAN	5	142	3
FIRST CAME HER DAMSELS A DECOROUS FILE	495	2	DON JUAN	5	146	1
AND APT TO BE TRANSFERRED TO THE FIRST BUYER	14	3	DON JUAN	6	16	6
AFTER THE FIRST INVESTIGATING VIEW	24	3	DON JUAN	6	37	3
WHEN FIRST SHE STARTS AND THEN RETURNS TO PEEP	36	3	DON JUAN	6	60	7
COULD NOT AT FIRST EXPOUND WHAT WAS AMISS	43	3	DON JUAN	6	74	8
HER FEET THAT HER FIRST MOVEMENT WAS TO STOOP	44	3	DON JUAN	6	77	3
AND POOR JUANNA TOO THE CHILD'S FIRST NIGHT	46	3	DON JUAN	6	81	1
FOR THIS FIRST FAULT AND THAT ON NO CONDITION	47	3	DON JUAN	6	82	5
WITH THE FIRST RAY OR RATHER GREY OF MORN	49	3	DON JUAN	6	87	1
THE FIRST WAS TO BOMBARD IT AND KNOCK DOWN	78	3	DON JUAN	7	23	3
THAT ONE WOULD THINK THE FIRST WHO BORE IT ADAM	79	3	DON JUAN	7	25	8
IS OF ALL DREAMS THE FIRST HALLUCINATION	88	3	DON JUAN	7	44	4
WAS MADE WITH ALL ALACRITY THE FIRST	91	3	DON JUAN	7	50	2
YOU WERE THE FIRST I' THE BREACH I WAS NOT SLACK	98	3	DON JUAN	7	61	3
BUT DEEMS HIMSELF THE FIRST IN GLORY'S VAN	108	3	DON JUAN	7	84	6
THOUGH 'TWAS DON JUAN'S FIRST OF FIELDS AND THOUGH	121	3	DON JUAN	8	21	1
FOR THE FIRST AND LAST TIME FOR LIKE A PAD	122	3	DON JUAN	8	22	5
JUST AT THE CLOSE OF THE FIRST BRIDAL YEAR	125	3	DON JUAN	8	27	4
THE FIRST TIME THOUGHT QUITE TERRIBLE ENOUGH	134	3	DON JUAN	8	42	2
FIRST ONE OR TWO THEN FIVE SIX AND A DOZEN	135	3	DON JUAN	8	45	1
THE GENTLEMEN THAT WERE THE FIRST TO SHOW	135	3	DON JUAN	8	45	6
AMONG THE FIRST--I WILL NOT SAY THE FIRST	136	3	DON JUAN	8	48	1
AMONG THE FIRST--I WILL NOT SAY THE FIRST	136	3	DON JUAN	8	48	1
AT FIRST IT GRUMBLES THEN IT SWEARS AND THEN	138	3	DON JUAN	8	51	1
BUT TO CONTINUE--I SAY NOT THE FIRST	138	3	DON JUAN	8	52	1
BUT OF THE FIRST OUR LITTLE FRIEND DON JUAN	138	3	DON JUAN	8	52	2
THE TOWN WAS ENTERED FIRST ONE COLUMN MADE	146	3	DON JUAN	8	69	1
THE TURKS AT FIRST PRETENDED TO HAVE SCAMPERED	149	3	DON JUAN	8	75	6
BY GOD WE'LL BE TOO LATE FOR THE FIRST CUT	162	3	DON JUAN	8	101	1
THE FIRST WITH SIGHS THE SECOND WITH AN OATH	166	3	DON JUAN	8	109	3
BUT BRAVELY RUSHED ON HIS FIRST HEAVENLY NIGHT	168	3	DON JUAN	8	114	3
A GLANCE ON THAT SLAIN SON HIS FIRST AND LAST	169	3	DON JUAN	8	116	8
WITH BLOODY HANDS HE WROTE HIS FIRST DISPATCH	178	3	DON JUAN	8	133	5
AS THE FIRST CANTO PROMISED YOU HAVE NOW	181	3	DON JUAN	8	138	2
NOW--THAT THE RABBLE'S FIRST VAIN SHOUTS ARE O'ER	187	3	DON JUAN	9	9	6
AS ALSO OF THE FIRST ACADEMICIANS	191	3	DON JUAN	9	17	2
TO BE THE FIRST OF WHAT WE USED TO CALL	198	3	DON JUAN	9	32	2
FIRST OUT OF AND THEN BACK AGAIN TO CHAOS	201	3	DON JUAN	9	37	7
SINCE FIRST HER MAJESTY WAS SINGLY CROWNED	205	3	DON JUAN	9	46	6
CALLS ILION'S THE FIRST DAMAGES ON RECORD	209	3	DON JUAN	9	53	8
OF HER FIRST FRUIT BUT HOW HE FALLS AND RISES	210	3	DON JUAN	9	55	7
GREAT JOY WAS HER'S OR RATHER JOYS THE FIRST	212	3	DON JUAN	9	59	1
THE TWO FIRST FEELINGS RAN THEIR COURSE COMPLETE	213	3	DON JUAN	9	61	1
AND LIGHTED FIRST HER EYE AND THEN HER MOUTH	213	3	DON JUAN	9	61	2
FIRST ISMAIL'S CAPTURE CAUGHT YOUR FANCY QUITE	215	3	DON JUAN	9	65	6
WITH THE FIRST DRAUGHT INTOXICATES APACE	216	3	DON JUAN	9	67	4
FOR SUCH ALL WOMEN ARE AT FIRST NO DOUBT	220	3	DON JUAN	9	75	4
(AS IT WILL LOOK SOMETIMES WITH THE FIRST STARE	224	3	DON JUAN	9	84	4
DRAINS ITS FIRST DRAUGHT OF LIPS--BUT AS I SAID	238	3	DON JUAN	10	28	7
JUAN DEMURRED AT THIS FIRST NOTICE TO	245	3	DON JUAN	10	43	1
WHO DID NOT LIKE AT FIRST TO LOSE HER MINION	246	3	DON JUAN	10	44	4
SHE COULD NOT FIND AT FIRST A FIT SUCCESSOR	247	3	DON JUAN	10	47	8
WHICH PASSED OR CATCH THE FIRST GLIMPSE OF THE CLIFFS	256	3	DON JUAN	10	64	8
AT THE FIRST SIGHT OF ALBION'S CHALKY BELT--	257	3	DON JUAN	10	65	4
WHO IS BUT FIRST OF SLAVES THE NATIONS ARE	258	3	DON JUAN	10	68	2
THE FIRST ATTACK AT ONCE PROVED THE DIVINITY	271	3	DON JUAN	11	6	1
MAY NOT THINK MUCH OF LONDON'S FIRST APPEARANCE--	271	3	DON JUAN	11	7	7
HIS POCKETS FIRST AND THEN HIS BODY RIDDLED	276	3	DON JUAN	11	17	8
THE FIRST THE EMBLEM (RARELY THOUGH) OF WHAT	290	3	DON JUAN	11	44	4
BUT MAKING MONEY SLOWLY FIRST THEN QUICKER	317	3	DON JUAN	12	4	3
FIRST SAVE IN CASE OF PIGEONS--HOW THE GROVE	322	3	DON JUAN	12	13	V5
SO FIRST THERE WAS A GENEROUS EMULATION	330	3	DON JUAN	12	30	1
MEANING A VIRGIN'S FIRST BLUSH AT A ROUT	330	3	DON JUAN	12	31	5
TASTES THEIR FIRST SEASON (MOSTLY IF THEY HAVE MONEY)	330	3	DON JUAN	12	31	8
BUT FIRST OF LITTLE LEILA WE'LL DISPOSE	335	3	DON JUAN	12	41	1
ADVERSITY IS THE FIRST PATH TO TRUTH	339	3	DON JUAN	12	50	5
THAT FROM THE FIRST OF CANTOS UP TO THIS	341	3	DON JUAN	12	54	3
THESE FIRST TWELVE BOOKS ARE MERELY FLOURISHES	341	3	DON JUAN	12	54	5
FOR THE FIRST SEASON SUCH A LIFE SCARCE PALLS	342	3	DON JUAN	12	57	8
AT FIRST HE DID NOT THINK THE WOMEN PRETTY	347	3	DON JUAN	12	68	8
I SAY AT FIRST--FOR HE FOUND OUT AT LAST	347	3	DON JUAN	12	69	1
AT THE FIRST BLUSH FOR A FAIR BRITON HIDES	350	3	DON JUAN	12	74	3
IF THAT THE WEEDS O'ERLIVE NOT THE FIRST CROP--	368	3	DON JUAN	13	22	7
THE FIRST YET FROWNED SUPERBLY O'ER THE SOIL	386	3	DON JUAN	13	59	5
NOR JUDGE AT FIRST IF ALL BE TRUE TO NATURE	390	3	DON JUAN	13	67	8
SMOOTH SPEECH HIS FIRST AND MAIDENLY TRANSGRESSION	400	3	DON JUAN	13	90	4
THE BEST FIRST SPEECH THAT EVER YET WAS MADE	400	3	DON JUAN	13	90	8
THE FIRST THING BOYS LIKE AFTER PLAY AND FRUIT	405	3	DON JUAN	13	101	3
FOR TOO MUCH TRUTH AT FIRST SIGHT NE'ER ATTRACTS	416	3	DON JUAN	14	13	6
BUT WHEN OF THE FIRST SIGHT YOU HAVE HAD YOUR FILL	417	3	DON JUAN	14	17	6
OF TUMBLING FIRST AND HAVING IN EXCHANGE	424	3	DON JUAN	14	32	3
AS THEY WILL DO LIKE LEAVES AT THE FIRST BREEZE	431	3	DON JUAN	14	48	6
OF DOCTORS' COMMONS BUT SHE DREADED FIRST	437	3	DON JUAN	14	62	5
AND FIRST IN THE O'ERFLOWING OF HER HEART	438	3	DON JUAN	14	65	1
WAS NOT AT FIRST TOO READILY IMPRESS'D	448	3	DON JUAN	14	88	8
KNOCKEST AT DOORS AT FIRST WITH MODEST TAP	459	3	DON JUAN	15	8	2

273

FIRST   (CONTINUED)
   THE FIRST IS RATHER MORE THAN MORTAL CAN DO . . . . 465 3 DON JUAN 15   21   3
   THOUGH AT THE FIRST I MIGHT PERCHANCE DERIDE . . . . . . 466 3 DON JUAN 15   23   5
   WHICH SEEMS AT FIRST TO NEED NO LOFTY WING . . . . 467 3 DON JUAN 15   25   3
   OPINIONS TWO WHICH AT FIRST SIGHT MAY LOOK . . . . 494 3 DON JUAN 15   87   3
   STRAINED ON THE SPOT WHERE FIRST THE FIGURE GLEAMED . . . 511 3 DON JUAN 16   25   3
   THE FIRST--BUT WHAT SHE COULD NOT WELL DIVINE . . . . . 513 3 DON JUAN 16   30   8
   AT FIRST THEN KINDLING INTO ANIMATION . . . . 518 3 DON JUAN 16   40   5
   GLIDING THE FIRST TIME TO A RENDEZVOUS . . . . 556 3 DON JUAN 16 112   7
   HE FIRST INCLINED TO THINK HE HAD BEEN MISTAKEN . . . . 558 3 DON JUAN 16 118   3
   THAT HE HAD MADE AT FIRST A SILLY BLUNDER . . . . 560 3 DON JUAN 16 122   6
   (I'LL TAKE THE LIKENESS I CAN FIRST COME AT) . . . . . 564 3 DON JUAN 17   4   5
FIRST-BORN'S
   SWEET TO THE FATHER IS HIS FIRST-BORN'S BIRTH . . . . . 88 2 DON JUAN 1 124   6
FIRSTLY
   FIRSTLY BEGIN WITH THE BEGINNING--(THOUGH . . . . 393 3 DON JUAN 13   73   5
   FIRSTLY THEY MUST ALLURE THE CONVERSATION . . . . 404 3 DON JUAN 13   98   1
   FIRSTLY HE SAID HE NEVER INTERFERED . . . . 439 3 DON JUAN 14   66   1
   THE WORLD IS FULL OF ORPHANS FIRSTLY THOSE . . . . . . 562 3 DON JUAN 17   1   1
FIRST'S
   AND THE TRUE HYMEN (THE FIRST'S BUT A SCREEN)-- . . . . 288 2 DON JUAN 3   25   4
FISH
   AND TUMBLE DOWNWARD LIKE THE FLYING FISH . . . . 10 2 DON JUAN D   3   6
   FOR BREAKFAST OF EGGS COFFEE BREAD AND FISH . . . . . . 226 2 DON JUAN 2 133   8
   BUT THERE WERE EGGS FRUIT COFFEE BREAD FISH HONEY . . . 233 2 DON JUAN 2 145   7
   AND FISH AND SOUP BY SOME SIDE DISHES BACKED . . . . . 428 2 DON JUAN 5   32   5
   YOU COULD GLIDE O'ER THEM LIKE A GOLDEN FISH . . . . . 449 2 DON JUAN 5   65   8
   OR THROWN TO LIONS OR MADE BAITS FOR FISH . . . . . . 492 2 DON JUAN 5 141   4
   OR MINCED IN PIECES AS SMALL BAITS FOR FISH . . . . . 492 2 DON JUAN 5 141 V4
   MORALS WERE BETTER AND THE FISH NO WORSE . . . . 496 2 DON JUAN 5 149   8
   BESIDES FISH BEASTS AND BIRDS THE SPARROW'S FALL . . . 192 3 DON JUAN 9   19   5
   WHICH ENCYCLOPEDIZE BOTH FLESH AND FISH . . . . 486 3 DON JUAN 15   68   6
   AMIDST THIS TUMULT OF FISH FLESH AND FOWL . . . . . . 488 3 DON JUAN 15   74   1
   (UNHEEDED TWICE) TO HAVE A FIN OF FISH . . . . 542 3 DON JUAN 16   87   8
   TO THE CONSUMERS OF FISH FOWL AND GAME . . . . 546 3 DON JUAN 16   95   3
FISH'D
   LIKE PETER THE APOSTLE--AND HE FISH'D . . . . 223 2 DON JUAN 2 126   2
FISHER
   A FISHER THEREFORE WAS HE--THOUGH OF MEN . . . . 223 2 DON JUAN 2 126   1
   BUT MANY A FISHER IN HIS RUGGED SONG . . . . 383 2 DON JUAN 4   73 V1
FISHERMAN
   A FISHERMAN HE HAD BEEN IN HIS YOUTH . . . . 222 2 DON JUAN 2 125   1
   AND STILL A SORT OF FISHERMAN WAS HE . . . . 222 2 DON JUAN 2 125   2
FISHERS
   FISHERS FOR MEN LIKE SIRENS WITH SOFT LUTES . . . . . 343 3 DON JUAN 12   59   6
FISHERY
   FISHERY AND FARM BOTH INTO HIS OWN HAND . . . . 198 3 DON JUAN 9   31   8
FISHES
   AND SAFFRON SOUPS AND SWEETBREADS AND THE FISHES . . . 307 2 DON JUAN 3   62   3
   AND TRUSTING JUAN MAY ESCAPE THE FISHES . . . . 65 3 DON JUAN 6 120   5
   BEGINNINGS ARE FAIR FACES ENDS MERE FISHES-- . . . . . 349 3 DON JUAN 12   73   2
FIST
   THE DOOR WAS FASTEN'D BUT WITH VOICE AND FIST . . . . 95 2 DON JUAN 1 136   7
FISTY
   LIKE TO THE CHAMPION IN THE FISTY RING . . . . 296 3 DON JUAN 11   55   2
FIT
   DEEMING THE CHAIN IT WEARS EVEN MEN MAY FIT . . . . . 18 2 DON JUAN D   15   4
   FIT FOR MY POEM (THAT IS FOR MY NEW ONE) . . . . 24 2 DON JUAN 1   5   7
   OF ARISTOTLE AND THE RULES 'TIS FIT . . . . 86 2 DON JUAN 1 120   7
   THAT ALL THE ISRAELITES ARE FIT TO MOB ITS . . . . . . 89 2 DON JUAN 1 125   7
   A SUDDEN FIT OF DRUNKENNESS OR SPLEEN . . . . 98 2 DON JUAN 1 142   6
   YOU'VE MADE THE APARTMENT IN A FIT CONDITION-- . . . . 104 2 DON JUAN 1 152   3
   ARE SUCH AS FIT WITH LADY'S FEET BUT THESE . . . . . . 121 2 DON JUAN 1 181   2
   AGUE IN ITS COLD FIT THEY FILL'D THEIR BOAT . . . . . 189 2 DON JUAN 2   63   7
   FIT FOR THE MODEL OF A STATUARY . . . . 218 2 DON JUAN 2 118   5
   FORSOOTH SCARCE FIT FOR BALLADS IN THE STREET . . . . 392 2 DON JUAN 4   89   6
   THEIR NAMES WHO REARED IT BUT HUGE HOUSES FIT ILL-- . . 444 2 DON JUAN 5   59   5
   A QUANTITY OF CLOTHES FIT FOR THE BACK . . . . 450 2 DON JUAN 5   67   3
   BUT SUCH AS FIT AN ASIATIC BREECH . . . . 451 2 DON JUAN 5   68   5
   TO USE ALL FIT AND PROPER COURTESIES . . . . 472 2 DON JUAN 5 105   5
   AS THOSE WHOSE WIVES HAVE MADE THEM FIT FOR HEAVEN . . 500 2 DON JUAN 5 154   8
   YET VERY FIT TO MURDER SLEEP IN THOSE . . . . 27 3 DON JUAN 6   42   2
   THOUGH AN UNUSUAL FIT OF LOVE OR DUTY . . . . 51 3 DON JUAN 6   91   7
   IN ONE THING NE'ERTHELESS 'TIS FIT TO PRAISE . . . . . 176 3 DON JUAN 8 128   1
   ALL FIT TO MAKE A PATAGONIAN JEALOUS . . . . 205 3 DON JUAN 9   46   8
   AND THOUGH AS YOU REMEMBER IN A FIT . . . . 234 3 DON JUAN 10   19   1
   SHE COULD NOT FIND AT FIRST A FIT SUCCESSOR . . . . . 247 3 DON JUAN 10   47   8
   'TWAS FIT THAT HERE AS IN THE HOLY LAND . . . . 262 3 DON JUAN 10   75 V2
   HER VOICE THOUGH SWEET IS NOT SO FIT TO WARBLE . . . . 350 3 DON JUAN 12   75   5
   FOR A YOUNG GENTLEMAN'S FIT EDUCATION . . . . 432 3 DON JUAN 14   52   6
   A FIGURE FIT TO WALK BEFORE A KING . . . . 440 3 DON JUAN 14   70   4
FITS
   AND FITS HER LOOSELY--LIKE AN EASY GLOVE . . . . 276 2 DON JUAN 3   3   4
   WHILE OTHERS HAVE A GENIUS TURNED FOR FITS . . . . . . 340 3 DON JUAN 12   52   4
   BUT WHETHER FITS OR WITS OR HARPSICHORDS . . . . 340 3 DON JUAN 12   53   1
   HIS FEELINGS HAD NOT THOSE STRANGE FITS LIKE TERTIANS . 366 3 DON JUAN 13   17   5
FITTED
   THE REST ARE HARDLY FITTED FOR A FAIR . . . . 390 2 DON JUAN 4   85   4
   IF THEY WERE FITTED FOR THE PURPOSED CAGE . . . . . . 424 2 DON JUAN 5   26   5

	PAGE	VOL		CANTO	STANZA	LN

FITTED (CONTINUED)
```
    THIS STRANGE SALOON MUCH FITTED FOR INSPIRING    . . . . .  469   2 DON JUAN  5    100   5
    SOFT WORDS TOO FITTED FOR THE PERORATION . .  . . . . .      74   3 DON JUAN  7     16   5
    ILL FITTED WITH HER IGNORANCE TO JOSTLE  . .  . . . . .     250   3 DON JUAN 10     52   5
    AGAINST HER BEING MENTION'D AS WELL FITTED   . . . . . .    477   3 DON JUAN 15     48   6
FITTER
    WERE FITTER FOR ME LOVE IS FOR THE FREE   . . . . . .      484   2 DON JUAN  5    127   4
    THROUGH ALL THE PURPLE AND FINE LINEN FITTER   . . . . .   237   3 DON JUAN 10     26   6
FITTEST
    AND THEREFORE FITTEST AS OF HIS PERSUASION   . . . . . .   478   3 DON JUAN 15     50   2
FITTING
    IS'T WISE OR FITTING CAUSELESS TO EXPLORE   . . . . .     101   2 DON JUAN  1    146   5
    WHICH SHALL BE SPECIFIED IN FITTING TIME . .  . . . .     135   2 DON JUAN  1    200  V7
    I ALSO WOULD SUGGEST THE FITTING TIME . .  . . . . . .    482   2 DON JUAN  5    123   1
    OF FITTING OUT HER FAVOURITES CONFERRED   . . . . . .     247   3 DON JUAN 10     46   2
FITZ-FRISKY
    LADY FITZ-FRISKY AND MISS MAEVIA MANNISH  . . . . . .     295   3 DON JUAN 11     53   7
FITZ-FULKE
    THE DUCHESS OF FITZ-FULKE THE COUNTESS CRABBEY .  . . . .  396   3 DON JUAN 13     79   3
    THE DUCHESS OF FITZ-FULKE WHO LOVED TRACASSERIE  . . . .   428   3 DON JUAN 14     41   7
    THE DUCHESS OF FITZ-FULKE PLAYED WITH HER VEIL  . . . .    514   3 DON JUAN 16     31   5
    THE FULL GROWN HEBE OF FITZ-FULKE WHOSE MIND  . . . .      525   3 DON JUAN 16     49   2
    THE FAIR FITZ-FULKE SEEMED VERY MUCH AT EASE  . . . .      548   3 DON JUAN 16    100   2
    THE PHANTOM OF HER FROLIC GRACE--FITZ-FULKE  . . . .       561   3 DON JUAN 16    123   8
FITZ-PLANTAGENET
    AND LORD AUGUSTUS FITZ-PLANTAGENET  . . . . . . . . .      399   3 DON JUAN 13     87   7
    AT LORD AUGUSTUS FITZ-PLANTAGENET   . . . . . . . . .      428   3 DON JUAN 14     42   8
    POOR LORD AUGUSTUS FITZ-PLANTAGENET   . . . . . . . .      429   3 DON JUAN 14     44   8
    WITH LORD AUGUSTUS FITZ-PLANTAGENET   . . . . . . . .      437   3 DON JUAN 14     62   8
FIVE
    (I THINK THE QUARTO HOLDS FIVE HUNDRED PAGES)    . . . .     11   2 DON JUAN  D      4   2
    'TWERE BETTER TO HAVE TWO OF FIVE AND TWENTY   . . . .      56   2 DON JUAN  1     62   4
    AND SOBER SUNS MUST SET AT FIVE O'CLOCK  . .  . . . .       94   2 DON JUAN  1    134   8
    WHEN AFTER SEARCHING IN FIVE HUNDRED NOOKS   . . . . .     110   2 DON JUAN  1    161   3
    TO PLAYS IN FIVE AND OPERAS IN THREE ACTS   . . . . .      138   2 DON JUAN  1    203   4
    AND MADE AT LEAST FIVE HUNDRED GOOD ZECCHINI   . . . .     390   2 DON JUAN  4     84   5
    THEY HAD SLAIN HIM WITH FIVE SLUGS AND LEFT HIM THERE   .  429   2 DON JUAN  5     34   2
    KILLED BY FIVE BULLETS FROM AN OLD GUN-BARREL   . . . .    429   2 DON JUAN  5     34   8
    AND THERE WE GO--BUT WHERE FIVE BITS OF LEAD  . . . .      432   2 DON JUAN  5     39   2
    FOUR WIVES AND TWICE FIVE HUNDRED MAIDS UNSEEN  . . .      496   2 DON JUAN  5    148   7
    FIRST ONE OR TWO THEN FIVE SIX AND A DOZEN  . . . .        135   3 DON JUAN  8     45   1
    BUT FLANKED BY FIVE BRAVE SONS (SUCH IS POLYGAMY   . .     164   3 DON JUAN  8    105   1
    WHO FOUGHT WITH HIS FIVE CHILDREN IN THE VAN  . . .        164   3 DON JUAN  8    105   8
    HIS FIVE BRAVE BOYS NO LESS THE FOE DEFIED  . . . .        165   3 DON JUAN  8    107   5
    OF ALL THE FIVE ON BAYONETS MET HIS LOT  . . . . .         166   3 DON JUAN  8    110   4
    OR FIVE OR ONE OR ZERO SHE COULD NEVER   . . . . .         241   3 DON JUAN 10     33   7
    IN TWICE FIVE YEARS THE GREATEST LIVING POET  . . .        296   3 DON JUAN 11     55   1
    WHERE ARE THOSE MARTYRED SAINTS THE FIVE PER CENTS   .     307   3 DON JUAN 11     77   7
    HIMSELF FOR FIVE FOUR THREE OR TWO YEAR'S SPACE  . .       329   3 DON JUAN 12     29   6
    FIVE AS THEY MIGHT DO IN A MODEST WAY  . . . . .           548   3 DON JUAN 16     99   3
FIVE-BAR
    AS IS THE HUNTER'S AT THE FIVE-BAR GATE  . . . . . .       140   3 DON JUAN  8     55   2
FIX
    NOT SCANDAL'S FANGS COULD FIX ON MUCH THAT'S SEIZABLE   .   66   2 DON JUAN  1     83   3
    A MORTAL MOTHER WOULD ON LETHE FIX . . . . . . .          346   2 DON JUAN  4      4   8
    BESIDES HE HAD SOME QUALITIES WHICH FIX  . . . . . .       230   3 DON JUAN 10     10   1
    NOT THAT SHE MEANT TO FIX AGAIN IN HASTE . . . . .         248   3 DON JUAN 10     48   5
    WHERE HE MAY FIX HIMSELF LIKE SMALL JACK HORNER   . .      303   3 DON JUAN 11     69   4
    OR ON THE WATCH THEIR LONGING EYES WOULD FIX  . . .        406   3 DON JUAN 13    102   7
    TO FIX THE DUE BOUNDS OF THIS DANGEROUS QUALITY   . . .    448   3 DON JUAN 14     89   8
FIX'D
    TO LENGTHEN FETTERS BY ANOTHER FIX'D  . . . . . .          16   2 DON JUAN  D     12   7
    AS VIBRATES MY FOND HEART TO MY FIX'D SOUL   . . . .       133   2 DON JUAN  1    196   8
    AND NOT THE FIX'D--HE KNEW THE WAY TO WHEEDLE   . . .      317   2 DON JUAN  3     80   4
    'TIS--'TIS HER FATHER'S--FIX'D UPON THE PAIR   . . .       363   2 DON JUAN  4     35   8
    A FAIRER MARK AND WITH A FIX'D EYE SCANN'D  . . . .        367   2 DON JUAN  4     43   7
    IN FIX'D FEROCITY WHEN JOYOUS TEARS   . . . . . .          368   2 DON JUAN  4     45   6
    BUT FIX'D AS MARBLE'S UNCHANGED ASPECT THROWS   . . .      377   2 DON JUAN  4     61   3
    WITH THEIR GREEN FACES FIX'D UPON THE FLOOD  . . . .       385   3 DON JUAN 13     57   8
    WHOSE HEART WAS FIX'D UPON A STAR OR BLUESTRING   . . .    474   3 DON JUAN 15     42   3
FIXED
    OR FASCINATE WHOME'ER THEY FIXED THEIR EYES ON  . . . .    463   2 DON JUAN  5     90   8
    JUST AT THIS INSTANT WHILE THEIR EYES WERE FIXED   . .     159   3 DON JUAN  8     96   1
    IN EGYPT'S RAYS TO HARP AT A FIXED HOUR)   . . . .         388   3 DON JUAN 13     64   4
    THIS MAY BE FIXED AT SOMEWHERE BEFORE THIRTY--  . . .      433   3 DON JUAN 14     53   1
    FAIR ADELINE WITH EYES FIXED ON THE GROUND  . . . .        518   3 DON JUAN 16     40   4
    BECAUSE HE FIXED IT AND TO STOP HIS TALKING  . . . .       565   3 DON JUAN 17      8   2
FLAG
    WITH HIS GREY SIGNAL FLAG AND THE PAST TENSE   . . . .     376   3 DON JUAN 13     40   5
FLAGS
    ALTHOUGH HE FLEECED THE FLAGS OF EVERY NATION   . . . .    283   2 DON JUAN  3     14   2
    MIRRORED THE CHRISTIAN FLAGS--AS MOONBEAMS ON THE WATER .  173   3 DON JUAN  8    122  V8
FLAIL
    THE TURKISH BATTERIES THRASHED THEM LIKE A FLAIL   . . .   134   3 DON JUAN  8     43   5
FLAKE
    FROM EVERY FLAKE AND YET ROLLS ON THE SAME  . . . . .      398   2 DON JUAN  4    100   6
FLAME
    WHILE THE SUN SMILED ON HER WITH HIS FIRST FLAME   . . .   232   2 DON JUAN  2    142   3
    FOR HEALTH AND IDLENESS TO PASSION'S FLAME  . . . . .      245   2 DON JUAN  2    169   5
```

275

FLAME   (CONTINUED)

	PAGE	VOL	CANTO	STANZA	LN
LIKE THE WIND O'ER A HARP-STRING OR A FLAME	355	2 DON JUAN	4	21	4
IN THE LARGE DARK EYE'S MUTUAL-DARTED FLAME	367	2 DON JUAN	4	44	4
WHO FAIN WOULD HAVE A MUTUAL FLAME CONFEST	14	3 DON JUAN	6	17	3
TO SWALLOW FLAME AND NEVER TAKE IT ILL	93	3 DON JUAN	7	52	6
TO SWALLOW FLAME AND NEITHER SWERVE NOR SPILL	93	3 DON JUAN	7	52	V6
NOUGHT TO BE SEEN SAVE THE ARTILLERY'S FLAME	115	3 DON JUAN	8	6	2
FLAME WAS SHOWERED FORTH ABOVE AS WELL'S BELOW	135	3 DON JUAN	8	45	4
HUMANITY MUST YIELD TO STEEL AND FLAME	139	3 DON JUAN	8	54	4
FOR A NEW FLAME A THOUGHT TO CAST OF GLOOM ENOUGH	206	3 DON JUAN	9	48	5
MIGHT SCATTER FIRE THROUGH ICE LIKE HECLA'S FLAME	254	3 DON JUAN	10	59	8
THOSE BRIGHT MOTHS FLUTTERING ROUND A DYING FLAME	349	3 DON JUAN	12	72	4

FLAMES

	PAGE	VOL	CANTO	STANZA	LN
TO KINDLE FIRE AND AS THE NEW FLAMES GAVE	216	2 DON JUAN	2	115	5
OLD FLAMES NEW WIVES BECOME OUR BITTEREST FOES--	231	3 DON JUAN	10	12	7

FLAMINGO'S

	PAGE	VOL	CANTO	STANZA	LN
AT LEAST AS RED AS THE FLAMINGO'S CREST	48	3 DON JUAN	6	85	V4

FLANK'D

	PAGE	VOL	CANTO	STANZA	LN
(FLANK'D BY THE HELLESPONT AND BY THE SEA)	385	2 DON JUAN	4	76	2
FLANK'D BY LARGE GROVES WHICH TOWER'D ON EITHER HAND	433	2 DON JUAN	5	41	4

FLANKED

	PAGE	VOL	CANTO	STANZA	LN
BY EUNUCHS FLANKED WHILE AT THEIR HEAD THERE STALKED	21	3 DON JUAN	6	30	4
BUT FLANKED BY FIVE BRAVE SONS (SUCH IS POLYGAMY	164	3 DON JUAN	8	105	1

FLANKS

	PAGE	VOL	CANTO	STANZA	LN
THE TURKS BEHIND THE TRAVERSES AND FLANKS	134	3 DON JUAN	8	44	1
THEIR FLANKS--BUT IT IS HARDLY WORTH MY WHILE	300	3 DON JUAN	11	63	2

FLASH

	PAGE	VOL	CANTO	STANZA	LN
BUT NOW THERE CAME A FLASH OF HOPE ONCE MORE	176	2 DON JUAN	2	38	1
HER EYE MIGHT FLASH ON HIS BUT FOUND IT DIM	396	2 DON JUAN	4	95	3
FULL FLASH ALL FANCY UNTIL FAIRLY DIDDLED	276	3 DON JUAN	11	17	7
ON THE HIGH TOBY-SPICE SO FLASH THE MUZZLE	277	3 DON JUAN	11	19	6
FLASH UP IN INGOTS FROM THE MINE OBSCURE	319	3 DON JUAN	12	8	5

FLASH'D

	PAGE	VOL	CANTO	STANZA	LN
FLASH'D AN EXPRESSION MORE OF PRIDE THAN IRE	54	2 DON JUAN	1	60	4
FLASH'D ON HER LITTLE HAND BUT WHAT WAS SHOCKING	220	2 DON JUAN	2	121	7
FLASH'D O'ER HIS SOUL A FEW HEROIC RAYS	303	2 DON JUAN	3	55	2
AND THUS SOME BODING FLASH'D THROUGH EITHER FRAME	355	2 DON JUAN	4	21	6
HER RECOLLECTION ON HER FLASH'D THE DREAM	380	2 DON JUAN	4	66	4

FLASHED

	PAGE	VOL	CANTO	STANZA	LN
OBJECT ON OBJECT FLASHED SO BRIGHT AND FAST	465	2 DON JUAN	5	93	6
BUT O'ER HER BRIGHT BROW FLASHED A TUMULT STRANGE	473	2 DON JUAN	5	108	3
IF I SAID FIRE FLASHED FROM GULBEYAZ' EYES	489	2 DON JUAN	5	134	1
'TWERE NOTHING--FOR HER EYES FLASHED ALWAYS FIRE	489	2 DON JUAN	5	134	2
SO FULLY FLASHED THE PHANTOM ON HIS EYES	169	3 DON JUAN	8	115	1
FAR FLASHED HER BURNING TOWERS O'ER DANUBE'S STREAM	175	3 DON JUAN	8	127	3
WHICH FLASHED AS FAR AS WHERE THE MUSK-BULL BROWSES	353	3 DON JUAN	12	82	6
THAT FLASHED AND AFTER DARKENED IN THE SHADE	507	3 DON JUAN	16	15	8

FLASHES

	PAGE	VOL	CANTO	STANZA	LN
FLASHES INTO THE HEART--ALL SUNNY LAND	160	2 DON JUAN	2	7	4
WHICH FLASHES O'ER A WASTE AND ICY CLIME	67	3 DON JUAN	7	2	4
THE EAR FAR MORE THAN THUNDER FOR HEAVEN'S FLASHES	115	3 DON JUAN	8	6	7

FLASHING

	PAGE	VOL	CANTO	STANZA	LN
SHE LAY HER DARK EYES FLASHING THROUGH THEIR TEARS	108	2 DON JUAN	1	158	2
ON HIM HER FLASHING EYES A MOMENT BENT	379	2 DON JUAN	4	65	4
IN ALL THE FLASHING OF THEIR FULL ARRAY	442	2 DON JUAN	5	56	4
AND THE DEEP PASSIONS FLASHING THROUGH HER FORM	489	2 DON JUAN	5	135	7
WITH FLASHING EYES AND STARTING TEARS AND FLUNG	101	3 DON JUAN	7	67	4
BUT SEEING FLASHING FORWARD LIKE THE DAY	126	3 DON JUAN	8	30	3
THE REEKING BAYONET AND THE FLASHING BLADE	146	3 DON JUAN	8	69	3
WITH FLASHING EYES AND WEAPONS MATCHED WITH THEM	157	3 DON JUAN	8	92	2
THROUGH STREET AND SQUARE FAST FLASHING CHARIOTS HURLED	302	3 DON JUAN	11	67	3

FLASK

	PAGE	VOL	CANTO	STANZA	LN
OR DUTCH WITH THIRST--WHAT HO A FLASK OF RHENISH	392	3 DON JUAN	13	72	8

FLASKS

	PAGE	VOL	CANTO	STANZA	LN
SIX FLASKS OF WINE AND THEY CONTRIVED TO GET	181	2 DON JUAN	2	47	4
AND FLASKS OF SAMIAN AND OF CHIAN WINE	291	2 DON JUAN	3	31	4

FLAT

	PAGE	VOL	CANTO	STANZA	LN
WHO QUEER A FLAT WHO (SPITE OF BOW-STREET'S BAN)	277	3 DON JUAN	11	19	5
AND MAKE A MUSIC WHETHER FLAT OR SHARP	402	3 DON JUAN	13	93	4

FLATTER

	PAGE	VOL	CANTO	STANZA	LN
BUT THEY HATE FLATTERY SO I NEVER FLATTER)	287	2 DON JUAN	3	22	6
HE BEING PAID TO SATIRISE OR FLATTER	316	2 DON JUAN	3	78	7
JUST AS A LANGUID SMILE BEGAN TO FLATTER	493	2 DON JUAN	5	143	6
THE NUMBERS ARE TOO GREAT FOR THEM TO FLATTER ALL	50	3 DON JUAN	6	88	8
DOGS OR MEN (FOR I FLATTER YOU IN SAYING	70	3 DON JUAN	7	7	1
O'ER SILENCED CITIES MERELY SERVED TO FLATTER	197	3 DON JUAN	9	29	5
AND WRINKLES (THE DAMNED DEMOCRATS) WON'T FLATTER	236	3 DON JUAN	10	24	8
THE FORMER'S HYMENEAL HOPES TO FLATTER	292	3 DON JUAN	11	46	3
THE INSOLENT SOLDIERY TO SOOTHE AND FLATTER	299	3 DON JUAN	11	62	4
IN ANYTHING HOWEVER SHE MIGHT FLATTER	448	3 DON JUAN	14	88	2

FLATTER'D

	PAGE	VOL	CANTO	STANZA	LN
SHE FLATTER'D JULIA WITH HER SAGE PROTECTION	58	2 DON JUAN	1	67	5

FLATTERED

	PAGE	VOL	CANTO	STANZA	LN
JUAN MUCH FLATTERED BY HER LOVE OR LUST--	221	3 DON JUAN	9	77	3

FLATTERER

	PAGE	VOL	CANTO	STANZA	LN
I AM NO FLATTERER--YOU'VE SUPPED FULL OF FLATTERY	185	3 DON JUAN	9	5	1

FLATTERERS

	PAGE	VOL	CANTO	STANZA	LN
THAT EVEN ITS GROSSEST FLATTERERS DARE NOT PRAISE	17	2 DON JUAN	D	13	3

FLATTERING

	PAGE	VOL	CANTO	STANZA	LN
AND IF IN FLATTERING STRAINS I DO NOT PREDICATE	20	2 DON JUAN	D	17	3

	PAGE	VOL		CANTO	STANZA	LN

FLATTERING   (CONTINUED)
WHOSE TEMPORARY PASSION WAS QUITE FLATTERING . . . . . 217 3 DON JUAN 9 70 3
NOR FLATTERING TO THEIR TEMPER OR THEIR TASTE . . . . . 230 3 DON JUAN 10 11 5
FLATTERS
WHICH FLATTERS BUT IS FLATTERY CONVEYED . . . . 372 3 DON JUAN 13 32 3
WHICH NEVER FLATTERS EITHER WHIG OR TORY . . . . 465 3 DON JUAN 15 20 V7
FLATTERY
A KIND OF FLATTERY THAT'S HARDLY FAIR . . . . 278 2 DON JUAN 3 6 3
BUT THEY HATE FLATTERY SO I NEVER FLATTER) . . . . 287 2 DON JUAN 3 22 6
OF BEAUTY FLATTERY THREATS A SHILLING--NO . . . . 439 2 DON JUAN 5 49 3
I AM NO FLATTERER--YOU'VE SUPPED FULL OF FLATTERY . . . 185 3 DON JUAN 9 5 1
MUCH FLATTERY--EVEN VOLTAIRE'S AND THAT'S A PITY . . . 194 3 DON JUAN 9 23 6
TO TURN HER HEAD WITH WALTZING AND WITH FLATTERY . . . . 331 3 DON JUAN 12 32 8
WHICH FLATTERS BUT IS FLATTERY CONVEYED . . . . 372 3 DON JUAN 13 32 3
TO FEEL THAT FLATTERY WHICH ATTRACTS THE PROUD . . . . 493 3 DON JUAN 15 83 6
FLAVOUR
IS SHARPEN'D FROM ITS HIGH CELESTIAL FLAVOUR . . . . 277 2 DON JUAN 3 5 7
FLAW
IN WHICH NOT ENVY'S SELF A FLAW DISCOVERS . . . . . . 29 2 DON JUAN 1 16 6
SOCIETY THAT CHINA WITHOUT FLAW . . . . . . 352 3 DON JUAN 12 78 5
MISS RAW MISS FLAW MISS SHOWMAN AND MISS KNOWMAN . . . 473 3 DON JUAN 15 40 4
FLAWS
THEY DREW CONSTRUCTED LADDERS REPAIRED FLAWS . . . . 89 3 DON JUAN 7 47 6
OR CHEERFUL WITHOUT ANY FLAWS OR STARTS . . . . 292 3 DON JUAN 11 47 5
SUCH CLASSIC PAS--SANS FLAWS--SET OFF OUR HERO . . . 427 3 DON JUAN 14 39 7
WHATE'ER MAY BE HER FOLLIES OR HER FLAWS . . . . 502 3 DON JUAN 16 2 6
FLAY
THAT LURES TO FLAY ALIVE THE YOUNG BEGINNER . . . . . 294 2 DON JUAN 3 36 6
FLAY'D
USED TO IT NO DOUBT AS EELS ARE TO BE FLAY'D . . . . 414 2 DON JUAN 5 7 8
FLED
HE FLED LIKE JOSEPH LEAVING IT BUT THERE . . . . 124 2 DON JUAN 1 186 7
THEY FOUND NO FAULT WITH TIME SAVE THAT HE FLED . . . 351 2 DON JUAN 4 13 3
UNTIL THE MEMORY OF AN AGE IS FLED . . . . . 399 2 DON JUAN 4 102 3
HAD FACED NAPOLEON'S FOES UNTIL THEY FLED-- . . . . . 431 2 DON JUAN 5 37 6
FLEE
PINIONS TO FLEE AWAY AND BE AT REST . . . . . . 228 3 DON JUAN 10 6 3
FLEECE
SUCH AS LIT ONWARD TO THE GOLDEN FLEECE . . . . . 303 2 DON JUAN 3 55 3
FLEECED
ALTHOUGH HE FLEECED THE FLAGS OF EVERY NATION . . . . 283 2 DON JUAN 3 14 2
PINNED LIKE A FLOCK AND FLEECED TOO IN THEIR FOLD . . . 468 3 DON JUAN 15 26 3
FLEECY
LIKE FLEECY CLOUDS ABOUT THE MOON FLOW'D ROUND HER . . 311 2 DON JUAN 3 70 8
LIKE FLEECY CLOUDS INTO THE SKY RETIRED . . . . . 504 3 DON JUAN 16 8 6
FLEET
WHEN THE SALE OF NEW BOOKS IS NOT SO FLEET . . . . . 79 3 DON JUAN 7 26 5
THE FLEET AND CAMP SALUTED WITH GREAT GRACE . . . . . 89 3 DON JUAN 7 47 3
FLEET-DITCH
TO HURL THESE FLEET-DITCH DIVERS DOWN THEIR LAKES . . . 334 2 DON JUAN 3 100 V8
FLEETING
OF SUCH TRANSCENDANT AND MORE FLEETING FLIGHT . . . . 66 3 DON JUAN 7 1 4
SO BEAUTIFUL SO FLEETING TO THE MUSE . . . . 108 3 DON JUAN 7 82 8
FLESH
RUIN'D ITS BLOOD BUT MUCH IMPROVED ITS FLESH . . . . 53 2 DON JUAN 1 58 2
THE FLESH IS FRAIL AND SO THE SOUL UNDONE . . . . 56 2 DON JUAN 1 63 6
AND FLESH (WHICH DEATH MOWS DOWN TO HAY) IS GRASS . . 147 2 DON JUAN 1 220 4
AND OUT THEY SPOKE OF LOTS FOR FLESH AND BLOOD . . . 194 2 DON JUAN 2 73 7
GOAT'S FLESH THERE IS NO DOUBT AND KID AND MUTTON . . 238 2 DON JUAN 2 154 2
FOR LOVE MUST BE SUSTAIN'D LIKE FLESH AND BLOOD-- . . 246 2 DON JUAN 2 170 4
TO HINT THAT FLESH IS FORM'D OF FIERY DUST . . . 269 2 DON JUAN 2 212 8
THIS SKIN MUST GO THE WAY TOO OF ALL FLESH . . . 422 2 DON JUAN 5 22 3
SELL FLESH AND BLOOD WHEN DINNER HAS OPPREST ONE . . . 426 2 DON JUAN 5 30 6
WE WOULD AGAINST THEM MAKE THE FLESH OBEY-- . . . 474 2 DON JUAN 5 110 7
IT TEACHES THEM THAT THEY ARE FLESH AND BLOOD . . . . 491 2 DON JUAN 5 138 1
THE GREATEST NUMBER FLESH HATH EVER KNOWN . . . . 255 3 DON JUAN 10 62 8
HAD NOT THE FLESH MADE SOME SMALL OPTION . . . . 467 3 DON JUAN 15 24 V4
WHICH ENCYCLOPEDIZE BOTH FLESH AND FISH . . . . 486 3 DON JUAN 15 68 6
AMIDST THIS TUMULT OF FISH FLESH AND FOWL . . . . 488 3 DON JUAN 15 74 1
FORTH INTO SOMETHING MUCH LIKE FLESH AND BLOOD . . . 561 3 DON JUAN 16 123 4
FLESH-COLOURED
A PAIR OF TROWSERS OF FLESH-COLOURED SILK . . . . 456 2 DON JUAN 5 77 2
FLESHY
IT LAUGHS NOT--THERE IS NOW NO FLESHY BAR . . . . . 188 3 DON JUAN 9 12 3
FLEW
HIM ALMOST MAN BUT SHE FLEW IN A RAGE . . . . 51 2 DON JUAN 1 54 5
AND THEN FLEW OUT INTO ANOTHER PASSION . . . . 121 2 DON JUAN 1 181 8
AND JULIA INSTANT TO THE CLOSET FLEW . . . . 121 2 DON JUAN 1 182 2
NE'ER WITH SUCH FORCE THE SWIFTEST ARROW FLEW . . . 218 2 DON JUAN 2 117 6
AND FLEW TO HER YOUNG MATE LIKE A YOUNG BIRD . . . 257 2 DON JUAN 2 190 6
HE FLEW INTO A PASSION AND IN FACT . . . . 296 2 DON JUAN 3 40 2
HIS ARMS WERE LIKE A SERPENT'S COIL THEN FLEW . . . 370 2 DON JUAN 4 48 5
AND FLEW AT ALL SHE MET AS ON HER FOES . . . 380 2 DON JUAN 4 67 4
MY PEN AND EASILY FLEW IN A RAGE . . . . 397 2 DON JUAN 4 98 V6
A BEE FLEW OUT AND STUNG HER TO THE HEART . . . 44 3 DON JUAN 6 77 7
BUT FLEW TO WHERE THE PLEASANT NOISE GREW LOUDER . . 129 3 DON JUAN 8 33 V8
FONDLY THE WHEELING FIRE-FLIES FLEW AROUND HER . . . 435 3 DON JUAN 14 57 1
THE DOOR FLEW WIDE NOT SWIFTLY--BUT AS FLY . . . 558 3 DON JUAN 16 117 1
FLICKERED
OF HEALTH BUT FLICKERED WITH A FAINT REFLECTION . . . 245 3 DON JUAN 10 43 6

FLIES
```
FLIES IN ONE'S FACE AND MAKES IT WEATHER-TOUGH  . . . .   162   2 DON JUAN  2     11    6
FORTH FROM ITS RAVEN FRINGE THE FULL GLANCE FLIES . . . . 218   2 DON JUAN  2    117    5
AND IN PERSPECTIVE MANY A SQUADRON FLIES . . . . . . .    461   2 DON JUAN  5     86    6
BUT STILL THE SPOUSELESS VIRGIN KNOWLEDGE FLIES  . . . .   37   3 DON JUAN  6     63    5
WHICH SATAN ANGLES WITH FOR SOULS LIKE FLIES . . . . .    154   3 DON JUAN  8     86    8
THE TWIGS WHICH SATAN LIMES FOR HUMAN FLIES  . . . . .    154   3 DON JUAN  8     86   V8
A WHOLE ONE AND MY HEART FLIES TO MY HEAD--  . . . . .    233   3 DON JUAN 10     17    8
THAN THEIR HE RELATIVES) LIKE FLIES O'ER CANDY . . . .    331   3 DON JUAN 12     32    6
BUT THESE ARE TRIFLES  DOWNWARD FLIES MY LORD . . . .     379   3 DON JUAN 13     46    1
A PAPER KITE WHICH FLIES 'TWIXT LIFE AND DEATH . . . .    414   3 DON JUAN 14      8    5
```
FLIGHT
```
THAT FLIGHT WAS BASE AND DASTARDLY AND NO MAN  . . . .     63   2 DON JUAN  1     77    3
OF SUCH TRANSCENDANT AND MORE FLEETING FLIGHT  . . . .     66   2 DON JUAN  7      1    4
OF HUMAN THOUGHTS WHICH JOSTLE IN THEIR FLIGHT . . . .    215   3 DON JUAN  9     65    4
SHE WAS A PITCH BEYOND A COXCOMB'S FLIGHT  . . . . .      435   3 DON JUAN 14     57    4
SUCH AS THE TIMES MAY FURNISH  'TIS A FLIGHT . . . .     467   3 DON JUAN 15     25    2
THE SEA-GULLS WITH A STEADY SOBER FLIGHT--  . . . . .     558   3 DON JUAN 16    117    2
```
FLIGHTS
```
ITS PETTY PASSIONS MARRIAGES AND FLIGHTS . . . . . .     353   2 DON JUAN  4     17    6
```
FLIGHTY
```
OR COLERIDGE LONG BEFORE HIS FLIGHTY PEN . . . . . .     329   2 DON JUAN  3     93    5
```
FLINCH
```
FOR ONE WOULD NOT RETREAT NOR T'OTHER FLINCH . . . .     150   3 DON JUAN  8     77    8
IF POSSIBLE AND THIRDLY NEVER FLINCH . . . . . . .       404   3 DON JUAN 13     98    6
```
FLING
```
CONTRIVED TO FLING THE BED-CLOTHES IN A HEAP . . . .      97   2 DON JUAN  1    140    5
FLING UP A STRAW 'TWILL SHOW THE WAY THE WIND BLOWS . .   414   3 DON JUAN 14      8    2
```
FLINGS
```
WHERE I CAN'T SAY OR GOLD OR DIAMOND FLINGS  . . . .     465   2 DON JUAN  5     94    5
LIKE DAVID FLINGS SMOOTH PEBBLES 'GAINST A GIANT . . .   138   3 DON JUAN  8     51    2
SO THAT THE BRANCH A GOODLY VERDURE FLINGS . . . . .     436   3 DON JUAN 14     59    3
```
FLINT
```
THEN LOOK'D CLOSE AT THE FLINT AS IF TO SEE-- . . . .    365   2 DON JUAN  4     40    6
AND WISHED HE HAD BEEN LESS HASTY WITH HIS FLINT . . .   275   3 DON JUAN 11     14    8
```
FLINTS
```
TO RUTS AND FLINTS AND LOVELY NATURE'S SKILL . . . .     198   3 DON JUAN  9     31    5
```
FLIRT
```
SOME FLIRT SOME READ AND SOME IN VICES GROVEL  . . . .   263   2 DON JUAN  2    201   V7
```
FLIRTATION
```
COMMIT--FLIRTATION WITH THE MUSE OF MOORE  . . . . .     139   2 DON JUAN  1    205    8
HER VILE AMBIGUOUS METHOD OF FLIRTATION  . . . . .       222   3 DON JUAN  9     81    7
BUT YET IS MERELY INNOCENT FLIRTATION . . . . . . .      345   3 DON JUAN 12     63    7
KNOW HOW TO END THIS HALF AND HALF FLIRTATION  . . . .   345   3 DON JUAN 12     63   V7
FLIRTATION--BUT DECOROUS THE MERE PRAISE . . . . . .     408   3 DON JUAN 13    108    5
A LITTLE BLACK UPON THIS NEW FLIRTATION  . . . . .       429   3 DON JUAN 14     43    2
```
FLIRTED
```
WHEN TIRED OF PLAY HE FLIRTED WITHOUT SIN  . . . . .     327   3 DON JUAN 12     25    5
```
FLITS
```
NOT STINGS AND FLITS THROUGH ETHER WITHOUT AIM . . . .   400   3 DON JUAN 13     89    6
HE FLITS ON THE BRIDAL EVE . . . . . . . . . .           519   3 DON JUAN 16  L   3    6
```
FLITTED
```
HE FLITTED TO AND FRO A DANCING LIGHT  . . . . . .        89   3 DON JUAN  7     46    7
```
FLOAT
```
AS FAST AS OARS COULD PULL AND WATER FLOAT . . . . .     432   2 DON JUAN  5     40    4
IT IS A PLEASANT VOYAGE PERHAPS TO FLOAT  . . . . .      191   3 DON JUAN  9     18    1
BUT STILL SEA-WORTHY SKIFF AND SHE MAY FLOAT . . . .     227   3 DON JUAN 10      4    7
WHAT THOUGH ON LETHE'S STREAM HE SEEM TO FLOAT . . . .   457   3 DON JUAN 15      4    5
```
FLOATING
```
THE FIFTH DAY AND THEIR BOAT LAY FLOATING THERE  . . .   193   2 DON JUAN  2     70    3
THEY LOOK'D UP TO THE SKY WHOSE FLOATING GLOW  . . . .   253   2 DON JUAN  2    185    1
DOWN HER WHITE NECK LONG FLOATING AUBURN CURLS-- . . .   291   2 DON JUAN  3     30    5
LIKE WATER-LILIES FLOATING DOWN A RILL . . . . . .        22   3 DON JUAN  6     33    6
WITH FLOATING DRAPERIES AND WITH FLYING HAIR . . . .      42   3 DON JUAN  6     72    2
LIKE BANQUO'S OFFSPRING--FLOATING PAST ME SEEMS  . . .   233   3 DON JUAN 10     18    6
A FLOATING BALANCE OF ACCOMPLISHMENT . . . . . . .       340   3 DON JUAN 12     52    2
```
FLOATS
```
FLOATS SCUMLIKE UPPERMOST AND THESE JACK CADES . . . .   334   2 DON JUAN  3    100    5
YOU KNOW HOW NEAR US THE DEEP BOSPHORUS FLOATS . . . .   464   2 DON JUAN  5     92    4
```
FLOCK
```
THE PATRIARCH OF THE FLOCK ALL GENTLY COWERS . . . .     292   2 DON JUAN  3     32    4
IS DREADFUL TO THE SHEPHERD AND THE FLOCK  . . . . .     305   2 DON JUAN  3     58    2
FLOCK O'ER THEIR CARRION JUST LIKE MEN BELOW . . . .     358   2 DON JUAN  4     28    8
PINNED LIKE A FLOCK AND FLEECED TOO IN THEIR FOLD  . .   468   3 DON JUAN 15     26    3
```
FLOCK'S
```
OR A BELL-WETHER FORM THE FLOCK'S CONNECTION  . . . .     90   3 DON JUAN  7     48    6
```
FLOG
```
I PRAY YE FLOG THEM UPON ALL OCCASIONS  . . . . .        157   2 DON JUAN  2      1    3
```
FLOOD
```
THE ROSY FLOOD OF TWILIGHT'S SKY ADMIRED--  . . . .      334   2 DON JUAN  3    101    6
WHICH TAKEN AT THE FLOOD--YOU KNOW THE REST  . . . .       6   3 DON JUAN  6      1    2
WHICH TAKEN AT THE FLOOD LEADS--GOD KNOWS WHERE  . . .     7   3 DON JUAN  6      2    2
AS FOR A BROOK TO COPE WITH OCEAN'S FLOOD  . . . . .     106   3 DON JUAN  7     80    7
THE LIVELIEST FIRE AND SAW THE FIERCEST FLOOD  . . . .   129   3 DON JUAN  8     33   V4
AND LOVE THE LAND OF MOUNTAIN AND OF FLOOD . . . . .     234   3 DON JUAN 10     19    8
WITH THEIR GREEN FACES FIX'D UPON THE FLOOD  . . . .     385   3 DON JUAN 13     57    8
```
FLOOR
```
HIS BLOOD WAS RUNNING ON THE VERY FLOOR  . . . . .       375   2 DON JUAN  4     58    3
LIKE HARNESSED METEORS THEN ALONG THE FLOOR  . . . .     302   3 DON JUAN 11     67    4
```

FLOOR'D
HIS MAN WAS FLOOR'D AND HELPLESS AT HIS FOOT . . . . . . 370 2 DON JUAN 4 49 5
FLOORED
OH JACK I'M FLOORED BY THAT 'ERE BLOODY FRENCHMAN . . . . 274 3 DON JUAN 11 13 8
FLOORS
OVER THE FLOORS WERE SPREAD GAZELLES AND CATS . . . . . 310 2 DON JUAN 3 68 4
THROUGH GLITTERING GALLERIES AND O'ER MARBLE FLOORS . . . 460 2 DON JUAN 5 85 3
FLORENTINE
SO SAID THE FLORENTINE YE MONARCHS HEARKEN . . . . . 264 3 DON JUAN 10 80 1
FLORID
HOURIS OR AUGHT EXCEPT HIS FLORID RACE . . . . . . 169 3 DON JUAN 8 116 3
FLOTILLA
THEY LOOKED UPON THE MUSCOVITE FLOTILLA . . 73 3 DON JUAN 7 13 7
TO ATTACK THE TURK'S FLOTILLA WHICH LAY NIGH . . . . 78 3 DON JUAN 7 24 3
THE RUSS FLOTILLA GETTING UNDER WAY . . . . . . 81 3 DON JUAN 7 29 2
FLOUNCED
WERE OF THE FINEST THAT E'ER FLOUNCED IN NETS . . . . 307 2 DON JUAN 3 62 4
FLOUNDERED
AND AS HE FLOUNDERED ON WITHOUT DUE SPEED . . . . . 56 3 DON JUAN 6 101 V6
FLOURISH
MERIDIAN-BORN TO FLOURISH IN THIS NATION . . . . . 246 3 DON JUAN 10 44 V2
FLOURISHED
FLOURISHED ITS SOPHISTRY FOR ARISTOCRACY . . . . . . 329 2 DON JUAN 3 93 V6
THE GENTLE JUAN FLOURISHED THOUGH AT TIMES . . . . 243 3 DON JUAN 10 37 1
FLOURISHES
THESE FIRST TWELVE BOOKS ARE MERELY FLOURISHES . . . 341 3 DON JUAN 12 54 5
IN HIS HARMONIOUS SETTLEMENT--(WHICH FLOURISHES . . . . 471 3 DON JUAN 15 35 2
FLOURISHING
AS FLOURISHING IN EVERY CHRISTIAN LAND . . . . . 220 3 DON JUAN 9 76 6
FLOW
AND BLOOD ('TWAS FROM THE NOSE) BEGAN TO FLOW . . . 124 2 DON JUAN 1 186 3
OF BLOOD AND TEARS MUST FLOW THE UNEBBING SEA . . . . 101 3 DON JUAN 7 68 8
THE BLOOD MAY GUSH OUT AS THE DANUBE'S FLOW . . . . 155 3 DON JUAN 8 87 3
WHICH MAKES ALL STYX THROUGH ONE SMALL LIVER FLOW . . . 190 3 DON JUAN 9 15 5
IN THE NEXT OCEAN WHICH MAY FLOW JUST THEN . . . . 217 3 DON JUAN 9 69 6
WHICH KNOWS NO EBB TO ITS IMPERIOUS FLOW . . . . . 366 3 DON JUAN 13 16 6
FLOW'D
FLOW'D IN HER VEIL AND MANY A PRECIOUS STONE . . . . 220 2 DON JUAN 2 121 6
A PLEASURE IN THE GENTLE STREAM THAT FLOW'D . . . . 304 2 DON JUAN 3 56 6
LIKE FLEECY CLOUDS ABOUT THE MOON FLOW'D ROUND HER . 311 2 DON JUAN 3 70 8
FLOW'D LIKE AN ALPINE TORRENT WHICH THE SUN . . . . 313 2 DON JUAN 3 73 2
ROOTED WHERE ONCE THE ADRIAN WAVE FLOW'D O'ER . . . 337 2 DON JUAN 3 105 4
WITNESS THE LANDS WHICH FLOW'D WITH MILK AND HONEY . . 405 3 DON JUAN 13 100 1
WHICH FLOW'D ON FOR A MOMENT IN THE BEAM . . . . . 480 3 DON JUAN 15 55 5
FLOWED
BUT NOW IT FLOWED IN NATURAL AND FAST . . . . . 490 2 DON JUAN 5 137 5
FLOWED FROM THEIR BLOOD-SHOT EYES ALL RED WITH STRIFE . 171 3 DON JUAN 8 119 7
FLOWER
AS SWEETNESS TO THE FLOWER OR SALT TO OCEAN . . . . 51 2 DON JUAN 1 55 6
TO DOUBLE EVEN THE SWEETNESS OF A FLOWER . . . . . 144 2 DON JUAN 1 214 8
ON WHICH LIKE A YOUNG FLOWER SNAPP'D FROM THE STALK . . 249 2 DON JUAN 2 176 5
THEIR HEARTS THE FLOWER FROM WHENCE THE HONEY SPRUNG . 254 2 DON JUAN 2 187 8
HER PASSIONS HAD ARISEN AND HER YOUTH'S FLOWER . . . 262 2 DON JUAN 2 198 V5
IN MARBLE FONTS THERE GRAIN AND FLOWER AND FRUIT . . . 373 2 DON JUAN 4 55 2
THE BLEEDING FLOWER AND BLASTED FRUIT OF LOVE . . . 382 2 DON JUAN 4 70 8
CALLED PARKS WHERE THERE IS NEITHER FRUIT NOR FLOWER . 301 3 DON JUAN 11 66 4
PEACE TO THE SLUMBERS OF EACH FOLDED FLOWER-- . . . 409 3 DON JUAN 13 111 5
THERE IS A FLOWER CALLED LOVE IN IDLENESS . . . . 442 3 DON JUAN 14 75 1
BUT THOUGH THE FLOWER IS DIFFERENT WITH THE FRENCH . . 442 3 DON JUAN 14 75 7
AS GROWS A FLOWER THUS QUIETLY SHE GREW . . . . 476 3 DON JUAN 15 47 3
WAS SUCH AS LIES BETWEEN A FLOWER AND GEM . . . . 481 3 DON JUAN 15 58 8
FLOWERS
HE PORED UPON THE LEAVES AND ON THE FLOWERS . . . . 72 2 DON JUAN 1 94 1
FLOWERS TO THE GRAVE) AND SOBBING OFTEN HE . . . . 165 2 DON JUAN 2 17 6
AS THOSE WHO DOTE ON ODOURS PLUCK THE FLOWERS . . . 275 2 DON JUAN 3 2 5
THERE WREATHE HIS VENERABLE HORNS WITH FLOWERS . . . 292 2 DON JUAN 3 32 2
PAST HIM IN CRYSTAL AND A JOY IN FLOWERS . . . . . 304 2 DON JUAN 3 56 7
AND THICK WITH DAMASK FLOWERS OF SILK INLAID . . . 308 2 DON JUAN 3 64 3
SOME HANDS UNSEEN STREW'D FLOWERS UPON HIS TOMB . . . 339 2 DON JUAN 3 109 5
TO PASS THEIR LIVES IN FOUNTAINS AND ON FLOWERS . . . 352 2 DON JUAN 4 15 7
(PLAIN TRUTH DEAR MURRAY NEEDS FEW FLOWERS OF SPEECH) . 470 2 DON JUAN 5 101 2
LIKE FLOWERS OF DIFFERENT HUE AND CLIME AND ROOT . . 38 3 DON JUAN 6 65 2
OF PORCELAIN HELD IN THE FETTERED FLOWERS . . . . 54 3 DON JUAN 6 97 7
LIKE FLOWERS WELL WATERED AFTER A LONG DROUTH-- . . . 213 3 DON JUAN 9 61 4
FLOWING
HERE HE EMBARKED AND WITH A FLOWING SAIL . . . . . 256 3 DON JUAN 10 64 1
AND SULKILY THE RIVER'S RIPPLE'S FLOWING . . . . . 422 3 DON JUAN 14 28 4
FLOWS
WE KNOW NOT THIS--THE BLOOD FLOWS ON TOO FAST . . . . 345 2 DON JUAN 4 2 6
FLUENT
AND BEING FLUENT (SAVE INDEED WHEN FEE'D ILL) . . . . 317 2 DON JUAN 3 80 6
FLUNG
AND THERE HE LAY FULL LENGTH WHERE HE WAS FLUNG . . . 213 2 DON JUAN 2 108 5
THEN WAS THE CORDIAL POUR'D AND MANTLE FLUNG . . . 216 2 DON JUAN 2 114 1
AND NIGHT IS FLUNG OFF LIKE A MOURNING SUIT . . . . 230 2 DON JUAN 2 139 7
HER GLANCES ON IT AND THEN LONGING FLUNG . . . . . 44 3 DON JUAN 6 76 4
WITH FLASHING EYES AND STARTING TEARS AND FLUNG . . . 101 3 DON JUAN 7 67 7
AND THIRTY THOUSAND MUSQUETS FLUNG THEIR PILLS . . . 117 3 DON JUAN 8 12 2
FLUNG HERE BY FATE OR CIRCUMSTANCE WHICH TAME . . . 139 3 DON JUAN 8 54 6

```
                                                     PAGE VOL    CANTO  STANZA  LN
FLUNG    (CONTINUED)
   UPON THE RUSSIAN STEEL HIS BREAST HE FLUNG . . . . . . 170  3 DON JUAN  8   118   2
   HE DASHED HIMSELF UPON HIS FOES AND FLUNG  . . . . . . 170  3 DON JUAN  8   118  V2
   FLUNG HOVERING GRACES O'ER HIM LIKE A BANNER  . . . . . 223  3 DON JUAN  9    83   8
   A MOSQUE SO NOBLE FLUNG LIKE PEARLS TO SWINE  . . . . . 262  3 DON JUAN 10    75   8
FLURRY
   PEEP OUT SOMETIMES WHEN THINGS ARE IN A FLURRY . . . . 237  3 DON JUAN 10    26   5
   FOR THE LESS CAUSE THERE IS FOR ALL THIS FLURRY  . . . 260  3 DON JUAN 10    72   6
FLUSH
   HER OWN WAS FRESHEST THOUGH A FEVERISH FLUSH  . . . . . 231  2 DON JUAN  2   141   2
   HER CHEEK BEGAN TO FLUSH HER EYES TO SPARKLE  . . . . .  56  2 DON JUAN  6   101   7
   IT IS ENOUGH THAT FORTUNE FOUND HIM FLUSH  . . . . . . 227  3 DON JUAN 10     5   6
FLUSHED
   ONE WITH HER FLUSHED CHEEK LAID ON HER WHITE ARM . . . .  39  3 DON JUAN  6    66   1
   FOR SHE SEEMED AGITATED FLUSHED AND FRIGHTENED . . . . .  42  3 DON JUAN  6    72   7
   FLUSHED WITH A PIOUS FURY TO SURVEY  . . . . . . . . . 262  3 DON JUAN 10    75  V7
   THOUGH SOMETIMES FAINTLY FLUSHED--AND ALWAYS CLEAR . . 545  3 DON JUAN 16    94   7
FLUTTER
   WHERE STILL WE FLUTTER ON FOR PENCE OR PRAISE  . . . . 422  2 DON JUAN  5    22   8
   MARCH MY MUSE  IF YOU CANNOT FLY YET FLUTTER  . . . . . 468  3 DON JUAN 15    27   2
FLUTTER'D
   IT CAME AND WENT AND FLUTTER'D ROUND THEM TILL . . . . 206  2 DON JUAN  2    94   7
FLUTTERERS
   OF FLUTTERERS THOUGH SHE DEEM'D HE HAD MORE SENSE . . . 493  2 DON JUAN 15    83   3
FLUTTERING
   WITH FLUTTERING DOUBTS IF ALL BE WELL OR ILL-- . . . . 286  2 DON JUAN  3    21   5
   WHILE STILL A FLUTTERING SIGH GULBEYAZ HEAVED  . . . . 500  2 DON JUAN  5   155   6
   THOSE BRIGHT MOTHS FLUTTERING ROUND A DYING FLAME  . . 349  3 DON JUAN 12    72   4
FLY
   WHEN PROUD GRENADA FELL AND FORCED TO FLY  . . . . . . .  52  2 DON JUAN  1    56   5
   WILL ALL BE HERE PERHAPS YE YET MAY FLY--  . . . . . . .  96  2 DON JUAN  1   137   7
   FLY JUAN FLY FOR HEAVEN'S SAKE--NOT A WORD--  . . . . . 121  2 DON JUAN  1   182   3
   FLY JUAN FLY FOR HEAVEN'S SAKE--NOT A WORD--  . . . . . 121  2 DON JUAN  1   182   3
   HERE IS THE GARDEN-KEY--FLY--FLY--ADIEU  . . . . . . . 121  2 DON JUAN  1   182   6
   HERE IS THE GARDEN-KEY--FLY--FLY--ADIEU  . . . . . . . 121  2 DON JUAN  1   182   6
   WHICH LEARN'D FROM THIS EXAMPLE NOT TO FLY . . . . . . 337  2 DON JUAN  3   106   7
   IN SOME SHAPE LET NONE THINK TO FLY THE DANGER . . . . 383  2 DON JUAN  4    73   7
   OH LOVE O GLORY WHAT ARE YE WHO FLY  . . . . . . . . . .  66  3 DON JUAN  7     1   1
   TO FLY FROM MALGRE ALL WHICH PEOPLE SAY  . . . . . . . 134  3 DON JUAN  8    42   3
   NONE SAVE THE SPANISH FLY AND ATTIC BEE  . . . . . . . 196  3 DON JUAN  9    28   7
   SOME DIE SOME FLY SOME LANGUISH ON THE CONTINENT . . . 308  3 DON JUAN 11    80   7
   'TIS THE POSTILLION'S PARADISE WHEELS FLY  . . . . . . 377  3 DON JUAN 13    42   3
   A BLEST HOUR FOR POSTILLIONS--CHARIOTS FLY  . . . . . . 377  3 DON JUAN 13    42  V3
   TO FLY FROM AS FROM HUNGRY PIKES A ROACH . . . . . . . 421  3 DON JUAN 14    26   3
   IF SO SHE WOULD HAVE HAD THE STRENGTH TO FLY . . . . . 449  3 DON JUAN 14    91   3
   MARCH MY MUSE  IF YOU CANNOT FLY YET FLUTTER . . . . . 468  3 DON JUAN 15    27   2
   THE DOOR FLEW WIDE NOT SWIFTLY--BUT AS FLY . . . . . . 558  3 DON JUAN 16   117   1
   THE WIND SHIFTS AND I FLY INTO A RAGE  . . . . . . . . 566  3 DON JUAN 17    10   8
FLYING
   AND TUMBLE DOWNWARD LIKE THE FLYING FISH . . . . . . . .  10  2 DON JUAN  D     3   6
   WITH FLOATING DRAPERIES AND WITH FLYING HAIR . . . . . .  42  3 DON JUAN  6    72   2
   MORE VIRGIN VALOUR NEVER DREAMT OF FLYING  . . . . . . 131  3 DON JUAN  8    36   3
   THERE MAILS FAST FLYING OFF LIKE A DELUSION  . . . . . 278  3 DON JUAN 11    22   4
   OR LIKE A FLYING HOUR BEFORE AURORA  . . . . . . . . . 428  3 DON JUAN 14    40   1
FOAM
   AND FOAM AND ROLL WITH STRANGE CONVULSIONS RACK'D  . . 198  2 DON JUAN  2    79   5
   HIS EYES FROM OFF HIS FACE BUT WIPED THE FOAM  . . . . 203  2 DON JUAN  2    89   2
   PALE AS THE FOAM THAT FROTH'D ON HIS DEAD BROW . . . . 362  2 DON JUAN  4    34   2
   AND SWEPT AS GALES SWEEP FOAM AWAY WHOLE RANKS . . . . 134  3 DON JUAN  8    44   3
   NOW) YOU MAY CROSS THE BLUE DEEP AND WHITE FOAM--  . . 290  3 DON JUAN 11    44   3
   SPARKLING WITH FOAM UNTIL AGAIN SUBSIDING  . . . . . . 385  3 DON JUAN 13    58   2
   LASH'D FROM THE FOAM OF AGES WHILE THE GRAVES  . . . . 500  3 DON JUAN 15    99   7
   THE FOAM WHICH MADE ITS VIRGIN BUMPER GAY  . . . . . . 504  3 DON JUAN 16     9   3
FOAMING
   FOAMING O'ER HER LONE HEAD SO FIERCE AND HIGH  . . . . 361  2 DON JUAN  4    31   7
   BROKE FOAMING O'ER THE BLUE SYMPLEGADES  . . . . . . . 413  2 DON JUAN  5     5   2
   AND THEN THERE WAS CHAMPAGNE WITH FOAMING WHIRLS . . . 484  3 DON JUAN 15    65   7
FOAMS
   WHICH RISES FOAMS AND BREAKS BUT NOT IN VAIN . . . . . .  60  3 DON JUAN  6   108  V7
FOCIS
   WOULD YOU DO LESS PRO FOCIS ET PRO ARIS  . . . . . . . 174  3 DON JUAN  8   124  V8
FOCUS
   INTO ONE FOCUS KINDLED FROM ABOVE  . . . . . . . . . . 254  2 DON JUAN  2   186   3
   WE LEFT HIM IN THE FOCUS OF SUCH GLORY . . . . . . . . 229  3 DON JUAN 10     9   2
FOE
   ALFONSO GRAPPLED TO DETAIN THE FOE . . . . . . . . . . 124  2 DON JUAN  1   186   1
   THE PEOPLE'S SYCOPHANT THE PRINCE'S FOE  . . . . . . . 151  2 DON JUAN  1  V  2   7
   OR KNOW WHO RESTED THERE A FOE TO REST . . . . . . . . 274  2 DON JUAN  3     1   6
   THOUGH FOE TO LOVE AND YET THEY COULD NOT BE . . . . . 348  2 DON JUAN  4     8   6
   ON THE FIRST FOE WHOM LAMBRO'S CALL MIGHT BRING  . . . 365  2 DON JUAN  4    39   8
   IF YOU HAVE GOT A FORMER FRIEND FOR FOE  . . . . . . . 366  2 DON JUAN  4    41   6
   AGAINST A FOE OR RAN A SABRE THROUGH SKIN  . . . . . . .  75  3 DON JUAN  7    17   4
   HOW PEACE SHOULD MAKE JOHN BULL THE FRENCHMAN'S FOE  . .  77  3 DON JUAN  7    22   8
   UPON THE FOE THE SECOND'S ORDINATION . . . . . . . . . .  91  3 DON JUAN  7    50   5
   AND I BECAME A PRISONER TO THE FOE-- . . . . . . . . . .  98  3 DON JUAN  7    61   6
   AND DOUBTLESS WOULD BE FOREMOST ON THE FOE . . . . . . .  98  3 DON JUAN  7    62   3
   HIS JEST ALIKE IN FACE OF FRIEND OR FOE  . . . . . . . 147  3 DON JUAN  8    70   6
   OF FOE O'ER HIM SNATCHED AT IT AND BIT . . . . . . . . 153  3 DON JUAN  8    84   2
   MORE THAN THE HEAD OF THE INVETERATE FOE . . . . . . . 154  3 DON JUAN  8    85   7
```

FOE   (CONTINUED)
      ACKNOWLEDGE AUGHT OF DREAD OF DEATH OR FOE 155   3 DON JUAN 8   87   5
      OF THE LAST FOE IS ECHOED BY HIS OWN 155   3 DON JUAN 8   87   8
      HIS FIVE BRAVE BOYS NO LESS THE FOE DEFIED 165   3 DON JUAN 8   107   5
      FOR THEM IN SAVING SUCH A DESPERATE FOE-- 165   3 DON JUAN 8   108   5
      DEAR JEFFREY ONCE MY MOST REDOUBTED FOE 232   3 DON JUAN 10   16   2
      WHO NOW THAT HE IS DEAD HAS NOT A FOE 254   3 DON JUAN 10   59 V3
      HOW ALL THE NATIONS DEEM HER WORST FOE 258   3 DON JUAN 10   67   5
      A VERDICT--GRIEVOUS FOE TO THOSE WHO CAUSE IT-- . . . 346   3 DON JUAN 12   65   5
      THAN STORMS IT AS A FOE WOULD TAKE A CITY 350   3 DON JUAN 12   74   6
      DETERMINED RIGHT OR WRONG ON FRIEND OR FOE 366   3 DON JUAN 13   16   4
FOE'S
      WHO HELD THE PLACE AND TO ASSIST THE FOE'S 71   3 DON JUAN 7   10   8
FOES
      NOR FOES--ALL NATIONS--CONDESCEND TO SMILE-- 17   2 DON JUAN D   13   4
      HIS TALE IF FOES BE FOOD IN HELL AT SEA 200   2 DON JUAN 2   83   5
      FOES FRIENDS MEN WOMEN NOW ARE NOUGHT TO ME 244   2 DON JUAN 2   166   7
      AND FLEW AT ALL SHE MET AS ON HER FOES 380   2 DON JUAN 4   67   4
      HAD FACED NAPOLEON'S FOES UNTIL THEY FLED-- 431   2 DON JUAN 5   37   6
      OF WAR'S MOST MORTAL ENGINES TO THEIR FOES 116   3 DON JUAN 8   8   3
      RUSHED WHERE THE THICKEST FIRE ANNOUNCED MOST FOES . 127   3 DON JUAN 8   32   8
      WITHOUT OR WITH OFFENCE TO FRIENDS OR FOES 156   3 DON JUAN 8   89   7
      HE DASHED HIMSELF UPON HIS FOES AND FLUNG 170   3 DON JUAN 8   118 V2
      THEIR FRIENDS FROM FOES--BESIDES SUCH THINGS FROM HASTE . 177   3 DON JUAN 8   130   4
      WITH THOUGHT--AND OF THOUGHT'S FOES BY FAR MOST RUDE . . 194   3 DON JUAN 9   24   3
      OLD FLAMES NEW WIVES BECOME OUR BITTEREST FOES-- . . 231   3 DON JUAN 10   12   7
      CONVERTED FOES SHOULD SCORN TO JOIN WITH THOSE . . . 231   3 DON JUAN 10   12   8
      THAT WORSE THAN WORST OF FOES THE ONCE ADORED 258   3 DON JUAN 10   67   6
      SUCH SMALL DISTINCTION BETWEEN FRIENDS AND FOES . . . 421   3 DON JUAN 14   25   4
      MORE FOES BY THIS SAME SCROLL WHEN I BEGAN IT I . . . 482   3 DON JUAN 15   60   6
FOG-BANKS
      THE FREQUENT FOG-BANKS GAVE THEM CAUSE TO DOUBT-- . . 207   2 DON JUAN 2   96   6
FOIBLE
      A MATRON WHO HER HUSBAND'S FOIBLE KNOWS 117   2 DON JUAN 1   175   3
      IT WAS HIS FOIBLE BUT BY NO MEANS SINISTER-- 368   3 DON JUAN 13   21   2
FOIBLES
      SUFFERING EACH OTHER'S FOIBLES BY ACCORD 57   2 DON JUAN 1   65   5
      OBSERVANT OF THE FOIBLES OF THE CROWD 462   3 DON JUAN 15   15   3
FOLD
      HER HAIR WAS STARR'D WITH GEMS HER VEIL'S FINE FOLD . . 312   2 DON JUAN 3   72   4
      HIS TURBAN FURL'D IN MANY A GRACEFUL FOLD 315   2 DON JUAN 3   77   5
      OTHERS IN WIGS OF MARLBOROUGH'S MARTIAL FOLD 391   3 DON JUAN 13   70   4
      PINNED LIKE A FLOCK AND FLEECED TOO IN THEIR FOLD . . 468   3 DON JUAN 15   26   3
FOLDED
      PEACE TO THE SLUMBERS OF EACH FOLDED FLOWER-- 409   3 DON JUAN 13   111   5
      A ROSE WITH ALL ITS SWEETEST LEAVES YET FOLDED . . . 475   3 DON JUAN 15   43   8
FOLDS
      A SHAWL WHOSE FOLDS IN CASHMIRE HAD BEEN NURST . . . 451   2 DON JUAN 5   68   6
      TO HEAVING BACK THE PORTAL FOLDS IT SCARED 463   2 DON JUAN 5   90   4
      BUT HIS EYES MAY BE SEEN FROM THE FOLDS BETWEEN . . . 519   3 DON JUAN 16 L 4   7
FOLKS
      FOLKS ARE DISCOURAGED AND MOST SURELY NO MEN 205   2 DON JUAN 2   93   5
      ARE NOT THESE PRETTY STANZAS--SOME FOLKS SAY-- . . . 336   2 DON JUAN 3   104 V1
      AFFLICTING YOUNG FOLKS WITH A SORT OF DIZZINESS . . . 108   3 DON JUAN 7   83   8
      FOR WIT HATH NO GREAT FRIEND IN AGUISH FOLKS 540   3 DON JUAN 16   83   3
      FOR LAUGHTER RARELY SHAKES THESE AGUISH FOLKS 540   3 DON JUAN 16   83 V3
FOLLIES
      OF PEERESSES WHOSE FOLLIES HAD RUN DRY 329   3 DON JUAN 12   29   8
      FOLLIES TRICK'D OUT SO BRIGHTLY THAT THEY BLIND-- . . 480   3 DON JUAN 15   57   6
      WHATE'ER MAY BE HER FOLLIES OR HER FLAWS 502   3 DON JUAN 16   2   6
FOLLOW
      TO FOLLOW JUAN'S WAKE LIKE SANCHO PANCA 175   2 DON JUAN 2   37   8
      AND FOLLOW FAR THE DISAPPEARING SUN 355   2 DON JUAN 4   22   2
      WILL FOLLOW ME NO TRIFLING SIR FOR WHEN 458   2 DON JUAN 5   81   4
      WE NEEDS MUST FOLLOW WHEN FATE PUTS FROM SHORE . . . 460   2 DON JUAN 5   84   5
      AT LEAST TO FOLLOW THOSE WHO MIGHT BE SO 98   3 DON JUAN 7   61   4
      AS TRAVELLERS FOLLOW OVER BOG AND BRAKE 127   3 DOV JUAN 8   32   4
      MAKES MEN LIKE CATTLE FOLLOW HIM WHO LEADS 132   3 DON JUAN 8   38   8
      TO FOLLOW HIM BEYOND THE DRAWING-ROOM 227   3 DON JUAN 10   5   5
      AH--WHAT SHOULD FOLLOW SLIPS FROM MY REFLECTION . . . 456   3 DON JUAN 15   1   1
      FURTHER I SHALL NOT FOLLOW THE RESEARCH 485   3 DON JUAN 15   67   6
FOLLOW'D
      PERHAPS IT MAY BE FOLLOW'D BY THE GREAT 92   2 DON JUAN 1   130   8
      'TWERE WELL IF OTHERS FOLLOW'D MY EXAMPLE 147   2 DON JUAN 1   221   8
      THE MAINMAST FOLLOW'D BUT THE SHIP STILL LAY 173   2 DON JUAN 2   32   3
      REGALED TWO SHARKS WHO FOLLOW'D O'ER THE BILLOW-- . . 197   2 DON JUAN 2   77   7
      THOUGH THE TWO SHARKS STILL FOLLOW'D THEM AND DASH'D . 209   2 DON JUAN 2   101   7
      AH IF YOU HAD BUT FOLLOW'D MY ADVICE 430   3 DON JUAN 14   47   8
      AS THOUGH THE LURKING THOUGHT HAD FOLLOW'D FREE . . . 456   3 DON JUAN 15   1   4
      FOLLOW'D BY PETITS PUITS D'AMOUR--A DISH 486   3 DON JUAN 15   68   2
FOLLOWED
      THEY FOLLOWED CLOSE BEHIND THEIR SABLE GUIDE 440   2 DON JUAN 5   51   2
      WHICH ALL WHO SAW IT FOLLOWED WRONG OR RIGHT 89   3 DON JUAN 7   46   8
      WHAT FOLLOWED--A SHOT LAID ME ON MY BACK 98   3 DON JUAN 7   61   5
      FOLLOWED IN HASTE BY VARIOUS GRENADIERS 147   3 DON JUAN 8   71   2
      AND THE PAUSE FOLLOWED WHICH WHEN SONG EXPIRES . . . 521   3 DON JUAN 16   41   3
      FOLLOWED HIS VEINS NO LONGER COLD BUT HEATED 559   3 DON JUAN 16   119   4
FOLLOWER
      UNTO HIS NEAREST FOLLOWER OR HENCHMAN 274   3 DON JUAN 11   13   7

PAGE VOL   CANTO STANZA LN

FOLLOWERS
   FOLLOWERS OF FAME NINE FARROW OF THAT SOW . . . . . . 22 2 DON JUAN 1   2 6
   BUT WORDSWORTH'S POEM AND HIS FOLLOWERS LIKE . . . . . 330 2 DON JUAN 3   95 3
   PICKED OUT AMONGST HIS FOLLOWERS WITH SOME SKILL . . . 162 3 DON JUAN 8   102 3
FOLLOWING
   FOLLOWING ANTONIA'S MOTIONS HERE AND THERE . . . . . . 109 2 DON JUAN 1   160 2
   SHOWN IN THE FOLLOWING COPY OF HER LETTER . . . . . . 129 2 DON JUAN 1   191 8
   WHEN HE AND SOUTHEY FOLLOWING THE SAME PATH . . . . . 329 2 DON JUAN 3   93 7
   SO JUAN FOLLOWING HONOUR AND HIS NOSE . . . . 127 3 DON JUAN 8   32 7
   FOLLOWING THE BENT OF BODY OR OF MIND) . . . . 193 3 DON JUAN 9   21 5
   WERE THEIR REWARD FOR FOLLOWING BILLY'S BANNERS . . . 242 3 DON JUAN 10   36 4
   HAVE TAKEN UP TO FILL THE FOLLOWING SERMON . . . . . 416 3 DON JUAN 14   15 2
   FOLLOWING THE IGNES FATUI OF MANKIND . . . . 479 3 DON JUAN 15   54 6
FOLLOWS
   AND HERE EXACTLY FOLLOWS WHAT HE SAID-- . . . . 178 3 DON JUAN 8   133 6
   WHATEVER FOLLOWS NE'ERTHELESS MAY BE . . . . 456 3 DON JUAN 15   1 2
FOLLY
   HE WONDERS AT THEIR VICE AND NOT HIS FOLLY . . . . . . 74 2 DON JUAN 1   99 8
   AND OF THE FOLLY OF ALL PRUDISH FEARS . . . . 78 2 DON JUAN 1   107 2
   OF HUMAN FRAILTY FOLLY ALSO CRIME . . . . 277 2 DON JUAN 3   5 2
   SHORTLY AND SWEETLY THE MASONIC FOLLY . . . . 448 2 DON JUAN 5   63 2
   THEIR FOLLY IN FORGETTING THERE ARE FOOLS . . . . . . 463 3 DON JUAN 15   17 8
   AND YET SUCH IS MY FOLLY OR MY FATE . . . . 496 3 DON JUAN 15   91 4
FOLLY'S
   OF FOLLY'S FRUIT FOR THOUGH YOUR FOOLS ABOUND . . . . 402 3 DON JUAN 13   95 5
FOND
   HER EYE (I'M VERY FOND OF HANDSOME EYES) . . . . 54 2 DON JUAN 1   60 1
   I'M FOND MYSELF OF SOLITUDE OR SO . . . . 68 2 DON JUAN 1   87 5
   FOND OF A LITTLE LOVE (WHICH I CALL LEISURE) . . . . . 85 2 DON JUAN 1   118 6
   I'M FOND OF FIRE AND CRICKETS AND ALL THAT . . . . . . 94 2 DON JUAN 1   135 7
   AS VIBRATES MY FOND HEART TO MY FIX'D SOUL . . . . . 133 2 DON JUAN 1   196 8
   PROSE POETS LIKE BLANK-VERSE I'M FOND OF RHYME . . . . 136 2 DON JUAN 1   201 5
   SOME PEOPLE LIKE BLANK VERSE I'M FOND OF RHYME . . . . 136 2 DON JUAN 1   201 V5
   (THERE'S ONE AT LEAST IS VERY FOND OF THIS) . . . . . 140 2 DON JUAN 1   206 4
   BUT I BEING FOND OF TRUE PHILOSOPHY . . . . 147 2 DON JUAN 1   220 1
   OF US DIES WITH THEM AS EACH FOND HOPE ENDS . . . . . 167 2 DON JUAN 2   21 6
   WHO WERE NOT QUITE SO FOND OF ANIMAL FOOD . . . . . . 198 2 DON JUAN 2   78 2
   WE KNOW TOO THEY ARE VERY FOND OF WAR . . . . 238 2 DON JUAN 2   156 5
   FOR JUAN WHO WAS SOMEWHAT FOND OF REST-- . . . . . . 245 2 DON JUAN 2   168 2
   MEN GROW ASHAMED OF BEING SO VERY FOND . . . . 278 2 DON JUAN 3   7 1
   DEFYING AUGURY WITH THAT FOND KISS . . . . 356 2 DON JUAN 4   24 4
   'TIS ALL THE SAME TO ME I'M FOND OF YIELDING . . . . 397 2 DON JUAN 4   98 1
   AND YOU WILL FIND US NOT TOO FOND OF JOKING . . . . . 454 2 DON JUAN 5   75 4
   DUDU WAS FOND OF KISSING--WHICH I'M SURE . . . . . . 35 3 DON JUAN 6   59 2
   IF FOND OF A CHANCE OGLE AT HER GLASS . . . . 36 3 DON JUAN 6   60 4
   A FOND HALLUCINATION AND A THEME . . . . 47 3 DON JUAN 6   83 5
   WITH BEARDS AND WHISKERS AND THE LIKE THE FOND . . . 209 3 DON JUAN 9   53 4
   I LEAVE TO THOSE WHO ARE FOND OF SOLVING DOUBT . . . 531 3 DON JUAN 16   62 4
   WAVED O'ER HIS COUCH HE MEDITATED FOND . . . . 555 3 DON JUAN 16   110 6
FONDLY
   THUS THE FRAIL BEINGS WE WOULD FONDLY CHERISH . . . . 275 2 DON JUAN 3   2 7
   ON SUCH AS THESE THE LIP TOO FONDLY LINGERS . . . . . 472 2 DON JUAN 5   106 4
   UPON THE TREE WHICH EVE SO FONDLY SEARCHED . . . . . 192 3 DON JUAN 9   19 8
   FONDLY THE WHEELING FIRE-FLIES FLEW AROUND HER . . . 435 3 DON JUAN 14   57 1
FONT
   THE ARTS OF WHICH THESE LANDS WERE ONCE THE FONT . . 436 2 DON JUAN 5   46 6
   AN AGE MAY COME FONT OF ETERNITY . . . . 411 3 DON JUAN 14   3 5
FONTS
   IN MARBLE FONTS THERE GRAIN AND FLOWER AND FRUIT . . 373 2 DON JUAN 4   55 2
FOOD
   OR REGENT WHO ADMIRES SUCH KIND OF FOOD-- . . . . . . 10 2 DON JUAN D   2 4
   FOR EARLY STOMACHS TO PROVE WHOLESOME FOOD . . . . . . 45 2 DON JUAN 1   43 2
   WATER AND WINE AND FOOD--AND YOU MIGHT SEE . . . . . 194 2 DON JUAN 2   72 6
   AND WHO SHOULD DIE TO BE HIS FELLOW'S FOOD . . . . . 194 2 DON JUAN 2   73 8
   WHO WERE NOT QUITE SO FOND OF ANIMAL FOOD . . . . . . 198 2 DON JUAN 2   78 2
   HIS TALE IF FOES BE FOOD IN HELL AT SEA . . . . . . 200 2 DON JUAN 2   83 5
   WITH FOOD AND RAIMENT AND THOSE SOFT ATTENTIONS . . . 221 2 DON JUAN 2   123 2
   AND LONG FOR FOOD BUT CHIEFLY A BEEF-STEAK . . . . . 237 2 DON JUAN 2   153 8
   EGGS OYSTERS TOO ARE AMATORY FOOD . . . . 246 2 DON JUAN 2   170 6
   AND LOVE WHICH ALSO MUCH DEPENDS ON FOOD . . . . . . 246 2 DON JUAN 2   170 V4
   OYSTERS AND EGGS ARE ALSO LOVING FOOD . . . . 246 2 DON JUAN 2   170 V6
   WITH TEMPERANCE IN PLEASURE AS IN FOOD . . . . 302 2 DON JUAN 3   53 4
   FOOD SHE REFUSED AND RAIMENT NO PRETENCE . . . . . . 381 2 DON JUAN 4   68 5
   OF FOOD I THINK WITH PHILIP'S SON OR RATHER . . . . . 427 2 DON JUAN 5   31 7
   TO BE PURSUED AS FOOD FOR INANITION . . . . 328 3 DON JUAN 12   27 6
FOOL
   OF HAVING PLAY'D THE FOOL THOUGH BOTH I SPURN HE . . 103 2 DON JUAN 1   151 5
   CAN MAKE THE FOOL OF WHICH THEY MADE BEFORE . . . . . 144 2 DON JUAN 1   216 3
   (LIKE TRUANT ROGUES) THE DEVIL OR THE FOOL . . . . . 162 2 DON JUAN 2   10 4
   THE LOVELIEST CHASTEST BEST BUT--QUITE A FOOL . . . . 405 2 DON JUAN 4   111 6
   BUT EVERY FOOL DESCRIBES IN THESE BRIGHT DAYS . . . . 440 2 DON JUAN 5   52 2
   YOU FOOL I TELL YOU NO ONE MEANS YOU HARM . . . . . 459 2 DON JUAN 5   82 5
   GREAT JOY TO LONDON NOW SAYS SOME GREAT FOOL . . . . 88 3 DON JUAN 7   44 1
   A FOOL WHOSE BELLS HAVE CEASED TO RING AT ALL-- . . . 267 3 DON JUAN 10   86 8
   WHO LIKE TO PLAY THE FOOL WITH CIRCUMSPECTION . . . . 304 3 DON JUAN 11   71 8
   I HAVE SEEN JOHN HALF DETECT HIMSELF A FOOL-- . . . . 310 3 DON JUAN 11   85 8
   BUT WHEN WE HOVER BETWEEN FOOL AND SAGE . . . . . . 315 3 DON JUAN 12   1 4
   THE FOOL WILL CALL SUCH MANIA A DISEASE-- . . . . . 321 3 DON JUAN 12   11 3
   THUS GENTLEMEN MAY SOMETIMES PLAY THE FOOL . . . . . 376 3 DON JUAN 13   39 V6

FOOL   (CONTINUED)
    WHEN CONGREVE'S FOOL COULD VIE WITH MOLIERE'S BETE . . . 402   3 DON JUAN 13   94   6
    SHALL FOOL ME TO THE TOP UP OF MY BENT-- 498   3 DON JUAN 15   94   3
FOOLING
    COME COME 'TIS NO TIME NOW FOR FOOLING THERE 114   2 DON JUAN 1   170   6
    EXCLAIMING FOOLING SWEARING AT THE INERT 96   3 DON JUAN 7   58   3
FOOLISH
    I THINK THE FOOLISH PEOPLE WERE POSSESS'D 34   2 DON JUAN 1   24   3
    AND TRUTH TO SAY HE MADE A FOOLISH FIGURE 110   2 DON JUAN 1   161   2
    A FOOLISH CLEVER FELLOW IDEM SEMPER 150   2 DON JUAN 1   V   1   8
    THEY HOPED THE WIND WOULD RISE THESE FOOLISH MEN . . . 192   2 DON JUAN 2   69   5
    BUT THESE ARE FOOLISH THINGS TO ALL THE WISE 37   3 DON JUAN 6   63   1
    'TWAS FOOLISH NERVOUS AS SHE MUST ALLOW 47   3 DON JUAN 6   83   4
    BECAUSE A FOOLISH OR IMPRUDENT ACT 58   3 DON JUAN 6   104   4
    OH FOOLISH MORTALS ALWAYS TAUGHT IN VAIN 101   3 DON JUAN 7   68   5
    KEEP MERELY FIRING AT A FOOLISH DISTANCE 151   3 DON JUAN 8   78   8
FOOL'S
    ON A FOOL'S HEAD--AND THERE IS LONDON TOWN 265   3 DON JUAN 10   82   8
    I HAVE SEEN CROWNS WORN INSTEAD OF A FOOL'S CAP-- . . . 310   3 DON JUAN 11   84   5
FOOLS
    THE MOMENT HE HAS SENT HIS FOOLS AWAY 114   2 DON JUAN 1   169   2
    WHICH MAKES SO MANY POETS AND SOME FOOLS 136   2 DON JUAN 1   201   4
    AND ALL HER FOOLS WHOM I COULD LAY THE LASH ON 244   2 DON JUAN 2   166   6
    FROM FOOLS WHO DREAD TO KNOW THE TRUTH OF LIFE 69   3 DON JUAN 7   6 V8
    DUKES--FOOLS BY BIRTH WHILE CLOGHER'S BISHOP SULLIES . . 314   3 DON JUAN 11   V 76   5
    NOT EVEN IN FOOLS--WHO--HOWSOEVER BLIND 372   3 DON JUAN 13   32 V6
    OF FOLLY'S FRUIT FOR THOUGH YOUR FOOLS ABOUND 402   3 DON JUAN 13   95   5
    THEIR FOLLY IN FORGETTING THERE ARE FOOLS 463   3 DON JUAN 15   17   8
FOOLSCAP
    A BALL-ROOM BARD A FOOLSCAP HOT-PRESS DARLING 404   2 DON JUAN 4   109   2
    A HUGE DUN CUPOLA LIKE A FOOLSCAP CROWN 265   3 DON JUAN 10   82   7
    NOR SOUGHT OF FOOLSCAP SUBJECTS TO BE KING-- 296   3 DON JUAN 11   55   6
    BLACK LETTER UPON FOOLSCAP WHILE OUR HAIR 315   3 DON JUAN 12   1   7
FOOT
    HIS MAN WAS FLOOR'D AND HELPLESS AT HIS FOOT 370   2 DON JUAN 4   49   5
    HIS MAN WAS PROSTRATE BLEEDING AT HIS FOOT 370   2 DON JUAN 4   49 V5
    AND LONG LONG DESERTS SCORCH THE CAMEL'S FOOT 373   2 DON JUAN 4   55   6
    GAVE IT A SLIGHT KICK WITH HIS CHRISTIAN FOOT 453   2 DON JUAN 5   73   6
    AND KISS THE LADY'S FOOT WHICH MAXIM WHEN 470   2 DON JUAN 5   102   4
    AT LENGTH PERCEIVING THE FOOT COULD NOT STAND 471   2 DON JUAN 5   104   7
    THIS FELLOW BEING SIX FOOT HIGH COULD RAISE-- 84   3 DON JUAN 7   37   5
    AND TALL AND STRONG AND SWIFT OF FOOT WERE THEY . . . 145   3 DON JUAN 8   66   1
    THE BREATH OF MORN AND MAN WHERE FOOT BY FOOT 146   3 DON JUAN 8   69   7
    THE BREATH OF MORN AND MAN WHERE FOOT BY FOOT 146   3 DON JUAN 8   69   7
    A DYING MOSLEM WHO HAD FELT THE FOOT 153   3 DON JUAN 8   84   1
    WHO NEVER HAD A FOOT OF LAND TILL NOW-- 237   3 DON JUAN 10   25   7
    THEIR PEAKS BENEATH YOUR HUMAN FOOT AND THERE 412   3 DON JUAN 14   5   5
FOOTING
    A THING IN FOOTING INDISPENSABLE 427   3 DON JUAN 14   38   5
FOOTMARKS
    HAD SIGNS OR FOOTMARKS BUT THE EARTH SAID NOUGHT . . . 100   2 DON JUAN 1   144   4
FOOTMEN
    TO PROVE THEIR PRIDE AS FOOTMEN TO A BEGGAR 537   3 DON JUAN 16   76   8
FOOTSTEP
    A FEELING IN EACH FOOTSTEP AS DISCLOSED 61   3 DON JUAN 6   111   5
FOOTSTEPS
    SOME BLOOD AND SEVERAL FOOTSTEPS BUT NO MORE 125   2 DON JUAN 1   187   6
    AND NEAR THE CAVE HER QUICK LIGHT FOOTSTEPS DREW . . . 232   2 DON JUAN 2   142   2
    OF YOUR OWN FOOTSTEPS--VOICES FROM THE URN 508   3 DON JUAN 16   18   4
    WITH AWFUL FOOTSTEPS REGULAR AS RHYME 556   3 DON JUAN 16   113   3
FOP
    OF BEING WITHOUT ALLOY OF FOP OR BEAU 354   3 DON JUAN 12   84   7
FOPLINGS
    THAN WHISPERING FOPLINGS OR THAN WITLINGS LOUD 493   3 DON JUAN 15   83   4
FORBADE
    BUT THE FAIR FACE WHICH MET HIS EYES FORBADE 235   2 DON JUAN 2   149   2
    BUT ETIQUETTE FORBADE THEM ALL TO GIGGLE 501   2 DON JUAN 5   156   8
FORBEAR
    AND DEEMS HE THAT WE ALWAYS WILL FORBEAR 153   2 DON JUAN 1   V   4   4
    WOULD BEAR SUCH OUTRAGE AND FORBEAR TO KILL 368   2 DON JUAN 4   46   6
    THE CAUSE OF THIS ODD TRAVESTY--FORBEAR 454   2 DON JUAN 5   74   5
    THOUGH SOMEWHAT GRIEVED COULD SCARCE FORBEAR A SMILE . . 459   2 DON JUAN 5   83   3
    AND ALL (EXCEPT MAHOMETANS) FORBEAR 12   3 DON JUAN 6   12   7
    AND (THOUGH I COULD NOT NOW AND THEN FORBEAR 193   3 DON JUAN 9   21   4
    ABOVE ALL I BEG ALL MEN TO FORBEAR 454   3 DON JUAN 14   99   1
FORBEARANCE
    I PRAISE YOUR VAST FORBEARANCE NOT TO BEAT 103   2 DON JUAN 1   150   5
FORBEARS
    BUT THERE ARE FORMS WHICH TIME TO TOUCH FORBEARS . . . 468   2 DON JUAN 5   98   3
FORBID
    BUT HEAVEN FORBID THAT SUCH A THOUGHT SHOULD CROSS . . . 67   2 DON JUAN 1   84   2
    FORBID BY HEAVENLY FINED BY HUMAN LAWS 113   2 DON JUAN 1   167   3
    THE COPIOUS USE OF CLARET IS FORBID TOO 144   2 DON JUAN 1   216   6
    I FIND THAT WINE OR BRANDY IS FORBID TOO 145   2 DON JUAN 1   216 V6
    (WHICH GOD FORBID) OR SOME OR A GREAT MANY 301   2 DON JUAN 3   50   2
FORBIDDEN
    BESIDES FORBIDDEN FRUITS FOR SHE NE'ER PAUSED 476   2 DON JUAN 5   113 V6
    FOR THAT SAD TEMPTER A FORBIDDEN WOMAN 10   3 DON JUAN 6   7   4
FORBIDDING
    YOU MAY DO RIGHT FORBIDDING THEM TO SHOW 'EM 403   2 DON JUAN 4   107   7

```
                                                      PAGE VOL      CANTO STANZA LN
FORBIDS
   FORBIDS ALL WANDERING AS THE WORST OF SINNING  . . . . .  25  2 DON JUAN  1      7    4
   FORBIDS  A GREAT IMPRESSION IN MY YOUTH  . . . . . .  403  3 DON JUAN 13     96    6
FORBORE
   THEN LAMBRO WHO TILL NOW FORBORE TO SPEAK  . . . . .  364  2 DON JUAN  4     37    5
FORCE
   PATRIOT BY FORCE AND COURTISAN BY CRAFT  . . . . . .  155  2 DON JUAN  1  V   6    6
   WIT WITHOUT SENSE--AND VIOLENCE WITHOUT FORCE  . . . .  155  2 DON JUAN  1  V   6   V7
   A STRANGE EXAMPLE OF THE FORCE OF LAW . . . . . . .  155  2 DON JUAN  1  V   7    1
   THEY TOOK BY FORCE FROM JUAN JULIA'S LETTER . . . . .  195  2 DON JUAN  2     74    8
   NE'ER WITH SUCH FORCE THE SWIFTEST ARROW FLEW  . . . .  218  2 DON JUAN  2    117    6
   BUT TURKISH FORCE AND LATIN FRAUD . . . . . . . .  325  2 DON JUAN  3  L  14    5
   BUT HER LARGE DARK EYE SHOW'D DEEP PASSION'S FORCE . .  374  2 DON JUAN  4     56    7
   WHOSE FORCE DESCRIPTION ONLY WOULD ABATE . . . . . .  467  2 DON JUAN  5     97    3
   HIS HEART TO FORCE IT OUT FOR (TO BE SHORTER) . . . .  479  2 DON JUAN  5    118    7
   WITH GENTLE FORCE HER WHITE ARMS HE UNWOUND . . . . .  484  2 DON JUAN  5    126    3
FORCED
   WERE FORCED TO MAKE AN ODD SORT OF APOLOGY . . . . .   44  2 DON JUAN  1     41    7
   WHEN PROUD GRENADA FELL AND FORCED TO FLY  . . . . .   52  2 DON JUAN  1     56    5
   FOR THEY WERE FORCED WITH STEERING TO DISPENSE . . . .  177  2 DON JUAN  2     40    3
FORCES
   A PATH TO ADD HIS OWN SLIGHT ARM AND FORCES  . . . .  126  3 DON JUAN  8     30    7
   REQUIRES ARITHMETIC BEYOND MY FORCES . . . . . .  486  3 DON JUAN 15     69    4
   THOSE WHO IN COUNTY INTEREST TRY THEIR FORCES . . . .  534. 3 DON JUAN 16     68   V6
FORE
   AND TOSSED ALONG THE VESSEL FORE AND AFT . . . . . .  155  2 DON JUAN  1  V   6    4
   A GALE AND IN THE FORE AND AFTER HOLD . . . . . . .  178  2 DON JUAN  2     42    2
FOREGO
   AND FOR WHICH NATURE MIGHT FOREGO HER DEBT-- . . . .  458  3 DON JUAN 15      7    6
   IF SOMEONE HAD NOT TOLD ME TO FOREGO IT . . . . . .  467  3 DON JUAN 15     24    8
   BUT I HAVE DINED AND MUST FOREGO ALAS . . . . . . .  487  3 DON JUAN 15     71    7
FOREHEAD
   PILLOW'D HIS DEATH-LIKE FOREHEAD THEN SHE WRUNG . . .  216  2 DON JUAN  2    114    5
   OF SUFFERANCE YET UPON HIS FOREHEAD LAY  . . . . . .  234  2 DON JUAN  2    147    4
   HER ATTIC FOREHEAD AND HER PHIDIAN NOSE . . . . . .   27  3 DON JUAN  6     42    4
FOREIGN
   FOR SHE GOT HOLD OF A YOUNG FOREIGN NINNY  . . . . .  390  2 DON JUAN  4     84   V5
   HIS WOND'ROUS JOURNEY TO SOME FOREIGN COURT  . . . .  440  2 DON JUAN  5     52    3
   AND TO THE BEAUTIES OF A FOREIGN DAME . . . . . . .  349  3 DON JUAN 12     72    6
   FROM FOREIGN YOKE TO FREE THE HELPLESS NATIVE-- . . .  363  3 DON JUAN 13     10    4
   OR DID WHAT THEY SHOULD NOT WITH FOREIGN GRACES  . .  368  3 DON JUAN 13     23    4
   (EXCUSE A FOREIGN SLIPSLOP NOW AND THEN . . . . . .  380  3 DON JUAN 13     47    6
   SHE TOOK UP WITH SOME FOREIGN YOUNGER BROTHER  . . .  474  3 DON JUAN 15     42    7
FOREIGNER
   TO FOREIGNER OR NATIVE SAVE SOME SILLY ONES  . . . .  263  3 DON JUAN 10     77    6
   A FOREIGNER OF RANK HAD GRACED OUR SHORE . . . . . .  283  3 DON JUAN 11     32    6
   ALSO A FOREIGNER OF HIGH CONDITION . . . . . . . .  382  3 DON JUAN 13     52    7
   A FOX-HUNT TO A FOREIGNER IS STRANGE . . . . . . .  424  3 DON JUAN 14     32    1
FOREIGNER'S
   OF A RICH FOREIGNER'S INITIATION  . . . . . . .  293  3 DON JUAN 11     49    6
FOREIGNERS
   THEN THERE WERE FOREIGNERS OF MUCH RENOWN  . . . . .   75  3 DON JUAN  7     18    1
   TO WELCOME FOREIGNERS IN THIS WAY NOW . . . . . . .  275  3 DON JUAN 11     15    2
   ESPECIALLY FOR FOREIGNERS--AND MOSTLY . . . . . . .  283  3 DON JUAN 11     31    2
   WHICH FOREIGNERS CAN NEVER UNDERSTAND . . . . . . .  326  3 DON JUAN 12     23    8
   AND THEN HE DANCED--ALL FOREIGNERS EXCEL . . . . . .  427  3 DON JUAN 14     38    1
   (FOR FOREIGNERS DON'T KNOW THAT A FAUX PAS  . . . .  436  3 DON JUAN 14     60    5
FOREMAST
   FOREMAST AND BOWSPRIT WERE CUT DOWN AND THEY . . . .  173  2 DON JUAN  2     32    5
FOREMOST
   AND GOING DOWN HEAD FOREMOST--SUNK IN SHORT  . . . .  183  2 DON JUAN  2     51    8
   THE FILE OF PIRATES SAVE THE FOREMOST WHO  . . . . .  370  2 DON JUAN  4     48    7
   THE FOREMOST IN THE CHARGE OR IN THE SALLY . . . . .  431  2 DON JUAN  5     37    7
   BUT STILL A FORTRESS OF THE FOREMOST RANK  . . . . .   70  3 DON JUAN  7      9    4
   AND DOUBTLESS WOULD BE FOREMOST ON THE FOE . . . . .   98  3 DON JUAN  7     62    3
   AMONG THE FOREMOST BUT IF YOU'D EXPRESS  . . . . . .  100  3 DON JUAN  7     65    6
   AMONG THE FOREMOST OFFERED HIM GOOD QUARTER  . . . .  152  3 DON JJAN  8     80    2
   THE MORNING POST WAS FOREMOST TO PROCLAIM-- . . . .  382  3 DON JUAN 13     51    6
   I HAVE NAMED A FEW NOT FOREMOST IN DEGREE  . . . . .  397  3 DON JUAN 13     83    5
FORE-PAWS
   AS A GREAT FAVOUR ONE OF THE FORE-PAWS . . . . . .  193  2 DON JUAN  2     71    6
FORERUNNERS
   THAN MY FORERUNNERS  CARELESSLY I SING . . . . . .  181  3 DON JUAN  8    138    7
FORESAW
   OWN THEY FORESAW THAT YOU WOULD FALL AT LAST . . . .  432  3 DON JUAN 14     50    6
FORESEEN
   THE CONSEQUENCE WAS EASILY FORESEEN-- . .  . . . .  192  2 DON JUAN  2     69    1
FOREST
   WHERE THE WILD BRANCH OF THE CORK FOREST GREW  . . .   70  2 DON JUAN  1     90    4
   AND YET THE FOREST LEAVES SEEM'D STIRR'D WITH PRAYER . .  335  2 DON JUAN  3    102    8
   OF THE PINE FOREST AND THE SILENT SHORE  . . . . .  337  2 DON JUAN  3    105    2
   EVERGREEN FOREST WHICH BOCCACIO'S LORE . . . . . .  337  2 DON JUAN  3    105    6
   CUT FROM ITS FOREST ROOT OF YEARS--THE RIVER . . . .  349  2 DON JUAN  4     10    4
   THE FREE-BORN FOREST FOUND AND KEPT THEM FREE  . . .  145  3 DON JUAN  8     65    7
   WHEN THE STRIPT FOREST BOWS TO THE BLEAK AIR . . . .  155  3 DON JUAN  8     88    4
FORESTALLED
   OR IF FORESTALLED GET OPPOSITE AND OGLE-- . . . . .  304  3 DON JUAN 11     72    2
FORESTERS
   WITH THE FREE FORESTERS DIVIDE NO SPOIL  . . . . . .  145  3 DON JUAN  8     67    6
   THE DAPPLED FORESTERS--AS DAY AWOKE  . . . . . . .  384  3 DON JUAN 13     56    6
```

	PAGE	VOL	CANTO	STANZA	LN
FORESTRY					
IN SIGHT THEN LOST AMIDST THE FORESTRY	265	3 DON JUAN	10	82	4
FOREST'S					
THAN OTHERS CROWDED IN THE FOREST'S MAZE--	562	3 DON JUAN	17	1	4
FORESTS					
IN DESERTS FORESTS CROWDS OR BY THE SHORE	443	2 DON JUAN	5	57	2
FOREST-TOPS					
THAT WAVED IN FOREST-TOPS AND SMOOTH'D THE AIR	210	2 DON JUAN	2	103	4
FORETELLS					
FORETELLS THE HEAVIEST TEMPEST IT DISPLAYS	61	2 DON JUAN	1	73	3
FOREVER					
TO LIVE WITH HIM FOREVER WERE TOO MUCH	247	2 DON JUAN	2	173	5
WHEREAS IF ONE SOLE LADY PLEASED FOREVER	270	2 DON JUAN	2	213	7
AND BREAST MATERNAL WEAN'D AT ONCE FOREVER	349	2 DON JUAN	4	10	6
WHEN IT'S LAST WEANING DRAUGHT IS DRAINED FOREVER	349	2 DON JUAN	4	10	V6
FOREVER AND ANON A SOMETHING SHOOK	359	2 DON JUAN	4	29	4
O'ER THE FAIR VENUS BUT FOREVER FAIR	377	2 DON JUAN	4	61	4
SENSES TO SLEEP--THE POWER SEEM'D GONE FOREVER	381	2 DON JUAN	4	68	8
RESTORE ME THOSE PURE FEELINGS GONE FOREVER	9	3 DON JUAN	6	5	8
OF THE GOOD FEUDAL TIMES FOREVER GONE	255	3 DON JUAN	10	62	3
FOREVER AND ANON COMES INDIGESTION	269	3 DON JUAN	11	3	1
WHICH SITS FOREVER UPON MEMORY'S CRUPPER	304	3 DON JUAN	11	72	5
FORGET					
SHE MARRIED (I FORGET THE PEDIGREE)	52	2 DON JUAN	1	57	1
WITH--SEVERAL OTHER THINGS WHICH I FORGET	73	2 DON JUAN	1	96	7
WE NE'ER FORGET THOUGH THERE WE ARE FORGOT	90	2 DON JUAN	1	126	8
MY HEART IS FEMININE NOR CAN FORGET--	133	2 DON JUAN	1	196	5
OF LOVE WHEN I FORGET YOU MAY I FAIL	160	2 DON JUAN	2	7	5
AND OH IF E'ER I SHOULD FORGET I SWEAR--	166	2 DON JUAN	2	19	1
AND MADE A SCENE MEN DO NOT SOON FORGET	172	2 DON JUAN	2	31	3
OF TWO SUCH LESSONS WHY FORGET	324	2 DON JUAN	3	L 10	3
HOWEVER STRANGE HE COULD NOT YET FORGET HER	483	2 DON JUAN	5	124	3
O'ERTHROWS THE SAME WE READILY FORGET	8	3 DON JUAN	6	4	3
OR IF THESE DO NOT MOVE YOU DON'T FORGET	174	3 DON JUAN	8	125	3
WHICH FEW WILL SING I TRUST BUT NONE FORGET IT--	179	3 DON JUAN	8	135	3
I QUITE FORGET THIS POEM'S MERELY QUIZZICAL	203	3 DON JUAN	9	41	3
I QUITE FORGET WHICH OF THEM WAS IN HAND	205	3 DON JUAN	9	46	3
HER NOTE SHE DON'T FORGET THE INFANT GIRL	249	3 DON JUAN	10	51	7
I'M AT MY OLD LUNES--DIGRESSION AND FORGET	364	3 DON JUAN	13	12	1
I HAD FORGOTTEN--BUT MUST NOT FORGET--	400	3 DON JUAN	13	90	1
AS I HAVE SAID IN--I FORGET WHAT PAGE	433	3 DON JUAN	14	54	5
I'VE ALSO SEEN SOME WIVES (NOT TO FORGET	452	3 DON JUAN	14	95	5
FORGETTING					
FORGETTING DUNCAN NELSON HOWE AND JERVIS	23	2 DON JUAN	1	4	8
FORGETTING EACH OMISSION IS A LOSS TO	331	2 DON JUAN	3	96	7
OF THOSE FORGETTING THE GREAT PLACE OF REST	448	2 DON JUAN	5	63	3
FORGETTING QUITE THE WOMAN (WHICH COMPOSED	211	3 DON JUAN	9	58	2
THEIR FOLLY IN FORGETTING THERE ARE FOOLS	463	3 DON JUAN	15	17	8
FORGIVE					
AND SO FAREWELL--FORGIVE ME LOVE ME--NO	132	2 DON JUAN	1	195	7
HE WILL FORGIVE US--YES--IT MUST BE--YES	364	2 DON JUAN	4	38	3
OR AT THE LEAST FORGIVE THE LOVING RASH ONE	8	3 DON JUAN	6	4	4
THEIR CHOICE THAN LIFE FORGIVE THEM AS BEGUILED	143	3 DON JUAN	8	62	5
HOWEVER I FORGIVE HIM AND I TRUST	230	3 DON JUAN	10	11	7
HE WILL FORGIVE HIMSELF--IF NOT I MUST	230	3 DON JUAN	10	11	8
BESIDES (ALAS HIS TASTE--FORGIVE AND PITY)	347	3 DON JUAN	12	68	7
FORGIVEN					
GREAT LUSTRE THERE IS MUCH TO BE FORGIVEN	465	2 DON JUAN	5	94	6
AND BE THY SINS FORGIVEN--BUT UPON THIS	352	3 DON JUAN	12	79	3
FORGIVENESS					
MIGHT MEET FROM MEN A LITTLE MORE FORGIVENESS	326	3 DON JUAN	12	22	8
FORGOT					
FORGOT WITH HIM HER VERY PRUDENT CARRIAGE	58	2 DON JUAN	1	66	8
HE MISS'D THE PATHWAY HE FORGOT THE HOURS	72	2 DON JUAN	1	94	5
(I HAVE FORGOT THE NUMBER AND THINK NO MAN	74	2 DON JUAN	1	98	5
WE NE'ER FORGET THOUGH THERE WE ARE FORGOT	90	2 DON JUAN	1	126	8
AND HALF FORGOT THEIR DANGER AND DESPAIR	114	2 DON JUAN	1	170	4
HE HAD PRONOUNCED HER NAME--BUT SHE FORGOT	228	2 DON JUAN	2	135	7
AND HELL AND PURGATORY--BUT FORGOT	258	2 DON JUAN	2	193	7
HAIDEE FORGOT THE ISLAND WAS HER SIRE'S	282	2 DON JUAN	3	13	4
THEY CHANGED FROM ROOM TO ROOM BUT ALL FORGOT	379	2 DON JUAN	4	64	5
OUR BARITONE I ALMOST HAD FORGOT	392	2 DON JUAN	4	89	1
INVENTED BY SOME NAME I HAVE FORGOT	406	2 DON JUAN	4	112	3
STILL HE FORGOT NOT HIS DISGUISE--ALONG	21	3 DON JUAN	6	30	1
RIGHT I WAS BUSY AND FORGOT WHY YOU	100	3 DON JUAN	7	66	1
HERE WAR FORGOT HIS OWN DESTRUCTIVE ART	152	3 DON JUAN	8	82	5
WITH HIS DISPATCH FORGOT TO BREAK THE SEAL	211	3 DON JUAN	9	57	8
OF ALL HIS FEELINGS--ONLY HE FORGOT 'EM	251	3 DON JUAN	10	54	8
BECAUSE I'D RATHER IT SHOULD BE FORGOT	499	3 DON JUAN	15	96	5
FORGOTTEN					
AND THERE WERE OTHERS SCARCE FORGOTTEN YET	22	2 DON JUAN	1	3	4
AND SO HAVE BEEN FORGOTTEN--I CONDEMN NONE	24	2 DON JUAN	1	5	5
BUT JUAN HAD HE QUITE FORGOTTEN JULIA	267	2 DON JUAN	2	208	1
AND SHOULD HE HAVE FORGOTTEN HER SO SOON	267	2 DON JUAN	2	208	2
I HAVE FORGOTTEN WHAT I MEANT TO SAY	200	3 DON JUAN	9	36	2
I HAD FORGOTTEN--BUT MUST NOT FORGET--	400	3 DON JUAN	13	90	1
FORKS					
WITH MASSY PLATE FOR ARMOUR KNIVES AND FORKS	482	3 DON JUAN	15	62	2
THOUGH KNIVES AND FORKS CLANGED ROUND AS IN A FRAY	542	3 DON JUAN	16	87	5

285

		PAGE	VOL	CANTO	STANZA	LN

FORLORN
FORLORN AND GAZING ON THE DEEP BLUE SURGE	387	2 DON JUAN	4	79	3
YOU LIKE TO BE THE HOPE OF THE FORLORN	98	3 DON JUAN	7	62	2
JUST AS KOUTOUSOW'S MOST FORLORN OF HOPES	148	3 DON JUAN	8	73	3

FORM
DEAD SCANDALS FORM GOOD SUBJECTS FOR DISSECTION	37	2 DON JUAN	1	31	8
BUT HEAR THESE FREEDOMS FORM THE UTMOST LIST	65	2 DON JUAN	1	80	5
I'VE GOT A PLAN TO FORM A TREATISE WHICH	138	2 DON JUAN	1	204	V2
IN THE THIRD FORM OR EVEN IN THE FOURTH	158	2 DON JUAN	2	2	2
FIRST PARTINGS FORM A LESSON HARD TO LEARN	164	2 DON JUAN	2	14	3
HER DOWRY AND HER VEIL IN FORM ALIKE	221	2 DON JUAN	2	122	5
AND THUS THEY FORM A GROUP THAT'S QUITE ANTIQUE	259	2 DON JUAN	2	194	7
THAT ALL THE REST CREEP IN AND FORM A JUNCTION	271	2 DON JUAN	2	215	4
THESE TWO FORM THE LAST GASP OF PASSION'S BREATH	280	2 DON JUAN	3	9	V3
INSTEAD OF SPEECH MAY FORM A LASTING LINK	327	2 DON JUAN	3	88	5
FORM NOT THE TRUE TEMPTATION WHICH ALLURES	332	2 DON JUAN	3	97	5
OH POWERS OF FORM--WHAT ASPECT SEES SHE THERE	363	2 DON JUAN	4	35	V7
IN SHORT ALL THINGS WHICH FORM A TURKISH DANDY	451	2 DON JUAN	5	68	8
HER FORM HAD ALL THE SOFTNESS OF HER SEX	474	2 DON JUAN	5	109	1
AND THE DEEP PASSIONS FLASHING THROUGH HER FORM	489	2 DON JUAN	5	135	7
BUT BID MY WOMEN FORM THE MILKY WAY	494	2 DON JUAN	5	145	3
WHICH FORM AN ORNAMENT BUT NO MORE PART	13	3 DON JUAN	6	14	7
IN THE FAIR FORM OF THEIR COMPANION NEW	24	3 DON JUAN	6	37	5
BUT RATHER SKIM THE EARTH WHILE DUDU'S FORM	26	3 DON JUAN	6	41	5
FEW ANGLES WERE THERE IN HER FORM 'TIS TRUE	27	3 DON JUAN	6	42	5
WHOSE HEADLONG PASSIONS FORM THEIR PROPER WOES	49	3 DON JUAN	6	87	8
OR A BELL-WETHER FORM THE FLOCK'S CONNECTION	90	3 DON JUAN	7	48	6
WOULD FORM A LENGTHY LEXICON OF GLORY	120	3 DON JUAN	8	17	7
INTENTIONS WHICH FORM ALL MANKIND'S TRUMP CARD	123	3 DON JUAN	8	25	3
WHO THUS COULD FORM A LINE AND FIGHT AGAIN	136	3 DON JUAN	8	47	5
SO MUCH LESS FIGHT AS MIGHT FORM AN APOLOGY	165	3 DON JUAN	8	108	4
AS WELL AS FURTHER DRAIN THE WITHERED FORM	243	3 DON JUAN	10	38	4
WHICH FORM THAT BITTER DRAUGHT THE HUMAN SPECIES	261	3 DON JUAN	10	73	8
CAN FORM A SLIGHT ACQUAINTANCE WITH FRESH AIR	301	3 DON JUAN	11	66	8
AND WHY SHOULD I NOT FORM MY SPECULATION	325	3 DON JUAN	12	21	2
CAN'T FORM A FRIENDSHIP BUT THE WORLD O'ERAWES IT	346	3 DON JUAN	12	65	3
BUT HIS ADVENTURES FORM A SORRY SIGHT--	363	3 DON JUAN	13	9	6
ITS SESSIONS FORM OUR ONLY ALMANACK	378	3 DON JUAN	13	43	8
OTHERS THAT SOME ORIGINAL SHAPE OR FORM	388	3 DON JUAN	13	64	1
APPEARANCES APPEAR TO FORM THE JOINT	396	3 DON JUAN	13	81	3
BUT FORM GOOD HOUSEKEEPERS TO BREED A NATION	420	3 DON JUAN	14	24	8
BUT BOTH TOGETHER FORM A KIND OF CENTAUR	442	3 DON JUAN	14	73	7
AS FEW WOULD EVER DREAM COULD FORM THE LINK	454	3 DON JUAN	14	100	5
OF MARRIAGE--(WHICH MIGHT FORM A PAINTER'S FAME	473	3 DON JUAN	15	39	7
HER BEAUTY ALSO SEEM'D TO FORM NO CLOG	477	3 DON JUAN	15	48	5
WITH ALL THE ADDED CHARM OF FORM AND FEATURE	478	3 DON JUAN	15	52	4
AS FORM A SCIENCE AND A NOMENCLATURE	486	3 DON JUAN	15	69	7
HIS FORM YOU MAY TRACE BUT NOT HIS FACE	519	3 DON JUAN	16	L 4	5
DRAPERIED HER FORM WITH CURIOUS FELICITY	550	3 DON JUAN	16	102	8

FORMAL
| THE SQUIRES FAMILIARLY FORMAL AND | 538 | 3 DON JUAN | 16 | 79 | 1 |

FORMALITY
| GREAT PLENTY MUCH FORMALITY SMALL CHEER | 538 | 3 DON JUAN | 16 | 78 | 7 |

FORM'D
AS FAIR A THING AS E'ER WAS FORM'D OF CLAY	214	2 DON JUAN	2	110	8
FOR WOMAN'S FACE WAS NEVER FORM'D IN VAIN	235	2 DON JUAN	2	149	5
TO HINT THAT FLESH IS FORM'D OF FIERY DUST	269	2 DON JUAN	2	212	4
GEMS GOLD AND SILVER FORM'D THE SERVICE MOSTLY	306	2 DON JUAN	3	61	7
WITH BUTTONS FORM'D OF PEARLS AS LARGE AS PEAS	311	2 DON JUAN	3	70	5
THE SITUATION SEEMS STILL FORM'D FOR FAME--	386	2 DON JUAN	4	77	5
FORM'D A WHOLE WHICH IRREGULAR IN PARTS	390	3 DON JUAN	13	67	4
FORM'D OF TWO MIGHTY TRIBES THE BORES AND BORED	402	3 DON JUAN	13	95	8
TALL STATELY FORM'D TO LEAD THE COURTLY VAN	440	3 DON JUAN	14	70	5
A LOVELY BEING SCARCELY FORM'D OR MOULDED	475	3 DON JUAN	15	43	7

FORMED
FORMED RATHER FOR INSTRUCTING THAN DELIGHTING	412	2 DON JUAN	5	2	5
AND IS THIS BLOOD THEN FORMED BUT TO BE SHED	432	2 DON JUAN	5	39	4
A RICH CONFUSION FORMED A DISARRAY	465	2 DON JUAN	5	93	3
THEY FORMED A VERY NYMPH-LIKE LOOKING CREW	469	2 DON JUAN	5	99	5
FORMED LIKE AN AMPHITHEATRE EACH DWELLING	78	3 DON JUAN	7	23	7
AND THUS THEY FORMED A RATHER CUROUS PAIR	252	3 DON JUAN	10	57	5
IN HAPPIER PLIGHT THAN IF THEY FORMED A PAIR	344	3 DON JUAN	12	61	8
AND FORMED A BASIS OF ESTEEM WHICH ENDS	365	3 DON JUAN	13	15	7
AND HE DID NOT SEEM FORMED OF CLAY	518	3 DON JUAN	16	L 2	6

FORMER
IS PHILOSOPHIC IN OUR FORMER FRIENDS	37	2 DON JUAN	1	30	2
TO MEND HIS FORMER MORALS AND GET NEW	129	2 DON JUAN	1	191	3
NOT EVEN A VISION OF HIS FORMER WOES	227	2 DON JUAN	2	134	5
UNWELCOME VISIONS OF OUR FORMER YEARS	227	2 DON JUAN	2	134	7
NO DOUBT WHATE'ER MIGHT BE THEIR FORMER STRIFE	301	2 DON JUAN	3	50	5
I CAN'T HELP THINKING THAT ALL FORMER STRIFE	301	2 DON JUAN	3	50	V5
IF YOU HAVE GOT A FORMER FRIEND FOR FOE	366	2 DON JUAN	4	41	6
THE FORMER IN A PALACE WHERE LIKE NUNS	498	2 DON JUAN	5	152	3
IN FORMER WORKS MADE NEW PREPARED FASCINES	89	3 DON JUAN	7	47	7
WILL JOIN YOUR FORMER REGIMENT WHICH SHOULD BE	100	3 DON JUAN	7	66	2
WITH OTHER RELICS OF A FORMER WORLD	201	3 DON JUAN	9	37	2
WHEN THIS WORLD SHALL BE FORMER UNDERGROUND	201	3 DON JUAN	9	37	3
THE FORMER KNOW WHAT'S WHAT WHILE NEW-FLEDGED CHICKS	230	3 DON JUAN	10	10	3
BY FORMER VOYAGES STOOD TO WATCH THE SKIFFS	256	3 DON JUAN	10	64	7

286

```
                                                          PAGE VOL      CANTO STANZA LN
FORMER   (CONTINUED)
  FOR ITS DECAYING FAME AND FORMER WORTH   . . . . . .  257  3 DON JUAN 10     66    5
  SWORE PRAISES AND RECALL'D THEIR FORMER FIRES  . . . . 425  3 DON JUAN 14     34    6
  THE LAST IS APT THE FORMER TO ACCUSE  . . . . . . .    564  3 DON JUAN 17      6    4
FORMER'S
  EXCEPTING ONLY WHEN THE FORMER'S PICK'D  . . . . . .   502  2 DON JUAN  5    158    3
  THE FORMER'S HYMENEAL HOPES TO FLATTER  . . . . . .    292  3 DON JUAN 11     46    3
FORMIDABLE
  AND GIRT BY FORMIDABLE WAVES BUT THEY . . . . . . .    211  2 DON JUAN  2    104    2
  HE THERE BUILDS UP A FORMIDABLE DYKE  . . . . . . .    330  2 DON JUAN  3     95    1
  OF DANUBE'S BANK TOOK FORMIDABLE CHARGE  . . . . .      72  2 DON JUAN  7     12    5
  JUDGES IN VERY FORMIDABLE ERMINE  . . . . . . . .     391  3 DON JUAN 13     69    1
FORMOSUM
  BEGINNING WITH FORMOSUM PASTOR CORYDON  . . . . . .     45  2 DON JUAN  1     42    8
FORMS
  WHICH FORMS IN FACT TRUE LOVE'S ANTITHESIS  . . . . .  279  2 DON JUAN  3      8    2
  THEIR ENERGY LIKE LIFE FORMS ALL THEIR FAME . . . .    377  2 DON JUAN  4     61    7
  OF FORMS AND FEATURES IT WOULD STRIKE YOU BLIND  . .   467  2 DON JUAN  5     97    6
  BUT THERE ARE FORMS WHICH TIME TO TOUCH FORBEARS  . .  468  2 DON JUAN  5     98    3
  BUT THERE ARE FORMS WHICH TIME ADORNS NOT WEARS  . .   468  2 DON JUAN  5     98   V3
  BUT HERE A SMALL DELAY FORMS A GREAT CRIME  . . . .    482  2 DON JUAN  5    123    5
  SO STYLED ACCORDING TO THE USUAL FORMS  . . . . .      12  3 DON JUAN  6     13    2
  THAT FORMS THIS DESK OF WHAT THEY MEAN--LYKANTHROPY . . 192  3 DON JJAN  9     20    6
  WHICH FORMS A PEDIGREE FROM MISS TO MISS . . . . .     340  3 DON JUAN 12     52    3
  FORMS A SAD CLIMAX TO ROMANTIC HOMAGES  . . . . .      346  3 DON JUAN 12     65    6
  OF MAN'S OPINIONS FORMS THEIR EDUCATION . . . . .      354  3 DON JUAN 12     83   V6
  FORMS THE MOST DIFFICULT IN PUNCTUATION . . . . .      396  3 DON JUAN 13     81    2
  AS PHIDIAN FORMS CUT OUT OF MARBLE ATTIC . . . . .     409  3 DON JUAN 13    110    3
  THE FORMS OF THE GRIM KNIGHT AND PICTURED SAINT  . .   508  3 DON JUAN 16     18    1
FORNICATION
  PLAIN SIMPLE FORNICATION--NOR BEHOLD  . . . . . .      314  3 DON JUAN 11   V 76    7
FORSOOK
  FORSOOK THE DIM EYES OF THESE SHIPWRECK'D MEN  . . .   204  2 DON JUAN  2     91    8
  WHOM HE FORSOOK TO FILL THE LAUREATE'S STY . . . . .   231  3 DON JUAN 10     13    4
FORSOOTH
  FORSOOTH SCARCE FIT FOR BALLADS IN THE STREET  . . .   392  2 DON JUAN  4     89    6
  PEOPLE ARE APT TO BLAME THE FATES FORSOOTH . . . .     339  3 DON JUAN 12     50    3
  TO LEAVE THE PARTIES TO THEMSELVES FORSOOTH . . . .    439  3 DON JUAN 14     67    3
FORTALICE
  WHEN EACH HOUSE WAS A FORTALICE--AS TELL . . . . .     386  3 DON JUAN 13     60    5
FORTE
  WITH ARGUMENTS ACCORDING TO THEIR FORTE . . . . .      437  2 DON JUAN  5     48    7
  I WON'T DESCRIBE DESCRIPTION IS MY FORTE . . . . .     440  2 DON JUAN  5     52    1
  A MODEST HOPE--BUT MODESTY'S MY FORTE . . . . . .      466  3 DON JUAN 15     22    1
FORTH
  WHEN EVERY YEAR AND MONTH SENDS FORTH A NEW ONE  . .    21  2 DON JUAN  1      1    2
  THEIR SENSES THEY'D HAVE SENT YOUNG MASTER FORTH  . .   34  2 DON JUAN  1     25    6
  WHERE THE SUBLIME SOARS FORTH ON WINGS MORE AMPLE  . .  45  2 DON JUAN  1     42    6
  THEY STAND FORTH MARSHALL'D IN A HANDSOME TROOP . .     46  2 DON JUAN  1     45    3
  SENDS SIN WITHOUT A RAG ON SHIVERING FORTH . . . .      57  2 DON JUAN  1     64    3
  AND SEND HIM LIKE A DOVE OF PROMISE FORTH  . . . .     161  2 DON JUAN  2      8    8
  BROUGHT FORTH IN PURPLE CRADLED IN VERMILLION  . . .   205  2 DON JUAN  2     92    3
  FORTH FROM ITS RAVEN FRINGE THE FULL GLANCE FLIES  . . 218  2 DON JUAN  2    117    5
  AND FORTH THEY WANDER'D HER SIRE BEING GONE  . . . .   252  2 DON JUAN  2    182    1
  AND THUS THEY WANDER'D FORTH AND HAND IN HAND . . .    253  2 DON JUAN  2    184    1
  POURS FORTH AT LAST THE HEART'S-BLOOD TURN'D TO TEARS . 270  2 DON JUAN  2    214    7
  AND SEND HIM FORTH LIKE SAMSON--STRONG IN BLINDNESS  . 304  2 DON JUAN  3     57   V8
  AND LIKE THE SOIL BENEATH IT WILL BRING FORTH  . . .   374  2 DON JUAN  4     56    5
  THE FIRE BURST FORTH FROM HER NUMIDIAN VEINS . . .     375  2 DON JUAN  4     57    7
  THE TEARS RUSH'D FORTH FROM HER O'ERCLOUDED BRAIN  . . 380  2 DON JUAN  4     66    7
  GO AND HE GOETH COME AND FORTH HE STEPP'D  . . . .     430  2 DON JUAN  5     36    6
  THROUGH ORANGE BOWERS AND JASMINE AND SO FORTH . . .   434  2 DON JUAN  5     42    2
  I SAY UNLOCKING THE RECESS PULLED FORTH . . . . .      450  2 DON JUAN  5     67    2
  HE WENT FORTH WITH THE LOVELY ODALISQUES . . . . .      20  3 DON JUAN  6     29    1
  THAN ARE YOUR MIGHTY PASSIONS AND SO FORTH . . . .      32  3 DON JUAN  6     53    5
  BY TINKLING SOUNDS WHEN THEY GO FORTH TO VICTUAL  . .   90  3 DON JUAN  7     48    7
  A PREACHER HAD HELD FORTH (WHO NOBLY SPURNED  . . .     99  3 DON JUAN  7     64    5
  MARCHED FORTH WITH NERVE AND SINEWS BENT TO SLAY--  . 113  3 DON JUAN  8      2    4
  FLAME WAS SHOWERED FORTH ABOVE AS WELL'S BELOW . . .   135  3 DON JUAN  8     45    4
  IN ONE WIDE WOUND POURED FORTH HIS SOUL AT ONCE  . .   170  3 DON JUAN  8    118    8
  BEAUTY SPRINGS FORTH AND NATURE'S SELF TURNS PALER .   204  3 DON JUAN  9     44    4
  DREW FORTH A POCKET-PISTOL FROM HIS VESTURE  . . . .   274  3 DON JUAN 11     13    3
  PALL MALL AND SO FORTH HAVE A CORUSCATION  . . . .     280  3 DON JUAN 11     26    2
  THEY REACHED THE HOTEL FORTH STREAMED FROM THE FRONT DOOR . 282  3 DON JUAN 11     30    1
  WHERE SCIENCE MARSHALS FORTH HER OWN QUADRILLE . . .   303  3 DON JUAN 11     70    8
  THUS FAR GO FORTH THOU LAY WHICH I WILL BACK . . .     312  3 DON JUAN 11     90    2
  FROM WHENCE POURED FORTH A TRIBE OF WELL-CLAD WAITERS . 313  3 DON JUAN 11   V 29    2
  I COULD SEND FORTH MY MANDATE LIKE A PRIMATE . . .     327  3 DON JUAN 12     24    3
  AND RATHER HELD IN THAN PUT FORTH HIS VIGOUR . . .     427  3 DON JUAN 14     39    4
  THAT COOKERY COULD HAVE CALL'D FORTH SUCH RESOURCES . 486  3 DON JUAN 15     69    6
  HIS CHAMBER DOOR WIDE OPEN--AND WENT FORTH . . . .     508  3 DON JUAN 16     17    2
  BY WHICH LORD HENRY'S GOOD TASTE WOULD GO FORTH IN .   529  3 DON JUAN 16     59    6
  FORTH INTO UNIVERSAL EPIGRAM . . . . . . . . .         552  3 DON JUAN 16    104    2
  JUAN PUT FORTH ONE ARM--ETERNAL POWERS  . . . . .      559  3 DON JUAN 16    120    1
  GLEAMED FORTH AS THROUGH THE CASEMENT'S IVY SHROUD  . 560  3 DON JUAN 16    121    7
  HIS OTHER ARM FORTH--WONDER UPON WONDER  . . . . .     560  3 DON JUAN 16    122    2
  FORTH INTO SOMETHING MUCH LIKE FLESH AND BLOOD . . .   561  3 DON JUAN 16    123    4
  ARE TUTORS GUARDIANS AND SO FORTH COMPARED . . . .     564  3 DON JUAN 17      4    2
FORTIFICATION
  WITHIN THE EXTENT OF THIS FORTIFICATION  . . . . .      71  3 DON JUAN  7     10    1
```

```
                                                        PAGE VOL      CANTO STANZA LN
FORTNIGHT
    BUT ONCE A WEEK OR FORTNIGHT UNINVITED    . . . . . .  534  3 DON JUAN 16      69    1
FORTRESS
    AND HOW TO SCALE A FORTRESS--OR A NUNNERY    . . . . .   42  2 DON JUAN  1      38    8
    TO WHERE THE LAST CESAREAN FORTRESS STOOD    . . . . .  337  2 DON JUAN  3     105    5
    THE FORTRESS IS CALLED ISMAIL AND IS PLACED  . . . . .   70  3 DON JUAN  7       9    1
    BUT STILL A FORTRESS OF THE FOREMOST RANK    . . . . .   70  3 DON JUAN  7       9    4
    A FORTRESS HARLEQUIN IN UNIFORM . . . . . . . . . . .    95  3 DON JUAN  7      55    8
FORTRESSES
    OF FORTRESSES BUT FIGHTING WHERE IT PLEASES  . . . . .  149  3 DON JUAN  8      74    7
FORTS
    TO SEE IN FORTS OF NETHERLANDS OR FRANCE--   . . . . .  136  3 DON JUAN  8      46    5
FORTUNATE
    THRICE FORTUNATE WHO OF THAT FRAGILE MOULD   . . . . .  350  2 DON JUAN  4      11    2
    SHE TOO WAS FORTUNATE LAST CARNIVAL   . . . . . . . .   390  2 DON JUAN  4      84    4
FORTUNE
    AND BY GOOD FORTUNE GLIDING SOFTLY CAUGHT HER    . . .  208  2 DON JUAN  2      99    3
    MAY NOT HAVE THE GOOD FORTUNE OF ULYSSES . . . . . . .  287  2 DON JUAN  3      23    2
    FORTUNE HAS PLAYED YOU HERE A PRETTY FREAK   . . . . .  418  2 DON JUAN  5      14    4
    BUT DROOP NOT FORTUNE AT YOUR TIME OF LIFE   . . . . .  419  2 DON JUAN  5      17    1
    HEAVEN HELP THE SCHOLAR WHOM HIS FORTUNE SENDS HERE  .  423  2 DON JUAN  5      24    4
    WHICH FORTUNE PLAINLY SEEMED TO RECOMMEND    . . . . .  451  2 DON JUAN  5      69    5
    THERE'S FORTUNE EVEN IN FAME WE MUST ALLOW   . . . . .   82  3 DON JUAN  7      33    6
    AND ALL PRESAGED GOOD FORTUNE TO THEIR CAUSE . . . . .   89  3 DON JUAN  7      47    4
    YOUR FORTUNE WAS IN A FAIR WAY TO SWELL  . . . . . . .  214  3 DON JUAN  9      63    6
    LOVE HAD MADE CATHERINE MAKE EACH LOVER'S FORTUNE . .   222  3 DON JUAN  9      81    1
    IT IS ENOUGH THAT FORTUNE FOUND HIM FLUSH    . . . . .  227  3 DON JUAN 10       5    6
    WHICH PUZZLES US TO KNOW WHAT FORTUNE MEANS  . . . . .  247  3 DON JUAN 10      47    3
    FOR THOSE WHOM FAVOUR OR WHOM FORTUNE SWELLS . . . . .  283  3 DON JUAN 11      31    3
    BUZZ ROUND THE FORTUNE WITH THEIR BUSY BATTERY  . . .   331  3 DON JUAN 12      32    7
    'TWAS NOT HER FORTUNE--HE HAS ENOUGH WITHOUT . . . . .  332  3 DON JUAN 12      35    2
    AND FORTUNE HAS AN AWKWARD PART TO PLAY   . . . . . .   342  3 DON JUAN 12      58    2
    IN BIRTH IN RANK IN FORTUNE LIKEWISE EQUAL   . . . . .  367  3 DON JUAN 13      20    1
    WHOM FRANCE AND FORTUNE LATELY DEIGN'D TO WAFT HERE  .  398  3 DON JUAN 13      86    4
    IF THAT A BONNE FORTUNE BE REALLY BONNE   . . . . . .   438  3 DON JUAN 14      64    8
FORTUNE'S
    BY ONE OF THOSE ODD TURNS OF FORTUNE'S TIDES . . . . .  125  3 DON JUAN  8      27    5
    (I MEAN IN FORTUNE'S MATRIMONIAL BOUNTIES)   . . . . .  312  3 DON JUAN 11      89    4
FORTUNES
    THEIR LIVES AND FORTUNES WERE EXTREMELY VARIOUS  . . .  266  2 DON JUAN  2     206    5
    WE WILL REVIVE OUR FORTUNES BEFORE LONG  . . . . . . .  389  2 DON JUAN  4      82    8
    OH YE WHO MAKE THE FORTUNES OF ALL BOOKS . . . . . . .  403  2 DON JUAN  4     108    1
FORTY
    (I WONDER WHAT IT WILL BE LIKE AT FORTY  . . . . . . .  143  2 DON JUAN  1     213    2
    HE DIED AT FIFTY FOR A QUEEN OF FORTY . . . . . . . .     9  3 DON JUAN  6       5    1
    FORTY FEET HIGH UPON A CAVALIERE . . . . . . . . . . .   72  3 DON JUAN  7      12    8
    OF FORTY THOUSAND WHO HAD MANNED THE WALL    . . . . .  175  3 DON JUAN  8     127    7
    (WIDOWS OF FORTY WERE THESE BIRDS LONG CAGED)   . . .   178  3 DON JUAN  8     132    3
    THESE FORTY DAYS' ADVANTAGE OF HER YEARS--   . . . . .  432  3 DON JUAN 14      52    1
FORTY-PARSON-POWER
    OH FOR A FORTY-PARSON-POWER TO CHAUNT . . . . . . . .   241  3 DON JUAN 10      34    1
FORTY'S
    A HAZY WIDOWER TURNED OF FORTY'S SURE . . . . . . . .   333  3 DON JUAN 12      37    5
    A DRUNKEN GENTLEMAN OF FORTY'S SURE   . . . . . . . .   333  3 DON JUAN 12      37   V5
FORWARD
    BUT SEEING FLASHING FORWARD LIKE THE DAY . . . . . . .  126  3 DON JUAN  8      30    3
    BACKWARD AND FORWARD TO THE ECHOES FAINT . . . . . . .  508  3 DON JUAN 16      18    3
FOSSILE
    AS RARE IN LIVING BEINGS AS A FOSSILE . . . . . . . .   250  3 DON JUAN 10      52    3
FOSTER-BABES
    OF TIME AND TONGUES THE FOSTER-BABES OF FAME . . . . .  398  2 DON JUAN  4     100    2
FOUGHT
    BUT HERE ARE MEN WHO FOUGHT IN GALLANT ACTIONS . . . .   83  3 DON JUAN  7      34    1
    AS GALLANTLY AS EVER HEROES FOUGHT . . . . . . . . . .   83  3 DON JUAN  7      34    2
    THEY FOUND THAT HE HAD FOUGHT BENEATH THEIR BANNER  .    95  3 DON JUAN  7      56    8
    SHADE OF LEONIDAS WHO FOUGHT SO HEARTY . . . . . . . .  108  3 DON JUAN  7      82    3
    AND FOUGHT AWAY WITH MIGHT AND MAIN NOT KNOWING  . . .  120  3 DON JUAN  8      19    2
    NO CAESAR BUT A FINE YOUNG LAD WHO FOUGHT    . . . . .  126  3 DON JUAN  8      29    2
    INTO THE HEARTS OF THOSE WHO FOUGHT TILL NOW . . . . .  137  3 DON JUAN  8      49    4
    WHO FOUGHT WITH HIS FIVE CHILDREN IN THE VAN . . . . .  164  3 DON JUAN  8     105    8
    HE FOUGHT BUT HAS NOT FED SO WELL OF LATE    . . . . .  185  3 DON JUAN  9       6    5
    THE GALLANT CAVALIERS WHO FOUGHT IN VAIN . . . . . . .  386  3 DON JUAN 13      60    7
    THE HUNTERS FOUGHT THEIR FOX-HUNT O'ER AGAIN . . . . .  408  3 DON JUAN 13     108    7
    WHO FOUGHT AND FIGHT IN ABSENCE TOO MY BATTLES  . . .   452  3 DON JUAN 14      96    7
FOUL
    HOWEVER THE POOR JACKALLS ARE LESS FOUL  . . . . . . .  196  3 DON JUAN  9      27    6
    BY FOUL CORRUPTION INTO STREAMS--EVEN THEY   . . . . .  287  3 DON JUAN 11      40    7
    OR WALKED IF FOUL THEY READ OR TOLD A TALE   . . . . .  406  3 DON JUAN 13     104    3
    HEAVEN SAIN HIM FAIR OR FOUL . . . . . . . . . . . . .  520  3 DON JUAN 16    L  6    6
FOUND
    IT WAS A TRYING MOMENT THAT WHICH FOUND HIM  . . . . .   41  2 DON JUAN  1      36    4
    HE PUZZLED OVER WHAT HE FOUND A NEW ONE   . . . . . .    68  2 DON JUAN  1      86    5
    AS ALL HAVE FOUND ON TRIAL OR MAY FIND   . . . . . . .   69  2 DON JUAN  1      89    4
    HE FOUND HOW MUCH OLD TIME HAD BEEN A WINNER--   . . .   72  2 DON JUAN  1      94    7
    HE ALSO FOUND THAT HE HAD LOST HIS DINNER    . . . . .   72  2 DON JUAN  1      94    8
    NOW JULIA FOUND AT LENGTH A VOICE AND CRIED  . . . . .   98  2 DON JUAN  1     142    1
    AND FOUND MUCH LINEN LACE AND SEVERAL PAIR   . . . . .   99  2 DON JUAN  1     143    3
    UNDER THE BED THEY SEARCH'D AND THERE THEY FOUND--  .   100  2 DON JUAN  1     144    1
    BUT FOUND MY VERY INNOCENCE PERPLEX   . . . . . . . .   101  2 DON JUAN  1     147    6

                                   288
```

FOUND   (CONTINUED)
AND WHEN 'TIS FOUND LET ME TOO HAVE THAT PLEASURE 104   2 DON JUAN 1   153   8
LIGHTS CAME AT LENGTH AND MEN AND MAIDS WHO FOUND 125   2 DON JUAN 1   187   1
WHO FAVOURS WHAT SHE SHOULD NOT FOUND HIS WAY 126   2 DON JUAN 1   188   3
FOUND--GOD KNOWS HOW--HIS SOLITARY WAY 126   2 DON JUAN 1   188   V3
THOUGH HEAVEN KNOWS HOW IT EVER FOUND A LODGEMENT 144   2 DON JUAN 1   215   8
FOR I HAVE FOUND IT ANSWER--SO MAY YOU 163   2 DON JUAN 2   13   8
THE PUMPS AND THERE WERE FOUR FEET WATER FOUND 170   2 DON JUAN 2   27   8
AND SO HE FOUND A WINE-AND-WATERY GRAVE 186   2 DON JUAN 2   57   5
WHICH I FOUND VERY TROUBLESOME TO PAY 190   2 DON JUAN 2   65   8
'TWAS BUT HIS OWN SUPPRESS'D TILL NOW HE FOUND 194   2 DON JUAN 2   73   6
UNTIL THEY FOUND A RAGGED PIECE OF SHEET 201   2 DON JUAN 2   85   2
AND TRIED TO AWAKEN THEM BUT FOUND THEM DEAD 208   2 DON JUAN 2   98   8
THEY FOUND A TURTLE OF THE HAWK'S-BILL KIND 208   2 DON JUAN 2   99   2
WHO DIED TWO DAYS BEFORE AND NOW HAD FOUND 213   2 DON JUAN 2   109   7
THE CLIFF TOWARDS SUNSET ON THAT DAY SHE FOUND 224   2 DON JUAN 2   129   2
THE MORN BROKE AND FOUND JUAN SLUMBERING STILL 229   2 DON JUAN 2   137   1
OF HIS FAIR FACE AND FOUND BY SYMPATHY 241   2 DON JUAN 2   162   4
WHEN JUAN WOKE HE FOUND SOME GOOD THINGS READY 246   2 DON JUAN 2   171   1
FOUND IN ONE SIGH THE BEST INTERPRETER 256   2 DON JUAN 2   189   6
OF SECRET TREASURES FOUND IN HIDDEN VALES 293   2 DON JUAN 3   34   3
HAVE FOUND THE FAME YOUR SHORES REFUSE 321   2 DON JUAN 3 L 2   3
OR GRAVEN STONE FOUND IN A BARRACK'S STATION 327   2 DON JUAN 3   89   6
THEY FOUND NO FAULT WITH TIME SAVE THAT HE FLED 351   2 DON JUAN 4   13   3
MOONS CHANGING HAD ROLL'D ON AND CHANGELESS FOUND . . . 352   2 DON JUAN 4   16   1
WHO NEVER FOUND A SINGLE HOUR TOO SLOW 353   2 DON JUAN 4   18   3
HE FOUND--BUT SOUGHT NOT I HAVE PLEDGED MY FAITH . . . 366   2 DON JUAN 4   42   6
AND WHEN HE DID HE FOUND HIMSELF AT SEA 384   2 DON JUAN 4   75   4
ARE WHAT I FOUND THERE--BUT THE DEVIL A PHRYGIAN . . . 387   2 DON JUAN 4   78   8
FROM HIS DULL CABIN FOUND HIMSELF A SLAVE 387   2 DON JUAN 4   79   2
FOUND ONLY ON THE STAGE AND EACH MORE PAIN'D 394   2 DON JUAN 4   93   3
HER EYE MIGHT FLASH ON HIS BUT FOUND IT DIM 396   2 DON JUAN 4   95   3
AFTER THE USUAL PROCESS MIGHT BE FOUND 407   2 DON JUAN 4   113   3
EXCEPT THAT I HAVE FOUND IT NOTHING NEW 418   2 DON JUAN 5   14   8
FOUND LIFE MOST TOLERABLE AFTER MEALS 427   2 DON JUAN 5   31   2
I FOUND THE MILITARY COMMANDANT 428   2 DON JUAN 5   33   7
WAS HARDLY LONG ENOUGH BUT BABA FOUND 457   2 DON JUAN 5   79   2
WE SHOULD HAVE FOUND OUT THE PERPETUAL MOTION . . . 475   2 DON JUAN 5   112   8
AND WHEN 'TWAS FOUND STRAIGHTWAY THE BARGAIN CLOSED . . 476   2 DON JUAN 5   113   4
THIS WAS AN AWKWARD TEST AS JUAN FOUND 484   2 DON JUAN 5   126   1
BECAUSE HE HAD JOURNEYED FIFTY MILES AND FOUND . . . 497   2 DON JUAN 5   150   3
SO THAT THE HEIR APPARENT STILL WAS FOUND 499   2 DON JUAN 5   153   7
AND MOST OF US HAVE FOUND IT NOW AND THEN 6   3 DON JUAN 6   1   3
THEY ALL FOUND OUT AS FEW OR FEWER SPECKS 24   3 DON JUAN 6   37   4
IN SOME EXOTIC GARDEN SOMETIMES FOUND 38   3 DON JUAN 6   65   3
A WOOD OBSCURE LIKE THAT WHERE DANTE FOUND 43   3 DON JUAN 6   75   3
HER NECK ALONE WAS SEEN BUT THAT WAS FOUND 48   3 DON JUAN 6   85   3
BUT ENDED IN HIS BEING FOUND OUT AND SACKED . . . 58   3 DON JUAN 6   104   6
FOR ANY FURTHER ANSWER THAT HE FOUND 58   3 DON JUAN 6   105   3
AND MORE MIGHT BE FOUND OUT IF I COULD POKE ENOUGH . . 74   3 DON JUAN 7   15   6
AT LENGTH THEY FOUND MERE CANNONADE ALONE . . . 81   3 DON JUAN 7   30   4
THEIR NAMES ARE RARELY FOUND NOR OFTEN SOUGHT . . . 83   3 DON JUAN 7   34   4
THEY FOUND THAT HE HAD FOUGHT BENEATH THEIR BANNER . . 95   3 DON JUAN 7   56   8
AND STRANGE TO SAY THEY FOUND SOME CONSOLATION . . . 105   3 DON JUAN 7   75   7
IF HOMER HAD FOUND MORTARS READY MADE 106   3 DON JUAN 7   78   4
UNLESS GUN-POWDER SHOULD BE FOUND TO HARM 106   3 DON JUAN 7   79   5
AND SUCH THEY ARE--AND SUCH THEY WILL BE FOUND . . . 114   3 DON JUAN 8   5   1
HE FOUND HIMSELF ALONE AND FRIENDS RETIRING . . . 125   3 DON JUAN 8   27   8
HE FOUND A NUMBER OF CHASSEURS ALL SCATTERED . . . 131   3 DON JUAN 8   37   7
EGAD THEY FOUND THE SECOND TIME WHAT THEY . . . 134   3 DON JUAN 8   42   1
THEY FOUND ON THEIR RETURN THE SELF-SAME WELCOME . . 134   3 DON JUAN 8   42   7
BUT THOSE WHO SCALED FOUND OUT THAT THEIR ADVANCE . . 136   3 DON JUAN 8   46   1
SO WAS HIS BLOOD STIRRED WHILE HE FOUND RESISTANCE . . 140   3 DON JUAN 8   55   1
THE FREE-BORN FOREST FOUND AND KEPT THEM FREE . . . 145   3 DON JUAN 8   65   7
AND FOUND THEIR LIVES WERE LET AT A SHORT LEASE-- . . 150   3 DON JUAN 8   76   4
OF MURDERED WOMEN WHO HAD FOUND THEIR WAY . . . 157   3 DON JUAN 8   91   3
BUT LET IT GO--IT WILL ONE DAY BE FOUND 201   3 DON JUAN 9   37   1
JUST THEN AS THEY ARE RATHER NUMEROUS FOUND . . . 205   3 DON JUAN 9   46   4
JUAN WHO FOUND HIMSELF HE KNEW NOT HOW . . . 223   3 DON JUAN 9   83   1
WHEN NEWTON SAW AN APPLE FALL HE FOUND . . . 225   3 DON JUAN 10   1   1
IT IS ENOUGH THAT FORTUNE FOUND HIM FLUSH . . . 227   3 DON JUAN 10   5   6
(THE SAME WHO PHYSICKED PETER) FOUND THE TICK . . . 244   3 DON JUAN 10   39   3
AND FOUND HIM NOT AMIDST THE VARIOUS PROGENIES . . . 281   3 DON JUAN 11   28   3
COMMODIOUS BUT IMMORAL THEY ARE FOUND 282   3 DON JUAN 11   30   6
HE FOUND HIMSELF EXTREMELY IN THE FASHION . . . 284   3 DON JUAN 11   33   7
IF HE FOUND NOT THIS SPAWN OF TAX-BORN RICHES . . . 288   3 DON JUAN 11   41   7
WHICH NOW HE FOUND WAS BLUE INSTEAD OF GREEN . . . 294   3 DON JUAN 11   51   8
AND HENCEFORTH FOUND HIMSELF MORE GAILY CLASSED . . . 300   3 DON JUAN 11   64   6
AND JUAN FOUND HIMSELF IN AN EXTENSIVE . . . 313   3 DON JUAN 11 V 29   7
TO BUILD A COLLEGE OR TO FOUND A RACE . . . 320   3 DON JUAN 12   10   2
BESIDES HE HAD FOUND OUT THAT HE WAS NO TUTOR . . . 336   3 DON JUAN 12   42   1
EXAMPLES MAY BE FOUND OF SUCH PURSUITS . . . 343   3 DON JUAN 12   59   2
I SAY AT FIRST--FOR HE FOUND OUT AT LAST . . . 347   3 DON JUAN 12   69   1
('TIS AN OLD NORMAN NAME AND TO BE FOUND . . . 359   3 DON JUAN 13   2   2
BUT THE CLUBS FOUND IT RATHER SERIOUS LAUGHTER . . . 398   3 DON JUAN 13   86   6
PROFESSIONS TOO ARE NO MORE TO BE FOUND . . . 402   3 DON JUAN 13   95   3
SOME WOULD NOT DEEM SUCH WOMEN COULD BE FOUND . . . 429   3 DON JUAN 14   44   4
EUREKA I HAVE FOUND IT WHAT I MEAN 443   3 DON JUAN 14   76   1
WITH SLOTH HATH FOUND IT DIFFICULT TO DWELL . . . 445   3 DON JUAN 14   81   6

	PAGE	VOL	CANTO	STANZA	LN

FOUND (CONTINUED)
BUT TILL THAT POINT D'APPUI IS FOUND ALAS . . . . . 446 3 DON JUAN 14 84 7
'TIS RARELY FOUND BUT WOULD REPAY ALL CHECKS . . . . 451 3 DON JUAN 14 93 V5
COLUMBUS FOUND A NEW WORLD IN A CUTTER . . . . . . 468 3 DON JUAN 15 27 6
WHO HITHERTO HAD FOUND THINGS NOT AMISS . . . . . 492 3 DON JUAN 15 81 V3
HE FOUND AS PEOPLE ON MOST TRIALS MUST . . . . . 560 3 DON JUAN 16 122 5
FOUND HIS OWN LEGS EMBARGOED FROM MERE WALKING . . . 565 3 DON JUAN 17 8 4

FOUNDATION
NO PERMANENT FOUNDATION CAN BE LAID . . . . . 268 2 DON JUAN 2 209 4
IN DIGGING THE FOUNDATION OF A CLOSET . . . . . . 327 2 DON JUAN 3 89 7

FOUNDED
AND FOUNDED DOCTORS' COMMONS--I HAVE CONNED . . . . 209 3 DON JUAN 9 53 6
YET AS THEY FOUNDED CHURCHES WITH THE PRODUCE . . . 242 3 DON JUAN 10 36 7
THOUGH OFT WELL FOUNDED WHICH CONFIRMED BUT MORE . . 366 3 DON JUAN 13 17 2

FOUNDERED
WHERE SHIPS HAVE FOUNDERED AS DOTH MANY A BOAT . . . 227 3 DON JUAN 10 4 8
IF THAT MY PEGASUS SHOULD NOT BE FOUNDERED . . . . 341 3 DON JUAN 12 55 7

FOUNT
HER TEARS TOO BEING RETURN'D INTO THEIR FOUNT . . . 295 2 DON JUAN 3 38 7
OF WHICH YOUR LAWFUL AWFUL WEDLOCK FOUNT IS-- . . . 312 3 DON JUAN 11 89 6

FOUNTAIN
AND CLOG THE FOUNTAIN OF ETERNAL TEARS . . . . . 275 2 DON JUAN 3 1 V8
DAMM'D FROM ITS FOUNTAIN--THE CHILD FROM THE KNEE . 349 2 DON JUAN 4 10 5
A MARBLE FOUNTAIN ECHOES THROUGH THE GLOOMS . . . . 442 2 DON JUAN 5 55 4
IN THY PERENNIAL FOUNTAIN--HOW MAN FELL I . . . . 210 3 DON JUAN 9 55 5
AMIDST THE COURT A GOTHIC FOUNTAIN PLAY'D . . . . 389 3 DON JUAN 13 65 1

FOUNTAINS
TO PASS THEIR LIVES IN FOUNTAINS AND ON FLOWERS . . 352 2 DON JUAN 4 15 7
IN LOVE DRINKS ALL LIFE'S FOUNTAINS (SAVE TEARS) DRY . 216 3 DON JUAN 9 67 8
TRUTH'S FOUNTAINS MAY BE CLEAR--HER STREAMS ARE MUDDY . 495 3 DON JUAN 15 88 6

FOUR
LIKE FOUR AND TWENTY BLACKBIRDS IN A PYE . . . . . 9 2 DON JUAN D 1 8
THE FOUR FIRST RHYMES ARE SOUTHEY'S EVERY LINE . . . 149 2 DON JUAN 1 222 7
A LECTURE AND SOME MONEY FOR FOUR SPRINGS . . . . 161 2 DON JUAN 2 9 3
THE PUMPS AND THERE WERE FOUR FEET WATER FOUND . . . 170 2 DON JUAN 2 27 8
THE SAILORS ATE HIM ALL SAVE THREE OR FOUR . . . . 198 2 DON JUAN 2 78 1
THEIR LIVING FREIGHT WAS NOW REDUCED TO FOUR . . . 209 2 DON JUAN 2 101 4
ENGRAVE UPON THE PLATE YOU ROSE AT FOUR . . . . . 230 2 DON JUAN 2 140 8
THREE OR FOUR THINGS FOR WHICH THE LORD HE PRAISED . 239 2 DON JUAN 2 157 5
YET TO THESE FOUR IN THREE THINGS THE SAME LUCK HOLDS . 266 2 DON JUAN 2 206 7
I'VE KNOWN THE ABSENT WRONG'D FOUR TIMES A DAY . . . 288 2 DON JUAN 3 25 8
I'VE SEEN A FRIEND BETRAYED FOUR TIMES A DAY . . . . 288 2 DON JUAN 3 25 V8
FOUR BLACKS WERE AT HIS ELBOW IN A TRICE . . . . 458 2 DON JUAN 5 80 8
SHE WAS OF COURSE THE FAVOURITE OF THE FOUR . . . . 495 2 DON JUAN 5 146 8
FOUR WIVES AND TWICE FIVE HUNDRED MAIDS UNSEEN . . . 496 2 DON JUAN 5 148 7
HE HAD FIFTY DAUGHTERS AND FOUR DOZEN SONS . . . . 498 2 DON JUAN 5 152 1
AND AS FOUR WIVES MUST HAVE QUADRUPLE CLAIMS . . . . 11 3 DON JUAN 6 11 7
THE FAVOURITE BUT WHAT'S FAVOUR AMONGST FOUR . . . . 12 3 DON JUAN 6 12 2
A PHANTOM UPON EACH OF THE FOUR POSTS . . . . . 30 3 DON JUAN 6 48 4
ONE TWO OR THREE--OR FOUR OR LESS OR MORE . . . . 51 3 DON JUAN 6 91 V5
THOUGHT NOT UPON THE CHARMS OF FOUR YOUNG BRIDES . . 168 3 DON JUAN 8 114 2
THAT I DEVOUTLY WISHED THE THREE WERE FOUR . . . . 271 3 DON JUAN 11 6 7
THESE FREEBORN SOUNDS PROCEEDED FROM FOUR PADS . . . 273 3 DON JUAN 11 11 1
HIMSELF FOR FIVE FOUR THREE OR TWO YEAR'S SPACE . . . 329 3 DON JUAN 12 29 6
THERE WERE FOUR HONOURABLE MISTERS WHOSE . . . . . 398 3 DON JUAN 13 86 1
THE FOUR MISS RAWBOLDS IN A GLEE WOULD SHINE . . . . 408 3 DON JUAN 13 107 5
HAVE PLAINLY MADE IT OUT THAT FOUR ARE THREE . . . . 548 3 DON JUAN 16 99 4

FOUR-AND-TWENTY
AND FOUR-AND-TWENTY HOURS AND TWICE THAT NUMBER . . . 248 3 DON JUAN 10 48 2

FOUR-POSTED
FOUR-POSTED AND SILK CURTAINED WHICH ARE GIVEN . . . 18 3 DON JUAN 6 25 3

FOURSCORE
FROM DAY-BREAK AND WHEN COFFIN'D AT FOURSCORE . . . 230 2 DON JUAN 2 140 7
AND FOURSCORE CANNON ON THE DANUBE'S BORDER . . . . 85 3 DON JUAN 7 38 7

FOURTH
IN THE THIRD FORM OR EVEN IN THE FOURTH . . . . . 158 2 DON JUAN 2 2 2
THE FOURTH DAY CAME BUT NOT A BREATH OF AIR . . . . 193 2 DON JUAN 2 70 1
TO MAKE A MISTRESS OR FOURTH WIFE OR VICTIM . . . . 409 2 DON JUAN 4 116 8
HER FOURTH TO RALLY HIM INTO REPENTANCE . . . . . 491 2 DON JUAN 5 139 4
HIS MAJESTY SALUTED HIS FOURTH SPOUSE . . . . . 500 2 DON JUAN 5 154 1
GULBEYAZ WAS THE FOURTH AND (AS I SAID) . . . . . 12 3 DON JUAN 6 12 1
A FOURTH AS MARBLE STATUE-LIKE AND STILL . . . . 40 3 DON JUAN 6 68 1
HIS THIRD WAS SABRED AND THE FOURTH MOST CHERISHED . 166 3 DON JUAN 8 110 3
THINK IF THEN GEORGE THE FOURTH SHOULD BE DUG UP . . 202 3 DON JUAN 9 39 1
THE FOURTH AT ONCE ESTABLISHED THE WHOLE TRINITY . . 271 3 DON JUAN 11 6 5
AND WHERE IS FUM THE FOURTH OUR ROYAL BIRD . . . . 307 3 DON JUAN 11 78 4
WHETHER HE MARRIED WITH THE THIRD OR FOURTH . . . . 312 3 DON JUAN 11 89 1
THE FOURTH WE HEAR AND SEE AND SAY TOO DAILY . . . . 465 3 DON JUAN 15 21 6

FOURTHLY
AND FOURTHLY WHAT NEED HARDLY BE SAID TWICE . . . . 439 3 DON JUAN 14 66 7

FOWL
AROUND THE WILD FOWL NESTLED IN THE BRAKE . . . . 385 3 DON JUAN 13 57 5
AMIDST THIS TUMULT OF FISH FLESH AND FOWL . . . . 488 3 DON JUAN 15 74 1
AND THE LOUD SHRIEK OF SAGE MINERVA'S FOWL . . . . 499 3 DON JUAN 15 97 3
TO THE CONSUMERS OF FISH FOWL AND GAME . . . . . 546 3 DON JUAN 16 95 3

FOWLS
FOWLS A LA CONDE SLICES EKE OF SALMON . . . . . 484 3 DON JUAN 15 65 1

FOX-HUNT
THE HUNTERS FOUGHT THEIR FOX-HUNT O'ER AGAIN . . . . 408 3 DON JUAN 13 108 7
A FOX-HUNT TO A FOREIGNER IS STRANGE . . . . . . 424 3 DON JUAN 14 32 1

	PAGE	VOL	CANTO	STANZA	LN
FOX'S					
BUT LEAPS AND BURSTS AND SOMETIMES FOX'S BRUSHES	425	3 DON JUAN	14	35	2
FOX-TERRIERS					
UNLESS THEY ARE GAME AS BULL-DOGS AND FOX-TERRIERS	78	3 DON JUAN	7	24	8
FRACTION					
THAN THE MERE PLODDING THROUGH EACH VULGAR FRACTION	321	3 DON JUAN	12	11	6
FRAGILE					
THRICE FORTUNATE WHO OF THAT FRAGILE MOULD	350	2 DON JUAN	4	11	2
THAT URNS AND PIPKINS ARE BUT FRAGILE BROTHERS	491	2 DON JUAN	5	138	4
FRAGILITY					
LOOKED GRAVE AND PALE TO SEE HER FRIEND'S FRAGILITY	430	3 DON JUAN	14	46	7
FRAGRANT					
FOR ALL WAS VAST STILL FRAGRANT AND DIVINE	460	2 DON JUAN	5	85	8
FOR HIM THE FRAGRANT PRODUCE OF EACH TRIP	320	3 DON JUAN	12	9	3
FRAIL					
THE FLESH IS FRAIL AND SO THE SOUL UNDONE	56	2 DON JUAN	1	63	6
THUS THE FRAIL BEINGS WE WOULD FONDLY CHERISH	275	2 DON JUAN	3	2	7
FRAIL MAN WHEN PAPER--EVEN A RAG LIKE THIS	327	2 DON JUAN	3	88	7
PROVING THAT TRITE OLD TRUTH THAT LIFE'S AS FRAIL	134	3 DON JUAN	8	43	3
ITSELF WITH BEAUTY'S FRAIL INANITY	219	3 DON JUAN	9	73	5
OF FRAIL HUMANITY--MUST MAKE US SELFISH	236	3 DON JUAN	10	23	7
NOR WISHED OF SUCH FRAIL REALMS TO BE THE KING	296	3 DON JUAN	11	55	V6
CHIEF IMPULSE WITH A FEW FRAIL PAPER PELLETS	298	3 DON JUAN	11	60	V8
OF HUNTING--FOR THE SAGEST YOUTH IS FRAIL	424	3 DON JUAN	14	33	6
FRAIL MARINERS AFLOAT WITHOUT A CHART	442	3 DON JUAN	14	74	5
THAN WHEN SOME SQUEAMISH PEOPLE DEEM HER FRAIL	483	3 DON JUAN	15	64	4
PERHAPS SHE WAS ASHAMED OF SEEMING FRAIL	532	3 DON JUAN	16	64	5
WHILE SCOUT THE PARISH GUARDIAN OF THE FRAIL	533	3 DON JUAN	16	67	2
FRAILER					
AND FRAILER SINCE WITHOUT A BREATH OF AIR	306	3 DON JUAN	11	76	V5
BECAUSE 'TIS FRAILER DOUBTLESS THAN A STANCH ONE	446	3 DON JUAN	14	85	6
FRAILTIES					
THEREFORE HIS FRAILTIES I'LL NO FURTHER SCAN	40	2 DON JUAN	1	35	3
FRAILTY					
OF HUMAN FRAILTY FOLLY ALSO CRIME	277	2 DON JUAN	3	5	2
FRAME					
HIS SLENDER FRAME AND PALLID ASPECT LAY	214	2 DON JUAN	2	110	7
'TWAS WELL BECAUSE HEALTH IN THE HUMAN FRAME	245	2 DON JUAN	2	169	3
AND THUS SOME BODING FLASH'D THROUGH EITHER FRAME	355	2 DON JUAN	4	21	6
JUAN AND SHUDDERING O'ER HIS FRAME WOULD CREEP	359	2 DON JUAN	4	29	5
IT NE'ER CAN BE REPLACED IN PROPER FRAME	502	2 DON JUAN	5	158	4
A PICTURE IS THE PAST EVEN ERE ITS FRAME	509	3 DON JUAN	16	19	7
FRAMED					
NOR MUCH TO CLIMB THROUGH LITTLE BOXES FRAMED	278	3 DON JUAN	11	21	4
FRAMES					
START FROM THE FRAMES WHICH FENCE THEIR ASPECTS STERN	508	3 DON JUAN	16	18	6
FRANCE					
FRANCE TOO HAD BUONAPARTE AND DEMOURIER	22	2 DON JUAN	1	2	7
ESPECIALLY IN FRANCE AND ITALY	129	2 DON JUAN	1	191	4
HOLLAND FRANCE ENGLAND GERMANY OR SPAIN	157	2 DON JUAN	2	1	2
WHICH SCARCE EVEN FRANCE THE PARAGON OF NATIONS	299	2 DON JUAN	3	46	3
IN FRANCE FOR INSTANCE HE WOULD WRITE A CHANSON	320	2 DON JUAN	3	86	1
TO SEE IN FORTS OF NETHERLANDS OR FRANCE--	136	3 DON JUAN	8	46	5
FRANCE COULD NOT EVEN CONQUER YOUR GREAT NAME	183	3 DON JUAN	9	1	3
WHOM FRANCE AND FORTUNE LATELY DEIGN'D TO WAFT HERE	398	3 DON JUAN	13	86	4
LADIES WHO HAVE STUDIED FRIENDSHIP BUT IN FRANCE	450	3 DON JUAN	14	92	4
FRANCESES					
WHERE ARE THE LADY CAROLINES AND FRANCESES	308	3 DON JUAN	11	80	1
FRANCIS'					
EVEN WERE SAINT FRANCIS' PARAMOUR THEIR GUEST	14	3 DON JUAN	6	17	5
FRANCS					
IT COSTS THREE FRANCS FOR EVERY MASS THAT'S SAID	185	2 DON JUAN	2	55	8
FRANK					
HE GAVE THE WORD ARREST OR SLAY THE FRANK	369	2 DON JUAN	4	47	8
FRANKINCENSE					
ITS FUMES ARE FRANKINCENSE TO HUMAN THOUGHT	402	2 DON JUAN	4	106	2
FRANKS					
HE HAD TRAVELL'D 'MONGST THE ARABS TURKS AND FRANKS	319	2 DON JUAN	3	84	1
TRUST NOT FOR FREEDOM TO THE FRANKS--	325	2 DON JUAN	3	L 14	1
FRANTIC					
AND ALWAYS ENVY THOUGH WE DEEM IT FRANTIC	353	2 DON JUAN	4	18	8
AND PASSION'S SELF MUST HAVE A SPICE OF FRANTIC	347	3 DON JUAN	12	68	3
FRAUD					
BUT TURKISH FORCE AND LATIN FRAUD	325	2 DON JUAN	3	L 14	5
FRAUGHT					
FRAUGHT WITH THIS FINE INTENTION AND WELL FENCED	64	2 DON JUAN	1	82	1
FRAY					
TO SOME DISTINGUISHED STRANGERS IN THAT FRAY	82	3 DON JUAN	7	32	6
THOSE WHO DISLIKE TO LOOK UPON A FRAY	126	3 DON JUAN	8	30	5
THOUGH KNIVES AND FORKS CLANGED ROUND AS IN A FRAY	542	3 DON JUAN	16	87	5
FREAK					
THEY KNEW NOT WHAT TO THINK OF SUCH A FREAK	229	2 DON JUAN	2	138	8
FORTUNE HAS PLAYED YOU HERE A PRETTY FREAK	418	2 DON JUAN	5	14	4
FRED					
WHY--WHY--BESIDES FRED REALLY WAS ATTACHED	332	3 DON JUAN	12	35	1
FREDERICK					
FREDERICK THE GREAT FROM MOLWITZ DEIGNED TO RUN	122	3 DON JUAN	8	22	4
POOR FREDERICK WHY DID SHE ACCORD PERUSALS	332	3 DON JUAN	12	34	6
AND AFTER ALL POOR FREDERICK MAY DO BETTER--	332	3 DON JUAN	12	35	7

291

```
                                                    PAGE VOL      CANTO STANZA LV
FREE
  A TRUE HIDALGO FREE FROM EVERY STAIN . . . . . . .   26  2 DON JUAN  1      9    2
  AND IF STILL FREE THAT SUCH OR SUCH A LOVER . . . .   64  2 DON JUAN  1     78    4
  WAX'D BROAD AND WAVING LIKE A BANNER FREE . . . . .  204  2 DON JUAN  2     91    6
  WAS COARSER AND HER AIR THOUGH FIRM LESS FREE . . .  221  2 DON JUAN  2    122    6
  FREE AS A MARRIED WOMAN OR SUCH OTHER . . . . . . .  248  2 DON JUAN  2    175    3
  OF FREE THOUGHTS IN HIS TRAVELS FOR VARIETY . . . .  318  2 DON JUAN  3     83    3
  I DREAM'D THAT GREECE MIGHT STILL BE FREE . . . . .  321  2 DON JUAN  3   L  3    4
  THIS IS A LIBERAL AGE AND THOUGHTS ARE FREE . . . .  347  2 DON JUAN  4      7    6
  JUAN REPLIED NOT WHILE THIS ARM IS FREE . . . . . .  365  2 DON JUAN  4     40    2
  DANCING ALL FREE AND HAPPY IN THE SUN) . . . . . .   393  2 DON JUAN  4     90    7
  THEY LEFT THIS BEING FREE AND NEUTRAL AS A SCOUT . .  394  2 DON JUAN  4     92   V5
  A SPELL FROM WHICH EVEN YET I AM NOT QUITE FREE . .  413  2 DON JUAN  5      4    6
  IF WE SHOULD STRIKE A STROKE TO SET US FREE . . . .  434  2 DON JUAN  5     43    6
  THE SUN HIMSELF WAS SCARCE MORE FREE FROM SPECKS . .  474  2 DON JUAN  5    109    6
  OUR SOULS AT LEAST ARE FREE AND 'TIS IN VAIN . . .   474  2 DON JUAN  5    110    6
  FELT MOST INDIGNANT STILL AT NOT BEING FREE . . . .  481  2 DON JUAN  5    121    8
  WERE FITTER FOR ME LOVE IS FOR THE FREE . . . . . .  484  2 DON JUAN  5    127    4
  THE STARS FROM OUT THE SKY THAN NOT BE FREE . . . .    7  3 DON JUAN  6      3    5
  BUT THAT YOU WON'T--THEN DON'T--I AM NOT LESS FREE    34  3 DON JUAN  6     56    8
  A WATCHWORD TILL THE FUTURE SHALL BE FREE . . . . .  114  3 DON JUAN  8      5    8
  THE FREE-BORN FOREST FOUND AND KEPT THEM FREE . . .  145  3 DON JUAN  8     65    7
  WITH THE FREE FORESTERS DIVIDE NO SPOIL . . . . . .  145  3 DON JUAN  8     67    6
  IN LEAVING VERSE MORE FREE FROM THE RESTRICTION . .  154  3 DON JUAN  8     86    4
  SHOWED WHAT THINGS WERE BEFORE THE WORLD WAS FREE .  179  3 DON JUAN  8    135    8
  TO FREE HIS COUNTRY PITT TOO HAD HIS PRIDE . . . .   186  3 DON JUAN  9      8    6
  I DO NOT KNOW--I WISH MEN TO BE FREE . . . . . . .   195  3 DON JUAN  9     25    7
  AS YET ARE STRONGLY STINGING TO BE FREE . . . . . .  196  3 DON JUAN  9     28    8
  WENT BOUNDING FOR THE ISLAND OF THE FREE . . . . .   256  3 DON JUAN 10     64    2
  WOULD SHE BE PROUD OR BOAST HERSELF THE FREE . . .   258  3 DON JUAN 10     68    1
  IS FREE THE RESPIRATION'S WORTH THE MONEY . . . . .  259  3 DON JUAN 10     70    8
  JUAN ADMIRED THESE HIGHWAYS OF FREE MILLIONS . . .   263  3 DON JUAN 10     77    4
  (SEE BILLINGSGATE) MADE EVEN THE TONGUE MORE FREE .  288  3 DON JUAN 11     42    8
  BUT WOULD NOT CHANGE MY FREE THOUGHTS FOR A THRONE .  312  3 DON JUAN 11     90    8
  MALTHUS AND WILBERFORCE--THE LAST SET FREE . . . .   325  3 DON JUAN 12     20    5
  THAT NOBLE SIGHT WHEN REALLY FREE THE NATION . . .   354  3 DON JUAN 12     83    2
  FROM FOREIGN YOKE TO FREE THE HELPLESS NATIVE-- . .  363  3 DON JUAN 13     10    4
  BECAUSE BOLD BRITONS HAVE A TONGUE AND FREE QUILL .  367  3 DON JUAN 13     20    5
  BEGAN TO THINK THE DUCHESS' CONDUCT FREE . . . . .   430  3 DON JUAN 14     46    4
  IF FREE FROM PASSION WHICH ALL FRIENDSHIP CHECKS .   451  3 DON JUAN 14     93    5
  AS THOUGH THE LURKING THOUGHT HAD FOLLOW'D FREE . .  456  3 DON JUAN 15      1    4
  AND TAUGHT HIM WHEN TO BE RESERVED OR FREE . . . .   492  3 DON JUAN 15     82    6
  HE WAS FREE TO CONFESS--(WHENCE COMES THIS PHRASE .  536  3 DON JUAN 16     73    1
  THE GLORIOUS--FREE--AND HAPPY CONSTITUTION . . . .   536  3 DON JUAN 16     74   V8
  THEREFORE I WOULD SOLICIT FREE DISCUSSION . . . . .  564  3 DON JUAN 17      6    1
FREEBORN
  HOW LONELY EVERY FREEBORN CREATURE BROODS . . . . .  358  2 DON JUAN  4     28    5
  THE FREE-BORN FOREST FOUND AND KEPT THEM FREE . . .  145  3 DON JUAN  8     65    7
  THESE FREEBORN SOUNDS PROCEEDED FROM FOUR PADS . . .  273  3 DON JUAN 11     11    1
  HAVE BEEN OBLIGED TO SLAY A FREEBORN NATIVE . . . .  277  3 DON JUAN 11     18    7
FREED
  OF NATIONS FREED AND THE WORLD OVERJOY'D . . . . .   339  2 DON JUAN  3    109    4
  UNLESS HE'S DRUNK AND THEN NO DOUBT HE'S FREED . . .  427  2 DON JUAN  5     31    5
  WHEN FREED FROM BONDS (WHICH ARE OF NO GREAT USE .    23  3 DON JUAN  6     34    4
  YOU MIGHT HAVE FREED FALL'N EUROPE FROM THE UNITY .  187  3 DON JUAN  9      9    3
  YOU HAVE FREED THE BLACKS--NOW PRAY SHUT UP THE WHITES 445  3 DON JUAN 14     82    8
FREEDOM
  TO WORTH AS FREEDOM WISDOM AS TO WIT . . . . . . .    18  2 DON JUAN  D     15    6
  THEN CAME HER FREEDOM FOR SHE HAD NO MOTHER . . . .  248  2 DON JUAN  2    175    1
  OF FREEDOM THAT THIS NOW INSPIRED TYRTAEUS . . . .   319  2 DON JUAN  3     84   V2
  TRUST NOT FOR FREEDOM TO THE FRANKS-- . . . . . . .  325  2 DON JUAN  3   L 14    1
  FROM FRIENDS AND HOME AND FREEDOM FAR ESTRANGED . .  414  2 DON JUAN  5      7    1
  EXCUSE MY FREEDOM WHEN I HERE ASSURE YOU . . . . .    63  3 DON JUAN  6    115    7
  DEFENCE OF FREEDOM COUNTRY OR OF LAWS . . . . . . .   86  3 DON JUAN  7     40    4
  WHICH NOW IS LEAGUED YOUNG FREEDOM TO ANNOY . . . .  106  3 DON JUAN  7     79    7
  FALSE FRIEND WHO HELD OUT FREEDOM TO MANKIND . . .   258  3 DON JUAN 10     67    7
  UPON THE CAPTIVE FREEDOM HE'S AS FAR . . . . . . .   258  3 DON JUAN 10     68    6
  TO FREEDOM HE APPLIED (A GRIEF AND A BORE) . . . .   288  3 DON JUAN 11     41    6
  OF FREEDOM SHALL COMPLETE THEIR EDUCATION . . . . .  354  3 DON JUAN 12     83    6
  A FRIEND TO FREEDOM AND FREEHOLDERS--YET . . . . .   535  3 DON JUAN 16     72    1
FREEDOM'S
  WAS FREEDOM'S BEST AND BRAVEST FRIEND . . . . . . .  325  2 DON JUAN  3   L 12    2
  YET IN THE END EXCEPT IN FREEDOM'S BATTLES . . . .   114  3 DON JUAN  8      4    7
  AND HERE HE CRIED IS FREEDOM'S CHOSEN STATION . . .  272  3 DON JUAN 11      9    5
FREEDOMS
  BUT HEAR THESE FREEDOMS FORM THE UTMOST LIST . . .    65  2 DON JUAN  1     80    5
  MERE FREEDOMS OF THE FEMALE CORPORATION . . . . . .  429  3 DON JUAN 14     43    4
FREEHOLDERS
  A FRIEND TO FREEDOM AND FREEHOLDERS--YET . . . . .   535  3 DON JUAN 16     72    1
FREEHOLDS
  HEAVEN'S FREEHOLDS IN A SORT OF DOOMSDAY SCROLL . .  242  3 DON JUAN 10     35    5
FREELY
  FEMALE AS WHERE SHE LIKES MAY FREELY PASS . . . . .  248  2 DON JUAN  2    175    4
  I THEREFORE IF YOU WISH ME TO FIGHT FREELY . . . .   103  3 DON JUAN  7     72    7
  MAY STILL EXPATIATE FREELY AS WILL I . . . . . . .   195  3 DON JUAN  9     26    7
  WHOSE DRAPERY HINTS WE MAY ADMIRE THEM FREELY . . .  390  3 DON JUAN 13     68    8
FREEMASONRY
  AS IN FREEMASONRY A HIGHER BROTHER . . . . . . . .   369  3 DON JUAN 13     24    4
FREEMASONS
  LOWER'D LEAVEN'D LIKE A HISTORY OF FREEMASONS . . .  419  3 DON JUAN 14     22    2
```

FREEST
    THE FREEST SHE THAT EVER GAZED ON GLASS 248   2 DON JUAN   2   175   6
FREETHINKER
    THERE WAS LORD PYRRHO TOO THE GREAT FREETHINKER   398   3 DON JUAN 13   84   7
FREE-WILL
    REMITS THE MATTER TO OUR OWN FREE-WILL   453   2 DON JUAN   5   72   8
FREEZE
    LIKE SAMUEL FROM THE GRAVE TO FREEZE ONCE MORE 15   2 DON JUAN   D   11   2
    MY TEETH BEGIN TO CHATTER MY VEINS FREEZE-- 121   2 DON JUAN   1   181   6
    BEWITCHING TORTURING AS THEY FREEZE OR GLOW 438   3 DON JUAN 14   63   7
FREEZING
    ASSUME THEN LEAVE US ON OUR FREEZING WAY 66   3 DON JUAN   7   1   8
FREIGHT
    THEIR LIVING FREIGHT WAS NOW REDUCED TO FOUR   209   2 DON JUAN   2   101   4
FRENCH
    WERE FRENCH AND FAMOUS PEOPLE AS WE KNOW 22   2 DON JUAN   1   3   3
    SHE READ SOME FRENCH ROMANCES HERE AND THERE   28   2 DON JUAN   1   13   3
    IN FRENCH BUT THEN THE RHYME WOULD GO FOR NOUGHT) . . . 67   2 DON JUAN   1   84   8
    FRENCH STUFFS LACE TWEEZERS TOOTHPICKS TEAPOT TRAY   . . 284   2 DON JUAN   3   17   5
    FRENCH STUFFS LACE TWEEZERS TOOTHPICKS A BIDET 284   2 DON JUAN   3   17   V5
    WHO NAME THE FRENCH IN ENGLISH SAVE TO SHEW 77   3 DON JUAN   7   22   7
    TO RUSSIAN TARTAR ENGLISH FRENCH COSSACQUE 89   3 DON JUAN   7   46   2
    AS WHEN THE FRENCH THAT DISSIPATED NATION 176   3 DON JUAN   8   129   4
    THE SPANISH AND THE FRENCH AS WELL AS DUTCH 184   3 DON JUAN   9   3   5
    THE FRENCH WERE NOT YET A LAMP-LIGHTING NATION 280   3 DON JUAN 11   26   6
    THEY TALKED BAD FRENCH OF SPANISH AND UPON ITS 294   3 DON JUAN 11   50   5
    THE FACT FOR WORDS AND LET THE FRENCH TRANSLATE   . . . 405   3 DON JUAN 13   101   7
    BUT THOUGH THE FLOWER IS DIFFERENT WITH THE FRENCH . . 442   3 DON JUAN 14   75   7
    YOUR STOMACH ERE YOU DINE THE FRENCH WILL DO   488   3 DON JUAN 15   72   4
FRENCHMAN
    OH JACK I'M FLOORED BY THAT 'ERE BLOODY FRENCHMAN 274   3 DON JUAN 11   13   8
    THE SULKY HUNTSMAN GRIMLY SAID THE FRENCHMAN   425   3 DON JUAN 14   34   V7
FRENCHMAN'S
    HOW PEACE SHOULD MAKE JOHN BULL THE FRENCHMAN'S FOE . . . 77   3 DON JUAN   7   22   8
FRENCHMEN
    THEN THERE WERE FRENCHMEN GALLANT YOUNG AND GAY 77   3 DON JUAN   7   22   1
FREQUENT
    THE FREQUENT FOG-BANKS GAVE THEM CAUSE TO DOUBT-- . . . 207   2 DON JUAN   2   96   6
    A FREQUENT MODEL AND IF E'ER SHE MUST 219   2 DON JUAN   2   119   5
FREQUENTLY
    POOR THING HOW FREQUENTLY BY ME AND OTHERS 374   3 DON JUAN 13   36   7
FRESCO
    IN GUIDO'S FAMOUS FRESCO WHICH ALONE 428   3 DON JUAN 14   40   2
FRESH
    SPRUNG UP A BRANCH AS BEAUTIFUL AS FRESH 53   2 DON JUAN   1   58   4
    THE WIND BLEW FRESH AGAIN AS IT GREW LATE   172   2 DON JUAN   2   30   5
    TO PAY HIM A FRESH VISIT WITH A DISH 226   2 DON JUAN   2   133   7
    ALTHOUGH THE MORTAL QUITE AS FRESH AND FAIR 232   2 DON JUAN   2   142   7
    ELSE HOW THE DEVIL IS IT THAT FRESH FEATURES 267   2 DON JUAN   2   208   7
    I SAW THE PRETTIEST CREATURE FRESH FROM MILAN 268   2 DON JUAN   2   209   7
    'TWAS FRESH--FOR HE HAD LATELY USED THE LOCK-- 365   2 DON JUAN   4   40   7
    'TIS TRUE IT GETS ANOTHER BRIGHT AND FRESH 422   2 DON JUAN   5   22   1
    AND FRESH AND BEAUTIFUL EXCEEDINGLY   24   3 DON JUAN   6   36   3
    IN HIS REPLIES SHE PUZZLED HIM FOR FRESH ONES   56   3 DON JUAN   6   101   5
    AND FRESH AS IS A TORRENT OR A TREE   145   3 DON JUAN   8   65   8
    FROM SOME FRESH PARADISE AND SET TO PLOUGH 202   3 DON JUAN   9   40   2
    NEXT OF NEW KNIGHTS THE FRESH AND GLORIOUS HATCH . . . 215   3 DON JUAN   9   65   7
    THEY CANNOT QUENCH YOUNG FEELINGS FRESH AND EARLY . . . 234   3 DON JUAN 10   19   6
    ON OUR FRESH FEELINGS BUT--AS BEING PARTICIPATED . . . 236   3 DON JUAN 10   23   5
    AND FOR THEIR PAINS GET ONLY A FRESH PUNCTURE   263   3 DON JUAN 10   77   8
    CAN FORM A SLIGHT ACQUAINTANCE WITH FRESH AIR   301   3 DON JUAN 11   66   8
    OTHERS HAVE LOST THEIR FRESH AND FAIRY LOOKS   308   3 DON JUAN 11   81   5
    OF ELEGANT ET CETERA IN FRESH BATCHES--   340   3 DON JUAN 12   53   7
    AT A LONG DATE--TILL THEY CAN GET A FRESH ONE-- 379   3 DON JUAN 13   45   6
    AWAY AWAY FRESH HORSES ARE THE WORD   379   3 DON JUAN 13   46   3
    IF BUT TO SET ITS EDGE TO A FRESH POLISH 433   3 DON JUAN 14   53   V7
    PARTLY PERHAPS BECAUSE A FRESH SENSATION 468   3 DON JUAN 15   28   4
    EXPECTANT OF THE GHOST'S FRESH OPERATIONS 555   3 DON JUAN 16   111   8
FRESHER
    OR FRESHER BRIGHTER BUT THE YEAR GONE THROUGH   422   2 DON JUAN   5   22   2
FRESHEST
    HER OWN WAS FRESHEST THOUGH A FEVERISH FLUSH   231   2 DON JUAN   2   141   2
    WILL FEED UPON THE FAIREST FRESHEST CHEEK   243   3 DON JUAN 10   38   3
FRESHLIER
    AND EVERY MORN HIS COLOUR FRESHLIER CAME   245   2 DON JUAN   2   169   1
FRESHLY
    BROAD AS TRANSPARENT DEEP AND FRESHLY FED 385   3 DON JUAN 13   57   2
FRESHNESS
    THE FRESHNESS OF THE HEART CAN FALL LIKE DEW   144   2 DON JUAN   1   214   2
    THEY FELT THE FRESHNESS OF ITS GROWING GREEN   210   2 DON JUAN   2   103   3
FRET
    BY SOME LOW ROCK OR SHELVE THAT MADE IT FRET   251   2 DON JUAN   2   181   7
    I'VE RARELY SEEN THE MAN THEY DID NOT FRET 16   3 DON JUAN   6   21   8
    AND NEXT A QUARREL (AS HE SEEMED TO FRET) 437   3 DON JUAN 14   62   7
FRETTED
    FRETTED WITH GOLD OR SILVER--BY COMMAND 310   2 DON JUAN   3   69   5
    AND ONLY FRETTED WHEN THE SCENT 'GAN FAIL   424   3 DON JUAN 14   33   4
FRETWORK
    THE GALE SWEEPS THROUGH ITS FRETWORK AND OFT SINGS   . . 387   3 DON JUAN 13   62   6

293

FRIAR
NOW LIKE FRIAR BACON'S BRAZEN HEAD I'VE SPOKEN 145   2 DON JUAN   1   217   5
JUST AS A FRIAR MAY ACCUSE HIS VOW 493   2 DON JUAN   5   142   6
BY THY HUMANE DISCOVERY FRIAR BACON 129   3 DON JUAN   8   33   8
OF FRIAR BACON'S BRIGHT INVENTION--SHARED 129   3 DON JUAN   8   33 V5
BROKE IN UPON BY THE BLACK FRIAR OF LATE 515   3 DON JUAN 16   35   4
WHAT FRIAR SAID JUAN AND HE DID HIS BEST 515   3 DON JUAN 16   35   5
OH HAVE YOU NEVER HEARD OF THE BLACK FRIAR 516   3 DON JUAN 16   36   1
THE FRIAR OF LATE HAS NOT BEEN OFT PERCEIVED 516   3 DON JUAN 16   36   8
THE AIR OF 'TWAS A FRIAR OF ORDERS GREY 517   3 DON JUAN 16   38   8
BEWARE BEWARE OF THE BLACK FRIAR 518   3 DON JUAN 16   L 1   1
AND EXPELLED THE FRIARS ONE FRIAR STILL 518   3 DON JUAN 16   L 1   7
BUT BEWARE BEWARE OF THE BLACK FRIAR 520   3 DON JUAN 16   L 5   1
THEN GRAMMERCY FOR THE BLACK FRIAR 520   3 DON JUAN 16   L 6   5
IT IS THE SABLE FRIAR AS BEFORE 556   3 DON JUAN 16   113   2
THE SABLE FRIAR IN HIS SOLEMN HOOD 558   3 DON JUAN 16   117   8
FRIAR'S
TO QUESTION THAT FRIAR'S RIGHT 520   3 DON JUAN 16   L 5   8
OF THIS SAME MYSTIC FRIAR'S CURIOUS DOINGS 527   3 DON JUAN 16   53   7
FRIARS
BUT THESE HAD FALLEN NOT WHEN THE FRIARS FELL 386   3 DON JUAN 13   60   3
AND EXPELLED THE FRIARS ONE FRIAR STILL 518   3 DON JUAN 16   L 1   7
FRIDAY
THE OTHER EVENING ('TWAS ON FRIDAY LAST)-- 428   2 DON JUAN   5   33   1
FRIED
BAKED FRIED OR BURNT TURNED INSIDE-OUT OR DROWNED . . . 201   3 DON JUAN   9   37   5
FRIEND
I'LL THEREFORE TAKE OUR ANCIENT FRIEND DON JUAN 21   2 DON JUAN   1   1   6
SO AS I SAID I'LL TAKE MY FRIEND DON JUAN 24   2 DON JUAN   1   5   8
I CAN'T SAY MUCH FOR FRIEND OR YET RELATION) 38   2 DON JUAN   1   32   5
WITH DONNA INEZ QUITE A FAVOURITE FRIEND 58   2 DON JUAN   1   66   2
BY HARBOURING SOME DEAR FRIEND EXTREMELY VICIOUS . . . 74   2 DON JUAN   1   99   5
AND WHEN THE SPOUSE AND FRIEND ARE GONE OFF WHOLLY . . 74   2 DON JUAN   1   99   7
PARTICULARLY WITH A TIRESOME FRIEND 90   2 DON JUAN   1   126   4
HER SPEECH OUT TO HER PROTEGE AND FRIEND 241   2 DON JUAN   2   161   6
BORN TO SOME FRIEND WHO HOLDS HIS WIFE AND RICHES . . . 287   2 DON JUAN   3   23   7
I'VE SEEN A FRIEND BETRAYED FOUR TIMES A DAY 288   2 DON JUAN   3   25 V8
AND MADE HIM A GOOD FRIEND BUT BAD ACQUAINTANCE 303   2 DON JUAN   3   54   8
WAS FREEDOM'S BEST AND BRAVEST FRIEND 325   2 DON JUAN   3   L 12   2
WHICH MIX'D ALL FEELINGS FRIEND CHILD LOVER BROTHER . . 357   2 DON JUAN   4   26   3
IF YOU HAVE GOT A FORMER FRIEND FOR FOE 366   2 DON JUAN   4   41   6
AY QUOTH HIS FRIEND I THOUGHT IT WOULD APPEAR 420   2 DON JUAN   5   19   3
HIS FRIEND TOO ADDING A NEW SAVING CLAUSE 437   2 DON JUAN   5   47   6
AND JUAN AND HIS FRIEND ALBEIT THEY HEARD 439   2 DON JUAN   5   50   2
A BOOK FRIEND SINGLE LADY OR A GLASS 444   2 DON JUAN   5   58   2
WHILE HE WAS DRESSING BABA THEIR BLACK FRIEND 451   2 DON JUAN   5   69   1
WHO LENT HIS LADY TO HIS FRIEND HORTENSIUS 10   3 DON JUAN   6   7   8
A PRETTY STRANGER WITHOUT FRIEND OR GUIDE 28   3 DON JUAN   6   45   5
EXPLICITLY OUR SEVERAL POSTS MY FRIEND 100   3 DON JUAN   7   65   7
OUR BRITISH FRIEND THESE ARE THE WIVES OF OTHERS . . . 103   3 DON JUAN   7   71   2
BUT OF THE FIRST OUR LITTLE FRIEND DON JUAN 138   3 DON JUAN   8   52   2
HIS JEST ALIKE IN FACE OF FRIEND OR FOE 147   3 DON JUAN   8   70   6
AS MY FRIEND JEFFREY WRITES WITH SUCH AN AIR 230   3 DON JUAN 10   11   6
FALSE FRIEND WHO HELD OUT FREEDOM TO MANKIND 258   3 DON JUAN 10   67   7
HOWE'ER OUR FRIEND DON JUAN MIGHT COMMAND 329   3 DON JUAN 12   29   5
FOR LIKE AN AGED AUNT OR TIRESOME FRIEND 334   3 DON JUAN 12   39   4
DETERMINED RIGHT OR WRONG ON FRIEND OR FOE 366   3 DON JUAN 13   16   4
WITHOUT A FRIEND WHAT WERE HUMANITY 430   3 DON JUAN 14   47   5
WAS NOT CONFINED TO FEELING FOR HER FRIEND 432   3 DON JUAN 14   51   2
THIS SORT OF CHASTE LIAISON FOR A FRIEND 438   3 DON JUAN 14   64   4
HER HUSBAND'S FRIEND HER OWN YOUNG AND A STRANGER . . . 449   3 DON JUAN 14   91   8
SHE WAS OR THOUGHT SHE WAS HIS FRIEND--AND THIS 450   3 DON JUAN 14   92   1
NO FRIEND LIKE TO A WOMAN EARTH DISCOVERS 451   3 DON JUAN 14   93   7
SOME HEIR TO A LARGE PROPERTY SOME FRIEND 470   3 DON JUAN 15   33   2
AND AS MY FRIEND SCOTT SAYS I SOUND MY WARISON 481   3 DON JUAN 15   59   3
BOTH IN THE CASE OF LOVER AND OF FRIEND 491   3 DON JUAN 15   79   4
THE FRIEND OF ARTISTS IF NOT ARTS--THE OWNER 528   3 DON JUAN 16   57   2
A FRIEND TO FREEDOM AND FREEHOLDERS--YET 535   3 DON JUAN 16   72   1
NO LESS A FRIEND TO GOVERNMENT--HE HELD 535   3 DON JUAN 16   72   2
FOR WIT HATH NO GREAT FRIEND IN AGUISH FOLKS 540   3 DON JUAN 16   83   3
HOW SWEET THE TASK TO SHIELD AN ABSENT FRIEND 552   3 DON JUAN 16   104   7
FRIENDLESS
TO FEEL IN FRIENDLESS PALACES A HOME 475   3 DON JUAN 15   44   7
FRIEND'S
LOOKED GRAVE AND PALE TO SEE HER FRIEND'S FRAGILITY . . 430   3 DON JUAN 14   46   7
FRIENDS
IS PHILOSOPHIC IN OUR FORMER FRIENDS 37   2 DON JUAN   1   30   2
THEIR FRIENDS HAD TRIED AT RECONCILIATION 38   2 DON JUAN   1   32   1
WITH TORCHES FRIENDS AND SERVANTS IN GREAT NUMBER . . . 96   2 DON JUAN   1   138   2
THE LOSS OF LOVE THE TREACHERY OF FRIENDS 167   2 DON JUAN   2   21   4
HIS SPANISH FRIENDS FOR THOSE IN ITALY 169   2 DON JUAN   2   24   8
WHEN PATIENTS NEITHER PLAGUED WITH FRIENDS NOR WIFE . . 190   2 DON JUAN   2   64   3
'TIS SURELY FAIR TO DINE UPON OUR FRIENDS 200   2 DON JUAN   2   83   6
FOES FRIENDS MEN WOMEN NOW ARE NOUGHT TO ME 244   2 DON JUAN   2   166   1
AMONG HIS FRIENDS THE MAINOTS SOME HE SOLD 284   2 DON JUAN   3   16   2
HE DEEM'D BEING IN A LONE ISLE AMONG FRIENDS 318   2 DON JUAN   3   83   1
WHEN THEY FROM THEIR SWEET FRIENDS ARE TORN APART . . . 338   2 DON JUAN   3   108   3
OF FRIENDS--AND OPIATE DRAUGHTS--THERE'S LOVE AND WINE . 343   2 DON JUAN   3   V 98   2
THE DEATH OF FRIENDS AND THAT WHICH SLAYS EVEN MORE-- . 350   2 DON JUAN   4   12   3

FRIENDS   (CONTINUED)

	PAGE	VOL	CANTO	STANZA	LN
FROM FRIENDS AND HOME AND FREEDOM FAR ESTRANGED	414	2 DON JUAN 5	7	6
HAVE YOU NO FRIENDS -- I HAD--BUT BY GOD'S BLESSING	419	2 DON JUAN 5	16	1
THEIR PRESENT LESSONS ON OUR PAGAN FRIENDS HERE	423	2 DON JUAN 5	24	2
SHOWS THAT HE THINKS HIS FRIENDS HAVE NOT BEEN SLEEPING	436	2 DON JUAN 5	45	4
OUR FRIENDS THE TURKS WHO WITH LOUD ALLA'S NOW	87	3 DON JUAN 7	42	1
FOR SOME WERE THINKING OF THEIR HOME AND FRIENDS	94	3 DON JUAN 7	54	7
WHILE THEIR BELOVED FRIENDS BEGAN TO ARM	105	3 DON JUAN 7	76	7
AS WIFE AND FRIENDS DID FOR THE BOILS OF JOB--	105	3 DON JUAN 7	77	7
HE FOUND HIMSELF ALONE AND FRIENDS RETIRING	125	3 DON JUAN 8	27	8
OUT BETWEEN FRIENDS AS WELL AS ALLIED NATIONS	136	3 DON JUAN 8	48	4
WITHOUT OR WITH OFFENCE TO FRIENDS OR FOES	156	3 DON JUAN 8	89	7
STRUCK AT HIS FRIENDS AS BABIES BEAT THEIR NURSES	165	3 DON JUAN 8	108	8
THEIR FRIENDS FROM FOES--BESIDES SUCH THINGS FROM HASTE	177	3 DON JUAN 8	130	4
HER FRIENDS LIKE THE SAD FAMILY OF HECTOR	182	3 DON JJAN 8	141	3
OLD ENEMIES WHO HAVE BECOME NEW FRIENDS	231	3 DON JUAN 10	12	1
IN PLACE OF WHAT HER HOME AND FRIENDS ONCE WERE	252	3 DON JUAN 10	57	3
MY FRIENDS THE WHIGS EXACTLY WHERE THEY WERE	308	3 DON JUAN 11	79	8
(FRIENDS OF THE PARTY) WHO BEGIN ACCUSALS	332	3 DON JUAN 12	34	4
HE HAD MANY FRIENDS WHO HAD MANY WIVES AND WAS	342	3 DON JUAN 12	57	1
IN MAKING MEN WHAT COURTESY CALLS FRIENDS	365	3 DON JUAN 13	15	8
AND NUMEROUS PARTY OF HIS NOBLE FRIENDS	382	3 DON JUAN 13	52	3
FOR SOME HAD ABSENT LOVERS ALL HAD FRIENDS	407	3 DON JUAN 13	105	1
TO THE GREAT PLEASURE OF OUR FRIENDS MANKIND	414	3 DON JUAN 14	9	5
SUCH SMALL DISTINCTION BETWEEN FRIENDS AND FOES	421	3 DON JUAN 14	25	4
FOR WHICH MOST FRIENDS RESERVE THEIR SENSIBILITY	430	3 DON JUAN 14	46	8
OH JOB YOU HAD TWO FRIENDS ONE'S QUITE ENOUGH	431	3 DON JUAN 14	48	1
LET NO MAN GRUMBLE WHEN HIS FRIENDS FALL OFF	431	3 DON JUAN 14	48	5
UTTER'D BY FRIENDS THOSE PROPHETS OF THE PAST	432	3 DON JUAN 14	50	4
I'VE ALSO SEEN SOME FEMALE FRIENDS ('TIS ODD	452	3 DON JUAN 14	96	1
GREW FRIENDS IN THIS OR ANY OTHER SENSE	453	3 DON JUAN 14	97	2
UPON HER FRIENDS AS EVERYBODY OUGHT	524	3 DON JUAN 16	47	4
HEAVEN AND HIS FRIENDS KNEW THAT A PRIVATE LIFE	536	3 DON JUAN 16	74	1
EVEN FROM OUR GRAMMAR UPWARDS FRIENDS OF YORE	542	3 DON JUAN 16	86	5

FRIENDS'

	PAGE	VOL	CANTO	STANZA	LN
'TIS IN ARRANGING ALL MY FRIENDS' AFFAIRS	33	2 DON JUAN 1	23	7

FRIENDSHIP

	PAGE	VOL	CANTO	STANZA	LN
AN HONEST FRIENDSHIP WITH A MARRIED LADY--	288	2 DON JUAN 3	25	3
THE DEATH OF FRIENDSHIP LOVE YOUTH ALL THAT IS	350	2 DON JUAN 4	12	4
OF AN IMPROPER FRIENDSHIP FOR HER HORSE	446	2 DON JUAN 5	61	3
A SENTIMENTAL FRIENDSHIP THROUGH AND THROUGH	25	3 DON JUAN 6	39	3
OF SENTIMENTAL FRIENDSHIP THERE WERE THREE	26	3 DON JUAN 6	40	2
OF FRIENDSHIP WHICH YOU MAY ACCEPT OR PASS	342	3 DON JUAN 12	57	3
CAN'T FORM A FRIENDSHIP BUT THE WORLD O'ERAWES IT	346	3 DON JUAN 12	65	3
AND ROBES SWEET FRIENDSHIP IN A BRUSSELS LACE	430	3 DON JUAN 14	47	4
WITHOUT THE FARCE OF FRIENDSHIP OR ROMANCE	450	3 DON JUAN 14	92	2
LADIES WHO HAVE STUDIED FRIENDSHIP BUT IN FRANCE	450	3 DON JUAN 14	92	4
BUT OF SUCH FRIENDSHIP AS MAN'S MAY TO MAN BE	450	3 DON JUAN 14	92	7
IF FREE FROM PASSION WHICH ALL FRIENDSHIP CHECKS	451	3 DON JUAN 14	93	5

FRIENDSHIPS

	PAGE	VOL	CANTO	STANZA	LN
HIS FRIENDSHIPS THEREFORE AND NO LESS AVERSIONS	366	3 DON JUAN 13	17	1

FRIGHT

	PAGE	VOL	CANTO	STANZA	LN
YOU MIGHT BE SURE SHE WAS A PERFECT FRIGHT	48	2 DON JUAN 1	48	6
WHAT WILL BECOME ON'T--I'M IN SUCH A FRIGHT	115	2 DON JUAN 1	171	3
THE HOARSE HARSH WAVES KEPT TIME FRIGHT CURED THE QUALMS	174	2 DON JUAN 2	34	5

FRIGHTEN

	PAGE	VOL	CANTO	STANZA	LN
TO FRIGHTEN THEM INTO CAPITULATION	78	3 DON JUAN 7	24	6
WHICH THOUGH 'TIS CERTAIN TO PERPLEX AND FRIGHTEN	281	3 DON JUAN 11	27	7

FRIGHTENED

	PAGE	VOL	CANTO	STANZA	LN
FOR SHE SEEMED AGITATED FLUSHED AND FRIGHTENED	42	3 DON JUAN 6	72	7
YET NEITHER FRIGHTENED BY A FEMALE FUSS	344	3 DON JUAN 12	61	5

FRIGHTS

	PAGE	VOL	CANTO	STANZA	LN
AND FRIGHTS--ESPECIALLY IF 'TIS A DAUGHTER	564	3 DON JUAN 17	4	7

FRINGE

	PAGE	VOL	CANTO	STANZA	LN
FORTH FROM ITS RAVEN FRINGE THE FULL GLANCE FLIES	218	2 DON JUAN 2	117	5

FRINGED

	PAGE	VOL	CANTO	STANZA	LN
FOR THOSE LARGE BLACK EYES WERE SO BLACKLY FRINGED	314	2 DON JUAN 3	75	3

FRINGES

	PAGE	VOL	CANTO	STANZA	LN
THE BLACK BOUGH) TEAR-DROPS THROUGH HER EYES' DARK FRINGES	40	3 DON JUAN 6	67	8
THEIR WAY THROUGH HER SEALED EYELIDS' GLOSSY FRINGES	40	3 DON JUAN 6	67	V7

FRISKS

	PAGE	VOL	CANTO	STANZA	LN
(ALTHOUGH THE CONSEQUENCES OF SUCH FRISKS	20	3 DON JUAN 6	29	5

FRO

	PAGE	VOL	CANTO	STANZA	LN
HE FLITTED TO AND FRO A DANCING LIGHT	89	3 DON JUAN 7	46	7

FROCK

	PAGE	VOL	CANTO	STANZA	LN
BACK FELL THE SABLE FROCK AND DREARY COWL	561	3 DON JUAN 16	123	5

FROID

	PAGE	VOL	CANTO	STANZA	LN
IN THE MEANTIME CROSS-LEGGED WITH GREAT SANG FROID	172	3 DON JUAN 8	121	1

FROLIC

	PAGE	VOL	CANTO	STANZA	LN
THE PHANTOM OF HER FROLIC GRACE--FITZ-FULKE	561	3 DON JUAN 16	123	8

FRONT

	PAGE	VOL	CANTO	STANZA	LN
WHICH OPENED ON THEIR VIEW AND O'ER THE FRONT	436	2 DON JUAN 5	46	2
O'ER HER FAIR FRONT LIKE MORNING'S ON A LILY	58	3 DON JUAN 6	105	8
IN LIEU OF A BARE BLADE AND BRAZEN FRONT	275	3 DON JUAN 11	15	5
THEY REACHED THE HOTEL FORTH STREAMED FROM THE FRONT DOOR	282	3 DON JUAN 11	30	1
OF POLITICIANS AND THEIR DOUBLE FRONT	285	3 DON JUAN 11	36	4
HIS CURLS FELL NEGLIGENTLY O'ER HIS FRONT	513	3 DON JUAN 16	29	5

FRONTIER

	PAGE	VOL	CANTO	STANZA	LN
LIFE'S SAD POST-HORSES O'ER THE DREARY FRONTIER	238	3 DON JUAN 10	27	7

		PAGE	VOL	CANTO	STANZA	LN

FROST
(WITH SOME ASSISTANCE FROM THE FROST AND SNOW) . . . . . 147 3 DON JUAN 8 70 2
TO LOSE BY SOME TWENTY YEARS . . . . . 253 3 DON JUAN 10 58 7
FOR IF THE POLE'S NOT OPEN BUT ALL FROST . . . . . . 376 3 DON JUAN 13 39 7
AND THE HARD FROST DESTROY'D THE SCENTING DAYS . . . . 407 3 DON JUAN 13 106 4

FROSTS
PERHAPS HE LONGED IN BITTER FROSTS FOR CLIMES . . . . 243 3 DON JUAN 10 37 5

FROSTY
BY THOUGHT OF FROSTY CAUCASUS BUT FEW . . . . . 396 2 DON JUAN 4 96 6

FROTH'D
PALE AS THE FOAM THAT FROTH'D ON HIS DEAD BROW . . . . 362 2 DON JUAN 4 34 2

FROWN
AT SUCH ALLIANCES HIS SIRES WOULD FROWN . . . . . 52 2 DON JUAN 1 57 4
WHICH IF WITHDRAWN WOULD BUT DISCLOSE THE FROWN . . . 182 2 DON JUAN 2 49 3
HE HEARD REPEATED JUAN WITH A FROWN . . . . . . 470 2 DON JUAN 5 102 5
WHOSE FROWN WOULD PUT THE SPHERES ALL OUT OF TUNE . . . 494 2 DON JUAN 5 144 3
A FROWN ON NATURE'S OR ON HUMAN FACE-- . . . . . 145 3 DON JUAN 8 65 6

FROWN'D
SHE BLUSH'D AND FROWN'D NOT BUT SHE STROVE TO SPEAK . . . 81 2 DON JUAN 1 112 7
THE MISSES BRIDLED AND THE MATRONS FROWN'D . . . . 429 3 DON JUAN 14 44 2

FROWNED
THE MATRON FROWNED WHY SO--FOR FEAR OF GHOSTS . . . . 30 3 DON JUAN 6 48 2
THE EMPRESS SMILED THE REIGNING FAVOURITE FROWNED-- . . . 205 3 DON JUAN 9 46 2
THE FIRST YET FROWNED SUPERBLY O'ER THE SOIL . . . . 386 3 DON JUAN 13 59 5

FROWNS
WHICH DRACHENFELS FROWNS OVER LIKE A SPECTRE . . . . 255 3 DON JUAN 10 62 2

FROWZY
A DROWSY FROWZY POEM CALL'D THE EXCURSION . . . . . 330 2 DON JUAN 3 94 7

FROZE
WHICH FROZE TO MARBLE AS IT FELL SHE THOUGHT . . . . 362 2 DON JUAN 4 33 8

FROZEN
WHITE COLD AND PURE AS LOOKS A FROZEN RILL . . . . 40 3 DON JUAN 6 68 3
SLIDING KNEE-DEEP IN LATELY FROZEN MUD . . . . . 148 3 DON JUAN 8 73 7
FROZEN INTO A VERY VINOUS ICE . . . . . . 375 3 DON JUAN 13 37 3

FRUGAL
I SAID BEFORE THE FRUGAL LIFE IS HIS . . . . . 319 3 DON JUAN 12 7 2

FRUIT
TO YOU I ENVY NEITHER FRUIT NOR BOUGHS-- . . . . . 13 2 DON JUAN D 7 3
WENT PLUCKING VARIOUS FRUIT WITHOUT HER LEAVE . . . 30 2 DON JUAN 1 18 8
BUT THERE WERE EGGS FRUIT COFFEE BREAD FISH HONEY . . . 233 2 DON JUAN 2 145 7
LIKE BRANCHES WHEN THE FRUIT BENEATH IS MELLOW . . . 311 2 DON JUAN 3 70 V4
IN MARBLE FONTS THERE GRAIN AND FLOWER AND FRUIT . . . 373 2 DON JUAN 4 55 2
THE BLEEDING FLOWER AND BLASTED FRUIT OF LOVE . . . 382 2 DON JUAN 4 70 8
AND FAIR BROWS GENTLY DROOPING AS THE FRUIT . . . . 38 3 DON JUAN 6 65 6
BRING DOWN THE FRUIT WHICH STILL PERVERSELY CLUNG . . . 44 3 DON JUAN 6 76 6
UPON THE GOLDEN FRUIT THE VISION BORE . . . . . 44 3 DON JUAN 6 77 6
LOVELY AS THOSE WHICH RIPENED EDEN'S FRUIT . . . . 86 3 DON JUAN 7 41 7
OF HER FIRST FRUIT BUT HOW HE FALLS AND RISES . . . 210 3 DON JUAN 9 55 7
(WHO LIKE SOUR FRUIT TO STIR THEIR VEINS' SALT TIDES . . 251 3 DON JUAN 10 54 3
CALLED PARKS WHERE THERE IS NEITHER FRUIT NOR FLOWER . . 301 3 DON JUAN 11 66 4
A FRUIT TO BLOOM UPON THEIR WITHERING BOUGH . . . . 330 3 DON JUAN 12 31 2
OF FOLLY'S FRUIT FOR THOUGH YOUR FOOLS ABOUND . . . 402 3 DON JUAN 13 95 5
THE FIRST THING BOYS LIKE AFTER PLAY AND FRUIT . . . 405 3 DON JUAN 13 101 3

FRUITFUL
OF LIFE'S STRANGE TREE SO FRUITFUL ON OCCASION . . . . 250 2 DON JUAN 2 179 6

FRUITS
AND FRUITS AND DATE-BREAD LOAVES CLOSED THE REPAST . . 307 2 DON JUAN 3 63 2
BESIDES FORBIDDEN FRUITS FOR SHE NE'ER PAUSED . . . 476 2 DON JUAN 5 113 V6
AND THAT THIS WOOD WAS FULL OF PLEASANT FRUITS . . . 43 3 DON JUAN 6 75 7
OF THESE BRIEF BLOSSOMS THE IMMEDIATE FRUITS . . . . 168 3 DON JUAN 8 113 8
AND FRUITS AND ICE AND ALL THAT ART REFINES . . . . 488 3 DON JUAN 15 72 1

FRY
BECAUSE THEY ARE SO--A MALE MRS FRY . . . . . 266 3 DON JUAN 10 84 6
OH MRS FRY WHY GO TO NEWGATE WHY . . . . . 266 3 DON JUAN 10 85 1
I THOUGHT YOU HAD MORE RELIGION MRS FRY . . . . . 267 3 DON JUAN 10 85 8

FRYING
BUT ZOE THE MEANTIME SOME EGGS WAS FRYING . . . . . 233 2 DON JUAN 2 144 5

FUDDLE
THEIR FARE AND ALSO PAUSE BESIDES TO FUDDLE . . . . 260 3 DON JUAN 10 71 6

FUEL
THAT THERE WAS FUEL TO HAVE FURNISH'D TWENTY . . . . 226 2 DON JUAN 2 132 8
TOO OFTEN ALL THE CLOTHING MEAT OR FUEL . . . . . 256 3 DON JUAN 10 63 7
LET ME DIE WHERE I AM AND AS THE FUEL . . . . . 276 3 DON JUAN 11 16 4

FUI
PARS PARVA FUI BUT STILL ART AND PART . . . . . 419 3 DON JUAN 14 21 2

FUIMUS
THE DREARY FUIMUS OF ALL THINGS HUMAN . . . . . 376 3 DON JUAN 13 40 6

FULFIL
AND YET I MAY AS WELL THE TASK FULFIL . . . . . 134 2 DON JUAN 1 197 3
THE LAW OF ALL AROUND HER TO FULFIL . . . . . 475 2 DON JUAN 5 112 2
IT IS NOT THAT I SHALL NOT ALL FULFIL . . . . . 62 3 DON JUAN 6 114 3
HIS TIME A CORPORAL'S DUTY TO FULFIL . . . . . 93 3 DON JUAN 7 52 4

FULL
IN GIVING TO HIS BRETHREN THEIR FULL MEED . . . . 14 2 DON JUAN D 8 6
A STILLNESS WHICH LEAVES ROOM FOR THE FULL SOUL . . . 82 2 DON JUAN 1 114 2
THE DEPOSITIONS AND THE CAUSE AT FULL . . . . . 127 2 DON JUAN 1 189 2
A DISAPPOINTED LAWYER AT FULL LENGTH . . . . . 155 2 DON JUAN 1 V 6 8
AS A FULL POT OF PORTER TO THEIR THINKING . . . . 201 2 DON JUAN 2 85 7
AND THERE HE LAY FULL LENGTH WHERE HE WAS FLUNG . . . 213 2 DON JUAN 2 108 5

FULL   (CONTINUED)
```
      FORTH FROM ITS RAVEN FRINGE THE FULL GLANCE FLIES  .  .  .  . 218  2 DON JUAN  2   117   5
      FULL MANY A MORSEL FOR THAT TURKISH TRADE     .  .  .  .  .   223  2 DON JUAN  2   126   7
      FULL OF BARBARIC CARVING PAINT AND GILDING  .  .  .  .  .     223  2 DON JUAN  2   127   8
      I'VE SEEN HIM RISE FULL OFT INDEED OF LATE  .  .  .  .  .     230  2 DON JUAN  2   140   2
      WAS THAT IN WHICH THE HEART IS ALWAYS FULL  .  .  .  .  .     258  2 DON JUAN  2   192   3
      ROMANCES PAINT AT FULL LENGTH PEOPLE'S WOOINGS .  .  .  .  .  279  2 DON JUAN  3     8   3
      ITS POWER UNCONSCIOUSLY FULL MANY A TIME--  .  .  .  .  .     304  2 DON JUAN  3    56   3
      HER ORANGE SILK FULL TURKISH TROWSERS FURL'D  .  .  .  .  .   312  2 DON JUAN  3    72   7
      THAT WITHOUT NOTICE FEW FULL MOONS SHALL PASS IT  .  .  .  .  317  2 DON JUAN  3    81   3
      HAD BEEN THE FAVOURITE OF FULL MANY A MESS  .  .  .  .  .  .  318  2 DON JUAN  3    82   3
      FULL OF DEEP RAPTURES AND OF BUMPERS THEY--  .  .  .  .  .    343  2 DON JUAN  3  V 98   7
      SHOW WHAT THE PASSIONS ARE IN THEIR FULL GROWTH  .  .  .  .   368  2 DON JUAN  4    45   8
      THE WORLD IS FULL OF STRANGE VICISSITUDES  .  .  .  .  .      371  2 DON JUAN  4    51   1
      HER HUMAN CLAY IS KINDLED FULL OF POWER  .  .  .  .  .  .     374  2 DON JUAN  4    56   2
      NEW THOUGHTS OF LIFE FOR IT SEEM'D FULL OF SOUL  .  .  .  .   377  2 DON JUAN  4    60   7
      BACK TO OLD THOUGHTS WAX'D FULL OF FEARFUL MEANING  .  .  .   379  2 DON JUAN  4    64   8
      JUAN WAS JUVENILE AND THUS WAS FULL  .  .  .  .  .  .  .      415  2 DON JUAN  5     8   1
      JUAN WAS YOUNG--HAD COURAGE--AND WAS FULL  .  .  .  .  .      415  2 DON JUAN  5     8  V1
      HE PAUSED AND HIS DARK EYE GREW FULL OF GLOOM  .  .  .  .  .  420  2 DON JUAN  5    18   3
      RECEIPTS IN FULL BEGAN TO THINK OF DINING  .  .  .  .  .      426  2 DON JUAN  5    29   8
      IN ALL THE FLASHING OF THEIR FULL ARRAY  .  .  .  .  .  .     442  2 DON JUAN  5    56   4
      THERE SOLITUDE WE KNOW HAS HER FULL GROWTH IN  .  .  .  .     443  2 DON JUAN  5    57   3
      THOUGH FULL OF ALL THINGS WHICH COULD BE DESIRED  .  .  .  .  448  2 DON JUAN  5    64   3
      COULD I DO JUSTICE TO THE FULL DETAIL  .  .  .  .  .  .       467  2 DON JUAN  5    97   7
      DREW HIMSELF UP TO HIS FULL HEIGHT AGAIN  .  .  .  .  .  .    470  2 DON JUAN  5   102   6
      BUT JUAN WHO HAD STILL HIS HEART QUITE FULL  .  .  .  .  .    478  2 DON JUAN  5   117  V2
      YET SHE WOULD MAKE FULL MANY A MANICHEAN  .  .  .  .  .  .      7  3 DON JUAN  6     3   8
      FULL OF EXPRESSION RIGHT OR WRONG THAT STRIKE  .  .  .  .  .   32  3 DON JUAN  6    52   7
      AND THAT THIS WOOD WAS FULL OF PLEASANT FRUITS  .  .  .  .    43  3 DON JUAN  6    75   7
      WOULD MAKE US THINK THE MOON IS AT ITS FULL  .  .  .  .  .    46  3 DON JUAN  6    80   5
      STANDS ON HER TRIPOD AGONIZED AND FULL  .  .  .  .  .  .      59  3 DON JUAN  6   107   2
      FOR ON THE SIXTEENTH AT FULL GALLOP DREW  .  .  .  .  .  .    87  3 DON JUAN  7    43   1
      SO THAT THE STREETS OF COLOURED LAMPS ARE FULL  .  .  .  .    88  3 DON JUAN  7    44   5
      A MODERATE PENSION SHAKES FULL MANY A SAGE  .  .  .  .  .    118  3 DON JUAN  8    14   4
      OF BURNING CITIES THOSE FULL MOONS OF SLAUGHTER  .  .  .  .  173  3 DON JUAN  8   122  V7
      I AM NO FLATTERER--YOU'VE SUPPED FULL OF FLATTERY  .  .  .   185  3 DON JUAN  9     5   1
      TO EXACT OF CUPID'S BILLS THE FULL AMOUNT  .  .  .  .  .      213  3 DON JUAN  9    62   7
      AND WHAT A WHIRLPOOL FULL OF DEPTH AND DANGER  .  .  .  .  .  214  3 DON JUAN  9    64   3
      EXPEDIENT OF FULL BUMPERS FOR THE EYE  .  .  .  .  .  .       216  3 DON JUAN  9    67   7
      WHICH IS FULL SOON (THOUGH LIFE IS BUT A SPAN)  .  .  .  .    222  3 DON JUAN  9    79   4
      WITH ALL KINDS OF MECHANICS AND FULL SOON  .  .  .  .  .      226  3 DON JUAN 10     2   7
      AS GOING AT FULL SPEED--NO MATTER WHERE ITS  .  .  .  .  .    260  3 DON JUAN 10    72   3
      WHERE LONDON STREETS FERMENT IN FULL ACTIVITY  .  .  .  .  .  272  3 DON JUAN 11     8   4
      FULL FLASH ALL FANCY UNTIL FAIRLY DIDDLED  .  .  .  .  .      276  3 DON JUAN 11    17   7
      THE BENCH TOO SEATS OR SUITS FULL MANY A DEBTOR  .  .  .  .  280  3 DON JUAN 11    25   5
      FULL MANY AN EAGER GENTLEMAN OFT RUES  .  .  .  .  .  .       304  3 DON JUAN 11    71   5
      AND FULL OF PROMISE AS THE SPRING OF PRIME  .  .  .  .  .    354  3 DON JUAN 12    84   4
      MORE QUIET WHEN OUR MOON'S NO MORE AT FULL  .  .  .  .  .    360  3 DON JUAN 13     4   3
      RESERVE AND PRIDE COULD MAKE HIM AND FULL SLOW  .  .  .  .   366  3 DON JUAN 13    16   2
      WHAT HOPE REMAINS  OF HOPE THE FULL POSSESSION  .  .  .  .   379  3 DON JUAN 13    45   4
      THE ANNALS OF FULL MANY A LINE UNDONE--  .  .  .  .  .  .     386  3 DON JUAN 13    60   6
      THE CORN IS CUT THE MANOR FULL OF GAME  .  .  .  .  .  .      394  3 DON JUAN 13    75   3
      FULL GROWS HIS BAG AND WONDERFUL HIS FEATS  .  .  .  .  .    394  3 DON JUAN 13    75   6
      BUT FULL OF CUNNING AS ULYSSES' WHISTLE  .  .  .  .  .  .     407  3 DON JUAN 13   105   6
      IN YOUTH I WROTE BECAUSE MY MIND WAS FULL  .  .  .  .  .      415  3 DON JUAN 14    10   7
      AND IF THEIR FULL CONTENTS I DO NOT GIVE YE  .  .  .  .  .    440  3 DON JUAN 14    68   5
      HE SIGHED--THE NEXT RESOURCE IS THE FULL MOON  .  .  .  .    506  3 DON JUAN 16    13   1
      THE FULL GROWN HEBE OF FITZ-FULKE WHOSE MIND  .  .  .  .     525  3 DON JUAN 16    49   2
      AT THE FULL BOARD AND SIT ALIKE DELIGHTED  .  .  .  .  .     534  3 DON JUAN 16    69   5
      QUITE FULL RIGHT DULL GUESTS HOT AND DISHES COLD  .  .  .    538  3 DON JUAN 16    78   6
      AND FULL OF SENTIMENTS SUBLIME AS BILLOWS  .  .  .  .  .     555  3 DON JUAN 16   110   1
      IN FULL VOLUPTUOUS BUT NOT O'ERGROWN BULK  .  .  .  .  .     561  3 DON JUAN 16   123   7
      THE WORLD IS FULL OF ORPHANS FIRSTLY THOSE  .  .  .  .  .    562  3 DON JUAN 17     1   1
FULL-BLOWN
      SHE WAS A FINE AND SOMEWHAT FULL-BLOWN BLONDE  .  .  .  .    428  3 DON JUAN 14    42   1
      WHO NOW ARE BASKING IN THEIR FULL-BLOWN PRIDE  .  .  .  .    466  3 DON JUAN 15    23   3
FULLEST
      HAVE FELT THAT MOMENT IN ITS FULLEST POWER  .  .  .  .  .    335  2 DON JUAN  3   102   3
FULL-GROWN
      A FULL-GROWN CUPID VERY MUCH ADMIRED  .  .  .  .  .  .  .    428  3 DON JUAN 14    41   2
FULLY
      WOULD FULLY SUIT A WIDOW OF CONDITION.  .  .  .  .  .  .  .    67  2 DON JUAN  1    85   3
      SO FULLY FLASHED THE PHANTOM ON HIS EYES  .  .  .  .  .  .    169  3 DON JUAN  8   115   1
      ALAS COULD SHE BUT FULLY TRULY KNOW  .  .  .  .  .  .  .      258  3 DON JUAN 10    67   1
      UNTIL THEIR ROYAL RIDDLE'S FULLY READ  .  .  .  .  .  .      287  3 DON JUAN 11    40   4
      AND YOUR TRUE FEELINGS FULLY UNDERSTOOD  .  .  .  .  .  .     451  3 DON JUAN 14    93   6
FUM
      AND WHERE IS FUM THE FOURTH OUR ROYAL BIRD  .  .  .  .  .    307  3 DON JUAN 11    78   4
FUMES
      MY BRAIN WITH BLEST FUMES TILL MY EYES GROW DIM  .  .  .    372  2 DON JUAN  4    53  V7
      ITS FUMES ARE FRANKINCENSE TO HUMAN THOUGHT  .  .  .  .  .   402  2 DON JUAN  4   106   2
FUNCTION
      BUT VERY RARELY EXECUTES ITS FUNCTION  .  .  .  .  .  .  .   271  2 DON JUAN  2   215   2
      FOR BABA'S FUNCTION STOPT SHORT AT THE DOOR  .  .  .  .  .    57  3 DON JUAN  6   103   4
FUND'S
      THE SINKING FUND S UNFATHOMABLE SEA  .  .  .  .  .  .  .     548  3 DON JUAN 16    99   6
FUNDS
      I HAVE SEEN THE FUNDS AT WAR WITH HOUSE AND LAND--  .  .  . 310  3 DON JUAN 11    85   3
```

FUNERAL
   NOT LEAVING EVEN HIS FUNERAL EXPENSES . . . . 186 3 DON JUAN 9   8   3
FURENS
   (WHO AT SIXTEEN TRANSLATED HERCULES FURENS . . . . . 294 3 DON JUAN 11   52   6
   MILD--BUT AT TIMES A SORT OF HERCULES FURENS . . . . 567 3 DON JUAN 17   11   6
FURIES
   FOR FOR A WHILE THE FURIES MADE A PAUSE . . . . . . 378 2 DON JUAN 4   62   8
FURIOUS
   ARE THEY--NOW FURIOUS AS THE SWEEPING WAVE . . . . . 164 3 DON JUAN 8   106   5
   INTO AS FURIOUS ENGLISH) WITH HER BEST LOOK . . . . 294 3 DON JUAN 11   52   7
FURIOUSLY
   WARRIORS THEREON WERE BATTLING FURIOUSLY . . . . . 461 2 DON JUAN 5   86   3
FURL'D
   HER ORANGE SILK FULL TURKISH TROWSERS FURL'D . . . . 312 2 DON JUAN 3   72   7
   HIS TURBAN FURL'D IN MANY A GRACEFUL FOLD . . . . . 315 2 DON JUAN 3   77   5
FURNACE
   OF SOME ALCHYMIC FURNACE FROM WHENCE BROKE . . . . . 266 3 DON JUAN 10   83   3
FURNISH
   THE MILLINERS WHO FURNISH DRAPERY MISSES . . . . . 293 3 DON JUAN 11   49   1
   TO FURNISH MATTER FOR THEIR MORAL GIBING . . . . . 418 3 DON JUAN 14   19   6
   TO FURNISH MATTER FOR SOME FUTURE LIVY . . . . . . 440 3 DON JUAN 14   68   3
   SUCH AS THE TIMES MAY FURNISH 'TIS A FLIGHT . . . . 467 3 DON JUAN 15   25   2
   AND NOW THAT WE MAY FURNISH WITH SOME MATTER ALL . . 497 3 DON JUAN 15   93   7
FURNISH'D
   THAT THERE WAS FUEL TO HAVE FURNISH'D TWENTY . . . . 225 2 DON JUAN 2   132   8
   THEY FURNISH'D HIM ENTIRE EXCEPT SOME STITCHES . . . 240 2 DON JUAN 2   160   7
FURNISHED
   'TWAS ON THE WHOLE A NOBLY FURNISHED HALL . . . . . 31 3 DON JUAN 6   51   6
   LONG FURNISHED WITH OLD PICTURES OF GREAT WORTH . . 508 3 DON JUAN 16   17   4
FURNISHING
   AND THAT'S THEIR MODE OF FURNISHING SUPPLY . . . . . 190 2 DON JUAN 2   65   6
FURNITURE
   WITH FURNITURE AN EXQUISITE APARTMENT . . . . 448 2 DON JUAN 5   64   7
   THE FURNITURE WAS MOST PROFUSELY RICH . . . . 449 2 DON JUAN 5   65 V4
   I SPARE YOU THEN THE FURNITURE AND PLATE . . . . . 393 3 DON JUAN 13   74   8
FURROW
   WHO FURROW SOME NEW SOIL TO SOW FOR JOYS . . . . . 228 3 DON JUAN 10   7   8
FURRY
   IN THIS GAY CLIME OF BEAR-SKINS BLACK AND FURRY-- . . 237 3 DON JUAN 10   26   3
FURS
   HE HAD A BED OF FURS AND A PELISSE . . . . 226 2 DON JUAN 2   133   1
FURTHER
   THEREFORE HIS FRAILTIES I'LL NO FURTHER SCAN . . . . 40 2 DON JUAN 1   35   3
   THAT NIGHT THE VIRGIN WAS NO FURTHER PRAY'D . . . . 63 2 DON JUAN 1   76   8
   AND LIFE YIELDS NOTHING FURTHER TO RECALL . . . . . 90 2 DON JUAN 1   127   5
   AND MAKE NO FURTHER NOISE TILL YOU DISCOVER . . . . 104 2 DON JUAN 1   153   6
   BESEECHING SHE NO FURTHER WOULD REFUSE . . . . . . 120 2 DON JUAN 1   180   7
   I HAVE NO FURTHER CLAIM ON YOUR YOUNG HEART . . . . 130 2 DON JUAN 1   192   3
   YOUR PATIENCE FURTHER THAN BY THIS SHORT SAMPLE-- . . 147 2 DON JUAN 1   221   7
   AND SEEM'D AS IF THEY HAD NO FURTHER CARE . . . . . 208 2 DON JUAN 2   98   4
   HAD FURTHER SLEEP A FURTHER PLEASURE MADE . . . . . 235 2 DON JUAN 2   149   4
   HAD FURTHER SLEEP A FURTHER PLEASURE MADE . . . . . 235 2 DON JUAN 2   149   4
   THEY HAD NO FURTHER FEELING HOPE NOR CARE-- . . . . 256 2 DON JUAN 2   189 V6
   AND HAVING O'ER ITSELF NO FURTHER POWER . . . . . . 258 2 DON JUAN 2   192   4
   ALL FURTHER IS A BLANK--I WON'T DISPARAGE . . . . . 280 2 DON JUAN 3   9 V4
   AND FURTHER ON A GROUP OF GRECIAN GIRLS . . . . . . 291 2 DON JUAN 3   30   1
   HE ASK'D NO FURTHER QUESTIONS AND PROCEEDED . . . . 300 2 DON JUAN 3   49   1
   TO SOUNDS WHICH ECHO FURTHER WEST . . . . 321 2 DON JUAN 3 L 2   5
   JUAN WOULD QUESTION FURTHER BUT SHE PRESS'D . . . . 356 2 DON JUAN 4   24   1
   TILL FURTHER ORDERS SHOULD HIS DOOM ASSIGN . . . . 371 2 DON JUAN 4   50 V4
   AND FURTHER DOWNWARD TALL AND TOWERING STILL IS . . 385 2 DON JUAN 4   76   5
   HIS SINGING I' NO FURTHER TRUST CAN PLACE IN . . . . 391 2 DON JUAN 4   86   6
   ALL THIS MUST BE RESERVED FOR FURTHER SONG . . . . 410 2 DON JUAN 4   117   1
   THE PARCAE THEN CUT SHORT THE FURTHER SPINNING . . . 414 2 DON JUAN 5   6   3
   A RANGE OR SUITE OF FURTHER CHAMBERS WHICH . . . . 449 2 DON JUAN 5   65   2
   FURTHER OLD BABA RATHER BRISKLY ENTERED . . . . . . 493 2 DON JUAN 5   143   8
   THE MOON BREAKS HALF UNVEILED EACH FURTHER CHARM . . 39 3 DON JUAN 6   66   5
   FOR ANY FURTHER ANSWER THAT HE FOUND . . . . 58 3 DON JUAN 6   105   3
   HIS OWN REMONSTRANCE FURTHER HE WELL KNEW . . . . . 63 3 DON JUAN 6   116   4
   'TIS STRANGE THAT HE SHOULD FURTHER DAMN HIS EYES . . 88 3 DON JUAN 7   45   1
   IS TO THE DEVIL NOW NO FURTHER PRIZE . . . . 88 3 DON JUAN 7   45   3
   AND THAT WHICH FURTHER AIDED THEM TO STRIVE . . . . 136 3 DON JUAN 8   47   6
   THE CITY WITHOUT BEING FURTHER HAMPER'D . . . . . . 149 3 DON JUAN 8   75   4
   WHAT FURTHER HATH BEFALLEN OR MAY BEFALL . . . . . 181 3 DON JUAN 8   139   2
   AS WELL AS FURTHER DRAIN THE WITHERED FORM . . . . 243 3 DON JUAN 10   38   4
   A FURTHER PROOF WE SHOULD NOT JUDGE IN HASTE . . . . 347 3 DON JUAN 12   69   5
   'TIS PITY THAT IT TAKES NO FURTHER HOLD . . . . . . 382 3 DON JUAN 13   51   3
   FURTHER I'D QUOTE BUT SCRIPTURE INTERVENING . . . . 403 3 DON JUAN 13   96   5
   THE FURTHER PROGRESS OF THIS SAD MISTAKE . . . . . 437 3 DON JUAN 14   61   3
   WILL GO MUCH FURTHER THAN THERE'S NEED TO MENTION . . 462 3 DON JUAN 15   14   8
   FURTHER I SHALL NOT FOLLOW THE RESEARCH . . . . . . 485 3 DON JUAN 15   67   6
   WHICH FURTHER TO EXPLAIN WOULD BE A TRUISM . . . . 506 3 DON JUAN 16   13   8
   FURTHER IT MIGHT OR IT MIGHT NOT BE SO . . . . . . 553 3 DON JUAN 16   106   5
FURY
   THEIR FURY BEING SPENT BY ITS OWN SHOCK . . . . . . 305 2 DON JUAN 3   58   6
   BUT THOU--OH SWEET FURY OF THE FIERY RILL . . . . . 372 2 DON JUAN 4   53 V2
   TOO OFTEN IN ITS FURY OVERCOMING ALL . . . . 399 2 DON JUAN 4   101   3
   TO MATCH A COMMON FURY WITH HER RAGE . . . . 490 2 DON JUAN 5   136   2
   FLUSHED WITH A PIOUS FURY TO SURVEY . . . . 262 3 DON JUAN 10   75 V7

FUSION
AT KESWICK AND THROUGH STILL CONTINUED FUSION . . . . . . 12 2 DON JUAN D 5 3
FUSS
YET NEITHER FRIGHTENED BY A FEMALE FUSS . . . . 344 3 DON JUAN 12 61 5
FUTURE
IS NOT THE CERTAIN PATH TO FUTURE PRAISE . . . . 14 2 DON JUAN D 8 8
TO MEET THE INGENUOUS YOUTH OF FUTURE AGES . . . . . . 46 2 DON JUAN 1 45 4
SHE FOR THE FUTURE OF HER STRENGTH CONVINCED . . . . . 66 2 DON JUAN 1 82 3
AND FOR THE FUTURE--(BUT I WRITE THIS REELING . . . . . 156 2 DON JUAN 1 V 8 4
I SAY--THE FUTURE IS A SERIOUS MATTER-- . . . . 156 2 DON JUAN 1 V 8 7
BETWEEN THEIR PRESENT AND THEIR FUTURE STATE . . . . . 278 2 DON JUAN 3 6 2
THE FUTURE STATES OF BOTH ARE LEFT TO FAITH . . . . . 280 2 DON JUAN 3 9 3
LEAVING THE FUTURE STATES OF LOVE AND LIFE . . . . . . 280 2 DON JUAN 3 9 V7
RESERVED FOR FUTURE RANSOM IN THE HOLD-- . . . . . . 284 2 DON JUAN 3 16 6
HER FUTURE DREAMS SHOULD ALL BE KEPT IN HAND . . . . . 47 3 DON JUAN 6 82 8
EACH MAN OF WISDOM FUTURE PAST OR PRESENT . . . . . . 69 3 DON JUAN 7 5 4
A WATCHWORD TILL THE FUTURE SHALL BE FREE . . . . . . 114 3 DON JUAN 8 5 8
HIS STUBBORN VALOUR WAS NO FUTURE SHIELD . . . . 172 3 DON JUAN 8 122 3
THAT FUTURE BRIDEGROOMS SWORE AND SIGHED AND PAID IT . . . 293 3 DON JUAN 11 49 8
BAPTIZE POSTERITY OR FUTURE CLAY-- . . . . 324 3 DON JUAN 12 18 4
DISCUSSED THE PAST AND FUTURE PARLIAMENT . . . . . . 409 3 DON JUAN 13 109 V2
TO FURNISH MATTER FOR SOME FUTURE LIVY . . . . 440 3 DON JUAN 14 68 3
ABOUT THE PRESENT PAST OR FUTURE STATE . . . . 496 3 DON JUAN 15 91 6
MORE JOY THAN FROM ALL FUTURE PRIDE OR PRAISE . . . . . 554 3 DON JUAN 16 108 5
FUTURITY
THE PLEASANT RIDDLES OF FUTURITY-- . . . . 180 3 DON JUAN 8 137 6
GADS
IN WHICH THE HEEDLESS GENTLEMAN WHO GADS . . . . . . 273 3 DON JUAN 11 11 5
GAGE
KINDLING RELIGION TILL SHE THROWS DOWN HER GAGE . . . . 530 3 DON JUAN 16 60 5
GAIETIES
HER GAIETIES NONE HAD A RIGHT TO STARE . . . . 430 3 DON JUAN 14 45 6
GAIETY
AND BORE HIM WITH SOME GAIETY AND GRACE . . . . 388 2 DON JUAN 4 81 6
GAILY
AND HENCEFORTH FOUND HIMSELF MORE GAILY CLASSED . . . . 300 3 DON JUAN 11 64 6
THE SECOND MAY BE SADLY DONE OR GAILY . . . . 465 3 DON JUAN 15 21 4
GAIN
SWORD GOWN GAIN GLORY OFFER IN EXCHANGE . . . . 131 2 DON JUAN 1 194 4
WITH THE QUICK WAVE AND GAIN ERE IT WAS DARK . . . . . 212 2 DON JUAN 2 106 3
THE CARGOES HE CONFISCATED AND GAIN . . . . 223 2 DON JUAN 2 126 5
THE LOVE OF POWER AND RAPID GAIN OF GOLD . . . . . . 303 2 DON JUAN 3 54 1
AND DWARFS AND BLACKS AND SUCH LIKE THINGS THAT GAIN . . . 310 2 DON JUAN 3 68 5
OF CARE OR GAIN THE GREEN WOODS WERE THEIR PORTIONS . . . 145 3 DON JUAN 8 66 4
FOR THEY WERE HEATED BY THE HOPE OF GAIN . . . . . . 163 3 DON JUAN 8 103 6
HE WHO HAS NOUGHT TO GAIN CAN HAVE SMALL ART HE . . . . 195 3 DON JUAN 9 26 5
TO THAT WHICH NONE WILL GAIN--OR NONE WILL KNOW . . . . 299 3 DON JUAN 11 61 2
AND GAIN AN INCH OF STAIRCASE AT A TIME . . . . . . 302 3 DON JUAN 11 68 8
HOW MUCH WOULD NOVELS GAIN BY THE EXCHANGE . . . . . . 455 3 DON JUAN 14 101 3
GAIN'D
THE GOAL IS GAIN'D WE DIE YOU KNOW--AND THEN-- . . . . 93 2 DON JUAN 1 133 8
HE GAIN'D NO POINT EXCEPT SOME SELF-REBUKES . . . . . 110 2 DON JUAN 1 161 5
JUAN THE GATE GAIN'D TURN'D THE KEY ABOUT . . . . . . 125 2 DON JUAN 1 187 7
SO THE END'S GAIN'D WHAT SIGNIFIES THE ROUTE . . . . . 478 3 DON JUAN 15 51 8
GAINED
I HAVE GAINED SCIENCE IN THE THINGS WHICH PASS . . . . 403 2 DON JUAN 4 107 V3
KNOWLEDGE AT LEAST IS GAINED FOR INSTANCE NOW . . . . 422 2 DON JUAN 5 23 6
HIS LITTLE CAPTIVE GAINED HIM SOME APPLAUSE . . . . . 182 3 DON JUAN 8 140 5
SAVE YOU AND YOURS HAVE GAINED BY WATERLOO . . . . . 184 3 DON JUAN 9 4 8
AS WHAT IS LOST IN GREEN IS GAINED IN YELLOW . . . . . 395 3 DON JUAN 13 77 8
I WISH THEY'D STATE HOW MANY THEY HAVE GAINED . . . . 505 3 DON JUAN 16 11 8
OF NICETY WHERE A FACT IS TO BE GAINED) . . . . . . 507 3 DON JUAN 16 16 4
SINCE HE HAD GAINED AT LEAST HER OBSERVATION . . . . . 545 3 DON JUAN 16 93 5
HE GAINED ESTEEM WHERE IT WAS WORTH THE MOST . . . . . 553 3 DON JUAN 16 107 4
GAINERS
FOR THEY WHO HAD BEEN GAINERS BY THE ACT . . . . . . 198 2 DON JUAN 2 79 V3
GAINING
IN GAINING ALL THAT USEFUL SORT OF KNOWLEDGE . . . . . 228 2 DON JUAN 2 136 7
OF DEAD AND DYING THOUSANDS--SOMETIMES GAINING . . . . 121 3 DON JUAN 8 20 2
GAINS
WITH GOD AND MAN'S ABHORRENCE FOR ITS GAINS . . . . . 18 2 DON JUAN D 14 8
WITH MORE THAN ONE PROFESSION GAINS BY ALL . . . . . 390 2 DON JUAN 4 84 2
AMBITION RENDS AND GAMING GAINS A LOSS . . . . 317 3 DON JUAN 12 4 2
GAINSAY
GLORY LIKE YOURS SHOULD ANY DARE GAINSAY . . . . . . 183 3 DON JUAN 9 1 7
I'LL NOT GAINSAY THE GENEROUS PUBLIC'S VOICE . . . . . 334 3 DON JUAN 12 38 7
I'LL NOT GAINSAY THEM IT IS NOT MY CUE . . . . 359 3 DON JUAN 13 3 1
'GAINST
'GAINST YOU THE QUESTION WITH POSTERITY . . . . 13 2 DON JUAN D 7 8
AND BEATING 'GAINST HIS BOSOM HAIDEE'S HEART . . . . . 257 2 DON JUAN 2 191 7
LIKE OCEAN WARRING 'GAINST A ROCKY ISLE . . . . . . 489 2 DON JUAN 5 135 6
OF CLOSING 'GAINST THE LIGHT THEIR ORBS OF VISION . . . 50 3 DON JUAN 6 88 5
THEIR VOICES 'GAINST EACH OTHER WHICH IS NATURAL . . . 50 3 DON JUAN 6 88 7
LIKE DAVID FLINGS SMOOTH PEBBLES 'GAINST A GIANT . . . 138 3 DON JUAN 8 51 2
CLASHED 'GAINST THE SCYMITAR AND BABE AND MOTHER . . . 146 3 DON JUAN 8 69 4
'GAINST REASON--REASON NE'ER WAS HAND-AND-GLOVE . . . . 219 3 DON JUAN 9 74 5
AND 'GAINST THE BODY MAKES A STRONG APPEAL . . . . . 234 3 DON JUAN 10 20 5
HE MADE 'GAINST COSSAQUE SABRES IN THE WIDE . . . . . 249 3 DON JUAN 10 51 5
TURN OUT SO WE'LL SAY NOTHING 'GAINST THE WORDING . . . 270 3 DON JUAN 11 4 3

	PAGE	VOL		CANTO	STANZA	LN
'GAINST (CONTINUED)						
OF DOORS 'GAINST DUNS AND TO AN EARLY DINNER	282	3	DON JUAN	11	29	4
AND 'GAINST THOSE FEW YOUR ANNALISTS HAVE THUNDERED	324	3	DON JUAN	12	19	6
AND MALTHUS DOES THE THING 'GAINST WHICH HE WRITES	325	3	DON JUAN	12	20	8
ARE WISER IN THEIR WARNINGS 'GAINST THE WOE	336	3	DON JUAN	12	44	7
HIS ONLY OBJECT AND 'GAINST ODDS TO FIGHT	363	3	DON JUAN	13	9	4
HIS HOST WITH BROAD ARMS 'GAINST THE THUNDER-STROKE	384	3	DON JUAN	13	56	4
AND SOLACE YOUR SLIGHT LAPSE 'GAINST BONOS MORES	432	3	DON JUAN	14	50	7
OUR FEELINGS 'GAINST THE NATURE OF THE SOIL	447	3	DON JUAN	14	86	4
'GAINST RHYME I NEVER SHOULD HAVE KNOCK'D MY BROWS	467	3	DON JUAN	15	24	5
'GAINST SUCH BELIEF THERE'S SOMETHING STRONGER STILL	504	3	DON JUAN	16	7	7
GALE						
THEIR SPELLS AND GIVE THEM TO THE PASSING GALE	72	2	DON JUAN	1	95	7
WITH LOVE AND WAR A HEAVY GALE AT SEA	135	2	DON JUAN	1	200	3
INCREASED AT NIGHT UNTIL IT BLEW A GALE	170	2	DON JUAN	2	26	2
A GALE AND IN THE FORE AND AFTER HOLD	178	2	DON JUAN	2	42	2
BEEN STOVE IN THE BEGINNING OF THE GALE	181	2	DON JUAN	2	48	2
OF THE CONTINUANCE OF THE GALE TO RUN	189	2	DON JUAN	2	62	2
MEANTIME THE CURRENT WITH A RISING GALE	209	2	DON JUAN	2	101	1
TOWARDS WHICH THE IMPATIENT WIND BLEW HALF A GALE	256	3	DON JUAN	10	64	3
THE GALE SWEEPS THROUGH ITS FRETWORK AND OFT SINGS	387	3	DON JUAN	13	62	6
GALES						
AND SWEPT AS GALES SWEEP FOAM AWAY WHOLE RANKS	134	3	DON JUAN	8	44	3
HIS BEARD HE PUFFED HIS PIPE'S AMBROSIAL GALES	172	3	DON JUAN	8	121	7
GALILEO						
GREAT GALILEO WAS DEBARRED THE SUN	565	3	DON JUAN	17	8	1
GALL						
AND SMEAR HIS PAGE WITH GALL INSTEAD OF HONEY	142	2	DON JUAN	1	210	7
WITH ONE GOOD HEARTY CURSE I VENT MY GALL	17	3	DON JUAN	6	22	3
GALLANT						
THEN THERE WERE FRENCHMEN GALLANT YOUNG AND GAY	77	3	DON JUAN	7	22	1
BUT HERE ARE MEN WHO FOUGHT IN GALLANT ACTIONS	83	3	DON JUAN	7	34	1
THE GALLANT CAVALIERS WHO FOUGHT IN VAIN	386	3	DON JUAN	13	60	7
GALLANTED						
AFTER A DECENT TIME MUST BE GALLANTED	276	2	DON JUAN	3	4	4
GALLANTLY						
AS GALLANTLY AS EVER HEROES FOUGHT	83	3	DON JUAN	7	34	2
GALLANTRY						
WHAT MEN CALL GALLANTRY AND GODS ADULTERY	56	2	DON JUAN	1	63	7
GALLANT'S						
A RIB'S A THORN IN A WED GALLANT'S SIDE	292	3	DON JUAN	11	46	6
GALLED						
AND GALLED THE RUSSIANS WITH A HEAVY FIRE	82	3	DON JUAN	7	31	4
GALLERIES						
I PASS MY EVENINGS IN LONG GALLERIES SOLELY	444	2	DON JUAN	5	58	7
THROUGH GLITTERING GALLERIES AND O'ER MARBLE FLOORS	460	2	DON JUAN	5	85	3
BACK TO THEIR CHAMBERS THOSE LONG GALLERIES	19	3	DON JUAN	6	26	5
THE GALLERIES FROM ROOM TO ROOM THEY WALKED	21	3	DON JUAN	6	30	2
HUGE HALLS LONG GALLERIES SPACIOUS CHAMBERS JOIN'D	390	3	DON JUAN	13	67	1
GALLERY						
BUT IN A MIGHTY HALL OR GALLERY BOTH IN	443	2	DON JUAN	5	57	5
HAD SATE BENEATH THE GALLERY AT NIGHTS	353	3	DON JUAN	12	82	3
INTO A GALLERY OF A SOMBRE HUE	508	3	DON JUAN	16	17	3
GALLIC						
THEIR GALLIC NAMES UPON A GLORIOUS DAY	77	3	DON JUAN	7	22	3
GALLIOTS						
UNTIL THEY REACH'D SOME GALLIOTS PLACED IN LINE	371	2	DON JUAN	4	50	6
GALLON						
WATER A TWENTY GALLON CASK OR SO	181	2	DON JUAN	2	47	3
GALLONS						
THEN THERE WAS RUM EIGHT GALLONS IN A PUNCHEON	181	2	DON JUAN	2	47	8
GALLOP						
FOR ON THE SIXTEENTH AT FULL GALLOP DREW	87	3	DON JUAN	7	43	1
GALVANISM						
AND GALVANISM HAS SET SOME CORPSES GRINNING	92	2	DON JUAN	1	130	2
HIS SOUL (LIKE GALVANISM UPON THE DEAD)	133	3	DON JUAN	8	41	6
GAME						
BUT PEOPLE'S ANCESTORS ARE HISTORY'S GAME	53	3	DON JUAN	6	94	5
BUT A MAN'S GRANDMOTHER IS DEEMED FAIR GAME	53	3	DON JUAN	6	94	V5
UNLESS THEY ARE GAME AS BULL-DOGS AND FOX-TERRIERS	78	3	DON JUAN	7	24	8
BECAUSE DEFORMED YET DIED ALL GAME AND BOTTOM	166	3	DON JUAN	8	110	7
FOR GOOD SOCIETY IS BUT A GAME	342	3	DON JUAN	12	58	3
THE ROYAL GAME OF GOOSE AS I MAY SAY	342	3	DON JUAN	12	58	4
THE CORN IS CUT THE MANOR FULL OF GAME	394	3	DON JUAN	13	75	3
PRESERVE OF BORES WHO OUGHT TO BE MADE GAME	395	3	DON JUAN	13	78	8
QUEENS BISHOPS KNIGHTS ROOKS PAWNS THE WORLD'S A GAME	400	3	DON JUAN	13	89	2
IT ALL SPRUNG FROM A HARMLESS GAME AT BILLIARDS	454	3	DON JUAN	14	100	8
OF MISCHIEF OF ALL KINDS AND KEEP THE GAME	531	3	DON JUAN	16	63	2
TO THE CONSUMERS OF FISH FOWL AND GAME	546	3	DON JUAN	16	95	3
GAMED						
AND HAVING VOTED DINED DRANK GAMED AND WHORED	306	3	DON JUAN	11	75	7
WHEN WE HAVE MADE OUR LOVE AND GAMED OUR GAMING	418	3	DON JUAN	14	18	1
GAMESTER'S						
THE GAMESTER'S COUNTER OR THE STATESMAN'S DROSS	317	3	DON JUAN	12	4	6
GAMING						
THAT FOR SO LONG OPPOSED THIS GAMING EVIL	102	2	DON JUAN	1	148	V4
AMBITION RENDS AND GAMING GAINS A LOSS	317	3	DON JUAN	12	4	2
WHEN WE HAVE MADE OUR LOVE AND GAMED OUR GAMING	418	3	DON JUAN	14	18	1
GAN						
AND ONLY FRETTED WHEN THE SCENT 'GAN FAIL	424	3	DON JUAN	14	33	4
SHE 'GAN TO PONDER HOW TO SAVE HIS SOUL	468	3	DON JUAN	15	28	8

300

GAN
    AND OPENING HER PIANO GAN TO PLAY 517   3 DON JUAN 16   38   V7
GANDER
    HAS TAKEN FOR A SWAN ROGUE SOUTHEY'S GANDER 298   3 DON JUAN 11   59   8
    TEACH THEM THAT SAUCE FOR GOOSE IS SAUCE FOR GANDER . . . 446   3 DON JUAN 14   83   3
GANG
    ONE GANG OF PEOPLE INSTANTLY WAS PUT 171   2 DON JUAN   2   28   1
GANGS
    IN GANGS OF FIFTY THIEVES COMMIT THEIR CRIMES 79   2 DON JUAN   1   108   5
GAPE
    THOUGH THEY MAY MAKE CORRUPTION GAPE OR STARE 114   3 DON JUAN   8   4   6
GAPED
    FOR WHICH THEIR MOUTHS GAPED LIKE THE CRACKS OF EARTH . . 201   2 DON JUAN   2   84   2
GAPING
    FOR GLORY GAPING O'ER A SEA OF SLAUGHTER 91   3 DON JUAN   7   50   7
    BETWEEN THE GAPING HEIR AND GNAWING GOUT 376   3 DON JUAN 13   40   8
GARB
    NO--NONE OF THESE WILL DO--AND THEN THEIR GARB 160   2 DON JUAN   2   6   3
    THE EFFEMINATE GARB--THUS AFTER A SHORT PAUSE 455   2 DON JUAN   5   76   4
    EXPLAINS THE GARB WHICH JUAN TOOK AMISS 477   2 DON JUAN   5   114   8
    IN THIS VILE GARB THE DISTAFF WEB AND WOOF 484   2 DON JUAN   5   127   3
    AND CENTAUR-NESSUS GARB OF MORTAL CLOTHING 301   3 DON JUAN 11   65   4
    NOR WEAR AS GRACEFULLY AS GAULS HER GARB 350   3 DON JUAN 12   75   3
    IN COWL AND BEADS AND DUSKY GARB APPEARED 510   3 DON JUAN 16   21   2
GARBLE
    VARIED EACH RAY--BUT ALL DESCRIPTIONS GARBLE 55   3 DON JUAN   6   98   5
GARBS
    OF COLOUR'D GARBS AS BRIGHT AS BUTTERFLIES 289   2 DON JUAN   3   27   8
GARCILASSO
    BOSCAN OR GARCILASSO--BY THE WIND 72   2 DON JUAN   1   95   2
GARDEN
    PALACE OR GARDEN PARADISE OR CAVERN 24   2 DON JUAN   1   6   7
    LIKE GARDEN GODS--AND NOT SO DECENT EITHER 46   2 DON JUAN   1   45   8
    HE STOOD LIKE ADAM LINGERING NEAR HIS GARDEN 120   2 DON JUAN   1   180   5
    HIS GARDEN TREES ALL SHADOWY AND GREEN 289   2 DON JUAN   3   27   2
    WHATEER THE GARDEN BORE OR MART DISCLOSED 476   2 DON JUAN   5   113   V4
    IN SOME EXOTIC GARDEN SOMETIMES FOUND 38   3 DON JUAN   6   65   3
    ON ON THROUGH MEADOWS MANAGED LIKE A GARDEN 262   3 DON JUAN 10   76   1
    FOR WHICH SEE SHAKSPEARE'S EVER BLOOMING GARDEN-- . . . 442   3 DON JUAN 14   75   2
GARDEN-GATE
    AND MIGHT HAVE DONE SO BY THE GARDEN-GATE 122   2 DON JUAN   1   183   6
GARDEN-KEY
    HERE IS THE GARDEN-KEY--FLY--FLY--ADIEU 121   2 DON JUAN   1   182   6
GARDENS
    A TOWN OF GARDENS WALLS AND WEALTH AMAZING 445   2 DON JUAN   5   60   2
    OR SAUNTERED THROUGH THE GARDENS PITEOUSLY 406   3 DON JUAN 13   102   3
GARLANDS
    WITH GARLANDS ROUND BY EVERY NATION HUNG 199   3 DON JUAN   9   34   V6
GARLIC
    LIKE GARLIC HOWSOEVER SHE EXTENDS 231   3 DON JUAN 10   12   5
GARMENT
    AND THEN HIS ONLY GARMENT QUITE GAVE WAY 124   2 DON JUAN   1   186   6
    A GARMENT OF A MYSTICAL SUBLIMITY 421   3 DON JUAN 14   26   7
GARMENT'S
    THY GARMENT'S HEM WITH TRANSPORT CAN IT BE 364   2 DON JUAN   4   38   6
    HIS GARMENT'S NOVELTY AND HIS BEING AWKWARD 456   2 DON JUAN   5   78   2
GARMENTS
    HE WITH THE BEARDLESS CHIN AND GARMENTS TORN 98   3 DON JUAN   7   62   6
    HIS GARMENTS ONLY A SLIGHT MURMUR MADE 510   3 DON JUAN 16   21   5
GARRISON
    HER GUARDIAN ANGEL HAD GIVEN UP HIS GARRISON 30   2 DON JUAN   1   17   4
    WHERE WIVES AT LEAST ARE SELDOM KEPT IN GARRISON 248   2 DON JUAN   2   175   8
GARTER'D
    TO SILKEN ROWS OF GAY AND GARTER'D EARLS 390   3 DON JUAN 13   68   2
GARTERS
    BLUE AS THE GARTERS WHICH SERENELY LIE 404   2 DON JUAN   4   110   6
GAS
    AS IS A THEATRE LIT UP BY GAS 444   2 DON JUAN   5   58   6
    O'ER WHOM SUWARROW SHONE LIKE A GAS LAMP 89   3 DON JUAN   7   46   3
    (FOR IN THOSE DAYS WE HAD NOT GOT TO GAS) -- 278   3 DON JUAN 11   22   8
    THEIR MOON THEIR SUN THEIR GAS THEIR FARTHING CANDLE . . 342   3 DON JUAN 12   56   8
GASHES
    FROM TWO SMART SABRE GASHES DEEP AND RED-- 370   2 DON JUAN   4   49   7
GASP
    THESE TWO FORM THE LAST GASP OF PASSION'S BREATH 280   2 DON JUAN   3   9   V3
GASPING
    GASPING ON DECK BECAUSE YOU SOAR TOO HIGH BOB 10   2 DON JUAN   D   3   7
GASPS
    GASPS AND WHATEVER ELSE THE OWNERS CHOOSE-- 110   2 DON JUAN   1   162   5
    HE HERS UNTIL THEY END IN BROKEN GASPS 259   2 DON JUAN   2   194   6
GASTRIC
    DEPENDS SO MUCH UPON THE GASTRIC JUICE 428   2 DON JUAN   5   32   8
GATE
    JUAN THE GATE GAIN'D TURN'D THE KEY ABOUT 125   2 DON JUAN   1   187   7
    OLD LAMBRO PASS'D UNSEEN A PRIVATE GATE 306   2 DON JUAN   3   61   1
    AND KNOCKING AT THE GATE 'TWAS OPENED WIDE 440   2 DON JUAN   5   51   6
    IN MOCKERY TO THE ENORMOUS GATE WHICH ROSE 462   2 DON JUAN   5   87   5
    THE GATE SO SPLENDID WAS IN ALL ITS FEATURES 462   2 DON JUAN   5   87   7
    AS IS THE HUNTER'S AT THE FIVE-BAR GATE 140   3 DON JUAN   8   55   2

GATE   (CONTINUED)
```
OPENED THE GATE CALLED KILIA TO THE GROUPS  . . . . .  148  3 DON JUAN  8   73   5
AND SEND THE SENTINEL BEFORE YOUR GATE  . . . . . . .  185  3 DON JUAN  9    6   3
THOU GATE OF LIFE AND DEATH--THOU NONDESCRIPT . . . .  210  3 DON JUAN  9   55   2
YET LEAVE THE GATE WHICH ELOQUENCE SLIPS THROUGH  . .  557  3 DON JUAN 16  115   3
```
GATHER
```
WHERE TWENTY AGES GATHER O'ER A NAME . . . . . . . .  398  2 DON JUAN  4  100   4
AND GENTLE READER WHEN YOU GATHER MEANING  . . . . .  403  3 DON JUAN 13   96   3
TO GATHER TO A SOMEWHAT LARGE AMOUNT HE  . . . . . .  535  3 DON JUAN 16   71   5
THE MOMENTS WHEN WE GATHER FROM A GLANCE .  . . . . .  554  3 DON JUAN 16  108   4
```
GATHER'D
```
ARE GATHER'D ROUND US BY THY LOOK OF REST  . . . . .  338  2 DON JUAN  3  107   7
AND GATHER'D AS THEY RUN LIKE GROWING WATER  . . . .  448  3 DON JUAN 14   88   6
```
GATHERED
```
AND RAVEN RINGLETS GATHERED IN DARK CROWD  . . . . .   39  3 DON JUAN  6   66   2
MY SIMILES ARE GATHERED IN A HEAP  . . . . . . . . .   40  3 DON JUAN  6   68   6
OF INSPIRATION GATHERED FROM DISTRESS  . . . . . . .   59  3 DON JUAN  6  107   3
STOOD AS THE UNPACKING GATHERED MORE SPECTATORS) . .  313  3 DON JUAN 11  V 29   6
HAD GATHERED A LARGE TEAR INTO ITS CORNER  . . . . .  532  3 DON JUAN 16   65   2
```
GATHERING
```
THE HUM OF ARMIES GATHERING RANK ON RANK . . . . . .  110  3 DON JUAN  7   86   2
```
GATHERS
```
ALL WHICH SELECTED FROM THE SPOIL HE GATHERS . . . .  284  2 DON JUAN  3   17   7
WELL NIGH THE SHORE WHERE ONE STOOPS DOWN AND GATHERS .  191  3 DON JUAN  9   18   7
A DREADFUL TRADE LIKE HIS WHO GATHERS SAMPHIRE . . .  299  3 DON JUAN 11   62   3
SHE GATHERS A REPERTORY OF FACTS . . . . . . . . . .  416  3 DON JUAN 14   13   2
```
GAUDY
```
A GAUDY TASTE FOR THEY ARE LITTLE SKILLED IN . . . .  436  2 DON JUAN  5   46   5
```
GAULS
```
NOR WEAR AS GRACEFULLY AS GAULS HER GARB . . . . . .  350  3 DON JUAN 12   75   3
```
GAUNT
```
AMIDST THE SKELETONS OF THAT GAUNT CREW  . . . . . .  210  2 DON JUAN  2  102   4
AND FAMINE WITH HER GAUNT AND BONY GROWTH  . . . . .   88  3 DON JUAN  7   45   6
GAUNT FAMINE NEVER SHALL APPROACH THE THRONE-- . . .  175  3 DON JUAN  8  126   7
AND WHEREFORE BLAME GAUNT WEALTH'S AUSTERITIES . . .  319  3 DON JUAN 12    7   6
GAUNT GOURMAND WITH WHOLE NATIONS FOR YOUR BOOTY . .  459  3 DON JUAN 15    9   5
```
GAUZE
```
AND THE STRIPED WHITE GAUZE BARACAN THAT BOUND HER .  311  2 DON JUAN  3   70   7
WHAT THE DEVIL SHALL I DO WITH ALL THIS GAUZE  . . .  455  2 DON JUAN  5   76   6
```
GAVE
```
AND GAVE NO OUTWARD SIGNS OF INWARD STRIFE . . . . .   35  2 DON JUAN  1   26   6
KEPT THIS HERSELF AND GAVE HER SON ANOTHER . . . . .   47  2 DON JUAN  1   46   8
AND THEN HIS ONLY GARMENT QUITE GAVE WAY . . . . . .  124  2 DON JUAN  1  186   6
A LETTER TOO SHE GAVE (HE NEVER READ IT)  . . . . .  161  2 DON JUAN  2    9   7
(HERE THE SHIP GAVE A LURCH AND HE GREW SEA-SICK)  .  166  2 DON JUAN  2   19   8
SHE GAVE A HEEL AND THEN A LURCH TO PORT . . . . . .  183  2 DON JUAN  2   51   7
AND GAVE NO SIGN OF LIFE SAVE HIS LIMBS QUIVERING  .  204  2 DON JUAN  2   90   8
THE FREQUENT FOG-BANKS GAVE THEM CAUSE TO DOUBT-- .  207  2 DON JUAN  2   96   6
TO KINDLE FIRE AND AS THE NEW FLAMES GAVE  . . . . .  216  2 DON JUAN  2  115   5
THEY ALSO GAVE A PETTICOAT APIECE  . . . . . . . . .  226  2 DON JUAN  2  133   5
I CAN'T SAY THAT SHE GAVE THEM ANY TEA . . . . . . .  233  2 DON JUAN  2  145   6
WHICH GAVE ME SOME SENSATIONS LIKE A VILLAIN . . . .  268  2 DON JUAN  2  209   8
THE PEASANTS GAVE THE POOR DUMB THING A PITTANCE . .  285  2 DON JUAN  3   18   6
HE GAVE THE DIFFERENT NATIONS SOMETHING NATIONAL . .  319  2 DON JUAN  3   85   2
YOU HAVE THE LETTERS CADMUS GAVE-- . . . . . . . . .  324  2 DON JUAN  3  L 10   5
HE LOOK'D UPON HER BUT GAVE NO REPLY . . . . . . . .  365  2 DON JUAN  4   39   4
HE GAVE THE WORD ARREST OR SLAY THE FRANK  . . . . .  369  2 DON JUAN  4   47   8
WERE TRIED IN VAIN BY THOSE WHO SERVED SHE GAVE  . .  378  2 DON JUAN  4   63   7
A FEW BRIEF QUESTIONS AND THE ANSWERS GAVE . . . . .  387  2 DON JUAN  4   79   6
GAVE LIGHT ENOUGH TO HINT THEIR FARTHER WAY  . . . .  442  2 DON JUAN  5   56   2
GAVE IT A SLIGHT KICK WITH HIS CHRISTIAN FOOT  . . .  453  2 DON JUAN  5   73   6
SHE THOUGHT HERS GAVE A DOUBLE RIGHT DIVINE  . . . .  485  2 DON JUAN  5  129   7
GAVE WHAT I HAD--A HEART--AS THE WORLD WENT I . . .    9  3 DON JUAN  6    5   6
GAVE WHAT WAS WORTH A WORLD FOR WORLDS COULD NEVER .    9  3 DON JUAN  6    5   7
AND NEXT SHE GAVE HER (I SAY HER BECAUSE . . . . . .   35  3 DON JUAN  6   58   1
AND THEN SHE GAVE JUANNA A CHASTE KISS . . . . . . .   35  3 DON JUAN  6   59   1
THE TROUBLE THAT THEY GAVE THEIR IMMORALITY  . . . .   64  3 DON JUAN  6  117   7
TO JACK HOWE'ER THIS GAVE BUT SLIGHT CONCERN . . . .  133  3 DON JUAN  8   41   5
IS SPECIAL PROVIDENCE THOUGH HOW IT GAVE . . . . . .  192  3 DON JUAN  9   19   6
NO DOUBT GAVE PAIN WHERE EACH NEW PAIR OF SHOULDERS  208  3 DON JUAN  9   52   7
WHICH GAVE HER DUKES THE GRACELESS NAME OF BIRON . .  253  3 DON JUAN 10   58   4
GAVE WAY TO'T SINCE HE COULD NOT OVERCOME IT . . . .  272  3 DON JUAN 11    9   4
NOT TO BE OVERLOOKED--AND GAVE SUCH CREDIT . . . . .  293  3 DON JUAN 11   49   7
THE WORLD GAVE GROUND BEFORE HER BRIGHT ARRAY  . . .  364  3 DON JUAN 13   11   5
FOR WHEN HIS PIOUS CONSORT GAVE HIM STONES . . . . .  410  3 DON JUAN 14    1   7
GAVE HER A RIGHT TO HAVE MATERNAL FEARS  . . . . . .  432  3 DON JUAN 14   52   5
I RECK NOT IF AN ACORN GAVE IT BIRTH . . . . . . . .  436  3 DON JUAN 14   59   4
NOR IF UNTO THE WORLD I EVER GAVE IT . . . . . . . .  444  3 DON JUAN 14   80   3
GAVE HIM TO LAY THE DEVIL WHO LOOKS O'ER LINCOLN . .  540  3 DON JUAN 16   82   7
```
GAY
```
THAT THIS IS NOT A MORAL TALE THOUGH GAY . . . . . .  140  2 DON JUAN  1  207   6
SEEM AT THE SAME TIME MYSTICAL AND GAY . . . . . . .  220  2 DON JUAN  2  120   8
THOSE GAY RECESSES--MANY A PRECIOUS STONE  . . . . .   54  3 DON JUAN  6   97   5
THEN THERE WERE FRENCHMEN GALLANT YOUNG AND GAY  . .   77  3 DON JUAN  7   22   1
THE GREAT AND GAY KOUTOUSOW MIGHT HAVE LAIN  . . . .  148  3 DON JUAN  8   72   7
SMOOTHED FOR A MONARCH'S SEAT OF HONOUR GAY  . . . .  235  3 DON JUAN 10   21   6
IN THIS GAY CLIME OF BEAR-SKINS BLACK AND FURRY-- .  237  3 DON JUAN 10   26   3
TO-MORROW SEES ANOTHER RACE AS GAY . . . . . . . . .  310  3 DON JUAN 11   86   2
THAT LADIES IN THEIR YOUTH A LITTLE GAY  . . . . . .  336  3 DON JUAN 12   44   4
```

GAY   (CONTINUED)

	PAGE	VOL	CANTO	STANZA	LN
SWEET ADELINE AMIDST THE GAY WORLD'S HUM	365	3 DON JUAN 13		13	4
OUR GAY RUSS SPANIARD WAS ORDAINED TO SHINE	383	3 DON JUAN 13		53	4
TO SILKEN ROWS OF GAY AND GARTER'D EARLS	390	3 DON JUAN 13		68	2
METHINKS GAY PUNCH HATH SOMETHING OF THE SAME	400	3 DON JUAN 13		89	4
NOW GRAVE NOW GAY BUT NEVER DULL OR PERT	426	3 DON JUAN 14		37	5
OF AN OLD FAMILY SOME GAY SIR JOHN	470	3 DON JUAN 15		33	3
TO HIS GAY NOTHINGS NOTHING WAS REPLIED	490	3 DON JUAN 15		78	1
HIS TACT TOO TEMPER'D HIM FROM GRAVE TO GAY	492	3 DON JUAN 15		82	5
THE FOAM WHICH MADE ITS VIRGIN BUMPER GAY	504	3 DON JUAN 16		9	3
NOT NIGH THE GAY SALOON OF LADIES GENT	533	3 DON JUAN 16		66	2
IMBIBED THE GAY BON MOT OR HAPPY HOAX	540	3 DON JUAN 16		83	5
IN GAY REMARK ON WHAT HE HAD HEARD OR SEEN	552	3 DON JUAN 16		105	5

GAZE

	PAGE	VOL	CANTO	STANZA	LN
SOMETIMES HE TURN'D TO GAZE UPON HIS BOOK	72	2 DON JUAN 1		95	1
PILAUS AND MEATS OF ALL SORTS MET THE GAZE	291	2 DON JUAN 3		31	3
TO GAZE ONCE MORE ON THE COMMANDING CLAY	431	2 DON JUAN 5		37	3
WHICH MEET THE GAZE WHAT'ER IT MAY REGARD--	118	3 DON JUAN 8		13	4
AS WE NOW GAZE UPON THE MAMMOTH'S BONES	180	3 DON JUAN 8		137	3
HER MAJESTY WHO LIKED TO GAZE ON YOUTH	213	3 DON JUAN 9		61	6
THE WORLD TO GAZE UPON THOSE NORTHERN LIGHTS	353	3 DON JUAN 12		82	5
AND GAZE WHERE'ER THE PALACE OR THE HOVEL IS	361	3 DON JUAN 13		7	7
A DULL AND DESOLATE APPENDAGE GAZE	373	3 DON JUAN 13		33	2
THE PRAISE OF PERSECUTION GAZE AGAIN	373	3 DON JUAN 13		33	5
WE GAZE UPON A GIANT FOR HIS STATURE	390	3 DON JUAN 13		67	7
THE GULF OF ROCK YAWNS--YOU CAN'T GAZE A MINUTE . . .	412	3 DON JUAN 14		5	7
FEEL SOME ABSTRACTION WHEN THEY GAZE ON HER	506	3 DON JUAN 16		14	3
TO GAZE INSTEAD OF PAVEMENT UPON GRASS	539	3 DON JUAN 16		81	3

GAZED

	PAGE	VOL	CANTO	STANZA	LN
GAZED DIM AND DESOLATE--TWELVE DAYS HAD FEAR	182	2 DON JUAN 2		49	V7
FROM HIS PALE LIPS AND EVER ON HIM GAZED	203	2 DON JUAN 2		89	3
AND AS HE GAZED HIS DIZZY BRAIN SPUN FAST	214	2 DON JUAN 2		110	1
HE WOKE AND GAZED AND WOULD HAVE SLEPT AGAIN	235	2 DON JUAN 2		149	1
AND JUAN GAZED AS ONE WHO IS AWOKE	237	2 DON JUAN 2		152	1
A SIGHT ON WHICH HE HAD NOT LATELY GAZED	239	2 DON JUAN 2		157	3
THE FREEST SHE THAT EVER GAZED ON GLASS	248	2 DON JUAN 2		175	6
THEY GAZED UPON THE GLITTERING SEA BELOW	253	2 DON JUAN 2		185	3
THEY GAZED UPON THE SUNSET 'TIS AN HOUR	354	2 DON JUAN 4		20	1
EVEN AS THEY GAZED A SUDDEN TREMOR CAME	355	2 DON JUAN 4		21	2
JUAN GAZED ON HER AS TO ASK HIS FATE--	355	2 DON JUAN 4		22	5
JUAN AND HAIDEE GAZED UPON EACH OTHER	357	2 DON JUAN 4		26	1
HER GLANCE NOR GRASP FOR STILL SHE GAZED AND GRASP'D . .	361	2 DON JUAN 4		32	7
HE GAZED ON HER AND SHE ON HIM 'TWAS STRANGE	367	2 DON JUAN 4		44	1
SHE GAZED BUT NONE SHE EVER COULD RETRACE	381	2 DON JUAN 4		68	4
I GAZED UPON HIM FOR I KNEW HIM WELL	430	2 DON JUAN 5		35	1
SO AS I GAZED ON HIM I THOUGHT OR SAID--	430	2 DON JUAN 5		35	8
FROM ME I GAZED (AS OFT I HAVE GAZED THE SAME)	431	2 DON JUAN 5		38	6
FROM ME I GAZED (AS OFT I HAVE GAZED THE SAME)	431	2 DON JUAN 5		38	6
AND GAZED AROUND THEM TO THE LEFT AND RIGHT	439	2 DON JUAN 5		50	7
HIS HIGHNESS GAZED UPON GULBEYAZ' CHARMS	12	3 DON JUAN 6		13	6
WHO GAZED UPON HER CHEEK'S TRANSCENDANT HUE	27	3 DON JUAN 6		42	3
AND GAZED ON JUAN WITH A WILD SURPRISE	159	3 DON JUAN 8		95	8
BEFORE THEY BUTCHER LITTLE LEILA GAZED	261	3 DON JUAN 10		74	7
CRACKED SHIVERED VANISHED SCARCELY GAZED ON ERE	306	3 DON JUAN 11		76	5
SHE GAZED UPON A WORLD SHE SCARCELY KNEW	476	3 DON JUAN 15		47	1
AND JUAN GAZED UPON IT WITH A STARE	510	3 DON JUAN 16		23	3

GAZELLE

	PAGE	VOL	CANTO	STANZA	LN
NEW BROKE A CAMELOPARD A GAZELLE	160	2 DON JUAN 2		6	2
THROWN BACK UPON ITS HAUNCHES--A GAZELLE	160	2 DON JUAN 2		6	V2

GAZELLE-EYED

	PAGE	VOL	CANTO	STANZA	LN
OF HIS GAZELLE-EYED DAUGHTERS SHE WAS ONE	264	2 DON JUAN 2		202	4

GAZELLES

	PAGE	VOL	CANTO	STANZA	LN
OVER THE FLOORS WERE SPREAD GAZELLES AND CATS	310	2 DON JUAN 3		68	4

GAZES

	PAGE	VOL	CANTO	STANZA	LN
AN INFANT WHEN IT GAZES ON A LIGHT	261	2 DON JUAN 2		196	1

GAZETTE

	PAGE	VOL	CANTO	STANZA	LN
PELL-MELL AND WITH A WHOLE GAZETTE OF SLAUGHTER . . .	82	3 DON JUAN 7		31	8
YOU CAN'T REPEAT NINE NAMES FROM EACH GAZETTE . . .	83	3 DON JUAN 7		34	8
THAN IN THY GREEK GAZETTE OF THAT CAMPAIGN . . .	106	3 DON JUAN 7		80	4
TO THE GAZETTE--WHICH DOUBTLESS FAIRLY DEALT . . .	120	3 DON JUAN 8		18	2
THINK HOW THE JOYS OF READING A GAZETTE	174	3 DON JUAN 8		125	1
THE WHOLE GAZETTE OF THOUSANDS WHOM HE SLEW	212	3 DON JUAN 9		60	4
THE VACANCIES ARE FILLED UP--SEE GAZETTE	383	3 DON JUAN 13		54	8
THAT LIVE GAZETTE HAD SCATTER'D TO DISFIGURE	460	3 DON JUAN 15		11	2

GAZETTES

	PAGE	VOL	CANTO	STANZA	LN
TILL AFTER CLOYING THE GAZETTES WITH CANT	21	2 DON JUAN 1		1	3
INTO GAZETTES BUT FAME (CAPRICIOUS STRUMPET)	74	3 DON JUAN 7		15	7
TRUTHS THAT YOU WILL NOT READ IN THE GAZETTES	187	3 DON JUAN 9		10	3

GAZING

	PAGE	VOL	CANTO	STANZA	LN
THEY OPEN'D WINDOWS GAZING IF THE GROUND	100	2 DON JUAN 1		144	3
WHEN GAZING ON THEM MYSTIFIED BY DISTANCE	163	2 DON JUAN 2		12	7
DON JUAN STOOD AND GAZING FROM THE STERN	164	2 DON JUAN 2		14	1
BUT GAZING ON EACH GLOWING MAID	326	2 DON JUAN 3	L 15	4
AND GAZING ON THE DEAD SHE THOUGHT HIS FACE	363	2 DON JUAN 4		35	1
FORLORN AND GAZING ON THE DEEP BLUE SURGE	387	2 DON JUAN 4		79	3
IN GAZING ON THAT VENERABLE ARCH	386	3 DON JUAN 13		59	8
AND HE STOOD GAZING OUT ON THE CASCADE	507	3 DON JUAN 16		15	7

GEAR

	PAGE	VOL	CANTO	STANZA	LN
WITH SUCH SMALL GEAR TO GIVE MYSELF CONCERN	300	3 DON JUAN 11		63	3

		PAGE	VOL	CANTO	STANZA	LN

GEM
JOY SPARKLING IN THEIR DARK EYES LIKE A GEM — 351 2 DON JUAN 4 13 6
OF EYES WHICH PUT OUT EACH SURROUNDING GEM — 466 2 DON JUAN 5 96 4
ARRAYED HERSELF WITH MANTLE GEM AND VEIL — 49 3 DON JUAN 6 87 4
TO SEE THE SULTAN RICH IN MANY A GEM — 104 3 DON JUAN 7 74 4
HAS FEELINGS PURE AND POLISHED AS A GEM— — 157 3 DON JUAN 8 92 4
WAS SUCH AS LIES BETWEEN A FLOWER AND GEM — 481 3 DON JUAN 15 58 8

GEMS
BUT THROUGH THEM GOLD AND GEMS PROFUSELY SHONE — 220 2 DON JUAN 2 121 4
GEMS GOLD AND SILVER FORM'D THE SERVICE MOSTLY — 306 2 DON JUAN 3 61 7
AND GEMS--AND GOLD--AND SILVER--GLITTERED MOSTLY — 306 2 DON JUAN 3 61 V7
HER HAIR WAS STARR'D WITH GEMS HER VEIL'S FINE FOLD — 312 2 DON JUAN 3 72 4
THE SPARKLING GEMS BENEATH YOU MIGHT BEHOLD — 315 2 DON JUAN 3 77 3
AND THIS ADDITION WITH SUCH GEMS WAS BOUND — 457 2 DON JUAN 5 79 6
A DAZZLING MASS OF GEMS AND GOLD AND GLITTER — 465 2 DON JUAN 5 93 7
OF GEMS AND PLUMES AND PEARLS AND SILKS TO WHERE — 303 3 DON JUAN 11 70 4
THERE IS A SAMENESS IN ITS GEMS AND ERMINE — 416 3 DON JUAN 14 15 6
SPANGLED WITH GEMS--THE MONK MADE HIS BLOOD CURDLE — 556 3 DON JUAN 16 113 8

GENDER
THE GENDER STILL WAS EPICENE AT LEAST — 35 3 DON JUAN 6 58 2

GENE
BUT NONE WERE GENE THE GREAT HOUR OF UNION — 406 3 DON JUAN 13 103 1

GENERAL
IS IT FOR THIS THAT GENERAL COUNT O'REILLY — 102 2 DON JUAN 1 148 7
BY GENERAL SUBSCRIPTION OF THE LADIES — 199 2 DON JUAN 2 81 8
(IN GENERAL HE SURPRISED MEN WITH THE SWORD) — 294 2 DON JUAN 3 37 3
THE LOVE OF OFFSPRING'S NATURE'S GENERAL LAW — 488 2 DON JUAN 5 133 1
THERE WAS A GENERAL WHISPER TOSS AND WRIGGLE — 501 2 DON JUAN 5 156 7
AND ALL ABASHED TOO AT THE GENERAL STARE — 28 3 DON JUAN 6 45 6
THE ODA IN A GENERAL COMMOTION — 42 3 DON JUAN 6 71 2
THE MOMENT OF THE GENERAL CONSTERNATION — 78 3 DON JUAN 7 24 2
A GENERAL COUNCIL IN WHICH UNANIMITY — 92 3 DON JUAN 7 51 2
WHY GENERAL IF HE HATH NO GREATER FAULT — 98 3 DON JUAN 7 62 7
ALSO THE GENERAL MARKOW BRIGADIER — 117 3 DON JUAN 8 11 1
THE GENERAL MARKOW WHO COULD THUS EVINCE — 117 3 DON JUAN 8 11 6
BUT HERE I LEAVE THE GENERAL CONCERN — 120 3 DON JUAN 8 17 1
UNDER THE ORDERS OF THE GENERAL LASCY — 130 3 DON JUAN 8 34 3
THE GENERAL LASCY WHO HAD BEEN HARD PREST — 140 3 DON JUAN 8 56 1
THE GENERAL WHO HELD HIM IN COMMAND — 141 3 DON JUAN 8 57 4
AS SOON AS THUNDER 'MIDST THE GENERAL NOISE — 142 3 DON JUAN 8 59 7
THE GENERAL BOON BACK-WOODSMAN OF KENTUCKY — 143 3 DON JUAN 8 61 4
('MONGST OTHER DEATHS THE GENERAL RIBAUPIERRE'S — 147 3 DON JUAN 8 71 6
A JUNCTION OF THE GENERAL MEKNOP'S MEN — 151 3 DON JUAN 8 79 1
(WITHOUT THE GENERAL WHO HAD FALLEN SOME TIME — 151 3 DON JUAN 8 79 2
A GENERAL OBJECT OF ATTENTION MADE — 223 3 DON JUAN 9 83 2
SUCH IS THE SHORTEST WAY TO GENERAL CURSES — 264 3 DON JUAN 10 79 4
AND MIEN EXCITED GENERAL ADMIRATION-- — 287 3 DON JUAN 11 39 2
ON GENERAL TOPICS POEMS MUST CONFINE — 290 3 DON JUAN 11 44 7
ABOUT SUCH GENERAL MATTERS--BUT PARTICULAR — 290 3 DON JUAN 11 44 V7
(A THING WITH POETRY IN GENERAL HARD) — 322 3 DON JUAN 12 13 4
AND NOW THERE WAS A GENERAL SENSATION — 329 3 DON JUAN 12 28 7
AND THEN THERE WAS A GENERAL COMPETITION — 330 3 DON JUAN 12 30 2
I DON'T MEAN THIS AS GENERAL BUT PARTICULAR — 343 3 DON JUAN 12 59 1
AND GENERAL FIREFACE FAMOUS IN THE FIELD — 399 3 DON JUAN 13 88 2
'TIS SAID--INDEED A GENERAL COMPLAINT-- — 418 3 DON JUAN 14 19 1
BUT ON THE WHOLE TO GENERAL ADMIRATION — 425 3 DON JUAN 14 34 1
AND REND'RING GENERAL THAT WHICH IS ESPECIAL — 467 3 DON JUAN 15 25 8
THAN MATCH-MAKING IN GENERAL 'TIS NO SIN — 470 3 DON JUAN 15 31 6
BOTH BUSY (AS A GENERAL IN HIS TENT — 533 3 DON JUAN 16 66 6
(THUS WE TRANSLATE A GENERAL INVITATION) — 534 3 DON JUAN 16 69 2
AND JUAN TOO IN GENERAL BEHIND NONE — 552 3 DON JUAN 16 105 4

GENERALITIES
I THEREFORE DEAL IN GENERALITIES — 444 3 DON JUAN 14 80 8

GENERALLY
HAS GENERALLY NO GREAT CROP TO SPARE IT HE — 14 2 DON JUAN D 9 3
FOR MUTES ARE GENERALLY USED FOR THAT — 463 2 DON JUAN 5 89 8
ARE GENERALLY PROSPEROUS IN REIGNING — 247 3 DON JUAN 10 47 2
THEY GENERALLY HAVE SOME ONLY SON — 470 3 DON JUAN 15 33 1
BOWS HAVE THEY GENERALLY WITH TWO STRINGS — 501 3 DON JUAN 16 1 5

GENERAL'S
AS IN A GENERAL'S LETTER WHEN WELL WHACKED — 107 3 DON JUAN 7 81 V5

GENERALS
SOULS OF IMMORTAL GENERALS PHOEBUS WATCHES — 107 3 DON JUAN 7 81 7
TO KILL AND GENERALS TURN IT INTO JEST — 212 3 DON JUAN 9 60 8
GENERALS SOME ALL IN ARMOUR OF THE OLD — 391 3 DON JUAN 13 70 1

GENERATION
IMPROVING STILL THROUGH EVERY GENERATION — 54 2 DON JUAN 1 59 2
SPURR'D HER TO TEACH ANOTHER GENERATION — 162 2 DON JUAN 2 10 8
HIS STATION GENERATION EVEN HIS NATION — 327 2 DON JUAN 3 89 2
STEEL BARONS MOLTEN THE NEXT GENERATION — 390 3 DON JUAN 13 68 1
THE NESTORS OF THE SPORTING GENERATION — 425 3 DON JUAN 14 34 5
WHO FAVOUR MALGRE MALTHUS GENERATION-- — 472 3 DON JUAN 15 37 2

GENERATIONS
THE VERY GENERATIONS OF THE DEAD — 399 2 DON JUAN 4 102 1
ALL GENERATIONS I SHOULD LIKE TO KNOW — 53 3 DON JUAN 6 94 7

GENEROUS
PERVADED HIM--ALTHOUGH A GENEROUS CREATURE — 138 3 DON JUAN 8 52 7
IF YOU HAVE ACTED ONCE A GENEROUS PART — 184 3 DON JUAN 9 4 5
CATHERINE WAS GENEROUS--ALL SUCH LADIES ARE — 222 3 DON JUAN 9 80 1

GENEROUS   (CONTINUED)
    SO FIRST THERE WAS A GENEROUS EMULATION 330   3 DON JUAN 12   30   1
    I'LL NOT GAINSAY THE GENEROUS PUBLIC'S VOICE 334   3 DON JUAN 12   38   7
    OR GENEROUS DRAFT CONCEDED AS A GIFT 379   3 DON JUAN 13   45   5
GENEROUSLY
    WHICH MORTALS GENEROUSLY WOULD DIVIDE 367   3 DON JUAN 13   19   7
GENETRIX
    STILL WE RESPECT THEE ALMA VENUS GENETRIX 554   3 DON JUAN 16   109   8
GENEVOISES
    WITH SAUCES GENEVOISES AND HAUNCH OF VENISON 484   3 DON JUAN 15   65   2
GENIAL
    AND NEARER AS THEY CAME A GENIAL SAVOUR 437   2 DON JUAN 5   47   1
    MOVES--FEMALE HEARTS ARE SUCH A GENIAL SOIL 480   2 DON JUAN 5   120   3
    OUR YOUNG LIEUTENANT TO THE GENIAL CARE 224   2 DON JUAN 9   84   2
    A LITTLE GENIAL SPRINKLING OF HYPOCRISY 346   3 DON JUAN 12   66   2
    A GENTLE GENIAL COURTESY OF MIND 372   3 DON JUAN 13   32   6
    PROFESSORS OF THAT GENIAL ART AND PATRONS 472   3 DON JUAN 15   37   3
    WITH NATURE'S GENIAL GENITORS SO THAT 564   3 DON JUAN 17   4   3
GENITORS
    WITH NATURE'S GENIAL GENITORS SO THAT 564   3 DON JUAN 17   4   3
GENIUS
    (SIGNS OF TRUE GENIUS AND OF EMPTY POCKETS) 91   2 DON JUAN 1   129   2
    A GENIUS WHO HAS DRUNK HIMSELF TO DEATH 309   2 DON JUAN 3   66   2
    BUT HE HAD GENIUS--WHEN A TURNCOAT HAS IT -. 317   2 DON JUAN 3   81   1
    BUT HE HAD GENIUS--MANY A SCOUNDREL HAS IT-- 317   2 DON JUAN 3   81   V1
    OF THOSE WHO HAD MOST GENIUS FOR THIS SORT 26   3 DON JUAN 6   40   1
    WHILE OTHERS HAVE A GENIUS TURNED FOR FITS 340   3 DON JUAN 12   52   8
    THAN FINDING THUS THEIR GENIUS STAND REBUKED 479   3 DON JUAN 15   53   6
GENSERIC'S
    SINCE RODERIC'S GOTH'S OR OLDER GENSERIC'S VANDALS . . . 129   2 DON JUAN 1   190   V4
GENT
    GENT READER NOTHING A MERE SPECULATION 413   3 DON JUAN 14   7   2
    NOT NIGH THE GAY SALOON OF LADIES GENT 533   3 DON JUAN 16   66   2
GENTEELLY
    REQUEST THAT THEY MAY BOTH BE USED GENTEELLY 103   3 DON JUAN 7   72   8
GENTLE
    AND TREMULOUSLY GENTLE HER SMALL HAND 60   2 DON JUAN 1   71   2
    COULD NOT ESCAPE THE GENTLE JULIA'S EYES 73   2 DON JUAN 1   97   2
    THE TEARS WERE GUSHING FROM HER GENTLE EYES 84   2 DON JUAN 1   117   3
    YET IF MY GENTLE MUSE HE PLEASE TO ROAST 142   2 DON JUAN 1   210   4
    BUT FOR THE PRESENT GENTLE READER AND 147   2 DON JUAN 1   221   1
    ITS GENTLE TOUCH AND TREMBLING CARE A SIGH 215   2 DON JUAN 2   113   7
    THE GENTLE GIRL AND HER ATTENDANT--ONE 216   2 DON JUAN 2   115   2
    SO GENTLE STIRLESS HELPLESS AND UNMOVED 261   2 DON JUAN 2   197   3
    A PLEASURE IN THE GENTLE STREAM THAT FLOW'D 304   2 DON JUAN 3   56   6
    WITH HIS RUDE SCYTHE SUCH GENTLE BOSOMS HE 348   2 DON JUAN 4   8   4
    THE GENTLE PRESSURE AND THE THRILLING TOUCH 351   2 DON JUAN 4   14   1
    A GENTLE SLUMBER BUT IT WAS NOT DEEP 359   2 DON JUAN 4   29   3
    GENTLE BUT WITHOUT MEMORY SHE LAY 379   2 DON JUAN 4   64   6
    WITH GENTLE FORCE HER WHITE ARMS HE UNWOUND 484   2 DON JUAN 5   126   3
    OF GENTLE FEMININE DELIGHT AND SHOWN 13   3 DON JUAN 6   15   2
    THAN IS THE CUSTOM OF THE GENTLE SEX 24   3 DON JUAN 6   37   6
    KATINKA TOO AND WITH A GENTLE BOW 31   3 DON JUAN 6   50   3
    AND THEREFORE WAS SHE KIND AND GENTLE AS 33   3 DON JUAN 6   55   1
    TO QUIT HER GENTLE PARTNER AND TO DWELL 48   3 DON JUAN 6   84   6
    BECAUSE ALL GENTLE READERS HAVE THE GIFT 50   3 DON JUAN 6   88   4
    WHILE GENTLE WRITERS ALSO LOVE TO LIFT 50   3 DON JUAN 6   88   6
    TOO GENTLE READER AND MOST SHOCKING SOUNDS 112   3 DON JUAN 8   1   3
    OH GENTLE LADIES SHOULD YOU SEEK TO KNOW 207   3 DON JUAN 9   49   1
    OF GENTLE DAMES AMONG WHOSE RECREATIONS 223   3 DON JUAN 9   82   6
    THE GENTLE JUAN FLOURISHED THOUGH AT TIMES 243   3 DON JUAN 10   37   1
    AND WITH THAT GENTLE SERIOUS CHARACTER 250   3 DON JUAN 10   52   2
    THERE'S GLORY AGAIN FOR YOU GENTLE READER ALL . . . 261   3 DON JUAN 10   73   5
    MY GENTLE COUNTRYMEN WE WILL RENEW 266   3 DON JUAN 10   84   3
    THAT'S RATHER FINE THE GENTLE SOUND OF THAMIS-- . . 279   3 DON JUAN 11   24   1
    THEN THERE'S MY GENTLE EUPHUES WHO THEY SAY 298   3 DON JUAN 11   59   1
    YE GENTLE READERS AND UNGENTLE WRITERS 325   3 DON JUAN 12   20   2
    AND NOW TO BUSINESS OH MY GENTLE JUAN 326   3 DON JUAN 12   23   1
    HIGH IN HIGH CIRCLES GENTLE IN HER OWN 338   3 DON JUAN 12   48   1
    SO GENTLE CHARMING CHARITABLE CHASTE-- 346   3 DON JUAN 12   66   7
    HE LIKED THE GENTLE SPANIARD FOR HIS GRAVITY 368   3 DON JUAN 13   22   1
    A GENTLE GENIAL COURTESY OF MIND 372   3 DON JUAN 13   32   6
    AND GENTLE READER WHEN YOU GATHER MEANING 403   3 DON JUAN 13   96   3
    BUT ALL WAS GENTLE AND ARISTOCRATIC 409   3 DON JUAN 13   110   1
    HIS INEXPERIENCE MOVED HER GENTLE RUTH 432   3 DON JUAN 14   51   7
    ANOTHER GENTLE COMMON-PLACE OR TWO 440   3 DON JUAN 14   69   2
    OUR GENTLE ADELINE HAD ONE DEFECT-- 446   3 DON JUAN 14   85   1
    AS FAR AS HER OWN GENTLE HEART ALLOW'D 476   3 DON JUAN 15   46   2
    FEW FEMALES WITHOUT SOME SUCH GENTLE LEAVEN 525   3 DON JUAN 16   49   7
GENTLEMAN
    OR GENTLEMAN OF SEVENTY YEARS COMPLETE 89   2 DON JUAN 1   125   3
    BY ALL MEANS LET THE GENTLEMAN PROCEED 104   2 DON JUAN 1   152   2
    THIS PRETTY GENTLEMAN WITHIN THE CLOSET 114   2 DON JUAN 1   170   8
    THE GOOD OLD GENTLEMAN WAS QUITE AGHAST 175   2 DON JUAN 2   37   1
    WAS URGENT THAT THE GENTLEMAN WHOSE FATE 240   2 DON JUMN 2   159   3
    THE GOOD OLD GENTLEMAN HAD BEEN DETAIN'D 283   2 DON JUAN 3   15   1
    AN HONEST GENTLEMAN AT HIS RETURN 287   2 DON JUAN 3   23   1
    WITH SUCH TRUE BREEDING OF A GENTLEMAN 296   2 DON JUAN 3   41   1
    A GENTLEMAN SO RICH IN THE WORLD'S GOODS 371   2 DON JUAN 4   51   3

305

	PAGE	VOL		CANTO	STANZA	LN

GENTLEMAN   (CONTINUED)

REPLIED OLD GENTLEMAN I'M NOT A LADY	453	2 DON JUAN	5	73	8
THE GENTLEMAN TO KISS THE LADY'S HANDS	472	2 DON JUAN	5	105	8
NATURE HAD WRITTEN GENTLEMAN HE SAID	223	3 DON JUAN	9	83	6
IN WHICH THE HEEDLESS GENTLEMAN WHO GADS	273	3 DON JUAN	11	11	5
SUCH AS NO GENTLEMAN CAN QUITE REFUSE	293	3 DON JUAN	11	48	6
FULL MANY AN EAGER GENTLEMAN OFT RUES	304	3 DON JUAN	11	71	5
SOME GENTLEMAN WHO FIGHTS OR WRITES OR DRIVES	333	3 DON JUAN	12	36	6
A DRUNKEN GENTLEMAN OF FORTY'S SURE	333	3 DON JUAN	12	37	V5
A FINISHED GENTLEMAN FROM TOP TO TOE	354	3 DON JUAN	12	84	8
THAT GENTLEMAN OF LORDS AND GENTLEMEN	380	3 DON JUAN	13	47	2
OF HIS DRILL'D NYMPHS BUT LIKE A GENTLEMAN	427	3 DON JUAN	14	38	8
WILL PIQUE A GENTLEMAN FOR HIS OWN CREDIT	491	3 DON JUAN	15	79	5

GENTLEMANLY

| A GENTLEMANLY DISTANCE NOT TOO NEAR | 366 | 2 DON JUAN | 4 | 41 | 5 |

GENTLEMAN'S

| BEYOND A SINGLE GENTLEMAN'S BELIEF | 301 | 2 DON JUAN | 3 | 51 | 8 |
| FOR A YOUNG GENTLEMAN'S FIT EDUCATION | 432 | 3 DON JUAN | 14 | 52 | 6 |

GENTLEMEN

YOU--GENTLEMEN BY DINT OF LONG SECLUSION	12	2 DON JUAN	D	5	1
THROUGH THE MOST GOTHIC GENTLEMEN OF SPAIN	26	2 DON JUAN	1	9	4
OR GENTLEMEN WHO THOUGH WELL-BORN AND BRED	33	2 DON JUAN	1	22	3
FOR INSTANCE--GENTLEMEN WHOSE LADIES TAKE	74	2 DON JUAN	1	98	2
I SAY WHEN THESE SAME GENTLEMEN ARE JEALOUS	74	2 DON JUAN	1	98	7
AND OH YE GENTLEMEN WHO HAVE ALREADY	288	2 DON JUAN	3	25	1
THE ONLY GENTLEMEN SEEM I AND YOU	417	2 DON JUAN	5	13	5
WILL PLEASE TO ACCOMPANY THOSE GENTLEMEN	458	2 DON JUAN	5	81	2
TO GENTLEMEN IN ANY SUCH LIKE CASE	482	2 DON JUAN	5	123	2
FOR GENTLEMEN MUST SOMETIMES RISK THEIR SKIN	10	3 DON JUAN	6	7	3
TO GENTLEMEN ENGAGED IN THE ASSAULT	119	3 DON JUAN	8	16	7
THE GENTLEMEN THAT WERE THE FIRST TO SHOW	135	3 DON JUAN	8	45	6
GENTLEMEN FARMERS--A RACE WORN OUT QUITE	198	3 DON JUAN	9	32	3
AND GENTLEMEN ARE IN A PITEOUS PLIGHT	198	3 DON JUAN	9	32	5
GIGANTIC GENTLEMEN YET HAD A TOUCH	209	3 DON JUAN	9	54	4
A ROW OF GENTLEMEN ALONG THE STREETS	281	3 DON JUAN	11	27	1
I'VE SEEN THE COUNTRY GENTLEMEN TURN SQUEAKERS--	310	3 DON JUAN	11	85	4
FOR GENTLEMEN WHOSE PASSIONS MAY BOIL OER	313	3 DON JUAN	11	V 29	5
MAY BE THE BAITS FOR GENTLEMEN OR LORDS	340	3 DON JUAN	12	53	3
THUS GENTLEMEN MAY RUN UPON A SHOAL	376	3 DON JUAN	13	39	6
THUS GENTLEMEN MAY SOMETIMES PLAY THE FOOL	376	3 DON JUAN	13	39	V6
THAT GENTLEMAN OF LORDS AND GENTLEMEN	380	3 DON JUAN	13	47	2
THE GENTLEMEN GOT UP BETIMES TO SHOOT	405	3 DON JUAN	13	101	1
FOR THEN THE GENTLEMEN WERE RATHER TIRED)	408	3 DON JUAN	13	108	2
BUT GENTLEMEN IN STAYS AS STIFF AS STONES	409	3 DON JUAN	13	110	8
AND ONCE O'ER SEVERAL COUNTRY GENTLEMEN	424	3 DON JUAN	14	33	8
OF SINGLE GENTLEMEN WHO WOULD BE DOUBLE	477	3 DON JUAN	15	48	8
ALL COUNTRY GENTLEMEN ESQUIRED OR KNIGHTED	534	3 DON JUAN	16	69	3

GENTLER

| STILL GENTLER PURCHASER THE BARD--THAT'S I-- | 147 | 2 DON JUAN | 1 | 221 | 2 |
| ALL MY BOY FEELINGS ALL MY GENTLER DREAMS | 233 | 3 DON JUAN | 10 | 18 | 4 |

GENTLEWOMAN

| ALSO MY LADY'S GENTLEWOMAN TRICKY | 380 | 3 DON JUAN | 13 | 47 | 3 |

GENTLY

GENTLY BUT PALPABLY CONFIRM'D ITS GRASP	81	2 DON JUAN	1	111	2
AND THEREFORE SIDE BY SIDE WERE GENTLY LAID	98	2 DON JUAN	1	141	5
PEDRILLO AND SO GENTLY EBB'D HIS BREATH	197	2 DON JUAN	2	76	3
BREATHING ALL GENTLY O'ER HIS CHEEK AND MOUTH	245	2 DON JUAN	2	168	7
THE PATRIARCH OF THE FLOCK ALL GENTLY COWERS	292	2 DON JUAN	3	32	4
IT ALSO GENTLY HINTS TO THEM THAT OTHERS	491	2 DON JUAN	5	138	2
AND FAIR BROWS GENTLY DROOPING AS THE FRUIT	38	3 DON JUAN	6	65	6
HIS STERN PHILOSOPHY BUT GENTLY STROKING	172	3 DON JUAN	8	121	6
I THINK TO CANTER GENTLY THROUGH A HUNDRED	341	3 DON JUAN	12	55	8
TO GENTLY SMOOTHE THE PROGRESS OF DECLINE	360	3 DON JUAN	13	5	V6
GIVE GENTLY WAY WHEN THERE'S TOO GREAT A PRESS	366	3 DON JUAN	13	18	5
GENTLY TO LULL DOWN THE SUBSIDING SOUL	484	3 DON JUAN	15	66	6

GEOFFRY'S

| TURPIN'S OR MONMOUTH GEOFFRY'S CHRONICLE | 503 | 3 DON JUAN | 16 | 5 | 2 |

GEOGRAPHERS

| AS GEOGRAPHERS LAY DOWN A SHOAL IN MAPS | 155 | 2 DON JUAN | 1 | V 7 | 8 |

GEOGRAPHY

THE VERY BOTANY BAY IN MORAL GEOGRAPHY	330	2 DON JUAN	3	94	2
STATISTICS TACTICS POLITICS AND GEOGRAPHY)--	149	3 DON JUAN	8	74	4
WHERE GEOGRAPHY FINDS NO ONE TO OBLIGE HER--	348	3 DON JUAN	12	70	4

GEORDI-AN

| THE GORDIAN OR THE GEORDI-AN KNOT WHOSE STRINGS | 536 | 3 DON JUAN | 16 | 74 | 7 |

GEORGE

IN MY HOT YOUTH--WHEN GEORGE THE THIRD WAS KING	143	2 DON JUAN	1	212	8
TWO BATTERIES CAP-A-PIE AS OUR SAINT GEORGE	72	3 DON JUAN	7	12	3
THOUGH IRELAND STARVE GREAT GEORGE WEIGHS TWENTY STONE	175	3 DON JUAN	8	126	8
GEORGE WASHINGTON HAD THANKS AND NOUGHT BESIDE	186	3 DON JUAN	9	8	4
THINK IF THEN GEORGE THE FOURTH SHOULD BE DUG UP	202	3 DON JUAN	9	39	1
WHERE'S WHITBREAD ROMILLY WHERE'S GEORGE THE THIRD	307	3 DON JUAN	11	78	2
OR GRAVE LORD GEORGE WITH WHOM PERHAPS MIGHT END	470	3 DON JUAN	15	33	4

GEORGE'S

| THAT YOU AND I WILL WIN SAINT GEORGE'S COLLAR | 160 | 3 DON JUAN | 8 | 97 | 8 |

GEORGIAN

KATINKA WAS A GEORGIAN WHITE AND RED	26	3 DON JUAN	6	41	2
NOR SHOW YOUR GEORGIAN IGNORANCE--FOR SHAME	28	3 DON JUAN	6	44	5
THE GEORGIAN AND HER PARAMOUR REPLIED	62	3 DON JUAN	6	113	1

306

GEORGIANS
     AND THERE WITH GEORGIANS RUSSIANS AND CIRCASSIANS . . . . 407 2 DON JUAN 4   113   7
     OF GEORGIANS RUSSIANS NUBIANS AND WHATNOT   . . . . . . 417 2 DON JUAN 5   13   2
     WHO WITH THE BRIGHTEST GEORGIANS MIGHT COMPARE . . . . . 24 3 DON JUAN 6   36   4
GERM
     LOVE BEARS WITHIN ITS BREAST THE VERY GERM . . . . . 451 3 DON JUAN 14   94   1
GERMAN
     JUAN TO WHOM HE SPOKE IN GERMAN KNEW   . . . . 141 3 DON JUAN 8   57   1
     AS MUCH OF GERMAN AS OF SANSCRIT AND   . . . . . . 141 3 DON JUAN 8   57   2
     BY GERMAN POSTBOYS DRIVEN A GERMAN MILE . . . . . 260 3 DON JUAN 10   71 V8
     BY GERMAN POSTBOYS DRIVEN A GERMAN MILE . . . . . 260 3 DON JUAN 10   71 V8
     OR WITH ITS MIST OF GERMAN MYSTERIES . . . . . . 450 3 DON JUAN 14   92 V5
GERMANY
     HOLLAND FRANCE ENGLAND GERMANY OR SPAIN . . . . . 157 2 DON JUAN 1   2   2
     IN GERMANY THE PEGASUS HE'D PRANCE ON . . . . . . 320 2 DON JUAN 3   86   5
     TO GERMANY WHOSE SOMEWHAT TARDY MILLIONS . . . . . 254 3 DON JUAN 10   60   7
     NOT LIKE SLOW GERMANY WHERIN THEY MUDDLE . . . . . 260 3 DON JUAN 10   71   4
     OR GERMANY WHERE PEOPLE PURELY KISS . . . . . . 450 3 DON JUAN 14   92   5
     BUT WHETHER REVEREND RAPP LEARN'D THIS IN GERMANY . . . 472 3 DON JUAN 15   36   3
GESTURE
     THE GESTURE WHICH ENCHANTS THE EYE THAT SPEAKS . . . 292 2 DON JUAN 3   33   4
     JUAN YET QUICKLY UNDERSTOOD THEIR GESTURE . . . . 274 3 DON JUAN 11   13   1
GET
     COME SIR GET IN)--MY MASTER MUST BE NEAR . . . . . 115 2 DON JUAN 1   172   5
     AND JUAN THROTTLED HIM TO GET AWAY . . . . 124 2 DON JUAN 1   186   2
     TO MEND HIS FORMER MORALS AND GET NEW . . . . . . 129 2 DON JUAN 1   191   3
     TO GET UP PART OF THE CARGO AND WHAT NOT . . . . . 171 2 DON JUAN 2   28   3
     AT LAST THEY DID GET AT IT REALLY BUT . . . . . . 171 2 DON JUAN 2   28   5
     'TWAS DIFFICULT TO GET OUT SUCH PROVISION . . . . 180 2 DON JUAN 2   46   3
     SIX FLASKS OF WINE AND THEY CONTRIVED TO GET . . . 181 2 DON JUAN 2   47   4
     BUT JUAN TRUSTING THEY MIGHT STILL GET THROUGH . . . 187 2 DON JUAN 2   59   6
     BUT UP SHE GOT AND UP SHE MADE THEM GET . . . . . 230 2 DON JUAN 2   139   1
     MAN BEING REASONABLE MUST GET DRUNK . . . . . . 250 2 DON JUAN 2   179   1
     BUT TO RETURN--GET VERY DRUNK AND WHEN . . . . . 250 2 DON JUAN 2   179   7
     (FOR WE MUST GET THEM ANYHOW OR GRIEVE) . . . . . 270 2 DON JUAN 2   213   6
     WHICH GROWS A HABIT SHE CAN NE'ER GET OVER . . . . 276 2 DON JUAN 3   3   3
     THEY SOMETIMES ALSO GET A LITTLE TIRED   . . . . . 278 2 DON JUAN 3   7   2
     AND AS A SERVANT SOME PREFERMENT GET . . . . . . 391 2 DON JUAN 4   86   5
     AND WITH HIS FELLOWS OF THE THIRD SEX GET . . . . 391 2 DON JUAN 4   86 V5
     AND SIGH I CAN'T GET OUT LIKE YORICK'S STARLING . . . 404 2 DON JUAN 4   109   4
     HOW GET OUT HOW THE DEVIL GOT WE IN . . . . . . 435 2 DON JUAN 5   44   2
     SAID IN HEAVEN'S NAME LET'S GET SOME SUPPER NOW . . . 437 2 DON JUAN 5   47   7
     AND WHEN THE OLD NEGRO TOLD HIM TO GET READY . . . 453 2 DON JUAN 5   73   7
     AND YET AT LAST HE MANAGED TO GET THROUGH . . . . 456 2 DON JUAN 5   78   3
     AND AS SHE ALSO RISKED HER LIFE TO GET . . . . . 482 2 DON JUAN 5   122   4
     AND BEGGED THEY WOULD EXCUSE HER SHE'D GET OVER . . . 47 3 DON JUAN 6   83   7
     AND THOUGH HE WISHED EXTREMELY TO GET THROUGH . . . 63 3 DON JUAN 6   116   6
     CONTRIVED TO GET ITSELF COMPRISED WITHIN IT . . . . 142 3 DON JUAN 8   59   4
     AT LAST MAY GET A LITTLE TIRED OF THUNDER . . . . 185 3 DON JUAN 9   5   4
     NOW WE'LL GET O'ER THE GROUND AT A GREAT RATE . . . 203 3 DON JUAN 9   42   4
     TO GET AT THEE NOT BATTER DOWN A WALL . . . . . . 210 3 DON JUAN 9   56   4
     WHICH MAKE ALL BODIES ANXIOUS TO GET OUT . . . . . 220 3 DON JUAN 9   75   2
     AND FOR THEIR PAINS GET ONLY A FRESH PUNCTURE . . . 263 3 DON JUAN 10   77   8
     AND FOR THEIR PAINS GET SMARTER PUNCTURATIONS . . . 263 3 DON JUAN 10   77 V8
     BUT IF YOU CAN CONTRIVE GET NEXT AT SUPPER . . . . 304 3 DON JUAN 11   72   1
     OR IF FORESTALLED GET OPPOSITE AND OGLE-- . . . . 304 3 DON JUAN 11   72   2
     REPUBLICS ALSO GET INVOLVED A BIT . . . . 318 3 DON JUAN 12   6   5
     MUST GET ITSELF DISCOUNTED BY A JEW . . . . . . 318 3 DON JUAN 12   6   8
     AND YOU MAY GET THE WEDDING DRESSES READY . . . . 343 3 DON JUAN 12   59   8
     AT A LONG DATE--TILL THEY CAN GET A FRESH ONE-- . . . 379 3 DON JUAN 13   45   6
     WHO COULD NOT GET THE PLACE FOR WHICH HE SUED . . . 391 3 DON JUAN 13   70   8
     HOW OUR VILLEGGIATURA WILL GET ON . . . . 397 3 DON JUAN 13   83   2
     WITH MEMORY EXCELLENT TO GET BY ROTE . . . . . . 401 3 DON JUAN 13   91   5
     SHE SERIOUSLY ADVISED HIM TO GET MARRIED . . . . . 469 3 DON JUAN 15   29   8
     HOW SHALL I GET THIS GOURMAND STANZA THROUGH . . . 483 3 DON JUAN 15   63   6
GETS
     'TIS TRUE IT GETS ANOTHER BRIGHT AND FRESH . . . . 422 2 DON JUAN 5   22   1
     AND WHEN AT LAST THE PRETTY CREATURE GETS . . . . 333 3 DON JUAN 12   36   5
GETTING
     OF GETTING HER LIEGE LORD INTO A SCRAPE . . . . . 32 2 DON JUAN 1   20   8
     GETTING THE BOATS OUT BEING WELL AWARE   . . . . . 180 2 DON JUAN 2   45   6
     WAS LOST BY GETTING AT SOME AQUA-VITA . . . . . . 186 2 DON JUAN 2   56   8
     IN GETTING OUT GOODS BALLAST GUNS AND TREASURE . . . 286 2 DON JUAN 3   20   8
     THE SERVANTS ALL WERE GETTING DRUNK OR IDLING . . . 295 2 DON JUAN 3   39   3
     OF GETTING INTO HEAVEN THE SHORTEST WAY . . . . . 336 2 DON JUAN 3   104   5
     SOME SAID HER YEARS WERE GETTING NIGH THEIR SUMMER . . 23 3 DON JUAN 6   35   5
     THE RUSS FLOTILLA GETTING UNDER WAY   . . . . . . 81 3 DON JUAN 7   29   2
     BUT GETTING NIGH GRIM DANTE'S OBSCURE WOOD . . . . 238 3 DON JUAN 10   27   3
     OF GETTING ON HIMSELF AND FINDING STATIONS . . . . 239 3 DON JUAN 10   30   3
     EXCEPT THE WHIGS NOT GETTING INTO PLACE . . . . . 309 3 DON JUAN 11   82   8
GHASTLY
     THERE WERE TWO FATHERS IN THIS GHASTLY CREW . . . . 202 2 DON JUAN 2   87   1
     A FIELD OF BATTLE'S GHASTLY WILDERNESS   . . . . . 167 3 DON JUAN 8   112   6
     HAVE SOMETHING GHASTLY DESOLATE AND DREAD . . . . 508 3 DON JUAN 16   17   8
GHOST
     THE GHOST OF VANISHED PLEASURES ONCE IN VOGUE ILL . . . 304 3 DON JUAN 11   72   6
     BUT NOW NO MORE THE GHOST OF SCANDAL STALKED ABOUT . . . 338 3 DON JUAN 12   47   3
     ALAS POOR GHOST--WHAT UNEXPECTED WOES . . . . . . 403 3 DON JUAN 13   97   7
     GRIM READER DID YOU EVER SEE A GHOST . . . . . . 498 3 DON JUAN 15   95   1

GHOST   (CONTINUED)

	PAGE	VOL		CANTO	STANZA	LN
I SAID IT WAS A STORY OF A GHOST--	502	3	DON JUAN	16	4	3
THAT HE THE NIGHT BEFORE HAD SEEN A GHOST	543	3	DON JUAN	16	90	2
BY LAST NIGHT'S GHOST BEEN DRIVEN FROM THEIR DEFENCES	545	3	DON JUAN	16	93	8
THE GHOST AT LEAST HAD DONE HIM THIS MUCH GOOD	553	3	DON JUAN	16	107	1
IN MAKING HIM AS SILENT AS A GHOST	553	3	DON JUAN	16	107	2
HIS OWN INTERNAL GHOST BEGAN TO AWAKEN	558	3	DON JUAN	16	118	5
THE GHOST STOPPED MENACED THEN RETIRED UNTIL	559	3	DON JUAN	16	119	7
THE GHOST HAD A REMARKABLY SWEET BREATH	560	3	DON JUAN	16	121	4
THE GHOST IF GHOST IT WERE SEEMED A SWEET SOUL	561	3	DON JUAN	16	123	1
THE GHOST IF GHOST IT WERE SEEMED A SWEET SOUL	561	3	DON JUAN	16	123	1
WHICH BEST IS TO ENCOUNTER--GHOST OR NONE	568	3	DON JUAN	17	14	1

GHOST'S

EXPECTANT OF THE GHOST'S FRESH OPERATIONS	555	3	DON JUAN	16	111	8

GHOSTS

THE MATRON FROWNED WHY SO--FOR FEAR OF GHOSTS	30	3	DON JUAN	6	48	2
AND SHOWN THEMSELVES AS GHOSTS OF BETTER TASTE	38	3	DON JUAN	6	64	7
THEIR TABLE WAS A BOARD TO TEMPT EVEN GHOSTS	404	3	DON JUAN	13	99	3
WHICH PASSES GHOSTS IN CURRENCY LIKE GOLD	510	3	DON JUAN	16	22	6

GIANT

THE GIANT DOOR WAS BROAD AND BRIGHT AND HIGH	461	2	DON JUAN	5	86	1
THE GIANT THOUGHT OF BEING A TITAN'S BRIDE	20	3	DON JUAN	6	28	4
LIKE DAVID FLINGS SMOOTH PEBBLES 'GAINST A GIANT	138	3	DON JUAN	8	51	2
WE GAZE UPON A GIANT FOR HIS STATURE	390	3	DON JUAN	13	67	7
IF SUCH DOOM WAITS EACH INTELLECTUAL GIANT	566	3	DON JUAN	17	10	1

GIANT'S

'TIS A GRAND SIGHT FROM OFF THE GIANT'S GRAVE	413	2	DON JUAN	5	5	3

GIANTS

TRUE KNIGHTS CHASTE DAMES HUGE GIANTS KINGS DESPOTIC	347	2	DON JUAN	4	6	6
OF TITANS GIANTS FELLOWS OF ABOUT	201	3	DON JUAN	9	38	6

GIAOUR

SUCH NOTICE OF A GIAOUR WHILE SCARCE TO ONE	501	2	DON JUAN	5	156	5

GIAOURS

BY REBEL PACHAS AND ENCROACHING GIAOURS	497	2	DON JUAN	5	150	7
OF GUEBRES GIAOURS AND GINNS AND GOULS IN HOSTS	30	3	DON JUAN	6	48	6

GIBBER

(THAT MAKE OLD EUROPE'S JOURNALS SQUEAK AND GIBBER ALL)	318	3	DON JUAN	12	5	4

GIBIER

ALAS I MUST LEAVE UNDESCRIBED THE GIBIER	487	3	DON JUAN	15	71	1

GIBING

TO FURNISH MATTER FOR THEIR MORAL GIBING	418	3	DON JUAN	14	19	6

GIBRALTAR

(THOUGH THESE TO OUR GIBRALTAR MUST KNOCK UNDER)--	136	3	DON JUAN	8	46	6

GIFT

BECAUSE ALL GENTLE READERS HAVE THE GIFT	50	3	DON JUAN	6	88	4
OR GENEROUS DRAFT CONCEDED AS A GIFT	379	3	DON JUAN	13	45	5

GIFTED

OR THAT OUR SIRES HAD A MORE GIFTED EYE	516	3	DON JUAN	16	36	6

GIFTGABBIT

BECAUSE THE NEIGHBOURING SCOTCH EARL OF GIFTGABBIT	534	3	DON JUAN	16	70	4

GIFTS

WAS LADEN WITH ALL KINDS OF GIFTS AND HONOURS	247	3	DON JUAN	10	46	7
WHO WOULD SUPPOSE THY GIFTS SOMETIMES OBDURATE)	540	3	DON JUAN	16	82	6

GIGANTIC

TILL A GIGANTIC PORTAL THROUGH THE GLOOM	460	2	DON JUAN	5	85	4
GIGANTIC GENTLEMEN YET HAD A TOUCH	209	3	DON JUAN	9	54	4
THERE WAS JACK JARGON THE GIGANTIC GUARDSMAN	399	3	DON JUAN	13	88	1

GIGGLE

BUT ETIQUETTE FORBADE THEM ALL TO GIGGLE	501	2	DON JUAN	5	156	8

GIGGLING

IS THIS A TIME FOR GIGGLING THIS A PLIGHT	115	2	DON JUAN	1	171	5

GILD

TO GILD REFINED GOLD OR PAINT THE LILY	314	2	DON JUAN	3	76	8

GILDED

OF WHICH SOME GILDED REMNANTS STILL WERE SEEN	415	2	DON JUAN	5	9	4
BORE OFF HIS BARGAINS TO A GILDED BOAT	432	2	DON JUAN	5	40	2
OF GILDED BRONZE AND CARVED IN CURIOUS GUISE	461	2	DON JUAN	5	86	2
ALL CARVED AND GILDED OR--AS IT WILL TELL	339	3	DON JUAN	12	51	V7
WHAT CAN YE RECOGNIZE--A GILDED CLOUD	373	3	DON JUAN	13	33	8

GILDING

FULL OF BARBARIC CARVING PAINT AND GILDING	223	2	DON JUAN	2	127	8
THERE SEEMED TO BE BESPRENT A DEAL OF GILDING	436	2	DON JUAN	5	46	3
THE GILDING WEARS SO SOON FROM OFF HER FETTER	421	3	DON JUAN	14	25	5

GILDS

ETERNAL SUMMER GILDS THEM YET	320	2	DON JUAN	3	L 1	5

GILES

A MAN AS GILES SAYS FOR THOUGH SHE WOULD WIDOW ALL	214	3	DON JUAN	9	63	7

GILLS

THE REST WERE JACKS AND GILLS AND WILLS AND BILLS	76	3	DON JUAN	7	20	1

GILT

BE GILT WHO SATE HATH CEASED TO BE THE SAME	509	3	DON JUAN	16	19	8

GILTBEDDING

AND THE TWO FAIR CO-HEIRESSES GILTBEDDING	473	3	DON JUAN	15	40	5

GILT-EDGED

THIS NOTE WAS WRITTEN UPON GILT-EDGED PAPER	134	2	DON JUAN	1	198	1

GINNS

OF GUEBRES GIAOURS AND GINNS AND GOULS IN HOSTS	30	3	DON JUAN	6	48	6

'GINS

BUT OFT DENIED AS PATIENCE 'GINS TO FAIL HE	459	3	DON JUAN	15	8	5

GIRD
   GIRD MORE DECEIT WITHIN A PETTICOAT . . . . 296 2 DON JUAN 3 41 6
GIRDLE
   HER GIRDLE SPARKLED AND THE RICHEST LACE . . . . . . 220 2 DON JUAN 2 121 5
   A PONIARD DECKED HER GIRDLE AS THE SIGN . . . . . . 475 2 DON JUAN 5 111 7
   THE STARRY DARKNESS ROUND HER LIKE A GIRDLE . . . . . 556 3 DON JUAN 16 113 7
GIRDS
   THAT STRETCHES TO THE STONY BELT WHICH GIRDS . . . . 49 3 DON JUAN 6 86 7
GIRL
   THE GENTLE GIRL AND HER ATTENDANT--ONE . . . . . . 216 2 DON JUAN 2 115 2
   FOR ONE CIRCASSIAN A SWEET GIRL WERE GIVEN . . . . . 407 2 DON JUAN 4 114 2
   I SEE YOU'VE BOUGHT ANOTHER GIRL 'TIS PITY . . . . . 500 2 DON JUAN 5 155 7
   HER NOTE SHE DON'T FORGET THE INFANT GIRL . . . . . 249 3 DON JUAN 10 51 7
   BEGGED TO BRING UP THE LITTLE GIRL AND OUT-- . . . . 330 3 DON JUAN 12 31 3
   OR ANDALUSIAN GIRL FROM MASS RETURNING . . . . . . 350 3 DON JUAN 12 75 2
   THE ISLAND GIRL BRED UP BY THE LONE SEA . . . . . . 481 3 DON JUAN 15 58 4
   THE DEVIL WAS IN THE GIRL COULD IT BE PRIDE . . . . 490 3 DON JUAN 15 78 4
   THERE WAS A COUNTRY GIRL IN A CLOSE CAP . . . . . . 530 3 DON JUAN 16 61 3
   BUT THIS POOR GIRL WAS LEFT IN THE GREAT HALL . . . . 533 3 DON JUAN 16 67 1
GIRLS
   OF BEES THE VOICE OF GIRLS THE SONG OF BIRDS . . . . 88 2 DON JUAN 1 123 7
   AND SUCH SWEET GIRLS--I MEAN SUCH GRACEFUL LADIES . . 159 2 DON JUAN 2 5 5
   AND SO IN SHORT THE GIRLS THEY REALLY WERE . . . . . 222 2 DON JUAN 2 124 5
   AND FURTHER ON A GROUP OF GRECIAN GIRLS . . . . . . 291 2 DON JUAN 3 30 1
   DWARFS DANCING GIRLS BLACK EUNUCHS AND A POET . . . . 316 2 DON JUAN 3 78 2
   THE DWARFS AND DANCING GIRLS HAD ALL RETIRED . . . . 334 2 DON JUAN 3 101 2
   COMPOSED A CHOIR OF GIRLS TEN OR A DOZEN . . . . . . 469 2 DON JUAN 5 99 2
   MEANTIME THESE TWO POOR GIRLS WITH SWIMMING EYES . . 104 3 DON JUAN 7 73 1
   WHO ONLY SAW THE BLACK-EYED GIRLS IN GREEN . . . . . 167 3 DON JUAN 8 111 4
   THE ONLY DANCE WHICH TEACHES GIRLS TO THINK . . . . 302 3 DON JUAN 11 68 3
   AND LADY MARYS BLOOMING INTO GIRLS . . . . 390 3 DON JUAN 13 68 4
   AND GIRLS OF SIXTEEN ARE THUS FAR SOCRATIC . . . . . 494 3 DON JUAN 15 86 1
GIRT
   AND GIRT BY FORMIDABLE WAVES BUT THEY . . . . . . 211 2 DON JUAN 2 104 2
   WHICH GIRT A SLIGHT CHEMISE AS WHITE AS MILK . . . . 456 2 DON JUAN 5 77 4
GIRTH
   HOW MANY MILES THE MOON MIGHT HAVE IN GIRTH . . . . . 71 2 DON JUAN 1 92 5
GIULETTA
   JULIET--OR--GIULETTA--WHICH LAST WAS . . . . 273 2 DON JUAN 2 V 2 1
GIVE
   THAT TURNS AND TURNS TO GIVE THE WORLD A NOTION . . . 17 2 DON JUAN D 13 7
   PRETTY WERE BUT TO GIVE A FEEBLE NOTION . . . . . . 51 2 DON JUAN 1 55 4
   SHOULD EVER GIVE HER HEART THE LEAST SENSATION . . . 63 2 DON JUAN 1 77 4
   THEIR SPELLS AND GIVE THEM TO THE PASSING GALE . . . 72 2 DON JUAN 1 95 7
   OF HIS POSITION I CAN GIVE NO NOTION . . . . 113 2 DON JUAN 1 168 1
   JUAN CONTRIVED TO GIVE AN AWKWARD BLOW . . . . . . 124 2 DON JUAN 1 186 5
   LET NOT A MONUMENT GIVE YOU OR ME HOPES . . . . . . 146 2 DON JUAN 1 219 7
   A DRESS THROUGH WHICH THE EYES GIVE SUCH A VOLLEY . . 160 2 DON JUAN 2 7 7
   GIVE US MORE GROG THEY CRIED FOR IT WILL BE . . . . . 175 2 DON JUAN 2 36 1
   BUT ONLY GIVE A BUST OF MARRIAGES . . . . 279 2 DON JUAN 3 8 4
   AND IF I HAD TO GIVE A CASTING VOICE . . . . 357 2 DON JUAN 4 25 5
   AND THEN GIVE WAY SUBDUED BECAUSE SURROUNDED . . . . 373 2 DON JUAN 4 54 6
   NOR TIME NOR SKILL NOR REMEDY COULD GIVE HER . . . . 381 2 DON JUAN 4 68 7
   ACQUIRE THE DEEP AND BITTER POWER TO GIVE . . . . . 402 2 DON JUAN 4 107 4
   IN THIS OUR WORLD--AND HAVE THE POWER TO GIVE . . . . 403 2 DON JUAN 4 107 V4
   AS OVID'S VERSE MAY GIVE TO UNDERSTAND . . . . . . 411 2 DON JUAN 5 1 6
   'TWOULD GIVE ME PLEASURE--PRAY WHAT IS YOUR NATION . . 417 2 DON JUAN 5 13 8
   CAN GIVE US EITHER PAIN OR PLEASURE WHO . . . . . . 428 2 DON JUAN 5 32 6
   WHO GIVE THEMSELVES TO ARCHITECTURE WHOLLY . . . . . 448 2 DON JUAN 5 63 4
   TO GIVE SOME REBEL PACHA A CRAVAT . . . . 463 2 DON JUAN 5 89 7
   HENCE MY OLD COMET GIVE THE STARS DUE WARNING-- . . . 494 2 DON JUAN 5 145 4
   AND I CAN GIVE MY WHOLE SOUL UP TO MIND . . . . . . 17 3 DON JUAN 6 22 6
   THIS CIRCUMSTANCE MAY SERVE TO GIVE A NOTION . . . . 72 3 DON JUAN 7 11 1
   MANY OF COMMON READERS GIVE A GUESS . . . . 82 3 DON JUAN 7 33 3
   AND THEREFORE WE MUST GIVE THE GREATER NUMBER . . . . 120 3 DON JUAN 8 18 1
   YOU SHOULD BUT GIVE FEW CARTRIDGES TO SUCH . . . . . 151 3 DON JUAN 8 78 3
   TO ANSWER RIBAS' SUMMONS TO GIVE WAY . . . . 171 3 DON JUAN 8 120 8
   BUT PRAY GIVE BACK A LITTLE TO THE NATION . . . . . 185 3 DON JUAN 9 6 8
   NOR GIVE MY VOICE TO SLAVERY'S JACKALL CRY . . . . . 195 3 DON JUAN 9 26 8
   OF AGE AND LOOKING BACK TO YOUTH GIVE ONE TEAR-- . . 238 3 DON JUAN 10 27 8
   SHE COULD NOT TOO MUCH GIVE HER APPROBATION . . . . 241 3 DON JUAN 10 33 1
   SAVE SUCH AS SOUTHEY CAN AFFORD TO GIVE . . . . . . 243 3 DON JUAN 10 37 4
   BEFORE THEY GIVE THEIR BROADSIDE BY-AND-BY . . . . . 266 3 DON JUAN 10 84 2
   A KERCHIEF CRYING GIVE SAL THAT--AND DIED . . . . . 276 3 DON JUAN 11 16 8
   WITH SUCH SMALL GEAR TO GIVE MYSELF CONCERN . . . . 300 3 DON JUAN 11 63 3
   WHICH TAKES SO MUCH--TO GIVE THE DEVIL HIS DUE-- . . 351 3 DON JUAN 12 76 3
   BUT THOUGH THE SOIL MAY GIVE YOU TIME AND TROUBLE . . 351 3 DON JUAN 12 76 7
   HINT THAT 'TIS TIME TO GIVE THE YOUNGER PLACE . . . . 360 3 DON JUAN 13 4 8
   GIVE GENTLY WAY WHEN THERE'S TOO GREAT A PRESS . . . 366 3 DON JUAN 13 18 5
   CONSISTED OF--WE GIVE THE SEX THE PAS-- . . . . . . 396 3 DON JUAN 13 79 2
   AND IF THEIR FULL CONTENTS I DO NOT GIVE YE . . . . 440 3 DON JUAN 14 68 5
   WOULD GIVE UP ARTLESSLY BOTH HEART AND HEAD . . . . 460 3 DON JUAN 15 10 6
   LIKE ALL WHO GIVE AND EKE RECEIVE IT GRATIS . . . . 469 3 DON JUAN 15 29 2
   AND NOW I WILL GIVE UP ALL ARGUMENT . . . . 498 3 DON JUAN 15 94 1
   WHO DO NOT GIVE PROFESSIONAL ATTENDANCE . . . . . . 537 3 DON JUAN 16 76 6
GIVEN
   HAS GIVEN A SAMPLE FROM THE VASTY VERSION . . . . . 11 2 DON JUAN D 4 3
   HER GUARDIAN ANGEL HAD GIVEN UP HIS GARRISON . . . . 30 2 DON JUAN 1 17 4
   AS E'ER TO MAN'S MATURER GROWTH WAS GIVEN . . . . . 48 2 DON JUAN 1 49 4

		PAGE	VOL	CANTO	STANZA	LN

GIVEN   (CONTINUED)

TO WHOM THE LYRE AND LAURELS HAVE BEEN GIVEN	77	2	DON JUAN	1	104	6
(SAINT PAUL SAYS 'TIS THE TOLL WHICH MUST BE GIVEN)	225	2	DON JUAN	2	131	8
JUAN REPLIED IT MUST BE WON NOT GIVEN	365	2	DON JUAN	4	40	V2
FOR ONE CIRCASSIAN A SWEET GIRL WERE GIVEN	407	2	DON JUAN	4	114	2
HE MUTTERED (BUT THE LAST WAS GIVEN ASIDE)	471	2	DON JUAN	5	103	3
WITH US THERE IS MORE LAW GIVEN TO THE CHASE	482	2	DON JUAN	5	123	4
TO NO MEN ARE SUCH CORDIAL GREETINGS GIVEN	500	2	DON JUAN	5	154	7
FOUR-POSTED AND SILK CURTAINED WHICH ARE GIVEN	18	3	DON JUAN	6	25	3
AT THE GIVEN SIGNAL JOINED TO THEIR ARRAY	20	3	DON JUAN	6	29	2
JUAN WAS GIVEN IN CHARGE AS HATH BEEN STATED	57	3	DON JUAN	6	102	6
SUCH AS HE THOUGHT THE LEAST GIVEN UP TO PREY	162	3	DON JUAN	8	102	4
AT HOME IT MIGHT HAVE GIVEN HER SOME VEXATION	241	3	DON JUAN	10	33	5
AND HUMBLY HOPE THAT THE SAME GOD WHICH HATH GIVEN	242	3	DON JUAN	10	36	V7
WAS GIVEN TO HER FAVOURITE AND NOW BORE HIS	248	3	DON JUAN	10	49	8
ON A BRASS PLATE WAS GIVEN TO KNOCKS AND FAME	283	3	DON JUAN	11	31	V8
AGAINST THE SAME GIVEN QUANTITY OF RHYME	312	3	DON JUAN	11	90	3
THEN SHE WAS GIVEN TO CHARITY AND PITY	338	3	DON JUAN	12	47	6
SOME DEEM IT BUT THE DISTANT ECHO GIVEN	388	3	DON JUAN	13	63	6
SHAPED BY DECAY PERCHANCE HATH GIVEN THE POWER	388	3	DON JUAN	13	64	2
HAS NOT YET GIVEN UP THE PRACTICE QUITE	420	3	DON JUAN	14	23	4
ALTHOUGH HER BIRTH AND WEALTH HAD GIVEN HER VOGUE	477	3	DON JUAN	15	48	3
BUT FOR THAT HOUR CALLED HALF-HOUR GIVEN TO DRESS	482	3	DON JUAN	15	61	7

GIVES

WHICH COURAGE GIVES WHILE POOR PEDRILLO'S PAIR	186	2	DON JUAN	2	56	5
WAS MUCH THE SAME AS FIRE GIVES A WET BLANKET	294	2	DON JUAN	3	36	V8
BUT IF IT GIVES THEM PLEASURE BE IT SO	347	2	DON JUAN	4	7	5
NOW THERE IS NOTHING GIVES A MAN SUCH SPIRITS	260	3	DON JUAN	10	72	1
GIVES WITH GREEK TRUTH THE GOOD OLD GREEK THE LIE	325	3	DON JUAN	12	19	8

GIVING

IN GIVING TO HIS BRETHREN THEIR FULL MEED	14	2	DON JUAN	D	8	6
OF HELL-FIRE--ALL PREPARED FOR PEOPLE GIVING	258	2	DON JUAN	2	192	7
AND ALL UNCONSCIOUS OF THE JOY 'TIS GIVING	261	2	DON JUAN	2	197	4
TO THE GREAT MARLBOROUGH'S SKILL IN GIVING KNOCKS	328	2	DON JUAN	3	90	7
DREW ALL EYES ON HIM GIVING THEM TO GUESS	415	2	DON JUAN	5	9	5
AND THEN THE MERCHANT GIVING CHANGE AND SIGNING	426	2	DON JUAN	5	29	7
AND GIVING UP ALL NOTIONS OF RESISTANCE	440	2	DON JUAN	5	51	1

GLACIERS

| GLACIERS VOLCANOS ORANGES AND ICES | 262 | 3 | DON JUAN | 10 | 76 | 8 |

GLACIS

| AND LEVELLED WEAPONS STILL AGAINST THE GLACIS | 130 | 3 | DON JUAN | 8 | 34 | 8 |
| KEPT ALWAYS PUSHING ONWARDS TO THE GLACIS | 130 | 3 | DON JUAN | 8 | 34 | V8 |

GLAD

BUT FOR THE PUMPS I'M GLAD TO MAKE THEM KNOWN	171	2	DON JUAN	2	29	4
ON SEEING HIS OWN CHIMNEY-SMOKE FELT GLAD	289	2	DON JUAN	3	26	3
OF CARNAGE--AND I THINK HE WAS MORE GLAD IN HER	182	3	DON JUAN	8	140	7
I SHOULD BE GLAD TO KNOW THAT WHICH IS BEING	190	3	DON JUAN	9	16	2
CATHERINE I SAY WAS VERY GLAD TO SEE	211	3	DON JUAN	9	57	5
REPLIED THAT SHE WAS GLAD TO SEE HIM THROUGH	240	3	DON JUAN	10	31	5
AT PRESENT I AM GLAD OF A PRETENCE	453	3	DON JUAN	14	97	4
YET SAW THIS MUCH WHICH HE WAS GLAD TO SEE	553	3	DON JUAN	16	106	8

GLADIATOR'S

| AND EVER-DYING GLADIATOR'S AIR | 377 | 2 | DON JUAN | 4 | 61 | 6 |

GLADLY

TOO MUCH AND WISHING GLADLY TO SURPRISE	294	2	DON JUAN	3	37	2
GLADLY ALL MATTERS DOWN TO STONE OR LEAD	268	3	DON JUAN	11	1	6
OUR HERO GLADLY SAW HIS LITTLE CHARGE	339	3	DON JUAN	12	51	2
THEY BREAK THEIR RANKS AND GLADLY LEAVE THE DRILL	417	3	DON JUAN	14	17	2

GLANCE

ONE GLANCE ON HIM AND SAID HEAVEN'S WILL BE DONE	202	2	DON JUAN	2	87	6
FORTH FROM ITS RAVEN FRINGE THE FULL GLANCE FLIES	218	2	DON JUAN	2	117	5
AND DARTS IN ONE QUICK GLANCE A LONG REPLY	241	2	DON JUAN	2	162	6
FROM HAIDEE'S GLANCE THAN ANY GRAVEN LETTER	242	2	DON JUAN	2	163	8
THE LEAST GLANCE BETTER UNDERSTOOD THAN WORDS	351	2	DON JUAN	4	14	2
HIS GLANCE INQUIRED OF HERS FOR SOME EXCUSE	355	2	DON JUAN	4	22	7
HER GLANCE NOR GRASP FOR STILL SHE GAZED AND GRASP'D	361	2	DON JUAN	4	32	7
WITHOUT A GROAN OR SIGH OR GLANCE TO SHOW	381	2	DON JUAN	4	69	2
A RUEFUL GLANCE UPON THE WAVES (WHICH BRIGHT ALL	393	2	DON JUAN	4	90	5
A GLANCE AT THAT WHICH WRAPT THE SLAVES IN WONDER	450	2	DON JUAN	5	66	2
WITH A FAR REACHING GLANCE--A PAPHIAN PAIR	466	2	DON JUAN	5	96	V3
PASSION AND POWER A GLANCE ON HIM SHE CAST	478	2	DON JUAN	5	116	6
THE PARTY A SLIGHT GLANCE THEN SAID I HAVE HEARD	97	3	DON JUAN	7	60	4
A GLANCE ON THE DULL CLOUDS (AS THICK AS STARCH	121	3	DON JUAN	8	21	6
UPON EACH OTHER WITH DILATED GLANCE	159	3	DON JUAN	8	96	2
A GLANCE AROUND--AND SHRUGGED--AND TWITCHED HIS SLEEVE	161	3	DON JUAN	8	99	6
A GLANCE ON THAT SLAIN SON HIS FIRST AND LAST	169	3	DON JUAN	8	116	8
NOR IN HER EYE AUSONIA'S GLANCE IS BURNING	350	3	DON JUAN	12	75	4
A SLIGHT GLANCE THROWN ON MEN OF EVERY STATION	416	3	DON JUAN	14	14	4
ALONG THE CANVAS THEIR EYES GLANCE LIKE DREAMS	509	3	DON JUAN	16	19	4
AND USUAL--JUAN WHEN HE CAST A GLANCE	546	3	DON JUAN	16	96	2
HER LAUGHING BLUE EYES WITH A GLANCE COULD SEIZE	548	3	DON JUAN	16	100	4
THE MOMENTS WHEN WE GATHER FROM A GLANCE	554	3	DON JUAN	16	108	4

GLANCED

THEN RISING HAUGHTILY HE GLANCED AROUND	484	2	DON JUAN	5	126	5
GLANCED MILDLY ALL THE WORLD WAS ON THE WATCH	213	3	DON JUAN	9	61	8
GLANCED FROM THE WALLS IN GOODLY PRESERVATION	390	3	DON JUAN	13	68	3
HE GLANCED LIKE A PERSONIFIED BOLERO	427	3	DON JUAN	14	39	8
AND HAVING CASUALLY GLANCED IT THROUGH	440	3	DON JUAN	14	69	6
GLANCED WITHOUT PAUSING ON HIM A BRIGHT EYE	510	3	DON JUAN	16	21	8

GLANCES
AND STOLEN GLANCES SWEETER FOR THE THEFT 62   2 DON JUAN 1   74   2
OF THEIR EXCHANGING GLANCES OF AFFECTION . . . . 351 2 DON JUAN 4   13   8
HER GLANCES ON IT AND THEN LONGING FLUNG 44   3 DON JUAN 6   76   4
GLANCING
THROWN BACK A MOMENT WITH THE GLANCING HAND . . . . . . 160 2 DON JUAN 2   7   2
THROUGH THE WAVED BRANCHES O'ER THE GREENSWARD GLANCING . . 290 2 DON JUAN 3   29   3
AND BOSOMS ARMS AND ANCLES GLANCING BARE 42   3 DON JUAN 6   72   4
GLARE
WHEREAS THE OTHER AFTER ALL ITS GLARE . . . . 114 3 DON JUAN 8   4   2
AND NOT BE DAZZLED BY ITS EARLY GLARE . . . . 224 3 DON JUAN 9   84 V6
OF WASTE AND HASTE AND GLARE AND GLOSS AND GLITTER . . . 237 3 DON JUAN 10   26   2
THEN GLARE THE LAMPS THEN WHIRL THE WHEELS THEN ROAR . . . 302 3 DON JUAN 11   67   2
GLARED
THEY GLARED UPON EACH OTHER--ALL WAS DONE   . . . . . . 194 2 DON JUAN 2   72   5
AND LOOKING LIKE TWO INCUBI THEY GLARED . . . . 463 2 DON JUAN 5   90   2
WITH INFANT TERRORS GLARED AS FROM A TRANCE . . . . . . 159 3 DON JUAN 8   96   6
SUNK AND THE CRIMSON CROSS GLARED O'ER THE FIELD . . . . 172 3 DON JUAN 8   122   5
BUT STILL THE SHADE REMAINED THE BLUE EYES GLARED . . . . 560 3 DON JUAN 16   121   1
GLASS
(ANTONIA LET ME HAVE A GLASS OF WATER)   . . . . 106 2 DON JUAN 1   155   4
(FOR GOD'S SAKE LET ME HAVE A GLASS OF LIQUOR . . . . . 167 2 DON JUAN 2   20   3
THE FREEST SHE THAT EVER GAZED ON GLASS . . . . 248 2 DON JUAN 2   175   6
THE QUESTIONER FILL'D UP A GLASS OF WINE . . . . 297 2 DON JUAN 3   42   8
THEIR IMAGES AGAIN AS IN A GLASS . . . . 402 2 DON JUAN 4   107   5
PREPARED FOR SUPPER WITH A GLASS OF RUM . . . . 441 2 DON JUAN 5   53   8
A BOOK FRIEND SINGLE LADY OR A GLASS . . . . 444 2 DON JUAN 5   58   2
IF FOND OF A CHANCE OGLE AT HER GLASS 36   3 DON JUAN 6   60   4
AND THE STAINED GLASS WHICH LIGHTED THIS FAIR GROT . . . 55   3 DON JUAN 6   98   4
TO THOSE WHO BY THE DINT OF GLASS AND VAPOUR . . . . . 226 3 DON JUAN 10   3   6
OH FOR A GLASS OF MAX WE'VE MISS'D OUR BOOTY-- . . . . . 276 3 DON JUAN 11   16   3
SLOWLY DISTILLED INTO THE GLIMMERING GLASS . . . . . . 278 3 DON JUAN 11   22   7
THE COTERIES AND AS IN BANQUO'S GLASS . . . . 295 3 DON JUAN 11   54   3
I LOOK FOR IT--'TIS GONE A GLOBE OF GLASS . . . . . . 306 3 DON JUAN 11   76   4
WAS THE QUEEN-BEE THE GLASS OF ALL THAT'S FAIR . . . . 365 3 DON JUAN 13   13   5
MY MUSE A GLASS OF WEATHEROLOGY . . . . 378 3 DON JUAN 13   43   5
SHORN OF ITS GLASS OF THOUSAND COLOURINGS . . . . . . 387 3 DON JUAN 13   62   2
THE RUBY GLASS THAT SHAKES WITHIN HIS HAND . . . . . . 457 3 DON JUAN 15   4   7
O'ER LIFE TOO SWEET AN IMAGE FOR SUCH GLASS . . . . . . 475 3 DON JUAN 15   43   6
IS LIKE THE LAST GLASS OF CHAMPAGNE WITHOUT . . . . . . 504 3 DON JUAN 16   9   2
IN CHISELLED STONE AND PAINTED GLASS AND ALL . . . . . 507 3 DON JUAN 16   16   7
A NOISE LIKE TO WET FINGERS DRAWN ON GLASS . . . . . . 556 3 DON JUAN 16   114   1
GLASSES
THE GLASSES JINGLED AND THE PALATES TINGLED . . . . . 487 3 DON JUAN 15   70   1
GLASSFUL
ABOUT A LIQUID GLASSFUL WILL REMAIN . . . . 375 3 DON JUAN 13   37   6
GLASSY
YOUNG JUAN WANDER'D BY THE GLASSY BROOKS 70   2 DON JUAN 1   90   1
THROUGH THE SERENE AND PLACID GLASSY DEEP . . . . . . 447 3 DON JUAN 14   87   7
GLAZED
AND THE BOY'S EYES WHICH THE DULL FILM HALF GLAZED . . . 203 2 DON JUAN 2   89   5
AND FELL UPON THEIR GLAZED EYES LIKE A SCREEN . . . . . 210 2 DON JUAN 2   103   5
GLAZED O'ER HER EYES--THE BEAUTIFUL THE BLACK-- . . . . 381 2 DON JUAN 4   69   7
THEY ALSO SET A GLAZED WESTPHALIAN HAM ON . . . . . . 484 3 DON JUAN 15   65   5
GLEAM
GLEAM IN THE MOONLIGHT AND HER WHITE ARM CLASPS . . . . 259 2 DON JUAN 2   194   2
YET SHE BETRAY'D AT TIMES A GLEAM OF SENSE . . . . . . 381 2 DON JUAN 4   68   1
SOPHIA'S CUPOLA WITH GOLDEN GLEAM . . . . 412 2 DON JUAN 5   3   4
THE LAMPS OF WESTMINSTER'S MORE REGULAR GLEAM . . . . . 279 3 DON JUAN 11   24   4
GLEAMED
AND NOTHING BRIGHTER GLEAMED THROUGH THE SALOON   . . . 504 3 DON JUAN 16   8   7
STRAINED ON THE SPOT WHERE FIRST THE FIGURE GLEAMED . . . 511 3 DON JUAN 16   25   3
GLEAMED FORTH AS THROUGH THE CASEMENT'S IVY SHROUD . . . 560 3 DON JUAN 16   121   7
GLEAMING
SOME FAINT LAMPS GLEAMING FROM THE LOFTY WALLS . . . . 442 2 DON JUAN 5   56   1
PURSUED ITS COURSE NOW GLEAMING AND NOW HIDING . . . . 385 3 DON JUAN 13   58   6
GLEAMS
TO EXPOUND THEIR VAIN AND VISIONARY GLEAMS 45   3 DON JUAN 6   78   4
GLEAMS ONLY THROUGH THE DAWN OF ITS CREATION . . . . . 316 3 DON JUAN 12   2   8
THE CHARMS OF OTHER DAYS IN STARLIGHT GLEAMS . . . . . 509 3 DON JUAN 16   19   2
GLEAN
BUT WHAT WE CAN WE GLEAN IN THIS VILE AGE . . . . . . 403 3 DON JUAN 13   97   1
THEY COULD NOT EVEN GLEAN THE SLIGHTEST SPLINTERS . . . 434 3 DON JUAN 14   56   5
GLEAN'D
SAVE A FEW GLEAN'D FROM THE SEPULCHRAL GLOOM . . . . . 399 2 DON JUAN 4   102   6
GLEANERS
BUT FROM BEING FARMERS WE TURN GLEANERS GLEANING . . . 403 3 DON JUAN 13   96   1
GLEANING
OF THAT WEAK WORDY HARVEST THE SOLE GLEANING . . . . . 207 3 DON JUAN 9   49   8
BUT FROM BEING FARMERS WE TURN GLEANERS GLEANING . . . 403 3 DON JUAN 13   96   1
GLEANINGS
OF CHAFF ALTHOUGH OUR GLEANINGS BE NOT GRIST . . . . . 403 3 DON JUAN 13   97   2
GLEE
AND HAVE A KIND OF WILD AND HORRID GLEE . . . . 183 2 DON JUAN 2   50   6
THE FOUR MISS RAWBOLDS IN A GLEE WOULD SHINE . . . . . 408 3 DON JUAN 13   107   5
GLIBBER
OR PLEASURE WHO MAKE POLITICS RUN GLIBBER ALL . . . . . 318 3 DON JUAN 12   5   6
ALL WHICH I USE TO MAKE MY RHYMES RUN GLIBBER . . . . . 487 3 DON JUAN 15   71   3
GLIBLY
WHICH GLIBLY GLIDES FROM EVERY VULGAR TONGUE . . . . . 564 3 DON JUAN 17   5   2

311

		PAGE	VOL		CANTO	STANZA	LN

GLIDE
FAREWELL WHERE GUADALQUIVIR'S WATERS GLIDE • • • • • 166 2 DON JUAN 2   18 5
YOU COULD GLIDE O'ER THEM LIKE A GOLDEN FISH • • • • • 449 2 DON JUAN 5   65 8
GLIDED
GLIDED ALONG THE SMOOTH AND HARDEN'D SAND • • • • • 253 2 DON JUAN 2 184 3
ABOVE THE ICE HAD LIKE A SKAITER GLIDED • • • • • • 327 3 DON JUAN 12   25 4
WITH THAT SHE ROSE AND GLIDED OFF AS SNOW • • • • • 517 3 DON JUAN 16   38 V5
GLIDES
AND GLIDES AWAY ASSURED SHE NEVER HURTS YE • • • • • 300 3 DON JUAN 11   63 8
AND RATHER CALMLY INTO THE HEART GLIDES • • • • • • 350 3 DON JUAN 12   74 5
WHICH GLIBLY GLIDES FROM EVERY VULGAR TONGUE • • • • • 564 3 DON JUAN 17   5 2
GLIDING
AND BY GOOD FORTUNE GLIDING SOFTLY CAUGHT HER • • • • • 208 2 DON JUAN 2   99 3
INSTEAD OF GLIDING GRACIOUSLY DOWN LETHE • • • • • • 245 3 DON JUAN 10   42 7
QUIET--SANK INTO SOFTER RIPPLES GLIDING • • • • • • 385 3 DON JUAN 13   58 4
GLIDING THE FIRST TIME TO A RENDEZVOUS • • • • • • 556 3 DON JUAN 16 112 7
GLIMMER
GLIMMER ON HIGH THEIR BURIED LOCKS STILL WAVE • • • • • 509 3 DON JUAN 16   19 3
GLIMMER'D
COME OUT AND GLIMMER'D AS A SIX-WEEKS' STAR • • • • • 398 3 DON JUAN 13   84 6
GLIMMERING
SLOWLY DISTILLED INTO THE GLIMMERING GLASS • • • • • • 278 3 DON JUAN 11   22 7
GLIMPSE
A GLIMPSE OF SUNSHINE SET SOME HANDS TO BALE-- • • • • 176 2 DON JUAN 2   38 7
IT LASTED 'TWAS LIKE A SHORT GLIMPSE OF HELL • • • • • 489 2 DON JUAN 5 135 3
WHEN JUAN CAUGHT A GLIMPSE OF THIS SAD SIGHT • • • • • 158 3 DON JUAN 8   93 4
I CARE NOT--'TIS A GLIMPSE OF AULD LANG SYNE • • • • • 233 3 DON JUAN 10   18 8
WHICH PASSED OR CATCH THE FIRST GLIMPSE OF THE CLIFFS • • • 256 3 DON JUAN 10   64 8
TO CATCH A GLIMPSE EVEN OF A PRETTY PEASANT • • • • • 422 3 DON JUAN 14   28 8
GLISTENING
FROM GLISTENING WAVES AND SKIES SO HOT AND BARE-- • • • • 210 2 DON JUAN 2 103 6
FELT AN ODD GLISTENING MOISTURE IN HER EYE • • • • • 480 2 DON JUAN 5 120 8
GLISTERS
AT MAKING MATCHES WHERE 'TIS GOLD THAT GLISTERS • • • • 331 3 DON JUAN 12   32 5
GLITTER
THE OUTSTRETCH'D OCEAN GLITTER LIKE A LAKE • • • • • 249 2 DON JUAN 2 177 8
A DAZZLING MASS OF GEMS AND GOLD AND GLITTER • • • • • 465 2 DON JUAN 5   93 7
OF WASTE AND HASTE AND GLARE AND GLOSS AND GLITTER • • • 237 3 DON JUAN 10   26 2
GLITTERED
AND GEMS--AND GOLD--AND SILVER--GLITTERED MOSTLY • • • • 306 2 DON JUAN 3   61 V7
THEIR SABRES GLITTERED O'ER HER LITTLE HEAD • • • • • 158 3 DON JUAN 8   93 1
GLITTERERS
THOSE LITTLE GLITTERERS OF THE LONDON NIGHT • • • • • 435 3 DON JUAN 14   57 2
GLITTERING
SWEET TO THE MISER ARE HIS GLITTERING HEAPS • • • • • • 88 2 DON JUAN 1 124 5
IS GLITTERING YOUTH WHICH I HAVE SPENT BETIMES-- • • • • 145 2 DON JUAN 1 217 7
GLITTERING LIKE CRESCENTS O'ER A TURK'S PAVILION • • • • 205 2 DON JUAN 2   92 5
THEY GAZED UPON THE GLITTERING SEA BELOW • • • • • • 253 2 DON JUAN 2 185 3
JOY OF ITS GLITTERING TREASURE AND REPEAT • • • • • • 264 2 DON JUAN 2 203 V5
THEIR CLASSICAL PROFILES AND GLITTERING DRESSES • • • • 292 2 DON JUAN 3   33 1
THE GLITTERING LIME-TWIGS OF OUR LATTER DAYS • • • • • 422 2 DON JUAN 5   22 7
THROUGH GLITTERING GALLERIES AND O'ER MARBLE FLOORS • • • 460 2 DON JUAN 5   85 3
(AS NIGHT DEW ON A CYPRESS GLITTERING TINGES • • • • • 40 3 DON JUAN 6   67 7
MUST STEER WITH CARE THROUGH ALL THAT GLITTERING SEA • • • 303 3 DON JUAN 11   70 3
A SILENT CHANGE DISSOLVES THE GLITTERING MASS • • • • • 306 3 DON JUAN 11   76 6
SOME LIKENESS WHICH THE GLITTERING CIRQUE CONFINES • • • 321 3 DON JUAN 12   12 6
GLOBE
I LOOK FOR IT--'TIS GONE A GLOBE OF GLASS • • • • • 306 3 DON JUAN 11   76 4
GLOOM
AND O'ER HIS EYE A MOMENTARY GLOOM • • • • • • • • 298 2 DON JUAN 3   44 3
SAVE A FEW GLEAN'D FROM THE SEPULCHRAL GLOOM • • • • • 399 2 DON JUAN 4 102 6
HE PAUSED AND HIS DARK EYE GREW FULL OF GLOOM • • • • • 420 2 DON JUAN 5   18 3
TILL A GIGANTIC PORTAL THROUGH THE GLOOM • • • • • • 460 2 DON JUAN 5   85 4
FOR A NEW FLAME A THOUGHT TO CAST OF GLOOM ENOUGH • • • • 206 3 DON JUAN 9   48 5
GLOOMIER
OR GLOOMY CARAVAGGIO'S GLOOMIER STAIN • • • • • • • 392 3 DON JUAN 13   72 3
GLOOMIEST
I THINK IT IS PERHAPS THE GLOOMIEST HOUR • • • • • • 426 2 DON JUAN 5   30 7
GLOOMS
A MARBLE FOUNTAIN ECHOES THROUGH THE GLOOMS • • • • • 442 2 DON JUAN 5   55 4
GLOOMY
WHILE SHE STILL SILVERS O'ER YOUR GLOOMY PATH • • • • • 70 3 DON JUAN 7   7 8
THE GLOOMY CLOUDS WHICH O'ER IT AS A YOKE • • • • • • 266 3 DON JUAN 10   83 5
OR GLOOMY CARAVAGGIO'S GLOOMIER STAIN • • • • • • • 392 3 DON JUAN 13   72 3
GLORIED
HE GLORIED IN THE NAME OF ENGLISHMAN • • • • • • • 537 3 DON JUAN 16   75 8
GLORIES
BESIDES THEIR RESURRECTION AIDS OUR GLORIES • • • • • • 37 2 DON JUAN 1   31 5
THROUGH WHICH THE DEEPEN'D GLORIES ONCE COULD ENTER • • • 387 3 DON JUAN 13   62 3
FATIGUED WITH THESE HEREDITARY GLORIES • • • • • • • 392 3 DON JUAN 13   71 2
GLORIOUS
AND ALTHOUGH HERE AND THERE SOME GLORIOUS RARITY • • • • 14 2 DON JUAN D   9 5
I SAY THE SUN IS A MOST GLORIOUS SIGHT • • • • • • • 230 2 DON JUAN 2 140 1
FOR INSTANCE--PASSION IN A LOVER'S GLORIOUS • • • • • 278 2 DON JUAN 3   6 7
THE GLORIOUS MEED OF POPULAR APPLAUSE • • • • • • • 318 2 DON JUAN 3   82 7
I SEE THEIR GLORIOUS BLACK EYES SHINE • • • • • • • 326 2 DON JUAN 3 L 15 3
THEIR GALLIC NAMES UPON A GLORIOUS DAY • • • • • • • 77 3 DON JUAN 7   22 3
OH GLORIOUS LAUREL SINCE FOR ONE SOLE LEAF • • • • • • 101 3 DON JUAN 7   68 6
NEXT OF NEW KNIGHTS THE FRESH AND GLORIOUS HATCH • • • • 215 3 DON JUAN 9   65 7

GLORIOUS   (CONTINUED)

MY BOSOM UNDERWENT A GLORIOUS GLOW	226	3	DON JUAN	10	3	3
YE GLORIOUS GOTHIC SCENES HOW MUCH YE STRIKE	255	3	DON JUAN	10	61	3
THE WORLD WHICH AT THE WORST'S A GLORIOUS BLUNDER--	269	3	DON JUAN	11	3	8
WHO SHOES THE GLORIOUS ANIMAL WITH STILTS	297	3	DON JUAN	11	57	7
JUST TO CONSOLE SAD GLORY FOR BEING GLORIOUS	372	3	DON JUAN	13	32	8
A GLORIOUS REMNANT OF THE GOTHIC PILE	386	3	DON JUAN	13	59	1
ON BIRTH-DAYS GLORIOUS WITH A STAR AND STRING	440	3	DON JUAN	14	70	6
OR GLORIOUS AS A DIAMOND RICHLY SET	458	3	DON JUAN	15	7	4
A HETEROGENEOUS MASS OF GLORIOUS BLAME	480	3	DON JUAN	15	57	3
THE GLORIOUS--FREE--AND HAPPY CONSTITUTION	536	3	DON JUAN	16	74	V8
WERE SOMETHING VERY GLORIOUS TO BEHOLD	538	3	DON JUAN	16	78	4

GLORIOUSLY

BUT AT THE LEAST YOU MAY DIE GLORIOUSLY--	161	3	DON JUAN	8	100	5
WHO GREW LIKE CEDARS ROUND HIM GLORIOUSLY--	169	3	DON JUAN	8	116	4

GLORY

FOR ALL THE GLORY YOUR CONVERSION BROUGHT	12	2	DON JUAN	D	6	3
BUT WHETHER GLORY POWER OR LOVE OR TREASURE	93	2	DON JUAN	1	133	6
SWORD GOWN GAIN GLORY OFFER IN EXCHANGE	131	2	DON JUAN	1	194	4
GLORY THE GRAPE LOVE GOLD IN THESE ARE SUNK	250	2	DON JUAN	2	179	3
AND GLORY LONG HAS MADE THE SAGES SMILE	328	2	DON JUAN	3	90	1
AND GLORY MAKES THE SAGES OFTEN SMILE	328	2	DON JUAN	3	90	V1
THEY DO NOT MUCH CONTRIBUTE TO HIS GLORY	329	2	DON JUAN	3	92	8
INSTINCT OF GORE AND GLORY EARTH HAS KNOWN	401	2	DON JUAN	4	105	7
AMBITION AVARICE VENGEANCE GLORY GLUE	422	2	DON JUAN	5	22	6
SAVE SOLYMAN THE GLORY OF THEIR LINE	495	2	DON JUAN	5	147	8
IN CATHERINE'S REIGN WHOM GLORY STILL ADORES	52	3	DON JUAN	6	92	7
OH LOVE O GLORY WHAT ARE YE WHO FLY	66	3	DON JUAN	7	1	1
BUT OH YE GODDESSES OF WAR AND GLORY	73	3	DON JUAN	7	14	2
SOMETIMES CALLS MURDER AND AT OTHERS GLORY	79	3	DON JUAN	7	26	8
IN SHORT THIS LAST ATTACK THOUGH RICH IN GLORY	83	3	DON JUAN	7	35	1
HIS GLORY MIGHT HALF EQUAL HIS ESTATE	84	3	DON JUAN	7	37	4
FOR GLORY GAPING O'ER A SEA OF SLAUGHTER	91	3	DON JUAN	7	50	7
GLORY BEGAN TO DAWN WITH DUE SUBLIMITY	92	3	DON JUAN	7	51	6
SO NOW MY LADS FOR GLORY--HERE HE TURNED	99	3	DON JUAN	7	64	1
NOTHING--THE WORK OF GLORY STILL WENT ON	106	3	DON JUAN	7	78	1
SHADOWS OF GLORY (LEST I BE CONFOUNDED)	108	3	DON JUAN	7	82	6
BUT GLORY'S GLORY AND IF YOU WOULD FIND	108	3	DON JUAN	7	84	7
YET I LOVE GLORY--GLORY'S A GREAT THING--	118	3	DON JUAN	8	14	1
WOULD FORM A LENGTHY LEXICON OF GLORY	120	3	DON JUAN	8	17	7
IN SEARCH OF GLORY SHOULD LOOK ON BEFORE	127	3	DON JUAN	8	31	7
OF GLORY AND ALL THAT IMMORTAL STUFF	134	3	DON JUAN	8	42	4
OF GLORY WHICH SO PIERCES THROUGH AND THROUGH ONE	138	3	DON JUAN	8	52	6
TROOPS AS ARE MEANT TO MARCH WITH GREATEST GLORY ON	151	3	DON JUAN	8	78	4
THEN FEED HER FAMINE FAT WITH WELLESLEY'S GLORY	174	3	DON JUAN	8	125	8
GLORY TO GOD AND TO THE EMPRESS (POWERS	178	3	DON JUAN	8	133	7
GLORY LIKE YOURS SHOULD ANY DARE GAINSAY	183	3	DON JUAN	9	1	7
EXCEPT THE ALL-CLOUDLESS GLORY (WHICH FEW MEN'S IS)	186	3	DON JUAN	9	8	5
PONDERING ON GLORY CHIVALRY AND KINGS	197	3	DON JUAN	9	30	4
GLORY AND TRIUMPH O'ER HER ASPECT BURST	212	3	DON JUAN	9	59	3
WE LEFT HIM IN THE FOCUS OF SUCH GLORY	229	3	DON JUAN	10	9	2
BAROUCHE WHICH HAD THE GLORY TO DISPLAY ONCE	248	3	DON JUAN	10	49	5
ALAS THAT GLORY SHOULD BE CHILLED BY SNOW	254	3	DON JUAN	10	59	5
THERE'S GLORY AGAIN FOR YOU GENTLE READER ALL	261	3	DON JUAN	10	73	5
THAT ALL THEIR GLORY AS A COMPOSITION	364	3	DON JUAN	13	11	7
JUST TO CONSOLE SAD GLORY FOR BEING GLORIOUS	372	3	DON JUAN	13	32	8
LIKE MAN'S VAIN GLORY AND HIS VAINER TROUBLES	389	3	DON JUAN	13	65	8
HE REVEL'D IN HIS CICERONIAN GLORY	401	3	DON JUAN	13	91	4
AND WERE HER OBJECT ONLY WHAT'S CALL'D GLORY	416	3	DON JUAN	14	13	7
WITH NO GREAT CARE FOR WHAT IS NICKNAMED GLORY	464	3	DON JUAN	15	19	3
RELIEVED ITSELF BY PORK FOR GREATER GLORY	483	3	DON JUAN	15	63	8
ITS GLORY THROUGH ALL AGES SHINING SUNNY	529	3	DON JUAN	16	59	7

GLORY'S

AND LOVE OF GLORY'S BUT AN AIRY LUST	399	2	DON JUAN	4	101	2
BUT DEEMS HIMSELF THE FIRST IN GLORY'S VAN	108	3	DON JUAN	7	84	6
BUT GLORY'S GLORY AND IF YOU WOULD FIND	108	3	DON JUAN	7	84	7
AND SO THEY ARE YET THUS IS GLORY'S DREAM	112	3	DON JUAN	8	1	4
YET I LOVE GLORY--GLORY'S A GREAT THING--	118	3	DON JUAN	8	14	1
WITHOUT WHICH GLORY'S BUT A TAVERN SONG--	144	3	DON JUAN	8	63	4
BEHOLD HIM PLACED IN YOUTH AND GLORY'S PILLORY	204	3	DON JUAN	9	44	V7

GLOSS

OF WASTE AND HASTE AND GLARE AND GLOSS AND GLITTER	237	3	DON JUAN	10	26	2
WHOSE CITIES NIGHT BY NO MEANS DEIGNS TO GLOSS	280	3	DON JUAN	11	26	5

GLOSSY

HER GLOSSY HAIR WAS CLUSTER'D O'ER A BROW	55	2	DON JUAN	1	61	1
TO HIDE THE GLOSSY SHOULDER WHICH UPREARS	108	2	DON JUAN	1	15B	6
THE GLOSSY REBELS MOCK'D THE JETTY STAIN	314	2	DON JUAN	3	75	4
THEIR WAY THROUGH HER SEALED EYELIDS' GLOSSY FRINGES	40	3	DON JUAN	6	67	V7

GLOVE

AND FITS HER LOOSELY--LIKE AN EASY GLOVE	276	2	DON JUAN	3	3	4

GLOVES

MY HAT AND GLOVES STILL LYING ON THE TABLE	428	2	DON JUAN	5	33	4

GLOW

SCOPE TO ALL SUCH AS FEEL THE INHERENT GLOW	13	2	DON JUAN	D	7	6
MOUNTING AT TIMES TO A TRANSPARENT GLOW	55	2	DON JUAN	1	61	5
NOR BURGUNDY IN ALL ITS SUNSET GLOW	251	2	DON JUAN	2	180	6
NOR WINE IN ALL THE PURPLE OF ITS GLOW	251	2	DON JUAN	2	180	V6
THEY LOOK'D UP TO THE SKY WHOSE FLOATING GLOW	253	2	DON JUAN	2	185	1
THE TWILIGHT GLOW WHICH MOMENTLY GREW LESS	255	2	DON JUAN	2	188	4

GLOW   (CONTINUED)
    NOT THAT HIS ANGER DID NOT SOMETIMES GLOW   . . . . . . 300 2 DON JUAN 3   48   V1
    AND SEE A SENTIMENTAL PASSION GLOW . . . . 14 3 DON JUAN 6   17   4
    IN THE CHILL DARK WHEN COURAGE DOES NOT GLOW   . . . . . 121 3 DON JUAN 8   21   3
    BUT RED WITH NO REDEEMING GORE THE GLOW . . . . . . 172 3 DON JUAN 8   122   6
    MY BOSOM UNDERWENT A GLORIOUS GLOW . . . . 226 3 DON JUAN 10   3   3
    OF LIFE REACH TEN O'CLOCK AND WHILE A GLOW   . . . . . 229 3 DON JUAN 10   8   5
    THE TURNPIKES GLOW WITH DUST AND ROTTEN ROW   . . . . . 378 3 DON JUAN 13   44   5
    BEWITCHING TORTURING AS THEY FREEZE OR GLOW   . . . . . 438 3 DON JUAN 14   63   7
GLOW'D
    GLOW'D IN HER CHEEK AND YET SHE FELT NO WRONG   . . . . . 78 2 DON JUAN 1   106   2
GLOWED
    FOR EVER SINCE IMMORTAL MAN HATH GLOWED . . . . . . 226 3 DON JUAN 10   2   6
    WHICH SET THE BEAUTY OFF IN WHICH HE GLOWED   . . . . . 239 3 DON JUAN 10   29   6
GLOWING
    NOR GLOWING REVERIE NOR POET'S LAY   . . . . 73 2 DON JUAN 1   96   3
    AND HALF RETIRING FROM THE GLOWING ARM   . . . . . . 83 2 DON JUAN 1   115   2
    SAW NOTHING HAPPIER THAN HER GLOWING FACE   . . . . . 262 2 DON JUAN 2   198   8
    WERE SCARLET FROM WHOSE GLOWING CENTER GREW   . . . . . 309 2 DON JUAN 3   67   6
    SURMOUNTED AS ITS CLASP--A GLOWING CRESCENT   . . . . . 315 2 DON JUAN 3   77   7
    BUT GAZING ON EACH GLOWING MAID . . . . 326 2 DON JUAN 3   L 15   4
    FELT THE WARM BLOOD WHICH IN HIS FACE WAS GLOWING   . . . 478 2 DON JUAN 5   117   4
    FIRING AND THRUSTING SLASHING SWEATING GLOWING . . . . . 120 2 DON JUAN 8   19   6
    THAN THE MORE GLOWING DAMES WHOSE LOT IS CAST   . . . . 347 3 DON JUAN 12   69   3
    UNTO THE GLOWING INDIA OF THE SOUL . . . . 376 3 DON JUAN 13   39   2
    THE SOBER SAD ANTITHESIS TO GLOWING-- . . . . . . 422 3 DON JUAN 14   28   6
    SINCE THEN SHE HAD SPARKLED THROUGH THREE GLOWING WINTERS 434 3 DON JUAN 14   56   1
    IT PRESSED UPON A HARD BUT GLOWING BUST   . . . . . 560 3 DON JUAN 16   122   3
GLOWS
    IS POESY ACCORDING AS THE MIND GLOWS . . . . . . 414 3 DON JUAN 14   8   4
GLOWWORM
    MUCH AS SHE WOULD HAVE SEEN A GLOWWORM SHINE   . . . . 480 3 DON JUAN 15   56   3
GLUE
    AMBITION AVARICE VENGEANCE GLORY GLUE . . . . 422 2 DON JUAN 5   22   6
GLUT
    THEY HAVE AT HAND A BLOOMING GLUT OF BRIDES   . . . . . 471 3 DON JUAN 15   33   8
GLUTTON
    THE INSULTS TOO OF EVERY SERVILE GLUTTON   . . . . . . 299 2 DON JUAN 3   46   7
GLUTTON'S
    WAS WONT TO BOAST--AS IF A GLUTTON'S TRAY   . . . . . 538 3 DON JUAN 16   78   3
GNASH'D
    AND GNASH'D THEIR TEETH AND HOWLING TORE THEIR HAIR   . . 180 2 DON JUAN 2   45   4
GNAW
    AND FEELING STILL THE FAMISH'D VULTURE GNAW   . . . . . 239 2 DON JUAN 2   157   6
GNAW'D
    'TWAS NATURE GNAW'D THEM TO THIS RESOLUTION   . . . . . 195 2 DON JUAN 2   75   6
GNAWING
    BETWEEN THE GAPING HEIR AND GNAWING GOUT . . . . . . 376 3 DON JUAN 13   40   8
GNAWS
    BUT AT SIXTEEN THE CONSCIENCE RARELY GNAWS   . . . . . 113 2 DON JUAN 1   167   5
GNEISENAU
    AND THAT IF BLUCHER BULOW GNEISENAU . . . . 137 3 DON JUAN 8   49   1
GO
    PERHAPS SOME VIRTUOUS BLUSHES--LET THEM GO--   . . . . 13 2 DON JUAN D   7   2
    THE MAJOR PART OF SUCH APPELLANTS GO . . . . 14 2 DON JUAN D   9   7
    WHO CHOSE TO GO WHERE'ER HE HAD A MIND   . . . . . . 31 2 DON JUAN 1   19   3
    IN CASE OUR LORD THE KING SHOULD GO TO WAR AGAIN   . . . 42 2 DON JUAN 1   38   6
    IF PEOPLE GO BEYOND 'TIS QUITE A CRIME   . . . . . . 65 2 DON JUAN 1   80   7
    IN FRENCH BUT THEN THE RHYME WOULD GO FOR NOUGHT)   . . . 67 2 DON JUAN 1   84   8
    AND THEN--GOD KNOWS WHAT NEXT--I CAN'T GO ON   . . . . 83 2 DON JUAN 1   115   7
    HOW DARE YOU THINK YOUR LADY WOULD GO ON SO . . . . . 101 2 DON JUAN 1   146   8
    THAT WORD IS IDLE NOW--BUT LET IT GO . . . . . . 132 2 DON JUAN 1   195   8
    THE VERY PLACE WHERE WICKED PEOPLE GO . . . . 140 2 DON JUAN 1   207   8
    GO LITTLE BOOK FROM THIS MY SOLITUDE . . . . 149 2 DON JUAN 1   222   1
    I CAST THEE ON THE WATERS GO THY WAYS . . . . . . 149 2 DON JUAN 1   222   2
    EVEN NATIONS FEEL THIS WHEN THEY GO TO WAR   . . . . . 164 2 DON JUAN 2   14   4
    TO BID MEN COME AND GO AND COME AGAIN-- . . . . . . 299 2 DON JUAN 3   47   2
    WHICH MIGHT GO FAR BUT SHE DON'T DANCE WITH VIGOUR   . . 390 2 DON JUAN 4   85   7
    BUT NEXT WHEN I'M ENGAGED TO SING THERE--DO GO   . . . 392 2 DON JUAN 4   88   8
    WHAT MUST I GO TO THE OBLIVIOUS COOKS . . . . 403 2 DON JUAN 4   108   5
    THIS SKIN MUST GO THE WAY TOO OF ALL FLESH   . . . . . 422 2 DON JUAN 5   22   3
    GO AND HE GOETH COME AND FORTH HE STEPP'D   . . . . . 430 2 DON JUAN 5   36   6
    AND THERE WE GO--BUT WHERE FIVE BITS OF LEAD   . . . . 432 2 DON JUAN 5   39   7
    HER FIFTH TO CALL HER MAIDS AND GO TO BED   . . . . . 491 2 DON JUAN 5   139   5
    WITH LADIES IT IS TIME TO GO TO REST . . . . . . 29 3 DON JUAN 6   46   2
    BUT GO THEY MUST AT ONCE AND WILL-I-NILL-I   . . . . 64 3 DON JUAN 6   118   8
    BY TINKLING SOUNDS WHEN THEY GO FORTH TO VICTUAL   . . . 90 3 DON JUAN 7   48   7
    BUT BY THE MASS WHO GO BELOW WITHOUT . . . . . . 124 3 DON JUAN 8   26   5
    MEN RUN AWAY MUCH RATHER THAN GO THROUGH . . . . . . 130 3 DON JUAN 8   35   3
    WHICH WAS CUT OFF AND SCARCE EVEN THEN LET GO   . . . . 154 3 DON JUAN 8   85   8
    I'VE DONE NOW GO AND DINE FROM OFF THE PLATE   . . . . 185 3 DON JUAN 9   6   1
    GO HEAR IT IN YOUR FAMISHED COUNTRY'S CRIES   . . . . 187 3 DON JUAN 9   9   7
    DEATH LAUGHS--GO PONDER O'ER THE SKELETON   . . . . . 188 3 DON JUAN 9   11   1
    (OR RATHER PEOPLES)--GO ON WITHOUT PAUSE   . . . . . 196 3 DON JUAN 9   28   4
    BUT LET IT GO--IT WILL ONE DAY BE FOUND . . . . . . 201 3 DON JUAN 9   37   1
    FROM THEE WE COME TO THEE WE GO AND WHY . . . . . . 210 3 DON JUAN 9   56   3
    OH MRS FRY WHY GO TO NEWGATE WHY . . . . 266 3 DON JUAN 10   85   1
    NOT LONG BEFORE THE MOST OF THEM GO HOME-- . . . . . 277 3 DON JUAN 11   20   3
    OR TO SOME LONELY ISLE OF JAILORS GO . . . . . . 296 3 DON JUAN 11   56   7

GO   (CONTINUED)

	PAGE	VOL	CANTO	STANZA	LN
THUS FAR GO FORTH THOU LAY WHICH I WILL BACK	312	3 DON JUAN	11	90	2
WHAT IS HIS OWN--GO LOOK AT EACH TRANSACTION	321	3 DON JUAN	12	11	4
AND OUGHT TO GO BY QUITE ANOTHER NAME	323	3 DON JUAN	12	15	8
AN AWKWARD INCLINATION TO GO WRONG	338	3 DON JUAN	12	48	4
I'VE NOT BEGUN WHAT WE HAVE TO GO THROUGH	341	3 DON JUAN	12	54	4
WITHIN--ET CAETERA SHALL I GO ON--NO	374	3 DON JUAN	13	36	4
SO LET THE OFTEN USED VOLCANO GO	374	3 DON JUAN	13	36	6
TO CONSTITUTE A READER THERE MUST GO	393	3 DON JUAN	13	73	3
GO TO THE COFFEE-HOUSE AND TAKE ANOTHER	431	3 DON JUAN	14	48	8
AND--WHAT IS WORST OF ALL--WON'T LET YOU GO	438	3 DON JUAN	14	63	8
WILL GO MUCH FURTHER THAN THERE'S NEED TO MENTION	462	3 DON JUAN	15	14	8
AND MIGHT GO ON IF WELL WOUND UP LIKE WATCHES	473	3 DON JUAN	15	40	8
AND THEN THERE WAS--BUT WHY SHOULD I GO ON	475	3 DON JUAN	15	43	1
UNLESS THE LADIES SHOULD GO OFF--THERE WAS	475	3 DON JUAN	15	43	2
GONE TO WHERE VICTORIES MUST LIKE DINNERS GO	485	3 DON JUAN	15	67	5
MIGHT COME OR GO BUT JUAN COULD NOT STATE	511	3 DON JUAN	16	24	7
BY WHICH LORD HENRY'S GOOD TASTE WOULD GO FORTH IN	529	3 DON JUAN	16	59	6
FOR HOW COULD IT GO ON EXPLAIN WHO CAN	537	3 DON JUAN	16	75	7
BUT NOT TO GO TOO FAR I HOLD IT LAW	563	3 DON JUAN	17	2	4

GOADED

	PAGE	VOL	CANTO	STANZA	LN
AND SHELLS OR HELLS IT COULD NOT MORE HAVE GOADED	119	3 DON JUAN	8	16	4

GOAL

	PAGE	VOL	CANTO	STANZA	LN
THE GOAL IS GAIN'D WE DIE YOU KNOW--AND THEN--	93	2 DON JUAN	1	133	8

GOAT'S

	PAGE	VOL	CANTO	STANZA	LN
GOAT'S FLESH THERE IS NO DOUBT AND KID AND MUTTON	238	2 DON JUAN	2	154	2

GO-BETWEEN

	PAGE	VOL	CANTO	STANZA	LN
AT BEST NO BETTER THAN A GO-BETWEEN	84	2 DON JUAN	1	116	8
A GO-BETWEEN YET BLUNDERING IN EXTREMES	155	2 DON JUAN	1	V 6	3
HARD LABOUR'S AN INDIFFERENT GO-BETWEEN	443	3 DON JUAN	14	76	5

GOBLET

	PAGE	VOL	CANTO	STANZA	LN
HIS BELL-MOUTHED GOBLET MAKES ME FEEL QUITE DANISH	392	3 DON JUAN	13	72	7

GOBLINS

	PAGE	VOL	CANTO	STANZA	LN
OF GOBLINS BUT STILL MORE OF MEN AFRAID	98	2 DON JUAN	1	141	3

GOD

	PAGE	VOL	CANTO	STANZA	LN
TO--GOD KNOWS WHERE--FOR NO ONE ELSE CAN KNOW	14	2 DON JUAN	D	9	8
WITH GOD AND MAN'S ABHORRENCE FOR ITS GAINS	18	2 DON JUAN	D	14	8
NELSON WAS ONCE BRITANNIA'S GOD OF WAR	23	2 DON JUAN	1	4	1
SAVE THAT HER DUTY BOTH TO MAN AND GOD	35	2 DON JUAN	1	27	7
TO SCHOOL (AS GOD BE PRAISED THAT I HAVE NONE)	50	2 DON JUAN	1	52	4
THINKING GOD MIGHT NOT UNDERSTAND HER CASE	62	2 DON JUAN	1	75	V8
AND HERE THOU ART A GOD INDEED DIVINE	69	2 DON JUAN	1	88	4
AND THEN--GOD KNOWS WHAT NEXT--I CAN'T GO ON	83	2 DON JUAN	1	115	7
BUT--GOD KNOWS HOW--THIS WISE RESOLVE TAKES WING	85	2 DON JUAN	1	119	V5
GOD GRANT YOU FEEL NOT THEN THE BITTEREST GRIEF	107	2 DON JUAN	1	157	7
FOUND--GOD KNOWS HOW--HIS SOLITARY WAY	126	2 DON JUAN	1	188	V3
TO LIFT OUR FATAL LOVE TO GOD FROM MAN	131	2 DON JUAN	1	194	V8
BUT IF YOU DON'T I'LL LAY IT ON BY GOD	140	2 DON JUAN	1	206	8
AS WHEN HE SWORE BY GOD HE'D SELL HIS SHIRT	154	2 DON JUAN	1	V 5	3
HIS THOUGHTS HOW WELL APPLIED THE NAME OF GOD	154	2 DON JUAN	1	V 5	V2
TO GOD KNOWS WHAT--BUT NEVER YET I SCANNED	161	2 DON JUAN	2	7	V6
ARE LONGER LIVED THAN OTHERS--GOD KNOWS WHY	190	2 DON JUAN	2	65	2
WHO SLEEP AT LAST PERHAPS (GOD ONLY KNOWS)	227	2 DON JUAN	2	134	3
OH LOVE THOU ART THE VERY GOD OF EVIL	266	2 DON JUAN	2	205	7
(WHICH GOD FORBID) OR SOME OR A GREAT MANY	301	2 DON JUAN	3	50	2
'TWAS ALL THE SAME TO HIM--GOD SAVE THE KING	319	2 DON JUAN	3	85	3
I WISH TO GOD THAT SOMEBODY WOULD BUY US	423	2 DON JUAN	5	24	8
EVE AND PAVED (GOD KNOWS HOW) THE ROAD TO EVIL	474	2 DON JUAN	5	109	4
(ENOUGH GOD KNOWS) WOULD MUCH FALL SHORT OF THIS	489	2 DON JUAN	5	134	8
WHICH TAKEN AT THE FLOOD LEADS--GOD KNOWS WHERE	7	3 DON JUAN	6	2	2
LIFE HAS NOUGHT LIKE IT GOD IS LOVE THEY SAY	9	3 DON JUAN	6	6	5
AND LOVE'S A GOD OR WAS BEFORE THE BROW	9	3 DON JUAN	6	6	6
I'M A PHILOSOPHER GOD DAMN THEM ALL	17	3 DON JUAN	6	22	V1
GOOD GOD I WONDER WHAT THEY WOULD BE AT	67	3 DON JUAN	7	3	6
I WONDER (ALTHOUGH MARS NO DOUBT'S A GOD I	77	3 DON JUAN	7	21	1
LET THERE BE LIGHT SAID GOD AND THERE WAS LIGHT	86	3 DON JUAN	7	41	1
WHO WERE ACCUSTOMED AS A SORT OF GOD	104	3 DON JUAN	7	74	3
AND GOD KNOWS WHO BESIDES IN AU AND OU	137	3 DON JUAN	8	49	2
BUT NEVER MIND--GOD SAVE THE KING AND KINGS	137	3 DON JUAN	8	50	1
GOD MADE THE COUNTRY AND MAN THE TOWN	142	3 DON JUAN	8	60	2
BY GOD WE'LL BE TOO LATE FOR THE FIRST CUT	162	3 DON JUAN	8	101	8
AT LEAST NINE-TENTHS OF WHAT WE CALL SO--GOD	163	3 DON JUAN	8	104	2
GLORY TO GOD AND TO THE EMPRESS (POWERS	178	3 DON JUAN	8	133	7
ON HER CANALS WHERE GOD TAKES SEA AND LAND	198	3 DON JUAN	9	31	7
OF GOD THE LOVE OF SENTIMENT THE LOVING	219	3 DON JUAN	9	74	2
SHE ALSO RECOMMENDED HIM TO GOD	240	3 DON JUAN	10	32	1
AND HUMBLY HOPE THAT THE SAME GOD WHICH HATH GIVEN	242	3 DON JUAN	10	36	V7
MY GUARD MY OLD GUARD EXCLAIMED THAT GOD OF CLAY--	254	3 DON JUAN	10	59	2
HAD SUCH BEEN CUT IN PHAETON'S TIME THE GOD	263	3 DON JUAN	10	78	5
OF ENGLISH SAVE THEIR SHIBBOLETH GOD DAMN	274	3 DON JUAN	11	12	2
OR GOD BE WITH YOU--AND 'TIS NOT ABSURD	274	3 DON JUAN	11	12	5
I HEARD THEM WISH GOD WITH YOU SAVE THAT WAY--	274	3 DON JUAN	11	12	8
GOD DAMN YOU LADS I'VE MISSED A HANDSOME BOOTY	276	3 DON JUAN	11	16	V3
WHERE IS NAPOLEON THE GRAND GOD KNOWS	307	3 DON JUAN	11	77	1
THOUGH GOD KNOWS WHENCE IT CAME FROM THERE WAS TOO	483	3 DON JUAN	15	63	2
THEN THERE WAS GOD KNOWS WHAT A L'ALLEMANDE	484	3 DON JUAN	15	66	1
I WISH TO GOD YOU'DE DRESS US SOME SUCH PARTRIDGES	485	3 DON JUAN	15	67	V8
GOD HELP US SINCE WE HAVE NEED ON OUR CAREER	496	3 DON JUAN	15	90	3
THAT SCARLET CLOAK--GOD HELP US--WHEN CLOSE WRAPPED	530	3 DON JUAN	16	61	V7

315

	PAGE	VOL	CANTO		STANZA	LN

GOD-BORN
THE VIRGIN MOTHER OF THE GOD-BORN CHILD . . . . 387 3 DON JUAN 13 61 2

GODDESS
OF THEIR OWN SAND-PITS TO MIX WITH A GODDESS . . . . 220 3 DON JUAN 9 75 3

GODDESSES
BECAUSE OF FILTHY LOVES OF GODS AND GODDESSES . . . . 44 2 DON JUAN 1 41 2
AND HOW THE GODDESSES CAME DOWN TO MEN . . . . . . 72 2 DON JUAN 1 94 4
BUT OH YE GODDESSES OF WAR AND GLORY . . . . 73 3 DON JUAN 7 14 2

GODFATHER'S
BUT SUCH A GODFATHER'S AS GOOD A CARD . . . . . 76 3 DON JUAN 7 19 4

GOD-KNOWS-WHAT
HIS GRACE HIS GOD-KNOWS-WHAT FOR CUPID'S CUP . . . . 216 3 DON JUAN 9 67 3

GODLY
OR NO 'TIS SAID HIS SECT IS RICH AND GODLY . . . . . 472 3 DON JUAN 15 36 4

GOD'S
FOR GOD'S SAKE MADAM--MADAM--HERE'S MY MASTER . . . . 96 2 DON JUAN 1 137 1
FOR GOD'S SAKE READER TAKE THEM NOT FOR MINE . . . 149 2 DON JUAN 1 222 8
(FOR GOD'S SAKE LET ME HAVE A GLASS OF LIQUOR . . . 167 2 DON JUAN 2 20 3
BUT BY GOD'S GRACE HERE WRECKS WERE IN SUCH PLENTY . . 226 2 DON JUAN 2 132 7
HAVE YOU NO FRIENDS -- I HAD--BUT BY GOD'S BLESSING . . 419 2 DON JUAN 5 16 1
CARNAGE (SO WORDSWORTH TELLS YOU) IS GOD'S DAUGHTER . . 116 3 DON JUAN 8 9 6
IN BEGGING HIM FOR GOD'S SAKE JUST TO SHOW . . . . . 165 3 DON JUAN 8 108 3
SMOOTHED EVEN THE SIMPLON'S STEEP AND BY GOD'S BLESSING . 215 3 DON JUAN 9 66 7
AND NO LESS TO GOD'S SON AS WELL AS MOTHER . . . . . 240 3 DON JUAN 10 32 2
AND BEING TOLD IT WAS GOD'S HOUSE SHE SAID . . . . . 262 3 DON JUAN 10 75 1
HEROES MUST DIE AND BY GOD'S BLESSING 'TIS . . . . . 277 3 DON JUAN 11 20 2

GODS
WHERE ALL HIS HOUSEHOLD GODS LAY SHIVER'D ROUND HIM . . 41 2 DON JUAN 1 36 6
BECAUSE OF FILTHY LOVES OF GODS AND GODDESSES . . . . 44 2 DON JUAN 1 41 2
LIKE GARDEN GODS--AND NOT SO DECENT EITHER . . . . . 46 2 DON JUAN 1 45 8
WHAT MEN CALL GALLANTRY AND GODS ADULTERY . . . . . 56 2 DON JUAN 1 63 7
WHATE'ER OUR HOUSEHOLD GODS PROTECT OF DEAR . . . . 338 2 DON JUAN 3 107 6
WHOM THE GODS LOVE DIE YOUNG WAS SAID OF YORE . . . 350 2 DON JUAN 4 12 1
QUITE DISAPPEARED--THE GODS KNOW HOW (I CAN'T . . . 127 3 DON JUAN 8 31 3
OH YE IMMORTAL GODS WHAT IS THEOGONY . . . . . . 192 3 DON JUAN 9 20 1
CONTRIVED TO TALK ABOUT THE GODS OF LATE . . . . . 298 3 DON JUAN 11 60 4
YE GODS I GROW A TALKER LET US PRATE . . . . . . 345 3 DON JUAN 12 64 1
BUT BY THE GODS I SWEAR THAT WHITE IS BLACK . . . . 348 3 DON JUAN 12 71 V2

GODSAKE
AND SO--FOR GODSAKE--HOCK AND SODA WATER . . . . . 156 2 DON JUAN 1 V 8 8

GODSHIP'S
AND BEG HIS BRITISH GODSHIP'S HUMBLE PARDON . . . . 442 3 DON JUAN 14 75 4

GOES
WHEN THEY SUSPECT THAT ANYONE GOES SHARES . . . . . 11 3 DON JUAN 6 10 7
I SKETCH YOUR WORLD EXACTLY AS IT GOES . . . . . . 156 3 DON JUAN 8 89 8
GOES WHEN SOME PERSON CONDESCENDS TO PRAISE . . . . 156 3 DON JUAN 8 90 V4
GOES WHEN SOME PERT PRETENDER DEALS HIS PRAISE . . . 156 3 DON JUAN 8 90 V4
THEIR CASH COMES FROM THEIR WEALTH GOES TO A JEW . . 306 3 DON JUAN 11 75 4
IF HE GOES AFTER DINNER TO A BALL . . . . 333 3 DON JUAN 12 37 V6

GOETH
GO AND HE GOETH COME AND FORTH HE STEPP'D . . . . . 430 2 DON JUAN 5 36 6

GOETHE'S
WOULD BE OLD GOETHE'S--(SEE WHAT SAYS DESTAEL) . . . 320 2 DON JUAN 3 86 6
MUCH IN THE MODE OF GOETHE'S MEPHISTOPHELES . . . . 361 3 DON JUAN 13 7 8

GOING
SHE FELT IT GOING AND RESOLVED TO MAKE . . . . . 62 2 DON JUAN 1 75 2
WAS GOING ON SOME PEOPLE WERE UNQUIET . . . . . . 173 2 DON JUAN 2 33 2
THEIR BEST CLOTHES AS IF GOING TO A FAIR . . . . . 180 2 DON JUAN 2 45 2
AND GOING DOWN HEAD FOREMOST--SUNK IN SHORT . . . . 183 2 DON JUAN 2 51 8
WHICH WAS AN ODD ONE A TROOP GOING TO ACT . . . . 388 2 DON JUAN 4 80 4
THAT THEY WERE GOING TO A MARRIAGE FEAST . . . . . 90 3 DON JUAN 7 49 2
BUT NOW THE TOWN IS GOING TO BE ATTACKED . . . . . 107 3 DON JUAN 7 81 5
AND STILL LESS GUESSING WHERE THEY MIGHT BE GOING . . 120 3 DON JUAN 8 19 4
WHEN A MAN'S COUNTRY'S GOING TO THE DEVIL . . . . . 257 3 DON JUAN 10 66 8
AS GOING AT FULL SPEED--NO MATTER WHERE ITS . . . . 260 3 DON JUAN 10 72 3
GOOD CHRISTIANS THAT TO WHICH THEY ALL ARE GOING . . 278 3 DON JUAN 11 21 V8
BUT NOW I'M GOING TO BE IMMORAL NOW . . . . . 335 3 DON JUAN 12 40 1
OF THE SAD CONSEQUENCE OF GOING ASTRAY . . . . . 336 3 DON JUAN 12 44 6
TO KEEP THE WHEELS GOING OF THE HIGHER CLASS . . . 342 3 DON JUAN 12 57 5
TASTES WE ARE GOING TO TRY THE SUPERNATURAL . . . . 497 3 DON JUAN 15 93 8

GOLD
SINCE GOLD ALONE SHOULD NOT HAVE BEEN ITS PRICE . . 12 2 DON JUAN D 6 4
BAPTIZED IN MOLTEN GOLD AND SWATHED IN DUN . . . 205 2 DON JUAN 2 92 4
HER BROW WAS OVERHUNG WITH COINS OF GOLD . . . . 217 2 DON JUAN 2 116 1
BUT THROUGH THEM GOLD AND GEMS PROFUSELY SHONE . . 220 2 DON JUAN 2 121 4
AND THE SEA SHINES WITH PURPLE--WHITE--AND GOLD . . 230 2 DON JUAN 2 139 V7
GLORY THE GRAPE LOVE GOLD IN THESE ARE SUNK . . . 250 2 DON JUAN 2 179 3
OF CHARMS TO MAKE GOOD GOLD AND CURE BAD AILS . . 293 2 DON JUAN 3 34 5
A DAY OF GOLD FROM OUT AN AGE OF IRON . . . . 294 2 DON JUAN 3 36 3
THE LOVE OF POWER AND RAPID GAIN OF GOLD . . . . 303 2 DON JUAN 3 54 1
GEMS GOLD AND SILVER FORM'D THE SERVICE MOSTLY . . 306 2 DON JUAN 3 61 7
AND GEMS--AND GOLD--AND SILVER--GLITTERED MOSTLY . 306 2 DON JUAN 3 61 V7
GOLD CUPS OF FILIGREE MADE TO SECURE . . . . 307 2 DON JUAN 3 63 5
A SUN EMBOSS'D IN GOLD WHOSE RAYS OF TISSUE . . 309 2 DON JUAN 3 67 7
FRETTED WITH GOLD OR SILVER--BY COMMAND . . . 310 2 DON JUAN 3 69 5
ALL GOLD AND CRIMSON SHONE HER JELICK'S FELLOW . 311 2 DON JUAN 3 70 6
FINISHED WITH BRIGHT GOLD LACE HER JACKET'S FELLOW . 311 2 DON JUAN 3 70 V4
ONE LARGE GOLD BRACELET CLASP'D EACH LOVELY ARM . 312 2 DON JUAN 3 71 1
LOCKLESS--SO PLIABLE FROM THE PURE GOLD . . . . 312 2 DON JUAN 3 71 2

GOLD (CONTINUED)

	PAGE	VOL	CANTO	STANZA	LN
A LIKE GOLD BAR ABOVE HER INSTEP ROLLED	312	2 DON JUAN	3	72	2
TO GILD REFINED GOLD OR PAINT THE LILY	314	2 DON JUAN	3	76	8
JUAN HAD ON A SHAWL OF BLACK AND GOLD	315	2 DON JUAN	3	77	1
I GRANT THE POWER OF PATHOS AND OF GOLD	439	2 DON JUAN	5	49	2
AND ATAGHAN OF GOLD AND SHOES OF YELLOW	451	2 DON JUAN	5	68	V7
A DAZZLING MASS OF GEMS AND GOLD AND GLITTER	465	2 DON JUAN	5	93	7
WHERE I CAN'T SAY OR GOLD OR DIAMOND FLINGS	465	2 DON JUAN	5	94	5
THE AGE OF GOLD (WHEN GOLD WAS YET UNKNOWN	33	3 DON JUAN	6	55	2
THE AGE OF GOLD (WHEN GOLD WAS YET UNKNOWN	33	3 DON JUAN	6	55	2
TO WASTE SO MUCH GOLD FOR A LITTLE DROSS	113	3 DON JUAN	8	3	5
LIKE GOLD AS IN COMPARISON TO DROSS	280	3 DON JUAN	11	26	3
OH GOLD WHY CALL WE MISERS MISERABLE	316	3 DON JUAN	12	3	1
OH GOLD I STILL PREFER THEE UNTO PAPER	317	3 DON JUAN	12	4	7
BUT) OF FINE UNCLIPT GOLD WHERE DULLY RESTS	321	3 DON JUAN	12	12	5
AT MAKING MATCHES WHERE 'TIS GOLD THAT GLISTERS	331	3 DON JUAN	12	32	5
LORDLINGS WITH STAVES OF WHITE OR KEYS OF GOLD	391	3 DON JUAN	13	70	5
WHICH PASSES GHOSTS IN CURRENCY LIKE GOLD	510	3 DON JUAN	16	22	6
BUT RARELY SEEN LIKE GOLD COMPARED WITH PAPER	510	3 DON JUAN	16	22	7

GOLDEN

	PAGE	VOL	CANTO	STANZA	LN
SUCH AS LIT ONWARD TO THE GOLDEN FLEECE	303	2 DON JUAN	3	55	3
SOPHIA'S CUPOLA WITH GOLDEN GLEAM	412	2 DON JUAN	5	3	4
YOU COULD GLIDE O'ER THEM LIKE A GOLDEN FISH	449	2 DON JUAN	5	65	8
AND IN THE MIDST A GOLDEN APPLE GREW--	44	3 DON JUAN	6	76	1
UPON THE GOLDEN FRUIT THE VISION BORE	44	3 DON JUAN	6	77	6
NATIONS ATHWART THE DEEP THE GOLDEN RAYS	319	3 DON JUAN	12	8	4
A GOLDEN SCABBARD ON A DAMASQUE SWORD	422	3 DON JUAN	14	27	5

GONDOLIER

	PAGE	VOL	CANTO	STANZA	LN
THE SONG AND OAR OF ADRIA'S GONDOLIER	87	2 DON JUAN	1	122	3

GONE

	PAGE	VOL	CANTO	STANZA	LN
AND WHEN THE SPOUSE AND FRIEND ARE GONE OFF WHOLLY	74	2 DON JUAN	1	99	7
I SAID THE SMALL-POX HAS GONE OUT OF LATE	92	2 DON JUAN	1	130	7
SHE LOITER'D AND HE TOLD HER TO BE GONE	116	2 DON JUAN	1	173	3
ME AND MY EPIC BRETHREN GONE BEFORE	137	2 DON JUAN	1	202	2
THE ILLUSION'S GONE FOR EVER AND THOU ART	144	2 DON JUAN	1	215	5
WOULD HAVE BEEN VAIN AND THEY MUST HAVE GONE DOWN	171	2 DON JUAN	2	29	2
DAY BROKE AND THE WIND LULL'D THE MASTS WERE GONE	176	2 DON JUAN	2	38	2
FAST BY THE HEAD AND ALL DISTINCTION GONE	179	2 DON JUAN	2	44	2
BUT HE DIED EARLY AND WHEN HE WAS GONE	202	2 DON JUAN	2	87	4
HE KNEW NOT FOR THE EARTH WAS GONE FOR HIM	214	2 DON JUAN	2	111	2
AND FORTH THEY WANDER'D HER SIRE BEING GONE	252	2 DON JUAN	2	182	1
WHERE IS THE PYRRHIC PHALANX GONE	324	2 DON JUAN	3	L 10	3
T' OUR TALE--THE FEAST WAS OVER THE SLAVES GONE	334	2 DON JUAN	3	101	1
WITH HIS BROAD BRIGHT AND DROPPING ORB WERE GONE	355	2 DON JUAN	4	22	4
SENSES TO SLEEP--THE POWER SEEM'D GONE FOREVER	381	2 DON JUAN	4	68	8
THAT TASTE IS GONE THAT FAME IS BUT A LOTTERY	404	2 DON JUAN	4	109	7
OR FRESHER BRIGHTER BUT THE YEAR GONE THROUGH	422	2 DON JUAN	5	22	2
THE MAN WAS GONE IN SOME ITALIAN QUARREL	429	2 DON JUAN	5	34	7
WHEN HE WAS GONE THERE WAS A SUDDEN CHANGE	473	2 DON JUAN	5	108	1
RESTORE ME THOSE PURE FEELINGS GONE FOREVER	9	3 DON JUAN	6	5	8
THEIR GUARDS BEING GONE AND AS IT WERE A TRUCE	23	3 DON JUAN	6	34	6
MEANTIME GULBEYAZ WHEN HER KING WAS GONE	54	3 DON JUAN	6	97	1
AS HE LOOKED DOWN UPON HIS CHILDREN GONE	170	3 DON JUAN	8	117	7
WHO WAS GONE TO HIS PLACE) AND PASSED FOR MUCH	209	3 DON JUAN	9	54	2
OF THE GOOD FEUDAL TIMES FOREVER GONE	255	3 DON JUAN	10	62	3
TELL THEM THAT YOUTH ONCE GONE RETURNS NO MORE	267	3 DON JUAN	10	86	3
THE DRUID'S GROVES ARE GONE--SO MUCH THE BETTER	280	3 DON JUAN	11	25	1
HAD GONE BEFORE HIM AND HIS WARS AND LOVES	284	3 DON JUAN	11	33	2
I LOOK FOR IT--'TIS GONE A GLOBE OF GLASS	306	3 DON JUAN	11	76	4
AND DANDIES ALL ARE GONE ON THE WIND'S WINGS	306	3 DON JUAN	11	76	8
GONE DOWN IT SEEMS TO SCOTLAND TO BE FIDDLED	307	3 DON JUAN	11	78	5
OTHERS FOR OTHER DIRTY WORK GONE THROUGH	314	3 DON JUAN	11	V 76	8
BUT GREY WAS NOT ARRIVED AND CHATHAM GONE	353	3 DON JUAN	12	82	8
I'VE DONE WITH MY TIRADE THE WORLD WAS GONE	381	3 DON JUAN	13	49	1
THE DAYS OF COMEDY ARE GONE ALAS	402	3 DON JUAN	13	94	5
GONE TO WHERE VICTORIES MUST LIKE DINNERS GO	485	3 DON JUAN	15	67	5
THE LAST THIN PETTICOATS WERE VANISHED GONE	504	3 DON JUAN	16	8	5
AND HIS MASS OF THE DAYS THAT ARE GONE	518	3 DON JUAN	16	L 1	4
OF WHAT SHE HAD GONE THROUGH WITH--SINCE A BRIDE	525	3 DON JUAN	16	50	6
SATE SILENT NOW HIS USUAL SPIRITS GONE	552	3 DON JUAN	16	105	6

GOOD

	PAGE	VOL	CANTO	STANZA	LN
(THIS OLD SONG AND NEW SIMILE HOLDS GOOD)	10	2 DON JUAN	D	2	2
EVIL AND GOOD HAVE HAD THEIR TITHE OF TALK	22	2 DON JUAN	1	2	3
A GOOD DEAL LIKE HIM TOO THOUGH QUITE THE SAME NONE	24	2 DON JUAN	1	5	3
AND EVEN THE GOOD WITH INWARD ENVY GROAN	26	2 DON JUAN	1	10	6
A GREAT OPINION OF HER OWN GOOD QUALITIES	32	2 DON JUAN	1	20	2
BESIDES HER GOOD OLD GRANDMOTHER (WHO DOTED)	36	2 DON JUAN	1	28	5
DEAD SCANDALS FORM GOOD SUBJECTS FOR DISSECTION	37	2 DON JUAN	1	31	8
LET'S OWN SINCE IT CAN DO NO GOOD ON EARTH	41	2 DON JUAN	1	36	3
I DON'T THINK SAPPHO'S ODE A GOOD EXAMPLE	45	2 DON JUAN	1	42	4
ALTHOUGH NO DOUBT HIS REAL INTENT WAS GOOD	45	2 DON JUAN	1	43	4
FROM SIRE TO SON TO AUGUR GOOD OR ILL	49	2 DON JUAN	1	51	5
NOTHING BUT WHAT WAS GOOD HER BREAST WAS PEACEABLE--	66	2 DON JUAN	1	83	5
TO THE GOOD SENSE AND SENSES OF MANKIND	69	2 DON JUAN	1	89	2
ACCORDING TO SOME GOOD OLD WOMAN'S TALE	72	2 DON JUAN	1	95	8
A GOOD DEAL MAY BE BOUGHT FOR FIFTY LOUIS	79	2 DON JUAN	1	108	8
AND SO GOOD NIGHT--RETURN WE TO OUR STORY	94	2 DON JUAN	1	134	2
'TIS NOT MY FAULT--I KEPT GOOD WATCH--ALACK	96	2 DON JUAN	1	137	4
DREST TO RECEIVE SO MUCH GOOD COMPANY	106	2 DON JUAN	1	156	8

GOOD   (CONTINUED)

	PAGE	VOL	CANTO		STANZA	LN
SO THAT A SUIT OR ACTION WERE MADE GOOD	109	2	DON JUAN	1	160	5
NOTHING SO DEAR AS AN UNFILCH'D GOOD NAME	112	2	DON JUAN	1	165	5
THE DEVIL'S IN THE URCHIN AND NO GOOD--	115	2	DON JUAN	1	171	4
AND NO GREAT GOOD SEEM'D ANSWER'D IF SHE STAID	116	2	DON JUAN	1	173	6
NONE CAN SAY THAT THIS WAS NOT GOOD ADVICE	122	2	DON JUAN	1	183	1
WITH GOOD DISCRETION AND IN CURRENT RHYME	135	2	DON JUAN	1	200	V8
GOOD WORKMEN NEVER QUARREL WITH THEIR TOOLS	136	2	DON JUAN	1	201	6
I'VE LAID IN TOO A STOCK OF GOOD MACHINERY	136	2	DON JUAN	1	201	V7
ALL THESE CONFIRM MY STATEMENT A GOOD DEAL	138	2	DON JUAN	1	203	5
TO THEIR OWN GOOD THIS WARNING TO DESPISE	141	2	DON JUAN	1	208	2
HINT THAT SOME SIX OR SEVEN GOOD YEARS AGO	143	2	DON JUAN	1	212	4
SO FOR A GOOD OLD-GENTLEMANLY VICE	144	2	DON JUAN	1	216	7
IT MATTERS NOT MUCH HOW BY GOOD OR ILL	146	2	DON JUAN	1	218	V3
AND SO YOUR HUMBLE SERVANT AND GOOD BYE	147	2	DON JUAN	1	221	4
AND IF AS I BELIEVE THY VEIN BE GOOD	149	2	DON JUAN	1	222	3
OF GOOD ADVICE--AND TWO OR THREE OF CREDIT	161	2	DON JUAN	2	9	8
THE GOOD OLD GENTLEMAN WAS QUITE AGHAST	175	2	DON JUAN	2	37	1
THE SHIP WOULD SWIM AN HOUR WHICH BY GOOD LUCK	177	2	DON JUAN	2	40	7
THREW IN BY GOOD LUCK OVER THE SHIP'S RAIL	181	2	DON JUAN	2	48	6
MEN REALLY KNOW NOT WHAT GOOD WATER'S WORTH	201	2	DON JUAN	2	84	4
OUR SHIPWRECK'D SEAMEN THOUGHT IT A GOOD OMEN--	205	2	DON JUAN	2	93	1
AND BY GOOD FORTUNE GLIDING SOFTLY CAUGHT HER	208	2	DON JUAN	2	99	3
BY WHICH NO DOUBT A GOOD DEAL MAY BE MADE	223	2	DON JUAN	2	126	8
BECAUSE THE GOOD OLD MAN HAD SO MUCH NOUS	225	2	DON JUAN	2	130	5
WHICH IS ACQUIRED IN NATURE'S GOOD OLD COLLEGE	228	2	DON JUAN	2	136	8
ALTHOUGH SHE TOLD HIM IN GOOD MODERN GREEK	236	2	DON JUAN	2	150	6
ARE OIL AND GUNPOWDER AND SOME GOOD LESSONS	245	2	DON JUAN	2	169	6
LOVE THOUGH GOOD ALWAYS IS NOT QUITE SO GOOD)	246	2	DON JUAN	2	170	2
LOVE THOUGH GOOD ALWAYS IS NOT QUITE SO GOOD)	246	2	DON JUAN	2	170	2
FOR WITHOUT HEART LOVE'S NOT QUITE SO GOOD)	246	2	DON JUAN	2	170	V2
WHEN JUAN WOKE HE FOUND SOME GOOD THINGS READY	246	2	DON JUAN	2	171	1
TO MAKE US UNDERSTAND EACH GOOD OLD MAXIM	264	2	DON JUAN	2	203	7
SO GOOD--I WONDER CASTLEREAGH DON'T TAX 'EM	264	2	DON JUAN	2	203	8
YET LOVE MAY MAKE MARRIAGE AS GOOD WHITE WINE	277	2	DON JUAN	3	5	V5
DECIDED THUS AND SHOW'D GOOD REASON WHY	281	2	DON JUAN	3	11	6
THE GOOD OLD GENTLEMAN HAD BEEN DETAIN'D	283	2	DON JUAN	3	15	1
MAY NOT HAVE THE GOOD FORTUNE OF ULYSSES	287	2	DON JUAN	3	23	2
OF CHARMS TO MAKE GOOD GOLD AND CURE BAD AILS	293	2	DON JUAN	3	34	5
TO FIND SO MUCH GOOD COMPANY INVITED	294	2	DON JUAN	3	37	8
HE WAS SO GREAT A LOSS TO GOOD SOCIETY	296	2	DON JUAN	3	41	8
BODED NO GOOD WHATEVER IT EXPRESS'D	297	2	DON JUAN	3	42	4
AND THAT GOOD WINE NE'ER WASH'D DOWN BETTER FARE	298	2	DON JUAN	3	45	4
IS GOOD TO GOVERN--ALMOST AS A GUELF	299	2	DON JUAN	3	47	8
(NUPTIAL EXAMPLES ARE AS GOOD AS ANY)	301	2	DON JUAN	3	50	4
FOR SOMETHING BETTER IF NOT WHOLLY GOOD	302	2	DON JUAN	3	53	6
AND MADE HIM A GOOD FRIEND BUT BAD ACQUAINTANCE	303	2	DON JUAN	3	54	8
BUT IN GOOD COMPANY--THE GOUT OR STONE	305	2	DON JUAN	3	59	8
AS THE PSALM SAYS INDITING A GOOD MATTER	316	2	DON JUAN	3	78	8
REVERSING THE GOOD CUSTOM OF OLD DAYS	316	2	DON JUAN	3	79	2
EVEN GOOD MEN LIKE TO MAKE THE PUBLIC STARE--	317	2	DON JUAN	3	81	4
ARE GOOD MANURE FOR THEIR MORE BARE BIOGRAPHY	330	2	DON JUAN	3	94	4
(WE'VE NOT SO GOOD A WORD BUT HAVE THE THING	332	2	DON JUAN	3	97	2
OH HESPERUS THOU BRINGEST ALL GOOD THINGS--	338	2	DON JUAN	3	107	1
GOOD TO THE SOUL WHICH WE NO MORE CAN BIND	360	2	DON JUAN	4	30	6
FOR GOOD OR EVIL BURNING FROM ITS BIRTH	374	2	DON JUAN	4	56	3
HAS SOME GOOD NOTES AND THEN THE TENOR'S WIFE	389	2	DON JUAN	4	83	4
AND MADE AT LEAST FIVE HUNDRED GOOD ZECCHINI	390	2	DON JUAN	4	84	5
POOR CREATURES THEIR GOOD LOOKS WERE SADLY CHANGED	414	2	DON JUAN	5	7	4
GOOD TEETH WITH CURLING RATHER DARK BROWN HAIR	416	2	DON JUAN	5	11	3
I WONDER IF HIS APPETITE WAS GOOD	426	2	DON JUAN	5	30	1
(OF WHICH I MIGHT HAVE A GOOD DEAL TO SAY	434	2	DON JUAN	5	42	3
AND PUT HIMSELF UPON HIS GOOD BEHAVIOUR	437	2	DON JUAN	5	47	5
BABA EYED JUAN AND SAID BE SO GOOD	453	2	DON JUAN	5	73	1
I WISH YOU A GOOD APPETITE--FAREWELL	460	2	DON JUAN	5	84	2
KEEP YOUR GOOD NAME THOUGH EVE HERSELF ONCE FELL	460	2	DON JUAN	5	84	6
A GOOD DEAL PRACTISED HERE UPON OCCASION	464	2	DON JUAN	5	92	8
AND TAKING HINTS IN GOOD PART ALL THE WHILE	473	2	DON JUAN	5	107	4
AS GOOD MEN WEAR WHO HAVE DONE A VIRTUOUS ACTION	473	2	DON JUAN	5	107	8
SHE WAS A GOOD DEAL SHOCKED NOT SHOCKED AT TEARS	479	2	DON JUAN	5	118	1
JUAN'S WAS GOOD AND MIGHT HAVE BEEN STILL BETTER	483	2	DON JUAN	5	124	1
OF GOOD EXAMPLES PITY THAT SO FEW BY	486	2	DON JUAN	5	131	4
IS SOMETIMES GOOD FOR PEOPLE IN HER STATION	490	2	DON JUAN	5	137	8
AND WORKS OF THE SAME POTTERY BAD OR GOOD	491	2	DON JUAN	5	138	6
HE WAS AS GOOD A SOVEREIGN OF THE SORT	495	2	DON JUAN	5	147	5
NOW IF THIS HOLDS GOOD IN A CHRISTIAN LAND	11	3	DON JUAN	6	11	1
WITH ONE GOOD HEARTY CURSE I VENT MY GALL	17	3	DON JUAN	6	22	3
I KNOW NOT HOW BUT GOOD AS ANY OTHER	21	3	DON JUAN	6	31	4
OF ONE GOOD MAN WITH STATELY MARCH AND SLOW	22	3	DON JUAN	6	33	5
AND YAWNED A GOOD DEAL WITH DISCREET SURPRIZE	42	3	DON JUAN	6	73	8
HIMSELF IN AT THE AGE WHEN ALL GROW GOOD	43	3	DON JUAN	6	75	4
WITH YOU DUDU A GOOD NIGHT'S REST HAVE KNOWN	46	3	DON JUAN	6	81	6
AND SO GOOD NIGHT TO THEM--OR IF YOU WILL	49	3	DON JUAN	6	86	1
GOOD MORROW--FOR THE COCK HAD CROWN AND LIGHT	49	3	DON JUAN	6	86	2
AND THEREFORE OF CIRCASSIANS HAD GOOD STORE	51	3	DON JUAN	6	91	5
PERHAPS PRECARIOUS HAD THEY BUT THOUGHT GOOD	53	3	DON JUAN	6	95	5
TO BODE HIM NO GREAT GOOD HE DEPRECATED	57	3	DON JUAN	6	102	2
GROWLING AND GRUMBLING IN GOOD TURKISH PHRASE	64	3	DON JUAN	6	117	2
I LEAVE THEM FOR THE PRESENT WITH GOOD WISHES	65	3	DON JUAN	6	120	1

GOOD (CONTINUED)

	PAGE	VOL		CANTO	STANZA	LN
GOOD GOD I WONDER WHAT THEY WOULD BE AT	67	3	DON JUAN	7	3	6
BUT SUCH A GODFATHER'S AS GOOD A CARD	76	3	DON JUAN	7	19	4
THUS EVEN GOOD FAME MAY SUFFER SAD CONTRACTIONS	83	3	DON JUAN	7	34	5
BEEN ONE TO WHICH A GOOD HEART COULD BE PARTIAL	86	3	DON JUAN	7	40	3
AND ALL PRESAGED GOOD FORTUNE TO THEIR CAUSE	89	3	DON JUAN	7	47	4
(THIS METAPHOR I THINK HOLDS GOOD AS AUGHT	90	3	DON JUAN	7	49	3
MAINTAINED AT THE EXPENSE OF YOUR GOOD KING	118	3	DON JUAN	8	14	3
IN SUCH GOOD COMPANY AS ALWAYS THRONG	123	3	DON JUAN	8	24	6
NOT BY THE NUMBERS GOOD INTENT HATH SAVED	124	3	DON JUAN	8	26	4
THOSE ANTIENT GOOD INTENTIONS WHICH ONCE SHAVED	124	3	DON JUAN	8	26	6
WHEN AFTER A GOOD DEAL OF HEAVY FIRING	125	3	DON JUAN	8	27	7
OR A GOOD BOXER INTO A SAD PICKLE	134	3	DON JUAN	8	43	6
NOT ONLY FAMOUS BUT OF THAT GOOD FAME	144	3	DON JUAN	8	63	3
ITS SANGUINARY WAY GOOD--THEN ANOTHER	146	3	DON JUAN	8	69	2
AMONG THE FOREMOST OFFERED HIM GOOD QUARTER	152	3	DON JUAN	8	80	2
WITH GOOD AND BAD AND WORSE ALIKE PROLIFIC	156	3	DON JUAN	8	89	4
AND ONE GOOD ACTION IN THE MIDST OF CRIMES	156	3	DON JUAN	8	90	1
TO THIS VAIN REFUGE MADE THE GOOD HEART DROOP	157	3	DON JUAN	8	91	4
OF PRESENT LIFE A GOOD DEAL MORE THAN WE--	161	3	DON JUAN	8	100	3
NEITHER--BUT A GOOD PLAIN OLD TEMPERATE MAN	164	3	DON JUAN	8	105	7
THE GOOD OLD KHAN WHO LONG HAD CEASED TO SEE	169	3	DON JUAN	8	116	2
ARE HINTS AS GOOD AS SERMONS OR AS RHYMES	174	3	DON JUAN	8	125	6
OF SINGLE BLESSEDNESS AND THOUGHT IT GOOD	177	3	DON JUAN	8	131	4
WITHOUT A STOMACH--WHAT WERE A GOOD NAME	189	3	DON JUAN	9	14	8
'TIS TIME WE SHOULD PROCEED WITH OUR GOOD POEM	193	3	DON JUAN	9	22	1
FOR I MAINTAIN THAT IT IS REALLY GOOD	193	3	DON JUAN	9	22	2
ARE USELESS MIND GOOD PEOPLE WHAT I SAY--	196	3	DON JUAN	9	28	3
MAKES US BELIEVE OURSELVES AS GOOD AS ANY	216	3	DON JUAN	9	68	8
(THE LAST IF THEY HAVE SOUL ARE QUITE AS GOOD	218	3	DON JUAN	9	71	3
THAT GOOD OLD STEAM-BOAT WHICH KEEPS VERSES MOVING	219	3	DON JUAN	9	74	4
OR THE EAR-TRUMPET OF MY GOOD OLD AUNT	241	3	DON JUAN	10	34	5
YOU'LL DEEM NO DOUBT THEY PUT IT TO A GOOD USE	242	3	DON JUAN	10	36	8
OF THE GOOD FEUDAL TIMES FOREVER GONE	255	3	DON JUAN	10	62	5
GOOD GOVERNMENT HAS LEFT THEM SEEMS BUT CRUEL	256	3	DON JUAN	10	63	8
TEACH THEM THE DECENCIES OF GOOD THREESCORE	267	3	DON JUAN	10	86	1
'TIS NOT SO TO BE GOOD AND BE IT STATED	267	3	DON JUAN	10	87	4
WHICH LOOKS ALONG THAT VALE OF GOOD AND ILL	272	3	DON JUAN	11	8	3
GOOD CHRISTIANS THAT TO WHICH THEY ALL ARE GOING	278	3	DON JUAN	11	21	V8
AFTER THE GOOD EXAMPLE OF GREEN ERIN	286	3	DON JUAN	11	38	7
AND PASSED FOR ARGUMENTS OF GOOD ENDURANCE	294	3	DON JUAN	11	52	4
NOW WERE I ONCE AT HOME AND IN GOOD SATIRE	299	3	DON JUAN	11	62	6
ALL KINDS OF TOIL SAVE FOR OUR COUNTRY'S GOOD--	301	3	DON JUAN	11	65	7
OF THE GOOD COMPANY CAN WIN A CORNER	303	3	DON JUAN	11	69	2
WHOM A GOOD MIEN ESPECIALLY IF NEW	305	3	DON JUAN	11	73	6
A SCOUNDREL AND YOU'LL HAVE GOOD COMPANY	310	3	DON JUAN	11	86	V8
FAR EASIER ENOUGH FOR THE GOOD TOWN OF MANCHESTER	314	3	DON JUAN	11	V 75	3
TO HERD WITH BOYS OR HOARD WITH GOOD THREESCORE--	316	3	DON JUAN	12	2	2
GIVES WITH GREEK TRUTH THE GOOD OLD GREEK THE LIE	325	3	DON JUAN	12	19	8
GOOD PEOPLE ALL OF EVERY DEGREE	325	3	DON JUAN	12	20	1
THOUGH THERE'S A SHORTER A GOOD DEAL THAN THIS	326	3	DON JUAN	12	22	4
SO GOOD AN OPPORTUNITY NO DOUBT--	332	3	DON JUAN	12	35	4
WHICH SHOWS HOW VERY USEFUL GOOD ADVICE IS	333	3	DON JUAN	12	37	V8
THE QUANTITY OF GOOD SHE DID'S UNKNOWN	338	3	DON JUAN	12	48	5
BECAUSE SHE THOUGHT HIM A GOOD HEART AT BOTTOM	338	3	DON JUAN	12	49	2
IT DOES NOR GOOD NOR HARM BEING MERELY MEANT	342	3	DON JUAN	12	57	4
A YOUNG UNMARRIED MAN WITH A GOOD NAME	342	3	DON JUAN	12	58	1
FOR GOOD SOCIETY IS BUT A GAME	342	3	DON JUAN	12	58	3
LIKE POPLARS WITH GOOD PRINCIPLES FOR ROOTS	343	3	DON JUAN	12	59	4
BUT HE HAD SEEN SO MUCH GOOD LOVE BEFORE	346	3	DON JUAN	12	67	4
THE TALENT AND GOOD HUMOUR HE DISPLAYED	355	3	DON JUAN	12	85	5
IN RIGHT GOOD EARNEST--ALSO AN APPEAL	357	3	DON JUAN	12	V 18	2
(FATE IS A GOOD EXCUSE FOR OUR OWN WILL)	364	3	DON JUAN	13	12	6
BECAUSE ITS OWN GOOD PLEASURE HATH DECIDED	366	3	DON JUAN	13	16	8
TO VIRTUE PROPER OR GOOD EDUCATION	372	3	DON JUAN	13	31	3
AND RASH ENTHUSIASM IN GOOD SOCIETY	374	3	DON JUAN	13	35	7
AND AS THE GOOD SHIPS SENT UPON THAT MESSAGE	376	3	DON JUAN	13	39	3
THE PASSEE AND THE PASSED FOR GOOD SOCIETY	396	3	DON JUAN	13	80	7
WHO LOVED PHILOSOPHY AND A GOOD DINNER	399	3	DON JUAN	13	87	2
GOOD AT ALL THINGS BUT BETTER AT A BET	399	3	DON JUAN	13	87	8
GOOD COMPANY'S A CHESS-BOARD--THERE ARE KINGS	400	3	DON JUAN	13	89	1
A MOMENT'S GOOD THING MAY HAVE COST THEM YEARS	408	3	DON JUAN	13	109	6
GOOD HOURS OF FAIR CHEEKS ARE THE FAIREST TINTERS	409	3	DON JUAN	13	111	7
BUT THEN 'TWOULD SPOIL MUCH GOOD PHILOSOPHY	410	3	DON JUAN	14	1	4
BUT FORM GOOD HOUSEKEEPERS TO BREED A NATION	420	3	DON JUAN	14	24	8
WITH EMPHASIS AND ALSO WITH GOOD SENSE--	427	3	DON JUAN	14	38	4
TO HUNT OUR ERRORS UP WITH A GOOD GRACE	430	3	DON JUAN	14	47	6
A WOMAN SO SHE'S GOOD WHAT DOES IT SIGNIFY	435	3	DON JUAN	14	57	8
THAT GOOD BUT RARELY CAME FROM GOOD ADVICE	439	3	DON JUAN	14	66	8
THAT GOOD BUT RARELY CAME FROM GOOD ADVICE	439	3	DON JUAN	14	66	8
HE WAS A COLD GOOD HONOURABLE MAN	440	3	DON JUAN	14	70	1
UNLESS GOOD COMPANY HE KEPT TOO LONG	443	3	DON JUAN	14	77	6
SHE HAD HEARD BUT WOMEN HEAR WITH MORE GOOD HUMOUR	460	3	DON JUAN	15	11	3
'TIS THUS THE GOOD WILL AMIABLY ERR	463	3	DON JUAN	15	17	3
SHE HAD A GOOD OPINION OF ADVICE	469	3	DON JUAN	15	29	1
A DASHING DEMOISELLE OF GOOD ESTATE	474	3	DON JUAN	15	42	2
A RUSS OR TURK--THE ONE'S AS GOOD AS T'OTHER	474	3	DON JUAN	15	42	8
CHILD TO THE CARE OF GUARDIANS GOOD AND KIND	475	3	DON JUAN	15	44	2
IF GOOD IS NONE THE WORSE FOR REPETITION	478	3	DON JUAN	15	51	2

PAGE VOL   CANTO STANZA LN

GOOD   (CONTINUED)
BUT THINKS LESS OF GOOD EATING THAN THE WHISPER . . . . 487 3 DON JUAN 15 70 7
LIKE A GOOD SHIP ENTANGLED AMONG ICE . . . . 490 3 DON JUAN 15 77 7
AND THEN HE HAD GOOD LOOKS--THAT POINT WAS CARRIED . . . 493 3 DON JUAN 15 84 1
AND ALWAYS HAVE DONE SOMEHOW THESE GOOD LOOKS . . . . . 493 3 DON JUAN 15 84 7
AND WHETHER FOR GOOD OR WHETHER FOR ILL . . . . . . 519 3 DON JUAN 16 L 3 1
BY WHICH LORD HENRY'S GOOD TASTE WOULD GO FORTH IN . . . 529 3 DON JUAN 16 59 6
TAKERS OF TITHES AND MAKERS OF GOOD MATCHES . . . . 539 3 DON JUAN 16 80 7
WERE GOOD SMALL-TALK FOR OTHERS STILL LESS GREAT)-- . . . 544 3 DON JUAN 16 91 8
THE GHOST AT LEAST HAD DONE HIM THIS MUCH GOOD . . . . 553 3 DON JUAN 16 107 1
YET ONE THING RATHER GOOD THE GRAVE HAD SPARED . . . . 560 3 DON JUAN 16 121 3
GOOD-FOR-NOTHING
A LITTLE CURLY-HEADED GOOD-FOR-NOTHING . . . . . . 34 2 DON JUAN 1 25 1
GOODLIEST
THE GOODLIEST SOIL OF BODY AND OF MIND . . . . . . 359 3 DON JUAN 13 2 8
GOODLINESS
YOUNG JUAN WAX'D IN GOODLINESS AND GRACE . . . . . . 48 2 DON JUAN 1 49 1
GOODLY
ON THROUGH A FARTHER RANGE OF GOODLY ROOMS . . . . . 442 2 DON JUAN 5 55 2
SO GOODLY WAS HER THIRST FOR SCIENCE GROWN . . . . . 476 2 DON JUAN 5 113 V7
A GOODLY SINECURE NO DOUBT BUT MADE . . . . 22 3 DON JUAN 6 32 1
CONTINUE AS I SAID THIS GOODLY ROW . . . . 22 3 DON JUAN 6 33 3
AND TREES OF GOODLY GROWTH AND SPREADING ROOTS . . . . 43 3 DON JUAN 6 75 8
A GOODLY GUARDIAN FOR HIS INFANT CHARGE . . . . . . 335 3 DON JUAN 12 41 7
GLANCED FROM THE WALLS IN GOODLY PRESERVATION . . . . 390 3 DON JUAN 13 68 3
IN MY YOUNG DAYS THAT CHASTE AND GOODLY VEIL . . . . 422 3 DON JUAN 14 27 2
SO THAT THE BRANCH A GOODLY VERDURE FLINGS . . . . . 436 3 DON JUAN 14 59 3
A GOODLY SPIRIT FOR A STATE DIVAN . . . . 440 3 DON JUAN 14 70 3
THERE WAS A GOODLY SOUPE A LA BONNE FEMME . . . . . 483 3 DON JUAN 15 63 1
THERE WAS A GOODLY MATCH TOO TO BE RUN . . . . . . 527 3 DON JUAN 16 55 5
GOODNESS
OF GOODNESS IN THUS LEAVING THEM A VOICE . . . . . . 452 2 DON JUAN 5 70 5
PROVIDED ALWAYS YOUR GREAT GOODNESS STILL . . . . . 453 2 DON JUAN 5 72 7
GOODS
IN GETTING OUT GOODS BALLAST GUNS AND TREASURE . . . . 286 2 DON JUAN 3 20 8
A GENTLEMAN SO RICH IN THE WORLD'S GOODS . . . . . 371 2 DON JUAN 4 51 3
ALL EARTHLY GOODS SAVE TITHES) AND BADE THEM PUSH ON . . 99 3 DON JUAN 7 64 6
THEIR GOODS AND EDICTS OUT FROM POLE TO POLE . . . . 257 3 DON JUAN 10 65 7
GOOSE
THE ROYAL GAME OF GOOSE AS I MAY SAY . . . . . . 342 3 DON JUAN 12 58 4
TEACH THEM THAT SAUCE FOR GOOSE IS SAUCE FOR GANDER . . . 446 3 DON JUAN 14 83 3
AND STUFF WITH SAGE THAT VERY VERDANT GOOSE . . . . . 497 3 DON JUAN 15 93 6
GORDIAN
HIS VERY NECKCLOTH'S GORDIAN KNOT WAS TIED . . . . . 513 3 DON JUAN 16 29 7
THE GORDIAN OR THE GEORDI-AN KNOT WHOSE STRINGS . . . . 536 3 DON JUAN 16 74 7
GORE
DABBLING ITS SLEEK YOUNG HANDS IN ERIN'S GORE . . . . 16 2 DON JUAN D 12 2
THE LAST SIGHT WHICH SHE SAW WAS JUAN'S GORE . . . . 375 2 DON JUAN 4 58 1
INSTINCT OF GORE AND GLORY EARTH HAS KNOWN . . . . . 401 2 DON JUAN 4 105 7
OF GORE DIVULGED THE CAUSE) THAT HE WAS DEAD . . . . 430 2 DON JUAN 5 35 7
OF HONEST FAME THAN SHEDDING SEAS OF GORE . . . . . 113 3 DON JUAN 8 3 8
A WOUNDED COMRADE SPRAWLING IN HIS GORE . . . . . . 121 3 DON JUAN 8 20 8
AND DEATH IS DRUNK WITH GORE THERE'S NOT A STREET . . . 152 3 DON JUAN 8 82 2
BUT RED WITH NO REDEEMING GORE THE GLOW . . . . . . 172 3 DON JUAN 8 122 6
BUT WHILE THE THIRST FOR GORE AND PLUNDER RAGED . . . . 178 3 DON JUAN 8 132 5
WHO PAINTED THEIR BARE LIMBS BUT NOT WITH GORE . . . . 180 3 DON JUAN 8 136 8
WHO FATTEN ON THEIR COUNTRY'S GORE AND DEBTS . . . . 187 3 DON JUAN 9 10 5
WITH GORE LIKE NADIR SHAH THAT COSTIVE SOPHY . . . . 199 3 DON JUAN 9 33 4
THAT E'ER WERE BREWED FROM ELEMENTS OR GORE . . . . . 356 3 DON JUAN 12 88 4
O'ER THE IRREGULARS IN LUST OR GORE . . . . 537 3 DON JUAN 16 76 5
GORGE
TRANSFERR'D TO GORGE UPON A SISTER SHORE . . . . . . 16 2 DON JUAN D 12 4
BUT A STONE BASTION WITH A NARROW GORGE . . . . . . 72 3 DON JUAN 7 12 1
GORGED
SAYING HE HAD GORGED ENOUGH TO MAKE A HORSE ILL . . . . 240 2 DON JUAN 2 159 8
GORME
AND BRILLIANT BREECHES BRIGHT AS A CAIRN GORME . . . . 204 3 DON JUAN 9 43 5
GORY
ACHILLES' SELF WAS NOT MORE GRIM AND GORY . . . . . 73 3 DON JUAN 7 14 6
AS HE TURNED O'ER EACH PALE AND GORY CHEEK . . . . . 158 3 DON JUAN 8 94 6
GOSPEL
RECEIVE AS GOSPEL AND WHICH GROW MORE ROOTED . . . . 503 3 DON JUAN 16 6 7
GOSPEL'S
A COMMENT ON THE GOSPEL'S SIN NO MORE . . . . . . 352 3 DON JUAN 12 79 2
GOT
OR BEING MOUNTED E'ER GOT DOWN AGAIN . . . . . . 26 2 DON JUAN 1 9 6
(I WONDER HOW THEY GOT THROUGH THE TWELVE HOURS) . . . 30 2 DON JUAN 1 18 6
AND WONDERS WHY THE DEVIL HE GOT HEIRS . . . . . . 75 2 DON JUAN 1 100 8
I'VE GOT NEW MYTHOLOGICAL MACHINERY . . . . 136 2 DON JUAN 1 201 7
I'VE GOT A PLAN TO FORM A TREATISE WHICH . . . . . 138 2 DON JUAN 1 204 V2
AND IN THY STEAD I'VE GOT A DEAL OF JUDGMENT . . . . 144 2 DON JUAN 1 215 7
HAVING GOT DRUNK EXCEEDINGLY TODAY . . . . 156 2 DON JUAN 1 V 8 5
THANK HEAVEN I'VE GOT NO METAPHOR QUITE READY . . . . 160 2 DON JUAN 2 6 7
JUAN EMBARK'D--THE SHIP GOT UNDER WAY . . . . . . 162 2 DON JUAN 2 11 1
BUT JUAN HAD GOT MANY THINGS TO LEAVE . . . . . . 164 2 DON JUAN 2 15 1
GOT TO THE SPIRIT-ROOM AND STOOD BEFORE . . . . . . 174 2 DON JUAN 2 35 3
THE BOATS AS STATED HAD GOT OFF BEFORE . . . . . . 185 2 DON JUAN 2 54 1
WERE COUNTED IN THEM WHEN THEY GOT AFLOAT . . . . . 185 2 DON JUAN 2 54 8
JUAN GOT INTO THE LONG-BOAT AND THERE . . . . . . 186 2 DON JUAN 2 56 1

GOT   (CONTINUED)

	PAGE	VOL	CANTO	STANZA	LN
HEAVEN KNOWS WHAT CASH HE GOT OR BLOOD HE SPILT	223	2 DON JUAN	2	127	5
BUT UP SHE GOT AND UP SHE MADE THEM GET	230	2 DON JUAN	2	139	1
WHICH GOT HIM A FEW PRESENTS AND SOME THANKS	319	2 DON JUAN	3	84	5
IF YOU HAVE GOT A FORMER FRIEND FOR FOE	366	2 DON JUAN	4	41	6
FOR SHE GOT HOLD OF A YOUNG FOREIGN NINNY	390	2 DON JUAN	4	84	V5
HAVE GOT A TRAVELL'D AIR WHICH SHOWS YOU ONE	392	2 DON JUAN	4	88	3
KINDNESS DESTROYS WHAT LITTLE WE HAD GOT	423	2 DON JUAN	5	25	6
BENEVOLENCE DESTROYS WHAT WE HAD GOT	423	2 DON JUAN	5	25	V6
HOW GET OUT HOW THE DEVIL GOT WE IN	435	2 DON JUAN	5	44	2
(THOUGH CLAUDIUS RICH ESQUIRE SOME BRICKS HAS GOT	447	2 DON JUAN	5	62	5
BUT HE HAD GOT HAIDEE INTO HIS HEAD	483	2 DON JUAN	5	124	2
BUT THIS IS HER SERAGLIO TITLE GOT	21	3 DON JUAN	6	31	3
OR GOT RID OF THE PARTIES ALTOGETHER	65	3 DON JUAN	6	119	4
IT SEEMS HAS GOT AN EAR AS WELL AS TRUMPET	74	3 DON JUAN	7	15	8
DON JUAN HAD GOT OUT ON SHOOTER'S HILL	272	3 DON JUAN	11	8	1
THE DYING MAN CRIED HOLD I'VE GOT MY GRUEL	276	3 DON JUAN	11	16	2
(FOR IN THOSE DAYS WE HAD NOT GOT TO GAS) --	278	3 DON JUAN	11	22	8
TO DRAW A HIGH PRIZE NOW HOWE'ER HE GOT HER I	333	3 DON JUAN	12	37	7
WHICH WAS A WONDER IF YOU THINK WHO GOT HIM	338	3 DON JUAN	12	49	4
AT THAT HIS HEART HAD GOT A TOUGHER RIND	353	3 DON JUAN	12	81	6
I'VE GOT A BETTER SIMILIE THAN THAT	375	3 DON JUAN	13	37	V1
THE GENTLEMEN GOT UP BETIMES TO SHOOT	405	3 DON JUAN	13	101	1
OF CHARACTER IN THOSE AT LEAST WHO HAVE GOT ANY	417	3 DON JUAN	14	16	8
HATH GOT BLUE DEVILS FOR HIS MORNING MIRRORS	457	3 DON JUAN	15	4	4
NOW HERE I HAVE GOT THE PREACHER AT A DEAD LOCK	471	3 DON JUAN	15	35	8
FOR YOU HAVE GOT THAT PLEASURE STILL TO COME	498	3 DON JUAN	15	95	4
SAID JUAN HAD NOT GOT HIS USUAL LOOK ELATE	515	3 DON JUAN	16	34	3
ONE CAN'T TELL HOW IT E'ER GOT IN OR OUT	531	3 DON JUAN	16	62	2

GOTH

	PAGE	VOL	CANTO	STANZA	LN
THERE WAS A MODERN GOTH I MEAN A GOTHIC	529	3 DON JUAN	16	58	1

GOTHIC

	PAGE	VOL	CANTO	STANZA	LN
THROUGH THE MOST GOTHIC GENTLEMEN OF SPAIN	26	2 DON JUAN	1	9	4
FROM THE MOST GOTHIC GOTHS OF GOTHIC SPAIN	26	2 DON JUAN	1	9	V4
FROM THE MOST GOTHIC GOTHS OF GOTHIC SPAIN	26	2 DON JUAN	1	9	V4
YE GLORIOUS GOTHIC SCENES HOW MUCH YE STRIKE	255	3 DON JUAN	10	61	3
ALONG THE LAST FIELDS OF THAT GOTHIC GROUND)--	359	3 DON JUAN	13	2	4
THE GOTHIC BABEL OF A THOUSAND YEARS	381	3 DON JUAN	13	50	4
MIXED GOTHIC SUCH AS ARTISTS ALL ALLOW	384	3 DON JUAN	13	55	4
A GLORIOUS REMNANT OF THE GOTHIC PILE	386	3 DON JUAN	13	59	1
AMIDST THE COURT A GOTHIC FOUNTAIN PLAY'D	389	3 DON JUAN	13	65	1
THE GOTHIC CHAMBER WHERE HE WAS ENCLOSED	507	3 DON JUAN	16	15	3
WHERE MANY A GOTHIC ORNAMENT REMAINED	507	3 DON JUAN	16	16	6
THERE WAS A MODERN GOTH I MEAN A GOTHIC	529	3 DON JUAN	16	58	1
FOR GOTHIC DARING SHOWN IN ENGLISH MONEY	529	3 DON JUAN	16	59	8
THE LIGHT THAT THROUGH THE GOTHIC WINDOWS SHONE	568	3 DON JUAN	17	14	5

GOTH'S

	PAGE	VOL	CANTO	STANZA	LN
SINCE RODERIC'S GOTH'S OR OLDER GENSERIC'S VANDALS	129	2 DON JUAN	1	190	V4

GOTHS

	PAGE	VOL	CANTO	STANZA	LN
FROM THE MOST GOTHIC GOTHS OF GOTHIC SPAIN	26	2 DON JUAN	1	9	V4

GOULS

	PAGE	VOL	CANTO	STANZA	LN
OF GUEBRES GIAOURS AND GINNS AND GOULS IN HOSTS	30	3 DON JUAN	6	48	6

GOURMAND

	PAGE	VOL	CANTO	STANZA	LN
GAUNT GOURMAND WITH WHOLE NATIONS FOR YOUR BOOTY	459	3 DON JUAN	15	9	5
HOW SHALL I GET THIS GOURMAND STANZA THROUGH	483	3 DON JUAN	15	63	6

GOURMANDISE

	PAGE	VOL	CANTO	STANZA	LN
CAN'T LIKE RIPE AGE IN GOURMANDISE EXCEL	487	3 DON JUAN	15	70	6

GOUT

	PAGE	VOL	CANTO	STANZA	LN
BUT IN GOOD COMPANY--THE GOUT OR STONE	305	2 DON JUAN	3	59	8
BETWEEN THE GAPING HEIR AND GNAWING GOUT	376	3 DON JUAN	13	40	8
BETWEEN OUR DUTEOUS OFFSPRING--AND THE GOUT	376	3 DON JUAN	13	40	V8
FROM NATURE FOR THE SERVICE OF THE GOUT--	488	3 DON JUAN	15	72	2
TASTE OR THE GOUT--PRONOUNCE IT AS INCLINES	488	3 DON JUAN	15	72	3
HAST EVER HAD THE GOUT I HAVE NOT HAD IT--	488	3 DON JUAN	15	72	7
OF GOUT WHICH RUSTS ARISTOCRATIC HINGES	515	3 DON JUAN	16	34	8

GOVERN

	PAGE	VOL	CANTO	STANZA	LN
THE ENGLISH ALWAYS USE TO GOVERN DAMN	28	2 DON JUAN	1	14	8
IS GOOD TO GOVERN--ALMOST AS A GUELF	299	2 DON JUAN	3	47	8
BY THOSE WHO GOVERN IN THE MOOD POTENTIAL	285	3 DON JUAN	11	35	4

GOVERNMENT

	PAGE	VOL	CANTO	STANZA	LN
WHETHER YOU'RE PAID BY GOVERNMENT IN BRIBES	200	2 DON JUAN	9	35	4
GOOD GOVERNMENT HAS LEFT THEM SEEMS BUT CRUEL	256	3 DON JUAN	10	63	8
NO LESS A FRIEND TO GOVERNMENT--HE HELD	535	3 DON JUAN	16	72	2

GOWN

	PAGE	VOL	CANTO	STANZA	LN
SWORD GOWN GAIN GLORY OFFER IN EXCHANGE	131	2 DON JUAN	1	194	4
AND WRESTLING BOTH HIS ARMS INTO A GOWN	456	2 DON JUAN	5	78	4
AND STITCHED ITS LEAVES INTO A DRESSING GOWN	476	2 DON JUAN	5	113	V8
AS CAESAR WORE HIS ROBE YOU WEAR YOUR GOWN	232	3 DON JUAN	10	15	8
WHEN NATURE WEARS THE GOWN THAT DOTH BECOME HER	380	3 DON JUAN	13	48	3
SAVING HIS NIGHT GOWN WHICH IS AN UNDRESS	555	3 DON JUAN	16	111	2

GRACCHUS

	PAGE	VOL	CANTO	STANZA	LN
GRACCHUS OF ALL MORTALITY WHO LEVELS	237	3 DON JUAN	10	25	2

GRACE

	PAGE	VOL	CANTO	STANZA	LN
YOUNG JUAN WAX'D IN GOODLINESS AND GRACE	48	2 DON JUAN	1	49	1
POSSESS'D AN AIR AND GRACE BY NO MEANS COMMON	55	2 DON JUAN	1	61	7
SHE PRAY'D THE VIRGIN MARY FOR HER GRACE	62	2 DON JUAN	1	75	7
WHICH BY THE VIRGIN'S GRACE LET IN ANOTHER	63	2 DON JUAN	1	76	4
THE CHARMING CREATURES LIE WITH SUCH A GRACE	119	2 DON JUAN	1	178	7
BUT BY GOD'S GRACE HERE WRECKS WERE IN SUCH PLENTY	226	2 DON JUAN	2	132	7

GRACE   (CONTINUED)

	PAGE	VOL	CANTO	STANZA	LN
WITH ALL HIS KEEN WORN LOOK AND GRECIAN GRACE	363	2 DON JUAN	4	35	5
AND BORE HIM WITH SOME GAIETY AND GRACE	388	2 DON JUAN	4	81	6
AND HE ADVANCED THOUGH WITH BUT A BAD GRACE	472	2 DON JUAN	5	106	1
YET EVEN HER TYRANNY HAD SUCH A GRACE	476	2 DON JUAN	5	113	7
SO RECOLLECT THAT THE EXTREMEST GRACE	482	2 DON JUAN	5	123	6
AND RICH WITH ALL CONTRIVANCES WHICH GRACE	54	3 DON JUAN	6	97	4
THE FLEET AND CAMP SALUTED WITH GREAT GRACE	89	3 DON JUAN	7	47	3
HER INWARD GRACE FOR OUTWARD SHOW AND MAKES	96	3 DON JUAN	7	57	7
WHEN HE BEHELD HIS LATEST HERO GRACE	169	3 DON JUAN	8	116	5
OF CARNAGE--HER FAIR AND INFANT GRACE	182	3 DON JUAN	8	140	V7
IN FACT YOUR GRACE IS STILL BUT A YOUNG HERO	184	3 DON JUAN	9	2	8
HIS GRACE HIS GOD-KNOWS-WHAT FOR CUPID'S CUP	216	3 DON JUAN	9	67	3
YOU HAD REASON--'TWAS THAT A YOUNG CHILD OF GRACE	329	3 DON JUAN	12	29	2
THAT I DISSERT LIKE GRACE BEFORE A FEAST	334	3 DON JUAN	12	39	3
IT ADDS AN OUTWARD GRACE UNTO THEIR CARRIAGE--	344	3 DON JUAN	12	62	6
HE HAD THEN THE GRACE TOO RARE IN EVERY CLIME	354	3 DON JUAN	12	84	6
AND RECONCILED ALL QUALITIES WHICH GRACE MAN	368	3 DON JUAN	13	21	7
GRACE OF THE SOFT IDEAL SELDOM SHOWN	428	3 DON JUAN	14	40	6
TO HUNT OUR ERRORS UP WITH A GOOD GRACE	430	3 DON JUAN	14	47	6
HIS GRACE WAS AN ENDURING MARRIED MAN	437	3 DON JUAN	14	62	2
HER GRACE TOO PASS'D FOR BEING AN INTRIGANTE	438	3 DON JUAN	14	63	1
THEN ASKED HER GRACE WHAT NEWS WERE OF THE DUKE OF LATE	515	3 DON JUAN	16	34	5
HER GRACE REPLIED HIS GRACE WAS RATHER PAINED	515	3 DON JUAN	16	34	6
HER GRACE REPLIED HIS GRACE WAS RATHER PAINED	515	3 DON JUAN	16	34	6
NOT SO HER GRACIOUS GRACEFUL GRACELESS GRACE	525	3 DON JUAN	16	49	1
HER GRACE TOO ALSO SEIZED THE SAME OCCASION	526	3 DON JUAN	16	53	4
AND GRACE IS SAID THE GRACE I SHOULD HAVE SUNG--	538	3 DON JUAN	16	77	8
AND GRACE IS SAID THE GRACE I SHOULD HAVE SUNG--	538	3 DON JUAN	16	77	8
SOME PRAISED HER BEAUTY OTHERS HER GREAT GRACE	550	3 DON JUAN	16	102	1
THE PHANTOM OF HER FROLIC GRACE--FITZ-FULKE	561	3 DON JUAN	16	123	8
THE GUESTS DROPPED IN--THE LAST BUT ONE HER GRACE	568	3 DON JUAN	17	13	7
HER GRACE TOO HAD A SORT OF AIR REBUKED--	568	3 DON JUAN	17	14	6

GRACED

| A FOREIGNER OF RANK HAD GRACED OUR SHORE | 283 | 3 DON JUAN | 11 | 32 | 6 |
| GRACED WITH SOME MERIT AND WITH MORE EFFRONTERY | 401 | 3 DON JUAN | 13 | 91 | 7 |

GRACEFUL

AND SUCH SWEET GIRLS--I MEAN SUCH GRACEFUL LADIES	159	2 DON JUAN	2	5	5
HIS TURBAN FURL'D IN MANY A GRACEFUL FOLD	315	2 DON JUAN	3	77	5
WITH GRACEFUL ACTION SCIENCE NOT A JOT	392	2 DON JUAN	4	89	3
HIS ANSWERS WITH A VERY GRACEFUL BOW	223	3 DON JUAN	9	83	3
THEY ADDED GRACEFUL NECKS WHITE HANDS AND ARMS	408	3 DON JUAN	13	107	8
GRACEFUL AS DIAN WHEN SHE DRAWS HER BOW	517	3 DON JUAN	16	38	5
WITH THAT SHE ROSE AS GRACEFUL AS A ROE	517	3 DON JUAN	16	38	V5
NOT SO HER GRACIOUS GRACEFUL GRACELESS GRACE	525	3 DON JUAN	16	49	1

GRACEFULLY

| NOR WEAR AS GRACEFULLY AS GAULS HER GARB | 350 | 3 DON JUAN | 12 | 75 | 3 |

GRACELESS

| WHICH GAVE HER DUKES THE GRACELESS NAME OF BIRON | 253 | 3 DON JUAN | 10 | 58 | 4 |
| NOT SO HER GRACIOUS GRACEFUL GRACELESS GRACE | 525 | 3 DON JUAN | 16 | 49 | 1 |

GRACE'S

| THE MAGIC OF HER GRACE'S TALISMAN | 437 | 3 DON JUAN | 14 | 62 | 6 |

GRACES

IN THE SAME OBJECT GRACES QUITE AS KILLING	270	2 DON JUAN	2	213	3
FLUNG HOVERING GRACES O'ER HIM LIKE A BANNER	223	3 DON JUAN	9	83	8
OR DID WHAT THEY SHOULD NOT WITH FOREIGN GRACES	368	3 DON JUAN	13	23	4
ADMIRING MORE MINERVA THAN THE GRACES	494	3 DON JUAN	15	85	3
FOR ANY DEVIATION FROM THE GRACES	539	3 DON JUAN	16	79	7
WHILE ADELINE DISPENSED HER AIRS AND GRACES	548	3 DON JUAN	16	100	1

GRACIOUS

HER FACE WAS NOBLE HER EYES FINE MOUTH GRACIOUS	211	3 DON JUAN	9	58	8
NOT SO HER GRACIOUS GRACEFUL GRACELESS GRACE	525	3 DON JUAN	16	49	1
HIS SUBJECTS BY HIS GRACIOUS ACCEPTATION)	528	3 DON JUAN	16	56	7

GRACIOUSLY

| INSTEAD OF GLIDING GRACIOUSLY DOWN LETHE | 245 | 3 DON JUAN | 10 | 42 | 7 |

GRADUALLY

| FOR SHORE IT WAS AND GRADUALLY GREW | 207 | 2 DON JUAN | 2 | 97 | 7 |

GRAFTED

| BUT AS THERE'S SAFETY GRAFTED IN THE NUMBER | 371 | 3 DON JUAN | 13 | 30 | 1 |

GRAIN

| IN MARBLE FONTS THERE GRAIN AND FLOWER AND FRUIT | 373 | 2 DON JUAN | 4 | 55 | 2 |

GRAINS

| R PULV COM THREE GRAINS IPECACUANHAE | 244 | 3 DON JUAN | 10 | 41 | 5 |

GRAMMAR

| (OR BEATEN IF YOU INSIST ON GRAMMAR THOUGH | 87 | 3 DON JUAN | 7 | 42 | 5 |
| EVEN FROM OUR GRAMMAR UPWARDS FRIENDS OF YORE | 542 | 3 DON JUAN | 16 | 86 | 5 |

GRAMMERCY

| THEN GRAMMERCY FOR THE BLACK FRIAR | 520 | 3 DON JUAN | 16 | L 6 | 5 |

GRANBY

| PRINCE FERDINAND GRANBY BURGOYNE KEPPEL HOWE | 22 | 2 DON JUAN | 1 | 2 | 2 |

GRAND

HOW GRAND HIS SENTIMENTS WHICH NEER RUN RIOT	154	2 DON JUAN	1	V 5	2
TO PROVE ITS GRAND INGREDIENT IS ENNUI	332	2 DON JUAN	3	97	8
'TIS A GRAND SIGHT FROM OFF THE GIANT'S GRAVE	413	2 DON JUAN	5	5	3
AND ONE BY ONE IN TURN SOME GRAND MISTAKE	421	2 DON JUAN	5	21	7
THOUGH CERTES BY NO MEANS SO GRAND A SIGHT	444	2 DON JUAN	5	58	5
THOUGH HORRIBLE TO SEE YET GRAND TO TELL	489	2 DON JUAN	5	135	5
THE LASH TO BABA--BUT HER GRAND RESOURCE	491	2 DON JUAN	5	139	7
WITH NOTHING VERY GRAND TO MAKE A RIOT	32	3 DON JUAN	6	53	V4

GRAND (CONTINUED)

		PAGE	VOL		CANTO	STANZA	LN
BUT OH THOU GRAND LEGITIMATE ALEXANDER		52	3	DON JUAN	6	93	1
DECLARED WITH ALL HIS GRAND DISCOVERIES RECENT		69	3	DON JUAN	7	5	6
WHEN LONDON HAD A GRAND ILLUMINATION		88	3	DON JUAN	7	44	2
AND FACT IS TRUTH THE GRAND DESIDERATUM		107	3	DON JUAN	7	81	2
OH YE LESS GRAND LONG LIST OF KILLED AND WOUNDED		108	3	DON JUAN	7	82	2
THE HERO OF THIS GRAND POETIC RIDDLE		181	3	DON JUAN	8	139	3
SEEING HOW ART CAN MAKE HER WORK MORE GRAND		204	3	DON JUAN	9	44	5
CATHERINE WHO WAS THE GRAND EPITOME		211	3	DON JUAN	9	57	1
TO END OR TO BEGIN WITH THE NEXT GRAND		220	3	DON JUAN	9	76	2
IF HISTORY THE GRAND LIAR EVER SAITH		222	3	DON JUAN	9	81	4
AND YET I SEEK NOT TO BE GRAND NOR WITTY--		233	3	DON JUAN	10	17	6
MAN 'MIDST THY MOULDY MAMMOTHS GRAND CULVIER		250	3	DON JUAN	10	52	4
TO ME APPEARS A STIFF YET GRAND ERECTION		280	3	DON JUAN	11	25	7
THE GRAND NAPOLEON OF THE REALMS OF RHYME		296	3	DON JUAN	11	55	8
WHERE IS NAPOLEON THE GRAND GOD KNOWS		307	3	DON JUAN	11	77	1
AS THUS ON THURSDAY THERE WAS A GRAND DINNER		383	3	DON JUAN	13	54	1
IN A GRAND ARCH WHICH ONCE SCREENED MANY AN AISLE		386	3	DON JUAN	13	59	3
YET LEFT A GRAND IMPRESSION ON THE MIND		390	3	DON JUAN	13	67	5
THE GRAND ARCANUM'S NOT FOR MEN TO SEE ALL		419	3	DON JUAN	14	22	5
FOR SEVERAL WINTERS IN THE GRAND GRAND MONDE		428	3	DON JUAN	14	42	3
FOR SEVERAL WINTERS IN THE GRAND GRAND MONDE		428	3	DON JUAN	14	42	3
THE GRAND ANTITHESIS TO GREAT ENNUI		457	3	DON JUAN	15	2	3
BUT I MUST CROWD ALL INTO ONE GRAND MESS		483	3	DON JUAN	15	64	1
AND INDIGESTION'S GRAND MULTIPLICATION		486	3	DON JUAN	15	69	3
AND AS THE ISTHMUS OF THE GRAND CONNECTION		534	3	DON JUAN	16	69	7
ON ADELINE WHILE PLAYING HER GRAND ROLE		546	3	DON JUAN	16	96	3

GRAND-DAD'S

TO THOSE RELATED IN MY GRAND-DAD'S NARRATIVE		229	2	DON JUAN	2	137	8

GRANDE

AND IF IN FACT SHE TAKES TO A GRANDE PASSION		351	3	DON JUAN	12	77	1

GRANDFATHER

SIGH LIKE HIS SON THAN COUGH LIKE HIS GRANDFATHER		228	3	DON JUAN	10	6	8

GRANDMAMMA

HER GREAT GREAT GRANDMAMMA CHOSE TO REMAIN		52	2	DON JUAN	1	56	8
'TIS SAID THAT DONNA JULIA'S GRANDMAMMA		53	2	DON JUAN	1	58	7

GRANDMOTHER

BESIDES HER GOOD OLD GRANDMOTHER (WHO DOTED)		36	2	DON JUAN	1	28	5
BUT A MAN'S GRANDMOTHER IS DEEMED FAIR GAME		53	3	DON JUAN	6	94	V5

GRANDMOTHER'S

I'VE BRIBED MY GRANDMOTHER'S REVIEW--THE BRITISH		141	2	DON JUAN	1	209	8

GRANDMOTHERS

READ--WERE IT BUT YOUR GRANDMOTHERS TO VEX		403	2	DON JUAN	4	108	V6

GRANDSON

OH THOU HER LAWFUL GRANDSON ALEXANDER		52	3	DON JUAN	6	93	V1

GRANITE

THE SPRING GUSH'D THROUGH GRIM MOUTHS OF GRANITE MADE		389	3	DON JUAN	13	65	5

GRANT

GOD GRANT YOU FEEL NOT THEN THE BITTEREST GRIEF		107	2	DON JUAN	1	157	7
OF THE THREE HUNDRED GRANT BUT THREE		323	2	DON JUAN	3	L 7	5
I GRANT THE POWER OF PATHOS AND OF GOLD		439	2	DON JUAN	5	49	2
I GRANT YOU IN A CHURCH 'TIS VERY WELL		444	2	DON JUAN	5	59	2
IN HISTORY BUT WE AT LEAST MAY GRANT		127	3	DON JUAN	8	31	5

GRANTED

AND HEAR THE HEART BEAT WITH THE LOVE IT GRANTED		73	2	DON JUAN	1	96	6
WHICH JULIA HALF WITHHELD AND THEN HALF GRANTED		120	2	DON JUAN	1	180	2
WITH ALL IT GRANTED AND WITH ALL IT GRANTS		260	2	DON JUAN	2	195	8
IS THAT TO WHICH HER HEART IS WHOLLY GRANTED		276	2	DON JUAN	3	4	6
THE MERCY HE HAD GRANTED OFT ABUSED		303	2	DON JUAN	3	54	4
'TIS GRANTED AND THE VALET MOUNTS THE DICKEY--		380	2	DON JUAN	13	47	1
AT EIGHTEEN SHE WITH DUE DEMUR HAD GRANTED		434	3	DON JUAN	14	55	V5
HE TAXED HIS TONGUE FOR WORDS WHICH WERE NOT GRANTED		511	3	DON JUAN	16	23	7
TO STATE THE CASE IT MIGHT BE TA'EN FOR GRANTED		514	3	DON JUAN	16	33	7

GRANTING

AS IF SHE RATHER ORDERED THAN WAS GRANTING--		474	2	DON JUAN	5	109	8

GRANTORS

UNLESS TO PLAGUE THE GRANTORS--YET SO TRUE IT IS		190	2	DON JUAN	2	65	3

GRANTS

WITH ALL IT GRANTED AND WITH ALL IT GRANTS		260	2	DON JUAN	2	195	8

GRAPE

GLORY THE GRAPE LOVE GOLD IN THESE ARE SUNK		250	2	DON JUAN	2	179	3
AND BY A FIRE OF MUSQUETRY AND GRAPE		81	3	DON JUAN	7	29	7
AND GRAPE IN VOLLEYS LIKE A VINEYARD SCATTERS		160	3	DON JUAN	8	98	8
AND THIS IS STRONGER THAN THE STRONGEST GRAPE		375	3	DON JUAN	13	37	7
THE RED GRAPE IN THE SUNNY LANDS OF SONG		394	3	DON JUAN	13	76	4
THE UNMINGLED ESSENCE OF THE GRAPE AND YET		458	3	DON JUAN	15	7	2

GRAPES

SWEET IS THE VINTAGE WHEN THE SHOWERING GRAPES		88	2	DON JUAN	1	124	1

GRAPPLE

AND THIS IS THE SOLE MORTAL WHO COULD GRAPPLE		225	3	DON JUAN	10	1	7

GRAPPLED

ALFONSO GRAPPLED TO DETAIN THE FOE		124	2	DON JUAN	1	186	1

GRAPPLES

LIKE ONE WHO GRAPPLES WITH HIS ENEMY		184	2	DON JUAN	2	52	7

GRASP

GENTLY BUT PALPABLY CONFIRM'D ITS GRASP		81	2	DON JUAN	1	111	2
WITHIN HIS GRASP HE CLUNG TO IT AND SORE		212	2	DON JUAN	2	107	5
HER GLANCE NOR GRASP FOR STILL SHE GAZED AND GRASP'D		361	2	DON JUAN	4	32	7
IN VAIN SHE STRUGGLED IN HER FATHER'S GRASP--		370	2	DON JUAN	4	48	4

```
                                             PAGE VOL      CANTO STANZA LN
GRASP'D
    HER GLANCE NOR GRASP FOR STILL SHE GAZED AND GRASP'D  . . . 361  2 DON JUAN  4    32    7
GRASPS
    HALF BURIED IN THE TRESSES WHICH IT GRASPS  . . . . .  . 259  2 DON JUAN  2   194    4
GRASS
    AND FLESH (WHICH DEATH MOWS DOWN TO HAY) IS GRASS  . . . . 147  2 DON JUAN  1   220    4
    THE GRASS UPON MY GRAVE WILL GROW AS LONG  . . . . . . 398  2 DON JUAN  4    99    7
    GRASS BEFORE SCYTHES OR CORN BELOW THE SICKLE  . . . . . 134  3 DON JUAN  8    43    2
    WHICH SCARCELY ROSE MUCH HIGHER THAN GRASS BLADES  . . . . 136  3 DON JUAN  8    47    8
    HIS LAST AWARD WILL HAVE THE LONG GRASS GROW  . . . . . 299  3 DON JUAN 11    61    4
    THE GRASS MY TABLE-CLOTH IN OPEN AIR  . . . . . . . 488  3 DON JUAN 15    73    6
    AS O'ER THE GRASS THE DEW  . . . . . . . . . 520  3 DON JUAN 16  L  6    4
    TO GAZE INSTEAD OF PAVEMENT UPON GRASS  . . . . . . 539  3 DON JUAN 16    81    3
GRASS-GROWN
    TO ONE SMALL GRASS-GROWN PATCH (WHICH MUST AWAIT  . . . . 237  3 DON JUAN 10    25    5
GRATE
    THE DYING EMBERS DWINDLE IN THE GRATE--  . . . . . . 499  3 DON JUAN 15    97    7
GRATEFUL
    GRATEFUL SHE WAS AND YET A LITTLE SORE--  . . . . . . 63  2 DON JUAN  1    76    5
    HIS YOUNG LIP THANK'D IT WITH A GRATEFUL KISS  . . . . . 81  2 DON JUAN  1   112    3
GRATIFY
    TO GRATIFY LIKE A HUGE MOTH THIS ONE SENSE  . . . . . 88  2 DON JUAN  7    44    8
    ENOUGH TO GRATIFY A BEE'S SLIGHT MUNCHINGS  . . . . . 301  3 DON JUAN 11    66    5
GRATIFYING
    THE TEETH STILL KEPT THEIR GRATIFYING HOLD  . . . . . 153  3 DON JUAN  8    83    7
GRATIS
    BY WHICH MEN ARE UNSUFFOCATED GRATIS  . . . . . . 92  2 DON JUAN  1   130    5
    THE LIBELLER'S GRATIS COUNSEL DIRTY SHIELD  . . . . . 151  2 DON JUAN  1  V  2    3
    RENOWNED FOR RUINING GREAT BRITAIN GRATIS  . . . . . 186  3 DON JUAN  9     8    8
    WHO EATS FIRE GRATIS (SINCE THE PAY'S BUT SMALL)  . . . . 446  3 DON JUAN 14    83    6
    LIKE ALL WHO GIVE AND EKE RECEIVE IT GRATIS  . . . . . 469  3 DON JUAN 15    29    2
GRATTAN
    WHERE GRATTAN CURRAN SHERIDAN ALL THOSE  . . . . . . 307  3 DON JUAN 11    77    3
GRAVE
    LIKE SAMUEL FROM THE GRAVE TO FREEZE ONCE MORE  . . . . . 15  2 DON JUAN  D    11    2
    FLOWERS TO THE GRAVE) AND SOBBING OFTEN HE  . . . . . 165  2 DON JUAN  2    17    6
    AS EAGER TO ANTICIPATE THEIR GRAVE  . . . . . . . 184  2 DON JUAN  2    52    4
    AND SO HE FOUND A WINE-AND-WATERY GRAVE  . . . . . . 186  2 DON JUAN  2    57    5
    SHOULD SUCK HIM BACK TO HER INSATIATE GRAVE  . . . . . 213  2 DON JUAN  2   108    4
    YOUNG YET HER ELDER AND OF BROW LESS GRAVE  . . . . . 216  2 DON JUAN  2   115    3
    SIMPLER AND YET OF COLOURS NOT SO GRAVE  . . . . . . 220  2 DON JUAN  2   120    3
    OR PEOPLE IN A TRANCE INTO THEIR GRAVE  . . . . . . 225  2 DON JUAN  2   130    4
    SAPPHO THE SAGE BLUE-STOCKING IN WHOSE GRAVE  . . . . . 266  2 DON JUAN  2   205    4
    TEARS SHED INTO THE GRAVE OF THE CONNEXION  . . . . . 301  2 DON JUAN  3    50    7
    FOR STANDING ON THE PERSIAN'S GRAVE  . . . . . . . 321  2 DON JUAN  3  L  3    5
    AND WHEN HIS BONES ARE DUST HIS GRAVE A BLANK  . . . . . 327  2 DON JUAN  3    89    1
    THE OLD ARCHER'S SHAFTS PERHAPS THE EARLY GRAVE  . . . . 350  2 DON JUAN  4    12    7
    NO SIGN SAVE BREATH OF HAVING LEFT THE GRAVE  . . . . . 378  2 DON JUAN  4    63    8
    AND WENT DOWN TO THE GRAVE UNBORN WHEREIN  . . . . . 382  2 DON JUAN  4    70    5
    NONE BUT HER OWN AND FATHER'S GRAVE IS THERE  . . . . . 383  2 DON JUAN  4    72    3
    O'ERSHADOW'D THERE BY MANY A HERO'S GRAVE  . . . . . 387  2 DON JUAN  4    79    4
    THE GRASS UPON MY GRAVE WILL GROW AS LONG  . . . . . 398  2 DON JUAN  4    99    7
    'TIS A GRAND SIGHT FROM OFF THE GIANT'S GRAVE  . . . . . 413  2 DON JUAN  5     5    3
    WHICH TUMBLED ALL MANKIND INTO THE GRAVE  . . . . . 192  3 DON JUAN  9    19    4
    WHICH PUTS MY PEGASUS TO THESE GRAVE PACES  . . . . . 334  3 DON JUAN 12    39    8
    OR SOMEONE FOR HIM IN SOME SAGE GRAVE MOOD  . . . . . 371  3 DON JUAN 13    29    3
    IN HIS GRAVE OFFICE SO COMPLETELY SKILL'D  . . . . . 399  3 DON JUAN 13    88    6
    NOW GRAVE NOW GAY BUT NEVER DULL OR PERT  . . . . . 426  3 DON JUAN 14    37    5
    LOOKED GRAVE AND PALE TO SEE HER FRIEND'S FRAGILITY  . . 430  3 DON JUAN 14    46    7
    OR GRAVE LORD GEORGE WITH WHOM PERHAPS MIGHT END  . . . . 470  3 DON JUAN 15    33    4
    RADIANT AND GRAVE--AS PITYING MAN'S DECLINE  . . . . . 476  3 DON JUAN 15    45    5
    HIS TACT TOO TEMPER'D HIM FROM GRAVE TO GAY  . . . . . 492  3 DON JUAN 15    82    5
    AND THE PALE SMILE OF BEAUTIES IN THE GRAVE  . . . . . 509  3 DON JUAN 16    19    1
    YET ONE THING RATHER GOOD THE GRAVE HAD SPARED  . . . . 560  3 DON JUAN 16   121    3
GRAVEL
    ALONG HIS WASTED CHEEK AND SEEMED TO GRAVEL  . . . . . 245  3 DON JUAN 10    43    7
GRAVEN
    FROM HAIDEE'S GLANCE THAN ANY GRAVEN LETTER  . . . . . 242  2 DON JUAN  2   163    8
    OR GRAVEN STONE FOUND IN A BARRACK'S STATION  . . . . . 327  2 DON JUAN  3    89    6
GRAVES
    OF SENSE AND SONG ABOVE YOUR GRAVES MAY HISS--  . . . . 334  2 DON JUAN  3   100    6
    LASH'D FROM THE FOAM OF AGES WHILE THE GRAVES  . . . . . 500  3 DON JUAN 15    99    7
GRAVITATION
    IN A MOST NATURAL WHIRL CALLED GRAVITATION  . . . . . 225  3 DON JUAN 10     1    6
GRAVITY
    HE LIKED THE GENTLE SPANIARD FOR HIS GRAVITY  . . . . . 368  3 DON JUAN 13    22    1
GRAY
    BUT NOW AT THIRTY YEARS MY HAIR IS GRAY--  . . . . . 143  2 DON JUAN  1   213    1
    WITH RESOLUTION IN HIS DARK GRAY EYE  . . . . . . 416  2 DON JUAN  5    10    7
    WHOSE COLOUR WAS NOT BLACK NOR WHITE NOR GRAY  . . . . . 462  2 DON JUAN  5    88    4
    AND THE SKY SHOWS THAT VERY ANCIENT GRAY  . . . . . 422  3 DON JUAN 14    28    5
GRAZING
    REIGN'D TILL ONE SUMMER'S DAY HE TOOK TO GRAZING  . . . . 445  2 DON JUAN  5    60    4
GREAT
    HAS GENERALLY NO GREAT CROP TO SPARE IT HE  . . . . . 14  2 DON JUAN  D     9    3
    FOR NATIVE SPANISH SHE HAD NO GREAT CARE  . . . . . 28  2 DON JUAN  1    13    5
    WITH NO GREAT LOVE FOR LEARNING OR THE LEARN'D  . . . . 31  2 DON JUAN  1    19    2
    A GREAT OPINION OF HER OWN GOOD QUALITIES  . . . . . 32  2 DON JUAN  1    20    2
    WAS MANIFESTED IN A GREAT SENSATION  . . . . . . . 38  2 DON JUAN  1    33    8
```

GREAT   (CONTINUED)

	PAGE	VOL	CANTO		STANZA	LN
HER GREAT GREAT GRANDMAMMA CHOSE TO REMAIN	52	2	DON JUAN	1	56	8
HER GREAT GREAT GRANDMAMMA CHOSE TO REMAIN	52	2	DON JUAN	1	56	8
HER RESOLUTIONS WERE MOST TRULY GREAT	62	2	DON JUAN	1	75	5
THE MISCHIEF AFTER ALL COULD NOT BE GREAT	67	2	DON JUAN	1	85	6
UNTIL HIS MIGHTY HEART IN ITS GREAT MOOD	70	2	DON JUAN	1	91	3
IN CASE HE THOUGHT HIS WIFE TOO GREAT A PRIZE	75	2	DON JUAN	1	101	8
AND THERE IS NO GREAT CAUSE TO QUAKE	86	2	DON JUAN	1	120	3
PERHAPS IT MAY BE FOLLOW'D BY THE GREAT	92	2	DON JUAN	1	130	8
'TIS SAID THE GREAT CAME FROM AMERICA	92	2	DON JUAN	1	131	1
WITH TORCHES FRIENDS AND SERVANTS IN GREAT NUMBER	96	2	DON JUAN	1	138	2
THERE IS THE SOFA THERE THE GREAT ARM-CHAIR	104	2	DON JUAN	1	153	3
SHE WHISPER'D IN GREAT WRATH--I MUST DEPOSIT	114	2	DON JUAN	1	170	7
AND NO GREAT GOOD SEEM'D ANSWER'D IF SHE STAID	116	2	DON JUAN	1	173	6
HAVE ALWAYS DONE SO 'TIS OF NO GREAT USE	119	2	DON JUAN	1	179	2
HIS TEMPER NOT BEING UNDER GREAT COMMAND	123	2	DON JUAN	1	185	4
AND NO GREAT MISCHIEF'S DONE BY THEIR CAPRICE	135	2	DON JUAN	1	199	6
THE GREAT SUCCESS OF JUAN'S EDUCATION	162	2	DON JUAN	2	10	7
I RECOLLECT GREAT BRITAIN'S COAST LOOKS WHITE	163	2	DON JUAN	2	12	5
WAS ALSO GREAT WITH WHICH THEY HAD TO COPE	178	2	DON JUAN	2	41	4
HAVING BEEN SEVERAL DAYS IN GREAT DISTRESS	180	2	DON JUAN	2	46	2
FOR YET THEY STROVE ALTHOUGH OF NO GREAT USE	183	2	DON JUAN	2	51	4
WITH NOTHING BUT THE SKY FOR A GREAT COAT	189	2	DON JUAN	2	63	8
AS A GREAT FAVOUR ONE OF THE FORE-PAWS	193	2	DON JUAN	2	71	6
AND MAY BECOME OF GREAT ADVANTAGE WHEN	205	2	DON JUAN	2	93	4
A PLEASURE WORTHY XERXES THE GREAT KING	251	2	DON JUAN	2	180	3
OH LOVE OF WHOM GREAT CAESAR WAS THE SUITOR	266	2	DON JUAN	2	205	1
HE WAS SO GREAT A LOSS TO GOOD SOCIETY	296	2	DON JUAN	3	41	8
(WHICH GOD FORBID) OR SOME OR A GREAT MANY	301	2	DON JUAN	3	50	2
WITH GREAT MAGNIFICENCE WERE SEEN TO ISSUE	309	2	DON JUAN	3	67	V8
THE LAST WAS OF GREAT FAME AND LIKED TO SHOW IT	316	2	DON JUAN	3	78	4
TO THE GREAT MARLBOROUGH'S SKILL IN GIVING KNOCKS	328	2	DON JUAN	3	90	7
WE'RE TOLD THIS GREAT HIGH PRIEST OF ALL THE NINE	328	2	DON JUAN	3	91	6
THE WORLD NOT QUITE SO GREAT AS ARIOSTO	331	2	DON JUAN	3	96	8
EARTH AIR STARS--ALL THAT SPRINGS FROM THE GREAT WHOLE	336	2	DON JUAN	3	104	7
PURE BLOOD TO STAGNATE THEIR GREAT HEARTS TO FAIL	348	2	DON JUAN	4	9	2
FOR HAIDEE'S KNOWLEDGE WAS BY NO MEANS GREAT	354	2	DON JUAN	4	19	5
AND THEN DECIDE WITHOUT GREAT WRONG TO EITHER	357	2	DON JUAN	4	25	7
WITH NO GREAT VOICE IS PLEASING TO BEHOLD	389	2	DON JUAN	4	83	5
A VOICE OF NO GREAT COMPASS AND NOT SWEET	392	2	DON JUAN	4	89	4
GREAT WISH TO PLEASE--A MOST ATTRACTIVE DOWER	395	2	DON JUAN	4	94	7
I ONCE HAD A GREAT ALACRITY IN WIELDING	397	2	DON JUAN	4	98	5
AND SO GREAT NAMES ARE NOTHING MORE THAN NOMINAL	399	2	DON JUAN	4	101	1
IN ALL WHO O'ER THE GREAT DEEP TAKE THEIR WAYS	414	2	DON JUAN	5	6	6
MOST MEN ARE SLAVES NONE MORE SO THAN THE GREAT	423	2	DON JUAN	5	25	3
JUST AS MY GREAT COAT WAS ABOUT ME CAST	428	2	DON JUAN	5	33	3
METHINKS--SAID HE--IT WOULD BE NO GREAT SHAME	434	2	DON JUAN	5	43	5
ALAS MAN MAKES THAT GREAT WHICH MAKES HIM LITTLE	444	2	DON JUAN	5	59	1
OF THOSE FORGETTING THE GREAT PLACE OF REST	448	2	DON JUAN	5	63	3
PROVIDED ALWAYS YOUR GREAT GOODNESS STILL	453	2	DON JUAN	5	72	7
IN WHICH A PRINCESS WITH GREAT PLEASURE WOULD	453	2	DON JUAN	5	73	3
GREAT LUSTRE THERE IS MUCH TO BE FORGIVEN	465	2	DON JUAN	5	94	6
GREAT HAPPINESS OF THE NIL ADMIRARI	469	2	DON JUAN	5	100	8
BUT HERE A SMALL DELAY FORMS A GREAT CRIME	482	2	DON JUAN	5	123	5
WHATE'ER THY POWER AND GREAT IT SEEMS TO BE	484	2	DON JUAN	5	127	6
BUT ALL HIS GREAT PREPARATIVES FOR DYING	492	2	DON JUAN	5	141	7
HIS HIGHNESS CAST AROUND HIS GREAT BLACK EYES	500	2	DON JUAN	5	155	1
REMEMBER WHEN THOUGH I HAD NO GREAT PLENTY	9	3	DON JUAN	6	5	4
IF TRUE 'TIS NO GREAT LEASE OF ITS OWN FIRE	14	3	DON JUAN	6	16	2
WHEN FREED FROM BONDS (WHICH ARE OF NO GREAT USE	23	3	DON JUAN	6	34	4
WITH GREAT BLUE EYES A LOVELY HAND AND ARM	26	3	DON JUAN	6	41	3
BUT WHAT IS STRANGE--AND A STRONG PROOF HOW GREAT	42	3	DON JUAN	6	73	1
AND SO--SHE WOKE WITH A GREAT SCREAM AND START	44	3	DON JUAN	6	77	8
THE DAMSELS WHO HAD THOUGHTS OF SOME GREAT HARM	45	3	DON JUAN	6	79	1
THE NUMBERS ARE TOO GREAT FOR THEM TO FLATTER ALL	50	3	DON JUAN	6	88	8
PERHAPS A LITTLE LATER HER GREAT LORD	51	3	DON JUAN	6	90	2
TO BODE HIM NO GREAT GOOD HE DEPRECATED	57	3	DON JUAN	6	102	2
PICKING UP SHELLS BY THE GREAT OCEAN--TRUTH	69	3	DON JUAN	7	5	8
A GREEK OF GREAT ESTEEM AMONGST HIS NATION	71	3	DON JUAN	7	10	V5
BUT THEN THERE WAS A GREAT WANT OF PRECAUTION	72	3	DON JUAN	7	11	5
HAD BEEN CALLED JEMMY AFTER THE GREAT BARD	76	3	DON JUAN	7	19	2
BUT I'M TOO GREAT A PATRIOT TO RECORD	77	3	DON JUAN	7	22	2
LAND BATTERIES WORKED THEIR GUNS WITH GREAT PRECISION	81	3	DON JUAN	7	30	3
NAMES GREAT AS ANY THAT THE ROLL OF FAME HAS	82	3	DON JUAN	7	32	8
THIS WAS POTEMKIN--A GREAT THING IN DAYS	84	3	DON JUAN	7	37	1
WHEN HOMICIDE AND HARLOTRY MADE GREAT	84	3	DON JUAN	7	37	2
WHEN STARS AND WHORES AND DESPOTS COULD MAKE GREAT	84	3	DON JUAN	7	37	V2
GREAT JOY TO LONDON NOW SAYS SOME GREAT FOOL	88	3	DON JUAN	7	44	1
GREAT JOY TO LONDON NOW SAYS SOME GREAT FOOL	88	3	DON JUAN	7	44	1
BUT TO THE TALE--GREAT JOY UNTO THE CAMP	89	3	DON JUAN	7	46	1
THE FLEET AND CAMP SALUTED WITH GREAT GRACE	89	3	DON JUAN	7	47	3
SUCH IS THE SWAY OF YOUR GREAT MEN O'ER LITTLE	90	3	DON JUAN	7	48	8
AS SOMETIMES HAPPENS IN A GREAT EXTREMITY	92	3	DON JUAN	7	51	4
FOR THIS GREAT CONQUEROR PLAYED THE CORPORAL	95	3	DON JUAN	7	56	2
THIS GREAT PHILOSOPHER WAS THUS INSTILLING	96	3	DON JUAN	7	58	6
GREAT DEEDS ARE DOING--HOW SHALL I RELATE 'EM	107	3	DON JUAN	7	81	6
OH YE GREAT BULLETINS OF BONAPARTE	108	3	DON JUAN	7	82	1
TURNS OUT TO BE A BUTCHER IN GREAT BUSINESS	108	3	DON JUAN	7	83	7
THOUGH LED BY ARSENIEW THAT GREAT SON OF SLAUGHTER	116	3	DON JUAN	8	9	4

GREAT (CONTINUED)

	PAGE	VOL		CANTO	STANZA	LN
YET I LOVE GLORY--GLORY'S A GREAT THING--	118	3	DON JUAN	8	14	1
FREDERICK THE GREAT FROM MOLWITZ DEIGNED TO RUN	122	3	DON JUAN	8	22	4
(START NOT KIND READER SINCE GREAT HOMER THOUGHT	126	3	DON JUAN	8	29	6
TO MARCH A GREAT CONVENIENCE TO OUR MEN	136	3	DON JUAN	8	47	3
OF THE GREAT NAMES WHICH IN OUR FACES STARE	143	3	DON JUAN	8	61	3
NOW BACK TO THY GREAT JOYS CIVILIZATION	146	3	DON JUAN	8	68	2
THE GREAT AND GAY KOUTOUSOW MIGHT HAVE LAIN	148	3	DON JUAN	8	72	7
AND NO GREAT DILETTANTI IN TOPOGRAPHY	149	3	DON JUAN	8	74	6
ON GREAT OCCASIONS SUCH AS AN ATTACK	160	3	DON JUAN	8	97	3
AS GREAT A SCORNER OF THE NAZARENE	167	3	DON JUAN	8	111	2
IN THE MEANTIME CROSS-LEGGED WITH GREAT SANG FROID	172	3	DON JUAN	8	121	1
THOUGH IRELAND STARVE GREAT GEORGE WEIGHS TWENTY STONE	175	3	DON JUAN	8	126	8
BUT ON THE WHOLE THEIR CONTINENCE WAS GREAT	177	3	DON JUAN	8	131	1
AND AS IN THE GREAT JOY OF YOUR MILLENNIUM	180	3	DON JUAN	8	136	2
FRANCE COULD NOT EVEN CONQUER YOUR GREAT NAME	183	3	DON JUAN	9	1	3
YOU HAVE OBTAINED GREAT PENSIONS AND MUCH PRAISE	183	3	DON JUAN	9	1	6
THEY SAY YOU LIKE IT TOO--'TIS NO GREAT WONDER	185	3	DON JUAN	9	5	2
I DON'T MEAN TO REFLECT--A MAN SO GREAT AS	186	3	DON JUAN	9	7	1
GREAT MEN HAVE ALWAYS SCORNED GREAT RECOMPENSES	186	3	DON JUAN	9	8	1
GREAT MEN HAVE ALWAYS SCORNED GREAT RECOMPENSES	186	3	DON JUAN	9	8	1
RENOWNED FOR RUINING GREAT BRITAIN GRATIS	186	3	DON JUAN	9	8	8
YOU DID GREAT THINGS BUT NOT BEING GREAT IN MIND	187	3	DON JUAN	9	10	7
YOU DID GREAT THINGS BUT NOT BEING GREAT IN MIND	187	3	DON JUAN	9	10	7
FOR THE GREAT BENEFIT OF THOSE WHO KNOW	190	3	DON JUAN	9	15	3
OH YE GREAT AUTHORS LUMINOUS VOLUMINOUS	200	3	DON JUAN	9	35	1
OH YE GREAT AUTHORS--APROPOS DES BOTTES--	200	3	DON JUAN	9	36	1
I SAY WILL THESE GREAT RELICS WHEN THEY SEE 'EM	202	3	DON JUAN	9	40	7
NOW WE'LL GET O'ER THE GROUND AT A GREAT RATE	203	3	DON JUAN	9	42	4
THAT GREAT ENCHANTER AT WHOSE ROD'S COMMAND	204	3	DON JUAN	9	44	3
BUT LUCKILY OF NO GREAT LENGTH OR WEIGHT	207	3	DON JUAN	9	50	5
THOU DOST REPLENISH WORLDS BOTH GREAT AND SMALL	210	3	DON JUAN	9	56	6
OF THAT GREAT CAUSE OF WAR OR PEACE OR WHAT	211	3	DON JUAN	9	57	7
AT LEAST THREE PARTS OF THIS GREAT WHOLE) SHE TORE	211	3	DON JUAN	9	58	3
GREAT JOY WAS HER'S OR RATHER JOYS THE FIRST	212	3	DON JUAN	9	59	1
('TIS POPE'S PHRASE) A GREAT LONGING THO' A RASH ONE	216	3	DON JUAN	9	68	6
WHO PROMISED TO BE GREAT IN SOME FEW HOURS	222	3	DON JUAN	9	79	1
LOVE THAT GREAT OPENER OF THE HEART AND ALL	222	3	DON JUAN	9	80	2
ABOVE BELOW BY TURNPIKES GREAT OR SMALL--	222	3	DON JUAN	9	80	4
DAMSELS GREAT WEALTH AND ILLUSTRIOUS ORDERS	235	3	DON JUAN	10	21	V7
AND DEATH THE SOVEREIGN'S SOVEREIGN THOUGH THE GREAT	237	3	DON JUAN	10	25	1
WITH WHICH GREAT STATES SUCH THINGS ARE APT TO PUSH ON	246	3	DON JUAN	10	45	5
WHICH SHOWED WHAT GREAT DISCERNMENT WAS THE DONOR'S	247	3	DON JUAN	10	46	8
SHE SHOWED A GREAT DISLIKE TO HOLY WATER	252	3	DON JUAN	10	56	4
HAS LATELY BEEN THE GREAT PROFESSOR KANT	254	3	DON JUAN	10	60	4
I HAVE NO GREAT CAUSE TO LOVE THAT SPOT OF EARTH	257	3	DON JUAN	10	66	1
HOW HER GREAT NAME IS NOW THROUGHOUT ABHORRED	258	3	DON JUAN	10	67	2
AT THE GREAT END OF TRAVEL--WHICH IS DRIVING	260	3	DON JUAN	10	72	8
WHO DIED IN THE THEN GREAT ATTEMPT TO CLIMB	261	3	DON JUAN	10	74	5
TOWARD THE GREAT CITY--YE WHO HAVE A SPARK IN	264	3	DON JUAN	10	80	5
TO SET UP VAIN PRETENCES OF BEING GREAT	267	3	DON JUAN	10	87	3
AND LOST IN WONDER OF SO GREAT A NATION	272	3	DON JUAN	11	9	3
HE FROM THE WORLD HAD CUT OFF A GREAT MAN	277	3	DON JUAN	11	19	1
IN THE GREAT WORLD--WHICH BEING INTERPRETED	290	3	DON JUAN	11	45	1
AND NOT IN LITERATURE A GREAT DRAWCANSIR	294	3	DON JUAN	11	51	4
AT GREAT ASSEMBLIES OR IN PARTIES SMALL	295	3	DON JUAN	11	54	4
JUST AS HE REALLY PROMISED SOMETHING GREAT	298	3	DON JUAN	11	60	2
AS FROM MY GREAT GREAT HUMOUR YOU MAY LEARN	300	3	DON JUAN	11	63	V5
AS FROM MY GREAT GREAT HUMOUR YOU MAY LEARN	300	3	DON JUAN	11	63	V5
I HAVE SEEN SMALL POETS AND GREAT PROSERS AND	310	3	DON JUAN	11	85	1
WHICH HOLD FAST OTHER PLEASURES GREAT AND SMALL	316	3	DON JUAN	12	3	4
PERHAPS HE HATH GREAT PROJECTS IN HIS MIND	320	3	DON JUAN	12	10	1
GREAT BRITAIN WHICH THE MUSE MAY PENETRATE	327	3	DON JUAN	12	24	6
AMONGST THE SEX IN LITTLE THINGS OR GREAT	329	3	DON JUAN	12	28	2
OF BEING APT TO TALK AT A GREAT RATE	329	3	DON JUAN	12	28	6
'TIS A GREAT MORAL LESSON THEY ARE READING	341	3	DON JUAN	12	55	4
YCLEPT THE GREAT WORLD FOR IT IS THE LEAST	342	3	DON JUAN	12	56	2
AND TELL ME WHAT YOU THINK OF YOUR GREAT THINKERS	357	3	DON JUAN	12	89	8
IS NO GREAT MATTER SO 'TIS IN REQUEST	359	3	DON JUAN	13	3	4
ROUGH JOHNSON THE GREAT MORALIST PROFESSED	361	3	DON JUAN	13	7	1
A SORRIER STILL IS THE GREAT MORAL TAUGHT	363	3	DON JUAN	13	9	7
GIVE GENTLY WAY WHEN THERE'S TOO GREAT A PRESS	366	3	DON JUAN	13	18	5
AS MOST MEN DO THE LITTLE OR THE GREAT	367	3	DON JUAN	13	19	2
AND THE LORD HENRY WAS A GREAT DEBATER	367	3	DON JUAN	13	20	7
THERE WAS LORD PYRRHO TOO THE GREAT FREETHINKER	398	3	DON JUAN	13	84	1
SIR HENRY SILVERCUP THE GREAT RACE-WINNER	399	3	DON JUAN	13	87	4
A GREAT TACTICIAN AND NO LESS A SWORDSMAN	399	3	DON JUAN	13	88	3
FORBIDS A GREAT IMPRESSION IN MY YOUTH	403	3	DON JUAN	13	96	6
BUT TAKE AN ELL--AND MAKE A GREAT SENSATION	404	3	DON JUAN	13	98	5
BUT NONE WERE GENE THE GREAT HOUR OF UNION	406	3	DON JUAN	13	103	1
IF FROM GREAT NATURE'S OR OUR OWN ABYSS	410	3	DON JUAN	14	1	1
YOU KNOW OR DON'T KNOW THAT GREAT BACON SAITH	414	3	DON JUAN	14	8	1
TO THE GREAT PLEASURE OF OUR FRIENDS MANKIND	414	3	DON JUAN	14	9	5
OF NO GREAT PROMISE FOR POETIC PAGES	416	3	DON JUAN	14	15	8
PETTICOAT INFLUENCE IS A GREAT REPROACH	421	3	DON JUAN	14	26	1
ALL DIFFICULTIES WHETHER GREAT OR SMALL	423	3	DON JUAN	14	30	5
I WILL NOT MAKE HIS GREAT DESCRIPTION LESS	442	3	DON JUAN	14	75	3
SAITH HORACE THE GREAT LITTLE POET'S WRONG	443	3	DON JUAN	14	77	2
THERE WAS NO GREAT DISPARITY OF YEARS	447	3	DON JUAN	14	87	1

GREAT   (CONTINUED)

	PAGE	VOL	CANTO	STANZA	LN
BUT GREAT THINGS SPRING FROM LITTLE--WOULD YOU THINK	454	3	DON JUAN 14	100	1
THE GRAND ANTITHESIS TO GREAT ENNUI	457	3	DON JUAN 15	2	3
WAS IT NOT SO GREAT LOCKE AND GREATER BACON	464	3	DON JUAN 15	18	1
GREAT SOCRATES AND THOU DIVINER STILL	464	3	DON JUAN 15	18	2
WITH NO GREAT CARE FOR WHAT IS NICKNAMED GLORY	464	3	DON JUAN 15	19	3
OR BRIGANTINE OR PINK OF NO GREAT TONNAGE	468	3	DON JUAN 15	27	7
BY WHICH SUCH SIRENS CAN ATTRACT OUR GREAT	474	3	DON JUAN 15	42	6
GREAT THINGS WERE NOW TO BE ACHIEVED AT TABLE	482	3	DON JUAN 15	62	1
WHILE GREAT LUCULLUS' ROBE TRIUMPHAL MUFFLES--	484	3	DON JUAN 15	66	7
COMMENCED (FROM SUCH SLIGHT THINGS WILL GREAT COMMENCE)	493	3	DON JUAN 15	83	5
ALSO OBSERVE THAT LIKE THE GREAT LORD COKE	494	3	DON JUAN 15	87	1
BUT SAINT AUGUSTINE HAS THE GREAT PRIORITY	503	3	DON JUAN 16	5	5
A GREAT RESOURCE TO ALL AND NE'ER DENIED	506	3	DON JUAN 16	12	7
GREAT THOUGHTS WE CATCH FROM THENCE (BESIDES A COLD	506	3	DON JUAN 16	14	4
LONG FURNISHED WITH OLD PICTURES OF GREAT WORTH	508	3	DON JUAN 16	17	4
WAS LONG AND THUS FAR THERE WAS NO GREAT CAUSE	511	3	DON JUAN 16	24	3
WAS GREAT BECAUSE HIS MASTER BROOKED NO LESS	512	3	DON JUAN 16	28	7
THE FAMILY PHYSICIAN HAD GREAT SKILL	514	3	DON JUAN 16	32	5
WAS WEAK ENOUGH TO DEEM POPE A GREAT POET	524	3	DON JUAN 16	47	7
BUT THIS POOR GIRL WAS LEFT IN THE GREAT HALL	533	3	DON JUAN 16	67	1
THOSE WHO IN COUNTIES HAVE GREAT LAND RESOURCES	534	3	DON JUAN 16	68	6
LORD HENRY WAS A GREAT ELECTIONEERER	534	3	DON JUAN 16	70	1
'TWAS A GREAT BANQUET SUCH AS ALBION OLD	538	3	DON JUAN 16	78	2
GREAT PLENTY MUCH FORMALITY SMALL CHEER	538	3	DON JUAN 16	78	7
FOR WIT HATH NO GREAT FRIEND IN AGUISH FOLKS	540	3	DON JUAN 16	83	3
AND YET GREAT HEROES HAVE BEEN BRED BY BOTH	541	3	DON JUAN 16	84	8
WERE GOOD SMALL-TALK FOR OTHERS STILL LESS GREAT)--	544	3	DON JUAN 16	91	8
LITTLE THAT'S GREAT BUT MUCH OF WHAT IS CLEVER	547	3	DON JUAN 16	98	4
SOME PRAISED HER BEAUTY OTHERS HER GREAT GRACE	550	3	DON JUAN 16	102	1
SO THAT EVEN THOSE WHOSE FAITH IS THE MOST GREAT	556	3	DON JUAN 16	114	7
TRANSGRESSES THE GREAT BOUNDS OF LOVE OR AWE	563	3	DON JUAN 17	2	6
MALGRE SIR MATTHEW HALES'S GREAT HUMANITY	565	3	DON JUAN 17	7	8
GREAT GALILEO WAS DEBARRED THE SUN	565	3	DON JUAN 17	8	1

GREATER

	PAGE	VOL	CANTO	STANZA	LN
ALL CALDERON AND GREATER PART OF LOPE	27	2	DON JUAN 1	11	2
HAD GREATER NEED TO NERVE THEMSELVES AGAIN	205	2	DON JUAN 2	93	6
THE GREATER PART OF THESE WERE READY SPREAD	310	2	DON JUAN 3	69	6
PROTECTS HIS TOMB BUT GREATER CARE IS PAID	400	2	DON JUAN 4	104	V3
THE GREATER THEIR SUCCESS THE WORSE IT PROVES	411	2	DON JUAN 5	1	5
AND THERE HE STOOD WITH SUCH SANG-FROID THAT GREATER	416	2	DON JUAN 5	11	7
WITH AMBER MOUTHS OF GREATER PRICE OR LESS	441	2	DON JUAN 5	53	6
WHY GENERAL IF HE HATH NO GREATER FAULT	98	3	DON JUAN 7	62	7
TO TEACH HIM GREATER HAD HIS OWN LEG BROKEN	117	3	DON JUAN 8	11	8
AND THEREFORE WE MUST GIVE THE GREATER NUMBER	120	3	DON JUAN 8	18	1
BE THAT THE GREATER PART WERE KILLED OR WOUNDED	125	3	DON JUAN 8	28	2
TO CORPS THE GREATER PART OF WHICH WERE CORSES	126	3	DON JUAN 8	30	8
AS SOMETIMES HAVE BEEN GREATER SAGES' LOTS--	200	3	DON JUAN 9	36	3
THE GREATER IS THE PLEASURE IN ARRIVING	260	3	DON JUAN 10	72	7
COUNTRIES OF GREATER HEAT BUT LESSER SUCTION	262	3	DON JUAN 10	76	4
WAS IT NOT SO GREAT LOCKE AND GREATER BACON	464	3	DON JUAN 15	18	1
RELIEVED ITSELF BY PORK FOR GREATER GLORY	483	3	DON JUAN 15	63	8
TRAMPLING ON PLATO'S PRIDE WITH GREATER PRIDE	522	3	DON JUAN 16	43	3
THAT THE FATIGUE WAS GREATER THAN THE PROFIT	536	3	DON JUAN 16	73	8
UPON THE WHOLE IS GREATER THAN THE DIFFERENCE	541	3	DON JUAN 16	85	2

GREATEST

	PAGE	VOL	CANTO	STANZA	LN
THE GREATEST DANGER HERE WAS FROM A SHARK	212	2	DON JUAN 2	106	5
THE GREATEST HEIRESS OF THE EASTERN ISLES	224	2	DON JUAN 2	128	2
THE GREATEST WISEST BRAVEST AS WAS BEST	12	2	DON JUAN 6	13	V2
AS GREATEST OF ALL SOVEREIGNS AND WHORES	52	3	DON JUAN 6	92	8
WHO WERE THUS HONOURED BY THE GREATEST CHIEF	101	3	DON JUAN 7	68	2
WHICH BEARS THE GREATEST LIKENESS TO PALL MALL	124	3	DON JUAN 8	26	8
TROOPS AS ARE MEANT TO MARCH WITH GREATEST GLORY ON	151	3	DON JUAN 8	78	4
HAVE LEFT UNDONE THE GREATEST--AND MANKIND	187	3	DON JUAN 9	10	8
THE GREATEST NUMBER FLESH HATH EVER KNOWN	255	3	DON JUAN 10	62	8
ALSO THE EIGHTY GREATEST LIVING POETS	295	3	DON JUAN 11	54	7
IN TWICE FIVE YEARS THE GREATEST LIVING POET	296	3	DON JUAN 11	55	1
WHOSE GREATEST FAULT WAS LEAVING FEW TO FIND	479	3	DON JUAN 15	54	4
IS ALWAYS GREATEST AT A MIRACLE	503	3	DON JUAN 16	5	4

GREATLY

	PAGE	VOL	CANTO	STANZA	LN
AND MERELY TEND TO SHOW HOW GREATLY LOVE IS	62	2	DON JUAN 1	74	7
'TWOULD GREATLY TEND TO BETTER THEIR CONDITION	451	2	DON JUAN 5	69	7
AND ADDED GREATLY TO THE MISSING LIST	80	3	DON JUAN 7	27	8
HE KNEW NOT WHERE HE WAS NOR GREATLY CARED	129	3	DON JUAN 8	33	1
WHOSE BLOOD THE PUDDLE GREATLY DID ENRICH	147	3	DON JUAN 8	71	3
YET EUROPE DOUBTLESS OWES YOU GREATLY MORE	184	3	DON JUAN 9	3	2
(IF THAT MY MEMORY DOTH NOT GREATLY ERR)	242	3	DON JUAN 10	36	3
AND GREATLY SHONE WHENEVER THERE HAD BEEN A STIR	368	3	DON JUAN 13	21	6
THAT ANYTHING HE VIEWS CAN GREATLY PLEASE	373	3	DON JUAN 13	34	7
AN ART ON WHICH THE ARTISTS GREATLY VARY	374	3	DON JUAN 13	35	3
WITH THOSE WHO POPE SAYS GREATLY DARING DINE	383	3	DON JUAN 13	53	6
THAT IS WHEN THEY SUCCEED BUT GREATLY BLAMED	448	3	DON JUAN 14	89	4

GRECIAN

	PAGE	VOL	CANTO	STANZA	LN
BEING NO GRECIAN BUT HE HAD AN EAR	236	2	DON JUAN 2	151	2
STOP CRIED PHILOSOPHY WITH AIR SO GRECIAN	268	2	DON JUAN 2	210	7
AND FURTHER ON A GROUP OF GRECIAN GIRLS	291	2	DON JUAN 3	30	1
WITH ALL HIS KEEN WORN LOOK AND GRECIAN GRACE	363	2	DON JUAN 4	35	5

GREECE

	PAGE	VOL	CANTO	STANZA	LN
BUT SOMETHING OF THE SPIRIT OF OLD GREECE	303	2	DON JUAN 3	55	1

	PAGE	VOL		CANTO	STANZA	LN

GREECE   (CONTINUED)

	PAGE	VOL		CANTO	STANZA	LN
OF CONDUCT WAS WHICH HE OBSERVED IN GREECE	319	2	DON JUAN	3	84	8
IN GREECE HE'D SING SOME SORT OF HYMN LIKE THIS T'YE	320	2	DON JUAN	3	86	8
THE ISLES OF GREECE THE ISLES OF GREECE	320	2	DON JUAN	3	L 1	1
THE ISLES OF GREECE THE ISLES OF GREECE	320	2	DON JUAN	3	L 1	1
I DREAM'D THAT GREECE MIGHT STILL BE FREE	321	2	DON JUAN	3	L 3	4
FOR GREEKS A BLUSH--FOR GREECE A TEAR	323	2	DON JUAN	3	L 6	6
IF NOT LIKE ORPHEUS QUITE WHEN GREECE WAS YOUNG	326	2	DON JUAN	3	87	3
MEKNOP SERGE LWOW ARSENIEW OF MODERN GREECE	74	3	DON JUAN	7	15	3
WHEN MY POOR GREECE WAS ONCE AS NOW SURROUNDED	108	3	DON JUAN	7	82	4
AND GREECE AND BOUND FAIR HELEN IN A BOND	209	3	DON JUAN	9	53	V6

GREEK

	PAGE	VOL		CANTO	STANZA	LN
AND GREEK--THE ALPHABET--I'M NEARLY SURE	28	2	DON JUAN	1	13	2
AS WELL AS ALL THE GREEK I SINCE HAVE LOST	50	2	DON JUAN	1	53	3
LIKE THE FIRST OLD GREEK PRIVATEER THE ARGO	191	2	DON JUAN	2	66	8
'TWAS AN OLD CUSTOM OF THE GREEK AND ROMAN	205	2	DON JUAN	2	93	3
HE WAS A GREEK AND ON HIS ISLE HAD BUILT	223	2	DON JUAN	2	127	1
IN SEVERAL OATHS--ARMENIAN TURK AND GREEK--	229	2	DON JUAN	2	138	7
ALTHOUGH SHE TOLD HIM IN GOOD MODERN GREEK	236	2	DON JUAN	2	150	6
OR GREEK--THAT IS ALTHOUGH IT NOT MUCH MATTER'D	240	2	DON JUAN	2	160	5
ALTHOUGH HE LISTEN'D SO THAT THE YOUNG GREEK IN	241	2	DON JUAN	2	161	3
THAT IS SOME WORDS OF SPANISH TURK AND GREEK	243	2	DON JUAN	2	165	1
HALF NAKED LOVING NATURAL AND GREEK	259	2	DON JUAN	2	194	8
THE VINOUS GREEK TO WHOM HE HAD ADDRESS'D	297	2	DON JUAN	3	42	6
THE MODERN GREEK IN TOLERABLE VERSE	326	2	DON JUAN	3	87	2
BUT MANY A GREEK MAID IN A LOVING SONG	383	2	DON JUAN	4	73	1
I THOUGHT IN FACT YOU COULD NOT BE A GREEK	418	2	DON JUAN	5	14	2
A GREEK HAD RAISED AROUND THIS ELEVATION	71	3	DON JUAN	7	10	5
A GREEK OF GREAT ESTEEM AMONGST HIS NATION	71	3	DON JUAN	7	10	V5
THAN IN THY GREEK GAZETTE OF THAT CAMPAIGN	106	3	DON JUAN	7	80	4
WHICH SETTLES ALL THINGS ROMAN GREEK OR RUNIC	122	3	DON JUAN	8	23	4
THE GREEK OR TURKISH COHORN'S IGNORANCE	136	3	DON JUAN	8	46	3
(HIS MAGGIOR DUOMO A SMART SUBTLE GREEK	259	3	DON JUAN	10	70	5
IF NOT INTELLIGIBLE--WITHOUT GREEK	298	3	DON JUAN	11	60	3
GIVES WITH GREEK TRUTH THE GOOD OLD GREEK THE LIE	325	3	DON JUAN	12	19	8
GIVES WITH GREEK TRUTH THE GOOD OLD GREEK THE LIE	325	3	DON JUAN	12	19-	8
TO THE GREEK KALENDS OF ANOTHER SESSION	379	3	DON JUAN	13	45	2
THE GREEK EVE HELEN FROM THE SPARTAN'S BED	441	3	DON JUAN	14	72	5

GREEKS

	PAGE	VOL		CANTO	STANZA	LN
MADE QUITE A PICTURE OF THESE LITTLE GREEKS	292	2	DON JUAN	3	33	6
THAT A REPORT (ESPECIALLY THE GREEKS)	295	2	DON JUAN	3	38	2
FOR GREEKS A BLUSH--FOR GREECE A TEAR	323	2	DON JUAN	3	L 6	6
(CURTSIES ARE NEITHER USED BY TURKS NOR GREEKS)	31	3	DON JUAN	6	50	4

GREEK-WORSHIP

	PAGE	VOL		CANTO	STANZA	LN
WARNED HIM AGAINST GREEK-WORSHIP WHICH LOOKS ODD	240	3	DON JUAN	10	32	3

GREEN

	PAGE	VOL		CANTO	STANZA	LN
THY CLANKING CHAIN AND ERIN'S YET GREEN WOUNDS	19	2	DON JUAN	D	16	5
THEY FELT THE FRESHNESS OF ITS GROWING GREEN	210	2	DON JUAN	2	103	3
HIS GARDEN TREES ALL SHADOWY AND GREEN	289	2	DON JUAN	3	27	2
MOVED BY THE CHINESE NYMPH OF TEARS GREEN TEA	372	2	DON JUAN	4	52	2
THERE ON THE GREEN AND VILLAGE-COTTED HILL IS	385	2	DON JUAN	4	76	1
THE SOIL OF THE GREEN PROVINCE HE HAD WASTED	84	3	DON JUAN	7	36	7
OF CARE OR GAIN THE GREEN WOODS WERE THEIR PORTIONS	145	3	DON JUAN	8	66	4
WHO ONLY SAW THE BLACK-EYED GIRLS IN GREEN	167	3	DON JUAN	8	111	4
STRIP YOUR GREEN FIELDS AND TO YOUR HARVESTS CLING	175	3	DON JUAN	8	126	6
TO TAKE A QUIET RIDE IN SOME GREEN LANE	224	3	DON JUAN	9	85	8
HE NOW WAS GROWING UP LIKE A GREEN TREE ABLE	235	3	DON JUAN	10	22	5
A GUARDIAN GREEN IN YEARS A WARD CONNECTED	252	3	DON JUAN	10	57	6
A GREY WALL A GREEN RUIN RUSTY PIKE	255	3	DON JUAN	10	61	5
A GREEN FIELD IS A SIGHT WHICH MAKES HIM PARDON	262	3	DON JUAN	10	76	5
AFTER THE GOOD EXAMPLE OF GREEN ERIN	286	3	DON JUAN	11	38	7
WHICH NOW HE FOUND WAS BLUE INSTEAD OF GREEN	294	3	DON JUAN	11	51	8
SCOTCH WITH BLUE GREEN RIBBONS--IRISH WITH A BLUE	314	3	DON JUAN	11	V 76	2
WITH THEIR GREEN FACES FIX'D UPON THE FLOOD	385	3	DON JUAN	13	57	8
AS WHAT IS LOST IN GREEN IS GAINED IN YELLOW	395	3	DON JUAN	13	77	8
HEART-BALLADS OF GREEN ERIN OR GREY HIGHLANDS	523	3	DON JUAN	16	46	2

GREENER

	PAGE	VOL		CANTO	STANZA	LN
MY HEART IS NOT MUCH GREENER AND IN SHORT I	143	2	DON JUAN	1	213	4

GREENEST

	PAGE	VOL		CANTO	STANZA	LN
FAR SWEETER THAN THE GREENEST LAURELS SPRUNG	199	3	DON JUAN	9	34	4

GREENSWARD

	PAGE	VOL		CANTO	STANZA	LN
THROUGH THE WAVED BRANCHES O'ER THE GREENSWARD GLANCING	290	2	DON JUAN	3	29	3

GREETINGS

	PAGE	VOL		CANTO	STANZA	LN
THEIR LOOKS CAST DOWN THEIR GREETINGS ALMOST DUMB	60	2	DON JUAN	1	70	3
TO NO MEN ARE SUCH CORDIAL GREETINGS GIVEN	500	2	DON JUAN	5	154	7

GRENADA

	PAGE	VOL		CANTO	STANZA	LN
WHEN PROUD GRENADA FELL AND FORCED TO FLY	52	2	DON JUAN	1	56	5

GRENADIER

	PAGE	VOL		CANTO	STANZA	LN
AND YET BUT MADE A MIDDLING GRENADIER	209	3	DON JUAN	9	54	8

GRENADIERS

	PAGE	VOL		CANTO	STANZA	LN
BEING GRENADIERS THEY MOUNTED ONE BY ONE	119	3	DON JUAN	8	15	5
FOLLOWED IN HASTE BY VARIOUS GRENADIERS	147	3	DON JUAN	8	71	2
WERE ALL DEFLOWERED BY DIFFERENT GRENADIERS	177	3	DON JUAN	8	130	8
OF CONQUEST AND HIS GUARD OF GRENADIERS	253	3	DON JUAN	10	58	8

GRENVILLES

	PAGE	VOL		CANTO	STANZA	LN
WHERE ARE THE GRENVILLES TURNED AS USUAL WHERE	308	3	DON JUAN	11	79	7

GREW

	PAGE	VOL		CANTO	STANZA	LN
HE STUDIED STEADILY AND GREW APACE	48	2	DON JUAN	1	49	5
CHANGED FOR THE DAME GREW DISTANT THE YOUTH SHY	60	2	DON JUAN	1	70	2

GREW   (CONTINUED)
    WHERE THE WILD BRANCH OF THE CORK FOREST GREW 70   2 DON JUAN 1   90   4
    WHEN OLD KING DAVID'S BLOOD GREW DULL IN MOTION 113   2 DON JUAN 1   168   5
    THINK'ST THOU THE HONEY WITH THOSE OBJECTS GREW 144   2 DON JUAN 1   214   6
    (HERE THE SHIP GAVE A LURCH AND HE GREW SEA-SICK) 166   2 DON JUAN 2   19   8
    (HERE HE GREW INARTICULATE WITH RETCHING) 167   2 DON JUAN 2   20   8
    THE WIND BLEW FRESH AGAIN AS IT GREW LATE 172   2 DON JUAN 2   30   5
    WHAT COULD THEY DO AND HUNGER'S RAGE GREW WILD 193   2 DON JUAN 2   70   6
    AND THEN INTO A HOARSER MURMUR GREW 194   2 DON JUAN 2   73   3
    FOR SHORE IT WAS AND GRADUALLY GREW 207   2 DON JUAN 2   97   7
    AND HIGHER GREW THE MOUNTAINS AS THEY DREW 209   2 DON JUAN 2   100   2
    SHE GREW TO WOMANHOOD AND BETWEEN WHILES 224   2 DON JUAN 2   128   6
    AND THEIR COMPASSION GREW TO SUCH A SIZE 225   2 DON JUAN 2   131   6
    THE TWILIGHT GLOW WHICH MOMENTLY GREW LESS   255   2 DON JUAN 2   188   4
    ABOVE THEM THEIR DESSERT GREW ON ITS VINE 291   2 DON JUAN 3   31   6
    WERE SCARLET FROM WHOSE GLOWING CENTER GREW 309   2 DON JUAN 3   67   6
    AND PURE AS PSYCHE ERE SHE GREW A WIFE-- 313   2 DON JUAN 3   74   5
    WHERE GREW THE ARTS OF WAR AND PEACE-- 320   2 DON JUAN 3 L 1   3
    THEY TOOK IT UP WHEN MY DAYS GREW MORE MELLOW 345   2 DON JUAN 4   3   3
    GREW AND EACH WAVE ROSE ROUGHLY THREATENING HER .   .   . 361   2 DON JUAN 4   31   4
    MORE LIKE AND LIKE TO LAMBRO'S ASPECT GREW-- 363   2 DON JUAN 4   35   4
    THE OLD MAN'S CHEEK GREW PALE BUT NOT WITH DREAD .   .   . 365   2 DON JUAN 4   40   3
    OF ANCIENT DAYS ERE TYRANNY GREW STRONG 379   2 DON JUAN 4   65   8
    OR AT LEAST WAS SO ERE IT GREW A FASHION 402   2 DON JUAN 4   106   8
    HE PAUSED AND HIS DARK EYE GREW FULL OF GLOOM 420   2 DON JUAN 5   18   3
    HER BROW GREW BLACK BUT SHE WOULD NOT UPBRAID 483   2 DON JUAN 5   125   5
    HERSELF UPON HIS BREAST AND THERE SHE GREW 483   2 DON JUAN 5   125   8
    HIS SONS WERE KEPT IN PRISON TILL THEY GREW 499   2 DON JUAN 5   153   1
    AND IN THE MIDST A GOLDEN APPLE GREW-- 44   3 DON JUAN 6   76   1
    AND AS HIS SPEECH GREW STILL MORE BROKEN-KNEED 56   3 DON JUAN 6   101   6
    THEIR SPEED ABATED OR THEIR STRENGTH GREW DULL 59   3 DON JUAN 6   107   6
    WHEN IT GREW RATHER LATE TO SET THINGS RIGHT   73   3 DON JUAN 7   13   5
    IMMEDIATELY IN OTHERS GREW AGAIN 113   3 DON JUAN 8   2   8
    BUT FLEW TO WHERE THE PLEASANT NOISE GREW LOUDER .   .   . 129   3 DON JUAN 8   33 V8
    GREW DUMB FOR YOU MIGHT ALMOST HEAR A LINNET   .   .   . 142   3 DON JUAN 8   59   6
    HE WAS NOT ALL ALONE AROUND HIM GREW 145   3 DON JUAN 8   65   1
    NO SINKING SPIRITS TOLD THEM THEY GREW GREY 145   3 DON JUAN 8   66   5
    WHEREON THE RUSSIAN PATHOS GREW LESS TENDER 165   3 DON JUAN 8   107   6
    WHO GREW LIKE CEDARS ROUND HIM GLORIOUSLY-- 169   3 DON JUAN 8   116   4
    DON JUAN GREW A VERY POLISHED RUSSIAN-- 235   3 DON JUAN 10   21   1
    DON JUAN GREW I FEAR A LITTLE DISSIPATED 236   3 DON JUAN 10   23   3
    WHO THOUGH HER SPECTACLES AT LAST GREW DIM   241   3 DON JUAN 10   34   6
    I DON'T KNOW HOW IT WAS BUT HE GREW SICK 244   3 DON JUAN 10   39   1
    AND WHEN THEY GREW SO--ON THEIR NEW-FOUND LANTHORN .   . 280   3 DON JUAN 11   26   7
    AND THUS ACQUAINTANCE GREW AT NOBLE ROUTS 369   3 DON JUAN 13   24   1
    GREW FRIENDS IN THIS OR ANY OTHER SENSE 453   3 DON JUAN 14   97   2
    BESIDES HIS CONDUCT SINCE IN ENGLAND GREW MORE 460   3 DON JUAN 15   11   5
    ALTHOUGH I WONDER HOW IT GREW HABITUAL 472   3 DON JUAN 15   36   8
    BUT WHETHER ENGLISH DUKES GREW RARE OF LATE 474   3 DON JUAN 15   42   4
    AS GROWS A FLOWER THUS QUIETLY SHE GREW 476   3 DON JUAN 15   47   3
    AND JUAN GREW CARNATION WITH VEXATION 545   3 DON JUAN 16   93   3
    YET GREW A LITTLE PALE--WITH WHAT CONCERN 545   3 DON JUAN 16   94   5
    AND THEN HIS DREAD GREW WRATH AND HIS WRATH FIERCE .   . 559   3 DON JUAN 16   119   1
GREY
    TO A SEDATE GREY CIRCLE OF OLD SMOKERS 293   2 DON JUAN 3   34   2
    THE BLANK GREY WAS NOT MADE TO BLAST THEIR HAIR .   .   . 348   2 DON JUAN 4   9   3
    OF THE GREY MORNING AND LOOK VAINLY FOR 18   3 DON JUAN 6   24   5
    WITH THE FIRST RAY OR RATHER GREY OF MORN 49   3 DON JUAN 6   87   1
    NO SINKING SPIRITS TOLD THEM THEY GREW GREY 145   3 DON JUAN 8   66   5
    IN ITS MERIDIAN HER BLUE EYES OR GREY-- 218   3 DON JUAN 9   71   2
    A GREY WALL A GREEN RUIN RUSTY PIKE 255   3 DON JUAN 10   61   5
    BUT GREY WAS NOT ARRIVED AND CHATHAM GONE 353   3 DON JUAN 12   82   8
    WITH HIS GREY SIGNAL FLAG AND THE PAST TENSE   .   .   . 376   3 DON JUAN 13   40   5
    TO THIS GREY RUIN WITH A VOICE TO CHARM 388   3 DON JUAN 13   64   5
    THE AIR OF 'TWAS A FRIAR OF ORDERS GREY 517   3 DON JUAN 16   38   8
    HEART-BALLADS OF GREEN ERIN OR GREY HIGHLANDS .   .   . 523   3 DON JUAN 16   46   2
    BROUGHT TO SURVEY THESE GREY WALLS WHICH THOUGH SO THICK . 529   3 DON JUAN 16   58   3
    THE MOON PEEPED JUST ESCAPED FROM A GREY CLOUD .   .   . 560   3 DON JUAN 16   121   8
GREYHOUNDS
    BETWEEN SOME GREYHOUNDS ON MY LORD'S ESTATE 527   3 DON JUAN 16   55   6
    WHOSE HOUNDS NE'ER ERRED NOR GREYHOUNDS DEIGNED TO LURCH . 539   3 DON JUAN 16   80   2
GRIEF
    HIS LIKE ALL DEEP GRIEF PLUNGED IN SOLITUDE 68   2 DON JUAN 1   87   4
    KNOWS NOUGHT OF GRIEF WHO HAS NOT SO BEEN WORRIED .   .   . 89   2 DON JUAN 1   125 V7
    GOD GRANT YOU FEEL NOT THEN THE BITTEREST GRIEF .   .   . 107   2 DON JUAN 1   157   7
    THE ASHES OF OUR HOPES IS A DEEP GRIEF 301   2 DON JUAN 3   51   7
    HE FELT A GRIEF BUT KNOWING CAUSE FOR NONE   355   2 DON JUAN 4   22   6
    OR PLUNGED A PROVINCE OR A REALM IN GRIEF 101   3 DON JUAN 7   68   4
    LESS THAN THEIR GRIEF (AND TRULY NOT LESS JUST) .   .   . 104   3 DON JUAN 7   73   4
    THE TRUTH AND THOUGH GRIEF HER OLD AGE MIGHT SHORTEN .   . 222   3 DON JUAN 9   81   5
    GRIEF A RICH FIELD WHICH NEVER WOULD LIE FALLOW .   .   . 228   3 DON JUAN 10   7   6
    WAS BENT WITH GRIEF THAT MAHOMET SHOULD RESIGN .   .   . 262   3 DON JUAN 10   75   7
    TO FREEDOM HE APPLIED (A GRIEF AND A BORE)   288   3 DON JUAN 11   41   6
    A CURE FOR GRIEF--FOR WHAT CAN EVER RANKLE   422   3 DON JUAN 14   27   7
GRIEFS
    THAT IS TILL DEEPER GRIEFS CONGEAL OUR TEARS   164   2 DON JUAN 2   15   8
    AND SUCH LIGHT GRIEFS ARE NOT A THING TO DIE ON .   .   . 165   2 DON JUAN 2   16   4
GRIEVE
    THE GUILELESS HEART IN SILENCE MAY GRIEVE O'ER 107   2 DON JUAN 1   157   3

329

GRIEVE   (CONTINUED)
	PAGE	VOL		CANTO	STANZA	LN
(NO ONE CAN TELL HOW MUCH I GRIEVE TO SAY)	121	2	DON JUAN	1	181	3
SO THAT HE HAD MUCH BETTER CAUSE TO GRIEVE	164	2	DON JUAN	2	15	3
(FOR WE MUST GET THEM ANYHOW OR GRIEVE)	270	2	DON JUAN	2	213	6
OF SAFETY WHERE SHE LESS MAY SHRINK AND GRIEVE	161	3	DON JUAN	8	99	4
IN FACT THERE'S NOTHING MAKES ME SO MUCH GRIEVE	336	3	DON JUAN	12	43	6
NEM CON AMONGST THE WOMEN WHICH I GRIEVE	493	3	DON JUAN	15	84	2
HE COMES--BUT NOT TO GRIEVE	519	3	DON JUAN	16	L 3	8

GRIEVED
	PAGE	VOL		CANTO	STANZA	LN
GRIEVED BUT PERHAPS HER FEELINGS MAY BE BETTER	129	2	DON JUAN	1	191	7
HE WAS TO TRAVEL AND THOUGH INEZ GRIEVED	161	2	DON JUAN	2	9	4
THEY GRIEVED FOR THOSE WHO PERISH'D WITH THE CUTTER	188	2	DON JUAN	2	61	7
THOUGH SOMEWHAT GRIEVED COULD SCARCE FORBEAR A SMILE	459	2	DON JUAN	5	83	3
AND SAID IT GRIEVED HIM BUT HE COULD NOT STOOP	470	2	DON JUAN	5	102	7
AT WHICH HE SEEMED NO WHIT SURPRISED NOR GRIEVED	500	2	DON JUAN	5	155	4
AND GRIEVED FOR THOSE WHO COULD RETURN NO MORE	476	3	DON JUAN	15	45	8

GRIEVES
	PAGE	VOL		CANTO	STANZA	LN
REPLIED THE OTHER THOUGH IT GRIEVES ME SORE	460	2	DON JUAN	5	84	3
AND GROANS AND THUS THE PEOPLED CITY GRIEVES	155	3	DON JUAN	8	88	5
THAT MANY OF THE ILLS O'ER WHICH MAN GRIEVES	444	3	DON JUAN	14	78	6

GRIEVOUS
	PAGE	VOL		CANTO	STANZA	LN
A DULL STORY'S DOUBLY GRIEVOUS WHEN 'TIS LONG	419	2	DON JUAN	5	16	V8
A VERDICT--GRIEVOUS FOE TO THOSE WHO CAUSE IT--	346	3	DON JUAN	12	65	5

GRIM
	PAGE	VOL		CANTO	STANZA	LN
ACHILLES' SELF WAS NOT MORE GRIM AND GORY	73	3	DON JUAN	7	14	6
WARRIOR FROM WARRIOR IN THEIR GRIM CAREER	125	3	DON JUAN	8	27	2
BUT GETTING NIGH GRIM DANTE'S OBSCURE WOOD	238	3	DON JUAN	10	27	3
MADE THE CHASTE CATHERINE LOOK A LITTLE GRIM	246	3	DON JUAN	10	44	3
THE SPRING GUSH'D THROUGH GRIM MOUTHS OF GRANITE MADE	389	3	DON JUAN	13	65	5
GRIM READER DID YOU EVER SEE A GHOST	498	3	DON JUAN	15	95	1
I WISH TO HEAVEN THEY WOULD NOT LOOK SO GRIM	499	3	DON JUAN	15	97	6
THE FORMS OF THE GRIM KNIGHT AND PICTURED SAINT	508	3	DON JUAN	16	18	1

GRIMACE
	PAGE	VOL		CANTO	STANZA	LN
AND WAS RECEIVED WITH ALL THE DUE GRIMACE	285	3	DON JUAN	11	35	3

GRIMLY
	PAGE	VOL		CANTO	STANZA	LN
AND GRIMLY DARKLED O'ER THEIR FACES PALE	182	2	DON JUAN	2	49	6
THE SULKY HUNTSMAN GRIMLY SAID THE FRENCHMAN	425	3	DON JUAN	14	34	V7

GRIN
	PAGE	VOL		CANTO	STANZA	LN
WHITE BLACK OR COPPER--THE DEAD BONES WILL GRIN	188	3	DON JUAN	9	12	8
THE HUNTSMAN'S SELF RELENTED TO A GRIN	425	3	DON JUAN	14	34	7

GRIND
	PAGE	VOL		CANTO	STANZA	LN
AND PLANT AND REAP AND SPIN AND GRIND AND SOW	202	3	DON JUAN	9	40	4

GRINDSTONE'S
	PAGE	VOL		CANTO	STANZA	LN
FROM THAT IXION GRINDSTONE'S CEASELESS TOIL	17	2	DON JUAN	D	13	6

GRINNING
	PAGE	VOL		CANTO	STANZA	LN
AND GALVANISM HAS SET SOME CORPSES GRINNING	92	2	DON JUAN	1	130	2
TEARING AND GRINNING HOWLING SCREECHING SWEARING	198	2	DON JUAN	2	79	7

GRINS
	PAGE	VOL		CANTO	STANZA	LN
MARK HOW ITS LIPLESS MOUTH GRINS WITHOUT BREATH	188	3	DON JUAN	9	11	8
BROADENING TO GRINS HE COLOURED MORE THAN ONCE	542	3	DON JUAN	16	88	3

GRISLY
	PAGE	VOL		CANTO	STANZA	LN
HE TURN'D FROM GRISLY SAINTS AND MARTYRS HAIRY	235	2	DON JUAN	2	149	7

GRIST
	PAGE	VOL		CANTO	STANZA	LN
OF CHAFF ALTHOUGH OUR GLEANINGS BE NOT GRIST	403	3	DON JUAN	13	97	2

GRIZZLED
	PAGE	VOL		CANTO	STANZA	LN
GROWS GRIZZLED AND WE ARE NOT WHAT WE WERE--	315	3	DON JUAN	12	1	8

GROAN
	PAGE	VOL		CANTO	STANZA	LN
AND EVEN THE GOOD WITH INWARD ENVY GROAN	26	2	DON JUAN	1	10	6
INTO THE DEEP WITHOUT A TEAR OR GROAN	202	2	DON JUAN	2	87	8
HER STRUGGLES CEASED WITH ONE CONVULSIVE GROAN	375	2	DON JUAN	4	58	6
WITHOUT A GROAN OR SIGH OR GLANCE TO SHOW	381	2	DON JUAN	4	69	2
THE GROAN THE ROLL IN DUST THE ALL-WHITE EYE	118	3	DON JUAN	8	13	5
AT TIMES WOULD CURDLE O'ER SOME HEAVY GROAN	140	3	DON JUAN	8	55	8
IN LIKE CHURCH BELLS WITH SIGH HOWL GROAN YELL PRAYER	141	3	DON JUAN	8	58	7
BY THE ADVANCING MUSCOVITE--THE GROAN	155	3	DON JUAN	8	87	7
BENEATH HIS CARS OF CERES GROAN THE ROADS	320	3	DON JUAN	12	9	4
AS MANY GUESTS OR MORE BEFORE WHOM GROAN	381	3	DON JUAN	13	49	5
TILL SOMEONE WITH A GROAN EXPREST A WISH	542	3	DON JUAN	16	87	7

GROANING
	PAGE	VOL		CANTO	STANZA	LN
AMIDST SOME GROANING THOUSANDS DYING NEAR--	117	3	DON JUAN	8	11	3
THE FELLOW TO LIE GROANING ON THE ROAD	275	3	DON JUAN	11	15	7

GROANS
	PAGE	VOL		CANTO	STANZA	LN
AND GROANS AND THUS THE PEOPLED CITY GRIEVES	155	3	DON JUAN	8	88	5
DULY ACCOMPANIED BY SHRIEKS AND GROANS	179	3	DON JUAN	8	135	2

GROG
	PAGE	VOL		CANTO	STANZA	LN
FOR GROG AND SOMETIMES DRINK RUM FROM THE CASK	173	2	DON JUAN	2	33	8
GIVE US MORE GROG THEY CRIED FOR IT WILL BE	175	2	DON JUAN	2	36	1

GROOM'D
	PAGE	VOL		CANTO	STANZA	LN
THAT BRIDEGROOMS AFTER THEY ARE FAIRLY GROOM'D	473	3	DON JUAN	15	39	5

GROPING
	PAGE	VOL		CANTO	STANZA	LN
GROPING ALL PATHS TO POWER AND ALL IN VAIN	150	2	DON JUAN	1	V 1	6

GROSE
	PAGE	VOL		CANTO	STANZA	LN
WAS PRINTED GROVE ALTHOUGH HIS NAME WAS GROSE	120	3	DON JUAN	8	18	8

GROSS
	PAGE	VOL		CANTO	STANZA	LN
SUWARROW--WHO BUT SAW THINGS IN THE GROSS	105	3	DON JUAN	7	77	1
BEING MUCH TOO GROSS TO SEE THEM IN DETAIL	105	3	DON JUAN	7	77	2
HISTORY CAN ONLY TAKE THINGS IN THE GROSS	113	3	DON JUAN	8	3	1

GROSSER
	PAGE	VOL		CANTO	STANZA	LN
THE GROSSER PARTS BUT FEARFUL TO DEFACE	46	2	DON JUAN	1	44	4

PAGE VOL CANTO STANZA LN

GROSSEST
THAT EVEN ITS GROSSEST FLATTERERS DARE NOT PRAISE . . . . 17 2 DON JUAN D 13 3
GROSSLY
SO THAT I DO NOT GROSSLY ERR IN FACTS . . . . 149 3 DON JUAN 8 74 3
GROT
A HERMIT'S WITH A HARAM FOR A GROT . . . . 68 2 DON JUAN 1 87 8
AND THE STAINED GLASS WHICH LIGHTED THIS FAIR GROT . . . 55 3 DON JUAN 6 98 4
GROTESCA
AND THEN THERE'S THE GROTESCA--SUCH A DANCER . . . . . 390 2 DON JUAN 4 84 7
GROTESQUES
KINDS OF GROTESQUES ILLUMINED AND HOW THEY . . . . . . 47 2 DON JUAN 1 46 4
GROUND
THEY OPEN'D WINDOWS GAZING IF THE GROUND . . . . . . 100 2 DON JUAN 1 144 3
SOME HALF-TORN DRAPERY SCATTER'D ON THE GROUND . . . . 125 2 DON JUAN 1 187 5
AN UNKNOWN BARREN BEACH FOR BURIAL GROUND . . . . . 213 2 DON JUAN 2 109 8
AND DRYDEN'S LAY MADE HAUNTED GROUND TO ME . . . . . 337 2 DON JUAN 3 105 7
NO--ONLY TWO AT PRESENT ABOVE GROUND . . . . . . 421 2 DON JUAN 5 20 3
WHOSE EVERY BATTLE-FIELD IS HOLY GROUND . . . . . 114 3 DON JUAN 8 5 3
A YARD OR TWO OF GROUND WHICH BROUGHT THEM NIGHER . . . 121 3 DON JUAN 8 20 3
NOW WE'LL GET O'ER THE GROUND AT A GREAT RATE . . . . 203 3 DON JUAN 9 42 4
MY PEGASUS SHALL TIRE OF TOUCHING GROUND . . . . . 224 3 DON JUAN 9 85 3
'TIS SAID (FOR I'LL NOT ANSWER ABOVE GROUND . . . . . 225 3 DON JUAN 10 1 3
HIGH GROUND AS VIRGIN CYNTHIA SWAYS THE TIDES . . . . 322 3 DON JUAN 12 14 6
ALONG THE LAST FIELDS OF THAT GOTHIC GROUND)-- . . . . 359 3 DON JUAN 13 2 4
THE WORLD GAVE GROUND BEFORE HER BRIGHT ARRAY . . . . 364 3 DON JUAN 13 11 5
SHE MADE THE EARTH BELOW SEEM HOLY GROUND . . . . . 387 3 DON JUAN 13 61 5
HAVE BUILT AND LAID OUT GROUND AT SUCH A RATE . . . . 393 3 DON JUAN 13 74 3
LIKE SWIFT CAMILLA HE SCARCE SKIMM'D THE GROUND . . . . 427 3 DON JUAN 14 39 3
OF HER EXPLOITS FOR THIS WERE TICKLISH GROUND . . . . 428 3 DON JUAN 14 42 5
FAIR ADELINE WITH EYES FIXED ON THE GROUND . . . . . 518 3 DON JUAN 16 40 4
GROUNDS
JULIA IN FACT HAD TOLERABLE GROUNDS . . . . 118 2 DON JUAN 1 176 1
GROUP
AND THUS THEY FORM A GROUP THAT'S QUITE ANTIQUE . . . . 259 2 DON JUAN 2 194 7
AND FURTHER ON A GROUP OF GRECIAN GIRLS . . . . . . 291 2 DON JUAN 3 30 1
AS RENEGADOES WHILE IN HAPLESS GROUP . . . . . . 409 2 DON JUAN 4 116 5
THOUSANDS OF SLAUGHTERED MEN A YET WARM GROUP . . . . 157 3 DON JUAN 8 91 2
GROUPE
OR WILDER GROUPE OF SAVAGE SALVATORE'S . . . . . . 392 3 DON JUAN 13 71 4
GROUPING
WOULD THAT I WERE A PAINTER TO BE GROUPING . . . . . 60 3 DON JUAN 6 109 5
GROUPS
WITH WHITES AND BLACKS IN GROUPS ON SHOW FOR SALE . . . 416 2 DON JUAN 5 10 2
GROUPS OF BAD STATUES TABLES CHAIRS AND PICTURES . . . 465 2 DON JUAN 5 94 7
OPENED THE GATE CALLED KILIA TO THE GROUPS . . . . . 148 3 DON JUAN 8 73 5
OF COURSE THESE GROUPS WERE SCATTERED HERE AND THERE . . 533 3 DON JUAN 16 66 1
GROUSE
BUT THERE'S NO SHOOTING (SAVE GROUSE) TILL SEPTEMBER . . 380 3 DON JUAN 13 48 8
GROVE
WAS PRINTED GROVE ALTHOUGH HIS NAME WAS GROSE . . . . 120 3 DON JUAN 8 18 8
LOVE RULES THE CAMP THE COURT THE GROVE--FOR LOVE . . . 322 3 DON JUAN 12 13 1
PERHAPS THERE MAY BE SOMETHING IN THE GROVE . . . . 322 3 DON JUAN 12 13 5
FIRST SAVE IN CASE OF PIGEONS--HOW THE GROVE . . . . 322 3 DON JUAN 12 13 V5
CASH RULES THE GROVE AND FELLS IT TOO BESIDES . . . . 322 3 DON JUAN 12 14 2
NOW IF THE COURT AND CAMP AND GROVE BE NOT . . . . . 323 3 DON JUAN 12 16 1
GROVEL
SOME FLIRT SOME READ AND SOME IN VICES GROVEL . . . . 263 2 DON JUAN 2 201 V7
GROVELING
IN GROVELING ON TO POWER SUCH STAINS NOW DYE IT . . . 154 2 DON JUAN 1 V 5 6
GROVES
THE CYPRESS GROVES OLYMPUS HIGH AND HOAR . . . . . 412 2 DON JUAN 5 3 5
FLANK'D BY LARGE GROVES WHICH TOWER'D ON EITHER HAND . . 433 2 DON JUAN 5 41 4
THROUGH GROVES SO CALLED AS BEING VOID OF TREES . . . 278 3 DON JUAN 11 21 1
THE DRUID'S GROVES ARE GONE--SO MUCH THE BETTER . . . 280 3 DON JUAN 11 25 1
GROW
GROW TIRED OF SCIENTIFIC CONVERSATION . . . . . . 33 2 DON JUAN 1 22 4
WAS EVER SUFFER'D LEST HE SHOULD GROW VICIOUS . . . . 44 2 DON JUAN 1 40 8
WHICH WITH A LITTLE PATIENCE MIGHT GROW CHARMING . . . 68 2 DON JUAN 1 86 8
FOR FEAR SOME PRUDISH READERS SHOULD GROW SKITTISH . . 141 2 DON JUAN 1 209 7
BEFORE THE SEA UNTIL IT SHOULD GROW FINE . . . . . 189 2 DON JUAN 2 62 3
MEN GROW ASHAMED OF BEING SO VERY FOND . . . . . . 278 2 DON JUAN 3 7 1
BEFORE THE CONSEQUENCES GROW TOO AWFUL . . . . . . 282 2 DON JUAN 3 12 7
WIVES IN THEIR HUSBANDS' ABSENCES GROW SUBTLER . . . . 287 2 DON JUAN 3 22 7
SIGH'D FOR THEIR SAKES--THAT THEY SHOULD E'ER GROW OLDER . 292 2 DON JUAN 3 33 8
WISHED FOR THEIR SAKES--THEY NEVER MIGHT GROW OLDER . . 292 2 DON JUAN 3 33 V8
MEANT TO GROW OLD BUT DIE IN HAPPY SPRING . . . . . 348 2 DON JUAN 4 8 7
HERE I MUST LEAVE HIM FOR I GROW PATHETIC . . . . . 372 2 DON JUAN 4 52 1
MY BRAIN WITH BLEST FUMES TILL MY EYES GROW DIM . . . 372 2 DON JUAN 4 53 V7
THE GRASS UPON MY GRAVE WILL GROW AS LONG . . . . . 398 2 DON JUAN 4 99 7
EVEN TILL AN ICEBERG IT MAY CHANCE TO GROW . . . . . 398 2 DON JUAN 4 100 7
BUT I GROW SAD--AND LET A TALE GROW COLD . . . . . 413 2 DON JUAN 5 4 7
BUT I GROW SAD--AND LET A TALE GROW COLD . . . . . 413 2 DON JUAN 5 4 7
OF THE BEST FEELINGS OF MANKIND WHICH GROW . . . . . 439 2 DON JUAN 5 49 5
CHARMS FROM THE CHARMER YET SOME NEVER GROW . . . . 468 2 DON JUAN 5 98 7
GROW DEADLY PALE AND THEN BLUSH BACK AGAIN . . . . . 483 2 DON JUAN 5 124 8
THE STRICTER DOUBTLESS GROW THE VESTAL DUTIES . . . . 35 3 DON JUAN 6 58 7
HIMSELF IN AT THE AGE WHEN ALL GROW GOOD . . . . . 43 3 DON JUAN 6 75 4
WHERE THOUSAND LOVES AND TIES AND DUTIES GROW . . . . 174 3 DON JUAN 8 124 6
BUT I AM APT TO GROW TOO METAPHYSICAL . . . . . . 203 3 DON JUAN 9 41 1

331

GROW   (CONTINUED)
	PAGE	VOL		CANTO	STANZA	LN
BUT SOON THEY GROW AGAIN AND LEAVE THEIR NEST	228	3	DON JUAN	10	6	1
WHILE COMMON MEN GROW IGNORANTLY OLD	232	3	DON JUAN	10	14	5
OF ILLNESS I GROW MUCH MORE ORTHODOX	270	3	DON JUAN	11	5	8
HIS LAST AWARD WILL HAVE THE LONG GRASS GROW	299	3	DON JUAN	11	61	4
YE GODS I GROW A TALKER LET US PRATE	345	3	DON JUAN	12	64	1
RECEIVE AS GOSPEL AND WHICH GROW MORE ROOTED	503	3	DON JUAN	16	6	7
AND GROW QUITE FIGURATIVE WITH THEIR FIGURES	547	3	DON JUAN	16	98	8
WHO GROW UP CHILDREN ONLY SINCE THE OLD SAW	563	3	DON JUAN	17	2	2

GROWING
	PAGE	VOL		CANTO	STANZA	LN
THE GROWING WATERS IT UNMANS ONE QUITE	163	2	DON JUAN	2	12	3
THEY FELT THE FRESHNESS OF ITS GROWING GREEN	210	2	DON JUAN	2	103	3
MAY QUARREL AND THE LADY GROWING WISER	288	2	DON JUAN	3	24	4
THE PRESENT CENTURY WAS GROWING BLIND	328	2	DON JUAN	3	90	6
HE NOW WAS GROWING UP LIKE A GREEN TREE ABLE	235	3	DON JUAN	10	22	5
WITH ALL HIS LAURELS GROWING UPON ONE TREE	401	3	DON JUAN	13	91	V7
AND NOW BECAUSE I FEEL IT GROWING DULL	415	3	DON JUAN	14	10	8
AND GATHER'D AS THEY RUN LIKE GROWING WATER	448	3	DON JUAN	14	88	6
AND HONOUR'D RAN A RISK OF GROWING LESS SO	458	3	DON JUAN	15	6	2
WHEN ADELINE IN ALL HER GROWING SENSE	468	3	DON JUAN	15	28	1
MORE (LIKE A STOCK-HOLDER IN GROWING PELF)	470	3	DON JUAN	15	31	5
TO HINDER HIM FROM GROWING STILL MORE PALLID	515	3	DON JUAN	16	35	8
AND IS NOT MUCH IMPROVED BY GROWING OLD	516	3	DON JUAN	16	37	8

GROWLING
	PAGE	VOL		CANTO	STANZA	LN
GROWLING AND GRUMBLING IN GOOD TURKISH PHRASE	64	3	DON JUAN	6	117	2

GROWN
	PAGE	VOL		CANTO	STANZA	LN
OF ONE ANOTHER'S MINDS AT LAST HAVE GROWN	12	2	DON JUAN	D	5	4
TO KEEP ONE CREED'S A TASK GROWN QUITE HERCULEAN	20	2	DON JUAN	D	17	7
BECAUSE THE ARMY'S GROWN MORE POPULAR	23	2	DON JUAN	1	4	5
HER YOUNG PHILOSOPHER WAS GROWN ALREADY	49	2	DON JUAN	1	50	8
INDIFFERENT FROM THE FIRST OR CALLOUS GROWN	59	2	DON JUAN	1	68	6
JUAN BEING THEN GROWN UP TO MAN'S ESTATE	67	2	DON JUAN	1	85	2
AND HELD HER TONGUE HER VOICE WAS GROWN SO WEAK	81	2	DON JUAN	1	112	8
'TIS GROWN HIGH TIME TO THIN IT IN ITS TURN	92	2	DON JUAN	1	131	4
THEIR DESPERATE EFFORTS SEEM'D ALL USELESS GROWN	176	2	DON JUAN	2	38	6
BUT MORE IMPRUDENT GROWN WITH EVERY VISIT	282	2	DON JUAN	3	13	3
THE DANGEROUS LIFE IN WHICH HE HAD GROWN OLD	303	2	DON JUAN	3	54	3
A BEAUTY AT THE SEASON'S CLOSE GROWN HECTIC	309	2	DON JUAN	3	66	1
AND I GROWN ONE OF MANY WOODEN SPOONS	341	2	DON JUAN	3	110	6
SO GOODLY WAS HER THIRST FOR SCIENCE GROWN	476	2	DON JUAN	5	113	V7
BUT WHAT WAS NOT A SORT OF STYLE THAT'S GROWN	33	3	DON JUAN	6	55	6
OUT OF THEIR HIDES IF PARCHMENT HAD GROWN DEAR	75	3	DON JUAN	7	17	7
AND ALL AROUND WERE GROWN EXCEEDING WROTH	166	3	DON JUAN	8	109	5
ROSE STILL BUT FAINTER WERE THE THUNDERS GROWN	175	3	DON JUAN	8	127	6
THE TRUTH IS I'VE GROWN LATELY RATHER PHTHISICAL	270	3	DON JUAN	11	5	5
BEFORE AND AFTER BUT NOW GROWN MORE HOLY	297	3	DON JUAN	11	57	2
SINCE I'VE GROWN MORAL STILL I MUST ACCUSE YOU ALL	329	3	DON JUAN	12	28	5
ARE GROWN OF THE BEAU MONDE A PART POTENTIAL	418	3	DON JUAN	14	20	2
WHETHER WITH TIME THE SPECTRE HAS GROWN SHYER	516	3	DON JUAN	16	36	5
THE FULL GROWN HEBE OF FITZ-FULKE WHOSE MIND	525	3	DON JUAN	16	49	2

GROWN-UP
	PAGE	VOL		CANTO	STANZA	LN
SAFE WITH A LADY WHOSE LAST GROWN-UP DAUGHTER	339	3	DON JUAN	12	51	3

GROWS
	PAGE	VOL		CANTO	STANZA	LN
THAT THERE ARE MONTHS WHICH NATURE GROWS MORE MERRY IN	76	2	DON JUAN	1	102	7
FOR THEN THEIR ELOQUENCE GROWS QUITE PROFUSE	119	2	DON JUAN	1	179	4
WHEN SHIPWRECK'S SHORT ALLOWANCE GROWS TOO SCANTY	200	2	DON JUAN	2	83	7
WHICH GROWS A HABIT SHE CAN NE'ER GET OVER	276	2	DON JUAN	3	3	3
TO LOSE ITSELF WHEN THE OLD WORLD GROWS DULL	353	2	DON JUAN	4	17	3
BUT LET ME CHANGE THIS THEME WHICH GROWS TOO SAD	384	2	DON JUAN	4	74	1
AND THE SAD SECOND MOON GROWS DIM AGAIN	168	3	DON JUAN	8	113	4
THE LIST GROWS LONG OF LIVE AND DEAD PRETENDERS	299	3	DON JUAN	11	61	1
WHICH GROWS NO BETTER THOUGH 'TIS TIME IT SHOULD	301	3	DON JUAN	11	65	6
YAWNING A LITTLE AS THE NIGHT GROWS LATER	303	3	DON JUAN	11	69	8
CHANGE GROWS TOO CHANGEABLE WITHOUT BEING NEW	309	3	DON JUAN	11	82	6
GROWS GRIZZLED AND WE ARE NOT WHAT WE WERE--	315	3	DON JUAN	12	1	8
IT GROWS AN ACT OF PATRIOTIC CHARITY	357	3	DON JUAN	12	89	5
AND WAIT UNTIL THE NIGHTINGALE GROWS DUMBER	380	3	DON JUAN	13	48	5
WHEN ERE THE INK BE DRY THE SOUND GROWS COLD	382	3	DON JUAN	13	51	5
FULL GROWS HIS BAG AND WONDERFUL HIS FEATS	394	3	DON JUAN	13	75	6
AND THERE'S A COURAGE WHICH GROWS OUT OF FEAR	412	3	DON JUAN	14	5	2
OF FAME OR PROFIT WHEN THE WORLD GROWS WEARY	415	3	DON JUAN	14	11	2
AS GROWS A FLOWER THUS QUIETLY SHE GREW	476	3	DON JUAN	15	47	3
THEIR SORT OF HALF PROFESSION FOR IT GROWS	522	3	DON JUAN	16	44	4
BUT MANY A LONELY TREE THE LOFTIER GROWS	562	3	DON JUAN	17	1	3

GROWTH
	PAGE	VOL		CANTO	STANZA	LN
AS E'ER TO MAN'S MATURER GROWTH WAS GIVEN	48	2	DON JUAN	1	49	4
WHICH ARE (AS I MUST OWN) OF FEMALE GROWTH	221	2	DON JUAN	2	123	3
BUT SEEM THE GROWTH OF A MOST DIFFERENT CLIME	277	2	DON JUAN	3	5	V4
SHOW WHAT THE PASSIONS ARE IN THEIR FULL GROWTH	368	2	DON JUAN	4	45	8
THERE SOLITUDE WE KNOW HAS HER FULL GROWTH IN	443	2	DON JUAN	5	57	3
THOUGH WHAT IS SOUL OR MIND THEIR BIRTH OR GROWTH	17	3	DON JUAN	6	22	7
AND TREES OF GOODLY GROWTH AND SPREADING ROOTS	43	3	DON JUAN	6	75	8
AND FAMINE WITH HER GAUNT AND BONY GROWTH	88	3	DON JUAN	7	45	6
FOR ENNUI IS A GROWTH OF ENGLISH ROOT	405	3	DON JUAN	13	101	5
SOMETHING LIKE ILLNESS OF A SUDDEN GROWTH	514	3	DON JUAN	16	33	4

GRUDGES
	PAGE	VOL		CANTO	STANZA	LN
SOME FOR AMUSEMENT OTHERS FOR OLD GRUDGES	36	2	DON JUAN	1	28	8

GRUEL
	PAGE	VOL		CANTO	STANZA	LN
THE DYING MAN CRIED HOLD I'VE GOT MY GRUEL	276	3	DON JUAN	11	16	2

GRUMBLE
   LET NO MAN GRUMBLE WHEN HIS FRIENDS FALL OFF . . . . . 431 3 DON JUAN 14   48   5
GRUMBLED
   AND WOKE HER MAID SO EARLY THAT SHE GRUMBLED . . . . . 229 2 DON JUAN 2   138   5
GRUMBLES
   AT FIRST IT GRUMBLES THEN IT SWEARS AND THEN . . . . . 138 3 DON JUAN 8   51   1
GRUMBLING
   BEARS VEGETABLES IN A GRUMBLING WAY . . . . . . 191 2 DON JUAN 2   67   6
   AT LAST THEY SETTLED INTO SIMPLE GRUMBLING . . . . . 426 2 DON JUAN 5   29   1
   GROWLING AND GRUMBLING IN GOOD TURKISH PHRASE . . . . . 64 3 DON JUAN 6   117   2
GUADALQUIVIR
   A NOBLE STREAM AND CALL'D THE GUADALQUIVIR . . . . . 25 2 DON JUAN 1   8   8
   BUT IN HIS NATIVE STREAM THE GUADALQUIVIR . . . . . 211 2 DON JUAN 2   105   1
GUADALQUIVIR'S
   FAREWELL WHERE GUADALQUIVIR'S WATERS GLIDE . . . . . 166 2 DON JUAN 2   18   5
GUARD
   OFT IN THE WRONG AND NEVER ON HIS GUARD . . . . . . 33 2 DON JUAN 1   21   2
   OF CONQUEST AND HIS GUARD OF GRENADIERS . . . . . 253 3 DON JUAN 10   58   8
   MY GUARD MY OLD GUARD EXCLAIMED THAT GOD OF CLAY-- . . 254 3 DON JUAN 10   59   2
   MY GUARD MY OLD GUARD EXCLAIMED THAT GOD OF CLAY-- . . 254 3 DON JUAN 10   59   2
   'MIDST MANY ROCKS WE GUARD MORE AGAINST WRECKS . . . . 371 3 DON JUAN 13   30   6
   TO SHIELD HIMSELF THAN PUT YOU ON YOUR GUARD . . . . . 462 3 DON JUAN 15   14   4
GUARDED
   ITS WORKINGS THROUGH THE VAINLY GUARDED EYE . . . . . 61 2 DON JUAN 1   73   4
   GUARDED BY SHOALS AND ROCKS AS BY AN HOST . . . . . 249 2 DON JUAN 2   177   3
GUARDIAN
   HER GUARDIAN ANGEL HAD GIVEN UP HIS GARRISON . . . . . 30 2 DON JUAN 1   17   4
   INEZ BECAME SOLE GUARDIAN WHICH WAS FAIR . . . . . . 42 2 DON JUAN 1   37   5
   AND MOTHER BROTHER GUARDIAN SHE HAD NONE . . . . . 252 2 DON JUAN 2   182   3
   A GUARDIAN GREEN IN YEARS A WARD CONNECTED . . . . . 252 3 DON JUAN 10   57   6
   A RIGID GUARDIAN OR A ZEALOUS PRIEST . . . . . 334 3 DON JUAN 12   39   5
   A GOODLY GUARDIAN FOR HIS INFANT CHARGE . . . . . 335 3 DON JUAN 12   41   7
   WHILE SCOUT THE PARISH GUARDIAN OF THE FRAIL . . . . . 533 3 DON JUAN 16   67   2
GUARDIANS
   FOR SILLY WARDS WILL BRING THEIR GUARDIANS BLAME . . . . 336 3 DON JUAN 12   42   4
   CHILD TO THE CARE OF GUARDIANS GOOD AND KIND . . . . . 475 3 DON JUAN 15   44   2
   ARE TUTORS GUARDIANS AND SO FORTH COMPARED . . . . . 564 3 DON JUAN 17   4   2
GUARDS
   AND GUARDS AND BOLTS AND WALLS AND NOW AND THEN . . . . 22 3 DON JUAN 6   32   4
   THEIR GUARDS BEING GONE AND AS IT WERE A TRUCE . . . . . 23 3 DON JUAN 6   34   6
   SHE TO DISMISS HER GUARDS AND HE HIS HAREM . . . . . 53 3 DON JUAN 6   95   7
GUARDSMAN
   THERE WAS JACK JARGON THE GIGANTIC GUARDSMAN . . . . . 399 3 DON JUAN 13   88   1
GUEBRES
   OF GUEBRES GIAOURS AND GINNS AND GOULS IN HOSTS . . . . 30 3 DON JUAN 6   48   6
GUELF
   IS GOOD TO GOVERN--ALMOST AS A GUELF . . . . . . 299 2 DON JUAN 3   47   8
GUERDON
   HIS GUERDON 'TIS HIS VIRTUE MAKES HIM MAD . . . . . 363 3 DON JUAN 13   9   5
GUESS
   AND THOUGH HIS MEANING THEY COULD RARELY GUESS . . . . 318 2 DON JUAN 3   82   5
   DREW ALL EYES ON HIM GIVING THEM TO GUESS . . . . . 415 2 DON JUAN 5   9   5
   JUST AS ONE VIEWS A HORSE TO GUESS HIS PRICE . . . . . 441 2 DON JUAN 5   54   6
   MANY OF COMMON READERS GIVE A GUESS . . . . . . 82 3 DON JUAN 7   33   3
   IN HEAVEN I KNOW NOT NOR PRETEND TO GUESS . . . . . 167 3 DON JUAN 8   112   2
   TAKE TOWNS BY STORM NO CAUSES CAN I GUESS . . . . . 176 3 DON JUAN 8   129   5
   WHICH IS THE ONLY CAUSE THAT WE CAN GUESS . . . . . 371 3 DON JUAN 13   29   7
   AT LEAST HIS MANNER SUFFERS NOT TO GUESS . . . . . 373 3 DON JUAN 13   34   6
   AN ACCESSARY AS I HAVE CAUSE TO GUESS . . . . . . 443 3 DON JUAN 14   76   4
   YOU'LL NEVER GUESS I'LL BET YOU MILLIONS MILLIARDS-- . . 454 3 DON JUAN 14   100   7
   WHEN ONCE DECANTED--I PRESUME TO GUESS SO . . . . . 458 3 DON JUAN 15   6   6
   THOUGH PROBABLY MUCH LESS A FACT THAN GUESS) . . . . . 491 3 DON JUAN 15   80   6
GUESS'D
   A WORLD OF WORDS AND THINGS AT WHICH SHE GUESS'D . . . 241 2 DON JUAN 2   162   8
   AT LEAST WE THINK SO THOUGH BUT FEW HAVE GUESS'D . . . .   6 3 DON JUAN 6   1   4
   MY MUSE DESPISES REFERENCE AS YOU HAVE GUESS'D . . . . 433 3 DON JUAN 14   54   6
   IMPRESSIONS WERE MUCH STRONGER THAN SHE GUESS'D . . . . 448 3 DON JUAN 14   88   5
GUESSED
   THEIR DRESS WAS MOSLEM BUT YOU MIGHT HAVE GUESSED . . . . 96 3 DON JUAN 7   57   3
GUESSING
   THE CAUSE BEING PAST HIS GUESSING OR UNRIDDLING . . . . 290 2 DON JUAN 3   28   6
   AND STILL LESS GUESSING WHERE THEY MIGHT BE GOING . . . 120 3 DON JUAN 8   19   4
   GUESSING AT WHAT SHALL HAPPILY BE HID . . . . . 180 3 DON JUAN 8   137   7
GUEST
   THEIR CHARITY INCREASED ABOUT THEIR GUEST . . . . . 225 2 DON JUAN 2   131   5
   WITHOUT DISTURBING HER YET SLUMBERING GUEST . . . . . 245 2 DON JUAN 2   168   6
   AN ARAB WITH A STRANGER FOR A GUEST . . . . . 261 2 DON JUAN 2   196   4
   LOVE CONSTANT LOVE HAS BEEN MY CONSTANT GUEST . . . . 268 2 DON JUAN 2   209   5
   TAPPING THE SHOULDER OF THE NIGHEST GUEST . . . . . 297 2 DON JUAN 3   42   2
   A HAPPY LOVER AND A WELCOME GUEST-- . . . . . 343 2 DON JUAN 3 V 98   5
   HAD DEIGNED THAT NIGHT TO BE GULBEYAZ' GUEST . . . . . 12 3 DON JUAN 6   13 V6
   EVEN WERE SAINT FRANCIS' PARAMOUR THEIR GUEST . . . . . 14 3 DON JUAN 6   17   5
   SHE ADDED TO JUANNA THEIR NEW GUEST . . . . . . 29 3 DON JUAN 6   46   4
   YOU LOVE THIS BOYISH NEW SERAGLIO GUEST . . . . . . 63 3 DON JUAN 6   115   5
   WAS JUAN A RECHERCHE WELCOME GUEST . . . . . . 370 3 DON JUAN 13   28   2
   OF SUCH DISCUSSION SHE WAS THERE A GUEST . . . . . 480 3 DON JUAN 15   55   2
   BUT APPREHENSIVE OF HIS SPECTRAL GUEST . . . . . 555 3 DON JUAN 16   111   5
GUESTS
   AS MANY GUESTS OR MORE BEFORE WHOM GROAN . . . . . . 381 3 DON JUAN 13   49   5

		PAGE	VOL		CANTO	STANZA	LN
GUESTS (CONTINUED)							
THE NOBLE GUESTS ASSEMBLED AT THE ABBEY		396	3	DON JUAN	13	79	1
THE PARTY WE HAVE TOUCH'D ON WERE THE GUESTS		404	3	DON JUAN	13	99	2
THE GUESTS WERE PLACED ACCORDING TO THEIR ROLL		488	3	DON JUAN	15	74	3
QUITE FULL RIGHT DULL GUESTS HOT AND DISHES COLD		538	3	DON JUAN	16	78	6
LONG BANQUETS AND TOO MANY GUESTS ALTHOUGH		542	3	DON JUAN	16	86	2
THE GUESTS DROPPED IN--THE LAST BUT ONE HER GRACE		568	3	DON JUAN	17	13	7
GUESTS'							
WHICH TURNED UPON THEIR LATE GUESTS' MIENS AND FACES		550	3	DON JUAN	16	103	5
GUIDE							
THEY FOLLOWED CLOSE BEHIND THEIR SABLE GUIDE		440	2	DON JUAN	5	51	2
TO JUAN SOME SLIGHT LESSONS AS HIS GUIDE		464	2	DON JUAN	5	91	2
SO LET US BACK TO LILLIPUT AND GUIDE		20	3	DON JUAN	6	28	6
A PRETTY STRANGER WITHOUT FRIEND OR GUIDE		28	3	DON JUAN	6	45	5
IN THIS PLAIN PAIR SUWARROW AND HIS GUIDE		87	3	DON JUAN	7	43	8
HIS HASTE IMPATIENCE IS A BLUNDERING GUIDE		304	3	DON JUAN	11	71	6
THOUGH ONCE SHE WAS SEEN READING THE BATH GUIDE		525	3	DON JUAN	16	50	2
GUIDE-BOOK'S							
UPON THE GUIDE-BOOK'S PRIVILEGE THE SUN		279	3	DON JUAN	11	23	6
GUIDE-BOOKS							
TO GUIDE-BOOKS RHYMES TOURS SKETCHES ILLUSTRATIONS		440	2	DON JUAN	5	52	8
GUIDED							
AND LOVES OR HATES DISDAINING TO BE GUIDED		366	3	DON JUAN	13	16	7
GUIDES							
ALTHOUGH ('TWILL HAPPEN AS OUR PLANET GUIDES)		251	3	DON JUAN	10	54	5
GUIDO'S							
IN GUIDO'S FAMOUS FRESCO WHICH ALONE		428	3	DON JUAN	14	40	2
GUILE							
WHICH REALLY KNEW OR THOUGHT IT KNEW NO GUILE		438	3	DON JUAN	14	65	2
GUILELESS							
THE GUILELESS HEART IN SILENCE MAY GRIEVE O'ER		107	2	DON JUAN	1	157	3
GUILLOTINE							
ONE MAKES NEW NOSES ONE A GUILLOTINE		91	2	DON JUAN	1	129	3
GUILT							
BUT WHETHER 'TWAS THAT ONE'S OWN GUILT CONFOUNDS		118	2	DON JUAN	1	176	3
YET IF I NAME MY GUILT 'TIS NOT TO BOAST		130	2	DON JUAN	1	193	5
A VERY HANDSOME HOUSE FROM OUT HIS GUILT		223	2	DON JUAN	2	127	3
TO SIT AMIDST THE RUINS OF THEIR GUILT		352	3	DON JUAN	12	78	7
GUINEA							
SHINE LIKE A GUINEA AND SEVEN SHILLING PIECES		306	2	DON JUAN	3	60	8
GUISE							
THE MEN WITHIN THE BOAT AND IN THIS GUISE		206	2	DON JUAN	2	94	6
OF GILDED BRONZE AND CARVED IN CURIOUS GUISE		461	2	DON JUAN	5	86	2
WHERE THEY MIGHT MEET IN MUCH MORE PEACEFUL GUISE		472	2	DON JUAN	5	105	3
IN SUCH GUISE THAT SHE COULD MAKE NOTHING OF IT		438	3	DON JUAN	14	65	8
GUITARS							
GUITARS AND CASTANETS FROM ALICANT		284	2	DON JUAN	3	17	6
GULBEYAZ							
AND THUS GULBEYAZ THOUGH SHE KNEW NOT WHY		480	2	DON JUAN	5	120	7
GULBEYAZ FOR THE FIRST TIME IN HER DAYS		482	2	DON JUAN	5	122	1
GULBEYAZ WHO LOOKED ON HIM AS HER DEBTOR		483	2	DON JUAN	5	124	5
IS IT EXCLAIMED GULBEYAZ AS YOU SAY		494	2	DON JUAN	5	145	1
WHILE STILL A FLUTTERING SIGH GULBEYAZ HEAVED		500	2	DON JUAN	5	155	6
I KNOW GULBEYAZ WAS EXTREMELY WRONG		10	3	DON JUAN	6	8	1
GULBEYAZ WAS THE FOURTH AND (AS I SAID)		12	3	DON JUAN	6	12	1
IF FAIR GULBEYAZ OVERDID HER PART		15	3	DON JUAN	6	19	1
GULBEYAZ AND HER LORD WERE SLEEPING OR		18	3	DON JUAN	6	24	1
GULBEYAZ WAS AN EMPRESS BUT HAD BEEN		18	3	DON JUAN	6	25	7
THEY WONDERED HOW GULBEYAZ TOO COULD BE		24	3	DON JUAN	6	36	5
GULBEYAZ ROSE FROM RESTLESSNESS AND PALE		49	3	DON JUAN	6	87	2
MEANTIME GULBEYAZ WHEN HER KING WAS GONE		54	3	DON JUAN	6	97	1
GULBEYAZ WAS NO MODEL OF TRUE PATIENCE		56	3	DON JUAN	6	101	1
GULBEYAZ PROVED IN THAT BRIEF AGONY		59	3	DON JUAN	6	106	7
GULBEYAZ STOPPED AND BECKONED BABA--SLAVE		62	3	DON JUAN	6	112	1
GULBEYAZ SHEWED THEM BOTH COMMISERATION		65	3	DON JUAN	6	119	3
GULBEYAZ'							
YOU CAN'T SUPPOSE GULBEYAZ' ANGRY BROW		486	2	DON JUAN	5	131	8
IF I SAID FIRE FLASHED FROM GULBEYAZ' EYES		489	2	DON JUAN	5	134	1
HIS HIGHNESS GAZED UPON GULBEYAZ' CHARMS		12	3	DON JUAN	6	13	6
HAD DEIGNED THAT NIGHT TO BE GULBEYAZ' GUEST		12	3	DON JUAN	6	13	V6
GULBEYAZ' TACITURN OR SPEAKING WILL		61	3	DON JUAN	6	110	4
GULBEYAZM							
SO DEEP AN ANGUISH WRUNG GULBEYAZM BROW		58	3	DON JUAN	6	105	4
GULF							
'TIS NOT SO PLEASANT IN THE GULF OF LYONS		176	2	DON JUAN	2	39	8
THE GULF OF ROCK YAWNS--YOU CAN'T GAZE A MINUTE		412	3	DON JUAN	14	5	7
GULL							
THE EAGLE SOARS ALONE THE GULL AND CROW		358	2	DON JUAN	4	28	7
GULLET							
THE QUAINT OLD CRUEL COXCOMB IN HIS GULLET		407	3	DON JUAN	13	106	7
GULLETS							
HARD WORDS WHICH STICK IN THE SOFT MUSES' GULLETS		106	3	DON JUAN	7	78	8
GUN-BARREL							
KILLED BY FIVE BULLETS FROM AN OLD GUN-BARREL		429	2	DON JUAN	5	34	8
GUNNERY							
HE LEARN'D THE ARTS OF RIDING FENCING GUNNERY		42	2	DON JUAN	1	38	7
GUNPOWDER							
ARE OIL AND GUNPOWDER AND SOME GOOD LESSONS		245	2	DON JUAN	2	169	6
UNLESS GUN-POWDER SHOULD BE FOUND TO HARM		106	3	DON JUAN	7	79	5
NO LONGER NOW RESIST THE ATTRACTION OF GUNPOWDER		129	3	DON JUAN	8	33	V7

334

GUNS
    A SQUALL CAME ON AND WHILE SOME GUNS BROKE LOOSE . . . . . 172 2 DON JUAN 2   30   6
    SOME SWORE THAT THEY HEARD BREAKERS OTHERS GUNS . . . . 207 2 DON JUAN 2   96   7
    IN GETTING OUT GOODS BALLAST GUNS AND TREASURE . . . . . 286 2 DON JUAN 3   20   8
    LAND BATTERIES WORKED THEIR GUNS WITH GREAT PRECISION . . . 81 3 DON JUAN 7   30   3
    BOMBS DRUMS GUNS BASTIONS BATTERIES BAYONETS BULLETS . . 106 3 DON JUAN 7   78   7
    UPON THE HEAD BEFORE THEIR GUNS WERE COCKED . . . . . 134 3 DON JUAN 8   43   8
GURNEY
    THE BEST IS THAT IN SHORTHAND TA'EN BY GURNEY . . . . . 127 2 DON JUAN 1   189   7
GUSH
    GUSH FROM THE EARTH UNTIL THE LAND RUNS O'ER . . . . . 373 2 DON JUAN 4   55   3
    THE BLOOD MAY GUSH OUT AS THE DANUBE'S FLOW . . . . . . 155 3 DON JUAN 8   87   3
GUSH'D
    OF BILLOWS BUT AT INTERVALS THERE GUSH'D . . . . . . 184 2 DON JUAN 2   53   5
    THE SPRING GUSH'D THROUGH GRIM MOUTHS OF GRANITE MADE . . 389 3 DON JUAN 13   65   5
GUSHED
    THE BLOOD GUSHED FROM HER LIPS AND EARS AND EYES . . . . 376 2 DON JUAN 4   59 V1
    THE SPOUTING BLOOD GUSHED THROUGH HER MOUTH HER EYES . . 376 2 DON JUAN 4   59 V1
GUSHING
    THE TEARS WERE GUSHING FROM HER GENTLE EYES . . . . . . 84 2 DON JUAN 1   117   3
    PURPLE AND GUSHING SWEET ARE OUR ESCAPES . . . . 88 2 DON JUAN 1   124   3
    THEIR LADY TO HER COUCH WITH GUSHING EYES . . . . . . 376 2 DON JUAN 4   59   5
    TO BE SO BEING IN A GUSHING STREAM . . . . 380 2 DON JUAN 4   66   6
    THERE'S MUSIC IN THE GUSHING OF A RILL . . . . 458 3 DON JUAN 15   5   6
GUST
    A GUST--WHICH ALL DESCRIPTIVE POWER TRANSCENDS-- . . . . 172 2 DON JUAN 2   30   7
GUSTS
    BY GUSTS AND MANY A SPARKLING HEARTH WAS BRIGHT . . . . 94 2 DON JUAN 1   135   3
    LIKE SHOWERS WHICH ON THE MIDNIGHT GUSTS WILL PASS . . 556 3 DON JUAN 16   114   3
GUTS
    YE RIGID GUTS OF REAPERS--I TRANSLATE . . . . 190 3 DON JUAN 9   15   2
GYNOCRASY
    THE LOVELIEST OLIGARCHS OF OUR GYNOCRASY . . . . . . 346 3 DON JUAN 12   66   4
    ON PAIN OF MUCH DISPLEASING THE GYNOCRASY . . . . . . 526 3 DON JUAN 16   52   8
H
    LORD H AMUNDEVILLE AND LADY A . . . . 382 3 DON JUAN 13   51   8
HA
    OR A HA HA OR BAH--A YAWN OR POOH . . . . 456 3 DON JUAN 15   1   7
    OR A HA HA OR BAH--A YAWN OR POOH . . . . 456 3 DON JUAN 15   1   7
HABEAS
    OF THE STAR CHAMBER THAN OF HABEAS CORPUS . . . . . 391 3 DON JUAN 13   69   8
HABIT
    WHICH GROWS A HABIT SHE CAN NE'ER GET OVER . . . . . 276 2 DON JUAN 3   3   3
    A HABIT RATHER BLAMEABLE WHICH IS . . . . 79 3 DON JUAN 7   25   1
    OF FEELING FOR HOWEVER HABIT SEARS . . . . 102 3 DON JUAN 7   69   5
    BY HABIT TO WHAT THEIR OWN HEARTS ABHOR-- . . . . . 143 3 DON JUAN 8   62   6
HABITANT
    HIM WHOM SHE DEEM'D A HABITANT WHERE DWELL . . . . . 363 2 DON JUAN 4   36   3
HABITS
    MODERATE IN ALL HIS HABITS AND CONTENT . . . . . . 302 2 DON JUAN 3   53   3
    IN ALL THEIR HABITS--NOT SO YOU I OWN . . . . 232 3 DON JUAN 10   15   7
    UNLESS HER HABITS SHOULD BEGIN TO MEND . . . . . . 432 3 DON JUAN 14   51   4
HABITUAL
    ALTHOUGH I WONDER HOW IT GREW HABITUAL . . . . . . 472 3 DON JUAN 15   36   8
HABITUDE
    THE HARDNESS BY LONG HABITUDE PRODUCED . . . . . . 303 2 DON JUAN 3   54   2
HACK
    AND WE ARE SICK OF ITS HACK SOUNDS AND SIGHTS . . . . 353 2 DON JUAN 4   17   4
    SO THAT HIS HORSE OR CHARGER HUNTER HACK . . . . . 424 3 DON JUAN 14   32   7
    WITH RUST SHOULD SURELY CEASE TO HACK AND HEW . . . . 433 3 DON JUAN 14   53   6
    'TIS SAD TO HACK INTO THE ROOTS OF THINGS . . . . . 436 3 DON JUAN 14   59   1
HACKNEY
    WOULD HE SUBSIDE INTO A HACKNEY LAUREAT . . . . . . 15 2 DON JUAN D   11 V7
    BY VARIOUS JOLTINGS OF LIFE'S HACKNEY COACH . . . . 421 3 DON JUAN 14   26   5
HACKS
    BUT ON THEY RODE UPON TWO UKRAINE HACKS . . . . . . 87 3 DON JUAN 7   43   6
HAGGARD
    AND HAGGARD WITH A DISSIPATED LIFE . . . . 389 2 DON JUAN 4   83   2
HAGGLED
    THEY HAGGLED WRANGLED SWORE TOO--SO THEY DID . . . . 425 2 DON JUAN 5   28   4
HAGUE
    FROM THENCE TO HOLLAND'S HAGUE AND HELVOETSLUYS . . . 256 3 DON JUAN 10   63   1
HAIDEE
    HE HAD AN ONLY DAUGHTER CALL'D HAIDEE . . . . . . 224 2 DON JUAN 2   128   1
    FOR HAIDEE STRIPP'D HER SABLES OFF TO MAKE . . . . 226 2 DON JUAN 2   133   2
    NOT SO HAIDEE SHE SADLY TOSS'D AND TUMBLED . . . . 229 2 DON JUAN 2   138   1
    AND HAIDEE MET THE MORNING FACE TO FACE . . . . . 231 2 DON JUAN 2   141   1
    AND WHEN INTO THE CAVERN HAIDEE STEPP'D . . . . . 232 2 DON JUAN 2   143   1
    BUT HAIDEE STOPP'D HER WITH HER QUICK SMALL HAND . . 234 2 DON JUAN 2   146   3
    BUT ZOE BEING OLDER THAN HAIDEE . . . . 239 2 DON JUAN 2   158   5
    AND THEN FAIR HAIDEE TRIED HER TONGUE AT SPEAKING . . 241 2 DON JUAN 2   161   1
    CAME ALWAYS BACK TO COFFEE AND HAIDEE . . . . . . 246 2 DON JUAN 2   171   8
    AND THUS A MOON ROLL'D ON AND FAIR HAIDEE . . . . 248 2 DON JUAN 2   174   1
    HAIDEE SPOKE NOT OF SCRUPLES ASK'D NO VOWS . . . . 257 2 DON JUAN 2   190   1
    ALAS FOR JUAN AND HAIDEE THEY WERE . . . . . . 258 2 DON JUAN 2   193   1
    AND HAIDEE BEING DEVOUT AS WELL AS FAIR . . . . . 258 2 DON JUAN 2   193   5
    HAIDEE WAS NATURE'S BRIDE AND KNEW NOT THIS . . . . 264 2 DON JUAN 2   202   1
    HAIDEE WAS PASSION'S CHILD BORN WHERE THE SUN . . . 264 2 DON JUAN 2   202   2
    LEAVING DON JUAN AND HAIDEE TO PLEAD . . . . . . 271 2 DON JUAN 2   216   7

HAIDEE   (CONTINUED)

	PAGE	VOL	CANTO	STANZA	LN
HAIDEE AND JUAN WERE NOT MARRIED BUT	282	2 DON JUAN	3	12	1
HAIDEE FORGOT THE ISLAND WAS HER SIRE'S	282	2 DON JUAN	3	13	4
COMPARED WITH WHAT HAIDEE DID WITH HIS TREASURE	295	2 DON JUAN	3	39	6
WHO SEEM'D TO HAVE TURN'D HAIDEE INTO A MATRON	298	2 DON JUAN	3	44	8
HAIDEE AND JUAN CARPETED THEIR FEET	309	2 DON JUAN	3	67	1
HAIDEE AND HER BELOVED HID THEIR FEET	309	2 DON JUAN	3	67	VI
HAIDEE AND JUAN THOUGHT NOT OF THE DEAD	351	2 DON JUAN	4	13	1
JUAN AND HAIDEE GAZED UPON EACH OTHER	357	2 DON JUAN	4	26	1
HAIDEE AND JUAN THEIR SIESTA TOOK	359	2 DON JUAN	4	29	2
DEAR AS HER FATHER HAD BEEN TO HAIDEE	363	2 DON JUAN	4	36	6
AND HAIDEE CLUNG AROUND HIM JUAN 'TIS--	364	2 DON JUAN	4	38	1
WHEN HAIDEE THREW HERSELF HER BOY BEFORE	366	2 DON JUAN	4	42	3
BUT HE HAD GOT HAIDEE INTO HIS HEAD	483	2 DON JUAN	5	124	2
HIGH YET RESEMBLING NOT HIS LOST HAIDEE	481	3 DON JUAN	15	58	2

HAIDEE'S

	PAGE	VOL	CANTO	STANZA	LN
FROM HAIDEE'S GLANCE THAN ANY GRAVEN LETTER	242	2 DON JUAN	2	163	8
AND BEATING 'GAINST HIS BOSOM HAIDEE'S HEART	257	2 DON JUAN	2	191	7
THE BLOOM TOO HAD RETURN'D TO HAIDEE'S CHEEKS	295	2 DON JUAN	3	38	6
FOR HAIDEE'S SAKE IS MORE THAN I CAN SAY	300	2 DON JUAN	3	49	6
OF ALL THE DRESSES I SELECT HAIDEE'S	311	2 DON JUAN	3	70	1
AN EMERALD AIGRETTE WITH HAIDEE'S HAIR IN'T	315	2 DON JUAN	3	77	6
FOR HAIDEE'S KNOWLEDGE WAS BY NO MEANS GREAT	354	2 DON JUAN	4	19	5
WHILE ONE NEW TEAR AROSE IN HAIDEE'S EYE	355	2 DON JUAN	4	21	8
AND HAIDEE'S SWEET LIPS MURMUR'D LIKE A BROOK	359	2 DON JUAN	4	29	6
UP JUAN SPRUNG TO HAIDEE'S BITTER SHRIEK	364	2 DON JUAN	4	37	1
OF THOSE WITH WHICH HIS HAIDEE'S BOSOM BOUNDED	373	2 DON JUAN	4	54	4
BEAUTY AND LOVE WERE HAIDEE'S MOTHER'S DOWER	374	2 DON JUAN	4	56	6
WITH HAIDEE'S ISLE AND SOFT IONIAN FACE	478	2 DON JUAN	5	117	3

HAIL

	PAGE	VOL	CANTO	STANZA	LN
HAIL MUSE ET CETERA--WE LEFT JUAN SLEEPING	274	2 DON JUAN	3	1	1
BUT LIKE THE CLIMES THAT KNOW NOR SNOW NOR HAIL	348	2 DON JUAN	4	9	4
LIKE HAIL TO MAKE A BLOODY DIURETIC	117	3 DON JUAN	8	12	3
THEY FELL AS THICK AS HARVESTS BENEATH HAIL	134	3 DON JUAN	8	43	1
HAIL THAMIS HAIL UPON THY VERGE IT IS	277	3 DON JUAN	11	20	4
HAIL THAMIS HAIL UPON THY VERGE IT IS	277	3 DON JUAN	11	20	4
TO CRITICS OR TO HAIL THE SETTING SUN	466	3 DON JUAN	15	22	6
TO HAIL HER WITH THE APOSTROPHE--OH THOU	506	3 DON JUAN	16	13	6

HAIL'D

	PAGE	VOL	CANTO	STANZA	LN
HAIL'D A STRANGE BRIG CORPO DI CAIO MARIO	389	2 DON JUAN	4	82	4

HAIR

	PAGE	VOL	CANTO	STANZA	LN
HER GLOSSY HAIR WAS CLUSTER'D O'ER A BROW	55	2 DON JUAN	1	61	1
WHICH PLAY'D WITHIN THE TANGLES OF HER HAIR	80	2 DON JUAN	1	110	2
HER STREAMING HAIR THE BLACK CURLS STRIVE BUT FAIL	108	2 DON JUAN	1	158	5
CALL'D BACK THE TANGLES OF HER WANDERING HAIR	114	2 DON JUAN	1	170	2
BUT NOW AT THIRTY YEARS MY HAIR IS GRAY--	143	2 DON JUAN	1	213	1
ABOVE HIM HANGING BY A SINGLE HAIR	153	2 DON JUAN	1	V 4	2
AND GNASH'D THEIR TEETH AND HOWLING TORE THEIR HAIR	180	2 DON JUAN	2	45	4
THAT SPARKLED O'ER THE AUBURN OF HER HAIR	217	2 DON JUAN	2	116	2
HER CLUSTERING HAIR WHOSE LONGER LOCKS WERE ROLL'D	217	2 DON JUAN	2	116	3
HER HAIR I SAID WAS AUBURN BUT HER EYES	218	2 DON JUAN	2	117	1
HER HAIR HAD SILVER ONLY BOUND TO BE	221	2 DON JUAN	2	122	4
HER HAIR WAS THICKER BUT LESS LONG HER EYES	221	2 DON JUAN	2	122	7
HER HAIR WAS STARR'D WITH GEMS HER VEIL'S FINE FOLD	312	2 DON JUAN	3	72	4
AN EMERALD AIGRETTE WITH HAIDEE'S HAIR IN'T	315	2 DON JUAN	3	77	6
THE BLANK GREY WAS NOT MADE TO BLAST THEIR HAIR	348	2 DON JUAN	4	9	3
HER HAIR WAS DRIPPING AND THE VERY BALLS	362	2 DON JUAN	4	33	5
GOOD TEETH WITH CURLING RATHER DARK BROWN HAIR	416	2 DON JUAN	5	11	3
ONE DIFFICULTY STILL REMAINED--HIS HAIR	457	2 DON JUAN	5	79	1
WHOSE CHARTS LAY DOWN ITS CURRENTS TO A HAIR	7	3 DON JUAN	6	2	4
HER SHAPE HER HAIR HER AIR HER EVERYTHING	23	3 DON JUAN	6	35	2
JUANNA PLAYING WITH HER VEIL OR HAIR	28	3 DON JUAN	6	45	2
WITH FLOATING DRAPERIES AND WITH FLYING HAIR	42	3 DON JUAN	6	72	2
HER FACE DECLINED AND WAS UNSEEN HER HAIR	60	3 DON JUAN	6	108	1
HER HEAD HUNG DOWN AND HER LONG HAIR IN STOOPING	60	3 DON JUAN	6	109	1
AND BEGGED BY EVERY HAIR OF MAHOMET'S BEARD	62	3 DON JUAN	6	113	7
AND ABOVE ALL BE COMBED EVEN TO A HAIR	64	3 DON JUAN	6	118	4
ARE THINGS THE TURNING OF A HAIR OR FEATHER	65	3 DON JUAN	6	119	6
THE WOMEN WITH THEIR HAIR ABOUT THEIR EARS	102	3 DON JUAN	7	69	3
WHENCE HER FAIR HAIR ROSE TWINING WITH AFFRIGHT	158	3 DON JUAN	8	93	2
BLACK LETTER UPON FOOLSCAP WHILE OUR HAIR	315	3 DON JUAN	12	1	7
AS STANDS A STATUE STOOD HE FELT HIS HAIR	510	3 DON JUAN	16	23	5

HAIR'S

	PAGE	VOL	CANTO	STANZA	LN
HER HAIR'S LONG AUBURN WAVES DOWN TO HER HEEL	313	2 DON JUAN	3	73	1
ALMOST AN HAIR'S BREADTH TOO MUCH ON ONE SIDE	513	3 DON JUAN	16	29	8

HAIRY

	PAGE	VOL	CANTO	STANZA	LN
HE TURN'D FROM GRISLY SAINTS AND MARTYRS HAIRY	235	2 DON JUAN	2	149	7

HAL

	PAGE	VOL	CANTO	STANZA	LN
THE WITLESS FALSTAFF OF A HOARY HAL	267	3 DON JUAN	10	86	7

HALE

	PAGE	VOL	CANTO	STANZA	LN
A MAN OF THIRTY RATHER STOUT AND HALE	416	2 DON JUAN	5	10	6
BY NATURE AS IN HIGHER DAMES LESS HALE	532	3 DON JUAN	16	64	3

HALES'S

	PAGE	VOL	CANTO	STANZA	LN
MALGRE SIR MATTHEW HALES'S GREAT HUMANITY	565	3 DON JUAN	17	7	8

HALF

	PAGE	VOL	CANTO	STANZA	LN
(ALTHOUGH IT COST ME HALF AN HOUR IN SPINNING)	25	2 DON JUAN	1	7	6
OVID'S A RAKE AS HALF HIS VERSES SHOW HIM	45	2 DON JUAN	1	42	1
FOR HALF HIS DAYS WERE PASS'D AT CHURCH THE OTHER	48	2 DON JUAN	1	49	7
WAS LARGE AND DARK SUPPRESSING HALF ITS FIRE	54	2 DON JUAN	1	60	2

HALF   (CONTINUED)

	PAGE	VOL	CANTO		STANZA	LN
SEES HALF THE BUSINESS IN A WICKED WAY	82	2	DON JUAN	1	113	6
AND JULIA SATE WITH JUAN HALF EMBRACED	83	2	DON JUAN	1	115	1
AND HALF RETIRING FROM THE GLOWING ARM	83	2	DON JUAN	1	115	2
WITH MORE THAN HALF THE CITY AT HIS BACK--	96	2	DON JUAN	1	137	2
AND HALF FORGOT THEIR DANGER AND DESPAIR	114	2	DON JUAN	1	170	4
WHICH JULIA HALF WITHHELD AND THEN HALF GRANTED	120	2	DON JUAN	1	180	2
WHICH JULIA HALF WITHHELD AND THEN HALF GRANTED	120	2	DON JUAN	1	180	2
YET HALF AFRAID TO VENTURE FOR THE DRAUGHT	155	2	DON JUAN	1	V 6	2
TO SAVE ONE HALF THE PEOPLE THEN ON BOARD	181	2	DON JUAN	2	48	8
HALF EPILEPTICAL AND HALF HYSTERICAL--	183	2	DON JUAN	2	50	7
HALF EPILEPTICAL AND HALF HYSTERICAL--	183	2	DON JUAN	2	50	7
THE BOATS PULLED OFF WITH THEIR HALF NAKED CREWS	183	2	DON JUAN	2	51	V6
ONE HALF SATE UP THOUGH NUMB'D WITH THE IMMERSION	189	2	DON JUAN	2	63	4
WHILE T'OTHER HALF WERE LAID DOWN IN THEIR PLACE	189	2	DON JUAN	2	63	5
AND THE BOY'S EYES WHICH THE DULL FILM HALF GLAZED	203	2	DON JUAN	2	89	5
ROLL'D ON THE BEACH HALF SENSELESS FROM THE SEA	212	2	DON JUAN	2	107	8
DON JUAN ALMOST FAMISH'D AND HALF DROWN'D	224	2	DON JUAN	2	129	4
IT OPEN'D HALF THE TURNPIKE-GATES TO HEAVEN--	225	2	DON JUAN	2	131	7
WITH THE FAR MOUNTAIN-CRESCENT HALF SURROUNDED	252	2	DON JUAN	2	183	5
HALF BURIED IN THE TRESSES WHICH IT GRASPS	259	2	DON JUAN	2	194	4
HALF NAKED LOVING NATURAL AND GREEK	259	2	DON JUAN	2	194	8
OF MEN AND MADE THEM SPEECHES WHEN HALF MELLOW	318	2	DON JUAN	3	82	4
HAD FALLEN WITH HIS RIGHT SHOULDER HALF CUT THROUGH	370	2	DON JUAN	4	48	8
YET COULD HIS CORPORAL PANGS AMOUNT TO HALF	373	2	DON JUAN	4	54	3
AND STILL IT HALF CALLS UP THE REALMS OF FAIRY	413	2	DON JUAN	5	4	3
SOFAS 'TWAS HALF A SIN TO SIT UPON	449	2	DON JUAN	5	65	5
ONE'S TURNED HALF MUSSULMAN AND ONE A MAID	459	2	DON JUAN	5	83	7
OF HALF-VOLUPTUOUSNESS AND HALF COMMAND	473	2	DON JUAN	5	108	8
A WOMAN'S TEAR-DROP MELTS A MAN'S HALF SEARS	479	2	DON JUAN	5	118	5
AND HALF OF THAT OPINION'S ALSO MINE	485	2	DON JUAN	5	129	8
THESE DON'T EXPRESS ONE HALF WHAT I SHOULD SAY	487	2	DON JUAN	5	132	6
THAT A MERE CHRISTIAN SHOULD BE HALF SO PRETTY	500	2	DON JUAN	5	155	8
THAN YOU WOULD MAKE THE HALF OF--DON'T SAY NO	29	3	DON JUAN	6	47	5
THE MOON BREAKS HALF UNVEILED EACH FURTHER CHARM	39	3	DON JUAN	6	66	5
HAVE HALF WITHDRAWN FROM HIM OBLIVION'S SCREEN	82	3	DON JUAN	7	33	8
HIS GLORY MIGHT HALF EQUAL HIS ESTATE	84	3	DON JUAN	7	37	4
MAY HAVE ANOTHER NAME FOR HALF WE SCAN	163	3	DON JUAN	8	104	3
AND HALF A MILLION FOR YOUR SABINE FARM	186	3	DON JUAN	9	7	7
FEEDS YOU BY PRINTING HALF THE REALM'S STARVATION--	200	3	DON JUAN	9	35	8
BUT I AM HALF A SCOT BY BIRTH AND BRED	233	3	DON JUAN	10	17	7
SODAE-SULPHAT SIX DRAMS HALF DRAM MANNAE OPTIM	244	3	DON JUAN	10	41	2
AQ FERVENT OUNCE AND A HALF TWO DRAMS TINCT SENNAE	244	3	DON JUAN	10	41	3
TOWARDS WHICH THE IMPATIENT WIND BLEW HALF A GALE	256	3	DON JUAN	10	64	3
WHO BUTCHERED HALF THE EARTH AND BULLIED T'OTHER	265	3	DON JUAN	10	81	8
TO THINK SO FOR HALF ENGLISH AS I AM	274	3	DON JUAN	11	12	6
I HAVE SEEN JOHN HALF DETECT HIMSELF A FOOL--	310	3	DON JUAN	11	85	8
THEY KNOW NOT HOW) THE ONE HALF THE PRESENT CASE	314	3	DON JUAN	11	V 75	7
KNOW HOW TO END THIS HALF AND HALF FLIRTATION	345	3	DON JUAN	12	63	V7
KNOW HOW TO END THIS HALF AND HALF FLIRTATION	345	3	DON JUAN	12	63	V7
INTO A COUNTRY WHERE 'TIS HALF A FASHION	347	3	DON JUAN	12	68	4
SEEMED TO HIM HALF COMMERCIAL HALF PEDANTIC	347	3	DON JUAN	12	68	5
SEEMED TO HIM HALF COMMERCIAL HALF PEDANTIC	347	3	DON JUAN	12	68	5
HALF HER ATTRACTIONS--PROBABLY FROM PITY--	350	3	DON JUAN	12	74	4
(WHILE YET THE CHURCH WAS ROME'S) STOOD HALF APART	386	3	DON JUAN	13	59	2
SOME NE'ER BELIEVED ONE HALF OF WHAT THEY HEARD	429	3	DON JUAN	14	44	5
AND SET THE OTHER HALF OF EARTH TO RIGHTS	445	3	DON JUAN	14	82	7
AS WOMEN HATE HALF MEASURES ON THE WHOLE	468	3	DON JUAN	15	28	7
THAT HALF ITS PRODUCE TENDS TO EMIGRATION	472	3	DON JUAN	15	37	6
THIS HE EXPRESS'D HALF SMILING AND HALF SERIOUS	477	3	DON JUAN	15	49	4
THIS HE EXPRESS'D HALF SMILING AND HALF SERIOUS	477	3	DON JUAN	15	49	4
HALF VIRTUES AND WHOLE VICES BEING COMBINED	480	3	DON JUAN	15	57	4
OF WHOM HALF MY PHILOSOPHY THE PROGENY IS	488	3	DON JUAN	15	73	8
HAS SPARKLED AND LET HALF ITS SPIRIT OUT	504	3	DON JUAN	16	9	6
BACK TO HIS CHAMBER SHORN OF HALF HIS STRENGTH	511	3	DON JUAN	16	25	8
FOR SUCH SIGHTS THOUGH THE TALE IS HALF BELIEVED	516	3	DON JUAN	16	36	7
FOR ADELINE IS HALF A POETESS	517	3	DON JUAN	16	39	2
THEIR SORT OF HALF PROFESSION FOR IT GROWS	522	3	DON JUAN	16	44	4
THE THEME HALF CREDITED THE STRANGE TRADITION	527	3	DON JUAN	16	54	4
HE HAD PAID HIS NEIGHBOUR'S PRAYER WITH HALF A TURBOT	543	3	DON JUAN	16	88	8
HALF LETTING IN LONG SHADOWS ON THE LIGHT	558	3	DON JUAN	16	117	4

HALF-CHASTE

	PAGE	VOL	CANTO		STANZA	LN
UNLIKE OUR OWN HALF-CHASTE ELIZABETH	222	3	DON JUAN	9	81	2

HALF-DEMON

	PAGE	VOL	CANTO		STANZA	LN
HERO BUFFOON HALF-DEMON AND HALF-DIRT	95	3	DON JUAN	7	55	5

HALF-DIRT

	PAGE	VOL	CANTO		STANZA	LN
HERO BUFFOON HALF-DEMON AND HALF-DIRT	95	3	DON JUAN	7	55	5

HALF-FORGAVE

	PAGE	VOL	CANTO		STANZA	LN
THE VERY WOMEN HALF-FORGAVE HER FACE	476	2	DON JUAN	5	113	V8

HALF-GIRLISH

	PAGE	VOL	CANTO		STANZA	LN
MY MISTRESS ALL FOR THAT HALF-GIRLISH FACE	115	2	DON JUAN	1	171	8

HALF-HOUR

	PAGE	VOL	CANTO		STANZA	LN
HAD POUR'D UPON HIM FOR THE LAST HALF-HOUR	110	2	DON JUAN	1	161	7
BUT FOR THAT HOUR CALLED HALF-HOUR GIVEN TO DRESS	482	3	DON JUAN	15	61	7

HALF-KILL'D

	PAGE	VOL	CANTO		STANZA	LN
WITH JUAN LEFT HALF-KILL'D SOME STANZAS BACK	384	2	DON JUAN	4	74	8

HALF-PAST

	PAGE	VOL	CANTO		STANZA	LN
OF HALF-PAST SIX--PERHAPS STILL NEARER SEVEN	77	2	DON JUAN	1	104	2
AT HALF-PAST EIGHT O'CLOCK BOOMS HENCOOPS SPARS	183	2	DON JUAN	2	51	1
THE WHOLE ODA FROM THEIR BEDS AT HALF-PAST THREE	46	3	DON JUAN	6	80	4

337

		PAGE	VOL		CANTO	STANZA	LN
HALF-PAY							
	HALF-PAY FOR LIFE MAKE MANKIND WORTH DESTROYING	118	3 DON JUAN	8	14	8
	NO HERO TRUSTETH WHOLLY TO HALF-PAY	163	3 DON JUAN	8	103	8
HALF-SEAS-OVER							
	UPON THEIR AIRY CONFINE HALF-SEAS-OVER	255	3 DON JUAN	10	61	8
HALF-SERIOUS							
	PULCI WAS SIRE OF THE HALF-SERIOUS RHYME	347	2 DON JUAN	4	6	3
HALF-SHUT							
	HER EYES WERE NOT TOO SPARKLING YET HALF-SHUT	27	3 DON JUAN	6	43	3
HALF-SMOTHER'D							
	YOUNG JUAN SLIPP'D HALF-SMOTHER'D FROM THE BED	112	2 DON JUAN	1	165	8
HALF-SOLVED							
	HALF-SOLVED INTO THOSE SODAS OR MAGNESIAS	261	3 DON JUAN	10	73	7
HALF-STARVED							
	A HALF-STARVED BABE A WRECK UPON LIFE'S OCEAN	563	3 DON JUAN	17	3	4
HALF-TORN							
	SOME HALF-TORN DRAPERY SCATTER'D ON THE GROUND	125	2 DON JUAN	1	187	5
HALF-UNQUENCHED							
	A HALF-UNQUENCHED VOLCANO O'ER A SPACE	265	3 DON JUAN	10	81	2
HALF-VOLUPTUOUSNESS							
	OF HALF-VOLUPTUOUSNESS AND HALF COMMAND	473	2 DON JUAN	5	108	8
HALF-WAY							
	A HALF-WAY HOUSE OF DIPLOMATIC REST	472	2 DON JUAN	5	105	2
	LIFE'S HALF-WAY HOUSE WHERE DAMES WITH VIRTUE CROWNED	43	3 DON JUAN	6	75	5
	OF HUMAN YEARS THAT HALF-WAY HOUSE THAT RUDE	238	3 DON JUAN	10	27	5
HALIFAX							
	AT HALIFAX BUT NOW HE SERVED THE TARTARS	76	3 DON JUAN	7	19	8
HALL							
	AND STOOD WITHIN HIS HALL AT EVENTIDE	306	2 DON JUAN	3	61	2
	THE WORDS WHICH SHOOK BELSHAZZAR IN HIS HALL	308	2 DON JUAN	3	65	5
	AND A MAGNIFICIENT LARGE HALL DISPLAYED	440	2 DON JUAN	5	51	7
	ALONG THIS HALL AND UP AND DOWN SOME SQUATTED	441	2 DON JUAN	5	53	1
	HE LEADS THEM THROUGH THE HALL AND WITHOUT STOPPING	442	2 DON JUAN	5	55	1
	BUT IN A MIGHTY HALL OR GALLERY BOTH IN	443	2 DON JUAN	5	57	5
	OF A HUGE HALL AND ON ITS EITHER SIDE	462	2 DON JUAN	5	87	2
	IN THIS IMPERIAL HALL AT DISTANCE LAY	466	2 DON JUAN	5	95	1
	'TWAS ON THE WHOLE A NOBLY FURNISHED HALL	31	3 DON JUAN	6	51	6
	ONE ON THE OTHER THROUGHOUT THE WHOLE HALL	42	3 DON JUAN	6	71	5
	SALOON ROOM HALL O'ERFLOW BEYOND THEIR BRINK	302	3 DON JUAN	11	68	5
	THAT TIME HAS LEFT OUR FATHERS OF THEIR HALL	507	3 DON JUAN	16	16	8
	THE SHADOW PASSED AWAY--BUT WHERE THE HALL	511	3 DON JUAN	16	24	2
	HE WALKS FROM HALL TO HALL	519	3 DON JUAN	16	L 4	4
	HE WALKS FROM HALL TO HALL	519	3 DON JUAN	16	L 4	4
	SAY NOUGHT TO HIM AS HE WALKS THE HALL	520	3 DON JUAN	16	L 6	1
	BUT THIS POOR GIRL WAS LEFT IN THE GREAT HALL	533	3 DON JUAN	16	67	1
	CHECQUERED WITH ALL THE TRACERY OF THE HALL	559	3 DON JUAN	16	120	4
HALLAM'S							
	WHOSE TALE BELONGS TO HALLAM'S MIDDLE AGES	330	3 DON JUAN	12	30	8
HALLELUJAHS							
	LIE WITH THEIR HALLELUJAHS QUENCH'D LIKE FIRE	387	3 DON JUAN	13	62	8
HALLOW'D							
	BY THEIR OWN FEELINGS HALLOW'D AND UNITED	265	2 DON JUAN	2	204	5
HALLOWING							
	THE SILVER LIGHT WHICH HALLOWING TREE AND TOWER	82	2 DON JUAN	1	114	5
HALLS							
	IN HOLLOW HALLS WITH SPARRY ROOFS AND CELLS	253	2 DON JUAN	2	184	6
	OF AGES ON ITS WATER-FRETTED HALLS	362	2 DON JUAN	4	33	3
	BUT NOT ENOUGH TO SHOW THE IMPERIAL HALLS	442	2 DON JUAN	5	56	3
	IN KINGLY CHAMBERS OR IMPERIAL HALLS	471	2 DON JUAN	5	103	7
	WITH A SOFT BESOM WILL I SWEEP YOUR HALLS	266	3 DON JUAN	10	84	7
	HUGE HALLS LONG GALLERIES SPACIOUS CHAMBERS JOIN'D	390	3 DON JUAN	13	67	1
	OF SUCH A SPIRIT IN THESE HALLS OF OLD	510	3 DON JUAN	16	22	2
HALLUCINATION							
	A FOND HALLUCINATION AND A THEME	47	3 DON JUAN	6	83	5
	IS OF ALL DREAMS THE FIRST HALLUCINATION	88	3 DON JUAN	7	44	4
	INSTEAD OF LOVE THAT MERE HALLUCINATION	360	3 DON JUAN	13	6	6
HALOS							
	OF SUNSET HALOS O'ER THE LAUREL-BROWED	373	3 DON JUAN	13	33	7
HALT							
	WHICH MADE A LONG DEBATE BUT I MUST HALT	83	3 DON JUAN	7	35	6
HALTS							
	AND LONG THE LATEST OF ARRIVALS HALTS	302	3 DON JUAN	11	68	6
HAM							
	THEY ALSO SET A GLAZED WESTPHALIAN HAM ON	484	3 DON JUAN	15	65	5
HAMLET							
	WHICH HAMLET TELLS US IS A PASS OF DREAD	133	3 DON JUAN	8	41	4
HAMLETS							
	SOME LITTLE HAMLETS WITH NEW NAMES UNCOUTH	387	2 DON JUAN	4	78	2
HAMMER							
	AT FIRST HE TRIED TO HAMMER AN EXCUSE	110	2 DON JUAN	1	162	1
	THE ANVIL OF HIS SPEECH RECEIVED THE HAMMER	111	2 DON JUAN	1	163	3
	TO HAMMER A HOARSE LAUGH FROM THE THICK THRONG	540	3 DON JUAN	16	83	8
HAMMOCK							
	AND ROCKING IN HIS HAMMOCK LONG'D FOR LAND	169	2 DON JUAN	2	25	5
HAMMOCKS							
	SOME LASH'D THEM IN THEIR HAMMOCKS SOME PUT ON	180	2 DON JUAN	2	45	1
HAMPER							
	HE CAGED IN ONE HUGE HAMPER ALTOGETHER	285	2 DON JUAN	3	18	8
HAMPER'D							
	THE CITY WITHOUT BEING FURTHER HAMPER'D	149	3 DON JUAN	8	75	4

338

HAMS
   UPON THEIR HAMS WERE OCCUPIED AT CHESS . . . . 441 2 DON JUAN 5   53   2
HAND
   AND TREMULOUSLY GENTLE HER SMALL HAND . . . . 60 2 DON JUAN 1   71   2
   A HAND MAY FIRST AND THEN A LIP BE KIST . . . . 65 2 DON JUAN 1   80   3
   ONE HAND ON JUAN'S CARLESSLY WAS THROWN . . . . 80 2 DON JUAN 1   109   7
   THE HAND WHICH STILL HELD JUAN'S BY DEGREES . . . . . 81 2 DON JUAN 1   111   1
   HE TURN'D HIS LIP TO HERS AND WITH HIS HAND . . . . . 114 2 DON JUAN 1   170   1
   AND THEY CONTINUED BATTLING HAND TO HAND . . . . . . 123 2 DON JUAN 1   185   2
   AND THEY CONTINUED BATTLING HAND TO HAND . . . . . . 123 2 DON JUAN 1   185   2
   HER SMALL WHITE HAND COULD HARDLY REACH THE TAPER . . . 134 2 DON JUAN 1   198   3
   MUST WITH PERMISSION SHAKE YOU BY THE HAND . . . . . 147 2 DON JUAN 1   221   3
   THROWN BACK A MOMENT WITH THE GLANCING HAND . . . . . 160 2 DON JUAN 2   7   2
   KEPT TWO HAND AND ONE CHAIN-PUMP STILL IN USE . . . . 172 2 DON JUAN 2   30   4
   ASLEEP THEY SHOOK THEM BY THE HAND AND HEAD . . . . . 208 2 DON JUAN 2   98   7
   AND QUIVERING HAND AND THEN HE LOOK'D FOR THOSE . . . . 213 2 DON JUAN 2   109   3
   HE FELL UPON HIS SIDE AND HIS STRETCH'D HAND . . . . . 214 2 DON JUAN 2   110   4
   AND CHAFING HIM THE SOFT WARM HAND OF YOUTH . . . . . 215 2 DON JUAN 2   113   3
   FLASH'D ON HER LITTLE HAND BUT WHAT WAS SHOCKING . . . 220 2 DON JUAN 2   121   7
   BUT HAIDEE STOPP'D HER WITH HER QUICK SMALL HAND . . . 234 2 DON JUAN 2   146   3
   AND THUS THEY WANDER'D FORTH AND HAND IN HAND . . . . 253 2 DON JUAN 2   184   1
   AND THUS THEY WANDER'D FORTH AND HAND IN HAND . . . . 253 2 DON JUAN 2   184   1
   LINK'D HAND IN HAND AND DANCING EACH TOO HAVING . . . 291 2 DON JUAN 3   30   4
   LINK'D HAND IN HAND AND DANCING EACH TOO HAVING . . . 291 2 DON JUAN 3   30   4
   TO SEE HIS ORDERS DONE TOO OUT OF HAND-- . . . . . . 299 2 DON JUAN 3   47   3
   THE HAND FROM BURNING UNDERNEATH THEM PLACED . . . . . 307 2 DON JUAN 3   63   6
   WITH MOTHER OF PEARL OR IVORY STOOD AT HAND . . . . . 310 2 DON JUAN 3   69   3
   THAT THE HAND STRETCH'D AND SHUT IT WITHOUT HARM . . . 312 2 DON JUAN 3   71   3
   ANNOUNCED HER RANK TWELVE RINGS WERE ON HER HAND . . . 312 2 DON JUAN 3   72   3
   HER FATHER'S FACE--BUT NEVER STOPP'D HIS HAND . . . . 367 2 DON JUAN 4   43   8
   EVEN TO THE DELICACY OF THEIR HAND . . . . 368 2 DON JUAN 4   45   3
   A TURK WITH BEADS IN HAND AND PIPE IN MOUTH . . . . . 387 2 DON JUAN 4   78   6
   AND THOUGH THUS CHAIN'D AS NATURAL HER HAND . . . . . 396 2 DON JUAN 4   95   4
   'TIS SAID NO ONE IN HAND CAN HOLD A FIRE . . . . . . 396 2 DON JUAN 4   96   5
   WHILE THE RIGHT HAND WHICH WROTE IT STILL IS ABLE . . . 398 2 DON JUAN 4   99   5
   THEY LITTLE THINK WHAT MISCHIEF IS IN HAND . . . . . 411 2 DON JUAN 5   1   4
   SOME DOWN AND WEIGHING OTHERS IN THEIR HAND . . . . . 426 2 DON JUAN 5   29   4
   FLANK'D BY LARGE GROVES WHICH TOWER'D ON EITHER HAND . . 433 2 DON JUAN 5   41   4
   BABA PROPOSED THAT HE SHOULD KISS THE HAND . . . . . 471 2 DON JUAN 5   104   8
   ALTHOUGH NO FAIRER--SMALLER--SOFTER HAND . . . . . . 472 2 DON JUAN 5   106 V2
   HER HAND ON HIS AND BENDING ON HIM EYES . . . . . . 483 2 DON JUAN 5   125   2
   ARE SIMILES AT HAND FOR THE DISTRESS . . . . 487 2 DON JUAN 5   132   3
   THE DAGGER CLOSE AT HAND WHICH MADE IT AWKWARD . . . . 492 2 DON JUAN 5   140   2
   ARE APT TO CARRY THINGS WITH A HIGH HAND . . . . . . 11 3 DON JUAN 6   11   3
   WOMEN ON T'OTHER HAND SEEM SOMEWHAT SILLY . . . . . . 14 3 DON JUAN 6   16   8
   WITH GREAT BLUE EYES A LOVELY HAND AND ARM . . . . . 26 3 DON JUAN 6   41   3
   SHE TOOK JUANNA BY THE HAND TO SHOW . . . . 31 3 DON JUAN 6   50   5
   OF THE UNPLEASANT KIND WITH NONE AT HAND . . . . . . 45 3 DON JUAN 6   78   3
   HER FUTURE DREAMS SHOULD ALL BE KEPT IN HAND . . . . . 47 3 DON JUAN 6   82   8
   AT HAND AS ONE MAY LIKE TO HAVE A FAN . . . . 51 3 DON JUAN 6   91   4
   AND ONE HAND O'ER THE OTTOMAN LAY DROOPING . . . . . 60 3 DON JUAN 6   109   3
   STARS MEDALS AND A BLOODY SWORD IN HAND . . . . . . 141 3 DON JUAN 8   57   6
   FISHERY AND FARM BOTH INTO HIS OWN HAND . . . . . . 198 3 DON JUAN 9   31   8
   SUPPOSE HIM SWORD BY SIDE AND HAT IN HAND . . . . . . 204 3 DON JUAN 9   44   1
   I QUITE FORGET WHICH OF THEM WAS IN HAND . . . . . . 205 3 DON JUAN 9   46   3
   A NERVOUS FAMILY TO WHOSE HEART OR HAND . . . . . . 205 3 DON JUAN 9   46 V3
   HE ON THE OTHER HAND IF NOT IN LOVE . . . . 216 3 DON JUAN 9   68   1
   BECAUSE THE CLERGY TAKE THE THING IN HAND . . . . . . 220 3 DON JUAN 9   76   4
   YOUR HAND AT HARDENED AND IMPERIAL SIN . . . . . . 266 3 DON JUAN 10   85   4
   A MORAL COUNTRY BUT I HOLD MY HAND-- . . . . 311 3 DON JUAN 11   87   4
   IT SEEMS THE VIRGIN'S HEART EXPECTS YOUR HAND . . . . 343 3 DON JUAN 12   60   6
   ESPECIALLY WITH POLITICS ON HAND . . . . 435 3 DON JUAN 14   58   4
   THE RUBY GLASS THAT SHAKES WITHIN HIS HAND . . . . . 457 3 DON JUAN 15   4   7
   THEY HAVE AT HAND A BLOOMING GLUT OF BRIDES . . . . . 471 3 DON JUAN 15   33   8
   NOR CANVASS WHAT SO EMINENT A HAND MEANT . . . . . . 472 3 DON JUAN 15   38   6
   AND ENTREMETS TO PIDDLE WITH AT HAND . . . . 484 3 DON JUAN 15   66   5
   THIS SAVOURED OF THIS WORLD BUT HIS HAND SHOOK-- . . . 512 3 DON JUAN 16   27   1
   WITH SWORD IN HAND AND TORCH TO LIGHT . . . . . . 518 3 DON JUAN 16 L 2   3
   THE VERY SERVANTS PUZZLING HOW TO HAND . . . . . . 538 3 DON JUAN 16   79   3
HAND-AND-GLOVE
   'GAINST REASON--REASON NE'ER WAS HAND-AND-GLOVE . . . . 219 3 DON JUAN 9   74   5
HANDED
   THE LOTS WERE MADE AND MARK'D AND MIX'D AND HANDED . . 195 2 DON JUAN 2   75   1
   HIS WAY TO--WHERE HE KNEW NOT--SINGLE HANDED . . . . 127 3 DON JUAN 8   32   3
HANDLE
   AT LEAST SHE LEFT IT A MORE SLENDER HANDLE . . . . . 58 2 DON JUAN 1   67   8
   MUST STILL OBEY THE HIGH--WHICH IS THEIR HANDLE . . . 342 3 DON JUAN 12   56   7
HANDMAID
   AND CHEERFULNESS THE HANDMAID OF THEIR TOIL . . . . . 145 3 DON JUAN 8   67   2
HANDMAIDS
   O'ERCHARGED WITH RAIN HER SUMMON'D HANDMAIDS BORE . . . 376 2 DON JUAN 4   59   4
   HER HANDMAIDS TENDED BUT SHE HEEDED NOT . . . . . . 379 2 DON JUAN 4   64   1
HANDS
   DABBLING ITS SLEEK YOUNG HANDS IN ERIN'S GORE . . . . 16 2 DON JUAN D   12   2
   AND FANS TURN INTO FALCHIONS IN FAIR HANDS . . . . . 33 2 DON JUAN 1   21   7
   PROMISED TO TURN OUT WELL IN PROPER HANDS . . . . . 42 2 DON JUAN 1   37   4
   A GLIMPSE OF SUNSHINE SET SOME HANDS TO BALE-- . . . . 176 2 DON JUAN 2   38   7
   PRESSURE OF HANDS PERHAPS EVEN A CHASTE KISS-- . . . . 242 2 DON JUAN 2   164   7
   WHILE BACCHUS POURS OUT WINE OR HANDS A JELLY . . . . 246 2 DON JUAN 2   170   5

HANDS   (CONTINUED)
    SO THAT ALL HANDS WERE BUSY BEYOND MEASURE . . . . . . 286 2 DON JUAN   3   20   7
    YIELDING TO THEIR SMALL HANDS DRAWS BACK AGAIN . . . . 292 2 DON JUAN   3   32   8
    DEGENERATE INTO HANDS LIKE MINE . . . . 322 2 DON JUAN   3   L 5   6
    AND TAKE ALL COLOURS--LIKE THE HANDS OF DYERS . . . . 326 2 DON JUAN   3   87   8
    SOME HANDS UNSEEN STREW'D FLOWERS UPON HIS TOMB . . . 339 2 DON JUAN   3   109   5
    THAT IS--THE LADY CLAPPING HIS HANDS TWICE . . . . . 458 2 DON JUAN   5   80   7
    THE GENTLEMAN TO KISS THE LADY'S HANDS . . . . . . 472 2 DON JUAN   5   105   8
    AND HANDS OBEY--OUR HEARTS ARE STILL OUR OWN . . . . 484 2 DON JUAN   5   127   8
    THEIR DIRTY DIPLOMATIC HANDS TO VENT . . . . 498 2 DON JUAN   5   151   5
    OH ENVIABLE BRIAREUS WITH THY HANDS . . . . 20 3 DON JUAN   6   28   1
    DON JUAN AT HIS HANDS AND INFORMATION . . . . 55 3 DON JUAN   6   99   2
    WITH BLOODY HANDS HE WROTE HIS FIRST DISPATCH . . . . 178 3 DON JUAN   8   133   5
    WHICH HANDS OR PENS HAVE EVER TRACED OF SWORDS . . . . 179 3 DON JUAN   8   134   3
    BLOOD ONLY SERVES TO WASH AMBITION'S HANDS . . . . . 212 3 DON JUAN   9   59   8
    HIS SERVICES HE KISSED HANDS THE NEXT DAY . . . . . 247 3 DON JUAN 10   46   5
    BUT KEEP YOUR HANDS OUT OF HIS BREECHES' POCKET . . . 264 3 DON JUAN 10   79   8
    KISS HANDS FEET ANY PART OF MAJESTY . . . . 286 3 DON JUAN 11   38   6
    THEY ADDED GRACEFUL NECKS WHITE HANDS AND ARMS . . . 408 3 DON JUAN 13   107   8
HANDSOME
    THEY STAND FORTH MARSHALL'D IN A HANDSOME TROOP . . . 46 2 DON JUAN   1   45   3
    TALL HANDSOME SLENDER BUT WELL KNIT HE SEEM'D . . . . 51 2 DON JUAN   1   54   2
    HER EYE (I'M VERY FOND OF HANDSOME EYES) . . . . . 54 2 DON JUAN   1   60   1
    THE LOVER WHO MUST PAY A HANDSOME PRICE . . . . . . 57 2 DON JUAN   1   64   7
    I HOPE HE'S YOUNG AND HANDSOME--IS HE TALL . . . . . 105 2 DON JUAN   1   154   6
    AND VERY HANDSOME SUPERNATURAL SCENERY . . . . . . 136 2 DON JUAN   1   201   8
    I'M FOR A HANDSOME ARTICLE HIS CREDITOR . . . . . . 142 2 DON JUAN   1   210   3
    A VERY HANDSOME HOUSE FROM OUT HIS GUILT . . . . . 223 2 DON JUAN   2   127   3
    AND HANDSOME CORPSES STREW'D UPON THE SHORE . . . . 229 2 DON JUAN   2   138   4
    THE ODDS ARE THAT HE FINDS A HANDSOME URN . . . . . 287 2 DON JUAN   3   23   5
    HANDSOME AND YOUNG ENJOYING ALL THE PRESENT . . . . 371 2 DON JUAN   4   51   4
    TOUCH'D HIS NOR THAT--NOR ANY HANDSOME LIMB . . . . 396 2 DON JUAN   4   95   5
    AND THEN THOUGH PALE HE WAS SO VERY HANDSOME . . . . 415 2 DON JUAN   5   9   7
    I OFFER YOU A HANDSOME SUIT OF CLOTHES . . . . . . 455 2 DON JUAN   5   76   1
    HE LIKED TO HAVE A HANDSOME PARAMOUR . . . . 51 3 DON JUAN   6   91   3
    YOU'LL FIND TEN THOUSAND HANDSOME COXCOMBS BLOODY . . 167 3 DON JUAN   8   112   8
    SUPPOSE HIM IN A HANDSOME UNIFORM . . . . 204 3 DON JUAN   9   43   1
    THE HANDSOME HERALD ON WHOSE PLUMAGE SAT . . . . . 211 3 DON JUAN   9   57   6
    THAT SHE WAS HANDSOME AND THOUGH FIERCE LOOKED LENIENT . 214 3 DON JUAN   9   63   5
    IT IS TO SPECULATE ON HANDSOME FACES . . . . . . 223 3 DON JUAN   9   82   7
    PERCEIVING HE WAS IN A HANDSOME WAY . . . . 239 3 DON JUAN 10   30   2
    HE HAD BROUGHT HIS SPENDING TO A HANDSOME ANCHOR-- . . 240 3 DON JUAN 10   31   4
    SO CATHERINE WHO HAD A HANDSOME WAY . . . . 247 3 DON JUAN 10   46   1
    GOD DAMN YOU LADS I'VE MISSED A HANDSOME BOOTY . . . 276 3 DON JUAN 11   16   V3
    YOUNG HANDSOME AND ACCOMPLISHED WHO WAS SAID . . . . 283 3 DON JUAN 11   32   7
    WHO SEEING A HANDSOME STRIPLING WITH SMOOTH FACE . . 285 3 DON JUAN 11   35   5
    OUR HERO AS A HERO YOUNG AND HANDSOME . . . . . . 305 3 DON JUAN 11   74   1
    HANDSOME BUT WASTED RICH WITHOUT A SOU . . . . . . 306 3 DON JUAN 11   75   2
    A HANDSOME MAN THAT HUMAN MIRACLE . . . . 441 3 DON JUAN 14   71   6
HANDSOMELY
    TO COME OFF HANDSOMELY IN THAT REGARD . . . . . . 235 3 DON JUAN 10   22   4
HANDY
    SLIPPERS OF SAFFRON DAGGER RICH AND HANDY . . . . . 451 2 DON JUAN   5   68   7
    AND NO MORE HANDY SUBSTITUTE BEEN NEAR . . . . . . 75 3 DON JUAN   7   17   8
    BEHIND HIS CARRIAGE AND LIKE HANDY LADS . . . . . 273 3 DON JUAN 11   11   3
    (WHO BY THE BY WHEN CLEVER ARE MORE HANDY . . . . . 331 3 DON JUAN 12   32   4
HANG
    SHAKESPEARE EXCLAIMS--HANG UP PHILOSOPHY . . . . . 272 2 DON JUAN   2   V 1   1
    THE RAMPART HIGHER THAN YOU'D WISH TO HANG . . . . 72 3 DON JUAN   7   11   4
HANGED
    NO LESS DESERVING TO BE HANGED THAN CROWNED . . . . 499 2 DON JUAN   5   153   8
HANGING
    ABOVE HIM HANGING BY A SINGLE HAIR . . . . 153 2 DON JUAN   1   V 4   2
HANGINGS
    THE HANGINGS OF THE ROOM WERE TAPESTRY MADE . . . . 308 2 DON JUAN   3   64   1
HANKER
    THOSE PLEASURES AFTER WHICH WILD YOUTH WILL HANKER . . 240 3 DON JUAN 10   31   6
HANKERING
    THEY SOMETIMES WITH A HANKERING FOR EXISTENCE . . . 151 3 DON JUAN   8   78   7
HANNIBAL
    WITH HANNIBAL AND WEARS THE TYRIAN TUNIC . . . . . 122 3 DON JUAN   8   23   6
HAP-HAZARD
    SNOW WELL 'TIS ALL HAP-HAZARD WHEN ONE WEDS . . . . 18 3 DON JUAN   6   25   6
HAPLESS
    AND THUS IT WAS WITH THIS OUR HAPLESS CREW . . . . 192 2 DON JUAN   2   68   1
    WAS HAPLESS IN THEIR NUPTIALS FOR SOME BAR . . . . 281 2 DON JUAN   3   10   4
    IN A FEW WORDS HE TOLD THEIR HAPLESS STORY . . . . 389 2 DON JUAN   4   82   1
    AS RENEGADOES WHILE IN HAPLESS GROUP . . . . . . 409 2 DON JUAN   4   116   5
    WHICH WELCOMES HAPLESS STRANGERS IN ALL PLACES . . . 28 3 DON JUAN   6   45   7
    THERE WAS AN END OF ISMAIL--HAPLESS TOWN . . . . . 175 3 DON JUAN   8   127   2
HAPPEN
    MY CHANCE SO HAPPEN--DEEDS) WITH ALL WHO WAR . . . 194 3 DON JUAN   9   24   2
    ALTHOUGH ('TWILL HAPPEN AS OUR PLANET GUIDES) . . . 251 3 DON JUAN 10   54   5
    FOR WHEN THEY HAPPEN AT A RIPER AGE . . . . 339 3 DON JUAN 12   50   2
HAPPEN'D
    WERE LINK'D TOGETHER AND IT HAPPEN'D THE MALE . . . 394 2 DON JUAN   4   92   6
    NOW IT SO HAPPEN'D IN THE CATALOGUE . . . . 477 3 DON JUAN 15   48   1
HAPPENED
    IF NOW AND THEN THERE HAPPENED A SLIGHT SLIP . . . . 496 2 DON JUAN   5   149   1

HAPPENED   (CONTINUED)
    IT HAPPENED WAS HIMSELF BEAT BACK JUST NOW . . . . . . 147 3 DON JUAN 8   70   4
    SOME ODD MISTAKES TOO HAPPENED IN THE DARK . . . . . . 177 3 DON JUAN 8   130   1
    IT HAPPENED LUCKILY THE CHASTE ORB SHONE . . . . 506 3 DON JUAN 16   13   3
    HAD IT NOT HAPPENED SCALDING HOT TO BE . . . . 513 3 DON JUAN 16   30   4
HAPPENS
    AS SOMETIMES HAPPENS IN A GREAT EXTREMITY . . . . 92 3 DON JUAN 7   51   4
    BUT AS IT HAPPENS TO BRAVE MEN THEY BLUNDERED-- . . . . 149 3 DON JUAN 8   75   5
    A THING WHICH HAPPENS EVERYWHERE EACH DAY-- . . . . . . 163 3 DON JUAN 8   103   7
    A THING WHICH HAPPENS RARELY THIS HE OWED . . . . 239 3 DON JUAN 10   29   2
    OCCURRED WHAT OFTEN HAPPENS I'M AFRAID . . . . 355 3 DON JUAN 12   85   3
HAPPIER
    HAPPIER THAN THEY WHO STILL PERCEIVED THEIR WOES . . . . 199 2 DON JUAN 2   80   4
    SAW NOTHING HAPPIER THAN HER GLOWING FACE . . . . . . 262 2 DON JUAN 2   198   8
    WOULD THEY HAVE BEEN THE HAPPIER FOR OBSCURITY . . . . . 470 2 DON JUAN 5   102 V1
    IN HAPPIER PLIGHT THAN IF THEY FORMED A PAIR . . . . . 344 3 DON JUAN 12   61   8
HAPPIEST
    THE HAPPIEST MORTALS EVEN AFTER DINNER-- . . . . 294 2 DON JUAN 3   36   2
    WAS HAPPIEST AMONGST MORTALS ANYWHERE . . . . 143 3 DON JUAN 8   61   5
    AND HAPPIEST THEY WHO HORSES CAN ENGAGE . . . . 378 3 DON JUAN 13   44   4
    THAT ADAM CALLED THE HAPPIEST OF MEN . . . . 434 3 DON JUAN 14   55   8
HAPPILY
    GUESSING AT WHAT SHALL HAPPILY BE HID . . . . 180 3 DON JUAN 8   137   7
HAPPINESS
    TO BE HER HAPPINESS AND WHOM SHE DEEM'D . . . . 247 2 DON JUAN 2   172   6
    MUST SHARE IT--HAPPINESS WAS BORN A TWIN . . . . 247 2 DON JUAN 2   172   8
    WHEN HAPPINESS HAD BEEN THEIR ONLY DOWER . . . . 354 2 DON JUAN 4   20   5
    GREAT HAPPINESS OF THE NIL ADMIRARI . . . . 469 2 DON JUAN 5   100   8
    WHICH IF NOT HAPPINESS IS MUCH MORE NIGH IT . . . . . . 32 3 DON JUAN 6   53   4
    OF DEEDS TO HUMAN HAPPINESS MOST DEAR . . . . 108 3 DON JUAN 7   83   6
    OF BRITAIN'S PRESENT WEALTH AND HAPPINESS-- . . . . . . 371 3 DON JUAN 13   29   8
    WAS WHAT HE CALLED THE ART OF HAPPINESS . . . . 374 3 DON JUAN 13   35   2
    THAT HAPPINESS FOR MAN--THE HUNGRY SINNER-- . . . . . . 404 3 DON JUAN 13   99   7
HAPPY
    WHICH SERVES THE HAPPY COUPLE FOR A TAVERN . . . . 24 2 DON JUAN 1   6   8
    HAPPY THE NATIONS OF THE MORAL NORTH . . . . 57 2 DON JUAN 1   64   1
    HAD BEEN THE HAPPY LOVER HE CONCLUDED . . . . 118 2 DON JUAN 1   177   4
    TO RENDER HAPPY ALL WHO JOY WOULD WIN . . . . 247 2 DON JUAN 2   172   7
    AND THEY WERE HAPPY FOR TO THEIR YOUNG EYES . . . . . . 265 2 DON JUAN 2   204   7
    BESIDES THAT WOULD.A HAPPY LOT INSURE US . . . . 267 2 DON JUAN 2   207 V3
    PILLOW'D UPON A FAIR AND HAPPY BREAST . . . . 274 2 DON JUAN 3   1   2
    YET THEY WERE HAPPY--HAPPY IN THE ILLICIT . . . . 282 2 DON JUAN 3   13   1
    YET THEY WERE HAPPY--HAPPY IN THE ILLICIT . . . . 282 2 DON JUAN 3   13   1
    BUT ALL THE BETTER FOR THE HAPPY PAIR . . . . 288 2 DON JUAN 3   24   3
    THE INNOCENCE WHICH HAPPY CHILDHOOD BLESSES . . . . . . 292 2 DON JUAN 3   33   5
    A LIFE WHICH MADE THEM HAPPY BEYOND MEASURE . . . . . . 295 2 DON JUAN 3   39   4
    A HAPPY LOVER AND A WELCOME GUEST-- . . . . 343 2 DON JUAN 3 V 98   5
    MEANT TO GROW OLD BUT DIE IN HAPPY SPRING . . . . 348 2 DON JUAN 4   8   7
    THE HEART--WHICH MAY BE BROKEN HAPPY THEY . . . . 350 2 DON JUAN 4   11   1
    AS IF THEIR LAST DAY OF A HAPPY DATE . . . . 355 2 DON JUAN 4   22   3
    DANCING ALL FREE AND HAPPY IN THE SUN) . . . . 393 2 DON JUAN 4   90   7
    TO MAKE MEN HAPPY OR TO KEEP THEM SO . . . . 470 2 DON JUAN 5   101   3
    NOT ALL THE CLAMOUR BROKE HER HAPPY STATE . . . . 42 3 DON JUAN 6   73   5
    THRICE HAPPY HE WHOSE NAME HAS BEEN WELL SPELT . . . . . 120 3 DON JUAN 8   18   6
    THOUSANDS BLAZE LOVE HOPE DIE--HOW HAPPY THEY-- . . . . 229 3 DON JUAN 10   8   8
    WHICH OPENS TO THE THOUSAND HAPPY FEW . . . . 302 3 DON JUAN 11   67   7
    THRICE HAPPY HE WHO AFTER A SURVEY . . . . 303 3 DON JUAN 11   69   1
    IT STOOD EMBOSOM'D IN A HAPPY VALLEY . . . . 384 3 DON JUAN 13   66   1
    BORN WITH THAT HAPPY SOUL WHICH SELDOM FAINTS . . . . . 424 3 DON JUAN 14   31   5
    THRICE HAPPY THEY WHO HAVE AN OCCUPATION . . . . 443 3 DON JUAN 14   77   8
    THE GLORIOUS--FREE--AND HAPPY CONSTITUTION . . . . . . 536 3 DON JUAN 16   74 V8
    THE THREE STRINGS OF OUR HAPPY CONSTITUTION . . . . . . 536 3 DON JUAN 16   74 V8
    IMBIBED THE GAY BON MOT OR HAPPY HOAX . . . . 540 3 DON JUAN 16   83   5
HARAM
    A HERMIT'S WITH A HARAM FOR A GROT . . . . 68 2 DON JUAN 1   87   8
    ALTHOUGH THEIR HARAM EDUCATION LED . . . . 101 3 DON JUAN 7   67   4
HARANGUE
    ON EACH HARANGUE DEPENDS SOME HOSTILE SWORDS . . . . . 153 2 DON JUAN 1 V 4   3
    OUTLINE OF AN HARANGUE--BUT I'LL TO BED . . . . 538 3 DON JUAN 16   77 V5
HARBOUR
    THY CLIFFS DEAR DOVER HARBOUR AND HOTEL . . . . 259 3 DON JUAN 10   69   2
HARBOURING
    BY HARBOURING SOME DEAR FRIEND EXTREMELY VICIOUS . . . . 74 2 DON JUAN 1   99   5
HARD
    AND SOMETIMES LADIES HIT EXCEEDING HARD . . . . 33 2 DON JUAN 1   21   6
    ('TWERE HARD TO TELL UPON A LIKE OCCASION . . . . 38 2 DON JUAN 1   32   3
    METHINKS THE REQUISITION'S RATHER HARD . . . . 85 2 DON JUAN 1   118   3
    AND LAID CONDITIONS HE THOUGHT VERY HARD ON . . . . . . 120 2 DON JUAN 1   180   3
    FIRST PARTINGS FORM A LESSON HARD TO LEARN . . . . . . 164 2 DON JUAN 2   14   3
    AND FIND A QUINSY VERY HARD TO TREAT . . . . 168 2 DON JUAN 2   22   4
    AND THE HARD WAVE O'ERWHELM'D HIM AS 'TWAS DASH'D . . . 212 2 DON JUAN 2   107   4
    WHEN WE HAVE WHAT WE LIKE 'TIS HARD TO MISS IT . . . . 282 2 DON JUAN 3   13   5
    IT IS A HARD ALTHOUGH A COMMON CASE . . . . 305 2 DON JUAN 3   59   1
    THE READER BUT 'TWOULD NOT BE HARD TO BRING . . . . . . 332 2 DON JUAN 3   97   6
    OUR SIN THE SAME AND HARD AS HIS TO MEND . . . . 344 2 DON JUAN 4   1   6
    HARD WORDS HARSH TRUTH A TRUTH WHICH MANY KNOW . . . . 353 2 DON JUAN 4   18   1
    WHEN SOME UNTOWARD PART OF RAIMENT STUCK HARD . . . . . 456 2 DON JUAN 5   78   6
    SO THAT A PONIARD PIERCES IF 'TIS STUCK HARD . . . . . 492 2 DON JUAN 5   140   4
    AMONGST THEM ALL HARD BLOWS TO INFLICT OR WARD . . . . . 76 3 DON JUAN 7   19   6

```
                                                          PAGE VOL   CANTO  STANZA  LN
HARD   (CONTINUED)
    HARD WORDS WHICH STICK IN THE SOFT MUSES' GULLETS  . . . .  106  3 DON JUAN   7     78     8
    UNTIL THEIR VERY NUMBER MAKES MEN HARD  . . . . . . .       118  3 DON JUAN   8     13     2
    THE GENERAL LASCY WHO HAD BEEN HARD PREST  . . . . . .      140  3 DON JUAN   8     56     1
    AND THOUGH THE DUTY WAXED A LITTLE HARD  . . . . . . .      235  3 DON JUAN  10     22     2
    ESTEEMING IT A LITTLE HARD HE SHOULD  . . . . . . . .       277  3 DON JUAN  11     18     5
    STILL HE EXCELS THAT ARTIFICIAL HARD  . . . . . . . .       297  3 DON JUAN  11     58     1
    (A THING WITH POETRY IN GENERAL HARD)  . . . . . . . .      322  3 DON JUAN  12     13     4
    THAT CLAUSE IS HARD) AND SECONDLY PROCEED  . . . . . .      393  3 DON JUAN  13     73     6
    AND THE HARD FROST DESTROY'D THE SCENTING DAYS  . . . .     407  3 DON JUAN  13    106     4
    HARD LABOUR'S AN INDIFFERENT GO-BETWEEN  . . . . . . .      443  3 DON JUAN  14     76     5
    AND NEVER STRAINING HARD TO VERSIFY  . . . . . . . .       464  3 DON JUAN  15     19     6
    AND LOOKED AT JUAN HARD BUT NOTHING UTTERED  . . . . . .    514  3 DON JUAN  16     31     6
    IT PRESSED UPON A HARD BUT GLOWING BUST  . . . . . . .      560  3 DON JUAN  16    122     3
HARDEN'D
    GLIDED ALONG THE SMOOTH AND HARDEN'D SAND  . . . . . .      253  2 DON JUAN   2    184     3
HARDENED
    YOUR HAND AT HARDENED AND IMPERIAL SIN  . . . . . . .       266  3 DON JUAN  10     85     4
    OR HARDENED FEELINGS WHICH PERHAPS IDEAL  . . . . . . .     553  3 DON JUAN  16    107     7
HARDER
    AND HARDER FOR THE HEART TO OVERCOME  . . . . . . . .       301  2 DON JUAN   3     51     3
HARDIEST
    HARDSHIPS WHICH HAVE THE HARDIEST OVERWORN  . . . . . .     420  2 DON JUAN   5     18     8
HARDLY
    HER SMALL WHITE HAND COULD HARDLY REACH THE TAPER  . . .    134  2 DON JUAN   1    198     3
    OR ELSE THE THING HAD HARDLY COME TO PASS)  . . . . .       158  2 DON JUAN   2      3     6
    AND YET THEIR PRESENT HOPE WAS HARDLY MORE  . . . . . .     185  2 DON JUAN   2     54     3
    YOU HARDLY COULD PERCEIVE WHEN HE WAS DEAD  . . . . . .     197  2 DON JUAN   2     76     4
    REFUSING HIS OWN SPANIEL HARDLY COULD  . . . . . . . .      198  2 DON JUAN   2     78     4
    A KIND OF FLATTERY THAT'S HARDLY FAIR  . . . . . . . .      278  2 DON JUAN   3      6     3
    SO THAT THE FEW WHO MET HIM HARDLY HEEDED  . . . . . .      300  2 DON JUAN   3     49     3
    BUT WHICH TO CHOOSE I REALLY HARDLY KNOW  . . . . . . .     357  2 DON JUAN   4     25     4
    THE REST ARE HARDLY FITTED FOR A FAIR  . . . . . . . .      390  2 DON JUAN   4     85     4
    WILL HARDLY LEAVE YOU (AS SHE'S NOT YOUR WIFE)  . . . .     419  2 DON JUAN   5     17     3
    THE BLACK HOWEVER WITHOUT HARDLY DEIGNING  . . . . . .      450  2 DON JUAN   5     66     1
    WAS HARDLY LONG ENOUGH BUT BABA FOUND  . . . . . . . .      457  2 DON JUAN   5     79     2
    COULD HARDLY CARRY ANYTHING AWAY  . . . . . . . .          465  2 DON JUAN   5     93     5
    SHE HARDLY KNEW TO SUCH PERFECTION BRINGS  . . . . . .      485  2 DON JUAN   5    128     6
    BUT ERE THE MIDDLE WATCH WAS HARDLY OVER  . . . . . . .      41  3 DON JUAN   6     70     4
    I DID--WHAT NEXT--I REALLY HARDLY KNOW  . . . . . . .        98  3 DON JUAN   7     61     2
    YOU HARDLY WILL BELIEVE SUCH THINGS WERE TRUE  . . . .      180  3 DON JUAN   8    136     3
    HEAVEN'S BRANDY--THOUGH OUR BRAIN CAN HARDLY BEAR IT  . .   269  3 DON JUAN  11      2     8
    THOUGH HARDLY HEARD THROUGH MULTIFARIOUS DAMME'S  . . .     279  3 DON JUAN  11     24     3
    WERE HARDLY RUDE ENOUGH TO EARN THEIR PAY  . . . . . .      287  3 DON JUAN  11     40     8
    THEIR FLANKS--BUT IT IS HARDLY WORTH MY WHILE  . . . .      300  3 DON JUAN  11     63     2
    BECAUSE THE TIMES HAVE HARDLY LEFT THEM ONE TENANT  . .     308  3 DON JUAN  11     80     8
    THAT MANNERS HARDLY DIFFER MORE THAN DRESS  . . . . . .     402  3 DON JUAN  13     94     8
    AND HARDLY HEAVEN--BECAUSE IT NEVER ENDS  . . . . . . .     407  3 DON JUAN  13    105     3
    I HARDLY COULD COMPOSE ANOTHER LINE  . . . . . . . .       415  3 DON JUAN  14     12     2
    AND FOURTHLY WHAT NEED HARDLY BE SAID TWICE  . . . . .      439  3 DON JUAN  14     66     7
    PERHAPS 'TWAS HARDLY QUITE ASSURED ENOUGH  . . . . . .      462  3 DON JUAN  15     14     5
    SCOTT--OF SUCH TALENT--I COULD HARDLY HAVE  . . . . . .     481  3 DON JUAN  15     59    V6
    COULD HARDLY BE UNITED BY A DUNCE  . . . . . . . .         517  3 DON JUAN  16     39     8
    IN SHORT HE HARDLY COULD BE CLOTHED WITH LESS  . . . .      555  3 DON JUAN  16    111     4
    BEING WAN AND WORN WITH EYES THAT HARDLY BROOKED  . . .     568  3 DON JUAN  17     14     4
HARDNESS
    THE HARDNESS BY LONG HABITUDE PRODUCED  . . . . . . .       303  2 DON JUAN   3     54     2
HARDSHIP
    AND HARDSHIP STILL HAS BEEN THE SAILOR'S LOT  . . . . .     191  2 DON JUAN   2     66     5
HARDSHIPS
    HAD SUFFER'D MORE--HIS HARDSHIPS WERE COMPARATIVE  . . .    229  2 DON JUAN   2    137     7
    HARDSHIPS WHICH HAVE THE HARDIEST OVERWORN  . . . . . .     420  2 DON JUAN   5     18     8
    AFTER THE HARDSHIPS YOU'VE ALREADY BORNE  . . . . . .        98  3 DON JUAN   7     62     4
HARDSMAN
    THERE WAS THE WAGGISH WELCH JUDGE JEFFERIES HARDSMAN  . .   399  3 DON JUAN  13     88     5
HARDY
    WAS MORE ROBUST AND HARDY TO THE VIEW  . . . . . . . .      202  2 DON JUAN   2     87     3
HAREM
    BY WHICH THE MORE A HAREM IS ENCREASED  . . . . . . .        35  3 DON JUAN   6     58     6
    SHE TO DISMISS HER GUARDS AND HE HIS HAREM  . . . . . .      53  3 DON JUAN   6     95     7
    THE DISCIPLINE OF THE WHOLE HAREM BORE  . . . . . . .        57  3 DON JUAN   6    103     2
    NOW I COULD MUCH MORE EASILY SKETCH A HAREM  . . . . .      419  3 DON JUAN  14     21     3
HARES
    MARCH HAS ITS HARES AND MAY MUST HAVE ITS HEROINE  . . .     76  2 DON JUAN   1    102     8
HARK
    HARK RISING TO THE IGNOBLE CALL--  . . . . . . . .         324  2 DON JUAN   3   L  9     5
    HARK THROUGH THE SILENCE OF THE COLD DULL NIGHT  . . .      110  3 DON JUAN   7     86     1
    VIBRATE TO THE ETERNAL NAME   HARK THROUGH  . . . . .       116  3 DON JUAN   8      8     7
    I NEVER SAW SUCH EYES--BUT HARK NOW CHOOSE  . . . . . .     162  3 DON JUAN   8    101     3
    HARK HOW THE ROAR INCREASES--NO EXCUSE  . . . . . . .       162  3 DON JUAN   8    101     5
HARLEQUIN
    A FORTRESS HARLEQUIN IN UNIFORM  . . . . . . . .            95  3 DON JUAN   7     55     8
HARLOT
    AS PURPLE TO THE BABYLONIAN HARLOT  . . . . . . . .        108  3 DON JUAN   7     84     3
    WHOSE LEISURE HOURS ARE WASTED ON A HARLOT  . . . . . .     109  3 DON JUAN   7     84    V3
    THE STATESMAN HERO HARLOT LAWYER--WARD  . . . . . . .       123  3 DON JUAN   8     25     5
    FOR BABYLON'S THAN RUSSIA'S ROYAL HARLOT--  . . . . . .     237  3 DON JUAN  10     26     7
    BUT TO DENOUNCE THE AMPHIBIOUS SORT OF HARLOT  . . . .      344  3 DON JUAN  12     62     7
HARLOTRY
    WHEN HOMICIDE AND HARLOTRY MADE GREAT  . . . . . . . .       84  3 DON JUAN   7     37     2
```

342

HARM
```
    YET STILL SHE MUST HAVE THOUGHT THERE WAS NO HARM  .  .  .  .  .  83   2 DON JUAN  1    115   4
    THAT THE HAND STRETCH'D AND SHUT IT WITHOUT HARM  .  .  .  .    312   2 DON JUAN  3     71   3
    YOU FOOL I TELL YOU NO ONE MEANS YOU HARM  .  .  .  .  .  .     459   2 DON JUAN  5     82   1
    THE DAMSELS WHO HAD THOUGHTS OF SOME GREAT HARM  .  .  .  .      45   3 DON JUAN  6     79   1
    THIS AWKWARD BUSINESS WITHOUT HARM TO OTHERS  .  .  .  .  .      63   3 DON JUAN  6    116   7
    TO BURN A TOWN WHICH NEVER DID THEM HARM  .  .  .  .  .  .  .   105   3 DON JUAN  7     76   8
    UNLESS GUN-POWDER SHOULD BE FOUND TO HARM  .  .  .  .  .  .     106   3 DON JUAN  7     79   5
    NO HARM UNTO A RIGHT LEGITIMATE HEAD  .  .  .  .  .  .  .  .    117   3 DON JUAN  8     10   7
    IS RATHER DEAR--I'M SURE I MEAN NO HARM  .  .  .  .  .  .  .    186   3 DON JUAN  9      7   8
    IT DOES NOR GOOD NOR HARM BEING MERELY MEANT  .  .  .  .  .     342   3 DON JUAN 12     57   4
    AND THEREFORE HAVE HIS VOLUMES DONE SUCH HARM  .  .  .  .  .    364   3 DON JUAN 13     11   6
HARMLESS
    QUITE INNOCENTLY DONE AND HARMLESS STYLED  .  .  .  .  .         59   2 DON JUAN  1     69   3
    APPEAR'D LIKE TWO POOR HARMLESS WOMEN WHO  .  .  .  .  .         98   2 DON JUAN  1    141   2
    ENJOYED THE LONELY VIGOROUS HARMLESS DAYS  .  .  .  .  .        143   3 DON JUAN  8     61   7
    WHOSE CHIEFLY HARMLESS TALENT WAS TO AMUSE  .  .  .  .  .       398   3 DON JUAN 13     86   5
    IT ALL SPRUNG FROM A HARMLESS GAME AT BILLIARDS  .  .  .  .     454   3 DON JUAN 14    100   8
    WAS DANGEROUS--I THINK SHE IS AS HARMLESS  .  .  .  .  .  .     498   3 DON JUAN 15     94   7
HARMONIOUS
    SOUNDS LESS HARMONIOUS UNDERNEATH THE SUN SOON  .  .  .  .      132   3 DON JUAN  8     39   3
    SETS TO SOFT MUSIC THE HARMONIOUS SIGH  .  .  .  .  .  .       430   3 DON JUAN 14     47   3
    MUST PERCH HARMONIOUS ON MY TUNEFUL QUILL  .  .  .  .  .  .     458   3 DON JUAN 15      5   4
    IN HIS HARMONIOUS SETTLEMENT--(WHICH FLOURISHES  .  .  .  .     471   3 DON JUAN 15     35   2
HARMONISED
    A PROLOGUE WHICH BUT SLIGHTLY HARMONISED  .  .  .  .  .  .      543   3 DON JUAN 16     90   3
HARMONIST
    WHEN RAPP THE HARMONIST EMBARGOED MARRIAGE  .  .  .  .  .       471   3 DON JUAN 15     35   1
HARMONIZED
    AND HARMONIZED BY THE OLD CHORAL WALL  .  .  .  .  .  .  .      388   3 DON JUAN 13     63   8
HARMONY
    WHERE ALL WAS HARMONY AND CALM AND QUIET  .  .  .  .  .          32   3 DON JUAN  6     53   2
    WHY CALL'D HE HARMONY A STATE SANS WEDLOCK  .  .  .  .  .       471   3 DON JUAN 15     35   7
    BECAUSE HE EITHER MEANT TO SNEER AT HARMONY  .  .  .  .  .      472   3 DON JUAN 15     36   1
HARNESS
    THE VERIEST JADE WILL WINCE WHOSE HARNESS WRINGS  .  .  .      137   3 DON JUAN  8     50   5
HARNESSED
    LIKE HARNESSED METEORS THEN ALONG THE FLOOR  .  .  .  .  .      302   3 DON JUAN 11     67   4
HARP
    THE HERO'S HARP THE LOVER'S LUTE  .  .  .  .  .  .  .  .        321   2 DON JUAN  3  L  2   2
    THE EPIC HARP--THE LYRIC LUTE--  .  .  .  .  .  .  .  .        321   2 DON JUAN  3  L  2  V2
    AND THEN A SLAVE BETHOUGHT HER OF A HARP  .  .  .  .  .  .      379   2 DON JUAN  4     65   1
    WITH WHICH I STILL CAN HARP AND CARP AND FIDDLE  .  .  .  .     181   3 DON JUAN  8    139   1
    THOUGH HYMNED BY EVERY HARP UNLESS WITHIN  .  .  .  .  .        199   3 DON JUAN  9     34   7
    IN EGYPT'S RAYS TO HARP AT A FIXED HOUR)  .  .  .  .  .  .      388   3 DON JUAN 13     64   4
    BUT LONGBOW WILD AS AN AEOLIAN HARP  .  .  .  .  .  .  .        402   3 DON JUAN 13     93   2
    DOWN TO THE HARP--BECAUSE TO MUSIC'S CHARMS  .  .  .  .  .      408   3 DON JUAN 13    107   7
    SHE SEIZED HER HARP WHOSE STRINGS WERE KINDLED SOON  .  .      517   3 DON JUAN 16     38   6
HARP'D
    OR THAT SHE HAD NOT HARP'D UPON THE TRUE STRING  .  .  .  .     474   3 DON JUAN 15     42   5
HARPER
    THE HARPER CAME AND TUNED HIS INSTRUMENT  .  .  .  .  .  .      379   2 DON JUAN  4     65   2
HARPER'S
    THE VOICE THE WORDS THE HARPER'S SKILL AT ONCE  .  .  .  .      517   3 DON JUAN 16     39   7
HARPSICHORD
    STRONGBOW WAS LIKE A NEW-TUNED HARPSICHORD  .  .  .  .  .       402   3 DON JUAN 13     93   1
HARPSICHORDS
    BUT WHETHER FITS OR WITS OR HARPSICHORDS  .  .  .  .  .  .      340   3 DON JUAN 12     53   1
HARP-STRING
    LIKE THE WIND O'ER A HARP-STRING OR A FLAME  .  .  .  .  .      355   2 DON JUAN  4     21   4
HARPY
    AND TRANSIENT AND DEVOURED BY THE SAME HARPY  .  .  .  .  .     310   3 DON JUAN 11     86   3
HARRISON
    AS THOSE OF THE BEST TIME-PIECE MADE BY HARRISON  .  .  .        30   2 DON JUAN  1     17   6
HARROW
    TO SEVERAL SAINTS THAT SHORTLY PLOUGH OR HARROW  .  .  .  .      99   3 DON JUAN  7     63   6
    BUT HARROW UP HIS FEELINGS TILL THEY WITHER  .  .  .  .  .      355   3 DON JUAN 12     86   6
HARSH
    THE HOARSE HARSH WAVES KEPT TIME FRIGHT CURED THE QUALMS  .    174   2 DON JUAN  2     34   5
    WAS WHIPT AT COLLEGE--A HARSH SIRE--ODD SPOUSE  .  .  .  .      328   2 DON JUAN  3     91   7
    HARD WORDS HARSH TRUTH A TRUTH WHICH MANY KNOW  .  .  .  .      353   2 DON JUAN  4     18   1
    MADE JUAN IN HIS HARSH INTENTIONS PAUSE  .  .  .  .  .  .       437   2 DON JUAN  5     47   4
    WHILE THE HARSH PRUDE INDEMNIFIES HER VIRTUE  .  .  .  .  .     337   3 DON JUAN 12     45   1
    THAT WHERE THEIR EDUCATION HARSH OR MILD  .  .  .  .  .  .      563   3 DON JUAN 17      2   5
HARSHLIER
    NONE CAN DEEM HARSHLIER OF ME THAN I DEEM  .  .  .  .  .  .     130   2 DON JUAN  1    193   6
HARTS
    PANTING FOR POWER AS HARTS FOR COOLING STREAMS  .  .  .  .      155   2 DON JUAN  1  V  6   1
HARVEST
    OF THAT WEAK WORDY HARVEST THE SOLE GLEANING  .  .  .  .  .     207   3 DON JUAN  9     49   8
HARVESTS
    THEY FELL AS THICK AS HARVESTS BENEATH HAIL  .  .  .  .  .      134   3 DON JUAN  8     43   1
    STRIP YOUR GREEN FIELDS AND TO YOUR HARVESTS CLING  .  .  .     175   3 DON JUAN  8    126   6
HASTE
    OF TWENTY-FIVE OR THIRTY--(COME MAKE HASTE)  .  .  .  .  .      115   2 DON JUAN  1    172   6
    HASTE--HASTE--I HEAR ALFONSO'S HURRYING FEET--  .  .  .  .      121   2 DON JUAN  1    182   7
    HASTE--HASTE--I HEAR ALFONSO'S HURRYING FEET--  .  .  .  .      121   2 DON JUAN  1    182   7
    I USED--I WRITE IN HASTE AND IF A STAIN  .  .  .  .  .  .       130   2 DON JUAN  1    192   6
    SNATCH'D DOWN HIS SABRE IN HOT HASTE TO WREAK  .  .  .  .       364   2 DON JUAN  4     37   3
```

HASTE   (CONTINUED)
```
    THEIR HASTE OR WASTE I NEITHER KNOW NOR CARE    . . . .    . .  80   3 DON JUAN  7    27   2
    FOLLOWED IN HASTE BY VARIOUS GRENADIERS    . . . . . . .    . . 147   3 DON JUAN  8    71   2
    THEIR FRIENDS FROM FOES--BESIDES SUCH THINGS FROM HASTE . .  . 177   3 DON JUAN  8   130   4
    SUSPICIOUS PEOPLE WHO FIND FAULT IN HASTE    . . . . . .    . . 230   3 DON JUAN 10    11   3
    OF WASTE AND HASTE AND GLARE AND GLOSS AND GLITTER    . .   . . 237   3 DON JUAN 10    26   2
    NOT THAT SHE MEANT TO FIX AGAIN IN HASTE    . . . . . .    . . 248   3 DON JUAN 10    48   5
    HIS HASTE IMPATIENCE IS A BLUNDERING GUIDE    . . . . .    . . 304   3 DON JUAN 11    71   6
    A FURTHER PROOF WE SHOULD NOT JUDGE IN HASTE    . . . .    . . 347   3 DON JUAN 12    69   5
    MEN LOVE IN HASTE BUT THEY DETEST AT LEISURE    . . . .    . . 361   3 DON JUAN 13     6   8
```
HASTENING
```
    BUT WHICH NEGLECT IS HASTENING TO DESTROY    . . . . .    . . 400   2 DON JUAN  4   103   6
```
HASTENS
```
    WHICH HASTENS AS PHYSICIANS SAY ONE'S FATE    . . . . .    . . 230   2 DON JUAN  2   140   4
```
HASTILY
```
    IS NOT TO BE PUT HASTILY TOGETHER    . . . . . . . . .    . . 355   3 DON JUAN 12    86   2
    HERSELF THEN HASTILY LOOKED DOWN AND MUTTERED    . . . .    . . 514   3 DON JUAN 16    31   2
    AND HASTILY--AS NOTHING CAN CONFOUND    . . . . . . .    . . 542   3 DON JUAN 16    88   4
```
HASTY
```
    AND HASTY TEMPER ON A KINDLING MIND    . . . . . . . .    . . 155   2 DON JUAN  1  V 7   2
    AND WISHED HE HAD BEEN LESS HASTY WITH HIS FLINT    . .    . . 275   3 DON JUAN 11    14   8
```
HAT
```
    MY HAT AND GLOVES STILL LYING ON THE TABLE    . . . .    . . 428   2 DON JUAN  5    33   4
    THEY ARE PUT ON AS EASILY AS A HAT    . . . . . . . .    . .  13   3 DON JUAN  6    14   4
    OVER A COCKED HAT IN A CROWDED ROOM    . . . . . . .    . . 204   3 DON JUAN  9    43   4
    SUPPOSE HIM SWORD BY SIDE AND HAT IN HAND    . . . .    . . 204   3 DON JUAN  9    44   1
    HIS BOW CONVERTED INTO A COCKED HAT    . . . . . . .    . . 205   3 DON JUAN  9    45   5
    SOME LAID ASIDE LIKE AN OLD OPERA HAT    . . . . . .    . . 308   3 DON JUAN 11    79   3
```
HATCH
```
    NEXT OF NEW KNIGHTS THE FRESH AND GLORIOUS HATCH    . .    . . 215   3 DON JUAN  9    65   7
    WITH WIT TO HATCH A PUN OR TELL A STORY    . . . . .    . . 401   3 DON JUAN 13    91   6
```
HATCHED
```
    BUT THE OLD MARCHIONESS SOME PLAN HAS HATCHED    . . .    . . 332   3 DON JUAN 12    35   5
```
HATCHES
```
    ON BOARD OF ONE OF THESE AND UNDER HATCHES    . . . .    . . 371   2 DON JUAN  4    50   7
```
HATCHING
```
    CAW ME CAW THEE--FOR SIX MONTHS HATH BEEN HATCHING    . .   . 307   3 DON JUAN 11    78   7
```
HATCHWAY
```
    AND THEN WENT DOWN THE HATCHWAY ONE BY ONE    . . . .    . . 393   2 DON JUAN  4    90   8
```
HATE
```
    HER STATURE TALL--I HATE A DUMPY WOMAN    . . . . . .    . .  55   2 DON JUAN  1    61   8
    COLDNESS OR ANGER EVEN DISDAIN OR HATE    . . . . . .    . .  61   2 DON JUAN  1    73   7
    OF ONE WHOSE HATE IS MASKED BUT TO ASSAIL    . . . .    . . 182   2 DON JUAN  2    49   4
    BESIDES I HATE ALL MYSTERY AND THAT AIR    . . . . .    . . 222   2 DON JUAN  2   124   3
    I HATE YOUR POETS SO READ NONE OF THOSE    . . . . .    . . 243   2 DON JUAN  2   165   8
    I HATE INCONSTANCY--I LOATHE DETEST    . . . . . . .    . . 268   2 DON JUAN  2   209   1
    RAGE FEAR HATE JEALOUSY REVENGE COMPUNCTION    . . . .    . . 271   2 DON JUAN  2   215   6
    BUT THEY HATE FLATTERY SO I NEVER FLATTER)    . . . .    . . 287   2 DON JUAN  3    22   6
    HATE TO THE WORLD AND WAR WITH EVERY NATION    . . .    . . 303   2 DON JUAN  3    55   7
    CALL'D SOCIAL HAUNTS OF HATE AND VICE AND CARE    . .   . . 358   2 DON JUAN  4    28   4
    THE TENOR THESE TWO HATED WITH A HATE    . . . . . .    . . 394   2 DON JUAN  4    93   2
    BESIDES I HATE TO SLEEP ALONE QUOTH SHE    . . . . .    . .  30   3 DON JUAN  6    48   1
    SAVE WED A YEAR I HATE RECRUITS WITH WIVES    . . . .    . . 102   3 DON JUAN  7    70   8
    HE HATED CRUELTY AS ALL MEN HATE    . . . . . . . .    . . 140   3 DON JUAN  8    55   6
    WHICH HATE NOR ENVY E'ER COULD TINGE WITH WRONG    . .    . 144   3 DON JUAN  8    63   6
    THEY HATE ME NOT I THEM--AND HERE WE'LL PAUSE    . . .    . . 193   3 DON JUAN  9    21   8
    WHICH (THOUGH I HATE TO SAY A THING THAT'S BITTER)    . .   . 237   3 DON JUAN 10    26   4
    THEY HATE A MURDERER MUCH LESS THAN A CLAIMANT    . .   . . 264   3 DON JUAN 10    79   5
    AND HATE ALL VICE EXCEPT ITS REPUTATION    . . . . .    . . 327   3 DON JUAN 12    25   8
    THE JOYS OF MUTUAL HATE TO KEEP THEM WARM    . . . .    . . 360   3 DON JUAN 13     6   5
    BUT NEITHER LOVE NOR HATE IN MUCH EXCESS    . . . .    . . 361   3 DON JUAN 13     8   1
    I HATE TO HUNT DOWN A TIRED METAPHOR    . . . . . .    . . 374   3 DON JUAN 13    36   5
    WHO DID NOT HATE SO MUCH THE SIN AS SINNER    . . . .    . . 399   3 DON JUAN 13    87   6
    I HATE A MOTIVE LIKE A LINGERING BOTTLE    . . . . .    . . 435   3 DON JUAN 14    58   1
    I HATE IT AS I HATE A DROVE OF CATTLE    . . . . . .    . . 435   3 DON JUAN 14    58   5
    I HATE IT AS I HATE A DROVE OF CATTLE    . . . . . .    . . 435   3 DON JUAN 14    58   5
    I HATE IT AS I HATE AN ARGUMENT    . . . . . . . .    . . 435   3 DON JUAN 14    58   7
    I HATE IT AS I HATE AN ARGUMENT    . . . . . . . .    . . 435   3 DON JUAN 14    58   7
    BECAUSE I HATE EVEN DEMOCRATIC ROYALTY    . . . . .    . . 466   3 DON JUAN 15    23   8
    AS WOMEN HATE HALF MEASURES ON THE WHOLE    . . . .    . . 468   3 DON JUAN 15    28   7
    AND HATE THOSE WHO WON'T LET THEM COME TO PASS    . .   . . 491   3 DON JUAN 15    79   8
    MYSELF WITH METAPHYSICS NONE CAN HATE    . . . . . .    . . 496   3 DON JUAN 15    91   2
    AND SCARLET CLOAK (I HATE THE SIGHT TO SEE SINCE--    . .   . 530   3 DON JUAN 16    61   4
```
HATED
```
    THE TENOR THESE TWO HATED WITH A HATE    . . . . . .    . . 394   2 DON JUAN  4    93   2
    HE HATED CRUELTY AS ALL MEN HATE    . . . . . . . .    . . 140   3 DON JUAN  8    55   6
    YOUNG MEN WHO--THOUGH THEY HATED TO DISCUSS    . . . .    . . 344   3 DON JUAN 12    61   3
    DISCUSSED (HE HATED BEER YCLEPT THE SMALL)    . . . .    . . 533   3 DON JUAN 16    67   3
```
HATEFUL
```
    THAT HORRID EQUINOX THAT HATEFUL SECTION    . . . . .    . . 238   3 DON JUAN 10    27   4
```
HATER
```
    THAT HATER OF MANKIND WOULD BE A SHAME    . . . . .    . .  53   3 DON JUAN  6    94   3
    RIGHT HONESTLY HE LIKED AN HONEST HATER--    . . . .    . . 361   3 DON JUAN 13     7   2
```
HATES
```
    AND LOVES OR HATES DISDAINING TO BE GUIDED    . . . .    . . 366   3 DON JUAN 13    16   7
```
HATING
```
    WHO HATING HOGS YET WISHED TO SAVE THEIR BACON    . .   . . .  87   3 DON JUAN  7    42   8
```
HATRED
```
    FOR A RETURN TO HATRED I WOULD SHUN HER    . . . . .    . . 231   3 DON JUAN 10    12   4
    NOW HATRED IS BY FAR THE LONGEST PLEASURE    . . . .    . . 361   3 DON JUAN 13     6   7
```

HAUD
    HAUD IGNARA LOQUOR THESE ARE NUGAE QUARUM 419   3 DON JUAN 14   21   1
HAUGHTILY
    THEN RISING HAUGHTILY HE GLANCED AROUND 484   2 DON JUAN 5   126   5
HAUGHTY
    AND RARELY CEASED THE HAUGHTY BILLOW'S ROAR 249   2 DON JUAN 2   177   6
    HAUGHTY AND HUGE ALONG THE DISTANCE LOWERS 460   2 DON JUAN 5   85   5
    HER VERY SMILE WAS HAUGHTY THOUGH SO SWEET 475   2 DON JUAN 5   111   1
    THOSE HAUGHTY SHOP-KEEPERS WHO STERNLY DEALT 257   3 DON JUAN 10   65   6
    AND TALENT ON HIS HAUGHTY SPIRIT WROUGHT 365   3 DON JUAN 13   15   6
    WHERE THE TRIUMPHAL CHARIOTS' HAUGHTY MARCH 485   3 DON JUAN 15   67   4
    TO SUCH PERFORMANCES WITH HAUGHTY SMILE 521   3 DON JUAN 16   42   7
HAUNCH
    WITH SAUCES GENEVOISES AND HAUNCH OF VENISON 484   3 DON JUAN 15   65   2
HAUNCHES
    THROWN BACK UPON ITS HAUNCHES--A GAZELLE 160   2 DON JUAN 2   6   V2
HAUNT
    ONE OF THOSE PRETTY PRECIOUS PLAGUES WHICH HAUNT 438   3 DON JUAN 14   63   3
HAUNTED
    WITH USELESS PENITENCE PERPLEX'D AND HAUNTED 120   2 DON JUAN 1   180   6
    WITH BASE SUSPICION NOW NO LONGER HAUNTED 120   2 DON JUAN 1   180   V6
    AND DRYDEN'S LAY MADE HAUNTED GROUND TO ME 337   2 DON JUAN 3   105   7
    I SAY I DO BELIEVE A HAUNTED SPOT 499   3 DON JUAN 15   96   3
HAUNTING
    THAN HAUNTING SOME OLD RUIN OR WILD WASTE 38   3 DON JUAN 6   64   8
HAUNTS
    CALL'D SOCIAL HAUNTS OF HATE AND VICE AND CARE 358   2 DON JUAN 4   28   4
HAUSTUS
    HAUSTUS (AND HERE THE SURGEON CAME AND CUPPED HIM) . . . 244   3 DON JUAN 10   41   4
    ET HAUSTUS TER IN DIE CAPIENDUS 244   3 DON JUAN 10   41   8
HAUTEUR
    SHE IN HER VIRTUE HE IN HIS HAUTEUR 365   3 DON JUAN 13   14   8
HAVING
    NOT HAVING OF MY OWN DOMESTIC CARES 33   2 DON JUAN 1   23   8
    OF HAVING PLAY'D THE FOOL THOUGH BOTH I SPURN HE 103   2 DON JUAN 1   151   5
    I AM ASHAMED OF HAVING SHED THESE TEARS 106   2 DON JUAN 1   155   5
    AND BREAK A PROMISE AFTER HAVING MADE IT HER 142   2 DON JUAN 1   210   5
    HAVING GOT DRUNK EXCEEDINGLY TODAY 156   2 DON JUAN 1 V 8   5
    HAVING BEEN SEVERAL DAYS IN GREAT DISTRESS 180   2 DON JUAN 2   46   2
    HAVING NO PAPER FOR THE WANT OF BETTER 195   2 DON JUAN 2   74   7
    FOR HAVING USED THEIR APPETITES SO SADLY 199   2 DON JUAN 2   80   8
    AND HAVING LEARNT TO SWIM IN THAT SWEET RIVER 211   2 DON JUAN 2   105   3
    BUT I HAVE DONE WITH KISSES--HAVING KISSED 232   2 DON JUAN 2   142   V7
    ITALIAN NOT AT ALL HAVING NO TEACHERS 243   2 DON JUAN 2   165   2
    AND NEVER HAVING DREAMT OF FALSEHOOD SHE 257   2 DON JUAN 2   190   7
    AND HAVING O'ER ITSELF NO FURTHER POWER 258   2 DON JUAN 2   192   4
    THEN HAVING SETTLED HIS MARINE AFFAIRS 285   2 DON JUAN 3   19   1
    HIS VESSEL HAVING NEED OF SOME REPAIRS 285   2 DON JUAN 3   19   3
    HAVING NO CUSTOM-HOUSE NOR QUARANTINE 286   2 DON JUAN 3   20   2
    LINK'D HAND IN HAND AND DANCING EACH TOO HAVING 291   2 DON JUAN 3   30   4
    AND HAVING PICKED UP SEVERAL ODDS AND ENDS 318   2 DON JUAN 3   83   2
    AND HAVING LIVED WITH PEOPLE OF ALL RANKS 319   2 DON JUAN 3   84   3
    NO SIGN SAVE BREATH OF HAVING LEFT THE GRAVE 378   2 DON JUAN 4   63   8
    AND HAVING LED A RATHER LOOSISH LIFE 389   2 DON JUAN 4   83   V2
    HAVING NO HEART TO SHOW HE SHOWS HIS TEETH 392   2 DON JUAN 4   89   8
    HAVING WITHSTOOD TEMPTATION IN MY YOUTH 397   2 DON JUAN 4   97   2
    AT THE FIRST TWO BOOKS HAVING TOO MUCH TRUTH 397   2 DON JUAN 4   97   4
    THE EUNUCH HAVING EYED THEM O'ER WITH CARE 425   2 DON JUAN 5   28   1
    HAVING NO EQUALS NOTHING WHICH HAD E'ER 480   2 DON JUAN 5   119   2
    AND NEVER HAVING DREAMT WHAT 'TWAS TO BEAR 480   2 DON JUAN 5   119   4
    WAS MUCH EMBARRASSED NEVER HAVING MET 482   2 DON JUAN 5   122   2
    FOR HAVING HAD HIM TO HER PALACE LED 483   2 DON JUAN 5   124   6
    TO CUTTING SHORT THEIR HOPES OF HAVING ANY 487   2 DON JUAN 5   132   8
    THE RUSSIANS HAVING BUILT TWO BATTERIES ON 78   3 DON JUAN 7   23   1
    FOR HAVING THROWN HIMSELF INTO A DITCH 147   3 DON JUAN 8   71   1
    HAVING BEEN USED TO SERVE ON HORSES' BACKS 149   3 DON JUAN 8   74   5
    DON JUAN HAVING DONE THE BEST HE COULD 277   3 DON JUAN 11   18   1
    AND HAVING VOTED DINED DRANK GAMED AND WHORED 306   3 DON JUAN 11   75   7
    SOME FOR HAVING TURNED CONVERTED CULLIES 314   3 DON JUAN 11 V 76   3
    AND ALL BY HAVING TACT AS WELL AS TASTE 346   3 DON JUAN 12   66   8
    COURT MYSTERIES HAVING BEEN HIMSELF A MINISTER 368   3 DON JUAN 13   21   4
    OF TUMBLING FIRST AND HAVING IN EXCHANGE 424   3 DON JUAN 14   32   3
    AND HAVING CASUALLY GLANCED IT THROUGH 440   3 DON JUAN 14   69   6
    HAVING WOUND UP WITH THIS SUBLIME COMPARISON 481   3 DON JUAN 15   59   1
    HE SHUT HIS DOOR AND AFTER HAVING READ 512   3 DON JUAN 16   27   2
    AND THEN THE MID-DAY HAVING WORN TO ONE 527   3 DON JUAN 16   55   1
HAWK
    BUT LIKE A HAWK ENCUMBER'D WITH HIS HOOD-- 10   2 DON JUAN D   2   6
    OR HAWK OR BRIDE MOST MORTALS AFTER ONE 122   3 DON JUAN 8   22   6
HAWKE
    VERNON THE BUTCHER CUMBERLAND WOLFE HAWKE 22   2 DON JUAN 1   2   1
HAWKED
    AND SEVERAL OF HER BEST BON-MOTS WERE HAWKED ABOUT . . . 338   3 DON JUAN 12   47   5
    HAWKED ABOUT AT A DISCOUNT SMALL OR LARGE-- 379   3 DON JUAN 13   45   7
HAWKS
    SOME COSSACQUES HOVERING LIKE HAWKS ROUND A HILL 95   3 DON JUAN 7   56   3
    AS HAWKS MAY POUNCE UPON A WOODLAND SONGSTER 285   3 DON JUAN 11   35   8
HAWK'S-BILL
    THEY FOUND A TURTLE OF THE HAWK'S-BILL KIND 208   2 DON JUAN 2   99   2

		PAGE	VOL	CANTO	STANZA	LN
HAY						
AND FLESH (WHICH DEATH MOWS DOWN TO HAY) IS GRASS		147	2 DON JUAN	1	220	4
HAYLEY'S						
AND HAYLEY'S TRIUMPHS WHICH SHE DEEMED PATHETIC		525	3 DON JUAN	16	50	3
HAZARD						
HOWEVER HE REPLIED AT HAZARD WITH		294	3 DON JUAN	11	52	1
BUT TA'EN AT HAZARD AS THE RHYME MAY RUN		397	3 DON JUAN	13	83	6
HAZARDS						
AS SEVERAL PEOPLE THINK SUCH HAZARDS RUDE		270	3 DON JUAN	11	4	4
HAZY						
A HAZY WIDOWER TURNED OF FORTY'S SURE		333	3 DON JUAN	12	37	5
HEAD						
I DON'T CHOOSE TO SAY MUCH UPON THIS HEAD		33	2 DON JUAN	1	22	5
A BOSOM WHEREON HE HIS HEAD MIGHT LAY		73	2 DON JUAN	1	96	5
COULD ENTER INTO DON ALFONSO'S HEAD		97	2 DON JUAN	1	139	2
NOW LIKE FRIAR BACON'S BRAZEN HEAD I'VE SPOKEN		145	2 DON JUAN	1	217	5
MY HEART IN PASSION AND MY HEAD ON RHYMES		145	2 DON JUAN	1	217	8
TO HEAD THE POLL I WONDER WHO WOULD BUY IT		154	2 DON JUAN	1	V 5	4
FAST BY THE HEAD AND ALL DISTINCTION GONE		179	2 DON JUAN	2	44	2
AND GOING DOWN HEAD FOREMOST--SUNK IN SHORT		183	2 DON JUAN	2	51	8
TO EAT THE HEAD OF HIS ARCH-ENEMY		200	2 DON JUAN	2	83	3
ASLEEP THEY SHOOK THEM BY THE HAND AND HEAD		208	2 DON JUAN	2	98	7
RAISED HIGHER THE FAINT HEAD WHICH O'ER IT HUNG		216	2 DON JUAN	2	114	3
JUST FOR THE PRESENT AND IN HIS LULL'D HEAD		227	2 DON JUAN	2	134	4
HIS HEAD UPON HIS ELBOW AND HE SAW		239	2 DON JUAN	2	157	2
ROUND JUAN'S HEAD AND HIS AROUND HERS LIES		259	2 DON JUAN	2	194	3
SUSTAIN'D HIS HEAD UPON HER BOSOM'S CHARMS		260	2 DON JUAN	2	195	4
HIS SOBER HEAD MAJESTICALLY TAME		292	2 DON JUAN	3	32	5
AND WITHOUT TURNING HIS FACETIOUS HEAD		297	2 DON JUAN	3	43	1
AND ANSWER LET ONE LIVING HEAD		323	2 DON JUAN	3	L 8	4
FOAMING O'ER HER LONE HEAD SO FIERCE AND HIGH		361	2 DON JUAN	4	31	7
REPLIED YOUR BLOOD BE THEN ON YOUR OWN HEAD		365	2 DON JUAN	4	40	5
LET HIM DISARM OR BY MY FATHER'S HEAD		369	2 DON JUAN	4	47	1
ONE ON THE ARM THE OTHER ON THE HEAD		370	2 DON JUAN	4	49	8
AND HER HEAD DROOP'D AS WHEN THE LILY LIES		376	2 DON JUAN	4	59	3
BESIDES I'VE NO MORE ON THIS HEAD TO ADD		384	2 DON JUAN	4	74	5
INTO DON JUAN'S HEAD A THOUGHT WHICH HE		434	2 DON JUAN	5	43	2
LET'S KNOCK THAT OLD BLACK FELLOW ON THE HEAD		434	2 DON JUAN	5	43	7
SOME FEMALE HEAD MOST CURIOUSLY PRESUMES		442	2 DON JUAN	5	55	6
BUT THEY AS SOON SHALL CIRCUMCISE MY HEAD		452	2 DON JUAN	5	71	8
THAT SOON HIS HEAD WAS MOST COMPLETELY CROWNED		457	2 DON JUAN	5	79	4
WHILE BABA MADE HIM COMB HIS HEAD AND OIL IT		457	2 DON JUAN	5	79	8
HIS HEAD UNTIL THE CEREMONY ENDED		466	2 DON JUAN	5	95	8
BUT HE HAD GOT HAIDEE INTO HIS HEAD		483	2 DON JUAN	5	124	2
HER FIRST THOUGHT WAS TO CUT OFF JUAN'S HEAD		491	2 DON JUAN	5	139	1
THE CUTTING OFF HIS HEAD WAS NOT THE ART		492	2 DON JUAN	5	140	7
MAN WITH HIS HEAD REFLECTS--(AS SPURZHEIM TELLS)		7	3 DON JUAN	6	2	V7
MAN'S PENSIVE PART IS NOW AND THEN THE HEAD		7	3 DON JUAN	6	2	V7
BY EUNUCHS FLANKED WHILE AT THEIR HEAD THERE STALKED		21	3 DON JUAN	6	30	4
AND BOWED HER THROBBING HEAD O'ER TREMBLING KNEES		59	3 DON JUAN	6	107	8
HER HEAD HUNG DOWN AND HER LONG HAIR IN STOOPING		60	3 DON JUAN	6	109	1
SHE STOPT AND RAISED HER HEAD TO SPEAK--BUT PAUSED		61	3 DON JUAN	6	111	1
PASSIVE OBEDIENCE--NOW RAISED UP THE HEAD		101	3 DON JUAN	7	67	6
HIS CAP AND HEAD WHICH PROVES THE HEAD TO BE		116	3 DON JUAN	8	10	3
HIS CAP AND HEAD WHICH PROVES THE HEAD TO BE		116	3 DON JUAN	8	10	3
NO HARM UNTO A RIGHT LEGITIMATE HEAD		117	3 DON JUAN	8	10	7
UPON THE HEAD BEFORE THEIR GUNS WERE COCKED		134	3 DON JUAN	8	43	8
ON SUCH OCCASIONS NOT A SINGLE HEAD		152	3 DON JUAN	8	81	6
SEIZED FAST AS IF 'TWERE BY THE SERPENT'S HEAD		153	3 DON JUAN	8	83	3
TO THE LIVE LEG STILL CLUNG THE SEVERED HEAD		153	3 DON JUAN	8	84	8
MORE THAN THE HEAD OF THE INVETERATE FOE		154	3 DON JUAN	8	85	7
THEIR SABRES GLITTERED O'ER HER LITTLE HEAD		158	3 DON JUAN	8	93	1
THE SERASKIER IS KNOCKED UPON THE HEAD		160	3 DON JUAN	8	98	1
IS WOMAN WHAT A WHIRLWIND IS HER HEAD		214	3 DON JUAN	9	64	2
A WHOLE ONE AND MY HEART FLIES TO MY HEAD--		233	3 DON JUAN	10	17	8
ON A FOOL'S HEAD--AND THERE IS LONDON TOWN		265	3 DON JUAN	10	82	8
TOO SUBTLE FOR THE AIRIEST HUMAN HEAD		268	3 DON JUAN	11	1	4
AND WEAR MY HEAD DENYING THAT I WEAR IT		268	3 DON JUAN	11	1	8
(IN WHISPERS) TO HAVE TURNED HIS SOVEREIGN'S HEAD		283	3 DON JUAN	11	32	8
THE CONTRARY BUT THEN 'TIS IN THE HEAD		284	3 DON JUAN	11	34	2
WHAT MATTERS IF THE ROAD BE HEAD OR HEART		284	3 DON JUAN	11	34	8
TO TURN HER HEAD WITH WALTZING AND WITH FLATTERY		331	3 DON JUAN	12	32	8
THIS BY HIS HEART--HIS RIVAL BY HIS HEAD		402	3 DON JUAN	13	93	8
(MY HEART OR HEAD ACHES WITH THE MEMORY YET)		408	3 DON JUAN	13	107	1
TO INTRODUCE A BON MOT HEAD AND EARS		408	3 DON JUAN	13	109	4
UPON MY HEAD HAVE BID THEIR THUNDERS BREAK		414	3 DON JUAN	14	10	3
THE SORT OF THING TO TURN A YOUNG MAN'S HEAD		438	3 DON JUAN	14	64	1
WOULD GIVE UP ARTLESSLY BOTH HEART AND HEAD		460	3 DON JUAN	15	10	6
NOR BROKEN MY OWN HEAD NOR THAT OF PRISCIAN		467	3 DON JUAN	15	24	6
WAS THERE CHASTE DAME WHO HAD NOT IN HER HEAD		470	3 DON JUAN	15	32	4
I ALWAYS KNOCK MY HEAD AGAINST SOME ANGLE		496	3 DON JUAN	15	91	5
AND WHAT IS STRANGEST UPON THIS STRANGE HEAD		504	3 DON JUAN	16	7	5
AND MUCH WAS TALKED ON ALL SIDES ON THAT HEAD		527	3 DON JUAN	16	54	5
HINTS FROM THE INDEPENDENT HEART OR HEAD		538	3 DON JUAN	16	77	5
OF PILLOWING ITS HEAD ON A PIN-CUSHION		565	3 DON JUAN	17	6	5
HEADACHE						
HIS HEADACHE BEING INCREASED BY EVERY BILLOW		169	2 DON JUAN	2	25	6
YOU WAKE WITH HEAD-ACHE YOU SHALL SEE WHAT THEN		250	2 DON JUAN	2	179	8
MAY CHOOSE BETWEEN THE HEADACHE AND THE HEARTACHE		356	2 DON JUAN	4	24	8
WOULD THIS DAMNED HEADACHE SUFFER ME TO BEAR IT		268	3 DON JUAN	11	1	V8

HEADLONG
    HAD DYED IT WITH THE HEADLONG BLOOD WHOSE RACE . . . . . 231 2 DON JUAN 2 141 3
    AND YET A HEADLONG HEADSTRONG DOWNRIGHT SHE . . . . . . 7 3 DON JUAN 6 3 1
    WHOSE HEADLONG PASSIONS FORM THEIR PROPER WOES . . . . 49 3 DON JUAN 6 87 8
    THOU ARE NO NOVICE IN THE HEADLONG CHASE . . . . 326 3 DON JUAN 12 23 6
    THE OLD HEN--BY RUNNING HEADLONG TO THE WATER . . . . . 564 3 DON JUAN 17 4 8
HEAD-QUARTERS
    THEY BROUGHT HIM AND HIS COMRADES TO HEAD-QUARTERS . . . 96 3 DON JUAN 7 57 2
HEADS
    AND ALL MANKIND TURN WITH IT HEADS OR TAILS . . . . . . 159 2 DON JUAN 2 4 2
    OR BREAKS THEIR HOPES OR HEARTS OR HEADS OR NECKS . . . 172 2 DON JUAN 2 31 6
    CUT OFF A THOUSAND HEADS BEFORE-- --NOW PRAY . . . . . 453 2 DON JUAN 5 72 1
    HEADS BOW KNEES BEND EYES WATCH AROUND A THRONE . . . . 484 2 DON JUAN 5 127 7
    MEN WITH THEIR HEADS REFLECT ON THIS AND THAT-- . . . . 7 3 DON JUAN 6 2 7
    TRIMMED EITHER HEADS OR HEARTS TO DECORATE . . . . . . 13 3 DON JUAN 6 14 6
    OF HEADS THAN THEIR CARESSES OF THE HEART . . . . 13 3 DON JUAN 6 14 8
    FOR RICH MEN AND THEIR BRIDES TO LAY THEIR HEADS . . . . 18 3 DON JUAN 6 25 4
    AND HEADS IF THOU HADST ALL THINGS MULTIPLIED . . . . . 20 3 DON JUAN 6 28 2
    WHOSE HEADS WERE HEROES WHICH CUT OFF IN VAIN . . . . . 113 3 DON JUAN 8 2 7
    LAUNCHED AT THEIR HEADS--JOG--JOG--JOG--JOG--JOG--JOG . . 260 3 DON JUAN 10 71 V8
    AND AS ROMANTIC HEADS ARE PRETTY PAINTERS . . . . 284 3 DON JUAN 11 33 3
    LINE THE INTERIOR OF THEIR HEADS OR BONNETS . . . . . . 294 3 DON JUAN 11 50 3
    (NOT OF OLD VICTORS ALL WHOSE HEADS AND CRESTS . . . . . 321 3 DON JUAN 12 12 3
HEADSTRONG
    AND YET A HEADLONG HEADSTRONG DOWNRIGHT SHE . . . . . . 7 3 DON JUAN 6 3 1
HEADY
    SOME ACIDS WITH THE SWEETS--FOR SHE WAS HEADY . . . . . 482 3 DON JUAN 15 61 4
HEALTH
    IN HEALTH AND PURSE BEGIN YOUR DAY TO DATE . . . . . . 230 2 DON JUAN 2 140 6
    'TWAS WELL BECAUSE HEALTH IN THE HUMAN FRAME . . . . . 245 2 DON JUAN 2 169 3
    FOR HEALTH AND IDLENESS TO PASSION'S FLAME . . . . . . 245 2 DON JUAN 2 169 5
    AS MOST AT HIS AGE ARE OF HOPE AND HEALTH . . . . 415 2 DON JUAN 5 8 2
    OF SOLITUDE HEALTH SHRANK NOT FROM HIM--FOR . . . . . . 143 3 DON JUAN 8 62 2
    WITH YOUTH AND HEALTH ALL KISSES ARE HEAVEN-KISSING . . 215 3 DON JUAN 9 66 8
    ARE OVER HERE'S A HEALTH TO AULD LANG SYNE . . . . . . 232 3 DON JUAN 10 16 5
    IN HEALTH--WHEN ILL WE CALL THEM TO ATTEND US . . . . . 245 3 DON JUAN 10 42 3
    OF HEALTH BUT FLICKERED WITH A FAINT REFLECTION . . . . 245 3 DON JUAN 10 43 6
HEAP
    CONTRIVED TO FLING THE BED-CLOTHES IN A HEAP . . . . . . 97 2 DON JUAN 1 140 5
    INSULT ON INSULT HEAP AND WRONG ON WRONG . . . . 100 2 DON JUAN 1 145 3
    FROM OUT THE HEAP A PETTICOAT OR TWO . . . . 455 2 DON JUAN 5 76 V8
    MY SIMILES ARE GATHERED IN A HEAP . . . . 40 3 DON JUAN 6 68 6
    BUT BURIED IN THE HEAP OF SUCH TRANSACTIONS . . . . . . 83 3 DON JUAN 7 34 3
    OVER A HEAP OF BODIES FELT HIS HEEL . . . . 153 3 DON JUAN 8 83 2
    THE HEAP A MOMENT MORE HAD MADE HER TOMB . . . . 158 3 DON JUAN 8 94 8
    AND SPARKLING ON FROM HEAP TO HEAP DISPLAYS . . . . . . 319 3 DON JUAN 12 8 2
    AND SPARKLING ON FROM HEAP TO HEAP DISPLAYS . . . . . . 319 3 DON JUAN 12 8 2
    IN FEMALE DATES STRIKES TIME ALL OF A HEAP . . . . . . 433 3 DON JUAN 14 52 8
HEAPED
    ALL HEAPED TOGETHER SOMEHOW IN A LITTER . . . . 465 2 DON JUAN 5 93 V8
    LEAVING AS LADDERS THEIR HEAPED CARCASES . . . . 150 3 DON JUAN 8 76 6
HEAPS
    SWEET TO THE MISER ARE HIS GLITTERING HEAPS . . . . . . 88 2 DON JUAN 1 124 5
HEAR
    BUT HEAR THESE FREEDOMS FORM THE UTMOST LIST . . . . . 65 2 DON JUAN 1 80 5
    AND HEAR THE HEART BEAT WITH THE LOVE IT GRANTED . . . 73 2 DON JUAN 1 96 6
    WE'LL TALK OF THAT ANON--'TIS SWEET TO HEAR . . . . . 87 2 DON JUAN 1 122 1
    'TIS SWEET TO HEAR THE WATCHDOG'S HONEST BARK . . . . 88 2 DON JUAN 1 123 1
    HASTE--HASTE--I HEAR ALFONSO'S HURRYING FEET-- . . . . 121 2 DON JUAN 1 182 7
    BELOVED JULIA HEAR ME STILL BESEECHING . . . . 167 2 DON JUAN 2 20 7
    TO HEAR NEW WORDS AND TO REPEAT THEM BUT . . . . 244 2 DON JUAN 2 167 2
    FOR NONE LIKES MORE TO HEAR HIMSELF CONVERSE . . . . . 298 2 DON JUAN 3 45 8
    MAY HEAR OUR MUTUAL MURMURS SWEEP . . . . 326 2 DON JUAN 3 L 16 3
    TO THOSE WHO HAVE CEASED TO HEAR SUCH OR NE'ER HEARD . . 351 2 DON JUAN 4 14 8
    THEY HIRED HIM THOUGH TO HEAR HIM YOU'D BELIEVE . . . . 391 2 DON JUAN 4 87 7
    THE TIME MAY COME WHEN YOU MAY HEAR ME TOO . . . . . . 392 2 DON JUAN 4 88 6
    BUT HEAR THAT SEVERAL PEOPLE TAKE EXCEPTION . . . . . . 397 2 DON JUAN 4 97 3
    TO HEAR AND TO OBEY HAD BEEN FROM BIRTH . . . . 475 2 DON JUAN 5 112 1
    BED FOR THE DREAM SHE HAD BEEN OBLIGED TO HEAR . . . . 45 3 DON JUAN 6 79 6
    AND THEN WITHDREW TO HEAR ABOUT THE RUSSIANS . . . . . 52 3 DON JUAN 6 92 5
    HER ANGER AND BESEECH'D SHE'D HEAR HIM THROUGH-- . . . 57 3 DON JUAN 6 102 3
    TO HEAR IS TO OBEY HE SAID BUT STILL . . . . 62 3 DON JUAN 6 114 1
    WHAT WAS'T TO HIM TO HEAR TWO WOMEN SOB . . . . 105 3 DON JUAN 7 77 8
    I THINK I HEAR A LITTLE BIRD WHO SINGS . . . . 137 3 DON JUAN 8 50 3
    GREW DUMB FOR YOU MIGHT ALMOST HEAR A LINNET . . . . . 142 3 DON JUAN 8 59 6
    WHEREAS IF ALL BE TRUE WE HEAR OF HEAVEN . . . . 168 3 DON JUAN 8 114 7
    ALL THAT WE READ HEAR DREAM OF MAN'S DISTRESSES . . . . 173 3 DON JUAN 8 123 3
    AND WHEN YOU HEAR HISTORIANS TALK OF THRONES . . . . . 180 3 DON JUAN 8 137 1
    GO HEAR IT IN YOUR FAMISHED COUNTRY'S CRIES . . . . . 187 3 DON JUAN 9 9 7
    SO CALLED THE ANTIC LONG HATH CEASED TO HEAR . . . . . 188 3 DON JUAN 9 12 4
    TO HEAR DEBATES WHOSE THUNDER ROUSED (NOT ROUSES) . . . 353 3 DON JUAN 12 82 4
    PROUD OF HIS HEAR HIMS PROUD TOO OF HIS VOTE . . . . . 401 3 DON JUAN 13 91 1
    SHE HAD HEARD BUT WOMEN HEAR WITH MORE GOOD HUMOUR . . 460 3 DON JUAN 15 11 3
    THE FOURTH WE HEAR AND SEE AND SAY TOO DAILY . . . . . 465 3 DON JUAN 15 21 6
    NOT THE LESS PRECIOUS THAT WE SELDOM HEAR IT . . . . . 518 3 DON JUAN 16 40 8
HEARD
    BUT THIS I HEARD HER SAY AND CAN'T BE WRONG . . . . . . 28 2 DON JUAN 1 14 5
    CALMLY SHE HEARD EACH CALUMNY THAT ROSE . . . . 36 2 DON JUAN 1 29 6
    AND HEARD A VOICE IN ALL THE WINDS AND THEN . . . . . . 72 2 DON JUAN 1 94 2

HEARD   (CONTINUED)
FIRST KNOCKS WERE HEARD THEN MADAM--MADAM--HIST . . . . . 95 2 DON JUAN 1   136   8
WAS EVER HEARD OF SUCH A CURST DISASTER . . . . . . 96 2 DON JUAN 1   137   3
OR IN THE DESERT HEARD THE CAMEL'S BELL . . . . 201 2 DON JUAN 2   84   7
AND TRIED TO PERCH ALTHOUGH IT SAW AND HEARD . . . . . 206 2 DON JUAN 2   94   5
SOME SWORE THAT THEY HEARD BREAKERS OTHERS GUNS . . . . 207 2 DON JUAN 2   96   5
THAT FINER SIMPLER MUSIC NE'ER WAS HEARD . . . . . 236 2 DON JUAN 2   151   5
THEY HEARD THE WAVE'S SPLASH AND THE WIND SO LOW . . . . 253 2 DON JUAN 2   185   5
NOR OFFER'D ANY SHE HAD NEVER HEARD . . . . . . 257 2 DON JUAN 2   190   2
HAD DOUBTLESS HEARD ABOUT THE STYGIAN RIVER . . . . . . 258 2 DON JUAN 2   193   6
HE HEARD HIS RIVULET'S LIGHT BUBBLING RUN . . . . . 289 2 DON JUAN 3   27   3
TO THOSE WHO HAVE CEASED TO HEAR SUCH OR NE'ER HEARD . . . 351 2 DON JUAN 4   14   8
BUT NO ONE EVER HEARD HER SPEAK OR SHRIEK . . . . . 380 2 DON JUAN 4   67   5
FROM THEM AT LEAST THEIR DESTINY HE HEARD . . . . . 388 2 DON JUAN 4   80   3
YOU'VE HEARD OF RAUCOCANTI--I'M THE MAN . . . . . 392 2 DON JUAN 4   88   5
THEY HEARD NEXT DAY--THAT IN THE DARDANELLES . . . . . 393 2 DON JUAN 4   91   1
AND HEARD TROY DOUBTED TIME WILL DOUBT OF ROME . . . . . 399 2 DON JUAN 4   101   3
I HEARD A SHOT--'TWAS EIGHT O'CLOCK SCARCE PAST-- . . . 428 2 DON JUAN 5   33   5
AND JUAN AND HIS FRIEND ALBEIT THEY HEARD . . . . . 439 2 DON JUAN 5   50   2
HE HEARD REPEATED JUAN WITH A FROWN . . . . . 470 2 DON JUAN 5   102   5
NOT SO TO HER WHO NE'ER HAD HEARD SUCH THINGS . . . . . 485 2 DON JUAN 5   128   2
LITTLE WAS HEARD OF CRIMINAL OR CRIME . . . . . 496 2 DON JUAN 5   149   2
AND NOTHING EVER HEARD OF SAVE STARVATION . . . . . 15 3 DON JUAN 6   19 V7
I'VE HEARD OF STORIES OF A COCK AND BULL . . . . . 46 3 DON JUAN 6   80   1
AND SINGING BIRDS WITHOUT WERE HEARD TO WARBLE . . . . . 55 3 DON JUAN 6   98   3
CAN NEVER BE DESCRIBED WE ALL HAVE HEARD . . . . . 59 3 DON JUAN 6   106   4
SHE WOULD REVOKE THE ORDER HE HAD HEARD . . . . . 62 3 DON JUAN 6   113   8
THE PARTY A SLIGHT GLANCE THEN SAID I HAVE HEARD . . . . 97 3 DON JUAN 7   60   4
BUT LET THAT PASS--I THINK I HAVE HEARD YOUR NAME . . . 97 3 DON JUAN 7   60   7
AND WHERE THE HOTTEST FIRE WAS SEEN AND HEARD . . . . . 129 3 DON JUAN 8   33   5
LIGHTENING ALONG HIS VEINS AND WHERE HE HEARD . . . . . 129 3 DON JUAN 8   33 V3
WITH DISTANT SHRIEKS WERE HEARD HEAVEN TO UPBRAID-- . . 146 3 DON JUAN 8   69   5
WERE ALSO HEARD TO WONDER IN THE DIN . . . . . 178 3 DON JUAN 8   132   2
TO PRAYER WAS HEARD NO MORE--AND JUAN WEPT . . . . . 182 3 DON JUAN 8   141   7
I'VE HEARD THEM IN THE EPHESIAN RUINS HOWL . . . . . 196 3 DON JUAN 9   27   2
ALSO THE SOFTER SILKS WERE HEARD TO RUSTLE . . . . . 223 3 DON JUAN 9   82   5
HEARD--AND THAT BEE-LIKE BUBBLING BUSY HUM . . . . . 272 3 DON JUAN 11   8   7
AND EVEN THAT HE HAD SO RARELY HEARD . . . . . 274 3 DON JUAN 11   12   3
I HEARD THEM WISH GOD WITH YOU SAVE THAT WAY-- . . . 274 3 DON JUAN 11   12   8
THOUGH HARDLY HEARD THROUGH MULTIFARIOUS DAMME'S . . . . 279 3 DON JUAN 11   24   3
UNTO BY SAWNEY'S VIOLIN WE HAVE HEARD . . . . . 307 3 DON JUAN 11   78   6
MIDST WHOM WE HAVE HEARD FROM SOURCES QUITE CORRECT . . 382 3 DON JUAN 13   52   4
THE FACT--I'VE HEARD IT--ONCE PERHAPS TOO MUCH . . . 388 3 DON JUAN 13   64   8
WITH DANDIES DINED HEARD SENATORS DECLAIMING . . . . . 418 3 DON JUAN 14   18   3
SOME NE'ER BELIEVED ONE HALF OF WHAT THEY HEARD . . . . 429 3 DON JUAN 14   44   5
LORD HENRY HEARD HER PLANS OF ARTLESS ART . . . . . 438 3 DON JUAN 14   65   5
(I MERELY QUOTE WHAT I HAVE HEARD FROM MANY) . . . . . 452 3 DON JUAN 14   95   2
SHE HAD HEARD BUT WOMEN HEAR WITH MORE GOOD HUMOUR . . 460 3 DON JUAN 15   11   3
'TIS WONDERFUL HOW OFT THE SEX HAVE HEARD . . . . . 489 3 DON JUAN 15   76   7
NO BUT YOU HAVE HEARD--I UNDERSTAND--BE DUMB . . . . . 498 3 DON JUAN 15   95   2
WHEN SUDDENLY HE HEARD OR THOUGHT SO NIGH . . . . . 509 3 DON JUAN 16   20   5
JUAN WAS PETRIFIED HE HAD HEARD A HINT . . . . . 510 3 DON JUAN 16   22   1
OH HAVE YOU NEVER HEARD OF THE BLACK FRIAR . . . . . 516 3 DON JUAN 16   36   1
WHEN AN HEIR IS BORN HE IS HEARD TO MOURN . . . . . 519 3 DON JUAN 16 L 4   1
WHO HAVE HEARD MISS THAT OR THIS OR LADY T'OTHER . . . 522 3 DON JUAN 16   44   7
I HAVE NOT HEARD SHE WAS AT ALL POETIC . . . . . 525 3 DON JUAN 16   50   1
FOR ALL OF US HAVE EITHER HEARD OR READ-- . . . . . 538 3 DON JUAN 16   77   5
IN GAY REMARK ON WHAT HE HAD HEARD OR SEEN . . . . . 552 3 DON JUAN 16   105   5
IN VAIN HE HEARD THE OTHERS RAIL OR RALLY . . . . . 552 3 DON JUAN 16   105   7
HEARER
IN SHORT THERE NEVER WAS A BETTER HEARER . . . . . . 426 3 DON JUAN 14   37   8
HEARERS
THE HEARERS OF HER CASE BECAME REPEATERS . . . . . 36 2 DON JUAN 1   28   8
NOR BATE (ABATE) THEIR HEARERS OF AN INCH . . . . . 404 3 DON JUAN 13   98   4
HEARKEN
SO SAID THE FLORENTINE YE MONARCHS HEARKEN . . . . . 264 3 DON JUAN 10   80   1
HEARS
THE PRINCE'S TYRANT--TILL HE HEARS THE DRUMS . . . . . 151 2 DON JUAN 1 V 2 V8
HE HEARS--ALAS NO MUSIC OF THE SPHERES . . . . . 290 2 DON JUAN 3   28   3
WHICH NO ONE HEARS SO LOUDLY THOUGH IT RINGS . . . . . 489 3 DON JUAN 15   76   6
HEARSAY
PERHAPS FROM HEARSAY OR FROM RECOLLECTION . . . . . 238 3 DON JUAN 10   27   2
HEART
HER MEMORY WAS A MINE SHE KNEW BY HEART . . . . . 27 2 DON JUAN 1   11   1
LIKE WHAT THIS LIGHT TOUCH LEFT ON JUAN'S HEART . . . . 60 2 DON JUAN 1   71   8
AS IF HER HEART HAD DEEPER THOUGHTS IN STORE . . . . . 61 2 DON JUAN 1   72   3
POOR JULIA'S HEART WAS IN AN AWKWARD STATE . . . . . 62 2 DON JUAN 1   75   1
SHOULD EVER GIVE HER HEART THE LEAST SENSATION . . . . 63 2 DON JUAN 1   77   4
UNTIL HIS MIGHTY HEART IN ITS GREAT MOOD . . . . . 70 2 DON JUAN 1   91   3
AND HEAR THE HEART BEAT WITH THE LOVE IT GRANTED . . . . 73 2 DON JUAN 1   96   6
HOW BEAUTIFUL SHE LOOK'D HER CONSCIOUS HEART . . . . . 78 2 DON JUAN 1   106   1
BREATHES ALSO TO THE HEART AND O'ER IT THROWS . . . . . 82 2 DON JUAN 1   114   7
SING AT MY HEART SIX MONTHS AT LEAST IN VAIN . . . . . 102 2 DON JUAN 1   149   2
THE GUILELESS HEART IN SILENCE MAY GRIEVE O'ER . . . . 107 2 DON JUAN 1   157   3
AND LOUDER THAN HER BREATHING BEATS HER HEART . . . . . 108 2 DON JUAN 1   158   8
I HAVE NO FURTHER CLAIM ON YOUR YOUNG HEART . . . . . 130 2 DON JUAN 1   192   3
PRIDE FAME AMBITION TO FILL UP HIS HEART . . . . . 131 2 DON JUAN 1   194   5
MY HEART IS FEMININE NOR CAN FORGET-- . . . . . 133 2 DON JUAN 1   196   5
AS VIBRATES MY FOND HEART TO MY FIX'D SOUL . . . . . 133 2 DON JUAN 1   196   8
MY HEART IS NOT MUCH GREENER AND IN SHORT I . . . . . 143 2 DON JUAN 1   213   4

348

HEART   (CONTINUED)

	PAGE	VOL	CANTO	STANZA	LN
THE FRESHNESS OF THE HEART CAN FALL LIKE DEW	144	2	DON JUAN 1	214	2
NO MORE--NO MORE--OH NEVER MORE MY HEART	144	2	DON JUAN 1	215	1
MY HEART IN PASSION AND MY HEAD ON RHYMES	145	2	DON JUAN 1	217	8
YOU'DE SWEAR HIS VERY HEART HAD SWEATED THROUGH	154	2	DON JUAN 1	V 5	8
FLASHES INTO THE HEART--ALL SUNNY LAND	160	2	DON JUAN 2	7	4
A KIND OF SHOCK THAT SETS ONE'S HEART AJAR	164	2	DON JUAN 2	14	6
NO DOUBT WE WEEP FOR THOSE THE HEART ENDEARS--	164	2	DON JUAN 2	15	7
BUT DIE AS MANY AN EXILED HEART HATH DIED	166	2	DON JUAN 2	18	3
HE FELT THAT CHILLING HEAVINESS OF HEART	167	2	DON JUAN 2	21	1
HE SAW INCREASING ON HIS FATHER'S HEART	203	2	DON JUAN 2	88	7
STIFF ON HIS HEART AND PULSE AND HOPE WERE PAST	204	2	DON JUAN 2	90	4
(THE HEART WILL SLIP EVEN AS THE TONGUE AND PEN)	228	2	DON JUAN 2	135	6
FROM HEART TO CHEEK IS CURB'D INTO A BLUSH	231	2	DON JUAN 2	141	4
WHILE VENUS FILLS THE HEART (WITHOUT HEART REALLY	246	2	DON JUAN 2	170	1
WHILE VENUS FILLS THE HEART (WITHOUT HEART REALLY	246	2	DON JUAN 2	170	1
WHILE VENUS FILLS THE HEART (WHICH QUITE AS WELL IS	246	2	DON JUAN 2	170	V1
FOR WITHOUT HEART LOVE'S NOT QUITE SO GOOD)	246	2	DON JUAN 2	170	V2
THAT EVER MADE A YOUTHFUL HEART LESS STEADY	246	2	DON JUAN 2	171	3
WHERE HEART AND SOUL AND SENSE IN CONCERT MOVE	254	2	DON JUAN 2	186	5
AND BEATING 'GAINST HIS BOSOM HAIDEE'S HEART	257	2	DON JUAN 2	191	7
WAS THAT IN WHICH THE HEART IS ALWAYS FULL	258	2	DON JUAN 2	192	3
PILLOW'D ON HER O'ERFLOWING HEART WHICH,PANTS	260	2	DON JUAN 2	195	7
HOPE CARE NOR LOVE BEYOND HER HEART BEAT HERE	264	2	DON JUAN 2	202	8
AND OH THAT QUICKENING OF THE HEART THAT BEAT	264	2	DON JUAN 2	203	1
HOW PLEASANT FOR THE HEART AS WELL AS LIVER	270	2	DON JUAN 2	213	8
THE HEART IS LIKE THE SKY A PART OF HEAVEN	270	2	DON JUAN 2	214	1
AND LOVED BY A YOUNG HEART TOO DEEPLY BLEST	274	2	DON JUAN 3	1	4
ONE MAN ALONE AT FIRST HER HEART CAN MOVE	276	2	DON JUAN 3	3	6
IS THAT TO WHICH HER HEART IS WHOLLY GRANTED	276	2	DON JUAN 3	4	6
ALL HAD BEEN OPEN HEART AND OPEN HOUSE	295	2	DON JUAN 3	39	V7
HIS OWN ANXIETY HIS HEART TOO BLEEDING	299	2	DON JUAN 3	46	6
AND HARDER FOR THE HEART TO OVERCOME	301	2	DON JUAN 3	51	3
THE ONLY THING WHICH KEPT HIS HEART UNCLOSED	304	2	DON JUAN 3	57	3
OF A STRONG HUMAN HEART AND IN A SIRE	305	2	DON JUAN 3	58	8
AND PERSIAN CARPETS WHICH THE HEART BLED TO STAIN	310	2	DON JUAN 3	68	3
SOFT HOUR WHICH WAKES THE WISH AND MELTS THE HEART	338	2	DON JUAN 3	108	1
PERHAPS THE WEAKNESS OF A HEART NOT VOID	339	2	DON JUAN 3	109	6
ALAS THERE IS NO INSTINCT LIKE THE HEART--	349	2	DON JUAN 4	10	8
THE HEART--WHICH MAY BE BROKEN HAPPY THEY	350	2	DON JUAN 4	11	1
MIX'D IN EACH OTHER'S ARMS AND HEART IN HEART	358	2	DON JUAN 4	27	1
MIX'D IN EACH OTHER'S ARMS AND HEART IN HEART	358	2	DON JUAN 4	27	1
OF HIS QUENCH'D HEART AND THE SEA DIRGES LOW	362	2	DON JUAN 4	34	6
I FEEL MY HEART BECOME SO SYMPATHETIC	372	2	DON JUAN 4	52	5
AND AS THE SOIL IS SO THE HEART OF MAN	373	2	DON JUAN 4	55	8
LAY AT HER HEART WHOSE EARLIEST BEAT STILL TRUE	378	2	DON JUAN 4	62	6
HER THOUGHTS FROM SORROW THROUGH HER HEART RE-SENT	379	2	DON JUAN 4	65	6
HAVING NO HEART TO SHOW HE SHOWS HIS TEETH	392	2	DON JUAN 4	89	8
OF THE WORLD'S STOICS--MEN WITHOUT A HEART	423	2	DON JUAN 5	25	8
SO CALM THOUGH PIERCED THROUGH STOMACH HEART AND LIVER	430	2	DON JUAN 5	35	4
RUSH BACK UPON HIS HEART WHICH FILLED APACE	478	2	DON JUAN 5	117	5
BUT JUAN WHO HAD STILL HIS HEART QUITE FULL	478	2	DON JUAN 5	117	V2
HIS HEART TO FORCE IT OUT FOR (TO BE SHORTER)	479	2	DON JUAN 5	118	7
MOST LIKELY TO ATTAIN HER AIM--HIS HEART	492	2	DON JUAN 5	140	8
BUT WOMAN WITH THE HEART--OR SOMETHING ELSE	7	3	DON JUAN 6	2	V8
WOMAN'S THE HEART--OR ANYTHING INSTEAD	7	3	DON JUAN 6	2	V8
GAVE WHAT I HAD--A HEART--AS THE WORLD WENT I	9	3	DON JUAN 6	5	6
SHE THOUGHT THAT HER LORD'S HEART (EVEN COULD SHE CLAIM IT)	10	3	DON JUAN 6	8	6
OF WHAT SHOULD BE MONOPOLY--THE HEART	10	3	DON JUAN 6	9	8
OF HEADS THAN THEIR CARESSES OF THE HEART	13	3	DON JUAN 6	14	8
IS MUCH IN MOST THINGS NOT LESS IN THE HEART	15	3	DON JUAN 6	19	3
A BEE FLEW OUT AND STUNG HER TO THE HEART	44	3	DON JUAN 6	77	7
IS LIGHTER FAR OF HEART AND VOICE THAN THOSE	49	3	DON JUAN 6	87	7
THE HEART ASUNDER--THEN AS MORE OR LESS	59	3	DON JUAN 6	107	5
A COURIER ON THE SPUR INSPIRED NEW HEART	85	3	DON JUAN 7	39	3
BEEN ONE TO WHICH A GOOD HEART COULD BE PARTIAL	86	3	DON JUAN 7	40	3
AS WARM IN HEART AS FEMININE IN FEATURE	138	3	DON JUAN 8	52	8
WHERE FIGHTS NOT TO THE LAST SOME DESPERATE HEART	152	3	DON JUAN 8	82	3
TO THIS VAIN REFUGE MADE THE GOOD HEART DROOP	157	3	DON JUAN 8	91	4
THAT WHEN THE VERY LANCE WAS IN HIS HEART	169	3	DON JUAN 8	115	2
THEIR PAUSE NOR SIGNS HIS HEART WAS OUT OF JOINT	170	3	DON JUAN 8	117	5
WAS SHOWN AND SOME MORE NOBLE HEART BROKE THROUGH	174	3	DON JUAN 8	124	2
YOUR HEART JOINS CHORUS FAME IS BUT A DIN	199	3	DON JUAN 9	34	8
A NERVOUS FAMILY TO WHOSE HEART OR HAND	205	3	DON JUAN 9	46	V3
LOVE THAT GREAT OPENER OF THE HEART AND ALL	222	3	DON JUAN 9	80	2
A WHOLE ONE AND MY HEART FLIES TO MY HEAD--	233	3	DON JUAN 10	17	8
OF LIFE SHRUNK IN HIS HEART AND THICK AND SOOTY	276	3	DON JUAN 11	16	5
AS IF THEY ACTED WITH THE HEART INSTEAD	284	3	DON JUAN 11	34	4
WHAT MATTERS IF THE ROAD BE HEAD OR HEART	284	3	DON JUAN 11	34	8
AGAINST HIS HEART PREFERRED THEIR USUAL CLAIMS	293	3	DON JUAN 11	48	5
(NOW HERE'S A WORD QUITE AFTER MY OWN HEART	326	3	DON JUAN 12	22	3
THAN THOSE BRED UP BY PRUDES WITHOUT A HEART	337	3	DON JUAN 12	46	8
BECAUSE SHE THOUGHT HIM A GOOD HEART AT BOTTOM	338	3	DON JUAN 12	49	2
IT SEEMS THE VIRGIN'S HEART EXPECTS YOUR HAND	343	3	DON JUAN 12	60	6
THEN SEES YOUR HEART WRECKED WITH AN INWARD SCOFFING	345	3	DON JUAN 12	63	4
THAT HE WAS NOT IN HEART SO VERY WEAK--I MEANT	346	3	DON JUAN 12	67	5
AND RATHER CALMLY INTO THE HEART GLIDES	350	3	DON JUAN 12	74	5
AT THAT HIS HEART HAD GOT A TOUGHER RIND	353	3	DON JUAN 12	81	6
TO EYE OR HEART--IT IS THE PEOPLE'S TRUST	354	3	DON JUAN 12	83	8

	PAGE	VOL		CANTO	STANZA	LN

HEART   (CONTINUED)
A VESTAL SHRINE OF INNOCENCE OF HEART	370	3	DON JUAN	13	27	7
AND KINDLED FEELINGS IN THE ROUGHEST HEART	386	3	DON JUAN	13	59	6
THIS BY HIS HEART--HIS RIVAL BY HIS HEAD	402	3	DON JUAN	13	93	8
(MY HEART OR HEAD ACHES WITH THE MEMORY YET)	408	3	DON JUAN	13	107	4
A BATTLE WRECK OR HISTORY OF THE HEART	419	3	DON JUAN	14	21	4
HE THOUGHT AT HEART LIKE COURTLY CHESTERFIELD . . .	425	3	DON JUAN	14	35	5
THAN WEAR A HEART A WOMAN LOVES TO REND	438	3	DON JUAN	14	64	6
AND FIRST IN THE O'ERFLOWING OF HER HEART	438	3	DON JUAN	14	65	1
A SOMETHING ALL-SUFFICIENT FOR THE HEART	442	3	DON JUAN	14	74	1
HER HEART WAS VACANT THOUGH A SPLENDID MANSION . . .	446	3	DON JUAN	14	85	2
SHE KNEW NOT HER OWN HEART THEN HOW SHOULD I	449	3	DON JUAN	14	91	1
CORRODING IN THE CAVERN OF THE HEART	457	3	DON JUAN	15	3	2
WOULD GIVE UP ARTLESSLY BOTH HEART AND HEAD	460	3	DON JUAN	15	10	6
AN ARROW FOR THE HEART LIKE A SWEET VOICE	461	3	DON JUAN	15	13	8
WHOSE HEART WAS FIX'D UPON A STAR OR BLUESTRING . .	474	3	DON JUAN	15	42	3
AS FAR AS HER OWN GENTLE HEART ALLOW'D	476	3	DON JUAN	15	46	2
AND KEPT HER HEART SERENE WITHIN ITS ZONE	476	3	DON JUAN	15	47	4
FOR MAN THEREIN WITH EYES AND HEART TO DINE	489	3	DON JUAN	15	75	4
HINTS FROM THE INDEPENDENT HEART OR HEAD	538	3	DON JUAN	16	77	5
WHICH MANY PEOPLE TAKE FOR WANT OF HEART	547	3	DON JUAN	16	97	3
THE HEART IN AN EXISTENCE OF ITS OWN	554	3	DON JUAN	16	108	7
THAT HATH A MEMORY OR THAT HAD A HEART	554	3	DON JUAN	16	109	2
WHICH BEAT AS IF THERE WAS A WARM HEART UNDER . . .	560	3	DON JUAN	16	122	4
WHICH LEAVES THEM ORPHANS OF THE HEART NO LESS . . .	562	3	DON JUAN	17	1	8
THE SUFFERERS--BE'T IN HEART OR INTELLECT--	563	3	DON JUAN	17	2	7
WHICH LEAVES THEM ORPHANS OF THE HEART NO LESS . . .	563	3	DON JUAN	17	2	8

HEART-ACHE
'TWOULD SAVE US MANY A HEART-ACHE MANY A SHILLING . . .	270	2	DON JUAN	2	213	5
MAY CHOOSE BETWEEN THE HEADACHE AND THE HEARTACHE . . .	356	2	DON JUAN	4	24	8

HEART-ACHES
SOME HEART-ACHES HAD BEEN SPARED ME YET I CARE NOT-- . . .	431	3	DON JUAN	14	49	2

HEART-BALLADS
HEART-BALLADS OF GREEN ERIN OR GREY HIGHLANDS	523	3	DON JUAN	16	46	2

HEART-BURNING
SAID JUAN--SWALLOWING A HEART-BURNING SIGH	423	2	DON JUAN	5	24	3

HEART-FELT
WITH MUCH HEART-FELT RELUCTANCE BE IT SAID	112	2	DON JUAN	1	165	7

HEARTH
STANDING ALONE BESIDE HIS DESOLATE HEARTH	41	2	DON JUAN	1	36	5
BY GUSTS AND MANY A SPARKLING HEARTH WAS BRIGHT . . .	94	2	DON JUAN	1	135	3

HEARTHSTONE
TO FIND OUR HEARTHSTONE TURN'D INTO A TOMB	301	2	DON JUAN	3	51	5
WHATE'ER OF PEACE ABOUT OUR HEARTHSTONE CLINGS	338	2	DON JUAN	3	107	5

HEARTLESS
AND HEARTLESS DAUGHTERS--WORN--AND PALE--AND POOR	15	2	DON JUAN	D	11	6

HEART-QUAKE
EACH KISS A HEART-QUAKE--FOR A KISS'S STRENGTH	254	2	DON JUAN	2	186	7
WITH SOME SLIGHT HEART-QUAKE OF DOMESTIC TREASON-- . . .	370	3	DON JUAN	13	26	5

HEART'S
ALFONSO POMMELL'D TO HIS HEART'S DESIRE	122	2	DON JUAN	1	184	4
MY SHAME AND SORROW DEEP IN MY HEART'S CORE	132	2	DON JUAN	1	195	4
THAT SPRING-DEW OF THE SPIRIT THE HEART'S RAIN	250	2	DON JUAN	2	178	4
AND TURN'D HER PURE HEART'S PUREST BLOOD TO TEARS . . .	274	2	DON JUAN	3	1	8
AND SWEPT AS 'TWERE ACROSS THEIR HEART'S DELIGHT . . .	355	2	DON JUAN	4	21	3
AND THE HEART'S DEW OF PAIN SPRANG FAST AND CHILLY . .	58	3	DON JUAN	6	105	7

HEARTS
OF HUMAN HEARTS THAN ALL THE LONG ARRAY	84	2	DON JUAN	1	116	5
OR BREAKS THEIR HOPES OR HEARTS OR HEADS OR NECKS . .	172	2	DON JUAN	2	31	6
THEIR HEARTS THE FLOWER FROM WHENCE THE HONEY SPRUNG . .	254	2	DON JUAN	2	187	8
TAUGHT TO CONCEAL THEIR BURSTING HEARTS DESPOND . . .	263	2	DON JUAN	2	200	4
THEIR HEARTS THE STARS THEIR NUPTIAL TORCHES SHED . .	265	2	DON JUAN	2	204	2
AND BRING OUR HEARTS BACK TO THEIR STARTING-POST . .	286	2	DON JUAN	3	21	8
FOR WITHOUT HEARTS THERE IS NO HOME--AND FELT . . .	302	2	DON JUAN	3	52	2
OUR HEARTS FIRST IN THE DEPTHS OF LETHE'S SPRING . .	346	2	DON JUAN	4	4	5
PURE BLOOD TO STAGNATE THEIR GREAT HEARTS TO FAIL . .	348	2	DON JUAN	4	9	2
NO NOVELS E'ER HAD SET THEIR YOUNG HEARTS BLEEDING . .	354	2	DON JUAN	4	19	4
WHEN TWO YOUNG HEARTS ARE POUR'D IN ONE ANOTHER . . .	357	2	DON JUAN	4	26	5
WHICH COLDER HEARTS ENDURE TILL THEY ARE LAID . . .	382	2	DON JUAN	4	71	4
MOVES--FEMALE HEARTS ARE SUCH A GENIAL SOIL	480	2	DON JUAN	5	120	3
AND HANDS OBEY--OUR HEARTS ARE STILL OUR OWN	484	2	DON JUAN	5	127	8
IF HEARTS LAY ON THE LEFT SIDE OR THE RIGHT	485	2	DON JUAN	5	128	5
BUT WOMEN WITH THEIR HEARTS OR HEAVEN KNOWS WHAT . .	7	3	DON JUAN	6	2	8
TRIMMED EITHER HEADS OR HEARTS TO DECORATE	13	3	DON JUAN	6	14	4
MEN'S HEARTS AGAINST WHOLE MILLIONS WHEN THEIR TRADE . .	102	3	DON JUAN	7	69	6
THE HEARTS OF THE HEROIC ON A CHARGE	103	3	DON JUAN	7	71	7
STRUCK FOR AN INSTANT ON THE HEARTS OF MEN	111	3	DON JUAN	7	87	3
INTO THE HEARTS OF THOSE WHO FOUGHT TILL NOW	137	3	DON JUAN	8	49	4
SNATCH WHEN DESPAIR MAKES HUMAN HEARTS LESS PLIANT . .	138	3	DON JUAN	8	51	4
BY HABIT TO WHAT THEIR OWN HEARTS ABHOR--	143	3	DON JUAN	8	62	6
CORRUPTION COULD NOT MAKE THEIR HEARTS HER SOIL . . .	145	3	DON JUAN	8	67	4
READ YOUR OWN HEARTS AND IRELAND'S PRESENT STORY . .	174	3	DON JUAN	8	125	7
AND PARTS AND HEARTS HE DANCED AND SUNG AND HAD . . .	292	3	DON JUAN	11	47	2
AFTER MALE LOSS OF TIME AND HEARTS AND BETS	333	3	DON JUAN	12	36	3
AND CHANGED AS QUICKLY AS HEARTS AFTER MARRIAGE . . .	379	3	DON JUAN	13	46	4
AT LEAST OF THOSE WHOSE EYES ARE IN THEIR HEARTS . .	390	3	DON JUAN	13	67	6
ALL SONG AND SENTIMENT WHOSE HEARTS WERE SET	398	3	DON JUAN	13	85	7
WHAT ICEBERGS IN THE HEARTS OF MIGHTY MEN	455	3	DON JUAN	14	102	3
AND ALSO HEARTS IF THERE BE TRUTH IN LAYS	506	3	DON JUAN	16	14	8

```
                                                      PAGE VOL     CANTO STANZA LN
HEARTS'
   TO THEIR OWN HEARTS' MOST SWEET SOCIETY  . . . . . .  . 348  2 DON JUAN  4      8   2
HEART'S-BLOOD
   POURS FORTH AT LAST THE HEART'S-BLOOD TURN'D TO TEARS  . 270  2 DON JUAN  2    214   7
HEART-STRINGS
   WHEN ALL THE HEART-STRINGS LIKE WILD HORSES PULL  . . .  59  3 DON JUAN  6    107   4
HEARTY
   THE LITTLE FELLOW REALLY LOOK'D QUITE HEARTY  . . . . . 388  2 DON JUAN  4     81   5
   WITH ONE GOOD HEARTY CURSE I VENT MY GALL  . . . . . .   17  3 DON JUAN  6     22   3
   SHADE OF LEONIDAS WHO FOUGHT SO HEARTY  . . . . . . .  108  3 DON JUAN  7     82   3
   MY WORDS AT LEAST ARE MORE SINCERE AND HEARTY  . . . . 195  3 DON JUAN  9     26   3
HEAT
   OUT THROUGH A FEVER CAUSED BY ITS OWN HEAT  . . . . . . 168  2 DON JUAN  2     22   2
   FAMINE DESPAIR COLD THIRST AND HEAT HAD DONE  . . . . . 210  2 DON JUAN  2    102   1
   I NEVER THINK ABOUT IT IN A HEAT)  . . . . . . . . .    87  3 DON JUAN  7     42   6
   IN MORE DESTROYING NATURE AND THE HEAT  . . . . . . . . 152  3 DON JUAN  8     82   6
   TO MAKE A TWILIGHT IN JUST AS SOLMS HEAT IS  . . . . .  217  3 DON JUAN  9     69   7
   COUNTRIES OF GREATER HEAT BUT LESSER SUCTION  . . . . . 262  3 DON JUAN 10     76   4
HEATED
   BLOOD UNTIL HEATED--AND EVEN THERE HIS OWN  . . . . .   140  3 DON JUAN  8     55   7
   FOR THEY WERE HEATED BY THE HOPE OF GAIN  . . . . . .   163  3 DON JUAN  8    103   6
   FOLLOWED HIS VEINS NO LONGER COLD BUT HEATED  . . . . . 559  3 DON JUAN 16    119   4
HEATHEN
   THE HEATHEN ALSO THOUGH WITH LESSER LATITUDE  . . . . .  11  3 DON JUAN  6     11   2
   WHEN THEY SURVEY WITH CHRISTIAN EYES OR HEATHEN  . . .   24  3 DON JUAN  6     37   7
HEATHENISH
   THIS HEATHENISH CROSS RESTORED THE BREED AGAIN  . . . .  53  3 DON JUAN  1     58   1
   AS E'ER HELD HOURI IN THAT HEATHENISH HEAVEN  . . . . .  77  2 DON JUAN  1    104   4
   AND HENCE SOME HEATHENISH PHILOSOPHERS  . . . . . . .  219  3 DON JUAN  9     73   7
HEAVE
   AND IF WE NOW AND THEN A SIGH MUST HEAVE  . . . . . . . 164  2 DON JUAN  2     15   5
   TO HEAVE INTO THE DEEP WITH THOSE BEFORE  . . . . . . . 209  2 DON JUAN  2    101   6
   A RUSSIAN VESSEL E'ER WOULD HEAVE IN SIGHT  . . . . .   73  3 DON JUAN  7     13   3
   OF EMPIRES HEAVE BUT LIKE SOME PASSING WAVES  . . . . . 500  3 DON JUAN 15     99   8
HEAVED
   A SIGH FROM HIS HEAVED BOSOM--AND HERS TOO  . . . . . . 216  2 DON JUAN  2    114   8
   NEATH WHICH HER BREAST HEAVED LIKE A LITTLE BILLOW  . . 311  2 DON JUAN  3     70   4
   WHILE STILL A FLUTTERING SIGH GULBEYAZ HEAVED  . . . .  500  2 DON JUAN  5    155   6
   THROUGH THE HEAVED BREAST THE DREAM OF SOME FAR SHORE  . 40  2 DON JUAN  6     67   5
HEAVEN
   AND SEEM'D AT LEAST IN THE RIGHT ROAD TO HEAVEN  . . .   48  2 DON JUAN  1     49   6
   BUT HEAVEN FORBID THAT SUCH A THOUGHT SHOULD CROSS  . .  67  2 DON JUAN  1     84   2
   AS E'ER HELD HOURI IN THAT HEATHENISH HEAVEN  . . . .   77  2 DON JUAN  1    104   4
   FIRE WHICH PROMETHEUS FILCH'D FOR US FROM HEAVEN  . . .  90  2 DON JUAN  1    127   8
   UNLESS THE WORLD AND HEAVEN ITSELF BE BLIND  . . . . . 112  2 DON JUAN  1    165  V4
   STATE STATION HEAVEN MANKIND'S MY OWN ESTEEM  . . . . . 130  2 DON JUAN  1    193   7
   THOUGH HEAVEN KNOWS HOW IT EVER FOUND A LODGEMENT  . . 144  2 DON JUAN  1    215   8
   I WOULD TO HEAVEN THAT I WERE SO MUCH CLAY--  . . . . . 156  2 DON JUAN  1   V  8   1
   THANK HEAVEN I'VE GOT NO METAPHOR QUITE READY  . . . . 160  2 DON JUAN  2      6   7
   SOONER SHALL HEAVEN KISS EARTH--(HERE HE FELL SICKER)  . 167  2 DON JUAN  2     20   1
   THERE WAS NO LIGHT IN HEAVEN BUT A FEW STARS  . . . . . 183  2 DON JUAN  2     51   5
   AND ALL THE REST WERE THIN ENOUGH HEAVEN KNOWS  . . . . 199  2 DON JUAN  2     80   2
   TO TASTE OF HEAVEN--IF THIS BE TRUE INDEED  . . . . .  202  2 DON JUAN  2     86   7
   HEAVEN KNOWS WHAT CASH HE GOT OR BLOOD HE SPILT  . . . 223  2 DON JUAN  2    127   5
   IT OPEN'D HALF THE TURNPIKE-GATES TO HEAVEN--  . . . .  225  2 DON JUAN  2    131   7
   AND THINKS HEAVEN BRIGHTER EVEN THAN NEWTON'S PAGE  . . 242  2 DON JUAN  2    163  V7
   HEAVEN KNOWS--IT MAY BE NEPTUNE PAN OR JOVE  . . . . . 246  2 DON JUAN  2    170   8
   HEAVEN KNOWS HOW LONG--NO DOUBT THEY NEVER RECKON'D  . 254  2 DON JUAN  2    187   2
   AND NOW AND THEN HER EYE TO HEAVEN IS CAST  . . . . .  260  2 DON JUAN  2    195   5
   BUT THEN HER TEETH AND THEN OH HEAVEN HER EYES  . . . . 268  2 DON JUAN  2    210   4
   THE HEART IS LIKE THE SKY A PART OF HEAVEN  . . . . .  270  2 DON JUAN  2    214   1
   HAVE SUNG OF HEAVEN AND HELL OR MARRIAGE ARE  . . . . . 281  2 DON JUAN  3     10   2
   THAT HEAVENLIEST HOUR OF HEAVEN IS WORTHIEST THEE  . . 334  2 DON JUAN  3    101   8
   OF GETTING INTO HEAVEN THE SHORTEST WAY  . . . . . . . 336  2 DON JUAN  3    104   5
   LIKE LUCIFER WHEN HURL'D FROM HEAVEN FOR SINNING  . . . 344  2 DON JUAN  4      1   5
   OH POWERS OF HEAVEN WHAT DARK EYE MEETS SHE THERE  . . 363  2 DON JUAN  4     35   7
   IN VAIN THE DEWS OF HEAVEN DESCEND ABOVE  . . . . . .  382  2 DON JUAN  4     70   7
   THE TUMULUS--OF WHOM HEAVEN KNOWS 'T MAY BE  . . . . . 385  2 DON JUAN  4     76   6
   THEY SAY YOUR STOCKINGS ARE SO (HEAVEN KNOWS WHY  . . . 404  2 DON JUAN  4    110   4
   HAD DECK'D HER OUT IN ALL THE HUES OF HEAVEN  . . . . . 407  2 DON JUAN  4    114   4
   HEAVEN HELP THE SCHOLAR WHOM HIS FORTUNE SENDS HERE  . 423  2 DON JUAN  5     24   4
   WHAT SPEAKS OF HEAVEN SHOULD BY NO MEANS BE BRITTLE  . 444  2 DON JUAN  5     59   3
   MIGHT LEAD TO HEAVEN KNOWS WHERE BUT IN THIS ONE  . . . 449  2 DON JUAN  5     65   3
   THE VERGE OF HEAVEN AND IN HER LARGE EYES WROUGHT  . . 473  2 DON JUAN  5    108   6
   SHE WAS A SULTAN'S BRIDE (THANK HEAVEN NOT MINE)  . . . 475  2 DON JUAN  5    111   8
   IT TEACHES--HEAVEN KNOWS ONLY WHAT IT TEACHES  . . . .  491  2 DON JUAN  5    138   7
   I WISH TO HEAVEN HE WOULD NOT SHINE TILL MORNING  . . . 494  2 DON JUAN  5    145   2
   AS THOSE WHOSE WIVES HAVE MADE THEM FIT FOR HEAVEN  . . 500  2 DON JUAN  5    154   8
   BUT WOMEN WITH THEIR HEARTS OR HEAVEN KNOWS WHAT  . . .   7  3 DON JUAN  6      2   8
   THESE ARE BENEATH THE CANOPY OF HEAVEN  . . . . . . .   18  3 DON JUAN  6     25   1
   INSTEAD OF HEAVEN THEY STUMBLED BACKWARDS O'ER  . . . . 121  3 DON JUAN  8     20   7
   WHICH STIFFENED HEAVEN) AS IF HE WISHED FOR DAY--  . .  121  3 DON JUAN  8     21   7
   HOWEVER HEAVEN KNOWS HOW THE FATE WHO LEVELS  . . . .  134  3 DON JUAN  8     44   4
   WITH DISTANT SHRIEKS WERE HEARD HEAVEN TO UPBRAID--  . 146  3 DON JUAN  8     69   5
   IN HEAVEN I KNOW NOT NOR PRETEND TO GUESS  . . . . . . 167  3 DON JUAN  8    112   2
   AS THOUGH THERE WERE ONE HEAVEN AND NONE BESIDES--  . . 168  3 DON JUAN  8    114   6
   WHEREAS IF ALL BE TRUE WE HEAR OF HEAVEN  . . . . . .  168  3 DON JUAN  8    114   7
   HEAVEN HELP ME  I'M BUT LITTLE OF A PARSON  . . . . .  179  3 DON JUAN  8    134   4
   BUT HEAVEN AS CASSIO SAYS IS ABOVE ALL--  . . . . . .  192  3 DON JUAN  9     19   1
```

	PAGE	VOL	CANTO	STANZA	LN
HEAVEN (CONTINUED)					
BUT WENT TO HEAVEN IN AS SINCERE A WAY	242	3 DON JUAN 10	35	2
US LAND ON EARTH WILL DO NO LESS IN HEAVEN	242	3 DON JUAN 10	36	V8
THE HUMBLEST INDIVIDUAL UNDER HEAVEN	309	3 DON JUAN 11	82	3
IS HEAVEN AND HEAVEN IS LOVE--SO SINGS THE BARD	322	3 DON JUAN 12	13	2
IS HEAVEN AND HEAVEN IS LOVE--SO SINGS THE BARD	322	3 DON JUAN 12	13	2
AND AS FOR HEAVEN BEING LOVE WHY NOT SAY HONEY	322	3 DON JUAN 12	14	7
IS WAX HEAVEN IS NOT LOVE 'TIS MATRIMONY	322	3 DON JUAN 12	14	8
BESIDES THE MOST SUBLIME OF--HEAVEN KNOWS WHAT ELSE--	356	3 DON JUAN 12	88	5
BUT HEAVEN MUST BE DIVERTED ITS DIVERSION	377	3 DON JUAN 13	41	1
THE WIND IS WINGED FROM ONE POINT OF HEAVEN	388	3 DON JUAN 13	63	2
WITH WHICH THE WINDS OF HEAVEN CAN CLAIM ACCORD	402	3 DON JUAN 13	93	3
AND HARDLY HEAVEN--BECAUSE IT NEVER ENDS	407	3 DON JUAN 13	105	3
BUT EVEN THIS IS DIFFICULT HEAVEN KNOWS	421	3 DON JUAN 14	25	2
AND TAKE AS MANY HEROES AS HEAVEN PLEASES	459	3 DON JUAN 15	9	8
HEAVEN KNOWS BUT ADELINE'S MALICIOUS EYES	490	3 DON JUAN 15	78	7
I WISH TO HEAVEN THEY WOULD NOT LOOK SO GRIM	499	3 DON JUAN 15	97	6
OR EARTH BENEATH OR HEAVEN OR T'OTHER PLACE	510	3 DON JUAN 16	23	2
HEAVEN SAIN HIM FAIR OR FOUL	520	3 DON JUAN 16	L 6	6
FOR FEAR WE SHOULD SUPPOSE US QUITE IN HEAVEN	525	3 DON JUAN 16	49	8
HEAVEN AND HIS FRIENDS KNEW THAT A PRIVATE LIFE	536	3 DON JUAN 16	74	1
I SATE NEXT THAT O'ERWHELMING SON OF HEAVEN	539	3 DON JUAN 16	81	6
HEAVEN-KISSING					
NEW LIGHTED ON A HEAVEN-KISSING HILL	215	3 DON JUAN 9	66	2
WITH YOUTH AND HEALTH ALL KISSES ARE HEAVEN-KISSING	215	3 DON JUAN 9	66	8
WE HAVE JUST LIT ON A HEAVEN-KISSING HILL	224	3 DON JUAN 9	85	4
HEAVENLIEST					
THAT HEAVENLIEST HOUR OF HEAVEN IS WORTHIEST THEE	334	2 DON JUAN 3	101	8
HEAVENLY					
FORBID BY HEAVENLY FINED BY HUMAN LAWS	113	2 DON JUAN 1	167	3
IT CHANGED OF COURSE A HEAVENLY CAMELEON	205	2 DON JUAN 2	92	1
ON MOUNTAINS TOPS MORE HEAVENLY WHITE THAN HER	314	2 DON JUAN 3	76	4
BUT BRAVELY RUSHED ON HIS FIRST HEAVENLY NIGHT	168	3 DON JUAN 8	114	3
BUT WITH A HEAVENLY RAPTURE ON HIS FACE	169	3 DON JUAN 8	116	1
THE UNBOUNDED HOPE AND HEAVENLY IGNORANCE	554	3 DON JUAN 16	108	2
HEAVEN'S					
IN HEAVEN'S NAME DON ALFONSO WHAT D'YE MEAN	98	2 DON JUAN 1	142	2
FLY JUAN FLY FOR HEAVEN'S SAKE--NOT A WORD--	121	2 DON JUAN 1	182	3
ONE GLANCE ON HIM AND SAID HEAVEN'S WILL BE DONE	202	2 DON JUAN 2	87	6
SAID IN HEAVEN'S NAME LET'S GET SOME SUPPER NOW	437	2 DON JUAN 5	47	7
THE EAR FAR MORE THAN THUNDER FOR HEAVEN'S FLASHES	115	2 DON JUAN 8	6	7
MAKES MOUNTAINS PASSABLE AND BY HEAVEN'S BLESSING	215	3 DON JUAN 9	66	V7
HEAVEN'S FREEHOLDS IN A SORT OF DOOMSDAY SCROLL	242	3 DON JUAN 10	35	5
HEAVEN'S BRANDY--THOUGH OUR BRAIN CAN HARDLY BEAR IT	269	3 DON JUAN 11	2	8
HEAVENS					
THE HEAVENS AND EARTH AND AIR SEEM'D MADE FOR THEM	351	2 DON JUAN 4	13	2
HEAVES					
AND HEAVES A LONELY SUBTERRAQUEOUS SIGH	445	3 DON JUAN 14	81	3
HEAVIEST					
FORETELLS THE HEAVIEST TEMPEST IT DISPLAYS	61	2 DON JUAN 1	73	3
AND LED THEM BACK INTO THE HEAVIEST FIRE	133	3 DON JUAN 8	41	8
WHICH ARE THE HEAVIEST THAT OUR HISTORY MENTIONS	137	3 DON JUAN 8	49	8
HEAVINESS					
HE FELT THAT CHILLING HEAVINESS OF HEART	167	2 DON JUAN 2	21	1
HEAVING					
OR HEAVING WHELM THE HELPLESS CARAVAN	373	2 DON JUAN 4	55	7
TO HEAVING BACK THE PORTAL FOLDS IT SCARED	463	2 DON JUAN 5	90	4
HEAVING BETWEEN THIS WORLD AND WORLDS BEYOND	555	3 DON JUAN 16	110	2
HEAVY					
QUICK THICK AND HEAVY--AS A THUNDER-SHOWER	110	2 DON JUAN 1	161	8
WITH LOVE AND WAR A HEAVY GALE AT SEA	135	2 DON JUAN 1	200	3
NOUGHT BUT THE HEAVY SEA AND COMING NIGHT	178	2 DON JUAN 2	41	8
BUT E'ER TWAS WELL BEGUN--A HEAVY SEA	183	2 DON JUAN 2	50	V2
AND HOW THIS HEAVY FAINTNESS PASS'D AWAY	214	2 DON JUAN 2	111	5
AT LEAST IT IS A HEAVY SOUND TO ME	237	2 DON JUAN 2	152	6
A LITTLE HEAVY BUT NO LESS DIVINE	328	2 DON JUAN 3	91	2
THE LONG YEAR LINK'D WITH HEAVY DAY ON DAY	350	2 DON JUAN 4	11	5
STRUCK NOT ON MEMORY THOUGH A HEAVY ACHE	378	2 DON JUAN 4	62	5
A HEAVY PRICE MUST ALL PAY WHO THUS ERR	383	2 DON JUAN 4	73	6
AT LEAST ONE OF THEM--OH THE HEAVY NIGHT	18	3 DON JUAN 6	24	2
SOMETIMES A LITTLE HEAVY ON THE BACKS	54	3 DON JUAN 6	96	7
AND GALLED THE RUSSIANS WITH A HEAVY FIRE	82	3 DON JUAN 7	31	4
WHEN AFTER A GOOD DEAL OF HEAVY FIRING	125	3 DON JUAN 8	27	7
AT TIMES WOULD CURDLE O'ER SOME HEAVY GROAN	140	3 DON JUAN 8	55	8
WITH STEPS THAT TROD AS HEAVY YET UNHEARD	510	3 DON JUAN 16	21	4
HEBE					
THE FULL GROWN HEBE OF FITZ-FULKE WHOSE MIND	525	3 DON JUAN 16	49	2
HEBREW					
OF MOOR OR HEBREW BLOOD HE TRACED HIS SOURCE	26	2 DON JUAN 1	9	3
SHE LIKED THE ENGLISH AND THE HEBREW TONGUE	28	2 DON JUAN 1	14	1
'TIS STRANGE--THE HEBREW NOUN WHICH MEANS I AM	28	2 DON JUAN 1	14	7
'TIS WRITTEN IN THE HEBREW CHRONICLE	113	2 DON JUAN 1	168	2
HEBREWS					
THE HOWLING HEBREWS OF CYBELE'S PRIEST--	297	3 DON JUAN 11	58	8
HECATOMB					
A HECATOMB OF SUITORS WITH DEVOTION	434	3 DON JUAN 14	55	6
HECLA					
IT MAKES MY BLOOD BOIL LIKE THE SPRINGS OF HECLA	497	3 DON JUAN 15	92	7
HECLA'S					
MIGHT SCATTER FIRE THROUGH ICE LIKE HECLA'S FLAME	254	3 DON JUAN 10	59	8

```
                                                                PAGE VOL    CANTO STANZA LN
HECTIC
    A PURPLE HECTIC PLAY'D LIKE DYING DAY . . . . . . . . 234  2 DON JUAN   2     147    2
    A BEAUTY AT THE SEASON'S CLOSE GROWN HECTIC . . . . . 309  2 DON JUAN   3      66    1
    HECTIC AND BRIEF AS SUMMER'S DAY NIGH DONE . . . . . 229  3 DON JUAN  10       8    6
    CONSTRUCTION ASYOUR CURES FOR HECTIC PHTHISICS . . . . 349  3 DON JUAN  12      72    3
HECTOR
    HER FRIENDS LIKE THE SAD FAMILY OF HECTOR  . . . . . 182  3 DON JUAN   8     141    3
HE'D
    SWORE LUSTILY HE'D BE REVENGED THIS NIGHT . . . . . . 122  2 DON JUAN   1     184    5
    AS WHEN HE SWORE BY GOD HE'D SELL HIS SHIRT . . . . . 154  2 DON JUAN   1    V  5    3
    IN SPAIN HE'D MAKE A BALLAD OR ROMANCE ON  . . . . . 320  2 DON JUAN   3      86    3
    IN GERMANY THE PEGASUS HE'D PRANCE ON . . . . . . . . 320  2 DON JUAN   3      86    5
    IN ITALY HE'D APE THE TRECENTISTI . . . . . . . . . 320  2 DON JUAN   3      86    7
    IN GREECE HE'D SING SOME SORT OF HYMN LIKE THIS T'YE . . 320  2 DON JUAN   3      86    8
    THAT STILL HE'D WED WITH SUCH OR SUCH A LADY . . . . 469  3 DON JUAN  15      30    7
HEDGE
    NOW THAT THE PUBLIC HEDGE HATH SCARCE A STAKE . . . . 357  3 DON JUAN  12      89    2
    HE CLEAR'D HEDGE DITCH AND DOUBLE POST AND RAIL  . . . 424  3 DON JUAN  14      33    2
HEED
    AS HE BEFORE HAD DONE  HE DID NOT HEED  . . . . . . 170  3 DON JUAN   8     117    4
HEEDED
    SO THAT THE FEW WHO MET HIM HARDLY HEEDED  . . . . . 300  2 DON JUAN   3      49    3
    HER HANDMAIDS TENDED BUT SHE HEEDED NOT . . . . . . . 379  2 DON JUAN   4      64    1
HEEDLESS
    IN WHICH THE HEEDLESS GENTLEMAN WHO GADS . . . . . . 273  3 DON JUAN  11      11    5
    HEEDLESS OF PRICKS BECAUSE IT WAS OBTUSE . . . . . . 565  3 DON JUAN  17       6    6
HEEL
    SHE GAVE A HEEL AND THEN A LURCH TO PORT . . . . . . 183  2 DON JUAN   2      51    7
    THEY NEARLY REACH'D HER HEEL AND IN HER AIR . . . . . 217  2 DON JUAN   2     116    6
    HER HAIR'S LONG AUBURN WAVES DOWN TO HER HEEL . . . . 313  2 DON JUAN   3      73    1
    OVER A HEAP OF BODIES FELT HIS HEEL  . . . . . . . 153  3 DON JUAN   8      83    2
    WITH CLOWNISH HEEL YOUR POPULAR CIRCULATION . . . . . 200  3 DON JUAN   9      35    7
HEIGHT
    SHE DREW UP TO HER HEIGHT AS IF TO SHOW  . . . . . . 367  2 DON JUAN   4      43    6
    DREW HIMSELF UP TO HIS FULL HEIGHT AGAIN . . . . . . 470  2 DON JUAN   5     102    6
    SOME THOUGHT HER RATHER MASCULINE IN HEIGHT . . . . . 23  3 DON JUAN   6      35    7
    BUT ALWAYS AT A MOST PROVOKING HEIGHT-- . . . . . . 44  3 DON JUAN   6      76    8
    OF DEWY DAWN WOUND SLOWLY ROUND EACH HEIGHT . . . . . 49  3 DON JUAN   6      86    6
    A BOROUGH IS COMPRISED ALONG THE HEIGHT  . . . . . . 71  3 DON JUAN   7      10    2
    SOME HUNDRED FEET IN HEIGHT NOT TO SAY MILES . . . . 201  3 DON JUAN   9      38    7
    TO MARSHALL ONWARDS TO THE DELPHIAN HEIGHT . . . . . 467  3 DON JUAN  15      25   V5
HEIGHTENED
    HER EYE DILATED AND HER COLOUR HEIGHTENED  . . . . . 42  3 DON JUAN   6      72    8
HEIGHTENING
    IS BUT HEIGHTENING OF THE BEAU IDEAL . . . . . . . 269  2 DON JUAN   2     211    8
HEIR
    DYING INTESTATE JUAN WAS SOLE HEIR . . . . . . . . 42  2 DON JUAN   1      37    1
    YOU'D BETTER ASK OUR MISTRESS WHO'S HIS HEIR  . . . . 297  2 DON JUAN   3      43    6
    SO THAT THE HEIR APPARENT STILL WAS FOUND  . . . . . 499  2 DON JUAN   5     153    7
    AND LEFT AT LARGE LIKE A YOUNG HEIR TO MAKE  . . . . 127  3 DON JUAN   8      32    2
    BETWEEN THE GAPING HEIR AND GNAWING GOUT . . . . . . 376  3 DON JUAN  13      40    8
    TO BEAR A SON AND HEIR--AND ONE MISCARRIAGE . . . . . 434  3 DON JUAN  14      56    8
    SOME HEIR TO A LARGE PROPERTY SOME FRIEND  . . . . . 470  3 DON JUAN  15      33    2
    OF ONE OR BOTH OF WHOM HE SEEMS THE HEIR . . . . . . 481  3 DON JUAN  15      59    8
    WHEN AN HEIR IS BORN HE IS HEARD TO MOURN  . . . . . 519  3 DON JUAN  16    L  4    1
    FOR HE IS YET THE CHURCH'S HEIR . . . . . . . . . 520  3 DON JUAN  16    L  5    3
HEIRESS
    THE GREATEST HEIRESS OF THE EASTERN ISLES  . . . . . 224  2 DON JUAN   2     128    2
    UPON AN HEIRESS OR HIS NEIGHBOUR'S BRIDE . . . . . . 304  3 DON JUAN  11      71    2
    I'VE KNOWN THEM COURT AN HEIRESS FOR THEIR LOVER . . . 331  3 DON JUAN  12      33    4
    FOR THIS AN HEIRESS AND FOR THAT A BEAUTY  . . . . . 471  3 DON JUAN  15      34    2
HEIRESSES
    SOME HEIRESSES HAVE BIT AT SHARPERS' HOOKS . . . . . 308  3 DON JUAN  11      81    3
HEIRS
    PRODUCED HER DON MORE HEIRS AT LOVE THAN LAW . . . . 53  2 DON JUAN   1      58    8
    AND WONDERS WHY THE DEVIL HE GOT HEIRS  . . . . . . 75  2 DON JUAN   1     100    8
    IN THAT TO WHICH THE LAW MAKES THEM SOLE HEIRS . . . . 11  3 DON JUAN   6      10    8
    LET SPENDTHRIFTS' HEIRS ENQUIRE OF YOURS--WHO'S WISER . . 321  3 DON JUAN  12      11    8
    HAS CAUSE TO WISH HER SIRE HAD HAD MALE HEIRS  . . . . 331  3 DON JUAN  12      33    8
HELD
    AS E'ER HELD HOURI IN THAT HEATHENISH HEAVEN  . . . . 77  2 DON JUAN   1     104    4
    THE HAND WHICH STILL HELD JUAN'S BY DEGREES . . . . . 81  2 DON JUAN   1     111    1
    AND HELD HER TONGUE HER VOICE WAS GROWN SO WEAK . . . 81  2 DON JUAN   1     112    8
    THE VESSEL SWAM YET STILL SHE HELD HER OWN . . . . . 176  2 DON JUAN   2      38    4
    AND THEN HELD OUT HIS JUGULAR AND WRIST  . . . . . . 197  2 DON JUAN   2      76    8
    AND PATIENT SPIRIT HELD ALOOF HIS FATE  . . . . . . 203  2 DON JUAN   2      88    4
    THE BOY EXPIRED--THE FATHER HELD THE CLAY  . . . . . 204  2 DON JUAN   2      90    1
    THAT E'ER BY PRECIOUS METAL WAS HELD IN  . . . . . . 312  2 DON JUAN   3      71    8
    AND WISH'D THAT OTHERS HELD THE SAME OPINION . . . . 345  2 DON JUAN   4       3    2
    HAD HELD TILL NOW HER SOFT AND MILKY WAY . . . . . . 375  2 DON JUAN   4      57    5
    ON HER SIRE'S ARM WHICH UNTIL NOW SCARCE HELD  . . . . 375  2 DON JUAN   4      58    7
    SHE DIED BUT NOT ALONE SHE HELD WITHIN  . . . . . . 382  2 DON JUAN   4      70    1
    FOR SORROW O'ER EACH SENSE HELD STERN COMMAND  . . . . 396  2 DON JUAN   4      95    2
    POLYGAMY MAY WELL BE HELD IN DREAD . . . . . . . . 12  3 DON JUAN   6      12    3
    OF DUDU THOUGH THEY HELD THEIR TONGUES FROM DEFERENCE . . 31  3 DON JUAN   6      50    8
    OF PORCELAIN HELD IN THE FETTERED FLOWERS  . . . . . 54  3 DON JUAN   6      97    7
    AND WHEN TO HOLD ITS TONGUE NOW HELD IT TILL . . . . 61  3 DON JUAN   6     110    7
    WHO HELD THE PLACE AND TO ASSIST THE FOE'S . . . . . 71  3 DON JUAN   7      10    8
    NEW BATTERIES WERE ERECTED AND WAS HELD  . . . . . . 92  3 DON JUAN   7      51    1
    A PREACHER HAD HELD FORTH (WHO NOBLY SPURNED . . . . 99  3 DON JUAN   7      64    5
```

353

354

HELPED
    THE NEGRO BABA HELPED A LITTLE TOO 456   2 DON JUAN 5   78   5
    WITH THE SAME THOUGHT THE TWO WORDS HAVE HELPED OUT . . . 323 3 DON JUAN 12   15   4
HELPLESS
    WITH TIME AND TRIALS AND THOSE HELPLESS EYES   15   2 DON JUAN D   11   5
    WHO CANNOT LEAVE ALONE OUR HELPLESS CLAY 56   2 DON JUAN 1   63   3
    DEAR IS THE HELPLESS CREATURE WE DEFEND 90   2 DON JUAN 1   126   6
    SO LONELY LOVING HELPLESS AND THE HOUR 258   2 DON JUAN 2   192   2
    SO GENTLE STIRLESS HELPLESS AND UNMOVED 261   2 DON JUAN 2   197   3
    HIS MAN WAS FLOOR'D AND HELPLESS AT HIS FOOT 370   2 DON JUAN 4   49   5
    OR HEAVING WHELM THE HELPLESS CARAVAN 373   2 DON JUAN 4   55   7
    CHILD OR AN AGED HELPLESS MAN OR TWO-- 174   3 DON JUAN 8   124   4
    FOR SHE WAS HOMELESS HOUSELESS HELPLESS ALL 182   3 DON JUAN 8   141   2
    FROM FOREIGN YOKE TO FREE THE HELPLESS NATIVE-- 363   3 DON JUAN 13   10   4
HELVOETSLUYS
    FROM THENCE TO HOLLAND'S HAGUE AND HELVOETSLUYS 256   3 DON JUAN 10   63   1
HEM
    THY GARMENT'S HEM WITH TRANSPORT CAN IT BE 364   2 DON JUAN 4   38   6
    SHE SIGNED TO BABA WHO FIRST KISSED THE HEM 466   2 DON JUAN 5   96   6
HEN
    THE OLD HEN--BY RUNNING HEADLONG TO THE WATER 564   3 DON JUAN 17   4   8
HENCE
    EVEN SEVEN YEARS HENCE IT WOULD NOT BE TOO LATE 67   2 DON JUAN 1   85   4
    PERHAPS THEY'LL HAVE SOME MORE ABOUT A YEAR HENCE . . . 135   2 DON JUAN 1   199   8
    TO ALL THE BROTHER TARS WHO MAY HAVE NEED HENCE 171   2 DON JUAN 2   29   5
    ALL ONE AN HOUR HENCE JUAN ANSWER'D NO 175   2 DON JUAN 2   36   2
    HENCE ALL THIS RICE MEAT DANCING WINE AND FIDDLING . . 295   2 DON JUAN 3   39   1
    HENCE MY OLD COMET GIVE THE STARS DUE WARNING-- . . . 494   2 DON JUAN 5   145   4
    AND HENCE SOME HEATHENISH PHILOSOPHERS 219   3 DON JUAN 9   73   7
    BUT ASK HIM WHAT HE THINKS OF IT A YEAR HENCE 271   3 DON JUAN 11   7   8
    THEIR FEE BUT ERE THE WATERED WHEELS MAY HISS HENCE . . 379   3 DON JUAN 13   46   7
    AND HENCE HIGH LIFE IS OFT A DREARY VOID 444   3 DON JUAN 14   79   1
    AND HENCE ARISE THE WOES OF SENTIMENT 444   3 DON JUAN 14   79   6
HENCEFORTH
    AND HENCEFORTH FOUND HIMSELF MORE GAILY CLASSED 300   3 DON JUAN 11   64   6
    AND POSITIVELY HENCEFORTH NO TEMPTATION 498   3 DON JUAN 15   94   2
HENCEFORWARD
    START NOT STILL CHASTER READER--SHE'LL BE NICE HENCEFORWARD 86 2 DON JUAN 1   120   2
HENCHMAN
    UNTO HIS NEAREST FOLLOWER OR HENCHMAN 274   3 DON JUAN 11   13   7
    WAS ALMOST WORTHY TO BECOME HIS HENCHMAN 425   3 DON JUAN 14   34   V8
HENCOOPS
    AT HALF-PAST EIGHT O'CLOCK BOOMS HENCOOPS SPARS 183   2 DON JUAN 2   51   1
HENNA
    HER NAILS WERE TOUCH'D WITH HENNA BUT AGAIN 314   2 DON JUAN 3   75   6
    THE HENNA SHOULD BE DEEPLY DYED TO MAKE 314   2 DON JUAN 3   76   1
HEN-PECK'D
    INFORM US TRULY HAVE THEY NOT HEN-PECK'D YOU ALL 33   2 DON JUAN 1   22   8
HENRY
    AND THUS LORD HENRY WHO WAS CAUTIOUS AS 366   3 DON JUAN 13   16   1
    LORD HENRY ALSO LIKED TO BE SUPERIOR 367   3 DON JUAN 13   19   1
    AND THE LORD HENRY WAS A GREAT DEBATER 367   3 DON JUAN 13   20   7
    OF COURSERS ALSO SPAKE THEY HENRY RID 368   3 DON JUAN 13   23   5
    UPON HIS TALENT HENRY HAD NO DOUBTS 369   3 DON JUAN 13   24   5
    LORD HENRY AND THE LADY ADELINE 381   3 DON JUAN 13   50   1
    SIR HENRY SILVERCUP THE GREAT RACE-WINNER 399   3 DON JUAN 13   87   4
    LORD HENRY AND HIS LADY WERE THE HOSTS 404   3 DON JUAN 13   99   1
    LORD HENRY HEARD HER PLANS OF ARTLESS ART 438   3 DON JUAN 14   65   5
    LORD HENRY WALK'D INTO HIS CABINET 440   3 DON JUAN 14   68   2
    LORD HENRY SAID HIS MUFFIN WAS ILL BUTTERED 514   3 DON JUAN 16   31   4
    LORD HENRY WHO HAD NOW DISCUSSED HIS CHOCOLATE 515   3 DON JUAN 16   34   1
    THEN HENRY TURNED TO JUAN AND ADDRESSED 515   3 DON JUAN 16   35   1
    BUT ADD THE WORDS CRIED HENRY WHICH YOU MADE 517   3 DON JUAN 16   39   1
    BUT AS LORD HENRY WAS A CONNOISSEUR-- 528   3 DON JUAN 16   57   1
    LORD HENRY WISHED TO RAISE FOR A NEW PURCHASE 530   3 DON JUAN 16   60   2
    FOR HENRY WAS A SORT OF SABINE SHOWMAN 530   3 DON JUAN 16   60   8
    LORD HENRY WAS A JUSTICE AND THAT SCOUT 531   3 DON JUAN 16   62   6
    FOR THE LORD HENRY LINKED WITH DOGS AND HORSES 534   3 DON JUAN 16   68   2
    LORD HENRY WAS A GREAT ELECTIONEERER 534   3 DON JUAN 16   70   1
    ALL THIS (SAVE THE LAST STANZA) HENRY SAID 538   3 DON JUAN 16   77   1
    LORD HENRY AT HIS TABLE SHOULD ENDURE 543   3 DON JUAN 16   89   6
HENRY'S
    LORD HENRY'S MANSION WAS IN BLANK-BLANK SQUARE 369   3 DON JUAN 13   25   8
    AT HENRY'S MANSION THEN IN BLANK-BLANK SQUARE 370   3 DON JUAN 13   28   1
    THOUGH HE CAME IN HIS MIGHT WITH KING HENRY'S RIGHT . . 518   3 DON JUAN 16 L 2   1
    BY WHICH LORD HENRY'S GOOD TASTE WOULD GO FORTH IN . . 529   3 DON JUAN 16   59   6
HENS
    THEIR ARMS AS HENS THEIR WINGS ABOUT THEIR YOUNG . . . 101   3 DON JUAN 7   67   8
HEPHAESTION
    I AM NEITHER ALEXANDER NOR HEPHAESTION 189   3 DON JUAN 9   14   3
HERACLEIDAN
    THE HERACLEIDAN BLOOD MIGHT OWN 325   2 DON JUAN 3 L 13   6
HERALD
    THE HANDSOME HERALD ON WHOSE PLUMAGE SAT 211   3 DON JUAN 9   57   6
    SHAKSPEARE TALKS OF THE HERALD MERCURY 215   3 DON JUAN 9   66   1
    WHILE HER YOUNG HERALD KNELT BEFORE HER STILL 215   3 DON JUAN 9   66   4
HERBS
    OF HERBS AND CORDIALS THEY PRODUCED THEIR STORE 376   2 DON JUAN 4   59   6
HERCULEAN
    TO KEEP ONE CREED'S A TASK GROWN QUITE HERCULEAN 20   2 DON JUAN D   17   7

HERCULES
    AS HERCULES MIGHT DEEM HIS OWN . . . . 325 2 DON JUAN 3 L 13 V6
    FOR HAD HE NOT BEEN HERCULES HIS SPAN . . . . 84 3 DON JUAN 7 36 3
    (WHO AT SIXTEEN TRANSLATED HERCULES FURENS . . . . . 294 3 DON JUAN 11 52 6
    MILD--BUT AT TIMES A SORT OF HERCULES FURENS . . . . 567 3 DON JUAN 17 11 6
HERD
    OR ROAMS THE HERD BENEATH THE BULL'S PROTECTION . . . . 90 3 DON JUAN 7 48 4
    TO HERD WITH BOYS OR HOARD WITH GOOD THREESCORE-- . . . 316 3 DON JUAN 12 2 2
    THE BRANCHING STAG SWEPT DOWN WITH ALL HIS HERD . . . . 384 3 DON JUAN 13 56 7
HEREAFTER
    PERHAPS BE WEIGHED HEREAFTER IF NOT NOW . . . . . . 9 3 DON JUAN 6 6 2
    WILL BE DISCUSS'D HEREAFTER I OPINE . . . . 453 3 DON JUAN 14 97 3
HEREDITARY
    FATIGUED WITH THESE HEREDITARY GLORIES . . . . . . 392 3 DON JUAN 13 71 2
    WITH SOME SLIGHT LIGHT HEREDITARY TWINGES . . . . . 515 3 DON JUAN 16 34 7
HERE'S
    FOR GOD'S SAKE MADAM--MADAM--HERE'S MY MASTER . . . . 96 2 DON JUAN 1 137 1
    ARE OVER HERE'S A HEALTH TO AULD LANG SYNE . . . . 232 3 DON JUAN 10 16 5
    (NOW HERE'S A WORD QUITE AFTER MY OWN HEART . . . . 326 3 DON JUAN 12 22 3
    IF YOU HAVE NOUGHT ELSE HERE'S AT LEAST SATIETY . . . 416 3 DON JUAN 14 14 5
HERESY
    (LOVE LIKE RELIGION SOMETIMES RUNS TO HERESY) . . . . 446 2 DON JUAN 5 61 4
HERETOFORE
    WAS HERE (AS HERETOFORE AND SINCE) LET LOOSE . . . . 173 3 DON JUAN 8 123 8
HERMIT
    AN ACTIVE HERMIT EVEN IN AGE THE CHILD . . . . . . 144 3 DON JUAN 8 63 7
    THE THEME OF PRAISE A HERMIT WOULD NOT MISS . . . . 319 3 DON JUAN 12 7 4
HERMIT'S
    A HERMIT'S WITH A HARAM FOR A GROT . . . . 68 2 DON JUAN 1 87 8
HERO
    I WANT A HERO AN UNCOMMON WANT . . . . 21 2 DON JUAN 1 1 1
    'TIS WITH OUR HERO QUIETLY INURN'D . . . . 23 2 DON JUAN 1 4 4
    AND THEN YOUR HERO TELLS WHENE'ER YOU PLEASE . . . . 24 2 DON JUAN 1 6 3
    THAN JOSE WHO BEGOT OUR HERO WHO . . . . 26 2 DON JUAN 1 9 7
    TO DO WITH THE TRANSACTIONS OF MY HERO . . . . . . 341 2 DON JUAN 3 110 3
    WE LEFT OUR HERO AND THIRD HEROINE IN . . . . . . 10 3 DON JUAN 6 7 1
    OUR HERO THROUGH THE LABYRINTH OF LOVE . . . . . . 20 3 DON JUAN 6 28 7
    HERO BUFFOON HALF-DEMON AND HALF-DIRT . . . . . . 95 3 DON JUAN 7 55 5
    SOME SUCKING HERO IS COMPELLED TO REAR . . . . . . 108 3 DON JUAN 7 83 4
    TO TRACK OUR HERO ON HIS PATH OF FAME . . . . . . 120 3 DON JUAN 8 17 2
    THE STATESMAN HERO HARLOT LAWYER--WARD . . . . . . 123 3 DON JUAN 8 25 5
    NO HERO TRUSTETH WHOLLY TO HALF-PAY . . . . 163 3 DON JUAN 8 103 8
    WHEN HE BEHELD HIS LATEST HERO GRACE . . . . . . 169 3 DON JUAN 8 116 5
    THE HERO OF THIS GRAND POETIC RIDDLE . . . . . . 181 3 DON JUAN 8 139 3
    IN FACT YOUR GRACE IS STILL BUT A YOUNG HERO . . . . 184 3 DON JUAN 9 2 8
    OUR HERO (AND I TRUST KIND READER YOUR'S) -- . . . . 194 3 DON JUAN 9 23 1
    WE LEFT OUR HERO JUAN IN THE BLOOM . . . . 227 3 DON JUAN 10 5 1
    YOU'LL MOUNT WITH OUR YOUNG HERO THE CONVEYANCE . . . 248 3 DON JUAN 10 49 3
    BUT I WILL FALL AT LEAST AS FELL MY HERO . . . . . 296 3 DON JUAN 11 56 5
    OUR HERO AS A HERO YOUNG AND HANDSOME . . . . . . 305 3 DON JUAN 11 74 1
    OUR HERO AS A HERO YOUNG AND HANDSOME . . . . . . 305 3 DON JUAN 11 74 1
    OF WHAT BEFELL OUR HERO IN THE LAND . . . . 311 3 DON JUAN 11 87 2
    OUR HERO GLADLY SAW HIS LITTLE CHARGE . . . . . . 339 3 DON JUAN 12 51 2
    SUCH CLASSIC PAS--SANS FLAWS--SET OFF OUR HERO . . . 427 3 DON JUAN 14 39 7
    HERO--FOR WHAT IS SUBSTANCE TO A SPIRIT . . . . . 557 3 DON JUAN 16 116 7
    OUR HERO WAS IN CANTO THE SIXTEENTH . . . . 567 3 DON JUAN 17 12 1
HERO-BOY
    WHERE PERISH'D IN HIS FAME THE HERO-BOY . . . . . 400 2 DON JUAN 4 103 2
HEROES
    FOR THIS MEN WRITE SPEAK PREACH AND HEROES KILL . . . 146 2 DON JUAN 1 218 5
    THEY ALL WERE HEROES CONQUERORS AND CUCKOLDS . . . . 266 2 DON JUAN 2 206 8
    WHEN ALL THY HEROES ARE NO MORE . . . . 322 2 DON JUAN 3 L 5 V4
    ALL HEROES WHO IF LIVING STILL WOULD SLAY US . . . . 385 2 DON JUAN 4 76 8
    ALL HEROES WHEN ALIVE QUITE PROMPT TO SLAY US . . . . 385 2 DON JUAN 4 76 V8
    AS GALLANTLY AS EVER HEROES FOUGHT . . . . 83 3 DON JUAN 7 34 2
    THAT EVER PEOPLED HELL WITH HEROES SLAIN . . . . . 101 3 DON JUAN 7 68 3
    WILL TOUCH EVEN HEROES AND SUCH WAS SUWARROW . . . . 102 3 DON JUAN 7 69 8
    WHOSE HEADS WERE HEROES WHICH CUT OFF IN VAIN . . . . 113 3 DON JUAN 8 2 7
    AND HEROES ARE BUT MADE FOR BARDS TO SING . . . . . 118 3 DON JUAN 8 14 5
    FOR FIFTY THOUSAND HEROES NAME BY NAME . . . . . . 120 3 DON JUAN 8 17 4
    THERE HAVE BEEN AND ARE HEROES WHO BEGUN . . . . . 122 3 DON JUAN 8 22 2
    OFT ARE SOON CLOSED ALL HEROES ARE NOT BLIND . . . . 133 3 DON JUAN 8 40 6
    OF BAFFLED HEROES WHO STOOD SHYLY NEAR . . . . . . 148 3 DON JUAN 8 73 6
    TO TOUGH OLD HEROES AND CAN DO NO LESS . . . . . . 167 3 DON JUAN 8 112 4
    HEROES MUST DIE AND BY GOD'S BLESSING 'TIS . . . . . 277 3 DON JUAN 11 20 2
    HISTORIANS HEROES LAWYERS PRIESTS TO PUT . . . . . 286 3 DON JUAN 11 37 3
    HAS SPAIN HAD HEROES WHILE ROMANCE COULD CHARM . . . 364 3 DON JUAN 13 11 4
    WHERE TIME THROUGH HEROES AND THROUGH BEAUTIES STEERS . 381 3 DON JUAN 13 50 6
    WE LEFT OUR HEROES AND OUR HEROINES . . . . 423 3 DON JUAN 14 29 1
    FIRMNESS YCLEPT IN HEROES KINGS AND SEAMEN . . . . . 448 3 DON JUAN 14 89 3
    AND TAKE AS MANY HEROES AS HEAVEN PLEASES . . . . . 459 3 DON JUAN 15 9 8
    BUT OH YE MODERN HEROES WITH YOUR CARTRIDGES . . . . 485 3 DON JUAN 15 67 7
    AND YET GREAT HEROES HAVE BEEN BRED BY BOTH . . . . 541 3 DON JUAN 16 84 8
    HEROES SOMETIMES THOUGH SELDOM--SAGES NEVER . . . . 547 3 DON JUAN 16 98 2
HEROIC
    (HORACE MAKES THIS THE HEROIC TURNPIKE ROAD) . . . . 24 2 DON JUAN 1 6 2
    FLASH'D O'ER HIS SOUL A FEW HEROIC RAYS . . . . . . 303 2 DON JUAN 3 55 2
    THE HEROIC LAY IS TUNELESS NOW-- . . . . 322 2 DON JUAN 3 L 5 3
    THE HEROIC BOSOM BEATS NO MORE . . . . 322 2 DON JUAN 3 L 5 4

HEROIC   (CONTINUED)
```
    WHO SHALL AWAKE THE HEROIC LAY . . . . . . . . . . . . 322   2 DON JUAN   3  L   5   V3
    HEROIC STOIC CATO THE SENTENTIOUS . . . . . . . . . .   10   3 DON JUAN   6      7    7
    UNTIL EACH HIGH HEROIC BOSOM BURNED . . . . . . . . .   99   3 DON JUAN   7     64    3
    THE HEARTS OF THE HEROIC ON A CHARGE . . . . . . . .   103   3 DON JUAN   7     71    7
    TROUBLE HEROIC STOMACHS THOUGH THEIR LIDS SO . . . .   123   3 DON JUAN   8     40    5
    SOUNDS THE HEROIC SYLLABLES BOTH WAYS . . . . . . .    183   3 DON JUAN   9      1    2
    WHO IN HIS TIME HAD MADE HEROIC BUSTLE . . . . . . .   277   3 DON JUAN  11     19    2
    SHUT UP EACH HIGH HEROIC SALAMANDER . . . . . . . .    446   3 DON JUAN  14     83    5
    OF KNIGHTS AND DAMES HEROIC AND CHASTE TOO . . . . .   508   3 DON JUAN  16     17    5
```
HEROICALLY
```
    LOVE WHO HEROICALLY BREATHES A VEIN . . . . . . .     168   2 DON JUAN   2     23    3
    AND THUS HEROICALLY STOOD RESIGNED . . . . . . . .    492   3 DON JUAN   5    141    5
```
HEROINE
```
    MARCH HAS ITS HARES AND MAY MUST HAVE ITS HEROINE . . .  76  2 DON JUAN   1    102    8
    WE LEFT OUR HERO AND THIRD HEROINE IN . . . . . . . .    10  3 DON JUAN   6      7    1
    WHO IN HER WAY TOO WAS A HEROINE . . . . . . . .        449  3 DON JUAN  14     90    8
```
HEROINES
```
    WE LEFT OUR HEROES AND OUR HEROINES . . . . . . .      423  3 DON JUAN  14     29    1
```
HEROISM
```
    OF HEROISM AND TOOK HIS PLACE WITH SOLEMN . . . . .    130  3 DON JUAN   8     34    6
    TOUCHED BY THE HEROISM OF HIM THEY SLEW . . . . .      171  3 DON JUAN   8    119    5
```
HERO'S
```
    THE HERO'S HARP THE LOVER'S LUTE . . . . . . .         321  2 DON JUAN   3  L   2    2
    AS MOST ESSENTIAL TO THEIR HERO'S STORY . . . . . .    329  2 DON JUAN   3     92    7
    O'ERSHADOW'D THERE BY MANY A HERO'S GRAVE . . . . .    387  2 DON JUAN   4     79    4
    ALSO OUR HERO'S LOT HOWE'ER UNPLEASANT . . . . . .     410  2 DON JUAN   4    117    2
    BECAUSE IT MAKES US SMILE HIS HERO'S RIGHT . . . . .   363  3 DON JUAN  13      9    2
```
HER'S
```
    UNTO HIS PROTEGEE WHILE HER'S TRANSFIXED . . . . .     159  3 DON JUAN   8     96    5
    GREAT JOY WAS HER'S OR RATHER JOYS THE FIRST . . . .   212  3 DON JUAN   9     59    1
    POOR THING EVE'S WAS A TRIFLING CASE TO HER'S . . .    345  3 DON JUAN  12     64    8
    AND HER'S WERE THOSE WHICH CAN FACE CALCULATION . . .  432  3 DON JUAN  14     52    2
```
HE'S
```
    I HOPE HE'S YOUNG AND HANDSOME--IS HE TALL . . . . .   105  2 DON JUAN   1    154    6
    THERE FOR THE PRESENT AT THE LEAST HE'S FAST . . . .   115  2 DON JUAN   1    172    6
    AGAINST ALL NOBLE MALADIES HE'S BOLD . . . . . . .     168  2 DON JUAN   2     22    5
    HE'S WRONG--UNLESS MAN WERE A PIG INDEED . . . . . .   427  2 DON JUAN   5     31    3
    UNLESS HE'S DRUNK AND THEN NO DOUBT HE'S FREED . . .   427  2 DON JUAN   5     31    5
    UNLESS HE'S DRUNK AND THEN NO DOUBT HE'S FREED . . .   427  2 DON JUAN   5     31    5
    A FAVOURITE HORSE FALLEN LAME JUST AS HE'S MOUNTED .    16  3 DON JUAN   6     21    4
    HE'S A FINE BOY THE WOMEN MAY BE SENT . . . . . . .    100  3 DON JUAN   7     66    7
    UPON THE CAPTIVE FREEDOM HE'S AS FAR . . . . . . .     258  3 DON JUAN  10     68    6
    FOR HE'S SEEN IN THE PORCH AND HE'S SEEN IN THE CHURCH . 518 3 DON JUAN  16  L  2    7
    FOR HE'S SEEN IN THE PORCH AND HE'S SEEN IN THE CHURCH . 518 3 DON JUAN  16  L  2    7
    BUT NOW IT SEEMS HE'S RIGHT--HIS NOTION JUST . . . .   565  3 DON JUAN  17      8    7
```
HESITATE
```
    A PAGE WHERE TIME SHOULD HESITATE TO PRINT AGE . . . . 458  3 DON JUAN  15      7    5
```
HESITATION
```
    WHICH HESITATION MORE BETRAYED THAN MASQUED-- . . . .   56  3 DON JUAN   6    100    6
    AFTER SOME FASCINATING HESITATION-- . . . . . . .      518  3 DON JUAN  16     40    1
```
HESPERIAN
```
    BENEATH HIS CEASELESS TOUCHES THE HESPERIAN . . . . .  208  3 DON JUAN   9     51    V7
```
HESPERUS
```
    OH HESPERUS THOU BRINGEST ALL GOOD THINGS-- . . . .    338  2 DON JUAN   3    107    1
```
HETEROGENEOUS
```
    IF ALL THESE SEEM AN HETEROGENEOUS MASS . . . . . .    402  3 DON JUAN  13     94    1
    A HETEROGENEOUS MASS OF GLORIOUS BLAME . . . . . .     480  3 DON JUAN  15     57    3
```
HEW
```
    AND HEW OUT A HUGE MONUMENT OF PATHOS . . . . . .      355  3 DON JUAN  12     86    7
    WITH RUST SHOULD SURELY CEASE TO HACK AND HEW . . . .  433  3 DON JUAN  14     53    6
```
HEWED
```
    HE HEWED AWAY LIKE DOCTORS OF THEOLOGY . . . . . .     165  3 DON JUAN   8    108    6
```
HEWN
```
    A BROKEN PILLAR NOT UNCOUTHLY HEWN . . . . . . . .     400  2 DON JUAN   4    103    5
```
HEXAMETERS
```
    AND NOT THE PINK OF OLD HEXAMETERS . . . . . . . .      14  3 DON JUAN   6     18    3
```
HIATUS
```
    AT THIS MOST STRANGE AND UNEXPLAIN'D HIATUS . . . . .  111  2 DON JUAN   1    164    5
    WHILE THAT HIATUS MAXIME DEFLENDUS . . . . . . . .     245  3 DON JUAN  10     42    5
```
HICCUP
```
    YET STILL THEY DEIGN'D TO HICCUP OR TO BELLOW . . . .  318  2 DON JUAN   3     82    6
    IF HE CAN HICCUP NONSENSE AT A BALL . . . . . . .      333  3 DON JUAN  12     37    V6
```
HICCUP'D
```
    A SECOND HICCUP'D OUR OLD MASTER'S DEAD . . . . . .    297  2 DON JUAN   3     43    5
```
HICCUPS
```
    THE RESTLESS TITAN HICCUPS IN HIS DEN . . . . . . .    115  3 DON JUAN   8      7    8
```
HID
```
    HE HAD BEEN HID--I DON'T PRETEND TO SAY . . . . . .    112  2 DON JUAN   1    166    1
    TO KEEP HIS MEMORY WHOLE AND MUMMY HID . . . . . .     146  2 DON JUAN   1    219    4
    HAIDEE AND HER BELOVED HID THEIR FEET . . . . . . .    309  2 DON JUAN   3     67    V1
    AND HID HER FACE WITHIN JUANNA'S BREAST . . . . . ;     48  3 DON JUAN   6     85    2
    BUT WHETHER THEY ESCAPED OR NO LIES HID . . . . . .    178  3 DON JUAN   8    132    7
    GUESSING AT WHAT SHALL HAPPILY BE HID . . . . . . .    180  3 DON JUAN   8    137    7
    THAN CAN BE HID BY ALTERING HIS SHIRT HE . . . . . .   232  3 DON JUAN  10     15    4
```
HIDALGO
```
    A TRUE HIDALGO FREE FROM EVERY STAIN . . . . . . .      26  2 DON JUAN   1      9    2
    WITH AN HIDALGO WHO TRANSMITTED DOWN . . . . . . .      52  2 DON JUAN   1     57    2
    AND NOW HIDALGO NOW THAT YOU HAVE THROWN . . . . . .   105  2 DON JUAN   1    154    1
```

HIDDEN
LIKE EARTHQUAKES FROM THE HIDDEN FIRE CALL'D CENTRAL	271	2 DON JUAN 2	215 8
OF SECRET TREASURES FOUND IN HIDDEN VALES	293	2 DON JUAN 3	34 3
BE HIDDEN BY THE ROLLING WAVES WHICH HIDE	63	3 DON JUAN 6	115 2
HER HIDDEN FACE WAS PLUNGED AMIDST THE DEAD	158	3 DON JUAN 8	93 3
BLUSHED TOO BUT IT WAS HIDDEN BY THEIR ROUGE	293	3 DON JUAN 11	48 V2
A HIDDEN NECTAR UNDER A COLD PRESENCE	375	3 DON JUAN 13	38 3

HIDE
YOUR BAYS MAY HIDE THE BALDNESS OF YOUR BROWS--	13	2 DON JUAN D	7 1
LOOK WHERE YOU PLEASE--WE'VE NOTHING SIR TO HIDE	106	2 DON JUAN 1	156 4
TO HIDE THE GLOSSY SHOULDER WHICH UPREARS	108	2 DON JUAN 1	158 6
FOR ME ON EARTH EXCEPT SOME YEARS TO HIDE	132	2 DON JUAN 1	195 3
SO BLACK THE LONG WORN LION'S HIDE IN HUE	154	2 DON JUAN 1	V 5 7
ON THE SIXTH DAY THEY FED UPON HIS HIDE	193	2 DON JUAN 2	71 1
RATHER TO HIDE WHAT PLEASES MOST UNKNOWN	13	3 DON JUAN 6	15 4
BUT THERE SEEMED SOMETHING THAT HE WISHED TO HIDE	56	3 DON JUAN 6	100 5
BE HIDDEN BY THE ROLLING WAVES WHICH HIDE	63	3 DON JUAN 6	115 2
AND HIDE HER LITTLE PALPITATING BREAST	157	3 DON JUAN 8	91 7

HIDEOUS
NO HIDEOUS SIGN PROCLAIM'D HER SURELY DEAD	377	2 DON JUAN 4	60 4
(AS HE BLED INWARDLY NO HIDEOUS RIVER	430	2 DON JUAN 5	35 6
OF ALL THE HORRID HIDEOUS NOTES OF WOE	432	2 DON JUAN 5	50 1
THEIR HIDEOUS WIVES THEIR HORRID SELVES AND DRESSES	550	3 DON JUAN 16	103 7

HIDEOUSNESS
THE WOND'ROUS HIDEOUSNESS OF THOSE SMALL MEN	462	2 DON JUAN 5	88 3

HIDES
OUT OF THEIR HIDES IF PARCHMENT HAD GROWN DEAR	75	3 DON JUAN 7	17 7
THAT HIDES THE PAST WORLD LIKE TO A SET SUN	188	3 DON JUAN 9	11 3
HIDES TRAIN-OIL TALLOW AND THE RIGHTS OF THETIS	246	3 DON JUAN 10	45 7
AT THE FIRST BLUSH FOR A FAIR BRITON HIDES	350	3 DON JUAN 12	74 3

HIDING
PURSUED ITS COURSE NOW GLEAMING AND NOW HIDING	385	3 DON JUAN 13	58 6

HIEROGLYPHIC
THAT MONSTROUS HIEROGLYPHIC--THAT LONG SPOUT	207	3 DON JUAN 9	50 5

HIEROGLYPHICS
OR HIEROGLYPHICS ON EGYPTIAN STONES	180	3 DON JUAN 8	137 5

HIGH
GASPING ON DECK BECAUSE YOU SOAR TOO HIGH BOB	10	2 DON JUAN D	3 7
HIS SELF-COMMUNION WITH HIS OWN HIGH SOUL	70	2 DON JUAN 1	91 2
LONGINGS SUBLIME AND ASPIRATIONS HIGH	71	2 DON JUAN 1	93 2
IN THE DESIGN AND AS I HAVE A HIGH SENSE	86	2 DON JUAN 1	120 6
FROM LEAF TO LEAF 'TIS SWEET TO VIEW ON HIGH	87	2 DON JUAN 1	122 7
'TIS GROWN HIGH TIME TO THIN IT IN ITS TURN	92	2 DON JUAN 1	131 4
SURELY THE WINDOW'S NOT SO VERY HIGH	96	2 DON JUAN 1	137 8
THE ONLY HIGH SOUND PRECEPTS OF THE TRUE SUBLIME	136	2 DON JUAN 1	201 V3
THE HIGH WIND MADE THE TREBLE AND AS BASS	174	2 DON JUAN 2	34 4
THOUGH ON THE WAVE'S HIGH TOP TOO MUCH TO SET	188	2 DON JUAN 2	60 3
DISTINCT AND HIGH AND PALPABLE TO VIEW	207	2 DON JUAN 2	97 8
THE LAND APPEAR'D A HIGH AND ROCKY COAST	209	2 DON JUAN 2	100 1
THE BEACH WHICH LAY BEFORE HIM HIGH AND DRY	212	2 DON JUAN 2	106 4
BUT ALWAYS DANGEROUS WHEN THE HIGH WINDS TORE	249	2 DON JUAN 2	177 V6
AND DARKNESS AND DESTRUCTION AS ON HIGH	270	2 DON JUAN 2	214 4
IS SHARPEN'D FROM ITS HIGH CELESTIAL FLAVOUR	277	2 DON JUAN 3	5 7
PURSUED O'ER THE HIGH SEAS HIS WATERY JOURNEY	283	2 DON JUAN 3	14 7
AND THAT PROCEEDING AT A VERY HIGH RATE	296	2 DON JUAN 3	40 7
BUT NOW BEING LIFTED INTO HIGH SOCIETY	318	2 DON JUAN 3	83 1
FROM THE HIGH LYRIC DOWN TO THE LOW RATIONAL	319	2 DON JUAN 3	85 6
FILL HIGH THE CUP WITH SAMIAN WINE	324	2 DON JUAN 3	L 9 2
FILL HIGH THE BOWL WITH SAMIAN WINE	324	2 DON JUAN 3	L 11 1
FILL HIGH THE BOWL WITH SAMIAN WINE	325	2 DON JUAN 3	L 13 1
FILL HIGH THE BOWL WITH SAMIAN WINE	326	2 DON JUAN 3	L 15 1
WE'RE TOLD THIS GREAT HIGH PRIEST OF ALL THE NINE	328	2 DON JUAN 3	91 6
FOAMING O'ER HER LONE HEAD SO FIERCE AND HIGH	361	2 DON JUAN 4	31 7
HIGH AND INSCRUTABLE THE OLD MAN STOOD	365	2 DON JUAN 4	39 1
HIGH BARROWS WITHOUT MARBLE OR A NAME	386	2 DON JUAN 4	77 1
BUT SOLD BY THE IMPRESARIO AT NO HIGH RATE	388	2 DON JUAN 4	80 8
WHO HAD BID HIGH AS HUNDREDS SIX OR SEVEN	407	2 DON JUAN 4	114 V6
THE CYPRESS GROVES OLYMPUS HIGH AND HOAR	412	2 DON JUAN 5	3 5
OF A HIGH SPIRIT EVIDENTLY THOUGH	417	2 DON JUAN 5	12 2
COMMENCE WITH FEELINGS WARM AND PROSPECTS HIGH	421	2 DON JUAN 5	21 5
THE GIANT DOOR WAS BROAD AND BRIGHT AND HIGH	461	2 DON JUAN 5	86 1
HER BLOOD WAS HIGH HER BEAUTY SCARCE OF EARTH	475	2 DON JUAN 5	112 5
ARE APT TO CARRY THINGS WITH A HIGH HAND	11	3 DON JUAN 6	11 3
RATHER TOO HIGH AND DISTANT THAT SHE THREW	44	3 DON JUAN 6	76 3
THE WIND WAS DOWN BUT STILL THE SEA RAN HIGH	61	3 DON JUAN 6	110 8
CHILL AND CHAINED TO COLD EARTH WE LIFT ON HIGH	66	3 DON JUAN 7	1 5
IT STANDS SOME EIGHTY VERSTS FROM THE HIGH SEA	71	3 DON JUAN 7	9 7
OF THE HIGH TALENTS OF THIS NEW VAUBAN	72	3 DON JUAN 7	11 2
FORTY FEET HIGH UPON A CAVALIERE	72	3 DON JUAN 7	12 8
ALL PROPER MEN OF WEAPONS AS E'ER SCOFFED HIGH	75	3 DON JUAN 7	17 3
THIS FELLOW BEING SIX FOOT HIGH COULD RAISE	84	3 DON JUAN 7	37 5
UNTIL EACH HIGH HEROIC BOSOM BURNED	99	3 DON JUAN 7	64 3
SUWARROW THOUGH ENGAGED WITH ACCENTS HIGH	100	3 DON JUAN 7	65 3
THE HIGH ROMAN FASHION TOO OF CINCINNATUS	186	3 DON JUAN 9	7 3
THEN HELD THAT HIGH OFFICIAL SITUATION	206	3 DON JUAN 9	48 8
'TWAS A HIGH PLACE THE HIGHEST IN THE NATION	208	3 DON JUAN 9	52 4
'TIS VERY TRUE THE HILL SEEMED RATHER HIGH	215	3 DON JUAN 9	66 5
ESPECIALLY WHEN SUCH LEAD TO HIGH PLACES	223	3 DON JUAN 9	82 8
WITH HIS AGRARIAN LAWS THE HIGH ESTATE	237	3 DON JUAN 10	25 3

HIGH   (CONTINUED)
```
    WHILE THIS HIGH POST OF HONOUR'S IN ABEYANCE     .   .   .   .   . 248   3 DON JUAN 10      49    1
    HIGH DASHED THE SPRAY THE BOWS DIPPED IN THE SEA   .   .   .   . 256   3 DON JUAN 10      64    4
    A PARADISE OF HOPS AND HIGH PRODUCTION    .   .   .   .   .   . 262   3 DON JUAN 10      76    2
    O'ER THE HIGH HILL WHICH LOOKS WITH PRIDE OR SCORN   .   .   . 264   3 DON JUAN 10      80    4
    ON THE HIGH TOBY-SPICE SO FLASH THE MUZZLE    .   .   .   .   . 277   3 DON JUAN 11      19    6
    'TWILL BE BECAUSE OUR NOTION IS NOT HIGH  .   .   .   .   .   . 285   3 DON JUAN 11      36    3
    KICK OFF THEIR BURTHENS--MEANING THE HIGH CLASSES   .   .   . 310   3 DON JUAN 11      84    8
    HIGH GROUND AS VIRGIN CYNTHIA SWAYS THE TIDES   .   .   .   . 322   3 DON JUAN 12      14    6
    TANTAENE SUCH THE VIRTUES OF HIGH STATION   .   .   .   .   . 331   3 DON JUAN 12      33    5
    TO DRAW A HIGH PRIZE NOW HOWE'ER HE GOT HER I   .   .   .   . 333   3 DON JUAN 12      37    7
    HIGH IN HIGH CIRCLES GENTLE IN HER OWN    .   .   .   .   .   . 338   3 DON JUAN 12      48    1
    HIGH IN HIGH CIRCLES GENTLE IN HER OWN    .   .   .   .   .   . 338   3 DON JUAN 12      48    1
    MUST STILL OBEY THE HIGH--WHICH IS THEIR HANDLE   .   .   .   . 342   3 DON JUAN 12      56    7
    AND SOME OF THEM HIGH NAMES I HAVE ALSO KNOWN   .   .   .   . 344   3 DON JUAN 12      61    2
    AND THEREFORE SHALL MY LAY SOAR HIGH AND SOLEMN   .   .   . 358   3 DON JUAN 13       1    7
    HIS MANNER SHOWED HIM SPRUNG FROM A HIGH MOTHER   .   .   . 369   3 DON JUAN 13      24    6
    HER CHIEF RESOURCE WAS IN HER OWN HIGH SPIRIT   .   .   .   . 372   3 DON JUAN 13      31    4
    ALSO A FOREIGNER OF HIGH CONDITION.   .   .   .   .   .   .   . 382   3 DON JUAN 13      52    7
    CROWN'D BY HIGH WOODLANDS WHERE THE DRUID OAK   .   .   . 384   3 DON JUAN 13      56    2
    AND HERE AND THERE SOME STERN HIGH PATRIOT STOOD   .   . 391   3 DON JUAN 13      70    7
    OR RODE A NAG WHICH TROTTED NOT TOO HIGH  .   .   .   .   . 406   3 DON JUAN 13     102    5
    THEY RUN BEFORE THE WIND THROUGH HIGH SEAS BREAKING   .   . 442   3 DON JUAN 14      74    6
    AND HENCE HIGH LIFE IS OFT A DREARY VOID  .   .   .   .   .   . 444   3 DON JUAN 14      79    1
    SHUT UP EACH HIGH HEROIC SALAMANDER   .   .   .   .   .   . 446   3 DON JUAN 14      83    5
    TO LIKE TOO READILY OR TOO HIGH BRED  .   .   .   .   .   .   . 460   3 DON JUAN 15      10    4
    HIGH YET RESEMBLING NOT HIS LOST HAIDEE   .   .   .   .   .   . 481   3 DON JUAN 15      58    2
    A LAMP BURNED HIGH WHILE HE LEANT FROM A NICHE   .   .   . 507   3 DON JUAN 16      16    5
    AS DOUBTLESS SHOULD BE PEOPLE OF HIGH BIRTH   .   .   .   . 508   3 DON JUAN 16      17    6
    GLIMMER ON HIGH THEIR BURIED LOCKS STILL WAVE   .   .   . 509   3 DON JUAN 16      19    3
    THOUGH FOR THE PUBLIC WEAL DISPOSED TO VENTURE HIGH   .   . 536   3 DON JUAN 16      73    6
    FROM THEIR HIGH PLACES BY THE SIDEBOARD'S STAND--  .   .   . 539   3 DON JUAN 16      79    5
    I KNOW NOT BUT HER COLOUR NE'ER WAS HIGH--  .   .   .   .   . 545   3 DON JUAN 16      94    6
    YES SHE WAS TRULY WORTHY HER HIGH PLACE   .   .   .   .   . 550   3 DON JUAN 16     102    5
    WHICH STILL IN JUAN'S CANDLESTICKS BURNED HIGH   .   .   . 558   3 DON JUAN 16     117    5
HIGH-BORN
    WAS HIGH-BORN WEALTHY BY HER FATHER'S WILL   .   .   .   .   . 359   3 DON JUAN 13       2    5
HIGHER
    AND JUAN TOO BLASPHEMED AN OCTAVE HIGHER  .   .   .   .   . 122   2 DON JUAN  1     184    6
    BECAUSE THE SEA RAN HIGHER EVERY MINUTE   .   .   .   .   . 186   2 DON JUAN  2      57    7
    AND HIGHER GREW THE MOUNTAINS AS THEY DREW   .   .   .   . 209   2 DON JUAN  2     100    2
    RAISED HIGHER THE FAINT HEAD WHICH O'ER IT HUNG   .   .   . 216   2 DON JUAN  2     114    3
    THE RAMPART HIGHER THAN YOU'D WISH TO HANG   .   .   .   .  72   3 DON JUAN  7      11    4
    A HIGHER TITLE OR A LOFTIER STATION   .   .   .   .   .   .   . 114   3 DON JUAN  8       4    5
    WHICH SCARCELY ROSE MUCH HIGHER THAN GRASS BLADES   .   . 136   3 DON JUAN  8      47    8
    AMONGST THE HIGHER SPIRITS OF THE DAY .   .   .   .   .   . 300   3 DON JUAN 11      64    7
    OR IF HE DANCE NOT BUT HATH HIGHER VIEWS  .   .   .   .   . 304   3 DON JUAN 11      71    1
    TO KEEP THE WHEELS GOING OF THE HIGHER CLASS   .   .   .   . 342   3 DON JUAN 12      57    5
    AS IN FREEMASONRY A HIGHER BROTHER    .   .   .   .   .   . 369   3 DON JUAN 13      24    4
    BUT IN A HIGHER NICHE ALONE BUT CROWN'D   .   .   .   .   . 387   3 DON JUAN 13      61    1
    ON WHICH IT HINGES IN A HIGHER STATION    .   .   .   .   .   . 396   3 DON JUAN 13      81    4
    BY NATURE AS IN HIGHER DAMES LESS HALE    .   .   .   .   . 532   3 DON JUAN 16      64    3
    THE LOVE OF HIGHER THINGS AND BETTER DAYS   .   .   .   . 554   3 DON JUAN 16     108    1
HIGHEST
    AND CARRY PRECEPT TO THE HIGHEST PITCH    .   .   .   .   . 138   2 DON JUAN  1     204    6
    EVEN OF THE HIGHEST FOR A FEMALE MOULD    .   .   .   .   . 217   2 DON JUAN  2     116    5
    I STUDY ALSO BLAIR THE HIGHEST REACHERS   .   .   .   .   . 243   2 DON JUAN  2     165    6
    'TWAS A HIGH PLACE THE HIGHEST IN THE NATION   .   .   .   . 208   3 DON JUAN  9      52    4
    ADVANCED IN ALL THEIR AZURE'S HIGHEST HUE   .   .   .   .   . 294   3 DON JUAN 11      50    4
    ALTHOUGH THE HIGHEST BUT AS SWORDS HAVE HILTS   .   .   . 342   3 DON JUAN 12      56    3
    OF HIGHEST CASTE--THE BRAHMINS OF THE TON   .   .   .   .   . 397   3 DON JUAN 13      83    4
    THE REAL PORTRAIT OF THE HIGHEST TRIBE    .   .   .   .   . 418   3 DON JUAN 14      20    7
    EVEN WHERE THE ARTICLE AT HIGHEST RATE IS   .   .   .   .   . 469   3 DON JUAN 15      29    4
HIGHLAND
    (A HIGHLAND WELCOME ALL THE WIDE WORLD OVER)   .   .   .   .  12   3 DON JUAN  6      13    8
    CURE THEM OF TOURS HUSSAR AND HIGHLAND DRESSES  .   .   . 267   3 DON JUAN 10      86    2
HIGHLANDS
    SOME THOUGHT IT WAS MOUNT AETNA SOME THE HIGHLANDS    .   . 209   2 DON JUAN  2     100    7
    HEART-BALLADS OF GREEN ERIN OR GREY HIGHLANDS   .   .   . 523   3 DON JUAN 16      46    2
HIGHNESS
    UNLESS HIS HIGHNESS PROMISES TO MARRY ME  .   .   .   .   . 460   2 DON JUAN  5      84    8
    HIS HIGHNESS WAS A MAN OF SOLEMN PORT .   .   .   .   .   . 495   2 DON JUAN  5     147    1
    HIS HIGHNESS CAST AROUND HIS GREAT BLACK EYES   .   .   . 500   2 DON JUAN  5     155    1
    HIS HIGHNESS THE SUBLIMEST OF MANKIND--   .   .   .   .   .  12   3 DON JUAN  6      13    1
    HIS HIGHNESS GAZED UPON GULBEYAZ' CHARMS  .   .   .   .   .  12   3 DON JUAN  6      13    6
    HIS HIGHNESS QUITE CONNUBIALLY INCLINED   .   .   .   .   .  12   3 DON JUAN  6      13   V5
    (IF THAT HIS HIGHNESS WEARIED OF HIS BRIDE)   .   .   .   .   .  24   3 DON JUAN  6      36    7
    BUT AS IT WAS HIS HIGHNESS HAD TO HOLD    .   .   .   .   .  54   3 DON JUAN  6      96    1
    WHAT SLAVES HER HIGHNESS WISHED TO INDICATE   .   .   .   .  62   3 DON JUAN  6     112    7
HIGHNESS'
    AND THEN HIS HIGHNESS' EUNUCHS BLACK AND WHITE  .   .   .   . 495   2 DON JUAN  5     146    2
    THAT ADDING TO THE ACCOUNT HIS HIGHNESS' YEARS  .   .   .   .  10   3 DON JUAN  6       9    4
HIGHNESS'S
    TO-MORROW WHAT HIS HIGHNESS'S PHYSICIAN   .   .   .   .   .  46   3 DON JUAN  6      80    7
HIGH-SOUL'D
    AND AS A HIGH-SOUL'D MINISTER OF STATE IS   .   .   .   .   . 186   3 DON JUAN  9       8    7
HIGHWAY'S
    TRAPS FOR THE TRAVELLER EVERY HIGHWAY'S CLEAR   .   .   .   . 273   3 DON JUAN 11      10    6
HIGHWAYS
    THAN HE IN THESE SAD HIGHWAYS LEFT AT LARGE   .   .   .   . 198   3 DON JUAN  9      31    4
    JUAN ADMIRED THESE HIGHWAYS OF FREE MILLIONS    .   .   .   . 263   3 DON JUAN 10      77    4
```

```
                                                              PAGE VOL      CANTO STANZA LN
HILL
        AND DULY SEATED ON THE IMMORTAL HILL . . . . . . .    12  2 DON JUAN  D     6    8
        SOME LIKEN IT TO CLIMBING UP A HILL  . . . . . . .   146  2 DON JUAN  1   218    3
        RED SUN SINKS DOWN BEHIND THE AZURE HILL . . . . . . 252  2 DON JUAN  2   183    2
        ARRIVING AT THE SUMMIT OF A HILL . . . . . . . . .   286  2 DON JUAN  3    21    1
        THERE ON THE GREEN AND VILLAGE-COTTED HILL IS . . . 385  2 DON JUAN  4    76    1
        BEGAN TO CLOTHE EACH ASIATIC HILL  . . . . . . . .    49  3 DON JUAN  6    86    3
        SOME COSSACQUES HOVERING LIKE HAWKS ROUND A HILL  .   95  3 DON JUAN  7    56    3
        NEW LIGHTED ON A HEAVEN-KISSING HILL . . . . . . .   215  3 DON JUAN  9    66    2
        'TIS VERY TRUE THE HILL SEEMED RATHER HIGH . . . .   215  3 DON JUAN  9    66    5
        WE HAVE JUST LIT ON A HEAVEN-KISSING HILL  . . . .   224  3 DON JUAN  9    85    4
        O'ER THE HIGH HILL WHICH LOOKS WITH PRIDE OR SCORN   264  3 DON JUAN 10    80    4
        BOLD BRITONS WE ARE NOW ON SHOOTER'S HILL  . . . .   264  3 DON JUAN 10    80    8
        DON JUAN HAD GOT OUT ON SHOOTER'S HILL . . . . . .   272  3 DON JUAN 11     8    1
        THE MUSES UPON SION'S HILL MUST RAMBLE . . . . . .   297  3 DON JUAN 11    57    3
        BECAUSE THE MONKS PREFERRED A HILL BEHIND  . . . .   384  3 DON JUAN 13    55    7
        WHEN THE LORD OF THE HILL AMUNDEVILLE . . . . . . . 518  3 DON JUAN 16  L  1    5
HILLS
        WHOSE SUMMIT LIKE ALL HILLS IS LOST IN VAPOUR . . . 146  2 DON JUAN  1   218    4
        ON THE SNOW-TOPS OF DISTANT HILLS THE STREAK . . .  234  2 DON JUAN  2   147    3
        WAS BORN IN CUMBERLAND AMONG THE HILLS . . . . . .   76  3 DON JUAN  7    20    3
        OVER THE HILLS A FIRE ENOUGH TO BLIND  . . . . . .  126  3 DON JUAN  8    30    4
        SCOTCH PLAIDS SCOTCH SNOODS THE BLUE HILLS AND CLEAR STREAMS 233 3 DON JUAN 10 18  2
        WHO AFTER A LONG CHASE O'ER HILLS DALES BUSHES . .  425  3 DON JUAN 14    35    6
HILTS
        A MODERN ANCIENT PISTOL--BY THE HILTS . . . . . .   297  3 DON JUAN 11    57    8
        ALTHOUGH THE HIGHEST BUT AS SWORDS HAVE HILTS . . . 342  3 DON JUAN 12    56    3
HIMS
        PROUD OF HIS HEAR HIMS PROUD TOO OF HIS VOTE . . .  401  3 DON JUAN 13    91    1
HIMSELF'S
        AND THAT'S THE REASON HE HIMSELF'S SO DIRTY . . .   232  3 DON JUAN 10    15    2
HINDER
        IF PINDAR SANG HORSE-RACES WHAT SHOULD HINDER . .   319  2 DON JUAN  3    85    7
        TO HINDER HIM FROM GROWING STILL MORE PALLID . . .  515  3 DON JUAN 16    35    8
HINDOSTAN
        WHO AFTER LEAVING HINDOSTAN A WILD . . . . . . . .  199  3 DON JUAN  9    33    5
HINGE
        VOI CHE ENTRATE THE HINGE SEEMED TO SPEAK . . . .   557  3 DON JUAN 16   116    3
HINGES
        THE HINGES BEING AS SMOOTH AS ROGERS' RHYMES . . .  463  2 DON JUAN  5    89    4
        ON WHICH IT HINGES IN A HIGHER STATION . . . . . .  396  3 DON JUAN 13    81    4
        OF GOUT WHICH RUSTS ARISTOCRATIC HINGES . . . . .   515  3 DON JUAN 16    34    8
HINT
        A HINT IN TENDER CASES IS ENOUGH . . . . . . . . .  119  2 DON JUAN  1   178    1
        HINT THAT SOME SIX OR SEVEN GOOD YEARS AGO . . . .  143  2 DON JUAN  1   212    4
        TO HINT THAT FLESH IS FORM'D OF FIERY DUST . . . .  269  2 DON JUAN  2   212    8
        GAVE LIGHT ENOUGH TO HINT THEIR FARTHER WAY . . .   442  2 DON JUAN  5    56    2
        BEFORE THEY ENTERED BABA PAUSED TO HINT  . . . . .  464  2 DON JUAN  5    91    1
        TO HINT THAT HE IS COMING UP THIS WAY  . . . . . .  494  2 DON JUAN  5   144    8
        TO HINT AT LEAST HERE IS NO THOROUGHFARE . . . . .   72  3 DON JUAN  7    11    8
        DREW QUIET CONSOLATION THROUGH ITS HINT  . . . . .  241  3 DON JUAN 10    34    7
        LATE AUTHORS ASKED HIM FOR A HINT OR TWO . . . . .  294  3 DON JUAN 11    50    6
        WILL HINT ALLUSIONS NEVER MEANT NE'ER DOUBT  . . .  311  3 DON JUAN 11    88    7
        THIS--WHEN I SPEAK I DON'T HINT BUT SPEAK OUT . .   311  3 DON JUAN 11    88    8
        HINT THAT 'TIS TIME TO GIVE THE YOUNGER PLACE . .   360  3 DON JUAN 13     4    8
        BUT ERE HE WENT HE ADDED A SLIGHT HINT . . . . . .  440  3 DON JUAN 14    69    1
        WHICH SEEMS TO HINT YOU ARE NOT WORTH A THOUGHT .   490  3 DON JUAN 15    77    4
        JUAN WAS PETRIFIED HE HAD HEARD A HINT . . . . . .  510  3 DON JUAN 16    22    1
HINTED
        HINTED THE VAST ADVANTAGES WHICH THEY . . . . . .   451  2 DON JUAN  5    69    2
HINTERS
        THAT SHE HAD PUZZLED ALL THE ACUTEST HINTERS . . .  434  3 DON JUAN 14    56    3
HINTING
        AS HINTING MORE (UNLESS OUR JUDGMENTS WARP US) . .  391  3 DON JUAN 13    69    7
        HINTING THAT SOUL AND BODY ON THE WHOLE  . . . . .  558  3 DON JUAN 16   118    7
HINTS
        ACCORDING TO ALL HINTS I COULD COLLECT  . . . . .    38  2 DON JUAN  1    33    2
        OR HINTS CONTINUATION OF THE SPECIES . . . . . . .   44  2 DON JUAN  1    40    7
        AND TAKING HINTS IN GOOD PART ALL THE WHILE . . .   473  2 DON JUAN  5   107    4
        IT ALSO GENTLY HINTS TO THEM THAT OTHERS . . . . .  491  2 DON JUAN  5   138    2
        MAY SERVE PERHAPS AS OUTLINES OR SLIGHT HINTS . .    60  3 DON JUAN  6   109    8
        ARE HINTS AS GOOD AS SERMONS OR AS RHYMES  . . . .  174  3 DON JUAN  8   125    6
        BUT THESE PRECAUTIONARY HINTS CAN TOUCH  . . . . .  305  3 DON JUAN 11    73    1
        WHOSE DRAPERY HINTS WE MAY ADMIRE THEM FREELY . .   390  3 DON JUAN 13    68    8
        HINTS FROM THE INDEPENDENT HEART OR HEAD . . . . .  538  3 DON JUAN 16    77    5
HIP
        ONE'S HIP HE SLASHED AND SPLIT THE OTHER'S SHOULDER 158  3 DON JUAN  8    94    1
HIPPOCRENE
        AND CAMPBELL'S HIPPOCRENE IS SOMEWHAT DROUTHY . .   139  2 DON JUAN  1   205    6
        HAD KEPT HIM FROM THE BRINK OF HIPPOCRENE  . . . .  294  3 DON JUAN 11    51    7
HIRED
        THE LEARNED TUTORS WHOM FOR HIM SHE HIRED  . . . .   43  2 DON JUAN  1    39    3
        THEY HIRED HIM THOUGH TO HEAR HIM YOU'D BELIEVE .   391  2 DON JUAN  4    87    7
        THAT HIRED HUZZAS REDEEM NO LAND'S DISTRESSES . .   267  3 DON JUAN 10    86    4
HIRELING
        BUT WHICH 'TIS TIME TO TEACH THE HIRELING TRIBE .   187  3 DON JUAN  9    10    4
HIRSUTE
        THE USUAL HIRSUTE SEASONS WHICH DESTROY  . . . . .  209  3 DON JUAN  9    53    3
HISS
        OF SENSE AND SONG ABOVE YOUR GRAVES MAY HISS-- . .  334  2 DON JUAN  3   100    6
        THEIR FEE BUT ERE THE WATERED WHEELS MAY HISS HENCE 379 3 DON JUAN 13   46    7
```

HISSED
    TO SEE IT--THE KING HISSED AND THEN CAREST . . . . . . 309 3 DON JUAN 11 83 7
HISSES
    WHERE ARE THE DUBLIN SHOUTS--AND LONDON HISSES . . . . . 308 2 DON JUAN 11 79 6
HIST
    FIRST KNOCKS WERE HEARD THEN MADAM--MADAM--HIST . . . . 95 2 DON JUAN 1 136 8
HISTORIAN
    IF (SAYS THE HISTORIAN HERE) I COULD REPORT . . . . . . 82 3 DON JUAN 7 32 1
    AND HERE WE MAY REMARK WITH THE HISTORIAN . . . . . . 151 3 DON JUAN 8 78 2
HISTORIAN'S
    DEPENDING MORE UPON THE HISTORIAN'S STYLE . . . . . . 328 2 DON JUAN 3 90 3
HISTORIANS
    AND WHEN YOU HEAR HISTORIANS TALK OF THRONES . . . . . 180 3 DON JUAN 8 137 1
    HISTORIANS HEROES LAWYERS PRIESTS TO PUT . . . . 286 3 DON JUAN 11 37 3
HISTORICAL
    MEN WHOSE HISTORICAL SUPERIORITY . . . . 503 3 DON JUAN 16 5 3
HISTORIES
    AS ANY MENTIONED IN THE HISTORIES . . . . 495 2 DON JUAN 5 147 6
HISTORY
    TO JUAN'S EYES EXCEPTING NATURAL HISTORY . . . . 43 2 DON JUAN 1 39 8
    CHANGE HORSES MAKING HISTORY CHANGE ITS TUNE . . . . . 76 2 DON JUAN 1 103 5
    TO HISTORY TRADITION AND TO FACTS . . . . 138 2 DON JUAN 1 203 2
    ANOTHER PART OF HISTORY FOR THE DISHES . . . . 65 2 DON JUAN 6 120 3
    HISTORY CAN ONLY TAKE THINGS IN THE GROSS . . . . . . 113 3 DON JUAN 8 3 1
    IN HISTORY BUT WE AT LEAST MAY GRANT . . . . 127 3 DON JUAN 8 31 5
    WHICH ARE THE HEAVIEST THAT OUR HISTORY MENTIONS . . . . 137 3 DON JUAN 8 49 8
    WITH MODERN HISTORY HAS BUT SMALL CONNECTION . . . . . 186 3 DON JUAN 9 7 4
    THE HISTORY OF DIVORCES WHICH THOUGH CHEQUERED . . . . 209 3 DON JUAN 9 53 7
    IF HISTORY THE GRAND LIAR EVER SAITH . . . . 222 3 DON JUAN 9 81 4
    HER CHARMING FIGURE AND ROMANTIC HISTORY . . . . 328 3 DON JUAN 12 27 7
    ALBEIT ALL HUMAN HISTORY ATTESTS . . . . 404 3 DON JUAN 13 99 6
    A BATTLE WRECK OR HISTORY OF THE HEART . . . . 419 3 DON JUAN 14 21 4
    LOWER'D LEAVEN'D LIKE A HISTORY OF FREEMASONS . . . . . 419 3 DON JUAN 14 22 2
    THE WORLD (AS SINCE THAT HISTORY LESS POLITE . . . . . 420 3 DON JUAN 14 23 2
    SOME PARTS OF JUAN'S HISTORY WHICH RUMOUR . . . . . . 460 3 DON JUAN 15 11 1
    AURORA AT THE LAST (SO HISTORY MENTIONS . . . . 491 3 DON JUAN 15 80 5
    THEREFORE THE PRESENT PIECE OF NATURAL HISTORY . . . . . 531 3 DON JUAN 16 62 3
HISTORY'S
    HAVE MUCH EMPLOY'D THE MUSE OF HISTORY'S PEN . . . . . 266 2 DON JUAN 2 206 4
    BUT PEOPLE'S ANCESTORS ARE HISTORY'S GAME . . . . . . 53 3 DON JUAN 6 94 5
HIT
    AND SOMETIMES LADIES HIT EXCEEDING HARD . . . . 33 2 DON JUAN 1 21 6
    OF HIS OWN CASE AND NEVER HIT THE TRUE ONE . . . . . . 68 2 DON JUAN 1 86 3
    WHICH THEY HIT OFF AT ONCE IN THE BEGINNING . . . . . . 32 3 DON JUAN 6 52 6
    FOR AUGHT WE KNOW) RENOWN'S ALL HIT OR MISS . . . . . . 82 3 DON JUAN 7 33 5
    THAT HE WHO NAMES ONE BOTH PERCHANCE MAY HIT ON . . . . 221 3 DON JUAN 9 77 6
    IS NOT A MERELY SPECULATIVE HIT . . . . 318 3 DON JUAN 12 6 3
    THAT HE EXACTLY THE JUST MEDIUM HIT . . . . 535 3 DON JUAN 16 72 3
HITHERTO
    AND WORSE OFF THAN WE HITHERTO HAVE BEEN . . . . 435 2 DON JUAN 5 44 6
    WHO HITHERTO HAD FOUND THINGS NOT AMISS . . . . 492 3 DON JUAN 15 81 V3
HITS
    ACCORDING TO THE ARTILLERY'S HITS OR MISSES . . . . . . 105 3 DON JUAN 7 76 3
HIVED
    HIVED IN OUR BOSOMS LIKE THE BAG O' THE BEE . . . . . . 144 2 DON JUAN 1 214 5
HO
    NOW UNDER ARMS HO KATSKOFF TAKE HIM TO-- . . . . 100 3 DON JUAN 7 66 3
    OR DUTCH WITH THIRST--WHAT HO A FLASK OF RHENISH . . . . 392 3 DON JUAN 13 72 8
    PROVOKE MY THIRST--WHAT--HO OF WINE A STOUP . . . . . . 392 3 DON JUAN 13 72 V8
HOAR
    OR BE ALIVE AGAIN--AGAIN ALL HOAR . . . . 15 2 DON JUAN D 11 4
    THE CYPRESS GROVES OLYMPUS HIGH AND HOAR . . . . 412 2 DON JUAN 5 3 5
HOARD
    TO HOARD UP WARMTH AGAINST A WINTRY DAY . . . . 229 3 DON JUAN 10 9 8
    TO HERD WITH BOYS OR HOARD WITH GOOD THREESCORE-- . . . 316 3 DON JUAN 12 2 2
    WHICH HOLDS A TREASURE LIKE A MISER'S HOARD . . . . . . 422 3 DON JUAN 14 27 3
HOARDED
    A MISER FILLING HIS MOST HOARDED CHEST . . . . 261 2 DON JUAN 2 196 6
HOARDER'S
    MAY BE THE HOARDER'S PRINCIPLE OF ACTION . . . . 321 3 DON JUAN 12 11 2
HOARDING
    INSTEAD OF HOARDING IT WITH DUE PRECISION . . . . . . 192 2 DON JUAN 2 68 8
    I AM QUITE OF THEIR OPINION--AND AM HOARDING . . . . . 270 3 DON JUAN 11 4 V5
HOARDS
    THE LAST YEAR TO THE NEW TRANSFERS ITS HOARDS . . . . . 340 3 DON JUAN 12 53 5
HOARSE
    THE HOARSE HARSH WAVES KEPT TIME FRIGHT CURED THE QUALMS . 174 2 DON JUAN 2 34 5
    TO HAMMER A HOARSE LAUGH FROM THE THICK THRONG . . . . 540 3 DON JUAN 16 83 8
HOARSER
    AND THEN INTO A HOARSER MURMUR GREW . . . . 194 2 DON JUAN 2 73 3
HOARSEST
    AND THE LOUD CANNON PEALED HIS HOARSEST STRAINS . . . . 129 3 DON JUAN 8 33 6
HOARY
    AND THE FAR MOUNTAINS WAX A LITTLE HOARY . . . . 94 2 DON JUAN 1 134 4
    IN WHICH HE WAS OPPOSED BY YOUNG AND HOARY . . . . . . 83 3 DON JUAN 7 35 5
    THOUGH HOARY NOW AND WITH A WITHERING BREAST . . . . . 228 3 DON JUAN 10 6 5
    BECAUSE DECEMBER WITH HIS BREATH SO HOARY . . . . . . 229 3 DON JUAN 10 9 6
    THE WITLESS FALSTAFF OF A HOARY HAL . . . . 267 3 DON JUAN 10 86 7
    WHICH RINGS WHAT'S UPPERMOST OF NEW OR HOARY . . . . . 465 3 DON JUAN 15 20 7

		PAGE	VOL		CANTO	STANZA	LN

HOAX
IMBIBED THE GAY BON MOT OR HAPPY HOAX . . . . 540 3 DON JUAN 16 83 5

HOBGOBLIN'S
HOW ODD A SINGLE HOBGOBLIN'S NON-ENTITY . . . . 559 3 DON JUAN 16 120 7

HOC
NON EGO HOC FERREM CALIDA JUVENTA . . . . 143 2 DON JUAN 1 212 1

HOCHE
JOUBERT HOCHE MARCEAU LANNES DESSAIX MOREAU . . . . . 22 2 DON JUAN 1 3 5

HOCK
AND SO--FOR GODSAKE--HOCK AND SODA WATER . . . . . . 156 2 DON JUAN 1 V 8 8
SOME HOCK AND SODA-WATER THEN YOU'LL KNOW . . . . . 251 2 DON JUAN 2 180 2
VIE WITH THAT DRAUGHT OF HOCK AND SODA-WATER . . . 251 2 DON JUAN 2 180 8

HOGS
WHO HATING HOGS YET WISHED TO SAVE THEIR BACON . . . . 87 3 DON JUAN 7 42 8

HOIST
BUT IT IS TIME THAT I SHOULD HOIST MY BLUE PETER . . . . 309 3 DON JUAN 11 83 5

HOISTED
SOME HOISTED OUT THE BOATS AND THERE WAS ONE . . . . 179 2 DON JUAN 2 44 6

HOLBEIN'S
LIKE HOLBEIN'S DANCE OF DEATH--BUT 'TIS THE SAME)-- . . . 473 3 DON JUAN 15 39 8

HOLD
PEOPLE SHOULD HOLD THEIR TONGUES IN ANY CASE . . . . . 77 2 DON JUAN 1 105 4
ARE QUITE ENOUGH FOR ME SO THEY BUT HOLD . . . . . . 85 2 DON JUAN 1 118 8
TO HOLD A LEVEE ROUND HIS LADY'S BED . . . . 97 2 DON JUAN 1 139 6
IS IT FOR THIS I HAVE DISDAIN'D TO HOLD . . . . . . 101 2 DON JUAN 1 147 1
THE CHIMNEY--WHICH WOULD REALLY HOLD A LOVER . . . 104 2 DON JUAN 1 153 4
LOVE'S A CAPRICIOUS POWER I'VE KNOWN IT HOLD . . . 168 2 DON JUAN 2 22 1
THE WATER LEFT THE HOLD AND WASH'D THE DECKS . . . 172 2 DON JUAN 2 31 4
A GALE AND IN THE FORE AND AFTER HOLD . . . . . . 178 2 DON JUAN 2 42 2
AND TWO BOATS COULD NOT HOLD FAR LESS BE STORED . . 181 2 DON JUAN 2 48 7
RESERVED FOR FUTURE RANSOM IN THE HOLD-- . . . . . 284 2 DON JUAN 3 16 6
AND CLINGING AS IF LOTH TO LOSE ITS HOLD . . . . . 312 2 DON JUAN 3 71 6
LIKE ONE LIFE COULD NOT HOLD NOR DEATH DESTROY . . 376 2 DON JUAN 4 59 8
FOR SHE GOT HOLD OF A YOUNG FOREIGN NINNY . . . . 390 2 DON JUAN 4 84 V5
'TIS SAID NO ONE IN HAND CAN HOLD A FIRE . . . . . 396 2 DON JUAN 4 96 5
YOU'RE RIGHT ON BOTH ACCOUNTS TO HOLD YOUR TONGUE . 419 2 DON JUAN 5 16 7
METHOD'S MORE SURE AT MOMENTS TO TAKE HOLD . . . . 439 2 DON JUAN 5 49 4
THEN IF I DO SAID JUAN I'LL BE-- HOLD . . . . . . 454 2 DON JUAN 5 75 1
BUT AS IT WAS HIS HIGHNESS HAD TO HOLD . . . . . . 54 3 DON JUAN 6 96 1
AND WHEN TO HOLD ITS TONGUE NOW HELD IT TILL . . . 61 3 DON JUAN 6 110 2
THE TEETH STILL KEPT THEIR GRATIFYING HOLD . . . . 153 3 DON JUAN 8 83 7
THE DYING MAN CRIED HOLD I'VE GOT MY GRUEL . . . . 276 3 DON JUAN 11 16 2
AND (SHOULD SHE NOT HOLD FAST BY LOVE OR PRIDE) . . 292 3 DON JUAN 11 46 4
A MORAL COUNTRY BUT I HOLD MY HAND-- . . . . . . 311 3 DON JUAN 11 87 4
WHICH HOLD FAST OTHER PLEASURES GREAT AND SMALL . . 316 3 DON JUAN 12 3 4
WHO HOLD THE BALANCE OF THE WORLD WHO REIGN . . . 318 3 DON JUAN 12 5 1
AND HOLD UP TO THE SUN MY LITTLE TAPER . . . . . 325 3 DON JUAN 12 21 3
'TIS PITY THAT IT TAKES NO FURTHER HOLD . . . . . 382 3 DON JUAN 13 51 3
OF THOSE WHO HOLD THE KINGDOMS IN CONTROUL . . . . 455 3 DON JUAN 14 102 6
TO HOLD SOME SINECURES HE WISHED ABOLISHED . . . . 535 3 DON JUAN 16 72 7
BUT NOT TO GO TOO FAR I HOLD IT LAW . . . . 563 3 DON JUAN 17 2 4

HOLDERS
IF RATHER BROAD MADE STOCKS RISE AND THEIR HOLDERS . . . 208 3 DON JUAN 9 52 8
COLUMBIA'S STOCK HATH HOLDERS NOT UNKNOWN . . . . . 318 3 DON JUAN 12 6 6

HOLDING
FROM HOLDING UP THE NOTHINGNESS OF LIFE . . . . 69 3 DON JUAN 7 6 8

HOLDS
(THIS OLD SONG AND NEW SIMILE HOLDS GOOD) . . . . . . 10 2 DON JUAN D 2 2
(I THINK THE QUARTO HOLDS FIVE HUNDRED PAGES) . . . . 11 2 DON JUAN D 4 2
YET TO THESE FOUR IN THREE THINGS THE SAME LUCK HOLDS . 266 2 DON JUAN 2 206 7
BORN TO SOME FRIEND WHO HOLDS HIS WIFE AND RICHES . . . 287 2 DON JUAN 3 23 7
NOW IF THIS HOLDS GOOD IN A CHRISTIAN LAND . . . . . 11 3 DON JUAN 6 11 1
(THIS METAPHOR I THINK HOLDS GOOD AS AUGHT . . . . . 90 3 DON JUAN 7 49 3
HOLDS BY THE ROCK OR AS A LOVER'S KISS . . . . . . 238 3 DON JUAN 10 28 6
WHICH HOLDS WHAT MIGHT HAVE BEEN THE NOBLEST NATION . . 257 3 DON JUAN 10 66 2
IN THUNDER HOLDS THE WAY IT CAN'T WELL MISS . . . . 277 3 DON JUAN 11 20 6
AS A VOLCANO HOLDS THE LAVA MORE . . . . 374 3 DON JUAN 13 36 3
WHICH HOLDS A TREASURE LIKE A MISER'S HOARD . . . . 422 3 DON JUAN 14 27 3

HOLIDAY
AND WHEN A HOLIDAY UPON THEM SMILES . . . . 238 2 DON JUAN 2 154 3
HE ASKED THE MEANING OF THIS HOLIDAY . . . . 297 2 DON JUAN 3 42 5

HOLIER
THOSE HOLIER MYSTERIES WHICH THE WISE AND JUST . . . . 503 3 DON JUAN 16 6 6

HOLLAND
HOLLAND FRANCE ENGLAND GERMANY OR SPAIN . . . . . . 157 2 DON JUAN 2 1 2

HOLLAND'S
FROM THENCE TO HOLLAND'S HAGUE AND HELVOETSLUYS . . . . 256 3 DON JUAN 10 63 1

HOLLOW
IN HOLLOW HALLS WITH SPARRY ROOFS AND CELLS . . . . . 253 2 DON JUAN 2 184 6
WITHIN AN ALPINE HOLLOW WHEN THE WIND . . . . 360 2 DON JUAN 4 30 2
WHAT WAS NO DIRGE EXCEPT THE HOLLOW SEA'S . . . . . 383 2 DON JUAN 4 72 7
NOT THAT I DEEM OUR CHIEF JUDGE IS A HOLLOW MAN--) . . 357 3 DON JUAN 12 V 18 8
A MIGHTY WINDOW HOLLOW IN THE CENTRE . . . . . . 387 3 DON JUAN 13 62 1

HOLY
I THINK THAT WITH THIS HOLY NEW ALLIANCE . . . . . . 142 2 DON JUAN 1 211 1
THE SHIP CALL'D THE MOST HOLY TRINIDADA . . . . . . 169 2 DON JUAN 2 24 1
THAT HOLY STATE--BUT CERTAINLY BENEATH . . . . . . 280 2 DON JUAN 3 9 V5
ONE PERSON THRICE IN HOLY WEDLOCK BOUND . . . . . . 421 2 DON JUAN 5 20 5
IN HOLY MATRIMONY SNORES AWAY . . . . 42 3 DON JUAN 6 73 4

HOLY   (CONTINUED)
THE HOLY CAMEL'S HUMP BESIDES THE KORAN . . . . 57 3 DON JUAN 6 102   8
WHOSE EVERY BATTLE-FIELD IS HOLY GROUND . . . . 114 3 DON JUAN 8   5   3
JUST NOW BEHAVED AS IN THE HOLY LAND . . . . 116 3 DON JUAN 8   9   8
SHE SHOWED A GREAT DISLIKE TO HOLY WATER . . . . 252 3 DON JUAN 10   56   4
HIS HOLY TEMPLES IN THE LANDS WHICH BRED . . . . 262 3 DON JUAN 10   75   5
'TWAS FIT THAT HERE AS IN THE HOLY LAND . . . . 262 3 DON JUAN 10   75 V2
BEFORE AND AFTER BUT NOW GROWN MORE HOLY . . . . 297 3 DON JUAN 11   57   2
SHE MADE THE EARTH BELOW SEEM HOLY GROUND . . . . 387 3 DON JUAN 13   61   5
SHIP OFF THE HOLY THREE TO SENEGAL . . . . 446 3 DON JUAN 14   83   2
TO KEEP OUR HOLY BEACONS ALWAYS BRIGHT . . . . 496 3 DON JUAN 15   90   4
AS EVER LURKED BENEATH A HOLY HOOD . . . . 561 3 DON JUAN 16 123   2
HOMAGE
TO OFFER WILLING HOMAGE AS HER FAN . . . . 313 2 DON JUAN 3   73 V8
THERE WAS AWE IN THE HOMAGE WHICH SHE DREW . . . . . . 477 3 DON JUAN 15   47   5
HOMAGES
FOR BEING TOO EXCURSIVE IN HIS HOMAGES-- . . . . 312 3 DON JUAN 11   89   8
FORMS A SAD CLIMAX TO ROMANTIC HOMAGES . . . . 346 3 DON JUAN 12   65   6
HOME
TO SCHOOL OR HAD HIM SOUNDLY WHIPP'D AT HOME . . . . . 34 2 DON JUAN 1   25   7
HIS HOME DESERTED FOR THE LONELY WOOD . . . . 58 2 DON JUAN 1   87   2
BAY DEEP-MOUTH'D WELCOME AS WE DRAW NEAR HOME . . . . . 88 2 DON JUAN 1 123   2
AND REACH'D HIS HOME IN AN UNSEEMLY PLIGHT . . . . . . 126 2 DON JUAN 1 188   4
WHICH OVERLOOK'D THE WHITE WALLS OF HIS HOME . . . . . 286 2 DON JUAN 3   21   2
THE APPROACH OF HOME TO HUSBANDS AND TO SIRES . . . . . 287 2 DON JUAN 3   22   1
HE ENTER'D IN THE HOUSE NO MORE HIS HOME . . . . 301 2 DON JUAN 3   51   1
HE ENTER'D IN THE HOUSE--HIS HOME NO MORE . . . . 302 2 DON JUAN 3   52   1
FOR WITHOUT HEARTS THERE IS NO HOME--AND FELT . . . . . 302 2 DON JUAN 3   52   2
HOME TO THE WEARY FROM THE HUNGRY CHEER . . . . 338 2 DON JUAN 3 107   2
HER SALE SENT HOME SOME DISAPPOINTED BAWLERS . . . . . 407 2 DON JUAN 4 114   5
FROM FRIENDS AND HOME AND FREEDOM FAR ESTRANGED . . . . 414 2 DON JUAN 5   7   6
WHOM IF THEY WERE AT HOME IN SWEET CIRCASSIA . . . . . 25 3 DON JUAN 6   39   7
FOR SOME WERE THINKING OF THEIR HOME AND FRIENDS . . . 94 3 DON JUAN 7   54   7
SAYS HOTSPUR LONG ERE THEY WILL LEAVE THEIR HOME . . . 132 3 DON JUAN 8   38   4
TO DEEM THE WOODS SHALL BE OUR HOME AT LAST-- . . . . . 142 3 DON JUAN 8   60   8
HER HOME IS IN THE RARELY-TRODDEN WILD . . . . 143 3 DON JUAN 8   62   3
AT HOME IT MIGHT HAVE GIVEN HER SOME VEXATION . . . . . 241 3 DON JUAN 10   33   5
IN PLACE OF WHAT HER HOME AND FRIENDS ONCE WERE . . . . 252 3 DON JUAN 10   57   3
BUT JUAN FELT THOUGH NOT APPROACHING HOME . . . . 265 3 DON JUAN 10   81   5
NOT LONG BEFORE THE MOST OF THEM GO HOME-- . . . . . . 277 3 DON JUAN 11   20   3
FOR DOWNRIGHT RUDENESS YE MAY STAY AT HOME . . . . . . 290 3 DON JUAN 11   44   1
NOW WERE I ONCE AT HOME AND IN GOOD SATIRE . . . . . . 299 3 DON JUAN 11   62   6
THAT LADY WHO SHOULD BE AT HOME TO ALL . . . . 352 3 DON JUAN 12   79   8
AT HOME FAR MORE THAN EVER YET WAS LOVE-- . . . . 452 3 DON JUAN 14   96   4
TO FEEL IN FRIENDLESS PALACES A HOME . . . . 475 3 DON JUAN 15   44   7
IN BABYLON'S BRAVURAS--AS THE HOME . . . . 523 3 DON JUAN 16   46   1
HOMELESS
FOR SHE WAS HOMELESS HOUSELESS HELPLESS ALL . . . . . . 182 3 DON JUAN 8 141   2
HOMELY
DOWN TO A VERY HOMELY HOUSEHOLD SAVOUR . . . . 277 2 DON JUAN 3   5   8
HOMER
AFTER THE STYLE OF VIRGIL AND OF HOMER . . . . 135 2 DON JUAN 1 200   7
TROY OWES TO HOMER WHAT WHIST OWES TO HOYLE . . . . . . 328 2 DON JUAN 3   90   5
WE LEARN FROM HORACE HOMER SOMETIMES SLEEPS . . . . . . 333 2 DON JUAN 3   98   1
MEANWHILE AS HOMER SOMETIMES SLEEPS PERHAPS . . . . . . 503 2 DON JUAN 5 159   7
IF HOMER HAD FOUND MORTARS READY MADE . . . . 106 3 DON JUAN 7   78   4
OH THOU ETERNAL HOMER WHO COULDST CHARM . . . . 106 3 DON JUAN 7   79   1
OH THOU ETERNAL HOMER I HAVE NOW . . . . 106 3 DON JUAN 7   80   1
(START NOT KIND READER SINCE GREAT HOMER THOUGHT . . . 126 3 DON JUAN 8   29   6
HOMER'S
BUT THE BEST DISH THAT E'ER WAS COOK'D SINCE HOMER'S . . 221 2 DON JUAN 2 123   7
BEFORE PELIDES' DEATH OR HOMER'S BIRTH . . . . 400 2 DON JUAN 4 104   8
BY HOMER'S CATALOGUE OF SHIPS IS CLEAR . . . . 393 3 DON JUAN 13   74   6
TO HOMER'S ILIAD SINCE IT DREW TO TROY . . . . 441 3 DON JUAN 14   72   4
FOR WEAPONS BUT WHAT MUSE SINCE HOMER'S ABLE . . . . . 482 3 DON JUAN 15   62   3
HOMESTEAD
HE SUFFERED INFIDELS IN HIS HOMESTEAD . . . . 262 3 DON JUAN 10   75   3
HOMICIDE
OF HOMICIDE BUT THERE WAS NO SOLIDITY . . . . 80 3 DON JUAN 7   27   5
WHEN HOMICIDE AND HARLOTRY MADE GREAT . . . . 84 3 DON JUAN 7   37   2
HOMILIES
AND HOMILIES AND LIVES OF ALL THE SAINTS . . . . 47 2 DON JUAN 1   47   2
HOMILY
EACH EYE A SERMON AND HER BROW A HOMILY . . . . 29 2 DON JUAN 1   15   2
HOMMES
WITNESS THOSE CI-DEVANT JEUNES HOMMES WHO STEM . . . . 418 3 DON JUAN 14   18   7
HONEST
IN HONEST SIMPLE VERSE THIS SONG TO YOU . . . . 20 2 DON JUAN D   17   2
'TIS SWEET TO HEAR THE WATCHDOG'S HONEST BARK . . . . . 88 2 DON JUAN 1 123   1
UNLIKE THE HONEST ARAB THIEVES SO BRAVE . . . . 225 2 DON JUAN 2 130   6
AN HONEST GENTLEMAN AT HIS RETURN . . . . 287 2 DON JUAN 3   23   1
AN HONEST FRIENDSHIP WITH A MARRIED LADY-- . . . . . . 288 2 DON JUAN 3   25   3
AND THAT HIS FATHER WAS AN HONEST BLACKSMITH . . . . . 76 3 DON JUAN 7   20   4
OF HONEST FAME THAN SHEDDING SEAS OF GORE . . . . 113 3 DON JUAN 8   3   8
AND HONEST MEN FROM ICELAND TO BARBADOES . . . . 231 3 DON JUAN 10   13   5
COULD RECOMMENCE TO HUNT HIS HONEST MAN . . . . 281 3 DON JUAN 11   28   2
RIGHT HONESTLY HE LIKED AN HONEST HATER-- . . . . 361 3 DON JUAN 13   7   2
HONESTER
OF LIFE AND IN AN HONESTER VOCATION . . . . 283 2 DON JUAN 3   14   6

HONESTLY
    RIGHT HONESTLY HE LIKED AN HONEST HATER-- 361   3 DON JUAN 13   7   2
HONEY
    AND SMEAR HIS PAGE WITH GALL INSTEAD OF HONEY 142   2 DON JUAN 1   210   7
    THINK'ST THOU THE HONEY WITH THOSE OBJECTS GREW 144   2 DON JUAN 1   214   6
    BUT THERE WERE EGGS FRUIT COFFEE BREAD FISH HONEY 233   2 DON JUAN 2   145   7
    THEIR HEARTS THE FLOWER FROM WHENCE THE HONEY SPRUNG . . . 254   2 DON JUAN 2   187   8
    SEEMED TAKING OUT THE STING TO LEAVE THE HONEY 217   3 DON JUAN 9   70   8
    AND AS FOR HEAVEN BEING LOVE WHY NOT SAY HONEY 322   3 DON JUAN 12   14   7
    AND I ASSURE YOU THAT LIKE VIRGIN HONEY 330   3 DON JUAN 12   31   7
    WITNESS THE LANDS WHICH FLOW'D WITH MILK AND HONEY . . . 405   3 DON JUAN 13   100   1
    THAT WE OURSELVES--'TWAS IN THE HONEY MOON-- 517   3 DON JUAN 16   38   2
    THAT HONEY OF YOUR FASHIONABLE BEES-- 548   3 DON JUAN 16   100   6
HONEYMOON'S
    OF PAYMENT ERE THE HONEYMOON'S LAST KISSES 293   3 DON JUAN 11   49   3
HONOUR
    AND THAT HER HONOUR WAS A ROCK OR MOLE 66   2 DON JUAN 1   82   4
    JULIA HAD HONOUR VIRTUE TRUTH AND LOVE 80   2 DON JUAN 1   109   1
    MY HONOUR THUS IT SHALL NOT BE IN VAIN 105   2 DON JUAN 1   154   8
    SO JUAN FOLLOWING HONOUR AND HIS NOSE 127   3 DON JUAN 8   32   7
    THIS SPECIAL HONOUR WAS CONFERRED BECAUSE 182   3 DON JUAN 8   140   1
    SHOULD SO CONTINUE--'TIS A POINT OF HONOUR 231   3 DON JUAN 10   12   2
    SMOOTHED FOR A MONARCH'S SEAT OF HONOUR GAY 235   3 DON JUAN 10   21   6
    BUT SINCE STEAM ENGINES PRAISE AND HONOUR VAPOUR . . . 317   3 DON JUAN 12   4 V8
    HONOUR WAS MORE BEFORE THEIR NAMES THAN AFTER 398   3 DON JUAN 13   86   2
    SAVE IN THE CLUBS NO MAN OF HONOUR PLAYS-- 407   3 DON JUAN 13   106   2
    SO MUCH HE DEEMED HIS PATRONAGE AN HONOUR 528   3 DON JUAN 16   57   6
HONOURABLE
    YET JOSE WAS AN HONOURABLE MAN 40   2 DON JUAN 1   35   1
    THOSE HONOURABLE SCARS WHICH BROUGHT HIM FAME 431   2 DON JUAN 5   38   2
    HERE WAS AN HONOURABLE COMPROMISE 472   2 DON JUAN 5   105   1
    THE HONOURABLE MISTRESSES AND MISSES 308   3 DON JUAN 11   79   2
    HOW ALL THE NEEDY HONOURABLE MISTERS 331   3 DON JUAN 12   32   1
    ALSO THE HONOURABLE MRS SLEEP 396   3 DON JUAN 13   79   7
    THERE WERE FOUR HONOURABLE MISTERS WHOSE 398   3 DON JUAN 13   86   1
    HE WAS A COLD GOOD HONOURABLE MAN 440   3 DON JUAN 14   70   1
    THE LADY ADELINE RIGHT HONOURABLE 458   3 DON JUAN 15   6   1
    HIS SON THE HONOURABLE DICK DICEDRABBIT 534   3 DON JUAN 16   70   6
HONOUR'D
    AND HONOUR'D RAN A RISK OF GROWING LESS SO 458   3 DON JUAN 15   6   2
HONOURED
    WHO WERE THUS HONOURED BY THE GREATEST CHIEF 101   3 DON JUAN 7   68   2
    THEY HONOURED SUCH DETERMINED SCORN OF LIFE 171   3 DON JUAN 8   119   8
    HE ALMOST HONOURED HIM FOR HIS DOCILITY 368   3 DON JUAN 13   22   2
HONOUR'S
    FOR HONOUR'S PRIDE'S RELIGION'S VIRTUE'S SAKE 62   2 DON JUAN 1   75   4
    WHILE THIS HIGH POST OF HONOUR'S IN ABEYANCE 248   3 DON JUAN 10   49   1
HONOURS
    TO DUB THE LAST OF HONOURS IN DEGREES) 341   2 DON JUAN 3   110   8
    WAS LADEN WITH ALL KINDS OF GIFTS AND HONOURS 247   3 DON JUAN 10   46   7
HOOD
    BUT LIKE A HAWK ENCUMBER'D WITH HIS HOOD-- 10   2 DON JUAN D   2   6
    THE SABLE FRIAR IN HIS SOLEMN HOOD 558   3 DON JUAN 16   117   8
    AS EVER LURKED BENEATH A HOLY HOOD 561   3 DON JUAN 16   123   2
HOOK
    SHOULD HAVE A HOOK AND A SMALL TROUT TO PULL IT . . . 407   3 DON JUAN 13   106   8
HOOKS
    SOME HEIRESSES HAVE BIT AT SHARPERS' HOOKS 308   3 DON JUAN 11   81   3
    TO BAIT THEIR TENDER OR THEIR TENTER HOOKS 453   3 DON JUAN 14   97   8
HOPE
    THIS LICENCE IS TO HOPE THE READER WILL 86   2 DON JUAN 1   121   1
    I HOPE HE'S YOUNG AND HANDSOME--IS HE TALL 105   2 DON JUAN 1   154   6
    BECAUSE THE FIRST IS CRAZED BEYOND ALL HOPE 139   2 DON JUAN 1   205   3
    THE CREDULOUS HOPE OF MUTUAL MINDS IS O'ER 144   2 DON JUAN 1   216   5
    OF US DIES WITH THEM AS EACH FOND HOPE ENDS 167   2 DON JUAN 2   21   6
    TO PART WITH ALL TILL EVERY HOPE WAS BLIGHTED) 173   2 DON JUAN 2   32   7
    BUT NOW THERE CAME A FLASH OF HOPE ONCE MORE 176   2 DON JUAN 2   38   1
    BUT THE SHIP LABOUR'D SO THEY SCARCE COULD HOPE . . . 178   2 DON JUAN 2   41   2
    WITH LITTLE HOPE IN SUCH A ROLLING SEA 183   2 DON JUAN 2   50   2
    AND YET THEIR PRESENT HOPE WAS HARDLY MORE 185   2 DON JUAN 2   54   3
    BECAUSE THEY STILL CAN HOPE NOR SHINES THE KNIFE . . . 190   2 DON JUAN 2   64   5
    THEY LAY LIKE CARCASSES AND HOPE WAS NONE 194   2 DON JUAN 2   72   3
    STIFF ON HIS HEART AND PULSE AND HOPE WERE PAST . . . 204   2 DON JUAN 2   90   4
    THAN THESE AND SO THIS RAINBOW LOOK'D LIKE HOPE-- . . . 205   2 DON JUAN 2   93   7
    AROUND THEM (WHAT I HOPE WILL NEVER VANISH) 220   2 DON JUAN 2   120   6
    THEY HAD NO FURTHER FEELING HOPE NOR CARE-- 256   2 DON JUAN 2   189 V6
    HOPE CARE NOR LOVE BEYOND HER HEART BEAT HERE 264   2 DON JUAN 2   202   8
    AND IN THE HOPE OF MORE AT SEA REMAIN'D 283   2 DON JUAN 3   15   3
    THE ONLY HOPE OF COURAGE DWELLS 325   2 DON JUAN 3 L 14   4
    MAN--AND AS WE WOULD HOPE--PERHAPS THE DEVIL 345   2 DON JUAN 4   2   3
    BEFORE ONE CHARM OR HOPE HAD TAKEN WING 348   2 DON JUAN 4   8   8
    WITH JOY AND SORROW HOPE AND FEAR TO SEE 363   2 DON JUAN 4   36   8
    ALL HOPE TO LOOK UPON HER SWEET FACE BRED 377   2 DON JUAN 4   60   6
    EVEN WHEN THEY SMOTE HER IN THE HOPE TO SAVE 380   2 DON JUAN 4   67   8
    AS MOST AT HIS AGE ARE OF HOPE AND HEALTH 415   2 DON JUAN 5   8   2
    THAT ON A SUDDEN WHEN SHE LEAST HAD HOPE 44   3 DON JUAN 6   77   1
    BUT NE'ER THE LESS I HOPE IT IS NO CRIME 67   3 DON JUAN 7   2   6
    I HOPE THIS LITTLE QUESTION IS NO SIN 77   3 DON JUAN 7   21   4
    YOU LIKE TO BE THE HOPE OF THE FORLORN 98   3 DON JUAN 7   62   2

HOPE   (CONTINUED)
```
      MUCH LESS THAN IS THE HOPE OF EVERY COURT   . . . . .  . 106  3 DON JUAN  7    79   6
      TO HIM AND I SHOULD HOPE TO MOST THE THIRST . . . . .  . 138  3 DON JUAN  8    52   5
      IN JUAN'S LOOK PAIN PLEASURE HOPE FEAR MIXED  . . . .  . 159  3 DON JUAN  8    96   3
      FOR THEY WERE HEATED BY THE HOPE OF GAIN  . . . . . .  . 163  3 DON JUAN  8   103   6
      IN DARKNESS--I CAN ONLY HOPE THEY DID . . . . .  . . . . 178  3 DON JUAN  8   132   8
      THOUSANDS BLAZE LOVE HOPE DIE--HOW HAPPY THEY--  . . .  . 229  3 DON JUAN 10     8   8
      AND HUMBLY HOPE THAT THE SAME GOD WHICH HATH GIVEN  . . . 242  3 DON JUAN 10    36  V7
      THOUGH THIS WE HOPE--HAS BEEN RESERVED FOR THIS AGE  . . 376  3 DON JUAN 13    39  V5
      WHAT HOPE REMAINS  OF HOPE THE FULL POSSESSION . . . . . 379  3 DON JUAN 13    45   4
      WHAT HOPE REMAINS  OF HOPE THE FULL POSSESSION . . . . . 379  3 DON JUAN 13    45   4
      AS APROPOS OF HOPE OR RETROSPECTION  . . . . . . .  . . 456  3 DON JUAN 15     1   3
      A MODEST HOPE--BUT MODESTY'S MY FORTE . . . . . .  . . . 466  3 DON JUAN 15    22   1
      A MAN LIKE WHOM I HOPE WE SHAN'T SEE MANY SOON  . . .  . 484  3 DON JUAN 15    65   4
      WHICH YOU MIGHT ELSEWHERE HOPE TO FIND IN VAIN . . . .  . 502  3 DON JUAN 16     3   4
      OR HOPE OR LOVE WITH ANY OF THE WILES . . . . . .  . . . 544  3 DON JUAN 16    92   7
      THE UNBOUNDED HOPE AND HEAVENLY IGNORANCE  . . . . .  . 554  3 DON JUAN 16   108   2
      EXPIRING IN THE HOPE OF SENSATION--  . . . . . . . . . . 569  3 DON JUAN 17  V 13   7
HOPED
      SHE HOPED HE WOULD IMPROVE--PERHAPS BELIEVED  . . . .  . 161  2 DON JUAN  2     9   6
      THEY HOPED THE WIND WOULD RISE THESE FOOLISH MEN  . . . 192  2 DON JUAN  2    69   5
      HE HOPED INDEED HE THOUGHT HE COULD BE SURE . . . . .  .  58  3 DON JUAN  6   104   1
      SOME HOPED THINGS MIGHT NOT TURN OUT AS THEY FEAR'D . . 429  3 DON JUAN 14    44   3
HOPEFUL
      EVEN IN THE HOPEFUL ISLE WHOSE OUTLET'S DOVER . . . .  . 331  3 DON JUAN 12    33   6
HOPEFUL'S
      YOUNG HOPEFUL'S MISTRESS OR MISS FANNY'S LOVER . . . .  .  75  2 DON JUAN  1   100   4
HOPELESS
      THUS TO THEIR HOPELESS EYES THE NIGHT WAS SHOWN  . . . 182  2 DON JUAN  2    49   5
      AND HOPELESS EYES WHICH ON THE DEEP ALONE  . . . . .  . 182  2 DON JUAN  2    49  V6
HOPES
      WHAT ARE THE HOPES OF MAN OLD EGYPT'S KING  . . . . .  . 146  2 DON JUAN  1   219   1
      LET NOT A MONUMENT GIVE YOU OR ME HOPES  . . . . . .  . 146  2 DON JUAN  1   219   7
      OR BREAKS THEIR HOPES OR HEARTS OR HEADS OR NECKS  . . . 172  2 DON JUAN  2    31   6
      SO THAT THEMSELVES AS WELL AS HOPES WERE DAMP'D  . . . 188  2 DON JUAN  2    60   7
      AND CARRY THEM TO SHORE THESE HOPES WERE FINE . . . .  . 192  2 DON JUAN  2    69   6
      COULD NOT YET SEPARATE THEIR HOPES FROM FEARS . . . .  . 208  2 DON JUAN  2    98   3
      THE HOPES OF ALL MEN AND OF EVERY NATION . . . . . .  . 250  2 DON JUAN  2   179   4
      THE ASHES OF OUR HOPES IS A DEEP GRIEF  . . . . . .  . 301  2 DON JUAN  3    51   7
      TO CUTTING SHORT THEIR HOPES OF HAVING ANY . . .  . . . 487  2 DON JUAN  5   132   8
      YOUR SLAVE BRINGS TIDINGS--HE HOPES NOT TOO SOON--  . . 494  2 DON JUAN  5   144   5
      HIS THANKS AND HOPES TO TAKE THE CITY SOON . . . . .  . 140  3 DON JUAN  8    56   6
      JUST AS KOUTOUSOW'S MOST FORLORN OF HOPES  . . . . .  . 148  3 DON JUAN  8    73   3
      THE FORMER'S HYMENEAL HOPES TO FLATTER  . . . . . .  . 292  3 DON JUAN 11    46   3
      OF HOPES AND FEARS WHICH SHAKE A SINGLE BALL . . . .  . 304  3 DON JUAN 11    72   8
      POSSESS'D THE ORE OF WHICH MERE HOPES ALLURE . . . .  . 319  3 DON JUAN 12     8   3
HOPING
      HOPING NO VERY OLD VIZIER MIGHT CHOOSE  . . . . . .  . 409  2 DON JUAN  4   116   6
HOPS
      A PARADISE OF HOPS AND HIGH PRODUCTION  . . . . . .  . 262  3 DON JUAN 10    76   2
HORACE
      (HORACE MAKES THIS THE HEROIC TURNPIKE ROAD)  . . . .  .  24  2 DON JUAN  1     6   2
      CONSULE PLANCO HORACE SAID AND SO . . . . . . .  . . . 143  2 DON JUAN  1   212   2
      HORACE CATULLUS SCHOLARS OVID TUTOR  . . . . . . .  . 266  2 DON JUAN  2   205   3
      WE LEARN FROM HORACE HOMER SOMETIMES SLEEPS  . . . .  . 333  2 DON JUAN  3    98   1
      YET LET THEM THINK THAT HORACE HAS EXPREST . . . . .  . 448  2 DON JUAN  5    63   1
      THUS HORACE WROTE WE ALL KNOW LONG AGO  . . . . . .  . 470  2 DON JUAN  5   101   5
      WOULD POPE HAVE SUNG OR HORACE BEEN INSPIRED  . . . .  . 470  2 DON JUAN  5   101   8
      PERHAPS FROM HORACE HIS NIL ADMIRARI  . . . . . . .  . 374  3 DON JUAN 13    35   1
      OR (TO THE POINT WITH HORACE AND WITH PULCI)  . . . .  . 396  3 DON JUAN 13    81   7
      SAITH HORACE THE GREAT LITTLE POET'S WRONG . . . . .  . 443  3 DON JUAN 14    77   2
HORATIAN
      HORATIAN MEDIO TU TUTISSIMUS IBIS  . . . . . . . .  .  14  3 DON JUAN  6    17   8
HORDE
      SOCIETY IS NOW ONE POLISH'D HORDE . . . . . . .  . . . 402  3 DON JUAN 13    95   7
HORDES
      LEAVE BATTLES TO THE TURKISH HORDES  . . . . . . .  . 324  2 DON JUAN  3   L 9   3
HORIZON
      WHICH ARCHED THE HORIZON LIKE A FIERY CLOUD . . . .  . 115  3 DON JUAN  8     6   3
HORIZON'S
      'TWIXT NIGHT AND MORN UPON THE HORIZON'S VERGE . . .  . 500  3 DON JUAN 15    99   2
HORN
      LIKE ROLAND'S HORN IN RONCEVALLES' BATTLE  . . . . .  . 267  3 DON JUAN 10    87   8
HORNE
      A PARAGRAPH I THINK ABOUT HORNE TOOKE . . . . . .  . . 512  3 DON JUAN 16    27   3
HORNER
      WHERE HE MAY FIX HIMSELF LIKE SMALL JACK HORNER  . . . 303  3 DON JUAN 11    69   4
HORNET
      ALIGHTING RARELY--WERE SHE BUT A HORNET  . . . . . .  . 400  3 DON JUAN 13    89   7
HORNS
      THERE WREATHE HIS VENERABLE HORNS WITH FLOWERS  . . . 292  2 DON JUAN  3    32   2
      RIFE WITH MORE HORNS THAN HOUNDS--SHE HATH THE CHASE . . 395  3 DON JUAN 13    78   2
HORRIBLE
      WITHOUT BEING MUCH MORE HORRIBLE THAN DANTE . . . .  . 200  2 DON JUAN  2    83   8
      THOUGH HORRIBLE TO SEE YET GRAND TO TELL . . . . . .  . 489  2 DON JUAN  5   135   5
      OF HORRIBLE OR LUDICROUS TO QUOTE . . . . . . .  . . . 156  3 DON JUAN  8    89  V5
HORRID
      BUT VIRGIL'S SONGS ARE PURE EXCEPT THAT HORRID ONE  . . .  45  2 DON JUAN  1    42   7
      AND HAVE A KIND OF WILD AND HORRID GLEE . . . . .  . . 183  2 DON JUAN  2    50   6
```

HORRID   (CONTINUED)
A HORRID THOUGHT--FOR WHO WOULD BE A WIDOWER 278   2 DON JUAN 3   7   V7
AND HORRID WAS THE CONTRAST TO THE VIEW-- 431   2 DON JUAN 5   38   3
THE HORRID WAR-WHOOP AND THE SHRILLER SCREAM 175   3 DON JUAN 8   127   5
THAT HORRID EQUINOX THAT HATEFUL SECTION 238   3 DON JUAN 10   27   4
THE HORRID SIN--AND WHAT'S STILL WORSE THE TROUBLE . . 292   3 DON JUAN 11   46   8
OF ALL THE HORRID HIDEOUS NOTES OF WOE 432   3 DON JUAN 14   50   1
THEIR HIDEOUS WIVES THEIR HORRID SELVES AND DRESSES . . 550   3 DON JUAN 16   103   7
HORROR
IN SILENT HORROR AND THEIR DISTRIBUTION 195   2 DON JUAN 2   75   2
YOU STARTED BACK IN HORROR TO SURVEY 462   2 DON JUAN 5   88   2
UPON THE EAR AND SOUNDS OF HORROR CHIME 141   3 DON JUAN 8   58   6
HORRORS
AND TALK IN TENDER HORRORS OF OUR LOATHING 301   3 DON JUAN 11   65   6
HORSE
A BETTER CAVALIER NE'ER MOUNTED HORSE 26   2 DON JUAN 1   9   5
AN ARAB HORSE A STATELY STAG A BARB 160   2 DON JUAN 2   6   1
SAYING HE HAD GORGED ENOUGH TO MAKE A HORSE ILL . . . 240   2 DON JUAN 2   159   8
HORSE BY A BLACKLEG BROADCLOTH BY A TAILOR 424   2 DON JUAN 5   26   7
JUST AS ONE VIEWS A HORSE TO GUESS HIS PRICE 441   2 DON JUAN 5   54   6
OF AN IMPROPER FRIENDSHIP FOR HER HORSE 446   2 DON JUAN 5   61   3
IN AN ERRATUM OF HER HORSE FOR COURIER 446   2 DON JUAN 5   61   V7
A FAVOURITE HORSE FALLEN LAME JUST AS HE'S MOUNTED . . 16   3 DON JUAN 6   21   4
WHETHER THEY COME BY HORSE OR CHAISE OR COACH 279   3 DON JUAN 11   23   3
COULD BACK A HORSE AS DESPOTS RIDE A RUSSIAN 368   3 DON JUAN 13   23   8
SO THAT HIS HORSE OR CHARGER HUNTER HACK 424   3 DON JUAN 14   32   7
HE ACQUITTED BOTH HIMSELF AND HORSE THE 'SQUIRES . . 425   3 DON JUAN 14   34   2
HORSEBACK
BY SLAVES ON HORSEBACK--I HAVE SEEN MALT LIQUORS . . . 310   3 DON JUAN 11   85   6
HORSEMEN
IN SIGHT TWO HORSEMEN WHO WERE DEEMED COSSACQUES . . . 87   3 DON JUAN 7   43   2
HORSE-RACES
IF PINDAR SANG HORSE-RACES WHAT SHOULD HINDER 319   2 DON JUAN 3   85   7
HORSES
CHANGE HORSES MAKING HISTORY CHANGE ITS TUNE 76   2 DON JUAN 1   103   5
TROOPS OF UNTENDED HORSES HERE AND THERE 387   2 DON JUAN 4   78   1
BILLS--WOMEN--WIVES DOGS HORSES--AND MANKIND 17   3 DON JUAN 6   22   V2
WHEN ALL THE HEART-STRINGS LIKE WILD HORSES PULL . . 59   3 DON JUAN 6   107   4
AND WISHING THAT POST HORSES HAD THE WINGS 197   3 DON JUAN 9   30   6
I LEFT DON JUAN WITH HIS HORSES BAITING-- 203   3 DON JUAN 9   42   3
ON WITH THE HORSES OFF TO CANTERBURY 260   3 DON JUAN 10   71   1
BUT FOR POST HORSES WHO FINDS SYMPATHY 377   3 DON JUAN 13   42   5
AND HAPPIEST THEY WHO HORSES CAN ENGAGE 378   3 DON JUAN 13   44   4
AWAY AWAY FRESH HORSES ARE THE WORD 379   3 DON JUAN 13   46   3
HORSES THEY RIDE WITHOUT REMORSE OR RUTH 501   3 DON JUAN 16   1   6
FOR THE LORD HENRY LINKED WITH DOGS AND HORSES . . . 534   3 DON JUAN 16   68   2
HORSES'
HAVING BEEN USED TO SERVE ON HORSES' BACKS 149   3 DON JUAN 8   74   5
HORTENSIUS
WHO LENT HIS LADY TO HIS FRIEND HORTENSIUS 10   3 DON JUAN 6   7   8
HOSPITABLE
CONTINUED STILL HER HOSPITABLE CARES 285   2 DON JUAN 3   19   5
HOSPITABLY
HE WOULD HAVE HOSPITABLY CURED THE STRANGER 225   2 DON JUAN 2   130   7
HOSPITAL
A HOSPITAL A CHURCH--AND LEAVE BEHIND 320   3 DON JUAN 12   10   3
HOSPITALITY
HER FATHER'S HOSPITALITY SEEM'D MIDDLING 295   2 DON JUAN 3   39   5
AND ALL MEN LIKE TO SHOW THEIR HOSPITALITY 369   3 DON JUAN 13   24   7
LET NONE ACCUSE OLD ENGLAND'S HOSPITALITY-- 381   3 DON JUAN 13   49   7
HOST
GUARDED BY SHOALS AND ROCKS AS BY AN HOST 249   2 DON JUAN 2   177   3
A DEVOTEE WHEN SOARS THE HOST IN SIGHT 261   2 DON JUAN 2   196   3
AND BAFFLED THE ASSAULTS OF ALL THEIR HOST 171   3 DON JUAN 8   120   4
WE UNDERSTAND THE SPLENDID HOST INTENDS 382   3 DON JUAN 13   52   1
DECKED BY THE RAYS REFLECTED FROM HIS HOST 383   3 DON JUAN 13   53   5
HIS HOST WITH BROAD ARMS 'GAINST THE THUNDER-STROKE . 384   3 DON JUAN 13   56   4
HAD FALLEN LAST MARKET COST HIS HOST THREE VOTES . . 543   3 DON JUAN 16   89   8
DELIGHTED WITH THE DINNER AND THEIR HOST 549   3 DON JUAN 16   101   7
ASSEMBLED WITH OUR HOSTESS AND MINE HOST 568   3 DON JUAN 17   13   6
HOSTESS
THERE STANDS THE NOBLE HOSTESS NOR SHALL SINK 302   3 DON JUAN 11   68   1
ASSEMBLED WITH OUR HOSTESS AND MINE HOST 568   3 DON JUAN 17   13   6
HOSTILE
ON EACH HARANGUE DEPENDS SOME HOSTILE SWORDS 153   2 DON JUAN 1   V 4   3
HOST'S
SHOULD CAUSE MORE FEAR THAN A WHOLE HOST'S IDENTITY . . 559   3 DON JUAN 16   120   8
HOSTS
OF GUEBRES GIAOURS AND GINNS AND GOULS IN HOSTS . . . 30   3 DON JUAN 6   48   6
LORD HENRY AND HIS LADY WERE THE HOSTS 404   3 DON JUAN 13   99   1
HOT
IN MY HOT YOUTH--WHEN GEORGE THE THIRD WAS KING . . . 143   2 DON JUAN 1   212   8
SHRINKS FROM THE APPLICATION OF HOT TOWELS 168   2 DON JUAN 2   23   4
FROM GLISTENING WAVES AND SKIES SO HOT AND BARE-- . . 210   2 DON JUAN 2   103   6
WHILE YOUTH'S HOT WISHES IN OUR RED VEINS REVEL . . . 345   2 DON JUAN 4   2   5
SNATCH'D DOWN HIS SABRE IN HOT HASTE TO WREAK 364   2 DON JUAN 4   37   3
AND THIS WAS ADMIRABLE FOR SO HOT 119   3 DON JUAN 8   16   1
OF HOT OR COLD MERCURIAL OR SEDATE 327   3 DON JUAN 12   24   2
LIKE RUSSIANS RUSHING FROM HOT BATHS TO SNOWS 349   3 DON JUAN 12   73   5

HOT   (CONTINUED)
      WHAT THEY SHOULD LAUGH AT--THE NOW HOT OR COLD 366   3 DON JUAN 13   17   V7
      HAD IT NOT HAPPENED SCALDING HOT TO BE   513   3 DON JUAN 16   30   4
      QUITE FULL RIGHT DULL GUESTS HOT AND DISHES COLD   538   3 DON JUAN 16   78   6
HOTBEDS
      THEIR WHILE TO REAR WHOLE HOTBEDS IN THEIR WORKS   434   2 DON JUAN 5   42   7
HOTEL
      THY CLIFFS DEAR DOVER HARBOUR AND HOTEL   259   3 DON JUAN 10   69   2
      THEY REACHED THE HOTEL FORTH STREAMED FROM THE FRONT DOOR . 282 3 DON JUAN 11   30   1
HOTELS
      PURSUED HIS PATH AND DROVE PAST SOME HOTELS   282   3 DON JUAN 11   29   7
      INTO ONE OF THE SWEETEST OF HOTELS   283   3 DON JUAN 11   31   1
HOT-HOUSE
      AND MADE UPON THE HOT-HOUSE SEVERAL STRICTURES   406   3 DON JUAN 13   102   4
HOT-PRESS
      A BALL-ROOM BARD A FOOLSCAP HOT-PRESS DARLING   404   2 DON JUAN 4   109   2
HOTSPUR
      LIKE MODERATE HOTSPUR ON THE IMMORTAL PAGE   490   2 DON JUAN 5   136   4
      SAYS HOTSPUR LONG ERE THEY WILL LEAVE THEIR HOME 132   3 DON JUAN 8   38   4
HOTTENTOT
      AND HOTTENTOT ADJUSTMENT OF THEIR TRESSES   550   3 DON JUAN 16   103   V8
HOTTEST
      AND WHERE THE HOTTEST FIRE WAS SEEN AND HEARD   129   3 DON JUAN 8   33   5
HOUNDS
      HOUNDS WHEN THE HUNTSMAN TUMBLES ARE AT FAULT   119   3 DON JUAN 8   16   8
      RIFE WITH MORE HORNS THAN HOUNDS--SHE HATH THE CHASE . .   395   3 DON JUAN 13   78   2
      RODE O'ER THE HOUNDS IT MAY BE NOW AND THEN   424   3 DON JUAN 14   33   7
      WHOSE HOUNDS NE'ER ERRED NOR GREYHOUNDS DEIGNED TO LURCH   539   3 DON JUAN 16   80   2
HOUR
      (ALTHOUGH IT COST ME HALF AN HOUR IN SPINNING)   25   2 DON JUAN 1   7   6
      EXCEEDING SAGELY FROM THAT HOUR DISPENSED   66   2 DON JUAN 1   82   5
      'TWAS ON THE SIXTH OF JUNE ABOUT THE HOUR   77   2 DON JUAN 1   104   1
      THERE IS A DANGEROUS SILENCE IN THAT HOUR   82   2 DON JUAN 1   114   1
      MY MOTHER DREAM'D NOT IN MY NATAL HOUR   106   2 DON JUAN 1   155   7
      THE PEOPLE'S SYCOPHANT--IN JUSTICE'S HOUR   151   2 DON JUAN 1   V 2   V7
      WITHOUT THE SENSE TO KEEP IT FOR AN HOUR   152   2 DON JUAN 1   V 3   8
      BY THEM PER HOUR AND THEY HAD ALL BEEN UNDONE   171   2 DON JUAN 2   29   7
      ALL ONE AN HOUR HENCE JUAN ANSWER'D NO   175   2 DON JUAN 2   36   2
      THE SHIP WOULD SWIM AN HOUR WHICH BY GOOD LUCK   177   2 DON JUAN 2   40   7
      THE SEA-SHORE AT THIS HOUR MUST LEAVE HIS PLATE   240   2 DON JUAN 2   159   5
      IT WAS THE COOLING HOUR JUST WHEN THE ROUNDED   252   2 DON JUAN 2   183   1
      SO LONELY LOVING HELPLESS AND THE HOUR   258   2 DON JUAN 2   192   2
      THE LADY WATCH'D HER LOVER--AND THAT HOUR   262   2 DON JUAN 2   198   1
      WHILE SHE HAD NOT ONE HOUR TO SPARE FROM LOVING   295   2 DON JUAN 3   39   8
      AND MUSING THERE AN HOUR ALONE   321   2 DON JUAN 3   L 3   3
      OH THAT THE PRESENT HOUR WOULD LEND   325   2 DON JUAN 3   L 12   4
      THAT HEAVENLIEST HOUR OF HEAVEN IS WORTHIEST THEE . . .   334   2 DON JUAN 3   101   8
      AVE MARIA BLESSED BE THE HOUR   335   2 DON JUAN 3   102   1
      AVE MARIA 'TIS THE HOUR OF PRAYER   336   2 DON JUAN 3   103   1
      AVE MARIA 'TIS THE HOUR OF LOVE   336   2 DON JUAN 3   103   2
      SWEET HOUR OF TWILIGHT--IN THE SOLITUDE   337   2 DON JUAN 3   105   1
      HOW HAVE I LOVED THE TWILIGHT HOUR AND THEE   337   2 DON JUAN 3   105   8
      SOFT HOUR WHICH WAKES THE WISH AND MELTS THE HEART . .   338   2 DON JUAN 3   108   1
      HAD LEFT THE WRETCH AN UNCORRUPTED HOUR   339   2 DON JUAN 3   109   8
      WHO NEVER FOUND A SINGLE HOUR TOO SLOW   353   2 DON JUAN 4   18   3
      THEY GAZED UPON THE SUNSET 'TIS AN HOUR   354   2 DON JUAN 4   20   1
      I KNOW NOT WHY BUT IN THAT HOUR TO-NIGHT   355   2 DON JUAN 4   21   1
      SHOULD AN HOUR COME TO BID THEM BREATHE APART   358   2 DON JUAN 4   27   3
      THIS HOUR WERE THINE--AND THY YOUNG MINION'S LAST . . .   368   2 DON JUAN 4   46   V8
      THE MOORISH BLOOD PARTAKES THE PLANET'S HOUR   374   2 DON JUAN 4   56   4
      SAILING SIX KNOTS AN HOUR BEFORE THE WIND   384   2 DON JUAN 4   75   5
      BUT AT THIS HOUR I WISH TO PART IN PEACE   398   2 DON JUAN 4   99   2
      I THINK IT IS PERHAPS THE GLOOMIEST HOUR   426   2 DON JUAN 5   30   7
      TO LOSE THE HOUR WOULD MAKE HER QUITE A MARTYR   482   2 DON JUAN 5   122   7
      HER BEAUTIES SEIZED THE UNCONSCIOUS HOUR OF NIGHT . . .   39   3 DON JUAN 6   66   7
      MORE EVIL IN AN HOUR THAN THIRTY BRIGHT   86   3 DON JUAN 7   41   5
      THE HOUR AS IS THE CASE WITH LIVELY BRAINS   129   3 DON JUAN 8   33   4
      THAT HOUR IS NOT FOR US BUT 'TIS FOR YOU   180   3 DON JUAN 8   136   1
      HAD SEIZED THE LUCKY HOUR TO RECONNOITRE   273   3 DON JUAN 11   11   4
      LOUNGING AND BOXING AND THE TWILIGHT HOUR   301   3 DON JUAN 11   66   2
      A BLEST HOUR FOR POSTILLIONS--CHARIOTS FLY   377   3 DON JUAN 13   42   V3
      IN EGYPT'S RAYS TO HARP AT A FIXED HOUR)   388   3 DON JUAN 13   64   4
      LONGING AT SIXTY FOR THE HOUR OF SIX   406   3 DON JUAN 13   102   8
      BUT NONE WERE GENE THE GREAT HOUR OF UNION   406   3 DON JUAN 13   103   1
      BEFORE THEY FIND AN HOUR TO INTRODUCE IT   408   3 DON JUAN 13   109   7
      THEY SEPARATED AT AN EARLY HOUR   409   3 DON JUAN 13   111   1
      WHY DRINK WHY READ--TO MAKE SOME HOUR LESS DREARY 415   3 DON JUAN 14   11   4
      OR LIKE A FLYING HOUR BEFORE AURORA   428   3 DON JUAN 14   40   1
      WHICH MAY ROUND OFF AN HOUR UPON A TIME   465   3 DON JUAN 15   20   4
      BUT FOR THAT HOUR CALLED HALF-HOUR GIVEN TO DRESS . . .   482   3 DON JUAN 15   61   7
      DON JUAN WHEN THE MIDNIGHT HOUR OF PILLOWS   555   3 DON JUAN 16   110   3
HOURI
      AS E'ER HELD HOURI IN THAT HEATHENISH HEAVEN   77   2 DON JUAN 1   104   4
      AND THUS YOUR HOURI (IT MAY BE) DISPUTES   168   3 DON JUAN 8   113   7
HOURIS
      THOSE HOURIS LIKE ALL OTHER PRETTY CREATURES   167   3 DON JUAN 8   111   7
      YOUR HOURIS ALSO HAVE A NATURAL PLEASURE   168   3 DON JUAN 8   113   1
      THUS THE YOUNG KHAN WITH HOURIS IN HIS SIGHT   168   3 DON JUAN 8   114   1
      WITH PROPHETS HOURIS ANGELS SAINTS DESCRIED   169   3 DON JUAN 8   115   7
      HOURIS OR AUGHT EXCEPT HIS FLORID RACE   169   3 DON JUAN 8   116   3

                                    367

```
                                                          PAGE VOL        CANTO STANZA LN
HOURLY
     THIS HOURLY DREAD OF ALL WHOSE THREATENED STING  . . .  188  3 DON JUAN   9      11    6
HOURS
     (I WONDER HOW THEY GOT THROUGH THE TWELVE HOURS)  . . .   30  2 DON JUAN   1      18    6
     HAVE MOMENTS HOURS AND DAYS SO UNPREPARED  . . . . . .   33  2 DON JUAN   1      21    4
     HE MISS'D THE PATHWAY HE FORGOT THE HOURS  . . . . . .   72  2 DON JUAN   1      94    5
     THUS WOULD HE WHILE HIS LONELY HOURS AWAY  . . . . . .   73  2 DON JUAN   1      96    1
     ON WHICH THREE SINGLE HOURS OF MOONSHINE SMILE--  . . .   82  2 DON JUAN   1     113    7
     UNTIL THE HOURS OF ABSENCE SHOULD RUN THROUGH  . . . .   98  2 DON JUAN   1     141    6
     BESIDES IT WANTED BUT FEW HOURS OF DAY  . . . . . .     114  2 DON JUAN   1     169    6
     IN THE MEANTIME TO PASS HER HOURS AWAY  . . . . .       162  2 DON JUAN   2      10    1
     BEDEW'D HIS SPIRIT IN HIS CALMER HOURS  . . . . .       304  2 DON JUAN   3      56    8
     AND SHOW THAT LATE HOURS WINE AND LOVE ARE ABLE  . . .  309  2 DON JUAN   3      66    7
     KEPT FOR ALL COMERS AT ALL HOURS TO DINE  . . . .      310  2 DON JUAN   3      69    8
     THESE AT SOME CERTAIN PORTIONED HOURS WERE SPREAD  . .  310  2 DON JUAN   3      69   V6
     SIGH'D TO BEHOLD THEM OF THEIR HOURS BEREFT  . . . .   348  2 DON JUAN   4       8    5
     AND NEVER KNOW THE WEIGHT OF HUMAN HOURS  . . . . .    352  2 DON JUAN   4      15    8
     HE DOUBTED NOT A FEW HOURS OF REFLECTION  . . . . .    452  2 DON JUAN   5      71    5
     THIS WEAKNESS IN A FEW HOURS AND RECOVER  . . . . .     47  3 DON JUAN   6      83    8
     THOSE CAPTIVE SOOTHERS OF A CAPTIVE'S HOURS  . . . .    54  3 DON JUAN   6      97    8
     FOR SIX HOURS BORE THEY WITHOUT INTERMISSION  . . .     81  3 DON JUAN   7      30    1
     WHOSE LEISURE HOURS ARE WASTED ON A HARLOT  . . . .    109  3 DON JUAN   7      84   V3
     BEFORE THE BRIDAL HOURS HAVE DANCED THEIR MEASURE  . .  168  3 DON JUAN   8     113    3
     SUCH TALES BEING FOR THE TEA HOURS OF SOME TABBY  . .   184  3 DON JUAN   9       2    6
     SUNS AS RAYS--WORLDS LIKE ATOMS--YEARS LIKE HOURS  . .  189  3 DON JUAN   9      13    8
     WHO PROMISED TO BE GREAT IN SOME FEW HOURS  . . . .    222  3 DON JUAN   9      79    3
     AND FOUR-AND-TWENTY HOURS AND TWICE THAT NUMBER  . .    248  3 DON JUAN  10      48    2
     THE HOURS WHICH HOW TO PASS IS BUT TO FEW KNOWN  . .    406  3 DON JUAN  13     103    5
     GOOD HOURS OF FAIR CHEEKS ARE THE FAIREST TINTERS  . .  409  3 DON JUAN  13     111    7
     SOME HOURS TO MAKE THE REMNANT WORTH ENJOYING  . . .    444  3 DON JUAN  14      78    8
HOURS'
     IN TWELVE HOURS' TIME AND VERY LITTLE SPACE  . . . . .  277  3 DON JUAN  11      18    6
HOUSE
     TO SEE A KINGDOM OR A HOUSE O'ERTURN'D  . . . . .        31  2 DON JUAN   1      19    6
     HIS HOUSE WAS SOLD HIS SERVANTS SENT AWAY  . . . . .     39  2 DON JUAN   1      34    3
     THE HOUSE OF COMMONS DAMOCLES OF WORDS  . . . . .       153  2 DON JUAN   1    V  4    1
     THERSITES OF THE HOUSE PAROLLES OF LAW  . . . . .       153  2 DON JUAN   1    V  4    7
     A VERY HANDSOME HOUSE FROM OUT HIS GUILT  . . . . .     223  2 DON JUAN   2     127    3
     BUT TAKING HIM INTO HER FATHER'S HOUSE  . . . . .       225  2 DON JUAN   2     130    1
     AND PENSIVE TO HER FATHER'S HOUSE SHE WENT  . . . .     228  2 DON JUAN   2     136    1
     AND PUT HIS HOUSE IN MOURNING SEVERAL WEEKS  . . . .    295  2 DON JUAN   3      38    4
     SHE NOW KEPT HOUSE UPON HER OWN ACCOUNT  . . . . .      295  2 DON JUAN   3      38    8
     ALL HAD BEEN OPEN HEART AND OPEN HOUSE  . . . . . .     295  2 DON JUAN   3      39   V7
     ON TO THE HOUSE BUT BY A PRIVATE WAY  . . . . . .       300  2 DON JUAN   3      49    2
     HE ENTER'D IN THE HOUSE NO MORE HIS HOME . . . . .      301  2 DON JUAN   3      51    1
     HE ENTER'D IN THE HOUSE--HIS HOME NO MORE  . . . .      302  2 DON JUAN   3      52    1
     THEIR LOVES AND FEASTS AND HOUSE AND DRESS AND MODE  .  317  2 DON JUAN   3      81    7
     FOR THE FIRST MRS MILTON LEFT HIS HOUSE  . . . . .      328  2 DON JUAN   3      91    8
     AND SUBJECT WHEN THE HOUSE IS THIN TO COLD  . . . .     389  2 DON JUAN   4      83    3
     HIM BORNE INTO THE HOUSE AND UP THE STAIR  . . . .      429  2 DON JUAN   5      34    4
     A HALF-WAY HOUSE OF DIPLOMATIC REST  . . . . . .        472  2 DON JUAN   5     105    2
     LIFE'S HALF-WAY HOUSE WHERE DAMES WITH VIRTUE CROWNED    43  3 DON JUAN   6      75    5
     RAMPART WALL CASEMENT HOUSE--FOR THERE WAS NOT . . .    131  3 DON JUAN   8      37    3
     OF HUMAN YEARS THAT HALF-WAY HOUSE THAT RUDE  . . .     238  3 DON JUAN  10      27    5
     AND BEING TOLD IT WAS GOD'S HOUSE SHE SAID  . . . .     262  3 DON JUAN  10      75    1
     THE MANSION HOUSE TOO (THOUGH SOME PEOPLE QUIZ IT)  .   280  3 DON JUAN  11      25    6
     OF OFFICE OR THE HOUSE OF OFFICE FED  . . . . . .       287  3 DON JUAN  11      40    6
     THE HOUSE OF COMMONS TURNED TO A TAX-TRAP--  . . . .    310  3 DON JUAN  11      84    3
     I HAVE SEEN THE FUNDS AT WAR WITH HOUSE AND LAND--      310  3 DON JUAN  11      85    3
     SO THAT FEW MEMBERS KEPT THE HOUSE UP LATER  . . . .    367  3 DON JUAN  13      20    8
     WHICH DOTH NOT SHAKE SOME VERY SPLENDID HOUSE  . . .    370  3 DON JUAN  13      26    4
     WHEN EACH HOUSE WAS A FORTALICE--AS TELL  . . . .       386  3 DON JUAN  13      60    5
     AND NOT TO ENCOURAGE WHISPERING IN THE HOUSE  . . .     439  3 DON JUAN  14      67   V4
     OR STEP RAN SADLY THROUGH THAT ANTIQUE HOUSE  . . .     509  3 DON JUAN  16      20    4
     BUT STILL TO THE HOUSE OF AMUNDEVILLE  . . . . .        519  3 DON JUAN  16    L  3    3
     THOUGH NOT EXACTLY WHAT'S CALLED OPEN HOUSE  . . . .    534  3 DON JUAN  16      68    8
HOUSEHOLD
     WHERE ALL HIS HOUSEHOLD GODS LAY SHIVER'D ROUND HIM  .   41  2 DON JUAN   1      36    6
     SOME MIND THEIR HOUSEHOLD OTHERS DISSIPATION  . . .     263  2 DON JUAN   2     201    1
     DOWN TO A VERY HOMELY HOUSEHOLD SAVOUR  . . . . .       277  2 DON JUAN   3       5    8
     WHATE'ER OUR HOUSEHOLD GODS PROTECT OF DEAR  . . . .    338  2 DON JUAN   3     107    6
HOUSE-KEEPER
     CARE LIKE A HOUSE-KEEPER BRINGS EVERY WEEK  . . . .     243  3 DON JUAN  10      38    5
HOUSEKEEPERS
     BUT FORM GOOD HOUSEKEEPERS TO BREED A NATION  . . .     420  3 DON JUAN  14      24    8
HOUSELESS
     FOR SHE WAS HOMELESS HOUSELESS HELPLESS ALL  . . . .    182  3 DON JUAN   8     141    2
HOUSEMAID'S
     A PAIL OF HOUSEMAID'S WATER UNAWARES  . . . . . .        34  2 DON JUAN   1      24    8
HOUSES
     THEIR NAMES WHO REARED IT BUT HUGE HOUSES FIT ILL--  .  444  2 DON JUAN   5      59    5
     WHERE THERE WERE FEWER HOUSES AND MORE EASE  . . . .    144  3 DON JUAN   8      64    4
     WITH CARLTON OR WITH OTHER HOUSES TRY  . . . . . .      266  3 DON JUAN  10      85    3
     THE PARLIAMENT AND ALL THE OTHER HOUSES  . . . . .      353  3 DON JUAN  12      82    2
HOVE
     HE LEFT HIS SHIP TO BE HOVE DOWN NEXT DAY  . . . .      286  2 DON JUAN   3      20    5
HOVEL
     FROM THE DULL PALACE TO THE DIRTY HOVEL  . . . . .      263  2 DON JUAN   2     201    7
     AND GAZE WHERE'ER THE PALACE OR THE HOVEL IS  . . .     361  3 DON JUAN  13       7    7
```

HOVER
    AND PHANTOMS HOVERED OR MIGHT SEEM TO HOVER 41   3 DON JUAN   6   70   6
    BETWEEN THE PRESENT AND PAST WORLDS AND HOVER 255   3 DON JUAN 10   61   7
    BUT WHEN WE HOVER BETWEEN FOOL AND SAGE 315   3 DON JUAN 12   1   4
HOVERED
    AND SLUMBER HOVERED O'ER EACH LOVELY LIMB 38   3 DON JUAN   6   64   3
    AND PHANTOMS HOVERED OR MIGHT SEEM TO HOVER 41   3 DON JUAN   6   70   6
HOVERING
    SOME COSSACQUES HOVERING LIKE HAWKS ROUND A HILL . . . 95   3 DON JUAN   7   56   3
    FLUNG HOVERING GRACES O'ER HIM LIKE A BANNER 223   3 DON JUAN   9   83   8
    TO LEAVE THEM HOVERING AS THE EFFECT IS FINE 453   3 DON JUAN 14   97   5
HOVERS
    AND THE SAD TRUTH WHICH HOVERS O'ER MY DESK 345   2 DON JUAN   4   3   7
    WHICH HOVERS OFT ABOUT SOME MARRIED BEAUTIES 208   3 DON JUAN   9   51   4
    IN SHAPE OF MOONSHINE HOVERS O'ER THE PILE-- 279   3 DON JUAN 11   24   7
    BETWEEN TWO WORLDS LIFE HOVERS LIKE A STAR 500   3 DON JUAN 15   99   1
HOWE
    PRINCE FERDINAND GRANBY BURGOYNE KEPPEL HOWE 22   2 DON JUAN   1   2   2
    FORGETTING DUNCAN NELSON HOWE AND JERVIS 23   2 DON JUAN   1   4   8
HOWL
    FROM OUT HER SKIES--THEN HOWL YOUR IDLE WRATH 70   3 DON JUAN   7   7   7
    IN LIKE CHURCH BELLS WITH SIGH HOWL GROAN YELL PRAYER . 141   3 DON JUAN   8   58   7
    I'VE HEARD THEM IN THE EPHESIAN RUINS HOWL 196   3 DON JUAN   9   27   2
HOWLED
    AND HOWLED FOR HELP AS WOLVES DO FOR A MEAL-- 153   3 DON JUAN   8   83   6
HOWLING
    AND GNASH'D THEIR TEETH AND HOWLING TORE THEIR HAIR . . 180   2 DON JUAN   2   45   4
    WITH TENDERNESS--STOOD HOWLING ON THE BRINK 187   2 DON JUAN   2   58   4
    TEARING AND GRINNING HOWLING SCREECHING SWEARING . . . 198   2 DON JUAN   2   79   7
    THE HOWLING HEBREWS OF CYBELE'S PRIEST-- 297   3 DON JUAN 11   58   8
HOWSOE'ER
    AND THUS WITH WOMEN HOWSOE'ER IT SHOCK SOME'S 371   3 DON JUAN 13   30   7
HOWSOEVER
    THAT HOWSOEVER PEOPLE FAST AND PRAY 56   2 DON JUAN   1   63   5
    LIKE GARLIC HOWSOEVER SHE EXTENDS 231   3 DON JUAN 10   12   5
    NOT EVEN IN FOOLS--WHO--HOWSOEVER BLIND 372   3 DON JUAN 13   32   V6
HOYLE
    TROY OWES TO HOMER WHAT WHIST OWES TO HOYLE 328   2 DON JUAN   3   90   5
HU
    ALL SOUNDS IT PIERCETH ALLAH ALLAH HU 116   3 DON JUAN   8   8   8
HUE
    THE WAX WAS SUPERFINE ITS HUE VERMILLION 134   2 DON JUAN   1   198   8
    SO BLACK THE LONG WORN LION'S HIDE IN HUE 154   2 DON JUAN   1   V 5   7
    CLEARER THAN THAT WITHOUT AND ITS WIDE HUE 204   2 DON JUAN   2   91   5
    WERE BLACK AS DEATH THEIR LASHES THE SAME HUE 218   2 DON JUAN   2   117   2
    OF VELVET PANNELS EACH OF DIFFERENT HUE 308   2 DON JUAN   3   64   2
    I HAVE EXAMINED FEW PAIR OF THAT HUE) 404   2 DON JUAN   4   110   5
    ALL RAGAMUFFINS DIFFERING BUT IN HUE 417   2 DON JUAN   5   13   3
    BUT TIME STRIPS OUR ILLUSIONS OF THEIR HUE 421   2 DON JUAN   5   21   6
    WHO GAZED UPON HER CHEEK'S TRANSCENDANT HUE 27   3 DON JUAN   6   42   3
    LIKE FLOWERS OF DIFFERENT HUE AND CLIME AND ROOT . . . 38   3 DON JUAN   6   65   2
    SELDOM HE VARIED FEATURE HUE OR MUSCLE 132   3 DON JUAN   8   39   7
    AND PALLAS ALSO SANCTIONS THE SAME HUE 218   3 DON JUAN   9   71   7
    BUT STILL HIS STATE WAS DELICATE THE HUE 245   3 DON JUAN 10   43   5
    ADVANCED IN ALL THEIR AZURE'S HIGHEST HUE 294   3 DON JUAN 11   50   4
    'TIS NONSENSE TO DISPUTE ABOUT A HUE-- 359   3 DON JUAN 13   3   5
    INTO A GALLERY OF A SOMBRE HUE 508   3 DON JUAN 16   17   3
    BUT STILL FROM THAT SUBLIMER AZURE HUE 524   3 DON JUAN 16   47   5
HUES
    BRIGHT HUES WHEN OUT OF DOORS AND YET WHILE WAVE . . . 220   2 DON JUAN   2   120   5
    HAD DECK'D HER OUT IN ALL THE HUES OF HEAVEN 407   2 DON JUAN   4   114   4
    AND VARIOUS HUES AS IS THE TURKISH WONT-- 436   2 DON JUAN   5   46   4
    A PORTION OF YOUR FADING TWILIGHT HUES 108   3 DON JUAN   7   82   7
    BLOOMED ALSO IN LESS TRANSITORY HUES 293   3 DON JUAN 11   48   2
HUGE
    HE CAGED IN ONE HUGE HAMPER ALTOGETHER 285   2 DON JUAN   3   18   8
    TRUE KNIGHTS CHASTE DAMES HUGE GIANTS KINGS DESPOTIC . . 347   2 DON JUAN   4   6   6
    YET SMELT ROAST-MEAT BEHELD A HUGE FIRE SHINE 439   2 DON JUAN   5   50   5
    THEIR NAMES WHO REARED IT BUT HUGE HOUSES FIT ILL-- . . 444   2 DON JUAN   5   59   5
    AND HUGE TOMBS WORSE--MANKIND SINCE ADAM FELL 444   2 DON JUAN   5   59   6
    HAUGHTY AND HUGE ALONG THE DISTANCE LOWERS 460   2 DON JUAN   5   85   5
    OF A HUGE HALL AND ON ITS EITHER SIDE 462   2 DON JUAN   5   87   2
    TO GRATIFY LIKE A HUGE MOTH THIS ONE SENSE 88   3 DON JUAN   7   44   8
    MEN ARE BUT MAGGOTS OF SOME HUGE EARTH'S BURIAL) . . . 202   3 DON JUAN   9   39   8
    A HUGE DUN CUPOLA LIKE A FOOLSCAP CROWN 265   3 DON JUAN 10   82   7
    AND HEW OUT A HUGE MONUMENT OF PATHOS 355   3 DON JUAN 12   86   7
    THROUGH THE HUGE ARCH WHICH SOARS AND SINKS AGAIN . . . 388   3 DON JUAN 13   63   5
    HUGE HALLS LONG GALLERIES SPACIOUS CHAMBERS JOIN'D . . . 390   3 DON JUAN 13   67   1
HUGER
    HUGER THAN TWELVE OF OUR DEGENERATE BREED 391   3 DON JUAN 13   70   4
HUM
    OR LULL'D BY FALLING WATERS SWEET THE HUM 88   2 DON JUAN   1   123   6
    THE HUM OF ARMIES GATHERING RANK ON RANK 110   3 DON JUAN   7   86   2
    HEARD--AND THAT BEE-LIKE BUBBLING BUSY HUM 272   3 DON JUAN 11   8   7
    SWEET ADELINE AMIDST THE GAY WORLD'S HUM 365   3 DON JUAN 13   13   4
    OF THAT SAME TUNE WHEN PEOPLE HUM IT LONG)-- 529   3 DON JUAN 16   59   3
HUMAN
    OF HUMAN HEARTS THAN ALL THE LONG ARRAY 84   2 DON JUAN   1   116   5
    FORBID BY HEAVENLY FINED BY HUMAN LAWS 113   2 DON JUAN   1   167   3

HUMAN   (CONTINUED)
```
LIKE HUMAN BEINGS DURING CIVIL WAR . . . . . . . . . . 178  2 DON JUAN  2    42  8
'TWAS WELL BECAUSE HEALTH IN THE HUMAN FRAME . . . . . . 245  2 DON JUAN  2   169  3
HAVE SUCH A CHARM FOR US POOR HUMAN CREATURES . . . . . 267  2 DON JUAN  2   208  8
OF HUMAN FRAILTY FOLLY ALSO CRIME . . . . . . . . . . . 277  2 DON JUAN  3     5  2
THESE TWO ARE LEVELLERS AND HUMAN BREATH . . . . . . . 280  2 DON JUAN  3     9 V3
SO THESE POINT THE EPIGRAM OF HUMAN BREATH . . . . . . 280  2 DON JUAN  3     9 V3
DREADING THAT CLIMAX OF ALL HUMAN ILLS . . . . . . . . 293  2 DON JUAN  3    35  7
A THING TO HUMAN FEELINGS THE MOST TRYING . . . . . . 301  2 DON JUAN  3    51  2
HIS FEELINGS FROM ALL MILK OF HUMAN KINDNESS . . . . . 304  2 DON JUAN  3    57  7
OF A STRONG HUMAN HEART AND IN A SIRE . . . . . . . . 305  2 DON JUAN  3    58  8
BUT THERE ARE HUMAN FEELINGS PAST ASSUAGING . . . . . 305  2 DON JUAN  3    58 V5
TOO PURE EVEN FOR THE PUREST HUMAN TIES . . . . . . . 313  2 DON JUAN  3    74  6
WHICH SHAKE SO MUCH THE HUMAN BRAIN AND BREAST-- . . . 343  2 DON JUAN  3  V 98  3
RESTORES ALL HUMAN FEELINGS TO BURLESQUE . . . . . . . 345  2 DON JUAN  4     3 V8
THE PRECIOUS PORCELAIN OF HUMAN CLAY . . . . . . . . . 350  2 DON JUAN  4    11  3
AND NEVER KNOW THE WEIGHT OF HUMAN HOURS . . . . . . . 352  2 DON JUAN  4    15  8
SHE STOOD AS ONE WHO CHAMPION'D HUMAN FEARS-- . . . . 367  2 DON JUAN  4    43  3
HER HUMAN CLAY IS KINDLED FULL OF POWER . . . . . . . 374  2 DON JUAN  4    56  2
AND NOTHING OUTWARD TELLS OF HUMAN CLAY . . . . . . . 383  2 DON JUAN  4    72  4
FOR HUMAN VANITY THE YOUNG DEFOIX . . . . . . . . . . 400  2 DON JUAN  4   103  4
WITH HUMAN BLOOD THAT COLUMN WAS CEMENTED . . . . . . 401  2 DON JUAN  4   105  1
WITH HUMAN FILTH THAT COLUMN IS DEFILED . . . . . . . 401  2 DON JUAN  4   105  2
ITS FUMES ARE FRANKINCENSE TO HUMAN THOUGHT . . . . . 402  2 DON JUAN  4   106  2
FOR THIS SUPERIOR YOKE OF HUMAN CATTLE . . . . . . . . 425  2 DON JUAN  5    28  8
AND ALL WHO HAVE SEEN A HUMAN NURSERY SAW . . . . . . 488  2 DON JUAN  5   133  5
AT HUMAN POWER AND VIRTUE AND ALL THAT . . . . . . . .  67  3 DON JUAN  7     3  4
FOR DEEMING HUMAN CLAY BUT COMMON DIRT . . . . . . . .  96  3 DON JUAN  7    58  5
OF DEEDS TO HUMAN HAPPINESS MOST DEAR . . . . . . . . 108  3 DON JUAN  7    83  6
A HUMAN HYDRA ISSUING FROM ITS FEN . . . . . . . . . 113  3 DON JUAN  8     2  5
SNATCH WHEN DESPAIR MAKES HUMAN HEARTS LESS PLIANT . . 138  3 DON JUAN  8    51  4
OF HUMAN NATURE'S AGONIZING VOICE . . . . . . . . . . 142  3 DON JUAN  8    59  8
A FROWN ON NATURE'S OR ON HUMAN FACE-- . . . . . . . 145  3 DON JUAN  8    65  6
NOW THAWED INTO A MARSH OF HUMAN BLOOD . . . . . . . . 148  3 DON JUAN  8    73  8
WHOSE FANGS EVE TAUGHT HER HUMAN SEED TO FEEL . . . . 153  3 DON JUAN  8    83  4
THE TWIGS WHICH SATAN LIMES FOR HUMAN FLIES . . . . . 154  3 DON JUAN  8    86 V8
AND HUMAN LIVES ARE LAVISHED EVERYWHERE . . . . . . . 155  3 DON JUAN  8    88  2
AND HUMAN BREATH IS POURED UPON THE AIR . . . . . . . 155  3 DON JUAN  8    88 V2
FOR CHECQUERED AS IS SEEN OUR HUMAN LOT . . . . . . . 156  3 DON JUAN  8    89  3
AS HUMAN BEINGS OR HIS WAYS ARE ODD . . . . . . . . . 163  3 DON JUAN  8   104  4
THAN HUMAN INSECTS CATERING FOR SPIDERS . . . . . . . 196  3 DON JUAN  9    27  8
FROM THE MANURE OF HUMAN CLAY THOUGH DECKED . . . . . 199  3 DON JUAN  9    34  5
OF HUMAN THOUGHTS WHICH JOSTLE IN THEIR FLIGHT . . . . 215  3 DON JUAN  9    65  4
AND THE TWO ARE SO MIXED WITH HUMAN DUST . . . . . . 221  3 DON JUAN  9    77  5
A THING TO COUNTERBALANCE HUMAN WOES . . . . . . . . 226  3 DON JUAN 10     2  5
OF HUMAN YEARS THAT HALF-WAY HOUSE THAT RUDE . . . . . 238  3 DON JUAN 10    27  5
WHICH FORM THAT BITTER DRAUGHT THE HUMAN SPECIES . . . 261  3 DON JUAN 10    73  8
TOO SUBTLE FOR THE AIRIEST HUMAN HEAD . . . . . . . . 268  3 DON JUAN 11     1  4
NOUGHT'S PERMANENT AMONG THE HUMAN RACE . . . . . . . 309  3 DON JUAN 11    82  7
WHICH IS THE CUD ESCHEWED BY HUMAN CATTLE . . . . . . 336  3 DON JUAN 12    43  8
THE DREARY FUIMUS OF ALL THINGS HUMAN . . . . . . . . 376  3 DON JUAN 13    40  6
ALBEIT ALL HUMAN HISTORY ATTESTS . . . . . . . . . . 404  3 DON JUAN 13    99  6
THEIR PEAKS BENEATH YOUR HUMAN FOOT AND THERE . . . . 412  3 DON JUAN 14     5  5
AND SUCH A STRAW BORNE ON BY HUMAN BREATH . . . . . . 414  3 DON JUAN 14     8  3
BUT MOSTLY SINGS OF HUMAN THINGS AND ACTS-- . . . . . 416  3 DON JUAN 14    13  4
A HANDSOME MAN THAT HUMAN MIRACLE . . . . . . . . . . 441  3 DON JUAN 14    71  6
WOULD BE DISCOVER'D IN THE HUMAN SOUL . . . . . . . . 455  3 DON JUAN 14   102  2
AND TURNING HUMAN NATURE TO AN ART . . . . . . . . . 457  3 DON JUAN 15     3  4
EXCEPT ITSELF--SUCH IS THE HUMAN BREAST . . . . . . . 505  3 DON JUAN 16    10  3
A HUMAN (WHAT THE ITALIANS NICKNAME) MULE . . . . . . 563  3 DON JUAN 17     3  5
```
HUMANE
```
OF THE HUMANE SOCIETY'S BEGINNING . . . . . . . . . .  92  2 DON JUAN  1   130  4
BY THY HUMANE DISCOVERY FRIAR BACON . . . . . . . . . 129  3 DON JUAN  8    33  8
```
HUMANITY
```
HUMANITY MUST YIELD TO STEEL AND FLAME . . . . . . . 139  3 DON JUAN  8    54  4
HE HAD BEHAVED WITH COURAGE AND HUMANITY-- . . . . . 182  3 DON JUAN  8   140  2
HUMANITY WOULD RISE AND THUNDER NAY . . . . . . . . . 183  3 DON JUAN  9     1  8
OF FRAIL HUMANITY--MUST MAKE US SELFISH . . . . . . . 236  3 DON JUAN 10    23  7
WITHOUT A FRIEND WHAT WERE HUMANITY . . . . . . . . . 430  3 DON JUAN 14    47  5
THAT WHICH HUMANITY MAY BEAR OR BEAR NOT . . . . . . 431  3 DON JUAN 14    49  6
TO PLAY UPON THE SURFACE OF HUMANITY . . . . . . . . 482  3 DON JUAN 15    60  2
MALGRE SIR MATTHEW HALES'S GREAT HUMANITY . . . . . . 565  3 DON JUAN 17     7  8
```
HUMANITY'S
```
A MORTGAGE ON HUMANITY'S ESTATE-- . . . . . . . . . 105  3 DON JUAN  7    76  6
```
HUMBLE
```
AND SO YOUR HUMBLE SERVANT AND GOOD BYE . . . . . . . 147  2 DON JUAN  1   221  4
IN PROSE I BEND MY HUMBLE VERSE) DOTH CALL . . . . . 163  3 DON JUAN  8   104  7
WITH HER THEN AS IN HUMBLE DUTY BOUND . . . . . . . . 224  3 DON JUAN  9    85  1
AND BEG HIS BRITISH GODSHIP'S HUMBLE PARDON . . . . . 442  3 DON JUAN 14    75  4
```
HUMBLED
```
FOR SHE FELT HUMBLED--AND HUMILIATION . . . . . . . . 490  2 DON JUAN  5   137  7
```
HUMBLER
```
BUT HE MORE MODEST TOOK AN HUMBLER RANGE . . . . . . 283  2 DON JUAN  3    14  5
AS EVEN IN A MUCH HUMBLER LOT HAD MADE . . . . . . . 485  2 DON JUAN  5   129  2
I PERCH UPON AN HUMBLER PROMONTORY . . . . . . . . . 464  3 DON JUAN 15    19  1
```
HUMBLEST
```
THE HUMBLEST INDIVIDUAL UNDER HEAVEN . . . . . . . . 309  3 DON JUAN 11    82  3
```
HUMBLY
```
AND HUMBLY HOPE THAT THE SAME GOD WHICH HATH GIVEN . . 242  3 DON JUAN 10    36 V7
```

		PAGE	VOL		CANTO	STANZA	LN
HUMBOLDT							
HUMBOLDT THE FIRST OF TRAVELLERS BUT NOT		406	2	DON JUAN	4	112	1
HUMBUG							
(A SET OF HUMBUG RASCALS WHEN ALL'S DONE)		219	2	DON JUAN	2	118	V6
HUMDRUM							
FOR 'TIS A LOW NEWSPAPER HUMDRUM LAW-SUIT		346	3	DON JUAN	12	65	1
IS BETTER THAN AN HUMDRUM TETE-A-TETE		402	3	DON JUAN	13	94	4
HUMILIATION							
FOR SHE FELT HUMBLED--AND HUMILIATION		490	2	DON JUAN	5	137	7
HUMILITY							
OR CONTRADICTED BUT WITH PROUD HUMILITY		368	3	DON JUAN	13	22	4
A PROUD HUMILITY IF SUCH THERE BE		492	3	DON JUAN	15	82	2
HUMMING							
HERE THEY WERE INTERRUPTED BY A HUMMING		494	2	DON JUAN	5	145	7
HUMOUR							
AS FROM MY GREAT GREAT HUMOUR YOU MAY LEARN		300	3	DON JUAN	11	63	V5
THE TALENT AND GOOD HUMOUR HE DISPLAYED		355	3	DON JUAN	12	85	5
SHE HAD HEARD BUT WOMEN HEAR WITH MORE GOOD HUMOUR . .		460	3	DON JUAN	15	11	3
HUMOURING							
BY HUMOURING ALWAYS WHAT THEY MIGHT ASSERT		426	3	DON JUAN	14	37	3
HUMOURS							
SOME SAID 'TWAS A CONCOCTION OF THE HUMOURS		244	3	DON JUAN	10	40	5
HUMP							
THE HOLY CAMEL'S HUMP BESIDES THE KORAN		57	3	DON JUAN	6	102	8
HUMPHREY							
SIR HUMPHREY DAVY'S LANTERN BY WHICH COALS		93	2	DON JUAN	1	132	4
HUNCHBACK							
BECAUSE A HUNCHBACK--MADE HIS BREAST THE SHIELD . . .		166	3	DON JUAN	8	110	V7
HUNDRED							
(I THINK THE QUARTO HOLDS FIVE HUNDRED PAGES) . . .		11	2	DON JUAN	D	4	2
WHEN AFTER SEARCHING IN FIVE HUNDRED NOOKS		110	2	DON JUAN	1	161	3
ALL THE REST PERISH'D NEAR TWO HUNDRED SOULS . . .		185	2	DON JUAN	2	55	1
TWO HUNDRED AND ODD STANZAS AS BEFORE		271	2	DON JUAN	2	216	3
AND AVERAGED EACH FROM TEN TO A HUNDRED DOLLARS . .		283	2	DON JUAN	3	15	8
THE DINNER MADE ABOUT A HUNDRED DISHES		307	2	DON JUAN	3	62	1
OF THE THREE HUNDRED GRANT BUT THREE		323	2	DON JUAN	3	L 7	5
A HUNDRED THOUSAND MEN MIGHT FIGHT AGAIN		386	2	DON JUAN	4	77	6
AND MADE AT LEAST FIVE HUNDRED GOOD ZECCHINI . . .		390	2	DON JUAN	4	84	5
SOME WENT OFF DEARLY FIFTEEN HUNDRED DOLLARS . . .		407	2	DON JUAN	4	114	1
FOUR WIVES AND TWICE FIVE HUNDRED MAIDS UNSEEN . .		496	2	DON JUAN	5	148	1
SHE COULD BUT CLAIM THE FIFTEENTH HUNDRED PART . . .		10	3	DON JUAN	6	9	7
ALL BAD PROPENSITIES IN FIFTEEN HUNDRED		21	3	DON JUAN	6	31	7
THREE HUNDRED CANNON THREW UP THEIR EMETIC . . .		117	3	DON JUAN	8	12	1
AS WERE SOME HUNDRED YOUNGSTERS ALL ABREAST . . .		140	3	DON JUAN	8	56	3
HE MOVED SOME HUNDRED MILES OFF FOR A STATION . . .		144	3	DON JUAN	8	64	3
YE TWICE TEN HUNDRED THOUSAND DAILY SCRIBES		200	3	DON JUAN	9	35	2
SOME HUNDRED FEET IN HEIGHT NOT TO SAY MILES . . .		201	3	DON JUAN	9	38	7
HER HUNDRED ARMS AND LEGS AND FAIN OUTRUN HER . .		231	3	DON JUAN	10	12	6
AND WHOM DO WE REMEMBER NOT A HUNDRED		324	3	DON JUAN	12	19	2
I THINK TO CANTER GENTLY THROUGH A HUNDRED		341	3	DON JUAN	12	55	8
BESIDES HE HAD NOT SEEN OF SEVERAL HUNDRED		353	3	DON JUAN	12	81	3
HUNDREDS							
WHO BADE ON TILL THE HUNDREDS REACH'D ELEVEN . . .		407	2	DON JUAN	4	114	6
WHO HAD BID HIGH AS HUNDREDS SIX OR SEVEN		407	2	DON JUAN	4	114	4
UP JOHNSON CAME WITH HUNDREDS AT HIS BACK		160	3	DON JUAN	8	97	5
THE OLD PACHA SITS AMONG SOME HUNDREDS DEAD . . .		160	3	DON JUAN	8	98	3
SOME HUNDREDS BREATHED--THE REST WERE SILENT ALL . .		175	3	DON JUAN	8	127	8
HUNDSFOT							
WITH SCHNAPPS--SAD DOGS WHOM HUNDSFOT OR FERFLUCTER .		260	3	DON JUAN	10	71	7
HUNG							
RAISED HIGHER THE FAINT HEAD WHICH O'ER IT HUNG . .		216	2	DON JUAN	2	114	3
WERE HUNG WITH MARBLE ICICLES THE WORK		362	2	DON JUAN	4	33	2
A MOST PRODIGIOUS PIPPIN--BUT IT HUNG		44	3	DON JUAN	6	76	2
HER HEAD HUNG DOWN AND HER LONG HAIR IN STOOPING . .		60	3	DON JUAN	6	109	1
WITH GARLANDS ROUND BY EVERY NATION HUNG		199	3	DON JUAN	9	34	V6
HUNGER							
LULL'D EVEN THE SAVAGE HUNGER WHICH DEMANDED . . .		195	2	DON JUAN	2	75	3
SOME HUNGER TOO THEY SAY THE PEOPLE FEELS--		185	3	DON JUAN	9	6	6
HUNGER'S							
WHAT COULD THEY DO AND HUNGER'S RAGE GREW WILD . . .		193	2	DON JUAN	2	70	6
HUNGRY							
MEN WILL PROVE HUNGRY EVEN WHEN NEXT PERDITION . . .		180	2	DON JUAN	2	46	V5
AND THAT A SHIPWRECK'D YOUTH WOULD HUNGRY BE . . .		233	2	DON JUAN	2	145	2
HOME TO THE WEARY TO THE HUNGRY CHEER		338	2	DON JUAN	3	107	2
BESIDES I'M HUNGRY AND JUST NOW WOULD TAKE . . .		435	2	DON JUAN	5	44	7
THINGS WHICH IN HUNGRY MORTALS' EYES FIND FAVOUR . .		437	2	DON JUAN	5	47	3
TO THOSE SAD HUNGRY JACOBINS THE WORMS		12	3	DON JUAN	6	13	4
(WHILE ON THE PAVEMENT MANY A HUNGRY WHORE		313	3	DON JUAN	11	V 29	3
THAT HAPPINESS FOR MAN--THE HUNGRY SINNER-- . . .		404	3	DON JUAN	13	99	7
HELD OUT UNTO THE HUNGRY ISRAELITES		405	3	DON JUAN	13	100	2
TO FLY FROM AS FROM HUNGRY PIKES A ROACH		421	3	DON JUAN	14	26	3
HUNT							
WHEREAS THE OTHERS HUNT FOR REGAL SPIDERS		196	3	DON JUAN	9	27	V8
COULD RECOMMENCE TO HUNT HIS HONEST MAN		281	3	DON JUAN	11	28	2
I HATE TO HUNT DOWN A TIRED METAPHOR		374	3	DON JUAN	13	36	5
OR HUNT THE YOUNG BECAUSE THEY LIKED THE SPORT-- . .		405	3	DON JUAN	13	101	2
TO HUNT OUR ERRORS UP WITH A GOOD GRACE		430	3	DON JUAN	14	47	6
HUNTED							
ASK'D NEXT DAY IF MEN EVER HUNTED TWICE		425	3	DON JUAN	14	35	8

371

HUNTER
    SO THAT HIS HORSE OR CHARGER HUNTER HACK . . . . 424 3 DON JUAN 14   32   7
HUNTER'S
    AS IS THE HUNTER'S AT THE FIVE-BAR GATE . . . . 140 3 DON JUAN 8   55   2
HUNTERS
    THE HUNTERS FOUGHT THEIR FOX-HUNT O'ER AGAIN . . . . 408 3 DON JUAN 13   108   7
    THERE WERE SOME HUNTERS BOLD AND COURSERS KEEN . . . . 539 3 DON JUAN 16   80   1
HUNTING
    CITE IS THAT BOON LIVED HUNTING UP TO NINETY . . . . 143 3 DON JUAN 8   62   8
    OFFSPRING OF SOME SAGE HUSBAND--HUNTING COUNTESS . . . . 312 3 DON JUAN 11   89   2
    OF HUNTING--FOR THE SAGEST YOUTH IS FRAIL . . . . . 424 3 DON JUAN 14   33   6
HUNTING-BOX
    BABEL WAS NIMROD'S HUNTING-BOX AND THEN . . . . 445 2 DON JUAN 5   60   1
HUNTSMAN
    THE SPECTRE HUNTSMAN OF ONESTI'S LINE . . . . . . 337 2 DON JUAN 3   106   5
    HOUNDS WHEN THE HUNTSMAN TUMBLES ARE AT FAULT . . . . 119 3 DON JUAN 8   16   8
    THE SULKY HUNTSMAN GRIMLY SAID THE FRENCHMAN . . . . 425 3 DON JUAN 14   34   V7
HUNTSMAN'S
    THE HUNTSMAN'S SELF RELENTED TO A GRIN . . . . . . 425 3 DON JUAN 14   34   7
HURL
    TO HURL THESE FLEET-DITCH DIVERS DOWN THEIR LAKES . . . 334 2 DON JUAN 3   100   V8
HURL'D
    THERE WINDS AND WAVES HAD HURL'D THEM AND FROM THENCE . . 177 2 DON JUAN 2   40   1
    LIKE LUCIFER WHEN HURL'D FROM HEAVEN FOR SINNING . . . 344 2 DON JUAN 4   1   5
HURLED
    LIKE ALL THE WORLDS BEFORE WHICH HAVE BEEN HURLED . . . 201 3 DON JUAN 9   37   6
    THROUGH STREET AND SQUARE FAST FLASHING CHARIOTS HURLED . 302 3 DON JUAN 11   67   3
HURLING
    HURLING DEFIANCE CITY STREAM AND SHORE . . . . . . 116 3 DON JUAN 8   8   4
HURLS
    AND HURLS AT ONCE HIS VENOM AND HIS STRENGTH . . . . 218 3 DON JUAN 2   117   8
    AS CARELESSLY AS HURLS THE MOTH HER WING . . . . . . 170 3 DON JUAN 8   118   3
HURRA
    HURRA AND ALLAH AND ONE MOMENT MORE . . . . . . 111 3 DON JUAN 7   87   7
HURRAH
    HURRAH HOW SWIFTLY SPEEDS THE POST SO MERRY . . . . . 260 3 DON JUAN 10   71   3
HURRIED
    WITH EAGER EYES AND LIGHT BUT HURRIED TREAD . . . . . 42 3 DON JUAN 6   72   3
    THE LOFTIEST HURRIED BY THE TIME AND PLACE . . . . . 139 3 DON JUAN 8   54   7
HURRY
    WE WERE TRANSFERR'D ON BOARD HER IN A HURRY . . . . . 389 2 DON JUAN 4   82   5
    BECAUSE THEY WERE CONSTRUCTED IN A HURRY . . . . . . 79 3 DON JUAN 7   26   2
    OF THE BRIGHT BAYONET AND THEY ALL SHOULD HURRY ON . . . 151 3 DON JUAN 8   78   6
    HE LIVED (NOT DEATH BUT JUAN) IN A HURRY . . . . . 237 3 DON JUAN 10   26   1
    DIRECTION BE SO 'TIS BUT IN A HURRY . . . . . . 260 3 DON JUAN 10   72   4
    AND WITH SUCH HURRY THAT ERE HE COULD CURB IT . . . 543 3 DON JUAN 16   88   2
HURRYING
    HASTE--HASTE--I HEAR ALFONSO'S HURRYING FEET-- . . . . 121 2 DON JUAN 1   182   7
HURT
    BUT THEN 'TIS NOT MY FAULT IF OTHERS HURT YOU . . . . 37 2 DON JUAN 1   30   8
    THAT THEY WILL NOT CRY OUT BEFORE THEY'RE HURT . . . . 140 2 DON JUAN 1   207   3
    A MOMENT MORE WOULD HURT YOUR REPUTATION . . . . . 482 2 DON JUAN 5   123   8
    SEEKING FAR LESS TO SAVE YOU THAN TO HURT YOU . . . 337 3 DON JUAN 12   45   3
HURTS
    AND GLIDES AWAY ASSURED SHE NEVER HURTS YE . . . . . 300 3 DON JUAN 11   63   8
HUSBAND
    AND IF IN THE MEANTIME HER HUSBAND DIED . . . . . 67 2 DON JUAN 1   84   1
    A REAL HUSBAND ALWAYS IS SUSPICIOUS . . . . . . 74 2 DON JUAN 1   99   1
    AND TRUANT HUSBAND SHOULD RETURN AND SAY . . . . . 98 2 DON JUAN 1   141   7
    A HUSBAND LIKE ALFONSO AT MY SIDE . . . . . . 100 2 DON JUAN 1   145   6
    YES DON ALFONSO HUSBAND NOW NO MORE . . . . . . 101 2 DON JUAN 1   146   1
    A HUSBAND RATHER OLD NOT MUCH IN UNITY . . . . . 158 2 DON JUAN 2   3   7
    WORN FOR A HUSBAND OR SOME OTHER BRUTE . . . . . 230 2 DON JUAN 2   139   8
    A THANKLESS HUSBAND NEXT A FAITHLESS LOVER . . . . 263 2 DON JUAN 2   200   7
    BUT IN A HUSBAND IS PRONOUNCED UXORIOUS . . . . . 278 2 DON JUAN 3   6   8
    FOR INSTANCE IF A HUSBAND OR HIS WIFE . . . . . 301 2 DON JUAN 3   50   3
    WHOSE HUSBAND ONLY KNOWS HER NOT A WHORE . . . . . 353 2 DON JUAN 4   17   8
    AS FAST AS EVER HUSBAND BY HIS MATE . . . . . . 42 3 DON JUAN 6   73   4
    A ROYAL HUSBAND IN ALL SAVE THE RING-- . . . . . 217 3 DON JUAN 9   70   6
    OFFSPRING OF SOME SAGE HUSBAND--HUNTING COUNTESS . . . 312 3 DON JUAN 11   89   2
    SHE CALLED HER HUSBAND NOW AND THEN APART . . . . 438 3 DON JUAN 14   65   3
HUSBAND'S
    WITH SUCH SERENITY HER HUSBAND'S WOES . . . . . . 36 2 DON JUAN 1   29   2
    SHE DID THIS DURING EVEN HER HUSBAND'S LIFE-- . . . . 48 2 DON JUAN 1   48   7
    BY STEALTH HER HUSBAND'S TEMPLES TO ENCUMBER . . . . 96 2 DON JUAN 1   138   6
    OR FOR SO YOUNG A HUSBAND'S JEALOUS FEARS-- . . . . 106 2 DON JUAN 1   155   3
    A MATRON WHO HER HUSBAND'S FOIBLE KNOWS . . . . . 117 2 DON JUAN 1   175   3
    HER HUSBAND'S FRIEND HER OWN YOUNG AND A STRANGER . . . 449 3 DON JUAN 14   91   8
HUSBANDS
    OF FIFTY AND SUCH HUSBANDS ARE IN PLENTY . . . . . 56 2 DON JUAN 1   62   2
    THE APPROACH OF HOME TO HUSBANDS AND TO SIRES . . . . 287 2 DON JUAN 3   22   1
    NOT ALL LONE MATRONS FOR THEIR HUSBANDS MOURN . . . . 287 2 DON JUAN 3   23   3
    EMPERORS ARE ONLY HUSBANDS IN WIVES' EYES . . . . . 477 2 DON JUAN 5   115   5
    WHEN THEIR LIEGE HUSBANDS TREAT THEM WITH INGRATITUDE . . 11 3 DON JUAN 6   11   6
    SAD RAKES TO SADDER HUSBANDS CHASTELY TAMING . . . . 418 3 DON JUAN 14   18   5
HUSBANDS'
    MUCH LONGER--THINK OF HUSBANDS' LOVERS' LIVES . . . . 123 2 DON JUAN 1   185   7
    WIVES IN THEIR HUSBANDS' ABSENCES GROW SUBTLER . . . . 287 2 DON JUAN 3   22   7
    LIKE CHASTEST WIVES FROM CONSTANT HUSBANDS' SIDES . . . 125 3 DON JUAN 8   27   3

		PAGE	VOL	CANTO	STANZA	LN

HUSH
BUT THERE'S A RUMOUR WHICH I FAIN WOULD HUSH . . . . . 53 2 DON JUAN 1 58 6
AND NOT IN VAIN HE LISTENED--HUSH WHAT'S THAT . . . . 556 3 DON JUAN 16 112 1
HUSH'D
OF ECHOING THUNDER AND THEN ALL WAS HUSH'D . . . . . 184 2 DON JUAN 2 53 3
BENT WITH HUSH'D LIPS THAT DRANK HIS SCARCE-DRAWN BREATH . 232 2 DON JUAN 2 143 8
HUSH'D AS THE BABE UPON ITS MOTHER'S BREAST . . . . . 235 2 DON JUAN 2 148 2
CIRCLING ALL NATURE HUSH'D AND DIM AND STILL . . . . . 252 2 DON JUAN 2 183 4
HUSH'D INTO DEPTHS BEYOND THE WATCHER'S DIVING . . . . 261 2 DON JUAN 2 197 6
HUSHED
LAY IN A BREATHLESS HUSHED AND STONY SLEEP . . . . . 40 3 DON JUAN 6 68 2
HUSSAR
CURE THEM OF TOURS HUSSAR AND HIGHLAND DRESSES . . . . 267 3 DON JUAN 10 86 2
HUSTINGS
OFF--OR UPON THE HUSTINGS--SOME SLIGHT SUCH . . . . . 538 3 DON JUAN 16 77 4
HUSTLE
AMBASSADORS BEGAN AS 'TWERE TO HUSTLE . . . . . 223 3 DON JUAN 9 82 3
BOOZE IN THE KEN OR AT THE SPELLKEN HUSTLE . . . . 277 3 DON JUAN 11 19 4
HUT
FOR SOME OF THESE ARE ROCKS WITH SCARCE A HUT ON . . . 238 2 DON JUAN 2 154 6
UNTO THE NEAREST HUT THEMSELVES BETAKE . . . . 127 3 DON JUAN 8 32 6
HUT WHENCE WISE TRAVELLERS DRIVE WITH CIRCUMSPECTION . . 238 3 DON JUAN 10 27 6
HUT WHERE WE TRAVELLERS BAIT WITH DIM REFLECTION . . 238 3 DON JUAN 10 27 V6
HUZZAS
THAT HIRED HUZZAS REDEEM NO LAND'S DISTRESSES . . . . 267 3 DON JUAN 10 86 4
HYAENA
AND WITH HYAENA LAUGHTER DIED DESPAIRING . . . . . . 198 2 DON JUAN 2 79 8
HYDES
TO STRIP THE SAXONS OF THEIR HYDES LIKE TANNERS . . . 242 3 DON JUAN 10 36 6
HYDRA
A HUMAN HYDRA ISSUING FROM ITS FEN . . . . 113 3 DON JUAN 8 2 5
HYMEN
AND THE TRUE HYMEN (THE FIRST'S BUT A SCREEN)-- . . . 288 2 DON JUAN 3 25 6
HYMENEAL
THE FORMER'S HYMENEAL HOPES TO FLATTER . . . . . 292 3 DON JUAN 11 46 3
HYMEN'S
WHERE HYMEN'S TORCH BUT BRANDS ONE STRUMPET MORE . . . 353 2 DON JUAN 4 17 7
WHERE HYMEN'S SHRINE BUT STAMPS ONE STRUMPET MORE . . . 353 2 DON JUAN 4 17 V7
HYMETTUS
ON SUNIUM OR HYMETTUS LIKE DIOGENES . . . . . . 488 3 DON JUAN 15 73 7
HYMN
ALTHOUGH LONGINUS TELLS US THERE IS NO HYMN . . . . . 45 2 DON JUAN 1 42 5
IN GREECE HE'D SING SOME SORT OF HYMN LIKE THIS T'YE . . 320 2 DON JUAN 3 86 8
THY PRAISE HYPOCRISY OH FOR A HYMN . . . . 241 3 DON JUAN 10 34 2
RATTLES AROUND ME HER DISCORDANT HYMN . . . . . . 499 3 DON JUAN 15 97 4
HYMNED
THOUGH HYMNED BY EVERY HARP UNLESS WITHIN . . . . . 199 3 DON JUAN 9 34 7
HYPOCRISY
AND LOVE IS TAUGHT HYPOCRISY FROM YOUTH . . . . . 61 2 DON JUAN 1 72 8
ITSELF 'TIS STILL THE SAME HYPOCRISY . . . . . . 61 2 DON JUAN 1 73 6
THY PRAISE HYPOCRISY OH FOR A HYMN . . . . . . 241 3 DON JUAN 10 34 2
A LITTLE GENIAL SPRINKLING OF HYPOCRISY . . . . . 346 3 DON JUAN 12 66 2
BUT WEAR THE NEWEST MANTLE OF HYPOCRISY . . . . . 526 3 DON JUAN 16 52 7
HYPOCRITE
SHE WAS NO HYPOCRITE AT LEAST POOR SOUL . . . . . . 242 3 DON JUAN 10 35 1
(THE HYPOCRITE) WILL BANISH THEM LIKE MARIUS . . . . 352 3 DON JUAN 12 78 6
HYPOCRITICAL
BE HYPOCRITICAL BE CAUTIOUS BE . . . . 310 3 DON JUAN 11 86 7
HYSTERIC
WILL SAY TO THIS HYSTERIC OF A VISION . . . . . 46 3 DON JUAN 6 80 8
HYSTERICAL
HALF EPILEPTICAL AND HALF HYSTERICAL-- . . . . . . 183 2 DON JUAN 2 50 7
HYSTERICS
AND INDICATIONS OF HYSTERICS WHOSE . . . . 110 2 DON JUAN 1 162 3
ANTONIA IN HYSTERICS JULIA SWOON'D . . . . . 125 2 DON JUAN 1 187 3
I
I WISH HE WOULD EXPLAIN HIS EXPLANATION . . . . 10 2 DON JUAN D 2 8
(I THINK THE QUARTO HOLDS FIVE HUNDRED PAGES) . . . . 11 2 DON JUAN D 4 2
I WOULD NOT IMITATE THE PETTY THOUGHT . . . . . . 12 2 DON JUAN D 6 1
TO YOU I ENVY NEITHER FRUIT NOR BOUGHS-- . . . . 13 2 DON JUAN D 7 3
I WISH YOUR FATE MAY YIELD YE WHEN SHE CHOOSES . . . 14 2 DON JUAN D 8 3
WHERE SHALL I TURN ME NOT TO VIEW ITS BONDS . . . 19 2 DON JUAN D 16 1
FOR I WILL NEVER FEEL THEM--ITALY . . . . . 19 2 DON JUAN D 16 2
MEANTIME--SIR LAUREATE--I PROCEED TO DEDICATE . . . 20 2 DON JUAN D 17 1
AND IF IN FLATTERING STRAINS I DO NOT PREDICATE . . . 20 2 DON JUAN D 17 3
'TIS THAT I STILL RETAIN MY BUFF AND BLUE . . . . 20 2 DON JUAN D 17 4
I WANT A HERO AN UNCOMMON WANT . . . . . 21 2 DON JUAN 1 1 1
OF SUCH AS THESE I SHOULD NOT CARE TO VAUNT . . . . 21 2 DON JUAN 1 1 5
AND SO HAVE BEEN FORGOTTEN--I CONDEMN NONE . . . . 24 2 DON JUAN 1 5 5
SO AS I SAID I'LL TAKE MY FRIEND DON JUAN . . . . 24 2 DON JUAN 1 5 8
AND THEREFORE I SHALL OPEN WITH A LINE . . . . 25 2 DON JUAN 1 7 5
SO SAYS THE PROVERB--AND I QUITE AGREE . . . . 25 2 DON JUAN 1 8 4
IN SHORT IN ALL THINGS SHE WAS FAIRLY WHAT I CALL . . 27 2 DON JUAN 1 12 5
AND OTHER STUFFS WITH WHICH I WON'T STAY PUZZLING . . . 27 2 DON JUAN 1 12 8
BUT I MUST LEAVE THE PROOFS TO THOSE WHO'VE SEEN 'EM . . 28 2 DON JUAN 1 14 4
BUT THIS I HEARD HER SAY AND CAN'T BE WRONG . . . . 28 2 DON JUAN 1 14 5
'TIS STRANGE--THE HEBREW NOUN WHICH MEANS I AM . . . 28 2 DON JUAN 1 14 7
(I WONDER HOW THEY GOT THROUGH THE TWELVE HOURS) . . . 30 2 DON JUAN 1 18 6
I DON'T CHOOSE TO SAY MUCH UPON THIS HEAD . . . . 33 2 DON JUAN 1 22 5

I   (CONTINUED)

	PAGE	VOL			CANTO	STANZA	LN
I LOATHE THAT LOW VICE CURIOSITY	33	2	DON	JUAN	1	23	5
BUT IF THERE'S ANY THING IN WHICH I SHINE	33	2	DON	JUAN	1	23	6
AND SO I INTERFERED AND WITH THE BEST	34	2	DON	JUAN	1	24	1
I THINK THE FOOLISH PEOPLE WERE POSSESS'D	34	2	DON	JUAN	1	24	3
FOR NEITHER OF THEM COULD I EVER FIND	34	2	DON	JUAN	1	24	4
I CAN'T SAY MUCH FOR FRIEND OR YET RELATION)	38	2	DON	JUAN	1	32	5
ACCORDING TO ALL HINTS I COULD COLLECT	38	2	DON	JUAN	1	33	2
I ASK'D THE DOCTORS AFTER HIS DISEASE	39	2	DON	JUAN	1	34	6
THAT I MUST SAY WHO KNEW HIM VERY WELL	40	2	DON	JUAN	1	35	2
I DON'T THINK SAPPHO'S ODE A GOOD EXAMPLE	45	2	DON	JUAN	1	42	4
I CAN'T HELP THINKING JUVENAL WAS WRONG	45	2	DON	JUAN	1	43	3
IS MORE THAN I KNOW--BUT DON JUAN'S MOTHER	47	2	DON	JUAN	1	46	7
I CAN'T BUT SAY THAT HIS MAMMA WAS RIGHT	48	2	DON	JUAN	1	48	2
I RECOMMEND AS MUCH TO EVERY WIFE	48	2	DON	JUAN	1	48	8
AT SIX I SAID HE WAS A CHARMING CHILD	49	2	DON	JUAN	1	50	1
I HAD MY DOUBTS PERHAPS I HAVE THEM STILL	49	2	DON	JUAN	1	51	1
I HAD MY DOUBTS PERHAPS I HAVE THEM STILL	49	2	DON	JUAN	1	51	1
BUT WHAT I SAY IS NEITHER HERE NOR THERE	49	2	DON	JUAN	1	51	2
I KNEW HIS FATHER WELL AND HAVE SOME SKILL	49	2	DON	JUAN	1	51	3
BUT SCANDAL'S MY AVERSION--I PROTEST	49	2	DON	JUAN	1	51	7
FOR MY PART I SAY NOTHING--NOTHING--BUT	50	2	DON	JUAN	1	52	1
THIS I WILL SAY--MY REASONS ARE MY OWN--	50	2	DON	JUAN	1	52	2
THAT IF I HAD AN ONLY SON TO PUT	50	2	DON	JUAN	1	52	3
TO SCHOOL (AS GOD BE PRAISED THAT I HAVE NONE)	50	2	DON	JUAN	1	52	4
'TIS NOT WITH DONNA INEZ I WOULD SHUT	50	2	DON	JUAN	1	52	5
FOR THERE IT WAS I PICK'D UP MY OWN KNOWLEDGE	50	2	DON	JUAN	1	52	8
THOUGH I ACQUIRED--BUT I PASS OVER THAT	50	2	DON	JUAN	1	53	2
THOUGH I ACQUIRED--BUT I PASS OVER THAT	50	2	DON	JUAN	1	53	2
AS WELL AS ALL THE GREEK I SINCE HAVE LOST	50	2	DON	JUAN	1	53	3
I SAY THAT THERE'S THE PLACE--BUT VERBUM SAT	50	2	DON	JUAN	1	53	4
I THINK I PICK'D UP TOO AS WELL AS MOST	50	2	DON	JUAN	1	53	5
I THINK I PICK'D UP TOO AS WELL AS MOST	50	2	DON	JUAN	1	53	5
I NEVER MARRIED--BUT I THINK I KNOW	50	2	DON	JUAN	1	53	7
I NEVER MARRIED--BUT I THINK I KNOW	50	2	DON	JUAN	1	53	7
I NEVER MARRIED--BUT I THINK I KNOW	50	2	DON	JUAN	1	53	7
SHE MARRIED (I FORGET THE PEDIGREE)	52	2	DON	JUAN	1	57	1
BUT THERE'S A RUMOUR WHICH I FAIN WOULD HUSH	53	2	DON	JUAN	1	58	6
I SHALL HAVE MUCH TO SPEAK ABOUT) AND SHE	54	2	DON	JUAN	1	59	7
HER STATURE TALL--I HATE A DUMPY WOMAN	55	2	DON	JUAN	1	61	8
AND YET I THINK INSTEAD OF SUCH A ONE	56	2	DON	JUAN	1	62	3
AND NOW I THINK ON'T MI VIEN IN MENTE	56	2	DON	JUAN	1	62	6
'TIS A SAD THING I CANNOT CHOOSE BUT SAY	56	2	DON	JUAN	1	63	1
JULIA WAS--YET I NEVER COULD SEE WHY--	58	2	DON	JUAN	1	66	1
I CAN'T TELL WHETHER JULIA SAW THE AFFAIR	59	2	DON	JUAN	1	68	1
BUT I AM NOT SO SURE I SHOULD HAVE SMILED	59	2	DON	JUAN	1	69	5
BUT I AM NOT SO SURE I SHOULD HAVE SMILED	59	2	DON	JUAN	1	69	5
I RECOMMEND YOUNG LADIES TO MAKE TRIAL	64	2	DON	JUAN	1	78	8
AND SO I'D HAVE HER THINK WERE I THE MAN	64	2	DON	JUAN	1	79	7
BUT NOT MY FAULT--I TELL THEM ALL IN TIME	65	2	DON	JUAN	1	80	8
I REALLY DON'T KNOW WHAT NOR JULIA EITHER	65	2	DON	JUAN	1	81	8
I ONLY SAY SUPPOSE IT--INTER NOS	67	2	DON	JUAN	1	84	6
I ONLY SAY SUPPOSE THIS SUPPOSITION	67	2	DON	JUAN	1	85	1
I MEAN THE SERAPH WAY OF THOSE ABOVE	67	2	DON	JUAN	1	85	8
BUT THEN I BEG IT MAY BE UNDERSTOOD	68	2	DON	JUAN	1	87	6
BY SOLITUDE I MEAN A SULTAN'S NOT	68	2	DON	JUAN	1	87	7
THE BARD I QUOTE FROM DOES NOT SING AMISS	69	2	DON	JUAN	1	88	5
OR LOVE--I WON'T SAY MORE ABOUT ENTWINED	69	2	DON	JUAN	1	89	6
I CAN'T HELP THINKING PUBERTY ASSISTED	71	2	DON	JUAN	1	93	8
WITH--SEVERAL OTHER THINGS WHICH I FORGET	73	2	DON	JUAN	1	96	7
OR WHICH AT LEAST I NEED NOT MENTION YET	73	2	DON	JUAN	1	96	8
(I HAVE FORGOT THE NUMBER AND THINK NO MAN	74	2	DON	JUAN	1	98	5
I SAY WHEN THESE SAME GENTLEMEN ARE JEALOUS	74	2	DON	JUAN	1	98	7
OF SIGHT THAT I MUST THINK ON THIS OCCASION	75	2	DON	JUAN	1	101	2
BUT WHAT MOTIVE WAS I SHA'N'T SAY HERE	75	2	DON	JUAN	1	101	5
I LIKE TO BE PARTICULAR IN DATES	76	2	DON	JUAN	1	103	2
SHE SATE BUT NOT ALONE I KNOW NOT WELL	77	2	DON	JUAN	1	105	1
AND EVEN IF I KNEW I SHOULD NOT TELL--	77	2	DON	JUAN	1	105	3
AND EVEN IF I KNEW I SHOULD NOT TELL--	77	2	DON	JUAN	1	105	3
I WISH THESE LAST HAD NOT OCCURR'D IN SOOTH	78	2	DON	JUAN	1	107	5
I CANNOT KNOW WHAT JUAN THOUGHT OF THIS	81	2	DON	JUAN	1	112	1
AND THEN--GOD KNOWS WHAT NEXT--I CAN'T GO ON	83	2	DON	JUAN	1	115	7
I'M ALMOST SORRY THAT I E'ER BEGUN	83	2	DON	JUAN	1	115	8
I WISH INDEED THEY HAD NOT HAD OCCASION	84	2	DON	JUAN	1	117	4
AND WHISPERING I WILL NE'ER CONSENT--CONSENTED	84	2	DON	JUAN	1	117	8
FOND OF A LITTLE LOVE (WHICH I CALL LEISURE)	85	2	DON	JUAN	1	118	6
I CARE NOT FOR NEW PLEASURES AS THE OLD	85	2	DON	JUAN	1	118	7
I MAKE A RESOLUTION EVERY SPRING	85	2	DON	JUAN	1	119	3
YET STILL I TRUST IT MAY BE KEPT THROUGHOUT	85	2	DON	JUAN	1	119	6
IN THE DESIGN AND AS I HAVE A HIGH SENSE	86	2	DON	JUAN	1	120	6
TO BEG HIS PARDON WHEN I ERR A BIT	86	2	DON	JUAN	1	120	8
I SAID THE SMALL-POX HAS GONE OUT OF LATE	92	2	DON	JUAN	1	130	7
WHAT THEN--I DO NOT KNOW NO MORE DO YOU--	94	2	DON	JUAN	1	134	1
'TIS NOT MY FAULT--I KEPT GOOD WATCH--ALACK	96	2	DON	JUAN	1	137	4
I CAN'T TELL HOW OR WHY OR WHAT SUSPICION	97	2	DON	JUAN	1	139	1
(MIND--THAT I DO NOT SAY--SHE HAD NOT SLEPT)	97	2	DON	JUAN	1	140	2
I CAN'T TELL WHY SHE SHOULD TAKE ALL THIS TROUBLE	97	2	DON	JUAN	1	140	7
MY DEAR I WAS THE FIRST WHO CAME AWAY	98	2	DON	JUAN	1	141	8
HAS MADNESS SEIZED YOU WOULD THAT I HAD DIED	98	2	DON	JUAN	1	142	3

I   (CONTINUED)

	PAGE	VOL		CANTO	STANZA	LN
ERE SUCH A MONSTER'S VICTIM I HAD BEEN	98	2	DON JUAN	1	142	4
SEARCH THEN THE ROOM ALFONSO SAID I WILL	98	2	DON JUAN	1	142	8
ERE I THE WIFE OF SUCH A WRETCH HAD BEEN	98	2	DON JUAN	1	142	V4
IT WAS FOR THIS THAT I BECAME A BRIDE	100	2	DON JUAN	1	145	4
FOR THIS IN SILENCE I HAVE SUFFER'D LONG	100	2	DON JUAN	1	145	5
IS IT FOR THIS I HAVE DISDAIN'D TO HOLD	101	2	DON JUAN	1	147	1
THAT I HAVE CHOSEN A CONFESSOR SO OLD	101	2	DON JUAN	1	147	3
SO MUCH HE ALWAYS DOUBTED I WAS MARRIED--	101	2	DON JUAN	1	147	7
I YET HAVE CHOSEN FROM OUT THE YOUTH OF SEVILLE	102	2	DON JUAN	1	148	2
IS IT FOR THIS I SCARCE WENT ANYWHERE	102	2	DON JUAN	1	148	3
I FAVOUR'D NONE--NAY WAS ALMOST UNCIVIL	102	2	DON JUAN	1	148	6
WHO TOOK ALGIERS DECLARES I USED HIM VILELY	102	2	DON JUAN	1	148	8
I SHUNNED THEM AS I WOULD DO THE DEVIL	102	2	DON JUAN	1	148	V6
I SHUNNED THEM AS I WOULD DO THE DEVIL	102	2	DON JUAN	1	148	V6
I SHUNNED THEM TO LEAVE NO CAUSE FOR CAVIL	102	2	DON JUAN	1	148	V6
THE COUNT STRONGSTROGANOFF I PUT IN PAIN	102	2	DON JUAN	1	149	6
HAVE I NOT HAD TWO BISHOPS AT MY FEET	103	2	DON JUAN	1	150	1
I WONDER IN WHAT QUARTER NOW THE MOON IS	103	2	DON JUAN	1	150	4
I PRAISE YOUR VAST FORBEARANCE NOT TO BEAT	103	2	DON JUAN	1	150	5
WHOM I SEE STANDING THERE AND LOOKING SENSIBLE	103	2	DON JUAN	1	151	4
OF HAVING PLAY'D THE FOOL THOUGH BOTH I SPURN HE . . .	103	2	DON JUAN	1	151	5
I WOULD NOT YOU FOR NOTHING SHOULD BE FEE'D--	104	2	DON JUAN	1	152	6
OH SOBB'D ANTONIA I COULD TEAR THEIR EYES OUT	104	2	DON JUAN	1	152	8
I WISH TO SLEEP AND BEG YOU WILL TAKE CARE	104	2	DON JUAN	1	153	5
I HOPE HE'S YOUNG AND HANDSOME--IS HE TALL	105	2	DON JUAN	1	154	6
I AM ASHAMED OF HAVING SHED THESE TEARS	106	2	DON JUAN	1	155	5
THAT I SHOULD FALL INTO A MONSTER'S POWER	106	2	DON JUAN	1	155	8
ONLY ANOTHER TIME I TRUST YOU'LL TELL US	106	2	DON JUAN	1	156	5
AND NOW SIR I HAVE DONE AND SAY NO MORE	107	2	DON JUAN	1	157	1
THE LITTLE I HAVE SAID MAY SERVE TO SHOW	107	2	DON JUAN	1	157	2
I LEAVE YOU TO YOUR CONSCIENCE AS BEFORE	107	2	DON JUAN	1	157	5
HE HAD BEEN HID--I DON'T PRETEND TO SAY	112	2	DON JUAN	1	166	1
HOW NOR CAN I INDEED DESCRIBE THE WHERE--	112	2	DON JUAN	1	166	2
BUT PITY HIM I NEITHER MUST NOR MAY	112	2	DON JUAN	1	166	5
AND SECONDLY I PITY NOT BECAUSE	113	2	DON JUAN	1	167	1
OF HIS POSITION I CAN GIVE NO NOTION	113	2	DON JUAN	1	168	1
SHE WHISPER'D IN GREAT WRATH--I MUST DEPOSIT	114	2	DON JUAN	1	170	7
YOU'LL LOSE YOUR LIFE AND I SHALL LOSE MY PLACE . . .	115	2	DON JUAN	1	171	7
(I REALLY MADAM WONDER AT YOUR TASTE--	115	2	DON JUAN	1	172	4
THEY BLUSH AND WE BELIEVE THEM AT LEAST I	119	2	DON JUAN	1	179	1
(NO ONE CAN TELL HOW MUCH I GRIEVE TO SAY)	121	2	DON JUAN	1	181	3
HASTE--HASTE--I HEAR ALFONSO'S HURRYING FEET-- . . .	121	2	DON JUAN	1	182	7
I DOUBT ALL LIKENESS ENDS BETWEEN THE PAIR	124	2	DON JUAN	1	186	8
HERE ENDS THIS CANTO--NEED I SING OR SAY	126	2	DON JUAN	1	188	1
I HAVE NO FURTHER CLAIM ON YOUR YOUNG HEART	130	2	DON JUAN	1	192	3
I USED--I WRITE IN HASTE AND IF A STAIN	130	2	DON JUAN	1	192	6
I USED--I WRITE IN HASTE AND IF A STAIN	130	2	DON JUAN	1	192	6
I LOVED I LOVE YOU FOR THIS LOVE HAVE LOST	130	2	DON JUAN	1	193	1
I LOVED I LOVE YOU FOR THIS LOVE HAVE LOST	130	2	DON JUAN	1	193	1
YET IF I NAME MY GUILT 'TIS NOT TO BOAST	130	2	DON JUAN	1	193	5
NONE CAN DEEM HARSHLIER OF ME THAN I DEEM	130	2	DON JUAN	1	193	6
I TRACE THIS SCRAWL BECAUSE I CANNOT REST--	130	2	DON JUAN	1	193	7
I TRACE THIS SCRAWL BECAUSE I CANNOT REST--	130	2	DON JUAN	1	193	7
THESE I COULD BEAR BUT CANNOT CAST ASIDE	132	2	DON JUAN	1	195	5
BUT STILL I THINK I CAN COLLECT MY MIND	133	2	DON JUAN	1	196	2
BUT STILL I THINK I CAN COLLECT MY MIND	133	2	DON JUAN	1	196	2
I STRUGGLE BUT CAN NOT COLLECT MY MIND	133	2	DON JUAN	1	196	V2
I HAVE NO MORE TO SAY BUT LINGER STILL	134	2	DON JUAN	1	197	1
AND YET I MAY AS WELL THE TASK FULFIL	134	2	DON JUAN	1	197	3
I HAD NOT LIVED TILL NOW COULD SORROW KILL	134	2	DON JUAN	1	197	5
AND I MUST EVEN SURVIVE THIS LAST ADIEU	134	2	DON JUAN	1	197	7
I SHALL PROCEED WITH HIS ADVENTURES IS	135	2	DON JUAN	1	199	2
AND HERE THE ADVANTAGE IS MY OWN I WEEN	137	2	DON JUAN	1	202	3
(NOT THAT I HAVE NOT SEVERAL MERITS MORE	137	2	DON JUAN	1	202	4
IF ANY PERSON DOUBT IT I APPEAL	138	2	DON JUAN	1	203	1
IF EVER I SHOULD CONDESCEND TO PROSE	138	2	DON JUAN	1	204	1
THAT WENT BEFORE IN THESE I SHALL ENRICH	138	2	DON JUAN	1	204	4
THOU SHALT NOT WRITE IN SHORT BUT WHAT I CHOOSE . . .	140	2	DON JUAN	1	206	5
THIS STORY IS NOT MORAL FIRST I PRAY	140	2	DON JUAN	1	207	2
BESIDES IN CANTO TWELFTH I MEAN TO SHOW	140	2	DON JUAN	1	207	7
I TELL HIM IF A CLERGYMAN HE LIES	141	2	DON JUAN	1	208	6
THE PUBLIC APPROBATION I EXPECT	141	2	DON JUAN	1	209	1
WHICH I WITH THEIR AMUSEMENT WILL CONNECT	141	2	DON JUAN	1	209	3
I SENT IT IN A LETTER TO THE EDITOR	142	2	DON JUAN	1	210	1
ALL I CAN SAY IS--THAT HE HAD THE MONEY	142	2	DON JUAN	1	210	8
I THINK THAT WITH THIS HOLY NEW ALLIANCE	142	2	DON JUAN	1	211	1
I MAY ENSURE THE PUBLIC AND DEFY	142	2	DON JUAN	1	211	2
DAILY OR MONTHLY OR THREE MONTHLY I	142	2	DON JUAN	1	211	4
SAY I BY WHICH QUOTATION THERE IS MEANT A	143	2	DON JUAN	1	212	3
(LONG ERE I DREAMT OF DATING FROM THE BRENTA)	143	2	DON JUAN	1	212	5
I WAS MOST READY TO RETURN A BLOW	143	2	DON JUAN	1	212	6
(I WONDER WHAT IT WILL BE LIKE AT FORTY	143	2	DON JUAN	1	213	2
I THOUGHT OF A PERUKE THE OTHER DAY)	143	2	DON JUAN	1	213	3
MY HEART IS NOT MUCH GREENER AND IN SHORT I	143	2	DON JUAN	1	213	4
AND FEEL NO MORE THE SPIRIT TO RETORT I	143	2	DON JUAN	1	213	6
AND DEEM NOT WHAT I DEEM'D MY SOUL INVINCIBLE	143	2	DON JUAN	1	213	8
I THOUGHT OF DYEING IT THE OTHER DAY	143	2	DON JUAN	1	213	V3
INSENSIBLE I TRUST BUT NONE THE WORSE	144	2	DON JUAN	1	215	6

I (CONTINUED)

	PAGE	VOL	CANTO		STANZA	LN
IN SHORT I MUST NOT LEAD THE LIFE I DID DO	144	2	DON JUAN	1	216	4
IN SHORT I MUST NOT LEAD THE LIFE I DID DO	144	2	DON JUAN	1	216	4
I THINK I MUST TAKE UP WITH AVARICE	144	2	DON JUAN	1	216	8
I THINK I MUST TAKE UP WITH AVARICE	144	2	DON JUAN	1	216	8
I FIND THAT WINE OR BRANDY IS FORBID TOO--	145	2	DON JUAN	1	216	V6
IS GLITTERING YOUTH WHICH I HAVE SPENT BETIMES--	145	2	DON JUAN	1	217	7
IS THAT SAME TIME WHICH I HAVE SPENT BETIMES	145	2	DON JUAN	1	217	V7
BUT I BEING FOND OF TRUE PHILOSOPHY	147	2	DON JUAN	1	220	1
STILL GENTLER PURCHASER THE BARD--THAT'S I--	147	2	DON JUAN	1	221	2
EACH OTHER AND IF NOT I SHALL NOT TRY	147	2	DON JUAN	1	221	6
I CAST THEE ON THE WATERS GO THY WAYS	149	2	DON JUAN	1	222	2
AND IF AS I BELIEVE THY VEIN BE GOOD	149	2	DON JUAN	1	222	3
I CAN'T HELP PUTTING IN MY CLAIM TO PRAISE--	149	2	DON JUAN	1	222	6
TO HEAD THE POLL I WONDER WHO WOULD BUY IT	154	2	DON JUAN	1	V 5	4
I WOULD TO HEAVEN THAT I WERE SO MUCH CLAY--	156	2	DON JUAN	1	V 8	1
I WOULD TO HEAVEN THAT I WERE SO MUCH CLAY--	156	2	DON JUAN	1	V 8	1
AS I AM BLOOD--BONE--MARROW PASSION--FEELING--	156	2	DON JUAN	1	V 8	2
AND FOR THE FUTURE--(BUT I WRITE THIS REELING	156	2	DON JUAN	1	V 8	4
SO THAT I SEEM TO STAND UPON THE CEILING)	156	2	DON JUAN	1	V 8	6
I SAY--THE FUTURE IS A SERIOUS MATTER--	156	2	DON JUAN	1	V 8	7
I PRAY YE FLOG THEM UPON ALL OCCASIONS	157	2	DON JUAN	2	1	3
I CAN'T SAY THAT IT PUZZLES ME AT ALL	158	2	DON JUAN	2	3	1
I SAID THAT JUAN HAD BEEN SENT TO CADIZ--	159	2	DON JUAN	2	5	1
A PRETTY TOWN I RECOLLECT IT WELL--	159	2	DON JUAN	2	5	2
AND SUCH SWEET GIRLS--I MEAN SUCH GRACEFUL LADIES	159	2	DON JUAN	2	5	5
I CAN'T DESCRIBE IT THOUGH SO MUCH IT STRIKE	159	2	DON JUAN	2	5	7
NOR LIKEN IT--I NEVER SAW THE LIKE	159	2	DON JUAN	2	5	8
BUT DAMN ME--IF I EVER SAW THE LIKE	159	2	DON JUAN	2	5	V8
OF LOVE WHEN I FORGET YOU MAY I FAIL	160	2	DON JUAN	2	7	5
OF LOVE WHEN I FORGET YOU MAY I FAIL	160	2	DON JUAN	2	7	5
TO GOD KNOWS WHAT--BUT NEVER YET I SCANNED	161	2	DON JUAN	2	7	V6
AS I WHO'VE CROSS'D IT OFT KNOW WELL ENOUGH	162	2	DON JUAN	2	11	4
I CAN'T BUT SAY IT IS AN AWKWARD SIGHT	163	2	DON JUAN	2	12	1
I RECOLLECT GREAT BRITAIN'S COAST LOOKS WHITE	163	2	DON JUAN	2	12	5
YOU SNEER AND I ASSURE YOU THIS IS TRUE	163	2	DON JUAN	2	13	7
FOR I HAVE FOUND IT ANSWER--SO MAY YOU	163	2	DON JUAN	2	13	8
FOR I HAVE FOUND IT WELL--AND SO MAY YOU	163	2	DON JUAN	2	13	V8
SWEETS TO THE SWEET (I LIKE SO MUCH TO QUOTE	165	2	DON JUAN	2	17	3
PERHAPS I MAY REVISIT THEE NO MORE	166	2	DON JUAN	2	18	2
AND OH IF E'ER I SHOULD FORGET I SWEAR--	166	2	DON JUAN	2	19	1
AND OH IF E'ER I SHOULD FORGET I SWEAR--	166	2	DON JUAN	2	19	1
THAN I RESIGN THINE IMAGE OH MY FAIR	166	2	DON JUAN	2	19	5
THAT SOME I REALLY THINK DO NEVER DIE	190	2	DON JUAN	2	65	4
WHICH I FOUND VERY TROUBLESOME TO PAY	190	2	DON JUAN	2	65	8
WITH THEIR ONE OAR (I WISH THEY HAD HAD A PAIR)	193	2	DON JUAN	2	70	5
I CAN DO NOTHING AND HE SAW HIM THROWN	202	2	DON JUAN	2	87	7
BUT IN THIS CASE I ALSO MUST REMARK	206	2	DON JUAN	2	95	1
LEANDER MR EKENHEAD AND I DID	211	2	DON JUAN	2	105	8
HER HAIR I SAID WAS AUBURN BUT HER EYES	218	2	DON JUAN	2	117	1
I'LL TELL YOU WHY I SAY SO FOR 'TIS JUST	219	2	DON JUAN	2	119	1
I NE'ER SAW JUSTICE DONE AND YET SHE WAS	219	2	DON JUAN	2	119	4
AROUND THEM (WHAT I HOPE WILL NEVER VANISH)	220	2	DON JUAN	2	120	6
WHICH ARE (AS I MUST OWN) OF FEMALE GROWTH	221	2	DON JUAN	2	123	3
BESIDES I HATE ALL MYSTERY AND THAT AIR	222	2	DON JUAN	2	124	3
BUT THIS I KNOW IT WAS A SPACIOUS BUILDING	223	2	DON JUAN	2	127	7
I SAY THE SUN IS A MOST GLORIOUS SIGHT	230	2	DON JUAN	2	140	1
I HAVE SAT UP ON PURPOSE ALL THE NIGHT	230	2	DON JUAN	2	140	3
AS AT THIS MOMENT I SHOULD LIKE TO DO	232	2	DON JUAN	2	142	V6
BUT I HAVE DONE WITH KISSES--HAVING KISSED	232	2	DON JUAN	2	142	V7
ALL THOSE THAT WOULD--REGRETTING THOSE I MISSED	232	2	DON JUAN	2	142	V8
I CAN'T SAY THAT SHE GAVE THEM ANY TEA	233	2	DON JUAN	2	145	6
I SAY THAT BEEF IS RARE AND CAN'T HELP THINKING	238	2	DON JUAN	2	155	1
FED UPON BEEF--I WON'T SAY MUCH OF BEER	238	2	DON JUAN	2	156	2
SO WERE THE CRETANS--FROM WHICH I INFER	238	2	DON JUAN	2	156	7
BY FEMALE LIPS AND EYES--THAT IS I MEAN	242	2	DON JUAN	2	164	1
AS WAS THE CASE AT LEAST WHERE I HAVE BEEN	242	2	DON JUAN	2	164	4
I LEARN'D THE LITTLE THAT I KNOW BY THIS	242	2	DON JUAN	2	164	8
I LEARN'D THE LITTLE THAT I KNOW BY THIS	242	2	DON JUAN	2	164	8
MUCH ENGLISH I CANNOT PRETEND TO SPEAK	243	2	DON JUAN	2	165	3
I STUDY ALSO BLAIR THE HIGHEST REACHERS	243	2	DON JUAN	2	165	6
I HATE YOUR POETS SO READ NONE OF THOSE	243	2	DON JUAN	2	165	8
AS FOR THE LADIES I HAVE NOUGHT TO SAY	244	2	DON JUAN	2	166	1
WHERE I LIKE OTHER DOGS HAVE HAD MY DAY	244	2	DON JUAN	2	166	3
AND ALL HER FOOLS WHOM I COULD LAY THE LASH ON	244	2	DON JUAN	2	166	6
BUT I HAVE SPOKEN OF ALL THIS ALREADY--	246	2	DON JUAN	2	171	5
I SPEAK OF CHRISTIAN LANDS IN THIS COMPARISON	248	2	DON JUAN	2	175	7
THE COAST--I THINK IT WAS THE COAST THAT I	251	2	DON JUAN	2	181	1
THE COAST--I THINK IT WAS THE COAST THAT I	251	2	DON JUAN	2	181	1
AS I HAVE SAID UPON AN EXPEDITION	252	2	DON JUAN	2	182	2
I THINK IT MUST BE RECKON'D BY ITS LENGTH	254	2	DON JUAN	2	186	8
BY LENGTH I MEAN DURATION THEIRS ENDURED	254	2	DON JUAN	2	187	1
THE BEST EXAMPLES WHICH I KNOW FOR LOVES	257	2	DON JUAN	2	191	V8
SO GOOD--I WONDER CASTLEREAGH DON'T TAX 'EM	264	2	DON JUAN	2	203	8
I CAN'T BUT SAY IT SEEMS TO ME MOST TRULY A	267	2	DON JUAN	2	208	3
I HATE INCONSTANCY--I LOATHE DETEST	268	2	DON JUAN	2	209	1
I HATE INCONSTANCY--I LOATHE DETEST	268	2	DON JUAN	2	209	1
I SAW THE PRETTIEST CREATURE FRESH FROM MILAN	268	2	DON JUAN	2	209	7
I WILL MY DEAR PHILOSOPHY I SAID	268	2	DON JUAN	2	210	3

	PAGE	VOL	CANTO	STANZA	LN
I WILL MY DEAR PHILOSOPHY I SAID	268	2	DON JUAN 2	210	3
AND SO I STOPPED TO TALK WITH A VENETIAN	268	2	DON JUAN 2	210	V8
STOP SO I STOPP'D--BUT TO RETURN THAT WHICH	269	2	DON JUAN 2	211	1
AND LAYING DOWN MY PEN I MAKE MY BOW	271	2	DON JUAN 2	216	6
LAST NIGHT I HAD ANOTHER PROOF HOW TRULY IT	272	2	DON JUAN 2	V 1	6
ANOTHER JULIET-- WHOM I WOULD NOT PASS--	273	2	DON JUAN 2	V 2	5
IS ROUSSEAU'S JULIETTA--I NEER KNEW	273	2	DON JUAN 2	V 2	7
ONE OF THE NAME BUT THAT I LOVED HER TOO	273	2	DON JUAN 2	V 2	8
I KNOW NOT IF THE FAULT BE MEN'S OR THEIRS	276	2	DON JUAN 3	4	1
ALL FURTHER IS A BLANK--I WON'T DISPARAGE	280	2	DON JUAN 3	9	V4
THOUGH LIFE AND LOVE I LIKE NOT TO DISPARAGE	280	2	DON JUAN 3	9	V4
BY BEATRICE AND NOT A MISTRESS--I	281	2	DON JUAN 3	11	2
I THINK THAT DANTE'S MORE ABSTRUSE ECSTATICS	281	2	DON JUAN 3	11	7
BUT THEY HATE FLATTERY SO I NEVER FLATTER)	287	2	DON JUAN 3	22	6
SOME CHASTE LIAISON OF THE KIND--I MEAN	288	2	DON JUAN 3	25	2
TALKING'S DRY WORK I HAVE NO TIME TO SPARE	297	2	DON JUAN 3	43	4
I KNOW NOT QUOTH THE FELLOW WHO OR WHAT	298	2	DON JUAN 3	45	1
BUT THIS I KNOW THAT THIS ROAST CAPON'S FAT	298	2	DON JUAN 3	45	3
I SAID THAT LAMBRO WAS A MAN OF PATIENCE	299	2	DON JUAN 3	46	1
YET SUCH THINGS ARE WHICH I CAN NOT EXPLAIN	299	2	DON JUAN 3	47	6
FOR HAIDEE'S SAKE IS MORE THAN I CAN SAY	300	2	DON JUAN 3	49	6
I CAN'T HELP THINKING THAT ALL FORMER STRIFE	301	2	DON JUAN 3	50	V5
UP WITH THE COFFEE WHICH (I THINK) THEY SPOIL'D	307	2	DON JUAN 3	63	8
OF ALL THE DRESSES I SELECT HAIDEE'S	311	2	DON JUAN 3	70	1
I KNOW NOT HOW--HER PRESENCE MADE YE FEEL	313	2	DON JUAN 3	74	V7
SHE WAS SO LIKE A VISION I MIGHT ERR	314	2	DON JUAN 3	76	6
WHEN DAZZLED WITH HER ASPECT I MIGHT ERR	314	2	DON JUAN 3	76	V6
I DREAM'D THAT GREECE MIGHT STILL BE FREE	321	2	DON JUAN 3	L 3	4
I COULD NOT DEEM MYSELF A SLAVE	321	2	DON JUAN 3	L 3	6
EVEN AS I SING SUFFUSE MY FACE	323	2	DON JUAN 3	L 6	4
I SEE THEIR GLORIOUS BLACK EYES SHINE	326	2	DON JUAN 3	L 15	3
WHERE NOTHING SAVE THE WAVES AND I	326	2	DON JUAN 3	L 16	2
BUT LET ME TO MY STORY I MUST OWN	331	2	DON JUAN 3	96	1
IF I HAVE ANY FAULT IT IS DIGRESSION	331	2	DON JUAN 3	96	2
WHILE I SOLILOQUIZE BEYOND EXPRESSION	331	2	DON JUAN 3	96	4
WHILE I AM CHATTERING BEYOND ALL EXPRESSION	331	2	DON JUAN 3	96	V4
I KNOW THAT WHAT OUR NEIGHBOURS CALL LONGUEURS	332	2	DON JUAN 3	97	1
THAT YOU WERE LIVING--OR I HAD YOUR ROD	334	2	DON JUAN 3	100	V7
THE TIME THE CLIME THE SPOT WHERE I SO OFT	335	2	DON JUAN 3	102	2
IN NAMELESS PRINT--THAT I HAVE NO DEVOTION	336	2	DON JUAN 3	104	2
HOW HAVE I LOVED THE TWILIGHT HOUR AND THEE	337	2	DON JUAN 3	105	8
AND I GROWN ONE OF MANY WOODEN SPOONS	341	2	DON JUAN 3	110	6
I FEEL THIS TEDIOUSNESS WILL NEVER DO--	342	2	DON JUAN 3	111	1
'TIS BEING TOO EPIC AND I MUST CUT DOWN	342	2	DON JUAN 3	111	2
THEY'LL NEVER FIND IT OUT UNLESS I OWN	342	2	DON JUAN 3	111	4
AS BOY I THOUGHT MYSELF A CLEVER FELLOW	345	2	DON JUAN 4	3	1
AND IF I LAUGH AT ANY MORTAL THING	346	2	DON JUAN 4	4	1
'TIS THAT I MAY NOT WEEP AND IF I WEEP	346	2	DON JUAN 4	4	2
'TIS THAT I MAY NOT WEEP AND IF I WEEP	346	2	DON JUAN 4	4	2
I DON'T PRETEND THAT I QUITE UNDERSTAND	346	2	DON JUAN 4	5	4
I DON'T PRETEND THAT I QUITE UNDERSTAND	346	2	DON JUAN 4	5	4
MY OWN MEANING WHEN I WOULD BE VERY FINE	346	2	DON JUAN 4	5	5
BUT THE FACT IS THAT I HAVE NOTHING PLANN'D	346	2	DON JUAN 4	5	6
I CHOSE A MODERN SUBJECT AS MORE MEET	347	2	DON JUAN 4	6	8
HOW I HAVE TREATED IT I DO NOT KNOW	347	2	DON JUAN 4	7	1
HOW I HAVE TREATED IT I DO NOT KNOW	347	2	DON JUAN 4	7	1
I KNOW NOT WHY BUT IN THAT HOUR TO-NIGHT	355	2	DON JUAN 4	21	1
OR I AT LEAST SHALL NOT SURVIVE TO SEE	356	2	DON JUAN 4	23	8
I HAVE TRIED BOTH SO THOSE WHO WOULD A PART TAKE	356	2	DON JUAN 4	24	7
BUT WHICH TO CHOOSE I REALLY HARDLY KNOW	357	2	DON JUAN 4	25	4
AND IF I HAD TO GIVE A CASTING VOICE	357	2	DON JUAN 4	25	5
FOR BOTH SIDES I COULD MANY REASONS SHOW	357	2	DON JUAN 4	25	6
I HAVE SEEN SUCH--BUT MUST NOT CALL TO MIND	363	2	DON JUAN 4	36	8
I HAVE SEEN SUCH--BUT THEY UNHINGED MY MIND	363	2	DON JUAN 4	36	V8
OF PLEASURE AND OF PAIN--EVEN WHILE I KISS	364	2	DON JUAN 4	38	5
HE FOUND--BUT SOUGHT NOT I HAVE PLEDGED MY FAITH	366	2	DON JUAN 4	42	6
I LOVE HIM--I WILL DIE WITH HIM I KNEW	366	2	DON JUAN 4	42	7
I LOVE HIM--I WILL DIE WITH HIM I KNEW	366	2	DON JUAN 4	42	7
I LOVE HIM--I WILL DIE WITH HIM I KNEW	366	2	DON JUAN 4	42	7
I SAID THEY WERE ALIKE THEIR FEATURES AND	368	2	DON JUAN 4	45	1
NOT I HE SAID HAVE SOUGHT THIS STRANGER'S ILL	368	2	DON JUAN 4	46	4
NOT I HAVE MADE THIS DESOLATION FEW	368	2	DON JUAN 4	46	5
BUT I MUST DO MY DUTY--HOW THOU HAST	368	2	DON JUAN 4	46	7
HERE I MUST LEAVE HIM FOR I GROW PATHETIC	372	2	DON JUAN 4	52	1
HERE I MUST LEAVE HIM FOR I GROW PATHETIC	372	2	DON JUAN 4	52	1
I FEEL MY HEART BECOME SO SYMPATHETIC	372	2	DON JUAN 4	52	5
THAT I MUST HAVE RECOURSE TO BLACK BOHEA	372	2	DON JUAN 4	52	6
I WOULD TAKE REFUGE IN WEAK PUNCH BUT RACK	372	2	DON JUAN 4	53	5
(IN EACH SENSE OF THE WORD) WHENE'ER I FILL	372	2	DON JUAN 4	53	6
I LEAVE DON JUAN FOR THE PRESENT SAFE--	373	2	DON JUAN 4	54	1
I DON'T MUCH LIKE DESCRIBING PEOPLE MAD	384	2	DON JUAN 4	74	3
WITH EASE BUT WHERE I SOUGHT FOR ILION'S WALLS	386	2	DON JUAN 4	77	7
ARE WHAT I FOUND THERE--BUT THE DEVIL A PHRYGIAN	387	2	DON JUAN 4	78	8
HIS SINGING I NO FURTHER TRUST CAN PLACE IN	391	2	DON JUAN 4	86	6
MY OWN MERITS AND THOUGH YOUNG--I SEE SIR--YOU	392	2	DON JUAN 4	88	2
OUR BARITONE I ALMOST HAD FORGOT	392	2	DON JUAN 4	89	1
I REALLY THINK YET JUAN'S THEN ORDEAL	396	2	DON JUAN 4	96	7
HERE I MIGHT ENTER ON A CHASTE DESCRIPTION	397	2	DON JUAN 4	97	1

```
    I ONCE HAD A GREAT ALACRITY IN WIELDING . . . . .  . . . 397  2 DON JUAN  4   98   5
    BUT AT THIS HOUR I WISH TO PART IN PEACE . . . . . . . . 398  2 DON JUAN  4   99   2
    I CANTER BY THE SPOT EACH AFTERNOON . . . . . . . . . . 400  2 DON JUAN  4  103   1
    I PASS EACH DAY WHERE DANTE'S BONES ARE LAID . . . . . 400  2 DON JUAN  4  104   1
    BUT SPOIL (I THINK) A VERY PRETTY POEM . . . . . . . . . 403  2 DON JUAN  4  107   8
    I HAVE GAINED SCIENCE IN THE THINGS WHICH PASS . . . . 403  2 DON JUAN  4  107   V3
    WHAT MUST I GO TO THE OBLIVIOUS COOKS . . . . . . . . . 403  2 DON JUAN  4  108   5
    AH MUST I THEN THE ONLY MINSTREL BE . . . . . . . . . . 403  2 DON JUAN  4  108   7
    WHAT CAN I PROVE A LION THEN NO MORE . . . . . . . . . 404  2 DON JUAN  4  109   1
    AND SIGH I CAN'T GET OUT LIKE YORICK'S STARLING . . . . 404  2 DON JUAN  4  109   4
    AND I YE LEARNED LADIES SAY OF YOU . . . . . . . . . . 404  2 DON JUAN  4  110   3
    I HAVE EXAMINED FEW PAIR OF THAT HUE) . . . . . . . . . 404  2 DON JUAN  4  110   5
    YOU READ MY STANZAS AND I READ YOUR FEATURES . . . . 405  2 DON JUAN  4  111   3
    STILL I HAVE NO DISLIKE TO LEARNED NATURES . . . . . . 405  2 DON JUAN  4  111   5
    I KNOW ONE WOMAN OF THAT PURPLE SCHOOL . . . . . . . 405  2 DON JUAN  4  111   7
    INVENTED BY SOME NAME I HAVE FORGOT . . . . . . . . . 406  2 DON JUAN  4  112   3
    AS I WILL MAKE YOU QUICKLY UNDERSTAND . . . . . . . . 411  2 DON JUAN  5    1   V6
    I THEREFORE DO DENOUNCE ALL AMOROUS WRITING . . . . 412  2 DON JUAN  5    2   1
    THE TWELVE ISLES AND THE MORE THAN I COULD DREAM . . 412  2 DON JUAN  5    3   6
    I HAVE A PASSION FOR THE NAME OF MARY . . . . . . . . 413  2 DON JUAN  5    4   1
    WHERE I BEHELD WHAT NEVER WAS TO BE . . . . . . . . . 413  2 DON JUAN  5    4   4
    A SPELL FROM WHICH EVEN YET I AM NOT QUITE FREE . . . 413  2 DON JUAN  5    4   6
    BUT I GROW SAD--AND LET A TALE GROW COLD . . . . . . 413  2 DON JUAN  5    4   7
    YET I MUST OWN HE LOOKED A LITTLE DULL . . . . . . . . 415  2 DON JUAN  5    8   3
    THE ONLY GENTLEMEN SEEM I AND YOU . . . . . . . . . . 417  2 DON JUAN  5   13   5
    IF I COULD YIELD YOU ANY CONSOLATION . . . . . . . . . 417  2 DON JUAN  5   13   7
    I THOUGHT IN FACT YOU COULD NOT BE A GREEK . . . . . 418  2 DON JUAN  5   14   2
    EXCEPT THAT I HAVE FOUND IT NOTHING NEW . . . . . . . 418  2 DON JUAN  5   14   8
    PRAY SIR SAID JUAN IF I MAY PRESUME . . . . . . . . . . 418  2 DON JUAN  5   15   1
    IS THAT WHICH I WOULD LEARN -- I SERVED FOR SOME . . 418  2 DON JUAN  5   15   5
    IS THAT WHICH I WOULD LEARN -- I SERVED FOR SOME . . 418  2 DON JUAN  5   15   5
    HAVE YOU NO FRIENDS -- I HAD--BUT BY GOD'S BLESSING . 419  2 DON JUAN  5   16   1
    I HAVE ANSWERED ALL YOUR QUESTIONS WITHOUT PRESSING 419  2 DON JUAN  5   16   3
    I MOURN BUT FOR THE PAST--I LOVED A MAID . . . . . . . 420  2 DON JUAN  5   18   2
    I MOURN BUT FOR THE PAST--I LOVED A MAID . . . . . . . 420  2 DON JUAN  5   18   2
    'TIS NOT MY PRESENT LOT AS I HAVE SAID . . . . . . . . 420  2 DON JUAN  5   18   6
    WHICH I DEPLORE SO MUCH FOR I HAVE BORNE . . . . . . 420  2 DON JUAN  5   18   7
    WHICH I DEPLORE SO MUCH FOR I HAVE BORNE . . . . . . 420  2 DON JUAN  5   18   7
    AY QUOTH HIS FRIEND I THOUGHT IT WOULD APPEAR . . . 420  2 DON JUAN  5   19   3
    SUCH AS I TOO WOULD SHED IF IN YOUR PLACE . . . . . . 420  2 DON JUAN  5   19   6
    I CRIED UPON MY FIRST WIFE'S DYING DAY . . . . . . . . 420  2 DON JUAN  5   19   7
    NO FAITH--WHAT THEN--I RAN AWAY FROM HER . . . . . . 421  2 DON JUAN  5   20   8
    SAID JUAN BUT I REALLY DON'T SEE HOW . . . . . . . . . 422  2 DON JUAN  5   23   2
    I WISH TO GOD THAT SOMEBODY WOULD BUY US . . . . . . 423  2 DON JUAN  5   24   8
    I WONDER IF HIS APPETITE WAS GOOD . . . . . . . . . . 426  2 DON JUAN  5   30   1
    I THINK IT IS PERHAPS THE GLOOMIEST HOUR . . . . . . . 426  2 DON JUAN  5   30   7
    OF FOOD I THINK WITH PHILIP'S SON OR RATHER . . . . . 427  2 DON JUAN  5   31   7
    I THINK WITH ALEXANDER THAT THE ACT . . . . . . . . . 428  2 DON JUAN  5   32   1
    I HEARD A SHOT--'TWAS EIGHT O'CLOCK SCARCE PAST-- . . 428  2 DON JUAN  5   33   5
    AND RUNNING OUT AS FAST AS I WAS ABLE . . . . . . . . 428  2 DON JUAN  5   33   6
    I FOUND THE MILITARY COMMANDANT . . . . . . . . . . . 428  2 DON JUAN  5   33   7
    TO PERISH ON THE PAVEMENT SO I HAD . . . . . . . . . . 429  2 DON JUAN  5   34   3
    AND STRIPPED AND LOOKED TO--BUT WHY SHOULD I ADD . . 429  2 DON JUAN  5   34   5
    I GAZED UPON HIM FOR I KNEW HIM WELL . . . . . . . . . 430  2 DON JUAN  5   35   1
    I GAZED UPON HIM FOR I KNEW HIM WELL . . . . . . . . . 430  2 DON JUAN  5   35   1
    AND THOUGH I HAVE SEEN MANY CORPSES NEVER . . . . . 430  2 DON JUAN  5   35   2
    SO AS I GAZED ON HIM I THOUGHT OR SAID-- . . . . . . . 430  2 DON JUAN  5   35   8
    SO AS I GAZED ON HIM I THOUGHT OR SAID-- . . . . . . . 430  2 DON JUAN  5   35   8
    FROM ME I GAZED (AS OFT I HAVE GAZED THE SAME) . . . . 431  2 DON JUAN  5   38   6
    FROM ME I GAZED (AS OFT I HAVE GAZED THE SAME) . . . . 431  2 DON JUAN  5   38   6
    TO TRY IF I COULD WRENCH AUGHT OUT OF DEATH . . . . . 431  2 DON JUAN  5   38   7
    I SCARCELY COULD BELIEVE THAT HE WAS DEAD . . . . . . 432  2 DON JUAN  5   39   V4
    (OF WHICH I MIGHT HAVE A GOOD DEAL TO SAY . . . . . . 434  2 DON JUAN  5   42   3
    BUT I DIGRESS OF ALL APPEALS--ALTHOUGH . . . . . . . . 439  2 DON JUAN  5   49   1
    I GRANT THE POWER OF PATHOS AND OF GOLD . . . . . . . 439  2 DON JUAN  5   49   2
    I WON'T DESCRIBE DESCRIPTION IS MY FORTE . . . . . . . 440  2 DON JUAN  5   52   1
    I PASS MY EVENINGS IN LONG GALLERIES SOLELY . . . . . 444  2 DON JUAN  5   58   7
    I GRANT YOU IN A CHURCH 'TIS VERY WELL . . . . . . . . 444  2 DON JUAN  5   59   2
    HAS BEEN ACCUSED (I DOUBT NOT BY CONSPIRACY) . . . . 446  2 DON JUAN  5   61   2
    (FOR SUCH EXAGGERATIONS HERE AND THERE I SEE) . . . . 446  2 DON JUAN  5   61   6
    I WISH THE CASE COULD COME BEFORE A JURY HERE . . . . 446  2 DON JUAN  5   61   8
    I WISH TO BE PERSPICUOUS AND THE BLACK . . . . . . . . 450  2 DON JUAN  5   67   1
    I SAY UNLOCKING THE RECESS PULLED FORTH . . . . . . . 450  2 DON JUAN  5   67   2
    AND YET THOUGH I HAVE SAID THERE WAS NO DEARTH . . . 450  2 DON JUAN  5   67   6
    YOU PUT ME OUT IN WHAT I HAD TO SAY . . . . . . . . . 453  2 DON JUAN  5   72   3
    SIR--AS I SAID AS SOON AS I HAVE SUPT . . . . . . . . . 453  2 DON JUAN  5   72   4
    SIR--AS I SAID AS SOON AS I HAVE SUPT . . . . . . . . . 453  2 DON JUAN  5   72   4
    I SHALL PERPEND IF YOUR PROPOSAL MAY . . . . . . . . 453  2 DON JUAN  5   72   5
    BE SUCH AS I CAN PROPERLY ACCEPT . . . . . . . . . . 453  2 DON JUAN  5   72   6
    WHAT YOU MAY BE I NEITHER KNOW NOR CARE . . . . . . . 454  2 DON JUAN  5   74   1
    SAID BABA BUT PRAY DO AS I DESIRE . . . . . . . . . . 454  2 DON JUAN  5   74   2
    I HAVE NO MORE TIME NOR MANY WORDS TO SPARE . . . . 454  2 DON JUAN  5   74   3
    AT LEAST SAID JUAN SURE I MAY INQUIRE . . . . . . . . 454  2 DON JUAN  5   74   4
    I HAVE NO AUTHORITY TO TELL THE REASON . . . . . . . . 454  2 DON JUAN  5   74   8
    THEN IF I DO SAID JUAN I'LL BE-- HOLD . . . . . . . . . 454  2 DON JUAN  5   75   1
    THAT I UNSEXED MY DRESS BUT BABA STROKING . . . . . . 454  2 DON JUAN  5   75   6
    THE THINGS DOWN SAID--INCENSE ME AND I CALL . . . . . 454  2 DON JUAN  5   75   7
    I OFFER YOU A HANDSOME SUIT OF CLOTHES . . . . . . . . 455  2 DON JUAN  5   76   1
```

I (CONTINUED)

	PAGE	VOL		CANTO	STANZA	LN
WHAT THE DEVIL SHALL I DO WITH ALL THIS GAUZE	455	2	DON JUAN	5	76	6
I SAY A THING IT MUST AT ONCE BE DONE	458	2	DON JUAN	5	81	5
YOU FOOL I TELL YOU NO ONE MEANS YOU HARM	459	2	DON JUAN	5	82	1
I YIELD THUS FAR BUT SOON WILL BREAK THE CHARM	459	2	DON JUAN	5	82	5
IF ANY TAKE ME FOR THAT WHICH I SEEM	459	2	DON JUAN	5	82	6
SO THAT I TRUST FOR EVERYBODY'S SAKE	459	2	DON JUAN	5	82	7
I WISH YOU A GOOD APPETITE--FAREWELL	460	2	DON JUAN	5	84	2
AND YOU AND I MAY CHANCE ERE MORNING RISE	464	2	DON JUAN	5	92	5
(OF WHICH I HAVE ALSO SEEN SOME SIX OR SEVEN)	465	2	DON JUAN	5	94	4
WHERE I CAN'T SAY OR GOLD OR DIAMOND FLINGS	465	2	DON JUAN	5	94	5
ON WHICH I CANNOT PAUSE TO MAKE MY STRICTURES	465	2	DON JUAN	5	94	8
THAN LESSEN IT BY WHAT I COULD RELATE	467	2	DON JUAN	5	97	5
COULD I DO JUSTICE TO THE FULL DETAIL	467	2	DON JUAN	5	97	7
THIS MUCH HOWEVER I MAY ADD--HER YEARS	468	2	DON JUAN	5	98	1
I WON'T BE BAIL FOR ANYTHING BEYOND	469	2	DON JUAN	5	99	8
AND I MUST SAY I NE'ER COULD SEE THE VERY	469	2	DON JUAN	5	100	7
AND I MUST SAY I NE'ER COULD SEE THE VERY	469	2	DON JUAN	5	100	7
NOT TO ADMIRE IS ALL THE ART I KNOW	470	2	DON JUAN	5	101	1
I KNOW NOT WHAT MIGHT BE THE LADY'S THOUGHT	473	2	DON JUAN	5	108	2
THIS I MUST LEAVE SULTANAS TO DECIDE	477	2	DON JUAN	5	115	4
I ALSO WOULD SUGGEST THE FITTING TIME	482	2	DON JUAN	5	123	1
THE PRISONED EAGLE WILL NOT PAIR NOR I	484	2	DON JUAN	5	126	7
THOU ASK'ST IF I CAN LOVE BE THIS THE PROOF	484	2	DON JUAN	5	127	1
HOW MUCH I HAVE LOVED--THAT I LOVE NOT THEE	484	2	DON JUAN	5	127	2
HOW MUCH I HAVE LOVED--THAT I LOVE NOT THEE	484	2	DON JUAN	5	127	2
I AM NOT DAZZLED BY THIS SPLENDID ROOF	484	2	DON JUAN	5	127	5
THESE DON'T EXPRESS ONE HALF WHAT I SHOULD SAY	487	2	DON JUAN	5	132	6
IF I SAID FIRE FLASHED FROM GULBEYAZ' EYES	489	2	DON JUAN	5	134	1
I SHOULD BUT BRING DISGRACE UPON THE DYER	489	2	DON JUAN	5	134	4
SO JUAN'S VIRTUE EBBED I KNOW NOT HOW	493	2	DON JUAN	5	142	2
I WISH TO HEAVEN HE WOULD NOT SHINE TILL MORNING	494	2	DON JUAN	5	145	2
I KNOW NOT IF HE HAD DOMESTIC CARES--	496	2	DON JUAN	5	148	5
I SEE YOU'VE BOUGHT ANOTHER GIRL 'TIS PITY	500	2	DON JUAN	5	155	7
I WISH THEIR YEARS HAD BEEN FIFTEEN AND TWENTY	9	3	DON JUAN	6	5	2
FOR THEN WEALTH KINGDOMS WORLDS ARE BUT A SPORT--I	9	3	DON JUAN	6	5	3
REMEMBER WHEN THOUGH I HAD NO GREAT PLENTY	9	3	DON JUAN	6	5	4
OF WORLDS TO LOSE YET STILL TO PAY MY COURT I	9	3	DON JUAN	6	5	5
GAVE WHAT I HAD--A HEART--AS THE WORLD WENT I	9	3	DON JUAN	6	5	6
GAVE WHAT I HAD--A HEART--AS THE WORLD WENT I	9	3	DON JUAN	6	5	6
I KNOW GULBEYAZ WAS EXTREMELY WRONG	10	3	DON JUAN	6	8	1
I OWN IT I DEPLORE IT I CONDEMN IT	10	3	DON JUAN	6	8	2
I OWN IT I DEPLORE IT I CONDEMN IT	10	3	DON JUAN	6	8	2
I OWN IT I DEPLORE IT I CONDEMN IT	10	3	DON JUAN	6	8	3
BUT I DETEST ALL FICTION EVEN IN SONG	10	3	DON JUAN	6	9	1
I AM NOT LIKE CASSIO AN ARITHMETICIAN	10	3	DON JUAN	6	9	1
GULBEYAZ WAS THE FOURTH AND (AS I SAID)	12	3	DON JUAN	6	12	1
WOULD LIKE (I THINK) TO TRUST ALL TO DESIRE	14	3	DON JUAN	6	16	4
I OWN NO PROSODY CAN EVER RATE IT	15	3	DON JUAN	6	18	7
I KNOW NOT--IT SUCCEEDED AND SUCCESS	15	3	DON JUAN	6	19	2
WITH ONE GOOD HEARTY CURSE I VENT MY GALL	17	3	DON JUAN	6	22	3
AND I CAN GIVE MY WHOLE SOUL UP TO MIND	17	3	DON JUAN	6	22	6
IS MORE THAN I KNOW--THE DEUCE TAKE THEM BOTH	17	3	DON JUAN	6	22	8
IS MORE THAN I KNOW AND SO DAMN THEM BOTH	17	3	DON JUAN	6	22	V8
I DOUBT IF ANY NOW COULD MAKE IT WORSE	17	3	DON JUAN	6	23	4
I LOVE THE SEX AND SOMETIMES WOULD REVERSE	19	3	DON JUAN	6	27	1
WHETHER SHE WAS A MOTHER I KNOW NOT	21	3	DON JUAN	6	31	1
I KNOW NOT HOW BUT GOOD AS ANY OTHER	21	3	DON JUAN	6	31	4
CONTINUE AS I SAID THIS GOODLY ROW	22	3	DON JUAN	6	33	3
YOU DON'T SLEEP SOUNDLY AND I CANNOT BEAR	29	3	DON JUAN	6	47	2
AND I OF YOUR YOUNG CHARGE WILL TAKE DUE CARE	29	3	DON JUAN	6	47	6
BESIDES I HATE TO SLEEP ALONE QUOTH SHE	30	3	DON JUAN	6	48	1
REPLIED KATINKA I AM SURE I SEE	30	3	DON JUAN	6	48	3
REPLIED KATINKA I AM SURE I SEE	30	3	DON JUAN	6	48	3
AND THEN I HAVE THE WORST DREAMS THAT CAN BE	30	3	DON JUAN	6	48	5
I FEAR JUANNA'S DREAMS WOULD BE BUT FEW	30	3	DON JUAN	6	48	8
AND I SHALL PLACE JUANNA WITH DUDU	30	3	DON JUAN	6	49	4
I MIGHT DESCRIBE AS I HAVE SEEN IT ALL	31	3	DON JUAN	6	51	4
I MIGHT DESCRIBE AS I HAVE SEEN IT ALL	31	3	DON JUAN	6	51	4
WHICH SOME CALL THE SUBLIME I WISH THEY'D TRY IT	32	3	DON JUAN	6	53	6
IS THE SUBLIME--I WISH THAT THEY WOULD TRY IT	32	3	DON JUAN	6	53	V6
I THINK IT MAY BE OF CORINTHIAN BRASS	34	3	DON JUAN	6	56	1
THIS LONG PARENTHESIS I COULD NOT SHUT	34	3	DON JUAN	6	56	4
BUT THAT YOU WON'T--THEN DON'T--I AM NOT LESS FREE	34	3	DON JUAN	6	56	8
I HAVE BUT ONE SIMILE AND THAT'S A BLUNDER	34	3	DON JUAN	6	57	7
AND NEXT SHE GAVE HER (I SAY HER BECAUSE	35	3	DON JUAN	6	58	1
I WISH IT NEVER LED TO SOMETHING WORSE	35	3	DON JUAN	6	59	8
I DID MY VERY BOYISH BEST TO SHINE	37	3	DON JUAN	6	62	5
AND I LOVE WISDOM MORE THAN SHE LOVES ME	37	3	DON JUAN	6	63	2
I KNOW NOT NEVER COUNTING PAST THEIR TEENS	41	3	DON JUAN	6	69	4
WITH STRICT ENQUIRY I COULD N'ER DISCOVER	41	3	DON JUAN	6	70	2
MORE THAN I HAVE MYSELF OF WHAT COULD MAKE	42	3	DON JUAN	6	71	7
WITH SUCH A CLAMOUR--I HAD THOUGHT IT RIGHT	46	3	DON JUAN	6	81	3
BUT NOW I MUST TRANSFER HER TO THE CHARGE	46	3	DON JUAN	6	81	7
I CAN'T TELL WHY SHE BLUSHED NOR CAN EXPOUND	48	3	DON JUAN	6	85	5
ALL THAT I KNOW IS THAT THE FACTS I STATE	48	3	DON JUAN	6	85	7
ALL THAT I KNOW IS THAT THE FACTS I STATE	48	3	DON JUAN	6	85	7
ALL GENERATIONS I SHOULD LIKE TO KNOW	53	3	DON JUAN	6	94	7
WHAT SHE COULD NE'ER EXPRESS--THEN HOW SHOULD I	59	3	DON JUAN	6	106	8

I   (CONTINUED)

	PAGE	VOL	CANTO	STANZA	LN
WOULD THAT I WERE A PAINTER TO BE GROUPING	60	3	DON JUAN	6	109	5
IT IS NOT THAT I SHALL NOT ALL FULFIL	62	3	DON JUAN	6	114	3
I DO NOT MEAN DESTRUCTION AND EXPOSURE	62	3	DON JUAN	6	114	7
EXCUSE MY FREEDOM WHEN I HERE ASSURE YOU	63	3	DON JUAN	6	115	7
AND HERE I LEAVE THEM AT THEIR PREPARATION	65	3	DON JUAN	6	119	1
I LEAVE THEM FOR THE PRESENT WITH GOOD WISHES	65	3	DON JUAN	6	120	1
BUT NE'ER THE LESS I HOPE IT IS NO CRIME	67	3	DON JUAN	7	2	6
TO LAUGH AT ALL THINGS--FOR I WISH TO KNOW	67	3	DON JUAN	7	2	7
THE PRESENT POEM--OF--I KNOW NOT WHAT--	67	3	DON JUAN	7	3	2
GOOD GOD I WONDER WHAT THEY WOULD BE AT	67	3	DON JUAN	7	3	6
I SAY NO MORE THAN HAS BEEN SAID IN DANTE'S	67	3	DON JUAN	7	3	7
FOR MY PART I PRETEND NOT TO BE CATO	68	3	DON JUAN	7	4	6
BUT WHICH IS BEST YOU KNOW NO MORE THAN I	68	3	DON JUAN	7	4	8
MUST I RESTRAIN ME THROUGH THE FEAR OF STRIFE	69	3	DON JUAN	7	6	7
DOGS OR MEN (FOR I FLATTER YOU IN SAYING	70	3	DON JUAN	7	7	1
READ OR READ NOT WHAT I AM NOW ESSAYING	70	3	DON JUAN	7	7	3
FIERCE LOVES AND FAITHLESS WARS--I AM NOT SURE	70	3	DON JUAN	7	8	1
THE FACT'S ABOUT THE SAME I AM SECURE	70	3	DON JUAN	7	8	3
I SING THEM BOTH AND AM ABOUT TO BATTER	70	3	DON JUAN	7	8	4
HOW SHALL I SPELL THE NAME OF EACH COSSACQUE	73	3	DON JUAN	7	14	3
AND MORE MIGHT BE FOUND OUT IF I COULD POKE ENOUGH	74	3	DON JUAN	7	15	6
I DON'T KNOW WHETHER THEY HAD ARMS OR CREST	76	3	DON JUAN	7	19	3
I'VE SAID ALL I KNOW OF A NAME THAT FILLS	76	3	DON JUAN	7	20	5
I WONDER (ALTHOUGH MARS NO DOUBT'S A GOD I	77	3	DON JUAN	7	21	1
I WONDER (ALTHOUGH MARS NO DOUBT'S A GOD I	77	3	DON JUAN	7	21	1
I HOPE THIS LITTLE QUESTION IS NO SIN	77	3	DON JUAN	7	21	4
BECAUSE THOUGH I AM BUT A SIMPLE NODDY	77	3	DON JUAN	7	21	5
I THINK ONE SHAKESPEAR PUTS THE SAME THOUGHT IN	77	3	DON JUAN	7	21	6
NOW I SHOULD LIKE TO KNOW BEING RATHER CURIOUS	77	3	DON JUAN	7	21	V1
THEIR HASTE OR WASTE I NEITHER KNOW NOR CARE	80	3	DON JUAN	7	27	2
WHICH WAS RETURNED WITH INTEREST I MAY SAY	81	3	DON JUAN	7	29	6
IF (SAYS THE HISTORIAN HERE) I COULD REPORT	82	3	DON JUAN	7	32	1
I THINK THAT SEVERAL VOLUMES WOULD FALL SHORT	82	3	DON JUAN	7	32	3
AND I SHOULD STILL HAVE MANY THINGS TO SAY	82	3	DON JUAN	7	32	4
OF ALL OUR MODERN BATTLES I WILL BET	83	3	DON JUAN	7	34	7
WHICH MADE A LONG DEBATE BUT I MUST HALT	83	3	DON JUAN	7	35	6
FOR IF I WROTE DOWN EVERY WARRIOR'S SPEECH	83	3	DON JUAN	7	35	7
I DOUBT FEW READERS E'ER WOULD MOUNT THE BREACH	83	3	DON JUAN	7	35	8
I CANNOT TELL THE WAY IN WHICH HE PLEADED	85	3	DON JUAN	7	38	4
I NEVER THINK ABOUT IT IN A HEAT)	87	3	DON JUAN	7	42	6
BUT HERE I SAY THE TURKS WERE MUCH MISTAKEN	87	3	DON JUAN	7	42	7
(THIS METAPHOR I THINK HOLDS GOOD AS AUGHT	90	3	DON JUAN	7	49	3
THE PARTY A SLIGHT GLANCE THEN SAID I HAVE HEARD	97	3	DON JUAN	7	60	4
BUT LET THAT PASS--I THINK I HAVE HEARD YOUR NAME	97	3	DON JUAN	7	60	7
BUT LET THAT PASS--I THINK I HAVE HEARD YOUR NAME	97	3	DON JUAN	7	60	7
I DID--WHAT NEXT--I REALLY HARDLY KNOW	98	3	DON JUAN	7	61	2
I DID--WHAT NEXT--I REALLY HARDLY KNOW	98	3	DON JUAN	7	61	2
YOU WERE THE FIRST I' THE BREACH I WAS NOT SLACK	98	3	DON JUAN	7	61	3
AND I BECAME A PRISONER TO THE FOE--	98	3	DON JUAN	7	61	6
WHERE WILL YOU SERVE--WHERE'ER YOU PLEASE--I KNOW	98	3	DON JUAN	7	62	1
OR IT MAY BE TO-NIGHT THE ASSAULT I HAVE VOWED	99	3	DON JUAN	7	63	5
IN HIS RESUMED AMUSEMENT I CONFESS	100	3	DON JUAN	7	65	4
RIGHT I WAS BUSY AND FORGOT WHY YOU	100	3	DON JUAN	7	66	1
HIS POST I MEAN THE REGIMENT NIKOLAIEW	100	3	DON JUAN	7	66	5
SAVE WED A YEAR I HATE RECRUITS WITH WIVES	102	3	DON JUAN	7	70	8
AND NOT OUR OWN I AM TOO QUALIFIED	103	3	DON JUAN	7	71	3
INTO A CAMP I KNOW THAT NOUGHT SO BOTHERS	103	3	DON JUAN	7	71	6
I THEREFORE IF YOU WISH ME TO FIGHT FREELY	103	3	DON JUAN	7	72	7
OH THOU ETERNAL HOMER I HAVE NOW	106	3	DON JUAN	7	80	1
AND YET LIKE ALL MEN ELSE I MUST ALLOW	106	3	DON JUAN	7	80	5
GREAT DEEDS ARE DOING--HOW SHALL I RELATE 'EM	107	3	DON JUAN	7	81	6
WHATEVER DEED BE DONE I WILL RELATE 'EM	107	3	DON JUAN	7	81	V6
SHADOWS OF GLORY (LEST I BE CONFOUNDED)	108	3	DON JUAN	7	82	6
WHEN I CALL FADING MARTIAL IMMORTALITY	108	3	DON JUAN	7	83	1
I MEAN THAT EVERY AGE AND EVERY YEAR	108	3	DON JUAN	7	83	2
YET I LOVE GLORY--GLORY'S A GREAT THING--	118	3	DON JUAN	8	14	1
BUT HERE I LEAVE THE GENERAL CONCERN	120	3	DON JUAN	8	17	1
IN THE DESPATCH I KNEW A MAN WHOSE LOSS	120	3	DON JUAN	8	18	7
I ALMOST LATELY HAVE BEGUN TO DOUBT	124	3	DON JUAN	8	26	1
I DON'T KNOW HOW THE THING OCCURRED--IT MIGHT	125	3	DON JUAN	8	28	1
QUITE DISAPPEARED--THE GODS KNOW HOW (I CAN'T	127	3	DON JUAN	8	31	3
AMONG THE FIRST--I WILL NOT SAY THE FIRST	136	3	DON JUAN	8	48	1
FOR IF HE DON'T I DOUBT IF MEN WILL LONGER--	137	3	DON JUAN	8	50	2
I THINK I HEAR A LITTLE BIRD WHO SINGS	137	3	DON JUAN	8	50	3
I THINK I HEAR A LITTLE BIRD WHO SINGS	137	3	DON JUAN	8	50	3
I RATHER DOUBT AND I WOULD FAIN SAY FIE ON'T	138	3	DON JUAN	8	51	6
I RATHER DOUBT AND I WOULD FAIN SAY FIE ON'T	138	3	DON JUAN	8	51	6
IF I HAD NOT PERCEIVED THAT REVOLUTION	138	3	DON JUAN	8	51	7
BUT TO CONTINUE--I SAY NOT THE FIRST	138	3	DON JUAN	8	52	1
TO HIM AND I SHOULD HOPE TO MOST THE THIRST	138	3	DON JUAN	8	52	5
SO COWPER SAYS--AND I BEGIN TO BE	142	3	DON JUAN	8	60	3
OF HIS OPINION WHEN I SEE CAST DOWN	142	3	DON JUAN	8	60	4
IN CITIES CAGED THE PRESENT CASE IN POINT I	143	3	DON JUAN	8	62	7
(I DON'T MUCH PIQUE MYSELF UPON ORTHOGRAPHY	149	3	DON JUAN	8	74	2
SO THAT I DO NOT GROSSLY ERR IN FACTS	149	3	DON JUAN	8	74	3
I SKETCH YOUR WORLD EXACTLY AS IT GOES	156	3	DON JUAN	8	89	8
I SHALL NOT SAY EXACTLY WHAT HE SAID	158	3	DON JUAN	8	93	5
IIP CAME JOHN JOHNSON (I WILL NOT SAY JACK	160	3	DON JUAN	8	97	1

I (CONTINUED)

	PAGE	VOL	CANTO	STANZA	LN
THAT YOU AND I WILL WIN SAINT GEORGE'S COLLAR	160	3	DON JUAN 8	97	8
UPON THIS CHILD--I SAVED HER--MUST NOT LEAVE	161	3	DON JUAN 8	99	2
AND I AM WITH YOU--WHEREON JOHNSON TOOK	161	3	DON JUAN 8	99	5
QUOTH JOHNSON--NEITHER WILL I QUITE ENSURE	161	3	DON JUAN 8	100	4
JUAN REPLIED--AT LEAST I WILL ENDURE	161	3	DON JUAN 8	100	6
I NEVER SAW SUCH EYES--BUT HARK NOW CHOOSE	162	3	DON JUAN 8	101	3
I SHOULD BE LOTH TO MARCH WITHOUT YOU BUT	162	3	DON JUAN 8	101	7
IN PROSE I BEND MY HUMBLE VERSE) DOTH CALL	163	3	DON JUAN 8	104	7
WHILE COURAGE CLUNG BUT TO A SINGLE TWIG--AM I	164	3	DON JUAN 8	105	5
IN HEAVEN I KNOW NOT NOR PRETEND TO GUESS	167	3	DON JUAN 8	112	2
TAKE TOWNS BY STORM NO CAUSES CAN I GUESS	176	3	DON JUAN 8	129	5
IN DARKNESS--I CAN ONLY HOPE THEY DID	178	3	DON JUAN 8	132	8
WHICH FEW WILL SING I TRUST BUT NONE FORGET IT--	179	3	DON JUAN 8	135	3
FOR I WILL TEACH IF POSSIBLE THE STONES	179	3	DON JUAN 8	135	4
AS NOW OCCUR I THOUGHT THAT I WOULD PEN YOU 'EM	180	3	DON JUAN 8	136	4
AS NOW OCCUR I THOUGHT THAT I WOULD PEN YOU 'EM	180	3	DON JUAN 8	136	4
READER I HAVE KEPT MY WORD--AT LEAST SO FAR	181	3	DON JUAN 8	138	1
FOR I HAVE DRAWN MUCH LESS WITH A LONG BOW	181	3	DON JUAN 8	138	6
THAN MY FORERUNNERS CARELESSLY I SING	181	3	DON JUAN 8	138	7
WITH WHICH I STILL CAN HARP AND CARP AND FIDDLE	181	3	DON JUAN 8	139	1
I BY-AND-BY MAY TELL YOU IF AT ALL	181	3	DON JUAN 8	139	4
BUT NOW I CHOOSE TO BREAK OFF IN THE MIDDLE	181	3	DON JUAN 8	139	5
OF CARNAGE--AND I THINK HE WAS MORE GLAD IN HER	182	3	DON JUAN 8	140	7
I DON'T THINK THAT YOU USED KINNAIRD QUITE WELL	184	3	DON JUAN 9	2	1
(I WISH YOUR BARDS WOULD SING IT RATHER BETTER)	184	3	DON JUAN 9	3	8
AND I SHALL BE DELIGHTED TO LEARN WHO	184	3	DON JUAN 9	4	7
I AM NO FLATTERER--YOU'VE SUPPED FULL OF FLATTERY	185	3	DON JUAN 9	5	1
I DON'T MEAN TO REFLECT--A MAN SO GREAT AS	186	3	DON JUAN 9	7	1
IS RATHER DEAR--I'M SURE I MEAN NO HARM	186	3	DON JUAN 9	7	8
I AM NEITHER ALEXANDER NOR HEPHAESTION	189	3	DON JUAN 9	14	3
THAN BUONAPARTE'S CANCER--COULD I DASH ON	189	3	DON JUAN 9	14	6
YE RIGID GUTS OF REAPERS--I TRANSLATE	190	3	DON JUAN 9	15	2
TO BE OR NOT TO BE--ERE I DECIDE	190	3	DON JUAN 9	16	1
I SHOULD BE GLAD TO KNOW THAT WHICH IS BEING	190	3	DON JUAN 9	16	2
UNTIL I SEE BOTH SIDES FOR ONCE AGREEING	190	3	DON JUAN 9	16	6
FOR ME I SOMETIMES THINK THAT LIFE IS DEATH	190	3	DON JUAN 9	16	7
THIS WORLD I DOUBT IF DOUBT ITSELF BE DOUBTING	191	3	DON JUAN 9	17	8
AND YET I KNOW NO MORE THAN THE MAHOGANY	192	3	DON JUAN 9	20	5
I COMPREHEND FOR WITHOUT TRANSFORMATION	192	3	DON JUAN 9	20	7
BUT I THE MILDEST MEEKEST OF MANKIND	193	3	DON JUAN 9	21	1
AND (THOUGH I COULD NOT NOW AND THEN FORBEAR	193	3	DON JUAN 9	21	4
THEY HATE ME NOT I THEM--AND HERE WE'LL PAUSE	193	3	DON JUAN 9	21	8
FOR I MAINTAIN THAT IT IS REALLY GOOD	193	3	DON JUAN 9	22	2
AND TILL SHE DOTH I FAIN MUST BE CONTENT	193	3	DON JUAN 9	22	7
OUR HERO (AND I TRUST KIND READER YOUR'S) --	194	3	DON JUAN 9	23	1
I KNOW ITS MIGHTY EMPIRE NOW ALLURES	194	3	DON JUAN 9	23	5
FOR ME I DEEM AN ABSOLUTE AUTOCRAT	194	3	DON JUAN 9	23	7
AND I WILL WAR AT LEAST IN WORDS (AND--SHOULD	194	3	DON JUAN 9	24	1
I KNOW NOT WHO MAY CONQUER IF I COULD	194	3	DON JUAN 9	24	5
I KNOW NOT WHO MAY CONQUER IF I COULD	194	3	DON JUAN 9	24	5
IT IS NOT THAT I ADULATE THE PEOPLE	195	3	DON JUAN 9	25	1
I DO NOT KNOW--I WISH MEN TO BE FREE	195	3	DON JUAN 9	25	7
I DO NOT KNOW--I WISH MEN TO BE FREE	195	3	DON JUAN 9	25	7
I SHALL OFFEND ALL PARTIES--NEVER MIND	195	3	DON JUAN 9	26	2
THAN IF I SOUGHT TO SAIL BEFORE THE WIND	195	3	DON JUAN 9	26	4
MAY STILL EXPATIATE FREELY AS WILL I	195	3	DON JUAN 9	26	7
ARE USELESS MIND GOOD PEOPLE WHAT I SAY--	196	3	DON JUAN 9	28	3
I HAVE FORGOTTEN WHAT I MEANT TO SAY	200	3	DON JUAN 9	36	2
I HAVE FORGOTTEN WHAT I MEANT TO SAY	200	3	DON JUAN 9	36	2
I SAY WILL THESE GREAT RELICS WHEN THEY SEE 'EM	202	3	DON JUAN 9	40	7
BUT I AM APT TO GROW TOO METAPHYSICAL	203	3	DON JUAN 9	41	1
THE TIME IS OUT OF JOINT--AND SO AM I	203	3	DON JUAN 9	41	2
I QUITE FORGET THIS POEM'S MERELY QUIZZICAL	203	3	DON JUAN 9	41	3
I NE'ER DECIDE WHAT I SHALL SAY AND THIS I CALL	203	3	DON JUAN 9	41	5
I NE'ER DECIDE WHAT I SHALL SAY AND THIS I CALL	203	3	DON JUAN 9	41	5
I NE'ER DECIDE WHAT I SHALL SAY AND THIS I CALL	203	3	DON JUAN 9	41	5
I NEVER KNOW THE WORD WHICH WILL COME NEXT	203	3	DON JUAN 9	41	8
SO ON I RAMBLE NOW AND THEN NARRATING	203	3	DON JUAN 9	42	1
I LEFT DON JUAN WITH HIS HORSES BAITING--	203	3	DON JUAN 9	42	3
I SHALL NOT BE PARTICULAR IN STATING	203	3	DON JUAN 9	42	5
I QUITE FORGET WHICH OF THEM WAS IN HAND	205	3	DON JUAN 9	46	3
I THINK I CAN EXPLAIN MYSELF WITHOUT	207	3	DON JUAN 9	50	1
I THINK I CAN EXPLAIN MYSELF WITHOUT	207	3	DON JUAN 9	50	1
AND HERE I MUST AN ANECDOTE RELATE	207	3	DON JUAN 9	50	7
WHOSE STATUES WARM (I FEAR ALAS TOO TRUE 'TIS)	208	3	DON JUAN 9	51	6
SAID--LADY I BESEECH YOU TO SUPPOSE THEM	208	3	DON JUAN 9	51	8
AND THUS I SUPPLICATE YOUR SUPPOSITION	208	3	DON JUAN 9	52	1
JUAN I SAID WAS A MOST BEAUTEOUS BOY	209	3	DON JUAN 9	53	1
AND FOUNDED DOCTORS' COMMONS--I HAVE CONNED	209	3	DON JUAN 9	53	6
WHENCE IS OUR EXIT AND OUR ENTRANCE--WELL I	210	3	DON JUAN 9	55	3
IN THY PERENNIAL FOUNTAIN--HOW MAN FELL I	210	3	DON JUAN 9	55	5
SOME CALL THEE THE WORST CAUSE OF WAR BUT I	210	3	DON JUAN 9	56	1
CATHERINE I SAY WAS VERY GLAD TO SEE	211	3	DON JUAN 9	57	5
OF FAITHFUL PAIRS--(I NEEDS MUST RHYME WITH DOVE	219	3	DON JUAN 9	74	5
I CANNOT STOP TO ALTER WORDS ONCE WRITTEN	221	3	DON JUAN 9	77	4
JUAN RETIRED--AND SO WILL I UNTIL	224	3	DON JUAN 9	85	2
SO LOFTY THAT I FEEL MY BRAIN TURN ROUND	224	3	DON JUAN 9	85	5
AND THOUGH SO MUCH INFERIOR AS I KNOW	226	3	DON JUAN 10	3	5

I   (CONTINUED)
    I WISH TO DO AS MUCH BY POESY . . . . 226 3 DON JUAN 10   3   8
    IN THE WIND'S EYE I HAVE SAILED AND SAIL BUT FOR . . . 227 3 DON JUAN 10   4   1
    THE STARS I OWN MY TELESCOPE IS DIM . . . . 227 3 DON JUAN 10   4   2
    BUT AT THE LEAST I HAVE SHUNNED THE COMMON SHORE . . . 227 3 DON JUAN 10   4   3
    (FOR I HAVE MORE THAN ONE MUSE AT A PUSH) . . . . . . 227 3 DON JUAN 10   5   4
    OH SAITH THE PSALMIST THAT I HAD A DOVE'S . .   . . . 228 3 DON JUAN 10   6   2
    I RATHER THINK THE MOON SHOULD DATE THE DEARS . . . . 230 3 DON JUAN 10   10   8
    I KNOW NO OTHER REASON WHATSOE'ER . . . . 230 3 DON JUAN 10   11   2
    HOWEVER I FORGIVE HIM AND I TRUST . . . . 230 3 DON JUAN 10   11   7
    HOWEVER I FORGIVE HIM AND I TRUST . . . . 230 3 DON JUAN 10   11   7
    HE WILL FORGIVE HIMSELF--IF NOT I MUST . . .   . . . 230 3 DON JUAN 10   11   8
    AND I KNOW NOTHING WHICH COULD MAKE AMENDS . . . . . 231 3 DON JUAN 10   12   3
    FOR A RETURN TO HATRED I WOULD SHUN HER . . .   . . 231 3 DON JUAN 10   12   4
    IN ALL THEIR HABITS--NOT SO YOU I OWN . . .   . . . 232 3 DON JUAN 10   15   7
    I DO NOT KNOW YOU AND MAY NEVER KNOW . . . . 232 3 DON JUAN 10   16   6
    MOST NOBLY AND I OWN IT FROM MY SOUL . . . . 232 3 DON JUAN 10   16   8
    AND WHEN I USE THE PHRASE OF AULD LANG SYNE . . . . . 233 3 DON JUAN 10   17   1
    FOR ME FOR I WOULD RATHER TAKE MY WINE . . .   . . . 233 3 DON JUAN 10   17   3
    AND YET I SEEK NOT TO BE GRAND NOR WITTY-- . .   . . 233 3 DON JUAN 10   17   6
    BUT I AM HALF A SCOT BY BIRTH AND BRED . . .   . . . 233 3 DON JUAN 10   17   7
    OF WHAT I THEN DREAMT CLOTHED IN THEIR OWN PALL . . . 233 3 DON JUAN 10   18   5
    I CARE NOT--'TIS A GLIMPSE OF AULD LANG SYNE . . . . 233 3 DON JUAN 10   18   8
    I RAILED AT SCOTS TO SHEW MY WRATH AND WIT . . . . . 234 3 DON JUAN 10   19   3
    I SCOTCHED NOT KILLED THE SCOTCHMAN IN MY BLOOD . . . 234 3 DON JUAN 10   19   7
    DON JUAN GREW I FEAR A LITTLE DISSIPATED . .   . . . 236 3 DON JUAN 10   23   3
    WHICH (THOUGH I HATE TO SAY A THING THAT'S BITTER) . . 237 3 DON JUAN 10   26   4
    I WON'T DESCRIBE--THAT IS IF I CAN HELP . . .   . . . 238 3 DON JUAN 10   28   1
    I WON'T DESCRIBE--THAT IS IF I CAN HELP . . .   . . . 238 3 DON JUAN 10   28   1
    DESCRIPTION AND I WON'T REFLECT--THAT IS . .   . . . 238 3 DON JUAN 10   28   2
    IF I CAN STAVE OFF THOUGHT WHICH AS A WHELP . . . . . 238 3 DON JUAN 10   28   3
    DRAINS ITS FIRST DRAUGHT OF LIPS--BUT AS I SAID . . . 238 3 DON JUAN 10   28   7
    I WON'T PHILOSOPHIZE AND WILL BE READ . . .   . . . 238 3 DON JUAN 10   28   8
    I CAN'T COMPLAIN WHOSE ANCESTORS ARE THERE . . . . . 242 3 DON JUAN 10   36   1
    AND THOUGH I CAN'T HELP THINKING 'TWAS SCARCE FAIR . . 242 3 DON JUAN 10   36   5
    I DON'T KNOW HOW IT WAS BUT HE GREW SICK . .   . . . 244 3 DON JUAN 10   39   1
    I CANNOT TELL EXACTLY WHAT IT WAS . . . . 250 3 DON JUAN 10   53   3
    ON WHICH I HAVE NOT TIME JUST NOW TO LECTURE . . . . 255 3 DON JUAN 10   62   4
    I HAVE NO GREAT CAUSE TO LOVE THAT SPOT OF EARTH . . . 257 3 DON JUAN 10   66   1
    BUT THOUGH I OWE IT LITTLE BUT MY BIRTH . . .   . . . 257 3 DON JUAN 10   66   3
    I FEEL A MIXED REGRET AND VENERATION . . . . 257 3 DON JUAN 10   66   4
    AND WHEN I THINK UPON A POT OF BEER-- . . .   . . . 263 3 DON JUAN 10   77   1
    BUT I WON'T WEEP--AND SO DRIVE ON POSTILLIONS . . . . 263 3 DON JUAN 10   77   2
    BUT--I WON'T WEEP--COME POSTBOYS WHIRL ALONG . . . . 263 3 DON JUAN 10   77   V2
    HE PAUSED--AND SO WILL I AS DOTH A CREW . . .   . . . 266 3 DON JUAN 10   84   1
    WITH A SOFT BESOM WILL I SWEEP YOUR HALLS . . . . . . 266 3 DON JUAN 10   84   7
    I THOUGHT YOU HAD MORE RELIGION MRS FRY . . .   . . . 267 3 DON JUAN 10   85   8
    AND TELL THEM--BUT YOU WON'T AND I HAVE PRATED . . . 267 3 DON JUAN 10   87   6
    AND YET WHO CAN BELIEVE IT I WOULD SHATTER . . . . . 268 3 DON JUAN 11   1   5
    AND WEAR MY HEAD DENYING THAT I WEAR IT . . .   . . . 268 3 DON JUAN 11   1   8
    BUT WHICH I DOUBT EXTREMELY--THOU SOLE PRISM . . . . 269 3 DON JUAN 11   2   6
    IS THAT I FIND NO SPOT WHERE MAN CAN REST EYE ON . . . 269 3 DON JUAN 11   3   5
    I AM QUITE OF THEIR OPINION--AND AM HOARDING . . . . 270 3 DON JUAN 11   4   V5
    AND THEREFORE WILL I LEAVE OFF METAPHYSICAL . . . . . 270 3 DON JUAN 11   5   1
    IF I AGREE THAT WHAT IS IS THEN THIS I CALL . . . . . 270 3 DON JUAN 11   5   3
    IF I AGREE THAT WHAT IS IS THEN THIS I CALL . . . . . 270 3 DON JUAN 11   5   3
    I DON'T KNOW WHAT THE REASON IS--THE AIR . .   . . . 270 3 DON JUAN 11   5   6
    PERHAPS BUT AS I SUFFER FROM THE SHOCKS . . .   . . . 270 3 DON JUAN 11   5   7
    OF ILLNESS I GROW MUCH MORE ORTHODOX . . . . 270 3 DON JUAN 11   5   8
    (BUT THAT I NEVER DOUBTED NOR THE DEVIL) . .   . . . 271 3 DON JUAN 11   6   2
    THAT I DEVOUTLY WISHED THE THREE WERE FOUR . . . . . 271 3 DON JUAN 11   6   7
    I SAY DON JUAN WRAPT IN CONTEMPLATION . . . . 272 3 DON JUAN 11   9   1
    TO THINK SO FOR HALF ENGLISH AS I AM . . . . 274 3 DON JUAN 11   12   6
    (TO MY MISFORTUNE) NEVER CAN I SAY . . . . 274 3 DON JUAN 11   12   7
    I HEARD THEM WHEN GOD WITH YOU SAVE THAT WAY-- . . . 274 3 DON JUAN 11   12   8
    I RECOLLECT SOME INNKEEPERS WHO DON'T . . .   . . . 275 3 DON JUAN 11   15   3
    BUT WHAT IS TO BE DONE I CAN'T ALLOW . . . . 275 3 DON JUAN 11   15   6
    LET ME DIE WHERE I AM AND AS THE FUEL . . .   . . . 276 3 DON JUAN 11   16   4
    I COULD SAY MORE BUT DO NOT CHOOSE TO ENCROACH . . . 279 3 DON JUAN 11   23   5
    YET UNDISCOVERED TREASURE WHAT I CAN . . . . 281 3 DON JUAN 11   28   6
    I DON'T MEAN THAT THEY ARE PASSIONLESS BUT QUITE . . . 284 3 DON JUAN 11   34   1
    NOW WHAT I LOVE IN WOMEN IS THEY WON'T . . .   . . . 285 3 DON JUAN 11   36   6
    THE TRUTH IN MASQUERADE AND I DEFY . . . . 286 3 DON JUAN 11   37   2
    I DON'T KNOW WHICH WAS MOST ADMIRED OR LESS . . . . . 287 3 DON JUAN 11   39   3
    THESE PHRASES OF REFINEMENT I MUST BORROW . . . . . . 288 3 DON JUAN 11   42   5
    SPIRIT WOULD NAME AND THEREFORE EVEN I WON'T ANENT . . 289 3 DON JUAN 11   43   4
    EVEN I--ALBEIT I'M SURE I DID NOT KNOW IT . . . . . . 296 3 DON JUAN 11   55   5
    EVEN I--ALBEIT I'M SURE I DID NOT KNOW IT . . . . . . 296 3 DON JUAN 11   55   5
    BUT I WILL FALL AT LEAST AS FELL MY HERO . .   . . . 296 3 DON JUAN 11   56   5
    IF I MIGHT AUGUR I SHOULD RATE BUT LOW . . .   . . . 299 3 DON JUAN 11   61   6
    IF I MIGHT AUGUR I SHOULD RATE BUT LOW . . .   . . . 299 3 DON JUAN 11   61   6
    NOW WERE I ONCE AT HOME AND IN GOOD SATIRE . . . . . 299 3 DON JUAN 11   62   6
    I THINK I KNOW A TRICK OR TWO WOULD TURN . .   . . . 300 3 DON JUAN 11   63   1
    I THINK I KNOW A TRICK OR TWO WOULD TURN . .   . . . 300 3 DON JUAN 11   63   1
    MY JUAN WHOM I LEFT IN DEADLY PERIL . . . . 300 3 DON JUAN 11   64   1
    I WISH THEY KNEW THE LIFE OF A YOUNG NOBLE . . . . . 305 3 DON JUAN 11   74   8
    I LOOK FOR IT--'TIS GONE A GLOBE OF GLASS . . . . . . 306 3 DON JUAN 11   76   4
    I HAVE SEEN MORE CHANGES DOWN FROM MONARCHS TO . . . 309 3 DON JUAN 11   82   2
    I KNEW THAT NOUGHT WAS LASTING BUT NOW EVEN . . . . . 309 3 DON JUAN 11   82   5

I (CONTINUED)

	PAGE	VOL	CANTO	STANZA	LN
I HAVE SEEN NAPOLEON WHO SEEMED QUITE A JUPITER	309	3 DON JUAN 11	83	1
SHRINK TO A SATURN I HAVE SEEN A DUKE	309	3 DON JUAN 11	83	2
BUT IT IS TIME THAT I SHOULD HOIST MY BLUE PETER	309	3 DON JUAN 11	83	5
AND SAIL FOR A NEW THEME--I HAVE SEEN--AND SHOOK	309	3 DON JUAN 11	83	6
I HAVE SEEN THE LANDHOLDERS WITHOUT A RAP--	310	3 DON JUAN 11	84	1
I HAVE SEEN JOHANNA SOUTHCOTE--I HAVE SEEN	310	3 DON JUAN 11	84	2
I HAVE SEEN JOHANNA SOUTHCOTE--I HAVE SEEN	310	3 DON JUAN 11	84	2
I HAVE SEEN THAT SAD AFFAIR OF THE LATE QUEEN--	310	3 DON JUAN 11	84	4
I HAVE SEEN CROWNS WORN INSTEAD OF A FOOL'S CAP--	310	3 DON JUAN 11	84	5
I HAVE SEEN A CONGRESS DOING ALL THAT'S MEAN--	310	3 DON JUAN 11	84	6
I HAVE SEEN SOME NATIONS LIKE O'ERLOADED ASSES	310	3 DON JUAN 11	84	7
I HAVE SEEN SMALL POETS AND GREAT PROSERS AND	310	3 DON JUAN 11	85	1
I HAVE SEEN THE FUNDS AT WAR WITH HOUSE AND LAND--	310	3 DON JUAN 11	85	3
BY SLAVES ON HORSEBACK--I HAVE SEEN MALT LIQUORS	310	3 DON JUAN 11	85	6
I HAVE SEEN JOHN HALF DETECT HIMSELF A FOOL--	310	3 DON JUAN 11	85	8
BUT HOW SHALL I RELATE IN OTHER CANTOS	311	3 DON JUAN 11	87	1
A MORAL COUNTRY BUT I HOLD MY HAND--	311	3 DON JUAN 11	87	4
FOR I DISDAIN TO WRITE AN ATALANTIS	311	3 DON JUAN 11	87	5
AND THAT I SING OF NEITHER MINE NOR ME	311	3 DON JUAN 11	88	5
THIS--WHEN I SPEAK I DON'T HINT BUT SPEAK OUT	311	3 DON JUAN 11	88	8
THIS--WHEN I SPEAK I DON'T HINT BUT SPEAK OUT	311	3 DON JUAN 11	88	8
(I MEAN IN FORTUNE'S MATRIMONIAL BOUNTIES)	312	3 DON JUAN 11	89	4
THUS FAR GO FORTH THOU LAY WHICH I WILL BACK	312	3 DON JUAN 11	90	2
SO MUCH THE BETTER--I MAY STAND ALONE	312	3 DON JUAN 11	90	7
OF MAN IT IS--I REALLY SCARCE KNOW WHAT	315	3 DON JUAN 12	1	3
I WONDER PEOPLE SHOULD BE LEFT ALIVE	316	3 DON JUAN 12	2	3
OH GOLD I STILL PREFER THEE UNTO PAPER	317	3 DON JUAN 12	4	7
I SAID BEFORE THE FRUGAL LIFE IS HIS	319	3 DON JUAN 12	7	2
I SAY THAT LINE'S A LAPSUS OF THE PEN--	323	3 DON JUAN 12	16	4
WELL IF I DON'T SUCCEED I HAVE SUCCEEDED	324	3 DON JUAN 12	17	1
WELL IF I DON'T SUCCEED I HAVE SUCCEEDED	324	3 DON JUAN 12	17	1
AND MY SUCCESS PRODUCED WHAT I IN SOOTH	324	3 DON JUAN 12	17	4
NO MORE OF THEM THAN THEY OF HER I TROW	324	3 DON JUAN 12	18	8
AS SERIOUS AS IF I HAD FOR INDITERS	325	3 DON JUAN 12	20	4
AND WHY SHOULD I NOT FORM MY SPECULATION	325	3 DON JUAN 12	21	2
I THINK THAT PHILO-GENITIVENESS IS--	326	3 DON JUAN 12	22	2
I SAY METHINKS THAT PHILO-GENITIVENESS	326	3 DON JUAN 12	22	7
I COULD SEND FORTH MY MANDATE LIKE A PRIMATE	327	3 DON JUAN 12	24	3
BUT I AM SICK OF POLITICS BEGIN	327	3 DON JUAN 12	25	1
THINK NOT FAIR CREATURES THAT I MEAN TO ABUSE YOU ALL--	329	3 DON JUAN 12	28	3
I HAVE ALWAYS LIKED YOU BETTER THAN I STATE	329	3 DON JUAN 12	28	4
I HAVE ALWAYS LIKED YOU BETTER THAN I STATE	329	3 DON JUAN 12	28	4
SINCE I'VE GROWN MORAL STILL I MUST ACCUSE YOU ALL	329	3 DON JUAN 12	28	5
AND I ASSURE YOU THAT LIKE VIRGIN HONEY	330	3 DON JUAN 12	31	7
TO HIS BILLETS WHY WALTZ WITH HIM WHY I PRAY	332	3 DON JUAN 12	34	7
TO DRAW A HIGH PRIZE NOW HOWE'ER HE GOT HER I	333	3 DON JUAN 12	37	7
I FOR MY PART--(ONE MODERN INSTANCE MORE	334	3 DON JUAN 12	38	1
BUT THOUGH I ALSO HAD REFORMED BEFORE	334	3 DON JUAN 12	38	5
THAT I DISSERT LIKE GRACE BEFORE A FEAST	334	3 DON JUAN 12	39	3
I MEAN TO SHOW THINGS REALLY AS THEY ARE	335	3 DON JUAN 12	40	2
NOT AS THEY OUGHT TO BE FOR I AVOW	335	3 DON JUAN 12	40	3
(I WISH THAT OTHERS WOULD FIND OUT THE SAME)	336	3 DON JUAN 12	42	2
VIRTUOUS SHE WAS--AND HAD BEEN I BELIEVE	336	3 DON JUAN 12	43	2
THAT--BUT I WILL NOT LISTEN BY YOUR LEAVE	336	3 DON JUAN 12	43	V4
MOREOVER I'VE REMARKED (AND I WAS ONCE	336	3 DON JUAN 12	44	1
I THINK YOU'LL FIND FROM MANY A FAMILY PICTURE	337	3 DON JUAN 12	46	3
I SAID THAT LADY PINCHBECK HAD BEEN TALKED ABOUT--	338	3 DON JUAN 12	47	1
I CALL SUCH THINGS TRANSMISSION FOR THERE IS	340	3 DON JUAN 12	52	1
BUT NOW I WILL BEGIN MY POEM--'TIS	341	3 DON JUAN 12	54	1
I THOUGHT AT SETTING OFF ABOUT TWO DOZEN	341	3 DON JUAN 12	55	5
I THINK TO CANTER GENTLY THROUGH A HUNDRED	341	3 DON JUAN 12	55	8
THE ROYAL GAME OF GOOSE AS I MAY SAY	342	3 DON JUAN 12	58	4
I DON'T MEAN THIS AS GENERAL BUT PARTICULAR	343	3 DON JUAN 12	59	1
AND SOME OF THEM HIGH NAMES I HAVE ALSO KNOWN	344	3 DON JUAN 12	61	2
IT IS--I MEANT AND MEAN NOT TO DISPARAGE	344	3 DON JUAN 12	62	4
YE GODS I GROW A TALKER LET US PRATE	345	3 DON JUAN 12	64	1
THE NEXT OF PERILS THOUGH I PLACE IT STERNEST	345	3 DON JUAN 12	64	2
FOR HE WAS SICK--NO 'TWAS NOT THE WORD SICK I MEANT--	346	3 DON JUAN 12	67	3
THAT HE WAS NOT IN HEART SO VERY WEAK--I MEANT	346	3 DON JUAN 12	67	5
I SAY AT FIRST--FOR HE FOUND OUT AT LAST	347	3 DON JUAN 12	69	1
THOUGH TRAVELLED I HAVE NEVER HAD THE LUCK TO	348	3 DON JUAN 12	70	1
BUT IF I HAD BEEN AT TIMBUCTOO THERE	348	3 DON JUAN 12	70	7
NO DOUBT I SHOULD BE TOLD THAT BLACK IS FAIR	348	3 DON JUAN 12	70	8
IT IS I WILL NOT SWEAR THAT BLACK IS WHITE	348	3 DON JUAN 12	71	1
BUT I SUSPECT IN FACT THAT WHITE IS BLACK	348	3 DON JUAN 12	71	2
BUT BY THE GODS I SWEAR THAT WHITE IS BLACK	348	3 DON JUAN 12	71	V2
I SAID THAT JUAN DID NOT THINK THEM PRETTY	350	3 DON JUAN 12	74	2
THOSE BRAVURAS (WHICH I STILL AM LEARNING	350	3 DON JUAN 12	75	6
TO LIKE THOUGH I HAVE BEEN SEVEN YEARS IN ITALY	350	3 DON JUAN 12	75	7
I LEAVE THE SAINTS TO SETTLE THEIR OWN SCORE	352	3 DON JUAN 12	79	4
FOR ME I LEAVE THE MATTER WHERE I FIND IT	352	3 DON JUAN 12	80	1
FOR ME I LEAVE THE MATTER WHERE I FIND IT	352	3 DON JUAN 12	80	1
(WHATEVER PEOPLE SAY) I DON'T KNOW WHETHER	355	3 DON JUAN 12	86	4
I CAN'T OBLIGE YOU READER TO READ ON	356	3 DON JUAN 12	87	6
MY PLAN (BUT I IF BUT FOR SINGULARITY	357	3 DON JUAN 12	89	5
THAT SUIT IN CHANCERY--(I HAVE A CHANCERY SUIT	357	3 DON JUAN 12	V 18	1
IN LAW THAN EQUITY--AS I CAN FEEL--	357	3 DON JUAN 12	V 18	4
NOT THAT I DEEM OUR CHIEF JUDGE IS A HOLLOW MAN--)	357	3 DON JUAN 12	V 18	8

I   (CONTINUED)
I NOW MEAN TO BE SERIOUS--IT IS TIME . . . .   358 3 DON JUAN 13   1 1
I LEAVE THEM TO THEIR TASTE NO DOUBT THE BEST . . . .   359 3 DON JUAN 13   3 2
I KNOW THAT SOME WOULD FAIN POSTPONE THIS ERA . . . .   360 3 DON JUAN 13   5 1
FOR MY PART I AM BUT A MERE SPECTATOR . . . .   361 3 DON JUAN 13   7 6
THOUGH 'TWAS NOT ONCE SO IF I SNEER SOMETIMES . . .   361 3 DON JUAN 13   8 2
IT IS BECAUSE I CANNOT WELL DO LESS . . . .   361 3 DON JUAN 13   8 3
I SHOULD BE VERY WILLING TO REDRESS . . . .   361 3 DON JUAN 13   8 5
I TELL THE TALE AS IT IS TOLD NOR DARE . . . . . .   365 3 DON JUAN 13   13 1
AND NOW I WILL PROCEED UPON THE PAIR . . . .   365 3 DON JUAN 13   13 3
THAT THEREFORE DO I PREVIOUSLY DECLARE . . . . . .   369 3 DON JUAN 13   25 7
SUCH I MIGHT STUMBLE OVER UNAWARES . . . .   370 3 DON JUAN 13   26 7
UNLESS I KNEW THE VERY CHASTEST SQUARES . . . . . .   370 3 DON JUAN 13   26 8
'TIS TRUE I MIGHT HAVE CHOSEN PICCADILLY . . . . . .   370 3 DON JUAN 13   27 1
BUT I HAVE MOTIVES WHETHER WISE OR SILLY . . . . . .   370 3 DON JUAN 13   27 3
THEREFORE I NAME NOT SQUARE STREET PLACE UNTIL I . .   370 3 DON JUAN 13   27 5
THEREFORE I NAME NOT SQUARE STREET PLACE UNTIL I . .   370 3 DON JUAN 13   27 5
SUCH ARE--BUT I HAVE LOST THE LONDON CHART . . . . .   370 3 DON JUAN 13   27 8
WITHIN--ET CAETERA SHALL I GO ON--NO . . . .   374 3 DON JUAN 13   36 4
I HATE TO HUNT DOWN A TIRED METAPHOR . . . .   374 3 DON JUAN 13   36 5
AND SUCH ARE MANY--THOUGH I ONLY MEANT HER . . . . .   375 3 DON JUAN 13   38 4
FROM WHOM I NOW DEDUCE THESE MORAL LESSONS . . . . .   375 3 DON JUAN 13   38 5
SOMETIMES A LITTLE LATER I DON'T ERR . . . . . .   378 3 DON JUAN 13   43 2
UPON MY SHOULDERS HERE I MUST AVER . . . .   378 3 DON JUAN 13   43 4
CAN PAINT COSI VIAGGINO I RICCHI . . . .   380 3 DON JUAN 13   47 5
THE CAUSE I KNOW NOT NOR CAN SOLVE BUT SUCH . . . .   388 3 DON JUAN 13   64 7
THE CELLS TOO AND REFECTORY I WEEN . . . .   389 3 DON JUAN 13   66 4
VIRTUES OF WHICH BOTH YOU AND I HAVE NEED . . . . .   393 3 DON JUAN 13   73 4
WHILE I WITHOUT REMORSE OF RHYME OR FEAR . . . . . .   393 3 DON JUAN 13   74 2
I SPARE YOU THEN THE FURNITURE AND PLATE . . . . . .   393 3 DON JUAN 13   74 8
I CAN'T EXACTLY TRACE THEIR RULE OF RIGHT . . . . .   397 3 DON JUAN 13   82 1
I HAVE SEEN MORE THAN I'LL SAY--BUT WE WILL SEE . .   397 3 DON JUAN 13   83 1
I HAVE NAMED A FEW NOT FOREMOST IN DEGREE . . . . .   397 3 DON JUAN 13   83 5
I HAD FORGOTTEN--BUT MUST NOT FORGET-- . . . . . .   400 3 DON JUAN 13   90 1
YOU MAY BE BOAZ AND I--MODEST RUTH . . . .   403 3 DON JUAN 13   96 4
I MUST NOT QUITE OMIT THE TALKING SAGE . . . . . .   403 3 DON JUAN 13   97 3
I WILL NOT DWELL UPON RAGOUTS OR ROASTS . . . . . .   404 3 DON JUAN 13   99 5
I LOVE THE MYSTERY OF A FEMALE MISSAL . . . .   407 3 DON JUAN 13   105 4
FOR ME I KNOW NOUGHT NOTHING I DENY . . . .   411 3 DON JUAN 14   3 1
FOR ME I KNOW NOUGHT NOTHING I DENY . . . .   411 3 DON JUAN 14   3 1
I WRITE WHAT'S UPPERMOST WITHOUT DELAY . . . . . .   413 3 DON JUAN 14   7 5
FOR I HAVE SEEN A PORTION OF THAT SAME . . . . . .   414 3 DON JUAN 14   9 2
OF PASSIONS TOO I HAVE PROVED ENOUGH TO BLAME . . .   414 3 DON JUAN 14   9 4
FOR I WAS RATHER FAMOUS IN MY TIME . . . .   414 3 DON JUAN 14   9 7
UNTIL I FAIRLY KNOCK'D IT UP WITH RHYME . . . . . .   414 3 DON JUAN 14   9 8
I HAVE BROUGHT THIS WORLD ABOUT MY EARS AND EKE . .   414 3 DON JUAN 14   10 1
AND YET I CAN'T HELP SCRIBBLING ONCE A WEEK . . . .   414 3 DON JUAN 14   10 5
IN YOUTH I WROTE BECAUSE MY MIND WAS FULL . . . . .   415 3 DON JUAN 14   10 7
AND NOW BECAUSE I FEEL IT GROWING DULL . . . . . .   415 3 DON JUAN 14   10 8
I ASK IN TURN--WHY DO YOU PLAY AT CARDS . . . . . .   415 3 DON JUAN 14   11 3
AND WHAT I WRITE I CAST UPON THE STREAM . . . . . .   415 3 DON JUAN 14   11 7
AND WHAT I WRITE I CAST UPON THE STREAM . . . . . .   415 3 DON JUAN 14   11 7
TO SWIM OR SINK--I HAVE HAD AT LEAST MY DREAM . . .   415 3 DON JUAN 14   11 8
I THINK THAT WERE I CERTAIN OF SUCCESS . . . . . .   415 3 DON JUAN 14   12 1
I THINK THAT WERE I CERTAIN OF SUCCESS . . . . . .   415 3 DON JUAN 14   12 1
I HARDLY COULD COMPOSE ANOTHER LINE . . . .   415 3 DON JUAN 14   12 2
AND YET 'TIS NOT AFFECTED I OPINE . . . .   415 3 DON JUAN 14   12 6
THE PORTION OF THIS WORLD WHICH I AT PRESENT . . . .   416 3 DON JUAN 14   15 1
NOW I COULD MUCH MORE EASILY SKETCH A HAREM . . . .   419 3 DON JUAN 14   21 3
THAN THESE THINGS AND BESIDES I WISH TO SPARE 'EM .   419 3 DON JUAN 14   21 5
FOR REASONS WHICH I CHOOSE TO KEEP APART . . . . . .   419 3 DON JUAN 14   21 6
AND THEREFORE WHAT I THROW OFF IS IDEAL-- . . . . .   419 3 DON JUAN 14   22 1
I FOR ONE VENERATE A PETTICOAT-- . . . .   421 3 DON JUAN 14   26 6
MUCH I RESPECT AND MUCH I HAVE ADORED . . . .   422 3 DON JUAN 14   27 1
MUCH I RESPECT AND MUCH I HAVE ADORED . . . .   422 3 DON JUAN 14   27 1
WITH WHICH I COULD NOT BREW A PASTORAL . . . . . .   423 3 DON JUAN 14   30 3
YET I MUST OWN--ALTHOUGH IN THIS I YIELD . . . . . .   425 3 DON JUAN 14   35 3
YET I MUST OWN--ALTHOUGH IN THIS I YIELD . . . . . .   425 3 DON JUAN 14   35 3
OF PANTOMIME--HE DANCED I SAY RIGHT WELL . . . . . .   427 3 DON JUAN 14   38 3
BUT OH THAT I SHOULD EVER PEN SO SAD A LINE . . . .   430 3 DON JUAN 14   46 1
SOME HEART-ACHES HAD BEEN SPARED ME YET I CARE NOT--   431 3 DON JUAN 14   49 2
I WOULD NOT BE A TORTOISE IN HIS SCREEN . . . . . .   431 3 DON JUAN 14   49 3
IS THAT PORTENTOUS PHRASE I TOLD YOU SO . . . . . .   432 3 DON JUAN 14   50 3
SAY SEVEN-AND-TWENTY FOR I NEVER KNEW . . . .   433 3 DON JUAN 14   53 2
AS I HAVE SAID IN--I FORGET WHAT PAGE . . . .   433 3 DON JUAN 14   54 4
AS I HAVE SAID IN--I FORGET WHAT PAGE . . . .   433 3 DON JUAN 14   54 5
I HATE A MOTIVE LIKE A LINGERING BOTTLE . . . . . .   435 3 DON JUAN 14   58 1
I HATE IT AS I HATE A DROVE OF CATTLE . . . .   435 3 DON JUAN 14   58 5
I HATE IT AS I HATE A DROVE OF CATTLE . . . .   435 3 DON JUAN 14   58 5
I HATE IT AS I HATE AN ARGUMENT . . . .   435 3 DON JUAN 14   58 7
I HATE IT AS I HATE AN ARGUMENT . . . .   435 3 DON JUAN 14   58 7
I RECK NOT IF AN ACORN GAVE IT BIRTH . . . .   436 3 DON JUAN 14   59 4
AND I REFER YOU TO WISE OXENSTIERN . . . .   436 3 DON JUAN 14   59 8
AND IF THEIR FULL CONTENTS I DO NOT GIVE YE . . . .   440 3 DON JUAN 14   68 5
IT IS BECAUSE I DO NOT KNOW THEM YET . . . .   440 3 DON JUAN 14   68 6
BUT I SHALL ADD THEM IN A BRIEF APPENDIX . . . . . .   440 3 DON JUAN 14   68 8
AND SUCH I MEAN TO MAKE HIM WHEN I REIGN . . . . . .   440 3 DON JUAN 14   70 8
AND SUCH I MEAN TO MAKE HIM WHEN I REIGN . . . . . .   440 3 DON JUAN 14   70 8
I DON'T KNOW WHAT AND THEREFORE CANNOT TELL-- . . .   441 3 DON JUAN 14   71 2

I   (CONTINUED)

	PAGE	VOL	CANTO	STANZA	LN
WHICH FOR WHAT I KNOW MAY OF YORE HAVE LED	441	3	DON JUAN 14	72	3
I WILL NOT MAKE HIS GREAT DESCRIPTION LESS	442	3	DON JUAN 14	75	3
I TOUCH A SINGLE LEAF WHERE HE IS WARDEN--	442	3	DON JUAN 14	75	6
EUREKA I HAVE FOUND IT WHAT I MEAN	443	3	DON JUAN 14	76	1
EUREKA I HAVE FOUND IT WHAT I MEAN	443	3	DON JUAN 14	76	1
AN ACCESSARY AS I HAVE CAUSE TO GUESS	443	3	DON JUAN 14	76	4
AS FAR AS I KNOW THAT THE CHURCH RECEIVES	444	3	DON JUAN 14	78	4
I DO DECLARE UPON AN AFFIDAVIT	444	3	DON JUAN 14	80	1
ROMANCES I NE'ER READ LIKE THOSE I HAVE SEEN	444	3	DON JUAN 14	80	2
ROMANCES I NE'ER READ LIKE THOSE I HAVE SEEN	444	3	DON JUAN 14	80	2
NOR IF UNTO THE WORLD I EVER GAVE IT	444	3	DON JUAN 14	80	3
BUT SUCH INTENT I NEVER HAD NOR HAVE IT	444	3	DON JUAN 14	80	5
I THEREFORE DEAL IN GENERALITIES	444	3	DON JUAN 14	80	8
BUT THERE'S ANOTHER LITTLE THING I OWN	445	3	DON JUAN 14	82	5
THIS I COULD PROVE BEYOND A SINGLE DOUBT	446	3	DON JUAN 14	84	5
LIKE ARCHIMEDES I LEAVE EARTH AS 'TWAS	446	3	DON JUAN 14	84	8
I LEAVE IT TO YOUR PEOPLE OF SAGACITY	449	3	DON JUAN 14	90	4
SHE KNEW NOT HER OWN HEART THEN HOW SHOULD I	449	3	DON JUAN 14	91	1
I THINK NOT SHE WAS THEN IN LOVE WITH JUAN	449	3	DON JUAN 14	91	2
(I WILL NOT SAY IT WAS A FALSE OR TRUE ONE)	449	3	DON JUAN 14	91	6
I HAVE SEARCHED THE WORLD AND MIDST SUCCESS OR CHECKS	451	3	DON JUAN 14	93	V5
(I MERELY QUOTE WHAT I HAVE HEARD FROM MANY)	452	3	DON JUAN 14	95	2
(I MERELY QUOTE WHAT I HAVE HEARD FROM MANY)	452	3	DON JUAN 14	95	2
I HAD A PARAMOUR--AND I'VE HAD MANY	452	3	DON JUAN 14	95	V2
WHOM I HAD NOT SOME REASON TO REGRET	452	3	DON JUAN 14	95	V3
BUT TRUE--AS IF EXPEDIENT I COULD PROVE)	452	3	DON JUAN 14	96	2
OR IF THE OATH SEEM STRONG--I SWEAR BY JOVE	452	3	DON JUAN 14	96	V2
WILL BE DISCUSS'D HEREAFTER I OPINE	453	3	DON JUAN 14	97	3
AT PRESENT I AM GLAD OF A PRETENCE	453	3	DON JUAN 14	97	4
OR SERIOUS ARE THE TOPICS I MUST BANISH	453	3	DON JUAN 14	98	5
TO THE NEXT CANTO WHERE PERHAPS I SHALL	453	3	DON JUAN 14	98	6
ABOVE ALL I BEG ALL MEN TO FORBEAR	454	3	DON JUAN 14	99	1
AND I SHALL TAKE A MUCH MORE SERIOUS AIR	454	3	DON JUAN 14	99	5
THAN I HAVE YET DONE IN THIS EPIC SATIRE	454	3	DON JUAN 14	99	6
IN THEIR RESOLVES--ALAS THAT I SHOULD SAY SO	458	3	DON JUAN 15	6	4
WHEN ONCE DECANTED--I PRESUME TO GUESS SO	458	3	DON JUAN 15	6	6
I PERCH UPON AN HUMBLER PROMONTORY	464	3	DON JUAN 15	19	1
BUT SPECULATING AS I CAST MINE EYE	464	3	DON JUAN 15	19	4
I RATTLE ON EXACTLY AS I'D TALK	464	3	DON JUAN 15	19	7
I DON'T KNOW THAT THERE MAY BE MUCH ABILITY	465	3	DON JUAN 15	20	1
JUST AS I FEEL THE IMPROVVISATORE	465	3	DON JUAN 15	20	8
THE WHOLE TOGETHER IS WHAT I COULD WISH	465	3	DON JUAN 15	21	7
I MEANT TO MAKE THIS POEM VERY SHORT	466	3	DON JUAN 15	22	3
BUT NOW I CAN'T TELL WHERE IT MAY NOT RUN	466	3	DON JUAN 15	22	4
NO DOUBT IF I HAD WISH'D TO PAY MY COURT	466	3	DON JUAN 15	22	5
WERE MORE--BUT I WAS BORN FOR OPPOSITION	466	3	DON JUAN 15	22	8
SO THAT I VERILY BELIEVE IF THEY	466	3	DON JUAN 15	23	2
THOUGH AT THE FIRST I MIGHT PERCHANCE DERIDE	466	3	DON JUAN 15	23	5
THEIR TUMBLE I SHOULD TURN THE OTHER WAY	466	3	DON JUAN 15	23	6
BECAUSE I HATE EVEN DEMOCRATIC ROYALTY	466	3	DON JUAN 15	23	8
I THINK I SHOULD HAVE MADE A DECENT SPOUSE	467	3	DON JUAN 15	24	1
I THINK I SHOULD HAVE MADE A DECENT SPOUSE	467	3	DON JUAN 15	24	1
IF I HAD NEVER PROVED THE SOFT CONDITION	467	3	DON JUAN 15	24	2
I THINK I SHOULD HAVE MADE MONASTIC VOWS	467	3	DON JUAN 15	24	3
I THINK I SHOULD HAVE MADE MONASTIC VOWS	467	3	DON JUAN 15	24	3
'GAINST RHYME I NEVER SHOULD HAVE KNOCK'D MY BROWS	467	3	DON JUAN 15	24	5
BUT LAISSEZ ALLER--KNIGHTS AND DAMES I SING	467	3	DON JUAN 15	25	1
NOW HERE I HAVE GOT THE PREACHER AT A DEAD LOCK	471	3	DON JUAN 15	35	8
PIOUS AND PURE BEYOND WHAT I CAN TERM ANY	472	3	DON JUAN 15	36	5
ALTHOUGH I WONDER HOW IT GREW HABITUAL	472	3	DON JUAN 15	36	8
WHICH LAST I LEAVE UNTO THE LORD'S SPIRITUAL	472	3	DON JUAN 15	36	V8
HAD ADELINE READ MALTHUS I CAN'T TELL	472	3	DON JUAN 15	38	1
I WISH SHE HAD HIS BOOK'S THE ELEVENTH COMMANDMENT	472	3	DON JUAN 15	38	2
THIS HE (AS FAR AS I CAN UNDERSTAND) MEANT	472	3	DON JUAN 15	38	4
HIS TALENT I WILL NOT DENY NOR DWELL	473	3	DON JUAN 15	38	V5
AND THEN THERE WAS--BUT WHY SHOULD I GO ON	475	3	DON JUAN 15	43	1
THAN I HAVE TIME OR WILL TO TAKE TO PIECES	478	3	DON JUAN 15	52	8
IT WAS NOT JEALOUSY I THINK BUT SHUN	479	3	DON JUAN 15	54	5
AND AS MY FRIEND SCOTT SAYS I SOUND MY WARISON	481	3	DON JUAN 15	59	3
SCOTT--OF SUCH TALENT--I COULD HARDLY HAVE	481	3	DON JUAN 15	59	V6
I SAY IN MY SLIGHT WAY I MAY PROCEED	482	3	DON JUAN 15	60	1
I SAY IN MY SLIGHT WAY I MAY PROCEED	482	3	DON JUAN 15	60	1
I WRITE THE WORLD NOR CARE IF THE WORLD READ	482	3	DON JUAN 15	60	3
AT LEAST FOR THIS I CANNOT SPARE ITS VANITY	482	3	DON JUAN 15	60	4
MORE FOES BY THIS SAME SCROLL WHEN I BEGAN IT I	482	3	DON JUAN 15	60	6
MORE FOES BY THIS SAME SCROLL WHEN I BEGAN IT I	482	3	DON JUAN 15	60	6
THOUGHT THAT IT MIGHT TURN OUT SO--NOW I KNOW IT	482	3	DON JUAN 15	60	7
BUT STILL I AM OR WAS A PRETTY POET	482	3	DON JUAN 15	60	8
THERE ALSO WAS--THE SINNER THAT I AM	483	3	DON JUAN 15	63	5
HOW SHALL I GET THIS GOURMAND STANZA THROUGH	483	3	DON JUAN 15	63	6
BUT I MUST CROWD ALL INTO ONE GRAND MESS	483	3	DON JUAN 15	64	1
OR MASS FOR SHOULD I STRETCH INTO DETAIL	483	3	DON JUAN 15	64	2
BUT THOUGH A BONNE VIVANTE I MUST CONFESS	483	3	DON JUAN 15	64	5
A MAN LIKE WHOM I HOPE WE SHAN'T SEE MANY SOON	484	3	DON JUAN 15	65	4
WITH THINGS I CAN'T WITHSTAND OR UNDERSTAND	484	3	DON JUAN 15	66	3
FURTHER I SHALL NOT FOLLOW THE RESEARCH	485	3	DON JUAN 15	67	6
I WISH TO GOD YOU'DE DRESS US SOME SUCH PARTRIDGES	485	3	DON JUAN 15	67	V8
IN THE FEAST PECKING LESS THAN I CAN TELL	487	3	DON JUAN 15	70	4

I (CONTINUED)

		PAGE	VOL	CANTO		STANZA	LN
ALAS I MUST LEAVE UNDESCRIBED THE GIBIER		487	3	DON JUAN	15	71	1
ALL WHICH I USE TO MAKE MY RHYMES RUN GLIBBER		487	3	DON JUAN	15	71	3
I MUST NOT INTRODUCE EVEN A SPARE RIB HERE		487	3	DON JUAN	15	71	5
BUT I HAVE DINED AND MUST FOREGO ALAS		487	3	DON JUAN	15	71	7
HAST EVER HAD THE GOUT I HAVE NOT HAD IT--		488	3	DON JUAN	15	72	7
BUT I MAY HAVE AND YOU TOO READER DREAD IT		488	3	DON JUAN	15	72	8
MUST I PASS OVER IN MY BILL OF FARE		488	3	DON JUAN	15	73	2
I MUST ALTHOUGH A FAVOURITE PLAT OF MINE		488	3	DON JUAN	15	73	3
A SITUATION DIFFICULT I WEEN		489	3	DON JUAN	15	75	3
I SOMETIMES ALMOST THINK THAT EYES HAVE EARS		489	3	DON JUAN	15	76	1
OF WHICH I CAN'T TELL WHENCE THEIR KNOWLEDGE SPRINGS . . .		489	3	DON JUAN	15	76	4
AND LOOK'D AS MUCH AS IF TO SAY I SAID IT--		491	3	DON JUAN	15	79	1
NEM CON AMONGST THE WOMEN WHICH I GRIEVE		493	3	DON JUAN	15	84	2
HAS SHOWN I KNOW NOT WHY THEY SHOULD DISPLEASE		494	3	DON JUAN	15	86	6
(SEE LITTLETON) WHENE'ER I HAVE EXPRESSED		494	3	DON JUAN	15	87	2
PERHAPS I HAVE A THIRD TOO IN A NOOK		494	3	DON JUAN	15	87	5
IF PEOPLE CONTRADICT THEMSELVES CAN I		495	3	DON JUAN	15	88	1
I NEVER DID SO NEVER WILL--HOW SHOULD I		495	3	DON JUAN	15	88	4
I NEVER DID SO NEVER WILL--HOW SHOULD I		495	3	DON JUAN	15	88	4
BUT HERE AGAIN WHY WILL I THUS ENTANGLE		496	3	DON JUAN	15	91	1
SO MUCH AS I DO ANY KIND OF WRANGLE		496	3	DON JUAN	15	91	3
I ALWAYS KNOCK MY HEAD AGAINST SOME ANGLE		496	3	DON JUAN	15	91	5
YET I WISH WELL TO TROJAN AND TO TYRIAN		496	3	DON JUAN	15	91	7
FOR I WAS BRED A MODERATE PRESBYTERIAN		496	3	DON JUAN	15	91	8
BUT THOUGH I AM A TEMPERATE THEOLOGIAN		497	3	DON JUAN	15	92	1
ARE TOPICS WHICH I SOMETIMES INTRODUCE		497	3	DON JUAN	15	93	2
AND NOW I WILL GIVE UP ALL ARGUMENT		498	3	DON JUAN	15	94	1
INDEED I NEVER KNEW WHAT PEOPLE MEANT		498	3	DON JUAN	15	94	5
WAS DANGEROUS--I THINK SHE IS AS HARMLESS		498	3	DON JUAN	15	94	7
NO BUT YOU HAVE HEARD--I UNDERSTAND--BE DUMB		498	3	DON JUAN	15	95	2
AND DO NOT THINK I MEAN TO SNEER AT MOST		498	3	DON JUAN	15	95	5
SERIOUS YOU LAUGH--YOU MAY THAT WILL I NOT		499	3	DON JUAN	15	96	1
I SAY I DO BELIEVE A HAUNTED SPOT		499	3	DON JUAN	15	96	3
I SAY I DO BELIEVE A HAUNTED SPOT		499	3	DON JUAN	15	96	3
EXISTS--AND WHERE THAT SHALL I NOT RECALL		499	3	DON JUAN	15	96	4
THE NIGHT (I SING BY NIGHT--SOMETIMES AN OWL		499	3	DON JUAN	15	97	1
I WISH TO HEAVEN THEY WOULD NOT LOOK SO GRIM		499	3	DON JUAN	15	97	6
I THINK TOO THAT I HAVE SATE UP TOO LATE		499	3	DON JUAN	15	97	8
I THINK TOO THAT I HAVE SATE UP TOO LATE		499	3	DON JUAN	15	97	8
TO RHYME AT NOON--WHEN I HAVE OTHER THINGS		500	3	DON JUAN	15	98	2
TO THINK OF IF I EVER THINK--I SAY		500	3	DON JUAN	15	98	3
TO THINK OF IF I EVER THINK--I SAY		500	3	DON JUAN	15	98	3
I FEEL SOME CHILLY MIDNIGHT SHUDDERINGS		500	3	DON JUAN	15	98	4
IS WHAT I HAVE NOT LEISURE TO INSPECT		502	3	DON JUAN	16	2	3
BUT THIS I MUST SAY IN MY OWN APPLAUSE		502	3	DON JUAN	16	2	4
OF ALL THE MUSES THAT I RECOLLECT		502	3	DON JUAN	16	2	5
I SAID IT WAS A STORY OF A GHOST--		502	3	DON JUAN	16	4	3
WHAT THEN I ONLY KNOW IT SO BEFELL		502	3	DON JUAN	16	4	4
I DO NOT SPEAK PROFANELY TO RECALL		503	3	DON JUAN	16	6	5
I MERELY MEAN TO SAY WHAT JOHNSON SAID		504	3	DON JUAN	16	7	1
OR NONE OR LIKE--LIKE NOTHING THAT I KNOW		505	3	DON JUAN	16	10	2
(I HAVE HAD OF BOTH SOME NOT TO BE DISDAINED)		505	3	DON JUAN	16	11	7
I WISH THEY'D STATE HOW MANY THEY HAVE GAINED		505	3	DON JUAN	16	11	8
(I STATE THIS FOR I AM CAUTIOUS TO A PITCH		507	3	DON JUAN	16	16	3
(I STATE THIS FOR I AM CAUTIOUS TO A PITCH		507	3	DON JUAN	16	16	3
A PARAGRAPH I THINK ABOUT HORNE TOOKE		512	3	DON JUAN	16	27	3
THE SPIRIT OF THESE WALLS--IN TRUTH NOT I		516	3	DON JUAN	16	36	2
THE LAST TIME WAS--I PRAY SAID ADELINE--		516	3	DON JUAN	16	37	1
I CAN'T TELL WHY TO THIS DISSIMULATION--		518	3	DON JUAN	16	40	3
WAS MORE SHAKESPEARIAN IF I DO NOT ERR		524	3	DON JUAN	16	48	4
I HAVE NOT HEARD SHE WAS AT ALL POETIC		525	3	DON JUAN	16	50	1
THOUGH WHY I CANNOT SAY--AT LEAST THIS MINUTE		526	3	DON JUAN	16	51	8
THERE WAS A MODERN GOTH I MEAN A GOTHIC		529	3	DON JUAN	16	58	1
AND SCARLET CLOAK (I HATE THE SIGHT TO SEE SINCE-- . .		530	3	DON JUAN	16	61	4
SINCE--SINCE--IN YOUTH I HAD THE SAD MISHAP-- . . .		530	3	DON JUAN	16	61	5
BUT LUCKILY I HAVE PAID FEW PARISH FEES SINCE)		530	3	DON JUAN	16	61	6
I LEAVE TO THOSE WHO ARE FOND OF SOLVING DOUBT . . .		531	3	DON JUAN	16	62	1
AND THOUGHT I SAY NO MORE--I'VE SAID TOO MUCH		538	3	DON JUAN	16	77	2
AND GRACE IS SAID THE GRACE I SHOULD HAVE SUNG-- . . .		538	3	DON JUAN	16	77	8
I SATE NEXT THAT O'ERWHELMING SON OF HEAVEN		539	3	DON JUAN	16	81	6
THE LOUDEST WIT I E'ER WAS DEAFENED WITH		539	3	DON JUAN	16	81	8
I KNEW HIM IN HIS LIVELIER LONDON DAYS		540	3	DON JUAN	16	82	1
I KNOW NOT BUT HER COLOUR NE'ER WAS HIGH--		545	3	DON JUAN	16	94	6
I ASK BUT THIS OF MINE TO--NOT DEFEND		552	3	DON JUAN	16	104	5
ARE SO DIVINE THAT I MUST DEEM THEM REAL--		553	3	DON JUAN	16	107	8
I SEE--I SEE--AH NO--'TIS NOT--YET 'TIS--		556	3	DON JUAN	16	112	2
I SEE--I SEE--AH NO--'TIS NOT--YET 'TIS--		556	3	DON JUAN	16	112	2
BUT NOT TO GO TOO FAR I HOLD IT LAW		563	3	DON JUAN	17	2	4
(I'LL TAKE THE LIKENESS I CAN FIRST COME AT)		564	3	DON JUAN	17	4	5
THEREFORE I WOULD SOLICIT FREE DISCUSSION		564	3	DON JUAN	17	6	1
AND SO FOR ONE WILL I--AS WELL I MAY--		566	3	DON JUAN	17	10	4
AND SO FOR ONE WILL I--AS WELL I MAY--		566	3	DON JUAN	17	10	4
WOULD THAT I WERE LESS BILIOUS--BUT OH FIE ON'T . . .		566	3	DON JUAN	17	10	5
JUST AS I MAKE MY MIND UP EVERY DAY		566	3	DON JUAN	17	10	6
THE WIND SHIFTS AND I FLY INTO A RAGE		566	3	DON JUAN	17	10	8
TEMPERATE I AM--YET NEVER HAD A TEMPER		567	3	DON JUAN	17	11	1
MODEST I AM--YET WITH SOME SLIGHT ASSURANCE		567	3	DON JUAN	17	11	2
SO THAT I ALMOST THINK THAT THE SAME SKIN		567	3	DON JUAN	17	11	7

I   (CONTINUED)
      IS MORE THAN I SHALL VENTURE TO DESCRIBE-- . . . . . . 567 3 DON JUAN 17   12   7
      I LEAVE THE THING A PROBLEM LIKE ALL THINGS-- . . . . . 568 3 DON JUAN 17   13   1
      BUT OH THAT I WERE DEAD--FOR WHILE ALIVE-- . . . . . . 569 3 DON JUAN 17 V 13   1
      WOULD THAT I NEER HAD LOVED--OH WOMAN--WOMAN-- . . . . 569 3 DON JUAN 17 V 13   2
      ALL THAT I WRITE OR WROTE CAN NE'ER REVIVE . . . . . . 569 3 DON JUAN 17 V 13   3
IBIS
      HORATIAN MEDIO TU TUTISSIMUS IBIS . . . .   14 3 DON JUAN 6   17   8
ICE
      FEARLESS--BECAUSE NO FEELING DWELLS IN ICE . . . . . . 18 2 DON JUAN D   15   7
      WITH VIANDS AND SHERBETS IN ICE--AND WINE-- . . . . . 310 2 DON JUAN 3   69   7
      THE SUN WHICH YEARLY MELTS THE POLAR ICE . . . . . . 501 2 DON JUAN 5   157   7
      MADE ICE SEEM PARADISE AND WINTER SUNNY . . . . 235 3 DON JUAN 10   21   8
      IN WHICH THE NEVA'S ICE WOULD CEASE TO LIVE . . . . . 243 3 DON JUAN 10   37   6
      MIGHT SCATTER FIRE THROUGH ICE LIKE HECLA'S FLAME . . 254 3 DON JUAN 10   59   8
      ABOVE THE ICE HAD LIKE A SKAITER GLIDED . . . . 327 3 DON JUAN 12   25   4
      THOSE POLAR SUMMERS ALL SUN AND SOME ICE . . . . . . 349 3 DON JUAN 12   72   8
      FROZEN INTO A VERY VINOUS ICE . . . . 375 3 DON JUAN 13   37   3
      WHEN ONCE YOU HAVE BROKEN THEIR CONFOUNDED ICE . . . . 375 3 DON JUAN 13   38   8
      BOATS WHEN 'TWAS WATER SKAITING WHEN 'TWAS ICE . . . . 407 3 DON JUAN 13   106   3
      AND FRUITS AND ICE AND ALL THAT ART REFINES . . . . . 488 3 DON JUAN 15   72   1
      LIKE A GOOD SHIP ENTANGLED AMONG ICE . . . . 490 3 DON JUAN 15   77   7
ICEBERG
      EVEN TILL AN ICEBERG IT MAY CHANCE TO GROW . . . . . 398 2 DON JUAN 4   100   7
ICEBERGS
      WHAT ICEBERGS IN THE HEARTS OF MIGHTY MEN . . . . . . 455 3 DON JUAN 14   102   3
ICELAND
      AND HONEST MEN FROM ICELAND TO BARBADOES . . . . . . 231 3 DON JUAN 10   13   5
ICES
      AND EATING ICES WERE O'ERHEARD TO SAY . . . . 239 3 DON JUAN 10   30   6
      GLACIERS VOLCANOS ORANGES AND ICES . . . . 262 3 DON JUAN 10   76   8
ICHAR
      THE DUKE OF ICHAR AND DON FERNAN NUNEZ . . . . 103 2 DON JUAN 1   150   2
ICICLES
      WERE HUNG WITH MARBLE ICICLES THE WORK . . . . 362 2 DON JUAN 4   33   2
ICY
      WHICH FLASHES O'ER A WASTE AND ICY CLIME . . . . . . 67 3 DON JUAN 7   2   4
I'D
      NO--NO--I'D SEND HIM OUT BETIMES TO COLLEGE . . . . . 50 2 DON JUAN 1   52   7
      AND SO I'D HAVE HER THINK WERE I THE MAN . . . . . . 64 2 DON JUAN 1   79   7
      I'D WEEP BUT MINE IS NOT A WEEPING MUSE . . . . . . 165 2 DON JUAN 2   16   3
      I'D RATHER LEAVE IT MUCH TO YOUR OWN MIND . . . . . 467 2 DON JUAN 5   97   4
      I'D RATHER TELL TEN LIES THAN SAY A WORD . . . . . . 77 3 DON JUAN 7   22   4
      I'D TRY CONCLUSIONS WITH THOSE JANIZARIES . . . . . 299 3 DON JUAN 11   62   7
      FURTHER I'D QUOTE BUT SCRIPTURE INTERVENING . . . . 403 3 DON JUAN 13   96   5
      I'D RATHER NOT SAY WHAT MIGHT BE RELATED . . . . . 428 3 DON JUAN 14   42   4
      I RATTLE ON EXACTLY AS I'D TALK . . . . 464 3 DON JUAN 15   19   7
      BECAUSE I'D RATHER IT SHOULD BE FORGOT . . . . . . 499 3 DON JUAN 15   96   5
ID
      ARCADES AMBO ID EST--BLACKGUARDS BOTH . . . . 394 2 DON JUAN 4   93   8
IDA
      AND IDA IN THE DISTANCE STILL THE SAME . . . . . . 386 2 DON JUAN 4   77   3
IDEA
      POOR LITTLE FELLOW HE HAD NO IDEA . . . . 68 2 DON JUAN 1   86   2
IDEAL
      THAN ALL THE NONSENSE OF THEIR STONE IDEAL) . . . . 218 2 DON JUAN 2   118   8
      IS BUT HEIGHTENING OF THE BEAU IDEAL . . . . 269 2 DON JUAN 2   211   8
      DON JUAN WHO WAS REAL OR IDEAL-- . . . . 234 3 DON JUAN 10   20   1
      THAT ALL'S IDEAL--ALL OURSELVES I'LL STAKE THE . . 269 3 DON JUAN 11   2   3
      AND THEREFORE WHAT I THROW OFF IS IDEAL-- . . . . . 419 3 DON JUAN 14   22   1
      GRACE OF THE SOFT IDEAL SELDOM SHOWN . . . . 428 3 DON JUAN 14   40   6
      OR HARDENED FEELINGS WHICH PERHAPS IDEAL . . . . . 553 3 DON JUAN 16   107   7
IDEM
      A FOOLISH CLEVER FELLOW IDEM SEMPER . . . . 150 2 DON JUAN 1 V 1   8
      CHANGEABLE TOO--YET SOMEHOW IDEM SEMPER . . . . . . 567 3 DON JUAN 17   11   3
IDENTIFY
      WHO WOULD AS 'TWERE IDENTIFY THEIR DUST . . . . . . 399 2 DON JUAN 4   101   4
IDENTITY
      SHOULD CAUSE MORE FEAR THAN A WHOLE HOST'S IDENTITY . . 559 3 DON JUAN 16   120   8
IDLE
      SILENT AND PENSIVE IDLE RESTLESS SLOW . . . . 68 2 DON JUAN 1   87   1
      THAT WORD IS IDLE NOW--BUT LET IT GO . . . . 132 2 DON JUAN 1   195   8
      WERE ONCE HER CARES HOW IDLE SEEM'D THEY NOW) . . . 362 2 DON JUAN 4   34   4
      FROM OUT HER SKIES--THEN HOWL YOUR IDLE WRATH . . . 70 3 DON JUAN 7   7   7
      OF IDLE APPRENSIONS WHICH LIKE WIND . . . . 133 3 DON JUAN 8   40   4
      IS IDLE LET US LIKE MOST OTHERS BOW . . . . 286 3 DON JUAN 11   38   5
      WHAT ANTRES VAST AND DESARTS IDLE THEN . . . . . . 455 3 DON JUAN 14   102   1
      AS THE MERE PASTIME OF AN IDLE DAY . . . . 521 3 DON JUAN 16   42   3
IDLENESS
      FOR HEALTH AND IDLENESS TO PASSION'S FLAME . . . . 245 2 DON JUAN 2   169   5
      THERE IS A FLOWER CALLED LOVE IN IDLENESS . . . . . 442 3 DON JUAN 14   75   1
      TO SAY IS NOT THAT LOVE IS IDLENESS . . . . 443 3 DON JUAN 14   76   2
      BUT THAT IN LOVE SUCH IDLENESS HAS BEEN . . . . . . 443 3 DON JUAN 14   76   3
IDLING
      SURPRISED AT THESE UNWONTED SIGNS OF IDLING . . . . 290 2 DON JUAN 3   28   2
      THE SERVANTS ALL WERE GETTING DRUNK OR IDLING . . . 295 2 DON JUAN 3   39   3
IDLY
      BECAUSE HE MOPETH IDLY IN HIS SHELL . . . . 445 3 DON JUAN 14   81   2
IDOL
      AMBITION WAS MY IDOL WHICH WAS BROKEN . . . . 145 2 DON JUAN 1   217   1

```
                                                         PAGE VOL     CANTO STANZA LN
IDOL   (CONTINUED)
    TO BE HER SOUL'S FIRST IDOL AND ITS LAST . . . . . . . 247  2 DON JUAN  2    173   V8
    OVER THEIR IDOL TILL SOME WEALTHIER LUST . . . . . . . 263  2 DON JUAN  2    200    5
    THAT PAINTING IS NO IDOL 'TIS TOO LIKE  . . . . . . .  336  2 DON JUAN  3    103    8
IDOLATRY
    IT WOULD NOT BE IDOLATRY TO KNEEL  . . . . . . . . .   313  2 DON JUAN  3     74    8
IFFSKCHY
    ENDING IN ISCHSKIN OUSCKIN IFFSKCHY OUSKI  . . . . .    74  3 DON JUAN  7     16    7
IGNARA
    HAUD IGNARA LOQUOR THESE ARE NUGAE QUARUM  . . . . .   419  3 DON JUAN 14     21    1
IGNES
    FOLLOWING THE IGNES FATUI OF MANKIND . . . . . . . .   479  3 DON JUAN 15     54    6
IGNIS
    AN IGNIS FATUUS OR AS SAILORS STRANDED  . . . . . .    127  3 DON JUAN  8     32    5
IGNIS-FATUUS
    A SORT OF IGNIS-FATUUS TO THE MIND . . . . . . . . .   281  3 DON JUAN 11     27    6
IGNOBLE
    HARK RISING TO THE IGNOBLE CALL--  . . . . . . . . .   324  2 DON JUAN  3   L  9    5
IGNORANCE
    SHE WAS ALL WHICH PURE IGNORANCE ALLOWS  . . . . . .   257  2 DON JUAN  2    190    5
    NOR SHOW YOUR GEORGIAN IGNORANCE--FOR SHAME . . . . .   28  3 DON JUAN  6     44    5
    FROM IGNORANCE OF DANGER WHICH INDUES . . . . . . .    131  3 DON JUAN  8     36    4
    THE GREEK OR TURKISH COHORN'S IGNORANCE . . . . . .    136  3 DON JUAN  8     46    3
    ILL FITTED WITH HER IGNORANCE TO JOSTLE . . . . . .    250  3 DON JUAN 10     52    5
    THE UNBOUNDED HOPE AND HEAVENLY IGNORANCE  . . . . .   554  3 DON JUAN 16    108    2
IGNORANT
    AN IGNORANT NOTELESS TIMELESS TUNELESS FELLOW  . . .   391  2 DON JUAN  4     87    4
IGNORANTLY
    WHILE COMMON MEN GROW IGNORANTLY OLD . . . . . . . .   232  3 DON JUAN 10     14    5
ILIA
    OH DURA ILIA MESSORUM--OH . . . . . . . . . . . . .    190  3 DON JUAN  9     15    1
ILIAD
    TO HOMER'S ILIAD SINCE IT DREW TO TROY  . . . . . .    441  3 DON JUAN 14     72    4
ILIADS
    AND FOR THEIR AENEIDS ILIADS AND ODYSSEYS  . . . . .    44  2 DON JUAN  1     41    6
ILION
    THE SHORES OF ILION LAY BENEATH THEIR LEE--  . . . .   384  2 DON JUAN  4     75    6
    AS TERRIBLE AS THAT OF ILION . . . . . . . . . . . .   106  3 DON JUAN  7     78    3
    AND WHETHER IN HIS TRAVELS HE SAW ILION  . . . . . .   294  3 DON JUAN 11     50    8
ILION'S
    WITH EASE BUT WHERE I SOUGHT FOR ILION'S WALLS . . .   386  2 DON JUAN  4     77    7
    CALLS ILION'S THE FIRST DAMAGES ON RECORD  . . . . .   209  3 DON JUAN  9     53    8
I'LL
    I'LL THEREFORE TAKE OUR ANCIENT FRIEND DON JUAN  . .    21  2 DON JUAN  1      1    6
    SO AS I SAID I'LL TAKE MY FRIEND DON JUAN  . . . . .    24  2 DON JUAN  1      5    8
    THEREFORE HIS FRAILTIES I'LL NO FURTHER SCAN . . . .    40  2 DON JUAN  1     35    3
    BUT NOW I'LL BEAR NO MORE NOR HERE REMAIN  . . . . .   100  2 DON JUAN  1    145    7
    I'LL WRITE POETICAL COMMANDMENTS WHICH  . . . . . .    138  2 DON JUAN  1    204    2
    I'LL CALL THE WORK LONGINUS O'ER A BOTTLE  . . . . .   138  2 DON JUAN  1    204    7
    BUT IF YOU DON'T I'LL LAY IT ON BY GOD . . . . . . .   140  2 DON JUAN  1    206    8
    I'LL TELL YOU WHY I SAY SO FOR 'TIS JUST . . . . . .   219  2 DON JUAN  2    119    1
    I'LL TELL YOU WHO THEY WERE THIS FEMALE PAIR . . . .   222  2 DON JUAN  2    124    1
    I'LL JUST INQUIRE IF SHE BE WIFE OR MAID . . . . . .   268  2 DON JUAN  2    210    5
    THAT BEING ABOUT THE NUMBER I'LL ALLOW  . . . . . .    271  2 DON JUAN  2    216    4
    THE READER--BUT THE RULE IS --AND I'LL BRING . . . .   332  2 DON JUAN  3     97   V6
    I'LL PROVE THAT SUCH THE OPINION OF THE CRITIC IS . .   342  2 DON JUAN  3    111    7
    THEREFORE I'LL MAKE DON JUAN LEAVE THE SHIP SOON . .    397  2 DON JUAN  4     97    5
    WHY THEN I'LL SWEAR AS POET WORDY SWORE . . . . . .    404  2 DON JUAN  4    109    5
    I'LL SWEAR--AS MOTHER WORDSWORTH SWORE . . . . . . .   404  2 DON JUAN  4    109   V5
    I'LL BET SOME PAIR OF STOCKINGS BEAT PERU  . . . . .   406  2 DON JUAN  4    112   V8
    I'LL NOT BE BULLIED DECENT OR INDECENT  . . . . . .    410  2 DON JUAN  4    117   V6
    I'LL MAKE THIS POEM QUITE A MORAL MODEL  . . . . . .   412  2 DON JUAN  5      2   V8
    PERHAPS THERE'S NOTHING--I'LL NOT SAY APPALS . . . .   442  2 DON JUAN  5     56    5
    THEN IF I DO SAID JUAN I'LL BE-- HOLD  . . . . . . .   454  2 DON JUAN  5     75    1
    I'LL TAKE JUANNA WE'RE A SLENDERER PAIR  . . . . . .    29  3 DON JUAN  6     47    4
    STILL I'LL RECORD A FEW IF BUT TO ENCREASE . . . . .    74  3 DON JUAN  7     15    1
    YOUR ARM AND I'LL BET MOSCOW TO A DOLLAR . . . . . .   160  3 DON JUAN  8     97    7
    DONE I'LL NOT QUIT HER TILL SHE SEEMS SECURE . . . .   161  3 DON JUAN  8    100    2
    FOR MY PART I'LL ENLIST ON NEITHER SIDE . . . . . .    190  3 DON JUAN  9     16    5
    'TIS SAID (FOR I'LL NOT ANSWER ABOVE GROUND  . . . .   225  3 DON JUAN 10      1    3
    OUR OLD ACQUAINTANCE AND AT LEAST I'LL TRY . . . . .   266  3 DON JUAN 10     84    2
    JUST NOW ENOUGH BUT BY-AND-BY I'LL PRATTLE . . . . .   267  3 DON JUAN 10     87    7
    THAT ALL'S IDEAL--ALL OURSELVES I'LL STAKE THE . . .   269  3 DON JUAN 11      2    3
    SO TAKE HIM UP I'LL HELP YOU WITH THE LOAD . . . . .   275  3 DON JUAN 11     15    8
    AS I'LL TELL AUREA AT TO-MORROW'S ROUT  . . . . . .    332  3 DON JUAN 12     35    6
    I'LL NOT GAINSAY THE GENEROUS PUBLIC'S VOICE . . . .   334  3 DON JUAN 12     38    7
    OR IF I'M WRONG I'LL NOT BE TA'EN ABACK--  . . . . .   348  3 DON JUAN 12     71    6
    I'LL LEAVE A SINGLE READER'S EYELID DRY . . . . . .    355  3 DON JUAN 12     86    5
    I'LL NOT GAINSAY THEM IT IS NOT MY CUE . . . . . . .   359  3 DON JUAN 13      3    1
    I'LL HAVE ANOTHER FIGURE IN A TRICE--  . . . . . . .   375  3 DON JUAN 13     37    1
    I HAVE SEEN MORE THAN I'LL SAY--BUT WE WILL SEE . . .   397  3 DON JUAN 13     83    1
    YOU'LL NEVER GUESS I'LL BET YOU MILLIONS MILLIARDS-- . . 454  3 DON JUAN 14    100    7
    A KIND OF TRIUMPH I'LL NOT RECOMMEND . . . . . . . .   491  3 DON JUAN 15     79    2
    YES I'LL BEGIN A THOROUGH REFORMATION . . . . . . .    498  3 DON JUAN 15     94    4
    BUT COME I'LL SET YOUR STORY TO A TUNE . . . . . . .   517  3 DON JUAN 16     38    4
    OF THE OFFICIAL CANDIDATE I'LL TOUCH . . . . . . . .   538  3 DON JUAN 16     77    6
    OUTLINE OF AN HARANGUE--BUT I'LL TO BED  . . . . . .   538  3 DON JUAN 16     77   V5
    (I'LL TAKE THE LIKENESS I CAN FIRST COME AT)  . . . .   564  3 DON JUAN 17      4    5
ILL
    AND SOUTHEY LIVES TO SING THEM VERY ILL  . . . . . .    19  2 DON JUAN  D     16    8
```

ILL (CONTINUED)
HE HAD BEEN ILL BROUGHT UP AND WAS BORN BILIOUS . . . . 40 2 DON JUAN 1 35 8
FROM SIRE TO SON TO AUGUR GOOD OR ILL . . . . 49 2 DON JUAN 1 51 5
SOUNDS ILL IN LOVE WHATE'ER IT MAY IN MONEY . . . . . 78 2 DON JUAN 1 107 8
IT MATTERS NOT MUCH HOW BY GOOD OR ILL . . . . . . 146 2 DON JUAN 1 218 V3
AND DEEMING THERE WERE REMEDIES FOR ANY ILL . . . . . 187 2 DON JUAN 2 59 7
TWO BLANKETS STITCH'D TOGETHER ANSWERING ILL . . . . . 188 2 DON JUAN 2 61 3
SAYING HE HAD GORGED ENOUGH TO MAKE A HORSE ILL . . . 240 2 DON JUAN 2 159 8
WITH FLUTTERING DOUBTS IF ALL BE WELL OR ILL-- . . . . 286 2 DON JUAN 3 21 5
AND BEING FLUENT (SAVE INDEED WHEN FEE'D ILL) . . . . 317 2 DON JUAN 3 80 6
NOT I HE SAID HAVE SOUGHT THIS STRANGER'S ILL . . . . 368 2 DON JUAN 4 46 4
AND MAKE LIKE OTHER NYMPHS THY LOVERS ILL . . . . . 372 2 DON JUAN 4 53 4
NOW IF MY PEGASUS SHOULD NOT BE SHOD ILL . . . . . . 412 2 DON JUAN 5 2 7
AMMON'S (ILL PLEASED WITH ONE WORLD AND ONE FATHER) . 427 2 DON JUAN 5 31 8
THEIR NAMES WHO REARED IT BUT HUGE HOUSES FIT ILL-- . 444 2 DON JUAN 5 59 5
AT A PER-CENTAGE A CHILD CROSS DOG ILL . . . . . . 16 3 DON JUAN 6 21 3
BUT SUCH PRECIPITATION MAY END ILL . . . . 62 3 DON JUAN 6 114 5
TO SWALLOW FLAME AND NEVER TAKE IT ILL . . . . . . 93 3 DON JUAN 7 52 6
ONE OF WHOM SPOKE THEIR TONGUE OR WELL OR ILL . . . 95 3 DON JUAN 7 56 5
AND SWEARING IF THE INFANT CAME TO ILL . . . . . . 162 3 DON JUAN 8 102 5
AS IF HE WISHED THAT SHE SHOULD FARE LESS ILL . . . 198 3 DON JUAN 9 31 3
WHICH YOUTH WOULD NOT ACT ILL TO KEEP IN MIND) . . . 224 3 DON JUAN 9 84 5
IN HEALTH--WHEN ILL WE CALL THEM TO ATTEND US . . . 245 3 DON JUAN 10 42 3
ILL FITTED WITH HER IGNORANCE TO JOSTLE . . . . . 250 3 DON JUAN 10 52 5
ACCORDING AS YOU TAKE THINGS WELL OR ILL-- . . . . 264 3 DON JUAN 10 80 7
WHICH LOOKS ALONG THAT VALE OF GOOD AND ILL . . . . 272 3 DON JUAN 11 8 3
THE DROPS FELL FROM HIS DEATH-WOUND AND HE DREW ILL . 276 3 DON JUAN 11 16 6
LEFT IT BEFORE HE HAD BEEN TREATED VERY ILL . . . . 300 3 DON JUAN 11 64 5
THE GHOST OF VANISHED PLEASURES ONCE IN VOGUE ILL . . 304 3 DON JUAN 11 72 6
ALTHOUGH SHE WAS NOT EVIL NOR MEANT ILL . . . . . 364 3 DON JUAN 13 12 4
ESPECIALLY WHEN WE ARE ILL AT EASE . . . . 431 3 DON JUAN 14 48 2
AND THY PURE CREED MADE SANCTION OF ALL ILL . . . . 464 3 DON JUAN 15 18 4
LORD HENRY SAID HIS MUFFIN WAS ILL BUTTERED . . . . 514 3 DON JUAN 16 31 4
FAIR ADELINE ENQUIRED IF HE WERE ILL . . . . . . 514 3 DON JUAN 16 32 3
AND WHETHER FOR GOOD OR WHETHER FOR ILL . . . . . 519 3 DON JUAN 16 L 3 1
ILL-BRED
IT SURELY WAS EXCEEDINGLY ILL-BRED . . . . 97 2 DON JUAN 1 139 4
WHICH MADE HIM SEEM EXCEEDINGLY ILL-BRED . . . . . 483 2 DON JUAN 5 124 4
ILL-BREEDING
TO SAY THE BEST IT WAS EXTREME ILL-BREEDING . . . . 116 2 DON JUAN 1 174 4
ILLE
BEATUS ILLE PROCUL FROM NEGOTIIS . . . . 443 3 DON JUAN 14 77 1
ILL-GOTTEN
OF AN ILL-GOTTEN MILLION OF PIASTRES . . . . . . 222 2 DON JUAN 2 125 8
ILLICIT
YET THEY WERE HAPPY--HAPPY IN THE ILLICIT . . . . . 282 2 DON JUAN 3 13 1
ILLNESS
MADE HIS LAST ILLNESS WHEN ALL WORN AND WAN . . . . 84 3 DON JUAN 7 36 5
OF ILLNESS I GROW MUCH MORE ORTHODOX . . . . . . 270 3 DON JUAN 11 5 8
SOMETHING LIKE ILLNESS OF A SUDDEN GROWTH . . . . . 514 3 DON JUAN 16 33 4
ILLNESSES
BUT VULGAR ILLNESSES DON'T LIKE TO MEET . . . . . 168 2 DON JUAN 2 22 6
ILLS
DREADING THAT CLIMAX OF ALL HUMAN ILLS . . . . . 293 2 DON JUAN 3 35 7
LIKE THE DEATH-WATCH WITHIN OUR EARS THE ILLS . . . 117 3 DON JUAN 8 12 6
THAT MANY OF THE ILLS O'ER WHICH MAN GRIEVES . . . 444 3 DON JUAN 14 78 6
ILL-SORTED
HE AND HIS WIFE WERE AN ILL-SORTED PAIR-- . . . . 49 2 DON JUAN 1 51 6
ILL-TIMED
BABA INDIGNANT AT THIS ILL-TIMED PRIDE . . . . . 471 2 DON JUAN 5 103 1
ILLUMINATE
SUSPENDED MAY ILLUMINATE MANKIND . . . . 281 3 DON JUAN 11 27 2
ILLUMINATION
WHEN LONDON HAD A GRAND ILLUMINATION . . . . . . 88 3 DON JUAN 7 44 2
MATCHED WITH THE CONTINENT'S ILLUMINATION . . . . 280 3 DON JUAN 11 26 4
ILLUMINE
WHOSE PAMPHLETS VOLUMES NEWSPAPERS ILLUMINE US . . . 200 3 DON JUAN 9 35 3
ILLUMINED
KINDS OF GROTESQUES ILLUMINED AND HOW THEY . . . . 47 2 DON JUAN 1 46 4
ILL-USED
HAD BEEN NEGLECTED ILL-USED AND WHAT NOT . . . . . 166 3 DON JUAN 8 110 6
ILLUSION
'TIS SOMETHING NOTHING WORDS ILLUSION WIND-- . . . 328 2 DON JUAN 3 90 2
ILLUSION'S
THE ILLUSION'S GONE FOR EVER AND THOU ART . . . . 144 2 DON JUAN 1 215 5
AND AS FOR OTHER LOVE THE ILLUSION'S O'ER . . . . 316 3 DON JUAN 12 2 6
ILLUSIONS
BUT TIME STRIPS OUR ILLUSIONS OF THEIR HUE . . . . 421 2 DON JUAN 5 21 6
ILLUSTRATING
EXPOUNDING AND ILLUSTRATING THE RIDDLE . . . . . 337 3 DON JUAN 12 45 7
ILLUSTRATION
WAS--PARDON THE PEDANTIC ILLUSTRATION-- . . . . . 522 3 DON JUAN 16 43 2
ILLUSTRATIONS
TO GUIDE-BOOKS RHYMES TOURS SKETCHES ILLUSTRATIONS . 440 2 DON JUAN 5 52 8
VOLUMES WITH SIMILAR SAD ILLUSTRATIONS . . . . . 464 3 DON JUAN 15 18 7
ILLUSTRIOUS
DAMSELS GREAT WEALTH AND ILLUSTRIOUS ORDERS . . . . 235 3 DON JUAN 10 21 V7
I'M
AND GREEK--THE ALPHABET--I'M NEARLY SURE . . . . . 28 2 DON JUAN 1 13 2

                                                      PAGE VOL   CANTO STANZA LN

I'M   (CONTINUED)
    I'M A PLAIN MAN AND IN A SINGLE STATION   33   2 DON JUAN 1   22   6
    I'M NOT TO BLAME AS YOU WELL KNOW NO MORE IS . . .   37   2 DON JUAN 1   31   3
    HER EYE (I'M VERY FOND OF HANDSOME EYES)   54   2 DON JUAN 1   60   1
    I'M REALLY PUZZLED WHAT TO THINK OR SAY   59   2 DON JUAN 1   68   7
    'TIS SURELY JUAN NOW--NO I'M AFRAID   63   2 DON JUAN 1   76   7
    FOR MY PART TO SUCH DOINGS I'M A STRANGER   65   2 DON JUAN 1   80   4
    I'M FOND MYSELF OF SOLITUDE OR SO   68   2 DON JUAN 1   87   5
    I'M VERY CERTAIN MINE WOULD NOT HAVE DONE SO . . .   80   2 DON JUAN 1   110   8
    I'M SURE SHE WOULD HAVE SHRUNK AS FROM AN ASP . . .   81   2 DON JUAN 1   111   V6
    I'M ALMOST SORRY THAT I E'ER BEGUN   83   2 DON JUAN 1   115   8
    FOR MY PART I'M A MODERATE-MINDED BARD   85   2 DON JUAN 1   118   5
    I'M VERY SORRY VERY MUCH ASHAMED   85   2 DON JUAN 1   119   7
    'TWAS IN NOVEMBER BUT I'M NOT SO SURE   86   2 DON JUAN 1   121   7
    I'M FOND OF FIRE AND CRICKETS AND ALL THAT   94   2 DON JUAN 1   135   7
    WHAT WILL BECOME ON'T--I'M IN SUCH A FRIGHT . . .   115   2 DON JUAN 1   171   3
    PROSE POETS LIKE BLANK-VERSE I'M FOND OF RHYME . .   136   2 DON JUAN 1   201   5
    SOME PEOPLE LIKE BLANK VERSE I'M FOND OF RHYME . .   136   2 DON JUAN 1   201   V5
    I'M FOR A HANDSOME ARTICLE HIS CREDITOR   142   2 DON JUAN 1   210   3
    I'M SORRY THUS TO PROBE A WOUND SO RAW   155   2 DON JUAN 1 V   7   5
    BUT FOR THE PUMPS I'M GLAD TO MAKE THEM KNOWN . .   171   2 DON JUAN 2   29   4
    BUT I'M DIGRESSING WHAT ON EARTH HAD NERO   341   2 DON JUAN 3   110   1
    YOU'VE HEARD OF RAUCOCANTI--I'M THE MAN   392   2 DON JUAN 4   88   5
    BUT NEXT WHEN I'M ENGAGED TO SING THERE--DO GO . .   392   2 DON JUAN 4   88   8
    'TIS ALL THE SAME TO ME I'M FOND OF YIELDING . . .   397   2 DON JUAN 4   98   1
    I'M SENSIBLE REDUNDANCY IS WRONG   410   2 DON JUAN 4   117   5
    BESIDES I'M HUNGRY AND JUST NOW WOULD TAKE . . .   435   2 DON JUAN 5   44   7
    AND THEN I'M WITH YOU IF YOU'RE FOR A ROW   437   2 DON JUAN 5   47   8
    AND THAT'S THE REASON I'M SO MELANCHOLY   444   2 DON JUAN 5   58   8
    MIGHT TEACH THEM THIS MUCH BETTER THAN I'M ABLE . .   444   2 DON JUAN 5   59   8
    REPLIED OLD GENTLEMAN I'M NOT A LADY   453   2 DON JUAN 5   73   8
    I'M A PHILOSOPHER CONFOUND THEM ALL   17   3 DON JUAN 6   22   1
    I'M A PHILOSOPHER GOD DAMN THEM ALL   17   3 DON JUAN 6   22   V1
    I'M PUZZLED WHAT TO DO WITH YOU MY DEAR   29   3 DON JUAN 6   46   3
    DUDU WAS FOND OF KISSING--WHICH I'M SURE   35   3 DON JUAN 6   59   2
    BUT I'M TOO GREAT A PATRIOT TO RECORD   77   3 DON JUAN 7   22   2
    POOR THING WHAT'S TO BE DONE I'M PUZZLED QUITE . .   161   3 DON JUAN 8   99   8
    HEAVEN HELP ME I'M BUT LITTLE OF A PARSON   179   3 DON JUAN 8   134   4
    IS RATHER DEAR--I'M SURE I MEAN NO HARM   186   3 DON JUAN 9   7   8
    OH JACK I'M FLOORED BY THAT 'ERE BLOODY FRENCHMAN .   274   3 DON JUAN 11   13   8
    EVEN I--ALBEIT I'M SURE I DID NOT KNOW IT   296   3 DON JUAN 11   55   5
    AT LEAST IT RHYMES TO LOVE BUT I'M PREPARED . . .   322   3 DON JUAN 12   13   6
    WHY I'M POSTERITY--AND SO ARE YOU   324   3 DON JUAN 12   19   1
    I'M SERIOUS--SO ARE ALL MEN UPON PAPER   325   3 DON JUAN 12   21   1
    BUT I'M RESOLVED TO SAY NOUGHT THAT'S AMISS)-- . .   326   3 DON JUAN 12   22   6
    BUT NOW I'M GOING TO BE IMMORAL NOW   335   3 DON JUAN 12   40   1
    PERHAPS THIS NEW POSITION--BUT I'M RIGHT   348   3 DON JUAN 12   71   5
    OR IF I'M WRONG I'LL NOT BE TA'EN ABACK--   348   3 DON JUAN 12   71   6
    BUT I'M RELAPSING INTO METAPHYSICS   349   3 DON JUAN 12   72   1
    OCCURRED WHAT OFTEN HAPPENS I'M AFRAID   355   3 DON JUAN 12   85   3
    I'M AT MY OLD LUNES--DIGRESSION AND FORGET . . .   364   3 DON JUAN 13   12   1
    BUT I'M NOT OEDIPUS AND LIFE'S A SPHINX   364   3 DON JUAN 13   12   8
    OF THIS I'M SURE AT LEAST THERE'S NO SERVILITY . .   465   3 DON JUAN 15   20   5
    BUT I'M TOO LATE AND THEREFORE MUST MAKE PLAY . . .   538   3 DON JUAN 16   78   1
IMAGE
    TO ALL EXCEPT ONE IMAGE MADLY BLIND   133   2 DON JUAN 1   196   6
    THAN I RESIGN THINE IMAGE OH MY FAIR   166   2 DON JUAN 2   19   5
    WHAT THOUGH 'TIS BUT A PICTURED IMAGE STRIKE-- . .   336   2 DON JUAN 3   103   7
    BEHOLDS HER OWN SHY SHADOWY IMAGE PASS   36   3 DON JUAN 6   60   6
    WITH WHICH MEN IMAGE OUT THE UNKNOWN THING   188   3 DON JUAN 9   11   2
    O'ER LIFE TOO SWEET AN IMAGE FOR SUCH GLASS . . .   475   3 DON JUAN 15   43   6
IMAGED
    WAS IMAGED BACK IN BLOOD THE SEA OF SLAUGHTER . .   172   3 DON JUAN 8   122   8
    BUT DEATH IS IMAGED IN THEIR SHADOWY BEAMS   509   3 DON JUAN 16   19   6
IMAGES
    THEIR IMAGES AGAIN AS IN A GLASS   402   2 DON JUAN 4   107   5
IMAGINARY
    OF THINE IMAGINARY DEATHLESS TREE   101   3 DON JUAN 7   68   7
    ALTHOUGH 'TIS AN IMAGINARY THING   296   3 DON JUAN 11   55   4
IMAGINATION
    FOR THE IMAGINATION OR THE SENSES   293   2 DON JUAN 3   35   2
    LEAF AND IMAGINATION DROOPS HER PINION   345   2 DON JUAN 4   3   6
    AND MONEY THAT MOST PURE IMAGINATION   316   3 DON JUAN 12   2   7
    LONGBOW WAS RICH IN AN IMAGINATION   401   3 DON JUAN 13   92   5
IMAGINATION'S
    IMAGINATION'S QUITE ENOUGH FOR THAT   463   3 DON JUAN 15   16   3
IMAGINE
    WITH ALL WE CAN IMAGINE OF THE SKIES   313   2 DON JUAN 3   74   4
    REMEMBER OR (IF YOU CAN NOT) IMAGINE   486   2 DON JUAN 5   130   1
IMAGINED
    BUT NOT AS YET IMAGINED IT COULD BE A   68   2 DON JUAN 1   86   6
    HAD SHE IMAGINED SUCH A THING COULD ROUSE   81   2 DON JUAN 1   111   7
IMBIBED
    IMBIBED THE GAY BON MOT OR HAPPY HOAX   540   3 DON JUAN 16   83   5
IMITATE
    I WOULD NOT IMITATE THE PETTY THOUGHT   12   2 DON JUAN D   6   1
IMITATING
    AT LAST FALL SICK OF IMITATING JOB   137   3 DON JUAN 8   50   8
IMMACULATE
    BRIGHT AND IMMACULATE UNMIX'D AND PURE   64   2 DON JUAN 1   79   2

                                          390

		PAGE	VOL		CANTO	STANZA	LN
IMMATERIALISM'S							
FOR IMMATERIALISM'S A SERIOUS MATTER		556	3	DON JUAN	16	114	6
IMMEDIATE							
BUT WHEN THEY LIGHT UPON IMMEDIATE DEATH		133	3	DON JUAN	8	40	7
OF THESE BRIEF BLOSSOMS THE IMMEDIATE FRUITS		168	3	DON JUAN	8	113	8
BUT THAT AT PRESENT WITH IMMEDIATE REFERENCE		469	3	DON JUAN	15	30	3
BUT SO FAR THE IMMEDIATE EFFECT		526	3	DON JUAN	16	52	1
IMMEDIATELY							
IMMEDIATELY THE MASTS WERE CUT AWAY		173	2	DON JUAN	2	32	1
WHEREON IMMEDIATELY AT HIS REQUEST		96	3	DON JUAN	7	57	1
IMMEDIATELY IN OTHERS GREW AGAIN		113	3	DON JUAN	8	2	8
THE WHOLE COURT LOOKED IMMEDIATELY MOST SWEET		213	3	DON JUAN	9	61	3
IMMEMOR							
AND ET SEPULCHRI IMMEMOR STRUIS DOMOS		448	2	DON JUAN	5	63	7
IMMEMORIAL							
WHICH BOUNDS RAVENNA'S IMMEMORIAL WOOD		337	2	DON JUAN	3	105	3
IMMENSE							
THE PRECIPICE SHE STOOD ON WAS IMMENSE		78	2	DON JUAN	1	106	7
THOU HAST STRUCK ONE IMMENSE COLOSSUS DOWN		445	3	DON JUAN	14	82	3
IMMERSION							
ARISE LIKE TITAN FROM THE SEA'S IMMERSION		14	2	DON JUAN	D	9	6
ONE HALF SATE UP THOUGH NUMB'D WITH THE IMMERSION		189	2	DON JUAN	2	63	4
IMMORAL							
IMMORAL CONDUCT BY THE FANCIED SWAY		84	2	DON JUAN	1	116	3
WHO TO IMMORAL COURSES WOULD ALLURE US		267	2	DON JUAN	2	207	3
COMMODIOUS BUT IMMORAL THEY ARE FOUND		282	3	DON JUAN	11	30	6
BUT NOW I'M GOING TO BE IMMORAL NOW		335	3	DON JUAN	12	40	1
IMMORALITY							
THE TROUBLE THAT THEY GAVE THEIR IMMORALITY		64	3	DON JUAN	6	117	7
AND KNEW NO BETTER IN HER IMMORALITY		532	3	DON JUAN	16	64	7
IMMORTAL							
AND DULY SEATED ON THE IMMORTAL HILL		12	2	DON JUAN	D	6	8
HE THOUGHT OF WOOD NYMPHS AND IMMORTAL BOWERS		72	2	DON JUAN	1	94	3
BY THE IMMORTAL WISH AND POWER TO BLESS		357	2	DON JUAN	4	26	8
LIKE MODERATE HOTSPUR ON THE IMMORTAL PAGE		490	2	DON JUAN	5	136	4
LIKE NATURAL SHAKESPEARE ON THE IMMORTAL PAGE		490	2	DON JUAN	5	136	V4
WHO WERE IMMORTAL COULD ONE TELL THEIR STORY		73	3	DON JUAN	7	14	4
HE FELL IMMORTAL IN A BULLETIN		76	3	DON JUAN	7	20	8
SOULS OF IMMORTAL GENERALS PHOEBUS WATCHES		107	3	DON JUAN	7	81	7
ARE THINGS IMMORTAL TO IMMORTAL MAN		108	3	DON JUAN	7	84	2
ARE THINGS IMMORTAL TO IMMORTAL MAN		108	3	DON JUAN	7	84	2
OF GLORY AND ALL THAT IMMORTAL STUFF		134	3	DON JUAN	8	42	4
OH YE IMMORTAL GODS WHAT IS THEOGONY		192	3	DON JUAN	9	20	1
OF THE IMMORTAL PETER'S POLISHED BOORS		194	3	DON JUAN	9	23	3
FOR EVER SINCE IMMORTAL MAN HATH GLOWED		226	3	DON JUAN	10	2	6
WHICH LEAVES FEW DROPS OF THAT IMMORTAL RAIN		375	3	DON JUAN	13	37	4
IN SOULS IMMORTAL SHUN THEM TETE A TETE		556	3	DON JUAN	16	114	8
IMMORTALITY							
WHEN I CALL FADING MARTIAL IMMORTALITY		108	3	DON JUAN	7	83	1
IMMOVEABLE							
BUT JUAN WAS IMMOVEABLE UNTIL		162	3	DON JUAN	8	102	1
IMP							
UPON THE MOST UNQUIET IMP ON EARTH		34	2	DON JUAN	1	25	4
IMPALED							
TO BE IMPALED OR QUARTERED AS A DISH		492	2	DON JUAN	5	141	2
IMPALEMENT							
WE FROM IMPALEMENT HAD ENSURED OUR SKIN		435	2	DON JUAN	5	44	V4
IMPART							
OH CAESAR'S COMMENTARIES NOW IMPART YE		108	3	DON JUAN	7	82	5
IMPARTIAL							
IMPARTIAL BETWEEN TYRIAN AND TROJAN		497	3	DON JUAN	15	92	3
BY AN IMPARTIAL INDEMNIFICATION		550	3	DON JUAN	16	103	2
IMPATIENCE							
HIS HASTE IMPATIENCE IS A BLUNDERING GUIDE		304	3	DON JUAN	11	71	6
IMPATIENT							
TOWARDS WHICH THE IMPATIENT WIND BLEW HALF A GALE		256	3	DON JUAN	10	64	3
IMPATIENTLY							
LETS OUT IMPATIENTLY HIS RUSHING BREATH		412	3	DON JUAN	14	4	7
IMPEDE							
SO PLACED AS TO IMPEDE THE FIRE OF THOSE		71	3	DON JUAN	7	10	7
SUCH MEASURES AS SHE THOUGHT MIGHT BEST IMPEDE		437	3	DON JUAN	14	61	2
IMPERATIVE							
THE MOST IMPERATIVE OF SOVEREIGN SPELLS		393	2	DON JUAN	4	91	3
MONARCHS ARE LESS IMPERATIVE THAN RHYMES)--		456	2	DON JUAN	5	77	8
EVEN AT YOUR OWN IMPERATIVE EXPENSE		62	3	DON JUAN	6	114	6
IMPERIAL							
BUT NOT ENOUGH TO SHOW THE IMPERIAL HALLS		442	2	DON JUAN	5	56	3
IN THIS IMPERIAL HALL AT DISTANCE LAY		466	2	DON JUAN	5	95	1
IN KINGLY CHAMBERS OR IMPERIAL HALLS		471	2	DON JUAN	5	103	7
SOMETHING IMPERIAL OR IMPERIOUS THREW		474	2	DON JUAN	5	110	1
AT LENGTH IN AN IMPERIAL WAY SHE LAID		483	2	DON JUAN	5	125	1
OF THEM HIS LIPS IMPERIAL EVER SPAKE		501	2	DON JUAN	5	156	6
HAD BOWED THEMSELVES BEFORE THE IMPERIAL EYES		19	3	DON JUAN	6	26	3
THINE EAR IMPERIAL AND JUST NOW RHYMES WANDER		52	3	DON JUAN	6	93	V3
THE IMPERIAL BRIDE--AND ADDED LET THE BOAT		62	3	DON JUAN	6	113	2
FOR THE IMPERIAL PRESENCE WHERIN WHETHER		65	3	DON JUAN	6	119	2
LIKE AN IMPERIAL PEACOCK STALK ABROAD		104	3	DON JUAN	7	74	5
OF THE IMPERIAL FAVOURITE'S CONDITION		208	3	DON JUAN	9	52	3
HER PLUMPNESS HER IMPERIAL CONDESCENSION		218	3	DON JUAN	9	72	2
YOUR HAND AT HARDENED AND IMPERIAL SIN		266	3	DON JUAN	10	85	4

391

		PAGE	VOL		CANTO	STANZA	LN
IMPERIOUS							
SOMETHING IMPERIAL OR IMPERIOUS THREW		474	2 DON JUAN		5	110	1
FELL INTO THAT NO LESS IMPERIOUS PASSION		216	3 DON JUAN		9	68	2
WHICH KNOWS NO EBB TO ITS IMPERIOUS FLOW		366	3 DON JUAN		13	16	6
AND WITH AN AIR TO SAY THE LEAST IMPERIOUS		477	3 DON JUAN		15	49	6
IMPERTURBABLE							
COOL AND QUITE ENGLISH IMPERTURBABLE		365	3 DON JUAN		13	14	4
IMPIOUS							
FIRING THE COUNTIES TILL THEY IMPIOUS WAR WAGE		530	3 DON JUAN		16	60	V5
IMPLORED							
IMPLORED THAT PRESENT PARDON MIGHT BE SHOWN		47	3 DON JUAN		6	82	4
IMPORT							
A THING OF MUCH LESS IMPORT IN THAT CLIME--		51	3 DON JUAN		6	90	5
THE IMPORT OF THIS DIPLOMATIC PHRASE		207	3 DON JUAN		9	49	2
OF IMPORT BOTH TO VIRGIN AND TO BRIDE		292	3 DON JUAN		11	46	2
IMPORTANT							
BY WINDS AND WAVES AND SOME IMPORTANT CAPTURES		283	2 DON JUAN		3	15	2
PRIVATE THOUGH PUBLICLY IMPORTANT BORE		283	2 DON JUAN		11	32	2
A MOST IMPORTANT OUTWORK OF THE CITY--		545	3 DON JUAN		16	93	6
IMPORTUNE							
WHOSE AVARICE ALL DISBURSEMENTS DID IMPORTUNE		222	3 DON JUAN		9	81	3
IMPORTUNITY							
WORN OUT WITH IMPORTUNITY OR FALL		333	3 DON JUAN		12	37	2
IMPOSE							
SOME PEOPLE WOULD IMPOSE NOW WITH AUTHORITY		503	3 DON JUAN		16	5	1
IMPOSED							
IMPOSED NOT UPON HER SHE SAW HER BLAZE		480	3 DON JUAN		15	56	2
IMPOSING							
AND TAKE WHAT KINGS CALL AN IMPOSING ATTITUDE		11	3 DON JUAN		6	11	4
IMPOSSIBILE							
QUIETS AT ONCE WITH QUIA IMPOSSIBILE		503	3 DON JUAN		16	5	8
IMPOSSIBLE							
BUT THAT'S IMPOSSIBLE AND CANNOT BE--		166	2 DON JUAN		2	19	2
WHO BIDS ALL MEN BELIEVE THE IMPOSSIBLE		503	3 DON JUAN		16	5	6
AND IF IT IS IMPOSSIBLE YOU SHALL		503	3 DON JUAN		16	6	3
IMPOSTORS							
(A RACE OF MERE IMPOSTORS WHEN ALL'S DONE--		218	2 DON JUAN		2	118	6
IMPOSTURE							
LABOUR THERE'S A SURE MARKET FOR IMPOSTURE		91	2 DON JUAN		1	128	8
IMPRACTICABLE							
TO THAT IMPRACTICABLE PLACE TIMBUCTOO		348	3 DON JUAN		12	70	3
TO THIS IMPRACTICABLE NOVEL-READING TRANCE		450	3 DON JUAN		14	92	V6
IMPRESARIO							
BUT SOLD BY THE IMPRESARIO AT NO HIGH RATE		388	2 DON JUAN		4	80	8
SAYING OUR MACHIAVELIAN IMPRESARIO		389	2 DON JUAN		4	82	2
SAYING OUR PORCO OF AN IMPRESARIO		389	2 DON JUAN		4	82	V2
IMPRESS							
THAT NOVELTIES PLEASE LESS THAN THEY IMPRESS		347	3 DON JUAN		12	69	8
IMPRESS'D							
WAS NOT AT FIRST TOO READILY IMPRESS'D		448	3 DON JUAN		14	88	8
IMPRESSION							
'TWAS STRANGE ENOUGH SHE SHOULD RETAIN THE IMPRESSION		252	3 DON JUAN		10	56	1
SECURE OF ADMIRATION ITS IMPRESSION		372	3 DON JUAN		13	31	7
YET LEFT A GRAND IMPRESSION ON THE MIND		390	3 DON JUAN		13	67	5
WITH THIS DEBUT WHICH MADE A STRONG IMPRESSION		400	3 DON JUAN		13	90	6
FORBIDS A GREAT IMPRESSION IN MY YOUTH		403	3 DON JUAN		13	96	6
RETIRE BUT LOOK INTO YOUR PAST IMPRESSION		413	3 DON JUAN		14	6	2
THESE SEALS UPON HER WAX MADE NO IMPRESSION		480	3 DON JUAN		15	57	7
MAKE MORE IMPRESSION THAN THE BEST OF BOOKS		493	3 DON JUAN		15	84	8
IMPRESSIONS							
IMPRESSIONS WERE MUCH STRONGER THAN SHE GUESS'D		448	3 DON JUAN		14	88	5
IMPRIMATUR							
YOUR IMPRIMATUR WILL YE NOT ANNEX		403	2 DON JUAN		4	108	4
IMPRINT							
AND FOR ONE KISS WOULD FAIN IMPRINT A BRACE		472	2 DON JUAN		5	106	5
IMPROBABLE							
BELIEVE--IF 'TIS IMPROBABLE YOU MUST		503	3 DON JUAN		16	6	2
IMPROPER							
OF AN IMPROPER FRIENDSHIP FOR HER HORSE		446	2 DON JUAN		5	61	3
IMPROVE							
SHE HOPED HE WOULD IMPROVE--PERHAPS BELIEVED		161	2 DON JUAN		2	9	6
IMPROVED							
RUIN'D ITS BLOOD BUT MUCH IMPROVED ITS FLESH		53	2 DON JUAN		1	58	2
AND IS NOT MUCH IMPROVED BY GROWING OLD		516	3 DON JUAN		16	37	8
IMPROVEMENT							
AND THEN AS AN IMPROVEMENT 'TWILL BE SHOWN		342	3 DON JUAN		3	111	6
FROM MUCH IMPROVEMENT WITH THAT VIRTUOUS PLOUGH		335	3 DON JUAN		12	40	5
IMPROVEMENTS							
THOSE MOVEMENTS THOSE IMPROVEMENTS IN OUR BODIES		220	3 DON JUAN		9	75	1
IMPROVING							
IMPROVING STILL THROUGH EVERY GENERATION		54	2 DON JUAN		1	59	2
'TWAS WONDERFUL HOW THINGS WENT ON IMPROVING		295	2 DON JUAN		3	39	7
WITH RHYME BUT ALWAYS LEANT LESS TO IMPROVING		219	3 DON JUAN		9	74	6
IMPROVVISATORE							
JUST AS I FEEL THE IMPROVVISATORE		465	3 DON JUAN		15	20	8
IMPRUDENT							
TO LEAVE TOGETHER THIS IMPRUDENT PAIR		80	2 DON JUAN		1	110	6
BUT MORE IMPRUDENT GROWN WITH EVERY VISIT		282	2 DON JUAN		3	13	3
BECAUSE A FOOLISH OR IMPRUDENT ACT		58	3 DON JUAN		6	104	4

392

		PAGE	VOL	CANTO	STANZA	LN
IMPS						
WERE SATE LIKE UGLY IMPS AS IF ALLIED		462	2 DON JUAN	5	87	4
IMPULSE						
A DREADFUL IMPULSE TO EACH LOUD MEANDER		52	3 DON JUAN	6	93	5
A THING OF IMPULSE AND A CHILD OF SONG		123	3 DON JUAN	8	24	2
AND THAT ODD IMPULSE WHICH IN WARS OR CREEDS		132	3 DON JUAN	8	38	7
CHIEF IMPULSE WITH A FEW FRAIL PAPER PELLETS		298	3 DON JUAN	11	60	V8
IMPUTED						
WHO HAVE IMPUTED SUCH DESIGNS AS SHOW		347	2 DON JUAN	4	7	3
IMPUTES						
FOR MALICE STILL IMPUTES SOME PRIVATE END)		58	2 DON JUAN	1	66	6
INANITION						
MEN EVEN WHEN DYING DISLIKE INANITION		180	2 DON JUAN	2	46	5
THE FAIR SULTANA ERRED FROM INANITION		10	3 DON JUAN	6	9	5
TO BE PURSUED AS FOOD FOR INANITION)		328	3 DON JUAN	12	27	6
INANITY						
AND IN THIS SCENE OF ALL-CONFESSED INANITY		69	3 DON JUAN	7	6	5
ITSELF WITH BEAUTY'S FRAIL INANITY		219	3 DON JUAN	9	73	5
OR MODESTY OR ABSENCE OR INANITY		490	3 DON JUAN	15	78	6
INARTICULATE						
(HERE HE GREW INARTICULATE WITH RETCHING)		167	2 DON JUAN	2	20	8
INCARNATE						
THAN EVEN THE TAILOR'S) HIS INCARNATE SKIN		188	3 DON JUAN	9	12	7
EVEN SHUFFLING SOUTHEY THAT INCARNATE LIE		231	3 DON JUAN	10	13	2
INCENSE						
THE THINGS DOWN SAID--INCENSE ME AND I CALL		454	2 DON JUAN	5	75	7
INCESSANT						
WHOSE RAYS SHONE EVER TREMBLING BUT INCESSANT		315	2 DON JUAN	3	77	8
ARE QUESTIONS ANSWERLESS AND YET INCESSANT		37	3 DON JUAN	6	63	8
INCH						
'TWAS BLOW FOR BLOW DISPUTING INCH BY INCH		150	3 DON JUAN	8	77	7
'TWAS BLOW FOR BLOW DISPUTING INCH BY INCH		150	3 DON JUAN	8	77	7
AND GAIN AN INCH OF STAIRCASE AT A TIME		302	3 DON JUAN	11	68	8
AYE EVERY INCH A DUKE THERE WERE TWELVE PEERS		398	3 DON JUAN	13	85	2
NOR BATE (ABATE) THEIR HEARERS OF AN INCH		404	3 DON JUAN	13	98	4
INCIDENTS						
AND THERE ARE OTHER INCIDENTS REMAINING		135	2 DON JUAN	1	200	V6
SOME YEARS BEFORE THE INCIDENTS RELATED		286	3 DON JUAN	11	37	8
INCISION						
CUT THROUGH AND THROUGH (OH DAMNABLE INCISION)		536	3 DON JUAN	16	74	6
INCLINATION						
HER VERY NOD WAS NOT AN INCLINATION		475	2 DON JUAN	5	111	2
IN ANSWER MADE AN INCLINATION TO		141	3 DON JUAN	8	57	3
HE HAD A KIND OF INCLINATION OR		249	3 DON JUAN	10	50	4
AN AWKWARD INCLINATION TO GO WRONG		338	3 DON JUAN	12	48	4
INCLINED						
THE WORLD AS USUAL WICKEDLY INCLINED		31	2 DON JUAN	1	19	5
HIS HIGHNESS QUITE CONNUBIALLY INCLINED		12	3 DON JUAN	6	13	V5
HE FIRST INCLINED TO THINK HE HAD BEEN MISTAKEN		558	3 DON JUAN	16	118	3
INCLINES						
TASTE OR THE GOUT--PRONOUNCE IT AS INCLINES		488	3 DON JUAN	15	72	3
INCLOSED						
THE PUREST ORE INCLOSED THE WHITEST SKIN		312	2 DON JUAN	3	71	7
INCOME						
ENQUIRED HIS INCOME AND IF HE HAD BROTHERS		293	3 DON JUAN	11	48	8
INCOMES						
AT LEAST TO THOSE OF INCOMES WHICH AFFORD		51	3 DON JUAN	6	90	6
INCOME-TAX						
A SORT OF INCOME-TAX LAID ON BY FATE		122	2 DON JUAN	1	183	4
INCOMPARABLE						
SAVE THINE INCOMPARABLE OIL MACASSAR		30	2 DON JUAN	1	17	8
INCOMPLETE						
THE RUSSIAN BATTERIES WERE INCOMPLETE		79	3 DON JUAN	7	26	1
INCONSTANCY						
I HATE INCONSTANCY--I LOATHE DETEST		268	2 DON JUAN	2	209	1
MEN CALL INCONSTANCY IS NOTHING MORE		269	2 DON JUAN	2	211	2
WRITE ODES ON THE INCONSTANCY OF WOMAN		288	2 DON JUAN	3	24	8
INCONTINENT						
YOUR CONTINENTAL OATHS ARE BUT INCONTINENT		289	3 DON JUAN	11	43	2
INCONVENIENCE						
THE INCONVENIENCE OF CIVILIZATION		144	3 DON JUAN	8	64	5
INCONVENIENT						
TO THOSE WHO HAD FELT THE INCONVENIENT STATE		177	3 DON JUAN	8	131	3
INCORRECT						
MADE ALL THEIR NAVAL MATTERS INCORRECT		80	3 DON JUAN	7	28	2
INCORRIGIBLE						
WITH ALL KINDS OF INCORRIGIBLE SAMPLES		236	3 DON JUAN	10	23	6
INCREASED						
HIS HEADACHE BEING INCREASED BY EVERY BILLOW		169	2 DON JUAN	2	25	6
INCREASED AT NIGHT UNTIL IT BLEW A GALE		170	2 DON JUAN	2	26	2
THE LEAK INCREASED SHOALS ROUND HER BUT NO SHORE		176	2 DON JUAN	2	38	3
FEEL NOW HIS APPETITE INCREASED MUCH MORE		198	2 DON JUAN	2	78	5
THEIR CHARITY INCREASED ABOUT THEIR GUEST		225	2 DON JUAN	2	131	5
WHOSE VICTORIES HAD RECENTLY INCREASED		52	3 DON JUAN	6	92	6
INCREASES						
WHICH ALWAYS SPOILS THE BREED IF IT INCREASES		52	2 DON JUAN	1	57	8
HARK HOW THE ROAR INCREASES--NO EXCUSE		162	3 DON JUAN	8	101	5
INCREASES TILL YOU SHALL MAKE COMMON CAUSE		196	3 DON JUAN	9	28	6
INCREASING						
HE SAW INCREASING ON HIS FATHER'S HEART		203	2 DON JUAN	2	88	7

```
                                                           PAGE VOL     CANTO  STANZA  LN
INCREMENT
    HIS MUSE MADE INCREMENT OF ANYTHING  . . . . . . . . 319  2 DON JUAN  3      85    5
INCUBI
    AND LOOKING LIKE TWO INCUBI THEY GLARED . . . . . . . 463  2 DON JUAN  5      90    2
INCUMBRANCE
    WITHOUT EVEN THE INCUMBRANCE OF A BROTHER . . . . . . 248  2 DON JUAN  2     175    5
INCURR'D
    OR PERILS BY A LOVING MAID INCURR'D  . . . . . . . . 257  2 DON JUAN  2     190    4
INDE
    FROM CEYLON INDE OR FAR CATHAY UNLOADS . . . . . . . 320  3 DON JUAN 12       9    2
INDECENT
    AND ALL THE FAULT OF THAT INDECENT SUN  . . . . . . . 56  2 DON JUAN  1      63    2
    I'LL NOT BE BULLIED DECENT OR INDECENT . . . . . . . 410  2 DON JUAN  4     117   V6
INDECISION
    THEIR OBSTINACY PRIDE AND INDECISION . . . . . . . .  64  3 DON JUAN  6     117    5
INDEED'S
    THE LAST INDEED'S INFALLIBLY THE CASE . . . . . . . . 74  2 DON JUAN  1      99    6
    OR EVEN MERE FASHION WHICH INDEED'S THE BEST . . . . 370  3 DON JUAN 13      28    6
INDEMNIFICATION
    BY AN IMPARTIAL INDEMNIFICATION . . . . . . . . . . . 550  3 DON JUAN 16     103    2
INDEMNIFIES
    WHILE THE HARSH PRUDE INDEMNIFIES HER VIRTUE . . . . 337  3 DON JUAN 12      45    1
INDENTURES
    INTO THE EXCURSIVE BREAKING THE INDENTURES . . . . . 284  3 DON JUAN 11      33    5
INDEPENDENCE
    THAN THOSE WHO WERE NOT PAID FOR INDEPENDENCE . . . . 537  3 DON JUAN 16      76    2
INDEPENDENT
    BY HIS SEEMING INDEPENDENT IN HIS LAYS . . . . . . . 316  2 DON JUAN  3      79    6
    AN INDEPENDENT BEING IN HIS DAY-- . . . . . . . . . . 328  2 DON JUAN  3      91    3
    QUITE INDEPENDENT OF THE ZODIAC'S SIGNS . . . . . . . 423  3 DON JUAN 14      29    3
    HE WAS AS INDEPENDENT--AYE MUCH MORE-- . . . . . . . 537  3 DON JUAN 16      76    1
    HINTS FROM THE INDEPENDENT HEART OR HEAD . . . . . . 538  3 DON JUAN 16      77    5
INDEX
    WHICH SAVES IN FACT THE TROUBLE OF AN INDEX . . . . . 46  2 DON JUAN  1      44    8
    TO COME BETWEEN MINE EPIC AND ITS INDEX . . . . . . . 440  3 DON JUAN 14      68    8
INDIA
    LOLAH WAS DUSK AS INDIA AND AS WARM  . . . . . . . .  26  3 DON JUAN  6      41    1
    UNTO THE GLOWING INDIA OF THE SOUL . . . . . . . . . 376  3 DON JUAN 13      39    2
INDIAN
    HAD DONE THEIR WORK OF SPLENDOUR INDIAN MATS . . . . 310  2 DON JUAN  3      68    2
    WHICH THE WEST INDIAN MARKET SCARCE WOULD BRING . . . 408  2 DON JUAN  4     115    2
    AS AN EAST INDIAN SUNRISE ON THE MAIN . . . . . . . . 212  3 DON JUAN  9      59    4
INDICATE
    WHAT SLAVES HER HIGHNESS WISHED TO INDICATE . . . . .  62  3 DON JUAN  6     112    7
    TO INDICATE A CUPIDON BROKE LOOSE . . . . . . . . . . 461  3 DON JUAN 15      12    6
INDICATIONS
    AND INDICATIONS OF HYSTERICS WHOSE . . . . . . . . . 110  2 DON JUAN  1     162    3
    'MIDST OTHER INDICATIONS OF FESTIVITY . . . . . . . . 290  2 DON JUAN  3      29    4
INDICATIVE
    WHILE ALL WITHOUT'S INDICATIVE OF REST . . . . . . . 457  3 DON JUAN 15       3   V3
    INDICATIVE OF SOME SURPRISE AND PITY . . . . . . . . 545  3 DON JUAN 16      93    2
INDIFFERENCE
    BECAUSE INDIFFERENCE BEGINS TO LULL  . . . . . . . . 360  3 DON JUAN 13       4    5
    THAT POLISH OF INDIFFERENCE--IN THE MANNER . . . . . 373  3 DON JUAN 13      34   V2
    INDIFFERENCE CERTES DON'T PRODUCE DISTRESS . . . . . 374  3 DON JUAN 13      35    6
    AURORA SAT WITH THAT INDIFFERENCE . . . . . . . . . . 490  3 DON JUAN 15      77    1
    AURORA WHO IN HER INDIFFERENCE . . . . . . . . . . . 493  3 DON JUAN 15      83    1
INDIFFERENT
    INDIFFERENT FROM THE FIRST OR CALLOUS GROWN . . . . .  59  2 DON JUAN  1      68    6
    BREAD HAS BEEN MADE (INDIFFERENT) FROM POTATOES . . .  92  2 DON JUAN  1     130    1
    BUT ADELINE WAS NOT INDIFFERENT FOR . . . . . . . . . 374  3 DON JUAN 13      36    1
    HARD LABOUR'S AN INDIFFERENT GO-BETWEEN . . . . . . . 443  3 DON JUAN 14      76    5
INDIGESTION
    HAD BEEN AS SHORT IN YOUTH AS INDIGESTION . . . . . .  84  3 DON JUAN  7      36    4
    WHAT INDIGESTION IS--THAT INWARD FATE . . . . . . . . 190  3 DON JUAN  9      15    4
    FOREVER AND ANON COMES INDIGESTION . . . . . . . . . 269  3 DON JUAN 11       3    1
INDIGESTION'S
    AND INDIGESTION'S GRAND MULTIPLICATION . . . . . . . 486  3 DON JUAN 15      69    3
INDIGNANT
    BABA INDIGNANT AT THIS ILL-TIMED PRIDE . . . . . . . 471  2 DON JUAN  5     103    1
    FELT MOST INDIGNANT STILL AT NOT BEING FREE . . . . . 481  2 DON JUAN  5     121    8
INDISPENSABLE
    A THING IN FOOTING INDISPENSABLE . . . . . . . . . . 427  3 DON JUAN 14      38    5
INDISPENSIBLE
    UNDER PRETENCE OF BUSINESS INDISPENSIBLE . . . . . . 103  2 DON JUAN  1     151    2
INDISPOSED
    HE HAD BEEN RATHER INDISPOSED OF LATE . . . . . . . . 199  2 DON JUAN  2      81    5
INDISTINCT
    'TWAS WHITE AND INDISTINCT NOR STOPP'D TO MEET . . . 361  2 DON JUAN  4      32    6
INDITERS
    AS SERIOUS AS IF I HAD FOR INDITERS  . . . . . . . . 325  3 DON JUAN 12      20    4
    WHY DO THEIR SKETCHES FAIL THEM AS INDITERS . . . . . 418  3 DON JUAN 14      20    5
INDITING
    AS THE PSALM SAYS INDITING A GOOD MATTER . . . . . . 316  2 DON JUAN  3      78    8
INDIVIDUAL
    BUT WHERE HE MET THE INDIVIDUAL MAN  . . . . . . . . 144  3 DON JUAN  8      64    7
    NATIONS SHE LIKED MAN AS AN INDIVIDUAL . . . . . . . 214  3 DON JUAN  9      63    8
    THE HUMBLEST INDIVIDUAL UNDER HEAVEN . . . . . . . . 309  3 DON JUAN 11      82    3
IN-DOOR
    OF IN-DOOR COMFORTS STILL SHE HATH A MINE-- . . . . . 395  3 DON JUAN 13      77    5
    AND IN-DOOR LIFE IS LESS POETICAL . . . . . . . . . . 423  3 DON JUAN 14      30    1
```

INDUCED
    THEIR BOSOMS WHO HAVE BEEN INDUCED TO ROAM 286   2 DON JUAN 3   21   4
    WITH COST AND CARE AND WARMTH INDUCED TO SHOOT 38   3 DON JUAN 6   65   4
INDUES
    FROM IGNORANCE OF DANGER WHICH INDUES 131   3 DON JUAN 8   36   4
INDULGE
    OR OLD INDULGE MAN WITH A SECOND SIGHT   496   3 DON JUAN 15   90   6
INDULGENCE
    INDULGENCE OF THEIR INNOCENT DESIRES 282   2 DON JUAN 3   13   2
INEBRIETY
    WERE NOTHING BUT A MORAL INEBRIETY 374   3 DON JUAN 13   35   8
INEFFABLY
    INEFFABLY--LEGITIMATELY VILE 17   2 DON JUAN 0   13   2
INERT
    EXCLAIMING FOOLING SWEARING AT THE INERT 96   3 DON JUAN 7   58   3
INEXPERIENCE
    YET INEXPERIENCE COULD NOT BE HIS BAR 347   3 DON JUAN 12   69   6
    HIS INEXPERIENCE MOVED HER GENTLE RUTH   432   3 DON JUAN 14   51   7
INEXPLICABLE
    THAT SAD INEXPLICABLE BEAST OF PREY-- 207   3 DON JUAN 9   50   2
    A TERM INEXPLICABLE TO THE MUSE 224   3 DON JUAN 9   84   8
INEZ
    THAT WHICH ADORN'D THE BRAIN OF DONNA INEZ 27   2 DON JUAN 1   11   8
    NOW DONNA INEZ HAD WITH ALL HER MERIT 32   2 DON JUAN 1   20   1
    DON JOSE AND THE DONNA INEZ LED 35   2 DON JUAN 1   26   1
    FOR INEZ CALL'D SOME DRUGGISTS AND PHYSICIANS 35   2 DON JUAN 1   27   1
    INEZ BECAME SOLE GUARDIAN WHICH WAS FAIR 42   2 DON JUAN 1   37   5
    BUT THAT WHICH DONNA INEZ MOST DESIRED 43   2 DON JUAN 1   39   1
    FOR DONNA INEZ DREADED THE MYTHOLOGY 44   2 DON JUAN 1   41   8
    'TIS NOT WITH DONNA INEZ I WOULD SHUT 50   2 DON JUAN 1   52   5
    WITH DONNA INEZ QUITE A FAVOURITE FRIEND 58   2 DON JUAN 1   66   2
    THAT INEZ HAD ERE DON ALFONSO'S MARRIAGE 58   2 DON JUAN 1   66   7
    IS THAT THE DONNA INEZ DID NOT TEASE 73   2 DON JUAN 1   97   5
    BUT INEZ WAS SO ANXIOUS AND SO CLEAR 75   2 DON JUAN 1   101   1
    ALFONSO'S LOVES WITH INEZ WERE WELL KNOWN 118   2 DON JUAN 1   176   2
    TO SPEAK OF INEZ NOW WERE ONE MAY SAY 118   2 DON JUAN 1   177   7
    BUT DONNA INEZ TO DIVERT THE TRAIN 128   2 DON JUAN 1   190   1
    BUT TO OUR TALE THE DONNA INEZ SENT 161   2 DON JUAN 2   8   1
    HE WAS TO TRAVEL AND THOUGH INEZ GRIEVED 161   2 DON JUAN 2   9   4
    BRAVE INEZ NOW SET UP A SUNDAY SCHOOL 162   2 DON JUAN 2   10   2
    HIS MOTHER DONNA INEZ FINDING TOO 240   3 DON JUAN 10   31   1
INFALLIBLE
    HE SCRATCHED HIS EAR THE INFALLIBLE RESOURCE 56   3 DON JUAN 6   100   7
INFALLIBLY
    THE LAST INDEED'S INFALLIBLY THE CASE 74   2 DON JUAN 1   99   6
INFANCY
    ALTHOUGH IN INFANCY A LITTLE WILD 49   2 DON JUAN 1   50   3
    AND TENDERNESS AND INFANCY BUT NOW 367   2 DON JUAN 4   43   2
INFANT
    THAT LIKE AN INFANT JUAN SWEETLY SLEPT   232   2 DON JUAN 2   143   3
    AN INFANT WHEN IT GAZES ON A LIGHT 261   2 DON JUAN 2   196   1
    WITH INFANT TERRORS GLARED AS FROM A TRANCE 159   3 DON JUAN 8   96   6
    AND SWEARING IF THE INFANT CAME TO ILL   162   3 DON JUAN 8   102   5
    OF CARNAGE--AND HER FAIR AND INFANT GRACE 182   3 DON JUAN 8   140   V7
    HER NOTE SHE DON'T FORGET THE INFANT GIRL 249   3 DON JUAN 10   51   7
    HE LOVED THE INFANT ORPHAN HE HAD SAVED 251   3 DON JUAN 10   55   2
    THE TRUE BELIEVERS--AND HER INFANT BROW 262   3 DON JUAN 10   75   6
    A GOODLY GUARDIAN FOR HIS INFANT CHARGE 335   3 DON JUAN 12   41   7
    ITS SHRILLER ECHOES--LIKE AN INFANT MADE 385   3 DON JUAN 13   58   3
    BUT JUST TO PLAY WITH AS AN INFANT PLAYS 414   3 DON JUAN 14   8   8
INFANTINE
    EARLY IN YEARS AND YET MORE INFANTINE 476   3 DON JUAN 15   45   1
INFANTS
    INFANTS OF THREE YEARS OLD WERE TAUGHT THAT DAY   . . . 162   2 DON JUAN 2   10   5
INFECTED
    INFECTED HER WITH SYMPATHY TILL NOW   480   2 DON JUAN 5   119   3
    THAT LEADS TO LASSITUDE THE MOST INFECTED   301   3 DON JUAN 11   65   3
INFER
    SO WERE THE CRETANS--FROM WHICH I INFER 238   2 DON JUAN 2   156   7
INFERIOR
    BUT OF INFERIOR MATERIALS SHE   221   2 DON JUAN 2   122   2
    AND THOUGH SO MUCH INFERIOR AS I KNOW 226   3 DON JUAN 10   3   5
    THE VERY LOWEST FIND OUT AN INFERIOR 367   3 DON JUAN 13   19   3
    WAS MUCH INFERIOR TO KING MENELAUS-- 441   3 DON JUAN 14   72   7
INFERNAL
    IT OPENED WITH A MOST INFERNAL CREAK 557   3 DON JUAN 16   116   1
INFIDEL
    AT SUCH A PERTINACIOUS INFIDEL 166   3 DON JUAN 8   109   6
INFIDELS
    OF PURCHASED INFIDELS SOME RAISED THEIR EYES   441   2 DON JUAN 5   54   2
    BE IN THESE DAYS) SOME INFIDELS WHO DON'T 447   2 DON JUAN 5   62   2
    AND INFIDELS TO PULL DOWN EVERY STEEPLE 195   3 DON JUAN 9   25   3
    HE SUFFERED INFIDELS IN HIS HOMESTEAD 262   3 DON JUAN 10   75   3
INFINITE
    AMIDST LIFE'S INFINITE VARIETY 464   3 DON JUAN 15   19   2
INFINITIES
    BY THE INFINITIES OF AGONY   118   3 DON JUAN 8   13   3
INFLAMMATION
    THE INFLAMMATION OF HIS WEEKLY BILLS 293   2 DON JUAN 3   35   8

INFLAMMATIONS
   NOR INFLAMMATIONS REDDEN HIS BLIND EYE . . . . 168 2 DON JUAN 2   22   8
INFLICT
   TORTURE IS THEIRS WHAT THEY INFLICT THEY FEEL . . . . . 262 2 DON JUAN 2   199   8
   AMONGST THEM ALL HARD BLOWS TO INFLICT OR WARD . . . . . 76 3 DON JUAN 7   19   6
INFLICTED
   ALL IT HATH FELT INFLICTED PASS'D AND PROVED . . . . 261 2 DON JUAN 2   197   5
   INFLICTED ON THE DISH A DEADLY WOUND . . . . 542 3 DON JUAN 16   88   6
INFLICTION
   THEIR NUMBERS WERE MUCH THINN'D BY THIS INFLICTION . . . 199 2 DON JUAN 2   80   1
INFLUENCE
   STILL O'ER HIS MIND THE INFLUENCE OF THE CLIME . . . . . 304 2 DON JUAN 3   56   1
   BENEATH THE INFLUENCE OF THE EASTERN STAR . . . . . . 347 3 DON JUAN 12   69   4
   PETTICOAT INFLUENCE IS A GREAT REPROACH . . . . 421 3 DON JUAN 14   26   1
   NO DOUBT THE SECRET INFLUENCE OF THE SEX . . . . 451 3 DON JUAN 14   93   1
   HAD ENGLISH INFLUENCE IN THE SELF-SAME SPHERE HERE . . . 534 3 DON JUAN 16   70   5
INFORM
   INFORM US TRULY HAVE THEY NOT HEN-PECK'D YOU ALL . . . . 33 2 DON JUAN 1   22   8
   KNOCKED TO INFORM HIM IT WAS TIME TO DRESS . . . . . . 512 3 DON JUAN 16   28   8
INFORMATION
   NO VERY SATISFACTORY INFORMATION . . . . 387 2 DON JUAN 4   79   7
   DON JUAN AT HIS HANDS AND INFORMATION . . . . 55 3 DON JUAN 6   99   2
INFORMED
   INFORMED HIM THAT HE HAD A LITTLE BROTHER . . . . . 240 3 DON JUAN 10   32   6
INFUSION
   IN WINDOWS HERE THE LAMPLIGHTER'S INFUSION . . . . . 278 3 DON JUAN 11   22   6
INGENUOUS
   TO MEET THE INGENUOUS YOUTH OF FUTURE AGES . . . . . . 46 2 DON JUAN 1   45   4
   OH YE WHO TEACH THE INGENUOUS YOUTH OF NATIONS . . . . 157 2 DON JUAN 2   1   1
   FAIR ADELINE THE MORE INGENUOUS . . . . 460 3 DON JUAN 15   10   1
INGLORIOUS
   REAPING ALLUSIONS PRIVATE AND INGLORIOUS . . . . . . 369 3 DON JUAN 13   25   4
INGOTS
   FLASH UP IN INGOTS FROM THE MINE OBSCURE . . . . 319 3 DON JUAN 12   8   5
   CONTAINING INGOTS BAGS OF DOLLARS COINS . . . . 321 3 DON JUAN 12   12   2
INGRATITUDE
   WHEN THEIR LIEGE HUSBANDS TREAT THEM WITH INGRATITUDE . . 11 3 DON JUAN 6   11   6
INGREDIENT
   TO PROVE ITS GRAND INGREDIENT IS ENNUI . . . . . . 332 2 DON JUAN 3   97   8
INGREDIENTS
   INTO THE OPENING BUT ALL SUCH INGREDIENTS . . . . . 171 2 DON JUAN 2   29   1
INHERENT
   SCOPE TO ALL SUCH AS FEEL THE INHERENT GLOW . . . . . 13 2 DON JUAN D   7   6
   THUS SUNG HE AND SUCH IS THE INHERENT FIRE . . . . 319 2 DON JUAN 3   84 V1
   INHERENT WHAT WE MORTALS CALL ROMANTIC . . . . . . 353 2 DON JUAN 4   18   7
INHERITS
   ARE SWEPT AWAY AND TOMB INHERITS TOMB . . . . 399 2 DON JUAN 4   102   2
INITIATION
   OF A RICH FOREIGNER'S INITIATION . . . . 293 3 DON JUAN 11   49   6
INJURED
   BEING ONLY INJURED BY HIS OWN ASSERTION . . . . . . 14 2 DON JUAN D   9   4
   SOME POUNDS OF BREAD THOUGH INJURED BY THE WET . . . . 181 2 DON JUAN 2   47   2
   THAT INJURED QUEEN BY CHRONICLERS SO COARSE . . . . . 446 2 DON JUAN 5   61   1
   DESPITE HER INJURED LOVE AND FIERY PRIDE . . . . . . 62 3 DON JUAN 6   113   5
INJURY
   BECAUSE IT THEN RECEIVED NO INJURY . . . . 117 2 DON JUAN 8   10   5
   REDRESSING INJURY REVENGING WRONG . . . . 363 3 DON JUAN 13   10   1
INK
   BY BLOOD OR INK 'TIS SWEET TO PUT AN END . . . . . . 90 2 DON JUAN 1   126   2
   THERE'S PEN AND INK FOR YOU SIR WHEN YOU NEED-- . . . 104 2 DON JUAN 1   152   4
   BUT WORDS ARE THINGS AND A SMALL DROP OF INK . . . . 327 2 DON JUAN 3   88   1
   WHEN ERE THE INK BE DRY THE SOUND GROWS COLD . . . . 382 3 DON JUAN 13   51   5
INKY
   THE SINGEING OF A SINGLE INKY WHISKER . . . . 498 2 DON JUAN 5   151   8
INLAID
   AN IVORY INLAID TABLE SPREAD WITH STATE . . . . . . 306 2 DON JUAN 3   61   5
   AND THICK WITH DAMASK FLOWERS OF SILK INLAID . . . . 308 2 DON JUAN 3   64   3
   THE TABLES MOST OF EBONY INLAID . . . . 310 2 DON JUAN 3   69   2
INLY
   FOR DON ALFONSO AND SHE INLY SWORE . . . . 80 2 DON JUAN 1   109   2
INNATE
   YOUNG INNATE FEELINGS ALL HAVE FELT BELOW . . . . . 353 2 DON JUAN 4   18   5
INNER
   THROUGH YEARS OR MOONS THE INNER WEIGHT TO BEAR . . . 382 2 DON JUAN 4   71   3
   ITS INNER CRASH IS LIKE AN EARTHQUAKE'S RUIN . . . . 446 3 DON JUAN 14   85   8
INNKEEPERS
   I RECOLLECT SOME INNKEEPERS WHO DON'T . . . . 275 3 DON JUAN 11   15   3
INNOCENCE
   WHERE ALL WAS PEACE AND INNOCENCE AND BLISS . . . . . 30 2 DON JUAN 1   18   5
   EVEN INNOCENCE ITSELF HAS MANY A WILE . . . . 61 2 DON JUAN 1   72   6
   SO WAS HER CREED IN HER OWN INNOCENCE . . . . 78 2 DON JUAN 1   106   8
   BUT FOUND MY VERY INNOCENCE PERPLEX . . . . . . 101 2 DON JUAN 1   147   6
   HIS EVE WITH ALL THE INNOCENCE SHE VAUNTED . . . . . 120 2 DON JUAN 1   180 V6
   THE INNOCENCE WHICH HAPPY CHILDHOOD BLESSES . . . . . 292 2 DON JUAN 3   33   5
   OVER THE INNOCENCE OF THAT SWEET CHILD . . . . . . 302 2 DON JUAN 3   52   7
   IN PERFECT INNOCENCE SHE THEN UNMADE . . . . 36 3 DON JUAN 6   60   1
   ITS VOTARIES LIKE INNOCENCE RELYING . . . . 131 3 DON JUAN 8   36   5
   A VESTAL SHRINE OF INNOCENCE OF HEART . . . . . . 370 3 DON JUAN 13   27   7
   BUT INNOCENCE IS BOLD EVEN AT THE STAKE . . . . . . 437 3 DON JUAN 14   61   5

INNOCENCE   (CONTINUED)
 OR THAT HE HAD AN AIR OF INNOCENCE 468   3 DON JUAN 15   28   5
 WHICH IS FOR INNOCENCE A SAD TEMPTATION-- 468   3 DON JUAN 15   28   6
INNOCENT
 SUCH LOVE IS INNOCENT AND MAY EXIST 65   2 DON JUAN 1   80   1
 WAS JULIA'S INNOCENT DETERMINATION 65   2 DON JUAN 1   81   2
 HER PLAN SHE DEEM'D BOTH INNOCENT AND FEASIBLE . . . 66   2 DON JUAN 1   83   1
 BOTH WERE SO YOUNG AND ONE SO INNOCENT 247   2 DON JUAN 2   172   1
 AND ONE WAS INNOCENT BUT BOTH TOO YOUNG 254   2 DON JUAN 2   187   V8
 SO INNOCENT AND BEAUTIFUL A PAIR 258   2 DON JUAN 2   193   V3
 INDULGENCE OF THEIR INNOCENT DESIRES 282   2 DON JUAN 3   13   2
 HERE WAS NO LACK OF INNOCENT DIVERSION 293   2 DON JUAN 3   35   1
 TO FIND RETORTS FOR INNOCENT BLOOD SHED 314   3 DON JUAN 11   V 75   4
 THEMSELVES ON INNOCENT TANTALIZATION 327   3 DON JUAN 12   25   7
 BUT YET IS MERELY INNOCENT FLIRTATION 345   3 DON JUAN 12   63   7
 AN INNOCENT PREDOMINANCE ANNEX 451   3 DON JUAN 14   93   3
 UNTO SUCH FEELINGS AS SEEM'D INNOCENT 460   3 DON JUAN 15   10   7
 SWEET SOUL--SHE WAS SO VERY INNOCENT 493   3 DON JUAN 15   83   V8
INNOCENTLY
 QUITE INNOCENTLY DONE AND HARMLESS STYLED 59   2 DON JUAN 1   69   3
 BUT INNOCENTLY SO AS SOCRATES 494   3 DON JUAN 15   86   2
INNOCENTS
 WHERE ARE TEN THOUSAND LOVELY INNOCENTS 307   3 DON JUAN 11   77   V7
INNOVATION'S
 THAT INNOVATION'S SPIRIT NOW-A-DAYS 536   3 DON JUAN 16   73   3
INOCULATION
 HERSELF EXTREMELY ON THE INOCULATION 478   3 DON JUAN 15   50   6
INOFFENSIVE
 WHO'S QUIET INOFFENSIVE SILENT SHY 30   3 DON JUAN 6   49   5
INQUIRE
 I'LL JUST INQUIRE IF SHE BE WIFE OR MAID 268   2 DON JUAN 2   210   5
 NO MATTER WE SHOULD NE'ER TOO MUCH INQUIRE 396   2 DON JUAN 4   96   1
 AT LEAST SAID JUAN SURE I MAY INQUIRE 454   2 DON JUAN 5   74   4
INQUIRED
 MUCH INTO ALL HIS STUDIES SHE INQUIRED 43   2 DON JUAN 1   39   5
 HIS GLANCE INQUIRED OF HERS FOR SOME EXCUSE 355   2 DON JUAN 4   22   7
 INQUIRED WHO WAS THIS VERY NEW YOUNG MAN 222   3 DON JUAN 9   79   2
INQUISITION
 DURING THIS INQUISITION JULIA'S TONGUE 100   2 DON JUAN 1   145   1
INQUISITIONS
 RACKS PRISONS INQUISITIONS RESURRECTION 272   3 DON JUAN 11   9   7
INQUISITORS
 THEN ADVOCATES INQUISITORS AND JUDGES 36   2 DON JUAN 1   28   7
INS
 FOR JUAN STOOD WELL BOTH WITH INS AND OUTS 369   3 DON JUAN 13   24   3
INSANITY
 (THE JURY BROUGHT THEIR VERDICT IN INSANITY) . . . 29   2 DON JUAN 1   15   8
 FOR SAVING HER AMIDST THE WILD INSANITY 182   3 DON JUAN 8   140   6
 EXCEPT WHERE 'TIS A MERE INSANITY 219   3 DON JUAN 9   73   3
INSATIATE
 SHOULD SUCK HIM BACK TO HER INSATIATE GRAVE 213   2 DON JUAN 2   108   4
INSCRIBE
 TO YOU THE UNFLATTERING MUSE DEIGNS TO INSCRIBE . . . 187   3 DON JUAN 9   10   2
INSCRUTABLE
 HIGH AND INSCRUTABLE THE OLD MAN STOOD 365   2 DON JUAN 4   39   1
INSECTS
 THAN HUMAN INSECTS CATERING FOR SPIDERS 196   3 DON JUAN 9   27   8
INSECURE
 WOULD NOT ALONE HAVE MADE HIM INSECURE 58   3 DON JUAN 6   104   5
INSENSIBLE
 INSENSIBLE I TRUST BUT NONE THE WORSE 144   2 DON JUAN 1   215   6
 INSENSIBLE--NOT DEAD BUT NEARLY SO-- 224   2 DON JUAN 2   129   3
INSERT
 OF WHOM WE CAN INSERT BUT ROUSAMOUSKI 74   3 DON JUAN 7   16   8
INSERTED
 BUT ONE THING'S ODD WHICH HERE MUST BE INSERTED . . . 251   3 DON JUAN 10   55   7
INSIDE
 AND LIKING NOT THE INSIDE LOCK'D THE OUT 125   2 DON JUAN 1   187   8
 BOTH BLACK AS IF YOU HAD TURNED HIM INSIDE OUT . . . 154   2 DON JUAN 1   V 5   V7
 DISSECTING THE WHOLE INSIDE OF A QUESTION 232   3 DON JUAN 10   14   7
INSIDE-OUT
 BAKED FRIED OR BURNT TURNED INSIDE-OUT OR DROWNED . . . 201   3 DON JUAN 9   37   5
INSINUATING
 INSINUATING WITHOUT INSINUATION 462   3 DON JUAN 15   15   2
INSINUATION
 INSINUATING WITHOUT INSINUATION 462   3 DON JUAN 15   15   2
INSIPID
 INSIPID IN THIS NAUGHTY WORLD OF OURS 30   2 DON JUAN 1   18   2
INSIST
 (OR BEATEN IF YOU INSIST ON GRAMMAR THOUGH 87   3 DON JUAN 7   42   5
INSISTING
 INSISTING ON REMOVAL OF THE PRINCE 117   3 DON JUAN 8   11   2
 WHEREAS INSISTING IN OR OUT OF SEASON 478   3 DON JUAN 15   51   5
INSISTS
 AND (IF LET IN) INSISTS IN TERMS UNHANDSOME 459   3 DON JUAN 15   8   7
INSOLENCE
 AND INSOLENCE NO DOUBT IS WHAT THEY ARE 288   3 DON JUAN 11   41   1
INSOLENT
 YOU BOB ARE RATHER INSOLENT YOU KNOW 10   2 DON JUAN D   3   1

```
                                                      PAGE VOL      CANTO   STANZA LN

INSOLENT   (CONTINUED)
    THE INSOLENT SOLDIERY TO SOOTHE AND FLATTER . . . . . . . 299  3 DON JUAN 11    62    4
    NOR INSOLENT ENOUGH TO SCORN THE SCORNER . . . . . . .  . 532  3 DON JUAN 16    65    6
INSPECT
    IS WHAT I HAVE NOT LEISURE TO INSPECT . . . . . . . .  . 502  3 DON JUAN 16     2    3
INSPECTOR
    A CITY WHICH PRESENTS TO THE INSPECTOR  . . . . . . .  . 255  3 DON JUAN 10    62    6
INSPIRATION
    OF INSPIRATION GATHERED FROM DISTRESS . . . . . . . .  .  59  3 DON JUAN  6   107    3
INSPIRED
    OF FREEDOM THAT THIS NOW INSPIRED TYRTAEUS . . . . .   . 319  2 DON JUAN  3    84   V2
    WOULD POPE HAVE SUNG OR HORACE BEEN INSPIRED . . . .   . 470  2 DON JUAN  5   101    8
    A COURIER ON THE SPUR INSPIRED NEW HEART . . . . . .   .  85  3 DON JUAN  7    39    3
    THE CHASTE AND THOSE WHO ARE NOT SO MUCH INSPIRED . .  . 428  3 DON JUAN 14    41    6
INSPIRERS
    SO BE THEY HER INSPIRERS CALL THEM MARS . . . . . .   .  112  3 DON JUAN  8     1    7
INSPIRES
    MOST NATURALLY SOME SMALL DOUBT INSPIRES-- . . . . .  .  287  2 DON JUAN  3    22    3
INSPIRING
    THIS STRANGE SALOON MUCH FITTED FOR INSPIRING . . . .  . 469  2 DON JUAN  5   100    5
INSTALMENTS
    AT ONCE WITHOUT INSTALMENTS (AN OLD WAY . . . . . .   .  412  3 DON JUAN 14     4    5
INSTANCE
    FOR INSTANCE--GENTLEMEN WHOSE LADIES TAKE . . . .   .  .  74  2 DON JUAN  1    98    2
    FOR INSTANCE--PASSION IN A LOVER'S GLORIOUS . . .  .  .  278  2 DON JUAN  3     6    7
    FOR INSTANCE IF A HUSBAND OR HIS WIFE . . . . . .   .  .  301  2 DON JUAN  3    50    3
    IN FRANCE FOR INSTANCE HE WOULD WRITE A CHANSON . .   .  320  2 DON JUAN  3    86    1
    KNOWLEDGE AT LEAST IS GAINED FOR INSTANCE NOW . . .   .  422  2 DON JUAN  5    23    6
    UGLY FOR INSTANCE--NINON DEL'ENCLOS . . . . . . .   .  .  468  2 DON JUAN  5    98    8
    I FOR MY PART--(ONE MODERN INSTANCE MORE . . . . .   .   334  3 DON JUAN 12    38    1
    BUT THE TENTH INSTANCE WILL BE A TORNADO . . . . .   .   351  3 DON JUAN 12    77    7
INSTANCES
    (BUT HERE PERHAPS THE INSTANCES ARE FEWER) . . . .   .   333  3 DON JUAN 12    37    3
INSTANT
    AND JULIA INSTANT TO THE CLOSET FLEW . . . . . .   .  .  121  2 DON JUAN  1   182    2
    LAMBRO PRESENTED AND ONE INSTANT MORE . . . . . .   .  .  366  2 DON JUAN  4    42    1
    THUS MUCH SHE VIEW'D AN INSTANT AND NO MORE-- . . .  .   375  2 DON JUAN  4    58    5
    THE VERY INSTANT TILL THE CHANGE THAT CAST . . . .   .   381  2 DON JUAN  4    69    5
    JUAN WHO FOR AN INSTANT HAD BEEN MOVED . . . . . .   .   481  2 DON JUAN  5   121    2
    STRUCK FOR AN INSTANT ON THE HEARTS OF MEN . . . .   .   111  3 DON JUAN  7    87    3
    JUST AT THIS INSTANT WHILE THEIR EYES WERE FIXED . .  .  159  3 DON JUAN  8    96    1
    WHICH FOR AN INSTANT CLIP ENJOYMENT'S WINGS . . . .  .   227  3 DON JUAN 10     5    8
    PURSUED AN INSTANT FOR HER OWN CONTENT . . . . . .   .   521  3 DON JUAN 16    42    4
INSTANTLY
    ONE GANG OF PEOPLE INSTANTLY WAS PUT . . . . . . .   .   171  2 DON JUAN  2    28    1
    AND SOLD HIM INSTANTLY WHEN OUT OF DANGER . . . . .  .   225  2 DON JUAN  2   130    8
    THAT THEY MUST INSTANTLY BE WELL ARRAYED . . . . .   .    64  3 DON JUAN  6   118    3
INSTEAD
    INSTEAD OF QUARRELLING HAD THEY BEEN BUT BOTH IN . .  .   34  2 DON JUAN  1    25    5
    INSTEAD OF BEING SCATTER'D THROUGH THE PAGES . . .  .  .  46  2 DON JUAN  1    45    2
    INSTEAD OF STANDING STARING ALTOGETHER . . . . . .  .  .  46  2 DON JUAN  1    45    7
    AND YET I THINK INSTEAD OF SUCH A ONE . . . . . .   .  .  56  2 DON JUAN  1    62    3
    AND SMEAR HIS PAGE WITH GALL INSTEAD OF HONEY . . .  .  142  2 DON JUAN  1   210    7
    INSTEAD OF SAIL WERE TO THE OAR MADE FAST . . . .   .  . 188  2 DON JUAN  2    61    4
    INSTEAD OF HOARDING IT WITH DUE PRECISION . . . .   .  . 192  2 DON JUAN  2    68    8
    INSTEAD OF SPEECH MAY FORM A LASTING LINK . . . .   .  . 327  2 DON JUAN  3    88    5
    INSTEAD OF BEARING UP WITHOUT DEBATE . . . . . .   .  .  394  2 DON JUAN  4    93    6
    A TOWN WAS TA'EN MYSELF INSTEAD OF WIDIN . . . .   .  .  418  2 DON JUAN  5    15    8
    WOMAN'S THE HEART--OR ANYTHING INSTEAD . . . . .   .  .    7  3 DON JUAN  6     2   V8
    BUT NOW INSTEAD OF SLAYING PRIAM'S SON . . . . .   .  .  106  3 DON JUAN  7    78    5
    INSTEAD OF HEAVEN THEY STUMBLED BACKWARDS O'ER . .  .  .  121  3 DON JUAN  8    20    7
    TO SIGH INSTEAD OF COUGHING--AND CRYING-- PISH . .  .  .  228  3 DON JUAN 10     6   V8
    JUAN INSTEAD OF COURTING COURTS WAS COURTED . . .  .  .  239  3 DON JUAN 10    29    1
    INSTEAD OF GLIDING GRACIOUSLY DOWN LETHE . . . .   .  .  245  3 DON JUAN 10    42    7
    INSTEAD OF WICKS THEY MADE A WICKED MAN TURN . .   .  .  280  3 DON JUAN 11    26    8
    AS IF THEY ACTED WITH THE HEART INSTEAD . . . .   .  .   284  3 DON JUAN 11    34    4
    WHICH NOW HE FOUND WAS BLUE INSTEAD OF GREEN . .   .  .  294  3 DON JUAN 11    51    8
    I HAVE SEEN CROWNS WORN INSTEAD OF A FOOL'S CAP-- .  .   310  3 DON JUAN 11    84    5
    INSTEAD OF LOVE THAT MERE HALLUCINATION . . . .   .  .   360  3 DON JUAN 13     6    6
    TO GAZE INSTEAD OF PAVEMENT UPON GRASS . . . . .   .  .  539  3 DON JUAN 16    81    3
    RATHER THAN REST INSTEAD OF POPPIES WILLOWS . . .  .  .  555  3 DON JUAN 16   110    5
    ONLY THE WALL INSTEAD OF WHAT HE SOUGHT . . . .   .  .   560  3 DON JUAN 16   122    8
INSTEP
    A LIKE GOLD BAR ABOVE HER INSTEP ROLLED . . . . . .  .   312  2 DON JUAN  3    72    2
INSTILLING
    THIS GREAT PHILOSOPHER WAS THUS INSTILLING . . . .  .     96  3 DON JUAN  7    58    6
INSTINCT
    ALAS THERE IS NO INSTINCT LIKE THE HEART-- . . . .  .    349  2 DON JUAN  4    10    8
    INSTINCT OF GORE AND GLORY EARTH HAS KNOWN . . . .  .    401  2 DON JUAN  4   105    7
    KNELT DOWN BY INSTINCT WONDERING IN HIS MIND . . .  .    466  2 DON JUAN  5    95    6
INSTRUCTING
    FORMED RATHER FOR INSTRUCTING THAN DELIGHTING . . .  .   412  2 DON JUAN  5     2    5
    PRAYING INSTRUCTING DESOLATING PLUNDERING . . . . .  .    95  3 DON JUAN  7    55    6
INSTRUCTIONS
    HAD HIS INSTRUCTIONS WHERE AND HOW TO DEAL . . . .  .    477  2 DON JUAN  5   114   V6
    RECEIVED INSTRUCTIONS HOW TO PLAY HIS CARD . . . .  .    247  3 DON JUAN 10    46    6
INSTRUCTOR
    TO YOUR INSTRUCTOR  JUAN NOW WAS BORNE . . . . . .  .    264  3 DON JUAN 10    80    2
INSTRUCTS
    THE PRIEST INSTRUCTS AND SO OUR LIFE EXHALES . . . .  .  159  2 DON JUAN  2     4    6
```

INSTRUMENT
 THE ,HARPER CAME AND TUNED HIS INSTRUMENT 379   2 DON JUAN 4   65   2
 AN AIRY INSTRUMENT WITH WHICH HE SOUGHT 406   2 DON JUAN 4   112   5
INSTRUMENTS
 THE SURGEON HAD HIS INSTRUMENTS AND BLED 197   2 DON JUAN 2   76   2
INSULAR
 OF LIVING IN THEIR INSULAR ABODE 317   2 DON JUAN 3   81   8
INSULT
 INSULT ON INSULT HEAP AND WRONG ON WRONG 100   2 DON JUAN 1   145   3
 INSULT ON INSULT HEAP AND WRONG ON WRONG 100   2 DON JUAN 1   145   3
INSULTS
 THE INSULTS TOO OF EVERY SERVILE GLUTTON 299   2 DON JUAN 3   46   7
INSURE
 IF ONLY FROM THE DEVIL THEY WOULD INSURE US 267   2 DON JUAN 2   207   5
 BESIDES THAT WOULD A HAPPY LOT INSURE US 267   2 DON JUAN 2   207 V3
INSURED
 BUT HOW FAITH IS ACQUIRED AND THEN INSURED 47   2 DON JUAN 1   47   5
 BUT OF ALL VERSE WHAT MOST INSURED HER PRAISE 525   3 DON JUAN 16   50   7
IN'T
 AN EMERALD AIGRETTE WITH HAIDEE'S HAIR IN'T 315   2 DON JUAN 3   77   6
 BUT COULD NOT FOR THE MUSE OF ME PUT LESS IN'T . . . 410   2 DON JUAN 4   117   6
 'TWOULD BE AS WELL AND--(THOUGH THERE'S NOT MUCH IN'T) . . 464   2 DON JUAN 5   91   5
 IN POLITESSE AND HAVE A SOUND AFFRONTING IN'T-- . . . 289   3 DON JUAN 11   43   6
 THEN BROKE HIS PACKET TO SEE WHAT WAS IN'T 440   3 DON JUAN 14   69   5
 SOLE CREDITOR WHOSE PROCESS DOTH INVOLVE IN'T . . . 458   3 DON JUAN 15   7   7
 BUT THOUGHT LIKE MOST MEN THERE WAS NOTHING IN'T . . 510   3 DON JUAN 16   22   3
INTEGRITY
 WITH ALL THEIR CHASTE INTEGRITY OF LAWS 35   3 DON JUAN 6   58   5
INTELLECT
 BETWEEN HIS OWN AND OTHERS' INTELLECT 330   2 DON JUAN 3   95   2
 AND INTELLECT THAT NEITHER EYES NOR EARS 398   3 DON JUAN 13   85   4
 OF INTELLECT EXPENDED ON TWO COURSES 486   3 DON JUAN 15   69   2
 THE SUFFERERS--BE'T IN HEART OR INTELLECT-- 563   3 DON JUAN 17   2   7
INTELLECTS
 THAT NEITHER OF THEIR INTELLECTS ARE VAST 345   2 DON JUAN 4   2   4
 WOULD PIQUE HIMSELF ON INTELLECTS WHOSE USE 428   2 DON JUAN 5   32   7
INTELLECTUAL
 THE INTELLECTUAL EUNUCH CASTLEREAGH 15   2 DON JUAN D   11   8
 BUT--OH YE LORDS OF LADIES INTELLECTUAL 33   2 DON JUAN 1   22   7
 KNOWING (DOGS HAVE SUCH INTELLECTUAL NOSES) 187   2 DON JUAN 2   58   5
 AND SHOW THEM WHAT AN INTELLECTUAL WAR IS 299   3 DON JUAN 11   62   8
 COMMANDS--THE INTELLECTUAL LORD OF ALL 320   3 DON JUAN 12   9   8
 IF SUCH DOOM WAITS EACH INTELLECTUAL GIANT 566   3 DON JUAN 17   10   1
INTELLIGENCE
 BRIGHT WITH INTELLIGENCE AND FAIR AND SMOOTH 55   2 DON JUAN 1   61   2
INTELLIGIBLE
 IF NOT INTELLIGIBLE--WITHOUT GREEK 298   3 DON JUAN 11   60   3
INTENDED
 AS IS A SLAVE BY HIS INTENDED BIDDER 425   2 DON JUAN 5   27   1
INTENDS
 WE UNDERSTAND THE SPLENDID HOST INTENDS 382   3 DON JUAN 13   52   1
 WHICH LIKE A CREED NE'ER SAYS ALL IT INTENDS 407   3 DON JUAN 13   105   5
INTENSE
 THEIR INTENSE SOULS INTO EACH OTHER POUR'D 257   2 DON JUAN 2   191   3
 LOVE WAS BORN WITH THEM IN THEM SO INTENSE 358   2 DON JUAN 4   27   7
 THOUGH ON ALL OTHER THINGS WITH LOOKS INTENSE 381   2 DON JUAN 4   68   3
 INTENSE INTENTIONS ARE A DANGEROUS MATTER 448   3 DON JUAN 14   88   4
 FELT ON THE WHOLE AN INTEREST INTENSE-- 468   3 DON JUAN 15   28   3
 SHE NEITHER DEEMED HIS FEELINGS WERE INTENSE 493   3 DON JUAN 15   83 V5
INTENSITY
 BY MEASURING THE INTENSITY OF BLUE 406   2 DON JUAN 4   112   7
INTENT
 ALTHOUGH NO DOUBT HIS REAL INTENT WAS GOOD 45   2 DON JUAN 1   43   4
 TO STAY THERE HAD NOT ANSWER'D HER INTENT 161   2 DON JUAN 2   8   3
 LIKE A MERE LOG AND BAFFLED OUR INTENT 173   2 DON JUAN 2   32   4
 AS IF OLD OCEAN BAFFLED OUR INTENT 173   2 DON JUAN 2   32 V4
 NOT BY THE NUMBERS GOOD INTENT HATH SAVED 124   3 DON JUAN 8   26   4
 BUT SUCH INTENT I NEVER HAD NOR HAVE IT 444   3 DON JUAN 14   80   5
INTENTION
 FRAUGHT WITH THIS FINE INTENTION AND WELL FENCED 66   2 DON JUAN 1   82   1
 HE LIED WITH SUCH A FERVOUR OF INTENTION-- 317   2 DON JUAN 3   80   7
INTENTIONS
 INTENTIONS BUT THEIR TREATMENT WAS NOT KIND 34   2 DON JUAN 1   24   2
 ALL PROPAGATED WITH THE BEST INTENTIONS 93   2 DON JUAN 1   132   3
 MADE JUAN IN HIS HARSH INTENTIONS PAUSE 437   2 DON JUAN 5   47   4
 INTENTIONS WHICH FORM ALL MANKIND'S TRUMP CARD 123   3 DON JUAN 8   25   3
 THOSE ANTIENT GOOD INTENTIONS WHICH ONCE SHAVED . . . 124   3 DON JUAN 8   26   6
 WHAT YOUR INTENTIONS ARE--ONE WAY OR OTHER 343   3 DON JUAN 12   60   5
 HERSELF THAT HER INTENTIONS WERE THE BEST-- 448   3 DON JUAN 14   88   3
 INTENSE INTENTIONS ARE A DANGEROUS MATTER 448   3 DON JUAN 14   88   4
INTER
 I ONLY SAY SUPPOSE IT--INTER NOS 67   2 DON JUAN 1   84   6
INTEREST
 HAVE SPENT MY LIFE BOTH INTEREST AND PRINCIPAL 143   2 DON JUAN 1   213   7
 WHICH WAS RETURNED WITH INTEREST I MAY SAY 81   3 DON JUAN 7   29   6
 WITH INTEREST AND IN TURN WAS WONT WITH RIGOUR 213   3 DON JUAN 9   62   6
 HAD RAISED AN INTEREST IN HER WHICH ENCREASED 338   3 DON JUAN 12   48   8
 NOW WHEN SHE ONCE HAD TA'EN AN INTEREST 448   3 DON JUAN 14   88   1
 FELT ON THE WHOLE AN INTEREST INTENSE-- 468   3 DON JUAN 15   28   3

		PAGE	VOL		CANTO	STANZA	LN
INTEREST (CONTINUED)							
THOSE WHO IN COUNTY INTEREST TRY THEIR FORCES	. . . .	534	3 DON JUAN	16	68	V6
WAS MEMBER FOR THE OTHER INTEREST (MEANING	. . .	535	3 DON JUAN	16	70	7
TO SOME SMALL PLAN OF INTEREST OR AMBITION--	. . .	541	3 DON JUAN	16	85	7
INTERESTED							
WHERE SHE WAS INTERESTED (AS WAS SAID)	. . . . .	460	3 DON JUAN	15	10	2
INTERESTING							
OR ANY INTERESTING BEAST OF PREY	. . . . . .	487	2 DON JUAN	5	132	2
INTERESTS							
THEIR OWN TRUE INTERESTS WHICH KINGS RARELY KNOW	. .	53	3 DON JUAN	6	95	2
INTERFERED							
AND SO I INTERFERED AND WITH THE BEST	. . . . .	34	2 DON JUAN	1	24	1
BUT HERE KATINKA INTERFERED AND SAID	. . . . .	29	3 DON JUAN	6	47	7
FIRSTLY HE SAID HE NEVER INTERFERED	. . . . .	439	3 DON JUAN	14	66	1
INTERIM							
AND IN THE INTERIM (TO PURSUE THIS VISION)	. . . .	67	2 DON JUAN	1	85	5
INTERIOR							
REACHED THE INTERIOR TALUS OF THE RAMPART	. . .	135	3 DON JUAN	8	44	8
LINE THE INTERIOR OF THEIR HEADS OR BONNETS	. . .	294	3 DON JUAN	11	50	3
INTERJECTION							
ALL PRESENT LIFE IS BUT AN INTERJECTION	. . . .	456	3 DON JUAN	15	1	5
INTERJECTIONS							
OH CATHERINE (FOR OF ALL INTERJECTIONS	. . . .	215	3 DON JUAN	9	65	1
INTERMINABLE							
INTERMINABLE--NOT ETERNAL--SPEAKERS--	. . . . .	310	3 DON JUAN	11	85	2
INTERMISSION							
FOR SIX HOURS BORE THEY WITHOUT INTERMISSION	. .	81	3 DON JUAN	7	30	1
ON WHICH THE REST WITHOUT MORE INTERMISSION	.	152	3 DON JUAN	8	81	3
INTERMISSIONS							
BUT AS HE HAD SOME LUCID INTERMISSIONS	. . . .	35	2 DON JUAN	1	27	3
INTERNAL							
AND MY INTERNAL SPIRIT CUT A CAPER .	. . . .	226	3 DON JUAN	10	3	4
HIS OWN INTERNAL GHOST BEGAN TO AWAKEN	. . . .	558	3 DON JUAN	16	118	5
INTERPOSED							
'TWIXT HER AND JUAN INTERPOSED THE CREW	. . . .	370	2 DON JUAN	4	48	3
HERE LOLAH INTERPOSED--MAMMA YOU KNOW .	. . .	29	3 DON JUAN	6	47	1
AND HERE JUANNA KINDLY INTERPOSED .	. . . . .	48	3 DON JUAN	6	84	1
INTERPRETATION							
AND MILDEST MATRON-LIKE INTERPRETATION	. . . . .	208	3 DON JUAN	9	52	2
INTERPRETED							
IN THE GREAT WORLD--WHICH BEING INTERPRETED	. . .	290	3 DON JUAN	11	45	1
INTERPRETER							
FOUND IN ONE SIGH THE BEST INTERPRETER	. . . .	256	2 DON JUAN	2	189	6
AND MADE THY BEST INTERPRETER A SIGH .	. . . .	275	2 DON JUAN	3	2	4
INTERRUPT							
NOR THAT A SNEEZE SHOULD INTERRUPT HIS SIGH	. . .	168	2 DON JUAN	2	22	7
REPLIED THE OTHER DO NOT INTERRUPT .	. . . .	453	2 DON JUAN	5	72	2
INTERRUPTED							
AND AS HE INTERRUPTED NOT WENT EKING	. . . .	241	2 DON JUAN	2	161	5
WAS INTERRUPTED BY THE PIRATE CREW .	. . . .	393	2 DON JUAN	4	90	2
HERE THEY WERE INTERRUPTED BY A HUMMING	. . . .	494	2 DON JUAN	5	145	7
HERE--HE WAS INTERRUPTED BY A KNIFE	. . . .	273	3 DON JUAN	11	10	7
INTERTWISTED							
THEY ARE SO MUCH INTERTWISTED WITH THE EARTH	. . .	436	3 DON JUAN	14	59	2
INTERVALS							
OF BILLOWS BUT AT INTERVALS THERE GUSH'D .	. . .	184	2 DON JUAN	2	53	5
A VISITANT AT INTERVALS APPEARS .	. . . . .	504	3 DON JUAN	16	7	4
INTERVENE							
THEY SMILE STILL MORE AND THEN THERE INTERVENE	. . .	242	2 DON JUAN	2	164	6
INTERVENES							
AS ERE THAT AWFUL PERIOD INTERVENES	. . . . .	41	3 DON JUAN	6	69	6
INTERVENING							
FURTHER I'D QUOTE BUT SCRIPTURE INTERVENING	. . .	403	3 DON JUAN	13	96	5
INTERVIEW							
HOW THIS SAME INTERVIEW HAD TAKEN PLACE	. . .	77	2 DON JUAN	1	105	2
NOR SETTLES ALL THINGS IN ONE INTERVIEW	. . . .	351	3 DON JUAN	12	76	5
INTESTATE							
DYING INTESTATE JUAN WAS SOLE HEIR .	. . . . .	42	2 DON JUAN	1	37	1
INTOXICATES							
WITH THE FIRST DRAUGHT INTOXICATES APACE	. . . .	216	3 DON JUAN	9	67	4
INTOXICATION							
THE BEST OF LIFE IS BUT INTOXICATION .	. . . .	250	2 DON JUAN	2	179	2
IN LOVE THERE'S SOMETHING OF INTOXICATION	. . . .	474	3 DON JUAN	15	41	V7
INTRIGANTE							
HER GRACE TOO PASS'D FOR BEING AN INTRIGANTE	. . .	438	3 DON JUAN	14	63	1
INTRIGUES							
INTRIGUES ADVENTURES OF THE COMMON SCHOOL	. . .	353	2 DON JUAN	4	17	5
THE USUAL PROGRESS OF INTRIGUES BETWEEN	. . . .	236	3 DON JUAN	10	24	2
INTRODUCE							
TO INTRODUCE A BON MOT HEAD AND EARS	. . . . .	408	3 DON JUAN	13	109	4
BEFORE THEY FIND AN HOUR TO INTRODUCE IT	. . . .	408	3 DON JUAN	13	109	7
I MUST NOT INTRODUCE EVEN A SPARE RIB HERE	. . .	487	3 DON JUAN	15	71	5
ARE TOPICS WHICH I SOMETIMES INTRODUCE	. . . .	497	3 DON JUAN	15	93	2
INTRODUCTION							
LETTER OF INTRODUCTION WHICH THE MORN .	. . . .	169	2 DON JUAN	2	24	6
HERE THE TWELFTH CANTO OF OUR INTRODUCTION	. . .	356	3 DON JUAN	12	87	1
INTRUDE							
WHERE NOUGHT UPON THEIR PASSION COULD INTRUDE	. . .	262	2 DON JUAN	2	198	6
METHINKS AT MEALS SOME ODD THOUGHTS MIGHT INTRUDE	. . .	426	2 DON JUAN	5	30	3

	PAGE	VOL	CANTO	STANZA	LN
INTRUSIVE					
TO SUCH A SORROW BY THE INTRUSIVE TONE	481	2	DON JUAN 5	121	3
INUNDATIONS					
WHICH THREATENS INUNDATIONS DEEP AND YELLOW	228	3	DON JUAN 10	7	4
INURBANITY					
HAS BEEN DECLARED AN ACT OF INURBANITY	565	3	DON JUAN 17	7	7
INURED					
TO JEROME AND TO CHRYSOSTOM INURED	47	2	DON JUAN 1	47	3
INURN'D					
'TIS WITH OUR HERO QUIETLY INURN'D	23	2	DON JUAN 1	4	4
INVADED					
AND SUCH THEIR CREED WAS TILL THEY WERE INVADED	73	3	DON JUAN 7	13	4
INVALID					
AND LEFT HIM 'MIDST THE INVALID AND MAIMED	154	3	DON JUAN 8	85	4
INVASION					
LIKE AN INVASION OF THEIR BABES AND SUCKLINGS	488	2	DON JUAN 5	133	4
INVENT					
TO THOSE WHO COULD INVENT HIM A NEW PLEASURE	85	2	DON JUAN 1	118	2
A RACK OF PLEASURES WHERE WE MUST INVENT	444	3	DON JUAN 14	79	2
INVENTED					
AS IF THE PEASANT'S SCORN THIS MODE INVENTED	401	2	DON JUAN 4	105	V3
INVENTED BY SOME NAME I HAVE FORGOT	406	2	DON JUAN 4	112	3
WHICH SURELY WERE INVENTED FOR OUR SINS--	36	3	DON JUAN 6	61	8
INVENTION					
SURE MY INVENTION MUST BE DOWN AT ZERO	341	2	DON JUAN 3	110	5
OF FRIAR BACON'S BRIGHT INVENTION--SHARED	129	3	DON JUAN 8	33	V5
TO THESE THE INVENTION OF CHAMPAGNE AND TRUFFLES	542	3	DON JUAN 16	86	7
INVENTIONS					
THIS IS THE PATENT AGE OF NEW INVENTIONS	93	2	DON JUAN 1	132	1
AND HAVE TEN THOUSAND DELICATE INVENTIONS	221	2	DON JUAN 2	123	4
INVESTIGATING					
AFTER THE FIRST INVESTIGATING VIEW	24	3	DON JUAN 6	37	3
INVESTIGATION					
AND NOW COMMENCED A STRICT INVESTIGATION	43	3	DON JUAN 6	74	1
INVETERATE					
MORE THAN THE HEAD OF THE INVETERATE FOE	154	3	DON JUAN 8	85	7
JUAN AS AN INVETERATE PATRICIAN	290	3	DON JUAN 11	45	7
INVINCIBLE					
AND DEEM NOT WHAT I DEEM'D MY SOUL INVINCIBLE	143	2	DON JUAN 1	213	8
INVIOLATE					
HERE LAWS ARE ALL INVIOLATE NONE LAY	273	3	DON JUAN 11	10	5
INVITATION					
(THUS WE TRANSLATE A GENERAL INVITATION)	534	3	DON JUAN 16	69	2
INVITE					
WHO CAME AT STATED MOMENTS TO INVITE ALL	393	2	DON JUAN 4	90	3
WERE THERE WITH BROWS THAT DID NOT MUCH INVITE	391	3	DON JUAN 13	69	2
INVITED					
TO FIND SO MUCH GOOD COMPANY INVITED	294	2	DON JUAN 3	37	8
AND SENATE WHEN INVITED ELSEWHERE TRULY	398	3	DON JUAN 13	84	3
INVITING					
PLAIN--SIMPLE--SHORT AND BY NO MEANS INVITING	412	2	DON JUAN 5	2	3
INVOLVE					
SOLE CREDITOR WHOSE PROCESS DOTH INVOLVE IN'T	458	3	DON JUAN 15	7	7
INVOLVED					
REPUBLICS ALSO GET INVOLVED A BIT	318	3	DON JUAN 12	6	5
INWARD					
AND EVEN THE GOOD WITH INWARD ENVY GROAN	26	2	DON JUAN 1	10	6
AND GAVE NO OUTWARD SIGNS OF INWARD STRIFE	35	2	DON JUAN 1	26	6
HER INWARD GRACE FOR OUTWARD SHOW AND MAKES	96	3	DON JUAN 7	57	7
WHAT INDIGESTION IS--THAT INWARD FATE	190	3	DON JUAN 9	15	4
THEN SEES YOUR HEART WRECKED WITH AN INWARD SCOFFING	345	3	DON JUAN 12	63	4
INWARDLY					
(AS HE BLED INWARDLY NO HIDEOUS RIVER	430	2	DON JUAN 5	35	6
IO					
NOT AS OF YORE TO CARRY OFF AN IO	248	2	DON JUAN 2	174	7
IONIAN					
WITH AN IONIAN ACCENT LOW AND SWEET	236	2	DON JUAN 2	150	7
SHED ITS IONIAN ELEGANCE WHICH SHOW'D	304	2	DON JUAN 3	56	2
WITH HAIDEE'S ISLE AND SOFT IONIAN FACE	478	2	DON JUAN 5	117	3
IPECACUANHAE					
R PULV COM THREE GRAINS IPECACUANHAE	244	3	DON JUAN 10	41	5
IPHIGENE					
(WHEN A NEW IPHIGENE SHE WENT TO TAURIS)	248	3	DON JUAN 10	49	7
IRA					
OR CA IRA ACCORDING TO THE FASHION ALL	319	2	DON JUAN 3	85	4
IRE					
FLASH'D AN EXPRESSION MORE OF PRIDE THAN IRE	54	2	DON JUAN 1	60	4
THAN THE STERN SINGLE DEEP AND WORDLESS IRE	305	2	DON JUAN 3	58	7
IRELAND					
THOUGH IRELAND STARVE GREAT GEORGE WEIGHS TWENTY STONE	175	3	DON JUAN 8	126	8
LONGBOW FROM IRELAND STRONGBOW FROM THE TWEED	401	3	DON JUAN 13	92	2
IRELAND'S					
READ YOUR OWN HEARTS AND IRELAND'S PRESENT STORY	174	3	DON JUAN 8	125	7
BID IRELAND'S LONDONDERRY'S MARQUESS SHOW	207	3	DON JUAN 9	49	3
IRISH					
AND LORD MOUNT COFFEEHOUSE THE IRISH PEER	102	2	DON JUAN 1	149	7
THERE WAS AN IRISH LADY TO WHOSE BUST	219	2	DON JUAN 2	119	3
THE EAR BECOMES MORE IRISH AND LESS NICE	366	2	DON JUAN 4	41	8
AFTER ALL) OR LIKE IRISH AT A FAIR	23	3	DON JUAN 6	34	5

IRISH   (CONTINUED)
     OLD ERSE OR IRISH OR IT MAY BE PUNIC--   122   3 DON JUAN 8   23   2
     SCOTCH WITH BLUE GREEN RIBBONS--IRISH WITH A BLUE 314   3 DON JUAN 11   V 76   2
     THERE ALSO WERE SOME IRISH ABSENTEES 397   3 DON JUAN 13   83   8
IRISHMAN
     THOUGH AS AN IRISHMAN YOU LOVE POTATOES 186   3 DON JUAN 9   7   5
IRON
     A DAY OF GOLD FROM OUT AN AGE OF IRON 294   2 DON JUAN 3   36   3
     OF A SMALL IRON DOOR 'TWAS OPENED AND 433   2 DON JUAN 5   41   2
     FAMOUS FOR MINES OF SALT AND YOKES OF IRON 253   3 DON JUAN 10   58   2
     BESIDES SOME VEINS OF IRON LEAD OR COPPER   254   3 DON JUAN 10   60   3
     YE BEAUTIFUL ROULEAUS YE IRON CASKETS 321   3 DON JUAN 12   12   V1
     AND IRON TIME ERE LEAD HAD TA'EN THE LEAD   391   3 DON JUAN 13   70   2
IRREGULAR
     AT THE FIRST NOTES IRREGULAR AND SHARP   379   2 DON JUAN 4   65   3
     FORM'D A WHOLE WHICH IRREGULAR IN PARTS 390   3 DON JUAN 13   67   4
IRREGULARITY
     WHICH SOME IRREGULARITY MAY MAKE 86   2 DON JUAN 1   120   5
     IN MINE IRREGULARITY OF CHIME 465   3 DON JUAN 15   20   6
IRREGULARLY
     THOUGH RATHER MORE IRREGULARLY SPOTTED   416   2 DON JUAN 5   10   3
IRREGULARS
     O'ER THE IRREGULARS IN LUST OR GORE   537   3 DON JUAN 16   76   5
IRRELIGION
     LUCRETIUS' IRRELIGION IS TOO STRONG   45   2 DON JUAN 1   43   1
IRREVOCABLE
     IRREVOCABLE VOW OF REFORMATION 175   2 DON JUAN 2   37   4
IRRIGATE
     TO IRRIGATE THE DRYNESS OF DECLINE 360   3 DON JUAN 13   5   6
IRRITABILIS
     THE VATES IRRITABILIS TAKES CARE   317   2 DON JUAN 3   81   2
ISAAC
     IN WHICH SIR ISAAC NEWTON COULD DISCLOSE 226   3 DON JUAN 10   2   3
     WHATEVER ISAAC WALTON SINGS OR SAYS 407   3 DON JUAN 13   106   6
ISCARIOT
     A SCRIBBLING SELF-SOLD SOUL-HIRED SCORNED ISCARIOT 15   2 DON JUAN D   11   V8
ISCHSKIN
     ENDING IN ISCHSKIN OUSCKIN IFFSKCHY OUSKI 74   3 DON JUAN 7   16   7
ISLAND
     AND DOWN THE CLIFF THE ISLAND VIRGIN CAME   232   2 DON JUAN 2   142   1
     HAIDEE FORGOT THE ISLAND WAS HER SIRE'S 282   2 DON JUAN 3   13   4
     AND HE BEGUN A LONG LOW ISLAND SONG 379   2 DON JUAN 4   65   7
     TO POOR KATINKA SPAIN'S AN ISLAND NEAR   28   3 DON JUAN 6   44   7
     WENT BOUNDING FOR THE ISLAND OF THE FREE   256   3 DON JUAN 10   64   2
     THE ISLAND GIRL BRED UP BY THE LONE SEA 481   3 DON JUAN 15   58   4
ISLANDER
     SIGHS O'ER HER NAME AND MANY AN ISLANDER 383   2 DON JUAN 4   73   2
ISLANDS
     OF CANDIA CYPRUS RHODES OR OTHER ISLANDS 209   2 DON JUAN 2   100   8
     THAN YOUR SIRES' ISLANDS OF THE BLEST 321   2 DON JUAN 3 L 2   6
     IN ISLANDS IS IT SEEMS DOWNRIGHT AND THOROUGH 288   3 DON JUAN 11   42   6
     O'ER FAR ATLANTIC CONTINENTS OR ISLANDS 523   3 DON JUAN 16   46   4
ISLE
     HE WAS A GREEK AND ON HIS ISLE HAD BUILT 223   2 DON JUAN 2   127   1
     HIS PORT LAY ON THE OTHER SIDE O' THE ISLE 285   2 DON JUAN 3   19   8
     WHICH TURN'D THE ISLE INTO A PLACE OF PLEASURE 295   2 DON JUAN 3   39   2
     HE DEEM'D BEING IN A LONE ISLE AMONG FRIENDS 318   2 DON JUAN 3   83   4
     THE TEIAN BARD OF SCIO'S ISLE 321   2 DON JUAN 3 L 2   V1
     THAT ISLE IS NOW ALL DESOLATE AND BARE   383   2 DON JUAN 4   72   1
     WITH HAIDEE'S ISLE AND SOFT IONIAN FACE 478   2 DON JUAN 5   117   3
     LIKE OCEAN WARRING 'GAINST A ROCKY ISLE 489   2 DON JUAN 5   135   6
     AN ISLE NEAR ISMAIL HAD TWO ENDS IN VIEW 78   3 DON JUAN 7   23   2
     MAY FIND HIMSELF WITHIN THAT ISLE OF RICHES 273   3 DON JUAN 11   11   7
     MAKE THIS A SACRED PART OF ALBION'S ISLE 279   3 DON JUAN 11   24   8
     OR TO SOME LONELY ISLE OF JAILORS GO 296   3 DON JUAN 11   56   7
     EVEN IN THE HOPEFUL ISLE WHOSE OUTLET'S DOVER 331   3 DON JUAN 12   33   6
ISLES
     THE GREATEST HEIRESS OF THE EASTERN ISLES   224   2 DON JUAN 2   128   2
     BUT BEEF IS RARE WITHIN THESE OXLESS ISLES 238   2 DON JUAN 2   154   1
     THE ISLES OF GREECE THE ISLES OF GREECE 320   2 DON JUAN 3 L 1   1
     THE ISLES OF GREECE THE ISLES OF GREECE 320   2 DON JUAN 3 L 1   1
     THE TWELVE ISLES AND THE MORE THAN I COULD DREAM 412   2 DON JUAN 5   3   6
     AND WHERE THE DAUGHTER WHOM THE ISLES LOVED WELL 307   3 DON JUAN 11   77   6
ISMAIL
     THE FORTRESS IS CALLED ISMAIL AND IS PLACED 70   3 DON JUAN 7   9   1
     AN ISLE NEAR ISMAIL HAD TWO ENDS IN VIEW 78   3 DON JUAN 7   23   2
     OFF ISMAIL AND COMMENCED A CANNONADE 81   3 DON JUAN 7   29   5
     YOU WILL TAKE ISMAIL AT WHATEVER PRICE   86   3 DON JUAN 7   40   8
     SHALL PASS O'ER WHAT WAS ISMAIL AND ITS TUSK   99   3 DON JUAN 7   63   7
     WALKED O'ER THE WALLS OF ISMAIL AS IF NURST 138   3 DON JUAN 8   52   3
     THERE WAS AN END OF ISMAIL--HAPLESS TOWN 175   3 DON JUAN 8   127   2
     SLAUGHTER OF ISMAIL   THOUGH MY WILD MUSE VARIES 249   3 DON JUAN 10   51   6
ISMAIL'S
     WITH ISMAIL'S STORM TO SOFTEN IT THE MORE   146   3 DON JUAN 8   68   8
     ISMAIL'S NO MORE   THE CRESCENT'S SILVER BOW 172   3 DON JUAN 8   122   4
     ETERNAL SUCH NAMES MINGLED) ISMAIL'S OUR'S 178   3 DON JUAN 8   133   8
     WORN OUT WITH BATTERING ISMAIL'S STUBBORN WALL 181   3 DON JUAN 8   139   6
     FIRST ISMAIL'S CAPTURE CAUGHT YOUR FANCY QUITE 215   3 DON JUAN 9   65   6
ISRAELITES
     THAT ALL THE ISRAELITES ARE FIT TO MOB ITS 89   2 DON JUAN 1   125   7
     HELD OUT UNTO THE HUNGRY ISRAELITES   . . . . ,.   . . . 405   3 DON JUAN 13   100   2

ISSUE
    MERIDIAN-LIKE WERE SEEN ALL LIGHT TO ISSUE . . . . . . 309 2 DON JUAN 3   67   8
    THE UPHOLSTERER'S FIAT LUX HAD BADE TO ISSUE . . . . . 309 2 DON JUAN 3   67 V8
    WITH GREAT MAGNIFICENCE WERE SEEN TO ISSUE . . . . . . 309 2 DON JUAN 3   67 V8
ISSUING
    A HUMAN HYDRA ISSUING FROM ITS FEN . . . . 113 3 DON JUAN 8   2   5
IS'T
    AND BREAK THE--WHICH COMMANDMENT IS'T THEY BREAK . . . 74 2 DON JUAN 1   98   4
    IS'T WORTHY OF YOUR YEARS--YOU HAVE THREESCORE . . . . 101 2 DON JUAN 1   146   3
    IS'T WISE OR FITTING CAUSELESS TO EXPLORE . . . . . . 101 2 DON JUAN 1   146   5
    IS'T ENGLISH NO--'TIS ONLY PARLIAMENTARY) . . . . . . 536 3 DON JUAN 16   73   2
    AGAIN--WHAT IS'T THE WIND NO NO--THIS TIME . . . . . . 556 3 DON JUAN 16   113   1
    OR HOW IS'T MATTER TREMBLES TO COME NEAR IT . . . . . 557 3 DON JUAN 16   116   8
ISTHMUS
    AND AS THE ISTHMUS OF THE GRAND CONNECTION . . . . . . 534 3 DON JUAN 16   69   7
ITALIAN
    DID NOT THE ITALIAN MUSICO CAZZANI . . . . 102 2 DON JUAN 1   149   1
    ITALIAN NOT AT ALL HAVING NO TEACHERS . . . . 243 2 DON JUAN 2   165   2
    THE MAN WAS GONE IN SOME ITALIAN QUARREL . . . . 429 2 DON JUAN 5   34   7
    BENT AN ITALIAN SKY-BLUE PAPHIAN PAIR . . . . 467 2 DON JUAN 5   96 V3
    OF BEAUTIES COOL AS AN ITALIAN CONVENT . . . . 22 2 DON JUAN 6   32   7
    AN ENGLISH LADY ASKED OF AN ITALIAN . . . . 208 3 DON JUAN 9   51   1
ITALIANS
    TO BE ITALIANS AS THEY WERE IN FACT . . . . 388 2 DON JUAN 4   80   2
    A HUMAN (WHAT THE ITALIANS NICKNAME) MULE . . . . . . 563 3 DON JUAN 17   3   5
ITALY
    FOR I WILL NEVER FEEL THEM--ITALY . . . . 19 2 DON JUAN 0   16   2
    ESPECIALLY IN FRANCE AND ITALY . . . . 129 2 DON JUAN 1   191   4
    HIS SPANISH FRIENDS FOR THOSE IN ITALY . . . . 169 2 DON JUAN 2   24   8
    IN ITALY HE'D APE THE TRECENTISTI . . . . 320 2 DON JUAN 3   86   7
    WHETHER IN CALEDON OR ITALY . . . . 231 3 DON JUAN 10   13   6
    TO LIKE THOUGH I HAVE BEEN SEVEN YEARS IN ITALY . . . 350 3 DON JUAN 12   75   7
    TO SOOTHE OUR EARS LEST ITALY SHOULD FAIL . . . . . . 523 3 DON JUAN 16   45   8
ITCH
    THIS SCENE OF ROYAL ITCH AND LOYAL SCRATCHING . . . . 307 3 DON JUAN 11   78   8
ITEMS
    AND CANNOT FIND A BILL'S SMALL ITEMS COSTLY . . . . . 283 3 DON JUAN 11   31   4
ITHACA
    WHO DYING ON THE COAST OF ITHACA . . . . 285 2 DON JUAN 3   18   5
IT'S
    RAILING AT POWER--BUT ENVYING ALL IT'S TOOLS . . . . . 152 2 DON JUAN 1 V 3 V7
    WHEN IT'S LAST WEANING DRAUGHT IS DRAINED FOREVER . . . 349 2 DON JUAN 4   10 V6
    AS EVERY PALTRY MAGAZINE CAN SHOW IT'S . . . . 295 3 DON JUAN 11   54   8
    'TIS STRANGE THE MIND SHOULD LET SUCH PHRASES QUELL IT'S 298 3 DON JUAN 11   60 V7
I'VE
    WHEN PEOPLE SAY I'VE TOLD YOU FIFTY TIMES . . . . . . 79 2 DON JUAN 1   108   1
    WHEN POETS SAY I'VE WRITTEN FIFTY RHYMES . . . . 79 2 DON JUAN 1   108   3
    HOW SORRY YOU WILL BE WHEN I'VE MISCARRIED . . . . . . 101 2 DON JUAN 1   147   8
    I'VE NOTHING TO REPROACH OR TO REQUEST . . . . 130 2 DON JUAN 1   193   8
    I'VE GOT NEW MYTHOLOGICAL MACHINERY . . . . 136 2 DON JUAN 1   201   7
    I'VE LAID IN TOO A STOCK OF GOOD MACHINERY . . . . . . 136 2 DON JUAN 1   201 V7
    I'VE GOT A PLAN TO FORM A TREATISE WHICH . . . . 138 2 DON JUAN 1   204 V2
    I'VE BRIBED MY GRANDMOTHER'S REVIEW--THE BRITISH . . . 141 2 DON JUAN 1   209   8
    AND IN THY STEAD I'VE GOT A DEAL OF JUDGMENT . . . . . 144 2 DON JUAN 1   215   7
    NOW LIKE FRIAR BACON'S BRAZEN HEAD I'VE SPOKEN . . . . 145 2 DON JUAN 1   217   5
    THANK HEAVEN I'VE GOT NO METAPHOR QUITE READY . . . . 160 2 DON JUAN 2   6   7
    LOVE'S A CAPRICIOUS POWER I'VE KNOWN IT HOLD . . . . . 168 2 DON JUAN 2   22   1
    I'VE SEEN MUCH FINER WOMEN RIPE AND REAL . . . . 218 2 DON JUAN 2   118   7
    I'VE SEEN HIM RISE FULL OFT INDEED OF LATE . . . . . . 230 2 DON JUAN 2   140   2
    I'VE CHANGED FOR SOME FEW YEARS THE DAY TO NIGHT . . . 230 2 DON JUAN 2   140 V3
    IN THIS ANATOMY I'VE FINISH'D NOW . . . . 271 2 DON JUAN 2   216   2
    I'VE KNOWN THE ABSENT WRONG'D FOUR TIMES A DAY . . . . 288 2 DON JUAN 3   25   8
    I'VE SEEN A FRIEND BETRAYED FOUR TIMES A DAY . . . . . 288 2 DON JUAN 3   25 V8
    BESIDES I'VE NO MORE ON THIS HEAD TO ADD . . . . 384 2 DON JUAN 4   74   5
    SAVE CHANGE I'VE STOOD UPON ACHILLES' TOMB . . . . . . 399 2 DON JUAN 4   101   7
    HAD SHE BUT BEEN A CHRISTIAN I'VE A NOTION . . . . . . 475 2 DON JUAN 5   112   7
    I'VE RARELY SEEN THE MAN THEY DID NOT FRET . . . . . . 16 3 DON JUAN 6   21   8
    I'VE SEEN YOUR STORMY SEAS AND STORMY WOMEN . . . . . . 32 3 DON JUAN 6   53   7
    I'VE KNOWN SOME ODD ONES WHICH SEEMED REALLY PLANNED . . 45 3 DON JUAN 6   78   5
    I'VE HEARD OF STORIES OF A COCK AND BULL . . . . 46 3 DON JUAN 6   80   1
    BUT WHEN I'VE ADDED THAT THE ELDER JACK SMITH . . . . . 76 3 DON JUAN 7   20   2
    I'VE SAID ALL I KNOW OF A NAME THAT FILLS . . . . 76 3 DON JUAN 7   20   5
    I'VE DONE NOW GO AND DINE FROM OFF THE PLATE . . . . . 185 3 DON JUAN 9   6   1
    I'VE HEARD THEM IN THE EPHESIAN RUINS HOWL . . . . . . 196 3 DON JUAN 9   27   2
    THE TRUTH IS I'VE GROWN LATELY RATHER PHTHISICAL . . . 270 3 DON JUAN 11   5   5
    THE DYING MAN CRIED HOLD I'VE GOT MY GRUEL . . . . . . 276 3 DON JUAN 11   16   2
    GOD DAMN YOU LADS I'VE MISSED A HANDSOME BOOTY . . . . 276 3 DON JUAN 11   16 V3
    I'VE DONE TO FIND THE SAME THROUGHOUT LIFE'S JOURNEY . 281 3 DON JUAN 11   28   7
    INDEED I'VE NOT THE NECESSARY BILE . . . . 300 3 DON JUAN 11   63   4
    I'VE SEEN THE COUNTRY GENTLEMEN TURN SQUEAKERS-- . . . 310 3 DON JUAN 11   85   4
    I'VE SEEN THE PEOPLE RIDDEN O'ER LIKE SAND . . . . . . 310 3 DON JUAN 11   85   5
    WHATE'ER IT WAS 'TWAS MINE I'VE PAID IN TRUTH . . . . 324 3 DON JUAN 12   17   6
    SINCE I'VE GROWN MORAL STILL I MUST ACCUSE YOU ALL . . 329 3 DON JUAN 12   28   5
    I'VE KNOWN THEM COURT AN HEIRESS FOR THEIR LOVER . . . 331 3 DON JUAN 12   33   4
    MOREOVER I'VE REMARKED (AND I WAS ONCE . . . . 336 3 DON JUAN 12   44   1
    I'VE NOT BEGUN WHAT WE HAVE TO GO THROUGH . . . . . . 341 3 DON JUAN 12   54   4
    I'VE KNOWN A DOZEN WEDDINGS MADE EVEN THUS . . . . . . 344 3 DON JUAN 12   61   1
    I'VE GOT A BETTER SIMILE THAN THAT . . . . 375 3 DON JUAN 13   37 V1
    IF BUT TO SHOW I'VE TRAVELL'D AND WHAT'S TRAVEL . . . 380 3 DON JUAN 13   47   7

403

I'VE   (CONTINUED)
```
    I'VE DONE WITH MY TIRADE  THE WORLD WAS GONE  . . . . . 381  3 DON JUAN 13    49   1
    THE FACT--I'VE HEARD IT--ONCE PERHAPS TOO MUCH . . . . . 388  3 DON JUAN 13    64   8
    I'VE SEEN A VIRTUOUS WOMAN PUT DOWN QUITE  . . . . . . . 397  3 DON JUAN 13    82   3
    ON WHAT I'VE SEEN OR PONDER'D SAD OR CHEERY . . . . . . 415  3 DON JUAN 14    11   6
    SO LONG I'VE BATTLED EITHER MORE OR LESS . . . . . . . . 415  3 DON JUAN 14    12   3
    I'VE SEEN THEM BALANCE EVEN THE SCALE WITH FIGHTERS . . . 418  3 DON JUAN 14    20   3
    STILL THERE WAS SOMETHING WANTING AS I'VE SAID-- . . . . 441  3 DON JUAN 14    72   1
    I'VE ALSO SEEN SOME WIVES (NOT TO FORGET . . . . . . . . 452  3 DON JUAN 14    95   5
    I HAD A PARAMOUR--AND I'VE HAD MANY . . . . . . . . . . 452  3 DON JUAN 14    95   V2
    I'VE ALSO SEEN SOME FEMALE FRIENDS ('TIS ODD  . . . . . 452  3 DON JUAN 14    96   1
    BECAUSE IT SOMETIMES AS I'VE SEEN OR READ IT  . . . . . 491  3 DON JUAN 15    79   3
    IN SHORT UPON THAT SUBJECT I'VE SOME QUALMS VERY . . . . 499  3 DON JUAN 15    96   7
    TITUS EXCLAIMED I'VE LOST A DAY OF ALL  . . . . . . . . 505  3 DON JUAN 16    11   5
    AND THOUGHT I SAY NO MORE--I'VE SAID TOO MUCH . . . . . 538  3 DON JUAN 16    77   2
```
IVORY
```
    AN IVORY INLAID TABLE SPREAD WITH STATE  . . . . . . . . 306  2 DON JUAN  3    61   5
    WITH MOTHER OF PEARL OR IVORY STOOD AT HAND . . . . . . 310  2 DON JUAN  3    69   3
    A DIMPLED CHIN A NECK OF IVORY STOLE . . . . . . . . . . 561  3 DON JUAN 16   123   3
```
IVRESSE
```
    WHICH CATHERINE IN A MOMENT OF IVRESSE . . . . . . . . . 287  3 DON JUAN 11    39   5
```
IVY
```
    GLEAMED FORTH AS THROUGH THE CASEMENT'S IVY SHROUD . . . 560  3 DON JUAN 16   121   7
```
IXION
```
    FROM THAT IXION GRINDSTONE'S CEASELESS TOIL . . . . . . .  17  2 DON JUAN  D    13   6
```
JACK
```
    FLOATS SCUMLIKE UPPERMOST AND THESE JACK CADES . . . . . 334  2 DON JUAN  3   100   5
    MIGHT END IN ACTING AS HIS OWN JACK KETCH  . . . . . . .  63  3 DON JUAN  6   116   5
    JACK THOMSON AND BILL THOMSON--ALL THE REST  . . . . . .  76  3 DON JUAN  7    19   1
    BUT WHEN I'VE ADDED THAT THE ELDER JACK SMITH  . . . . .  76  3 DON JUAN  7    20   2
    TO JACK HOWE'ER THIS GAVE BUT SLIGHT CONCERN . . . . . . 133  3 DON JUAN  8    41   5
    UP CAME JOHN JOHNSON (I WILL NOT SAY JACK  . . . . . . . 160  3 DON JUAN  8    97   1
    OH JACK I'M FLOORED BY THAT 'ERE BLOODY FRENCHMAN  . . . 274  3 DON JUAN 11    13   8
    ON WHICH JACK AND HIS TRAIN SET OFF AT SPEED . . . . . . 275  3 DON JUAN 11    14   1
    WHERE HE MAY FIX HIMSELF LIKE SMALL JACK HORNER  . . . . 303  3 DON JUAN 11    69   4
    THERE WAS JACK JARGON THE GIGANTIC GUARDSMAN . . . . . . 399  3 DON JUAN 13    88   1
```
JACKALL
```
    NOR GIVE MY VOICE TO SLAVERY'S JACKALL CRY . . . . . . . 195  3 DON JUAN  9    26   8
    THAT'S AN APPROPRIATE SIMILE THAT JACKALL-- . . . . . . 196  3 DON JUAN  9    27   1
```
JACKALLS
```
    HOWEVER THE POOR JACKALLS ARE LESS FOUL  . . . . . . . . 196  3 DON JUAN  9    27   6
```
JACKET
```
    AND THEN HIS TATTERED JACKET OFF HE STRIPPED . . . . . . 456  2 DON JUAN  5    77   V3
    IN RUSSET JACKET--LYNX-LIKE IS HIS AIM . . . . . . . . . 394  3 DON JUAN 13    75   5
    AND WEAR THE MELTON JACKET FOR A SPACE-- . . . . . . . . 395  3 DON JUAN 13    78   6
```
JACKET'S
```
    FINISHED WITH BRIGHT GOLD LACE HER JACKET'S FELLOW . . . 311  2 DON JUAN  3    70   V4
```
JACKETS
```
    WHILE THEY THRUST SHEETS SHIRTS JACKETS BALES OF MUSLIN . 171  2 DON JUAN  2    28   8
```
JACKS
```
    THE REST WERE JACKS AND GILLS AND WILLS AND BILLS . . . .  76  3 DON JUAN  7    20   1
```
JACOB
```
    NOT ALL THE REVERIES OF JACOB BEHMEN . . . . . . . . . .   7  3 DON JUAN  6     2   5
```
JACOBINS
```
    TO THOSE SAD HUNGRY JACOBINS THE WORMS . . . . . . . . .  12  3 DON JUAN  6    13   4
```
JACOB'S
```
    WAS NOT LIKE JACOB'S) OR TO CROSS A DITCH  . . . . . . .  93  3 DON JUAN  7    52   8
```
JADE
```
    THE VERIEST JADE WILL WINCE WHOSE HARNESS WRINGS . . . . 137  3 DON JUAN  8    50   5
```
JADED
```
    ALL SAVE THE BLACKS SEEM'D JADED WITH VEXATION . . . . . 414  2 DON JUAN  5     7   5
    ON LIFE'S WORN CONFINE JADED BLOATED SATED . . . . . . . 267  3 DON JUAN 10    87   2
```
JAIL
```
    READY FOR JAIL THEIR PLACE OF CONVALESCENCE  . . . . . . 530  3 DON JUAN 16    61   2
```
JAILOR
```
    FEE BY A COUNSEL FELON BY A JAILOR . . . . . . . . . . . 424  2 DON JUAN  5    26   8
    (WHEN SHE DON'T PIN MEN'S LIMBS IN LIKE A JAILOR)-- . . . 204  3 DON JUAN  9    44   6
    IN PRISON--BUT THE JAILOR WHAT IS HE . . . . . . . . . . 258  3 DON JUAN 10    68   3
```
JAILORS
```
    OR TO SOME LONELY ISLE OF JAILORS GO . . . . . . . . . . 296  3 DON JUAN 11    56   7
```
JAMES'S
```
    SAINT JAMES'S PALACE AND SAINT JAMES'S HELLS . . . . . . 282  3 DON JUAN 11    29   8
    SAINT JAMES'S PALACE AND SAINT JAMES'S HELLS . . . . . . 282  3 DON JUAN 11    29   8
```
JANIZARIES
```
    I'D TRY CONCLUSIONS WITH THOSE JANIZARIES  . . . . . . . 299  3 DON JUAN 11    62   7
```
JAR
```
    IT HAS A STRANGE QUICK JAR UPON THE EAR  . . . . . . . . 366  2 DON JUAN  4    41   1
```
JARGON
```
    A JARGON A MERE PHILANTHROPIC DIN  . . . . . . . . . . . 266  3 DON JUAN 10    85   6
    THERE WAS JACK JARGON THE GIGANTIC GUARDSMAN . . . . . . 399  3 DON JUAN 13    88   1
```
JASMINE
```
    THROUGH ORANGE BOWERS AND JASMINE AND SO FORTH . . . . . 434  2 DON JUAN  5    42   2
```
JASON
```
    THEE WITCH OR EACH MEDEA HAS HER JASON . . . . . . . . . 396  3 DON JUAN 13    81   6
```
JASON'S
```
    AS CAPTAIN PARRY'S VOYAGE MAY DO TO JASON'S  . . . . . . 419  3 DON JUAN 14    22   4
```
JAUNT
```
    ABOUT PHILOSOPHY PURSUED HIS JAUNT . . . . . . . . . . . 254  3 DON JUAN 10    60   6
```
JAWS
```
    NOW FEELING ALL THE VULTURE IN HIS JAWS  . . . . . . . . 193  2 DON JUAN  2    71   4
```

JAWS   (CONTINUED)
   DESTRUCTION'S JAWS INTO THE DEVIL'S DEN 130   3 DON JUAN 8   35   4
   HAVE VENTURED PAST THE JAWS OF MOOR AND TIGER 348   3 DON JUAN 12   70 V6
JE
   THAT UNDEFINABLE JE NE SCAIS QUOI 441   3 DON JUAN 14   72   2
JEALOUS
   YET HE WAS JEALOUS THOUGH HE DID NOT SHOW IT 57   2 DON JUAN 1   65   7
   I SAY WHEN THESE SAME GENTLEMEN ARE JEALOUS 74   2 DON JUAN 1   98   7
   JEALOUS OF SOME ONE WHO HAD NO SUCH WISHES 74   2 DON JUAN 1   99   3
   OR FOR SO YOUNG A HUSBAND'S JEALOUS FEARS-- 106   2 DON JUAN 1 155   3
   PERHAPS 'TIS OF ANTONIA YOU ARE JEALOUS 106   2 DON JUAN 1 156   1
   ALL FIT TO MAKE A PATAGONIAN JEALOUS 205   3 DON JUAN 9   46   8
JEALOUSIES
   THE TIGRIS HATH ITS JEALOUSIES LIKE THAMES 11   3 DON JUAN 6   11   8
   AND YET THEY HAD THEIR LITTLE JEALOUSIES 25   3 DON JUAN 6   38   1
JEALOUSY
   FOR JEALOUSY DISLIKES THE WORLD TO KNOW IT 57   2 DON JUAN 1   65   8
   MENTION'D HIS JEALOUSY BUT NEVER WHO 118   2 DON JUAN 1 177   3
   RAGE FEAR HATE JEALOUSY REVENGE COMPUNCTION 271   2 DON JUAN 2 215   6
   IT WAS NOT JEALOUSY I THINK BUT SHUN 479   3 DON JUAN 15   54   5
JEAN
   MY LEIPSIC AND MY MONT SAINT JEAN SEEMS CAIN 296   3 DON JUAN 11   56   2
JEER
   WITHOUT THE LEAST PROPENSITY TO JEER 245   3 DON JUAN 10   42   4
JEFFERIES
   THERE WAS THE WAGGISH WELCH JUDGE JEFFERIES HARDSMAN . . 399   3 DON JUAN 13   88   5
JEFFREY
   AS MY FRIEND JEFFREY WRITES WITH SUCH AN AIR 230   3 DON JUAN 10   11   6
   DEAR JEFFREY ONCE MY MOST REDOUBTED FOE 232   3 DON JUAN 10   16   2
   MY JEFFREY HELD HIM UP AS AN EXAMPLE 323   3 DON JUAN 12   16   7
JELICK'S
   ALL GOLD AND CRIMSON SHONE HER JELICK'S FELLOW 311   2 DON JUAN 3   70   6
JELICKS
   SHE WORE TWO JELICKS--ONE WAS OF PALE YELLOW 311   2 DON JUAN 3   70   2
JELLIES
   WHILE BACCHUS WILL PURVEY WITH WINES AND JELLIES . . . 246   2 DON JUAN 2 170 V5
JELLY
   WHILE BACCHUS POURS OUT WINE OR HANDS A JELLY 246   2 DON JUAN 2 170   5
JEMMY
   HAD BEEN CALLED JEMMY AFTER THE GREAT BARD 76   3 DON JUAN 7   19   2
JEOPARDY
   HERSELF FROM OUT HER PRESENT JEOPARDY 170   2 DON JUAN 2   27   6
JEROME
   TO JEROME AND TO CHRYSOSTOM INURED 47   2 DON JUAN 1   47   3
JERVIS
   FORGETTING DUNCAN NELSON HOWE AND JERVIS 23   2 DON JUAN 1   4   8
JEST
   AGAINST ALL EVIL SPEAKING EVEN IN JEST 49   2 DON JUAN 1   51   8
   HIS JEST ALIKE IN FACE OF FRIEND OR FOE 147   3 DON JUAN 8   70   6
   TO KILL AND GENERALS TURN IT INTO JEST 212   3 DON JUAN 9   60   8
   A JEST AT VICE BY VIRTUE'S CALLED A CRIME 358   3 DON JUAN 13   1   3
   PERHAPS THE FINE OLD FELLOW SPOKE IN JEST-- 361   3 DON JUAN 13   7   5
   A JEST A RIDDLE FAME THROUGH THIN AND THICK SOUGHT . . 363   3 DON JUAN 13   10   7
   TO BRING WHAT WAS A JEST TO A SERIOUS END 491   3 DON JUAN 15   79   6
   OR NONE AT ALL--WHICH SEEMS A SORRY JEST 494   3 DON JUAN 15   87   6
   TO JEST YOU'LL CHOOSE SOME OTHER THEME JUST NOW 516   3 DON JUAN 16   37   6
   JEST QUOTH MILOR WHY ADELINE YOU KNOW 517   3 DON JUAN 16   38   1
   TO JEST UPON SUCH THEMES IN MANY A SALLY 526   3 DON JUAN 16   53   3
JESTEST
   AND JESTEST WITH THE BROWS OF MIGHTIEST MEN 266   2 DON JUAN 2 206   2
JESTING
   SURVEYING DRILLING ORDERING JESTING PONDERING 95   3 DON JUAN 7   55   2
   SOME PLEASANT JESTING AT THE AWKWARD STRANGER 424   3 DON JUAN 14   32   4
JET
   SOME BOUGHT THE JET WHILE OTHERS CHOSE THE PALE 416   2 DON JUAN 5   10   4
JETTY
   THE GLOSSY REBELS MOCK'D THE JETTY STAIN 314   2 DON JUAN 3   75   4
JEUNES
   WITNESS THOSE CI-DEVANT JEUNES HOMMES WHO STEM 418   3 DON JUAN 14   18   7
JEW
   A JEW TOOK ONE OF HIS TWO MISTRESSES 39   2 DON JUAN 1   34   4
   OF ANY CREDITORS THE WORST A JEW IT IS 190   2 DON JUAN 2   65   5
   THEIR CASH COMES FROM THEIR WEALTH GOES TO A JEW . . . 306   3 DON JUAN 11   75   4
   JEW ROTHSCHILD AND HIS FELLOW CHRISTIAN BARING 318   3 DON JUAN 12   5   8
   MUST GET ITSELF DISCOUNTED BY A JEW 318   3 DON JUAN 12   6   8
JEWELS
   O'ER WHOM AN EMPRESS HER CROWN JEWELS SCATTERING . . . 217   3 DON JUAN 9   70 V5
JEWS
   SO JUAN WEPT AS WEPT THE CAPTIVE JEWS 165   2 DON JUAN 2   16   1
   HOW SOME WERE BOUGHT BY PACHAS SOME BY JEWS 409   2 DON JUAN 4 116   2
   BELIEVE THE JEWS THOSE UNBELIEVERS WHO 447   2 DON JUAN 5   62   7
JINGLED
   THE GLASSES JINGLED AND THE PALATES TINGLED 487   3 DON JUAN 15   70   1
JOANNA
   JOANNA SOUTHCOTE'S SHILOH AND HER SECT 330   2 DON JUAN 3   95   4
JOB
   FINE TRUTHS EVEN CONSCIENCE TOO HAS A TOUGH JOB . . . 264   2 DON JUAN 2 203   6
   AS WIFE AND FRIENDS DID FOR THE BOILS OF JOB-- 105   3 DON JUAN 7   77   7
   AT LAST FALL SICK OF IMITATING JOB 137   3 DON JUAN 8   50   8
   OH JOB YOU HAD TWO FRIENDS ONE'S QUITE ENOUGH 431   3 DON JUAN 14   48   1

JOB'S
    ALFONSO SAW HIS WIFE AND THOUGHT OF JOB'S . . . . . . 110 2 DON JUAN 1   162   6
JOCUND
    SAINT FROM HIS BEADS TO JOIN THE JOCUND RACE . . . . . 395 3 DON JUAN 13   78   4
JOG
    LAUNCHED AT THEIR HEADS--JOG--JOG--JOG--JOG--JOG--JOG . 260 3 DON JUAN 10   71 V8
    LAUNCHED AT THEIR HEADS--JOG--JOG--JOG--JOG--JOG--JOG . 260 3 DON JUAN 10   71 V8
    LAUNCHED AT THEIR HEADS--JOG--JOG--JOG--JOG--JOG--JOG . 260 3 DON JUAN 10   71 V8
    LAUNCHED AT THEIR HEADS--JOG--JOG--JOG--JOG--JOG--JOG . 260 3 DON JUAN 10   71 V8
    LAUNCHED AT THEIR HEADS--JOG--JOG--JOG--JOG--JOG--JOG . 260 3 DON JUAN 10   71 V8
    LAUNCHED AT THEIR HEADS--JOG--JOG--JOG--JOG--JOG--JOG . 260 3 DON JUAN 10   71 V8
JOHANNA
    I HAVE SEEN JOHANNA SOUTHCOTE--I HAVE SEEN . . . . . . 310 3 DON JUAN 11   84   2
JOHN
    HOW PEACE SHOULD MAKE JOHN BULL THE FRENCHMAN'S FOE . . . 77 3 DON JUAN 7   22   8
    AND THROWS A CLOUD O'ER LONGMAN AND JOHN MURRAY . . . . 79 3 DON JUAN 7   26   4
    WHICH TO THAT BOTTLE-CONJURER JOHN BULL . . . . 88 3 DON JUAN 7   44   3
    THAT SAGE (SAID JOHN) SURRENDERS AT DISCRETION . . . . 88 3 DON JUAN 7   44   6
    SINCE JOHN HAS LATELY LOST THE USE OF BOTH . . . . . . 88 3 DON JUAN 7   45   4
    JOHN JOHNSON SEEING THEIR EXTREME DISMAY . . . . . . 105 3 DON JUAN 7   75   1
    PUT TO SUCH TRIAL JOHN BULL'S PARTIAL PATIENCE . . . . 136 3 DON JUAN 8   48   6
    UP CAME JOHN JOHNSON (I WILL NOT SAY JACK . . . . . . 160 3 DON JUAN 8   97   1
    LIKE MANY PUBLICATIONS OF JOHN MURRAY . . . . 237 3 DON JUAN 10   26 V3
    JOHN KEATS WHO WAS KILLED OFF BY ONE CRITIQUE . . . . 298 3 DON JUAN 11   60   1
    EXCHANGED FOR THIN POTATIONS BY JOHN BULL-- . . . . . 310 3 DON JUAN 11   85   7
    I HAVE SEEN JOHN HALF DETECT HIMSELF A FOOL-- . . . . 310 3 DON JUAN 11   85   8
    AND SIR JOHN POTTLEDEEP THE MIGHTY DRINKER . . . . . 398 3 DON JUAN 13   84   8
    OF AN OLD FAMILY SOME GAY SIR JOHN . . . . 470 3 DON JUAN 15   33   3
    THAN COULD ROAST BEEF IN OUR ROUGH JOHN BULL WAY . . . 487 3 DON JUAN 15   71   4
    IN POLITICS MY DUTY IS TO SHOW JOHN . . . . 497 3 DON JUAN 15   92   5
JOHNSON
    YOUR NAMES--MINE'S JOHNSON AND MY COMRADE'S JUAN . . . . 97 3 DON JUAN 7   60   1
    JOHNSON WHO KNEW BY THIS LONG COLLOQUY . . . . 100 3 DON JUAN 7   65   1
    WHY JOHNSON WHAT THE DEVIL DO YOU MEAN . . . . 102 3 DON JUAN 7   70   2
    JOHN JOHNSON SEEING THEIR EXTREME DISMAY . . . . . . 105 3 DON JUAN 7   75   1
    JUAN AND JOHNSON JOINED A CERTAIN CORPS . . . . 120 3 DON JUAN 8   19   1
    JUST AT THIS CRISIS UP CAME JOHNSON TOO . . . . 130 3 DON JUAN 8   35   1
    BUT JOHNSON WAS A CLEVER FELLOW WHO . . . . 130 3 DON JUAN 8   35   5
    JOHNSON RETIRED A LITTLE JUST TO RALLY . . . . 131 3 DON JUAN 8   36   7
    BY JOVE HE WAS A NOBLE FELLOW JOHNSON . . . . 132 3 DON JUAN 8   39   1
    BUT JOHNSON ONLY RAN OFF TO RETURN . . . . 133 3 DON JUAN 8   41   1
    THAT JOHNSON AND SOME FEW WHO HAD NOT SCAMPERED . . . 135 3 DON JUAN 8   44   7
    JUAN AND JOHNSON AND SOME VOLUNTEERS . . . . 152 3 DON JUAN 8   80   1
    UP CAME JOHN JOHNSON (I WILL NOT SAY JACK . . . . . . 160 3 DON JUAN 8   97   1
    UP JOHNSON CAME WITH HUNDREDS AT HIS BACK . . . . . . 160 3 DON JUAN 8   97   5
    AND I AM WITH YOU--WHEREON JOHNSON TOOK . . . . . . 161 3 DON JUAN 8   99   5
    QUOTH JOHNSON--NEITHER WILL I QUITE ENSURE . . . . . 161 3 DON JUAN 8   100   4
    JOHNSON SAID--JUAN WE'VE NO TIME TO LOSE . . . . . . 162 3 DON JUAN 8   101   1
    JOHNSON WHO REALLY LOVED HIM IN HIS WAY . . . . . . 162 3 DON JUAN 8   102   2
    AND SPITE OF JOHNSON AND OF JUAN WHO . . . . 165 3 DON JUAN 8   108   1
    JUAN AND JOHNSON WHEREUPON THEY FELL . . . . 166 3 DON JUAN 8   109   2
    ROUGH JOHNSON THE GREAT MORALIST PROFESSED . . . . . 361 3 DON JUAN 13   7   1
    I MERELY MEAN TO SAY WHAT JOHNSON SAID . . . . 504 3 DON JUAN 16   7   1
JOHNSON'S
    BUT HIS LIFE FALLING INTO JOHNSON'S WAY . . . . . . 328 2 DON JUAN 3   91   5
JOIN
    WILL JOIN YOUR FORMER REGIMENT WHICH SHOULD BE . . . . 100 3 DON JUAN 7   66   2
    THOUGH PRIESTS AND SLAVES MAY JOIN IN THE SERVILE CRY . 195 3 DON JUAN 9   26 V8
    CONVERTED FOES SHOULD SCORN TO JOIN WITH THOSE . . . . 231 3 DON JUAN 10   12   8
    WOULD SCARCELY JOIN AGAIN THE REFORMADOES . . . . . 231 3 DON JUAN 10   13   3
    SAINT FROM HIS BEADS TO JOIN THE JOCUND RACE . . . . 395 3 DON JUAN 13   78   4
    HE WOULD NOT JOIN THEM IN A SINGLE SALLY . . . . . . 552 3 DON JUAN 16   105   8
JOIN'D
    WHICH BEING JOIN'D LIKE SWARMING BEES THEY CLUNG-- . . 254 2 DON JUAN 2   187   7
    HUGE HALLS LONG GALLERIES SPACIOUS CHAMBERS JOIN'D . . 390 3 DON JUAN 13   67   1
JOINED
    AT THE GIVEN SIGNAL JOINED TO THEIR ARRAY . . . . . . 20 3 DON JUAN 6   29   2
    JUAN AND JOHNSON JOINED A CERTAIN CORPS . . . . . . 120 3 DON JUAN 8   19   1
JOINS
    YOUR HEART JOINS CHORUS FAME IS BUT A DIN . . . . . 199 3 DON JUAN 9   34   8
JOINT
    A JOINT UPON THEIR BARBAROUS SPITS THEY PUT ON . . . . 238 2 DON JUAN 2   154   4
    THEIR PAUSE NOR SIGNS HIS HEART WAS OUT OF JOINT . . . 170 3 DON JUAN 8   117   5
    THE TIME IS OUT OF JOINT--AND SO AM I . . . . 203 3 DON JUAN 9   41   2
    APPEARANCES APPEAR TO FORM THE JOINT . . . . 396 3 DON JUAN 13   81   3
JOKE
    OF ALL SAVE DUDU'S DREAM WHICH WAS NO JOKE . . . . . . 58 3 DON JUAN 6   104   8
    HE HAD HIS JUDGE'S JOKE FOR CONSOLATION . . . . . . 399 3 DON JUAN 13   88   8
    AND NOT A JOKE HE CUT BUT EARNED ITS PRAISE . . . . . 540 3 DON JUAN 16   82   3
    HER OWN BUT SERVED TO SET OFF EVERY JOKE . . . . . . 552 3 DON JUAN 16   104   5
JOKERS
    OF WONDERFUL REPLIES FROM ARAB JOKERS . . . . 293 2 DON JUAN 3   34   4
JOKES
    BUT HERE IT SEEMED HIS JOKES HAD CEASED TO TAKE . . . 147 3 DON JUAN 8   70   8
    HIS JOKES WERE SERMONS AND HIS SERMONS JOKES . . . . 540 3 DON JUAN 16   83   1
    HIS JOKES WERE SERMONS AND HIS SERMONS JOKES . . . . 540 3 DON JUAN 16   83   1
JOKING
    AND YOU WILL FIND US NOT TOO FOND OF JOKING . . . . . 454 2 DON JUAN 5   75   4
JOLLY
    HE WAS A JOLLY FELLOW AND COULD CRACK . . . . 147 3 DON JUAN 8   70   5

JOLT
 AT EVERY JOLT--AND THEY WERE MANY--STILL . . . . 198 3 DON JUAN 9 31 1
JOLTINGS
 BY VARIOUS JOLTINGS OF LIFE'S HACKNEY COACH . . . . . . 421 3 DON JUAN 14 26 5
JONES
 WE HAVE NO ACCOMPLISH'D BLACKGUARDS LIKE TOM JONES . . . 409 3 DON JUAN 13 110 7
JOSE
 HIS FATHER'S NAME WAS JOSE--DON OF COURSE . . . . . . 26 2 DON JUAN 1 9 1
 THAN JOSE WHO BEGOT OUR HERO WHO . . . . 26 2 DON JUAN 1 9 7
 DON JOSE LIKE A LINEAL SON OF EVE . . . . 30 2 DON JUAN 1 18 7
 DON JOSE AND HIS LADY QUARRELL'D--WHY . . . . 33 2 DON JUAN 1 23 1
 DON JOSE AND THE DONNA INEZ LED . . . . 35 2 DON JUAN 1 26 1
 BEFORE UNLUCKILY DON JOSE DIED . . . . 38 2 DON JUAN 1 32 8
 YET JOSE WAS AN HONOURABLE MAN . . . . 40 2 DON JUAN 1 35 1
JOSEPH
 HE FLED LIKE JOSEPH LEAVING IT BUT THERE . . . . . . 124 2 DON JUAN 1 186 7
JOSE'S
 A SMALL OLD SPANIEL--WHICH HAD BEEN DON JOSE'S . . . . 187 2 DON JUAN 2 58 1
JOSTLE
 OF HUMAN THOUGHTS WHICH JOSTLE IN THEIR FLIGHT . . . . 215 3 DON JUAN 9 65 4
 ILL FITTED WITH HER IGNORANCE TO JOSTLE . . . . . 250 3 DON JUAN 10 52 5
JOT
 WITH GRACEFUL ACTION SCIENCE NOT A JOT . . . . . 392 2 DON JUAN 4 89 3
 WERE THERE A JOT OF SENSE AMONG MANKIND . . . . . 446 3 DON JUAN 14 84 6
JOUBERT
 JOUBERT HOCHE MARCEAU LANNES DESSAIX MOREAU . . . . . 22 2 DON JUAN 1 3 5
JOURNAL
 SHE KEPT A JOURNAL WHERE HIS FAULTS WERE NOTED . . . . 36 2 DON JUAN 1 28 1
JOURNALS
 (THAT MAKE OLD EUROPE'S JOURNALS SQUEAK AND GIBBER ALL) . 318 3 DON JUAN 12 5 4
JOURNEY
 WAS IT FOR THIS YOU TOOK YOUR SUDDEN JOURNEY . . . . 103 2 DON JUAN 1 151 1
 WHO TO MADRID ON PURPOSE MADE A JOURNEY . . . . . 127 2 DON JUAN 1 189 8
 PURSUED O'ER THE HIGH SEAS HIS WATERY JOURNEY . . . . 283 2 DON JUAN 3 14 7
 HIS WOND'ROUS JOURNEY TO SOME FOREIGN COURT . . . . 440 2 DON JUAN 5 52 3
 HIS JOURNEY WE'VE SO MANY TOURS OF LATE . . . . . 203 3 DON JUAN 9 42 6
 I'VE DONE TO FIND THE SAME THROUGHOUT LIFE'S JOURNEY . . 281 3 DON JUAN 11 28 7
JOURNEYED
 BECAUSE HE HAD JOURNEYED FIFTY MILES AND FOUND . . . . 497 2 DON JUAN 5 150 3
 THEY JOURNEYED ON THROUGH POLAND AND THROUGH WARSAW . . 253 3 DON JUAN 10 58 1
JOVE
 HEAVEN KNOWS--IT MAY BE NEPTUNE PAN OR JOVE . . . . 246 2 DON JUAN 2 170 8
 BY JOVE A NOBLE PALACE--LIGHTED TOO . . . . . . 436 2 DON JUAN 5 45 8
 BY JOVE HE WAS A NOBLE FELLOW JOHNSON . . . . . 132 3 DON JUAN 8 39 1
 OR IF THE OATH SEEM STRONG--I SWEAR BY JOVE . . . . 452 3 DON JUAN 14 96 V2
JOVE'S
 DESCRIBING PRIAM'S PELEUS' OR JOVE'S SON . . . . . 164 3 DON JUAN 8 105 6
JOY
 AT LEAST IT SEEM'D SO AND HIS MOTHER'S JOY . . . . 49 2 DON JUAN 1 50 6
 AND THEN ABASH'D AT ITS OWN JOY WITHDREW . . . . . 81 2 DON JUAN 1 112 4
 TO RENDER HAPPY ALL WHO JOY WOULD WIN . . . . . . 247 2 DON JUAN 2 172 7
 FEEL RAPTURE BUT NOT SUCH TRUE JOY ARE REAPING . . . . 261 2 DON JUAN 2 196 7
 AND ALL UNCONSCIOUS OF THE JOY 'TIS GIVING . . . . . 261 2 DON JUAN 2 197 4
 JOY OF ITS ALCHYMY AND TO REPEAT . . . . 264 2 DON JUAN 2 203 5
 JOY OF ITS GLITTERING TREASURE AND REPEAT . . . . . 264 2 DON JUAN 2 203 V5
 PAST HIM IN CRYSTAL AND A JOY IN FLOWERS . . . . . 304 2 DON JUAN 3 56 7
 JOY SPARKLING IN THEIR DARK EYES LIKE A GEM . . . . 351 2 DON JUAN 4 13 6
 WITH JOY AND SORROW HOPE AND FEAR TO SEE . . . . . 363 2 DON JUAN 4 36 2
 THAT DOUBT SHOULD MINGLE WITH MY FILIAL JOY . . . . 364 2 DON JUAN 4 38 7
 ALL PHANTASIES WHICH YIELDED JOY OR MIRTH . . . . . 475 2 DON JUAN 5 112 3
 GREAT JOY TO LONDON NOW SAYS SOME GREAT FOOL . . . . 88 3 DON JUAN 7 44 1
 BUT TO THE TALE--GREAT JOY UNTO THE CAMP . . . . . 89 3 DON JUAN 7 46 1
 THE WHOLE CAMP RUNG WITH JOY YOU WOULD HAVE THOUGHT . . 90 3 DON JUAN 7 49 1
 NOW SWIMMING IN THE SENTIMENT OF JOY . . . . . . 123 3 DON JUAN 8 24 3
 WITH JOY TO SAVE AND DREAD OF SOME MISCHANCE . . . . 159 3 DON JUAN 8 96 4
 AND AS IN THE GREAT JOY OF YOUR MILLENNIUM . . . . 180 3 DON JUAN 8 136 2
 GREAT JOY WAS HER'S OR RATHER JOYS THE FIRST . . . . 212 3 DON JUAN 9 59 1
 THERE IS A MOVE SET DOWN FOR JOY OR SORROW . . . . 288 3 DON JUAN 11 42 4
 AN OH OR AH OF JOY OR MISERY . . . . 456 3 DON JUAN 15 1 6
 MORE JOY THAN FROM ALL FUTURE PRIDE OR PRAISE . . . . 554 3 DON JUAN 16 108 5
JOYOUS
 IN FIX'D FEROCITY WHEN JOYOUS TEARS . . . . . . 368 2 DON JUAN 4 45 6
 THE EVAPORATION OF A JOYOUS DAY . . . . 504 3 DON JUAN 16 9 1
JOYS
 THEY NE'ER TILL NOW HAD KNOWN THE JOYS OF DRINKING . . 201 2 DON JUAN 2 85 8
 THOSE THEIR BRIGHT RISE HAD LIGHTED TO SUCH JOYS . . . 352 2 DON JUAN 4 16 2
 BOTH MALADIES ARE TAXES ON OUR JOYS . . . . . . 357 2 DON JUAN 4 25 3
 WHATE'ER THEIR DREAMS BE IF OF JOYS OR WOES . . . . 16 3 DON JUAN 6 20 3
 YET DISAPPOINTED JOYS ARE WOES AS DEEP . . . . . 16 3 DON JUAN 6 20 4
 NOW BACK TO THY GREAT JOYS CIVILIZATION . . . . . 146 3 DON JUAN 8 68 2
 THINK HOW THE JOYS OF READING A GAZETTE . . . . . 174 3 DON JUAN 8 125 1
 GREAT JOY WAS HER'S OR RATHER JOYS THE FIRST . . . . 212 3 DON JUAN 9 59 1
 WHO FURROW SOME NEW SOIL TO SOW FOR JOYS . . . . . 228 3 DON JUAN 10 7 8
 OR REVEL IN THE JOYS OF CALCULATION . . . . . . 320 3 DON JUAN 12 10 8
 THE JOYS OF MUTUAL HATE TO KEEP THEM WARM . . . . 360 3 DON JUAN 13 6 5
JUAN
 I'LL THEREFORE TAKE OUR ANCIENT FRIEND DON JUAN . . . 21 2 DON JUAN 1 1 6
 SO AS I SAID I'LL TAKE MY FRIEND DON JUAN . . . . 24 2 DON JUAN 1 5 8
 FOR LITTLE JUAN O'ER ME THREW DOWN STAIRS . . . . . 34 2 DON JUAN 1 24 7

JUAN (CONTINUED)

	PAGE	VOL	CANTO	STANZA	LN
DYING INTESTATE JUAN WAS SOLE HEIR	42	2 DON JUAN	1	37	1
RESOLVED THAT JUAN SHOULD BE QUITE A PARAGON	42	2 DON JUAN	1	38	2
JUAN WAS TAUGHT FROM OUT THE BEST EDITION	46	2 DON JUAN	1	44	1
THIS TOO WAS A SEAL'D BOOK TO LITTLE JUAN--	48	2 DON JUAN	1	48	1
YOUNG JUAN WAX'D IN GOODLINESS AND GRACE	48	2 DON JUAN	1	49	1
YOUNG JUAN NOW WAS SIXTEEN YEARS OF AGE	51	2 DON JUAN	1	54	1
JUAN SHE SAW AND AS A PRETTY CHILD	59	2 DON JUAN	1	69	1
BUT AS FOR JUAN HE HAD NO MORE NOTION	60	2 DON JUAN	1	70	7
SHE VOW'D SHE NEVER WOULD SEE JUAN MORE	63	2 DON JUAN	1	76	1
'TIS SURELY JUAN NOW--NO I'M AFRAID	63	2 DON JUAN	1	76	7
JUAN BEING THEN GROWN UP TO MAN'S ESTATE	67	2 DON JUAN	1	85	2
SO MUCH FOR JULIA NOW WE'LL TURN TO JUAN	68	2 DON JUAN	1	86	1
YOUNG JUAN WANDER'D BY THE GLASSY BROOKS	70	2 DON JUAN	1	90	1
HE JUAN (AND NOT WORDSWORTH) SO PURSUED	70	2 DON JUAN	1	91	1
SHE SAW THAT JUAN WAS NOT AT HIS EASE	73	2 DON JUAN	1	97	3
FOR LEAVING JUAN TO THIS NEW TEMPTATION	75	2 DON JUAN	1	101	4
BUT THERE WERE SHE AND JUAN FACE TO FACE--	77	2 DON JUAN	1	105	6
I CANNOT KNOW WHAT JUAN THOUGHT OF THIS	81	2 DON JUAN	1	112	1
AND JULIA SATE WITH JUAN HALF EMBRACED	83	2 DON JUAN	1	115	1
BUT KEEPING JULIA AND DON JUAN STILL	86	2 DON JUAN	1	121	5
YOUNG JUAN SLIPP'D HALF-SMOTHER'D FROM THE BED	112	2 DON JUAN	1	165	8
FOR DAVID LIVED BUT JUAN NEARLY DIED	113	2 DON JUAN	1	168	8
OUR COUNSEL--(JUAN MIND YOU MUST NOT SLEEP)	115	2 DON JUAN	1	172	8
ALFONSO NE'ER TO JUAN HAD ALLUDED	118	2 DON JUAN	1	177	2
LIKE THROWING JUAN IN ALFONSO'S WAY	118	2 DON JUAN	1	177	8
FLY JUAN FLY FOR HEAVEN'S SAKE--NOT A WORD--	121	2 DON JUAN	1	182	3
JUAN HAD REACH'D THE ROOM-DOOR IN A TRICE	122	2 DON JUAN	1	183	5
WHO THREATEN'D DEATH--SO JUAN KNOCK'D HIM DOWN	122	2 DON JUAN	1	183	8
AND JUAN TOO BLASPHEMED AN OCTAVE HIGHER	122	2 DON JUAN	1	184	6
FOR JUAN VERY LUCKILY NE'ER SAW IT	123	2 DON JUAN	1	185	3
AND JUAN THROTTLED HIM TO GET AWAY	124	2 DON JUAN	1	186	2
JUAN CONTRIVED TO GIVE AN AWKWARD BLOW	124	2 DON JUAN	1	186	5
JUAN THE GATE GAIN'D TURN'D THE KEY ABOUT	125	2 DON JUAN	1	187	7
HOW JUAN NAKED FAVOUR'D BY THE NIGHT	126	2 DON JUAN	1	188	2
I SAID THAT JUAN HAD BEEN SENT TO CADIZ--	159	2 DON JUAN	2	5	1
DON JUAN BADE HIS VALET PACK HIS THINGS	161	2 DON JUAN	2	9	1
JUAN EMBARK'D--THE SHIP GOT UNDER WAY	162	2 DON JUAN	2	11	1
SO JUAN STOOD BEWILDER'D ON THE DECK	163	2 DON JUAN	2	13	1
DON JUAN STOOD AND GAZING FROM THE STERN	164	2 DON JUAN	2	14	1
BUT JUAN HAD GOT MANY THINGS TO LEAVE	164	2 DON JUAN	2	15	1
SO JUAN WEPT AS WEPT THE CAPTIVE JEWS	165	2 DON JUAN	2	16	1
AND JUAN WEPT AND MUCH HE SIGH'D AND THOUGHT	165	2 DON JUAN	2	17	1
OUR JUAN WHO WITH SENSE BEYOND HIS YEARS	174	2 DON JUAN	2	35	2
ALL ONE AN HOUR HENCE JUAN ANSWER'D NO	175	2 DON JUAN	2	36	2
JUAN GOT INTO THE LONG-BOAT AND THERE	186	2 DON JUAN	2	56	1
FOR JUAN WORE THE MAGISTERIAL FACE	186	2 DON JUAN	2	56	4
AND JUAN CAUGHT HIM UP AND ERE HE STEPP'D	187	2 DON JUAN	2	58	7
BUT JUAN TRUSTING THEY MIGHT STILL GET THROUGH	187	2 DON JUAN	2	59	6
AND JUAN WHO HAD STILL REFUSED BECAUSE	193	2 DON JUAN	2	71	2
THEY TOOK BY FORCE FROM JUAN JULIA'S LETTER	195	2 DON JUAN	2	74	8
TO THESE WAS ADDED JUAN WHO BEFORE	198	2 DON JUAN	2	78	3
ALL EXCEPT JUAN WHO THROUGHOUT ABSTAIN'D	200	2 DON JUAN	2	82	5
JUAN TO LAVE HIS YOUTHFUL LIMBS WAS WONT	211	2 DON JUAN	2	105	2
HOW LONG IN HIS DAMP TRANCE YOUNG JUAN LAY	214	2 DON JUAN	2	111	1
DON JUAN ALMOST FAMISH'D AND HALF DROWN'D	224	2 DON JUAN	2	129	4
JUAN SLEPT LIKE A TOP OR LIKE THE DEAD	227	2 DON JUAN	2	134	2
YOUNG JUAN SLEPT ALL DREAMLESS--BUT THE MAID	228	2 DON JUAN	2	135	1
THAT AT THIS MOMENT JUAN KNEW IT NOT	228	2 DON JUAN	2	135	8
THE MORN BROKE AND FOUND JUAN SLUMBERING STILL	229	2 DON JUAN	2	137	1
THAT LIKE AN INFANT JUAN SWEETLY SLEPT	232	2 DON JUAN	2	143	3
THE COFFEE MADE WOULD FAIN HAVE WAKEN'D JUAN	234	2 DON JUAN	2	146	2
FOR JUAN SO THAT EVEN WHEN HE PRAY'D	235	2 DON JUAN	2	149	6
NOW JUAN COULD NOT UNDERSTAND A WORD	236	2 DON JUAN	2	151	1
AND JUAN GAZED AS ONE WHO IS AWOKE	237	2 DON JUAN	2	152	1
AND JUAN TOO WAS HELP'D OUT FROM HIS DREAM	237	2 DON JUAN	2	153	1
BUT TO RESUME THE LANGUID JUAN RAISED	239	2 DON JUAN	2	157	1
BUT NOT A WORD COULD JUAN COMPREHEND	241	2 DON JUAN	2	161	2
THUS JUAN LEARN'D HIS ALPHA BETA BETTER	242	2 DON JUAN	2	163	7
RETURN WE TO DON JUAN HE BEGUN	244	2 DON JUAN	2	167	1
FOR JUAN WHO WAS SOMEWHAT FOND OF REST--	245	2 DON JUAN	2	168	2
WHEN JUAN WOKE HE FOUND SOME GOOD THINGS READY	246	2 DON JUAN	2	171	1
WELL--JUAN AFTER BATHING IN THE SEA	246	2 DON JUAN	2	171	7
THAT BATHING PASS'D FOR NOTHING JUAN SEEM'D	247	2 DON JUAN	2	172	1
ALAS FOR JUAN AND HAIDEE THEY WERE	258	2 DON JUAN	2	193	1
AND JUAN SUNK TO SLEEP WITHIN HER ARMS	260	2 DON JUAN	2	195	2
BUT JUAN HAD HE QUITE FORGOTTEN JULIA	267	2 DON JUAN	2	208	1
LEAVING DON JUAN AND HAIDEE TO PLEAD	271	2 DON JUAN	2	216	7
HAIL MUSE ET CETERA--WE LEFT JUAN SLEEPING	274	2 DON JUAN	3	1	1
HAIDEE AND JUAN WERE NOT MARRIED BUT	282	2 DON JUAN	3	12	1
EVER SINCE JUAN SERVED HER FOR A SPOUSE	295	2 DON JUAN	3	39	V8
HAIDEE AND JUAN CARPETED THEIR FEET	309	2 DON JUAN	3	67	1
JUAN HAD ON A SHAWL OF BLACK AND GOLD	315	2 DON JUAN	3	77	1
YOUNG JUAN AND HIS LADY-LOVE WERE LEFT	348	2 DON JUAN	4	8	1
HAIDEE AND JUAN THOUGHT NOT OF THE DEAD	351	2 DON JUAN	4	13	1
AND JUAN WAS A BOY OF SAINTLY BREEDING	354	2 DON JUAN	4	19	6
JUAN GAZED ON HER AS TO ASK HIS FATE--	355	2 DON JUAN	4	22	5
WHEN JUAN SPOKE TOO--IT MIGHT BE IN SPORT--	356	2 DON JUAN	4	23	5
JUAN WOULD QUESTION FURTHER BUT SHE PRESS'D	356	2 DON JUAN	4	24	1

JUAN   (CONTINUED)

	PAGE	VOL	CANTO	STANZA	LN
JUAN AND HAIDEE GAZED UPON EACH OTHER	357	2 DON JUAN	4	26	1
HAIDEE AND JUAN THEIR SIESTA TOOK	359	2 DON JUAN	4	29	2
JUAN AND SHUDDERING O'ER HIS FRAME WOULD CREEP	359	2 DON JUAN	4	29	5
LAY JUAN NOR COULD AUGHT RENEW THE BEAT	362	2 DON JUAN	4	34	5
UP JUAN SPRUNG TO HAIDEE'S BITTER SHRIEK	364	2 DON JUAN	4	37	1
AND HAIDEE CLUNG AROUND HIM JUAN 'TIS--	364	2 DON JUAN	4	38	1
THEN TURN'D TO JUAN IN WHOSE CHEEK THE BLOOD	365	2 DON JUAN	4	39	5
JUAN REPLIED NOT WHILE THIS ARM IS FREE	365	2 DON JUAN	4	40	2
JUAN REPLIED IT MUST BE WON NOT GIVEN	365	2 DON JUAN	4	40	V2
'TWIXT HER AND JUAN INTERPOSED THE CREW	370	2 DON JUAN	4	48	3
JUAN FROM THE APARTMENT WITH A SIGN	371	2 DON JUAN	4	50	2
I LEAVE DON JUAN FOR THE PRESENT SAFE--	373	2 DON JUAN	4	54	1
WITH JUAN LEFT HALF-KILL'D SOME STANZAS BACK	384	2 DON JUAN	4	74	8
DON JUAN HERE PERMITTED TO EMERGE	387	2 DON JUAN	4	79	1
JUAN WAS TOLD ABOUT THEIR CURIOUS CASE	388	2 DON JUAN	4	81	2
WAS JUAN WHO--AN AWKWARD THING AT HIS AGE	394	2 DON JUAN	4	92	7
THEREFORE I'LL MAKE DON JUAN LEAVE THE SHIP SOON	397	2 DON JUAN	4	97	5
AND NOW DELAY THE PROGRESS OF DON JUAN	410	2 DON JUAN	4	117	7
JUAN WAS JUVENILE AND THUS WAS FULL	415	2 DON JUAN	5	8	1
JUAN WAS YOUNG--HAD COURAGE--AND WAS FULL	415	2 DON JUAN	5	8	V1
NEXT JUAN STOOD TILL SOME MIGHT CHOOSE TO BUY	416	2 DON JUAN	5	10	8
WHEN JUAN ANSWERED SPANISH HE REPLIED	418	2 DON JUAN	5	14	1
PRAY SIR SAID JUAN IF I MAY PRESUME	418	2 DON JUAN	5	15	1
ALAS SAID JUAN 'TWERE A TALE DISTRESSING	419	2 DON JUAN	5	16	5
'TIS NOT SAID JUAN FOR MY PRESENT DOOM	420	2 DON JUAN	5	18	1
MY THIRD-- --YOUR THIRD QUOTH JUAN TURNING ROUND	421	2 DON JUAN	5	20	1
WELL THEN YOUR THIRD SAID JUAN WHAT DID SHE	421	2 DON JUAN	5	20	6
YOU TAKE THINGS COOLLY SIR SAID JUAN WHY	421	2 DON JUAN	5	21	1
SAID JUAN BUT I REALLY DON'T SEE HOW	422	2 DON JUAN	5	23	2
SAID JUAN--SWALLOWING A HEART-BURNING SIGH	423	2 DON JUAN	5	24	3
THE PURCHASER OF JUAN AND ACQUAINTANCE	432	2 DON JUAN	5	40	1
MADE JUAN IN HIS HARSH INTENTIONS PAUSE	437	2 DON JUAN	5	47	4
AND JUAN AND HIS FRIEND ALBEIT THEY HEARD	439	2 DON JUAN	5	50	2
WILL IT SAID JUAN SHARPLY STRIKE ME DEAD	452	2 DON JUAN	5	71	7
BABA EYED JUAN AND SAID BE SO GOOD	453	2 DON JUAN	5	73	1
ARRAY HER LIMBS BUT JUAN STANDING MUTE	453	2 DON JUAN	5	73	4
AT LEAST SAID JUAN SURE I MAY INQUIRE	454	2 DON JUAN	5	74	4
THEN IF I DO SAID JUAN I'LL BE-- HOLD	454	2 DON JUAN	5	75	1
WHAT SIR SAID JUAN SHALL IT E'ER BE TOLD	454	2 DON JUAN	5	75	5
SIGHED JUAN MUTTERING ALSO SOME SLIGHT OATHS	455	2 DON JUAN	5	76	5
SO MUCH THE BETTER JUAN SAID FOR THEM	459	2 DON JUAN	5	82	2
DON JUAN TURNING TO HIS COMRADE WHO	459	2 DON JUAN	5	83	2
FAREWELL SAID JUAN SHOULD WE MEET NO MORE	460	2 DON JUAN	5	84	1
BABA LED JUAN ONWARD ROOM BY ROOM	460	2 DON JUAN	5	85	2
JUAN A MOMENT AS THIS PAIR SO SMALL	463	2 DON JUAN	5	90	5
TO JUAN SOME SLIGHT LESSONS AS HIS GUIDE	464	2 DON JUAN	5	91	2
TO JUAN WHO THOUGH NOT MUCH USED TO PRAY	466	2 DON JUAN	5	95	5
POINTED TO JUAN WHO REMAINED BELOW	466	2 DON JUAN	5	96	8
AND WERE ALL CLAD ALIKE LIKE JUAN TOO	469	2 DON JUAN	5	99	3
BABA AND JUAN WHICH LAST STOOD ADMIRING	469	2 DON JUAN	5	100	3
MOTIONED TO JUAN TO APPROACH AND THEN	470	2 DON JUAN	5	102	2
HE HEARD REPEATED JUAN WITH A FROWN	470	2 DON JUAN	5	102	5
WOULD JUAN BEND THOUGH 'TWERE TO MAHOMET'S BRIDE	471	2 DON JUAN	5	103	5
AND JUAN NOW HIS WILLINGNESS EXPREST	472	2 DON JUAN	5	105	4
HE WHISPERED JUAN NOT TO BE AFRAID	473	2 DON JUAN	5	107	5
JUAN THE LATEST OF HER WHIMS HAD CAUGHT	477	2 DON JUAN	5	114	1
EXPLAINS THE GARB WHICH JUAN TOOK AMISS	477	2 DON JUAN	5	114	8
BUT JUAN WHO HAD STILL HIS MIND O'ERFLOWING	478	2 DON JUAN	5	117	2
BUT JUAN WHO HAD STILL HIS HEART QUITE FULL	478	2 DON JUAN	5	117	V2
JUAN WHO FOR AN INSTANT HAD BEEN MOVED	481	2 DON JUAN	5	121	2
THIS WAS AN AWKWARD TEST AS JUAN FOUND	484	2 DON JUAN	5	126	1
SHE THOUGHT OF KILLING JUAN--BUT POOR LAD	492	2 DON JUAN	5	140	5
JUAN WAS MOVED HE HAD MADE UP HIS MIND	492	2 DON JUAN	5	141	1
JUAN AMONGST THE DAMSELS IN DISGUISE	500	2 DON JUAN	5	155	3
DON JUAN IN HIS FEMININE DISGUISE	19	3 DON JUAN	6	26	1
SHEWED JUAN OR JUANNA THROUGH AND THROUGH	34	3 DON JUAN	6	57	4
DON JUAN AT HIS HANDS AND INFORMATION	55	3 DON JUAN	6	99	2
JUAN WAS GIVEN IN CHARGE AS HATH BEEN STATED	57	3 DON JUAN	6	102	6
JUAN HAD NOT BETRAYED HIMSELF IN FACT	58	3 DON JUAN	6	104	2
AT WHICH DUDU LOOKED STRANGE AND JUAN SILLY	64	3 DON JUAN	6	118	7
AND TRUSTING JUAN MAY ESCAPE THE FISHES	65	3 DON JUAN	6	120	5
YOUR NAMES--MINE'S JOHNSON AND MY COMRADE'S JUAN	97	3 DON JUAN	7	60	1
HE SHALL IF THAT HE DARE HERE JUAN BOWED	99	3 DON JUAN	7	63	1
DON JUAN WHO WAS MUCH MORE SENTIMENTAL	105	3 DON JUAN	7	75	4
JUAN AND JOHNSON JOINED A CERTAIN CORPS	120	3 DON JUAN	8	19	1
BUT JUAN WAS QUITE A BROTH OF A BOY	123	3 DON JUAN	8	24	1
JUAN BY SOME STRANGE CHANCE WHICH OFT DIVIDES	125	3 DON JUAN	8	27	1
JUAN WHO HAD NO SHIELD TO SNATCH AND WAS	126	3 DON JUAN	8	29	1
THIS SIMILE ENOUGH FOR AJAX JUAN	126	3 DON JUAN	8	29	7
SO JUAN FOLLOWING HONOUR AND HIS NOSE	127	3 DON JUAN	8	32	7
EXCEPT DON JUAN--A MERE NOVICE WHOSE	131	3 DON JUAN	8	36	2
BUT OF THE FIRST OUR LITTLE FRIEND DON JUAN	138	3 DON JUAN	8	52	2
BUT JUAN NEVER LEFT THEM WHILE THEY HAD CHARMS	139	3 DON JUAN	8	53	8
TO JUAN WHO WAS NEAREST HIM ADDRESSED	140	3 DON JUAN	8	56	5
JUAN TO WHOM HE SPOKE IN GERMAN KNEW	141	3 DON JUAN	8	57	1
JUAN AND JOHNSON AND SOME VOLUNTEERS	152	3 DON JUAN	8	80	1
WHEN JUAN CAUGHT A GLIMPSE OF THIS SAD SIGHT	158	3 DON JUAN	8	93	4
DON JUAN RAISED HIS LITTLE CAPTIVE FROM	158	3 DON JUAN	8	94	7

JUAN   (CONTINUED)

	PAGE	VOL		CANTO	STANZA	LN
AND GAZED ON JUAN WITH A WILD SURPRISE	159	3	DON JUAN	8	95	8
EXCLAIMING--JUAN JUAN ON BOY BRACE	160	3	DON JUAN	8	97	6
EXCLAIMING--JUAN JUAN ON BOY BRACE	160	3	DON JUAN	8	97	6
THEN UP WITH ME--BUT JUAN ANSWERED LOOK	161	3	DON JUAN	8	99	1
SAID JUAN--WHATSOEVER IS TO BE	161	3	DON JUAN	8	100	1
JUAN REPLIED--AT LEAST I WILL ENDURE	161	3	DON JUAN	8	100	6
JOHNSON SAID--JUAN WE'VE NO TIME TO LOSE	162	3	DON JUAN	8	101	1
BUT JUAN WAS IMMOVEABLE UNTIL	162	3	DON JUAN	8	102	1
JUAN CONSENTED TO MARCH ON THROUGH THUNDER	163	3	DON JUAN	8	103	3
AND SPITE OF JOHNSON AND OF JUAN WHO	165	3	DON JUAN	8	108	1
JUAN AND JOHNSON WHEREUPON THEY FELL	166	3	DON JUAN	8	109	2
WHILE JUAN IS SENT OFF WITH THE DISPATCH	181	3	DON JUAN	8	139	7
TO PRAYER WAS HEARD NO MORE--AND JUAN WEPT	182	3	DON JUAN	8	141	7
DON JUAN WHO HAD SHONE IN THE LATE SLAUGHTER	197	3	DON JUAN	9	29	1
BUT JUAN TURNED HIS EYES ON THE SWEET CHILD	199	3	DON JUAN	9	33	1
I LEFT DON JUAN WITH HIS HORSES BAITING--	203	3	DON JUAN	9	42	3
JUAN WAS NONE OF THESE BUT SLIGHT AND SLIM	206	3	DON JUAN	9	47	1
JUAN I SAID WAS A MOST BEAUTEOUS BOY	209	3	DON JUAN	9	53	1
JUAN MUCH FLATTERED BY HER LOVE OR LUST--	221	3	DON JUAN	9	77	3
JUAN WHO FOUND HIMSELF HE KNEW NOT HOW	223	3	DON JUAN	9	83	1
JUAN RETIRED--AND SO WILL I UNTIL	224	3	DON JUAN	9	85	2
WE LEFT OUR HERO JUAN IN THE BLOOM	227	3	DON JUAN	10	5	1
BUT JUAN WAS NOT MEANT TO DIE SO SOON	229	3	DON JUAN	10	9	1
DON JUAN WHO WAS REAL OR IDEAL--	234	3	DON JUAN	10	20	1
DON JUAN GREW A VERY POLISHED RUSSIAN--	235	3	DON JUAN	10	21	1
DON JUAN GREW I FEAR A LITTLE DISSIPATED	236	3	DON JUAN	10	23	3
HE LIVED (NOT DEATH BUT JUAN) IN A HURRY	237	3	DON JUAN	10	26	1
JUAN INSTEAD OF COURTING COURTS WAS COURTED	239	3	DON JUAN	10	29	1
THE GENTLE JUAN FLOURISHED THOUGH AT TIMES	243	3	DON JUAN	10	37	1
(WITH MORE BESIDE IF JUAN HAD NOT STOPPED'EM)	244	3	DON JUAN	10	41	6
JUAN DEMURRED AT THIS FIRST NOTICE TO	245	3	DON JUAN	10	43	1
THIS SECRET CHARGE ON JUAN TO DISPLAY	247	3	DON JUAN	10	46	3
ALL PRIVATE FAVOURITES OF DON JUAN FOR	249	3	DON JUAN	10	50	2
DON JUAN LOVED HER AND SHE LOVED HIM AS	250	3	DON JUAN	10	53	1
WAS JUAN WHOM SHE SEEMED TO HAVE SELECTED	252	3	DON JUAN	10	57	2
JUAN WHO CARED NOT A TOBACCO-STOPPER	254	3	DON JUAN	10	60	5
BUT JUAN POSTED ON THROUGH MANHEIM BONN	255	3	DON JUAN	10	62	1
BUT JUAN SEASONED AS WELL MIGHT BE	256	3	DON JUAN	10	64	6
THE BLUE SEA'S BORDER AND DON JUAN FELT--	257	3	DON JUAN	10	65	2
DON JUAN NOW SAW ALBION'S EARLIEST BEAUTIES--	259	3	DON JUAN	10	69	1
JUAN THOUGH CARELESS YOUNG AND MAGNIFIQUE	259	3	DON JUAN	10	70	1
THE EFFECT ON JUAN WAS OF COURSE SUBLIME	261	3	DON JUAN	10	74	1
JUAN ADMIRED THESE HIGHWAYS OF FREE MILLIONS	263	3	DON JUAN	10	77	4
TO YOUR INSTRUCTOR JUAN NOW WAS BORNE	264	3	DON JUAN	10	80	2
BUT JUAN FELT THOUGH NOT APPROACHING HOME	265	3	DON JUAN	10	81	5
BUT JUAN SAW NOT THIS EACH WREATH OF SMOKE	266	3	DON JUAN	10	83	1
DON JUAN HAD GOT OUT ON SHOOTER'S HILL	272	3	DON JUAN	11	8	1
I SAY DON JUAN WRAPT IN CONTEMPLATION	272	3	DON JUAN	11	9	1
JUAN WHO DID NOT UNDERSTAND A WORD	274	3	DON JUAN	11	12	1
JUAN YET QUICKLY UNDERSTOOD THEIR GESTURE	274	3	DON JUAN	11	13	1
JUAN WHO SAW THE MOON'S LATE MINION BLEED	275	3	DON JUAN	11	14	5
DON JUAN HAVING DONE THE BEST HE COULD	277	3	DON JUAN	11	18	1
DON JUAN OUR YOUNG DIPLOMATIC SINNER	282	3	DON JUAN	11	29	6
BUT JUAN NOW IS STEPPING FROM HIS CARRIAGE	282	3	DON JUAN	11	30	8
JUAN WHOSE WAS A DELICATE COMMISSION	283	3	DON JUAN	11	32	1
JUAN PRESENTED IN THE PROPER PLACE	285	3	DON JUAN	11	35	1
DON JUAN WAS PRESENTED AND HIS DRESS	287	3	DON JUAN	11	39	1
BUT JUAN WAS RECEIVED WITH MUCH EMPRESSEMENT --	288	3	DON JUAN	11	42	1
JUAN AS AN INVETERATE PATRICIAN	290	3	DON JUAN	11	45	7
BUT JUAN WAS A BACHELOR--OF ARTS	292	3	DON JUAN	11	47	1
JUAN WHO WAS A LITTLE SUPERFICIAL	294	3	DON JUAN	11	51	1
JUAN KNEW SEVERAL LANGUAGES--AS WELL	295	3	DON JUAN	11	53	1
BUT JUAN WAS MY MOSCOW AND FALIERO	296	3	DON JUAN	11	56	1
MY JUAN WHOM I LEFT IN DEADLY PERIL	300	3	DON JUAN	11	64	1
WHO LIKE DON JUAN TAKES AN ACTIVE SHARE	303	3	DON JUAN	11	70	2
BUT CARPE DIEM JUAN CARPE CARPE	310	3	DON JUAN	11	86	1
WHAT JUAN SAW AND UNDERWENT SHALL BE	311	3	DON JUAN	11	88	1
AND JUAN FOUND HIMSELF IN AN EXTENSIVE	313	3	DON JUAN	11	V 29	7
JUAN AS A VOLUPTUARY WAS NEW	314	3	DON JUAN	11	V 75	V1
AND NOW TO BUSINESS OH MY GENTLE JUAN	326	3	DON JUAN	12	23	1
PAULO MAJORA JUAN UNDECIDED	327	3	DON JUAN	12	25	2
HOWE'ER OUR FRIEND DON JUAN MIGHT COMMAND	329	3	DON JUAN	12	29	5
AS JUAN WAS A PERSON OF CONDITION	330	3	DON JUAN	12	30	4
DON JUAN WAS DELIGHTED TO SECURE	335	3	DON JUAN	12	41	6
JUAN TOO WAS A SORT OF FAVOURITE WITH HER	338	3	DON JUAN	12	49	1
DON JUAN SAW THAT MICROCOSM ON STILTS	342	3	DON JUAN	12	56	1
JUAN WHO DID NOT STAND IN THE PREDICAMENT	346	3	DON JUAN	12	67	1
I SAID THAT JUAN DID NOT THINK THEM PRETTY	350	3	DON JUAN	12	74	2
BUT JUAN WAS NO CASUIST NOR HAD PONDERED	353	3	DON JUAN	12	81	1
AND JUAN WAS RECEIVED AS HATH BEEN SAID	355	3	DON JUAN	12	85	1
THE FAIR MOST FATAL JUAN EVER MET	364	3	DON JUAN	13	12	3
HIMSELF AND JUAN IN THEIR MUTUAL STATIONS	365	3	DON JUAN	13	15	3
O'ER JUAN HE COULD NO DISTINCTION CLAIM	367	3	DON JUAN	13	20	2
AND JUAN LIKE A TRUE-BORN ANDALUSIAN	368	3	DON JUAN	13	23	7
FOR JUAN STOOD WELL BOTH WITH INS AND OUTS	369	3	DON JUAN	13	24	3
WAS JUAN A RECHERCHE WELCOME GUEST	370	3	DON JUAN	13	28	2
JUAN--IN THIS RESPECT AT LEAST LIKE SAINTS--	424	3	DON JUAN	14	31	1
BUT JUAN HAD BEEN EARLY TAUGHT TO RANGE	424	3	DON JUAN	14	32	5

JUAN   (CONTINUED)
    BUT JUAN ALSO SHARED IN HER AUSTERITY 432   3 DON JUAN 14   51   5
    THAT JUAN WAS UNLIKELY TO RESIST-- 436   3 DON JUAN 14   60   4
    AND BADE HIM COUNSEL JUAN WITH A SMILE 438   3 DON JUAN 14   65   4
    TO WEAN DON JUAN FROM THE SIREN'S WILE 438   3 DON JUAN 14   65   6
    THIRDLY THAT JUAN HAD MORE BRAIN THAN BEARD 439   3 DON JUAN 14   66   5
    I THINK NOT SHE WAS THEN IN LOVE WITH JUAN 449   3 DON JUAN 14   91   2
    WHETHER DON JUAN AND CHASTE ADELINE 453   3 DON JUAN 14   97   1
    AND JUAN TOO ESPECIALLY THE LATTER 454   3 DON JUAN 14   99   4
    IT IS NOT CLEAR THAT ADELINE AND JUAN 454   3 DON JUAN 14   99   7
    BUT RIGHT OR WRONG DON JUAN WAS WITHOUT IT 461   3 DON JUAN 15   13   3
    JUAN REPLIED WITH ALL BECOMING DEFERENCE 469   3 DON JUAN 15   30   1
    THAT JUAN HAD ENOUGH OF MAINTENANCE 473   3 DON JUAN 15   39   2
    MADE JUAN WONDER AS NO DOUBT HE MUST 477   3 DON JUAN 15   49   3
    JUAN REJOINED--SHE WAS A CATHOLIC 478   3 DON JUAN 15   50   1
    JUAN WAS SOMETHING SHE COULD NOT DIVINE 480   3 DON JUAN 15   56   5
    JUAN KNEW NOUGHT OF SUCH A CHARACTER-- 481   3 DON JUAN 15   58   1
    ADELINE AND DON JUAN RATHER BLENDED 482   3 DON JUAN 15   61   3
    DON JUAN SAT NEXT AN A L'ESPAGNOLE-- 488   3 DON JUAN 15   74   5
    NOW JUAN THOUGH NO COXCOMB IN PRETENCE 490   3 DON JUAN 15   77   5
    JUAN WAS DRAWN THUS INTO SOME ATTENTIONS 491   3 DON JUAN 15   80   1
    BUT JUAN HAD A SORT OF WINNING WAY 492   3 DON JUAN 15   82   1
    AND JUAN ON RETIRING FOR THE NIGHT 506   3 DON JUAN 16   12   1
    TILL WANTED THEREFORE JUAN ONLY SIGHED 506   3 DON JUAN 16   12   8
    JUAN FELT SOMEWHAT PENSIVE AND DISPOSED 507   3 DON JUAN 16   15   1
    AS JUAN MUSED ON MUTABILITY 509   3 DON JUAN 16   20   1
    BUT SLOWLY AND AS HE PASSED JUAN BY 510   3 DON JUAN 16   21   7
    JUAN WAS PETRIFIED HE HAD HEARD A HINT 510   3 DON JUAN 16   22   1
    AND JUAN GAZED UPON IT WITH A STARE 510   3 DON JUAN 16   23   3
    MIGHT COME OR GO BUT JUAN COULD NOT STATE 511   3 DON JUAN 16   24   7
    AND LOOKED AT JUAN HARD BUT NOTHING UTTERED 514   3 DON JUAN 16   31   6
    THE CAUSE BUT JUAN SAID HE WAS QUITE WELL 514   3 DON JUAN 16   32   8
    SAID JUAN HAD NOT GOT HIS USUAL LOOK ELATE 515   3 DON JUAN 16   34   3
    THEN HENRY TURNED TO JUAN AND ADDRESSED 515   3 DON JUAN 16   35   1
    WHAT FRIAR SAID JUAN AND HE DID HIS BEST 515   3 DON JUAN 16   35   5
    AND THEREFORE JUAN NOW BEGAN TO RALLY 526   3 DON JUAN 16   53   1
    BUT JUAN WHEN CROSS-QUESTIONED ON THE VISION 527   3 DON JUAN 16   54   6
    AND JUAN TOOK HIS PLACE HE KNEW NOT WHERE 542   3 DON JUAN 16   87   2
    AND JUAN GREW CARNATION WITH VEXATION 545   3 DON JUAN 16   93   3
    AS JUAN SHOULD HAVE KNOWN HAD NOT HIS SENSES 545   3 DON JUAN 16   93   7
    AND USUAL--JUAN WHEN HE CAST A GLANCE 546   3 DON JUAN 16   96   2
    AND JUAN TOO IN GENERAL BEHIND NONE 552   3 DON JUAN 16   105   4
    BUT JUAN SITTING SILENT IN HIS NOOK 553   3 DON JUAN 16   106   6
    DON JUAN WHEN THE MIDNIGHT HOUR OF PILLOWS 555   3 DON JUAN 16   110   3
    DON JUAN SHOOK AS ERST HE HAD BEEN SHAKEN 558   3 DON JUAN 16   118   1
    BUT JUAN EAGER NOW THE TRUTH TO PIERCE 559   3 DON JUAN 16   119   3
    JUAN PUT FORTH ONE ARM--ETERNAL POWERS 559   3 DON JUAN 16   120   1
    AND JUAN PUZZLED BUT STILL CURIOUS THRUST 560   3 DON JUAN 16   122   1
    THE LATEST JUAN WITH HIS VIRGIN FACE 568   3 DON JUAN 17   13   8
    'TWERE DIFFICULT TO SAY--BUT JUAN LOOKED 568   3 DON JUAN 17   14   2
JUANNA
    JUANNA--WELL A PRETTY NAME ENOUGH 28   3 DON JUAN 6   44   2
    JUANNA PLAYING WITH HER VEIL OR HAIR 28   3 DON JUAN 6   45   2
    SHE ADDED TO JUANNA THEIR NEW GUEST 29   3 DON JUAN 6   46   4
    I'LL TAKE JUANNA WE'RE A SLENDERER PAIR 29   3 DON JUAN 6   47   4
    AND I SHALL PLACE JUANNA WITH DUDU 30   3 DON JUAN 6   49   4
    SHE TOOK JUANNA BY THE HAND TO SHOW 31   3 DON JUAN 6   50   5
    SHEWED JUAN OR JUANNA THROUGH AND THROUGH 34   3 DON JUAN 6   57   4
    AND THEN SHE GAVE JUANNA A CHASTE KISS 35   3 DON JUAN 6   59   1
    HER AID TO FAIR JUANNA WHOSE EXCESS 36   3 DON JUAN 6   61   3
    A BLESSING IS SOUND SLEEP--JUANNA LAY 42   3 DON JUAN 6   73   2
    AND POOR JUANNA TOO THE CHILD'S FIRST NIGHT 46   3 DON JUAN 6   81   1
    JUANNA SHOULD BE TAKEN FROM HER AND 47   3 DON JUAN 6   82   7
    AND HERE JUANNA KINDLY INTERPOSED 48   3 DON JUAN 6   84   1
    AS THUS JUANNA SPOKE DUDU TURNED ROUND 48   3 DON JUAN 6   85   1
JUANNA'S
    I FEAR JUANNA'S DREAMS WOULD BE BUT FEW 30   3 DON JUAN 6   48   8
    AND HID HER FACE WITHIN JUANNA'S BREAST 48   3 DON JUAN 6   85   2
JUAN'S
    NARRATING SOMEWHAT OF DON JUAN'S FATHER 25   2 DON JUAN 1   7   7
    DON JUAN'S PARENTS LIVED BESIDE THE RIVER 25   2 DON JUAN 1   8   7
    TO JUAN'S EYES EXCEPTING NATURAL HISTORY 43   2 DON JUAN 1   39   8
    IS MORE THAN I KNOW--BUT DON JUAN'S MOTHER 47   2 DON JUAN 1   46   7
    LIKE WHAT THIS LIGHT TOUCH LEFT ON JUAN'S HEART . . . 60   2 DON JUAN 1   71   8
    IN YOUNG DON JUAN'S FAVOUR AND TO HIM ITS 65   2 DON JUAN 1   81   3
    PERHAPS TO FINISH JUAN'S EDUCATION 75   2 DON JUAN 1   101   6
    SHE THOUGHT OF HER OWN STRENGTH AND JUAN'S YOUTH . . 78   2 DON JUAN 1   107   1
    ONE HAND ON JUAN'S CARLESSLY WAS THROWN 80   2 DON JUAN 1   109   7
    'TWAS SURELY VERY WRONG IN JUAN'S MOTHER 80   2 DON JUAN 1   110   5
    THE HAND WHICH STILL HELD JUAN'S BY DEGREES 81   2 DON JUAN 1   111   1
    BUT PRESS'D HER BLOODLESS LIP TO JUAN'S CHEEK 114   2 DON JUAN 1   169   8
    FROM DELICACY TO DON JUAN'S EAR 118   2 DON JUAN 1   176   7
    THIS WAS DON JUAN'S EARLIEST SCRAPE BUT WHETHER . . . 135   2 DON JUAN 1   199   1
    SAW JUAN'S LAST ELOPEMENT WITH THE DEVIL 138   2 DON JUAN 1   203   8
    IN JUAN'S CASE WERE BUT EMPLOY'D IN VAIN 157   2 DON JUAN 2   1   6
    THE GREAT SUCCESS OF JUAN'S EDUCATION 162   2 DON JUAN 2   10   7
    COULD JUAN'S PASSION WHILE THE BILLOWS ROAR 168   2 DON JUAN 2   23   7
    WERE SETTLED LONG ERE JUAN'S SIRE WAS BORN 169   2 DON JUAN 2   24   4
    TO FOLLOW JUAN'S WAKE LIKE SANCHO PANCA 175   2 DON JUAN 2   37   8

	PAGE	VOL	CANTO	STANZA	LN
JUAN'S (CONTINUED)					
SO JUAN'S SPANIEL SPITE OF HIS ENTREATING	193	2 DON JUAN	2	70	7
AND THE LOT FELL ON JUAN'S LUCKLESS TUTOR	195	2 DON JUAN	2	75	8
ROUND JUAN'S HEAD AND HIS AROUND HERS LIES	259	2 DON JUAN	2	194	3
AND CALLED FROM JUAN'S BREAST A FAINT LOW SIGH	355	2 DON JUAN	4	21	7
HAD STOPP'D THIS CANTO AND DON JUAN'S BREATH	366	2 DON JUAN	4	42	2
THE LAST SIGHT WHICH SHE SAW WAS JUAN'S GORE	375	2 DON JUAN	4	58	1
JUAN'S COMPANION WAS A ROMAGNOLE	395	2 DON JUAN	4	94	1
I REALLY THINK YET JUAN'S THEN ORDEAL	396	2 DON JUAN	4	96	7
INTO DON JUAN'S HEAD A THOUGHT WHICH HE	434	2 DON JUAN	5	43	2
JUAN'S WAS GOOD AND MIGHT HAVE BEEN STILL BETTER	483	2 DON JUAN	5	124	1
HER FIRST THOUGHT WAS TO CUT OFF JUAN'S HEAD	491	2 DON JUAN	5	139	1
SO JUAN'S VIRTUE EBBED I KNOW NOT HOW	493	2 DON JUAN	5	142	2
THOUGH 'TWAS DON JUAN'S FIRST OF FIELDS AND THOUGH	121	3 DON JUAN	8	21	1
IN JUAN'S LOOK PAIN PLEASURE HOPE FEAR MIXED	159	3 DON JUAN	8	96	3
SO MUCH DID JUAN'S SETTING OFF DISTRESS HER	247	3 DON JUAN	10	47	7
AND JUAN'S SUITE LATE SCATTERED AT A DISTANCE	275	3 DON JUAN	11	14	2
BEFORE DON JUAN'S FEET HE COULD NOT TELL	276	3 DON JUAN	11	17	2
THAT JUAN'S CHARIOT ROLLING LIKE A DRUM	277	3 DON JUAN	11	20	5
BY SPECIOUS SEEMING JUAN'S YOUTH AND PATIENCE	365	3 DON JUAN	13	15	5
THAT TIME WOULD TEMPER JUAN'S FAULTS OF YOUTH	439	3 DON JUAN	14	67	5
SOME PARTS OF JUAN'S HISTORY WHICH RUMOUR	460	3 DON JUAN	15	11	1
OF JUAN'S MERITS AND HIS SITUATION	468	3 DON JUAN	15	28	2
BUT ADELINE DETERMINED JUAN'S WEDDING	473	3 DON JUAN	15	40	1
AND JUAN'S MIND WAS IN THE PROPER TONE	506	3 DON JUAN	16	13	5
(WHO WATCHED THE CHANGES OF DON JUAN'S BROW	516	3 DON JUAN	16	37	2
OF JUAN'S NERVOUS FEELINGS ON THAT DAY	526	3 DON JUAN	16	51	4
CAME OVER JUAN'S EAR WHICH THROBBED ALAS	556	3 DON JUAN	16	114	5
WHICH STILL IN JUAN'S CANDLESTICKS BURNED HIGH	558	3 DON JUAN	16	117	5
JUDGE					
IF WE MAY JUDGE OF MATTER BY THE MIND	18	2 DON JUAN	D	15	1
AS BEING THE BEST JUDGE OF A LADY'S CASE	62	2 DON JUAN	1	75	8
JUDGE THEN IF HER CAPRICES E'ER STOOD STILL	475	2 DON JUAN	5	112	6
A FURTHER PROOF WE SHOULD NOT JUDGE IN HASTE	347	3 DON JUAN	12	69	5
ASK A BLIND MAN THE BEST JUDGE YOU'LL ATTACK	348	3 DON JUAN	12	71	4
NOT THAT I DEEM OUR CHIEF JUDGE IS A HOLLOW MAN--)	357	3 DON JUAN	12 V	18	8
NOR JUDGE AT FIRST IF ALL BE TRUE TO NATURE	390	3 DON JUAN	13	67	4
THERE WAS THE WAGGISH WELCH JUDGE JEFFERIES HARDSMAN	399	3 DON JUAN	13	88	5
ADELINE NO DEEP JUDGE OF CHARACTER	463	3 DON JUAN	15	17	1
NOW JUSTICES OF PEACE MUST JUDGE ALL PIECES	531	3 DON JUAN	16	63	1
IF WE MAY JUDGE FROM EACH NEW YEAR'S DISPLAY	548	3 DON JUAN	16	99	V5
JUDGED					
EVEN PETRARCH'S SELF IF JUDGED WITH DUE SEVERITY	411	2 DON JUAN	5	1	7
HE JUDGED THEM PROPER TO ASSAIL THE WORKS	93	3 DON JUAN	7	53	4
WHICH JUDGED MANKIND AT THEIR DUE ESTIMATION	372	3 DON JUAN	13	31	5
NEXT THAT HE NEVER JUDGED FROM WHAT APPEAR'D	439	3 DON JUAN	14	66	3
JUDGE'S					
HE HAD HIS JUDGE'S JOKE FOR CONSOLATION	399	3 DON JUAN	13	88	8
JUDGES					
THEN ADVOCATES INQUISITORS AND JUDGES	36	2 DON JUAN	1	28	7
JUDGES IN VERY FORMIDABLE ERMINE	391	3 DON JUAN	13	69	1
JUDGING					
IN JUDGING MEN--WHEN ONCE HIS JUDGMENT WAS	366	3 DON JUAN	13	16	3
JUDGING BY WHAT THEY TAKE AND WHAT THEY PAY	548	3 DON JUAN	16	99	5
JUDGMENT					
AND IN THY STEAD I'VE GOT A DEAL OF JUDGMENT	144	2 DON JUAN	1	215	7
WHICH PORTIONS OUT UPON THE JUDGMENT DAY	242	3 DON JUAN	10	35	4
IN JUDGING MEN--WHEN ONCE HIS JUDGMENT WAS	366	3 DON JUAN	13	16	3
BUT FOR HIS JUDGMENT--NEVER KNOWN TO FAIL	528	3 DON JUAN	16	57	8
JUDGMENTS					
AND ALL MAY THINK WHICH WAY THEIR JUDGMENTS LEAN 'EM	28	2 DON JUAN	1	14	6
AS HINTING MORE (UNLESS OUR JUDGMENTS WARP US)	391	3 DON JUAN	13	69	7
JUDICIOUSLY					
JUDICIOUSLY FROM OUT THE SCHOOLBOY'S VISION	46	2 DON JUAN	1	44	3
JUGULAR					
AND THEN HELD OUT HIS JUGULAR AND WRIST	197	2 DON JUAN	2	76	8
JUICE					
OF RAISIN ORANGE AND POMEGRANATE JUICE	307	2 DON JUAN	3	62	7
DEPENDS SO MUCH UPON THE GASTRIC JUICE	428	2 DON JUAN	5	32	8
WHERE JUNIPER EXPRESSES ITS BEST JUICE	256	3 DON JUAN	10	63	3
JUICY					
HER PRIME OF LIFE JUST NOW IN JUICY VIGOUR	218	3 DON JUAN	9	72	5
JULIA					
THERE WAS THE DONNA JULIA WHOM TO CALL	51	2 DON JUAN	1	55	3
COULD BE BUT JULIA (WHOM ON THIS OCCASION	54	2 DON JUAN	1	59	6
JULIA WAS--YET I NEVER COULD SEE WHY--	58	2 DON JUAN	1	66	1
FOR NOT A LINE HAD JULIA EVER PENN'D	58	2 DON JUAN	1	66	4
SHE FLATTER'D JULIA WITH HER SAGE PROTECTION	58	2 DON JUAN	1	67	5
I CAN'T TELL WHETHER JULIA SAW THE AFFAIR	59	2 DON JUAN	1	68	1
WHEN HE WAS SIXTEEN JULIA TWENTY-THREE	59	2 DON JUAN	1	69	6
THAT DONNA JULIA KNEW THE REASON WHY	60	2 DON JUAN	1	70	6
THUS JULIA SAID--AND THOUGHT SO TO BE SURE	64	2 DON JUAN	1	79	6
I REALLY DON'T KNOW WHAT NOR JULIA EITHER	65	2 DON JUAN	1	81	8
BUT WHETHER JULIA TO THE TASK WAS EQUAL	66	2 DON JUAN	1	82	7
(THIS SHOULD BE ENTRE NOUS FOR JULIA THOUGHT	67	2 DON JUAN	1	84	7
SO MUCH FOR JULIA NOW WE'LL TURN TO JUAN	68	2 DON JUAN	1	86	1
WHEN JULIA SATE WITHIN AS PRETTY A BOWER	77	2 DON JUAN	1	104	3
JULIA HAD HONOUR VIRTUE TRUTH AND LOVE	80	2 DON JUAN	1	109	1
AND JULIA SATE WITH JUAN HALF EMBRACED	83	2 DON JUAN	1	115	1

412

```
                                                      PAGE VOL   CANTO STANZA LN
JULIA   (CONTINUED)
   BUT KEEPING JULIA AND DON JUAN STILL  . . . . . . . .  86  2 DON JUAN  1    121   5
   'TWAS MIDNIGHT--DONNA JULIA WAS IN BED  . . . . . . .  95  2 DON JUAN  1    136   1
   POOR DONNA JULIA STARTING AS FROM SLEEP . . . . . . .  97  2 DON JUAN  1    140   1
   BUT JULIA MISTRESS AND ANTONIA MAID  . . . . . . . .   98  2 DON JUAN  1    141   1
   NOW JULIA FOUND AT LENGTH A VOICE AND CRIED . . . . .  98  2 DON JUAN  1    142   1
   ANTONIA PUZZLED JULIA DID NOT SPEAK  . . . . . . . . 114  2 DON JUAN  1    169   7
   JULIA SAID NOUGHT THOUGH ALL THE WHILE THERE ROSE . . 117  2 DON JUAN  1    175   1
   JULIA IN FACT HAD TOLERABLE GROUNDS  . . . . . . . . 118  2 DON JUAN  1    176   1
   WHICH JULIA HALF WITHHELD AND THEN HALF GRANTED  . . 120  2 DON JUAN  1    180   2
   AND JULIA INSTANT TO THE CLOSET FLEW . . . . . . . . 121  2 DON JUAN  1    182   2
   ANTONIA CRIED OUT RAPE AND JULIA FIRE  . . . . . . . 122  2 DON JUAN  1    184   2
   ANTONIA IN HYSTERICS JULIA SWOON'D . . . . . . . . . 125  2 DON JUAN  1    187   3
   JULIA WAS SENT INTO A CONVENT SHE  . . . . . . . . . 129  2 DON JUAN  1    191   6
   JULIA WAS SENT INTO A NUNNERY  . . . . . . . . . . . 129  2 DON JUAN  1    191   V6
   FAREWELL TOO DEAREST JULIA--(HERE HE DREW  . . . . . 166  2 DON JUAN  2     18   7
   OH JULIA WHAT IS EVERY OTHER WOE--  . . . . . . . . . 167  2 DON JUAN  2     20   2
   JULIA MY LOVE--(YOU RASCAL PEDRO QUICKER)--  . . . . 167  2 DON JUAN  2     20   5
   OH JULIA--(THIS CURST VESSEL PITCHES SO)--  . . . . . 167  2 DON JUAN  2     20   6
   BELOVED JULIA HEAR ME STILL BESEECHING  . . . . . . . 167  2 DON JUAN  2     20   7
   BUT JUAN HAD HE QUITE FORGOTTEN JULIA  . . . . . . . 267  2 DON JUAN  2    208   1
JULIA'S
   BOABDIL WEPT OF DONNA JULIA'S KIN  . . . . . . . . .   52  2 DON JUAN  1     56   6
   'TIS SAID THAT DONNA JULIA'S GRANDMAMMA  . . . . . .   53  2 DON JUAN  1     58   7
   ALFONSO WAS THE NAME OF JULIA'S LORD . . . . . . . .   57  2 DON JUAN  1     65   1
   YET JULIA'S VERY COLDNESS STILL WAS KIND . . . . . .   60  2 DON JUAN  1     71   1
   POOR JULIA'S HEART WAS IN AN AWKWARD STATE  . . . . .  62  2 DON JUAN  1     75   1
   WAS JULIA'S INNOCENT DETERMINATION . . . . . . . . .   65  2 DON JUAN  1     81   2
   AND THEN HE THOUGHT OF DONNA JULIA'S EYES  . . . . .   71  2 DON JUAN  1     92   8
   COULD NOT ESCAPE THE GENTLE JULIA'S EYES . . . . . .   73  2 DON JUAN  1     97   2
   AND JULIA'S VOICE WAS LOST EXCEPT IN SIGHS . . . . .   84  2 DON JUAN  1    117   1
   DURING THIS INQUISITION JULIA'S TONGUE . . . . . . . 100  2 DON JUAN  1    145   1
   THEY TOOK BY FORCE FROM JUAN JULIA'S LETTER . . . . . 195  2 DON JUAN  2     74   8
JULIET
   UNLESS PHILOSOPHY CAN MAKE A JULIET  . . . . . . . . 272  2 DON JUAN  2  V   1    2
   NIGHT WAS A JULIET TO THE VERY NAME  . . . . . . . . 272  2 DON JUAN  2  V   1    8
   JULIET--OR--GIULETTA--WHICH LAST WAS . . . . . . . . 273  2 DON JUAN  2  V   2    1
   ANOTHER JULIET-- WHOM I WOULD NOT PASS--  . . . . . . 273  2 DON JUAN  2  V   2    5
JULIETTA
   IS ROUSSEAU'S JULIETTA--I NEER KNEW  . . . . . . . . 273  2 DON JUAN  2  V   2    7
JULY
   THE ENGLISH WINTER--ENDING IN JULY . . . . . . . . . 377  3 DON JUAN 13     42   1
   THE LONDON WINTER'S ENDED IN JULY--  . . . . . . . . 378  3 DON JUAN 13     43   1
JUMBLING
   AND BY MISTAKE SEQUINS WITH PARAS JUMBLING . . . . . 426  2 DON JUAN  5     29   5
JUMP'D
   LEFT HIM SO DRUNK HE JUMP'D INTO THE WAVE  . . . . . 186  2 DON JUAN  2     57   3
JUNCTION
   THAT ALL THE REST CREEP IN AND FORM A JUNCTION . . . 271  2 DON JUAN  2    215   4
   A JUNCTION OF THE GENERAL MEKNOP'S MEN . . . . . . . 151  3 DON JUAN  8     79   1
JUNCTURE
   WHO KICK AGAINST THE PRICKS JUST AT THIS JUNCTURE  . 263  3 DON JUAN 10     77   7
JUNE
   'TWAS ON A SUMMER'S DAY--THE SIXTH OF JUNE--  . . . .  76  2 DON JUAN  1    103   1
   'TWAS ON THE SIXTH OF JUNE ABOUT THE HOUR  . . . . .   77  2 DON JUAN  1    104   1
   THE LONGEST NOT THE TWENTY-FIRST OF JUNE . . . . . .   82  2 DON JUAN  1    113   5
   SUPPOSE FROM JUNE THE SIXTH (THE FATAL DAY . . . . .   86  2 DON JUAN  1    121   2
   PERHAPS BUT WHO WOULD SCORN THE MONTH OF JUNE  . . . 229  2 DON JUAN 10      9   5
   SLIPS FROM THE MOUNTAIN IN THE MONTH OF JUNE . . . . 517  3 DON JUAN 16     38   V6
JUNGLE
   THE CUBLESS TIGRESS IN HER JUNGLE RAGING . . . . . . 305  2 DON JUAN  3     58   1
JUNIOR
   AND (AS HER JUNIOR BY SIX WEEKS) HIS YOUTH . . . . . 432  3 DON JUAN 14     51   8
JUNIPER
   WHERE JUNIPER EXPRESSES ITS BEST JUICE . . . . . . . 256  3 DON JUAN 10     63   3
JUPITER
   I HAVE SEEN NAPOLEON WHO SEEMED QUITE A JUPITER  . . 309  3 DON JUAN 11     83   1
JURIES
   WHERE JURIES CAST UP WHAT A WIFE IS WORTH  . . . . .   57  2 DON JUAN  1     64   5
   FROM THOSE OF OTHER LANDS UNBLEST WITH JURIES  . . . 436  3 DON JUAN 14     60   7
   A CASE WHICH TO THE JURIES WE MAY LEAVE  . . . . . . 493  3 DON JUAN 15     84   4
JURY
   (THE JURY BROUGHT THEIR VERDICT IN INSANITY) . . . .   29  2 DON JUAN  1     15   8
   I WISH THE CASE COULD COME BEFORE A JURY HERE  . . . 446  2 DON JUAN  5     61   8
   JURY OF MATRONS SCARCE KNEW WHAT TO ANSWER . . . . . 294  3 DON JUAN 11     51   4
JURYMAST
   A JURYMAST OR RUDDER OR COULD SAY  . . . . . . . . . 177  2 DON JUAN  2     40   6
   DROOP'D DRIPPING ON THE OAR (THEIR JURY-MAST)  . . . 214  2 DON JUAN  2    110   5
JUST
   WITH JUST ENOUGH OF TALENT AND NO MORE . . . . . . .   16  2 DON JUAN  D     12   6
   JUST AS THE SPARTAN LADIES DID OF YORE  . . . . . . .  36  2 DON JUAN  1     29   3
   BY CONTRAST WHICH IS WHAT WE JUST WERE WISHING ALL . . 37  2 DON JUAN  1     31   6
   AND ANSWER'D BUT TO NATURE'S JUST DEMANDS  . . . . .   42  2 DON JUAN  1     37   6
   PLATONIC PERFECT JUST SUCH LOVE AS MINE  . . . . . .   64  2 DON JUAN  1     79   5
   BUT JUST SUPPOSE THAT MOMENT SHOULD BETIDE . . . . .   67  2 DON JUAN  1     84   5
   THEY'RE ON THE STAIR JUST NOW AND IN A CRACK . . . .   96  2 DON JUAN  1    137   6
   AS IF SHE HAD JUST NOW FROM OUT THEM CREPT . . . . .   97  2 DON JUAN  1    140   6
   IN DON ALFONSO'S FACTS WHICH JUST NOW WORE . . . . . 111  2 DON JUAN  1    164   6
   AND LARGEST THINKING IT WAS JUST THE THING . . . . . 146  2 DON JUAN  1    219   3
```

413

JUST   (CONTINUED)

	PAGE	VOL	CANTO	STANZA	LN
JUST LIKE A BLACK EYE IN A RECENT SCUFFLE	205	2 DON JUAN	2	92	7
JUST AS HIS FEEBLE ARMS COULD STRIKE NO MORE	212	2 DON JUAN	2	107	3
WITH JUST ENOUGH OF LIFE TO FEEL ITS PAIN	213	2 DON JUAN	2	108	7
I'LL TELL YOU WHY I SAY SO FOR 'TIS JUST	219	2 DON JUAN	2	119	1
REJECTED SEVERAL SUITORS JUST TO LEARN	224	2 DON JUAN	2	128	7
JUST FOR THE PRESENT AND IN HIS LULL'D HEAD	227	2 DON JUAN	2	134	4
SWEET SKIES JUST WHEN HE RISES OR IS SET	230	2 DON JUAN	2	139	3
TAKING HER FOR A SISTER JUST THE SAME	232	2 DON JUAN	2	142	5
FAIR AS THE ROSE JUST PLUCKED TO CROWN THE WREATH	235	2 DON JUAN	2	148	V5
JUST IN THE WAY WE VERY OFTEN SEE	244	2 DON JUAN	2	167	8
WAS JUST DESCRIBING--YES IT WAS THE COAST--	251	2 DON JUAN	2	181	7
IT WAS THE COOLING HOUR JUST WHEN THE ROUNDED	252	2 DON JUAN	2	183	1
JUST IN THE VERY CRISIS SHE SHOULD NOT	258	2 DON JUAN	2	193	8
I'LL JUST INQUIRE IF SHE BE WIFE OR MAID	268	2 DON JUAN	2	210	5
WITH ONE OR TWO SMALL SENSES ADDED JUST	269	2 DON JUAN	2	212	7
SMALL SOCIAL PARTIES JUST BEGUN TO DINE	291	2 DON JUAN	3	31	2
JUST AS OLD AGE IS CREEPING ON APACE	305	2 DON JUAN	3	59	5
FLOCK O'ER THEIR CARRION JUST LIKE MEN BELOW	358	2 DON JUAN	4	28	5
JUST AT THE VERY TIME WHEN HE LEAST BROODS	371	2 DON JUAN	4	51	5
LEAVES NOTHING TILL THE COMING OF THE JUST--	399	2 DON JUAN	4	101	6
JUST NOW A BLACK OLD NEUTRAL PERSONAGE	424	2 DON JUAN	5	26	1
JUST AS MY GREAT COAT WAS ABOUT ME CAST	428	2 DON JUAN	5	33	3
JUST KILLED AND SCARCELY COMPETENT TO PANT	429	2 DON JUAN	5	33	V8
BESIDES I'M HUNGRY AND JUST NOW WOULD TAKE	435	2 DON JUAN	5	44	7
JUST AS ONE VIEWS A HORSE TO GUESS HIS PRICE	441	2 DON JUAN	5	54	6
IF YOU COULD JUST CONTRIVE HE SAID TO STINT	464	2 DON JUAN	5	91	3
IS JUST TWO MINUTES FOR YOUR DECLARATION--	482	2 DON JUAN	5	123	7
JUST AS A FRIAR MAY ACCUSE HIS VOW	493	2 DON JUAN	5	142	6
JUST AS A LANGUID SMILE BEGAN TO FLATTER	493	2 DON JUAN	5	143	6
BUT JUST REMARKED WITH AIR SEDATE AND WISE	500	2 DON JUAN	5	155	5
FOR WERE THE SULTAN JUST TO ALL HIS DEARS	10	3 DON JUAN	6	9	6
A FAVOURITE HORSE FALLEN LAME JUST AS HE'S MOUNTED	16	3 DON JUAN	6	21	4
AS DOTH A RAINBOW THE JUST CLEARING AIR	17	3 DON JUAN	6	23	8
A SLIGHT EXAMPLE JUST TO CAST A SHADE	22	3 DON JUAN	6	32	5
WHO WISHED THEY HAD A BROTHER JUST LIKE HER	25	3 DON JUAN	6	39	6
SHE LOOKED (THIS SIMILE'S QUITE NEW) JUST CUT	27	3 DON JUAN	6	43	5
JUST WHEN THE FADING LAMPS WANED DIM AND BLUE	41	3 DON JUAN	6	70	5
THAT JUST AS HER YOUNG LIP BEGAN TO OPE	44	3 DON JUAN	6	77	5
AT LEAST TO DREAM SO LOUDLY AS JUST NOW	47	3 DON JUAN	6	83	2
THINE EAR IMPERIAL AND JUST NOW RHYMES WANDER	52	3 DON JUAN	6	93	V3
(THE AFORESAID BABA) JUST THEN TO DO MORE	57	3 DON JUAN	6	103	6
JUST AS YOU'D BREAK A SUCKING SALAMANDER	93	3 DON JUAN	7	52	5
CAPTIVES JUST NOW ESCAPED WAS THE REPLY	97	3 DON JUAN	7	59	5
LESS THAN THEIR GRIEF (AND TRULY NOT LESS JUST)	104	3 DON JUAN	7	73	4
JUST NOW BEHAVED AS IN THE HOLY LAND	116	3 DON JUAN	8	9	8
JUST AT THE CLOSE OF THE FIRST BRIDAL YEAR	125	3 DON JUAN	8	27	4
JUST AT THIS CRISIS UP CAME JOHNSON TOO	130	3 DON JUAN	8	35	1
JOHNSON RETIRED A LITTLE JUST TO RALLY	131	3 DON JUAN	8	36	7
JUST NAMED THESE PALISADES WERE PRIMLY SET	136	3 DON JUAN	8	46	8
WHO CAME AS IF JUST DROPPED DOWN FROM THE MOON	140	3 DON JUAN	8	56	4
IT HAPPENED WAS HIMSELF BEAT BACK JUST NOW	147	3 DON JUAN	8	70	4
JUST AS KOUTOUSOW'S MOST FORLORN OF HOPES	148	3 DON JUAN	8	73	3
BEFORE BEING BADLY SECONDED JUST THEN)	151	3 DON JUAN	8	79	3
JUST AT THIS INSTANT WHILE THEIR EYES WERE FIXED	159	3 DON JUAN	8	96	1
IN BEGGING HIM FOR GOD'S SAKE JUST TO SHOW	165	3 DON JUAN	8	108	3
DO JUST WHATE'ER THEY PLEASE BY DINT OF FEATURES	167	3 DON JUAN	8	111	6
JUST PONDER WHAT A PIOUS PASTIME WAR IS	174	3 DON JUAN	8	124	8
SAYS SHAKESPEARE WHO JUST NOW IS MUCH IN FASHION	189	3 DON JUAN	9	14	2
JUST NOW--BUT BY AND BY THE TRUTH WILL SHOW 'EM	193	3 DON JUAN	9	22	5
HOW WILL--TO THESE YOUNG PEOPLE JUST THRUST OUT	202	3 DON JUAN	9	40	1
JUST THEN AS THEY ARE RATHER NUMEROUS FOUND	205	3 DON JUAN	9	46	4
AND HAD JUST BURIED THE FAIR FACED LANSKOI	206	3 DON JUAN	9	47	8
JUST NOW YOUR'S WERE CUT OUT IN DIFFERENT SECTIONS	215	3 DON JUAN	9	65	5
IN THE NEXT OCEAN WHICH MAY FLOW JUST THEN	217	3 DON JUAN	9	69	6
TO MAKE A TWILIGHT IN JUST AS SOLMS HEAT IS	217	3 DON JUAN	9	69	7
HER PRIME OF LIFE JUST NOW IN JUICY VIGOUR	218	3 DON JUAN	9	72	5
WE HAVE JUST LIT ON A HEAVEN-KISSING HILL	224	3 DON JUAN	9	85	4
AND WHEREFORE THIS EXORDIUM--WHY JUST NOW	226	3 DON JUAN	10	3	1
BUT HIS JUST NOW WERE SPREAD AS IS A CUSHION	235	3 DON JUAN	10	21	5
THERE WAS JUST THEN A KIND OF A DISCUSSION	246	3 DON JUAN	10	45	1
JUST NOW THERE WAS NO PERIL OF TEMPTATION	251	3 DON JUAN	10	55	1
ON WHICH I HAVE NOT TIME JUST NOW TO LECTURE	255	3 DON JUAN	10	62	4
WHO KICK AGAINST THE PRICKS JUST AT THIS JUNCTURE	263	3 DON JUAN	10	77	7
JUST AS THE DAY BEGAN TO WANE AND DARKEN	264	3 DON JUAN	10	80	3
COULD REACH WITH HERE AND THERE A SAIL JUST SKIPPING	265	3 DON JUAN	10	82	3
JUST NOW ENOUGH BUT BY-AND-BY I'LL PRATTLE	267	3 DON JUAN	10	87	7
JUST AT THE PROPER TIME AND THOUGH A LAD	292	3 DON JUAN	11	47	6
JUST AS HE REALLY PROMISED SOMETHING GREAT	298	3 DON JUAN	11	60	2
MANKIND JUST NOW SEEM WRAPT IN MEDITATION	325	3 DON JUAN	12	21	4
PRELUDIOS TRYING JUST A STRING OR TWO	341	3 DON JUAN	12	54	6
JUST TO CONSOLE SAD GLORY FOR BEING GLORIOUS	372	3 DON JUAN	13	32	8
JUST AS A MANDARIN FINDS NOTHING FINE--	373	3 DON JUAN	13	34	5
PROUD OF HIS LEARNING (JUST ENOUGH TO QUOTE)	401	3 DON JUAN	13	91	3
BUT JUST TO PLAY WITH AS AN INFANT PLAYS	414	3 DON JUAN	14	8	8
BUT THIS CAN'T WELL BE TRUE JUST NOW FOR WRITERS	418	3 DON JUAN	14	20	1
HE DID NOT FALL ASLEEP JUST AFTER DINNER	426	3 DON JUAN	14	36	8
JUST AS I FEEL THE IMPROVVISATORE	465	3 DON JUAN	15	20	8
OR--WHAT IS JUST THE SAME--IT WEARIES OUT	478	3 DON JUAN	15	51	7

```
                                                           PAGE VOL       CANTO   STANZA LV
JUST  (CONTINUED)
     JUST TO RELIEVE HER SPIRITS FROM DEJECTION  . . . . .   483  3 DON JUAN 15     64   8
     SLIGHT BUT SELECT AND JUST ENOUGH TO EXPRESS   . . . .   491  3 DON JUAN 15     80   2
     THOSE HOLIER MYSTERIES WHICH THE WISE AND JUST  . . .    503  3 DON JUAN 16      6   6
     TO JEST YOU'LL CHOOSE SOME OTHER THEME JUST NOW   . . .  516  3 DON JUAN 16     37   6
     'TIS WHITE AT LEAST WHEN THEY JUST RISE FROM BED  . .    532  3 DON JUAN 16     64   4
     THAT HE EXACTLY THE JUST MEDIUM HIT  . . . . . . .       535  3 DON JUAN 16     72   3
     JUST AS A REGULAR COMMON SOLDIER OR A WHORE . . . . .    537  3 DON JUAN 16     76  V3
     THE MOON PEEPED JUST ESCAPED FROM A GREY CLOUD . . . .   560  3 DON JUAN 16    121   8
     BUT NOW IT SEEMS HE'S RIGHT--HIS NOTION JUST   . . . .   565  3 DON JUAN 17      8   7
     JUST AS I MAKE MY MIND UP EVERY DAY  . . . . . .         566  3 DON JUAN 17     10   6
JUSTEST
     WHEN NERO PERISH'D BY THE JUSTEST DOOM  . . . . . .      339  2 DON JUAN  3    109   1
JUSTICE
     I NE'ER SAW JUSTICE DONE AND YET SHE WAS . . . . .       219  2 DON JUAN  2    119   4
     COULD I DO JUSTICE TO THE FULL DETAIL . . . . . .        467  2 DON JUAN  5     97   7
     HIS LORDSHIP'S JUSTICE--SEEMS NOT THAT OF SOLOMON--  . . 357  3 DON JUAN 12   V 18   7
     LORD HENRY WAS A JUSTICE AND THAT SCOUT  . . . . .       531  3 DON JUAN 16     62   6
     SHE WAITED UNTIL JUSTICE COULD RECALL  . . . . .         533  3 DON JUAN 16     67   5
JUSTICE'S
     THE PEOPLE'S SYCOPHANT--IN JUSTICE'S HOUR  . . . . .     151  2 DON JUAN  1    V 2  V7
JUSTICES
     NOW JUSTICES OF PEACE MUST JUDGE ALL PIECES  . . . . .   531  3 DON JUAN 16     63   1
JUSTIFY
     HE WOULD NOT JUSTIFY WHAT HE HAD DONE . . . . . . .      116  2 DON JUAN  1    174   3
JUSTLY
     AND DON'T KNOW JUSTLY WHAT WE WOULD BE AT--  . . . . .   315  3 DON JUAN 12      1   5
JUVENAL
     I CAN'T HELP THINKING JUVENAL WAS WRONG  . . . . .        45  2 DON JUAN  1     43   3
JUVENILE
     JUAN WAS JUVENILE AND THUS WAS FULL  . . . . .           415  2 DON JUAN  5      8   1
     OF WRATH AND RHYME WHEN JUVENILE AND CURLY  . . . . .    234  3 DON JUAN 10     19   2
JUVENTA
     NON EGO HOC FERREM CALIDA JUVENTA  . . . . . . .         143  2 DON JUAN  1    212   1
KAFF
     ASIA WHERE KAFF LOOKS DOWN UPON THE KURDS  . . . . .      49  3 DON JUAN  6     86   8
KALEIDOSCOPE
     QUITE A CELESTIAL KALEIDOSCOPE . . . . . . . . .         205  2 DON JUAN  2     93   8
KALENDS
     TO THE GREEK KALENDS OF ANOTHER SESSION  . . . . . .     379  3 DON JUAN 13     45   2
KANT
     HAS LATELY BEEN THE GREAT PROFESSOR KANT . . . . . .     254  3 DON JUAN 10     60   4
KATINKA
     LOLAH KATINKA AND DUDU IN SHORT . . . . . . .            26  3 DON JUAN  6     40   3
     KATINKA WAS A GEORGIAN WHITE AND RED . . . . . .         26  3 DON JUAN  6     41   3
     KATINKA ASKED HER ALSO WHENCE SHE CAME--  . . . . .      28  3 DON JUAN  6     44   3
     TO POOR KATINKA SPAIN'S AN ISLAND NEAR . . . . .         28  3 DON JUAN  6     44   7
     BUT HERE KATINKA INTERFERED AND SAID . . . . . .         29  3 DON JUAN  6     47   7
     REPLIED KATINKA I AM SURE I SEE . . . . . . . .          30  3 DON JUAN  6     48   3
     THE SAME KATINKA UNTIL BY-AND-BY . . . . . . .           30  3 DON JUAN  6     49   3
     KATINKA TOO AND WITH A GENTLE BOW  . . . . . . .         31  3 DON JUAN  6     50   3
KATSKOFF
     NOW UNDER ARMS HO KATSKOFF TAKE HIM TO--  . . . . . .    100  3 DON JUAN  7     66   3
KEATS
     JOHN KEATS WHO WAS KILLED OFF BY ONE CRITIQUE  . . . .   298  3 DON JUAN 11     60   1
KEEL
     UNDER THE VESSEL'S KEEL THE SAIL WAS PAST  . . . . .     176  2 DON JUAN  2     39   1
KEEN
     THERE HIS WORN BOSOM AND KEEN EYE WOULD MELT   . . .     302  2 DON JUAN  3     52   6
     WITH ALL HIS KEEN WORN LOOK AND GRECIAN GRACE  . . .     363  2 DON JUAN  4     35   5
     (AS BEING THE BRAVE LIONS' KEEN PROVIDERS)  . . . .      196  2 DON JUAN  9     27   7
     THERE WERE SOME HUNTERS BOLD AND COURSERS KEEN . . .     539  3 DON JUAN 16     80   1
     THERE WERE BUT TWO EXCEPTIONS TO THIS KEEN  . . . .      552  3 DON JUAN 16    105   1
KEEP
     TO KEEP ONE CREED'S A TASK GROWN QUITE HERCULEAN  . . .   20  2 DON JUAN  D     17   7
     BUT WILL KEEP BAKING BROILING BURNING ON . . . . .       56  2 DON JUAN  1     63   4
     TO KEEP THEM BEAUTIFUL OR LEAVE THEM NEAT  . . . . .      99  2 DON JUAN  1    143   6
     HOW CAN YOU DO SUCH THINGS AND KEEP YOUR FAME  . . .     112  2 DON JUAN  1    165   3
     PRAY KEEP YOUR NONSENSE FOR SOME LUCKIER NIGHT--  . .    115  2 DON JUAN  1    171   1
     AND IF WE CAN BUT TILL THE MORNING KEEP  . . . . .       115  2 DON JUAN  1    172   7
     BUT IT WILL SERVE TO KEEP MY VERSE COMPACT)  . . . .     119  2 DON JUAN  1    178   4
     TO KEEP HIS MEMORY WHOLE AND MUMMY HID . . . . .         146  2 DON JUAN  1    219   4
     WITHOUT THE SENSE TO KEEP IT FOR AN HOUR . . . . .       152  2 DON JUAN  1    V 3   8
     AND KEEP THE SHIP AFLOAT THOUGH THREE FEET YET . . .     172  2 DON JUAN  2     30   3
     THAT STILL COULD KEEP AFLOAT THE STRUGGLING TARS   . .   183  2 DON JUAN  2     51   3
     YET FOR ALL THAT KEEP NOT TOO LONG AWAY  . . . .         288  2 DON JUAN  3     25   7
     KEEP YOUR GOOD NAME THOUGH EVE HERSELF ONCE FELL   . .   460  2 DON JUAN  5     84   6
     TO MAKE MEN HAPPY OR TO KEEP THEM SO . . . . .           470  2 DON JUAN  5    101   3
     'TIS NOT HIS CONQUESTS KEEP HIS NAME IN FASHION  . .       8  3 DON JUAN  6      4   6
     YET HE COULD NOT AT TIMES KEEP BY THE WAY  . . . .        20  3 DON JUAN  6     29   4
     HER OFFICE WAS TO KEEP ALOOF OR SMOTHER  . . . . .        21  3 DON JUAN  6     31   6
     ALONG THE REST CONTRIVED TO KEEP THIS DEN  . . . .        22  3 DON JUAN  6     32   6
     KEEP MERELY FIRING AT A FOOLISH DISTANCE . . . . .       151  3 DON JUAN  8     78   8
     WHICH YOUTH WOULD NOT ACT ILL TO KEEP IN MIND) . . .     224  3 DON JUAN  9     84   5
     BUT KEEP YOUR HANDS OUT OF HIS BREECHES' POCKET  . .     264  3 DON JUAN 10     79   8
     YE VILLAINS AND ABOVE ALL KEEP A SHARP EYE . . . .       310  3 DON JUAN 11     86   5
     WHO KEEP THE WORLD BOTH OLD AND NEW IN PAIN  . . . .     318  3 DON JUAN 12      5   5
     ONLY TO KEEP ITS CORN AT THE OLD PRICE  . . . .          335  3 DON JUAN 12     40   8
     TO KEEP THE WHEELS GOING OF THE HIGHER CLASS   . . .     342  3 DON JUAN 12     57   5
```

415

		PAGE	VOL	CANTO	STANZA	LN

KEEP   (CONTINUED)
	PAGE	VOL	CANTO	STANZA	LN
THOUGH SEVERAL ALSO KEEP THEIR PERPENDICULAR	343	3	DON JUAN 12	59	3
THEY WARM INTO A SCRAPE BUT KEEP OF COURSE	349	3	DON JUAN 12	73	7
THE JOYS OF MUTUAL HATE TO KEEP THEM WARM	360	3	DON JUAN 13	6	5
AND QUITE ENOUGH FOR ME TO KEEP IN MIND--	414	3	DON JUAN 14	9	3
FOR REASONS WHICH I CHOOSE TO KEEP APART	419	3	DON JUAN 14	21	6
IF BUT TO KEEP THY CREDIT AS A MOWER	433	3	DON JUAN 14	53	8
WAS SUCH AS RATHER SEEM'D TO KEEP ALOOF	462	3	DON JUAN 15	14	3
TO KEEP EXTREMES FROM MEETING WHEN ONCE SET	492	3	DON JUAN 15	81	6
TO KEEP OUR HOLY BEACONS ALWAYS BRIGHT	496	3	DON JUAN 15	90	4
AS IF TO ASK HOW YOU CAN DARE TO KEEP	508	3	DON JUAN 16	18	7
OF MISCHIEF OF ALL KINDS AND KEEP THE GAME	531	3	DON JUAN 16	63	2
AND CHAMPION HIM TO THE UTMOST--HE WOULD KEEP IT	536	3	DON JUAN 16	75	2

KEEPING
	PAGE	VOL	CANTO	STANZA	LN
AND THAT STILL KEEPING UP THE OLD CONNEXION	58	2	DON JUAN 1	67	1
BUT KEEPING JULIA AND DON JUAN STILL	86	2	DON JUAN 1	121	5
(KEEPING THE DUE PROPORTIONS STILL IN SIGHT)	467	3	DON JUAN 15	25	6
BUT WHAT WITH KEEPING SOME AND BREAKING OTHERS	535	3	DON JUAN 16	71	7

KEEPS
	PAGE	VOL	CANTO	STANZA	LN
WHICH KEEPS WHEN PUSH'D BY QUESTIONS RATHER ROUGH	119	2	DON JUAN 1	178	5
AND PLACES ONE KEEPS LOOKING AT THE STEEPLE	164	2	DON JUAN 2	14	8
THAT GOOD OLD STEAM-BOAT WHICH KEEPS VERSES MOVING	219	3	DON JUAN 9	74	4
AND WON'T SAY YES AND KEEPS YOU ON AND OFF-ING.	345	3	DON JUAN 12	63	2
SHE KEEPS IT FOR YOU LIKE A TRUE ALLY	350	3	DON JUAN 12	74	8
AND KEEPS THE ATROCIOUS READER IN SUSPENSE	453	3	DON JUAN 14	97	6

KEG
	PAGE	VOL	CANTO	STANZA	LN
TWO CASKS OF BISCUIT AND A KEG OF BUTTER	180	2	DON JUAN 2	46	7

KELP
	PAGE	VOL	CANTO	STANZA	LN
OF THIS ODD LABYRINTH OR AS THE KELP	238	3	DON JUAN 10	28	5

KEN
	PAGE	VOL	CANTO	STANZA	LN
BOOZE IN THE KEN OR AT THE SPELLKEN HUSTLE	277	3	DON JUAN 11	19	4

KENNINGTON
	PAGE	VOL	CANTO	STANZA	LN
THROUGH KENNINGTON AND ALL THE OTHER TONS	277	3	DON JUAN 11	20	7

KENTUCKY
	PAGE	VOL	CANTO	STANZA	LN
THE GENERAL BOON BACK-WOODSMAN OF KENTUCKY	143	3	DON JUAN 8	61	4

KEPPEL
	PAGE	VOL	CANTO	STANZA	LN
PRINCE FERDINAND GRANBY BURGOYNE KEPPEL HOWE	22	2	DON JUAN 1	2	2

KEPT
	PAGE	VOL	CANTO	STANZA	LN
FROM BETTER COMPANY HAVE KEPT YOUR OWN	12	2	DON JUAN D	5	2
SHE KEPT A JOURNAL WHERE HIS FAULTS WERE NOTED	36	2	DON JUAN 1	28	1
KEPT THIS HERSELF AND GAVE HER SON ANOTHER	47	2	DON JUAN 1	46	8
SHE KEPT HER COUNSEL IN SO CLOSE A WAY	59	2	DON JUAN 1	68	8
YET STILL I TRUST IT MAY BE KEPT THROUGHOUT	85	2	DON JUAN 1	119	6
'TIS NOT MY FAULT--I KEPT GOOD WATCH--ALACK	96	2	DON JUAN 1	137	4
HIS DAILY TASK HAD KEPT HIS FANCY COOL	158	2	DON JUAN 2	2	3
KEPT TWO HAND AND ONE CHAIN-PUMP STILL IN USE	172	2	DON JUAN 2	30	4
THE HOARSE HARSH WAVES KEPT TIME FRIGHT CURED THE QUALMS	174	2	DON JUAN 2	34	5
KEPT STILL ALOOF THE CREW WHO ERE THEY SUNK	174	2	DON JUAN 2	35	7
LIKE BRUTES--AND THUS HIS DANGEROUS POST KEPT HE	175	2	DON JUAN 2	36	5
AND FOR THE BOAT--THE CREW KEPT CROWDING IN IT	186	2	DON JUAN 2	57	8
EACH SEA CURL'D O'ER THE STERN AND KEPT THEM WET	188	2	DON JUAN 2	60	5
KEPT ABOVE WATER WITH AN OAR FOR MAST	188	2	DON JUAN 2	61	2
OF THE NEW FIRE WHICH ZOE KEPT UP KNEELING	237	2	DON JUAN 2	153	6
WHERE WIVES AT LEAST ARE SELDOM KEPT IN GARRISON	248	2	DON JUAN 2	175	8
SHE NOW KEPT HOUSE UPON HER OWN ACCOUNT	295	2	DON JUAN 3	38	8
THE ONLY THING WHICH KEPT HIS HEART UNCLOSED	304	2	DON JUAN 3	57	3
KEPT FOR ALL COMERS AT ALL HOURS TO DINE	310	2	DON JUAN 3	69	8
STILL KEPT HIS SPIRITS UP--AT LEAST HIS FACE	388	2	DON JUAN 4	81	4
A THOUSAND WARRIORS BY HIS WORD WERE KEPT	430	2	DON JUAN 5	36	4
YE WHO HAVE KEPT YOUR CHASTITY WHEN YOUNG	486	2	DON JUAN 5	130	2
BECAUSE HE KEPT THEM QUIET IN HIS CLOSET HE	496	2	DON JUAN 5	148	V6
HIS SONS WERE KEPT IN PRISON TILL THEY GREW	499	2	DON JUAN 5	153	1
A DAME WHO KEPT UP DISCIPLINE AMONG	21	3	DON JUAN 6	30	5
HER FUTURE DREAMS SHOULD ALL BE KEPT IN HAND	47	3	DON JUAN 6	82	8
KEPT UP AND ABOVE ALL THE WHERE AND HOW	55	3	DON JUAN 6	99	7
THIS HE DISCREETLY KEPT IN THE BACKGROUND	58	3	DON JUAN 6	105	1
AIR 'MIDST THE REST WHO KEPT THEIR VALIANT FACES	130	3	DON JUAN 8	34	7
KEPT ALWAYS PUSHING ONWARDS TO THE GLACIS	130	3	DON JUAN 8	34	V8
THE FREE-BORN FOREST FOUND AND KEPT THEM FREE	145	3	DON JUAN 8	65	7
THE TEETH STILL KEPT THEIR GRATIFYING HOLD	153	3	DON JUAN 8	83	7
BUT THE STONE BASTION STILL KEPT UP ITS FIRE	171	3	DON JUAN 8	120	1
READER I HAVE KEPT MY WORD--AT LEAST SO FAR	181	3	DON JUAN 8	138	1
AND MADE A VOW TO SHIELD HER WHICH HE KEPT	182	3	DON JUAN 8	141	8
KEPT THE PLACE OPEN FOR THEIR EMULATION	248	3	DON JUAN 10	48	8
HAD KEPT HIM FROM THE BRINK OF HIPPOCRENE	294	3	DON JUAN 11	51	7
SO THAT FEW MEMBERS KEPT THE HOUSE UP LATER	367	3	DON JUAN 13	20	8
WITH FAIR LONG LOCKS HAD ALSO KEPT THEIR STATION	390	3	DON JUAN 13	68	5
OUR RIDICULES ARE KEPT IN THE BACK-GROUND--	402	3	DON JUAN 13	95	1
CHASTE WERE HIS STEPS EACH KEPT WITHIN DUE BOUND	427	3	DON JUAN 14	39	1
AT LEAST HE KEPT HIS VANITY RETIRED	428	3	DON JUAN 14	41	4
UNLESS GOOD COMPANY HE KEPT TOO LONG	443	3	DON JUAN 14	77	6
SOME TRUTHS ARE BETTER KEPT BEHIND A SCREEN	444	3	DON JUAN 14	80	6
AND KEPT HER HEART SERENE WITHIN ITS ZONE	476	3	DON JUAN 15	47	4
SEEMED PALE AND SHIVERED AS IF SHE HAD KEPT	568	3	DON JUAN 17	14	7

KERCHIEF
	PAGE	VOL	CANTO	STANZA	LN
THE FIRST AND TALLEST HER WHITE KERCHIEF WAVING	291	2	DON JUAN 3	30	2
A KERCHIEF CRYING GIVE SAL THAT--AND DIED	276	3	DON JUAN 11	16	8

KESWICK
	PAGE	VOL	CANTO	STANZA	LN
AT KESWICK AND THROUGH STILL CONTINUED FUSION	12	2	DON JUAN D	5	3

				PAGE	VOL		CANTO	STANZA	LN

KETCH
    MIGHT END IN ACTING AS HIS OWN JACK KETCH . . . . . . 63 3 DON JUAN 6 116 5
KETTLE
    UNLESS TO MAKE THEIR KETTLE DRUMS A NEW SKIN . . . . . 75 3 DON JUAN 7 17 6
KEY
    JUAN THE GATE GAIN'D TURN'D THE KEY ABOUT . . . . . . 125 2 DON JUAN 1 187 7
    IS THE POOR PRIVILEGE TO TURN THE KEY . . . . 258 3 DON JUAN 10 68 5
KEYS
    LORDLINGS WITH STAVES OF WHITE OR KEYS OF GOLD . . . . . 391 3 DON JUAN 13 70 5
KHAN
    BUT TO OUR SUBJECT A BRAVE TARTAR KHAN-- . . . . . . 163 3 DON JUAN 8 104 5
    AND WHAT THEY PLEASED TO DO WITH THE YOUNG KHAN . . . 167 3 DON JUAN 8 112 1
    THUS THE YOUNG KHAN WITH HOURIS IN HIS SIGHT . . . . 168 3 DON JUAN 8 114 1
    THE GOOD OLD KHAN WHO LONG HAD CEASED TO SEE . . . . 169 3 DON JUAN 8 116 2
KIBES
    OR ROUGHLY TREADING ON THE COURTIER'S KIBES . . . . . 200 3 DON JUAN 9 35 6
KIBITKA
    AND THERE IN A KIBITKA HE ROLLED ON . . . . 197 3 DON JUAN 9 30 1
KICK
    GAVE IT A SLIGHT KICK WITH HIS CHRISTIAN FOOT . . . . 453 2 DON JUAN 5 73 6
    WAS THAT THEY COULD KICK DOWN THE PALISADES . . . . . 136 3 DON JUAN 8 47 7
    WHO KICK AGAINST THE PRICKS JUST AT THIS JUNCTURE . . . 263 3 DON JUAN 10 77 7
    KICK OFF THEIR BURTHENS--MEANING THE HIGH CLASSES . . . 310 3 DON JUAN 11 84 8
KICKED
    IN VAIN HE KICKED AND SWORE AND WRITHED AND BLED . . . 153 3 DON JUAN 8 83 5
KICKS
    FROM CROWNS TO KICKS ACCORDING TO THEIR VICES . . . . 425 2 DON JUAN 5 27 8
KID
    GOAT'S FLESH THERE IS NO DOUBT AND KID AND MUTTON . . . 238 2 DON JUAN 2 154 2
    CHEAPENING AN OX AN ASS A LAMB OR KID . . . . 425 2 DON JUAN 5 28 6
KIDDY
    POOR TOM WAS ONCE A KIDDY UPON TOWN . . . . . . 276 3 DON JUAN 11 17 5
KILIA
    OPENED THE GATE CALLED KILIA TO THE GROUPS . . . . . 148 3 DON JUAN 8 73 5
KILL
    DARE YOU SUSPECT ME WHOM THE THOUGHT WOULD KILL . . . 98 2 DON JUAN 1 142 7
    I HAD NOT LIVED TILL NOW COULD SORROW KILL . . . . . 134 2 DON JUAN 1 197 5
    FOR THIS MEN WRITE SPEAK PREACH AND HEROES KILL . . . 146 2 DON JUAN 1 218 5
    WOULD BEAR SUCH OUTRAGE AND FORBEAR TO KILL . . . . . 368 2 DON JUAN 4 46 6
    CORRUPTION CAME NOT IN EACH MIND TO KILL . . . . . . 377 2 DON JUAN 4 60 5
    HER WISH WAS BUT TO KILL KILL KILL LIKE LEAR'S . . . 490 2 DON JUAN 5 136 7
    HER WISH WAS BUT TO KILL KILL KILL LIKE LEAR'S . . . 490 2 DON JUAN 5 136 7
    HER WISH WAS BUT TO KILL KILL KILL LIKE LEAR'S . . . 490 2 DON JUAN 5 136 7
    WE SHALL NOT SEE HIS LIKENESS HE COULD KILL HIS . . . 132 3 DON JUAN 8 39 4
    TO KILL AND GENERALS TURN IT INTO JEST . . . . . . 212 3 DON JUAN 9 60 8
    KILL A MAN'S FAMILY AND HE MAY BROOK IT . . . . . . 264 3 DON JUAN 10 79 7
KILL'D
    WHO SAW THEIR SPOUSES KILL'D AND NOBLY CHOSE . . . 36 2 DON JUAN 1 29 4
    WHO KILL'D HIMSELF FOR LOVE (WITH WINE) LAST YEAR . . . 102 2 DON JUAN 1 149 8
    WAS KILL'D AND PORTION'D OUT FOR PRESENT EATING . . . 193 2 DON JUAN 2 70 8
    WHO ATE LAST WAR MORE YANKEES THAN HE KILL'D . . . 399 3 DON JUAN 13 88 4
KILLED
    JUST KILLED AND SCARCELY COMPETENT TO PANT . . . . . 429 2 DON JUAN 5 33 V8
    KILLED BY FIVE BULLETS FROM AN OLD GUN-BARREL . . . . 429 2 DON JUAN 5 34 8
    OF KILLED AND WOUNDED WHO WILL NOT BE MISSED . . . . 107 3 DON JUAN 7 81 V8
    OH YE LESS GRAND LONG LIST OF KILLED AND WOUNDED . . . 108 3 DON JUAN 7 82 2
    BE THAT THE GREATER PART WERE KILLED OR WOUNDED . . . 125 3 DON JUAN 8 28 2
    THIS VALIANT MAN KILLED ALL THE TURKS HE MET . . . . 150 3 DON JUAN 8 77 1
    OUR KILLED ALREADY PILED UP TO THE CHIN . . . . . 160 3 DON JUAN 8 98 6
    KILLED BECAUSE WHAT HE SWALLOWED WOULD NOT PASS . . . 199 3 DON JUAN 9 33 V8
    I SCOTCHED NOT KILLED THE SCOTCHMAN IN MY BLOOD . . . 234 3 DON JUAN 10 19 7
    JOHN KEATS WHO WAS KILLED OFF BY ONE CRITIQUE . . . . 298 3 DON JUAN 11 60 1
    MORE WITH THESE DINNERS THAN THE KILLED OR WOUNDED-- . . 383 3 DON JUAN 13 53 8
KILLING
    FOR KILLING BODIES AND FOR SAVING SOULS . . . . . . 93 2 DON JUAN 1 132 2
    IN THE SAME OBJECT GRACES QUITE AS KILLING . . . . . 270 2 DON JUAN 2 213 3
    SHE THOUGHT OF KILLING JUAN--BUT POOR LAD . . . . . 492 2 DON JUAN 5 140 5
    THAT KILLING HIM IS NOT THE WAY TO CURE YOU . . . . 63 3 DON JUAN 6 115 8
    THE CAUSE OF KILLING TCHITCHITZKOFF AND SMITH . . . 79 3 DON JUAN 7 25 4
    AND LECTURING ON THE NOBLE ART OF KILLING-- . . . . 96 3 DON JUAN 7 58 4
    FOR KILLING NOTHING BUT A BEAR OR BUCK HE . . . . . 143 3 DON JUAN 8 61 6
KIN
    BOABDIL WEPT OF DONNA JULIA'S KIN . . . . . . 52 2 DON JUAN 1 56 6
    EXHAUSTION OR DISORDERS OF THE SAME KIN . . . . . 244 3 DON JUAN 10 40 4
    WHICH WITH THE BLOOD TOO READILY WILL CLAIM KIN . . . 244 3 DON JUAN 10 40 6
    AND DAUGHTERS BROTHERS SISTERS KITH OR KIN . . . . . 470 3 DON JUAN 15 31 2
KIND
    OR REGENT WHO ADMIRES SUCH KIND OF FOOD-- . . . . . 10 2 DON JUAN D 2 4
    HE WAS A MORTAL OF THE CARELESS KIND . . . . . . 31 2 DON JUAN 1 19 1
    INTENTIONS BUT THEIR TREATMENT WAS NOT KIND . . . . 34 2 DON JUAN 1 24 2
    AND PUT THE BUSINESS PAST ALL KIND OF DOUBT . . . . 35 2 DON JUAN 1 26 8
    YET JULIA'S VERY COLDNESS STILL WAS KIND . . . . . 60 2 DON JUAN 1 71 1
    WITH ANY KIND OF TROUBLESOME CONTROL . . . . . . 66 2 DON JUAN 1 82 6
    A KIND ANTITHESIS TO CONGREVE'S ROCKETS . . . . . 91 2 DON JUAN 1 129 6
    EXAMPLES OF THIS KIND ARE SO CONTAGIOUS . . . . . 96 2 DON JUAN 1 138 7
    (AS EVERY KIND OF PARTING HAS ITS STINGS) . . . . . 161 2 DON JUAN 2 9 5
    A KIND OF SHOCK THAT SETS ONE'S HEART AJAR . . . . 164 2 DON JUAN 2 14 6
    FOR SAILORS ARE IN FACT A DIFFERENT KIND . . . . . 170 2 DON JUAN 2 26 5
    AND HAVE A KIND OF WILD AND HORRID GLEE . . . . . 183 2 DON JUAN 2 50 6

417

KIND   (CONTINUED)

	PAGE	VOL		CANTO	STANZA	LN
THEY FOUND A TURTLE OF THE HAWK'S-BILL KIND	208	2 DON JUAN	2	99	2
TO THESE KIND EFFORTS MADE A LOW REPLY	215	2 DON JUAN	2	113	8
TO HER AS 'TWERE THE KIND OF BEING SENT	247	2 DON JUAN	2	172	3
A KIND OF FLATTERY THAT'S HARDLY FAIR	278	2 DON JUAN	3	6	3
SOME CHASTE LIAISON OF THE KIND--I MEAN	288	2 DON JUAN	3	25	2
QUITE COMMON IN THOSE COUNTIES ARE A KIND	308	2 DON JUAN	3	65	2
ANOTHER DESPOT OF THE KIND	325	2 DON JUAN	3 L	12	5
TO THE KIND READER OF OUR SOBER CLIME	347	2 DON JUAN	4	6	1
AND THESE WERE NOT OF THE VAIN KIND WHICH CLOYS	352	2 DON JUAN	4	16	4
IT WAS A MOMENT OF THAT AWFUL KIND--	363	2 DON JUAN	4	36	7
YET HAS A SENTIMENTAL KIND OF AIR	390	2 DON JUAN	4	85	6
YET HAS A KIND OF SOFT AND SILLY AIR	390	2 DON JUAN	4	85	V6
A KIND OF BLUNT COMPASSION FOR THE SAD	417	2 DON JUAN	5	12	5
A KIND OF DEATH COMES O'ER US ALL ALONE	443	2 DON JUAN	5	57	7
HER BEAUTY OF THAT OVERPOWERING KIND	467	2 DON JUAN	5	97	2
IN ANY KIND OF MISCHIEF TO BE WROUGHT	477	2 DON JUAN	5	114	5
AUGHT OF A SERIOUS SORROWING KIND ALTHOUGH	480	2 DON JUAN	5	119	5
A KIND OF STATE MORE AWKWARD THAN UNCOMMON	10	3 DON JUAN	6	7	2
A SLIGHT BLUSH A SOFT TREMOR A CALM KIND	13	3 DON JUAN	6	15	1
ALL FELT A SOFT KIND OF CONCATENATION	25	3 DON JUAN	6	38	6
A KIND OF SLEEPY VENUS SEEMED DUDU	27	3 DON JUAN	6	42	1
WITH KIND REMARKS UPON THEIR MIEN AND FACES	28	3 DON JUAN	6	45	8
AND THEREFORE WAS SHE KIND AND GENTLE AS	33	3 DON JUAN	6	55	1
THE BRAZEN UPPERMOST) KIND READER PASS	34	3 DON JUAN	6	56	3
A KIND CONSTRUCTION UPON THEM AND ME	34	3 DON JUAN	6	56	7
OF THE UNPLEASANT KIND WITH NONE AT HAND	45	3 DON JUAN	6	78	3
A KIND OF PHANTASY PROPORTIONATE	84	3 DON JUAN	7	37	6
AWARE THIS KIND OF BAGGAGE NEVER THRIVES	102	3 DON JUAN	7	70	7
TO ME THIS KIND OF LIFE IS NOT SO NEW	103	3 DON JUAN	7	72	5
TO BATTLES SIEGES AND THAT KIND OF PLEASURE	123	3 DON JUAN	8	24	7
(START NOT KIND READER SINCE GREAT HOMER THOUGHT	126	3 DON JUAN	8	29	6
WAS NOTHING BUT A VALOUROUS KIND OF CUNNING	130	3 DON JUAN	8	35	8
HE SHEWED HIMSELF AS KIND AS MORTAL CAN	144	3 DON JUAN	8	64	8
OUR HERO (AND I TRUST KIND READER YOUR'S) --	194	3 DON JUAN	9	23	1
THOUGH BOLD AND BLOODY WAS THE KIND OF THING	217	3 DON JUAN	9	70	2
THE NOBLEST KIND OF LOVE IS LOVE PLATONICAL	220	3 DON JUAN	9	76	1
OF THOSE IN OFFICE ALL THE WORLD LOOKED KIND	224	3 DON JUAN	9	84	3
THERE WAS JUST THEN A KIND OF A DISCUSSION	246	3 DON JUAN	10	45	1
HE HAD A KIND OF INCLINATION OR	249	3 DON JUAN	10	50	4
A KIND OF PRIDE THAT HE SHOULD BE AMONG	257	3 DON JUAN	10	65	5
TO ME SEEMS BUT A DUBIOUS KIND OF REED	324	3 DON JUAN	12	18	5
WHERE EVERY KIND OF MISCHIEF'S DAILY BREWING	326	3 DON JUAN	12	23	3
WITH THE KIND WORLD'S AMEN--WHO WOULD HAVE THOUGHT IT	328	3 DON JUAN	12	26	8
BECAME A KIND OF FASHIONABLE MYSTERY	328	3 DON JUAN	12	27	8
TO SOME SHE SHOWED ATTENTION OF THAT KIND	372	3 DON JUAN	13	32	2
(IF BUT FOR COMFORT) THAT ALL THINGS ARE KIND	377	3 DON JUAN	13	41	4
A KIND OF COMMON-PLACE EVEN IN THEIR CRIMES	417	3 DON JUAN	14	16	4
WITH THE KIND VIEW OF SAVING AN ECLAT	436	3 DON JUAN	14	60	1
BUT BOTH TOGETHER FORM A KIND OF CENTAUR	442	3 DON JUAN	14	73	7
WHETHER THEIR TALK WAS OF THE KIND CALL'D SMALL	453	3 DON JUAN	14	98	4
CHILD TO THE CARE OF GUARDIANS GOOD AND KIND	475	3 DON JUAN	15	44	2
HIS FAME TOO--FOR HE HAD THAT KIND OF FAME	480	3 DON JUAN	15	57	1
A KIND OF TRIUMPH I'LL NOT RECOMMEND	491	3 DON JUAN	15	79	2
AURORA'S SPIRIT WAS NOT OF THAT KIND	492	3 DON JUAN	15	81	8
SO MUCH AS I DO ANY KIND OF WRANGLE	496	3 DON JUAN	15	91	3
SURVEYED HIM WITH A KIND OF CALM SURPRISE	514	3 DON JUAN	16	31	8
AND THAT WAS OF A FASCINATING KIND	525	3 DON JUAN	16	49	4
ITS KIND ATTENTIONS TO THEIR PROPER PALE	533	3 DON JUAN	16	67	6
AND THIS AT PRESENT WAS HER KIND EMPLOYMENT	548	3 DON JUAN	16	100	8

KINDER

SOME KINDER CASUISTS ARE PLEASED TO SAY	336	2 DON JUAN	3	104	1
FOR KINDER FEELINGS WHATSOE'ER THEIR NATION	480	2 DON JUAN	5	120	4
THE KINDER VETERAN WITH CALM WORDS WILL COURT YOU	337	3 DON JUAN	12	45	5

KINDEST

ENQUIRIES AFTER THEM WITH KINDEST CARE	64	3 DON JUAN	6	118	6
HE SAID--AND IN THE KINDEST CALMUCK TONE--	102	3 DON JUAN	7	70	1
THE KINDEST MAY BE TAKEN AS A TEST	359	3 DON JUAN	13	3	6

KINDLE

| TO KINDLE FIRE AND AS THE NEW FLAMES GAVE | 216 | 2 DON JUAN | 2 | 115 | 5 |
| WHICH KINDLE MANHOOD BUT CAN NE'ER ENTRANCE | 554 | 3 DON JUAN | 16 | 108 | 6 |

KINDLED

INTO ONE FOCUS KINDLED FROM ABOVE	254	2 DON JUAN	2	186	3
HER HUMAN CLAY IS KINDLED FULL OF POWER	374	2 DON JUAN	4	56	2
AND KINDLED FEELINGS IN THE ROUGHEST HEART	386	3 DON JUAN	13	59	6
SHE SEIZED HER HARP WHOSE STRINGS WERE KINDLED SOON	517	3 DON JUAN	16	38	6
DIED FROM THE TOUCH THAT KINDLED THEM TO SOUND	521	3 DON JUAN	16	41	2

KINDLES

| WHICH KINDLES SUNLIKE O'ER THE LAUREL-BROWED | 373 | 3 DON JUAN | 13 | 33 | V7 |

KINDLING

AND HASTY TEMPER ON A KINDLING MIND	155	2 DON JUAN	1 V	7	2
UPON HIS SENSES AND THE KINDLING BEAM	237	2 DON JUAN	2	153	5
BEGONE SHE CRIED WITH KINDLING EYES--AND DO	63	3 DON JUAN	6	116	2
AT FIRST THEN KINDLING INTO ANIMATION	518	3 DON JUAN	16	40	5
KINDLING RELIGION TILL SHE THROWS DOWN HER GAGE	530	3 DON JUAN	16	60	5
HIS VICE--FOR HE WAS OF A KINDLING NATION--	567	3 DON JUAN	17	12	6

KINDLY

| THEY KINDLY LEAVE US THOUGH NOT QUITE ALONE | 305 | 2 DON JUAN | 3 | 59 | 7 |
| AND HERE JUANNA KINDLY INTERPOSED | 48 | 3 DON JUAN | 6 | 84 | 1 |

```
                                                        PAGE VOL    CANTO STANZA LN
KINDNESS
     HIS FEELINGS FROM ALL MILK OF HUMAN KINDNESS   . . . . .  304  2 DON JUAN  3    57   7
     OF FEELING FOR SOME KINDNESS DONE WHEN POWER   . . . . .  339  2 DON JUAN  3   109   7
     KINDNESS DESTROYS WHAT LITTLE WE HAD GOT .  . . . . . .   423  2 DON JUAN  5    25   6
     WITH EVERY KINDNESS SHORT OF OSTENTATION .  . . . . . .    34  3 DON JUAN  6    57   3
KINDS
     FROM COUNSEL LEARNED IN THOSE KINDS OF LAWS  . . . . . .   38  2 DON JUAN  1    33   3
     KINDS OF GROTESQUES ILLUMINED AND HOW THEY   . . . . . .   47  2 DON JUAN  1    46   4
     AND ALL KINDS OF BENEVOLENT MACHINES .  . . . . . . . .    89  3 DON JUAN  7    47   8
     WITH ALL KINDS OF MECHANICS AND FULL SOON   . . . . . .  226  3 DON JUAN 10     2   7
     WITH ALL KINDS OF INCORRIGIBLE SAMPLES   . . . . . . .   236  3 DON JUAN 10    23   6
     WAS LADEN WITH ALL KINDS OF GIFTS AND HONOURS  . . . .   247  3 DON JUAN 10    46   7
     ALL KINDS OF TOIL SAVE FOR OUR COUNTRY'S GOOD--  . . .   301  3 DON JUAN 11    65   7
     OF TYRANNY OF ALL KINDS MY CONCISION .  . . . . . . .    466  3 DON JUAN 15    22   7
     OF MISCHIEF OF ALL KINDS AND KEEP THE GAME  . . . . .    531  3 DON JUAN 16    63   2
KING
     A DAINTY DISH TO SET BEFORE THE KING . . . . . . . .     10  2 DON JUAN  D     2   3
     IN CASE OUR LORD THE KING SHOULD GO TO WAR AGAIN  . . .   42  2 DON JUAN  1    38   6
     WHEN OLD KING DAVID'S BLOOD GREW DULL IN MOTION   . . .  113  2 DON JUAN  1   168   5
     IN MY HOT YOUTH--WHEN GEORGE THE THIRD WAS KING   . . .  143  2 DON JUAN  1   212   8
     WHAT ARE THE HOPES OF MAN OLD EGYPT'S KING  . . . . .    146  2 DON JUAN  1   219   1
     THE KING COMMANDS US AND THE DOCTOR QUACKS US  . . . .   159  2 DON JUAN  2     4   5
     A PLEASURE WORTHY XERXES THE GREAT KING  . . . . . . .   251  2 DON JUAN  2   180   3
     'TWAS ALL THE SAME TO HIM--GOD SAVE THE KING  . . . .    319  2 DON JUAN  3    85   3
     A KING SATE ON THE ROCKY BROW  . . . . . . . . .        322  2 DON JUAN  3  L 4   1
     THEY HAVE A KING WHO BUYS AND SELLS  . . . . . . . .    325  2 DON JUAN  3  L 14   2
     IS ALWAYS MUCH MORE SPLENDID THAN A KING . . . . . .    408  2 DON JUAN  4   115   6
     WHERE NABUCHADONOSOR KING OF MEN .  . . . . . . . .     445  2 DON JUAN  5    60   3
     MEANTIME GULBEYAZ WHEN HER KING WAS GONE .  . . . .      54  3 DON JUAN  6    97   1
     MAINTAINED AT THE EXPENSE OF YOUR GOOD KING  . . . . .  118  3 DON JUAN  8    14   3
     BUT NEVER MIND--GOD SAVE THE KING AND KINGS  . . . . .  137  3 DON JUAN  8    50   1
     WHICH LOVES SO WELL ITS COUNTRY AND ITS KING   . . . .  175  3 DON JUAN  8   126   2
     OF EVERY KING THAT EVER CURST A NATION   . . . . . .    194  3 DON JUAN  9    24  V8
     BECAUSE EACH LOVER LOOKED A SORT OF KING .  . . . . .   217  3 DON JUAN  9    70   4
     NOR SOUGHT OF FOOLSCAP SUBJECTS TO BE KING--  . . . .   296  3 DON JUAN 11    55   6
     NOR WISHED OF SUCH FRAIL REALMS TO BE THE KING  . . .   296  3 DON JUAN 11    55  V6
     TO SEE IT--THE KING HISSED AND THEN CAREST  . . . . .   309  3 DON JUAN 11    83   7
     A KING IN CONSTITUTIONAL POSSESSION  . . . . . . . .    354  3 DON JUAN 12    83   3
     A FIGURE FIT TO WALK BEFORE A KING . . . . . . . . .    440  3 DON JUAN 14    70   4
     WAS MUCH INFERIOR TO KING MENELAUS--  . . . . . . .     441  3 DON JUAN 14    72   7
     SHUT UP--NO NOT THE KING BUT THE PAVILION   . . . . .   446  3 DON JUAN 14    83   7
     HE READ AN ARTICLE THE KING ATTACKING  . . . . . . .    512  3 DON JUAN 16    26   7
     THOUGH HE CAME IN HIS MIGHT WITH KING HENRY'S RIGHT  .  518  3 DON JUAN 16  L 2   1
     THE KING HIMSELF HAD CHEAPENED IT BUT THOUGHT  . . . .  528  3 DON JUAN 16    56   5
     BUT COULD HE QUIT HIS KING IN TIMES OF STRIFE  . . . .  536  3 DON JUAN 16    74   3
KINGDOM
     TO SEE A KINGDOM OR A HOUSE O'ERTURN'D   . . . . . .     31  2 DON JUAN  1    19   6
     AND TOOK HIS KINGDOM FROM HIM YOU WILL FIND  . . . . .  308  2 DON JUAN  3    65   6
     A KINGDOM OR CONFUSION ANYWHERE .  . . . . . . . . .    485  2 DON JUAN  5   129   3
KINGDOMS
     FOR THEN WEALTH KINGDOMS WORLDS ARE BUT A SPORT--I  . .   9  3 DON JUAN  6     5   3
     MASTER OF THIRTY KINGDOMS SO SUBLIME .  . . . . . .      51  3 DON JUAN  6    90   3
     OF THOSE WHO HOLD THE KINGDOMS IN CONTROUL  . . . . .   455  3 DON JUAN 14   102   6
KINGLY
     IN KINGLY CHAMBERS OR IMPERIAL HALLS   . . . . . . .    471  2 DON JUAN  5   103   7
     THE KINGLY SCOURGE THE LUST OF NOTORIETY .  . . . . .   146  3 DON JUAN  8    68   5
KING'S
     IN ANYBODY'S BUSINESS BUT THE KING'S   . . . . . . .    439  3 DON JUAN 14    66   2
KINGS
     EUROPE HAS SLAVES--ALLIES--KINGS--ARMIES STILL .  . . .  19  2 DON JUAN  D    16   7
     A LIST OF SHIPS AND CAPTAINS AND KINGS REIGNING   . . . 135  2 DON JUAN  1   200   4
     TRUE KNIGHTS CHASTE DAMES HUGE GIANTS KINGS DESPOTIC  .  347  2 DON JUAN  4     6   6
     IN THE MORE CHASTENED DOMES OF WESTERN KINGS   . . . .  465  2 DON JUAN  5    94   3
     AND KINGS AND CONSORTS OFT ARE MYSTIFIED .  . . . . .   477  2 DON JUAN  5   115   6
     EARTH BEING ONLY MADE FOR QUEENS AND KINGS  . . . . .   485  2 DON JUAN  5   128   4
     AND TAKE WHAT KINGS CALL AN IMPOSING ATTITUDE  . . . .   11  3 DON JUAN  6    11   4
     WHO ON THE VERY LOFTIEST KINGS HAVE DINED--  . . . . .   12  3 DON JUAN  6    13   5
     THEIR OWN TRUE INTERESTS WHICH KINGS RARELY KNOW  . . .  53  3 DON JUAN  6    95   2
     BUT NEVER MIND--GOD SAVE THE KING AND KINGS  . . . . .  137  3 DON JUAN  8    50   1
     AS MUCH FROM MOBS AS KINGS--FROM YOU AS ME  . . . . .   195  3 DON JUAN  9    25   8
     PONDERING ON GLORY CHIVALRY AND KINGS .  . . . . . .    197  3 DON JUAN  9    30   4
     O'ER KINGS WHO NOW AT LEAST MUST TALK OF LAW   . . . .  261  3 DON JUAN 10    74   6
     THE WORTHIEST KINGS HAVE EVER LOVED LEAST STATE  . . .  267  3 DON JUAN 10    87   5
     DIPLOMATISTS OF RATHER WAVERING KINGS  . . . . . . .    287  3 DON JUAN 11    40   3
     STATESMEN CHIEFS ORATORS QUEENS PATRIOTS KINGS   . . .  306  3 DON JUAN 11    76   7
     GOOD COMPANY'S A CHESS-BOARD--THERE ARE KINGS  . . . .  400  3 DON JUAN 13    89   1
     FIRMNESS YCLEPT IN HEROES KINGS AND SEAMEN  . . . . .   448  3 DON JUAN 14    89   3
     THIS WAS THE MODE OF CYRUS BEST OF KINGS--   . . . . .  501  3 DON JUAN 16     1   3
     HAVE TIED TOGETHER COMMONS LORDS AND KINGS  . . . . .   536  3 DON JUAN 16    74   8
KINGS'
     HIS VERY CELLARS MIGHT BE KINGS' ABODES  . . . . . .    320  3 DON JUAN 12     9   6
KINNAIRD
     I DON'T THINK THAT YOU USED KINNAIRD QUITE WELL   . . .  184  3 DON JUAN  9     2   1
KISS
     WHERE OUR FIRST PARENTS NEVER LEARN'D TO KISS  . . . .   30  2 DON JUAN  1    18   3
     WHO SAW THOSE FIGURES ON THE MARGIN KISS ALL   . . . .   47  2 DON JUAN  1    46   5
     HIS YOUNG LIP THANK'D IT WITH A GRATEFUL KISS  . . . .   81  2 DON JUAN  1   112   3
     THIS IS TRUE CRITICISM AND YOU MAY KISS--  . . . . .    140  2 DON JUAN  1   206   6
     SOONER SHALL HEAVEN KISS EARTH--(HERE HE FELL SICKER)  . 167  2 DON JUAN  2    20   1
```

419

	PAGE	VOL		CANTO	STANZA	LN
KISS (CONTINUED)						
PRESSURE OF HANDS PERHAPS EVEN A CHASTE KISS--	242	2 DON JUAN	2	164	7
THEIR LIPS DREW NEAR AND CLUNG INTO A KISS	253	2 DON JUAN	2	185	8
A LONG LONG KISS A KISS OF YOUTH AND LOVE	254	2 DON JUAN	2	186	1
A LONG LONG KISS A KISS OF YOUTH AND LOVE	254	2 DON JUAN	2	186	1
EACH KISS A HEART-QUAKE--FOR A KISS'S STRENGTH	254	2 DON JUAN	2	186	7
SHOWERS TRIPLE LIGHT AND SCORCHES EVEN THE KISS	264	2 DON JUAN	2	202	3
AND REALLY LONGED TO KISS HER--LIKE A VILLAIN	268	2 DON JUAN	2	209	V8
THERE'S NOTHING WRONG IN A CONNUBIAL KISS	279	2 DON JUAN	3	8	6
DEFYING AUGURY WITH THAT FOND KISS	356	2 DON JUAN	4	24	4
OF PLEASURE AND OF PAIN--EVEN WHILE I KISS	364	2 DON JUAN	4	38	5
AND KISS THE LADY'S FOOT WHICH MAXIM WHEN	470	2 DON JUAN	5	102	4
BABA PROPOSED THAT HE SHOULD KISS THE HAND	471	2 DON JUAN	5	104	8
THE GENTLEMAN TO KISS THE LADY'S HANDS	472	2 DON JUAN	5	105	8
AND FOR ONE KISS WOULD FAIN IMPRINT A BRACE	472	2 DON JUAN	5	106	5
TO KISS THEM ALL AT ONCE FROM NORTH TO SOUTH	19	3 DON JUAN	6	27	8
AND THEN SHE GAVE JUANNA A CHASTE KISS	35	3 DON JUAN	6	59	1
KISS RHYMES TO BLISS IN FACT AS WELL AS VERSE--	35	3 DON JUAN	6	59	7
HOLDS BY THE ROCK OR AS A LOVER'S KISS	238	3 DON JUAN	10	28	6
KISS HANDS FEET ANY PART OF MAJESTY	286	3 DON JUAN	11	38	6
WILL KISS NOT IN SAD METAPHOR--BUT EARNEST--	286	3 DON JUAN	11	38	V7
OR GERMANY WHERE PEOPLE PURELY KISS	450	3 DON JUAN	14	92	5
UNLESS SOME BEAUTY WITH A KISS SHOULD BRIBE	567	3 DON JUAN	17	12	8
KISS'D						
AND FIRST A LITTLE CRUCIFIX HE KISS'D	197	2 DON JUAN	2	76	7
AND YOUNG AURORA KISS'D HER LIPS WITH DEW	232	2 DON JUAN	2	142	4
KISSED						
BUT I HAVE DONE WITH KISSES--HAVING KISSED	232	2 DON JUAN	2	142	V7
THEY TWINED LIKE SERPENTS AND THEY KISSED LIKE DOVES	257	2 DON JUAN	2	191	V7
SHE SIGNED TO BABA WHO FIRST KISSED THE HEM	466	2 DON JUAN	5	96	6
BUT SHE ROSE UP AND KISSED THE MATRON'S BROW	31	3 DON JUAN	6	50	1
HIS SERVICES HE KISSED HANDS THE NEXT DAY	247	3 DON JUAN	10	46	5
RETIRED AND AS HE WENT OUT CALMLY KISSED HER	440	3 DON JUAN	14	69	7
KISSES						
BUT I HAVE DONE WITH KISSES--HAVING KISSED	232	2 DON JUAN	2	142	V7
SUCH KISSES AS BELONG TO EARLY DAYS	254	2 DON JUAN	2	186	4
OR SHOW THE SAME DISLIKE TO SUITORS' KISSES	287	2 DON JUAN	3	23	4
KISSES SWEET WORDS EMBRACES AND ALL THAT	13	3 DON JUAN	6	14	2
AND THEN WITH TEARS AND SIGHS AND SOME SLIGHT KISSES	105	3 DON JUAN	7	76	1
WITH YOUTH AND HEALTH ALL KISSES ARE HEAVEN-KISSING	215	3 DON JUAN	9	66	8
OF PAYMENT ERE THE HONEYMOON'S LAST KISSES	293	3 DON JUAN	11	49	3
KISSING						
DUDU WAS FOND OF KISSING--WHICH I'M SURE	35	3 DON JUAN	6	59	2
KISS'S						
EACH KISS A HEART-QUAKE--FOR A KISS'S STRENGTH	254	2 DON JUAN	2	186	7
KIST						
A HAND MAY FIRST AND THEN A LIP BE KIST	65	2 DON JUAN	1	80	3
KIT-CAT						
KIT-CAT THE FAMOUS CONVERSATIONIST	403	3 DON JUAN	13	97	4
KITE						
A PAPER KITE WHICH FLIES 'TWIXT LIFE AND DEATH	414	3 DON JUAN	14	8	5
KITH						
AND DAUGHTERS BROTHERS SISTERS KITH OR KIN	470	3 DON JUAN	15	31	2
KITTENS						
TWO PARROTS WITH A PERSIAN CAT AND KITTENS	285	2 DON JUAN	3	18	2
KNEAD						
WHY DON'T THEY KNEAD TWO VIRTUOUS SOULS FOR LIFE	502	2 DON JUAN	5	158	7
KNEE						
BUT SUNK AGAIN UPON HIS BLEEDING KNEE	213	2 DON JUAN	2	109	2
SHE SITS UPON HIS KNEE AND DRINKS HIS SIGHS	259	2 DON JUAN	2	194	5
DAMM'D FROM ITS FOUNTAIN--THE CHILD FROM THE KNEE	349	2 DON JUAN	4	10	5
A CANDIOTE CLOAK WHICH TO THE KNEE MIGHT REACH	451	2 DON JUAN	5	68	3
THE PRINCE DELIGNE WAS WOUNDED IN THE KNEE	116	3 DON JUAN	8	10	1
KNEE-DEEP						
SLIDING KNEE-DEEP IN LATELY FROZEN MUD	148	3 DON JUAN	8	73	7
KNEEL						
IT WOULD NOT BE IDOLATRY TO KNEEL	313	2 DON JUAN	3	74	8
'TWAS TREASON TO BEHOLD HER AND NOT KNEEL	313	2 DON JUAN	3	74	V8
'TIS LAMBRO--'TIS MY FATHER KNEEL WITH ME--	364	2 DON JUAN	4	38	2
A SECOND TIME DESIRED HIM TO KNEEL DOWN	470	2 DON JUAN	5	102	3
VICTORY AND PAUSING AS SHE SAW HIM KNEEL	211	3 DON JUAN	9	57	7
KNEELING						
OF THE NEW FIRE WHICH ZOE KEPT UP KNEELING	237	2 DON JUAN	2	153	6
A LADY BABA STOPPED AND KNEELING SIGNED	466	2 DON JUAN	5	95	4
KNEES						
HEADS BOW KNEES BEND EYES WATCH AROUND A THRONE	484	2 DON JUAN	5	127	7
O'ER HIS WORST ENEMY WHEN AT HIS KNEES	17	3 DON JUAN	6	23	5
AND BOWED HER THROBBING HEAD O'ER TREMBLING KNEES	59	3 DON JUAN	6	107	8
KNELL						
THAN THAT ALL-SOFTENING OVER-POWERING KNELL	439	2 DON JUAN	5	49	7
WAS RUNG BY DINNER'S KNELL TILL THEN ALL WERE	406	3 DON JUAN	13	103	2
KNELT						
KNELT DOWN BY INSTINCT WONDERING IN HIS MIND	466	2 DON JUAN	5	95	6
WHILE HER YOUNG HERALD KNELT BEFORE HER STILL	215	3 DON JUAN	9	66	4
KNEW						
HER MEMORY WAS A MINE SHE KNEW BY HEART	27	2 DON JUAN	1	11	1
SHE KNEW THE LATIN--THAT IS THE LORD'S PRAYER	28	2 DON JUAN	1	13	1
THAT I MUST SAY WHO KNEW HIM VERY WELL	40	2 DON JUAN	1	35	2
I KNEW HIS FATHER WELL AND HAVE SOME SKILL	49	2 DON JUAN	1	51	3

420

KNEW   (CONTINUED)
    THAT DONNA JULIA KNEW THE REASON WHY 60   2 DON JUAN 1   70 6
    OR TRANSPORT AS WE KNEW ALL THAT BEFORE 69   2 DON JUAN 1   89 7
    AND EVEN IF I KNEW I SHOULD NOT TELL-- 77   2 DON JUAN 1   105 3
    HE KNEW NOT WHEREFORE THAT WHICH HE WAS BID . . . . . . 111 2 DON JUAN 1   163 8
    TO WHOM SHE KNEW HIS MOTHER'S FAME WAS DEAR . . . . . . 118 2 DON JUAN 1   176 8
    WATER APPEAR'D YET THOUGH THE PEOPLE KNEW . . . . 178 2 DON JUAN 2   42 3
    AND WHEN HIS COMRADE'S THOUGHT EACH SUFFERER KNEW . . . . 194 2 DON JUAN 2   73 5
    THEY KNEW NOT WHERE NOR WHAT THEY WERE ABOUT . . . . . . 207 2 DON JUAN 2   96 4
    IN VARIOUS CONJECTURES FOR NONE KNEW . . . . 209 2 DON JUAN 2   100 4
    HE KNEW NOT FOR THE EARTH WAS GONE FOR HIM . . . . 214 2 DON JUAN 2   111 2
    HE KNEW NOT TILL EACH PAINFUL PULSE AND LIMB . . . . . . 214 2 DON JUAN 2   111 6
    THAT AT THIS MOMENT JUAN KNEW IT NOT . . . . 228 2 DON JUAN 2   135 8
    BETTER THAN HER KNEW WHAT IN FACT SHE MEANT . . . . . . 228 2 DON JUAN 2   136 3
    THEY KNEW NOT WHAT TO THINK OF SUCH A FREAK . . . . . . 229 2 DON JUAN 2   138 8
    SHE KNEW THAT THE BEST FEELINGS MUST HAVE VICTUAL . . . . 233 2 DON JUAN 2   145 1
    KNEW (BY TRADITION FOR SHE NE'ER HAD READ) . . . . . . 239 2 DON JUAN 2   158 6
    HAIDEE WAS NATURE'S BRIDE AND KNEW NOT THIS . . . . . . 264 2 DON JUAN 2   202 1
    IS ROUSSEAU'S JULIETTA--I NEER KNEW . . . . 273 2 DON JUAN 2 V 2 7
    AND WATCH'D BY EYES THAT NEVER YET KNEW WEEPING . . . . . 274 2 DON JUAN 3   1 3
    BUT KNEW THE CAUSE NO MORE THAN A PHILOSOPHER . . . . . 289 2 DON JUAN 3   26 8
    THESE RASCALS BEING NEW COMERS KNEW NOT WHOM . . . . . . 298 2 DON JUAN 3   44 1
    AND NOT THE FIX'D--HE KNEW THE WAY TO WHEEDLE . . . . . 317 2 DON JUAN 3   80 4
    AND KNEW THE SELF-LOVES OF THE DIFFERENT NATIONS . . . . 319 2 DON JUAN 3   84 2
    AND KNEW SUCH BRIGHTNESS WAS BUT THE REFLECTION . . . . . 351 2 DON JUAN 4   13 7
    CHAIN'D TO A ROCK SHE KNEW NOT HOW BUT STIR . . . . . . 361 2 DON JUAN 4   31 2
    I LOVE HIM--I WILL DIE WITH HIM I KNEW . . . . 366 2 DON JUAN 4   42 7
    BUT WHEN THE OFFER WENT BEYOND THEY KNEW . . . . 407 2 DON JUAN 4   114 7
    I GAZED UPON HIM FOR I KNEW HIM WELL . . . . 430 2 DON JUAN 5   35 1
    AT ALL SUCH AUCTIONS KNEW HOW TO PREVAIL . . . . 477 2 DON JUAN 5   114 6
    AND SHE WOULD HAVE CONSOLED BUT KNEW NOT HOW . . . . . . 480 2 DON JUAN 5   119 1
    AND THUS GULBEYAZ THOUGH SHE KNEW NOT WHY . . . . 480 2 DON JUAN 5   120 7
    SHE HARDLY KNEW TO SUCH PERFECTION BRINGS . . . . 485 2 DON JUAN 5   128 6
    FOR NE'ER TILL NOW SHE KNEW A CHECKED DESIRE . . . . . . 489 2 DON JUAN 5   134 6
    THE PUBLIC KNEW NO MORE THAN DOES THIS RHYME . . . . . . 496 2 DON JUAN 5   149 6
    AND EVEN THOSE WERE NEARER THAN THEY KNEW 31   3 DON JUAN 6   51 8
    WHEN BABA SAW THESE SYMPTOMS WHICH HE KNEW 57   3 DON JUAN 6   102 1
    BABA WHO KNEW BY EXPERIENCE WHEN TO TALK 61   3 DON JUAN 6   110 1
    (THOUGH HE WELL KNEW THE MEANING) TO BE SHOWN 62   3 DON JUAN 6   112 6
    HIS OWN REMONSTRANCE FURTHER HE WELL KNEW 63   3 DON JUAN 6   116 4
    WHO KNEW THIS LIFE WAS NOT WORTH A POTATO 68   3 DON JUAN 7   4 6
    THIS DIALOGUE FOR HE WHO ANSWERED KNEW 97   3 DON JUAN 7   59 7
    JOHNSON WHO KNEW BY THIS LONG COLLOQUY . . . . 100 3 DON JUAN 7   65 1
    IN THE DESPATCH I KNEW A MAN WHOSE LOSS . . . . 120 3 DON JUAN 8   18 7
    HE KNEW NOT WHY ARRIVING AT THIS PASS . . . . 126 3 DON JUAN 8   29 3
    HIS WAY TO--WHERE HE KNEW NOT--SINGLE HANDED . . . . . . 127 3 DON JUAN 8   32 3
    HE KNEW NOT WHERE HE WAS NOR GREATLY CARED . . . . 129 3 DON JUAN 8   33 1
    KNEW WHEN AND HOW TO CUT AND COME AGAIN . . . . 130 3 DON JUAN 8   35 6
    JUAN TO WHOM HE SPOKE IN GERMAN KNEW . . . . 141 3 DON JUAN 8   57 1
    THEY KNEW NOT WHERE BEING CARRIED BY THE STREAM . . . . . 148 3 DON JUAN 8   72 2
    JUAN WHO FOUND HIMSELF HE KNEW NOT HOW . . . . 223 3 DON JUAN 9   83 1
    WAS TRANQUIL THOUGH SHE KNEW NOT WHY OR WHEREFORE . . . . 250 3 DON JUAN 10   52 8
    JURY OF MATRONS SCARCE KNEW WHAT TO ANSWER . . . . 294 3 DON JUAN 11   51 4
    JUAN KNEW SEVERAL LANGUAGES--AS WELL . . . . 295 3 DON JUAN 11   53 1
    I WISH THEY KNEW THE LIFE OF A YOUNG NOBLE . . . . 305 3 DON JUAN 11   74 8
    I KNEW THAT NOUGHT WAS LASTING BUT NOW EVEN . . . . . . 309 3 DON JUAN 11   82 5
    AND HOW HE HAD BEEN TOSSED HE SCARCE KNEW WHITHER . . . . 338 3 DON JUAN 12   49 5
    HE KNEW THE WORLD AND WOULD NOT SEE DEPRAVITY . . . . . 368 3 DON JUAN 13   22 5
    UNLESS I KNEW THE VERY CHASTEST SQUARES . . . . 370 3 DON JUAN 13   26 8
    FOR THOSE WHO KNEW NOT TO RESIGN OR REIGN . . . . 386 3 DON JUAN 13   60 8
    KNEW THAT HE HAD A RIDER ON HIS BACK . . . . 424 3 DON JUAN 14   32 8
    SAY SEVEN-AND-TWENTY FOR I NEVER KNEW . . . . 433 3 DON JUAN 14   53 2
    WHICH REALLY KNEW OR THOUGHT IT KNEW NO GUILE . . . . . 438 3 DON JUAN 14   65 2
    WHICH REALLY KNEW OR THOUGHT IT KNEW NO GUILE . . . . . 438 3 DON JUAN 14   65 2
    SHE KNEW NOT HER OWN HEART THEN HOW SHOULD I . . . . . . 449 3 DON JUAN 14   91 1
    SO AS TO MAKE THEM FEEL HE KNEW HIS STATION . . . . . . 462 3 DON JUAN 15   15 6
    SHE GAZED UPON A WORLD SHE SCARCELY KNEW . . . . 476 3 DON JUAN 15   47 1
    JUAN KNEW NOUGHT OF SUCH A CHARACTER-- . . . . 481 3 DON JUAN 15   58 1
    INDEED I NEVER KNEW WHAT PEOPLE MEANT . . . . 498 3 DON JUAN 15   94 5
    HE STOOD--HOW LONG HE KNEW NOT BUT IT SEEMED . . . . . . 511 3 DON JUAN 16   25 1
    AND KNEW NO BETTER IN HER IMMORALITY . . . . 532 3 DON JUAN 16   64 7
    HEAVEN AND HIS FRIENDS KNEW THAT A PRIVATE LIFE . . . . . 536 3 DON JUAN 16   74 1
    I KNEW HIM IN HIS LIVELIER LONDON DAYS . . . . 540 3 DON JUAN 16   82 1
    AND JUAN TOOK HIS PLACE HE KNEW NOT WHERE . . . . 542 3 DON JUAN 16   87 2
    THEY LITTLE KNEW OR MIGHT HAVE SYMPATHISED . . . . 543 3 DON JUAN 16   90 1
    THAT ONE SCARCE KNEW AT WHAT TO MARVEL MOST . . . . . . 543 3 DON JUAN 16   90 6
    MISCHIEF IN FAMILIES AS SOME KNOW OR KNEW . . . . 565 3 DON JUAN 17   7 5
KNIFE
    BECAUSE THEY STILL CAN HOPE NOR SHINES THE KNIFE . . . . 190 2 DON JUAN 2   64 5
    THE LAWYER'S BRIEF IS LIKE THE SURGEON'S KNIFE . . . . . 232 3 DON JUAN 10   14 6
    HERE--HE WAS INTERRUPTED BY A KNIFE . . . . 273 3 DON JUAN 11   10 7
    WHEN DEMAGOGUES WOULD WITH A BUTCHER'S KNIFE . . . . . . 536 3 DON JUAN 16   74 5
KNIGHT
    A BLOTTED SHIELD NO SHIRE'S TRUE KNIGHT WOULD WEAR . . . 153 2 DON JUAN 1 V 4 6
    BUT FACTS ARE FACTS NO KNIGHT COULD BE MORE TRUE . . . . 396 2 DON JUAN 4   96 2
    SCOTT WHO CAN PAINT YOUR CHRISTIAN KNIGHT OR SARACEN . . . 481 3 DON JUAN 15   59 5
    THE FORMS OF THE GRIM KNIGHT AND PICTURED SAINT . . . . 508 3 DON JUAN 16   18 1
KNIGHTED
    ALL COUNTRY GENTLEMEN ESQUIRED OR KNIGHTED . . . . . . 534 3 DON JUAN 16   69 3

		PAGE	VOL		CANTO	STANZA	LN

KNIGHTS
      A SORT OF BLOTTED SHIELD FEW KNIGHTS WOULD WEAR . . . . . 153 2 DON JUAN 1 V 4 V6
      TRUE KNIGHTS CHASTE DAMES HUGE GIANTS KINGS DESPOTIC . . . 347 2 DON JUAN 4   6   6
      NEXT OF NEW KNIGHTS THE FRESH AND GLORIOUS HATCH . . . . . 215 3 DON JUAN 9   65   7
      HIS KNIGHTS WITH LOTTING OTHERS' PROPERTIES . . . . 242 3 DON JUAN 10   35   7
      QUEENS BISHOPS KNIGHTS ROOKS PAWNS THE WORLD'S A GAME . . . 400 3 DON JUAN 13   89   2
      BUT LAISSEZ ALLER--KNIGHTS AND DAMES I SING . . . . 467 3 DON JUAN 15   25   1
      OF KNIGHTS AND DAMES HEROIC AND CHASTE TOO . . . . 508 3 DON JUAN 16   17   5
KNIGHTS'
      INTO SOME SIXTY THOUSAND NEW KNIGHTS' FEES . . . . 242 3 DON JUAN 10   35   8
KNIT
      TALL HANDSOME SLENDER BUT WELL KNIT HE SEEM'D . . . . . . 51 2 DON JUAN 1   54   2
KNITS
      WHICH KNITS SOCIETY--THE DINNER BELL . . . . 439 2 DON JUAN 5   49   V8
KNIVES
      WITH MASSY PLATE FOR ARMOUR KNIVES AND FORKS . . . . . . 482 3 DON JUAN 15   62   2
      THOUGH KNIVES AND FORKS CLANGED ROUND AS IN A FRAY . . . . 542 3 DON JUAN 16   87   5
KNOCK
      OR BY ONE'S EARLY VALET'S CURSED KNOCK . . . . 237 2 DON JUAN 2   152   5
      LET'S KNOCK THAT OLD BLACK FELLOW ON THE HEAD . . . . . . 434 2 DON JUAN 5   43   7
      THE FIRST WAS TO BOMBARD IT AND KNOCK DOWN . . . . 78 3 DON JUAN 7   23   3
      (THOUGH THESE TO OUR GIBRALTAR MUST KNOCK UNDER)-- . . . . 136 3 DON JUAN 8   46   6
      I ALWAYS KNOCK MY HEAD AGAINST SOME ANGLE . . . . 496 3 DON JUAN 15   91   5
KNOCK'D
      WHO THREATEN'D DEATH--SO JUAN KNOCK'D HIM DOWN . . . . . 122 2 DON JUAN 1   183   8
      UNTIL I FAIRLY KNOCK'D IT UP WITH RHYME . . . . 414 3 DON JUAN 14   9   8
      'GAINST RHYME I NEVER SHOULD HAVE KNOCK'D MY BROWS . . . . 467 3 DON JUAN 15   24   5
KNOCKED
      PUTTING THE VERY BRAVEST WHO WERE KNOCKED . . . . 134 3 DON JUAN 8   43   7
      THE SERASKIER IS KNOCKED UPON THE HEAD . . . . 160 3 DON JUAN 8   98   1
      KNOCKED TO INFORM HIM IT WAS TIME TO DRESS . . . . 512 3 DON JUAN 16   28   8
KNOCKERS
      OF ROCKS BEWITCH'D THAT OPEN TO THE KNOCKERS . . . . . . 293 2 DON JUAN 3   34   6
      AS THUNDERED KNOCKERS BROKE THE LONG-SEALED SPELL . . . . 282 3 DON JUAN 11   29   3
KNOCKEST
      KNOCKEST AT DOORS AT FIRST WITH MODEST TAP . . . . 459 3 DON JUAN 15   8   2
KNOCKING
      AND KNOCKING AT THE GATE 'TWAS OPENED WIDE . . . . 440 2 DON JUAN 5   51   6
KNOCKINGS
      TITHES TAXES DUNS AND DOORS WITH DOUBLE KNOCKINGS . . . . 346 3 DON JUAN 12   67   8
KNOCKS
      FIRST KNOCKS WERE HEARD THEN MADAM--MADAM--HIST . . . . . 95 2 DON JUAN 1   136   8
      TO THE GREAT MARLBOROUGH'S SKILL IN GIVING KNOCKS . . . . 328 2 DON JUAN 3   90   7
      ON A BRASS PLATE WAS GIVEN TO KNOCKS AND FAME . . . . . . 283 3 DON JUAN 11   31   V8
KNOLL
      NO CHRISTIAN KNOLL TO TABLE SAW NO LINE . . . . 439 2 DON JUAN 5   50   3
KNOLLES
      OF CANTEMIR OR KNOLLES WHERE FEW SHINE . . . . 495 2 DON JUAN 5   147   7
KNOT
      TWINE LIKE A KNOT OF SNAKES AROUND HIS FACE . . . . 510 3 DON JUAN 16   23   6
      HIS VERY NECKCLOTH'S GORDIAN KNOT WAS TIED . . . . 513 3 DON JUAN 16   29   7
      THE GORDIAN OR THE GEORDI-AN KNOT WHOSE STRINGS . . . . . 536 3 DON JUAN 16   74   7
      WHICH TIED IN ONE FIRM KNOT WITHOUT CONFUSION . . . . . . 536 3 DON JUAN 16   74   V7
KNOTS
      LIKE KNOTS OF VIPERS ON A DUNGHILL'S SOIL . . . . 271 2 DON JUAN 2   215   5
      SAILING SIX KNOTS AN HOUR BEFORE THE WIND . . . . 384 2 DON JUAN 4   75   5
KNOW
      YOU BOB ARE RATHER INSOLENT YOU KNOW . . . . 10 2 DON JUAN D   3   1
      TO--GOD KNOWS WHERE--FOR NO ONE ELSE CAN KNOW . . . . . . 14 2 DON JUAN D   9   8
      WERE FRENCH AND FAMOUS PEOPLE AS WE KNOW . . . . 22 2 DON JUAN 1   3   3
      I'M NOT TO BLAME AS YOU WELL KNOW NO MORE IS . . . . . . 37 2 DON JUAN 1   31   3
      IS MORE THAN I KNOW--BUT DON JUAN'S MOTHER . . . . 47 2 DON JUAN 1   46   7
      I NEVER MARRIED--BUT I THINK I KNOW . . . . 50 2 DON JUAN 1   53   7
      IN SPAIN YOU KNOW THIS IS A SORT OF SIN) . . . . 52 2 DON JUAN 1   56   4
      FOR JEALOUSY DISLIKES THE WORLD TO KNOW IT . . . . 57 2 DON JUAN 1   65   8
      PERHAPS SHE DID NOT KNOW OR DID NOT CARE . . . . 59 2 DON JUAN 1   68   5
      I REALLY DON'T KNOW WHAT NOR JULIA EITHER . . . . 65 2 DON JUAN 1   81   8
      TORMENTED WITH A WOUND HE COULD NOT KNOW . . . . 68 2 DON JUAN 1   87   3
      TO PLAGUE THEMSELVES WITHAL THEY KNOW NOT WHY . . . . . . 71 2 DON JUAN 1   93   4
      SHE SATE BUT NOT ALONE I KNOW NOT WELL . . . . 77 2 DON JUAN 1   105   1
      I CANNOT KNOW WHAT JUAN THOUGHT OF THIS . . . . 81 2 DON JUAN 1   112   1
      'TIS SWEET TO KNOW THERE IS AN EYE WILL MARK . . . . . . 88 2 DON JUAN 1   123   3
      FEW MORTALS KNOW WHAT END THEY WOULD BE AT . . . . 93 2 DON JUAN 1   133   5
      THE GOAL IS GAIN'D WE DIE YOU KNOW--AND THEN-- . . . . . 93 2 DON JUAN 1   133   8
      WHAT THEN--I DO NOT KNOW NO MORE DO YOU-- . . . . 94 2 DON JUAN 1   134   1
      WHY DON'T YOU KNOW THAT IT MAY END IN BLOOD . . . . . . 115 2 DON JUAN 1   171   6
      TO NEWSPAPERS WHOSE TRUTH ALL KNOW AND FEEL . . . . . . 138 2 DON JUAN 1   203   3
      AS I WHO'VE CROSS'D IT OFT KNOW WELL ENOUGH . . . . . . 162 2 DON JUAN 2   11   4
      BECAUSE TILL PEOPLE KNOW WHAT'S COME TO PASS . . . . . . 185 2 DON JUAN 2   55   6
      MEN REALLY KNOW NOT WHAT GOOD WATER'S WORTH . . . . . . 201 2 DON JUAN 2   84   4
      FOR AS YOU KNOW THE SPANISH WOMEN BANISH . . . . 220 2 DON JUAN 2   120   4
      BUT THIS I KNOW IT WAS A SPACIOUS BUILDING . . . . 223 2 DON JUAN 2   127   7
      BUT BEING NAKED SHE WAS SHOCK'D YOU KNOW . . . . 224 2 DON JUAN 2   129   5
      FOR WE ALL KNOW THAT ENGLISH PEOPLE ARE . . . . 238 2 DON JUAN 2   156   1
      WE KNOW TOO THEY ARE VERY FOND OF WAR . . . . 238 2 DON JUAN 2   156   5
      I LEARN'D THE LITTLE THAT I KNOW BY THIS . . . . 242 2 DON JUAN 2   164   8
      SOME HOCK AND SODA-WATER THEN YOU'LL KNOW . . . . 251 2 DON JUAN 2   180   2
      THE BEST EXAMPLES WHICH I KNOW FOR LOVES . . . . 257 2 DON JUAN 2   191   V8
      OR KNOW WHO RESTED THERE A FOE TO REST . . . . 274 2 DON JUAN 3   1   6

422

KNOW   (CONTINUED)
    I KNOW NOT IF THE FAULT BE MEN'S OR THEIRS 276   2 DON JUAN 3   4   1
    HE DID NOT KNOW (ALAS HOW MEN WILL LIE) 295   2 DON JUAN 3   38   1
    I KNOW NOT QUOTH THE FELLOW WHO OR WHAT 298   2 DON JUAN 3   45   1
    BUT THIS I KNOW THAT THIS ROAST CAPON'S FAT 298   2 DON JUAN 3   45   3
    I KNOW NOT HOW--HER PRESENCE MADE YE FEEL 313   2 DON JUAN 3   74 V7
    I KNOW THAT WHAT OUR NEIGHBOURS CALL LONGUEURS 332   2 DON JUAN 3   97   1
    WE KNOW NOT THIS--THE BLOOD FLOWS ON TOO FAST 345   2 DON JUAN 4   2   6
    HOW I HAVE TREATED IT I DO NOT KNOW 347   2 DON JUAN 4   7   1
    BUT LIKE THE CLIMES THAT KNOW NOR SNOW NOR HAIL 348   2 DON JUAN 4   9   4
    AND NEVER KNOW THE WEIGHT OF HUMAN HOURS 352   2 DON JUAN 4   15   8
    HARD WORDS HARSH TRUTH A TRUTH WHICH MANY KNOW 353   2 DON JUAN 4   18   1
    I KNOW NOT WHY BUT IN THAT HOUR TO-NIGHT 355   2 DON JUAN 4   21   1
    BUT WHICH TO CHOOSE I REALLY HARDLY KNOW 357   2 DON JUAN 4   25   4
    AND WHO CAN KNOW ALL FALSE WHAT THEN WE SEE 360   2 DON JUAN 4   30 V8
    THAT COCKING OF A PISTOL WHEN YOU KNOW 366   2 DON JUAN 4   41   2
    YOUR NATURE'S FIRMNESS--KNOW YOUR DAUGHTER'S TOO 366   2 DON JUAN 4   42   8
    AND THEY WHO WATCH'D HER NEAREST COULD NOT KNOW 381   2 DON JUAN 4   69   4
    YE COULD NOT KNOW WHERE LIES A THING SO FAIR 383   2 DON JUAN 4   72   5
    I KNOW ONE WOMAN OF THAT PURPLE SCHOOL 405   2 DON JUAN 4   111   7
    WE KNOW WHAT SLAVERY IS AND OUR DISASTERS 422   2 DON JUAN 5   23   7
    THERE SOLITUDE WE KNOW HAS HER FULL GROWTH IN 443   2 DON JUAN 5   57   3
    WE KNOW WHERE THINGS AND MEN MUST END AT BEST 448   2 DON JUAN 5   63   5
    WHICH PUZZLED NATURE MUCH TO KNOW WHAT ART MEANT 448   2 DON JUAN 5   64   8
    WHAT YOU MAY BE I NEITHER KNOW NOR CARE 454   2 DON JUAN 5   74   1
    YOU KNOW HOW NEAR US THE DEEP BOSPHORUS FLOATS 464   2 DON JUAN 5   92   4
    NOT TO ADMIRE IS ALL THE ART I KNOW 470   2 DON JUAN 5   101   1
    THUS HORACE WROTE WE ALL KNOW LONG AGO 470   2 DON JUAN 5   101   5
    I KNOW NOT WHAT MIGHT BE THE LADY'S THOUGHT 473   2 DON JUAN 5   108   2
    BUT WHEN YOU HAVE SUPPOSED THE FEW WE KNOW 486   2 DON JUAN 5   131   7
    EVEN YE WHO KNOW WHAT A CHECKED WOMAN IS 489   2 DON JUAN 5   134   7
    SO JUAN'S VIRTUE EBBED I KNOW NOT HOW 493   2 DON JUAN 5   142   2
    I KNOW NOT IF HE HAD DOMESTIC CARES-- 496   2 DON JUAN 5   148   5
    WHICH TAKEN AT THE FLOOD--YOU KNOW THE REST   6   3 DON JUAN 6   1   2
    I KNOW GULBEYAZ WAS EXTREMELY WRONG   10   3 DON JUAN 6   8   1
    I KNOW NOT--IT SUCCEEDED AND SUCCESS   15   3 DON JUAN 6   19   2
    IS MORE THAN I KNOW--THE DEUCE TAKE THEM BOTH   17   3 DON JUAN 6   22   8
    IS MORE THAN I KNOW AND SO DAMN THEM BOTH   17   3 DON JUAN 6   22 V8
    WHETHER SHE WAS A MOTHER I KNOW NOT   21   3 DON JUAN 6   31   1
    I KNOW NOT HOW BUT GOOD AS ANY OTHER   21   3 DON JUAN 6   31   4
    HERE LOLAH INTERPOSED--MAMMA YOU KNOW   29   3 DON JUAN 6   47   1
    I KNOW NOT NEVER COUNTING PAST THEIR TEENS   41   3 DON JUAN 6   69   4
    ALL THAT I KNOW IS THAT THE FACTS I STATE   48   3 DON JUAN 6   85   7
    ALL GENERATIONS I SHOULD LIKE TO KNOW   53   3 DON JUAN 6   94   7
    THEIR OWN TRUE INTERESTS WHICH KINGS RARELY KNOW   53   3 DON JUAN 6   95   2
    HE HAD PASSED THE NIGHT WAS WHAT SHE WISHED TO KNOW . . .   55   3 DON JUAN 6   99   8
    YOU KNOW THE REST THE WORDS STUCK IN HER THROAT   62   3 DON JUAN 6   113   4
    WHAT DOST THOU KNOW OF LOVE OR FEELING--WRETCH   63   3 DON JUAN 6   116   1
    WHEN WE KNOW WHAT ALL ARE WE MUST BEWAIL US   67   3 DON JUAN 7   2   5
    TO LAUGH AT ALL THINGS--FOR I WISH TO KNOW   67   3 DON JUAN 7   2   7
    THE PRESENT POEM--OF--I KNOW NOT WHAT--   67   3 DON JUAN 7   3   2
    BUT WHICH IS BEST YOU KNOW NO MORE THAN I   68   3 DON JUAN 7   4   8
    TO KNOW THAT NOTHING COULD BE KNOWN A PLEASANT   69   3 DON JUAN 7   5   2
    IN SHORT ALL KNOW OR VERY SOON MAY KNOW IT   69   3 DON JUAN 7   6   4
    IN SHORT ALL KNOW OR VERY SOON MAY KNOW IT   69   3 DON JUAN 7   6   4
    FROM FOOLS WHO DREAD TO KNOW THE TRUTH OF LIFE   69   3 DON JUAN 7   6 V8
    I DON'T KNOW WHETHER THEY HAD ARMS OR CREST   76   3 DON JUAN 7   19   3
    I'VE SAID ALL I KNOW OF A NAME THAT FILLS   76   3 DON JUAN 7   20   5
    NOW I SHOULD LIKE TO KNOW BEING RATHER CURIOUS   77   3 DON JUAN 7   21 V1
    THEIR HASTE OR WASTE I NEITHER KNOW NOR CARE   80   3 DON JUAN 7   27   2
    FOR AUGHT WE KNOW) RENOWN'S ALL HIT OR MISS   82   3 DON JUAN 7   33   5
    I DID--WHAT NEXT--I REALLY HARDLY KNOW   98   3 DON JUAN 7   61   2
    WHERE WILL YOU SERVE--WHERE'ER YOU PLEASE--I KNOW   98   3 DON JUAN 7   62   1
    AND SELF WOULD KNOW WHAT DUTY TO ATTEND 100   3 DON JUAN 7   65   8
    INTO A CAMP I KNOW THAT NOUGHT SO BOTHERS 103   3 DON JUAN 7   71   6
    BUT COULD WE KNOW THEM IN DETAIL PERCHANCE 113   3 DON JUAN 8   3   2
    I DON'T KNOW HOW THE THING OCCURRED--IT MIGHT 125   3 DON JUAN 8   28   1
    QUITE DISAPPEARED--THE GODS KNOW HOW (I CAN'T 127   3 DON JUAN 8   31   3
    WHICH MADE SOME THINK AND OTHERS KNOW A HELL COME 134   3 DON JUAN 8   42   8
    ALL WALLS WE KNOW AND MANY NEVER KNOWN 142   3 DON JUAN 8   60   6
    IN HEAVEN I KNOW NOT NOR PRETEND TO GUESS 167   3 DON JUAN 8   112   2
    FOR THE GREAT BENEFIT OF THOSE WHO KNOW 190   3 DON JUAN 9   15   3
    I SHOULD BE GLAD TO KNOW THAT WHICH IS BEING 190   3 DON JUAN 9   16   2
    SO LITTLE DO WE KNOW WHAT WE'RE ABOUT IN 191   3 DON JUAN 9   17   7
    YOUR WISE MEN DON'T KNOW MUCH OF NAVIGATION 191   3 DON JUAN 9   18   4
    OFFENCE WE KNOW NOT PROBABLY IT PERCHED 192   3 DON JUAN 9   19   7
    AND YET I KNOW NO MORE THAN THE MAHOGANY 192   3 DON JUAN 9   20   5
    I KNOW ITS MIGHTY EMPIRE NOW ALLURES 194   3 DON JUAN 9   23   5
    I KNOW NOT WHO MAY CONQUER IF I COULD 194   3 DON JUAN 9   24   5
    I DO NOT KNOW--I WISH MEN TO BE FREE 195   3 DON JUAN 9   25   7
    MUCH TOO POETICAL MEN SHOULD KNOW WHY 203   3 DON JUAN 9   41   6
    I NEVER KNOW THE WORD WHICH WILL COME NEXT 203   3 DON JUAN 9   41   8
    OH GENTLE LADIES SHOULD YOU SEEK TO KNOW 207   3 DON JUAN 9   49   1
    KNOW NOT SINCE KNOWLEDGE SAW HER BRANCHES STRIPT 210   3 DON JUAN 9   55   6
    AND THOUGH SO MUCH INFERIOR AS I KNOW 226   3 DON JUAN 10   3   5
    THE FORMER KNOW WHAT'S WHAT WHILE NEW-FLEDGED CHICKS . . . 230   3 DON JUAN 10   10   3
    KNOW LITTLE MORE OF LOVE THAN WHAT IS SUNG 230   3 DON JUAN 10   10   4
    I KNOW NO OTHER REASON WHATSOE'ER 230   3 DON JUAN 10   11   2
    AND I KNOW NOTHING WHICH COULD MAKE AMENDS 231   3 DON JUAN 10   12   3

KNOW   (CONTINUED)
    I DO NOT KNOW YOU AND MAY NEVER KNOW . . . . 232 3 DON JUAN 10   16   6
    I DO NOT KNOW YOU AND MAY NEVER KNOW . . . . 232 3 DON JUAN 10   16   6
    AND KNOW NO MORE OF WHAT IS HERE THAN THERE-- . . . . 234 3 DON JUAN 10   20   8
    I DON'T KNOW HOW IT WAS BUT HE GREW SICK . . . . . . 244 3 DON JUAN 10   39   1
    WHICH PUZZLES US TO KNOW WHAT FORTUNE MEANS . . . . . 247 3 DON JUAN 10   47   3
    ALAS COULD SHE BUT FULLY TRULY KNOW . . . . 258 3 DON JUAN 10   67   1
    TO KNOW MYSELF AND ALL BESIDES MERE SPIRIT . . . . . 268 3 DON JUAN 11   1   V7
    KNOW VERY CLEARLY--OR AT LEAST LIE STILL . . . . . . 270 3 DON JUAN 11   4   8
    I DON'T KNOW WHAT THE REASON IS--THE AIR . . . . . . 270 3 DON JUAN 11   5   6
    I DON'T KNOW WHICH WAS MOST ADMIRED OR LESS . . . . . 287 3 DON JUAN 11   39   3
    EVEN I--ALBEIT I'M SURE I DID NOT KNOW IT . . . . . 296 3 DON JUAN 11   55   5
    TO THAT WHICH NONE WILL GAIN--OR NONE WILL KNOW . . . 299 3 DON JUAN 11   61   2
    I THINK I KNOW A TRICK OR TWO WOULD TURN . . . . . . 300 3 DON JUAN 11   63   1
    THEY ARE YOUNG BUT KNOW NOT YOUTH--IT IS ANTICIPATED . 306 3 DON JUAN 11   75   1
    YOU ARE NOT A MORAL PEOPLE AND YOU KNOW IT . . . . . 311 3 DON JUAN 11   87   7
    THEY KNOW NOT HOW) THE ONE HALF THE PRESENT CASE . . 314 3 DON JUAN 11 V 75   7
    OF MAN IT IS--I REALLY SCARCE KNOW WHAT . . . . . . 315 3 DON JUAN 12   1   3
    AND DON'T KNOW JUSTLY WHAT WE WOULD BE AT-- . . . . 315 3 DON JUAN 12   1   5
    KNOW NOT WHAT VISIONS SPRING FROM EACH CHEESE-PARING . 316 3 DON JUAN 12   3   8
    SINCE ODDS ARE THAT POSTERITY WILL KNOW . . . . . . 324 3 DON JUAN 12   18   7
    WHICH THE MERE PASSIONLESS CAN NEVER KNOW . . . . . . 336 3 DON JUAN 12   44   8
    THAT DAUGHTERS OF SUCH MOTHERS AS MAY KNOW . . . . . 337 3 DON JUAN 12   46   4
    KNOW HOW TO END THIS HALF AND HALF FLIRTATION . . . . 345 3 DON JUAN 12   63   V7
    THOUGH DESPOTS KNOW IT NOT--TILL THE PROGRESSION . . 354 3 DON JUAN 12   83   5
    (WHATEVER PEOPLE SAY) I DON'T KNOW WHETHER . . . . . 355 3 DON JUAN 12   86   4
    I KNOW THAT SOME WOULD FAIN POSTPONE THIS ERA . . . . 360 3 DON JUAN 13   5   1
    THE CAUSE I KNOW NOT NOR CAN SOLVE BUT SUCH . . . . . 388 3 DON JUAN 13   64   1
    OH READER   IF THAT THOU CANST READ--AND KNOW . . . . 393 3 DON JUAN 13   73   1
    FOR ME I KNOW NOUGHT NOTHING I DENY . . . . 411 3 DON JUAN 14   3   1
    ADMIT REJECT CONTEMN AND WHAT KNOW YOU . . . . 411 3 DON JUAN 14   3   2
    THE WORST TO KNOW IT--WHEN THE MOUNTAINS REAR . . . . 412 3 DON JUAN 14   5   4
    TO PLUNGE WITH ALL YOUR FEARS--BUT WHERE YOU KNOW NOT . 413 3 DON JUAN 14   6   7
    YOU KNOW OR DON'T KNOW THAT GREAT BACON SAITH . . . . 414 3 DON JUAN 14   8   1
    YOU KNOW OR DON'T KNOW THAT GREAT BACON SAITH . . . . 414 3 DON JUAN 14   8   1
    (FOR FOREIGNERS DON'T KNOW THAT A FAUX PAS . . . . . 436 3 DON JUAN 14   60   5
    IT IS BECAUSE I DO NOT KNOW THEM YET . . . . 440 3 DON JUAN 14   68   6
    I DON'T KNOW WHAT AND THEREFORE CANNOT TELL-- . . . . 441 3 DON JUAN 14   71   2
    WHICH FOR WHAT I KNOW MAY OF YORE HAVE LED . . . . . 441 3 DON JUAN 14   72   3
    AS FAR AS I KNOW THAT THE CHURCH RECEIVES . . . . . . 444 3 DON JUAN 14   78   4
    I DON'T KNOW THAT THERE MAY BE MUCH ABILITY . . . . . 465 3 DON JUAN 15   20   1
    AS SEEKING NOT TO KNOW IT SILENT LONE . . . . 476 3 DON JUAN 15   47   2
    THOUGHT THAT IT MIGHT TURN OUT SO--NOW I KNOW IT . . 482 3 DON JUAN 15   60   7
    NOW THOUGH WE KNOW OF OLD THAT LOOKS DECEIVE . . . . 493 3 DON JUAN 15   84   6
    HAS SHOWN I KNOW NOT WHY THEY SHOULD DISPLEASE . . . 494 3 DON JUAN 15   86   6
    HOW LITTLE DO WE KNOW THAT WHICH WE ARE . . . . . . 500 3 DON JUAN 15   99   3
    WHAT THEN I ONLY KNOW IT SO BEFELL . . . . 502 3 DON JUAN 16   4   4
    OR NONE OR LIKE--LIKE NOTHING THAT I KNOW . . . . . 505 3 DON JUAN 16   10   2
    JEST QUOTH MILOR WHY ADELINE YOU KNOW . . . . 517 3 DON JUAN 16   38   1
    BACCHUS AND CERES BEING AS WE KNOW . . . . 542 3 DON JUAN 16   86   4
    I KNOW NOT BUT HER COLOUR NE'ER WAS HIGH-- . . . . . 545 3 DON JUAN 16   94   6
    MISCHIEF IN FAMILIES AS SOME KNOW OR KNEW . . . . . . 565 3 DON JUAN 17   7   5
KNOWING
    DISSATISFIED NOR KNOWING WHAT HE WANTED . . . . 73 2 DON JUAN 1   96   2
    KNOWING THEY MUST BE SETTLED BY THE LAWS . . . . . . 109 2 DON JUAN 1   159   8
    KNOWING (DOGS HAVE SUCH INTELLECTUAL NOSES) . . . . . 187 2 DON JUAN 2   58   5
    NOT KNOWING WHAT HIMSELF TO SAY OR DO . . . . 187 2 DON JUAN 2   59   4
    WITHOUT KNOWING WHY--AN OVERPOWERING TONE . . . . . . 236 2 DON JUAN 2   151   7
    BUT NOT KNOWING METAPHYSICS HAD NO NOTION . . . . . . 289 2 DON JUAN 3   26   4
    HE FELT A GRIEF BUT KNOWING CAUSE FOR NONE . . . . . 355 2 DON JUAN 4   22   6
    ON MANY A TOKEN WITHOUT KNOWING WHAT . . . . 378 2 DON JUAN 4   63   2
    THEIR NEVER KNOWING THEIR OWN MIND TWO DAYS . . . . . 64 3 DON JUAN 6   117   6
    AND FOUGHT AWAY WITH MIGHT AND MAIN NOT KNOWING . . . 120 3 DON JUAN 8   19   2
    UPON REFLECTION KNOWING THAT BEHIND . . . . 133 3 DON JUAN 8   40   2
    SO PRIME SO SWELL SO NUTTY AND SO KNOWING . . . . . . 277 3 DON JUAN 11   19   8
    AS BETTER KNOWING WHY THEY SHOULD BE SO . . . . . . 337 3 DON JUAN 12   46   2
    KNOWING THAT SUCH UNEASY VIRTUE LEADS . . . . 352 3 DON JUAN 12   80   2
    THE EARLIEST KNOWLEDGE FROM THE TREE SO KNOWING . . . 444 3 DON JUAN 14   78   3
    AND THIS AND HIS NOT KNOWING HOW MUCH OATS . . . . . 543 3 DON JUAN 16   89   7
KNOWLEDGE
    FOR THERE IT WAS I PICK'D UP MY OWN KNOWLEDGE . . . . 50 2 DON JUAN 1   52   8
    KNOWLEDGE OF MATTERS--BUT NO MATTER WHAT-- . . . . . 50 2 DON JUAN 1   53   6
    TO PERFECT KNOWLEDGE OF THE BOUNDLESS SKIES . . . . . 71 2 DON JUAN 1   92   7
    THE TREE OF KNOWLEDGE HAS BEEN PLUCK'D--ALL'S KNOWN-- . 90 2 DON JUAN 1   127   4
    IN GAINING ALL THAT USEFUL SORT OF KNOWLEDGE . . . . 228 2 DON JUAN 2   136   7
    UNLESS INDEED IT WAS FROM HIS OWN KNOWLEDGE HE . . . 281 2 DON JUAN 3   11   5
    FOR HAIDEE'S KNOWLEDGE WAS BY NO MEANS GREAT . . . . 354 2 DON JUAN 4   19   5
    KNOWLEDGE AT LEAST IS GAINED FOR INSTANCE NOW . . . . 422 2 DON JUAN 5   23   6
    UNTIL THE TREE OF KNOWLEDGE WAS PULLED DOWN . . . . . 476 2 DON JUAN 5   113   V8
    SHE WOULD HAVE CUT THE TREE OF KNOWLEDGE DOWN . . . . 476 2 DON JUAN 5   113   V7
    WITHOUT OUR KNOWLEDGE OR OUR APPROBATION . . . . . . 25 3 DON JUAN 6   38   4
    BUT STILL THE SPOUSELESS VIRGIN KNOWLEDGE FLIES . . . 37 3 DON JUAN 6   63   5
    SOCRATES SAID OUR ONLY KNOWLEDGE WAS . . . . 69 3 DON JUAN 7   5   1
    KNOW NOT SINCE KNOWLEDGE SAW HER BRANCHES STRIPT . . 210 3 DON JUAN 9   55   6
    BESIDES THEIR KNOWLEDGE OF THE WORLD AND SENSE . . . 336 3 DON JUAN 12   44   5
    HAS NOT CONTRACTED MUCH MORE DEBT THAN KNOWLEDGE . . 377 3 DON JUAN 13   42   8
    THE EARLIEST KNOWLEDGE FROM THE TREE SO KNOWING . . . 444 3 DON JUAN 14   78   3
    OF WHICH I CAN'T TELL WHENCE THEIR KNOWLEDGE SPRINGS . 489 3 DON JUAN 15   76   4
KNOWMAN
    MISS RAW MISS FLAW MISS SHOWMAN AND MISS KNOWMAN . . 473 3 DON JUAN 15   40   4

KNOWN

	PAGE	VOL	CANTO	STANZA	LN
FOR EVERY BRANCH OF EVERY SCIENCE KNOWN--	26	2 DON JUAN	1	10	2
THE TREE OF KNOWLEDGE HAS BEEN PLUCK'D--ALL'S KNOWN--	90	2 DON JUAN	1	127	4
PRAY HAVE THE COURTESY TO MAKE IT KNOWN	105	2 DON JUAN	1	154	3
ALFONSO'S LOVES WITH INEZ WERE WELL KNOWN	118	2 DON JUAN	1	176	2
THAT HAD FOR CENTURIES BEEN KNOWN IN SPAIN	128	2 DON JUAN	1	190	3
LOVE'S A CAPRICIOUS POWER I'VE KNOWN IT HOLD	168	2 DON JUAN	2	22	1
BUT FOR THE PUMPS I'M GLAD TO MAKE THEM KNOWN	171	2 DON JUAN	2	29	4
THEY NE'ER TILL NOW HAD KNOWN THE JOYS OF DRINKING	201	2 DON JUAN	2	85	8
SUCH THINGS A MOTHER HAD NOT KNOWN HER SON	210	2 DON JUAN	2	102	3
ALAS THE LOVE OF WOMEN IT IS KNOWN	262	2 DON JUAN	2	199	1
I'VE KNOWN THE ABSENT WRONG'D FOUR TIMES A DAY	288	2 DON JUAN	3	25	8
KNOWN BUT TO THEM AT LEAST APPEARING SUCH	351	2 DON JUAN	4	14	5
INSTINCT OF GORE AND GLORY EARTH HAS KNOWN	401	2 DON JUAN	4	105	7
AND BABA WHO HAD NE'ER BEEN KNOWN TO FAIL	477	2 DON JUAN	5	114	4
COULD YET BE KNOWN UNTO THE FATES ALONE	499	2 DON JUAN	5	153	4
I'VE KNOWN SOME ODD ONES WHICH SEEMED REALLY PLANNED	45	3 DON JUAN	6	78	5
WITH YOU DUDU A GOOD NIGHT'S REST HAVE KNOWN	46	3 DON JUAN	6	81	6
TO KNOW THAT NOTHING COULD BE KNOWN A PLEASANT	69	3 DON JUAN	7	5	2
AND ADMIRAL RIBAS (KNOWN IN RUSSIAN STORY)	83	3 DON JUAN	7	35	3
ALL WALLS MEN KNOW AND MANY NEVER KNOWN	142	3 DON JUAN	8	60	6
THE GREATEST NUMBER FLESH HATH EVER KNOWN	255	3 DON JUAN	10	62	8
'TWAS MERELY KNOWN THAT ON A SECRET MISSION	283	3 DON JUAN	11	32	5
ALTHOUGH HE HAD KNOWN PLEASURE IN EXCESS	314	3 DON JUAN	11	V 75	V2
I'VE KNOWN THEM COURT AN HEIRESS FOR THEIR LOVER	331	3 DON JUAN	12	33	4
I'VE KNOWN A DOZEN WEDDINGS MADE EVEN THUS	344	3 DON JUAN	12	61	1
AND SOME OF THEM HIGH NAMES I HAVE ALSO KNOWN	344	3 DON JUAN	12	61	2
A MAN KNOWN IN THE COUNCILS OF THE NATION	365	3 DON JUAN	13	14	3
THE SLAP-DASH REGIMENT SO WELL KNOWN TO FAME	383	3 DON JUAN	13	54	6
THE HOURS WHICH HOW TO PASS IS BUT TO FEW KNOWN	406	3 DON JUAN	13	103	5
BUT SADDEST WHEN HIS SCIENCE IS WELL KNOWN	463	3 DON JUAN	15	17	6
HAD SHE KNOWN THIS SHE WOULD HAVE CALMLY SMILED--	480	3 DON JUAN	15	55	7
IF HE HAD KNOWN EXACTLY HIS OWN PLIGHT	506	3 DON JUAN	16	12	5
BUT FOR HIS JUDGMENT--NEVER KNOWN TO FAIL	528	3 DON JUAN	16	57	8
AS JUAN SHOULD HAVE KNOWN HAD NOT HIS SENSES	545	3 DON JUAN	16	93	7

KNOW'S

	PAGE	VOL	CANTO	STANZA	LN
WHY FAME--BUT FAME YOU KNOW'S SOMETIMES A LIAR--	516	3 DON JUAN	16	36	3

KNOWS

	PAGE	VOL	CANTO	STANZA	LN
TO--GOD KNOWS WHERE--FOR NO ONE ELSE CAN KNOW	14	2 DON JUAN	D	9	8
AND THEN--GOD KNOWS WHAT NEXT--I CAN'T GO ON	83	2 DON JUAN	1	115	7
BUT--GOD KNOWS HOW--THIS WISE RESOLVE TAKES WING	85	2 DON JUAN	1	119	V5
KNOWS NOUGHT OF GRIEF WHO HAS NOT SO BEEN WORRIED	89	2 DON JUAN	1	125	V7
MAN'S A PHENOMENON ONE KNOWS NOT WHAT	93	2 DON JUAN	1	133	1
A MATRON WHO HER HUSBAND'S FOIBLE KNOWS	117	2 DON JUAN	1	175	3
FOUND--GOD KNOWS HOW--HIS SOLITARY WAY	126	2 DON JUAN	1	188	V3
MY TEXT WITH MANY THINGS THAT NO ONE KNOWS	138	2 DON JUAN	1	204	5
THOUGH HEAVEN KNOWS HOW IT EVER FOUND A LODGEMENT	144	2 DON JUAN	1	215	8
TO GOD KNOWS WHAT--BUT NEVER YET I SCANNED	161	2 DON JUAN	2	7	V6
ARE LONGER LIVED THAN OTHERS--GOD KNOWS WHY	190	2 DON JUAN	2	65	2
AND ALL THE REST WERE THIN ENOUGH HEAVEN KNOWS	199	2 DON JUAN	2	80	2
HEAVEN KNOWS WHAT CASH HE GOT OR BLOOD HE SPILT	223	2 DON JUAN	2	127	5
WHO SLEEP AT LAST PERHAPS (GOD ONLY KNOWS)	227	2 DON JUAN	2	134	3
HEAVEN KNOWS--IT MAY BE NEPTUNE PAN OR JOVE	246	2 DON JUAN	2	170	8
HEAVEN KNOWS HOW LONG--NO DOUBT THEY NEVER RECKON'D	254	2 DON JUAN	2	187	2
OF WHICH THE FIRST NE'ER KNOWS THE SECOND CAUSE	318	2 DON JUAN	3	82	8
WHOSE HUSBAND ONLY KNOWS HER NOT A WHORE	353	2 DON JUAN	4	17	8
THE TUMULUS--OF WHOM HEAVEN KNOWS 'T MAY BE	385	2 DON JUAN	4	76	6
THEY SAY YOUR STOCKINGS ARE SO (HEAVEN KNOWS WHY	404	2 DON JUAN	4	110	4
MIGHT LEAD TO HEAVEN KNOWS WHERE BUT IN THIS ONE	449	2 DON JUAN	5	65	3
EVE AND PAVED (GOD KNOWS HOW) THE ROAD TO EVIL	474	2 DON JUAN	5	109	4
(ENOUGH GOD KNOWS) WOULD MUCH FALL SHORT OF THIS	489	2 DON JUAN	5	134	8
IT TEACHES--HEAVEN KNOWS ONLY WHAT IT TEACHES	491	2 DON JUAN	5	138	7
WHICH TAKEN AT THE FLOOD LEADS--GOD KNOWS WHERE	7	3 DON JUAN	6	2	2
BUT WOMEN WITH THEIR HEARTS OR HEAVEN KNOWS WHAT	7	3 DON JUAN	6	2	8
OF--BUT CHRONOLOGY BEST KNOWS THE YEARS	9	3 DON JUAN	6	6	8
HOWEVER HEAVEN KNOWS HOW THE FATE WHO LEVELS	134	3 DON JUAN	8	44	4
AND GOD KNOWS WHO BESIDES IN AU AND OU	137	3 DON JUAN	8	49	2
WHERE IS NAPOLEON THE GRAND GOD KNOWS	307	3 DON JUAN	11	77	1
LIKE MANY PEOPLE EVERYBODY KNOWS	335	3 DON JUAN	12	41	5
BESIDES THE MOST SUBLIME OF--HEAVEN KNOWS WHAT ELSE--	356	3 DON JUAN	12	88	5
WHICH KNOWS NO EBB TO ITS IMPERIOUS FLOW	366	3 DON JUAN	13	16	6
BUT EVEN THIS IS DIFFICULT HEAVEN KNOWS	421	3 DON JUAN	14	25	2
THOUGH GOD KNOWS WHENCE IT CAME FROM THERE WAS TOO	483	3 DON JUAN	15	63	2
THEN THERE WAS GOD KNOWS WHAT A L'ALLEMANDE	484	3 DON JUAN	15	66	1
HEAVEN KNOWS BUT ADELINE'S MALICIOUS EYES	490	3 DON JUAN	15	78	7
AND THAT IT IS SO EVERYBODY KNOWS	522	3 DON JUAN	16	44	6

KOCLOBSKI

	PAGE	VOL	CANTO	STANZA	LN
KOCLOBSKI KOURAKIN AND MOUSKIN POUSKIN	75	3 DON JUAN	7	17	2

KOKLOPHTI

	PAGE	VOL	CANTO	STANZA	LN
SCHEREMATOFF AND CHREMATOFF KOKLOPHTI	75	3 DON JUAN	7	17	1

KONINGSBERG

	PAGE	VOL	CANTO	STANZA	LN
AND KONINGSBERG THE CAPITAL WHOSE VAUNT	254	3 DON JUAN	10	60	2

KORAN

	PAGE	VOL	CANTO	STANZA	LN
THE HOLY CAMEL'S HUMP BESIDES THE KORAN	57	3 DON JUAN	6	102	8

KOSCIUSKO'S

	PAGE	VOL	CANTO	STANZA	LN
THROUGH POLAND THERE IS KOSCIUSKO'S NAME	254	3 DON JUAN	10	59	7

KOURAKIN

	PAGE	VOL	CANTO	STANZA	LN
KOCLOBSKI KOURAKIN AND MOUSKIN POUSKIN	75	3 DON JUAN	7	17	2

KOUTOUSOW

	PAGE	VOL	CANTO	STANZA	LN
KOUTOUSOW HE WHO AFTERWARDS BEAT BACK	147	3 DON JUAN	8	70	1
THE GREAT AND GAY KOUTOUSOW MIGHT HAVE LAIN	148	3 DON JUAN	8	72	7

		PAGE	VOL	CANTO	STANZA	LN
KOUTOUSOW'S	JUST AS KOUTOUSOW'S MOST FORLORN OF HOPES	148	3	DON JUAN	8	73	3
KOZAKS	THE KOZAKS OR IF SO YOU PLEASE COSSACQUES--	149	3	DON JUAN	8	74	1
KURDS	ASIA WHERE KAFF LOOKS DOWN UPON THE KURDS	49	3	DON JUAN	6	86	8
KUTHEREIAN	WHO WOULD NOT SIGH AI AI TAN KUTHEREIAN	554	3	DON JUAN	16	109	1
LA	LA BELLE ALLIANCE OF DUNCES DOWN AT ZERO	296	3	DON JUAN	11	56	3
	THERE WAS THE PREUX CHEVALIER DE LA RUSE	398	3	DON JUAN	13	86	3
	OR SWISS ROUSSEAU CRY VOILA LA PERVENCHE	442	3	DON JUAN	14	75	8
	THERE WAS A GOODLY SOUPE A LA BONNE FEMME	483	3	DON JUAN	15	63	1
	RELIEVED WITH DINDON A LA PERIGUEUX	483	3	DON JUAN	15	63	4
	SOUPE A LA BEAUVEAU WHOSE RELIEF WAS DORY	483	3	DON JUAN	15	63	7
	FOWLS A LA CONDE SLICES EKE OF SALMON	484	3	DON JUAN	15	65	1
LABLE	THEY DIFFER AS WINE DIFFERS FROM ITS LABLE	458	3	DON JUAN	15	6	5
LABORIOUS	WAS LIKE ALL BUSINESS A LABORIOUS NOTHING	301	3	DON JUAN	11	65	2
LABOUR	LABOUR THERE'S A SURE MARKET FOR IMPOSTURE	91	2	DON JUAN	1	128	8
	EMPLOYED FOR SINCE IT IS THEIR DAILY LABOUR	288	3	DON JUAN	11	41	2
	AS SOME WHO LABOUR MORE AND YET MAY CHARM LESS	498	3	DON JUAN	15	94	8
LABOUR'D	BUT THE SHIP LABOUR'D SO THEY SCARCE COULD HOPE	178	2	DON JUAN	2	41	2
LABOURER	LABOURER IN THE SAME VINEYARD THOUGH THE VINE	297	3	DON JUAN	11	58	2
LABOURING	YOUR LABOURING PEOPLE THINK BEYOND ALL QUESTION	191	2	DON JUAN	2	67	7
LABOUR'S	HARD LABOUR'S AN INDIFFERENT GO-BETWEEN	443	3	DON JUAN	14	76	5
LABYRINTH	THEIR LABYRINTH OF FABLES TO THREAD THROUGH	137	2	DON JUAN	1	202	7
	OUR HERO THROUGH THE LABYRINTH OF LOVE	20	3	DON JUAN	6	28	7
	THIS LABYRINTH OF FEMALES AND EACH STATION	34	3	DON JUAN	6	57	5
	OF THIS ODD LABYRINTH OR AS THE KELP	238	3	DON JUAN	10	28	5
	THAT LABYRINTH WHOSE CLUE IS OF THE SAME	349	3	DON JUAN	12	72	2
LACE	AND FOUND MUCH LINEN LACE AND SEVERAL PAIR	99	2	DON JUAN	1	143	3
	HER GIRDLE SPARKLED AND THE RICHEST LACE	220	2	DON JUAN	2	121	5
	FRENCH STUFFS LACE TWEEZERS TOOTHPICKS TEAPOT TRAY	284	2	DON JUAN	3	17	5
	FRENCH STUFFS LACE TWEEZERS TOOTHPICKS A BIDET	284	2	DON JUAN	3	17	V5
	FINISHED WITH BRIGHT GOLD LACE HER JACKET'S FELLOW	311	2	DON JUAN	3	70	V4
	THUS HE PROFANELY TERMED THE FINEST LACE	455	2	DON JUAN	5	76	7
	MEDALS RANKS RIBBONS LACE EMBROIDERY SCARLET	108	3	DON JUAN	7	84	1
	AND ROBES SWEET FRIENDSHIP IN A BRUSSELS LACE	430	3	DON JUAN	14	47	4
LACES	BUT VIRTUE'S SELF WITH ALL HER TIGHTEST LACES	494	3	DON JUAN	15	85	5
LACING	TO HELP THE LADIES IN THEIR DRESS AND LACING	391	2	DON JUAN	4	86	V6
LACK	AND FALL FOR LACK OF MOISTURE QUITE A-DRY BOB	10	2	DON JUAN	D	3	8
	HERE WAS NO LACK OF INNOCENT DIVERSION	293	2	DON JUAN	3	35	1
	OH TO POSSESS SUCH LUSTRE--AND THEN LACK	381	2	DON JUAN	4	69	8
	AND OF VARIETY THERE WAS NO LACK--	450	2	DON JUAN	5	67	5
	ALAS WHAT TO THEIR MEMORY CAN LACK	73	3	DON JUAN	7	14	5
	AND EVERYBODY SEES THAT WHAT THEY LACK	348	3	DON JUAN	12	71	V4
LACKEYS	AND SUMMON LACKEYS ARM'D WITH FIRE AND SWORD	97	2	DON JUAN	1	139	7
LACQUEYS	OF LACQUEYS USHER TO THE FEAST PREPARED	439	2	DON JUAN	5	50	4
LAD	A LAD OF SIXTEEN CAUSING A DIVORCE	158	2	DON JUAN	2	2	7
	AND ONE OAR FOR A MAST WHICH A YOUNG LAD	181	2	DON JUAN	2	48	5
	A PRETTY LAD BUT BURSTING WITH CONCEIT	392	2	DON JUAN	4	89	2
	BUT SEEING AT HIS ELBOW A MERE LAD	417	2	DON JUAN	5	12	1
	SHE THOUGHT OF KILLING JUAN--BUT POOR LAD	492	2	DON JUAN	5	140	5
	IT BEING (NOT NOW BUT ONLY WHILE A LAD)	19	3	DON JUAN	6	27	6
	NO CAESAR BUT A FINE YOUNG LAD WHO FOUGHT	126	3	DON JUAN	8	29	2
	IT WAS NOT MARVELLOUS THAT A MERE LAD	127	3	DON JUAN	8	31	6
	JUST AT THE PROPER TIME AND THOUGH A LAD	292	3	DON JUAN	11	47	6
LADDER	HE SHOWED THEM HOW TO MOUNT A LADDER (WHICH	93	3	DON JUAN	7	52	7
LADDERS	THEY DREW CONSTRUCTED LADDERS REPAIRED FLAWS	89	3	DON JUAN	7	47	6
	LEAVING AS LADDERS THEIR HEAPED CARCASES	150	3	DON JUAN	8	76	6
LADEN	WAS LADEN WITH ALL KINDS OF GIFTS AND HONOURS	247	3	DON JUAN	10	46	7
LADIES	AND SOMETIMES LADIES HIT EXCEEDING HARD	33	2	DON JUAN	1	21	6
	BUT--OH YE LORDS OF LADIES INTELLECTUAL	33	2	DON JUAN	1	22	7
	JUST AS THE SPARTAN LADIES DID OF YORE	36	2	DON JUAN	1	29	3
	LADIES EVEN OF THE MOST UNEASY VIRTUE	56	2	DON JUAN	1	62	7
	I RECOMMEND YOUNG LADIES TO MAKE TRIAL	64	2	DON JUAN	1	78	8
	FOR INSTANCE--GENTLEMEN WHOSE LADIES TAKE	74	2	DON JUAN	1	98	2
	THEY MAKE SOME BLUNDER WHICH THEIR LADIES TELL US	74	2	DON JUAN	1	98	8
	WITH OTHER ARTICLES OF LADIES FAIR	99	2	DON JUAN	1	143	5
	AND THEN BY THE ADVICE OF SOME OLD LADIES	128	2	DON JUAN	1	190	7

426

LADIES   (CONTINUED)
```
    A NAME THE LADIES MUST NOT TAKE AMISS . . . . . .  . .  140   2 DON JUAN   1    206  V4
    AND SUCH SWEET GIRLS--I MEAN SUCH GRACEFUL LADIES .  . .  159   2 DON JUAN   2      5   5
    BY GENERAL SUBSCRIPTION OF THE LADIES . . . . . .   . .  199   2 DON JUAN   2     81   8
    BY LIKING A VARIETY OF LADIES . . . . . . . . . .   . .  199   2 DON JUAN   2     81  V8
    A PRESENT LIBERALLY MADE BY LADIES . . . . . . . .  . .  199   2 DON JUAN   2     81  V8
    AS FOR THE LADIES I HAVE NOUGHT TO SAY . . . . .    . .  244   2 DON JUAN   2    166   1
    OF MAGIC LADIES WHO BY ONE SOLE ACT . . . . . . .   . .  293   2 DON JUAN   3     34   7
    TO HELP THE LADIES IN THEIR DRESS AND LACING . . .  . .  391   2 DON JUAN   4     86  V6
    AND I YE LEARNED LADIES SAY OF YOU . . . . . . . .  . .  404   2 DON JUAN   4    110   3
    OF LADIES WHO CANNOT HAVE THEIR OWN WAY . . . . .   . .  487   2 DON JUAN   5    132   4
    IT IS OBSERVED THAT LADIES ARE LITIGIOUS . . . . .  . .   11   3 DON JUAN   6     10   1
    IN THE SERAGLIO WHERE THE LADIES LAY . . . . . .    . .   19   3 DON JUAN   6     26   6
    OF LADIES OF ALL COUNTRIES AT THE WILL . . . . .    . .   22   3 DON JUAN   6     33   4
    WITH LADIES IT.IS TIME TO GO TO REST . . . . . .    . .   29   3 DON JUAN   6     46   2
    WITH ALL THINGS LADIES WANT SAVE ONE OR TWO . . .   . .   31   3 DON JUAN   6     51   7
    LIKE OTHER ANGRY LADIES OF HER NATION-- . . . . .   . .   65   3 DON JUAN   6    119   5
    THE LADIES--WHO BY NO MEANS HAD BEEN BRED . . . .   . .  101   3 DON JUAN   7     67   2
    BUT THESE ARE BUT TWO TURKISH LADIES WHO . . . . .  . .  103   3 DON JUAN   7     72   1
    BUT ALL THE LADIES SAVE SOME TWENTY SCORE . . . .   . .  176   3 DON JUAN   8    129   7
    THE COURTIERS STARED THE LADIES WHISPERED AND . .   . .  205   3 DON JUAN   9     46   1
    OH GENTLE LADIES SHOULD YOU SEEK TO KNOW . . . .    . .  207   3 DON JUAN   9     49   1
    CATHERINE WAS GENEROUS--ALL SUCH LADIES ARE . . .   . .  222   3 DON JUAN   9     80   1
    MIDDLE-AGED LADIES EVEN MORE THAN YOUNG . . . . .   . .  230   3 DON JUAN  10     10   2
    AND LADIES LIKE A LITTLE SPICE OF MARS . . . . .    . .  284   3 DON JUAN  11     33  V4
    AMONGST LIVE POETS AND BLUE LADIES PAST . . . . .   . .  300   3 DON JUAN  11     64   2
    THAT LADIES IN THEIR YOUTH A LITTLE GAY . . . . .   . .  336   3 DON JUAN  12     44   4
    THE SINGLE LADIES WISHING TO BE DOUBLE . . . . .    . .  342   3 DON JUAN  12     58   7
    THE LADIES SCILLY BUSEY--MISS ECLAT . . . . . . .   . .  396   3 DON JUAN  13     79   4
    THE LADIES--SOME ROUGED SOME A LITTLE PALE-- . . .  . .  406   3 DON JUAN  13    104   1
    BUT IN THE COUNTRY LADIES SEEK THEIR BOWER . . . .  . .  409   3 DON JUAN  13    111   3
    LADIES WHO HAVE STUDIED FRIENDSHIP BUT IN FRANCE .  . .  450   3 DON JUAN  14     92   4
    THE SUREST WAY FOR LADIES AND FOR BOOKS . . . . .   . .  453   3 DON JUAN  14     97   7
    UNLESS THE LADIES SHOULD GO OFF--THERE WAS . . . .  . .  475   3 DON JUAN  15     43   2
    THE LADIES WITH MORE MODERATION MINGLED . . . . .   . .  487   3 DON JUAN  15     70   3
    NOT NIGH THE GAY SALOON OF LADIES GENT . . . . .    . .  533   3 DON JUAN  16     66   2
    MY LORDS AND LADIES PROUDLY CONDESCENDING . . . .   . .  538   3 DON JUAN  16     79   2
    EACH CARRIAGE WAS ANNOUNCED AND LADIES ROSE . . .   . .  549   3 DON JUAN  16    101   3
LADIES'
    THE ELDER LADIES' WRINKLES CURLED MUCH CRISPER . .  . .  221   3 DON JUAN   9     78   3
    OR LADIES' FANCIES--RATHER TRANSITORY . . . . . .   . .  229   3 DON JUAN  10      9   4
    OF LADIES' LUCUBRATIONS SO THEY LEAD . . . . . .    . .  284   3 DON JUAN  11     34   6
    THOUGH LADIES' ROBES SEEM SCANT ENOUGH FOR LESS .   . .  482   3 DON JUAN  15     61   8
    WHICH SOME PRETEND TO TRACE IN LADIES' SMILES . .   . .  544   3 DON JUAN  16     92   8
LADS
    SO NOW MY LADS FOR GLORY--HERE HE TURNED . . . .    . .   99   3 DON JUAN   7     64   1
    BEHIND HIS CARRIAGE AND LIKE HANDY LADS . . . . .   . .  273   3 DON JUAN  11     11   3
    GOD DAMN YOU LADS I'VE MISSED A HANDSOME BOOTY .    . .  276   3 DON JUAN  11     16  V3
LADY
    HIS MOTHER WAS A LEARNED LADY FAMED . . . . . . .   . .   26   2 DON JUAN   1     10   1
    AND NEVER DREAM'D HIS LADY WAS CONCERN'D . . . .    . .   31   2 DON JUAN   1     19   4
    DON JOSE AND HIS LADY QUARRELL'D--WHY . . . . . .   . .   33   2 DON JUAN   1     23   1
    SHE TOOK HIS LADY ALSO IN AFFECTION . . . . . . .   . .   58   2 DON JUAN   1     67   3
    THE UNEXPECTED DEATH OF SOME OLD LADY . . . . . .   . .   89   2 DON JUAN   1    125   2
    HOW DARE YOU THINK YOUR LADY WOULD GO ON SO . . .   . .  101   2 DON JUAN   1    146   8
    ADDED TO THOSE HIS LADY WITH SUCH VIGOUR . . . .    . .  110   2 DON JUAN   1    161   6
    A LADY WITH APOLOGIES ABOUNDS . . . . . . . . . .   . .  118   2 DON JUAN   1    176   5
    A LADY ALWAYS DISTANT FROM THE FACT-- . . . . . .   . .  119   2 DON JUAN   1    178   6
    AS ONE WHO WAS A LADY IN THE LAND . . . . . . . .   . .  217   2 DON JUAN   2    116   8
    THERE WAS AN IRISH LADY TO WHOSE BUST . . . . . .   . .  219   2 DON JUAN   2    119   3
    AND SUCH WAS SHE THE LADY OF THE CAVE . . . . . .   . .  220   2 DON JUAN   2    120   1
    AND LOOK'D UPON THE LADY IN WHOSE CHEEK . . . . .   . .  236   2 DON JUAN   2    150   2
    SHE WAITED ON HER LADY WITH THE SUN . . . . . . .   . .  252   2 DON JUAN   2    182   5
    THE LADY WATCH'D HER LOVER--AND THAT HOUR . . . .   . .  262   2 DON JUAN   2    198   1
    WHEREAS IF ONE SOLE LADY PLEASED FOREVER . . . .    . .  270   2 DON JUAN   2    213   7
    THEY SAY NO MORE OF DEATH OR OF THE LADY . . . .    . .  280   2 DON JUAN   3      9   8
    MAY QUARREL AND THE LADY GROWING WISER . . . . .    . .  288   2 DON JUAN   3     24   4
    AN HONEST FRIENDSHIP WITH A MARRIED LADY-- . . .    . .  288   2 DON JUAN   3     25   3
    A LADY WITH HER DAUGHTERS OR HER NIECES . . . . .   . .  306   2 DON JUAN   3     60   7
    MEANTIME THE LADY AND HER LOVER SATE . . . . . .    . .  306   2 DON JUAN   3     61   3
    THE LADY AND HER LOVER LEFT ALONE . . . . . . . .   . .  334   2 DON JUAN   3    101   5
    AND ALL BECAUSE A LADY FELL IN LOVE . . . . . . .   . .  371   2 DON JUAN   4     51   8
    THEIR LADY TO HER COUCH WITH GUSHING EYES . . . .   . .  376   2 DON JUAN   4     59   5
    LADY TO LADY WELL AS MAN TO MAN . . . . . . . . .   . .  393   2 DON JUAN   4     91   6
    LADY TO LADY WELL AS MAN TO MAN . . . . . . . . .   . .  393   2 DON JUAN   4     91   6
    OH LADY DAPHNE LET ME MEASURE YOU . . . . . . . .   . .  406   2 DON JUAN   4    112   8
    THAT THERE HAD BEEN A LADY IN THE CASE . . . . .    . .  420   2 DON JUAN   5     19   4
    NO LADY E'ER IS OGLED BY A LOVER . . . . . . . . .  . .  424   2 DON JUAN   5     26   6
    A BOOK FRIEND SINGLE LADY OR A GLASS . . . . . . .  . .  444   2 DON JUAN   5     58   2
    REPLIED OLD GENTLEMAN I'M NOT A LADY . . . . . .    . .  453   2 DON JUAN   5     73   8
    THAT IS--THE LADY CLAPPING HIS HANDS TWICE . . . .  . .  458   2 DON JUAN   5     80   7
    A LADY BABA STOPPED AND KNEELING SIGNED . . . . .   . .  466   2 DON JUAN   5     95   4
    THE LADY RISING UP WITH SUCH AN AIR . . . . . .    . .  466   2 DON JUAN   5     96   1
    THE LADY EYED HIM O'ER AND O'ER AND BADE . . . .    . .  473   2 DON JUAN   5    107   1
    THE SPOUSE OF POTIPHAR THE LADY BOOBY . . . . . .   . .  486   2 DON JUAN   5    131   2
    WHO LENT HIS LADY TO HIS FRIEND HORTENSIUS . . .    . .   10   3 DON JUAN   6      7   8
    WITH A CARVED LADY ON A MONUMENT . . . . . . . . .  . .   40   3 DON JUAN   6     68   8
    A LADY OF A CERTAIN AGE WHICH MEANS . . . . . . .   . .   41   3 DON JUAN   6     69   2
    AN ENGLISH LADY ASKED OF AN ITALIAN . . . . . . .   . .  208   3 DON JUAN   9     51   1
```

LADY   (CONTINUED)
    SAID--LADY I BESEECH YOU TO SUPPOSE THEM 208   3 DON JUAN   9   51   8
    LADY FITZ-FRISKY AND MISS MAEVIA MANNISH 295   3 DON JUAN 11   53   7
    WHERE IS LORD THIS AND WHERE MY LADY THAT 308   3 DON JUAN 11   79   1
    WHERE ARE THE LADY CAROLINES AND FRANCESES 308   3 DON JUAN 11   80   1
    THAT THE YOUNG LADY MADE A MONSTROUS CHOICE 334   3 DON JUAN 12   38   8
    SUPPRESSION LADY PINCHBECK WAS HIS CHOICE 336   3 DON JUAN 12   42   8
    I SAID THAT LADY PINCHBECK HAD BEEN TALKED ABOUT-- . . 338   3 DON JUAN 12   47   1
    SAFE WITH A LADY WHOSE LAST GROWN-UP DAUGHTER 339   3 DON JUAN 12   51   3
    FOR TALK SIX TIMES WITH THE SAME SINGLE LADY 343   3 DON JUAN 12   59   7
    BUT SHOULD A LADY ASK ME TO OBLIGE HER 348   3 DON JUAN 12   70   V4
    THAT LADY WHO SHOULD BE AT HOME TO ALL 352   3 DON JUAN 12   79   8
    A LADY ALTOGETHER TO HIS MIND 353   3 DON JUAN 12   81   4
    THE LADY ADELINE AMUNDEVILLE 359   3 DON JUAN 13   2   1
    THE LADY ADELINE AMUNDEVILLE 364   3 DON JUAN 13   12   2
    NODDING BESIDE MY LADY IN HIS CARRIAGE 379   3 DON JUAN 13   46   2
    LORD HENRY AND THE LADY ADELINE 381   3 DON JUAN 13   50   1
    LORD H AMUNDEVILLE AND LADY A 382   3 DON JUAN 13   51   8
    AND LADY MARYS BLOOMING INTO GIRLS 390   3 DON JUAN 13   68   4
    LORD HENRY AND HIS LADY WERE THE HOSTS 404   3 DON JUAN 13   99   1
    MY DIAN OF THE EPHESIANS LADY ADELINE 430   3 DON JUAN 14   46   3
    THE LADY ADELINE'S SERENE SEVERITY 432   3 DON JUAN 14   51   1
    THE LADY ADELINE AS SOON'S SHE SAW 436   3 DON JUAN 14   60   3
    THE LADY ADELINE RESOLVED TO TAKE 437   3 DON JUAN 14   61   1
    MY BUSINESS IS WITH LADY ADELINE 449   3 DON JUAN 14   90   7
    THE LADY ADELINE AMUNDEVILLE 458   3 DON JUAN 15   5   2
    THE LADY ADELINE RIGHT HONOURABLE 458   3 DON JUAN 15   6   1
    THAT STILL HE'D WED WITH SUCH OR SUCH A LADY 469   3 DON JUAN 15   30   7
    FOR THIS A LADY NO ONE CAN REJECT 471   3 DON JUAN 15   34   5
    AS CONGRESSES OF LATE DO) OF THE LADY 482   3 DON JUAN 15   61   2
    BUT SO FAR LIKE A LADY THAT 'TWAS DREST 488   3 DON JUAN 15   74   7
    AURORA AND THE LADY ADELINE-- 489   3 DON JUAN 15   75   2
    WHO HAVE HEARD MISS THAT OR THIS OR LADY T'OTHER . . 522   3 DON JUAN 16   44   7
    BUT WITH THE LADY ADELINE THE MOST 549   3 DON JUAN 16   101   8
LADYE-LOVE
    AND FIRMER FAITH NO LADYE-LOVE DESIRE 396   2 DON JUAN   4   96   3
LADY-LOVE
    YOUNG JUAN AND HIS LADY-LOVE WERE LEFT 348   2 DON JUAN   4   8   1
LADY-MOTHER
    HIS LADY-MOTHER MATHEMATICAL 158   2 DON JUAN   2   3   3
LADY'S
    THAT YOU MIGHT BRAIN THEM WITH THEIR LADY'S FAN . . . 33   2 DON JUAN   1   21   5
    AS BEING THE BEST JUDGE OF A LADY'S CASE 62   2 DON JUAN   1   75   8
    TO HOLD A LEVEE ROUND HIS LADY'S BED 97   2 DON JUAN   1   139   6
    ARE SUCH AS FIT WITH LADY'S FEET BUT THESE 121   2 DON JUAN   1   181   2
    CONDEMN THE ROYAL LADY'S TASTE WHO WORE 238   2 DON JUAN   2   155   4
    AND KISS THE LADY'S FOOT WHICH MAXIM WHEN 470   2 DON JUAN   5   102   4
    THE GENTLEMAN TO KISS THE LADY'S HANDS 472   2 DON JUAN   5   105   8
    I KNOW NOT WHAT MIGHT BE THE LADY'S THOUGHT 473   2 DON JUAN   5   108   2
    IN EARLY YOUTH TO TURN A LADY'S MAID-- 37   3 DON JUAN   6   62   4
    AND IF ONE LADY'S SLIP COULD LEAVE A CRIME ON . . . 53   3 DON JUAN   6   94   6
    ALSO MY LADY'S GENTLEWOMAN TRICKY 380   3 DON JUAN 13   47   3
    MY LADY'S PRATTLE FILTER'D THROUGH HER WOMAN 418   3 DON JUAN 14   19   8
    THE LADY'S VOICE CEASED AND THE THRILLING WIRES . . 521   3 DON JUAN 16   41   1
LAFAYETTE
    PETION CLOOTZ DANTON MARAT LAFAYETTE 22   2 DON JUAN   1   3   2
LAFITTE
    THOSE AND THE TRULY LIBERAL LAFITTE 318   3 DON JUAN 12   6   1
LAID
    AND THEREFORE SIDE BY SIDE WERE GENTLY LAID 98   2 DON JUAN   1   141   5
    AND LAID CONDITIONS HE THOUGHT VERY HARD ON 120   2 DON JUAN   1   180   3
    A SORT OF INCOME-TAX LAID ON BY FATE 122   2 DON JUAN   1   183   4
    I'VE LAID IN TOO A STOCK OF GOOD MACHINERY 136   2 DON JUAN   1   201   V7
    LAID WITH ONE BLAST THE SHIP ON HER BEAM ENDS . . . 172   2 DON JUAN   2   30   8
    WHILE T'OTHER HALF WERE LAID DOWN IN THEIR PLACE . . 189   2 DON JUAN   2   63   5
    NO PERMANENT FOUNDATION CAN BE LAID 268   2 DON JUAN   2   209   4
    ARE LAID WITHIN OUR BOSOMS BUT TO PERISH 275   2 DON JUAN   3   2   8
    THE SECOND HAD HIS CHEEK LAID OPEN BUT 370   2 DON JUAN   4   49   1
    THEY LAID HIM IN A BOAT AND PLIED THE OAR 371   2 DON JUAN   4   50   5
    WHICH COLDER HEARTS ENDURE TILL THEY ARE LAID . . . 382   2 DON JUAN   4   71   4
    I PASS EACH DAY WHERE DANTE'S BONES ARE LAID 400   2 DON JUAN   4   104   1
    AT LENGTH IN AN IMPERIAL WAY SHE LAID 483   2 DON JUAN   5   125   1
    AND ALSO AS MAY BE PRESUMED SHE LAID 485   2 DON JUAN   5   129   4
    WERE LAID ASIDE BUT NOT BEFORE SHE OFFERED 36   3 DON JUAN   6   61   2
    ONE WITH HER FLUSHED CHEEK LAID ON HER WHITE ARM . . 39   3 DON JUAN   6   66   1
    WHAT FOLLOWED--A SHOT LAID ME ON MY BACK 98   3 DON JUAN   7   61   5
    WAS FROM A PISTOL SHOT THAT LAID HIM DEAD 152   3 DON JUAN   8   81   2
    FOR THE SAME BLOW WHICH LAID HER MOTHER HERE 159   3 DON JUAN   8   95   4
    THE CRUEL NAZARENES WHO HAD LAID LOW 262   3 DON JUAN 10   75   4
    IN AMBUSH LAID WHO HAD PERCEIVED HIM LOITER 273   3 DON JUAN 11   11   2
    SOME LAID ASIDE LIKE AN OLD OPERA HAT 308   3 DON JUAN 11   79   3
    AS MANY COVERS DULY DAILY LAID 381   3 DON JUAN 13   49   6
    HAVE BUILT AND LAID OUT GROUND AT SUCH A RATE . . . 393   3 DON JUAN 13   74   3
LAIN
    THE GREAT AND GAY KOUTOUSOW MIGHT HAVE LAIN 148   3 DON JUAN   8   72   7
LAISSEZ
    BUT LAISSEZ ALLER--KNIGHTS AND DAMES I SING 467   3 DON JUAN 15   25   1
LAKE
    CHECKS TO A LAKE WHOSE WAVES IN CIRCLES SPREAD . . . 231   2 DON JUAN   2   141   7

```
                                                        PAGE VOL   CANTO   STANZA  LN
LAKE    (CONTINUED)
    THE OUTSTRETCH'D OCEAN GLITTER LIKE A LAKE  . . . . . . 249  2 DON JUAN  2     177   8
    OR RATHER LAKE--FOR RILLS DO NOT RUN SLOWLY--  . . . .  22  3 DON JUAN  6      33   7
    'TWAS LIKE THE FAWN WHICH IN THE LAKE DISPLAYED  . . .  36  3 DON JUAN  6      60   5
    BEFORE THE MANSION LAY A LUCID LAKE  . . . . . . . . . 385  3 DON JUAN 13      57   1
    THE RIVER FROM THE LAKE ALL BLUELY DASH'D  . . . . . . 447  3 DON JUAN 14      87   6
LAKE-LIKE
    WILL BRING THE OTHER ERE THE LAKE-LIKE BROW  . . . . . 229  3 DON JUAN 10       8   3
LAKERS
    WITH ALL THE LAKERS IN AND OUT OF PLACE  . . . . . . .   9  2 DON JUAN  D       1   6
LAKE'S
    LET IN THE RIPPLING SOUND OF THE LAKE'S BILLOW  . . . . 507  3 DON JUAN 16     15   4
LAKES
    WHICH MAKES ME WISH YOU'D CHANGE YOUR LAKES FOR OCEAN  .  12  2 DON JUAN  D      5   8
    WITH HIS DEAR WAGGONERS AROUND HIS LAKES  . . . . . . . 333  2 DON JUAN  3     98   4
    TO HURL THESE FLEET-DITCH DIVERS DOWN THEIR LAKES . . . 334  2 DON JUAN  3    100  V8
L'ALLEMANDE
    THEN THERE WAS GOD KNOWS WHAT A L'ALLEMANDE  . . . . . 484  3 DON JUAN 15      66   1
LAMB
    WHILE PEACEFUL AS IF STILL AN UNWEAN'D LAMB  . . . . . 292  2 DON JUAN  3      32   3
    LAMB AND PISTACHIO NUTS--IN SHORT ALL MEATS  . . . . . 307  2 DON JUAN  3      62   2
    CHEAPENING AN OX AN ASS A LAMB OR KID  . . . . . . . . 425  2 DON JUAN  5      28   6
    WHO LOOK'D A WHITE LAMB YET WAS A BLACK SHEEP  . . . . 396  3 DON JUAN 13      79   8
LAMBRO
    LAMBRO OUR SEA-SOLICITOR WHO HAD  . . . . . . . . . . 289  2 DON JUAN  3      26   1
    BUT LAMBRO SAW ALL THESE THINGS WITH AVERSION  . . . . 293  2 DON JUAN  3      35   5
    I SAID THAT LAMBRO WAS A MAN OF PATIENCE  . . . . . . 299  2 DON JUAN  3      46   1
    OLD LAMBRO PASS'D UNSEEN A PRIVATE GATE  . . . . . . . 306  2 DON JUAN  3      61   1
    THEN LAMBRO WHO TILL NOW FORBORE TO SPEAK  . . . . . . 364  2 DON JUAN  4      37   5
    'TIS LAMBRO--'TIS MY FATHER KNEEL WITH ME--  . . . . . 364  2 DON JUAN  4      38   2
    YOUNG MAN YOUR SWORD SO LAMBRO ONCE MORE SAID  . . . . 365  2 DON JUAN  4      40   1
    LAMBRO PRESENTED AND ONE INSTANT MORE  . . . . . . . . 366  2 DON JUAN  4      42   1
    OLD LAMBRO BADE THEM TAKE HIM TO THE SHORE  . . . . . 371  2 DON JUAN  4      50   3
LAMBRO'S
    LAMBRO'S RECEPTION AT HIS PEOPLE'S BANQUET  . . . . . 294  2 DON JUAN  3      36   7
    THEY THUS ADDRESS'D--AND LAMBRO'S VISAGE FELL--  . . . 298  2 DON JUAN  3      44   2
    MORE LIKE AND LIKE TO LAMBRO'S ASPECT GREW--  . . . . 363  2 DON JUAN  4      35   4
    ON THE FIRST FOE WHOM LAMBRO'S CALL MIGHT BRING  . . . 365  2 DON JUAN  4      39   8
LAME
    A FAVOURITE HORSE FALLEN LAME JUST AS HE'S MOUNTED  . .  16  3 DON JUAN  6      21   4
LAMED
    THE RUSSIAN OFFICER FOR LIFE WAS LAMED  . . . . . . . 154  3 DON JUAN  8      85   2
LAMENTATION
    AND MADE A LOUD AND PIOUS LAMENTATION  . . . . . . . . 175  2 DON JUAN  2      37   2
LAMENTED
    LIKE THE LAMENTED LATE SIR SAMUEL ROMILLY  . . . . . .  29  2 DON JUAN  1      15   4
    THUS IS THE TROPHY USED AND THUS LAMENTED  . . . . . . 401  2 DON JUAN  4     105   5
    WAS THE LAMENTED LANSKOI WHO WAS SUCH  . . . . . . . . 209  3 DON JUAN  9      54   6
LAMP
    O'ER WHOM SUWARROW SHONE LIKE A GAS LAMP  . . . . . .  89  3 DON JUAN  7      46   3
    YES READY MONEY IS ALADDIN'S LAMP  . . . . . . . . . . 321  3 DON JUAN 12      12   8
    A LAMP BURNED HIGH WHILE HE LEANT FROM A NICHE  . . . 507  3 DON JUAN 16      16   5
LAMPLIGHTER'S
    IN WINDOWS HERE THE LAMPLIGHTER'S INFUSION  . . . . . 278  3 DON JUAN 11      22   6
LAMP-LIGHTING
    THE FRENCH WERE NOT YET A LAMP-LIGHTING NATION  . . . 280  3 DON JUAN 11      26   6
LAMPS
    SOME FAINT LAMPS GLEAMING FROM THE LOFTY WALLS  . . . 442  2 DON JUAN  5      56   1
    'TWAS NIGHT BUT THERE WERE LAMPS AS HATH BEEN SAID  . .  40  3 DON JUAN  6      67   2
    JUST WHEN THE FADING LAMPS WANED DIM AND BLUE  . . . .  41  3 DON JUAN  6      70   5
    SO THAT THE CRESTFALLEN COLOURED LAMPS ARE FULL  . . .  88  3 DON JUAN  7      44   5
    THE LAMPS OF WESTMINSTER'S MORE REGULAR GLEAM  . . . . 279  3 DON JUAN 11      24   4
    'TWERE NOT FOR WANT OF LAMPS TO AID HIS DODGING HIS  . 281  3 DON JUAN 11      28   5
    THEN GLARE THE LAMPS THEN WHIRL THE WHEELS THEN ROAR  . 302  3 DON JUAN 11      67   2
LANCE
    THAT WHEN THE VERY LANCE WAS IN HIS HEART  . . . . . . 169  3 DON JUAN  8     115   2
LAND
    ALFONSO'S DAYS HAD NOT BEEN IN THE LAND  . . . . . . . 123  2 DON JUAN  1     185   6
    ALL EUROPEAN CLIMES BY LAND OR SEA  . . . . . . . . . 129  2 DON JUAN  1     191   2
    FLASHES INTO THE HEART--ALL SUNNY LAND  . . . . . . . 160  2 DON JUAN  2       7   4
    TO SEE ONE'S NATIVE LAND RECEDING THROUGH  . . . . . . 163  2 DON JUAN  2      12   2
    AND ROCKING IN HIS HAMMOCK LONG'D FOR LAND  . . . . . 169  2 DON JUAN  2      25   5
    SOME FANCIED THEY SAW LAND AND SOME SAID NO  . . . . . 207  2 DON JUAN  2      96   5
    IF 'TWAS NOT LAND THAT ROSE WITH THE SUN'S RAY  . . . 207  2 DON JUAN  2      97   3
    HE WISH'D THAT LAND HE NEVER MIGHT SEE MORE  . . . . . 207  2 DON JUAN  2      97   4
    THE LAND APPEAR'D A HIGH AND ROCKY COAST  . . . . . . 209  2 DON JUAN  2     100   1
    AS THEY DREW NIGH THE LAND WHICH NOW WAS SEEN  . . . . 210  2 DON JUAN  2     103   1
    WERE MAD FOR LAND AND THUS THEIR COURSE THEY RAN  . . 211  2 DON JUAN  2     104   3
    AND LIKE A WITHER'D LILY ON THE LAND  . . . . . . . . 214  2 DON JUAN  2     110   6
    AS ONE WHO WAS A LADY IN THE LAND  . . . . . . . . . . 217  2 DON JUAN  2     116   8
    AFTER LONG TRAVELLING BY LAND OR WATER  . . . . . . . 287  2 DON JUAN  3      22   2
    MUCH LESS EXPERIENCE OF DRY LAND THAN OCEAN  . . . . . 289  2 DON JUAN  3      26   2
    AROUND AS PRINCESS OF HER FATHER'S LAND  . . . . . . . 312  2 DON JUAN  3      72   1
    A LAND OF SLAVES SHALL NE'ER BE MINE--  . . . . . . . 326  2 DON JUAN  3    L 16   5
    AGAINST THE CREED AND MORALS OF THE LAND  . . . . . . 346  2 DON JUAN  4       5   2
    GUSH FROM THE EARTH UNTIL THE LAND RUNS O'ER  . . . . 373  2 DON JUAN  4      55   3
    FOR NIGHT WAS CLOSING ERE THEY CAME TO LAND  . . . . . 433  2 DON JUAN  5      41   6
    NOW IF THIS HOLDS GOOD IN A CHRISTIAN LAND  . . . . . .  11  3 DON JUAN  6      11   1
    AND WAS BELEAGUER'D BOTH BY LAND AND WATER  . . . . . .  70  3 DON JUAN  7       8   6
```

429

	PAGE	VOL	CANTO	STANZA	LN
LAND (CONTINUED)					
LAND BATTERIES WORKED THEIR GUNS WITH GREAT PRECISION	81	3	DON JUAN 7	30	3
AS E'ER WAS LOCUST ON THE LAND IT BLASTED	84	3	DON JUAN 7	36	8
JUST NOW BEHAVED AS IN THE HOLY LAND	116	3	DON JUAN 8	9	8
ON HER CANALS WHERE GOD TAKES SEA AND LAND	198	3	DON JUAN 9	31	7
ARE OR WOULD BE THOU SEA OF LIFE'S DRY LAND	210	3	DON JUAN 9	56	8
AS FLOURISHING IN EVERY CHRISTIAN LAND	220	3	DON JUAN 9	76	6
AND LEAVING LAND FAR OUT OF SIGHT WOULD SKIM	227	3	DON JUAN 10	4	4
AND LOVE THE LAND OF MOUNTAIN AND OF FLOOD	234	3	DON JUAN 10	19	8
WHO NEVER HAD A FOOT OF LAND TILL NOW--	237	3	DON JUAN 10	25	7
US LAND ON EARTH WILL DO NO LESS IN HEAVEN	242	3	DON JUAN 10	36	V8
THAT WATER LAND OF DUTCHMEN AND OF DITCHES	256	3	DON JUAN 10	63	2
TO THOSE WHO UPON LAND OR WATER DWELL	259	3	DON JUAN 10	69	6
'TWAS FIT THAT HERE AS IN THE HOLY LAND	262	3	DON JUAN 10	75	V2
FROM OUR NEXT NEIGHBOUR'S LAND WHERE LIKE A CHESSMAN	288	3	DON JUAN 11	42	3
I HAVE SEEN THE FUNDS AT WAR WITH HOUSE AND LAND--	310	3	DON JUAN 11	85	3
OF WHAT BEFELL OUR HERO IN THE LAND	311	3	DON JUAN 11	87	2
OF EARLY LIFE BUT THIS IS A NEW LAND	326	3	DON JUAN 12	23	7
AS BEAUTIFUL AS HER OWN NATIVE LAND	329	3	DON JUAN 12	29	3
BY THOSE WHO SOW THEM IN A LAND THAT'S ARABLE	495	3	DON JUAN 15	89	3
THOSE WHO IN COUNTIES HAVE GREAT LAND RESOURCES	534	3	DON JUAN 16	68	6
LANDED					
WERE LANDED IN THE MARKET ONE AND ALL	407	2	DON JUAN 4	113	6
WHO LANDED LOWER DOWN THEIR LANDING DONE	119	3	DON JUAN 8	15	3
THE LANDED AND THE MONIED SPECULATION	360	3	DON JUAN 13	6	4
LANDHOLDERS					
I HAVE SEEN THE LANDHOLDERS WITHOUT A RAP--	310	3	DON JUAN 11	84	1
LANDING					
BUT FINDING NO PLACE FOR THEIR LANDING BETTER	211	2	DON JUAN 2	104	7
AND TRIED TO MAKE A LANDING ON THE MAIN	82	3	DON JUAN 7	31	5
WHO LANDED LOWER DOWN THEIR LANDING DONE	119	3	DON JUAN 8	15	3
AND HAD IT NOT BEEN FOR SOME STRAY TROOPS LANDING	148	3	DON JUAN 8	72	1
LANDLORD					
THE OBSEQUIOUS LANDLORD HATH THE CHANGE RESTORED	379	3	DON JUAN 13	46	5
WHICH WITH THE LANDLORD MAKES TOO LONG A STAND	435	3	DON JUAN 14	58	2
LANDLORDS					
TO DOUBT (NO LESS THAN LANDLORDS OF THEIR RENTAL)	322	3	DON JUAN 12	13	7
LANDOR					
AND THAT DEEP-MOUTHED BOEOTIAN SAVAGE LANDOR	298	3	DON JUAN 11	59	7
LAND'S					
THAT HIRED HUZZAS REDEEM NO LAND'S DISTRESSES	267	3	DON JUAN 10	86	4
WAS DEARLY PURCHASED BY HIS LAND'S PERDITION	364	3	DON JUAN 13	11	8
LANDS					
TO A CHANCERY SUIT AND MESSUAGES AND LANDS	42	2	DON JUAN 1	37	2
I SPEAK OF CHRISTIAN LANDS IN THIS COMPARISON	248	2	DON JUAN 2	175	7
THE ARTS OF WHICH THESE LANDS WERE ONCE THE FONT	436	2	DON JUAN 5	46	6
OR TRAVELLING IN PATAGONIAN LANDS	20	3	DON JUAN 6	28	5
HIS HOLY TEMPLES IN THE LANDS WHICH BRED	262	3	DON JUAN 10	75	5
THE LANDS ON EITHER SIDE ARE HIS THE SHIP	320	3	DON JUAN 12	9	1
BUT COMING YOUNG FROM LANDS AND SCENES ROMANTIC	347	3	DON JUAN 12	68	1
THE RED GRAPE IN THE SUNNY LANDS OF SONG	394	3	DON JUAN 13	76	4
WITNESS THE LANDS WHICH FLOW'D WITH MILK AND HONEY	405	3	DON JUAN 13	100	1
FROM THOSE OF OTHER LANDS UNBLEST WITH JURIES	436	3	DON JUAN 14	60	7
TO TURN CHURCH LANDS TO LAY	518	3	DON JUAN 16	L 2	2
ALL MOUNTAINEERS WITH DREAMS THAT THEY ARE NIGH LANDS	523	3	DON JUAN 16	46	6
LANDSCAPE					
BUT SHE WAS A SOFT LANDSCAPE OF MILD EARTH	32	3	DON JUAN 6	53	1
'TIS THE SAME LANDSCAPE WHICH THE MODERN MARS SAW	253	3	DON JUAN 10	58	5
HERE SWEETLY SPREAD A LANDSCAPE OF LORRAINE	392	3	DON JUAN 13	72	1
LAND-SERVICE					
BESIDES THE PRINCE IS ALL FOR THE LAND-SERVICE	23	2	DON JUAN 1	4	7
LANDSMEN					
SOME LANDSMEN WOULD HAVE LOOK'D A LITTLE PALE	170	2	DON JUAN 2	26	4
LANDSMEN'S					
OF ALL THE LUCKLESS LANDSMEN'S SEA-SICK MAWS	174	2	DON JUAN 2	34	6
LANE					
TO TAKE A QUIET RIDE IN SOME GREEN LANE	224	3	DON JUAN 9	85	8
LANG					
ARE OVER HERE'S A HEALTH TO AULD LANG SYNE	232	3	DON JUAN 10	16	5
AND WHEN I USE THE PHRASE OF AULD LANG SYNE	233	3	DON JUAN 10	17	1
AS AULD LANG SYNE BRINGS SCOTLAND ONE AND ALL	233	3	DON JUAN 10	18	1
I CARE NOT--'TIS A GLIMPSE OF AULD LANG SYNE	233	3	DON JUAN 10	18	8
LANGERON					
THE PRINCE DELIGNE AND LANGERON AND DAMAS	82	3	DON JUAN 7	32	7
LANGUAGE					
IN EVERY CHRISTIAN LANGUAGE EVER NAMED	26	2	DON JUAN 1	10	3
HOW NOBLE IS HIS LANGUAGE NEVER PERT	154	2	DON JUAN 1	V 5	1
NO DOUBT LESS OF HER LANGUAGE THAN HER LOOK	242	2	DON JUAN 2	163	4
LEARNING THAT LANGUAGE CHIEFLY FROM ITS PREACHERS	243	2	DON JUAN 2	165	4
WAS BROKEN WORDS THEY THOUGHT A LANGUAGE THERE--	256	2	DON JUAN 2	189	4
A LANGUAGE TOO BUT LIKE TO THAT OF BIRDS	351	2	DON JUAN 4	14	4
AND THIS THEY SAY IN LANGUAGE RATHER ROUGH	67	3	DON JUAN 7	3	5
SWEAR THAT PAT'S LANGUAGE SPRUNG FROM THE SAME CLIME	122	3	DON JUAN 8	23	5
NO COMMON LANGUAGE AND BESIDES IN TIME	141	3	DON JUAN 8	58	2
OF HIM WHO IN THE LANGUAGE OF HIS STATION	206	3	DON JUAN 9	48	7
THOUGH NAMELESS IN OUR LANGUAGE--WE RETORT	405	3	DON JUAN 13	101	6
LANGUAGES					
THE LANGUAGES ESPECIALLY THE DEAD	44	2	DON JUAN 1	40	1
WHO SEVERAL LANGUAGES DID UNDERSTAND	169	2	DON JUAN 2	25	3
JUAN KNEW SEVERAL LANGUAGES--AS WELL	295	3	DON JUAN 11	53	1

LANGUID
  AND CAST THEIR LANGUID EYES DOWN AND LET LOOSE 119   2 DON JUAN 1   179   6
  BUT TO RESUME THE LANGUID JUAN RAISED 239   2 DON JUAN 2   157   1
  JUST AS A LANGUID SMILE BEGAN TO FLATTER 493   2 DON JUAN 5   143   6
  THAT FEVER WHICH PRECEDES THE LANGUID ROUT 220   3 DON JUAN 9   75   6
LANGUISH
  SOME DIE SOME FLY SOME LANGUISH ON THE CONTINENT 308   3 DON JUAN 11   80   7
  BUT EN AVANT THE LIGHT LOVES LANGUISH O'ER 542   3 DON JUAN 16   86   1
LANGUISHING
  BEING SOMEWHAT LARGE AND LANGUISHING AND LAZY 26   3 DON JUAN 6   41   7
LANGUOR
  A LOVING LANGUOR WHICH IS NOT REPOSE 82   2 DON JUAN 1   114   8
  MUST END IN LANGUOR--MEN WON'T SLEEP LIKE SWINE-- 343   2 DON JUAN 3 V 98   4
LANNES
  JOUBERT HOCHE MARCEAU LANNES DESSAIX MOREAU 22   2 DON JUAN 1   3   5
LANSKOI
  AND HAD JUST BURIED THE FAIR FACED LANSKOI 206   3 DON JUAN 9   47   8
  WAS THE LAMENTED LANSKOI WHO WAS SUCH 209   3 DON JUAN 9   54   6
LANTERN
  SIR HUMPHREY DAVY'S LANTERN BY WHICH COALS 93   2 DON JUAN 1   132   4
LANTHORN
  AND WHEN THEY GREW SO--ON THEIR NEW-FOUND LANTHORN . . . 280   3 DON JUAN 11   26   7
LANTHORNS
  WHICH SHOWED A WANT OF LANTHORNS OR OF TASTE-- 177   3 DON JUAN 8   130   2
LAOCOON'S
  O'ER THE LAOCOON'S ALL ETERNAL THROES 377   2 DON JUAN 4   61   5
LAP
  QUENCHED IN THE LAP OF THE SALT SEA OR THETIS 217   3 DON JUAN 9   69   8
  A SECRETARY--LAP DOG AND A BULL DOG--AND 249   3 DON JUAN 10   50 V1
LAP-DOGS
  LIKE LAP-DOGS THE LEAST CIVIL SONS OF BITCHES 288   3 DON JUAN 11   41   8
LAPS
  DROPP'D IN THEIR LAPS SCARCE PLUCK'D THEIR MELLOW STORE . 291   2 DON JUAN 3   31   8
LAPSE
  AND SOLACE YOUR SLIGHT LAPSE 'GAINST BONOS MORES . . . 432   3 DON JUAN 14   50   7
LAPSED
  NOW IN THE MOONLIGHT AND NOW LAPSED IN SHADE 510   3 DON JUAN 16   21   3
LAPSUS
  I SAY THAT LINE'S A LAPSUS OF THE PEN-- 323   3 DON JUAN 12   16   4
LARGE
  WAS LARGE AND DARK SUPPRESSING HALF ITS FIRE 54   2 DON JUAN 1   60   2
  THIS THOUGH NOT LARGE WAS ONE OF THE MOST RICH 238   2 DON JUAN 2   154   8
  HAD A LARGE ORDER FROM THE DEY OF TRIPOLI 284   2 DON JUAN 3   16   8
  THEIR LARGE BLACK EYES AND SOFT SERAPHIC CHEEKS 292   2 DON JUAN 3   33   2
  WITH BUTTONS FORM'D OF PEARLS AS LARGE AS PEAS 311   2 DON JUAN 3   70   5
  ONE LARGE GOLD BRACELET CLASP'D EACH LOVELY ARM 312   2 DON JUAN 3   71   1
  HER PERSON IF ALLOW'D AT LARGE TO RUN 313   2 DON JUAN 3   73   4
  FOR THOSE LARGE BLACK EYES WERE SO BLACKLY FRINGED . . . 314   2 DON JUAN 3   75   3
  THAT LARGE BLACK PROPHET EYE SEEM'D TO DILATE 355   2 DON JUAN 4   22   1
  IN THE LARGE DARK EYE'S MUTUAL-DARTED FLAME 367   2 DON JUAN 4   44   4
  THERE THE LARGE OLIVE RAINS ITS AMBER STORE 373   2 DON JUAN 4   55   1
  BUT HER LARGE DARK EYE SHOW'D DEEP PASSION'S FORCE . . . 374   2 DON JUAN 4   56   7
  FLANK'D BY LARGE GROVES WHICH TOWER'D ON EITHER HAND . . 433   2 DON JUAN 5   41   4
  AND A MAGNIFICIENT LARGE HALL DISPLAYED 440   2 DON JUAN 5   51   7
  THE VERGE OF HEAVEN AND IN HER LARGE EYES WROUGHT . . . 473   2 DON JUAN 5   108   6
  BEING SOMEWHAT LARGE AND LANGUISHING AND LAZY 26   3 DON JUAN 6   41   7
  OF LOLAH--THOUGH HER COUCH IS NOT SO LARGE 46   3 DON JUAN 6   81   8
  BUT POOR DUDU WITH LARGE DROPS IN HER OWN 47   3 DON JUAN 6   82   2
  AS LEAVING A SMALL FAMILY AT LARGE 103   3 DON JUAN 7   71   8
  AND LEFT AT LARGE LIKE A YOUNG HEIR TO MAKE 127   3 DON JUAN 8   32   2
  AND THE SWEET CONSEQUENCE OF LARGE SOCIETY 146   3 DON JUAN 8   68   3
  BUT ELSE UNHURT SHE OPENED HER LARGE EYES 159   3 DON JUAN 8   95   7
  THAN HE IN THESE SAD HIGHWAYS LEFT AT LARGE 198   3 DON JUAN 9   31   4
  THOUGH SOMEWHAT LARGE EXUBERANT AND TRUCULENT 213   3 DON JUAN 9   62   1
  WHO MIGHT NOT PROFIT MUCH BY BEING AT LARGE 335   3 DON JUAN 12   41   8
  BEING LONG MARRIED AND THUS SET AT LARGE 339   3 DON JUAN 12   51   4
  A LARGE ACQUAINTANCE LETS NOT VIRTUE SLUMBER 371   3 DON JUAN 13   30   3
  HAWKED ABOUT AT A DISCOUNT SMALL OR LARGE-- 379   3 DON JUAN 13   45   7
  SHUT UP THE WORLD AT LARGE LET BEDLAM OUT 446   3 DON JUAN 14   84   1
  SOME HEIR TO A LARGE PROPERTY SMALL OR FRIEND 470   3 DON JUAN 15   33   2
  AURORA RABY WITH HER LARGE DARK EYES 514   3 DON JUAN 16   31   7
  HAD GATHERED A LARGE TEAR INTO ITS CORNER 532   3 DON JUAN 16   65   2
  TO GATHER TO A SOMEWHAT LARGE AMOUNT HE 535   3 DON JUAN 16   71   5
LARGEST
  AND LARGEST THINKING IT WAS JUST THE THING 146   2 DON JUAN 1   219   3
LARK
  'TIS SWEET TO BE AWAKEN'D BY THE LARK 88   2 DON JUAN 1   123   5
  WHO ON A LARK WITH BLACK-EYED SAL (HIS BLOWING) . . . 277   3 DON JUAN 11   19   7
LASCIAMI'S
  THE LASCIAMI'S AND QUAVERING ADDIO'S 523   3 DON JUAN 16   45   5
LASCIATE
  LIKE THAT OF HELL LASCIATE OGNI SPERANZA 557   3 DON JUAN 16   116   2
LASCY
  UNDER THE ORDERS OF THE GENERAL LASCY 130   3 DON JUAN 8   34   3
  THE GENERAL LASCY WHO HAD BEEN HARD PREST 140   3 DON JUAN 8   56   1
LASH
  AND ALL HER FOOLS WHOM I COULD LAY THE LASH ON 244   2 DON JUAN 2   166   6
  BETWEEN THE BOSPHORUS AS THEY LASH AND LAVE 413   2 DON JUAN 5   5   5
  SOME SPEAKERS WHINE AND OTHERS LAY THE LASH ON 437   2 DON JUAN 5   48   5
  THE LASH TO BABA--BUT HER GRAND RESOURCE 491   2 DON JUAN 5   139   7

431

		PAGE	VOL	CANTO	STANZA	LN
LASH'D						
SOME LASH'D THEM IN THEIR HAMMOCKS SOME PUT ON		180	2 DON JUAN	2	45	1
THE WATERS BEAT WHILE HE THERETO WAS LASH'D		212	2 DON JUAN	2	107	6
LASH'D FROM THE FOAM OF AGES WHILE THE GRAVES		500	3 DON JUAN	15	99	7
LASHES						
WERE BLACK AS DEATH THEIR LASHES THE SAME HUE		218	2 DON JUAN	2	117	2
LASSITUDE						
THAT LEADS TO LASSITUDE THE MOST INFECTED		301	3 DON JUAN	11	65	3
LAST						
LAST--YOURS HAS LATELY BEEN A COMMON CASE--		9	2 DON JUAN	D	1	4
OF ONE ANOTHER'S MINDS AT LAST HAVE GROWN		12	2 DON JUAN	D	5	4
(BUT THIS LAST SIMILE IS TRITE AND STUPID)		51	2 DON JUAN	1	55	8
THE LAST INDEED 'S INFALLIBLY THE CASE		74	2 DON JUAN	1	99	6
LEAVING AT LAST NOT MUCH BESIDES CHRONOLOGY		76	2 DON JUAN	1	103	7
I WISH THESE LAST HAD NOT OCCURR'D IN SOOTH		78	2 DON JUAN	1	107	5
WHO KILL'D HIMSELF FOR LOVE (WITH WINE) LAST YEAR		102	2 DON JUAN	1	149	8
HAD POUR'D UPON HIM FOR THE LAST HALF-HOUR		110	2 DON JUAN	1	161	7
THE ATTORNEY LAST WHO LINGER'D NEAR THE DOOR		111	2 DON JUAN	1	164	2
AT LAST AS THEY MORE FAINTLY WRESTLING LAY		124	2 DON JUAN	1	186	4
AND I MUST EVEN SURVIVE THIS LAST ADIEU		134	2 DON JUAN	1	197	7
SAW JUAN'S LAST ELOPEMENT WITH THE DEVIL		138	2 DON JUAN	1	203	8
AND THE TWO LAST HAVE LEFT ME MANY A TOKEN		145	2 DON JUAN	1	217	3
HIS FIRST--PERHAPS HIS LAST--FAREWELL OF SPAIN		162	2 DON JUAN	2	11	8
AT LAST THEY DID GET AT IT REALLY BUT		171	2 DON JUAN	2	28	5
EASED HER AT LAST (ALTHOUGH WE NEVER MEANT		173	2 DON JUAN	2	32	6
REPENTED ALL HIS SINS AND MADE A LAST		175	2 DON JUAN	2	37	3
BUT STILL 'TIS BEST TO STRUGGLE TO THE LAST		176	2 DON JUAN	2	39	5
THEN CAME THE CARPENTER AT LAST WITH TEARS		179	2 DON JUAN	2	43	1
AND LOOK'D UPON IT LONG AND WHEN AT LAST		204	2 DON JUAN	2	90	2
AT LAST WITH SWIMMING WADING SCRAMBLING HE		212	2 DON JUAN	2	107	7
LEFT HIM AT LAST THE SOLE OF MANY MASTERS		222	2 DON JUAN	2	125	7
AND WHEN AT LAST HE OPEN'D HIS BLACK EYES		225	2 DON JUAN	2	131	4
WHO SLEEP AT LAST PERHAPS (GOD ONLY KNOWS)		227	2 DON JUAN	2	134	3
TILL PAUSING AT THE LAST HER BREATH TO TAKE		241	2 DON JUAN	2	161	7
LIKE A RICH WRECK--HER FIRST LOVE AND HER LAST		247	2 DON JUAN	2	173	8
TO BE HER SOUL'S FIRST IDOL AND ITS LAST		247	2 DON JUAN	2	173	V8
AT LAST HER FATHER'S PROWS PUT OUT TO SEA		248	2 DON JUAN	2	174	5
AT LAST HER FATHER TOOK A VOYAGE TO SEA		248	2 DON JUAN	2	174	V5
AND YET LAST NIGHT BEING AT A MASQUERADE		268	2 DON JUAN	2	209	6
POURS FORTH AT LAST THE HEART'S-BLOOD TURN'D TO TEARS		270	2 DON JUAN	2	214	7
LAST NIGHT I HAD ANOTHER PROOF HOW TRULY IT		272	2 DON JUAN	2	V 1	6
JULIET--OR--GIULETTA--WHICH LAST WAS		273	2 DON JUAN	2	V 2	1
THESE TWO FORM THE LAST GASP OF PASSION'S BREATH		280	2 DON JUAN	3	9	V3
TO LAST--OF ALL CONNEXIONS THE MOST STEADY		288	2 DON JUAN	3	25	5
IN SMALL FINE CHINA CUPS CAME IN AT LAST		307	2 DON JUAN	3	63	4
THE LAST WAS OF GREAT FAME AND LIKED TO SHOW IT		316	2 DON JUAN	3	78	4
AN EASTERN ANTIJACOBIN AT LAST		316	2 DON JUAN	3	79	3
THE LAST WAR--MUCH THE SAME IN PORTUGAL		320	2 DON JUAN	3	86	4
WORDSWORTH'S LAST QUARTO BY THE WAY IS BIGGER		330	2 DON JUAN	3	94	5
THE ROSY SKY WITH THE LAST SUNLIGHT FIRED		335	2 DON JUAN	3	101	V6
TO WHERE THE LAST CESAREAN FORTRESS STOOD		337	2 DON JUAN	3	105	5
TO DUB THE LAST OF HONOURS IN DEGREES)		341	2 DON JUAN	3	110	8
MUST SINK AT LAST INTO A SWOON DIVINE--		343	2 DON JUAN	3	V 98	6
AND SHARP ADVERSITY WILL TEACH AT LAST		345	2 DON JUAN	4	2	2
BUT ALL THESE SAVE THE LAST BEING OBSOLETE		347	2 DON JUAN	4	6	7
WHEN IT'S LAST WEANING DRAUGHT IS DRAINED FOREVER		349	2 DON JUAN	4	10	V6
AWAITS AT LAST EVEN THOSE WHOM LONGEST MISS		350	2 DON JUAN	4	12	6
AS IF THEIR LAST DAY OF A HAPPY DATE		355	2 DON JUAN	4	22	3
THIS HOUR WERE THINE--AND THY YOUNG MINION'S LAST		368	2 DON JUAN	4	46	V8
THE LAST SIGHT WHICH SHE SAW WAS JUAN'S GORE		375	2 DON JUAN	4	58	1
TWELVE DAYS AND NIGHTS SHE WITHER'D THUS AT LAST		381	2 DON JUAN	4	69	1
LAST CARNIVAL SHE MADE A DEAL OF STRIFE		389	2 DON JUAN	4	83	6
SHE TOO WAS FORTUNATE LAST CARNIVAL		390	2 DON JUAN	4	84	4
YOU WAS NOT LAST YEAR AT THE FAIR OF LUGO		392	2 DON JUAN	4	88	7
AS ON THE BEACH THE WAVES AT LAST ARE BROKE		402	2 DON JUAN	4	106	5
THUS TO THEIR LAST SANDS ARE THE PASSIONS BROUGHT		402	2 DON JUAN	4	106	V6
THE LAST IF LATE ACCOUNTS BE ACCURATE		406	2 DON JUAN	4	112	2
THOUGH WILBERFORCE AT LAST HAS MADE IT TWICE		408	2 DON JUAN	4	115	3
ALL FEELINGS CHANGED BUT THIS WAS LAST TO VARY		413	2 DON JUAN	5	4	5
ON THE ROUGH DEEP BUT THIS LAST BLOW--AND HERE		420	2 DON JUAN	5	19	1
AT LAST THEY SETTLED INTO SIMPLE GRUMBLING		426	2 DON JUAN	5	29	1
THE OTHER EVENING ('TWAS ON FRIDAY LAST)--		428	2 DON JUAN	5	33	1
WHICH FOR THE LAST THOUGH NOT THE FIRST TIME BLED		431	2 DON JUAN	5	37	4
THE LAST OF THESE WAS NEVER MUCH THE FASHION		437	2 DON JUAN	5	48	3
AT LAST THEY REACHED A QUARTER MOST RETIRED		448	2 DON JUAN	5	64	1
AND YET AT LAST HE MANAGED TO GET THROUGH		456	2 DON JUAN	5	78	3
INTO A ROOM STILL NOBLER THAN THE LAST		465	2 DON JUAN	5	93	2
BABA AND JUAN WHICH LAST STOOD ADMIRING		469	2 DON JUAN	5	100	3
HE MUTTERED (BUT THE LAST WAS GIVEN ASIDE)		471	2 DON JUAN	5	103	3
WHEN BEING MADE HER PROPERTY AT LAST		478	2 DON JUAN	5	116	4
WHEN SEEING HIM PLACED BY HER SIDE AT LAST		478	2 DON JUAN	5	116	V4
THAT BEING THE LAST THING A PROUD WOMAN TRIES		483	2 DON JUAN	5	125	6
AND THEN HER SEX'S SHAME BROKE IN AT LAST		490	2 DON JUAN	5	137	3
FOR BEING THE LAST WIFE OF THE EMPEROR		495	2 DON JUAN	5	146	7
IN THE LAST LINE WHICH CANNOT WELL BE WORSE		14	3 DON JUAN	6	18	5
HER SON'S SON LET NOT THIS LAST PHRASE OFFEND		52	3 DON JUAN	6	93	2
IN SHORT THIS LAST ATTACK THOUGH RICH IN GLORY		83	3 DON JUAN	7	35	1
MADE HIS LAST ILLNESS WHEN ALL WORN AND WAN		84	3 DON JUAN	7	36	5
WHENCE COME YE--FROM CONSTANTINOPLE LAST		97	3 DON JUAN	7	59	4

432

LAST   (CONTINUED)
    THOUSANDS OF WHOM WERE DRAWING THEIR LAST BREATH . . . . 111 3 DON JUAN 7   87 4
    WHEN UP THE BRISTLING MOSLEM ROSE AT LAST   . . . . . . 115 3 DON JUAN 8   7 3
    THEIR CLAY FOR THE LAST TIME THEIR SOULS ENCUMBER-- . . . 120 3 DON JUAN 8   18 5
    FOR THE FIRST AND LAST TIME FOR LIKE A PAD . . . . . . 122 3 DON JUAN 8   22 5
    AT LAST FALL SICK OF IMITATING JOB . . . . 137 3 DON JUAN 8   50 8
    AT LAST IT TAKES TO WEAPONS SUCH AS MEN . . . . 138 3 DON JUAN 8   51 3
    TO DEEM THE WOODS SHALL BE OUR HOME AT LAST-- . . . . . 142 3 DON JUAN 8   60 8
    WHERE FIGHTS NOT TO THE LAST SOME DESPERATE HEART . . . . 152 3 DON JUAN 8   82 3
    OF THE LAST FOE IS ECHOED BY HIS OWN . . . . 155 3 DON JUAN 8   87 8
    AND WHOM FOR THIS AT LAST MUST WE CONDEMN . . . . . . 157 3 DON JUAN 8   92 6
    AS THE LAST LINK WITH ALL SHE HAD HELD DEAR . . . . . . 159 3 DON JUAN 8   95 6
    THAT DRINKS AND STILL IS DRY AT LAST THEY PERISHED-- . . 166 3 DON JUAN 8   110 1
    A GLANCE ON THAT SLAIN SON HIS FIRST AND LAST . . . . . 169 3 DON JUAN 8   116 8
    WHICH LAST MEN LIKE WHEN THEY HAVE TIME TO PAUSE . . . . 182 3 DON JUAN 8   140 3
    AT LAST MAY GET A LITTLE TIRED OF THUNDER   . . . . . . 185 3 DON JUAN 9   5 4
    (THE LAST IF THEY HAVE SOUL ARE QUITE AS GOOD . . . . . 218 3 DON JUAN 9   71 3
    WHO THOUGH HER SPECTACLES AT LAST GREW DIM . . . . . . 241 3 DON JUAN 10   34 6
    'TWAS ONLY THE FATIGUE OF LAST CAMPAIGN . . . . 244 3 DON JUAN 10   40 8
    BUT TIME THE COMFORTER WILL COME AT LAST . . . . 248 3 DON JUAN 10   48 1
    THE LAST EXPIRED IN CUT THROAT CASTLEREAGH . . . . . . 254 3 DON JUAN 10   59 V4
    AND LAST NOT LEAST TO STRANGERS UNINSTRUCTED . . . . . 259 3 DON JUAN 10   69 7
    OF PAYMENT ERE THE HONEYMOON'S LAST KISSES . . . . . . 293 3 DON JUAN 11   49 3
    AND WITH THE PAGES OF THE LAST REVIEW . . . . 294 3 DON JUAN 11   50 2
    HIS LAST AWARD WILL HAVE THE LONG GRASS GROW   . . . . . 299 3 DON JUAN 11   61 4
    BEING TIRED IN TIME AND NEITHER LEAST NOR LAST . . . . . 300 3 DON JUAN 11   64 4
    FOR FAME IS DROSS OR WORSE--AND AT THE LAST . . . . . . 317 3 DON JUAN 12   4 V7
    MALTHUS AND WILBERFORCE--THE LAST SET FREE . . . . . . 325 3 DON JUAN 12   20 5
    AND FAR AWAY THE LAST BUD OF HER RACE . . . . 329 3 DON JUAN 12   29 4
    LOOK YES LAST NIGHT AND YET SAY NO TO-DAY   . . . . . . 332 3 DON JUAN 12   34 8
    AND WHEN AT LAST THE PRETTY CREATURE GETS   . . . . . . 333 3 DON JUAN 12   36 5
    SAFE WITH A LADY WHOSE LAST GROWN-UP DAUGHTER . . . . . 339 3 DON JUAN 12   51 3
    THE LAST YEAR TO THE NEW TRANSFERS ITS HOARDS . . . . . 340 3 DON JUAN 12   53 5
    I SAY AT FIRST--FOR HE FOUND OUT AT LAST . . . . 347 3 DON JUAN 12   69 1
    ALONG THE LAST FIELDS OF THAT GOTHIC GROUND)-- . . . . . 359 3 DON JUAN 13   2 4
    'TIS ODD BUT TRUE--LAST WAR THE NEWS ABOUNDED . . . . . 383 3 DON JUAN 13   53 7
    THESE LAST HAD DISAPPEAR'D--A LOSS TO ART   . . . . . . 386 3 DON JUAN 13   59 4
    WHO ATE LAST WAR MORE YANKEES THAN HE KILL'D   . . . . . 399 3 DON JUAN 13   88 4
    BUT SEIZE THE LAST WORD WHICH NO DOUBT'S THE BEST . . . . 404 3 DON JUAN 13   98 8
    SUNG OR REHEARSED THE LAST DANCE FROM ABROAD   . . . . . 406 3 DON JUAN 13   104 4
    WOULD RISK TO PLEASE IT MY LAST RAG OF BREECHES   . . . . 421 3 DON JUAN 14   26 V8
    OWN THEY FORESAW THAT YOU WOULD FALL AT LAST   . . . . . 432 3 DON JUAN 14   50 6
    OF THE LAST AXIOM HE ADVISED HIS SPOUSE . . . . 439 3 DON JUAN 14   67 2
    WHICH LAST I LEAVE UNTO THE LORD'S SPIRITUAL   . . . . . 472 3 DON JUAN 15   36 V8
    TO NOVEL POWER AND AS SHE WAS THE LAST   . . . . 476 3 DON JUAN 15   46 7
    AURORA AT THE LAST (SO HISTORY MENTIONS . . . . 491 3 DON JUAN 15   80 5
    THE LAST THIN PETTICOATS WERE VANISHED GONE . . . . . . 504 3 DON JUAN 16   8 5
    IS LIKE THE LAST GLASS OF CHAMPAGNE WITHOUT . . . . . . 504 3 DON JUAN 16   9 2
    THE LAST TIME--I PRAY SAID ADELINE-- . . . . 516 3 DON JUAN 16   37 1
    AND PROMISES TO ALL--WHICH LAST COMMENCED   . . . . . . 535 3 DON JUAN 16   71 4
    HAD MADE MORE PROGRESS THAN FOR THE LAST CENTURY . . . . 536 3 DON JUAN 16   73 4
    ALL THIS (SAVE THE LAST STANZA) HENRY SAID . . . . . . 538 3 DON JUAN 16   77 1
    EARLIEST TO RISE AND LAST TO QUIT THE SEARCH   . . . . . 539 3 DON JUAN 16   80 4
    HAD FALLEN LAST MARKET COST HIS HOST THREE VOTES . . . . 543 3 DON JUAN 16   89 8
    BY LAST NIGHT'S GHOST BEEN DRIVEN FROM THEIR DEFENCES . . 545 3 DON JUAN 16   93 8
    AND FAMILIES EVEN TO THE LAST RELATION . . . . 550 3 DON JUAN 16   103 6
    THE LAST IS APT THE FORMER TO ACCUSE . . . . 564 3 DON JUAN 17   6 4
    THE GUESTS DROPPED IN--THE LAST BUT ONE HER GRACE . . . . 568 3 DON JUAN 17   13 7
LASTED
    IT LASTED 'TWAS LIKE A SHORT GLIMPSE OF HELL   . . . . . 489 2 DON JUAN 5   135 3
LASTING
    INSTEAD OF SPEECH MAY FORM A LASTING LINK   . . . . . . 327 2 DON JUAN 3   88 5
    BUT STRONG AND LASTING TILL NO TONGUE CAN TELL . . . . . 444 2 DON JUAN 5   59 4
    I KNEW THAT NOUGHT WAS LASTING BUT NOW EVEN . . . . . . 309 3 DON JUAN 11   82 5
LAST'S
    THE LAST'S A MIRACLE AND SUCH WAS RECKONED . . . . . . 365 3 DON JUAN 13   13 7
LATE
    THY LATE REVIVING ROMAN SOUL DESPONDS . . . . 19 2 DON JUAN D   16 3
    LIKE THE LAMENTED LATE SIR SAMUEL ROMILLY   . . . . . . 29 2 DON JUAN 1   15 4
    ARE MASKS IT OFTEN WEARS AND STILL TOO LATE . . . . . . 61 2 DON JUAN 1   73 8
    EVEN SEVEN YEARS HENCE IT WOULD NOT BE TOO LATE   . . . . 67 2 DON JUAN 1   85 4
    UNTIL TOO LATE FOR USEFUL CONVERSATION   . . . . 84 2 DON JUAN 1   117 2
    WHAT WONDROUS NEW MACHINES HAVE LATE BEEN SPINNING   . . . 92 2 DON JUAN 1   130 6
    I SAID THE SMALL-POX HAS GONE OUT OF LATE   . . . . . . 92 2 DON JUAN 1   130 7
    RELUCTANTLY STILL TARRYING THERE AS LATE AS . . . . . . 111 2 DON JUAN 1   164 3
    SOME STRANGE EXCUSES FOR HIS LATE PROCEEDING   . . . . . 116 2 DON JUAN 1   174 2
    THE ONLY MISCHIEF WAS IT CAME TOO LATE   . . . . 122 2 DON JUAN 1   183 2
    THE WIND BLEW FRESH AGAIN AS IT GREW LATE   . . . . . . 172 2 DON JUAN 2   30 5
    'TIS NEVER TOO LATE TO BE WHOLLY WRECK'D . . . . 176 2 DON JUAN 2   39 6
    HE HAD BEEN RATHER INDISPOSED OF LATE . . . . 199 2 DON JUAN 2   81 5
    'TIS AS THE SNAKE LATE COIL'D WHO POURS HIS LENGTH   . . . 218 2 DON JUAN 2   117 7
    I'VE SEEN HIM RISE INDEED OFT INDEED OF LATE   . . . . . 230 2 DON JUAN 2   140 2
    IS USED UNTIL THE TRUTH ARRIVES TOO LATE-- . . . . . . 278 2 DON JUAN 3   6 4
    AND SHOW THAT LATE HOURS WINE AND LOVE ARE ABLE   . . . . 309 2 DON JUAN 3   66 7
    UNTIL HIS LATE LIFE BY ARCHDEACON COXE   . . . . 328 2 DON JUAN 3   90 8
    WHERE LATE HE TROD HER BEAUTIFUL HER OWN . . . . 375 2 DON JUAN 4   58 4
    FOR SOON ARE LOVE IS HIS OWN AVENGER . . . . 383 2 DON JUAN 4   73 8
    THE LAST IF LATE ACCOUNTS BE ACCURATE . . . . 406 2 DON JUAN 4   112 2
    BUT THAT OF LATE YOUR SCRIBBLERS THINK IT WORTH   . . . . 434 2 DON JUAN 5   42 6

433

PAGE VOL   CANTO STANZA LV

LATE   (CONTINUED)

	PAGE	VOL	CANTO	STANZA	LV
THE MOMENT TILL TOO LATE TO COME AGAIN	6	3 DON JUAN	6	1	5
ARE TRUE AS TRUTH HAS EVER BEEN OF LATE	48	3 DON JUAN	6	85	8
FOR FEAR OF ANY ERROR LIKE THE LATE	62	3 DON JUAN	6	112	8
WHEN IT GREW RATHER LATE TO SET THINGS RIGHT	73	3 DON JUAN	7	13	5
OUT OF THOSE NINETEEN WHO LATE RHYMED TO PITH	79	3 DON JUAN	7	25	6
FELL IN WITH WHAT WAS LATE THE SECOND COLUMN	130	3 DON JUAN	8	34	2
BY GOD WE'LL BE TOO LATE FOR THE FIRST CUT	162	3 DON JUAN	8	101	8
HE FOUGHT BUT HAS NOT FED SO WELL OF LATE	185	3 DON JUAN	9	6	5
DON JUAN WHO HAD SHONE IN THE LATE SLAUGHTER	197	3 DON JUAN	9	29	1
HIS JOURNEY WE'VE SO MANY TOURS OF LATE	203	3 DON JUAN	9	42	6
TELL THEM THOUGH IT MAY BE PERHAPS TOO LATE	267	3 DON JUAN	10	87	1
AND JUAN'S SUITE LATE SCATTERED AT A DISTANCE	275	3 DON JUAN	11	14	2
AND OFFERING AS USUAL LATE ASSISTANCE	275	3 DON JUAN	11	14	4
JUAN WHO SAW THE MOON'S LATE MINION BLEED	275	3 DON JUAN	11	14	5
LATE AUTHORS ASKED HIM FOR A HINT OR TWO	294	3 DON JUAN	11	50	6
CONTRIVED TO TALK ABOUT THE GODS OF LATE	298	3 DON JUAN	11	60	4
AN EVOLUTION OFT PERFORMED OF LATE)	308	3 DON JUAN	11	79	5
I HAVE SEEN THAT SAD AFFAIR OF THE LATE QUEEN--	310	3 DON JUAN	11	84	4
LOVE LINGERS STILL ALTHOUGH 'TWERE LATE TO WIVE	316	3 DON JUAN	12	2	5
OF LATE THE PENALTY OF SUCH SUCCESS	324	3 DON JUAN	12	17	7
WHOSE LOSS IN THE LATE ACTION WE REGRET	383	3 DON JUAN	13	54	7
BUT READER THOU HAST PATIENT BEEN OF LATE	393	3 DON JUAN	13	74	1
HER LATE PERFORMANCE HAD BEEN A DEAD SET	428	3 DON JUAN	14	42	7
BUT WHETHER ENGLISH DUKES GREW RARE OF LATE	474	3 DON JUAN	15	42	4
AS USUAL--THE SAME REASON WHICH SHE LATE DID	478	3 DON JUAN	15	50	8
AND ADDS A THIRD TO WHAT WAS LATE A PAIR	481	3 DON JUAN	15	59	V8
AS CONGRESSES OF LATE DO) OF THE LADY	482	3 DON JUAN	15	61	2
I THINK TOO THAT I HAVE SATE UP TOO LATE	499	3 DON JUAN	15	97	8
THEN ASKED HER GRACE WHAT NEWS WERE OF THE DUKE OF LATE	515	3 DON JUAN	16	34	5
BROKE IN UPON BY THE BLACK FRIAR OF LATE	515	3 DON JUAN	16	35	4
THE FRIAR OF LATE HAS NOT BEEN OFT PERCEIVED	516	3 DON JUAN	16	36	8
SOME WONDERING 'TWAS SO EARLY SOME SO LATE	527	3 DON JUAN	16	55	4
BUT I'M TOO LATE AND THEREFORE MUST MAKE PLAY	538	3 DON JUAN	16	78	1
A BEGGAR AND A QUEEN OR WAS (OF LATE	541	3 DON JUAN	16	84	2
OF LATE YEARS TO DISPENSE WITH COCKER'S RIGOURS	547	3 DON JUAN	16	98	7
WHICH TURNED UPON THEIR LATE GUESTS' MIENS AND FACES	550	3 DON JUAN	16	103	5
AND WITCHES UNTO NONE THOUGH SOMEWHAT LATE	565	3 DON JUAN	17	7	2

LATELY

	PAGE	VOL	CANTO	STANZA	LV
LAST--YOURS HAS LATELY BEEN A COMMON CASE--	9	2 DON JUAN	D	1	4
AND COLERIDGE TOO HAS LATELY TAKEN WING	10	2 DON JUAN	D	2	5
WHICH TIME HAD LATELY RENDER'D MUCH MORE CHASTE	58	2 DON JUAN	1	67	2
A SIGHT ON WHICH HE HAD NOT LATELY GAZED	239	2 DON JUAN	2	157	3
'TWAS FRESH--FOR HE HAD LATELY USED THE LOCK--	365	2 DON JUAN	4	40	7
AND TAKING LATELY BY SUWARROW'S BIDDING	418	2 DON JUAN	5	15	7
HAVE NOT BEEN TROUBLED WITH THEM LATELY NOW	419	2 DON JUAN	5	16	2
AND WRITTEN LATELY TWO MEMOIRS UPON'T)	447	2 DON JUAN	5	62	6
HIS LATELY BOWSTRUNG BROTHER CAUSED HIS RISE	495	2 DON JUAN	5	147	4
HAD MADE HIM LATELY BASK IN HIS BRIDE'S BEAUTY	51	3 DON JUAN	6	91	8
SINCE JOHN HAS LATELY LOST THE USE OF BOTH	88	3 DON JUAN	7	45	4
I ALMOST LATELY HAVE BEGUN TO DOUBT	124	3 DON JUAN	8	26	1
SLIDING KNEE-DEEP IN LATELY FROZEN MUD	148	3 DON JUAN	8	73	7
IN LOPPING OFF YOUR LATELY MARRIED MEN	168	3 DON JUAN	8	113	2
SINCE LATELY THERE HAVE BEEN NO RENTS AT ALL	198	3 DON JUAN	9	32	4
HAS LATELY BEEN THE GREAT PROFESSOR KANT	254	3 DON JUAN	10	60	4
THE TRUTH IS I'VE GROWN LATELY RATHER PHTHISICAL	270	3 DON JUAN	11	5	5
COLUMN DATE FALMOUTH THERE HAS LATELY BEEN HERE	383	3 DON JUAN	13	54	5
WHOM FRANCE AND FORTUNE LATELY DEIGN'D TO WAFT HERE	398	3 DON JUAN	13	86	4
IN HIM SOME FEELINGS HE HAD LATELY LOST	553	3 DON JUAN	16	107	6

LATER

	PAGE	VOL	CANTO	STANZA	LV
PERHAPS A LITTLE LATER HER GREAT LORD	51	3 DON JUAN	6	90	2
YAWNING A LITTLE AS THE NIGHT GROWS LATER	303	3 DON JUAN	11	69	8
WITHIN THESE LATEST THOUSAND YEARS OR LATER	361	3 DON JUAN	13	7	4
SO THAT FEW MEMBERS KEPT THE HOUSE UP LATER	367	3 DON JUAN	13	20	8
SOMETIMES A LITTLE LATER I DON'T ERR	378	3 DON JUAN	13	43	2

LATEST

	PAGE	VOL	CANTO	STANZA	LV
JUAN THE LATEST OF HER WHIMS HAD CAUGHT	477	2 DON JUAN	5	114	1
WHEN HE BEHELD HIS LATEST HERO GRACE	169	3 DON JUAN	8	116	5
AND LONG THE LATEST OF ARRIVALS HALTS	302	3 DON JUAN	11	68	6
WITHIN THESE LATEST THOUSAND YEARS OR LATER	361	3 DON JUAN	13	7	4
AN ORATOR THE LATEST OF THE SESSION	400	3 DON JUAN	13	90	2
THE LATEST JUAN WITH HIS VIRGIN FACE	568	3 DON JUAN	17	13	8

LATIN

	PAGE	VOL	CANTO	STANZA	LV
SHE KNEW THE LATIN--THAT IS THE LORD'S PRAYER	28	2 DON JUAN	1	13	1
BUT TURKISH FORCE AND LATIN FRAUD	325	2 DON JUAN	3	L 14	5

LATITUDE

	PAGE	VOL	CANTO	STANZA	LV
THE HEATHEN ALSO THOUGH WITH LESSER LATITUDE	11	3 DON JUAN	6	11	2

LATTER

	PAGE	VOL	CANTO	STANZA	LV
AND ALL MISTOOK ABOUT THE LATTER ONCE	207	2 DON JUAN	2	96	8
AS ALL HIS LATTER MEALS HAD BEEN QUITE RAW	239	2 DON JUAN	2	157	4
THE GLITTERING LIME-TWIGS OF OUR LATTER DAYS	422	2 DON JUAN	5	22	7
LET NOT THE LATTER QUALITY OFFEND	52	3 DON JUAN	6	93	V2
AND OTHERS OF THEMSELVES AND LATTER ENDS	94	3 DON JUAN	7	54	8
AND BEING TOLD THE LATTER SENT A BEY	171	3 DON JUAN	8	120	7
WITH HER THE LATTER THOUGH AT TIMES CONVENIENT	214	3 DON JUAN	9	63	1
'TIS ALSO OF SOME MOMENT TO THE LATTER	292	3 DON JUAN	11	46	5
AND PASSED (AT LEAST THE LATTER YEARS OF LIFE)	338	3 DON JUAN	12	47	7
BUT WHEN THE LATTER WORKS ITS OWN UNDOING	446	3 DON JUAN	14	85	7
AND JUAN TOO ESPECIALLY THE LATTER	454	3 DON JUAN	14	99	4

434

LATTER   (CONTINUED)
    OF WHICH PERHAPS THE LATTER IS MOST TRUE 456   3 DON JUAN 15   1   8
    THE LATTER WORSE USED OF THE TWO WE'VE SEEN-- 541   3 DON JUAN 16   84   3
    OF WHICH THE LATTER MERITS EVERY PREFERENCE 541   3 DON JUAN 16   85   4
LATTERLY
    MUST NOT HAVE LATTERLY BEEN QUITE WORN OUT 124   3 DON JUAN 8   26   3
LATTICE
    TO THRUST ITS BLACK EYES THROUGH THE DOOR OR LATTICE . . . 442   2 DON JUAN 5   55   7
    ITS TWINKLE THROUGH THE LATTICE DUSKY QUITE 18   3 DON JUAN 6   24   6
LAUD
    HE DID NOT LOATHE THE SIRE TO LAUD THE SON 15   2 DON JUAN D   10   7
LAUDANUM
    A QUINTESSENTIAL LAUDANUM OR BLACK DROP 216   3 DON JUAN 9   67   5
LAUGH
    AND IF I LAUGH AT ANY MORTAL THING 346   2 DON JUAN 4   4   1
    TO LAUGH AT ALL THINGS--FOR I WISH TO KNOW 67   3 DON JUAN 7   2   7
    BEATING OR BEATEN SHE WILL LAUGH THE SAME)-- 183   3 DON JUAN 9   1   5
    A SINGLE LAUGH DEMOLISHED THE RIGHT ARM 364   3 DON JUAN 13   11   2
    WHAT THEY SHOULD LAUGH AT--THE MERE AGUE STILL 366   3 DON JUAN 13   17   7
    WHAT THEY SHOULD LAUGH AT--THE NOW HOT OR COLD 366   3 DON JUAN 13   17 V7
    SERIOUS YOU LAUGH--YOU MAY THAT WILL I NOT 499   3 DON JUAN 15   96   1
    TO LAUGH HIM OUT OF HIS SUPPOSED DISMAY 526   3 DON JUAN 16   51   6
    TO HAMMER A HOARSE LAUGH FROM THE THICK THRONG 540   3 DON JUAN 16   83   8
LAUGH'D
    A SORT OF THING AT WHICH ONE WOULD HAVE LAUGH'D 183   2 DON JUAN 2   50   3
LAUGHING
    THEN THERE'S THAT LAUGHING SLUT THE PELEGRINI 390   2 DON JUAN 4   84   3
    HER LAUGHING BLUE EYES WITH A GLANCE COULD SEIZE 548   3 DON JUAN 16   100   4
LAUGHS
    DEATH LAUGHS--GO PONDER O'ER THE SKELETON 188   3 DON JUAN 9   11   1
    DEATH LAUGHS AT ALL YOU WEEP FOR--LOOK UPON 188   3 DON JUAN 9   11   5
    MARK HOW IT LAUGHS AND SCORNS AT ALL YOU ARE 188   3 DON JUAN 9   12   1
    IT LAUGHS NOT--THERE IS NOW NO FLESHY BAR 188   3 DON JUAN 9   12   3
    AND THUS DEATH LAUGHS--IT IS SAD MERRIMENT 189   3 DON JUAN 9   13   1
LAUGHTER
    IF ANY LAUGHTER AT SUCH TIMES COULD BE 183   2 DON JUAN 2   50   4
    AND WITH HYAENA LAUGHTER DIED DESPAIRING 198   2 DON JUAN 2   79   8
    LET US HAVE WINE AND WOMAN MIRTH AND LAUGHTER 250   2 DON JUAN 2   178   7
    A MOST UNORIENTAL ROAR OF LAUGHTER 290   2 DON JUAN 3   28   8
    FOR LAUGHTER--BUT SHE FELT HER SPIRITS LOW 47   3 DON JUAN 6   83   6
    SINCE LAUGHTER NOW-A-DAYS IS DEEMED TOO SERIOUS 358   3 DON JUAN 13   1   2
    BUT THE CLUBS FOUND IT RATHER SERIOUS LAUGHTER 398   3 DON JUAN 13   86   6
    FOR LAUGHTER RARELY SHAKES THESE AGUISH FOLKS 540   3 DON JUAN 16   83 V3
    A WISE MAN MORE THAN LAUGHTER FROM A DUNCE-- 542   3 DON JUAN 16   98   5
LAUNCHED
    LAUNCHED AT THEIR HEADS--JOG--JOG--JOG--JOG--JOG--JOG . . 260   3 DON JUAN 10   71 V8
LAURA
    THINK YOU IF LAURA HAD BEEN PETRARCH'S WIFE 279   2 DON JUAN 3   8   7
LAUREAT
    WOULD HE SUBSIDE INTO A HACKNEY LAUREAT 15   2 DON JUAN D   11 V7
LAUREATE
    MEANTIME--SIR LAUREATE--I PROCEED TO DEDICATE 20   2 DON JUAN D   17   1
    THERE WAS NO DOUBT HE EARN'D HIS LAUREATE PENSION . . . 317   2 DON JUAN 3   80   8
LAUREATE'S
    WHOM HE FORSOOK TO FILL THE LAUREATE'S STY 231   3 DON JUAN 10   13   4
    A LAUREATE'S ODE OR SERVILE PEER'S CONTENT 435   3 DON JUAN 14   58   8
LAUREL
    MY EPICAL PRETENSIONS TO THE LAUREL 141   2 DON JUAN 1   209   6
    OH GLORIOUS LAUREL SINCE FOR ONE SOLE LEAF 101   3 DON JUAN 7   68   6
LAUREL-BROWED
    OF SUNSET HALOS O'ER THE LAUREL-BROWED 373   3 DON JUAN 13   33   7
    WHICH KINDLES SUNLIKE O'ER THE LAUREL-BROWED 373   3 DON JUAN 13   33 V7
LAURELS
    HE THAT RESERVES HIS LAURELS FOR POSTERITY 14   2 DON JUAN D   9   1
    TO WHOM THE LYRE AND LAURELS HAVE BEEN GIVEN 77   2 DON JUAN 1   104   6
    'TIS SWEET TO WIN NO MATTER HOW ONE'S LAURELS 90   2 DON JUAN 1   126   1
    HE MUST HIS LAURELS SEPARATELY EARN 120   3 DON JUAN 8   17   3
    FAR SWEETER THAN THE GREENEST LAURELS SPRUNG 199   3 DON JUAN 9   34   4
    WITH ALL HIS LAURELS GROWING UPON ONE TREE 401   3 DON JUAN 13   91 V7
LAVA
    AND THE BLOOD'S LAVA AND THE PULSE A BLAZE 254   2 DON JUAN 2   186   6
    BESIDES ITS LAVA WITH ALL SORTS OF SHOT 119   3 DON JUAN 8   16   3
    AS A VOLCANO HOLDS THE LAVA MORE 374   3 DON JUAN 13   36   3
LAVE
    JUAN TO LAVE HIS YOUTHFUL LIMBS WAS WONT 211   2 DON JUAN 2   105   2
    BETWEEN THE BOSPHORUS AS THEY LASH AND LAVE 413   2 DON JUAN 5   5   5
LAVES
    MY OWN THE BURNING TEAR-DROP LAVES 326   2 DON JUAN 3 L 15   5
LAVEST
    ARE OR WOULD BE THOU SEA WHICH LAVEST LIFE'S SAND . . . 210   3 DON JUAN 9   56 V8
LAVISH
    OF WHICH WE ARE LAVISH FIRST AND THEN RAPACIOUS 145   2 DON JUAN 1   217 V8
    OF LAVISH PEARLS WHOSE WORTH COULD SCARCE BE TOLD . . . 312   2 DON JUAN 3   72   6
LAVISHED
    AND HUMAN LIVES ARE LAVISHED EVERYWHERE 155   3 DON JUAN 8   88   2
LAW
    PRODUCED HER DON MORE HEIRS AT LOVE THAN LAW 53   2 DON JUAN 1   58   8
    IF THERE BE LAW OR LAWYERS IN ALL SPAIN 100   2 DON JUAN 1   145   8
    'TWAS A FINE CAUSE FOR THOSE IN LAW DELIGHTING 150   2 DON JUAN 1   V 1   1

	PAGE	VOL		CANTO	STANZA	LN

LAW (CONTINUED)

	PAGE	VOL		CANTO	STANZA	LN
WHICH LAW AFFORDS TO MANY A DIRTY DEED	151	2	DON JUAN	1	V 2	4
THERSITES OF THE HOUSE PAROLLES OF LAW	153	2	DON JUAN	1	V 4	7
A STRANGE EXAMPLE OF THE FORCE OF LAW	155	2	DON JUAN	1	V 7	1
THE LAW OF ALL AROUND HER TO FULFIL	475	2	DON JUAN	5	112	2
WITH US THERE IS MORE LAW GIVEN TO THE CHASE	482	2	DON JUAN	5	123	4
THE LOVE OF OFFSPRING'S NATURE'S GENERAL LAW	488	2	DON JUAN	5	133	1
TO THE TRUE LAW OF NATIONS WHICH NE'ER MEANT	498	2	DON JUAN	5	151	3
MUST MAKE A PRESENT TO HIS SIRE IN LAW	498	2	DON JUAN	5	152	8
IN THAT TO WHICH THE LAW MAKES THEM SOLE HEIRS	11	3	DON JUAN	6	10	8
O'ER KINGS WHO NOW AT LEAST MUST TALK OF LAW	261	3	DON JUAN	10	74	6
THE LAW AT LEAST UNTIL THE BENCH REVERT TO TRUE	314	3	DON JUAN	11	V 76	6
AND WHEN THE DELICACIES OF THE LAW	352	3	DON JUAN	12	78	3
IN LAW THAN EQUITY--AS I CAN FEEL--	357	3	DON JUAN	12	V 18	4
TO SEE MEN LET THESE SCOUNDREL SOVEREIGNS BREAK LAW	497	3	DON JUAN	15	92	8
BUT THAT WITH THEM ALL LAW WOULD BE DEMOLISHED	535	3	DON JUAN	16	72	8
BUT NOT TO GO TOO FAR I HOLD IT LAW	563	3	DON JUAN	17	2	4

LAWFUL

	PAGE	VOL		CANTO	STANZA	LN
LEST THEIR TOO LAWFUL BED-FELLOW SHOULD WAKE	18	3	DON JUAN	6	24	8
OH THOU HER LAWFUL GRANDSON ALEXANDER	52	3	DON JUAN	6	93	V1
OF WHICH YOUR LAWFUL AWFUL WEDLOCK FOUNT IS--	312	3	DON JUAN	11	89	6
BY NO QUITE LAWFUL MARRIAGE OF THE ARTS	390	3	DON JUAN	13	67	2

LAW'S

	PAGE	VOL		CANTO	STANZA	LN
THE LAW'S EXPOUNDER AND THE STATE'S CORRECTOR	29	2	DON JUAN	1	15	5

LAWS

	PAGE	VOL		CANTO	STANZA	LN
FROM COUNSEL LEARNED IN THOSE KINDS OF LAWS	38	2	DON JUAN	1	33	3
KNOWING THEY MUST BE SETTLED BY THE LAWS	109	2	DON JUAN	1	159	8
FORBID BY HEAVENLY FINED BY HUMAN LAWS	113	2	DON JUAN	1	167	3
YIELD TO STERN TIME AND NATURE'S WRINKLING LAWS	219	2	DON JUAN	2	119	6
ACCORDING TO THE ANCIENT EPIC LAWS	503	2	DON JUAN	5	159	3
WITH ALL THEIR CHASTE INTEGRITY OF LAWS	35	3	DON JUAN	6	58	5
DEFENCE OF FREEDOM COUNTRY OR OF LAWS	86	3	DON JUAN	7	40	4
WITH HIS AGRARIAN LAWS THE HIGH ESTATE	237	3	DON JUAN	10	25	3
HERE LAWS ARE ALL INVIOLATE NONE LAY	273	3	DON JUAN	11	10	5
BY ALL THE LAWS THE STRICTEST LAWYER PLEADS	352	3	DON JUAN	12	80	6
HIS PREPOSSESSIONS LIKE THE LAWS OF PERSIANS	366	3	DON JUAN	13	17	3
HE BROKE 'TIS TRUE SOME STATUTES OF THE LAWS	424	3	DON JUAN	14	33	5
DOORS THERE WERE MANY THROUGH WHICH BY THE LAWS	511	3	DON JUAN	16	24	5

LAW-SUIT

	PAGE	VOL		CANTO	STANZA	LN
FOR 'TIS A LOW NEWSPAPER HUMDRUM LAW-SUIT	346	3	DON JUAN	12	65	1
ALSO A LAWSUIT UPON TENURES BURGAGE	530	3	DON JUAN	16	60	3

LAW-SUITS

	PAGE	VOL		CANTO	STANZA	LN
WHERE LIVES NOT LAW-SUITS MUST BE RISKED FOR PASSION	347	3	DON JUAN	12	68	2

LAWYER

	PAGE	VOL		CANTO	STANZA	LN
LAWYER BY TRADE--AND ORATOR BY CHANCE	152	2	DON JUAN	1	V 3	V5
A DISAPPOINTED LAWYER AT FULL LENGTH	155	2	DON JUAN	1	V 6	8
THE STATESMAN HERO HARLOT LAWYER--WARD	123	3	DON JUAN	8	25	5
THE LAWYER AND THE CRITIC BUT BEHOLD	232	3	DON JUAN	10	14	1
BY ALL THE LAWS THE STRICTEST LAWYER PLEADS	352	3	DON JUAN	12	80	6

LAWYER'S

	PAGE	VOL		CANTO	STANZA	LN
THE LAWYER'S BRIEF IS LIKE THE SURGEON'S KNIFE	232	3	DON JUAN	10	14	6

LAWYERS

	PAGE	VOL		CANTO	STANZA	LN
AND WHAT THE LAWYERS CALL A MALUS ANIMUS	37	2	DON JUAN	1	30	5
THE LAWYERS DID THEIR UTMOST FOR DIVORCE	38	2	DON JUAN	1	32	6
IF THERE BE LAW OR LAWYERS IN ALL SPAIN	100	2	DON JUAN	1	145	8
HISTORIANS HEROES LAWYERS PRIESTS TO PUT	286	3	DON JUAN	11	37	3
BOTH LAWYERS AND BOTH MEN OF EDUCATION	401	3	DON JUAN	13	92	3
THERE WERE TWO LAWYERS BUSY ON A MORTGAGE	530	3	DON JUAN	16	60	1
THE LAWYERS IN THE STUDY AND IN AIR	533	3	DON JUAN	16	66	3

LAWYERS'

	PAGE	VOL		CANTO	STANZA	LN
THE PUBLIC FEELING AND THE LAWYERS' FEES	39	2	DON JUAN	1	34	2

LAY

	PAGE	VOL		CANTO	STANZA	LN
BUT AH HE DIED AND BURIED WITH HIM LAY	39	2	DON JUAN	1	34	1
WHERE ALL HIS HOUSEHOLD GODS LAY SHIVER'D ROUND HIM	41	2	DON JUAN	1	36	6
NOR GLOWING REVERIE NOR POET'S LAY	73	2	DON JUAN	1	96	3
A BOSOM WHEREON HE HIS HEAD MIGHT LAY	73	2	DON JUAN	1	96	5
SHE LAY HER DARK EYES FLASHING THROUGH THEIR TEARS	108	2	DON JUAN	1	158	2
BUT BEAUTIFUL SHE LAY--HER EYES SHED TEARS	108	2	DON JUAN	1	158	V2
YOUNG SLENDER AND PACK'D EASILY HE LAY	112	2	DON JUAN	1	166	3
AT LAST AS THEY MORE FAINTLY WRESTLING LAY	124	2	DON JUAN	1	186	4
BUT IF YOU DON'T I'LL LAY IT ON BY GOD	140	2	DON JUAN	1	206	8
AS GEOGRAPHERS LAY DOWN A SHOAL IN MAPS	155	2	DON JUAN	1	V 7	8
BUT NOW LAY SICK AND SPEECHLESS ON HIS PILLOW	169	2	DON JUAN	2	25	4
THERE SHE LAY MOTIONLESS AND SEEM'D UPSET	172	2	DON JUAN	2	31	1
THE MAINMAST FOLLOW'D BUT THE SHIP STILL LAY	173	2	DON JUAN	2	32	3
THEY WON'T LAY OUT THEIR MONEY ON THE DEAD--	185	2	DON JUAN	2	55	7
THE FIFTH DAY AND THEIR BOAT LAY FLOATING THERE	193	2	DON JUAN	2	70	3
THEY LAY LIKE CARCASSES AND HOPE WAS NONE	194	2	DON JUAN	2	72	3
DEATH LEFT NO DOUBT AND THE DEAD BURTHEN LAY	204	2	DON JUAN	2	90	3
THOUGH RIGHT AHEAD THE ROARING BREAKERS LAY	211	2	DON JUAN	2	104	4
THE BEACH WHICH LAY BEFORE HIM HIGH AND DRY	212	2	DON JUAN	2	106	4
AND THERE HE LAY FULL LENGTH WHERE HE WAS FLUNG	213	2	DON JUAN	2	108	5
HIS SLENDER FRAME AND PALLID ASPECT LAY	214	2	DON JUAN	2	110	7
LAY DROOPING OER THE OAR WHICH SERVED FOR MAST	214	2	DON JUAN	2	110	V5
HOW LONG IN HIS DAMP TRANCE YOUNG JUAN LAY	214	2	DON JUAN	2	111	1
AS FAR AS IN HER LAY TO TAKE HIM IN	224	2	DON JUAN	2	129	7
WERE NEARLY TINDER SINCE SO LONG THEY LAY	226	2	DON JUAN	2	132	5
AS O'ER HIM LAY THE CALM AND STIRLESS AIR	233	2	DON JUAN	2	144	4
FOR STILL HE LAY AND ON HIS THIN·WORN CHEEK	234	2	DON JUAN	2	147	1

LAY   (CONTINUED)

	PAGE	VOL			CANTO	STANZA	LN
OF SUFFERANCE YET UPON HIS FOREHEAD LAY	234	2	DON	JUAN	2	147	4
AND SHE BENT O'ER HIM AND HE LAY BENEATH	235	2	DON	JUAN	2	148	1
AND ALL HER FOOLS WHOM I COULD LAY THE LASH ON	244	2	DON	JUAN	2	166	6
DROOPING AND DEWY ON THE BEACH HE LAY--	249	2	DON	JUAN	2	176	6
LAY AT THIS PERIOD QUIET AS THE SKY	251	2	DON	JUAN	2	181	3
THE VOICELESS SANDS AND DROPPING CAVES THAT LAY	255	2	DON	JUAN	2	188	5
HIS PORT LAY ON THE OTHER SIDE O' THE ISLE	285	2	DON	JUAN	3	19	8
HE LAY COILED LIKE THE BOA IN THE WOOD	300	2	DON	JUAN	3	48	4
HE LAY DARK AS THE SCORPION IN YOUR PATH	300	2	DON	JUAN	3	48	V4
AND SHIPS BY THOUSANDS LAY BELOW	322	2	DON	JUAN	3	L 4	3
THE HEROIC LAY IS TUNELESS NOW--	322	2	DON	JUAN	3	L 5	3
WHO SHALL AWAKE THE HEROIC LAY	322	2	DON	JUAN	3	L 5	V3
AND DRYDEN'S LAY MADE HAUNTED GROUND TO ME	337	2	DON	JUAN	3	105	7
LAY JUAN NOR COULD AUGHT RENEW THE BEAT	362	2	DON	JUAN	4	34	5
WHERE LAY SOME SHIPS WHICH WERE TO SAIL AT NINE	371	2	DON	JUAN	4	50	4
DAYS LAY SHE IN THAT STATE UNCHANGED THOUGH CHILL	377	2	DON	JUAN	4	60	1
WHEN EXQUISITELY CHISELL'D STILL LAY THERE	377	2	DON	JUAN	4	61	2
LAY AT HER HEART WHOSE EARLIEST BEAT STILL TRUE	378	2	DON	JUAN	4	62	6
GENTLE BUT WITHOUT MEMORY SHE LAY	379	2	DON	JUAN	4	64	6
AND LAY THIS SHEAF OF SORROWS ON THE SHELF	384	2	DON	JUAN	4	74	2
THE SHORES OF ILION LAY BENEATH THEIR LEE--	384	2	DON	JUAN	4	75	6
SOME SPEAKERS WHINE AND OTHERS LAY THE LASH ON	437	2	DON	JUAN	5	48	5
IN THIS IMPERIAL HALL AT DISTANCE LAY	466	2	DON	JUAN	5	95	1
IF HEARTS LAY ON THE LEFT SIDE OR THE RIGHT	485	2	DON	JUAN	5	128	5
WHOSE CHARTS LAY DOWN ITS CURRENTS TO A HAIR	7	3	DON	JUAN	6	2	4
FOR RICH MEN AND THEIR BRIDES TO LAY THEIR HEADS	18	3	DON	JUAN	6	25	4
IN THE SERAGLIO WHERE THE LADIES LAY	19	3	DON	JUAN	6	26	6
MANY AND BEAUTIFUL LAY THOSE AROUND	38	3	DON	JUAN	6	65	1
ABOVE HER BROW LAY DREAMING SOFT AND WARM	39	3	DON	JUAN	6	66	3
LAY IN A BREATHLESS HUSHED AND STONY SLEEP	40	3	DON	JUAN	6	68	2
A BLESSING IS SOUND SLEEP--JUANNA LAY	42	3	DON	JUAN	6	73	2
OF THOSE WHO CANNOT LAY ON A NEW TAX	54	3	DON	JUAN	6	96	8
AND ONE HAND O'ER THE OTTOMAN LAY DROOPING	60	3	DON	JUAN	6	109	3
TO ATTACK THE TURK'S FLOTILLA WHICH LAY NIGH	78	3	DON	JUAN	7	24	3
WITHIN A CABLE'S LENGTH THEIR VESSELS LAY	81	3	DON	JUAN	7	29	4
BEGAN TO LAY ABOUT WITH STEEL AND LEAD--	152	3	DON	JUAN	8	81	4
UPON A TAKEN BASTION WHERE THERE LAY	157	3	DON	JUAN	8	91	1
BUT WHAT HE DID WAS TO LAY ON THEIR BACKS	158	3	DON	JUAN	8	93	7
AND LAY BEFORE THEM WITH HIS CHILDREN NEAR	171	3	DON	JUAN	8	119	4
AND CARCASES THAT LAY AS THICK AS THATCH	197	3	DON	JUAN	9	29	4
OF ABSENCE LAY ONE'S OLD RESENTMENTS LEVEL	257	3	DON	JUAN	10	66	7
WHICH SHALL LAY BARE HER BOSOM TO THE SWORD	258	3	DON	JUAN	10	67	4
HERE LAWS ARE ALL INVIOLATE NONE LAY	273	3	DON	JUAN	11	10	5
THUS FAR GO FORTH THOU LAY WHICH I WILL BACK	312	3	DON	JUAN	11	90	2
AN END TO ANSWER OR A PLAN TO LAY--	342	3	DON	JUAN	12	58	6
AND THEREFORE SHALL MY LAY SOAR HIGH AND SOLEMN	358	3	DON	JUAN	13	1	7
BEFORE THE MANSION LAY A LUCID LAKE	385	3	DON	JUAN	13	57	1
BUBBLE AND SQUEAK WOULD SPOIL MY LIQUID LAY	487	3	DON	JUAN	15	71	6
TO TURN CHURCH LANDS TO LAY	518	3	DON	JUAN	16	L 2	2
WHOEVER MAY BE THE LAY	520	3	DON	JUAN	16	L 5	4
OF ADELINE IN BRINGING THIS SAME LAY	526	3	DON	JUAN	16	51	2
GAVE HIM TO LAY THE DEVIL WHO LOOKS O'ER LINCOLN	540	3	DON	JUAN	16	82	7

LAYING

	PAGE	VOL			CANTO	STANZA	LN
BY LAYING WHATE'ER SUM IN MULCT THEY PLEASE ON	57	2	DON	JUAN	1	64	6
AND LAYING DOWN MY PEN I MAKE MY BOW	271	2	DON	JUAN	2	216	6

LAYS

	PAGE	VOL			CANTO	STANZA	LN
BY HIS SEEMING INDEPENDENT IN HIS LAYS	316	2	DON	JUAN	3	79	6
WHICH LAYS BOTH MEN AND WOMEN ON THE SHELF	41	3	DON	JUAN	6	69	7
AND ALSO HEARTS IF THERE BE TRUTH IN LAYS	506	3	DON	JUAN	16	14	8

LAZARET

	PAGE	VOL			CANTO	STANZA	LN
THE LIVER IS THE LAZARET OF BILE	271	2	DON	JUAN	2	215	1

LAZY

	PAGE	VOL			CANTO	STANZA	LN
BEING SOMEWHAT LARGE AND LANGUISHING AND LAZY	26	3	DON	JUAN	6	41	7

LEAD

	PAGE	VOL			CANTO	STANZA	LN
IN SHORT I MUST NOT LEAD THE LIFE I DID DO	144	2	DON	JUAN	1	216	4
CHEWING A PIECE OF BAMBOO AND SOME LEAD	200	2	DON	JUAN	2	82	6
AND THERE WE GO--BUT WHERE FIVE BITS OF LEAD	432	2	DON	JUAN	5	39	2
MIGHT LEAD TO HEAVEN KNOWS WHERE BUT IN THIS ONE	449	2	DON	JUAN	5	65	3
THAT THIS DISGUISE' MAY LEAD TO NO MISTAKE	459	2	DON	JUAN	5	82	8
LIKE MOLTEN LEAD AS IF YOU THRUST A PIKE IN	479	2	DON	JUAN	5	118	6
OR AS A LITTLE DOG WILL LEAD THE BLIND	90	3	DON	JUAN	7	48	5
STRIPT TO HIS SHIRT WAS COME TO LEAD THE VAN	90	3	DON	JUAN	7	49	8
IN WAR THAN LOVE HE HAD BETTER LEAD THE ASSAULT	98	3	DON	JUAN	7	62	8
BY SPECIAL PROVIDENCE TO LEAD TO-MORROW	99	3	DON	JUAN	7	63	4
ASHES TO ASHES--WHY NOT LEAD TO LEAD	117	3	DON	JUAN	8	10	8
ASHES TO ASHES--WHY NOT LEAD TO LEAD	117	3	DON	JUAN	8	10	8
BEGAN TO LAY ABOUT WITH STEEL AND LEAD--	152	3	DON	JUAN	8	81	4
THE WAYS THAT LEAD THERE BE THEY NEAR OR FAR	222	3	DON	JUAN	9	80	3
ESPECIALLY WHEN SUCH LEAD TO HIGH PLACES	223	3	DON	JUAN	9	82	8
BESIDES SOME VEINS OF IRON LEAD OR COPPER	254	3	DON	JUAN	10	60	3
GLADLY ALL MATTERS DOWN TO STONE OR LEAD	268	3	DON	JUAN	11	1	6
WHO IN A ROW LIKE TOM COULD LEAD THE VAN	277	3	DON	JUAN	11	19	3
OF LADIES' LUCUBRATIONS SO THEY LEAD	284	3	DON	JUAN	11	34	6
OF RANK ENOUGH TO SET IN STONE OR LEAD	314	3	DON	JUAN	11	V 75	2
COQUETRY OR A WISH TO TAKE THE LEAD	351	3	DON	JUAN	12	77	4
AND IRON TIME ERE LEAD HAD TA'EN THE LEAD	391	3	DON	JUAN	13	70	2
AND IRON TIME ERE LEAD HAD TA'EN THE LEAD	391	3	DON	JUAN	13	70	2
TALL STATELY FORM'D TO LEAD THE COURTLY VAN	440	3	DON	JUAN	14	70	5

LEADEN
    OF BLOOD AND WATER LEADEN CASTLEREAGH . . . . 207 3 DON JUAN 9   50 6
LEADER
    THEIR LEADER SANG--AND BOUNDED TO HER SONG . . . . . . 291 2 DON JUAN 3   30 7
    ARE BOUGHT UP OTHERS BY A WARLIKE LEADER . . . . 425 2 DON JUAN 5   27 5
LEADING
    AND WAS NOT TO BE HELD IN LEADING STRINGS . . . . . . 439 3 DON JUAN 14   66 6
LEADS
    BEING PRIDE WHICH LEADS THE MIND TO SOAR TOO FAR . . . 344 2 DON JUAN 4   1 7
    HE LEADS THEM THROUGH THE HALL AND WITHOUT STOPPING . . 442 2 DON JUAN 5   55 1
    WHICH TAKEN AT THE FLOOD LEADS--GOD KNOWS WHERE . . . .   7 3 DON JUAN 6   2 2
    WHICH LEADS BEHOLDERS ON A BOGGY WALK . . . . 89 3 DON JUAN 7   46 6
    MAKES MEN LIKE CATTLE FOLLOW HIM WHO LEADS . . . . . 132 3 DON JUAN 8   38 8
    THAT LEADS TO LASSITUDE THE MOST INFECTED . . . . . 301 3 DON JUAN 11   65 3
    KNOWING THAT SUCH UNEASY VIRTUE LEADS . . . . 352 3 DON JUAN 12   80 2
    OF PLATONISM WHICH LEADS SO OFT AMISS . . . . 450 3 DON JUAN 14   92 3
    TO SAY LEADS OFT TO CRIM CON WITH THE MARRIED-- . . . 493 3 DON JUAN 15   84 3
LEAF
    OVER THE MYSTIC LEAF HIS SOUL WAS SHOOK . . . . . . 72 2 DON JUAN 1   95 5
    FROM LEAF TO LEAF 'TIS SWEET TO VIEW ON HIGH . . . . 87 2 DON JUAN 1   122 7
    FROM LEAF TO LEAF 'TIS SWEET TO VIEW ON HIGH . . . . 87 2 DON JUAN 1   122 7
    LEAF AND IMAGINATION DROOPS HER PINION . . . . . . 345 2 DON JUAN 4   3 6
    OH GLORIOUS LAUREL SINCE FOR ONE SOLE LEAF . . . . 101 3 DON JUAN 7   68 6
    I TOUCH A SINGLE LEAF WHERE HE IS WARDEN-- . . . . 442 3 DON JUAN 14   75 6
LEAFY
    HIMSELF AT LENGTH WITHIN THE LEAFY NOOKS . . . . . . 70 2 DON JUAN 1   90 3
LEAGUED
    WHICH NOW IS LEAGUED YOUNG FREEDOM TO ANNOY . . . . 106 3 DON JUAN 7   79 7
LEAGUERED
    ALONG THE LEAGUERED WALL AND BRISTLING BANK . . . . 110 3 DON JUAN 7   86 4
LEAK
    BUT THEY COULD NOT COME AT THE LEAK AS YET . . . . 171 2 DON JUAN 2   28 4
    AND THEN THE LEAK THEY RECKON'D TO REDUCE . . . . 172 2 DON JUAN 2   30 2
    THE LEAK INCREASED SHOALS ROUND HER BUT NO SHORE . 176 2 DON JUAN 2   38 3
    BUT WITH A LEAK AND NOT A STICK OF MAST . . . . . 176 2 DON JUAN 2   39 3
    AS WATER THROUGH AN UNEXPECTED LEAK . . . . 490 2 DON JUAN 5   137 6
    ROUSED BY REPULSE--THROUGH A TOLERABLE LEAK . . . 490 2 DON JUAN 5   137 V6
LEAN
    AND ALL MAY THINK WHICH WAY THEIR JUDGMENTS LEAN 'EM . . 28 2 DON JUAN 1   14 6
    OR DO THEY BENEFIT MANKIND LEAN MISER . . . . . . 321 3 DON JUAN 12   11 7
    TO LEAN ON FOR SUPPORT IN ANY WAY . . . . 324 3 DON JUAN 12   18 6
    BRONZED O'ER SOME LEAN AND STOIC ANCHORITE-- . . . 392 3 DON JUAN 13   72 4
LEAN'D
    UNCONSCIOUSLY SHE LEAN'D UPON THE OTHER . . . . . . 80 2 DON JUAN 1   110 1
    WHO DIE IN RIGHTEOUSNESS SHE LEAN'D AND THERE . . . 233 2 DON JUAN 2   144 2
LEANDER
    LEANDER MR EKENHEAD AND I DID . . . . 211 2 DON JUAN 2   105 8
LEANING
    ALFONSO LEANING BREATHLESS BY THE DOOR . . . . . . 125 2 DON JUAN 1   187 4
    HIS CAUSE BY LEANING MUCH FROM MIGHT TO RIGHT . . . 391 3 DON JUAN 13   69 4
    WHICH HATH A LITTLE LEANING TO A LOTTERY . . . . . 397 3 DON JUAN 13   82 2
    THE SAME SELF-INTEREST WITH A DIFFERENT LEANING) . . 535 3 DON JUAN 16   70 8
LEANS
    OF ALL THE PILLARS OF THE STATE WHICH LEANS . . . . 54 3 DON JUAN 6   96 6
LEANT
    WITH RHYME BUT ALWAYS LEANT LESS TO IMPROVING . . . 219 3 DON JUAN 9   74 6
    A LAMP BURNED HIGH WHILE HE LEANT FROM A NICHE . . . 507 3 DON JUAN 16   16 5
LEAP
    AND DOLPHIN'S LEAP AND LITTLE BILLOW CROST . . . . 251 2 DON JUAN 2   181 6
    ALL THOSE MAY LEAP WHO RATHER WOULD BE NEUTER-- . . 266 2 DON JUAN 2   205 5
    THOUGH SHE WAS FAR FROM THAT LEAP YEAR WHOSE LEAP . 433 3 DON JUAN 14   52 7
    THOUGH SHE WAS FAR FROM THAT LEAP YEAR WHOSE LEAP . 433 3 DON JUAN 14   52 7
LEAP'D
    THEN SOME LEAP'D OVERBOARD WITH DREADFUL YELL . . . 184 2 DON JUAN 2   52 3
    OFF THREW HIM IN THEN AFTER HIM HE LEAP'D . . . . . 187 2 DON JUAN 2   58 8
LEAPING
    'TIS THEREFORE BETTER LOOKING BEFORE LEAPING-- . . . 436 2 DON JUAN 5   45 6
LEAPS
    BUT LEAPS AND BURSTS AND SOMETIMES FOX'S BRUSHES . . 425 3 DON JUAN 14   35 2
LEARN
    HIM UP TO LEARN HIS CATECHISM ALONE . . . . 50 2 DON JUAN 1   52 6
    FOR HE WOULD LEARN THE RUDIMENTS OF LOVE . . . . . 67 2 DON JUAN 1   85 7
    WHICH SOME ARE BORN WITH BUT THE MOST PART LEARN . . 71 2 DON JUAN 1   93 3
    SO THAT CIVILISATION THEY MAY LEARN . . . . 92 2 DON JUAN 1   131 6
    FIRST PARTINGS FORM A LESSON HARD TO LEARN . . . . 164 2 DON JUAN 2   14 3
    REJECTED SEVERAL SUITORS JUST TO LEARN . . . . . . 224 2 DON JUAN 2   128 7
    WE LEARN FROM HORACE HOMER SOMETIMES SLEEPS . . . . 333 2 DON JUAN 3   98 1
    IS THAT WHICH I WOULD LEARN -- I SERVED FOR SOME . . 418 2 DON JUAN 5   15 5
    AND I SHALL BE DELIGHTED TO LEARN WHO . . . . . . 184 3 DON JUAN 9   4 7
    AS FROM MY GREAT GREAT HUMOUR YOU MAY LEARN . . . . 300 3 DON JUAN 11   63 V5
    AND FOR YOUR CONSCIENCE ONLY LEARN TO NERVE IT-- . . 366 3 DON JUAN 13   18 6
    BEFORE YOU LEARN TO CALL THIS SUPERSTITION . . . . 500 3 DON JUAN 15   98 8
LEARN'D
    WHERE OUR FIRST PARENTS NEVER LEARN'D TO KISS . . . . 30 2 DON JUAN 1   18 3
    WITH NO GREAT LOVE FOR LEARNING OR THE LEARN'D . . . 31 2 DON JUAN 1   19 2
    HE LEARN'D THE ARTS OF RIDING FENCING GUNNERY . . . 42 2 DON JUAN 1   38 7
    OF RHETORIC WHICH THE LEARN'D CALL RIGMAROLE . . . 116 2 DON JUAN 1   174 8
    (OR WAS BEFORE PERU LEARN'D TO REBEL) . . . . . . 159 2 DON JUAN 2   5 4
    THUS JUAN LEARN'D HIS ALPHA BETA BETTER . . . . . 242 2 DON JUAN 2   163 7

LEARN'D   (CONTINUED)
```
    I LEARN'D THE LITTLE THAT I KNOW BY THIS  . . . . . . . 242   2 DON JUAN  2     164    8
    LEARN'D PIOUS TEMPERATE IN LOVE AND WINE  . . . . . . . 328   2 DON JUAN  3      91    4
    WHICH LEARN'D FROM THIS EXAMPLE NOT TO FLY  . . . . . . 337   2 DON JUAN  3     106    7
    BUT WHETHER REVEREND RAPP LEARN'D THIS IN GERMANY  . . . 472  3 DON JUAN 15      36    3
LEARNED
    HIS MOTHER WAS A LEARNED LADY FAMED  . . . . . . . . .  26   2 DON JUAN  1      10    1
    'TIS PITY LEARNED VIRGINS EVER WED  . . . . . . . . .   33   2 DON JUAN  1      22    1
    FROM COUNSEL LEARNED IN THOSE KINDS OF LAWS  . . . . .  38   2 DON JUAN  1      33    3
    THE LEARNED TUTORS WHOM FOR HIM SHE HIRED  . . . . . .  43   2 DON JUAN  1      39    3
    EXPURGATED BY LEARNED MEN WHO PLACE  . . . . . . . . .  46   2 DON JUAN  1      44    2
    AND I YE LEARNED LADIES SAY OF YOU  . . . . . . . . .  404   2 DON JUAN  4     110    3
    STILL I HAVE NO DISLIKE TO LEARNED NATURES  . . . . .  405   2 DON JUAN  4     111    5
    BESTOWED UPON HIM AS THE PUBLIC LEARNED  . . . . . . . 287   3 DON JUAN 11      39    7
    EXAMINED BY THIS LEARNED AND ESPECIAL  . . . . . . . . 294   3 DON JUAN 11      51    3
    WHICH LENT HIS LEARNED LUCUBRATIONS PITH  . . . . . .  294   3 DON JUAN 11      52    3
    BUT HAVE NOT LEARNED TO WISH IT ANY LESS  . . . . . .  324   3 DON JUAN 12      17    8
LEARNEDLY
    OTHERS TALKED LEARNEDLY OF CERTAIN TUMOURS  . . . . .  244   3 DON JUAN 10      40    3
LEARNEST
    (SUCH EARLY TRAVELLER IS THE TRUTH THOU LEARNEST)--  .  345   3 DON JUAN 12      64    6
LEARNING
    WITH NO GREAT LOVE FOR LEARNING OR THE LEARN'D  . . .   31   2 DON JUAN  1      19    2
    LEARNING THAT LANGUAGE CHIEFLY FROM ITS PREACHERS  . .  243   2 DON JUAN  2     165    4
    IS LEARNING TO REDUCE HIS PAST EXPENSES  . . . . . . . 240   3 DON JUAN 10      31    8
    THOSE BRAVURAS (WHICH I STILL AM LEARNING  . . . . . . 350   3 DON JUAN 12      75    6
    PROUD OF HIS LEARNING (JUST ENOUGH TO QUOTE)  . . . .  401   3 DON JUAN 13      91    3
LEARNS
    FOR THERE ONE LEARNS--'TIS NOT FOR ME TO BOAST  . . .   50   2 DON JUAN  1      53    1
LEARNT
    AND HAVING LEARNT TO SWIM IN THAT SWEET RIVER  . . . . 211   2 DON JUAN  2     105    3
    ARE ALSO LEARNT FROM CERES AND FROM BACCHUS  . . . . . 245   2 DON JUAN  2     169    7
    (FOR THEY MUST TALK) AND HE HAD LEARNT TO SAY  . . . . 249   2 DON JUAN  2     176    2
LEAR'S
    HER WISH WAS BUT TO KILL KILL KILL LIKE LEAR'S  . . .  490   2 DON JUAN  5     136    7
LEASE
    OR OF SOME CENTURIES TO TAKE A LEASE  . . . . . . . .  398   2 DON JUAN  4      99    6
    IF TRUE 'TIS NO GREAT LEASE OF ITS OWN FIRE  . . . . .  14   3 DON JUAN  6      16    2
    AND FOUND THEIR LIVES WERE LET AT A SHORT LEASE--  . .  150   3 DON JUAN  8      76    4
LEASES
    AND OF ALL THINGS EXCEPTING TITHES AND LEASES  . . . . 531   3 DON JUAN 16      63    5
LEAST
    'TIS POETRY--AT LEAST BY HIS ASSERTION  . . . . . . .   11   2 DON JUAN  D       4    5
    AT LEAST HER CONVERSATION WAS OBSCURE  . . . . . . . .  28   2 DON JUAN  1      13    6
    A PRIEST THE OTHER--AT LEAST SO THEY SAY  . . . . . .   39   2 DON JUAN  1      34    5
    THE ARTS AT LEAST ALL SUCH AS COULD BE SAID  . . . . .  44   2 DON JUAN  1      40    3
    AND SEEM'D AT LEAST IN THE RIGHT ROAD TO HEAVEN  . . .  48   2 DON JUAN  1      49    6
    AT LEAST IT SEEM'D SO AND HIS MOTHER'S JOY  . . . . .   49   2 DON JUAN  1      50    6
    AT LEAST SHE LEFT IT A MORE SLENDER HANDLE  . . . . .   58   2 DON JUAN  1      67    8
    OF THIS AT LEAST NO SYMPTOM E'ER WAS SHOWN  . . . . .   59   2 DON JUAN  1      68    4
    SHOULD EVER GIVE HER HEART THE LEAST SENSATION  . . .   63   2 DON JUAN  1      77    4
    OR WHICH AT LEAST I NEED NOT MENTION YET  . . . . . .   73   2 DON JUAN  1      96    8
    AND ARE TO BE SO AT THE LEAST ONCE MORE--  . . . . . .  95   2 DON JUAN  1     136    6
    SING AT MY HEART SIX MONTHS AT LEAST IN VAIN  . . . .  102   2 DON JUAN  1     149    2
    AT LEAST PERHAPS HE HAS NOT SIXTY YEARS  . . . . . .   106   2 DON JUAN  1     155    1
    AT LEAST 'TWAS RATHER EARLY TO BEGIN  . . . . . . . .  113   2 DON JUAN  1     167    4
    THERE FOR THE PRESENT AT THE LEAST HE'S FAST  . . . .  115   2 DON JUAN  1     172    6
    THEY BLUSH AND WE BELIEVE THEM AT LEAST I  . . . . .   119   2 DON JUAN  1     179    1
    AT LEAST SINCE THE RETIREMENT OF THE VANDALS  . . . .  128   2 DON JUAN  1     190    4
    (AT LEAST THIS IS THE THING MOST PEOPLE DO)  . . . . . 129   2 DON JUAN  1     191    5
    (THERE'S ONE AT LEAST IS VERY FOND OF THIS)  . . . .   140   2 DON JUAN  1     206    4
    BECAUSE AT LEAST THE PAST WERE PAST AWAY--  . . . . .  156   2 DON JUAN  1    V  8    3
    AT LEAST HAD HE BEEN NURTURED IN THE NORTH  . . . . .  158   2 DON JUAN  2       2    4
    AND MUST HAVE MEALS AT LEAST ONE MEAL A DAY  . . . .   191   2 DON JUAN  2      67    2
    HE SLUMBER'D YET SHE THOUGHT AT LEAST SHE SAID  . . .  228   2 DON JUAN  2     135    5
    AND THOSE WHO ARE NOT DROWNED AT LEAST MAY SLEEP  . .  229   2 DON JUAN  2     137   V8
    AT LEAST IT IS A HEAVY SOUND TO ME  . . . . . . . . .  237   2 DON JUAN  2     152    6
    AS WAS THE CASE AT LEAST WHERE I HAVE BEEN  . . . . .  242   2 DON JUAN  2     164    4
    WHERE WIVES AT LEAST ARE SELDOM KEPT IN GARRISON  . .  248   2 DON JUAN  2     175    8
    AT LEAST IN THE BEGINNING ERE ONE TIRES  . . . . . .   282   2 DON JUAN  3      13    6
    (THE LEAST OF WHICH WOULD SET TEN POETS RAVING)  . . . 291   2 DON JUAN  3      30    6
    PLEASURE (WHENE'ER SHE SINGS AT LEAST) 'S A SIREN  . . 294   2 DON JUAN  3      36    5
    THE WHIP THE RACK OR DUNGEON AT THE LEAST  . . . . .   296   2 DON JUAN  3      40    5
    TO FEEL AT LEAST A PATRIOT'S SHAME  . . . . . . . . .  323   2 DON JUAN  3    L  6    3
    WERE STILL AT LEAST OUR COUNTRYMEN  . . . . . . . . .  324   2 DON JUAN  3    L 11    6
    ERE WHAT WE LEAST WISH TO BEHOLD WILL SLEEP  . . . . . 346   2 DON JUAN  4       4    6
    THE LEAST GLANCE BETTER UNDERSTOOD THAN WORDS  . . . . 351   2 DON JUAN  4      14    2
    KNOWN BUT TO THEM AT LEAST APPEARING SUCH  . . . . .   351   2 DON JUAN  4      14    5
    FOR FEELINGS CAUSELESS OR AT LEAST ABSTRUSE  . . . . . 355   2 DON JUAN  4      22    8
    OR I AT LEAST SHALL NOT SURVIVE TO SEE  . . . . . . .  356   2 DON JUAN  4      23    8
    IN ARMS AT LEAST HE STOOD IN ACT TO SPRING  . . . . .  365   2 DON JUAN  4      39    7
    JUST AT THE VERY TIME WHEN HE LEAST BROODS  . . . . .  371   2 DON JUAN  4      51    5
    FROM THEM AT LEAST THEIR DESTINY HE HEARD  . . . . . . 388   2 DON JUAN  4      80    3
    STILL KEPT HIS SPIRITS UP--AT LEAST HIS FACE  . . . .  388   2 DON JUAN  4      81    4
    AND MADE AT LEAST FIVE HUNDRED GOOD ZECCHINI  . . . .  390   2 DON JUAN  4      84    5
    OR AT LEAST WAS SO ERE IT GREW A FASHION  . . . . . .  402   2 DON JUAN  4     106    8
    KNOWLEDGE AT LEAST IS GAINED FOR INSTANCE NOW  . . . . 422   2 DON JUAN  5      23    6
    AT LEAST SAID JUAN SURE I MAY INQUIRE  . . . . . . .   454   2 DON JUAN  5      74    4
    TWO LITTLE DWARFS THE LEAST YOU COULD SUPPOSE  . . . . 462   2 DON JUAN  5      87    3
```

LEAST   (CONTINUED)

	PAGE	VOL	CANTO		STANZA	LN
OUR SOULS AT LEAST ARE FREE AND 'TIS IN VAIN	474	2	DON JUAN	5	110	6
SHE DEEMED HER LEAST COMMAND MUST YIELD DELIGHT	485	2	DON JUAN	5	128	3
THE TURKS DO WELL TO SHUT--AT LEAST SOMETIMES--	501	2	DON JUAN	5	157	1
AT LEAST WE THINK SO THOUGH BUT FEW HAVE GUESS'D	6	3	DON JUAN	6	1	4
OR AT THE LEAST FORGIVE THE LOVING RASH ONE	8	3	DON JUAN	6	4	4
AND NOT THE LEAST SO WHEN THEY ARE RELIGIOUS	11	3	DON JUAN	6	10	3
IN THE DAMNED LINE ('TIS WORTH AT LEAST A CURSE)	15	3	DON JUAN	6	18	V5
OUR LEAST OF SORROWS ARE SUCH AS WE WEEP	16	3	DON JUAN	6	20	6
AT LEAST ONE OF THEM--OH THE HEAVY NIGHT	18	3	DON JUAN	6	24	2
HER THOUGHTS AT LEAST TILL NOW APPEAR TO HAVE BEEN	33	3	DON JUAN	6	54	4
THE GENDER STILL WAS EPICENE AT LEAST	35	3	DON JUAN	6	58	2
ALL TREMBLING WONDERING WITHOUT THE LEAST NOTION	42	3	DON JUAN	6	71	6
AT LEAST--AND THEN SHE TOO UNCLOSED HER EYES	42	3	DON JUAN	6	73	7
THAT ON A SUDDEN WHEN SHE LEAST HAD HOPE	44	3	DON JUAN	6	77	1
AT LEAST TO DREAM SO LOUDLY AS JUST NOW	47	3	DON JUAN	6	83	2
SHE DID NOT FIND HERSELF THE LEAST DISPOSED	48	3	DON JUAN	6	84	5
AT LEAST AS RED AS THE FLAMINGO'S CREST	48	3	DON JUAN	6	85	V4
AT LEAST TO THOSE OF INCOMES WHICH AFFORD	51	3	DON JUAN	6	90	6
HE DRANK SIX CUPS OF COFFEE AT THE LEAST	52	3	DON JUAN	6	92	4
OR WAS AT LEAST UNLESS 'TIS SINCE DEFACED	71	3	DON JUAN	7	9	5
TO HINT AT LEAST HERE IS NO THOROUGHFARE	72	3	DON JUAN	7	11	8
SINCE THERE IS DISCORD AFTER BOTH AT LEAST)	90	3	DON JUAN	7	49	4
AT LEAST TO FOLLOW THOSE WHO MIGHT BE SO	98	3	DON JUAN	7	61	4
IF NOT IN POETRY AT LEAST IN FACT	107	3	DON JUAN	7	81	1
AT LEAST HE FEELS IT AND SOME SAY HE SEES	109	3	DON JUAN	7	85	1
AT LEAST THE SHARP POINTS OF THAT BURNING MARLE	124	3	DON JUAN	8	26	V7
IN HISTORY BUT WE AT LEAST MAY GRANT	127	3	DON JUAN	8	31	5
AT LEAST TO ALL THOSE WHO WERE LEFT ALIVE	136	3	DON JUAN	8	47	4
OR AT LEAST SUITED NOT THIS VALIANT TARTAR	152	3	DON JUAN	8	80	4
BUT AT THE LEAST YOU MAY DIE GLORIOUSLY--	161	3	DON JUAN	8	100	5
JUAN REPLIED--AT LEAST I WILL ENDURE	161	3	DON JUAN	8	100	6
SUCH AS HE THOUGHT THE LEAST GIVEN UP TO PREY	162	3	DON JUAN	8	102	4
THEY SHOULD AT LEAST HAVE FIFTY ROUBLES ROUND	162	3	DON JUAN	8	102	8
AT LEAST NINE-TENTHS OF WHAT WE CALL SO--GOD	163	3	DON JUAN	8	104	2
AND HELL THERE MUST AT LEAST BE SIX OR SEVEN	168	3	DON JUAN	8	114	8
READER I HAVE KEPT MY WORD--AT LEAST SO FAR	181	3	DON JJAN	8	138	1
AND I WILL WAR AT LEAST IN WORDS (AND--SHOULD	194	3	DON JUAN	9	24	1
MY WORDS AT LEAST ARE MORE SINCERE AND HEARTY	195	3	DON JUAN	9	26	3
OF PEGASUS--OR AT THE LEAST POST CHAISES	197	3	DON JUAN	9	30	7
AT LEAST HE PAYS NO RENT AND HAS BEST RIGHT	198	3	DON JUAN	9	32	1
(FOR THEY THEMSELVES WILL BE BUT OF THE LEAST	202	3	DON JUAN	9	39	4
AT LEAST THREE PARTS OF THIS GREAT WHOLE) SHE TORE	211	3	DON JUAN	9	58	3
BUT AT THE LEAST I HAVE SHUNNED THE COMMON SHORE	227	3	DON JUAN	10	4	3
AT LEAST SOME TWENTY-NINE DO OUT OF THIRTY	232	3	DON JUAN	10	15	6
AND ALL OUR LITTLE FEUDS AT LEAST ALL MINE	232	3	DON JUAN	10	16	1
SHE WAS NO HYPOCRITE AT LEAST POOR SOUL	242	3	DON JUAN	10	35	1
WITHOUT THE LEAST PROPENSITY TO JEER	245	3	DON JUAN	10	42	4
AND LAST NOT LEAST TO STRANGERS UNINSTRUCTED	259	3	DON JUAN	10	69	7
O'ER KINGS WHO NOW AT LEAST MUST TALK OF LAW	261	3	DON JUAN	10	74	6
OUR OLD ACQUAINTANCE AND AT LEAST I'LL TRY	266	3	DON JUAN	10	84	4
THE WORTHIEST KINGS HAVE EVER LOVED LEAST STATE	267	3	DON JUAN	10	87	5
KNOW VERY CLEARLY--AT LEAST LIE STILL	270	3	DON JUAN	11	4	8
LIKE LAP-DOGS THE LEAST CIVIL SONS OF BITCHES	288	3	DON JUAN	11	41	8
BUT I WILL FALL AT LEAST AS FELL MY HERO	296	3	DON JUAN	11	56	5
WHOSE STRAINS--WHATE'ER THEY BE--SURPASS AT LEAST	297	3	DON JUAN	11	57	V7
CAMBYSES' ROARING ROMANS BEAT AT LEAST	297	3	DON JUAN	11	58	7
THE CONQUEROR AT LEAST WHO ERE TIME RENDERS	299	3	DON JUAN	11	61	3
BEING TIRED IN TIME AND NEITHER LEAST NOR LAST	300	3	DON JUAN	11	64	4
THE LAW AT LEAST UNTIL THE BENCH REVERT TO TRUE	314	3	DON JUAN	11	V 76	6
AT LEAST IT RHYMES TO LOVE BUT I'M PREPARED	322	3	DON JUAN	12	13	6
AT LEAST IN A COLD COUNTRY MAY AWARD	322	3	DON JJAN	12	13	V6
OH PARDON ME DIGRESSION--OR AT LEAST	334	3	DON JUAN	12	39	1
AND PASSED (AT LEAST THE LATTER YEARS OF LIFE)	338	3	DON JUAN	12	47	7
OR AT THE LEAST WOULD LENGTHEN OUT MY SONG--	338	3	DON JUAN	12	48	6
AT LEAST ENTIRELY FOR HE HAD SEEN TOO MANY	338	3	DON JUAN	12	49	7
YCLEPT THE GREAT WORLD FOR IT IS THE LEAST	342	3	DON JUAN	12	56	2
AT LEAST THEY THINK SO TO EXERT THEIR STATE	367	3	DON JUAN	13	19	4
BUT ADELINE HAD NOT THE LEAST OCCASION	372	3	DON JUAN	13	31	1
AT LEAST HIS MANNER SUFFERS NOT TO GUESS	373	3	DON JUAN	13	34	6
AT LEAST OF THOSE WHOSE EYES ARE IN THEIR HEARTS	390	3	DON JUAN	13	67	6
IN THIS SORT END AT LEAST WITH THE BEGINNING	393	3	DON JUAN	13	73	8
AND LOWER THE PRICE OF ROUGE--AT LEAST SOME WINTERS	409	3	DON JUAN	13	111	8
TO SWIM OR SINK--I HAVE HAD AT LEAST MY DREAM	415	3	DON JUAN	14	11	8
IF YOU HAVE NOUGHT ELSE HERE'S AT LEAST SATIETY	416	3	DON JUAN	14	14	5
OF CHARACTER IN THOSE AT LEAST WHO HAVE GOT ANY	417	3	DON JUAN	14	16	8
IT PALLS--AT LEAST IT DID SO UPON ME	417	3	DON JUAN	14	17	7
JUAN--IN THIS RESPECT AT LEAST LIKE SAINTS--	424	3	DON JUAN	14	31	1
AT LEAST HE KEPT HIS VANITY RETIRED	428	3	DON JUAN	14	41	4
AT LEAST AS FAR AS BIENSEANCE ALLOWS	439	3	DON JUAN	14	67	4
YET MADE THE MISERY OF AT LEAST TWO LIVES	452	3	DON JUAN	14	95	8
OR MINIATURE AT LEAST AS IS MY NOTION	457	3	DON JUAN	15	2	6
IS THAT WHICH PASSES WITH LEAST CONTRADICTION	457	3	DON JUAN	15	3	8
SINCERE HE WAS--AT LEAST YOU COULD NOT DOUBT IT	461	3	DON JUAN	15	13	5
OF THIS I'M SURE AT LEAST THERE'S NO SERVILITY	465	3	DON JUAN	15	20	5
AT LEAST NINE AND A NINTH BESIDE OF TEN	468	3	DON JUAN	15	26	4
AND WITH AN AIR TO SAY THE LEAST IMPERIOUS	477	3	DON JUAN	15	49	6
AT LEAST FOR THIS I CANNOT SPARE ITS VANITY	482	3	DON JUAN	15	60	4
THOUGH WHY I CANNOT SAY--AT LEAST THIS MINUTE	526	3	DON JUAN	16	51	8

PAGE VOL   CANTO STANZA LN

LEAST   (CONTINUED)
'TIS WHITE AT LEAST WHEN THEY JUST RISE FROM BED . . . . . 532 3 DON JUAN 16   64   4
SINCE HE HAD GAINED AT LEAST HER OBSERVATION . . . . . 545 3 DON JUAN 16   93   5
THE GHOST AT LEAST HAD DONE HIM THIS MUCH GOOD . . . . . 553 3 DON JUAN 16   107   1
LEATHERN
SOME LEATHER CAPS AND WHAT REMAIN'D OF SHOES . . . . . 195 2 DON JUAN 2   74   2
LEATHERS
UNTIL THE CHAINS AND LEATHERS WERE WORN THROUGH . . . . 178 2 DON JUAN 2   42   5
LEAVE
BUT I MUST LEAVE THE PROOFS TO THOSE WHO'VE SEEN 'EM . . . 28 2 DON JUAN 1   14   4
WENT PLUCKING VARIOUS FRUIT WITHOUT HER LEAVE . . . . . 30 2 DON JUAN 1   18   8
WHO CANNOT LEAVE ALONE OUR HELPLESS CLAY . . . . 56 2 DON JUAN 1   63   3
LEAVE TO O'ERSTEP THE WRITTEN RIGHTS OF WOMAN . . . . . 74 2 DON JUAN 1   98   3
NOR LEAVE A WISH WHICH WISDOM MIGHT REPROVE . . . . . . 80 2 DON JUAN 1   109   5
TO LEAVE TOGETHER THIS IMPRUDENT PAIR . . . . 80 2 DON JUAN 1   110   6
TO KEEP THEM BEAUTIFUL OR LEAVE THEM NEAT . . . . 99 2 DON JUAN 1   143   6
I SHUNNED THEM TO LEAVE NO CAUSE FOR CAVIL . . . . . . 102 2 DON JUAN 1   148   V6
I LEAVE YOU TO YOUR CONSCIENCE AS BEFORE . . . . 107 2 DON JUAN 1   157   5
WITH PRAY SIR LEAVE THE ROOM AND SAY NO MORE . . . . . 111 2 DON JUAN 1   163   4
BUT WHY--WE LEAVE THE READER IN THE DARK-- . . . . . . 161 2 DON JUAN 2   8   4
BUT JUAN HAD GOT MANY THINGS TO LEAVE . . . . 164 2 DON JUAN 2   15   1
AND LEAVE LIKE OPENING HELL UPON THE MIND . . . . . . 227 2 DON JUAN 2   134   V7
THE SEA-SHORE AT THIS HOUR MUST LEAVE HIS PLATE . . . . 240 2 DON JUAN 2   159   5
THEY KINDLY LEAVE US THOUGH NOT QUITE ALONE . . . . . 305 2 DON JUAN 3   59   7
LEAVE BATTLES TO THE TURKISH HORDES . . . . 324 2 DON JUAN 3 L 9   3
HERE I MUST LEAVE HIM FOR I GROW PATHETIC . . . . . . 372 2 DON JUAN 4   52   1
FOR TEA AND COFFEE LEAVE US MUCH MORE SERIOUS . . . . . 372 2 DON JUAN 4   52   8
I LEAVE DON JUAN FOR THE PRESENT SAFE-- . . . . 373 2 DON JUAN 4   54   1
THEREFORE I'LL MAKE DON JUAN LEAVE THE SHIP SOON . . . . 397 2 DON JUAN 4   97   5
AND THEREFORE LEAVE THEM TO THE PURER PAGE . . . . . . 397 2 DON JUAN 4   98   2
WILL HARDLY LEAVE YOU (AS SHE'S NOT YOUR WIFE) . . . . . 419 2 DON JUAN 5   17   3
WOULD LEAVE HIS PROPOSITION TO THEIR CHOICE . . . . . . 452 2 DON JUAN 5   70   3
THOSE WHO WILL LEAVE YOU OF NO SEX AT ALL . . . . . . 454 2 DON JUAN 5   75   8
I'D RATHER LEAVE IT MUCH TO YOUR OWN MIND . . . . . . 467 2 DON JUAN 5   97   4
TOOK LEAVE WITH SUCH A FACE OF SATISFACTION . . . . . . 473 2 DON JUAN 5   107   7
THIS I MUST LEAVE SULTANAS TO DECIDE . . . . 477 2 DON JUAN 5   115   4
WE LEAVE THIS ROYAL COUPLE TO REPOSE . . . . 16 3 DON JUAN 6   20   1
THE MATRON TOO WAS WROTH TO LEAVE HER WARM . . . . . . 45 3 DON JUAN 6   79   5
AND IF ONE LADY'S SLIP COULD LEAVE A CRIME ON . . . . . 53 3 DON JUAN 6   94   6
TO PROVE RELUCTANT AND BEGGED LEAVE TO CRAVE . . . . . 62 3 DON JUAN 6   112   5
AND HERE I LEAVE THEM AT THEIR PREPARATION . . . . . . 65 3 DON JUAN 6   119   1
I LEAVE THEM FOR THE PRESENT WITH GOOD WISHES . . . . . 65 3 DON JUAN 6   120   1
ASSUME THEN LEAVE US ON OUR FREEZING WAY . . . . 66 3 DON JUAN 7   1   8
BUT HERE I LEAVE THE GENERAL CONCERN . . . . 120 3 DON JUAN 8   17   1
SAYS HOTSPUR LONG ERE THEY WILL LEAVE THEIR HOME . . . . 132 3 DON JUAN 8   38   4
UPON THIS CHILD--I SAVED HER--MUST NOT LEAVE . . . . . 161 3 DON JUAN 8   99   2
SEEMED TAKING OUT THE STING TO LEAVE THE HONEY . . . . . 217 3 DON JUAN 9   70   8
BUT SOON THEY GROW AGAIN AND LEAVE THEIR NEST . . . . . 228 3 DON JUAN 10   6   1
AND THEREFORE WILL I LEAVE OFF METAPHYSICAL . . . . . . 270 3 DON JUAN 11   5   1
YOU LEAVE BEHIND--THE NEXT OF MUCH YOU COME . . . . . . 290 3 DON JUAN 11   44   5
A HOSPITAL A CHURCH--AND LEAVE BEHIND . . . . 320 3 DON JUAN 12   10   3
THAT--BUT I WILL NOT LISTEN BY YOUR LEAVE . . . . . . 336 3 DON JUAN 12   43   V4
I LEAVE THE SAINTS TO SETTLE THEIR OWN SCORE . . . . . 352 3 DON JUAN 12   79   4
FOR ME I LEAVE THE MATTER WHERE I FIND IT . . . . . . 352 3 DON JUAN 12   80   1
I'LL LEAVE A SINGLE READER'S EYELID DRY . . . . 355 3 DON JUAN 12   86   5
I LEAVE THEM TO THEIR TASTE NO DOUBT THE BEST . . . . . 359 3 DON JUAN 13   3   2
IN SUCH A SORT AS CANNOT LEAVE BEHIND . . . . 372 3 DON JUAN 13   32   4
EVEN NIMROD'S SELF MIGHT LEAVE THE PLAINS OF DURA . . . . 395 3 DON JUAN 13   78   5
THEY BREAK THEIR RANKS AND GLADLY LEAVE THE DRILL . . . . 417 3 DON JUAN 14   17   2
THE STREAM NOR LEAVE THE WORLD WHICH LEAVETH THEM . . . . 418 3 DON JUAN 14   18   8
TO LEAVE THE PARTIES TO THEMSELVES FORSOOTH . . . . . 439 3 DON JUAN 14   67   3
LIKE ARCHIMEDES I LEAVE EARTH AS 'TWAS . . . . 446 3 DON JUAN 14   84   8
I LEAVE IT TO YOUR PEOPLE OF SAGACITY . . . . 449 3 DON JUAN 14   90   4
TO LEAVE THEM HOVERING AS THE EFFECT IS FINE . . . . . 453 3 DON JUAN 14   97   5
BUT LEAVE THEM TO THE CONSCIENCE OF THE NATIONS . . . . 464 3 DON JUAN 15   18   8
A LINE AND LEAVE POSTERITY UNDONE . . . . 470 3 DON JUAN 15   33   5
WHICH LAST I LEAVE UNTO THE LORD'S SPIRITUAL . . . . . 472 3 DON JUAN 15   36   V8
ALAS I MUST LEAVE UNDESCRIBED THE GIBIER . . . . 487 3 DON JUAN 15   71   1
A CASE WHICH TO THE JURIES WE MAY LEAVE . . . . 493 3 DON JUAN 15   84   4
I LEAVE TO THOSE WHO ARE FOND OF SOLVING DOUBT . . . . . 531 3 DON JUAN 16   62   4
YET LEAVE THE GATE WHICH ELOQUENCE SLIPS THROUGH . . . . 557 3 DON JUAN 16   115   3
I LEAVE THE THING A PROBLEM LIKE ALL THINGS-- . . . . . 568 3 DON JUAN 17   13   1
LEAVEN
A FACT WITHOUT SOME LEAVEN OF A LIE . . . . 286 3 DON JUAN 11   37   4
FEW FEMALES WITHOUT SOME SUCH GENTLE LEAVEN . . . . . . 525 3 DON JUAN 16   49   7
LEAVEN'D
LOWER'D LEAVEN'D LIKE A HISTORY OF FREEMASONS . . . . . 419 3 DON JUAN 14   22   2
LEAVENING
LEAVENING HIS BLOOD AS CAYENNE DOTH A CURRY . . . . . . 260 3 DON JUAN 10   72   2
LEAVES
HE PORED UPON THE LEAVES AND ON THE FLOWERS . . . . . . 72 2 DON JUAN 1   94   1
A STILLNESS WHICH LEAVES ROOM FOR THE FULL SOUL . . . . 82 2 DON JUAN 1   114   2
THAN ON THE NAME A PERSON LEAVES BEHIND . . . . 328 2 DON JUAN 3   90   4
AND YET THE FOREST LEAVES SEEM'D STIRR'D WITH PRAYER . . . 335 2 DON JUAN 3   102   8
LEAVES NOTHING TILL THE COMING OF THE JUST-- . . . . . 399 2 DON JUAN 4   101   6
AND STITCHED ITS LEAVES INTO A DRESSING GOWN . . . . . 476 2 DON JUAN 5   113   V8
WHICH LEAVES YOU MINUS OF THE CASH YOU COUNTED . . . . . 16 3 DON JUAN 6   21   5
AND THEN MY STOICISM LEAVES NOUGHT BEHIND . . . . . . 17 3 DON JUAN 6   22   4
THICKER THAN LEAVES THE LIVES BEGAN TO FALL . . . . . . 116 3 DON JUAN 8   9   3

LEAVES   (CONTINUED)
```
    OBSERVE YOUR LOVER WHEN HE LEAVES YOUR ARMS  . . .  . .  139  3 DON JUAN  8    53   7
    AS THE YEAR CLOSING WHIRLS THE SCARLET LEAVES  . . .  . .  155  3 DON JUAN  8    88   3
    AS AUTUMN WINDS DISPERSE THE YELLOW LEAVES  . . .  . .  155  3 DON JUAN  8    88   V3
    WHICH ON ROUGH ROADS LEAVES SCARCELY A WHOLE BONE)  . .  . .  197  3 DON JUAN  9    30   3
    FOR SUCH A SHIELD WHICH LEAVES BUT LITTLE MERIT  . . .  . .  372  3 DON JUAN 13    31   2
    WHICH LEAVES FEW DROPS OF THAT IMMORTAL RAIN  . . .  . .  375  3 DON JUAN 13    37   4
    OF THE TWO PRINCIPLES BUT LEAVES BEHIND  .  . .  . .  377  3 DON JUAN 13    41   6
    YOUTH FADES AND LEAVES OUR DAYS NO LONGER SUNNY  . . .  . .  405  3 DON JUAN 13   100   5
    AS THEY WILL DO LIKE LEAVES AT THE FIRST BREEZE  . . .  . .  431  3 DON JUAN 14    48   6
    EVE MADE UP MILLINERY WITH FIG LEAVES--  . .  . .  . .  444  3 DON JUAN 14    78   2
    LEAVES A SAD SEDIMENT OF TIME'S WORST SAND  . . .  . .  457  3 DON JUAN 15     4   8
    A ROSE WITH ALL ITS SWEETEST LEAVES YET FOLDED  . .  . .  475  3 DON JUAN 15    43   8
    THAT MOST UNLIQUIDATING LIQUID LEAVES  . . .  . .  548  3 DON JUAN 16    99   7
    WHICH LEAVES THEM ORPHANS OF THE HEART NO LESS  . .  . .  562  3 DON JUAN 17     1   8
    WHICH LEAVES THEM ORPHANS OF THE HEART NO LESS  . .  . .  563  3 DON JUAN 17     2   8
LEAVETH
    THE STREAM NOR LEAVE THE WORLD WHICH LEAVETH THEM  . .  . .  418  3 DON JUAN 14    18   8
LEAVING
    AND BOTCHING PATCHING LEAVING STILL BEHIND  . . .  . .   18  2 DON JUAN  D    14   2
    FOR LEAVING JUAN TO THIS NEW TEMPTATION  . . .  . .   75  2 DON JUAN  1   101   4
    LEAVING AT LAST NOT MUCH BESIDES CHRONOLOGY  . . .  . .   76  2 DON JUAN  1   103   7
    HOW THE PHYSICIANS LEAVING PILL AND POTION  . . .  . .  113  2 DON JUAN  1   168   3
    HE FLED LIKE JOSEPH LEAVING IT BUT THERE  . . .  . .  124  2 DON JUAN  1   186   7
    AT LEAVING EVEN THE MOST UNPLEASANT PEOPLE  . . .  . .  164  2 DON JUAN  2    14   7
    LEAVING DON JUAN AND HAIDEE TO PLEAD  . . .  . .  271  2 DON JUAN  2   216   7
    SO LEAVING EACH THEIR PRIEST AND PRAYER-BOOK READY  . .  . .  280  2 DON JUAN  3     9   7
    LEAVING THE FUTURE STATES OF LOVE AND LIFE  . . .  . .  280  2 DON JUAN  3     9  V7
    LEAVING MY PEOPLE TO PROCEED ALONE  .  . .  . .  331  2 DON JUAN  3    96   3
    LEAVING SUCH TO THE LITERARY RABBLE  .  . .  . .  398  2 DON JUAN  4    99   3
    WHO ROWED OFF LEAVING THEM WITHOUT A WORD  . . .  . .  433  2 DON JUAN  5    41   8
    OF GOODNESS IN THUS LEAVING THEM A VOICE  . . .  . .  452  2 DON JUAN  5    70   5
    AS LEAVING A SMALL FAMILY AT LARGE  . . .  . .  103  3 DON JUAN  7    71   8
    LEAVING AS LADDERS THEIR HEAPED CARCASES  . . .  . .  150  3 DON JUAN  8    76   6
    IN LEAVING VERSE MORE FREE FROM THE RESTRICTION  . . .  . .  154  3 DON JUAN  8    86   4
    NOT LEAVING EVEN HIS FUNERAL EXPENSES  . . .  . .  186  3 DON JUAN  9     8   3
    WHO AFTER LEAVING HINDOSTAN A WILD  . . .  . .  199  3 DON JUAN  9    33   5
    AND LEAVING LAND FAR OUT OF SIGHT WOULD SKIM  . .  . .  227  3 DON JUAN 10     4   4
    WHICH SKIMS THE SURFACE LEAVING SCARCE A SCAR  . . .  . .  335  3 DON JUAN 12    40   6
    LEAVING ALL CLARETLESS THE UNMOISTENED THROTTLE  . . .  . .  435  3 DON JUAN 14    58   3
    WHOSE GREATEST FAULT WAS LEAVING FEW TO FIND  . .  . .  479  3 DON JUAN 15    54   4
LECTURE
    SOME WOMEN USE THEIR TONGUES--SHE LOOK'D A LECTURE  . .  . .   29  2 DON JUAN  1    15   1
    A LECTURE AND SOME MONEY FOR FOUR SPRINGS  . . .  . .  161  2 DON JUAN  2     9   3
    ON WHICH I HAVE NOT TIME JUST NOW TO LECTURE  . . .  . .  255  2 DON JUAN 10    62   4
    THE WORLD BY EXPERIENCE RATHER THAN BY LECTURE  . .  . .  337  3 DON JUAN 12    46   5
LECTURES
    SERMONS HE READ AND LECTURES HE ENDURED  . . .  . .   47  2 DON JUAN  1    47   1
    OR ON THE MORNING PAPERS READ THEIR LECTURES  . . .  . .  406  3 DON JUAN 13   102   6
LECTURING
    AND LECTURING ON THE NOBLE ART OF KILLING--  . . .  . .   96  3 DON JUAN  7    58   4
LED
    DON JOSE AND THE DONNA INEZ LED  . . .  . .   35  2 DON JUAN  1    26   1
    OF MORTALS WHOM THY LURE HATH LED ALONG--  .  . .  . .   78  2 DON JUAN  1   106   6
    LED BY SOME TORTUOSITY OF MIND  .  . .  . .  141  2 DON JUAN  1   208   3
    HAD PETRARCH'S PASSION LED TO PETRARCH'S WEDDING  . .  . .  279  2 DON JUAN  3     8  V7
    AND RUSHING IN DISORDERLY THOUGH LED  . . .  . .  369  2 DON JUAN  4    47   5
    SOME SHEPHERDS (UNLIKE PARIS) LED TO STARE  . . .  . .  387  2 DON JUAN  4    78   3
    AND HAVING LED A RATHER LOOSISH LIFE  . . .  . .  389  2 DON JUAN  4    83  V2
    THEY LOOKED LIKE PERSONS BEING LED TO SENTENCE  . .  . .  432  2 DON JUAN  5    40   5
    HE LED THEM ONWARD FIRST THROUGH A LOW THICKET  . .  . .  433  2 DON JUAN  5    41   3
    BABA LED JUAN ONWARD ROOM BY ROOM  . . .  . .  460  2 DON JUAN  5    85   2
    THERE CAPTIVES LED IN TRIUMPH DROOP THE EYE  . . .  . .  461  2 DON JUAN  5    86   5
    WITH THIS ENCOURAGEMENT HE LED THE WAY  . . .  . .  465  2 DON JUAN  5    93   1
    FOR HAVING HAD HIM TO HER PALACE LED  . . .  . .  483  2 DON JUAN  5   124   6
    I WISH IT NEVER LED TO SOMETHING WORSE  . . .  . .   35  3 DON JUAN  6    59   8
    YOU SERVED AT WIDIN--YES--YOU LED THE ATTACK  . .  . .   98  3 DON JUAN  7    61   1
    ALTHOUGH THEIR HARAM EDUCATION LED  . . .  . .  101  3 DON JUAN  7    67   4
    THOUGH LED BY ARSENIEW THAT GREAT SON OF SLAUGHTER  . .  . .  116  3 DON JUAN  8     9   4
    AND LED THEM BACK INTO THE HEAVIEST FIRE  . . .  . .  133  3 DON JUAN  8    41   8
    WHO MARCHED TO MOSCOW LED BY FAME THE SYREN  . . .  . .  253  3 DON JUAN 10    58   6
    WHICH FOR WHAT I KNOW MAY OF YORE HAVE LED  . . .  . .  441  3 DON JUAN 14    72   3
LEE
    UNLESS WITH BREAKERS CLOSE BENEATH HER LEE  . . .  . .  180  2 DON JUAN  2    45   8
    THE SHORES OF ILION LAY BENEATH THEIR LEE--  . . .  . .  384  2 DON JUAN  4    75   6
    ON A LEE SHORE TILL IT BEGINS TO BLOW--  . . .  . .  345  3 DON JUAN 12    63   3
LEERS
    AS THEY BEHELD THE YOUNGER CAST SOME LEERS  . . .  . .  221  3 DON JUAN  9    78   4
LEFT
    AND LEFT HIS WIDOW TO HER OWN AVERSION  .  . .  . .   39  2 DON JUAN  1    34   8
    NO CHOICE WAS LEFT HIS FEELINGS OR HIS PRIDE  . .  . .   41  2 DON JUAN  1    36   7
    AN ONLY SON LEFT WITH AN ONLY MOTHER  . . .  . .   42  2 DON JUAN  1    37   7
    WHO LEFT AN ONLY DAUGHTER MY NARRATION  . . .  . .   54  2 DON JUAN  1    59   4
    AT LEAST SHE LEFT IT A MORE SLENDER HANDLE  . . .  . .   58  2 DON JUAN  1    67   8
    WITHDREW ITSELF FROM HIS BUT LEFT BEHIND  . . .  . .   60  2 DON JUAN  1    71   3
    LIKE WHAT THIS LIGHT TOUCH LEFT ON JUAN'S HEART  . . .  . .   60  2 DON JUAN  1    71   8
    TREMBLINGS WHEN MET AND RESTLESSNESS WHEN LEFT  . .  . .   62  2 DON JUAN  1    74   4
    HE LEFT THE ROOM FOR HIS RELINQUISH'D SWORD  . . .  . .  121  2 DON JUAN  1   182   1
    AND THE TWO LAST HAVE LEFT ME MANY A TOKEN  . . .  . .  145  2 DON JUAN  1   217   3
```

		PAGE	VOL	CANTO	STANZA	LN

LEFT   (CONTINUED)

THE WATER LEFT THE HOLD AND WASH'D THE DECKS	172	2 DON JUAN	2	31	2
HAD LEFT THEIR BODIES AND WHAT'S WORSE ALAS	185	2 DON JUAN	2	55	2
LEFT HIM SO DRUNK HE JUMP'D INTO THE WAVE	186	2 DON JUAN	2	57	3
WHICH LEFT SCARCE ROOM FOR MOTION OR EXERTION	189	2 DON JUAN	2	63	2
AND THEN THEY LEFT OFF EATING THE DEAD BODY	200	2 DON JUAN	2	82	8
DEATH LEFT NO DOUBT AND THE DEAD BURTHEN LAY	204	2 DON JUAN	2	90	3
BECAUSE IT LEFT ENCOURAGEMENT BEHIND	208	2 DON JUAN	2	99	6
LEFT HIM AT LAST THE SOLE OF MANY MASTERS	222	2 DON JUAN	2	125	7
AND THUS THEY LEFT HIM TO HIS LONE REPOSE	227	2 DON JUAN	2	134	1
WHO SMOOTH'D HIS PILLOW AS SHE LEFT THE DEN	228	2 DON JUAN	2	135	2
WHICH EVE HAS LEFT HER DAUGHTERS SINCE HER FALL	256	2 DON JUAN	2	189	8
HAIL MUSE ET CETERA--WE LEFT JUAN SLEEPING	274	2 DON JUAN	3	1	1
THE FUTURE STATES OF BOTH ARE LEFT TO FAITH	280	2 DON JUAN	3	9	3
HE LEFT HIS SHIP TO BE HOVE DOWN NEXT DAY	286	2 DON JUAN	3	20	5
AND HIS ONE BLOW LEFT LITTLE WORK FOR TWO	300	2 DON JUAN	3	48	8
FOR WHAT IS LEFT THE POET HERE	323	2 DON JUAN	3	L 6	5
FOR THE FIRST MRS MILTON LEFT HIS HOUSE	328	2 DON JUAN	3	91	8
THE LADY AND HER LOVER LEFT ALONE	334	2 DON JUAN	3	101	5
HAD LEFT THE WRETCH AN UNCORRUPTED HOUR	339	2 DON JUAN	3	109	8
YOUNG JUAN AND HIS LADY-LOVE WERE LEFT	348	2 DON JUAN	4	8	1
NO SIGN SAVE BREATH OF HAVING LEFT THE GRAVE	378	2 DON JUAN	4	63	8
WITH JUAN LEFT HALF-KILL'D SOME STANZAS BACK	384	2 DON JUAN	4	74	8
OR SHOULD BE LEFT WITH FETTERS OR WITHOUT	394	2 DON JUAN	4	92	V5
THEY LEFT THIS BEING FREE AND NEUTRAL AS A SCOUT	394	2 DON JUAN	4	92	V5
THEY HAD SLAIN HIM WITH FIVE SLUGS AND LEFT HIM THERE	429	2 DON JUAN	5	34	2
AND NOW NOUGHT LEFT HIM BUT THE MUFFLED DRUM	430	2 DON JUAN	5	36	8
AND GAZED AROUND THEM TO THE LEFT AND RIGHT	439	2 DON JUAN	5	50	7
NO LIPS E'ER LEFT THEIR TRANSITORY TRACE	472	2 DON JUAN	5	106	3
AND LEFT HIS CHEEKS AS PALE AS SNOWDROPS BLOWING	478	2 DON JUAN	5	117	6
IF HEARTS LAY ON THE LEFT SIDE OR THE RIGHT	485	2 DON JUAN	5	128	5
HE LEFT TO HIS VIZIER ALL STATE AFFAIRS	496	2 DON JUAN	5	148	3
WE LEFT OUR HERO AND THIRD HEROINE IN	10	3 DON JUAN	6	7	1
IN WHICH WE LEFT HIM SEVERAL LINES ABOVE	20	3 DON JUAN	6	28	8
THEIR PLACE OF REST AND LEFT TO BOTH THEIR PIQUES	31	3 DON JUAN	6	50	6
UPON THE DANUBE'S LEFT BRANCH AND LEFT BANK	70	3 DON JUAN	7	9	2
UPON THE DANUBE'S LEFT BRANCH AND LEFT BANK	70	3 DON JUAN	7	9	2
UPON THE LEFT WHICH FROM ITS LOFTIER STATION	71	3 DON JUAN	7	10	3
WHICH (IT MAY BE) HAS NOT MUCH LEFT TO SPARE	114	3 DON JUAN	8	4	4
AND LEFT AT LARGE LIKE A YOUNG HEIR TO MAKE	127	3 DON JUAN	8	32	2
PACES WERE LEFT WHEREON YOU COULD CONTRIVE	136	3 DON JUAN	8	47	2
AT LEAST TO ALL THOSE WHO WERE LEFT ALIVE	136	3 DON JUAN	8	47	4
BUT JUAN NEVER LEFT THEM WHILE THEY HAD CHARMS	139	3 DON JUAN	8	53	8
AND WHAT'S STILL STRANGER LEFT BEHIND A NAME	144	3 DON JUAN	8	63	1
NOR SWORD NOR SORROW YET HAD LEFT A TRACE	145	3 DON JUAN	8	65	4
AND LEFT HIM 'MIDST THE INVALID AND MAIMED	154	3 DON JUAN	8	85	4
SHORN OF ITS BEST AND LOVELIEST AND LEFT BARE	155	3 DON JUAN	8	88	6
HAD SCARRED HER BROW AND LEFT ITS CRIMSON TRACE	159	3 DON JUAN	8	95	6
HAVE LEFT UNDONE THE GREATEST--AND MANKIND	187	3 DON JUAN	9	10	8
WAS LEFT UPON HIS WAY TO THE CHIEF CITY	194	3 DON JUAN	9	23	2
WAS LEFT UPON HIS WAY WITH THE DISPATCH	197	3 DON JUAN	9	29	2
THAN HE IN THESE SAD HIGHWAYS LEFT AT LARGE	198	3 DON JUAN	9	31	4
OF THINGS DESTROYED AND LEFT IN AIRY DOUBT	201	3 DON JUAN	9	38	4
I LEFT DON JUAN WITH HIS HORSES BAITING--	203	3 DON JUAN	9	42	3
WE LEFT OUR HERO JUAN IN THE BLOOM	227	3 DON JUAN	10	5	1
WE LEFT HIM IN THE FOCUS OF SUCH GLORY	229	3 DON JUAN	10	9	2
GOOD GOVERNMENT HAS LEFT THEM SEEMS BUT CRUEL	256	3 DON JUAN	10	63	8
MY JUAN WHOM I LEFT IN DEADLY PERIL	300	3 DON JUAN	11	64	1
LEFT IT BEFORE HE HAD BEEN TREATED VERY ILL	300	3 DON JUAN	11	64	5
BECAUSE THE TIMES HAVE HARDLY LEFT THEM ONE TENANT	308	3 DON JUAN	11	80	8
I WONDER PEOPLE SHOULD BE LEFT ALIVE	316	3 DON JUAN	12	2	3
HAD LEFT ALL THE ACCOMPLISHMENTS SHE TAUGHT HER	339	3 DON JUAN	12	51	5
THEY AND THEIR BILLS ARCADIANS BOTH ARE LEFT	379	3 DON JUAN	13	45	1
FEW SPECIMENS YET LEFT US CAN COMPARE	384	3 DON JUAN	13	55	5
YET LEFT A GRAND IMPRESSION ON THE MIND	390	3 DON JUAN	13	67	5
BISHOPS WHO HAD NOT LEFT A SINGLE SERMON	391	3 DON JUAN	13	69	5
THERE'S LITTLE LEFT BUT TO BE BORED OR BORE	418	3 DON JUAN	14	18	6
WE LEFT OUR HEROES AND OUR HEROINES	423	3 DON JUAN	14	29	1
HAD NOTHING LEFT IT BUT A DESPERATE LOYALTY	466	3 DON JUAN	15	23	V8
RICH NOBLE BUT AN ORPHAN LEFT AN ONLY	475	3 DON JUAN	15	44	1
BY DEATH WHEN WE ARE LEFT ALAS BEHIND	475	3 DON JUAN	15	44	6
OR LIKE A BILLOW LEFT BY STORMS BEHIND	504	3 DON JUAN	16	9	7
THAT TIME HAS LEFT OUR FATHERS OF THEIR HALL	507	3 DON JUAN	16	16	8
ALL THERE WAS AS HE LEFT IT STILL HIS TAPER	512	3 DON JUAN	16	26	1
BUT THIS POOR GIRL WAS LEFT IN THE GREAT HALL	533	3 DON JUAN	16	67	1
BUT OTHERS WHO WERE LEFT WITH SCARCE A THIRD	543	3 DON JUAN	16	89	3
LEFT IN A TENDER MOONLIGHT SITUATION	567	3 DON JUAN	17	12	2

LEFT-LEGS

| ROUND THE PATRICIAN LEFT-LEGS WHICH ADORN | 404 | 2 DON JUAN | 4 | 110 | 7 |

LEG

| TO TEACH HIM GREATER HAD HIS OWN LEG BROKEN | 117 | 3 DON JUAN | 8 | 11 | 8 |
| TO THE LIVE LEG STILL CLUNG THE SEVERED HEAD | 153 | 3 DON JUAN | 8 | 84 | 8 |

LEGACY

| SWEET IS A LEGACY AND PASSING SWEET | 89 | 2 DON JUAN | 1 | 125 | 1 |

LEGAL

THE DOOR WAS FASTEN'D IN HIS LEGAL FACE	111	2 DON JUAN	1	164	8
UPON ALL LEGAL OBJECTS OF POSSESSION	11	3 DON JUAN	6	10	2
A LEGAL BROOM'S A MORAL CHIMNEY-SWEEPER	232	3 DON JUAN	10	15	1
THERE WAS PAROLLES TOO THE LEGAL BULLY	398	3 DON JUAN	13	84	1

	PAGE	VOL	CANTO	STANZA	LN

LEGEND
WITH THIS SAME LEGEND)--IF YOU BUT DESIGN . . . . . . 516 3 DON JUAN 16 37 5
LEGHORN
WAS STEERING DULY FOR THE PORT LEGHORN . . . . . . 169 2 DON JUAN 2 24 2
BY NAME--WAS DESTINED FOR THE PORT LEGHORN . . . . . 169 2 DON JUAN 2 24 V2
LEGITIMACY
LEGITIMACY ITS BORN VOTARIES WHEN . . . . 485 2 DON JUAN 5 128 7
LEGITIMACY'S
YOU HAVE REPAIRED LEGITIMACY'S CRUTCH-- . . . . . . 184 3 DON JUAN 9 3 3
LEGITIMATE
BUT OH THOU GRAND LEGITIMATE ALEXANDER . . . . . . 52 3 DON JUAN 6 93 1
NO HARM UNTO A RIGHT LEGITIMATE HEAD . . . . 117 3 DON JUAN 8 10 7
LEGITIMATELY
INEFFABLY--LEGITIMATELY VILE . . . . 17 2 DON JUAN 0 13 2
LEGS
HER HUNDRED ARMS AND LEGS AND FAIN OUTRUN HER . . . . 231 3 DON JUAN 10 12 6
FOUND HIS OWN LEGS EMBARGOED FROM MERE WALKING . . . . 565 3 DON JUAN 17 8 4
LEILA
SAT LITTLE LEILA WHO SURVIVED THE PARRIES . . . . . 249 3 DON JUAN 10 51 4
BEFORE THEY BUTCHER LITTLE LEILA GAZED . . . . . . 261 3 DON JUAN 10 74 7
THE LITTLE LEILA WITH HER ORIENT EYES . . . . . . 328 3 DON JUAN 12 27 1
BUT FIRST OF LITTLE LEILA WE'LL DISPOSE . . . . . . 335 3 DON JUAN 12 41 1
LEILA'S
AMONGST YOU ABOUT LEILA'S EDUCATION . . . . 329 3 DON JUAN 12 28 8
LEIPSIC
MY LEIPSIC AND MY MONT SAINT JEAN SEEMS CAIN . . . . 296 3 DON JUAN 11 56 2
LEISURE
FOND OF A LITTLE LOVE (WHICH I CALL LEISURE) . . . . 85 2 DON JUAN 1 118 6
O'ER WHICH REFLECTION MAY BE MADE AT LEISURE . . . . 145 2 DON JUAN 1 217 4
WHOSE LEISURE HOURS ARE WASTED ON A HARLOT . . . . . 109 3 DON JUAN 7 84 V3
NO LESS DELIGHTED TO EMPLOY HIS LEISURE . . . . . . 123 3 DON JUAN 8 24 8
OR DULL REPENTANCE HATH HAD DREARY LEISURE . . . . . 168 3 DON JUAN 8 113 5
THERE WAS SMALL LEISURE FOR SUPERFLUOUS SIN . . . . . 178 3 DON JUAN 8 132 6
MEN LOVE IN HASTE BUT THEY DETEST AT LEISURE . . . . 361 3 DON JUAN 13 6 8
IS WHAT I HAVE NOT LEISURE TO INSPECT . . . . . . 502 3 DON JUAN 16 2 3
LELY
ALSO SOME BEAUTIES OF SIR PETER LELY . . . . . . 390 3 DON JUAN 13 68 7
LEMAN'S
OR LIKE THE RHONE BY LEMAN'S WATERS WASH'D . . . . . 447 3 DON JUAN 14 87 4
LEND
OH THAT THE PRESENT HOUR WOULD LEND . . . . 325 2 DON JUAN 3 L 12 4
ALMOST AS FAR AS PETERSBURGH AND LEND . . . . . . 52 3 DON JUAN 6 93 4
LEND TO THAT COLOUR A TRANSCENDANT RAY . . . . . . 218 3 DON JUAN 9 71 6
WHEN WILL YOUR NAMES LEND LUSTRE EVEN TO PARTRIDGES . . 485 3 DON JUAN 15 67 8
LENDS
BUT PHOEBUS LENDS ME NOW AND THEN A STRING . . . . . 181 3 DON JUAN 8 138 8
LENGTH
UNTIL AT LENGTH THE SMOTHER'D FIRE BROKE OUT . . . . 35 2 DON JUAN 1 26 7
HIMSELF AT LENGTH WITHIN THE LEAFY NOOKS . . . . . . 70 2 DON JUAN 1 90 3
NOW JULIA FOUND AT LENGTH A VOICE AND CRIED . . . . . 98 2 DON JUAN 1 142 1
AND WHEN AT LENGTH THEY'RE OUT OF BREATH THEY SIGH . . 119 2 DON JUAN 1 179 5
LIGHTS CAME AT LENGTH AND MEN AND MAIDS WHO FOUND . . 125 2 DON JUAN 1 187 1
A DISAPPOINTED LAWYER AT FULL LENGTH . . . . 155 2 DON JUAN 1 V 6 8
AND IF HE WEPT AT LENGTH THEY WERE NOT FEARS . . . . 179 2 DON JUAN 2 43 5
AT LENGTH ONE WHISPER'D HIS COMPANION WHO . . . . . 194 2 DON JUAN 2 73 1
AT LENGTH THE LOTS WERE TORN UP AND PREPARED . . . . 195 2 DON JUAN 2 74 5
AT LENGTH THEY CAUGHT TWO BOOBIES AND A NODDY . . . . 200 2 DON JUAN 2 82 7
AND WHEN THE WISH'D-FOR SHOWER AT LENGTH WAS COME . . 203 2 DON JUAN 2 89 4
AND THERE HE LAY FULL LENGTH WHERE HE WAS FLUNG . . . 213 2 DON JUAN 2 108 5
OF DOWNCAST LENGTH IN WHOSE SILK SHADOW LIES . . . . 218 2 DON JUAN 2 117 3
'TIS AS THE SNAKE LATE COIL'D WHO POURS HIS LENGTH . . 218 2 DON JUAN 2 117 7
I THINK IT MUST BE RECKON'D BY ITS LENGTH . . . . . 254 2 DON JUAN 2 186 8
BY LENGTH I MEAN DURATION THEIRS ENDURED . . . . . 254 2 DON JUAN 2 187 1
FOR ANY LENGTH--CONTRIVED TO MAKE EACH OTHER CEASE . . 277 2 DON JUAN 3 5 V4
ROMANCES PAINT AT FULL LENGTH PEOPLE'S WOOINGS . . . 279 2 DON JUAN 3 8 3
ACCORDING TO THEIR SIZE AND AGE AND LENGTH . . . . . 283 2 DON JUAN 3 15 V7
SHE WOKE AT LENGTH BUT NOT AS SLEEPERS WAKE . . . . 378 2 DON JUAN 4 62 1
AT LENGTH THOSE EYES WHICH THEY WOULD FAIN BE WEANING . 379 2 DON JUAN 4 64 7
LIKE MOUNTAIN MISTS AT LENGTH DISSOLVED IN RAIN . . . 380 2 DON JUAN 4 66 8
FOR ANY LENGTH OF DAYS IN SUCH A PICKLE . . . . . . 419 2 DON JUAN 5 17 4
AT LENGTH PERCEIVING THE FOOT COULD NOT STAND . . . . 471 2 DON JUAN 5 104 7
AT LENGTH IN AN IMPERIAL WAY SHE LAID . . . . . . 483 2 DON JUAN 5 125 1
AT LENGTH SHE SAID THAT IN A SLUMBER SOUND . . . . . 43 3 DON JUAN 6 75 1
THEN OUT IT CAME AT LENGTH THAT TO DUDU . . . . . . 57 3 DON JUAN 6 102 5
AT LENGTH SHE ROSE UP AND BEGAN TO WALK . . . . . . 61 3 DON JUAN 6 110 5
WITHIN A CABLE'S LENGTH THEIR VESSELS LAY . . . . . 81 3 DON JUAN 7 29 4
AT LENGTH THEY FOUND MERE CANNONADE ALONE . . . . . 81 3 DON JUAN 7 30 4
TILL IN APPROACHING WERE AT LENGTH DESCRIED . . . . 87 3 DON JUAN 7 43 7
WITHIN A CANNON-SHOT LENGTH OF THE PLACE . . . . . 89 3 DON JUAN 7 47 5
(SO THAT THEIR EFFORTS SHOULD AT LENGTH PREVAIL) . . 105 3 DON JUAN 7 77 6
WAS MADE AT LENGTH WITH THOSE WHO DARED TO CLIMB . . 151 3 DON JUAN 8 79 4
AT LENGTH HE CONDESCENDED TO ENQUIRE . . . . 171 3 DON JUAN 8 120 5
TILL ALL THE ARTS AT LENGTH ARE BROUGHT ABOUT . . . 202 3 DON JUAN 9 40 5
BUT LUCKILY OF NO GREAT LENGTH OR WEIGHT . . . . . 207 3 DON JUAN 9 50 8
UNTIL A ROYAL SMILE AT LENGTH DISCLOSED . . . . . . 211 3 DON JUAN 9 58 6
AT LENGTH THEY ROSE LIKE A WHITE WALL ALONG . . . . 257 3 DON JUAN 10 65 1
HAVE TAKEN UP AT LENGTH WITH YOUNGER BROTHERS . . . . 308 3 DON JUAN 11 81 2
AT LENGTH THE BOYS DREW UP BEFORE A DOOR . . . . . 313 3 DON JUAN 11 V 29 1
WAKING ALREADY AND RETURNED AT LENGTH . . . . . . 511 3 DON JUAN 16 25 7
WHETHER HIS VIRTUE TRIUMPHED--OR AT LENGTH . . . . . 567 3 DON JUAN 17 12 5

LENGTHEN
    TO LENGTHEN FETTERS BY ANOTHER FIX'D . . . . 16 2 DON JUAN D   12   7
    OR AT THE LEAST WOULD LENGTHEN OUT MY SONG-- . . . . . 338 3 DON JUAN 12   48   6
LENGTHENING
    THOSE LONELY WALKS AND LENGTHENING REVERIES . . . . . . 73 2 DON JUAN 1   97   1
LENGTHY
    WOULD FORM A LENGTHY LEXICON OF GLORY . . . . 120 3 DON JUAN 8   17   7
LENIENT
    THAT SHE WAS HANDSOME AND THOUGH FIERCE LOOKED LENIENT . 214 3 DON JUAN 9   63   3
LENT
    IN MY YOUNG DAYS THEY LENT ME CASH THAT WAY . . . . . . 190 2 DON JUAN 2   65   7
    WHO LENT HIS LADY TO HIS FRIEND HORTENSIUS . . . . 10 3 DON JUAN 6   7   8
    SHE COULD REPAY EACH AMATORY LOOK YOU LENT . . . . . . 213 3 DON JUAN 9   62   5
    WHICH LENT HIS LEARNED LUCUBRATIONS PITH . . . . 294 3 DON JUAN 11   52   3
LEONIDAS
    SHADE OF LEONIDAS WHO FOUGHT SO HEARTY . . . . 108 3 DON JUAN 7   82   3
    NOT SO LEONIDAS AND WASHINGTON . . . . 114 3 DON JUAN 8   5   2
L'EPROUVEUSE
    NAMED FROM HER MYSTIC OFFICE L'EPROUVEUSE . . . . . . 224 3 DON JUAN 9   84   7
LESBIAN
    THE LESBIAN SAPPHO AND THE BLIND OLD MAN . . . . 320 2 DON JUAN 3 L 1 V2
L'ESPAGNOLE
    A L'ESPAGNOLE TIMBALLE AND SALPICON-- . . . . 484 3 DON JUAN 15   66   2
    DON JUAN SAT NEXT AN A L'ESPAGNOLE-- . . . . 488 3 DON JUAN 15   74   5
LESSEN
    THAN LESSEN IT BY WHAT I COULD RELATE . . . . 467 2 DON JUAN 5   97   5
LESSER
    THE HEATHEN ALSO THOUGH WITH LESSER LATITUDE . . . . . 11 3 DON JUAN 6   11   2
    COUNTRIES OF GREATER HEAT BUT LESSER SUCTION . . . . . 262 3 DON JUAN 10   76   4
    WE LITTLE PEOPLE IN OUR LESSER WAY . . . . 566 3 DON JUAN 17   10   2
LESSON
    FIRST PARTINGS FORM A LESSON HARD TO LEARN . . . . . . 164 2 DON JUAN 2   14   3
    A LESSON IN HER TONGUE BUT BY SURMISE . . . . 242 2 DON JUAN 2   163   3
    BY WAY OF LESSON AGAINST ACTUAL TURKS . . . . 93 3 DON JUAN 7   53   4
    'TIS A GREAT MORAL LESSON THEY ARE READING . . . . . . 341 3 DON JUAN 12   55   4
LESSONS
    ARE OIL AND GUNPOWDER AND SOME GOOD LESSONS . . . . . . 245 2 DON JUAN 2   169   6
    OF TWO SUCH LESSONS WHY FORGET . . . . 324 2 DON JUAN 3 L 10   3
    THEIR PRESENT LESSONS ON OUR PAGAN FRIENDS HERE . . . 423 2 DON JUAN 5   24   2
    TO JUAN SOME SLIGHT LESSONS AS HIS GUIDE . . . . 464 2 DON JUAN 5   91   2
    UNTIL 'TIS TAUGHT BY LESSONS RATHER RUDE . . . . 53 3 DON JUAN 6   95   3
    UPON THE MORAL LESSONS OF MANKIND . . . . 353 3 DON JUAN 12   81   2
    FROM WHOM I NOW DEDUCE THESE MORAL LESSONS . . . . . . 375 3 DON JUAN 13   38   5
LEST
    WAS EVER SUFFER'D LEST HE SHOULD GROW VICIOUS . . . . . 44 2 DON JUAN 1   40   8
    IN DEEP DESPAIR LEST HE HAD DONE AMISS . . . . 81 2 DON JUAN 1   112   5
    FAST TO THE SAND LEST THE RETURNING WAVE . . . . 213 2 DON JUAN 2   108   2
    LEST THEY SHOULD SEEM PRINCESSES IN DISGUISE . . . . . 222 2 DON JUAN 2   124   2
    AND WRAPT HIM CLOSER LEST THE AIR TOO RAW . . . . . . 232 2 DON JUAN 2   143   6
    MUST BREAKFAST AND BETIMES--LEST THEY SHOULD ASK IT . . 233 2 DON JUAN 2   144   7
    LEST THEIR TOO LAWFUL BED-FELLOW SHOULD WAKE . . . . . 18 3 DON JUAN 6   24   8
    SHADOWS OF GLORY (LEST I BE CONFOUNDED) . . . . 108 3 DON JUAN 7   82   6
    TO THE OLD TEXT STILL BETTER--LEST IT SHOULD . . . . . 270 3 DON JUAN 11   4   2
    TO SOOTHE OUR EARS LEST ITALY SHOULD FAIL . . . . . . 523 3 DON JUAN 16   45   8
LETHE
    A MORTAL MOTHER WOULD ON LETHE FIX . . . . 346 2 DON JUAN 4   4   8
    INSTEAD OF GLIDING GRACIOUSLY DOWN LETHE . . . . 245 3 DON JUAN 10   42   7
LETHE'S
    OUR HEARTS FIRST IN THE DEPTHS OF LETHE'S SPRING . . . 346 2 DON JUAN 4   4   5
    WHAT THOUGH ON LETHE'S STREAM HE SEEM TO FLOAT . . . . 457 3 DON JUAN 15   4   5
LET'S
    LET'S OWN SINCE IT CAN DO NO GOOD ON EARTH . . . . . . 41 2 DON JUAN 1   36   3
    (AND SO MY SOBER MUSE--COME LET'S BE STEADY-- . . . . . 160 2 DON JUAN 2   6   8
    LET'S KNOCK THAT OLD BLACK FELLOW ON THE HEAD . . . . 434 2 DON JUAN 5   43   7
    SAID IN HEAVEN'S NAME LET'S GET SOME SUPPER NOW . . . 437 2 DON JUAN 5   47   7
LETTER
    SHOWN IN THE FOLLOWING COPY OF HER LETTER . . . . . . 129 2 DON JUAN 1   191   8
    I SENT IT IN A LETTER TO THE EDITOR . . . . 142 2 DON JUAN 1   210   1
    A LETTER TOO SHE GAVE (HE NEVER READ IT) . . . . 161 2 DON JUAN 2   9   7
    HER LETTER OUT AGAIN AND READ IT THROUGH) . . . . . . 166 2 DON JUAN 2   18   8
    LETTER OF INTRODUCTION WHICH THE MORN . . . . 169 2 DON JUAN 2   24   6
    THEY TOOK FORCE FROM JUAN JULIA'S LETTER . . . . 195 2 DON JUAN 2   74   8
    FROM HAIDEE'S GLANCE THAN ANY GRAVEN LETTER . . . . . 242 2 DON JUAN 2   163   8
    'TIS STRANGE THE SHORTEST LETTER WHICH MAN USES . . . 327 2 DON JUAN 3   88   4
    THE LETTER OF THE PRINCE TO THE SAME MARSHAL . . . . . 86 3 DON JUAN 7   40   1
    AS IN A GENERAL'S LETTER WHEN WELL WHACKED . . . . . 107 3 DON JUAN 7   81 V5
    THE LETTER OPEN WITH AN AIR WHICH POSED . . . . 211 3 DON JUAN 9   58   4
    BLACK LETTER UPON FOOLSCAP WHILE OUR HAIR . . . . . . 315 3 DON JUAN 12   1   7
    PRAY DID YOU SEE HER ANSWER TO HIS LETTER . . . . . . 332 3 DON JUAN 12   35   8
    PERHAPS YOU'LL HAVE A LETTER FROM THE MOTHER . . . . . 343 3 DON JUAN 12   60   1
    OR CRAMM'D TWELVE SHEETS INTO ONE LITTLE LETTER . . . 406 3 DON JUAN 13   104   7
    TAKE CARE WHAT YOU REPLY TO SUCH A LETTER . . . . . . 407 3 DON JUAN 13   105   8
    A LOVING LETTER WITH A MYSTIC SEAL . . . . 422 3 DON JUAN 14   27   6
LETTERS
    AND OPEN'D CERTAIN TRUNKS OF BOOKS AND LETTERS . . . . . 36 2 DON JUAN 1   28   2
    SOFT PERSIAN SENTENCES IN LILAC LETTERS . . . . 308 2 DON JUAN 3   64   7
    YOU HAVE THE LETTERS CADMUS GAVE-- . . . . 324 2 DON JUAN 3 L 10   5
LETTING
    FOR LETTING THAT PURE SANCTUARY ALONE . . . . 370 3 DON JUAN 13   27   4
    HALF LETTING IN LONG SHADOWS ON THE LIGHT . . . . . . 558 3 DON JUAN 16   117   4

```
                                                            PAGE VOL      CANTO STANZA LN
LEUCADIA'S
    (LEUCADIA'S ROCK STILL OVERLOOKS THE WAVE)  . . . . . . 266  2 DON JUAN  2   205   6
LEVANT
    PIECED OUT FOR DIFFERENT MARTS IN THE LEVANT  . . . . . 284  2 DON JUAN  3    17   2
LEVANTINES
    TO WHICH THE LEVANTINES ARE VERY PARTIAL . . . . . . . 290  2 DON JUAN  3    29   8
LEVEE
    TO HOLD A LEVEE ROUND HIS LADY'S BED . . . . . . .      97  2 DON JUAN  1   139   6
    THE FESTAL MIDNIGHT AND THE LEVEE MORN  . . . . . .    404  2 DON JUAN  4   110   8
    BUT WHEN THE LEVEE ROSE AND ALL WAS BUSTLE  . . . . .  223  3 DON JUAN  9    82   1
LEVEES
    THE ORNAMENTS OF LEVEES AND A ROUT . . . . . . . .     404  2 DON JUAN  4   110  V8
LEVEL
    BUT TIME WHICH BRINGS ALL BEINGS TO THEIR LEVEL  . . . 345  2 DON JUAN  4     2   1
    OF ABSENCE LAY ONE'S OLD RESENTMENTS LEVEL  . . . . .  257  3 DON JUAN 10    66   7
    SO SMOOTH SO LEVEL SUCH A MODE OF SHAVING  . . . . .   263  3 DON JUAN 10    78   2
    ON SO UNCONTROVERTIBLE A LEVEL . . . . . . . . .       271  3 DON JUAN 11     6   6
LEVELLED
    AND LEVELLED WEAPONS STILL AGAINST THE GLACIS  . . . . 130  3 DON JUAN  8    34   8
    HIS SECOND SON WAS LEVELLED BY A SHOT . . . . . . .    166  3 DON JUAN  8   110   2
LEVELLERS
    THESE TWO ARE LEVELLERS AND HUMAN BREATH . . . . . .   280  2 DON JUAN  3     9  V3
LEVELS
    SCIENCE ENOUGH WHICH LEVELS TO AN ASS . . . . . .      69   3 DON JUAN  7     5   3
    HOWEVER HEAVEN KNOWS HOW THE FATE WHO LEVELS  . . . .  134  3 DON JUAN  8    44   4
    GRACCHUS OF ALL MORTALITY WHO LEVELS . . . . . . .     237  3 DON JUAN 10    25   2
LEXICON
    WOULD FORM A LENGTHY LEXICON OF GLORY . . . . . . .    120  3 DON JUAN  8    17   7
LIAISON
    SOME CHASTE LIAISON OF THE KIND--I MEAN  . . . . . .   288  2 DON JUAN  3    25   2
    THIS SORT OF CHASTE LIAISON FOR A FRIEND . . . . . .   438  3 DON JUAN 14    64   4
LIAR
    IF HISTORY THE GRAND LIAR EVER SAITH . . . . . . .     222  3 DON JUAN  9    81   4
    WHY FAME--BUT FAME YOU KNOW'S SOMETIMES A LIAR--  . . 516  3 DON JUAN 16    36   3
LIARS
    OF OTHERS' FEELING BUT THEY ARE SUCH LIARS . . . . .   326  2 DON JUAN  3    87   7
    PRAISED BE ALL LIARS AND ALL LIES WHO NOW  . . . . .  286  3 DON JUAN 11    38   1
LIBATIONS
    FOR IF MY PURE LIBATIONS EXCEED THREE . . . . . .      372  2 DON JUAN  4    52   4
LIBEL
    A LIBEL OR WHATE'ER YOU PLEASE TO RHYME ON . . . . .   53   3 DON JUAN  6    94   4
LIBELLER'S
    THE LIBELLER'S GRATIS COUNSEL DIRTY SHIELD . . . . .   151  2 DON JUAN  1  V  2   3
LIBELS
    IN PIOUS LIBELS BY NO MEANS A FEW . . . . . . . .      414  3 DON JUAN 14    10   4
LIBERAL
    THIS IS A LIBERAL AGE AND THOUGHTS ARE FREE . . . . . 347  2 DON JUAN  4     7   6
    O'ER CONGRESS WHETHER ROYALIST OR LIBERAL  . . . . .  318  3 DON JUAN 12     5   2
    THOSE AND THE TRULY LIBERAL LAFITTE  . . . . . . .    318  3 DON JUAN 12     6   1
    SINCE ADELINE WAS LIBERAL BY NATURE  . . . . . . .    478  3 DON JUAN 15    52   6
LIBERALLY
    A PRESENT LIBERALLY MADE BY LADIES . . . . . . . .     199  2 DON JUAN  2    81  V8
LIBERATE
    PERHAPS HE FAIN WOULD LIBERATE MANKIND . . . . . .     320  3 DON JUAN 12    10   5
LIBERATED
    AMIDST THE ROAR OF LIBERATED ROME . . . . . . . .     339  2 DON JUAN  3   109   3
LIBERATOR
    AND EUROPE'S LIBERATOR--STILL ENSLAVED . . . . . .     185  3 DON JUAN  9     5   8
LIBERTY
    HERE MY CHASTE MUSE A LIBERTY MUST TAKE--  . . . . .   86   2 DON JUAN  1   120   1
    THIS LIBERTY IS A POETIC LICENCE . . . . . . . .       86   2 DON JUAN  1   120   4
    AND SO SHE TOOK THE LIBERTY TO STATE . . . . . . .    240  2 DON JUAN  2   159   1
    BUT THEY WILL NOT FIND LIBERTY A TROY--  . . . . . .  106  3 DON JUAN  7    79   8
LIBERTY'S
    OF MURMURING LIBERTY'S WIDE WAVES WHICH BLEND  . . .  52   3 DON JUAN  6    93   6
LIBRARY
    THE ELDERLY WALKED THROUGH THE LIBRARY . . . . . .    406  3 DON JUAN 13   102   1
LICENCE
    THIS LIBERTY IS A POETIC LICENCE . . . . . . . .       86   2 DON JUAN  1   120   4
    THIS LICENCE IS TO HOPE THE READER WILL . . . . . .    86   2 DON JUAN  1   121   1
    OF THOSE WHO HAVE NOT A LICENCE FOR THE SAME . . . .  531  3 DON JUAN 16    63   4
LICENCES
    BUT SUCH SMALL LICENCES MUST LOVERS BROOK  . . . . .  429  3 DON JUAN 14    43   3
LICENTIATE
    A TUTOR THE LICENTIATE PEDRILLO . . . . . . . . .      169  2 DON JUAN  2    25   2
LID
    BURGLARIOUSLY BROKE HIS COFFIN'S LID . . . . . . .     146  2 DON JUAN  1   219   6
LIDS
    TROUBLE HEROIC STOMACHS THOUGH THEIR LIDS SO . . . .  133  3 DON JUAN  8    40   5
LIE
    BENEATH THE LIE THIS STATE THING BREATHED O'ER THEE  . 19   2 DON JUAN  D    16   4
    AND HELP THEM WITH A LIE OR TWO ADDITIONAL . . . . .   37   2 DON JUAN  1    31   2
    SOME PEOPLE WHISPER (BUT NO DOUBT THEY LIE . . . . .   58   2 DON JUAN  1    66   5
    ITS SNOW THROUGH ALL--HER SOFT LIPS LIE APART . . . . 108  2 DON JUAN  1   158   7
    THE CHARMING CREATURES LIE WITH SUCH A GRACE . . . .  119  2 DON JUAN  1   178   7
    THEY ALSO LIE TOO--UNDER A MISTAKE . . . . . . .      141  2 DON JUAN  1   208   8
    HE DID NOT KNOW (ALAS HOW MEN WILL LIE)  . . . . .    295  2 DON JUAN  3    38   1
    WHILE LIFE'S STRANGE PRINCIPLE WILL OFTEN LIE . . . . 350  2 DON JUAN  4    11   7
    BLOSSOM AND BOUGH LIE WITHER'D WITH ONE BLIGHT . . .  382  2 DON JUAN  4    70   6
```

446

LIE   (CONTINUED)

	PAGE	VOL	CANTO	STANZA	LN
WHICH ONCE-NAMED MYRIADS NAMELESS LIE BENEATH	399	2 DON JUAN	4	102	7
WILL SINK WHERE LIE THE SONGS AND WARS OF EARTH	400	2 DON JUAN	4	104	7
BLUE AS THE GARTERS WHICH SERENELY LIE	404	2 DON JUAN	4	110	6
THEY LIE WE LIE ALL LIE BUT LOVE NO LESS	15	3 DON JUAN	6	19	6
THEY LIE WE LIE ALL LIE BUT LOVE NO LESS	15	3 DON JUAN	6	19	6
THEY LIE WE LIE ALL LIE BUT LOVE NO LESS	15	3 DON JUAN	6	19	6
LIE DOWN IN DUDGEON TO SIGH FOR THE LIGHT	18	3 DON JUAN	6	24	4
YOU LOLAH MUST CONTINUE STILL TO LIE	30	3 DON JUAN	6	49	1
THAT THE YOUNG STRANGER SHOULD NOT LIE ALONE	46	3 DON JUAN	6	81	4
BY THE DECEASED WHO LIE IN FAMOUS SLUMBER	120	3 DON JUAN	8	18	3
EVEN WITH HIS LIFE--FOR (BUT THEY LIE) 'TIS SAID	153	3 DON JUAN	8	84	7
LIE ROUND THE BATTERY BUT STILL IT BATTERS	160	3 DON JUAN	8	98	7
GRIEF A RICH FIELD WHICH NEVER WOULD LIE FALLOW	228	3 DON JUAN	10	7	6
EVEN SHUFFLING SOUTHEY THAT INCARNATE LIE	231	3 DON JUAN	10	13	2
KNOW VERY CLEARLY--OR AT LEAST LIE STILL	270	3 DON JUAN	11	4	8
THE FELLOW TO LIE GROANING ON THE ROAD	275	3 DON JUAN	11	15	7
(THE DEN OF MANY A DIPLOMATIC LOST LIE)	283	3 DON JUAN	11	31	6
WHO LIVE BY LIES YET DARE NOT BOLDLY LIE	285	3 DON JUAN	11	36	5
OR CAN'T DO OTHERWISE THAN LIE BUT DO IT	285	3 DON JUAN	11	36	7
AND AFTER ALL WHAT IS A LIE 'TIS BUT	286	3 DON JUAN	11	37	1
A FACT WITHOUT SOME LEAVEN OF A LIE	286	3 DON JUAN	11	37	4
BUT TO SIT UP WHILE OTHERS LIE IN BED	290	3 DON JUAN	11	45	5
AND ON OUR SOPHAS MAKES US LIE DEJECTED	301	3 DON JUAN	11	65	5
WHICH 'TIS THE COMMON CRY AND LIE TO VAUNT AS	311	3 DON JUAN	11	87	3
GIVES WITH GREEK TRUTH THE GOOD OLD GREEK THE LIE	325	3 DON JUAN	12	19	8
IN THIS WHATEVER OTHER BLUNDERS LIE	378	3 DON JUAN	13	43	3
LIE WITH THEIR HALLELUJAHS QUENCH'D LIKE FIRE	387	3 DON JUAN	13	62	8
AT ONCE THE LIE AND THE ELITE OF CROWDS	396	3 DON JUAN	13	80	2
TO HIS OWN CIRCUMSTANCES THERE MIGHT LIE	469	3 DON JUAN	15	30	4
FEELINGS OF YOUTH LIKE THOSE WHICH OVERTHROWN LIE	475	3 DON JUAN	15	44	5
EVEN MY VERACIOUS SELF--BUT THAT'S A LIE	495	3 DON JUAN	15	88	3

LIED

	PAGE	VOL	CANTO	STANZA	LN
HE LIED WITH SUCH A FERVOUR OF INTENTION--	317	2 DON JUAN	3	80	7

LIEGE

	PAGE	VOL	CANTO	STANZA	LN
OF GETTING HER LIEGE LORD INTO A SCRAPE	32	2 DON JUAN	1	20	8
WHEN THEIR LIEGE HUSBANDS TREAT THEM WITH INGRATITUDE	11	3 DON JUAN	6	11	6

LIES

	PAGE	VOL	CANTO	STANZA	LN
I TELL HIM IF A CLERGYMAN HE LIES	141	2 DON JUAN	1	208	6
OF DOWNCAST LENGTH IN WHOSE SILK SHADOW LIES	218	2 DON JUAN	2	117	3
ROUND JUAN'S HEAD AND HIS AROUND HERS LIES	259	2 DON JUAN	2	194	3
FOR THERE IT LIES SO TRANQUIL SO BELOVED	261	2 DON JUAN	2	197	1
THERE LIES THE THING WE LOVE WITH ALL ITS ERRORS	261	2 DON JUAN	2	197	7
AND HER HEAD DROOP'D AS WHEN THE LILY LIES	376	2 DON JUAN	4	59	3
YE COULD NOT KNOW WHERE LIES A THING SO FAIR	383	2 DON JUAN	4	72	5
HERE STALKS THE VICTOR THERE THE VANQUISHED LIES	461	2 DON JUAN	5	86	4
THEIR LIES YCLEPED DESPATCHES WITHOUT RISK OR	498	2 DON JUAN	5	151	7
I'D RATHER TELL TEN LIES THAN SAY A WORD	77	3 DON JUAN	7	22	4
AND THAT OUTRAGEOUS APPETITE FOR LIES	154	3 DON JUAN	8	86	7
BUT WHETHER THEY ESCAPED OR NO LIES HID	178	3 DON JUAN	8	132	7
WHO LIVE BY LIES YET DARE NOT BOLDLY LIE	285	3 DON JUAN	11	36	5
PRAISED BE ALL LIARS AND ALL LIES WHO NOW	286	3 DON JUAN	11	38	1
WITHAL IT LIES PERHAPS A LITTLE LOW	384	3 DON JUAN	13	55	6
WHOSE VIRTUE LIES IN NEVER BEING DETECTED	437	3 DON JUAN	14	61	8
THERE LIES THE RUB--AND THIS THEY ARE BUT WEAK IN	442	3 DON JUAN	14	74	4
ESPECIALLY WHEN THEY WOULD LOOK LIKE LIES	444	3 DON JUAN	14	80	7
THE DIFFICULTY LIES IN COLOURING	467	3 DON JUAN	15	25	5
WAS SUCH AS LIES BETWEEN A FLOWER AND GEM	481	3 DON JUAN	15	58	8

LIEU

	PAGE	VOL	CANTO	STANZA	LN
THAT IN THE LIEU OF DRAWING ON HIS BANKER	240	3 DON JUAN	10	31	2
IN LIEU OF A BARE BLADE AND BRAZEN FRONT	275	3 DON JUAN	11	15	5
IN LIEU OF SONS OF THESE HE MADE NO BONES	410	3 DON JUAN	14	1	8
AND RISE AT NINE IN LIEU OF LONG ELEVEN	539	3 DON JUAN	16	81	4

LIEUTENANT

	PAGE	VOL	CANTO	STANZA	LN
O'ER WHICH LIEUTENANT COLONEL YESOUSKOI	150	3 DON JUAN	8	76	7
SEEMS LOVE TURNED A LIEUTENANT OF ARTILLERY	204	3 DON JUAN	9	44	8
BUT WHEN ON THE LIEUTENANT AT HER FEET	213	3 DON JUAN	9	61	5
FOR A LIEUTENANT TO CLIMB UP BUT SKILL	215	3 DON JUAN	9	66	6
OUR YOUNG LIEUTENANT TO THE GENIAL CARE	224	3 DON JUAN	9	84	2

LIEUTENANT'S

	PAGE	VOL	CANTO	STANZA	LN
A YOUNG LIEUTENANT'S WITH A NOT OLD QUEEN	236	3 DON JUAN	10	24	4

LIFE

	PAGE	VOL	CANTO	STANZA	LN
FOR SOME TIME AN UNHAPPY SORT OF LIFE	35	2 DON JUAN	1	26	2
SHE DID THIS DURING EVEN HER HUSBAND'S LIFE--	48	2 DON JUAN	1	48	7
AND LIFE YIELDS NOTHING FURTHER TO RECALL	90	2 DON JUAN	1	127	5
YOU'LL LOSE YOUR LIFE AND I SHALL LOSE MY PLACE	115	2 DON JUAN	1	171	7
MAN'S LOVE IS OF MAN'S LIFE A THING APART	131	2 DON JUAN	1	194	1
AND BEAR WITH LIFE TO LOVE AND PRAY FOR YOU	134	2 DON JUAN	1	197	8
HAVE SPENT MY LIFE BOTH INTEREST AND PRINCIPAL	143	2 DON JUAN	1	213	7
IN SHORT I MUST NOT LEAD THE LIFE I DID DO	144	2 DON JUAN	1	216	4
THE PRIEST INSTRUCTS AND SO OUR LIFE EXHALES	159	2 DON JUAN	2	4	6
ESPECIALLY WHEN LIFE IS RATHER NEW	163	2 DON JUAN	2	12	4
THAN MANY PERSONS MORE ADVANCED IN LIFE	164	2 DON JUAN	2	15	4
'TIS VERY CERTAIN THE DESIRE OF LIFE	190	2 DON JUAN	2	64	1
THEY LIVE UPON THE LOVE OF LIFE AND BEAR	191	2 DON JUAN	2	66	2
AND GAVE NO SIGN OF LIFE SAVE HIS LIMBS QUIVERING	204	2 DON JUAN	2	90	8
WHICH YIELDED A DAY'S LIFE AND TO THEIR MIND	208	2 DON JUAN	2	99	4
FROM WHOSE RELUCTANT ROAR HIS LIFE HE WRUNG	213	2 DON JUAN	2	108	3
WITH JUST ENOUGH OF LIFE TO FEEL ITS PAIN	213	2 DON JUAN	2	108	7

LIFE   (CONTINUED)

	PAGE	VOL	CANTO	STANZA	LN
AND TINGLING VEIN SEEM'D THROBBING BACK TO LIFE	214	2 DON JUAN	2	111	7
THE BEST OF LIFE IS BUT INTOXICATION	250	2 DON JUAN	2	179	2
AS IF THERE WERE NO LIFE BENEATH THE SKY	255	2 DON JUAN	2	188	7
SAVE THEIRS AND THAT THEIR LIFE COULD NEVER DIE	255	2 DON JUAN	2	188	8
ALL THAT IT HATH OF LIFE WITH US IS LIVING	261	2 DON JUAN	2	197	5
AND IF 'TIS LOST LIFE HATH NO MORE TO BRING	262	2 DON JUAN	2	199	4
WITHOUT WHICH LIFE WOULD BE EXTREMELY DULL	269	2 DON JUAN	2	212	5
(UNLESS AT ONCE SHE PLUNGE FOR LIFE IN PRAYERS)--	276	2 DON JUAN	3	4	3
HE WOULD HAVE WRITTEN SONNETS ALL HIS LIFE	279	2 DON JUAN	3	8	8
THOUGH LIFE AND LOVE I LIKE NOT TO DISPARAGE	280	2 DON JUAN	3	9	V4
SO DRAMAS CLOSE WITH DEATH OR SETTLEMENT FOR LIFE	280	2 DON JUAN	3	9	V7
LEAVING THE FUTURE STATES OF LOVE AND LIFE	280	2 DON JUAN	3	9	V7
THE PARADISE BEYOND LIKE THAT OF LIFE	280	2 DON JUAN	3	9	V7
OF LIFE AND IN AN HONESER VOCATION	283	2 DON JUAN	3	14	6
IS ALL THAT LIFE ALLOWS THE LUCKIEST SINNER	294	2 DON JUAN	3	36	4
A LIFE WHICH MADE THEM HAPPY BEYOND MEASURE	295	2 DON JUAN	3	39	4
IF ALL THE DEAD COULD NOW RETURN TO LIFE	301	2 DON JUAN	3	50	1
THE DANGEROUS LIFE IN WHICH HE HAD GROWN OLD	303	2 DON JUAN	3	54	3
ROUND HER SHE MADE AN ATMOSPHERE OF LIFE	313	2 DON JUAN	3	74	1
UNTIL HIS LATE LIFE BY ARCHDEACON COXE	328	2 DON JUAN	3	90	8
BUT HIS LIFE FALLING INTO JOHNSON'S WAY	328	2 DON JUAN	3	91	5
A LONG AND SNAKE-LIKE LIFE OF DULL DECAY	348	2 DON JUAN	4	9	7
AND THAT BRIEF DREAM APPEAR'D A LIFE TOO LONG	362	2 DON JUAN	4	34	8
LIKE ONE LIFE COULD NOT HOLD NOR DEATH DESTROY	376	2 DON JUAN	4	59	8
NEW THOUGHTS OF LIFE FOR IT SEEM'D FULL OF SOUL	377	2 DON JUAN	4	60	7
THEIR ENERGY LIKE LIFE FORMS ALL THEIR FAME	377	2 DON JUAN	4	61	7
YET LOOKS NOT LIFE FOR THEY ARE STILL THE SAME	377	2 DON JUAN	4	61	8
RATHER THE DEAD FOR LIFE SEEM'D SOMETHING NEW	378	2 DON JUAN	4	62	2
A SECOND PRINCIPLE OF LIFE WHICH MIGHT	382	2 DON JUAN	4	70	2
IF SHE LOVED RASHLY HER LIFE PAID FOR WRONG--	383	2 DON JUAN	4	73	5
AND HAGGARD WITH A DISSIPATED LIFE	389	2 DON JUAN	4	83	2
AND HAVING LED A RATHER LOOSISH LIFE	389	2 DON JUAN	4	83	V2
LIFE SEEMS THE SMALLEST PORTION OF EXISTENCE	398	2 DON JUAN	4	100	3
IF IN THE COURSE OF SUCH A LIFE AS WAS	402	2 DON JUAN	4	107	1
BUT DROOP NOT FORTUNE AT YOUR TIME OF LIFE	419	2 DON JUAN	5	17	1
BUT MINE HAVE VANISHED ALL WHEN LIFE IS NEW	421	2 DON JUAN	5	21	4
FOUND LIFE MOST TOLERABLE AFTER MEALS	427	2 DON JUAN	5	31	2
CAN THIS BE DEATH THEN WHAT IS LIFE OR DEATH	430	2 DON JUAN	5	36	1
IN ALL HER LIFE WITH AUGHT SAVE PRAYERS AND PRAISE	482	2 DON JUAN	5	122	3
AND AS SHE ALSO RISKED HER LIFE TO GET	482	2 DON JUAN	5	122	4
WHY DON'T THEY KNEAD TWO VIRTUOUS SOULS FOR LIFE	502	2 DON JUAN	5	158	7
LIFE HAS NOUGHT LIKE IT GOD IS LOVE THEY SAY	9	3 DON JUAN	6	6	5
AND TIMIDLY EXPANDING INTO LIFE	27	3 DON JUAN	6	43	8
WHO KNEW THIS LIFE WAS NOT WORTH A POTATO	68	3 DON JUAN	7	4	4
FROM HOLDING UP THE NOTHINGNESS OF LIFE	69	3 DON JUAN	7	6	8
FROM FOOLS WHO DREAD TO KNOW THE TRUTH OF LIFE	69	3 DON JUAN	7	6	V8
TO ME THIS KIND OF LIFE IS NOT SO NEW	103	3 DON JUAN	7	72	5
WHO CALCULATED LIFE AS SO MUCH DROSS	105	3 DON JUAN	7	77	3
THAT AWFUL PAUSE DIVIDING LIFE FROM DEATH	111	3 DON JUAN	7	87	2
A MOMENT AND ALL WILL BE LIFE AGAIN	111	3 DON JUAN	7	87	5
HALF-PAY FOR LIFE MAKE MANKIND WORTH DESTROYING	118	3 DON JUAN	8	14	8
WHO PASSES FOR IN LIFE AND DEATH MOST LUCKY	143	3 DON JUAN	8	61	2
THEIR CHOICE THAN LIFE FORGIVE THEM AS BEGUILED	143	3 DON JUAN	8	62	5
THOUGH LIFE AND DEATH AND VICTORY WERE AT STAKE	147	3 DON JUAN	8	70	1
EVEN WITH HIS LIFE--FOR (BUT THEY LIE) 'TIS SAID	153	3 DON JUAN	8	84	7
THE RUSSIAN OFFICER FOR LIFE WAS LAMED	154	3 DON JUAN	8	85	2
HER LIFE TO CHANCE BUT POINT ME OUT SOME NOOK	161	3 DON JUAN	8	99	3
OF PRESENT LIFE A GOOD DEAL MORE THAN WE--	161	3 DON JUAN	8	100	3
AND FELT--THOUGH DONE WITH LIFE--HE WAS ALONE	170	3 DON JUAN	8	117	8
THEY HONOURED SUCH DETERMINED SCORN OF LIFE	171	3 DON JUAN	8	119	8
HE WHOSE WHOLE LIFE HAS BEEN ASSAULT AND BATTERY	185	3 DON JUAN	9	5	3
TURNS LIFE TO TERROR EVEN THOUGH IN ITS SHEATH	188	3 DON JUAN	9	11	7
STINGS IN LIFE WITH APPREHENSION IN ITS SHEATH	188	3 DON JUAN	9	11	V7
WHY SHOULD NOT LIFE BE EQUALLY CONTENT	189	3 DON JUAN	9	13	3
FOR ME I SOMETIMES THINK THAT LIFE IS DEATH	190	3 DON JUAN	9	16	7
RATHER THAN LIFE A MERE AFFAIR OF BREATH	190	3 DON JUAN	9	16	8
THAT ONE LIFE SAVED ESPECIALLY IF YOUNG	199	3 DON JUAN	9	34	2
THOU GATE OF LIFE AND DEATH--THOU NONDESCRIPT	210	3 DON JUAN	9	55	2
DARK RIDDLE OF ALL LIFE EARTH'S LIFELESS END	210	3 DON JUAN	9	56	V7
HER PRIME OF LIFE JUST NOW IN JUICY VIGOUR	218	3 DON JUAN	9	72	5
WHICH IS FULL SOON (THOUGH LIFE IS BUT A SPAN)	222	3 DON JUAN	9	79	4
OF LIFE REACH TEN O'CLOCK AND WHILE A GLOW	229	3 DON JUAN	10	8	5
THE BASER SIDES OF LITERATURE AND LIFE	232	3 DON JUAN	10	14	2
YOUNG PEOPLE AT HIS TIME OF LIFE SHOULD BE ABLE	235	3 DON JUAN	10	22	3
WITH DAMN YOUR EYES YOUR MONEY OR YOUR LIFE	273	3 DON JUAN	11	10	8
EXPOSED TO LOSE HIS LIFE AS WELL AS BREECHES	273	3 DON JUAN	11	11	8
OF LIFE SHRUNK IN HIS HEART AND THICK AND SOOTY	276	3 DON JUAN	11	16	5
I WISH THEY KNEW THE LIFE OF A YOUNG NOBLE	305	3 DON JUAN	11	74	8
I SAID BEFORE THE FRUGAL LIFE IS HIS	319	3 DON JUAN	12	7	2
OF EARLY LIFE BUT THIS IS A NEW LAND	326	3 DON JUAN	12	23	7
AND PASSED (AT LEAST THE LATTER YEARS OF LIFE)	338	3 DON JUAN	12	47	7
FOR THE FIRST SEASON SUCH A LIFE SCARCE PALLS	342	3 DON JUAN	12	57	8
AND YET A THIRD OF LIFE IS PASS'D IN SLEEP	411	3 DON JUAN	14	3	8
LESS FROM DISGUST OF LIFE THAN DREAD OF DEATH	412	3 DON JUAN	14	4	8
A PAPER KITE WHICH FLIES 'TWIXT LIFE AND DEATH	414	3 DON JUAN	14	8	5
AND IN-DOOR LIFE IS LESS POETICAL	423	3 DON JUAN	14	30	1
AND HENCE HIGH LIFE IS OFT A DREARY VOID	444	3 DON JUAN	14	79	1
ALL PRESENT LIFE IS BUT AN INTERJECTION	456	3 DON JUAN	15	1	5

LIFE   (CONTINUED)
        O'ER LIFE TOO SWEET AN IMAGE FOR SUCH GLASS . . . . 475 3 DON JUAN 15   43   6
        BETWEEN TWO WORLDS LIFE HOVERS LIKE A STAR . . . . . .   500 3 DON JUAN 15   99   1
        HEAVEN AND HIS FRIENDS KNEW THAT A PRIVATE LIFE . . . .   536 3 DON JUAN 16   74   1
LIFELESS
        AND WET AND COLD AND LIFELESS AT HER FEET . . . . . .   362 2 DON JUAN 4   34   1
        TO BREAK THE LIFELESS SPLENDOR OF THE WHOLE . . . . . .   442 2 DON JUAN 5   56   8
        DARK RIDDLE OF ALL LIFE EARTH'S LIFELESS END . . . . .   210 3 DON JUAN 9   56 V7
LIFE'S
        OF LIFE'S STRANGE TREE SO FRUITFUL ON OCCASION . . . .   250 2 DON JUAN 2   179   6
        PITY HE LOVED ADVENTUROUS LIFE'S VARIETY . . . . . .   296 2 DON JUAN 3   41   7
        WHILE LIFE'S STRANGE PRINCIPLE WILL OFTEN LIE . . . . . 350 2 DON JUAN 4   11   7
        LIFE'S HALF-WAY HOUSE WHERE DAMES WITH VIRTUE CROWNED . . 43 3 DON JUAN 6   75   5
        PROVING THAT TRITE OLD TRUTH THAT LIFE'S AS FRAIL . . .   134 3 DON JUAN 8   43   3
        ARE OR WOULD BE THOU SEA OF LIFE'S DRY LAND . . . . .   210 3 DON JUAN 9   56   8
        ARE OR WOULD BE THOU SEA WHICH LAVEST LIFE'S SAND . . .   210 3 DON JUAN 9   56 V8
        IN LOVE DRINKS ALL LIFE'S FOUNTAINS (SAVE TEARS) DRY . . 216 3 DON JUAN 9   67   8
        LIFE'S SAD POST-HORSES O'ER THE DREARY FRONTIER . . .   238 3 DON JUAN 10   27   7
        ON LIFE'S WORN CONFINE JADED BLOATED SATED . . . . .   267 3 DON JUAN 10   87   2
        I'VE DONE TO FIND THE SAME THROUGHOUT LIFE'S JOURNEY . . 281 3 DON JUAN 11   28   7
        LIFE'S A POOR PLAYER --THEN PLAY OUT THE PLAY . . . . .   310 3 DON JUAN 11   86   4
        FOR THEY HAVE PASSED LIFE'S EQUINOCTIAL LINE . . . . .   360 3 DON JUAN 13   5   4
        BUT I'M NOT OEDIPUS AND LIFE'S A SPHINX . . . .   364 3 DON JUAN 13   12   8
        MUST BE DECLINED WHILE LIFE'S THIN THREAD'S SPUN OUT . . 376 3 DON JUAN 13   40   7
        BY VARIOUS JOLTINGS OF LIFE'S HACKNEY COACH . . . . .   421 3 DON JUAN 14   26   5
        AMIDST LIFE'S INFINITE VARIETY . . . .   464 3 DON JUAN 15   19   2
        A HALF-STARVED BABE A WRECK UPON LIFE'S OCEAN . . . . .   563 3 DON JUAN 17   3   4
        TO LIFE'S SMALL RUBS SHOULD SURELY BE MORE PLIANT . . .   566 3 DON JUAN 17   10   3
LIFE-TIME
        WHO IN HIS LIFE-TIME EACH WAS DEEMED A BORE . . . . .   566 3 DON JUAN 17   9   4
LIFT
        TO LIFT OUR FATAL LOVE TO GOD FROM MAN . . . .   131 2 DON JUAN 1   194 V8
        WHOLE OF HER STERN-FRAME AND ERE SHE COULD LIFT . . . . 170 2 DON JUAN 2   27   5
        WHILE GENTLE WRITERS ALSO LOVE TO LIFT . . . .   50 3 DON JUAN 6   88   6
        CHILL AND CHAINED TO COLD EARTH WE LIFT ON HIGH . . . .   66 3 DON JUAN 7   1   5
LIFTED
        BUT NOW BEING LIFTED INTO HIGH SOCIETY . . . .   318 2 DON JUAN 3   83   1
LIFTING
        AND LIFTING HIM WITH CARE INTO THE CAVE . . . .   216 2 DON JUAN 2   115   1
LIGHT
        LIKE WHAT THIS LIGHT TOUCH LEFT ON JUAN'S HEART . . .   60 2 DON JUAN 1   71   8
        THE SILVER LIGHT WHICH HALLOWING TREE AND TOWER . . . .   82 2 DON JUAN 1   114   5
        THERE'S SOMETHING CHEERFUL IN THAT SORT OF LIGHT . . .   94 2 DON JUAN 1   135   5
        DIRE WAS THE SCUFFLE AND OUT WENT THE LIGHT . . . . .   122 2 DON JUAN 1   184   1
        THE NINE DAYS' WONDER WHICH WAS BROUGHT TO LIGHT . . .   126 2 DON JUAN 1   188   6
        AND SUCH LIGHT GRIEFS ARE NOT A THING TO DIE ON . . . .   165 2 DON JUAN 2   16   4
        THERE WAS NO LIGHT IN HEAVEN BUT A FEW STARS . . . .   183 2 DON JUAN 2   51   5
        AS MORNING BROKE THE LIGHT WIND DIED AWAY . . . . .   207 2 DON JUAN 2   97   1
        LIGHT TO THE ROCKS THAT ROOF'D THEM WHICH THE SUN . . .   216 2 DON JUAN 2   115   6
        AND NEAR THE CAVE HER QUICK LIGHT FOOTSTEPS DREW . . .   232 2 DON JUAN 2   142   2
        SHOWS STARS AND WOMEN IN A BETTER LIGHT . . . . . .   237 2 DON JUAN 2   152   8
        AND SAW EACH OTHER'S DARK EYES DARTING LIGHT . . . .   253 2 DON JUAN 2   185   6
        AN INFANT WHEN IT GAZES ON A LIGHT . . . .   261 2 DON JUAN 2   196   1
        SHOWERS TRIPLE LIGHT AND SCORCHES EVEN THE KISS . . . .   264 2 DON JUAN 2   202   3
        LIGHT CLASSIC ARTICLES OF FEMALE WANT . . . .   284 2 DON JUAN 3   17   4
        HE HEARD HIS RIVULET'S LIGHT BUBBLING RUN . . . . . .   289 2 DON JUAN 3   27   3
        MERIDIAN-LIKE WERE SEEN ALL LIGHT TO ISSUE . . . . .   309 2 DON JUAN 3   67   8
        DYES WITH HIS MORNING LIGHT--AND WOULD CONCEAL . . . .   313 2 DON JUAN 3   73   3
        BUT CLOSED ITS LITTLE BEING WITHOUT LIGHT . . . . . .   382 2 DON JUAN 4   70   4
        SHALL SORROW LIGHT OR SHAME SHE WAS NOT MADE . . . .   382 2 DON JUAN 4   71   2
        GAVE LIGHT ENOUGH TO HINT THEIR FARTHER WAY . . . . .   442 2 DON JUAN 5   56   2
        WHICH IS NOT QUITE SO LIGHT AS YOU MAY DEEM . . . . .   459 2 DON JUAN 5   82   4
        LIE DOWN IN DUDGEON TO SIGH FOR THE LIGHT . . . . . .   18 3 DON JUAN 6   24   4
        ALL BASHFULLY TO STRUGGLE INTO LIGHT . . . .   39 3 DON JUAN 6   66   8
        WITH EAGER EYES AND LIGHT BUT HURRIED TREAD . . . . .   42 3 DON JUAN 6   72   3
        GOOD MORROW--FOR THE COCK HAD CROWN AND LIGHT . . . .   49 3 DON JUAN 6   86   2
        OF CLOSING 'GAINST THE LIGHT THEIR ORBS OF VISION . . .   50 3 DON JUAN 6   88   5
        OUR EYES IN SEARCH OF EITHER LOVELY LIGHT . . . . . .   66 3 DON JUAN 7   1   6
        LET THERE BE LIGHT SAID GOD AND THERE WAS LIGHT . . . .   86 3 DON JUAN 7   41   1
        LET THERE BE LIGHT SAID GOD AND THERE WAS LIGHT . . . .   86 3 DON JUAN 7   41   1
        HE FLITTED TO AND FRO A DANCING LIGHT . . . .   89 3 DON JUAN 7   46   7
        OF THE ARMED RIVER WHILE WITH STRAGGLING LIGHT . . . .   110 3 DON JUAN 7   86   5
        BUT WHEN THEY LIGHT UPON IMMEDIATE DEATH . . . . . .   133 3 DON JUAN 8   40   7
        AGAINST THE LIGHT WHEREIN SHE DIES HE CLUNG . . . . .   170 3 DON JUAN 8   118   4
        OF LIGHT TO SAVE THE VENERABLY CHASTE-- . . . . . .   177 3 DON JUAN 8   130   6
        OR DONE IS LIGHT TO WHAT SHE'LL SAY OR DO-- . . . . .   214 3 DON JUAN 9   64   7
        (LIKE LUCUS FROM NO LIGHT) THROUGH PROSPECTS NAMED . .   278 3 DON JUAN 11   21   2
        THERE REMBRANDT MADE HIS DARKNESS EQUAL LIGHT . . . .   392 3 DON JUAN 13   72   2
        THE CLARET LIGHT AND THE MADEIRA STRONG . . . . . .   394 3 DON JUAN 13   76   6
        BUT LIGHT AND AIRY STOOD ON THE ALERT . . . .   426 3 DON JUAN 14   37   1
        IT WAS NOT SCORN--WHICH COULD NOT LIGHT ON ONE . . . .   479 3 DON JUAN 15   54   3
        DEEP SECRETS TO HER ROLLING LIGHT ARE TOLD . . . . .   506 3 DON JUAN 16   14   6
        WITH SOME SLIGHT LIGHT HEREDITARY TWINGES . . . . . .   515 3 DON JUAN 16   34   7
        WITH SWORD IN HAND AND TORCH TO LIGHT . . . .   518 3 DON JUAN 16 L 2   3
        BUT EN AVANT THE LIGHT LOVES LANGUISH O'ER . . . . .   542 3 DON JUAN 16   86   1
        HALF LETTING IN LONG SHADOWS ON THE LIGHT . . . . . .   558 3 DON JUAN 16   117   4
        WHEN ANY DARE A NEW LIGHT TO PRESENT . . . .   564 3 DON JUAN 17   5   3
        THE LIGHT THAT THROUGH THE GOTHIC WINDOWS SHONE . . . .   568 3 DON JUAN 17   14   5
LIGHTED
        AND LIGHTED AT TOO PURE A SHRINE TO DIM ITS . . . . .   65 2 DON JUAN 1   81   5

449

		PAGE	VOL		CANTO	STANZA	LN

LIGHTED   (CONTINUED)
   BEAUTY UPON THE BEAUTIFUL THEY LIGHTED . . . . 265 2 DON JUAN 2 204 3
   THOSE THEIR BRIGHT RISE HAD LIGHTED TO SUCH JOYS . . . 352 2 DON JUAN 4 16 2
   BY JOVE A NOBLE PALACE--LIGHTED TOO . . . . 436 2 DON JUAN 5 45 8
   AND THE STAINED GLASS WHICH LIGHTED THIS FAIR GROT . . 55 3 DON JUAN 6 98 4
   LIKE TO A LIGHTED ALABASTER VASE-- . . . . 159 3 DON JUAN 8 96 8
   AND LIGHTED FIRST HER EYE AND THEN HER MOUTH . . . . 213 3 DON JUAN 9 61 2
   NEW LIGHTED ON A HEAVEN-KISSING HILL . . . . 215 3 DON JUAN 9 66 2
LIGHTEN
   LIKE SKIES THAT RAIN AND LIGHTEN AS A VEIL . . . . . 108 2 DON JUAN 1 158 3
LIGHTENING
   LIGHTENING ALONG HIS VEINS AND WHERE HE HEARD . . . . 129 3 DON JUAN 8 33 V3
LIGHTER
   THE VERY AIR SEEM'D LIGHTER FROM HER EYES . . . . . 313 3 DON JUAN 3 74 2
   IS LIGHTER FAR OF HEART AND VOICE THAN THOSE . . . . 49 3 DON JUAN 6 87 7
LIGHTEST
   THE LIGHTEST BEING THE SAFEST AT A DISTANCE . . . . . 140 3 DON JUAN 8 55 5
LIGHTLY
   ONE WITH HER AUBURN TRESSES LIGHTLY BOUND . . . . . 38 3 DON JUAN 6 65 5
LIGHTNING
   AS IF HER VEINS RAN LIGHTNING SHE IN SOOTH . . . . . 55 2 DON JUAN 1 61 6
   THEY WERE ALL SUMMER LIGHTNING MIGHT ASSAIL . . . . 348 2 DON JUAN 4 9 5
   FILLED AS WITH LIGHTNING--FOR HIS SPIRIT SHARED . . . 129 3 DON JUAN 8 33 3
   AFFECT NO MORE THAN LIGHTNING A CONDUCTOR . . . . . 260 3 DON JUAN 10 71 8
   WOULD YOU HAVE ENDLESS LIGHTNING IN THE SKIES . . . . 451 3 DON JUAN 14 94 6
LIGHTS
   LIGHTS CAME AT LENGTH AND MEN AND MAIDS WHO FOUND . . . 125 2 DON JUAN 1 187 1
   AND DISTANT FROM EACH OTHER BURNED THE LIGHTS . . . . 38 2 DON JUAN 6 64 2
   THE LINE OF LIGHTS TOO UP TO CHARING CROSS . . . . . 280 3 DON JUAN 11 26 1
   THE WORLD TO GAZE UPON THOSE NORTHERN LIGHTS . . . . 353 3 DON JUAN 12 82 5
   IN VERNET'S OCEAN LIGHTS AND THERE THE STORIES . . . 392 3 DON JUAN 13 71 6
   BUT BY DIM LIGHTS THE PORTRAITS OF THE DEAD . . . . . 508 3 DON JUAN 16 17 7
LIKE
   LIKE FOUR AND TWENTY BLACKBIRDS IN A PYE . . . . . . 9 2 DON JUAN D 1 8
   BUT LIKE A HAWK ENCUMBER'D WITH HIS HOOD-- . . . . . 10 2 DON JUAN D 2 6
   AND TUMBLE DOWNWARD LIKE THE FLYING FISH . . . . . . 10 2 DON JUAN D 3 6
   ARISE LIKE TITAN FROM THE SEA'S IMMERSION . . . . . 14 2 DON JUAN D 9 6
   LIKE SAMUEL FROM THE GRAVE TO FREEZE ONCE MORE . . . 15 2 DON JUAN D 11 2
   AND FILL'D THEIR SIGN-POSTS THEN LIKE WELLESLEY NOW . 22 2 DON JUAN 1 2 4
   EACH IN THEIR TURN LIKE BANQUO'S MONARCHS STALK . . . 22 2 DON JUAN 1 2 5
   A GOOD DEAL LIKE HIM TOO THOUGH QUITE THE SAME NONE . 24 2 DON JUAN 1 5 3
   LIKE THE LAMENTED LATE SIR SAMUEL ROMILLY . . . . . 29 2 DON JUAN 1 15 4
   DON JOSE LIKE A LINEAL SON OF EVE . . . . 30 2 DON JUAN 1 18 7
   CONDUCT LIKE THIS BY NO MEANS COMPREHENDS . . . . . 37 2 DON JUAN 1 30 6
   ('TWERE HARD TO TELL UPON A LIKE OCCASION . . . . . 38 2 DON JUAN 1 32 3
   LIKE GARDEN GODS--AND NOT SO DECENT EITHER . . . . . 46 2 DON JUAN 1 45 8
   HER EYEBROW'S SHAPE WAS LIKE THE AERIAL BOW . . . . 55 2 DON JUAN 1 61 3
   LIKE WHAT THIS LIGHT TOUCH LEFT ON JUAN'S HEART . . . 60 2 DON JUAN 1 71 8
   HIS LIKE ALL DEEP GRIEF PLUNGED IN SOLITUDE . . . . 68 2 DON JUAN 1 87 4
   UNLESS LIKE WORDSWORTH THEY PROVE UNINTELLIGIBLE . . . 70 2 DON JUAN 1 90 8
   LIKE COLERIDGE INTO A METAPHYSICIAN . . . . 70 2 DON JUAN 1 91 8
   IN THOUGHTS LIKE THESE TRUE WISDOM MAY DISCERN . . . 71 2 DON JUAN 1 93 1
   OR LIKE ALL VERY CLEVER PEOPLE COULD NOT . . . . . 73 2 DON JUAN 1 97 8
   I LIKE TO BE PARTICULAR IN DATES . . . . 76 2 DON JUAN 1 103 2
   WHICH TREMBLED LIKE THE BOSOM WHERE 'TWAS PLACED . . . 83 2 DON JUAN 1 115 3
   'TIS STRANGE OLD PEOPLE DONT LIKE TO BE BURIED . . . 89 2 DON JUAN 1 125 V8
   LIKE ADAM'S RECOLLECTION OF HIS FALL . . . . 90 2 DON JUAN 1 127 3
   BUT HAS NOT ANSWER'D LIKE THE APPARATUS . . . . . . 92 2 DON JUAN 1 130 3
   APPEAR'D LIKE TWO POOR HARMLESS WOMEN WHO . . . . . 98 2 DON JUAN 1 141 2
   A HUSBAND LIKE ALFONSO AT MY SIDE . . . . 100 2 DON JUAN 1 145 6
   LIKE SKIES THAT RAIN AND LIGHTEN AS A VEIL . . . . . 108 2 DON JUAN 1 158 3
   HE LIKE ACHATES FAITHFUL TO THE TOMB . . . . 109 2 DON JUAN 1 159 6
   LIKE THROWING JUAN IN ALFONSO'S WAY . . . . 118 2 DON JUAN 1 177 8
   HE STOOD LIKE ADAM LINGERING NEAR HIS GARDEN . . . . 120 2 DON JUAN 1 180 5
   HE FLED LIKE JOSEPH LEAVING IT BUT THERE . . . . . 124 2 DON JUAN 1 186 7
   IF YOU WOULD LIKE TO SEE THE WHOLE PROCEEDINGS . . . 127 2 DON JUAN 1 189 1
   PROSE POETS LIKE BLANK-VERSE I'M FOND OF RHYME . . . 136 2 DON JUAN 1 201 5
   SOME PEOPLE LIKE BLANK VERSE I'M FOND OF RHYME . . . 136 2 DON JUAN 1 201 V5
   THOU SHALT NOT BEAR FALSE WITNESS LIKE THE BLUES . . . 140 2 DON JUAN 1 206 3
   (I WONDER WHAT IT WILL BE LIKE AT FORTY . . . . . . 143 2 DON JUAN 1 213 2
   THE FRESHNESS OF THE HEART CAN FALL LIKE DEW . . . . 144 2 DON JUAN 1 214 2
   HIVED IN OUR BOSOMS LIKE THE BAG O' THE BEE . . . . 144 2 DON JUAN 1 214 5
   NOW LIKE FRIAR BACON'S BRAZEN HEAD I'VE SPOKEN . . . 145 2 DON JUAN 1 217 1
   WHOSE SUMMIT LIKE ALL HILLS IS LOST IN VAPOUR . . . . 146 2 DON JUAN 1 218 4
   NOR LIKEN IT--I NEVER SAW THE LIKE . . . . 159 2 DON JUAN 2 5 8
   BUT DAMN ME--IF I EVER SAW THE LIKE . . . . 159 2 DON JUAN 2 5 V8
   AND SEND HIM LIKE A DOVE OF PROMISE FORTH . . . . . 161 2 DON JUAN 2 8 8
   (LIKE TRUANT ROGUES) THE DEVIL OR THE FOOL . . . . . 162 2 DON JUAN 2 10 4
   SWEETS TO THE SWEET (I LIKE SO MUCH TO QUOTE . . . . 165 2 DON JUAN 2 17 3
   BUT VULGAR ILLNESSES DON'T LIKE TO MEET . . . . . . 168 2 DON JUAN 2 22 6
   LIKE A MERE LOG AND BAFFLED OUR INTENT . . . . . . 173 2 DON JUAN 2 32 4
   BUT LET US DIE LIKE MEN NOT SINK BELOW . . . . . . 175 2 DON JUAN 2 36 4
   LIKE BRUTES--AND THUS HIS DANGEROUS POST KEPT HE . . . 175 2 DON JUAN 2 36 5
   TO FOLLOW JUAN'S WAKE LIKE SANCHO PANCA . . . . . . 175 2 DON JUAN 2 37 8
   STILL SWAM--THOUGH NOT EXACTLY LIKE A DUCK . . . . . 177 2 DON JUAN 2 40 8
   LIKE HUMAN BEINGS DURING CIVIL WAR . . . . 178 2 DON JUAN 2 42 8
   OVER THE WASTE OF WATERS LIKE A VEIL . . . . 182 2 DON JUAN 2 49 2
   AND THE SEA YAWN'D AROUND HER LIKE A HELL . . . . . 184 2 DON JUAN 2 52 5
   LIKE ONE WHO GRAPPLES WITH HIS ENEMY . . . . 184 2 DON JUAN 2 52 7

LIKE   (CONTINUED)

	PAGE	VOL	CANTO	STANZA	LN
LOUDER THAN THE LOUD OCEAN LIKE A CRASH	184	2	DON JUAN	2	53	2
AT WATCH AND WATCH THUS SHIVERING LIKE THE TERTIAN	189	2	DON JUAN	2	63	6
AND STAND LIKE ROCKS THE TEMPEST'S WEAR AND TEAR	191	2	DON JUAN	2	66	4
LIKE THE FIRST OLD GREEK PRIVATEER THE ARGO	191	2	DON JUAN	2	66	8
HE CANNOT LIVE LIKE WOODCOCKS UPON SUCTION	191	2	DON JUAN	2	67	3
BUT LIKE THE SHARK AND TIGER MUST HAVE PREY	191	2	DON JUAN	2	67	4
AND LYING ON THEIR WEARINESS LIKE BALM	192	2	DON JUAN	2	68	4
LULL'D THEM LIKE TURTLES SLEEPING ON THE BLUE	192	2	DON JUAN	2	68	5
AND OCEAN SLUMBER'D LIKE AN UNWEAN'D CHILD	193	2	DON JUAN	2	70	2
THEY LAY LIKE CARCASSES AND HOPE WAS NONE	194	2	DON JUAN	2	72	3
LIKE THE PROMETHEAN VULTURE THIS POLLUTION	195	2	DON JUAN	2	75	4
LIKE MOST IN THE BELIEF IN WHICH THEY'RE BRED	197	2	DON JUAN	2	76	6
DRINKING SALT-WATER LIKE A MOUNTAIN-STREAM	198	2	DON JUAN	2	79	6
FOR WHICH THEIR MOUTHS GAPED LIKE THE CRACKS OF EARTH	201	2	DON JUAN	2	84	2
SUCK'D IN THE MOISTURE WHICH LIKE NECTAR STREAM'D	202	2	DON JUAN	2	86	2
WAX'D BROAD AND WAVING LIKE A BANNER FREE	204	2	DON JUAN	2	91	6
THEN CHANGED LIKE TO A BOW THAT'S BENT AND THEN	204	2	DON JUAN	2	91	7
GLITTERING LIKE CRESCENTS O'ER A TURK'S PAVILION	205	2	DON JUAN	2	92	5
JUST LIKE A BLACK EYE IN A RECENT SCUFFLE	205	2	DON JUAN	2	92	7
THAN THESE AND SO THIS RAINBOW LOOK'D LIKE HOPE--	205	2	DON JUAN	2	93	7
LIKE CHARON'S BARK OF SPECTRES DULL AND PALE	209	2	DON JUAN	2	101	3
AND FELL UPON THEIR GLAZED EYES LIKE A SCREEN	210	2	DON JUAN	2	103	5
AND LIKE A WITHER'D LILY ON THE LAND	214	2	DON JUAN	2	110	6
LIKE TWILIGHT ROSY STILL WITH THE SET SUN	218	2	DON JUAN	2	118	2
LIKE PETER THE APOSTLE--AND HE FISH'D	223	2	DON JUAN	2	126	2
STILL IN HER TEENS AND LIKE A LOVELY TREE	224	2	DON JUAN	2	128	5
BUT LIKE CONVEYING TO THE CAT THE MOUSE	225	2	DON JUAN	2	130	3
JUAN SLEPT LIKE A TOP OR LIKE THE DEAD	227	2	DON JUAN	2	134	2
JUAN SLEPT LIKE A TOP OR LIKE THE DEAD	227	2	DON JUAN	2	134	2
AND LEAVE LIKE OPENING HELL UPON THE MIND	227	2	DON JUAN	2	134	V7
AND NIGHT IS FLUNG OFF LIKE A MOURNING SUIT	230	2	DON JUAN	2	139	7
AND NIGHT IS BACKWARD LIKE A MANTLE ROLLED	230	2	DON JUAN	2	139	V8
LIKE TO A TORRENT WHICH A MOUNTAIN'S BASE	231	2	DON JUAN	2	141	5
AS AT THIS MOMENT I SHOULD LIKE TO DO	232	2	DON JUAN	2	142	V6
THAT LIKE AN INFANT JUAN SWEETLY SLEPT	232	2	DON JUAN	2	143	3
AND THUS LIKE TO AN ANGEL O'ER THE DYING	233	2	DON JUAN	2	144	1
A PURPLE HECTIC PLAY'D LIKE DYING DAY	234	2	DON JUAN	2	147	2
LULL'D LIKE THE DEPTH OF OCEAN WHEN AT REST	235	2	DON JUAN	2	148	4
WHO LIKE A MORNING SLUMBER--FOR THE NIGHT	237	2	DON JUAN	2	152	7
A PLEASURE--LIKE ALL PLEASURES--RATHER DEAR	238	2	DON JUAN	2	156	6
HE FELL UPON WHATE'ER WAS OFFER'D LIKE	239	2	DON JUAN	2	157	7
WHO WATCH'D HIM LIKE A MOTHER WOULD HAVE FED	239	2	DON JUAN	2	158	2
AND DRESS'D HIM FOR THE PRESENT LIKE A TURK	240	2	DON JUAN	2	160	4
WHERE I LIKE OTHER DOGS HAVE HAD MY DAY	244	2	DON JUAN	2	166	3
LIKE OTHER MEN TOO MAY HAVE HAD MY PASSION--	244	2	DON JUAN	2	166	4
BUT THAT LIKE OTHER THINGS HAS PASS'D AWAY	244	2	DON JUAN	2	166	5
FOR LOVE MUST BE SUSTAIN'D LIKE FLESH AND BLOOD--	246	2	DON JUAN	2	170	4
LIKE A RICH WRECK--HER FIRST LOVE AND HER LAST	247	2	DON JUAN	2	173	8
ON WHICH LIKE A YOUNG FLOWER SNAPP'D FROM THE STALK	249	2	DON JUAN	2	176	5
THE OUTSTRETCH'D OCEAN GLITTER LIKE A LAKE	249	2	DON JUAN	2	177	8
WITH ONE STAR SPARKLING THROUGH IT LIKE AN EYE	252	2	DON JUAN	2	183	8
SPREAD LIKE A ROSY OCEAN VAST AND BRIGHT	253	2	DON JUAN	2	185	2
AND BEAUTY ALL CONCENTRATING LIKE RAYS	254	2	DON JUAN	2	186	2
WHICH BEING JOIN'D LIKE SWARMING BEES THEY CLUNG--	254	2	DON JUAN	2	187	7
AND FLEW TO HER YOUNG MATE LIKE A YOUNG BIRD	257	2	DON JUAN	2	190	6
THEY TWINED LIKE SERPENTS AND THEY KISSED LIKE DOVES	257	2	DON JUAN	2	191	V7
THEY TWINED LIKE SERPENTS AND THEY KISSED LIKE DOVES	257	2	DON JUAN	2	191	V7
AND ALL ITS CHARM LIKE DEATH WITHOUT ITS TERRORS	261	2	DON JUAN	2	197	8
WHICH GAVE ME SOME SENSATIONS LIKE A VILLAIN	268	2	DON JUAN	2	209	8
AND REALLY LONGED TO KISS HER--LIKE A VILLAIN	268	2	DON JUAN	2	209	V8
AS WHEN SHE ROSE UPON US LIKE AN EVE	270	2	DON JUAN	2	213	4
THE HEART IS LIKE THE SKY A PART OF HEAVEN	270	2	DON JUAN	2	214	1
BUT CHANGES NIGHT AND DAY TOO LIKE THE SKY	270	2	DON JUAN	2	214	2
LIKE KNOTS OF VIPERS ON A DUNGHILL'S SOIL	271	2	DON JUAN	2	215	5
LIKE EARTHQUAKES FROM THE HIDDEN FIRE CALL'D CENTRAL	271	2	DON JUAN	2	215	8
AND FITS HER LOOSELY--LIKE AN EASY GLOVE	276	2	DON JUAN	3	3	4
AS YOU MAY FIND WHENE'ER YOU LIKE TO PROVE HER	276	2	DON JUAN	3	3	5
MARRIAGE FROM LOVE LIKE VINEGAR FROM WINE--	277	2	DON JUAN	3	5	5
THOUGH LIFE AND LOVE I LIKE NOT TO DISPARAGE	280	2	DON JUAN	3	9	V4
THE PARADISE BEYOND LIKE THAT OF LIFE	280	2	DON JUAN	3	9	V7
WHEN WE HAVE WHAT WE LIKE 'TIS HARD TO MISS IT	282	2	DON JUAN	3	13	5
HIS PRISONERS DIVIDING THEM LIKE CHAPTERS	283	2	DON JUAN	3	15	6
A SOFA LIKE A BED MAY COME BY WRONG	288	2	DON JUAN	3	25	V8
LIKE DERVISES WHO TURN AS ON A PIVOT HE	290	2	DON JUAN	3	29	6
WERE STRUNG TOGETHER LIKE A ROW OF PEARLS	291	2	DON JUAN	3	30	3
HE LAY COILED LIKE THE BOA IN THE WOOD	300	2	DON JUAN	3	48	4
AND TURN HIM LIKE THE CYCLOPS MAD WITH BLINDNESS	304	2	DON JUAN	3	57	8
AND SEND HIM FORTH LIKE SAMSON--STRONG IN BLINDNESS	304	2	DON JUAN	3	57	V8
LIKE CHERUBS ROUND AN ALTAR-PIECE THEY CLING	306	2	DON JUAN	3	60	5
SHINE LIKE A GUINEA AND SEVEN SHILLING PIECES	306	2	DON JUAN	3	60	8
LIKE SKULLS AT MEMPHIAN BANQUETS TO THE MIND	308	2	DON JUAN	3	65	4
(FOR THAT'S THE NAME THEY LIKE TO PRAY BENEATH)--	309	2	DON JUAN	3	66	4
AND DWARFS AND BLACKS AND SUCH LIKE THINGS THAT GAIN	310	2	DON JUAN	3	68	5
NEATH WHICH HER BREAST HEAVED LIKE A LITTLE BILLOW	311	2	DON JUAN	3	70	4
LIKE FLEECY CLOUDS ABOUT THE MOON FLOW'D ROUND HER	311	2	DON JUAN	3	70	8
LIKE BRANCHES WHEN THE FRUIT BENEATH IS MELLOW	311	2	DON JUAN	3	70	V4
A LIKE GOLD BAR ABOVE HER INSTEP ROLLED	312	2	DON JUAN	3	72	2
FLOW'D LIKE AN ALPINE TORRENT WHICH THE SUN	313	2	DON JUAN	3	73	2

451

	PAGE	VOL		CANTO	STANZA	LN
LIKE (CONTINUED)						
SHE WAS SO LIKE A VISION I MIGHT ERR	314	2	DON JUAN	3	76	6
LIKE SMALL STARS THROUGH THE MILKY WAY APPARENT	315	2	DON JUAN	3	77	4
WITH TRUTH LIKE SOUTHEY AND WITH VERSE LIKE CRASHAW	316	2	DON JUAN	3	79	8
WITH TRUTH LIKE SOUTHEY AND WITH VERSE LIKE CRASHAW	316	2	DON JUAN	3	79	8
BELIEVED LIKE SOUTHEY--AND PERUSED LIKE CRASHAW	316	2	DON JUAN	3	79	V8
BELIEVED LIKE SOUTHEY--AND PERUSED LIKE CRASHAW	316	2	DON JUAN	3	79	V8
EVEN GOOD MEN LIKE TO MAKE THE PUBLIC STARE--	317	2	DON JUAN	3	81	4
IN GREECE HE'D SING SOME SORT OF HYMN LIKE THIS T'YE	320	2	DON JUAN	3	86	8
DEGENERATE INTO HANDS LIKE MINE	322	2	DON JUAN	3	L 5	6
SOUND LIKE A DISTANT TORRENT'S FALL	323	2	DON JUAN	3	L 8	3
WE WILL NOT THINK OF THEMES LIKE THESE	324	2	DON JUAN	3	L 11	2
IF NOT LIKE ORPHEUS QUITE WHEN GREECE WAS YOUNG	326	2	DON JUAN	3	87	3
AND TAKE ALL COLOURS--LIKE THE HANDS OF DYERS	326	2	DON JUAN	3	87	8
FALLING LIKE DEW UPON A THOUGHT PRODUCES	327	2	DON JUAN	3	88	2
FRAIL MAN WHEN PAPER--EVEN A RAG LIKE THIS	327	2	DON JUAN	3	88	7
LIKE SHAKSPEARE'S STEALING DEER LORD BACON'S BRIBES	329	2	DON JUAN	3	92	2
LIKE TITUS' YOUTH AND CAESAR'S EARLIEST ACTS	329	2	DON JUAN	3	92	3
LIKE BURNS (WHOM DOCTOR CURRIE WELL DESCRIBES)	329	2	DON JUAN	3	92	4
LIKE CROMWELL'S PRANKS--BUT ALTHOUGH TRUTH EXACTS	329	2	DON JUAN	3	92	5
ALL ARE NOT MORALISTS LIKE SOUTHEY WHEN	329	2	DON JUAN	3	93	1
BUT WORDSWORTH'S POEM AND HIS FOLLOWERS LIKE	330	2	DON JUAN	3	95	3
THAT PAINTING IS NO IDOL 'TIS TOO LIKE	336	2	DON JUAN	3	103	8
OR ANY SUCH LIKE SOVEREIGN BUFFOONS	341	2	DON JUAN	3	110	2
MUST END IN LANGUOR--MEN WON'T SLEEP LIKE SWINE--	343	2	DON JUAN	3	V 98	4
LIKE LUCIFER WHEN HURL'D FROM HEAVEN FOR SINNING	344	2	DON JUAN	4	1	5
BUT LIKE THE CLIMES THAT KNOW NOR SNOW NOR HAIL	348	2	DON JUAN	4	9	4
ALAS THERE IS NO INSTINCT LIKE THE HEART--	349	2	DON JUAN	4	10	8
JOY SPARKLING IN THEIR DARK EYES LIKE A GEM	351	2	DON JUAN	4	13	6
A LANGUAGE TOO BUT LIKE TO THAT OF BIRDS	351	2	DON JUAN	4	14	4
BUT LIKE TWO BEINGS BORN FROM OUT A RILL	352	2	DON JUAN	4	15	5
LIKE THE WIND O'ER A HARP-STRING OR A FLAME	355	2	DON JUAN	4	21	4
FLOCK O'ER THEIR CARRION JUST LIKE MEN BELOW	358	2	DON JUAN	4	28	8
AND HAIDEE'S SWEET LIPS MURMUR'D LIKE A BROOK	359	2	DON JUAN	4	29	6
RANG IN HER SAD EARS LIKE A MERMAID'S SONG	362	2	DON JUAN	4	34	7
LIKE TO HER FATHER'S FEATURES TILL EACH TRACE	363	2	DON JUAN	4	35	3
MORE LIKE AND LIKE TO LAMBRO'S ASPECT GREW--	363	2	DON JUAN	4	35	4
MORE LIKE AND LIKE TO LAMBRO'S ASPECT GREW--	363	2	DON JUAN	4	35	4
HOW LIKE THEY LOOKED THE EXPRESSION WAS THE SAME	367	2	DON JUAN	4	44	2
HIS OWN SHALL ROLL BEFORE YOU LIKE A BALL	369	2	DON JUAN	4	47	2
HIS ARMS WERE LIKE A SERPENT'S COIL THEN FLEW	370	2	DON JUAN	4	48	5
WITH THE BLOOD RUNNING LIKE A LITTLE BROOK	370	2	DON JUAN	4	49	6
AND MAKE LIKE OTHER NYMPHS THY LOVERS ILL	372	2	DON JUAN	4	53	4
AND LIKE THE SOIL BENEATH IT WILL BRING FORTH	374	2	DON JUAN	4	56	5
THOUGH SLEEPING LIKE A LION NEAR A SOURCE	374	2	DON JUAN	4	56	8
LIKE SUMMER CLOUDS ALL SILVERY SMOOTH AND FAIR	375	2	DON JUAN	4	57	2
HER WRITHING FELL SHE LIKE A CEDAR FELL'D	375	2	DON JUAN	4	58	8
LIKE ONE LIFE COULD NOT HOLD NOR DEATH DESTROY	376	2	DON JUAN	4	59	8
THEIR ENERGY LIKE LIFE FORMS ALL THEIR FAME	377	2	DON JUAN	4	61	7
LIKE MOUNTAIN MISTS AT LENGTH DISSOLVED IN RAIN	380	2	DON JUAN	4	66	8
I DON'T MUCH LIKE DESCRIBING PEOPLE MAD	384	2	DON JUAN	4	74	3
AS FOR THE FIGURANTI ARE LIKE	390	2	DON JUAN	4	85	1
AND SIGH I CAN'T GET OUT LIKE YORICK'S STARLING	404	2	DON JUAN	4	109	4
LIKE A BACKGAMMON BOARD THE PLACE WAS DOTTED	416	2	DON JUAN	5	10	1
CASTS OFF ITS BRIGHT SKIN YEARLY LIKE THE SNAKE	421	2	DON JUAN	5	21	8
SO THAT THEIR BARGAIN SOUNDED LIKE A BATTLE	425	2	DON JUAN	5	28	7
THEY LOOKED LIKE PERSONS BEING LED TO SENTENCE	432	2	DON JUAN	5	40	4
LIKE ESAU FOR MY BIRTHRIGHT A BEEF-STEAK	435	2	DON JUAN	5	44	8
(LOVE LIKE RELIGION SOMETIMES RUNS TO HERESY)	446	2	DON JUAN	5	61	4
A MORAL (LIKE ALL MORALS) MELANCHOLY	448	2	DON JUAN	5	63	6
YOU COULD GLIDE O'ER THEM LIKE A GOLDEN FISH	449	2	DON JUAN	5	65	8
WERE SATE LIKE UGLY IMPS AS IF ALLIED	462	2	DON JUAN	5	87	4
O'ER THEM LIKE DEATH UPON A MONARCH'S PRIDE	462	2	DON JUAN	5	87	V6
AND LOOKING LIKE TWO INCUBI THEY GLARED	463	2	DON JUAN	5	90	2
LIKE NEEDLES WHICH MAY PIERCE THOSE PETTICOATS	464	2	DON JUAN	5	92	2
BENT LIKE AN ANTELOPE A PAPHIAN PAIR	466	2	DON JUAN	5	96	3
AND WERE ALL CLAD ALIKE LIKE JUAN TOO	469	2	DON JUAN	5	99	3
THERE'S NOTHING IN THE WORLD LIKE ETIQUETTE	471	2	DON JUAN	5	103	6
HE STOOD LIKE ATLAS WITH A WORLD OF WORDS	471	2	DON JUAN	5	104	1
WITH AUGHT WHICH LOOKS LIKE DESPOTISM IN VIEW	474	2	DON JUAN	5	110	5
THESE WORDS WENT THROUGH HIS SOUL LIKE ARAB-SPEARS	478	2	DON JUAN	5	117	7
LIKE MOLTEN LEAD AS IF YOU THRUST A PIKE IN	479	2	DON JUAN	5	118	6
BUT TEARS MUST STOP LIKE ALL THINGS ELSE AND SOON	481	2	DON JUAN	5	121	1
TO GENTLEMEN IN ANY SUCH LIKE CASE	482	2	DON JUAN	5	123	2
LIKE AN INVASION OF THEIR BABES AND SUCKLINGS	488	2	DON JUAN	5	133	4
IT LASTED 'TWAS LIKE A SHORT GLIMPSE OF HELL	489	2	DON JUAN	5	135	3
LIKE OCEAN WARRING 'GAINST A ROCKY ISLE	489	2	DON JUAN	5	135	6
LIKE MODERATE HOTSPUR ON THE IMMORTAL PAGE	490	2	DON JUAN	5	136	4
HER WISH WAS BUT TO KILL KILL KILL LIKE LEAR'S	490	2	DON JUAN	5	136	7
LIKE NATURAL SHAKESPEARE ON THE IMMORTAL PAGE	490	2	DON JUAN	5	136	V4
A STORM IT RAGED AND LIKE THE STORM IT PASSED	490	2	DON JUAN	5	137	1
DISSOLVED LIKE SNOW BEFORE A WOMAN CRYING	492	2	DON JUAN	5	141	8
THE SUN HIMSELF HAS SENT ME LIKE A RAY	494	2	DON JUAN	5	144	7
THE FORMER IN A PALACE WHERE LIKE NUNS	498	2	DON JUAN	5	152	3
'TWAS THE BOY'S MITE AND LIKE THE WIDOW'S MAY	9	3	DON JUAN	6	6	1
LIFE HAS NOUGHT LIKE IT GOD IS LOVE THEY SAY	9	3	DON JUAN	6	6	5
I AM NOT LIKE CASSIO AN ARITHMETICIAN	10	3	DON JUAN	6	9	1
THE TIGRIS HATH ITS JEALOUSIES LIKE THAMES	11	3	DON JUAN	6	11	8
MAY LOOK LIKE WHAT IS--NEITHER HERE NOR THERE	13	3	DON JUAN	6	14	3

452

LIKE (CONTINUED)

```
WOULD LIKE (I THINK) TO TRUST ALL TO DESIRE . . . . . .  14  3 DON JUAN  6   16   4
THE SOUL OUT (LIKE THE STONE) WITH PETTY CARES . . . . .  16  3 DON JUAN  6   20   8
LIKE WATER-LILIES FLOATING DOWN A RILL . . . . . . . . .  22  3 DON JUAN  6   33   6
LIKE BIRDS OR BOYS OR BEDLAMITES BROKE LOOSE . . . . . .  23  3 DON JUAN  6   34   2
AFTER ALL) OR LIKE IRISH AT A FAIR . . . . . . . . . . .  23  3 DON JUAN  6   34   5
LIKE ALL THE REST BUT UPON THIS OCCASION . . . . . . . .  25  3 DON JUAN  6   38   2
LIKE MAGNETISM OR DEVILISM OR WHAT . . . . . . . . . . .  25  3 DON JUAN  6   38   7
WHICH MADE THEM LIKE THEIR NEW COMPANION . . . . . . . .  25  3 DON JUAN  6   38  V7
WHO WISHED THEY HAD A BROTHER JUST LIKE HER . . . . . . .  25  3 DON JUAN  6   39   6
STOLE ON YOUR SPIRIT LIKE A MAY-DAY BREAKING . . . . . .  27  3 DON JUAN  6   43   2
FROM MARBLE LIKE PYGMALION'S STATUE WAKING . . . . . . .  27  3 DON JUAN  6   43   6
WHICH PAINTERS CANNOT CATCH LIKE FACES SINNING . . . . .  32  3 DON JUAN  6   52   4
AND PLEASING OR UNPLEASING STILL ARE LIKE . . . . . . .  32  3 DON JUAN  6   52   8
'TWAS LIKE THE FAWN WHICH IN THE LAKE DISPLAYED . . . . .  36  3 DON JUAN  6   60   5
MAKING A WOMAN LIKE A PORCUPINE . . . . . . . . . . . .  37  3 DON JUAN  6   62   1
LIKE FLOWERS OF DIFFERENT HUE AND CLIME AND ROOT . . . .  38  3 DON JUAN  6   65   2
TO THOSE WHO LIKE THEIR COMPANY ABOUT . . . . . . . . .  41  3 DON JUAN  6   70   7
NEITHER CAME CROWDING LIKE THE WAVES OF OCEAN . . . . . .  42  3 DON JUAN  6   71   4
A WOOD OBSCURE LIKE THAT WHERE DANTE FOUND . . . . . . .  43  3 DON JUAN  6   75   3
WHEN ALL AROUND RANG LIKE A TOCSIN BELL . . . . . . . .  48  3 DON JUAN  6   84   4
AT HAND AS ONE MAY LIKE TO HAVE A FAN . . . . . . . . .  51  3 DON JUAN  6   91   4
ALL GENERATIONS I SHOULD LIKE TO KNOW . . . . . . . . .  53  3 DON JUAN  6   94   7
AND WHEN SHE SAW HIM STUMBLING LIKE A STEED . . . . . .  56  3 DON JUAN  6  101   4
O'ER HER FAIR FRONT LIKE MORNING'S ON A LILY . . . . . .  58  3 DON JUAN  6  105   8
WHEN ALL THE HEART-STRINGS LIKE WILD HORSES PULL . . . .  59  3 DON JUAN  6  107   4
FELL IN LONG TRESSES LIKE THE WEEPING WILLOW . . . . . .  60  3 DON JUAN  6  108   2
STIRRED UP AND DOWN HER BOSOM LIKE A BILLOW . . . . . .  60  3 DON JUAN  6  108   6
BUT ONE WHICH BABA DID NOT LIKE TO BRAVE . . . . . . . .  62  3 DON JUAN  6  112   3
FOR FEAR OF ANY ERROR LIKE THE LATE . . . . . . . . . .  62  3 DON JUAN  6  112   8
LIKE OTHER ANGRY LADIES OF HER NATION-- . . . . . . . .  65  3 DON JUAN  6  119   5
THAT HE HIMSELF FELT ONLY LIKE A YOUTH . . . . . . . . .  69  3 DON JUAN  7    5   7
NOW I SHOULD LIKE TO KNOW BEING RATHER CURIOUS . . . . .  77  3 DON JUAN  7   21  V1
FORMED LIKE AN AMPHITHEATRE EACH DWELLING . . . . . . .  78  3 DON JUAN  7   23   7
TO GRATIFY LIKE A HUGE MOTH THIS ONE SENSE . . . . . . .  88  3 DON JUAN  7   44   8
O'ER WHOM SUWARROW SHONE LIKE A GAS LAMP . . . . . . . .  89  3 DON JUAN  7   46   3
OR LIKE A WISP ALONG THE MARSH SO DAMP . . . . . . . . .  89  3 DON JUAN  7   46   5
WAS NOT LIKE JACOB'S) OR TO CROSS A DITCH . . . . . . .  93  3 DON JUAN  7   52   8
LIKE MEN WITH TURBANS SCYMITARS AND DIRKS . . . . . . .  93  3 DON JUAN  7   53   2
SOME COSSACQUES HOVERING LIKE HAWKS ROUND A HILL . . . .  95  3 DON JUAN  7   56   3
YOU LIKE TO BE THE HOPE OF THE FORLORN . . . . . . . . .  98  3 DON JUAN  7   62   2
LIKE AN IMPERIAL PEACOCK STALK ABROAD . . . . . . . . . 104  3 DON JUAN  7   74   5
IN THIS FOR FEMALES LIKE EXAGGERATION . . . . . . . . . 105  3 DON JUAN  7   75   8
AND YET LIKE ALL MEN ELSE I MUST ALLOW . . . . . . . . . 106  3 DON JUAN  7   80   5
AN UNIFORM TO BOYS IS LIKE A FAN . . . . . . . . . . . . 108  3 DON JUAN  7   84   4
BECAUSE HE RUNS BEFORE IT LIKE A PIG . . . . . . . . . . 109  3 DON JUAN  7   85   2
SAY THAT HE SCUDS BEFORE IT LIKE A BRIG . . . . . . . . 109  3 DON JUAN  7   85   4
LIKE A BOB-MAJOR FROM A VILLAGE STEEPLE . . . . . . . . 109  3 DON JUAN  7   85   8
THE ARMY LIKE A LION FROM HIS DEN . . . . . . . . . . . 113  3 DON JUAN  8    2   3
WHICH ARCHED THE HORIZON LIKE A FIERY CLOUD . . . . . . 115  3 DON JUAN  8    6   3
ANSWERING THE CHRISTIAN THUNDERS WITH LIKE VOICES . . . 115  3 DON JUAN  8    7   4
WHILE THE WHOLE RAMPART BLAZED LIKE ETNA WHEN . . . . . 115  3 DON JUAN  8    7   7
LIKE HAIL TO MAKE A BLOODY DIURETIC . . . . . . . . . . 117  3 DON JUAN  8   12   3
LIKE THE DEATH-WATCH WITHIN OUR EARS THE ILLS . . . . . 117  3 DON JUAN  8   12   6
FOR THE FIRST AND LAST TIME FOR LIKE A PAD . . . . . . . 122  3 DON JUAN  8   22   5
AND FIGHT LIKE FIENDS FOR PAY OR POLITICS . . . . . . . 122  3 DON JUAN  8   22   8
LIKE CHASTEST WIVES FROM CONSTANT HUSBANDS' SIDES . . . 125  3 DON JUAN  8   27   3
FOR A MUCH LONGER TIME THEN LIKE AN ASS-- . . . . . . . 126  3 DON JUAN  8   29   5
THEN LIKE AN ASS HE WENT UPON HIS WAY . . . . . . . . . 126  3 DON JUAN  8   30   1
BUT SEEING FLASHING FORWARD LIKE THE DAY . . . . . . . . 126  3 DON JUAN  8   30   3
AND LEFT AT LARGE LIKE A YOUNG HEIR TO MAKE . . . . . . 127  3 DON JUAN  8   32   2
ITS VOTARIES LIKE INNOCENCE RELYING . . . . . . . . . . 131  3 DON JUAN  8   36   5
WHICH DID NOT COMBAT LIKE THE DEVIL AS YET-- . . . . . . 131  3 DON JUAN  8   37   6
MAKES MEN LIKE CATTLE FOLLOW HIM WHO LEADS . . . . . . . 132  3 DON JUAN  8   38   8
OF IDLE APPRENSIONS WHICH LIKE WIND . . . . . . . . . . 133  3 DON JUAN  8   40   4
HIS SOUL (LIKE GALVANISM UPON THE DEAD) . . . . . . . . 133  3 DON JUAN  8   41   6
THE TURKISH BATTERIES THRASHED THEM LIKE A FLAIL . . . . 134  3 DON JUAN  8   43   5
OF THE NEXT BASTION FIRED AWAY LIKE DEVILS . . . . . . . 134  3 DON JUAN  8   44   2
ALL NECK OR NOTHING AS LIKE PITCH OR ROSIN . . . . . . . 135  3 DON JUAN  8   45   3
LIKE DAVID FLINGS SMOOTH PEBBLES 'GAINST A GIANT . . . . 138  3 DON JUAN  8   51   2
EVEN FROM A CHILD FELT LIKE A CHILD HOWE'ER . . . . . . 139  3 DON JUAN  8   53   2
DASHED ON LIKE A SPURRED BLOOD-HORSE IN A RACE . . . . . 139  3 DON JUAN  8   54   8
IN LIKE CHURCH BELLS WITH SIGH HOWL GROAN YELL PRAYER . 141  3 DON JUAN  8   58   7
THE SCENES LIKE CATHERINE'S BOUDOIR AT THREE-SCORE . . . 146  3 DON JUAN  8   68   7
TOOK LIKE CAMELIONS SOME SLIGHT TINGE OF FEAR . . . . . 148  3 DON JUAN  8   73   4
OF CARNAGE LIKE THE NILE'S SUN-SODDEN SLIME . . . . . . 152  3 DON JUAN  8   82   7
WHICH SATAN ANGLES WITH FOR SOULS LIKE FLIES . . . . . . 154  3 DON JUAN  8   86   8
LIKE TO A LIGHTED ALABASTER VASE-- . . . . . . . . . . 159  3 DON JUAN  8   96   8
AND GRAPE IN VOLLEYS LIKE A VINEYARD SCATTERS . . . . . 160  3 DON JUAN  8   98   8
AS BEING A VIRTUE LIKE TERRESTRIAL PATIENCE . . . . . . 165  3 DON JUAN  8  107   7
HE HEWED AWAY LIKE DOCTORS OF THEOLOGY . . . . . . . . . 165  3 DON JUAN  8  108   6
AND POURED UPON HIM AND HIS SONS LIKE RAIN . . . . . . . 166  3 DON JUAN  8  109   7
WHICH THEY RESISTED LIKE A SANDY PLAIN . . . . . . . . . 166  3 DON JUAN  8  109   8
THOSE HOURIS LIKE ALL OTHER PRETTY CREATURES . . . . . . 167  3 DON JUAN  8  111   7
ON HIS SOUL LIKE A CEASELESS SUNRISE DART-- . . . . . . 169  3 DON JUAN  8  115   6
WHO GREW LIKE CEDARS ROUND HIM GLORIOUSLY-- . . . . . . 169  3 DON JUAN  8  116   4
THE EARTH WHICH HE BECAME LIKE A FELLED TREE . . . . . . 169  3 DON JUAN  8  116   6
AND SHOOK (TILL NOW UNSHAKEN) LIKE A REED . . . . . . . 170  3 DON JUAN  8  117   6
SAW NOTHING LIKE THE SCENE AROUND--YET LOOKING . . . . . 172  3 DON JUAN  8  121   4
```

LIKE   (CONTINUED)

	PAGE	VOL	CANTO		STANZA	LN
OF BURNING STREETS LIKE MOONLIGHT ON THE WATER	172	3	DON JUAN	8	122	7
WHILE MOSQUES AND STREETS BENEATH HIS EYES LIKE THATCH	178	3	DON JUAN	8	133	3
COULD RHYME LIKE NERO O'ER A BURNING CITY	179	3	DON JUAN	8	134	8
WHICH LAST MEN LIKE WHEN THEY HAVE TIME TO PAUSE	182	3	DON JUAN	8	140	3
HER FRIENDS LIKE THE SAD FAMILY OF HECTOR	182	3	DON JUAN	8	141	3
GLORY LIKE YOURS SHOULD ANY DARE GAINSAY	183	3	DON JUAN	9	1	7
AND LIKE SOME OTHER THINGS WON'T DO TO TELL	184	3	DON JUAN	9	2	3
THEY SAY YOU LIKE IT TOO--'TIS NO GREAT WONDER	185	3	DON JUAN	9	5	2
MAY LIKE BEING PRAISED FOR EVERY LUCKY BLUNDER	185	3	DON JUAN	9	5	6
THAT HIDES THE PAST WORLD LIKE TO A SET SUN	188	3	DON JUAN	9	11	3
LIKE BUBBLES ON AN OCEAN MUCH LESS AMPLE	189	3	DON JUAN	9	13	6
SUNS AS RAYS--WORLDS LIKE ATOMS--YEARS LIKE HOURS	189	3	DON JUAN	9	13	8
SUNS AS RAYS--WORLDS LIKE ATOMS--YEARS LIKE HOURS	189	3	DON JUAN	9	13	8
LIKE PYRRHO ON A SEA OF SPECULATION	191	3	DON JUAN	9	18	2
LIKE MOSES OR MELANCTHON WHO HAVE NE'ER	193	3	DON JUAN	9	21	2
LIKE MOSES OR LIKE COBBETT WHO HAVE NE'ER	193	3	DON JUAN	9	21	V2
LIKE MOSES OR LIKE COBBETT WHO HAVE NE'ER	193	3	DON JUAN	9	21	V2
WHEREIN SHE LIKED HER OWN TO STAND LIKE ROCKS	197	3	DON JUAN	9	29	8
WITH GORE LIKE NADIR SHAH THAT COSTIVE SOPHY	199	3	DON JUAN	9	33	4
LIKE ALL THE WORLDS BEFORE WHICH HAVE BEEN HURLED	201	3	DON JUAN	9	37	6
LIKE TO THE NOTIONS WE NOW ENTERTAIN	201	3	DON JUAN	9	38	5
LOOK LIKE THE MONSTERS OF A NEW MUSEUM	202	3	DON JUAN	9	40	8
WAVING LIKE SAILS NEW SHIVERED IN A STORM	204	3	DON JUAN	9	43	3
(WHEN SHE DON'T PIN MEN'S LIMBS IN LIKE A JAILOR)--	204	3	DON JUAN	9	44	6
BUT STILL SO LIKE THAT PSYCHE WERE MORE CLEVER	205	3	DON JUAN	9	45	6
WITH BEARDS AND WHISKERS AND THE LIKE THE FOND	209	3	DON JUAN	9	53	4
LIKE FLOWERS WELL WATERED AFTER A LONG DROUTH--	213	3	DON JUAN	9	61	4
AS THOSE WHO LIKE THINGS ROSY RIPE AND SUCCULENT	213	3	DON JUAN	9	62	3
MIND LIKE THE WIND WHATEVER SHE HAS SAID	214	3	DON JUAN	9	64	6
FLUNG HOVERING GRACES O'ER HIM LIKE A BANNER	223	3	DON JUAN	9	83	8
AND ALL MY FANCIES WHIRLING LIKE A MILL	224	3	DON JUAN	9	85	6
SIGH LIKE HIS SON THAN COUGH LIKE HIS GRANDFATHER	228	3	DON JUAN	10	6	8
SIGH LIKE HIS SON THAN COUGH LIKE HIS GRANDFATHER	228	3	DON JUAN	10	6	8
LIKE ARNO IN THE SUMMER TO A SHALLOW	228	3	DON JUAN	10	7	2
LIKE GARLIC HOWSOEVER SHE EXTENDS	231	3	DON JUAN	10	12	5
THE LAWYER'S BRIEF IS LIKE THE SURGEON'S KNIFE	232	3	DON JUAN	10	14	6
LIKE BANQUO'S OFFSPRING--FLOATING PAST ME SEEMS	233	3	DON JUAN	10	18	6
HE NOW WAS GROWING UP LIKE A GREEN TREE ABLE	235	3	DON JUAN	10	22	5
AND SHUT OUR SOULS UP IN US LIKE A SHELL-FISH	236	3	DON JUAN	10	23	8
LIKE MANY PUBLICATIONS OF JOHN MURRAY	237	3	DON JUAN	10	26	V3
LIKE A RACE-HORSE MUCH TO EACH DRESS HE SPORTED	239	3	DON JUAN	10	29	5
TO STRIP THE SAXONS OF THEIR HYDES LIKE TANNERS	242	3	DON JUAN	10	36	6
HE FELT LIKE OTHER PLANTS CALLED SENSITIVE	243	3	DON JUAN	10	37	2
CARE LIKE A HOUSE-KEEPER BRINGS EVERY WEEK	243	3	DON JUAN	10	38	5
WHO DID NOT LIKE AT FIRST TO LOSE HER MINION	246	3	DON JUAN	10	44	4
AND DROOPING LIKE AN EAGLE'S WITH CLIPT PINION	246	3	DON JUAN	10	44	6
HER CLIMACTERIC TEASED HER LIKE HER TEENS	247	3	DON JUAN	10	47	5
(WHO LIKE SOUR FRUIT TO STIR THEIR VEINS' SALT TIDES	251	3	DON JUAN	10	54	3
MIGHT SCATTER FIRE THROUGH ICE LIKE HECLA'S FLAME	254	3	DON JUAN	10	59	6
AND THENCE THROUGH BERLIN DRESDEN AND THE LIKE	255	3	DON JUAN	10	61	1
WHICH DRACHENFELS FROWNS OVER LIKE A SPECTRE	255	3	DON JUAN	10	62	2
AT LENGTH THEY ROSE LIKE A WHITE WALL ALONG	257	3	DON JUAN	10	65	1
NOT LIKE SLOW GERMANY WHERIN THEY MUDDLE	260	3	DON JUAN	10	71	4
A MOSQUE SO NOBLE FLUNG LIKE PEARLS TO SWINE	262	3	DON JUAN	10	75	8
ON ON THROUGH MEADOWS MANAGED LIKE A GARDEN	262	3	DON JUAN	10	76	1
A HUGE DUN CUPOLA LIKE A FOOLSCAP CROWN	265	3	DON JUAN	10	82	7
ARE BOWED AND PUT THE SUN OUT LIKE A TAPER	266	3	DON JUAN	10	83	6
LIKE ROLAND'S HORN IN RONCEVALLES' BATTLE	267	3	DON JUAN	10	87	8
LIKE TO A ROMAN TRUMPET LIKE A BATTLE	267	3	DON JUAN	10	87	V8
BEHIND HIS CARRIAGE AND LIKE HANDY LADS	273	3	DON JUAN	11	11	3
WHO IN A ROW LIKE TOM COULD LEAD THE VAN	277	3	DON JUAN	11	19	3
THAT JUAN'S CHARIOT ROLLING LIKE A DRUM	277	3	DON JUAN	11	20	5
(LIKE LUCUS FROM NO LIGHT) THROUGH PROSPECTS NAMED	278	3	DON JUAN	11	21	2
THERE MAILS FAST FLYING OFF LIKE A DELUSION	278	3	DON JUAN	11	22	4
LIKE GOLD AS IN COMPARISON TO DROSS	280	3	DON JUAN	11	26	3
THE OTHER LOOKS LIKE PHOSPHORUS ON SHEETS	281	3	DON JUAN	11	27	5
USEFUL LIKE MALTHUS IN PROMOTING MARRIAGE--	282	3	DON JUAN	11	30	7
AND LADIES LIKE A LITTLE SPICE OF MARS	284	3	DON JUAN	11	33	V4
IS IDLE LET US LIKE MOST OTHERS BOW	286	3	DON JUAN	11	38	5
LIKE LAP-DOGS THE LEAST CIVIL SONS OF BITCHES	288	3	DON JUAN	11	41	8
FROM OUR NEXT NEIGHBOUR'S LAND WHERE LIKE A CHESSMAN	288	3	DON JUAN	11	42	3
THEMSELVES TO UNITY LIKE THIS OF MINE	290	3	DON JUAN	11	44	8
LIKE TO THE CHAMPION IN THE FISTY RING	296	3	DON JUAN	11	55	5
THEIR CHANCES--THEY'RE TOO NUMEROUS LIKE THE THIRTY	299	3	DON JUAN	11	61	7
A DREADFUL TRADE LIKE HIS WHO GATHERS SAMPHIRE	299	3	DON JUAN	11	62	3
WAS LIKE ALL BUSINESS A LABORIOUS NOTHING	301	3	DON JUAN	11	65	2
LIKE HARNESSED METEORS THEN ALONG THE FLOOR	302	3	DON JUAN	11	67	4
WHERE HE MAY FIX HIMSELF LIKE SMALL JACK HORNER	303	3	DON JUAN	11	69	4
WHO LIKE DON JUAN TAKES AN ACTIVE SHARE	303	3	DON JUAN	11	70	2
WHO LIKE TO PLAY THE FOOL WITH CIRCUMSPECTION	304	3	DON JUAN	11	71	8
LIKE OTHER SLAVES OF COURSE MUST PAY HIS RANSOM	305	3	DON JUAN	11	74	3
SOME LAID ASIDE LIKE AN OLD OPERA HAT	308	3	DON JUAN	11	79	3
I HAVE SEEN SOME NATIONS LIKE O'ERLOADED ASSES	310	3	DON JUAN	11	84	7
I'VE SEEN THE PEOPLE RIDDEN O'ER LIKE SAND	310	3	DON JUAN	11	85	5
A PERIOD SOMETHING LIKE A PRINTED PAGE	315	3	DON JUAN	12	1	6
WHICH MAKES BANK CREDIT LIKE A BARK OF VAPOUR	317	3	DON JUAN	12	4	8
AND THE VINE BLUSHES LIKE AURORA'S LIP	320	3	DON JUAN	12	9	5
I COULD SEND FORTH MY MANDATE LIKE A PRIMATE	327	3	DON JUAN	12	24	3

LIKE   (CONTINUED)

		PAGE	VOL	CANTO	STANZA	LN

ABOVE THE ICE HAD LIKE A SKAITER GLIDED 327   3 DON JUAN 12   25   4
AND I ASSURE YOU THAT LIKE VIRGIN HONEY 330   3 DON JUAN 12   31   7
THAN THEIR HE RELATIVES) LIKE FLIES O'ER CANDY 331   3 DON JUAN 12   32   6
THAT I DISSERT LIKE GRACE BEFORE A FEAST 334   3 DON JUAN 12   39   3
FOR LIKE AN AGED AUNT OR TIRESOME FRIEND 334   3 DON JUAN 12   39   4
FOR LIKE A DAY-DAWN SHE WAS YOUNG AND PURE 335   3 DON JUAN 12   41   2
OR LIKE THE OLD COMPARISON OF SNOWS 335   3 DON JUAN 12   41   3
LIKE MANY PEOPLE EVERYBODY KNOWS 335   3 DON JUAN 12   41   5
TO BE TRANSMITTED LIKE THE LORD MAYOR'S BARGE 339   3 DON JUAN 12   51   6
MORE MUSE-LIKE--SAY LIKE CYTHEREA'S SHELL 339   3 DON JUAN 12   51   8
LIKE POPLARS WITH GOOD PRINCIPLES FOR ROOTS 343   3 DON JUAN 12   59   4
FISHERS FOR MEN LIKE SIRENS WITH SOFT LUTES 343   3 DON JUAN 12   59   6
A PERIL--NOT INDEED LIKE LOVE OR MARRIAGE 344   3 DON JUAN 12   62   2
FOR EUROPE PLOUGHS IN AFRIC LIKE BOS PIGER 348   3 DON JUAN 12   70   6
OR SAY THEY ARE LIKE VIRTUOUS MERMAIDS WHOSE 349   3 DON JUAN 12   73   1
LIKE RUSSIANS RUSHING FROM HOT BATHS TO SNOWS 349   3 DON JUAN 12   73   5
SHE KEEPS IT FOR YOU LIKE A TRUE ALLY 350   3 DON JUAN 12   74   8
TO LIKE THOUGH I HAVE BEEN SEVEN YEARS IN ITALY 350   3 DON JUAN 12   75   7
(THE HYPOCRITE) WILL BANISH THEM LIKE MARIUS 352   3 DON JUAN 12   78   6
ALAS   MUST NOBLEST VIEWS LIKE AN OLD SONG 363   3 DON JUAN 13   10   5
HIS PREPOSSESSIONS LIKE THE LAWS OF PERSIANS 366   3 DON JUAN 13   17   3
HIS FEELINGS HAD NOT THOSE STRANGE FITS LIKE TERTIANS . . 366   3 DON JUAN 13   17   5
FOR LIKE A RACER OR A BOXER TRAINING 366   3 DON JUAN 13   18   7
WELL LIKE MOST ENGLISHMEN AND LOVED THE RACES 368   3 DON JUAN 13   23   6
AND JUAN LIKE A TRUE-BORN ANDALUSIAN 368   3 DON JUAN 13   23   7
AND ALL MEN LIKE TO SHOW THEIR HOSPITALITY 369   3 DON JUAN 13   24   7
DEPARTED LIKE THE REST OF THEIR COMPEERS 381   3 DON JUAN 13   50   2
(WHOSE ARTICLES ARE LIKE THE THIRTY NINE 383   3 DON JUAN 13   53   2
STOOD LIKE CARACTACUS IN ACT TO RALLY 384   3 DON JUAN 13   56   3
TO QUAFF A BROOK WHICH MURMURED LIKE A BIRD 384   3 DON JUAN 13   56   8
ITS SHRILLER ECHOES--LIKE AN INFANT MADE 385   3 DON JUAN 13   58   3
STREAMING FROM OFF THE SUN LIKE SERAPH'S WINGS 387   3 DON JUAN 13   62   4
LIE WITH THEIR HALLELUJAHS QUENCH'D LIKE FIRE 387   3 DON JUAN 13   62   8
STRANGE FACES LIKE TO MEN IN MASQUERADE 389   3 DON JUAN 13   65   3
LIKE MAN'S VAIN GLORY AND HIS VAINER TROUBLES 389   3 DON JUAN 13   65   8
WHO PASS LIKE WATER FILTERED IN A TANK 396   3 DON JUAN 13   80   3
LIKE CHARLEMAGNE'S--AND ALL SUCH PEERS IN LOOK 398   3 DON JUAN 13   85   3
STRONGBOW WAS LIKE A NEW-TUNED HARPSICHORD 402   3 DON JUAN 13   93   1
THE FIRST THING BOYS LIKE AFTER PLAY AND FRUIT 405   3 DON JUAN 13   101   3
THE EARTH HAS NOTHING LIKE A SHE EPISTLE 407   3 DON JUAN 13   105   2
WHICH LIKE A CREED NE'ER SAYS ALL IT INTENDS 407   3 DON JUAN 13   105   5
WE HAVE NO ACCOMPLISH'D BLACKGUARDS LIKE TOM JONES . . . 409   3 DON JUAN 13   110   7
WHO LIKE TO MIX SOME SLIGHT ALLOY WITH FAME 414   3 DON JUAN 14   9   6
SOMETIMES INDEED LIKE SOLDIERS OFF PARADE 417   3 DON JUAN 14   17   1
LOWER'D LEAVEN'D LIKE A HISTORY OF FREEMASONS 419   3 DON JUAN 14   22   1
WHICH HOLDS A TREASURE LIKE A MISER'S HOARD 422   3 DON JUAN 14   27   3
AND WORK AWAY LIKE SPIRIT UPON MATTER 423   3 DON JUAN 14   30   7
JUAN--IN THIS RESPECT AT LEAST LIKE SAINTS-- 424   3 DON JUAN 14   31   1
HE THOUGHT AT HEART LIKE COURTLY CHESTERFIELD 425   3 DON JUAN 14   35   5
AND WHATNOT--THOUGH HE HAD RIDDEN LIKE A CENTAUR 425   3 DON JUAN 14   35   V7
NOT LIKE A BALLET-MASTER IN THE VAN 427   3 DON JUAN 14   38   7
OF HIS DRILL'D NYMPHS BUT LIKE A GENTLEMAN 427   3 DON JUAN 14   38   8
LIKE SWIFT CAMILLA HE SCARCE SKIMM'D THE GROUND 427   3 DON JUAN 14   39   3
HE GLANCED LIKE A PERSONIFIED BOLERO 427   3 DON JUAN 14   39   8
OR LIKE A FLYING HOUR BEFORE AURORA 428   3 DON JUAN 14   40   1
THERE'S NOUGHT IN THIS BAD WORLD LIKE SYMPATHY 430   3 DON JUAN 14   47   1
AS THEY WILL DO LIKE LEAVES AT THE FIRST BREEZE 431   3 DON JUAN 14   48   6
I HATE A MOTIVE LIKE A LINGERING BOTTLE 435   3 DON JUAN 14   58   1
THAT LIKE TO MAKE A QUARREL WHEN THEY CAN'T 438   3 DON JUAN 14   63   5
AND ANSWER'D LIKE A STATESMAN OR A PROPHET 438   3 DON JUAN 14   65   7
LESS LIKE A YOUNG WIFE THAN AN AGED SISTER 440   3 DON JUAN 14   69   8
UNLESS LIKE WISE TIRESIAS WE HAD PROVED 442   3 DON JUAN 14   73   2
REDUCED TO PRACTICE AND PERFORM'D LIKE DANCES 444   3 DON JUAN 14   79   8
ROMANCES I NE'ER READ LIKE THOSE I HAVE SEEN 444   3 DON JUAN 14   80   2
ESPECIALLY WHEN THEY WOULD LOOK LIKE LIES 444   3 DON JUAN 14   80   7
AND ASK THEM HOW THEY LIKE TO BE IN THRALL 446   3 DON JUAN 14   83   4
LIKE ARCHIMEDES I LEAVE EARTH AS 'TWAS 446   3 DON JUAN 14   84   8
ITS INNER CRASH IS LIKE AN EARTHQUAKE'S RUIN 446   3 DON JUAN 14   85   8
THEY MOVED LIKE STARS UNITED IN THEIR SPHERES 447   3 DON JUAN 14   87   3
OR LIKE THE RHONE BY LEMAN'S WATERS WASH'D 447   3 DON JUAN 14   87   4
AND GATHER'D AS THEY RUN LIKE GROWING WATER 448   3 DON JUAN 14   88   6
NO FRIEND LIKE TO A WOMAN EARTH DISCOVERS 451   3 DON JUAN 14   93   7
LIKE A MEEK TRADESMAN WHEN APPROACHING PALELY 459   3 DON JUAN 15   8   3
BECAUSE SHE WAS NOT APT LIKE SOME OF US 460   3 DON JUAN 15   10   3
TO LIKE TOO READILY OR TOO HIGH BRED 460   3 DON JUAN 15   10   4
BECAUSE HE HAD LIKE ALCIBIADES 460   3 DON JUAN 15   11   7
AN ARROW FOR THE HEART LIKE A SWEET VOICE 461   3 DON JUAN 15   13   8
LIKE VIRTUE AND THE ABSENCE OF PRETENSION 462   3 DON JUAN 15   14   7
PINNED LIKE A FLOCK AND FLEECED TOO IN THEIR FOLD . . . 468   3 DON JUAN 15   26   3
LIKE ALL WHO GIVE AND EKE RECEIVE IT GRATIS 469   3 DON JUAN 15   29   2
ARRANGING THEM LIKE BOOKS ON THE SAME SHELF 470   3 DON JUAN 15   31   3
MORE (LIKE A STOCK-HOLDER IN GROWING PELF) 470   3 DON JUAN 15   31   5
LIKE HOLBEIN'S DANCE OF DEATH--BUT 'TIS THE SAME)-- . . 473   3 DON JUAN 15   39   8
AND MIGHT GO ON IF WELL WOUND UP LIKE WATCHES 473   3 DON JUAN 15   40   8
FEELINGS OF YOUTH LIKE THOSE WHICH OVERTHROWN LIE . . . 475   3 DON JUAN 15   44   5
AND THIS OMISSION LIKE THAT OF THE BUST 477   3 DON JUAN 15   49   1
PERHAPS SHE DID NOT LIKE THE QUIET WAY 479   3 DON JUAN 15   53   1
LIKE ANTHONY'S BY CAESAR BY THE FEW 479   3 DON JUAN 15   53   7

LIKE   (CONTINUED)
```
        A MAN LIKE WHOM I HOPE WE SHAN'T SEE MANY SOON .  .  .  .  .  484   3 DON JUAN 15    65    4
        GONE TO WHERE VICTORIES MUST LIKE DINNERS GO  .  .  .  .  .  485   3 DON JUAN 15    67    5
        CAN'T LIKE RIPE AGE IN GOURMANDISE EXCEL .  .  .  .  .  .  .  487   3 DON JUAN 15    70    6
        ON SUNIUM OR HYMETTUS LIKE DIOGENES  .  .  .  .  .  .  .  .  488   3 DON JUAN 15    73    7
        BUT SO FAR LIKE A LADY THAT 'TWAS DREST .  .  .  .  .  .  .  488   3 DON JUAN 15    74    7
        LIKE THAT SAME MYSTIC MUSIC OF THE SPHERES  .  .  .  .  .  .  489   3 DON JUAN 15    76    5
        LIKE A GOOD SHIP ENTANGLED AMONG ICE .  .  .  .  .  .  .  .  490   3 DON JUAN 15    77    7
        AT SEVENTY YEARS HAD PHANTASIES LIKE THESE  .  .  .  .  .  .  494   3 DON JUAN 15    86    4
        ALSO OBSERVE THAT LIKE THE GREAT LORD COKE  .  .  .  .  .  .  494   3 DON JUAN 15    87    1
        IT MAKES MY BLOOD BOIL LIKE THE SPRINGS OF HECLA  .  .  .  .  497   3 DON JUAN 15    92    7
        LIKE THOSE OF THE PHILOSOPHER OF MALMSBURY  .  .  .  .  .  .  499   3 DON JUAN 15    96    8
        BETWEEN TWO WORLDS LIFE HOVERS LIKE A STAR  .  .  .  .  .  .  500   3 DON JUAN 15    99    1
        OF EMPIRES HEAVE BUT LIKE SOME PASSING WAVES  .  .  .  .  .  500   3 DON JUAN 15    99    8
        LIKE FLEECY CLOUDS INTO THE SKY RETIRED  .  .  .  .  .  .  .  504   3 DON JUAN 16     8    6
        IS LIKE THE LAST GLASS OF CHAMPAGNE WITHOUT .  .  .  .  .  .  504   3 DON JUAN 16     9    2
        OR LIKE A SYSTEM COUPLED WITH A DOUBT .  .  .  .  .  .  .  .  504   3 DON JUAN 16     9    4
        OR LIKE A SODA BOTTLE WHEN ITS SPRAY  .  .  .  .  .  .  .  .  504   3 DON JUAN 16     9    5
        OR LIKE A BILLOW LEFT BY STORMS BEHIND  .  .  .  .  .  .  .  504   3 DON JUAN 16     9    7
        OR LIKE AN OPIATE WHICH BRINGS TROUBLED REST  .  .  .  .  .  505   3 DON JUAN 16    10    1
        OR NONE OR LIKE--LIKE NOTHING THAT I KNOW  .  .  .  .  .  .  505   3 DON JUAN 16    10    2
        OR NONE OR LIKE--LIKE NOTHING THAT I KNOW  .  .  .  .  .  .  505   3 DON JUAN 16    10    2
        NO REAL LIKENESS--LIKE THE OLD TYRIAN VEST  .  .  .  .  .  .  505   3 DON JUAN 16    10    5
        MAY SIT LIKE THAT OF NESSUS AND RECALL  .  .  .  .  .  .  .  505   3 DON JUAN 16    11    3
        SITS LIKE A SEDATIVE WHILE WE RECALL  .  .  .  .  .  .  .  .  505   3 DON JUAN 16    11   V3
        ALONG THE CANVAS THEIR EYES GLANCE LIKE DREAMS .  .  .  .  .  509   3 DON JUAN 16    19    4
        BUT THOUGHT LIKE MOST MEN THERE WAS NOTHING IN'T  .  .  .  .  510   3 DON JUAN 16    22    3
        WHICH PASSES GHOSTS IN CURRENCY LIKE GOLD  .  .  .  .  .  .  510   3 DON JUAN 16    22    6
        BUT RARELY SEEN LIKE GOLD COMPARED WITH PAPER  .  .  .  .  .  510   3 DON JUAN 16    22    7
        TWINE LIKE A KNOT OF SNAKES AROUND HIS FACE .  .  .  .  .  .  510   3 DON JUAN 16    23    6
        HE DRESSED AND LIKE YOUNG PEOPLE HE WAS WONT  .  .  .  .  .  513   3 DON JUAN 16    29    1
        SOMETHING LIKE ILLNESS OF A SUDDEN GROWTH  .  .  .  .  .  .  514   3 DON JUAN 16    33    4
        AS DID THE CYNIC ON SOME LIKE OCCASION .  .  .  .  .  .  .  .  522   3 DON JUAN 16    43    4
        TO SOMETHING LIKE THIS WHEN TOO OFT DISPLAYED  .  .  .  .  .  522   3 DON JUAN 16    44    5
        BURROWING FOR BOROUGHS LIKE A RAT OR RABBIT .  .  .  .  .  .  534   3 DON JUAN 16    70    2
        YET LIKE THEIR MASTERS FEARFUL OF OFFENDING .  .  .  .  .  .  539   3 DON JUAN 16    79    6
        AND SOMETHING LIKE A SMILE UPON HER CHEEK  .  .  .  .  .  .  544   3 DON JUAN 16    92    2
        LIKE ADDISON'S FAINT PRAISE SO WONT TO DAMN .  .  .  .  .  .  552   3 DON JUAN 16   104    4
        ALAS HER STAR MUST WANE LIKE THAT OF DIAN  .  .  .  .  .  .  554   3 DON JUAN 16   109    3
        SO LIKE A SPIRITUAL PIT-A-PAT .  .  .  .  .  .  .  .  .  .  556   3 DON JUAN 16   112    5
        THE STARRY DARKNESS ROUND HER LIKE A GIRDLE .  .  .  .  .  .  556   3 DON JUAN 16   113    7
        A NOISE LIKE TO WET FINGERS DRAWN ON GLASS .  .  .  .  .  .  556   3 DON JUAN 16   114    1
        LIKE SHOWERS WHICH ON THE MIDNIGHT GUSTS WILL PASS  .  .  .  556   3 DON JUAN 16   114    3
        SOUNDING LIKE VERY SUPERNATURAL WATER .  .  .  .  .  .  .  .  556   3 DON JUAN 16   114    4
        LIKE THAT OF HELL LASCIATE OGNI SPERANZA  .  .  .  .  .  .  557   3 DON JUAN 16   116    2
        FORTH INTO SOMETHING MUCH LIKE FLESH AND BLOOD  .  .  .  .  561   3 DON JUAN 16   123    4
        IS LIKE--A DUCKLING BY DAME PARTLETT REARED .  .  .  .  .  .  564   3 DON JUAN 17     4    6
        A SOMETHING LIKE IT--AS BEAR WITNESS LUTHER .  .  .  .  .  .  565   3 DON JUAN 17     6    8
        I LEAVE THE THING A PROBLEM LIKE ALL THINGS--  .  .  .  .  .  568   3 DON JUAN 17    13    1
```
LIKED
```
        SHE LIKED THE ENGLISH AND THE HEBREW TONGUE  .  .  .  .  .   28   2 DON JUAN  1    14    1
        AND NONE LIKED TO ANTICIPATE THE BLOW .  .  .  .  .  .  .  .  175   2 DON JUAN  2    36    6
        THE LAST WAS OF GREAT FAME AND LIKED TO SHOW IT .  .  .  .  316   2 DON JUAN  3    78    4
        ANOTHER TIME HE MIGHT HAVE LIKED TO SEE 'EM .  .  .  .  .  .  384   2 DON JUAN  4    75    7
        MY PEN AND LIKED POETIC WAR TO WAGE  .  .  .  .  .  .  .  .  397   2 DON JUAN  4    98    6
        AS BOYS LOVE ROWS MY BOYHOOD LIKED A SQUABBLE  .  .  .  .  .  398   2 DON JUAN  4    99    1
        HE LIKED TO HAVE A HANDSOME PARAMOUR  .  .  .  .  .  .  .  .   51   3 DON JUAN  6    91    3
        SHE LIKED QUICK ANSWERS IN ALL CONVERSATIONS  .  .  .  .  .   56   3 DON JUAN  6   101    3
        WHEREIN SHE LIKED HER OWN TO STAND LIKE ROCKS  .  .  .  .  .  197   3 DON JUAN  9    29    8
        BESIDES THE EMPRESS SOMETIMES LIKED A BOY  .  .  .  .  .  .  206   3 DON JUAN  9    47    7
        HER MAJESTY WHO LIKED TO GAZE ON YOUTH .  .  .  .  .  .  .  .  213   3 DON JUAN  9    61    6
        NATIONS SHE LIKED MAN AS AN INDIVIDUAL  .  .  .  .  .  .  .  214   3 DON JUAN  9    63    8
        I HAVE ALWAYS LIKED YOU BETTER THAN I STATE .  .  .  .  .  .  329   3 DON JUAN 12    28    4
        RIGHT HONESTLY HE LIKED AN HONEST HATER--  .  .  .  .  .  .  361   3 DON JUAN 13     7    2
        LORD HENRY ALSO LIKED TO BE SUPERIOR .  .  .  .  .  .  .  .  367   3 DON JUAN 13    19    1
        HE LIKED TO TEACH THAT WHICH HE HAD BEEN TAUGHT  .  .  .  .  368   3 DON JUAN 13    21    5
        HE LIKED THE GENTLE SPANIARD FOR HIS GRAVITY  .  .  .  .  .  368   3 DON JUAN 13    22    1
        OR HUNT THE YOUNG BECAUSE THEY LIKED THE SPORT--  .  .  .  .  405   3 DON JUAN 13   101    2
```
LIKELY
```
        MOST LIKELY TO ATTAIN HER AIM--HIS HEART .  .  .  .  .  .  .  492   2 DON JUAN  5   140    8
        AND WAS NOT LIKELY ALL AT ONCE TO BURST  .  .  .  .  .  .  .  437   3 DON JUAN 14    62    3
```
LIKEN
```
        SOME LIKEN IT TO CLIMBING UP A HILL  .  .  .  .  .  .  .  .  146   2 DON JUAN  1   218    3
        NOR LIKEN IT--I NEVER SAW THE LIKE .  .  .  .  .  .  .  .  .  159   2 DON JUAN  2     5    8
```
LIKENESS
```
        I DOUBT ALL LIKENESS ENDS BETWEEN THE PAIR .  .  .  .  .  .  124   2 DON JUAN  1   186    8
        WHICH BEARS THE GREATEST LIKENESS TO PALL MALL .  .  .  .  .  124   3 DON JUAN  8    26    8
        WE SHALL NOT SEE HIS LIKENESS HE COULD KILL HIS .  .  .  .  132   3 DON JUAN  8    39    4
        SOME LIKENESS WHICH THE GLITTERING CIRQUE CONFINES  .  .  .  321   3 DON JUAN 12    12    6
        A DULL AND FAMILY LIKENESS THROUGH ALL AGES .  .  .  .  .  .  416   3 DON JUAN 14    15    7
        NO REAL LIKENESS--LIKE THE OLD TYRIAN VEST  .  .  .  .  .  .  505   3 DON JUAN 16    10    5
        (I'LL TAKE THE LIKENESS I CAN FIRST COME AT) .  .  .  .  .  564   3 DON JUAN 17     4    5
```
LIKES
```
        THAT NO ONE LIKES TO BE DISTURB'D AT MEALS .  .  .  .  .  .   69   2 DON JUAN  1    89    5
        AND LIKES PARTICULARLY TO PRODUCE .  .  .  .  .  .  .  .  .   91   2 DON JUAN  1   128    3
        FEMALE AS WHERE SHE LIKES MAY FREELY PASS  .  .  .  .  .  .  248   2 DON JUAN  2   175    4
        FOR NONE LIKES MORE TO HEAR HIMSELF CONVERSE  .  .  .  .  .  298   2 DON JUAN  3    45    8
        WHO LIKES A LISTENER WHETHER SAINT OR SINNER--  .  .  .  .  426   3 DON JUAN 14    36    7
```
LIKEWISE
```
        MAY LIKEWISE PUT OFF FOR A TIME WHAT STORY .  .  .  .  .  .   79   3 DON JUAN  7    26    7
```

456

		PAGE	VOL	CANTO	STANZA	LV

LIKEWISE (CONTINUED)

IN BIRTH IN RANK IN FORTUNE LIKEWISE EQUAL . . . . . . 367 3 DON JUAN 13 20 1
HE LIKEWISE COULD BE MOST THINGS TO ALL WOMEN . . . . . 424 3 DON JUAN 14 31 7

LIKING

AND LIKING NOT THE INSIDE LOCK'D THE OUT . . . . 125 2 DON JUAN 1 187 8
BY LIKING A VARIETY OF LADIES . . . . 199 2 DON JUAN 2 81 V8
FOR WOMEN SHED AND USE THEM AT THEIR LIKING . . . . . 479 2 DON JUAN 5 118 2

LIKINGS

OF COMMON LIKINGS WHICH MAKE SOME DEPLORE . . . . . . 366 3 DON JUAN 13 17 6

LILAC

SOFT PERSIAN SENTENCES IN LILAC LETTERS . . . . 308 2 DON JUAN 3 64 7

LILLIPUT

SO LET US BACK TO LILLIPUT AND GUIDE . . . . 20 3 DON JUAN 6 28 6

LILY

AND LIKE A WITHER'D LILY ON THE LAND . . . . 214 2 DON JUAN 2 110 6
TO GILD REFINED GOLD OR PAINT THE LILY . . . . 314 2 DON JUAN 3 76 8
AND HER HEAD DROOP'D AS WHEN THE LILY LIES . . . . . 376 2 DON JUAN 4 59 3
O'ER HER FAIR FRONT LIKE MORNING'S ON A LILY . . . . . 58 3 DON JUAN 6 105 8

LIMB

HE KNEW NOT TILL EACH PAINFUL PULSE AND LIMB . . . . . 214 2 DON JUAN 2 111 6
THE LIMB WHICH IT ADORN'D ITS ONLY MOULD . . . . . . 312 2 DON JUAN 3 71 4
TOUCH'D HIS NOR THAT--NOR ANY HANDSOME LIMB . . . . . 396 2 DON JUAN 4 95 5
AND SLUMBER HOVERED O'ER EACH LOVELY LIMB . . . . . . 38 3 DON JUAN 6 64 3
THERE WAS A SOMETHING IN HIS TURN OF LIMB . . . . . . 206 3 DON JUAN 9 47 3

LIMBS

AND GAVE NO SIGN OF LIFE SAVE HIS LIMBS QUIVERING . . . 204 2 DON JUAN 2 90 8
JUAN TO LAVE HIS YOUTHFUL LIMBS WAS WONT . . . . . . 211 2 DON JUAN 2 105 2
HE BUOY'D HIS BOYISH LIMBS AND STROVE TO PLY . . . . . 212 2 DON JUAN 2 106 2
AROUND HIS SCARCE-CLAD LIMBS AND THE FAIR ARM . . . . 216 2 DON JUAN 2 114 2
ARRAY HER LIMBS BUT JUAN STANDING MUTE . . . . 453 2 DON JUAN 5 73 4
THEIR DELICATE LIMBS A THOUSAND BOSOMS THERE . . . . . 19 3 DON JUAN 6 26 7
WHO PAINTED THEIR BARE LIMBS BUT NOT WITH GORE . . . . 180 3 DON JUAN 8 136 8
O'ER LIMBS WHOSE SYMMETRY SET OFF THE SILK . . . . . 204 3 DON JUAN 9 43 8
(WHEN SHE DON'T PIN MEN'S LIMBS IN LIKE A JAILOR)-- . . 204 3 DON JUAN 9 44 6

LIMES

THE TWIGS WHICH SATAN LIMES FOR HUMAN FLIES . . . . . 154 3 DON JUAN 8 86 V8

LIME-TWIGS

THE GLITTERING LIME-TWIGS OF OUR LATTER DAYS . . . . 422 2 DON JUAN 5 22 7

LIMIT

WHO DID NOT LIMIT MUCH HIS BILLS PER WEEK . . . . . . 259 3 DON JUAN 10 70 3

LIMITED

BOTH WHICH ARE LIMITED TO NO CONDITION . . . . 541 3 DON JUAN 16 85 8

LIMITS

LOVE THEN BUT LOVE WITHIN ITS PROPER LIMITS . . . . . 65 2 DON JUAN 1 81 1
WHO LIMITS ALL HIS BATTLES TO THE BAR . . . . 398 3 DON JUAN 13 84 2
HAVE YOU EXPLORED THE LIMITS OF THE COAST . . . . . 502 3 DON JUAN 16 4 5

LINCOLN

GAVE HIM TO LAY THE DEVIL WHO LOOKS O'ER LINCOLN . . . 540 3 DON JUAN 16 82 7

LINE

AND THEREFORE I SHALL OPEN WITH A LINE . . . . 25 2 DON JUAN 1 7 5
FOR NOT A LINE HAD JULIA EVER PENN'D . . . . 58 2 DON JUAN 1 66 4
WITH THE EXCEPTION OF THE SECOND LINE . . . . 69 2 DON JUAN 1 88 6
THE FOUR FIRST RHYMES ARE SOUTHEY'S EVERY LINE . . . . 149 2 DON JUAN 1 222 7
EXISTS THE REMNANT OF A LINE . . . . 325 2 DON JUAN 3 L 13 3
THE SPECTRE HUNTSMAN OF ONESTI'S LINE . . . . 337 2 DON JUAN 3 106 5
AND TRACE IT IN THIS POEM EVERY LINE . . . . 346 2 DON JUAN 4 5 3
UNTIL THEY REACH'D SOME GALLIOTS PLACED IN LINE . . . 371 2 DON JUAN 4 50 6
NO CHRISTIAN KNOLL TO TABLE SAW NO LINE . . . . . . 439 2 DON JUAN 5 50 3
IT SEEMS THE WORK OF TIMES BEFORE THE LINE . . . . . 461 2 DON JUAN 5 86 7
SAVE SOLYMAN THE GLORY OF THEIR LINE . . . . 495 2 DON JUAN 5 147 8
IN THE LAST LINE WHICH CANNOT WELL BE WORSE . . . . . 14 3 DON JUAN 6 18 5
IN THE DAMNED LINE ('TIS WORTH AT LEAST A CURSE) . . . 15 3 DON JUAN 6 18 V5
WHO THUS COULD FORM A LINE AND FIGHT AGAIN . . . . . 136 3 DON JUAN 8 47 5
IN THE OTHER LINE--BUT NOT TO SUCH EXCESS . . . . . 176 3 DON JUAN 8 129 3
MAKE MY SOUL PASS THE EQUINOCTIAL LINE . . . . 255 3 DON JUAN 10 61 6
THE LINE OF LIGHTS TOO UP TO CHARING CROSS . . . . . 280 3 DON JUAN 11 26 1
LINE THE INTERIOR OF THEIR HEADS OR BONNETS . . . . . 294 3 DON JUAN 11 50 3
THAT OX OF VERSE WHO PLOUGHS FOR EVERY LINE-- . . . . 297 3 DON JUAN 11 58 6
FOR THEY HAVE PASSED LIFE'S EQUINOCTIAL LINE . . . . 360 3 DON JUAN 13 5 4
WHICH NE'ER CAN PASS THE EQUINOCTIAL LINE . . . . . 373 3 DON JUAN 13 34 3
NONE THAN THEMSELVES COULD BOAST A LONGER LINE . . . 381 3 DON JUAN 13 50 5
THE ANNALS OF FULL MANY A LINE UNDONE-- . . . . . . 386 3 DON JUAN 13 60 6
I HARDLY COULD COMPOSE ANOTHER LINE . . . . 415 3 DON JUAN 14 12 2
AND THOUGH THESE LINES SHOULD ONLY LINE PORTMANTEAUS . . 416 3 DON JUAN 14 14 7
BUT OH THAT I SHOULD EVER PEN SO SAD A LINE . . . . . 430 3 DON JUAN 14 46 1
REGRETTING MUCH THAT SHE HAD CHOSEN SO BAD A LINE . . . 430 3 DON JUAN 14 46 5
TO DRAW THE LINE BETWEEN THE FALSE AND TRUE . . . . . 449 3 DON JUAN 14 90 5
A LINE AND LEAVE POSTERITY UNDONE . . . . 470 3 DON JUAN 15 33 5
THAT ANCIENT LINE IN THE PALE MOONSHINE . . . . . . 519 3 DON JUAN 16 L 4 3

LINEAGE

HIM WHAT'S HIS LINEAGE LET HIM BUT BE SHOWN-- . . . . 105 2 DON JUAN 1 154 5

LINEAL

DON JOSE LIKE A LINEAL SON OF EVE . . . . 30 2 DON JUAN 1 18 7

LINED

PERHAPS IT MAY BE LINED WITH THIS MY CANTO . . . . . 165 2 DON JUAN 2 16 8

LINEN

AND FOUND MUCH LINEN LACE AND SEVERAL PAIR . . . . . 99 2 DON JUAN 1 143 3
THROUGH ALL THE PURPLE AND FINE LINEN FITTER . . . . 237 3 DON JUAN 10 26 6

LINE'S

THE BLOOD OF ALL HIS LINE'S CASTILIAN LORDS . . . . . 471 2 DON JUAN 5 104 3
I SAY THAT LINE'S A LAPSUS OF THE PEN-- . . . . . . 323 3 DON JUAN 12 16 4

	PAGE	VOL		CANTO	STANZA	LN

LINES
AND READ (THE ONLY BOOK SHE COULD) THE LINES . . . . . . 241 2 DON JUAN 2 162 3
IN LIQUID LINES MELLIFLUOUSLY BLAND . . . . 411 2 DON JUAN 5 1 2
IN WHICH WE LEFT HIM SEVERAL LINES ABOVE . . . . . . 20 3 DON JUAN 6 28 8
THREE LINES OF THE DISPATCH IN TAKING SCHMACKSMITH . . 76 3 DON JUAN 7 20 6
AND THOUGH THESE LINES SHOULD ONLY LINE PORTMANTEAUS . . 416 3 DON JUAN 14 14 7
LINGER
I HAVE NO MORE TO SAY BUT LINGER STILL . . . . . . 134 2 DON JUAN 1 197 1
LINGER'D
THE ATTORNEY LAST WHO LINGER'D NEAR THE DOOR . . . . 111 2 DON JUAN 1 164 2
LINGERING
HE STOOD LIKE ADAM LINGERING NEAR HIS GARDEN . . . . 120 2 DON JUAN 1 180 5
I HATE A MOTIVE LIKE A LINGERING BOTTLE . . . . . . 435 3 DON JUAN 14 58 1
LINGERS
ON SUCH AS THESE THE LIP TOO FONDLY LINGERS . . . . 472 2 DON JUAN 5 106 4
LOVE LINGERS STILL ALTHOUGH 'TWERE LATE TO WIVE . . . . 316 3 DON JUAN 12 2 5
LINK
INSTEAD OF SPEECH MAY FORM A LASTING LINK . . . . . 327 2 DON JUAN 3 88 5
AS THE LAST LINK WITH ALL SHE HAD HELD DEAR . . . . 159 3 DON JUAN 8 95 6
AS FEW WOULD EVER DREAM COULD FORM THE LINK . . . . 454 3 DON JUAN 14 100 5
LINK'D
WERE LINK'D ALIKE AS FOR THE COMMON PEOPLE HE . . . . 284 2 DON JUAN 3 16 7
LINK'D HAND IN HAND AND DANCING EACH TOO HAVING . . . 291 2 DON JUAN 3 30 4
THOUGH LINK'D AMONG A FETTER'D RACE . . . . . . 323 2 DON JUAN 3 L 6 2
THE LONG YEAR LINK'D WITH HEAVY DAY ON DAY . . . . 350 2 DON JUAN 4 11 5
AND TWILIGHT SAW THEM LINK'D IN PASSION'S TIES . . . . 354 2 DON JUAN 4 20 6
WERE LINK'D TOGETHER AND IT HAPPEN'D THE MALE . . . . 394 2 DON JUAN 4 92 6
LINKED
FOR THE LORD HENRY LINKED WITH DOGS AND HORSES . . . . 534 3 DON JUAN 16 68 2
LINNET
GREW DUMB FOR YOU MIGHT ALMOST HEAR A LINNET . . . . 142 3 DON JUAN 8 59 6
LINT
STOOD CALLING OUT FOR BANDAGES AND LINT . . . . . . 275 3 DON JUAN 11 14 7
LION
THOUGH SLEEPING LIKE A LION NEAR A SOURCE . . . . 374 2 DON JUAN 4 56 8
WHAT CAN I PROVE A LION THEN NO MORE . . . . . . 404 2 DON JUAN 4 109 1
THE ARMY LIKE A LION FROM HIS DEN . . . . . . 113 3 DON JUAN 8 2 3
AND CLIMATE--STOPPED THE LION SCANDAL'S DEN . . . . 241 3 DON JUAN 10 33 V4
LIONESS
IF CAUSE SHOULD BE--A LIONESS THOUGH TAME . . . . 367 2 DON JUAN 4 44 6
A TIGRESS ROBBED OF YOUNG A LIONESS . . . . . . 487 2 DON JUAN 5 132 1
LION'S
SO BLACK THE LONG WORN LION'S HIDE IN HUE . . . . 154 2 DON JUAN 1 V 5 7
AND MIDNIGHT LISTENS TO THE LION'S ROAR . . . . 373 2 DON JUAN 4 55 5
WHAT FEAR YOU THINK YOU THIS A LION'S DEN . . . . 458 2 DON JUAN 5 81 6
AS BOLD AS DANIEL IN THE LION'S DEN . . . . . 217 3 DON JUAN 9 69 4
NOW THAT THE LION'S FALL'N MAY RISE AGAIN . . . . . 296 3 DON JUAN 11 56 4
LIONS
AND DANIEL TAMED THE LIONS IN THEIR DEN . . . . . 445 2 DON JUAN 5 60 5
OR THROWN TO LIONS OR MADE BAITS FOR FISH . . . . 492 2 DON JUAN 5 141 4
ALL COUNTRIES HAVE THEIR LIONS BUT IN THEE . . . . 327 3 DON JUAN 12 24 7
LIONS'
(AS BEING THE BRAVE LIONS' KEEN PROVIDERS) . . . . . 196 3 DON JUAN 9 27 7
LIP
A HAND MAY FIRST AND THEN A LIP BE KIST . . . . . 65 2 DON JUAN 1 80 3
HIS YOUNG LIP THANK'D IT WITH A GRATEFUL KISS . . . 81 2 DON JUAN 1 112 3
BUT PRESS'D HER BLOODLESS LIP TO JUAN'S CHEEK . . . 114 2 DON JUAN 1 169 8
HE TURN'D HIS LIP TO HERS AND WITH HIS HAND . . . 114 2 DON JUAN 1 170 1
SHORT UPPER LIP--SWEET LIPS THAT MAKE US SIGH . . . 218 2 DON JUAN 2 118 3
HER LIP WHICH ZOE NEEDS MUST UNDERSTAND . . . . 234 2 DON JUAN 2 146 5
HIS LIP TO HERS AND SILENCED HIM WITH THIS . . . . 356 2 DON JUAN 4 24 2
AND O'ER HER UPPER LIP THEY SEEM'D TO POUR . . . . 361 2 DON JUAN 4 31 5
ON SUCH AS THESE THE LIP TOO FONDLY LINGERS . . . . 472 2 DON JUAN 5 106 4
THE STORY SCARCELY PASSED A SINGLE LIP-- . . . . 496 2 DON JUAN 5 149 3
THAT JUST AS HER YOUNG LIP BEGAN TO OPE . . . . 44 3 DON JUAN 6 77 5
AND THE VINE BLUSHES LIKE AURORA'S LIP . . . . . 320 3 DON JUAN 12 9 5
A RED LIP WITH TWO ROWS OF PEARLS BENEATH . . . . 560 3 DON JUAN 16 121 6
LIPLESS
MARK HOW ITS LIPLESS MOUTH GRINS WITHOUT BREATH . . . . 188 3 DON JUAN 9 11 8
LIPS
AND BIT HER LIPS (FOR ELSE SHE MIGHT HAVE SCREAM'D) . . . 51 2 DON JUAN 1 54 6
ITS SNOW THROUGH ALL--HER SOFT LIPS LIE APART . . . . 108 2 DON JUAN 1 158 7
AND THEIR BAKED LIPS WITH MANY A BLOODY CRACK . . . . 202 2 DON JUAN 2 86 1
FROM HIS PALE LIPS AND EVER ON HIM GAZED . . . . . 203 2 DON JUAN 2 89 3
SHORT UPPER LIP--SWEET LIPS THAT MAKE US SIGH . . . . 218 2 DON JUAN 2 118 3
AND YOUNG AURORA KISS'D HER LIPS WITH DEW . . . . 232 2 DON JUAN 2 142 4
BENT WITH HUSH'D LIPS THAT DRANK HIS SCARCE-DRAWN BREATH . 232 2 DON JUAN 2 143 8
BY FEMALE LIPS AND EYES--THAT IS I MEAN . . . . 242 2 DON JUAN 2 164 2
THEIR LIPS DREW NEAR AND CLUNG INTO A KISS . . . . 253 2 DON JUAN 2 185 8
AS IF THEIR SOULS AND LIPS EACH OTHER BECKON'D . . . 254 2 DON JUAN 2 187 6
BUT NOW THEIR EYES AND ALSO LIPS WERE DRY . . . . 295 2 DON JUAN 3 38 5
AND HAIDEE'S SWEET LIPS MURMUR'D LIKE A BROOK . . . . 359 2 DON JUAN 4 29 6
THE BLOOD GUSHED FROM HER LIPS AND EARS AND EYES . . . 376 2 DON JUAN 4 59 V1
WITH NOTHING LIVID STILL HER LIPS WERE RED . . . . 377 2 DON JUAN 4 60 2
NO LIPS E'ER LEFT THEIR TRANSITORY TRACE . . . . 472 2 DON JUAN 5 106 3
OF THEM HIS LIPS IMPERIAL EVER SPAKE . . . . . 501 2 DON JUAN 5 156 6
THEY BIT THEIR LIPS AND WHISPERED WITH A WRIGGLE . . . 501 2 DON JUAN 5 156 V7
AND LIPS APART WHICH SHOWED THE PEARLS BENEATH . . . 38 3 DON JUAN 6 65 8
AND ALL LIPS WERE APPLIED UNTO ALL EARS . . . . 221 3 DON JUAN 9 78 2
DRAINS ITS FIRST DRAUGHT OF LIPS--BUT AS I SAID . . . 238 3 DON JUAN 10 28 7

458

LIPS'
   A VEIN HAD BURST AND HER SWEET LIPS' PURE DYES . . . . . 376 2 DON JUAN 4   59   1
LIQUID
   IN LIQUID LINES MELLIFLUOUSLY BLAND . . . . 411 2 DON JUAN 5   1   2
   ABOUT A LIQUID GLASSFUL WILL REMAIN . . . . 375 3 DON JUAN 13   37   6
   AND SEDGES BROODING IN THEIR LIQUID BED . . . . 385 3 DON JUAN 13   57   6
   WHEN HER SOFT LIQUID WORDS RUN ON APACE . . . . . . 426 3 DON JUAN 14   36   6
   BUBBLE AND SQUEAK WOULD SPOIL MY LIQUID LAY . . . . . 487 3 DON JUAN 15   71   6
   THAT MOST UNLIQUIDATING LIQUID LEAVES . . . . 548 3 DON JUAN 16   99   7
LIQUOR
   (FOR GOD'S SAKE LET ME HAVE A GLASS OF LIQUOR . . . . . 167 2 DON JUAN 2   20   3
   BECAUSE 'TIS LIQUOR ONLY AND BEING FAR . . . . . . 238 2 DON JUAN 2   156   3
   (WHICH WILL COME OVER THINGS) BEATS LOVE OR LIQUOR . . 317 3 DON JUAN 12   4   5
LIQUORS
   BY SLAVES ON HORSEBACK--I HAVE SEEN MALT LIQUORS . . . 310 3 DON JUAN 11   85   6
LISP
   THE LISP OF CHILDREN AND THEIR EARLIEST WORDS . . . . . 88 2 DON JUAN 1   123   8
LISPER
   ON ONE ANOTHER AND EACH LOVELY LISPER . . . . 221 3 DON JUAN 9   78   5
   (WHEN SEATED NEXT HIM) OF SOME PRETTY LISPER . . . . 487 3 DON JUAN 15   70   8
LIST
   BUT HEAR THESE FREEDOMS FORM THE UTMOST LIST . . . . . 65 2 DON JUAN 1   80   5
   A LIST OF SHIPS AND CAPTAINS AND KINGS REIGNING . . . 135 2 DON JUAN 1   200   4
   AND ADDED GREATLY TO THE MISSING LIST . . . . 80 3 DON JUAN 7   27   8
   WITH SOME SMALL VARIATIONS IN THE LIST . . . . . . 107 3 DON JUAN 7   81 V7
   OH YE LESS GRAND LONG LIST OF KILLED AND WOUNDED . . . 108 3 DON JUAN 7   82   2
   THE LIST GROWS LONG OF LIVE AND DEAD PRETENDERS . . . 299 3 DON JUAN 11   61   1
   SO BRILLIANT WHERE THE LIST OF ROUTS AND DANCES IS-- . . 308 3 DON JUAN 11   80   3
   IN SHORT THE LIST OF ALTERATIONS BOTHERS . . . . . . 308 3 DON JUAN 11   81   6
   YOU'LL ADD TO MATRIMONY'S LIST OF CURES . . . . . . 343 3 DON JUAN 12   60   8
   PREPARED EACH MORN FOR EVENINGS LIST OH LIST-- . . . . 403 3 DON JUAN 13   97   6
   PREPARED EACH MORN FOR EVENINGS LIST OH LIST-- . . . . 403 3 DON JUAN 13   97   6
   BOLDLY REFERRING TO THE LIST OF PEERS . . . . 432 3 DON JUAN 14   52   3
   IN ENGLAND RANKS QUITE ON A DIFFERENT LIST . . . . . 436 3 DON JUAN 14   60   6
   THE CIVIL LIST (HE DEIGNS TO ACCEPT OBLIGING ALL . . . 528 3 DON JUAN 16   56   6
   SOONER COME PLACE INTO THE CIVIL LIST . . . . 536 3 DON JUAN 16   75   1
LISTEN
   'TIS SWEET TO LISTEN AS THE NIGHTWINDS CREEP . . . . . 87 2 DON JUAN 1   122   6
   THAT--BUT I WILL NOT LISTEN BY YOUR LEAVE . . . . . 336 3 DON JUAN 12   43 V4
   AS ONCE OR TWICE TO SMILE IF NOT TO LISTEN . . . . . 491 3 DON JUAN 15   80   8
   PERVADES A MOMENT THOSE WHO LISTEN ROUND . . . . . . 521 3 DON JUAN 16   41   4
LISTEN'D
   ALTHOUGH HE LISTEN'D SO THAT THE YOUNG GREEK IN . . . . 241 2 DON JUAN 2   161   3
LISTENED
   AND NOT IN VAIN HE LISTENED--HUSH WHAT'S THAT . . . . 556 3 DON JUAN 16   112   1
LISTENER
   WHO LIKES A LISTENER WHETHER SAINT OR SINNER-- . . . . 426 3 DON JUAN 14   36   7
LISTENING
   LISTENING DEBATES NOT VERY WISE OR WITTY . . . . . . 380 3 DON JUAN 13   48   6
   AND LISTENING TO THE TOPICS MOST IN VOGUE . . . . . 426 3 DON JUAN 14   37   4
   IN LISTENING MERELY TO HIS VOICE'S TONE . . . . . . 461 3 DON JUAN 15   13   6
LISTENS
   AND MIDNIGHT LISTENS TO THE LION'S ROAR . . . . . . 373 2 DON JUAN 4   55   5
LIT
   SUCH AS LIT ONWARD TO THE GOLDEN FLEECE . . . . . . 303 2 DON JUAN 3   55   3
   AS IS A THEATRE LIT UP BY GAS . . . . 444 2 DON JUAN 5   58   6
   THE MATCH WAS LIT TOO SOON AND NO ASSISTANCE . . . . 80 3 DON JUAN 7   28   5
   WE HAVE JUST LIT ON A HEAVEN-KISSING HILL . . . . . 224 3 DON JUAN 9   85   4
   BUT LONDON'S SO WELL LIT THAT IF DIOGENES . . . . . 281 3 DON JUAN 11   28   1
LITERARY
   LEAVING SUCH TO THE LITERARY RABBLE . . . . 398 3 DON JUAN 4   99   3
   THIS IS THE LITERARY LOWER EMPIRE . . . . 299 3 DON JUAN 11   62   1
LITERATURE
   THE BASER SIDES OF LITERATURE AND LIFE . . . . . . 232 3 DON JUAN 10   14   2
   AND NOT IN LITERATURE A GREAT DRAWCANSIR . . . . . . 294 3 DON JUAN 11   51   2
LITIGIOUS
   IT IS OBSERVED THAT LADIES ARE LITIGIOUS . . . . . . 11 3 DON JUAN 6   10   1
LITTER
   MAGNIFICENTLY MINGLED IN A LITTER . . . . 465 2 DON JUAN 5   93   8
   ALL HEAPED TOGETHER SOMEHOW IN A LITTER . . . . . . 465 2 DON JUAN 5   93 V8
LITTLE
   FOR LITTLE JUAN O'ER ME THREW DOWN STAIRS . . . . . 34 2 DON JUAN 1   24   7
   A LITTLE CURLY-HEADED GOOD-FOR-NOTHING . . . . . . 34 2 DON JUAN 1   25   1
   HIS CLASSIC STUDIES MADE A LITTLE PUZZLE . . . . . . 44 2 DON JUAN 1   41   1
   THIS TOO WAS A SEAL'D BOOK TO LITTLE JUAN-- . . . . . 48 2 DON JUAN 1   48   1
   ALTHOUGH IN INFANCY A LITTLE WILD . . . . 49 2 DON JUAN 1   50   3
   THERE SURELY WILL BE LITTLE DOUBT WITH SOME . . . . . 60 2 DON JUAN 1   70   5
   A LITTLE PRESSURE THRILLING AND SO BLAND . . . . . . 60 2 DON JUAN 1   71   4
   ALL THESE ARE LITTLE PRELUDES TO POSSESSION . . . . . 62 2 DON JUAN 1   74   5
   GRATEFUL SHE WAS AND YET A LITTLE SORE-- . . . . . . 63 2 DON JUAN 1   76   5
   POOR LITTLE FELLOW HE HAD NO IDEA . . . . 68 2 DON JUAN 1   86   2
   WHICH WITH A LITTLE PATIENCE MIGHT GROW CHARMING . . . 68 2 DON JUAN 1   86   8
   A LITTLE STILL SHE STROVE AND MUCH REPENTED . . . . . 84 2 DON JUAN 1   117   7
   FOND OF A LITTLE LOVE (WHICH I CALL LEISURE) . . . . . 85 2 DON JUAN 1   118   6
   AND THE FAR MOUNTAINS WAX A LITTLE HOARY . . . . . . 94 2 DON JUAN 1   134   4
   DO PRAY UNDO THE BOLT A LITTLE FASTER-- . . . . . . 96 2 DON JUAN 1   137   5
   THE LITTLE I HAVE SAID MAY SERVE TO SHOW . . . . . . 107 2 DON JUAN 1   157   2
   FOR REPUTATIONS HE HAD LITTLE CARE . . . . 109 2 DON JUAN 1   160   4
   ANTONIA LET HIM--NOT A LITTLE SORE . . . . 111 2 DON JUAN 1   164   4

LITTLE (CONTINUED)

	PAGE	VOL	CANTO	STANZA	LN
NO DOUBT IN LITTLE COMPASS ROUND OR SQUARE	112	2	DON JUAN 1	166	4
DENYING SEVERAL LITTLE THINGS HE WANTED	120	2	DON JUAN 1	180	4
WITH A NEAT LITTLE CROW-QUILL SLIGHT AND NEW	134	2	DON JUAN 1	198	2
GO LITTLE BOOK FROM THIS MY SOLITUDE	149	2	DON JUAN 1	222	1
A LITTLE BREATH LOVE WINE AMBITION FAME	159	2	DON JUAN 2	4	7
HIS BERTH A LITTLE DAMP AND HIM AFRAID	169	2	DON JUAN 2	25	8
SOME LANDSMEN WOULD HAVE LOOK'D A LITTLE PALE	170	2	DON JUAN 2	26	4
WITH LITTLE HOPE IN SUCH A ROLLING SEA	183	2	DON JUAN 2	50	2
AND THE POOR LITTLE CUTTER QUICKLY SWAMP'D	188	2	DON JUAN 2	60	8
AND MOST OF THEM HAD LITTLE CLOTHES BUT RAGS	189	2	DON JUAN 2	62	8
AND FIRST A LITTLE CRUCIFIX HE KISS'D	197	2	DON JUAN 2	76	7
OR BUT AT TIMES A LITTLE SUPPER MADE	200	2	DON JUAN 2	82	4
LITTLE HE SAID AND NOW AND THEN HE SMILED	203	2	DON JUAN 2	88	5
FLASH'D ON HER LITTLE HAND BUT WHAT WAS SHOCKING	220	2	DON JUAN 2	121	7
A LITTLE SMUGGLING AND SOME PIRACY	222	2	DON JUAN 2	125	6
BESIDES BEING LESS IN LOVE SHE YAWN'D A LITTLE	233	2	DON JUAN 2	145	3
I LEARN'D THE LITTLE THAT I KNOW BY THIS	242	2	DON JUAN 2	164	8
FOR LITTLE HAD HE WANDER'D SINCE THE DAY	249	2	DON JUAN 2	176	4
AND DOLPHIN'S LEAP AND LITTLE BILLOW CROST	251	2	DON JUAN 2	181	6
THEY SOMETIMES ALSO GET A LITTLE TIRED	278	2	DON JUAN 3	7	2
MADE QUITE A PICTURE OF THESE LITTLE GREEKS	292	2	DON JUAN 3	33	6
HE IS NOR WHENCE HE CAME--AND LITTLE CARE	298	2	DON JUAN 3	45	2
AND HIS ONE BLOW LEFT LITTLE WORK FOR TWO	300	2	DON JUAN 3	48	8
SO LITTLE THEY EXPECTED HIM THAT DAY	300	2	DON JUAN 3	49	4
OUR LITTLE SELVES RE-FORM'D IN FINER CLAY	305	2	DON JUAN 3	59	4
NEATH WHICH HER BREAST HEAVED LIKE A LITTLE BILLOW	311	2	DON JUAN 3	70	4
A LITTLE HEAVY BUT NO LESS DIVINE	328	2	DON JUAN 3	91	2
ANOTHER OUTCRY FOR A LITTLE BOAT	333	2	DON JUAN 3	98	7
THE LITTLE BOATMAN AND HIS PETER BELL	334	2	DON JUAN 3	100	7
WAS NOT FOR THEM--THEY HAD TOO LITTLE CLAY	348	2	DON JUAN 4	9	8
SERENELY SAVAGE WITH A LITTLE CHANGE	367	2	DON JUAN 4	44	3
WITH THE BLOOD RUNNING LIKE A LITTLE BROOK	370	2	DON JUAN 4	49	6
BUT CLOSED ITS LITTLE BEING WITHOUT LIGHT	382	2	DON JUAN 4	70	4
SOME LITTLE HAMLETS WITH NEW NAMES UNCOUTH	387	2	DON JUAN 4	78	2
THE LITTLE FELLOW REALLY LOOK'D QUITE HEARTY	388	2	DON JUAN 4	81	5
THE PRIMA-DONNA THOUGH A LITTLE OLD	389	2	DON JUAN 4	83	1
PERHAPS HIS RECENT WOUNDS MIGHT HELP A LITTLE	396	2	DON JUAN 4	95	8
A LITTLE CUPOLA MORE NEAT THAN SOLEMN	400	2	DON JUAN 4	104	2
THEY LITTLE THINK WHAT MISCHIEF IS IN HAND	411	2	DON JUAN 5	1	4
YET I MUST OWN HE LOOKED A LITTLE DULL	415	2	DON JUAN 5	8	3
AN OPEN BROW A LITTLE MARKED WITH CARE	416	2	DON JUAN 5	11	5
KINDNESS DESTROYS WHAT LITTLE WE HAD GOT	423	2	DON JUAN 5	25	6
UP IN A LITTLE CREEK BELOW A WALL	432	2	DON JUAN 5	40	7
A GAUDY TASTE FOR THEY ARE LITTLE SKILLED IN	436	2	DON JUAN 5	46	5
WHO LITTLE THOUGHT THAT HIS OWN CRACKED EXISTENCE	440	2	DON JUAN 5	51	3
TWO OR THREE SEEM SO LITTLE ONE SEEMS NOTHING	443	2	DON JUAN 5	57	1
ALAS MAN MAKES THAT GREAT WHICH MAKES HIM LITTLE	444	2	DON JUAN 5	59	1
HIS TOILET THOUGH NO DOUBT A LITTLE BACKWARD	456	2	DON JUAN 5	78	4
THE NEGRO BABA HELPED A LITTLE TOO	456	2	DON JUAN 5	78	5
TWO LITTLE DWARFS THE LEAST YOU COULD SUPPOSE	462	2	DON JUAN 5	87	3
YOU NEVER THOUGHT ABOUT THOSE LITTLE CREATURES	462	2	DON JUAN 5	87	8
THEY LOOKED SO LITTLE DID STRONG THINGS AT TIMES--	463	2	DON JUAN 5	89	2
IT WAS AS IF THEIR LITTLE LOOKS COULD POISON	463	2	DON JUAN 5	90	7
TO SWING A LITTLE LESS FROM SIDE TO SIDE	464	2	DON JUAN 5	91	6
AND ALSO COULD YOU LOOK A LITTLE MODEST	464	2	DON JUAN 5	91	8
AUGHT SAVE SOME LITTLE POUTING PETTY CARE	480	2	DON JUAN 5	119	V5
FOR EASTERN STAYS ARE LITTLE MADE TO PAD	492	2	DON JUAN 5	140	3
AND SHOWED BUT LITTLE ROYAL CURIOSITY	496	2	DON JUAN 5	148	4
LITTLE WAS HEARD OF CRIMINAL OR CRIME	496	2	DON JUAN 5	149	2
'TIS TRUE A LITTLE TROUBLED HERE AND THERE	497	2	DON JUAN 5	150	6
AND YET THEY HAD THEIR LITTLE JEALOUSIES	25	3	DON JUAN 6	38	1
BUT IT SUFFICES--LITTLE WAS AMISS	31	3	DON JUAN 6	51	5
HER TOILET WHICH COST LITTLE FOR SHE WAS	36	3	DON JUAN 6	60	2
TO SCOLD A LITTLE AT THE FALSE ALARM	45	3	DON JUAN 6	79	3
SO BEAUTIFUL THAT ART COULD LITTLE MEND HER	50	3	DON JUAN 6	89	5
PERHAPS A LITTLE LATER HER GREAT LORD	51	3	DON JUAN 6	90	2
SOMETIMES A LITTLE HEAVY ON THE BACKS	54	3	DON JUAN 6	96	7
THE MUSE WILL TAKE A LITTLE TOUCH AT WARFARE	65	3	DON JUAN 6	120	8
AS LITTLE AS THE MOON STOPS FOR THE BAYING	70	3	DON JUAN 7	7	5
OF DANUBE--WITH SOME STRENGTH BUT LITTLE TASTE	71	3	DON JUAN 7	9	V3
LITTLE CARED THEY FOR MAHOMET OR MUFTI	75	3	DON JUAN 7	17	5
I HOPE THIS LITTLE QUESTION IS NO SIN	77	3	DON JUAN 7	21	4
THEY HAD BUT LITTLE BAGGAGE AT THEIR BACKS	87	3	DON JUAN 7	43	4
OR AS A LITTLE DOG WILL LEAD THE BLIND	90	3	DON JUAN 7	48	5
SUCH IS THE SWAY OF YOUR GREAT MEN O'ER LITTLE	90	3	DON JUAN 7	48	8
AND WHY BECAUSE A LITTLE--ODD--OLD MAN	90	3	DON JUAN 7	49	7
THAT ALL IS SETTLED--THERE WAS LITTLE DIN	94	3	DON JUAN 7	54	6
THOUGH LITTLE VERSED IN FEELINGS ORIENTAL	105	3	DON JUAN 7	75	2
AND CARED AS LITTLE FOR HIS ARMY'S LOSS	105	3	DON JUAN 7	77	5
TO WASTE SO MUCH GOLD FOR A LITTLE DROSS	113	3	DON JUAN 8	3	5
JOHNSON RETIRED A LITTLE JUST TO RALLY	131	3	DON JUAN 8	36	7
AND THERE A LITTLE SHELTERED FROM THE SHOT	131	3	DON JUAN 8	37	1
RETIRE A LITTLE MERELY TO TAKE BREATH	133	3	DON JUAN 8	40	4
I THINK I HEAR A LITTLE BIRD WHO SINGS	137	3	DON JUAN 8	50	3
BUT OF THE FIRST OUR LITTLE FRIEND DON JUAN	138	3	DON JUAN 8	52	2
TWO LONG OCTAVES PASSED IN A LITTLE MINUTE	142	3	DON JUAN 8	59	2
A WORD WHICH LITTLE SUITS WITH SERASKIERS	152	3	DON JUAN 8	80	3
WHENE'ER HE CAN FOR THERE IS LITTLE ART	154	3	DON JUAN 8	86	3

		PAGE	VOL		CANTO	STANZA	LN
LITTLE (CONTINUED)							
A LITTLE SCORCHED AT PRESENT WITH THE BLAZE		156	3	DON JUAN	8	90	6
AND HIDE HER LITTLE PALPITATING BREAST		157	3	DON JUAN	8	91	7
THEIR SABRES GLITTERED O'ER HER LITTLE HEAD		158	3	DON JUAN	8	93	1
DON JUAN RAISED HIS LITTLE CAPTIVE FROM		158	3	DON JUAN	8	94	7
TOBACCO ON A LITTLE CARPET--TROY		172	3	DON JUAN	8	121	3
HIMSELF OR BASTION LITTLE MATTERED NOW		172	3	DON JUAN	8	122	2
HAD MADE THEM CHASTE--THEY RAVISHED VERY LITTLE		176	3	DON JUAN	8	128	8
HEAVEN HELP ME I'M BUT LITTLE OF A PARSON		179	3	DON JUAN	8	134	4
HIS LITTLE CAPTIVE GAINED HIM SOME APPLAUSE		182	3	DON JUAN	8	140	5
AT LAST MAY GET A LITTLE TIRED OF THUNDER		185	3	DON JUAN	9	5	4
BUT PRAY GIVE BACK A LITTLE TO THE NATION		185	3	DON JUAN	9	6	8
SO LITTLE DO WE KNOW WHAT WE'RE ABOUT IN		191	3	DON JUAN	9	17	7
HOWEVER LITTLE BOTH ARE UNDERSTOOD		193	3	DON JUAN	9	22	4
HE TURNED HIS EYES UPON HIS LITTLE CHARGE		198	3	DON JUAN	9	31	2
LITTLE BUT TO THE PURPOSE AND HIS MANNER		223	3	DON JUAN	9	83	7
KNOW LITTLE MORE OF LOVE THAN WHAT IS SUNG		230	3	DON JUAN	10	10	4
AND ALL OUR LITTLE FEUDS AT LEAST ALL MINE		232	3	DON JUAN	10	16	1
AND THOUGH THE DUTY WAXED A LITTLE HARD		235	3	DON JUAN	10	22	2
DON JUAN GREW I FEAR A LITTLE DISSIPATED		236	3	DON JUAN	10	23	3
INFORMED HIM THAT HE HAD A LITTLE BROTHER		240	3	DON JUAN	10	32	6
MADE THE CHASTE CATHERINE LOOK A LITTLE GRIM		246	3	DON JUAN	10	44	3
SAT LITTLE LEILA WHO SURVIVED THE PARRIES		249	3	DON JUAN	10	51	4
POOR LITTLE THING SHE WAS AS FAIR AS DOCILE		250	3	DON JUAN	10	52	1
THE LITTLE TURK REFUSED TO BE CONVERTED		251	3	DON JUAN	10	55	8
WHATE'ER THE CAUSE THE CHURCH MADE LITTLE OF IT--		252	3	DON JUAN	10	56	7
WHAT EVEN YOUNG STRANGERS FEEL A LITTLE STRONG		257	3	DON JUAN	10	65	3
BUT THOUGH I OWE IT LITTLE BUT MY BIRTH		257	3	DON JUAN	10	66	3
YET STARED AT THIS A LITTLE THOUGH HE PAID IT--		259	3	DON JUAN	10	70	4
BEFORE THEY BUTCHER LITTLE LEILA GAZED		261	3	DON JUAN	10	74	7
ESTEEMING IT A LITTLE HARD HE SHOULD		277	3	DON JUAN	11	18	5
IN TWELVE HOURS' TIME AND VERY LITTLE SPACE		277	3	DON JUAN	11	18	6
NOR MUCH TO CLIMB THROUGH LITTLE BOXES FRAMED		278	3	DON JUAN	11	21	4
AND LADIES LIKE A LITTLE SPICE OF MARS		284	3	DON JUAN	11	33	V4
JUAN WHO WAS A LITTLE SUPERFICIAL		294	3	DON JUAN	11	51	1
YAWNING A LITTLE AS THE NIGHT GROWS LATER		303	3	DON JUAN	11	69	8
OR LITTLE OVERTURNS AND NOT THE FEW		305	3	DON JUAN	11	73	4
WHERE LITTLE CASTLEREAGH THE DEVIL CAN TELL		307	3	DON JUAN	11	77	2
THERE'S LITTLE STRANGE IN THIS BUT SOMETHING STRANGE IS		309	3	DON JUAN	11	81	7
AND ADDING STILL A LITTLE THROUGH EACH CROSS		317	3	DON JUAN	12	4	4
AND HOLD UP TO THE SUN MY LITTLE TAPER		325	3	DON JUAN	12	21	3
MIGHT MEET FROM MEN A LITTLE MORE FORGIVENESS		326	3	DON JUAN	12	22	8
THE LITTLE LEILA WITH HER ORIENT EYES		328	3	DON JUAN	12	27	1
AMONGST THE SEX IN LITTLE THINGS OR GREAT		329	3	DON JUAN	12	28	2
BEGGED TO BRING UP THE LITTLE GIRL AND OUT--		330	3	DON JUAN	12	31	3
BUT FIRST OF LITTLE LEILA WE'LL DISPOSE		335	3	DON JUAN	12	41	1
TO MAKE HIS LITTLE WILD ASIATIC TAME		336	3	DON JUAN	12	42	6
THAT LADIES IN THEIR YOUTH A LITTLE GAY		336	3	DON JUAN	12	44	4
IN BRIEF THE LITTLE ORPHAN OF THE EAST		338	3	DON JUAN	12	48	7
A LITTLE SPOILED BUT NOT SO ALTOGETHER		338	3	DON JUAN	12	49	3
OUR HERO GLADLY SAW HIS LITTLE CHARGE		339	3	DON JUAN	12	51	2
PERHAPS A LITTLE STRANGE IF NOT QUITE NEW		341	3	DON JUAN	12	54	2
BUT THOSE WHO HAVE BEEN A LITTLE USED TO ROUGHING		345	3	DON JUAN	12	63	V6
A LITTLE GENIAL SPRINKLING OF HYPOCRISY		346	3	DON JUAN	12	66	2
A LITTLE BLASE--'TIS NOT TO BE WONDERED		353	3	DON JUAN	12	81	5
ALTHOUGH WHEN LONG A LITTLE APT TO WEARY US		358	3	DON JUAN	13	1	6
AS MOST MEN DO THE LITTLE OR THE GREAT		367	3	DON JUAN	13	19	2
FOR SUCH A SHIELD WHICH LEAVES BUT LITTLE MERIT		372	3	DON JUAN	13	31	2
SOMETIMES A LITTLE LATER I DON'T ERR		378	3	DON JUAN	13	43	2
WITHAL IT LIES PERHAPS A LITTLE LOW		384	3	DON JUAN	13	55	6
ITS LITTLE TORRENT IN A THOUSAND BUBBLES		389	3	DON JUAN	13	65	7
WHICH HATH A LITTLE LEANING TO A LOTTERY		397	3	DON JUAN	13	82	2
THE LADIES--SOME ROUGED SOME A LITTLE PALE--		406	3	DON JUAN	13	104	1
OR CRAMM'D TWELVE SHEETS INTO ONE LITTLE LETTER		406	3	DON JUAN	13	104	7
A LITTLE EARLIER THAN THE WANING MOON		409	3	DON JUAN	13	111	4
WITH MUCH TO EXCITE THERE'S LITTLE TO EXALT		417	3	DON JUAN	14	16	1
THERE'S LITTLE LEFT BUT TO BE BORED OR BORE		418	3	DON JUAN	14	18	6
'TIS THAT IN FACT THERE'S LITTLE TO DESCRIBE		418	3	DON JUAN	14	20	8
A LITTLE SPOILT BUT BY NO MEANS SO QUITE		428	3	DON JUAN	14	41	3
A LITTLE BLACK UPON THIS NEW FLIRTATION		429	3	DON JUAN	14	43	2
THOSE LITTLE GLITTERERS OF THE LONDON NIGHT		435	3	DON JUAN	14	57	2
SAITH HORACE THE GREAT LITTLE PEOPLE'S WRONG		443	3	DON JUAN	14	77	2
BUT THERE'S ANOTHER LITTLE THING I OWN		445	3	DON JUAN	14	82	5
BUT GREAT THINGS SPRING FROM LITTLE--WOULD YOU THINK		454	3	DON JUAN	14	100	1
MAY RETROGRADE A LITTLE IN THE DANCE		473	3	DON JUAN	15	39	6
LITTLE AURORA DEEM'D SHE WAS THE THEME		480	3	DON JUAN	15	55	1
SHE HAD SO MUCH OR LITTLE OF THE CHILD		480	3	DON JUAN	15	55	8
HOW LITTLE DO WE KNOW THAT WHICH WE ARE		500	3	DON JUAN	15	99	3
WHOSE LITTLE NIBBLING RUSTLE WILL EMBARRASS		509	3	DON JUAN	16	20	7
A LITTLE TURN FOR MISCHIEF YOU MIGHT TRACE		525	3	DON JUAN	16	49	5
THEY LITTLE KNEW OR MIGHT HAVE SYMPATHISED		543	3	DON JUAN	16	90	1
(FOR LITTLE THINGS UPON MY LORD'S ESTATE		544	3	DON JUAN	16	91	7
YET GREW A LITTLE PALE--WITH WHAT CONCERN		545	3	DON JUAN	16	94	5
LITTLE THAT'S GREAT BUT MUCH OF WHAT IS CLEVER		547	3	DON JUAN	16	98	4
TRUE SHE SAID LITTLE--'TWAS THE REST THAT BROKE		552	3	DON JUAN	16	104	1
OBSERVING LITTLE IN HIS REVERIE		553	3	DON JUAN	16	106	7
WE LITTLE PEOPLE IN OUR LESSER WAY		566	3	DON JUAN	17	10	2
LITTLETON							
(SEE LITTLETON) WHENE'ER I HAVE EXPRESSED		494	3	DON JUAN	15	87	2

```
                                                        PAGE VOL      CANTO STANZA LN
LIVE
    AND LIVE AND DIE MAKE LOVE AND PAY OUR TAXES   . . . . .  159  2 DON JUAN   2      4   3
    THAT A TIGHT BOAT WILL LIVE IN A ROUGH SEA  . . . . . .   180  2 DON JUAN   2     45   7
    THEY LIVE UPON THE LOVE OF LIFE AND BEAR . . . . . . .    191  2 DON JUAN   2     66   2
    HE CANNOT LIVE LIKE WOODCOCKS UPON SUCTION . . . . . .    191  2 DON JUAN   2     67   3
    TO LIVE WITH HIM FOREVER WERE TOO MUCH  . . . . . . .     247  2 DON JUAN   2    173   5
    AND IN SUCH COLOURS THAT THEY SEEM TO LIVE  . . . . .     402  2 DON JUAN   4    107   6
    AND AIR--EARTH--WATER--FIRE LIVE--AND WE DEAD  . . . .    432  2 DON JUAN   5     39   6
    NOR EVEN DIOGENES--WE LIVE AND DIE . . . . . . . .        68   3 DON JUAN   7      4   7
    THAT SUCH EXISTED (AND THEY MAY LIVE NOW . . . . . .      82   3 DON JUAN   7     33   4
    TO THE LIVE LEG STILL CLUNG THE SEVERED HEAD . . . . .    153  3 DON JUAN   8     84   8
    IN WHICH THE NEVA'S ICE WOULD CEASE TO LIVE . . . . .     243  3 DON JUAN  10     37   6
    LIVE ANIMALS AN OLD MAID OF THREESCORE  . . . . . .       249  3 DON JUAN  10     50   6
    WHO LIVE BY LIES YET DARE NOT BOLDLY LIE . . . . . .      285  3 DON JUAN  11     36   5
    THE LIST GROWS LONG OF LIVE AND DEAD PRETENDERS . . .     299  3 DON JUAN  11     61   1
    AMONGST LIVE POETS AND BLUE LADIES PAST . . . . . .       300  3 DON JUAN  11     64   2
    THAT LIVE GAZETTE HAD SCATTER'D TO DISFIGURE  . . . .     460  3 DON JUAN  15     11   2
    AND BEING CONSUMPTIVE LIVE ON A MILK DIET  . . . . . .    474  3 DON JUAN  15     41   8
LIVED
    DON JUAN'S PARENTS LIVED BESIDE THE RIVER  . . . . . .    25   2 DON JUAN   1      8   7
    THEY LIVED RESPECTABLY AS MAN AND WIFE  . . . . . .       35   2 DON JUAN   1     26   4
    THEY LIVED TOGETHER AS MOST PEOPLE DO . . . . . . .       57   2 DON JUAN   1     65   4
    FOR DAVID LIVED BUT JUAN NEARLY DIED  . . . . . . .       113  2 DON JUAN   1    168   8
    I HAD NOT LIVED TILL NOW COULD SORROW KILL . . . . . .    134  2 DON JUAN   1    197   5
    ARE LONGER LIVED THAN OTHERS--GOD KNOWS WHY . . . . .     190  2 DON JUAN   2     65   2
    OF AN OLD MAN WHO LIVED UPON THE WATER  . . . . . .       222  2 DON JUAN   2    124   8
    AND THERE HE LIVED EXCEEDINGLY AT EASE  . . . . . .       223  2 DON JUAN   2    127   4
    AND HAVING LIVED WITH PEOPLE OF ALL RANKS  . . . . .      319  2 DON JUAN   3     84   3
    WHY DID THEY NOT THEN DIE--THEY HAD LIVED TOO LONG  . .   358  2 DON JUAN   4     27   2
    THEY SHOULD HAVE LIVED TOGETHER DEEP IN WOODS  . . .      358  2 DON JUAN   4     28   1
    THUS LIVED--THUS DIED SHE NEVER MORE ON HER . . . .       382  2 DON JUAN   4     71   1
    WHO LIVED TOO LONG FOR MEN BUT DIED TOO SOON  . . .       400  2 DON JUAN   4    103   3
    THEY LIVED TILL SOME BASHAW WAS SENT ABROAD . . . .       498  2 DON JUAN   5    152   4
    CITE IS THAT BOON LIVED HUNTING UP TO NINETY . . . .      143  3 DON JUAN   8     62   8
    HE LIVED (NOT DEATH BUT JUAN) IN A HURRY . . . . . .      237  3 DON JUAN  10     26   1
    AND LIVED AS DID THE BROKEN-HEARTED FAIR . . . . .        344  3 DON JUAN  12     61   7
    AND LIVED CONTENTEDLY WITHOUT COMPLAINTS . . . . .        424  3 DON JUAN  14     31   3
LIVELIER
    YOUR EYES TO REVEL IN A LIVELIER SIGHT  . . . . . .       392  3 DON JUAN  13     72   6
    I KNEW HIM IN HIS LIVELIER LONDON DAYS  . . . . . .       540  3 DON JUAN  16     82   1
LIVELIEST
    THE LIVELIEST FIRE AND SAW THE FIERCEST FLOOD . . . .     129  3 DON JUAN   8     33  V4
LIVELY
    SHE WAS NOT VIOLENTLY LIVELY BUT  . . . . . . .          27   3 DON JUAN   6     43   1
    A LIVELY READER'S FANCY DOES THE REST . . . . . .        55   3 DON JUAN   6     98   8
    THE HOUR AS IS THE CASE WITH LIVELY BRAINS  . . . .      129  3 DON JUAN   8     33   4
LIVER
    HOW PLEASANT FOR THE HEART AS WELL AS LIVER  . . . . .    270  2 DON JUAN   2    213   8
    THE LIVER IS THE LAZARET OF BILE . . . . . . . .         271  2 DON JUAN   2    215   1
    AH WHY THE LIVER WILT THOU THUS ATTACK  . . . . . .      372  2 DON JUAN   4     53   3
    SO CALM THOUGH PIERCED THROUGH STOMACH HEART AND LIVER .  430  2 DON JUAN   5     35   4
    WHICH MAKES ALL STYX THROUGH ONE SMALL LIVER FLOW  . .    190  3 DON JUAN   9     15   5
LIVES
    AND SOUTHEY LIVES TO SING THEM VERY ILL . . . . .        19   2 DON JUAN   D     16   8
    AND HOMILIES AND LIVES OF ALL THE SAINTS . . . . .       47   2 DON JUAN   1     47   2
    MUCH LONGER--THINK OF HUSBANDS' LOVERS' LIVES . . . .    123  2 DON JUAN   1    185   7
    TO LOSE THEIR LIVES AS WELL AS SPOIL THEIR DIET . . .    173  2 DON JUAN   2     33   4
    THEIR LIVES AND FORTUNES WERE EXTREMELY VARIOUS  . . .    266  2 DON JUAN   2    206   5
    MAKING THEIR SUMMER LIVES ONE CEASELESS SONG . . . .     337  2 DON JUAN   3    106   2
    TO PASS THEIR LIVES IN FOUNTAINS AND ON FLOWERS  . .      352  2 DON JUAN   4     15   7
    THEY VOW TO AMEND THEIR LIVES AND YET THEY DON'T . . .    414  2 DON JUAN   5      6   7
    THICKER THAN LEAVES THE LIVES BEGAN TO FALL . . . .      116  3 DON JUAN   8      9   3
    AND FOUND THEIR LIVES WERE LET AT A SHORT LEASE-- . .    150  3 DON JUAN   8     76   4
    AND HUMAN LIVES ARE LAVISHED EVERYWHERE  . . . . .       155  3 DON JUAN   8     88   2
    AS IF HE HAD THREE LIVES AS WELL AS TAILS  . . . .       172  3 DON JUAN   8    121   8
    TAKE LIVES TAKE WIVES TAKE AUGHT EXCEPT MEN'S PURSES  .   264  3 DON JUAN  10     79   2
    HERE ARE CHASTE WIVES PURE LIVES HERE PEOPLE PAY  . .     273  3 DON JUAN  11     10   1
    EVEN PLUTARCH'S LIVES HAVE BUT PICKED OUT A FEW  . .      324  3 DON JUAN  12     19   5
    WHERE LIVES NOT LAW-SUITS MUST BE RISKED FOR PASSION .    347  3 DON JUAN  12     68   2
    YET MADE THE MISERY OF AT LEAST TWO LIVES  . . . . .      452  3 DON JUAN  14     95   8
    BUT CERTES IT CONDUCTS TO LIVES ASCETIC  . . . . .        472  3 DON JUAN  15     38   7
LIVID
    WITH NOTHING LIVID STILL HER LIPS WERE RED  . . . . .     377  2 DON JUAN   4     60   2
LIVING
    BRAVE MEN WERE LIVING BEFORE AGAMEMNON  . . . . . .       24   2 DON JUAN   1      5   1
    'TIS SAID THAT PERSONS LIVING ON ANNUITIES  . . . . .     190  2 DON JUAN   2     65   1
    THEIR LIVING FREIGHT WAS NOW REDUCED TO FOUR . . . .      209  2 DON JUAN   2    101   4
    PLEASURE OR PAIN TO ONE ANOTHER LIVING  . . . . .        258  2 DON JUAN   2    192   8
    ALL THAT IT HATH OF LIFE WITH US IS LIVING  . . . .      261  2 DON JUAN   2    197   2
    OF LIVING IN THEIR INSULAR ABODE . . . . . . . .        317  2 DON JUAN   3     81   8
    AND ANSWER LET ONE LIVING HEAD . . . . . . . .         323  2 DON JUAN   3   L  8   4
    'TIS BUT THE LIVING WHO ARE DUMB  . . . . . . .         323  2 DON JUAN   3   L  8   6
    OH POPE WOULD THAT THOU WERT LIVING FOR THEIR SAKES  .    334  2 DON JUAN   3    100  V7
    THAT YOU WERE LIVING--OR I HAD YOUR ROD . . . . .        334  2 DON JUAN   3    100  V7
    ALL HEROES WHO IF LIVING STILL WOULD SLAY US . . . .     385  2 DON JUAN   4     76   8
    ACTED UPON THE LIVING AS ON WIRE  . . . . . . .         133  3 DON JUAN   8     41   7
    WHOM HE PRESERVED--A PURE AND LIVING PEARL . . . .       249  3 DON JUAN  10     51   8
    AS RARE IN LIVING BEINGS AS A FOSSILE . . . . . .        250  3 DON JUAN  10     52   3
    HE SAW TEN THOUSAND LIVING AUTHORS PASS  . . . . .       295  3 DON JUAN  11     54   5
```

462

LIVING   (CONTINUED)
  ALSO THE EIGHTY GREATEST LIVING POETS 295   3 DON JUAN 11   54   7
  IN TWICE FIVE YEARS THE GREATEST LIVING POET   296   3 DON JUAN 11   55   1
  THE ART OF LIVING IN ALL CLIMES WITH EASE   460   3 DON JUAN 15   11   8
  LOOK LIVING IN THE MOON AND AS YOU TURN 508   3 DON JUAN 16   18   2
LIVONIAN
  (AS PISTOL CALLS IT) BUT A YOUNG LIVONIAN   140   3 DON JUAN 8   56   8
LIVORNO
  IN SAILING FROM LIVORNO BY THE PIRATE 388   2 DON JUAN 4   80   7
LIVY
  TO FURNISH MATTER FOR SOME FUTURE LIVY   440   3 DON JUAN 14   68   3
LO
  WHEN LO HE STUMBLED O'ER A PAIR OF SHOES 120   2 DON JUAN 1   180   8
  AND LO A FIFTH APPEARS--AND WHAT IS SHE   41   3 DON JUAN 6   69   1
  LO DUSKY MASSES 'STEAL IN DUBIOUS SIGHT   110   3 DON JUAN 7   86   3
  WHEN ITS QUICKSILVER'S DOWN AT ZERO--LO 378   3 DON JUAN 13   44   1
  BUT LO A TENIERS WOOS AND NOT IN VAIN 392   3 DON JUAN 13   72   5
  IT WAS NO MOUSE BUT LO A MONK ARRAYED 510   3 DON JUAN 16   21   1
  AND LO UPON THAT DAY IT CAME TO PASS   539   3 DON JUAN 16   81   5
LOAD
  SO TAKE HIM UP I'LL HELP YOU WITH THE LOAD 275   3 DON JUAN 11   15   8
LOADED
  THE FIRE WAS THAT WERE RED VESUVIUS LOADED 119   3 DON JUAN 8   16   2
LOAM
  UPON THE BLACK LOAM LONG MANURED BY VICE 335   3 DON JUAN 12   40   7
LOAN
  COULD HE NOT BEG THE LOAN OF CHARLES WAIN   333   2 DON JUAN 3   99   3
  ARE THE TRUE LORDS OF EUROPE EVERY LOAN 318   3 DON JUAN 12   6   2
LOATHE
  HE DID NOT LOATHE THE SIRE TO LAUD THE SON 15   2 DON JUAN D   10   7
  I LOATHE THAT LOW VICE CURIOSITY   33   2 DON JUAN 1   23   5
  I HATE INCONSTANCY--I LOATHE DETEST   268   2 DON JUAN 2   209   1
LOATHES
  WHY YOU SHOULD WEAR THEM--WHAT THOUGH MY SOUL LOATHES   . 455   2 DON JUAN 5   76   3
LOATHING
  TO SHOW HIS LOATHING OF THE SPOT HE SOIL'D   401   2 DON JUAN 4   105   4
  AND TALK IN TENDER HORRORS OF OUR LOATHING   301   3 DON JUAN 11   65   6
LOATHSOME
  AND WHICH IN RAVAGE THE MORE LOATHSOME EVIL IS--   . . . 92   2 DON JUAN 1   131   7
  THEIR LOATHSOME PHANTASMAGORIA OER THE MIND 227   2 DON JUAN 2   134   V7
LOAVES
  AND FRUITS AND DATE-BREAD LOAVES CLOSED THE REPAST   . . 307   2 DON JUAN 3   63   2
LOBSTER
  A LOBSTER SALAD AND CHAMPAIGNE AND CHAT   94   2 DON JUAN 1   135   8
LOCHABER
  THAT BRINGS LOCHABER BACK TO EYES THAT ROAM 523   3 DON JUAN 16   46   3
LOCK
  'TWAS FRESH--FOR HE HAD LATELY USED THE LOCK--   365   2 DON JUAN 4   40   7
  NOW HERE I HAVE GOT THE PREACHER AT A DEAD LOCK   . . . 471   3 DON JUAN 15   35   8
LOCK'D
  AND LIKING NOT THE INSIDE LOCK'D THE OUT 125   2 DON JUAN 1   187   8
LOCKE
  WAS IT NOT SO GREAT LOCKE AND GREATER BACON 464   3 DON JUAN 15   18   1
  PYTHAGORAS LOCKE SOCRATES--BUT PAGES 566   3 DON JUAN 17   9   1
LOCKLESS
  LOCKLESS--SO PLIABLE FROM THE PURE GOLD 312   2 DON JUAN 3   71   2
LOCKS
  HER CLUSTERING HAIR WHOSE LONGER LOCKS WERE ROLL'D   . . 217   2 DON JUAN 2   116   3
  HER LOCKS CURL'D NEGLIGENTLY ROUND HER FACE   220   2 DON JUAN 2   121   3
  AND SHE WOULD SOFTLY STIR HIS LOCKS SO CURLY   245   2 DON JUAN 2   168   5
  WITH FAIR LONG LOCKS HAD ALSO KEPT THEIR STATION . . . 390   3 DON JUAN 13   68   5
  GLIMMER ON HIGH THEIR BURIED LOCKS STILL WAVE   509   3 DON JUAN 16   19   3
LOCUST
  AS E'ER WAS LOCUST ON THE LAND IT BLASTED   84   3 DON JUAN 7   36   8
  HOWE'ER THE MIGHTY LOCUST DESOLATION 175   3 DON JUAN 8   126   5
LODGE
  TO LODGE THERE WHEN A WAR BROKE OUT ACCORDING 498   2 DON JUAN 5   151   2
LODGED
  HE WAS WELL LODGED BUT ONLY WONDERED HOW 262   3 DON JUAN 10   75   2
LODGEMENT
  THOUGH HEAVEN KNOWS HOW IT EVER FOUND A LODGEMENT   . . 144   2 DON JUAN 1   215   8
LOFTIER
  UPON THE LEFT WHICH FROM ITS LOFTIER STATION   71   3 DON JUAN 7   10   3
  A HIGHER TITLE OR A LOFTIER STATION   114   3 DON JUAN 8   4   5
  THEN TURN'D UNTO THE STARS FOR LOFTIER RAYS 480   3 DON JUAN 15   56   4
  BUT MANY A LONELY TREE THE LOFTIER GROWS 562   3 DON JUAN 17   1   3
LOFTIEST
  WHO ON THE VERY LOFTIEST KINGS HAVE DINED--   12   3 DON JUAN 6   13   5
  THE LOFTIEST HURRIED BY THE TIME AND PLACE 139   3 DON JUAN 8   54   7
  THE LOFTIEST MINDS OUTRUN THEIR TARDY AGES   566   3 DON JUAN 17   9   5
LOFTY
  THERE WAS NO WANT OF LOFTY MIRRORS AND   310   2 DON JUAN 3   69   1
  SOME FAINT LAMPS GLEAMING FROM THE LOFTY WALLS   . . . 442   2 DON JUAN 5   56   1
  HER PRESENCE WAS AS LOFTY AS HER STATE   467   2 DON JUAN 5   97   1
  SO LOFTY THAT I FEEL MY BRAIN TURN ROUND 224   3 DON JUAN 9   85   5
  WHICH SEEMS AT FIRST TO NEED NO LOFTY WING   467   3 DON JUAN 15   25   3
LOG
  LIKE A MERE LOG AND BAFFLED OUR INTENT   173   2 DON JUAN 2   32   4
LOGICAL
  TO DEEM AS A MOST LOGICAL CONCLUSION 12   2 DON JUAN D   5   5

463

		PAGE	VOL	CANTO	STANZA	LN

LOITER
IN AMBUSH LAID WHO HAD PERCEIVED HIM LOITER . . . . . . 273 3 DON JUAN 11 11 2
LOITER'D
SHE LOITER'D AND HE TOLD HER TO BE GONE . . . . 116 2 DON JUAN 1 173 3
LOLAH
LOLAH KATINKA AND DUDU IN SHORT . . . . . . 26 3 DON JUAN 6 40 3
LOLAH WAS DUSK AS INDIA AND AS WARM . . . . 26 3 DON JUAN 6 41 1
LOLAH DEMANDED THE NEW DAMSEL'S NAME-- . . . . . . 28 3 DON JUAN 6 44 1
SAID LOLAH WITH AN ACCENT RATHER ROUGH . . . . . . 28 3 DON JUAN 6 44 6
HERE LOLAH INTERPOSED--MAMMA YOU KNOW . . . . 29 3 DON JUAN 6 47 1
YOU LOLAH MUST CONTINUE STILL TO LIE . . . . 30 3 DON JUAN 6 49 1
BETWEEN THE EYES AND LOLAH ON BOTH CHEEKS . . . . . 31 3 DON JUAN 6 50 2
OF LOLAH--THOUGH HER COUCH IS NOT SO LARGE . . . . . 46 3 DON JUAN 6 81 8
LOLAH'S
LOLAH'S EYES SPARKLED AT THE PROPOSITION . . . . . . 47 3 DON JUAN 6 82 1
LONDON
BUT FOR THE MAKER MR MANN OF LONDON . . . . . . 171 2 DON JUAN 2 29 8
A LONDON BAS WILL BEAT THY SKY PERU . . . . 406 2 DON JUAN 4 112 V8
GREAT JOY TO LONDON NOW SAYS SOME GREAT FOOL . . . . 88 3 DON JUAN 7 44 1
WHEN LONDON HAD A GRAND ILLUMINATION . . . . 88 3 DON JUAN 7 44 2
COCKNEYS OF LONDON MUSCADINS OF PARIS . . . . . . 174 3 DON JUAN 8 124 7
ON A FOOL'S HEAD--AND THERE IS LONDON TOWN . . . . . 265 3 DON JUAN 10 82 8
WHERE LONDON STREETS FERMENT IN FULL ACTIVITY . . . . 272 3 DON JUAN 11 8 4
IN DECENT LONDON WHEN THE DAYLIGHT'S O'ER . . . . . 282 3 DON JUAN 11 30 5
WHERE ARE THE DUBLIN SHOUTS--AND LONDON HISSES . . . 308 3 DON JUAN 11 79 6
THOU ART IN LONDON--IN THAT PLEASANT PLACE . . . . . 326 3 DON JUAN 12 23 2
SUCH ARE--BUT I HAVE LOST THE LONDON CHART . . . . . 370 3 DON JUAN 13 27 8
THE LONDON WINTER'S ENDED IN JULY-- . . . . 378 3 DON JUAN 13 43 1
THE LONDON WINTER AND THE COUNTRY SUMMER . . . . . 380 3 DON JUAN 13 48 1
THOSE LITTLE GLITTERERS OF THE LONDON NIGHT . . . . . 435 3 DON JUAN 14 57 2
I KNEW HIM IN HIS LIVELIER LONDON DAYS . . . . . . 540 3 DON JUAN 16 82 1
LONDONDERRY
OF LONDONDERRY DRAWLING AGAINST TIME . . . . 74 3 DON JUAN 7 16 6
LONDONDERRY'S
BID IRELAND'S LONDONDERRY'S MARQUESS SHOW . . . . . 207 3 DON JUAN 9 49 3
LONDON'S
MAY NOT THINK MUCH OF LONDON'S FIRST APPEARANCE-- . . 271 3 DON JUAN 11 7 7
BUT LONDON'S SO WELL LIT THAT IF DIOGENES . . . . . 281 3 DON JUAN 11 28 1
THAT IS ERE MIDNIGHT--WHICH IS LONDON'S NOON . . . . 409 3 DON JUAN 13 111 2
LONE
AND THUS THEY LEFT HIM TO HIS LONE REPOSE . . . . . 227 2 DON JUAN 2 134 1
THEY FEAR'D NO EYES NOR EARS ON THAT LONE BEACH . . . 256 2 DON JUAN 2 189 1
AND NOW 'TWAS DONE--ON THE LONE SHORE WERE PLIGHTED . 265 2 DON JUAN 2 204 1
NOT ALL LONE MATRONS FOR THEIR HUSBANDS MOURN . . . . 287 2 DON JUAN 3 23 3
HE DEEM'D BEING IN A LONE ISLE AMONG FRIENDS . . . . 318 2 DON JUAN 3 83 4
FOAMING O'ER HER LONE HEAD SO FIERCE AND HIGH . . . . 361 2 DON JUAN 4 31 7
FOR LOVE OR BREAKFAST PRIVATE PLEASING LONE . . . . . 54 2 DON JUAN 6 97 3
AS SEEKING NOT TO KNOW IT SILENT LONE . . . . . . 476 3 DON JUAN 15 47 4
THE ISLAND GIRL BRED UP BY THE LONE SEA . . . . . . 481 3 DON JUAN 15 58 4
LONELINESS
WHO SHUT IN CHAMBERS THINK IT LONELINESS . . . . . . 255 2 DON JUAN 2 188 2
LONELY
HIS HOME DESERTED FOR THE LONELY WOOD . . . . . . 68 2 DON JUAN 1 87 2
THUS WOULD HE WHILE HIS LONELY HOURS AWAY . . . . . 73 2 DON JUAN 1 96 1
THOSE LONELY WALKS AND LENGTHENING REVERIES . . . . . 73 2 DON JUAN 1 97 1
SO LONELY LOVING HELPLESS AND THE HOUR . . . . . . 258 2 DON JUAN 2 192 2
A LONELY PURE AFFECTION UNOPPOSED . . . . . . 304 2 DON JUAN 3 57 5
HOW LONELY EVERY FREEBORN CREATURE BROODS . . . . . 358 2 DON JUAN 4 28 5
ENJOYED THE LONELY VIGOROUS HARMLESS DAYS . . . . . 143 3 DON JUAN 8 61 7
OR TO SOME LONELY ISLE OF JAILORS GO . . . . 296 3 DON JUAN 11 56 7
AND HEAVES A LONELY SUBTERRAQUEOUS SIGH . . . . . . 445 3 DON JUAN 14 81 3
BUT STILL HER ASPECT HAD AN AIR SO LONELY . . . . . 475 3 DON JUAN 15 44 3
BUT MANY A LONELY TREE THE LOFTIER GROWS . . . . . . 562 3 DON JUAN 17 1 3
LONG
AND WORDSWORTH IN A RATHER LONG EXCURSION . . . . . 11 2 DON JUAN D 4 1
YOU--GENTLEMEN BY DINT OF LONG SECLUSION . . . . . 12 2 DON JUAN D 5 1
AND OFFER POISON LONG ALREADY MIX'D . . . . 16 2 DON JUAN D 12 8
WHICH WITH A LONG MINORITY AND CARE . . . . 42 2 DON JUAN 1 37 3
HE WON THEM WELL AND MAY HE WEAR THEM LONG . . . . . 77 2 DON JUAN 1 104 8
OF HUMAN HEARTS THAN ALL THE LONG ARRAY . . . . . . 84 2 DON JUAN 1 116 5
WHO'VE MADE US YOUTH WAIT TOO--TOO LONG ALREADY . . . 89 2 DON JUAN 1 125 4
THE MAJOR PART OF THEM HAD LONG BEEN WIVED . . . . . 96 2 DON JUAN 1 138 3
FOR THIS IN SILENCE I HAVE SUFFER'D LONG . . . . . . 100 2 DON JUAN 1 145 5
THAT FOR SO LONG OPPOSED THIS GAMING EVIL . . . . . 102 2 DON JUAN 1 148 V4
(LONG ERE I DREAMT OF DATING FROM THE BRENTA) . . . . 143 2 DON JUAN 1 212 5
SO BLACK THE LONG WORN LION'S HIDE IN HUE . . . . . 154 2 DON JUAN 1 V 5 7
FAREWELL MY SPAIN A LONG FAREWELL HE CRIED . . . . . 166 2 DON JUAN 2 18 1
WERE SETTLED LONG ERE JUAN'S SIRE WAS BORN . . . . . 169 2 DON JUAN 2 24 4
AND LONG HAD VOYAGED THROUGH MANY A STORMY SEA . . . 179 2 DON JUAN 2 43 4
AS NOW MIGHT RENDER THEIR LONG SUFFERING LESS . . . . 180 2 DON JUAN 2 46 4
BUT THE BOY BORE UP LONG AND WITH A MILD . . . . . 203 2 DON JUAN 2 88 3
AND LOOK'D UPON IT LONG AND WHEN AT LAST . . . . . 204 2 DON JUAN 2 90 2
WHO LONG HAD BEEN HIS MATES UPON THE SEA . . . . . . 213 2 DON JUAN 2 109 4
HOW LONG IN HIS DAMP TRANCE YOUNG JUAN LAY . . . . . 214 2 DON JUAN 2 111 5
HIS DEWY CURLS LONG DRENCH'D BY EVERY STORM . . . . . 216 2 DON JUAN 2 114 6
HER HAIR WAS THICKER BUT LESS LONG HER EYES . . . . . 221 2 DON JUAN 2 122 7
WERE NEARLY TINDER SINCE SO LONG THEY LAY . . . . . 226 2 DON JUAN 2 132 5
AND LONG FOR FOOD BUT CHIEFLY A BEEF-STEAK . . . . . 237 2 DON JUAN 2 153 8
AND DARTS IN ONE QUICK GLANCE A LONG REPLY . . . . . 241 2 DON JUAN 2 162 6

464

LONG   (CONTINUED)
	PAGE	VOL	CANTO	STANZA	LN
WITHOUT WHOM VENUS WILL NOT LONG ATTACK US	245	2 DON JUAN	2	169	8
SAVE ON THE DEAD LONG SUMMER DAYS WHICH MAKE	249	2 DON JUAN	2	177	7
AFTER LONG TRAVEL ENNUI LOVE OR SLAUGHTER	251	2 DON JUAN	2	180	7
BRINGING WARM WATER WREATHING HER LONG TRESSES . . .	252	2 DON JUAN	2	182	7
A LONG LONG KISS A KISS OF YOUTH AND LOVE	254	2 DON JUAN	2	186	1
A LONG LONG KISS A KISS OF YOUTH AND LOVE	254	2 DON JUAN	2	186	1
HEAVEN KNOWS HOW LONG--NO DOUBT THEY NEVER RECKON'D .	254	2 DON JUAN	2	187	2
ALL FEELINGS WHICH O'ERLEAP THE YEARS LONG LOST . . .	286	2 DON JUAN	3	21	7
AFTER LONG TRAVELLING BY LAND OR WATER	287	2 DON JUAN	3	22	2
YET FOR ALL THAT KEEP NOT TOO LONG AWAY	288	2 DON JUAN	3	25	7
DOWN HER WHITE NECK LONG FLOATING AUBURN CURLS-- . .	291	2 DON JUAN	3	30	5
CRIMSON AS CLEFT POMEGRANATES THEIR LONG TRESSES . .	292	2 DON JUAN	3	33	3
AND LONG HE PAUSED TO RE-ASSURE HIS EYES	294	2 DON JUAN	3	37	6
WITHOUT A WELCOME THERE HE LONG HAD DWELT	302	2 DON JUAN	3	52	4
THE HARDNESS BY LONG HABITUDE PRODUCED	303	2 DON JUAN	3	54	2
HAD COST HIS ENEMIES A LONG REPENTANCE	303	2 DON JUAN	3	54	7
HER HAIR'S LONG AUBURN WAVES DOWN TO HER HEEL . . .	313	2 DON JUAN	3	73	1
MIGHT FOR LONG LYING MAKE HIMSELF AMENDS	318	2 DON JUAN	3	83	6
AND MUST THY LYRE SO LONG DIVINE	322	2 DON JUAN	3	L 5	5
SOME DULL MS OBLIVION LONG HAS SANK	327	2 DON JUAN	3	89	5
AND GLORY LONG HAS MADE THE SAGES SMILE	328	2 DON JUAN	3	90	1
OR COLERIDGE LONG BEFORE HIS FLIGHTY PEN	329	2 DON JUAN	3	93	5
(IN COPYING) THIS LONG CANTO INTO TWO	342	2 DON JUAN	3	111	3
A LONG AND SNAKE-LIKE LIFE OF DULL DECAY	348	2 DON JUAN	4	9	7
THE LONG YEAR LINK'D WITH HEAVY DAY ON DAY	350	2 DON JUAN	4	11	5
DEEPEST IN THOSE WHO LONG THE MOST TO DIE	350	2 DON JUAN	4	11	8
WHY DID THEY NOT THEN DIE--THEY HAD LIVED TOO LONG .	358	2 DON JUAN	4	27	2
AND THAT BRIEF DREAM APPEAR'D A LIFE TOO LONG . . .	362	2 DON JUAN	4	34	8
AND LONG LONG DESERTS SCORCH THE CAMEL'S FOOT . . .	373	2 DON JUAN	4	55	6
AND LONG LONG DESERTS SCORCH THE CAMEL'S FOOT . . .	373	2 DON JUAN	4	55	6
AND HE BEGUN A LONG LOW ISLAND SONG	379	2 DON JUAN	4	65	7
LONG WITH HER DESTINY BUT SHE SLEEPS WELL	382	2 DON JUAN	4	71	7
WITH HER SIRE'S STORY MAKES THE NIGHT LESS LONG . .	383	2 DON JUAN	4	73	3
WE WILL REVIVE OUR FORTUNES BEFORE LONG	389	2 DON JUAN	4	82	8
THE GRASS UPON MY GRAVE WILL GROW AS LONG	398	2 DON JUAN	4	99	7
WHO LIVED TOO LONG FOR MEN BUT DIED TOO SOON . . .	400	2 DON JUAN	4	103	3
OF SILENCE WOULD NOT LONG BE BORNE BY THOUGHT . . .	402	2 DON JUAN	4	106	V4
(BECAUSE THIS CANTO HAS BECOME TOO LONG)	410	2 DON JUAN	4	117	3
AND LONG BESIDES -- OH IF 'TIS REALLY SO	419	2 DON JUAN	5	16	6
A SAD TALE SADDENS DOUBLY WHEN 'TIS LONG	419	2 DON JUAN	5	16	8
A DULL STORY'S DOUBLY GRIEVOUS WHEN 'TIS LONG . . .	419	2 DON JUAN	5	16	V8
I PASS MY EVENINGS IN LONG GALLERIES SOLELY	444	2 DON JUAN	5	58	7
WHERE ECHO WOKE AS IF FROM A LONG SLUMBER	448	2 DON JUAN	5	64	2
WAS HARDLY LONG ENOUGH BUT BABA FOUND	457	2 DON JUAN	5	79	2
SO MANY FALSE LONG TRESSES ALL TO SPARE	457	2 DON JUAN	5	79	3
THUS HORACE WROTE WE ALL KNOW LONG AGO	470	2 DON JUAN	5	101	5
AS TO ANNOUNCE HIS VISITS A LONG WHILE	495	2 DON JUAN	5	146	5
WITH ALL THE DAMSELS IN THEIR LONG ARRAY	19	3 DON JUAN	6	26	2
BACK TO THEIR CHAMBERS THOSE LONG GALLERIES	19	3 DON JUAN	6	26	5
THIS LONG PARENTHESIS I COULD NOT SHUT	34	3 DON JUAN	6	56	4
OF THE LONG CARAVAN WHICH IN THE CHILL	49	3 DON JUAN	6	86	5
TO THIS LONG CATECHISM OF QUESTIONS ASKED	56	3 DON JUAN	6	100	2
FELL IN LONG TRESSES LIKE THE WEEPING WILLOW . . .	60	3 DON JUAN	6	108	2
HER HEAD HUNG DOWN AND HER LONG HAIR IN STOOPING . .	60	3 DON JUAN	6	109	1
WHICH MADE A LONG DEBATE BUT I MUST HALT	83	3 DON JUAN	7	35	6
IF STARS AND TITLES COULD ENTAIL LONG PRAISE . . .	84	3 DON JUAN	7	37	3
JOHNSON WHO KNEW BY THIS LONG COLLOQUY	100	3 DON JUAN	7	65	1
ALL EARS THOUGH LONG ALL AGES THOUGH SO SHORT . . .	106	3 DON JUAN	7	79	2
OH YE LESS GRAND LONG LIST OF KILLED AND WOUNDED . .	108	3 DON JUAN	7	82	2
LONG BOOMING OF EACH PEAL ON PEAL O'ERCAME	115	3 DON JUAN	8	6	6
AIR MIDST THE REST WHOSE SHORT BREATH AND LONG FACES .	130	3 DON JUAN	8	34	V7
SAYS HOTSPUR LONG ERE THEY WILL LEAVE THEIR HOME . .	132	3 DON JUAN	8	38	4
TWO LONG OCTAVES PASSED IN A LITTLE MINUTE	142	3 DON JUAN	8	59	2
THE GOOD OLD KHAN WHO LONG HAD CEASED TO SEE . . .	169	3 DON JUAN	8	116	2
PERHAPS THE SEASON'S CHILL AND THEIR LONG STATION . .	176	3 DON JUAN	8	128	6
(WIDOWS OF FORTY WERE THESE BIRDS LONG CAGED) . . .	178	3 DON JUAN	8	132	3
FOR I HAVE DRAWN MUCH LESS WITH A LONG BOW	181	3 DON JUAN	8	138	6
SO CALLED THE ANTIC LONG HATH CEASED TO HEAR . . .	188	3 DON JUAN	9	12	4
AND SWIMMING LONG IN THE ABYSS OF THOUGHT	191	3 DON JUAN	9	18	5
A SCARLET COAT BLACK FACINGS A LONG PLUME	204	3 DON JUAN	9	43	2
THAT MONSTROUS HIEROGLYPHIC--THAT LONG SPOUT . . .	207	3 DON JUAN	9	50	5
LIKE FLOWERS WELL WATERED AFTER A LONG DROUTH-- . .	213	3 DON JUAN	9	61	4
THY LONG LONG BILLS WHENCE NOTHING IS DEDUCTED . . .	259	3 DON JUAN 10		69	8
THY LONG LONG BILLS WHENCE NOTHING IS DEDUCTED . . .	259	3 DON JUAN 10		69	8
NOT LONG BEFORE THE MOST OF THEM GO HOME--	277	3 DON JUAN 10		20	3
THE LIST GROWS LONG OF LIVE AND DEAD PRETENDERS . .	299	3 DON JUAN 11		61	1
HIS LAST AWARD WILL HAVE THE LONG GRASS GROW . . .	299	3 DON JUAN 11		61	4
AND LONG THE LATEST OF ARRIVALS HALTS	302	3 DON JUAN 11		68	6
PERMITS WHATE'ER THEY PLEASE OR DID NOT LONG SINCE .	305	3 DON JUAN 11		73	8
WHERE'S BRUMMELL DISHED WHERE'S LONG POLE WELLESLEY DIDDLED	307	3 DON JUAN 11		78	1
FOR SOMETIMES THEY ACCEPT SOME LONG PURSUER	333	3 DON JUAN 12		37	1
UPON THE BLACK LOAM LONG MANURED BY VICE	335	3 DON JUAN 12		40	7
BEING LONG MARRIED AND THUS SET AT LARGE	339	3 DON JUAN 12		51	4
ALTHOUGH WHEN LONG A LITTLE APT TO WEARY US	358	3 DON JUAN 13		1	6
HE WHO WILL COMBAT EVIL LONG IN USE	363	3 DON JUAN 13		10	V1
AND TRADESMEN WITH LONG BILLS AND LONGER FACES . . .	378	3 DON JUAN 13		44	7
AT A LONG DATE--TILL THEY CAN GET A FRESH ONE-- . .	379	3 DON JUAN 13		45	6
HUGE HALLS LONG GALLERIES SPACIOUS CHAMBERS JOIN'D . .	390	3 DON JUAN 13		67	1

LONG (CONTINUED)

	PAGE	VOL	CANTO	STANZA	LN
WITH FAIR LONG LOCKS HAD ALSO KEPT THEIR STATION	390	3 DON JUAN	13	68	5
SO LONG I'VE BATTLED EITHER MORE OR LESS	415	3 DON JUAN	14	12	3
WHO AFTER A LONG CHASE O'ER HILLS DALES BUSHES	425	3 DON JUAN	14	35	6
TO EARLY RISERS AFTER A LONG CHASE	426	3 DON JUAN	14	36	2
WITH A LONG MEMORANDUM OF OLD STORIES	432	3 DON JUAN	14	50	8
WHICH WITH THE LANDLORD MAKES TOO LONG A STAND	435	3 DON JUAN	14	58	2
UNLESS GOOD COMPANY HE KEPT TOO LONG	443	3 DON JUAN	14	77	6
LONG DIALOGUES WHICH PASS'D WITHOUT A WORD	489	3 DON JUAN	15	76	8
SINCE WITH DIGRESSIONS WE TOO LONG HAVE TARRIED	493	3 DON JUAN	15	84	5
BUT DRAW THE LONG BOW BETTER NOW THAN EVER	501	3 DON JUAN	16	1	8
LONG FURNISHED WITH OLD PICTURES OF GREAT WORTH	508	3 DON JUAN	16	17	4
WAS LONG AND THUS FAR THERE WAS NO GREAT CAUSE	511	3 DON JUAN	16	24	3
HE STOOD--HOW LONG HE KNEW NOT BUT IT SEEMED	511	3 DON JUAN	16	25	1
AND A LONG EULOGY OF PATENT BLACKING	512	3 DON JUAN	16	26	8
SAW--WELL NO MATTER 'TWAS SO LONG AGO	517	3 DON JUAN	16	38	3
OH THE LONG EVENINGS OF DUETS AND TRIOS	523	3 DON JUAN	16	45	1
OF THAT SAME TUNE WHEN PEOPLE HUM IT LONG)--	529	3 DON JUAN	16	59	3
AND RISE AT NINE IN LIEU OF LONG ELEVEN	539	3 DON JUAN	16	81	4
OR TO COARSE EFFORTS VERY LOUD AND LONG	540	3 DON JUAN	16	83	7
LONG BANQUETS AND TOO MANY GUESTS ALTHOUGH	542	3 DON JUAN	16	86	2
TEMPERANCE DELIGHTS HER BUT LONG FASTING RUFFLES	542	3 DON JUAN	16	86	8
AS WIDE AS IF A LONG SPEECH WERE TO COME	557	3 DON JUAN	16	115	4
HALF LETTING IN LONG SHADOWS ON THE LIGHT	558	3 DON JUAN	16	117	4
SO OFTEN URGED SO LOUDLY AND SO LONG	564	3 DON JUAN	17	5	6

LONG-BOAT

	PAGE	VOL	CANTO	STANZA	LN
BUT IN THE LONG-BOAT THEY CONTRIVED TO STOW	181	2 DON JUAN	2	47	1
JUAN GOT INTO THE LONG-BOAT AND THERE	186	2 DON JUAN	2	56	1
NINE SOULS MORE WENT IN HER THE LONG-BOAT STILL	188	2 DON JUAN	2	61	1

LONG-BOAT'S

	PAGE	VOL	CANTO	STANZA	LN
AND THE LONG-BOAT'S CONDITION WAS BUT BAD	181	2 DON JUAN	2	48	3

LONGBOW

	PAGE	VOL	CANTO	STANZA	LN
LONGBOW FROM IRELAND STRONGBOW FROM THE TWEED	401	3 DON JUAN	13	92	2
LONGBOW WAS RICH IN AN IMAGINATION	401	3 DON JUAN	13	92	5
BUT LONGBOW WILD AS AN AEOLIAN HARP	402	3 DON JUAN	13	93	2

LONGBOW'S

	PAGE	VOL	CANTO	STANZA	LN
AT LONGBOW'S PHRASES YOU MIGHT SOMETIMES CARP	402	3 DON JUAN	13	93	6

LONG'D

	PAGE	VOL	CANTO	STANZA	LN
AND ROCKING IN HIS HAMMOCK LONG'D FOR LAND	169	2 DON JUAN	2	25	5

LONGED

	PAGE	VOL	CANTO	STANZA	LN
AND REALLY LONGED TO KISS HER--LIKE A VILLAIN	268	2 DON JUAN	2	209	V8
PERHAPS HE LONGED IN BITTER FROSTS FOR CLIMES	243	3 DON JUAN	10	37	5
BOTH LONGED EXTREMELY TO BE SUNG IN SPANISH	295	3 DON JUAN	11	53	8

LONGER

	PAGE	VOL	CANTO	STANZA	LN
WITH BASE SUSPICION NOW NO LONGER HAUNTED	120	2 DON JUAN	1	180	V6
MUCH LONGER--THINK OF HUSBANDS' LOVERS' LIVES	123	2 DON JUAN	1	185	7
TO WEATHER OUT MUCH LONGER THE DISTRESS	178	2 DON JUAN	2	41	3
ARE LONGER LIVED THAN OTHERS--GOD KNOWS WHY	190	2 DON JUAN	2	65	2
HER CLUSTERING HAIR WHOSE LONGER LOCKS WERE ROLL'D	217	2 DON JUAN	2	116	3
AND THIS EXTREME EFFECT (TO TIRE NO LONGER	488	2 DON JUAN	5	133	7
AND THIS STRONG SECOND CAUSE (TO TIRE NO LONGER	488	2 DON JUAN	5	133	V7
AND WHAT IS WORSE STILL A MUCH LONGER STORY	120	3 DON JUAN	8	17	8
FOR A MUCH LONGER TIME THEN LIKE AN ASS--	126	3 DON JUAN	8	29	5
NO LONGER NOW RESIST THE ATTRACTION OF GUNPOWDER	129	3 DON JUAN	8	33	V7
FOR IF HE DON'T I DOUBT IF MEN WILL LONGER--	137	3 DON JUAN	8	50	2
AND PALSIED FANCY WHICH NO LONGER ROVES	228	3 DON JUAN	10	6	6
AND TRADESMEN WITH LONG BILLS AND LONGER FACES	378	3 DON JUAN	13	44	7
NONE THAN THEMSELVES COULD BOAST A LONGER LINE	381	3 DON JUAN	13	50	5
YOUTH FADES AND LEAVES OUR DAYS NO LONGER SUNNY	405	3 DON JUAN	13	100	5
THE THIRD TIME AFTER A STILL LONGER PAUSE	511	3 DON JUAN	16	24	1
NO LONGER READY EARS AND SHORT-HAND PENS	540	3 DON JUAN	16	83	4
FOLLOWED HIS VEINS NO LONGER COLD BUT HEATED	559	3 DON JUAN	16	119	4

LONGEST

	PAGE	VOL	CANTO	STANZA	LN
THE LONGEST NOT THE TWENTY-FIRST OF JUNE	82	2 DON JUAN	1	113	5
AWAITS AT LAST EVEN THOSE WHOM LONGEST MISS	350	2 DON JUAN	4	12	6
NOW HATRED IS BY FAR THE LONGEST PLEASURE	361	3 DON JUAN	13	6	7

LONGEVITY

	PAGE	VOL	CANTO	STANZA	LN
DESPAIR OF ALL RECOVERY SPOILS LONGEVITY	190	2 DON JUAN	2	64	7

LONGING

	PAGE	VOL	CANTO	STANZA	LN
DEVOUR'D IT LONGING FOR THE OTHER TOO	193	2 DON JUAN	2	71	8
HER GLANCES ON IT AND THEN LONGING FLUNG	44	3 DON JUAN	6	76	4
('TIS POPE'S PHRASE) A GREAT LONGING THO' A RASH ONE	216	3 DON JUAN	9	68	6
OR ON THE WATCH THEIR LONGING EYES WOULD FIX	406	3 DON JUAN	13	102	7
LONGING AT SIXTY FOR THE HOUR OF SIX	406	3 DON JUAN	13	102	8

LONGINGS

	PAGE	VOL	CANTO	STANZA	LN
LONGINGS SUBLIME AND ASPIRATIONS HIGH	71	2 DON JUAN	1	93	2
THE LONGINGS OF THE CANNIBAL ARISE	194	2 DON JUAN	2	72	7

LONGINUS

	PAGE	VOL	CANTO	STANZA	LN
ALTHOUGH LONGINUS TELLS US THERE IS NO HYMN	45	2 DON JUAN	1	42	5
I'LL CALL THE WORK LONGINUS O'ER A BOTTLE	138	2 DON JUAN	1	204	7
PLUMED BY LONGINUS OR THE STAGYRITE	467	3 DON JUAN	15	25	4

LONGMAN

	PAGE	VOL	CANTO	STANZA	LN
AND THROWS A CLOUD O'ER LONGMAN AND JOHN MURRAY	79	3 DON JUAN	7	26	4

LONG-SEALED

	PAGE	VOL	CANTO	STANZA	LN
AS THUNDERED KNOCKERS BROKE THE LONG-SEALED SPELL	282	3 DON JUAN	11	29	3

LONGUEURS

	PAGE	VOL	CANTO	STANZA	LN
I KNOW THAT WHAT OUR NEIGHBOURS CALL LONGUEURS	332	2 DON JUAN	3	97	1

LOOK

	PAGE	VOL	CANTO	STANZA	LN
EVEN AS THE PAGE IS RUSTLED WHILE WE LOOK	72	2 DON JUAN	1	95	3

LOOK   (CONTINUED)
	PAGE	VOL		CANTO	STANZA	LN
OUR COMING AND LOOK BRIGHTER WHEN WE COME	88	2	DON JUAN	1	123	4
LOOK WHERE YOU PLEASE--WE'VE NOTHING SIR TO HIDE	106	2	DON JUAN	1	156	4
HE CAST A RUEFUL LOOK OR TWO AND DID	111	2	DON JUAN	1	163	7
AN AWKWARD LOOK AS HE REVOLVED THE CASE	111	2	DON JUAN	1	164	7
AND THUS IN EVERY LOOK SHE SAW EXPREST	241	2	DON JUAN	2	162	7
NO DOUBT LESS OF HER LANGUAGE THAN HER LOOK	242	2	DON JUAN	2	163	4
FOR CERTAIN MERCHANTMEN UPON THE LOOK	248	2	DON JUAN	2	174	6
THEY LOOK UPON EACH OTHER AND THEIR EYES	259	2	DON JUAN	2	194	1
THEY COULD NOT LOOK MORE ROSY THAN BEFORE	314	2	DON JUAN	3	75	8
THE MOUNTAINS LOOK ON MARATHON--	321	2	DON JUAN	3	L 3	1
LOOK UP TO THINE AND TO THY SON'S ABOVE	336	2	DON JUAN	3	103	4
ARE GATHER'D ROUND US BY THY LOOK OF REST	338	2	DON JUAN	3	107	7
WITH ALL HIS KEEN WORN LOOK AND GRECIAN GRACE	363	2	DON JUAN	4	35	5
AND LOOKING ON HER AS TO LOOK HER THROUGH	368	2	DON JUAN	4	46	3
HIS OWN WELL IN SO WELL ERE YOU COULD LOOK	370	2	DON JUAN	4	49	4
ALL HOPE TO LOOK UPON HER SWEET FACE BRED	377	2	DON JUAN	4	60	6
HE HAD AN ENGLISH LOOK THAT IS WAS SQUARE	416	2	DON JUAN	5	11	1
AND ALSO COULD YOU LOOK A LITTLE MODEST	464	2	DON JUAN	5	91	8
MAY LOOK LIKE WHAT IS--NEITHER HERE NOR THERE	13	3	DON JUAN	6	14	3
OF THE GREY MORNING AND LOOK VAINLY FOR	18	3	DON JUAN	6	24	5
SHE DID NOT EVEN LOOK INTO THE MIRROR	50	3	DON JUAN	6	89	8
THOSE WHO DISLIKE TO LOOK UPON A FRAY	126	3	DON JUAN	8	30	5
ACCOUNT FOR EVERYTHING WHICH MAY LOOK BAD	127	3	DON JUAN	8	31	4
IN SEARCH OF GLORY SHOULD LOOK ON BEFORE	127	3	DON JUAN	8	31	7
IN JUAN'S LOOK PAIN PLEASURE HOPE FEAR MIXED	159	3	DON JUAN	8	96	3
THEN UP WITH ME--BUT JUAN ANSWERED LOOK	161	3	DON JUAN	8	99	1
AND THROWING BACK A DIM LOOK ON HIS SONS	170	3	DON JUAN	8	118	7
DEATH LAUGHS AT ALL YOU WEEP FOR--LOOK UPON	188	3	DON JUAN	9	11	5
LOOK LIKE THE MONSTERS OF A NEW MUSEUM	202	3	DON JUAN	9	40	8
AND HAD RETAINED HIS BOYISH LOOK BEYOND	209	3	DON JUAN	9	53	2
THE COURT THAT WATCHED EACH LOOK HER VISAGE WORE	211	3	DON JUAN	9	58	5
WOULD WISH TO LOOK ON WHILE THEY ARE IN VIGOUR	213	3	DON JUAN	9	62	4
SHE COULD REPAY EACH AMATORY LOOK YOU LENT	213	3	DON JUAN	9	62	5
TOO WISE TO LOOK THROUGH OPTICS BLACK OR BLUE)--	218	3	DON JUAN	9	71	8
(AS IT WILL LOOK SOMETIMES WITH THE FIRST STARE	224	3	DON JUAN	9	84	4
OUTWARD DISLIKE WHICH DON'T LOOK WELL ABROAD	240	3	DON JUAN	10	32	5
MADE THE CHASTE CATHERINE LOOK A LITTLE GRIM	246	3	DON JUAN	10	44	3
AND LOOK DOWN ON THE UNIVERSE WITH PITY--	290	3	DON JUAN	11	45	6
INTO AS FURIOUS ENGLISH) WITH HER BEST LOOK	294	3	DON JUAN	11	52	7
AND LOOK ON AS A MOURNER OR A SCORNER	303	3	DON JUAN	11	69	6
I LOOK FOR IT--'TIS GONE A GLOBE OF GLASS	306	3	DON JUAN	11	76	4
IF THAT CAN WELL BE THAN HIS WOODEN LOOK	309	3	DON JUAN	11	83	4
WHAT IS HIS OWN--GO LOOK AT EACH TRANSACTION	321	3	DON JUAN	12	11	4
LOOK YES LAST NIGHT AND YET SAY NO TO-DAY	332	3	DON JUAN	12	34	8
(THOUGH PARRY'S EFFORTS LOOK A LUCKY PRESAGE)	376	3	DON JUAN	13	39	5
LIKE CHARLEMAGNE'S--AND ALL SUCH PEERS IN LOOK	398	3	DON JUAN	13	85	3
LOOK BACK O'ER AGES ERE UNTO THE STAKE FAST	411	3	DON JUAN	14	2	5
YOU LOOK DOWN O'ER THE PRECIPICE AND DREAR	412	3	DON JUAN	14	5	6
RETIRE BUT LOOK INTO YOUR PAST IMPRESSION	413	3	DON JUAN	14	6	2
THIS NOBLE PERSONAGE BEGAN TO LOOK	429	3	DON JUAN	14	43	1
ESPECIALLY WHEN THEY WOULD LOOK LIKE LIES	444	3	DON JUAN	14	80	7
WHO LOOK UPON THEM AS THEY OUGHT TO DO	479	3	DON JUAN	15	53	8
WITH TWO TRANSCENDANT EYES SEEMED TO LOOK THROUGH HIM	489	3	DON JUAN	15	75	8
OPINIONS TWO WHICH AT FIRST SIGHT MAY LOOK	494	3	DON JUAN	15	87	3
I WISH TO HEAVEN THEY WOULD NOT LOOK SO GRIM	499	3	DON JUAN	15	97	6
LOOK LIVING IN THE MOON AND AS YOU TURN	508	3	DON JUAN	16	18	2
SAID JUAN HAD NOT GOT HIS USUAL LOOK ELATE	515	3	DON JUAN	16	34	3
YOU LOOK QUOTH HE AS IF YOU HAD HAD YOUR REST	515	3	DON JUAN	16	35	3
BY A LOOK SCARCE PERCEPTIBLY ASKANCE	546	3	DON JUAN	16	96	6
'TIS TRUE HE SAW AURORA LOOK AS THOUGH	553	3	DON JUAN	16	106	1
BUT SELDOM PAY THE ABSENT NOR WOULD LOOK	553	3	DON JUAN	16	106	4

LOOK'D
	PAGE	VOL		CANTO	STANZA	LN
SOME WOMEN USE THEIR TONGUES--SHE LOOK'D A LECTURE	29	2	DON JUAN	1	15	1
SHE LOOK'D A SADNESS SWEETER THAN HER SMILE	61	2	DON JUAN	1	72	2
AND LOOK'D EXTREMELY AT THE OPENING DOOR	63	2	DON JUAN	1	76	3
AND WHEN HE LOOK'D UPON HIS WATCH AGAIN	72	2	DON JUAN	1	94	6
HOW BEAUTIFUL SHE LOOK'D HER CONSCIOUS HEART	78	2	DON JUAN	1	106	1
SOME LANDSMEN WOULD HAVE LOOK'D A LITTLE PALE	170	2	DON JUAN	2	26	4
TO PAY THEM WITH AND SOME LOOK'D O'ER THE BOW	179	2	DON JUAN	2	44	5
AND THEN THEY LOOK'D AROUND THEM AND DESPAIR'D	195	2	DON JUAN	2	74	3
AND LOOK'D UPON IT LONG AND WHEN AT LAST	204	2	DON JUAN	2	90	2
THAN THESE AND SO THIS RAINBOW LOOK'D LIKE HOPE--	205	2	DON JUAN	2	93	7
THE SHORE LOOK'D WILD WITHOUT A TRACE OF MAN	211	2	DON JUAN	2	104	1
AND QUIVERING HAND AND THEN HE LOOK'D FOR THOSE	213	2	DON JUAN	2	109	3
LOOK'D BACK UPON HIM AND A MOMENT STAID	228	2	DON JUAN	2	135	3
WHERE THE BLUE VEINS LOOK'D SHADOWY SHRUNK AND WEAK	234	2	DON JUAN	2	147	5
AND LOOK'D UPON THE LADY IN WHOSE CHEEK	236	2	DON JUAN	2	150	2
THEY LOOK'D UP TO THE SKY WHOSE FLOATING GLOW	253	2	DON JUAN	2	185	1
THE SHARP ROCKS LOOK'D BELOW EACH DROP THEY CAUGHT	362	2	DON JUAN	4	33	7
HE LOOK'D ON HER BUT GAVE NO REPLY	365	2	DON JUAN	4	39	4
THEN LOOK'D CLOSE AT THE FLINT AS IF TO SEE	365	2	DON JUAN	4	40	6
SHE LOOK'D ON MANY A FACE WITH VACANT EYE	378	2	DON JUAN	4	63	1
THE LITTLE FELLOW REALLY LOOK'D QUITE HEARTY	388	2	DON JUAN	4	81	5
WITH EYES THAT LOOK'D INTO THE VERY SOUL	395	2	DON JUAN	4	94	3
WITH HER SON IN HER BLESSED ARMS LOOK'D ROUND	387	3	DON JUAN	13	61	3
WHO LOOK'D A WHITE LAMB YET WAS A BLACK SHEEP	396	3	DON JUAN	13	79	8
SOME LOOK'D PERPLEK'D AND OTHERS LOOK'D PROFOUND	429	3	DON JUAN	14	44	6
SOME LOOK'D PERPLEK'D AND OTHERS LOOK'D PROFOUND	429	3	DON JUAN	14	44	6

LOOK'D   (CONTINUED)
    SHE LOOK'D AS IF SHE SAT BY EDEN'S DOOR . . . . 476 3 DON JUAN 15   45   7
    WITH WHICH AURORA ON THOSE BAUBLES LOOK'D . . . . . . 479 3 DON JUAN 15   53   2
    REQUIRED   AURORA SCARCELY LOOK'D ASIDE . . . . 490 3 DON JUAN 15   78   3
    AND LOOK'D AS MUCH AS IF TO SAY I SAID IT-- . . . . . 491 3 DON JUAN 15   79   1
    AURORA WHO LOOK'D MORE ON BOOKS THAN FACES . . . . . 494 3 DON JUAN 15   85   1
LOOKED
    HOW LIKE THEY LOOKED THE EXPRESSION WAS THE SAME . . . 367 2 DON JUAN 4   44   2
    YET I MUST OWN HE LOOKED A LITTLE DULL   . . . . 415 2 DON JUAN 5   8   3
    AND STRIPPED AND LOOKED TO--BUT WHY SHOULD I ADD . . . 429 2 DON JUAN 5   34   5
    THEY LOOKED LIKE PERSONS BEING LED TO SENTENCE . . . . 432 2 DON JUAN 5   40   5
    HE LOOKED IN ALMOST ALL RESPECTS A MAID . . . . 458 2 DON JUAN 5   80   3
    HE LOOKED--IN ALL SAVE MODESTY--A MAID . . . . 458 2 DON JUAN 5   80 V3
    THEY LOOKED SO LITTLE DID STRONG THINGS AT TIMES-- . . 463 2 DON JUAN 5   89   2
    GULBEYAZ WHO LOOKED ON HIM AS HER DEBTOR . . . . . . 483 2 DON JUAN 5   124   5
    LOOKED INTO HIS FOR LOVE WHERE NONE REPLIES . . . . . 483 2 DON JUAN 5   125   4
    AND LOOKING AS HE ALWAYS LOOKED PERCEIVED . . . . . . 500 2 DON JUAN 5   155   2
    LOOKED MORE ADAPTED TO BE PUT TO BED . . . . 26 3 DON JUAN 6   41   6
    SHE LOOKED (THIS SIMILE'S QUITE NEW) JUST CUT . . . . 27 3 DON JUAN 6   43   5
    AT WHICH DUDU LOOKED STRANGE AND JUAN SILLY . . . . . 64 3 DON JUAN 6   118   7
    THEY LOOKED UPON THE MUSCOVITE FLOTILLA . . . . 73 3 DON JUAN 7   13   7
    LOOKED ON AS IF IN DOUBT IF THEY COULD TRUST . . . . 104 3 DON JUAN 7   73   2
    AND WHAT WAS STRANGER NEVER LOOKED BEHIND . . . . . . 126 3 DON JUAN 8   30   2
    AS HE LOOKED DOWN UPON HIS CHILDREN GONE . . . . . . 170 3 DON JUAN 8   117   7
    FAIR CATHERINE'S PASTIME--WHO LOOKED ON THE MATCH . . 197 3 DON JUAN 9   29   6
    THAT THOUGH HE LOOKED ONE OF THE SERAPHIM . . . . . . 206 3 DON JUAN 9   47   5
    THE WHOLE COURT LOOKED IMMEDIATELY MOST SWEET . . . . 213 3 DON JUAN 9   61   3
    THAT SHE WAS HANDSOME AND THOUGH FIERCE LOOKED LENIENT . 214 3 DON JUAN 9   63   1
    HER MAJESTY LOOKED DOWN THE YOUTH LOOKED UP-- . . . . 216 3 DON JUAN 9   67   1
    HER MAJESTY LOOKED DOWN THE YOUTH LOOKED UP-- . . . . 216 3 DON JUAN 9   67   1
    BECAUSE EACH LOVER LOOKED A SORT OF KING . . . . . . 217 3 DON JUAN 9   70   4
    OF THOSE IN OFFICE ALL THE WORLD LOOKED KIND . . . . 224 3 DON JUAN 9   84   3
    AND LOOKED DOWN OVER ATTICA OR HE . . . . 271 3 DON JUAN 11   7   2
    WELL LOOKED UPON BY BOTH TO THAT EXTENT . . . . 342 3 DON JUAN 12   57   2
    LOOKED GRAVE AND PALE TO SEE HER FRIEND'S FRAGILITY . . 430 3 DON JUAN 14   46   7
    SHE LOOKED AND SAW HIM PALE AND TURNED AS PALE . . . . 514 3 DON JUAN 16   31   1
    HERSELF THEN HASTILY LOOKED DOWN AND MUTTERED . . . . 514 3 DON JUAN 16   31   2
    AND LOOKED AT JUAN HARD BUT NOTHING UTTERED . . . . . 514 3 DON JUAN 16   31   6
    'TWERE DIFFICULT TO SAY--BUT JUAN LOOKED . . . . . . 568 3 DON JUAN 17   14   2
LOOKING
    A MAN WELL LOOKING FOR HIS YEARS AND WHO . . . . . . 57 2 DON JUAN 1   65   2
    OF LOOKING IN THE BED AS WELL AS UNDER . . . . 100 2 DON JUAN 1   144   8
    WHOM I SEE STANDING THERE AND LOOKING SENSIBLE . . . . 103 2 DON JUAN 1   151   4
    AND PLACES ONE KEEPS LOOKING AT THE STEEPLE . . . . . 164 2 DON JUAN 2   14   8
    AND OTHERS LOOKING WITH A STUPID STARE . . . . 208 2 DON JUAN 2   98   2
    AND LOOKING ON HER AS TO LOOK HER THROUGH . . . . . . 368 2 DON JUAN 4   46   3
    'TIS THEREFORE BETTER LOOKING BEFORE LEAPING-- . . . . 436 2 DON JUAN 5   45   6
    AND LOOKING LIKE TWO INCUBI THEY GLARED . . . . 463 2 DON JUAN 5   90   2
    THEY FORMED A VERY NYMPH-LIKE LOOKING CREW . . . . . 469 2 DON JUAN 5   99   5
    AND LOOKING ON HIM WITH A SORT OF SMILE . . . . 473 2 DON JUAN 5   107   6
    AND LOOKING COLDLY IN HER FACE HE CRIED . . . . 484 2 DON JUAN 5   126   6
    AND LOOKING AS HE ALWAYS LOOKED PERCEIVED . . . . . . 500 2 DON JUAN 5   155   2
    AND LOOKING AT HER STEADFASTLY SHE SIGHED . . . . . . 28 3 DON JUAN 6   45   3
    SAW NOTHING LIKE THE SCENE AROUND--YET LOOKING . . . . 172 3 DON JUAN 8   121   4
    OF AGE AND LOOKING BACK TO YOUTH GIVE ONE TEAR-- . . . 238 3 DON JUAN 10   27   8
LOOKS
    THEIR LOOKS CAST DOWN THEIR GREETINGS ALMOST DUMB . . . 60 2 DON JUAN 1   70   3
    AND THEN SHE LOOKS SO MODEST ALL THE WHILE . . . . . 82 2 DON JUAN 1   113   8
    AND TURNING UP HER NOSE WITH LOOKS ABUSED . . . . . . 109 2 DON JUAN 1   159   3
    BUT DON ALFONSO STOOD WITH DOWNCAST LOOKS . . . . . . 110 2 DON JUAN 1   161   1
    I RECOLLECT GREAT BRITAIN'S COAST LOOKS WHITE . . . . 163 2 DON JUAN 2   12   5
    AND MARATHON LOOKS ON THE SEA . . . . 321 2 DON JUAN 3 L 3   2
    WHICH LOOKS O'ER SEA-BORN SALAMIS . . . . 322 2 DON JUAN 3 L 4   2
    WITH SWIMMING LOOKS OF SPEECHLESS TENDERNESS . . . . 357 2 DON JUAN 4   26   2
    YET LOOKS NOT LIFE FOR THEY ARE STILL THE SAME . . . . 377 2 DON JUAN 4   61   8
    THOUGH ON ALL OTHER THINGS WITH LOOKS INTENSE . . . . 381 2 DON JUAN 4   68   3
    WHO ADVERTISE NEW POEMS BY YOUR LOOKS . . . . 403 2 DON JUAN 4   108   3
    POOR CREATURES THEIR GOOD LOOKS WERE SADLY CHANGED . . 414 2 DON JUAN 5   7   4
    THE CAPTIVES SEEMED TO MARK THEIR LOOKS AND AGE . . . 424 2 DON JUAN 5   26   3
    EACH VILLA ON THE BOSPHORUS LOOKS A SCREEN . . . . . 436 2 DON JUAN 5   46   7
    IT WAS AS IF THEIR LITTLE LOOKS COULD POISON . . . . 463 2 DON JUAN 5   90   7
    WITH AUGHT WHICH LOOKS LIKE DESPOTISM IN VIEW . . . . 474 2 DON JUAN 5   110   5
    WHITE COLD AND PURE AS LOOKS A FROZEN RILL . . . . . 40 3 DON JUAN 6   68   3
    ASIA WHERE KAFF LOOKS DOWN UPON THE KURDS . . . . . . 49 3 DON JUAN 6   86   8
    WARNED HIM AGAINST GREEK-WORSHIP WHICH LOOKS ODD . . . 240 3 DON JUAN 10   32   3
    O'ER THE HIGH HILL WHICH LOOKS WITH PRIDE OR SCORN . . 264 3 DON JUAN 10   80   4
    WHICH LOOKS ALONG THAT VALE OF GOOD AND ILL . . . . . 272 3 DON JUAN 11   8   3
    THE OTHER LOOKS LIKE PHOSPHORUS ON SHEETS . . . . . . 281 3 DON JUAN 11   27   5
    OTHERS HAVE LOST THEIR FRESH AND FAIRY LOOKS . . . . 308 3 DON JUAN 11   81   5
    WHEN EVEN THE SEA LOOKS DIM WITH ALL ITS SPRAY . . . . 422 3 DON JUAN 14   28   3
    AND THEN HE HAD GOOD LOOKS--THAT POINT WAS CARRIED . . 493 3 DON JUAN 15   84   1
    NOW THOUGH WE KNOW OF OLD THAT LOOKS DECEIVE . . . . 493 3 DON JUAN 15   84   6
    AND ALWAYS HAVE DONE SOMEHOW THESE GOOD LOOKS . . . . 493 3 DON JUAN 15   84   7
    AND YET HIS LOOKS APPEARED TO SANCTION BOTH . . . . . 514 3 DON JUAN 16   33   2
    GAVE HIM TO LAY THE DEVIL WHO LOOKS O'ER LINCOLN . . . 540 3 DON JUAN 16   82   7
LOOP-HOLE
    THE WITS WATCHED EVERY LOOP-HOLE FOR THEIR ART . . . . 408 3 DON JUAN 13   109   3
LOOSE
    BUT NOT A PAGE OF ANY THING THAT'S LOOSE . . . . . . 44 2 DON JUAN 1   40   6

	PAGE	VOL	CANTO	STANZA	LN

LOOSE (CONTINUED)
THIS IS THE AGE OF ODDITIES LET LOOSE . . . . 91 2 DON JUAN 1 128 5
AND CAST THEIR LANGUID EYES DOWN AND LET LOOSE . . . . . 119 2 DON JUAN 1 179 5
A SQUALL CAME ON AND WHILE SOME GUNS BROKE LOOSE . . . . 172 2 DON JUAN 2 30 6
AND ALL THINGS FOR A CHANCE HAD BEEN CAST LOOSE . . . . 183 2 DON JUAN 2 51 2
LIKE BIRDS OR BOYS OR BEDLAMITES BROKE LOOSE . . . . . 23 3 DON JUAN 6 34 2
WAS HERE (AS HERETOFORE AND SINCE) LET LOOSE . . . . . 173 3 DON JUAN 8 123 8
TO INDICATE A CUPIDON BROKE LOOSE . . . . 461 3 DON JUAN 15 12 6
LOOSELY
AND FITS HER LOOSELY--LIKE AN EASY GLOVE . . . . . . 276 2 DON JUAN 3 3 4
LOOSISH
AND HAVING LED A RATHER LOOSISH LIFE . . . . 389 2 DON JUAN 4 83 V2
LOPE
ALL CALDERON AND GREATER PART OF LOPE . . . . 27 2 DON JUAN 1 11 2
LOPPING
IN LOPPING OFF YOUR LATELY MARRIED MEN . . . . . . 168 3 DON JUAN 8 113 2
LOQUOR
HAUD IGNARA LOQUOR THESE ARE NUGAE QUARUM . . . . . 419 3 DON JUAN 14 21 1
LORD
OF GETTING HER LIEGE LORD INTO A SCRAPE . . . . . . 32 2 DON JUAN 1 20 8
AND TRIED TO PROVE HER LOVING LORD WAS MAD . . . . . 35 2 DON JUAN 1 27 2
IN CASE OUR LORD THE KING SHOULD GO TO WAR AGAIN . . . 42 2 DON JUAN 1 38 6
ALFONSO WAS THE NAME OF JULIA'S LORD . . . . 57 2 DON JUAN 1 65 1
AND LORD MOUNT COFFEEHOUSE THE IRISH PEER . . . . . 102 2 DON JUAN 1 149 7
WENT RAGING MAD--LORD HOW THEY DID BLASPHEME . . . . 198 2 DON JUAN 2 79 4
THREE OR FOUR THINGS FOR WHICH THE LORD HE PRAISED . . . 239 2 DON JUAN 2 157 5
LIKE SHAKSPEARE'S STEALING DEER LORD BACON'S BRIBES . . . 329 2 DON JUAN 3 92 2
GULBEYAZ AND HER LORD WERE SLEEPING OR . . . . . . 18 3 DON JUAN 6 24 1
PERHAPS A LITTLE LATER HER GREAT LORD . . . . 51 3 DON JUAN 6 90 2
YOU MY LORD DUKE IS FAR ABOVE REFLECTION . . . . . . 186 3 DON JUAN 9 7 2
AND CATHERINE WHO LOVED ALL THINGS (SAVE HER LORD . . . 209 3 DON JUAN 9 54 1
THE FAMILY VAULT RECEIVES ANOTHER LORD . . . . . . 306 3 DON JUAN 11 75 8
WHERE IS LORD THIS AND WHERE MY LADY THAT . . . . . 308 3 DON JUAN 11 79 1
COMMANDS--THE INTELLECTUAL LORD OF ALL . . . . . . 320 3 DON JUAN 12 9 8
TO BE TRANSMITTED LIKE THE LORD MAYOR'S BARGE . . . . 339 3 DON JUAN 12 51 6
AND THUS LORD HENRY WHO WAS CAUTIOUS AS . . . . . . 366 3 DON JUAN 13 16 1
LORD HENRY ALSO LIKED TO BE SUPERIOR . . . . 367 3 DON JUAN 13 19 1
AND THE LORD HENRY WAS A GREAT DEBATER . . . . . . 367 3 DON JUAN 13 20 7
LORD HENRY'S MANSION WAS IN BLANK-BLANK SQUARE . . . . 369 3 DON JUAN 13 25 8
BUT THESE ARE TRIFLES DOWNWARD FLIES MY LORD . . . . 379 3 DON JUAN 13 46 1
LORD HENRY AND THE LADY ADELINE . . . . 381 3 DON JUAN 13 50 1
LORD H AMUNDEVILLE AND LADY A . . . . 382 3 DON JUAN 13 51 8
THERE WAS LORD PYRRHO TOO THE GREAT FREETHINKER . . . . 398 3 DON JUAN 13 84 7
AND LORD AUGUSTUS FITZ-PLANTAGENET . . . . 399 3 DON JUAN 13 87 7
LORD HENRY AND HIS LADY WERE THE HOSTS . . . . . . 404 3 DON JUAN 13 99 1
AT LORD AUGUSTUS FITZ-PLANTAGENET . . . . 428 3 DON JUAN 14 42 8
POOR LORD AUGUSTUS FITZ-PLANTAGENET . . . . 429 3 DON JUAN 14 44 8
WITH LORD AUGUSTUS FITZ-PLANTAGENET . . . . 437 3 DON JUAN 14 62 8
LORD HENRY HEARD HER PLANS OF ARTLESS ART . . . . . 438 3 DON JUAN 14 65 5
LORD HENRY WALK'D INTO HIS CABINET . . . . 440 3 DON JUAN 14 68 2
SHE LOVED HER LORD OR THOUGHT SO BUT THAT LOVE . . . . 447 3 DON JUAN 14 86 1
OR GRAVE LORD GEORGE WITH WHOM PERHAPS MIGHT END . . . 470 3 DON JUAN 15 33 4
SERF LORD MAN WITH SUCH SKILL AS NONE WOULD SHARE IT IF . 481 3 DON JUAN 15 59 6
ALSO OBSERVE THAT LIKE THE GREAT LORD COKE . . . . . 494 3 DON JUAN 15 87 1
LORD HENRY SAID HIS MUFFIN WAS ILL BUTTERED . . . . . 514 3 DON JUAN 16 31 4
LORD HENRY WHO HAD NOW DISCUSSED HIS CHOCOLATE . . . . 515 3 DON JUAN 16 34 1
WHEN THE LORD OF THE HILL AMUNDEVILLE . . . . 518 3 DON JUAN 16 L 1 5
AMUNDEVILLE IS LORD BY DAY . . . . 520 3 DON JUAN 16 L 5 5
BUT THE MONK IS LORD BY NIGHT . . . . 520 3 DON JUAN 16 L 5 6
BUT AS LORD HENRY WAS A CONNOISSEUR-- . . . . 528 3 DON JUAN 16 57 1
BY WHICH LORD HENRY'S GOOD TASTE WOULD GO FORTH IN . . . 529 3 DON JUAN 16 59 6
LORD HENRY WISHED TO RAISE FOR A NEW PURCHASE . . . . 530 3 DON JUAN 16 60 2
LORD HENRY WAS A JUSTICE AND THAT SCOUT . . . . . . 531 3 DON JUAN 16 62 6
FOR THE LORD HENRY LINKED WITH DOGS AND HORSES . . . . 534 3 DON JUAN 16 68 2
LORD HENRY WAS A GREAT ELECTIONEERER . . . . 534 3 DON JUAN 16 70 1
LORD HENRY AT HIS TABLE SHOULD ENDURE . . . . 543 3 DON JUAN 16 89 6
LORDLINGS
LORDLINGS WITH STAVES OF WHITE OR KEYS OF GOLD . . . . 391 3 DON JUAN 13 70 5
LORD'S
SHE KNEW THE LATIN--THAT IS THE LORD'S PRAYER . . . . 28 2 DON JUAN 1 13 1
SHE THOUGHT THAT HER LORD'S HEART (EVEN COULD SHE CLAIM IT) 10 3 DON JUAN 6 8 6
WHAT DANIEL READ WAS SHORT-HAND OF THE LORD'S . . . . 179 3 DON JUAN 8 134 5
A PEASANT'S SWEAT IS WORTH HIS LORD'S ESTATE . . . . . 190 3 DON JUAN 9 15 6
WHICH LAST I LEAVE UNTO THE LORD'S SPIRITUAL . . . . . 472 3 DON JUAN 15 36 V8
BETWEEN SOME GREYHOUNDS ON MY LORD'S ESTATE . . . . . 527 3 DON JUAN 16 55 6
(FOR LITTLE THINGS UPON MY LORD'S ESTATE . . . . . . 544 3 DON JUAN 16 91 7
AT THEIR LORD'S SON'S OR SIMILAR CONNECTION'S . . . . 546 3 DON JUAN 16 95 7
LORDS
BUT--OH YE LORDS OF LADIES INTELLECTUAL . . . . . . 33 2 DON JUAN 1 22 7
TRANSFORM'D THEIR LORDS TO BEASTS (BUT THAT'S A FACT) . . 293 2 DON JUAN 3 34 8
THE BLOOD OF ALL HIS LINE'S CASTILIAN LORDS . . . . . 471 3 DON JUAN 5 104 3
ARE THE TRUE LORDS OF EUROPE EVERY LOAN . . . . . . 318 3 DON JUAN 12 6 2
MAY BE THE BAITS FOR GENTLEMEN OR LORDS . . . . . . 340 3 DON JUAN 12 53 3
MAY BE THE TRAPS FOR THEIR CONNUBIAL LORDS . . . . . 340 3 DON JUAN 12 53 V3
BEFORE THE LORDS--WHOSE CHANCELLOR'S MORE ACUTE . . . . 357 3 DON JUAN 13 V 18 7
THAT GENTLEMAN OF LORDS AND GENTLEMEN . . . . 380 3 DON JUAN 13 47 2
PRESENT LORDS A B C--EARLS DUKES BY NAME . . . . . . 383 3 DON JUAN 13 54 2
BY THE MARRIAGE BED OF THEIR LORDS 'TIS SAID . . . . . 519 3 DON JUAN 16 L 3 5
HAVE TIED TOGETHER COMMONS LORDS AND KINGS . . . . . 536 3 DON JUAN 16 74 8

```
                                                         PAGE VOL      CANTO STANZA LN
LORDS   (CONTINUED)
      MY LORDS AND LADIES PROUDLY CONDESCENDING   .  .  .  . 538  3 DON JUAN 16      79   2
      AND CURTSIED OFF THE STAGE--THEIR LORDS THE SAME  .  .  . 549  3 DON JUAN 16     101  V4
LORDSHIP
      THAT IS IF SAME LORDSHIP HAS AN ANCESTOR .  .  .  .  .  . 314  3 DON JUAN 11    V 75   1
      BECAUSE MY CASES PUT HIS LORDSHIP TO'T--  .  .  .  .  .  . 357  3 DON JUAN 12    V 18   5
LORDSHIP'S
      HIS LORDSHIP'S JUSTICE--SEEMS NOT THAT OF SOLOMON--  .  . 357  3 DON JUAN 12    V 18   7
LORDSHIPS
      THE ACCUSED TO THINK THEIR LORDSHIPS WOULD DETERMINE .  . 391  3 DON JUAN 13      69   3
LORE
      THE ARAB LORE AND POET'S SONG WERE DONE  .  .  .  .  .  . 334  2 DON JUAN  3     101   3
      EVERGREEN FOREST WHICH BOCCACIO'S LORE  .  .  .  .  .  . 337  2 DON JUAN  3     105   6
LORRAINE
      HERE SWEETLY SPREAD A LANDSCAPE OF LORRAINE .  .  .  .  . 392  3 DON JUAN 13      72   1
LOSE
      AND LOSE IN SHINING SNOW THEIR SUMMITS BLUE .  .  .  .  .  94  2 DON JUAN  1     134  V5
      YOU'LL LOSE YOUR LIFE AND I SHALL LOSE MY PLACE  .  .  .  . 115  2 DON JUAN  1     171   7
      YOU'LL LOSE YOUR LIFE AND I SHALL LOSE MY PLACE  .  .  .  . 115  2 DON JUAN  1     171   7
      TO LOSE THEIR LIVES AS WELL AS SPOIL THEIR DIET  .  .  .  . 173  2 DON JUAN  2      33   4
      SAD THOUGHT TO LOSE THE SPOUSE THAT WAS ADORNING .  .  . 278  2 DON JUAN  3       7   7
      AND CLINGING AS IF LOTH TO LOSE ITS HOLD .  .  .  .  .  . 312  2 DON JUAN  3      71   6
      TO LOSE ITSELF WHEN THE OLD WORLD GROWS DULL .  .  .  .  . 353  2 DON JUAN  4      17   3
      AND LOSE THEIR OWN IN UNIVERSAL DEATH  .  .  .  .  .  . 399  2 DON JUAN  4     102   8
      TO LOSE THE HOUR WOULD MAKE HER QUITE A MARTYR .  .  .  . 482  2 DON JUAN  5     122   7
      OF WORLDS TO LOSE YET STILL TO PAY MY COURT I  .  .  .  .   9  3 DON JUAN  6       5   5
      THINNER SHE MIGHT HAVE BEEN AND YET SCARCE LOSE  .  .  .  .  27  3 DON JUAN  6      42   6
      JOHNSON SAID--JUAN WE'VE NO TIME TO LOSE .  .  .  .  .  . 162  3 DON JUAN  8     101   1
      WHO DID NOT LIKE AT FIRST TO LOSE HER MINION  .  .  .  .  . 246  3 DON JUAN 10      44   4
      TO LOSE BY ONE MONTH'S FROST SOME TWENTY YEARS  .  .  .  . 253  3 DON JUAN 10      58   7
      EXPOSED TO LOSE HIS LIFE AS WELL AS BREECHES  .  .  .  .  . 273  3 DON JUAN 11      11   8
      THEY LOSE THEIR CASTE AT ONCE AS DO THE PARIAS  .  .  .  . 352  3 DON JUAN 12      78   2
      TO LOSE THOSE BEST MONTHS IN A SWEATY CITY .  .  .  .  .  . 380  3 DON JUAN 13      48   4
      BUT OH AMBROSIAL CASH AH WHO WOULD LOSE THEE  .  .  .  . 405  3 DON JUAN 13     100   7
      AND THEN EVEN THEN SOME BORE MAY MAKE THEM LOSE IT  .  . 408  3 DON JUAN 13     109   8
      AND AMPLIFY YOU LOSE MUCH BY CONCISION  .  .  .  .  .  . 478  3 DON JUAN 15      51   4
      THE NEXT ARE SUCH AS ARE NOT DOOMED TO LOSE  .  .  .  . 562  3 DON JUAN 17       1   5
LOSES
      AND RECOLLECT A POET NOTHING LOSES .  .  .  .  .  .  .  .  14  2 DON JUAN  D       8   5
LOSING
      LOSING ELECTIONS CHARACTER AND TEMPER  .  .  .  .  .  . 150  2 DON JUAN  1     V 1   7
      LOSING THE ADVANTAGE OF A VIRTUOUS STATION .  .  .  .  . 263  2 DON JUAN  2     201   4
      THUS SHE CAME OFTEN NOT A MOMENT LOSING  .  .  .  .  .  . 282  2 DON JUAN  3      13   7
      THE ONE IS WINNING AND THE OTHER LOSING  .  .  .  .  .  . 415  3 DON JUAN 14      12   8
LOSS
      NEVER COULD SHE SURVIVE THAT COMMON LOSS .  .  .  .  .  .  67  2 DON JUAN  1      84   4
      THE LOSS OF LOVE THE TREACHERY OF FRIENDS  .  .  .  .  . 167  2 DON JUAN  2      21   4
      BUT THE SAME CAUSE CONDUCIVE TO HIS LOSS .  .  .  .  .  . 186  2 DON JUAN  2      57   2
      HE LOVED HIS CHILD AND WOULD HAVE WEPT THE LOSS OF HER  .  . 289  2 DON JUAN  3      26   7
      HE WAS SO GREAT A LOSS TO GOOD SOCIETY  .  .  .  .  .  . 296  2 DON JUAN  3      41   8
      THERE WANTED BUT THE LOSS OF THIS TO WEAN  .  .  .  .  . 304  2 DON JUAN  3      57   6
      FORGETTING EACH OMISSION IS A LOSS TO  .  .  .  .  .  .  . 331  2 DON JUAN  3      96   7
      WEAK STILL WITH LOSS OF BLOOD HE SCARCE COULD URGE  .  . 387  2 DON JUAN  4      79   5
      PERHAPS HIS RECENT LOSS OF BLOOD MIGHT PULL  .  .  .  . 415  2 DON JUAN  5       8   5
      HIS SPIRIT DOWN AND THEN THE LOSS OF WEALTH  .  .  .  . 415  2 DON JUAN  5       8   6
      AND CARED AS LITTLE FOR HIS ARMY'S LOSS  .  .  .  .  .  . 105  3 DON JUAN  7      77   5
      IN BALANCING THE PROFIT AND THE LOSS .  .  .  .  .  .  . 113  3 DON JUAN  8       3   3
      IN THE DESPATCH I KNEW A MAN WHOSE LOSS  .  .  .  .  .  . 120  3 DON JUAN  8      18   7
      AMBITION RENDS AND GAMING GAINS A LOSS  .  .  .  .  .  . 317  3 DON JUAN 12       4   2
      AFTER MALE LOSS OF TIME AND HEARTS AND BETS  .  .  .  . 333  3 DON JUAN 12      36   3
      WHOSE LOSS IN THE LATE ACTION WE REGRET  .  .  .  .  .  . 383  3 DON JUAN 13      54   7
      THESE LAST HAD DISAPPEAR'D--A LOSS TO ART  .  .  .  .  . 386  3 DON JUAN 13      59   4
LOST
      AS WELL AS ALL THE GREEK I SINCE HAVE LOST .  .  .  .  .  .  50  2 DON JUAN  1      53   3
      HE ALSO FOUND THAT HE HAD LOST HIS DINNER  .  .  .  .  .  .  72  2 DON JUAN  1      94   8
      AND JULIA'S VOICE WAS LOST EXCEPT IN SIGHS .  .  .  .  .  .  84  2 DON JUAN  1     117   1
      YOU'D BEST BEGIN WITH TRUTH AND WHEN YOU'VE LOST YOUR  .  .  91  2 DON JUAN  1     128   7
      I LOVED I LOVE YOU FOR THIS LOVE HAVE LOST .  .  .  .  .  . 130  2 DON JUAN  1     193   1
      WHOSE SUMMIT LIKE ALL HILLS IS LOST IN VAPOUR  .  .  .  . 146  2 DON JUAN  1     218   4
      LOST THAT MOST PRECIOUS STONE OF STONES--HIS MODESTY  .  . 157  2 DON JUAN  2       1  V8
      WAS LOST BY GETTING AT SOME AQUA-VITA .  .  .  .  .  .  . 186  2 DON JUAN  2      56   8
      AND SOME OF THEM HAD LOST THEIR RECOLLECTION  .  .  .  . 199  2 DON JUAN  2      80   3
      SET BY A CURRENT TOWARD IT THEY WERE LOST  .  .  .  .  . 209  2 DON JUAN  2     100   3
      AND IF 'TIS LOST LIFE HATH NO MORE TO BRING  .  .  .  .  . 262  2 DON JUAN  2     199   4
      ALL FEELINGS WHICH O'ERLEAP THE YEARS LONG LOST  .  .  . 286  2 DON JUAN  3      21   7
      THEY ALMOST LOST THEIR WAY AND HAD TO PICK IT--  .  .  .  . 433  2 DON JUAN  5      41   5
      BUT ACTIUM LOST FOR CLEOPATRA'S EYES  .  .  .  .  .  .  .   8  3 DON JUAN  6       4   7
      THREE FIRESHIPS LOST THEIR AMIABLE EXISTENCE  .  .  .  .  80  3 DON JUAN  7      28   3
      THE MOSLEM TOO HAD LOST BOTH SHIPS AND MEN  .  .  .  .  82  3 DON JUAN  7      31   1
      SINCE JOHN HAS LATELY LOST THE USE OF BOTH .  .  .  .  .  88  3 DON JUAN  7      45   4
      LOST FOR HIS REPARTEE WAS TAKING CITIES  .  .  .  .  .  .  93  3 DON JUAN  7      53  V8
      TO SOME SPOT WHERE THEY LOST THEIR UNDERSTANDING  .  . 148  3 DON JUAN  8      72   3
      IF YET THE CITY'S REST WERE WON OR LOST  .  .  .  .  .  . 171  3 DON JUAN  8     120   6
      AND THAT'S ONE COMFORT FOR MY LOST ADVICE  .  .  .  .  . 200  3 DON JUAN  9      36   7
      IN SIGHT THEN LOST AMIDST THE FORESTRY  .  .  .  .  .  . 265  3 DON JUAN 10      82   4
      AND LOST IN WONDER OF SO GREAT A NATION  .  .  .  .  .  . 272  3 DON JUAN 11       9   3
      (THE DEN OF MANY A DIPLOMATIC LOST LIE)  .  .  .  .  .  . 283  3 DON JUAN 11      31   6
      OTHERS HAVE LOST THEIR FRESH AND FAIRY LOOKS .  .  .  . 308  3 DON JUAN 11      81   5
      SUCH ARE--BUT I HAVE LOST THE LONDON CHART  .  .  .  . 370  3 DON JUAN 13      27   8
```

470

		PAGE	VOL	CANTO	STANZA	LN
LOST (CONTINUED)						
(A CHANCE STILL) 'TIS A VOYAGE OR VESSEL LOST		376	3 DON JUAN	13	39	8
AS WHAT IS LOST IN GREEN IS GAINED IN YELLOW		395	3 DON JUAN	13	77	8
AND LOST VIRGINITY OF ORATORY		401	3 DON JUAN	13	91	2
HAD SUPERSTITION LOST HER TALISMAN		467	3 DON JUAN	15	24	V4
HIGH YET RESEMBLING NOT HIS LOST HAIDEE		481	3 DON JUAN	15	58	2
THE MIND IS LOST IN MIGHTY CONTEMPLATION		486	3 DON JUAN	15	69	1
AND DON'T REGRET THE TIME YOU MAY HAVE LOST		498	3 DON JUAN	15	95	3
TITUS EXCLAIMED I'VE LOST A DAY OF ALL		505	3 DON JUAN	16	11	5
IN HIM SOME FEELINGS HE HAD LATELY LOST		553	3 DON JUAN	16	107	6
LOT						
AND HARDSHIP STILL HAS BEEN THE SAILOR'S LOT		191	2 DON JUAN	2	66	5
AND THE LOT FELL ON JUAN'S LUCKLESS TUTOR		195	2 DON JUAN	2	75	8
BESIDES THAT WOULD A HAPPY LOT INSURE US		267	2 DON JUAN	2	207	V3
FOR SOME FEW YEARS HIS LOT HAD BEEN O'ERCAST		316	2 DON JUAN	3	79	5
HE ALWAYS IS COMPLAINING OF HIS LOT		392	2 DON JUAN	4	89	5
ALSO OUR HERO'S LOT HOWE'ER UNPLEASANT		410	2 DON JUAN	4	117	2
LOT OF SO YOUNG A PARTNER IN THE WOE		417	2 DON JUAN	5	12	6
WITH WHOM IT IS OUR LUCK TO CAST OUR LOT		417	2 DON JUAN	5	13	4
'TIS NOT MY PRESENT LOT AS I HAVE SAID		420	2 DON JUAN	5	18	6
'TIS BAD AND MAY BE BETTER--ALL MEN'S LOT		423	2 DON JUAN	5	25	2
AS EVEN IN A MUCH HUMBLER LOT HAD MADE		485	2 DON JUAN	5	129	2
FOR CHECQUERED AS IS SEEN OUR HUMAN LOT		156	3 DON JUAN	8	89	3
OF ALL THE FIVE ON BAYONETS MET HIS LOT		166	3 DON JUAN	8	110	4
WHO NEVER COVETED THEIR NEIGHBOUR'S LOT		323	3 DON JUAN	12	16	3
TO THE LOT OF HIM WHO SCARCE PURSUED AT ALL		333	3 DON JUAN	12	37	4
THAN THE MORE GLOWING DAMES WHOSE LOT IS CAST		347	3 DON JUAN	12	69	3
WHOSE LOT IT IS BY MAN TO BE MISTAKEN		464	3 DON JUAN	15	18	3
LOTH						
AND CLINGING AS IF LOTH TO LOSE ITS HOLD		312	2 DON JUAN	3	71	6
I SHOULD BE LOTH TO MARCH WITHOUT YOU BUT		162	3 DON JUAN	8	101	7
BUT FOR THE REST AS HE HIMSELF SEEMED LOTH		514	3 DON JUAN	16	33	6
LOT'S						
OR LOT'S WIFE DONE IN SALT--OR WHAT YOU WILL		40	3 DON JUAN	6	68	5
LOTS						
AND OUT THEY SPOKE OF LOTS FOR FLESH AND BLOOD		194	2 DON JUAN	2	73	7
AT LENGTH THE LOTS WERE TORN UP AND PREPARED		195	2 DON JUAN	2	74	5
THE LOTS WERE MADE AND MARK'D AND MIX'D AND HANDED		195	2 DON JUAN	2	75	1
IN NUMBER'D LOTS THEY ALL HAD CUFFS AND COLLARS		283	2 DON JUAN	3	15	7
AS SOMETIMES HAVE BEEN GREATER SAGES' LOTS--		200	3 DON JUAN	9	36	3
LOTTED						
WERE TO BE CHAIN'D AND LOTTED OUT PER COUPLE		393	2 DON JUAN	4	91	7
IT CHANCED AMONGST THE OTHER PEOPLE LOTTED		416	2 DON JUAN	5	10	5
LOTTERY						
THAT TASTE IS GONE THAT FAME IS BUT A LOTTERY		404	2 DON JUAN	4	109	7
SEE NOUGHT MORE STRANGE IN THIS THAN T'OTHER LOTTERY		333	3 DON JUAN	12	37	8
WHICH HATH A LITTLE LEANING TO A LOTTERY		397	3 DON JUAN	13	82	2
LOTTING						
HIS KNIGHTS WITH LOTTING OTHERS' PROPERTIES		242	3 DON JUAN	10	35	7
LOUD						
AND THE LOUD BREAKER BOILS AGAINST THE ROCK		94	2 DON JUAN	1	134	7
NO MOON NO STARS THE WIND WAS LOW OR LOUD		94	2 DON JUAN	1	135	2
AND MADE A LOUD AND PIOUS LAMENTATION		175	2 DON JUAN	2	37	2
LOUDER THAN THE LOUD OCEAN LIKE A CRASH		184	2 DON JUAN	2	53	2
SHE COULD NOT FROM THE SPOT AND THE LOUD ROAR		361	2 DON JUAN	4	31	3
OF SEAMEN'S FATES AND THE LOUD TEMPESTS RAISE		414	2 DON JUAN	5	6	4
A DREADFUL IMPULSE TO EACH LOUD MEANDER		52	3 DON JUAN	6	93	5
OUR FRIENDS THE TURKS WHO WITH LOUD ALLA'S NOW		87	3 DON JUAN	7	42	1
A MIRRORED HELL THE VOLLEYING ROAR AND LOUD		115	3 DON JUAN	8	6	5
IN THE SAME MOMENT LOUD AS EVEN THE ROAR		116	3 DON JUAN	8	8	2
AND THE LOUD CANNON PEALED HIS HOARSEST STRAINS		129	3 DON JUAN	8	33	6
LOUD AS THE VIRTUES THOU DOST LOUDLY VAUNT		241	3 DON JUAN	10	34	3
NOW YAWNS ALL DESOLATE NOW LOUD NOW FAINTER		387	3 DON JUAN	13	62	5
DESPITE THE SNAKE SOCIETY'S LOUD RATTLES		452	3 DON JUAN	14	96	8
SERENE ACCOMPLISH'D CHEERFUL BUT NOT LOUD		462	3 DON JUAN	15	15	1
THAN WHISPERING FOPLINGS OR THAN WITLINGS LOUD		493	3 DON JUAN	15	83	4
AND THE LOUD SHRIEK OF SAGE MINERVA'S FOWL		499	3 DON JUAN	15	97	3
OR TO COARSE EFFORTS VERY LOUD AND LONG		540	3 DON JUAN	16	83	7
LOUDER						
AND LOUDER THAN HER BREATHING BEATS HER HEART		108	2 DON JUAN	1	158	8
LOUDER THAN THE LOUD OCEAN LIKE A CRASH		184	2 DON JUAN	2	53	2
BUT FLEW TO WHERE THE PLEASANT NOISE GREW LOUDER		129	3 DON JUAN	8	33	V8
LOUDEST						
THE LOUDEST WIT I E'ER WAS DEAFENED WITH		539	3 DON JUAN	16	81	8
LOUDLY						
AND THAT SO LOUDLY THAT UPSTARTED ALL		42	3 DON JUAN	6	71	1
AT LEAST TO DREAM SO LOUDLY AS JUST NOW		47	3 DON JUAN	6	83	2
LOUD AS THE VIRTUES THOU DOST LOUDLY VAUNT		241	3 DON JUAN	10	34	3
WHICH NO ONE HEARS SO LOUDLY THOUGH IT RINGS		489	3 DON JUAN	15	76	6
SO OFTEN URGED SO LOUDLY AND SO LONG		564	3 DON JUAN	17	5	6
LOUIS						
A GOOD DEAL MAY BE BOUGHT FOR FIFTY LOUIS		79	2 DON JUAN	1	108	8
LOUNGING						
LOUNGING AND BOXING AND THE TWILIGHT HOUR		301	3 DON JUAN	11	66	2
LOVE						
WITH NO GREAT LOVE FOR LEARNING OR THE LEARN'D		31	2 DON JUAN	1	19	2
PRODUCED HER DON MORE HEIRS AT LOVE THAN LAW		53	2 DON JUAN	1	58	8
AND LOVE THAN EITHER AND THERE WOULD ARISE		54	2 DON JUAN	1	60	5
AND LOVE IS TAUGHT HYPOCRISY FROM YOUTH		61	2 DON JUAN	1	72	8

471

LOVE   (CONTINUED)

	PAGE	VOL			CANTO	STANZA	LN
AND MERELY TEND TO SHOW HOW GREATLY LOVE IS	62	2	DON	JUAN	1	74	7
AND THEN THERE ARE SUCH THINGS AS LOVE DIVINE	64	2	DON	JUAN	1	79	1
PLATONIC PERFECT JUST SUCH LOVE AS MINE	64	2	DON	JUAN	1	79	5
SUCH LOVE IS INNOCENT AND MAY EXIST	65	2	DON	JUAN	1	80	1
OF ALL O'ER WHICH SUCH LOVE MAY BE A RANGER	65	2	DON	JUAN	1	80	6
LOVE THEN BUT LOVE WITHIN ITS PROPER LIMITS	65	2	DON	JUAN	1	81	1
LOVE THEN BUT LOVE WITHIN ITS PROPER LIMITS	65	2	DON	JUAN	1	81	1
HE MIGHT BE TAUGHT BY LOVE AND HER TOGETHER--	65	2	DON	JUAN	1	81	7
FOR HE WOULD LEARN THE RUDIMENTS OF LOVE	67	2	DON	JUAN	1	85	7
OH LOVE IN SUCH A WILDERNESS AS THIS	69	2	DON	JUAN	1	88	1
OR LOVE--I WON'T SAY MORE ABOUT ENTWINED	69	2	DON	JUAN	1	89	6
AND HEAR THE HEART BEAT WITH THE LOVE IT GRANTED	73	2	DON	JUAN	1	96	6
OH LOVE HOW PERFECT IS THY MYSTIC ART	78	2	DON	JUAN	1	106	3
SOUNDS ILL IN LOVE WHATE'ER IT MAY IN MONEY	78	2	DON	JUAN	1	107	8
AT FIFTY LOVE FOR LOVE IS RARE 'TIS TRUE	79	2	DON	JUAN	1	108	6
AT FIFTY LOVE FOR LOVE IS RARE 'TIS TRUE	79	2	DON	JUAN	1	108	6
JULIA HAD HONOUR VIRTUE TRUTH AND LOVE	80	2	DON	JUAN	1	109	1
LOVE IS SO VERY TIMID WHEN 'TIS NEW	81	2	DON	JUAN	1	112	6
BUT WHO ALAS CAN LOVE AND THEN BE WISE	84	2	DON	JUAN	1	117	5
FOND OF A LITTLE LOVE (WHICH I CALL LEISURE)	85	2	DON	JUAN	1	118	6
IS FIRST AND PASSIONATE LOVE--IT STANDS ALONE	90	2	DON	JUAN	1	127	2
BUT WHETHER GLORY POWER OR LOVE OR TREASURE	93	2	DON	JUAN	1	133	6
WHO KILL'D HIMSELF FOR LOVE (WITH WINE) LAST YEAR	102	2	DON	JUAN	1	149	8
AND NOT FROM ANY LOVE TO YOU NOR ME	103	2	DON	JUAN	1	151	8
EVEN THEN THEIR LOVE THEY COULD NOT ALL COMMAND	114	2	DON	JUAN	1	170	3
TO LOVE TOO MUCH HAS BEEN THE ONLY ART	130	2	DON	JUAN	1	192	5
I LOVED I LOVE YOU FOR THIS LOVE HAVE LOST	130	2	DON	JUAN	1	193	1
I LOVED I LOVE YOU FOR THIS LOVE HAVE LOST	130	2	DON	JUAN	1	193	1
MAN'S LOVE IS OF MAN'S LIFE A THING APART	131	2	DON	JUAN	1	194	1
TO LOVE AGAIN AND BE AGAIN UNDONE	131	2	DON	JUAN	1	194	8
TO MOURN ALONE THE LOVE WHICH HAS UNDONE	131	2	DON	JUAN	1	194	V8
TO LIFT OUR FATAL LOVE TO GOD FROM MAN	131	2	DON	JUAN	1	194	V8
AND SO FAREWELL--FORGIVE ME LOVE ME--NO	132	2	DON	JUAN	1	195	7
AND BEAR WITH LIFE TO LOVE AND PRAY FOR YOU	134	2	DON	JUAN	1	197	8
WITH LOVE AND WAR A HEAVY GALE AT SEA	135	2	DON	JUAN	1	200	3
MY DAYS OF LOVE ARE OVER ME NO MORE	144	2	DON	JUAN	1	216	1
AND LIVE AND DIE MAKE LOVE AND PAY OUR TAXES	159	2	DON	JUAN	2	4	3
A LITTLE BREATH LOVE WINE AMBITION FAME	159	2	DON	JUAN	2	4	7
OF LOVE WHEN I FORGET YOU MAY I FAIL	160	2	DON	JUAN	2	7	5
JULIA MY LOVE--(YOU RASCAL PEDRO QUICKER)--	167	2	DON	JUAN	2	20	5
THE LOSS OF LOVE THE TREACHERY OF FRIENDS	167	2	DON	JUAN	2	21	4
LOVE WHO HEROICALLY BREATHES A VEIN	168	2	DON	JUAN	2	23	3
SEA-SICKNESS DEATH HIS LOVE WAS PERFECT HOW ELSE	168	2	DON	JUAN	2	23	6
THEY LIVE UPON THE LOVE OF LIFE AND BEAR	191	2	DON	JUAN	2	66	2
BESIDES BEING LESS IN LOVE SHE YAWN'D A LITTLE	233	2	DON	JUAN	2	145	3
WITH SCIO WINE--AND ALL FOR LOVE NOT MONEY	233	2	DON	JUAN	2	145	8
HE WAS IN LOVE--AS YOU WOULD BE NO DOUBT	244	2	DON	JUAN	2	167	6
LOVE THOUGH GOOD ALWAYS IS NOT QUITE SO GOOD)	246	2	DON	JUAN	2	170	2
FOR LOVE MUST BE SUSTAIN'D LIKE FLESH AND BLOOD--	246	2	DON	JUAN	2	170	4
AND LOVE WHICH ALSO MUCH DEPENDS ON FOOD	246	2	DON	JUAN	2	170	V4
LIKE A RICH WRECK--HER FIRST LOVE AND HER LAST	247	2	DON	JUAN	2	173	8
GLORY THE GRAPE LOVE GOLD IN THESE ARE SUNK	250	2	DON	JUAN	2	179	3
AFTER LONG TRAVEL ENNUI LOVE OR SLAUGHTER	251	2	DON	JUAN	2	180	7
A LONG LONG KISS A KISS OF YOUTH AND LOVE	254	2	DON	JUAN	2	186	1
OF NATURE'S ORACLE--FIRST LOVE--THAT ALL	256	2	DON	JUAN	2	189	7
AS THEY WHO WATCH O'ER WHAT THEY LOVE WHILE SLEEPING	261	2	DON	JUAN	2	196	8
THERE LIES THE THING WE LOVE WITH ALL ITS ERRORS	261	2	DON	JUAN	2	197	7
SHE AND HER WAVE-WORN LOVE HAD MADE THEIR BOWER	262	2	DON	JUAN	2	198	5
ALAS THE LOVE OF WOMEN IT IS KNOWN	262	2	DON	JUAN	2	199	1
MADE BUT TO LOVE TO FEEL THAT SHE WAS HIS	264	2	DON	JUAN	2	202	5
HOPE CARE LOVE BEYOND HER HEART BEAT HERE	264	2	DON	JUAN	2	202	8
OH LOVE OF WHOM GREAT CAESAR WAS THE SUITOR	266	2	DON	JUAN	2	205	1
OH LOVE THOU ART THE VERY GOD OF EVIL	266	2	DON	JUAN	2	205	7
EAT DRINK AND LOVE WHAT CAN THE REST AVAIL US	267	2	DON	JUAN	2	207	7
LOVE CONSTANT LOVE HAS BEEN MY CONSTANT GUEST	268	2	DON	JUAN	2	209	5
LOVE CONSTANT LOVE HAS BEEN MY CONSTANT GUEST	268	2	DON	JUAN	2	209	5
OER WHOSE SAD TALE LOVE ECHOS STILL ALAS--	273	2	DON	JUAN	2	V 2	3
OH LOVE WHAT IS IT IN THIS WORLD OF OURS	275	2	DON	JUAN	3	2	1
IN ALL THE OTHERS ALL SHE LOVES IS LOVE	276	2	DON	JUAN	3	3	2
ALTHOUGH NO DOUBT HER FIRST OF LOVE AFFAIRS	276	2	DON	JUAN	3	4	5
THAT LOVE AND MARRIAGE RARELY CAN COMBINE	277	2	DON	JUAN	3	5	3
MARRIAGE FROM LOVE LIKE VINEGAR FROM WINE--	277	2	DON	JUAN	3	5	5
YET LOVE MAY MAKE MARRIAGE AS GOOD WHITE WINE	277	2	DON	JUAN	3	5	V5
THOUGH LIFE AND LOVE I LIKE NOT TO DISPARAGE	280	2	DON	JUAN	3	9	V4
LEAVING THE FUTURE STATES OF LOVE AND LIFE	280	2	DON	JUAN	3	9	V7
WITH LOVE FOR MANY AND WITH FEARS FOR SOME	286	2	DON	JUAN	3	21	6
IF LOVE PATERNAL IN HIS BOSOM PLEADED	300	2	DON	JUAN	3	49	5
THE LOVE OF POWER AND RAPID GAIN OF GOLD	303	2	DON	JUAN	3	54	1
'TIS TRUE HE HAD NO ARDENT LOVE FOR PEACE--	303	2	DON	JUAN	3	55	5
A LOVE OF MUSIC AND OF SCENES SUBLIME	304	2	DON	JUAN	3	56	5
BUT WHATSOE'ER HE HAD OF LOVE REPOSED	304	2	DON	JUAN	3	57	1
AND SHOW THAT LATE HOURS WINE AND LOVE ARE ABLE	309	2	DON	JUAN	3	66	7
LEARN'D PIOUS TEMPERATE IN LOVE AND WINE	328	2	DON	JUAN	3	91	4
AVE MARIA 'TIS THE HOUR OF LOVE	336	2	DON	JUAN	3	103	2
OR FILLS WITH LOVE THE PILGRIM ON HIS WAY	338	2	DON	JUAN	3	108	4
OF FRIENDS--AND OPIATE DRAUGHTS--THERE'S LOVE AND WINE	343	2	DON	JUAN	3	V 98	2
THOUGH FOE TO LOVE AND YET THEY COULD NOT BE	348	2	DON	JUAN	4	8	6
WHOM THE GODS LOVE DIE YOUNG WAS SAID OF YORE	350	2	DON	JUAN	4	12	1

LOVE   (CONTINUED)

	PAGE	VOL	CANTO		STANZA	LN
THE DEATH OF FRIENDSHIP LOVE YOUTH ALL THAT IS	350	2	DON JUAN	4	12	4
MOST LOVE POSSESSION UNTO THEM APPEAR'D	352	2	DON JUAN	4	16	7
BUT THEIRS WAS LOVE IN WHICH THE MIND DELIGHTS	353	2	DON JUAN	4	17	2
OF LOVE HAD FIRST O'ERWHELM'D THEM FROM SUCH SKIES	354	2	DON JUAN	4	20	4
AND LOVE TOO MUCH AND YET CAN NOT LOVE LESS	357	2	DON JUAN	4	26	6
AND LOVE TOO MUCH AND YET CAN NOT LOVE LESS	357	2	DON JUAN	4	26	6
LOVE WAS BORN WITH THEM IN THEM SO INTENSE	358	2	DON JUAN	4	27	7
I LOVE HIM--I WILL DIE WITH HIM I KNEW	366	2	DON JUAN	4	42	7
AND ALL BECAUSE A LADY FELL IN LOVE	371	2	DON JUAN	4	51	8
BEAUTY AND LOVE WERE HAIDEE'S MOTHER'S DOWER	374	2	DON JUAN	4	56	6
AND SUNG OF LOVE THE FIERCE NAME STRUCK THROUGH ALL	380	2	DON JUAN	4	66	3
THE BLEEDING FLOWER AND BLASTED FRUIT OF LOVE	382	2	DON JUAN	4	70	8
FOR SOON OR LATE LOVE IS HIS OWN AVENGER	383	2	DON JUAN	4	73	8
AS BOYS LOVE ROWS MY BOYHOOD LIKED A SQUABBLE	398	2	DON JUAN	4	99	1
AND LOVE OF GLORY'S BUT AN AIRY LUST	399	2	DON JUAN	4	101	2
AND SOME SEEMED MUCH IN LOVE WITH THEIR OWN DRESS	441	2	DON JUAN	5	53	4
(LOVE LIKE RELIGION SOMETIMES RUNS TO HERESY)	446	2	DON JUAN	5	61	4
AND LOVE DESTROY AND SAPPING SORROW WRINGS	468	2	DON JUAN	5	98	6
AS YOU WILL SEE IF SHE YOU LOVE SHALL BRING HERS	472	2	DON JUAN	5	106	6
AND MERELY SAYING CHRISTIAN CANST THOU LOVE	478	2	DON JUAN	5	116	7
LOOKED INTO HIS FOR LOVE WHERE NONE REPLIES	483	2	DON JUAN	5	125	4
THOU ASK'ST IF I CAN LOVE BE THIS THE PROOF	484	2	DON JUAN	5	127	1
HOW MUCH I HAVE LOVED--THAT I LOVE NOT THEE	484	2	DON JUAN	5	127	2
WERE FITTER FOR ME LOVE IS FOR THE FREE	484	2	DON JUAN	5	127	4
LOVE WITH YOU AND BEEN IN THE DOG-DAYS STUNG	486	2	DON JUAN	5	130	4
THE LOVE OF OFFSPRING'S NATURE'S GENERAL LAW	488	2	DON JUAN	5	133	1
HOW MOTHERS LOVE THEIR CHILDREN'S SQUALLS AND CHUCKLINGS	488	2	DON JUAN	5	133	6
ALL WHO HAVE LOVED OR LOVE WILL STILL ALLOW	9	3	DON JUAN	6	6	4
LIFE HAS NOUGHT LIKE IT GOD IS LOVE THEY SAY	9	3	DON JUAN	6	6	5
OF LOVE WHEN SEATED ON HIS LOVELIEST THRONE	13	3	DON JUAN	6	15	6
THEY LIE WE LIE ALL LIE BUT LOVE NO LESS	15	3	DON JUAN	6	19	6
WHEN WICKED WIVES WHO LOVE SOME BACHELOR	18	3	DON JUAN	6	24	3
BEATING FOR LOVE AS THE CAGED BIRDS FOR AIR	19	3	DON JUAN	6	26	8
I LOVE THE SEX AND SOMETIMES WOULD REVERSE	19	3	DON JUAN	6	27	1
OUR HERO THROUGH THE LABYRINTH OF LOVE	20	3	DON JUAN	6	28	7
AND I LOVE WISDOM MORE THAN SHE LOVES ME	37	3	DON JUAN	6	63	2
WHILE GENTLE WRITERS ALSO LOVE TO LIFT	50	3	DON JUAN	6	88	6
THOUGH PALE WITH CONFLICTS BETWEEN LOVE AND PRIDE--	50	3	DON JUAN	6	89	6
THOUGH AN UNUSUAL FIT OF LOVE OR DUTY	51	3	DON JUAN	6	91	7
FOR LOVE OR BREAKFAST PRIVATE PLEASING LONE	54	3	DON JUAN	6	97	3
DESPITE HER INJURED LOVE AND FIERY PRIDE	62	3	DON JUAN	6	113	5
YOU LOVE THIS BOYISH NEW SERAGLIO GUEST	63	3	DON JUAN	6	115	5
WHAT DOST THOU KNOW OF LOVE OR FEELING--WRETCH	63	3	DON JUAN	6	116	1
OH LOVE O GLORY WHAT ARE YE WHO FLY	66	3	DON JUAN	7	1	1
IN WAR THAN LOVE HE HAD BETTER LEAD THE ASSAULT	98	3	DON JUAN	7	62	8
YET I LOVE GLORY--GLORY'S A GREAT THING--	118	3	DON JUAN	8	14	1
HAD SKETCHES OF LOVE TEMPEST TRAVEL WAR--	181	3	DON JUAN	8	138	3
THOUGH AS AN IRISHMAN YOU LOVE POTATOES	186	3	DON JUAN	9	7	5
SEEMS LOVE TURNED A LIEUTENANT OF ARTILLERY	204	3	DON JUAN	9	44	8
IN LOVE AND WAR) HOW ODD ARE THE CONNECTIONS	215	3	DON JUAN	9	65	3
AND SO THEY FELL IN LOVE--SHE WITH HIS FACE	216	3	DON JUAN	9	67	2
IN LOVE DRINKS ALL LIFE'S FOUNTAINS (SAVE TEARS) DRY	216	3	DON JUAN	9	67	8
HE ON THE OTHER HAND IF NOT IN LOVE	216	3	DON JUAN	9	68	1
AND THAT'S ENOUGH FOR LOVE IS VANITY	219	3	DON JUAN	9	73	1
MAKE LOVE THE MAIN SPRING OF THE UNIVERSE	219	3	DON JUAN	9	73	8
BESIDES PLATONIC LOVE BESIDES THE LOVE	219	3	DON JUAN	9	74	1
BESIDES PLATONIC LOVE BESIDES THE LOVE	219	3	DON JUAN	9	74	1
OF GOD THE LOVE OF SENTIMENT THE LOVING	219	3	DON JUAN	9	74	2
TO LOVE THERE ARE THOSE THINGS WHICH WORDS NAME SENSES--	219	3	DON JUAN	9	74	8
THE NOBLEST KIND OF LOVE IS LOVE PLATONICAL	220	3	DON JUAN	9	76	1
THE NOBLEST KIND OF LOVE IS LOVE PLATONICAL	220	3	DON JUAN	9	76	1
IS THAT WHICH MAY BE CHRISTENED LOVE CANONICAL	220	3	DON JUAN	9	76	3
JUAN MUCH FLATTERED BY HER LOVE OR LUST--	221	3	DON JUAN	9	77	3
LOVE THAT GREAT OPENER OF THE HEART AND ALL	222	3	DON JUAN	9	80	2
LOVE--(THOUGH SHE HAD A CURSED TASTE FOR WAR	222	3	DON JUAN	9	80	5
LOVE HAD MADE CATHERINE MAKE EACH LOVER'S FORTUNE	222	3	DON JUAN	9	81	1
THOUSANDS BLAZE LOVE HOPE DIE--HOW HAPPY THEY--	229	3	DON JUAN	10	8	8
KNOW LITTLE MORE OF LOVE THAN WHAT IS SUNG	230	3	DON JUAN	10	10	4
IN VISIONS OF THOSE SKIES FROM WHENCE LOVE SPRUNG	230	3	DON JUAN	10	10	6
AND LOVE THE LAND OF MOUNTAIN AND OF FLOOD	234	3	DON JUAN	10	19	8
FOR LOVE WAR OR AMBITION WHICH REWARD	235	3	DON JUAN	10	22	6
ALL PRAISED THE EMPRESS'S MATERNAL LOVE	240	3	DON JUAN	10	32	8
NOR BROTHER FATHER SISTER DAUGHTER LOVE	250	3	DON JUAN	10	53	2
AS PATRIOTS (NOW AND THEN) MAY LOVE A NATION	251	3	DON JUAN	10	55	3
I HAVE NO GREAT CAUSE TO LOVE THAT SPOT OF EARTH	257	3	DON JUAN	10	66	1
'TIS ONLY THAT THEY LOVE TO THROW AWAY	273	3	DON JUAN	11	10	3
NOW WHAT I LOVE IN WOMEN IS THEY WON'T	285	3	DON JUAN	11	36	6
(IN LOVE OR BRANDY'S FERVENT FERMENTATION)	287	3	DON JUAN	11	39	6
AND (SHOULD SHE NOT HOLD FAST BY LOVE OR PRIDE)	292	3	DON JUAN	11	46	4
MAKES ONE IN LOVE EVEN WITH ITS VERY FAULTS	302	3	DON JUAN	11	68	4
BY THOSE WHO LOVE TO SAY THAT WHITE IS BLACK	312	3	DON JUAN	11	90	6
LOVE LINGERS STILL ALTHOUGH 'TWERE LATE TO WIVE	316	3	DON JUAN	12	2	5
AND AS FOR OTHER LOVE THE ILLUSION'S O'ER	316	3	DON JUAN	12	2	6
LOVE OR LUST MAKES MAN SICK AND WINE MUCH SICKER	317	3	DON JUAN	12	4	1
(WHICH WILL COME OVER THINGS) BEATS LOVE OR LIQUOR	317	3	DON JUAN	12	4	5
LOVE RULES THE CAMP THE COURT THE GROVE--FOR LOVE	322	3	DON JUAN	12	13	1
LOVE RULES THE CAMP THE COURT THE GROVE FOR LOVE	322	3	DON JUAN	12	13	1
IS HEAVEN AND HEAVEN IS LOVE--SO SINGS THE BARD	322	3	DON JUAN	12	13	2

LOVE   (CONTINUED)

<pre>
                                                           PAGE VOL   CANTO STANZA LV
  AT LEAST IT RHYMES TO LOVE BUT I'M PREPARED . . . . . . 322 3 DON JUAN 12   13   6
  BUT IF LOVE DON'T CASH DOES AND CASH ALONE . . . . . . 322 3 DON JUAN 12   14   1
  SO CASH RULES LOVE THE RULER ON HIS OWN . . . . 322 3 DON JUAN 12   14   5
  AND AS FOR HEAVEN BEING LOVE WHY NOT SAY HONEY . . . . . 322 3 DON JUAN 12   14   7
  IS WAX HEAVEN IS NOT LOVE 'TIS MATRIMONY . . . . 322 3 DON JUAN 12   14   8
  IS NOT ALL LOVE PROHIBITED WHATEVER . . . . 323 3 DON JUAN 12   15   1
  EXCEPTING MARRIAGE WHICH IS LOVE NO DOUBT . . . . 323 3 DON JUAN 12   15   2
  LOVE MAY EXIST WITH MARRIAGE AND SHOULD EVER . . . . . . 323 3 DON JUAN 12   15   5
  BUT LOVE SANS BANNS IS BOTH A SIN AND SHAME . . . . . . 323 3 DON JUAN 12   15   7
  HE PLAYED AND PAID MADE LOVE WITHOUT MUCH SIN . . . . . 327 3 DON JUAN 12   25   V5
  A PERIL--NOT INDEED LIKE LOVE OR MARRIAGE . . . . 344 3 DON JUAN 12   62   2
  A WIFE MAKES OR TAKES LOVE IN UPRIGHT EARNEST . . . . . 345 3 DON JUAN 12   64   4
  BUT HE HAD SEEN SO MUCH GOOD LOVE BEFORE . . . . 346 3 DON JUAN 12   67   4
  INSTEAD OF LOVE THAT MERE HALLUCINATION . . . . 360 3 DON JUAN 13   6   6
  MEN LOVE IN HASTE BUT THEY DETEST AT LEISURE . . . . . . 361 3 DON JUAN 13   6   8
  BUT NEITHER LOVE NOR HATE IN MUCH EXCESS . . . . 361 3 DON JUAN 13   8   1
  TO THIS WE HAVE ADDED SINCE THE LOVE OF MONEY . . . . . 405 3 DON JUAN 13   100   3
  I LOVE THE MYSTERY OF A FEMALE MISSAL . . . . 407 3 DON JUAN 13   105   4
  LOVE WAR A TEMPEST--SURELY THERE'S VARIETY . . . . 416 3 DON JUAN 14   14   1
  WHEN WE HAVE MADE OUR LOVE AND GAMED OUR GAMING . . . . 418 3 DON JUAN 14   18   1
  THEIR LOVE THEIR VIRTUE BEAUTY EDUCATION . . . . 420 3 DON JUAN 14   24   7
  FIRED WITH AN ABSTRACT LOVE OF VIRTUE SHE . . . . 430 3 DON JUAN 14   46   2
  AND IN EACH CIRCUMSTANCE OF LOVE OR WAR . . . . 441 3 DON JUAN 14   71   7
  THERE IS A FLOWER CALLED LOVE IN IDLENESS . . . . 442 3 DON JUAN 14   75   1
  TO SAY IS NOT THAT LOVE IS IDLENESS . . . . 443 3 DON JUAN 14   76   2
  BUT THAT IN LOVE SUCH IDLENESS HAS BEEN . . . . 443 3 DON JUAN 14   76   3
  AN OYSTER MAY BE CROSS'D IN LOVE--AND WHY . . . . 445 3 DON JUAN 14   81   1
  SHE LOVED HER LORD OR THOUGHT SO BUT THAT LOVE . . . . . 447 3 DON JUAN 14   86   1
  I THINK NOT SHE WAS THEN IN LOVE WITH JUAN . . . . 449 3 DON JUAN 14   91   2
  LOVE BEARS WITHIN ITS BREAST THE VERY GERM . . . . 451 3 DON JUAN 14   94   1
  AT HOME FAR MORE THAN EVER YET WAS LOVE-- . . . . 452 3 DON JUAN 14   96   4
  AND AS FOR LOVE--OH LOVE--WE WILL PROCEED . . . . 458 3 DON JUAN 15   5   1
  AND AS FOR LOVE--OH LOVE--WE WILL PROCEED . . . . 458 3 DON JUAN 15   5   1
  THERE'S NOTHING WOMEN LOVE TO DABBLE IN . . . . 470 3 DON JUAN 15   31   4
  IN LOVE THERE'S SOMETHING OF INTOXICATION . . . . 474 3 DON JUAN 15   41   V7
  A SLIGHT REPAST MAKES PEOPLE LOVE MUCH MORE . . . . . . 542 3 DON JUAN 16   86   3
  OR HOPE OR LOVE WITH ANY OF THE WILES . . . . 544 3 DON JUAN 16   92   7
  THE LOVE OF HIGHER THINGS AND BETTER DAYS . . . . 554 3 DON JUAN 16   108   1
  TRANSGRESSES THE GREAT BOUNDS OF LOVE OR AWE . . . . . . 563 3 DON JUAN 17   2   6
LOVE-BEATEN
  ALREADY MANY A ONCE LOVE-BEATEN BREAST . . . . 63 3 DON JUAN 6   115   3
LOVE-BEGOTTEN
  TO CALL MEN LOVE-BEGOTTEN OR PROCLAIM . . . . 53 3 DON JUAN 6   94   1
LOVED
  I LOVED I LOVE YOU FOR THIS LOVE HAVE LOST . . . . . .   130 2 DON JUAN 1   193   1
  HIS FATHER'S HE LOVED AS YE WHOM MAY THINK . . . . . .   187 2 DON JUAN 2   58   2
  A SOMETHING TO BE LOVED A CREATURE MEANT . . . .   247 2 DON JUAN 2   172   5
  SHE LOVED AND WAS BELOVED--SHE ADORED . . . .   257 2 DON JUAN 2   191   1
  ONE OF THE NAME BUT THAT I LOVED HER TOO . . . .   273 2 DON JUAN 2   V 2   8
  AND LOVED BY A YOUNG HEART TOO DEEPLY BLEST . . . . .   274 2 DON JUAN 3   1   4
  WHICH MAKES IT FATAL TO BE LOVED AH WHY . . . .   275 2 DON JUAN 3   2   2
  HE LOVED HIS CHILD AND WOULD HAVE WEPT THE LOSS OF HER . 289 2 DON JUAN 3   26   7
  PITY HE LOVED ADVENTUROUS LIFE'S VARIETY . . . .   296 2 DON JUAN 3   41   7
  WHERE BURNING SAPPHO LOVED AND SUNG . . . .   320 2 DON JUAN 3   L 1   2
  HOW HAVE I LOVED THE TWILIGHT HOUR AND THEE . . . . .   337 2 DON JUAN 3   105   8
  PERCHANCE THE DEATH OF ONE SHE LOVED TOO WELL . . . .   363 2 DON JUAN 4   36   5
  BY THE SEA SHORE WHEREON SHE LOVED TO DWELL . . . . .   382 2 DON JUAN 4   71   8
  IF SHE LOVED RASHLY HER LIFE PAID FOR WRONG-- . . . .   383 2 DON JUAN 4   73   5
  I MOURN BUT FOR THE PAST--I LOVED A MAID . . . .   420 2 DON JUAN 5   18   2
  OF ONE WHO DARED TO ASK IF HE HAD LOVED . . . .   481 2 DON JUAN 5   121   4
  HOW MUCH I HAVE LOVED--THAT I LOVE NOT THEE . . . . .   484 2 DON JUAN 5   127   2
  ALL WHO HAVE LOVED OR LOVE WILL STILL ALLOW . . . . .   9 3 DON JUAN 6   6   4
  WHO LOVED BLOOD AS AN ALDERMAN LOVES MARROW . . . . .   70 3 DON JUAN 7   8   8
  OR LOVED IT WAS WITH WHAT WE CALL THE BEST . . . . . .   123 3 DON JUAN 8   25   2
  JOHNSON WHO REALLY LOVED HIM IN HIS WAY . . . .   162 3 DON JUAN 8   102   2
  AND CATHERINE WHO LOVED ALL THINGS (SAVE HER LORD . .   209 3 DON JUAN 9   54   1
  DON JUAN LOVED HER AND SHE LOVED HIM AS . . . .   250 3 DON JUAN 10   53   1
  DON JUAN LOVED HER AND SHE LOVED HIM AS . . . .   250 3 DON JUAN 10   53   1
  HE LOVED THE INFANT ORPHAN HE HAD SAVED . . . .   251 3 DON JUAN 10   55   2
  HE NATURALLY LOVED WHAT HE PROTECTED . . . .   252 3 DON JUAN 10   57   4
  THE WORTHIEST KINGS HAVE EVER LOVED LEAST STATE . . .   267 3 DON JUAN 10   87   5
  AND WHERE THE DAUGHTER WHOM THE ISLES LOVED WELL . . .   307 3 DON JUAN 11   77   6
  AND WEDDED UNTO ONE SHE HAD LOVED WELL . . . .   365 3 DON JUAN 13   14   2
  WELL LIKE MOST ENGLISHMEN AND LOVED THE RACES . . . .   368 3 DON JUAN 13   23   6
  WHO LOVED PHILOSOPHY AND A GOOD DINNER . . . .   399 3 DON JUAN 13   87   2
  BUT THE TWO YOUNGEST LOVED MORE TO BE SET . . . . . .   408 3 DON JUAN 13   107   6
  THE DUCHESS OF FITZ-FULKE WHO LOVED TRACASSERIE . . .   428 3 DON JUAN 14   41   7
  NEITHER CAN SHOW QUITE HOW THEY WOULD BE LOVED . . . .   442 3 DON JUAN 14   73   4
  SHE LOVED HER LORD OR THOUGHT SO BUT THAT LOVE . . . .   447 3 DON JUAN 14   86   1
  WOULD THAT I NEER HAD LOVED--OH WOMAN--WOMAN-- . . . .   569 3 DON JUAN 17   V 13   2
LOVELIEST
  THE LOVELIEST CHASTEST BEST BUT--QUITE A FOOL . . . .   405 2 DON JUAN 4   111   8
  OF LOVE WHEN SEATED ON HIS LOVELIEST THRONE . . . . .   13 3 DON JUAN 6   15   6
  SHORN OF ITS BEST AND LOVELIEST AND LEFT BARE . . . .   155 3 DON JUAN 8   88   6
  THE LOVELIEST OLIGARCHS OF OUR GYNOCRASY . . . .   346 3 DON JUAN 12   66   4
LOVELY
  WHICH OUT OF ALL THE LOVELY THINGS WE SEE . . . . . .   144 2 DON JUAN 1   214   3
  LOVELY SEEM'D ANY OBJECT THAT SHOULD SWEEP . . . . . .   210 2 DON JUAN 2   103   7
</pre>

474

LOVELY   (CONTINUED)
      A LOVELY FEMALE FACE OF SEVENTEEN . . . . 215 2 DON JUAN 2   112   8
      STILL IN HER TEENS AND LIKE A LOVELY TREE . . . . . . 224 2 DON JUAN 2   128   5
      SO LOVING AND SO LOVELY --TILL THEN NEVER . . . . . . 258 2 DON JUAN 2   193   2
      TO BE A LOVELY AND A FEARFUL THING . . . . 262 2 DON JUAN 2   199   2
      A LOVELY STATUE WE ALMOST ADORE . . . . 269 2 DON JUAN 2   211   6
      ONE LARGE GOLD BRACELET CLASP'D EACH LOVELY ARM . . . 312 2 DON JUAN 3   71   1
      HE WENT FORTH WITH THE LOVELY ODALISQUES . . . . 20 3 DON JUAN 6   29   1
      WITH GREAT BLUE EYES A LOVELY HAND AND ARM . . . . . . 26 3 DON JUAN 6   41   3
      AND SLUMBER HOVERED O'ER EACH LOVELY LIMB . . . . 38 3 DON JUAN 6   64   3
      OUR EYES IN SEARCH OF EITHER LOVELY LIGHT . . . . 66 3 DON JUAN 7   1   6
      LOVELY AS THOSE WHICH RIPENED EDEN'S FRUIT . . . . 86 3 DON JUAN 7   41   7
      TO RUTS AND FLINTS AND LOVELY NATURE'S SKILL . . . . . 198 3 DON JUAN 9   31   5
      ON ONE ANOTHER AND EACH LOVELY LISPER . . . . 221 3 DON JUAN 9   78   5
      WHERE ARE TEN THOUSAND LOVELY INNOCENTS . . . . 307 3 DON JUAN 11   77   V7
      A LOVELY BEING SCARCELY FORM'D OR MOULDED . . . . . . 475 3 DON JUAN 15   43   7
      MORE WARM AS LOVELY AND NOT LESS SINCERE . . . . 481 3 DON JUAN 15   58   5
LOVER
      THE LOVER WHO MUST PAY A HANDSOME PRICE . . . . 57 2 DON JUAN 1   64   7
      AND IF STILL FREE THAT SUCH OR SUCH A LOVER . . . . . . 64 2 DON JUAN 1   78   4
      YOUNG HOPEFUL'S MISTRESS OR MISS FANNY'S LOVER . . . . . 75 2 DON JUAN 1   100   4
      THE CHIMNEY--WHICH WOULD REALLY HOLD A LOVER . . . . . 104 2 DON JUAN 1   153   4
      HAD BEEN THE HAPPY LOVER HE CONCLUDED . . . . 118 2 DON JUAN 1   177   4
      THE LADY WATCH'D HER LOVER--AND THAT HOUR . . . . . . 262 2 DON JUAN 2   198   1
      A THANKLESS HUSBAND NEXT A FAITHLESS LOVER . . . . . . 263 2 DON JUAN 2   200   7
      SOME TAKE A LOVER SOME TAKE DRAMS OR PRAYERS . . . . . 263 2 DON JUAN 2   201   1
      IN HER FIRST PASSION WOMAN LOVES HER LOVER . . . . . . 276 2 DON JUAN 3   3   1
      MEANTIME THE LADY AND HER LOVER SATE . . . . 306 2 DON JUAN 3   61   3
      THE LADY AND HER LOVER LEFT ALONE . . . . 334 2 DON JUAN 3   101   5
      FROM A TRUE LOVER SHADOW'D MY MIND'S EYE . . . . 337 2 DON JUAN 3   106   8
      A HAPPY LOVER AND A WELCOME GUEST-- . . . . 343 2 DON JUAN 3 V 98   5
      WHICH MIX'D ALL FEELINGS FRIEND CHILD LOVER BROTHER . 357 2 DON JUAN 4   26   3
      BUT TIMES ARE ALTER'D SINCE A RHYMING LOVER . . . . . 405 2 DON JUAN 4   111   2
      NO LADY E'ER IS OGLED BY A LOVER . . . . 424 2 DON JUAN 5   26   6
      EXPECTING ALL THE WELCOME OF A LOVER . . . . 12 3 DON JUAN 6   13   7
      ANNOUNCING THE APPOINTMENT OF THAT LOVER OF . . . . . . 85 3 DON JUAN 7   39   7
      OBSERVE YOUR LOVER WHEN HE LEAVES YOUR ARMS . . . . . 139 3 DON JUAN 8   53   7
      A LOVER AS HAD COST HER MANY A TEAR . . . . 209 3 DON JUAN 9   54   7
      BECAUSE EACH LOVER LOOKED A SORT OF KING . . . . 217 3 DON JUAN 9   70   4
      I'VE KNOWN THEM COURT AN HEIRESS FOR THEIR LOVER . . . 331 3 DON JUAN 12   33   4
      A LOVER WITH CAPRICES SOFT AND DEAR . . . . 438 3 DON JUAN 14   63   4
      BOTH IN THE CASE OF LOVER AND OF FRIEND . . . . 491 3 DON JUAN 15   79   4
      BUT LOVER POET OR ASTRONOMER . . . . 506 3 DON JUAN 16   14   1
LOVER'S
      FOR INSTANCE--PASSION IN A LOVER'S GLORIOUS . . . . . 278 2 DON JUAN 3   6   7
      THE HERO'S HARP THE LOVER'S LUTE . . . . 321 2 DON JUAN 3 L 2   2
      LOVE HAD MADE CATHERINE MAKE EACH LOVER'S FORTUNE . . . 222 3 DON JUAN 9   81   1
      HOLDS BY THE ROCK OR AS A LOVER'S KISS . . . . 238 3 DON JUAN 10   28   6
LOVERS
      OR COELEBS' WIFE SET OUT IN QUEST OF LOVERS . . . . . . 29 2 DON JUAN 1   16   4
      AS BUT TO LOVERS A TRUE SENSE AFFORDS . . . . 351 2 DON JUAN 4   14   6
      AND MAKE LIKE OTHER NYMPHS THY LOVERS ILL . . . . . . 372 2 DON JUAN 4   53   4
      FOR SO IT SEEMS TO LOVERS SWIFT OR SLOW . . . . 14 3 DON JUAN 6   17   2
      AND PITY LOVERS RATHER MORE THAN SEAMEN . . . . 32 3 DON JUAN 6   53   8
      RUN MUCH LESS RISK OF LOVERS TURNING RUDE . . . . 43 3 DON JUAN 6   75   6
      FOR SOME HAD ABSENT LOVERS ALL HAD FRIENDS . . . . . . 407 3 DON JUAN 13   105   1
      BUT SUCH SMALL LICENCES MUST LOVERS BROOK . . . . . . 429 3 DON JUAN 14   43   3
      SO THAT YOU HAVE NOT BEEN NOR WILL BE LOVERS . . . . . 451 3 DON JUAN 14   93   8
      HAD LOVERS NOT SOME REASON TO REGRET . . . . 452 3 DON JUAN 14   95   3
LOVERS'
      MUCH LONGER--THINK OF HUSBANDS' LOVERS' LIVES . . . . 123 2 DON JUAN 1   185   7
      IN LOVERS' PARTS HIS PASSION MORE TO BREATHE . . . . . 392 2 DON JUAN 4   89   7
LOVE'S
      LOVE'S A CAPRICIOUS POWER I'VE KNOWN IT HOLD . . . . . 168 2 DON JUAN 2   22   1
      IS PLEASANT BESIDES BEING TRUE LOVE'S ESSENCE . . . . 245 2 DON JUAN 2   169   4
      FOR WITHOUT HEART LOVE'S NOT QUITE SO GOOD) . . . . . 246 2 DON JUAN 2   170   V2
      OF LOVE'S AND NIGHT'S AND OCEAN'S SOLITUDE . . . . . . 262 2 DON JUAN 2   198   2
      WHICH FORMS IN FACT TRUE LOVE'S ANTITHESIS . . . . . . 279 2 DON JUAN 3   8   2
      LOVE'S THE FIRST NET WHICH SPREADS ITS DEADLY MESH . . 422 2 DON JUAN 5   22   5
      HIM WHOM SHE MEANT TO TUTOR IN LOVE'S WAYS . . . . . . 482 2 DON JUAN 5   122   5
      AND LOVE'S A GOD OR WAS BEFORE THE BROW . . . . 9 3 DON JUAN 6   6   6
      OF EPIC LOVE'S BEGINNING END AND MIDDLE . . . . 337 3 DON JUAN 12   45   8
      WHERE NONE WERE DREAMT OF UNTO LOVE'S AFFAIRS . . . . 369 3 DON JUAN 13   25   5
      METHINKS LOVE'S VERY TITLE SAYS ENOUGH . . . . 451 3 DON JUAN 14   94   7
      LOVE'S RIOTOUS BUT MARRIAGE SHOULD HAVE QUIET . . . . 474 3 DON JUAN 15   41   7
LOVES
      BECAUSE OF FILTHY LOVES OF GODS AND GODDESSES . . . . . 44 2 DON JUAN 1   41   2
      ALFONSO'S LOVES WITH INEZ WERE WELL KNOWN . . . . . . 118 2 DON JUAN 1   176   2
      THE BEST EXAMPLES WHICH I KNOW FOR LOVES . . . . 257 2 DON JUAN 2   191   V8
      IN HER FIRST PASSION WOMAN LOVES HER LOVER . . . . . . 276 2 DON JUAN 3   3   1
      IN ALL THE OTHERS ALL SHE LOVES IS LOVE . . . . 276 2 DON JUAN 3   3   2
      'TIS DANGEROUS TO READ OF LOVES UNLAWFUL . . . . 282 2 DON JUAN 3   12   8
      THEIR LOVES AND FEASTS AND HOUSE AND DRESS AND MODE . 317 2 DON JUAN 3   81   7
      SO THAT THERE WAS NO REASON FOR THEIR LOVES . . . . . 354 2 DON JUAN 4   19   7
      WHEN AMATORY POETS SING THEIR LOVES . . . . 411 2 DON JUAN 5   1   1
      AND I LOVE WISDOM MORE THAN SHE LOVES ME . . . . 37 3 DON JUAN 6   63   2
      FIERCE LOVES AND FAITHLESS WARS--I AM NOT SURE . . . . . 70 3 DON JUAN 7   8   1
      WHO LOVED BLOOD AS AN ALDERMAN LOVES MARROW . . . . . . 70 3 DON JUAN 7   8   8
      WHERE THOUSAND LOVES AND TIES AND DUTIES GROW . . . . 174 3 DON JUAN 8   124   6

		PAGE	VOL		CANTO	STANZA	LN
LOVES	**(CONTINUED)**						
WHICH LOVES SO WELL ITS COUNTRY AND ITS KING		175	3	DON JUAN	8	126	2
AND WHO THAT RECOLLECTS YOUNG YEARS AND LOVES--		228	3	DON JUAN	10	6	4
HAD GONE BEFORE HIM AND HIS WARS AND LOVES		284	3	DON JUAN	11	33	2
WARS REVELS LOVES--DO THESE BRING MEN MORE EASE		321	3	DON JUAN	12	11	5
AND STOCKINGS VIRTUES LOVES AND CHASTITIES		347	3	DON JUAN	12	67	V8
AND LOVES OR HATES DISDAINING TO BE GUIDED		366	3	DON JUAN	13	16	7
THAN WEAR A HEART A WOMAN LOVES TO REND		438	3	DON JUAN	14	64	6
BUT EN AVANT THE LIGHT LOVES LANGUISH O'ER		542	3	DON JUAN	16	86	1
LOVING							
AND TRIED TO PROVE HER LOVING LORD WAS MAD		35	2	DON JUAN	1	27	2
A LOVING LANGUOR WHICH IS NOT REPOSE		82	2	DON JUAN	1	114	8
BELOVED AND LOVING MANY ALL IS O'ER		132	2	DON JUAN	1	195	2
OYSTERS AND EGGS ARE ALSO LOVING FOOD		246	2	DON JUAN	2	170	V6
OR PERILS BY A LOVING MAID INCURR'D		257	2	DON JUAN	2	190	4
SO LONELY LOVING HELPLESS AND THE HOUR		258	2	DON JUAN	2	192	2
SO LOVING AND SO LOVELY --TILL THEN NEVER		258	2	DON JUAN	2	193	2
HALF NAKED LOVING NATURAL AND GREEK		259	2	DON JUAN	2	194	8
WHILE SHE HAD NOT ONE HOUR TO SPARE FROM LOVING		295	2	DON JUAN	3	39	8
NOW PILLOW'D CHEEK TO CHEEK IN LOVING SLEEP		359	2	DON JUAN	4	29	1
BUT MANY A GREEK MAID IN A LOVING SONG		383	2	DON JUAN	4	73	1
OR AT THE LEAST FORGIVE THE LOVING RASH ONE		8	3	DON JUAN	6	4	4
OF GOD THE LOVE OF SENTIMENT THE LOVING		219	3	DON JUAN	9	74	2
HIS DUTIES WARLIKE LOVING OR OFFICIAL		294	3	DON JUAN	11	51	5
A LOVING LETTER WITH A MYSTIC SEAL		422	3	DON JUAN	14	27	6
LOW							
I LOATHE THAT LOW VICE CURIOSITY		33	2	DON JUAN	1	23	5
NO MOON NO STARS THE WIND WAS LOW OR LOUD		94	2	DON JUAN	1	135	2
THE BOAT MADE WAY YET NOW THEY WERE SO LOW		207	2	DON JUAN	2	96	3
TO THESE KIND EFFORTS MADE A LOW REPLY		215	2	DON JUAN	2	113	8
HER BROW WAS WHITE AND LOW HER CHEEK'S PURE DYE		218	2	DON JUAN	2	118	1
WITH AN IONIAN ACCENT LOW AND SWEET		236	2	DON JUAN	2	150	7
BY SOME LOW ROCK OR SHELVE THAT MADE IT FRET		251	2	DON JUAN	2	181	7
THEY HEARD THE WAVE'S SPLASH AND THE WIND SO LOW		253	2	DON JUAN	2	185	5
FROM THE HIGH LYRIC DOWN TO THE LOW RATIONAL		319	2	DON JUAN	3	85	6
AND CALLED FROM JUAN'S BREAST A FAINT LOW SIGH		355	2	DON JUAN	4	21	7
OF HIS QUENCH'D HEART AND THE SEA DIRGES LOW		362	2	DON JUAN	4	34	6
AND HE BEGUN A LONG LOW ISLAND SONG		379	2	DON JUAN	4	65	7
HE LED THEM ONWARD FIRST THROUGH A LOW THICKET		433	2	DON JUAN	5	41	3
OF HER DEEP-PURPLE ROBE AND SPEAKING LOW		466	2	DON JUAN	5	96	7
FOR LAUGHTER--BUT SHE FELT HER SPIRITS LOW		47	3	DON JUAN	6	83	6
A LOW SOFT OTTOMAN) AND BLACK DESPAIR		60	3	DON JUAN	6	108	5
BRING THE TWO SLAVES SHE SAID IN A LOW TONE		62	3	DON JUAN	6	112	2
LOW AS THE COMPLIMENT DESERVED SUWARROW		99	3	DON JUAN	7	63	2
LOW WERE THE WHISPERS MANIFOLD THE RUMOURS		244	3	DON JUAN	10	40	1
THE CRUEL NAZARENES WHO HAD LAID LOW		262	3	DON JUAN	10	75	4
IF I MIGHT AUGUR I SHOULD RATE BUT LOW		299	3	DON JUAN	11	61	6
THUS THE LOW WORLD NORTH SOUTH OR WEST OR EAST		342	3	DON JUAN	12	56	6
FOR 'TIS A LOW NEWSPAPER HUMDRUM LAW-SUIT		346	3	DON JUAN	12	65	1
WITHAL IT LIES PERHAPS A LITTLE LOW		384	3	DON JUAN	13	55	6
TOO SCANTY IN THESE TIMES OF LOW TAXATION		528	3	DON JUAN	16	56	8
LOWE							
WITH TURNCOAT SOUTHEY FOR MY TURNKEY LOWE		296	3	DON JUAN	11	56	8
LOWER							
ABOUT THE LOWER REGION OF THE BOWELS		168	2	DON JUAN	2	23	2
HER ANGER PITCHED INTO A LOWER TUNE		490	2	DON JUAN	5	136	5
WHO LANDED LOWER DOWN THEIR LANDING DONE		119	3	DON JUAN	8	15	3
THIS IS THE LITERARY LOWER EMPIRE		299	3	DON JUAN	11	62	1
AND LOWER THE PRICE OF ROUGE--AT LEAST SOME WINTERS		409	3	DON JUAN	13	111	8
BULL SOMETHING OF THE LOWER WORLD'S CONDITION		497	3	DON JUAN	15	92	6
LOWER'D							
LOWER'D LEAVEN'D LIKE A HISTORY OF FREEMASONS		419	3	DON JUAN	14	22	2
LOWERS							
OR EATS FROM OUT THE PALM OR PLAYFUL LOWERS		292	2	DON JUAN	3	32	6
HAUGHTY AND HUGE ALONG THE DISTANCE LOWERS		460	2	DON JUAN	5	85	5
LOWEST							
THE VERY LOWEST FIND OUT AN INFERIOR		367	3	DON JUAN	13	19	3
LOYAL							
THEIR LOYAL TREASON RENEGADO RIGOUR		330	2	DON JUAN	3	94	3
THEIR LOYAL ZEAL AND RENEGADO VIGOUR		330	2	DON JUAN	3	94	V3
THIS SCENE OF ROYAL ITCH AND LOYAL SCRATCHING		307	3	DON JUAN	11	78	8
LOYALTY							
AND WAX AN ULTRA-ROYALIST IN LOYALTY		466	3	DON JUAN	15	23	7
HAD NOTHING LEFT IT BUT A DESPERATE LOYALTY		466	3	DON JUAN	15	23	V8
LUBBERLY							
COULD REMEDY THIS LUBBERLY DEFECT		80	3	DON JUAN	7	28	6
LUCCA							
IN SPAIN AND LUCCA ATHENS EVERYWHERE		488	3	DON JUAN	15	73	4
LUCENDO							
LUCUS A NON LUCENDO NOT WHAT WAS		33	3	DON JUAN	6	55	5
LUCID							
BUT AS HE HAD SOME LUCID INTERMISSIONS		35	2	DON JUAN	1	27	3
BEFORE THE MANSION LAY A LUCID LAKE		385	3	DON JUAN	13	57	1
LUCIFER							
LIKE LUCIFER WHEN HURL'D FROM HEAVEN FOR SINNING		344	2	DON JUAN	4	1	5
LUCK							
THE SHIP WOULD SWIM AN HOUR WHICH BY GOOD LUCK		177	2	DON JUAN	2	40	7
THREW IN BY GOOD LUCK OVER THE SHIP'S RAIL		181	2	DON JUAN	2	48	6
YET TO THESE FOUR IN THREE THINGS THE SAME LUCK HOLDS		266	2	DON JUAN	2	206	7

	PAGE	VOL		CANTO	STANZA	LN

LUCK   (CONTINUED)
WITH WHOM IT IS OUR LUCK TO CAST OUR LOT 417   2 DON JUAN   5   13   4
REJOINED THE OTHER WHEN OUR BAD LUCK MENDS HERE   423   2 DON JUAN   5   24   6
THOUGH TRAVELLED I HAVE NEVER HAD THE LUCK TO 348   3 DON JUAN 12   70   1
THE LUCK OF FINDING EVERYBODY SOLVENT 458   3 DON JUAN 15   7   8
ON THEM AND BREAD 'TWAS OFT MY LUCK TO DINE 488   3 DON JUAN 15   73   5
LUCKIER
PRAY KEEP YOUR NONSENSE FOR SOME LUCKIER NIGHT-- 115   2 DON JJAN   1   171   1
THEIR LUCKIER VOTARIES TILL OLD AGE'S TEDIUM 235   3 DOV JUAN 10   22   7
LUCKIEST
IS ALL THAT LIFE ALLOWS THE LUCKIEST SINNER 294   2 DON JUAN   3   36   4
LUCKILY
FOR JUAN VERY LUCKILY NE'ER SAW IT 123   2 DON JUAN   1   185   3
SO LUCKILY FOR BOTH MY PHRASES FAIL 467   2 DON JUAN   5   97   8
BUT LUCKILY OF NO GREAT LENGTH OR WEIGHT 207   3 DJN JUAN   9   50   8
IT HAPPENED LUCKILY THE CHASTE ORB SHONE 506   3 DON JUAN 16   13   3
BUT LUCKILY I HAVE PAID FEW PARISH FEES SINCE) 530   3 DON JUAN 16   61   6
LUCKLESS
OF ALL THE LUCKLESS LANDSMEN'S SEA-SICK MAWS 174   2 DON JUAN   2   34   6
AND THE LOT FELL ON JUAN'S LUCKLESS TUTOR 195   2 DON JUAN   2   75   8
THE YOUNGER PORTION STOOD--A LUCKLESS VICTIM 409   2 DON JUAN   4   116   V7
LUCKLESSLY
WITH RAUCOCANTI LUCKLESSLY WAS CHAIN'D 394   2 DON JUAN   4   93   1
LUCK'S
BUT SHE WAS LUCKY AND LUCK'S ALL   YOUR QUEENS 247   3 DON JUAN 10   47   1
LUCKY
WHO PASSES FOR IN LIFE AND DEATH MOST LUCKY 143   3 DON JUAN   8   61   2
MAY LIKE BEING PRAISED FOR EVERY LUCKY BLUNDER 185   3 DJN JUAN   9   5   6
BUT SHE WAS LUCKY AND LUCK'S ALL   YOUR QUEENS 247   3 DON JUAN 10   47   1
HAD SEIZED THE LUCKY HOUR TO RECONNOITRE 273   3 DON JUAN 11   11   4
(THOUGH PARRY'S EFFORTS LOOK A LUCKY PRESAGE) 376   3 DON JUAN 13   39   5
LUCRETIUS'
LUCRETIUS' IRRELIGION IS TOO STRONG   45   2 DON JUAN   1   43   1
LUCUBRATION
ALSO A SEASONING SLIGHT OF LUCUBRATION   416   3 DON JUAN 14   14   2
LUCUBRATIONS
OF LADIES' LUCUBRATIONS SO THEY LEAD 284   3 DON JUAN 11   34   6
WHICH LENT HIS LEARNED LUCUBRATIONS PITH 294   3 DON JUAN 11   52   3
EXULTING IN THEIR BRILLIANT LUCUBRATIONS 533   3 DON JUAN 16   66   8
LUCULLUS'
WHILE GREAT LUCULLUS' ROBE TRIUMPHAL MUFFLES-- 484   3 DON JUAV 15   66   7
LUCUS
LUCUS A NON LUCENDO NOT WHAT WAS 33   3 DON JUAN   6   55   5
(LIKE LUCUS FROM NO LIGHT) THROUGH PROSPECTS NAMED . . 278   3 DON JUAN 11   21   2
LUDICROUS
OF HORRIBLE OR LUDICROUS TO QUOTE 156   3 DON JUAN   8   89   V5
LUES
THEIR REAL LUES OR OUR PSEUDO-SYPHILIS 92   2 DON JUAV   1   131   8
LUGGAGE
THERE WAS NOT NOW A LUGGAGE BOY BUT SOUGHT 90   3 DON JUAN   7   49   5
COACH CHARIOT LUGGAGE BAGGAGE EQUIPAGE 378   3 DJN JUAN 13   44   2
LUGO
YOU WAS NOT LAST YEAR AT THE FAIR OF LUGO 392   2 DON JUAN   4   88   7
LULL
BECAUSE INDIFFERENCE BEGINS TO LULL 360   3 DON JUAN 13   4   5
WHICH FAIN WOULD LULL ITS RIVER-CHILD TO SLEEP 447   3 DON JUAN 14   87   8
GENTLY TO LULL DOWN THE SUBSIDING SOUL 484   3 DON JUAN 15   66   6
LULLABY
NO DOUBT CAN SOOTHE THEM WITH A LULLABY-- 272   2 DON JUAN   2   V   1   5
LULL'D
OR LULL'D BY FALLING WATERS SWEET THE HUM 88   2 DON JUAN   1   123   6
DAY BROKE AND THE WIND LULL'D THE MASTS WERE GONE . . . 176   2 DON JUAN   2   38   2
LULL'D THEM LIKE TURTLES SLEEPING ON THE BLUE 192   2 DON JUAN   2   68   5
LULL'D EVEN THE SAVAGE HUNGER WHICH DEMANDED 195   2 DON JUAN   2   75   3
JUST FOR THE PRESENT AND IN HIS LULL'D HEAD 227   2 DON JUAN   2   134   4
LULL'D LIKE THE DEPTH OF OCEAN WHEN AT REST 235   2 DON JUAN   2   148   4
LULLED
AMIDST THE BODIES LULLED IN BLOODY REST 157   3 DON JUAN   8   91   8
LUMINOUS
PRESAGING A MOST LUMINOUS ATTACK 89   3 DON JUAN   7   46   4
OH YE GREAT AUTHORS LUMINOUS VOLUMINOUS 200   3 DON JUAN   9   35   1
LUNATIC
AS ELDON ON A LUNATIC COMMISSION-- 497   3 DON· JUAN 15   92   4
LUNCHEON
BUT SCARCE ENOUGH TO SERVE THEM FOR A LUNCHEON-- 181   2 DON JUAN   2   47   7
LUNCHEONS
HIS AFTERNOONS HE PASSED IN VISITS LUNCHEONS 301   3 DON JUAN 11   66   1
LUNES
I'M AT MY OLD LUNES--DIGRESSION AND FORGET 364   3 DON JUAN 13   12   1
LURCH
(HERE THE SHIP GAVE A LURCH AND HE GREW SEA-SICK) . . . 166   2 DON JUAN   2   19   8
SHE GAVE A HEEL AND THEN A LURCH TO PORT 183   2 DON JUAN   2   51   7
WHOSE HOUNDS NE'ER ERRED NOR GREYHOUNDS DEIGNED TO LURCH 539   3 DON JUAN 16   80   2
LURE
OF MORTALS WHOM THY LURE HATH LED ALONG-- 78   2 DON JUAN   1   106   6
LURES
THAT LURES TO FLAY ALIVE THE YOUNG BEGINNER 294   2 DON JUAN   3   36   6
LURK
WHERE WAVES MIGHT WASH AND SEALS MIGHT BREED AND LURK . 362   2 DON JUAN   4   33   4

477

		PAGE	VOL	CANTO	STANZA	LN

LURKED
LURKED CHRISTIANITY WHICH SOMETIMES BARTERS . . . . . . 96 3 DON JUAN 7 57 6
THERE LURKED A MAN BENEATH THE SPIRIT'S DRESS . . . . . 206 3 DON JUAN 9 47 6
AS EVER LURKED BENEATH A HOLY HOOD . . . . 561 3 DON JUAN 16 123 2
LURKING
THE SECRET CAVERN OF THIS LURKING TREASURE-- . . . . . 104 2 DON JUAN 1 153 7
THE LURKING BIAS BE IT TRUTH OR ERROR . . . . 413 3 DON JUAN 14 6 5
BUT WHEN IT WAS SHE HAD THAT LURKING DEMON . . . . . 448 3 DON JUAN 14 89 1
AS THOUGH THE LURKING THOUGHT HAD FOLLOW'D FREE . . . 456 3 DON JUAN 15 1 4
LURKS
OF MODERN DINNERS WHERE MORE MYSTERY LURKS . . . . . 482 3 DON JUAN 15 62 6
LUST
THE PRINCE'S TYRANT--THROUGH LUST OF POWER . . . . . 151 2 DON JUAN 1 V 2 V8
OVER THEIR IDOL TILL SOME WEALTHIER LUST . . . . . 263 2 DON JUAN 2 200 5
AND LOVE OF GLORY'S BUT AN AIRY LUST . . . . 399 2 DON JUAN 4 101 2
BUT AS IT WAS MERE LUST OF POWER TO O'ER-ARCH ALL . . 86 3 DON JUAN 7 40 5
THE LUST WHICH STINGS THE SPLENDOUR WHICH ENCUMBERS . 145 3 DON JUAN 8 67 5
THE KINGLY SCOURGE THE LUST OF NOTORIETY . . . . . . 146 3 DON JUAN 8 68 5
JUAN MUCH FLATTERED BY HER LOVE OR LUST-- . . . . . 221 3 DON JUAN 9 77 3
LOVE OR LUST MAKES MAN SICK AND WINE MUCH SICKER . . 317 3 DON JUAN 12 4 1
O'ER THE IRREGULARS IN LUST OR GORE . . . . 537 3 DON JUAN 16 76 5
LUSTILY
SWORE LUSTILY HE'D BE REVENGED THIS NIGHT . . . . . 122 2 DON JUAN 1 184 5
LUSTRE
ETHERIAL LUSTRE WITH WHAT SWEET PERSUASION . . . . . 65 2 DON JUAN 1 81 6
OH TO POSSESS SUCH LUSTRE--AND THEN LACK . . . . . 381 2 DON JUAN 4 69 8
GREAT LUSTRE THERE IS MUCH TO BE FORGIVEN . . . . . 465 2 DON JUAN 5 94 6
WHEN WILL YOUR NAMES LEND LUSTRE EVEN TO PARTRIDGES . 485 3 DON JUAN 15 67 8
LUTE
THE HERO'S HARP THE LOVER'S LUTE . . . . 321 2 DON JUAN 3 L 2 2
THE EPIC HARP--THE LYRIC LUTE-- . . . . 321 2 DON JUAN 3 L 2 V2
LUTES
FISHERS FOR MEN LIKE SIRENS WITH SOFT LUTES . . . . 343 3 DON JUAN 12 59 6
LUTHER
BY FENELON BY LUTHER AND BY PLATO . . . . 68 3 DON JUAN 7 4 2
A SOMETHING LIKE IT--AS BEAR WITNESS LUTHER . . . . 565 3 DON JUAN 17 6 8
LUX
THE UPHOLSTERER'S FIAT LUX HAD BADE TO ISSUE . . . . 309 2 DON JUAN 3 67 V8
LUXURIANT
LUXURIANT BUDDING CHEERFUL WITHOUT MIRTH . . . . . . 32 3 DON JUAN 6 53 3
LUXURIOUS
A SLICE OR TWO FROM YOUR LUXURIOUS MEALS . . . . . 185 3 DON JUAN 9 6 4
LWOW
MEKNOP SERGE LWOW ARSENIEW OF MODERN GREECE . . . . 74 3 DON JUAN 7 15 3
LYING
AND LYING ON THEIR WEARINESS LIKE BALM . . . . . . 192 2 DON JUAN 2 68 4
ALL TRANQUILLY THE SHIPWRECK'D BOY WAS LYING . . . . 233 2 DON JUAN 2 144 3
AND ROUND ITS ONCE WARM PRECINCTS PALELY LYING . . . 301 2 DON JUAN 3 51 6
MIGHT FOR LONG LYING MAKE HIMSELF AMENDS . . . . . 318 2 DON JUAN 3 83 6
MY HAT AND GLOVES STILL LYING ON THE TABLE . . . . 428 2 DON JUAN 5 33 4
LYKANTHROPY
THAT FORMS THIS DESK OF WHAT THEY MEAN--LYKANTHROPY . 192 3 DON JUAN 9 20 6
LYNX
THOUGH WATCHFUL AS THE LYNX THEY NE'ER DISCOVER . . . 75 2 DON JUAN 1 100 2
LYNX-LIKE
IN RUSSET JACKET--LYNX-LIKE IS HIS AIM . . . . . . 394 3 DON JUAN 13 75 5
LYONS
'TIS NOT SO PLEASANT IN THE GULF OF LYONS . . . . . 176 2 DON JUAN 2 39 8
LYRE
TO WHOM THE LYRE AND LAURELS HAVE BEEN GIVEN . . . . 77 2 DON JUAN 1 104 6
AND MUST THY LYRE SO LONG DIVINE . . . . 322 2 DON JUAN 3 L 5 5
UPON MY LYRE OR MAKING THE PEGS SURE . . . . . . 341 3 DON JUAN 12 54 7
MY TREMBLING LYRE ALREADY SEVERAL STRINGS . . . . . 568 3 DON JUAN 17 13 5
LYRIC
FROM THE HIGH LYRIC DOWN TO THE LOW RATIONAL . . . . 319 2 DON JUAN 3 85 6
THE EPIC HARP--THE LYRIC LUTE-- . . . . 321 2 DON JUAN 3 L 2 V2
ADDED HER SWEET VOICE TO THE LYRIC SOUND . . . . . 518 3 DON JUAN 16 40 6
MACASSAR
SAVE THINE INCOMPARABLE OIL MACASSAR . . . . . . 30 2 DON JUAN 1 17 8
MACHIAVEL
BY SWIFT BY MACHIAVEL BY ROCHEFOUCAULT . . . . . 68 3 DON JUAN 7 4 1
AS MACHIAVEL SHOWS THOSE IN PURPLE RAIMENT . . . . 264 3 DON JUAN 10 79 3
MACHIAVELIAN
SAYING OUR MACHIAVELIAN IMPRESARIO . . . . 389 2 DON JUAN 4 82 2
MACHINERY
I'VE GOT NEW MYTHOLOGICAL MACHINERY . . . . 136 2 DON JUAN 1 201 7
I'VE LAID IN TOO A STOCK OF GOOD MACHINERY . . . . 136 2 DON JUAN 1 201 V7
MACHINES
WHAT WONDROUS NEW MACHINES HAVE LATE BEEN SPINNING . 92 2 DON JUAN 1 130 6
AND ALL KINDS OF BENEVOLENT MACHINES . . . . . . 89 3 DON JUAN 7 47 8
AND MADE THEM CHARGE WITH BAYONET THESE MACHINES . . 93 3 DON JUAN 7 53 3
MACKAW
A MONKEY A DUTCH MASTIFF A MACKAW . . . . 285 2 DON JUAN 3 18 1
MACKSTAY
MISS BOMBAZEEN MISS MACKSTAY MISS O'TABBEY . . . . 396 3 DON JUAN 13 79 5
MAD
AND TRIED TO PROVE HER LOVING LORD WAS MAD . . . . 35 2 DON JUAN 1 27 4
WENT RAGING MAD--LORD HOW THEY DID BLASPHEME . . . . 198 2 DON JUAN 2 79 4
WERE MAD FOR LAND AND THUS THEIR COURSE THEY RAN . . 211 2 DON JUAN 2 104 3

MAD   (CONTINUED)
		PAGE	VOL		CANTO	STANZA	LN
AND TURN HIM LIKE THE CYCLOPS MAD WITH BLINDNESS		304	2	DON JUAN	3	57	8
I DON'T MUCH LIKE DESCRIBING PEOPLE MAD		384	2	DON JUAN	4	74	3
ALL THAT THE DEVIL WOULD DO IF RUN STARK MAD		173	3	DON JUAN	8	123	4
SHE SMILED AT MAD SUWARROW'S RHYMES WHO THREW		212	3	DON JUAN	9	60	2
HIS GUERDON 'TIS HIS VIRTUE MAKES HIM MAD		363	3	DON JUAN	13	9	5

MADAM
		PAGE	VOL		CANTO	STANZA	LN
FIRST KNOCKS WERE HEARD THEN MADAM--MADAM--HIST		95	2	DON JUAN	1	136	8
FIRST KNOCKS WERE HEARD THEN MADAM--MADAM--HIST		95	2	DON JUAN	1	136	8
FOR GOD'S SAKE MADAM--MADAM--HERE'S MY MASTER		96	2	DON JUAN	1	137	1
FOR GOD'S SAKE MADAM--MADAM--HERE'S MY MASTER		96	2	DON JUAN	1	137	1
OR MADAM DIES--ALFONSO MUTTER'D DAMN HER		111	2	DON JUAN	1	163	5
(I REALLY MADAM WONDER AT YOUR TASTE--		115	2	DON JUAN	1	172	4
BUT 'TIS A NAME SO SPREAD O'ER SIR AND MADAM		79	3	DON JUAN	7	25	7

MADDENED
		PAGE	VOL		CANTO	STANZA	LN
THE MADDENED TURKS THEIR CITY STILL DISPUTE		146	3	DON JUAN	8	69	8

MADDENING
		PAGE	VOL		CANTO	STANZA	LN
A MADDENING SPIRIT WHICH WOULD STRIVE TO BLEND		219	3	DON JUAN	9	73	4

MADE
		PAGE	VOL		CANTO	STANZA	LN
CONSPIRACY OR CONGRESS TO BE MADE--		18	2	DON JUAN	D	14	5
SHE MADE THE CLEVEREST PEOPLE QUITE ASHAMED		26	2	DON JUAN	1	10	5
AS THOSE OF THE BEST TIME-PIECE MADE BY HARRISON		30	2	DON JUAN	1	17	6
THEN THEIR RELATIONS WHO MADE MATTERS WORSE		38	2	DON JUAN	1	32	2
ARTS SCIENCES NO BRANCH WAS MADE A MYSTERY		43	2	DON JUAN	1	39	7
HIS CLASSIC STUDIES MADE A LITTLE PUZZLE		44	2	DON JUAN	1	41	1
DISCOVERIES MADE BUT NONE COULD BE AWARE		59	2	DON JUAN	1	68	3
AND ALMOST MIGHT HAVE MADE A TARQUIN QUAKE		62	2	DON JUAN	1	75	6
WHO'VE MADE US YOUTH WAIT TOO--TOO LONG ALREADY		89	2	DON JUAN	1	125	4
BREAD HAS BEEN MADE (INDIFFERENT) FROM POTATOES		92	2	DON JUAN	1	130	1
YOU'VE MADE THE APARTMENT IN A FIT CONDITION--		104	2	DON JUAN	1	152	3
SO THAT A SUIT OR ACTION WERE MADE GOOD		109	2	DON JUAN	1	160	5
AND TRUTH TO SAY HE MADE A FOOLISH FIGURE		110	2	DON JUAN	1	161	2
WHO TO MADRID ON PURPOSE MADE A JOURNEY		127	2	DON JUAN	1	189	8
AND BREAK A PROMISE AFTER HAVING MADE IT HER		142	2	DON JUAN	1	210	5
CAN MAKE THE FOOL OF WHICH THEY MADE BEFORE		144	2	DON JUAN	1	216	3
O'ER WHICH REFLECTION MAY BE MADE AT LEISURE		145	2	DON JUAN	1	217	4
AND THE WAVES OOZING THROUGH THE PORT-HOLE MADE		169	2	DON JUAN	2	25	7
WHICH STRUCK HER AFT AND MADE AN AWKWARD RIFT		170	2	DON JUAN	2	27	3
AND MADE A SCENE MEN DO NOT SOON FORGET		172	2	DON JUAN	2	31	3
THE HIGH WIND MADE THE TREBLE AND AS BASS		174	2	DON JUAN	2	34	4
AND MADE A LOUD AND PIOUS LAMENTATION		175	2	DON JUAN	2	37	2
REPENTED ALL HIS SINS AND MADE A LAST		175	2	DON JUAN	2	37	3
THAT MADE HIS EYELIDS AS A WOMAN'S BE		179	2	DON JUAN	2	43	6
SOME WENT TO PRAYERS AGAIN AND MADE A VOW		179	2	DON JUAN	2	44	3
AND MADE THEM BALE WITHOUT A MOMENT'S EASE		188	2	DON JUAN	2	60	6
INSTEAD OF SAIL WERE TO THE OAR MADE FAST		188	2	DON JUAN	2	61	4
THE LOTS WERE MADE AND MARK'D AND MIX'D AND HANDED		195	2	DON JUAN	2	75	1
WAS A SMALL PRESENT MADE TO HIM AT CADIZ		199	2	DON JUAN	2	81	7
A PRESENT LIBERALLY MADE BY LADIES		199	2	DON JUAN	2	81	V8
OR BUT AT TIMES A LITTLE SUPPER MADE		200	2	DON JUAN	2	82	4
THE BOAT MADE WAY YET NOW THEY WERE SO LOW		207	2	DON JUAN	2	96	3
TO THESE KIND EFFORTS MADE A LOW REPLY		215	2	DON JUAN	2	113	8
THEY MADE A MOST SUPERIOR MESS OF BROTH		221	2	DON JUAN	2	123	5
BY WHICH NO DOUBT A GOOD DEAL MAY BE MADE		223	2	DON JUAN	2	126	8
THEY MADE A FIRE BUT SUCH A FIRE AS THEY		226	2	DON JUAN	2	132	1
BUT UP SHE GOT AND UP SHE MADE THEM GET		230	2	DON JUAN	2	139	1
MISTAKE YOU WOULD HAVE MADE ON SEEING THE TWO		232	2	DON JUAN	2	142	6
THE COFFEE MADE WOULD FAIN HAVE WAKEN'D JUAN		234	2	DON JUAN	2	146	2
HAD FURTHER SLEEP A FURTHER PLEASURE MADE		235	2	DON JUAN	2	149	4
TO STIR HER VIANDS MADE HIM QUITE AWAKE		237	2	DON JUAN	2	153	7
HAD MADE HER MISTRESS QUIT HER BED TO TRACE		240	2	DON JUAN	2	159	4
HER EARNESTNESS WOULD NE'ER HAVE MADE AN END		241	2	DON JUAN	2	161	4
THAT EVER MADE A YOUTHFUL HEART LESS STEADY		246	2	DON JUAN	2	171	3
BUT THEN THE THOUGHT OF PARTING MADE HER QUAKE		247	2	DON JUAN	2	173	6
BY SOME LOW ROCK OR SHELVE THAT MADE IT FRET		251	2	DON JUAN	2	181	7
AROUND THEM MADE THEM TO EACH OTHER PRESS		255	2	DON JUAN	2	188	6
SHE AND HER WAVE-WORN LOVE HAD MADE THEIR BOWER		262	2	DON JUAN	2	198	5
MADE BUT TO LOVE TO FEEL THAT SHE WAS HIS		264	2	DON JUAN	2	202	5
ABHOR CONDEMN ABJURE THE MORTAL MADE		268	2	DON JUAN	2	209	2
CAN CALM--FOR WHAT IT MADE ME ON THAT SAME		272	2	DON JUAN	2	V 1	7
AND MADE THY BEST INTERPRETER A SIGH		275	2	DON JUAN	3	2	4
A MELODY WHICH MADE HIM DOUBT HIS EARS		290	2	DON JUAN	3	28	5
MADE QUITE A PICTURE OF THESE LITTLE GREEKS		292	2	DON JUAN	3	33	6
A LIFE WHICH MADE THEM HAPPY BEYOND MEASURE		295	2	DON JUAN	3	39	4
AND MADE HIM A GOOD FRIEND BUT BAD ACQUAINTANCE		303	2	DON JUAN	3	54	8
THE DINNER MADE ABOUT A HUNDRED DISHES		307	2	DON JUAN	3	62	1
GOLD CUPS OF FILIGREE MADE TO SECURE		307	2	DON JUAN	3	63	5
THE HANGINGS OF THE ROOM WERE TAPESTRY MADE		308	2	DON JUAN	3	64	1
OR WERE OF TORTOISE-SHELL OR RARE WOODS MADE		310	2	DON JUAN	3	69	4
ROUND HER SHE MADE AN ATMOSPHERE OF LIFE		313	2	DON JUAN	3	74	1
HER OVERPOWERING PRESENCE MADE YOU FEEL		313	2	DON JUAN	3	74	7
I KNOW NOT HOW--HER PRESENCE MADE YE FEEL		313	2	DON JUAN	3	74	V7
WHICH MADE THEIR NEW ESTABLISHMENT COMPLETE		316	2	DON JUAN	3	78	3
OF MEN AND MADE THEM SPEECHES WHEN HALF MELLOW		318	2	DON JUAN	3	82	4
HIS MUSE MADE INCREMENT OF ANYTHING		319	2	DON JUAN	3	85	5
IT MADE ANACREON'S SONG DIVINE		324	2	DON JUAN	3	L 11	3
AND GLORY LONG HAS MADE THE SAGES SMILE		328	2	DON JUAN	3	90	1
AND DRYDEN'S LAY MADE HAUNTED GROUND TO ME		337	2	DON JUAN	3	105	7
THEIR FACES WERE NOT MADE FOR WRINKLES THEIR		348	2	DON JUAN	4	9	1

MADE   (CONTINUED)

	PAGE	VOL	CANTO	STANZA	LN
THE BLANK GREY WAS NOT MADE TO BLAST THEIR HAIR	348	2 DON JUAN	4	9	3
THE HEAVENS AND EARTH AND AIR SEEM'D MADE FOR THEM	351	2 DON JUAN	4	13	2
THEY WERE NOT MADE IN THE REAL WORLD TO FILL	352	2 DON JUAN	4	15	3
WHAT WAS IT MADE THEM THUS EXEMPT FROM CARE	353	2 DON JUAN	4	18	4
FOR IT HAD MADE THEM WHAT THEY WERE THE POWER	354	2 DON JUAN	4	20	3
AND STUMBLED ALMOST EVERY STEP SHE MADE	361	2 DON JUAN	4	32	3
NOT I HAVE MADE THIS DESOLATION FEW	368	2 DON JUAN	4	46	5
FOR FOR A WHILE THE FURIES MADE A PAUSE	378	2 DON JUAN	4	62	8
SHALL SORROW LIGHT OR SHAME SHE WAS NOT MADE	382	2 DON JUAN	4	71	2
LAST CARNIVAL SHE MADE A DEAL OF STRIFE	389	2 DON JUAN	4	83	6
AND MADE AT LEAST FIVE HUNDRED GOOD ZECCHINI	390	2 DON JUAN	4	84	5
IT SEEMS WHEN THIS ALLOTMENT WAS MADE OUT	394	2 DON JUAN	4	92	1
THOUGH WILBERFORCE AT LAST HAS MADE IT TWICE	408	2 DON JUAN	4	115	3
THE EUNUCH MADE A SIGN TO THOSE ON BOARD	433	2 DON JUAN	5	41	7
MADE JUAN IN HIS HARSH INTENTIONS PAUSE	437	2 DON JUAN	5	47	4
PERHAPS BECAUSE OUR APPELLANTS MADE OUT OF SEASON	437	2 DON JUAN	5	48	V4
OF WORKMANSHIP SO RARE THEY MADE YOU WISH	449	2 DON JUAN	5	65	7
WHILE BABA MADE HIM COMB HIS HEAD AND OIL IT	457	2 DON JUAN	5	79	8
AS BABA WITH HIS FINGERS MADE THEM FALL	463	2 DON JUAN	5	90	3
MADE FIERCE REMONSTRANCES AND THEN A THREAT	471	2 DON JUAN	5	103	2
A THOUSAND TIMES OF HIM HAD MADE AN END	471	2 DON JUAN	5	104	6
WHEN BEING MADE HER PROPERTY AT LAST	478	2 DON JUAN	5	116	4
WHICH MADE HIM SEEM EXCEEDINGLY ILL-BRED	483	2 DON JUAN	5	124	4
EARTH BEING ONLY MADE FOR QUEENS AND KINGS	485	2 DON JUAN	5	128	4
AS EVEN IN A MUCH HUMBLER LOT HAD MADE	485	2 DON JUAN	5	129	2
MADE HER A BEAUTIFUL EMBODIED STORM	489	2 DON JUAN	5	135	8
THE DAGGER CLOSE AT HAND WHICH MADE IT AWKWARD	492	2 DON JUAN	5	140	2
FOR EASTERN STAYS ARE LITTLE MADE TO PAD	492	2 DON JUAN	5	140	3
JUAN WAS MOVED HE HAD MADE UP HIS MIND	492	2 DON JUAN	5	141	1
OR THROWN TO LIONS OR MADE BAITS FOR FISH	492	2 DON JUAN	5	141	4
AND THEN IF MATTERS COULD BE MADE UP NOW	493	2 DON JUAN	5	142	4
NO SCANDALS MADE THE DAILY PRESS A CURSE--	496	2 DON JUAN	5	149	7
AS THOSE WHOSE WIVES HAVE MADE THEM FIT FOR HEAVEN	500	2 DON JUAN	5	154	8
THE NEW-BOUGHT VIRGIN MADE HER BLUSH AND SHAKE	501	2 DON JUAN	5	156	2
A GOODLY SINECURE NO DOUBT BUT MADE	22	3 DON JUAN	6	32	1
WHICH MADE THEM LIKE THEIR NEW COMPANION	25	3 DON JUAN	6	38	V7
EXTREMELY PURE WHICH MADE THEM ALL CONCUR	25	3 DON JUAN	6	39	4
AND FEET SO SMALL THEY SCARCE SEEMED MADE TO TREAD	26	3 DON JUAN	6	41	4
WHICH MADE HIM WONDER MORE THAN ANY WONDER	34	3 DON JUAN	6	57	V7
HAD MADE HIM LATELY BASK IN HIS BRIDE'S BEAUTY	51	3 DON JUAN	6	91	8
WOULD NOT ALONE HAVE MADE HIM INSECURE	58	3 DON JUAN	6	104	5
WHICH MADE HIM DAILY BLESS HIS OWN NEUTRALITY	64	3 DON JUAN	6	117	8
AND BROUGHT BEFORE THE EMPRESS WHO HAD MADE	64	3 DON JUAN	6	118	5
MADE ALL THEIR NAVAL MATTERS INCORRECT	80	3 DON JUAN	7	28	2
AND THOUGH AS YET THE TURKS MADE NO RESISTANCE	80	3 DON JUAN	7	28	V5
AND MADE A SIGNAL TO RETREAT AT ONE	81	3 DON JUAN	7	30	6
WHICH MADE A LONG DEBATE BUT I MUST HALT	83	3 DON JUAN	7	35	6
MADE HIS LAST ILLNESS WHEN ALL WORN AND WAN	84	3 DON JUAN	7	36	5
WHEN HOMICIDE AND HARLOTRY MADE GREAT	84	3 DON JUAN	7	37	2
IN FORMER WORKS MADE NEW PREPARED FASCINES	89	3 DON JUAN	7	47	7
WAS MADE WITH ALL ALACRITY THE FIRST	91	3 DON JUAN	7	50	2
AND MADE THEM CHARGE WITH BAYONET THESE MACHINES	93	3 DON JUAN	7	53	3
HE MADE NO ANSWER BUT HE TOOK THE CITY	93	3 DON JUAN	7	53	8
TO WHOM HE SPOKE AND MADE HIS WORDS BUT FEW	97	3 DON JUAN	7	59	8
IF HOMER HAD FOUND MORTARS READY MADE	106	3 DON JUAN	7	78	4
AND HEROES ARE BUT MADE FOR BARDS TO SING	118	3 DON JUAN	8	14	5
WHICH MADE SOME THINK AND OTHERS KNOW A HELL COME	134	3 DON JUAN	8	42	8
IN ANSWER MADE AN INCLINATION TO	141	3 DON JUAN	8	57	3
GOD MADE THE COUNTRY AND MAN MADE THE TOWN	142	3 DON JUAN	8	60	2
GOD MADE THE COUNTRY AND MAN MADE THE TOWN	142	3 DON JUAN	8	60	2
NO FASHION MADE THEM APES OF HER DISTORTIONS	145	3 DON JUAN	8	66	6
THE TOWN WAS ENTERED FIRST ONE COLUMN MADE	146	3 DON JUAN	8	69	1
WAS MADE AT LENGTH WITH THOSE WHO DARED TO CLIMB	151	3 DON JUAN	8	79	4
HE MADE THE TEETH MEET NOR RELINQUISHED IT	153	3 DON JUAN	8	84	6
TO THIS VAIN REFUGE MADE THE GOOD HEART DROOP	157	3 DON JUAN	8	91	4
THE HEAP A MOMENT MORE HAD MADE HER TOMB	158	3 DON JUAN	8	94	8
BECAUSE A HUNCHBACK--MADE HIS BREAST THE SHIELD	166	3 DON JUAN	8	110	V7
SOME TWENTY TIMES HE MADE THE RUSS RETIRE	171	3 DON JUAN	8	120	3
HAD MADE THEM CHASTE--THEY RAVISHED VERY LITTLE	176	3 DON JUAN	8	128	8
AND MADE A VOW TO SHIELD HER WHICH HE KEPT	182	3 DON JUAN	8	141	8
AND WATERLOO HAS MADE THE WORLD YOUR DEBTOR--	184	3 DON JUAN	9	3	7
MADE UP BY YOUTH FAME AND AN ARMY TAILOR--	204	3 DON JUAN	9	44	2
IF RATHER BROAD MADE STOCKS RISE AND THEIR HOLDERS	208	3 DON JUAN	9	52	8
AND YET BUT MADE A MIDDLING GRENADIER	209	3 DON JUAN	9	54	8
MADE UP UPON AN AMATORY PATTERN	217	3 DON JUAN	9	70	5
LOVE HAD MADE CATHERINE MAKE EACH LOVER'S FORTUNE	222	3 DON JUAN	9	81	1
A GENERAL OBJECT OF ATTENTION MADE	223	3 DON JUAN	9	83	2
MADE ICE SEEM PARADISE AND WINTER SUNNY	235	3 DON JUAN	10	21	8
MADE THE CHASTE CATHERINE LOOK A LITTLE GRIM	246	3 DON JUAN	10	44	3
MADE CATHERINE TASTE NEXT NIGHT A QUIET SLUMBER--	248	3 DON JUAN	10	48	4
HE MADE 'GAINST COSSAQUE SABRES IN THE WIDE	249	3 DON JUAN	10	51	5
WHATE'ER THE CAUSE THE CHURCH MADE LITTLE OF IT--	252	3 DON JUAN	10	56	7
AND YET THIS WANT OF TIES MADE THEIR'S MORE TENDER	252	3 DON JUAN	10	57	8
AND MADE THE VERY BILLOWS PAY THEM TOLL	257	3 DON JUAN	10	65	8
IN SELF-DEFENCE--THIS MADE HIM MEDITATIVE	277	3 DON JUAN	11	18	8
WHO IN HIS TIME HAD MADE HEROIC BUSTLE	277	3 DON JUAN	11	19	2
INSTEAD OF WICKS THEY MADE A WICKED MAN TURN	280	3 DON JUAN	11	26	8
AS ALSO BONFIRES MADE OF COUNTRY SEATS	281	3 DON JUAN	11	27	3

MADE   (CONTINUED)
```
    (SEE BILLINGSGATE) MADE EVEN THE TONGUE MORE FREE  . . . .  288  3 DON JUAN 11     42   8
    SOME MAIDS HAVE BEEN MADE WIVES SOME MERELY MOTHERS  . . .  308  3 DON JUAN 11     81   4
    HE PLAYED AND PAID MADE LOVE WITHOUT MUCH SIN  . . . . .    327  3 DON JUAN 12     25  V5
    THAT THE YOUNG LADY MADE A MONSTROUS CHOICE  . . . . . .    334  3 DON JUAN 12     38   8
    I'VE KNOWN A DOZEN WEDDINGS MADE EVEN THUS  . . . . . .     344  3 DON JUAN 12     61   1
    WHOSE CHARMS MADE ALL MEN SPEAK AND WOMEN DUMB  . . . . .   365  3 DON JUAN 13     13   6
    THE TWICE TWO THOUSAND FOR WHOM EARTH WAS MADE  . . . . .   381  3 DON JUAN 13     49   2
    ITS SHRILLER ECHOES--LIKE AN INFANT MADE  . . . . . .      385  3 DON JUAN 13     58   3
    SHE MADE THE EARTH BELOW SEEM HOLY GROUND  . . . . . .     387  3 DON JUAN 13     61   5
    THE SPRING GUSH'D THROUGH GRIM MOUTHS OF GRANITE MADE  . . 389  3 DON JUAN 13     65   5
    THERE REMBRANDT MADE HIS DARKNESS EQUAL LIGHT  . . . . .    392  3 DON JUAN 13     72   2
    PRESERVE OF BORES WHO OUGHT TO BE MADE GAME  . . . . .      395  3 DON JUAN 13     78   8
    WITH THIS DEBUT WHICH MADE A STRONG IMPRESSION  . . . . .   400  3 DON JUAN 13     90   6
    THE BEST FIRST SPEECH THAT EVER YET WAS MADE  . . . . .     400  3 DON JUAN 13     90   8
    WAS MADE BY MRS ADAMS WHERE SHE CRIES  . . . . . .         403  3 DON JUAN 13     96   7
    AND MADE UPON THE HOT-HOUSE SEVERAL STRICTURES  . . . . .   406  3 DON JUAN 13    102   4
    IN LIEU OF SONS OF THESE HE MADE NO BONES  . . . . . .     410  3 DON JUAN 14      1   8
    WHEN WE HAVE MADE OUR LOVE AND GAMED OUR GAMING  . . . .    418  3 DON JUAN 14     18   1
    AND NEVER CRANED AND MADE BUT FEW FAUX PAS  . . . . .      424  3 DON JUAN 14     33   3
    'TWAS RATHER HER EXPERIENCE MADE HER SAGE  . . . . . .     433  3 DON JUAN 14     54   3
    THAT YOUNG MEN RARELY MADE MONASTIC VOWS  . . . . . .      439  3 DON JUAN 14     67   6
    AND WHEN THEY HAVE MADE THE SHORE THROUGH EV'RY SHOCK  . . 442  3 DON JUAN 14     74   7
    EVE MADE UP MILLINERY WITH FIG LEAVES--  . . . . . .       444  3 DON JUAN 14     78   2
    THE PASSION WHICH MADE SOLOMON A ZANY  . . . . . . .       452  3 DON JUAN 14     95   4
    YET MADE THE MISERY OF AT LEAST TWO LIVES  . . . . . .     452  3 DON JUAN 14     95   8
    AND THY PURE CREED MADE SANCTION OF ALL ILL  . . . . .      464  3 DON JUAN 15     18   4
    I THINK I SHOULD HAVE MADE A DECENT SPOUSE  . . . . .      467  3 DON JUAN 15     24   1
    I THINK I SHOULD HAVE MADE MONASTIC VOWS  . . . . . .      467  3 DON JUAN 15     24   3
    HAD NOT THE FLESH MADE SOME SMALL OPTION  . . . . . .      467  3 DON JUAN 15     24  V4
    MEN MADE THE MANNERS MANNERS NOW MAKE MEN--  . . . . .      468  3 DON JUAN 15     26   2
    MADE JUAN WONDER AS NO DOUBT HE MUST  . . . . . . .        477  3 DON JUAN 15     49   3
    THESE SEALS UPON HER WAX MADE NO IMPRESSION  . . . . .      480  3 DON JUAN 15     57   7
    WHERE ALL THE PONTIC SPOILS MADE SUCH A SHOW  . . . . .     485  3 DON JUAN 15     67  V3
    THE FOAM WHICH MADE ITS VIRGIN BUMPER GAY  . . . . . .     504  3 DON JUAN 16      9   3
    HIS GARMENTS ONLY A SLIGHT MURMUR MADE  . . . . . . .      510  3 DON JUAN 16     21   5
    WHICH MADE HIM HAVE RECOURSE UNTO HIS SPOON  . . . . .      513  3 DON JUAN 16     30   5
    BUT ADD THE WORDS CRIED HENRY WHICH YOU MADE  . . . . .     517  3 DON JUAN 16     39   1
    MADE NORMAN CHURCH HIS PREY  . . . . . . . . .             518  3 DON JUAN 16  L   1   6
    MADE EPIGRAMS OCCASIONALLY TOO  . . . . . . . . .          524  3 DON JUAN 16     47   3
    HAD CAUSED HIS NERVES--MADE ANSWERS RATHER CLOUDED  . . .   527  3 DON JUAN 16     54  V8
    HAD MADE MORE PROGRESS THAN FOR THE LAST CENTURY  . . . .   536  3 DON JUAN 16     73   4
    HAVE PLAINLY MADE IT OUT THAT FOUR ARE THREE  . . . . .     548  3 DON JUAN 16     99   4
    SPANGLED WITH GEMS--THE MONK MADE HIS BLOOD CURDLE  . . .   556  3 DON JUAN 16    113   8
    THAT HE HAD MADE AT FIRST A SILLY BLUNDER  . . . . . .     560  3 DON JUAN 16    122   6
MADEIRA
    BUT THEN HAVE THEIR CLARET AND MADEIRA  . . . . . . .      360  3 DON JUAN 13      5   5
    THE CLARET LIGHT AND THE MADEIRA STRONG  . . . . . .       394  3 DON JUAN 13     76   6
MADLY
    TO ALL EXCEPT ONE IMAGE MADLY BLIND  . . . . . . .        133  2 DON JUAN  1    196   6
    WHO HAD ALREADY PERISH'D SUFFERING MADLY  . . . . . .      199  2 DON JUAN  2     80   7
MADMEN
    THAT MADMEN MAY NOT BITE YOU ON A VISIT  . . . . . .       280  3 DON JUAN 11     25   4
MADMEN'S
    MORE THAN SUCH MADMEN'S FELLOW MAN--THE MOON'S  . . . .     341  2 DON JUAN  3    110   4
MADNESS
    HAS MADNESS SEIZED YOU WOULD THAT I HAD DIED  . . . . .     98  2 DON JUAN  1    142   3
    AND WHIRL'D HER BRAIN TO MADNESS SHE AROSE  . . . . .      380  2 DON JUAN  4     67   2
MADRID
    WHO TO MADRID ON PURPOSE MADE A JOURNEY  . . . . . .       127  2 DON JUAN  1    189   8
    AND THEN HE TALKED WITH HIM ABOUT MADRID  . . . . . .      368  3 DON JUAN 13     23   1
MADRID'S
    MADRID'S AND MOSCOW'S CLIMES WERE OF A PIECE  . . . . .     239  3 DON JUAN 10     30   8
MAEVIA
    LADY FITZ-FRISKY AND MISS MAEVIA MANNISH  . . . . . .      295  3 DON JUAN 11     53   7
MAGAZINE
    AS EVERY PALTRY MAGAZINE CAN SHOW IT'S  . . . . . .        295  3 DON JUAN 11     54   8
MAGAZINES
    ALL OTHER MAGAZINES OF ART OR SCIENCE  . . . ' . . . .     142  2 DON JUAN  1    211   3
MAGGIOR
    (HIS MAGGIOR DUOMO A SMART SUBTLE GREEK  . . . . . .       259  3 DON JUAN 10     70   5
MAGGOTS
    MEN ARE BUT MAGGOTS OF SOME HUGE EARTH'S BURIAL)  . . . .   202  3 DON JUAN  9     39   8
MAGIC
    OF MAGIC LADIES WHO BY ONE SOLE ACT  . . . . . .          293  2 DON JUAN  3     34   7
    FOR ONCE IT WAS A MAGIC SOUND TO ME  . . . . . .          413  2 DON JUAN  5      4   2
    APPEARED TO HIM BUT AS THE MAGIC VAPOUR  . . . . . .       266  2 DON JUAN 10     83   2
    BECAUSE--SUCH WAS HIS MAGIC POWER TO PLEASE--  . . . . .    399  3 DON JUAN 13     86   7
    THE MAGIC OF HER GRACE'S TALISMAN  . . . . . . . .         437  3 DON JUAN 14     62   6
MAGICIAN'S
    'TWAS BUT A DOUBT BUT NE'ER MAGICIAN'S WAND  . . . . .      60  2 DON JUAN  1     71   6
MAGICIANS
    AS IF 'TWERE ONE WHEREON MAGICIANS BIND  . . . . . .        72  2 DON JUAN  1     95   6
MAGISTERIAL
    FOR JUAN WORE THE MAGISTERIAL FACE  . . . . . . .         186  2 DON JUAN  2     56   4
MAGNANIMITY
    HER NOBLEST VIRTUE WAS HER MAGNANIMITY  . . . . . .         27  2 DON JUAN  1     12   2
    THAT ALL THE WORLD EXCLAIM'D WHAT MAGNANIMITY  . . . .      36  2 DON JUAN  1     29   8
    FOR ONCE BY SOME ODD SORT OF MAGNANIMITY  . . . . . .       92  3 DON JUAN  7     51  V4
```

481

	PAGE	VOL	CANTO	STANZA	LN
MAGNANIMOUS					
'TIS ALSO PLEASANT TO BE DEEM'D MAGNANIMOUS	37	2	DON JUAN 1	30	3
MAGNESIAS					
HALF-SOLVED INTO THOSE SODAS OR MAGNESIAS	261	3	DON JUAN 10	73	7
MAGNETIC					
IT TREMBLED AS MAGNETIC NEEDLES DO	134	2	DON JUAN 1	198	4
MAGNETISM					
LIKE MAGNETISM OR DEVILISM OR WHAT	25	3	DON JUAN 6	38	7
MAGNIFICENCE					
WITH GREAT MAGNIFICENCE WERE SEEN TO ISSUE	309	2	DON JUAN 3	67	V8
MAGNIFICENTLY					
MAGNIFICENTLY MINGLED IN A LITTER	465	2	DON JUAN 5	93	8
MAGNIFICIENT					
AND A MAGNIFICIENT LARGE HALL DISPLAYED	440	2	DON JUAN 5	51	7
MAGNIFIQUE					
JUAN THOUGH CARELESS YOUNG AND MAGNIFIQUE	259	3	DON JUAN 10	70	1
MAHOGANY					
AND YET I KNOW NO MORE THAN THE MAHOGANY	192	3	DON JUAN 9	20	5
MAHOMET					
DESCRIBED BY MAHOMET AND ANACREON MOORE	77	2	DON JUAN 1	104	5
CAESAR AND POMPEY MAHOMET BELISARIUS	266	2	DON JUAN 2	206	3
OH MAHOMET THAT HIS MAJESTY SHOULD TAKE	501	2	DON JUAN 5	156	4
LITTLE CARED THEY FOR MAHOMET OR MUFTI	75	3	DON JUAN 7	17	5
AS EVER MAHOMET PICKED OUT FOR A MARTYR	167	3	DON JUAN 8	111	3
SHE STILL HELD OUT THAT MAHOMET WAS A PROPHET	252	3	DON JUAN 10	56	8
WAS BENT WITH GRIEF THAT MAHOMET SHOULD RESIGN	262	3	DON JUAN 10	75	7
MAHOMETANS					
AND ALL (EXCEPT MAHOMETANS) FORBEAR	12	3	DON JUAN 6	12	7
MAHOMET'S					
WOULD JUAN BEND THOUGH 'TWERE TO MAHOMET'S BRIDE	471	2	DON JUAN 5	103	5
AND BEGGED BY EVERY HAIR OF MAHOMET'S BEARD	62	3	DON JUAN 6	113	7
MAID					
HER MAID ANTONIA WHO WAS AN ADEPT	97	2	DON JUAN 1	140	4
BUT JULIA MISTRESS AND ANTONIA MAID	98	2	DON JUAN 1	141	1
CLOSED THE ORATION OF THE TRUSTY MAID	116	2	DON JUAN 1	173	2
THE CHARMS OF MAID WIFE AND STILL LESS OF WIDOW	144	2	DON JUAN 1	216	2
HAD NEVER SEEN THE MAID OR WHATSOE'ER	216	2	DON JUAN 2	115	7
MISTRESS AND MAID THE FIRST WAS ONLY DAUGHTER	222	2	DON JUAN 2	124	7
AND THEREFORE WITH HER MAID SHE THOUGHT IT BEST	225	2	DON JUAN 2	131	1
(A VIRGIN ALWAYS ON HER MAID RELIES)	225	2	DON JUAN 2	131	2
SHE AND HER MAID AND PROMISED BY DAY-BREAK	226	2	DON JUAN 2	133	6
YOUNG JUAN SLEPT ALL DREAMLESS--BUT THE MAID	228	2	DON JUAN 2	135	1
AND WOKE HER MAID SO EARLY THAT SHE GRUMBLED	229	2	DON JUAN 2	138	5
OR PERILS BY A LOVING MAID INCURR'D	257	2	DON JUAN 2	190	4
I'LL JUST INQUIRE IF SHE BE WIFE OR MAID	268	2	DON JUAN 2	210	5
BUT GAZING ON EACH GLOWING MAID	326	2	DON JUAN 3	L 15	4
HER MOTHER WAS A MOORISH MAID FROM FEZ	373	2	DON JUAN 4	54	7
BUT MANY A GREEK MAID IN A LOVING SONG	383	2	DON JUAN 4	73	1
I MOURN BUT FOR THE PAST--I LOVED A MAID	420	2	DON JUAN 5	18	2
HE LOOKED IN ALMOST ALL RESPECTS A MAID	458	2	DON JUAN 5	80	3
HE LOOKED--IN ALL SAVE MODESTY--A MAID	458	2	DON JUAN 5	80	V3
ONE'S TURNED HALF MUSSULMAN AND ONE A MAID	459	2	DON JUAN 5	83	7
NAY QUOTH THE MAID THE SULTAN'S SELF SHAN'T CARRY ME	460	2	DON JUAN 5	84	7
IN EARLY YOUTH TO TURN A LADY'S MAID--	37	3	DON JUAN 6	62	4
OR WIDOW MAID OR MOTHER SHE CAN CHANGE HER	214	3	DON JUAN 9	64	5
LIVE ANIMALS AN OLD MAID OF THREESCORE	249	3	DON JUAN 10	50	6
ALTHOUGH HE WAS NOT OLD NOR EVEN A MAID--	249	3	DON JUAN 10	50	8
A TRACE UNWORTHY EITHER WIFE OR MAID--	372	3	DON JUAN 13	32	5
MAIDENHEADS					
ELEVEN THOUSAND MAIDENHEADS OF BONE	255	3	DON JUAN 10	62	7
MAIDEN-LIKE					
PACED ON MOST MAIDEN-LIKE AND MELANCHOLY	22	3	DON JUAN 6	33	8
MAIDENLY					
SMOOTH SPEECH HIS FIRST AND MAIDENLY TRANSGRESSION	400	3	DON JUAN 13	90	4
MAID'S					
BUT AS MY MAID'S UNDREST PRAY TURN YOUR SPIES OUT	104	2	DON JUAN 1	152	7
BESIDES HER MAID'S AS PRETTY FOR THEIR SIZE	246	2	DON JUAN 2	171	4
MAIDS					
HER MAIDS WERE OLD AND IF SHE TOOK A NEW ONE	48	2	DON JUAN 1	48	5
LIGHTS CAME AT LENGTH AND MEN AND MAIDS WHO FOUND	125	2	DON JUAN 1	187	1
HER FIFTH TO CALL HER MAIDS AND GO TO BED	491	2	DON JUAN 5	139	5
FOUR WIVES AND TWICE FIVE HUNDRED MAIDS UNSEEN	496	2	DON JUAN 5	148	7
HER TITLE WAS THE MOTHER OF THE MAIDS	21	3	DON JUAN 6	30	8
OR WHETHER THEY WERE MAIDS WHO CALLED HER MOTHER	21	3	DON JUAN 6	31	2
BUT HERE THE MOTHER OF THE MAIDS DREW NEAR	29	3	DON JUAN 6	46	1
MATRONS AND MAIDS AND THOSE WHOM YOU MAY CALL	42	3	DON JUAN 6	71	3
SOME MAIDS HAVE BEEN MADE WIVES SOME MERELY MOTHERS	308	3	DON JUAN 11	81	4
MAIL					
IN MAIL OF PROOF--HER PURITY OF SOUL	66	2	DON JUAN 1	82	2
WITH THE YORK MAIL--BUT ONWARD AS WE ROLL	263	3	DON JUAN 10	78	7
BY DRIVING THE YORK MAIL--BUT AH MY SINKING SOUL	263	3	DON JUAN 10	78	V7
MAILS					
THERE MAILS FAST FLYING OFF LIKE A DELUSION	278	3	DON JUAN 11	22	4
MAIMED					
AND LEFT HIM 'MIDST THE INVALID AND MAIMED	154	3	DON JUAN 8	85	4
MAIN					
BOTH MAIN AND MIZEN FIRST THE MIZEN WENT	173	2	DON JUAN 2	32	2
BUT TO THE MAIN POINT WHERE WE HAVE BEEN TENDING--	478	2	DON JUAN 5	116	1
AND TRIED TO MAKE A LANDING ON THE MAIN	82	3	DON JUAN 7	31	5

MAIN   (CONTINUED)

	PAGE	VOL	CANTO		STANZA	LN
AND FOUGHT AWAY WITH MIGHT AND MAIN NOT KNOWING	120	3	DON JUAN	8	19	2
BETWEEN THESE NATIONS AS A MAIN OF COCKS	197	3	DON JUAN	9	29	7
BETWEEN YOUR TURK AND RUSSIAN AS A MAIN	197	3	DON JUAN	9	29	V7
AS AN EAST INDIAN SUNRISE ON THE MAIN	212	3	DON JUAN	9	59	4
MAKE LOVE THE MAIN SPRING OF THE UNIVERSE	219	3	DON JUAN	9	73	8

MAINMAST

	PAGE	VOL	CANTO		STANZA	LN
THE MAINMAST FOLLOW'D BUT THE SHIP STILL LAY	173	2	DON JUAN	2	32	3

MAINOTS

	PAGE	VOL	CANTO		STANZA	LN
AMONG HIS FRIENDS THE MAINOTS SOME HE SOLD	284	2	DON JUAN	3	16	2

MAINTAIN

	PAGE	VOL	CANTO		STANZA	LN
FOR I MAINTAIN THAT IT IS REALLY GOOD	193	3	DON JUAN	9	22	2
MAINTAIN THOU ART THE BEST FOR AFTER ALL	210	3	DON JUAN	9	56	2
OTHERS AGAIN WERE READY TO MAINTAIN	244	3	DON JUAN	10	40	7

MAINTAINED

	PAGE	VOL	CANTO		STANZA	LN
MAINTAINED AT THE EXPENSE OF YOUR GOOD KING	118	3	DON JUAN	8	14	3
MAINTAINED WITH ALL THE DUE PREVARICATION	246	3	DON JUAN	10	45	4

MAINTENANCE

	PAGE	VOL	CANTO		STANZA	LN
THAT JUAN HAD ENOUGH OF MAINTENANCE	473	3	DON JUAN	15	39	2
OR SEPARATE MAINTENANCE IN CASE 'TWAS DOOM'D--	473	3	DON JUAN	15	39	3

MAJESTIC

	PAGE	VOL	CANTO		STANZA	LN
HER SWEET SMILE AND HER THEN MAJESTIC FIGURE	218	3	DON JUAN	9	72	1

MAJESTICALLY

	PAGE	VOL	CANTO		STANZA	LN
HIS SOBER HEAD MAJESTICALLY TAME	292	2	DON JUAN	3	32	5

MAJESTY

	PAGE	VOL	CANTO		STANZA	LN
AND MUST HAVE COST HIS MAJESTY A TREASURE	85	2	DON JUAN	1	118	4
THAT SOMEWHAT MANLY MAJESTY OF STRIDE	464	2	DON JUAN	5	91	4
HIS MAJESTY WAS ALWAYS SO POLITE	495	2	DON JUAN	5	146	4
HIS MAJESTY SALUTED HIS FOURTH SPOUSE	500	2	DON JUAN	5	154	1
OH MAHOMET THAT HIS MAJESTY SHOULD TAKE	501	2	DON JUAN	5	156	4
EXCEPT HIS MAJESTY WHO WITH HER AID	22	3	DON JUAN	6	32	3
SINCE FIRST HER MAJESTY WAS SINGLY CROWNED	205	3	DON JUAN	9	46	6
OR ON MIGHT DREAD HER MAJESTY HAD NOT ROOM ENOUGH	206	3	DON JUAN	9	48	3
HER MAJESTY WHO LIKED TO GAZE ON YOUTH	213	3	DON JUAN	9	61	6
AND SOME SUCH VISIONS CROSSED HER MAJESTY	215	3	DON JUAN	9	66	3
HER MAJESTY LOOKED DOWN THE YOUTH LOOKED UP--	216	3	DON JUAN	9	67	1
AN ORDER FROM HER MAJESTY CONSIGNED	224	3	DON JUAN	9	84	1
KISS HANDS FEET ANY PART OF MAJESTY	286	3	DON JUAN	11	38	6

MAJOR

	PAGE	VOL	CANTO		STANZA	LN
THE MAJOR PART OF SUCH APPELLANTS GO	14	2	DON JUAN	D	9	7
THE MAJOR PART OF THEM HAD LONG BEEN WIVED	96	2	DON JUAN	1	138	3

MAJORA

	PAGE	VOL	CANTO		STANZA	LN
PAULO MAJORA JUAN UNDECIDED	327	3	DON JUAN	12	25	2

MAKE

	PAGE	VOL	CANTO		STANZA	LN
COULD NEVER MAKE A MEMORY SO FINE AS	27	2	DON JUAN	1	11	7
WERE FORCED TO MAKE AN ODD SORT OF APOLOGY	44	2	DON JUAN	1	41	7
WHICH MAKE THE READER ENVY HIS TRANSGRESSIONS	47	2	DON JUAN	1	47	8
THESE FEW SHORT YEARS MAKE WOND'ROUS ALTERATIONS	59	2	DON JUAN	1	69	7
SHE FELT IT GOING AND RESOLVED TO MAKE	62	2	DON JUAN	1	75	2
I RECOMMEND YOUNG LADIES TO MAKE TRIAL	64	2	DON JUAN	1	78	8
THEY MAKE SOME BLUNDER WHICH THEIR LADIES TELL US	74	2	DON JUAN	1	98	8
THEY MAKE YOU DREAD THAT THEY'LL RECITE THEM TOO	79	2	DON JUAN	1	108	4
I MAKE A RESOLUTION EVERY SPRING	85	2	DON JUAN	1	119	3
WHICH SOME IRREGULARITY MAY MAKE	86	2	DON JUAN	1	120	5
AND MAKE NO FURTHER NOISE TILL YOU DISCOVER	104	2	DON JUAN	1	153	6
PRAY HAVE THE COURTESY TO MAKE IT KNOWN	105	2	DON JUAN	1	154	3
OF TWENTY-FIVE OR THIRTY--(COME MAKE HASTE)	115	2	DON JUAN	1	172	2
A TEAR OR TWO AND THEN WE MAKE IT UP	119	2	DON JUAN	1	179	7
SHOULD CAPTAINS THE REMARK OR CRITICS MAKE	141	2	DON JUAN	1	208	7
CAN MAKE THE FOOL OF WHICH THEY MADE BEFORE	144	2	DON JUAN	1	216	3
AND LIVE AND DIE MAKE LOVE AND PAY OUR TAXES	159	2	DON JUAN	2	4	3
THEIR VERY WALK WOULD MAKE YOUR BOSOM SWELL	159	2	DON JUAN	2	5	6
BUT FOR THE PUMPS I'M GLAD TO MAKE THEM KNOWN	171	2	DON JUAN	2	29	4
SHORT UPPER LIP--SWEET LIPS THAT MAKE US SIGH	218	2	DON JUAN	2	118	3
FOR HAIDEE STRIPP'D HER SABLES OFF TO MAKE	226	2	DON JUAN	2	133	2
TO MAKE THE CRETANS BLOODIER IN BATTLE	238	2	DON JUAN	2	155	8
SAYING HE HAD GORGED ENOUGH TO MAKE A HORSE ILL	240	2	DON JUAN	2	159	8
SAVE ON THE DEAD LONG SUMMER DAYS WHICH MAKE	249	2	DON JUAN	2	177	7
TO MAKE US UNDERSTAND EACH GOOD OLD MAXIM	264	2	DON JUAN	2	203	7
WHICH MAKE THE ENGLISH CLIMATE OF OUR YEARS	270	2	DON JUAN	2	214	8
AND LAYING DOWN MY PEN I MAKE MY BOW	271	2	DON JUAN	2	216	6
UNLESS PHILOSOPHY CAN MAKE A JULIET	272	2	DON JUAN	2	V 1	2
FOR ANY LENGTH--CONTRIVED TO MAKE EACH OTHER CEASE	277	2	DON JUAN	3	5	V4
YET LOVE MAY MAKE MARRIAGE AS GOOD WHITE WINE	277	2	DON JUAN	3	5	V5
OF CHARMS TO MAKE GOOD GOLD AND CURE BAD AILS	293	2	DON JUAN	3	34	5
AND MAKE HIM SAMSONLIKE--MORE FIERCE WITH BLINDNESS	304	2	DON JUAN	3	57	V8
THE HENNA SHOULD BE DEEPLY DYED TO MAKE	314	2	DON JUAN	3	76	1
EVEN GOOD MEN LIKE TO MAKE THE PUBLIC STARE--	317	2	DON JUAN	3	81	4
MIGHT FOR LONG LYING MAKE HIMSELF AMENDS	318	2	DON JUAN	3	83	6
IN SPAIN HE'D MAKE A BALLAD OR ROMANCE ON	320	2	DON JUAN	3	86	3
TO MAKE A NEW THERMOPYLAE	323	2	DON JUAN	3	L 7	6
AND MAKE LIKE OTHER NYMPHS THY LOVERS ILL	372	2	DON JUAN	4	53	4
NOTHING COULD MAKE HER MEET HER FATHER'S FACE	381	2	DON JUAN	4	68	2
COULD STIR HIS PULSE OR MAKE HIS FAITH FEEL BRITTLE	396	2	DON JUAN	4	95	7
THEREFORE I'LL MAKE DON JUAN LEAVE THE SHIP SOON	397	2	DON JUAN	4	97	5
OH YE WHO MAKE THE FORTUNES OF ALL BOOKS	403	2	DON JUAN	4	108	1
TO MAKE A MISTRESS OR FOURTH WIFE OR VICTIM	409	2	DON JUAN	4	116	8
AS I WILL MAKE YOU QUICKLY UNDERSTAND	411	2	DON JUAN	5	1	V6
I'LL MAKE THIS POEM QUITE A MORAL MODEL	412	2	DON JUAN	5	2	V8

MAKE (CONTINUED)

	PAGE	VOL		CANTO	STANZA	LN
IN MAKE OF A COMPLEXION WHITE AND RUDDY	416	2	DON JUAN	5	11	2
WHICH SHOULD CONFIRM OR SHAKE OR MAKE A FAITH	431	2	DON JUAN	5	38	8
ARE THINGS WHICH MAKE AN ENGLISH EVENING PASS	444	2	DON JUAN	5	58	4
ON WHICH I CANNOT PAUSE TO MAKE MY STRICTURES	465	2	DON JUAN	5	94	8
WERE RIPE THEY MIGHT MAKE SIX AND TWENTY SPRINGS	468	2	DON JUAN	5	98	2
TO MAKE MEN HAPPY OR TO KEEP THEM SO	470	2	DON JUAN	5	101	3
WE WOULD AGAINST THEM MAKE THE FLESH OBEY--	474	2	DON JUAN	5	110	7
TO LOSE THE HOUR WOULD MAKE HER QUITE A MARTYR	482	2	DON JUAN	5	122	7
MUST MAKE A PRESENT TO HIS SIRE IN LAW	498	2	DON JUAN	5	152	8
YET SHE WOULD MAKE FULL MANY A MANICHEAN	7	3	DON JUAN	6	3	8
AND FOR THEIR RIGHTS CONNUBIAL MAKE A STAND	11	3	DON JUAN	6	11	5
TO MAKE THE NUPTIAL COUCH A BED OF WARE	12	3	DON JUAN	6	12	8
I DOUBT IF ANY NOW COULD MAKE IT WORSE	17	3	DON JUAN	6	23	4
THAN YOU WOULD MAKE THE HALF OF--DON'T SAY NO	29	3	DON JUAN	6	47	5
WITH NOTHING VERY GRAND TO MAKE A RIOT	32	3	DON JUAN	6	53	V4
MORE THAN I HAVE MYSELF OF WHAT COULD MAKE	42	3	DON JUAN	6	71	7
WOULD MAKE US THINK THE MOON IS AT ITS FULL	46	3	DON JUAN	6	80	5
MIGHT MAKE THE MATTER STILL WORSE THAN IT WAS	57	3	DON JUAN	6	103	8
UNLESS TO MAKE THEIR KETTLE DRUMS A NEW SKIN	75	3	DON JUAN	7	17	6
MAY MAKE UP FOR A BULLET IN HIS BODY	77	3	DON JUAN	7	21	3
HOW PEACE SHOULD MAKE JOHN BULL THE FRENCHMAN'S FOE	77	3	DON JUAN	7	22	8
AND TRIED TO MAKE A LANDING ON THE MAIN	82	3	DON JUAN	7	31	5
WHEN STARS AND WHORES AND DESPOTS COULD MAKE GREAT	84	3	DON JUAN	7	37	V2
THOUGH THEY MAY MAKE CORRUPTION GAPE OR STARE	114	3	DON JUAN	8	4	6
SPARE OR SMITE RARELY--MAN'S MAKE MILLIONS ASHES	115	3	DON JUAN	8	6	8
LIKE HAIL TO MAKE A BLOODY DIURETIC	117	3	DON JUAN	8	12	3
HALF-PAY FOR LIFE MAKE MANKIND WORTH DESTROYING	118	3	DON JUAN	8	14	8
PERHAPS MIGHT MAKE HIM SHIVER YAWN OR THROW	121	3	DON JUAN	8	21	5
AND LEFT AT LARGE LIKE A YOUNG HEIR TO MAKE	127	3	DON JUAN	8	32	2
WILL OFTENTIMES MAKE DEADLY QUARRELS BURST	136	3	DON JUAN	8	48	3
CORRUPTION COULD NOT MAKE THEIR HEARTS HER SOIL	145	3	DON JUAN	8	67	4
TO MAKE HIM PRISONER WAS ALSO DISHED	152	3	DON JUAN	8	80	8
MAKE EPIC POESY SO RARE AND RICH	156	3	DON JUAN	8	90	8
WHO MAKE THE BEDS OF THOSE WHO WON'T TAKE QUARTER	167	3	DON JUAN	8	111	5
THESE BLACK-EYED VIRGINS MAKE THE MOSLEMS FIGHT	168	3	DON JUAN	8	114	5
TO MAKE A ROMAN SORT OF SABINE WEDDING	177	3	DON JUAN	8	131	7
INCREASES TILL YOU SHALL MAKE COMMON CAUSE	196	3	DON JUAN	9	28	6
SEEING HOW ART CAN MAKE HER WORK MORE GRAND	204	3	DON JUAN	9	44	5
THAN SOME WIVES (WHO MAKE BLUNDERS NO LESS STUPID)	205	3	DON JUAN	9	45	7
ALL FIT TO MAKE A PATAGONIAN JEALOUS	205	3	DON JUAN	9	46	8
TO MAKE A TWILIGHT IN JUST AS SOLMS HEAT IS	217	3	DON JUAN	9	69	7
ENOUGH TO MAKE A STRIPLING VERY VAIN	218	3	DON JUAN	9	72	8
MAKE LOVE THE MAIN SPRING OF THE UNIVERSE	219	3	DON JUAN	9	73	8
WHICH MAKE ALL BODIES ANXIOUS TO GET OUT	220	3	DON JUAN	9	75	2
LOVE HAD MADE CATHERINE MAKE EACH LOVER'S FORTUNE	222	3	DON JUAN	9	81	1
SUCH DIFFERENCE DOTH A FEW MONTHS MAKE YOU'D THINK	228	3	DON JUAN	10	7	5
AND I KNOW NOTHING WHICH COULD MAKE AMENDS	231	3	DON JUAN	10	12	3
TO MAKE SUCH PUPPETS OF US THINGS BELOW)	232	3	DON JUAN	10	16	4
MAKE SOME PREFER THE CIRCULATING MEDIUM	235	3	DON JUAN	10	22	8
OF FRAIL HUMANITY--MUST MAKE US SELFISH	236	3	DON JUAN	10	23	7
MAKE MY SOUL PASS THE EQUINOCTIAL LINE	255	3	DON JUAN	10	61	6
UNLESS YOU MAKE THEIR BETTERS BETTER--FIE	267	3	DON JUAN	10	85	7
WHAT A SUBLIME DISCOVERY 'TWAS TO MAKE THE	269	3	DON JUAN	11	2	1
WHICH MAKE US WISH OURSELVES IN TOWN AT ONCE--	277	3	DON JUAN	11	20	8
MAKE THIS A SACRED PART OF ALBION'S ISLE	279	3	DON JUAN	11	24	8
(THAT MAKE OLD EUROPE'S JOURNALS SQUEAK AND GIBBER ALL)	318	3	DON JUAN	12	5	4
OR PLEASURE WHO MAKE POLITICS RUN GLIBBER ALL	318	3	DON JUAN	12	5	6
BUT THESE ARE FEW AND IN THE END THEY MAKE	328	3	DON JUAN	12	26	1
TO MAKE HIS LITTLE WILD ASIATIC TAME	336	3	DON JUAN	12	42	6
OR WISH TO MAKE A RIVAL'S BOSOM BLEED	351	3	DON JUAN	12	77	6
RESERVE AND PRIDE COULD MAKE HIM AND FULL SLOW	366	3	DON JUAN	13	16	2
OF COMMON LIKINGS WHICH MAKE SOME DEPLORE	366	3	DON JUAN	13	17	6
'TWILL MAKE IF PROVED VAST EFFORTS WITHOUT PAINING	366	3	DON JUAN	13	18	8
ENOUGH TO MAKE FOR PORT ERE TIME SHALL SUMMON	376	3	DON JUAN	13	40	4
AND MAKE A MUSIC WHETHER FLAT OR SHARP	402	3	DON JUAN	13	93	4
BUT TAKE AN ELL--AND MAKE A GREAT SENSATION	404	3	DON JUAN	13	98	5
THE MIDDLE-AGED TO MAKE THE DAY MORE SHORT	405	3	DON JUAN	13	101	4
TO MAKE EACH CORRESPONDENT A NEW DEBTOR	406	3	DON JUAN	13	104	8
AND THEN EVEN THEN SOME BORE MAY MAKE THEM LOSE IT	408	3	DON JUAN	13	109	8
IS DIFFICULT PRAY TELL ME CAN YOU MAKE FAST	411	3	DON JUAN	14	2	3
WHY DRINK WHY READ--TO MAKE SOME HOUR LESS DREARY	415	3	DON JUAN	14	11	4
HE NE'ER PRESUMED TO MAKE AN ERROR CLEARER--	426	3	DON JUAN	14	37	7
WOULD MAKE INDEED SOME MELANCHOLY MIRTH	436	3	DON JUAN	14	59	6
THAT LIKE TO MAKE A QUARREL WHEN THEY CAN'T	438	3	DON JUAN	14	63	5
OR MAKE A WERTER OF HIM IN THE END	438	3	DON JUAN	14	64	2
IN SUCH GUISE THAT SHE COULD MAKE NOTHING OF IT	438	3	DON JUAN	14	65	8
AND SUCH I MEAN TO MAKE HIM WHEN I REIGN	440	3	DON JUAN	14	70	8
I WILL NOT MAKE HIS GREAT DESCRIPTION LESS	442	3	DON JUAN	14	75	3
SOME HOURS TO MAKE THE REMNANT WORTH ENJOYING	444	3	DON JUAN	14	78	8
THEY'LL ONLY MAKE MISTAKES ABOUT THE FAIR	454	3	DON JUAN	14	99	3
SO AS TO MAKE THEM FEEL HE KNEW HIS STATION	462	3	DON JUAN	15	15	6
THEY PLEASED OR TAKE HIM FOR AND THEIR	463	3	DON JUAN	15	16	2
I MEANT TO MAKE THIS POEM VERY SHORT	466	3	DON JUAN	15	22	8
MEN MADE THE MANNERS MANNERS NOW MAKE MEN--	468	3	DON JUAN	15	26	2
WE'LL DO OUR BEST TO MAKE THE BEST ON'T--MARCH	468	3	DON JUAN	15	27	1
ALL WHICH I USE TO MAKE MY RHYMES RUN GLIBBER	487	3	DON JUAN	15	71	3
THAT HE WOULD RATHER MAKE THEM MORE THAN LESS	491	3	DON JUAN	15	80	4
MAKE MORE IMPRESSION THAN THE BEST OF BOOKS	493	3	DON JUAN	15	84	8

MAKE   (CONTINUED)
```
    AND THESE DISSENTIONS MAKE A SORRY SIGHT . . . . . . .  496   3 DON JUAN 15     90   V4
    BUT I'M TOO LATE AND THEREFORE MUST MAKE PLAY  . . . . .  538   3 DON JUAN 16     78    1
    AND MAKE THE WORLDING SNEER THE YOUNGLING WEEP . . . . .  555   3 DON JUAN 16    110    8
    SURPRISE HAS THIS EFFECT--TO MAKE ONE DUMB . . . . . . .  557   3 DON JUAN 16    115    2
    AS FAR AS WORDS MAKE RULES--OUR COMMON NOTION  . . . . .  563   3 DON JUAN 17      3    2
    JUST AS I MAKE MY MIND UP EVERY DAY  . . . . . . .  566   3 DON JUAN 17     10    6
MAKER
    BUT FOR THE MAKER MR MANN OF LONDON   . . . . . . .  171   2 DON JUAN  2     29    8
MAKERS
    TAKERS OF TITHES AND MAKERS OF GOOD MATCHES . . . . . .  539   3 DON JUAN 16     80    7
MAKES
    WHICH MAKES ME WISH YOU'D CHANGE YOUR LAKES FOR OCEAN . .   12   2 DON JUAN  D      5    8
    AND MAKES THE WORD MILTONIC MEAN SUBLIME . . . . . . .   15   2 DON JUAN  D     10    4
    (HORACE MAKES THIS THE HEROIC TURNPIKE ROAD) . . . . .   24   2 DON JUAN  1      6    2
    A QUIET CONSCIENCE MAKES ONE SO SERENE . . . . . . .   66   2 DON JUAN  1     83    6
    MAN'S A STRANGE ANIMAL AND MAKES STRANGE USE . . . . .   91   2 DON JUAN  1    128    1
    ONE MAKES NEW NOSES ONE A GUILLOTINE . . . . . . .   91   2 DON JUAN  1    129    3
    THERE MIGHT BE ONE MORE MOTIVE WHICH MAKES TWO . . . . .  118   2 DON JUAN  1    177    1
    WHICH MAKES SO MANY POETS AND SOME FOOLS . . . . . .  136   2 DON JUAN  1    201    4
    FLIES IN ONE'S FACE AND MAKES IT WEATHER-TOUGH . . . . .  162   2 DON JUAN  2     11    6
    AND MAKES MEN'S MISERIES OF ALARMING BREVITY . . . . .  190   2 DON JUAN  2     64    8
    WITH SOME PRETENCE ABOUT THE SUN THAT MAKES . . . . . .  230   2 DON JUAN  2    139    2
    WHICH MAKES IT FATAL TO BE LOVED AH WHY  . . . . . . .  275   2 DON JUAN  3      2    2
    SQUEEZED THROUGH THE RIND WHICH MAKES IT BEST FOR USE . .  307   2 DON JUAN  3     62    8
    THAT WHICH MAKES THOUSANDS PERHAPS MILLIONS THINK . . . .  327   2 DON JUAN  3     88    3
    AND GLORY MAKES THE SAGES OFTEN SO SMILE . . . . . . .  328   2 DON JUAN  3     90   V1
    OF OCEAN--NO OF AIR AND THEN HE MAKES . . . . . . .  333   2 DON JUAN  3     98    6
    AS THE FAR BELL OF VESPER MAKES HIM START . . . . . .  338   2 DON JUAN  3    108    5
    WHICH MAKES NOT OTHERS SMILE THEN TURN'D ASIDE . . . . .  356   2 DON JUAN  4     23    2
    WITH HER SIRE'S STORY MAKES THE NIGHT LESS LONG . . . .  383   2 DON JUAN  4     73    3
    FROM ALL THE POPE MAKES YEARLY 'TWOULD PERPLEX . . . . .  391   2 DON JUAN  4     86    7
    MAKES US FEEL OUR MORTALITY IN FACT  . . . . . . .  428   2 DON JUAN  5     32    3
    ALAS MAN MAKES THAT GREAT WHICH MAKES HIM LITTLE . . . .  444   2 DON JUAN  5     59    1
    ALAS MAN MAKES THAT GREAT WHICH MAKES HIM LITTLE . . . .  444   2 DON JUAN  5     59    1
    WHOSE SMILE MAKES ALL THE PLANETS DANCE WITH MIRTH . . .  494   2 DON JUAN  5    144    4
    AND MAKES OUR SNOW LESS PURE THAN OUR MORALITY . . . . .  501   2 DON JUAN  5    157    6
    IN THAT TO WHICH THE LAW MAKES THEM SOLE HEIRS . . . . .   11   3 DON JUAN  6     10    8
    THUS THE SAME CAUSE WHICH MAKES A VERSE WANT FEET . . . .   79   3 DON JUAN  7     26    3
    MAKES THAT OF MULTITUDES TAKE ONE DIRECTION . . . . . .   90   3 DON JUAN  7     48    2
    HER INWARD GRACE FOR OUTWARD SHOW AND MAKES . . . . . .   96   3 DON JUAN  7     57    7
    UNTIL THEIR VERY NUMBER MAKES MEN HARD . . . . . . .  118   3 DON JUAN  8     13    2
    MAKES MEN LIKE CATTLE FOLLOW HIM WHO LEADS . . . . . .  132   3 DON JUAN  8     38    8
    THAT DAILY SHILLING WHICH MAKES WARRIORS TOUGH)-- . . . .  134   3 DON JUAN  8     42    6
    SNATCH WHEN DESPAIR MAKES HUMAN HEARTS LESS PLIANT . . .  138   3 DON JUAN  8     51    4
    WHICH MAKES ALL STYX THROUGH ONE SMALL LIVER FLOW . . . .  190   3 DON JUAN  9     15    5
    MAKES MOUNTAINS PASSABLE AND BY HEAVEN'S BLESSING . . . .  215   3 DON JUAN  9     66   V7
    WHICH MAKES ONE DRUNK AT ONCE WITHOUT THE BASE . . . . .  216   3 DON JUAN  9     67    6
    MAKES US BELIEVE OURSELVES AS GOOD AS ANY  . . . . . .  216   3 DON JUAN  9     68    8
    WHICH MAKES ALL FEMALE AGES EQUAL--WHEN  . . . . . . .  217   3 DON JUAN  9     69    2
    AND 'GAINST THE BODY MAKES A STRONG APPEAL . . . . . .  234   3 DON JUAN 10     20    5
    A GREEN FIELD IS A SIGHT WHICH MAKES HIM PARDON . . . .  262   3 DON JUAN 10     76    5
    AND ON OUR SOPHAS MAKES US LIE DEJECTED  . . . . . . .  301   3 DON JUAN 11     65    5
    MAKES ONE IN LOVE EVEN WITH ITS VERY FAULTS  . . . . .  302   3 DON JUAN 11     68    4
    LOVE OR LUST MAKES MAN SICK AND WINE MUCH SICKER . . . .  317   3 DON JUAN 12      4    1
    WHICH MAKES BANK CREDIT LIKE A BARK OF VAPOUR  . . . . .  317   3 DON JUAN 12      4    8
    EVEN WITH THE VERY ORE WHICH MAKES THEM BASE   . . . . .  320   3 DON JUAN 12     10    6
    IN FACT THERE'S NOTHING MAKES ME SO MUCH GRIEVE . . . .  336   3 DON JUAN 12     43    6
    A WIFE MAKES OR TAKES LOVE IN UPRIGHT EARNEST . . . . .  345   3 DON JUAN 12     64    4
    'TIS NOT MERE SPLENDOUR MAKES THE SHOW AUGUST  . . . . .  354   3 DON JUAN 12     83    7
    BECAUSE IT MAKES US SMILE HIS HERO'S RIGHT . . . . . .  363   3 DON JUAN 13      9    2
    HIS GUERDON 'TIS HIS VIRTUE MAKES HIM MAD  . . . . . .  363   3 DON JUAN 13      9    5
    HIS BELL-MOUTHED GOBLET MAKES ME FEEL QUITE DANISH . . .  392   3 DON JUAN 13     72    7
    WHICH MAKES THE SOUTHERN AUTUMN'S DAY APPEAR   . . . . .  395   3 DON JUAN 13     77    2
    DEATH SO CALL'D IS A THING WHICH MAKES MEN WEEP . . . .  411   3 DON JUAN 14      3    7
    WHICH WITH THE LANDLORD MAKES TOO LONG A STAND . . . . .  435   3 DON JUAN 14     58    2
    WHICH MAKES A DANDY WHILE IT SPOILS A MAN  . . . . . .  461   3 DON JUAN 15     12    8
    'TIS SAID IT MAKES REALITY MORE BEARABLE . . . . . . .  495   3 DON JUAN 15     89    5
    IT MAKES MY BLOOD BOIL LIKE THE SPRINGS OF HECLA . . . .  497   3 DON JUAN 15     92    7
    A SLIGHT REPAST MAKES PEOPLE LOVE MUCH MORE . . . . . .  542   3 DON JUAN 16     86    3
    THIS MAKES YOUR ACTORS ARTISTS AND ROMANCERS   . . . . .  547   3 DON JUAN 16     98    1
MAKING
    CHANGE HORSES MAKING HISTORY CHANGE ITS TUNE   . . . . .   76   2 DON JUAN  1    103    5
    SOME TRIAL HAD BEEN MAKING AT A RAFT . . . . . . .  183   2 DON JUAN  2     50    1
    MAKING THEIR SUMMER LIVES ONE CEASELESS SONG . . . . .  337   2 DON JUAN  3    106    2
    MAKING HER STATURE TALL EVEN TALLER--NEAR  . . . . . .  367   2 DON JUAN  4     43   V5
    MAKING A SIGNAL OFF SOME PROMONTORY  . . . . . . .  389   2 DON JUAN  4     82    3
    HIS PEACE WAS MAKING BUT BEFORE HE VENTURED  . . . . .  493   2 DON JUAN  5    143    7
    THEIR SPLEEN IN MAKING STRIFE AND SAFELY WORDING . . . .  498   2 DON JUAN  5    151    6
    A BAD OLD WOMAN MAKING A WORSE WILL   . . . . . . .   16   3 DON JUAN  6     21    5
    MAKING A WOMAN LIKE A PORCUPINE. . . . . . .   37   3 DON JUAN  6     62    1
    BUT MAKING MONEY SLOWLY FIRST THEN QUICKER . . . . . .  317   3 DON JUAN 12      4    3
    AT MAKING MATCHES WHERE 'TIS GOLD THAT GLISTERS  . . . .  331   3 DON JUAN 12     32    5
    UPON MY LYRE OR MAKING THE PEGS SURE . . . . . . .  341   3 DON JUAN 12     54    7
    IN MAKING MEN WHAT COURTESY CALLS FRIENDS  . . . . . .  365   3 DON JUAN 13     15    8
    FOR MAKING SQUARES AND STREETS ANONYMOUS . . . . . .  370   3 DON JUAN 13     26    2
    MAKING THE COUNTENANCE A MASQUE OF REST  . . . . . .  457   3 DON JUAN 15      3    3
    NEXT TO THE MAKING MATCHES FOR HERSELF . . . . . . .  470   3 DON JUAN 15     31    1
    IN MAKING HIM AS SILENT AS A GHOST . . . . . . . .  553   3 DON JUAN 16    107    2
```

485

	PAGE	VOL		CANTO	STANZA	LN

MAK'ST
THOU MAK'ST THE CHASTE CONNUBIAL STATE PRECARIOUS . . . . 266 2 DON JUAN 2 206 1
THOU MAK'ST PHILOSOPHERS THERE'S EPICURUS . . . . . 267 2 DON JUAN 2 207 1
MALADIES
AGAINST ALL NOBLE MALADIES HE'S BOLD . . . . 168 2 DON JUAN 2 22 5
BOTH MALADIES ARE TAXES ON OUR JOYS . . . . 357 2 DON JUAN 4 25 3
MAL-A-PROPOS
SAVE THAT OF DREAMING ONCE MAL-A-PROPOS . . . . . . 48 3 DON JUAN 6 84 8
MALE
THERE CHANCED TO BE AN ODD MALE AND ODD FEMALE . . . . 394 2 DON JUAN 4 92 2
IF THE SOPRANO MIGHT BE DEEM'D TO BE MALE . . . . . 394 2 DON JUAN 4 92 4
WERE LINK'D TOGETHER AND IT HAPPEN'D THE MALE . . . . 394 2 DON JUAN 4 92 6
BECAUSE THEY ARE SO--A MALE MRS FRY . . . . . 266 3 DON JUAN 10 84 6
HAS CAUSE TO WISH HER SIRE HAD HAD MALE HEIRS . . . . 331 3 DON JUAN 12 33 8
AFTER MALE LOSS OF TIME AND HEARTS AND BETS . . . . 333 3 DON JUAN 12 36 3
FEMALE OR MALE A SCHOOL-BOY OR A QUEEN . . . . . 421 3 DON JUAN 14 25 8
ET BENE DIC NEUTRUM DIC ALIQUANDO MALE . . . . . 465 3 DON JUAN 15 21 2
MALGRE
TO FLY FROM MALGRE ALL WHICH PEOPLE SAY . . . . . 134 3 DON JUAN 8 42 3
WHO FAVOUR MALGRE MALTHUS GENERATION-- . . . . . 472 3 DON JUAN 15 37 2
MALGRE SIR MATTHEW HALES'S GREAT HUMANITY . . . . . 565 3 DON JUAN 17 7 8
MALICE
FOR MALICE STILL IMPUTES SOME PRIVATE END) . . . . . 58 2 DON JUAN 1 66 6
BUT ALWAYS WITHOUT MALICE IF HE WARR'D . . . . . 123 3 DON JUAN 8 25 1
MALICIOUS
HEAVEN KNOWS BUT ADELINE'S MALICIOUS EYES . . . . . 490 3 DON JUAN 15 78 7
MALL
WHICH BEARS THE GREATEST LIKENESS TO PALL MALL . . . . 124 3 DON JUAN 8 26 8
PALL MALL AND SO FORTH HAVE A CORUSCATION . . . . 280 3 DON JUAN 11 26 2
OVER THE STONES STILL RATTLING UP PALL MALL . . . . 282 3 DON JUAN 11 29 1
MALMSBURY
LIKE THOSE OF THE PHILOSOPHER OF MALMSBURY . . . . . 499 3 DON JUAN 15 96 8
MALMSEY
WITH MAUDLIN CLARENCE IN HIS MALMSEY BUTT . . . . . 112 2 DON JUAN 1 166 8
IN PREFERENCE SURE TO CLARENCE' MALMSEY BUTT . . . . 112 2 DON JUAN 1 166 V8
MALT
BY SLAVES ON HORSEBACK--I HAVE SEEN MALT LIQUORS . . . 310 3 DON JUAN 11 85 6
MALTHUS
USEFUL LIKE MALTHUS IN PROMOTING MARRIAGE-- . . . . 282 3 DON JUAN 11 30 7
WITHOUT CASH MALTHUS TELLS YOU TAKE NO BRIDES . . . . 322 3 DON JUAN 12 14 4
MALTHUS AND WILBERFORCE--THE LAST SET FREE . . . . 325 3 DON JUAN 12 20 5
AND MALTHUS DOES THE THING 'GAINST WHICH HE WRITES . . 325 3 DON JUAN 12 20 8
WHO FAVOUR MALGRE MALTHUS GENERATION-- . . . . . 472 3 DON JUAN 15 37 2
HAD ADELINE READ MALTHUS I CAN'T TELL . . . . . 472 3 DON JUAN 15 38 1
MALUS
AND WHAT THE LAWYERS CALL A MALUS ANIMUS . . . . . 37 2 DON JUAN 1 30 5
MAMMA
I CAN'T BUT SAY THAT HIS MAMMA WAS RIGHT . . . . . 48 2 DON JUAN 1 48 2
HERE LOLAH INTERPOSED--MAMMA YOU KNOW . . . . . 29 3 DON JUAN 6 47 1
THE MAMMA MIA'S AND THE AMOR MIO'S . . . . . 523 3 DON JUAN 16 45 3
MAMMOTH'S
AS WE NOW GAZE UPON THE MAMMOTH'S BONES . . . . . 180 3 DON JUAN 8 137 3
MAMMOTHS
AND MAMMOTHS AND YOUR WINGED CROCODILES . . . . . 201 3 DON JUAN 9 38 8
MAN 'MIDST THY MOULDY MAMMOTHS GRAND CULVIER . . . . 250 3 DON JUAN 10 52 4
MAN
THINK'ST THOU COULD HE--THE BLIND OLD MAN--ARISE . . . 15 2 DON JUAN D 11 1
THIS WAS AN EASY MATTER WITH A MAN . . . . 33 2 DON JUAN 1 21 1
I'M A PLAIN MAN AND IN A SINGLE STATION . . . . . 33 2 DON JUAN 1 22 6
THEY LIVED RESPECTABLY AS MAN AND WIFE . . . . . 35 2 DON JUAN 1 26 4
SAVE THAT HER DUTY BOTH TO MAN AND GOD . . . . . 35 2 DON JUAN 1 27 7
YET JOSE WAS AN HONOURABLE MAN . . . . 40 2 DON JUAN 1 35 1
HIM ALMOST MAN BUT SHE FLEW IN A RAGE . . . . . . 51 2 DON JUAN 1 54 5
WEDDED SHE WAS SOME YEARS AND TO A MAN . . . . . 56 2 DON JUAN 1 62 1
A MAN WELL LOOKING FOR HIS YEARS AND WHO . . . . . 57 2 DON JUAN 1 65 2
THAT FLIGHT WAS BASE AND DASTARDLY AND NO MAN . . . . 63 2 DON JUAN 1 77 3
AND IF THE MAN SHOULD ASK 'TIS BUT DENIAL . . . . . 64 2 DON JUAN 1 78 7
AND SO I'D HAVE HER THINK WERE I THE MAN . . . . . 64 2 DON JUAN 1 79 7
OF MAN THE WONDERFUL AND OF THE STARS . . . . . 71 2 DON JUAN 1 92 2
(I HAVE FORGOT THE NUMBER AND THINK NO MAN . . . . . 74 2 DON JUAN 1 98 5
HAD THOUGHT ONE MAN MIGHT BE DETERR'D BY TWO . . . . 98 2 DON JUAN 1 141 4
OH VALIANT MAN WITH SWORD DRAWN AND COCK'D TRIGGER . . 103 2 DON JUAN 1 150 7
WHO IS THE MAN YOU SEARCH FOR HOW D'YE CALL . . . . 105 2 DON JUAN 1 154 4
'TIS WOMAN'S WHOLE EXISTENCE MAN MAY RANGE . . . . 131 2 DON JUAN 1 194 2
TO LIFT OUR FATAL LOVE TO GOD FROM MAN . . . . . 131 2 DON JUAN 1 194 V8
WHAT ARE THE HOPES OF MAN OLD EGYPT'S KING . . . . 146 2 DON JUAN 1 219 1
'TWAS FOR A VOYAGE THAT THE YOUNG MAN WAS MEANT . . . 161 2 DON JUAN 2 8 5
AND THOUGH 'TIS TRUE THAT MAN CAN ONLY DIE ONCE . . . 176 2 DON JUAN 2 39 7
COULD DO NO MORE HE WAS A MAN IN YEARS . . . . . 179 2 DON JUAN 2 43 3
BETTER PERHAPS FOR MAN THAT AN EMBARGO . . . . . 191 2 DON JUAN 2 66 V7
BUT MAN IS A CARNIVOROUS PRODUCTION . . . . . 191 2 DON JUAN 2 67 1
THE SHORE LOOK'D WILD WITHOUT A TRACE OF MAN . . . . 211 2 DON JUAN 2 104 1
OF AN OLD MAN WHO LIVED UPON THE WATER . . . . . 222 2 DON JUAN 2 124 8
BECAUSE THE GOOD OLD MAN HAD SO MUCH NOUS . . . . 225 2 DON JUAN 2 130 5
MAN BEING REASONABLE MUST GET DRUNK . . . . . 250 2 DON JUAN 2 179 1
THEY ARE RIGHT FOR MAN TO MAN SO OFT UNJUST . . . . 263 2 DON JUAN 2 200 1
THEY ARE RIGHT FOR MAN TO MAN SO OFT UNJUST . . . . 263 2 DON JUAN 2 200 1
ONE MAN ALONE AT FIRST HER HEART CAN MOVE . . . . 276 2 DON JUAN 3 3 6
TO HIS TUNIS CORRESPONDENTS SAVE ONE MAN . . . . . 284 2 DON JUAN 3 16 3

MAN   (CONTINUED)

	PAGE	VOL	CANTO	STANZA	LN
AH WHAT IS MAN WHAT PERILS STILL ENVIRON	294	2	DON JUAN	3	36	1
HE--BEING A MAN WHO SELDOM USED A WORD	294	2	DON JUAN	3	37	1
YOU'RE WRONG--HE WAS THE MILDEST MANNER'D MAN	296	2	DON JUAN	3	41	1
I SAID THAT LAMBRO WAS A MAN OF PATIENCE	299	2	DON JUAN	3	46	1
HE WAS A MAN OF A STRANGE TEMPERAMENT	302	2	DON JUAN	3	53	1
HE WAS A MAN WHO HAD SEEN MANY CHANGES	317	2	DON JUAN	3	80	1
THE LESBIAN SAPPHO AND THE BLIND OLD MAN	320	2	DON JUAN	3	L 1	V2
'TIS STRANGE THE SHORTEST LETTER WHICH MAN USES	327	2	DON JUAN	3	88	4
FRAIL MAN WHEN PAPER--EVEN A RAG LIKE THIS	327	2	DON JUAN	3	88	7
MORE THAN SUCH MADMEN'S FELLOW MAN--THE MOON'S	341	2	DON JUAN	3	110	4
MAN--AND AS WE WOULD HOPE--PERHAPS THE DEVIL	345	2	DON JUAN	4	2	3
PUT UP YOUNG MAN PUT UP YOUR SILLY SWORD	364	2	DON JUAN	4	37	8
HIGH AND INSCRUTABLE THE OLD MAN STOOD	365	2	DON JUAN	4	39	1
YOUNG MAN YOUR SWORD SO LAMBRO ONCE MORE SAID	365	2	DON JUAN	4	40	1
HIS MAN WAS FLOOR'D AND HELPLESS AT HIS FOOT	370	2	DON JUAN	4	49	5
HIS MAN WAS PROSTRATE BLEEDING AT HIS FOOT	370	2	DON JUAN	4	49	V5
AND AS THE SOIL IS SO THE HEART OF MAN	373	2	DON JUAN	4	55	8
YOU'VE HEARD OF RAUCOCANTI--I'M THE MAN	392	2	DON JUAN	4	88	5
LADY TO LADY WELL AS MAN TO MAN	393	2	DON JUAN	4	91	6
LADY TO LADY WELL AS MAN TO MAN	393	2	DON JUAN	4	91	6
THAT HE A MAN OF RANK AND BIRTH HAD BEEN	415	2	DON JUAN	5	9	V6
A MAN OF THIRTY RATHER STOUT AND HALE	416	2	DON JUAN	5	10	6
REPLIED THE OTHER WHAT CAN A MAN DO	421	2	DON JUAN	5	21	2
HE'S WRONG--UNLESS MAN WERE A PIG INDEED	427	2	DON JUAN	5	31	3
THE MAN WAS GONE IN SOME ITALIAN QUARREL	429	2	DON JUAN	5	34	7
ALAS MAN MAKES THAT GREAT WHICH MAKES HIM LITTLE	444	2	DON JUAN	5	59	1
HIS HIGHNESS WAS A MAN OF SOLEMN PORT	495	2	DON JUAN	5	147	1
INTO THAT MORAL CENTAUR MAN AND WIFE	502	2	DON JUAN	5	158	8
MAN WITH HIS HEAD REFLECTS--(AS SPURZHEIM TELLS)	7	3	DON JUAN	6	2	V7
SELF-LOVE IN MAN TOO BEATS ALL FEMALE ART	15	3	DON JUAN	6	19	5
I'VE RARELY SEEN THE MAN THEY DID NOT FRET	16	3	DON JUAN	6	21	8
OF ONE GOOD MAN WITH STATELY MARCH AND SLOW	22	3	DON JUAN	6	33	5
INDEED ON ANY OTHER AS A MAN	51	3	DON JUAN	6	91	2
TO CALL A MAN A WHORESON--OR TO SAY	53	3	DON JUAN	6	94	V1
EACH MAN OF WISDOM FUTURE PAST OR PRESENT	69	3	DON JUAN	7	5	4
THERE WAS A MAN IF THAT HE WAS A MAN	84	3	DON JUAN	7	36	1
THERE WAS A MAN IF THAT HE WAS A MAN	84	3	DON JUAN	7	36	1
LET THERE BE BLOOD SAYS MAN AND THERE'S A SEA	86	3	DON JUAN	7	41	2
AND WHY BECAUSE A LITTLE--ODD--OLD MAN	90	3	DON JUAN	7	49	7
FOR THE MAN WAS WE SAFELY MAY ASSERT	95	3	DON JUAN	7	55	3
IS NEITHER MAN NOR WOMAN THE CHIEF THREW ON	97	3	DON JUAN	7	60	3
TO SEE AN OLD MAN RATHER WILD THAN WISE	104	3	DON JUAN	7	73	5
ARE THINGS IMMORTAL TO IMMORTAL MAN	108	3	DON JUAN	7	84	2
IN THE DESPATCH I KNEW A MAN WHOSE LOSS	120	3	DON JUAN	8	18	7
MAN QUITE AS QUIETLY AS BLOWS THE MONSOON	132	3	DON JUAN	8	39	5
THE MAN IN ALL THE REST MIGHT BE CONFEST	139	3	DON JUAN	8	53	3
GOD MADE THE COUNTRY AND MAN MADE THE TOWN	142	3	DON JUAN	8	60	2
OF NATURE OR THE MAN OF ROSS RUN WILD	144	3	DON JUAN	8	63	8
BUT WHERE HE MET THE INDIVIDUAL MAN	144	3	DON JUAN	8	64	7
THE BREATH OF MORN AND MAN WHERE FOOT BY FOOT	146	3	DON JUAN	8	69	7
THIS VALIANT MAN KILLED ALL THE TURKS HE MET	150	3	DON JUAN	8	77	1
AND SUCH IS VICTORY AND SUCH IS MAN	163	3	DON JUAN	8	104	1
NEITHER--BUT A GOOD PLAIN OLD TEMPERATE MAN	164	3	DON JUAN	8	105	7
BUT DOUBTLESS THEY PREFER A FINE YOUNG MAN	167	3	DON JUAN	8	112	3
OF CARNAGE WHEN THIS OLD MAN WAS PIERCED THROUGH	171	3	DON JUAN	8	119	3
CHILD OR AN AGED HELPLESS MAN OF TWO--	174	3	DON JUAN	8	124	4
BUT THOUGH YOUR YEARS AS MAN TEND FAST TO ZERO	184	3	DON JUAN	9	2	7
I DON'T MEAN TO REFLECT--A MAN SO GREAT AS	186	3	DON JUAN	9	7	1
NEVER HAD MORTAL MAN SUCH OPPORTUNITY	187	3	DON JUAN	9	9	1
HE STRIPS FROM MAN THAT MANTLE (FAR MORE DEAR	188	3	DON JUAN	9	12	6
THAT ALL IS DUBIOUS WHICH MAN MAY ATTAIN	191	3	DON JUAN	9	17	3
OH THOU TOO MORTAL MAN WHAT IS PHILANTHROPY	192	3	DON JUAN	9	20	2
THERE LURKED A MAN BENEATH THE SPIRIT'S DRESS	206	3	DON JUAN	9	47	6
IN THY PERENNIAL FOUNTAIN--HOW MAN FELL I	210	3	DON JUAN	9	55	5
A MAN AS GILES SAYS FOR THOUGH SHE WOULD WIDOW ALL	214	3	DON JUAN	9	63	7
NATIONS SHE LIKED MAN AS AN INDIVIDUAL	214	3	DON JUAN	9	63	8
WHAT A STRANGE THING IS MAN AND WHAT A STRANGER	214	3	DON JUAN	9	64	1
INQUIRED WHO WAS THIS VERY NEW YOUNG MAN	222	3	DON JUAN	9	79	2
ROUND THE YOUNG MAN WITH THEIR CONGRATULATIONS	223	3	DON JUAN	9	82	4
MAN FELL WITH APPLES AND WITH APPLES ROSE	226	3	DON JUAN	10	2	1
FOR EVER SINCE IMMORTAL MAN HATH GLOWED	226	3	DON JUAN	10	2	6
MAN 'MIDST THY MOULDY MAMMOTHS GRAND CULVIER	250	3	DON JUAN	10	52	4
NOW THERE IS NOTHING GIVES A MAN SUCH SPIRITS	260	3	DON JUAN	10	72	1
IS THAT I FIND NO SPOT WHERE MAN CAN REST EYE ON	269	3	DON JUAN	11	3	5
TO OUR THEME--THE MAN WHO HAS STOOD ON THE ACROPOLIS	271	3	DON JUAN	11	7	1
THE DYING MAN CRIED HOLD I'VE GOT MY GRUEL	276	3	DON JUAN	11	16	2
HE FROM THE WORLD HAD CUT OFF A GREAT MAN	277	3	DON JUAN	11	19	1
INSTEAD OF WICKS THEY MADE A WICKED MAN TURN	280	3	DON JUAN	11	26	8
COULD RECOMMENCE TO HUNT HIS HONEST MAN	281	3	DON JUAN	11	28	2
NOT ONLY IN MERE TALKING BUT THE PRESS MAN	288	3	DON JUAN	11	42	5
THAT SWARTHY SPORUS NEITHER MAN NOR BARD	297	3	DON JUAN	11	58	5
AS WILL ENVIRON A CONSPICUOUS MAN SOME	305	3	DON JUAN	11	74	5
THE WORLD IN WHICH A MAN WAS BORN ALAS	306	3	DON JUAN	11	76	2
OF MAN IT IS--I REALLY SCARCE KNOW WHAT	315	3	DON JUAN	12	1	3
YE WHO BUT SEE THE SAVING MAN AT TABLE	316	3	DON JUAN	12	3	5
LOVE OR LUST MAKES MAN SICK AND WINE MUCH SICKER	317	3	DON JUAN	12	4	1
UNLESS A MAN CAN CALCULATE HIS MEANS	325	3	DON JUAN	12	21	7
WHEN MAN IN BATTLE OR IN QUARREL TILTS	342	3	DON JUAN	12	56	5

MAN   (CONTINUED)

			PAGE	VOL			CANTO	STANZA	LN
A YOUNG UNMARRIED MAN WITH A GOOD NAME	.	.	342	3	DON JUAN	12		58	1
ASK A BLIND MAN THE BEST JUDGE YOU'LL ATTACK	.	.	348	3	DON JUAN	12		71	4
NOT THAT I DEEM OUR CHIEF JUDGE IS A HOLLOW MAN--)	.	.	357	3	DON JUAN	12	V	18	8
THE FAIR SEX SHOULD BE ALWAYS FAIR AND NO MAN	.	.	359	3	DON JUAN	13		3	7
A MAN KNOWN IN THE COUNCILS OF THE NATION	.	.	365	3	DON JUAN	13		14	3
AND RECONCILED ALL QUALITIES WHICH GRACE MAN	.	.	368	3	DON JUAN	13		21	7
THAT HAPPINESS FOR MAN--THE HUNGRY SINNER--	.	.	404	3	DON JUAN	13		99	7
SAVE IN THE CLUBS NO MAN OF HONOUR PLAYS--	.	.	407	3	DON JUAN	13		106	2
WOE TO THE MAN WHO VENTURES A REBUKE	.	.	429	3	DON JUAN	14		43	5
LET NO MAN GRUMBLE WHEN HIS FRIENDS FALL OFF	.	.	431	3	DON JUAN	14		48	5
HIS GRACE WAS AN ENDURING MARRIED MAN	.	.	437	3	DON JUAN	14		62	2
HE WAS A COLD GOOD HONOURABLE MAN	.	.	440	3	DON JUAN	14		70	1
A HANDSOME MAN THAT HUMAN MIRACLE	.	.	441	3	DON JUAN	14		71	6
THAT MANY OF THE ILLS O'ER WHICH MAN GRIEVES	.	.	444	3	DON JUAN	14		78	6
OH WILBERFORCE THOU MAN OF BLACK RENOWN	.	.	445	3	DON JUAN	14		82	1
BUT OF SUCH FRIENDSHIP AS MAN'S MAY TO MAN BE	.	.	450	3	DON JUAN	14		92	7
AS E'ER BROUGHT MAN AND WOMAN TO THE BRINK	.	.	454	3	DON JUAN	14		100	3
WHICH MAKES A DANDY WHILE IT SPOILS A MAN	.	.	461	3	DON JUAN	15		12	8
WHOSE LOT IT IS BY MAN TO BE MISTAKEN	.	.	464	3	DON JUAN	15		18	3
SERF LORD MAN WITH SUCH SKILL AS NONE WOULD SHARE IT IF	.	.	481	3	DON JUAN	15		59	6
A MAN LIKE WHOM I HOPE WE SHAN'T SEE MANY SOON	.	.	484	3	DON JUAN	15		65	4
FOR MAN THEREIN WITH EYES AND HEART TO DINE	.	.	489	3	DON JUAN	15		75	4
OR OLD INDULGE MAN WITH A SECOND SIGHT	.	.	496	3	DON JUAN	15		90	6
A WISE MAN MORE THAN LAUGHTER FROM A DUNCE--	.	.	542	3	DON JUAN	16		88	5
THEY WONDERED HOW A YOUNG MAN SO ABSURD	.	.	543	3	DON JUAN	16		89	5
THE MAN WAS WELL-NIGH DEAD ERE MEN BEGUN	.	.	565	3	DON JUAN	17		8	5
SUCH AS ENABLES MAN TO SHOW HIS STRENGTH	.	.	567	3	DON JUAN	17		12	3

MANACLES

COBBLING AT MANACLES FOR ALL MANKIND--	.	.	18	2	DON JUAN	D		14	6

MANAGED

AND YET AT LAST HE MANAGED TO GET THROUGH	.	.	456	2	DON JUAN	5		78	3
IF MATTERS HAD BEEN MANAGED AS DESIRED	.	.	55	3	DON JUAN	6		99	5
ON ON THROUGH MEADOWS MANAGED LIKE A GARDEN	.	.	262	3	DON JUAN	10		76	1

MANCHESTER

| FAR EASIER THOUGH FOR THE GOOD TOWN OF MANCHESTER | . | . | 314 | 3 | DON JUAN | 11 | V | 75 | 3 |

MANDARIN

| JUST AS A MANDARIN FINDS NOTHING FINE-- | . | . | 373 | 3 | DON JUAN | 13 | | 34 | 5 |

MANDATE

| I COULD SEND FORTH MY MANDATE LIKE A PRIMATE | . | . | 327 | 3 | DON JUAN | 12 | | 24 | 3 |

MANGER

| TALK ABOUT POETRY AND RACK AND MANGER | . | . | 305 | 3 | DON JUAN | 11 | | 74 | 6 |

MANHEIM

| BUT JUAN POSTED ON THROUGH MANHEIM BONN | . | . | 255 | 3 | DON JUAN | 10 | | 62 | 1 |

MANHOOD

| NOT THAT HIS MANHOOD COULD BE CALLED IN QUESTION | . | . | 84 | 3 | DON JUAN | 7 | | 36 | 2 |
| WHICH KINDLE MANHOOD BUT CAN NE'ER ENTRANCE | . | . | 554 | 3 | DON JUAN | 16 | | 108 | 6 |

MANIA

| THE FOOL WILL CALL SUCH MANIA A DISEASE-- | . | . | 321 | 3 | DON JUAN | 12 | | 11 | 3 |

MANICHEAN

| YET SHE WOULD MAKE FULL MANY A MANICHEAN | . | . | 7 | 3 | DON JUAN | 6 | | 3 | 8 |

MANIFESTED

| WAS MANIFESTED IN A GREAT SENSATION | . | . | 38 | 2 | DON JUAN | 1 | | 33 | 8 |

MANIFOLD

| LOW WERE THE WHISPERS MANIFOLD THE RUMOURS | . | . | 244 | 3 | DON JUAN | 10 | | 40 | 1 |

MANKIND

COBBLING AT MANACLES FOR ALL MANKIND--	.	.	18	2	DON JUAN	D		14	6
TO THE GOOD SENSE AND SENSES OF MANKIND	.	.	69	2	DON JUAN	1		89	2
ARE WAYS TO BENEFIT MANKIND AS TRUE	.	.	93	2	DON JUAN	1		132	7
BUT THEN AS BARD MY DUTY TO MANKIND	.	.	155	2	DON JUAN	1	V	7	6
AND ALL MANKIND TURN WITH IT HEADS OR TAILS	.	.	159	2	DON JUAN	2		4	2
OF THE BEST FEELINGS OF MANKIND WHICH GROW	.	.	439	2	DON JUAN	5		49	5
AND HUGE TOMBS WORSE--MANKIND SINCE ADAM FELL	.	.	444	2	DON JUAN	5		59	6
HIS HIGHNESS THE SUBLIMEST OF MANKIND--	.	.	12	3	DON JUAN	6		13	1
BILLS--WOMEN--WIVES DOGS HORSES--AND MANKIND	.	.	17	3	DON JUAN	6		22	V2
THE TYRANT'S WISH THAT MANKIND ONLY HAD	.	.	19	3	DON JUAN	6		27	2
THAT HATER OF MANKIND WOULD BE A SHAME	.	.	53	3	DON JUAN	6		94	3
HALF-PAY FOR LIFE MAKE MANKIND WORTH DESTROYING	.	.	118	3	DON JUAN	8		14	8
HAVE LEFT UNDONE THE GREATEST--AND MANKIND	.	.	187	3	DON JUAN	9		10	8
WHICH TUMBLED ALL MANKIND INTO THE GRAVE	.	.	192	3	DON JUAN	9		19	4
BUT I THE MILDEST MEEKEST OF MANKIND	.	.	193	3	DON JUAN	9		21	1
FALSE FRIEND WHO HELD OUT FREEDOM TO MANKIND	.	.	258	3	DON JUAN	10		67	7
SUSPENDED MAY ILLUMINATE MANKIND	.	.	281	3	DON JUAN	11		27	2
PERHAPS HE FAIN WOULD LIBERATE MANKIND	.	.	320	3	DON JUAN	12		10	5
OR DO THEY BENEFIT MANKIND LEAN MISER	.	.	321	3	DON JUAN	12		11	7
MANKIND JUST NOW SEEM WRAPT IN MEDITATION	.	.	325	3	DON JUAN	12		21	4
UPON THE MORAL LESSONS OF MANKIND	.	.	353	3	DON JUAN	12		81	2
WHICH JUDGED MANKIND AT THEIR DUE ESTIMATION	.	.	372	3	DON JUAN	13		31	5
PERHAPS MANKIND MIGHT FIND THE PATH THEY MISS--	.	.	410	3	DON JUAN	14		1	3
TO THE GREAT PLEASURE OF OUR FRIENDS MANKIND	.	.	414	3	DON JUAN	14		9	5
WERE THERE A JOT OF SENSE AMONG MANKIND	.	.	446	3	DON JUAN	14		84	6
WOULD SHOW MANKIND THEIR SOUL'S ANTIPODES	.	.	455	3	DON JUAN	14		101	8
FOR THERE ARE FEW THINGS BY MANKIND LESS BROOK'D	.	.	479	3	DON JUAN	15		53	4
FOLLOWING THE IGNES FATUI OF MANKIND	.	.	479	3	DON JUAN	15		54	6

MANKIND'S

| STATE STATION HEAVEN MANKIND'S MY OWN ESTEEM | . | . | 130 | 2 | DON JUAN | 1 | | 193 | 2 |
| INTENTIONS WHICH FORM ALL MANKIND'S TRUMP CARD | . | . | 123 | 3 | DON JUAN | 8 | | 25 | 3 |

MANLIER

| THE NOBLER AND THE MANLIER ONE | . | . | 324 | 2 | DON JUAN | 3 | L | 10 | 4 |
| STRICT AND HIS MIND ASSUMED A MANLIER VIGOUR | . | . | 460 | 3 | DON JUAN | 15 | | 11 | 6 |

MANLY
          THAT SOMEWHAT MANLY MAJESTY OF STRIDE 464   2 DON JUAN 5   91   4
MANN
          BUT FOR THE MAKER MR MANN OF LONDON   171   2 DON JUAN 2   29   8
MANNAE
          SODAE-SULPHAT   SIX DRAMS   HALF DRAM MANNAE OPTIM 244   3 DON JUAN 10   41   2
MANNED
          THEIR DELHIS MANNED SOME BOATS AND SAILED AGAIN   82   3 DON JUAN 7   31   3
          OF FORTY THOUSAND WHO HAD MANNED THE WALL 175   3 DON JJAN 8   127   7
MANNER
          WRIT IN A MANNER WHICH IS MY AVERSION 330   2 DON JUAN 3   94   8
          AFTER THE MANNER THEN IN FASHION THERE 457   3 DON JUAN 5   79   5
          BUT WHETHER FROM HIS VOICE OR SPEECH OR MANNER 95   3 DON JUAN 7   56   7
          LITTLE BUT TO THE PURPOSE AND HIS MANNER 223   3 DON JUAN 9   83   7
          HIS MANNER SHOWED HIM SPRUNG FROM A HIGH MOTHER 369   3 DON JUAN 13   24   6
          AT LEAST HIS MANNER SUFFERS NOT TO GUESS 373   3 DON JUAN 13   34   6
          THAT POLISH OF INDIFFERENCE--IN THE MANNER 373   3 DON JUAN 13   34   V2
          IN ANY MANNER BY THE UNINITIATED   419   3 DON JUAN 14   22   8
          HIS MANNER WAS PERHAPS THE MORE SEDUCTIVE   461   3 DON JUAN 15   12   1
          IN FACT HIS MANNER WAS HIS OWN ALONE 461   3 DON JUAN 15   13   4
MANNER'D
          YOU'RE WRONG--HE WAS THE MILDEST MANNER'D MAN 296   2 DON JUAN 3   41   1
MANNERS
          TO TEACH HIM MANNERS FOR THE TIME TO COME   34   2 DON JUAN 1   25   8
          THEIR MANNERS MENDING AND THEIR MORALS CURING   162   2 DON JUAN 2   10   V7
          IT MAY SEEM STRANGE TO FIND HIS MANNERS BLAND   299   2 DON JUAN 3   47   5
          THAT MANNERS HARDLY DIFFER MORE THAN DRESS 402   3 DON JUAN 13   94   8
          WITH NATURE MANNERS WHICH ARE ARTIFICIAL 467   3 DON JUAN 15   25   7
          MEN MADE THE MANNERS MANNERS NOW MAKE MEN-- 468   3 DON JUAN 15   26   2
          MEN MADE THE MANNERS MANNERS NOW MAKE MEN-- 468   3 DON JUAN 15   26   2
MANNISH
          LADY FITZ-FRISKY AND MISS MAEVIA MANNISH 295   3 DON JJAN 11   53   7
MANOR
          THE CORN IS CUT THE MANOR FULL OF GAME 394   3 DON JUAN 13   75   3
          HAD BAGGED THIS POACHER UPON NATURE'S MANOR 531   3 DON JUAN 16   62   8
MANORS
          ERNEIS RADULPHUS--EIGHT-AND-FORTY MANORS 242   3 DON JUAV 10   36   2
MAN'S
          WITH GOD AND MAN'S ABHORRENCE FOR ITS GAINS 18   2 DON JUAN D   14   8
          AS E'ER TO MAN'S MATURER GROWTH WAS GIVEN   48   2 DON JUAN 1   49   4
          JUAN BEING THEN GROWN UP TO MAN'S ESTATE 67   2 DON JUAN 1   85   2
          MAN'S A STRANGE ANIMAL AND MAKES STRANGE USE   91   2 DON JUAN 1   128   1
          MAN'S A PHENOMENON ONE KNOWS NOT WHAT 93   2 DON JUAN 1   133   1
          MAN'S LOVE IS OF MAN'S LIFE A THING APART   131   2 DON JUAN 1   194   1
          MAN'S LOVE IS OF MAN'S LIFE A THING APART   131   2 DON JUAN 1   194   1
          AS THE RICH MAN'S IN HELL WHO VAINLY SCREAM'D 202   2 DON JUAN 2   86   4
          THE OLD MAN'S CHEEK GREW PALE BUT NOT WITH DREAD 365   2 DON JUAN 4   40   3
          WE MUST BE NEAR SOME PLACE OF MAN'S ABODE-- 436   2 DON JUAN 5   45   1
          BUT THERE IS SOMETHING WHEN MAN'S EYE APPEARS   479   2 DON JUAN 5   118   3
          A WOMAN'S TEAR-DROP MELTS A MAN'S HALF SEARS   479   2 DON JUAN 5   118   5
          MAN'S PENSIVE PART IS NOW AND THEN THE HEAD   7   3 DON JUAN 6   2   V7
          AS ANY MAN'S CLAY MIXTURE UNDERGOES 16   3 DON JUAN 6   20   5
          BUT A MAN'S GRANDMOTHER IS DEEMED FAIR GAME 53   3 DON JUAN 6   94   V5
          PRAISE) IF A MAN'S NAME IN A BULLETIN 77   3 DON JUAN 7   21   2
          SPARE OR SMITE RARELY--MAN'S MAKE MILLIONS ASHES   115   3 DON JUAN 8   6   8
          ALL THAT WE READ HEAR DREAM OF MAN'S DISTRESSES 173   3 DON JUAN 8   123   3
          AS THE SOLE SIGN OF MAN'S BEING IN HIS SENSES   240   3 DON JUAN 10   31   7
          THE POOR MAN'S SPARKLING SUBSTITUTE FOR RICHES 256   3 DON JUAN 10   63   4
          WHEN A MAN'S COUNTRY'S GOING TO THE DEVIL   257   3 DON JUAN 10   66   8
          KILL A MAN'S FAMILY AND HE MAY BROOK IT 264   3 DON JUAN 10   79   7
          NOR WHAT THE MEANING OF THE MAN'S FAREWELL 276   3 DON JUAN 11   17   4
          OF MAN'S OPINIONS FORMS THEIR EDUCATION 354   3 DON JUAN 12   83   V6
          MAN'S PITY'S FOR HIMSELF OR FOR HIS SON 377   3 DON JUAN 13   42   6
          LIKE MAN'S VAIN GLORY AND HIS VAINER TROUBLES   389   3 DON JUAN 13   65   8
          MAN'S VERY SYMPATHY WITH THEIR ESTATE 420   3 DON JUAN 14   24   5
          THE SORT OF THING TO TURN A YOUNG MAN'S HEAD   438   3 DON JUAN 14   64   1
          IF SUCH CAN E'ER BE DRAWN BY MAN'S CAPACITY 449   3 DON JUAN 14   90   6
          BUT OF SUCH FRIENDSHIP AS MAN'S MAY TO MAN BE   450   3 DON JUAN 14   92   7
          RADIANT AND GRAVE--AS PITYING MAN'S DECLINE 476   3 DON JUAN 15   45   5
          THE WISE MAN'S SURE WHEN HE NO MORE CAN SHARE IT HE . . . 566   3 DON JUAN 17   9   7
MANSION
          THE MANSION HOUSE TOO (THOUGH SOME PEOPLE QUIZ IT)   . . . 280   3 DON JUAN 11   25   6
          LORD HENRY'S MANSION WAS IN BLANK-BLANK SQUARE 369   3 DON JUAN 13   25   8
          AT HENRY'S MANSION THEN IN BLANK-BLANK SQUARE   370   3 DON JUAN 13   28   1
          THE PEERAGE TO A MANSION VERY FINE. 381   3 DON JUAN 13   50   3
          STILL OLDER MANSION OF A RICH AND RARE 384   3 DON JUAN 13   55   3
          BEFORE THE MANSION LAY A LUCID LAKE 385   3 DON JUAN 13   57   1
          HER HEART WAS VACANT THOUGH A SPLENDID MANSION 446   3 DON JUAN 14   85   2
MANSION'S
          THE MANSION'S SELF WAS VAST AND VENERABLE   389   3 DON JUAN 13   66   1
MAN-SLAYER
          OF ALL MEN SAVING SYLLA THE MAN-SLAYER 143   3 DON JUAN 8   61   1
MANTILLA
          THE BASQUINA AND THE MANTILLA THEY. 220   2 DON JUAN 2   120   7
MANTLE
          THEN WAS THE CORDIAL POUR'D AND MANTLE FLUNG   216   2 DON JUAN 2   114   1
          AND NIGHT IS BACKWARD LIKE A MANTLE ROLLED 230   2 DON JUAN 2   139   V8
          ARRAYED HERSELF WITH MANTLE GEM AND VEIL 49   3 DON JUAN 6   87   4
          HE STRIPS FROM MAN THAT MANTLE (FAR MORE DEAR   188   3 DON JUAN 9   12   6

489

		PAGE	VOL		CANTO	STANZA	LN
MANTLE (CONTINUED)							
NOR WORN THE MOTLEY MANTLE OF A POET	. . . .	467	3	DON JUAN	15	24	7
BUT WEAR THE NEWEST MANTLE OF HYPOCRISY	. . . . . .	526	3	DON JUAN	16	52	7
MANTLES							
AND CLAP A WHITE CAPE ON THEIR MANTLES BLUE	. . . . .	94	2	DON JUAN	1	134	5
MANURE							
ARE GOOD MANURE FOR THEIR MORE BARE BIOGRAPHY	. . . .	330	2	DON JUAN	3	94	4
FROM THE MANURE OF HUMAN CLAY THOUGH DECKED	. . . . .	199	3	DON JUAN	9	34	5
MANURED							
UPON THE BLACK LOAM LONG MANURED BY VICE	. . . . . .	335	3	DON JUAN	12	40	7
MANY							
EUTROPIUS OF ITS MANY MASTERS--BLIND	. . . . .	18	2	DON JUAN	D	15	5
WITH MANY OF THE MILITARY SET	. . . .	22	2	DON JUAN	1	3	6
NOT ANY OF THE MANY COULD DIVINE	. . . .	33	2	DON JUAN	1	23	2
INDEED THERE WERE NOT MANY MORE TO TELL	. . . .	40	2	DON JUAN	1	35	4
POOR FELLOW HE HAD MANY THINGS TO WOUND HIM	. . . .	41	2	DON JUAN	1	36	2
OF MANY CHARMS IN HER AS NATURAL	. . . . .	51	2	DON JUAN	1	55	5
EVEN INNOCENCE ITSELF HAS MANY A WILE	. . . . .	61	2	DON JUAN	1	72	6
BUT THEN THEY ONLY SEEM SO MANY BROTHERS	. . . .	63	2	DON JUAN	1	77	8
HOW MANY MILES THE MOON MIGHT HAVE IN GIRTH	. . . .	71	2	DON JUAN	1	92	5
OF AIR-BALLOONS AND OF THE MANY BARS	. . . . .	71	2	DON JUAN	1	92	6
SHE WHO FOR MANY YEARS HAD WATCH'D HER SON SO--	. . .	80	2	DON JUAN	1	110	7
BY GUSTS AND MANY A SPARKLING HEARTH WAS BRIGHT	. . .	94	2	DON JUAN	1	135	3
WERE THERE NOT ALSO RUSSIANS ENGLISH MANY	. . . .	102	2	DON JUAN	1	149	5
BELOVED AND LOVING MANY ALL IS O'ER	. . . . .	132	2	DON JUAN	1	195	2
WHICH MAKES SO MANY POETS AND SOME FOOLS	. . . .	136	2	DON JUAN	1	201	4
MY TEXT WITH MANY THINGS THAT NO ONE KNOWS	. . . .	138	2	DON JUAN	1	204	5
AND THE TWO LAST HAVE LEFT ME MANY A TOKEN	. . . .	145	2	DON JUAN	1	217	1
THE WORLD WILL FIND THEE AFTER MANY DAYS	. . . .	149	2	DON JUAN	1	222	4
WHICH LAW AFFORDS TO MANY A DIRTY DEED	. . . . .	151	2	DON JUAN	1	V 2	4
BUT JUAN HAD GOT MANY THINGS TO LEAVE	. . . . .	164	2	DON JUAN	2	15	1
THAN MANY PERSONS MORE ADVANCED IN LIFE	. . . .	164	2	DON JUAN	2	15	4
BUT DIE AS MANY AN EXILED HEART HATH DIED	. . . .	166	2	DON JUAN	2	18	3
AND LONG HAD VOYAGED THROUGH MANY A STORMY SEA	. . .	179	2	DON JUAN	2	43	4
AND THEN THEY WERE TOO MANY THOUGH SO FEW--	. . .	185	2	DON JUAN	2	54	6
AND THEIR BAKED LIPS WITH MANY A BLOODY CRACK	. . .	202	2	DON JUAN	2	86	1
FLOW'D IN HER VEIL AND MANY A PRECIOUS STONE	. . .	220	2	DON JUAN	2	121	6
HAD NOT SO MANY ORNAMENTS TO STRIKE	. . . .	221	2	DON JUAN	2	122	3
LEFT HIM AT LAST THE SOLE OF MANY MASTERS	. . . .	222	2	DON JUAN	2	125	7
AND SOMETIMES CAUGHT AS MANY AS HE WISH'D	. . . .	223	2	DON JUAN	2	126	4
FULL MANY A MORSEL FOR THAT TURKISH TRADE	. . . .	223	2	DON JUAN	2	126	7
'TWOULD SAVE US MANY A HEART-ACHE MANY A SHILLING	. .	270	2	DON JUAN	2	213	5
'TWOULD SAVE US MANY A HEART-ACHE MANY A SHILLING	. .	270	2	DON JUAN	2	213	5
HOW MANY SONNETS HAD ENSUED THE BEDDING	. . . .	279	2	DON JUAN	3	8	V8
AND ROUGH WITH REEFS WHICH RAN OUT MANY A MILE	. . .	285	2	DON JUAN	3	19	7
WITH LOVE FOR MANY AND WITH FEARS FOR SOME	. . . .	286	2	DON JUAN	3	21	6
(WHICH GOD FORBID) OR SOME OR A GREAT MANY	. . . .	301	2	DON JUAN	3	50	2
ITS POWER UNCONSCIOUSLY FULL MANY A TIME--	. . .	304	2	DON JUAN	3	56	3
HIS TURBAN FURL'D IN MANY A GRACEFUL FOLD	. . . .	315	2	DON JUAN	3	77	5
HE WAS A MAN WHO HAD SEEN MANY CHANGES	. . . .	317	2	DON JUAN	3	80	1
BUT HE HAD GENIUS--MANY A SCOUNDREL HAS IT--	. . .	317	2	DON JUAN	3	81	V1
HAD BEEN THE FAVOURITE OF FULL MANY A MESS	. . . .	318	2	DON JUAN	3	82	3
AND I GROWN ONE OF MANY WOODEN SPOONS	. . . . .	341	2	DON JUAN	3	110	6
AND MANY DEATHS DO THEY ESCAPE BY THIS	. . . . .	350	2	DON JUAN	4	12	2
HARD WORDS HARSH TRUTH A TRUTH WHICH MANY KNOW	. . .	353	2	DON JUAN	4	18	1
FOR BOTH SIDES I COULD MANY REASONS SHOW	. . . .	357	2	DON JUAN	4	25	6
BUT THERE TOO MANY A POISON-TREE HAS ROOT	. . . .	373	2	DON JUAN	4	55	4
SHE LOOK'D ON MANY A FACE WITH VACANT EYE	. . . .	378	2	DON JUAN	4	63	1
ON MANY A TOKEN WITHOUT KNOWING WHAT	. . . . .	378	2	DON JUAN	4	63	2
BUT MANY A GREEK MAID IN A LOVING SONG	. . . . .	383	2	DON JUAN	4	73	1
SIGHS O'ER HER NAME AND MANY AN ISLANDER	. . . .	383	2	DON JUAN	4	73	2
BUT MANY A FISHER IN HIS RUGGED SONG	. . . . .	383	2	DON JUAN	4	73	V1
O'ERSHADOW'D THERE BY MANY A HERO'S GRAVE	. . . .	387	2	DON JUAN	4	79	4
THAT EACH PULL'D DIFFERENT WAYS WITH MANY AN OATH	. .	394	2	DON JUAN	4	93	7
TO BEAR THE COMPLIMENTS OF MANY A BORE	. . . . .	404	2	DON JUAN	4	109	3
THERE STILL ARE MANY RAINBOWS IN YOUR SKY	. . . .	421	2	DON JUAN	5	21	3
AND THOUGH I HAVE SEEN MANY CORPSES NEVER	. . . .	430	2	DON JUAN	5	35	2
AND SUCH AN END THAT HE WHO MANY A DAY	. . . . .	431	2	DON JUAN	5	37	5
SEEING WHAT'S MEANT FOR MANY WITH BUT ONE	. . . .	443	2	DON JUAN	5	57	8
I HAVE NO MORE TIME NOR MANY WORDS TO SPARE	. . . .	454	2	DON JUAN	5	74	3
SO MANY FALSE LONG TRESSES ALL TO SPARE	. . . .	457	2	DON JUAN	5	79	3
AND IN PERSPECTIVE MANY A SQUADRON FLIES	. . . .	461	2	DON JUAN	5	86	6
FOR WHAT IS STEALING YOUNG ONES FEW OR MANY	. . . .	487	2	DON JUAN	5	132	7
THUS ENDED MANY A FAIR SULTANA'S TRIP	. . . . .	496	2	DON JUAN	5	149	V5
YET SHE WOULD MAKE FULL MANY A MANICHEAN	. . . .	7	3	DON JUAN	6	3	8
AS THE TRIBUNALS SHOW THROUGH MANY A SESSION	. . .	11	3	DON JUAN	6	10	6
AND THOUGH HE CERTAINLY RAN MANY RISKS	. . . . .	20	3	DON JUAN	6	29	3
MANY AND BEAUTIFUL LAY THOSE AROUND	. . . . .	38	3	DON JUAN	6	65	1
THOSE GAY RECESSES--MANY A PRECIOUS STONE	. . . .	54	3	DON JUAN	6	97	5
SPARKLED ALONG ITS ROOF AND MANY A VASE	. . . .	54	3	DON JUAN	6	97	6
ALREADY MANY A ONCE LOVE-BEATEN BREAST	. . . . .	63	3	DON JUAN	6	115	3
WHICH MANY PEOPLE PASS FOR WITS BY QUOTING	. . . .	77	3	DON JUAN	7	21	8
COMMON IN MANY CASES WAS IN THIS	. . . . .	79	3	DON JUAN	7	25	3
AND I SHOULD STILL HAVE MANY THINGS TO SAY	. . . .	82	3	DON JUAN	7	32	4
MANY OF COMMON READERS GIVE A GUESS	. . . . .	82	3	DON JUAN	7	33	3
TO SEE THE SULTAN RICH IN MANY A GEM	. . . . .	104	3	DON JUAN	7	74	4
UNCERTAINTY IS ONE OF MANY BLISSES	. . . . .	105	3	DON JUAN	7	76	5
A MODERATE PENSION SHAKES FULL MANY A SAGE	. . . .	118	3	DON JUAN	8	14	4
WITH MANY OTHER WARRIORS AS WE SAID	. . . . .	133	3	DON JUAN	8	41	2

490

MANY   (CONTINUED)
OF WAR AND TAKING TOWNS WHEN MANY A SHRIEK . . . . . . 141 3 DON JUAN 8   58   3
RINGS O'ER THE DIALOGUE AND MANY A CRIME . . . . 141 3 DON JUAN 8   58   4
ALL WALLS MEN KNOW AND MANY NEVER KNOWN . . . . 142 3 DON JUAN 8   60   6
NOR YET TOO MANY NOR TOO FEW THEIR NUMBERS . . . . . . 145 3 DON JUAN 8   67   3
AT EVERY JOLT--AND THEY WERE MANY--STILL . . . . 198 3 DON JUAN 9   31   1
HIS JOURNEY WE'VE SO MANY TOURS OF LATE . . . . 203 3 DON JUAN 9   42   6
A LOVER AS HAD COST HER MANY A TEAR . . . . 209 3 DON JUAN 9   54   7
FOR ONE ESPECIAL PERSON OUT OF MANY . . . . 216 3 DON JUAN 9   68   7
WHERE SHIPS HAVE FOUNDERED AS DOTH MANY A BOAT . . . . 227 3 DON JUAN 10   4   8
LIKE MANY PUBLICATIONS OF JOHN MURRAY . . . . 237 3 DON JUAN 10   26 V3
BUT HERE IS ONE PRESCRIPTION OUT OF MANY . . . . 244 3 DON JUAN 10   41   1
THE BENCH TOO SEATS OR SUITS FULL MANY A DEBTOR . . . . 280 3 DON JUAN 11   25   5
THERE MANY AN ENVOY EITHER DWELT OR DWELLS . . . . . . 283 3 DON JUAN 11   31   5
(THE DEN OF MANY A DIPLOMATIC LOST LIE) . . . . 283 3 DON JUAN 11   31   6
FULL MANY AN EAGER GENTLEMAN OFT RUES . . . . 304 3 DON JUAN 11   71   5
OR MANY (FOR THE NUMBER'S SOMETIMES SUCH) . . . . . . 305 3 DON JUAN 11   73   5
(WHILE ON THE PAVEMENT MANY A HUNGRY WHORE . . . . . . 313 3 DON JUAN 11 V 29   3
LIKE MANY PEOPLE EVERYBODY KNOWS . . . . 335 3 DON JUAN 12   41   5
I THINK YOU'LL FIND FROM MANY A FAMILY PICTURE . . . . 337 3 DON JUAN 12   46   3
AT LEAST ENTIRELY FOR HE HAD SEEN TOO MANY . . . . . . 338 3 DON JUAN 12   49   7
HE HAD MANY FRIENDS WHO HAD MANY WIVES AND WAS . . . . 342 3 DON JUAN 12   57   1
HE HAD MANY FRIENDS WHO HAD MANY WIVES AND WAS . . . . 342 3 DON JUAN 12   57   1
YET MANY HAVE A METHOD MORE RETICULAR-- . . . . 343 3 DON JUAN 12   59   5
THOUGH MANY THOUSANDS BOTH OF PITH AND PLUCK TOO . . . 348 3 DON JUAN 12   70 V5
AS MANY OTHER NOBLE SCIONS WERE . . . . 370 3 DON JUAN 13   28   3
'MIDST MANY ROCKS WE GUARD MORE AGAINST WRECKS . . . . 371 3 DON JUAN 13   30   6
AND SUCH ARE MANY--THOUGH I ONLY MEANT HER . . . . . . 375 3 DON JUAN 13   38   4
AS MANY DOUBTS AS ANY OTHER DOCTRINE . . . . 377 3 DON JUAN 13   41   7
AS MANY GUESTS OR MORE BEFORE WHOM GROAN . . . . 381 3 DON JUAN 13   49   5
AS MANY COVERS DULY DAILY LAID . . . . 381 3 DON JUAN 13   49   6
WITH MANY MORE BY RANK AND FASHION DECKED . . . . . . 382 3 DON JUAN 13   52   6
IN A GRAND ARCH WHICH ONCE SCREENED MANY AN AISLE . . . 386 3 DON JUAN 13   59   3
THE ANNALS OF FULL MANY A LINE UNDONE-- . . . . 386 3 DON JUAN 13   60   6
BY MANY WINDINGS TO THEIR CLEVER CLINCH . . . . 404 3 DON JUAN 13   98   2
SO MANY TROUBLES FROM HER BIRTH BESET HER . . . . . . 421 3 DON JUAN 14   25   3
THAT MANY OF THE ILLS O'ER WHICH MAN GRIEVES . . . . . 444 3 DON JUAN 14   78   6
(I MERELY QUOTE WHAT I HAVE HEARD FROM MANY) . . . . . 452 3 DON JUAN 14   95   2
I HAD A PARAMOUR--AND I'VE HAD MANY . . . . 452 3 DON JUAN 14   95 V2
AND TAKE AS MANY HEROES AS HEAVEN PLEASES . . . . . . 459 3 DON JUAN 15   9   8
BY MANY VIRTUES TO BE WORTH THE TROUBLE . . . . 477 3 DON JUAN 15   48   7
A MAN LIKE WHOM I HOPE WE SHAN'T SEE MANY SOON . . . . 484 3 DON JUAN 15   65   4
I WISH THEY'D STATE HOW MANY THEY HAVE GAINED . . . . 505 3 DON JUAN 16   11   8
WHERE MANY A GOTHIC ORNAMENT REMAINED . . . . 507 3 DON JUAN 16   16   6
DOORS THERE WERE MANY THROUGH WHICH BY THE LAWS . . . . 511 3 DON JUAN 16   24   5
TO JEST UPON SUCH THEMES IN MANY A SALLY . . . . 526 3 DON JUAN 16   53   3
LONG BANQUETS AND TOO MANY GUESTS ALTHOUGH . . . . . . 542 3 DON JUAN 16   86   2
WHICH MANY PEOPLE TAKE FOR WANT OF HEART . . . . 547 3 DON JUAN 16   97   3
OF EROS BUT THOUGH THOU HAST PLAYED US MANY TRICKS . . . 554 3 DON JUAN 16   109   7
BUT MANY A LONELY TREE THE LOFTIER GROWS . . . . 562 3 DON JUAN 17   1   3
MANY-COLOUR'D
HER DRESS WAS MANY-COLOUR'D FINELY SPUN . . . . 220 2 DON JUAN 2   121   2
MAPS
AS GEOGRAPHERS LAY DOWN A SHOAL IN MAPS . . . . 155 2 DON JUAN 1 V 7   8
MAR
(SUCH THINGS IN FACT IT DON'T ASK MUCH TO MAR) . . . . 281 2 DON JUAN 3   10   6
CAN EVERY ELEMENT OUR ELEMENTS MAR . . . . 432 2 DON JUAN 5   39   5
MARAT
PETION CLOOTZ DANTON MARAT LAFAYETTE . . . . 22 2 DON JUAN 1   3   2
MARATHON
THE MOUNTAINS LOOK ON MARATHON-- . . . . 321 2 DON JUAN 3 L 3   1
AND MARATHON LOOKS ON THE SEA . . . . 321 2 DON JUAN 3 L 3   2
MARBLE
CRYSTAL AND MARBLE PLATE AND PORCELAIN . . . . 310 2 DON JUAN 3   68   1
CANOVA'S MARBLE OR THE WORDS OF BURKE . . . . 315 2 DON JUAN 3   76 V8
WERE HUNG WITH MARBLE ICICLES THE WORK . . . . 362 2 DON JUAN 4   33   2
WHICH FROZE TO MARBLE AS IT FELL SHE THOUGHT . . . . . 362 2 DON JUAN 4   33   8
IN MARBLE FONTS THERE GRAIN AND FLOWER AND FRUIT . . . 373 2 DON JUAN 4   55   2
THE RULING PASSION SUCH AS MARBLE SHOWS . . . . 377 2 DON JUAN 4   61   1
HIGH BARROWS WITHOUT MARBLE OR A NAME . . . . 386 2 DON JUAN 4   77   1
A MARBLE FOUNTAIN ECHOES THROUGH THE GLOOMS . . . . . 442 2 DON JUAN 5   55   4
THROUGH GLITTERING GALLERIES AND O'ER MARBLE FLOORS . . 460 2 DON JUAN 5   85   3
FROM MARBLE LIKE PYGMALION'S STATUE WAKING . . . . . 27 3 DON JUAN 6   43   6
THE MORTAL AND THE MARBLE STILL AT STRIFE . . . . . . 27 3 DON JUAN 6   43   7
A FOURTH AS MARBLE STATUE-LIKE AND STILL . . . . . . 40 3 DON JUAN 6   68   1
MOTHER OF PEARL AND PORPHYRY AND MARBLE . . . . 55 3 DON JUAN 6   98   1
SWEEPING THE MARBLE UNDERNEATH HER CHAIR . . . . . . 60 3 DON JUAN 6   108   3
AS PHIDIAN FORMS CUT OUT OF MARBLE ATTIC . . . . . . 409 3 DON JUAN 13   110   3
FROM OFF THE MARBLE WHICH HAD NO DEFECT . . . . 434 3 DON JUAN 14   56   6
MARBLED
PLACE ME ON SUNIUM'S MARBLED STEEP . . . . 326 2 DON JUAN 3 L 16   1
MARBLE'S
BUT FIX'D AS MARBLE'S UNCHANGED ASPECT THROWS . . . . 377 2 DON JUAN 4   61   3
MARCEAU
JOUBERT HOCHE MARCEAU LANNES DESSAIX MOREAU . . . . . 22 2 DON JUAN 1   3   5
MARCH
MARCH HAS ITS HARES AND MAY MUST HAVE ITS HEROINE . . . 76 2 DON JUAN 1   102   8
BUT BRED WITHIN THE MARCH OF OLD ANCONA . . . . 395 2 DON JUAN 4   94   2
AND MARCH AWAY--'TWERE EASIER DONE THAN SAID . . . . . 434 2 DON JUAN 5   43   8

MARCH   (CONTINUED)
OF ONE GOOD MAN WITH STATELY MARCH AND SLOW	22	3	DON JUAN	6	33	5
THEN SLACKENED IT WHICH IS THE MARCH MOST CAUSED . . .	61	3	DON JUAN	6	111	3
THE MARCH THE CHARGE THE SHOUTS OF EITHER FAITH . . .	111	3	DON JUAN	7	87	6
THE NIGHTLY MUSTER AND THE SILENT MARCH	121	3	DON JUAN	8	21	2
TO MARCH A GREAT CONVENIENCE TO OUR MEN	136	3	DON JUAN	8	47	3
TROOPS AS ARE MEANT TO MARCH WITH GREATEST GLORY ON . .	151	3	DON JUAN	8	78	4
I SHOULD BE LOTH TO MARCH WITHOUT YOU BUT	162	3	DON JUAN	8	101	7
JUAN CONSENTED TO MARCH ON THROUGH THUNDER	163	3	DON JUAN	8	103	3
WHICH MOURN'D THE POWER OF TIME'S OR TEMPEST'S MARCH . .	386	3	DON JUAN	13	59	7
WE'LL DO OUR BEST TO MAKE THE BEST ON'T--MARCH . .	468	3	DON JUAN	15	27	1
MARCH MY MUSE IF YOU CANNOT FLY YET FLUTTER . .	468	3	DON JUAN	15	27	2
WHERE THE TRIUMPHAL CHARIOTS' HAUGHTY MARCH . .	485	3	DON JUAN	15	67	4

MARCHED
MARCHED FORTH WITH NERVE AND SINEWS BENT TO SLAY-- . .	113	3	DON JUAN	8	2	4
BUT ON THEY MARCHED DEAD BODIES TRAMPLING O'ER	120	3	DON JUAN	8	19	5
MARCHED WITH THE BRAVE BATTALION OF POLOUZKI-- . .	150	3	DON JUAN	8	76	8
WHO MARCHED TO MOSCOW LED BY FAME THE SYREN	253	3	DON JUAN	10	58	6

MARCHES
TO HIM WHOSE BREEDING MARCHES WITH HIS QUALITY	369	3	DON JUAN	13	24	8

MARCHIONESS
BUT THE OLD MARCHIONESS SOME PLAN HAS HATCHED . .	332	3	DON JUAN	12	35	5

MARGIN
WHO SAW THOSE FIGURES ON THE MARGIN KISS ALL	47	2	DON JUAN	1	46	5

MARIA
AVE MARIA O'ER THE EARTH AND SEA	334	2	DON JUAN	3	101	7
AVE MARIA BLESSED BE THE HOUR	335	2	DON JUAN	3	102	1
AVE MARIA 'TIS THE HOUR OF PRAYER	336	2	DON JUAN	3	103	1
AVE MARIA 'TIS THE HOUR OF LOVE	336	2	DON JUAN	3	103	2
AVE MARIA MAY OUR SPIRITS DARE	336	2	DON JUAN	3	103	3
AVE MARIA OH THAT FACE SO FAIR	336	2	DON JUAN	3	103	5

MARINE
THEN HAVING SETTLED HIS MARINE AFFAIRS	285	2	DON JUAN	3	19	1

MARINERS
FRAIL MARINERS AFLOAT WITHOUT A CHART	442	3	DON JUAN	14	74	5

MARINET'S
IN MARINET'S AFFAIR--IN FACT 'TWAS SHABBY	184	3	DON JUAN	9	2	2

MARIO
HAIL'D A STRANGE BRIG CORPO DI CAIO MARIO	389	2	DON JUAN	4	82	4

MARIUS
(THE HYPOCRITE) WILL BANISH THEM LIKE MARIUS . . .	352	3	DON JUAN	12	78	6

MARK
'TIS SWEET TO KNOW THERE IS AN EYE WILL MARK . .	88	2	DON JUAN	1	123	3
A FAIRER MARK AND WITH A FIX'D EYE SCANN'D . . .	367	2	DON JUAN	4	43	7
THE CAPTIVES SEEMED TO MARK THEIR LOOKS AND AGE . .	424	2	DON JUAN	5	26	3
PRESENTED A FINE MARK TO THROW A SHELL IN . .	78	3	DON JUAN	7	23	8
INDEED THE SMOKE WAS SUCH THEY SCARCE COULD MARK . .	177	3	DON JUAN	8	130	3
MARK HOW ITS LIPLESS MOUTH GRINS WITHOUT BREATH . .	188	3	DON JUAN	9	11	8
MARK HOW IT LAUGHS AND SCORNS AT ALL YOU ARE . .	188	3	DON JUAN	9	12	1

MARK'D
THE LOTS WERE MADE AND MARK'D AND MIX'D AND HANDED . .	195	2	DON JUAN	2	75	1

MARKED
AN OPEN BROW A LITTLE MARKED WITH CARE	416	2	DON JUAN	5	11	5
BESIDES THE MARKED DISTINCTION OF HIS AIR	355	3	DON JUAN	12	85	6

MARKET
LABOUR THERE'S A SURE MARKET FOR IMPOSTURE . . .	91	2	DON JUAN	1	128	8
FOR THE SLAVE MARKET OF CONSTANTINOPLE	393	2	DON JUAN	4	91	8
WERE LANDED IN THE MARKET ONE AND ALL	407	2	DON JUAN	4	113	6
WHICH THE WEST INDIAN MARKET SCARCE WOULD BRING . .	408	2	DON JUAN	4	115	2
AND AGE AND SEX WERE IN THE MARKET RANGED . . .	414	2	DON JUAN	5	7	2
SEEN BEAUTIES BROUGHT TO MARKET BY THE SCORE . . .	418	3	DON JUAN	14	18	4
FOR WHICH SMALL THANKS ARE STILL THE MARKET PRICE . .	469	3	DON JUAN	15	29	3
HAD FALLEN LAST MARKET COST HIS HOST THREE VOTES . .	543	3	DON JUAN	16	89	8

MARKETABLE
BECAUSE IT IS A MARKETABLE VICE	57	2	DON JUAN	1	64	8

MARKOW
ALSO THE GENERAL MARKOW BRIGADIER	117	3	DON JUAN	8	11	1
THE GENERAL MARKOW WHO COULD THUS EVINCE	117	3	DON JUAN	8	11	6

MARLBOROUGH'S
TO THE GREAT MARLBOROUGH'S SKILL IN GIVING KNOCKS . .	328	2	DON JUAN	3	90	7
OTHERS IN WIGS OF MARLBOROUGH'S MARTIAL FOLD . . .	391	3	DON JUAN	13	70	3

MARLE
AT LEAST THE SHARP POINTS OF THAT BURNING MARLE . .	124	3	DON JUAN	8	26	V7

MARMORA
TO FIND OUR WAY TO MARMORA WITHOUT BOATS	464	2	DON JUAN	5	92	6

MARQUESS
BID IRELAND'S LONDONDERRY'S MARQUESS SHOW	207	3	DON JUAN	9	49	3

MARR'D
OF HIS ATTRACTIONS MARR'D THE FAIR PERSPECTIVE . .	461	3	DON JUAN	15	12	5
BUT ERE THE MATTER COULD BE MARR'D OR MENDED . .	482	3	DON JUAN	15	61	5

MARRIAGE
THAT INEZ HAD ERE DON ALFONSO'S MARRIAGE . . .	58	2	DON JUAN	1	66	7
BUYS THEM IN MARRIAGE--AND WHAT RESTS BEYOND . .	263	2	DON JUAN	2	200	6
THAT LOVE AND MARRIAGE RARELY CAN COMBINE . .	277	2	DON JUAN	3	5	3
MARRIAGE FROM LOVE LIKE VINEGAR FROM WINE-- . .	277	2	DON JUAN	3	5	5
YET LOVE MAY MAKE MARRIAGE AS GOOD WHITE WINE . .	277	2	DON JUAN	3	5	V5
ALL COMEDIES ARE ENDED BY A MARRIAGE	280	2	DON JUAN	3	9	2
HAVE SUNG OF HEAVEN AND HELL OR MARRIAGE ARE . .	281	2	DON JUAN	3	10	2
THAT THEY WERE GOING TO A MARRIAGE FEAST . . .	90	3	DON JUAN	7	49	2

MARRIAGE   (CONTINUED)

	PAGE	VOL	CANTO		STANZA	LN
ADD WHAT MAY BE CALLED MARRIAGE IN DISGUISE	220	3	DON JUAN	9	76	8
USEFUL LIKE MALTHUS IN PROMOTING MARRIAGE--	282	3	DON JUAN	11	30	7
EXCEPTING MARRIAGE WHICH IS LOVE NO DOUBT	323	3	DON JUAN	12	15	2
LOVE MAY EXIST WITH MARRIAGE AND SHOULD EVER	323	3	DON JUAN	12	15	5
AND MARRIAGE ALSO MAY EXIST WITHOUT	323	3	DON JUAN	12	15	6
OF VESTALS BROUGHT INTO THE MARRIAGE MART	337	3	DON JUAN	12	46	7
A PERIL--NOT INDEED LIKE LOVE OR MARRIAGE	344	3	DON JUAN	12	62	2
AND CHANGED AS QUICKLY AS HEARTS AFTER MARRIAGE	379	3	DON JUAN	13	46	4
BY NO QUITE LAWFUL MARRIAGE OF THE ARTS	390	3	DON JUAN	13	67	2
SHE HAD ALSO SNATCH'D A MOMENT SINCE HER MARRIAGE	434	3	DON JUAN	14	56	7
THE MARRIAGE STATE THE BEST OR WORST OF ANY)	452	3	DON JUAN	14	95	6
FOR MORALS MARRIAGE AND THIS QUESTION CARRIED	469	3	DON JUAN	15	29	7
SOME DRAMA OF THE MARRIAGE UNITIES	470	3	DON JUAN	15	32	5
UNLESS A MARRIAGE WAS APPLIED TO MEND	470	3	DON JUAN	15	33	6
WHEN RAPP THE HARMONIST EMBARGOED MARRIAGE	471	3	DON JUAN	15	35	1
OR MARRIAGE BY DIVORCING THEM THUS ODDLY	472	3	DON JUAN	15	36	2
OR TURNING MARRIAGE INTO ARITHMETIC	472	3	DON JUAN	15	38	8
OF MARRIAGE--(WHICH MIGHT FORM A PAINTER'S FAME	473	3	DON JUAN	15	39	7
LOVE'S RIOTOUS BUT MARRIAGE SHOULD HAVE QUIET	474	3	DON JUAN	15	41	7
BY THE MARRIAGE BED OF THEIR LORDS 'TIS SAID	519	3	DON JUAN	16	L 3	5

MARRIAGE-MORNING

WHICH E'ER SET OFF A MARRIAGE-MORNING FACE	455	2	DON JUAN	5	76	8

MARRIAGES

BUT ONLY GIVE A BUST OF MARRIAGES	279	2	DON JUAN	3	8	4
ITS PETTY PASSIONS MARRIAGES AND FLIGHTS	353	2	DON JUAN	4	17	6

MARRIED

I NEVER MARRIED--BUT I THINK I KNOW	50	2	DON JUAN	1	53	7
SHE MARRIED (I FORGET THE PEDIGREE)	52	2	DON JUAN	1	57	1
WAS MARRIED CHARMING CHASTE AND TWENTY-THREE	54	2	DON JUAN	1	59	8
SO MUCH HE ALWAYS DOUBTED I WAS MARRIED--	101	2	DON JUAN	1	147	7
FREE AS A MARRIED WOMAN OR SUCH OTHER	248	2	DON JUAN	2	175	3
HAIDEE AND JUAN WERE NOT MARRIED BUT	282	2	DON JUAN	3	12	1
AN HONEST FRIENDSHIP WITH A MARRIED LADY--	288	2	DON JUAN	3	25	3
THAT WOULD HAVE SET TOM MOORE THOUGH MARRIED RAVING	291	2	DON JUAN	3	30	V6
IN LOPPING OFF YOUR LATELY MARRIED MEN	168	3	DON JUAN	8	113	2
WHICH HOVERS OFT ABOUT SOME MARRIED BEAUTIES	208	3	DON JUAN	9	51	4
MARRIED UNMARRIED AND REMARRIED (THIS IS	308	3	DON JUAN	11	79	4
WHETHER HE MARRIED WITH THE THIRD OR FOURTH	312	3	DON JUAN	11	89	1
RECRUITED ALL WITH CONSTANT MARRIED MEN	323	3	DON JUAN	12	16	2
NAY MARRIED DAMES WILL NOW AND THEN DISCOVER	331	3	DON JUAN	12	33	2
BEING LONG MARRIED AND THUS SET AT LARGE	339	3	DON JUAN	12	51	4
THE MARRIED ONES TO SAVE THE VIRGINS TROUBLE	342	3	DON JUAN	12	58	8
HIS GRACE WAS AN ENDURING MARRIED MAN	437	3	DON JUAN	14	62	2
SHE SERIOUSLY ADVISED HIM TO GET MARRIED	469	3	DON JUAN	15	29	8
IF THAT THEY WERE NOT MARRIED ALL ALREADY	469	3	DON JUAN	15	30	8
TO SAY LEADS OFT TO CRIM CON WITH THE MARRIED--	493	3	DON JUAN	15	84	3

MARROW

EMASCULATED TO THE MARROW IT	18	2	DON JUAN	D	15	2
AS I AM BLOOD--BONE--MARROW PASSION--FEELING--	156	2	DON JUAN	1 V	8	2
WHO LOVED BLOOD AS AN ALDERMAN LOVES MARROW	70	3	DON JUAN	7	8	8

MARRY

UNLESS HIS HIGHNESS PROMISES TO MARRY ME	460	2	DON JUAN	5	84	8
WHICH SAYS THOU SHALT NOT MARRY UNLESS WELL	472	3	DON JUAN	15	38	3

MARRYING

MARRYING THEIR COUSINS--NAY THEIR AUNTS AND NIECES	52	2	DON JUAN	1	57	7

MARS

I WONDER (ALTHOUGH MARS NO DOUBT'S A GOD I	77	3	DON JUAN	7	21	1
NOW MARS NOW MOMUS AND WHEN BENT TO STORM	95	3	DON JUAN	7	55	7
SO BE THEY HER INSPIRERS CALL THEM MARS	112	3	DON JUAN	8	1	7
'TIS THE SAME LANDSCAPE WHICH THE MODERN MARS SAW	253	3	DON JUAN	10	58	5
AND LADIES LIKE A LITTLE SPICE OF MARS	284	3	DON JUAN	11	33	V4

MARSH

OR LIKE A WISP ALONG THE MARSH SO DAMP	89	3	DON JUAN	7	46	5
NOW THAWED INTO A MARSH OF HUMAN BLOOD	148	3	DON JUAN	8	73	8

MARSHAL

BATTLES TO THE COMMAND FIELD MARSHAL SOUVAROFF	85	3	DON JUAN	7	39	8
THE LETTER OF THE PRINCE TO THE SAME MARSHAL	86	3	DON JUAN	7	40	1

MARSHALL

TO MARSHALL ONWARDS TO THE DELPHIAN HEIGHT	467	3	DON JUAN	15	25	V5

MARSHALL'D

THEY STAND FORTH MARSHALL'D IN A HANDSOME TROOP	46	2	DON JUAN	1	45	3

MARSHALS

WHERE SCIENCE MARSHALS FORTH HER OWN QUADRILLE	303	3	DON JUAN	11	70	8

MART

THE COURT CAMP CHURCH THE VESSEL AND THE MART	131	2	DON JUAN	1	194	3
'TIS THERE THE MART OF THE COLONIAL TRADE IS	159	2	DON JUAN	2	5	3
FOR ALTHOUGH DESTINED TO THE TURKISH MART HE	388	2	DON JUAN	4	81	3
WHATEER THE GARDEN BORE OR MART DISCLOSED	476	2	DON JUAN	5	113	V4
OF TRUTH THAN PROSE UNLESS TO SUIT THE MART	154	2	DON JUAN	8	86	5
OF VESTALS BROUGHT INTO THE MARRIAGE MART	337	3	DON JUAN	12	46	7

MARTIAL

TO ALL THOSE NAUSEOUS EPIGRAMS OF MARTIAL	45	2	DON JUAN	1	43	8
PERCEIVED IT WAS THE PYRRHIC DANCE SO MARTIAL	290	2	DON JUAN	3	29	7
HOW TO ENCOUNTER WITH THIS MARTIAL SCOLD	54	3	DON JUAN	6	96	3
INTO ALL ASPIRANTS FOR MARTIAL PRAISE	85	3	DON JUAN	7	39	V4
HIS MAXIMS WHICH TO MARTIAL COMPREHENSION	96	3	DON JUAN	7	58	7
WHEN I CALL FADING MARTIAL IMMORTALITY	108	3	DON JUAN	7	83	1
THEIR MARTIAL FACES ON THE PARAPET	135	3	DON JUAN	8	45	7

```
                                                              PAGE VOL        CANTO STANZA LN

MARTIAL   (CONTINUED)
    A RUSSIAN OFFICER IN MARTIAL TREAD . . . . . . . .   153  3 DON JUAN  8    83    1
    WITH MARTIAL STOICISM NOUGHT SEEMED TO ANNOY . . .   172  3 DON JUAN  8   121    5
    OTHERS IN WIGS OF MARLBOROUGH'S MARTIAL FOLD . . .   391  3 DON JUAN 13    70    3
MARTS
    WHERE DIFFERENT TALENTS FIND THEIR DIFFERENT MARTS . . .  91  2 DON JUAN  1   128    6
    PIECED OUT FOR DIFFERENT MARTS IN THE LEVANT . . .   284  2 DON JUAN  3    17    2
MARTYR
    AND NOT AT ALL DISPOSED TO PROVE A MARTYR . . . .   122  2 DON JUAN  1   184    8
    TO LOSE THE HOUR WOULD MAKE HER QUITE A MARTYR . .   482  2 DON JUAN  5   122    7
    A SAVAGE SORT OF MILITARY MARTYR . . . . . . .   152  3 DON JUAN  8    80    6
    AS EVER MAHOMET PICKED OUT FOR A MARTYR . . . .   167  3 DON JUAN  8   111    3
    VICTIM WHEN WRONG AND MARTYR OFT WHEN RIGHT . . .   420  3 DON JUAN 14    23    6
MARTYRED
    WHERE ARE THOSE MARTYRED SAINTS THE FIVE PER CENTS . . .  307  3 DON JUAN 11    77    7
MARTYRLY
    TREAT A DISSENTING AUTHOR VERY MARTYRLY . . . . .   142  2 DON JUAN  1   211    8
MARTYRS
    HE TURN'D FROM GRISLY SAINTS AND MARTYRS HAIRY . .   235  2 DON JUAN  2   149    7
    OF MARTYRS AWED AS SPAGNOLETTO TAINTED . . . . .   392  3 DON JUAN 13    71    7
MARVEL
    MARVEL AND PRAISE FOR BOTH OR NONE THINGS WIN . .   469  2 DON JUAN  5   100    6
    NO MARVEL THEN HE WAS A FAVOURITE . . . . . .   428  3 DON JUAN 14    41    1
    THAT ONE SCARCE KNEW AT WHAT TO MARVEL MOST . . .   543  3 DON JUAN 16    90    6
MARVELL'D
    MARVELL'D AT MERIT OF ANOTHER NATION . . . . . .   425  3 DON JUAN 14    34    3
    SHE MARVELL'D WHAT HE SAW IN SUCH A BABY . . . .   477  3 DON JUAN 15    49    7
MARVELLED
    AT WHICH HE MARVELLED SINCE IT HAD NOT RAINED . .   515  3 DON JUAN 16    34    4
MARVELLING
    CAME UP ALL MARVELLING AT SUCH A DEED . . . . .   275  3 DON JUAN 11    14    3
MARVELLOUS
    IT WAS NOT MARVELLOUS THAT A MERE LAD . . . . .   127  3 DON JUAN  8    31    6
MARY
    SHE PRAY'D THE VIRGIN MARY FOR HER GRACE . . . .    62  2 DON JUAN  1    75    7
    TO VIRGIN MARY SEVERAL POUNDS OF CANDLES . . . .   128  2 DON JUAN  1   190    6
    TO THE SWEET PORTRAITS OF THE VIRGIN MARY . . . .   235  2 DON JUAN  2   149    8
    WHICH CHARMED THE CHARMING MARY MONTAGU . . . . .   412  2 DON JUAN  5     3    8
    I HAVE A PASSION FOR THE NAME OF MARY . . . . .   413  2 DON JUAN  5     4    1
MARY'S
    SUCH AS WAS MARY'S QUEEN OF SCOTS TRUE--TEARS . .   468  2 DON JUAN  5    98    5
    NAPOLEON'S MARY'S (QUEEN OF SCOTLAND) SHOULD . . .   218  3 DON JUAN  9    71    5
MARYS
    AND LADY MARYS BLOOMING INTO GIRLS . . . . . . .   390  3 DON JUAN 13    68    4
MASCULINE
    WERE MASCULINE TO SEE THEM AND TO SEIZE . . . .   121  2 DON JUAN  1   181    4
    SOME THOUGHT HER RATHER MASCULINE IN HEIGHT . . .    23  3 DON JUAN  6    35    7
MASK
    A COW'S SHAPE FOR A MASK--WAS ONLY (SINKING . . .   238  2 DON JUAN  2   155    5
MASKED
    OF ONE WHOSE HATE IS MASKED BUT TO ASSAIL . . . .   182  2 DON JUAN  2    49    4
MASKS
    ARE MASKS IT OFTEN WEARS AND STILL TOO LATE . . .    61  2 DON JUAN  1    73    8
MASONIC
    SHORTLY AND SWEETLY THE MASONIC FOLLY . . . . .   448  2 DON JUAN  5    63    2
MASQUE
    MAKING THE COUNTENANCE A MASQUE OF REST . . . . .   457  3 DON JUAN 15     3    3
MASQUED
    (THOUGH SHE WAS MASQUED THEN AS A FAIR VENETIAN) .   268  2 DON JUAN  2   210    8
    WHICH HESITATION MORE BETRAYED THAN MASQUED-- . .    56  3 DON JUAN  6   100    6
MASQUERADE
    AND YET LAST NIGHT BEING AT A MASQUERADE . . . .   268  2 DON JUAN  2   209    6
    IN TRICKING HER OUT FOR A MASQUERADE . . . . . .    37  3 DON JUAN  6    62    6
    THE TRUTH IN MASQUERADE AND I DEFY . . . . . .   286  3 DON JUAN 11    37    2
    STRANGE FACES LIKE TO MEN IN MASQUERADE . . . .   389  3 DON JUAN 13    65    3
    DOUBTLESS IT IS A BRILLIANT MASQUERADE . . . . .   417  3 DON JUAN 14    17    5
    AND VEGETABLES ALL IN MASQUERADE . . . . . . .   488  3 DON JUAN 15    74    2
MASQUERADES
    AND WHAT WITH MASQUERADES AND FETES AND BALLS . .   342  3 DON JUAN 12    57    7
MASQUERADING
    AS NOT BEING IN A MASQUERADING MOOD . . . . . .   453  2 DON JUAN  5    73    5
    THAT THESE WERE MERELY MASQUERADING TARTARS . . .    96  3 DON JUAN  7    57    4
MASS
    EXCEPT TO BULL-FIGHTS MASS PLAY ROUT AND REVEL . .   102  2 DON JUAN  1   148    4
    THEY MUST WAIT SEVERAL WEEKS BEFORE A MASS . . .   185  2 DON JUAN  2    55    4
    IT COSTS THREE FRANCS FOR EVERY MASS THAT'S SAID .   185  2 DON JUAN  2    55    8
    A DAZZLING MASS OF GEMS AND GOLD AND GLITTER . .   465  2 DON JUAN  5    93    7
    BUT BY THE MASS WHO GO BELOW WITHOUT . . . . .   124  3 DON JUAN  8    26    5
    A MIGHTY MASS OF BRICK AND SMOKE AND SHIPPING . .   265  3 DON JUAN 10    82    1
    A SILENT CHANGE DISSOLVES THE GLITTERING MASS . .   306  3 DON JUAN 11    76    6
    OR ANDALUSIAN GIRL FROM MASS RETURNING . . . . .   350  3 DON JUAN 12    75    2
    IF ALL THESE SEEM AN HETEROGENEOUS MASS . . . .   402  3 DON JUAN 13    94    1
    A HETEROGENEOUS MASS OF GLORIOUS BLAME . . . . .   480  3 DON JUAN 15    57    3
    OR MASS FOR SHOULD I STRETCH INTO DETAIL . . . .   483  3 DON JUAN 15    64    2
    AND HIS MASS OF THE DAYS THAT ARE GONE . . . . .   518  3 DON JUAN 16  L  1    4
MASS-BOOKS
    WHICH ANCIENT MASS-BOOKS OFTEN ARE AND THIS ALL .    47  2 DON JUAN  1    46    3
MASSES
    LO DUSKY MASSES STEAL IN DUBIOUS SIGHT . . . . .   110  3 DON JUAN  7    86    3
```

MASSY
    THIS MASSY PORTAL STOOD AT THE WIDE CLOSE   . . . . . . 462 2 DON JUAN 5   87   1
    INTO AN ELEGANT EXTRACT (MUCH LESS MASSY)   . . . . . 130 3 DON JUAN 8   34   5
    WITH MASSY PLATE FOR ARMOUR KNIVES AND FORKS . . . . 482 3 DON JUAN 15   62   2
    THERE WERE SOME MASSY MEMBERS OF THE CHURCH . . . . 539 3 DON JUAN 16   80   6
MAST
    AND CARRY AWAY PERHAPS A MAST OR SO   . . . . . 170 2 DON JUAN 2   26   8
    BUT WITH A LEAK AND NOT A STICK OF MAST . . . . 176 2 DON JUAN 2   39   3
    AND ONE OAR FOR A MAST WHICH A YOUNG LAD . . . . 181 2 DON JUAN 2   48   5
    KEPT ABOVE WATER WITH AN OAR FOR MAST . . . . 188 2 DON JUAN 2   61   2
    LAY DROOPING OER THE OAR WHICH SERVED FOR MAST . . 214 2 DON JUAN 2 110   V5
    A MAST WAS ALMOST CRUMBLED TO A CRUTCH . . . . 226 2 DON JUAN 2 132   6
MASTER
    THEIR SENSES THEY'D HAVE SENT YOUNG MASTER FORTH . . . 34 2 DON JUAN 1   25   6
    FOR GOD'S SAKE .MADAM--MADAM--HERE'S MY MASTER . . . 96 2 DON JUAN 1 137   1
    HER MASTER AND HIS MYRMIDONS OF WHOM . . . . 109 2 DON JUAN 1 159   4
    WHO CAN HAVE PUT MY MASTER IN THIS MOOD . . . 115 2 DON JUAN 1 171   2
    COME SIR GET IN)--MY MASTER MUST BE NEAR . . . 115 2 DON JUAN 1 172   5
    DINE WITH THEM ON HIS PASTOR AND HIS MASTER . . . 198 2 DON JUAN 2   78   8
    TITUS THE MASTER ANTONY THE SLAVE . . . . 266 2 DON JUAN 2 205   2
    YOU MEAN OUR MASTER--NOT THE OLD BUT NEW . . . 297 2 DON JUAN 3   43   8
    MASTER OF THIRTY KINGDOMS SO SUBLIME . . . . 51 3 DON JUAN 6   90   3
    HE WAS YOUR MASTER OF YOUR STUPID COLLEGE . . . 264 3 DON JUAN 10   80   V2
    WAS GREAT BECAUSE HIS MASTER BROOKED NO LESS . . . 512 3 DON JUAN 16   28   7
    MIGHT COST BOTH MEN AND MASTER TOO--THEIR PLACES . . 539 3 DON JUAN 16   79   8
MASTER'D
    AND MASTER'D BY HER WISDOM OR HER PRIDE . . . . 356 2 DON JUAN 4   23   4
MASTERPIECE
    BUT WISH THIS MASTERPIECE OF NATURE'S WORK . . . . 315 2 DON JUAN 3   76   V7
MASTER'S
    AND NEXT THEY THOUGHT UPON THE MASTER'S MATE . . . . 199 2 DON JUAN 2   81   1
    A SECOND HICCUP'D OUR OLD MASTER'S DEAD . . . . 297 2 DON JUAN 3   43   5
MASTERS
    SOMETHING OF WHICH ITS MASTERS ARE AFRAID . . . . 18 2 DON JUAN D   14   3
    EUTROPIUS OF ITS MANY MASTERS--BLIND . . . . 18 2 DON JUAN D   15   5
    LEFT HIM AT LAST THE SOLE OF MANY MASTERS . . . 222 2 DON JUAN 2 125   7
    A TYRANT BUT OUR MASTERS THEN . . . . . 324 3 DON JUAN 3 L 11   2
    MAY TEACH US BETTER TO BEHAVE WHEN MASTERS . . . 422 2 DON JUAN 5   23   8
    WOULD WE WERE MASTERS NOW IF BUT TO TRY . . . . 423 2 DON JUAN 5   24   1
    THE WORLD NOT THE WORLD'S MASTERS WILL DECIDE . . 184 3 DON JUAN 9   4   6
    AND SCENT THE PREY THEIR MASTERS WOULD ATTACK ALL . . 196 3 DON JUAN 9   27   5
    MASTERS OF THEIR OWN TIME--OR IN COMMUNION . . . 406 3 DON JUAN 13 103   3
    YET LIKE THEIR MASTERS FEARFUL OF OFFENDING . . . 539 3 DON JUAN 16   79   6
MASTIFF
    A MONKEY A DUTCH MASTIFF A MACKAW . . . . . 285 2 DON JUAN 3   18   1
MASTS
    IMMEDIATELY THE MASTS WERE CUT AWAY . . . . 173 2 DON JUAN 2   32   1
    DAY BROKE AND THE WIND LULL'D THE MASTS WERE GONE . . 176 2 DON JUAN 2   38   2
    OF MASTS A WILDERNESS OF STEEPLES PEEPING . . . 265 3 DON JUAN 10   82   5
MATAPAN
    SOME HE DISPOSED OF OFF CAPE MATAPAN . . . . . 284 2 DON JUAN 3   16   1
MATCH
    TO MATCH A COMMON FURY WITH HER RAGE . . . . 490 2 DON JUAN 5 136   2
    THE MATCH WAS LIT TOO SOON AND NO ASSISTANCE . . . 80 3 DON JUAN 7   28   5
    SUWARROW NOW WAS CONQUEROR--A MATCH . . . . 178 3 DON JUAN 8 133   1
    FAIR CATHERINE'S PASTIME--WHO LOOKED ON THE MATCH . . 197 3 DON JUAN 9   29   6
    THERE WAS A GOODLY MATCH TOO TO BE RUN . . . . 527 3 DON JUAN 16   55   5
MATCHED
    WITH FLASHING EYES AND WEAPONS MATCHED WITH THEM . . 157 3 DON JUAN 8   92   2
    MATCHED WITH THE CONTINENT'S ILLUMINATION . . . 280 3 DON JUAN 11   26   4
    MATCHED FOR THE SPRING WHOM SEVERAL WENT TO SEE . . 527 3 DON JUAN 16   55   8
MATCHES
    UNEQUAL MATCHES SUCH AS ARE ALAS . . . . . 236 3 DON JUAN 10   24   3
    AT MAKING MATCHES WHERE 'TIS GOLD THAT GLISTERS . . 331 3 DON JUAN 12   32   5
    ALL MATCHLESS CREATURES AND YET BENT ON MATCHES . . 340 3 DON JUAN 12   53   8
    NEXT TO THE MAKING MATCHES FOR HERSELF . . . . 470 3 DON JUAN 15   31   1
    ALL THESE WERE UNOBJECTIONABLE MATCHES . . . . 473 3 DON JUAN 15   40   7
    TAKERS OF TITHES AND MAKERS OF GOOD MATCHES . . . 539 3 DON JUAN 16   80   7
MATCHLESS
    ALL MATCHLESS CREATURES AND YET BENT ON MATCHES . . 340 3 DON JUAN 12   53   8
MATCH-MAKING
    THAN MATCH-MAKING IN GENERAL 'TIS NO SIN . . . . 470 3 DON JUAN 15   31   6
MATE
    THE NOBLEST EFFORTS FOR HERSELF AND MATE . . . . 62 2 DON JUAN 1   75   3
    AND NEXT THEY THOUGHT UPON THE MASTER'S MATE . . . 199 2 DON JUAN 2   81   1
    AND FLEW TO HER YOUNG MATE LIKE A YOUNG BIRD . . . 257 2 DON JUAN 2 190   6
    AS FAST AS EVER HUSBAND BY HIS MATE . . . . 42 3 DON JUAN 6   73   3
MATERIAL
    AND ARISTIPPUS A MATERIAL CREW . . . . . 267 2 DON JUAN 2 207   2
    IN SIZE FROM OVERWORKING THE MATERIAL-- . . . . 202 3 DON JUAN 9   39   7
MATERIALISED
    BY MATTER AND SO MUCH MATERIALISED . . . . 543 3 DON JUAN 16   90   5
MATERIALS
    THERE POETS FIND MATERIALS FOR THEIR BOOKS . . . . 70 2 DON JUAN 1   90   5
    BUT OF MATERIALS THAT MUCH SHOCK THE MUSE-- . . . 195 2 DON JUAN 2   74   6
    BUT OF INFERIOR MATERIALS SHE . . . . . 221 2 DON JUAN 2 122   2
    MATERIALS AS WERE CAST UP ROUND THE BAY . . . . 226 2 DON JUAN 2 132   3
    SOVEREIGNS MAY SWAY MATERIALS BUT NOT MATTER . . . 236 3 DON JUAN 10   24   7
MATERNAL
    AND BREAST MATERNAL WEAN'D AT ONCE FOREVER . . . . 349 2 DON JUAN 4   10   6

MATERNAL   (CONTINUED)
   ALL PRAISED THE EMPRESS'S MATERNAL LOVE . . . . 240 3 DON JUAN 10   32   8
   GAVE HER A RIGHT TO HAVE MATERNAL FEARS . . . . 432 3 DON JUAN 14   52   5
MATES
   WHO LONG HAD BEEN HIS MATES UPON THE SEA . . . . 213 2 DON JUAN 2   109   4
MATHEMATICAL
   HER FAVOURITE SCIENCE WAS THE MATHEMATICAL . . . . 27 2 DON JUAN 1   12   1
   HIS LADY-MOTHER MATHEMATICAL . . . . 158 2 DON JUAN 2   3   3
MATHEMATICIAN
   ANGLE THE SOI-DISANT MATHEMATICIAN . . . . 399 3 DON JUAN 13   87   3
MATHEMATICS
   MEANT TO PERSONIFY THE MATHEMATICS . . . . 281 2 DON JUAN 3   11   8
MATHO
   OMNIA VULT BELLE MATHO DICERE--DIC ALIQUANDO . . . . . 465 3 DON JUAN 15   21   1
MATRIMONIAL
   FOR NO ONE CARES FOR MATRIMONIAL COOINGS . . . . 279 2 DON JUAN 3   8   5
   (I MEAN IN FORTUNE'S MATRIMONIAL BOUNTIES) . . . . . . 312 3 DON JUAN 11   89   4
MATRIMONY
   IN HOLY MATRIMONY SNORES AWAY . . . . 42 3 DON JUAN 6   73   4
   WHICH BEING THE DAMN'DEST PART OF MATRIMONY . . . . . . 217 3 DON JUAN 9   70   7
   IS WAX HEAVEN IS NOT LOVE 'TIS MATRIMONY . . . . 322 3 DON JUAN 12   14   8
MATRIMONY'S
   YOU'LL ADD TO MATRIMONY'S LIST OF CURES . . . . 343 3 DON JUAN 12   60   8
MATRON
   A MATRON WHO HER HUSBAND'S FOIBLE KNOWS . . . . 117 2 DON JUAN 1   175   3
   WHO SEEM'D TO HAVE TURN'D HAIDEE INTO A MATRON . . . . 298 2 DON JUAN 3   44   8
   'TIS BEAUTIFUL TO SEE A MATRON BRING . . . . 306 2 DON JUAN 3   60   3
   AS SUITS A MATRON WHO HAS PLAYED A PRANK . . . . 500 2 DON JUAN 5   154   4
   THE MATRON FROWNED WHY SO--FOR FEAR OF GHOSTS . . . . . 30 3 DON JUAN 6   48   2
   THE MATRON TOO WAS WROTH TO LEAVE HER WARM . . . . . . 45 3 DON JUAN 6   79   5
   ALSO A SO-SO MATRON BOLDLY FIGHT . . . . 397 3 DON JUAN 13   82   5
MATRON-LIKE
   AND MILDEST MATRON-LIKE INTERPRETATION . . . . 208 3 DON JUAN 9   52   2
MATRON'S
   BUT SHE ROSE UP AND KISSED THE MATRON'S BROW . . . . . 31 3 DON JUAN 6   50   1
   THE OTHERS POUTING AT THE MATRON'S PREFERENCE . . . . . 31 3 DON JUAN 6   50   7
MATRONS
   AND MATRONS WHO WOULD BE NO LESS SECURE . . . . 64 2 DON JUAN 1   79   4
   NOT ALL LONE MATRONS FOR THEIR HUSBANDS MOURN . . . . . 287 2 DON JUAN 3   23   3
   MATRONS AND MAIDS AND THOSE WHOM YOU MAY CALL . . . . . 42 3 DON JUAN 6   71   3
   IS WHEN CHASTE MATRONS TO THEIR OTHER TIES . . . . . . 220 3 DON JUAN 9   76   7
   JURY OF MATRONS SCARCE KNEW WHAT TO ANSWER . . . . . . 294 3 DON JUAN 11   51   4
   THE MISSES BRIDLED AND THE MATRONS FROWN'D . . . . . . 429 3 DON JUAN 14   44   2
   BUT RAPP IS THE REVERSE OF ZEALOUS MATRONS . . . . . . 472 3 DON JUAN 15   37   1
MATS
   HAD DONE THEIR WORK OF SPLENDOUR INDIAN MATS . . . . . 310 2 DON JUAN 3   68   2
MATTER
   IF WE MAY JUDGE OF MATTER BY THE MIND . . . . 18 2 DON JUAN D   15   1
   THIS WAS AN EASY MATTER WITH A MAN . . . . 33 2 DON JUAN 1   21   1
   BUT THAT'S NO MATTER AND THE WORST'S BEHIND . . . . . . 34 2 DON JUAN 1   24   6
   KNOWLEDGE OF MATTERS--BUT NO MATTER WHAT-- . . . . . . 50 2 DON JUAN 1   53   6
   NO MATTER HOW OR WHY THE THING BEFELL . . . . 77 2 DON JUAN 1   105   5
   'TIS SWEET TO WIN NO MATTER HOW ONE'S LAURELS . . . . . 90 2 DON JUAN 1   126   1
   NO MATTER WHAT--IT WAS NOT THAT THEY SOUGHT . . . . . . 100 2 DON JUAN 1   144   2
   I SAY--THE FUTURE IS A SERIOUS MATTER-- . . . . 156 2 DON JUAN 1   V 8   7
   PROVED EVEN STILL A MORE NUTRITIOUS MATTER . . . . . . 208 2 DON JUAN 2   99   5
   A FEMALE FAMILY'S A SERIOUS MATTER . . . . 287 2 DON JUAN 3   22   4
   AS THE PSALM SAYS INDITING A GOOD MATTER . . . . 316 2 DON JUAN 3   78   8
   NO MATTER WE SHOULD NE'ER TOO MUCH INQUIRE . . . . . . 396 2 DON JUAN 4   96   1
   AND--BUT NO MATTER ALL THOSE THINGS ARE OVER . . . . . 405 2 DON JUAN 4   111   4
   REMITS THE MATTER TO OUR OWN FREE-WILL . . . . 453 2 DON JUAN 5   72   8
   BUT WORDS ARE NOT ENOUGH IN SUCH A MATTER . . . . . . 493 2 DON JUAN 5   143   2
   THOUGH NOT FOR WANT OF MATTER BUT 'TIS TIME . . . . . . 503 2 DON JUAN 5   159   2
   ALONE FOR REASONS WHICH DON'T MATTER YOU . . . . 30 3 DON JUAN 6   49   2
   HE DID NOT THINK MUCH ON THE MATTER NOR . . . . 51 3 DON JUAN 6   91   1
   MIGHT MAKE THE MATTER STILL WORSE THAN IT WAS . . . . . 57 3 DON JUAN 6   103   8
   IF THIS BE THE RIGHT READING--'TIS NO MATTER . . . . . 70 3 DON JUAN 7   8   2
   NO MATTER WHAT POOR SOULS MIGHT BE UNDONE . . . . 78 3 DON JUAN 7   23   5
   SMILED AS SHE TALKED THE MATTER O'ER BUT TEARS . . . . 221 3 DON JUAN 9   78   6
   SOVEREIGNS MAY SWAY MATERIALS BUT NOT MATTER . . . . . 236 3 DON JUAN 10   24   7
   OR SEVEN AND TWENTY--BUT IT DOES NOT MATTER . . . . . . 236 3 DON JUAN 10   24   V7
   PERHAPS SHE HAD NOTHING TO CONFESS--NO MATTER . . . . . 252 3 DON JUAN 10   56   6
   AS GOING AT FULL SPEED--NO MATTER WHERE ITS . . . . . 260 3 DON JUAN 10   72   3
   WHEN BISHOP BERKELEY SAID THERE WAS NO MATTER . . . . . 268 3 DON JUAN 11   1   1
   AND PROVED IT--'TWAS NO MATTER WHAT HE SAID . . . . . . 268 3 DON JUAN 11   1   2
   HE WAS A BACHELOR WHICH IS A MATTER . . . . 292 3 DON JUAN 11   46   1
   WHERE THE PRAETORIAN BANDS TAKE UP THE MATTER-- . . . . 299 3 DON JUAN 11   62   2
   (NO MATTER WHICH) TURN POLITICIAN STUPIDER . . . . . . 309 3 DON JUAN 11   83   3
   HOW FAR IT PROFITS IS ANOTHER MATTER-- . . . . 339 3 DON JUAN 12   51   1
   AND THE WHOLE MATTER RESTS UPON EYE-SIGHT . . . . 348 3 DON JUAN 12   71   3
   FOR ME I LEAVE THE MATTER WHERE I FIND IT . . . . 352 3 DON JUAN 12   80   1
   IS NO GREAT MATTER SO 'TIS IN REQUEST . . . . 359 3 DON JUAN 13   3   4
   NO MATTER HOW OR WHY THE PASSPORT SHROUDS . . . . 396 3 DON JUAN 13   80   6
   TO FURNISH MATTER FOR THEIR MORAL GIBING . . . . 418 3 DON JUAN 14   19   6
   NO MATTER WHETHER RUSSET SILK OR DIMITY . . . . 421 3 DON JUAN 14   26   8
   AND WORK AWAY LIKE SPIRIT UPON MATTER . . . . 423 3 DON JUAN 14   30   7
   TO FURNISH MATTER FOR SOME FUTURE LIVY . . . . 440 3 DON JUAN 14   68   3
   INTENSE INTENTIONS ARE A DANGEROUS MATTER . . . . 448 3 DON JUAN 14   88   4
   ANTICIPATING AUGHT ABOUT THE MATTER . . . . 454 3 DON JUAN 14   99   2

MATTER (CONTINUED)

	PAGE	VOL	CANTO	STANZA	LN
BENEATH THE SURFACE BUT WHAT DID IT MATTER	474	3 DON JUAN	15	41	6
BUT ERE THE MATTER COULD BE MARR'D OR MENDED	482	3 DON JUAN	15	61	5
AND NOW THAT WE MAY FURNISH WITH SOME MATTER ALL	497	3 DON JUAN	15	93	7
THAT SOMETHING WAS THE MATTER--ADELINE	513	3 DON JUAN	16	30	7
SAW--WELL NO MATTER 'TWAS SO LONG AGO	517	3 DON JUAN	16	38	3
BY MATTER AND SO MUCH MATERIALISED	543	3 DON JUAN	16	90	5
FOR IMMATERIALISM'S A SERIOUS MATTER	556	3 DON JUAN	16	114	6
OR HOW IS'T MATTER TREMBLES TO COME NEAR IT	557	3 DON JUAN	16	116	8
UPON ALL POINTS-- NO MATTER WHAT OR WHOSE--	564	3 DON JUAN	17	6	2

MATTER'D

	PAGE	VOL	CANTO	STANZA	LN
OR GREEK--THAT IS ALTHOUGH IT NOT MUCH MATTER'D	240	2 DON JUAN	2	160	5

MATTERED

	PAGE	VOL	CANTO	STANZA	LN
HIMSELF OR BASTION LITTLE MATTERED NOW	172	3 DON JUAN	8	122	2

MATTERS

	PAGE	VOL	CANTO	STANZA	LN
THEN THEIR RELATIONS WHO MADE MATTERS WORSE	38	2 DON JUAN	1	32	2
KNOWLEDGE OF MATTERS--BUT NO MATTER WHAT--	50	2 DON JUAN	1	53	6
IT MATTERS NOT MUCH HOW BY GOOD OR ILL	146	2 DON JUAN	1	218	V3
SO THANK YOUR STARS THAT MATTERS ARE NO WORSE	147	2 DON JUAN	1	220	7
AND THEN IF MATTERS COULD BE MADE UP NOW	493	2 DON JUAN	5	142	4
AND FOR THEIR OTHER MATTERS MEET AND SHARE 'EM	53	3 DON JUAN	6	95	8
IF MATTERS HAD BEEN MANAGED AS DESIRED	55	3 DON JUAN	6	99	5
MADE ALL THEIR NAVAL MATTERS INCORRECT	80	3 DON JUAN	7	28	2
IN ORDERING MATTERS AFTER HIS OWN BENT	85	3 DON JUAN	7	38	3
BUT CERTES MATTERS TOOK A DIFFERENT FACE	89	3 DON JUAN	7	47	1
WHEN MATTERS MUST BE CARRIED BY THE TOUCH	151	3 DON JUAN	8	78	5
AND DEVIATE INTO MATTERS RATHER DRY	203	3 DON JUAN	9	41	4
BUT IN SUCH MATTERS RUSSIA'S MIGHTY EMPRESS	221	3 DON JUAN	9	77	7
GLADLY ALL MATTERS DOWN TO STONE OR LEAD	268	3 DON JUAN	11	1	6
MOST WILLINGLY ALL EVER SEEN OR READ MATTERS	268	3 DON JUAN	11	1	V6
OF WORLDS AND SPECIES--MATTERS--SOULS AND BODY	269	3 DON JUAN	11	3	V7
WHAT MATTERS IF THE ROAD BE HEAD OR HEART	284	3 DON JUAN	11	34	8
ABOUT SUCH GENERAL MATTERS--BUT PARTICULAR	290	3 DON JUAN	11	44	V7
IN SEEING MATTERS WHICH ARE OUT OF SIGHT	457	3 DON JUAN	15	2	8

MATTHEW

	PAGE	VOL	CANTO	STANZA	LN
MALGRE SIR MATTHEW HALES'S GREAT HUMANITY	565	3 DON JUAN	17	7	8

MATTOCK'S

	PAGE	VOL	CANTO	STANZA	LN
TO BE FILLED UP BY SPADE OR MATTOCK'S NEAR	245	3 DON JUAN	10	42	6

MATURE

	PAGE	VOL	CANTO	STANZA	LN
AND COUNTESSES MATURE IN ROBES AND PEARLS	390	3 DON JUAN	13	68	6

MATURER

	PAGE	VOL	CANTO	STANZA	LN
AS E'ER TO MAN'S MATURER GROWTH WAS GIVEN	48	2 DON JUAN	1	49	4

MAUDLIN

	PAGE	VOL	CANTO	STANZA	LN
WITH MAUDLIN CLARENCE IN HIS MALMSEY BUTT	112	2 DON JUAN	1	166	8

MAWS

	PAGE	VOL	CANTO	STANZA	LN
OF ALL THE LUCKLESS LANDSMEN'S SEA-SICK MAWS	174	2 DON JUAN	2	34	6

MAX

	PAGE	VOL	CANTO	STANZA	LN
OH FOR A GLASS OF MAX WE'VE MISS'D OUR BOOTY--	276	3 DON JUAN	11	16	3

MAXIM

	PAGE	VOL	CANTO	STANZA	LN
TO MAKE US UNDERSTAND EACH GOOD OLD MAXIM	264	2 DON JUAN	2	203	7
HOW PLEASANT WERE THE MAXIM (NOT QUITE NEW)	267	2 DON JUAN	2	207	6
AND KISS THE LADY'S FOOT WHICH MAXIM WHEN	470	2 DON JUAN	5	102	4
IN SHORT THE MAXIM FOR THE AMOROUS TRIBE IS	14	3 DON JUAN	6	17	7
BUT THIS IS NOT MY MAXIM HAD IT BEEN	431	3 DON JUAN	14	49	1
HIS OTHER MAXIM NOSCITUR A SOCIIS	443	3 DON JUAN	14	77	3

MAXIME

	PAGE	VOL	CANTO	STANZA	LN
WHILE THAT HIATUS MAXIME DEFLENDUS	245	3 DON JUAN	10	42	5

MAXIMS

	PAGE	VOL	CANTO	STANZA	LN
HIS MAXIMS WHICH TO MARTIAL COMPREHENSION	96	3 DON JUAN	7	58	7

MAY

	PAGE	VOL	CANTO	STANZA	LN
AND SO IS SPRING ABOUT THE END OF MAY	76	2 DON JUAN	1	102	3
MARCH HAS ITS HARES AND MAY MUST HAVE ITS HEROINE	76	2 DON JUAN	1	102	8
HAVE SQUANDER'D MY WHOLE SUMMER WHILE 'TWAS MAY	143	2 DON JUAN	1	213	5
AND SHUDDER--WHILE AS BEAUTIFUL AS MAY	157	3 DON JUAN	8	91	5

MAYBE

	PAGE	VOL	CANTO	STANZA	LN
DREST VOTED SHONE AND MAYBE SOMETHING MORE	418	3 DON JUAN	14	18	2

MAY-DAY

	PAGE	VOL	CANTO	STANZA	LN
STOLE ON YOUR SPIRIT LIKE A MAY-DAY BREAKING	27	3 DON JUAN	6	43	2
BEFORE MAY-DAY PERHAPS DESPITE HIS DUTY	243	3 DON JUAN	10	37	7

MAYOR'S

	PAGE	VOL	CANTO	STANZA	LN
TO BE TRANSMITTED LIKE THE LORD MAYOR'S BARGE	339	3 DON JUAN	12	51	6

MAZE

	PAGE	VOL	CANTO	STANZA	LN
OF HIS OLD AGE IN WILDS OF DEEPEST MAZE	143	3 DON JUAN	8	61	8
DISPLAY'D SOME SYLPH-LIKE FIGURES IN ITS MAZE	408	3 DON JUAN	13	108	3
THAN OTHERS CROWDED IN THE FOREST'S MAZE--	562	3 DON JUAN	17	1	4

ME

	PAGE	VOL	CANTO	STANZA	LN
WHICH MAKES ME WISH YOU'D CHANGE YOUR LAKES FOR OCEAN	12	2 DON JUAN	D	5	8
FOR ME WHO WANDERING WITH PEDESTRIAN MUSES	14	2 DON JUAN	D	8	1
WHERE SHALL I TURN ME NOT TO VIEW ITS BONDS	19	2 DON JUAN	D	16	1
HAVE VOICES--TONGUES TO CRY ALOUD FOR ME	19	2 DON JUAN	D	16	6
(ALTHOUGH IT COST ME HALF AN HOUR IN SPINNING)	25	2 DON JUAN	1	7	6
FOR LITTLE JUAN O'ER ME THREW DOWN STAIRS	34	2 DON JUAN	1	24	7
FOR THERE ONE LEARNS--'TIS NOT FOR ME TO BOAST	50	2 DON JUAN	1	53	1
AS IF IT SAID DETAIN ME IF YOU PLEASE	81	2 DON JUAN	1	111	3
ARE QUITE ENOUGH FOR ME SO THEY BUT HOLD	85	2 DON JUAN	1	118	8
DARE YOU SUSPECT ME WHOM THE THOUGHT WOULD KILL	98	2 DON JUAN	1	142	7
AND SEEMS TO ME ALMOST A SORT OF BLUNDER	100	2 DON JUAN	1	144	7
YOU NEVER YET TO ANY SAW ME CIVIL	102	2 DON JUAN	1	148	V6
CALL ME THE ONLY VIRTUOUS WIFE IN SPAIN	102	2 DON JUAN	1	149	4

	PAGE	VOL	CANTO	STANZA	LN
ME ALSO SINCE THE TIME SO OPPORTUNE IS--	103	2 DON JUAN	1	150	6
NOW TELL ME DON'T YOU CUT A PRETTY FIGURE	103	2 DON JUAN	1	150	8
AND NOT FROM ANY LOVE TO YOU NOR ME	103	2 DON JUAN	1	151	8
AND WHEN 'TIS FOUND LET ME TOO HAVE THAT PLEASURE	104	2 DON JUAN	1	153	8
DOUBT UPON ME CONFUSION OVER ALL	105	2 DON JUAN	1	154	2
TELL ME--AND BE ASSURED THAT SINCE YOU STAIN	105	2 DON JUAN	1	154	7
(ANTONIA LET ME HAVE A GLASS OF WATER)	106	2 DON JUAN	1	155	4
'TWILL ONE DAY ASK YOU WHY YOU USED ME SO	107	2 DON JUAN	1	157	6
(THAT MODERN PHRASE APPEARS TO ME SAD STUFF	119	2 DON JUAN	1	178	3
THEY TELL ME 'TIS DECIDED YOU DEPART	130	2 DON JUAN	1	192	1
NONE CAN DEEM HARSHLIER OF ME THAN I DEEM	130	2 DON JUAN	1	193	6
FOR ME ON EARTH EXCEPT SOME YEARS TO HIDE	132	2 DON JUAN	1	195	3
AND SO FAREWELL--FORGIVE ME LOVE ME--NO	132	2 DON JUAN	1	195	7
AND SO FAREWELL--FORGIVE ME LOVE ME--NO	132	2 DON JUAN	1	195	7
ME AND MY EPIC BRETHREN GONE BEFORE	137	2 DON JUAN	1	202	2
WHO THANK'D ME DULY BY RETURN OF POST--	142	2 DON JUAN	1	210	2
BECAUSE THEY TELL ME 'TWERE IN VAIN TO TRY	142	2 DON JUAN	1	211	6
NO MORE--NO MORE--OH NEVER MORE ON ME	144	2 DON JUAN	1	214	1
MY DAYS OF LOVE ARE OVER ME NO MORE	144	2 DON JUAN	1	216	1
AND THE TWO LAST HAVE LEFT ME MANY A TOKEN	145	2 DON JUAN	1	217	3
LET NOT A MONUMENT GIVE YOU OR ME HOPES	146	2 DON JUAN	1	219	7
I CAN'T SAY THAT IT PUZZLES ME AT ALL	158	2 DON JUAN	2	3	1
BUT DAMN ME--IF I EVER SAW THE LIKE	159	2 DON JUAN	2	5	V8
(FOR GOD'S SAKE LET ME HAVE A GLASS OF LIQUOR	167	2 DON JUAN	2	20	3
PEDRO BATTISTA HELP ME DOWN BELOW)	167	2 DON JUAN	2	20	4
BELOVED JULIA HEAR ME STILL BESEECHING	167	2 DON JUAN	2	20	7
'TIS TRUE THAT DEATH AWAITS BOTH YOU AND ME	175	2 DON JUAN	2	36	3
IN MY YOUNG DAYS THEY LENT ME CASH THAT WAY	190	2 DON JUAN	2	65	7
AT LEAST IT IS A HEAVY SOUND TO ME	237	2 DON JUAN	2	152	6
FOES FRIENDS MEN WOMEN NOW ARE NOUGHT TO ME	244	2 DON JUAN	2	166	7
I CAN'T BUT SAY IT SEEMS TO ME MOST TRULY A	267	2 DON JUAN	2	208	3
WHICH GAVE ME SOME SENSATIONS LIKE A VILLAIN	268	2 DON JUAN	2	209	8
CAN CALM--FOR WHAT IT MADE ME ON THAT SAME	272	2 DON JUAN	2	V 1	7
THE BLAME ON ME UNLESS YOU WISH THEY WERE	282	2 DON JUAN	3	12	4
BUT TO MY SUBJECT--LET ME SEE--WHAT WAS IT--	317	2 DON JUAN	3	81	5
PLACE ME ON SUNIUM'S MARBLED STEEP	326	2 DON JUAN	3	L 16	1
THERE SWAN-LIKE LET ME SING AND DIE	326	2 DON JUAN	3	L 16	4
BUT LET ME TO MY STORY I MUST OWN	331	2 DON JUAN	3	96	1
BUT SET THOSE PERSONS DOWN WITH ME TO PRAY	336	2 DON JUAN	3	104	3
AND DRYDEN'S LAY MADE HAUNTED GROUND TO ME	337	2 DON JUAN	3	105	7
SOME HAVE ACCUSED ME OF A STRANGE DESIGN	346	2 DON JUAN	4	5	1
PERHAPS NO BETTER THAN THEY HAVE TREATED ME	347	2 DON JUAN	4	7	2
MEANTIME APOLLO PLUCKS ME BY THE EAR	347	2 DON JUAN	4	7	7
AND TELLS ME TO RESUME MY STORY HERE	347	2 DON JUAN	4	7	8
'TIS LAMBRO--'TIS MY FATHER KNEEL WITH ME--	364	2 DON JUAN	4	38	2
DEAL WITH ME AS THOU WILT BUT SPARE THIS BOY	364	2 DON JUAN	4	38	8
STERN AS HER SIRE ON ME SHE CRIED LET DEATH	366	2 DON JUAN	4	42	4
WAKES ME NEXT MORNING WITH ITS SYNONYM	372	2 DON JUAN	4	53	8
BUT LET ME CHANGE THIS THEME WHICH GROWS TOO SAD	384	2 DON JUAN	4	74	1
THE TIME MAY COME WHEN YOU MAY HEAR ME TOO	392	2 DON JUAN	4	88	6
'TIS ALL THE SAME TO ME I'M FOND OF YIELDING	397	2 DON JUAN	4	98	1
OH LADY DAPHNE LET ME MEASURE YOU	406	2 DON JUAN	4	112	8
BUT COULD NOT FOR THE MUSE OF ME PUT LESS IN'T	410	2 DON JUAN	4	117	6
BEING PIQUED BY CRITICS WHO HAVE DONE ME WRONG	410	2 DON JUAN	4	117	V5
FOR ONCE IT WAS A MAGIC SOUND TO ME	413	2 DON JUAN	5	4	2
'TWOULD GIVE ME PLEASURE--PRAY WHAT IS YOUR NATION	417	2 DON JUAN	5	13	8
SHE HAS SERVED ME ALSO MUCH THE SAME AS YOU	418	2 DON JUAN	5	14	7
IT BETTERS PRESENT TIMES WITH ME OR YOU	422	2 DON JUAN	5	23	3
JUST AS MY GREAT COAT WAS ABOUT ME CAST	428	2 DON JUAN	5	33	3
BUT LET ME QUIT THE THEME AS SUCH THINGS CLAIM	431	2 DON JUAN	5	38	4
FROM ME I GAZED (AS OFT I HAVE GAZED THE SAME)	431	2 DON JUAN	5	38	6
WHICH MIGHT HAVE THEN OCCURRED TO YOU OR ME	434	2 DON JUAN	5	43	4
OR IF YOU DON'T THE FAULT IS NOT IN ME	450	2 DON JUAN	5	66	8
WILL IT SAID JUAN SHARPLY STRIKE ME DEAD	452	2 DON JUAN	5	71	7
YOU PUT ME OUT IN WHAT I HAD TO SAY	453	2 DON JUAN	5	72	3
THE THINGS DOWN SAID--INCENSE ME AND I CALL	454	2 DON JUAN	5	75	7
(THE RHYME OBLIGES ME TO THIS SOMETIMES	456	2 DON JUAN	5	77	7
AND NOW THEN YOU MUST COME ALONG WITH ME SIRS	458	2 DON JUAN	5	80	6
WILL FOLLOW ME NO TRIFLING SIR FOR WHEN	458	2 DON JUAN	5	81	4
IF ANY TAKE ME FOR THAT WHICH I SEEM	459	2 DON JUAN	5	82	6
REPLIED THE OTHER THOUGH IT GRIEVES ME SORE	460	2 DON JUAN	5	84	3
NAY QUOTH THE MAID THE SULTAN'S SELF SHAN'T CARRY ME	460	2 DON JUAN	5	84	7
UNLESS HIS HIGHNESS PROMISES TO MARRY ME	460	2 DON JUAN	5	84	8
WERE FITTER FOR ME LOVE IS FOR THE FREE	484	2 DON JUAN	5	127	4
THE SUN HIMSELF HAS SENT ME LIKE A RAY	494	2 DON JUAN	5	144	7
AND AS YOU'D HAVE ME PARDON YOUR PAST SCORNING--	494	2 DON JUAN	5	145	6
RESTORE ME THOSE PURE FEELINGS GONE FOREVER	9	3 DON JUAN	6	5	8
IT SOONER FOR THE SOUL OF ME AND CLASS	34	3 DON JUAN	6	56	5
A KIND CONSTRUCTION UPON THEM AND ME	34	3 DON JUAN	6	56	7
AND I LOVE WISDOM MORE THAN SHE LOVES ME	37	3 DON JUAN	6	63	2
YOUR FATHER'S SON 'TIS QUITE ENOUGH FOR ME	52	3 DON JUAN	6	93	8
MAY SETTLE BUT FAR BE'T FROM ME TO ANTICIPATE	65	3 DON JUAN	6	119	7
THEY ACCUSE ME--ME--THE PRESENT WRITER OF	67	3 DON JUAN	7	3	1
THEY ACCUSE ME--ME--THE PRESENT WRITER OF	67	3 DON JUAN	7	3	1
MUST I RESTRAIN ME THROUGH THE FEAR OF STRIFE	69	3 DON JUAN	7	6	7
WHAT FOLLOWED--A SHOT LAID ME ON MY BACK	98	3 DON JUAN	7	61	5
THE STRANGER STRIPLING MAY REMAIN WITH ME	100	3 DON JUAN	7	66	6
TO ME THIS KIND OF LIFE IS NOT SO NEW	103	3 DON JUAN	7	72	5

498

ME   (CONTINUED)

	PAGE	VOL	CANTO	STANZA	LN
I THEREFORE IF YOU WISH ME TO FIGHT FREELY	103	3 DON JUAN	7	72	7
THEN UP WITH ME--BUT JUAN ANSWERED LOOK	161	3 DON JUAN	8	99	1
HER LIFE TO CHANCE BUT POINT ME OUT SOME NOOK	161	3 DON JUAN	8	99	3
BUT LET ME PUT AN END UNTO MY THEME	175	3 DON JUAN	8	127	1
HEAVEN HELP ME I'M BUT LITTLE OF A PARSON	179	3 DON JUAN	8	134	4
BUT PHOEBUS LENDS ME NOW AND THEN A STRING	181	3 DON JUAN	8	138	8
FOR ME I SOMETIMES THINK THAT LIFE IS DEATH	190	3 DON JUAN	9	16	7
SOME PEOPLE HAVE ACCUSED ME OF MISANTHROPY	192	3 DON JUAN	9	20	4
WHY DO THEY CALL ME MISANTHROPE BECAUSE	193	3 DON JUAN	9	21	7
THEY HATE ME NOT I THEM--AND HERE WE'LL PAUSE	193	3 DON JUAN	9	21	8
FOR ME I DEEM AN ABSOLUTE AUTOCRAT	194	3 DON JUAN	9	23	7
WITHOUT ME THERE ARE DEMAGOGUES ENOUGH	195	3 DON JUAN	9	25	2
AS MUCH FROM MOBS AS KINGS--FROM YOU AS ME	195	3 DON JUAN	9	25	8
MAY CHOOSE TO TAX ME WITH WHICH IS NOT FAIR	230	3 DON JUAN	10	11	4
FOR ME FOR I WOULD RATHER TAKE MY WINE	233	3 DON JUAN	10	17	3
LIKE BANQUO'S OFFSPRING--FLOATING PAST ME SEEMS	233	3 DON JUAN	10	18	6
CLINGS TO ITS TEAT STICKS TO ME THROUGH THE ABYSS	238	3 DON JUAN	10	28	4
WOULD THIS DAMNED HEADACHE SUFFER ME TO BEAR IT	268	3 DON JUAN	11	1	V8
LET ME DIE WHERE I AM AND AS THE FUEL	276	3 DON JUAN	11	16	4
TO ME APPEARS A STIFF YET GRAND ERECTION	280	3 DON JUAN	11	25	7
SIR WALTER REIGNED BEFORE ME MOORE AND CAMPBELL	297	3 DON JUAN	11	57	1
SETS UP FOR BEING A SORT OF MORAL ME	298	3 DON JUAN	11	59	2
CAW ME CAW THEE--FOR SIX MONTHS HATH BEEN HATCHING	307	3 DON JUAN	11	78	7
AND THAT I SING OF NEITHER MINE NOR ME	311	3 DON JUAN	11	88	5
TO ME--OF WHICH THESE MORALS ARE A SAMPLE	323	3 DON JUAN	12	16	8
TO ME SEEMS BUT A DUBIOUS KIND OF REED	324	3 DON JUAN	12	18	5
OH PARDON ME DIGRESSION--OR AT LEAST	334	3 DON JUAN	12	39	1
IN FACT THERE'S NOTHING MAKES ME SO MUCH GRIEVE	336	3 DON JUAN	12	43	6
BUT SHOULD A LADY ASK ME TO OBLIGE HER	348	3 DON JUAN	12	70	V4
AND THIS REFLECTION BRINGS ME TO PLAIN PHYSICS	349	3 DON JUAN	12	72	5
AND HAVE OR HAD AN EAR THAT SERVED ME PRETTILY)--	350	3 DON JUAN	12	75	8
FOR ME I LEAVE THE MATTER WHERE I FIND IT	352	3 DON JUAN	12	80	1
AND TELL ME WHAT YOU THINK OF YOUR GREAT THINKERS	357	3 DON JUAN	12	89	8
POOR THING HOW FREQUENTLY BY ME AND OTHERS	374	3 DON JUAN	13	36	7
HIS BELL-MOUTHED GOBLET MAKES ME FEEL QUITE DANISH	392	3 DON JUAN	13	72	7
DAN PHOEBUS TAKES ME FOR AN AUCTIONEER	393	3 DON JUAN	13	74	4
IS DIFFICULT PRAY TELL ME CAN YOU MAKE FAST	411	3 DON JUAN	14	2	3
FOR ME I KNOW NOUGHT NOTHING I DENY	411	3 DON JUAN	14	3	1
THE WORLD IS ALL BEFORE ME OR BEHIND	414	3 DON JUAN	14	9	1
AND QUITE ENOUGH FOR ME TO KEEP IN MIND--	414	3 DON JUAN	14	9	3
IT OCCUPIES ME TO TURN BACK REGARDS	415	3 DON JUAN	14	11	5
THAT NO DEFEAT CAN DRIVE ME FROM THE NINE	415	3 DON JUAN	14	12	4
IT PALLS--AT LEAST IT DID SO UPON ME	417	3 DON JUAN	14	17	7
SOME HEART-ACHES HAD BEEN SPARED ME YET I CARE NOT--	431	3 DON JUAN	14	49	2
WHO DID NOT QUIT ME WHEN OPPRESSION TROD	452	3 DON JUAN	14	96	5
UPON ME WHOM NO SCANDAL COULD REMOVE	452	3 DON JUAN	14	96	6
IF SOMEONE HAD NOT TOLD ME TO FOREGO IT	467	3 DON JUAN	15	24	8
FOR ME APPEARS A QUESTION FAR TOO NICE	478	3 DON JUAN	15	52	5
SHALL FOOL ME TO THE TOP UP OF MY BENT--	498	3 DON JUAN	15	94	3
RATTLES AROUND ME HER DISCORDANT HYMN	499	3 DON JUAN	15	97	4
OLD PORTRAITS FROM OLD WALLS UPON ME SCOWL--	499	3 DON JUAN	15	97	5
SHOULD STILL BE SINGED BUT SLIGHTLY LET ME STATE)	565	3 DON JUAN	17	7	6
MY SOUL FROM OUT ME AT THY SINGLE SUMMON	569	3 DON JUAN	17	V 13	6

MEADOWS

	PAGE	VOL	CANTO	STANZA	LN
ON ON THROUGH MEADOWS MANAGED LIKE A GARDEN	262	3 DON JUAN	10	76	1

MEAGRE

	PAGE	VOL	CANTO	STANZA	LN
SOME DOME SURMOUNTED BY HIS MEAGRE FACE	320	3 DON JUAN	12	10	4

MEAL

	PAGE	VOL	CANTO	STANZA	LN
AND MUST HAVE MEALS AT LEAST ONE MEAL A DAY	191	2 DON JUAN	2	67	2
AND HOWLED FOR HELP AS WOLVES DO FOR A MEAL--	153	3 DON JUAN	8	83	6

MEALS

	PAGE	VOL	CANTO	STANZA	LN
THAT NO ONE LIKES TO BE DISTURB'D AT MEALS	69	2 DON JUAN	1	89	5
AND MUST HAVE MEALS AT LEAST ONE MEAL A DAY	191	2 DON JUAN	2	67	2
AS ALL HIS LATTER MEALS HAD BEEN QUITE RAW	239	2 DON JUAN	2	157	4
METHINKS AT MEALS SOME ODD THOUGHTS MIGHT INTRUDE	426	2 DON JUAN	5	30	3
FOUND LIFE MOST TOLERABLE AFTER MEALS	427	2 DON JUAN	5	31	2
A SLICE OR TWO FROM YOUR LUXURIOUS MEALS	185	3 DON JUAN	9	6	4

MEAN

	PAGE	VOL	CANTO	STANZA	LN
AND MAKES THE WORD MILTONIC MEAN SUBLIME	15	2 DON JUAN	D	10	4
OR IF THEY DID SO SATISFIED TO MEAN	66	2 DON JUAN	1	83	4
I MEAN THE SERAPH WAY OF THOSE ABOVE	67	2 DON JUAN	1	85	8
BY SOLITUDE I MEAN A SULTAN'S NOT	68	2 DON JUAN	1	87	7
THEY MEAN TO SCOLD AND VERY OFTEN DO	79	2 DON JUAN	1	108	2
AND MEAN NEXT WINTER TO BE QUITE RECLAIM'D	85	2 DON JUAN	1	119	8
IN HEAVEN'S NAME DON ALFONSO WHAT D'YE MEAN	98	2 DON JUAN	1	142	2
BESIDES IN CANTO TWELFTH I MEAN TO SHOW	140	2 DON JUAN	1	207	7
AND SUCH SWEET GIRLS--I MEAN SUCH GRACEFUL LADIES	159	2 DON JUAN	2	5	5
BY FEMALE LIPS AND EYES--THAT IS I MEAN	242	2 DON JUAN	2	164	2
BY LENGTH I MEAN DURATION THEIRS ENDURED	254	2 DON JUAN	2	187	1
SOME CHASTE LIAISON OF THE KIND--I MEAN	288	2 DON JUAN	3	25	2
YOU MEAN OUR MASTER--NOT THE OLD BUT NEW	297	2 DON JUAN	3	43	8
AND WEDLOCK AND A PADLOCK MEAN THE SAME	502	2 DON JUAN	5	158	2
I DO NOT MEAN DESTRUCTION AND EXPOSURE	62	3 DON JUAN	6	114	7
HIS POST I MEAN THE REGIMENT NIKOLAIEW	100	3 DON JUAN	7	66	5
WHY JOHNSON WHAT THE DEVIL DO YOU MEAN	102	3 DON JUAN	7	70	2
I MEAN THAT EVERY AGE AND EVERY YEAR	108	3 DON JUAN	7	83	2
BELLONA WHAT YOU WILL--THEY MEAN BUT WARS	112	3 DON JUAN	8	1	8
MORE THAN THE CAP IN FACT THE BALL COULD MEAN	117	3 DON JUAN	8	10	6

499

MEAN   (CONTINUED)
```
    I DON'T MEAN TO REFLECT--A MAN SO GREAT AS  . . . . .    186  3 DON JUAN   9      7  1
    IS RATHER DEAR--I'M SURE I MEAN NO HARM  . . . . . .     186  3 DON JUAN   9      7  8
    THAT FORMS THIS DESK OF WHAT THEY MEAN--LYKANTHROPY  . .  192  3 DON JUAN   9     20  6
    I DON'T MEAN THAT THEY ARE PASSIONLESS BUT QUITE  . .    284  3 DON JUAN  11     34  1
    I HAVE SEEN A CONGRESS DOING ALL THAT'S MEAN--  . .      310  3 DON JUAN  11     84  6
    (I MEAN IN FORTUNE'S MATRIMONIAL BOUNTIES)  . . . . .    312  3 DON JUAN  11     89  4
    THINK NOT FAIR CREATURES THAT I MEAN TO ABUSE YOU ALL--  329  3 DON JUAN  12     28  3
    I MEAN TO SHOW THINGS REALLY AS THEY ARE  . . . . .      335  3 DON JUAN  12     40  2
    I DON'T MEAN THIS AS GENERAL BUT PARTICULAR  . . . .     343  3 DON JUAN  12     59  1
    IT IS--I MEANT AND MEAN NOT TO DISPARAGE  . . . . .      344  3 DON JUAN  12     62  4
    I NOW MEAN TO BE SERIOUS--IT IS TIME  . . . . . .        358  3 DON JUAN  13      1  1
    AND SUCH I MEAN TO MAKE HIM WHEN I REIGN  . . . . .      440  3 DON JUAN  14     70  8
    EUREKA I HAVE FOUND IT WHAT I MEAN  . . . . . . .        443  3 DON JUAN  14     76  1
    AND DO NOT THINK I MEAN TO SNEER AT MOST  . . . . .      498  3 DON JUAN  15     95  5
    I MERELY MEAN TO SAY WHAT JOHNSON SAID  . . . . . .      504  3 DON JUAN  16      7  1
    THERE WAS A MODERN GOTH I MEAN A GOTHIC  . . . . .       529  3 DON JUAN  16     58  1
MEANDER
    A DREADFUL IMPULSE TO EACH LOUD MEANDER  . . . . . .      52  3 DON JUAN   6     93  5
MEANETH
    MY FAULTS EVEN WITH YOUR OWN WHICH MEANETH PUT  . . . .   34  3 DON JUAN   6     56  6
    MEANETH THE WEST OR WORST END OF A CITY  . . . . . .     290  3 DON JUAN  11     45  2
MEANING
    HE ASKED THE MEANING OF THIS HOLIDAY  . . . . . .        297  2 DON JUAN   3     42  5
    AND THOUGH HIS MEANING THEY COULD RARELY GUESS  . . .    318  2 DON JUAN   3     82  5
    MY OWN MEANING WHEN I WOULD BE VERY FINE  . . . . .      346  2 DON JUAN   4      5  5
    BACK TO OLD THOUGHTS WAX'D FULL OF FEARFUL MEANING  . .  379  2 DON JUAN   4     64  8
    (THOUGH HE WELL KNEW THE MEANING) TO BE SHOWN  . . .      62  3 DON JUAN   6    112  6
    'TIS PITY THAT SUCH MEANING SHOULD PAVE HELL  . . . .    123  3 DON JUAN   8     25  8
    NOR WHAT THE MEANING OF THE MAN'S FAREWELL  . . . .      276  3 DON JUAN  11     17  4
    KICK OFF THEIR BURTHENS--MEANING THE HIGH CLASSES  . .   310  3 DON JUAN  11     84  8
    MEANING A VIRGIN'S FIRST BLUSH AT A ROUT  . . . . .      330  3 DON JUAN  12     31  5
    AND GENTLE READER WHEN YOU GATHER MEANING  . . . . .     403  3 DON JUAN  13     96  3
    WAS MEMBER FOR THE OTHER INTEREST (MEANING  . . . . .    535  3 DON JUAN  16     70  7
MEANS
    'TIS STRANGE--THE HEBREW NOUN WHICH MEANS I AM  . . .     28  2 DON JUAN   1     14  7
    CONDUCT LIKE THIS BY NO MEANS COMPREHENDS  . . . . .      37  2 DON JUAN   1     30  6
    POSSESS'D AN AIR AND GRACE BY NO MEANS COMMON  . . .      55  2 DON JUAN   1     61  7
    BY ALL MEANS LET THE GENTLEMAN PROCEED  . . . . . .      104  2 DON JUAN   1    152  2
    FOR HAIDEE'S KNOWLEDGE WAS BY NO MEANS GREAT  . . . .    354  2 DON JUAN   4     19  5
    BUT SHE DEFIED ALL MEANS THEY COULD EMPLOY  . . . .      376  2 DON JUAN   4     59  7
    TO WHOM THE OPERA IS BY NO MEANS NEW  . . . . . .        392  2 DON JUAN   4     88  4
    PLAIN--SIMPLE--SHORT AND BY NO MEANS INVITING  . . .     412  2 DON JUAN   5      2  3
    THOUGH CERTES BY NO MEANS SO GRAND A SIGHT  . . . .      444  2 DON JUAN   5     58  5
    WHAT SPEAKS OF HEAVEN SHOULD BY NO MEANS BE BRITTLE  . . 444  2 DON JUAN   5     59  3
    YOU FOOL I TELL YOU NO ONE MEANS YOU HARM  . . . . .     459  2 DON JUAN   5     82  1
    AND BETWEEN FEMALES MEANS NO MORE THAN THIS--  . . .      35  3 DON JUAN   6     59  5
    A LADY OF A CERTAIN AGE WHICH MEANS  . . . . . . .        41  3 DON JUAN   6     69  2
    HIS DAILY COUNCIL UPON WAYS AND MEANS . . . . . .         54  3 DON JUAN   6     96  2
    BY NO MEANS WOULD PRODUCE THE TOWN'S SUBMISSION  . .      81  3 DON JUAN   7     30  5
    THE LADIES--WHO BY NO MEANS HAD BEEN BRED  . . . . .     101  3 DON JUAN   7     67  2
    WAR'S MERIT IT BY NO MEANS MIGHT ENHANCE  . . . . .      113  3 DON JUAN   8      3  4
    A THING WHICH VICTORY BY NO MEANS BODED  . . . . .       119  3 DON JUAN   8     16  6
    WHICH PUZZLES US TO KNOW WHAT FORTUNE MEANS  . . . .     247  3 DON JUAN  10     47  3
    THROUGH HIS MEANS AND THE CHURCH'S MIGHT BE PAVED  . .   251  3 DON JUAN  10     55  6
    WHOSE CITIES NIGHT BY NO MEANS DEIGNS TO GLOSS  . . .    280  3 DON JUAN  11     26  5
    BY NO MEANS TO BE VERY WISE OR WITTY  . . . . . .        290  3 DON JUAN  11     45  4
    UNLESS A MAN CAN CALCULATE HIS MEANS  . . . . . .        325  3 DON JUAN  12     21  7
    MY MUSE BY EXHORTATION MEANS TO MEND  . . . . . .        334  3 DON JUAN  12     39  6
    WHENEVER--WHICH MEANS EVERY DAY--THEY'D SHOWN  . . .     338  3 DON JUAN  12     48  3
    IT WAS HIS FOIBLE BUT BY NO MEANS SINISTER--  . . .      368  3 DON JUAN  13     21  2
    IN PIOUS LIBELS BY NO MEANS A FEW  . . . . . . .         414  3 DON JUAN  14     10  4
    BESIDES MY MUSE BY NO MEANS DEALS IN FICTION  . . . .    416  3 DON JUAN  14     13  1
    WHICH MEANS THAT VULGAR PEOPLE MUST NOT SHARE IT  . .    419  3 DON JUAN  14     21  8
    AND THOUGH--BY NO MEANS OVERPOWERED WITH RICHES  . .     421  3 DON JUAN  14     26 V7
    A LITTLE SPOILT BUT BY NO MEANS SO QUITE  . . . . .      428  3 DON JUAN  14     41  3
    CONTENTED WHEN TRANSLATED MEANS BUT CLOYED  . . . .      444  3 DON JUAN  14     79  5
    AND THEREFORE THOUGH 'TIS BY NO MEANS MY WAY  . . .      500  3 DON JUAN  15     98  1
    WEIGHED ON HIS SPIRIT THOUGH BY NO MEANS SERIOUS  . .    514  3 DON JUAN  16     33  5
MEANT
    THE POET MEANT NO DOUBT AND THUS APPEALS  . . . . .       69  2 DON JUAN   1     89  1
    YET THERE'S NO DOUBT SHE ONLY MEANT TO CLASP  . . .       81  2 DON JUAN   1    111  4
    MY POEM'S EPIC AND IS MEANT TO BE  . . . . . . .         135  2 DON JUAN   1    200  1
    SAY I BY WHICH QUOTATION THERE IS MEANT A  . . . .       143  2 DON JUAN   1    212  3
    'TWAS FOR A VOYAGE THAT THE YOUNG MAN WAS MEANT  . .     161  2 DON JUAN   2      8  5
    EASED HER AT LAST (ALTHOUGH WE NEVER MEANT  . . . .      173  2 DON JUAN   2     32  6
    BETTER THAN HER KNEW WHAT IN FACT SHE MEANT  . . . .     228  2 DON JUAN   2    136  3
    A SOMETHING TO BE LOVED A CREATURE MEANT  . . . . .      247  2 DON JUAN   2    172  5
    SOME PERSONS SAY THAT DANTE MEANT THEOLOGY  . . . .      281  2 DON JUAN   3     11  1
    MEANT TO PERSONIFY THE MATHEMATICS  . . . . . .          281  2 DON JUAN   3     11  8
    QUICK TO PERCEIVE AND STRONG TO BEAR AND MEANT  . . .    302  2 DON JUAN   3     28  7
    THINK YE HE MEANT THEM FOR A SLAVE  . . . . . . .        324  2 DON JUAN   3  L 10  6
    MEANT TO GROW OLD BUT DIE IN HAPPY SPRING  . . . . .     348  2 DON JUAN   4      8  7
    WHICH MEN WEEP OVER MAY BE MEANT TO SAVE  . . . . .      350  2 DON JUAN   4     12  8
    SEEING WHAT'S MEANT FOR MANY WITH BUT ONE  . . . . .     443  2 DON JUAN   5     57  8
    WHICH PUZZLED NATURE MUCH TO KNOW WHAT ART MEANT  . .    448  2 DON JUAN   5     64  8
    WHAT ALL THIS WHILE BABA BOWED AND BENDED  . . . . .     466  2 DON JUAN   5     95  7
    SHE MEANT TO BE EXTREMELY CONDESCENDING  . . . . .       475  2 DON JUAN   5    112 V1
    HIM WHOM SHE MEANT TO TUTOR IN LOVE'S WAYS  . . . .      482  2 DON JUAN   5    122  5
```

```
MEANT    (CONTINUED)
     TO THE TRUE LAW OF NATIONS WHICH NE'ER MEANT    .  .  .  .  .  498  2 DON JUAN  5    151   3
     OF THEIR DESIGNS BY SAYING THEY MEANT WELL  .  .  .  .  .  .  123  3 DON JUAN  8     25   7
     TROOPS AS ARE MEANT TO MARCH WITH GREATEST GLORY ON   .  .  .  151  3 DON JUAN  8     78   4
     I HAVE FORGOTTEN WHAT I MEANT TO SAY .  .  .  .  .  .  .     200  3 DON JUAN  9     36   2
     BUT JUAN WAS NOT MEANT TO DIE SO SOON .  .  .  .  .  .  .    229  3 DON JUAN 10      9   1
     NOT THAT SHE MEANT TO FIX AGAIN IN HASTE .  .  .  .  .  .    248  3 DON JUAN 10     48   5
     WILL HINT ALLUSIONS NEVER MEANT NE'ER DOUBT .  .  .  .  .    311  3 DON JUAN 11     88   7
     SUCH AS--UNLESS MISS (BLANK) MEANT TO HAVE CHOSEN .  .  .    332  3 DON JUAN 12     34   5
     IT DOES NOR GOOD NOR HARM BEING MERELY MEANT  .  .  .  .     342  3 DON JUAN 12     57   4
     IT IS--I MEANT AND MEAN NOT TO DISPARAGE .  .  .  .  .  .    344  3 DON JUAN 12     62   4
     FOR HE WAS SICK--NO 'TWAS NOT THE WORD SICK I MEANT--  .     346  3 DON JUAN 12     67   3
     THAT HE WAS NOT IN HEART SO VERY WEAK--I MEANT  .  .  .      346  3 DON JUAN 12     67   5
     ALTHOUGH SHE WAS NOT EVIL NOR MEANT ILL  .  .  .  .  .  .    364  3 DON JUAN 13     12   4
     AND SUCH ARE MANY--THOUGH I ONLY MEANT HER  .  .  .  .  .    375  3 DON JUAN 13     38   4
     THIS NARRATIVE IS NOT MEANT FOR NARRATION  .  .  .  .  .     413  3 DON JUAN 14      7   6
     I MEANT TO MAKE THIS POEM VERY SHORT .  .  .  .  .  .  .     466  3 DON JUAN 15     22   3
     BECAUSE HE EITHER MEANT TO SNEER AT HARMONY .  .  .  .  .    472  3 DON JUAN 15     36   1
     THIS HE (AS FAR AS I CAN UNDERSTAND) MEANT  .  .  .  .  .    472  3 DON JUAN 15     38   4
     NOR CANVASS WHAT SO EMINENT A HAND MEANT .  .  .  .  .  .    472  3 DON JUAN 15     38   6
     INDEED I NEVER KNEW WHAT PEOPLE MEANT .  .  .  .  .  .  .    498  3 DON JUAN 15     94   5
MEANTIME
     MEANTIME--SIR LAUREATE--I PROCEED TO DEDICATE  .  .  .  .     20  2 DON JUAN  D     17   1
     AND IF IN THE MEANTIME HER HUSBAND DIED  .  .  .  .  .  .     67  2 DON JUAN  1     84   1
     MEANTIME THEY'LL DOUBTLESS PLEASE TO RECOLLECT  .  .  .      141  2 DON JUAN  1    209   5
     IN THE MEANTIME TO PASS HER HOURS AWAY   .  .  .  .  .  .    162  2 DON JUAN  2     10   1
     MEANTIME THE CURRENT WITH A RISING GALE  .  .  .  .  .  .    209  2 DON JUAN  2    101   1
     BUT ZOE THE MEANTIME SOME EGGS WAS FRYING   .  .  .  .  .    233  2 DON JUAN  2    144   5
     IN THE MEANTIME WITHOUT PROCEEDING MORE  .  .  .  .  .  .    271  2 DON JUAN  2    216   1
     MEANTIME THE LADY AND HER LOVER SATE .  .  .  .  .  .  .     306  2 DON JUAN  3     61   3
     MEANTIME APOLLO PLUCKS ME BY THE EAR .  .  .  .  .  .  .     347  2 DON JUAN  4      7   7
     MEANTIME (YON OLD BLACK EUNUCH SEEMS TO EYE US)  .  .  .     423  2 DON JUAN  5     24   7
     MEANTIME THE EDUCATION THEY WENT THROUGH .  .  .  .  .  .    499  2 DON JUAN  5    153   5
     MEANTIME GULBEYAZ WHEN HER KING WAS GONE .  .  .  .  .  .     54  3 DON JUAN  6     97   1
     IN THE MEANTIME THE BATTERIES PROCEEDED  .  .  .  .  .  .     85  3 DON JUAN  7     38   6
     MEANTIME THESE TWO POOR GIRLS WITH SWIMMING EYES  .  .  .    104  3 DON JUAN  7     73   1
     IN THE MEANTIME CROSS-LEGGED WITH GREAT SANG FROID  .  .    172  3 DON JUAN  8    121   1
     MEANTIME THE TAXES CASTLEREAGH AND DEBT  .  .  .  .  .  .    174  3 DON JUAN  8    125   5
     MEANTIME READ ALL THE NATIONAL DEBT SINKERS .  .  .  .  .    357  3 DON JUAN 12     89   7
     IN THE MEANTIME HIS VALET WHOSE PRECISION   .  .  .  .  .    512  3 DON JUAN 16     28   6
MEANWHILE
     MEANWHILE AS HOMER SOMETIMES SLEEPS PERHAPS .  .  .  .  .    503  2 DON JUAN  5    159   7
     MEANWHILE SWEET ADELINE DESERVED THEIR PRAISES  .  .  .     550  3 DON JUAN 16    103   1
MEASURE
     AND WONDERFUL BEYOND ALL WONDROUS MEASURE   .  .  .  .  .     93  2 DON JUAN  1    133   2
     SO THAT ALL HANDS WERE BUSY BEYOND MEASURE  .  .  .  .  .    286  2 DON JUAN  3     20   7
     A LIFE WHICH MADE THEM HAPPY BEYOND MEASURE .  .  .  .  .    295  2 DON JUAN  3     39   4
     OH LADY DAPHNE LET ME MEASURE YOU .  .  .  .  .  .  .  .     406  2 DON JUAN  4    112   8
     BEFORE THE BRIDAL HOURS HAVE DANCED THEIR MEASURE .  .  .    168  3 DON JUAN  8    113   3
MEASURED
     WHO MEASURED MEN AS YOU WOULD DO A STEEPLE  .  .  .  .  .     84  3 DON JUAN  7     37   8
MEASURES
     AND MEASURES ROUND OF TOISES THOUSANDS THREE  .  .  .  .     71  3 DON JUAN  7      9   8
     SUCH MEASURES AS SHE THOUGHT MIGHT BEST IMPEDE  .  .  .     437  3 DON JUAN 14     61   2
     AS WOMEN HATE HALF MEASURES ON THE WHOLE .  .  .  .  .  .    468  3 DON JUAN 15     28   7
MEASURING
     BY MEASURING THE INTENSITY OF BLUE .  .  .  .  .  .  .  .    406  2 DON JUAN  4    112   7
MEAT
     HENCE ALL THIS RICE MEAT DANCING WINE AND FIDDLING  .  .    295  2 DON JUAN  3     39   1
     TOO OFTEN ALL THE CLOTHING MEAT OR FUEL  .  .  .  .  .  .    256  3 DON JUAN 10     63   7
MEATS
     PILAUS AND MEATS OF ALL SORTS MET THE GAZE  .  .  .  .  .    291  2 DON JUAN  3     31   3
     LAMB AND PISTACHIO NUTS--IN SHORT ALL MEATS .  .  .  .  .    307  2 DON JUAN  3     62   2
     BUT VARIOUS AS THE VARIOUS MEATS DISPLAY'D  .  .  .  .  .    488  3 DON JUAN 15     74   4
MECHANICS
     WITH ALL KINDS OF MECHANICS AND FULL SOON   .  .  .  .  .    226  3 DON JUAN 10      2   7
MECHANTE
     AND SOMEWHAT MECHANTE IN HER AMOROUS SPHERE .  .  .  .  .    438  3 DON JUAN 14     63   2
MECUM
     THE VADE MECUM OF THE TRUE SUBLIME .  .  .  .  .  .  .  .    136  2 DON JUAN  1    201   3
MEDALS
     MEDALS RANKS RIBBONS LACE EMBROIDERY SCARLET  .  .  .  .    108  3 DON JUAN  7     84   1
     STARS MEDALS AND A BLOODY SWORD IN HAND  .  .  .  .  .  .    141  3 DON JUAN  8     57   6
MEDEA
     IN FEELINGS QUICK AS OVID'S MISS MEDEA   .  .  .  .  .  .     68  2 DON JUAN  1     86   4
     OR PRAY MEDEA FOR A SINGLE DRAGON .  .  .  .  .  .  .  .     333  2 DON JUAN  3     99   4
     THEE WITCH OR EACH MEDEA HAS HER JASON   .  .  .  .  .  .    396  3 DON JUAN 13     81   6
     CONVEY'D MEDEA AS HER SUPERCARGO  .  .  .  .  .  .  .  .     443  3 DON JUAN 14     76   8
MEDES
     AND MEDES WOULD NE'ER REVOKE WHAT WENT BEFORE  .  .  .  .    366  3 DON JUAN 13     17   4
MEDIAS
     MOST EPIC POETS PLUNGE IN MEDIAS RES  .  .  .  .  .  .  .     24  2 DON JUAN  1      6   1
MEDICINE
     AND THAT THE MEDICINE ANSWER'D VERY WELL .  .  .  .  .  .    113  2 DON JUAN  1    168   6
MEDICINES
     SHE TOOK THEIR MEDICINES WITHOUT ASKING WHY .  .  .  .  .    378  2 DON JUAN  4     63  V3
     THE SOVEREIGN SHOCKED AND ALL HIS MEDICINES DOUBLED  .  .    244  3 DON JUAN 10     39   8
MEDIO
     HORATIAN MEDIO TU TUTISSIMUS IBIS .  .  .  .  .  .  .  .      14  3 DON JUAN  6     17   8
```

                                 501

MEDITATE
   TO MEDITATE UPON THEIR SINS AND SELF . . . . 41 3 DON JUAN 6   69   8
MEDITATED
   WAVED O'ER HIS COUCH HE MEDITATED FOND . . . . . . 555 3 DON JUAN 16   110   6
MEDITATION
   MANKIND JUST NOW SEEM WRAPT IN MEDITATION . . . . . 325 3 DON JUAN 12   21   4
MEDITATIVE
   IN SELF-DEFENCE--THIS MADE HIM MEDITATIVE . . . . . 277 3 DON JUAN 11   18   8
MEDIUM
   MAKE SOME PREFER THE CIRCULATING MEDIUM . . . . . . 235 3 DON JUAN 10   22   8
   THAT HE EXACTLY THE JUST MEDIUM HIT . . . . 535 3 DON JUAN 16   72   3
MEED
   IN GIVING TO HIS BRETHREN THEIR FULL MEED . . . . . 14 2 DON JUAN D   8   6
   THE GLORIOUS MEED OF POPULAR APPLAUSE . . . . 318 2 DON JUAN 3   82   7
MEEK
   LIKE A MEEK TRADESMAN WHEN APPROACHING PALELY . . . . 459 3 DON JUAN 15   8   3
   AND ALSO MEEK AS A METAPHYSICIAN . . . . 497 3 DON JUAN 15   92   2
MEEKEST
   AND THEN THIS BEST AND MEEKEST WOMAN BORE . . . . . 36 2 DON JUAN 1   29   1
   BUT I THE MILDEST MEEKEST OF MANKIND . . . . . . 193 3 DON JUAN 9   21   1
MEET
   TO MEET THE INGENUOUS YOUTH OF FUTURE AGES . . . . . 46 2 DON JUAN 1   45   4
   DEATH SHUNS THE WRETCH WHO FAIN THE BLOW WOULD MEET . . 134 2 DON JUAN 1   197   6
   WE MEET AGAIN IF WE SHOULD UNDERSTAND . . . . . . 147 2 DON JUAN 1   221   5
   BUT VULGAR ILLNESSES DON'T LIKE TO MEET . . . . . 168 2 DON JUAN 2   22   6
   THE VELVET CUSHIONS--(FOR A THRONE MORE MEET)-- . . . 309 2 DON JUAN 3   67   5
   I CHOSE A MODERN SUBJECT AS MORE MEET . . . . . . 347 2 DON JUAN 4   6   8
   'TWAS WHITE AND INDISTINCT NOR STOPP'D TO MEET . . . 361 2 DON JUAN 4   32   6
   NOTHING COULD MAKE HER MEET HER FATHER'S FACE . . . . 381 2 DON JUAN 4   68   2
   FAREWELL SAID JUAN SHOULD WE MEET NO MORE . . . . . 460 2 DON JUAN 5   84   1
   WHEN WE NEXT MEET WE'LL HAVE A TALE TO TELL . . . . 460 2 DON JUAN 5   84   4
   WHERE THEY MIGHT MEET IN MUCH MORE PEACEFUL GUISE . . . 472 2 DON JUAN 5   105   3
   LET THIS FIFTH CANTO MEET WITH DUE APPLAUSE . . . . . 503 2 DON JUAN 5   159   5
   AND FOR THEIR OTHER MATTERS MEET AND SHARE 'EM . . . 53 3 DON JUAN 6   95   8
   WHICH MEET THE GAZE WHAT'ER IT MAY REGARD-- . . . . 118 3 DON JUAN 8   13   4
   HE MADE THE TEETH MEET NOR RELINQUISHED IT . . . . . 153 3 DON JUAN 8   84   6
   TO MEET HOWEVER 'TIS NO TIME TO CHAT . . . . . . 290 3 DON JUAN 11   44   6
   MIGHT MEET FROM MEN A LITTLE MORE FORGIVENESS . . . . 326 3 DON JUAN 12   22   8
   BUT BE IT AS IT MAY A BARD MUST MEET . . . . . . 423 3 DON JUAN 14   30   4
MEETING
   AWAITS IT EACH NEW MEETING OR ELECTION . . . . . . 272 3 DON JUAN 11   9   8
   TO KEEP EXTREMES FROM MEETING WHEN ONCE SET . . . . . 492 3 DON JUAN 15   81   6
MEETINGS
   AND COUNTY MEETINGS AND THE PARLIAMENT . . . . . . 360 3 DON JUAN 13   5   7
MEETS
   OH POWERS OF HEAVEN WHAT DARK EYE MEETS SHE THERE . . . 363 2 DON JUAN 4   35   7
   AND THAT'S ONE CAUSE SHE MEETS WITH CONTRADICTION . . . 416 3 DON JUAN 14   13   5
   WHICH NEVER MEETS AND THEREFORE CAN'T FALL OUT . . . . 430 3 DON JUAN 14   45   8
MEKNOP
   MEKNOP SERGE LWOW ARSENIEW OF MODERN GREECE . . . . . 74 3 DON JUAN 7   15   3
MEKNOP'S
   A JUNCTION OF THE GENERAL MEKNOP'S MEN . . . . . . 151 3 DON JUAN 8   79   1
MELANCHOLY
   'TIS MELANCHOLY AND A FEARFUL SIGN . . . . 277 2 DON JUAN 3   5   1
   AND THAT'S THE REASON I'M SO MELANCHOLY . . . . . 444 2 DON JUAN 5   58   8
   A MORAL (LIKE ALL MORALS) MELANCHOLY . . . . . . 448 2 DON JUAN 5   63   6
   PACED ON MOST MAIDEN-LIKE AND MELANCHOLY . . . . . 22 3 DON JUAN 6   33   8
   BUT SHE WAS PENSIVE MORE THAN MELANCHOLY . . . . . 33 3 DON JUAN 6   54   1
   OF MELANCHOLY MERRIMENT TO QUOTE . . . . 156 3 DON JUAN 8   89   5
   WOULD MAKE INDEED SOME MELANCHOLY MIRTH . . . . . . 436 3 DON JUAN 14   59   6
MELANCTHON
   LIKE MOSES OR MELANCTHON WHO HAVE NE'ER . . . . . . 193 3 DON JUAN 9   21   2
MELLIFLUOUSLY
   IN LIQUID LINES MELLIFLUOUSLY BLAND . . . . 411 2 DON JUAN 5   1   2
MELLOW
   DROPP'D IN THEIR LAPS SCARCE PLUCK'D THEIR MELLOW STORE . 291 2 DON JUAN 3   31   8
   LIKE BRANCHES WHEN THE FRUIT BENEATH IS MELLOW . . . . 311 2 DON JUAN 3   70   V4
   OF MEN AND MADE THEM SPEECHES WHEN HALF MELLOW . . . . 318 2 DON JUAN 3   82   4
   THEY TOOK IT UP WHEN MY DAYS GREW MORE MELLOW . . . . 345 2 DON JUAN 4   3   3
   WHO SWORE HIS VOICE WAS VERY RICH AND MELLOW . . . . 391 2 DON JUAN 4   87   6
   THEY TOOK HER WORD THAT HIS DULL ROAR WAS MELLOW . . . 391 2 DON JUAN 4   87   V6
   THE MELLOW AUTUMN CAME AND WITH IT CAME . . . . . . 394 3 DON JUAN 13   75   1
   WITHOUT DOORS TOO SHE MAY COMPETE IN MELLOW . . . . . 395 3 DON JUAN 13   77   7
MELLOW'D
   BY DISTANCE MELLOW'D O'ER THE WATERS SWEEP . . . . . 87 2 DON JUAN 1   122   4
MELODIES
   SOFTEST OF MELODIES AND COULD BE SAD . . . . 292 3 DON JUAN 11   47   4
MELODRAME
   AS MUSIC CHIMES IN WITH A MELODRAME . . . . 552 3 DON JUAN 16   104   6
MELODRAMES
   THEY TURN OUT MELODRAMES OR PANTOMIMES . . . . . . 470 3 DON JUAN 15   32   8
MELODY
   WHENCE MELODY DESCENDS AS FROM A THRONE . . . . . . 236 2 DON JUAN 2   151   8
   A MELODY WHICH MADE HIM DOUBT HIS EARS . . . . . . 290 2 DON JUAN 3   28   5
   HE WROTE THIS POLAR MELODY AND SET IT . . . . . . 179 3 DON JUAN 8   135   1
MELT
   SOONER SHALL THIS BLUE OCEAN MELT TO AIR . . . . . . 166 2 DON JUAN 2   19   3
   THERE HIS WORN BOSOM AND KEEN EYE WOULD MELT . . . . 302 2 DON JUAN 3   52   6
MELTED
   WERE MELTED FOR A MOMENT THOUGH NO TEAR . . . . . . 171 3 DON JUAN 8   119   6

```
                                                                      PAGE VOL    CANTO  STANZA  LN
MELTED   (CONTINUED)
      THE WHOLE COURT MELTED INTO ONE WIDE WHISPER   . . . . . . 221  3 DON JUAN   9      78    1
      AS WHITE AS CLEOPATRA'S MELTED PEARLS . . . . . . . . . 484  3 DON JUAN  15      65    8
MELTON
      AND WEAR THE MELTON JACKET FOR A SPACE--  . . . . . . . 395  3 DON JUAN  13      78    6
MELTS
      SOFT HOUR WHICH WAKES THE WISH AND MELTS THE HEART   . . . 338  2 DON JUAN   3     108    1
      A WOMAN'S TEAR-DROP MELTS A MAN'S HALF SEARS   . . . . . 479  2 DON JUAN   5     118    5
      THE SUN WHICH YEARLY MELTS THE POLAR ICE . . . . . . 501  2 DON JUAN   5     157    7
MEMBER
      WAS MEMBER FOR THE OTHER INTEREST (MEANING   . . . . . 535  3 DON JUAN  16      70    7
MEMBERS
      SO THAT FEW MEMBERS KEPT THE HOUSE UP LATER . . . . . 367  3 DON JUAN  13      20    8
      THERE WERE SOME MASSY MEMBERS OF THE CHURCH . . . . . 539  3 DON JUAN  16      80    6
MEMNON'S
      (THOUGH LESS THAN THAT OF MEMNON'S STATUE WARM   . . . 388  3 DON JUAN  13      64    3
MEMOIRS
      AND WRITTEN LATELY TWO MEMOIRS UPON'T)   . . . . . . . 447  2 DON JUAN   5      62    6
      'TIS TRUE THE MEMOIRS OF THE PRINCE DELIGNE   . . . . .  82  3 DON JUAN   7      33    7
MEMORANDUM
      WITH A LONG MEMORANDUM OF OLD STORIES   . . . . . . . 432  3 DON JUAN  14      50    8
MEMORY
      HER MEMORY WAS A MINE SHE KNEW BY HEART   . . . . . .  27  2 DON JUAN   1      11    1
      COULD NEVER MAKE A MEMORY SO FINE AS . . . . . . . .  27  2 DON JUAN   1      11    7
      SO DEAR IS STILL THE MEMORY OF THAT DREAM   . . . . . 130  2 DON JUAN   1     193    4
      TO KEEP HIS MEMORY WHOLE AND MUMMY HID   . . . . . . 146  2 DON JUAN   1     219    4
      FOR ON SUCH THINGS THE MEMORY REPOSES . . . . . . . 187  2 DON JUAN   2      58    3
      TO HIS MEMORY AND TWO OR THREE YOUNG MISSES . . . . . 287  2 DON JUAN   3      23    6
      STRUCK NOT ON MEMORY THOUGH A HEAVY ACHE . . . . . . 378  2 DON JUAN   4      62    5
      GENTLE BUT WITHOUT MEMORY SHE LAY . . . . . . . . . 379  2 DON JUAN   4      64    6
      UNTIL THE MEMORY OF AN AGE IS FLED . . . . . . . . 399  2 DON JUAN   4     102    3
      ALAS WHAT TO THEIR MEMORY CAN LACK . . . . . . . .  73  3 DON JUAN   7      14    5
      BUT MAY THEIR VERY MEMORY PERISH TOO--  . . . . . . 180  3 DON JUAN   8     136    5
      (IF THAT MY MEMORY DOTH NOT GREATLY ERR)   . . . . . 242  3 DON JUAN  10      36    3
      WERE EVERY MEMORY WRITTEN DOWN ALL TRUE   . . . . . 324  3 DON JUAN  12      19    3
      WITH MEMORY EXCELLENT TO GET BY ROTE  . . . . . . . 401  3 DON JUAN  13      91    5
      (MY HEART OR HEAD ACHES WITH THE MEMORY YET)   . . . 408  3 DON JUAN  13     107    4
      THAT HATH A MEMORY OR THAT HAD A HEART   . . . . . . 554  3 DON JUAN  16     109    2
MEMORY'S
      WHICH SITS FOREVER UPON MEMORY'S CRUPPER . . . . . . 304  3 DON JUAN  11      72    5
MEMPHIAN
      LIKE SKULLS AT MEMPHIAN BANQUETS TO THE MIND   . . . 308  2 DON JUAN   3      65    4
MEN
      DEEMING THE CHAIN IT WEARS EVEN MEN MAY FIT . . . . .  18  2 DON JUAN   D      15    4
      BRAVE MEN WERE LIVING BEFORE AGAMEMNON   . . . . . .  24  2 DON JUAN   1       5    1
      EXPURGATED BY LEARNED MEN WHO PLACE   . . . . . . .  46  2 DON JUAN   1      44    2
      WHAT MEN CALL GALLANTRY AND GODS ADULTERY   . . . .  56  2 DON JUAN   1      63    7
      AND HOW THE GODDESSES CAME DOWN TO MEN   . . . . . .  72  2 DON JUAN   1      94    4
      BY WHICH MEN ARE UNSUFFOCATED GRATIS . . . . . . .  92  2 DON JUAN   1     130    5
      OF GOBLINS BUT STILL MORE OF MEN AFRAID   . . . . .  98  2 DON JUAN   1     141    3
      LIGHTS CAME AT LENGTH AND MEN AND MAIDS WHO FOUND . . . 125  2 DON JUAN   1     187    1
      MEN HAVE ALL THESE RESOURCES WE BUT ONE  . . . . . . 131  2 DON JUAN   1     194    7
      OF PIOUS MEN HAVE PUBLISHED ON HIS ACTS   . . . . . 138  2 DON JUAN   1     203   V4
      FOR THIS MEN WRITE SPEAK PREACH AND HEROES KILL . . . 146  2 DON JUAN   1     218    5
      YOUNG MEN SHOULD TRAVEL IF BUT TO AMUSE   . . . . . 165  2 DON JUAN   2      16    5
      AND MADE A SCENE MEN DO NOT SOON FORGET   . . . . . 172  2 DON JUAN   2      31    3
      BUT LET US DIE LIKE MEN NOT SINK BELOW   . . . . . . 175  2 DON JUAN   2      36    4
      MEN EVEN WHEN DYING DISLIKE INANITION   . . . . . . 180  2 DON JUAN   2      46    5
      MEN WILL PROVE HUNGRY EVEN WHEN NEXT PERDITION . . . 180  2 DON JUAN   2      46   V5
      THEY HOPED THE WIND WOULD RISE THESE FOOLISH MEN . . . 192  2 DON JUAN   2      69    5
      MEN REALLY KNOW NOT WHAT GOOD WATER'S WORTH   . . . 201  2 DON JUAN   2      84    4
      FORSOOK THE DIM EYES OF THESE SHIPWRECK'D MEN   . . . 204  2 DON JUAN   2      91    8
      FOLKS ARE DISCOURAGED AND MOST SURELY NO MEN   . . . 205  2 DON JUAN   2      93    5
      THE MEN WITHIN THE BOAT AND IN THIS GUISE   . . . . 206  2 DON JUAN   2      94    6
      A FISHER THEREFORE WAS HE--THOUGH OF MEN . . . . . . 223  2 DON JUAN   2     126    1
      LIKE OTHER MEN TOO MAY HAVE HAD MY PASSION--   . . . 244  2 DON JUAN   2     166    4
      FOES FRIENDS MEN WOMEN NOW ARE NOUGHT TO ME . . . . 244  2 DON JUAN   2     166    7
      THE HOPES OF ALL MEN AND OF EVERY NATION   . . . . . 250  2 DON JUAN   2     179    4
      AND JESTEST WITH THE BROWS OF MIGHTIEST MEN . . . . 266  2 DON JUAN   2     206    2
      MEN CALL INCONSTANCY IS NOTHING MORE   . . . . . . 269  2 DON JUAN   2     211    2
      MEN GROW ASHAMED OF BEING SO VERY FOND   . . . . . . 278  2 DON JUAN   3       7    1
      (IN GENERAL MEN I SURPRISED MEN WITH THE SWORD)   . . 294  2 DON JUAN   3      37    3
      HE DID NOT KNOW (ALAS HOW MEN WILL LIE)   . . . . . 295  2 DON JUAN   3      38    1
      TO BID MEN COME AND GO AND COME AGAIN--  . . . . . . 299  2 DON JUAN   3      47    2
      THE WILD SEAS AND WILD MEN WITH WHOM HE CRUISED   . . 303  2 DON JUAN   3      54    6
      EVEN GOOD MEN LIKE TO MAKE THE PUBLIC STARE--   . . . 317  2 DON JUAN   3      81    4
      OF MEN AND MADE THEM SPEECHES WHEN HALF MELLOW . . . 318  2 DON JUAN   3      82    4
      AND MEN IN NATIONS--ALL WERE HIS . . . . . . . . . 322  2 DON JUAN   3   L   4    4
      MUST END IN LANGUOR--MEN WON'T SLEEP LIKE SWINE--   . 343  2 DON JUAN   3   V  98    4
      WHICH MEN WEEP OVER MAY BE MEANT TO SAVE   . . . . . 350  2 DON JUAN   4      12    8
      FLOCK O'ER THEIR CARRION JUST LIKE MEN BELOW . . . . 358  2 DON JUAN   4      28    8
      A HUNDRED THOUSAND MEN MIGHT FIGHT AGAIN . . . . . . 386  2 DON JUAN   4      77    6
      WHERE MEN HAVE SOULS OR BODIES SHE MUST ANSWER . . . 390  2 DON JUAN   4      84    8
      AS FOR THE MEN THEY ARE A MIDDLING SET   . . . . . . 391  2 DON JUAN   4      86    1
      WHO LIVED TOO LONG FOR MEN BUT DIED TOO SOON   . . . 400  2 DON JUAN   4     103    3
      MEN WHO PARTAKE ALL PASSIONS AS THEY PASS   . . . . 402  2 DON JUAN   4     107    5
      O'ERTHROWN EVEN MEN HE SOON BEGAN TO SHOW   . . . . 417  2 DON JUAN   5      12    4
      BUT THAT'S HER WAY WITH ALL MEN TILL THEY'RE TRIED   . 418  2 DON JUAN   5      14    5
      MEN ARE THE SPORT OF CIRCUMSTANCES WHEN   . . . . . 419  2 DON JUAN   5      17    7
```

MEN   (CONTINUED)

	PAGE	VOL	CANTO	STANZA	LN
THE CIRCUMSTANCES SEEM THE SPORT OF MEN	419	2	DON JUAN 5	17	8
MOST MEN ARE SLAVES NONE MORE SO THAN THE GREAT	423	2	DON JUAN 5	25	3
OF THE WORLD'S STOICS--MEN WITHOUT A HEART	423	2	DON JUAN 5	25	8
TURKEY CONTAINS NO BELLS AND YET MEN DINE	439	2	DON JUAN 5	50	1
WHERE NABUCHADONOSOR KING OF MEN	445	2	DON JUAN 5	60	3
WE KNOW WHERE THINGS AND MEN MUST END AT BEST	448	2	DON JUAN 5	63	5
THE WOND'ROUS HIDEOUSNESS OF THOSE SMALL MEN	462	2	DON JUAN 5	88	3
TO MAKE MEN HAPPY OR TO KEEP THEM SO	470	2	DON JUAN 5	101	3
AS GOOD MEN WEAR WHO HAVE DONE A VIRTUOUS ACTION	473	2	DON JUAN 5	107	8
AWARE OF THEIR DUE ROYAL RIGHTS O'ER MEN	485	2	DON JUAN 5	128	8
TO NO MEN ARE SUCH CORDIAL GREETINGS GIVEN	500	2	DON JUAN 5	154	7
THERE IS A TIDE IN THE AFFAIRS OF MEN	6	3	DON JUAN 6	1	1
MEN WITH THEIR HEADS REFLECT ON THIS AND THAT--	7	3	DON JUAN 6	2	7
MOST WISE MEN WITH ONE MODERATE WOMAN WED	12	3	DON JUAN 6	12	5
BILLS BEASTS AND MEN AND--NO NOT WOMANKIND	17	3	DON JUAN 6	22	2
FOR RICH MEN AND THEIR BRIDES TO LAY THEIR HEADS	18	3	DON JUAN 6	25	4
ARE WORSE THAN THE WORST DAMAGES MEN PAY	20	3	DON JUAN 6	29	6
MORE EASY BY THE ABSENCE OF ALL MEN	22	3	DON JUAN 6	32	2
WHICH LAYS BOTH MEN AND WOMEN ON THE SHELF	41	3	DON JUAN 6	69	7
TO CALL MEN LOVE-BEGOTTEN OR PROCLAIM	53	3	DON JUAN 6	94	1
DOGS OR MEN (FOR I FLATTER YOU IN SAYING	70	3	DON JUAN 7	7	1
ALL PROPER MEN OF WEAPONS AS E'ER SCOFFED HIGH	75	3	DON JUAN 7	17	3
A PLEASANT THING TO YOUNG MEN AT THEIR YEARS	75	3	DON JUAN 7	18	6
THE MOSLEM TOO HAD LOST BOTH SHIPS AND MEN	82	3	DON JUAN 7	31	1
BUT HERE ARE MEN WHO FOUGHT IN GALLANT ACTIONS	83	3	DON JUAN 7	34	1
WHO MEASURED MEN AS YOU WOULD DO A STEEPLE	84	3	DON JUAN 7	37	8
SUCH IS THE SWAY OF YOUR GREAT MEN O'ER LITTLE	90	3	DON JUAN 7	48	8
LIKE MEN WITH TURBANS SCYMITARS AND DIRKS	93	3	DON JUAN 7	53	2
AT WHICH YOUR WISE MEN SNEERED IN PHRASES WITTY	93	3	DON JUAN 7	53	7
YET MEN RESOLVED TO DASH THROUGH THICK AND THIN	94	3	DON JUAN 7	54	4
O'ER THE PROMOTED COUPLE OF BRAVE MEN	101	3	DON JUAN 7	68	1
ARMS TO WHICH MEN WILL NEVER MORE RESORT	106	3	DON JUAN 7	79	4
TO PAINT A SIEGE WHEREIN MORE MEN WERE SLAIN	106	3	DON JUAN 7	80	2
AND YET LIKE ALL MEN ELSE I MUST ALLOW	106	3	DON JUAN 7	80	5
STRUCK FOR AN INSTANT ON THE HEARTS OF MEN	111	3	DON JUAN 7	87	3
ALL WAS PREPARED--THE FIRE THE SWORD THE MEN	113	3	DON JUAN 8	2	1
UNTIL THEIR VERY NUMBER MAKES MEN HARD	118	3	DON JUAN 8	13	2
MEN RUN AWAY MUCH RATHER THAN GO THROUGH	130	3	DON JUAN 8	35	3
MAKES MEN LIKE CATTLE FOLLOW HIM WHO LEADS	132	3	DON JUAN 8	38	8
AS ANY OTHER BOON FOR WHICH MEN STICKLE	134	3	DON JUAN 8	43	4
TO MARCH A GREAT CONVENIENCE TO OUR MEN	136	3	DON JUAN 8	47	3
FOR IF HE DON'T I DOUBT IF MEN WILL LONGER--	137	3	DON JUAN 8	50	2
AT LAST IT TAKES TO WEAPONS SUCH AS MEN	138	3	DON JUAN 8	51	3
HE HATED CRUELTY AS ALL MEN HATE	140	3	DON JUAN 8	55	6
SHORT SPEECHES PASS BETWEEN TWO MEN WHO SPEAK	141	3	DON JUAN 8	58	1
ALL WALLS MEN KNOW AND MANY NEVER KNOWN	142	3	DON JUAN 8	60	6
OF ALL MEN SAVING SYLLA THE MAN-SLAYER	143	3	DON JUAN 8	61	1
WHERE IF MEN SEEK HER NOT AND DEATH BE MORE	143	3	DON JUAN 8	62	4
FOR WHICH MEN VAINLY DECIMATE THE THRONG	144	3	DON JUAN 8	63	2
'TIS TRUE HE SHRANK FROM MEN EVEN OF HIS NATION	144	3	DON JUAN 8	64	1
WAS MUCH REGRETTED) FOR THE MOSLEM MEN	147	3	DON JUAN 8	71	7
BUT AS IT HAPPENS TO BRAVE MEN THEY BLUNDERED--	149	3	DON JUAN 8	75	5
A JUNCTION OF THE GENERAL MEKNOP'S MEN	151	3	DON JUAN 8	79	1
THOUSANDS OF SLAUGHTERED MEN A YET WARM GROUP	157	3	DON JUAN 8	91	2
WHICH THINNED AT EVERY STEP THEIR RANKS OF MEN	163	3	DON JUAN 8	103	4
IN LOPPING OFF YOUR LATELY MARRIED MEN	168	3	DON JUAN 8	113	2
WHICH LAST MEN LIKE WHEN THEY HAVE TIME TO PAUSE	182	3	DON JUAN 8	140	3
GREAT MEN HAVE ALWAYS SCORNED GREAT RECOMPENSES	186	3	DON JUAN 9	8	1
WITH WHICH MEN IMAGE OUT THE UNKNOWN THING	188	3	DON JUAN 9	11	2
YOUR WISE MEN DON'T KNOW MUCH OF NAVIGATION	191	3	DON JUAN 9	18	4
MEN BECOME WOLVES ON ANY SLIGHT OCCASION	192	3	DON JUAN 9	20	8
I DO NOT KNOW--I WISH MEN TO BE FREE	195	3	DON JUAN 9	25	7
MEN ARE BUT MAGGOTS OF SOME HUGE EARTH'S BURIAL)	202	3	DON JUAN 9	39	8
MUCH TOO POETICAL MEN SHOULD KNOW WHY	203	3	DON JUAN 9	41	6
HER PREFERENCE OF A BOY TO MEN MUCH BIGGER	218	3	DON JUAN 9	72	3
AND HONEST MEN FROM ICELAND TO BARBADOES	231	3	DON JUAN 10	13	5
WHILE COMMON MEN GROW IGNORANTLY OLD	232	3	DON JUAN 10	14	5
FOR BOTH ARE MUCH THE SAME SINCE WHAT MEN THINK	234	3	DON JUAN 10	20	2
DEATH'S A REFORMER ALL MEN MUST ALLOW	237	3	DON JUAN 10	25	8
UNTO AN EMPRESS WHO PREFERRED YOUNG MEN	241	3	DON JUAN 10	33	2
THEY ERRED AS AGED MEN WILL DO BUT BY	285	3	DON JUAN 11	36	1
WARS REVELS LOVES--DO THESE BRING MEN MORE EASE	321	3	DON JUAN 12	11	5
RECRUITED ALL WITH CONSTANT MARRIED MEN	323	3	DON JUAN 12	16	2
I'M SERIOUS--SO ARE ALL MEN UPON PAPER	325	3	DON JUAN 12	21	1
MIGHT MEET FROM MEN A LITTLE MORE FORGIVENESS	326	3	DON JUAN 12	22	8
AND THEN MEN STARE AS IF A NEW ASS SPAKE	328	3	DON JUAN 12	26	5
FISHERS FOR MEN LIKE SIRENS WITH SOFT LUTES	343	3	DON JUAN 12	59	6
YOUNG MEN WHO--THOUGH THEY HATED TO DISCUSS	344	3	DON JUAN 12	61	3
TO TASTE--THE TRUTH IS IF MEN WOULD CONFESS	347	3	DON JUAN 12	69	7
MEN LOVE IN HASTE BUT THEY DETEST AT LEISURE	361	3	DON JUAN 13	6	8
WHOSE CHARMS MADE ALL MEN SPEAK AND WOMEN DUMB	365	3	DON JUAN 13	13	6
IN MAKING MEN WHAT COURTESY CALLS FRIENDS	365	3	DON JUAN 13	15	8
IN JUDGING MEN--WHEN ONCE HIS JUDGMENT WAS	366	3	DON JUAN 13	16	3
AS MOST MEN DO THE LITTLE OR THE GREAT	367	3	DON JUAN 13	19	2
AND ALL MEN LIKE TO SHOW THEIR HOSPITALITY	369	3	DON JUAN 13	24	7
BY NAMING STREETS SINCE MEN ARE SO CENSORIOUS	369	3	DON JUAN 13	25	2
OF COUNSELLORS FOR MEN--THUS FOR THE SEX	371	3	DON JUAN 13	30	2
UPON THE SHADES OF THOSE DISTINGUISHED MEN	373	3	DON JUAN 13	33	3

```
                                                          PAGE VOL    CANTO STANZA LN
MEN   (CONTINUED)
    STRANGE FACES LIKE TO MEN IN MASQUERADE . . . . .   . . 389  3 DON JUAN 13     65   3
    BOTH LAWYERS AND BOTH MEN OF EDUCATION   . . . . . . . 401  3 DON JUAN 13     92   3
    DEATH SO CALL'D IS A THING WHICH MAKES MEN WEEP  . . . 411  3 DON JUAN 14      3   7
    A SLIGHT GLANCE THROWN ON MEN OF EVERY STATION   . . . 416  3 DON JUAN 14     14   4
    NOTHING THAT SPEAKS TO ALL MEN AND ALL TIMES  . . . . 417  3 DON JUAN 14     16   2
    THE GRAND ARCANUM'S NOT FOR MEN TO SEE ALL  . . . . . 419  3 DON JUAN 14     22   5
    CONDEMN'D TO CHILD-BED AS MEN FOR THEIR SINS  . . . . 420  3 DON JUAN 14     23   7
    WITHOUT THE COXCOMBRY OF CERTAIN SHE MEN . . . . . .  424  3 DON JUAN 14     31   8
    ASK'D NEXT DAY IF MEN EVER HUNTED TWICE  . . . . . .  425  3 DON JUAN 14     35   8
    THAT ADAM CALLED THE HAPPIEST OF MEN . . . . . . .   434  3 DON JUAN 14     55   8
    THAT YOUNG MEN RARELY MADE MONASTIC VOWS . . . . . . 439  3 DON JUAN 14     67   6
    YOUR MEN OF BUSINESS ARE NOT APT TO EXPRESS  . . . . 443  3 DON JUAN 14     76   6
    AS OBSTINACY BOTH IN MEN AND WOMEN . . . . . . . .  448  3 DON JUAN 14     89   5
    ABOVE ALL I BEG ALL MEN TO FORBEAR . . . . . . . . 454  3 DON JUAN 14     99   1
    HOW DIFFERENTLY THE WORLD WOULD MEN BEHOLD  . . . .  455  3 DON JUAN 14    101   4
    WHAT ICEBERGS IN THE HEARTS OF MIGHTY MEN  . . . .   455  3 DON JUAN 14    102   3
    FEW MEN DARE SHOW THEIR THOUGHTS OF WORST OR BEST  . 457  3 DON JUAN 15      3   5
    THERE'S MUSIC IN ALL THINGS IF MEN HAD EARS  . . .  458  3 DON JUAN 15      5   7
    SUCH ABERRATIONS THAN WE MEN OF RIGOUR . . . . . .  460  3 DON JUAN 15     11   4
    THAT IS WITH MEN WITH WOMEN HE WAS WHAT  . . . . .  463  3 DON JUAN 15     16   1
    MEN MADE THE MANNERS MANNERS NOW MAKE MEN-- . . .   468  3 DON JUAN 15     26   2
    MEN MADE THE MANNERS MANNERS NOW MAKE MEN--  . . .  468  3 DON JUAN 15     26   2
    CONVINCES ALL MEN EVEN A POLITICIAN  . . . . . .    478  3 DON JUAN 15     51   6
    ALSO THE YOUNGER MEN TOO FOR A SPRINGALD . . . . .  487  3 DON JUAN 15     70   5
    FOR ALL MEN PROPHESY WHAT IS OR WAS  . . . . . . .  491  3 DON JUAN 15     79   7
    TO SEE MEN LET THESE SCOUNDREL SOVEREIGNS BREAK LAW . 497  3 DON JUAN 15     92   8
    MEN WHOSE HISTORICAL SUPERIORITY . . . . . . . .    503  3 DON JUAN 16      5   3
    WHO BIDS ALL MEN BELIEVE THE IMPOSSIBLE . . . . .   503  3 DON JUAN 16      5   6
    BUT THOUGHT LIKE MOST MEN THERE WAS NOTHING IN'T  . 510  3 DON JUAN 16     22   3
    THE PRIZE PIG PLOUGHMAN POACHERS THE MEN SENT   . . 533  3 DON JUAN 16     66   4
    HAVE PUBLIC DAYS WHEN ALL MEN MAY CAROUSE  . . . .  534  3 DON JUAN 16     68   7
    HE WAS ALL THINGS TO ALL MEN AND DISPENSED  . . .   535  3 DON JUAN 16     71   2
    MIGHT COST BOTH MEN AND MASTER TOO--THEIR PLACES  . 539  3 DON JUAN 16     79   8
    THOUGH TOO WELL BRED TO QUIZ MEN TO THEIR FACES  .  548  3 DON JUAN 16    100   3
    WHEN DEEP SLEEP FELL ON MEN AND THE WORLD WORE . .  556  3 DON JUAN 16    113   6
    THE MAN WAS WELL-NIGH DEAD ERE MEN BEGUN . . . .    565  3 DON JUAN 17      8   5
    OF WHICH MOST MEN PARTAKE BUT NO ONE SINGS . . . .  568  3 DON JUAN 17     13   3
MENACED
    THE GHOST STOPPED MENACED THEN RETIRED UNTIL  . . . . 559  3 DON JUAN 16    119   7
MENACING
    THOUGH EVERY WAVE ROLL'D MENACING TO FILL  . . . . . 188  2 DON JUAN  2     61   5
MENAGERIE
    THERE IS BUT ONE SUPERB MENAGERIE . . . . . . . . . 327  3 DON JUAN 12     24   8
MEND
    TO MEND HIS FORMER MORALS AND GET NEW . . . . . . . 129  2 DON JUAN  1    191   3
    OUR SIN THE SAME AND HARD AS HIS TO MEND . . . . .  344  2 DON JUAN  4      1   6
    BUT SOMETIMES IT MAY MEND AND OFTEN REACHES . . .   491  2 DON JUAN  5    138   8
    WHEN THINGS ARE AT THE WORST THEY SOMETIMES MEND  .   6  3 DON JUAN  6      1   8
    SO BEAUTIFUL THAT ART COULD LITTLE MEND HER . . .   50  3 DON JUAN  6     89   5
    THIS IS THE WAY PHYSICIANS MEND OR END US  . . . .  245  3 DON JUAN 10     42   1
    TO MEND THE PEOPLE'S AN ABSURDITY . . . . . . .    266  3 DON JUAN 10     85   5
    MY MUSE BY EXHORTATION MEANS TO MEND  . . . . . .   334  3 DON JUAN 12     39   6
    UNLESS HER HABITS SHOULD BEGIN TO MEND . . . . .    432  3 DON JUAN 14     51   4
    UNLESS A MARRIAGE WAS APPLIED TO MEND . . . . . .   470  3 DON JUAN 15     33   6
MENDED
    BUT ERE THE MATTER COULD BE MARR'D OR MENDED  . . . . 482  3 DON JUAN 15     61   5
MENDING
    THEIR MANNERS MENDING AND THEIR MORALS CURING . . . . 162  2 DON JUAN  2     10   V7
MENDS
    A TINKERING SLAVE-MAKER WHO MENDS OLD CHAINS  . . . .  18  2 DON JUAN  D     14   7
    IT MENDS THEIR MORALS NEVER MIND THE PAIN  . . . .  157  2 DON JUAN  2      1   4
    REJOINED THE OTHER WHEN OUR BAD LUCK MENDS HERE . .  423  2 DON JUAN  5     24   6
MENE
    SINCE MENE MENE TEKEL AND UPHARSIN . . . . . . . . . 179  3 DON JUAN  8    134   2
    SINCE MENE MENE TEKEL AND UPHARSIN . . . . . . . . . 179  3 DON JUAN  8    134   2
MENELAUS
    WAS MUCH INFERIOR TO KING MENELAUS--  . . . . . . . . 441  3 DON JUAN 14     72   7
MEN'S
    AND MAKES MEN'S MISERIES OF ALARMING BREVITY  . . . . 190  2 DON JUAN  2     64   8
    I KNOW NOT IF THE FAULT BE MEN'S OR THEIRS  . . . .  276  2 DON JUAN  3      4   1
    'TIS BAD AND MAY BE BETTER--ALL MEN'S LOT  . . . .  423  2 DON JUAN  5     25   2
    SOME TO MEN'S FEELINGS OTHERS TO THEIR REASON  . .   437  2 DON JUAN  5     48   2
    MEN'S HEARTS AGAINST WHOLE MILLIONS WHEN THEIR TRADE .  102  3 DON JUAN  7     69   6
    EXCEPT THE ALL-CLOUDLESS GLORY (WHICH FEW MEN'S IS) . 186  3 DON JUAN  9      8   5
    (WHEN SHE DON'T PIN MEN'S LIMBS IN LIKE A JAILOR)--  . 204  3 DON JUAN  9     44   6
    TAKE LIVES TAKE WIVES TAKE AUGHT EXCEPT MEN'S PURSES . 264  3 DON JUAN 10     79   2
    NEW VESTALS CLAIM MEN'S EYES WITH THE SAME PRAISE . . 340  3 DON JUAN 12     53   6
    MEN'S WRONGS AND RATHER CHECK THAN PUNISH CRIMES . . 361  3 DON JUAN 13      8   6
    OF MEN'S REGARD THE FEVER OR THE CHILL  . . . . .   366  3 DON JUAN 13     17   8
MENTAL
    PERHAPS THAN EVEN THE MENTAL PANGS OF DYING . . . . . 301  2 DON JUAN  3     51   4
MENTE
    AND NOW I THINK ON'T MI VIEN IN MENTE . . . . . . .  56  2 DON JUAN  1     62   6
MENTION
    OR WHICH AT LEAST I NEED NOT MENTION YET . . . . . .  73  2 DON JUAN  1     96   8
    WITH OTHER EXTRAS WHICH WE NEED NOT MENTION-- . . .  218  3 DON JUAN  9     72   6
    HOW WE WON'T MENTION WHY WE NEED NOT SAY . . . . .   235  3 DON JUAN 10     21   2
    WILL GO MUCH FURTHER THAN THERE'S NEED TO MENTION . . 462  3 DON JUAN 15     14   8
```

		PAGE	VOL		CANTO	STANZA	LN

MENTION'D
  IS THAT WHICH MUST BE MENTION'D IN THE SEQUEL . . . . . . 66 2 DON JUAN 1 82 8
  MENTION'D HIS JEALOUSY BUT NEVER WHO . . . . 118 2 DON JUAN 1 177 3
  AGAINST HER BEING MENTION'D AS WELL FITTED . . . . . . 477 3 DON JUAN 15 48 6
MENTIONED
  AS ANY MENTIONED IN THE HISTORIES . . . . 495 2 DON JUAN 5 147 6
MENTIONS
  ARE SAFELY MINED FOR IN THE MODE HE MENTIONS . . . . . 93 2 DON JUAN 1 132 5
  A THING WHICH POESY BUT SELDOM MENTIONS . . . . . . 221 2 DON JUAN 2 123 6
  WHICH ARE THE HEAVIEST THAT OUR HISTORY MENTIONS . . . 137 3 DON JUAN 8 49 8
  AURORA AT THE LAST (SO HISTORY MENTIONS . . . . . . 491 3 DON JUAN 15 80 5
MEPHISTOPHELES
  MUCH IN THE MODE OF GOETHE'S MEPHISTOPHELES . . . . . 361 3 DON JUAN 13 7 8
MERCENARY
  BY NIGHT AS DO THAT MERCENARY PACK ALL . . . . . . 196 3 DON JUAN 9 27 3
MERCHANDISE
  THE MERCHANDISE WAS SERVED IN THE SAME WAY . . . . . 284 2 DON JUAN 3 17 1
MERCHANT
  FOR WANDERING MERCHANT VESSELS NOW AND THEN . . . . . 223 2 DON JUAN 2 126 3
  EACH BEVY WITH THE MERCHANT IN HIS STATION . . . . . 414 2 DON JUAN 5 7 3
  TURN'D TO THE MERCHANT AND BEGUN TO BID . . . . . . 425 2 DON JUAN 5 28 2
  AND THEN THE MERCHANT GIVING CHANGE AND SIGNING . . . 426 2 DON JUAN 5 29 7
MERCHANTMEN
  FOR CERTAIN MERCHANTMEN UPON THE LOOK . . . . 248 2 DON JUAN 2 174 6
MERCHANT-SHIP
  MUCH PASSION SINCE THE MERCHANT-SHIP THE ARGO . . . . 443 3 DON JUAN 14 76 7
MERCIES
  AT MERCY OF THE WAVES WHOSE MERCIES ARE . . . . . . 178 2 DON JUAN 2 42 7
MERCURIAL
  OR PROUDLIER PRANCING WITH MERCURIAL SKILL . . . . . 303 3 DON JUAN 11 70 7
  OF HOT OR COLD MERCURIAL OR SEDATE . . . . 327 3 DON JUAN 12 24 2
MERCURY
  SHAKSPEARE TALKS OF THE HERALD MERCURY . . . . 215 3 DON JUAN 9 66 1
MERCY
  AT MERCY OF THE WAVES WHOSE MERCIES ARE . . . . . . 178 2 DON JUAN 2 42 7
  THE MERCY HE HAD GRANTED OFT ABUSED . . . . 303 2 DON JUAN 3 54 4
MERE
  LIKE A MERE LOG AND BAFFLED OUR INTENT . . . . 173 2 DON JUAN 2 32 4
  (A RACE OF MERE IMPOSTORS WHEN ALL'S DONE-- . . . . . 218 2 DON JUAN 2 118 6
  THE ALLEGORY) A MERE TYPE NO MORE . . . . 238 2 DON JUAN 2 155 6
  EXCEPT MERE BREATH AND SINCE THE SILENT SHORE . . . . 350 2 DON JUAN 4 12 5
  BY THE MERE SENSES AND THAT WHICH DESTROYS . . . . . 352 2 DON JUAN 4 16 6
  COULD SCARCE BE SHOWN EVEN BY A MERE SPECTATOR . . . . 416 2 DON JUAN 5 11 8
  BUT SEEING AT HIS ELBOW A MERE LAD . . . . 417 2 DON JUAN 5 12 1
  AS THOUGH THEY WERE IN A MERE CHRISTIAN FAIR . . . . . 425 2 DON JUAN 5 28 5
  THAT A MERE CHRISTIAN SHOULD BE HALF SO PRETTY . . . . 500 2 DON JUAN 5 155 8
  AT LENGTH THEY FOUND MERE CANNONADE ALONE . . . . . . 81 3 DON JUAN 7 30 4
  BUT AS IT WAS MERE LUST OF POWER TO O'ER-ARCH ALL . . 86 3 DON JUAN 7 40 5
  AS HATH BEEN DONE MERE CONQUEST TO ADVANCE . . . . . 113 3 DON JUAN 8 3 6
  WHILE THE MERE VICTOR'S MAY APPAL OR STUN . . . . . . 114 3 DON JUAN 8 5 6
  IT WAS NOT MARVELLOUS THAT A MERE LAD . . . . 127 3 DON JUAN 8 31 6
  EXCEPT DON JUAN--A MERE NOVICE WHOSE . . . . 131 3 DON JUAN 8 36 2
  AS HELL--MERE MORTALS WHO THEIR POWER ABUSE-- . . . . 173 3 DON JUAN 8 123 7
  RATHER THAN LIFE A MERE AFFAIR OF BREATH . . . . . . 190 3 DON JUAN 9 16 8
  WHEREAS YOUR MODERN MONARCHS ARE MERE SPIDERS . . . . 196 3 DON JUAN 9 27 V8
  THAT MONSTROUS MYSTAGOGUE--THAT MERE SPOUT . . . . . 207 3 DON JUAN 9 50 V5
  EXCEPT WHERE 'TIS A MERE INSANITY . . . . 219 3 DON JUAN 9 73 3
  WEAKNESS FOR WHAT MOST PEOPLE DEEM MERE VERMIN-- . . . 249 3 DON JUAN 10 50 5
  A JARGON A MERE PHILANTHROPIC DIN . . . . 266 3 DON JUAN 10 85 6
  TO KNOW MYSELF AND ALL BESIDES MERE SPIRIT . . . . . 268 3 DON JUAN 11 1 V7
  NOT ONLY IN MERE TALKING BUT THE PRESS MAN . . . . . 288 3 DON JUAN 11 42 5
  OR AN APPROVER OR A MERE SPECTATOR . . . . 303 3 DON JUAN 11 69 7
  POSSESS'D THE ORE OF WHICH MERE HOPES ALLURE . . . . . 319 3 DON JUAN 12 8 3
  THAN THE MERE PLODDING THROUGH EACH VULGAR FRACTION . . 321 3 DON JUAN 12 11 6
  WHICH THE MERE PASSIONLESS CAN NEVER KNOW . . . . . . 336 3 DON JUAN 12 44 8
  OF A MERE NOVICE HAD ONE SAFEGUARD MORE . . . . . . 346 3 DON JUAN 12 67 2
  BEGINNINGS ARE FAIR FACES ENDS MERE FISHES-- . . . . 349 3 DON JUAN 12 73 2
  THE PRIDE OF A MERE CHILD WITH A NEW SASH ON . . . . 351 3 DON JUAN 12 77 5
  'TIS NOT MERE SPLENDOUR MAKES THE SHOW AUGUST . . . . 354 3 DON JUAN 12 83 7
  INSTEAD OF LOVE THAT MERE HALLUCINATION . . . . . . 360 3 DON JUAN 13 6 6
  FOR MY PART I AM BUT A MERE SPECTATOR . . . . 361 3 DON JUAN 13 7 6
  BE FOR MERE FANCY'S SPORT A THEME CREATIVE . . . . . 363 3 DON JUAN 13 10 6
  WHAT THEY SHOULD LAUGH AT--THE MERE AGUE STILL . . . . 366 3 DON JUAN 13 17 7
  OR EVEN MERE FASHION WHICH INDEED'S THE BEST . . . . 370 3 DON JUAN 13 28 6
  BUT A MERE MODERN MUST BE MODERATE-- . . . . 393 3 DON JUAN 13 74 7
  BY THE MERE COMBINATION OF A COTERIE . . . . 397 3 DON JUAN 13 82 4
  FLIRTATION--BUT DECOROUS THE MERE PRAISE . . . . . . 408 3 DON JUAN 13 108 5
  GENT READER NOTHING A MERE SPECULATION . . . . 413 3 DON JUAN 14 7 2
  BUT A MERE AIRY AND FANTASTIC BASIS . . . . 413 3 DON JUAN 14 7 7
  MERE FREEDOMS OF THE FEMALE CORPORATION . . . . . . 429 3 DON JUAN 14 43 4
  AS THE MERE PASTIME OF AN IDLE DAY . . . . 521 3 DON JUAN 16 42 3
  'TWAS A MERE QUIET SMILE OF CONTEMPLATION . . . . . 545 3 DON JUAN 16 93 1
  FOUND HIS OWN LEGS EMBARGOED FROM MERE WALKING . . . . 565 3 DON JUAN 17 8 4
MERELY
  AND MERELY TEND TO SHOW HOW GREATLY LOVE IS . . . . . 62 2 DON JUAN 1 74 7
  SHE CAME INTO THE CAVE BUT IT WAS MERELY . . . . . . 245 2 DON JUAN 2 168 3
  AND MERELY PRACTISED AS A SEA-ATTORNEY . . . . 283 2 DON JUAN 3 14 8
  AND MERELY SAYING CHRISTIAN CANST THOU LOVE . . . . . 478 2 DON JUAN 5 116 7
  THAT THESE WERE MERELY MASQUERADING TARTARS . . . . . 96 3 DON JUAN 7 57 4

MERELY   (CONTINUED)
```
        BY MERELY WIELDING WITH POETIC ARM . . . . . . . . 106   3 DON JUAN   7      79     3
        RETIRE A LITTLE MERELY TO TAKE BREATH . . . . . . . 133   3 DON JUAN   8      40     8
        KEEP MERELY FIRING AT A FOOLISH DISTANCE . . . . . . 151   3 DON JUAN   8      78     8
        O'ER SILENCED CITIES MERELY SERVED TO FLATTER . . . 197   3 DON JUAN   9      29     5
        I QUITE FORGET THIS POEM'S MERELY QUIZZICAL . . . . 203   3 DON JUAN   9      41     3
        AND MERELY FOR THE SAKE OF ITS OWN MERITS . . . . . 260   3 DON JUAN  10      72     5
        'TWAS MERELY KNOWN THAT ON A SECRET MISSION . . . . 283   3 DON JUAN  11      32     5
        SOME MAIDS HAVE BEEN MADE WIVES SOME MERELY MOTHERS . 308  3 DON JUAN  11      81     4
        IS NOT A MERELY SPECULATIVE HIT . . . . . . . . . . 318   3 DON JUAN  12       6     3
        SHE MERELY WAS DEEMED AMIABLE AND WITTY . . . . . . 338   3 DON JUAN  12      47     4
        THESE FIRST TWELVE BOOKS ARE MERELY FLOURISHES . . . 341   3 DON JUAN  12      54     5
        IT DOES NOR GOOD NOR HARM BEING MERELY MEANT . . . . 342   3 DON JUAN  12      57     4
        BUT YET IS MERELY INNOCENT FLIRTATION . . . . . . . 345   3 DON JUAN  12      63     7
        THEIR POST BUT THEIR'S IS MERELY A CHIMERA . . . . . 360   3 DON JUAN  13       5     3
        SHE MERELY FELT A COMMON SYMPATHY . . . . . . . . . 449   3 DON JUAN  14      91     5
        (I MERELY QUOTE WHAT I HAVE HEARD FROM MANY) . . . . 452   3 DON JUAN  14      95     2
        IN LISTENING MERELY TO HIS VOICE'S TONE . . . . . . 461   3 DON JUAN  15      13     6
        I MERELY MEAN TO SAY WHAT JOHNSON SAID . . . . . . . 504   3 DON JUAN  16       7     1
        PERHAPS SHE MERELY HAD THE SIMPLE PROJECT . . . . . 526   3 DON JUAN  16      51     5
        BUT MERELY AS A CRITICAL REGALE . . . . . . . . . . 528   3 DON JUAN  16      57    V8
        AND MERELY STATE THOUGH NOT FOR THE CONSISTORY . . . 531   3 DON JUAN  16      62     5
        THEY ERR--'TIS MERELY WHAT IS CALLED MOBILITY . . . 547   3 DON JUAN  16      97     4
        BUT MERELY THEIR PARENTAL TENDERNESS . . . . . . . . 562   3 DON JUAN  17       1     7
MERIDIAN
        THAT IS TO SAY--IN A MERIDIAN CLIME . . . . . . . . 482   2 DON JUAN   5     123     3
        IN ITS MERIDIAN HER BLUE EYES OR GREY-- . . . . . . 218   3 DON JUAN   9      71     2
MERIDIAN-BORN
        MERIDIAN-BORN TO BLOOM IN  THIS OPINION . . . . . . 246   3 DON JUAN  10      44     2
        MERIDIAN-BORN TO FLOURISH IN THIS NATION . . . . . . 246   3 DON JUAN  10      44    V2
MERIDIAN-LIKE
        MERIDIAN-LIKE WERE SEEN ALL LIGHT TO ISSUE . . . . . 309   2 DON JUAN   3      67     8
MERIT
        OF MERIT AND COMPLAINT OF PRESENT DAYS . . . . . . . 14    2 DON JUAN   D       8     7
        NOW DONNA INEZ HAD WITH ALL HER MERIT . . . . . . . 32    2 DON JUAN   1      20     1
        THERE'S MERIT IN THIS SORT OF RESURRECTION . . . . . 37    2 DON JUAN   1      31    V7
        WAR'S MERIT IT BY NO MEANS MIGHT ENHANCE . . . . . . 113   3 DON JUAN   8       3     4
        THEN THERE'S MORE MERIT IN HIS SELF-DENIAL . . . . . 319   3 DON JUAN  12       7     8
        FOR SUCH A SHIELD WHICH LEAVES BUT LITTLE MERIT . . 372   3 DON JUAN  13      31     2
        GRACED WITH SOME MERIT AND WITH MORE EFFRONTERY . . 401   3 DON JUAN  13      91     7
        MARVELL'D AT MERIT OF ANOTHER NATION . . . . . . . . 425   3 DON JUAN  14      34     3
        WHOSE MERIT NONE ENOUGH CAN SING OR SAY . . . . . . 445   3 DON JUAN  14      82     2
        AND SANG WITH MUCH SIMPLICITY--A MERIT . . . . . . . 518   3 DON JUAN  16      40     7
MERITED
        THE WOUNDS THEY RICHLY MERITED AND SHRIEK . . . . . 158   3 DON JUAN   8      94     4
MERITORIOUS
        TO THOSE WHO WERE OR PASSED FOR MERITORIOUS . . . . 372   3 DON JUAN  13      32     7
MERITS
        (NOT THAT I HAVE NOT SEVERAL MERITS MORE . . . . . . 137   2 DON JUAN   1     202     4
        MY OWN MERITS AND THOUGH YOUNG--I SEE SIR--YOU . . . 392   2 DON JUAN   4      88     2
        WITH ITS PROUD BROW IT MERITS SLIGHT APPLAUSE . . . 86    3 DON JUAN   7      40     6
        (FOR DAY NE'ER SAW HIS MERITS) COULD DECREE . . . . 86    3 DON JUAN   7      41     4
        AND MERELY FOR THE SAKE OF ITS OWN MERITS . . . . . 260   3 DON JUAN  10      72     5
        OF JUAN'S MERITS AND HIS SITUATION . . . . . . . . . 468   3 DON JUAN  15      28     2
        SHE DEEMED HIS MERITS SOMETHING MORE THAN COMMON . . 473   3 DON JUAN  15      40     6
        OF WHICH THE LATTER MERITS EVERY PREFERENCE . . . . 541   3 DON JUAN  16      85     4
MERMAID'S
        RANG IN HER SAD EARS LIKE A MERMAID'S SONG . . . . . 362   2 DON JUAN   4      34     7
MERMAIDS
        OR SAY THEY ARE LIKE VIRTUOUS MERMAIDS WHOSE . . . . 349   3 DON JUAN  12      73     1
MERRIMENT
        OF MELANCHOLY MERRIMENT TO QUOTE . . . . . . . . . . 156   3 DON JUAN   8      89     5
        AND THUS DEATH LAUGHS--IT IS SAD MERRIMENT . . . . . 189   3 DON JUAN   9      13     1
MERRY
        THAT THERE ARE MONTHS WHICH NATURE GROWS MORE MERRY IN . 76  2 DON JUAN  1    102     7
        HIS QUESTION MUCH TOO MERRY TO DIVINE . . . . . . . 297   2 DON JUAN   3      42     7
        UNLESS IT WERE TO BE A MOMENT MERRY . . . . . . . . 346   2 DON JUAN   4       5     7
        HURRAH HOW SWIFTLY SPEEDS THE POST SO MERRY . . . . 260   3 DON JUAN  10      71     3
ME'S
        OBSERVE FOR THAT WITH ME'S A SINE QUA . . . . . . . 494   3 DON JUAN  15      86     8
MESH
        LOVE'S THE FIRST NET WHICH SPREADS ITS DEADLY MESH . 422   2 DON JUAN   5      22     5
MESS
        FOR WANT OF WATER AND THEIR SOLID MESS . . . . . . . 178   2 DON JUAN   2      41     5
        THEY MADE A MOST SUPERIOR MESS OF BROTH . . . . . . 221   2 DON JUAN   2     123     5
        HAD BEEN THE FAVOURITE OF FULL MANY A MESS . . . . . 318   2 DON JUAN   3      82     3
        BUT I MUST CROWD ALL INTO ONE GRAND MESS . . . . . . 483   3 DON JUAN  15      64     1
MESSAGE
        AND AS THE GOOD SHIPS SENT UPON THAT MESSAGE . . . . 376   3 DON JUAN  13      39     3
MESSALINA'S
        (FELLOWS WHOM MESSALINA'S SELF WOULD PENSION) . . . 218   3 DON JUAN   9      72     4
MESSENGER
        BUT HERE A MESSENGER BROUGHT IN DISPATCHES . . . . . 439   3 DON JUAN  14      67     8
MESSMATE
        HIS NEAREST MESSMATE TOLD HIS SIRE WHO THREW . . . . 202   2 DON JUAN   2      87     5
MESSORUM
        OH DURA ILIA MESSORUM--OH . . . . . . . . . . . . . 190   3 DON JUAN   9      15     1
MESSUAGES
        TO A CHANCERY SUIT AND MESSUAGES AND LANDS . . . . . 42    2 DON JUAN   1      37     2
```

507

MET
    AND IF SHE MET HIM THOUGH SHE SMILED NO MORE . . . . . . 61 2 DON JUAN 1   72   1
    TREMBLINGS WHEN MET AND RESTLESSNESS WHEN LEFT . . . . . 62 2 DON JUAN 1   74   4
    BUT MET ALFONSO IN HIS DRESSING-GOWN . . . . 122 2 DON JUAN 1 183   7
    AND WITH A PIECE OF PORK MOREOVER MET . . . . 181 2 DON JUAN 2   47   6
    AND HAIDEE MET THE MORNING FACE TO FACE . . . . 231 2 DON JUAN 2 141   1
    BUT THE FAIR FACE WHICH MET HIS EYES FORBADE . . . . . . 235 2 DON JUAN 2 149   2
    PILAUS AND MEATS OF ALL SORTS MET THE GAZE . . . . 291 2 DON JUAN 3   31   3
    SO THAT THE FEW WHO MET HIM HARDLY HEEDED . . . . 300 2 DON JUAN 3   49   3
    PERFORCE SINCE WHATSOEVER MET HER VIEW . . . . 378 2 DON JUAN 4   62   4
    AND FLEW AT ALL SHE MET AS ON HER FOES . . . . 380 2 DON JUAN 4   67   4
    WAS MUCH EMBARRASSED NEVER HAVING MET . . . . 482 2 DON JUAN 5 122   2
    HAD MET A PARTY TOWARDS THE TWILIGHT'S FALL . . . . . . 95 3 DON JUAN 7   56   4
    BUT WHERE HE MET THE INDIVIDUAL MAN . . . . 144 3 DON JUAN 8   64   7
    THIS VALIANT MAN KILLED ALL THE TURKS HE MET . . . . . 150 3 DON JUAN 8   77   1
    OF ALL THE FIVE ON BAYONETS MET HIS LOT . . . . 166 3 DON JUAN 8 110   4
    THE SENATE WHICH TIBERIUS MET OF OLD-- . . . . 314 3 DON JUAN 11 V 76   8
    THE FAIR MOST FATAL JUAN EVER MET . . . . 364 3 DON JUAN 13   12   3
    MET THE MORN AS THEY MIGHT IF FINE THEY RODE . . . . . 406 3 DON JUAN 13 104   2
METAL
    THAT E'ER BY PRECIOUS METAL WAS HELD IN . . . . 312 2 DON JUAN 3   71   8
    EXTREMELY COMMON IN THIS AGE WHOSE METAL . . . . 33 3 DON JUAN 6   55   7
METALS
    WHICH WAS A MIXTURE OF ALL METALS BUT . . . . 34 3 DON JUAN 6   56   2
    THE PIOUS METALS MOST IN REQUISITION . . . . 152 3 DON JUAN 8   81   5
METAMORPHOSIS
    UPON THE METAMORPHOSIS IN VIEW . . . . 459 2 DON JUAN 5   83   4
METAPHOR
    THANK HEAVEN I'VE GOT NO METAPHOR QUITE READY . . . . 160 2 DON JUAN 2   6   7
    (THIS METAPHOR I THINK HOLDS GOOD AS AUGHT . . . . . . 90 3 DON JUAN 7   49   3
    WILL KISS NOT IN SAD METAPHOR--BUT EARNEST-- . . . . . 286 3 DON JUAN 11   38 V7
    I HATE TO HUNT DOWN A TIRED METAPHOR . . . . 374 3 DON JUAN 13   36   5
METAPHYSICAL
    BUT I AM APT TO GROW TOO METAPHYSICAL . . . . 203 3 DON JUAN 9   41   1
    AND THEREFORE WILL I LEAVE OFF METAPHYSICAL . . . . . 270 3 DON JUAN 11   5   1
METAPHYSICIAN
    LIKE COLERIDGE INTO A METAPHYSICIAN . . . . 70 2 DON JUAN 1   91   8
    THERE WAS DICK DUBIOUS THE METAPHYSICIAN . . . . . . 399 3 DON JUAN 13   87   1
    AND ALSO MEEK AS A METAPHYSICIAN . . . . 497 3 DON JUAN 15   92   2
METAPHYSICS
    EXPLAINING METAPHYSICS TO THE NATION-- . . . . 10 2 DON JUAN D   2   7
    BUT NOT KNOWING METAPHYSICS HAD NO NOTION . . . . . . 289 2 DON JUAN 3   26   4
    OF METAPHYSICS OTHERS ARE CONTENT . . . . 340 3 DON JUAN 12   52   6
    BUT I'M RELAPSING INTO METAPHYSICS . . . . 349 3 DON JUAN 12   72   1
    MYSELF WITH METAPHYSICS NONE CAN HATE . . . . 496 3 DON JUAN 15   91   2
METEOR
    AND BRIGHT AS ANY METEOR EVER BRED . . . . 42 3 DON JUAN 6   72   5
    THERE'S NOT A METEOR IN THE POLAR SKY . . . . 66 3 DON JUAN 7   1   3
    YET SHE WAS NOTHING DAZZLED BY THE METEOR . . . . . . 480 3 DON JUAN 15   56   7
METEORS
    LIKE HARNESSED METEORS THEN ALONG THE FLOOR . . . . . 302 3 DON JUAN 11   67   4
METHINKS
    WHO CALL'D HER CHASTE METHINKS BEGAN TOO SOON . . . . 82 2 DON JUAN 1 113   3
    METHINKS THE REQUISITION'S RATHER HARD . . . . 85 2 DON JUAN 1 118   3
    METHINKS AT MEALS SOME ODD THOUGHTS MIGHT INTRUDE . . 426 2 DON JUAN 5   30   3
    METHINKS--SAID HE--IT WOULD BE NO GREAT SHAME . . . . 434 2 DON JUAN 5   43   5
    METHINKS THE STORY OF THE TOWER OF BABEL . . . . . . 444 2 DON JUAN 5   59   7
    METHINKS THESE ARE THE MOST TREMENDOUS WORDS . . . . 179 3 DON JUAN 8 134   1
    I SAY METHINKS THAT PHILO-GENITIVENESS . . . . 326 3 DON JUAN 12   22   7
    AND CAUGHT THEM--WHAT DO THEY NOT CATCH METHINKS . . 364 3 DON JUAN 13   12   7
    METHINKS GAY PUNCH HATH SOMETHING OF THE SAME . . . . 400 3 DON JUAN 13   89   4
    METHINKS LOVE'S VERY TITLE SAYS ENOUGH . . . . 451 3 DON JUAN 14   94   7
    METHINKS WE MAY PROCEED UPON OUR NARRATIVE . . . . . 481 3 DON JUAN 15   59   2
METHOD
    THAT IS THE USUAL METHOD BUT NOT MINE-- . . . . 25 2 DON JUAN 1   7   1
    HER VILE AMBIGUOUS METHOD OF FLIRTATION . . . . . . 222 3 DON JUAN 9   81   7
    YET MANY HAVE A METHOD MORE RETICULAR-- . . . . . . 343 3 DON JUAN 12   59   5
METHODISTIC
    A RAKE TURN'D METHODISTIC OR ECLECTIC-- . . . . . . 309 2 DON JUAN 3   66   3
METHOD'S
    METHOD'S MORE SURE AT MOMENTS TO TAKE HOLD . . . . . 439 2 DON JUAN 5   49   4
METHODS
    AND NO DOUBT OF ALL METHODS 'TIS THE BEST . . . . . 356 2 DON JUAN 4   24   5
METROPOLIS
    IN SMALL-EYED CHINA'S CROCKERY-WARE METROPOLIS . . . 271 3 DON JUAN 11   7   5
MI
    AND NOW I THINK ON'T MI VIEN IN MENTE . . . . 56 2 DON JUAN 1   62   6
    WITH TU MI CHAMAS'S FROM PORTINGALE . . . . 523 3 DON JUAN 16   45   7
MIA'S
    THE MAMMA MIA'S AND THE AMOR MIO'S . . . . 523 3 DON JUAN 16   45   3
MICROCOSM
    DON JUAN SAW THAT MICROCOSM ON STILTS . . . . 342 3 DON JUAN 12   56   1
MID-DAY
    AND PRUDENTLY POSTPONE UNTIL MID-DAY . . . . 500 3 DON JUAN 15   98   5
    AND THEN THE MID-DAY HAVING WORN TO ONE . . . . . . 527 3 DON JUAN 16   55   1
MIDDLE
    BUT ERE THE MIDDLE WATCH WAS HARDLY OVER . . . . . . 41 3 DON JUAN 6   70   4
    THEY BLEW UP IN THE MIDDLE OF THE RIVER . . . . . . 80 3 DON JUAN 7   28   7
    RIGHT IN THE MIDDLE OF THE PARAPET . . . . 136 3 DON JUAN 8   46   7

MIDDLE   (CONTINUED)
```
    BUT NOW I CHOOSE TO BREAK OFF IN THE MIDDLE . . . . . . . 181  3 DON JUAN  8   139   5
    OF ALL THE BARBAROUS MIDDLE AGES THAT . . . . . . . . 315  3 DON JUAN 12    1   1
    WHICH IS THE MOST BARBAROUS IS THE MIDDLE AGE . . . . . 315  3 DON JUAN 12    1   2
    WHOSE TALE BELONGS TO HALLAM'S MIDDLE AGES . . . . . . . 330  3 DON JUAN 12   30   8
    OF EPIC LOVE'S BEGINNING END AND MIDDLE . . . . . . . . 337  3 DON JUAN 12   45   8
MIDDLE-AGED
    SOME VOICES OF THE BUXOM MIDDLE-AGED . . . . . . . . 178  3 DON JUAN  8   132   1
    MIDDLE-AGED LADIES EVEN MORE THAN YOUNG . . . . . . . 230  3 DON JUAN 10   10   2
    THE MIDDLE-AGED TO MAKE THE DAY MORE SHORT . . . . . 405  3 DON JUAN 13   101   4
MIDDLING
    HER FATHER'S HOSPITALITY SEEM'D MIDDLING . . . . . . . 295  2 DON JUAN  3   39   5
    AS FOR THE MEN THEY ARE A MIDDLING SET . . . . . . . 391  2 DON JUAN  4   86   1
    AND YET BUT MADE A MIDDLING GRENADIER . . . . . . . . 209  2 DON JUAN  9   54   8
MIDNIGHT
    AT MIDNIGHT ON THE BLUE AND MOONLIT DEEP . . . . . . . 87  2 DON JUAN  1   122   2
    'TWAS MIDNIGHT--DARK AND SOMBRE WAS THE NIGHT . . . . . 94  2 DON JUAN  1   135  V1
    'TWAS MIDNIGHT--DONNA JULIA WAS IN BED . . . . . . . 95  2 DON JUAN  1   136   1
    WHAT MAY THIS MIDNIGHT VIOLENCE BETIDE . . . . . . . 98  2 DON JUAN  1   142   5
    AND BARDS BURN WHAT THEY CALL THEIR MIDNIGHT TAPER . . 146  2 DON JUAN  1   218   6
    MY MILD AND MIDNIGHT BEAKERS TO THE BRIM . . . . . . 372  2 DON JUAN  4   53   7
    AND MIDNIGHT LISTENS TO THE LION'S ROAR . . . . . . . 373  2 DON JUAN  4   55   5
    AND SIGH TO MIDNIGHT WINDS BUT NOT TO SONG . . . . . 398  2 DON JUAN  4   99   8
    THE FESTAL MIDNIGHT AND THE LEVEE MORN . . . . . . 404  2 DON JUAN  4   110   8
    THAT IS ERE MIDNIGHT--WHICH IS LONDON'S NOON . . . . . 409  3 DON JUAN 13   111   2
    SADDER THAN OWL-SONGS OR THE MIDNIGHT BLAST . . . . . 432  3 DON JUAN 14   50   2
    I FEEL SOME CHILLY MIDNIGHT SHUDDERINGS . . . . . . . 500  3 DON JUAN 15   98   4
    WITH ALL THE MYSTERY BY MIDNIGHT CAUSED . . . . . . 507  3 DON JUAN 16   15   5
    FOR HE MUTTERS HIS PRAYER IN THE MIDNIGHT AIR . . . . 518  3 DON JUAN 16  L  1   3
    DON JUAN WHEN THE MIDNIGHT HOUR OF PILLOWS . . . . . 555  3 DON JUAN 16   110   3
    LIKE SHOWERS WHICH ON THE MIDNIGHT GUSTS WILL PASS . . 556  3 DON JUAN 16   114   3
'MIDST
    'MIDST OTHER INDICATIONS OF FESTIVITY . . . . . . . . 290  2 DON JUAN  3   29   4
    AIR 'MIDST THE REST WHO KEPT THEIR VALIANT FACES . . . 130  3 DON JUAN  8   34   7
    AS SOON AS THUNDER 'MIDST THE GENERAL NOISE . . . . . 142  3 DON JUAN  8   59   7
    AND LEFT HIM 'MIDST THE INVALID AND MAIMED . . . . . 154  3 DON JUAN  8   85   4
    SMOKING HIS PIPE QUITE CALMLY 'MIDST THE DIN . . . . 160  3 DON JUAN  8   98   4
    MAN 'MIDST THY MOULDY MAMMOTHS GRAND CULVIER . . . . 250  3 DON JUAN 10   52   4
    'MIDST ROYAL DUKES AND DAMES CONDEMNED TO CLIMB . . . 302  3 DON JUAN 11   68   7
    'MIDST MANY ROCKS WE GUARD MORE AGAINST WRECKS . . . . 371  3 DON JUAN 13   30   6
MIDST
    NOW SHRINKING BACK NOW MIDST THE FIRST HE SEEMS . . . 155  2 DON JUAN  1  V 6   5
    AND IN THE MIDST A GOLDEN APPLE GREW-- . . . . . . . 44  3 DON JUAN  6   76   1
    AIR MIDST THE REST WHOSE SHORT BREATH AND LONG FACES . . 130  3 DON JUAN  8   34  V7
    AND ONE GOOD ACTION IN THE MIDST OF CRIMES . . . . . 156  3 DON JUAN  8   90   1
    MIDST WHOM WE HAVE HEARD FROM SOURCES QUITE CORRECT . . 382  3 DON JUAN 13   52   4
    I HAVE SEARCHED THE WORLD AND MIDST SUCCESS OR CHECKS . 451  3 DON JUAN 14   93  V5
MIEN
    HE WAS ABOVE THE VULGAR BY HIS MIEN . . . . . . . . 415  2 DON JUAN  5    9   6
    WITH KIND REMARKS UPON THEIR MIEN AND FACES . . . . . 28  3 DON JUAN  6   45   8
    AND MIEN EXCITED GENERAL ADMIRATION-- . . . . . . . . 287  3 DON JUAN 11   39   2
    WHOM A GOOD MIEN ESPECIALLY IF NEW . . . . . . . . 305  3 DON JUAN 11   73   6
    AURORA WITH HER PURE AND PLACID MIEN . . . . . . . . 552  3 DON JUAN 16   105   3
MIENS
    WHICH TURNED UPON THEIR LATE GUESTS' MIENS AND FACES . . 550  3 DON JUAN 16   103   5
MIGHT
    AND FOUGHT AWAY WITH MIGHT AND MAIN NOT KNOWING . . . . 120  3 DON JUAN  8   19   2
    HIS CAUSE BY LEANING MUCH FROM MIGHT TO RIGHT . . . . 391  3 DON JUAN 13   69   4
    THOUGH HE CAME IN HIS MIGHT WITH KING HENRY'S RIGHT . . 518  3 DON JUAN 16  L  2   1
MIGHTIER
    BUT YESTERDAY AND WHO HAD MIGHTIER BREATH . . . . . 430  2 DON JUAN  5   36   3
MIGHTIEST
    AND JESTEST WITH THE BROWS OF MIGHTIEST MEN . . . . . 266  2 DON JUAN  2   206   2
MIGHTY
    UNTIL HIS MIGHTY HEART IN ITS GREAT MOOD . . . . . . 70  2 DON JUAN  1   91   3
    THERE WAS NO MIGHTY REASON TO BE PLEASED . . . . . . 296  2 DON JUAN  3   40   3
    BUT IN A MIGHTY HALL OR GALLERY BOTH IN . . . . . . 443  2 DON JUAN  5   57   5
    THAN ARE YOUR MIGHTY PASSIONS AND SO FORTH . . . . . 32  3 DON JUAN  6   53   5
    WHICH ROCKED AS 'TWERE BENEATH THE MIGHTY NOISES . . . 115  3 DON JUAN  8    7   6
    HOWE'ER THE MIGHTY LOCUST DESOLATION . . . . . . . . 175  3 DON JUAN  8   126   5
    I KNOW ITS MIGHTY EMPIRE NOW ALLURES . . . . . . . . 194  3 DON JUAN  9   23   5
    BUT IN SUCH MATTERS RUSSIA'S MIGHTY EMPRESS . . . . . 221  3 DON JUAN  9   77   7
    A MIGHTY MASS OF BRICK AND SMOKE AND SHIPPING . . . . 265  3 DON JUAN 10   82   1
    OF TRAVELLERS TO MIGHTY BABYLON . . . . . . . . . 279  3 DON JUAN 11   23   2
    A MIGHTY WINDOW HOLLOW IN THE CENTRE . . . . . . . 387  3 DON JUAN 13   62   1
    AND SIR JOHN POTTLEDEEP THE MIGHTY DRINKER . . . . . 398  3 DON JUAN 13   84   8
    FORM'D OF TWO MIGHTY TRIBES THE BORES AND BORED . . . 402  3 DON JUAN 13   95   8
    WHAT ICEBERGS IN THE HEARTS OF MIGHTY MEN . . . . . 455  3 DON JUAN 14   102   3
    THE MIND IS LOST IN MIGHTY CONTEMPLATION . . . . . . 486  3 DON JUAN 15   69   1
    A MIGHTY MUG OF MORAL DOUBLE ALE . . . . . . . . . 533  3 DON JUAN 16   67   4
MILAN
    I SAW THE PRETTIEST CREATURE FRESH FROM MILAN . . . . . 268  2 DON JUAN  2   209   7
MILD
    THE SEA AND SKY WERE BLUE AND CLEAR AND MILD-- . . . . 193  2 DON JUAN  2   70   4
    BUT THE BOY BORE UP LONG AND WITH A MILD . . . . . . 203  2 DON JUAN  2   88   3
    OF MILD DEMEANOUR THOUGH OF SAVAGE MOOD . . . . . . 302  2 DON JUAN  3   53   2
    MY MILD AND MIDNIGHT BEAKERS TO THE BRIM . . . . . . 372  2 DON JUAN  4   53   7
    BUT SHE WAS A SOFT LANDSCAPE OF MILD EARTH . . . . . 32  3 DON JUAN  6   53   1
    THE BEAR IS CIVILIZED THE WOLF IS MILD . . . . . . . 157  3 DON JUAN  8   92   5
```

509

```
                                                        PAGE VOL      CANTO STANZA LN
MILD   (CONTINUED)
    MILD CATHERINE OWED THE CHANCE OF BEING CROWN'D  . . . . 205  3 DON JUAN   9    46  V4
    WE TEASE MILD BAILLIE OR SOFT ABERNETHY . . . . . . . 245  3 DON JUAN  10    42   8
    CAN TAX MY MILD MUSE WITH MISANTHROPY . . . . . . . . 286  3 DON JUAN  11    38   2
    WHILE THE MILD EMERALD'S BEAM SHADES DOWN THE DYES  . . . 319  3 DON JUAN  12     8   7
    SHE WAS THE MILD REPROVER OF THE YOUNG  . . . . . . . 338  3 DON JUAN  12    48   2
    THAT WHERE THEIR EDUCATION HARSH OR MILD . . . . . . . 563  3 DON JUAN  17     2   5
    MILD--BUT AT TIMES A SORT OF HERCULES FURENS  . . . . . 567  3 DON JUAN  17    11   6
MILDER
    HER DAUGHTER TEMPER'D WITH A MILDER RAY . . . . . . . 375  2 DON JUAN   4    57   1
MILDEST
    YOU'RE WRONG--HE WAS THE MILDEST MANNER'D MAN . . . . . 296  2 DON JUAN   3    41   1
    BUT I THE MILDEST MEEKEST OF MANKIND  . . . . . . . . 193  3 DON JUAN   9    21   1
    AND MILDEST MATRON-LIKE INTERPRETATION  . . . . . . . 208  3 DON JUAN   9    52   2
MILDLY
    GLANCED MILDLY ALL THE WORLD WAS ON THE WATCH . . . . . 213  3 DON JUAN   9    61   8
    MUST BURN MORE MILDLY ERE IT CAN ENLIGHTEN  . . . . . . 281  3 DON JUAN  11    27   8
MILE
    AND ROUGH WITH REEFS WHICH RAN OUT MANY A MILE  . . . . 285  2 DON JUAN   3    19   7
    THE TRAIN MIGHT REACH A QUARTER OF A MILE  . . . . . . 495  2 DON JUAN   5   146   3
    BY GERMAN POSTBOYS DRIVEN A GERMAN MILE  . . . . . . . 260  3 DON JUAN  10    71  V8
MILES
    HOW MANY MILES THE MOON MIGHT HAVE IN GIRTH . . . . .  71  2 DON JUAN   1    92   5
    BECAUSE HE HAD JOURNEYED FIFTY MILES AND FOUND . . . . 497  2 DON JUAN   5   150   3
    HE MOVED SOME HUNDRED MILES OFF FOR A STATION . . . . . 144  3 DON JUAN   8    64   3
    SOME HUNDRED FEET IN HEIGHT NOT TO SAY MILES  . . . . . 201  3 DON JUAN   9    38   7
MILITARY
    WITH MANY OF THE MILITARY SET . . . . . . . . . .  22  2 DON JUAN   1     3   6
    I FOUND THE MILITARY COMMANDANT . . . . . . . . . . 428  2 DON JUAN   5    33   7
    BY SERVICE WITH MY MILITARY BROTHERS  . . . . . . . . 103  3 DON JUAN   7    71   4
    A SAVAGE SORT OF MILITARY MARTYR  . . . . . . . . . 152  3 DON JUAN   8    80   6
MILK
    HIS FEELINGS FROM ALL MILK OF HUMAN KINDNESS  . . . . . 304  2 DON JUAN   3    57   7
    WHICH GIRT A SLIGHT CHEMISE AS WHITE AS MILK  . . . . . 456  3 DON JUAN   5    77   4
    WHITE STOCKINGS DRAWN UNCURDLED AS NEW MILK . . . . . . 204  3 DON JUAN   9    43   7
    WITNESS THE LANDS WHICH FLOW'D WITH MILK AND HONEY . . . 405  3 DON JUAN  13   100   1
    TILL SKIMM'D--AND THEN THERE WAS SOME MILK AND WATER  . . 474  3 DON JUAN  15    41   4
    AND BEING CONSUMPTIVE LIVE ON A MILK DIET . . . . . . 474  3 DON JUAN  15    41   8
MILK-AND-WATER
    WITH ALL THEIR PRETTY MILK-AND-WATER WAYS . . . . . . 156  3 DON JUAN   8    90   4
MILKY
    LIKE SMALL STARS THROUGH THE MILKY WAY APPARENT . . . . 315  2 DON JUAN   3    77   4
    HAD HELD TILL NOW HER SOFT AND MILKY WAY . . . . . . . 375  2 DON JUAN   4    57   5
    AS IF THE MILKY WAY THEIR FEET WAS UNDER . . . . . . . 450  2 DON JUAN   5    66   4
    BUT BID MY WOMEN FORM THE MILKY WAY . . . . . . . . 494  2 DON JUAN   5   145   3
MILL
    AND ALL MY FANCIES WHIRLING LIKE A MILL . . . . . . . 224  3 DON JUAN   9    85   6
MILLAH
    AND ONLY SHOUTED ALLA AND BIS MILLAH  . . . . . . .  73  3 DON JUAN   7    13   8
MILLENNIUM
    AND AS IN THE GREAT JOY OF YOUR MILLENNIUM  . . . . . . 180  3 DON JUAN   8   136   2
MILLIARDS
    YOU'LL NEVER GUESS I'LL BET YOU MILLIONS MILLIARDS-- . . . 454  3 DON JUAN  14   100   7
MILLINERS
    ESPOUSED TWO PARTNERS (MILLINERS OF BATH)  . . . . . . 329  2 DON JUAN   3    93   8
    THE MILLINERS WHO FURNISH DRAPERY MISSES . . . . . . . 293  3 DON JUAN  11    49   1
MILLINERY
    EVE MADE UP MILLINERY WITH FIG LEAVES--  . . . . . . . 444  3 DON JUAN  14    78   2
MILLION
    OF AN ILL-GOTTEN MILLION OF PIASTRES  . . . . . . . . 222  2 DON JUAN   2   125   8
    AND HALF A MILLION FOR YOUR SABINE FARM . . . . . . . 186  3 DON JUAN   9     7   7
    THE NEGROES AND IS WORTH A MILLION FIGHTERS . . . . . . 325  3 DON JUAN  12    20   6
    OR ELSE 'TWILL COST US ALL ANOTHER MILLION  . . . . . . 446  3 DON JUAN  14    83   8
MILLIONS
    THAT WHICH MAKES THOUSANDS PERHAPS MILLIONS THINK . . . . 327  3 DON JUAN   3    88   3
    MEN'S HEARTS AGAINST WHOLE MILLIONS WHEN THEIR TRADE  . . 102  3 DON JUAN   7    69   6
    SPARE OR SMITE RARELY--MAN'S MAKE MILLIONS ASHES . . . . 115  3 DON JUAN   8     6   8
    THE MILLIONS SLAIN BY SOLDIERS FOR THEIR RATION . . . . 146  3 DON JUAN   8    68   6
    TO GERMANY WHOSE SOMEWHAT TARDY MILLIONS . . . . . . . 254  3 DON JUAN  10    60   7
    JUAN ADMIRED THESE HIGHWAYS OF FREE MILLIONS  . . . . . 263  3 DON JUAN  10    77   4
    YOU'LL NEVER GUESS I'LL BET YOU MILLIONS MILLIARDS-- . . . 454  3 DON JUAN  14   100   7
    SOME MILLIONS MUST BE WRONG THAT'S PRETTY CLEAR  . . . . 496  3 DON JUAN  15    90   1
MILLPOND
    THERE WAS MISS MILLPOND SMOOTH AS SUMMER'S SEA . . . . . 474  3 DON JUAN  15    41   1
MILOR
    JEST QUOTH MILOR WHY ADELINE YOU KNOW . . . . . . . . 517  3 DON JUAN  16    38   1
MILTIADES
    THAT TYRANT WAS MILTIADES . . . . . . . . . . . 325  2 DON JUAN   3  L 12   3
MILTON
    MILTON APPEAL'D TO THE AVENGER TIME . . . . . . . .  15  2 DON JUAN   D    10   2
    THOU SHALT BELIEVE IN MILTON DRYDEN POPE . . . . . . . 139  2 DON JUAN   1   205   1
    DANTE AND MILTON AND OF BOTH THE AFFECTION  . . . . . . 281  2 DON JUAN   3    10   3
    FOR THE FIRST MRS MILTON LEFT HIS HOUSE . . . . . . . 328  2 DON JUAN   3    91   8
MILTONIC
    AND MAKES THE WORD MILTONIC MEAN SUBLIME . . . . . .  15  2 DON JUAN   D    10   4
MILTON'S
    BUT DANTE'S BEATRICE AND MILTON'S EVE . . . . . . . . 281  2 DON JUAN   3    10   7
    MILTON'S THE PRINCE OF POETS--SO WE SAY . . . . . . . 328  2 DON JUAN   3    91   1
MIMIC
    AND WHEN WELL PRACTISED IN THESE MIMIC SCENES . . . . .  93  3 DON JUAN   7    53   5
```

MIMICS
     CHALK MIMICS PAINTING THEN FESTOONS ARE TWIRLED . . . . . 302 3 DON JUAN 11   67   5
MINARET
     OR THE SNOW MINARET ON AN ALPINE STEEP . . . . 40 3 DON JUAN 6   68   4
MINCED
     OR MINCED IN PIECES AS SMALL BAITS FOR FISH . . . . . . 492 2 DON JUAN 5   141   V4
MIND
     IF WE MAY JUDGE OF MATTER BY THE MIND . . . . 18 2 DON JUAN D   15   1
     WHO CHOSE TO GO WHERE'ER HE HAD A MIND . . . . 31 2 DON JUAN 1   19   3
     AND SLIGHT SO VERY SLIGHT THAT TO THE MIND . . . . . . 60 2 DON JUAN 1   71   5
     SO BY THE POESY OF HIS OWN MIND . . . . 72 2 DON JUAN 1   95   4
     (MIND--THAT I DO NOT SAY--SHE HAD NOT SLEPT) . . . . . 97 2 DON JUAN 1   140   2
     OUR COUNSEL--(JUAN MIND YOU MUST NOT SLEEP) . . . . . 115 2 DON JUAN 1   172   8
     HIS MIND THE MORE O'ER THIS ITS MYSTERY BROODED . . . . 118 2 DON JUAN 1   177   6
     BUT STILL I THINK I CAN COLLECT MY MIND . . . . . . 133 2 DON JUAN 1   196   2
     I STRUGGLE BUT CAN NOT COLLECT MY MIND . . . . 133 2 DON JUAN 1   196   V2
     LED BY SOME TORTUOSITY OF MIND . . . . 141 2 DON JUAN 1   208   3
     AND READ YOUR BIBLE SIR AND MIND YOUR PURSE . . . . . 147 2 DON JUAN 1   220   8
     AND HASTY TEMPER ON A KINDLING MIND . . . . 155 2 DON JUAN 1 V 7   2
     IT MENDS THEIR MORALS NEVER MIND THE PAIN . . . . . 157 2 DON JUAN 2   1   4
     A--NEVER MIND HIS TUTOR AN OLD ASS . . . . 158 2 DON JUAN 2   3   4
     A MIND DISEASED NO REMEDY CAN PHYSIC-- . . . . 166 2 DON JUAN 2   19   7
     AND THOUGH 'TWAS NOT MUCH TO A NAVAL MIND . . . . . 170 2 DON JUAN 2   26   3
     WHICH YIELDED A DAY'S LIFE AND TO THEIR MIND . . . . 208 2 DON JUAN 2   99   4
     THEIR LOATHSOME PHANTASMAGORIA OER THE MIND . . . . . 227 2 DON JUAN 2   134 V7
     AND LEAVE LIKE OPENING HELL UPON THE MIND . . . . . 227 2 DON JUAN 2   134 V7
     SOME MIND THEIR HOUSEHOLD OTHERS DISSIPATION . . . . 263 2 DON JUAN 2   201   2
     STILL O'ER HIS MIND THE INFLUENCE OF THE CLIME . . . 304 2 DON JUAN 3   56   1
     LIKE SKULLS AT MEMPHIAN BANQUETS TO THE MIND . . . . 308 2 DON JUAN 3   65   4
     THE PUBLIC MIND SO FEW ARE THE ELECT . . . . 330 2 DON JUAN 3   95   6
     BEING PRIDE WHICH LEADS THE MIND TO SOAR TOO FAR . . . 344 2 DON JUAN 4   1   7
     BUT THEIRS WAS LOVE IN WHICH THE MIND DELIGHTS . . . 353 2 DON JUAN 4   17   2
     THE MYSTICAL USURPER OF THE MIND-- . . . . 360 2 DON JUAN 4   30   4
     I HAVE SEEN SUCH--BUT MUST NOT CALL TO MIND . . . . 363 2 DON JUAN 4   36   8
     I HAVE SEEN SOME SUCH--BUT THEY UNHINGED MY MIND . . . 363 2 DON JUAN 4   36 V8
     CORRUPTION CAME NOT IN EACH MIND TO KILL . . . . . . 377 2 DON JUAN 4   60   5
     COULD ALTOGETHER CALL THE PAST TO MIND . . . . 384 2 DON JUAN 4   75   3
     BUT NEVER MIND--SHE'LL TURN PERHAPS NEXT WEEK . . . . 418 2 DON JUAN 5   14   6
     KNELT DOWN BY INSTINCT WONDERING IN HIS MIND . . . . 466 2 DON JUAN 5   95   6
     I'D RATHER LEAVE IT MUCH TO YOUR OWN MIND . . . . . 467 2 DON JUAN 5   97   4
     BUT JUAN WHO HAD STILL HIS MIND O'ERFLOWING . . . . 478 2 DON JUAN 5   117   2
     JUAN WAS MOVED HE HAD MADE UP HIS MIND . . . . 492 2 DON JUAN 5   141   1
     ARE THE BEST TOKENS (TO A MODEST MIND) . . . . 13 3 DON JUAN 6   15   5
     AND I CAN GIVE MY WHOLE SOUL UP TO MIND . . . . . . 17 3 DON JUAN 6   22   6
     THOUGH WHAT IS SOUL OR MIND THEIR BIRTH OR GROWTH . . 17 3 DON JUAN 6   22   7
     THEIR NEVER KNOWING THEIR OWN MIND TWO DAYS . . . . 64 3 DON JUAN 6   117   6
     NEWTON (THAT PROVERB OF THE MIND) ALAS . . . . 69 3 DON JUAN 7   5   5
     'TIS THUS THE SPIRIT OF A SINGLE MIND . . . . 90 3 DON JUAN 7   48   1
     BUT NEVER MIND--GOD SAVE THE KING AND KINGS . . . . . 137 3 DON JUAN 8   50   1
     AND HE WHOSE VERY BODY WAS ALL MIND . . . . 139 3 DON JUAN 8   54   5
     COMPASSION BREATHES ALONG THE SAVAGE MIND . . . . . 164 3 DON JUAN 8   106   8
     ALL THAT THE MIND WOULD SHRINK FROM OF EXCESSES . . . 173 3 DON JUAN 8   123   1
     YOU DID GREAT THINGS BUT NOT BEING GREAT IN MIND . . . 187 3 DON JUAN 9   10   7
     FOLLOWING THE BENT OF BODY OR OF MIND) . . . . . . 193 3 DON JUAN 9   21   5
     I SHALL OFFEND ALL PARTIES--NEVER MIND . . . . 195 3 DON JUAN 9   26   2
     ARE USELESS MIND GOOD PEOPLE WHAT I SAY-- . . . . . . 196 3 DON JUAN 9   28   3
     MIND LIKE THE WIND WHATEVER SHE HAS SAID . . . . . 214 3 DON JUAN 9   64   6
     WHICH YOUTH WOULD NOT ACT ILL TO KEEP IN MIND) . . . . 224 3 DON JUAN 9   84   5
     THAN WHAT THEY THOUGHT FOR MIND CAN NEVER SINK . . . 234 3 DON JUAN 10   20   4
     AND NOW WOULD CHAIN THEM TO THE VERY MIND-- . . . . . 258 3 DON JUAN 10   67   8
     A SORT OF IGNIS-FATUUS TO THE MIND . . . . 281 3 DON JUAN 11   27   6
     'TIS STRANGE THE MIND THAT VERY FIERY PARTICLE . . . 298 3 DON JUAN 11   60   7
     'TIS STRANGE THE MIND SHOULD LET SUCH PHRASES QUELL IT'S 298 3 DON JUAN 11   60 V7
     IN MIND A SORT OF SENTIMENTAL BOGLE . . . . 304 3 DON JUAN 11   72   4
     PERHAPS HE HATH GREAT PROJECTS IN HIS MIND . . . . . 320 3 DON JUAN 12   10   1
     PEOPLE SOME TEN TIMES LESS IN FACT TO MIND IT . . . 352 3 DON JUAN 12   80   3
     A LADY ALTOGETHER TO HIS MIND . . . . 353 3 DON JUAN 12   81   4
     THE GOODLIEST SOIL OF BODY AND OF MIND . . . . 359 3 DON JUAN 13   2   8
     A GENTLE GENIAL COURTESY OF MIND . . . . 372 3 DON JUAN 13   32   6
     IS SOMETIMES TRUCULENT--BUT NEVER MIND . . . . . . 377 3 DON JUAN 13   41   2
     YET LEFT A GRAND IMPRESSION ON THE MIND . . . . . . 390 3 DON JUAN 13   67   5
     IS POESY ACCORDING AS THE MIND GLOWS . . . . 414 3 DON JUAN 14   8   4
     AND QUITE ENOUGH FOR ME TO KEEP IN MIND-- . . . . . 414 3 DON JUAN 14   9   3
     IN YOUTH I WROTE BECAUSE MY MIND WAS FULL . . . . . 415 3 DON JUAN 14   10   7
     AS NOW WITH THOSE OF SOI-DISANT SOUND MIND . . . . . 446 3 DON JUAN 14   84   4
     UPON HER MIND THE MORE SO AS HER BREAST . . . . . . 448 3 DON JUAN 14   88   7
     STRICT AND HIS MIND ASSUMED A MANLIER VIGOUR . . . . 460 3 DON JUAN 15   11   6
     IN HER OWN MIND AND THAT'S ENOUGH FOR WOMAN . . . . . 473 3 DON JUAN 15   40   2
     HER PLACE WAS FAR BEYOND IT AND HER MIND . . . . . . 479 3 DON JUAN 15   54   2
     THE MIND IS LOST IN MIGHTY CONTEMPLATION . . . . . 486 3 DON JUAN 15   69   1
     AND JUAN'S MIND WAS IN THE PROPER TONE . . . . . . 506 3 DON JUAN 16   13   5
     THE MORE HE THOUGHT THE MORE HIS MIND WAS POSED . . . 512 3 DON JUAN 16   28   5
     THE FULL GROWN HEBE OF FITZ-FULKE WHOSE MIND . . . . 525 3 DON JUAN 16   49   2
     JUST AS I MAKE MY MIND UP EVERY DAY . . . . 566 3 DON JUAN 17   10   6
MINDFUL
     THESE MUST SEEM DOUBLY MINDFUL OF THEIR VOWS . . . . 500 2 DON JUAN 5   154   5
MIND'S
     FROM A TRUE LOVER SHADOW'D MY MIND'S EYE . . . . . . 337 2 DON JUAN 3   106   8
MINDS
     OF ONE ANOTHER'S MINDS AT LAST HAVE GROWN . . . . . 12 2 DON JUAN D   5   4

MINDS   (CONTINUED)
      THE CREDULOUS HOPE OF MUTUAL MINDS IS O'ER 144   2 DON JUAN 1   216   5
      AND OTHER MINDS ACKNOWLEDGED MY DOMINION 345   2 DON JUAN 4   3   4
      WE WHOSE MINDS COMPREHEND ALL THINGS NO MORE 432   2 DON JUAN 5   39   7
      FEW YOUTHFUL MINDS CAN STAND THE STRONG CONCUSSION . . . 235   3 DON JUAN 10   21   3
      ACCORDING AS THEIR MINDS OR BACKS ARE BENT 340   3 DON JUAN 12   52   4
      THE LOFTIEST MINDS OUTRUN THEIR TARDY AGES 566   3 DON JUAN 17   9   5
MINE
      THAT IS THE USUAL METHOD BUT NOT MINE-- 25   2 DON JUAN 1   7   1
      HER MEMORY WAS A MINE SHE KNEW BY HEART 27   2 DON JUAN 1   11   1
      'TWAS SURELY NO CONCERN OF THEIRS NOR MINE 33   2 DON JUAN 1   23   4
      PLATONIC PERFECT JUST SUCH LOVE AS MINE 64   2 DON JUAN 1   79   5
      I'M VERY CERTAIN MINE WOULD NOT HAVE DONE SO 80   2 DON JUAN 1   110   8
      MINE IS THE VICTIM AND WOULD BE AGAIN 130   2 DON JUAN 1   192   4
      FOR GOD'S SAKE READER TAKE THEM NOT FOR MINE . . . . . . 149 2 DON JUAN 1   222   8
      I'D WEEP BUT MINE IS NOT A WEEPING MUSE 165   2 DON JUAN 2   16   3
      THE FAULT WAS THEIRS NOT MINE IT IS NOT FAIR . . . . . . 282 2 DON JUAN 3   12   2
      DEGENERATE INTO HANDS LIKE MINE 322   2 DON JUAN 3 L 5   6
      A LAND OF SLAVES SHALL NE'ER BE MINE-- 326   2 DON JUAN 3 L 16   5
      WERE THE SOLE ECHOS SAVE MY STEED'S AND MINE . . . . . . 337 2 DON JUAN 3   106   3
      DESCEND--THE FAULT IS MINE THIS FATAL SHORE 366   2 DON JUAN 4   42   5
      BUT MINE HAVE VANISHED ALL WHEN LIFE IS NEW 421   2 DON JUAN 5   21   4
      SHE WAS A SULTAN'S BRIDE (THANK HEAVEN NOT MINE) . . . . 475 2 DON JUAN 5   111   8
      AND HALF OF THAT OPINION'S ALSO MINE . . . . 485 2 DON JUAN 5   129   8
      PARTAKE OF MINE BUT BY TO-MORROW EARLY 29   3 DON JUAN 6   46   7
      OH YE WHOSE FATE IT IS AS ONCE 'TWAS MINE 37   3 DON JUAN 6   62   3
      'TIS NOT THEIR FAULT NOR MINE IF THIS BE SO-- 68   3 DON JUAN 7   4   5
      THIS CHILD WHO IS PARENTLESS AND THEREFORE MINE 161   3 DON JUAN 8   100   8
      AND ALL OUR LITTLE FEUDS AT LEAST ALL MINE . . . . 232 3 DON JUAN 10   16   1
      MY CHILDHOOD IN THIS CHILDISHNESS OF MINE 233   3 DON JUAN 10   18   7
      ALL PHANTASIES NOT EVEN EXCEPTING MINE . . . . 255 3 DON JUAN 10   61   4
      THEMSELVES TO UNITY LIKE THIS OF MINE 290   3 DON JUAN 11   44   8
      AND THAT I SING OF NEITHER MINE NOR ME . . . . 311 3 DON JUAN 11   88   5
      FLASH UP IN INGOTS FROM THE MINE OBSCURE . . . . 319 3 DON JUAN 12   8   5
      WHATE'ER IT WAS 'TWAS MINE I'VE PAID IN TRUTH 324   3 DON JUAN 12   17   6
      THAT'S YOUR AFFAIR NOT MINE A REAL SPIRIT 356   3 DON JUAN 12   87   7
      OF IN-DOOR COMFORTS STILL SHE HATH A MINE-- 395   3 DON JUAN 13   77   5
      TO COME BETWEEN MINE EPIC AND ITS INDEX 440   3 DON JUAN 14   68   8
      BUT SPECULATING AS I CAST MINE EYE 464   3 DON JUAN 15   19   4
      IN MINE IRREGULARITY OF CHIME 465   3 DON JUAN 15   20   6
      I MUST ALTHOUGH A FAVOURITE PLAT OF MINE . . . . 488 3 DON JUAN 15   73   3
      IT IS NOT MINE TO SAY 519   3 DON JUAN 16 L 3   2
      I ASK BUT THIS OF MINE TO--NOT DEFEND 552   3 DON JUAN 16   104   8
      ASSEMBLED WITH OUR HOSTESS AND MINE HOST . . . . 568 3 DON JUAN 17   13   6
MINED
      ARE SAFELY MINED FOR IN THE MODE HE MENTIONS . . . . . . 93 2 DON JUAN 1   132   5
MINERVA
      ADMIRING MORE MINERVA THAN THE GRACES 494   3 DON JUAN 15   85   3
MINERVA'S
      AND THE LOUD SHRIEK OF SAGE MINERVA'S FOWL . . . . 499 3 DON JUAN 15   97   3
MINE'S
      YOUR NAMES--MINE'S JOHNSON AND MY COMRADE'S JUAN . . . . 97 3 DON JUAN 7   60   1
      AND MINE'S A BUBBLE NOT BLOWN UP FOR PRAISE 414   3 DON JUAN 14   8   7
      IN SOME THINGS MINE'S BEYOND ALL CONTRADICTION . . . . . 502 3 DON JUAN 16   2   7
MINES
      FAMOUS FOR MINES OF SALT AND YOKES OF IRON . . . . 253 3 DON JUAN 10   58   2
MINGLE
      ALL THAT THE BEST CAN MINGLE AND EXPRESS . . . . 357 2 DON JUAN 4   26   4
      THAT DOUBT SHOULD MINGLE WITH MY FILIAL JOY 364   2 DON JUAN 4   38   7
      AND CHRISTIAN MINGLE WITH THEM AS YOU MAY 494   2 DON JUAN 5   145   5
MINGLED
      WAS MINGLED WITH HIS EVIL DEEDS AND WAYS 303   2 DON JUAN 3   55 V2
      TO SAY BY DEGRADATION)-- MINGLED THERE 310   2 DON JUAN 3   68   7
      MAGNIFICENTLY MINGLED IN A LITTER 465   2 DON JUAN 5   93   8
      ETERNAL SUCH NAMES MINGLED) ISMAIL'S OUR'S . . . . 178 3 DON JUAN 8   133   8
      WHERE MINGLED AND YET SEPARATE APPEARS 447   3 DON JUAN 14   87   5
      THE LADIES WITH MORE MODERATION MINGLED 487   3 DON JUAN 15   70   3
MINGLING
      AND MINGLING MODESTLY IN TOILS OR SPORTS . . . . 424 3 DON JUAN 14   31   6
MINIATURE
      OR MINIATURE AT LEAST AS IS MY NOTION 457   3 DON JUAN 15   2   6
MINION
      WHO DID NOT LIKE AT FIRST TO LOSE HER MINION . . . . . . 246 3 DON JUAN 10   44   4
      JUAN WHO SAW THE MOON'S LATE MINION BLEED 275   3 DON JUAN 11   14   5
MINION'S
      THIS HOUR WERE THINE--AND THY YOUNG MINION'S LAST . . . 368   2 DON JUAN 4   46 V8
MINISTER
      FOR INTO A PRIME MINISTER BUT CHANGE 283   2 DON JUAN 3   14   3
      AND AS A HIGH-SOUL'D MINISTER OF STATE IS 186   3 DON JUAN 9   8   7
      COURT MYSTERIES HAVING BEEN HIMSELF A MINISTER . . . . . 368 3 DON JUAN 13   21   4
MINISTERIAL
      AS IF BORN FOR THE MINISTERIAL TRADE 223   3 DON JUAN 9   83   4
MINISTERS
      THEIR BREAD AS MINISTERS AND FAVOURITES--(THAT'S . . . . 310 2 DON JUAN 3   68   6
      BESIDES THE MINISTERS AND UNDERLINGS 287   3 DON JUAN 11   40   1
      WHICH MINISTERS UNTO THE SOUL'S DELIGHT 457   3 DON JUAN 15   2   7
MINORITY
      WHICH WITH A LONG MINORITY AND CARE 42   2 DON JUAN 1   37   3
MINOTAUR
      THAT THE OLD FABLE OF THE MINOTAUR-- . . . . 238 2 DON JUAN 2   155   2

512

MINSTREL
    AH MUST I THEN THE ONLY MINSTREL BE   . . . . 403 2 DON JUAN 4   108   7
MINT
    SUCH AS ARE COINED IN CONVERSATION'S MINT   . . . . . 440 3 DON JUAN 14   69   3
    COINED FROM SURVIVING SUPERSTITION'S MINT . . . . . 510 3 DON JUAN 16   22   5
MINTAGE
    BRIGHT AS A NEW NAPOLEON FROM ITS MINTAGE . . . . . 458 3 DON JUAN 15   7   3
MINUS
    WHICH LEAVES YOU MINUS OF THE CASH YOU COUNTED . . . . 16 3 DON JUAN 6   21   6
MINUTE
    ALFONSO PAUSED A MINUTE--THEN BEGUN   . . . . 116 2 DON JUAN 1   174   1
    BECAUSE THE SEA RAN HIGHER EVERY MINUTE . . . . . . 186 2 DON JUAN 2   57   7
    A MINUTE PAST AND SHE HAD BEEN ALL TEARS . . . . . . 367 2 DON JUAN 4   43   1
    BE TOO MINUTE AN OUTLINE IS THE BEST   . . . . . . 55 3 DON JUAN 6   98   7
    STOPPED FOR A MINUTE AS PERHAPS HE OUGHT . . . . . . 126 3 DON JUAN 8   29   4
    TWO LONG OCTAVES PASSED IN A LITTLE MINUTE . . . . . 142 3 DON JUAN 8   59   2
    BUT IN THE SAME SMALL MINUTE EVERY SIN . . . . . . 142 3 DON JUAN 8   59   3
    THE GULF OF ROCK YAWNS--YOU CAN'T GAZE A MINUTE . . . 412 3 DON JUAN 14   5   7
    THOUGH WHY I CANNOT SAY--AT LEAST THIS MINUTE . . . . 526 3 DON JUAN 16   51   8
MINUTE'S
    HER RAGE WAS BUT A MINUTE'S AND 'TWAS WELL--   . . . . 489 2 DON JUAN 5   135   1
MINUTES
    IS JUST TWO MINUTES FOR YOUR DECLARATION-- . . . . . 482 2 DON JUAN 5   123   7
MINUTEST
    EVEN HER MINUTEST MOTIONS WENT AS WELL   . . . . . . 30 2 DON JUAN 1   17   5
MIO'S
    THE MAMMA MIA'S AND THE AMOR MIO'S . . . . 523 3 DON JUAN 16   45   3
MIRABEAU
    BARNAVE BRISSOT CONDORCET MIRABEAU . . . . 22 2 DON JUAN 1   3   1
MIRACLE
    THEIR PRESERVATION WOULD HAVE BEEN A MIRACLE   . . . . 183 2 DON JUAN 2   50   8
    THE LAST'S A MIRACLE AND SUCH WAS RECKONED . . . . . 365 2 DON JUAN 13   13   7
    A HANDSOME MAN THAT HUMAN MIRACLE . . . . 441 3 DON JUAN 14   71   6
    IS ALWAYS GREATEST AT A MIRACLE . . . . 503 3 DON JUAN 16   5   4
MIRE
    THUS ON THEY WALLOWED IN THE BLOODY MIRE . . . . . . 121 3 DON JUAN 8   20   1
MIRROR
    EACH WAS THE OTHER'S MIRROR AND BUT READ . . . . . . 351 2 DON JUAN 4   13   5
    SHE DID NOT EVEN LOOK INTO THE MIRROR . . . . 50 3 DON JUAN 6   89   8
    AND YOU WILL FIND THOUGH SHUDDERING AT THE MIRROR . . . 413 3 DON JUAN 14   6   3
    ASIDE HIS VERY MIRROR SOON WAS PUT . . . . 513 3 DON JUAN 16   29   4
MIRRORED
    A MIRRORED HELL THE VOLLEYING ROAR AND LOUD . . . . . 115 3 DON JUAN 8   6   5
    MIRRORED THE CHRISTIAN FLAGS--AS MOONBEAMS ON THE WATER . 173 3 DON JUAN 8   122   V8
MIRRORS
    THERE WAS NO WANT OF LOFTY MIRRORS AND   . . . . . . 310 2 DON JUAN 3   69   1
    HATH GOT BLUE DEVILS FOR HIS MORNING MIRRORS . . . . 457 3 DON JUAN 15   4   4
MIRTH
    FROM CIVIC REVELRY TO RURAL MIRTH . . . . 88 2 DON JUAN 1   124   4
    LET US HAVE WINE AND WOMAN MIRTH AND LAUGHTER . . . . 250 2 DON JUAN 2   178   9
    ALL PHANTASIES WHICH YIELDED JOY OR MIRTH . . . . . . 475 2 DON JUAN 5   112   3
    WHOSE SMILE MAKES ALL THE PLANETS DANCE WITH MIRTH . . 494 2 DON JUAN 5   144   4
    LUXURIANT BUDDING CHEERFUL WITHOUT MIRTH . . . . . . 32 3 DON JUAN 6   53   3
    WOULD MAKE INDEED SOME MELANCHOLY MIRTH . . . . . . 436 3 DON JUAN 14   59   6
MIRTH-MOVING
    A SOMETHING MUCH MIRTH-MOVING--AND IN THIS . . . . . 544 3 DON JUAN 16   92   V5
MISANTHROPE
    WHY DO THEY CALL ME MISANTHROPE BECAUSE . . . . . . 193 3 DON JUAN 9   21   7
MISANTHROPY
    SOME PEOPLE HAVE ACCUSED ME OF MISANTHROPY . . . . . 192 3 DON JUAN 9   20   4
    CAN TAX MY MILD MUSE WITH MISANTHROPY . . . . 286 3 DON JUAN 11   38   2
MISAPPLIED
    THE PHRASE IS SHAKSPEARE'S AND NOT MISAPPLIED-- . . . 184 3 DON JUAN 9   4   2
MISCALCULATION
    A SAD MISCALCULATION ABOUT DISTANCE   . . . . 80 3 DON JUAN 7   28   1
MISCARRIAGE
    AND THEN BOTH WORLDS WOULD PUNISH THEIR MISCARRIAGE . . 280 2 DON JUAN 3   9   6
    TO BEAR A SON AND HEIR--AND ONE MISCARRIAGE . . . . . 434 3 DON JUAN 14   56   8
    STRANGELY ENOUGH AS YET WITHOUT MISCARRIAGE . . . . . 471 3 DON JUAN 15   35   3
MISCARRIED
    HOW SORRY YOU WILL BE WHEN I'VE MISCARRIED . . . . . 101 2 DON JUAN 1   147   8
MISCARRY
    EVEN WORLDS MISCARRY WHEN TOO OFT THEY PUP . . . . . 202 3 DON JUAN 9   39   5
MISCHANCE
    WITH JOY TO SAVE AND DREAD OF SOME MISCHANCE   . . . . 159 3 DON JUAN 8   96   4
MISCHIEF
    THE MISCHIEF AFTER ALL COULD NOT BE GREAT . . . . . 67 2 DON JUAN 1   85   6
    THE DEVIL'S IN THE MOON FOR MISCHIEF THEY . . . . . 82 2 DON JUAN 1   113   2
    THE ONLY MISCHIEF WAS IT CAME TOO LATE   . . . . . . 122 2 DON JUAN 1   183   2
    PERHAPS MORE MISCHIEF HAD BEEN DONE BUT FOR   . . . . 174 2 DON JUAN 2   35   1
    THEY LITTLE THINK WHAT MISCHIEF IS IN HAND . . . . . 411 2 DON JUAN 5   1   4
    IN ANY KIND OF MISCHIEF TO BE WROUGHT . . . . 477 2 DON JUAN 5   114   5
    BY WHICH THEIR POWER OF MISCHIEF IS ENCREASED . . . . 342 3 DON JUAN 12   56   4
    A LITTLE TURN FOR MISCHIEF YOU MIGHT TRACE . . . . . 525 3 DON JUAN 16   49   5
    OF MISCHIEF OF ALL KINDS AND KEEP THE GAME . . . . . 531 3 DON JUAN 16   63   2
    MISCHIEF IN FAMILIES AS SOME KNOW OR KNEW . . . . . . 565 3 DON JUAN 17   7   5
MISCHIEF-MAKING
    AND MISCHIEF-MAKING MONKEY FROM HIS BIRTH . . . . . 34 2 DON JUAN 1   25   2
MISCHIEF'S
    AND NO GREAT MISCHIEF'S DONE BY THEIR CAPRICE . . . . 135 2 DON JUAN 1   199   6
    WHERE EVERY KIND OF MISCHIEF'S DAILY BREWING   . . . . 326 3 DON JUAN 12   23   3

	PAGE	VOL	CANTO	STANZA	LN

MISCHIEFS
SO THAT ALL MISCHIEFS SPRING UP FROM THIS ENTRAIL 271   2 DON JUAN   2   215   7
MISCHIEVOUS
AND STORE IT UP FOR MISCHIEVOUS ENJOYMENT   548   3 DON JUAN 16   100   7
MISCREANT
COLD-BLOODED SMOOTH-FACED PLACID MISCREANT 16   2 DON JUAN D   12   1
MISCUIT
OMNE TULIT PUNCTUM QUAE MISCUIT UTILE DULCI 396   3 DON JUAN 13   81   8
MISER
SWEET TO THE MISER ARE HIS GLITTERING HEAPS 88   2 DON JUAN 1   124   5
A MISER FILLING HIS MOST HOARDED CHEST   261   2 DON JUAN 2   196   6
HAS IN HIS ABSENCE WEDDED SOME RICH MISER 288   2 DON JUAN 3   24   2
WHY CALL THE MISER MISERABLE AS 319   3 DON JUAN 12   7   1
OR DO THEY BENEFIT MANKIND LEAN MISER 321   3 DON JUAN 12   11   7
MISERABLE
OH GOLD WHY CALL WE MISERS MISERABLE 316   3 DON JUAN 12   3   1
WHY CALL THE MISER MISERABLE AS 319   3 DON JUAN 12   7   1
MISERIES
AND MAKES MEN'S MISERIES OF ALARMING BREVITY 190   2 DON JUAN 2   64   8
MISER'S
OF OTHER STONES TO SOOTHE THE MISER'S EYES 319   3 DON JUAN 12   8   8
WHICH HOLDS A TREASURE LIKE A MISER'S HOARD 422   3 DON JUAN 14   27   3
MISERS
OH GOLD WHY CALL WE MISERS MISERABLE 316   3 DON JUAN 12   3   1
MISERY
MY MISERY CAN SCARCE BE MORE COMPLETE 134   2 DON JUAN 1   197   4
YET MADE THE MISERY OF AT LEAST TWO LIVES 452   3 DON JUAN 14   95   8
AN OH OR AH OF JOY OR MISERY 456   3 DON JUAN 15   1   6
MISFORTUNE
(TO MY MISFORTUNE) NEVER CAN I SAY 274   3 DON JUAN 11   12   7
MISHAP
SINCE--SINCE--IN YOUTH I HAD THE SAD MISHAP-- 530   3 DON JUAN 16   61   5
MISNOMER
SO THAT MY NAME OF EPIC'S NO MISNOMER 135   2 DON JUAN 1   200   8
MISS
MISS EDGEWORTH'S NOVELS STEPPING FROM THEIR COVERS   . . . 29   2 DON JUAN 1   16   2
IN FEELINGS QUICK AS OVID'S MISS MEDEA   68   2 DON JUAN 1   86   4
YOUNG HOPEFUL'S MISTRESS OR MISS FANNY'S LOVER 75   2 DON JUAN 1   100   4
WHEN WE HAVE WHAT WE LIKE 'TIS HARD TO MISS IT 282   2 DON JUAN 3   13   5
AWAITS AT LAST EVEN THOSE WHOM LONGEST MISS 350   2 DON JUAN 4   12   6
ONE OF THE VALOUROUS SMITHS WHOM WE SHALL MISS . . . 79   3 DON JUAN 7   25   5
FOR AUGHT WE KNOW) RENOWN'S ALL HIT OR MISS 82   3 DON JUAN 7   33   5
AS ALSO DID MISS PROTASOFF THEN THERE 224   3 DON JUAN 9   84   6
IN THUNDER HOLDS THE WAY IT CAN'T WELL MISS 277   3 DON JUAN 11   20   6
THAT PRODIGY MISS ARAMINTA SMITH 294   3 DON JUAN 11   52   5
LADY FITZ-FRISKY AND MISS MAEVIA MANNISH 295   3 DON JUAN 11   53   7
THE THEME OF PRAISE A HERMIT WOULD NOT MISS 319   3 DON JUAN 12   7   4
SUCH AS--UNLESS MISS (BLANK) MEANT TO HAVE CHOSEN . . 332   3 DON JUAN 12   34   5
WHICH FORMS A PEDIGREE FROM MISS TO MISS 340   3 DON JUAN 12   52   3
WHICH FORMS A PEDIGREE FROM MISS TO MISS 340   3 DON JUAN 12   52   3
THE LADIES SCILLY BUSEY--MISS ECLAT   396   3 DON JUAN 13   79   4
MISS BOMBAZEEN MISS MACKSTAY MISS O'TABBEY 396   3 DON JUAN 13   79   5
MISS BOMBAZEEN MISS MACKSTAY MISS O'TABBEY 396   3 DON JUAN 13   79   5
MISS BOMBAZEEN MISS MACKSTAY MISS O'TABBEY 396   3 DON JUAN 13   79   5
THERE WERE THE SIX MISS RAWBOLDS--PRETTY DEARS 398   3 DON JUAN 13   85   6
THE FOUR MISS RAWBOLDS IN A GLEE WOULD SHINE 408   3 DON JUAN 13   107   5
PERHAPS MANKIND MIGHT FIND THE PATH THEY MISS-- . . . 410   3 DON JUAN 14   1   3
BUT NEVER YET (EXCEPT OF COURSE A MISS 470   3 DON JUAN 15   32   1
BUT THEN WITH WHOM THERE WAS THE SAGE MISS READING . . 473   3 DON JUAN 15   40   3
MISS RAW MISS FLAW MISS SHOWMAN AND MISS KNOWMAN . . . 473   3 DON JUAN 15   40   4
MISS RAW MISS FLAW MISS SHOWMAN AND MISS KNOWMAN . . . 473   3 DON JUAN 15   40   4
MISS RAW MISS FLAW MISS SHOWMAN AND MISS KNOWMAN . . . 473   3 DON JUAN 15   40   4
MISS RAW MISS FLAW MISS SHOWMAN AND MISS KNOWMAN . . . 473   3 DON JUAN 15   40   4
THERE WAS MISS MILLPOND SMOOTH AS SUMMER'S SEA 474   3 DON JUAN 15   41   1
AND THEN THERE WAS THE MISS AUDACIA SHOESTRING 474   3 DON JUAN 15   42   1
WHO HAVE HEARD MISS THAT OR THIS OR LADY T'OTHER . . 522   3 DON JUAN 16   44   7
OR TIPTOE OF AN AMATORY MISS 556   3 DON JUAN 16   112   6
MISSAL
THE MISSAL TOO (IT WAS THE FAMILY MISSAL)   47   2 DON JUAN 1   46   1
THE MISSAL TOO (IT WAS THE FAMILY MISSAL)   47   2 DON JUAN 1   46   1
I LOVE THE MYSTERY OF A FEMALE MISSAL 407   3 DON JUAN 13   105   4
MISS'D
SO THAT IF ANY ACTOR MISS'D HIS PART 27   2 DON JUAN 1   11   3
HE MISS'D THE PATHWAY HE FORGOT THE HOURS   . . . 72   2 DON JUAN 1   94   5
OH FOR A GLASS OF MAX WE'VE MISS'D OUR BOOTY-- . . . 276   3 DON JUAN 11   16   3
MISSED
ALL THOSE THAT WOULD--REGRETTING THOSE I MISSED   . . . 232   2 DON JUAN 2   142   V8
THEY EITHER MISSED OR THEY WERE NEVER MISSED   80   3 DON JUAN 7   27   7
THEY EITHER MISSED OR THEY WERE NEVER MISSED   80   3 DON JUAN 7   27   7
OF KILLED AND WOUNDED WHO WILL NOT BE MISSED 107   3 DON JUAN 7   81   V8
AH IF HE HAD HOW MUCH HE WOULD HAVE MISSED HER 250   3 DON JUAN 10   53   8
GOD DAMN YOU LADS I'VE MISSED A HANDSOME BOOTY 276   3 DON JUAN 11   16   V3
MISSES
TO HIS MEMORY AND TWO OR THREE YOUNG MISSES 287   2 DON JUAN 3   23   6
DRAWN BY THE BLUE-COAT MISSES OF A COTERIE 404   3 DON JUAN 4   109   8
ACCORDING TO THE ARTILLERY'S HITS OR MISSES 105   3 DON JUAN 7   76   3
THE MILLINERS WHO FURNISH DRAPERY MISSES 293   3 DON JUAN 11   49   1
THE HONOURABLE MISTRESSES AND MISSES 308   3 DON JUAN 11   79   2
THE MISSES BRIDLED AND THE MATRONS FROWN'D 429   3 DON JUAN 14   44   2

514

MISSHAPEN
THEY WERE MISSHAPEN PIGMIES DEAF AND DUMB-- . . . . . . 462 2 DON JUAN 5   88   7
MISSING
AND ADDED GREATLY TO THE MISSING LIST . . . . 80 3 DON JUAN 7   27   8
MISSION
THOUGHT DAILY SERVICE WAS HER ONLY MISSION . . . . . . 252 2 DON JUAN 2   182   6
SHE THEN RESOLVED TO SEND HIM ON A MISSION . . . . . . 246 2 DON JUAN 10   44   7
'TWAS MERELY KNOWN THAT ON A SECRET MISSION . . . . . . 283 3 DON JUAN 11   32   5
THE ENVOY OF THE SECRET RUSSIAN MISSION . . . . 382 3 DON JUAN 13   52   8
MIST
WITH MIST AND EVERY BIRD WITH HIM AWAKES . . . . 230 2 DON JUAN 2   139   6
THE NIGHT WAS DARK AND THE THICK MIST ALLOWED . . . . 115 3 DON JUAN 8   6   1
OR WITH ITS MIST OF GERMAN MYSTERIES . . . . 450 3 DON JUAN 14   92   V5
MISTAKE
SHOULD RASHLY QUOTE FOR FEAR OF A MISTAKE) . . . . . . 74 2 DON JUAN 1   98   6
QUITE BY MISTAKE--SHE THOUGHT IT WAS HER OWN . . . . . 80 2 DON JUAN 1   109   8
THEY ALSO LIE TOO--UNDER A MISTAKE . . . . 141 2 DON JUAN 1   208   6
MISTAKE YOU WOULD HAVE MADE ON SEEING THE TWO . . . . 232 2 DON JUAN 2   142   6
AND ONE BY ONE IN TURN SOME GRAND MISTAKE . . . . . . 421 2 DON JUAN 5   21   7
AND BY MISTAKE SEQUINS WITH PARAS JUMBLING . . . . . . 426 2 DON JUAN 5   29   5
IN WRITING COURSER BY MISTAKE FOR COURIER . . . . . . 446 2 DON JUAN 5   61   7
THAT THIS DISGUISE MAY LEAD TO NO MISTAKE . . . . . . 459 2 DON JUAN 5   82   8
THAT EVEN THE PUREST PEOPLE MAY MISTAKE . . . . 328 3 DON JUAN 12   26   3
THE FURTHER PROGRESS OF THIS SAD MISTAKE . . . . 437 3 DON JUAN 14   61   3
THIS WAS NO BAD MISTAKE AS IT OCCURRED . . . . 543 3 DON JUAN 16   89   1
MISTAKEN
WERE DAMNABLY MISTAKEN FEW ARE SLOW . . . . 87 3 DON JUAN 7   42   3
BUT HERE I SAY THE TURKS WERE MUCH MISTAKEN . . . . . 87 3 DON JUAN 7   42   7
IF SHE HAD NOT MISTAKEN HIM FOR CUPID . . . . 205 3 DON JUAN 9   45   8
WHOSE LOT IT IS BY MAN TO BE MISTAKEN . . . . 464 3 DON JUAN 15   18   3
HE FIRST INCLINED TO THINK HE HAD BEEN MISTAKEN . . . 558 3 DON JUAN 16   118   3
MISTAKES
IT DIFFICULT TO SHUN SOME STRANGE MISTAKES . . . . . . 96 3 DON JUAN 7   57   8
SOME ODD MISTAKES TOO HAPPENED IN THE DARK . . . . . . 177 3 DON JUAN 8   130   1
THEY'LL ONLY MAKE MISTAKES ABOUT THE FAIR . . . . . . 454 3 DON JUAN 14   99   3
MISTAKING
AND THEN TO BE ASHAMED OF SUCH MISTAKING . . . . . . 558 3 DON JUAN 16   118   4
MISTERS
HOW ALL THE NEEDY HONOURABLE MISTERS . . . . 331 3 DON JUAN 12   32   1
THERE WERE FOUR HONOURABLE MISTERS WHOSE . . . . 398 3 DON JUAN 13   86   1
MISTOOK
AND ALL MISTOOK ABOUT THE LATTER ONCE . . . . 207 2 DON JUAN 2   96   8
FOR COMMONERS HAD EVER THEM MISTOOK . . . . 398 3 DON JUAN 13   85   5
SHE APPROVED HIS SILENCE SHE PERHAPS MISTOOK . . . . . 553 3 DON JUAN 16   106   2
MISTRESS
BESIDE HIS MISTRESS IN SOME SOFT ABODE . . . . 24 2 DON JUAN 1   6   6
WHISPER'D HE HAD A MISTRESS SOME SAID TWO . . . . . . 31 2 DON JUAN 1   19   7
YOUNG HOPEFUL'S MISTRESS OR MISS FANNY'S LOVER . . . . 75 2 DON JUAN 1   100   4
TO PROVE HER MISTRESS HAD BEEN SLEEPING DOUBLE . . . . 97 2 DON JUAN 1   140   8
BUT JULIA MISTRESS AND ANTONIA MAID . . . . 98 2 DON JUAN 1   141   1
MY MISTRESS ALL FOR THAT HALF-GIRLISH FACE . . . . . 115 2 DON JUAN 1   171   8
HIS MOTHER AND A MISTRESS AND NO WIFE . . . . 164 2 DON JUAN 2   15   2
MISTRESS AND MAID THE FIRST WAS ONLY DAUGHTER . . . . 222 2 DON JUAN 2   124   7
BECAUSE HER MISTRESS WOULD NOT LET HER BREAK . . . . . 234 2 DON JUAN 2   146   7
HAD MADE HER MISTRESS QUIT HER BED TO TRACE . . . . . 240 2 DON JUAN 2   159   4
BY BEATRICE AND NOT A MISTRESS--I . . . . 281 2 DON JUAN 3   11   2
YOU'D BETTER ASK OUR MISTRESS WHO'S HIS HEIR . . . . . 297 2 DON JUAN 3   43   6
OUR MISTRESS QUOTH A THIRD OUR MISTRESS--POOH-- . . . 297 2 DON JUAN 3   43   7
OUR MISTRESS QUOTH A THIRD OUR MISTRESS--POOH-- . . . 297 2 DON JUAN 3   43   7
TO MAKE A MISTRESS OR FOURTH WIFE OR VICTIM . . . . . 409 2 DON JUAN 4   116   8
A MISTRESS AND SUCH COMFORTABLE QUARTERS . . . . . . 415 2 DON JUAN 5   8   7
UNWED OR MISTRESS NEVER TO BE WED . . . . 470 3 DON JUAN 15   32   2
OR ON HIS MISTRESS--TERMS SYNONIMOUS-- . . . . 509 3 DON JUAN 16   20   2
MISTRESSES
A JEW TOOK ONE OF HIS TWO MISTRESSES . . . . 39 2 DON JUAN 1   34   4
THE HONOURABLE MISTRESSES AND MISSES . . . . 308 3 DON JUAN 11   79   2
WE TIRE OF MISTRESSES AND PARASITES . . . . 405 3 DON JUAN 13   100   6
MISTS
LIKE MOUNTAIN MISTS AT LENGTH DISSOLVED IN RAIN . . . 380 2 DON JUAN 4   66   8
AND OUT OF DOOR HATH SHOWERS AND MISTS AND SLEET . . . 423 3 DON JUAN 14   30   2
MISTY
UNTO THAT RATHER SOMEWHAT MISTY BOURN . . . . 133 3 DON JUAN 8   41   3
MITE
'TWAS THE BOY'S MITE AND LIKE THE WIDOW'S MAY . . . .   9 3 DON JUAN 6   6   1
MITFORD
AND MITFORD IN THE NINETEENTH CENTURY . . . . 325 3 DON JUAN 12   19   7
MITIGATED
HAD MITIGATED PART THOUGH NOT THE WHOLE . . . . 70 2 DON JUAN 1   91   4
MIX
UNFIT TO MIX IN THESE THICK SOLITUDES . . . . 358 2 DON JUAN 4   28   3
OF THEIR OWN SAND-PITS TO MIX WITH A GODDESS . . . . . 220 3 DON JUAN 9   75   3
WHO LIKE TO MIX SOME SLIGHT ALLOY WITH FAME . . . . . 414 3 DON JUAN 14   9   6
MIX'D
AND OFFER POISON LONG ALREADY MIX'D . . . . 16 2 DON JUAN D   12   8
AND SOMETIMES MIX'D UP FANCIES WITH REALITIES . . . . 32 2 DON JUAN 1   20   6
THE LOTS WERE MADE AND MARK'D AND MIX'D AND HANDED . . 195 2 DON JUAN 2   75   1
MIX'D WITH THE STONY VAPOURS OF THE VAULT . . . . . . 234 2 DON JUAN 2   147   8
WHICH MIX'D ALL FEELINGS FRIEND CHILD LOVER BROTHER . . 357 2 DON JUAN 4   26   3
MIX'D IN EACH OTHER'S ARMS AND HEART IN HEART . . . . 358 2 DON JUAN 4   27   1
BUT MIX'D WITH PITY PURE AS E'ER WAS PENN'D . . . . . 432 3 DON JUAN 14   51   6

		PAGE	VOL		CANTO	STANZA	LN

MIXED
AND MIXED UNTIL THE VERY PLEASURE STUNG . . . . . . 254 2 DON JUAN 2 187 V8
IN JUAN'S LOOK PAIN PLEASURE HOPE FEAR MIXED . . . . . 159 3 DON JUAN 8 96 3
AND THE TWO ARE SO MIXED WITH HUMAN DUST . . . . . . 221 3 DON JUAN 9 77 5
I FEEL A MIXED REGRET AND VENERATION . . . . 257 3 DON JUAN 10 66 4
MIXED GOTHIC SUCH AS ARTISTS ALL ALLOW . . . . . . 384 3 DON JUAN 13 55 4
YET MIXED SO SLIGHTLY THAT YOU CAN'T COMPLAIN . . . . 502 3 DON JUAN 16 3 6
MIXES
WHICH MIXES UP VINES OLIVES PRECIPICES . . . . . . 262 3 DON JUAN 10 76 7
MIXTURE
BUT AN EXTRANEOUS MIXTURE WHICH NO PEN . . . . . . 462 2 DON JUAN 5 88 5
A MIXTURE OF SENSATIONS MIGHT BE SCANNED . . . . . . 473 2 DON JUAN 5 108 7
AS ANY MAN'S CLAY MIXTURE UNDERGOES . . . . 16 3 DON JUAN 6 20 5
WHICH WAS A MIXTURE OF ALL METALS BUT . . . . . . 34 3 DON JUAN 6 56 2
A MIXTURE OF WILD BEASTS AND DEMI-GODS . . . . . . 164 3 DON JUAN 8 106 4
MIZEN
BOTH MAIN AND MIZEN FIRST THE MIZEN WENT . . . . . . 173 2 DON JUAN 2 32 2
BOTH MAIN AND MIZEN FIRST THE MIZEN WENT . . . . . . 173 2 DON JUAN 2 32 2
MOANS
THERE MOANS A STRANGE UNEARTHLY SOUND WHICH THEN . . . . 388 3 DON JUAN 13 63 3
MOB
THAT ALL THE ISRAELITES ARE FIT TO MOB ITS . . . . . 89 2 DON JUAN 1 125 7
BEYOND THE RULES OF POSTING--AND THE MOB . . . . . . 137 3 DON JUAN 8 50 7
BUT TO DENY THE MOB A CORDIAL WHICH IS . . . . . . 256 3 DON JUAN 10 63 6
THE MOB STOOD AND AS USUAL SEVERAL SCORE . . . . . . 282 3 DON JUAN 11 30 3
THUS ON THE MOB ALL STATESMEN ARE AS EAGER . . . . . 537 3 DON JUAN 16 76 7
MOBILITY
THEY ERR--'TIS MERELY WHAT IS CALLED MOBILITY . . . . 547 3 DON JUAN 16 97 4
MOBS
AS MUCH FROM MOBS AS KINGS--FROM YOU AS ME . . . . . 195 3 DON JUAN 9 25 8
MOCHA'S
AND MOCHA'S BERRY FROM ARABIA PURE . . . . 307 2 DON JUAN 3 63 3
MOCK
MOCK TYRANTS WHEN ROME'S ANNALS WAXED BUT DIRTY . . . . 299 3 DON JUAN 11 61 8
MOCK'D
THE GLOSSY REBELS MOCK'D THE JETTY STAIN . . . . . . 314 2 DON JUAN 3 75 4
MOCKERIES
TO THEM BUT MOCKERIES OF THE PAST ALONE . . . . . . 262 2 DON JUAN 2 199 5
MOCKERY
IN MOCKERY TO THE ENORMOUS GATE WHICH ROSE . . . . . 462 2 DON JUAN 5 87 5
MODE
ALTHOUGH HER MODE OF SPEAKING WAS NOT PURE . . . . . 28 2 DON JUAN 1 13 4
ARE SAFELY MINED FOR IN THE MODE HE MENTIONS . . . . 93 2 DON JUAN 1 132 5
IF DEAD HIS MODE OF DYING MIGHT BE PUT . . . . . . 112 2 DON JUAN 1 166 V7
A MODE SO BEAUTIFUL AND SO UNHOLY . . . . 161 2 DON JUAN 2 7 V7
AND THAT'S THEIR MODE OF FURNISHING SUPPLY . . . . . 190 2 DON JUAN 2 65 6
LET NOT HIS MODE OF RAISING CASH SEEM STRANGE . . . . 283 2 DON JUAN 3 14 1
THIS REVEL SEEM'D A CURIOUS MODE OF MOURNING . . . . 300 2 DON JUAN 3 49 8
THEIR LOVES AND FEASTS AND HOUSE AND DRESS AND MODE . . . 317 2 DON JUAN 3 81 7
AS IF THE PEASANT'S SCORN THIS MODE INVENTED . . . . 401 2 DON JUAN 4 105 V3
STITCHED UP IN SACKS--A MODE OF NAVIGATION . . . . . 464 2 DON JUAN 5 92 7
A MODE OF PROVING THAT THE EARTH TURNED ROUND . . . . 225 3 DON JUAN 10 1 5
IF THIS BE TRUE FOR WE MUST DEEM THE MODE . . . . . 226 3 DON JUAN 10 2 2
SO SMOOTH SO LEVEL SUCH A MODE OF SHAVING . . . . . 263 3 DON JUAN 10 78 2
MUCH IN THE MODE OF GOETHE'S MEPHISTOPHELES . . . . . 361 3 DON JUAN 13 7 8
YOU BIND YOURSELF AND CALL SOME MODE THE BEST ONE . . . 411 3 DON JUAN 14 2 6
THIS WAS THE MODE OF CYRUS BEST OF KINGS-- . . . . . 501 3 DON JUAN 16 1 3
A MODE ADOPTED SINCE BY MODERN YOUTH . . . . 501 3 DON JUAN 16 1 4
WHETHER THE MODE BE PERSIFLAGE OR PIETY . . . . . . 526 3 DON JUAN 16 52 6
MODEL
FIT FOR THE MODEL OF A STATUARY . . . . 218 2 DON JUAN 2 118 5
A FREQUENT MODEL AND IF E'ER SHE MUST . . . . . . 219 2 DON JUAN 2 119 5
THIS POEM WILL BECOME A MORAL MODEL . . . . 412 2 DON JUAN 5 2 8
I'LL MAKE THIS POEM QUITE A MORAL MODEL . . . . . . 412 2 DON JUAN 5 2 V8
GULBEYAZ WAS NO MODEL OF TRUE PATIENCE . . . . . . 56 3 DON JUAN 6 101 1
THE VERY MODEL OF A CHAMBERLAIN-- . . . . 440 3 DON JUAN 14 70 7
THEIR UNION WAS A MODEL TO BEHOLD . . . . 447 3 DON JUAN 14 86 7
AND SOCRATES THAT MODEL OF ALL DUTY . . . . 494 3 DON JUAN 15 85 7
MODERATE
MODERATE IN ALL HIS HABITS AND CONTENT . . . . . . 302 2 DON JUAN 3 53 3
LIKE MODERATE HOTSPUR ON THE IMMORTAL PAGE . . . . . 490 2 DON JUAN 5 136 4
MOST WISE MEN WITH ONE MODERATE WOMAN WED . . . . . 12 3 DON JUAN 6 12 5
A MODERATE PENSION SHAKES FULL MANY A SAGE . . . . . 118 3 DON JUAN 8 14 4
SOME PRETTY SHELL IS BEST FOR MODERATE BATHERS . . . . 191 3 DON JUAN 9 18 8
THAN MIGHT SUFFICE A MODERATE CENTURY THROUGH . . . . 309 3 DON JUAN 11 82 4
WITH MUSIC THE MOST MODERATE SHINE AS WITS . . . . . 340 3 DON JUAN 12 52 7
BUT A MERE MODERN MUST BE MODERATE-- . . . . . . 393 3 DON JUAN 13 74 7
FOR I WAS BRED A MODERATE PRESBYTERIAN . . . . . . 496 3 DON JUAN 15 91 8
MODERATELY
ALTHOUGH A FEMALE MODERATELY FICKLE . . . . 419 2 DON JUAN 5 17 2
MODERATE-MINDED
FOR MY PART I'M A MODERATE-MINDED BARD . . . . . . 85 2 DON JUAN 1 118 5
MODERATION
THE LADIES WITH MORE MODERATION MINGLED . . . . . . 487 3 DON JUAN 15 70 3
MODERN
OF ANY MODERN FEMALE SAINT'S COMPARISON . . . . . . 30 2 DON JUAN 1 17 2
(THAT MODERN PHRASE APPEARS TO ME SAD STUFF . . . . . 119 2 DON JUAN 1 178 3
ALTHOUGH SHE TOLD HIM IN GOOD MODERN GREEK . . . . . 236 2 DON JUAN 2 150 6
FROM WHICH OUR MODERN MORALS RIGHTLY SHRINKING . . . . 238 2 DON JUAN 2 155 3

```
                                                       PAGE VOL    CANTO  STANZA LV
MODERN   (CONTINUED)
    THE MODERN GREEK IN TOLERABLE VERSE  . . . . . . .  326  2 DON JUAN  3     87   2
    I CHOSE A MODERN SUBJECT AS MORE MEET . . . . . . .  347  2 DON JUAN  4      6   8
    MORE MODERN BUILDINGS AND THOSE BUILT OF YORE  . . . . .  443  2 DON JUAN  5     57   6
    MY MODERN MUSE MAY BE ALLOWED TO SNORE  . . . . .  503  2 DON JUAN  5    159  V8
    THIS MODERN AMAZON AND QUEEN OF QUEANS  . . . . .  54  3 DON JUAN  6     96   4
    MOST MODERN PREACHERS SAY THE SAME OR SHOW IT  . . . . .  69  3 DON JUAN  7      6   2
    MEKNOP SERGE LWOW ARSENIEW OF MODERN GREECE  . . . . .  74  3 DON JUAN  7     15   3
    OF ALL OUR MODERN BATTLES I WILL BET  . . . . . .  83  3 DON JUAN  7     34   7
    (THAT WHICH SOME ANCIENT MUSE OR MODERN WIT . . . .  153  3 DON JUAN  8     84   4
    WITH MODERN HISTORY HAS BUT SMALL CONNECTION  . . . . .  186  3 DON JUAN  9      7   4
    WHEREAS YOUR MODERN MONARCHS ARE MERE SPIDERS  . . . .  196  3 DON JUAN  9     27  V8
    'TIS THE SAME LANDSCAPE WHICH THE MODERN MARS SAW  . . .  253  3 DON JUAN 10     58   5
    A MODERN ANCIENT PISTOL--BY THE HILTS . . . . . .  297  3 DON JUAN 11     57   8
    AND THEN SHE DROPS A BRIEF AND MODERN CURTSY  . . . . .  300  3 DON JUAN 11     63   7
    OF MODERN REIGNING STERLING STUPID STAMP--  . . . . .  321  3 DON JUAN 12     12   7
    I FOR MY PART--(ONE MODERN INSTANCE MORE  . . . . .  334  3 DON JUAN 12     38   1
    AT WHICH ALL MODERN NATIONS VAINLY AIM  . . . . .  367  3 DON JUAN 13     20   6
    OF THEIR DEPARTURE SUCH IS MODERN FAME  . . . . .  382  3 DON JUAN 13     51   2
    BUT A MERE MODERN MUST BE MODERATE--  . . . . . .  393  3 DON JUAN 13     74   7
    OF MODERN DINNERS WHERE MORE MYSTERY LURKS  . . . . .  482  3 DON JUAN 15     62   6
    BUT OH YE MODERN HEROES WITH YOUR CARTRIDGES  . . . . .  485  3 DON JUAN 15     67   7
    A MODE ADOPTED SINCE BY MODERN YOUTH  . . . . . .  501  3 DON JUAN 16      1   4
    THERE WAS A MODERN GOTH I MEAN A GOTHIC  . . . . .  529  3 DON JUAN 16     58   1
MODERNS
    ANTIENTS AND MODERNS ALSO NOT A FEW  . . . . . . .  267  2 DON JUAN  2    207  V6
    BUT STILL WE MODERNS EQUAL YOU IN BLOOD . . . . . .  106  3 DON JUAN  7     80   8
MODEST
    TOO MUCH THEIR MODEST BARD BY THIS OMISSION . . . .  46  2 DON JUAN  1     44   5
    AND THEN SHE LOOKS SO MODEST ALL THE WHILE  . . . . .  82  2 DON JUAN  1    113   8
    BUT HE MORE MODEST TOOK AN HUMBLER RANGE . . . . .  283  2 DON JUAN  3     14   5
    AND ALSO COULD YOU LOOK A LITTLE MODEST . . . . . .  464  2 DON JUAN  5     91   8
    ARE THE BEST TOKENS (TO A MODEST MIND)  . . . . . .  13  3 DON JUAN  6     15   5
    THOUGH MODEST ON HIS UNEMBARRASSED BROW . . . . . .  223  3 DON JUAN  9     83   5
    A MODEST CONFIDENCE AND CALM ASSURANCE . . . . . .  294  3 DON JUAN 11     52   2
    A SLIGHT OBSERVER IN A MODEST WAY) . . . . . . .  336  3 DON JUAN 12     44   2
    TRICKED OUT BUT MODEST MORE THAN POET'S PEN . . . .  380  3 DON JUAN 13     47   4
    YOU MAY BE BOAZ AND I--MODEST RUTH . . . . . . .  403  3 DON JUAN 13     96   4
    KNOCKEST AT DOORS AT FIRST WITH MODEST TAP . . . . .  459  3 DON JUAN 15      8   2
    YOU SHOULD BE CIVIL IN A MODEST WAY . . . . . . .  459  3 DON JUAN 15      9   6
    A MODEST HOPE--BUT MODESTY'S MY FORTE . . . . . .  466  3 DON JUAN 15     22   1
    OF ALL THE MODEST PART OF PROPAGATION . . . . . .  472  3 DON JUAN 15     37   4
    IN VIRGINS--ALWAYS IN A MODEST WAY . . . . . . .  494  3 DON JUAN 15     86   7
    BURNT AND NOT BLUE AS MODEST TAPERS USE . . . . . .  512  3 DON JUAN 16     26   2
    FIVE AS THEY MIGHT DO IN A MODEST WAY . . . . . .  548  3 DON JUAN 16     99   3
    MODEST I AM--YET WITH SOME SLIGHT ASSURANCE . . . .  567  3 DON JUAN 17     11   2
MODESTLY
    THROUGH ROWS MOST MODESTLY CALLED PARADISE . . . . .  278  3 DON JUAN 11     21   7
    AND MINGLING MODESTLY IN TOILS OR SPORTS . . . . .  424  3 DON JUAN 14     31   6
    HE ADDED MODESTLY WHEN REBELS RAILED) . . . . . .  535  3 DON JUAN 16     72   6
MODESTY
    BECAME DIVESTED OF HIS NATIVE MODESTY . . . . . .  157  2 DON JUAN  2      1   8
    LOST THAT MOST PRECIOUS STONE OF STONES--HIS MODESTY . .  157  2 DON JUAN  2      1  V8
    HE LOOKED--IN ALL SAVE MODESTY--A MAID  . . . . . .  458  2 DON JUAN  5     80  V3
    OF MODESTY DECLINED THE ASSISTANCE PROFFERED  . . . .  36  3 DON JUAN  6     61   4
    OR MODESTY OR ABSENCE OR INANITY  . . . . . . .  490  3 DON JUAN 15     78   6
MODESTY'S
    BUT MODESTY'S AT TIMES ITS OWN REWARD . . . . . .  462  3 DON JUAN 15     14   6
    A MODEST HOPE--BUT MODESTY'S MY FORTE . . . . . .  466  3 DON JUAN 15     22   1
MODIFY
    THEY DID THEIR BEST TO MODIFY THEIR CASE  . . . . . .  189  2 DON JUAN  2     63   3
MOGUL
    AND SCARCE TO THE MOGUL A CUP OF COFFEE  . . . . .  199  3 DON JUAN  9     33   6
MOISTURE
    AND FALL FOR LACK OF MOISTURE QUITE A-DRY BOB . . . .  10  2 DON JUAN  D      3   8
    AND WHEN THEY DEEM'D ITS MOISTURE WAS COMPLETE . . . .  201  2 DON JUAN  2     85   4
    SUCK'D IN THE MOISTURE WHICH LIKE NECTAR STREAM'D . . .  202  2 DON JUAN  2     86   2
    FELT AN ODD GLISTENING MOISTURE IN HER EYE  . . . . .  480  2 DON JUAN  5    120   8
MOLDAVIA'S
    A VILLAGE OF MOLDAVIA'S WASTE WHEREIN . . . . . .  76  3 DON JUAN  7     20   7
MOLE
    AND THAT HER HONOUR WAS A ROCK OR MOLE . . . . . .  66  2 DON JUAN  1     82   4
MOLIERE'S
    WHEN CONGREVE'S FOOL COULD VIE WITH MOLIERE'S BETE  . .  402  3 DON JUAN 13     94   6
MOLTEN
    BAPTIZED IN MOLTEN GOLD AND SWATHED IN DUN  . . . . .  205  2 DON JUAN  2     92   4
    LIKE MOLTEN LEAD AS IF YOU THRUST A PIKE IN . . . .  479  2 DON JUAN  5    118   6
    STEEL BARONS MOLTEN THE NEXT GENERATION . . . . . .  390  3 DON JUAN 13     68   1
MOLU
    AN EARTHLY PARADISE OF OR MOLU . . . . . . . .  302  3 DON JUAN 11     67   8
MOLWITZ
    FREDERICK THE GREAT FROM MOLWITZ DEIGNED TO RUN  . . . .  122  3 DON JUAN  8     22   4
MOMENT
    IT WAS A TRYING MOMENT THAT WHICH FOUND HIM . . . . .  41  2 DON JUAN  1     36   4
    BUT JUST SUPPOSE THAT MOMENT SHOULD BETIDE  . . . . .  67  2 DON JUAN  1     84   5
    A MOMENT AT THE DOOR THAT WE MAY BE  . . . . . .  106  2 DON JUAN  1    156   7
    THE MOMENT HAS SENT HIS FOOLS AWAY . . . . . . .  114  2 DON JUAN  1    169   2
    IF AT THAT MOMENT HE HAD CHANCED TO CLAW IT . . . .  123  2 DON JUAN  1    185   5
    THROWN BACK A MOMENT WITH THE GLANCING HAND . . . .  160  2 DON JUAN  2      7   2
```

		PAGE	VOL		CANTO	STANZA	LN

MOMENT   (CONTINUED)

	PAGE	VOL		CANTO	STANZA	LN
AND FOR THE MOMENT IT HAD SOME EFFECT	176	2 DON JUAN	2	39	2
BUT BEING THIRSTIEST AT THE MOMENT HE	197	2 DON JUAN	2	77	3
THE MOMENT AFTER HE POLITELY ENDS	200	2 DON JUAN	2	83	4
BRIGHTEN'D AND FOR A MOMENT SEEM'D TO ROAM	203	2 DON JUAN	2	89	6
WHICH IN THEIR WAY THAT MOMENT CHANCED TO FALL	206	2 DON JUAN	2	95	7
UPON THE MOMENT COULD CONTRIVE WITH SUCH	226	2 DON JUAN	2	132	2
LOOK'D BACK UPON HIM AND A MOMENT STAID	228	2 DON JUAN	2	135	3
THAT AT THIS MOMENT JUAN KNEW IT NOT	228	2 DON JUAN	2	135	8
AS AT THIS MOMENT I SHOULD LIKE TO DO	232	2 DON JUAN	2	142	V6
A CHILD THE MOMENT WHEN IT DRAINS THE BREAST	261	2 DON JUAN	2	196	2
THUS SHE CAME OFTEN NOT A MOMENT LOSING	282	2 DON JUAN	3	13	7
HAVE FELT THAT MOMENT IN ITS FULLEST POWER	335	2 DON JUAN	3	102	3
UNLESS IT WERE TO BE A MOMENT MERRY	346	2 DON JUAN	4	5	7
IT WAS A MOMENT OF THAT AWFUL KIND--	363	2 DON JUAN	4	36	7
A MOMENT MORE WILL BRING THE SIGHT TO BEAR	366	2 DON JUAN	4	41	3
THE FATHER PAUSED A MOMENT THEN WITHDREW	368	2 DON JUAN	4	46	1
ON HIM HER FLASHING EYES A MOMENT BENT	379	2 DON JUAN	4	65	4
A MOMENT AT THE EUROPEAN YOUTH	387	2 DON JUAN	4	78	4
A MOMENT AND THEN DROPPED BUT TO RESUME	420	2 DON JUAN	5	18	5
A MOMENT WITHOUT SLACKENING FROM THEIR PACE	441	2 DON JUAN	5	54	3
JUAN A MOMENT AS THIS PAIR SO SMALL	463	2 DON JUAN	5	90	5
A MOMENT MORE WOULD HURT YOUR REPUTATION	482	2 DON JUAN	5	123	8
SHE ROSE AND PAUSING ONE CHASTE MOMENT THREW	483	2 DON JUAN	5	125	7
THE MOMENT TILL TOO LATE TO COME AGAIN	6	3 DON JUAN	6	1	5
SHE STOOD A MOMENT AS A PYTHONESS	59	3 DON JUAN	6	107	1
THE MOMENT OF THE GENERAL CUNSTERNATION	78	3 DON JUAN	7	24	2
A MOMENT AND ALL WILL BE LIFE AGAIN	111	3 DON JUAN	7	87	5
HURRA AND ALLAH AND ONE MOMENT MORE	111	3 DON JUAN	7	87	7
IN THE SAME MOMENT LOUD AS EVEN THE ROAR	116	3 DON JUAN	8	8	2
THE HEAP A MOMENT MORE HAD MADE HER TOMB	158	3 DON JUAN	8	94	8
PAUSED FOR A MOMENT FROM THE FIGHT AND CAST	169	3 DON JUAN	8	116	7
WERE MELTED FOR A MOMENT THOUGH NO TEAR	171	3 DON JUAN	8	119	6
THESE QUENCHED A MOMENT HER AMBITION'S THIRST--	212	3 DON JUAN	9	59	5
HOW BEAUTIFUL THAT MOMENT AND HOW ODD IS	220	3 DON JUAN	9	75	5
TO PAIN THE MOMENT WHEN YOU CEASE TO PLEASE	231	3 DON JUAN	10	13	8
WHO VINDICATES A MOMENT TOO HIS STREAM--	279	3 DON JUAN	11	24	2
WHICH CATHERINE IN A MOMENT OF IVRESSE	287	3 DON JUAN	11	39	5
'TIS ALSO OF SOME MOMENT TO THE LATTER	292	3 DON JUAN	11	46	5
OF FEEDING BRATS THE MOMENT HIS WIFE WEANS	325	3 DON JUAN	12	21	8
SHE HAD ALSO SNATCH'D A MOMENT SINCE HER MARRIAGE	434	3 DON JUAN	14	56	7
WHICH FLOW'D ON FOR A MOMENT IN THE BEAM	480	3 DON JUAN	15	55	5
TIME SHEDS A MOMENT O'ER EACH SPARKLING CREST	480	3 DON JUAN	15	55	6
PERVADES A MOMENT THOSE WHO LISTEN ROUND	521	3 DON JUAN	16	41	4

MOMENTARY

	PAGE	VOL		CANTO	STANZA	LN
AND O'ER HIS EYE A MOMENTARY GLOOM	298	2 DON JUAN	3	44	3

MOMENTLY

	PAGE	VOL		CANTO	STANZA	LN
THE TWILIGHT GLOW WHICH MOMENTLY GREW LESS	255	2 DON JUAN	2	188	4

MOMENT'S

	PAGE	VOL		CANTO	STANZA	LN
WAS BUT A MOMENT'S ACT--AH WELL-A-DAY	121	2 DON JUAN	1	181	5
AND MADE THEM BALE WITHOUT A MOMENT'S EASE	188	2 DON JUAN	2	60	6
A MOMENT'S MORE HAD SLAIN HER BUT THE WHILE	489	2 DON JUAN	5	135	2
A MOMENT'S GOOD THING MAY HAVE COST THEM YEARS	408	3 DON JUAN	13	109	6

MOMENTS

	PAGE	VOL		CANTO	STANZA	LN
HAVE MOMENTS HOURS AND DAYS SO UNPREPARED	33	2 DON JUAN	1	21	4
BUT PAYS OFF MOMENTS IN AN ENDLESS SHOWER	258	2 DON JUAN	2	192	6
AND WHEN THOSE DEEP AND BURNING MOMENTS PASS'D	260	2 DON JUAN	2	195	1
WHO CAME AT STATED MOMENTS TO INVITE ALL	393	2 DON JUAN	4	90	3
WE FOR SOME MOMENTS HAD SECURED OUR SKIN	435	2 DON JUAN	5	44	V4
METHOD'S MORE SURE AT MOMENTS TO TAKE HOLD	439	2 DON JUAN	5	49	4
OH YE AMBROSIAL MOMENTS ALWAYS UPPER	304	3 DON JUAN	11	72	3
THE MOMENTS WHEN WE GATHER FROM A GLANCE	554	3 DON JUAN	16	108	4

MOMONOFF

	PAGE	VOL		CANTO	STANZA	LN
NO WONDER THEN THAT YERMOLOFF OR MOMONOFF	206	3 DON JUAN	9	48	1

MOMUS

	PAGE	VOL		CANTO	STANZA	LN
NOW MARS NOW MOMUS AND WHEN BENT TO STORM	95	3 DON JUAN	7	55	7

MONARCH

	PAGE	VOL		CANTO	STANZA	LN
OF EVERY MONARCH TILL THEY ARE CONSIGNED	12	3 DON JUAN	6	13	3
NOR REIGN AT ALL OR AS A MONARCH REIGN	296	3 DON JUAN	11	56	6

MONARCH'S

	PAGE	VOL		CANTO	STANZA	LN
O'ER THEM LIKE DEATH UPON A MONARCH'S PRIDE	462	2 DON JUAN	5	87	V6
SMOOTHED FOR A MONARCH'S SEAT OF HONOUR GAY	235	3 DON JUAN	10	21	6

MONARCHS

	PAGE	VOL		CANTO	STANZA	LN
THE BLOOD OF MONARCHS WITH HIS PROPHECIES	15	2 DON JUAN	D	11	3
EACH IN THEIR TURN LIKE BANQUO'S MONARCHS STALK	22	2 DON JUAN	1	2	5
MONARCHS ARE LESS IMPERATIVE THAN RHYMES)--	456	2 DON JUAN	5	77	8
WHEREAS YOUR MODERN MONARCHS ARE MERE SPIDERS	196	3 DON JUAN	9	27	V8
WHICH SHRINK FROM TOUCH AS MONARCHS DO FROM RHYMES	243	3 DON JUAN	10	37	3
SO SAID THE FLORENTINE YE MONARCHS HEARKEN	264	3 DON JUAN	10	80	1
I HAVE SEEN MORE CHANGES DOWN FROM MONARCHS TO	309	3 DON JUAN	11	82	2

MONASTERY

	PAGE	VOL		CANTO	STANZA	LN
AN OLD OLD MONASTERY ONCE AND NOW	384	3 DON JUAN	13	55	2

MONASTIC

	PAGE	VOL		CANTO	STANZA	LN
IN HIS MONASTIC CONCUBINE OF SNOW--	14	3 DON JUAN	6	17	6
WITH MORE OF THE MONASTIC THAN HAS BEEN	389	3 DON JUAN	13	66	2
THAT YOUNG MEN RARELY MADE MONASTIC VOWS	439	3 DON JUAN	14	67	6
I THINK I SHOULD HAVE MADE MONASTIC VOWS	467	3 DON JUAN	15	24	3

MONCADA

	PAGE	VOL		CANTO	STANZA	LN
FOR THERE THE SPANISH FAMILY MONCADA	169	2 DON JUAN	2	24	3

```
                                                          PAGE VOL    CANTO STANZA LN
MONDE
    THE MONDE EXACTLY AS THEY OUGHT TO PAINT . . . . . .   418  3 DON JUAN 14    19   3
    ARE GROWN OF THE BEAU MONDE A PART POTENTIAL  . . . .  418  3 DON JUAN 14    20   2
    FOR SEVERAL WINTERS IN THE GRAND GRAND MONDE  . . . .  428  3 DON JUAN 14    42   3
MONEY
    SOUNDS ILL IN LOVE WHATE'ER IT MAY IN MONEY . . . . .   78  2 DON JUAN  1   107   8
    ALL I CAN SAY IS--THAT HE HAD THE MONEY . . . . . .    142  2 DON JUAN  1   210   8
    A LECTURE AND SOME MONEY FOR FOUR SPRINGS  . . . . .   161  2 DON JUAN  2     9   3
    THEY WON'T LAY OUT THEIR MONEY ON THE DEAD--  . . . .  185  2 DON JUAN  2    55   7
    HE ALSO STUFF'D HIS MONEY WHERE HE COULD . . . . . .   187  2 DON JUAN  2    59   1
    WITH SCIO WINE--AND ALL FOR LOVE NOT MONEY . . . . .   233  2 DON JUAN  2   145   8
    DAMSELS AND DANCES REVELS READY MONEY . . . . . . .    235  3 DON JUAN 10    21   7
    IS FREE THE RESPIRATION'S WORTH THE MONEY  . . . . .   259  3 DON JUAN 10    70   8
    WITH DAMN YOUR EYES YOUR MONEY OR YOUR LIFE . . . . .  273  3 DON JUAN 11    10   8
    AND MONEY THAT MOST PURE IMAGINATION  . . . . . . .    316  3 DON JUAN 12     2   7
    BUT MAKING MONEY SLOWLY FIRST THEN QUICKER . . . . .   317  3 DON JUAN 12     4   3
    YES READY MONEY IS ALADDIN'S LAMP . . . . . . .       321  3 DON JUAN 12    12   8
    TASTES THEIR FIRST SEASON (MOSTLY IF THEY HAVE MONEY)  330  3 DON JUAN 12    31   8
    OR PAPER TURNED TO MONEY BY THE BANK . . . . . . .     396  3 DON JUAN 13    80   5
    TO THIS WE HAVE ADDED SINCE THE LOVE OF MONEY  . . .   405  3 DON JUAN 13   100   3
    ON READY MONEY OR A DRAFT ON RANSOM  . . . . . . .     459  3 DON JUAN 15     8   8
    FOR GOTHIC DARING SHOWN IN ENGLISH MONEY . . . . . .   529  3 DON JUAN 16    59   8
MONGERS
    BANKERS--CONTRACTORS--BOROUGH MONGERS--BULLIES . . . . 314  3 DON JUAN 11  V 76   1
'MONGST
    HE HAD TRAVELL'D 'MONGST THE ARABS TURKS AND FRANKS . 319  2 DON JUAN  3    84   1
    BECAUSE ONE POET TRAVELLED 'MONGST THE TURKS) . . . .  434  2 DON JUAN  5    42   8
    'MONGST THEM WERE SEVERAL ENGLISHMEN OF PITH . . . .    75  3 DON JUAN  7    18   7
    ('MONGST OTHER DEATHS THE GENERAL RIBAUPIERRE'S  . . . 147  3 DON JUAN  8    71   6
MONIED
    THE LANDED AND THE MONIED SPECULATION . . . . . . .    360  3 DON JUAN 13     6   4
MONITEUR
    RECORDED IN THE MONITEUR AND COURIER . . . . . . .     22  2 DON JUAN  1     2   8
MONITORS
    OF MONITORS ADAPTED TO RECALL  . . . . . . . .        308  2 DON JUAN  3    65   3
MONK
    AND SPOKE MORE OF THE BARON THAN THE MONK  . . . . .   389  3 DON JUAN 13    66   8
    MUCH AS A MONK MAY DO WITHIN HIS CELL . . . . . . .    445  3 DON JUAN 14    81   4
    IT WAS NO MOUSE BUT LO A MONK ARRAYED . . . . . . .    510  3 DON JUAN 16    21   1
    A MONK REMAINED UNCHASED UNCHAINED . . . . . . . .     518  3 DON JUAN 16  L  2   5
    BUT THE MONK IS LORD BY NIGHT . . . . . . . .         520  3 DON JUAN 16  L  5   6
    SPANGLED WITH GEMS--THE MONK MADE HIS BLOOD CURDLE . . 556  3 DON JUAN 16   113   8
MONKEY
    AND MISCHIEF-MAKING MONKEY FROM HIS BIRTH  . . . . .    34  2 DON JUAN  1    25   2
    A MONKEY A DUTCH MASTIFF A MACKAW  . . . . . . .      285  2 DON JUAN  3    18   1
MONKS
    BECAUSE THE MONKS PREFERRED A HILL BEHIND  . . . . .   384  3 DON JUAN 13    55   7
    AND A PROPOS OF MONKS THEIR PIETY . . . . . . .       445  3 DON JUAN 14    81   5
MONMOUTH
    TURPIN'S OR MONMOUTH GEOFFRY'S CHRONICLE . . . . . .   503  3 DON JUAN 16     5   2
MONOPOLY
    OF WHAT SHOULD BE MONOPOLY--THE HEART . . . . . . .     10  3 DON JUAN  6     9   8
MONOSYLLABLE
    OTHERS IN MONOSYLLABLE TALK CHATTED  . . . . . . .    441  2 DON JUAN  5    53   3
MONOTONY
    WHATE'ER IT SHOWS WITH TRUTH A SMOOTH MONOTONY . . . . 417  3 DON JUAN 14    16   7
MONSOON
    MAN QUITE AS QUIETLY AS BLOWS THE MONSOON  . . . . .   132  3 DON JUAN  8    39   5
MONSTER
    AND HERE PERHAPS A MONSTER THERE A SAINT . . . . . .   389  3 DON JUAN 13    65   4
MONSTER'S
    ERE SUCH A MONSTER'S VICTIM I HAD BEEN  . . . . . .     98  2 DON JUAN  1   142   4
    THAT I SHOULD FALL INTO A MONSTER'S POWER . . . . .    106  2 DON JUAN  1   155   8
MONSTERS
    MONSTERS WHO COST A NO LESS MONSTROUS SUM  . . . . .   462  2 DON JUAN  5    88   8
    LOOK LIKE THE MONSTERS OF A NEW MUSEUM  . . . . . .    202  3 DON JUAN  9    40   8
MONSTROUS
    THIS MONSTROUS TALE HAD PROBABLY ITS SOURCE . . . . . 446  2 DON JUAN  5    61   5
    MONSTERS WHO COST A NO LESS MONSTROUS SUM  . . . . .   462  2 DON JUAN  5    88   8
    ENGENDERED MONSTROUS SHAPES OF EVERY CRIME . . . . .   152  3 DON JUAN  8    82   8
    THAT MONSTROUS HIEROGLYPHIC--THAT LONG SPOUT . . . .   207  3 DON JUAN  9    50   8
    THAT MONSTROUS MYSTAGOGUE--THAT MERE SPOUT . . . . .   207  3 DON JUAN  9    50  V5
    ONE MONSTROUS DIAMOND DREW MUCH OBSERVATION . . . . . 287  3 DON JUAN 11    39   4
    THAT THE YOUNG LADY MADE A MONSTROUS CHOICE . . . . . 334  3 DON JUAN 12    38   8
MONT
    MY LEIPSIC AND MY MONT SAINT JEAN SEEMS CAIN . . . .   296  3 DON JUAN 11    56   2
MONTAGU
    WHICH CHARMED THE CHARMING MARY MONTAGU  . . . . .    412  2 DON JUAN  5     3   8
MONTAIGNE
    QUE SCAIS-JE WAS THE MOTTO OF MONTAIGNE . . . . . .    191  3 DON JUAN  9    17   1
MONTH
    WHEN EVERY YEAR AND MONTH SENDS FORTH A NEW ONE  . .    21  2 DON JUAN  1     1   2
    PERHAPS BUT WHO WOULD SCORN THE MONTH OF JUNE  . . .   229  3 DON JUAN 10     9   5
    SLIPS FROM THE MOUNTAIN IN THE MONTH OF JUNE . . . .   517  3 DON JUAN 16    38  V6
MONTHLY
    DAILY OR MONTHLY OR THREE MONTHLY I  . . . . . . .    142  2 DON JUAN  1   211   4
    DAILY OR MONTHLY OR THREE MONTHLY I  . . . . . . .    142  2 DON JUAN  1   211   4
    MORTALITY THOU HAST THY MONTHLY BILLS . . . . . . .    117  3 DON JUAN  8    12   4
MONTH'S
    TO LOSE BY ONE MONTH'S FROST SOME TWENTY YEARS . . . . 253  3 DON JUAN 10    58   7
```

		PAGE	VOL	CANTO	STANZA	LN
MONTHS						
THAT THERE ARE MONTHS WHICH NATURE GROWS MORE MERRY IN		76	2 DON JUAN	1	102	7
IN SIGHT THAT SEVERAL MONTHS HAVE PASS'D WE'LL SAY		86	2 DON JUAN	1	121	6
SING AT MY HEART SIX MONTHS AT LEAST IN VAIN		102	2 DON JUAN	1	149	2
MONTHS WITH THE RUSSIAN ARMY HERE AND THERE		418	2 DON JUAN	5	15	6
HER STEADY BREATH (WHICH SOME MONTHS THE SAME STILL IS)		132	3 DON JUAN	8	39	6
SUCH DIFFERENCE DOTH A FEW MONTHS MAKE YOU'D THINK		228	3 DON JUAN	10	7	5
CAW ME CAW THEE--FOR SIX MONTHS HATH BEEN HATCHING		307	3 DON JUAN	11	78	7
TO LOSE THOSE BEST MONTHS IN A SWEATY CITY		380	3 DON JUAN	13	48	4
MONUMENT						
LET NOT A MONUMENT GIVE YOU OR ME HOPES		146	2 DON JUAN	1	219	7
WITH A CARVED LADY ON A MONUMENT		40	3 DON JUAN	6	68	8
AND HEW OUT A HUGE MONUMENT OF PATHOS		355	3 DON JUAN	12	86	7
MONUMENTS						
OH YE WHO BUILD UP MONUMENTS DEFILED		199	3 DON JUAN	9	33	3
MOOD						
UNTIL HIS MIGHTY HEART IN ITS GREAT MOOD		70	2 DON JUAN	1	91	3
WHO CAN HAVE PUT MY MASTER IN THIS MOOD		115	2 DON JUAN	1	171	2
BUT NEVER IN HIS REAL AND SERIOUS MOOD		300	2 DON JUAN	3	48	2
OF MILD DEMEANOUR THOUGH OF SAVAGE MOOD		302	2 DON JUAN	3	53	2
NOT ALWAYS SIGNS WITH HIM OF CALMEST MOOD		365	2 DON JUAN	4	39	3
AS NOT BEING IN A MASQUERADING MOOD		453	2 DON JUAN	5	73	5
BY THOSE WHO GOVERN IN THE MOOD POTENTIAL		285	3 DON JUAN	11	35	4
OR SOMEONE FOR HIM IN SOME SAGE GRAVE MOOD		371	3 DON JUAN	13	29	3
AND TUNE THE CONCORD TO A FINER MOOD		451	3 DON JUAN	14	93	4
MOON						
HOW MANY MILES THE MOON MIGHT HAVE IN GIRTH		71	2 DON JUAN	1	92	5
NOT ONLY OF THE AGE AND YEAR BUT MOON		76	2 DON JUAN	1	103	3
THE SUN SET AND UP ROSE THE YELLOW MOON		82	2 DON JUAN	1	113	1
THE DEVIL'S IN THE MOON FOR MISCHIEF THEY		82	2 DON JUAN	1	113	2
NO MOON NO STARS THE WIND WAS LOW OR LOUD		94	2 DON JUAN	1	135	2
I WONDER IN WHAT QUARTER NOW THE MOON IS		103	2 DON JUAN	1	150	4
AND THUS A MOON ROLL'D ON AND FAIR HAIDEE		248	2 DON JUAN	2	174	1
AND SAW THE SUN SET OPPOSITE THE MOON		249	2 DON JUAN	2	176	8
WHENCE THE BROAD MOON ROSE CIRCLING INTO SIGHT		253	2 DON JUAN	2	185	4
PERPLEXING QUESTION BUT NO DOUBT THE MOON		267	2 DON JUAN	2	208	4
LIKE FLEECY CLOUDS ABOUT THE MOON FLOW'D ROUND HER		311	2 DON JUAN	3	70	8
AND HE MUST NEEDS MOUNT NEARER TO THE MOON		333	2 DON JUAN	3	99	7
AND YET SHE DID NOT WANT TO REACH THE MOON		490	2 DON JUAN	5	136	3
BRIDE OF THE SUN AND SISTER OF THE MOON		494	2 DON JUAN	5	144	1
HE SAW WITH HIS OWN EYES THE MOON WAS ROUND		497	2 DON JUAN	5	150	1
THE MOON BREAKS HALF UNVEILED EACH FURTHER CHARM		39	3 DON JUAN	6	66	5
WOULD MAKE US THINK THE MOON IS AT ITS FULL		46	3 DON JUAN	6	80	5
AS LITTLE AS THE MOON STOPS FOR THE BAYING		70	3 DON JUAN	7	7	5
WHO CAME AS IF JUST DROPPED DOWN FROM THE MOON		140	3 DON JUAN	8	56	4
AND THE SAD SECOND MOON GROWS DIM AGAIN		168	3 DON JUAN	8	113	4
STEAM-ENGINES WILL CONDUCT HIM TO THE MOON		226	3 DON JUAN	10	2	8
AS MAY BE WON BY FAVOUR OF THE MOON		229	3 DON JUAN	10	9	3
I RATHER THINK THE MOON SHOULD DATE THE DEARS		230	3 DON JUAN	10	10	8
THEIR MOON THEIR SUN THEIR GAS THEIR FARTHING CANDLE		342	3 DON JUAN	12	56	8
BUT IN THE NOONTIDE OF THE MOON AND WHEN		388	3 DON JUAN	13	63	1
A LITTLE EARLIER THAN THE WANING MOON		409	3 DON JUAN	13	111	4
THAN DYING TAPERS--AND THE PEEPING MOON		504	3 DON JUAN	16	8	8
HE SIGHED--THE NEXT RESOURCE IS THE FULL MOON		506	3 DON JUAN	16	13	1
LOOK LIVING IN THE MOON AND AS YOU TURN		508	3 DON JUAN	16	18	2
THAT WE OURSELVES--'TWAS IN THE HONEY MOON--		517	3 DON JUAN	16	38	2
THE MOON PEEPED JUST ESCAPED FROM A GREY CLOUD		560	3 DON JUAN	16	121	8
MOONBEAMS						
MIRRORED THE CHRISTIAN FLAGS--AS MOONBEAMS ON THE WATER		173	3 DON JUAN	8	122	V8
ON WHICH THE MOONBEAMS FELL IN SILVERY SHOWERS		559	3 DON JUAN	16	120	3
MOONLIGHT						
GLEAM IN THE MOONLIGHT AND HER WHITE ARM CLASPS		259	2 DON JUAN	2	194	2
AND RAISING UP AN ARM AS MOONLIGHT FAIR		466	2 DON JUAN	5	96	5
OF BURNING STREETS LIKE MOONLIGHT ON THE WATER		172	3 DON JUAN	8	122	7
NOW IN THE MOONLIGHT AND NOW LAPSED IN SHADE		510	3 DON JUAN	16	21	3
LEFT IN A TENDER MOONLIGHT SITUATION		567	3 DON JUAN	17	12	2
MOONLIT						
AT MIDNIGHT ON THE BLUE AND MOONLIT DEEP		87	2 DON JUAN	1	122	2
MOON'S						
MORE THAN SUCH MADMEN'S FELLOW MAN--THE MOON'S		341	2 DON JUAN	3	110	4
JUAN WHO SAW THE MOON'S LATE MINION BLEED		275	3 DON JUAN	11	14	5
MORE QUIET WHEN OUR MOON'S NO MORE AT FULL		360	3 DON JUAN	13	4	3
MOONS						
THAT WITHOUT NOTICE FEW FULL MOONS SHALL PASS IT		317	2 DON JUAN	3	81	3
MOONS CHANGING HAD ROLL'D ON AND CHANGELESS FOUND		352	2 DON JUAN	4	16	1
THROUGH YEARS OR MOONS THE INNER WEIGHT TO BEAR		382	2 DON JUAN	4	71	3
OF BURNING CITIES THOSE FULL MOONS OF SLAUGHTER		173	3 DON JUAN	8	122	V7
MOONSHINE						
ON WHICH THREE SINGLE HOURS OF MOONSHINE SMILE--		82	2 DON JUAN	1	113	7
IN SHAPE OF MOONSHINE HOVERS O'ER THE PILE--		279	3 DON JUAN	11	24	7
THAT ANCIENT LINE IN THE PALE MOONSHINE		519	3 DON JUAN	16	L 4	3
MOOR						
OF MOOR OR HEBREW BLOOD HE TRACED HIS SOURCE		26	2 DON JUAN	1	9	3
HAVE VENTURED PAST THE JAWS OF MOOR AND TIGER		348	3 DON JUAN	12	70	V6
MOORE						
SCOTT ROGERS CAMPBELL MOORE AND CRABBE WILL TRY		13	2 DON JUAN	D	7	7
DESCRIBED BY MAHOMET AND ANACREON MOORE		77	2 DON JUAN	1	104	5
COMMIT--FLIRTATION WITH THE MUSE OF MOORE		139	2 DON JUAN	1	205	8
COMMIT ADULTERY WITH THOMAS MOORE		139	2 DON JUAN	1	205	V8

MOORE   (CONTINUED)

	PAGE	VOL	CANTO		STANZA	LN
THAT WOULD HAVE SET TOM MOORE THOUGH MARRIED RAVING . . .	291	2	DON JUAN	3	30	V6
SIR WALTER REIGNED BEFORE ME MOORE AND CAMPBELL	297	3	DON JUAN	11	57	1

MOORE'S
	PAGE	VOL	CANTO		STANZA	LN
(IN MOORE'S PHRASE) WHERE THE FASHIONABLE FAIR	301	3	DON JUAN	11	66	7

MOORISH
	PAGE	VOL	CANTO		STANZA	LN
ACCORDED WITH HER MOORISH ORIGIN	52	2	DON JUAN	1	56	2
HER MOTHER WAS A MOORISH MAID FROM FEZ	373	2	DON JUAN	4	54	7
THE MOORISH BLOOD PARTAKES THE PLANET'S HOUR	374	2	DON JUAN	4	56	4

MOPETH
	PAGE	VOL	CANTO		STANZA	LN
BECAUSE HE MOPETH IDLY IN HIS SHELL	445	3	DON JUAN	14	81	2

MORAL
	PAGE	VOL	CANTO		STANZA	LN
WAS THAT HIS BREEDING SHOULD BE STRICTLY MORAL	43	2	DON JUAN	1	39	4
HAPPY THE NATIONS OF THE MORAL NORTH	57	2	DON JUAN	1	64	1
THIS STORY IS NOT MORAL FIRST I PRAY	140	2	DON JUAN	1	207	2
THAT THIS IS NOT A MORAL TALE THOUGH GAY	140	2	DON JUAN	1	207	6
AND CRY THAT THEY THE MORAL CANNOT FIND	141	2	DON JUAN	1	208	5
AND BEG THEY'LL TAKE MY WORD ABOUT THE MORAL	141	2	DON JUAN	1	209	2
AND BEG THEY'LL WAIT WITH PATIENCE FOR THE MORAL . . .	141	2	DON JUAN	1	209	V2
THE VERY BOTANY BAY IN MORAL GEOGRAPHY	330	2	DON JUAN	3	94	2
BUT A MORAL TO EACH ERROR TACKED	412	2	DON JUAN	5	2	4
THIS POEM WILL BECOME A MORAL MODEL	412	2	DON JUAN	5	2	8
I'LL MAKE THIS POEM QUITE A MORAL MODEL	412	2	DON JUAN	5	2	V8
A MORAL (LIKE ALL MORALS) MELANCHOLY	448	2	DON JUAN	5	63	6
INTO THAT MORAL CENTAUR MAN AND WIFE	502	2	DON JUAN	5	158	8
IN MORAL ENGLAND WHERE THE THING'S A TAX)	20	3	DON JUAN	6	29	7
AND THAT'S THE MORAL OF THIS COMPOSITION	50	3	DON JUAN	6	88	1
A LEGAL BROOM'S A MORAL CHIMNEY-SWEEPER	232	3	DON JUAN	10	15	1
SETS UP FOR BEING A SORT OF MORAL ME	298	3	DON JUAN	11	59	2
A MORAL COUNTRY BUT I HOLD MY HAND--	311	3	DON JUAN	11	87	4
YOU ARE NOT A MORAL PEOPLE AND YOU KNOW IT	311	3	DON JUAN	11	87	7
SINCE I'VE GROWN MORAL STILL I MUST ACCUSE YOU ALL . .	329	3	DON JUAN	12	28	5
PERUSE 'TIS ALWAYS WITH A MORAL END	334	3	DON JUAN	12	39	2
'TIS A GREAT MORAL LESSON THEY ARE READING	341	3	DON JUAN	12	55	4
HOWE'ER HE MIGHT ESTEEM THIS MORAL NATION	347	3	DON JUAN	12	68	6
UPON THE MORAL LESSONS OF MANKIND	353	3	DON JUAN	12	81	2
A SORRIER STILL IS THE GREAT MORAL TAUGHT	363	3	DON JUAN	13	9	7
WERE NOTHING BUT A MORAL INEBRIETY	374	3	DON JUAN	13	35	8
FROM WHOM I NOW DEDUCE THESE MORAL LESSONS	375	3	DON JUAN	13	38	5
TO FURNISH MATTER FOR THEIR MORAL GIBING	418	3	DON JUAN	14	19	6
THOU MORAL WASHINGTON OF AFRICA	445	3	DON JUAN	14	82	4
IF SOME COLUMBUS OF THE MORAL SEAS	455	3	DON JUAN	14	101	7
BUT AS SUBSERVIENT TO A MORAL USE	497	3	DON JUAN	15	93	4
A MIGHTY MUG OF MORAL DOUBLE ALE	533	3	DON JUAN	16	67	4
MORAL OR PHYSICAL ON THIS OCCASION	567	3	DON JUAN	17	12	4

MORALEST
	PAGE	VOL	CANTO		STANZA	LN
WITH WHICH THIS MORALEST OF CITIES CATERS	313	3	DON JUAN	11	V 29	4

MORALIST
	PAGE	VOL	CANTO		STANZA	LN
THERE IS NO STERNER MORALIST THAN PLEASURE	308	2	DON JUAN	3	65	8
ROUGH JOHNSON THE GREAT MORALIST PROFESSED	361	3	DON JUAN	13	7	1

MORALISTS
	PAGE	VOL	CANTO		STANZA	LN
FROM POETS OR THE MORALISTS THEIR BETTERS	308	2	DON JUAN	3	64	8
ALL ARE NOT MORALISTS LIKE SOUTHEY WHEN	329	2	DON JUAN	3	93	1

MORALITIES
	PAGE	VOL	CANTO		STANZA	LN
AND SUCH INDEED SHE WAS IN HER MORALITIES	32	2	DON JUAN	1	20	4

MORALITY
	PAGE	VOL	CANTO		STANZA	LN
AND MAKES OUR SNOW LESS PURE THAN OUR MORALITY	501	2	DON JUAN	5	157	6
AND AS MY OBJECT IS MORALITY	355	3	DON JUAN	12	86	3
AND 'TWILL PERPLEX THE CASUISTS IN MORALITY	448	3	DON JUAN	14	89	7

MORALITY'S
	PAGE	VOL	CANTO		STANZA	LN
MORALITY'S PRIM PERSONIFICATION	29	2	DON JUAN	1	16	5

MORALLY
	PAGE	VOL	CANTO		STANZA	LN
AND MORALLY DECIDED THE BEST STATE IS	469	3	DON JUAN	15	29	6

MORALS
	PAGE	VOL	CANTO		STANZA	LN
ANACREON'S MORALS ARE A STILL WORSE SAMPLE	45	2	DON JUAN	1	42	2
TO MEND HIS FORMER MORALS AND GET NEW	129	2	DON JUAN	1	191	3
IT MENDS THEIR MORALS NEVER MIND THE PAIN	157	2	DON JUAN	2	1	4
THEIR MANNERS MENDING AND THEIR MORALS CURING	162	2	DON JUAN	2	10	V7
FROM WHICH OUR MODERN MORALS RIGHTLY SHRINKING	238	2	DON JUAN	2	155	3
AGAINST THE CREED AND MORALS OF THE LAND	346	2	DON JUAN	4	5	2
A MORAL (LIKE ALL MORALS) MELANCHOLY	448	2	DON JUAN	5	63	6
MORALS WERE BETTER AND THE FISH NO WORSE	496	2	DON JUAN	5	149	8
SO CELEBRATED FOR HIS MORALS WHEN	323	3	DON JUAN	12	16	6
TO ME--OF WHICH THESE MORALS ARE A SAMPLE	323	3	DON JUAN	12	16	8
FOR MORALS MARRIAGE AND THIS QUESTION CARRIED	469	3	DON JUAN	15	29	7
THE PROSPECT AND THEIR MORALS AND BESIDES	471	3	DON JUAN	15	33	7
AND MORALS OF THE COUNTRY FROM CAPRICES	531	3	DON JUAN	16	63	3

MOREAU
	PAGE	VOL	CANTO		STANZA	LN
JOUBERT HOCHE MARCEAU LANNES DESSAIX MOREAU	22	2	DON JUAN	1	3	5

MOREOVER
	PAGE	VOL	CANTO		STANZA	LN
AND WITH A PIECE OF PORK MOREOVER MET	181	2	DON JUAN	2	47	6
MOREOVER I'VE REMARKED (AND I WAS ONCE	336	3	DON JUAN	12	44	1

MORE'S
	PAGE	VOL	CANTO		STANZA	LN
THE MORE'S THE PITY WITH HER FACE AND FIGURE	390	2	DON JUAN	4	85	8
'TIS NOT ADDRESSED TO YOU--THE MORE'S THE PITY	233	3	DON JUAN	10	17	2
THE MORE'S THE REASON WHY YOU OUGHT TO STAY	459	3	DON JUAN	15	9	4

MORES
	PAGE	VOL	CANTO		STANZA	LN
AND SOLACE YOUR SLIGHT LAPSE 'GAINST BONOS MORES . . .	432	3	DON JUAN	14	50	7

MORN
	PAGE	VOL	CANTO		STANZA	LN
LETTER OF INTRODUCTION WHICH THE MORN	169	2	DON JUAN	2	24	6

```
                                                        PAGE VOL        CANTO STANZA LN
MORN   (CONTINUED)
    THE MORN BROKE AND FOUND JUAN SLUMBERING STILL . . . . .  229   2 DON JUAN   2   137   1
    AND EVERY MORN HIS COLOUR FRESHLIER CAME . . . . . . .    245   2 DON JUAN   2   169   1
    THE FESTAL MIDNIGHT AND THE LEVEE MORN . . . . . .        404   2 DON JUAN   4   110   8
    WITH THE FIRST RAY OR RATHER GREY OF MORN . . . . . .      49   3 DON JUAN   6    87   1
    THE BREATH OF MORN AND MAN WHERE FOOT BY FOOT . . . .     146   3 DON JUAN   8    69   7
    HE HATH NO MORN NOR NIGHT BUT ALL IS DARK . . . . . .     348   3 DON JUAN  12    71   7
    PREPARED EACH MORN FOR EVENINGS LIST OH LIST-- . . . .    403   3 DON JUAN  13    97   6
    MET THE MORN AS THEY MIGHT IF FINE THEY RODE . . . . .    406   3 DON JUAN  13   104   2
    'TWIXT NIGHT AND MORN UPON THE HORIZON'S VERGE . . . .    500   3 DON JUAN  15    99   2
MORNING
    A PRODIGY--HER MORNING DRESS WAS DIMITY . . . . . .        27   2 DON JUAN   1    12   6
    AND IF WE CAN BUT TILL THE MORNING KEEP . . . . . .       115   2 DON JUAN   1   172   7
    AS MORNING BROKE THE LIGHT WIND DIED AWAY . . . . . .     207   2 DON JUAN   2    97   1
    AND HAIDEE MET THE MORNING FACE TO FACE . . . . .         231   2 DON JUAN   2   141   1
    WHO LIKE A MORNING SLUMBER--FOR THE NIGHT . . . . . .     237   2 DON JUAN   2   152   7
    DYES WITH HIS MORNING LIGHT--AND WOULD CONCEAL . . . .    313   2 DON JUAN   3    73   3
    LET TO THE MORNING POST ITS ARISTOCRACY . . . . . .       329   2 DON JUAN   3    93   6
    WAKES ME NEXT MORNING WITH ITS SYNONYM . . . . . .        372   2 DON JUAN   4    53   8
    AND YOU AND I MAY CHANCE ERE MORNING RISE . . . . .       464   2 DON JUAN   5    92   5
    I WISH TO HEAVEN HE WOULD NOT SHINE TILL MORNING . . .    494   2 DON JUAN   5   145   2
    OF THE GREY MORNING AND LOOK VAINLY FOR . . . .           18   3 DON JUAN   6    24   5
    THOU MORNING POST SOLE RECORD OF THE PANNELS . . . .      308   3 DON JUAN  11    80   4
    THE MORNING POST WAS FOREMOST TO PROCLAIM-- . . . .       382   3 DON JUAN  13    51   6
    AND THUS WE SEE--WHO DOUBTS THE MORNING POST . . . .      383   3 DON JUAN  13    53   1
    OR ON THE MORNING PAPERS READ THEIR LECTURES . . . .      406   3 DON JUAN  13   102   6
    HATH GOT BLUE DEVILS FOR HIS MORNING MIRRORS . . . .      457   3 DON JUAN  15     4   4
    THIS MORNING RATHER SPENT LESS TIME UPON'T . . . .        513   3 DON JUAN  16    29   3
    THE MORNING CAME--AND BREAKFAST TEA AND TOAST . . . .     568   3 DON JUAN  17    13   2
MORNING'S
    O'ER HER FAIR FRONT LIKE MORNING'S ON A LILY . . . .       58   3 DON JUAN   6   105   8
MORNS
    HIS MORNS HE PASSED IN BUSINESS--WHICH DISSECTED . . . .  301   3 DON JUAN  11    65   1
MOROCCO
    MOROCCO BETWIXT EGYPT AND TANGIER . . . . . . . .          28   3 DON JUAN   6    44   8
MORROW
    GOOD MORROW--FOR THE COCK HAD CROWN AND LIGHT . . . .      49   3 DON JUAN   6    86   2
MORSEL
    FULL MANY A MORSEL FOR THAT TURKISH TRADE . . . . .       223   2 DON JUAN   2   126   7
    SHE SNATCH'D IT AND REFUSED ANOTHER MORSEL . . . .        240   2 DON JUAN   2   159   7
MORSELS
    HAD HIS FIRST CHOICE OF MORSELS FOR HIS PAINS . . . .     197   2 DON JUAN   2    77   2
MORTAL
    HE WAS A MORTAL OF THE CARELESS KIND . . . . . .          31   2 DON JUAN   1    19   1
    THEY WILL DESTROY A FACE WHICH MORTAL THOUGHT . . . .     219   2 DON JUAN   2   119   7
    NE'ER COMPASS'D NOR LESS MORTAL CHISEL WROUGHT . . . .    219   2 DON JUAN   2   119   8
    ALTHOUGH THE MORTAL QUITE AS FRESH AND FAIR . . . .       232   2 DON JUAN   2   142   7
    ABHOR CONDEMN ABJURE THE MORTAL MADE . . . . . .          268   2 DON JUAN   2   209   4
    AND IF I LAUGH AT ANY MORTAL THING . . . . . .            346   2 DON JUAN   4     4   1
    THETIS BAPTIZED HER MORTAL SON IN STYX . . . . .          346   2 DON JUAN   4     4   7
    A MORTAL MOTHER WOULD ON LETHE FIX . . . . .              346   2 DON JUAN   4     4   8
    THE MORTAL AND THE MARBLE STILL AT STRIFE . . . . .        27   3 DON JUAN   6    43   7
    OF WAR'S MOST MORTAL ENGINES TO THEIR FOES . . . .        116   3 DON JUAN   8     8   3
    HE SHEWED HIMSELF AS KIND AS MORTAL CAN . . . . .         144   3 DON JUAN   8    64   8
    NEVER HAD MORTAL MAN SUCH OPPORTUNITY . . . . .           187   3 DON JUAN   9     9   1
    OH THOU TOO MORTAL MAN WHAT IS PHILANTHROPY . . . .       192   3 DON JUAN   9    20   2
    AND THIS IS THE SOLE MORTAL WHO COULD GRAPPLE . . . .     225   3 DON JUAN  10     1   7
    AND CENTAUR-NESSUS GARB OF MORTAL CLOTHING . . . .        301   3 DON JUAN  11    65   4
    IF THAT A MORTAL EITHER COULD OR WOULD . . . . .          451   3 DON JUAN  14    93   V6
    THE FIRST IS RATHER MORE THAN MORTAL CAN DO . . . .       465   3 DON JUAN  15    21   3
    TREMENDOUS TO A MORTAL TYMPANUM . . . . . . .             557   3 DON JUAN  16   115   6
MORTALITY
    MAKES US FEEL OUR MORTALITY IN FACT . . . . .             428   2 DON JUAN   5    32   3
    MORTALITY THOU HAST THY MONTHLY BILLS . . . . .           117   3 DON JUAN   8    12   4
    GRACCHUS OF ALL MORTALITY WHO LEVELS . . . . . .          237   3 DON JUAN  10    25   2
MORTALITY'S
    AS ANY OF MORTALITY'S CONDITIONS . . . . . . .            191   3 DON JUAN   9    17   6
MORTAL'S
    THE OCEAN'S TIDES AND MORTAL'S BRAINS SHE SWAYS . . . .   506   3 DON JUAN  16    14   7
MORTALS
    OF MORTALS WHOM THY LURE HATH LED ALONG-- . . . .         78   2 DON JUAN   1   106   6
    FEW MORTALS KNOW WHAT END THEY WOULD BE AT . . . .        93   2 DON JUAN   1   133   5
    THE HAPPIEST MORTALS EVEN AFTER DINNER-- . . . .         294   2 DON JUAN   3    36   2
    TO HELP THE TASTE OF MORTALS FOR ENNUI . . . . .         332   2 DON JUAN   3    97   V8
    INHERENT WHAT WE MORTALS CALL ROMANTIC . . . . .         353   2 DON JUAN   4    18   7
    OH FOOLISH MORTALS ALWAYS TAUGHT IN VAIN . . . .         101   3 DON JUAN   7    68   5
    OR HAWK OR BRIDE MOST MORTALS AFTER ONE . . . . .        122   3 DON JUAN   8    22   6
    WAS HAPPIEST AMONGST MORTALS ANYWHERE . . . . .          143   3 DON JUAN   8    61   5
    AS HELL--MERE MORTALS WHO THEIR POWER ABUSE-- . . . .    173   3 DON JUAN   8   123   7
    'TIS NOT IN MORTALS TO COMMAND SUCCESS . . . .           366   3 DON JUAN  13    18   1
    WHICH MORTALS GENEROUSLY WOULD DIVIDE . . . . .          367   3 DON JUAN  13    19   7
    AND THEREFORE MORTALS CAVIL NOT AT ALL . . . . .         503   3 DON JUAN  16     6   1
MORTALS'
    THINGS WHICH IN HUNGRY MORTALS' EYES FIND FAVOUR . . . . 437   2 DON JUAN   5    47   3
MORTARS
    IF HOMER HAD FOUND MORTARS READY MADE . . . . . .        106   3 DON JUAN   7    78   4
MORTGAGE
    A MORTGAGE ON HUMANITY'S ESTATE-- . . . . . . .          105   3 DON JUAN   7    76   6
    THERE WERE TWO LAWYERS BUSY ON A MORTGAGE . . . . .      530   3 DON JUAN  16    60   1
```

	PAGE	VOL	CANTO	STANZA	LV
MORTIFIED					
DEEMING THE SAGE WOULD BE MUCH MORTIFIED	522	3	DON JUAN 16	43	5
MOSCOW					
WHICH MAY BE NAMES AT MOSCOW INTO RHYME	74	3	DON JUAN 7	16	2
YOUR ARM AND I'LL BET MOSCOW TO A DOLLAR	160	3	DON JUAN 8	97	7
WHO MARCHED TO MOSCOW LED BY FAME THE SYREN	253	3	DON JUAN 10	58	6
BUT JUAN WAS MY MOSCOW AND FALIERO	296	3	DON JUAN 11	56	1
MOSCOW'S					
MADRID'S AND MOSCOW'S CLIMES WERE OF A PIECE	239	3	DON JUAN 10	30	8
MOSES					
LIKE MOSES OR MELANCTHON WHO HAVE NE'ER	193	3	DON JUAN 9	21	2
LIKE MOSES OR LIKE COBBETT WHO HAVE NE'ER	193	3	DON JUAN 9	21	V2
MOSLEM					
THE MOSLEM TOO HAD LOST BOTH SHIPS AND MEN	82	3	DON JUAN 7	31	1
THEIR DRESS WAS MOSLEM BUT YOU MIGHT HAVE GUESSED	96	3	DON JUAN 7	57	3
WHEN UP THE BRISTLING MOSLEM ROSE AT LAST	115	3	DON JUAN 8	7	3
WAS MUCH REGRETTED) FOR THE MOSLEM MEN	147	3	DON JUAN 8	71	7
A DYING MOSLEM WHO HAD FELT THE FOOT	153	3	DON JUAN 8	84	1
THERE'S NOT A MOSLEM THAT HATH YIELDED SWORD	155	3	DON JUAN 8	87	2
THE MOSLEM ORPHAN WENT WITH HER PROTECTOR	182	3	DON JUAN 8	141	1
MOSLEMS					
WAS SPARED--THREE THOUSAND MOSLEMS PERISHED HERE	152	3	DON JUAN 8	81	7
THESE BLACK-EYED VIRGINS MAKE THE MOSLEMS FIGHT	168	3	DON JUAN 8	114	5
MOSQUE					
HE WENT TO MOSQUE IN STATE AND SAID HIS PRAYERS	496	2	DON JUAN 5	148	1
AND THE MOSQUE CRESCENT STRUGGLED INTO SIGHT	49	3	DON JUAN 6	86	4
BE UNIMPEDED BY THE PROUDEST MOSQUE	99	3	DON JUAN 7	63	8
A MOSQUE SO NOBLE FLUNG LIKE PEARLS TO SWINE	262	3	DON JUAN 10	75	8
MOSQUES					
WHILE MOSQUES AND STREETS BENEATH HIS EYES LIKE THATCH	178	3	DON JUAN 8	133	3
MOSTLY					
GEMS GOLD AND SILVER FORM'D THE SERVICE MOSTLY	306	2	DON JUAN 3	61	7
AND GEMS--AND GOLD--AND SILVER--GLITTERED MOSTLY	306	2	DON JUAN 3	61	V7
WHICH MOSTLY ENDS IN SOME SMALL BREACH OF BOTH	493	2	DON JUAN 5	142	8
BUT THEY WERE MOSTLY NERVOUS SIX-FOOT FELLOWS	205	3	DON JUAN 9	46	7
ESPECIALLY FOR FOREIGNERS--AND MOSTLY	283	3	DON JUAN 11	31	2
TASTES THEIR FIRST SEASON (MOSTLY IF THEY HAVE MONEY)	330	3	DON JUAN 12	31	8
PROFESSIONAL--ALL CLASSES MOSTLY PULL	403	3	DON JUAN 13	95	V4
BUT MOSTLY SINGS OF HUMAN THINGS AND ACTS--	416	3	DON JUAN 14	13	4
BUT THEN 'TIS MOSTLY ON THE WEAKER SIDE	466	3	DON JUAN 15	23	1
MOT					
TO INTRODUCE A BON MOT HEAD AND EARS	408	3	DON JUAN 13	109	4
IMBIBED THE GAY BON MOT OR HAPPY HOAX	540	3	DON JUAN 16	83	5
MOTH					
TO GRATIFY LIKE A HUGE MOTH THIS ONE SENSE	88	3	DON JUAN 7	44	8
AS CARELESSLY AS HURLS THE MOTH HER WING	170	3	DON JUAN 8	118	3
MOTHER					
AND ALSO OF HIS MOTHER IF YOU'D RATHER	25	2	DON JUAN 1	7	8
HIS MOTHER WAS A LEARNED LADY FAMED	26	2	DON JUAN 1	10	1
AN ONLY SON LEFT WITH AN ONLY MOTHER	42	2	DON JUAN 1	37	7
IS MORE THAN I KNOW--BUT DON JUAN'S MOTHER	47	2	DON JUAN 1	46	7
BETWEEN HIS TUTORS CONFESSOR AND MOTHER	48	2	DON JUAN 1	49	8
AND EVERYBODY BUT HIS MOTHER DEEM'D	51	2	DON JUAN 1	54	4
AND NEXT DAY PAID A VISIT TO HIS MOTHER	63	2	DON JUAN 1	76	2
AND THEN THE MOTHER CRIES THE FATHER SWEARS	75	2	DON JUAN 1	100	7
'TWAS SURELY VERY WRONG IN JUAN'S MOTHER	80	2	DON JUAN 1	110	5
MY MOTHER DREAM'D NOT IN MY NATAL HOUR	106	2	DON JUAN 1	155	7
HIS MOTHER AND A MISTRESS NONE ALIVE	164	2	DON JUAN 2	15	2
FAREWELL MY MOTHER AND SINCE ALL IS O'ER	166	2	DON JUAN 2	18	6
SUCH THINGS A MOTHER HAD NOT KNOWN HER SON	210	2	DON JUAN 2	102	3
WHO WATCH'D HIM LIKE A MOTHER WOULD HAVE FED	239	2	DON JUAN 2	158	2
THEN CAME HER FREEDOM FOR SHE HAD NO MOTHER	248	2	DON JUAN 2	175	1
AND MOTHER BROTHER GUARDIAN SHE HAD NONE	252	2	DON JUAN 2	182	3
MOTHER OF PEARL AND CORAL THE LESS COSTLY	306	2	DON JUAN 3	61	8
WITH MOTHER OF PEARL OR IVORY STOOD AT HAND	310	2	DON JUAN 3	69	3
A MORTAL MOTHER WOULD ON LETHE FIX	346	2	DON JUAN 4	4	8
HER MOTHER WAS A MOORISH MAID FROM FEZ	373	2	DON JUAN 4	54	7
I'LL SWEAR--AS MOTHER WORDSWORTH SWORE	404	2	DON JUAN 4	109	V5
PRESERVE YOUR STATE--THOUGH EVE EARTH'S MOTHER FELL	460	2	DON JUAN 5	84	V6
HER TITLE WAS THE MOTHER OF THE MAIDS	21	3	DON JUAN 6	30	8
WHETHER SHE WAS A MOTHER I KNOW NOT	21	3	DON JUAN 6	31	1
OR WHETHER THEY WERE MAIDS WHO CALLED HER MOTHER	21	3	DON JUAN 6	31	2
BUT HERE THE MOTHER OF THE MAIDS DREW NEAR	29	3	DON JUAN 6	46	1
MOTHER OF PEARL AND PORPHYRY AND MARBLE	55	3	DON JUAN 6	98	1
CLASHED 'GAINST THE SCYMITAR AND BABE AND MOTHER	146	3	DON JUAN 8	69	4
FOR THE SAME BLOW WHICH LAID HER MOTHER HERE	159	3	DON JUAN 8	95	4
THE FIFTH WHO BY A CHRISTIAN MOTHER NOURISHED	166	3	DON JUAN 8	110	5
OR WIDOW MAID OR MOTHER SHE CAN CHANGE HER	214	3	DON JUAN 9	64	5
HIS MOTHER DONNA INEZ FINDING TOO	240	3	DON JUAN 10	31	1
AND NO LESS TO GOD'S SON AS WELL AS MOTHER	240	3	DON JUAN 10	32	2
REVERED THE SOIL OF THOSE TRUE SONS THE MOTHER	265	3	DON JUAN 10	81	7
PERHAPS YOU'LL HAVE A LETTER FROM THE MOTHER	343	3	DON JUAN 12	60	1
HIS MANNER SHOWED HIM SPRUNG FROM A HIGH MOTHER	369	3	DON JUAN 13	24	6
THE VIRGIN MOTHER OF THE GOD-BORN CHILD	387	3	DON JUAN 13	61	2
SINCE HE WAS SURE HIS MOTHER WOULD FALL SICK	478	3	DON JUAN 15	50	3
SHOW OFF--TO PLEASE THEIR COMPANY OR MOTHER	522	3	DON JUAN 16	44	8
MOTHER'S					
HIS MOTHER'S FAMILY CAME OUT OF ARRAGON	43	2	DON JUAN 1	38	V4
AT LEAST IT SEEM'D SO AND HIS MOTHER'S JOY	49	2	DON JUAN 1	50	6

MOTHER'S   (CONTINUED)
```
    TO WHOM SHE KNEW HIS MOTHER'S FAME WAS DEAR . . . . . .  118  2 DON JUAN  1  176   8
    HUSH'D AS THE BABE UPON ITS MOTHER'S BREAST . . . . . .  235  2 DON JUAN  2  148   2
    THOU BRING'ST THE CHILD TOO TO THE MOTHER'S BREAST . . .  338  2 DON JUAN  3  107   8
    BEAUTY AND LOVE WERE HAIDEE'S MOTHER'S DOWER  . . . .    374  2 DON JUAN  4   56   6
MOTHERS
    THE BEST OF MOTHERS AND OF EDUCATIONS . . . . . . . .    157  2 DON JUAN  2    1   5
    SUCH AS THE DORIC MOTHERS BORE . . . . . . . . . .       325  2 DON JUAN  3 L 13   4
    HOW MOTHERS LOVE THEIR CHILDREN'S SQUALLS AND CHUCKLINGS  488  2 DON JUAN  5  133   6
    THOUGH NOT ALL BORN OF THE SAME SIRES AND MOTHERS . . .  491  2 DON JUAN  5  138   6
    THEIR MOTHERS AS THE ANTIPODES OF TIMON . . . . . .      53   3 DON JUAN  6   94   2
    CHEERFUL AS CHILDREN CLIMB THE BREASTS OF MOTHERS . . .  119  3 DON JUAN  8   15   6
    DAUGHTERS ADMIRED HIS DRESS AND PIOUS MOTHERS . . . .    293  3 DON JUAN 11   48   7
    SOME MAIDS HAVE BEEN MADE WIVES SOME MERELY MOTHERS . .  308  3 DON JUAN 11   81   4
    THE WATCHFUL MOTHERS AND THE CAREFUL SISTERS . . . .     331  3 DON JUAN 12   32   3
    THAT DAUGHTERS OF SUCH MOTHERS AS MAY KNOW . . . . .     337  3 DON JUAN 12   46   4
MOTHS
    THOSE BRIGHT MOTHS FLUTTERING ROUND A DYING FLAME . . .  349  3 DON JUAN 12   72   4
MOTION
    OF ENDLESS TORMENTS AND PERPETUAL MOTION . . . . . .     17   2 DON JUAN  D   13   8
    WHEN OLD KING DAVID'S BLOOD GREW DULL IN MOTION . . .    113  2 DON JUAN  1  168   5
    WHICH LEFT SCARCE ROOM FOR MOTION OR EXERTION . . . .    189  2 DON JUAN  2   63   2
    AND COOKS IN MOTION WITH THEIR CLEAN ARMS BARED . . .    439  2 DON JUAN  5   50   6
    WE SHOULD HAVE FOUND OUT THE PERPETUAL MOTION . . . .    475  2 DON JUAN  5  112   8
    MOTION WAS IN THEIR DAYS REST IN THEIR SLUMBERS . . .    145  3 DON JUAN  8   67   1
    IN MOTION BUT SHE HERE TOO MUCH REFINED-- . . . . . .    492  3 DON JUAN 15   81   7
MOTIONED
    HE MOTIONED THEM TO STOP AT SOME SMALL DISTANCE  . . .   440  2 DON JUAN  5   51   5
    MOTIONED TO JUAN TO APPROACH AND THEN . . . . . . .      470  2 DON JUAN  5  102   2
MOTIONLESS
    THERE SHE LAY MOTIONLESS AND SEEM'D UPSET . . . . . .    172  2 DON JUAN  2   31   1
MOTIONS
    EVEN HER MINUTEST MOTIONS WENT AS WELL  . . . . . .      30   2 DON JUAN  1   17   5
    FOLLOWING ANTONIA'S MOTIONS HERE AND THERE . . . . .     109  2 DON JUAN  1  160   2
MOTIVE
    SHE HAD SOME OTHER MOTIVE MUCH MORE NEAR . . . . . .     75   2 DON JUAN  1  101   3
    BUT WHAT THAT MOTIVE WAS I SHA'N'T SAY HERE . . . . .    75   2 DON JUAN  1  101   5
    THERE MIGHT BE ONE MORE MOTIVE WHICH MAKES TWO . . . .   118  2 DON JUAN  1  177   1
    BUT A THIRD MOTIVE WAS AS PROBABLY . . . . . . . .       78   3 DON JUAN  7   24   5
    I HATE A MOTIVE LIKE A LINGERING BOTTLE . . . . . .      435  3 DON JUAN 14   58   1
    A STRONG EXTERNAL MOTIVE AND IN THIS . . . . . . .       544  3 DON JUAN 16   92   5
    ITS MOTIVE FOR THAT CHARITY WE OWE . . . . . . . .       553  3 DON JUAN 16  106   3
MOTIVES
    BUT I HAVE MOTIVES WHETHER WISE OR SILLY . . . . . .     370  3 DON JUAN 13   27   3
    WITH MOTIVES THE MOST CLASSICAL AND PURE . . . . . .     528  3 DON JUAN 16   57   3
MOTLEY
    MY BOY --SAID HE AMIDST THIS MOTLEY CREW . . . . . .     417  2 DON JUAN  5   13   1
    NOR WORN THE MOTLEY MANTLE OF A POET . . . . . . .       467  3 DON JUAN 15   24   7
MOTS
    AWAIT THOSE WHO HAVE STUDIED THEIR BON MOTS . . . . .    403  3 DON JUAN 13   97   8
MOTTO
    THE MOTTO CUT UPON A WHITE CORNELIAN . . . . . . .       134  2 DON JUAN  1  198   7
    QUE SCAIS-JE WAS THE MOTTO OF MONTAIGNE . . . . . .      191  3 DON JUAN  9   17   1
MOULD
    EVEN OF THE HIGHEST FOR A FEMALE MOULD  . . . . . .      217  2 DON JUAN  2  116   5
    THE LIMB WHICH IT ADORN'D ITS ONLY MOULD . . . . . .     312  2 DON JUAN  3   71   4
    THRICE FORTUNATE WHO OF THAT FRAGILE MOULD . . . . .     350  2 DON JUAN  4   11   2
MOULDED
    A LOVELY BEING SCARCELY FORM'D OR MOULDED  . . . . .     475  3 DON JUAN 15   43   7
MOULDY
    MAN 'MIDST THY MOULDY MAMMOTHS GRAND CULVIER . . . .     250  3 DON JUAN 10   52   4
MOUNT
    AND LORD MOUNT COFFEEHOUSE THE IRISH PEER . . . . .      102  2 DON JUAN  1  149   7
    SOME THOUGHT IT WAS MOUNT AETNA SOME THE HIGHLANDS . .   209  2 DON JUAN  2  100   7
    AND HE MUST NEEDS MOUNT NEARER TO THE MOON . . . . .     333  2 DON JUAN  3   99   7
    I DOUBT FEW READERS E'ER WOULD MOUNT THE BREACH . . .    83   3 DON JUAN  7   35   8
    HE SHOWED THEM HOW TO MOUNT A LADDER (WHICH . . . .      93   3 DON JUAN  7   52   7
    YOU'LL MOUNT WITH OUR YOUNG HERO THE CONVEYANCE  . .     248  3 DON JUAN 10   49   3
    MOUNT PLEASANT AS CONTAINING NOUGHT TO PLEASE . . . .    278  3 DON JUAN 11   21   3
MOUNTAIN
    LIKE MOUNTAIN MISTS AT LENGTH DISSOLVED IN RAIN . . .    380  2 DON JUAN  4   66   8
    AND LOVE THE LAND OF MOUNTAIN AND OF FLOOD . . . . .     234  3 DON JUAN 10   19   8
    SLIPS FROM THE MOUNTAIN IN THE MONTH OF JUNE . . . .     517  3 DON JUAN 16   38   V6
MOUNTAIN-CRESCENT
    WITH THE FAR MOUNTAIN-CRESCENT HALF SURROUNDED . . . .   252  2 DON JUAN  2  183   5
MOUNTAINEERS
    ALL MOUNTAINEERS WITH DREAMS THAT THEY ARE NIGH LANDS  . 523  3 DON JUAN 16   46   6
MOUNTAIN'S
    LIKE TO A TORRENT WHICH A MOUNTAIN'S BASE . . . . .      231  2 DON JUAN  2  141   5
MOUNTAINS
    AND THE FAR MOUNTAINS WAX A LITTLE HOARY . . . . . .     94   2 DON JUAN  1  134   4
    AND HIGHER GREW THE MOUNTAINS AS THEY DREW . . . . .     209  2 DON JUAN  2  100   2
    BRIGHT PHOEBUS WHILE THE MOUNTAINS STILL ARE WET . . .   230  2 DON JUAN  2  139   5
    ON MOUNTAINS TOPS MORE HEAVENLY WHITE THAN HER . . .     314  2 DON JUAN  3   76   4
    THE MOUNTAINS LOOK ON MARATHON-- . . . . . . . .         321  2 DON JUAN  3 L  3   1
    MY ALTARS ARE THE MOUNTAINS AND THE OCEAN . . . . .      336  2 DON JUAN  3  104   6
    MAKES MOUNTAINS PASSABLE AND BY HEAVEN'S BLESSING . . .  215  3 DON JUAN  9   66   V7
    THE WORST TO KNOW IT--WHEN THE MOUNTAINS REAR . . . .    412  3 DON JUAN 14    5   4
    MOUNTAINS AND ALL WE CAN BE MOST SUBLIME AT . . . . .    423  3 DON JUAN 14   29   6
```

```
                                                            PAGE VOL     CANTO  STANZA LN
MOUNTAIN-SKIRTED
    A VAST UNTILL'D AND MOUNTAIN-SKIRTED PLAIN  . . . . .  . 386  2 DON JUAN  4    77   2
MOUNTAIN-STREAM
    DRINKING SALT-WATER LIKE A MOUNTAIN-STREAM  . . . . .  . 198  2 DON JUAN  2    79   6
MOUNTED
    A BETTER CAVALIER NE'ER MOUNTED HORSE . . . . . . .   .  26  2 DON JUAN  1     9   5
    OR BEING MOUNTED E'ER GOT DOWN AGAIN . . . . . . .   .   26  2 DON JUAN  1     9   6
    A FAVOURITE HORSE FALLEN LAME JUST AS HE'S MOUNTED  . . .  16  3 DON JUAN  6    21   4
    BEING GRENADIERS THEY MOUNTED ONE BY ONE . . . . . .  . 119  3 DON JUAN  8    15   5
MOUNTING
    MOUNTING AT TIMES TO A TRANSPARENT GLOW . . . . . .   .  55  2 DON JUAN  1    61   5
    CAME MOUNTING QUICKLY UP FOR IT WAS NOW . . . . . .   . 135  3 DON JUAN  8    45   2
MOUNTS
    'TIS GRANTED AND THE VALET MOUNTS THE DICKEY--  . . .  . 380  3 DON JUAN 13    47   1
MOURN
    TO MOURN ALONE THE LOVE WHICH HAS UNDONE . . . . .   . 131  2 DON JUAN  1   194 V8
    NOT ALL LONE MATRONS FOR THEIR HUSBANDS MOURN . . . . . 287  2 DON JUAN  3    23   3
    I MOURN BUT FOR THE PAST--I LOVED A MAID . . . .  . . . 420  2 DON JUAN  5    18   2
    WHICH OF THE ARMIES WOULD HAVE CAUSE TO MOURN . . .  . 150  3 DON JUAN  8    77   6
    YOUR VEINS OF COCKNEY SPIRIT SMILE OR MOURN . . . .   . 264  3 DON JUAN 10    80   6
    IF BRITAIN MOURN HER BLEAKNESS WE CAN TELL HER . .  . . 394  3 DON JUAN 13    76   7
    PERHAPS THERE MIGHT BE VICES WHICH WOULD MOURN IT . . . 400  3 DON JUAN 13    89   8
    WHEN AN HEIR IS BORN HE IS HEARD TO MOURN . . . .  . . 519  3 DON JUAN 16  L  4   1
MOURN'D
    WHICH MOURN'D THE POWER OF TIME'S OR TEMPEST'S MARCH . . 386  3 DON JUAN 13    59   7
MOURNER
    AND LOOK ON AS A MOURNER OR A SCORNER . . . . . . .  . 303  3 DON JUAN 11    69   6
    FOR SHE WAS NOT A SENTIMENTAL MOURNER . . . . . .   . 532  3 DON JUAN 16    65   4
MOURNFUL
    MOURNFUL--BUT MOURNFUL OF ANOTHER'S CRIME . . . .  . . 476  3 DON JUAN 15    45   6
    MOURNFUL--BUT MOURNFUL OF ANOTHER'S CRIME . . . .  . . 476  3 DON JUAN 15    45   6
MOURNING
    AND NIGHT IS FLUNG OFF LIKE A MOURNING SUIT . . . .   . 230  2 DON JUAN  2   139   7
    OUR DAYS AND PUT ONE'S SERVANTS INTO MOURNING . . .  . 278  2 DON JUAN  3     7   8
    AND PUT HIS HOUSE IN MOURNING SEVERAL WEEKS . . . .   . 295  2 DON JUAN  3    38   4
    THIS REVEL SEEM'D A CURIOUS MODE OF MOURNING . . . .  . 300  2 DON JUAN  3    49   8
MOURNS
    AH SURELY NOTHING DIES BUT SOMETHING MOURNS . . . .  . 338  2 DON JUAN  3   108   8
    MOURNS O'ER THE BEAUTY OF THE CYCLADES . . . . . .   . 383  2 DON JUAN  4    72   8
MOUSE
    BUT LIKE CONVEYING TO THE CAT THE MOUSE . . . . . .  . 225  2 DON JUAN  2   130   3
    A SUPERNATURAL AGENT--OR A MOUSE  . . . . . . . .   . 509  3 DON JUAN 16    20   6
    IT WAS NO MOUSE BUT LO A MONK ARRAYED . . . . . .  . . 510  3 DON JUAN 16    21   1
MOUSKIN
    KOCLOBSKI KOURAKIN AND MOUSKIN POUSKIN . . . . . .   .  75  3 DON JUAN  7    17   2
MOUTH
    INTO HIS DYING CHILD'S MOUTH--BUT IN VAIN . . . .  . . 203  2 DON JUAN  2    89   8
    'TWAS BENDING CLOSE O'ER HIS AND THE SMALL MOUTH  . . . 215  2 DON JUAN  2   113   1
    BREATHING ALL GENTLY O'ER HIS CHEEK AND MOUTH . . .  . 245  2 DON JUAN  2   168   7
    THE SPOUTING BLOOD GUSHED THROUGH HER MOUTH HER EYES . . 376  2 DON JUAN  4    59 V1
    A TURK WITH BEADS IN HAND AND PIPE IN MOUTH . . . .   . 387  2 DON JUAN  4    78   6
    THAT WOMANKIND HAD BUT ONE ROSY MOUTH . . . . . .   .  19  3 DON JUAN  6    27   7
    THE MOUTH OF SOME ONE IN HIS PLAYS SO DOATING  . . .  .  77  3 DON JUAN  7    21   7
    MARK HOW ITS LIPLESS MOUTH GRINS WITHOUT BREATH . . . . 188  3 DON JUAN  9    11   8
    HER FACE WAS NOBLE HER EYES FINE MOUTH GRACIOUS . . . . 211  3 DON JUAN  9    58   8
    AND LIGHTED FIRST HER EYE AND THEN HER MOUTH . . . .  . 213  3 DON JUAN  9    61   2
    WERE HIS EYES OPEN--YES AND HIS MOUTH TOO . . . .  . . 557  3 DON JUAN 16   115   1
    STATED) HIS MOUTH WHAT OPENED NEXT--THE DOOR . . . .  . 557  3 DON JUAN 16   115   8
MOUTHEY
    THE SECOND DRUNK THE THIRD SO QUAINT AND MOUTHEY . . . . 139  2 DON JUAN  1   205   4
MOUTHS
    FOR WHICH THEIR MOUTHS GAPED LIKE THE CRACKS OF EARTH . . 201  2 DON JUAN  2    84   2
    WITH AMBER MOUTH'S OF GREATER PRICE OR LESS . . . .   . 441  2 DON JUAN  5    53   6
    THE SPRING GUSH'D THROUGH GRIM MOUTHS OF GRANITE MADE . . 389  3 DON JUAN 13    65   5
    BECAUSE IT BREEDS NO MORE MOUTHS THAN IT NOURISHES . . . 471  3 DON JUAN 15    35   4
MOVE
    WHERE HEART AND SOUL AND SENSE IN CONCERT MOVE . . . . 254  2 DON JUAN  2   186   5
    ONE MAN ALONE AT FIRST HER HEART CAN MOVE  . . . . .  . 276  2 DON JUAN  3     3   6
    WOUNDED AND CHAIN'D SO THAT HE CANNOT MOVE . . . .  . . 371  2 DON JUAN  4    51   7
    CONCEIVED THAT PHRASE WAS QUITE ENOUGH TO MOVE  . . .  . 478  2 DON JUAN  5   116   8
    OR IF THESE DO NOT MOVE YOU DON'T FORGET  . . . . .   . 174  3 DON JUAN  8   125   3
    CALLED BROTHERLY AFFECTION COULD NOT MOVE . . . . .   . 250  3 DON JUAN 10    53   6
    THERE IS A MOVE SET DOWN FOR JOY OR SORROW . . . .  . . 288  3 DON JUAN 11    42   4
    THE STONE OF SYSIPHUS IF ONCE WE MOVE . . . . . .   . 447  3 DON JUAN 14    86   3
    YET COULD NOT SPEAK OR MOVE BUT ON ITS BASE . . . .   . 510  3 DON JUAN 16    23   4
MOVEABLES
    THE MOVEABLES WERE PRODIGALLY RICH . . . . . . .   . 449  2 DON JUAN  5    65   4
MOVED
    MOVED BY THE CHINESE NYMPH OF TEARS GREEN TEA . . . . . 372  2 DON JUAN  4    52   2
    JUAN WHO FOR AN INSTANT HAD BEEN MOVED  . . . . . .   . 481  2 DON JUAN  5   121   2
    JUAN WAS MOVED HE HAD MADE UP HIS MIND  . . . . . .   . 492  2 DON JUAN  5   141   1
    AND THEN MOVED ON AGAIN WITH RAPID PACE . . . . . .  .  61  3 DON JUAN  6   111   2
    HE MOVED SOME HUNDRED MILES OFF FOR A STATION . . . . . 144  3 DON JUAN  8    64   3
    NOW MOVED WITH PITY EVEN AS SOMETIMES NODS . . . .  . . 164  3 DON JUAN  8   106   6
    NOR BY MUSTACHIOS MOVED WERE LET ALONE  . . . . . .   . 344  3 DON JUAN 12    61   6
    HIS INEXPERIENCE MOVED HER GENTLE RUTH  . . . . . .   . 432  3 DON JUAN 14    51   7
    THEY MOVED LIKE STARS UNITED IN THEIR SPHERES . . . . . 447  3 DON JUAN 14    87   3
    HE MOVED AS SHADOWY AS THE SISTERS WEIRD . . . . .  . . 510  3 DON JUAN 16    21   6
MOVEMENT
    THEN WITH A SUDDEN MOVEMENT HE WITHDREW . . . . . .  . 370  2 DON JUAN  4    48   1
```

	PAGE	VOL		CANTO	STANZA	LN

MOVEMENT   (CONTINUED)
    HER FEET THAT HER FIRST MOVEMENT WAS TO STOOP . . . . . . 44 3 DON JUAN 6 77 3
    THE COLUMNS WERE IN MOVEMENT ONE AND ALL . . . . . . 116 3 DON JUAN 8 9 1
MOVEMENTS
    THOSE MOVEMENTS THOSE IMPROVEMENTS IN OUR BODIES . . . . 220 3 DON JUAN 9 75 1
    THE TOUT ENSEMBLE OF HIS MOVEMENTS WORE A . . . . . 428 3 DON JUAN 14 40 5
MOVES
    MOVES--FEMALE HEARTS ARE SUCH A GENIAL SOIL . . . . . 480 2 DON JUAN 5 120 3
    OF SOBER REASON WHERESOE'ER IT MOVES . . . . . . 284 3 DON JUAN 11 33 6
MOVING
    THE MOVING FIGURES AND THE SPARKLING SHEEN . . . . . 289 2 DON JUAN 3 27 6
    THAT GOOD OLD STEAM-BOAT WHICH KEEPS VERSES MOVING . . 219 3 DON JUAN 9 74 4
MOWER
    IF BUT TO KEEP THY CREDIT AS A MOWER . . . . 433 3 DON JUAN 14 53 8
MOWING
    BY MOWING CHRISTIANS DOWN ON EVERY SIDE . . . . . . 165 3 DON JUAN 8 107 3
MOWS
    AND FLESH (WHICH DEATH MOWS DOWN TO HAY) IS GRASS . . . 147 2 DON JUAN 1 220 4
MOZART'S
    AN AIR AS SENTIMENTAL AS MOZART'S . . . . 292 3 DON JUAN 11 47 3
MR
    THOU SHALT NOT COVET MR SOTHEBY'S MUSE . . . . . . 140 2 DON JUAN 1 206 1
    BUT FOR THE MAKER MR MANN OF LONDON . . . . 171 2 DON JUAN 2 29 8
    LEANDER MR EKENHEAD AND I DID . . . . 211 2 DON JUAN 2 105 8
MRS
    OR MRS TRIMMER'S BOOKS ON EDUCATION . . . . 29 2 DON JUAN 1 16 3
    FOR THE FIRST MRS MILTON LEFT HIS HOUSE . . . . . . 328 2 DON JUAN 3 91 8
    BECAUSE THEY ARE SO--A MALE MRS FRY . . . . 266 3 DON JUAN 10 84 6
    OH MRS FRY WHY GO TO NEWGATE WHY . . . . 266 3 DON JUAN 10 85 1
    I THOUGHT YOU HAD MORE RELIGION MRS FRY . . . . . . 267 3 DON JUAN 10 85 8
    AND MRS RABBI THE RICH BANKER'S SQUAW . . . . . . 396 3 DON JUAN 13 79 6
    ALSO THE HONOURABLE MRS SLEEP . . . . 396 3 DON JUAN 13 79 7
    WAS MADE BY MRS ADAMS WHERE SHE CRIES . . . . 403 3 DON JUAN 13 96 7
MS
    SOME DULL MS OBLIVION LONG HAS SANK . . . . 327 2 DON JUAN 3 89 5
MUCH
    WHO HAS NOT SEEN IT WILL BE MUCH TO PITY . . . . . . 25 2 DON JUAN 1 8 3
    FINDING THEMSELVES SO VERY MUCH EXCEEDED . . . . . . 26 2 DON JUAN 1 10 7
    I DON'T CHOOSE TO SAY MUCH UPON THIS HEAD . . . . . 33 2 DON JUAN 1 22 5
    I CAN'T SAY MUCH FOR FRIEND OR YET RELATION) . . . . . 38 2 DON JUAN 1 32 5
    IS BROUGHT UP MUCH MORE WISELY THAN ANOTHER . . . . . 42 2 DON JUAN 1 37 8
    MUCH INTO ALL HIS STUDIES SHE INQUIRED . . . . . . 43 2 DON JUAN 1 39 5
    IN ALL THESE HE WAS MUCH AND DEEPLY READ . . . . . . 44 2 DON JUAN 1 40 5
    SO MUCH INDEED AS TO BE DOWNRIGHT RUDE . . . . . . 45 2 DON JUAN 1 43 6
    TOO MUCH THEIR MODEST BARD BY THIS OMISSION . . . . . 46 2 DON JUAN 1 44 5
    I RECOMMEND AS MUCH TO EVERY WIFE . . . . . . 48 2 DON JUAN 1 48 8
    RUIN'D ITS BLOOD BUT MUCH IMPROVED ITS FLESH . . . . . 53 2 DON JUAN 1 58 2
    I SHALL HAVE MUCH TO SPEAK ABOUT) AND SHE . . . . . 54 2 DON JUAN 1 59 7
    IS MUCH MORE COMMON WHERE THE CLIMATE'S SULTRY . . . . 56 2 DON JUAN 1 63 8
    WAS NEITHER MUCH BELOVED NOR YET ABHORR'D . . . . . 57 2 DON JUAN 1 65 3
    WHICH TIME HAD LATELY RENDER'D MUCH MORE CHASTE . . . . 58 2 DON JUAN 1 67 2
    AND CERTAINLY THIS COURSE WAS MUCH THE BEST . . . . . 58 2 DON JUAN 1 67 4
    AND MUCH EMBARRASSMENT IN EITHER EYE . . . . 60 2 DON JUAN 1 70 4
    NOT SCANDAL'S FANGS COULD FIX ON MUCH THAT'S SEIZABLE . . 66 2 DON JUAN 1 83 3
    SO MUCH FOR JULIA NOW WE'LL TURN TO JUAN . . . . . . 68 2 DON JUAN 1 86 1
    HE FOUND HOW MUCH OLD TIME HAD BEEN A WINNER-- . . . . 72 2 DON JUAN 1 94 7
    SHE HAD SOME OTHER MOTIVE MUCH MORE NEAR . . . . . . 75 2 DON JUAN 1 101 3
    LEAVING AT LAST NOT MUCH BESIDES CHRONOLOGY . . . . . 76 2 DON JUAN 1 103 7
    BECAUSE THAT NUMBER RARELY MUCH ENDEARS . . . . . 78 2 DON JUAN 1 107 5
    AND WHILE SHE PONDER'D THIS BESIDES MUCH MORE . . . . 80 2 DON JUAN 1 109 6
    BUT WHAT HE DID IS MUCH WHAT YOU WOULD DO . . . . . 81 2 DON JUAN 1 112 2
    A LITTLE STILL SHE STROVE AND MUCH REPENTED . . . . . 84 2 DON JUAN 1 117 7
    I'M VERY SORRY VERY MUCH ASHAMED . . . . . . 85 2 DON JUAN 1 119 7
    AND FOUND MUCH LINEN LACE AND SEVERAL PAIR . . . . . 99 2 DON JUAN 1 143 5
    SO MUCH HE ALWAYS DOUBTED I WAS MARRIED-- . . . . . 101 2 DON JUAN 1 147 7
    DREST TO RECEIVE SO MUCH GOOD COMPANY . . . . . . 106 2 DON JUAN 1 156 8
    WITH MUCH SUSPICION IN HIS ATTITUDE . . . . . . 109 2 DON JUAN 1 160 3
    AND TREATING A YOUNG WIFE WITH SO MUCH RIGOUR . . . . 110 2 DON JUAN 1 161 4
    WITH MUCH HEART-FELT RELUCTANCE BE IT SAID . . . . . 112 2 DON JUAN 1 165 7
    SO MUCH AS WHEN WE CALL OUR OLD DEBTS IN . . . . . 113 2 DON JUAN 1 167 6
    A PAIR OF SHOES--WHAT THEN NOT MUCH IF THEY . . . . . 121 2 DON JUAN 1 181 1
    (NO ONE CAN TELL HOW MUCH I GRIEVE TO SAY) . . . . . 121 2 DON JUAN 1 181 3
    MUCH LONGER--THINK OF HUSBANDS' LOVERS' LIVES . . . . 123 2 DON JUAN 1 185 7
    TO LOVE TOO MUCH HAS BEEN THE ONLY ART . . . . . . 130 2 DON JUAN 1 192 5
    MY HEART IS NOT MUCH GREENER AND IN SHORT I . . . . . 143 2 DON JUAN 1 213 4
    IT MATTERS NOT MUCH HOW BY GOOD OR ILL . . . . . . 146 2 DON JUAN 1 218 V3
    I WOULD TO HEAVEN THAT I WERE SO MUCH CLAY-- . . . . 156 2 DON JUAN 1 V 8 1
    PUZZLED HIS TUTORS VERY MUCH OF COURSE . . . . . 158 2 DON JUAN 2 2 8
    A HUSBAND RATHER OLD NOT MUCH IN UNITY . . . . . . 158 2 DON JUAN 2 3 7
    I CAN'T DESCRIBE IT THOUGH SO MUCH IT STRIKE . . . . . 159 2 DON JUAN 2 5 7
    SO THAT HE HAD MUCH BETTER CAUSE TO GRIEVE . . . . . 164 2 DON JUAN 2 15 3
    AND JUAN WEPT AND MUCH HE SIGH'D AND THOUGHT . . . . 165 2 DON JUAN 2 17 1
    SWEETS TO THE SWEET (I LIKE SO MUCH TO QUOTE . . . . 165 2 DON JUAN 2 17 3
    NO DOUBT HE WOULD HAVE BEEN MUCH MORE PATHETIC . . . . 167 2 DON JUAN 2 21 1
    BUT BE MUCH PUZZLED BY A COUGH AND COLD . . . . . 168 2 DON JUAN 2 22 3
    AND THOUGH 'TWAS NOT MUCH TO A NAVAL MIND . . . . . 170 2 DON JUAN 2 26 3
    THUS DROWNINGS ARE MUCH TALK'D OF BY THE DIVERS . . . . 172 2 DON JUAN 2 31 7
    THAT PASSENGERS WOULD FIND IT MUCH AMISS . . . . . 173 2 DON JUAN 2 33 3
    THERE'S NOUGHT NO DOUBT SO MUCH THE SPIRIT CALMS . . . 174 2 DON JUAN 2 34 1

MUCH   (CONTINUED)

TO WEATHER OUT MUCH LONGER THE DISTRESS . . . . . . 178 2 DON JUAN 2   41   3
UNLESS WITH PEOPLE WHO TOO MUCH HAVE QUAFF'D . . . . 183 2 DON JUAN 2   50   5
THOUGH ON THE WAVE'S HIGH TOP TOO MUCH TO SET . . . . 188 2 DON JUAN 2   60   3
BUT OF MATERIALS THAT MUCH SHOCK THE MUSE-- . . . . . 195 2 DON JUAN 2   74   6
FEEL NOW HIS APPETITE INCREASED MUCH MORE . . . . . . 198 2 DON JUAN 2   78   5
THEIR NUMBERS WERE MUCH THINN'D BY THIS INFLICTION . . 199 2 DON JUAN 2   80   1
BESIDES BEING MUCH AVERSE FROM SUCH A FATE . . . . . 199 2 DON JUAN 2   81   3
WITHOUT BEING MUCH MORE HORRIBLE THAN DANTE . . . . . 200 2 DON JUAN 2   83   8
I'VE SEEN MUCH FINER WOMEN RIPE AND REAL . . . . . . 218 2 DON JUAN 2   118   7
BECAUSE THE GOOD OLD MAN HAD SO MUCH NOUS . . . . . . 225 2 DON JUAN 2   130   5
FED UPON BEEF--I WON'T SAY MUCH OF BEER . . . . 238 2 DON JUAN 2   156   2
OR GREEK--THAT IS ALTHOUGH IT NOT MUCH MATTER'D . . . 240 2 DON JUAN 2   160   5
MUCH ENGLISH I CANNOT PRETEND TO SPEAK . . . . 243 2 DON JUAN 2   165   3
AND LOVE WHICH ALSO MUCH DEPENDS ON FOOD . . . . . . 246 2 DON JUAN 2   170 V4
TO LIVE WITH HIM FOREVER WERE TOO MUCH . . . . 247 2 DON JUAN 2   173   5
SO MUCH AS TO PROPOSE TO TAKE A WALK-- . . . . 249 2 DON JUAN 2   176   3
HOW MUCH IT COSTS US YET EACH RISING THROB . . . . . 264 2 DON JUAN 2   203   2
HAVE MUCH EMPLOY'D THE MUSE OF HISTORY'S PEN . . . . 266 2 DON JUAN 2   206   4
HER TALE IS TOLD WITH SO MUCH SIMPLE EASE-- . . . . . 273 2 DON JUAN 2 V 2   6
NOT FINDING THAT THE ADDITIONS MUCH ENCUMBER . . . . 276 2 DON JUAN 3   3   8
AND DON'T SAY MUCH OF PARADISE OR WIFE . . . . 280 2 DON JUAN 3   9 V8
(SUCH THINGS IN FACT IT DON'T ASK MUCH TO MAR) . . . 281 2 DON JUAN 3   10   6
DISPLAYED MUCH MORE OF NERVE PERHAPS OF WIT . . . . . 283 2 DON JUAN 3   14 V7
(NONE TRUSTS THE SEX MORE OR SO MUCH ADMIRES-- . . . 287 2 DON JUAN 3   22   5
MUCH LESS EXPERIENCE OF DRY LAND THAN OCEAN . . . . . 289 2 DON JUAN 3   26   2
WAS MUCH THE SAME AS FIRE GIVES A WET BLANKET . . . . 294 2 DON JUAN 3   36 V8
TOO MUCH AND WISHING GLADLY TO SURPRISE . . . . 294 2 DON JUAN 3   37   2
IN FACT MUCH MORE ASTONISH'D THAN DELIGHTED . . . . . 294 2 DON JUAN 3   37   7
TO FIND SO MUCH GOOD COMPANY INVITED . . . . 294 2 DON JUAN 3   37   8
HIS QUESTION MUCH TOO MERRY TO DIVINE . . . . 297 2 DON JUAN 3   42   7
NOW IN A PERSON USED TO MUCH COMMAND-- . . . . 299 2 DON JUAN 3   47   1
BUT IN HIS SILENCE THERE WAS MUCH TO RUE . . . . . . 300 2 DON JUAN 3   48   7
THE PRESENT WEATHER WOULD BE MUCH MORE RAINY-- . . . 301 2 DON JUAN 3   50   6
TO DO NOT MUCH LESS DAMAGE THAN THE TABLE . . . . . . 309 2 DON JUAN 3   66   8
THE LAST WAR--MUCH THE SAME IN PORTUGAL . . . . 320 2 DON JUAN 3   86   4
YET IN THESE TIMES HE MIGHT HAVE DONE MUCH WORSE . . 326 2 DON JUAN 3   87   4
THEY DO NOT MUCH CONTRIBUTE TO HIS GLORY . . . . . . 329 2 DON JUAN 3   92   8
WHICH SHAKE SO MUCH THE HUMAN BRAIN AND BREAST-- . . 343 2 DON JUAN 3 V 98   3
WHICH STILL SAID ALL AND NE'ER COULD SAY TOO MUCH . . 351 2 DON JUAN 4   14   3
AN OPIUM DREAM OF TOO MUCH YOUTH AND READING . . . . 354 2 DON JUAN 4   19   2
IT WERE MUCH BETTER TO HAVE BOTH THAN NEITHER . . . . 357 2 DON JUAN 4   25   8
AND LOVE TOO MUCH AND YET CAN NOT LOVE LESS . . . . . 357 2 DON JUAN 4   26   6
FOR TEA AND COFFEE LEAVE US MUCH MORE SERIOUS . . . . 372 2 DON JUAN 4   52   8
THUS MUCH SHE VIEW'D AN INSTANT AND NO MORE-- . . . . 375 2 DON JUAN 4   58   5
SHE HAD SO MUCH EARTH COULD NOT CLAIM THE WHOLE . . . 377 2 DON JUAN 4   60   8
I DON'T MUCH LIKE DESCRIBING PEOPLE MAD . . . . 384 2 DON JUAN 4   74   3
BUT NOW WAS NOT MUCH PLEASED WITH CAPE SIGAEUM . . . 384 2 DON JUAN 4   75   8
SHOWING A MUCH MORE RECONCIL'D DEMEANOUR . . . . . . 388 2 DON JUAN 4   81   7
NO MATTER WE SHOULD NE'ER TOO MUCH INQUIRE . . . . . 396 2 DON JUAN 4   96   1
WAS MORE TRIUMPHANT AND NOT MUCH LESS REAL . . . . . 396 2 DON JUAN 4   96   8
AT THE FIRST TWO BOOKS HAVING TOO MUCH TRUTH . . . . 397 2 DON JUAN 4   97   4
IS ALWAYS MUCH MORE SPLENDID THAN A KING . . . . . . 408 2 DON JUAN 4   115   6
SHE HAS SERVED ME ALSO MUCH THE SAME AS YOU . . . . . 418 2 DON JUAN 5   14   7
WHICH I DEPLORE SO MUCH FOR I HAVE BORNE . . . . . . 420 2 DON JUAN 5   18   7
DEPENDS SO MUCH UPON THE GASTRIC JUICE . . . . 428 2 DON JUAN 5   32   8
THE LAST OF THESE WAS NEVER MUCH THE FASHION . . . . 437 2 DON JUAN 5   48   3
AND SOME SEEMED MUCH IN LOVE WITH THEIR OWN DRESS . . 441 2 DON JUAN 5   53   4
MIGHT TEACH THEM THIS MUCH BETTER THAN I'M ABLE . . . 444 2 DON JUAN 5   59   8
WHICH PUZZLED NATURE MUCH TO KNOW WHAT ART MEANT . . 448 2 DON JUAN 5   64   8
SO MUCH THE BETTER JUAN SAID FOR THEM . . . . 459 2 DON JUAN 5   82   2
'TWOULD BE AS WELL AND--(THOUGH THERE'S NOT MUCH IN'T) 464 2 DON JUAN 5   91   5
WEALTH HAD DONE WONDERS--TASTE NOT MUCH SUCH THINGS . 465 2 DON JUAN 5   94   1
GREAT LUSTRE THERE IS MUCH TO BE FORGIVEN . . . . . . 465 2 DON JUAN 5   94   6
TO JUAN WHO THOUGH NOT MUCH USED TO PRAY . . . . . . 466 2 DON JUAN 5   95   5
I'D RATHER LEAVE IT MUCH TO YOUR OWN MIND . . . . . . 467 2 DON JUAN 5   97   4
THIS MUCH HOWEVER I MAY ADD--HER YEARS . . . . 468 2 DON JUAN 5   98   1
THIS STRANGE SALOON MUCH FITTED FOR INSPIRING . . . . 469 2 DON JUAN 5   100   5
WHERE THEY MIGHT MEET IN MUCH MORE PEACEFUL GUISE . . 472 2 DON JUAN 5   105   3
WAS MUCH EMBARRASSED NEVER HAVING MET . . . . 482 2 DON JUAN 5   122   2
HOW MUCH I HAVE LOVED--THAT I LOVE NOT THEE . . . . . 484 2 DON JUAN 5   127   2
AS EVEN IN A MUCH HUMBLER LOT HAD MADE . . . . 485 2 DON JUAN 5   129   2
(ENOUGH GOD KNOWS) WOULD MUCH FALL SHORT OF THIS . . 489 2 DON JUAN 5   134   8
SULTANS TOO MUCH ABHOR THIS SORT OF SIN . . . . 10 3 DON JUAN 6   7   5
THE TU'S TOO MUCH--BUT LET IT STAND--THE VERSE . . . 14 3 DON JUAN 6   18   1
IS MUCH IN MOST THINGS NOT LESS IN THE HEART . . . . 15 3 DON JUAN 6   19   3
WHICH DOTH YOUR TRUE BELIEVER SO MUCH PLEASE . . . . 17 3 DON JUAN 6   23   3
AND MUCH MORE TENDER ON THE WHOLE THAN FIERCE . . . . 19 3 DON JUAN 6   27   5
SOME THOUGHT HER DRESS DID NOT SO MUCH BECOME HER . . 23 3 DON JUAN 6   35   3
WERE COUCHES TOILETS--AND MUCH MORE THAN THIS . . . . 31 3 DON JUAN 6   51   3
WHICH IF NOT HAPPINESS IS MUCH MORE NIGH IT . . . . . 32 3 DON JUAN 6   53   4
RUN MUCH LESS RISK OF LOVERS TURNING RUDE . . . . . . 43 3 DON JUAN 6   75   6
A THING OF MUCH LESS IMPORT IN THAT CLIME-- . . . . . 51 3 DON JUAN 6   90   5
HE DID NOT THINK MUCH ON THE MATTER NOR . . . . 51 3 DON JUAN 6   91   1
NOR MUCH DISPOSED TO WAIT IN WORD OR DEED . . . . . . 56 3 DON JUAN 6   101   2
THEN THERE WERE FOREIGNERS OF MUCH RENOWN . . . . . . 75 3 DON JUAN 7   18   1
HE DIED BENEATH A TREE AS MUCH UNBLEST ON . . . . . . 84 3 DON JUAN 7   36   6
BUT HERE I SAY THE TURKS WERE MUCH MISTAKEN . . . . . 87 3 DON JUAN 7   42   7
THERE WAS ENTHUSIASM AND MUCH APPLAUSE . . . . 89 3 DON JUAN 7   47   2

MUCH   (CONTINUED)

	PAGE	VOL	CANTO		STANZA	LN
DANGER AND SPOIL WITH ARDOUR MUCH ENCREASED	90	3	DON JUAN	7	49	6
'TWAS MUCH THAT HE WAS UNDERSTOOD AT ALL	95	3	DON JUAN	7	56	6
AND NOT MUCH SYMPATHY FOR BLOOD SURVEYED	102	3	DON JUAN	7	69	2
DON JUAN WHO WAS MUCH MORE SENTIMENTAL	105	3	DON JUAN	7	75	4
BEING MUCH TOO GROSS TO SEE THEM IN DETAIL	105	3	DON JUAN	7	77	2
WHO CALCULATED LIFE AS SO MUCH DROSS	105	3	DON JUAN	7	77	3
MUCH LESS THAN IS THE HOPE OF EVERY COURT	106	3	DON JUAN	7	79	6
TO WASTE SO MUCH GOLD FOR A LITTLE DROSS	113	3	DON JUAN	8	3	5
WHICH (IT MAY BE) HAS NOT MUCH LEFT TO SPARE	114	3	DON JUAN	8	4	4
AND WHAT IS WORSE STILL A MUCH LONGER STORY	120	3	DON JUAN	8	17	8
SO MUCH AS UNDER A TRIUMPHAL ARCH	121	3	DON JUAN	8	21	5
WITH SOMETHING NOT MUCH BETTER OR AS BAD	122	3	DON JUAN	8	22	3
OF HIS WHOLE ARMY WHICH SO MUCH ABOUNDED	125	3	DON JUAN	8	28	6
FOR A MUCH LONGER TIME THEN LIKE AN ASS--	126	3	DON JUAN	8	29	5
INTO AN ELEGANT EXTRACT (MUCH LESS MASSY)	130	3	DON JUAN	8	34	5
MEN RUN AWAY MUCH RATHER THAN GO THROUGH	130	3	DON JUAN	8	35	3
WHICH SCARCELY ROSE MUCH HIGHER THAN GRASS BLADES	136	3	DON JUAN	8	47	8
SO MUCH INTO THE RAW AS QUITE TO WRONG HER	137	3	DON JUAN	8	50	6
OR NEAR RELATIONS WHO ARE MUCH THE SAME	139	3	DON JUAN	8	54	2
AS MUCH OF GERMAN AS OF SANSCRIT AND	141	3	DON JUAN	8	57	7
THERE CANNOT BE MUCH CONVERSATÏON THERE	141	3	DON JUAN	8	58	8
SO MUCH FOR NATURE--BY WAY OF VARIETY	146	3	DON JUAN	8	68	1
WAS MUCH REGRETTED) FOR THE MOSLEM MEN	147	3	DON JUAN	8	71	7
(I DON'T MUCH PIQUE MYSELF UPON ORTHOGRAPHY	149	3	DON JUAN	8	74	2
ANOTHER COLUMN ALSO SUFFERED MUCH--	151	3	DON JUAN	8	78	1
TOO MUCH OF ONE SORT WOULD BE SOPORIFIC--	156	3	DON JUAN	8	89	6
SO MUCH LESS FIGHT AS MIGHT FORM AN APOLOGY	165	3	DON JUAN	8	108	4
A VIRTUE IN FASHION NOW-A-DAYS	176	3	DON JUAN	8	128	3
MUCH DID THEY SLAY MORE PLUNDER AND NO LESS	176	3	DON JUAN	8	129	1
WERE ALMOST AS MUCH VIRGINS AS BEFORE	176	3	DON JUAN	8	129	8
FOR I HAVE DRAWN MUCH LESS WITH A LONG BOW	181	3	DON JUAN	8	138	6
YOU HAVE OBTAINED GREAT PENSIONS AND MUCH PRAISE	183	3	DON JUAN	9	1	6
THOUGH BRITAIN OWES (AND PAYS YOU TOO) SO MUCH	184	3	DON JUAN	9	3	1
AND SWALLOWING EULOGY MUCH MORE THAN SATIRE HE	185	3	DON JUAN	9	5	5
LIKE BUBBLES ON AN OCEAN MUCH LESS AMPLE	189	3	DON JUAN	9	13	6
SAYS SHAKESPEARE WHO JUST NOW IS MUCH IN FASHION	189	3	DON JUAN	9	14	1
NOR EVER HAD FOR ABSTRACT FAME MUCH PASSION	189	3	DON JUAN	9	14	4
BUT WOULD MUCH RATHER HAVE A SOUND DIGESTION	189	3	DON JUAN	9	14	5
YOUR WISE MEN DON'T KNOW MUCH OF NAVIGATION	191	3	DON JUAN	9	18	4
MUCH FLATTERY--EVEN VOLTAIRE'S AND THAT'S A PITY	194	3	DON JUAN	9	23	6
NOT A BARBARIAN BUT MUCH WORSE THAN THAT	194	3	DON JUAN	9	23	8
AS MUCH FROM MOBS AS KINGS--FROM YOU AS ME	195	3	DON JUAN	9	25	8
MUCH TOO POETICAL MEN SHOULD KNOW WHY	203	3	DON JUAN	9	41	6
WHO WAS GONE TO HIS PLACE) AND PASSED FOR MUCH	209	3	DON JUAN	9	54	2
ALMOST AS MUCH AS ON A NEW DISPATCH	213	3	DON JUAN	9	61	7
OURSELVES A SINGER DANCER MUCH IN FASHION	216	3	DON JUAN	9	68	4
WE DON'T MUCH CARE WITH WHOM WE MAY ENGAGE	217	3	DON JUAN	9	69	3
AND CATHERINE (WE MUST SAY THUS MUCH FOR CATHERINE)	217	3	DON JUAN	9	70	1
HER PREFERENCE OF A BOY TO MEN MUCH BIGGER	218	3	DON JUAN	9	72	3
JUAN MUCH FLATTERED BY HER LOVE OR LUST--	221	3	DON JUAN	9	77	3
THE ELDER LADIES' WRINKLES CURLED MUCH CRISPER	221	3	DON JUAN	9	78	3
AND THOUGH SO MUCH INFERIOR AS I KNOW	226	3	DON JUAN	10	3	5
I WISH TO DO AS MUCH BY POESY	226	3	DON JUAN	10	3	8
BEYOND ITS DIMMED EYE'S SPHERE--BUT WOULD MUCH RATHER	228	3	DON JUAN	10	6	7
MUST COME MUCH RATHER SHOULD HE COURT THE RAY	229	3	DON JUAN	10	9	7
AND NOUGHT REMAINS UNSEEN BUT MUCH UNTOLD	232	3	DON JUAN	10	14	7
FOR BOTH ARE MUCH THE SAME SINCE WHAT MEN THINK	234	3	DON JUAN	10	20	2
MUCH TO HIS YOUTH AND MUCH TO HIS REPORTED	239	3	DON JUAN	10	29	3
MUCH TO HIS YOUTH AND MUCH TO HIS REPORTED	239	3	DON JUAN	10	29	3
VALOUR MUCH ALSO TO THE BLOOD HE SHOWED	239	3	DON JUAN	10	29	4
LIKE A RACE-HORSE MUCH TO EACH DRESS HE SPORTED	239	3	DON JUAN	10	29	5
SHE COULD NOT TOO MUCH GIVE HER APPROBATION	241	3	DON JUAN	10	33	1
SO MUCH DID JUAN'S SETTING OFF DISTRESS HER	247	3	DON JUAN	10	47	7
AH IF HE HAD HOW MUCH HE WOULD HAVE MISSED HER	250	3	DON JUAN	10	53	8
YE GLORIOUS GOTHIC SCENES HOW MUCH YE STRIKE	255	3	DON JUAN	10	61	3
WHO DID NOT LIMIT MUCH HIS BILLS PER WEEK	259	3	DON JUAN	10	70	3
THEY HATE A MURDERER MUCH LESS THAN A CLAIMANT	264	3	DON JUAN	10	79	5
OF ILLNESS I GROW MUCH MORE ORTHODOX	270	3	DON JUAN	11	5	8
ON PURPOSE TO BELIEVE SO MUCH THE MORE	271	3	DON JUAN	11	6	8
MAY NOT THINK MUCH OF LONDON'S FIRST APPEARANCE--	271	3	DON JUAN	11	7	7
THEIR CASH TO SHOW HOW MUCH THEY HAVE A YEAR	273	3	DON JUAN	11	10	4
NOR MUCH TO CLIMB THROUGH LITTLE BOXES FRAMED	278	3	DON JUAN	11	21	4
WHICH EVE MIGHT QUIT WITHOUT MUCH SACRIFICE--	278	3	DON JUAN	11	21	8
THROUGH THIS AND MUCH AND MORE IS THE APPROACH	279	3	DON JUAN	11	23	1
THE DRUID'S GROVES ARE GONE--SO MUCH THE BETTER	280	3	DON JUAN	11	25	1
ONE MONSTROUS DIAMOND DREW MUCH OBSERVATION	287	3	DON JUAN	11	39	4
BUT JUAN WAS RECEIVED WITH MUCH EMPRESSEMENT --	288	3	DON JUAN	11	42	1
YOU LEAVE BEHIND--THE NEXT OF MUCH YOU COME	290	3	DON JUAN	11	44	5
AND VERY MUCH UNLIKE WHAT PEOPLE WRITE	292	3	DON JUAN	11	47	8
MUCH AS THEY MIGHT HAVE BEEN SUPPOSED TO SPEAK	298	3	DON JUAN	11	60	5
AND WATCH AND WARD WHOSE PLANS A WORD TOO MUCH	305	3	DON JUAN	11	73	3
BEFORE HE CAN ESCAPE FROM SO MUCH DANGER	305	3	DON JUAN	11	74	4
MUCH LESS ON WHAT YOU DO THAN WHAT YOU SAY	310	3	DON JUAN	11	86	6
FOR BEING AS MUCH THE SUBJECT OF ATTACK	312	3	DON JUAN	11	90	4
SO MUCH THE BETTER--I MAY STAND ALONE	312	3	DON JUAN	11	90	7
LOVE OR LUST MAKES MAN SICK AND WINE MUCH SICKER	317	3	DON JUAN	12	4	1
THE ONLY TIME WHEN MUCH SUCCESS IS NEEDED	324	3	DON JUAN	12	17	3
HE PLAYED AND PAID MADE LOVE WITHOUT MUCH SIN	327	3	DON JUAN	12	25	V5

MUCH   (CONTINUED)

	PAGE	VOL	CANTO	STANZA	LN
THE WOMEN MUCH DIVIDED--AS IS USUAL	329	3	DON JUAN 12	28	1
WOULD BE MUCH BETTER TAUGHT BENEATH THE EYE	329	3	DON JUAN 12	29	7
FROM MUCH IMPROVEMENT WITH THAT VIRTUOUS PLOUGH	335	3	DON JUAN 12	40	5
WHO MIGHT NOT PROFIT MUCH BY BEING AT LARGE	335	3	DON JUAN 12	41	8
IN FACT THERE'S NOTHING MAKES ME SO MUCH GRIEVE	336	3	DON JUAN 12	43	6
TURN OUT MUCH BETTER FOR THE SMITHFIELD SHOW	337	3	DON JUAN 12	46	6
BUT HE HAD SEEN SO MUCH GOOD LOVE BEFORE	346	3	DON JUAN 12	67	4
BUT THUS MUCH AND NO SNEER AGAINST THE SHORE	346	3	DON JUAN 12	67	6
WHICH TAKES SO MUCH--TO GIVE THE DEVIL HIS DUE--	351	3	DON JUAN 12	76	3
ABROAD THOUGH DOUBTLESS THEY DO MUCH AMISS	352	3	DON JUAN 12	79	5
AN USURER COULD SCARCE EXPECT MUCH MORE--	356	3	DON JUAN 12	88	6
MUCH IN THE MODE OF GOETHE'S MEPHISTOPHELES	361	3	DON JUAN 13	7	8
BUT NEITHER LOVE NOR HATE IN MUCH EXCESS	361	3	DON JUAN 13	8	1
AND AS HE THOUGHT IN COUNTRY MUCH THE SAME--	367	3	DON JUAN 13	20	4
AND HAVE NOT YET ATTAINED TO MUCH SUCCESS	374	3	DON JUAN 13	35	4
HAS NOT CONTRACTED MUCH MORE DEBT THAN KNOWLEDGE	377	3	DON JUAN 13	42	8
THAN AN ADVERTISEMENT OR MUCH THE SAME	382	3	DON JUAN 13	51	4
THE FACT--I'VE HEARD IT--ONCE PERHAPS TOO MUCH	388	3	DON JUAN 13	64	8
WERE THERE WITH BROWS THAT DID NOT MUCH INVITE	391	3	DON JUAN 13	69	2
HIS CAUSE BY LEANING MUCH FROM MIGHT TO RIGHT	391	3	DON JUAN 13	69	4
WHO DID NOT HATE SO MUCH THE SIN AS SINNER	399	3	DON JUAN 13	87	6
SINCE EVE ATE APPLES MUCH DEPENDS ON DINNER	404	3	DON JUAN 13	99	8
BUT THEN 'TWOULD SPOIL MUCH GOOD PHILOSOPHY	410	3	DON JUAN 14	1	4
MUCH AS OLD SATURN ATE HIS PROGENY	410	3	DON JUAN 14	1	6
FOR TOO MUCH TRUTH AT FIRST SIGHT NE'ER ATTRACTS	416	3	DON JUAN 14	13	6
WITH MUCH TO EXCITE THERE'S LITTLE TO EXALT	417	3	DON JUAN 14	16	1
FACTITIOUS PASSIONS WIT WITHOUT MUCH SALT	417	3	DON JUAN 14	16	5
NOW I COULD MUCH MORE EASILY SKETCH A HAREM	419	3	DON JUAN 14	21	3
AND THERE IS MUCH WHICH COULD NOT BE APPRECIATED	419	3	DON JUAN 14	22	7
HAS MUCH OF SELFISHNESS AND MORE SUSPICION	420	3	DON JUAN 14	24	6
MUCH I RESPECT AND MUCH I HAVE ADORED	422	3	DON JUAN 14	27	1
MUCH I RESPECT AND MUCH I HAVE ADORED	422	3	DON JUAN 14	27	1
A FULL-GROWN CUPID VERY MUCH ADMIRED	428	3	DON JUAN 14	41	2
THE CHASTE AND THOSE WHO ARE NOT SO MUCH INSPIRED	428	3	DON JUAN 14	41	6
REGRETTING MUCH THAT SHE HAD CHOSEN SO BAD A LINE	430	3	DON JUAN 14	46	5
THEY ARE SO MUCH INTERTWISTED WITH THE EARTH	436	3	DON JUAN 14	59	2
IT WERE MUCH BETTER TO BE WED OR DEAD	438	3	DON JUAN 14	64	5
WAS MUCH INFERIOR TO KING MENELAUS--	441	3	DON JUAN 14	72	7
THERE IS AN AWKWARD THING WHICH MUCH PERPLEXES	442	3	DON JUAN 14	73	1
MUCH PASSION SINCE THE MERCHANT-SHIP THE ARGO	443	3	DON JUAN 14	76	7
IS MUCH MORE TO THE PURPOSE OF HIS SONG	443	3	DON JUAN 14	77	4
AND SINCE THAT TIME IT NEED NOT COST MUCH SHOWING	444	3	DON JUAN 14	78	5
MUCH AS A MONK MAY DO WITHIN HIS CELL	445	3	DON JUAN 14	81	4
THOUGH MUCH IN TEMPER BUT THEY NEVER CLASH'D	447	3	DON JUAN 14	87	2
IMPRESSIONS WERE MUCH STRONGER THAN SHE GUESS'D	448	3	DON JUAN 14	88	5
TO THUS MUCH ADELINE WOULD NOT ADVANCE	450	3	DON JUAN 14	92	6
AND I SHALL TAKE A MUCH MORE SERIOUS AIR	454	3	DON JUAN 14	99	5
HOW MUCH WOULD NOVELS GAIN BY THE EXCHANGE	455	3	DON JUAN 14	101	1
SHE IS SO RARE AND THOU HAST SO MUCH PREY	459	3	DON JUAN 15	9	2
WILL GO MUCH FURTHER THAN THERE'S NEED TO MENTION	462	3	DON JUAN 15	14	8
I DON'T KNOW THAT THERE MAY BE MUCH ABILITY	465	3	DON JUAN 15	20	1
FOR T'OTHER ONE WHO PROMISES MUCH DUTY	471	3	DON JUAN 15	34	4
AND AMPLIFY YOU LOSE MUCH BY CONCISION	478	3	DON JUAN 15	51	4
SHE HAD SO MUCH OR LITTLE OF THE CHILD	480	3	DON JUAN 15	55	8
MUCH AS SHE WOULD HAVE SEEN A GLOWWORM SHINE	480	3	DON JUAN 15	56	3
MY MUSE WOULD RUN MUCH MORE INTO EXCESS	483	3	DON JUAN 15	64	3
THOUGH SWALLOW'D WITH MUCH ZEST UPON THE WHOLE	484	3	DON JUAN 15	66	4
THIS MUCH IS SURE THAT OUT OF EARSHOT THINGS	489	3	DON JUAN 15	76	2
AND AFTER SO MUCH EXCELLENT ADVICE	490	3	DON JUAN 15	77	8
AND LOOK'D AS MUCH AS IF TO SAY I SAID IT--	491	3	DON JUAN 15	79	1
THOUGH PROBABLY MUCH LESS A FACT THAN GUESS)	491	3	DON JUAN 15	80	6
THOUGHT HER PREDICTIONS WENT NOT MUCH AMISS	492	3	DON JUAN 15	81	3
IN MOTION BUT SHE HERE TOO MUCH REFINED--	492	3	DON JUAN 15	81	7
PHILOSOPHY NO SHE TOO MUCH REJECTS	495	3	DON JUAN 15	89	7
SO MUCH AS I DO ANY KIND OF WRANGLE	496	3	DON JUAN 15	91	3
ALMOST AN HAIR'S BREADTH TOO MUCH ON ONE SIDE	513	3	DON JUAN 16	29	8
SO MUCH DISTRAIT HE WAS THAT ALL COULD SEE	513	3	DON JUAN 16	30	6
AND IS NOT MUCH IMPROVED BY GROWING OLD	516	3	DON JUAN 16	37	8
AND SANG WITH MUCH SIMPLICITY--A MERIT	518	3	DON JUAN 16	40	7
AND THEN OF COURSE THE CIRCLE MUCH ADMIRES	521	3	DON JUAN 16	41	5
DEEMING THE SAGE WOULD BE MUCH MORTIFIED	522	3	DON JUAN 16	43	5
WAS MUCH CONSOLED BY HIS OWN REPARTEE	522	3	DON-JUAN 16	43	8
SO MUCH THE PRESENT DYE SHE WAS REMOTE	524	3	DON JUAN 16	47	6
ALSO THEREON--BUT THAT'S NOT MUCH WE FIND	525	3	DON JUAN 16	49	6
SO MUCH THE BARD HAD REALLY BEEN PROPHETIC	525	3	DON JUAN 16	50	5
ON PAIN OF MUCH DISPLEASING THE GYNOCRASY	526	3	DON JUAN 16	52	8
AND MUCH WAS TALKED ON ALL SIDES ON THAT HEAD	527	3	DON JUAN 16	54	5
SO MUCH HE DEEMED HIS PATRONAGE AN HONOUR	528	3	DON JUAN 16	57	6
THERE WAS MUCH BUSTLE TOO AND PREPARATION	534	3	DON JUAN 16	68	3
NOT CALCULATING HOW MUCH THEY CONDENSED	535	3	DON JUAN 16	71	6
HE WAS AS INDEPENDENT--AYE MUCH MORE--	537	3	DON JUAN 16	76	1
AND THOUGHT I SAY NO MORE--I'VE SAID TOO MUCH	538	3	DON JUAN 16	77	2
GREAT PLENTY MUCH FORMALITY SMALL CHEER	538	3	DON JUAN 16	78	7
THEIR PLATES--WITHOUT IT MIGHT BE TOO MUCH BENDING	538	3	DON JUAN 16	79	4
A SLIGHT REPAST MAKES PEOPLE LOVE MUCH MORE	542	3	DON JUAN 16	86	3
AND THIS AND HIS NOT KNOWING HOW MUCH OATS	543	3	DON JUAN 16	89	7
BY MATTER AND SO MUCH MATERIALISED	543	3	DON JUAN 16	90	5
A SOMETHING MUCH MIRTH-MOVING--AND IN THIS	544	3	DON JUAN 16	92	V5

MUCH   (CONTINUED)
    SOME DOUBT HOW MUCH OF ADELINE WAS REAL 546   3 DON JUAN 16   96   8
    LITTLE THAT'S GREAT BUT MUCH OF WHAT IS CLEVER 547   3 DON JUAN 16   98   4
    THE FAIR FITZ-FULKE SEEMED VERY MUCH AT EASE 548   3 DON JUAN 16   100   2
    YET SAW THIS MUCH WHICH HE WAS GLAD TO SEE 553   3 DON JUAN 16   106   8
    THE GHOST AT LEAST HAD DONE HIM THIS MUCH GOOD . . . 553   3 DON JUAN 16   107   1
    OR (AS RHYMES MAY BE IN THESE DAYS) MUCH MORE 556   3 DON JUAN 16   113   4
    FORTH INTO SOMETHING MUCH LIKE FLESH AND BLOOD . . . 561   3 DON JUAN 16   123   4
    THIS THEY MUST BEAR WITH AND PERHAPS MUCH MORE 566   3 DON JUAN 17   9   6
MUCKS
    THY WAITERS RUNNING MUCKS AT EVERY BELL 259   3 DON JUAN 10   69   4
MUD
    ALTHOUGH OF CLAY ARE YET NOT QUITE OF MUD 491   2 DON JUAN 5   138   3
    SLIDING KNEE-DEEP IN LATELY FROZEN MUD 148   3 DON JUAN 8   73   7
    AND ROARED OUT AS HE WRITHED HIS NATIVE MUD IN . . . 274   3 DON JUAN 11   13   6
MUDDLE
    NOT LIKE SLOW GERMANY WHERIN THEY MUDDLE 260   3 DON JUAN 10   71   4
MUDDY
    TRUTH'S FOUNTAINS MAY BE CLEAR--HER STREAMS ARE MUDDY . 495   3 DON JUAN 15   88   6
MUEZZIN'S
    OF WHAT IT HAD BEEN THERE THE MUEZZIN'S CALL 182   3 DON JUAN 8   141   6
MUFFIN
    LORD HENRY SAID HIS MUFFIN WAS ILL BUTTERED 514   3 DON JUAN 16   31   4
    ALSO THE MUFFIN WHEREOF HE COMPLAINED 515   3 DON JUAN 16   34   2
MUFFLE
    (FOR SOMETIMES WE MUST BOX WITHOUT THE MUFFLE) 205   2 DON JUAN 2   92   8
MUFFLED
    AND NOW NOUGHT LEFT HIM BUT THE MUFFLED DRUM 430   2 DON JUAN 5   36   8
MUFFLES
    WHILE GREAT LUCULLUS' ROBE TRIUMPHAL MUFFLES-- 484   3 DON JUAN 15   66   7
MUFTI
    LITTLE CARED THEY FOR MAHOMET OR MUFTI 75   3 DON JUAN 7   17   5
MUG
    A MIGHTY MUG OF MORAL DOUBLE ALE 533   3 DON JUAN 16   67   4
MULCT
    BY LAYING WHATE'ER SUM IN MULCT THEY PLEASE ON 57   2 DON JUAN 1   64   6
MULE
    A HUMAN (WHAT THE ITALIANS NICKNAME) MULE 563   3 DON JUAN 17   3   5
MULTIFARIOUS
    THOUGH HARDLY HEARD THROUGH MULTIFARIOUS DAMME'S . . . 279   3 DON JUAN 11   24   3
MULTIPLICATION
    AND INDIGESTION'S GRAND MULTIPLICATION 486   3 DON JUAN 15   69   3
MULTIPLIED
    AND HEADS IF THOU HADST ALL THINGS MULTIPLIED 20   3 DON JUAN 6   28   2
MULTIPLY
    HAVE NOT ESSAY'D TO MULTIPLY THEIR CLIENTS 142   2 DON JUAN 1   211   5
    THERE THE STILL VARYING PANGS WHICH MULTIPLY 118   3 DON JUAN 8   13   1
MULTITUDE
    AND SINCE THERE'S SAFETY IN A MULTITUDE 371   3 DON JUAN 13   29   1
MULTITUDES
    MAKES THAT OF MULTITUDES TAKE ONE DIRECTION 90   3 DON JUAN 7   48   2
MUMMY
    TO KEEP HIS MEMORY WHOLE AND MUMMY HID 146   2 DON JUAN 1   219   4
MUNCHINGS
    ENOUGH TO GRATIFY A BEE'S SLIGHT MUNCHINGS 301   3 DON JUAN 11   66   5
MURDER
    YET VERY FIT TO MURDER SLEEP IN THOSE 27   3 DON JUAN 6   42   2
    SOMETIMES CALLS MURDER AND AT OTHERS GLORY 79   3 DON JUAN 7   26   8
MURDERED
    OF MURDERED WOMEN WHO HAD FOUND THEIR WAY 157   3 DON JUAN 8   91   3
MURDERER
    THEY HATE A MURDERER MUCH LESS THAN A CLAIMANT . . . 264   3 DON JUAN 10   79   5
MURDER'S
    ARE NOTHING BUT A CHILD OF MURDER'S RATTLES 114   3 DON JUAN 8   4   8
MURK
    OF HER BLACK EYES SEEM'D TURN'D TO TEARS AND MURK . . . 362   2 DON JUAN 4   33   6
MURMUR
    AND THEN INTO A HOARSER MURMUR GREW 194   2 DON JUAN 2   73   3
    HIS GARMENTS ONLY A SLIGHT MURMUR MADE 510   3 DON JUAN 16   21   5
MURMUR'D
    AND HAIDEE'S SWEET LIPS MURMUR'D LIKE A BROOK 359   2 DON JUAN 4   29   6
MURMURED
    TO QUAFF A BROOK WHICH MURMURED LIKE A BIRD 384   3 DON JUAN 13   56   8
MURMURING
    OF MURMURING LIBERTY'S WIDE WAVES WHICH BLEND 52   3 DON JUAN 6   93   6
MURMURS
    MAY HEAR OUR MUTUAL MURMURS SWEEP 326   2 DON JUAN 3 L 16   3
MURRAY
    (PLAIN TRUTH DEAR MURRAY NEEDS FEW FLOWERS OF SPEECH) . 470   2 DON JUAN 5   101   2
    AND THROWS A CLOUD O'ER LONGMAN AND JOHN MURRAY . . . 79   3 DON JUAN 7   26   4
    LIKE MANY PUBLICATIONS OF JOHN MURRAY 237   3 DON JUAN 10   26 V3
MUSCADINS
    COCKNEYS OF LONDON MUSCADINS OF PARIS 174   3 DON JUAN 8   124   7
MUSCLE
    SELDOM HE VARIED FEATURE HUE OR MUSCLE 132   3 DON JUAN 8   39   7
MUSCOVITE
    THEY LOOKED UPON THE MUSCOVITE FLOTILLA 73   3 DON JUAN 7   13   7
    BY THE ADVANCING MUSCOVITE--THE GROAN 155   3 DON JUAN 8   87   7
MUSE
    HERE MY CHASTE MUSE A LIBERTY MUST TAKE-- 86   2 DON JUAN 1   120   1

MUSE   (CONTINUED)

	PAGE	VOL	CANTO	STANZA	LN
COMMIT--FLIRTATION WITH THE MUSE OF MOORE	139	2 DON JUAN	1	205	8
THOU SHALT NOT COVET MR SOTHEBY'S MUSE	140	2 DON JUAN	1	206	1
YET IF MY GENTLE MUSE HE PLEASE TO ROAST	142	2 DON JUAN	1	210	4
(AND SO MY SOBER MUSE--COME LET'S BE STEADY--	160	2 DON JUAN	2	6	8
CHASTE MUSE--(WELL IF YOU MUST YOU MUST)--THE VEIL	160	2 DON JUAN	2	7	1
I'D WEEP BUT MINE IS NOT A WEEPING MUSE	165	2 DON JUAN	2	16	3
BUT OF MATERIALS THAT MUCH SHOCK THE MUSE--	195	2 DON JUAN	2	74	6
HAVE MUCH EMPLOY'D THE MUSE OF HISTORY'S PEN	266	2 DON JUAN	2	206	4
HAIL MUSE ET CETERA--WE LEFT JUAN SLEEPING	274	2 DON JUAN	3	1	1
HIS MUSE MADE INCREMENT OF ANYTHING	319	2 DON JUAN	3	85	5
THE SCIAN AND THE TEIAN MUSE	321	2 DON JUAN	3	L 2	1
AND AS MY MUSE IS A CAPRICIOUS ELF	384	2 DON JUAN	4	74	6
BUT COULD NOT FOR THE MUSE OF ME PUT LESS IN'T	410	2 DON JUAN	4	117	6
YOU'LL PARDON TO MY MUSE A FEW SHORT NAPS	503	2 DON JUAN	5	159	8
MY MODERN MUSE MAY BE ALLOWED TO SNORE	503	2 DON JUAN	5	159	V8
IN SUCH PROPORTION--BUT MY MUSE WITHSTANDS	20	3 DON JUAN	6	28	3
THE MUSE WILL TAKE A LITTLE TOUCH AT WARFARE	65	3 DON JUAN	6	120	8
OF WOLVES WILL THE BRIGHT MUSE WITHDRAW ONE RAY	70	3 DON JUAN	7	7	6
OF WHICH HOWE'ER THE MUSE DESCRIBES EACH ACT	107	3 DON JUAN	7	81	3
SO BEAUTIFUL SO FLEETING TO THE MUSE	108	3 DON JUAN	7	82	8
THIS CANTO ERE MY MUSE PERCEIVES FATIGUE	109	3 DON JUAN	7	85	6
UNRIDDLED AND AS MY TRUE MUSE EXPOUNDS	112	3 DON JUAN	8	1	5
(THAT WHICH SOME ANCIENT MUSE OR MODERN WIT	153	3 DON JUAN	8	84	4
AND NOW--WHAT IS YOUR FAME SHALL THE MUSE TUNE IT YE	187	3 DON JUAN	9	9	5
TO YOU THE UNFLATTERING MUSE DEIGNS TO INSCRIBE	187	3 DON JUAN	9	10	2
A TERM INEXPLICABLE TO THE MUSE	224	3 DON JUAN	9	84	8
(FOR I HAVE MORE THAN ONE MUSE AT A PUSH)	227	3 DON JUAN	10	5	4
SLAUGHTER OF ISMAIL THOUGH MY WILD MUSE VARIES	249	3 DON JUAN	10	51	6
CAN TAX MY MILD MUSE WITH MISANTHROPY	286	3 DON JUAN	11	38	2
GREAT BRITAIN WHICH THE MUSE MAY PENETRATE	327	3 DON JUAN	12	24	6
MY MUSE BY EXHORTATION MEANS TO MEND	334	3 DON JUAN	12	39	6
ON WHICH THE MUSE HAS ALWAYS SOUGHT TO ENTER--	375	3 DON JUAN	13	38	6
MY MUSE A GLASS OF WEATHEROLOGY	378	3 DON JUAN	13	43	5
MY MUSE THE BUTTERFLY HATH BUT HER WINGS	400	3 DON JUAN	13	89	5
BESIDES MY MUSE BY NO MEANS DEALS IN FICTION	416	3 DON JUAN	14	13	1
MY MUSE DESPISES REFERENCE AS YOU HAVE GUESS'D	433	3 DON JUAN	14	54	6
MARCH MY MUSE IF YOU CANNOT FLY YET FLUTTER	468	3 DON JUAN	15	27	2
MY MUSE HATH BRED AND STILL PERHAPS MAY BREED	482	3 DON JUAN	15	60	5
FOR WEAPONS BUT WHAT MUSE SINCE HOMER'S ABLE	482	3 DON JUAN	15	62	3
MY MUSE WOULD RUN MUCH MORE INTO EXCESS	483	3 DON JUAN	15	64	3

MUSED

	PAGE	VOL	CANTO	STANZA	LN
AS JUAN MUSED ON MUTABILITY	509	3 DON JUAN	16	20	1

MUSE-LIKE

	PAGE	VOL	CANTO	STANZA	LN
MORE MUSE-LIKE--SAY LIKE CYTHEREA'S SHELL	339	3 DON JUAN	12	51	8

MUSE'S

	PAGE	VOL	CANTO	STANZA	LN
AND EVEN MY MUSE'S WORST REPROOF'S A SMILE	300	3 DON JUAN	11	63	6
BY DEEMING THAT MY MUSE'S CONVERSATION	498	3 DON JUAN	15	94	6

MUSES

	PAGE	VOL	CANTO	STANZA	LN
FOR ME WHO WANDERING WITH PEDESTRIAN MUSES	14	2 DON JUAN	D	8	1
ALTHOUGH YOU BORROWED ALL THAT E'ER THE MUSES	493	2 DON JUAN	5	143	3
BEAR IT YE MUSES ON YOUR BRIGHTEST WING	175	3 DON JUAN	8	126	4
AND FAR BE IT FROM MY MUSES TO PRESUME	227	3 DON JUAN	10	5	3
THE MUSES UPON SION'S HILL MUST RAMBLE	297	3 DON JUAN	11	57	3
MY MUSES DO NOT CARE A PINCH OF ROSIN	341	3 DON JUAN	12	55	1
OF ALL THE MUSES THAT I RECOLLECT	502	3 DON JUAN	16	2	5

MUSES'

	PAGE	VOL	CANTO	STANZA	LN
HARD WORDS WHICH STICK IN THE SOFT MUSES' GULLETS	106	3 DON JUAN	7	78	8

MUSEUM

	PAGE	VOL	CANTO	STANZA	LN
LOOK LIKE THE MONSTERS OF A NEW MUSEUM	202	3 DON JUAN	9	40	8

MUSIC

	PAGE	VOL	CANTO	STANZA	LN
THAT FINER SIMPLER MUSIC NE'ER WAS HEARD	236	2 DON JUAN	2	151	5
HE HEARS--ALAS NO MUSIC OF THE SPHERES	290	2 DON JUAN	3	28	3
SONG DANCE WINE MUSIC STORIES FROM THE PERSIAN	293	2 DON JUAN	3	35	3
A LOVE OF MUSIC AND OF SCENES SUBLIME	304	2 DON JUAN	3	56	5
A WORDLESS MUSIC AND HER FACE SO FAIR	359	2 DON JUAN	4	29	7
WITH MUSIC THE MOST MODERATE SHINE AS WITS	340	3 DON JUAN	12	52	7
AND MAKE A MUSIC WHETHER FLAT OR SHARP	402	3 DON JUAN	13	93	4
HAD MUSIC--WALKING--RIDING--BOOKS--AND TALK	407	3 DON JUAN	13	104	V2
MY MUSIC HAS SOME MYSTIC DIAPASONS	419	3 DON JUAN	14	22	6
SETS TO SOFT MUSIC THE HARMONIOUS SIGH	430	3 DON JUAN	14	47	3
THERE'S MUSIC IN THE SIGHING OF A REED	458	3 DON JUAN	15	5	5
THERE'S MUSIC IN THE GUSHING OF A RILL	458	3 DON JUAN	15	5	6
THERE'S MUSIC IN ALL THINGS IF MEN HAD EARS	458	3 DON JUAN	15	5	7
LIKE THAT SAME MYSTIC MUSIC OF THE SPHERES	489	3 DON JUAN	15	76	5
THE CALENTURES OF MUSIC WHICH O'ERCOME	523	3 DON JUAN	16	46	5
AS MUSIC CHIMES IN WITH A MELODRAME	552	3 DON JUAN	16	104	6

MUSICAL

	PAGE	VOL	CANTO	STANZA	LN
IS MUSICAL--A DYING ACCENT DRIVEN	388	3 DON JUAN	13	63	4
AMONGST OUR OWN MOST MUSICAL OF NATIONS	523	3 DON JUAN	16	45	6

MUSICO

	PAGE	VOL	CANTO	STANZA	LN
DID NOT THE ITALIAN MUSICO CAZZANI	102	2 DON JUAN	1	149	1
THE MUSICO IS BUT A CRACK'D OLD BASIN	391	2 DON JUAN	4	86	2

MUSIC'S

	PAGE	VOL	CANTO	STANZA	LN
WHOSE ACCENTS ARE THE STEPS OF MUSIC'S THRONE	237	2 DON JUAN	2	151	V8
DOWN TO THE HARP--BECAUSE TO MUSIC'S CHARMS	408	3 DON JUAN	13	107	7
AND THEN HE HAD AN EAR FOR MUSIC'S SOUND	427	3 DON JUAN	14	39	5

MUSING

	PAGE	VOL	CANTO	STANZA	LN
AND MUSING THERE AN HOUR ALONE	321	2 DON JUAN	3	L 3	3

```
                                                        PAGE VOL    CANTO STANZA LN
MUSK-BULL
    WHICH FLASHED AS FAR AS WHERE THE MUSK-BULL BROWSES  . . . 353  3 DON JUAN 12    82   6
MUSLIN
    HER EVENING SILK OR IN THE SUMMER MUSLIN . . . . . . .  27  2 DON JUAN  1    12   7
    WHILE THEY THRUST SHEETS SHIRTS JACKETS BALES OF MUSLIN . . 171  2 DON JUAN  2    28   8
MUSQUETRY
    AND BY A FIRE OF MUSQUETRY AND GRAPE . . . . . . . .  81  3 DON JUAN  7    29   7
MUSQUETS
    AND THIRTY THOUSAND MUSQUETS FLUNG THEIR PILLS . . . . . 117  3 DON JUAN  8    12   2
MUSSULMAN
    OF ANY MUSSULMAN WHATE'ER HIS WORTH  . . . . . . . . 450  2 DON JUAN  5    67   4
    ONE'S TURNED HALF MUSSULMAN AND ONE A MAID . . . . . 459  2 DON JUAN  5    83   7
MUSSULMANS
    SLAIN BY SOME MUSSULMANS WHO WOULD NOT YET . . . . . 150  3 DON JUAN  8    77   3
MUSTACHIOS
    NOR BY MUSTACHIOS MOVED WERE LET ALONE  . . . . . . 344  3 DON JUAN 12    61   6
MUSTER
    AND THEN HE TRIED TO MUSTER ALL HIS PATIENCE . . . . . 110  2 DON JUAN  1   162   8
    THE NIGHTLY MUSTER AND THE SILENT MARCH . . . . . . 121  3 DON JUAN  8    21   2
MUTABILITY
    AS JUAN MUSED ON MUTABILITY . . . . . . . . . . 509  3 DON JUAN 16    20   1
MUTE
    THEIR PLACE OF BIRTH ALONE IS MUTE . . . . . . . . 321  2 DON JUAN  3  L  2   4
    ARRAY HER LIMBS BUT JUAN STANDING MUTE  . . . . . . 453  2 DON JUAN  5    73   4
MUTES
    FOR MUTES ARE GENERALLY USED FOR THAT . . . . . . . 463  2 DON JUAN  5    89   8
    'TWOULD BE CONVENIENT FOR THESE MUTES HAVE EYES . . . . 464  2 DON JUAN  5    92   1
MUTILATED
    AND PITYING SORE HIS MUTILATED CASE . . . . . . .  46  2 DON JUAN  1    44   6
MUTTER'D
    OR MADAM DIES--ALFONSO MUTTER'D DAMN HER . . . . . . 111  2 DON JUAN  1   163   5
MUTTERED
    HE MUTTERED (BUT THE LAST WAS GIVEN ASIDE) . . . . . 471  2 DON JUAN  5   103   3
    HERSELF THEN HASTILY LOOKED DOWN AND MUTTERED . . . . 514  3 DON JUAN 16    31   2
MUTTERING
    SIGHED JUAN MUTTERING ALSO SOME SLIGHT OATHS . . . . . 455  2 DON JUAN  5    76   5
MUTTERS
    FOR HE MUTTERS HIS PRAYER IN THE MIDNIGHT AIR . . . . 518  3 DON JUAN 16  L  1   3
MUTTON
    BEEF VEAL AND MUTTON BETTER FOR DIGESTION  . . . . . 191  2 DON JUAN  2    67   8
    GOAT'S FLESH THERE IS NO DOUBT AND KID AND MUTTON . . . 238  2 DON JUAN  2   154   2
    WHO ALL THE TIME WERE EATING UP HIS MUTTON . . . . . 299  2 DON JUAN  3    46   8
MUTUAL
    THE CREDULOUS HOPE OF MUTUAL MINDS IS O'ER . . . . . 144  2 DON JUAN  1   216   5
    MAY HEAR OUR MUTUAL MURMURS SWEEP . . . . . . . 326  2 DON JUAN  3  L 16   3
    OF THIS THEIR MUTUAL FEELING SHE REPLIED-- . . . . . 356  2 DON JUAN  4    23   6
    WHO FAIN WOULD HAVE A MUTUAL FLAME CONFEST . . . . .  14  3 DON JUAN  6    17   3
    THE JOYS OF MUTUAL HATE TO KEEP THEM WARM . . . . . 360  3 DON JUAN 13     6   5
    HIMSELF AND JUAN IN THEIR MUTUAL STATIONS . . . . . 365  3 DON JUAN 13    15   3
MUTUAL-DARTED
    IN THE LARGE DARK EYE'S MUTUAL-DARTED FLAME . . . . . 367  2 DON JUAN  4    44   4
MUTUALLY
    FAREWELL THEY MUTUALLY EXCLAIMED THIS SOIL . . . . . 459  2 DON JUAN  5    83   5
MUZZLE
    ON THE HIGH TOBY-SPICE SO FLASH THE MUZZLE . . . . . 277  3 DON JUAN 11    19   6
MY
    AND NOW MY EPIC RENEGADE WHAT ARE YE AT . . . . . .   9  2 DON JUAN  D     1   5
    A NEST OF TUNEFUL PERSONS TO MY EYE  . . . . . . .   9  2 DON JUAN  D     1   7
    NOR COIN MY SELF-LOVE TO SO BASE A VICE . . . . . .  12  2 DON JUAN  D     6   2
    'TIS THAT I STILL RETAIN MY BUFF AND BLUE . . . . .  20  2 DON JUAN  D    17   4
    MY POLITICS AS YET ARE ALL TO EDUCATE . . . . . .  20  2 DON JUAN  D    17   5
    IS IT NOT SO MY TORY ULTRA-JULIAN . . . . . . .  20  2 DON JUAN  D    17   8
    BUT NOT AT ALL ADAPTED TO MY RHYMES . . . . . . .  22  2 DON JUAN  1     3   8
    FIT FOR MY POEM (THAT IS FOR MY NEW ONE) . . . . .  24  2 DON JUAN  1     5   7
    FIT FOR MY POEM (THAT IS FOR MY NEW ONE) . . . . .  24  2 DON JUAN  1     5   7
    SO AS I SAID I'LL TAKE MY FRIEND DON JUAN . . . . .  24  2 DON JUAN  1     5   8
    MY WAY IS TO BEGIN WITH THE BEGINNING . . . . . .  25  2 DON JUAN  1     7   2
    THE REGULARITY OF MY DESIGN . . . . . . . . .  25  2 DON JUAN  1     7   3
    'TIS IN ARRANGING ALL MY FRIENDS' AFFAIRS . . . . .  33  2 DON JUAN  1    23   7
    NOT HAVING OF MY OWN DOMESTIC CARES . . . . . . .  33  2 DON JUAN  1    23   8
    BUT THEN 'TIS NOT MY FAULT IF OTHERS HURT YOU . . . .  37  2 DON JUAN  1    30   8
    I HAD MY DOUBTS PERHAPS I HAVE THEM STILL . . . . .  49  2 DON JUAN  1    51   1
    BUT SCANDAL'S MY AVERSION--I PROTEST . . . . . .  49  2 DON JUAN  1    51   7
    FOR MY PART I SAY NOTHING--NOTHING--BUT . . . . . .  50  2 DON JUAN  1    52   1
    THIS I WILL SAY--MY REASONS ARE MY OWN-- . . . . .  50  2 DON JUAN  1    52   2
    THIS I WILL SAY--MY REASONS ARE MY OWN-- . . . . .  50  2 DON JUAN  1    52   2
    FOR THERE IT WAS I PICK'D UP MY OWN KNOWLEDGE . . . .  50  2 DON JUAN  1    52   8
    WHO LEFT AN ONLY DAUGHTER MY NARRATION . . . . . .  54  2 DON JUAN  1    59   4
    FOR MY PART TO SUCH DOINGS I'M A STRANGER . . . . .  65  2 DON JUAN  1    80   4
    BUT NOT MY FAULT--I TELL THEM ALL IN TIME . . . . .  65  2 DON JUAN  1    80   8
    FOR MY PART I'M A MODERATE-MINDED BARD . . . . . .  85  2 DON JUAN  1   118   5
    BUT SOMEHOW THIS MY VESTAL VOW TAKES WING . . . . .  85  2 DON JUAN  1   119   5
    HERE MY CHASTE MUSE A LIBERTY MUST TAKE-- . . . . .  86  2 DON JUAN  1   120   1
    WITHOUT WHOSE EPOCH MY POETIC SKILL . . . . . . .  86  2 DON JUAN  1   121   7
    FOR GOD'S SAKE MADAM--MADAM--HERE'S MY MASTER . . . .  96  2 DON JUAN  1   137   1
    'TIS NOT MY FAULT--I KEPT GOOD WATCH--ALACK . . . . .  96  2 DON JUAN  1   137   4
    MY DEAR I WAS THE FIRST WHO CAME AWAY . . . . . .  98  2 DON JUAN  1   141   8
    A HUSBAND LIKE ALFONSO AT MY SIDE . . . . . . . 100  2 DON JUAN  1   145   6
    THE COMMON PRIVILEGES OF MY SEX . . . . . . . . 101  2 DON JUAN  1   147   2
```

MY (CONTINUED)

	PAGE	VOL	CANTO	STANZA	LN
BUT FOUND MY VERY INNOCENCE PERPLEX	101	2	DON JUAN	1	147	6
IS IT FOR THIS WHATE'ER MY SUITORS WERE	102	2	DON JUAN	1	148	5
SING AT MY HEART SIX MONTHS AT LEAST IN VAIN	102	2	DON JUAN	1	149	2
HAVE I NOT HAD TWO BISHOPS AT MY FEET	103	2	DON JUAN	1	150	1
BUT AS MY MAID'S UNDREST PRAY TURN YOUR SPIES OUT	104	2	DON JUAN	1	152	7
MY HONOUR THUS IT SHALL NOT BE IN VAIN	105	2	DON JUAN	1	154	8
THEY ARE UNWORTHY OF MY FATHER'S DAUGHTER	106	2	DON JUAN	1	155	6
MY MOTHER DREAM'D NOT IN MY NATAL HOUR	106	2	DON JUAN	1	155	7
MY MOTHER DREAM'D NOT IN MY NATAL HOUR	106	2	DON JUAN	1	155	7
YOU SAW THAT SHE WAS SLEEPING BY MY SIDE	106	2	DON JUAN	1	156	2
ANTONIA WHERE'S MY POCKET-HANDKERCHIEF	107	2	DON JUAN	1	157	8
WHO CAN HAVE PUT MY MASTER IN THIS MOOD	115	2	DON JUAN	1	171	2
YOU'LL LOSE YOUR LIFE AND I SHALL LOSE MY PLACE	115	2	DON JUAN	1	171	7
MY MISTRESS ALL FOR THAT HALF-GIRLISH FACE	115	2	DON JUAN	1	171	8
COME SIR GET IN)--MY MASTER MUST BE NEAR	115	2	DON JUAN	1	172	5
BUT IT WILL SERVE TO KEEP MY VERSE COMPACT)	119	2	DON JUAN	1	178	4
MY TEETH BEGIN TO CHATTER MY VEINS FREEZE--	121	2	DON JUAN	1	181	6
MY TEETH BEGIN TO CHATTER MY VEINS FREEZE--	121	2	DON JUAN	1	181	6
MY EYEBALLS BURN AND THROB BUT HAVE NO TEARS	130	2	DON JUAN	1	192	8
STATE STATION HEAVEN MANKIND'S MY OWN ESTEEM	130	2	DON JUAN	1	193	2
YET IF I NAME MY GUILT 'TIS NOT TO BOAST	130	2	DON JUAN	1	193	5
MY SHAME AND SORROW DEEP IN MY HEART'S CORE	132	2	DON JUAN	1	195	4
MY SHAME AND SORROW DEEP IN MY HEART'S CORE	132	2	DON JUAN	1	195	4
MY BREAST HAS BEEN ALL WEAKNESS IS SO YET	133	2	DON JUAN	1	196	1
BUT STILL I THINK I CAN COLLECT MY MIND	133	2	DON JUAN	1	196	2
MY BLOOD STILL RUSHES WHERE MY SPIRIT'S SET	133	2	DON JUAN	1	196	3
MY BLOOD STILL RUSHES WHERE MY SPIRIT'S SET	133	2	DON JUAN	1	196	3
MY HEART IS FEMININE NOR CAN FORGET--	133	2	DON JUAN	1	196	5
AS VIBRATES MY FOND HEART TO MY FIX'D SOUL	133	2	DON JUAN	1	196	8
AS VIBRATES MY FOND HEART TO MY FIX'D SOUL	133	2	DON JUAN	1	196	8
I STRUGGLE BUT CAN NOT COLLECT MY MIND	133	2	DON JUAN	1	196	V2
IT NE'ER CAN REACH SO TURNS TO YOU MY SOUL	133	2	DON JUAN	1	196	V8
AND DARE NOT SET MY SEAL UPON THIS SHEET	134	2	DON JUAN	1	197	2
MY MISERY CAN SCARCE BE MORE COMPLETE	134	2	DON JUAN	1	197	4
MY POEM'S EPIC AND IS MEANT TO BE	135	2	DON JUAN	1	200	1
SO THAT MY NAME OF EPIC'S NO MISNOMER	135	2	DON JUAN	1	200	8
AND DEVILS FOR MY SUPERNATURAL SCENERY	136	2	DON JUAN	1	201	V8
ME AND MY EPIC BRETHREN GONE BEFORE	137	2	DON JUAN	1	202	2
AND HERE THE ADVANTAGE IS MY OWN I WEEN	137	2	DON JUAN	1	202	3
ALL THESE CONFIRM MY STATEMENT A GOOD DEAL	138	2	DON JUAN	1	203	5
MY TEXT WITH MANY THINGS THAT NO ONE KNOWS	138	2	DON JUAN	1	204	5
NOT TO BELIEVE MY VERSE AND THEIR OWN EYES	141	2	DON JUAN	1	208	4
AND BEG THEY'LL TAKE MY WORD ABOUT THE MORAL	141	2	DON JUAN	1	209	2
MY EPICAL PRETENSIONS TO THE LAUREL	141	2	DON JUAN	1	209	6
I'VE BRIBED MY GRANDMOTHER'S REVIEW--THE BRITISH	141	2	DON JUAN	1	209	8
YET IF MY GENTLE MUSE HE PLEASE TO ROAST	142	2	DON JUAN	1	210	4
IN MY HOT YOUTH--WHEN GEORGE THE THIRD WAS KING	143	2	DON JUAN	1	212	8
BUT NOW AT THIRTY YEARS MY HAIR IS GRAY--	143	2	DON JUAN	1	213	1
MY HEART IS NOT MUCH GREENER AND IN SHORT I	143	2	DON JUAN	1	213	4
HAVE SQUANDER'D MY WHOLE SUMMER WHILE 'TWAS MAY	143	2	DON JUAN	1	213	5
HAVE SPENT MY LIFE BOTH INTEREST AND PRINCIPAL	143	2	DON JUAN	1	213	7
AND DEEM NOT WHAT I DEEM'D MY SOUL INVINCIBLE	143	2	DON JUAN	1	213	8
NO MORE--NO MORE--OH NEVER MORE MY HEART	144	2	DON JUAN	1	215	1
CANST THOU BE MY SOLE WORLD MY UNIVERSE	144	2	DON JUAN	1	215	2
CANST THOU BE MY SOLE WORLD MY UNIVERSE	144	2	DON JUAN	1	215	2
THOU CANST NOT BE MY BLESSING OR MY CURSE	144	2	DON JUAN	1	215	4
THOU CANST NOT BE MY BLESSING OR MY CURSE	144	2	DON JUAN	1	215	4
MY DAYS OF LOVE ARE OVER ME NO MORE	144	2	DON JUAN	1	216	1
AMBITION WAS MY IDOL WHICH WAS BROKEN	145	2	DON JUAN	1	217	1
MY HEART IN PASSION AND MY HEAD ON RHYMES	145	2	DON JUAN	1	217	8
MY HEART IN PASSION AND MY HEAD ON RHYMES	145	2	DON JUAN	1	217	8
'TWERE WELL IF OTHERS FOLLOW'D MY EXAMPLE	147	2	DON JUAN	1	221	8
GO LITTLE BOOK FROM THIS MY SOLITUDE	149	2	DON JUAN	1	222	1
I CAN'T HELP PUTTING IN MY CLAIM TO PRAISE--	149	2	DON JUAN	1	222	6
BUT THEN AS BARD MY DUTY TO MANKIND	155	2	DON JUAN	1	V 7	6
(AND SO MY SOBER MUSE--COME LET'S BE STEADY--	160	2	DON JUAN	2	6	8
TO--SAY MY PRAYERS--BUT NEVER WAS THERE PLANN'D	160	2	DON JUAN	2	7	6
PERHAPS IT MAY BE LINED WITH THIS MY CANTO	165	2	DON JUAN	2	16	8
FAREWELL MY SPAIN A LONG FAREWELL HE CRIED	166	2	DON JUAN	2	18	1
FAREWELL MY MOTHER AND SINCE ALL IS O'ER	166	2	DON JUAN	2	18	6
THAN I RESIGN THINE IMAGE OH MY FAIR	166	2	DON JUAN	2	19	5
JULIA MY LOVE--(YOU RASCAL PEDRO QUICKER)--	167	2	DON JUAN	2	20	5
IN MY YOUNG DAYS THEY LENT ME CASH THAT WAY	190	2	DON JUAN	2	65	7
TO THOSE RELATED IN MY GRAND-DAD'S NARRATIVE	229	2	DON JUAN	2	137	8
FROM THIS MY SUBJECT HAS NO BUSINESS HERE	238	2	DON JUAN	2	156	4
WHERE I LIKE OTHER DOGS HAVE HAD MY DAY	244	2	DON JUAN	2	166	3
LIKE OTHER MEN TOO MAY HAVE HAD MY PASSION--	244	2	DON JUAN	2	166	4
LOVE CONSTANT LOVE HAS BEEN MY CONSTANT GUEST	268	2	DON JUAN	2	209	5
BUT SOON PHILOSOPHY CAME TO MY AID	268	2	DON JUAN	2	210	1
I WILL MY DEAR PHILOSOPHY I SAID	268	2	DON JUAN	2	210	3
'TIS BUT MY CURIOSITY THAT CRIES	268	2	DON JUAN	2	210	V6
AND LAYING DOWN MY PEN I MAKE MY BOW	271	2	DON JUAN	2	216	6
AND LAYING DOWN MY PEN I MAKE MY BOW	271	2	DON JUAN	2	216	6
THE ONLY TWO THAT IN MY RECOLLECTION	281	2	DON JUAN	3	10	1
ALTHOUGH MY OPINION MAY REQUIRE APOLOGY	281	2	DON JUAN	3	11	3
DIRECT YOUR QUESTIONS TO MY NEIGHBOUR THERE	298	2	DON JUAN	3	45	6
BUT TO MY SUBJECT--LET ME SEE--WHAT WAS IT--	317	2	DON JUAN	3	81	5
MY COUNTRY ON THY VOICELESS SHORE	322	2	DON JUAN	3	L 5	2

```
EVEN AS I SING SUFFUSE MY FACE . . . . . . . . .  323  2 DON JUAN  3  L  6    4
MY OWN THE BURNING TEAR-DROP LAVES . . . . . . .  326  2 DON JUAN  3  L 15    5
WRIT IN A MANNER WHICH IS MY AVERSION . . . . . .  330  2 DON JUAN  3    94    8
BUT LET ME TO MY STORY I MUST OWN . . . . . . . .  331  2 DON JUAN  3    96    1
LEAVING MY PEOPLE TO PROCEED ALONE . . . . . . .  331  2 DON JUAN  3    96    3
BUT THESE ARE MY ADDRESSES FROM THE THRONE . . .  331  2 DON JUAN  3    96    5
MY ALTARS ARE THE MOUNTAINS AND THE OCEAN . . . .  336  2 DON JUAN  3   104    6
WERE THE SOLE ECHOS SAVE MY STEED'S AND MINE . .  337  2 DON JUAN  3   106    3
FROM A TRUE LOVER SHADOW'D MY MIND'S EYE . . . .  337  2 DON JUAN  3   106    8
TO DO WITH THE TRANSACTIONS OF MY HERO . . . . .  341  2 DON JUAN  3   110    3
SURE MY INVENTION MUST BE DOWN AT ZERO . . . . .  341  2 DON JUAN  3   110    5
THEY TOOK IT UP WHEN MY DAYS GREW MORE MELLOW . .  345  2 DON JUAN  4     3    3
AND OTHER MINDS ACKNOWLEDGED MY DOMINION . . . .  345  2 DON JUAN  4     3    4
NOW MY SERE FANCY FALLS INTO THE YELLOW . . . . .  345  2 DON JUAN  4     3    5
AND THE SAD TRUTH WHICH HOVERS O'ER MY DESK . . .  345  2 DON JUAN  4     3    7
MY OWN MEANING WHEN I WOULD BE VERY FINE . . . .  346  2 DON JUAN  4     5    5
A NOVEL WORD IN MY VOCABULARY . . . . . . . . . .  346  2 DON JUAN  4     5    8
AND TELLS ME TO RESUME MY STORY HERE . . . . . .  347  2 DON JUAN  4     7    8
I HAVE SEEN SOME SUCH--BUT THEY UNHINGED MY MIND    363  2 DON JUAN  4    36   V8
SMILED SCORNFULLY AND SAID WITHIN MY CALL . . . .  364  2 DON JUAN  4    37    6
'TIS LAMBRO--'TIS MY FATHER KNEEL WITH ME-- . . .  364  2 DON JUAN  4    38    2
THAT DOUBT SHOULD MINGLE WITH MY FILIAL JOY . . .  364  2 DON JUAN  4    38    7
HE FOUND--BUT SOUGHT NOT I HAVE PLEDGED MY FAITH    366  2 DON JUAN  4    42    6
BUT I MUST DO MY DUTY--HOW THOU HAST . . . . . .  368  2 DON JUAN  4    46    7
LET HIM DISARM OR BY MY FATHER'S HEAD . . . . . .  369  2 DON JUAN  4    47    1
FOR IF MY PURE LIBATIONS EXCEED THREE . . . . . .  372  2 DON JUAN  4    52    4
I FEEL MY HEART BECOME SO SYMPATHETIC . . . . . .  372  2 DON JUAN  4    52    5
MY MILD AND MIDNIGHT BEAKERS TO THE BRIM . . . .  372  2 DON JUAN  4    53    7
MY BRAIN WITH BLEST FUMES TILL MY EYES GROW DIM    372  2 DON JUAN  4    53   V7
MY BRAIN WITH BLEST FUMES TILL MY EYES GROW DIM    372  2 DON JUAN  4    53   V7
AND AS MY MUSE IS A CAPRICIOUS ELF . . . . . . .  384  2 DON JUAN  4    74    6
MY OWN MERITS AND THOUGH YOUNG--I SEE SIR--YOU .  392  2 DON JUAN  4    88    2
HAVING WITHSTOOD TEMPTATION IN MY YOUTH . . . . .  397  2 DON JUAN  4    97    2
MY PEN AND LIKED POETIC WAR TO WAGE . . . . . .  397  2 DON JUAN  4    98    6
MY PEN AND EASILY FLEW IN A RAGE . . . . . . . .  397  2 DON JUAN  4    98   V6
AS BOYS LOVE ROWS MY BOYHOOD LIKED A SQUABBLE . .  398  2 DON JUAN  4    99    1
WHETHER MY VERSE'S FAME BE DOOM'D TO CEASE . . .  398  2 DON JUAN  4    99    4
THE GRASS UPON MY GRAVE WILL GROW AS LONG . . . .  398  2 DON JUAN  4    99    7
YOU READ MY STANZAS AND I READ YOUR FEATURES . .  405  2 DON JUAN  4   111    3
NOW IF MY PEGASUS SHOULD NOT BE SHOD ILL . . . .  412  2 DON JUAN  5     2    7
MY BOY --SAID HE AMIDST THIS MOTLEY CREW . . . .  417  2 DON JUAN  5    13    1
'TIS NOT SAID JUAN FOR MY PRESENT DOOM . . . . .  420  2 DON JUAN  5    18    1
'TIS NOT MY PRESENT LOT AS I HAVE SAID . . . . .  420  2 DON JUAN  5    18    6
I CRIED UPON MY FIRST WIFE'S DYING DAY . . . . .  420  2 DON JUAN  5    19    7
AND ALSO WHEN MY SECOND RAN AWAY . . . . . . . .  420  2 DON JUAN  5    19    8
MY THIRD-- --YOUR THIRD QUOTH JUAN TURNING ROUND   421  2 DON JUAN  5    20    1
JUST AS MY GREAT COAT WAS ABOUT ME CAST . . . . .  428  2 DON JUAN  5    33    3
MY HAT AND GLOVES STILL LYING ON THE TABLE . . .  428  2 DON JUAN  5    33    4
LIKE ESAU FOR MY BIRTHRIGHT A BEEF-STEAK . . . .  435  2 DON JUAN  5    44    8
I WON'T DESCRIBE DESCRIPTION IS MY FORTE . . . .  440  2 DON JUAN  5    52    1
I PASS MY EVENINGS IN LONG GALLERIES SOLELY . . .  444  2 DON JUAN  5    58    7
BUT THEY AS SOON SHALL CIRCUMCISE MY HEAD . . . .  452  2 DON JUAN  5    71    8
THAT I UNSEXED MY DRESS BUT BABA STROKING . . . .  454  2 DON JUAN  5    75    6
WHY YOU SHOULD WEAR THEM--WHAT THOUGH MY SOUL LOATHES  455  2 DON JUAN  5    76    3
ELSE THEY SHALL FEEL THE WEIGHT OF THIS MY ARM .  459  2 DON JUAN  5    82    3
ON WHICH I CANNOT PAUSE TO MAKE MY STRICTURES . .  465  2 DON JUAN  5    94    8
SO LUCKILY FOR BOTH MY PHRASES FAIL . . . . . . .  467  2 DON JUAN  5    97    8
BUT THOUGH MY TURN WILL NOT BE SERVED WITH LESS    487  2 DON JUAN  5   132    5
BUT BID MY WOMEN FORM THE MILKY WAY . . . . . . .  494  2 DON JUAN  5   145    3
HENCE MY OLD COMET GIVE THE STARS DUE WARNING--    494  2 DON JUAN  5   145    4
YOU'LL PARDON TO MY MUSE A FEW SHORT NAPS . . . .  503  2 DON JUAN  5   159    8
MY MODERN MUSE MAY BE ALLOWED TO SNORE . . . . .  503  2 DON JUAN  5   159   V8
OF WORLDS TO LOSE YET STILL TO PAY MY COURT I . .    9  3 DON JUAN  6     5    5
WITH ONE GOOD HEARTY CURSE I VENT MY GALL . . . .   17  3 DON JUAN  6    22    3
AND THEN MY STOICISM LEAVES NOUGHT BEHIND . . . .   17  3 DON JUAN  6    22    4
AND I CAN GIVE MY WHOLE SOUL UP TO MIND . . . . .   17  3 DON JUAN  6    22    6
MY WISH IS QUITE AS WIDE BUT NOT SO BAD . . . . .   19  3 DON JUAN  6    27    4
IN SUCH PROPORTION--BUT MY MUSE WITHSTANDS . . .   20  3 DON JUAN  6    28    3
I'M PUZZLED WHAT TO DO WITH YOU MY DEAR . . . . .   29  3 DON JUAN  6    46    3
MY FAULTS EVEN WITH YOUR OWN WHICH MEANETH PUT .   34  3 DON JUAN  6    56    6
AND THUS MY NARRATIVE PROCEEDS--DUDU . . . . . .   34  3 DON JUAN  6    57    2
I DID MY VERY BOYISH BEST TO SHINE . . . . . . .   37  3 DON JUAN  6    62    5
MY TENDENCY IS TO PHILOSOPHIZE . . . . . . . . .   37  3 DON JUAN  6    63    3
MY SIMILES ARE GATHERED IN A HEAP . . . . . . . .   40  3 DON JUAN  6    68    6
OH THAT MY WORDS WERE COLOURS BUT THEIR TINTS . .   60  3 DON JUAN  6   109    7
EXCUSE MY FREEDOM WHEN I HERE ASSURE YOU . . . .   63  3 DON JUAN  6   115    7
MY BIDDING BABA VANISHED FOR TO STRETCH . . . . .   63  3 DON JUAN  6   116    3
AND SUCH AS THEY ARE SUCH MY PRESENT TALE IS . .   67  3 DON JUAN  7     2    1
FOR MY PART I PRETEND NOT TO BE CATO . . . . . .   68  3 DON JUAN  7     4    6
YOUR NAMES--MINE'S JOHNSON AND MY COMRADE'S JUAN   97  3 DON JUAN  7    60    1
WHAT FOLLOWED--A SHOT LAID ME ON MY BACK . . . .   98  3 DON JUAN  7    61    5
SO NOW MY LADS FOR GLORY--HERE HE TURNED . . . .   99  3 DON JUAN  7    64    1
MY DEBT IN BEING THUS ALLOWED TO DIE . . . . . .  100  3 DON JUAN  7    65    5
EXPLICITLY OUR SEVERAL POSTS MY FRIEND . . . . .  100  3 DON JUAN  7    65    7
BY SERVICE WITH MY MILITARY BROTHERS . . . . . .  103  3 DON JUAN  7    71    4
WHEN MY POOR GREECE WAS ONCE AS NOW SURROUNDED .  108  3 DON JUAN  7    82    4
THIS CANTO ERE MY MUSE PERCEIVES FATIGUE . . . .  109  3 DON JUAN  7    85    6
UNRIDDLED AND AS MY TRUE MUSE EXPOUNDS . . . . .  112  3 DON JUAN  8     1    5
```

MY (CONTINUED)

	PAGE	VOL	CANTO	STANZA	LN
MY CUE FOR ANY TIME TO BE TERRIFIC	156	3	DON JUAN 8	89	2
IN PROSE I BEND MY HUMBLE VERSE) DOTH CALL	163	3	DON JUAN 8	104	7
BUT LET ME PUT AN END UNTO MY THEME	175	3	DON JUAN 8	127	1
THE TOPIC'S TENDER SO SHALL BE MY PHRASE--	176	3	DON JUAN 8	128	5
READER I HAVE KEPT MY WORD--AT LEAST SO FAR	181	3	DON JUAN 8	138	1
THAN MY FORERUNNERS CARELESSLY I SING	181	3	DON JUAN 8	138	7
YOU MY LORD DUKE IS FAR ABOVE REFLECTION	186	3	DON JUAN 9	7	2
FOR MY PART I'LL ENLIST ON NEITHER SIDE	190	3	DON JUAN 9	16	5
MY CHANCE SO HAPPEN--DEEDS) WITH ALL WHO WAR	194	3	DON JUAN 9	24	2
TO THIS MY PLAIN SWORN DOWNRIGHT DETESTATION	194	3	DON JUAN 9	24	7
MY WORDS AT LEAST ARE MORE SINCERE AND HEARTY	195	3	DON JUAN 9	26	3
NOR GIVE MY VOICE TO SLAVERY'S JACKALL CRY	195	3	DON JUAN 9	26	8
AND THAT'S ONE COMFORT FOR MY LOST ADVICE	200	3	DON JUAN 9	36	7
MY PEGASUS SHALL TIRE OF TOUCHING GROUND	224	3	DON JUAN 9	85	3
SO LOFTY THAT I FEEL MY BRAIN TURN ROUND	224	3	DON JUAN 9	85	5
AND ALL MY FANCIES WHIRLING LIKE A MILL	224	3	DON JUAN 9	85	6
WHICH IS A SIGNAL TO MY NERVES AND BRAIN	224	3	DON JUAN 9	85	7
MY BOSOM UNDERWENT A GLORIOUS GLOW	226	3	DON JUAN 10	3	3
AND MY INTERNAL SPIRIT CUT A CAPER	226	3	DON JUAN 10	3	4
THE STARS I OWN MY TELESCOPE IS DIM	227	3	DON JUAN 10	4	2
OF BREAKERS HAS NOT DAUNTED MY SLIGHT TRIM	227	3	DON JUAN 10	4	6
AND FAR BE IT FROM MY MUSES TO PRESUME	227	3	DON JUAN 10	5	3
AS MY FRIEND JEFFREY WRITES WITH SUCH AN AIR	230	3	DON JUAN 10	11	6
DEAR JEFFREY ONCE MY MOST REDOUBTED FOE	232	3	DON JUAN 10	16	2
MOST NOBLY AND I OWN IT FROM MY SOUL	232	3	DON JUAN 10	16	8
FOR ME FOR I WOULD RATHER TAKE MY WINE	233	3	DON JUAN 10	17	3
A WHOLE ONE AND MY HEART FLIES TO MY HEAD--	233	3	DON JUAN 10	17	7
A WHOLE ONE AND MY HEART FLIES TO MY HEAD--	233	3	DON JUAN 10	17	8
ALL MY BOY FEELINGS ALL MY GENTLER DREAMS	233	3	DON JUAN 10	18	4
ALL MY BOY FEELINGS ALL MY GENTLER DREAMS	233	3	DON JUAN 10	18	4
MY CHILDHOOD IN THIS CHILDISHNESS OF MINE	233	3	DON JUAN 10	18	7
I RAILED AT SCOTS TO SHEW MY WRATH AND WIT	234	3	DON JUAN 10	19	3
I SCOTCHED NOT KILLED THE SCOTCHMAN IN MY BLOOD	234	3	DON JUAN 10	19	7
OR THE EAR-TRUMPET OF MY GOOD OLD AUNT	241	3	DON JUAN 10	34	5
(IF THAT MY MEMORY DOTH NOT GREATLY ERR)	242	3	DON JUAN 10	36	3
SLAUGHTER OF ISMAIL THOUGH MY WILD MUSE VARIES	249	3	DON JUAN 10	51	6
MY GUARD MY OLD GUARD EXCLAIMED THAT GOD OF CLAY--	254	3	DON JUAN 10	59	2
MY GUARD MY OLD GUARD EXCLAIMED THAT GOD OF CLAY--	254	3	DON JUAN 10	59	2
MAKE MY SOUL PASS THE EQUINOCTIAL LINE	255	3	DON JUAN 10	61	6
BUT THOUGH I OWE IT LITTLE BUT MY BIRTH	257	3	DON JUAN 10	66	3
BY DRIVING THE YORK MAIL--BUT AH MY SINKING SOUL	263	3	DON JUAN 10	78	V7
MY GENTLE COUNTRYMEN WE WILL RENEW	266	3	DON JUAN 10	84	3
AND WEAR MY HEAD DENYING THAT I WEAR IT	268	3	DON JUAN 11	1	8
OF THE TRUTH'S RAYS SPOIL NOT MY DRAUGHT OF SPIRIT	269	3	DON JUAN 11	2	7
AND THAT WHICH AFTER ALL MY SPIRIT VEXES	269	3	DON JUAN 11	3	4
(TO MY MISFORTUNE) NEVER CAN I SAY	274	3	DON JUAN 11	12	7
THE DYING MAN CRIED HOLD I'VE GOT MY GRUEL	276	3	DON JUAN 11	16	2
CAN TAX MY MILD MUSE WITH MISANTHROPY	286	3	DON JUAN 11	38	2
BUT JUAN WAS MY MOSCOW AND FALIERO	296	3	DON JUAN 11	56	1
MY LEIPSIC AND MY MONT SAINT JEAN SEEMS CAIN	296	3	DON JUAN 11	56	2
MY LEIPSIC AND MY MONT SAINT JEAN SEEMS CAIN	296	3	DON JUAN 11	56	2
BUT I WILL FALL AT LEAST AS FELL MY HERO	296	3	DON JUAN 11	56	5
WITH TURNCOAT SOUTHEY FOR MY TURNKEY LOWE	296	3	DON JUAN 11	56	8
THEN THERE'S MY GENTLE EUPHUES WHO THEY SAY	298	3	DON JUAN 11	59	1
THEIR FLANKS--BUT IT IS HARDLY WORTH MY WHILE	300	3	DON JUAN 11	63	2
MY NATURAL TEMPER'S REALLY AUGHT BUT STERN	300	3	DON JUAN 11	63	5
AND EVEN MY MUSE'S WORST REPROOF'S A SMILE	300	3	DON JUAN 11	63	6
AS FROM MY GREAT GREAT HUMOUR YOU MAY LEARN	300	3	DON JUAN 11	63	V5
MY JUAN WHOM I LEFT IN DEADLY PERIL	300	3	DON JUAN 11	64	1
WHERE IS LORD THIS AND WHERE MY LADY THAT	308	3	DON JUAN 11	79	1
MY FRIENDS THE WHIGS EXACTLY WHERE THEY WERE	308	3	DON JUAN 11	79	8
BUT IT IS TIME THAT I SHOULD HOIST MY BLUE PETER	309	3	DON JUAN 11	83	5
A MORAL COUNTRY BUT I HOLD MY HAND--	311	3	DON JUAN 11	87	4
MY TOPIC WITH OF COURSE THE DUE RESTRICTION	311	3	DON JUAN 11	88	2
BUT WOULD NOT CHANGE MY FREE THOUGHTS FOR A THRONE	312	3	DON JUAN 11	90	8
STRANGE TOO IN MY BUON CAMERADO SCOTT	323	3	DON JUAN 12	16	5
MY JEFFREY HELD HIM UP AS AN EXAMPLE	323	3	DON JUAN 12	16	7
AND THAT'S ENOUGH SUCCEEDED IN MY YOUTH	324	3	DON JUAN 12	17	2
AND MY SUCCESS PRODUCED WHAT I IN SOOTH	324	3	DON JUAN 12	17	4
IN THIS TWELFTH CANTO 'TIS MY WISH TO BE	325	3	DON JUAN 12	20	3
AND WHY SHOULD I NOT FORM MY SPECULATION	325	3	DON JUAN 12	21	2
AND HOLD UP TO THE SUN MY LITTLE TAPER	325	3	DON JUAN 12	21	3
THAT'S NOBLE THAT'S ROMANTIC FOR MY PART	326	3	DON JUAN 12	22	1
(NOW HERE'S A WORD QUITE AFTER MY OWN HEART	326	3	DON JUAN 12	22	3
AND NOW TO BUSINESS OH MY GENTLE JUAN	326	3	DON JUAN 12	23	1
I COULD SEND FORTH MY MANDATE LIKE A PRIMATE	327	3	DON JUAN 12	24	3
I FOR MY PART--(ONE MODERN INSTANCE MORE	334	3	DON JUAN 12	38	1
ALBEIT MY YEARS WERE LESS DISCREET THAN FEW	334	3	DON JUAN 12	38	4
MY MUSE BY EXHORTATION MEANS TO MEND	334	3	DON JUAN 12	39	6
WHICH PUTS MY PEGASUS TO THESE GRAVE PACES	334	3	DON JUAN 12	39	8
THAT--BUT MY CHASTER EAR WILL NOT RECEIVE	336	3	DON JUAN 12	43	4
OR AT THE LEAST WOULD LENGTHEN OUT MY SONG--	338	3	DON JUAN 12	48	6
BUT NOW I WILL BEGIN MY POEM--'TIS	341	3	DON JUAN 12	54	1
UPON MY LYRE OR MAKING THE PEGS SURE	341	3	DON JUAN 12	54	7
UPON MY FIDDLE--SEEING IF ALL'S SURE	341	3	DON JUAN 12	54	V7
MY MUSES DO NOT CARE A PINCH OF ROSIN	341	3	DON JUAN 12	55	1
IF THAT MY PEGASUS SHOULD NOT BE FOUNDERED	341	3	DON JUAN 12	55	7
AND AS MY OBJECT IS MORALITY	355	3	DON JUAN 12	86	3

MY   (CONTINUED)

	PAGE	VOL	CANTO	STANZA	LV
AND IF MY THUNDERBOLT NOT ALWAYS RATTLES	356	3	DON JUAN 12	88	1
BUT MY BEST CANTO SAVE ONE ON ASTRONOMY	356	3	DON JUAN 12	88	7
MY PLAN (BUT I IF BUT FOR SINGULARITY	357	3	DON JUAN 12	89	5
BECAUSE MY CASES PUT HIS LORDSHIP TO'T--	357	3	DON JUAN 12	V 18	1
AND THEREFORE SHALL MY LAY SOAR HIGH AND SOLEMN	358	3	DON JUAN 13	1	7
I'LL NOT GAINSAY THEM IT IS NOT MY CUE	359	3	DON JUAN 13	3	1
FOR MY PART I AM BUT A MERE SPECTATOR	361	3	DON JUAN 13	7	6
AND NOW AND THEN IT ALSO SUITS MY RHYMES	361	3	DON JUAN 13	8	4
I'M AT MY OLD LUNES--DIGRESSION AND FORGET	364	3	DON JUAN 13	12	1
AND TAKE MY WORD YOU WON'T HAVE ANY LESS	366	3	DON JUAN 13	18	3
UPON MY SHOULDERS HERE I MUST AVER	378	3	DON JUAN 13	43	4
MY MUSE A GLASS OF WEATHEROLOGY	378	3	DON JUAN 13	43	5
BUT THESE ARE TRIFLES DOWNWARD FLIES MY LORD	379	3	DON JUAN 13	46	1
NODDING BESIDE MY LADY IN HIS CARRIAGE	379	3	DON JUAN 13	46	2
ALSO MY LADY'S GENTLEWOMAN TRICKY	380	3	DON JUAN 13	47	3
I'VE DONE WITH MY TIRADE THE WORLD WAS GONE	381	3	DON JUAN 13	49	1
PROVOKE MY THIRST--WHAT--HO OF WINE A STOUP	392	3	DON JUAN 13	72	V8
MY MUSE THE BUTTERFLY HATH BUT HER WINGS	400	3	DON JUAN 13	89	5
FORBIDS A GREAT IMPRESSION IN MY YOUTH	403	3	DON JUAN 13	96	6
(MY HEART OR HEAD ACHES WITH THE MEMORY YET)	408	3	DON JUAN 13	107	4
FOR WHICH MY SOLE EXCUSE IS--'TIS MY WAY	413	3	DON JUAN 14	7	3
FOR WHICH MY SOLE EXCUSE IS--'TIS MY WAY	413	3	DON JUAN 14	7	3
FOR I WAS RATHER FAMOUS IN MY TIME	414	3	DON JUAN 14	9	7
I HAVE BROUGHT THIS WORLD ABOUT MY EARS AND EKE	414	3	DON JUAN 14	10	1
UPON MY HEAD HAVE BID THEIR THUNDERS BREAK	414	3	DON JUAN 14	10	3
IN YOUTH I WROTE BECAUSE MY MIND WAS FULL	415	3	DON JUAN 14	10	7
TO SWIM OR SINK--I HAVE HAD AT LEAST MY DREAM	415	3	DON JUAN 14	11	8
BESIDES MY MUSE BY NO MEANS DEALS IN FICTION	416	3	DON JUAN 14	13	1
MY LADY'S PRATTLE FILTER'D THROUGH HER WOMAN	418	3	DON JUAN 14	19	8
MY MUSIC HAS SOME MYSTIC DIAPASONS	419	3	DON JUAN 14	22	6
WOULD RISK TO PLEASE IT MY LAST RAG OF BREECHES	421	3	DON JUAN 14	26	V8
IN MY YOUNG DAYS THAT CHASTE AND GOODLY VEIL	422	3	DON JUAN 14	27	2
MY DIAN OF THE EPHESIANS LADY ADELINE	430	3	DON JUAN 14	46	3
AH IF YOU HAD BUT FOLLOW'D MY ADVICE	430	3	DON JUAN 14	47	4
BUT THIS IS NOT MY MAXIM HAD IT BEEN	431	3	DON JUAN 14	49	1
MY MUSE DESPISES REFERENCE AS YOU HAVE GUESS'D	433	3	DON JUAN 14	54	6
BUT THIS IS NOT AT PRESENT MY CONCERN	436	3	DON JUAN 14	59	7
IF IN MY EXTREMITY OF RHYME'S DISTRESS	442	3	DON JUAN 14	75	5
MY BUSINESS IS WITH LADY ADELINE	449	3	DON JUAN 14	90	7
WHO FOUGHT AND FIGHT IN ABSENCE TOO MY BATTLES	452	3	DON JUAN 14	96	7
CONSIDERABLE TALENT IN MY WAY	453	3	DON JUAN 14	98	8
AH--WHAT SHOULD FOLLOW SLIPS FROM MY REFLECTION	456	3	DON JUAN 15	1	1
OR MINIATURE AT LEAST AS IS MY NOTION	457	3	DON JUAN 15	2	6
MUST PERCH HARMONIOUS ON MY TUNEFUL QUILL	458	3	DON JUAN 15	5	4
ON WHAT MAY SUIT OR MAY NOT SUIT MY STORY	464	3	DON JUAN 15	19	5
A MODEST HOPE--BUT MODESTY'S MY FORTE	466	3	DON JUAN 15	22	1
AND PRIDE MY FEEBLE--LET US RAMBLE ON	466	3	DON JUAN 15	22	4
NO DOUBT IF I HAD WISH'D TO PAY MY COURT	466	3	DON JUAN 15	22	5
OF TYRANNY OF ALL KINDS MY CONCISION	466	3	DON JUAN 15	22	7
BUT FOR MY OWN PECULIAR SUPERSTITION	467	3	DON JUAN 15	24	4
'GAINST RHYME I NEVER SHOULD HAVE KNOCK'D MY BROWS	467	3	DON JUAN 15	24	5
NOR BROKEN MY OWN HEAD NOR THAT OF PRISCIAN	467	3	DON JUAN 15	24	6
MARCH MY MUSE IF YOU CANNOT FLY YET FLUTTER	468	3	DON JUAN 15	27	2
MY OBJECTION'S TO HIS TITLE NOT HIS RITUAL	472	3	DON JUAN 15	36	7
'TIS NOT MY PURPOSE ON HIS VIEWS TO DWELL	472	3	DON JUAN 15	38	5
AND AS MY FRIEND SCOTT SAYS I SOUND MY WARISON	481	3	DON JUAN 15	59	3
AND AS MY FRIEND SCOTT SAYS I SOUND MY WARISON	481	3	DON JUAN 15	59	3
SCOTT THE SUPERLATIVE OF MY COMPARATIVE--	481	3	DON JUAN 15	59	4
I SAY IN MY SLIGHT WAY I MAY PROCEED	482	3	DON JUAN 15	60	1
MY MUSE HATH BRED AND STILL PERHAPS MAY BREED	482	3	DON JUAN 15	60	5
MY MUSE WOULD RUN MUCH MORE INTO EXCESS	483	3	DON JUAN 15	64	3
REQUIRES ARITHMETIC BEYOND MY FORCES	486	3	DON JUAN 15	69	4
ALL WHICH I USE TO MAKE MY RHYMES RUN GLIBBER	487	3	DON JUAN 15	71	3
BUBBLE AND SQUEAK WOULD SPOIL MY LIQUID LAY	487	3	DON JUAN 15	71	6
MUST I PASS OVER IN MY BILL OF FARE	488	3	DON JUAN 15	73	2
ON THEM AND BREAD 'TWAS OFT MY LUCK TO DINE	488	3	DON JUAN 15	73	5
THE GRASS MY TABLE-CLOTH IN OPEN AIR	488	3	DON JUAN 15	73	6
OF WHOM HALF MY PHILOSOPHY THE PROGENY IS	488	3	DON JUAN 15	73	8
EVEN MY VERACIOUS SELF--BUT THAT'S A LIE	495	3	DON JUAN 15	88	3
AND YET SUCH IS MY FOLLY OR MY FATE	496	3	DON JUAN 15	91	4
AND YET SUCH IS MY FOLLY OR MY FATE	496	3	DON JUAN 15	91	4
I ALWAYS KNOCK MY HEAD AGAINST SOME ANGLE	496	3	DON JUAN 15	91	5
IN POLITICS MY DUTY IS TO SHOW JOHN	497	3	DON JUAN 15	92	5
IT MAKES MY BLOOD BOIL LIKE THE SPRINGS OF HECLA	497	3	DON JUAN 15	92	7
BECAUSE MY BUSINESS IS TO DRESS SOCIETY	497	3	DON JUAN 15	93	5
SHALL FOOL ME TO THE TOP UP OF MY BENT--	498	3	DON JUAN 15	94	3
BY DEEMING THAT MY MUSE'S CONVERSATION	498	3	DON JUAN 15	94	6
FOR CERTAIN REASONS MY BELIEF IS SERIOUS	498	3	DON JUAN 15	95	8
MY SMILES MUST BE SINCERE OR NOT AT ALL	499	3	DON JUAN 15	96	2
AND THEREFORE THOUGH 'TIS BY NO MEANS MY WAY	500	3	DON JUAN 15	98	1
SHADOWS--BUT YOU MUST BE IN MY CONDITION	500	3	DON JUAN 15	98	7
BUT THIS I MUST SAY IN MY OWN APPLAUSE	502	3	DON JUAN 16	2	4
BUT WONDER THEY SO FEW ARE SINCE MY TALE IS	502	3	DON JUAN 16	3	7
SOMETIMES UNLESS MY FEELINGS RATHER ERR)	506	3	DON JUAN 16	14	5
SOMETHING BUT WHAT'S NOT STATED IN MY TALE	514	3	DON JUAN 16	31	3
BETWEEN SOME GREYHOUNDS ON MY LORD'S ESTATE	527	3	DON JUAN 16	55	6
MY LORDS AND LADIES PROUDLY CONDESCENDING	538	3	DON JUAN 16	79	2
(FOR LITTLE THINGS UPON MY LORD'S ESTATE	544	3	DON JUAN 16	91	7

                                                                    PAGE VOL   CANTO STANZA LN
MY   (CONTINUED)
    JUST AS I MAKE MY MIND UP EVERY DAY   . . . . 566 3 DON JUAN 17   10   6
    MY TREMBLING LYRE ALREADY SEVERAL STRINGS   . . . . . . 568 3 DON JUAN 17   13   5
    MY SOUL FROM OUT ME AT THY SINGLE SUMMON . . . . 569 3 DON JUAN 17 V 13   6
MYRIADS
    WHICH ONCE-NAMED MYRIADS NAMELESS LIE BENEATH   . . . . . 399 2 DON JUAN 4   102   7
MYRMIDONS
    HER MASTER AND HIS MYRMIDONS OF WHOM   . . . . 109 2 DON JUAN 1   159   4
MYRTLE
    UNWITHERING MYRTLE ROUND THE UNBLUNTED DART . . . . . . 554 3 DON JUAN 16   109   6
MYSELF
    I'M FOND MYSELF OF SOLITUDE OR SO   . . . . 68 2 DON JUAN 1   87   5
    IS THAT MYSELF AND SEVERAL NOW IN SEVILLE   . . . . . . 138 2 DON JUAN 1   203   7
    SAY VERY OFTEN TO MYSELF ALAS   . . . . 147 2 DON JUAN 1   220   1
    I COULD NOT DEEM MYSELF A SLAVE . . . . 321 2 DON JUAN 3 L 3   6
    AS BOY I THOUGHT MYSELF A CLEVER FELLOW . . . . . . 345 2 DON JUAN 4   3   1
    FOR FEAR OF SEEMING RATHER TOUCH'D MYSELF-- . . . . . . 384 2 DON JUAN 4   74   4
    'TWOULD NOT BECOME MYSELF TO DWELL UPON . . . . . . 392 2 DON JUAN 4   88   1
    A TOWN WAS TA'EN MYSELF INSTEAD OF WIDIN . . . . . . 418 2 DON JUAN 5   15   8
    MORE THAN I HAVE MYSELF OF WHAT COULD MAKE . . . . . . 42 3 DON JUAN 6   71   7
    (I DON'T MUCH PIQUE MYSELF UPON ORTHOGRAPHY . . . . . . 149 3 DON JUAN 8   74   2
    I THINK I CAN EXPLAIN MYSELF WITHOUT . . . . 207 3 DON JUAN 9   50   1
    TO KNOW MYSELF AND ALL BESIDES MERE SPIRIT . . . . . . 268 3 DON JUAN 11   1   V7
    WITH SUCH SMALL GEAR TO GIVE MYSELF CONCERN . . . . . . 300 3 DON JUAN 11   63   3
    MYSELF WITH METAPHYSICS NONE CAN HATE . . . . 496 3 DON JUAN 15   91   2
MYSTAGOGUE
    THAT MONSTROUS MYSTAGOGUE--THAT MERE SPOUT . . . . . . 207 3 DON JUAN 9   50   V5
MYSTERIES
    COURT MYSTERIES HAVING BEEN HIMSELF A MINISTER . . . . . 368 3 DON JUAN 13   21   4
    OR WITH ITS MIST OF GERMAN MYSTERIES . . . . 450 3 DON JUAN 14   92   V5
    THOSE HOLIER MYSTERIES WHICH THE WISE AND JUST . . . . . 503 3 DON JUAN 16   6   6
MYSTERIOUS
    THAT SOURCE OF THE SUBLIME AND THE MYSTERIOUS-- . . . . . 498 3 DON JUAN 15   95   7
    QUITE WELL YES NO--THESE ANSWERS WERE MYSTERIOUS . . . . 514 3 DON JUAN 16   33   1
MYSTERY
    AS IF SHE DEEM'D THAT MYSTERY WOULD ENNOBLE 'EM . . . . . 28 2 DON JUAN 1   13   8
    ARTS SCIENCES NO BRANCH WAS MADE A MYSTERY . . . . . . 43 2 DON JUAN 1   39   7
    HIS MIND THE MORE O'ER THIS ITS MYSTERY BROODED . . . . . 118 2 DON JUAN 1   177   6
    BESIDES I HATE ALL MYSTERY AND THAT AIR . . . . . . 222 2 DON JUAN 2   124   3
    BUT IT WAS ALL A MYSTERY HERE WE ARE . . . . 432 2 DON JUAN 5   39   1
    THE MYSTERY OF THIS RUPTURE OF THEIR REST . . . . . . 48 3 DON JUAN 6   85   6
    WITH ALL ITS VEIL OF MYSTERY DRAWN APART . . . . . . 169 3 DON JUAN 8   115   4
    BECAME A KIND OF FASHIONABLE MYSTERY . . . . 328 3 DON JUAN 12   27   8
    I LOVE THE MYSTERY OF A FEMALE MISSAL . . . . 407 3 DON JUAN 13   105   4
    OF MODERN DINNERS WHERE MORE MYSTERY LURKS . . . . . . 482 3 DON JUAN 15   62   6
    WITH ALL THE MYSTERY BY MIDNIGHT CAUSED . . . . . . 507 3 DON JUAN 16   15   5
    A REEL WITHIN A BOTTLE IS A MYSTERY . . . . 531 3 DON JUAN 16   62   1
    RESOLVED TO THRUST THE MYSTERY CARTE AND TIERCE . . . . . 559 3 DON JUAN 16   119   5
MYSTIC
    OVER THE MYSTIC LEAF HIS SOUL WAS SHOOK . . . . 72 2 DON JUAN 1   95   5
    OH LOVE HOW PERFECT IS THY MYSTIC ART . . . . 78 2 DON JUAN 1   106   3
    FROM OUR OLD CRASH SOME MYSTIC ANCIENT STRAIN . . . . . 201 3 DON JUAN 9   38   3
    NAMED FROM HER MYSTIC OFFICE L'EPROUVEUSE . . . . . . 224 3 DON JUAN 9   84   7
    MY MUSIC HAS SOME MYSTIC DIAPASONS . . . . 419 3 DON JUAN 14   22   6
    A LOVING LETTER WITH A MYSTIC SEAL . . . . 422 3 DON JUAN 14   27   6
    LIKE THAT SAME MYSTIC MUSIC OF THE SPHERES . . . . . . 489 3 DON JUAN 15   76   5
    OF THIS SAME MYSTIC FRIAR'S CURIOUS DOINGS . . . . . . 527 3 DON JUAN 16   53   7
MYSTICAL
    SEEM AT THE SAME TIME MYSTICAL AND GAY . . . . 220 2 DON JUAN 2   120   8
    THE MYSTICAL USURPER OF THE MIND-- . . . . 360 2 DON JUAN 4   30   4
    THE NEXT THE VIRGIN'S MYSTICAL VIRGINITY . . . . . . 271 3 DON JUAN 11   6   3
    A GARMENT OF A MYSTICAL SUBLIMITY . . . . 421 3 DON JUAN 14   26   7
MYSTIFIED
    WHEN GAZING ON THEM MYSTIFIED BY DISTANCE . . . . . . 163 2 DON JUAN 2   12   7
    AND KINGS AND CONSORTS OFT ARE MYSTIFIED . . . . . . 477 2 DON JUAN 5   115   6
MYTHOLOGICAL
    I'VE GOT NEW MYTHOLOGICAL MACHINERY . . . . 136 2 DON JUAN 1   201   7
MYTHOLOGY
    FOR DONNA INEZ DREADED THE MYTHOLOGY . . . . 44 2 DON JUAN 1   41   8
NABUCHADONOSOR
    WHERE NABUCHADONOSOR KING OF MEN . . . . 445 2 DON JUAN 5   60   3
NADIR
    WITH GORE LIKE NADIR SHAH THAT COSTIVE SOPHY . . . . . 199 3 DON JUAN 9   33   4
NAG
    HE FEAR'D HIS NECK TO VENTURE SUCH A NAG ON . . . . . . 333 2 DON JUAN 3   99   6
    OR RODE A NAG WHICH TROTTED NOT TOO HIGH . . . . . . 406 3 DON JUAN 13   102   5
NAIAD
    SWEET NAIAD OF THE PHLEGETHONTIC RILL . . . . 372 2 DON JUAN 4   53   2
NAILED
    AND SITTING AS IF NAILED UPON HIS CHAIR . . . . . . 542 3 DON JUAN 16   87   4
NAILS
    THERE BREATHLESS WITH HIS DIGGING NAILS HE CLUNG . . . . 213 2 DON JUAN 2   108   1
    HER NAILS WERE TOUCH'D WITH HENNA BUT AGAIN . . . . . . 314 2 DON JUAN 3   75   6
NAKED
    HOW JUAN NAKED FAVOUR'D BY THE NIGHT . . . . 126 2 DON JUAN 1   188   2
    THE BOATS PULLED OFF WITH THEIR HALF NAKED CREWS . . . . 183 2 DON JUAN 2   51   V6
    BUT BEING NAKED SHE WAS SHOCK'D YOU KNOW . . . . . . 224 2 DON JUAN 2   129   5
    NEXT THEY--HE BEING NAKED SAVE A TATTER'D . . . . . . 240 2 DON JUAN 2   160   1
    HALF NAKED LOVING NATURAL AND GREEK . . . . 259 2 DON JUAN 2   194   8

NAME
HIS FATHER'S NAME WAS JOSE--DON OF COURSE	26	2 DON JUAN	1	9	1
ALFONSO WAS THE NAME OF JULIA'S LORD	57	2 DON JUAN	1	65	1
IN HEAVEN'S NAME DON ALFONSO WHAT D'YE MEAN	98	2 DON JUAN	1	142	2
IF EVER YOU INDEED DESERVED THE NAME	101	2 DON JUAN	1	146	2
NOTHING SO DEAR AS AN UNFILCH'D GOOD NAME	112	2 DON JUAN	1	165	5
YET IF I NAME MY GUILT 'TIS NOT TO BOAST	130	2 DON JUAN	1	193	5
SO THAT MY NAME OF EPIC'S NO MISNOMER	135	2 DON JUAN	1	200	8
A NAME THE LADIES MUST NOT TAKE AMISS	140	2 DON JUAN	1	206	V4
A NAME A WRETCHED PICTURE AND WORSE BUST	146	2 DON JUAN	1	218	8
HIS THOUGHTS HOW WELL APPLIED THE NAME OF GOD	154	2 DON JUAN	1	V 5	V2
FIGHTING DEVOTION DUST--PERHAPS A NAME	159	2 DON JUAN	2	4	8
BY NAME--WAS DESTINED FOR THE PORT LEGHORN	169	2 DON JUAN	2	24	V2
BATTISTA THOUGH (A NAME CALL'D SHORTLY TITA)	186	2 DON JUAN	2	56	7
HE HAD PRONOUNCED HER NAME--BUT SHE FORGOT	228	2 DON JUAN	2	135	7
NIGHT WAS A JULIET TO THE VERY NAME	272	2 DON JUAN	2	V 1	8
THE REAL NAME OF THE FAIR VERONESE--	273	2 DON JUAN	2	V 2	2
ONE OF THE NAME BUT THAT I LOVED HER TOO	273	2 DON JUAN	2	V 2	8
THE NAME AND QUALITY OF HIS NEW PATRON	298	2 DON JUAN	3	44	7
(FOR THAT'S THE NAME THEY LIKE TO PRAY BENEATH)--	309	2 DON JUAN	3	66	4
MAY TURN HIS NAME UP AS A RARE DEPOSIT	327	2 DON JUAN	3	89	8
THAN ON THE NAME A PERSON LEAVES BEHIND	328	2 DON JUAN	3	90	4
OF VERSE (THE NAME WITH WHICH WE CANTABS PLEASE	341	2 DON JUAN	3	110	7
AND SUNG OF LOVE THE FIERCE NAME STRUCK THROUGH ALL	380	2 DON JUAN	4	66	3
SIGHS O'ER HER NAME AND MANY AN ISLANDER	383	2 DON JUAN	4	73	2
HIGH BARROWS WITHOUT MARBLE OR A NAME	386	2 DON JUAN	4	77	1
WHERE TWENTY AGES GATHER O'ER A NAME	398	2 DON JUAN	4	100	4
INVENTED BY SOME NAME I HAVE FORGOT	406	2 DON JUAN	4	112	3
I HAVE A PASSION FOR THE NAME OF MARY	413	2 DON JUAN	5	4	1
SAID IN HEAVEN'S NAME LET'S GET SOME SUPPER NOW	437	2 DON JUAN	5	47	7
KEEP YOUR GOOD NAME THOUGH EVE HERSELF ONCE FELL	460	2 DON JUAN	5	84	6
'TIS NOT HIS CONQUESTS KEEP HIS NAME IN FASHION	8	3 DON JUAN	6	4	6
LOLAH DEMANDED THE NEW DAMSEL'S NAME--	28	3 DON JUAN	6	44	1
JUANNA--WELL A PRETTY NAME ENOUGH	28	3 DON JUAN	6	44	2
HOW SHALL I SPELL THE NAME OF EACH COSSACQUE	73	3 DON JUAN	7	14	3
I'VE SAID I KNOW OF A NAME THAT FILLS	76	3 DON JUAN	7	20	5
PRAISE) IF A MAN'S NAME IN A BULLETIN	77	3 DON JUAN	7	21	2
WHO NAME THE FRENCH IN ENGLISH SAVE TO SHEW	77	3 DON JUAN	7	22	7
BUT 'TIS A NAME SO SPREAD O'ER SIR AND MADAM	79	3 DON JUAN	7	25	7
YOUR NAME BEFORE THE SECOND IS A NEW ONE	97	3 DON JUAN	7	60	5
BUT LET THAT PASS--I THINK I HAVE HEARD YOUR NAME	97	3 DON JUAN	7	60	7
VIBRATE TO THE ETERNAL NAME HARK THROUGH	116	3 DON JUAN	8	8	7
FOR FIFTY THOUSAND HEROES NAME BY NAME	120	3 DON JUAN	8	17	4
FOR FIFTY THOUSAND HEROES NAME BY NAME	120	3 DON JUAN	8	17	4
THRICE HAPPY HE WHOSE NAME HAS BEEN WELL SPELT	120	3 DON JUAN	8	18	6
WAS PRINTED GROVE ALTHOUGH HIS NAME WAS GROSE	120	3 DON JUAN	8	18	8
AND THOUGH HIS NAME THAN AJAX OR ACHILLES	132	3 DON JUAN	8	39	2
AND WHAT'S STILL STRANGER LEFT BEHIND A NAME	144	3 DON JUAN	8	63	1
MAY HAVE ANOTHER NAME FOR HALF WE SCAN	163	3 DON JUAN	8	104	3
FRANCE COULD NOT EVEN CONQUER YOUR GREAT NAME	183	3 DON JUAN	9	1	3
WITHOUT A STOMACH--WHAT WERE A GOOD NAME	189	3 DON JUAN	9	14	8
TO LOVE THERE ARE THOSE THINGS WHICH WORDS NAME SENSES--	219	3 DON JUAN	9	74	8
WHICH GAVE HER DUKES THE GRACELESS NAME OF BIRON	253	3 DON JUAN	10	58	4
THROUGH POLAND THERE IS KOSCIUSKO'S NAME	254	3 DON JUAN	10	59	7
HOW HER GREAT NAME IS NOW THROUGHOUT ABHORRED	258	3 DON JUAN	10	67	2
SPIRIT WOULD NAME AND THEREFORE EVEN I WON'T ANENT	289	3 DON JUAN	11	43	4
OR FAME OR NAME FOR WIT WAR SENSE OR NONSENSE	305	3 DON JUAN	11	73	2
AND OUGHT TO GO BY QUITE ANOTHER NAME	323	3 DON JUAN	12	15	8
THE TENTH OR TWENTIETH NAME WOULD BE BUT BLUNDERED	324	3 DON JUAN	12	19	4
A YOUNG UNMARRIED MAN WITH A GOOD NAME	342	3 DON JUAN	12	58	1
('TIS AN OLD NORMAN NAME AND TO BE FOUND	359	3 DON JUAN	13	2	2
THEREFORE I NAME NOT SQUARE STREET PLACE UNTIL I	370	3 DON JUAN	13	27	5
PRESENT LORDS A B C--EARLS DUKES BY NAME	383	3 DON JUAN	13	54	2
WERE THINGS BUT ONLY CALL'D BY THEIR RIGHT NAME	455	3 DON JUAN	14	102	7
A PRETTY NAME AS ONE WOULD WISH TO READ	458	3 DON JUAN	15	5	3
TO NAME A THING IN NOMENCLATURE RATHER	533	3 DON JUAN	16	67	7
HE GLORIED IN THE NAME OF ENGLISHMAN	537	3 DON JUAN	16	75	8

NAMED
IN EVERY CHRISTIAN LANGUAGE EVER NAMED	26	2 DON JUAN	1	10	3
AS NUMA'S (WHO WAS ALSO NAMED POMPILIUS)	40	2 DON JUAN	1	35	7
SIXTEEN CALLED THOMSON AND NINETEEN NAMED SMITH	75	3 DON JUAN	7	18	8
JUST NAMED THESE PALISADES WERE PRIMLY SET	136	3 DON JUAN	8	46	8
NAMED AFTER THEE ACHILLES) AND QUITE THROUGH'T	153	3 DON JUAN	8	84	5
NAMED FROM HER MYSTIC OFFICE L'EPROUVEUSE	224	3 DON JUAN	9	84	1
(LIKE LUCUS FROM NO LIGHT) THROUGH PROSPECTS NAMED	278	3 DON JUAN	11	21	2
I HAVE NAMED A FEW NOT FOREMOST IN DEGREE	397	3 DON JUAN	13	83	5
BUT WHAT IS ODD NONE EVER NAMED THE DUKE	430	3 DON JUAN	14	45	1
OF DOUBLE NATURE AND THUS DOUBLY NAMED--	448	3 DON JUAN	14	89	2

NAMELESS
IN NAMELESS PRINT--THAT I HAVE NO DEVOTION	336	2 DON JUAN	3	104	2
WHICH ONCE-NAMED MYRIADS NAMELESS LIE BENEATH	399	2 DON JUAN	4	102	7
THOUGH NAMELESS IN OUR LANGUAGE--WE RETORT	405	3 DON JUAN	13	101	6

NAMES
THE NAMES OF ALL THE WITNESSES THE PLEADINGS	127	2 DON JUAN	1	189	3
FOR CALLING NAMES AND TAKING THEM AGAIN	150	2 DON JUAN	1	V 1	4
THE SAME THINGS CHANGE THEIR NAMES AT SUCH A RATE	278	2 DON JUAN	3	6	6
SUCH NAMES AT PRESENT CUT A CONVICT FIGURE	330	2 DON JUAN	3	94	1
SOME LITTLE HAMLETS WITH NEW NAMES UNCOUTH	387	2 DON JUAN	4	78	2
AND SO GREAT NAMES ARE NOTHING MORE THAN NOMINAL	399	2 DON JUAN	4	101	1

NAMES   (CONTINUED)

	PAGE	VOL		CANTO	STANZA	LN
THEIR NAMES WHO REARED IT BUT HUGE HOUSES FIT ILL--	444	2	DON JUAN	5	59	5
WHOSE NAMES WANT NOTHING BUT--PRONUNCIATION	73	3	DON JUAN	7	14	8
WHICH MAY BE NAMES AT MOSCOW INTO RHYME	74	3	DON JUAN	7	16	2
THEIR GALLIC NAMES UPON A GLORIOUS DAY	77	3	DON JUAN	7	22	3
NAMES GREAT AS ANY THAT THE ROLL OF FAME HAS	82	3	DON JUAN	7	32	8
THEIR NAMES ARE RARELY FOUND NOR OFTEN SOUGHT	83	3	DON JUAN	7	34	4
YOU CAN'T REPEAT NINE NAMES FROM EACH GAZETTE	83	3	DON JUAN	7	34	8
YOUR NAMES--MINE'S JOHNSON AND MY COMRADE'S JUAN	97	3	DON JUAN	7	60	1
THE SERVILE AND THE VAIN SUCH NAMES WILL BE	114	3	DON JUAN	8	5	7
OF THE GREAT NAMES WHICH IN OUR FACES STARE	143	3	DON JUAN	8	61	3
ETERNAL SUCH NAMES MINGLED) ISMAIL'S OUR'S	178	3	DON JUAN	8	133	8
THAT HE WHO NAMES ONE BOTH PERCHANCE MAY HIT ON	221	3	DON JUAN	9	77	6
AND BLAZON O'ER THE DOOR THEIR NAMES IN BRASS	283	3	DON JUAN	11	31	8
AND SOME OF THEM HIGH NAMES I HAVE ALSO KNOWN	344	3	DON JUAN	12	61	2
HONOUR WAS MORE BEFORE THEIR NAMES THAN AFTER	398	3	DON JUAN	13	86	2
WHEN WILL YOUR NAMES LEND LUSTRE EVEN TO PARTRIDGES	485	3	DON JUAN	15	67	8

NAMING

BY NAMING STREETS SINCE MEN ARE SO CENSORIOUS	369	3	DON JUAN	13	25	2

NAPLES

OR ROME ON TIBER--NAPLES ON THE SEA	271	3	DON JUAN	11	7	V6

NAPOLEON

NAPOLEON ON HIS BOLD AND BLOODY TRACK	147	3	DON JUAN	8	70	3
EXCEPT NAPOLEON OR ABUSED IT MORE	187	3	DON JUAN	9	9	2
THE GRAND NAPOLEON OF THE REALMS OF RHYME	296	3	DON JUAN	11	55	8
WHERE IS NAPOLEON THE GRAND GOD KNOWS	307	3	DON JUAN	11	77	1
I HAVE SEEN NAPOLEON WHO SEEMED QUITE A JUPITER	309	3	DON JUAN	11	83	1
BRIGHT AS A NEW NAPOLEON FROM ITS MINTAGE	458	3	DON JUAN	15	7	3

NAPOLEON'S

HAD FACED NAPOLEON'S FOES UNTIL THEY FLED--	431	2	DON JUAN	5	37	6
NAPOLEON'S MARY'S (QUEEN OF SCOTLAND) SHOULD	218	3	DON JUAN	9	71	5

NAPS

YOU'LL PARDON TO MY MUSE A FEW SHORT NAPS	503	2	DON JUAN	5	159	8

NARRATE

NOW PONDERING--IT IS TIME WE SHOULD NARRATE	203	3	DON JUAN	9	42	2

NARRATING

NARRATING SOMEWHAT OF DON JUAN'S FATHER	25	2	DON JUAN	1	7	7
SO ON I RAMBLE NOW AND THEN NARRATING	203	3	DON JUAN	9	42	1

NARRATION

WHO LEFT AN ONLY DAUGHTER MY NARRATION	54	2	DON JUAN	1	59	4
'TIS TIME WE SHOULD RETURN TO PLAIN NARRATION	34	3	DON JUAN	6	57	1
CONJECTURING WONDERING ASKING A NARRATION	43	3	DON JUAN	6	74	3
AND CANNOT TUNE THOSE DISCORDS OF NARRATION	74	3	DON JUAN	7	16	1
THIS NARRATIVE IS NOT MEANT FOR NARRATION	413	3	DON JUAN	14	7	6
BUT WISHED FOR A STILL MORE DETAILED NARRATION	526	3	DON JUAN	16	53	6

NARRATIVE

TO THOSE RELATED IN MY GRAND-DAD'S NARRATIVE	229	2	DON JUAN	2	137	8
BUT TO THE NARRATIVE THE VESSEL BOUND	407	2	DON JUAN	4	113	1
AND THUS MY NARRATIVE PROCEEDS--DUDU	34	3	DON JUAN	6	57	2
THIS NARRATIVE IS NOT MEANT FOR NARRATION	413	3	DON JUAN	14	7	6
METHINKS WE MAY PROCEED UPON OUR NARRATIVE	481	3	DON JUAN	15	59	2

NARROW

BUT A STONE BASTION WITH A NARROW GORGE	72	3	DON JUAN	7	12	1
SO NARROW AS TO SHAME THEIR WINTRY BRINK	228	3	DON JUAN	10	7	3
EVEN IN THE COUNTRY CIRCLE'S NARROW BOUND--	544	3	DON JUAN	16	91	6

NARROWNESS

THERE IS A NARROWNESS IN SUCH A NOTION	12	2	DON JUAN	D	5	7

NATAL

MY MOTHER DREAM'D NOT IN MY NATAL HOUR	106	2	DON JUAN	1	155	7

NATHLESS

ABOUT HIS EARS AND NATHLESS WOULD NOT BEND	471	2	DON JUAN	5	104	2

NATION

EXPLAINING METAPHYSICS TO THE NATION--	10	2	DON JUAN	D	2	7
THE HOPES OF ALL MEN AND OF EVERY NATION	250	2	DON JUAN	2	179	4
ALTHOUGH HE FLEECED THE FLAGS OF EVERY NATION	283	2	DON JUAN	3	14	2
HATE TO THE WORLD AND WAR WITH EVERY NATION	303	2	DON JUAN	3	55	7
HIS STATION GENERATION EVEN HIS NATION	327	2	DON JUAN	3	89	2
A CROWD OF SHIVERING SLAVES OF EVERY NATION	414	2	DON JUAN	5	7	1
'TWOULD GIVE ME PLEASURE--PRAY WHAT IS YOUR NATION	417	2	DON JUAN	5	13	8
OF ALL THE CUSTOMS OF THIS POLISHED NATION	452	2	DON JUAN	5	70	8
HER STATE (IT IS THE CUSTOM OF HER NATION)	475	2	DON JUAN	5	111	6
FOR KINDER FEELINGS WHATSOE'ER THEIR NATION	480	2	DON JUAN	5	120	4
LIKE OTHER ANGRY LADIES OF HER NATION--	65	3	DON JUAN	6	119	5
A GREEK OF GREAT ESTEEM AMONGST HIS NATION	71	3	DON JUAN	7	10	V5
THAN THOUSANDS OF THIS NEW AND POLISHED NATION	73	3	DON JUAN	7	14	7
SHOUTS BRIDGES ARCHES PENSIONS FROM A NATION	114	3	DON JUAN	8	4	3
'TIS TRUE HE SHRANK FROM MEN EVEN OF HIS NATION	144	3	DON JUAN	8	64	1
BUT STILL THERE IS UNTO A PATRIOT NATION	175	3	DON JUAN	8	126	1
AS WHEN THE FRENCH THAT DISSIPATED NATION	176	3	DON JUAN	8	129	4
BUT PRAY GIVE BACK A LITTLE TO THE NATION	185	3	DON JUAN	9	6	8
BUT NOT AT THE EXPENCE OF A WHOLE NATION	185	3	DON JUAN	9	6	V8
OF EVERY DESPOTISM IN EVERY NATION	194	3	DON JUAN	9	24	8
OF EVERY KING THAT EVER CURST A NATION	194	3	DON JUAN	9	24	V8
WITH GARLANDS ROUND BY EVERY NATION HUNG	199	3	DON JUAN	9	34	V6
'TWAS A HIGH PLACE THE HIGHEST IN THE NATION	208	3	DON JUAN	9	52	4
AND AVARICE--DISGUST A POLISHED NATION	223	3	DON JUAN	9	81	V8
WHOSE AGE AND WHAT WAS BETTER STILL WHOSE NATION	241	3	DON JUAN	10	33	3
MERIDIAN-BORN TO FLOURISH IN THIS NATION	246	3	DON JUAN	10	44	V2
AS PATRIOTS (NOW AND THEN) MAY LOVE A NATION	251	3	DON JUAN	10	55	3

NATION   (CONTINUED)

	PAGE	VOL	CANTO	STANZA	LV
WHICH HOLDS WHAT MIGHT HAVE BEEN THE NOBLEST NATION	257	3 DON JUAN 10	66	2
AND LOST IN WONDER OF SO GREAT A NATION	272	3 DON JUAN 11	9	3
THE FRENCH WERE NOT YET A LAMP-LIGHTING NATION	280	3 DON JUAN 11	26	6
BUT SEATS A NATION OR UPSETS A THRONE	318	3 DON JUAN 12	6	4
PERHAPS HE WOULD BE WEALTHIEST OF HIS NATION	320	3 DON JUAN 12	10	7
HOWE'ER HE MIGHT ESTEEM THIS MORAL NATION	347	3 DON JUAN 12	68	6
THAT NOBLE SIGHT WHEN REALLY FREE THE NATION	354	3 DON JUAN 12	83	2
PEACE WAR THE TAXES AND WHAT'S CALLED THE NATION	360	3 DON JUAN 13	6	2
A MAN KNOWN IN THE COUNCILS OF THE NATION	365	3 DON JUAN 13	14	3
BUT FORM GOOD HOUSEKEEPERS TO BREED A NATION	420	3 DON JUAN 14	24	8
MARVELL'D AT MERIT OF ANOTHER NATION	425	3 DON JUAN 14	34	3
HIS VICE--FOR HE WAS OF A KINDLING NATION--	567	3 DON JUAN 17	12	6

NATIONAL

HE GAVE THE DIFFERENT NATIONS SOMETHING NATIONAL	319	2 DON JUAN 3	85	2
AS ANY OTHER NOTION AND NOT NATIONAL)--	122	3 DON JUAN 8	23	8
MEANTIME READ ALL THE NATIONAL DEBT SINKERS	357	3 DON JUAN 12	89	7

NATION'S

AND AS THE WIND A WIDOWED NATION'S WAIL	105	3 DON JUAN 7	77	4
TO TELL HOW HE REDUCED THE NATION'S DEBT	440	3 DON JUAN 14	68	4
WHICH NODDED TO THE NATION'S SPOILS BELOW	485	3 DON JUAN 15	67	3

NATIONS

NOR FOES--ALL NATIONS--CONDESCEND TO SMILE--	17	2 DON JUAN D	13	4
HAPPY THE NATIONS OF THE MORAL NORTH	57	2 DON JUAN 1	64	1
PARTICULARLY AMONGST SUN-BURNT NATIONS	59	2 DON JUAN 1	69	8
OH YE WHO TEACH THE INGENUOUS YOUTH OF NATIONS	157	2 DON JUAN 2	1	1
EVEN NATIONS FEEL THIS WHEN THEY GO TO WAR	164	2 DON JUAN 2	14	4
WHICH SCARCE EVEN FRANCE THE PARAGON OF NATIONS	299	2 DON JUAN 3	46	3
AND KNEW THE SELF-LOVES OF THE DIFFERENT NATIONS	319	2 DON JUAN 3	84	2
HE GAVE THE DIFFERENT NATIONS SOMETHING NATIONAL	319	2 DON JUAN 3	85	2
AND MEN IN NATIONS--ALL WERE HIS	322	2 DON JUAN 3	L 4	4
OF NATIONS FREED AND THE WORLD OVERJOY'D	339	2 DON JUAN 3	109	4
TO THE TRUE LAW OF NATIONS WHICH NE'ER MEANT	498	2 DON JUAN 5	151	3
OF VARIOUS NATIONS AND ALL VOLUNTEERS	75	3 DON JUAN 7	18	2
WHICH BREATHES OF NATIONS SAVED NOT WORLDS UNDONE	114	3 DON JUAN 8	5	4
TOWNS NATIONS WORLDS IN HER REVOLVING PRANKS	135	3 DON JUAN 8	44	5
OUT BETWEEN FRIENDS AS WELL AS ALLIED NATIONS	136	3 DON JUAN 8	48	4
THE FATE OF NATIONS--BUT THIS RUSS SO WITTY	179	3 DON JUAN 8	134	7
CALLED SAVIOUR OF THE NATIONS--NOT YET SAVED	185	3 DON JUAN 9	5	7
BETWEEN THESE NATIONS AS A MAIN OF COCKS	197	3 DON JUAN 9	29	7
NATIONS SHE LIKED MAN AS AN INDIVIDUAL	214	3 DON JUAN 9	63	8
HOW ALL THE NATIONS DEEM HER THEIR WORST FOE	258	3 DON JUAN 10	67	5
WHO IS BUT FIRST OF SLAVES THE NATIONS ARE	258	3 DON JUAN 10	68	2
I HAVE SEEN SOME NATIONS LIKE O'ERLOADED ASSES	310	3 DON JUAN 11	84	7
NATIONS ATHWART THE DEEP THE GOLDEN RAYS	319	3 DON JUAN 12	8	4
AT WHICH ALL MODERN NATIONS VAINLY AIM	367	3 DON JUAN 13	20	6
GAUNT GOURMAND WITH WHOLE NATIONS FOR YOUR BOOTY	459	3 DON JUAN 15	9	5
BUT LEAVE THEM TO THE CONSCIENCE OF THE NATIONS	464	3 DON JUAN 15	18	8
OF NATIONS AND HAD NEVER BENT OR BOW'D	476	3 DON JUAN 15	46	6
ALL NATIONS HAVE BELIEVED THAT FROM THE DEAD	504	3 DON JUAN 16	7	3
AMONGST OUR OWN MOST MUSICAL OF NATIONS	523	3 DON JUAN 16	45	6

NATIONS'

| IN THE DISSOLVING CIRCLE ALL THE NATIONS' | 223 | 3 DON JUAN 9 | 82 | 2 |

NATIVE

FOR NATIVE SPANISH SHE HAD NO GREAT CARE	28	2 DON JUAN 1	13	5
BECAME DIVESTED OF HIS NATIVE MODESTY	157	2 DON JUAN 2	1	8
TO SEE ONE'S NATIVE LAND RECEDING THROUGH	163	2 DON JUAN 2	12	2
BEHELD HIS NATIVE SPAIN RECEDING FAR	164	2 DON JUAN 2	14	2
BUT IN HIS NATIVE STREAM THE GUADALQUIVIR	211	2 DON JUAN 2	105	1
AND IN THEIR NATIVE BEAUTY STOOD AVENGED	314	2 DON JUAN 3	75	5
IN NATIVE SWORDS AND NATIVE RANKS	325	2 DON JUAN 3	L 14	3
IN NATIVE SWORDS AND NATIVE RANKS	325	2 DON JUAN 3	L 14	3
ADMIRING THIS NEW NATIVE OF THE DEEP	36	3 DON JUAN 6	60	8
SO THAT WE CAN OUR NATIVE SUN ASSUAGE	217	3 DON JUAN 9	69	5
TO FOREIGNER OR NATIVE SAVE SOME SILLY ONES	263	3 DON JUAN 10	77	6
AND ROARED OUT AS HE WRITHED HIS NATIVE MUD IN	274	3 DON JUAN 11	13	6
HAVE BEEN OBLIGED TO SLAY A FREEBORN NATIVE	277	3 DON JUAN 11	18	7
AS BEAUTIFUL AS HER OWN NATIVE LAND	329	3 DON JUAN 12	29	3
FROM FOREIGN YOKE TO FREE THE HELPLESS NATIVE--	363	3 DON JUAN 13	10	4
ALL PURGED AND PIOUS FROM THEIR NATIVE CLOUDS	396	3 DON JUAN 13	80	4

NATURAL

TO JUAN'S EYES EXCEPTING NATURAL HISTORY	43	2 DON JUAN 1	39	8
HIS NATURAL SPIRIT NOT IN VAIN THEY TOIL'D	49	2 DON JUAN 1	50	5
OF MANY CHARMS IN HER AS NATURAL	51	2 DON JUAN 1	55	5
A PRETTY WOMAN--(THAT'S QUITE NATURAL	158	2 DON JUAN 2	3	5
HALF NAKED LOVING NATURAL AND GREEK	259	2 DON JUAN 2	194	8
AND THOUGH THUS CHAIN'D AS NATURAL HER HAND	396	2 DON JUAN 4	95	4
LIKE NATURAL SHAKESPEARE ON THE IMMORTAL PAGE	490	2 DON JUAN 5	136	V4
BUT NOW IT FLOWED IN NATURAL AND FAST	490	2 DON JUAN 5	137	5
TO TAKE US FROM OUR NATURAL REST AND PULL	46	3 DON JUAN 6	80	3
THEIR VOICES 'GAINST EACH OTHER WHICH IS NATURAL	50	3 DON JUAN 6	88	7
AND NATURAL AGONIES WITH A SLIGHT SHADE	102	3 DON JUAN 7	69	4
YOUR HOURIS ALSO HAVE A NATURAL PLEASURE	168	3 DON JUAN 8	113	1
IN A MOST NATURAL WHIRL CALLED GRAVITATION	225	3 DON JUAN 10	1	6
WERE NOTHING BUT THE NATURAL ATMOSPHERE	266	3 DON JUAN 10	83	7
MY NATURAL TEMPER'S REALLY AUGHT BUT STERN	300	3 DON JUAN 11	63	5
EXPOSED HIM AS WAS NATURAL TO TEMPTATION	355	3 DON JUAN 12	85	7
HAS NOT THE NATURAL STAYS OF STRICT OLD AGE	494	3 DON JUAN 15	85	6
THEREFORE THE PRESENT PIECE OF NATURAL HISTORY	531	3 DON JUAN 16	62	3

540

NATURALLY
```
    MOST NATURALLY SOME SMALL DOUBT INSPIRES--  . . . . . . 287  2 DON JUAN  3    22   3
    THEY NATURALLY POUR THE WINE AND OIL  . . . . . . . . 480  2 DON JUAN  5   120   5
    AND NATURALLY THOUGHT THEY COULD HAVE PLUNDERED  . . . 149  3 DON JUAN  8    75   3
    THE SHUDDER WHICH RUNS NATURALLY THROUGH . . . . . . . 212  3 DON JUAN  9    60   6
    HE NATURALLY LOVED WHAT HE PROTECTED . . . . . . . . . 252  3 DON JUAN 10    57   4
    WHAT NATURE NATURALLY MOST ENCOURAGES)-- . . . . . . . 471  3 DON JUAN 15    35   6
```
NATURE
```
    THAT THERE ARE MONTHS WHICH NATURE GROWS MORE MERRY IN  . 76  2 DON JUAN  1   102   7
    OF HIS OWN NATURE AND THE VARIOUS ARTS  . . . . . . .  91  2 DON JUAN  1   128   2
    'TWAS NATURE GNAW'D THEM TO THIS RESOLUTION . . . . . 195  2 DON JUAN  2    75   6
    NATURE WITH HIM TO THRILL BENEATH HIS TOUCH . . . . . 247  2 DON JUAN  2   173   3
    CIRCLING ALL NATURE HUSH'D AND DIM AND STILL . . . . . 252  2 DON JUAN  2   183   4
    'TIS THAT OUR NATURE CANNOT ALWAYS BRING . . . . . . . 346  2 DON JUAN  4     4   3
    BUT WAS IN THEM THEIR NATURE OR THEIR FATE . . . . . . 354  2 DON JUAN  4    19   3
    WHILE NATURE TORTURED TWENTY THOUSAND WAYS . . . . . . 440  2 DON JUAN  5    52   6
    WHICH PUZZLED NATURE MUCH TO KNOW WHAT ART MEANT . . . 448  2 DON JUAN  5    64   8
    BEING A TRUE WOMAN IN A STATE OF NATURE . . . . . . . 476  2 DON JUAN  5   113  V7
    BUT NATURE TEACHES MORE THAN POWER CAN SPOIL . . . . . 480  2 DON JUAN  5   120   1
    AGAINST PROPORTION--THE WILD STROKES OF NATURE . . . .  32  3 DON JUAN  6    52   5
    A CHILD OF NATURE CARELESSLY ARRAYED . . . . . . . .   36  3 DON JUAN  6    60   3
    OF NATURE OR THE MAN OF ROSS RUN WILD . . . . . . . . 144  3 DON JUAN  8    63   8
    SO MUCH FOR NATURE--BY WAY OF VARIETY . . . . . . . . 146  3 DON JUAN  8    68   1
    IN MORE DESTROYING NATURE AND THE HEAT . . . . . . . . 152  3 DON JUAN  8    82   6
    NATURE HAD WRITTEN GENTLEMAN HE SAID . . . . . . . . . 223  3 DON JUAN  9    83   6
    OF ANYTHING WHICH NATURE WOULD EXPRESS . . . . . . . . 373  3 DON JUAN 13    34   4
    WHEN NATURE WEARS THE GOWN THAT DOTH BECOME HER . . . . 380  3 DON JUAN 13    48   3
    NOR JUDGE AT FIRST IF ALL BE TRUE TO NATURE . . . . . 390  3 DON JUAN 13    67   8
    A WANT OF THAT TRUE NATURE WHICH SUBLIMES . . . . . . 417  3 DON JUAN 14    16   6
    OUR FEELINGS 'GAINST THE NATURE OF THE SOIL . . . . . 447  3 DON JUAN 14    86   4
    OF DOUBLE NATURE AND THUS DOUBLY NAMED-- . . . . . . . 448  3 DON JUAN 14    89   2
    AND TURNING HUMAN NATURE TO AN ART . . . . . . . . . . 457  3 DON JUAN 15     3   4
    AND FOR WHICH NATURE MIGHT FOREGO HER DEBT-- . . . . . 458  3 DON JUAN 15     7   6
    BY NATURE SOFT HIS WHOLE ADDRESS HELD OFF . . . . . . 462  3 DON JUAN 15    14   1
    WITH NATURE MANNERS WHICH ARE ARTIFICIAL . . . . . . . 467  3 DON JUAN 15    25   7
    WHAT NATURE NATURALLY MOST ENCOURAGES)-- . . . . . . . 471  3 DON JUAN 15    35   6
    SINCE ADELINE WAS LIBERAL BY NATURE . . . . . . . . . 478  3 DON JUAN 15    52   6
    BUT NATURE'S NATURE AND HAS MORE CAPRICES . . . . . . 478  3 DON JUAN 15    52   7
    FROM OUT THE COMMONEST DEMANDS OF NATURE . . . . . . . 486  3 DON JUAN 15    69   8
    FROM NATURE FOR THE SERVICE OF THE GOUT-- . . . . . . 488  3 DON JUAN 15    72   2
    BY NATURE AS IN HIGHER DAMES LESS HALE . . . . . . . . 532  3 DON JUAN 16    64   3
```
NATURE'S
```
    AND ANSWER'D BUT TO NATURE'S JUST DEMANDS . . . . . .  42  2 DON JUAN  1    37   6
    YIELD TO STERN TIME AND NATURE'S WRINKLING LAWS . . . 219  2 DON JUAN  2   119   6
    WHICH IS ACQUIRED IN NATURE'S GOOD OLD COLLEGE . . . . 228  2 DON JUAN  2   136   8
    OF NATURE'S ORACLE--FIRST LOVE--THAT ALL . . . . . . . 256  2 DON JUAN  2   189   7
    AND SHE WAS WORSHIPP'D AFTER NATURE'S FASHION . . . . 257  2 DON JUAN  2   191   2
    HAIDEE WAS NATURE'S BRIDE AND KNEW NOT THIS . . . . . 264  2 DON JUAN  2   202   1
    THAN ADMIRATION DUE WHERE NATURE'S RICH . . . . . . . 269  2 DON JUAN  2   211   3
    BUT WISH THIS MASTERPIECE OF NATURE'S WORK . . . . . . 315  2 DON JUAN  3    76  V7
    BUT THOUGHT HOW WORTHY ALTHOUGH NATURE'S WORK . . . . 315  2 DON JUAN  3    76  V7
    YOUR NATURE'S FIRMNESS--KNOW YOUR DAUGHTER'S TOO . . . 366  2 DON JUAN  4    42   8
    THE LOVE OF OFFSPRING'S NATURE'S GENERAL LAW . . . . . 488  2 DON JUAN  5   133   1
    OF HUMAN NATURE'S AGONIZING VOICE . . . . . . . . . . 142  3 DON JUAN  8    59   8
    A FROWN ON NATURE'S OR ON HUMAN FACE-- . . . . . . . . 145  3 DON JUAN  8    65   6
    TO RUTS AND FLINTS AND LOVELY NATURE'S SKILL . . . . . 198  3 DON JUAN  9    31   5
    BEAUTY SPRINGS FORTH AND NATURE'S SELF TURNS PALER . . 204  3 DON JUAN  9    44   4
    IF FROM GREAT NATURE'S OR OUR OWN ABYSS . . . . . . . 410  3 DON JUAN 14     1   1
    IS SHOWN THROUGH NATURE'S WHOLE ANALOGIES . . . . . . 451  3 DON JUAN 14    94   4
    BUT NATURE'S NATURE AND HAS MORE CAPRICES . . . . . . 478  3 DON JUAN 15    52   7
    WAS NATURE'S ALL AURORA COULD NOT BE . . . . . . . . . 481  3 DON JUAN 15    58   6
    HAD BAGGED THIS POACHER UPON NATURE'S MANOR . . . . . 531  3 DON JUAN 16    62   8
    BUT OF ALL NATURE'S DISCREPANCIES NONE . . . . . . . . 541  3 DON JUAN 16    85   1
    WITH NATURE'S GENIAL GENITORS SO THAT . . . . . . . . 564  3 DON JUAN 17     4   3
```
NATURES
```
    STILL I HAVE NO DISLIKE TO LEARNED NATURES . . . . . . 405  2 DON JUAN  4   111   5
    SOME BY A PLACE--AS TEND THEIR YEARS OR NATURES . . . 425  2 DON JUAN  5    27   6
    THEIR NATURES OR THEIR SOVEREIGNS WHO EMPLOY . . . . . 157  3 DON JUAN  8    92   7
```
NAUGHT
```
    A PLEASURE NAUGHT BUT DRUNKENNESS CAN BRING . . . . . 251  2 DON JUAN  2   180  V3
```
NAUGHTY
```
    INSIPID IN THIS NAUGHTY WORLD OF OURS . . . . . . . .  30  2 DON JUAN  1    18   2
    FOR NAUGHTY CHILDREN WHO WOULD RATHER PLAY . . . . . . 162  2 DON JUAN  2    10   3
    FIND ONE WHERE NOTHING NAUGHTY CAN BE SHOWN . . . . . 370  3 DON JUAN 13    27   6
```
NAUSEA
```
    BUT WORST OF ALL IS NAUSEA OR A PAIN . . . . . . . . . 168  2 DON JUAN  2    23   1
```
NAUSEOUS
```
    TO ALL THOSE NAUSEOUS EPIGRAMS OF MARTIAL . . . . . .  45  2 DON JUAN  1    43   8
```
NAUTICAL
```
    WE ENTER ON OUR NAUTICAL EXISTENCE . . . . . . . . . . 163  2 DON JUAN  2    12   8
```
NAVAL
```
    AT WHICH THE NAVAL PEOPLE ARE CONCERN'D . . . . . . .  23  2 DON JUAN  1     4   6
    AND THOUGH 'TWAS NOT MUCH TO A NAVAL MIND . . . . . . 170  2 DON JUAN  2    26   3
    MORE TO SECURE THEM IN THEIR NAVAL CELLS . . . . . . . 393  2 DON JUAN  4    91   5
    MADE ALL THEIR NAVAL MATTERS INCORRECT . . . . . . .   80  3 DON JUAN  7    28   2
    AN ENGLISH NAVAL OFFICER WHO WISHED . . . . . . . . . 152  3 DON JUAN  8    80   7
```
NAVIGATE
```
    THAT SHE MUST OFTEN NAVIGATE O'ER FICTION . . . . . . 495  3 DON JUAN 15    88   8
```
NAVIGATION
```
    STITCHED UP IN SACKS--A MODE OF NAVIGATION . . . . . . 464  2 DON JUAN  5    92   7
```

```
                                                           PAGE VOL        CANTO STANZA LN
NAVIGATION   (CONTINUED)
     YOUR WISE MEN DON'T KNOW MUCH OF NAVIGATION . . . . .  191  3 DON JUAN  9     18    4
     SOMETHING ABOUT THE BALTIC'S NAVIGATION . . . . . . .  246  3 DON JUAN 10     45    6
NAVIGATORS
     THOSE NAVIGATORS MUST BE ABLE SEAMEN . . . . . . . .     7  3 DON JUAN  6      2    3
NAY
     MARRYING THEIR COUSINS--NAY THEIR AUNTS AND NIECES . .   52  2 DON JUAN  1     57    7
     I FAVOUR'D NONE--NAY WAS ALMOST UNCIVIL . . . . . . .  102  2 DON JUAN  1    148    6
     NAY QUOTH THE MAID THE SULTAN'S SELF SHAN'T CARRY ME .  460  2 DON JUAN  5     84    7
     NAY HE HAD WOUNDED THOUGH BUT SLIGHTLY BOTH . . . . .  166  3 DON JUAN  8    109    1
     HUMANITY WOULD RISE AND THUNDER NAY . . . . . . . . .  183  3 DON JUAN  9      1    8
     NAY MARRIED DAMES WILL NOW AND THEN DISCOVER . . . . .  331  3 DON JUAN 12     33    2
     THEIR WALLS IF THEY SAID NAY . . . . . . . . . . . .   518  3 DON JUAN 16   L  2    4
NAZARENE
     AS GREAT A SCORNER OF THE NAZARENE . . . . . . . . .   167  3 DON JUAN  8    111    2
NAZARENES
     THE CRUEL NAZARENES WHO HAD LAID LOW . . . . . . . .   262  3 DON JUAN 10     75    4
NE
     THAT UNDEFINABLE JE NE SCAIS QUOI . . . . . . . . . .  441  3 DON JUAN 14     72    2
NEAR
     ESPECIALLY IN COUNTRIES NEAR THE SUN . . . . . . .      56  2 DON JUAN  1     62    5
     SHE HAD SOME OTHER MOTIVE MUCH MORE NEAR . . . . .      75  2 DON JUAN  1    101    3
     BAY DEEP-MOUTH'D WELCOME AS WE DRAW NEAR HOME . . . .    88  2 DON JUAN  1    123    2
     THE ATTORNEY LAST WHO LINGER'D NEAR THE DOOR . . . .   111  2 DON JUAN  1    164    2
     COME SIR GET IN)--MY MASTER MUST BE NEAR . . . . .     115  2 DON JUAN  1    172    5
     HE STOOD LIKE ADAM LINGERING NEAR HIS GARDEN . . . .   120  2 DON JUAN  1    180    5
     UPON SUCH THINGS WOULD VERY NEAR ABSORB . . . . . .    160  2 DON JUAN  2      6    5
     ALL THE REST PERISH'D NEAR TWO HUNDRED SOULS . . . .   185  2 DON JUAN  2     55    1
     AND NEAR THE CAVE HER QUICK LIGHT FOOTSTEPS DREW . .   232  2 DON JUAN  2    142    2
     THEIR LIPS DREW NEAR AND CLUNG INTO A KISS . . . . .   253  2 DON JUAN  2    185    8
     HE BORE THESE SNEERS AGAINST HIS NEAR RELATIONS . . .  299  2 DON JUAN  3     46    5
     IS AWFUL TO THE VESSEL NEAR THE ROCK . . . . .        305  2 DON JUAN  3     58    4
     A GENTLEMANLY DISTANCE NOT TOO NEAR . . . . . .       366  2 DON JUAN  4     41    5
     MAKING HER STATURE TALL EVEN TALLER--NEAR . . . . .   367  2 DON JUAN  4     43   V5
     THOUGH SLEEPING LIKE A LION NEAR A SOURCE . . . . .   374  2 DON JUAN  4     56    8
     BUT BEING THE PRIMA-DONNA'S NEAR RELATION . . . . .   391  2 DON JUAN  4     87    5
     THE SCARS OF HIS OLD WOUNDS WERE NEAR HIS NEW . . .   431  2 DON JUAN  5     38    1
     WE MUST BE NEAR SOME PLACE OF MAN'S ABODE-- . . . .   436  2 DON JUAN  5     45    1
     YOU KNOW HOW NEAR US THE DEEP BOSPHORUS FLOATS . . .  464  2 DON JUAN  5     92    4
     TO CROSS HER BROW SHE WONDERED HOW SO NEAR . . . .    480  2 DON JUAN  5    119    7
     TO POOR KATINKA SPAIN'S AN ISLAND NEAR . . . . . .     28  3 DON JUAN  6     44    7
     BUT HERE THE MOTHER OF THE MAIDS DREW NEAR . . . . .    29  3 DON JUAN  6     46    1
     THAT THEY HAVE NOTHING BETTER NEAR OR NEWER . . . .     35  3 DON JUAN  6     59    6
     AND NO MORE HANDY SUBSTITUTE BEEN NEAR . . . . . .      75  3 DON JUAN  7     17    8
     AN ISLE NEAR ISMAIL HAD TWO ENDS IN VIEW . . . . .      78  3 DON JUAN  7     23    2
     ONE BARK BLEW UP A SECOND NEAR THE WORKS . . . . .      81  3 DON JUAN  7     30    7
     AMIDST SOME GROANING THOUSANDS DYING NEAR-- . . . .    117  3 DON JUAN  8     11    3
     OR NEAR RELATIONS WHO ARE MUCH THE SAME . . . . .     139  3 DON JUAN  8     54    2
     CRIME CAME NOT NEAR HIM--SHE IS NOT THE CHILD . . .   143  3 DON JUAN  8     62    1
     OF BAFFLED HEROES WHO STOOD SHYLY NEAR . . . . . .    148  3 DON JUAN  8     73    6
     A SLENDER STREAK OF BLOOD ANNOUNCED HOW NEAR . . .    159  3 DON JUAN  8     95    2
     AND LAY BEFORE THEM WITH HIS CHILDREN NEAR . . . .    171  3 DON JUAN  8    119    4
     BUT STILL HE SMILES AND WHETHER NEAR OR FAR . . . .   188  3 DON JUAN  9     12    5
     THE WAYS THAT LEAD THERE BE THEY NEAR OR FAR . . .    222  3 DON JUAN  9     80    3
     HE WROTE TO SPAIN--AND ALL HIS NEAR RELATIONS . . .   239  3 DON JUAN 10     30    1
     TO BE FILLED UP BY SPADE OR MATTOCK'S NEAR . . . .    245  3 DON JUAN 10     42    6
     'TIS ROUND HIM NEAR HIM HERE THERE EVERYWHERE . . .   412  3 DON JUAN 14      5    1
     OR HOW IS'T MATTER TREMBLES TO COME NEAR IT . . . .   557  3 DON JUAN 16    116    8
NEARER
     OF HALF-PAST SIX--PERHAPS STILL NEARER SEVEN . . .     77  2 DON JUAN  1    104    2
     AND HE MUST NEEDS MOUNT NEARER TO THE MOON . . . .    333  2 DON JUAN  3     99    7
     AND NEARER AS THEY CAME A GENIAL SAVOUR . . . . .     437  2 DON JUAN  5     47    1
     AND EVEN THOSE WERE NEARER THAN THEY KNEW . . . .      31  3 DON JUAN  6     51    8
     FOR SOME TIME TILL THEY CAME IN NEARER VIEW . . . .    87  3 DON JUAN  7     43    3
NEAREST
     HIS NEAREST MESSMATE TOLD HIS SIRE WHO THREW . . .    202  2 DON JUAN  2     87    5
     ADVANCING TO THE NEAREST DINNER TRAY . . . . . .      297  2 DON JUAN  3     42    1
     AND THEY WHO WATCH'D HER NEAREST COULD NOT KNOW . .   381  2 DON JUAN  4     69    4
     UNTO THE NEAREST HUT THEMSELVES BETAKE . . . . .      127  3 DON JUAN  8     32    6
     TO JUAN WHO WAS NEAREST HIM ADDRESSED . . . . . .     140  3 DON JUAN  8     56    5
     UNTO HIS NEAREST FOLLOWER OR HENCHMAN . . . . . .     274  3 DON JUAN 11     13    7
     WHO ARE STRONGLY ACTED ON BY WHAT IS NEAREST . . .    547  3 DON JUAN 16     97    8
NEARLY
     AND GREEK--THE ALPHABET--I'M NEARLY SURE . . . . .     28  2 DON JUAN  1     13    2
     FOR DAVID LIVED BUT JUAN NEARLY DIED . . . . . .      113  2 DON JUAN  1    168    8
     DAYS NEARLY O'ER MIGHT BE DISPOSED TO RIOT . . . .    173  2 DON JUAN  2     33    6
     THEY NEARLY REACH'D HER HEEL AND IN HER AIR . . . .   217  2 DON JUAN  2    116    6
     INSENSIBLE--NOT DEAD BUT NEARLY SO-- . . . . . .      224  2 DON JUAN  2    129    3
     WERE NEARLY TINDER SINCE SO LONG THEY LAY . . . .     226  2 DON JUAN  2    132    5
     AND STILL MORE NEARLY TO THE PLACE ADVANCING . . .    290  2 DON JUAN  3     29    1
     UNTIL YOU NEARLY TROD ON THEM AND THEN . . . . .      462  2 DON JUAN  5     88    1
NEARS
     AND AS THE SPOT WHERE THEY APPEAR HE NEARS . . . .    290  2 DON JUAN  3     28    1
NEAT
     TO KEEP THEM BEAUTIFUL OR LEAVE THEM NEAT . . . .      99  2 DON JUAN  1    143    6
     WITH A NEAT LITTLE CROW-QUILL SLIGHT AND NEW . . .    134  2 DON JUAN  1    198    2
     A LITTLE CUPOLA MORE NEAT THAN SOLEMN . . . . . .     400  2 DON JUAN  4    104    2
     A NEAT SNUG STUDY ON A WINTER'S NIGHT . . . . .       444  2 DON JUAN  5     58    1
NEATH
     NEATH WHICH HER BREAST HEAVED LIKE A LITTLE BILLOW . .  311  2 DON JUAN  3     70    4
```

542

NECESSARY
    AS THEY WHO PRINT THEM THINK IS NECESSARY   79   3 DON JUAN 7   26   6
    WAS NOT SO NECESSARY FOR THEY TELL   214   3 DON JUAN 9   63   2
    INDEED I'VE NOT THE NECESSARY BILE   300   3 DON JUAN 11   63   4
    A THING QUITE NECESSARY TO THE ELECT   526   3 DON JUAN 16   52   3
NECK
    DOWN HER WHITE NECK LONG FLOATING AUBURN CURLS--   .   291   2 DON JUAN 3   30   5
    HE FEAR'D HIS NECK TO VENTURE SUCH A NAG ON . .   .   333   2 DON JUAN 3   99   6
    WAS THROWN AS 'TWERE ABOUT THE NECK OF YOU-- .   . .   474   2 DON JUAN 5   110   3
    ONE NECK WHICH HE WITH ONE FELL STROKE MIGHT PIERCE   .   19   3 DON JUAN 6   27   3
    HER NECK ALONE WAS SEEN BUT THAT WAS FOUND   .   .   48   3 DON JUAN 6   85   3
    HE STILL PREFERRED HIS OWN NECK TO ANOTHER'S   .   .   63   3 DON JUAN 6   116   8
    ALL NECK OR NOTHING AS LIKE PITCH OR ROSIN   .   .   135   3 DON JUAN 8   45   3
    A DIMPLED CHIN A NECK OF IVORY STOLE   561   3 DON JUAN 16   123   3
NECKCLOTH
    AND BLACK SILK NECKCLOTH--AND REPLIED YOU'RE RIGHT   . . 161   3 DON JUAN 8   99   7
NECKCLOTH'S
    HIS VERY NECKCLOTH'S GORDIAN KNOT WAS TIED   513   3 DON JUAN 16   29   7
NECKS
    OR BREAKS THEIR HOPES OR HEARTS OR HEADS OR NECKS   . . .   172   2 DON JUAN 2   31   6
    THEY TROD AS UPON NECKS AND TO COMPLETE   475   2 DON JUAN 5   111   5
    OF WHITE CLIFFS WHITE NECKS BLUE EYES BLUER STOCKINGS   .   346   3 DON JUAN 12   67   7
    THEY ADDED GRACEFUL NECKS WHITE HANDS AND ARMS   408   3 DON JUAN 13   107   8
NECTAR
    SUCK'D IN THE MOISTURE WHICH LIKE NECTAR STREAM'D   . . .   202   2 DON JUAN 2   86   2
    A HIDDEN NECTAR UNDER A COLD PRESENCE   375   3 DON JUAN 13   38   3
NEED
    THE FAME YOU ENVY AND THE SKILL YOU NEED   14   2 DON JUAN D   8   4
    OR WHICH AT LEAST I NEED NOT MENTION YET   73   2 DON JUAN 1   96   8
    THERE'S PEN AND INK FOR YOU SIR WHEN YOU NEED--   .   104   2 DON JUAN 1   152   4
    HERE ENDS THIS CANTO--NEED I SING OR SAY   126   2 DON JUAN 1   188   1
    TO ALL THE BROTHER TARS WHO MAY HAVE NEED HENCE   .   171   2 DON JUAN 2   29   5
    HAD GREATER NEED TO NERVE THEMSELVES AGAIN   205   2 DON JUAN 2   93   6
    AND NEED HE HAD OF SLUMBER YET FOR NONE   229   2 DON JUAN 2   137   6
    HIS VESSEL HAVING NEED OF SOME REPAIRS   285   2 DON JUAN 3   19   3
    SHE HAD NO NEED OF THIS DAY NE'ER WILL BREAK   . . .   314   2 DON JUAN 3   76   3
    NEED NOT SEEM VERY WONDERFUL FOR VICE   408   2 DON JUAN 4   115   5
    YOU NEED NOT TAKE THEM UNDER YOUR DIRECTION   186   3 DON JUAN 9   7   6
    WITH OTHER EXTRAS WHICH WE NEED NOT MENTION--   . . .   218   3 DON JUAN 9   72   6
    HOW WE WON'T MENTION WHY WE NEED NOT SAY   235   3 DON JUAN 10   21   2
    PERHAPS--BUT SANS PERHAPS WE NEED NOT SEEK   243   3 DON JUAN 10   38   1
    CARED MOST ABOUT IT NEED NOT NOW BE PLEADED--   . . .   324   3 DON JUAN 12   17   5
    VIRTUES OF WHICH BOTH YOU AND I HAVE NEED   393   3 DON JUAN 13   73   4
    AND SIMPLE IN THE WORLD AND DOTH NOT NEED   437   3 DON JUAN 14   61   6
    AND FOURTHLY WHAT NEED HARDLY BE SAID TWICE   439   3 DON JUAN 14   66   7
    AND SINCE THAT TIME IT NEED NOT COST MUCH SHOWING   .   444   3 DON JUAN 14   78   5
    TO SHOW IT--(POINTS WE NEED NOT NOW DISCUSS)--   .   460   3 DON JUAN 15   10   5
    WILL GO MUCH FURTHER THAN THERE'S NEED TO MENTION   .   462   3 DON JUAN 15   14   8
    WHICH SEEMS AT FIRST TO NEED NO LOFTY WING   . . .   467   3 DON JUAN 15   25   3
    GOD HELP US SINCE WE HAVE NEED ON OUR CAREER   . . .   496   3 DON JUAN 15   90   3
    TO THINK HIS SKULL HAD NOT SOME NEED OF CAULKING   .   565   3 DON JUAN 17   8   6
NEEDED
    WHICH NEEDED NOT AN EMPIRE TO PERSUADE   483   2 DON JUAN 5   125   3
    THE ONLY TIME WHEN MUCH SUCCESS IS NEEDED   324   3 DON JUAN 12   17   3
NEEDLE
    SO SHAKES THE NEEDLE AND SO STANDS THE POLE   133   2 DON JUAN 1   196   7
    AS TURNS THE NEEDLE TREMBLING TO THE POLE   133   2 DON JUAN 1   196   V7
    AND ALWAYS CHANGED AS TRUE AS ANY NEEDLE   317   2 DON JUAN 3   80   2
NEEDLES
    IT TREMBLED AS MAGNETIC NEEDLES DO   134   2 DON JUAN 1   198   4
    LIKE NEEDLES WHICH MAY PIERCE THOSE PETTICOATS   464   2 DON JUAN 5   92   2
NEEDLES'
    THROUGH NEEDLES' EYES IT EASIER FOR THE CAMEL IS   . . .   397   2 DON JUAN 4   97   7
NEEDS
    HER LIP WHICH ZOE NEEDS MUST UNDERSTAND   234   2 DON JUAN 2   146   5
    AND HE MUST NEEDS MOUNT NEARER TO THE MOON   333   2 DON JUAN 3   99   7
    AND THEN HE ADDED THAT HE NEEDS MUST SAY   451   2 DON JUAN 5   69   6
    WE NEEDS MUST FOLLOW WHEN FATE PUTS FROM SHORE   . . .   460   2 DON JUAN 5   84   5
    (PLAIN TRUTH DEAR MURRAY NEEDS FEW FLOWERS OF SPEECH)   .   470   2 DON JUAN 5   101   2
    AND AFTERWARDS IF HE MUST NEEDS DESTROY   123   3 DON JUAN 8   24   5
    OF FAITHFUL PAIRS--(I NEEDS MUST RHYME WITH DOVE   . .   219   3 DON JUAN 9   74   3
NEEDY
    HOW ALL THE NEEDY HONOURABLE MISTERS   331   3 DON JUAN 12   32   1
NE'ER
    A BETTER CAVALIER NE'ER MOUNTED HORSE   26   2 DON JUAN 1   9   5
    HIS PARENTS NE'ER AGREED EXCEPT IN DOTING   34   2 DON JUAN 1   25   3
    'TWAS BUT A DOUBT BUT NE'ER MAGICIAN'S WAND   60   2 DON JUAN 1   71   6
    THOUGH WATCHFUL AS THE LYNX THEY NE'ER DISCOVER   . .   75   2 DON JUAN 1   100   2
    AND WHISPERING I WILL NE'ER CONSENT--CONSENTED   . . .   84   2 DON JUAN 1   117   8
    WE NE'ER FORGET THOUGH THERE WE ARE FORGOT   90   2 DON JUAN 1   126   8
    AND NE'ER BELIEVED IN NEGATIVES TILL THESE   109   2 DON JUAN 1   160   7
    ALFONSO NE'ER TO JUAN HAD ALLUDED   118   2 DON JUAN 1   177   2
    FOR JUAN VERY LUCKILY NE'ER SAW IT   123   2 DON JUAN 1   185   3
    IT NE'ER CAN REACH SO TURNS TO YOU MY SOUL   133   2 DON JUAN 1   196   V8
    RESIST HIS STOMACH NE'ER AT SEA BEFORE   168   2 DON JUAN 2   23   8
    THEY NE'ER TILL NOW HAD KNOWN THE JOYS OF DRINKING   .   201   2 DON JUAN 2   85   8
    NE'ER WITH SUCH FORCE THE SWIFTEST ARROW FLEW   . . .   218   2 DON JUAN 2   117   6
    I NE'ER SAW JUSTICE DONE AND YET SHE WAS   219   2 DON JUAN 2   119   4
    NE'ER COMPASS'D NOR LESS MORTAL CHISEL WROUGHT   . . .   219   2 DON JUAN 2   119   8

543

NE'ER   (CONTINUED)
    THAT SLEEP WHICH SEEM'D AS IT WOULD NE'ER AWAKE . . . . 234 2 DON JUAN 2   146   8
    THAT FINER SIMPLER MUSIC NE'ER WAS HEARD . . . . 236 2 DON JUAN 2   151   5
    KNEW (BY TRADITION FOR SHE NE'ER HAD READ) . . . . . . 239 2 DON JUAN 2   158   6
    HER EARNESTNESS WOULD NE'ER HAVE MADE AN END . . . . . 241 2 DON JUAN 2   161   4
    WHICH GROWS A HABIT SHE CAN NE'ER GET OVER . . . . . . 276 2 DON JUAN 3   3   3
    BUT THOSE WHO HAVE NE'ER END WITH ONLY ONE . . . . . . 276 2 DON JUAN 3   4   8
    AND THAT GOOD WINE NE'ER WASH'D DOWN BETTER FARE . . . 298 2 DON JUAN 3   45   4
    SHE HAD NO NEED OF THIS DAY NE'ER WILL BREAK . . . . . 314 2 DON JUAN 3   76   3
    OF WHICH THE FIRST NE'ER KNOWS THE SECOND CAUSE . . . . 318 2 DON JUAN 3   82   8
    A LAND OF SLAVES SHALL NE'ER BE MINE-- . . . . 326 2 DON JUAN 3 L 16   5
    BREAK WITH THE FIRST FALL THEY CAN NE'ER BEHOLD . . . . 350 2 DON JUAN 4   11   4
    WHICH STILL SAID ALL AND NE'ER COULD SAY TOO MUCH . . . 351 2 DON JUAN 4   14   3
    TO THOSE WHO HAVE CEASED TO HEAR SUCH OR NE'ER HEARD . . 351 2 DON JUAN 4   14   8
    AS ONE WHO NE'ER HAD DWELT AMONG THE SICK . . . . 380 2 DON JUAN 4   67   3
    NO MATTER WE SHOULD NE'ER TOO MUCH INQUIRE . . . . . . 396 2 DON JUAN 4   96   1
    BUT THOSE WHO SATE NE'ER STIRRED IN ANY WISE . . . . . 441 2 DON JUAN 5   54   4
    AND I MUST SAY I NE'ER COULD SEE THE VERY . . . . 469 2 DON JUAN 5   100   7
    BESIDES FORBIDDEN FRUITS FOR SHE NE'ER PAUSED . . . . . 476 2 DON JUAN 5   113 V6
    AND BABA WHO HAD NE'ER BEEN KNOWN TO FAIL . . . . 477 2 DON JUAN 5   114   4
    NOT SO TO HER WHO NE'ER HAD HEARD SUCH THINGS . . . . . 485 2 DON JUAN 5   128   2
    FOR NE'ER TILL NOW SHE KNEW A CHECKED DESIRE . . . . . 489 2 DON JUAN 5   134   6
    TO THE TRUE LAW OF NATIONS WHICH NE'ER MEANT . . . . . 498 2 DON JUAN 5   151   3
    IT NE'ER CAN BE REPLACED IN PROPER FRAME . . . . 502 2 DON JUAN 5   158   4
    WHAT SHE COULD NE'ER EXPRESS--THEN HOW SHOULD I . . . . 59 3 DON JUAN 6   106   8
    BUT NE'ER THE LESS I HOPE IT IS NO CRIME . . . . 67 3 DON JUAN 7   2   6
    (FOR DAY NE'ER SAW HIS MERITS) COULD DECREE . . . . . . 86 3 DON JUAN 7   41   4
    LIKE MOSES OR MELANCTHON WHO HAVE NE'ER . . . . 193 3 DON JUAN 9   21   2
    LIKE MOSES OR LIKE COBBETT WHO HAVE NE'ER . . . . 193 3 DON JUAN 9   21 V2
    I NE'ER DECIDE WHAT I SHALL SAY AND THIS I CALL . . . . 203 3 DON JUAN 9   41   5
    'GAINST REASON--REASON NE'ER WAS HAND-AND-GLOVE . . . . 219 3 DON JUAN 9   74   5
    FOR CATS AND BIRDS MORE PENCHANT NE'ER DISPLAYED . . . 249 3 DON JUAN 10   50   7
    WILL HINT ALLUSIONS NEVER MEANT NE'ER DOUBT . . . . . . 311 3 DON JUAN 11   88   7
    AND MEDES WOULD NE'ER REVOKE WHAT WENT BEFORE . . . . . 366 3 DON JUAN 13   17   4
    WHICH NE'ER CAN PASS THE EQUINOCTIAL LINE . . . . 373 3 DON JUAN 13   34   3
    WHICH LIKE A CREED NE'ER SAYS ALL IT INTENDS . . . . . 407 3 DON JUAN 13   105   5
    FOR TOO MUCH TRUTH AT FIRST SIGHT NE'ER ATTRACTS . . . 416 3 DON JUAN 14   13   6
    HE NE'ER PRESUMED TO MAKE AN ERROR CLEARER-- . . . . . 426 3 DON JUAN 14   37   7
    AND NE'ER TO BE DESCRIBED FOR TO THE DOLOUR . . . . . . 428 3 DON JUAN 14   40   7
    SOME NE'ER BELIEVED ONE HALF OF WHAT THEY HEARD . . . . 429 3 DON JUAN 14   44   5
    ROMANCES I NE'ER READ LIKE THOSE I HAVE SEEN . . . . . 444 3 DON JUAN 14   80   2
    BECAUSE HE NE'ER SEEM'D ANXIOUS TO SEDUCE . . . . 461 3 DON JUAN 15   12   2
    YET NE'ER BETRAYING THIS IN CONVERSATION . . . . 462 3 DON JUAN 15   15   4
    AND AS SHE TREATS ALL THINGS AND NE'ER RETREATS . . . . 502 3 DON JUAN 16   3   1
    A GREAT RESOURCE TO ALL AND NE'ER DENIED . . . . 506 3 DON JUAN 16   12   7
    WHOSE HOUNDS NE'ER ERRED NOR GREYHOUNDS DEIGNED TO LURCH 539 3 DON JUAN 16   80   2
    I KNOW NOT BUT HER COLOUR NE'ER WAS HIGH-- . . . . . . 545 3 DON JUAN 16   94   6
    WHICH KINDLE MANHOOD BUT CAN NE'ER ENTRANCE . . . . . . 554 3 DON JUAN 16   108   6
    ALL THAT I WRITE OR WROTE CAN NE'ER REVIVE . . . . . . 569 3 DON JUAN 17   V 13   3
NEER
    FAMOUS FOR ALWAYS TALKING AND NEER FIGHTING . . . . . . 150 2 DON JUAN 1   V 1   3
    HOW GRAND HIS SENTIMENTS WHICH NEER RUN RIOT . . . . . 154 2 DON JUAN 1   V 5   2
    IS ROUSSEAU'S JULIETTA--I NEER KNEW . . . . 273 2 DON JUAN 2   V 2   7
    WOULD THAT I NEER HAD LOVED--OH WOMAN--WOMAN-- . . . . 569 3 DON JUAN 17   V 13   2
NE'ERTHELESS
    WERE THINGS TO SHAKE A STOIC NE'ERTHELESS . . . . 415 2 DON JUAN 5   9   1
    THERE SHOULD BE NE'ERTHELESS A SLIGHT SUBSTRATUM . . . 107 3 DON JUAN 7   81   4
    UPON THEM NE'ERTHELESS HAD REACHED THE RAMPART . . . . 149 3 DON JUAN 8   75   2
    IN ONE THING NE'ERTHELESS 'TIS FIT TO PRAISE . . . . . 176 3 DON JUAN 8   128   1
    BLUSHING AND BEARDLESS AND YET NE'ERTHELESS . . . . . . 206 3 DON JUAN 9   47   1
    WHATEVER FOLLOWS NE'ERTHELESS MAY BE . . . . 456 3 DON JUAN 15   1   2
NEGATIVES
    AND NE'ER BELIEVED IN NEGATIVES TILL THESE . . . . . . 109 2 DON JUAN 1   160   7
NEGLECT
    NEGLECT INDEED REQUIRES A SAINT TO BEAR IT . . . . . . 32 2 DON JUAN 1   20   3
    BUT WHICH NEGLECT IS HASTENING TO DESTROY . . . . 400 2 DON JUAN 4   103   6
    SHOULD NEITHER COURT NEGLECT NOR DREAD TO BEAR IT . . . 356 3 DON JUAN 12   87   8
NEGLECTED
    HAD BEEN NEGLECTED ILL-USED AND WHAT NOT . . . . 166 3 DON JUAN 8   110   6
NEGLIGENTLY
    HER LOCKS CURL'D NEGLIGENTLY ROUND HER FACE . . . . . . 220 2 DON JUAN 2   121   3
    HIS CURLS FELL NEGLIGENTLY O'ER HIS FRONT . . . . 513 3 DON JUAN 16   29   5
NEGOCIATION
    A SORT OF TREATY OR NEGOCIATION . . . . 246 3 DON JUAN 10   45   2
NEGOTIIS
    BEATUS ILLE PROCUL FROM NEGOTIIS . . . . 443 3 DON JUAN 14   77   1
NEGRESSES
    TWELVE NEGRESSES FROM NUBIA BROUGHT A PRICE . . . . . . 408 2 DON JUAN 4   115   1
NEGRO
    SOME NODDED TO THE NEGRO FROM THEIR STATION . . . . . . 441 2 DON JUAN 5   54   7
    AND WHEN THE OLD NEGRO TOLD HIM TO GET READY . . . . . 453 2 DON JUAN 5   73   7
    REJOINED THE NEGRO PRAY BE NOT PROVOKING . . . . 454 2 DON JUAN 5   75   2
    THE NEGRO BABA HELPED A LITTLE TOO . . . . 456 2 DON JUAN 5   78   5
NEGROES
    THE NEGROES MORE PHILOSOPHY DISPLAY'D-- . . . . 414 2 DON JUAN 5   7   7
    THE NEGROES AND IS WORTH A MILLION FIGHTERS . . . . . . 325 3 DON JUAN 12   20   6
    TRACE UP THOSE SHUFFLING NEGROES NILE OR NIGER . . . . 348 3 DON JUAN 12   70   2
NEGRO'S
    FOR THE OLD NEGRO'S CONFIDENCE IN CREEPING . . . . . . 436 2 DON JUAN 5   45   2

	PAGE	VOL	CANTO	STANZA	LN
NEIGHBOUR					
THAT CARRIED OFF HIS NEIGHBOUR BY THE THIGH	212	2 DON JUAN	2	106	6
DIRECT YOUR QUESTIONS TO MY NEIGHBOUR THERE	298	2 DON JUAN	3	45	6
WITH THIS HIS TUNEFUL NEIGHBOUR THAN HIS FATE	394	2 DON JUAN	4	93	4
AND SHOULD YOU DOUBT PRAY ASK OF YOUR NEXT NEIGHBOUR	288	3 DON JUAN	11	41	4
A SNEER OR SHORT REPLY UNTO THEIR NEIGHBOUR	288	3 DON JUAN	11	41	V4
NEIGHBOURING					
HIS REST THE RUSHING OF THE NEIGHBOURING RILL	229	2 DON JUAN	2	137	3
AND FELT HER VEINS CHILL'D BY THE NEIGHBOURING SEA	233	2 DON JUAN	2	145	4
BECAUSE THE NEIGHBOURING SCOTCH EARL OF GIFTGABBIT	534	3 DON JUAN	16	70	4
NEIGHBOUR'S					
FROM OUR NEXT NEIGHBOUR'S LAND WHERE LIKE A CHESSMAN	288	3 DON JUAN	11	42	3
UPON AN HEIRESS OR HIS NEIGHBOUR'S BRIDE	304	3 DON JUAN	11	71	2
WHO NEVER COVETED THEIR NEIGHBOUR'S LOT	323	3 DON JUAN	12	16	3
HE HAD PAID HIS NEIGHBOUR'S PRAYER WITH HALF A TURBOT	543	3 DON JUAN	16	88	8
NEIGHBOURS					
I KNOW THAT WHAT OUR NEIGHBOURS CALL LONGUEURS	332	2 DON JUAN	3	97	1
NELSON					
NELSON WAS ONCE BRITANNIA'S GOD OF WAR	23	2 DON JUAN	1	4	1
FORGETTING DUNCAN NELSON HOWE AND JERVIS	23	2 DON JUAN	1	4	8
NEM					
NEM CON AMONGST THE WOMEN WHICH I GRIEVE	493	3 DON JUAN	15	84	2
NEPTUNE					
HEAVEN KNOWS--IT MAY BE NEPTUNE PAN OR JOVE	246	2 DON JUAN	2	170	8
N'ER					
WITH STRICT ENQUIRY I COULD N'ER DISCOVER	41	3 DON JUAN	6	70	2
NERO					
WHEN NERO PERISH'D BY THE JUSTEST DOOM	339	2 DON JUAN	3	109	1
BUT I'M DIGRESSING WHAT ON EARTH HAD NERO	341	2 DON JUAN	3	110	1
COULD RHYME LIKE NERO O'ER A BURNING CITY	179	3 DON JUAN	8	134	8
NERVE					
HAD GREATER NEED TO NERVE THEMSELVES AGAIN	205	2 DON JUAN	2	93	6
DISPLAYED MUCH MORE OF NERVE PERHAPS OF WIT	283	2 DON JUAN	3	14	V7
MARCHED FORTH WITH NERVE AND SINEWS BENT TO SLAY--	113	2 DON JUAN	8	2	4
AND FOR YOUR CONSCIENCE ONLY LEARN TO NERVE IT--	366	3 DON JUAN	13	18	6
BEAR A BOLD BROW AND FOR YOUR BOSOM NERVE IT	367	3 DON JUAN	13	18	V4
NERVES					
ON ITS OWN STRENGTH WITH CARELESS NERVES AND THEWS--	131	3 DON JUAN	8	36	6
WHICH IS A SIGNAL TO MY NERVES AND BRAIN	224	3 DON JUAN	9	85	7
HAD CAUSED HIS NERVES--MADE ANSWERS RATHER CLOUDED	527	3 DON JUAN	16	54	V8
NERVOUS					
'TWAS FOOLISH NERVOUS AS SHE MUST ALLOW	47	3 DON JUAN	6	83	4
BUT THEY WERE MOSTLY NERVOUS SIX-FOOT FELLOWS	205	3 DON JUAN	9	46	7
A NERVOUS FAMILY TO WHOSE HEART OR HAND	205	3 DON JUAN	9	46	V3
OF JUAN'S NERVOUS FEELINGS ON THAT DAY	526	3 DON JUAN	16	51	4
NESSUS					
MAY SIT LIKE THAT OF NESSUS AND RECALL	505	3 DON JUAN	16	11	3
NEST					
A NEST OF TUNEFUL PERSONS TO MY EYE	9	2 DON JUAN	D	1	7
SOFT AS THE CALLOW CYGNET IN ITS NEST	235	2 DON JUAN	2	148	6
TO SEE HER BIRD REPOSING IN HIS NEST	245	2 DON JUAN	2	168	4
BUT SOON THEY GROW AGAIN AND LEAVE THEIR NEST	228	3 DON JUAN	10	6	1
NESTLE					
THE SWEETEST SONG-BIRDS NESTLE IN A PAIR	358	2 DON JUAN	4	28	6
NESTLED					
AROUND THE WILD FOWL NESTLED IN THE BRAKE	385	3 DON JUAN	13	57	5
NESTORS					
THE NESTORS OF THE SPORTING GENERATION	425	3 DON JUAN	14	34	5
NET					
LOVE'S THE FIRST NET WHICH SPREADS ITS DEADLY MESH	422	2 DON JUAN	5	22	5
BUT DESTINY AND PASSION SPREAD THE NET	364	3 DON JUAN	13	12	5
NETHERLANDS					
TO SEE IN FORTS OF NETHERLANDS OR FRANCE--	136	3 DON JUAN	8	46	5
NETS					
WERE OF THE FINEST THAT E'ER FLOUNCED IN NETS	307	2 DON JUAN	3	62	4
NEUTER					
BY WHICH NONE WERE PERMITTED TO BE NEUTER--	195	2 DON JUAN	2	75	7
ALL THOSE MAY LEAP WHO RATHER WOULD BE NEUTER--	266	2 DON JUAN	2	205	5
AND RATHER WISHED IN SUCH THINGS TO STAND NEUTER	336	3 DON JUAN	12	42	3
NEUTRAL					
THEY LEFT THIS BEING FREE AND NEUTRAL AS A SCOUT	394	2 DON JUAN	4	92	V5
JUST NOW A BLACK OLD NEUTRAL PERSONAGE	424	2 DON JUAN	5	26	1
NEUTRALISED					
THAT NEUTRALISED DULL DORUS OF THE NINE	297	3 DON JUAN	11	58	4
NEUTRALITY					
WHICH MADE HIM DAILY BLESS HIS OWN NEUTRALITY	64	3 DON JUAN	6	117	8
NEUTRALIZE					
AND NEUTRALIZE HER OUTWARD SHOW OF SCARLET	237	3 DON JUAN	10	26	8
NEUTRUM					
ET BENE DIC NEUTRUM DIC ALIQUANDO MALE	465	3 DON JUAN	15	21	2
NEVA'S					
IN WHICH THE NEVA'S ICE WOULD CEASE TO LIVE	243	3 DON JUAN	10	37	6
NEW					
(THIS OLD SONG AND NEW SIMILE HOLDS GOOD)	10	2 DON JUAN	D	2	2
OF HIS NEW SYSTEM TO PERPLEX THE SAGES	11	2 DON JUAN	D	4	4
WHEN EVERY YEAR AND MONTH SENDS FORTH A NEW ONE	21	2 DON JUAN	1	1	2
FIT FOR MY POEM (THAT IS FOR MY NEW ONE)	24	2 DON JUAN	1	5	7
HER MAIDS WERE OLD AND IF SHE TOOK A NEW ONE	48	2 DON JUAN	1	48	5
HE PUZZLED OVER WHAT HE FOUND A NEW ONE	68	2 DON JUAN	1	86	5

545

NEW   (CONTINUED)

	PAGE	VOL	CANTO		STANZA	LN
FOR LEAVING JUAN TO THIS NEW TEMPTATION	75	2	DON JUAN	1	101	4
LOVE IS SO VERY TIMID WHEN 'TIS NEW	81	2	DON JUAN	1	112	6
TO THOSE WHO COULD INVENT HIM A NEW PLEASURE	85	2	DON JUAN	1	118	2
I CARE NOT FOR NEW PLEASURES AS THE OLD	85	2	DON JUAN	1	118	7
SOME NEW EXPERIMENT TO SHOW HIS PARTS	91	2	DON JUAN	1	128	4
ONE MAKES NEW NOSES ONE A GUILLOTINE	91	2	DON JUAN	1	129	3
BY BORROWING A NEW ONE FROM AN OX	91	2	DON JUAN	1	129	8
WHAT WONDROUS NEW MACHINES HAVE LATE BEEN SPINNING	92	2	DON JUAN	1	130	6
THIS IS THE PATENT AGE OF NEW INVENTIONS	93	2	DON JUAN	1	132	1
TO MEND HIS FORMER MORALS AND GET NEW	129	2	DON JUAN	1	191	3
WITH A NEAT LITTLE CROW-QUILL SLIGHT AND NEW	134	2	DON JUAN	1	198	2
NEW CHARACTERS THE EPISODES ARE THREE	135	2	DON JUAN	1	200	5
I'VE GOT NEW MYTHOLOGICAL MACHINERY	136	2	DON JUAN	1	201	7
I THINK THAT WITH THIS HOLY NEW ALLIANCE	142	2	DON JUAN	1	211	1
EXTRACTS EMOTIONS BEAUTIFUL AND NEW	144	2	DON JUAN	1	214	4
NEW BROKE A CAMELOPARD A GAZELLE	160	2	DON JUAN	2	6	2
ESPECIALLY WHEN LIFE IS RATHER NEW	163	2	DON JUAN	2	12	4
BEHIND THEIR CARRIAGES THEIR NEW PORTMANTEAU	165	2	DON JUAN	2	16	7
BUT OTHERS PONDER'D ON A NEW DISSECTION	199	2	DON JUAN	2	80	5
TO KINDLE FIRE AND AS THE NEW FLAMES GAVE	216	2	DON JUAN	2	115	5
ACHILLES ORDER'D DINNER FOR NEW COMERS	221	2	DON JUAN	2	123	8
AND THE FIRST BREAKFAST SPOILT PREPARED A NEW ONE	234	2	DON JUAN	2	146	6
OF THE NEW FIRE WHICH ZOE KEPT UP KNEELING	237	2	DON JUAN	2	153	6
TO HEAR NEW WORDS AND TO REPEAT THEM BUT	244	2	DON JUAN	2	167	2
HOW PLEASANT WERE THE MAXIM (NOT QUITE NEW)	267	2	DON JUAN	2	207	6
YOU MEAN OUR MASTER--NOT THE OLD BUT NEW	297	2	DON JUAN	3	43	8
THESE RASCALS BEING NEW COMERS KNEW NOT WHOM	298	2	DON JUAN	3	44	1
THE NAME AND QUALITY OF HIS NEW PATRON	298	2	DON JUAN	3	44	7
OF THE APARTMENT--AND APPEAR'D QUITE NEW	309	2	DON JUAN	3	67	4
WHICH MADE THEIR NEW ESTABLISHMENT COMPLETE	316	2	DON JUAN	3	78	3
TO MAKE A NEW THERMOPYLAE	323	2	DON JUAN	3 L	7	6
IN DIGGING DRAINS FOR A NEW WATER CLOSET	327	2	DON JUAN	3	89	V7
AND THE NEW BIRTHS OF BOTH THEIR STALE VIRGINITIES	330	2	DON JUAN	3	95	7
WHILE ONE NEW TEAR AROSE IN HAIDEE'S EYE	355	2	DON JUAN	4	21	8
FADED OR ALTER'D INTO SOMETHING NEW--	363	2	DON JUAN	4	35	2
NEW THOUGHTS OF LIFE FOR IT SEEM'D FULL OF SOUL	377	2	DON JUAN	4	60	7
RATHER THE DEAD FOR LIFE SEEM'D SOMETHING NEW	378	2	DON JUAN	4	62	2
SOME LITTLE HAMLETS WITH NEW NAMES UNCOUTH	387	2	DON JUAN	4	78	2
TO WHOM THE OPERA IS BY NO MEANS NEW	392	2	DON JUAN	4	88	4
WHO ADVERTISE NEW POEMS BY YOUR LOOKS	403	2	DON JUAN	4	108	3
EXCEPT THAT I HAVE FOUND IT NOTHING NEW	418	2	DON JUAN	5	14	8
BUT MINE HAVE VANISHED ALL WHEN LIFE IS NEW	421	2	DON JUAN	5	21	4
THE SCARS OF HIS OLD WOUNDS WERE NEAR HIS NEW	431	2	DON JUAN	5	38	1
NEW PAINTED OR A PRETTY OPERA-SCENE	436	2	DON JUAN	5	46	8
HIS FRIEND TOO ADDING A NEW SAVING CLAUSE	437	2	DON JUAN	5	47	6
SEEMS FERTILE IN ADVENTURES STRANGE AND NEW	459	2	DON JUAN	5	83	6
THEIR TALK OF COURSE RAN MOST ON THE NEW COMER	23	3	DON JUAN	6	35	1
IN THE FAIR FORM OF THEIR COMPANION NEW	24	3	DON JUAN	6	37	5
IN A NEW FACE THE UGLIEST CREATURE BREATHING	24	3	DON JUAN	6	37	8
WHICH MADE THEM LIKE THEIR NEW COMPANION	25	3	DON JUAN	6	38	V7
BUT CERTAIN 'TIS THEY ALL FELT FOR THEIR NEW	25	3	DON JUAN	6	39	1
THEY ALL ALIKE ADMIRED THEIR NEW CONNEXION	26	3	DON JUAN	6	40	8
SHE LOOKED (THIS SIMILE'S QUITE NEW) JUST CUT	27	3	DON JUAN	6	43	5
LOLAH DEMANDED THE NEW DAMSEL'S NAME--	28	3	DON JUAN	6	44	1
SHE ADDED TO JUANNA THEIR NEW GUEST	29	3	DON JUAN	6	46	4
ADMIRING THIS NEW NATIVE OF THE DEEP	36	3	DON JUAN	6	60	8
OF THOSE WHO CANNOT LAY ON A NEW TAX	54	3	DON JUAN	6	96	8
YOU LOVE THIS BOYISH NEW SERAGLIO GUEST	63	3	DON JUAN	6	115	5
OF THE HIGH TALENTS OF THIS NEW VAUBAN	72	3	DON JUAN	7	11	2
THAN THOUSANDS OF THIS NEW AND POLISHED NATION	73	3	DON JUAN	7	14	7
UNLESS TO MAKE THEIR KETTLE DRUMS A NEW SKIN	75	3	DON JUAN	7	17	6
WHEN THE SALE OF NEW BOOKS IS NOT SO FLEET	79	3	DON JUAN	7	26	5
IN THE NEW BATTERIES ERECTED THERE	80	3	DON JUAN	7	27	6
A COURIER ON THE SPUR INSPIRED NEW HEART	85	3	DON JUAN	7	39	3
IN FORMER WORKS MADE NEW PREPARED FASCINES	89	3	DON JUAN	7	47	7
NEW BATTERIES WERE ERECTED AND WAS HELD	92	3	DON JUAN	7	51	1
YOUR NAME BEFORE THE SECOND IS A NEW ONE	97	3	DON JUAN	7	60	5
TO BE DISPOSED OF IN A WAY SO NEW	101	3	DON JUAN	7	67	3
TO ME THIS KIND OF LIFE IS NOT SO NEW	103	3	DON JUAN	7	72	5
WARM BOUT ARE BROKEN INTO THEIR NEW TRICKS	122	3	DON JUAN	8	22	7
PERHAPS MAY FIND IT BETTER THAN A NEW ONE)--	126	3	DON JUAN	8	29	8
AMIDST SUCH SCENES--THOUGH THIS WAS QUITE A NEW ONE	138	3	DON JUAN	8	52	4
WHOSE YOUNG UNWAKENED WORLD WAS EVER NEW	145	3	DON JUAN	8	65	3
SAFETY THAN HIS NEW ORDER OF SAINT VLADIMIR	182	3	DON JUAN	8	140	8
AS THESE NEW CANTOS TOUCH ON WARLIKE FEATS	187	3	DON JUAN	9	10	1
UNTO THE NEW CREATION RISING OUT	201	3	DON JUAN	9	38	2
HOW THE NEW WORLDINGS OF THE THEN NEW EAST	202	3	DON JUAN	9	39	2
HOW THE NEW WORLDINGS OF THE THEN NEW EAST	202	3	DON JUAN	9	39	2
AND EVERY NEW CREATION HATH DECREASED	202	3	DON JUAN	9	39	6
LOOK LIKE THE MONSTERS OF A NEW MUSEUM	202	3	DON JUAN	9	40	8
WAVING LIKE SAILS NEW SHIVERED IN A STORM	204	3	DON JUAN	9	43	3
WHITE STOCKINGS DRAWN UNCURDLED AS NEW MILK	204	3	DON JUAN	9	43	7
FOR A NEW FLAME A THOUGHT TO CAST OF GLOOM ENOUGH	206	3	DON JUAN	9	48	5
NO DOUBT GAVE PAIN WHERE EACH NEW PAIR OF SHOULDERS	208	3	DON JUAN	9	52	7
ALMOST AS MUCH AS ON A NEW DISPATCH	213	3	DON JUAN	9	61	7
THE OLDEST THING ON RECORD AND YET NEW	214	3	DON JUAN	9	64	8
NEXT OF NEW KNIGHTS THE FRESH AND GLORIOUS HATCH	215	3	DON JUAN	9	65	7
NEW LIGHTED ON A HEAVEN-KISSING HILL	215	3	DON JUAN	9	66	2

NEW   (CONTINUED)

	PAGE	VOL	CANTO	STANZA	LN
INQUIRED WHO WAS THIS VERY NEW YOUNG MAN	222	3 DON JUAN	9	79	2
WHO FURROW SOME NEW SOIL TO SOW FOR JOYS	228	3 DON JUAN	10	7	8
OLD ENEMIES WHO HAVE BECOME NEW FRIENDS	231	3 DON JUAN	10	12	1
OLD FLAMES NEW WIVES BECOME OUR BITTEREST FOES--	231	3 DON JUAN	10	12	7
INTO SOME SIXTY THOUSAND NEW KNIGHTS' FEES	242	3 DON JUAN	10	35	8
AND SENT THE DOCTORS IN A NEW DIRECTION	245	3 DON JUAN	10	43	4
(WHEN A NEW IPHIGENE SHE WENT TO TAURIS)	248	3 DON JUAN	10	49	7
AWAITS IT EACH NEW MEETING OR ELECTION	272	3 DON JUAN	11	9	8
WHOM A GOOD MIEN ESPECIALLY IF NEW	305	3 DON JUAN	11	73	6
CHANGE GROWS TOO CHANGEABLE WITHOUT BEING NEW	309	3 DON JUAN	11	82	6
AND SAIL FOR A NEW THEME--I HAVE SEEN--AND SHOOK	309	3 DON JUAN	11	83	6
JUAN AS A VOLUPTUARY WAS NEW	314	3 DON JUAN	11	V 75	V1
WHO KEEP THE WORLD BOTH OLD AND NEW IN PAIN	318	3 DON JUAN	12	5	5
'TIS TRUE THAT THY CAREER IS NOT A NEW ONE	326	3 DON JUAN	12	23	5
OF EARLY LIFE BUT THIS IS A NEW LAND	326	3 DON JUAN	12	23	7
AND THEN MEN STARE AS IF A NEW ASS SPAKE	328	3 DON JUAN	12	26	5
THE LAST YEAR TO THE NEW TRANSFERS ITS HOARDS	340	3 DON JUAN	12	53	5
NEW VESTALS CLAIM MEN'S EYES WITH THE SAME PRAISE	340	3 DON JUAN	12	53	6
PERHAPS A LITTLE STRANGE IF NOT QUITE NEW	341	3 DON JUAN	12	54	2
AND SENDS NEW WERTERS YEARLY TO THEIR COFFIN	345	3 DON JUAN	12	63	6
PERHAPS THIS NEW POSITION--BUT I'M RIGHT	348	3 DON JUAN	12	71	5
THE PRIDE OF A MERE CHILD WITH A NEW SASH ON	351	3 DON JUAN	12	77	5
TO MAKE EACH CORRESPONDENT A NEW DEBTOR	406	3 DON JUAN	13	104	8
WHEN NOTHING SHALL BE EITHER OLD OR NEW	411	3 DON JUAN	14	3	6
TIRING OLD READERS NOR DISCOVERING NEW	414	3 DON JUAN	14	10	6
AND NOW IN THIS NEW FIELD WITH SOME APPLAUSE	424	3 DON JUAN	14	33	1
A LITTLE BLACK UPON THIS NEW FLIRTATION	429	3 DON JUAN	14	43	2
ADVANCE BEYOND WHILE THEY COULD PASS FOR NEW	433	3 DON JUAN	14	53	4
WITH THE NEW VENUS OF THEIR BRILLIANT OCEAN	434	3 DON JUAN	14	55	4
AND PASS FOR WANT OF BETTER THOUGH NOT NEW	440	3 DON JUAN	14	69	4
THE WILD SENSATION UNTO HER A NEW ONE	449	3 DON JUAN	14	91	4
THE NEW WORLD WOULD BE NOTHING TO THE OLD	455	3 DON JUAN	14	101	6
BRIGHT AS A NEW NAPOLEON FROM ITS MINTAGE	458	3 DON JUAN	15	7	3
WHICH RINGS WHAT'S UPPERMOST OF NEW OR HOARY	465	3 DON JUAN	15	20	7
COLUMBUS FOUND A NEW WORLD IN A CUTTER	468	3 DON JUAN	15	27	6
BEING NO SIBYL IN THE NEW WORLD'S WAYS	480	3 DON JUAN	15	56	6
'TIS TIME THAT SOME NEW PROPHET SHOULD APPEAR	496	3 DON JUAN	15	90	5
OUR BUBBLES AS THE OLD BURST NEW EMERGE	500	3 DON JUAN	15	99	6
NEW BUILDINGS OF CORRECTEST CONFORMATION	529	3 DON JUAN	16	58	7
LORD HENRY WISHED TO RAISE FOR A NEW PURCHASE	530	3 DON JUAN	16	60	2
IF WE MAY JUDGE FROM EACH NEW YEAR'S DISPLAY	548	3 DON JUAN	16	99	V5
WHEN ANY DARE A NEW LIGHT TO PRESENT	564	3 DON JUAN	17	5	3

NEW-BOUGHT

| THE NEW-BOUGHT VIRGIN MADE HER BLUSH AND SHAKE | 501 | 2 DON JUAN | 5 | 156 | 2 |

NEWER

| COMPANION SOMETHING NEWER STILL AS 'TWERE | 25 | 3 DON JUAN | 6 | 39 | 2 |
| THAT THEY HAVE NOTHING BETTER NEAR OR NEWER | 35 | 3 DON JUAN | 6 | 59 | 6 |

NEWEST

| AND SETTLED BONNETS BY THE NEWEST CODE | 406 | 3 DON JUAN | 13 | 104 | 6 |
| BUT WEAR THE NEWEST MANTLE OF HYPOCRISY | 526 | 3 DON JUAN | 16 | 52 | 7 |

NEW-FLEDGED

| THE FORMER KNOW WHAT'S WHAT WHILE NEW-FLEDGED CHICKS | 230 | 3 DON JUAN | 10 | 10 | 3 |

NEW-FOUND

| AND WHEN THEY GREW SO--ON THEIR NEW-FOUND LANTHORN | 280 | 3 DON JUAN | 11 | 26 | 7 |

NEWGATE

| OH MRS FRY WHY GO TO NEWGATE WHY | 266 | 3 DON JUAN | 10 | 85 | 1 |

NEWLY

| DOES THESE THINGS FOR US AND WHENEVER NEWLY A | 267 | 2 DON JUAN | 2 | 208 | 5 |
| THERE WAS THE YOUNG BARD RACKRHYME WHO HAD NEWLY | 398 | 3 DON JUAN | 13 | 84 | 5 |

NEWS

| 'TIS ODD BUT TRUE--LAST WAR THE NEWS ABOUNDED | 383 | 3 DON JUAN | 13 | 53 | 7 |
| THEN ASKED HER GRACE WHAT NEWS WERE OF THE DUKE OF LATE | 515 | 3 DON JUAN | 16 | 34 | 5 |

NEWSPAPER

INTO ALL PANTERS FOR NEWSPAPER PRAISE	85	3 DON JUAN	7	39	4
FOR 'TIS A LOW NEWSPAPER HUMDRUM LAW-SUIT	346	3 DON JUAN	12	65	1
THEIR OFFICE HE TOOK UP AN OLD NEWSPAPER	512	3 DON JUAN	16	26	5

NEWSPAPERS

WERE IN THE ENGLISH NEWSPAPERS OF COURSE	126	2 DON JUAN	1	188	8
TO NEWSPAPERS WHOSE TRUTH ALL KNOW AND FEEL	138	2 DON JUAN	1	203	3
TO NEWSPAPERS--SERMONS WHICH THE ZEAL	138	2 DON JUAN	1	203	V3
WHOSE PAMPHLETS VOLUMES NEWSPAPERS ILLUMINE US	200	3 DON JUAN	9	35	3

NEWTON

NEWTON (THAT PROVERB OF THE MIND) ALAS	69	3 DON JUAN	7	5	5
WHEN NEWTON SAW AN APPLE FALL HE FOUND	225	3 DON JUAN	10	1	1
IN WHICH SIR ISAAC NEWTON COULD DISCLOSE	226	3 DON JUAN	10	2	3

NEWTON'S

| AND THINKS HEAVEN BRIGHTER EVEN THAN NEWTON'S PAGE | 242 | 2 DON JUAN | 2 | 163 | V7 |

NEW-TUNED

| STRONGBOW WAS LIKE A NEW-TUNED HARPSICHORD | 402 | 3 DON JUAN | 13 | 93 | 1 |

NEXT

SHE NEXT DECIDED HE WAS ONLY BAD	35	2 DON JUAN	1	27	4
AND NEXT DAY PAID A VISIT TO HIS MOTHER	63	2 DON JUAN	1	76	2
AND THEN--GOD KNOWS WHAT NEXT--I CAN'T GO ON	83	2 DON JUAN	1	115	7
AND MEAN NEXT WINTER TO BE QUITE RECLAIM'D	85	2 DON JUAN	1	119	8
NEXT OWNER FOR THEIR DOUBLE-DAMN'D POST-OBITS	89	2 DON JUAN	1	125	8
THE PLEASANT SCANDAL WHICH AROSE NEXT DAY	126	2 DON JUAN	1	188	5
THEMSELVES AND THE NEXT TIME THEIR SERVANTS TIE ON	165	2 DON JUAN	2	16	6
MEN WILL PROVE HUNGRY EVEN WHEN NEXT PERDITION	180	2 DON JUAN	2	46	V5

NEXT   (CONTINUED)
ON WHAT IN FACT NEXT DAY WERE THEY TO DINE . . . . . 192 2 DON JUAN 2   69   4
AND NEXT THEY THOUGHT UPON THE MASTER'S MATE . . . . . 199 2 DON JUAN 2   81   1
NEXT THEY--HE BEING NAKED SAVE A TATTER'D . . . . . 240 2 DON JUAN 2   160   1
A THANKLESS HUSBAND NEXT A FAITHLESS LOVER . . . . . 263 2 DON JUAN 2   200   7
HE LEFT HIS SHIP TO BE HOVE DOWN NEXT DAY . . . . . 286 2 DON JUAN 3   20   5
ARE SOMEWHAT SICK AND SORRY THE NEXT DAY . . . . . 343 2 DON JUAN 3 V 98   8
AND NEXT PROCEEDED QUIETLY TO COCK . . . . . . 365 2 DON JUAN 4   40   8
WAKES ME NEXT MORNING WITH ITS SYNONYM . . . . . 372 2 DON JUAN 4   53   8
BUT NEXT WHEN I'M ENGAGED TO SING THERE--DO GO . . . . 392 2 DON JUAN 4   88   8
THEY HEARD NEXT DAY--THAT IN THE DARDANELLES . . . . 393 2 DON JUAN 4   91   1
NEXT JUAN STOOD TILL SOME MIGHT CHOOSE TO BUY . . . . 416 2 DON JUAN 5   10   8
BUT NEVER MIND--SHE'LL TURN PERHAPS NEXT WEEK . . . . 418 2 DON JUAN 5   14   6
WONDERING WHAT NEXT TILL THE CAIQUE WAS BROUGHT . . . 432 2 DON JUAN 5   40   6
NEXT WITH A VIRGIN ZONE HE WAS EQUIPPED . . . . . 456 2 DON JUAN 5   77   3
WHEN WE NEXT MEET WE'LL HAVE A TALE TO TELL . . . . . 460 2 DON JUAN 5   84   4
AND NEXT HIS SAVAGE VIRTUE HE ACCUSED . . . . . 493 2 DON JUAN 5   142   5
AND NEXT SHE GAVE HER (I SAY HER BECAUSE . . . . . 35 3 DON JUAN 6   58   1
I DID--WHAT NEXT--I REALLY HARDLY KNOW . . . . . 98 3 DON JUAN 7   61   2
THE NEXT SHALL RING A PEAL TO SHAKE ALL PEOPLE . . . 109 3 DON JUAN 7   85   7
OF THE NEXT BASTION FIRED AWAY LIKE DEVILS . . . . 134 3 DON JUAN 8   44   2
THAT THEY SHOULD ALL BE SHOT ON THE NEXT DAY . . . . 162 3 DON JUAN 8   102   6
I NEVER KNOW THE WORD WHICH WILL COME NEXT . . . . 203 3 DON JUAN 9   41   8
HER NEXT AMUSEMENT WAS MORE FANCIFUL . . . . . 212 3 DON JUAN 9   60   1
NEXT OF NEW KNIGHTS THE FRESH AND GLORIOUS HATCH . . . 215 3 DON JUAN 9   65   7
IN THE NEXT OCEAN WHICH MAY FLOW JUST THEN . . . . 217 3 DON JUAN 9   69   6
TO END OR TO BEGIN WITH THE NEXT GRAND . . . . . 220 3 DON JUAN 9   76   2
HIS SERVICES HE KISSED HANDS THE NEXT DAY . . . . 247 3 DON JUAN 10   46   7
MADE CATHERINE TASTE NEXT NIGHT A QUIET SLUMBER-- . . 248 3 DON JUAN 10   48   4
THE NEXT THE VIRGIN'S MYSTICAL VIRGINITY . . . . . 271 3 DON JUAN 11   6   3
AND SHOULD YOU DOUBT PRAY ASK OF YOUR NEXT NEIGHBOUR . 288 3 DON JUAN 11   41   4
FROM OUR NEXT NEIGHBOUR'S LAND WHERE LIKE A CHESSMAN . 288 3 DON JUAN 11   42   3
YOU LEAVE BEHIND--THE NEXT OF MUCH YOU COME . . . . 290 3 DON JUAN 11   44   5
BUT IF YOU CAN CONTRIVE GET NEXT AT SUPPER . . . . 304 3 DON JUAN 11   72   1
TO THE NEXT COMER OR--AS IT WILL TELL . . . . . 339 3 DON JUAN 12   51   7
THE NEXT OF PERILS THOUGH I PLACE IT STERNEST . . . 345 3 DON JUAN 12   64   2
STEEL BARONS MOLTEN THE NEXT GENERATION . . . . . 390 3 DON JUAN 13   68   1
DISCUSSED THE FASHION WHICH MIGHT NEXT PREVAIL . . . 406 3 DON JUAN 13   104   5
ASK'D NEXT DAY IF MEN EVER HUNTED TWICE . . . . . 425 3 DON JUAN 14   35   8
WHEN CALLED NEXT DAY DECLINED THE ROUGH ADVENTURE . . 425 3 DON JUAN 14   35 V8
AND NEXT A QUARREL (AS HE SEEMED TO FRET) . . . . 437 3 DON JUAN 14   62   7
NEXT THAT HE NEVER JUDGED FROM WHAT APPEAR'D . . . . 439 3 DON JUAN 14   66   3
TO THE NEXT CANTO WHERE PERHAPS I SHALL . . . . . 453 3 DON JUAN 14   98   6
NEXT TO THE MAKING MATCHES FOR HERSELF . . . . . 470 3 DON JUAN 15   31   1
(WHEN SEATED NEXT HIM) OF SOME PRETTY LISPER . . . . 487 3 DON JUAN 15   70   8
DON JUAN SAT NEXT AN A L'ESPAGNOLE-- . . . . . 488 3 DON JUAN 15   74   5
BUT NEXT TO DRESSING FOR A ROUT OR BALL . . . . . 505 3 DON JUAN 16   11   1
HE SIGHED--THE NEXT RESOURCE IS THE FULL MOON . . . 506 3 DON JUAN 16   13   1
TALK O'ER THEMSELVES THE PAST AND NEXT ELECTION . . . 534 3 DON JUAN 16   69   8
I SATE NEXT THAT O'ERWHELMING SON OF HEAVEN . . . . 539 3 DON JUAN 16   81   4
STATED) HIS MOUTH WHAT OPENED NEXT--THE DOOR . . . . 557 3 DON JUAN 16   115   8
THE NEXT ARE SUCH AS ARE NOT DOOMED TO LOSE . . . . 562 3 DON JUAN 17   1   5
THE NEXT ARE ONLY CHILDREN AS THEY ARE STYLED . . . 563 3 DON JUAN 17   2   1
NIBBLE
BECAUSE 'TIS SO WHO NIBBLE SCRIBBLE QUIBBLE HE . . . 503 3 DON JUAN 16   5   7
NIBBLING
WHOSE LITTLE NIBBLING RUSTLE WILL EMBARRASS . . . . 509 3 DON JUAN 16   20   7
NICE
START NOT STILL CHASTER READER--SHE'LL BE NICE HENCEFORWARD 86 2 DON JUAN 1   120   2
THE EAR BECOMES MORE IRISH AND LESS NICE . . . . . 366 2 DON JUAN 4   41   8
FOR ME APPEARS A QUESTION FAR TOO NICE . . . . . 478 3 DON JUAN 15   52   5
NICETY
OF NICETY WHERE A FACT IS TO BE GAINED) . . . . . 507 3 DON JUAN 16   16   4
NICHE
SOME FAVOUR'D OBJECT AND AS IN THE NICHE . . . . . 269 2 DON JUAN 2   211   5
WITHIN A NICHE NIGH TO ITS PINNACLE . . . . . . 386 3 DON JUAN 13   60   1
BUT IN A HIGHER NICHE ALONE BUT CROWN'D . . . . . 387 3 DON JUAN 13   61   1
A LAMP BURNED HIGH WHILE HE LEANT FROM A NICHE . . . 507 3 DON JUAN 16   16   5
NICHED
A CERTAIN PRESS OR CUPBOARD NICHED IN YONDER . . . 450 2 DON JUAN 5   66   6
NICKNAME
A HUMAN (WHAT THE ITALIANS NICKNAME) MULE . . . . 563 3 DON JUAN 17   3   5
NICKNAMED
WITH NO GREAT CARE FOR WHAT IS NICKNAMED GLORY . . . 464 3 DON JUAN 15   19   3
NIECES
MARRYING THEIR COUSINS--NAY THEIR AUNTS AND NIECES . . 52 2 DON JUAN 1   57   7
A LADY WITH HER DAUGHTERS OR HER NIECES . . . . 306 2 DON JUAN 3   60   7
NIGER
TRACE UP THOSE SHUFFLING NEGROES NILE OR NIGER . . . 348 3 DON JUAN 12   70   2
NIGH
AS THEY DREW NIGH THE LAND WHICH NOW WAS SEEN . . . 210 2 DON JUAN 2   103   1
SOME SAID HER YEARS WERE GETTING NIGH THEIR SUMMER . . 23 3 DON JUAN 6   35   5
WHICH IF NOT HAPPINESS IS MUCH MORE NIGH IT . . . . 32 3 DON JUAN 6   53   4
TO ATTACK THE TURK'S FLOTILLA WHICH LAY NIGH . . . . 78 3 DON JUAN 7   24   3
WELL NIGH THE SHORE WHERE ONE STOOPS DOWN AND GATHERS 191 3 DON JUAN 9   18   7
HECTIC AND BRIEF AS SUMMER'S DAY NIGH DONE . . . . 229 3 DON JUAN 10   8   7
BUT GETTING NIGH GRIM DANTE'S OBSCURE WOOD . . . . 238 3 DON JUAN 10   27   3
WERE WELL NIGH OVER 'TIS PERHAPS A PITY . . . . 380 3 DON JUAN 13   48   2
WITHIN A NICHE NIGH TO ITS PINNACLE . . . . . . 386 3 DON JUAN 13   60   1

	PAGE	VOL	CANTO	STANZA	LN
NIGH (CONTINUED)					
WHEN SUDDENLY HE HEARD OR THOUGHT SO NIGH	509	3 DON JUAN 16	20	5
ALL MOUNTAINEERS WITH DREAMS THAT THEY ARE NIGH LANDS	523	3 DON JUAN 16	46	6
NOT NIGH THE GAY SALOON OF LADIES GENT	533	3 DON JUAN 16	66	2
NIGH AND MORE NIGH THE AWFUL ECHOES DREW	557	3 DON JUAN 16	115	5
NIGH AND MORE NIGH THE AWFUL ECHOES DREW	557	3 DON JUAN 16	115	5
NIGHER					
A YARD OR TWO OF GROUND WHICH BROUGHT THEM NIGHER	121	3 DON JUAN 8	20	3
NIGHEST					
TAPPING THE SHOULDER OF THE NIGHEST GUEST	297	2 DON JUAN 3	42	2
NIGHT					
THAT NIGHT THE VIRGIN WAS NO FURTHER PRAY'D	63	2 DON JUAN 1	76	8
AND SO GOOD NIGHT--RETURN WE TO OUR STORY	94	2 DON JUAN 1	134	2
'TWAS AS THE WATCHMEN SAY A CLOUDY NIGHT	94	2 DON JUAN 1	135	1
'TWAS MIDNIGHT--DARK AND SOMBRE WAS THE NIGHT	94	2 DON JUAN 1	135	V1
PRAY KEEP YOUR NONSENSE FOR SOME LUCKIER NIGHT--	115	2 DON JUAN 1	171	1
SWORE LUSTILY HE'D BE REVENGED THIS NIGHT	122	2 DON JUAN 1	184	5
HOW JUAN NAKED FAVOUR'D BY THE NIGHT	126	2 DON JUAN 1	188	2
INCREASED AT NIGHT UNTIL IT BLEW A GALE	170	2 DON JUAN 2	26	2
NOUGHT BUT THE HEAVY SEA AND COMING NIGHT	178	2 DON JUAN 2	41	8
THUS TO THEIR HOPELESS EYES THE NIGHT WAS SHOWN	182	2 DON JUAN 2	49	5
'TWAS A ROUGH NIGHT AND BLEW SO STIFFLY YET	188	2 DON JUAN 2	60	1
AND THE SAME NIGHT THERE FELL A SHOWER OF RAIN	201	2 DON JUAN 2	84	1
NIGHT FELL--THIS SEEM'D A BETTER OMEN STILL	206	2 DON JUAN 2	94	8
BY NIGHT CHILL'D BY DAY SCORCH'D THUS ONE BY ONE	210	2 DON JUAN 2	102	5
CHILLED BY THE NIGHT--AND BLACKENED BY THE SUN	210	2 DON JUAN 2	102	V5
AND TIME HAD NOTHING MORE OF NIGHT NOR DAY	214	2 DON JUAN 2	111	3
AND NIGHT IS FLUNG OFF LIKE A MOURNING SUIT	230	2 DON JUAN 2	139	7
AND NIGHT IS BACKWARD LIKE A MANTLE ROLLED	230	2 DON JUAN 2	139	V8
I HAVE SAT UP ON PURPOSE ALL THE NIGHT	230	2 DON JUAN 2	140	3
I'VE CHANGED FOR SOME FEW YEARS THE DAY TO NIGHT	230	2 DON JUAN 2	140	V3
WHO LIKE A MORNING SLUMBER--FOR THE NIGHT	237	2 DON JUAN 2	152	7
THEY FELT NO TERRORS FROM THE NIGHT THEY WERE	256	2 DON JUAN 2	189	2
AND YET LAST NIGHT BEING AT A MASQUERADE	268	2 DON JUAN 2	209	6
BUT CHANGES NIGHT AND DAY TOO LIKE THE SKY	270	2 DON JUAN 2	214	2
LAST NIGHT I HAD ANOTHER PROOF HOW TRULY IT	272	2 DON JUAN 2	V 1	6
NIGHT WAS A JULIET TO THE VERY NAME	272	2 DON JUAN 2	V 1	8
HER EYELASHES THOUGH DARK AS NIGHT WERE TINGED	314	2 DON JUAN 3	75	1
WITH HER SIRE'S STORY MAKES THE NIGHT LESS LONG	383	2 DON JUAN 4	73	3
FOR NIGHT WAS CLOSING ERE THEY CAME TO LAND	433	2 DON JUAN 5	41	6
OF NIGHT WHICH ROBE THE CHAMBER OR WHERE POPPING	442	2 DON JUAN 5	55	5
BUT SADDENS MORE BY NIGHT AS WELL AS DAY	442	2 DON JUAN 5	56	6
A NEAT SNUG STUDY ON A WINTER'S NIGHT	444	2 DON JUAN 5	58	1
BEFORE HE CAME ESPECIALLY AT NIGHT	495	2 DON JUAN 5	146	6
HAD DEIGNED THAT NIGHT TO BE GULBEYAZ' GUEST	12	3 DON JUAN 6	13	V6
AT LEAST ONE OF THEM--OH THE HEAVY NIGHT	18	3 DON JUAN 6	24	2
AND WILL NOT TOSS AND CHATTER THE NIGHT THROUGH	30	3 DON JUAN 6	49	6
HER BEAUTIES SEIZED THE UNCONSCIOUS HOUR OF NIGHT	39	3 DON JUAN 6	66	7
'TWAS NIGHT BUT THERE WERE LAMPS AS HATH BEEN SAID	40	3 DON JUAN 6	67	2
(AS NIGHT DEW ON A CYPRESS GLITTERING TINGES	40	3 DON JUAN 6	67	7
AND POOR JUANNA TOO THE CHILD'S FIRST NIGHT	46	3 DON JUAN 6	81	1
AND SO GOOD NIGHT TO THEM--OR IF YOU WILL	49	3 DON JUAN 6	86	1
HE HAD PASSED THE NIGHT WAS WHAT SHE WISHED TO KNOW	55	3 DON JUAN 6	99	8
THE FIAT OF THIS SPOILED CHILD OF THE NIGHT	86	3 DON JUAN 7	41	3
HARK THROUGH THE SILENCE OF THE COLD DULL NIGHT	110	3 DON JUAN 7	86	1
THE NIGHT WAS DARK AND THE THICK MIST ALLOWED	115	3 DON JUAN 8	6	1
BUT BRAVELY RUSHED ON HIS FIRST HEAVENLY NIGHT	168	3 DON JUAN 8	114	3
BY NIGHT AS DO THAT MERCENARY PACK ALL	196	3 DON JUAN 9	27	3
MADE CATHERINE TASTE NEXT NIGHT A QUIET SLUMBER--	248	3 DON JUAN 10	48	4
HAD SET SOME TIME AND NIGHT WAS ON THE RIDGE	279	3 DON JUAN 11	23	7
WHOSE CITIES NIGHT BY NO MEANS DEIGNS TO GLOSS	280	3 DON JUAN 11	26	5
ADMITTED A SMALL PARTY AS NIGHT FELL--	282	3 DON JUAN 11	29	5
YAWNING A LITTLE AS THE NIGHT GROWS LATER	303	3 DON JUAN 11	69	8
LOOK YES LAST NIGHT AND YET SAY NO TO-DAY	332	3 DON JUAN 12	34	8
HE HATH NO MORN NOR NIGHT BUT ALL IS DARK	348	3 DON JUAN 12	71	7
BACK TO THE NIGHT WIND BY THE WATERFALL	388	3 DON JUAN 13	63	7
THOSE LITTLE GLITTERERS OF THE LONDON NIGHT	435	3 DON JUAN 14	57	2
THE NIGHT (I SING BY NIGHT--SOMETIMES AN OWL	499	3 DON JUAN 15	97	1
THE NIGHT (I SING BY NIGHT--SOMETIMES AN OWL	499	3 DON JUAN 15	97	1
'TWIXT NIGHT AND MORN UPON THE HORIZON'S VERGE	500	3 DON JUAN 15	99	2
AND JUAN ON RETIRING FOR THE NIGHT	506	3 DON JUAN 16	12	1
THEN AS THE NIGHT WAS CLEAR THOUGH COLD HE THREW	508	3 DON JUAN 16	17	1
HE ABIDETH NIGHT AND DAY	519	3 DON JUAN 16	L 3	4
BUT THE MONK IS LORD BY NIGHT	520	3 DON JUAN 16	L 5	6
THAT HE THE NIGHT BEFORE HAD SEEN A GHOST	543	3 DON JUAN 16	90	2
THE NIGHT WAS AS BEFORE HE WAS UNDREST	555	3 DON JUAN 16	111	1
SAVING HIS NIGHT GOWN WHICH IS AN UNDRESS	555	3 DON JUAN 16	111	2
AGAIN THROUGH SHADOWS OF THE NIGHT SUBLIME	556	3 DON JUAN 16	113	5
THE NIGHT BEFORE BUT BEING SICK OF SHAKING	558	3 DON JUAN 16	118	2
NIGHTINGALE					
UNSEEN AS SINGS THE NIGHTINGALE THEY WERE	358	2 DON JUAN 4	28	2
AND WAIT UNTIL THE NIGHTINGALE GROWS DUMBER	380	3 DON JUAN 13	48	5
AND NOW AND THEN A NIGHTINGALE)--IS DIM	499	3 DON JUAN 15	97	2
NIGHTINGALES					
MORE THAN FOR THOSE OF NIGHTINGALES OR DOVES	354	2 DON JUAN 4	19	8
NIGHTINGLE					
THE NIGHTINGLE THAT SINGS WITH THE DEEP THORN	49	3 DON JUAN 6	87	5
NIGHTLY					
OF WHOM THESE TWO YEARS SHE HAD NIGHTLY DREAM'D	247	2 DON JUAN 2	172	4

	PAGE	VOL	CANTO	STANZA	LN
NIGHTLY (CONTINUED)					
THE NIGHTLY MUSTER AND THE SILENT MARCH	121	3 DON JUAN	8	21	2
BOTH SENATES SEE THEIR NIGHTLY VOTES PARTICIPATED . . .	306	3 DON JUAN	11	75	5
AND DRAW THEM NIGHTLY WHEN A TICKET'S SENT	342	3 DON JUAN	12	57	6
THERE'S ALSO NIGHTLY TO THE UNINITIATED	344	3 DON JUAN	12	62	1
NIGHT'S					
OF LOVE'S AND NIGHT'S AND OCEAN'S SOLITUDE	262	2 DON JUAN	2	198	2
WITH YOU DUDU A GOOD NIGHT'S REST HAVE KNOWN	46	3 DON JUAN	6	81	6
BY LAST NIGHT'S GHOST BEEN DRIVEN FROM THEIR DEFENCES .	545	3 DON JUAN	16	93	8
NIGHTS					
TWELVE DAYS AND NIGHTS SHE WITHER'D THUS AT LAST . . .	381	2 DON JUAN	4	69	1
SOME DAYS AND NIGHTS ELAPSED BEFORE THAT HE	384	2 DON JUAN	4	75	2
WHEN NIGHTS ARE EQUAL BUT NOT SO THE DAYS	414	2 DON JUAN	5	6	2
HAD SATE BENEATH THE GALLERY AT NIGHTS	353	3 DON JUAN	12	82	3
THE NIGHTS AND DAYS MOST PEOPLE CAN REMEMBER	505	3 DON JUAN	16	11	6
NIGHTWINDS					
'TIS SWEET TO LISTEN AS THE NIGHTWINDS CREEP	87	2 DON JUAN	1	122	6
NIKOLAIEW					
IN THE NIKOLAIEW REGIMENT--THE SAME	97	3 DON JUAN	7	60	8
HIS POST I MEAN THE REGIMENT NIKOLAIEW	100	3 DON JUAN	7	66	5
NIL					
GREAT HAPPINESS OF THE NIL ADMIRARI	469	2 DON JUAN	5	100	8
PERHAPS FROM HORACE HIS NIL ADMIRARI	374	3 DON JUAN	13	35	1
NILE					
TRACE UP THOSE SHUFFLING NEGROES NILE OR NIGER	348	3 DON JUAN	12	70	2
NILE'S					
OF CARNAGE LIKE THE NILE'S SUN-SODDEN SLIME	152	3 DON JUAN	8	82	7
NIMROD'S					
BABEL WAS NIMROD'S HUNTING-BOX AND THEN	445	2 DON JUAN	5	60	1
EVEN NIMROD'S SELF MIGHT LEAVE THE PLAINS OF DURA . . .	395	3 DON JUAN	13	78	5
NIMRODS					
NIMRODS WHOSE CANVAS SCARCE CONTAIN'D THE STEED	391	2 DON JUAN	13	70	6
NINE					
FOLLOWERS OF FAME NINE FARROW OF THAT SOW	22	2 DON JUAN	1	2	6
THE NINE DAYS' WONDER WHICH WAS BROUGHT TO LIGHT . . .	126	2 DON JUAN	1	188	6
NINE IN THE CUTTER THIRTY IN THE BOAT	185	2 DON JUAN	2	54	7
NINE SOULS MORE WENT IN HER THE LONG-BOAT STILL . . .	188	2 DON JUAN	2	61	1
WE'RE TOLD THIS GREAT HIGH PRIEST OF ALL THE NINE . . .	328	2 DON JUAN	3	91	6
WHERE LAY SOME SHIPS WHICH WERE TO SAIL AT NINE . . .	371	2 DON JUAN	4	50	4
'TWAS NINE WHEN STILL ADVANCING UNDISMAYED	81	3 DON JUAN	7	29	3
YOU CAN'T REPEAT NINE NAMES FROM EACH GAZETTE	83	3 DON JUAN	7	34	8
SO THAT ON EITHER SIDE SOME NINE OR TEN	136	3 DON JUAN	8	47	1
THAT NEUTRALISED DULL DORUS OF THE NINE	297	3 DON JUAN	11	58	4
NINE TIMES IN TEN 'TIS BUT CAPRICE OR FASHION	351	3 DON JUAN	12	77	3
(WHOSE ARTICLES ARE LIKE THE THIRTY NINE	383	3 DON JUAN	13	53	2
THAT NO DEFEAT CAN DRIVE ME FROM THE NINE	415	3 DON JUAN	14	12	4
WHAT ANTHROPOPHAGI IN NINE OF TEN	455	3 DON JUAN	14	102	5
AT LEAST NINE AND A NINTH BESIDE OF TEN	468	3 DON JUAN	15	26	4
AND RISE AT NINE IN LIEU OF LONG ELEVEN	539	3 DON JUAN	16	81	4
NINETEEN					
SIXTEEN CALLED THOMSON AND NINETEEN NAMED SMITH	75	3 DON JUAN	7	18	8
OUT OF THOSE NINETEEN WHO LATE RHYMED TO PITH	79	3 DON JUAN	7	25	6
NINETEENTH					
AND MITFORD IN THE NINETEENTH CENTURY	325	3 DON JUAN	12	19	7
NINE-TENTHS					
AT LEAST NINE-TENTHS OF WHAT WE CALL SO--GOD	163	3 DON JUAN	8	104	2
NINETY					
CITE IS THAT BOON LIVED HUNTING UP TO NINETY	143	3 DON JUAN	8	62	8
NINEVEH					
ROME BABYLON TYRE CARTHAGE NINEVEH	142	3 DON JUAN	8	60	5
OR SAT AMIDST THE BRICKS OF NINEVEH	271	3 DON JUAN	11	7	6
NINI					
AND THEN THERE ARE THE DANCERS THERE'S THE NINI . . .	390	2 DON JUAN	4	84	1
NINNY					
FOR SHE GOT HOLD OF A YOUNG FOREIGN NINNY	390	2 DON JUAN	4	84	V5
NINON					
UGLY FOR INSTANCE--NINON DEL'ENCLOS	468	2 DON JUAN	5	98	8
NINTH					
AT LEAST NINE AND A NINTH BESIDE OF TEN	468	3 DON JUAN	15	26	4
NOAH'S					
AS IF A SPANISH SHIP WERE NOAH'S ARK	161	2 DON JUAN	2	8	6
SINCE NOAH'S ARK WENT CRUISING HERE AND THERE	191	2 DON JUAN	2	66	6
AND HAD IT BEEN THE DOVE FROM NOAH'S ARK	206	2 DON JUAN	2	95	5
NOBLE					
A NOBLE STREAM AND CALL'D THE GUADALQUIVIR	25	2 DON JUAN	1	8	8
HIS BLOOD LESS NOBLE THAN SUCH BLOOD SHOULD BE	52	2 DON JUAN	1	57	3
HOW NOBLE IS HIS LANGUAGE NEVER PERT	154	2 DON JUAN	1	V 5	1
AGAINST ALL NOBLE MALADIES HE'S BOLD	168	2 DON JUAN	2	22	5
BY JOVE A NOBLE PALACE--LIGHTED TOO	436	2 DON JUAN	5	45	8
AND LECTURING ON THE NOBLE ART OF KILLING--	96	3 DON JUAN	7	58	4
BY JOVE HE WAS A NOBLE FELLOW JOHNSON	132	3 DON JUAN	8	39	1
WAS SHOWN AND SOME MORE NOBLE HEART BROKE THROUGH . . .	174	3 DON JUAN	8	124	2
YET YOU'RE A NOBLE FELLOW AND BUT WAIT	185	3 DON JUAN	9	6	V1
HER FACE WAS NOBLE HER EYES FINE MOUTH GRACIOUS . . .	211	3 DON JUAN	9	58	8
A MOSQUE SO NOBLE FLUNG LIKE PEARLS TO SWINE	262	3 DON JUAN	10	75	8
THERE STANDS THE NOBLE HOSTESS NOR SHALL SINK	302	3 DON JUAN	11	68	1
NOBLE RICH CELEBRATED AND A STRANGER	305	3 DON JUAN	11	74	2
I WISH THEY KNEW THE LIFE OF A YOUNG NOBLE	305	3 DON JUAN	11	74	8
THE SHADE OF BONAPARTE'S NOBLE DARING--	318	3 DON JUAN	12	5	7

	PAGE	VOL	CANTO	STANZA	LN
NOBLE (CONTINUED)					
THAT'S NOBLE THAT'S ROMANTIC FOR MY PART	326	3 DON JUAN	12	22	1
THAT NOBLE SIGHT WHEN REALLY FREE THE NATION	354	3 DON JUAN	12	83	2
AND THUS ACQUAINTANCE GREW AT NOBLE ROUTS	369	3 DON JUAN	13	24	1
AS MANY OTHER NOBLE SCIONS WERE	370	3 DON JUAN	13	28	3
AND NUMEROUS PARTY OF HIS NOBLE FRIENDS	382	3 DON JUAN	13	52	3
TO NORMAN ABBEY WHIRLED THE NOBLE PAIR--	384	3 DON JUAN	13	55	1
THE NOBLE GUESTS ASSEMBLED AT THE ABBEY	396	3 DON JUAN	13	79	1
THIS NOBLE PERSONAGE BEGAN TO LOOK	429	3 DON JUAN	14	43	1
AND NOBLE BIRTHS NOR DREAD THE ENUMERATION--	432	3 DON JUAN	14	52	4
SERENE AND NOBLE--CONJUGAL BUT COLD	447	3 DON JUAN	14	86	8
RICH NOBLE BUT AN ORPHAN LEFT AN ONLY	475	3 DON JUAN	15	44	1
NOBLER					
THE NOBLER AND THE MANLIER ONE	324	2 DON JUAN	3	L 10	4
INTO A ROOM STILL NOBLER THAN THE LAST	465	2 DON JUAN	5	93	2
NOBLEST					
HER NOBLEST VIRTUE WAS HER MAGNANIMITY	27	2 DON JUAN	1	12	2
AND WORTHY OF THE NOBLEST PEDIGREE	42	2 DON JUAN	1	38	3
THE NOBLEST EFFORTS FOR HERSELF AND MATE	62	2 DON JUAN	1	75	3
THE NOBLEST KIND OF LOVE IS LOVE PLATONICAL	220	2 DON JUAN	9	76	1
WHICH HOLDS WHAT MIGHT HAVE BEEN THE NOBLEST NATION	257	3 DON JUAN	10	66	2
ALAS MUST NOBLEST VIEWS LIKE AN OLD SONG	363	3 DON JUAN	13	10	5
NOBLY					
WHO SAW THEIR SPOUSES KILL'D AND NOBLY CHOSE	36	2 DON JUAN	1	29	4
'TWAS ON THE WHOLE A NOBLY FURNISHED HALL	31	3 DON JUAN	6	51	6
A PREACHER HAD HELD FORTH (WHO NOBLY SPURNED	99	3 DON JUAN	7	64	5
MOST NOBLY AND I OWN IT FROM MY SOUL	232	3 DON JUAN	10	16	8
NOBODY					
(BUT DOUBTLESS NOBODY WILL BE SO PERT)	140	2 DON JUAN	1	207	5
SO NOBODY ARRIVED ON SHORE BUT HIM	212	2 DON JUAN	2	106	8
OF ARTICLES WHICH NOBODY REQUIRED	448	2 DON JUAN	5	64	5
FROM WHICH THE SECRET NOBODY COULD RIP	496	2 DON JUAN	5	149	5
THAT NOBODY CAN EVER TAKE AMISS	35	3 DON JUAN	6	59	3
NOD					
HER VERY NOD WAS NOT AN INCLINATION	475	2 DON JUAN	5	111	2
FOR EVERYTHING SEEMED RESTING ON HIS NOD	104	3 DON JUAN	7	74	1
OR SULTAN AS THE AUTHOR (TO WHOSE NOD	163	3 DON JUAN	8	104	6
NODDED					
SOME NODDED TO THE NEGRO FROM THEIR STATION	441	2 DON JUAN	5	54	7
WHICH NODDED TO THE NATION'S SPOILS BELOW	485	3 DON JUAN	15	67	3
NODDING					
THE ORANGE AND POMEGRANATE NODDING O'ER	291	3 DON JUAN	3	31	7
YOU SIR SAID BABA NODDING TO THE ONE	458	2 DON JUAN	5	81	1
NODDING BESIDE MY LADY IN HIS CARRIAGE	379	3 DON JUAN	13	46	2
NODDY					
AT LENGTH THEY CAUGHT TWO BOOBIES AND A NODDY	200	2 DON JUAN	2	82	7
BECAUSE THOUGH I AM BUT A SIMPLE NODDY	77	3 DON JUAN	7	21	5
NODS					
AND THEN SHE HAD RECOURSE TO NODS AND SIGNS	241	2 DON JUAN	2	162	1
NODS FROM THE TREE WAS SLUMBERING WITH SOFT BREATH	38	3 DON JUAN	6	65	7
NOW MOVED WITH PITY EVEN AS SOMETIMES NODS	164	3 DON JUAN	8	106	6
NOISE					
AND MAKE NO FURTHER NOISE TILL YOU DISCOVER	104	2 DON JUAN	1	153	6
AS WONDERING WHAT THE DEVIL NOISE THAT IS	442	2 DON JUAN	5	55	8
BUT FLEW TO WHERE THE PLEASANT NOISE GREW LOUDER	129	3 DON JUAN	8	33	V8
AS SOON AS THUNDER 'MIDST THE GENERAL NOISE	142	3 DON JUAN	8	59	7
A NOISE LIKE TO WET FINGERS DRAWN ON GLASS	556	3 DON JUAN	16	114	1
NOISES					
WHICH ROCKED AS 'TWERE BENEATH THE MIGHTY NOISES	115	3 DON JUAN	8	7	6
NO-MEANING					
PERHAPS YOU MAY PICK OUT SOME QUEER NO-MEANING	207	3 DON JUAN	9	49	7
NOMENCLATURE					
THEIR NOMENCLATURE THERE IS NOT A DAY	82	2 DON JUAN	1	113	4
BY WHICH ITS NOMENCLATURE CAME TO PASS	33	3 DON JUAN	6	55	3
AS FORM A SCIENCE AND A NOMENCLATURE	486	3 DON JUAN	15	69	7
TO NAME A THING IN NOMENCLATURE RATHER	533	3 DON JUAN	16	67	7
NOMINAL					
AND SO GREAT NAMES ARE NOTHING MORE THAN NOMINAL	399	2 DON JUAN	4	101	1
NOMINATED					
YET 'TIS SO NOMINATED IN THE BOND	278	2 DON JUAN	3	7	5
NON					
NON EGO HOC FERREM CALIDA JUVENTA	143	2 DON JUAN	1	212	1
LUCUS A NON LUCENDO NOT WHAT WAS	33	3 DON JUAN	6	55	5
NON-AGE					
WHILE YET AMERICA WAS IN HER NON-AGE	468	3 DON JUAN	15	27	8
NONCE					
ALSO HE DRESSED UP FOR THE NONCE FASCINES	93	3 DON JUAN	7	53	1
NON-DESCRIPT					
A NON-DESCRIPT AND EVER VARYING RHYME	67	3 DON JUAN	7	2	2
THOU GATE OF LIFE AND DEATH--THOU NONDESCRIPT	210	3 DON JUAN	9	55	2
NONE					
A GOOD DEAL LIKE HIM TOO THOUGH QUITE THE SAME NONE	24	2 DON JUAN	1	5	3
AND SO HAVE BEEN FORGOTTEN--I CONDEMN NONE	24	2 DON JUAN	1	5	5
OF ALL THE SPANISH TOWNS IS NONE MORE PRETTY	25	2 DON JUAN	1	8	5
TO SCHOOL (AS GOD BE PRAISED THAT I HAVE NONE)	50	2 DON JUAN	1	52	4
DISCOVERIES MADE BUT NONE COULD BE AWARE	59	2 DON JUAN	1	68	3
I FAVOUR'D NONE--NAY WAS ALMOST UNCIVIL	102	2 DON JUAN	1	148	6
HOWEVER PRESENT REMEDY WAS NONE	116	2 DON JUAN	1	173	5
BUT THERE WERE AMPLE REASONS FOR IT NONE	116	2 DON JUAN	1	174	5

		PAGE	VOL	CANTO	STANZA	LN

NONE   (CONTINUED)

	PAGE	VOL	CANTO	STANZA	LN
NONE CAN SAY THAT THIS WAS NOT GOOD ADVICE	122	2 DON JUAN	1	183	1
ARE VARIOUS BUT THEY NONE OF THEM ARE DULL	127	2 DON JUAN	1	189	6
NONE CAN DEEM HARSHLIER OF ME THAN I DEEM	130	2 DON JUAN	1	193	6
INSENSIBLE I TRUST BUT NONE THE WORSE	144	2 DON JUAN	1	215	6
NO--NONE OF THESE WILL DO--AND THEN THEIR GARB	160	2 DON JUAN	2	6	3
AND NONE LIKED TO ANTICIPATE THE BLOW	175	2 DON JUAN	2	36	6
OF CANDLES TO THEIR SAINTS--BUT THERE WERE NONE	179	2 DON JUAN	2	44	4
THEY LAY LIKE CARCASSES AND HOPE WAS NONE	194	2 DON JUAN	2	72	3
AND NONE TO BE THE SACRIFICE WOULD CHOOSE	195	2 DON JUAN	2	74	4
NONE IN PARTICULAR HAD SOUGHT OR PLANN'D IT	195	2 DON JUAN	2	75	5
BY WHICH NONE WERE PERMITTED TO BE NEUTER--	195	2 DON JUAN	2	75	7
IN VARIOUS CONJECTURES FOR NONE KNEW	209	2 DON JUAN	2	100	4
BUT NONE OF THEM APPEAR'D TO SHARE HIS WOES	213	2 DON JUAN	2	109	5
AND NEED HE HAD OF SLUMBER YET FOR NONE	229	2 DON JUAN	2	137	6
I HATE YOUR POETS SO READ NONE OF THOSE	243	2 DON JUAN	2	165	8
AND MOTHER BROTHER GUARDIAN SHE HAD NONE	252	2 DON JUAN	2	182	3
YET THERE ARE SOME THEY SAY WHO HAVE HAD NONE	276	2 DON JUAN	3	4	7
(NONE TRUSTS THE SEX MORE OR SO MUCH ADMIRES--	287	2 DON JUAN	3	22	5
FOR NONE LIKES MORE TO HEAR HIMSELF CONVERSE	298	2 DON JUAN	3	45	8
HE FELT A GRIEF BUT KNOWING CAUSE FOR NONE	355	2 DON JUAN	4	22	6
SHE GAZED BUT NONE SHE EVER COULD RETRACE	381	2 DON JUAN	4	68	4
NONE BUT HER OWN AND FATHER'S GRAVE IS THERE	383	2 DON JUAN	4	72	3
IN SOME SHAPE LET NONE THINK TO FLY THE DANGER	383	2 DON JUAN	4	73	7
MOST MEN ARE SLAVES NONE MORE SO THAN THE GREAT	423	2 DON JUAN	5	25	3
TO FEEL FOR NONE IS THE TRUE SOCIAL ART	423	2 DON JUAN	5	25	7
MARVEL AND PRAISE FOR BOTH OR NONE THINGS WIN	469	2 DON JUAN	5	100	6
FROM HIS TRANSLATION BUT HAD NONE ADMIRED	470	2 DON JUAN	5	101	7
LOOKED INTO HIS FOR LOVE WHERE NONE REPLIES	483	2 DON JUAN	5	125	4
THE FEMALE RANKS SO THAT NONE STIRRED OR TALKED	21	3 DON JUAN	6	30	6
OF THE UNPLEASANT KIND WITH NONE AT HAND	45	3 DON JUAN	6	78	3
THAT SHE SPAWNS WARRIORS BY THE SCORE WHERE NONE	164	3 DON JUAN	8	105	2
AS THOUGH THERE WERE ONE HEAVEN AND NONE BESIDES--	168	3 DON JUAN	8	114	6
WHICH FEW WILL SING I TRUST BUT NONE FORGET IT--	179	3 DON JUAN	8	135	3
NONE SAVE THE SPANISH FLY AND ATTIC BEE	196	3 DON JUAN	9	28	7
JUAN WAS NONE OF THESE BUT SLIGHT AND SLIM	206	3 DON JUAN	9	47	1
WHICH NONE DIVINE AND EVERYONE OBEYS	207	3 DON JUAN	9	49	6
THOU RIDDLE--WHICH ALL READ--NONE UNDERSTAND	210	3 DON JUAN	9	56	V7
HERE LAWS ARE ALL INVIOLATE NONE LAY	273	3 DON JUAN	11	10	5
TO THAT WHICH NONE WILL GAIN--OR NONE WILL KNOW	299	3 DON JUAN	11	61	2
TO THAT WHICH NONE WILL GAIN--OR NONE WILL KNOW	299	3 DON JUAN	11	61	2
AND SCORN HIS TEMPERATE BOARD AS NONE AT ALL	316	3 DON JUAN	12	3	6
BUT WHETHER ALL OR EACH OR NONE OF THESE	321	3 DON JUAN	12	11	1
WITHOUT CASH CAMPS WERE THIN AND COURTS WERE NONE	322	3 DON JUAN	12	14	3
THAT FEW OR NONE MORE THAN HIMSELF HAD CAUGHT	368	3 DON JUAN	13	21	3
WHERE NONE WERE DREAMT OF UNTO LOVE'S AFFAIRS	369	3 DON JUAN	13	25	5
LET NONE ACCUSE OLD ENGLAND'S HOSPITALITY--	381	3 DON JUAN	13	49	7
NONE THAN THEMSELVES COULD BOAST A LONGER LINE	381	3 DON JUAN	13	50	5
BUT NONE WERE GENE THE GREAT HOUR OF UNION	406	3 DON JUAN	13	103	1
BUT WHAT IS ODD NONE EVER NAMED THE DUKE	430	3 DON JUAN	14	45	1
HER GAIETIES NONE HAD A RIGHT TO STARE	430	3 DON JUAN	14	45	6
BUT NONE OF THESE POSSESS'D A STING TO WOUND HER--	435	3 DON JUAN	14	57	3
WHOSE MERIT NONE ENOUGH CAN SING OR SAY	445	3 DON JUAN	14	82	2
IF GOOD IS NONE THE WORSE FOR REPETITION	478	3 DON JUAN	15	51	2
IT WAS NOT ENVY--ADELINE HAD NONE	479	3 DON JUAN	15	54	1
SERF LORD MAN WITH SUCH SKILL AS NONE WOULD SHARE IT IF	481	3 DON JUAN	15	59	6
OR NONE AT ALL--WHICH SEEMS A SORRY JEST	494	3 DON JUAN	15	87	6
MYSELF WITH METAPHYSICS NONE CAN HATE	496	3 DON JUAN	15	91	2
OR NONE OR LIKE--LIKE NOTHING THAT I KNOW	505	3 DON JUAN	16	10	2
DYED PURPLE NONE AT PRESENT CAN TELL HOW	505	3 DON JUAN	16	10	6
SOME TO THEIR SEVERAL PASTIMES OR TO NONE	527	3 DON JUAN	16	55	3
BUT OF ALL NATURE'S DISCREPANCIES NONE	541	3 DON JUAN	16	85	1
AND JUAN TOO IN GENERAL BEHIND NONE	552	3 DON JUAN	16	105	4
AND WITCHES UNTO NONE THOUGH SOMEWHAT LATE	565	3 DON JUAN	17	7	2
WHICH BEST IS TO ENCOUNTER--GHOST OR NONE	568	3 DON JUAN	17	14	1

NON-ENTITY

	PAGE	VOL	CANTO	STANZA	LN
HOW ODD A SINGLE HOBGOBLIN'S NON-ENTITY	559	3 DON JUAN	16	120	7

NONSENSE

	PAGE	VOL	CANTO	STANZA	LN
PRAY KEEP YOUR NONSENSE FOR SOME LUCKIER NIGHT--	115	2 DON JUAN	1	171	1
THAN ALL THE NONSENSE OF THEIR STONE IDEAL)	218	2 DON JUAN	2	118	8
HIS PURSE HIS SOUL HIS SENSE AND EVEN HIS NONSENSE	88	3 DON JUAN	7	44	7
OR FAME OR NAME FOR WIT WAR SENSE OR NONSENSE	305	3 DON JUAN	11	73	7
IF HE CAN HICCUP NONSENSE AT A BALL	333	3 DON JUAN	12	37	V6
'TIS NONSENSE TO DISPUTE ABOUT A HUE--	359	3 DON JUAN	13	3	1

NONSUIT

	PAGE	VOL	CANTO	STANZA	LN
OF COUNSEL TO NONSUIT OR TO ANNUL	127	2 DON JUAN	1	189	4

NOOK

	PAGE	VOL	CANTO	STANZA	LN
REMAIN'D UNKNOWN WITHIN HIS CRAGGY NOOK	248	2 DON JUAN	2	174	4
HER LIFE TO CHANCE BUT POINT ME OUT SOME NOOK	161	3 DON JUAN	8	99	3
THE POLITICIANS IN A NOOK APART	408	3 DON JUAN	13	109	1
PERHAPS I HAVE A THIRD TOO IN A NOOK	494	3 DON JUAN	15	87	5
THERE COUCHED ALL SNUGLY ON HIS PILLOW'S NOOK	512	3 DON JUAN	16	27	5
BUT JUAN SITTING SILENT IN HIS NOOK	553	3 DON JUAN	16	106	6

NOOKS

	PAGE	VOL	CANTO	STANZA	LN
HIMSELF AT LENGTH WITHIN THE LEAFY NOOKS	70	2 DON JUAN	1	90	3
WHEN AFTER SEARCHING IN FIVE HUNDRED NOOKS	110	2 DON JUAN	1	161	3

NOON

	PAGE	VOL	CANTO	STANZA	LN
THAT IS ERE MIDNIGHT--WHICH IS LONDON'S NOON	409	3 DON JUAN	13	111	2
TO RHYME AT NOON--WHEN I HAVE OTHER THINGS	500	3 DON JUAN	15	98	2

NOONTIDE
    BUT IN THE NOONTIDE OF THE MOON AND WHEN . . . . 388 3 DON JUAN 13   63   1
NORMAN
    ('TIS AN OLD NORMAN NAME AND TO BE FOUND . . . . . . 359 3 DON JUAN 13   2   2
    TO NORMAN ABBEY WHIRLED THE NOBLE PAIR-- . . . . . . 384 3 DON JUAN 13   55   1
    WHO SITTETH BY NORMAN STONE . . . . 518 3 DON JUAN 16 L 1   2
    MADE NORMAN CHURCH HIS PREY . . . . 518 3 DON JUAN 16 L 1   6
NORTH
    HAPPY THE NATIONS OF THE MORAL NORTH . . . . 57 2 DON JUAN 1   64   1
    AT LEAST HAD HE BEEN NURTURED IN THE NORTH . . . . . 158 2 DON JUAN 2   2   4
    THERE BEING NO SUCH PROFUSION IN THE NORTH . . . . . 434 2 DON JUAN 5   42   4
    WHICH IN THE NORTH PREVENTS PRECOCIOUS CRIMES . . . . 501 2 DON JUAN 5 157   5
    TO KISS THEM ALL AT ONCE FROM NORTH TO SOUTH . . . . 19 3 DON JUAN 6   27   8
    BY THE NORTH POLE--THEY SOUGHT HER CAUSE OF CARE . . . 42 3 DON JUAN 6   72   6
    THUS THE LOW WORLD NORTH SOUTH OR WEST OR EAST . . . . 342 3 DON JUAN 12   56   6
    ON ROADS EAST SOUTH NORTH WEST THERE IS A RUN . . . . 377 3 DON JUAN 13   42   4
NORTHERN
    THE WORLD TO GAZE UPON THOSE NORTHERN LIGHTS . . . . 353 3 DON JUAN 12   82   5
NORTH-WEST
    BUT AFTER ALL THEY ARE A NORTH-WEST PASSAGE . . . . . 376 3 DON JUAN 13   39   1
NOS
    I ONLY SAY SUPPOSE IT--INTER NOS . . . . 67 2 DON JUAN 1   84   6
NOSCITUR
    HIS OTHER MAXIM NOSCITUR A SOCIIS . . . . 443 3 DON JUAN 14   77   3
NOSE
    AND TURNING UP HER NOSE WITH LOOKS ABUSED . . . . 109 2 DON JUAN 1 159   3
    AND BLOOD ('TWAS FROM THE NOSE) BEGAN TO FLOW . . . 124 2 DON JUAN 1 186   3
    SHAWLED TO THE NOSE AND BEARDED TO THE EYES . . . . 495 2 DON JUAN 5 147   2
    HER ATTIC FOREHEAD AND HER PHIDIAN NOSE . . . . . . 27 3 DON JUAN 6   42   4
    SO JUAN FOLLOWING HONOUR AND HIS NOSE . . . . . . 127 3 DON JUAN 8   32   7
NOSES
    ONE MAKES NEW NOSES ONE A GUILLOTINE . . . . 91 2 DON JUAN 1 129   3
    KNOWING (DOGS HAVE SUCH INTELLECTUAL NOSES) . . . . 187 2 DON JUAN 2   58   5
NOTE
    THIS NOTE WAS WRITTEN UPON GILT-EDGED PAPER . . . . 134 2 DON JUAN 1 198   1
    AND OF THIS BABA WILLINGLY TOOK NOTE . . . . . . 62 3 DON JUAN 6 113   6
    THEY WRITE AND FOR WHAT END BUT NOTE OR TEXT . . . . 203 3 DON JUAN 9   41   7
    HER NOTE SHE DON'T FORGET THE INFANT GIRL . . . . 249 3 DON JUAN 10   51   7
    QUICK SILVER SMALL TALK ENDING (IF YOU NOTE IT) . . . 328 3 DON JUAN 12   26   7
NOTED
    SHE KEPT A JOURNAL WHERE HIS FAULTS WERE NOTED . . . . 36 2 DON JUAN 1   28   1
    LET EVERYTHING BE NOTED WITH PRECISION . . . . . . 104 2 DON JUAN 1 152   5
    THE THIRD SORT TO BE NOTED IN OUR CHRONICLE . . . . . 220 3 DON JUAN 9   76   5
NOTELESS
    AN IGNORANT NOTELESS TIMELESS TUNELESS FELLOW . . . . 391 2 DON JUAN 4   87   4
NOTES
    AT THE FIRST NOTES IRREGULAR AND SHARP . . . . . 379 2 DON JUAN 4   65   3
    HAS SOME GOOD NOTES AND THEN THE TENOR'S WIFE . . . . 389 2 DON JUAN 4   83   4
    OF ALL THE HORRID HIDEOUS NOTES OF WOE . . . . . 432 3 DON JUAN 14   50   1
NOTHING
    AND RECOLLECT A POET NOTHING LOSES . . . . 14 2 DON JUAN D   8   5
    IN VIRTUES NOTHING EARTHLY COULD SURPASS HER . . . . 30 2 DON JUAN 1   17   7
    FOR MY PART I SAY NOTHING--NOTHING--BUT . . . . . . 50 2 DON JUAN 1   52   1
    FOR MY PART I SAY NOTHING--NOTHING--BUT . . . . . . 50 2 DON JUAN 1   52   1
    NOTHING BUT WHAT WAS GOOD HER BREAST WAS PEACEABLE-- . . 66 2 DON JUAN 1   83   5
    AND LIFE YIELDS NOTHING FURTHER TO RECALL . . . . . 90 2 DON JUAN 1 127   5
    I WOULD NOT YOU FOR NOTHING SHOULD BE FEE'D-- . . . . 104 2 DON JUAN 1 152   6
    LOOK WHERE YOU PLEASE--WE'VE NOTHING SIR TO HIDE . . . 106 2 DON JUAN 1 156   4
    BUT NOTHING ELSE THE TIME OF WORDS WAS O'ER . . . . . 111 2 DON JUAN 1 163   6
    NOTHING SO DEAR AS AN UNFILCH'D GOOD NAME . . . . . 112 2 DON JUAN 1 165   5
    THERE'S NOTHING SO BECOMING TO THE FACE . . . . . 119 2 DON JUAN 1 178   8
    I'VE NOTHING TO REPROACH OR TO REQUEST . . . . . 130 2 DON JUAN 1 193   8
    NOTHING SHOULD TEMPT HIM MORE (THIS PERIL PAST) . . . 175 2 DON JUAN 2   37   5
    WITH NOTHING BUT THE SKY FOR A GREAT COAT . . . . . 189 2 DON JUAN 2   63   8
    I CAN DO NOTHING AND HE SAW HIM THROWN . . . . . 202 2 DON JUAN 2   87   7
    AND TIME HAD NOTHING MORE OF NIGHT NOR DAY . . . . 214 2 DON JUAN 2 111   3
    HER DOWRY WAS AS NOTHING TO HER SMILES . . . . . 224 2 DON JUAN 2 128   4
    FAST IN HIS CAVE AND NOTHING CLASH'D UPON . . . . . 229 2 DON JUAN 2 137   2
    THAT BATHING PASS'D FOR NOTHING JUAN SEEM'D . . . . 247 2 DON JUAN 2 172   2
    SAW NOTHING HAPPIER THAN HER GLOWING FACE . . . . . 262 2 DON JUAN 2 198   8
    ELSEWHERE WAS NOTHING--SHE HAD NOUGHT TO FEAR . . . . 264 2 DON JUAN 2 202   7
    MEN CALL INCONSTANCY IS NOTHING MORE . . . . . . 269 2 DON JUAN 2 211   2
    THERE'S NOTHING WRONG IN A CONNUBIAL KISS . . . . . 279 2 DON JUAN 3   8   6
    HIS TITLE AND 'TIS NOTHING BUT TAXATION . . . . . 283 2 DON JUAN 3   14   4
    THE POWER OF ART WAS TURN'D TO NOTHING FOR . . . . . 314 2 DON JUAN 3   75   7
    WHERE NOTHING SAVE THE WAVES AND I . . . . . . 326 2 DON JUAN 3 L 16   2
    BECOME A THING OR NOTHING SAVE TO RANK . . . . . 327 2 DON JUAN 3   89   3
    'TIS SOMETHING NOTHING WORDS ILLUSION WIND-- . . . . 328 2 DON JUAN 3   90   2
    AH SURELY NOTHING DIES BUT SOMETHING MOURNS . . . . 338 2 DON JUAN 3 108   8
    NOTHING SO DIFFICULT AS A BEGINNING . . . . . . 344 2 DON JUAN 4   1   1
    BUT THE FACT IS THAT I HAVE NOTHING PLANN'D . . . . 346 2 DON JUAN 4   5   6
    WITH NOTHING LIVID STILL HER LIPS WERE RED . . . . . 377 2 DON JUAN 4   60   2
    NOTHING COULD MAKE HER MEET HER FATHER'S FACE . . . . 381 2 DON JUAN 4   68   2
    AND NOTHING OUTWARD TELLS OF HUMAN CLAY . . . . . 383 2 DON JUAN 4   72   4
    BUT AFTER ALL 'TIS NOTHING BUT COLD SNOW . . . . . 398 2 DON JUAN 4 100   8
    AND SO GREAT NAMES ARE NOTHING MORE THAN NOMINAL . . . 399 2 DON JUAN 4 101   1
    LEAVES NOTHING TILL THE COMING OF THE JUST-- . . . . 399 2 DON JUAN 4 101   6
    ARE SAVING--VICE SPARES NOTHING FOR A RARITY . . . . 408 2 DON JUAN 4 115   8
    EXCEPT THAT I HAVE FOUND IT NOTHING NEW . . . . . 418 2 DON JUAN 5   14   8

	PAGE	VOL		CANTO	STANZA	LV
NOTHING (CONTINUED)						
WHAT BROUGHT YOU HERE--OH NOTHING VERY RARE--	418	2 DON JUAN	5	15	2
SURELY 'TIS NOTHING WONDERFUL TO SEE	421	2 DON JUAN	5	20	4
PERHAPS THERE'S NOTHING--I'LL NOT SAY APPALS	442	2 DON JUAN	5	56	5
TWO OR THREE SEEM SO LITTLE ONE SEEMS NOTHING	443	2 DON JUAN	5	57	1
THERE'S NOTHING IN THE WORLD LIKE ETIQUETTE	471	2 DON JUAN	5	103	6
HAVING NO EQUALS NOTHING WHICH HAD E'ER	480	2 DON JUAN	5	119	2
THERE'S NOTHING WHETS THE BEAK OR ARMS THE CLAW	488	2 DON JUAN	5	133	3
'TWERE NOTHING--FOR HER EYES FLASHED ALWAYS FIRE	489	2 DON JUAN	5	134	2
AND NOTHING EVER HEARD OF SAVE STARVATION	15	3 DON JUAN	6	19	V7
DUDU SAID NOTHING BUT SAT DOWN BESIDE	28	3 DON JUAN	6	45	1
WHAT SAY YOU CHILD--DUDU SAID NOTHING AS	30	3 DON JUAN	6	49	7
WITH NOTHING VERY GRAND TO MAKE A RIOT	32	3 DON JUAN	6	53	V4
THAT THEY HAVE NOTHING BETTER NEAR OR NEWER	35	3 DON JUAN	6	59	6
THAT BROKE FOR NOTHING ON THEIR SLEEPING EAR	45	3 DON JUAN	6	79	4
TO KNOW THAT NOTHING COULD BE KNOWN A PLEASANT	69	3 DON JUAN	7	5	2
WHOSE NAMES WANT NOTHING BUT--PRONUNCIATION	73	3 DON JUAN	7	14	8
NOTHING--THE WORK OF GLORY STILL WENT ON	106	3 DON JUAN	7	78	1
ARE NOTHING BUT A CHILD OF MURDER'S RATTLES	114	3 DON JUAN	8	4	8
WAS NOTHING BUT A VALOUROUS KIND OF CUNNING	130	3 DON JUAN	8	35	8
ALL NECK OR NOTHING AS LIKE PITCH OR ROSIN	135	3 DON JUAN	8	45	3
FOR KILLING NOTHING BUT A BEAR OR BUCK HE	143	3 DON JUAN	8	61	6
SAW NOTHING LIKE THE SCENE AROUND--YET LOOKING	172	3 DON JUAN	8	121	4
AND I KNOW NOTHING WHICH COULD MAKE AMENDS	231	3 DON JUAN	10	12	3
PERHAPS SHE HAD NOTHING TO CONFESS--NO MATTER	252	3 DON JUAN	10	56	6
THY LONG LONG BILLS WHENCE NOTHING IS DEDUCTED	259	3 DON JUAN	10	69	8
NOW THERE IS NOTHING GIVES A MAN SUCH SPIRITS	260	3 DON JUAN	10	72	1
WERE NOTHING BUT THE NATURAL ATMOSPHERE	266	3 DON JUAN	10	83	7
TURN OUT SO WE'LL SAY NOTHING 'GAINST THE WORDING	270	3 DON JUAN	11	4	3
WAS LIKE ALL BUSINESS A LABURIOUS NOTHING	301	3 DON JUAN	11	65	2
IN FACT THERE'S NOTHING MAKES ME SO MUCH GRIEVE	336	3 DON JUAN	12	43	6
FIND ONE WHERE NOTHING NAUGHTY CAN BE SHOWN	370	3 DON JUAN	13	27	6
JUST AS A MANDARIN FINDS NOTHING FINE--	373	3 DON JUAN	13	34	5
WERE NOTHING BUT A MORAL INEBRIETY	374	3 DON JUAN	13	35	8
THE EARTH HAS NOTHING LIKE A SHE EPISTLE	407	3 DON JUAN	13	105	2
NOTHING MORE TRUE THAN NOT TO TRUST YOUR SENSES	411	3 DON JUAN	14	2	7
FOR ME I KNOW NOUGHT NOTHING I DENY	411	3 DON JUAN	14	3	1
WHEN NOTHING SHALL BE EITHER OLD OR NEW	411	3 DON JUAN	14	3	6
GENT READER NOTHING A MERE SPECULATION	413	3 DON JUAN	14	7	2
NOTHING THAT SPEAKS TO ALL MEN AND ALL TIMES	417	3 DON JUAN	14	16	2
IN SUCH GUISE THAT SHE COULD MAKE NOTHING OF IT	438	3 DON JUAN	14	65	8
SHE HAD NOTHING TO COMPLAIN OF OR REPROVE	447	3 DON JUAN	14	86	5
THE NEW WORLD WOULD BE NOTHING TO THE OLD	455	3 DON JUAN	14	101	6
NOTHING AFFECTED STUDIED OR CONSTRUCTIVE	461	3 DON JUAN	15	12	3
HAD NOTHING LEFT IT BUT A DESPERATE LOYALTY	466	3 DON JUAN	15	23	V8
THERE'S NOTHING WOMEN LOVE TO DABBLE IN	470	3 DON JUAN	15	31	4
YET SHE WAS NOTHING DAZZLED BY THE METEOR	480	3 DON JUAN	15	56	7
TO HIS GAY NOTHINGS NOTHING WAS REPLIED	490	3 DON JUAN	15	78	1
OR SOMETHING WHICH WAS NOTHING AS URBANITY	490	3 DON JUAN	15	78	2
HE WHO DOUBTS ALL THINGS NOTHING CAN DENY	495	3 DON JUAN	15	88	5
AND NOTHING BRIGHTER GLEAMED THROUGH THE SALOON	504	3 DON JUAN	16	8	7
OR NONE OR LIKE--LIKE NOTHING THAT I KNOW	505	3 DON JUAN	16	10	2
BUT THOUGHT LIKE MOST MEN THERE WAS NOTHING IN'T	510	3 DON JUAN	16	22	3
AND LOOKED AT JUAN HARD BUT NOTHING UTTERED	514	3 DON JUAN	16	31	6
BUT WE'LL SAY NOTHING OF AFFAIRS OF STATE)	541	3 DON JUAN	16	84	4
AND HASTILY--AS NOTHING CAN CONFOUND	542	3 DON JUAN	16	88	4
NOTHINGNESS						
FROM HOLDING UP THE NOTHINGNESS OF LIFE	69	3 DON JUAN	7	6	8
NOTHINGS						
UPON THE NOTHINGS WHICH ARE DAILY SPENT	189	3 DON JUAN	9	13	5
TO HIS GAY NOTHINGS NOTHING WAS REPLIED	490	3 DON JUAN	15	78	1
NOTICE						
THAT WITHOUT NOTICE FEW FULL MOONS SHALL PASS IT	317	2 DON JUAN	3	81	3
SUCH NOTICE OF A GIAOUR WHILE SCARCE TO ONE	501	2 DON JUAN	5	156	5
JUAN DEMURRED AT THIS FIRST NOTICE TO	245	3 DON JUAN	10	43	1
NOTION						
THERE IS A NARROWNESS IN SUCH A NOTION	12	2 DON JUAN	D	5	7
THAT TURNS AND TURNS TO GIVE THE WORLD A NOTION	17	2 DON JUAN	D	13	7
PRETTY WERE BUT TO GIVE A FEEBLE NOTION	51	2 DON JUAN	1	55	4
BUT AS FOR JUAN HE HAD NO MORE NOTION	60	2 DON JUAN	1	70	7
OF HIS POSITION I CAN GIVE NO NOTION	113	2 DON JUAN	1	168	1
BUT NOT KNOWING METAPHYSICS HAD NO NOTION	289	2 DON JUAN	3	26	4
AND YOU SHALL SEE WHO HAS THE PROPEREST NOTION	336	2 DON JUAN	3	104	4
HAD SHE BUT BEEN A CHRISTIAN I'VE A NOTION	475	2 DON JUAN	5	112	7
ALL TREMBLING WONDERING WITHOUT THE LEAST NOTION	42	3 DON JUAN	6	71	6
THIS CIRCUMSTANCE MAY SERVE TO GIVE A NOTION	72	3 DON JUAN	7	11	1
AS ANY OTHER NOTION AND NOT NATIONAL)--	122	3 DON JUAN	8	23	8
'TWILL BE BECAUSE OUR NOTION IS NOT HIGH	285	3 DON JUAN	11	36	3
OR MINIATURE AT LEAST AS IS MY NOTION	457	3 DON JUAN	15	2	6
AS FAR AS WORDS MAKE RULES--OUR COMMON NOTION	563	3 DON JUAN	17	3	2
BUT NOW IT SEEMS HE'S RIGHT--HIS NOTION JUST	565	3 DON JUAN	17	8	7
NOTIONS						
AND GIVING UP ALL NOTIONS OF RESISTANCE	440	2 DON JUAN	5	51	1
LIKE TO THE NOTIONS WE NOW ENTERTAIN	201	3 DON JUAN	9	38	5
NOTORIETY						
THE KINGLY SCOURGE THE LUST OF NOTORIETY	146	3 DON JUAN	8	68	5
NOTORIOUS						
WHICH WERE OR ARE OR ARE TO BE NOTORIOUS	369	3 DON JUAN	13	25	6
NOUGHT						
IN FRENCH BUT THEN THE RHYME WOULD GO FOR NOUGHT)	67	2 DON JUAN	1	84	8

554

NOUGHT   (CONTINUED)
KNOWS NOUGHT OF GRIEF WHO HAS NOT SO BEEN WORRIED   89   2 DON JUAN   1   125 V7
HAD SIGNS OR FOOTMARKS BUT THE EARTH SAID NOUGHT   100   2 DON JUAN   1   144   4
JULIA SAID NOUGHT THOUGH ALL THE WHILE THERE ROSE   117   2 DON JUAN   1   175   1
THERE'S NOUGHT NO DOUBT SO MUCH THE SPIRIT CALMS   174   2 DON JUAN   2   34   1
NOUGHT BUT THE HEAVY SEA AND COMING NIGHT   178   2 DON JUAN   2   41   8
AS FOR THE LADIES I HAVE NOUGHT TO SAY   244   2 DON JUAN   2   166   1
FOES FRIENDS MEN WOMEN NOW ARE NOUGHT TO ME   244   2 DON JUAN   2   166   7
WHERE NOUGHT UPON THEIR PASSION COULD INTRUDE   262   2 DON JUAN   2   198   6
ELSEWHERE WAS NOTHING--SHE HAD NOUGHT TO FEAR   264   2 DON JUAN   2   202   7
AND NOW NOUGHT LEFT HIM BUT THE MUFFLED DRUM   430   2 DON JUAN   5   36   8
LIFE HAS NOUGHT LIKE IT GOD IS LOVE THEY SAY   9   3 DON JUAN   6   6   5
AND THEN MY STOICISM LEAVES NOUGHT BEHIND   17   3 DON JUAN   6   22   4
INTO A CAMP I KNOW THAT NOUGHT SO BOTHERS   103   3 DON JUAN   7   71   6
NOUGHT TO BE SEEN SAVE THE ARTILLERY'S FLAME   115   3 DON JUAN   8   6   2
WITH MARTIAL STOICISM NOUGHT SEEMED TO ANNOY   172   3 DON JUAN   8   121   5
GEORGE WASHINGTON HAD THANKS AND NOUGHT BESIDE   186   3 DON JUAN   9   8   4
HE WHO HAS NOUGHT TO GAIN CAN HAVE SMALL ART HE   195   3 DON JUAN   9   26   5
AND NOUGHT REMAINS UNSEEN BUT MUCH UNTOLD   232   3 DON JUAN 10   14   3
MOUNT PLEASANT AS CONTAINING NOUGHT TO PLEASE   278   3 DON JUAN 11   21   3
I KNEW THAT NOUGHT WAS LASTING BUT NOW EVEN   309   3 DON JUAN 11   82   5
BECAUSE YOU'LL SAY NOUGHT CALLS FOR SUCH A TRIAL-- . . .   319   3 DON JUAN 12   7   7
BUT I'M RESOLVED TO SAY NOUGHT THAT'S AMISS)--   326   3 DON JUAN 12   22   6
SEE NOUGHT MORE STRANGE IN THIS THAN T'OTHER LOTTERY . . .   333   3 DON JUAN 12   37   8
BUT THIS HAS NOUGHT TO DO WITH THEIR OUTSIDES   350   3 DON JUAN 12   74   1
NOUGHT AGAINST EITHER AND BOTH SEEMED SECURE--   365   3 DON JUAN 13   14   7
PROFESSIONAL AND THERE IS NOUGHT TO CULL   402   3 DON JUAN 13   95   4
FOR ME I KNOW NOUGHT NOTHING I DENY   411   3 DON JUAN 14   3   1
IF YOU HAVE NOUGHT ELSE HERE'S AT LEAST SATIETY   416   3 DON JUAN 14   15   5
THERE'S NOUGHT IN THIS BAD WORLD LIKE SYMPATHY   430   3 DON JUAN 14   47   1
AS SHE HAD SEEN NOUGHT CLAIMING ITS EXPANSION   446   3 DON JUAN 14   85   4
JUAN KNEW NOUGHT OF SUCH A CHARACTER--   481   3 DON JUAN 15   58   1
SAY NOUGHT TO HIM AS HE WALKS THE HALL   520   3 DON JUAN 16   L 6   1
AND HE'LL SAY NOUGHT TO YOU   520   3 DON JUAN 16   L 6   2
A FAT FEN VICARAGE AND NOUGHT TO THINK ON   540   3 DON JUAN 16   82   8
SMILE OF AURORA'S THERE WAS NOUGHT TO PIQUE   544   3 DON JUAN 16   92   6
NOUGHT'S
NOUGHT'S MORE SUBLIME THAN ENERGETIC BILE   489   2 DON JUAN   5   135   4
NOUGHT'S PERMANENT AMONG THE HUMAN RACE   309   3 DON JUAN 11   82   7
NOUN
'TIS STRANGE--THE HEBREW NOUN WHICH MEANS I AM   28   2 DON JUAN   1   14   7
NOURISHED
THE FIFTH WHO BY A CHRISTIAN MOTHER NOURISHED   166   3 DON JUAN   8   110   5
NOURISHES
BECAUSE IT BREEDS NO MORE MOUTHS THAN IT NOURISHES   . .   471   3 DON JUAN 15   35   4
NOUS
(THIS SHOULD BE ENTRE NOUS FOR JULIA THOUGHT   67   2 DON JUAN   1   84   7
BECAUSE THE GOOD OLD MAN HAD SO MUCH NOUS   225   2 DON JUAN   2   130   5
NOVEL
SOME PLAY THE DEVIL AND THEN WRITE A NOVEL   263   2 DON JUAN   2   201   8
A NOVEL WORD IN MY VOCABULARY   346   2 DON JUAN   4   5   8
TO NOVEL POWER AND AS SHE WAS THE LAST   476   3 DON JUAN 15   46   7
NOVEL-READING
TO THIS IMPRACTICABLE NOVEL-READING TRANCE   450   3 DON JUAN 14   92 V6
NOVELS
MISS EDGEWORTH'S NOVELS STEPPING FROM THEIR COVERS   . .   29   2 DON JUAN   1   16   2
NO NOVELS E'ER HAD SET THEIR YOUNG HEARTS BLEEDING   . .   354   2 DON JUAN   4   19   4
HOW MUCH WOULD NOVELS GAIN BY THE EXCHANGE   455   3 DON JUAN 14   101   3
NOVELTIES
WHO THINK THAT NOVELTIES ARE BUTTERFLIES   328   3 DON JUAN 12   27   5
THAT NOVELTIES PLEASE LESS THAN THEY IMPRESS   347   3 DON JUAN 12   69   8
NOVELTY
HIS GARMENT'S NOVELTY AND HIS BEING AWKWARD   456   2 DON JUAN   5   78   2
NOVEMBER
'TWAS IN NOVEMBER BUT I'M NOT SO SURE   86   2 DON JUAN   1   121   7
'TWAS IN NOVEMBER WHEN FINE DAYS ARE FEW   94   2 DON JUAN   1   134   3
NOVICE
EMBARRASS'D AT FIRST STARTING WITH A NOVICE   62   2 DON JUAN   1   74   8
EXCEPT DON JUAN--A MERE NOVICE WHOSE   131   3 DON JUAN   8   36   2
THOU ARE NO NOVICE IN THE HEADLONG CHASE   326   3 DON JUAN 12   23   6
OF A MERE NOVICE HAD ONE SAFEGUARD MORE   346   3 DON JUAN 12   67   2
NOW-A-DAYS
BY WHICH SUCH THINGS ARE SETTLED NOW-A-DAYS   45   3 DON JUAN   6   78   8
A VIRTUE MUCH IN FASHION NOW-A-DAYS   176   3 DON JUAN   8   128   3
SINCE LAUGHTER NOW-A-DAYS IS DEEMED TOO SERIOUS   358   3 DON JUAN 13   1   2
WHICH NOW-A-DAYS IS THE THERMOMETER   524   3 DON JUAN 16   48   2
THAT INNOVATION'S SPIRIT NOW-A-DAYS   536   3 DON JUAN 16   73   3
NUBIA
TWELVE NEGRESSES FROM NUBIA BROUGHT A PRICE   408   2 DON JUAN   4   115   1
NUBIANS
OF GEORGIANS RUSSIANS NUBIANS AND WHATNOT   417   2 DON JUAN   5   13   2
NUGAE
HAUD IGNARA LOQUOR THESE ARE NUGAE QUARUM   419   3 DON JUAN 14   21   1
NUMA'S
AS NUMA'S (WHO WAS ALSO NAMED POMPILIUS)   40   2 DON JUAN   1   35   7
NUMB'D
ONE HALF SATE UP THOUGH NUMB'D WITH THE IMMERSION . . .   189   2 DON JUAN   2   63   4
NUMBER
(I HAVE FORGOT THE NUMBER AND THINK NO MAN   74   2 DON JUAN   1   98   5

555

NUMBER   (CONTINUED)

	PAGE	VOL	CANTO		STANZA	LN
BECAUSE THAT NUMBER RARELY MUCH ENDEARS	78	2 DON JUAN	1		107	6
WITH TORCHES FRIENDS AND SERVANTS IN GREAT NUMBER	96	2 DON JUAN	1		138	2
THAT BEING ABOUT THE NUMBER I'LL ALLOW	271	2 DON JUAN	2		216	4
SHE THEN PREFERS HIM IN THE PLURAL NUMBER	276	2 DON JUAN	3		3	7
ONE WONDERED WHAT TO DO WITH SUCH A NUMBER	448	2 DON JUAN	5		64	4
UNTIL THEIR VERY NUMBER MAKES MEN HARD	118	3 DON JUAN	8		13	2
AND THEREFORE WE MUST GIVE THE GREATER NUMBER	120	3 DON JUAN	8		18	1
HE FOUND A NUMBER OF CHASSEURS ALL SCATTERED	131	3 DON JUAN	8		37	7
AND FOUR-AND-TWENTY HOURS AND TWICE THAT NUMBER	248	3 DON JUAN	10		48	2
THE GREATEST NUMBER FLESH HATH EVER KNOWN	255	3 DON JUAN	10		62	8
BUT AS THERE'S SAFETY GRAFTED IN THE NUMBER	371	3 DON JUAN	13		30	1

NUMBER'D

IN NUMBER'D LOTS THEY ALL HAD CUFFS AND COLLARS	283	2 DON JUAN	3		15	7

NUMBER'S

OR MANY (FOR THE NUMBER'S SOMETIMES SUCH)	305	3 DON JUAN	11		73	5

NUMBERS

THEIR NUMBERS WERE MUCH THINN'D BY THIS INFLICTION	199	2 DON JUAN	2		80	1
THE NUMBERS ARE TOO GREAT FOR THEM TO FLATTER ALL	50	3 DON JUAN	6		88	8
NOT BY THE NUMBERS GOOD INTENT HATH SAVED	124	3 DON JUAN	8		26	4
NOR YET TOO MANY NOR TOO FEW THEIR NUMBERS	145	3 DON JUAN	8		67	3

NUMERAL

THAT BEING ABOUT THEIR AVERAGE NUMERAL	295	3 DON JUAN	11		54	6

NUMEROUS

AMONGST HER NUMEROUS ACQUAINTANCE ALL	51	2 DON JUAN	1		55	1
JUST THEN AS THEY ARE RATHER NUMEROUS FOUND	205	3 DON JUAN	9		46	4
THEIR CHANCES--THEY'RE TOO NUMEROUS LIKE THE THIRTY	299	3 DON JUAN	11		61	7
AND NUMEROUS PARTY OF HIS NOBLE FRIENDS	382	3 DON JUAN	13		52	3

NUMIDIAN

THE FIRE BURST FORTH FROM HER NUMIDIAN VEINS	375	2 DON JUAN	4		57	7

NUN

MORE THAN WITHIN THE BOSOM OF A NUN	244	2 DON JUAN	2		167	5
TO SUPPER BUT YOU WORTHY CHRISTIAN NUN	458	2 DON JUAN	5		81	3

NUNEZ

THE DUKE OF ICHAR AND DON FERNAN NUNEZ	103	2 DON JUAN	1		150	2

NUNNERY

AND HOW TO SCALE A FORTRESS--OR A NUNNERY	42	2 DON JUAN	1		38	8
JULIA WAS SENT INTO A NUNNERY	129	2 DON JUAN	1		191	V6

NUNS

THE FORMER IN A PALACE WHERE LIKE NUNS	498	2 DON JUAN	5		152	3

NUPTIAL

THEIR HEARTS THE STARS THEIR NUPTIAL TORCHES SHED	265	2 DON JUAN	2		204	2
(NUPTIAL EXAMPLES ARE AS GOOD AS ANY)	301	2 DON JUAN	3		50	4
TO MAKE THE NUPTIAL COUCH A BED OF WARE	12	3 DON JUAN	6		12	8
AS ERE WAS VIRGIN OF A NUPTIAL CHIME	74	3 DON JUAN	7		16	4

NUPTIALS

WAS HAPLESS IN THEIR NUPTIALS FOR SOME BAR	281	2 DON JUAN	3		10	4

NURSERY

AND ALL WHO HAVE SEEN A HUMAN NURSERY SAW	488	2 DON JUAN	5		133	5

NURSES

STRUCK AT HIS FRIENDS AS BABIES BEAT THEIR NURSES	165	3 DON JUAN	8		108	8
ON THAT SWEET ORE WHICH EVERYBODY NURSES	264	3 DON JUAN	10		79	6

NURSING

THEN DRESSING NURSING PRAYING AND ALL'S OVER	263	2 DON JUAN	2		200	8
HER CHILDREN UP (IF NURSING THEM DON'T THIN HER)	306	2 DON JUAN	3		60	4

NURST

THAT FAMISH'D PEOPLE MUST BE SLOWLY NURST	239	2 DON JUAN	2		158	7
A SHAWL WHOSE FOLDS IN CASHMIRE HAD BEEN NURST	451	2 DON JUAN	5		68	6
WALKED O'ER THE WALLS OF ISMAIL AS IF NURST	138	3 DON JUAN	8		52	3

NURTURE

TORY BY NURTURE WHIG BY CIRCUMSTANCE	152	2 DON JUAN	1	V	3	1

NURTURED

AT LEAST HAD HE BEEN NURTURED IN THE NORTH	158	2 DON JUAN	2		2	4

NUTBROWN

AH NUTBROWN PARTRIDGES AH BRILLIANT PHEASANTS	394	3 DON JUAN	13		75	7

NUTRITIOUS

PROVED EVEN STILL A MORE NUTRITIOUS MATTER	208	2 DON JUAN	2		99	5

NUTS

LAMB AND PISTACHIO NUTS--IN SHORT ALL MEATS	307	2 DON JUAN	3		62	2

NUTTY

SO PRIME SO SWELL SO NUTTY AND SO KNOWING	277	3 DON JUAN	11		19	8

NYMPH

A NYMPH AND HER BELOVED ALL UNSEEN	352	2 DON JUAN	4		15	6
MOVED BY THE CHINESE NYMPH OF TEARS GREEN TEA	372	2 DON JUAN	4		52	2

NYMPH-LIKE

THEY FORMED A VERY NYMPH-LIKE LOOKING CREW	469	2 DON JUAN	5		99	5

NYMPHS

HE THOUGHT OF WOOD NYMPHS AND IMMORTAL BOWERS	72	2 DON JUAN	1		94	3
AND MAKE LIKE OTHER NYMPHS THY LOVERS ILL	372	2 DON JUAN	4		53	4
OF HIS DRILL'D NYMPHS BUT LIKE A GENTLEMAN	427	3 DON JUAN	14		38	8

OAK

CROWN'D BY HIGH WOODLANDS WHERE THE DRUID OAK	384	3 DON JUAN	13		56	2

OAKS

AS OAKS BLOWN DOWN WITH ALL THEIR THOUSAND WINTERS	155	3 DON JUAN	8		88	8
AND OAKS AS OLDEN AS THEIR PEDIGREE	381	3 DON JUAN	13		50	7

OAR

THE SONG AND OAR OF ADRIA'S GONDOLIER	87	2 DON JUAN	1		122	3
AND ONE OAR FOR A MAST WHICH A YOUNG LAD	181	2 DON JUAN	2		48	5
KEPT ABOVE WATER WITH AN OAR FOR MAST	188	2 DON JUAN	2		61	2

OAR   (CONTINUED)
```
        INSTEAD OF SAIL WERE TO THE OAR MADE FAST     . . . . . . 188  2 DON JUAN  2     61   4
        BUT AS THEY HAD BUT ONE OAR AND THAT BRITTLE  . . . . . . 192  2 DON JUAN  2     69   7
        WITH THEIR ONE OAR (I WISH THEY HAD HAD A PAIR) . . . . . 193  2 DON JUAN  2     70   5
        NOR YET HAD HE ARRIVED BUT FOR THE OAR   . .  . . . . . . 212  2 DON JUAN  2    107   1
        DROOP'D DRIPPING ON THE OAR (THEIR JURY-MAST) . . . . . . 214  2 DON JUAN  2    110   5
        LAY DROOPING OER THE OAR WHICH SERVED FOR MAST . . . . . . 214  2 DON JUAN  2    110  V5
        THEY LAID HIM IN A BOAT AND PLIED THE OAR  . . . . . . . . 371  2 DON JUAN  4     50   5
OARS
        SOME BROKEN PLANKS AND OARS THAT TO THE TOUCH  . . . . . . 226  2 DON JUAN  2    132   4
        AS FAST AS OARS COULD PULL AND WATER FLOAT . . . . . . . . 432  2 DON JUAN  5     40   4
OATH
        THAT EACH PULL'D DIFFERENT WAYS WITH MANY AN OATH . . . . 394  2 DON JUAN  4     93   7
        TO THE SOFT OATH OF ANA-SEING SIKTUM  . . . . . . . . . . 409  2 DON JUAN  4    116  V8
        OR AS A DAME REPENTS HER OF HER OATH  . . . . . . . . . . 493  2 DON JUAN  5    142   7
        FOR THEY ARE DAMNED THAT ONCE ALL FAMOUS OATH  . . . . . . 88  3 DON JUAN  7     45   2
        THE FIRST WITH SIGHS THE SECOND WITH AN OATH   . . . . . . 166  3 DON JUAN  8    109   3
        OR IF THE OATH SEEM STRONG--I SWEAR BY JOVE  . . . . . . . 452  3 DON JUAN 14     96  V2
OATHS
        OF FIRE THAN WATER SPITE OF OATHS AND TEARS . . . . . . . 174  2 DON JUAN  2     35   6
        IN SEVERAL OATHS--ARMENIAN TURK AND GREEK--  . . . . . . . 229  2 DON JUAN  2    138   7
        SIGHED JUAN MUTTERING ALSO SOME SLIGHT OATHS  . . . . . . 455  2 DON JUAN  5     76   5
        THESE ARE BUT VULGAR OATHS AS YOU MAY DEEM   . . . . . . . 112  3 DON JUAN  8      1   2
        YOUR CONTINENTAL OATHS ARE BUT INCONTINENT   . . . . . . . 289  3 DON JUAN 11     43   2
OATS
        ARISE WHEN WE SEE EMPERORS FALL WITH OATS   . . . . . . . 198  3 DON JUAN  9     32   8
        AND THIS AND HIS NOT KNOWING HOW MUCH OATS . . . . . . . . 543  3 DON JUAN 16     89   7
OBDURATE
        WHO WOULD SUPPOSE THY GIFTS SOMETIMES OBDURATE)  . . . . . 540  3 DON JUAN 16     82   6
OBEDIENCE
        PASSIVE OBEDIENCE--NOW RAISED UP THE HEAD   . . . . . . . 101  3 DON JUAN  7     67   6
OBEISANCE
        THEY BOWED OBEISANCE AND WITHDREW RETIRING   . . . . . . . 469  2 DON JUAN  5    100   1
OBEY
        WOULD HE ADORE A SULTAN HE OBEY . . . . . . . . . . . . .  15  2 DON JUAN  D     11   7
        WE WOULD AGAINST THEM MAKE THE FLESH OBEY--  . . . . . . . 474  2 DON JUAN  5    110   7
        TO HEAR AND TO OBEY HAD BEEN FROM BIRTH  . . . . . . . . . 475  2 DON JUAN  5    112   1
        AND HANDS OBEY--OUR HEARTS ARE STILL OUR OWN . . . . . . . 484  2 DON JUAN  5    127   8
        HIS BEST TO OBEY IN WHAT HE HAD BEEN TASKED  . . . . . . .  56  3 DON JUAN  6    100   4
        TO HEAR IS TO OBEY HE SAID BUT STILL   . . . . . . . . . .  62  3 DON JUAN  6    114   1
        MUST STILL OBEY THE HIGH--WHICH IS THEIR HANDLE . . . . . 342  3 DON JUAN 12     56   7
        WHICH EVEN THOSE WHO OBEY WOULD FAIN BE THOUGHT  . . . . . 421  3 DON JUAN 14     26   2
OBEY'D
        AN ORDER SOMEWHAT SULLENLY OBEY'D . . . . . . . . . . . . 116  2 DON JUAN  1    173   4
OBEYED
        BABA RETIRE WHICH HE OBEYED IN STYLE  . . . . . . . . . . 473  2 DON JUAN  5    107   2
OBEYS
        WHICH NONE DIVINE AND EVERYONE OBEYS  . . . . . . . . . . 207  3 DON JUAN  9     49   6
OBIT
        WILL HAVE A FIRM POST OBIT ON POSTERITY  . . . . . . . . . 566  3 DON JUAN 17      9   8
OBJECT
        WITH BUT THE SINGLE OBJECT--TO ADVANCE   .   . . . . . . . 152  2 DON JUAN  1  V  3  V3
        LOVELY SEEM'D ANY OBJECT THAT SHOULD SWEEP   . . . . . . . 210  2 DON JUAN  2    103   7
        SOME FAVOUR'D OBJECT AND AS IN THE NICHE   . . . . . . . . 269  2 DON JUAN  2    211   5
        IN THE SAME OBJECT GRACES QUITE AS KILLING   . . . . . . . 270  2 DON JUAN  2    213   3
        OBJECT ON OBJECT FLASHED SO BRIGHT AND FAST  . . . . . . . 465  2 DON JUAN  5     93   6
        OBJECT ON OBJECT FLASHED SO BRIGHT AND FAST  . . . . . . . 465  2 DON JUAN  5     93   6
        THE SECOND OBJECT WAS TO PROFIT BY . . . . . . . . . . . .  78  3 DON JUAN  7     24   1
        A GENERAL OBJECT OF ATTENTION MADE . . . . . . . . . . . . 223  3 DON JUAN  9     83   2
        WHILE THE POOR RICH WRETCH OBJECT OF THESE CARES  . . . . 331  3 DON JUAN 12     33   7
        AND AS MY OBJECT IS MORALITY . . . . . . . . . . . . . . . 355  3 DON JUAN 12     86   3
        HIS ONLY OBJECT AND 'GAINST ODDS TO FIGHT   . . . . . . . 363  3 DON JUAN 13      9   4
        AND WERE HER OBJECT ONLY WHAT'S CALL'D GLORY . . . . . . . 416  3 DON JUAN 14     13   7
        UPON AN OBJECT WHETHER SAD OR PLAYFUL  . . . . . . . . . . 463  3 DON JUAN 15     16   7
        OR WED ALREADY WHO OBJECT TO THIS  . . . . . . . . . . . . 470  3 DON JUAN 15     32   3
        'TWERE DIFFICULT TO SAY WHAT WAS THE OBJECT  . . . . . . . 526  3 DON JUAN 16     51   1
OBJECTION
        FOR HIS OWN SHARE--HE SAW BUT SMALL OBJECTION . . . . . . 452  2 DON JUAN  5     71   1
OBJECTION'S
        MY OBJECTION'S TO HIS TITLE NOT HIS RITUAL . . . . . . . . 472  3 DON JUAN 15     36   7
OBJECTIONS
        A THIRD BECAUSE THERE CAN BE NO OBJECTIONS . . . . . . . . 471  3 DON JUAN 15     34   8
OBJECTS
        HATH BUT TWO OBJECTS HOW TO SERVE AND BIND   . . . . . . .  18  2 DON JUAN  D     15   3
        THINK'ST THOU THE HONEY WITH THOSE OBJECTS GREW . . . . . 144  2 DON JUAN  1    214   6
        UPON ALL LEGAL OBJECTS OF POSSESSION . . . . . . . . . . .  11  3 DON JUAN  6     10   2
        FOR OBJECTS WORTHY OF THE SENTIMENT  . . . . . . . . . . . 460  3 DON JUAN 15     10   8
OBLIGE
        WHERE GEOGRAPHY FINDS NO ONE TO OBLIGE HER   . . . . . . . 348  3 DON JUAN 12     70   4
        BUT SHOULD A LADY ASK ME TO OBLIGE HER   . . . . . . . . . 348  3 DON JUAN 12     70  V4
        I CAN'T OBLIGE YOU READER TO READ ON . . . . . . . . . . . 356  3 DON JUAN 12     87   6
OBLIGED
        AND HE HIMSELF OBLIGED TO SHUT UP SHOP--HE   . . . . . . .  27  2 DON JUAN  1     11   6
        HOW SOME TO BURDENS WERE OBLIGED TO STOOP  . . . . . . . . 409  2 DON JUAN  4    116   3
        BED FOR THE DREAM SHE HAD BEEN OBLIGED TO HEAR . . . . . .  45  3 DON JUAN  6     79   6
        IN COURAGE WAS OBLIGED TO SNATCH A SHIELD  . . . . . . . . 125  3 DON JUAN  8     28   7
        HAVE BEEN OBLIGED TO SLAY A FREEBORN NATIVE  . . . . . . . 277  3 DON JUAN 11     18   7
OBLIGES
        (THE RHYME OBLIGES ME TO THIS SOMETIMES  . . . . . . . . . 456  2 DON JUAN  5     77   7
```

```
                                                             PAGE VOL      CANTO STANZA LN

OBLIGING
    THE CIVIL LIST (HE DEIGNS TO ACCEPT OBLIGING ALL   . . . .  528  3 DON JUAN 16    56    6
OBLIVION
    SOME DULL MS OBLIVION LONG HAS SANK     . . . . . . .  327  2 DON JUAN  3    89    5
    THE DRAINER OF OBLIVION EVEN THE SOT  . . . . . . . .  457  3 DON JUAN 15     4    3
OBLIVION'S
    HAVE HALF WITHDRAWN FROM HIM OBLIVION'S SCREEN  . . . . .   82  3 DON JUAN  7    33    8
OBLIVIOUS
    WHAT MUST I GO TO THE OBLIVIOUS COOKS  . . . . . . .  403  2 DON JUAN  4   108    5
OBSCURE
    AT LEAST HER CONVERSATION WAS OBSCURE  . . . .        28  2 DON JUAN  1    13    6
    (ALTHOUGH THEIR TALK'S OBSCURE AND CIRCUMSPECT)  . . .    38  2 DON JUAN  1    33    4
    ABOUT THE DAY--THE ERA'S MORE OBSCURE  . . . .        86  2 DON JUAN  1   121    8
    A WOOD OBSCURE LIKE THAT WHERE DANTE FOUND  . . . .     43  3 DON JUAN  6    75    3
    BUT GETTING NIGH GRIM DANTE'S OBSCURE WOOD  . . . .    238  3 DON JUAN 10    27    3
    FLASH UP IN INGOTS FROM THE MINE OBSCURE  . . . . .    319  3 DON JUAN 12     8    5
OBSCURITY
    ARE TWISTED TO A PHRASE OF SOME OBSCURITY  . . . . .    69  2 DON JUAN  1    88    8
    WOULD THEY HAVE BEEN THE HAPPIER FOR OBSCURITY  . .   470  2 DON JUAN  5   102   V1
OBSEQUIOUS
    THE OBSEQUIOUS LANDLORD HATH THE CHANGE RESTORED  . . .  379  3 DON JUAN 13    46    5
OBSERVANT
    OBSERVANT OF THE FOIBLES OF THE CROWD  . . . . . .    462  3 DON JUAN 15    15    3
OBSERVATION
    ONE MONSTROUS DIAMOND DREW MUCH OBSERVATION .  . . . .  287  3 DON JUAN 11    39    4
    SINCE HE HAD GAINED AT LEAST HER OBSERVATION  . . . .  545  3 DON JUAN 16    93    5
OBSERVE
    OBSERVE YOUR LOVER WHEN HE LEAVES YOUR ARMS  . . . .   139  3 DON JUAN  8    53    7
    OBSERVE FOR THAT WITH ME'S A SINE QUA .  . . . .      494  3 DON JUAN 15    86    8
    ALSO OBSERVE THAT LIKE THE GREAT LORD COKE  . . . .   494  3 DON JUAN 15    87    1
OBSERVED
    OF CONDUCT WAS WHICH HE OBSERVED IN GREECE  . . . .   319  2 DON JUAN  3    84    8
    IT IS OBSERVED THAT LADIES ARE LITIGIOUS  . . . . .    11  3 DON JUAN  6    10    1
    OBSERVED AS STRICTLY BOTH AT BOARD AND BED  . . . .   470  3 DON JUAN 15    32    6
OBSERVER
    A SLIGHT OBSERVER IN A MODEST WAY)  . . . . . . .    336  3 DON JUAN 12    44    2
OBSERVING
    OBSERVING LITTLE IN HIS REVERIE . . . . . . . .     553  3 DON JUAN 16   106    7
OBSOLETE
    BUT ALL THESE SAVE THE LAST BEING OBSOLETE  . . . .   347  2 DON JUAN  4     6    7
OBSTACLE
    THE SLIGHTEST OBSTACLE WHICH MAY ENCUMBER  . . . .    371  3 DON JUAN 13    30   V5
OBSTINACY
    THEIR OBSTINACY PRIDE AND INDECISION  . . . . . .     64  3 DON JUAN  6   117    5
    AS OBSTINACY BOTH IN MEN AND WOMEN . . . . . . .     448  3 DON JUAN 14    89    5
OBSTINATE
    AS OBSTINATE AS SWEDISH CHARLES AT BENDER  . . . .    165  3 DON JUAN  8   107    4
OBSTINATELY
    AND TO WHICH BEAUTY OBSTINATELY CLINGS  . . . . .     468  2 DON JUAN  5    98   V4
OBTAIN
    MIGHT PROBABLY OBTAIN BOTH IN THE END . . . . .       451  2 DON JUAN  5    69    3
    WHILE SOUVAROFF DETERMINED TO OBTAIN IT  . . . . .     92  3 DON JUAN  7    51    7
OBTAINED
    YOU HAVE OBTAINED GREAT PENSIONS AND MUCH PRAISE  . . .  183  3 DON JUAN  9     1    6
OBTAINING
    THE MORE SO IN OBTAINING OUR OWN ENDS . . . . . .     37  2 DON JUAN  1    30    4
OBTUSE
    HEEDLESS OF PRICKS BECAUSE IT WAS OBTUSE  . . . . .   565  3 DON JUAN 17     6    6
OBVIOUS
    PROLONGS IT THIS IS OBVIOUS TO PHYSICIANS  . . . .    190  2 DON JUAN  2    64    2
    THE REASON'S OBVIOUS IF THERE'S AN ECLAT  . . . .    352  3 DON JUAN 12    78    1
    WAS OBVIOUS IN EACH FEATURE OF HER FACE  . . . . .    550  3 DON JUAN 16   102    3
OCCASION
    ALL WHICH MIGHT IF OCCASION SERVED BE QUOTED  . . . .   36  2 DON JUAN  1    28    3
    ('TWERE HARD TO TELL UPON A LIKE OCCASION  . . . .     38  2 DON JUAN  1    32    3
    TO PUBLIC FEELING WHICH ON THIS OCCASION .  . . . .    38  2 DON JUAN  1    33    7
    COULD BE BUT JULIA (WHOM ON THIS OCCASION  . . . .     54  2 DON JUAN  1    59    6
    PREFERENCE THAT WE MUST FEEL UPON OCCASION  . . . .     63  2 DON JUAN  1    77    6
    EXERTION MIGHT BE USEFUL ON OCCASION  . . . .         65  2 DON JUAN  1    81    4
    OF SIGHT THAT I MUST THINK ON THIS OCCASION  . . . .    75  2 DON JUAN  1   101    2
    I WISH INDEED THEY HAD NOT HAD OCCASION  . . . . .     84  2 DON JUAN  1   117    4
    OF LIFE'S STRANGE TREE SO FRUITFUL ON OCCASION  . . .  250  2 DON JUAN  2   179    6
    A GOOD DEAL PRACTISED HERE UPON OCCASION  . . . . .   464  2 DON JUAN  5    92    8
    LIKE ALL THE REST BUT UPON THIS OCCASION  . . . . .    25  3 DON JUAN  6    38    2
    THE RUSSIAN ARMY UPON THIS OCCASION  . . . . .       176  3 DON JUAN  8   128    2
    MEN BECOME WOLVES ON ANY SLIGHT OCCASION  . . . . .   192  3 DON JUAN  9    20    8
    IT HAD BEEN AN AFFRONT ON THIS OCCASION  . . . . .   330  3 DON JUAN 12    30    5
    EVEN THOUGH HIMSELF AVOIDED THE OCCASION  . . . . .   355  3 DON JUAN 12    85    8
    THOUGH APT TO ACT WITH FIRE UPON OCCASION  . . . .   365  3 DON JUAN 13    14    5
    BUT ADELINE HAD NOT THE LEAST OCCASION  . . . . .   372  3 DON JUAN 13    31    1
    AND SECONDLY MUST LET SLIP NO OCCASION  . . . . .   404  3 DON JUAN 13    98    3
    SOMETIMES WITH AND SOMETIMES WITHOUT OCCASION  . . .  413  3 DON JUAN 14     7    4
    OF RUIN ROSE FROM SUCH A SLIGHT OCCASION  . . . .   454  3 DON JUAN 14   100    4
    BUT WILL NOT SWEAR YET BOTH UPON OCCASION  . . . .   458  3 DON JUAN 15     6    7
    AS DID THE CYNIC ON SOME LIKE OCCASION  . . . .     522  3 DON JUAN 16    43    4
    HER GRACE TOO ALSO SEIZED THE SAME OCCASION  . . . .  526  3 DON JUAN 16    53    4
    MORAL OR PHYSICAL ON THIS OCCASION  . . . . .       567  3 DON JUAN 17    12    4
OCCASIONALLY
    MADE EPIGRAMS OCCASIONALLY TOO . . . . . . . . .     524  3 DON JUAN 16    47    3
```

		PAGE	VOL	CANTO	STANZA	LN

OCCASIONS
  I PRAY YE FLOG THEM UPON ALL OCCASIONS . . . . 157 2 DON JUAN 2   1 3
  AS UPON SUCH OCCASIONS TARS WILL ASK . . . . 173 2 DON JUAN 2   33 7
  HAD SOMETHING READY UPON MOST OCCASIONS-- . . . . . . 319 2 DON JUAN 3   84 4
  FOR SUCH PRECEDENCE UPON SUCH OCCASIONS . . . . 136 3 DON JUAN 8   48 2
  ON SUCH OCCASIONS NOT A SINGLE HEAD . . . . 152 3 DON JUAN 8   81 6
  ON GREAT OCCASIONS SUCH AS AN ATTACK . . . . 160 3 DON JUAN 8   97 3
  THE TANTI PALPITI'S ON SUCH OCCASIONS . . . . 523 3 DON JUAN 16   45 4
OCCUPANTS
  OF THE FAIR OCCUPANTS IF THERE BE SPRITES . . . . . . 38 3 DON JUAN 6   64 4
OCCUPATION
  TO QUIT HIS ACADEMIC OCCUPATION . . . . 175 2 DON JUAN 2   37 6
  THRICE HAPPY THEY WHO HAVE AN OCCUPATION . . . . . . 443 3 DON JUAN 14   77 8
  YOU SEE HERE WAS ENOUGH OF OCCUPATION . . . . 534 3 DON JUAN 16   68 1
OCCUPIED
  THEIR SOFA OCCUPIED THREE PARTS COMPLETE . . . . . . 309 2 DON JUAN 3   67 3
  UPON THEIR HAMS WERE OCCUPIED AT CHESS . . . . 441 2 DON JUAN 5   53 2
  AND EVERY COUCH IS OCCUPIED YOU HAD BEST . . . . 29 3 DON JUAN 6   46 6
  AND WHETHER HE HAD OCCUPIED THEIR STATION . . . . . . 55 3 DON JUAN 6   99 4
  THE ANIMALS AFORESAID OCCUPIED . . . . 249 3 DON JUAN 10   51 1
  BUT ADELINE WAS OCCUPIED BY FAME . . . . 546 3 DON JUAN 16   95 1
OCCUPIES
  IT OCCUPIES ME TO TURN BACK REGARDS . . . . 415 3 DON JUAN 14   11 5
OCCUR
  OCCUR IN ORIENT PALACES AND EVEN . . . . 465 2 DON JUAN 5   94 2
  MIGHT HERE AND THERE OCCUR SOME VIOLATION . . . . . . 176 3 DON JUAN 8 129 2
  OCCUR THOUGH RARELY WHEN THERE IS A SPARK . . . . . . 177 3 DON JUAN 8 130 5
  AS NOW OCCUR I THOUGHT THAT I WOULD PEN YOU 'EM . . . 180 3 DON JUAN 8 136 4
OCCURR'D
  I WISH THESE LAST HAD NOT OCCURR'D IN SOOTH . . . . . 78 2 DON JUAN 1 107 5
OCCURRED
  WHICH MIGHT HAVE THEN OCCURRED TO YOU OR ME . . . . . 434 2 DON JUAN 5   43 4
  WHEN THINGS BEYOND THE COMMON HAVE OCCURRED-- . . . . 59 3 DON JUAN 6 106 6
  I DON'T KNOW HOW THE THING OCCURRED--IT MIGHT . . . . 125 3 DON JUAN 8   28 1
  OCCURRED WHAT OFTEN HAPPENS I'M AFRAID . . . . 355 3 DON JUAN 12   85 3
  THIS WAS NO BAD MISTAKE AS IT OCCURRED . . . . 543 3 DON JUAN 16   89 1
OCCURS
  BUT THIS OCCURS BUT SELDOM BETWEEN WHILES . . . . . . 238 2 DON JUAN 2 154 5
OCEAN
  WHICH MAKES ME WISH YOU'D CHANGE YOUR LAKES FOR OCEAN . . 12 2 DON JUAN D   5 8
  AS SWEETNESS TO THE FLOWER OR SALT TO OCEAN . . . . . 51 2 DON JUAN 1   55 6
  THAN HE WHO NEVER SAW THE SEA OF OCEAN . . . . 60 2 DON JUAN 1   70 8
  THE RAINBOW BASED ON OCEAN SPAN THE SKY . . . . 87 2 DON JUAN 1 122 8
  SOONER SHALL THIS BLUE OCEAN MELT TO AIR . . . . . . 166 2 DON JUAN 2   19 3
  AS IF OLD OCEAN BAFFLED OUR INTENT . . . . 173 2 DON JUAN 2   32 V4
  CLAMOUR'D IN CHORUS TO THE ROARING OCEAN . . . . . . 174 2 DON JUAN 2   34 8
  LOUDER THAN THE LOUD OCEAN LIKE A CRASH . . . . 184 2 DON JUAN 2   53 2
  WHEN OVER CATHOLICS THE OCEAN ROLLS . . . . 185 2 DON JUAN 2   55 3
  OF OCEAN WHEN THEY WOKE THEY FELT A QUALM . . . . . . 192 2 DON JUAN 2   68 6
  AND OCEAN SLUMBER'D LIKE AN UNWEAN'D CHILD . . . . . 193 2 DON JUAN 2   70 2
  LULL'D LIKE THE DEPTH OF OCEAN WHEN AT REST . . . . . 235 2 DON JUAN 2 148 4
  THE OUTSTRETCH'D OCEAN GLITTER LIKE A LAKE . . . . . 249 2 DON JUAN 2 177 8
  SPREAD LIKE A ROSY OCEAN VAST AND BRIGHT . . . . . . 253 2 DON JUAN 2 185 2
  THE SILENT OCEAN AND THE STARLIGHT BAY . . . . 255 2 DON JUAN 2 188 3
  OCEAN THEIR WITNESS AND THE CAVE THEIR BED . . . . . 265 2 DON JUAN 2 204 4
  MUCH LESS EXPERIENCE OF DRY LAND THAN OCEAN . . . . . 289 2 DON JUAN 3   26 2
  THE OCEAN WHEN ITS YEASTY WAR IS WAGING . . . . 305 2 DON JUAN 3   58 3
  OF OCEAN--NO OF AIR AND THEN HE MAKES . . . . 333 2 DON JUAN 3   98 6
  MY ALTARS ARE THE MOUNTAINS AND THE OCEAN . . . . . . 336 2 DON JUAN 3 104 6
  BUT AS THE TORRENT WIDENS TOWARDS THE OCEAN . . . . . 345 2 DON JUAN 4   2 7
  SPRINKLED WITH PALACES THE OCEAN STREAM . . . . 412 2 DON JUAN 5   3 2
  LIKE OCEAN WARRING 'GAINST A ROCKY ISLE . . . . 489 2 DON JUAN 5 135 6
  NEITHER CAME CROWDING LIKE THE WAVES OF OCEAN . . . . 42 3 DON JUAN 6   71 4
  PICKING UP SHELLS BY THE GREAT OCEAN--TRUTH . . . . . 69 3 DON JUAN 7   5 8
  BUT THE TOWN DITCH BELOW WAS DEEP AS OCEAN . . . . . . 72 3 DON JUAN 7   11 3
  LIKE BUBBLES ON AN OCEAN MUCH LESS AMPLE . . . . . . 189 3 DON JUAN 9   13 6
  IN THE NEXT OCEAN WHICH MAY FLOW JUST THEN . . . . . 217 3 DON JUAN 9   69 6
  THE OCEAN OF ETERNITY THE ROAR . . . . 227 3 DON JUAN 10   4 5
  WITH QUIET CRUIZING O'ER THE OCEAN WOMAN . . . . . . 376 3 DON JUAN 13   40 2
  IN VERNET'S OCEAN LIGHTS AND THERE THE STORIES . . . 392 3 DON JUAN 13   71 6
  AND NOT TO POUR THEIR OCEAN IN A SIEVE . . . . 431 3 DON JUAN 14   49 8
  WITH THE NEW VENUS OF THEIR BRILLIANT OCEAN . . . . . 434 3 DON JUAN 14   55 4
  WHEREWITH WE BREAK OUR BUBBLES ON THE OCEAN . . . . . 457 3 DON JUAN 15   2 4
  A HALF-STARVED BABE A WRECK UPON LIFE'S OCEAN . . . . 563 3 DON JUAN 17   3 4
OCEAN-BURIED
  THE OCEAN-BURIED RISEN FROM DEATH TO BE . . . . 363 2 DON JUAN 4   36 4
OCEAN'S
  OF LOVE'S AND NIGHT'S AND OCEAN'S SOLITUDE . . . . . 262 2 DON JUAN 2 198 2
  AS FOR A BROOK TO COPE WITH OCEAN'S FLOOD . . . . . . 106 3 DON JUAN 7   80 7
  THE OCEAN'S TIDES AND MORTAL'S BRAINS SHE SWAYS . . . 506 3 DON JUAN 16   14 7
OCEAN-TREASURE
  HE WAS HER OWN HER OCEAN-TREASURE CAST . . . . 247 2 DON JUAN 2 173 7
O'CLOCK
  AND SOBER SUNS MUST SET AT FIVE O'CLOCK . . . . 94 2 DON JUAN 1 134 8
  AT ONE O'CLOCK THE WIND WITH SUDDEN SHIFT . . . . . . 170 2 DON JUAN 2   27 1
  AT HALF-PAST EIGHT O'CLOCK BOOMS HENCOOPS SPARS . . . 183 2 DON JUAN 2   51 1
  I HEARD A SHOT--'TWAS EIGHT O'CLOCK SCARCE PAST-- . . 428 2 DON JUAN 5   33 5
  OF LIFE REACH TEN O'CLOCK AND WHILE A GLOW . . . . . 229 3 DON JUAN 10   8 5
OCTAVE
  AND JUAN TOO BLASPHEMED AN OCTAVE HIGHER . . . . . . 122 2 DON JUAN 1 184 6

PAGE VOL   CANTO STANZA LN

OCTAVE'S
AND WAS THRUST IN TO CLOSE THE OCTAVE'S CHIME . . . . . 14 3 DON JUAN 6 18 6
OCTAVES
TWO LONG OCTAVES PASSED IN A LITTLE MINUTE . . . . . . 142 3 DON JUAN 8 59 2
ODA
IT WAS A SPACIOUS CHAMBER (ODA IS . . . . 31 3 DON JUAN 6 51 1
THE ODA IN A GENERAL COMMOTION . . . . 42 3 DON JUAN 6 71 2
THE WHOLE ODA FROM THEIR BEDS AT HALF-PAST THREE . . 46 3 DON JUAN 6 80 4
THE CHIEF DAME OF THE ODA UPON WHOM . . . . . 57 3 DON JUAN 6 103 1
ODALISQUES
HE WENT FORTH WITH THE LOVELY ODALISQUES . . . . 20 3 DON JUAN 6 29 1
ODD
REQUIRED THIS CONDUCT--WHICH SEEM'D VERY ODD . . . . 35 2 DON JUAN 1 27 8
WERE FORCED TO MAKE AN ODD SORT OF APOLOGY . . . . 44 2 DON JUAN 1 41 7
'TIS ODD NOT ONE OF ALL THESE SEEKERS THOUGHT . . . 100 2 DON JUAN 1 144 6
TWO HUNDRED AND ODD STANZAS AS BEFORE . . . . . . 271 2 DON JUAN 2 216 3
WAS WHIPT AT COLLEGE--A HARSH SIRE--ODD SPOUSE . . . 328 2 DON JUAN 3 91 7
WHICH WAS AN ODD ONE A TROOP GOING TO ACT . . . . 388 2 DON JUAN 4 80 4
THERE CHANCED TO BE AN ODD MALE AND ODD FEMALE . . 394 2 DON JUAN 4 92 2
THERE CHANCED TO BE AN ODD MALE AND ODD FEMALE . . 394 2 DON JUAN 4 92 2
METHINKS AT MEALS SOME ODD THOUGHTS MIGHT INTRUDE . . 426 2 DON JUAN 5 30 3
THE CAUSE OF THIS ODD TRAVESTY--FORBEAR . . . . . . 454 2 DON JUAN 5 74 5
FELT AN ODD GLISTENING MOISTURE IN HER EYE . . . . 480 2 DON JUAN 5 120 8
SOMETIMES AT SIX YEARS OLD--THOUGH THIS SEEMS ODD . . 498 2 DON JUAN 5 152 6
I'VE KNOWN SOME ODD ONES WHICH SEEMED REALLY PLANNED . 45 3 DON JUAN 6 78 5
AND WHY BECAUSE A LITTLE--ODD--OLD MAN . . . . . . 90 3 DON JUAN 7 49 7
FOR ONCE BY SOME ODD SORT OF MAGNANIMITY . . . . . 92 3 DON JUAN 7 51 V4
TO SOME ODD ANGLE FOR WHICH ALL WERE STRAINING . . . 121 3 DON JUAN 8 20 4
BY ONE OF THOSE ODD TURNS OF FORTUNE'S TIDES . . . . 125 3 DON JUAN 8 27 5
AND THAT ODD IMPULSE WHICH IN WARS OR CREEDS . . . 132 3 DON JUAN 8 38 7
AS HUMAN BEINGS OR HIS WAYS ARE ODD . . . . 163 3 DON JUAN 8 104 4
SOME ODD MISTAKES TOO HAPPENED IN THE DARK . . . . 177 3 DON JUAN 8 130 1
OF THAT ODD STRING OF WORDS ALL IN A ROW . . . . . 207 3 DON JUAN 9 49 5
IN LOVE AND WAR) HOW ODD ARE THE CONNECTIONS . . . 215 3 DON JUAN 9 65 3
HOW BEAUTIFUL THAT MOMENT AND HOW ODD IS . . . . . 220 3 DON JUAN 9 75 5
OF THIS ODD LABYRINTH OR AS THE KELP . . . . . . 238 3 DON JUAN 10 28 5
WARNED HIM AGAINST GREEK-WORSHIP WHICH LOOKS ODD . . 240 3 DON JUAN 10 32 3
BUT ONE THING'S ODD WHICH HERE MUST BE INSERTED . . 251 3 DON JUAN 10 55 7
'TIS ODD BUT TRUE--LAST WAR THE NEWS ABOUNDED . . . 383 3 DON JUAN 13 53 7
BUT WHAT IS ODD NONE EVER NAMED THE DUKE . . . . . 430 3 DON JUAN 14 45 1
'TIS ODD OR ODDS IT MAY TURN OUT A ROCK . . . . . 442 3 DON JUAN 14 74 8
I'VE ALSO SEEN SOME FEMALE FRIENDS ('TIS ODD . . . 452 3 DON JUAN 14 96 1
BY SOME ODD CHANCE TOO HE WAS PLACED BETWEEN . . . 489 3 DON JUAN 15 75 1
TELLS AN ODD STORY OF WHICH BY THE BYE . . . . 516 3 DON JUAN 16 36 4
OF TWO THINGS--HOW (THE QUESTION RATHER ODD IS) . . 543 3 DON JUAN 16 90 7
HOW ODD A SINGLE HOBGOBLIN'S NON-ENTITY . . . . . 559 3 DON JUAN 16 120 7
ODDEST
SINCE IN A WAY THAT'S RATHER OF THE ODDEST HE . . . . 157 2 DON JUAN 2 1 7
WHICH HAS AT TIMES AN ASPECT OF THE ODDEST . . . . 464 2 DON JUAN 5 91 7
ODDITIES
THIS IS THE AGE OF ODDITIES LET LOOSE . . . . . . 91 2 DON JUAN 1 128 5
ODDLY
OR MARRIAGE BY DIVORCING THEM THUS ODDLY . . . . . 472 3 DON JUAN 15 36 2
ODDS
THE ODDS ARE THAT HE FINDS A HANDSOME URN . . . . 287 2 DON JUAN 3 23 5
AND HAVING PICKED UP SEVERAL ODDS AND ENDS . . . . 318 2 DON JUAN 3 83 2
WHEN THEY BEHOLD THE BRAVE OPPRESSED WITH ODDS . . . 164 3 DON JUAN 8 106 2
SINCE ODDS ARE THAT POSTERITY WILL KNOW . . . . 324 3 DON JUAN 12 18 7
HIS ONLY OBJECT AND 'GAINST ODDS TO FIGHT . . . . 363 3 DON JUAN 13 9 4
'TIS ODD OR ODDS IT MAY TURN OUT A ROCK . . . . . 442 3 DON JUAN 14 74 8
WERE ODDS AGAINST A DISEMBODIED SOUL . . . . . . 558 3 DON JUAN 16 118 8
ODE
I DON'T THINK SAPPHO'S ODE A GOOD EXAMPLE . . . . 45 2 DON JUAN 1 42 4
A LAUREATE'S ODE OR SERVILE PEER'S CONTENT . . . . 435 3 DON JUAN 14 58 8
ODES
WRITE ODES ON THE INCONSTANCY OF WOMAN . . . . . 288 2 DON JUAN 3 24 8
ODOURS
AS THOSE WHO DOTE ON ODOURS PLUCK THE FLOWERS . . . 275 2 DON JUAN 3 2 5
ODYSSEYS
AND FOR THEIR AENEIDS ILIADS AND ODYSSEYS . . . . 44 2 DON JUAN 1 41 6
OEDIPUS
BUT I'M NOT OEDIPUS AND LIFE'S A SPHINX . . . . . 364 3 DON JUAN 13 12 8
OER
LAY DROOPING OER THE OAR WHICH SERVED FOR MAST . . . 214 2 DON JUAN 2 110 V5
THEIR LOATHSOME PHANTASMAGORIA OER THE MIND . . . . 227 2 DON JUAN 2 134 V7
OER WHOSE SAD TALE LOVE ECHOS STILL ALAS-- . . . 273 2 DON JUAN 2 V 2 3
FOR GENTLEMEN WHOSE PASSIONS MAY BOIL OER . . . 313 3 DON JUAN 11 V 29 5
O'ER-ARCH
BUT AS IT WAS MERE LUST OF POWER TO O'ER-ARCH ALL . . 86 3 DON JUAN 7 40 5
O'ERAWES
CAN'T FORM A FRIENDSHIP BUT THE WORLD O'ERAWES IT . . 346 3 DON JUAN 12 65 3
O'ERCAME
LONG BOOMING OF EACH PEAL ON PEAL O'ERCAME . . . . 115 3 DON JUAN 8 6 6
O'ERCAST
FOR SOME FEW YEARS HIS LOT HAD BEEN O'ERCAST . . . 316 2 DON JUAN 3 79 5
O'ERCHARGED
O'ERCHARGED WITH RAIN HER SUMMON'D HANDMAIDS BORE . . 376 2 DON JUAN 4 59 4
O'ERCLOUDED
THE TEARS RUSH'D FORTH FROM HER O'ERCLOUDED BRAIN . . 380 2 DON JUAN 4 66 7

	PAGE	VOL	CANTO	STANZA	LN

O'ERCOME
AGAIN TO BE O'ERCOME AGAIN TO DASH ON . . . . . . 257 2 DON JUAN 2 191 6
THE CALENTURES OF MUSIC WHICH O'ERCOME . . . . . . 523 3 DON JUAN 16 46 5
O'ERCROWDED
THE BOATS PUT OFF O'ERCROWDED WITH THEIR CREWS . . . . . 183 2 DON JUAN 2 51 6
O'ERFLOW
SALOON ROOM HALL O'ERFLOW BEYOND THEIR BRINK . . . . . 302 3 DON JUAN 11 68 5
O'ERFLOW'D
O'ERFLOW'D HER SOUL WITH THEIR UNITED POWER . . . . . . 262 2 DON JUAN 2 198 3
O'ERFLOWING
PILLOW'D ON HER O'ERFLOWING HEART WHICH PANTS . . . . . . 260 2 DON JUAN 2 195 7
PRESENTED THE O'ERFLOWING CUP AND SAID . . . . 297 2 DON JUAN 3 43 3
BUT JUAN WHO HAD STILL HIS MIND O'ERFLOWING . . . . . . 478 2 DON JUAN 5 117 2
AND FIRST IN THE O'ERFLOWING OF HER HEART . . . . . . 438 3 DON JUAN 14 65 1
O'ERFLOWS
TO BALAAM AND FROM TONGUE TO EAR O'ERFLOWS . . . . . . 328 3 DON JUAN 12 26 6
O'ERGROWN
IN FULL VOLUPTUOUS BUT NOT O'ERGROWN BULK . . . . . . 561 3 DON JUAN 16 123 7
O'ERHEARD
AND EATING ICES WERE O'ERHEARD TO SAY . . . . 239 3 DON JUAN 10 30 6
O'ERLABOUR'D
THE WELCOME STALL TO THE O'ERLABOUR'D STEER . . . . . . 338 2 DON JUAN 3 107 4
O'ERLEAP
ALL FEELINGS WHICH O'ERLEAP THE YEARS LONG LOST . . . . 286 2 DON JUAN 3 21 7
O'ERLIVE
IF THAT THE WEEDS O'ERLIVE NOT THE FIRST CROP-- . . . . 368 3 DON JUAN 13 22 7
O'ERLOADED
I HAVE SEEN SOME NATIONS LIKE O'ERLOADED ASSES . . . . . 310 3 DON JUAN 11 84 7
O'ERMASTER'D
AND HE HIMSELF O'ERMASTER'D AND CUT DOWN . . . . . . 375 2 DON JUAN 4 58 2
O'ERPASS'D
SCARCELY O'ERPASS'D THE CREAM OF YOUR CHAMPAIGNE . . . . 250 2 DON JUAN 2 178 2
O'ERPOWERING
WHILE THE O'ERPOWERING EYE THAT TURNS YOU PALE . . . . 160 2 DON JUAN 2 7 3
O'ERPOWERING US TO BE WHATE'ER MAY SEEM . . . . . . 360 2 DON JUAN 4 30 5
O'ERSHADING
WAVED AND O'ERSHADING HER WAN CHEEK APPEARS . . . . . . 108 2 DON JUAN 1 158 4
O'ERSHADOW'D
O'ERSHADOW'D THERE BY MANY A HERO'S GRAVE . . . . . . 387 2 DON JUAN 4 79 4
O'ERSPREADS
O'ERSPREADS THE CHEEK WHICH SEEMS TOO PURE FOR CLAY . . . 229 3 DON JUAN 10 8 7
O'ERSTEP
LEAVE TO O'ERSTEP THE WRITTEN RIGHTS OF WOMAN . . . . . 74 2 DON JUAN 1 98 3
O'ERTHROWN
O'ERTHROWN EVEN MEN HE SOON BEGAN TO SHOW . . . . . . 417 2 DON JUAN 5 12 4
O'ERTHROWS
O'ERTHROWS THE SAME WE READILY FORGET . . . . 8 3 DON JUAN 6 4 3
O'ERTOPPED
O'ERTOPPED WITH CYPRESSES DARK-GREEN AND TALL . . . . . 432 2 DON JUAN 5 40 8
O'ERTURN'D
TO SEE A KINGDOM OR A HOUSE O'ERTURN'D . . . . 31 2 DON JUAN 1 19 6
O'ERWHELM'D
AND THE HARD WAVE O'ERWHELM'D HIM AS 'TWAS DASH'D . . . 212 2 DON JUAN 2 107 4
OF LOVE HAD FIRST O'ERWHELM'D THEM FROM SUCH SKIES . . . 354 2 DON JUAN 4 20 4
O'ERWHELMING
WITH THIS O'ERWHELMING WORLD WHERE ALL MUST ERR . . . . 250 3 DON JUAN 10 52 6
I SATE NEXT THAT O'ERWHELMING SON OF HEAVEN . . . . . 539 3 DON JUAN 16 81 6
O'ERWROUGHT
AND FELT AGAIN WITH HIS DESPAIR O'ERWROUGHT . . . . . . 215 2 DON JUAN 2 112 4
OFFENCE
ALL PRETTY PASTIMES IN WHICH NO OFFENCE IS . . . . . . 293 2 DON JUAN 3 35 4
WITHOUT OR WITH OFFENCE TO FRIENDS OR FOES . . . . . . 156 3 DON JUAN 8 89 7
OFFENCE WE KNOW NOT PROBABLY IT PERCHED . . . . . . 192 3 DON JUAN 9 19 7
OF ALL OFFENCES THAT'S THE WORST OFFENCE . . . . . . 490 3 DON JUAN 15 77 3
OFFENCES
OF ALL OFFENCES THAT'S THE WORST OFFENCE . . . . . . 490 3 DON JUAN 15 77 3
OFFEND
HER SON'S SON LET NOT THIS LAST PHRASE OFFEND . . . . . 52 3 DON JUAN 6 93 2
LET NOT THE LATTER QUALITY OFFEND . . . . 52 3 DON JUAN 6 93 V2
I SHALL OFFEND ALL PARTIES--NEVER MIND . . . . 195 3 DON JUAN 9 26 2
OFFENDING
YET LIKE THEIR MASTERS FEARFUL OF OFFENDING . . . . . . 539 3 DON JUAN 16 79 6
OFFER
AND OFFER POISON LONG ALREADY MIX'D . . . . 16 2 DON JUAN D 12 8
SWORD GOWN GAIN GLORY OFFER IN EXCHANGE . . . . . . 131 2 DON JUAN 1 194 4
TO OFFER HIS YOUNG PINION AS HER FAN . . . . 313 2 DON JUAN 3 73 8
TO OFFER WILLING HOMAGE AS HER FAN . . . . 313 2 DON JUAN 3 73 V8
BUT WHEN THE OFFER WENT BEYOND THEY KNEW . . . . . . 407 2 DON JUAN 4 114 7
I OFFER YOU A HANDSOME SUIT OF CLOTHES . . . . 455 2 DON JUAN 5 76 1
OFFER'D
'TIS SAID THAT XERXES OFFER'D A REWARD . . . . . . 85 2 DON JUAN 1 118 1
HE FELL UPON WHATE'ER WAS OFFER'D LIKE . . . . 239 2 DON JUAN 2 157 7
NOR OFFER'D ANY SHE HAD NEVER HEARD . . . . 257 2 DON JUAN 2 190 2
OFFERED
WERE LAID ASIDE BUT NOT BEFORE SHE OFFERED . . . . . . 36 3 DON JUAN 6 61 2
A THIRD'S ALL PALLID ASPECT OFFERED MORE . . . . . . 40 3 DON JUAN 6 67 3
AMONG THE FOREMOST OFFERED HIM GOOD QUARTER . . . . . . 152 3 DON JUAN 8 80 2
OFFERING
AND OFFERING AS USUAL LATE ASSISTANCE . . . . 275 3 DON JUAN 11 14 4

561

OFF-HAND
    OTHERS IN THAT OFF-HAND AND DASHING STYLE . . . . . . 351 3 DON JUAN 12   76   2
OFFICE
    HER OFFICE WAS TO KEEP ALOOF OR SMOTHER . . . .   21 3 DON JUAN 6   31   6
    OF THOSE IN OFFICE ALL THE WORLD LOOKED KIND . . . . 224 3 DON JUAN 9   84   3
    NAMED FROM HER MYSTIC OFFICE L'EPROUVEUSE . . . . .   224 3 DON JUAN 9   84   7
    OF OFFICE OR THE HOUSE OF OFFICE FED . . . .   287 3 DON JUAN 11   40   6
    OF OFFICE OR THE HOUSE OF OFFICE FED . . . .   287 3 DON JUAN 11   40   6
    IN HIS GRAVE OFFICE SO COMPLETELY SKILL'D . . . . .   399 3 DON JUAN 13   88   6
    THEIR OFFICE HE TOOK UP AN OLD NEWSPAPER . . . . . .   512 3 DON JUAN 16   26   5
OFFICER
    HE RECOGNIZED AN OFFICER OF RANK . . . .   141 3 DON JUAN 8   57   8
    AN ENGLISH NAVAL OFFICER WHO WISHED . . . .   152 3 DON JUAN 8   80   7
    A RUSSIAN OFFICER IN MARTIAL TREAD . . . .   153 3 DON JUAN 8   83   1
    THE RUSSIAN OFFICER FOR LIFE WAS LAMED . . . . . .   154 3 DON JUAN 8   85   2
OFFICERS
    OF OFFICERS A THIRD FELL ON THE SPOT . . . .   119 3 DON JUAN 8   16   5
OFFICES
    IN THE DEAR OFFICES OF PEACE OR WAR . . . .   288 3 DON JUAN 11   41   3
OFFICIAL
    THEN HELD THAT HIGH OFFICIAL SITUATION . . . . . .   206 3 DON JUAN 9   48   8
    WHAT WERE THE ACTUAL AND OFFICIAL DUTIES . . . . . .   208 3 DON JUAN 9   51   2
    HIS DUTIES WARLIKE LOVING OR OFFICIAL . . . .   294 3 DON JUAN 11   51   5
    OF THE OFFICIAL CANDIDATE I'LL TOUCH . . . .   538 3 DON JUAN 16   77   6
OFF-ING
    AND WON'T SAY YES AND KEEPS YOU ON AND OFF-ING . . . . 345 3 DON JUAN 12   63   2
OFFSPRING
    LIKE BANQUO'S OFFSPRING--FLOATING PAST ME SEEMS . . . 233 3 DON JUAN 10   18   6
    OFFSPRING OF SOME SAGE HUSBAND--HUNTING COUNTESS . . . 312 3 DON JUAN 11   89   2
    BETWEEN OUR DUTEOUS OFFSPRING--AND THE GOUT . . . . . 376 3 DON JUAN 13   40   V8
OFFSPRING'S
    AND BURIED SINKS BENEATH ITS OFFSPRING'S DOOM . . . . 399 2 DON JUAN 4   102   4
    THE LOVE OF OFFSPRING'S NATURE'S GENERAL LAW . . . . . 488 2 DON JUAN 5   133   1
OFT
    OFT IN THE WRONG AND NEVER ON HIS GUARD . . . .   33 2 DON JUAN 1   21   2
    ALTHOUGH DEFIANCE OFT DECLINED AFFORDS . . . . 153 2 DON JUAN 1 V 4   5
    AS I WHO'VE CROSS'D IT OFT KNOW WELL ENOUGH . . . . . 162 2 DON JUAN 2   11   4
    UPON ITS COURSE) PASS'D OFT BEFORE THEIR EYES . . . . 206 2 DON JUAN 2   94   4
    I'VE SEEN HIM RISE FULL OFT INDEED OF LATE . . . . . . 230 2 DON JUAN 2   140   2
    THEY ARE RIGHT FOR MAN TO MAN SO OFT UNJUST . . . . . 263 2 DON JUAN 2   200   1
    THE MERCY HE HAD GRANTED OFT ABUSED . . . . 303 2 DON JUAN 3   54   4
    SO VILE HE 'SCAPED THE DOOM WHICH OFT AVENGES . . . . 317 2 DON JUAN 3   80   5
    THE TIME THE CLIME THE SPOT WHERE I SO OFT . . . . . 335 2 DON JUAN 3   102   2
    OFT CAME AND WENT AS THERE RESOLVED TO DIE . . . . . . 365 2 DON JUAN 4   39   6
    FROM ME I GAZED (AS OFT I HAVE GAZED THE SAME) . . . . 431 2 DON JUAN 5   38   6
    AND KINGS AND CONSORTS OFT ARE MYSTIFIED . . . . . . 477 2 DON JUAN 5   115   6
    THRONES WORLDS ET CETERA ARE SO OFT UPSET . . . . .   8 3 DON JUAN 6   4   1
    JUAN BY SOME STRANGE CHANCE WHICH OFT DIVIDES . . . 125 3 DON JUAN 8   27   1
    OFT ARE SOON CLOSED ALL HEROES ARE NOT BLIND . . . . 133 3 DON JUAN 8   40   6
    EVEN WORLDS MISCARRY WHEN TOO OFT THEY PUP . . . . . 202 3 DON JUAN 9   39   5
    WHICH HOVERS OFT ABOUT SOME MARRIED BEAUTIES . . . . 208 3 DON JUAN 9   51   4
    AND THEN BEFORE SIGHS CEASE FOR OFT THE ONE . . . . 229 3 DON JUAN 10   8   2
    FULL MANY AN EAGER GENTLEMAN OFT RUES . . . .   304 3 DON JUAN 11   71   5
    AN EVOLUTION OFT PERFORMED OF LATE) . . . .   308 3 DON JUAN 11   79   5
    THOUGH OFT WELL FOUNDED WHICH CONFIRMED BUT MORE . . 366 3 DON JUAN 13   17   2
    THE GALE SWEEPS THROUGH ITS FRETWORK AND OFT SINGS . . 387 3 DON JUAN 13   62   6
    VICTIM WHEN WRONG AND MARTYR OFT WHEN RIGHT . . . . 420 3 DON JUAN 14   23   6
    ARE THEY OFT DULL AND DREARY AS A DUN-- . . . . 423 3 DON JUAN 14   29   7
    AND HENCE HIGH LIFE IS OFT A DREARY VOID-- . . . . . 444 3 DON JUAN 14   79   1
    OF PLATONISM WHICH LEADS SO OFT AMISS . . . .   450 3 DON JUAN 14   92   3
    HOW OFT WOULD VICE AND VIRTUE PLACES CHANGE . . . . 455 3 DON JUAN 14   101   5
    BUT OFT DENIED AS PATIENCE 'GINS TO FAIL HE . . . . . 459 3 DON JUAN 15   8   5
    ON THEM AND BREAD 'TWAS OFT MY LUCK TO DINE . . . . 488 3 DON JUAN 15   73   5
    'TIS WONDERFUL HOW OFT THE SEX HAVE HEARD . . . . . 489 3 DON JUAN 15   76   7
    TO SAY LEADS OFT TO CRIM CON WITH THE MARRIED-- . . 493 3 DON JUAN 15   84   3
    THE FRIAR OF LATE HAS NOT BEEN OFT PERCEIVED . . . . 516 3 DON JUAN 16   36   8
    BECAUSE THE PRESENT TALE HAS OFT BEEN TOLD . . . . . 516 3 DON JUAN 16   37   7
    TO SOMETHING LIKE THIS WHEN TOO OFT DISPLAYED . . . 522 3 DON JUAN 16   44   5
OFTEN
    (WHO DOES NOT OFTEN CLAIM THE BRIGHT REVERSION) . . . 14 2 DON JUAN D   9   2
    WHICH ANCIENT MASS-BOOKS OFTEN ARE AND THIS ALL . .   47 2 DON JUAN 1   46   3
    CARESS'D HIM OFTEN SUCH A THING MIGHT BE . . . . . .   59 2 DON JUAN 1   69   2
    ARE MASKS IT OFTEN WEARS AND STILL TOO LATE . . . .   61 2 DON JUAN 1   73   8
    THEY MEAN TO SCOLD AND VERY OFTEN DO . . . .   79 2 DON JUAN 1   108   2
    BUT THAT CAN'T BE AS HAS BEEN OFTEN SHOWN . . . . . 118 2 DON JUAN 1   176   4
    THE PASSAGE YOU SO OFTEN HAVE EXPLORED-- . . . . . . 121 2 DON JUAN 1   182   5
    SAY VERY OFTEN TO MYSELF ALAS . . . .   147 2 DON JUAN 1   220   2
    FLOWERS TO THE GRAVE) AND SOBBING OFTEN HE . . . . . 165 2 DON JUAN 2   17   6
    HAD OFTEN TURN'D THE ART TO SOME ACCOUNT . . . . . . 211 2 DON JUAN 2   105   4
    JUST IN THE WAY WE VERY OFTEN SEE . . . .   244 2 DON JUAN 2   167   8
    THUS SHE CAME OFTEN NOT A MOMENT LOSING . . . . . . 282 2 DON JUAN 3   13   7
    AND GLORY MAKES THE SAGES OFTEN SMILE . . . .   328 2 DON JUAN 3   90   V1
    WHILE LIFE'S STRANGE PRINCIPLE WILL OFTEN LIE . . . 350 2 DON JUAN 4   11   7
    TOO OFTEN IN ITS FURY OVERCOMING ALL . . . .   399 2 DON JUAN 4   101   3
    BUT SOMETIMES IT MAY MEND AND OFTEN REACHES . . . . 491 2 DON JUAN 5   138   8
    THEIR NAMES ARE RARELY FOUND NOR OFTEN SOUGHT . . .   83 3 DON JUAN 7   34   4
    TOO OFTEN ALL THE CLOTHING MEAT OR FUEL . . . . . . 256 3 DON JUAN 10   63   7
    OCCURRED WHAT OFTEN HAPPENS I'M AFRAID . . . . . .   355 3 DON JUAN 12   85   3
    ARISING OUT OF BUSINESS OFTEN BROUGHT . . . .   365 3 DON JUAN 13   15   2

```
                                                            PAGE VOL      CANTO    STANZA  LN
OFTEN   (CONTINUED)
    WILL VERY OFTEN SUPERSEDE THE REST . . . . . . . . . . . 371  3 DON JUAN 13        28    8
    SO LET THE OFTEN USED VOLCANO GO . . . . . . . . . . . . 374  3 DON JUAN 13        36    6
    AND EKE THE WISE AS HAS BEEN OFTEN SHOWN . . . . . . . . 463  3 DON JUAN 15        17    4
    THAT SHE MUST OFTEN NAVIGATE O'ER FICTION . . . . . . . . 495  3 DON JUAN 15        88    8
    SO OFTEN URGED SO LOUDLY AND SO LONG . . . . . . . . . . 564  3 DON JUAN 17         5    6
OFTENER
    TURNS OFTENER TO THE STARS THAN TO HIS BOOK . . . . . . . 242  2 DON JUAN  2       163    6
OFTENTIMES
    FOR OFTENTIMES WHEN PEGASUS SEEMS WINNING . . . . . . . . 344  2 DON JUAN  4         1    3
    WILL OFTENTIMES MAKE DEADLY QUARRELS BURST . . . . . . . 136  3 DON JUAN  8        48    3
OGLE
    IF FOND OF A CHANCE OGLE AT HER GLASS . . . . . . . . . .  36  3 DON JUAN  6        60    4
    OR IF FORESTALLED GET OPPOSITE AND OGLE-- . . . . . . . . 304  3 DON JUAN 11        72    2
OGLED
    NO LADY E'ER IS OGLED BY A LOVER . . . . . . . . . . . . 424  2 DON JUAN  5        26    6
OGLING
    FROM OGLING ALL THEIR CHARMS FROM BREASTS TO BACKS . . .  20  3 DON JUAN  6        29    8
OGNI
    LIKE THAT OF HELL LASCIATE OGNI SPERANZA . . . . . . . . 557  3 DON JUAN 16       116    2
OIL
    SAVE THINE INCOMPARABLE OIL MACASSAR . . . . . . . . . .  30  2 DON JUAN  1        17    8
    ARE OIL AND GUNPOWDER AND SOME GOOD LESSONS . . . . . . . 245  2 DON JUAN  2       169    6
    WHILE BABA MADE HIM COMB HIS HEAD AND OIL IT . . . . . . 457  2 DON JUAN  5        79    8
    THEY NATURALLY POUR THE WINE AND OIL . . . . . . . . . . 480  2 DON JUAN  5       120    5
OLD
    (THIS OLD SONG AND NEW SIMILE HOLDS GOOD) . . . . . . . .  10  2 DON JUAN  D         2    2
    THINK'ST THOU COULD HE--THE BLIND OLD MAN--ARISE . . . .  15  2 DON JUAN  D        11    1
    A TINKERING SLAVE-MAKER WHO MENDS OLD CHAINS . . . . . .  18  2 DON JUAN  D        14    7
    BESIDES HER GOOD OLD GRANDMOTHER (WHO DOTED) . . . . . .  36  2 DON JUAN  1        28    5
    SOME FOR AMUSEMENT OTHERS FOR OLD GRUDGES . . . . . . . .  36  2 DON JUAN  1        28    8
    AND IF OUR QUARRELS SHOULD RIP UP OLD STORIES . . . . . .  37  2 DON JUAN  1        31    1
    HER MAIDS WERE OLD AND IF SHE TOOK A NEW ONE . . . . . .  48  2 DON JUAN  1        48    5
    FOR FROM A ROOT THE UGLIEST IN OLD SPAIN . . . . . . . .  53  2 DON JUAN  1        58    3
    AND THAT STILL KEEPING UP THE OLD CONNEXION . . . . . . .  58  2 DON JUAN  1        67    1
    HE FOUND HOW MUCH OLD TIME HAD BEEN A WINNER-- . . . . .  72  2 DON JUAN  1        94    7
    ACCORDING TO SOME GOOD OLD WOMAN'S TALE . . . . . . . . .  72  2 DON JUAN  1        95    8
    I CARE NOT FOR NEW PLEASURES AS THE OLD . . . . . . . . .  85  2 DON JUAN  1       118    7
    THE UNEXPECTED DEATH OF SOME OLD LADY . . . . . . . . . .  89  2 DON JUAN  1       125    2
    'TIS STRANGE OLD PEOPLE DONT LIKE TO BE BURIED . . . . .  89  2 DON JUAN  1       125   V8
    SWEET IS OLD WINE IN BOTTLES ALE IN BARRELS . . . . . . .  90  2 DON JUAN  1       126    5
    WITH WHICH THE DOCTOR PAID OFF AN OLD POX . . . . . . . .  91  2 DON JUAN  1       129    7
    THAT I HAVE CHOSEN A CONFESSOR SO OLD . . . . . . . . . . 101  2 DON JUAN  1       147    3
    AT THAT AGE HE WOULD BE TOO OLD FOR SLAUGHTER . . . . . . 106  2 DON JUAN  1       155    2
    SO MUCH AS WHEN WE CALL OUR OLD DEBTS IN . . . . . . . . 113  2 DON JUAN  1       167    6
    WHEN OLD KING DAVID'S BLOOD GREW DULL IN MOTION . . . . . 113  2 DON JUAN  1       168    5
    AND THEN BY THE ADVICE OF SOME OLD LADIES . . . . . . . . 128  2 DON JUAN  1       190    7
    WHAT ARE THE HOPES OF MAN OLD EGYPT'S KING . . . . . . . 146  2 DON JUAN  1       219    1
    A--NEVER MIND HIS TUTOR AN OLD ASS . . . . . . . . . . . 158  2 DON JUAN  2         3    4
    A HUSBAND RATHER OLD NOT MUCH IN UNITY . . . . . . . . . 158  2 DON JUAN  2         3    7
    INFANTS OF THREE YEARS OLD WERE TAUGHT THAT DAY . . . . . 162  2 DON JUAN  2        10    5
    AND THEN WITH VIOLENCE THE OLD SHIP RIGHTED . . . . . . . 173  2 DON JUAN  2        32    8
    AS IF OLD OCEAN BAFFLED OUR INTENT . . . . . . . . . . . 173  2 DON JUAN  2        32   V4
    THE GOOD OLD GENTLEMAN WAS QUITE AGHAST . . . . . . . . . 175  2 DON JUAN  2        37    1
    A SMALL OLD SPANIEL--WHICH HAD BEEN DON JOSE'S . . . . . 187  2 DON JUAN  2        58    1
    LIKE THE FIRST OLD GREEK PRIVATEER THE ARGO . . . . . . . 191  2 DON JUAN  2        66    8
    'TWAS AN OLD CUSTOM OF THE GREEK AND ROMAN . . . . . . . 205  2 DON JUAN  2        93    3
    OF AN OLD MAN WHO LIVED UPON THE WATER . . . . . . . . . 222  2 DON JUAN  2       124    8
    A SAD OLD FELLOW WAS HE IF YOU PLEASE . . . . . . . . . . 223  2 DON JUAN  2       127    6
    BECAUSE THE GOOD OLD MAN HAD SO MUCH NOUS . . . . . . . . 225  2 DON JUAN  2       130    5
    WHICH IS ACQUIRED IN NATURE'S GOOD OLD COLLEGE . . . . . 228  2 DON JUAN  2       136    8
    AND CALL'D HER FATHER'S OLD SLAVES UP WHO SWORE . . . . . 229  2 DON JUAN  2       138    6
    THAT THE OLD FABLE OF THE MINOTAUR-- . . . . . . . . . . 238  2 DON JUAN  2       155    2
    FEW THINGS SURPASS OLD WINE AND THEY MAY PREACH . . . . . 250  2 DON JUAN  2       178    5
    TO MAKE US UNDERSTAND EACH GOOD OLD MAXIM . . . . . . . . 264  2 DON JUAN  2       203    7
    THE GOOD OLD GENTLEMAN HAD BEEN DETAIN'D . . . . . . . . 283  2 DON JUAN  3        15    1
    TOSSED OVERBOARD UNSALEABLE (BEING OLD) . . . . . . . . . 284  2 DON JUAN  3        16    4
    TO A SEDATE GREY CIRCLE OF OLD SMOKERS . . . . . . . . . 293  2 DON JUAN  3        34    2
    A SECOND HICCUP'D OUR OLD MASTER'S DEAD . . . . . . . . . 297  2 DON JUAN  3        43    5
    YOU MEAN OUR MASTER--NOT THE OLD BUT NEW . . . . . . . . 297  2 DON JUAN  3        43    8
    THE DANGEROUS LIFE IN WHICH HE HAD GROWN OLD . . . . . . 303  2 DON JUAN  3        54    3
    BUT SOMETHING OF THE SPIRIT OF OLD GREECE . . . . . . . . 303  2 DON JUAN  3        55    1
    MIGHT CARRY OUT TO COLCHIS IN OLD DAYS . . . . . . . . . 303  2 DON JUAN  3        55   V4
    JUST AS OLD AGE IS CREEPING ON APACE . . . . . . . . . . 305  2 DON JUAN  3        59    5
    OLD LAMBRO PASS'D UNSEEN A PRIVATE GATE . . . . . . . . . 306  2 DON JUAN  3        61    1
    REVERSING THE GOOD CUSTOM OF OLD DAYS . . . . . . . . . . 316  2 DON JUAN  3        79    2
    WOULD BE OLD GOETHE'S--(SEE WHAT SAYS DESTAEL) . . . . . 320  2 DON JUAN  3        86    6
    THE LESBIAN SAPPHO AND THE BLIND OLD MAN . . . . . . . . 320  2 DON JUAN  3     L   1   V2
    OF AGES TO WHAT STRAITS OLD TIME REDUCES . . . . . . . . 327  2 DON JUAN  3        88    6
    MEANT TO GROW OLD BUT DIE IN HAPPY SPRING . . . . . . . . 348  2 DON JUAN  4         8    7
    THE OLD ARCHER'S SHAFTS PERHAPS THE EARLY GRAVE . . . . . 350  2 DON JUAN  4        12    7
    TO LOSE ITSELF WHEN THE OLD WORLD GROWS DULL . . . . . . 353  2 DON JUAN  4        17    3
    HIGH AND INSCRUTABLE THE OLD MAN STOOD . . . . . . . . . 365  2 DON JUAN  4        39    1
    THE OLD MAN'S CHEEK GREW PALE BUT NOT WITH DREAD . . . . 365  2 DON JUAN  4        40    3
    THE THIRD A WARY COOL OLD SWORDER TOOK . . . . . . . . . 370  2 DON JUAN  4        49    2
    OLD LAMBRO BADE THEM TAKE HIM TO THE SHORE . . . . . . . 371  2 DON JUAN  4        50    3
    BACK TO OLD THOUGHTS WAX'D FULL OF FEARFUL MEANING . . . 379  2 DON JUAN  4        64    8
    IN TIME TO HIS OLD TUNE HE CHANGED THE THEME . . . . . . 380  2 DON JUAN  4        66    2
    AND OLD SCAMANDER (IF 'TIS HE) REMAIN . . . . . . . . . . 386  2 DON JUAN  4        77    4
```

OLD (CONTINUED)

	PAGE	VOL	CANTO	STANZA	LN
THE PRIMA-DONNA THOUGH A LITTLE OLD	389	2 DON JUAN	4	83	1
FROM AN OLD ROMAN PRINCESS AT BOLOGNA	389	2 DON JUAN	4	83	8
THE MUSICO IS BUT A CRACK'D OLD BASIN	391	2 DON JUAN	4	86	2
BUT BRED WITHIN THE MARCH OF OLD ANCONA	395	2 DON JUAN	4	94	2
HOPING NO VERY OLD VIZIER MIGHT CHOOSE	409	2 DON JUAN	4	116	6
MEANTIME (YON OLD BLACK EUNUCH SEEMS TO EYE US)	423	2 DON JUAN	5	24	7
JUST NOW A BLACK OLD NEUTRAL PERSONAGE	424	2 DON JUAN	5	26	1
KILLED BY FIVE BULLETS FROM AN OLD GUN-BARREL	429	2 DON JUAN	5	34	8
THE SCARS OF HIS OLD WOUNDS WERE NEAR HIS NEW	431	2 DON JUAN	5	38	1
LET'S KNOCK THAT OLD BLACK FELLOW ON THE HEAD	434	2 DON JUAN	5	43	7
FOR THE OLD NEGRO'S CONFIDENCE IN CREEPING	436	2 DON JUAN	5	45	2
AND WHEN THE OLD NEGRO TOLD HIM TO GET READY	453	2 DON JUAN	5	73	7
REPLIED OLD GENTLEMAN I'M NOT A LADY	453	2 DON JUAN	5	73	8
BY THIS OLD BLACK ENCHANTER'S UNSOUGHT AID	459	2 DON JUAN	5	83	8
FURTHER OLD BABA RATHER BRISKLY ENTERED	493	2 DON JUAN	5	143	8
HENCE MY OLD COMET GIVE THE STARS DUE WARNING--	494	2 DON JUAN	5	145	4
SOMETIMES AT SIX YEARS OLD--THOUGH THIS SEEMS ODD	498	2 DON JUAN	5	152	6
AND NOT THE PINK OF OLD HEXAMETERS	14	3 DON JUAN	6	18	3
A BAD OLD WOMAN MAKING A WORSE WILL	16	3 DON JUAN	6	21	5
THAN HAUNTING SOME OLD RUIN OR WILD WASTE	38	3 DON JUAN	6	64	8
AND WHY BECAUSE A LITTLE--ODD--OLD MAN	90	3 DON JUAN	7	49	7
CONTINUED YOUR OLD REGIMENT'S ALLOWED	99	3 DON JUAN	7	63	3
TO SEE AN OLD MAN RATHER WILD THAN WISE	104	3 DON JUAN	7	73	5
THINK WHAT IT IS TO BE IN YOUR OLD AGE	118	3 DON JUAN	8	14	2
OLD ERSE OR IRISH OR IT MAY BE PUNIC--	122	3 DON JUAN	8	23	2
PROVING THAT TRITE OLD TRUTH THAT LIFE'S AS FRAIL	134	3 DON JUAN	8	43	3
OF HIS OLD AGE IN WILDS OF DEEPEST MAZE	143	3 DON JUAN	8	61	8
AS DO THE SUBTLE SNAKES DESCRIBED OF OLD	153	3 DON JUAN	8	83	8
THE OLD PACHA SITS AMONG SOME HUNDREDS DEAD	160	3 DON JUAN	8	98	3
NEITHER--BUT A GOOD PLAIN OLD TEMPERATE MAN	164	3 DON JUAN	8	105	7
TO TOUGH OLD HEROES AND CAN DO NO LESS	167	3 DON JUAN	8	112	4
IN BATTLE TO OLD AGE AND UGLINESS	167	3 DON JUAN	8	112	V4
THE GOOD OLD KHAN WHO LONG HAD CEASED TO SEE	169	3 DON JUAN	8	116	2
OF CARNAGE WHEN THIS OLD MAN WAS PIERCED THROUGH	171	3 DON JUAN	8	119	3
BUT SIX OLD DAMSELS EACH OF SEVENTY YEARS	177	3 DON JUAN	8	130	7
AND WONDER WHAT OLD WORLD SUCH THINGS COULD SEE	180	3 DON JUAN	8	137	4
UPON YOUR TOMB IN WESTMINSTER'S OLD ABBEY	184	3 DON JUAN	9	2	4
FROM OUR OLD CRASH SOME MYSTIC ANCIENT STRAIN	201	3 DON JUAN	9	38	3
PARISIAN ASPECT WHICH UPSET OLD TROY	209	3 DON JUAN	9	53	5
THAT GOOD OLD STEAM-BOAT WHICH KEEPS VERSES MOVING	219	3 DON JUAN	9	74	4
THE TRUTH AND THOUGH GRIEF HER OLD AGE MIGHT SHORTEN	222	3 DON JUAN	9	81	5
OLD ENEMIES WHO HAVE BECOME NEW FRIENDS	231	3 DON JUAN	10	12	1
OLD FLAMES NEW WIVES BECOME OUR BITTEREST FOES--	231	3 DON JUAN	10	12	7
WHILE COMMON MEN GROW IGNORANTLY OLD	232	3 DON JUAN	10	14	5
THEIR LUCKIER VOTARIES TILL OLD AGE'S TEDIUM	235	3 DON JUAN	10	22	7
A YOUNG LIEUTENANT'S WITH A NOT OLD QUEEN	236	3 DON JUAN	10	24	4
HE OWED TO AN OLD WOMAN AND HIS POST	239	3 DON JUAN	10	29	8
OR THE EAR-TRUMPET OF MY GOOD OLD AUNT	241	3 DON JUAN	10	34	5
FOR CAUSES YOUNG OR OLD THE CANKER-WORM	243	3 DON JUAN	10	38	2
LIVE ANIMALS AN OLD MAID OF THREESCORE	249	3 DON JUAN	10	50	6
ALTHOUGH HE WAS NOT OLD NOR EVEN A MAID--	249	3 DON JUAN	10	50	8
BUT SHE WAS YET BUT TEN YEARS OLD AND THEREFORE	250	3 DON JUAN	10	52	7
HE WAS NOT YET QUITE OLD ENOUGH TO PROVE	250	3 DON JUAN	10	53	4
MY GUARD MY OLD GUARD EXCLAIMED THAT GOD OF CLAY--	254	3 DON JUAN	10	59	2
OF ABSENCE LAY ONE'S OLD RESENTMENTS LEVEL	257	3 DON JUAN	10	66	7
OUR OLD ACQUAINTANCE AND AT LEAST I'LL TRY	266	3 DON JUAN	10	84	6
TO THE OLD TEXT STILL BETTER--LEST IT SHOULD	270	3 DON JUAN	11	4	2
BUT THE OLD WAY IS BEST FOR THE PURBLIND	281	3 DON JUAN	11	27	4
SOME LAID ASIDE LIKE AN OLD OPERA HAT	308	3 DON JUAN	11	79	3
THE SENATE WHICH TIBERIUS MET OF OLD--	314	3 DON JUAN	11	V 76	8
TOO OLD FOR YOUTH--TOO YOUNG AT THIRTY-FIVE	316	3 DON JUAN	12	2	1
(THAT MAKE OLD EUROPE'S JOURNALS SQUEAK AND GIBBER ALL)	318	3 DON JUAN	12	5	4
WHO KEEP THE WORLD BOTH OLD AND NEW IN PAIN	318	3 DON JUAN	12	5	5
(NOT OF OLD VICTORS ALL WHOSE HEADS AND CRESTS	321	3 DON JUAN	12	12	3
GIVES WITH GREEK TRUTH THE GOOD OLD GREEK THE LIE	325	3 DON JUAN	12	19	6
BUT THE OLD MARCHIONESS SOME PLAN HAS HATCHED	332	3 DON JUAN	12	35	5
ONLY TO KEEP ITS CORN AT THE OLD PRICE	335	3 DON JUAN	12	40	7
OR LIKE THE OLD COMPARISON OF SNOWS	335	3 DON JUAN	12	41	3
BUT IN OLD ENGLAND WHEN A YOUNG BRIDE ERRS	345	3 DON JUAN	12	64	7
AS AN OLD TEMPLE DWINDLED TO A COLUMN	358	3 DON JUAN	13	1	8
('TIS AN OLD NORMAN NAME AND TO BE FOUND	359	3 DON JUAN	13	2	2
PERHAPS THE FINE OLD FELLOW SPOKE IN JEST--	361	3 DON JUAN	13	7	5
ALAS MUST NOBLEST VIEWS LIKE AN OLD SONG	363	3 DON JUAN	13	10	5
I'M AT MY OLD LUNES--DIGRESSION AND FORGET	364	3 DON JUAN	13	12	1
LET NONE ACCUSE OLD ENGLAND'S HOSPITALITY--	381	3 DON JUAN	13	49	7
AN OLD OLD MONASTERY ONCE AND NOW	384	3 DON JUAN	13	55	2
AN OLD OLD MONASTERY ONCE AND NOW	384	3 DON JUAN	13	55	2
AND HARMONIZED BY THE OLD CHORAL WALL	388	3 DON JUAN	13	63	8
GENERALS SOME ALL IN ARMOUR OF THE OLD	391	3 DON JUAN	13	70	1
THE QUAINT OLD CRUEL COXCOMB IN HIS GULLET	407	3 DON JUAN	13	106	7
THERE NOW ARE NO 'SQUIRE WESTERNS AS OF OLD	409	3 DON JUAN	13	110	4
MUCH AS OLD SATURN ATE HIS PROGENY	410	3 DON JUAN	14	1	6
WHEN NOTHING SHALL BE EITHER OLD OR NEW	411	3 DON JUAN	14	3	6
AT ONCE WITHOUT INSTALMENTS (AN OLD WAY	412	3 DON JUAN	14	4	5
TIRING OLD READERS NOR DISCOVERING NEW	414	3 DON JUAN	14	10	6
REMNANT WERE THERE OF THE OLD WORLD'S SOLE THRONE	428	3 DON JUAN	14	40	4
WITH A LONG MEMORANDUM OF OLD STORIES	432	3 DON JUAN	14	50	8
THE NEW WORLD WOULD BE NOTHING TO THE OLD	455	3 DON JUAN	14	101	6

OLD   (CONTINUED)

	PAGE	VOL	CANTO	STANZA	LN
TILL OLD MAY UNDERGO ADULTERATION	458	3	DON JUAN 15	6	8
OLD SKELETON WITH AGES FOR YOUR BOOTY	459	3	DON JUAN 15	9	V5
THE DIFFERENCE IS THAT IN THE DAYS OF OLD	468	3	DON JUAN 15	26	1
OF AN OLD FAMILY SOME GAY SIR JOHN	470	3	DON JUAN 15	33	3
SHE HELD THEIR OLD FAITH AND OLD FEELINGS FAST	476	3	DON JUAN 15	46	8
SHE HELD THEIR OLD FAITH AND OLD FEELINGS FAST	476	3	DON JUAN 15	46	8
NOW THOUGH WE KNOW OF OLD THAT LOOKS DECEIVE	493	3	DON JUAN 15	84	6
HAS NOT THE NATURAL STAYS OF STRICT OLD AGE	494	3	DON JUAN 15	85	6
SOME OLD--SOME PAST--SOME PRESENT--SOME TO BE	495	3	DON JUAN 15	89	V7
OR OLD INDULGE MAN WITH A SECOND SIGHT	496	3	DON JUAN 15	90	6
OLD PORTRAITS FROM OLD WALLS UPON ME SCOWL--	499	3	DON JUAN 15	97	5
OLD PORTRAITS FROM OLD WALLS UPON ME SCOWL--	499	3	DON JUAN 15	97	5
OUR BUBBLES AS THE OLD BURST NEW EMERGE	500	3	DON JUAN 15	99	6
NO REAL LIKENESS--LIKE THE OLD TYRIAN VEST	505	3	DON JUAN 16	10	5
LONG FURNISHED WITH OLD PICTURES OF GREAT WORTH	508	3	DON JUAN 16	17	4
OF SUCH A SPIRIT IN THESE HALLS OF OLD	510	3	DON JUAN 16	22	2
THEIR OFFICE HE TOOK UP AN OLD NEWSPAPER	512	3	DON JUAN 16	26	5
AND IS NOT MUCH IMPROVED BY GROWING OLD	516	3	DON JUAN 16	37	8
AND A YOUNG RACE-HORSE OF OLD PEDIGREE	527	3	DON JUAN 16	55	7
AND THROW DOWN OLD WHICH HE CALLED RESTORATION	529	3	DON JUAN 16	58	8
THE COST WOULD BE A TRIFLE--AN OLD SONG	529	3	DON JUAN 16	59	1
'TWAS A GREAT BANQUET SUCH AS ALBION OLD	538	3	DON JUAN 16	78	2
WHO GROW UP CHILDREN ONLY SINCE THE OLD SAW	563	3	DON JUAN 17	2	2
THE OLD HEN--BY RUNNING HEADLONG TO THE WATER	564	3	DON JUAN 17	4	8
OLDEN					
OLDEN SHE WAS--BUT HAD BEEN VERY YOUNG	336	3	DON JUAN 12	43	1
AND OAKS AS OLDEN AS THEIR PEDIGREE	381	3	DON JUAN 13	50	7
OLDER					
SINCE RODERIC'S GOTH'S OR OLDER GENSERIC'S VANDALS	129	2	DON JUAN 1	190	V4
BUT ZOE BEING OLDER THAN HAIDEE	239	2	DON JUAN 2	158	5
SIGH'D FOR THEIR SAKES--THAT THEY SHOULD E'ER GROW OLDER	292	2	DON JUAN 3	33	8
WISHED FOR THEIR SAKES--THEY NEVER MIGHT GROW OLDER	292	2	DON JUAN 3	33	V8
STILL OLDER MANSION OF A RICH AND RARE	384	3	DON JUAN 13	55	3
OLDEST					
THE OLDEST THING ON RECORD AND YET NEW	214	3	DON JUAN 9	64	8
OLD-GENTLEMANLY					
SO FOR A GOOD OLD-GENTLEMANLY VICE	144	2	DON JUAN 1	216	7
OLIGARCHS					
THE LOVELIEST OLIGARCHS OF OUR GYNOCRASY	346	3	DON JUAN 12	66	4
OLIVE					
THERE THE LARGE OLIVE RAINS ITS AMBER STORE	373	2	DON JUAN 4	55	1
OLIVE-BRANCH					
THEY WOULD HAVE EAT HER OLIVE-BRANCH AND ALL	206	2	DON JUAN 2	95	8
OLIVES					
WHICH MIXES UP VINES OLIVES PRECIPICES	262	3	DON JUAN 10	76	7
THE SIMPLE OLIVES BEST ALLIES OF WINE	488	3	DON JUAN 15	73	1
OLYMPUS					
THE CYPRESS GROVES OLYMPUS HIGH AND HOAR	412	2	DON JUAN 5	3	5
OMEN					
OUR SHIPWRECK'D SEAMEN THOUGHT IT A GOOD OMEN--	205	2	DON JUAN 2	93	1
NIGHT FELL--THIS SEEM'D A BETTER OMEN STILL	206	2	DON JUAN 2	94	8
AND THEN DISMISS'D THE OMEN FROM HER BREAST	356	2	DON JUAN 4	24	3
OMINOUS					
AN OMINOUS AND WILD AND DESPERATE SOUND	194	2	DON JUAN 2	73	4
OMISSION					
TOO MUCH THEIR MODEST BARD BY THIS OMISSION	46	2	DON JUAN 1	44	5
FORGETTING EACH OMISSION IS A LOSS TO	331	2	DON JUAN 3	96	7
AND THIS OMISSION LIKE THAT OF THE BUST	477	3	DON JUAN 15	49	1
OMIT					
WE WILL OMIT THE PROOFS SAVE ONE OR TWO	396	2	DON JUAN 4	96	4
I MUST NOT QUITE OMIT THE TALKING SAGE	403	3	DON JUAN 13	97	3
OMITTED					
OF ADELINE AURORA WAS OMITTED	477	3	DON JUAN 15	48	2
OMITTING					
OMITTING TURBAN SLIPPERS PISTOLS DIRK--	240	2	DON JUAN 2	160	6
OMNE					
OMNE TULIT PUNCTUM QUAE MISCUIT UTILE DULCI	396	3	DON JUAN 13	81	8
OMNIA					
OMNIA VULT BELLE MATHO DICERE--DIC ALIQUANDO	465	3	DON JUAN 15	21	1
ONCE					
LIKE SAMUEL FROM THE GRAVE TO FREEZE ONCE MORE	15	2	DON JUAN D	11	2
NELSON WAS ONCE BRITANNIA'S GOD OF WAR	23	2	DON JUAN 1	4	1
AND ARE TO BE SO AT THE LEAST ONCE MORE--	95	2	DON JUAN 1	136	6
BEGAN AT ONCE TO SCREAM AND YAWN AND WEEP	97	2	DON JUAN 1	140	3
AND NEVER ONCE HE HAS HAD CAUSE TO SCOLD	101	2	DON JUAN 1	147	5
A READY ANSWER WHICH AT ONCE ENABLES	117	2	DON JUAN 1	175	2
ONCE ALL IN ALL BUT NOW A THING APART	144	2	DON JUAN 1	215	3
A DEMOCRAT SOME ONCE OR TWICE A YEAR	152	2	DON JUAN 1	V 3	2
BUT NOW THERE CAME A FLASH OF HOPE ONCE MORE	176	2	DON JUAN 2	38	1
AND THOUGH 'TIS TRUE THAT MAN CAN ONLY DIE ONCE	176	2	DON JUAN 2	39	7
AND ALL MISTOOK ABOUT THE LATTER ONCE	207	2	DON JUAN 2	96	8
AS ONCE (A FEAT ON WHICH OURSELVES WE PRIDED)	211	2	DON JUAN 2	105	7
AND THEN ONCE MORE HIS FEELINGS BACK WERE BROUGHT	215	2	DON JUAN 2	112	6
AND HURLS AT ONCE HIS VENOM AND HIS STRENGTH	218	2	DON JUAN 2	117	8
(UNLESS AT ONCE SHE PLUNGE FOR LIFE IN PRAYERS)--	276	2	DON JUAN 3	4	3
A TERRIER TOO WHICH ONCE HAD BEEN A BRITON'S	285	2	DON JUAN 3	18	4
HIS ANGRY WORD ONCE O'ER HE SHED NO BLOOD	300	2	DON JUAN 3	48	6
AND ROUND ITS ONCE WARM PRECINCTS PALELY LYING	301	2	DON JUAN 3	51	6

ONCE   (CONTINUED)

	PAGE	VOL		CANTO	STANZA	LN
ROOTED WHERE ONCE THE ADRIAN WAVE FLOW'D O'ER	337	2 DON JUAN	3	105	4
TURNS WHAT WAS ONCE ROMANTIC TO BURLESQUE	345	2 DON JUAN	4	3	8
THEY WERE ALONE ONCE MORE FOR THEM TO BE	349	2 DON JUAN	4	10	1
AND BREAST MATERNAL WEAN'D AT ONCE FOREVER	349	2 DON JUAN	4	10	6
WERE ONCE HER CARES HOW IDLE SEEM'D THEY NOW)	362	2 DON JUAN	4	34	4
YOUNG MAN YOUR SWORD SO LAMBRO ONCE MORE SAID	365	2 DON JUAN	4	40	1
BUT AFTER BEING FIRED AT ONCE OR TWICE	366	2 DON JUAN	4	41	7
I ONCE HAD A GREAT ALACRITY IN WIELDING	397	2 DON JUAN	4	98	5
THOSE SUFFERINGS ONCE RESERVED FOR HELL ALONE	401	2 DON JUAN	4	105	V8
AT ONCE ADVENTUROUS AND CONTEMPLATIVE	402	2 DON JUAN	4	107	2
'TWAS FOR THE SULTAN AND AT ONCE WITHDREW	407	2 DON JUAN	4	114	8
FOR ONCE IT WAS A MAGIC SOUND TO ME	413	2 DON JUAN	5	4	2
AND THEY WHO WAITED ONCE AND WORSHIPPED--THEY	431	2 DON JUAN	5	37	1
TO GAZE ONCE MORE ON THE COMMANDING CLAY	431	2 DON JUAN	5	37	3
AND WHEN WE ONCE WERE FAIRLY OUT AND WHEN	435	2 DON JUAN	5	44	3
THE ARTS OF WHICH THESE LANDS WERE ONCE THE FONT	436	2 DON JUAN	5	46	6
I SAY A THING IT MUST AT ONCE BE DONE	458	2 DON JUAN	5	81	5
KEEP YOUR GOOD NAME THOUGH EVE HERSELF ONCE FELL	460	2 DON JUAN	5	84	6
WHEN SHE WHOSE TURN IT WAS WAS WED AT ONCE	498	2 DON JUAN	5	152	5
TO KISS THEM ALL AT ONCE FROM NORTH TO SOUTH	19	3 DON JUAN	6	27	8
WHICH THEY HIT OFF AT ONCE IN THE BEGINNING	32	3 DON JUAN	6	52	6
OH YE WHOSE FATE IT IS AS ONCE 'TWAS MINE	37	3 DON JUAN	6	62	3
WHICH AS ALL SPOKE AT ONCE AND MORE THAN ONCE	43	3 DON JUAN	6	74	2
WHICH AS ALL SPOKE AT ONCE AND MORE THAN ONCE	43	3 DON JUAN	6	74	2
SAVE THAT OF DREAMING ONCE MAL-A-PROPOS	48	3 DON JUAN	6	84	8
ALREADY MANY A ONCE LOVE-BEATEN BREAST	63	3 DON JUAN	6	115	3
BUT GO THEY MUST AT ONCE AND WILL-I-NILL-I	64	3 DON JUAN	6	118	8
FOR THEY ARE DAMNED THAT ONCE ALL FAMOUS OATH	88	3 DON JUAN	7	45	2
FOR ONCE BY SOME ODD SORT OF MAGNANIMITY	92	3 DON JUAN	7	51	V4
ARE VERY SILENT WHEN THEY ONCE BELIEVE	94	3 DON JUAN	7	54	5
WHEN MY POOR GREECE WAS ONCE AS NOW SURROUNDED	108	3 DON JUAN	7	82	4
THOSE ANTIENT GOOD INTENTIONS WHICH ONCE SHAVED	124	3 DON JUAN	8	26	6
THE DEATH-DISGORGING RAMPART ONCE AGAIN	151	3 DON JUAN	8	79	5
ON EARTH IN PARADISE AND WHEN ONCE SEEN	167	3 DON JUAN	8	111	6
STOPPED AS IF ONCE MORE WILLING TO CONCEDE	170	3 DON JUAN	8	117	2
IN ONE WIDE WOUND POURED FORTH HIS SOUL AT ONCE	170	3 DON JUAN	8	118	8
IF YOU HAVE ACTED ONCE A GENEROUS PART	184	3 DON JUAN	9	4	5
UNTIL I SEE BOTH SIDES FOR ONCE AGREEING	190	3 DON JUAN	9	16	6
IF ONCE BEYOND HER BOUDOIR'S PRECINCTS IN YE WENT	214	3 DON JUAN	9	63	5
WHICH MAKES ONE DRUNK AT ONCE WITHOUT THE BASE	216	3 DON JUAN	9	67	6
I CANNOT STOP TO ALTER WORDS ONCE WRITTEN	221	3 DON JUAN	9	77	4
DEAR JEFFREY ONCE MY MOST REDOUBTED FOE	232	3 DON JUAN	10	16	2
EXISTS WHEN THE ONCE THINKERS ARE LESS REAL	234	3 DON JUAN	10	20	3
AT ONCE HER ROYAL SPLENDOUR AND REWARD	247	3 DON JUAN	10	46	4
BAROUCHE WHICH HAD THE GLORY TO DISPLAY ONCE	248	3 DON JUAN	10	49	5
IN PLACE OF WHAT HER HOME AND FRIENDS ONCE WERE	252	3 DON JUAN	10	57	3
THAT WORSE THAN WORST OF FOES THE ONCE ADORED	258	3 DON JUAN	10	67	6
TELL THEM THAT YOUTH ONCE GONE RETURNS NO MORE	267	3 DON JUAN	10	86	3
THE FIRST ATTACK AT ONCE PROVED THE DIVINITY	271	3 DON JUAN	11	6	1
THE FOURTH AT ONCE ESTABLISHED THE WHOLE TRINITY	271	3 DON JUAN	11	6	5
POOR TOM WAS ONCE A KIDDY UPON TOWN	276	3 DON JUAN	11	17	5
WHICH MAKE US WISH OURSELVES IN TOWN AT ONCE--	277	3 DON JUAN	11	20	8
NOW WERE I ONCE AT HOME AND IN GOOD SATIRE	299	3 DON JUAN	11	62	6
IS NOT AT ONCE TOO PALPABLY DESCRIED	304	3 DON JUAN	11	71	4
THE GHOST OF VANISHED PLEASURES ONCE IN VOGUE ILL	304	3 DON JUAN	11	72	6
SOME WHO ONCE SET THEIR CAPS AT CAUTIOUS DUKES	308	3 DON JUAN	11	81	1
BUT 'TIS AS WELL AT ONCE TO UNDERSTAND	311	3 DON JUAN	11	87	6
MOREOVER I'VE REMARKED (AND I WAS ONCE	336	3 DON JUAN	12	44	1
BUT ONCE THERE (IF YOU DOUBT THIS PRITHEE TRY)	350	3 DON JUAN	12	74	7
THEY LOSE THEIR CASTE AT ONCE AS DO THE PARIAS	352	3 DON JUAN	12	78	2
THOUGH 'TWAS NOT ONCE SO IF I SNEER SOMETIMES	361	3 DON JUAN	13	8	2
IN JUDGING MEN--WHEN ONCE HIS JUDGMENT WAS	366	3 DON JUAN	13	16	3
WHEN ONCE YOU HAVE BROKEN THEIR CONFOUNDED ICE	375	3 DON JUAN	13	38	8
AN OLD OLD MONASTERY ONCE AND NOW	384	3 DON JUAN	13	55	2
IN A GRAND ARCH WHICH ONCE SCREENED MANY AN AISLE	386	3 DON JUAN	13	59	3
TWELVE SAINTS HAD ONCE STOOD SANCTIFIED IN STONE	386	3 DON JUAN	13	60	2
THROUGH WHICH THE DEEPEN'D GLORIES ONCE COULD ENTER	387	3 DON JUAN	13	62	3
THE FACT--I'VE HEARD IT--ONCE PERHAPS TOO MUCH	388	3 DON JUAN	13	64	8
AT ONCE THE LIE AND THE ELITE OF CROWDS	396	3 DON JUAN	13	80	2
AT ONCE WITHOUT INSTALMENTS (AN OLD WAY	412	3 DON JUAN	14	4	5
AND YET I CAN'T HELP SCRIBBLING ONCE A WEEK	414	3 DON JUAN	14	10	5
AND ONCE O'ER SEVERAL COUNTRY GENTLEMEN	424	3 DON JUAN	14	33	8
AND WAS NOT LIKELY ALL AT ONCE TO BURST	437	3 DON JUAN	14	62	3
THE STONE OF SYSIPHUS IF ONCE WE MOVE	447	3 DON JUAN	14	86	3
NOW WHEN SHE ONCE HAD TA'EN AN INTEREST	448	3 DON JUAN	14	88	1
WHEN ONCE DECANTED--I PRESUME TO GUESS SO	458	3 DON JUAN	15	6	6
IF ONCE THEIR PHANTASIES BE BROUGHT TO BEAR	463	3 DON JUAN	15	16	6
AS ONCE OR TWICE TO SMILE IF NOT TO LISTEN	491	3 DON JUAN	15	80	8
TO KEEP EXTREMES FROM MEETING WHEN ONCE SET	492	3 DON JUAN	15	81	6
QUIETS AT ONCE WITH QUIA IMPOSSIBILE	503	3 DON JUAN	16	5	8
ONCE TWICE THRICE PASSED REPASSED--THE THING OF AIR	510	3 DON JUAN	16	23	1
THE VOICE THE WORDS THE HARPER'S SKILL AT ONCE	517	3 DON JUAN	16	39	7
THOUGH ONCE SHE WAS SEEN READING THE BATH GUIDE	525	3 DON JUAN	16	50	2
BUT ONCE A WEEK OR FORTNIGHT UNINVITED	534	3 DON JUAN	16	69	1
BROADENING TO GRINS HE COLOURED MORE THAN ONCE	542	3 DON JUAN	16	88	3
OF ORPHANS PAINTS AT ONCE A PARISH SCHOOL	563	3 DON JUAN	17	3	3

ONCE-NAMED

	PAGE	VOL		CANTO	STANZA	LN
WHICH ONCE-NAMED MYRIADS NAMELESS LIE BENEATH	399	2 DON JUAN	4	102	7

	PAGE	VOL	CANTO	STANZA	LN
OF ONE ANOTHER'S MINDS AT LAST HAVE GROWN	12	2	DON JUAN	D	5	4
TO--GOD KNOWS WHERE--FOR NO ONE ELSE CAN KNOW	14	2	DON JUAN	D	9	8
TO KEEP ONE CREED'S A TASK GROWN QUITE HERCULEAN	20	2	DON JUAN	D	17	7
WHEN EVERY YEAR AND MONTH SENDS FORTH A NEW ONE	21	2	DON JUAN	1	1	2
THE AGE DISCOVERS HE IS NOT THE TRUE ONE	21	2	DON JUAN	1	1	4
FIT FOR MY POEM (THAT IS FOR MY NEW ONE)	24	2	DON JUAN	1	5	7
ONE SAD EXAMPLE MORE THAT ALL IS VANITY	29	2	DON JUAN	1	15	7
FOR SHE HAD NOT EVEN ONE--THE WORST OF ALL	29	2	DON JUAN	1	16	8
BUT FOR DOMESTIC QUARRELS ONE WILL DO	31	2	DON JUAN	1	19	8
AND WHY AND WHEREFORE NO ONE UNDERSTANDS	33	2	DON JUAN	1	21	8
ANY ONE ELSE--THEY WERE BECOME TRADITIONAL	37	2	DON JUAN	1	31	4
A JEW TOOK ONE OF HIS TWO MISTRESSES	39	2	DON JUAN	1	34	4
BUT VIRGIL'S SONGS ARE PURE EXCEPT THAT HORRID ONE	45	2	DON JUAN	1	42	7
FOR THERE WE HAVE THEM ALL AT ONE FELL SWOOP	46	2	DON JUAN	1	45	1
SO WELL NOT ONE OF THE AFORESAID PAINTS	47	2	DON JUAN	1	47	6
IF SUCH AN EDUCATION WAS THE TRUE ONE	48	2	DON JUAN	1	48	3
HER MAIDS WERE OLD AND IF SHE TOOK A NEW ONE	48	2	DON JUAN	1	48	5
FOR THERE ONE LEARNS--'TIS NOT FOR ME TO BOAST	50	2	DON JUAN	1	53	1
MAY HAVE SUGGESTED THAT THIS SINGLE ONE	54	2	DON JUAN	1	59	5
AND YET I THINK INSTEAD OF SUCH A ONE	56	2	DON JUAN	1	62	3
AND NOT EXACTLY EITHER ONE OR TWO	57	2	DON JUAN	1	65	6
A QUIET CONSCIENCE MAKES ONE SO SERENE	66	2	DON JUAN	1	83	6
OF HIS OWN CASE AND NEVER HIT THE TRUE ONE	68	2	DON JUAN	1	86	3
HE PUZZLED OVER WHAT HE FOUND A NEW ONE	68	2	DON JUAN	1	86	5
THAT NO ONE LIKES TO BE DISTURB'D AT MEALS	69	2	DON JUAN	1	89	5
'TWAS STRANGE THAT ONE SO YOUNG SHOULD THUS CONCERN	71	2	DON JUAN	1	93	5
AS IF 'TWERE ONE WHEREON MAGICIANS BIND	72	2	DON JUAN	1	95	6
JEALOUS OF SOME ONE WHO HAD NO SUCH WISHES	74	2	DON JUAN	1	99	3
BUT WHATSOE'ER THE CAUSE IS ONE MAY SAY	76	2	DON JUAN	1	102	5
ONE HAND ON JUAN'S CARLESSLY WAS THROWN	80	2	DON JUAN	1	109	7
ALTHOUGH ONE MUST BE DAMN'D FOR YOU NO DOUBT	85	2	DON JUAN	1	119	2
ONE MAKES NEW NOSES ONE A GUILLOTINE	91	2	DON JUAN	1	129	3
ONE MAKES NEW NOSES ONE A GUILLOTINE	91	2	DON JUAN	1	129	3
ONE BREAKS YOUR BONES ONE SETS THEM IN THEIR SOCKETS	91	2	DON JUAN	1	129	4
ONE BREAKS YOUR BONES ONE SETS THEM IN THEIR SOCKETS	91	2	DON JUAN	1	129	4
BY BORROWING A NEW ONE FROM AN OX	91	2	DON JUAN	1	129	8
MAN'S A PHENOMENON ONE KNOWS NOT WHAT	93	2	DON JUAN	1	133	1
WERE ONE NOT PUNISH'D ALL WOULD BE OUTRAGEOUS	96	2	DON JUAN	1	138	8
HAD THOUGHT ONE MAN MIGHT BE DETERR'D BY TWO	98	2	DON JUAN	1	141	4
'TIS ODD NOT ONE OF ALL THESE SEEKERS THOUGHT	100	2	DON JUAN	1	144	6
'TWILL ONE DAY ASK YOU WHY YOU USED ME SO	107	2	DON JUAN	1	157	6
NOT ONE EXCEPT THE ATTORNEY WAS AMUSED	109	2	DON JUAN	1	159	5
SUSPECTS WITH ONE DO YOU REPROACH WITH THREE	117	2	DON JUAN	1	175	8
THERE MIGHT BE ONE MORE MOTIVE WHICH MAKES TWO	118	2	DON JUAN	1	177	1
TO SPEAK OF INEZ NOW WERE ONE MAY SAY	118	2	DON JUAN	1	177	7
(NO ONE CAN TELL HOW MUCH I GRIEVE TO SAY)	121	2	DON JUAN	1	181	3
DAY HAS NOT BROKE--THERE'S NO ONE IN THE STREET	121	2	DON JUAN	1	182	8
THERE'S MORE THAN ONE EDITION AND THE READINGS	127	2	DON JUAN	1	189	5
OF ONE OF THE MOST CIRCULATING SCANDALS	128	2	DON JUAN	1	190	2
MEN HAVE ALL THESE RESOURCES WE BUT ONE	131	2	DON JUAN	1	194	7
TO ALL EXCEPT ONE IMAGE MADLY BLIND	133	2	DON JUAN	1	196	6
AND YET SHE DID NOT LET ONE TEAR ESCAPE HER	134	2	DON JUAN	1	198	5
THERE'S ONLY ONE SLIGHT DIFFERENCE BETWEEN	137	2	DON JUAN	1	202	1
MY TEXT WITH MANY THINGS THAT NO ONE KNOWS	138	2	DON JUAN	1	204	5
(THERE'S ONE AT LEAST IS VERY FOND OF THIS)	140	2	DON JUAN	1	206	4
THE GROWING WATERS IT UNMANS ONE QUITE	163	2	DON JUAN	2	12	3
AND PLACES ONE KEEPS LOOKING AT THE STEEPLE	164	2	DON JUAN	2	14	8
AT ONE O'CLOCK THE WIND WITH SUDDEN SHIFT	170	2	DON JUAN	2	27	1
ONE GANG OF PEOPLE INSTANTLY WAS PUT	171	2	DON JUAN	2	28	1
KEPT TWO HAND AND ONE CHAIN-PUMP STILL IN USE	172	2	DON JUAN	2	30	4
LAID WITH ONE BLAST THE SHIP ON HER BEAM ENDS	172	2	DON JUAN	2	30	8
ALL ONE AN HOUR HENCE JUAN ANSWER'D NO	175	2	DON JUAN	2	36	2
SOME HOISTED OUT THE BOATS AND THERE WAS ONE	179	2	DON JUAN	2	44	6
AND ONE OAR FOR A MAST WHICH A YOUNG LAD	181	2	DON JUAN	2	48	5
TO SAVE ONE HALF THE PEOPLE THEN ON BOARD	181	2	DON JUAN	2	48	8
OF ONE WHOSE HATE IS MASKED BUT TO ASSAIL	182	2	DON JUAN	2	49	4
A SORT OF THING AT WHICH ONE WOULD HAVE LAUGH'D	183	2	DON JUAN	2	50	3
LIKE ONE WHO GRAPPLES WITH HIS ENEMY	184	2	DON JUAN	2	52	7
AND FIRST ONE UNIVERSAL SHRIEK THERE RUSH'D	184	2	DON JUAN	2	53	1
TAKES OFF ONE PECK OF PURGATORIAL COALS	185	2	DON JUAN	2	55	5
ONE HALF SATE UP THOUGH NUMB'D WITH THE IMMERSION	189	2	DON JUAN	2	63	4
AND MUST HAVE MEALS AT LEAST ONE MEAL A DAY	191	2	DON JUAN	2	67	2
BUT AS THEY HAD BUT ONE OAR AND THAT BRITTLE	192	2	DON JUAN	2	69	7
WITH THEIR ONE OAR (I WISH THEY HAD HAD A PAIR)	193	2	DON JUAN	2	70	5
AS A GREAT FAVOUR ONE OF THE FORE-PAWS	193	2	DON JUAN	2	71	6
AT LENGTH ONE WHISPER'D HIS COMPANION WHO	194	2	DON JUAN	2	73	1
AND WITH THEM THEIR TWO SONS OF WHOM THE ONE	202	2	DON JUAN	2	87	2
ONE GLANCE ON HIM AND SAID HEAVEN'S WILL BE DONE	202	2	DON JUAN	2	87	6
AND BLENDING EVERY COLOUR INTO ONE	205	2	DON JUAN	2	92	6
BY NIGHT CHILL'D BY DAY SCORCH'D THUS ONE BY ONE	210	2	DON JUAN	2	102	5
BY NIGHT CHILL'D BY DAY SCORCH'D THUS ONE BY ONE	210	2	DON JUAN	2	102	5
SAVE ONE A CORPSE FROM OUT THE FAMISH'D THREE	213	2	DON JUAN	2	109	6
THE GENTLE GIRL AND HER ATTENDANT--ONE	216	2	DON JUAN	2	115	2
AS ONE WHO WAS A LADY IN THE LAND	217	2	DON JUAN	2	116	8
EVER TO HAVE SEEN SUCH FOR SHE WAS ONE	218	2	DON JUAN	2	118	4
ONE SHOULD NOT RAIL WITHOUT A DECENT CAUSE	219	2	DON JUAN	2	119	2
(ONE OF THE WILD AND SMALLER CYCLADES)	223	2	DON JUAN	2	127	2
AND THE FIRST BREAKFAST SPOILT PREPARED A NEW ONE	234	2	DON JUAN	2	146	6

ONE   (CONTINUED)

	PAGE	VOL	CANTO	STANZA	LN
AND JUAN GAZED AS ONE WHO IS AWOKE	237	2 DON JUAN	2	152	1
THIS THOUGH NOT LARGE WAS ONE OF THE MOST RICH	238	2 DON JUAN	2	154	8
SUCH APPETITE IN ONE SHE HAD DEEM'D DEAD	239	2 DON JUAN	2	158	4
AND DARTS IN ONE QUICK GLANCE A LONG REPLY	241	2 DON JUAN	2	162	6
BOTH WERE SO YOUNG AND ONE SO INNOCENT	247	2 DON JUAN	2	172	1
ON ONE SIDE AND THE DEEP SEA CALM AND CHILL	252	2 DON JUAN	2	183	6
WITH ONE STAR SPARKLING THROUGH IT LIKE AN EYE	252	2 DON JUAN	2	183	8
INTO ONE FOCUS KINDLED FROM ABOVE	254	2 DON JUAN	2	186	3
WITH SOMETIMES MORE WITHIN THEM THAN ONE TONGUE	254	2 DON JUAN	2	187	V8
AND ONE WAS INNOCENT BUT BOTH TOO YOUNG	254	2 DON JUAN	2	187	V8
FOUND IN ONE SIGH THE BEST INTERPRETER	256	2 DON JUAN	2	189	6
HAD NOT ONE WORD TO SAY OF CONSTANCY	257	2 DON JUAN	2	190	8
PLEASURE OR PAIN TO ONE ANOTHER LIVING	258	2 DON JUAN	2	192	8
IS ALWAYS SO TO WOMEN ONE SOLE BOND	263	2 DON JUAN	2	200	2
OF HIS GAZELLE-EYED DAUGHTERS SHE WAS ONE	264	2 DON JUAN	2	202	4
WITH ONE OR TWO SMALL SENSES ADDED JUST	269	2 DON JUAN	2	212	7
WHEREAS IF ONE SOLE LADY PLEASED FOREVER	270	2 DON JUAN	2	213	7
ONE OF THE NAME BUT THAT I LOVED HER TOO	273	2 DON JUAN	2	V 2	8
ONE MAN ALONE AT FIRST HER HEART CAN MOVE	276	2 DON JUAN	3	3	6
BUT ONE THING'S PRETTY SURE A WOMAN PLANTED--	276	2 DON JUAN	3	4	2
BUT THOSE WHO HAVE NE'ER END WITH ONLY ONE	276	2 DON JUAN	3	4	8
THAT BOTH ARE TIED TILL ONE SHALL HAVE EXPIRED	278	2 DON JUAN	3	7	6
FOR NO ONE CARES FOR MATRIMONIAL COOINGS	279	2 DON JUAN	3	8	5
AT LEAST IN THE BEGINNING ERE ONE TIRES	282	2 DON JUAN	3	13	6
BY SWAMPING ONE OF THE PRIZES HE HAD CHAIN'D	283	2 DON JUAN	3	15	5
TO HIS TUNIS CORRESPONDENTS SAVE ONE MAN	284	2 DON JUAN	3	16	3
THE REST--SAVE HERE AND THERE SOME RICHER ONE	284	2 DON JUAN	3	16	5
HE CAGED IN ONE HUGE HAMPER ALTOGETHER	285	2 DON JUAN	3	18	8
AND THAT HIS SORROW MAY NOT BE A DUMB ONE	288	2 DON JUAN	3	24	7
OF MAGIC LADIES WHO BY ONE SOLE ACT	293	2 DON JUAN	3	34	7
OF HIS ARRIVAL SO THAT NO ONE STIRRED	294	2 DON JUAN	3	37	5
WHILE SHE HAD NOT ONE HOUR TO SPARE FROM LOVING	295	2 DON JUAN	3	39	8
HIS SMILE REQUESTED ONE OF THEM TO TELL	298	2 DON JUAN	3	44	6
AND HIS ONE BLOW LEFT LITTLE WORK FOR TWO	300	2 DON JUAN	3	48	8
BUT CERTAINLY TO ONE DEEM'D DEAD RETURNING	300	2 DON JUAN	3	49	7
SHE WORE TWO JELICKS--ONE WAS OF PALE YELLOW	311	2 DON JUAN	3	70	2
ONE LARGE GOLD BRACELET CLASP'D EACH LOVELY ARM	312	2 DON JUAN	3	71	1
HIS POLAR STAR BEING ONE WHICH RATHER RANGES	317	2 DON JUAN	3	80	3
AND ANSWER LET ONE LIVING HEAD	323	2 DON JUAN	3	L 8	4
BUT ONE ARISE--WE COME WE COME	323	2 DON JUAN	3	L 8	5
THE NOBLER AND THE MANLIER ONE	324	2 DON JUAN	3	L 10	4
MAKING THEIR SUMMER LIVES ONE CEASELESS SONG	337	2 DON JUAN	3	106	2
AND I GROWN ONE OF MANY WOODEN SPOONS	341	2 DON JUAN	3	110	6
BEFORE ONE CHARM OR HOPE HAD TAKEN WING	348	2 DON JUAN	4	8	8
WHERE HYMEN'S TORCH BUT BRANDS ONE STRUMPET MORE	353	2 DON JUAN	4	17	7
WHERE HYMEN'S SHRINE BUT STAMPS ONE STRUMPET MORE	353	2 DON JUAN	4	17	V7
WHEN ONE IS SHOOK IN SOUND AND ONE IN SIGHT	355	2 DON JUAN	4	21	5
WHEN ONE IS SHOOK IN SOUND AND ONE IN SIGHT	355	2 DON JUAN	4	21	5
WHILE ONE NEW TEAR AROSE IN HAIDEE'S EYE	355	2 DON JUAN	4	21	8
ONE OF THE TWO ACCORDING TO YOUR CHOICE	357	2 DON JUAN	4	25	1
WHEN TWO PURE HEARTS ARE POUR'D IN ONE ANOTHER	357	2 DON JUAN	4	26	5
PERCHANCE THE DEATH OF ONE SHE LOVED TOO WELL	363	2 DON JUAN	4	36	5
LAMBRO PRESENTED AND ONE INSTANT MORE	366	2 DON JUAN	4	42	1
SHE STOOD AS ONE WHO CHAMPION'D HUMAN FEARS--	367	2 DON JUAN	4	43	3
FOR SHE TOO WAS AS ONE WHO COULD AVENGE	367	2 DON JUAN	4	44	5
AND ARM'D FROM BOOT TO TURBAN ONE AND ALL	369	2 DON JUAN	4	47	5
ONE ON THE ARM THE OTHER ON THE HEAD	370	2 DON JUAN	4	49	8
ON BOARD OF ONE OF THESE AND UNDER HATCHES	371	2 DON JUAN	4	50	7
AND HERE WAS ONE EXCEEDINGLY UNPLEASANT	371	2 DON JUAN	4	51	2
SHE WAS NOT ONE TO WEEP AND RAVE AND CHAFE	373	2 DON JUAN	4	54	5
HER STRUGGLES CEASED WITH ONE CONVULSIVE GROAN	375	2 DON JUAN	4	58	6
LIKE ONE LIFE COULD NOT HOLD NOR DEATH DESTROY	376	2 DON JUAN	4	59	8
AS ONE WHO NE'ER HAD DWELT AMONG THE SICK	380	2 DON JUAN	4	67	3
BUT NO ONE EVER HEARD HER SPEAK OR SHRIEK	380	2 DON JUAN	4	67	5
BLOSSOM AND BOUGH LIE WITHER'D WITH ONE BLIGHT	382	2 DON JUAN	4	70	6
WHICH WAS AN ODD ONE A TROOP GOING TO ACT	388	2 DON JUAN	4	80	4
BY ONE OF THESE THE BUFFO OF THE PARTY	388	2 DON JUAN	4	81	1
WITH MORE THAN ONE PROFESSION GAINS BY ALL	390	2 DON JUAN	4	84	2
THERE'S ONE THOUGH TALL AND STIFFER THAN A PIKE	390	2 DON JUAN	4	85	5
BUT BEING QUALIFIED IN ONE WAY YET	391	2 DON JUAN	4	86	3
HAVE GOT A TRAVELL'D AIR WHICH SHOWS YOU ONE	392	2 DON JUAN	4	88	3
AND THEN WENT DOWN THE HATCHWAY ONE BY ONE	393	2 DON JUAN	4	90	8
AND THEN WENT DOWN THE HATCHWAY ONE BY ONE	393	2 DON JUAN	4	90	8
WE WILL OMIT THE PROOFS SAVE ONE OR TWO	396	2 DON JUAN	4	96	4
'TIS SAID NO ONE IN HAND CAN HOLD A FIRE	396	2 DON JUAN	4	96	5
I KNOW ONE WOMAN OF THAT PURPLE SCHOOL	405	2 DON JUAN	4	111	7
WERE LANDED IN THE MARKET ONE AND ALL	407	2 DON JUAN	4	113	6
FOR ONE CIRCASSIAN A SWEET GIRL WERE GIVEN	407	2 DON JUAN	4	114	2
THE FEMALES STOOD AS ONE BY ONE THEY PICK'D 'EM	409	2 DON JUAN	4	116	7
THE FEMALES STOOD AS ONE BY ONE THEY PICK'D 'EM	409	2 DON JUAN	4	116	7
ONE ARM HAD ON A BANDAGE RATHER BLOODY	416	2 DON JUAN	5	11	6
ONE PERSON THRICE IN HOLY WEDLOCK BOUND	421	2 DON JUAN	5	20	5
AND ONE BY ONE IN TURN SOME GRAND MISTAKE	421	2 DON JUAN	5	21	7
AND ONE BY ONE IN TURN SOME GRAND MISTAKE	421	2 DON JUAN	5	21	7
PERHAPS WE SHALL BE ONE DAY BY AND BY	423	2 DON JUAN	5	24	5
FIRST BUT FOR ONE AND AFTER FOR THE PAIR	425	2 DON JUAN	5	28	3
SELL FLESH AND BLOOD WHEN DINNER HAS OPPREST ONE	426	2 DON JUAN	5	30	6
AMMON'S (ILL PLEASED WITH ONE WORLD AND ONE FATHER)	427	2 DON JUAN	5	31	8

568

ONE   (CONTINUED)

	PAGE	VOL		CANTO	STANZA	LN
AMMON'S (ILL PLEASED WITH ONE WORLD AND ONE FATHER)	427	2	DON JUAN	5	31	8
OR AMMON'S--FOR TWO FATHERS CLAIMED THIS ONE	427	2	DON JUAN	5	31	V8
SAW ONE WHOM SUCH AN ACCIDENT BEFELL	430	2	DON JUAN	5	35	3
OR THREE OR TWO OR ONE SEND VERY FAR	432	2	DON JUAN	5	39	3
BECAUSE ONE POET TRAVELLED 'MONGST THE TURKS)	434	2	DON JUAN	5	42	8
BUT NO ONE EVER DREAMS OF BEING SHORT--	437	2	DON JUAN	5	48	8
ONE OR TWO STARED THE CAPTIVES IN THE FACE	441	2	DON JUAN	5	54	5
JUST AS ONE VIEWS A HORSE TO GUESS HIS PRICE	441	2	DON JUAN	5	54	6
BUT NO ONE TROUBLED HIM WITH CONVERSATION	441	2	DON JUAN	5	54	8
SPLENDID BUT SILENT SAVE IN ONE WHERE DROPPING	442	2	DON JUAN	5	55	3
TWO OR THREE SEEM SO LITTLE ONE SEEMS NOTHING	443	2	DON JUAN	5	57	1
SEEING WHAT'S MEANT FOR MANY WITH BUT ONE	443	2	DON JUAN	5	57	8
REIGN'D TILL ONE SUMMER'S DAY HE TOOK TO GRAZING	445	2	DON JUAN	5	60	4
ONE WONDERED WHAT TO DO WITH SUCH A NUMBER	448	2	DON JUAN	5	64	4
MIGHT LEAD TO HEAVEN KNOWS WHERE BUT IN THIS ONE	449	2	DON JUAN	5	65	3
ONE DIFFICULTY STILL REMAINED--HIS HAIR	457	2	DON JUAN	5	79	1
YOU SIR SAID BABA NODDING TO THE ONE	458	2	DON JUAN	5	81	1
YOU FOOL I TELL YOU NO ONE MEANS YOU HARM	459	2	DON JUAN	5	82	1
ONE'S TURNED HALF MUSSULMAN AND ONE A MAID	459	2	DON JUAN	5	83	7
AND FOR ONE KISS WOULD FAIN IMPRINT A BRACE	472	2	DON JUAN	5	106	5
OF ONE WHO DARED TO ASK IF HE HAD LOVED	481	2	DON JUAN	5	121	4
SHE ROSE AND PAUSING ONE CHASTE MOMENT THREW	483	2	DON JUAN	5	125	7
THESE DON'T EXPRESS ONE HALF WHAT I SHOULD SAY	487	2	DON JUAN	5	132	6
ONE OR THE OTHER BUT WHICH OF THE TWO	499	2	DON JUAN	5	153	3
SUCH NOTICE OF A GIAOUR WHILE SCARCE TO ONE	501	2	DON JUAN	5	156	5
THOUGH SUCH A SHE'S A DEVIL (IF THAT THERE BE ONE)	7	3	DON JUAN	6	3	7
OR AT THE LEAST FORGIVE THE LOVING RASH ONE	8	3	DON JUAN	6	4	4
MOST WISE MEN WITH ONE MODERATE WOMAN WED	12	3	DON JUAN	6	12	5
FOR NO ONE SAVE IN VERY EARLY YOUTH	14	3	DON JUAN	6	16	3
AND NO ONE VIRTUE YET EXCEPT STARVATION	17	3	DON JUAN	6	19	7
WITH ONE GOOD HEARTY CURSE I VENT MY GALL	17	3	DON JUAN	6	22	3
SO NOW ALL THINGS ARE DAMN'D ONE FEELS AT EASE	17	3	DON JUAN	6	23	1
AT LEAST ONE OF THEM--OH THE HEAVY NIGHT	18	3	DON JUAN	6	24	2
SNOW WELL 'TIS ALL HAP-HAZARD WHEN ONE WEDS	18	3	DON JUAN	6	25	6
ONE NECK WHICH HE WITH ONE FELL STROKE MIGHT PIERCE	19	3	DON JUAN	6	27	3
ONE NECK WHICH HE WITH ONE FELL STROKE MIGHT PIERCE	19	3	DON JUAN	6	27	3
THAT WOMANKIND HAD BUT ONE ROSY MOUTH	19	3	DON JUAN	6	27	7
WHERE ALL THE PASSIONS HAVE ALAS BUT ONE VENT	22	3	DON JUAN	6	32	8
OF ONE GOOD MAN WITH STATELY MARCH AND SLOW	22	3	DON JUAN	6	33	5
BUT NO ONE DOUBTED ON THE WHOLE THAT SHE	24	3	DON JUAN	6	36	1
WITH ALL THINGS LADIES WANT SAVE ONE OR TWO	31	3	DON JUAN	6	51	7
I HAVE BUT ONE SIMILE AND THAT'S A BLUNDER	34	3	DON JUAN	6	57	7
AND ONE BY ONE HER ARTICLES OF DRESS	36	3	DON JUAN	6	61	1
AND ONE BY ONE HER ARTICLES OF DRESS	36	3	DON JUAN	6	61	1
ONE WITH HER AUBURN TRESSES LIGHTLY BOUND	38	3	DON JUAN	6	65	5
ONE WITH HER FLUSHED CHEEK LAID ON HER WHITE ARM	39	3	DON JUAN	6	66	1
ONE ON THE OTHER THROUGHOUT THE WHOLE HALL	42	3	DON JUAN	6	71	5
PROPHETICALLY OR THAT WHICH ONE DEEMS	45	3	DON JUAN	6	78	6
APART FROM ONE WHO HAD NO SIN TO SHOW	48	3	DON JUAN	6	84	7
AT HAND AS ONE MAY LIKE TO HAVE A FAN	51	3	DON JUAN	6	91	4
ONE TWO OR THREE--OR FOUR OR LESS OR MORE	51	3	DON JUAN	6	91	V5
AND IF ONE LADY'S SLIP COULD LEAVE A CRIME ON	53	3	DON JUAN	6	94	6
AND ONE HAND O'ER THE OTTOMAN LAY DROOPING	60	3	DON JUAN	6	109	3
BUT ONE WHICH BABA DID NOT LIKE TO BRAVE	62	3	DON JUAN	6	112	3
AND SENT ONE ON A SUMMONS TO THE PAIR	64	3	DON JUAN	6	118	2
OF WOLVES WILL THE BRIGHT MUSE WITHDRAW ONE RAY	70	3	DON JUAN	7	7	6
CASE-MATED ONE AND T'OTHER A BARBETTE	72	3	DON JUAN	7	12	4
WHO WERE IMMORTAL COULD ONE TELL THEIR STORY	73	3	DON JUAN	7	14	4
BUT WISHING TO BE ONE DAY BRIGADIERS	75	3	DON JUAN	7	18	4
I THINK ONE SHAKESPEAR PUTS THE SAME THOUGHT IN	77	3	DON JUAN	7	21	6
THE MOUTH OF SOME ONE IN HIS PLAYS SO DOATING	77	3	DON JUAN	7	21	7
ONE OF THE VALOUROUS SMITHS WHOM WE SHALL MISS	79	3	DON JUAN	7	25	5
THAT ONE WOULD THINK THE FIRST WHO BORE IT ADAM	79	3	DON JUAN	7	25	8
AND MADE A SIGNAL TO RETREAT AT ONE	81	3	DON JUAN	7	30	6
ONE BARK BLEW UP A SECOND NEAR THE WORKS	81	3	DON JUAN	7	30	7
BEEN ONE TO WHICH A GOOD HEART COULD BE PARTIAL	86	3	DON JUAN	7	40	3
TO GRATIFY LIKE A HUGE MOTH THIS ONE SENSE	88	3	DON JUAN	7	44	8
MAKES THAT OF MULTITUDES TAKE ONE DIRECTION	90	3	DON JUAN	7	48	2
ONE OF WHOM SPOKE THEIR TONGUE OR WELL OR ILL	95	3	DON JUAN	7	56	5
YOUR NAME BEFORE THE SECOND IS A NEW ONE	97	3	DON JUAN	7	60	5
OH GLORIOUS LAUREL SINCE FOR ONE SOLE LEAF	101	3	DON JUAN	7	68	6
UNCERTAINTY IS ONE OF MANY BLISSES	105	3	DON JUAN	7	76	5
HURRA AND ALLAH AND ONE MOMENT MORE	111	3	DON JUAN	7	87	7
THEN ONE VAST FIRE AIR EARTH AND STREAM EMBRACED	115	3	DON JUAN	8	7	5
AND ONE ENORMOUS SHOUT OF ALLAH ROSE	116	3	DON JUAN	8	8	1
THE COLUMNS WERE IN MOVEMENT ONE AND ALL	116	3	DON JUAN	8	9	1
TO THE TRUE PORTRAIT OF ONE BATTLE-FIELD	117	3	DON JUAN	8	12	8
BEING GRENADIERS THEY MOUNTED ONE BY ONE	119	3	DON JUAN	8	15	5
BEING GRENADIERS THEY MOUNTED ONE BY ONE	119	3	DON JUAN	8	15	5
TO THEIR TWO SELVES ONE WHOLE BRIGHT BULLETIN	121	3	DON JUAN	8	19	8
OR HAWK OR BRIDE MOST MORTALS AFTER ONE	122	3	DON JUAN	8	22	6
BY ONE OF THOSE ODD TURNS OF FORTUNE'S TIDES	125	3	DON JUAN	8	27	5
PERHAPS MAY FIND IT BETTER THAN A NEW ONE)--	126	3	DON JUAN	8	29	8
FIRST ONE OR TWO THEN FIVE SIX AND A DOZEN	135	3	DON JUAN	8	45	1
AMIDST SUCH SCENES--THOUGH THIS WAS QUITE A NEW ONE	138	3	DON JUAN	8	52	4
OF GLORY WHICH SO PIERCES THROUGH AND THROUGH ONE	138	3	DON JUAN	8	52	6
FOR SEEING ONE WITH RIBBONS BLACK AND BLUE	141	3	DON JUAN	8	57	5
THE TOWN WAS ENTERED FIRST ONE COLUMN MADE	146	3	DON JUAN	8	69	1

ONE   (CONTINUED)

	PAGE	VOL	CANTO	STANZA	LN
FOR ONE WOULD NOT RETREAT NOR T'OTHER FLINCH	150	3	DON JUAN 8	77	8
TOO MUCH OF ONE SORT WOULD BE SOPORIFIC--	156	3	DON JUAN 8	89	6
AND ONE GOOD ACTION IN THE MIDST OF CRIMES	156	3	DON JUAN 8	90	1
FOR ONE ROUGH WEATHER-BEATEN VETERAN BODY	167	3	DON JUAN 8	112	7
AS THOUGH THERE WERE ONE HEAVEN AND NONE BESIDES--	168	3	DON JUAN 8	114	6
IN ONE VOLUPTUOUS BLAZE--AND THEN HE DIED	169	3	DON JUAN 8	115	8
IN ONE WIDE WOUND POURED FORTH HIS SOUL AT ONCE	170	3	DON JUAN 8	118	8
WHAT'S THIS IN ONE ANNIHILATED CITY	174	3	DON JUAN 8	124	5
IN ONE THING NE'ERTHELESS 'TIS FIT TO PRAISE	176	3	DON JUAN 8	128	1
WHICH MAKES ALL STYX THROUGH ONE SMALL LIVER FLOW	190	3	DON JUAN 9	15	5
LET THIS ONE TOIL FOR BREAD--THAT RACK FOR RENT	190	3	DON JUAN 9	15	7
WAS ONE OF THEIR MOST FAVOURITE POSITIONS	191	3	DON JUAN 9	17	4
WELL NIGH THE SHORE WHERE ONE STOOPS DOWN AND GATHERS	191	3	DON JUAN 9	18	7
THAT ONE LIFE SAVED ESPECIALLY IF YOUNG	199	3	DON JUAN 9	34	2
AND THAT'S ONE COMFORT FOR MY LOST ADVICE	200	3	DON JUAN 9	36	7
BUT LET IT GO--IT WILL ONE DAY BE FOUND	201	3	DON JUAN 9	37	1
THAT THOUGH HE LOOKED ONE OF THE SERAPHIM	206	3	DON JUAN 9	47	5
OR WASTE A WORLD SINCE NO ONE CAN DENY	210	3	DON JUAN 9	56	5
WHICH MAKES ONE DRUNK AT ONCE WITHOUT THE BASE	216	3	DON JUAN 9	67	6
('TIS POPE'S PHRASE) A GREAT LONGING THO' A RASH ONE	216	3	DON JUAN 9	68	6
FOR ONE ESPECIAL PERSON OUT OF MANY	216	3	DON JUAN 9	68	7
ALL THESE OR ANY ONE OF THESE EXPLAIN	218	3	DON JUAN 9	72	7
THAT HE WHO NAMES ONE BOTH PERCHANCE MAY HIT ON	221	3	DON JUAN 9	77	6
THE WHOLE COURT MELTED INTO ONE WIDE WHISPER	221	3	DON JUAN 9	78	1
ON ONE ANOTHER AND EACH LOVELY LISPER	221	3	DON JUAN 9	78	5
THAT ONE SHOULD DIE THAN TWO DRAG ON THE FETTER)	222	3	DON JUAN 9	80	8
(FOR I HAVE MORE THAN ONE MUSE AT A PUSH)	227	3	DON JUAN 10	5	4
AND THEN BEFORE SIGHS CEASE FOR OFT THE ONE	229	3	DON JUAN 10	8	2
A WHOLE ONE AND MY HEART FLIES TO MY HEAD--	233	3	DON JUAN 10	17	8
AS AULD LANG SYNE BRINGS SCOTLAND ONE AND ALL	233	3	DON JUAN 10	18	1
BUT ONE WHO IS NOT SO YOUTHFUL AS SHE WAS	236	3	DON JUAN 10	24	5
TO ONE SMALL GRASS-GROWN PATCH (WHICH MUST AWAIT	237	3	DON JUAN 10	25	5
OF AGE AND LOOKING BACK TO YOUTH GIVE ONE TEAR--	238	3	DON JUAN 10	27	4
OR FIVE OR ONE OR ZERO SHE COULD NEVER	241	3	DON JUAN 10	33	7
BUT HERE IS ONE PRESCRIPTION OUT OF MANY	244	3	DON JUAN 10	41	1
FOR ONE OR TWO DAYS READER WE REQUEST	248	3	DON JUAN 10	49	2
BUT ONE THING'S ODD WHICH HERE MUST BE INSERTED	251	3	DON JUAN 10	55	7
TO LOSE BY ONE MONTH'S FROST SOME TWENTY YEARS	253	3	DON JUAN 10	58	7
AS ONE WHO THOUGH HE WERE NOT OF THE RACE	265	3	DON JUAN 10	81	6
SPACE TO DISPUTE WHAT NO ONE EVER COULD	270	3	DON JUAN 11	4	6
DECIDE AND EVERYBODY ONE DAY WILL	270	3	DON JUAN 11	4	7
AND FIRED IT INTO ONE ASSAILANT'S PUDDING--	274	3	DON JUAN 11	13	4
WITH SLIGHT EXCEPTIONS ALL THE WAYS SEEM ONE	279	3	DON JUAN 11	23	4
BUT SEE THE WORLD IS ONLY ONE ATTORNEY	281	3	DON JUAN 11	28	8
INTO ONE OF THE SWEETEST OF HOTELS	283	3	DON JUAN 11	31	1
ONE MONSTROUS DIAMOND DREW MUCH OBSERVATION	287	3	DON JUAN 11	39	4
JOHN KEATS WHO WAS KILLED OFF BY ONE CRITIQUE	298	3	DON JUAN 11	60	1
MAKES ONE IN LOVE EVEN WITH ITS VERY FAULTS	302	3	DON JUAN 11	68	4
BECAUSE THE TIMES HAVE HARDLY LEFT THEM ONE TENANT	308	3	DON JUAN 11	80	8
THEY KNOW NOT HOW) THE ONE HALF THE PRESENT CASE	314	3	DON JUAN 11	V 75	7
'TIS TRUE THAT THY CAREER IS NOT A NEW ONE	326	3	DON JUAN 12	23	5
THERE IS BUT ONE SUPERB MENAGERIE	327	3	DON JUAN 12	24	8
IN ONE POINT ONLY WERE YOU SETTLED--AND	329	3	DON JUAN 12	29	1
AND ONE OR TWO SAD SEPARATE WIVES WITHOUT	330	3	DON JUAN 12	31	1
I FOR MY PART--(ONE MODERN INSTANCE MORE	334	3	DON JUAN 12	38	1
THOSE BECAME ONE WHO SOON WERE TO BE TWO	334	3	DON JUAN 12	38	6
WHAT YOUR INTENTIONS ARE--ONE WAY OR OTHER	343	3	DON JUAN 12	60	5
OF A MERE NOVICE HAD ONE SAFEGUARD MORE	346	3	DON JUAN 12	67	2
WHERE GEOGRAPHY FINDS NO ONE TO OBLIGE HER	348	3	DON JUAN 12	70	4
SHE CANNOT DO THESE THINGS NOR ONE OR TWO	351	3	DON JUAN 12	76	1
NOR SETTLES ALL THINGS IN ONE INTERVIEW	351	3	DON JUAN 12	76	5
BUT MY BEST CANTO SAVE ONE ON ASTRONOMY	356	3	DON JUAN 12	88	7
AND WEDDED UNTO ONE SHE HAD LOVED WELL	365	3	DON JUAN 13	14	2
FIND ONE WHERE NOTHING NAUGHTY CAN BE SHOWN	370	3	DON JUAN 13	27	6
AT A LONG DATE--TILL THEY CAN GET A FRESH ONE--	379	3	DON JUAN 13	45	6
UNLESS IT TEACHES ONE TO QUOTE AND CAVIL)	380	3	DON JUAN 13	47	8
THE WIND IS WINGED FROM ONE POINT OF HEAVEN	388	3	DON JUAN 13	63	2
WITH ALL HIS LAURELS GROWING UPON ONE TREE	401	3	DON JUAN 13	91	V7
BOTH WITS--ONE BORN SO AND THE OTHER BRED	402	3	DON JUAN 13	93	7
SOCIETY IS NOW ONE POLISH'D HORDE	402	3	DON JUAN 13	95	7
OR CRAMM'D TWELVE SHEETS INTO ONE LITTLE LETTER	406	3	DON JUAN 13	104	7
ONE SYSTEM EATS ANOTHER UP AND THIS	410	3	DON JUAN 14	1	5
YOU BIND YOURSELF AND CALL SOME MODE THE BEST ONE	411	3	DON JUAN 14	2	6
THE ONE IS WINNING AND THE OTHER LOSING	415	3	DON JUAN 14	12	8
AND THAT'S ONE CAUSE SHE MEETS WITH CONTRADICTION	416	3	DON JUAN 14	13	5
IS ONE OF WHICH THERE'S NO DESCRIPTION RECENT	416	3	DON JUAN 14	15	3
THAT NO ONE HAS SUCCEEDED IN DESCRIBING	418	3	DON JUAN 14	19	2
AND THAT THEIR BOOKS HAVE BUT ONE STYLE IN COMMON--	418	3	DON JUAN 14	19	7
I FOR ONE VENERATE A PETTICOAT--	421	3	DON JUAN 14	26	6
WHETHER A SKY'S OR TRADESMAN'S IS ALL ONE	423	3	DON JUAN 14	29	8
SOME NE'ER BELIEVED ONE HALF OF WHAT THEY HEARD	429	3	DON JUAN 14	44	5
WHO ONE MIGHT THINK WAS SOMETHING IN THE AFFAIR	430	3	DON JUAN 14	45	2
WHEN YOUR AFFAIRS COME ROUND ONE WAY OR T'OTHER	431	3	DON JUAN 14	48	7
TO ONE OF SEVENTY SUITORS HIS PROMOTION	434	3	DON JUAN 14	55	V6
TO BEAR A SON AND HEIR--AND ONE MISCARRIAGE	434	3	DON JUAN 14	56	6
ONE OF THOSE PRETTY PRECIOUS PLAGUES WHICH HAUNT	438	3	DON JUAN 14	63	3
FIND ONE EACH DAY OF THE DELIGHTFUL YEAR	438	3	DON JUAN 14	63	6
THOU HAST STRUCK ONE IMMENSE COLOSSUS DOWN	445	3	DON JUAN 14	82	3

ONE   (CONTINUED)

	PAGE	VOL	CANTO	STANZA	LN
OUR GENTLE ADELINE HAD ONE DEFECT--	446	3	DON JUAN 14	85	1
BECAUSE 'TIS FRAILER DOUBTLESS THAN A STANCH ONE	446	3	DON JUAN 14	85	6
THE WILD SENSATION UNTO HER A NEW ONE	449	3	DON JUAN 14	91	4
(I WILL NOT SAY IT WAS A FALSE OR TRUE ONE)	449	3	DON JUAN 14	91	6
A PRETTY NAME AS ONE WOULD WISH TO READ	458	3	DON JUAN 15	5	3
FOR ONE A SONGSTRESS WHO HATH NO DEFECT	471	3	DON JUAN 15	34	3
FOR T'OTHER ONE WHO PROMISES MUCH DUTY	471	3	DON JUAN 15	34	4
FOR THIS A LADY NO ONE CAN REJECT	471	3	DON JUAN 15	34	5
INDEED A CERTAIN FAIR AND FAIRY ONE	475	3	DON JUAN 15	43	3
IN ITS OWN STRENGTH--MOST STRANGE IN ONE SO YOUNG	477	3	DON JUAN 15	47	8
IT WAS NOT SCORN--WHICH COULD NOT LIGHT ON ONE	479	3	DON JUAN 15	54	3
THERE HAD NOT BEEN ONE SHAKESPEARE AND VOLTAIRE	481	3	DON JUAN 15	59	7
OF ONE OR BOTH OF WHOM HE SEEMS THE HEIR	481	3	DON JUAN 15	59	8
BUT I MUST CROWD ALL INTO ONE GRAND MESS	483	3	DON JUAN 15	64	1
WHICH NO ONE HEARS SO LOUDLY THOUGH IT RINGS	489	3	DON JUAN 15	76	6
THE BANQUETEERS HAD DROPPED OFF ONE BY ONE--	504	3	DON JUAN 16	8	3
THE BANQUETEERS HAD DROPPED OFF ONE BY ONE--	504	3	DON JUAN 16	8	3
ALMOST AN HAIR'S BREADTH TOO MUCH ON ONE SIDE	513	3	DON JUAN 16	29	8
BY ONE THREE TALENTS FOR THERE WERE NO LESS--	517	3	DON JUAN 16	39	6
AND EXPELLED THE FRIARS ONE FRIAR STILL	518	3	DON JUAN 16	L 1	7
AND THEN THE MID-DAY HAVING WORN TO ONE	527	3	DON JUAN 16	55	1
AND ONE ON TITHES WHICH SURE ARE DISCORD'S TORCHES	530	3	DON JUAN 16	60	4
ONE CAN'T TELL HOW IT E'ER GOT IN OR OUT	531	3	DON JUAN 16	62	2
WHICH TIED IN ONE FIRM KNOT WITHOUT CONFUSION	536	3	DON JUAN 16	74	V7
THAT ONE SCARCE KNEW AT WHAT TO MARVEL MOST	543	3	DON JUAN 16	90	6
NO ONE COULD ENVY HER DESERVED PROSPERITY	550	3	DON JUAN 16	102	6
SKIRMISH OF WITS O'ER THE DEPARTED ONE	552	3	DON JUAN 16	105	2
SURPRISE HAS THIS EFFECT--TO MAKE ONE DUMB	557	3	DON JUAN 16	115	2
JUAN PUT FORTH ONE ARM--ETERNAL POWERS	559	3	DON JUAN 16	120	1
YET ONE THING RATHER GOOD THE GRAVE HAD SPARED	560	3	DON JUAN 16	121	3
AND SO FOR ONE WILL I--AS WELL I MAY--	566	3	DON JUAN 17	10	4
FOR ONE WITHOUT--HAS TWO OR THREE WITHIN	567	3	DON JUAN 17	11	8
OF WHICH MOST MEN PARTAKE BUT NO ONE SINGS	568	3	DON JUAN 17	13	3
THE GUESTS DROPPED IN--THE LAST BUT ONE HER GRACE	568	3	DON JUAN 17	13	7
AS IF HE HAD COMBATED WITH MORE THAN ONE	568	3	DON JUAN 17	14	3

ONE'S

	PAGE	VOL	CANTO	STANZA	LN
'TIS SWEET TO WIN NO MATTER HOW ONE'S LAURELS	90	2	DON JUAN 1	126	1
BUT WHETHER 'TWAS THAT ONE'S OWN GUILT CONFOUNDS	118	2	DON JUAN 1	176	3
FLIES IN ONE'S FACE AND MAKES IT WEATHER-TOUGH	162	2	DON JUAN 2	11	6
TO SEE ONE'S NATIVE LAND RECEDING THROUGH	163	2	DON JUAN 2	12	2
A KIND OF SHOCK THAT SETS ONE'S HEART AJAR	164	2	DON JUAN 2	14	6
WHICH HASTENS AS PHYSICIANS SAY ONE'S FATE	230	2	DON JUAN 2	140	4
OR BY ONE'S EARLY VALET'S CURSED KNOCK	237	2	DON JUAN 2	152	5
THEY SMILE SO WHEN ONE'S RIGHT AND WHEN ONE'S WRONG	242	2	DON JUAN 2	164	5
THEY SMILE SO WHEN ONE'S RIGHT AND WHEN ONE'S WRONG	242	2	DON JUAN 2	164	5
OUR DAYS AND PUT ONE'S SERVANTS INTO MOURNING	278	2	DON JUAN 3	7	8
ONE'S TURNED HALF MUSSULMAN AND ONE A MAID	459	2	DON JUAN 5	83	7
TO BREAK THE RULES BY BRINGING ONE'S OWN BRIDE	103	3	DON JUAN 7	71	5
ONE'S HIP HE SLASHED AND SPLIT THE OTHER'S SHOULDER	158	3	DON JUAN 8	94	1
OF ABSENCE LAY ONE'S OLD RESENTMENTS LEVEL	257	3	DON JUAN 10	66	7
OH JOB YOU HAD TWO FRIENDS ONE'S QUITE ENOUGH	431	3	DON JUAN 14	48	1
A RUSS OR TURK--THE ONE'S AS GOOD AS T'OTHER	474	3	DON JUAN 15	42	8

ONES

	PAGE	VOL	CANTO	STANZA	LN
FOR WHAT IS STEALING YOUNG ONES FEW OR MANY	487	2	DON JUAN 5	132	7
I'VE KNOWN SOME ODD ONES WHICH SEEMED REALLY PLANNED	45	3	DON JUAN 6	78	5
IN HIS REPLIES SHE PUZZLED HIM FOR FRESH ONES	56	3	DON JUAN 6	101	5
TO FOREIGNER OR NATIVE SAVE SOME SILLY ONES	263	3	DON JUAN 10	77	6
THE MARRIED ONES TO SAVE THE VIRGINS TROUBLE	342	3	DON JUAN 12	58	8

ONESTI'S

	PAGE	VOL	CANTO	STANZA	LN
THE SPECTRE HUNTSMAN OF ONESTI'S LINE	337	2	DON JUAN 3	106	5

ON'T

	PAGE	VOL	CANTO	STANZA	LN
AND NOW I THINK ON'T MI VIEN IN MENTE	56	2	DON JUAN 1	62	6
WHAT WILL BECOME ON'T--I'M IN SUCH A FRIGHT	115	2	DON JUAN 1	171	3
I RATHER DOUBT AND I WOULD FAIN SAY FIE ON'T	138	3	DON JUAN 8	51	6
WE'LL DO OUR BEST TO MAKE THE BEST ON'T--MARCH	468	3	DON JUAN 15	27	1
WOULD THAT I WERE LESS BILIOUS--BUT OH FIE ON'T	566	3	DON JUAN 17	10	5

ONWARD

	PAGE	VOL	CANTO	STANZA	LN
SUCH AS LIT ONWARD TO THE GOLDEN FLEECE	303	2	DON JUAN 3	55	3
HE LED THEM ONWARD FIRST THROUGH A LOW THICKET	433	2	DON JUAN 5	41	3
BABA LED JUAN ONWARD ROOM BY ROOM	460	2	DON JUAN 5	85	2
WITH THE YORK MAIL--BUT ONWARD AS WE ROLL	263	3	DON JUAN 10	78	7
A SHADOW WHICH THE ONWARD SOUL BEHIND THROWS	414	3	DON JUAN 14	8	6

ONWARDS

	PAGE	VOL	CANTO	STANZA	LN
STILL SET THEM ONWARDS TO THE WELCOME SHORE	209	2	DON JUAN 2	101	2
KEPT ALWAYS PUSHING ONWARDS TO THE GLACIS	130	3	DON JUAN 8	34	V8
FROM THENCE HE WAS DRAWN ONWARDS TO COLOGNE	255	3	DON JUAN 10	62	5
TO MARSHALL ONWARDS TO THE DELPHIAN HEIGHT	467	3	DON JUAN 15	25	V5

OOZED

	PAGE	VOL	CANTO	STANZA	LN
AS THROUGH HIS PALMS BOB ACRES' VALOUR OOZED	493	2	DON JUAN 5	142	1

OOZING

	PAGE	VOL	CANTO	STANZA	LN
AND THE WAVES OOZING THROUGH THE PORT-HOLE MADE	169	2	DON JUAN 2	25	7

OPE

	PAGE	VOL	CANTO	STANZA	LN
TO OPE THIS DOOR WHICH THEY COULD REALLY DO	463	2	DON JUAN 5	89	3
THAT JUST AS HER YOUNG LIP BEGAN TO OPE	44	3	DON JUAN 6	77	5

OPEN

	PAGE	VOL	CANTO	STANZA	LN
AND THEREFORE I SHALL OPEN WITH A LINE	25	2	DON JUAN 1	7	5
PERHAPS TO OPEN DON ALFONSO'S EYES	75	2	DON JUAN 1	101	7
TO OPEN ALL ITSELF WITHOUT THE POWER	82	2	DON JUAN 1	114	3

571

```
                                                              PAGE VOL      CANTO STANZA LN

OPEN   (CONTINUED)
        THE DOOR IS OPEN--YOU MAY YET SLIP THROUGH  . . . . .  121  2 DON JUAN  1    182   1
        'TIS THUS WITH PEOPLE IN AN OPEN BOAT . . . . . . .    191  2 DON JUAN  2     66   1
        OF ROCKS BEWITCH'D THAT OPEN TO THE KNOCKERS . . . .   293  2 DON JUAN  3     34   6
        ALL HAD BEEN OPEN HEART AND OPEN HOUSE  . . . . . .    295  2 DON JUAN  3     39  V7
        ALL HAD BEEN OPEN HEART AND OPEN HOUSE  . . . . . .    295  2 DON JUAN  3     39  V7
        THE SECOND HAD HIS CHEEK LAID OPEN BUT  . . . . . .    370  2 DON JUAN  4     49   1
        AN OPEN BROW A LITTLE MARKED WITH CARE  . . . . . .    416  2 DON JUAN  5     11   5
        IT SEEMED HOWEVER BUT TO OPEN ON  . . . . . . .        449  2 DON JUAN  5     65   1
        BUT FROM THE RIVER THE TOWN'S OPEN QUITE  . . . . .     73  3 DON JUAN  7     13   1
        THE LETTER OPEN WITH AN AIR WHICH POSED  . . . . .     211  3 DON JUAN  9     58   4
        KEPT THE PLACE OPEN FOR THEIR EMULATION . . . . . .    248  3 DON JUAN 10     48   3
        FOR IF THE POLE'S NOT OPEN BUT ALL FROST  . . . . .    376  3 DON JUAN 13     39   7
        THE GRASS MY TABLE-CLOTH IN OPEN AIR  . . . . . .      488  3 DON JUAN 15     73   6
        HIS CHAMBER DOOR WIDE OPEN--AND WENT FORTH  . . . .    508  3 DON JUAN 16     17   2
        THOUGH NOT EXACTLY WHAT'S CALLED OPEN HOUSE . . . .    534  3 DON JUAN 16     68   8
        WERE HIS EYES OPEN--YES AND HIS MOUTH TOO . . . . .    557  3 DON JUAN 16    115   1
        HIS EYES WERE OPEN AND (AS WAS BEFORE . . . . . .     557  3 DON JUAN 16    115   7
OPEN'D
        WHICH PYE BEING OPEN'D THEY BEGAN TO SING . . . . .     10  2 DON JUAN  D      2   1
        AND OPEN'D CERTAIN TRUNKS OF BOOKS AND LETTERS . . .    36  2 DON JUAN  1     28   2
        THEY OPEN'D WINDOWS GAZING IF THE GROUND  . . . . .    100  2 DON JUAN  1    144   3
        HIS EYES HE OPEN'D SHUT AGAIN UNCLOSED  . . . . . .    215  2 DON JUAN  2    112   1
        AND WHEN AT LAST HE OPEN'D HIS BLACK EYES . . . . .    225  2 DON JUAN  2    131   4
        IT OPEN'D HALF THE TURNPIKE-GATES TO HEAVEN-- . . .    225  2 DON JUAN  2    131   7
OPENED
        OF A SMALL IRON DOOR 'TWAS OPENED AND . . . . . .     433  2 DON JUAN  5     41   2
        WHICH OPENED ON THEIR VIEW AND O'ER THE FRONT . . .    436  2 DON JUAN  5     46   2
        AND KNOCKING AT THE GATE 'TWAS OPENED WIDE  . . . .    440  2 DON JUAN  5     51   6
        OPENED THE GATE CALLED KILIA TO THE GROUPS  . . . .    148  3 DON JUAN  8     73   5
        BUT ELSE UNHURT SHE OPENED HER LARGE EYES . . . . .    159  3 DON JUAN  8     95   7
        STATED) HIS MOUTH WHAT OPENED NEXT--THE DOOR  . . .    557  3 DON JUAN 16    115   8
        IT OPENED WITH A MOST INFERNAL CREAK  . . . . . .     557  3 DON JUAN 16    116   1
OPENER
        LOVE THAT GREAT OPENER OF THE HEART AND ALL  . . . .   222  3 DON JUAN  9     80   2
        AN ERRING WOMAN FINDS AN OPENER DOOR  . . . . . .     352  3 DON JUAN 12     79   6
OPENING
        AND LOOK'D EXTREMELY AT THE OPENING DOOR  . . . . .     63  2 DON JUAN  1     76   3
        INTO THE OPENING BUT ALL SUCH INGREDIENTS . . . . .    171  2 DON JUAN  2     29   1
        AND LEAVE LIKE OPENING HELL UPON THE MIND . . . . .    227  2 DON JUAN  2    134  V7
        AND OPENING HER PIANO GAN TO PLAY . . . . . .         517  3 DON JUAN 16     38  V7
OPENS
        AGAIN IT OPENS IT CAN BE NO OTHER . . . . . .          63  2 DON JUAN  1     76   6
        TILL THE EYE CHEATED OPENS THICK WITH TEARS . . . .    227  2 DON JUAN  2    134   8
        WHICH OPENS TO THE THOUSAND HAPPY FEW . . . . . .      302  3 DON JUAN 11     67   7
OPERA
        TO WHOM THE OPERA IS BY NO MEANS NEW  . . . . . .      392  2 DON JUAN  4     88   4
        SOME LAID ASIDE LIKE AN OLD OPERA HAT . . . . . .      308  3 DON JUAN 11     79   3
OPERAS
        TO PLAYS IN FIVE AND OPERAS IN THREE ACTS . . . . .    138  2 DON JUAN  1    203   4
OPERA-SCENE
        NEW PAINTED OR A PRETTY OPERA-SCENE . . . . . .       436  2 DON JUAN  5     46   8
OPERATIONS
        EXPECTANT OF THE GHOST'S FRESH OPERATIONS . . . . .    555  3 DON JUAN 16    111   8
OPHELIA
        THE QUEEN OF DENMARK FOR OPHELIA BROUGHT  . . . . .    165  2 DON JUAN  2     17   5
OPIATE
        OF FRIENDS--AND OPIATE DRAUGHTS--THERE'S LOVE AND WINE . 343  2 DON JUAN  3   V 98   2
        OR LIKE AN OPIATE WHICH BRINGS TROUBLED REST  . . .    505  3 DON JUAN 16     10   1
        AND THOUGH IT WAS NO OPIATE SLUMBER CREPT . . . . .    512  3 DON JUAN 16     27   7
OPINE
        AND YET 'TIS NOT AFFECTED I OPINE . . . . . .         415  3 DON JUAN 14     12   6
        WILL BE DISCUSS'D HEREAFTER I OPINE . . . . . .       453  3 DON JUAN 14     97   3
OPINION
        A GREAT OPINION OF HER OWN GOOD QUALITIES  . . . . .    32  2 DON JUAN  1     20   2
        ALTHOUGH MY OPINION MAY REQUIRE APOLOGY . . . . . .    281  2 DON JUAN  3     11   3
        I'LL PROVE THAT SUCH THE OPINION OF THE CRITIC IS . .  342  2 DON JUAN  3    111   7
        AND WISH'D THAT OTHERS HELD THE SAME OPINION . . . .   345  2 DON JUAN  4      3   2
        OF HIS OPINION WHEN I SEE CAST DOWN  . . . . . .      142  2 DON JUAN  8     60   4
        MERIDIAN-BORN TO BLOOM IN  THIS OPINION . . . . . .    246  3 DON JUAN 10     44   2
        I AM QUITE OF THEIR OPINION--AND AM HOARDING  . . .    270  3 DON JUAN 11      4  V5
        SHE HAD A GOOD OPINION OF ADVICE  . . . . . .         469  3 DON JUAN 15     29   1
OPINION'S
        AND HALF OF THAT OPINION'S ALSO MINE  . . . . . .     485  2 DON JUAN  5    129   8
OPINIONS
        OF MAN'S OPINIONS FORMS THEIR EDUCATION . . . . . .    354  3 DON JUAN 12     83  V6
        OF OTHERS WITH HER OWN OPINIONS STATED-- . . . . .     478  3 DON JUAN 15     50   7
        OPINIONS TWO WHICH AT FIRST SIGHT MAY LOOK  . . . .    494  3 DON JUAN 15     87   3
        OPINIONS WEAR OUT IN SOME THOUSAND YEARS . . . . .     496  3 DON JUAN 15     90   7
OPIUM
        AN OPIUM DREAM OF TOO MUCH YOUTH AND READING . . . .   354  2 DON JUAN  4     19   2
OPPORTUNE
        ME ALSO SINCE THE TIME SO OPPORTUNE IS-- . . . . .     103  2 DON JUAN  1    150   6
        SEEING ARRIVE AN AID SO OPPORTUNE . . . . . .         140  3 DON JUAN  8     56   2
OPPORTUNITIES
        AND LET FEW OPPORTUNITIES ESCAPE  . . . . . .          32  2 DON JUAN  1     20   7
OPPORTUNITY
        WITH HIS YOUNG WIFE--A TIME AND OPPORTUNITY . . . . .  158  2 DON JUAN  2      3   8
        NEVER HAD MORTAL MAN SUCH OPPORTUNITY  . . . . . .    187  3 DON JUAN  9      9   1
```

OPPORTUNITY   (CONTINUED)

PAGE VOL   CANTO STANZA LN

THOUGHT SUCH AN OPPORTUNITY AS THIS IS . . . . 293 3 DON JUAN 11   49   5
SO GOOD AN OPPORTUNITY NO DOUBT-- . . . . 332 3 DON JUAN 12   35   4
OPPOSE
NOT THAT REMORSE DID NOT OPPOSE TEMPTATION . . . . . 84 2 DON JUAN 1   117   6
AS IF THE CORN-SHEAF SHOULD OPPOSE THE SICKLE . . . . 419 2 DON JUAN 5   17   6
OPPOSED
THAT FOR SO LONG OPPOSED THIS GAMING EVIL . . . . . 102 2 DON JUAN 1   148   V4
IN WHICH HE WAS OPPOSED BY YOUNG AND HOARY . . . . . . 83 3 DON JUAN 7   35   5
OPPOSING
OPPOSING SINGLY THE UNITED STRONG . . . . 363 3 DON JUAN 13   10   3
OPPOSITE
WHAT OPPOSITE DISCOVERIES WE HAVE SEEN . . . . . . 91 2 DON JUAN 1   129   1
AND SAW THE SUN SET OPPOSITE THE MOON . . . . 249 2 DON JUAN 2   176   8
OR IF FORESTALLED GET OPPOSITE AND OGLE-- . . . . . 304 3 DON JUAN 11   72   2
OPPOSITES
TWIN OPPOSITES THE SECOND IS THE BEST . . . . 494 3 DON JUAN 15   87   4
OPPOSITION
THAT OPPOSITION ONLY MORE ATTACHES-- . . . . 439 3 DON JUAN 14   67   7
WERE MORE--BUT I WAS BORN FOR OPPOSITION . . . . . . 466 3 DON JUAN 15   22   8
OPPRESSED
WHEN THEY BEHOLD THE BRAVE OPPRESSED WITH ODDS . . . . 164 3 DON JUAN 8   106   2
OPPRESSION
FROM HIS OWN BRAIN'S OPPRESSION WHILE IT REELS . . . . 427 2 DON JUAN 5   31   6
WHO DID NOT QUIT ME WHEN OPPRESSION TROD . . . . . . 452 3 DON JUAN 14   96   5
OPPRESSIVE
THAN SOLITARY PRIDE'S OPPRESSIVE WEIGHT . . . . . . 367 3 DON JUAN 13   19   6
OPPREST
SELL FLESH AND BLOOD WHEN DINNER HAS OPPREST ONE . . . 426 2 DON JUAN 5   30   6
OPTICS
COULD TURN THEIR OPTICS TO THE TEXT AND PRAY . . . . 47 2 DON JUAN 1   46   6
WITH SHRINKING SERPENT OPTICS ON HIM STARED . . . . 463 2 DON JUAN 5   90   6
TOO WISE TO LOOK THROUGH OPTICS BLACK OR BLUE)-- . . . 218 3 DON JUAN 9   71   8
OPTIM
SODAE-SULPHAT SIX DRAMS HALF DRAM MANNAE OPTIM . . . 244 3 DON JUAN 10   41   2
OPTION
HAD NOT THE FLESH MADE SOME SMALL OPTION . . . . . . 467 3 DON JUAN 15   24   V4
ORACLE
OF NATURE'S ORACLE--FIRST LOVE--THAT ALL . . . . . 256 2 DON JUAN 2   189   7
ORANGE
THE ORANGE AND POMEGRANATE NODDING O'ER . . . . . 291 2 DON JUAN 3   31   7
OF RAISIN ORANGE AND POMEGRANATE JUICE . . . . . 307 2 DON JUAN 3   62   7
HER ORANGE SILK FULL TURKISH TROWSERS FURL'D . . . . 312 2 DON JUAN 3   72   7
THROUGH ORANGE BOWERS AND JASMINE AND SO FORTH . . . . 434 2 DON JUAN 5   42   2
ORANGES
FAMOUS FOR ORANGES AND WOMEN--HE . . . . 25 2 DON JUAN 1   8   2
GLACIERS VOLCANOS ORANGES AND ICES . . . . 262 3 DON JUAN 10   76   8
ORATION
CLOSED THE ORATION OF THE TRUSTY MAID . . . . . 116 2 DON JUAN 1   173   2
TO ANSWER IN A VERY CLEAR ORATION . . . . 43 3 DON JUAN 6   74   5
ORATOR
AN ORATOR OF SUCH SET TRASH OF PHRASE . . . . . . 17 2 DON JUAN D   13   1
A SORT OF ORATOR BY SUFFERANCE . . . . 152 2 DON JUAN 1 V 3   5
LAWYER BY TRADE--AND ORATOR BY CHANCE . . . . . 152 2 DON JUAN 1 V 3   V5
BUT BEING NO ORATOR AS BRUTUS IS . . . . 43 3 DON JUAN 6   74   7
AN ORATOR THE LATEST OF THE SESSION . . . . . . 400 3 DON JUAN 13   90   2
ORATORS
STATESMEN CHIEFS ORATORS QUEENS PATRIOTS KINGS . . . . 306 3 DON JUAN 11   76   7
MOST ORATORS BUT VERY FEW FINANCIERS . . . . . 547 3 DON JUAN 16   98   5
ORATORY
AND LOST VIRGINITY OF ORATORY . . . . . . 401 3 DON JUAN 13   91   2
ORB
WITH HIS BROAD BRIGHT AND DROPPING ORB WERE GONE . . . 355 2 DON JUAN 4   22   4
IT HAPPENED LUCKILY THE CHASTE ORB SHONE . . . . 506 3 DON JUAN 16   13   3
ORBIT
HOW EARTH COULD ROUND THE SOLAR ORBIT RUN . . . . . 565 3 DON JUAN 17   8   3
ORBS
OF CLOSING 'GAINST THE LIGHT THEIR ORBS OF VISION . . . 50 3 DON JUAN 6   88   5
ORDAINED
OUR GAY RUSS SPANIARD WAS ORDAINED TO SHINE . . . . 383 3 DON JUAN 13   53   4
ORDEAL
I REALLY THINK YET JUAN'S THEN ORDEAL . . . . . 396 2 DON JUAN 4   96   7
ORDER
AN ORDER SOMEWHAT SULLENLY OBEY'D . . . . . 116 2 DON JUAN 1   173   4
HAD A LARGE ORDER FROM THE DEY OF TRIPOLI . . . . . 284 2 DON JUAN 3   16   8
SHE WOULD REVOKE THE ORDER HE HAD HEARD . . . . . 62 3 DON JUAN 6   113   8
WERE BRISKLY FIRED AND ANSWERED IN DUE ORDER . . . . 85 3 DON JUAN 7   38   8
THEIR CHIEFS TO ORDER--WERE ALL CUT TO PIECES . . . . 149 3 DON JUAN 8   74   8
SAFETY THAN HIS NEW ORDER OF SAINT VLADIMIR . . . . 182 3 DON JUAN 8   140   8
AN ORDER FROM HER MAJESTY CONSIGNED . . . . . 224 3 DON JUAN 9   84   1
ORDER'D
ACHILLES ORDER'D DINNER FOR NEW COMERS . . . . . . 221 2 DON JUAN 2   123   8
ORDERED
AS IF SHE RATHER ORDERED THAN WAS GRANTING-- . . . . 474 2 DON JUAN 5   109   8
SHE ORDERED HIM DIRECTLY TO BE BOUGHT . . . . . 477 2 DON JUAN 5   114   3
THE COLUMN ORDERED ON THE ASSAULT SCARCE PASSED . . . 115 3 DON JUAN 8   7   1
SO ORDERED IT AMIDST THESE SULPHURY REVELS . . . . 135 3 DON JUAN 8   44   6
ORDERING
IN ORDERING MATTERS AFTER HIS OWN BENT . . . . . 85 3 DON JUAN 7   38   3
SURVEYING DRILLING ORDERING JESTING PONDERING . . . . 95 3 DON JUAN 7   55   2

573

		PAGE	VOL		CANTO	STANZA	LN
ORDERLY							
(HERE HE CALLED UP A POLISH ORDERLY)		100	3	DON JUAN	7	66	4
QUITE ORDERLY AS IF UPON PARADE		119	3	DON JUAN	8	15	8
ORDERS							
WITH ORDERS TO THE PEOPLE TO CAREEN		286	2	DON JUAN	3	20	6
TO SEE HIS ORDERS DONE TOO OUT OF HAND--		299	2	DON JUAN	3	47	3
THEY STOWED HIM WITH STRICT ORDERS TO THE WATCHES		371	2	DON JUAN	4	50	8
TILL FURTHER ORDERS SHOULD HIS DOOM ASSIGN		371	2	DON JUAN	4	50	V4
YOUR ORDERS EVEN IN THEIR SEVEREST SENSE		62	3	DON JUAN	6	114	4
UNDER THE ORDERS OF THE GENERAL LASCY		130	3	DON JUAN	8	34	3
HIS ORDERS ALSO TO RECEIVE HIS PENSIONS		137	3	DON JUAN	8	49	7
AND ORDERS AND ON ALL THAT HE HAD DONE--		197	3	DON JUAN	9	30	5
DAMSELS GREAT WEALTH AND ILLUSTRIOUS ORDERS		235	3	DON JUAN	10	21	V7
DAMSELS AND RUBLES AND CHIVALRIC ORDERS		235	3	DON JUAN	10	21	V7
THE AIR OF 'TWAS A FRIAR OF ORDERS GREY		517	3	DON JUAN	16	38	8
ORDINATION							
UPON THE FOE THE SECOND'S ORDINATION		91	3	DON JUAN	7	50	5
ORDURE							
WHILE WEEDS AND ORDURE RANKLE ROUND THE BASE		400	2	DON JUAN	4	103	8
ORE							
THE PUREST ORE INCLOSED THE WHITEST SKIN		312	2	DON JUAN	3	71	7
ON THAT SWEET ORE WHICH EVERYBODY NURSES		264	3	DON JUAN	10	79	6
POSSESS'D THE ORE OF WHICH MERE HOPES ALLURE		319	3	DON JUAN	12	8	3
EVEN WITH THE VERY ORE WHICH MAKES THEM BASE		320	3	DON JUAN	12	10	6
WEIGH NOT THE THIN ORE WHERE THEIR VISAGE SHINES		321	3	DON JUAN	12	12	4
O'REILLY							
IS IT FOR THIS THAT GENERAL COUNT O'REILLY		102	2	DON JUAN	1	148	7
ORGAN							
BY A DISTANT ORGAN DOUBTING IF HE BE		237	2	DON JUAN	2	152	2
ORIENT							
OCCUR IN ORIENT PALACES AND EVEN		465	2	DON JUAN	5	94	2
THE LITTLE LEILA WITH HER ORIENT EYES		328	3	DON JUAN	12	27	1
ORIENTAL							
THE DARKNESS OF HER ORIENTAL EYE		52	2	DON JUAN	1	56	1
THESE ORIENTAL WRITINGS ON THE WALL		308	2	DON JUAN	3	65	1
OF ORIENTAL PLANTS ET CETERA		434	2	DON JUAN	5	42	5
WITH MORE THAN ORIENTAL SCRUPULOSITY		496	2	DON JUAN	5	148	2
WITH BUILDINGS IN THE ORIENTAL TASTE		70	3	DON JUAN	7	9	3
THOUGH LITTLE VERSED IN FEELINGS ORIENTAL		105	3	DON JUAN	7	75	2
ORIGIN							
ACCORDED WITH HER MOORISH ORIGIN		52	2	DON JUAN	1	56	2
THE THIRD THE USUAL ORIGIN OF EVIL		271	3	DON JUAN	11	6	4
ORIGINAL							
TO HAVE WHEN THE ORIGINAL IS DUST		146	2	DON JUAN	1	218	7
OTHERS THAT SOME ORIGINAL SHAPE OR FORM		388	3	DON JUAN	13	64	1
TO READ DON QUIXOTE IN THE ORIGINAL		453	3	DON JUAN	14	98	2
A SPECIAL TITIAN WARRANTED ORIGINAL		528	3	DON JUAN	16	56	2
ORNAMENT							
WHICH FORM AN ORNAMENT BUT NO MORE PART		13	3	DON JUAN	6	14	7
WHERE MANY A GOTHIC ORNAMENT REMAINED		507	3	DON JUAN	16	16	6
ORNAMENTED							
WAS ORNAMENTED IN A SORT OF WAY		47	2	DON JUAN	1	46	2
ORNAMENTS							
HAD NOT SO MANY ORNAMENTS TO STRIKE		221	2	DON JUAN	2	122	3
THE ORNAMENTS OF LEVEES AND A ROUT		404	2	DON JUAN	4	110	V8
ORPHAN							
THE MOSLEM ORPHAN WENT WITH HER PROTECTOR		182	3	DON JUAN	8	141	1
HE LOVED THE INFANT ORPHAN HE HAD SAVED		251	3	DON JUAN	10	55	2
IN BRIEF THE LITTLE ORPHAN OF THE EAST		338	3	DON JUAN	12	48	7
RICH NOBLE BUT AN ORPHAN LEFT AN ONLY		475	3	DON JUAN	15	44	1
ORPHAN'S							
TO UNDERTAKE THE ORPHAN'S EDUCATION		330	3	DON JUAN	12	30	3
ORPHANS							
THE WORLD IS FULL OF ORPHANS FIRSTLY THOSE		562	3	DON JUAN	17	1	1
WHICH LEAVES THEM ORPHANS OF THE HEART NO LESS		562	3	DON JUAN	17	1	8
WHICH LEAVES THEM ORPHANS OF THE HEART NO LESS		563	3	DON JUAN	17	2	8
OF ORPHANS PAINTS AT ONCE A PARISH SCHOOL		563	3	DON JUAN	17	3	3
THE WEALTHIEST ORPHANS ARE TO BE MORE PITIED		563	3	DON JUAN	17	3	8
ORPHEUS							
IF NOT LIKE ORPHEUS QUITE WHEN GREECE WAS YOUNG		326	2	DON JUAN	3	87	3
ORTHODOX							
OF ILLNESS I GROW MUCH MORE ORTHODOX		270	3	DON JUAN	11	5	8
ORTHOGRAPHY							
(I DON'T MUCH PIQUE MYSELF UPON ORTHOGRAPHY		149	3	DON JUAN	8	74	2
OSSIAN							
TILL WHAT IS CALL'D IN OSSIAN THE FIFTH DUAN		410	2	DON JUAN	4	117	8
OSTENTATION							
WITH EVERY KINDNESS SHORT OF OSTENTATION		34	3	DON JUAN	6	57	3
OSTLER							
THE OSTLER PLEADS FOR A SMALL REMINISCENCE		379	3	DON JUAN	13	46	8
O'TABBEY							
MISS BOMBAZEEN MISS MACKSTAY MISS O'TABBEY		396	3	DON JUAN	13	79	5
OTHERS'							
TO OTHERS' SHARE LET FEMALE ERRORS FALL		29	2	DON JUAN	1	16	7
AND THEN THEY STARED EACH OTHERS' FACES ROUND		100	2	DON JUAN	1	144	5
OF OTHERS' FEELING BUT THEY ARE SUCH LIARS		326	2	DON JUAN	3	87	7
BETWEEN HIS OWN AND OTHERS' INTELLECT		330	2	DON JUAN	3	95	2
HIS KNIGHTS WITH LOTTING OTHERS' PROPERTIES		242	3	DON JUAN	10	35	7
OTHERWISE							
OR CAN'T DO OTHERWISE THAN LIE BUT DO IT		285	3	DON JUAN	11	36	7
OF CHANGE AND HOW SHOULD THIS BE OTHERWISE		451	3	DON JUAN	14	94	2

OTTOMAN

		PAGE	VOL		CANTO	STANZA	LN
THE ASIAN POMP OF OTTOMAN PARADE	. . . .	440	2 DON JUAN	5	51	8
A LOW SOFT OTTOMAN) AND BLACK DESPAIR	. . . . . .	60	3 DON JUAN	6	108	5
AND ONE HAND O'ER THE OTTOMAN LAY DROOPING	. . . .	60	3 DON JUAN	6	109	3

OU
| AND GOD KNOWS WHO BESIDES IN AU AND OU | . . . | 137 | 3 DON JUAN | 8 | 49 | 2 |

OUGHT
SO LET US BE ACQUAINTED AS WE OUGHT	. .	417	2 DON JUAN	5	13	6
AND IS EXTINGUISHED SOONER THAN SHE OUGHT	. . . .	83	3 DON JUAN	7	34	6
STOPPED FOR A MINUTE AS PERHAPS HE OUGHT	. . . .	126	3 DON JUAN	8	29	4
AND OUGHT TO GO BY QUITE ANOTHER NAME	. . . .	323	3 DON JUAN	12	15	8
NOT AS THEY OUGHT TO BE FOR I AVOW	. . . .	335	3 DON JUAN	12	40	3
PRESERVE OF BORES WHO OUGHT TO BE MADE GAME	. . .	395	3 DON JUAN	13	78	8
THE MONDE EXACTLY AS THEY OUGHT TO PAINT	. . . .	418	3 DON JUAN	14	19	3
THE MORE'S THE REASON WHY YOU OUGHT TO STAY	. . .	459	3 DON JUAN	15	9	4
WHO LOOK UPON THEM AS THEY OUGHT TO DO	. . . .	479	3 DON JUAN	15	53	8
WHICH PIQUES A PREUX CHEVALIER--AS IT OUGHT	. . .	490	3 DON JUAN	15	77	2
AND WHETHER IT OUGHT NOT TO BE DISCLOSED	. . . .	512	3 DON JUAN	16	28	3
UPON HER FRIENDS AS EVERYBODY OUGHT	. . . .	524	3 DON JUAN	16	47	4

OUNCE
| AQ FERVENT OUNCE AND A HALF TWO DRAMS TINCT SENNAE | . . | 244 | 3 DON JUAN | 10 | 41 | 3 |

OUR
I'LL THEREFORE TAKE OUR ANCIENT FRIEND DON JUAN	. . . .	21	2 DON JUAN	1	1	6
'TIS WITH OUR HERO QUIETLY INURN'D	. . . .	23	2 DON JUAN	1	4	4
THAN JOSE WHO BEGOT OUR HERO WHO	. . . .	26	2 DON JUAN	1	9	7
WHERE OUR FIRST PARENTS NEVER LEARN'D TO KISS	. . .	30	2 DON JUAN	1	18	3
IS PHILOSOPHIC IN OUR FORMER FRIENDS	. . . .	37	2 DON JUAN	1	30	2
THE MORE SO IN OBTAINING OUR OWN ENDS	. . . .	37	2 DON JUAN	1	30	4
AND IF OUR QUARRELS SHOULD RIP UP OLD STORIES	. . .	37	2 DON JUAN	1	31	1
BESIDES THEIR RESURRECTION AIDS OUR GLORIES	. . .	37	2 DON JUAN	1	31	5
IN CASE OUR LORD THE KING SHOULD GO TO WAR AGAIN	. .	42	2 DON JUAN	1	38	6
WHO CANNOT LEAVE ALONE OUR HELPLESS CLAY	. . . .	56	2 DON JUAN	1	63	3
OUR COMING AND LOOK BRIGHTER WHEN WE COME	. . . .	88	2 DON JUAN	1	123	4
PURPLE AND GUSHING SWEET ARE OUR ESCAPES	. . . .	88	2 DON JUAN	1	124	3
TO STRIFE 'TIS SOMETIMES SWEET TO HAVE OUR QUARRELS	. .	90	2 DON JUAN	1	126	3
THEIR REAL LUES OR OUR PSEUDO-SYPHILIS	. . . .	92	2 DON JUAN	1	131	8
AND SO GOOD NIGHT--RETURN WE TO OUR STORY	. . . .	94	2 DON JUAN	1	134	2
SO MUCH AS WHEN WE CALL OUR OLD DEBTS IN	. . . .	113	2 DON JUAN	1	167	6
OUR COUNSEL--(JUAN MIND YOU MUST NOT SLEEP)	. . .	115	2 DON JUAN	1	172	8
TO LIFT OUR FATAL LOVE TO GOD FROM MAN	. . . .	131	2 DON JUAN	1	194	V8
HIVED IN OUR BOSOMS LIKE THE BAG O' THE BEE	. . .	144	2 DON JUAN	1	214	5
AND LIVE AND DIE MAKE LOVE AND PAY OUR TAXES	. . .	159	2 DON JUAN	2	4	3
AND AS THE VEERING WIND SHIFTS SHIFT OUR SAILS	. . .	159	2 DON JUAN	2	4	4
THE PRIEST INSTRUCTS AND SO OUR LIFE EXHALES	. . .	159	2 DON JUAN	2	4	6
BUT TO OUR TALE THE DONNA INEZ SENT	. . . .	161	2 DON JUAN	2	8	1
WE ENTER ON OUR NAUTICAL EXISTENCE	. . . .	163	2 DON JUAN	2	12	8
THAT IS TILL DEEPER GRIEFS CONGEAL OUR TEARS	. . .	164	2 DON JUAN	2	15	8
LIKE A MERE LOG AND BAFFLED OUR INTENT	. . . .	173	2 DON JUAN	2	32	4
AS IF OLD OCEAN BAFFLED OUR INTENT	. . . .	173	2 DON JUAN	2	32	V4
OUR JUAN WHO WITH SENSE BEYOND HIS YEARS	. . . .	174	2 DON JUAN	2	35	2
OF ALL OUR PUMPS--A WRECK COMPLETE SHE ROLL'D	. . .	178	2 DON JUAN	2	42	6
AND THUS IT WAS WITH THIS OUR HAPLESS CREW	. . . .	192	2 DON JUAN	2	68	1
'TIS SURELY FAIR TO DINE UPON OUR FRIENDS	. . . .	200	2 DON JUAN	2	83	6
OUR SHIPWRECK'D SEAMEN THOUGHT IT A GOOD OMEN--	. . .	205	2 DON JUAN	2	93	1
BECAUSE THE TACKLE OF OUR SHATTER'D BARK	. . . .	206	2 DON JUAN	2	95	3
BUT WITH OUR DAMSEL THIS WAS NOT THE CASE	. . . .	220	2 DON JUAN	2	121	1
UNWELCOME VISIONS OF OUR FORMER YEARS	. . . .	227	2 DON JUAN	2	134	7
FROM WHICH OUR MODERN MORALS RIGHTLY SHRINKING	. . .	238	2 DON JUAN	2	155	3
CERES IS COMMISSARY TO OUR BELLIES	. . . .	246	2 DON JUAN	2	170	V3
EXCEPTING OUR FIRST PARENTS SUCH A PAIR	. . . .	258	2 DON JUAN	2	193	3
IN SHORT IT IS THE USE OF OUR OWN EYES	. . . .	269	2 DON JUAN	2	212	6
WHICH MAKE THE ENGLISH CLIMATE OF OUR YEARS	. . .	270	2 DON JUAN	2	214	8
WHICH RAIN DOWN ON THE DUST OF OUR YEARS	. . . .	270	2 DON JUAN	2	214	V8
ARE LAID WITHIN OUR BOSOMS BUT TO PERISH	. . . .	275	2 DON JUAN	3	2	8
OUR DAYS AND PUT ONE'S SERVANTS INTO MOURNING	. . .	278	2 DON JUAN	3	7	8
AND BRING OUR HEARTS BACK TO THEIR STARTING-POST	. .	286	2 DON JUAN	3	21	8
LAMBRO OUR SEA-SOLICITOR WHO HAD	. . . .	289	2 DON JUAN	3	26	1
A SECOND HICCUP'D OUR OLD MASTER'S DEAD	. . . .	297	2 DON JUAN	3	43	5
YOU'D BETTER ASK OUR MISTRESS WHO'S HIS HEIR	. . .	297	2 DON JUAN	3	43	6
OUR MISTRESS QUOTH A THIRD OUR MISTRESS--POOH--	. . .	297	2 DON JUAN	3	43	7
OUR MISTRESS QUOTH A THIRD OUR MISTRESS--POOH--	. . .	297	2 DON JUAN	3	43	7
YOU MEAN OUR MASTER--NOT THE OLD BUT NEW	. . . .	297	2 DON JUAN	3	43	8
TO FIND OUR HEARTHSTONE TURN'D INTO A TOMB	. . . .	301	2 DON JUAN	3	51	5
THE ASHES OF OUR HOPES IS A DEEP GRIEF	. . . .	301	2 DON JUAN	3	51	7
TO FIND OUR CHILDREN RUNNING RESTIVE--THEY	. . . .	305	2 DON JUAN	3	59	2
IN WHOM OUR BRIGHTEST DAYS WE WOULD RETRACE	. . . .	305	2 DON JUAN	3	59	3
OUR LITTLE SELVES RE-FORM'D IN FINER CLAY	. . . .	305	2 DON JUAN	3	59	4
AND CLOUDS COME O'ER THE SUNSET OF OUR DAY	. . . .	305	2 DON JUAN	3	59	6
MUST WE BUT BLUSH--OUR FATHERS BLED	. . . .	323	2 DON JUAN	3	L 7	2
A REMNANT OF OUR SPARTAN DEAD	. . . .	323	2 DON JUAN	3	L 7	4
A TYRANT BUT OUR MASTERS THEN	. . . .	324	2 DON JUAN	3	L 11	5
WERE STILL AT LEAST OUR COUNTRYMEN	. . . .	324	2 DON JUAN	3	L 11	6
OUR VIRGINS DANCE BENEATH THE SHADE--	. . . .	326	2 DON JUAN	3	L 15	2
MAY HEAR OUR MUTUAL MURMURS SWEEP	. . . .	326	2 DON JUAN	3	L 16	3
I KNOW THAT WHAT OUR NEIGHBOURS CALL LONGUEURS	. . .	332	2 DON JUAN	3	97	1
T' OUR TALE--THE FEAST WAS OVER THE SLAVES GONE	. . .	334	2 DON JUAN	3	101	1
AVE MARIA MAY OUR SPIRITS DARE	. . . .	336	2 DON JUAN	3	103	3
WHATE'ER OF PEACE ABOUT OUR HEARTHSTONE CLINGS	. . .	338	2 DON JUAN	3	107	5
WHATE'ER OUR HOUSEHOLD GODS PROTECT OF DEAR	. . . .	338	2 DON JUAN	3	107	6

OUR (CONTINUED)

	PAGE	VOL	CANTO	STANZA	LN
IS THIS A FANCY WHICH OUR REASON SCORNS	338	2	DON JUAN 3	108	7
OUR SIN THE SAME AND HARD AS HIS TO MEND	344	2	DON JUAN 4	1	6
TILL OUR OWN WEAKNESS SHOWS US WHAT WE ARE	344	2	DON JUAN 4	1	8
WHILE YOUTH'S HOT WISHES IN OUR RED VEINS REVEL	345	2	DON JUAN 4	2	5
'TIS THAT OUR NATURE CANNOT ALWAYS BRING	346	2	DON JUAN 4	4	3
OUR HEARTS FIRST IN THE DEPTHS OF LETHE'S SPRING	346	2	DON JUAN 4	4	5
TO THE KIND READER OF OUR SOBER CLIME	347	2	DON JUAN 4	6	1
BOTH MALADIES ARE TAXES ON OUR JOYS	357	2	DON JUAN 4	25	3
SAYING OUR MACHIAVELIAN IMPRESARIO	389	2	DON JUAN 4	82	2
WE WILL REVIVE OUR FORTUNES BEFORE LONG	389	2	DON JUAN 4	82	8
SAYING OUR PORCO OF AN IMPRESARIO	389	2	DON JUAN 4	82	V2
OUR BARITONE I ALMOST HAD FORGOT	392	2	DON JUAN 4	89	1
WHERE ARE THE EPITAPHS OUR FATHERS READ	399	2	DON JUAN 4	102	5
IN THIS OUR WORLD--AND HAVE THE POWER TO GIVE	403	2	DON JUAN 4	107	V4
ALSO OUR HERO'S LOT HOWE'ER UNPLEASANT	410	2	DON JUAN 4	117	2
WITH WHOM IT IS OUR LUCK TO CAST OUR LOT	417	2	DON JUAN 5	13	4
WITH WHOM IT IS OUR LUCK TO CAST OUR LOT	417	2	DON JUAN 5	13	4
TO STRIVE TOO WITH OUR FATE WERE SUCH A STRIFE	419	2	DON JUAN 5	17	5
BUT TIME STRIPS OUR ILLUSIONS OF THEIR HUE	421	2	DON JUAN 5	21	6
THE GLITTERING LIME-TWIGS OF OUR LATTER DAYS	422	2	DON JUAN 5	22	7
WE KNOW WHAT SLAVERY IS AND OUR DISASTERS	422	2	DON JUAN 5	23	7
THEIR PRESENT LESSONS ON OUR PAGAN FRIENDS HERE	423	2	DON JUAN 5	24	2
REJOINED THE OTHER WHEN OUR BAD LUCK MENDS HERE	423	2	DON JUAN 5	24	6
BUT AFTER ALL WHAT IS OUR PRESENT STATE	423	2	DON JUAN 5	25	1
'TIS PLEASANT PURCHASING OUR FELLOW CREATURES	425	2	DON JUAN 5	27	2
MAKES US FEEL OUR MORTALITY IN FACT	428	2	DON JUAN 5	32	3
CAN EVERY ELEMENT OUR ELEMENTS MAR	432	2	DON JUAN 5	39	5
FROM SAINT BARTHOLOMEW WE HAVE SAVED OUR SKIN	435	2	DON JUAN 5	44	4
WE FOR SOME MOMENTS HAD SECURED OUR SKIN	435	2	DON JUAN 5	44	V4
WE FROM IMPALEMENT HAD ENSURED OUR SKIN	435	2	DON JUAN 5	44	V4
PERHAPS BECAUSE OUR APPELLANTS MADE OUT OF SEASON	437	2	DON JUAN 5	48	V4
REMITS THE MATTER TO OUR OWN FREE-WILL	453	2	DON JUAN 5	72	8
TO FIND OUR WAY TO MARMORA WITHOUT BOATS	464	2	DON JUAN 5	92	6
OUR SOULS AT LEAST ARE FREE AND 'TIS IN VAIN	474	2	DON JUAN 5	110	6
AND HANDS OBEY--OUR HEARTS ARE STILL OUR OWN	484	2	DON JUAN 5	127	8
AND HANDS OBEY--OUR HEARTS ARE STILL OUR OWN	484	2	DON JUAN 5	127	8
AND MAKES OUR SNOW LESS PURE THAN OUR MORALITY	501	2	DON JUAN 5	157	6
AND MAKES OUR SNOW LESS PURE THAN OUR MORALITY	501	2	DON JUAN 5	157	6
THUS FAR OUR CHRONICLE AND NOW WE PAUSE	503	2	DON JUAN 5	159	1
TO SLACKEN SAIL AND ANCHOR WITH OUR RHYME	503	2	DON JUAN 5	159	4
WE LEFT OUR HERO AND THIRD HEROINE IN	10	3	DON JUAN 6	7	1
OUR LEAST OF SORROWS ARE SUCH AS WE WEEP	16	3	DON JUAN 6	20	6
OUR HERO THROUGH THE LABYRINTH OF LOVE	20	3	DON JUAN 6	28	7
WITHOUT OUR KNOWLEDGE OR OUR APPROBATION	25	3	DON JUAN 6	38	4
WITHOUT OUR KNOWLEDGE OR OUR APPROBATION	25	3	DON JUAN 6	38	4
WHICH SURELY WERE INVENTED FOR OUR SINS--	36	3	DON JUAN 6	61	8
OUR ULTIMATE EXISTENCE WHAT'S OUR PRESENT	37	3	DON JUAN 6	63	7
OUR ULTIMATE EXISTENCE WHAT'S OUR PRESENT	37	3	DON JUAN 6	63	7
TO TAKE US FROM OUR NATURAL REST AND PULL	46	3	DON JUAN 6	80	3
OF THIS OUR BANQUET WE MUST SOMETIMES CHANGE	65	3	DON JUAN 6	120	4
OUR EYES IN SEARCH OF EITHER LOVELY LIGHT	66	3	DON JUAN 7	1	6
ASSUME THEN LEAVE US ON OUR FREEZING WAY	66	3	DON JUAN 7	1	8
SOCRATES SAID OUR ONLY KNOWLEDGE WAS	69	3	DON JUAN 7	5	1
TWO BATTERIES CAP-A-PIE AS OUR SAINT GEORGE	72	3	DON JUAN 7	12	3
OUR EUPHONY--THERE WAS STRONGENOFF AND STROKONOFF	74	3	DON JUAN 7	15	2
OF ALL OUR MODERN BATTLES I WILL BET	83	3	DON JUAN 7	34	7
OUR FRIENDS THE TURKS WHO WITH LOUD ALLA'S NOW	87	3	DON JUAN 7	42	1
EXPLICITLY OUR SEVERAL POSTS MY FRIEND	100	3	DON JUAN 7	65	7
OUR BRITISH FRIEND THESE ARE THE WIVES OF OTHERS	103	3	DON JUAN 7	71	2
AND NOT OUR OWN I AM TOO QUALIFIED	103	3	DON JUAN 7	71	3
WITH THEIR ATTENDANT AIDED OUR ESCAPE	103	3	DON JUAN 7	72	2
LIKE THE DEATH-WATCH WITHIN OUR EARS THE ILLS	117	3	DON JUAN 8	12	6
TO TRACK OUR HERO ON HIS PATH OF FAME	120	3	DON JUAN 8	17	2
(THOUGH THESE TO OUR GIBRALTAR MUST KNOCK UNDER)--	136	3	DON JUAN 8	46	6
TO MARCH A GREAT CONVENIENCE TO OUR MEN	136	3	DON JUAN 8	47	3
WHICH ARE THE HEAVIEST THAT OUR HISTORY MENTIONS	137	3	DON JUAN 8	49	8
BUT OF THE FIRST OUR LITTLE FRIEND DON JUAN	138	3	DON JUAN 8	52	2
TO DEEM THE WOODS SHALL BE OUR HOME AT LAST--	142	3	DON JUAN 8	60	8
OF THE GREAT NAMES WHICH IN OUR FACES STARE	143	3	DON JUAN 8	61	3
FOR CHECQUERED AS IS SEEN OUR HUMAN LOT	156	3	DON JUAN 8	89	3
OF OUR ARTILLERY AND HIS OWN 'TIS SAID	160	3	DON JUAN 8	98	5
OUR KILLED ALREADY PILED UP TO THE CHIN	160	3	DON JUAN 8	98	6
BUT TO OUR SUBJECT A BRAVE TARTAR KHAN--	163	3	DON JUAN 8	104	5
IN SHORT HOWE'ER OUR BETTER FAITH DERIDES	168	3	DON JUAN 8	114	4
BUT YE--OUR CHILDREN'S CHILDREN THINK HOW WE	179	3	DON JUAN 8	135	7
'TIS TIME WE SHOULD PROCEED WITH OUR GOOD POEM	193	3	DON JUAN 9	22	1
OUR HERO (AND I TRUST KIND READER YOUR'S) --	194	3	DON JUAN 9	23	1
FROM OUR OLD CRASH SOME MYSTIC ANCIENT STRAIN	201	3	DON JUAN 9	38	3
WHENCE IS OUR EXIT AND OUR ENTRANCE--WELL I	210	3	DON JUAN 9	55	3
WHENCE IS OUR EXIT AND OUR ENTRANCE--WELL I	210	3	DON JUAN 9	55	3
OUR VEINS WHEN THINGS CALLED SOVEREIGNS THINK IT BEST	212	3	DON JUAN 9	60	7
SO THAT WE CAN OUR NATIVE SUN ASSUAGE	217	3	DON JUAN 9	69	5
THOSE MOVEMENTS THOSE IMPROVEMENTS IN OUR BODIES	220	3	DON JUAN 9	75	7
OF OUR SENSATIONS WHAT A CURIOUS WAY	220	3	DON JUAN 9	75	7
THE THIRD SORT TO BE NOTED IN OUR CHRONICLE	220	3	DON JUAN 9	76	5
WELL WE WON'T ANALYZE--OUR STORY MUST	221	3	DON JUAN 9	77	1
UNLIKE OUR OWN HALF-CHASTE ELIZABETH	222	3	DON JUAN 9	81	2
OUR YOUNG LIEUTENANT TO THE GENIAL CARE	224	3	DON JUAN 9	84	2

OUR   (CONTINUED)

Entry	PAGE	VOL	CANTO		STANZA	LN
WE LEFT OUR HERO JUAN IN THE BLOOM	227	3	DON JUAN	10	5	1
OLD FLAMES NEW WIVES BECOME OUR BITTEREST FOES--	231	3	DON JUAN	10	12	7
AND ALL OUR LITTLE FEUDS AT LEAST ALL MINE	232	3	DON JUAN	10	16	1
ON OUR FRESH FEELINGS BUT--AS BEING PARTICIPATED	236	3	DON JUAN	10	23	5
AND SHUT OUR SOULS UP IN US LIKE A SHELL-FISH	236	3	DON JUAN	10	23	8
YOU'LL MOUNT WITH OUR YOUNG HERO THE CONVEYANCE	248	3	DON JUAN	10	49	3
ALTHOUGH ('TWILL HAPPEN AS OUR PLANET GUIDES)	251	3	DON JUAN	10	54	5
BUT SHOULD WE WISH TO WARM US ON OUR WAY	254	3	DON JUAN	10	59	6
OUR OLD ACQUAINTANCE AND AT LEAST I'LL TRY	266	3	DON JUAN	10	84	4
HEAVEN'S BRANDY--THOUGH OUR BRAIN CAN HARDLY BEAR IT	269	3	DON JUAN	11	2	8
OUR SOARINGS WITH ANOTHER SORT OF QUESTION	269	3	DON JUAN	11	3	3
THEY'RE RIGHT OUR DAYS ARE TOO BRIEF FOR AFFORDING	270	3	DON JUAN	11	4	5
TO OUR THEME--THE MAN WHO HAS STOOD ON THE ACROPOLIS	271	3	DON JUAN	11	7	1
OH FOR A GLASS OF MAX WE'VE MISS'D OUR BOOTY--	276	3	DON JUAN	11	16	3
DON JUAN OUR YOUNG DIPLOMATIC SINNER	282	3	DON JUAN	11	29	6
A FOREIGNER OF RANK HAD GRACED OUR SHORE	283	3	DON JUAN	11	32	6
WHICH SERVES OUR THINKING PEOPLE FOR A PASSION	284	3	DON JUAN	11	33	8
'TWILL BE BECAUSE OUR NOTION IS NOT HIGH	285	3	DON JUAN	11	36	3
FROM OUR NEXT NEIGHBOUR'S LAND WHERE LIKE A CHESSMAN	288	3	DON JUAN	11	42	3
AND ON OUR SOPHAS MAKES US LIE DEJECTED	301	3	DON JUAN	11	65	5
AND TALK IN TENDER HORRORS OF OUR LOATHING	301	3	DON JUAN	11	65	6
ALL KINDS OF TOIL SAVE FOR OUR COUNTRY'S GOOD--	301	3	DON JUAN	11	65	7
OUR HERO AS A HERO YOUNG AND HANDSOME	305	3	DON JUAN	11	74	1
AND WHERE IS FUM THE FOURTH OUR ROYAL BIRD	307	3	DON JUAN	11	78	4
OF WHAT BEFELL OUR HERO IN THE LAND	311	3	DON JUAN	11	87	2
BLACK LETTER UPON FOOLSCAP WHILE OUR HAIR	315	3	DON JUAN	12	1	7
HOWE'ER OUR FRIEND DON JUAN MIGHT COMMAND	329	3	DON JUAN	12	29	5
OUR HERO GLADLY SAW HIS LITTLE CHARGE	339	3	DON JUAN	12	51	2
WITH REGULAR DESCENT IN THESE OUR DAYS	340	3	DON JUAN	12	53	4
THE LOVELIEST OLIGARCHS OF OUR GYNOCRASY	346	3	DON JUAN	12	66	4
AMONG THE PROUDEST OF OUR ARISTOCRACY	346	3	DON JUAN	12	66	6
FOR BOTH OUR PREJUDICES HE MUST BACK	349	3	DON JUAN	12	71	V6
COMPARED WITH THOSE OF OUR PURE PEARLS OF PRICE	349	3	DON JUAN	12	72	7
HERE THE TWELFTH CANTO OF OUR INTRODUCTION	356	3	DON JUAN	12	87	1
NOT THAT I DEEM OUR CHIEF JUDGE IS A HOLLOW MAN--)	357	3	DON JUAN	12	V 18	8
MORE QUIET WHEN OUR MOON'S NO MORE AT FULL	360	3	DON JUAN	13	4	3
OUR PASSIONS AND WE WALK IN WISDOM'S WAYS	360	3	DON JUAN	13	4	6
(FATE IS A GOOD EXCUSE FOR OUR OWN WILL)	364	3	DON JUAN	13	12	6
BETWEEN OUR DUTEOUS OFFSPRING--AND THE GOUT	376	3	DON JUAN	13	40	V8
FOR PARLIAMENT IS OUR BAROMETER	378	3	DON JUAN	13	43	6
ITS SESSIONS FORM OUR ONLY ALMANACK	378	3	DON JUAN	13	43	8
OUR GAY RUSS SPANIARD WAS ORDAINED TO SHINE	383	3	DON JUAN	13	53	4
AS HINTING MORE (UNLESS OUR JUDGMENTS WARP US)	391	3	DON JUAN	13	69	7
HUGER THAN TWELVE OF OUR DEGENERATE BREED	391	3	DON JUAN	13	70	4
HOW OUR VILLEGGIATURA WILL GET ON	397	3	DON JUAN	13	83	2
OUR RIDICULES ARE KEPT IN THE BACK-GROUND--	402	3	DON JUAN	13	95	1
OF CHAFF ALTHOUGH OUR GLEANINGS BE NOT GRIST	403	3	DON JUAN	13	97	2
YOUTH FADES AND LEAVES OUR DAYS NO LONGER SUNNY	405	3	DON JUAN	13	100	5
THOUGH NAMELESS IN OUR LANGUAGE--WE RETORT	405	3	DON JUAN	13	101	6
IN THIS OUR PARTY POLISH'D SMOOTH AND COLD	409	3	DON JUAN	13	110	2
AND OUR SOPHIAS ARE NOT SO EMPHATIC	409	3	DON JUAN	13	110	5
IF FROM GREAT NATURE'S OR OUR OWN ABYSS	410	3	DON JUAN	14	1	1
TO THE GREAT PLEASURE OF OUR FRIENDS MANKIND	414	3	DON JUAN	14	9	5
WHEN WE HAVE MADE OUR LOVE AND GAMED OUR GAMING	418	3	DON JUAN	14	18	1
WHEN WE HAVE MADE OUR LOVE AND GAMED OUR GAMING	418	3	DON JUAN	14	18	1
WE LEFT OUR HEROES AND OUR HEROINES	423	3	DON JUAN	14	29	1
WE LEFT OUR HEROES AND OUR HEROINES	423	3	DON JUAN	14	29	1
SUCH CLASSIC PAS--SANS FLAWS--SET OFF OUR HERO	427	3	DON JUAN	14	39	7
TO HUNT OUR ERRORS UP WITH A GOOD GRACE	430	3	DON JUAN	14	47	6
OUR GENTLE ADELINE HAD ONE DEFECT--	446	3	DON JUAN	14	85	1
OUR FEELINGS 'GAINST THE NATURE OF THE SOIL	447	3	DON JUAN	14	86	4
THAT IN OUR YOUTH AS DANGEROUS A PASSION	454	3	DON JUAN	14	100	2
WHEREWITH WE BREAK OUR BUBBLES ON THE OCEAN	457	3	DON JUAN	15	2	4
WE'LL DO OUR BEST TO MAKE THE BEST ON'T--MARCH	468	3	DON JUAN	15	27	1
TWO WEEDS WHICH POSE OUR ECONOMIC CATOS	472	3	DON JUAN	15	37	8
BY WHICH SUCH SIRENS CAN ATTRACT OUR GREAT	474	3	DON JUAN	15	42	6
IS WANTING AND OUR BEST TIES IN THE TOMB	475	3	DON JUAN	15	44	8
METHINKS WE MAY PROCEED UPON OUR NARRATIVE	481	3	DON JUAN	15	59	2
THAN COULD ROAST BEEF IN OUR ROUGH JOHN BULL WAY	487	3	DON JUAN	15	71	4
GOD HELP US SINCE WE HAVE NEED ON OUR CAREER	496	3	DON JUAN	15	90	3
TO KEEP OUR HOLY BEACONS ALWAYS BRIGHT	496	3	DON JUAN	15	90	4
OUR BUBBLES AS THE OLD BURST NEW EMERGE	500	3	DON JUAN	15	99	6
UNDRESSING IS A WOE OUR ROBE DE CHAMBRE	505	3	DON JUAN	16	11	2
THAT TIME HAS LEFT OUR FATHERS OF THEIR HALL	507	3	DON JUAN	16	16	8
OR THAT OUR SIRES HAD A MORE GIFTED EYE	516	3	DON JUAN	16	36	6
AMONGST OUR OWN MOST MUSICAL OF NATIONS	523	3	DON JUAN	16	45	6
TO SOOTHE OUR EARS LEST ITALY SHOULD FAIL	523	3	DON JUAN	16	45	8
THE THREE STRINGS OF OUR HAPPY CONSTITUTION	536	3	DON JUAN	16	74	V8
EVEN FROM OUR GRAMMAR UPWARDS FRIENDS OF YORE	542	3	DON JUAN	16	86	5
AS FAR AS WORDS MAKE RULES--OUR COMMON NOTION	563	3	DON JUAN	17	3	2
WE LITTLE PEOPLE IN OUR LESSER WAY	566	3	DON JUAN	17	10	2
OUR HERO WAS IN CANTO THE SIXTEENTH	567	3	DON JUAN	17	12	1
ASSEMBLED WITH OUR HOSTESS AND MINE HOST	568	3	DON JUAN	17	13	6

OUR'S

Entry	PAGE	VOL	CANTO		STANZA	LN
ETERNAL SUCH NAMES MINGLED) ISMAIL'S OUR'S	178	3	DON JUAN	8	133	8

OURS

Entry	PAGE	VOL	CANTO		STANZA	LN
INSIPID IN THIS NAUGHTY WORLD OF OURS	30	2	DON JUAN	1	18	2
OH LOVE WHAT IS IT IN THIS WORLD OF OURS	275	2	DON JUAN	3	2	1

	PAGE	VOL	CANTO	STANZA	LN
OURS (CONTINUED)					
OF OURS ALTHOUGH THEY PROPAGATE MORE BROADLY	472	3	DON JUAN 15	36	6
ON OURS OR SPARS WITHIN SOME DUSKY CAVE	509	3	DON JUAN 16	19	5
LET OURS BE FOR HIS SOUL	520	3	DON JUAN 16	L 6	8
OURSELVES					
AS ONCE (A FEAT ON WHICH OURSELVES WE PRIDED)	211	2	DON JUAN 2	105	7
OURSELVES A SINGER DANCER MUCH IN FASHION	216	3	DON JUAN 9	68	4
MAKES US BELIEVE OURSELVES AS GOOD AS ANY	216	3	DON JUAN 9	68	8
THAT ALL'S IDEAL--ALL OURSELVES I'LL STAKE THE	269	3	DON JUAN 11	2	3
WHICH MAKE US WISH OURSELVES IN TOWN AT ONCE--	277	3	DON JUAN 11	20	8
THAT WE OURSELVES--'TWAS IN THE HONEY MOON--	517	3	DON JUAN 16	38	2
OUSCKIN					
ENDING IN ISCHSKIN OUSCKIN IFFSKCHY OUSKI	74	3	DON JUAN 7	16	7
OUSKI					
ENDING IN ISCHSKIN OUSCKIN IFFSKCHY OUSKI	74	3	DON JUAN 7	16	7
OUT-AT-ELBOW					
EACH OUT-AT-ELBOW PEER OR DESPERATE DANDY	331	3	DON JUAN 12	32	2
OUTBALANCE					
OUTBALANCE ALL THE CAESAR'S VICTORIES	8	3	DON JUAN 6	4	8
OUTCRY					
ANOTHER OUTCRY FOR A LITTLE BOAT	333	2	DON JUAN 3	98	7
OUTLET					
ITS OUTLET DASH'D INTO A STEEP CASCADE	385	3	DON JUAN 13	58	1
OUTLET'S					
EVEN IN THE HOPEFUL ISLE WHOSE OUTLET'S DOVER	331	3	DON JUAN 12	33	6
OUTLINE					
AN OUTLINE OF THE CUSTOMS OF THE EAST	35	3	DON JUAN 6	58	4
BE TOO MINUTE AN OUTLINE IS THE BEST	55	3	DON JUAN 6	98	7
THAT WATERY OUTLINE OF ETERNITY	457	3	DON JUAN 15	2	5
OUTLINE OF AN HARANGUE--BUT I'LL TO BED	538	3	DON JUAN 16	77	V5
OUTLINE'S					
SO THAT THE OUTLINE'S TOLERABLY FAIR	463	3	DON JUAN 15	16	4
OUTLINES					
MAY SERVE PERHAPS AS OUTLINES OR SLIGHT HINTS	60	3	DON JUAN 6	109	8
OUTRAGE					
WOULD BEAR SUCH OUTRAGE AND FORBEAR TO KILL	368	2	DON JUAN 4	46	6
OUTRAGEOUS					
WERE ONE NOT PUNISH'D ALL WOULD BE OUTRAGEOUS	96	2	DON JUAN 1	138	8
AND THAT OUTRAGEOUS APPETITE FOR LIES	154	3	DON JUAN 8	86	7
OUTRAN					
AND IF HIS PASSIONS NOW AND THEN OUTRAN	40	2	DON JUAN 1	35	5
OUTRUN					
HER HUNDRED ARMS AND LEGS AND FAIN OUTRUN HER	231	3	DON JUAN 10	12	6
THE LOFTIEST MINDS OUTRUN THEIR TARDY AGES	566	3	DON JUAN 17	9	5
OUTS					
FOR JUAN STOOD WELL BOTH WITH INS AND OUTS	369	3	DON JUAN 13	24	3
OUTSIDES					
BUT THIS HAS NOUGHT TO DO WITH THEIR OUTSIDES	350	3	DON JUAN 12	74	1
OUTSTRETCH'D					
THE OUTSTRETCH'D OCEAN GLITTER LIKE A LAKE	249	2	DON JUAN 2	177	8
OUTWARD					
AND GAVE NO OUTWARD SIGNS OF INWARD STRIFE	35	2	DON JUAN 1	26	6
AND NOTHING OUTWARD TELLS OF HUMAN CLAY	383	2	DON JUAN 4	72	4
AS FAR AS OUTWARD SHOW MAY CORRESPOND	469	2	DON JUAN 5	99	7
IN OUTWARD SHOW WHICH IS A SAVING CLAUSE)	35	3	DON JUAN 6	58	3
HER INWARD GRACE FOR OUTWARD SHOW AND MAKES	96	3	DON JUAN 7	57	7
AND NEUTRALIZE HER OUTWARD SHOW OF SCARLET	237	3	DON JUAN 10	26	8
OUTWARD DISLIKE WHICH DON'T LOOK WELL ABROAD	240	3	DON JUAN 10	32	5
IT ADDS AN OUTWARD GRACE UNTO THEIR CARRIAGE--	344	3	DON JUAN 12	62	6
OUTWORK					
A MOST IMPORTANT OUTWORK OF THE CITY--	545	3	DON JUAN 16	93	6
OVENS					
THEIR THROATS WERE OVENS THEIR SWOLN TONGUES WERE BLACK	202	2	DON JUAN 2	86	3
OVERBOARD					
THEN SOME LEAP'D OVERBOARD WITH DREADFUL YELL	184	2	DON JUAN 2	52	3
TOSSED OVERBOARD UNSALEABLE (BEING OLD)	284	2	DON JUAN 3	16	4
OVERCHARGE					
ALSO THE SOLACE OF AN OVERCHARGE	379	3	DON JUAN 13	45	8
OVER-CHILLY					
AT A SAD DISCOUNT WHILE YOUR OVER-CHILLY	14	3	DON JUAN 6	16	7
OVER-COLD					
OR OVER-COLD ANNIHILATES THE CHARM	13	3	DON JUAN 6	15	8
OVERCOME					
SHOULD RATHER FACE AND OVERCOME TEMPTATION	63	2	DON JUAN 1	77	2
AND HARDER FOR THE HEART TO OVERCOME	301	2	DON JUAN 3	51	3
GAVE WAY TO'T SINCE HE COULD NOT OVERCOME IT	272	3	DON JUAN 11	9	4
OVERCOMING					
TOO OFTEN IN ITS FURY OVERCOMING ALL	399	2	DON JUAN 4	101	3
OVERDID					
IF FAIR GULBEYAZ OVERDID HER PART	15	3	DON JUAN 6	19	1
OVERHEAD					
NOW OVERHEAD A RAINBOW BURSTING THROUGH	204	2	DON JUAN 2	91	1
OVERHUNG					
HER BROW WAS OVERHUNG WITH COINS OF GOLD	217	2	DON JUAN 2	116	1
OVERJOY'D					
OF NATIONS FREED AND THE WORLD OVERJOY'D	339	2	DON JUAN 3	109	4
OVERLAY					
THE SUPERSTRATUM WHICH WILL OVERLAY US	201	3	DON JUAN 9	37	8
OVERLOOK'D					
WHICH OVERLOOK'D THE WHITE WALLS OF HIS HOME	286	2	DON JUAN 3	21	2

OVERLOOKED
    NOT TO BE OVERLOOKED--AND GAVE SUCH CREDIT . . . . . . 293 3 DON JUAN 11   49   7
OVERLOOKS
    (LEUCADIA'S ROCK STILL OVERLOOKS THE WAVE) . . . . . . 266 2 DON JUAN 2   205   6
OVERPOWERED
    AND THOUGH--BY NO MEANS OVERPOWERED WITH RICHES . . . . 421 3 DON JUAN 14   26 V7
OVERPOWERING
    WITHOUT KNOWING WHY--AN OVERPOWERING TONE . . . . . 236 2 DON JUAN 2   151   7
    HER OVERPOWERING PRESENCE MADE YOU FEEL . . . . . . 313 2 DON JUAN 3   74   7
    THAN THAT ALL-SOFTENING OVER-POWERING KNELL . . . . . 439 2 DON JUAN 5   49   7
    HER BEAUTY OF THAT OVERPOWERING KIND . . . . 467 2 DON JUAN 5   97   2
OVERPOWERS
    THAT OVERPOWERS SOME ALPINE RIVER'S RUSH . . . . . . 231 2 DON JUAN 2   141   6
OVERSET
    THEY RAN THE BOAT FOR SHORE AND OVERSET HER . . . . . 211 2 DON JUAN 2   104   8
OVERSTRAIN
    AND THEN YOU OVERSTRAIN YOURSELF OR SO . . . . . . 10 2 DON JUAN D   3   5
OVERTHROWN
    FEELINGS OF YOUTH LIKE THOSE WHICH OVERTHROWN LIE . . . 475 3 DON JUAN 15   44   5
OVERTURE
    AND WHEN SO YOU SHALL HAVE THE OVERTURE . . . . . . 341 3 DON JUAN 12   54   8
OVERTURNS
    OR LITTLE OVERTURNS AND NOT THE FEW . . . . 305 3 DON JUAN 11   73   4
OVER-WARM
    A SINCERE WOMAN'S BREAST--FOR OVER-WARM . . . . . . 13 3 DON JUAN 6   15   7
OVER-WARMTH
    FOR OVER-WARMTH IF FALSE IS WORSE THAN TRUTH . . . . . 14 3 DON JUAN 6   16   1
OVERWORKING
    IN SIZE FROM OVERWORKING THE MATERIAL-- . . . . . . 202 3 DON JUAN 9   39   7
OVERWORN
    HARDSHIPS WHICH HAVE THE HARDIEST OVERWORN . . . . . 420 2 DON JUAN 5   18   8
OVERWROUGHT
    BUT OVERWROUGHT WITH PASSION AND DESPAIR . . . . . . 375 2 DON JUAN 4   57   6
OVID
    HORACE CATULLUS SCHOLARS OVID TUTOR . . . . 266 2 DON JUAN 2   205   3
OVID'S
    OVID'S A RAKE AS HALF HIS VERSES SHOW HIM . . . . . 45 2 DON JUAN 1   42   1
    IN FEELINGS QUICK AS OVID'S MISS MEDEA . . . . . . 68 2 DON JUAN 1   86   4
    AS OVID'S VERSE MAY GIVE TO UNDERSTAND . . . . . . 411 2 DON JUAN 5   1   6
OWE
    BUT THOUGH I OWE IT LITTLE BUT MY BIRTH . . . . . . 257 3 DON JUAN 10   66   3
    WITH VIVIFYING VENUS WHO DOTH OWE . . . . 542 3 DON JUAN 16   86   6
    ITS MOTIVE FOR THAT CHARITY WE OWE . . . . 553 3 DON JUAN 16   106   3
OWED
    MILD CATHERINE OWED THE CHANCE OF BEING CROWN'D . . . . 205 3 DON JUAN 9   46 V4
    A THING WHICH HAPPENS RARELY THIS HE OWED . . . . . 239 3 DON JUAN 10   29   2
    HE OWED TO AN OLD WOMAN AND HIS POST . . . . . . 239 3 DON JUAN 10   29   8
OWES
    TROY OWES TO HOMER WHAT WHIST OWES TO HOYLE . . . . . 328 2 DON JUAN 3   90   5
    TROY OWES TO HOMER WHAT WHIST OWES TO HOYLE . . . . . 328 2 DON JUAN 3   90   5
    THOUGH BRITAIN OWES (AND PAYS YOU TOO) SO MUCH . . . . 184 3 DON JUAN 9   3   1
    YET EUROPE DOUBTLESS OWES YOU GREATLY MORE . . . . . 184 3 DON JUAN 9   3   2
OWING
    THAT BEEF AND BATTLES BOTH WERE OWING TO HER . . . . . 238 2 DON JUAN 2   156   8
    WHILK WHICH (OR WHAT YOU PLEASE) WAS OWING TO . . . . 456 2 DON JUAN 5   78   1
    OWING TO HIM--AS ALSO HER SALVATION . . . . 251 3 DON JUAN 10   55   5
OWL
    THE OWL HIS ANTHEM WHERE THE SILENCED QUIRE . . . . . 387 3 DON JUAN 13   62   7
    THE NIGHT (I SING BY NIGHT--SOMETIMES AN OWL . . . . . 499 3 DON JUAN 15   97   1
OWL-SONGS
    SADDER THAN OWL-SONGS OR THE MIDNIGHT BLAST . . . . . 432 3 DON JUAN 14   50   2
OWN
    FROM BETTER COMPANY HAVE KEPT YOUR OWN . . . . . . 12 2 DON JUAN D   5   2
    BEING ONLY INJURED BY HIS OWN ASSERTION . . . . . . 14 2 DON JUAN D   9   4
    IN THEIR OWN WAY BY ALL THE THINGS THAT S"E DID . . . . 26 2 DON JUAN 1   10   8
    A GREAT OPINION OF HER OWN GOOD QUALITIES . . . . . 32 2 DON JUAN 1   20   2
    NOT HAVING OF MY OWN DOMESTIC CARES . . . . 33 2 DON JUAN 1   23   8
    THE MORE SO IN OBTAINING OUR OWN ENDS . . . . . . 37 2 DON JUAN 1   30   4
    AND LEFT HIS WIDOW TO HER OWN AVERSION . . . . . . 39 2 DON JUAN 1   34   8
    LET'S OWN SINCE IT CAN DO NO GOOD ON EARTH . . . . . 41 2 DON JUAN 1   36   3
    THIS I WILL SAY--MY REASONS ARE MY OWN-- . . . . . 50 2 DON JUAN 1   52   2
    FOR THERE IS I PICK'D UP MY OWN KNOWLEDGE . . . . . 50 2 DON JUAN 1   52   8
    WITH OTHER PEOPLE'S EYES OR IF HER OWN . . . . . . 59 2 DON JUAN 1   68   2
    SHE MUST NOT OWN BUT CHERISH'D MORE THE WHILE . . . . 61 2 DON JUAN 1   72   4
    OF HIS OWN CASE AND NEVER HIT THE TRUE ONE . . . . . 68 2 DON JUAN 1   86   3
    HIS SELF-COMMUNION WITH HIS OWN HIGH SOUL . . . . . 70 2 DON JUAN 1   91   2
    SO BY THE POESY OF HIS OWN MIND . . . . 72 2 DON JUAN 1   95   4
    OR PANDERING BLINDLY TO HIS OWN DISGRACE . . . . . . 74 2 DON JUAN 1   99   4
    SO WAS HER CREED IN HER OWN INNOCENCE . . . . . . 78 2 DON JUAN 1   106   8
    SHE THOUGHT OF HER OWN STRENGTH AND JUAN'S YOUTH . . . 78 2 DON JUAN 1   107   1
    QUITE BY MISTAKE--SHE THOUGHT IT WAS HER OWN . . . . . 80 2 DON JUAN 1   109   8
    AND THEN ABASH'D AT ITS OWN JOY WITHDREW . . . . . . 81 2 DON JUAN 1   112   4
    OF HIS OWN NATURE AND THE VARIOUS ARTS . . . . . . 91 2 DON JUAN 1   128   2
    BUT WHETHER 'TWAS THAT ONE'S OWN GUILT CONFOUNDS . . . 118 2 DON JUAN 1   176   3
    STATE STATION HEAVEN MANKIND'S MY OWN ESTEEM . . . . . 130 2 DON JUAN 1   193   2
    AND HERE THE ADVANTAGE IS MY OWN I WEEN . . . . . . 137 2 DON JUAN 1   202   3
    OR EVERY POET HIS OWN ARISTOTLE . . . . 138 2 DON JUAN 1   204   8
    TO THEIR OWN GOOD THIS WARNING TO DESPISE . . . . . 141 2 DON JUAN 1   208   2
    NOT TO BELIEVE MY VERSE AND THEIR OWN EYES . . . . . 141 2 DON JUAN 1   208   4
    OF ITS OWN THIRST TO SEE AGAIN THY SHORE . . . . . . 166 2 DON JUAN 2   18   4

OWN (CONTINUED)

	PAGE	VOL	CANTO		STANZA	LN
OUT THROUGH A FEVER CAUSED BY ITS OWN HEAT	168	2	DON JUAN	2	22	2
THE VESSEL SWAM YET STILL SHE HELD HER OWN	176	2	DON JUAN	2	38	4
'TWAS BUT HIS OWN SUPPRESS'D TILL NOW HE FOUND	194	2	DON JUAN	2	73	6
REFUSING HIS OWN SPANIEL HARDLY COULD	198	2	DON JUAN	2	78	4
WHICH ARE (AS I MUST OWN) OF FEMALE GROWTH	221	2	DON JUAN	2	123	3
HER OWN WAS FRESHEST THOUGH A FEVERISH FLUSH	231	2	DON JUAN	2	141	2
HE WAS HER OWN HER OCEAN-TREASURE CAST	247	2	DON JUAN	2	173	7
BY THEIR OWN FEELINGS HALLOW'D AND UNITED	265	2	DON JUAN	2	204	5
IN SHORT IT IS THE USE OF OUR OWN EYES	269	2	DON JUAN	2	212	6
UNLESS INDEED IT WAS FROM HIS OWN KNOWLEDGE HE	281	2	DON JUAN	3	11	5
ON SEEING HIS OWN CHIMNEY-SMOKE FELT GLAD	289	2	DON JUAN	3	26	3
SHE NOW KEPT HOUSE UPON HER OWN ACCOUNT	295	2	DON JUAN	3	38	8
HIS OWN ANXIETY HIS HEART TOO BLEEDING	299	2	DON JUAN	3	46	6
THE SOLITUDE OF PASSING HIS OWN DOOR	302	2	DON JUAN	3	52	3
THEIR FURY BEING SPENT BY ITS OWN SHOCK	305	2	DON JUAN	3	58	6
THE HERACLEIDAN BLOOD MIGHT OWN	325	2	DON JUAN	3	L 13	6
AS HERCULES MIGHT DEEM HIS OWN	325	2	DON JUAN	3	L 13	V6
MY OWN THE BURNING TEAR-DROP LAVES	326	2	DON JUAN	3	L 15	5
BETWEEN HIS OWN AND OTHERS' INTELLECT	330	2	DON JUAN	3	95	2
BUT LET ME TO MY STORY I MUST OWN	331	2	DON JUAN	3	96	1
THEY'LL NEVER FIND IT OUT UNLESS I OWN	342	2	DON JUAN	3	111	4
TILL OUR OWN WEAKNESS SHOWS US WHAT WE ARE	344	2	DON JUAN	4	1	8
MY OWN MEANING WHEN I WOULD BE VERY FINE	346	2	DON JUAN	4	5	5
TO THEIR OWN HEARTS' MOST SWEET SOCIETY	348	2	DON JUAN	4	8	2
REPLIED YOUR BLOOD BE THEN ON YOUR OWN HEAD	365	2	DON JUAN	4	40	5
HIS OWN SHALL ROLL BEFORE YOU LIKE A BALL	369	2	DON JUAN	4	47	2
HIS OWN WELL IN SO WELL ERE YOU COULD LOOK	370	2	DON JUAN	4	49	4
WHERE LATE HE TROD HER BEAUTIFUL HER OWN	375	2	DON JUAN	4	58	4
NONE BUT HER OWN AND FATHER'S GRAVE IS THERE	383	2	DON JUAN	4	72	3
FOR SOON OR LATE LOVE IS HIS OWN AVENGER	383	2	DON JUAN	4	73	8
EXTREMELY TAKEN WITH HIS OWN RELIGION	387	2	DON JUAN	4	78	7
MY OWN MERITS AND THOUGH YOUNG--I SEE SIR--YOU	392	2	DON JUAN	4	88	2
AND LOSE THEIR OWN IN UNIVERSAL DEATH	399	2	DON JUAN	4	102	8
YET I MUST OWN HE LOOKED A LITTLE DULL	415	2	DON JUAN	5	8	3
TO THEIR OWN WHIMS AND PASSIONS AND WHATNOT	423	2	DON JUAN	5	25	4
FROM HIS OWN BRAIN'S OPPRESSION WHILE IT REELS	427	2	DON JUAN	5	31	6
WHO LITTLE THOUGHT THAT HIS OWN CRACKED EXISTENCE	440	2	DON JUAN	5	51	3
AND SOME SEEMED MUCH IN LOVE WITH THEIR OWN DRESS	441	2	DON JUAN	5	53	4
FOR HIS OWN PART HE REALLY SHOULD REJOICE	452	2	DON JUAN	5	70	1
FOR HIS OWN SHARE--HE SAW BUT SMALL OBJECTION	452	2	DON JUAN	5	71	1
REMITS THE MATTER TO OUR OWN FREE-WILL	453	2	DON JUAN	5	72	8
I'D RATHER LEAVE IT MUCH TO YOUR OWN MIND	467	2	DON JUAN	5	97	4
AND HANDS OBEY--OUR HEARTS ARE STILL OUR OWN	484	2	DON JUAN	5	127	8
OF LADIES WHO CANNOT HAVE THEIR OWN WAY	487	2	DON JUAN	5	132	4
RATHER THAN SIN--EXCEPT TO HIS OWN WISH	492	2	DON JUAN	5	141	6
HE SAW WITH HIS OWN EYES THE MOON WAS ROUND	497	2	DON JUAN	5	150	1
BUT THEN THEIR OWN POLYGAMY'S TO BLAME	502	2	DON JUAN	5	158	6
BELOVED IN HER OWN WAY AND RATHER WHISK	7	3	DON JUAN	6	3	4
I OWN IT I DEPLORE IT I CONDEMN IT	10	3	DON JUAN	6	8	2
IF TRUE 'TIS NO GREAT LEASE OF ITS OWN FIRE	14	3	DON JUAN	6	16	2
I OWN NO PROSODY CAN EVER RATE IT	15	3	DON JUAN	6	18	7
BUT WHEN THEY REACHED THEIR OWN APARTMENTS THERE	23	3	DON JUAN	6	34	1
MY FAULTS EVEN WITH YOUR OWN WHICH MEANETH PUT	34	3	DON JUAN	6	56	6
BEHOLDS HER OWN SHY SHADOWY IMAGE PASS	36	3	DON JUAN	6	60	6
TO ITS OWN BOUGH AND DANGLED YET IN SIGHT	44	3	DON JUAN	6	76	7
IT FELL DOWN OF ITS OWN ACCORD BEFORE	44	3	DON JUAN	6	77	2
BUT POOR DUDU WITH LARGE DROPS IN HER OWN	47	3	DON JUAN	6	82	2
THEIR OWN TRUE INTERESTS WHICH KINGS RARELY KNOW	53	3	DON JUAN	6	95	2
AS SOON AS THEY RE-ENTERED THEIR OWN ROOM	57	3	DON JUAN	6	103	3
EVEN AT YOUR OWN IMPERATIVE EXPENSE	62	3	DON JUAN	6	114	6
BUT YOUR OWN FEELINGS EVEN SHOULD ALL THE REST	63	3	DON JUAN	6	115	1
HIS OWN REMONSTRANCE FURTHER HE WELL KNEW	63	3	DON JUAN	6	116	4
MIGHT END IN ACTING AS HIS OWN JACK KETCH	63	3	DON JUAN	6	116	5
HE STILL PREFERRED HIS OWN NECK TO ANOTHER'S	63	3	DON JUAN	6	116	8
THEIR NEVER KNOWING THEIR OWN MIND TWO DAYS	64	3	DON JUAN	6	117	6
WHICH MADE HIM DAILY BLESS HIS OWN NEUTRALITY	64	3	DON JUAN	6	117	8
THE TURKISH FIRE AND AIDED BY THEIR OWN	81	3	DON JUAN	7	30	2
IN ORDERING MATTERS AFTER HIS OWN BENT	85	3	DON JUAN	7	38	3
AND NOT OUR OWN I AM TOO QUALIFIED	103	3	DON JUAN	7	71	3
TO BREAK THE RULES BY BRINGING ONE'S OWN BRIDE	103	3	DON JUAN	7	71	5
THEIR OWN PROTECTORS--NOR WAS THEIR SURPRISE	104	3	DON JUAN	7	73	3
TO TEACH HIM GREATER HAD HIS OWN LEG BROKEN	117	3	DON JUAN	8	11	8
A PATH TO ADD HIS OWN SLIGHT ARM AND FORCES	126	3	DON JUAN	8	30	7
OF HIS OWN CORPS NOR EVEN THE CORPS WHICH HAD	127	3	DON JUAN	8	31	2
ON ITS OWN STRENGTH WITH CARELESS NERVES AND THEWS--	131	3	DON JUAN	8	36	6
BLOOD UNTIL HEATED--AND EVEN THERE HIS OWN	140	3	DON JUAN	8	55	7
BY HABIT TO WHAT THEIR OWN HEARTS ABHOR--	143	3	DON JUAN	8	62	6
HERE WAR FORGOT HIS OWN DESTRUCTIVE ART	152	3	DON JUAN	8	82	5
OF THE LAST FOE IS ECHOED BY HIS OWN	155	3	DON JUAN	8	87	8
OF OUR ARTILLERY AND HIS OWN 'TIS SAID	160	3	DON JUAN	8	98	5
SUCH DOOM MAY BE YOUR OWN IN AFTER TIMES	174	3	DON JUAN	8	125	4
READ YOUR OWN HEARTS AND IRELAND'S PRESENT STORY	174	3	DON JUAN	8	125	7
WHEREIN SHE LIKED HER OWN TO STAND LIKE ROCKS	197	3	DON JUAN	9	29	8
FISHERY AND FARM BOTH INTO HIS OWN HAND	198	3	DON JUAN	9	31	8
OF THEIR OWN SAND-PITS TO MIX WITH A GODDESS	220	3	DON JUAN	9	75	3
UNLIKE OUR OWN HALF-CHASTE ELIZABETH	222	3	DON JUAN	9	81	2
THE STARS I OWN MY TELESCOPE IS DIM	227	3	DON JUAN	10	4	2
IN ALL THEIR HABITS--NOT SO YOU I OWN	232	3	DON JUAN	10	15	7

```
                                                             PAGE VOL     CANTO  STANZA  LN
OWN   (CONTINUED)
      MOST NOBLY AND I OWN IT FROM MY SOUL . . . . . .    . 232   3 DON JUAN 10     16      8
      OF WHAT I THEN DREAMT CLOTHED IN THEIR OWN PALL  . . . . 233   3 DON JJAN 10     18      5
      AND MERELY FOR THE SAKE OF ITS OWN MERITS  . . . . . . 260   3 DON JUAN 10     72      5
      WHERE SCIENCE MARSHALS FORTH HER OWN QUADRILLE . . . . . 303   3 DON JJAN 11     70      8
      WHAT IS HIS OWN--GO LOOK AT EACH TRANSACTION . . . . . 321   3 DON JUAN 12     11      4
      SO CASH RULES LOVE THE RULER ON HIS OWN . . . . . . . 322   3 DON JUAN 12     14      5
      (NOW HERE'S A WORD QUITE AFTER MY OWN HEART . . . . . 326   3 DON JUAN 12     22      3
      AS BEAUTIFUL AS HER OWN NATIVE LAND  . . . . . . . 329   3 DON JUAN 12     29      3
      HIGH IN HIGH CIRCLES GENTLE IN HER OWN . . . . . . . 338   3 DON JUAN 12     48      1
      WHO HAVE A DUE RESPECT FOR THEIR OWN WISHES . . . . . 349   3 DON JUAN 12     73      4
      I LEAVE THE SAINTS TO SETTLE THEIR OWN SCORE . . . . . 352   3 DON JUAN 12     79      4
      OF HIS OWN COUNTRY--SELDOM SINCE THAT DAY  . . . . . 364   3 DON JJAN 13     11      3
      (FATE IS A GOOD EXCUSE FOR OUR OWN WILL) . . . . . . 364   3 DON JUAN 13     12      6
      BECAUSE ITS OWN GOOD PLEASURE HATH DECIDED . . . . . 366   3 DON JUAN 13     16      8
      HER CHIEF RESOURCE WAS IN HER OWN HIGH SPIRIT  . . . . 372   3 DON JUAN 13     31      4
      SAVE THAT THE PUPPETS PULL AT THEIR OWN STRINGS  . . . 400   3 DON JUAN 13     89      3
      MASTERS OF THEIR OWN TIME--OR IN COMMUNION . . . . . 406   3 DON JUAN 13    103      3
      EACH ROSE UP AT HIS OWN AND HAD TO SPARE . . . . . . 406   3 DON JUAN 13    103      6
      IF FROM GREAT NATURE'S OR OUR OWN ABYSS  . . . . . . 410   3 DON JUAN 14      1      1
      OF YOUR OWN THOUGHTS IN ALL THEIR SELF CONFESSION  . . . 413   3 DON JUAN 14      6      4
      YET I MUST OWN--ALTHOUGH IN THIS I YIELD .  . . . . . 425   3 DON JUAN 14     35      3
      OWN THEY FORESAW THAT YOU WOULD FALL AT LAST . . . . . 432   3 DON JUAN 14     50      6
      BUT THERE'S ANOTHER LITTLE THING I OWN  . . . . . . 445   3 DON JJAN 14     82      5
      BUT WHEN THE LATTER WORKS ITS OWN UNDOING  . . . . . 446   3 DON JUAN 14     85      7
      SHE KNEW NOT HER OWN HEART THEN HOW SHOULD I  . . . . . 449   3 DJN JUAN 14     91      1
      HER HUSBAND'S FRIEND HER OWN YOUNG AND A STRANGER  . . . 449   3 DON JUAN 14     91      8
      IN FACT HIS MANNER WAS HIS OWN ALONE . . . . . . . 461   3 DON JUAN 15     13      4
      BUT MODESTY'S AT TIMES ITS OWN REWARD .  . . . . . . 462   3 DON JUAN 15     14      6
      WAS APT TO ADD A COLOURING FROM HER OWN  . . . . . . 463   3 DON JUAN 15     17      2
      BUT FOR MY OWN PECULIAR SUPERSTITION . . . . . . . 467   3 DON JUAN 15     24      4
      NOR BROKEN MY OWN HEAD NOR THAT OF PRISCIAN . . . . . 467   3 DON JUAN 15     24      6
      TO HIS OWN CIRCUMSTANCES THERE MIGHT LIE . . . . . . 469   3 DJN JUAN 15     30      4
      SOME DIFFICULTIES AS IN HIS OWN PREFERENCE . . . . . 469   3 DON JUAN 15     30      5
      IN HER OWN MIND AND THAT'S ENOUGH FOR WOMAN . . . . . 473   3 DON JUAN 15     40      2
      AS FAR AS HER OWN GENTLE HEART ALLOW'D . . . . . . . 476   3 DON JUAN 15     46      2
      IN ITS OWN STRENGTH--MOST STRANGE IN ONE SO YOUNG  . . . 477   3 DON JUAN 15     47      8
      OF OTHERS WITH HER OWN OPINIONS STATED--  . . . . . 478   3 DON JUAN 15     50      7
      WILL PIQUE A GENTLEMAN FOR HIS OWN CREDIT  . . . . . 491   3 DON JUAN 15     79      5
      BUT THIS I MUST SAY IN MY OWN APPLAUSE  . . . . . . 502   3 DON JUAN 16      2      4
      IF HE HAD KNOWN EXACTLY HIS OWN PLIGHT  . . . . . . 506   3 DON JUAN 16     12      5
      OF YOUR OWN FOOTSTEPS--VOICES FROM THE URN . . . . . 508   3 DON JUAN 16     18      4
      PURSUED AN INSTANT FOR HER OWN CONTENT . . . . . . . 521   3 DON JUAN 16     42      4
      WAS MUCH CONSOLED BY HIS OWN REPARTEE . . . . . . . 522   3 DON JUAN 16     43      8
      AMONGST OUR OWN MOST MUSICAL OF NATIONS  . . . . . . 523   3 DON JUAN 16     45      6
      AND EVERYBODY OUT OF THEIR OWN SPHERE . . . . . . . 538   3 DON JUAN 16     78      8
      FROM THOSE WHO HAVE FEW RESOURCES OF THEIR OWN  . . . . 541   3 DON JUAN 16     85      5
      HER OWN BUT SERVED TO SET OFF EVERY JOKE . . . . . . 552   3 DON JUAN 16    104      5
      THE HEART IN AN EXISTENCE OF ITS OWN  . . . . . . . 554   3 DON JUAN 16    108      7
      HIS OWN INTERNAL GHOST BEGAN TO AWAKEN  . . . . . . 558   3 DON JUAN 16    118      5
      FOUND HIS OWN LEGS EMBARGOED FROM MERE WALKING . . . . 565   3 DON JUAN 17      8      4
OWN'D
      WHERE'S CHARLOTTE (THAT'S NOT EASILY OWN'D) . . . . . 307   3 DON JUAN 11     78     V3
      OWN'D TO A PENCHANT THOUGH DISCREET FOR BEAUTY . . . . 494   3 DON JUAN 15     85      8
OWNED
      FOR WHICH HE OWNED A PRESENT APPETITE . . . . . . . 452   2 DON JUAN  5     71      4
      WHICH MUST BE OWNED WAS SENSITIVE AND SURLY . . . . . 234   3 DON JUAN 10     19      4
OWNER
      NEXT OWNER FOR THEIR DOUBLE-DAMN'D POST-OBITS . . . . . 89    2 DON JUAN  1    125      8
      THE FRIEND OF ARTISTS IF NOT ARTS--THE OWNER . . . . . 528   3 DON JUAN 16     57      2
OWNER'S
      OF EYES WERE CRYING FOR THEIR OWNER'S CASE . . . . . 186   2 DON JUAN  2     56      6
OWNERS
      GASPS AND WHATEVER ELSE THE OWNERS CHOOSE-- . . . . . 110   2 DON JUAN  1    162      5
OX
      BY BORROWING A NEW ONE FROM AN OX . . . . . . . . 91    2 DON JUAN  1    129      8
      HIS OX--HIS ASS--NOR ANYTHING THAT'S HIS . . . . . . 140   2 DON JUAN  1    206     V2
      CHEAPENING AN OX AN ASS A LAMB OR KID .  . . . . . . 425   2 DON JUAN  5     28      6
      WHO FELL AS ROLLS AN OX O'ER IN HIS PASTURE . . . . . 274   3 DON JUAN 11     13      5
      THAT OX OF VERSE WHO PLOUGHS FOR EVERY LINE--  . . . . 297   3 DON JUAN 11     58      6
      THERE WAS A PRIZE OX A PRIZE PIG AND PLOUGHMAN . . . . 530   3 DON JUAN 16     60      7
OXENSTIERN
      AND I REFER YOU TO WISE OXENSTIERN . . . . . . . . 436   3 DON JUAN 14     59      8
OXLESS
      BUT BEEF IS RARE WITHIN THESE OXLESS ISLES . . . . . 238   2 DON JUAN  2    154      1
OYSTER
      AN OYSTER MAY BE CROSS'D IN LOVE--AND WHY  . . . . . 445   3 DON JUAN 14     81      1
OYSTERS
      EGGS OYSTERS TOO ARE AMATORY FOOD . . . . . . . . 246   2 DON JUAN  2    170      6
      OYSTERS AND EGGS ARE ALSO LOVING FOOD .  . . . . . . 246   2 DON JUAN  2    170     V6
PACE
      A MOMENT WITHOUT SLACKENING FROM THEIR PACE . . . . . 441   2 DON JUAN  5     54      3
      AND THEN MOVED ON AGAIN WITH RAPID PACE  . . . . . . 61    3 DON JUAN  6    111      2
      THE DEVIL MAY TAKE THAT STEALTHY PACE OF HIS . . . . . 556   3 DON JUAN 16    112      4
PACED
      PACED ON MOST MAIDEN-LIKE AND MELANCHOLY . . . . . . 22    3 DON JUAN  6     33      8
PACES
      PACES WERE LEFT WHEREON YOU COULD CONTRIVE . . . . . 136   3 DON JUAN  8     47      2
      WHICH PUTS MY PEGASUS TO THESE GRAVE PACES . . . . . 334   3 DON JUAN 12     39      8
```

PACHA
    BUT NOW HE SUNG THE SULTAN AND THE PACHA . . . . 316 2 DON JUAN 3   79   7
    TO GIVE SOME REBEL PACHA A CRAVAT . . . . 463 2 DON JUAN 5   89   7
    THEY WOULD PREFER TO PADISHA OR PACHA . . . . 25 3 DON JUAN 6   39   8
    THE OLD PACHA SITS AMONG SOME HUNDREDS DEAD . . . . . 160 3 DON JUAN 8   98   3
    WHERE THE CHIEF PACHA CALMLY HELD HIS POST . . . . . 171 3 DON JUAN 8 120   2
PACHAS
    HOW SOME WERE BOUGHT BY PACHAS SOME BY JEWS . . . . . 409 2 DON JUAN 4 116   2
    BY REBEL PACHAS AND ENCROACHING GIAOURS . . . . . . 497 2 DON JUAN 5 150   7
PACK
    EVEN IF IT SHOULD COMPRISE A PACK OF FABLES . . . . . 117 2 DON JUAN 1 175   6
    DON JUAN BADE HIS VALET PACK HIS THINGS . . . . . . 161 2 DON JUAN 2   9   1
    BY NIGHT AS DO THAT MERCENARY PACK ALL . . . . . . 196 3 DON JUAN 9   27   3
PACK'D
    YOUNG SLENDER AND PACK'D EASILY HE LAY . . . . 112 2 DON JUAN 1 166   3
PACKET
    THEN BROKE HIS PACKET TO SEE WHAT WAS IN'T . . . . . 440 3 DON JUAN 14   69   5
PACKETS
    THY PACKETS ALL WHOSE PASSENGERS ARE BOOTIES . . . . 259 3 DON JUAN 10   69   5
PAD
    FOR EASTERN STAYS ARE LITTLE MADE TO PAD . . . . . . 492 2 DON JUAN 5 140   3
    FOR THE FIRST AND LAST TIME FOR LIKE A PAD . . . . . 122 3 DON JUAN 8   22   5
PADISHA
    THEY WOULD PREFER TO PADISHA OR PACHA . . . . 25 3 DON JUAN 6   39   8
PADLOCK
    AND WEDLOCK AND A PADLOCK MEAN THE SAME . . . . . . 502 2 DON JUAN 5 158   2
PADS
    THESE FREEBORN SOUNDS PROCEEDED FROM FOUR PADS . . . . 273 3 DON JUAN 11   11   1
PAGAN
    THEIR PRESENT LESSONS ON OUR PAGAN FRIENDS HERE . . . 423 2 DON JUAN 5   24   2
PAGANS
    TO SLAY THE PAGANS WHO RESISTED BATTERING . . . . . 99 3 DON JUAN 7   64   7
PAGE
    BUT THEN THEY SHONE NOT ON THE POET'S PAGE . . . . . 24 2 DON JUAN 1   5   4
    BUT NOT A PAGE OF ANY THING THAT'S LOOSE . . . . . . 44 2 DON JUAN 1   40   6
    ACTIVE THOUGH NOT SO SPRIGHTLY AS A PAGE . . . . . . 51 2 DON JUAN 1   54   3
    EVEN AS THE PAGE IS RUSTLED WHILE WE LOOK . . . . . 72 2 DON JUAN 1   95   3
    AND SMEAR HIS PAGE WITH GALL INSTEAD OF HONEY . . . . 142 2 DON JUAN 1 210   7
    AND THINKS HEAVEN BRIGHTER EVEN THAN NEWTON'S PAGE . . 242 2 DON JUAN 2 163 V7
    AND THEREFORE LEAVE THEM TO THE PURER PAGE . . . . . 397 2 DON JUAN 4   98   2
    LIKE MODERATE HOTSPUR ON THE IMMORTAL PAGE . . . . . 490 2 DON JUAN 5 136   4
    LIKE NATURAL SHAKESPEARE ON THE IMMORTAL PAGE . . . . 490 2 DON JUAN 5 136 V4
    A PERIOD SOMETHING LIKE A PRINTED PAGE . . . . . . 315 3 DON JUAN 12   1   6
    WHO IN HIS COMMON-PLACE BOOK HAD A PAGE . . . . . . 403 3 DON JUAN 13   97   5
    AS I HAVE SAID IN--I FORGET WHAT PAGE . . . . 433 3 DON JUAN 14   54   5
    A PAGE WHERE TIME SHOULD HESITATE TO PRINT AGE . . . 458 3 DON JUAN 15   7   5
    ESPECIALLY UPON A PRINTED PAGE . . . . 494 3 DON JUAN 15   85   4
PAGEANT
    OF BRUTUS AT THE PAGEANT OF TIBERIUS . . . . 477 3 DON JUAN 15   49   2
PAGES
    (I THINK THE QUARTO HOLDS FIVE HUNDRED PAGES) . . . . 11 2 DON JUAN D   4   2
    INSTEAD OF BEING SCATTER'D THROUGH THE PAGES . . . . 46 2 DON JUAN 1   45   2
    AND WITH THE PAGES OF THE LAST REVIEW . . . . 294 3 DON JUAN 11   50   2
    OF NO GREAT PROMISE FOR POETIC PAGES . . . . 416 3 DON JUAN 14   15   8
    PYTHAGORAS LOCKE SOCRATES--BUT PAGES . . . . 566 3 DON JUAN 17   9   1
PAID
    BUT SCARCE A FEE WAS PAID ON EITHER SIDE . . . . . . 38 2 DON JUAN 1   32   7
    AND NEXT DAY PAID A VISIT TO HIS MOTHER . . . . . . 63 2 DON JUAN 1   76   2
    WITH WHICH THE DOCTOR PAID OFF AN OLD POX . . . . . 91 2 DON JUAN 1 129   7
    PAID DAILY VISITS TO HER BOY AND TOOK . . . . 248 2 DON JUAN 2 174   2
    HE BEING PAID TO SATIRISE OR FLATTER . . . . 316 2 DON JUAN 3   78   7
    IF SHE LOVED RASHLY HER LIFE PAID FOR WRONG-- . . . . 383 2 DON JUAN 4   73   5
    PROTECTS HIS DUST BUT REVERENCE HERE IS PAID . . . . 400 2 DON JUAN 4 104   3
    PROTECTS HIS TOMB BUT GREATER CARE IS PAID . . . . . 400 2 DON JUAN 4 104 V3
    WHETHER YOU'RE PAID BY GOVERNMENT IN BRIBES . . . . . 200 3 DON JUAN 9   35   4
    THEY MUST BE PAID THOUGH SIX DAYS SMOOTHLY RUN . . . 243 3 DON JUAN 10   38   7
    YET STARED AT THIS A LITTLE THOUGH HE PAID IT-- . . . 259 3 DON JUAN 10   70   4
    THAT FUTURE BRIDEGROOMS SWORE AND SIGHED AND PAID IT . 293 3 DON JUAN 11   49   8
    WHATE'ER IT WAS 'TWAS MINE I'VE PAID IN TRUTH . . . . 324 3 DON JUAN 12   17   6
    HE PLAYED AND PAID MADE LOVE WITHOUT MUCH SIN . . . . 327 3 DON JUAN 12   25 V5
    BUT LUCKILY I HAVE PAID FEW PARISH FEES SINCE) . . . 530 3 DON JUAN 16   61   6
    THAN THOSE WHO WERE NOT PAID FOR INDEPENDENCE . . . . 537 3 DON JUAN 16   76   2
    HE HAD PAID HIS NEIGHBOUR'S PRAYER WITH HALF A TURBOT . 543 3 DON JUAN 16   88   8
PAIL
    A PAIL OF HOUSEMAID'S WATER UNAWARES . . . . 34 2 DON JUAN 1   24   8
PAIN
    THE COUNT STRONGSTROGANOFF I PUT IN PAIN . . . . . . 102 2 DON JUAN 1 149   6
    'TIS WISE--'TIS WELL BUT NOT THE LESS A PAIN . . . . 130 2 DON JUAN 1 192   2
    IT MENDS THEIR MORALS NEVER MIND THE PAIN . . . . . 157 2 DON JUAN 2   1   4
    BUT WORST OF ALL IS NAUSEA OR A PAIN . . . . 168 2 DON JUAN 2   23   1
    WHEN DRIED TO SUMMER DUST TILL TAUGHT BY PAIN . . . . 201 2 DON JUAN 2   84   3
    WITH JUST ENOUGH OF LIFE TO FEEL ITS PAIN . . . . . 213 2 DON JUAN 2 108   7
    THOSE EYES TO CLOSE THOUGH WEARINESS AND PAIN . . . . 235 2 DON JUAN 2 149   3
    PLEASURE OR PAIN TO ONE ANOTHER LIVING . . . . . . 258 2 DON JUAN 2 192   8
    OF PLEASURE AND OF PAIN--EVEN WHILE I KISS . . . . . 364 2 DON JUAN 4   38   5
    BROUGHT BACK THE SENSE OF PAIN WITHOUT THE CAUSE . . 378 2 DON JUAN 4   62   7
    CAN GIVE US EITHER PAIN OR PLEASURE WHO . . . . . . 428 2 DON JUAN 5   32   6
    AND RAPTURE'S SELF WILL SEEM ALMOST A PAIN . . . . . 474 2 DON JUAN 5 110   4
    WHICH IT CAN EITHER PAIN OR EVIL CALL . . . . 17 3 DON JUAN 6   22   5

	PAGE	VOL		CANTO	STANZA	LN
PAIN (CONTINUED)						
AND THE HEART'S DEW OF PAIN SPRANG FAST AND CHILLY	58	3	DON JUAN	6	105	7
THEIR BAFFLED RAGE AND PAIN WHILE WAXING COLDER	158	3	DON JUAN	8	94	5
IN JUAN'S LOOK PAIN PLEASURE HOPE FEAR MIXED	159	3	DON JUAN	8	96	3
NO DOUBT GAVE PAIN WHERE EACH NEW PAIR OF SHOULDERS	208	3	DON JUAN	9	52	7
TO PAIN THE MOMENT WHEN YOU CEASE TO PLEASE	231	3	DON JUAN	10	13	8
WHO KEEP THE WORLD BOTH OLD AND NEW IN PAIN	318	3	DON JUAN	12	5	5
ON PAIN OF MUCH DISPLEASING THE GYNOCRASY	526	3	DON JUAN	16	52	8
PAIN'D						
FOUND ONLY ON THE STAGE AND EACH MORE PAIN'D	394	2	DON JUAN	4	93	3
PAINED						
HER GRACE REPLIED HIS GRACE WAS RATHER PAINED	515	3	DON JUAN	16	34	6
PAINFUL						
HE KNEW NOT TILL EACH PAINFUL PULSE AND LIMB	214	2	DON JUAN	2	111	6
YET 'TIS A PAINFUL FEELING AND UNWILLING	270	2	DON JUAN	2	213	1
ALAS HOW DEEPLY PAINFUL IS ALL PAYMENT	264	3	DON JUAN	10	79	1
PAINING						
'TWILL MAKE IF PROVED VAST EFFORTS WITHOUT PAINING	366	3	DON JUAN	13	18	8
PAINS						
HAD HIS FIRST CHOICE OF MORSELS FOR HIS PAINS	197	2	DON JUAN	2	77	2
AND FOR THEIR PAINS GET ONLY A FRESH PUNCTURE	263	3	DON JUAN	10	77	8
AND FOR THEIR PAINS GET SMARTER PUNCTURATIONS	263	3	DON JUAN	10	77	V8
THEY'RE BARREN AND NOT WORTH THE PAINS TO PULL	402	3	DON JUAN	13	95	6
PAINT						
FULL OF BARBARIC CARVING PAINT AND GILDING	223	2	DON JUAN	2	127	8
ROMANCES PAINT AT FULL LENGTH PEOPLE'S WOOINGS	279	2	DON JUAN	3	8	3
TO GILD REFINED GOLD OR PAINT THE LILY	314	2	DON JUAN	3	76	8
WITH SOME SMALL AID FROM SCISSORS PAINT AND TWEEZERS	458	2	DON JUAN	5	80	2
TO PAINT A SIEGE WHEREIN MORE MEN WERE SLAIN	106	3	DON JUAN	7	80	2
CAN PAINT COSI VIAGGINO I RICCHI	380	3	DON JUAN	13	47	5
THE MONDE EXACTLY AS THEY OUGHT TO PAINT	418	3	DON JUAN	14	19	3
SCOTT WHO CAN PAINT YOUR CHRISTIAN KNIGHT OR SARACEN	481	3	DON JUAN	15	59	5
TO PAINT A SOLE SENSATION--THOUGH QUITE COMMON--	569	3	DON JUAN	17	V 13	4
PAINTED						
NEW PAINTED OR A PRETTY OPERA-SCENE	436	2	DON JUAN	5	46	8
WHO PAINTED THEIR BARE LIMBS BUT NOT WITH GORE	180	3	DON JUAN	8	136	8
THAT PLEASANT CAPITAL OF PAINTED SNOWS	203	3	DON JUAN	9	42	8
THE PAINTING AND THE PAINTED YOUTH CERUSE	293	3	DON JUAN	11	48	4
IN CHISELLED STONE AND PAINTED GLASS AND ALL	507	3	DON JUAN	16	16	7
PALE AS IF PAINTED SO HER CHEEK BEING RED	532	3	DON JUAN	16	64	2
PAINTER						
WOULD THAT I WERE A PAINTER TO BE GROUPING	60	3	DON JUAN	6	109	5
PAINTER'S						
OF MARRIAGE--(WHICH MIGHT FORM A PAINTER'S FAME	473	3	DON JUAN	15	39	7
PAINTERS						
WHICH PAINTERS CANNOT CATCH LIKE FACES SINNING	32	3	DON JUAN	6	52	4
AND AS ROMANTIC HEADS ARE PRETTY PAINTERS	284	3	DON JUAN	11	33	3
PAINTING						
THAT PAINTING IS NO IDOL 'TIS TOO LIKE	336	2	DON JUAN	3	103	8
THE PAINTING AND THE PAINTED YOUTH CERUSE	293	3	DON JUAN	11	48	4
CHALK MIMICS PAINTING THEN FESTOONS ARE TWIRLED	302	3	DON JUAN	11	67	5
PAINTS						
SO WELL NOT ONE OF THE AFORESAID PAINTS	47	2	DON JUAN	1	47	6
OF ORPHANS PAINTS AT ONCE A PARISH SCHOOL	563	3	DON JUAN	17	3	3
PAIR						
HE AND HIS WIFE WERE AN ILL-SORTED PAIR--	49	2	DON JUAN	1	51	6
TO LEAVE TOGETHER THIS IMPRUDENT PAIR	80	2	DON JUAN	1	110	6
AND FOUND MUCH LINEN LACE AND SEVERAL PAIR	99	2	DON JUAN	1	143	3
IS IT FOR THIS WE WERE THE ONLY PAIR	102	2	DON JUAN	1	148	V3
HIS SUFFOCATION BY THAT PRETTY PAIR	112	2	DON JUAN	1	166	6
WHEN LO HE STUMBLED O'ER A PAIR OF SHOES	120	2	DON JUAN	1	180	8
A PAIR OF SHOES--WHAT THEN NOT MUCH IF THEY	121	2	DON JUAN	1	181	1
I DOUBT ALL LIKENESS ENDS BETWEEN THE PAIR	124	2	DON JUAN	1	186	8
IT WITH A PAIR OF PISTOLS AND THEIR FEARS	174	2	DON JUAN	2	35	4
WHICH COURAGE GIVES WHILE POOR PEDRILLO'S PAIR	186	2	DON JUAN	2	56	5
WITH THEIR ONE OAR (I WISH THEY HAD HAD A PAIR)	193	2	DON JUAN	2	70	5
I'LL TELL YOU WHO THEY WERE THIS FEMALE PAIR	222	2	DON JUAN	2	124	1
SINCE AFTER ALL NO DOUBT THE YOUTHFUL PAIR	233	2	DON JUAN	2	144	6
PAIR OF SCARCE DECENT TROWSERS--WENT TO WORK	240	2	DON JUAN	2	160	2
EXCEPTING OUR FIRST PARENTS SUCH A PAIR	258	2	DON JUAN	2	193	3
SO INNOCENT AND BEAUTIFUL A PAIR	258	2	DON JUAN	2	193	V3
THE BOOK WHICH TREATS OF THIS ERRONEOUS PAIR	282	2	DON JUAN	3	12	6
BUT ALL THE BETTER FOR THE HAPPY PAIR	288	2	DON JUAN	3	24	3
OH--THE THIRD CANTO--AND THE PRETTY PAIR--	317	2	DON JUAN	3	81	6
ENOUGH--THE FAITHFUL AND THE FAIRY PAIR	353	2	DON JUAN	4	18	2
THE SWEETEST SONG-BIRDS NESTLE IN A PAIR	358	2	DON JUAN	4	28	6
'TIS--'TIS HER FATHER'S--FIX'D UPON THE PAIR	363	2	DON JUAN	4	35	8
I HAVE EXAMINED FEW PAIR OF THAT HUE)	404	2	DON JUAN	4	110	5
I'LL BET SOME PAIR OF STOCKINGS BEAT PERU	406	2	DON JUAN	4	112	V8
AND PAIR THEIR RHYMES AS VENUS YOKES HER DOVES	411	2	DON JUAN	5	1	3
FIRST BUT FOR ONE AND AFTER FOR THE PAIR	425	2	DON JUAN	5	28	3
A PAIR OF TROWSERS OF FLESH-COLOURED SILK	456	2	DON JUAN	5	77	2
A PAIR OF DRAWERS--OF FINE CRIMSON SATIN	456	2	DON JUAN	5	77	V2
JUAN A MOMENT AS THIS PAIR SO SMALL	463	2	DON JUAN	5	90	5
BENT LIKE AN ANTELOPE A PAPHIAN PAIR	466	2	DON JUAN	5	96	3
WITH A FAR REACHING GLANCE--A PAPHIAN PAIR	466	2	DON JUAN	5	96	V3
BENT AN ITALIAN SKY-BLUE PAPHIAN PAIR	467	2	DON JUAN	5	96	V3
THE PRISONED EAGLE WILL NOT PAIR NOR I	484	2	DON JUAN	5	126	7
I'LL TAKE JUANNA WE'RE A SLENDERER PAIR	29	3	DON JUAN	6	47	4

583

PAIR   (CONTINUED)
AND SENT ONE ON A SUMMONS TO THE PAIR 64   3 DON JUAN 6   118   2
IN THIS PLAIN PAIR SUWARROW AND HIS GUIDE 87   3 DON JUAN 7   43   8
NO DOUBT GAVE PAIN WHERE EACH NEW PAIR OF SHOULDERS . . 208 3 DON JUAN 9   52   7
AND THUS THEY FORMED A RATHER CUROUS PAIR . . . . . . 252 3 DON JUAN 10   57   5
IN HAPPIER PLIGHT THAN IF THEY FORMED A PAIR . . . . . 344 3 DON JUAN 12   61   8
AND NOW I WILL PROCEED UPON THE PAIR . . . . 365 3 DON JUAN 13   13   3
TO NORMAN ABBEY WHIRLED THE NOBLE PAIR-- . . . . . . 384 3 DON JUAN 13   55   1
AND ADDS A THIRD TO WHAT WAS LATE A PAIR . . . . . . 481 3 DON JUAN 15   59 V8
PAIR'D
PAIR'D OFF WITH A BACCHANTE BLOOMING VISAGE . . . . . 394 2 DON JUAN 4   92   8
PAIRS
OF FAITHFUL PAIRS--(I NEEDS MUST RHYME WITH DOVE . . . 219 3 DON JUAN 9   74   3
PALACE
PALACE OR GARDEN PARADISE OR CAVERN 24   2 DON JUAN 1   6   7
FROM THE DULL PALACE TO THE DIRTY HOVEL . . . . 263 2 DON JUAN 2   201   7
BY JOVE A NOBLE PALACE--LIGHTED TOO . . . . 436 2 DON JUAN 5   45   8
WHY 'TIS A PALACE WHERE THE TRULY WISE . . . . 458 2 DON JUAN 5   81   7
FOR HAVING HAD HIM TO HER PALACE LED . . . . 483 2 DON JUAN 5   124   6
THE FORMER IN A PALACE WHERE LIKE NUNS . . . . 498 2 DON JUAN 5   152   3
SAINT JAMES'S PALACE AND SAINT JAMES'S HELLS . . . . . 282 3 DON JUAN 11   29   8
AND GAZE WHERE'ER THE PALACE OR THE HOVEL IS . . . . . 361 3 DON JUAN 13   7   7
WHEELS WHIRL FROM CARLTON PALACE TO SOHO . . . . . . 378 3 DON JUAN 13   44   3
PALACES
SPRINKLED WITH PALACES THE OCEAN STREAM . . . . 412 2 DON JUAN 5   3   2
OCCUR IN ORIENT PALACES AND EVEN . . . . 465 2 DON JUAN 5   94   2
ALL WRATH IN BARRACKS PALACES OR COTS . . . . 200 3 DON JUAN 9   36   5
TO FEEL IN FRIENDLESS PALACES A HOME . . . . 475 3 DON JUAN 15   44   7
PALATES
THE GLASSES JINGLED AND THE PALATES TINGLED . . . . . 487 3 DON JUAN 15   70   1
PALE
AND HEARTLESS DAUGHTERS--WORN--AND PALE--AND POOR . . . 15   2 DON JUAN D   11   6
SHE CEASED AND TURN'D UPON HER PILLOW PALE . . . . . 108 2 DON JUAN 1   158   1
WHILE THE O'ERPOWERING EYE THAT TURNS YOU PALE . . . . 160 2 DON JUAN 2   7   3
SOME LANDSMEN WOULD HAVE LOOK'D A LITTLE PALE . . . . 170 2 DON JUAN 2   26   4
AND GRIMLY DARKLED O'ER THEIR FACES PALE . . . . . . 182 2 DON JUAN 2   49   6
FROM HIS PALE LIPS AND EVER ON HIM GAZED . . . . . . 203 2 DON JUAN 2   89   3
LIKE CHARON'S BARK OF SPECTRES DULL AND PALE . . . . . 209 2 DON JUAN 2   101   3
THE PALE CONTENDED WITH THE PURPLE ROSE . . . . 236 2 DON JUAN 2   150   3
AND THEN ON THE PALE CHEEK HER BREAST NOW WARMS . . . 260 2 DON JUAN 2   195   6
ON CRIMSON SATIN BORDER'D WITH PALE BLUE . . . . . . 309 2 DON JUAN 3   67   2
SHE WORE TWO JELICKS--ONE WAS OF PALE YELLOW . . . . . 311 2 DON JUAN 3   70   2
PALE AS THE FOAM THAT FROTH'D ON HIS DEAD BROW . . . . 362 2 DON JUAN 4   34   2
THE OLD MAN'S CHEEK GREW PALE BUT NOT WITH DREAD . . . 365 2 DON JUAN 4   40   3
PALE STATUE-LIKE AND STERN SHE WOO'D THE BLOW . . . . 367 2 DON JUAN 4   43   4
AND THEN THOUGH PALE HE WAS SO VERY HANDSOME . . . . . 415 2 DON JUAN 5   9   7
SOME BOUGHT THE JET WHILE OTHERS CHOSE THE PALE . . . 416 2 DON JUAN 5   10   4
AND LEFT HIS CHEEKS AS PALE AS SNOWDROPS BLOWING . . . 478 2 DON JUAN 5   117   6
GROW DEADLY PALE AND THEN BLUSH BACK AGAIN . . . . . 483 2 DON JUAN 5   124   8
GULBEYAZ ROSE FROM RESTLESSNESS AND PALE 49   3 DON JUAN 6   87   2
THOUGH PALE WITH CONFLICTS BETWEEN LOVE AND PRIDE-- . . 50   3 DON JUAN 6   89   6
WHITE WAXEN AND AS ALABASTER PALE 60   3 DON JUAN 6   109   4
BEYOND THE DWARFING CITY'S PALE ABORTIONS . . . . . . 145 3 DON JUAN 8   66   2
AS HE TURNED O'ER EACH PALE AND GORY CHEEK . . . . . 158 3 DON JUAN 8   94   6
A PURE TRANSPARENT PALE YET RADIANT FACE . . . . . . 159 3 DON JUAN 8   96   7
AND SEA-SICK PASSENGERS TURNED SOMEWHAT PALE . . . . . 256 3 DON JUAN 10   64   5
THE LADIES--SOME ROUGED SOME A LITTLE PALE-- . . . . . 406 3 DON JUAN 13   104   1
'TIS TRUE YOU DON'T--BUT PALE AND STRUCK WITH TERROR . . 413 3 DON JUAN 14   6   1
LOOKED GRAVE AND PALE TO SEE HER FRIEND'S FRAGILITY . . 430 3 DON JUAN 14   46   7
AND THE PALE SMILE OF BEAUTIES IN THE GRAVE . . . . . 509 3 DON JUAN 16   19   1
SHE LOOKED AND SAW HIM PALE AND TURNED AS PALE . . . . 514 3 DON JUAN 16   31   1
SHE LOOKED AND SAW HIM PALE AND TURNED AS PALE . . . . 514 3 DON JUAN 16   31   1
THAT ANCIENT LINE IN THE PALE MOONSHINE . . . . . . 519 3 DON JUAN 16 L 4   3
THE PRESENT CULPRIT WAS EXTREMELY PALE . . . . 532 3 DON JUAN 16   64   1
PALE AS IF PAINTED SO HER CHEEK BEING RED . . . . . . 532 3 DON JUAN 16   64   2
ITS KIND ATTENTIONS TO THEIR PROPER PALE . . . . . . 533 3 DON JUAN 16   67   6
YET GREW A LITTLE PALE--WITH WHAT CONCERN . . . . . . 545 3 DON JUAN 16   94   5
SEEMED PALE AND SHIVERED AS IF SHE HAD KEPT . . . . . 568 3 DON JUAN 17   14   7
PALELY
AND ROUND ITS ONCE WARM PRECINCTS PALELY LYING . . . 301 2 DON JUAN 3   51   6
LIKE A MEEK TRADESMAN WHEN APPROACHING PALELY . . . . 459 3 DON JUAN 15   8   3
PALER
BEAUTY SPRINGS FORTH AND NATURE'S SELF TURNS PALER . . 204 3 DON JUAN 9   44   4
PALES
WHENE'ER THEIR TRIUMPH PALES OR STAR IS TAMED-- . . . 448 3 DON JUAN 14   89   6
PALISADE
O'ER THE ENTRENCHMENT AND THE PALISADE . . . . 119 3 DON JUAN 8   15   7
PALISADES
A QUANTITY OF PALISADES UPRIGHT 71   3 DON JUAN 7   10   6
JUST NAMED THESE PALISADES WERE PRIMLY SET . . . . . 136 3 DON JUAN 8   46   8
WAS THAT THEY COULD KICK DOWN THE PALISADES . . . . . 136 3 DON JUAN 8   47   7
NOR USE THOSE PALISADES BY DAMES ERECTED . . . . . . 437 3 DON JUAN 14   61   7
PALISADOED
HAD PALISADOED IN A WAY YOU'D WONDER . . . . 136 3 DON JUAN 8   46   4
PALL
OF HELL SHALL PALL THEM IN A DEEPER CLOAK . . . . . . 110 3 DON JUAN 7   86   8
WHICH BEARS THE GREATEST LIKENESS TO PALL MALL . . . . 124 3 DON JUAN 8   26   8
OF WHAT I THEN DREAMT CLOTHED IN THEIR OWN PALL . . . 233 3 DON JUAN 10   18   5
PALL MALL AND SO FORTH HAVE A CORUSCATION . . . . . . 280 3 DON JUAN 11   26   2

PALL   (CONTINUED)
    OVER THE STONES STILL RATTLING UP PALL MALL 282   3 DON JUAN 11   29   1
    THEIRS IS THE PLEASURE THAT CAN NEVER PALL 316   3 DON JUAN 12   3   2
    HE SWEEPS ALONG IN HIS DUSKY PALL 520   3 DON JUAN 16   L 6   3
PALLAS
    AND PALLAS ALSO SANCTIONS THE SAME HUE 218   3 DON JUAN 9   71   7
PALLID
    HIS SLENDER FRAME AND PALLID ASPECT LAY 214   2 DON JUAN 2   110   7
    A THIRD'S ALL PALLID ASPECT OFFERED MORE 40   3 DON JUAN 6   67   3
    A SPECTRAL RESIDENT--WHOSE PALLID BEAM 279   3 DON JUAN 11   24   6
    TO HINDER HIM FROM GROWING STILL MORE PALLID 515   3 DON JUAN 16   35   8
PALLS
    FOR THE FIRST SEASON SUCH A LIFE SCARCE PALLS 342   3 DON JUAN 12   57   8
    IT PALLS--AT LEAST IT DID SO UPON ME 417   3 DON JUAN 14   17   7
PALM
    OR EATS FROM OUT THE PALM OR PLAYFUL LOWERS 292   2 DON JUAN 3   32   6
PALMS
    AS THROUGH HIS PALMS BOB ACRES' VALOUR OOZED 493   2 DON JUAN 5   142   1
PALPABLE
    DISTINCT AND HIGH AND PALPABLE TO VIEW 207   2 DON JUAN 2   97   8
PALPABLY
    GENTLY BUT PALPABLY CONFIRM'D ITS GRASP 81   2 DON JUAN 1   111   2
    IS NOT AT ONCE TOO PALPABLY DESCRIED 304   3 DON JUAN 11   71   4
PALPITATING
    AND HIDE HER LITTLE PALPITATING BREAST 157   3 DON JUAN 8   91   7
PALPITATION
    STRONG PALPITATION RISES 'TIS HER BOON 267   2 DON JUAN 2   208   6
PALPITI'S
    THE TANTI PALPITI'S ON SUCH OCCASIONS 523   3 DON JUAN 16   45   4
PALSIED
    AND PALSIED FANCY WHICH NO LONGER ROVES 228   3 DON JUAN 10   6   6
PALTRY
    AS CERTAIN--THESE ARE PALTRY THINGS AND YET 16   3 DON JUAN 6   21   7
    IN TAKING UP THIS PALTRY SHEET OF PAPER 226   3 DON JUAN 10   3   2
    AS EVERY PALTRY MAGAZINE CAN SHOW IT'S 295   3 DON JUAN 11   54   8
PAMPER'D
    DREST TO A SYBARITE'S MOST PAMPER'D WISHES 307   2 DON JUAN 3   62   5
PAMPHLETS
    WHOSE PAMPHLETS VOLUMES NEWSPAPERS ILLUMINE US 200   3 DON JUAN 9   35   3
PAN
    HEAVEN KNOWS--IT MAY BE NEPTUNE PAN OR JOVE 246   2 DON JUAN 2   170   8
PANCA
    TO FOLLOW JUAN'S WAKE LIKE SANCHO PANCA 175   2 DON JUAN 2   37   8
PANDERING
    OR PANDERING BLINDLY TO HIS OWN DISGRACE 74   2 DON JUAN 1   99   4
PANG
    A PARTING PANG THE SPIRIT FROM HER PAST 381   2 DON JUAN 4   69   3
PANGS
    PERHAPS THAN EVEN THE MENTAL PANGS OF DYING 301   2 DON JUAN 3   51   4
    YET COULD HIS CORPORAL PANGS AMOUNT TO HALF 373   2 DON JUAN 4   54   3
    FOR DOGS OR TO BE SLAIN WITH PANGS REFINED 492   2 DON JUAN 5   141   3
    THERE THE STILL VARYING PANGS WHICH MULTIPLY 118   3 DON JUAN 8   13   1
PANNELS
    OF VELVET PANNELS EACH OF DIFFERENT HUE 308   2 DON JUAN 3   64   2
    THOU MORNING POST SOLE RECORD OF THE PANNELS 308   3 DON JUAN 11   80   4
PANORAMA
    A PANORAMA VIEW OF HELL'S IN TRAINING 135   2 DON JUAN 1   200   6
PANT
    AND THUS FOR WIDER CARNAGE TAUGHT TO PANT 16   2 DON JUAN 0   12   3
    STRETCHED IN THE STREET AND ABLE SCARCE TO PANT 428   2 DON JUAN 5   33   8
    JUST KILLED AND SCARCELY COMPETENT TO PANT 429   2 DON JUAN 5   33   V8
PANTALOONS
    BUT NEVER PUT ON PANTALOONS OR BODDICES 44   2 DON JUAN 1   41   4
PANTED
    COULD YIELD HIS SPIRIT THAT FOR WHICH IT PANTED 73   2 DON JUAN 1   96   4
    AT EIGHTEEN THOUGH BELOW HER FEET STILL PANTED 434   3 DON JUAN 14   55   5
PANTERS
    INTO ALL PANTERS FOR NEWSPAPER PRAISE 85   3 DON JUAN 7   39   4
PANTING
    PANTING FOR POWER AS HARTS FOR COOLING STREAMS 155   2 DON JUAN 1   V 6   1
    PANTING FOR POWER AS TANTALUS FOR WATER 155   2 DON JUAN 1   V 6   V1
PANTISOCRASY
    HE PRATED TO THE WORLD OF PANTISOCRASY 329   2 DON JUAN 3   93   2
PANTOMIME
    WE ALL HAVE SEEN HIM IN THE PANTOMIME 21   2 DON JUAN 1   1   7
    OF PANTOMIME--HE DANCED I SAY RIGHT WELL 427   3 DON JUAN 14   38   3
PANTOMIMES
    THEY TURN OUT MELODRAMES OR PANTOMIMES 470   3 DON JUAN 15   32   8
PANTS
    PILLOW'D ON HER O'ERFLOWING HEART WHICH PANTS 260   2 DON JUAN 2   195   7
PAPA
    WHILST HER PIRATICAL PAPA WAS CRUISING 282   2 DON JUAN 3   13   8
PAPER
    THIS NOTE WAS WRITTEN UPON GILT-EDGED PAPER 134   2 DON JUAN 1   198   1
    A CERTAIN PORTION OF UNCERTAIN PAPER 146   2 DON JUAN 1   218   2
    HAVING NO PAPER FOR THE WANT OF BETTER 195   2 DON JUAN 2   74   7
    FRAIL MAN WHEN PAPER--EVEN A RAG LIKE THIS 327   2 DON JUAN 3   88   7
    IN TAKING UP THIS PALTRY SHEET OF PAPER 226   3 DON JUAN 10   3   2
    THE WEALTH OF WORLDS (A WEALTH OF TAX AND PAPER) . . . 266   3 DON JUAN 10   83   4

PAPER   (CONTINUED)

	PAGE	VOL		CANTO	STANZA	LN
CHIEF IMPULSE WITH A FEW FRAIL PAPER PELLETS	298	3 DON JJAN	11	60	V8
OH GOLD I STILL PREFER THEE UNTO PAPER	317	3 DON JUAN	12	4	7
I'M SERIOUS--SO ARE ALL MEN UPON PAPER	325	3 DON JUAN	12	21	1
A PARAGRAPH IN EVERY PAPER TOLD	382	3 DON JUAN	13	51	1
OR PAPER TURNED TO MONEY BY THE BANK	396	3 DON JUAN	13	80	5
A PAPER KITE WHICH FLIES 'TWIXT LIFE AND DEATH	414	3 DON JUAN	14	8	5
BUT RARELY SEEN LIKE GOLD COMPARED WITH PAPER	510	3 DON JUAN	16	22	7
THE PAPER WAS RIGHT EASY TO PERUSE	512	3 DON JUAN	16	26	6

PAPERS

HAVE FILLED THEIR PAPERS WITH THEIR COMMENTS VARIOUS	352	3 DON JUAN	12	78	4
UPON DEBATE THE PAPERS ECHOED YET	400	3 DON JUAN	13	90	5
OR ON THE MORNING PAPERS READ THEIR LECTURES	406	3 DON JUAN	13	102	6

PAPHIAN

BENT LIKE AN ANTELOPE A PAPHIAN PAIR	466	2 DON JUAN	5	96	3
WITH A FAR REACHING GLANCE--A PAPHIAN PAIR	466	2 DON JUAN	5	96	V3
BENT AN ITALIAN SKY-BLUE PAPHIAN PAIR	467	2 DON JUAN	5	96	V3

PAPHIANS

OF THOSE PEDESTRIAN PAPHIANS WHO ABOUND	282	3 DON JUAN	11	30	4

PARABLE

APOLOGUE FABLE POESY AND PARABLE	495	3 DON JUAN	15	89	1

PARADE

THE ASIAN POMP OF OTTOMAN PARADE	440	2 DON JUAN	5	51	8
QUITE ORDERLY AS IF UPON PARADE	119	3 DON JUAN	8	15	8
WHERE'ER COLLECTIVE WISDOM CAN PARADE	371	3 DON JUAN	13	29	6
TO ALL SHE WAS POLITE WITHOUT PARADE	372	3 DON JUAN	13	32	1
THAT IS WITH THIRTY SERVANTS FOR PARADE	381	3 DON JUAN	13	49	4
SOMETIMES INDEED LIKE SOLDIERS OFF PARADE	417	3 DON JUAN	14	17	1
WHAT DILETTANTI DO WITH VAST PARADE)	522	3 DON JUAN	16	44	3

PARADING

PARADING ALL HER SENSIBILITY	532	3 DON JUAN	16	65	5

PARADISE

PALACE OR GARDEN PARADISE OR CAVERN	24	2 DON JUAN	1	6	7
EACH WAS AN ANGEL AND EARTH PARADISE	265	2 DON JUAN	2	204	8
THE PARADISE BEYOND LIKE THAT OF LIFE	280	2 DON JUAN	3	9	V7
AND DON'T SAY MUCH OF PARADISE OR WIFE	280	2 DON JUAN	3	9	V8
ANTICIPATE THE PROPHET'S PARADISE	458	2 DON JUAN	5	81	8
HAD PARADISE ITSELF TO HER BEEN SHOWN	476	2 DON JUAN	5	113	V7
DEBT HE CALLS WEALTH AND TAXES PARADISE	88	3 DON JUAN	7	45	5
ON EARTH IN PARADISE AND WHEN ONCE SEEN	167	3 DON JUAN	8	111	6
HE SHOUTED ALLAH AND SAW PARADISE	169	3 DON JUAN	8	115	3
FROM SOME FRESH PARADISE AND SET TO PLOUGH	202	3 DON JUAN	9	40	2
MADE ICE SEEM PARADISE AND WINTER SUNNY	235	3 DON JUAN	10	21	8
A PARADISE OF HOPS AND HIGH PRODUCTION	262	3 DON JUAN	10	76	2
THROUGH ROWS MOST MODESTLY CALLED PARADISE	278	3 DON JUAN	11	21	7
AN EARTHLY PARADISE OF OR MOLU	302	3 DON JUAN	11	67	8
'TIS THE POSTILLION'S PARADISE WHEELS FLY	377	3 DON JUAN	13	42	3
THIS PARADISE OF PLEASURE AND ENNUI	417	3 DON JUAN	14	17	8
ADAM EXCHANGED HIS PARADISE FOR PLOUGHING	444	3 DON JUAN	14	78	1

PARADOX

WHAT WAS A PARADOX BECOMES A TRUTH OR	565	3 DON JUAN	17	6	7

PARAGON

RESOLVED THAT JUAN SHOULD BE QUITE A PARAGON	42	2 DON JUAN	1	38	2
WHICH SCARCE EVEN FRANCE THE PARAGON OF NATIONS	299	2 DON JUAN	3	46	3
THAT USUAL PARAGON AN ONLY DAUGHTER	474	3 DON JUAN	15	41	2

PARAGONS

WHO WERE THE VERY PARAGONS OF WIVES	452	3 DON JUAN	14	95	7

PARAGRAPH

A PARAGRAPH IN EVERY PAPER TOLD	382	3 DON JUAN	13	51	1
A PARAGRAPH I THINK ABOUT HORNE TOOKE	512	3 DON JUAN	16	27	3

PARALLEL

OH SHE WAS PERFECT PAST ALL PARALLEL	30	2 DON JUAN	1	17	1

PARAMOUR

EVEN WERE SAINT FRANCIS' PARAMOUR THEIR GUEST	14	3 DON JUAN	6	17	5
HE LIKED TO HAVE A HANDSOME PARAMOUR	51	3 DON JUAN	6	91	3
THE GEORGIAN AND HER PARAMOUR REPLIED	62	3 DON JUAN	6	113	1
I HAD A PARAMOUR--AND I'VE HAD MANY	452	3 DON JUAN	14	95	V2

PARAPET

WHICH RAINED FROM BASTION BATTERY PARAPET	131	3 DON JUAN	8	37	2
THEIR MARTIAL FACES ON THE PARAPET	135	3 DON JUAN	8	45	7
RIGHT IN THE MIDDLE OF THE PARAPET	136	3 DON JUAN	8	46	7
HE CLIMBED TO WHERE THE PARAPET APPEARS	147	3 DON JUAN	8	71	4

PARAS

AND BY MISTAKE SEQUINS WITH PARAS JUMBLING	426	2 DON JUAN	5	29	5

PARASITES

WE TIRE OF MISTRESSES AND PARASITES	405	3 DON JUAN	13	100	6

PARCAE

THE PARCAE THEN CUT SHORT THE FURTHER SPINNING	414	2 DON JUAN	5	6	3

PARCHMENT

OUT OF THEIR HIDES IF PARCHMENT HAD GROWN DEAR	75	3 DON JUAN	7	17	7

PARDON

TO BEG HIS PARDON WHEN I ERR A BIT	86	2 DON JUAN	1	120	8
ALFONSO CLOSED HIS SPEECH AND BEGG'D HER PARDON	120	2 DON JUAN	1	180	1
AND AS YOU'D HAVE ME PARDON YOUR PAST SCORNING--	494	2 DON JUAN	5	145	6
YOU'LL PARDON TO MY MUSE A FEW SHORT NAPS	503	2 DON JUAN	5	159	8
THAT IS WE CANNOT PARDON THEIR BAD TASTE	14	3 DON JUAN	6	17	1
IMPLORED THAT PRESENT PARDON MIGHT BE SHOWN	47	3 DON JUAN	6	82	4
A GREEN FIELD IS A SIGHT WHICH MAKES HIM PARDON	262	3 DON JUAN	10	76	5
OH PARDON ME DIGRESSION--OR AT LEAST	334	3 DON JUAN	12	39	1

PARDON   (CONTINUED)
AND BEG HIS BRITISH GODSHIP'S HUMBLE PARDON 442   3 DON JUAN 14   75   4
WAS--PARDON THE PEDANTIC ILLUSTRATION-- 522   3 DON JUAN 16   43   2
PARDONED
THE WOMEN PARDONED ALL EXCEPT HER FACE   476   2 DON JUAN 5   113   8
PARE
IT WOULD NOT SPOIL SOME SEPARATE CHARM TO PARE 27   3 DON JUAN 6   42   8
PARENTAL
PARENTAL FEELINGS AND THE OTHER CLASS 250   3 DON JUAN 10   53   5
BUT MERELY THEIR PARENTAL TENDERNESS 562   3 DON JUAN 17   1   7
PARENTHESIS
THIS LONG PARENTHESIS I COULD NOT SHUT   34   3 DON JUAN 6   56   4
PARENTLESS
THIS CHILD WHO IS PARENTLESS AND THEREFORE MINE   161   3 DON JUAN 8   100   8
PARENT'S
TO THE YOUNG BIRD THE PARENT'S BROODING WINGS 338   2 DON JUAN 3   107   3
PARENTS
DON JUAN'S PARENTS LIVED BESIDE THE RIVER   25   2 DON JUAN 1   8   7
WHERE OUR FIRST PARENTS NEVER LEARN'D TO KISS   30   2 DON JUAN 1   18   3
HIS PARENTS NE'ER AGREED EXCEPT IN DOTING   34   2 DON JUAN 1   25   3
THUS PARENTS ALSO ARE AT TIMES SHORT-SIGHTED   75   2 DON JUAN 1   100   1
EXCEPTING OUR FIRST PARENTS SUCH A PAIR 258   2 DON JUAN 2   193   3
AND EATS HER PARENTS ALBEIT THE DIGESTION   411   3 DON JUAN 14   2   2
THEIR TENDER PARENTS IN THEIR BUDDING DAYS 562   3 DON JUAN 17   1   6
TOO SOON THEY ARE PARENTS TO THEMSELVES FOR WHAT   564   3 DON JUAN 17   4   1
PARGA'S
ON SULI'S ROCK AND PARGA'S SHORE   325   2 DON JUAN 3 L 13   2
PARIAN
PROUDEST OF PARIAN PATRICIAN (BRED 314   3 DON JUAN 11 V 75   6
PARIAS
THEY LOSE THEIR CASTE AT ONCE AS DO THE PARIAS 352   3 DON JUAN 12   78   2
PARIS
SOME SHEPHERDS (UNLIKE PARIS) LED TO STARE 387   2 DON JUAN 4   78   3
COCKNEYS OF LONDON MUSCADINS OF PARIS 174   3 DON JUAN 8   124   7
PARISH
BUT LUCKILY I HAVE PAID FEW PARISH FEES SINCE) 530   3 DON JUAN 16   61   6
WHILE SCOUT THE PARISH GUARDIAN OF THE FRAIL   533   3 DON JUAN 16   67   2
OF ORPHANS PAINTS AT ONCE A PARISH SCHOOL   563   3 DON JUAN 17   3   3
PARISIAN
PARISIAN ASPECT WHICH UPSET OLD TROY 209   3 DON JUAN 9   53   5
PARKS
CALLED PARKS WHERE THERE IS NEITHER FRUIT NOR FLOWER . . . 301   3 DON JUAN 11   66   4
PARLIAMENT
THE PARLIAMENT AND ALL THE OTHER HOUSES   353   3 DON JUAN 12   82   2
AND COUNTY MEETINGS AND THE PARLIAMENT   360   3 DON JUAN 13   5   7
FOR PARLIAMENT IS OUR BAROMETER 378   3 DON JUAN 13   43   6
DISCUSSED THE PAST AND FUTURE PARLIAMENT 409   3 DON JUAN 13   109 V2
PARLIAMENTARY
IS'T ENGLISH NO--'TIS ONLY PARLIAMENTARY)   536   3 DON JUAN 16   73   2
PARNASSIAN
THOSE CORNISH PLUNDERERS OF PARNASSIAN WRECKS 403   2 DON JUAN 4   108   6
PARODIES
THAN ANY OF THE PARODIES OF PITT   283   2 DON JUAN 3   14 V8
PAROLLES
THERSITES OF THE HOUSE PAROLLES OF LAW   153   2 DON JUAN 1 V 4   7
THERE WAS PAROLLES TOO THE LEGAL BULLY   398   3 DON JUAN 13   84   1
PAROXYSM
ALTHOUGH HER PAROXYSM DREW TOWARDS ITS CLOSE   380   2 DON JUAN 4   67   6
PARRIES
SAT LITTLE LEILA WHO SURVIVED THE PARRIES   249   3 DON JUAN 10   51   4
PARROTS
TWO PARROTS WITH A PERSIAN CAT AND KITTENS 285   2 DON JUAN 3   18   2
PARRY
AND HOW TO PARRY THE RENEW'D ATTACK   114   2 DON JUAN 1   169   5
PARRY'S
(THOUGH PARRY'S EFFORTS LOOK A LUCKY PRESAGE) 376   3 DON JUAN 13   39   5
AS CAPTAIN PARRY'S VOYAGE MAY DO TO JASON'S 419   3 DON JUAN 14   22   4
PARS
PARS PARVA FUI BUT STILL ART AND PART 419   3 DON JUAN 14   21   2
PARSON
HEAVEN HELP ME   I'M BUT LITTLE OF A PARSON   179   3 DON JUAN 8   134   4
THE VERY POWERFUL PARSON PETER PITH   539   3 DON JUAN 16   81   7
PART
THE MAJOR PART OF SUCH APPELLANTS GO   14   2 DON JUAN D   9   7
ALL CALDERON AND GREATER PART OF LOPE 27   2 DON JUAN 1   11   2
SO THAT IF ANY ACTOR MISS'D HIS PART 27   2 DON JUAN 1   11   3
FOR MY PART I SAY NOTHING--NOTHING--BUT 50   2 DON JUAN 1   52   1
FOR MY PART TO SUCH DOINGS I'M A STRANGER   65   2 DON JUAN 1   80   4
HAD MITIGATED PART THOUGH NOT THE WHOLE   70   2 DON JUAN 1   91   4
WHICH SOME ARE BORN WITH BUT THE MOST PART LEARN 71   2 DON JUAN 1   93   3
HOW SELF-DECEITFUL IS THE SAGEST PART 78   2 DON JUAN 1   106   5
FOR MY PART I'M A MODERATE-MINDED BARD   85   2 DON JUAN 1   118   5
THE MAJOR PART OF THEM HAD LONG BEEN WIVED 96   2 DON JUAN 1   138   3
OR DEATH OF THOSE WE DOTE ON WHEN A PART 167   2 DON JUAN 2   21   5
TO GET UP PART OF THE CARGO AND WHAT NOT 171   2 DON JUAN 2   28   3
TO PART WITH ALL TILL EVERY HOPE WAS BLIGHTED) 173   2 DON JUAN 2   32   7
PART WAS DIVIDED PART THROWN IN THE SEA 197   2 DON JUAN 2   77   5
PART WAS DIVIDED PART THROWN IN THE SEA 197   2 DON JUAN 2   77   5
AS IF TO WIN A PART FROM OFF THE WEIGHT 203   2 DON JUAN 2   88   6

```
                                                          PAGE VOL        CANTO STANZA LN
PART   (CONTINUED)
     WITH THE DEEP DEADLY THOUGHT THAT THEY MUST PART  .  .  .  .  . 203   2 DON JUAN  2     88    8
     AND THEN OF THESE SOME PART BURST INTO TEARS     .  .  .  .  . 208   2 DON JUAN  2     98    1
     TO WHAT PART OF THE EARTH THEY HAD BEEN TOST     .  .  .  .  . 209   2 DON JUAN  2    100    5
     THE HEART IS LIKE THE SKY A PART OF HEAVEN   .  .  .  .  .  . 270   2 DON JUAN  2    214    1
     BUT THAT PART OF THE COAST BEING SHOAL AND BARE  .  .  .  .  . 285   2 DON JUAN  3     19    6
     THE GREATER PART OF THESE WERE READY SPREAD  .  .  .  .  .  . 310   2 DON JUAN  3     69    6
     I HAVE TRIED BOTH SO THOSE WHO WOULD A PART TAKE  .  .  .  .  . 356   2 DON JUAN  4     24    7
     BUT AT THIS HOUR I WISH TO PART IN PEACE  .  .  .  .  .  .  . 398   2 DON JUAN  4     99    2
     FOR HIS OWN PART HE REALLY SHOULD REJOICE   .  .  .  .  .  . 452   2 DON JUAN  5     70    1
     WHEN SOME UNTOWARD PART OF RAIMENT STUCK HARD .  .  .  .  .  . 456   2 DON JUAN  5     78    6
     AND TAKING HINTS IN GOOD PART ALL THE WHILE .  .  .  .  .  . 473   2 DON JUAN  5    107    4
     MAN'S PENSIVE PART IS NOW AND THEN THE HEAD .  .  .  .  .  .    7   3 DON JUAN  6      2   V7
     SHE COULD BUT CLAIM THE FIFTEENTH HUNDRED PART .  .  .  .  .   10   3 DON JUAN  6      9    7
     WHICH FORM AN ORNAMENT BUT NO MORE PART  .  .  .  .  .  .  .   13   3 DON JUAN  6     14    7
     IF FAIR GULBEYAZ OVERDID HER PART .  .  .  .  .  .  .  .  .   15   3 DON JUAN  6     19    1
     ANOTHER PART OF HISTORY FOR THE DISHES  .  .  .  .  .  .  .   65   3 DON JUAN  6    120    3
     FOR MY PART I PRETEND NOT TO BE CATO  .  .  .  .  .  .  .  .   68   3 DON JUAN  7      4    6
     BUT ON THE THIRTEENTH WHEN ALREADY PART  .  .  .  .  .  .  .   85   3 DON JUAN  7     39    1
     BE THAT THE GREATER PART WERE KILLED OR WOUNDED  .  .  .  .  . 125   3 DON JUAN  8     28    2
     TO CORPS THE GREATER PART OF WHICH WERE CORSES .  .  .  .  . 126   3 DON JUAN  8     30    8
     THE CITY'S TAKEN--ONLY PART BY PART--  .  .  .  .  .  .  .  . 152   3 DON JUAN  8     82    1
     THE CITY'S TAKEN--ONLY PART BY PART--  .  .  .  .  .  .  .  . 152   3 DON JUAN  8     82    1
     BUT THEN THE FACT'S A FACT--AND 'TIS THE PART .  .  .  .  .  . 154   3 DON JUAN  8     86    1
     IF YOU HAVE ACTED ONCE A GENEROUS PART  .  .  .  .  .  .  .  . 184   3 DON JUAN  9      4    5
     FOR MY PART I'LL ENLIST ON NEITHER SIDE  .  .  .  .  .  .  .  . 190   3 DON JUAN  9     16    5
     WHICH BEING THE DAMN'DEST PART OF MATRIMONY .  .  .  .  .  . 217   3 DON JUAN  9     70    7
     MAKE THIS A SACRED PART OF ALBION'S ISLE  .  .  .  .  .  .  . 279   3 DON JUAN 11     24    8
     KISS HANDS FEET ANY PART OF MAJESTY .  .  .  .  .  .  .  .  . 286   3 DON JUAN 11     38    6
     THAT'S NOBLE THAT'S ROMANTIC FOR MY PART  .  .  .  .  .  .  . 326   3 DON JUAN 12     22    1
     I FOR MY PART--(ONE MODERN INSTANCE MORE  .  .  .  .  .  .  . 334   3 DON JUAN 12     38    1
     AND FORTUNE HAS AN AWKWARD PART TO PLAY  .  .  .  .  .  .  . 342   3 DON JUAN 12     58    2
     FOR MY PART I AM BUT A MERE SPECTATOR  .  .  .  .  .  .  .  . 361   3 DON JUAN 13      7    6
     ARE GROWN OF THE BEAU MONDE A PART POTENTIAL  .  .  .  .  .  . 418   3 DON JUAN 14     20    2
     PARS PARVA FUI BUT STILL ART AND PART  .  .  .  .  .  .  .  . 419   3 DON JUAN 14     21    2
     AND SHONE IN THE BEST PART OF DIALOGUE  .  .  .  .  .  .  .  . 426   3 DON JUAN 14     37    2
     BUT HOW TO FILL UP THAT SAME VACANT PART  .  .  .  .  .  .  . 442   3 DON JUAN 14     74    3
     OF ALL THE MODEST PART OF PROPAGATION .  .  .  .  .  .  .  . 472   3 DON JUAN 15     37    4
     (HIS FEASTS ARE NOT THE WORST PART OF HIS WORKS)  .  .  .  .  . 482   3 DON JUAN 15     62    4
     HER STOMACH'S NOT HER PECCANT PART THIS TALE  .  .  .  .  .  . 483   3 DON JUAN 15     64    6
     AS ALL MUST BLEND WHOSE PART IT IS TO AIM  .  .  .  .  .  .  . 546   3 DON JUAN 16     95    5
     SO WELL SHE ACTED ALL AND EVERY PART  .  .  .  .  .  .  .  . 547   3 DON JUAN 16     97    1
PARTAKE
     ENLARGEMENT OF EXISTENCE TO PARTAKE  .  .  .  .  .  .  .  . 247   2 DON JUAN  2    173    2
     A STRANGE SENSATION WHICH SHE MUST PARTAKE  .  .  .  .  .  . 378   2 DON JUAN  4     62    3
     MEN WHO PARTAKE ALL PASSIONS AS THEY PASS  .  .  .  .  .  .  . 402   2 DON JUAN  4    107    3
     PARTAKE OF MINE BUT BY TO-MORROW EARLY  .  .  .  .  .  .  .   29   3 DON JUAN  6     46    7
     OF WHICH MOST MEN PARTAKE BUT NO ONE SINGS  .  .  .  .  .  . 568   3 DON JUAN 17     13    3
PARTAKES
     THE MOORISH BLOOD PARTAKES THE PLANET'S HOUR  .  .  .  .  . 374   2 DON JUAN  4     56    4
PARTED
     AND THUS THEY PARTED EACH BY SEPARATE DOORS .  .  .  .  .  . 460   2 DON JUAN  5     85    1
     THEY PARTED FOR THE PRESENT THESE TO AWAIT  .  .  .  .  .  . 105   3 DON JUAN  7     76    2
     AND THEY SEEM OF A PARTED SOUL  .  .  .  .  .  .  .  .  .  . 519   3 DON JUAN 16   L  4    8
PARTIAL
     AND THEN WHAT PROPER PERSON CAN BE PARTIAL  .  .  .  .  .  .   45   2 DON JUAN  1     43    7
     TO WHICH THE LEVANTINES ARE VERY PARTIAL .  .  .  .  .  .  . 290   2 DON JUAN  3     29    8
     BEEN ONE TO WHICH A GOOD HEART COULD BE PARTIAL  .  .  .  .   86   3 DON JUAN  7     40    3
     PUT TO SUCH TRIAL JOHN BULL'S PARTIAL PATIENCE .  .  .  .  . 136   3 DON JUAN  8     48    6
PARTICIPATED
     ON OUR FRESH FEELINGS BUT--AS BEING PARTICIPATED  .  .  .  . 236   3 DON JUAN 10     23    5
     BOTH SENATES SEE THEIR NIGHTLY VOTES PARTICIPATED  .  .  .  . 306   3 DON JUAN 11     75    5
PARTICLE
     'TIS STRANGE THE MIND THAT VERY FIERY PARTICLE  .  .  .  .  . 298   3 DON JUAN 11     60    7
PARTICULAR
     I LIKE TO BE PARTICULAR IN DATES  .  .  .  .  .  .  .  .  .   76   2 DON JUAN  1    103    2
     NONE IN PARTICULAR HAD SOUGHT OR PLANN'D IT  .  .  .  .  .  . 195   2 DON JUAN  2     75    5
     I SHALL NOT BE PARTICULAR IN STATING .  .  .  .  .  .  .  . 203   3 DON JUAN  9     42    5
     ABOUT SUCH GENERAL MATTERS--BUT PARTICULAR  .  .  .  .  .  . 290   3 DON JUAN 11     44   V7
     I DON'T MEAN THIS AS GENERAL BUT PARTICULAR  .  .  .  .  .  . 343   3 DON JUAN 12     59    1
PARTICULARLY
     PARTICULARLY AMONGST SUN-BURNT NATIONS  .  .  .  .  .  .  .   59   2 DON JUAN  1     69    8
     PARTICULARLY WITH A TIRESOME FRIEND  .  .  .  .  .  .  .  .   90   2 DON JUAN  1    126    4
     AND LIKES PARTICULARLY TO PRODUCE  .  .  .  .  .  .  .  .  .   91   2 DON JUAN  1    128    3
PARTIES
     SMALL SOCIAL PARTIES JUST BEGUN TO DINE  .  .  .  .  .  .  . 291   2 DON JUAN  3     31    2
     OR GOT RID OF THE PARTIES ALTOGETHER  .  .  .  .  .  .  .  .   65   3 DON JUAN  6    119    4
     I SHALL OFFEND ALL PARTIES--NEVER MIND  .  .  .  .  .  .  . 195   3 DON JUAN  9     26    2
     AT GREAT ASSEMBLIES OR IN PARTIES SMALL  .  .  .  .  .  .  . 295   3 DON JUAN 11     54    4
     TO LEAVE THE PARTIES TO THEMSELVES FORSOOTH .  .  .  .  .  . 439   3 DON JUAN 14     67    3
PARTING
     (AS EVERY KIND OF PARTING HAS ITS STINGS)  .  .  .  .  .  . 161   2 DON JUAN  2      9    5
     BUT THEN THE THOUGHT OF PARTING MADE HER QUAKE  .  .  .  .  . 247   2 DON JUAN  2    173    6
     A PARTING PANG THE SPIRIT FROM HER PAST  .  .  .  .  .  .  . 381   2 DON JUAN  4     69    3
PARTINGS
     FIRST PARTINGS FORM A LESSON HARD TO LEARN  .  .  .  .  .  . 164   2 DON JUAN  2     14    3
PARTLETT
     IS LIKE--A DUCKLING BY DAME PARTLETT REARED .  .  .  .  .  . 564   3 DON JUAN 17      4    6
PARTLY
     PARTLY PERHAPS BECAUSE A FRESH SENSATION .  .  .  .  .  .  . 468   3 DON JUAN 15     28    4
```

```
                                                        PAGE VOL     CANTO  STANZA LN
PARTNER
    LOT OF SO YOUNG A PARTNER IN THE WOE . . . . . . . . . 417  2 DON JUAN  5     12   6
    TO QUIT HER GENTLE PARTNER AND TO DWELL . . . . . .  48  3 DON JUAN  6     84   6
PARTNERS
    ESPOUSED TWO PARTNERS (MILLINERS OF BATH) . . . . . 329  2 DON JUAN  3     93   8
PARTOUT
    THE SEAL A SUNFLOWER ELLE VOUS SUIT PARTOUT . . . . . 134  2 DON JUAN  1    198   6
PARTRIDGE
    OF THE POOR PARTRIDGE THROUGH HIS STUBBLE SCREEN . . . 539  3 DON JUAN 16     80   5
PARTRIDGE'
    (THERE'S FAME) YOUNG PARTRIDGE' FILLETS DECK'D WITH TRUFFLES 484  3 DON JUAN 15     66   8
PARTRIDGES
    AH NUTBROWN PARTRIDGES  AH BRILLIANT PHEASANTS . .  . . 394  3 DON JUAN 13     75   7
    WHEN WILL YOUR NAMES LEND LUSTRE EVEN TO PARTRIDGES . . 485  3 DON JUAN 15     67   8
    I WISH TO GOD YOU'DE DRESS US SOME SUCH PARTRIDGES . . 485  3 DON JUAN 15     67  V8
    PRESERVING PARTRIDGES AND PRETTY WENCHES . . . . . 531  3 DON JUAN 16     63   7
PARTS
    THE GROSSER PARTS BUT FEARFUL TO DEFACE . . . . .  46  2 DON JUAN  1     44   4
    SOME NEW EXPERIMENT TO SHOW HIS PARTS . . . . .  91  2 DON JUAN  1    128   4
    THEIR SOFA OCCUPIED THREE PARTS COMPLETE . . . . . 309  2 DON JUAN  3     67   3
    IN LOVERS' PARTS HIS PASSION MORE TO BREATHE . . . 392  3 DON JUAN  4     89   7
    WHERE THREE PARTS OF HIS COLUMN YET REMAIN . . . 148  3 DON JUAN  8     72   8
    HIS PARTS OF SPEECH AND IN THE STRANGE DISPLAYS . . . 207  3 DON JUAN  9     49   4
    AT LEAST THREE PARTS OF THIS GREAT WHOLE) SHE TORE . . 211  3 DON JUAN  9     58   3
    AND PARTS AND HEARTS HE DANCED AND SUNG AND HAD . . 292  3 DON JUAN 11     47   2
    FORM'D A WHOLE WHICH IRREGULAR IN PARTS . . . 390  3 DON JUAN 13     67   4
    SOME PARTS OF JUAN'S HISTORY WHICH RUMOUR . . . 460  3 DON JUAN 15     11   1
    HAVE IN THEIR SEVERAL ARTS OR PARTS ASCENDENCE . . . 537  3 DON JUAN 16     76   4
PARTURITION
    MAY AVERAGE ON THE WHOLE WITH PARTURITION . . . . . 420  3 DON JUAN 14     24   2
PARTY
    BY ONE OF THESE THE BUFFO OF THE PARTY . . . . 388  2 DON JUAN  4     81   1
    HAD MET A PARTY TOWARDS THE TWILIGHT'S FALL . . . .  95  3 DON JUAN  7     56   4
    THE PARTY A SLIGHT GLANCE THEN SAID I HAVE HEARD . .  97  3 DON JUAN  7     60   4
    THE CONSEQUENCE IS BEING OF NO PARTY . . . . . 195  3 DON JUAN  9     26   1
    OF TWILIGHT AS THE PARTY CROSSED THE BRIDGE . . . 279  3 DON JUAN 11     23   8
    ADMITTED A SMALL PARTY AS NIGHT FELL-- . . . . 282  3 DON JUAN 11     29   5
    (FRIENDS OF THE PARTY) WHO BEGIN ACCUSALS . . . 332  3 DON JUAN 12     34   4
    AND NUMEROUS PARTY OF HIS NOBLE FRIENDS . . . 382  3 DON JUAN 13     52   3
    THE PROMISED PARTY TO ENJOY ITS SWEETS . . . . 394  3 DON JUAN 13     75   2
    THE PARTY MIGHT CONSIST OF THIRTY-THREE . . . . 397  3 DON JUAN 13     83   3
    THE PARTY WE HAVE TOUCH'D ON WERE THE GUESTS . . . 404  3 DON JUAN 13     99   2
    IN THIS OUR PARTY POLISH'D SMOOTH AND COLD . . . 409  3 DON JUAN 13    110   2
PARVA
    PARS PARVA FUI BUT STILL ART AND PART . . . . . 419  3 DON JUAN 14     21   2
PAS
    CONSISTED OF--WE GIVE THE SEX THE PAS-- . . . . 396  3 DON JUAN 13     79   2
    AND NEVER CRANED AND MADE BUT FEW FAUX PAS . . . 424  3 DON JUAN 14     33   3
    SUCH CLASSIC PAS--SANS FLAWS--SET OFF OUR HERO . . 427  3 DON JUAN 14     39   7
    (FOR FOREIGNERS DON'T KNOW THAT A FAUX PAS . . . 436  3 DON JUAN 14     60   5
PASIPHAE
    THAT PASIPHAE PROMOTED BREEDING CATTLE . . . . . 238  2 DON JUAN  2    155   7
PASS
    THOUGH I ACQUIRED--BUT I PASS OVER THAT . . . .  50  2 DON JUAN  1     53   2
    AND IF YOU HAD IT O'ER AGAIN--'TWOULD PASS-- . . . 147  2 DON JUAN  1    220   6
    OR ELSE THE THING HAD HARDLY COME TO PASS) . . . 158  2 DON JUAN  2      3   6
    IN THE MEANTIME TO PASS HER HOURS AWAY . . . . 162  2 DON JUAN  2     10   1
    BECAUSE TILL PEOPLE KNOW WHAT'S COME TO PASS . . . 185  2 DON JUAN  2     55   6
    FEMALE AS WHERE SHE LIKES MAY FREELY PASS . . . 248  2 DON JUAN  2    175   4
    ANOTHER JULIET-- WHOM I WOULD NOT PASS-- . . . . 273  2 DON JUAN  2   V  2   5
    BUT THEN THIS WRATH WILL PASS AND TIME ASSUAGING . . 305  2 DON JUAN  3     58  V5
    THAT WITHOUT NOTICE FEW FULL MOONS SHALL PASS IT . . 317  2 DON JUAN  3     81   3
    TO PASS THEIR LIVES IN FOUNTAINS AND ON FLOWERS . . 352  2 DON JUAN  4     15   7
    TO PASS THAN THOSE TWO CANTOS INTO FAMILIES . . . 397  2 DON JUAN  4     97   8
    I PASS EACH DAY WHERE DANTE'S BONES ARE LAID . . . 400  2 DON JUAN  4    104   1
    MEN WHO PARTAKE ALL PASSIONS AS THEY PASS . . . 402  2 DON JUAN  4    107   3
    I HAVE GAINED SCIENCE IN THE THINGS WHICH PASS . . 403  2 DON JUAN  4    107  V3
    ARE THINGS WHICH MAKE AN ENGLISH EVENING PASS . . 444  2 DON JUAN  5     58   4
    I PASS MY EVENINGS IN LONG GALLERIES SOLELY . . . 444  2 DON JUAN  5     58   7
    BY WHICH ITS NOMENCLATURE CAME TO PASS . . . . .  33  3 DON JUAN  6     55   3
    THE BRAZEN UPPERMOST) KIND READER PASS . . . . .  34  3 DON JUAN  6     56   5
    BEHOLDS HER OWN SHY SHADOWY IMAGE PASS . . . . .  36  3 DON JUAN  6     60   6
    WHICH MANY PEOPLE PASS FOR WITS BY QUOTING . . .  77  3 DON JUAN  7     21   8
    BUT LET THAT PASS--I THINK I HAVE HEARD YOUR NAME . .  97  3 DON JUAN  7     60   7
    SHALL PASS O'ER WHAT WAS ISMAIL AND ITS TUSK . . .  99  3 DON JUAN  7     63   7
    HE KNEW NOT THY ARRIVING AT THIS PASS . . . . . 126  3 DON JUAN  8     29   3
    AND AS HE RUSHED ALONG IT CAME TO PASS HE . . . 130  3 DON JUAN  8     34   1
    WHICH HAMLET TELLS US IS A PASS OF DREAD . . . . 133  3 DON JUAN  8     41   4
    SHORT SPEECHES PASS BETWEEN TWO MEN WHO SPEAK . . 141  3 DON JUAN  8     58   1
    KILLED BECAUSE WHAT HE SWALLOWED WOULD NOT PASS . . 199  3 DON JUAN  9     33  V8
    THIS WE PASS OVER  WE WILL ALSO PASS . . . . . 236  3 DON JUAN 10     24   1
    THIS WE PASS OVER  WE WILL ALSO PASS . . . . . 236  3 DON JUAN 10     24   1
    MAKE MY SOUL PASS THE EQUINOCTIAL LINE . . . . 255  3 DON JUAN 10     61   6
    UNTIL TO SOME CONSPICUOUS SQUARE THEY PASS . . . 283  3 DON JUAN 11     31   7
    HE SAW TEN THOUSAND LIVING AUTHORS PASS . . . . 295  3 DON JUAN 11     54   5
    OF FRIENDSHIP WHICH YOU MAY ACCEPT OR PASS . . . 342  3 DON JUAN 12     57   3
    WHICH NE'ER CAN PASS THE EQUINOCTIAL LINE . . . . 373  3 DON JUAN 13     34   3
    WHO PASS LIKE WATER FILTERED IN A TANK . . . . 396  3 DON JUAN 13     80   3
    TO PASS THE STYX FOR MORE SUBSTANTIAL FEASTS . . . 404  3 DON JUAN 13     99   4
```

PASS   (CONTINUED)

	PAGE	VOL	CANTO	STANZA	LN
THE HOURS WHICH HOW TO PASS IS BUT TO FEW KNOWN	406	3 DON JUAN	13	103	5
ADVANCE BEYOND WHILE THEY COULD PASS FOR NEW	433	3 DON JUAN	14	53	4
AND PASS FOR WANT OF BETTER THOUGH NOT NEW	440	3 DON JUAN	14	69	4
MUST I PASS OVER IN MY BILL OF FARE	488	3 DON JUAN	15	73	2
AND HATE THOSE WHO WON'T LET THEM COME TO PASS	491	3 DON JUAN	15	79	8
AND LO UPON THAT DAY IT CAME TO PASS	539	3 DON JUAN	16	81	5
LIKE SHOWERS WHICH ON THE MIDNIGHT GUSTS WILL PASS	556	3 DON JUAN	16	114	3

PASSABLE

	PAGE	VOL	CANTO	STANZA	LN
MAKES MOUNTAINS PASSABLE AND BY HEAVEN'S BLESSING	215	3 DON JUAN	9	66	V7

PASSAGE

	PAGE	VOL	CANTO	STANZA	LN
THE PASSAGE YOU SO OFTEN HAVE EXPLORED--	121	2 DON JUAN	1	182	5
BUT AFTER ALL THEY ARE A NORTH-WEST PASSAGE	376	3 DON JUAN	13	39	1

PASS'D

	PAGE	VOL	CANTO	STANZA	LN
FOR HALF HIS DAYS WERE PASS'D AT CHURCH THE OTHER	48	2 DON JUAN	1	49	7
IN SIGHT THAT SEVERAL MONTHS HAVE PASS'D WE'LL SAY	86	2 DON JUAN	1	121	6
YOU'VE PASS'D YOUR YOUTH NOT SO UNPLEASANTLY	147	2 DON JUAN	1	220	5
UPON ITS COURSE) PASS'D OFT BEFORE THEIR EYES	206	2 DON JUAN	2	94	4
HE COULD PERHAPS HAVE PASS'D THE HELLESPONT	211	2 DON JUAN	2	105	6
SWAM ROUND AND ROUND AND ALL HIS SENSES PASS'D	214	2 DON JUAN	2	110	3
AND HOW THIS HEAVY FAINTNESS PASS'D AWAY	214	2 DON JUAN	2	111	5
BUT THAT LIKE OTHER THINGS HAS PASS'D AWAY	244	2 DON JUAN	2	166	5
THAT BATHING PASS'D FOR NOTHING JUAN SEEM'D	247	2 DON JUAN	2	172	2
AND WHEN THOSE DEEP AND BURNING MOMENTS PASS'D	260	2 DON JUAN	2	195	1
ALL IT HATH FELT INFLICTED PASS'D AND PROVED	261	2 DON JUAN	2	197	5
PASS'D BUT HE STROVE QUITE COURTEOUSLY TO QUELL	298	2 DON JUAN	3	44	4
OLD LAMBRO PASS'D UNSEEN A PRIVATE GATE	306	2 DON JUAN	3	61	1
AND YET A THIRD OF LIFE IS PASS'D IN SLEEP	411	3 DON JUAN	14	3	8
HER GRACE TOO PASS'D FOR BEING AN INTRIGANTE	438	3 DON JUAN	14	63	1
LONG DIALOGUES WHICH PASS'D WITHOUT A WORD	489	3 DON JUAN	15	76	8

PASSED

	PAGE	VOL	CANTO	STANZA	LN
THE SKIN HAS PASSED THROUGH SUCH A DEAL OF DIRT	154	2 DON JUAN	1	V 5	5
A STORM IT RAGED AND LIKE THE STORM IT PASSED	490	2 DON JUAN	5	137	1
PASSED WITHOUT WORDS--IN FACT SHE COULD NOT SPEAK	490	2 DON JUAN	5	137	2
THE STORY SCARCELY PASSED A SINGLE LIP--	496	2 DON JUAN	5	149	3
DUDU HAD NEVER PASSED FOR WANTING SENSE	43	3 DON JUAN	6	74	6
HE HAD PASSED THE NIGHT WAS WHAT SHE WISHED TO KNOW	55	3 DON JUAN	6	99	8
THE COLUMN ORDERED ON THE ASSAULT SCARCE PASSED	115	3 DON JUAN	8	7	1
TWO LONG OCTAVES PASSED IN A LITTLE MINUTE	142	3 DON JUAN	8	59	2
WHO WAS GONE TO HIS PLACE) AND PASSED FOR MUCH	209	3 DON JUAN	9	54	2
WHICH PASSED OR CATCH THE FIRST GLIMPSE OF THE CLIFFS	256	3 DON JUAN	10	64	8
AND PASSED FOR ARGUMENTS OF GOOD ENDURANCE	294	3 DON JUAN	11	52	4
HIS MORNS HE PASSED IN BUSINESS--WHICH DISSECTED	301	3 DON JUAN	11	65	1
HIS AFTERNOONS HE PASSED IN VISITS LUNCHEONS	301	3 DON JUAN	11	66	1
AND PASSED (AT LEAST THE LATTER YEARS OF LIFE)	338	3 DON JUAN	12	47	7
FOR THEY HAVE PASSED LIFE'S EQUINOCTIAL LINE	360	3 DON JUAN	13	5	4
TO THOSE WHO WERE OR PASSED FOR MERITORIOUS	372	3 DON JUAN	13	32	7
THE PASSEE AND THE PASSED FOR GOOD SOCIETY	396	3 DON JUAN	13	80	7
BUT SLOWLY AND AS HE PASSED JUAN BY	510	3 DON JUAN	16	21	7
ONCE TWICE THRICE PASSED REPASSED--THE THING OF AIR	510	3 DON JUAN	16	23	1
THE SHADOW PASSED AWAY--BUT WHERE THE HALL	511	3 DON JUAN	16	24	2
AND WOULD HAVE PASSED THE WHOLE OFF AS A DREAM	511	3 DON JUAN	16	25	5
THEY PASSED AS SUCH THINGS DO FOR SUPERSTITION	527	3 DON JUAN	16	54	2

PASSEE

	PAGE	VOL	CANTO	STANZA	LN
THE PASSEE AND THE PASSED FOR GOOD SOCIETY	396	3 DON JUAN	13	80	7

PASSENGER

	PAGE	VOL	CANTO	STANZA	LN
THERE'S NOT A SEA THE PASSENGER E'ER PUKES IN	413	2 DON JUAN	5	5	7

PASSENGERS

	PAGE	VOL	CANTO	STANZA	LN
THAT PASSENGERS WOULD FIND IT MUCH AMISS	173	2 DON JUAN	2	33	3
AND SEA-SICK PASSENGERS TURNED SOMEWHAT PALE	256	3 DON JUAN	10	64	5
THY PACKETS ALL WHOSE PASSENGERS ARE BOOTIES	259	3 DON JUAN	10	69	5

PASSES

	PAGE	VOL	CANTO	STANZA	LN
WHO PASSES FOR IN LIFE AND DEATH MOST LUCKY	143	3 DON JUAN	8	61	2
IS THAT WHICH PASSES WITH LEAST CONTRADICTION	457	3 DON JUAN	15	3	8
WHICH PASSES GHOSTS IN CURRENCY LIKE GOLD	510	3 DON JUAN	16	22	6

PASSIM

	PAGE	VOL	CANTO	STANZA	LN
FROM ARISTOTLE PASSIM--SEE POIETIKES	342	2 DON JUAN	3	111	8

PASSING

	PAGE	VOL	CANTO	STANZA	LN
THEIR SPELLS AND GIVE THEM TO THE PASSING GALE	72	2 DON JUAN	1	95	7
SWEET IS A LEGACY AND PASSING SWEET	89	2 DON JUAN	1	125	1
THE WIND WAS FAIR THE WATER PASSING ROUGH	162	2 DON JUAN	2	11	2
THE SOLITUDE OF PASSING HIS OWN DOOR	302	2 DON JUAN	3	52	3
HER EYE IN PASSING ON HIS WAY TO SALE	477	2 DON JUAN	5	114	2
OF EMPIRES HEAVE BUT LIKE SOME PASSING WAVES	500	3 DON JUAN	15	99	8
HE SEEMED UNCONSCIOUS OF ALL PASSING THERE	542	3 DON JUAN	16	87	6

PASSION

	PAGE	VOL	CANTO	STANZA	LN
BUT PASSION MOST DISSEMBLES YET BETRAYS	61	2 DON JUAN	1	73	1
OF WHICH YOUNG PASSION CANNOT BE BEREFT	62	2 DON JUAN	1	74	6
A PASSION WHICH PURSUES THOUGH IN DESPAIR	114	2 DON JUAN	1	170	V4
AND THEN FLEW OUT INTO ANOTHER PASSION	121	2 DON JUAN	1	181	8
THE PASSION WHICH STILL RAGES AS BEFORE	132	2 DON JUAN	1	195	6
MY HEART IN PASSION AND MY HEAD ON RHYMES	145	2 DON JUAN	1	217	8
AS I AM BLOOD--BONE--MARROW PASSION--FEELING--	156	2 DON JUAN	1	V 8	2
COULD JUAN'S PASSION WHILE THE BILLOWS ROAR	168	2 DON JUAN	2	23	7
LIKE OTHER MEN TOO MAY HAVE HAD MY PASSION--	244	2 DON JUAN	2	166	4
AND ALL THE BURNING TONGUES THE PASSION TEACH	256	2 DON JUAN	2	189	5
IF SOULS COULD DIE HAD PERISH'D IN THAT PASSION	257	2 DON JUAN	2	191	4
WHERE NOUGHT UPON THEIR PASSION COULD INTRUDE	262	2 DON JUAN	2	198	6
FOR THE FIRST PASSION STAYS THERE SUCH A WHILE	271	2 DON JUAN	2	215	3

PASSION   (CONTINUED)

	PAGE	VOL		CANTO	STANZA	LN
IN HER FIRST PASSION WOMAN LOVES HER LOVER	276	2 DON JUAN	3	3	1
FOR INSTANCE--PASSION IN A LOVER'S GLORIOUS	278	2 DON JUAN	3	6	7
HAD PETRARCH'S PASSION LED TO PETRARCH'S WEDDING	279	2 DON JUAN	3	8	V7
HE FLEW INTO A PASSION AND IN FACT	296	2 DON JUAN	3	40	2
BUT OVERWROUGHT WITH PASSION AND DESPAIR	375	2 DON JUAN	4	57	6
THE RULING PASSION SUCH AS MARBLE SHOWS	377	2 DON JUAN	4	61	1
IN LOVERS' PARTS HIS PASSION MORE TO BREATHE	392	2 DON JUAN	4	89	7
DASH INTO POETRY WHICH IS BUT PASSION	402	2 DON JUAN	4	106	7
I HAVE A PASSION FOR THE NAME OF MARY	413	2 DON JUAN	5	4	1
SOME TALK OF AN APPEAL UNTO SOME PASSION	437	2 DON JUAN	5	48	1
PASSION AND POWER A GLANCE ON HIM SHE CAST	478	2 DON JUAN	5	116	6
BY COMMONEST AMBITION THAT WHEN PASSION	8	3 DON JUAN	6	4	2
AND SEE A SENTIMENTAL PASSION GLOW	14	3 DON JUAN	6	17	4
AS PASSION RISES WITH ITS BOSOM WORN	49	3 DON JUAN	6	87	3
THIS PASSION MIGHT BLOW O'ER NOR DARED TO BALK	61	3 DON JUAN	6	110	3
NOR EVER HAD FOR ABSTRACT FAME MUCH PASSION	189	3 DON JUAN	9	14	4
FELL INTO THAT NO LESS IMPERIOUS PASSION	216	3 DON JUAN	9	68	2
WHOSE TEMPORARY PASSION WAS QUITE FLATTERING	217	3 DON JUAN	9	70	3
SHE ALSO HAD NO PASSION FOR CONFESSION	252	3 DON JUAN	10	56	5
WHICH SERVES OUR THINKING PEOPLE FOR A PASSION	284	3 DON JUAN	11	33	8
HE IS YOUR ONLY POET--PASSION PURE	319	3 DON JUAN	12	8	1
SUCH PURE DISINTERESTEDNESS OF PASSION	331	3 DON JUAN	12	33	3
BY RAILING AT THE UNKNOWN AND ENVIED PASSION	337	3 DON JUAN	12	45	2
WHERE LIVES NOT LAW-SUITS MUST BE RISKED FOR PASSION	347	3 DON JUAN	12	68	2
AND IF IN FACT SHE TAKES TO A GRANDE PASSION	351	3 DON JUAN	12	77	1
BUT DESTINY AND PASSION SPREAD THE NET	364	3 DON JUAN	13	12	5
MUCH PASSION SINCE THE MERCHANT-SHIP THE ARGO	443	3 DON JUAN	14	76	7
IF FREE FROM PASSION WHICH ALL FRIENDSHIP CHECKS	451	3 DON JUAN	14	93	5
HOW SHOULD THE TENDER PASSION E'ER BE TOUGH	451	3 DON JUAN	14	94	8
THE PASSION WHICH MADE SOLOMON A ZANY	452	3 DON JUAN	14	95	4
THAT IN OUR YOUTH AS DANGEROUS A PASSION	454	3 DON JUAN	14	100	2
OR THROWN INTO A PHILOSOPHIC PASSION	522	3 DON JUAN	16	43	6

PASSIONATE

IS FIRST AND PASSIONATE LOVE--IT STANDS ALONE	90	2 DON JUAN	1	127	2
FOR BEINGS PASSIONATE AS SAPPHO'S SONG	358	2 DON JUAN	4	27	6

PASSIONLESS

I DON'T MEAN THAT THEY ARE PASSIONLESS BUT QUITE	284	3 DON JUAN	11	34	1
WHICH THE MERE PASSIONLESS CAN NEVER KNOW	336	3 DON JUAN	12	44	8

PASSION'S

FOR HEALTH AND IDLENESS TO PASSION'S FLAME	245	2 DON JUAN	2	169	5
HAIDEE WAS PASSION'S CHILD BORN WHERE THE SUN	264	2 DON JUAN	2	202	2
THESE TWO FORM THE LAST GASP OF PASSION'S BREATH	280	2 DON JUAN	3	9	V3
AND TWILIGHT SAW THEM LINK'D IN PASSION'S TIES	354	2 DON JUAN	4	20	6
BUT HER LARGE DARK EYE SHOW'D DEEP PASSION'S FORCE	374	2 DON JUAN	4	56	7
SO SUPERNATURAL WAS HER PASSION'S RISE	489	2 DON JUAN	5	134	5
ON WHICH THE PASSION'S SELF SEEMS TO DEPEND	219	3 DON JUAN	9	73	6
AND PASSION'S SELF MUST HAVE A SPICE OF FRANTIC	347	3 DON JUAN	12	68	3
REMEMBER WITHOUT TELLING PASSION'S ERRORS	457	3 DON JUAN	15	4	2

PASSIONS

AND IF HIS PASSIONS NOW AND THEN OUTRAN	40	2 DON JUAN	1	35	5
HER PASSIONS HAD ARISEN AND HER YOUTH'S FLOWER	262	2 DON JUAN	2	198	V5
FOR WHEN THE TURBID PASSIONS ARE UNRULY IT	272	2 DON JUAN	2	V 1	4
ITS PETTY PASSIONS MARRIAGES AND FLIGHTS	353	2 DON JUAN	4	17	6
SHOW WHAT THE PASSIONS ARE IN THEIR FULL GROWTH	368	2 DON JUAN	4	45	8
THUS TO THEIR EXTREME VERGE THE PASSIONS BROUGHT	402	2 DON JUAN	4	106	6
THUS TO THEIR LAST SANDS ARE THE PASSIONS BROUGHT	402	2 DON JUAN	4	106	V6
MEN WHO PARTAKE ALL PASSIONS AS THEY PASS	402	2 DON JUAN	4	107	3
BOUGHT UP FOR DIFFERENT PURPOSES AND PASSIONS	407	2 DON JUAN	4	113	8
AND WITH ALL PASSIONS IN THEIR TURN ATTACKED	412	2 DON JUAN	5	2	6
TO THEIR OWN WHIMS AND PASSIONS AND WHATNOT	423	2 DON JUAN	5	25	4
THEIR PASSIONS AND ARE DEXT'ROUS SOME BY FEATURES	425	2 DON JUAN	5	27	4
AND THE DEEP PASSIONS FLASHING THROUGH HER FORM	489	2 DON JUAN	5	135	7
HER REASON BEING WEAK HER PASSIONS STRONG	10	3 DON JUAN	6	8	5
WHERE ALL THE PASSIONS HAVE ALAS BUT ONE VENT	22	3 DON JUAN	6	32	8
THAN ARE YOUR MIGHTY PASSIONS AND SO FORTH	32	3 DON JUAN	6	53	5
WHOSE HEADLONG PASSIONS FORM THEIR PROPER WOES	49	3 DON JUAN	6	87	8
BY ALL THE DEMONS OF ALL PASSIONS SHOWED	61	3 DON JUAN	6	111	7
FOR GENTLEMEN WHOSE PASSIONS MAY BOIL OER	313	3 DON JUAN	11	V 29	5
OUR PASSIONS AND WE WALK IN WISDOM'S WAYS	360	3 DON JUAN	13	4	6
OF PASSIONS TOO I HAVE PROVED ENOUGH TO BLAME	414	3 DON JUAN	14	9	4
FACTITIOUS PASSIONS WIT WITHOUT MUCH SALT	417	3 DON JUAN	14	16	5
THAT SAD RESULT OF PASSIONS AND POTATOES--	472	3 DON JUAN	15	37	7

PASSIVE

PASSIVE OBEDIENCE--NOW RAISED UP THE HEAD	101	3 DON JUAN	7	67	6

PASSPORT

WHEN FOR A PASSPORT OR SOME OTHER BAR	288	3 DON JUAN	11	41	5
OR WEALTH WHICH IS A PASSPORT EVERYWHERE	370	3 DON JUAN	13	28	5
NO MATTER HOW OR WHY THE PASSPORT SHROUDS	396	3 DON JUAN	13	80	6

PAST

OH SHE WAS PERFECT PAST ALL PARALLEL	30	2 DON JUAN	1	17	1
AND PUT THE BUSINESS PAST ALL KIND OF DOUBT	35	2 DON JUAN	1	26	8
RELUCTANT PAST HER BRIGHT EYES ROLLED--AS A VEIL	108	2 DON JUAN	1	158	V3
TIME IS TIME WAS TIME'S PAST A CHYMIC TREASURE	145	2 DON JUAN	1	217	6
BECAUSE AT LEAST THE PAST WERE PAST AWAY--	156	2 DON JUAN	1	V 8	3
BECAUSE AT LEAST THE PAST WERE PAST AWAY--	156	2 DON JUAN	1	V 8	3
NOTHING SHOULD TEMPT HIM MORE (THIS PERIL PAST)	175	2 DON JUAN	2	37	5
UNDER THE VESSEL'S KEEL THE SAIL WAS PAST	176	2 DON JUAN	2	39	1
STIFF ON HIS HEART AND PULSE AND HOPE WERE PAST	204	2 DON JUAN	2	90	4

```
                                                            PAGE VOL      CANTO STANZA LN
PAST    (CONTINUED)
    HIM PAST ALL BOUNDS BECAUSE SHE SMILED TO SEE  . . . . . . 239   2 DON JUAN  2   158   3
    TO THEM BUT MOCKERIES OF THE PAST ALONE  . . . . . . . . . 262   2 DON JUAN  2   199   5
    THE CAUSE BEING PAST HIS GUESSING OR UNRIDDLING  . . . . . 290   2 DON JUAN  3    28   6
    PAST HIM IN CRYSTAL AND A JOY IN FLOWERS  . . . . . . . . . 304   2 DON JUAN  3    56   7
    BUT THERE ARE HUMAN FEELINGS PAST ASSUAGING  . . . . . . . 305   2 DON JUAN  3    58  V5
    HE PRAISED THE PRESENT AND ABUSED THE PAST  . . . . . . . . 316   2 DON JUAN  3    79   1
    WE PONDER DEEPLY ON EACH PAST EMOTION  . . . . . . . . . . 345   2 DON JUAN  4     2   8
    THE PAST STILL WELCOME AS THE PRESENT THOUGHT  . . . . . . 354   2 DON JUAN  4    20   8
    A MINUTE PAST AND SHE HAD BEEN ALL TEARS  . . . . . . . . . 367   2 DON JUAN  4    43   1
    DONE THINE THE PRESENT VOUCHES FOR THE PAST  . . . . . . . 368   2 DON JUAN  4    46   8
    A PARTING PANG THE SPIRIT FROM HER PAST  . . . . . . . . . 381   2 DON JUAN  4    69   3
    ITS DWELLINGS DOWN ITS TENANTS PAST AWAY  . . . . . . . . . 383   2 DON JUAN  4    72   2
    COULD ALTOGETHER CALL THE PAST TO MIND  . . . . . . . . . . 384   2 DON JUAN  4    75   3
    ABOUT HIS PAST OR PRESENT SITUATION  . . . . . . . . . . . 387   2 DON JUAN  4    79   8
    THE WATERS AND REPENTANCE FOR PAST SINNING  . . . . . . . . 414   2 DON JUAN  5     6   5
    I MOURN BUT FOR THE PAST--I LOVED A MAID  . . . . . . . . . 420   2 DON JUAN  5    18   2
    I HEARD A SHOT--'TWAS EIGHT O'CLOCK SCARCE PAST--  . . . . 428   2 DON JUAN  5    33   5
    SHE NOW CONCEIVED ALL DIFFICULTIES PAST  . . . . . . . . . 478   2 DON JUAN  5   116   2
    AND AS YOU'D HAVE ME PARDON YOUR PAST SCORNING--  . . . . . 494   2 DON JUAN  5   145   6
    WHICH PAST WELL OFF--AS SHE COULD DO NO LESS  . . . . . . .  36   3 DON JUAN  6    61   5
    I KNOW NOT NEVER COUNTING PAST THEIR TEENS  . . . . . . . .  41   3 DON JUAN  6    69   4
    OF WHAT HAD PAST SINCE ALL THE SLAVES RETIRED  . . . . . .  55   3 DON JUAN  6    99   3
    EACH MAN OF WISDOM FUTURE PAST OR PRESENT  . . . . . . . .  69   3 DON JUAN  7     5   4
    WHAT ARE YE--WHAT YOU SEE US BRIEFLY PAST  . . . . . . . .  97   3 DON JUAN  7    59   6
    PAST PRESENT AND TO COME--BUT ALL MAY YIELD  . . . . . . . 117   3 DON JUAN  8    12   7
    AND PONDERING ON THE PRESENT AND THE PAST  . . . . . . . . 142   3 DON JUAN  8    60   7
    THAT HIDES THE PAST WORLD LIKE TO A SET SUN  . . . . . . . 188   3 DON JUAN  9    11   3
    LIKE BANQUO'S OFFSPRING--FLOATING PAST ME SEEMS  . . . . . 233   3 DON JUAN 10    18   6
    IS LEARNING TO REDUCE HIS PAST EXPENSES  . . . . . . . . . 240   3 DON JUAN 10    31   8
    BETWEEN THE PRESENT AND PAST WORLDS AND HOVER  . . . . . . 255   3 DON JUAN 10    61   7
    PURSUED HIS PATH AND DROVE PAST SOME HOTELS  . . . . . . . 282   3 DON JUAN 11    29   7
    AMONGST LIVE POETS AND BLUE LADIES PAST  . . . . . . . . . 300   3 DON JUAN 11    64   2
    WHERE IS THE WORLD OF EIGHT YEARS PAST 'TWAS THERE--  . . . 306   3 DON JUAN 11    76   3
    HAVE VENTURED PAST THE JAWS OF MOOR AND TIGER  . . . . . . 348   3 DON JUAN 12    70  V6
    AND THOUGH NOT VAINER FROM HIS PAST SUCCESS  . . . . . . . 353   3 DON JUAN 12    81   7
    YET IN THE VERY CENTRE PAST ALL PRICE  . . . . . . . . . . 375   3 DON JUAN 13    37   5
    WITH HIS GREY SIGNAL FLAG AND THE PAST TENSE  . . . . . . . 376   3 DON JUAN 13    40   5
    DISCUSSED THE PAST AND FUTURE PARLIAMENT  . . . . . . . . . 409   3 DON JUAN 13   109  V2
    RETIRE BUT LOOK INTO YOUR PAST IMPRESSION  . . . . . . . . 413   3 DON JUAN 14     6   2
    THEIRS WAS THAT BEST OF UNIONS PAST ALL DOUBT  . . . . . . 430   3 DON JUAN 14    45   7
    UTTER'D BY FRIENDS THOSE PROPHETS OF THE PAST  . . . . . . 432   3 DON JUAN 14    50   4
    SOME OLD--SOME PAST--SOME PRESENT--SOME TO BE  . . . . . . 495   3 DON JUAN 15    89  V7
    ABOUT THE PRESENT PAST OR FUTURE STATE  . . . . . . . . . . 496   3 DON JUAN 15    91   6
    A PICTURE IS THE PAST EVEN ERE ITS FRAME  . . . . . . . . . 509   3 DON JUAN 16    19   7
    TALK O'ER THEMSELVES THE PAST AND NEXT ELECTION  . . . . . 534   3 DON JUAN 16    69   8
    DULLY PAST O'ER THE DINNER OF THE DAY  . . . . . . . . . . 542   3 DON JUAN 16    87   1
    FOR ALL HER PAST EXERTION AND SOFT PHRASES  . . . . . . . . 550   3 DON JUAN 16   103   3
PASTIME
    JUST PONDER WHAT A PIOUS PASTIME WAR IS  . . . . . . . . . 174   3 DON JUAN  8   124   8
    FAIR CATHERINE'S PASTIME--WHO LOOKED ON THE MATCH  . . . . 197   3 DON JUAN  9    29   6
    AS THE MERE PASTIME OF AN IDLE DAY  . . . . . . . . . . . . 521   3 DON JUAN 16    42   3
PASTIMES
    ALL PRETTY PASTIMES IN WHICH NO OFFENCE IS  . . . . . . . . 293   2 DON JUAN  3    35   4
    SOME TO THEIR SEVERAL PASTIMES OR TO NONE  . . . . . . . . 527   3 DON JUAN 16    55   3
PASTOR
    BEGINNING WITH FORMOSUM PASTOR CORYDON  . . . . . . . . . .  45   2 DON JUAN  1    42   8
    DINE WITH THEM ON HIS PASTOR AND HIS MASTER  . . . . . . . 198   2 DON JUAN  2    78   8
PASTORAL
    WITH WHICH I COULD NOT BREW A PASTORAL  . . . . . . . . . . 423   3 DON JUAN 14    30   3
PASTURE
    WHO FELL AS ROLLS AN OX O'ER IN HIS PASTURE  . . . . . . . 274   3 DON JUAN 11    13   5
PATAGONIAN
    OR TRAVELLING IN PATAGONIAN LANDS  . . . . . . . . . . . .  20   3 DON JUAN  6    28   5
    ALL FIT TO MAKE A PATAGONIAN JEALOUS  . . . . . . . . . . . 205   3 DON JUAN  9    46   8
PATCH
    TO ONE SMALL GRASS-GROWN PATCH (WHICH MUST AWAIT  . . . . . 237   3 DON JUAN 10    25   5
PATCHING
    AND BOTCHING PATCHING LEAVING STILL BEHIND  . . . . . . . .  18   2 DON JUAN  D    14   2
PATENT
    THIS IS THE PATENT AGE OF NEW INVENTIONS  . . . . . . . . .  93   2 DON JUAN  1   132   1
    AND A LONG EULOGY OF PATENT BLACKING  . . . . . . . . . . . 512   3 DON JUAN 16    26   8
PATERNAL
    IF LOVE PATERNAL IN HIS BOSOM PLEADED  . . . . . . . . . . 300   2 DON JUAN  3    49   5
PATH
    IS NOT THE CERTAIN PATH TO FUTURE PRAISE  . . . . . . . . .  14   2 DON JUAN  D     8   8
    THE PATH IS THROUGH PERPLEXING WAYS AND WHEN  . . . . . . .  93   2 DON JUAN  1   133   7
    HE LAY DARK AS THE SCORPION IN YOUR PATH  . . . . . . . . . 300   2 DON JUAN  3    48  V4
    ALAS HIS COUNTRY SHOW'D NO PATH TO PRAISE  . . . . . . . . 303   2 DON JUAN  3    55   6
    WHEN HE AND SOUTHEY FOLLOWING THE SAME PATH  . . . . . . . 329   2 DON JUAN  3    93   7
    WHILE SHE STILL SILVERS O'ER YOUR GLOOMY PATH  . . . . . .  70   3 DON JUAN  7     7   8
    TO TRACK OUR HERO ON HIS PATH OF FAME  . . . . . . . . . . 120   3 DON JUAN  8    17   2
    A PATH TO ADD HIS OWN SLIGHT ARM AND FORCES  . . . . . . . 126   3 DON JUAN  8    30   7
    PURSUED HIS PATH AND DROVE PAST SOME HOTELS  . . . . . . . 282   3 DON JUAN 11    29   7
    ADVERSITY IS THE FIRST PATH TO TRUTH  . . . . . . . . . . . 339   3 DON JUAN 12    50   5
    PERHAPS MANKIND MIGHT FIND THE PATH THEY MISS--  . . . . . 410   3 DON JUAN 14     1   3
    HE WOULD NOT TREAD A FACTIOUS PATH TO PRAISE  . . . . . . . 536   3 DON JUAN 16    73   5
PATHETIC
    NO DOUBT HE WOULD HAVE BEEN MUCH MORE PATHETIC  . . . . . . 167   2 DON JUAN  2    21   7
```

```
                                                          PAGE VOL    CANTO STANZA  LN
PATHETIC   (CONTINUED)
    HERE I MUST LEAVE HIM FOR I GROW PATHETIC      .   .   .   .   . 372  2 DON JUAN  4      52    1
    AND HAYLEY'S TRIUMPHS WHICH SHE DEEMED PATHETIC   .   .   .   . 525  3 DON JUAN 16      50    3
PATHETICALLY
    WHICH MUST NOT BE PATHETICALLY TOLD     .   .   .   .   .   .   . 413  2 DON JUAN  5       4    8
PATHOS
    I GRANT THE POWER OF PATHOS AND OF GOLD   .   .   .   .   .   . 439  2 DON JUAN  5      49    2
    WHEREON THE RUSSIAN PATHOS GREW LESS TENDER .   .   .   .   . 165  3 DON JUAN  8     107    6
    AND HEW OUT A HUGE MONUMENT OF PATHOS .   .   .   .   .   .   . 355  3 DON JUAN 12      86    7
PATHS
    GROPING ALL PATHS TO POWER AND ALL IN VAIN   .   .   .   .   . 150  2 DON JUAN  1  V  1    6
    AMONGST THE PATHS OF BEING TAKEN IN    .   .   .   .   .   .   . 327  3 DON JUAN 12      25    3
    THEIR WAY THROUGH VIRTUE'S PRIMROSE PATHS OF SNOWS   .   .   . 328  3 DON JUAN 12      26    4
    THE PATHS O'ER WHICH THE FAR FESTOON ENTWINES   .   .   .   . 394  3 DON JUAN 13      76    3
PATHWAY
    HE MISS'D THE PATHWAY HE FORGOT THE HOURS    .   .   .   .   .  72  2 DON JUAN  1      94    5
PATIENCE
    NO DOUBT THIS PATIENCE WHEN THE WORLD IS DAMNING US   .   .   .  37  2 DON JUAN  1      30    1
    WHICH WITH A LITTLE PATIENCE MIGHT GROW CHARMING    .   .   .  68  2 DON JUAN  1      86    8
    AND THEN HE TRIED TO MUSTER ALL HIS PATIENCE .   .   .   .   . 110  2 DON JUAN  1     162    8
    ANTONIA'S PATIENCE NOW WAS AT A STAND--   .   .   .   .   .   . 114  2 DON JUAN  1     170    5
    AND BEG THEY'LL WAIT WITH PATIENCE FOR THE MORAL    .   .   . 141  2 DON JUAN  1     209   V2
    YOUR PATIENCE FURTHER THAN BY THIS SHORT SAMPLE--   .   .   . 147  2 DON JUAN  1     221    7
    I SAID THAT LAMBRO WAS A MAN OF PATIENCE  .   .   .   .   .   . 299  2 DON JUAN  3      46    1
    RESIGNS HERSELF WITH EXEMPLARY PATIENCE   .   .   .   .   .   . 440  2 DON JUAN  5      52    7
    YOUR PATIENCE) SHOWS THE CAUSE MUST STILL BE STRONGER   .   . 488  2 DON JUAN  5     133    8
    GULBEYAZ WAS NO MODEL OF TRUE PATIENCE  .   .   .   .   .   .  56  3 DON JUAN  6     101    1
    PUT TO SUCH TRIAL JOHN BULL'S PARTIAL PATIENCE  .   .   .   . 136  3 DON JUAN  8      48    6
    AS BEING A VIRTUE LIKE TERRESTRIAL PATIENCE .   .   .   .   . 165  3 DON JUAN  8     107    7
    BY SPECIOUS SEEMING JUAN'S YOUTH AND PATIENCE   .   .   .   . 365  3 DON JUAN 13      15    5
    BUT OFT DENIED AS PATIENCE 'GINS TO FAIL HE .   .   .   .   . 459  3 DON JUAN 15       8    5
PATIENT
    ALL THIS THE MOST WERE PATIENT AND SOME BOLD    .   .   .   . 178  2 DON JUAN  2      42    4
    AND PATIENT SPIRIT HELD ALOOF HIS FATE  .   .   .   .   .   .   . 203  2 DON JUAN  2      88    4
    HIS PATIENT AND PERHAPS WAS TO BE BLAMED  .   .   .   .   .   . 154  3 DON JUAN  8      85    6
    BUT READER THOU HAST PATIENT BEEN OF LATE   .   .   .   .   . 393  3 DON JUAN 13      74    1
    BUT STOOD IN TREMBLING PATIENT TRIBULATION  .   .   .   .   . 532  3 DON JUAN 16      65    7
    PATIENT--BUT NOT ENAMOURED OF ENDURANCE   .   .   .   .   .   . 567  3 DON JUAN 17      11    4
PATIENTS
    WHEN PATIENTS NEITHER PLAGUED WITH FRIENDS NOR WIFE .   .   . 190  2 DON JUAN  2      64    3
PATRIARCH
    THE PATRIARCH OF THE FLOCK ALL GENTLY COWERS    .   .   .   . 292  2 DON JUAN  3      32    4
PATRICIAN
    ROUND THE PATRICIAN LEFT-LEGS WHICH ADORN   .   .   .   .   . 404  2 DON JUAN  4     110    7
    JUAN AS AN INVETERATE PATRICIAN    .   .   .   .   .   .   .   . 290  3 DON JUAN 11      45    7
    PROUDEST OF PARIAN PATRICIAN (BRED .   .   .   .   .   .   .   . 314  3 DON JUAN 11  V 75    6
    THAT CALM PATRICIAN POLISH IN THE ADDRESS   .   .   .   .   . 373  3 DON JUAN 13      34    2
PATRIOT
    PATRIOT BY FORCE AND COURTISAN BY CRAFT   .   .   .   .   .   . 155  2 DON JUAN  1  V  6    6
    BUT I'M TOO GREAT A PATRIOT TO RECORD .   .   .   .   .   .   .  77  3 DON JUAN  7      22    2
    BUT STILL THERE IS UNTO A PATRIOT NATION  .   .   .   .   .   . 175  3 DON JUAN  8     126    1
    ALWAYS A PATRIOT AND SOMETIMES A PLACEMAN   .   .   .   .   . 368  3 DON JUAN 13      21    8
    AND HERE AND THERE SOME STERN HIGH PATRIOT STOOD    .   .   . 391  3 DON JUAN 13      70    7
    TO PATRIOT SYMPATHY A BRITON'S BLUSHES--  .   .   .   .   .   . 425  3 DON JUAN 14      35    4
PATRIOTIC
    IT GROWS AN ACT OF PATRIOTIC CHARITY    .   .   .   .   .   . 357  3 DON JUAN 12      89    3
PATRIOTISM
    'TWIXT PLACE AND PATRIOTISM--ALBEIT COMPELLED   .   .   .   . 535  3 DON JUAN 16      72    4
PATRIOT'S
    TO FEEL AT LEAST A PATRIOT'S SHAME    .   .   .   .   .   .   . 323  2 DON JUAN  3  L  6    3
PATRIOTS
    AS PATRIOTS (NOW AND THEN) MAY LOVE A NATION    .   .   .   . 251  3 DON JUAN 10      55    3
    STATESMEN CHIEFS ORATORS QUEENS PATRIOTS KINGS  .   .   .   . 306  3 DON JUAN 11      76    7
    WHO ROUSE THE SHIRTLESS PATRIOTS OF SPAIN   .   .   .   .   . 318  3 DON JUAN 12       5    3
    IN BRITAIN--WHICH OF COURSE TRUE PATRIOTS FIND  .   .   .   . 359  3 DON JUAN 13       2    7
    ERE PATRIOTS THEIR TRUE COUNTRY CAN REMEMBER--  .   .   .   . 380  3 DON JUAN 13      48    7
PATROCLUS
    PATROCLUS AJAX OR PROTESILAUS   .   .   .   .   .   .   .   .   . 385  2 DON JUAN  4      76    7
PATRON
    THE NAME AND QUALITY OF HIS NEW PATRON  .   .   .   .   .   . 298  2 DON JUAN  3      44    7
PATRONAGE
    SO MUCH HE DEEMED HIS PATRONAGE AN HONOUR   .   .   .   .   . 528  3 DON JUAN 16      57    6
PATRONS
    PROFESSORS OF THAT GENIAL ART AND PATRONS   .   .   .   .   . 472  3 DON JUAN 15      37    3
PAT'S
    SWEAR THAT PAT'S LANGUAGE SPRUNG FROM THE SAME CLIME   .   . 122  3 DON JUAN  8      23    5
PATTERN
    MADE UP UPON AN AMATORY PATTERN    .   .   .   .   .   .   .   . 217  3 DON JUAN  9      70    5
PAUL
    (SAINT PAUL SAYS 'TIS THE TOLL WHICH MUST BE GIVEN)   .   .   . 225  2 DON JUAN  2     131    8
    BUT SPENDS SO FAST SHE HAS NOT NOW A PAUL   .   .   .   .   . 390  2 DON JUAN  4      84    6
PAULO
    PAULO MAJORA JUAN UNDECIDED     .   .   .   .   .   .   .   .   . 327  3 DON JUAN 12      25    2
PAUSE
    FOR FOR A WHILE THE FURIES MADE A PAUSE   .   .   .   .   .   . 378  2 DON JUAN  4      62    8
    MADE JUAN IN HIS HARSH INTENTIONS PAUSE   .   .   .   .   .   . 437  2 DON JUAN  5      47    4
    THE EFFEMINATE GARB--THUS AFTER A SHORT PAUSE   .   .   .   . 455  2 DON JUAN  5      76    4
    ON WHICH I CANNOT PAUSE TO MAKE MY STRICTURES   .   .   .   . 465  2 DON JUAN  5      94    8
    THUS FAR OUR CHRONICLE AND NOW WE PAUSE   .   .   .   .   .   . 503  2 DON JUAN  5     159    1
```

		PAGE	VOL	CANTO	STANZA	LV

PAUSE   (CONTINUED)
HERE PAUSE WE FOR THE PRESENT--AS EVEN THEN	111	3 DON JUAN	7	87	1
THAT AWFUL PAUSE DIVIDING LIFE FROM DEATH	111	3 DON JUAN	7	87	2
THEIR PAUSE NOR SIGNS HIS HEART WAS OUT OF JOINT	170	3 DON JUAN	8	117	5
WHICH LAST MEN LIKE WHEN THEY HAVE TIME TO PAUSE	182	3 DON JUAN	8	140	3
THEY HATE ME NOT I THEM--AND HERE WE'LL PAUSE	193	3 DON JUAN	9	21	8
(OR RATHER PEOPLES)--GO ON WITHOUT PAUSE	196	3 DON JUAN	9	28	4
MAY PAUSE IN PONDERING HOW ALL SOULS ARE DIPT	210	3 DON JUAN	9	55	4
THEIR FARE AND ALSO PAUSE BESIDES TO FUDDLE	260	3 DON JUAN	10	71	6
ENTREATING YOU TO PAUSE BEFORE YOU DASH ON	337	3 DON JUAN	12	45	6
OH TIME WHY DOST NOT PAUSE THY SCYTHE SO DIRTY	433	3 DON JUAN	14	53	5
'TIS BEST TO PAUSE AND THINK ERE YOU RUSH ON	438	3 DON JUAN	14	64	7
HERE LET US PAUSE--WE ARE NOT PREST FOR TIME	455	3 DON JUAN	14	102	V1
THE THIRD TIME AFTER A STILL LONGER PAUSE	511	3 DON JUAN	16	24	1
AND THE PAUSE FOLLOWED WHICH WHEN SONG EXPIRES	521	3 DON JUAN	16	41	3

PAUSED
AND THEREFORE PAUSED NOT TO DISTURB THE SLUMBER	96	2 DON JUAN	1	138	4
ALFONSO PAUSED A MINUTE--THEN BEGUN	116	2 DON JUAN	1	174	1
AND LONG HE PAUSED TO RE-ASSURE HIS EYES	294	2 DON JUAN	3	37	6
THE FATHER PAUSED A MOMENT THEN WITHDREW	368	2 DON JUAN	4	46	1
HE PAUSED AND HIS DARK EYE GREW FULL OF GLOOM	420	2 DON JUAN	5	18	3
HE PAUSED AND TOOK A SURVEY UP AND DOWN	456	2 DON JUAN	5	78	8
BEFORE THEY ENTERED BABA PAUSED TO HINT	464	2 DON JUAN	5	91	1
BESIDES FORBIDDEN FRUITS FOR SHE NE'ER PAUSED	476	2 DON JUAN	5	113	V6
SHE STOPT AND RAISED HER HEAD TO SPEAK--BUT PAUSED	61	3 DON JUAN	6	111	1
PAUSED FOR A MOMENT FROM THE FIGHT AND CAST	169	3 DON JUAN	8	116	7
HE PAUSED--AND SO WILL I AS DOTH A CREW	266	3 DON JUAN	10	84	1

PAUSING
TILL PAUSING AT THE LAST HER BREATH TO TAKE	241	2 DON JUAN	2	161	7
SHE ROSE AND PAUSING ONE CHASTE MOMENT THREW	483	2 DON JUAN	5	125	1
VICTORY AND PAUSING AS SHE SAW HIM KNEEL	211	3 DON JUAN	9	57	7
GLANCED WITHOUT PAUSING ON HIM A BRIGHT EYE	510	3 DON JUAN	16	21	8

PAVE
| 'TIS PITY THAT SUCH MEANING SHOULD PAVE HELL | 123 | 3 DON JUAN | 8 | 25 | 8 |

PAVED
OH PLATO PLATO YOU HAVE PAVED THE WAY	84	2 DON JUAN	1	116	1
EVE AND PAVED (GOD KNOWS HOW) THE ROAD TO EVIL	474	2 DON JUAN	5	109	4
WHETHER HELL'S PAVEMENT--IF IT BE SO PAVED--	124	3 DON JUAN	8	26	2
THROUGH HIS MEANS AND THE CHURCH'S MIGHT BE PAVED	251	3 DON JUAN	10	55	6

PAVEMENT
TO PERISH ON THE PAVEMENT SO I HAD	429	2 DON JUAN	5	34	3
WHETHER HELL'S PAVEMENT--IF IT BE SO PAVED--	124	3 DON JUAN	8	26	2
THE BREADTH OF PAVEMENT AND YON SHRINE WHERE FAME IS	279	3 DON JUAN	11	24	5
(WHILE ON THE PAVEMENT MANY A HUNGRY WHORE	313	3 DON JUAN	11	V 29	3
TO GAZE INSTEAD OF PAVEMENT UPON GRASS	539	3 DON JUAN	16	81	3

PAVILION
| GLITTERING LIKE CRESCENTS O'ER A TURK'S PAVILION | 205 | 2 DON JUAN | 2 | 92 | 5 |
| SHUT UP--NO NOT THE KING BUT THE PAVILION | 446 | 3 DON JUAN | 14 | 83 | 7 |

PAVIOUR
| WHO IS NO PAVIOUR NOR ADMITS A BARGE | 198 | 3 DON JUAN | 9 | 31 | 6 |

PAWNS
| QUEENS BISHOPS KNIGHTS ROOKS PAWNS THE WORLD'S A GAME | 400 | 3 DON JUAN | 13 | 89 | 2 |

PAY
THE LOVER WHO MUST PAY A HANDSOME PRICE	57	2 DON JUAN	1	64	7
AND LIVE AND DIE MAKE LOVE AND PAY OUR TAXES	159	2 DON JUAN	2	4	3
TO PAY THEM WITH AND SOME LOOK'D O'ER THE BOW	179	2 DON JUAN	2	44	5
WHICH I FOUND VERY TROUBLESOME TO PAY	190	2 DON JUAN	2	65	8
TO PAY HIM A FRESH VISIT WITH A DISH	226	2 DON JUAN	2	133	7
A HEAVY PRICE MUST ALL PAY WHO THUS ERR	383	2 DON JUAN	4	73	6
OF WORLDS TO LOSE YET STILL TO PAY MY COURT I	9	3 DON JUAN	6	5	5
TO PAY UNPAID PROTESTED OR DISCOUNTED	16	3 DON JUAN	6	21	2
ARE WORSE THAN THE WORST DAMAGES MEN PAY	20	3 DON JUAN	6	29	6
AND FIGHT LIKE FIENDS FOR PAY OR POLITICS	122	3 DON JUAN	8	22	8
WHICH FILLS A REGIMENT (BESIDES THEIR PAY	134	3 DON JUAN	8	42	5
AND MADE THE VERY BILLOWS PAY THEM TOLL	257	3 DON JUAN	10	65	8
HERE ARE CHASTE WIVES PURE LIVES HERE PEOPLE PAY	273	3 DON JUAN	11	10	1
WERE HARDLY RUDE ENOUGH TO EARN THEIR PAY	287	3 DON JUAN	11	40	8
LIKE OTHER SLAVES OF COURSE MUST PAY HIS RANSOM	305	3 DON JUAN	11	74	3
NO DOUBT IF I HAD WISH'D TO PAY MY COURT	466	3 DON JUAN	15	22	5
JUDGING BY WHAT THEY TAKE AND WHAT THEY PAY	548	3 DON JUAN	16	99	5
BUT SELDOM PAY THE ABSENT NOR WOULD LOOK	553	3 DON JUAN	16	106	4

PAYING
| OF PAYING DEBTS WHICH CREDITORS REGRET) | 412 | 3 DON JUAN | 14 | 4 | 6 |

PAYMENT
| ALAS HOW DEEPLY PAINFUL IS ALL PAYMENT | 264 | 3 DON JUAN | 10 | 79 | 1 |
| OF PAYMENT ERE THE HONEYMOON'S LAST KISSES | 293 | 3 DON JUAN | 11 | 49 | 3 |

PAY'S
| WHO EATS FIRE GRATIS (SINCE THE PAY'S BUT SMALL) | 446 | 3 DON JUAN | 14 | 83 | 6 |

PAYS
BUT PAYS OFF MOMENTS IN AN ENDLESS SHOWER	258	2 DON JUAN	2	192	6
AND SO HE SAYS NO MORE--BUT PAYS HIS COURT	82	2 DON JUAN	7	32	5
THOUGH BRITAIN OWES (AND PAYS YOU TOO) SO MUCH	184	3 DON JUAN	9	3	1
AT LEAST HE PAYS NO RENT AND HAS BEST RIGHT	198	3 DON JUAN	9	32	1
THE VERY SUICIDE THAT PAYS HIS DEBT	412	3 DON JUAN	14	4	4

PEACE
WHERE ALL WAS PEACE AND INNOCENCE AND BLISS	30	2 DON JUAN	1	18	5
'TIS TRUE HE HAD NO ARDENT LOVE FOR PEACE--	303	2 DON JUAN	3	55	5
WHERE GREW THE ARTS OF WAR AND PEACE--	320	2 DON JUAN	3	L 1	3
WHATE'ER OF PEACE ABOUT OUR HEARTHSTONE CLINGS	338	2 DON JUAN	3	107	5

PEACE   (CONTINUED)
    BUT AT THIS HOUR I WISH TO PART IN PEACE 398   2 DON JUAN   4   99   2
    HIS PEACE WAS MAKING BUT BEFORE HE VENTURED 493   2 DON JUAN   5   143   7
    HOW PEACE SHOULD MAKE JOHN BULL THE FRENCHMAN'S FOE . . . 77   3 DON JUAN   7   22   8
    OF THAT GREAT CAUSE OF WAR OR PEACE OR WHAT 211   3 DON JUAN   9   57   2
    IN THE DEAR OFFICES OF PEACE OR WAR 288   3 DON JUAN 11   41   3
    PEACE WAR THE TAXES AND WHAT'S CALLED THE NATION . . . 360   3 DON JUAN 13   6   2
    PEACE TO THE SLUMBERS OF EACH FOLDED FLOWER-- 409   3 DON JUAN 13   111   5
    NOW JUSTICES OF PEACE MUST JUDGE ALL PIECES 531   3 DON JUAN 16   63   1
PEACEABLE
    DISCRETION AND WERE NOT SO PEACEABLE 40   2 DON JUAN   1   35   6
    NOTHING BUT WHAT WAS GOOD HER BREAST WAS PEACEABLE-- . . 66   2 DON JUAN   1   83   5
PEACEFUL
    WHILE PEACEFUL AS IF STILL AN UNWEAN'D LAMB 292   2 DON JUAN   3   32   3
    THERE HIS FEW PEACEFUL DAYS TIME HAD SWEPT O'ER 302   2 DON JUAN   3   52   5
    WHERE THEY MIGHT MEET IN MUCH MORE PEACEFUL GUISE . . . 472   2 DON JUAN   5   105   3
PEACOCK
    LIKE AN IMPERIAL PEACOCK STALK ABROAD 104   3 DON JUAN   7   74   5
PEAKS
    THEIR PEAKS BENEATH YOUR HUMAN FOOT AND THERE 412   3 DON JUAN 14   5   5
PEAL
    THE NEXT SHALL RING A PEAL TO SHAKE ALL PEOPLE 109   3 DON JUAN   7   85   7
    LONG BOOMING OF EACH PEAL ON PEAL O'ERCAME 115   3 DON JUAN   8   6   6
    LONG BOOMING OF EACH PEAL ON PEAL O'ERCAME 115   3 DON JUAN   8   6   6
PEALED
    AND THE LOUD CANNON PEALED HIS HOARSEST STRAINS . . . 129   3 DON JUAN   8   33   6
PEALS
    HERE PEALS THE PEOPLE'S VOICE NOR CAN ENTOMB IT . . . 272   3 DON JUAN 11   9   6
PEARL
    MOTHER OF PEARL AND CORAL THE LESS COSTLY 306   2 DON JUAN   3   61   8
    WITH MOTHER OF PEARL OR IVORY STOOD AT HAND 310   2 DON JUAN   3   69   3
    MOTHER OF PEARL AND PORPHYRY AND MARBLE 55   3 DON JUAN   6   98   1
    WHOM HE PRESERVED--A PURE AND LIVING PEARL 249   3 DON JUAN 10   51   8
PEARLS
    WERE STRUNG TOGETHER LIKE A ROW OF PEARLS 291   2 DON JUAN   3   30   3
    WITH BUTTONS FORM'D OF PEARLS AS LARGE AS PEAS 311   2 DON JUAN   3   70   5
    OF LAVISH PEARLS WHOSE WORTH COULD SCARCE BE TOLD . . . 312   2 DON JUAN   3   72   6
    AND LIPS APART WHICH SHOWED THE PEARLS BENEATH 38   3 DON JUAN   6   65   8
    A MOSQUE SO NOBLE FLUNG LIKE PEARLS TO SWINE 262   3 DON JUAN 10   75   8
    OF GEMS AND PLUMES AND PEARLS AND SILKS TO WHERE . . . 303   3 DON JUAN 11   70   4
    COMPARED WITH THOSE OF OUR PURE PEARLS OF PRICE . . . 349   3 DON JUAN 12   72   7
    AND COUNTESSES MATURE IN ROBES AND PEARLS 390   3 DON JUAN 13   68   6
    AS WHITE AS CLEOPATRA'S MELTED PEARLS 484   3 DON JUAN 15   65   8
    A RED LIP WITH TWO ROWS OF PEARLS BENEATH 560   3 DON JUAN 16   121   6
PEAS
    WITH BUTTONS FORM'D OF PEARLS AS LARGE AS PEAS 311   2 DON JUAN   3   70   5
PEASANT
    TO CATCH A GLIMPSE EVEN OF A PRETTY PEASANT 422   3 DON JUAN 14   28   8
PEASANT'S
    AS IF THE PEASANT'S COARSE CONTEMPT WERE VENTED . . . 401   2 DON JUAN   4   105   3
    AS IF THE PEASANT'S SCORN THIS MODE INVENTED 401   2 DON JUAN   4   105   V3
    PERHAPS AS WRETCHED IF A PEASANT'S QUEAN 18   3 DON JUAN   6   25   8
    A PEASANT'S SWEAT IS WORTH HIS LORD'S ESTATE 190   3 DON JUAN   9   15   6
PEASANTS
    THE PEASANTS GAVE THE POOR DUMB THING A PITTANCE . . . 285   2 DON JUAN   3   18   6
    OF SEVERAL RIBBONS AND SOME THOUSAND PEASANTS 222   3 DON JUAN   9   79   8
    AND AH YE POACHERS--'TIS NO SPORT FOR PEASANTS 394   3 DON JUAN 13   75   8
PEBBLE
    TRAMP TRAMP O'ER PEBBLE AND SPLASH SPLASH THRO PUDDLE . . 260   3 DON JUAN 10   71   2
PEBBLES
    OVER THE SHINING PEBBLES AND THE SHELLS 253   2 DON JUAN   2   184   2
    LIKE DAVID FLINGS SMOOTH PEBBLES 'GAINST A GIANT . . . 138   3 DON JUAN   8   51   2
PECCADILLOS
    A PLACE WHERE PECCADILLOS ARE UNKNOWN 370   3 DON JUAN 13   27   2
PECCANT
    HER STOMACH'S NOT HER PECCANT PART THIS TALE 483   3 DON JUAN 15   64   6
PECK
    TAKES OFF ONE PECK OF PURGATORIAL COALS 185   2 DON JUAN   2   55   5
PECKING
    IN THE FEAST PECKING LESS THAN I CAN TELL 487   3 DON JUAN 15   70   4
PECULIAR
    WITH A PECULIAR SMILE WHICH BY THE WAY 297   2 DON JUAN   3   42   3
    BUT FOR MY OWN PECULIAR SUPERSTITION 467   3 DON JUAN 15   24   4
PECULIARLY
    BUT THIS WILL MORE PECULIARLY BE SEEN) 137   2 DON JUAN   1   202   5
PEDANTIC
    SEEMED TO HIM HALF COMMERCIAL HALF PEDANTIC 347   3 DON JUAN 12   68   5
    WAS--PARDON THE PEDANTIC ILLUSTRATION-- 522   3 DON JUAN 16   43   2
PEDESTRIAN
    FOR ME WHO WANDERING WITH PEDESTRIAN MUSES 14   2 DON JUAN   D   8   1
    OF THOSE PEDESTRIAN PAPHIANS WHO ABOUND 282   3 DON JUAN 11   30   4
PEDIGREE
    AND WORTHY OF THE NOBLEST PEDIGREE 42   2 DON JUAN   1   38   3
    SHE MARRIED (I FORGET THE PEDIGREE) 52   2 DON JUAN   1   57   1
    TO STAIN HIS PEDIGREE A THOUSAND SWORDS 471   2 DON JUAN   5   104   5
    WHAT PEDIGREE THE BEST WOULD HAVE TO SHOW 53   3 DON JUAN   6   94   8
    WHICH FORMS A PEDIGREE FROM MISS TO MISS 340   3 DON JUAN 12   52   3
    AND OAKS AS OLDEN AS THEIR PEDIGREE 381   3 DON JUAN 13   50   7
    AND A YOUNG RACE-HORSE OF OLD PEDIGREE 527   3 DON JUAN 16   55   7

		PAGE	VOL	CANTO	STANZA	LN

PEDIGREES
IN PEDIGREES BY THOSE WHO WANDER STILL . . . . 359 3 DON JUAN 13 2 3
PEDLAR
SEASON'D HIS PEDLAR POEMS WITH DEMOCRACY . . . . 329 2 DON JUAN 3 93 4
PEDLARS
PEDLARS AND BOATS AND WAGGONS OH YE SHADES . . . . . 334 2 DON JUAN 3 100 1
PEDRILLO
A TUTOR THE LICENTIATE PEDRILLO . . . . 169 2 DON JUAN 2 25 2
AND EVEN PEDRILLO HIS MOST REVEREND TUTOR . . . . . 175 2 DON JUAN 2 36 7
THAT BEGG'D PEDRILLO FOR AN ABSOLUTION . . . . . . 179 2 DON JUAN 2 44 7
CONTRIVED TO HELP PEDRILLO TO A PLACE . . . . . . 186 2 DON JUAN 2 56 2
WHICH HE DIVIDED WITH PEDRILLO WHO . . . . 193 2 DON JUAN 2 71 7
PEDRILLO AND SO GENTLY EBB'D HIS BREATH . . . . . 197 2 DON JUAN 2 76 3
THE SAILORS ATE THE REST OF POOR PEDRILLO . . . . 197 2 DON JUAN 2 77 8
OF POOR PEDRILLO SOMETHING STILL REMAIN'D . . . . 200 2 DON JUAN 2 82 1
IN WASHING DOWN PEDRILLO WITH SALT WATER . . . . . 210 2 DON JUAN 2 102 8
PEDRILLO'S
WHICH COURAGE GIVES WHILE POOR PEDRILLO'S PAIR . . . . 186 2 DON JUAN 2 56 5
ABOUT HIS PERSON AND PEDRILLO'S TOO . . . . . . 187 2 DON JUAN 2 59 2
AND IF PEDRILLO'S FATE SHOULD SHOCKING BE . . . . . 200 2 DON JUAN 2 83 1
PEDRO
PEDRO BATTISTA HELP ME DOWN BELOW) . . . . 167 2 DON JUAN 2 20 4
JULIA MY LOVE--(YOU RASCAL PEDRO QUICKER)-- . . . . . 167 2 DON JUAN 2 20 5
PEDRO HIS VALET TOO HE TRIED TO SAVE . . . . 186 2 DON JUAN 2 57 1
PEEP
WHEN FIRST SHE STARTS AND THEN RETURNS TO PEEP . . . . 36 3 DON JUAN 6 60 7
THE STARS PEEP THROUGH THE VAPOURS DIM AND DANK . . . 110 3 DON JUAN 7 86 6
PEEP OUT SOMETIMES WHEN THINGS ARE IN A FLURRY . . . . 237 3 DON JUAN 10 26 5
PEEPED
THE MOON PEEPED JUST ESCAPED FROM A GREY CLOUD . . . . 560 3 DON JUAN 16 121 8
PEEPING
OF MASTS A WILDERNESS OF STEEPLES PEEPING . . . . . 265 3 DON JUAN 10 82 5
BEFORE A PETTICOAT AND PEEPING ANCLE . . . . . . 422 3 DON JUAN 14 27 8
THAN DYING TAPERS--AND THE PEEPING MOON . . . . . 504 3 DON JUAN 16 8 8
PEER
AND LORD MOUNT COFFEEHOUSE THE IRISH PEER . . . . . 102 2 DON JUAN 1 149 7
EACH OUT-AT-ELBOW PEER OR DESPERATE DANDY . . . . 331 3 DON JUAN 12 32 2
PEERAGE
THE PEERAGE TO A MANSION VERY FINE . . . . 381 3 DON JUAN 13 50 3
PEERESSES
OF PEERESSES WHOSE FOLLIES HAD RUN DRY . . . . . 329 3 DON JUAN 12 29 8
PEERING
OF THE THIRD SEX STEPT UP AND PEERING OVER . . . . 424 2 DON JUAN 5 26 2
PEER'S
A LAUREATE'S ODE OR SERVILE PEER'S CONTENT . . . . 435 3 DON JUAN 14 58 8
PEERS
OF PEERS TO PROVE THEIR TITLE NO DISGRACE . . . . 314 3 DON JUAN 11 V 75 8
AYE EVERY INCH A DUKE THERE WERE TWELVE PEERS . . . 398 3 DON JUAN 13 85 2
LIKE CHARLEMAGNE'S--AND ALL SUCH PEERS IN LOOK . . . 398 3 DON JUAN 13 85 3
BOLDLY REFERRING TO THE LIST OF PEERS . . . . . 432 3 DON JUAN 14 52 3
PEGASUS
HIS PEGASUS NOR ANYTHING THAT'S HIS . . . . . . 140 2 DON JUAN 1 206 2
IN GERMANY THE PEGASUS HE'D PRANCE ON . . . . . 320 2 DON JUAN 3 86 5
AND PEGASUS RUNS RESTIVE IN HIS WAGGON . . . . . 333 2 DON JUAN 3 99 2
FOR OFTENTIMES WHEN PEGASUS SEEMS WINNING . . . . 344 2 DON JUAN 4 1 3
NOW IF MY PEGASUS SHOULD NOT BE SHOD ILL . . . . . 412 2 DON JUAN 5 2 7
OF PEGASUS--OR AT THE LEAST POST CHAISES . . . . 197 3 DON JUAN 9 30 7
MY PEGASUS SHALL TIRE OF TOUCHING GROUND . . . . 224 3 DON JUAN 9 85 3
AND PEGASUS HATH A PSALMODIC AMBLE . . . . . . 297 3 DON JUAN 11 57 5
WHICH PUTS MY PEGASUS TO THESE GRAVE PACES . . . 334 3 DON JUAN 12 39 8
IF THAT MY PEGASUS SHOULD NOT BE FOUNDERED . . . 341 3 DON JUAN 12 55 7
PEGS
UPON MY LYRE OR MAKING THE PEGS SURE . . . . . . 341 3 DON JUAN 12 54 7
PELEGRINI
THEN THERE'S THAT LAUGHING SLUT THE PELEGRINI . . . . 390 2 DON JUAN 4 84 3
PELEUS'
DESCRIBING PRIAM'S PELEUS' OR JOVE'S SON . . . . . 164 3 DON JUAN 8 105 6
PELF
MORE (LIKE A STOCK-HOLDER IN GROWING PELF) . . . . . 470 3 DON JUAN 15 31 5
PELIDES'
BEFORE PELIDES' DEATH OR HOMER'S BIRTH . . . . . 400 2 DON JUAN 4 104 8
PELISSE
HE HAD A BED OF FURS AND A PELISSE . . . . 226 2 DON JUAN 2 133 1
THAT WITH THE ADDITION OF A SLIGHT PELISSE . . . . 239 3 DON JUAN 10 30 7
PELLETS
CHIEF IMPULSE WITH A FEW FRAIL PAPER PELLETS . . . . 298 3 DON JUAN 11 60 V8
PELL-MELL
PELL-MELL AND WITH A WHOLE GAZETTE OF SLAUGHTER . . . 82 3 DON JUAN 7 31 8
UPON HIS ANGRY SULTANSHIP PELL-MELL . . . . . . 166 3 DON JUAN 8 109 4
PEN
THERE'S PEN AND INK FOR YOU SIR WHEN YOU NEED-- . . . 104 2 DON JUAN 1 152 4
(THE HEART WILL SLIP EVEN AS THE TONGUE AND PEN) . . . 228 2 DON JUAN 2 135 6
HAVE MUCH EMPLOY'D THE MUSE OF HISTORY'S PEN . . . . 266 2 DON JUAN 2 206 4
AND LAYING DOWN MY PEN I MAKE MY BOW . . . . . . 271 2 DON JUAN 2 216 6
OR COLERIDGE LONG BEFORE HIS FLIGHTY PEN . . . . . 329 2 DON JUAN 3 93 5
MY PEN AND LIKED POETIC WAR TO WAGE . . . . . . 397 2 DON JUAN 4 98 6
MY PEN AND EASILY FLEW IN A RAGE . . . . 397 2 DON JUAN 4 98 V6
BUT AN EXTRANEOUS MIXTURE WHICH NO PEN . . . . . 462 2 DON JJAN 5 88 5
ALL THAT DEFIES THE WORST WHICH PEN EXPRESSES . . . . 173 3 DON JUAN 8 123 5

	PAGE	VOL		CANTO	STANZA	LN
PEN (CONTINUED)						
AS NOW OCCUR I THOUGHT THAT I WOULD PEN YOU 'EM	180	3	DON JUAN	8	136	4
I SAY THAT LINE'S A LAPSUS OF THE PEN--	323	3	DON JUAN	12	16	4
TRICKED OUT BUT MODEST MORE THAN POET'S PEN	380	3	DON JUAN	13	47	4
BUT OH THAT I SHOULD EVER PEN SO SAD A LINE	430	3	DON JUAN	14	46	1
PENALTY						
OF LATE THE PENALTY OF SUCH SUCCESS	324	3	DON JUAN	12	17	7
PENCE						
WHERE STILL WE FLUTTER ON FOR PENCE OR PRAISE	422	2	DON JUAN	5	22	8
PENCHANT						
FOR CATS AND BIRDS MORE PENCHANT NE'ER DISPLAYED	249	3	DON JUAN	10	50	7
OWN'D TO A PENCHANT THOUGH DISCREET FOR BEAUTY	494	3	DON JUAN	15	85	8
PENCHANTS						
HE SHOW'D THE ROYAL PENCHANTS OF A PIRATE	296	2	DON JUAN	3	40	8
PENCIL						
CAN TRACE ALTHOUGH PERHAPS THE PENCIL MAY	462	2	DON JUAN	5	88	6
PENETRATE						
GREAT BRITAIN WHICH THE MUSE MAY PENETRATE	327	3	DON JUAN	12	24	6
BUT AS TO WOMEN WHO CAN PENETRATE	420	3	DON JUAN	14	24	3
PENITENCE						
WITH USELESS PENITENCE PERPLEX'D AND HAUNTED	120	2	DON JUAN	1	180	6
PENN'D						
FOR NOT A LINE HAD JULIA EVER PENN'D	58	2	DON JUAN	1	66	4
BUT MIX'D WITH PITY PURE AS E'ER WAS PENN'D	432	3	DON JUAN	14	51	6
PENS						
WHICH HANDS OR PENS HAVE EVER TRACED OF SWORDS	179	3	DON JUAN	8	134	3
NO LONGER READY EARS AND SHORT-HAND PENS	540	3	DON JUAN	16	83	4
PENSION						
THERE WAS NO DOUBT HE EARN'D HIS LAUREATE PENSION	317	2	DON JUAN	3	80	8
PROVED DEATH IN BATTLE EQUAL TO A PENSION--	96	3	DON JUAN	7	58	8
A MODERATE PENSION SHAKES FULL MANY A SAGE	118	3	DON JUAN	8	14	4
(FELLOWS WHOM MESSALINA'S SELF WOULD PENSION)	218	3	DON JUAN	9	72	4
PENSIONS						
SHOUTS BRIDGES ARCHES PENSIONS FROM A NATION	114	3	DON JUAN	8	4	3
HIS ORDERS ALSO TO RECEIVE HIS PENSIONS	137	3	DON JUAN	8	49	7
YOU HAVE OBTAINED GREAT PENSIONS AND MUCH PRAISE	183	3	DON JUAN	9	1	6
PENSIVE						
SILENT AND PENSIVE IDLE RESTLESS SLOW	68	2	DON JUAN	1	87	1
AND PENSIVE TO HER FATHER'S HOUSE SHE WENT	228	2	DON JUAN	2	136	1
MAN'S PENSIVE PART IS NOW AND THEN THE HEAD	7	3	DON JUAN	6	2	V7
BUT SHE WAS PENSIVE MORE THAN MELANCHOLY	33	3	DON JUAN	6	54	1
AND SERIOUS MORE THAN PENSIVE AND SERENE	33	3	DON JUAN	6	54	2
JUAN FELT SOMEWHAT PENSIVE AND DISPOSED	507	3	DON JUAN	16	15	1
HE SATE HIM PENSIVE O'ER A DISH OF TEA	513	3	DON JUAN	16	30	2
PEOPLE						
WERE FRENCH AND FAMOUS PEOPLE AS WE KNOW	22	2	DON JUAN	1	3	3
AT WHICH THE NAVAL PEOPLE ARE CONCERN'D	23	2	DON JUAN	1	4	6
SHE MADE THE CLEVEREST PEOPLE QUITE ASHAMED	26	2	DON JUAN	1	10	5
THOUGH SEVERAL THOUSAND PEOPLE CHOSE TO TRY	33	2	DON JUAN	1	23	3
I THINK THE FOOLISH PEOPLE WERE POSSESS'D	34	2	DON JUAN	1	24	3
THAT HOWSOEVER PEOPLE FAST AND PRAY	56	2	DON JUAN	1	63	5
THEY LIVED TOGETHER AS MOST PEOPLE DO	57	2	DON JUAN	1	65	4
SOME PEOPLE WHISPER (BUT NO DOUBT THEY LIE	58	2	DON JUAN	1	66	5
FOR PEOPLE WHO ARE PLEASANTER THAN OTHERS	63	2	DON JUAN	1	77	7
IF PEOPLE GO BEYOND 'TIS QUITE A CRIME	65	2	DON JUAN	1	80	7
OR LIKE ALL VERY CLEVER PEOPLE COULD NOT	73	2	DON JUAN	1	97	8
PEOPLE SHOULD HOLD THEIR TONGUES IN ANY CASE	77	2	DON JUAN	1	105	4
WHEN PEOPLE SAY I'VE TOLD YOU FIFTY TIMES	79	2	DON JUAN	1	108	1
'TIS STRANGE OLD PEOPLE DONT LIKE TO BE BURIED	89	2	DON JUAN	1	125	V8
(AT LEAST THIS IS THE THING MOST PEOPLE DO)	129	2	DON JUAN	1	191	5
SOME PEOPLE LIKE BLANK VERSE I'M FOND OF RHYME	136	2	DON JUAN	1	201	V5
THE VERY PLACE WHERE WICKED PEOPLE GO	140	2	DON JUAN	1	207	8
AT LEAVING EVEN THE MOST UNPLEASANT PEOPLE	164	2	DON JUAN	2	14	7
ONE GANG OF PEOPLE INSTANTLY WAS PUT	171	2	DON JUAN	2	28	1
WAS GOING ON SOME PEOPLE WERE UNQUIET	173	2	DON JUAN	2	33	2
WATER APPEAR'D YET THOUGH THE PEOPLE KNEW	178	2	DON JUAN	2	42	3
TWO THINGS FOR DYING PEOPLE QUITE BEWILDERING	179	2	DON JUAN	2	43	8
TO SAVE ONE HALF THE PEOPLE THEN ON BOARD	181	2	DON JUAN	2	48	8
UNLESS WITH PEOPLE WHO TOO MUCH HAVE QUAFF'D	183	2	DON JUAN	2	50	5
BECAUSE TILL PEOPLE KNOW WHAT'S COME TO PASS	185	2	DON JUAN	2	55	6
WAS SERVED OUT TO THE PEOPLE WHO BEGUN	189	2	DON JUAN	2	62	6
'TIS THUS WITH PEOPLE IN AN OPEN BOAT	191	2	DON JUAN	2	66	1
YOUR LABOURING PEOPLE THINK BEYOND ALL QUESTION	191	2	DON JUAN	2	67	7
OR PEOPLE IN A TRANCE INTO THEIR GRAVE	225	2	DON JUAN	2	130	4
FOR WE ALL KNOW THAT ENGLISH PEOPLE ARE	238	2	DON JUAN	2	156	1
THAT FAMISH'D PEOPLE MUST BE SLOWLY NURST	239	2	DON JUAN	2	158	7
OF HELL-FIRE--ALL PREPARED FOR PEOPLE GIVING	258	2	DON JUAN	2	192	7
YET WHAT CAN PEOPLE DO EXCEPT DESPAIR	278	2	DON JUAN	3	6	5
WERE LINK'D ALIKE AS FOR THE COMMON PEOPLE HE	284	2	DON JUAN	3	16	7
WITH ORDERS TO THE PEOPLE TO CAREEN	286	2	DON JUAN	3	20	6
AVOUCH'D HIS DEATH (SUCH PEOPLE NEVER DIE)	295	2	DON JUAN	3	38	3
TO TEACH HIS PEOPLE TO BE MORE EXACT	296	2	DON JUAN	3	40	6
AND HAVING LIVED WITH PEOPLE OF ALL RANKS	319	2	DON JUAN	3	84	3
LEAVING MY PEOPLE TO PROCEED ALONE	331	2	DON JUAN	3	96	3
THE SHRILL CICALAS PEOPLE OF THE PINE	337	2	DON JUAN	3	106	1
SOME PEOPLE PREFER WINE--'TIS NOT AMISS	356	2	DON JUAN	4	24	6
I DON'T MUCH LIKE DESCRIBING PEOPLE MAD	384	2	DON JUAN	4	74	3
BUT HEAR THAT SEVERAL PEOPLE TAKE EXCEPTION	397	2	DON JUAN	4	97	3
IT CHANCED AMONGST THE OTHER PEOPLE LOTTED	416	2	DON JUAN	5	10	5

PEOPLE   (CONTINUED)
   IS SOMETIMES GOOD FOR PEOPLE IN HER STATION . . . . . . 490 2 DON JUAN 5 137 8
   OF ALL THE ELEMENTS WHICH PEOPLE SAY . . . . 32 3 DON JUAN 6   53 V5
   IF PEOPLE WOULD BUT SEE ITS REAL DRIFT-- . . . . 50 3 DON JUAN 6   88 2
   TO WHICH EMBARRASSED PEOPLE HAVE RECOURSE . . . . . . 56 3 DON JUAN 6 100 8
   WHICH MANY PEOPLE PASS FOR WITS BY QUOTING . . . . . . 77 3 DON JUAN 7   21 8
   IN THE THEN SOVEREIGN OF THE RUSSIAN PEOPLE . . . . . 84 3 DON JUAN 7   37 7
   THE NEXT SHALL RING A PEAL TO SHAKE ALL PEOPLE . . . . 109 3 DON JUAN 7   85 7
   OFF EACH ATTACK WHEN PEOPLE ARE IN QUEST . . . . 123 3 DON JUAN 8   25 6
   TO FLY FROM MALGRE ALL WHICH PEOPLE SAY . . . . 134 3 DON JUAN 8   42 3
   THE PEOPLE BY-AND-BY WILL BE THE STRONGER . . . . . . 137 3 DON JUAN 8   50 4
   OF THIS UNSIGHING PEOPLE OF THE WOODS . . . . 145 3 DON JUAN 8   67 8
   SOME HUNGER TOO THEY SAY THE PEOPLE FEELS-- . . . . . 185 3 DON JUAN 9   6 6
   SOME PEOPLE HAVE ACCUSED ME OF MISANTHROPY . . . . . . 192 3 DON JUAN 9   20 4
   IT IS NOT THAT I ADULATE THE PEOPLE . . . . 195 3 DON JUAN 9   25 1
   ARE USELESS MIND GOOD PEOPLE WHAT I SAY-- . . . . . . 196 3 DON JUAN 9   28 3
   HOW WILL--TO THESE YOUNG PEOPLE JUST THRUST OUT . . . 202 3 DON JUAN 9   40 1
   SUSPICIOUS PEOPLE WHO FIND FAULT IN HASTE . . . . . . 230 3 DON JUAN 10   11 3
   YOUNG PEOPLE AT HIS TIME OF LIFE SHOULD BE ABLE . . . 235 3 DON JUAN 10   22 3
   WEAKNESS FOR WHAT MOST PEOPLE DEEM MERE VERMIN-- . . . 249 3 DON JUAN 10   50 5
   AS SEVERAL PEOPLE THINK SUCH HAZARDS RUDE . . . . . . 270 3 DON JUAN 11   4 4
   HERE ARE CHASTE WIVES PURE LIVES HERE PEOPLE PAY . . . 273 3 DON JUAN 11   10 1
   THE MANSION HOUSE TOO (THOUGH SOME PEOPLE QUIZ IT) . . 280 3 DON JUAN 11   25 6
   WHICH SERVES OUR THINKING PEOPLE FOR A PASSION . . . . 284 3 DON JUAN 11   33 8
   AND ABOUT TWICE TWO THOUSAND PEOPLE BRED . . . . 290 3 DON JUAN 11   45 3
   AND VERY MUCH UNLIKE WHAT PEOPLE WRITE . . . . 292 3 DON JUAN 11   47 8
   AMONGST A PEOPLE FAMOUS FOR REFLECTION . . . . 304 3 DON JUAN 11   71 7
   I'VE SEEN THE PEOPLE RIDDEN O'ER LIKE SAND . . . . . . 310 3 DON JUAN 11   85 5
   YOU ARE NOT A MORAL PEOPLE AND YOU KNOW IT . . . . . . 311 3 DON JUAN 11   87 7
   I WONDER PEOPLE SHOULD BE LEFT ALIVE . . . . 316 3 DON JUAN 12   2 3
   AFTER A SORT BUT SOMEHOW PEOPLE NEVER . . . . 323 3 DON JUAN 12   15 3
   GOOD PEOPLE ALL OF EVERY DEGREE . . . . 325 3 DON JUAN 12   20 1
   THAT EVEN THE PUREST PEOPLE MAY MISTAKE . . . . 328 3 DON JUAN 12   26 3
   TO THE SURPRISE OF PEOPLE OF CONDITION . . . . 328 3 DON JUAN 12   27 4
   ALL PEOPLE AT ALL TIMES AND IN MOST PLACES . . . . . . 334 3 DON JUAN 12   39 7
   LIKE MANY PEOPLE EVERYBODY KNOWS . . . . 335 3 DON JUAN 12   41 5
   PEOPLE ARE APT TO BLAME THE FATES FORSOOTH . . . . . . 339 3 DON JUAN 12   50 3
   PEOPLE SOME TEN TIMES LESS IN FACT TO MIND IT . . . . 352 3 DON JUAN 12   80 3
   (WHATEVER PEOPLE SAY) I DON'T KNOW WHETHER . . . . . . 355 3 DON JUAN 12   86 4
   FROM WHAT SOME PEOPLE SAY 'TWILL BE WHEN DONE . . . . 356 3 DON JUAN 12   87 4
   TO SHOW THE PEOPLE THE BEST WAY TO BREAK . . . . 357 3 DON JUAN 12   89 4
   WHERE PEOPLE ALWAYS DID AS THEY WERE BID . . . . 368 3 DON JUAN 13   23 3
   AND YOUR COLD PEOPLE ARE BEYOND ALL PRICE . . . . . . 375 3 DON JUAN 13   38 7
   WHICH MEANS THAT VULGAR PEOPLE MUST NOT SHAKE IT . . . 419 3 DON JUAN 14   21 8
   WAS ALL THINGS UNTO PEOPLE OF ALL SORTS . . . . 424 3 DON JUAN 14   31 2
   I LEAVE IT TO YOUR PEOPLE OF SAGACITY . . . . 449 3 DON JUAN 14   90 4
   OR GERMANY WHERE PEOPLE PURELY KISS . . . . 450 3 DON JUAN 14   92 5
   WHICH CHARM MOST PEOPLE IN THEIR EARLIER DAY . . . . . 479 3 DON JUAN 15   53 3
   THAN WHEN SOME SQUEAMISH PEOPLE DEEM HER FRAIL . . . . 483 3 DON JUAN 15   64 4
   HE HAD THE ART OF DRAWING PEOPLE OUT . . . . 492 3 DON JUAN 15   82 7
   IF PEOPLE CONTRADICT THEMSELVES CAN I . . . . 495 3 DON JUAN 15   88 1
   INDEED I NEVER KNEW WHAT PEOPLE MEANT . . . . 498 3 DON JUAN 15   94 5
   SOME PEOPLE WOULD IMPOSE NOW WITH AUTHORITY . . . . . 503 3 DON JUAN 16   5 1
   THE NIGHTS AND DAYS MOST PEOPLE CAN REMEMBER . . . . . 505 3 DON JUAN 16   11 6
   AS DOUBTLESS SHOULD ·BE PEOPLE OF HIGH BIRTH . . . . . 508 3 DON JUAN 16   17 6
   MOST PEOPLE AS IT PLAYS ALONG THE ARRAS . . . . 509 3 DON JUAN 16   20 8
   HE DRESSED AND LIKE YOUNG PEOPLE HE WAS WONT . . . . . 513 3 DON JUAN 16   29 1
   OF THAT SAME TUNE WHEN PEOPLE HUM IT LONG)-- . . . . . 529 3 DON JUAN 16   59 3
   A SLIGHT REPAST MAKES PEOPLE LOVE MUCH MORE . . . . . 542 3 DON JUAN 16   86 3
   WHICH MANY PEOPLE TAKE FOR WANT OF HEART . . . . 547 3 DON JUAN 16   97 3
   THE RIDICULES OF PEOPLE IN ALL PLACES-- . . . . 548 3 DON JUAN 16 100 5
   HE FOUND AS PEOPLE ON MOST TRIALS MUST . . . . 560 3 DON JUAN 16 122 5
   WE LITTLE PEOPLE IN OUR LESSER WAY . . . . 566 3 DON JUAN 17   10 2
PEOPLED
   THAT EVER PEOPLED HELL WITH HEROES SLAIN . . . . 101 3 DON JUAN 7   68 3
   AND GROANS AND THUS THE PEOPLED CITY GRIEVES . . . . . 155 3 DON JUAN 8   88 5
   ALL BY WHICH HELL IS PEOPLED OR AS SAD . . . . 173 3 DON JUAN 8 123 6
PEOPLE'S
   WITH OTHER PEOPLE'S EYES OR IF HER OWN . . . . 59 2 DON JUAN 1   68 2
   THE PEOPLE'S SYCOPHANT THE PRINCE'S FOE . . . . 151 2 DON JUAN 1 V 2 7
   THE PEOPLE'S SYCOPHANT--TILL DANGER COMES . . . . . . 151 2 DON JUAN 1 V 2 V7
   THE PEOPLE'S SYCOPHANT--IN JUSTICE'S HOUR . . . . . . 151 2 DON JUAN 1 V 2 V7
   ROMANCES PAINT AT FULL LENGTH PEOPLE'S WOOINGS . . . . 279 2 DON JUAN 3   8 3
   LAMBRO'S RECEPTION AT HIS PEOPLE'S BANQUET . . . . . . 294 2 DON JUAN 3   36 7
   THE PEOPLE'S AWE AND ADMIRATION RAISING . . . . 445 2 DON JUAN 5   60 6
   BUT PEOPLE'S ANCESTORS ARE HISTORY'S GAME . . . . . . 53 3 DON JUAN 6   94 5
   TO MEND THE PEOPLE'S AN ABSURDITY . . . . 266 3 DON JUAN 10   85 5
   HERE PEALS THE PEOPLE'S VOICE NOR CAN ENTOMB IT . . . 272 3 DON JUAN 11   9 6
   TO EYE OR HEART--IT IS THE PEOPLE'S TRUST . . . . . . 354 3 DON JUAN 12   83 8
PEOPLES
   (OR RATHER PEOPLES)--GO ON WITHOUT PAUSE . . . . 196 3 DON JUAN 9   28 4
PEOPLING
   HE TOOK TO REGULARLY PEOPLING EARTH . . . . 312 3 DON JUAN 11   89 5
PER
   BY THEM PER HOUR AND THEY HAD ALL BEEN UNDONE . . . . 171 2 DON JUAN 2   29 7
   WERE TO BE CHAIN'D AND LOTTED OUT PER COUPLE . . . . . 393 2 DON JUAN 4   91 7
   WHO DID NOT LIMIT MUCH HIS BILLS PER WEEK . . . . . . 259 3 DON JUAN 10   70 3
   WHERE ARE THOSE MARTYRED SAINTS THE FIVE PER CENTS . . 307 3 DON JUAN 11   77 7
PERCEIVE
   YOU HARDLY COULD PERCEIVE WHEN HE WAS DEAD . . . . . . 197 2 DON JUAN 2   76 4

PERCEIVE   (CONTINUED)
   FOR SURELY IF WE ALWAYS COULD PERCEIVE   270   2 DON JUAN   2   213   2
   QUICK TO PERCEIVE AND STRONG TO BEAR AND MEANT 302   2 DON JUAN   3   53   5
   TILL THIRTY SHOULD PERCEIVE THERE'S A PLAIN WOMAN 359   3 DON JUAN 13   3   8
PERCEIVED
   HAPPIER THAN THEY WHO STILL PERCEIVED THEIR WOES 199   2 DON JUAN   2   80   4
   THE DISTANT DOG-BARK AND PERCEIVED BETWEEN 289   2 DON JUAN   3   27   4
   PERCEIVED IT WAS THE PYRRHIC DANCE SO MARTIAL 290   2 DON JUAN   3   29   7
   AND LOOKING AS HE ALWAYS LOOKED PERCEIVED 500   2 DON JUAN   5   155   2
   IF I HAD NOT PERCEIVED THAT REVOLUTION 138   3 DON JUAN   8   51   7
   IN AMBUSH LAID WHO HAD PERCEIVED HIM LOITER 273   3 DON JUAN 11   11   2
   THE FRIAR OF LATE HAS NOT BEEN OFT PERCEIVED 516   3 DON JUAN 16   36   8
PERCEIVES
   THIS CANTO ERE MY MUSE PERCEIVES FATIGUE 109   2 DON JUAN   7   35   6
PERCEIVING
   AND TURN'D WITHOUT PERCEIVING HIS CONDITION 70   2 DON JUAN   1   91   7
   PERCEIVING IN HIS ABSENCE SUCH EXPENSES 293   2 DON JUAN   3   35   6
   AT LENGTH PERCEIVING THE FOOT COULD NOT STAND 471   2 DON JUAN   5   104   7
   PERCEIVING THEN NO MORE THE COMMANDANT 127   3 DON JUAN   8   31   1
   PERCEIVING NOR COMMANDER NOR COMMANDED 127   3 DON JUAN   8   32   1
   PERCEIVING HE WAS IN A HANDSOME WAY 239   3 DON JUAN 10   30   2
   HE STARTED AND PERCEIVING SMILES AROUND 542   3 DON JUAN 16   88   2
PER-CENTAGE
   AT A PER-CENTAGE A CHILD CROSS DOG ILL 16   3 DON JUAN   6   21   3
PERCEPTIBLY
   BY A LOOK SCARCE PERCEPTIBLY ASKANCE 546   3 DON JUAN 16   96   6
PERCEPTION
   'TIS THE PERCEPTION OF THE BEAUTIFUL 269   2 DON JUAN   2   212   1
PERCH
   AND TRIED TO PERCH ALTHOUGH IT SAW AND HEARD 206   2 DON JUAN   2   94   5
   'TWAS WELL THIS BIRD OF PROMISE DID NOT PERCH 206   2 DON JUAN   2   95   2
   MUST PERCH HARMONIOUS ON MY TUNEFUL QUILL 458   3 DON JUAN 15   5   4
   I PERCH UPON AN HUMBLER PROMONTORY 464   3 DON JUAN 15   19   1
PERCHANCE
   PERCHANCE THE DEATH OF ONE SHE LOVED TOO WELL 363   2 DON JUAN   4   36   5
   BUT COULD WE KNOW THEM IN DETAIL PERCHANCE 113   3 DON JUAN   8   3   2
   YET IF PERCHANCE REMEMBERED STILL DISDAIN YOU 'EM . . . 180   3 DON JUAN   8   136   6
   THAT HE WHO NAMES ONE BOTH PERCHANCE MAY HIT ON . . . 221   3 DON JUAN   9   77   6
   SHAPED BY DECAY PERCHANCE HATH GIVEN THE POWER . . . 388   3 DON JUAN 13   64   2
   THOUGH AT THE FIRST I MIGHT PERCHANCE DERIDE 466   3 DON JUAN 15   23   5
PERCHED
   OFFENCE WE KNOW NOT PROBABLY IT PERCHED 192   3 DON JUAN   9   19   7
PERDITION
   MEN WILL PROVE HUNGRY EVEN WHEN NEXT PERDITION 180   2 DON JUAN   2   46 V5
   WAS DEARLY PURCHASED BY HIS LAND'S PERDITION 364   3 DON JUAN 13   11   8
   WHICH THREATENED THE WHOLE COUNTRY WITH PERDITION . . . 536   3 DON JUAN 16   74   4
PERENNIAL
   IN THY PERENNIAL FOUNTAIN--HOW MAN FELL I 210   3 DON JUAN   9   55   5
PERFECT
   OH SHE WAS PERFECT PAST ALL PARALLEL 30   2 DON JUAN   1   17   1
   PERFECT SHE WAS BUT A PERFECTION IS 30   2 DON JUAN   1   18   1
   YOU MIGHT BE SURE SHE WAS A PERFECT FRIGHT 48   2 DON JUAN   1   48   6
   PLATONIC PERFECT JUST SUCH LOVE AS MINE 64   2 DON JUAN   1   79   5
   HERE IS THE EMPIRE OF THY PERFECT BLISS 69   2 DON JUAN   1   88   3
   TO PERFECT KNOWLEDGE OF THE BOUNDLESS SKIES 71   2 DON JUAN   1   92   7
   OH LOVE HOW PERFECT IS THY MYSTIC ART 78   2 DON JUAN   1   106   3
   SEA-SICKNESS DEATH HIS LOVE WAS PERFECT HOW ELSE . . . 168   2 DON JUAN   2   23   6
   TO FIND THREE PERFECT PIPES OF THE THIRD SEX 391   2 DON JUAN   4   86   8
   A PERFECT TRANSFORMATION HERE DISPLAYED 458   2 DON JUAN   5   80   5
   IN PERFECT INNOCENCE SHE THEN UNMADE 36   3 DON JUAN   6   60   1
PERFECTION
   PERFECT SHE WAS BUT A PERFECTION IS 30   2 DON JUAN   1   18   1
   IN THAT COMPLETE PERFECTION WHICH ENSURES 332   2 DON JUAN   3   97   3
   SHE HARDLY KNEW TO SUCH PERFECTION BRINGS 485   2 DON JUAN   5   128   6
PERFECTLY
   HER CONDUCT HAD BEEN PERFECTLY CORRECT 446   3 DON JUAN 14   85   3
PERFORCE
   PERFORCE SINCE WHATSOEVER MET HER VIEW 378   2 DON JUAN   4   62   4
PERFORM
   BUT ERE THEY COULD PERFORM THIS PIOUS DUTY 276   3 DON JUAN 11   16   1
PERFORMANCE
   BOTH IN PERFORMANCE AND IN PREPARATION 416   3 DON JUAN 14   14   6
   HER LATE PERFORMANCE HAD BEEN A DEAD SET 428   3 DON JUAN 14   42   7
PERFORMANCES
   TO SUCH PERFORMANCES WITH HAUGHTY SMILE 521   3 DON JUAN 16   42   7
PERFORM'D
   REDUCED TO PRACTICE AND PERFORM'D LIKE DANCES 444   3 DON JUAN 14   79   8
PERFORMED
   AN EVOLUTION OFT PERFORMED OF LATE) 308   3 DON JUAN 11   79   5
PERFORMER'S
   TO THE PERFORMER'S DIFFIDENT CONFUSION 521   3 DON JUAN 16   41   8
PERFUME
   AND WAFTED FAR AROSE A RICH PERFUME 460   2 DON JUAN   5   85   6
PERHAPS
   PERHAPS SOME VIRTUOUS BLUSHES--LET THEM GO-- 13   2 DON JUAN   D   7   2
   CADIZ PERHAPS--BUT THAT YOU SOON MAY SEE-- 25   2 DON JUAN   1   8   6
   I HAD MY DOUBTS PERHAPS I HAVE THEM STILL 49   2 DON JUAN   1   51   1
   BUT WOULD HAVE BEEN PERHAPS BUT FOR THE SOUL 54   2 DON JUAN   1   60   7
   PERHAPS SHE DID NOT KNOW OR DID NOT CARE 59   2 DON JUAN   1   68   5

PERHAPS   (CONTINUED)

	PAGE	VOL	CANTO	STANZA	LN
MIGHT PLEASE PERHAPS A VIRTUOUS WIFE CAN QUELL	64	2 DON JUAN	1	78	5
PERHAPS TO FINISH JUAN'S EDUCATION	75	2 DON JUAN	1	101	6
PERHAPS TO OPEN DON ALFONSO'S EYES	75	2 DON JUAN	1	101	7
OF HALF-PAST SIX--PERHAPS STILL NEARER SEVEN	77	2 DON JUAN	1	104	2
PERHAPS IT MAY BE FOLLOW'D BY THE GREAT	92	2 DON JUAN	1	130	8
PERHAPS IT MAY SET OUT ON ITS RETURN--	92	2 DON JUAN	1	131	2
PERHAPS AS SHOOTING THEM AT WATERLOO	93	2 DON JUAN	1	132	8
WILL ALL BE HERE PERHAPS HE YET MAY FLY--	96	2 DON JUAN	1	137	7
AT LEAST PERHAPS HE HAS NOT SIXTY YEARS	106	2 DON JUAN	1	155	1
PERHAPS 'TIS OF ANTONIA YOU ARE JEALOUS	106	2 DON JUAN	1	156	1
PERHAPS 'TWAS IN A DIFFERENT WAY APPLIED	113	2 DON JUAN	1	168	7
GRIEVED BUT PERHAPS HER FEELINGS MAY BE BETTER	129	2 DON JUAN	1	191	7
PERHAPS THEY'LL HAVE SOME MORE ABOUT A YEAR HENCE	135	2 DON JUAN	1	199	8
FIGHTING DEVOTION DUST--PERHAPS A NAME	159	2 DON JUAN	2	4	8
SHE HOPED HE WOULD IMPROVE--PERHAPS BELIEVED	161	2 DON JUAN	2	9	6
HIS FIRST--PERHAPS HIS LAST--FAREWELL OF SPAIN	162	2 DON JUAN	2	11	8
PERHAPS IT MAY BE LINED WITH THIS MY CANTO	165	2 DON JUAN	2	16	8
PERHAPS I MAY REVISIT THEE NO MORE	166	2 DON JUAN	2	18	2
AND CARRY AWAY PERHAPS A MAST OR SO	170	2 DON JUAN	2	26	8
PERHAPS MORE MISCHIEF HAD BEEN DONE BUT FOR	174	2 DON JUAN	2	35	1
THE WIND IN FACT PERHAPS WAS RATHER LESS	178	2 DON JUAN	2	41	1
BETTER PERHAPS FOR MAN THAT AN EMBARGO	191	2 DON JUAN	2	66	V7
HE COULD PERHAPS HAVE PASS'D THE HELLESPONT	211	2 DON JUAN	2	105	6
AND DEEM THAT IT WAS SAVED PERHAPS IN VAIN	213	2 DON JUAN	2	108	8
PERHAPS NOT SO RESPECTABLE IN TRUTH	222	2 DON JUAN	2	125	5
WHO SLEEP AT LAST PERHAPS (GOD ONLY KNOWS)	227	2 DON JUAN	2	134	3
PRESSURE OF HANDS PERHAPS EVEN A CHASTE KISS--	242	2 DON JUAN	2	164	7
DISPLAYED MUCH MORE OF NERVE PERHAPS OF WIT	283	2 DON JUAN	3	14	V7
PERHAPS YOU THINK IN STUMBLING ON THIS FEAST	296	2 DON JUAN	3	40	1
PERHAPS YOU PROPHESY SOME SUDDEN ACT	296	2 DON JUAN	3	40	4
PERHAPS THAN EVEN THE MENTAL PANGS OF DYING	301	2 DON JUAN	3	51	4
AND THERE PERHAPS SOME SEED IS SOWN	325	2 DON JUAN	3	L 13	5
THAT WHICH MAKES THOUSANDS PERHAPS MILLIONS THINK	327	2 DON JUAN	3	88	3
PERHAPS THE WEAKNESS OF A HEART NOT VOID	339	2 DON JUAN	3	109	6
IN POESY UNLESS PERHAPS THE END	344	2 DON JUAN	4	1	2
MAN--AND AS WE WOULD HOPE--PERHAPS THE DEVIL	345	2 DON JUAN	4	2	3
PERHAPS NO BETTER THAN THEY HAVE TREATED ME	347	2 DON JUAN	4	7	2
THE OLD ARCHER'S SHAFTS PERHAPS THE EARLY GRAVE	350	2 DON JUAN	4	12	7
A PRETTY PERSON WHICH PERHAPS MAY STRIKE	390	2 DON JUAN	4	85	3
PERHAPS HIS RECENT WOUNDS MIGHT HELP A LITTLE	396	2 DON JUAN	4	95	8
PERHAPS HIS RECENT LOSS OF BLOOD MIGHT PULL	415	2 DON JUAN	5	8	5
BUT NEVER MIND--SHE'LL TURN PERHAPS NEXT WEEK	418	2 DON JUAN	5	14	6
PERHAPS WE SHALL BE ONE DAY BY AND BY	423	2 DON JUAN	5	24	5
I THINK IT IS PERHAPS THE GLOOMIEST HOUR	426	2 DON JUAN	5	30	7
PERHAPS EVEN MORE ATTENTION THAN IS DUE	431	2 DON JUAN	5	38	5
PERHAPS BECAUSE OUR APPELLANTS MADE OUT OF SEASON	437	2 DON JUAN	5	48	V4
PERHAPS THERE'S NOTHING--I'LL NOT SAY APPALS	442	2 DON JUAN	5	56	5
CAN TRACE ALTHOUGH PERHAPS THE PENCIL MAY	462	2 DON JUAN	5	88	6
PERHAPS THE FAULT OF HER SOFT SEX AND AGE--	490	2 DON JUAN	5	136	6
MEANWHILE AS HOMER SOMETIMES SLEEPS PERHAPS	503	2 DON JUAN	5	159	7
PERHAPS BE WEIGHED HEREAFTER IF NOT NOW	9	3 DON JUAN	6	6	2
PERHAPS AS WRETCHED IF A PEASANT'S QUEAN	18	3 DON JUAN	6	25	8
SO PICK AND CHUSE--PERHAPS YOU'LL BE CONTENT	40	3 DON JUAN	6	68	7
PERHAPS A LITTLE LATER HER GREAT LORD	51	3 DON JUAN	6	90	2
PERHAPS PRECARIOUS HAD THEY BUT THOUGHT GOOD	53	3 DON JUAN	6	95	5
MAY SERVE PERHAPS AS OUTLINES OR SLIGHT HINTS	60	3 DON JUAN	6	109	4
MAY WIN PERHAPS A RIBBON AT THE BREAST	118	3 DON JUAN	8	13	8
PERHAPS MIGHT MAKE HIM SHIVER YAWN OR THROW	121	3 DON JUAN	8	21	5
STOPPED FOR A MINUTE AS PERHAPS HE OUGHT	126	3 DON JUAN	8	29	4
PERHAPS MAY FIND IT BETTER THAN A NEW ONE)--	126	3 DON JUAN	8	29	8
HIS PATIENT AND PERHAPS WAS TO BE BLAMED	154	3 DON JUAN	8	85	6
ITS BLOODY BOND AND SAVED PERHAPS SOME PRETTY	174	3 DON JUAN	8	124	3
PERHAPS THE SEASON'S CHILL AND THEIR LONG STATION	176	3 DON JUAN	8	128	6
IT IS A PLEASANT VOYAGE PERHAPS TO FLOAT	191	3 DON JUAN	9	18	1
PERHAPS YOU MAY PICK OUT SOME QUEER NO-MEANING	207	3 DON JUAN	9	49	7
SUCH CLYTEMNESTRA THOUGH PERHAPS 'TIS BETTER	222	3 DON JUAN	9	80	7
PERHAPS BUT WHO WOULD SCORN THE MONTH OF JUNE	229	3 DON JUAN	10	9	5
PERHAPS FROM HEARSAY OR FROM RECOLLECTION	238	3 DON JUAN	10	27	2
PERHAPS HE LONGED IN BITTER FROSTS FOR CLIMES	243	3 DON JUAN	10	37	5
BEFORE MAY-DAY PERHAPS DESPITE HIS DUTY	243	3 DON JUAN	10	37	7
PERHAPS--BUT SANS PERHAPS WE NEED NOT SEEK	243	3 DON JUAN	10	38	1
PERHAPS--BUT SANS PERHAPS WE NEED NOT SEEK	243	3 DON JUAN	10	38	1
PERHAPS SHE HAD NOTHING TO CONFESS--NO MATTER	252	3 DON JUAN	10	56	6
TELL THEM THOUGH IT MAY BE PERHAPS TOO LATE	267	3 DON JUAN	10	87	1
PERHAPS BUT AS I SUFFER FROM THE SHOCKS	270	3 DON JUAN	11	5	7
PERHAPS THOUGHT HE IT IS THE COUNTRY'S WONT	275	3 DON JUAN	11	15	1
PERHAPS HE HATH GREAT PROJECTS IN HIS MIND	320	3 DON JUAN	12	10	1
PERHAPS HE FAIN WOULD LIBERATE MANKIND	320	3 DON JUAN	12	10	5
PERHAPS HE WOULD BE WEALTHIEST OF HIS NATION	320	3 DON JUAN	12	10	7
PERHAPS THERE MAY BE SOMETHING IN THE GROVE	322	3 DON JUAN	12	13	5
(BUT HERE PERHAPS THE INSTANCES ARE FEWER)	333	3 DON JUAN	12	37	3
PERHAPS A LITTLE STRANGE IF NOT QUITE NEW	341	3 DON JUAN	12	54	2
PERHAPS YOU'LL HAVE A LETTER FROM THE MOTHER	343	3 DON JUAN	12	60	1
PERHAPS YOU'LL HAVE A VISIT FROM THE BROTHER	343	3 DON JUAN	12	60	3
PERHAPS THIS NEW POSITION--BUT I'M RIGHT	348	3 DON JUAN	12	71	6
PERHAPS THIS IS AS IT SHOULD BE--IT IS	352	3 DON JUAN	12	79	1
PERHAPS THE FINE OLD FELLOW SPOKE IN JEST--	361	3 DON JUAN	13	7	5
PERHAPS WE HAVE BORROWED THIS FROM THE CHINESE--	373	3 DON JUAN	13	34	8

PERHAPS   (CONTINUED)
     PERHAPS FROM HORACE HIS NIL ADMIRARI . . . . . .   374 3 DON JUAN 13   35   1
     WERE WELL NIGH OVER 'TIS PERHAPS A PITY . . . . .   380 3 DON JUAN 13   48   2
     WITHAL IT LIES PERHAPS A LITTLE LOW . . . .   384 3 DON JUAN 13   55   6
     THE FACT--I'VE HEARD IT--ONCE PERHAPS TOO MUCH . . .   388 3 DON JUAN 13   64   8
     AND HERE PERHAPS A MONSTER THERE A SAINT . . . . .   389 3 DON JUAN 13   65   4
     PERHAPS THERE MIGHT BE VICES WHICH WOULD MOURN IT . .   400 3 DON JUAN 13   89   8
     PERHAPS MANKIND MIGHT FIND THE PATH THEY MISS-- . .   410 3 DON JUAN 14   1   3
     EXCEPT PERHAPS THAT YOU WERE BORN TO DIE . . . . .   411 3 DON JUAN 14   3   3
     PERHAPS OF ALL MOST DESPERATE WHICH WILL DARE . . .   412 3 DON JUAN 14   5   3
     PERHAPS SHE WISH'D AN ASPIRANT PROFOUNDER . . . . .   435 3 DON JUAN 14   57   5
     AND YOU WILL BE PERHAPS SURPRISED TO FIND . . . . .   446 3 DON JUAN 14   84   2
     TO THE NEXT CANTO WHERE PERHAPS I SHALL . . . . .   453 3 DON JUAN 14   98   6
     OF WHICH PERHAPS THE LATTER IS MOST TRUE . . . . .   456 3 DON JUAN 15   1   8
     HIS MANNER WAS PERHAPS THE MORE SEDUCTIVE . . . . .   461 3 DON JUAN 15   12   1
     PERHAPS 'TWAS HARDLY QUITE ASSURED ENOUGH . . . . .   462 3 DON JUAN 15   14   5
     PARTLY PERHAPS BECAUSE A FRESH SENSATION . . . . .   468 3 DON JUAN 15   28   4
     OR GRAVE LORD GEORGE WITH WHOM PERHAPS MIGHT END . .   470 3 DON JUAN 15   33   4
     PERHAPS BECAUSE 'TWAS FALLEN HER SIRES WERE PROUD . .   476 3 DON JUAN 15   46   8
     PERHAPS SHE DID NOT LIKE THE QUIET WAY . . . . . .   479 3 DON JUAN 15   53   1
     MY MUSE HATH BRED AND STILL PERHAPS MAY BREED . . .   482 3 DON JUAN 15   60   5
     OF WHICH PERHAPS THE COOKERY RATHER VARIES . . . .   486 3 DON JUAN 15   68   3
     PERHAPS I HAVE A THIRD TOO IN A NOOK . . . . . .   494 3 DON JUAN 15   87   5
     PERHAPS IT MAY TURN OUT THAT ALL WERE RIGHT . . . .   496 3 DON JUAN 15   90   2
     AT SPEAKING TRUTH PERHAPS THEY ARE LESS CLEVER . . .   501 3 DON JUAN 16   1   7
     WHICH HE PERHAPS HAD NOT DISCOVERED SOON . . . . .   513 3 DON JUAN 16   30   3
     PERHAPS SHE MERELY HAD THE SIMPLE PROJECT . . . . .   526 3 DON JUAN 16   51   5
     PERHAPS SHE MIGHT WISH TO CONFIRM HIM IN IT . . . .   526 3 DON JUAN 16   51   7
     PERHAPS THESE ARE MOST DIFFICULT TO TAME . . . . .   531 3 DON JUAN 16   63   6
     PERHAPS SHE WAS ASHAMED OF SEEMING FRAIL . . . . .   532 3 DON JUAN 16   64   5
     SHE APPROVED HIS SILENCE SHE PERHAPS MISTOOK . . .   553 3 DON JUAN 16   106   2
     OR HARDENED FEELINGS WHICH PERHAPS IDEAL . . . . .   553 3 DON JUAN 16   107   7
     THIS THEY MUST BEAR WITH AND PERHAPS MUCH MORE . . .   566 3 DON JUAN 17   9   6
PERIGUEUX
     RELIEVED WITH DINDON A LA PERIGUEUX . . . .   483 3 DON JUAN 15   63   4
PERIL
     NOTHING SHOULD TEMPT HIM MORE (THIS PERIL PAST) . .   175 2 DON JUAN 2   37   5
     AND PRESENT PERIL ALL BEFORE SURPASS'D . . . . . .   188 2 DON JUAN 2   61   6
     JUST NOW THERE WAS NO PERIL OF TEMPTATION . . . .   251 3 DON JUAN 10   55   1
     MY JUAN WHOM I LEFT IN DEADLY PERIL . . . .   300 3 DON JUAN 11   64   1
     A PERIL--NOT INDEED LIKE LOVE OR MARRIAGE . . . . .   344 3 DON JUAN 12   62   2
PERILS
     THEY THOUGHT THAT IN SUCH PERILS MORE THAN CHANCE . .   208 2 DON JUAN 2   99   7
     OR PERILS BY A LOVING MAID INCURR'D . . . .   257 2 DON JUAN 2   190   4
     AH WHAT IS MAN WHAT PERILS STILL ENVIRON . . . . .   294 2 DON JUAN 3   36   1
     A THOUSAND PERILS IN THIS DUBIOUS SHAPE . . . . .   103 3 DON JUAN 7   72   4
     THE NEXT OF PERILS THOUGH I PLACE IT STERNEST . . .   345 3 DON JUAN 12   64   2
PERIOD
     LAY AT THIS PERIOD QUIET AS THE SKY . . . .   251 2 DON JUAN 2   181   3
     AS ERE THAT AWFUL PERIOD INTERVENES . . . .   41 3 DON JUAN 6   69   6
     A PERIOD SOMETHING LIKE A PRINTED PAGE . . . . . .   315 3 DON JUAN 12   1   6
PERISH
     ARE LAID WITHIN OUR BOSOMS BUT TO PERISH . . . . .   275 2 DON JUAN 3   2   8
     WHICH PERISH IN THE REST BUT IN THEM WERE . . . .   353 2 DON JUAN 4   18   6
     THESE SMILE AND WRITHE AND PERISH STILL THE SAME . .   377 2 DON JUAN 4   61 V7
     TO PERISH ON THE PAVEMENT SO I HAD . . . .   429 2 DON JUAN 5   34   3
     BUT MAY THEIR VERY MEMORY PERISH TOO-- . . . . . .   180 3 DON JUAN 8   136   5
     SO PERISH EVERY TYRANT'S ROBE PIECE-MEAL . . . . .   505 3 DON JUAN 16   10   8
PERISH'D
     ALL THE REST PERISH'D NEAR TWO HUNDRED SOULS . . .   185 2 DON JUAN 2   55   1
     THEY GRIEVED FOR THOSE WHO PERISH'D WITH THE CUTTER .   188 2 DON JUAN 2   61   7
     WHO HAD ALREADY PERISH'D SUFFERING MADLY . . . . .   199 2 DON JUAN 2   80   7
     THEY PERISH'D UNTIL WITHER'D TO THESE FEW . . . .   210 2 DON JUAN 2   102   6
     IF SOULS COULD DIE HAD PERISH'D IN THAT PASSION . .   257 2 DON JUAN 2   191   4
     WHEN NERO PERISH'D BY THE JUSTEST DOOM . . . . . .   339 2 DON JUAN 3   109   1
     WHERE PERISH'D IN HIS FAME THE HERO-BOY . . . . .   400 2 DON JUAN 4   103   2
PERISHED
     BUT PERISHED WITHOUT SHIVERING OR SHAKING . . . . .   150 3 DON JUAN 8   76   5
     WAS SPARED--THREE THOUSAND MOSLEMS PERISHED HERE . .   152 3 DON JUAN 8   81   7
     THAT DRINKS AND STILL IS DRY   AT LAST THEY PERISHED--   166 3 DON JUAN 8   110   1
     HAD PERISHED IN THE FIELD OR BY THE WALL . . . . .   182 3 DON JUAN 8   141   4
PERIWIGS
     THERE BARBER'S BLOCKS WITH PERIWIGS IN CURL . . . .   278 3 DON JUAN 11   22   5
PERJURED
     UNGRATEFUL PERJURED BARBAROUS DON ALFONSO . . . . .   101 2 DON JUAN 1   146   7
PERMANENT
     NO PERMANENT FOUNDATION CAN BE LAID . . . .   268 2 DON JUAN 2   209   4
     NOUGHT'S PERMANENT AMONG THE HUMAN RACE . . . . .   309 3 DON JUAN 11   82   7
PERMISSION
     MUST WITH PERMISSION SHAKE YOU BY THE HAND . . . .   147 2 DON JUAN 1   221   3
PERMIT
     AT SIGHT NOR WOULD PERMIT YOU TO DISCOUNT . . . .   213 3 DON JUAN 9   62   8
     YET 'TIS IN VAIN SUCH SALLIES TO PERMIT . . . . .   234 3 DON JUAN 10   19   5
PERMITS
     PERMITS WHATE'ER THEY PLEASE OR DID NOT LONG SINCE . .   305 3 DON JUAN 11   73   8
PERMITTED
     BY WHICH NONE WERE PERMITTED TO BE NEUTER-- . . . .   195 2 DON JUAN 2   75   7
     DON JUAN HERE PERMITTED TO EMERGE . . . .   387 2 DON JUAN 4   79   1
PERORATION
     SOFT WORDS TOO FITTED FOR THE PERORATION . . . . .   74 3 DON JUAN 7   16   5

		PAGE	VOL	CANTO	STANZA	LN
PERPEND						
I SHALL PERPEND IF YOUR PROPOSAL MAY		453	2	DON JUAN 5	72	5
PERPENDICULAR						
A POEM'S PROGRESS SHOULD BE PERPENDICULAR		290	3	DON JUAN 11	44	V8
THOUGH SEVERAL ALSO KEEP THEIR PERPENDICULAR		343	3	DON JUAN 12	59	3
HAD STILL PRESERVED HIS PERPENDICULAR		441	3	DON JUAN 14	71	8
PERPETRATE						
WHICH YOU SHOULD PERPETRATE SOME SUMMER'S DAY		445	3	DON JUAN 14	82	6
PERPETRATED						
IS PERPETRATED ERE A WORD CAN BREAK		141	3	DON JUAN 8	58	5
PERPETRATES						
ALL THAT THE BODY PERPETRATES OF BAD		173	3	DON JUAN 8	123	2
PERPETUAL						
OF ENDLESS TORMENTS AND PERPETUAL MOTION		17	2	DON JUAN D	13	8
WE SHOULD HAVE FOUND OUT THE PERPETUAL MOTION		475	2	DON JUAN 5	112	8
PERPLEX						
OF HIS NEW SYSTEM TO PERPLEX THE SAGES		11	2	DON JUAN D	4	4
BUT FOUND MY VERY INNOCENCE PERPLEX		101	2	DON JUAN 1	147	6
FROM ALL THE POPE MAKES YEARLY 'TWOULD PERPLEX		391	2	DON JUAN 4	86	7
WHEN HE PUT ON THE CHERUB TO PERPLEX		474	2	DON JUAN 5	109	3
WHICH THOUGH 'TIS CERTAIN TO PERPLEX AND FRIGHTEN		281	3	DON JUAN 11	27	7
OR SHOULD IT SHAKE THE CHOICE WILL MORE PERPLEX--		371	3	DON JUAN 13	30	4
AND 'TWILL PERPLEX THE CASUISTS IN MORALITY		448	3	DON JUAN 14	89	7
PERPLEX'D						
WITH USELESS PENITENCE PERPLEX'D AND HAUNTED		120	2	DON JUAN 1	180	6
SOME LOOK'D PERPLEX'D AND OTHERS LOOK'D PROFOUND		429	3	DON JUAN 14	44	6
PERPLEXED						
FELT RESTLESS AND PERPLEXED AND COMPROMISED		506	3	DON JUAN 16	12	2
PERPLEXES						
(NOT THE MOST DAINTY ARIEL) AND PERPLEXES		269	3	DON JUAN 11	3	2
THERE IS AN AWKWARD THING WHICH MUCH PERPLEXES		442	3	DON JUAN 14	73	1
PERPLEXING						
THE PATH IS THROUGH PERPLEXING WAYS AND WHEN		93	2	DON JUAN 1	133	7
PERPLEXING QUESTION BUT NO DOUBT THE MOON		267	3	DON JUAN 2	208	4
THE WORLDS BEYOND THIS WORLD'S PERPLEXING WASTE		524	3	DON JUAN 16	48	5
PERPLEXING FOR MOST VIRGINS--A CHILD'S FATHER		533	3	DON JUAN 16	67	8
PERPLEXITY						
AND THE PERPLEXITY COULD NOT BE TOLD		54	3	DON JUAN 6	96	5
PERSECUTED						
AND PERSECUTED SAGES TEACH THE SCHOOLS		463	3	DON JUAN 15	17	7
PERSECUTION						
THE PRAISE OF PERSECUTION GAZE AGAIN		373	3	DON JUAN 13	33	5
PERSIAN						
TWO PARROTS WITH A PERSIAN CAT AND KITTENS		285	2	DON JUAN 3	18	2
SONG DANCE WINE MUSIC STORIES FROM THE PERSIAN		293	2	DON JUAN 3	35	3
SOFT PERSIAN SENTENCES IN LILAC LETTERS		308	2	DON JUAN 3	64	7
AND PERSIAN CARPETS WHICH THE HEART BLED TO STAIN		310	2	DON JUAN 3	68	3
AND THAT SAME DEVILISH DOCTRINE OF THE PERSIAN		377	3	DON JUAN 13	41	5
PERSIAN'S						
FOR STANDING ON THE PERSIAN'S GRAVE		321	2	DON JUAN 3	L 3	5
PERSIANS						
HIS PREPOSSESSIONS LIKE THE LAWS OF PERSIANS		366	3	DON JUAN 13	17	3
THE ANTIQUE PERSIANS TAUGHT THREE USEFUL THINGS		501	3	DON JUAN 16	1	1
PERSIFLAGE						
WHETHER THE MODE BE PERSIFLAGE OR PIETY		526	3	DON JUAN 16	52	6
PERSON						
AND THEN WHAT PROPER PERSON CAN BE PARTIAL		45	2	DON JUAN 1	43	7
IF ANY PERSON DOUBT IT I APPEAL		138	2	DON JUAN 1	203	1
IF ANY PERSON SHOULD PRESUME TO ASSERT		140	2	DON JUAN 1	207	1
ABOUT HIS PERSON AND PEDRILLO'S TOO		187	2	DON JUAN 2	59	2
NOW IN A PERSON USED TO MUCH COMMAND--		299	2	DON JUAN 3	47	1
HER PERSON IF ALLOW'D AT LARGE TO RUN		313	2	DON JUAN 3	73	4
THAN ON THE NAME A PERSON LEAVES BEHIND		328	2	DON JUAN 3	90	4
UPON YOUR PERSON TWELVE YARDS OFF OR SO		366	2	DON JUAN 4	41	4
A PRETTY PERSON WHICH PERHAPS MAY STRIKE		390	2	DON JUAN 4	85	3
ONE PERSON THRICE IN HOLY WEDLOCK BOUND		421	2	DON JUAN 5	20	5
IN CHIEF IN PROPER PERSON DEIGNED TO DRILL		93	3	DON JUAN 7	52	2
GOES WHEN SOME PERSON CONDESCENDS TO PRAISE		156	3	DON JUAN 8	90	V4
FOR ONE ESPECIAL PERSON OUT OF MANY		216	3	DON JUAN 9	68	7
AS JUAN WAS A PERSON OF CONDITION		330	3	DON JUAN 12	30	4
TO ASK THE REVEREND PERSON WHAT HE WANTED		511	3	DON JUAN 16	23	8
PERSONAGE						
JUST NOW A BLACK OLD NEUTRAL PERSONAGE		424	2	DON JUAN 5	26	1
THIS NOBLE PERSONAGE BEGAN TO LOOK		429	3	DON JUAN 14	43	1
PERSONAL						
OR SOME CONTRACTOR'S PERSONAL CUPIDITY		80	3	DON JUAN 7	27	3
PERSONIFICATION						
MORALITY'S PRIM PERSONIFICATION		29	2	DON JUAN 1	16	5
PERSONIFIED						
HE GLANCED LIKE A PERSONIFIED BOLERO		427	3	DON JUAN 14	39	8
PERSONIFY						
MEANT TO PERSONIFY THE MATHEMATICS		281	2	DON JUAN 3	11	8
PERSON'S						
REVENGE IN PERSON'S CERTAINLY NO VIRTUE		37	2	DON JUAN 1	30	7
PERSONS						
A NEST OF TUNEFUL PERSONS TO MY EYE		9	2	DON JUAN D	1	7
WITH PERSONS OF NO SORT OF EDUCATION		33	2	DON JUAN 1	22	2
BETWEEN YOUNG PERSONS WITHOUT ANY DANGER		65	2	DON JUAN 1	80	2
THAN MANY PERSONS MORE ADVANCED IN LIFE		164	2	DON JUAN 2	15	4

PERSONS (CONTINUED)
```
PERSONS   (CONTINUED)
    'TIS SAID THAT PERSONS LIVING ON ANNUITIES . . . . . . 190   2 DON JUAN  2     65    1
    SOME PERSONS SAY THAT DANTE MEANT THEOLOGY . . . . . . 281   2 DON JUAN  3     11    1
    BUT SET THOSE PERSONS DOWN WITH ME TO PRAY . . . . . . 336   2 DON JUAN  3    104    3
    THEY LOOKED LIKE PERSONS BEING LED TO SENTENCE . . . . 432   2 DON JUAN  5     40    5
    WAS WELL RECEIVED BY PERSONS OF CONDITION  . . . . . . 290   3 DON JUAN 11     45    8
    SOME PERSONS THINK THAT COLERIDGE HATH THE SWAY  . . . 298   3 DON JUAN 11     59    5
    THAT SUIT IN CHANCERY--WHICH SOME PERSONS PLEAD  . . . 324   3 DON JUAN 12     18    1
PERSPECTIVE
    HE SAW TOO IN PERSPECTIVE HER RELATIONS . . . . . . . 110   2 DON JUAN  1    162    7
    AND IN PERSPECTIVE MANY A SQUADRON FLIES . . . . . . . 461   2 DON JUAN  5     86    6
    OF HIS ATTRACTIONS MARR'D THE FAIR PERSPECTIVE . . . . 461   3 DON JUAN 15     12    5
PERSPICUOUS
    I WISH TO BE PERSPICUOUS AND THE BLACK  . . . . . . . 450   2 DON JUAN  5     67    1
    BEING QUITE PERSPICUOUS AND EXTREMELY FAIR  . . . . . 270   3 DON JUAN 11      5    4
    TO FEMALES OF PERSPICUOUS COMPREHENSIONS . . . . . . . 491   3 DON JUAN 15     80    3
PERSUADE
    WHICH NEEDED NOT AN EMPIRE TO PERSUADE  . . . . . . . 483   2 DON JUAN  5    125    3
    INTO THEIR ANNALS AND PERSUADE POOR FAME . . . . . . .  74   3 DON JUAN  7     15   V7
PERSUADED
    CHRISTIANS HAVE BURNT EACH OTHER QUITE PERSUADED . . .  66   2 DON JUAN  1     83    7
    BECAUSE THE TURKS COULD NEVER BE PERSUADED . . . . . .  73   3 DON JUAN  7     13    2
PERSUASION
    ETHERIAL LUSTRE WITH WHAT SWEET PERSUASION . . . . . .  65   2 DON JUAN  1     81    6
    AND THEREFORE FITTEST AS OF HIS PERSUASION . . . . . . 478   3 DON JUAN 15     50    2
PERT
    (BUT DOUBTLESS NOBODY WILL BE SO PERT) . . . . . . . . 140   2 DON JUAN  1    207    5
    HOW NOBLE IS HIS LANGUAGE NEVER PERT . . . . . . . . . 154   2 DON JUAN  1  V 5    1
    GOES WHEN SOME PERT PRETENDER DEALS HIS PRAISE . . . . 156   3 DON JUAN  8     90   V4
    NOW GRAVE NOW GAY BUT NEVER DULL OR PERT . . . . . . . 426   3 DON JUAN 14     37    5
PERTINACIOUS
    AT SUCH A PERTINACIOUS INFIDEL . . . . . . . . . . . . 166   3 DON JUAN  8    109    6
PERTINACITY
    HAD ALL THE PERTINACITY PRIDE HAS . . . . . . . . . . 366   3 DON JUAN 13     16    5
    IT HAD BEEN FIRMNESS NOW 'TIS PERTINACITY . . . . . . 449   3 DON JUAN 14     90    2
PERU
    (OR WAS BEFORE PERU LEARN'D TO REBEL) . . . . . . . . 159   2 DON JUAN  2      5    4
    A LONDON BAS WILL BEAT THY SKY PERU  . . . . . . . . . 406   2 DON JUAN  4    112   V8
    I'LL BET SOME PAIR OF STOCKINGS BEAT PERU  . . . . . . 406   2 DON JUAN  4    112   V8
    ON 'CHANGE AND EVEN THY SILVER SOIL PERU . . . . . . . 318   3 DON JUAN 12      6    7
PERUKE
    I THOUGHT OF A PERUKE THE OTHER DAY) . . . . . . . . . 143   2 DON JUAN  1    213    3
PERUSALS
    POOR FREDERICK WHY DID SHE ACCORD PERUSALS . . . . . . 332   3 DON JUAN 12     34    6
PERUSE
    PERUSE 'TIS ALWAYS WITH A MORAL END  . . . . . . . . . 334   3 DON JUAN 12     39    2
    THE PAPER WAS RIGHT EASY TO PERUSE . . . . . . . . . . 512   3 DON JUAN 16     26    6
PERUSED
    BELIEVED LIKE SOUTHEY--AND PERUSED LIKE CRASHAW  . . . 316   2 DON JUAN  3     79   V8
PERVADED
    PERVADED HIM--ALTHOUGH A GENEROUS CREATURE . . . . . . 138   3 DON JUAN  8     52    7
PERVADES
    PERVADES A MOMENT THOSE WHO LISTEN ROUND . . . . . . . 521   3 DON JUAN 16     41    4
PERVENCHE
    OR SWISS ROUSSEAU CRY VOILA LA PERVENCHE . . . . . . . 442   3 DON JUAN 14     75    8
PERVERSELY
    BRING DOWN THE FRUIT WHICH STILL PERVERSELY CLUNG . . .  44   3 DON JUAN  6     76    6
PESTILENCE
    WAR PESTILENCE THE DESPOT'S DESOLATION  . . . . . . . 146   3 DON JUAN  8     68    4
PETER
    LIKE PETER THE APOSTLE--AND HE FISH'D  . . . . . . . . 223   2 DON JUAN  2    126    2
    THE LITTLE BOATMAN AND HIS PETER BELL . . . . . . . . 334   2 DON JUAN  3    100    7
    (THE SAME WHO PHYSICKED PETER) FOUND THE TICK  . . . . 244   3 DON JUAN 10     39    3
    BUT IT IS TIME THAT I SHOULD HOIST MY BLUE PETER . . . 309   3 DON JUAN 11     83    5
    ALSO SOME BEAUTIES OF SIR PETER LELY . . . . . . . . . 390   3 DON JUAN 13     68    7
    THE VERY POWERFUL PARSON PETER PITH  . . . . . . . . . 539   3 DON JUAN 16     81    7
PETER'S
    OF THE IMMORTAL PETER'S POLISHED BOORS  . . . . . . . 194   3 DON JUAN  9     23    3
PETERS
    THREE OF THE SMITHS WERE PETERS BUT THE BEST . . . . .  76   3 DON JUAN  7     19    5
PETERSBURGH
    ALMOST AS FAR AS PETERSBURGH AND LEND  . . . . . . . .  52   3 DON JUAN  6     93    4
    FOR WHICH ALL PETERSBURGH IS ON THE WATCH  . . . . . . 181   3 DON JUAN  8    139    8
    SUPPOSE HIM THEN AT PETERSBURGH SUPPOSE  . . . . . . . 203   3 DON JUAN  9     42    7
    WHICH WAFTED HIM FROM PETERSBURGH THE BEST . . . . . . 248   3 DON JUAN 10     49    4
PETION
    PETION CLOOTZ DANTON MARAT LAFAYETTE . . . . . . . . .  22   2 DON JUAN  1      3    2
PETITION
    TO TALK OF A SUBSCRIPTION OR PETITION . . . . . . . . 330   3 DON JUAN 12     30    6
PETITS
    FOLLOW'D BY PETITS PUITS D'AMOUR--A DISH . . . . . . . 486   3 DON JUAN 15     68    2
    THERE'S PRETTY PICKING IN THOSE PETITS PUITS . . . . . 486   3 DON JUAN 15     68    8
PETRARCH'S
    THINK YOU IF LAURA HAD BEEN PETRARCH'S WIFE . . . . . 279   2 DON JUAN  3      8    7
    HAD PETRARCH'S PASSION LED TO PETRARCH'S WEDDING . . . 279   2 DON JUAN  3      8   V7
    HAD PETRARCH'S PASSION LED TO PETRARCH'S WEDDING . . . 279   2 DON JUAN  3      8   V7
    EVEN PETRARCH'S SELF IF JUDGED WITH DUE SEVERITY . . . 411   2 DON JUAN  5      1    7
PETRIFIED
    JUAN WAS PETRIFIED HE HAD HEARD A HINT . . . . . . . . 510   3 DON JUAN 16     22    1
```

			PAGE	VOL		CANTO	STANZA	LN
PETTICOAT								
THEIR VEIL AND PETTICOAT--ALAS TO DWELL	. . .	. .	.	160	2 DON JUAN	2	6	4
THEY ALSO GAVE A PETTICOAT APIECE	. . .	. .	.	226	2 DON JUAN	2	133	5
GIRD MORE DECEIT WITHIN A PETTICOAT	. . .	. .	.	296	2 DON JUAN	3	41	6
FROM OUT THE HEAP A PETTICOAT OR TWO	. .	. .	.	455	2 DON JUAN	5	76	V8
BUT TUGGING ON HIS PETTICOAT HE TRIPPED	.	. .	.	456	2 DON JUAN	5	77	5
PETTICOAT INFLUENCE IS A GREAT REPROACH	.	. .	.	421	3 DON JUAN	14	26	1
I FOR ONE VENERATE A PETTICOAT--	. . .	. .	.	421	3 DON JUAN	14	26	6
BEFORE A PETTICOAT AND PEEPING ANCLE	. .	. .	.	422	3 DON JUAN	14	27	8
PETTICOATS								
LIKE NEEDLES WHICH MAY PIERCE THOSE PETTICOATS	. .	.	464	2 DON JUAN	5	92	2
THE LAST THIN PETTICOATS WERE VANISHED GONE	. .	.	504	3 DON JUAN	16	8	5
PETTY								
I WOULD NOT IMITATE THE PETTY THOUGHT	. . .	.	.	12	2 DON JUAN	D	6	1
ITS PETTY PASSIONS MARRIAGES AND FLIGHTS	.	. .	.	353	2 DON JUAN	4	17	6
THERE MIGHT ARISE SOME POUTING PETTY CARE	.	. .	.	480	2 DON JUAN	5	119	6
AUGHT SAVE SOME LITTLE POUTING PETTY CARE	.	. .	.	480	2 DON JUAN	5	119	V5
THE SOUL OUT (LIKE THE STONE) WITH PETTY CARES	. .	.	16	3 DON JUAN	6	20	8
PHAETON'S								
HAD SUCH BEEN CUT IN PHAETON'S TIME THE GOD	. .	.	263	3 DON JUAN	10	78	5
PHALANX								
WHERE IS THE PYRRHIC PHALANX GONE	. . .	. .	.	324	2 DON JUAN	3	L 10	2
PHANTASIES								
ALL PHANTASIES WHICH YIELDED JOY OR MIRTH	.	. .	.	475	2 DON JUAN	5	112	3
COULD RISK OR COMPASS SUCH STRANGE PHANTASIES	.	.	.	477	2 DON JUAN	5	115	3
ALL PHANTASIES NOT EVEN EXCEPTING MINE	.	. .	.	255	3 DON JUAN	10	61	4
BROKEN IN CARRIAGES AND ALL THE PHANTASIES	.	.	.	308	3 DON JUAN	11	80	5
IF ONCE THEIR PHANTASIES BE BROUGHT TO BEAR	.	.	.	463	3 DON JUAN	15	16	6
AT SEVENTY YEARS HAD PHANTASIES LIKE THESE	.	.	.	494	3 DON JUAN	15	86	4
PHANTASMAGORIA								
THEIR LOATHSOME PHANTASMAGORIA OER THE MIND	. .	.	227	2 DON JUAN	2	134	V7
PHANTASY								
DEEM THIS A COMMENTATOR'S PHANTASY	. . .	.	.	281	2 DON JUAN	3	11	4
SERVE A SULTANA'S SENSUAL PHANTASY	. . .	.	.	484	2 DON JUAN	5	126	8
A PHANTASY WHICH SOMETIMES SEIZES WARRIORS	.	.	.	78	3 DON JUAN	7	24	7
A KIND OF PHANTASY PROPORTIONATE	. . .	.	.	84	3 DON JUAN	7	37	6
WITH WHAT HE HAD SEEN HIS PHANTASY HE FED	.	.	.	512	3 DON JUAN	16	27	6
PHANTOM								
A PHANTOM UPON EACH OF THE FOUR POSTS	. .	.	.	30	3 DON JUAN	6	48	4
SO FULLY FLASHED THE PHANTOM ON HIS EYES	.	.	.	169	3 DON JUAN	8	115	1
THE PHANTOM OF HER FROLIC GRACE--FITZ-FULKE	.	.	.	561	3 DON JUAN	16	123	8
PHANTOMS								
AND PHANTOMS HOVERED OR MIGHT SEEM TO HOVER	. .	.	41	3 DON JUAN	6	70	6
PHARISAIC								
OF THESE AMBROSIAL PHARISAIC TIMES	. . .	.	.	156	3 DON JUAN	8	90	3
PHEASANTS								
AH NUTBROWN PARTRIDGES AH BRILLIANT PHEASANTS	. .	.	394	3 DON JUAN	13	75	7
PHEDRA								
PHEDRA AND ALL WHICH STORY HAS DISCLOSED	.	. .	.	486	2 DON JUAN	5	131	3
PHENOMENON								
MAN'S A PHENOMENON ONE KNOWS NOT WHAT	. .	.	.	93	2 DON JUAN	1	133	1
PHIDIAN								
HER ATTIC FOREHEAD AND HER PHIDIAN NOSE	.	. .	.	27	3 DON JUAN	6	42	4
AS PHIDIAN FORMS CUT OUT OF MARBLE ATTIC	.	.	.	409	3 DON JUAN	13	110	3
PHILANTHROPIC								
A JARGON A MERE PHILANTHROPIC DIN	. . .	.	.	266	3 DON JUAN	10	85	6
PHILANTHROPY								
OH THOU TOO MORTAL MAN WHAT IS PHILANTHROPY	. .	.	192	3 DON JUAN	9	20	2
PHILIP'S								
OF FOOD I THINK WITH PHILIP'S SON OR RATHER	.	.	.	427	2 DON JUAN	5	31	7
AS PHILIP'S SON PROPOSED TO DO WITH ATHOS	.	.	.	355	3 DON JUAN	12	86	8
PHILO-GENITIVENESS								
I THINK THAT PHILO-GENITIVENESS IS--	. . .	.	.	326	3 DON JUAN	12	22	2
I SAY METHINKS THAT PHILO-GENITIVENESS	. .	.	.	326	3 DON JUAN	12	22	7
PHILOSOPHER								
HER YOUNG PHILOSOPHER WAS GROWN ALREADY	.	. .	.	49	2 DON JUAN	1	50	8
BUT KNEW THE CAUSE NO MORE THAN A PHILOSOPHER	.	.	.	289	2 DON JUAN	3	26	8
I'M A PHILOSOPHER CONFOUND THEM ALL	. .	.	.	17	3 DON JUAN	6	22	1
I'M A PHILOSOPHER GOD DAMN THEM ALL	. .	.	.	17	3 DON JUAN	6	22	V1
THIS GREAT PHILOSOPHER WAS THUS INSTILLING	.	.	.	96	3 DON JUAN	7	58	6
BUT SHE WAS A PHILOSOPHER WHOSE CAUTION	.	.	.	246	3 DON JUAN	10	44	V4
EXPERIENCE IS THE CHIEF PHILOSOPHER	. .	.	.	463	3 DON JUAN	15	17	5
LIKE THOSE OF THE PHILOSOPHER OF MALMSBURY	.	.	.	499	3 DON JUAN	15	96	8
PHILOSOPHERS								
THOU MAK'ST PHILOSOPHERS THERE'S EPICURUS	.	.	.	267	2 DON JUAN	2	207	1
AND HENCE SOME HEATHENISH PHILOSOPHERS	.	.	.	219	3 DON JUAN	9	73	7
PHILOSOPHIC								
IS PHILOSOPHIC IN OUR FORMER FRIENDS	. .	.	.	37	2 DON JUAN	1	30	2
OR THROWN INTO A PHILOSOPHIC PASSION	. .	.	.	522	3 DON JUAN	16	43	6
PHILOSOPHICAL								
SO THAT THE PHILOSOPHICAL BEHOLDER	. . .	.	.	292	2 DON JUAN	3	33	7
PHILOSOPHISED								
HE PROBABLY WOULD HAVE PHILOSOPHISED	. .	.	.	506	3 DON JUAN	16	12	6
PHILOSOPHIZE								
MY TENDENCY IS TO PHILOSOPHIZE	. . .	.	.	37	3 DON JUAN	6	63	3
I WON'T PHILOSOPHIZE AND WILL BE READ	. .	.	.	238	3 DON JUAN	10	28	8
PHILOSOPHY								
IF YOU THINK 'TWAS PHILOSOPHY THAT THIS DID	.	.	.	71	2 DON JUAN	1	93	7
BUT I BEING FOND OF TRUE PHILOSOPHY	. .	.	.	147	2 DON JUAN	1	220	1

604

	PAGE	VOL	CANTO	STANZA	LN

PHILOSOPHY (CONTINUED)

	PAGE	VOL	CANTO	STANZA	LN
BUT SOON PHILOSOPHY CAME TO MY AID	268	2 DON JUAN	2	210	1
I WILL MY DEAR PHILOSOPHY I SAID	268	2 DON JUAN	2	210	3
STOP CRIED PHILOSOPHY WITH AIR SO GRECIAN	268	2 DON JUAN	2	210	7
SHAKESPEARE EXCLAIMS--HANG UP PHILOSOPHY	272	2 DON JUAN	2	V 1	1
UNLESS PHILOSOPHY CAN MAKE A JULIET	272	2 DON JUAN	2	V 1	2
THE NEGROES MORE PHILOSOPHY DISPLAY'D--	414	2 DON JUAN	5	7	7
WILL SCARCELY FIND PHILOSOPHY FOR MORE	12	3 DON JUAN	6	12	6
HIS STERN PHILOSOPHY BUT GENTLY STROKING	172	3 DON JUAN	8	121	6
ABOUT PHILOSOPHY PURSUED HIS JAUNT	254	3 DON JUAN	10	60	6
OF FAIR PHILOSOPHY OR WHERE 'TIS THEY TREAD	284	3 DON JUAN	11	34	V6
WHO LOVED PHILOSOPHY AND A GOOD DINNER	399	3 DON JUAN	13	87	2
BUT THEN 'TWOULD SPOIL MUCH GOOD PHILOSOPHY	410	3 DON JUAN	14	1	4
OF WHOM HALF MY PHILOSOPHY THE PROGENY IS	488	3 DON JUAN	15	73	8
PHILOSOPHY NO SHE TOO MUCH REJECTS	495	3 DON JUAN	15	89	7

PHLEGETHONTIC

| SWEET NAIAD OF THE PHLEGETHONTIC RILL | 372 | 2 DON JUAN | 4 | 53 | 2 |

PHOEBUS

BRIGHT PHOEBUS WHILE THE MOUNTAINS STILL ARE WET	230	2 DON JUAN	2	139	5
WHERE DELOS ROSE AND PHOEBUS SPRUNG	320	2 DON JUAN	3	L 1	4
SOULS OF IMMORTAL GENERALS PHOEBUS WATCHES	107	3 DON JUAN	7	81	7
BUT PHOEBUS LENDS ME NOW AND THEN A STRING	181	3 DON JUAN	8	138	8
DAN PHOEBUS TAKES ME FOR AN AUCTIONEER	393	3 DON JUAN	13	74	4

PHOSPHORUS

| THE OTHER LOOKS LIKE PHOSPHORUS ON SHEETS | 281 | 3 DON JUAN | 11 | 27 | 5 |

PHRASE

AN ORATOR OF SUCH SET TRASH OF PHRASE	17	2 DON JUAN	D	13	1
ARE TWISTED TO A PHRASE OF SOME OBSCURITY	69	2 DON JUAN	1	88	8
(THAT MODERN PHRASE APPEARS TO ME SAD STUFF	119	2 DON JUAN	1	178	3
CONCEIVED THAT PHRASE WAS QUITE ENOUGH TO MOVE	478	2 DON JUAN	5	116	8
A STRANGE COINCIDENCE TO USE A PHRASE	45	3 DON JUAN	6	78	7
HER SON'S SON LET NOT THIS LAST PHRASE OFFEND	52	3 DON JUAN	6	93	2
GROWLING AND GRUMBLING IN GOOD TURKISH PHRASE	64	3 DON JUAN	6	117	2
BY HIS DISPATCHES COUCHED IN PITHY PHRASE	85	3 DON JUAN	7	39	6
OR THE SENSATION (IF THAT PHRASE SEEM WRONG)	123	3 DON JUAN	8	24	4
WHO HAD RETREATED AS THE PHRASE IS WHEN	130	3 DON JUAN	8	35	2
IS QUITE REFRESHING IN THE AFFECTED PHRASE	156	3 DON JUAN	8	90	2
THE TOPIC'S TENDER SO SHALL BE MY PHRASE--	176	3 DON JUAN	8	128	5
BUT PUNNED IT DOWN TO THIS FACETIOUS PHRASE--	183	3 DON JUAN	9	1	4
THE PHRASE IS SHAKSPEARE'S AND NOT MISAPPLIED--	184	3 DON JUAN	9	4	2
THE IMPORT OF THIS DIPLOMATIC PHRASE	207	3 DON JUAN	9	49	2
('TIS POPE'S PHRASE) A GREAT LONGING THO' A RASH ONE	216	3 DON JUAN	9	68	6
AND WHEN I USE THE PHRASE OF AULD LANG SYNE	233	3 DON JUAN	10	17	1
(IN MOORE'S PHRASE) WHERE THE FASHIONABLE FAIR	301	3 DON JUAN	11	66	7
FOR THAT'S THE PHRASE THAT SETTLES ALL THINGS NOW	330	3 DON JUAN	12	31	4
IS THAT PORTENTOUS PHRASE I TOLD YOU SO	432	3 DON JUAN	14	50	3
HE WAS FREE TO CONFESS--(WHENCE COMES THIS PHRASE	536	3 DON JUAN	16	73	1
WHO ARE SO IN THE STRICT SENSE OF THE PHRASE	562	3 DON JUAN	17	1	2

PHRASEOLOGY

| EXPENDED ALL THEIR EASTERN PHRASEOLOGY | 165 | 3 DON JUAN | 8 | 108 | 2 |

PHRASES

SWEET PLAYFUL PHRASES WHICH WOULD SEEM ABSURD	351	2 DON JUAN	4	14	7
SO LUCKILY FOR BOTH MY PHRASES FAIL	467	2 DON JUAN	5	97	8
AT WHICH YOUR WISE MEN SNEERED IN PHRASES WITTY	93	3 DON JUAN	7	53	7
THESE PHRASES OF REFINEMENT I MUST BORROW	288	3 DON JUAN	11	42	2
'TIS STRANGE THE MIND SHOULD LET SUCH PHRASES QUELL IT'S	298	3 DON JUAN	11	60	V7
AT LONGBOW'S PHRASES YOU MIGHT SOMETIMES CARP	402	3 DON JUAN	13	93	6
FOR ALL HER PAST EXERTION AND SOFT PHRASES	550	3 DON JUAN	16	103	3

PHRENSY

| HERS WAS A PHRENSY WHICH DISDAIN'D TO RAVE | 380 | 2 DON JUAN | 4 | 67 | 7 |

PHRYGIAN

| ARE WHAT I FOUND THERE--BUT THE DEVIL A PHRYGIAN | 387 | 2 DON JUAN | 4 | 78 | 8 |

PHTHISICAL

| THE TRUTH IS I'VE GROWN LATELY RATHER PHTHISICAL | 270 | 3 DON JUAN | 11 | 5 | 5 |

PHTHISICS

| CONSTRUCTION ASYOUR CURES FOR HECTIC PHTHISICS | 349 | 3 DON JUAN | 12 | 72 | 3 |

PHYSIC

| A MIND DISEASED NO REMEDY CAN PHYSIC-- | 166 | 2 DON JUAN | 2 | 19 | 7 |

PHYSICAL

| MORAL OR PHYSICAL ON THIS OCCASION | 567 | 3 DON JUAN | 17 | 12 | 4 |

PHYSICIAN

TO-MORROW WHAT HIS HIGHNESS'S PHYSICIAN	46	3 DON JUAN	6	80	7
THE EMPRESS WAS ALARMED AND HER PHYSICIAN	244	3 DON JUAN	10	39	2
THE FAMILY PHYSICIAN HAD GREAT SKILL	514	3 DON JUAN	16	32	5
IT WAS NOT THE PHYSICIAN THAT HE WANTED	514	3 DON JUAN	16	33	8

PHYSICIANS

FOR INEZ CALL'D SOME DRUGGISTS AND PHYSICIANS	35	2 DON JUAN	1	27	1
HOW THE PHYSICIANS LEAVING PILL AND POTION	113	2 DON JUAN	1	168	3
PROLONGS IT THIS IS OBVIOUS TO PHYSICIANS	190	2 DON JUAN	2	64	2
WHICH HASTENS AS PHYSICIANS SAY ONE'S FATE	230	2 DON JUAN	2	140	4
THY PLAGUES THY FAMINES THY PHYSICIANS YET TICK	117	3 DON JUAN	8	12	5
THIS IS THE WAY PHYSICIANS MEND OR END US	245	3 DON JUAN	10	42	1
THAN WITCHES BITCHES OR PHYSICIANS BREW	482	3 DON JUAN	15	62	8

PHYSICKED

| (THE SAME WHO PHYSICKED PETER) FOUND THE TICK | 244 | 3 DON JUAN | 10 | 39 | 3 |

PHYSICS

| AND THIS REFLECTION BRINGS ME TO PLAIN PHYSICS | 349 | 3 DON JUAN | 12 | 72 | 5 |
| OF PHYSICS BODIES WHETHER SHORT OR TALL | 511 | 3 DON JUAN | 16 | 24 | 6 |

PIANO

| AND OPENING HER PIANO GAN TO PLAY | 517 | 3 DON JUAN | 16 | 38 | V7 |

605

	PAGE	VOL	CANTO	STANZA	LN
PIASTRES					
OF AN ILL-GOTTEN MILLION OF PIASTRES	222	2 DON JUAN	2	125	8
PICCADILLY					
'TIS TRUE I MIGHT HAVE CHOSEN PICCADILLY	370	3 DON JUAN	13	27	1
PICK					
THEY ALMOST LOST THEIR WAY AND HAD TO PICK IT--	433	2 DON JUAN	5	41	5
SO PICK AND CHUSE--PERHAPS YOU'LL BE CONTENT	40	3 DON JUAN	6	68	7
STONES AND WHATEVER SHE COULD PICK UP TO	44	3 DON JUAN	6	76	5
AND PICK IT UP AND BITE IT TO THE CORE	44	3 DON JUAN	6	77	4
PERHAPS YOU MAY PICK OUT SOME QUEER NO-MEANING	207	3 DON JUAN	9	49	7
PICK'D					
FOR THERE IT WAS I PICK'D UP MY OWN KNOWLEDGE	50	2 DON JUAN	1	52	8
I THINK I PICK'D UP TOO AS WELL AS MOST	50	2 DON JUAN	1	53	5
THE FEMALES STOOD AS ONE BY ONE THEY PICK'D 'EM	409	2 DON JUAN	4	116	7
EXCEPTING ONLY WHEN THE FORMER'S PICK'D	502	2 DON JUAN	5	158	3
PICKED					
AND HAVING PICKED UP SEVERAL ODDS AND ENDS	318	2 DON JUAN	3	83	2
PICKED OUT AMONGST HIS FOLLOWERS WITH SOME SKILL	162	3 DON JUAN	8	102	3
AS EVER MAHOMET PICKED OUT FOR A MARTYR	167	3 DON JUAN	8	111	3
EVEN PLUTARCH'S LIVES HAVE BUT PICKED OUT A FEW	324	3 DON JUAN	12	19	5
PICKING					
PICKING UP SHELLS BY THE GREAT OCEAN--TRUTH	69	3 DON JUAN	7	5	8
THERE'S PRETTY PICKING IN THOSE PETITS PUITS	486	3 DON JUAN	15	68	8
PICKINGS					
POWER'S BASE PURVEYORS WHO FOR PICKINGS PROWL	196	3 DON JUAN	9	27	4
PICKLE					
FOR ANY LENGTH OF DAYS IN SUCH A PICKLE	419	2 DON JUAN	5	17	4
OR A GOOD BOXER INTO A SAD PICKLE	134	3 DON JUAN	8	43	6
PICTURE					
A NAME A WRETCHED PICTURE AND WORSE BUST	146	2 DON JUAN	1	218	8
A BOOK--A DAMNED BAD PICTURE AND WORSE BUST	146	2 DON JUAN	1	218	V8
MADE QUITE A PICTURE OF THESE LITTLE GREEKS	292	2 DON JUAN	3	33	6
I THINK YOU'LL FIND FROM MANY A FAMILY PICTURE	337	3 DON JUAN	12	46	3
A PICTURE IS THE PAST EVEN ERE ITS FRAME	509	3 DON JUAN	16	19	7
THERE WAS A PICTURE DEALER WHO HAD BROUGHT	528	3 DON JUAN	16	56	1
PICTURED					
WHAT THOUGH 'TIS BUT A PICTURED IMAGE STRIKE--	336	2 DON JUAN	3	103	7
THE FORMS OF THE GRIM KNIGHT AND PICTURED SAINT	508	3 DON JUAN	16	18	1
PICTURES					
GROUPS OF BAD STATUES TABLES CHAIRS AND PICTURES	465	2 DON JUAN	5	94	7
AND TUMBLED BOOKS OR CRITICISED THE PICTURES	406	3 DON JUAN	13	102	2
LONG FURNISHED WITH OLD PICTURES OF GREAT WORTH	508	3 DON JUAN	16	17	4
PICTURESQUE					
WHO HAS SAILED WHERE PICTURESQUE CONSTANTINOPLE IS	271	3 DON JUAN	11	7	3
PIDDLE					
AND ENTREMETS TO PIDDLE WITH AT HAND	484	3 DON JUAN	15	66	5
PIECE					
BUT FOR A CHILD WHAT PIECE OF WORK IS HERE	115	2 DON JUAN	1	172	3
AND WITH A PIECE OF PORK MOREOVER MET	181	2 DON JUAN	2	47	6
CHEWING A PIECE OF BAMBOO AND SOME LEAD	200	2 DON JUAN	2	82	6
UNTIL THEY FOUND A RAGGED PIECE OF SHEET	201	2 DON JUAN	2	85	2
TO DO AT ROME AS ROMANS DO A PIECE	319	2 DON JUAN	3	84	7
TURNING EACH PIECE OF SILVER O'ER AND TUMBLING	426	2 DON JUAN	5	29	3
MADRID'S AND MOSCOW'S CLIMES WERE OF A PIECE	239	3 DON JUAN	10	30	8
THEREFORE THE PRESENT PIECE OF NATURAL HISTORY	531	3 DON JUAN	16	62	3
PIECED					
PIECED OUT FOR DIFFERENT MARTS IN THE LEVANT	284	2 DON JUAN	3	17	2
PIECE-MEAL					
SO PERISH EVERY TYRANT'S ROBE PIECE-MEAL	505	3 DON JUAN	16	10	8
PIECES					
SHINE LIKE A GUINEA AND SEVEN SHILLING PIECES	306	2 DON JUAN	3	60	8
OR MINCED IN PIECES AS SMALL BAITS FOR FISH	492	2 DON JUAN	5	141	V4
THEIR CHIEFS TO ORDER--WERE ALL CUT TO PIECES	149	3 DON JUAN	8	74	8
THAN I HAVE TIME OR WILL TO TAKE TO PIECES	478	3 DON JUAN	15	52	8
NOW JUSTICES OF PEACE MUST JUDGE ALL PIECES	531	3 DON JUAN	16	63	1
PIERCE					
LIKE NEEDLES WHICH MAY PIERCE THOSE PETTICOATS	464	2 DON JUAN	5	92	2
ONE NECK WHICH HE WITH ONE FELL STROKE MIGHT PIERCE	19	3 DON JUAN	6	27	3
BUT JUAN EAGER NOW THE TRUTH TO PIERCE	559	3 DON JUAN	16	119	3
PIERCED					
BUT WHEN IT HATH BEEN SCORCH'D AND PIERCED AND RIVEN	270	2 DON JUAN	2	214	5
SO CALM THOUGH PIERCED THROUGH STOMACH HEART AND LIVER	430	2 DON JUAN	5	35	4
AND SIXTEEN BAYONETS PIERCED THE SERASKIER	152	3 DON JUAN	8	81	4
UNTO THE BAYONETS WHICH HAD PIERCED HIS YOUNG	170	3 DON JUAN	8	118	6
OF CARNAGE WHEN THIS OLD MAN WAS PIERCED THROUGH	171	3 DON JUAN	8	119	3
PIERCES					
SO THAT A PONIARD PIERCES IF 'TIS STUCK HARD	492	2 DON JUAN	5	140	4
OF GLORY WHICH SO PIERCES THROUGH AND THROUGH ONE	138	3 DON JUAN	8	52	6
THE BAYONET PIERCES AND THE SABRE CLEAVES	155	3 DON JUAN	8	88	1
PIERCETH					
ALL SOUNDS IT PIERCETH ALLAH ALLAH HU	116	3 DON JUAN	8	8	8
PIERCING					
UPON THEM HIS SLOW BROW AND PIERCING EYE--	97	3 DON JUAN	7	59	3
PIETY					
OF ELOQUENCE IN PIETY AND PROSE--	243	2 DON JUAN	2	165	7
IS NO LESS FAMED FOR TOLERANCE THAN PIETY	396	3 DON JUAN	13	80	8
AND A PROPOS OF MONKS THEIR PIETY	445	3 DON JUAN	14	81	5
BUT POLITICS AND POLICY AND PIETY	497	3 DON JUAN	15	93	1
WHETHER THE MODE BE PERSIFLAGE OR PIETY	526	3 DON JUAN	16	52	6

606

	PAGE	VOL	CANTO	STANZA	LN
PIG
HE'S WRONG--UNLESS MAN WERE A PIG INDEED	427	2 DON JUAN	5	31	3
WHAT THAT IS--ASK THE PIG WHO SEES THE WIND	108	3 DON JUAN	7	84	8
BECAUSE HE RUNS BEFORE IT LIKE A PIG	109	3 DON JUAN	7	85	2
THERE WAS A PRIZE OX A PRIZE PIG AND PLOUGHMAN	530	3 DON JUAN	16	60	7
THE PRIZE PIG PLOUGHMAN POACHERS THE MEN SENT	533	3 DON JUAN	16	66	4
PIGEONS
FIRST SAVE IN CASE OF PIGEONS--HOW THE GROVE	322	3 DON JUAN	12	13	V5
PIGER
FOR EUROPE PLOUGHS IN AFRIC LIKE BOS PIGER	348	3 DON JUAN	12	70	6
PIGMIES
THEY WERE MISSHAPEN PIGMIES DEAF AND DUMB--	462	2 DON JUAN	5	88	7
PIKE
A PRIEST A SHARK AN ALDERMAN OR PIKE	239	2 DON JUAN	2	157	8
THERE'S ONE THOUGH TALL AND STIFFER THAN A PIKE . . .	390	2 DON JUAN	4	85	5
LIKE MOLTEN LEAD AS IF YOU THRUST A PIKE IN	479	2 DON JUAN	5	118	6
A GREY WALL A GREEN RUIN RUSTY PIKE	255	3 DON JUAN	10	61	5
PIKES
TO FLY FROM AS FROM HUNGRY PIKES A ROACH	421	3 DON JUAN	14	26	3
PILAUS
PILAUS AND MEATS OF ALL SORTS MET THE GAZE	291	2 DON JUAN	3	31	3
OF CERTAIN STEWS AND ROAST-MEATS AND PILAUS	437	2 DON JUAN	5	47	2
PILE
IN SHAPE OF MOONSHINE HOVERS O'ER THE PILE--	279	3 DON JUAN	11	24	7
A GLORIOUS REMNANT OF THE GOTHIC PILE	386	3 DON JUAN	13	59	1
PILED
WITH THE PILED WOOD ROUND WHICH THE FAMILY CROWD . . .	94	2 DON JUAN	1	135	4
OUR KILLED ALREADY PILED UP TO THE CHIN	160	3 DON JUAN	8	98	6
PILGRIM
OR FILLS WITH LOVE THE PILGRIM ON HIS WAY	338	2 DON JUAN	3	108	4
PILL
HOW THE PHYSICIANS LEAVING PILL AND POTION	113	2 DON JUAN	1	168	3
PILLAGE
PILLAGE TO SOLDIERS PRIZE-MONEY TO SEAMEN	88	2 DON JUAN	1	124	8
PILLAR
A BROKEN PILLAR NOT UNCOUTHLY HEWN	400	2 DON JUAN	4	103	5
BEHOLD HIM PLACED AS IF UPON A PILLAR HE	204	3 DON JUAN	9	44	7
PILLARS
OF ALL THE PILLARS OF THE STATE WHICH LEANS	54	3 DON JUAN	6	96	6
PILLORY
BEHOLD HIM PLACED IN YOUTH AND GLORY'S PILLORY	204	3 DON JUAN	9	44	V7
PILLOW
SHE CEASED AND TURN'D UPON HER PILLOW PALE	108	2 DON JUAN	1	158	1
BUT NOW LAY SICK AND SPEECHLESS ON HIS PILLOW . . .	169	2 DON JUAN	2	25	4
WHO SMOOTH'D HIS PILLOW AS SHE LEFT THE DEN	228	2 DON JUAN	2	135	2
AND RECK'D NOT WHO AROUND HER PILLOW SAT	378	2 DON JUAN	4	63	4
OR RATHER SOFA (FOR IT WAS ALL PILLOW	60	3 DON JUAN	6	108	4
FOR CONTEMPLATION RATHER THAN HIS PILLOW	507	3 DON JUAN	16	15	2
PILLOW'D
PILLOW'D HIS DEATH-LIKE FOREHEAD THEN SHE WRUNG . . .	216	2 DON JUAN	2	114	5
PILLOW'D ON HER O'ERFLOWING HEART WHICH PANTS	260	2 DON JUAN	2	195	7
PILLOW'D UPON A FAIR AND HAPPY BREAST	274	2 DON JUAN	3	1	2
NOW PILLOW'D CHEEK TO CHEEK IN LOVING SLEEP	359	2 DON JUAN	4	29	1
PILLOWING
OF PILLOWING ITS HEAD ON A PIN-CUSHION	565	3 DON JUAN	17	6	5
PILLOW'S
THERE COUCHED ALL SNUGLY ON HIS PILLOW'S NOOK	512	3 DON JUAN	16	27	5
PILLOWS
DON JUAN WHEN THE MIDNIGHT HOUR OF PILLOWS	555	3 DON JUAN	16	110	3
PILLS
AND THIRTY THOUSAND MUSQUETS FLUNG THEIR PILLS	117	3 DON JUAN	8	12	2
PILOTS
THE STRUGGLE TO BE PILOTS IN A STORM	360	3 DON JUAN	13	6	3
THEY ARE BUT BAD PILOTS WHEN THE WEATHER'S ROUGH . . .	431	3 DON JUAN	14	48	3
PIMP
IS THE PLATONIC PIMP OF ALL POSTERITY	411	2 DON JUAN	5	1	8
PIN
(WHEN SHE DON'T PIN MEN'S LIMBS IN LIKE A JAILOR)-- . . .	204	3 DON JUAN	9	44	6
BECAUSE SHE DID NOT PIN HER FAITH ON FEATURE	480	3 DON JUAN	15	56	8
PINCH
SINCE NOT A PINCH OF DUST REMAINS OF CHEOPS	146	2 DON JUAN	1	219	8
NOR CARE A PINCH OF SNUFF ABOUT HIS CORPS)--	127	3 DON JUAN	8	31	8
MY MUSES DO NOT CARE A PINCH OF ROSIN	341	3 DON JUAN	12	55	1
PINCHBECK
SUPPRESSION LADY PINCHBECK WAS HIS CHOICE	336	3 DON JUAN	12	42	8
I SAID THAT LADY PINCHBECK HAD BEEN TALKED ABOUT-- . .	338	3 DON JUAN	12	47	1
PIN-CUSHION
OF PILLOWING ITS HEAD ON A PIN-CUSHION	565	3 DON JUAN	17	6	5
PINDAR
IF PINDAR SANG HORSE-RACES WHAT SHOULD HINDER	319	2 DON JUAN	3	85	7
HIMSELF FROM BEING AS PLIABLE AS PINDAR	319	2 DON JUAN	3	85	8
PINE
OF THE PINE FOREST AND THE SILENT SHORE	337	2 DON JUAN	3	105	2
THE SHRILL CICALAS PEOPLE OF THE PINE	337	2 DON JUAN	3	106	1
PINION
TO OFFER HIS YOUNG PINION AS HER FAN	313	2 DON JUAN	3	73	8
LEAF AND IMAGINATION DROOPS HER PINION	345	2 DON JUAN	4	3	6
AND DROOPING LIKE AN EAGLE'S WITH CLIPT PINION	246	3 DON JUAN	10	44	6
PINIONS
PINIONS TO FLEE AWAY AND BE AT REST	228	3 DON JUAN	10	6	3

	PAGE	VOL	CANTO	STANZA	LV
PINK					
OF AZURE PINK AND WHITE WAS HER CHEMISE--	311	2 DON JUAN	3	70	3
AND NOT THE PINK OF OLD HEXAMETERS	14	3 DON JUAN	6	18	3
OR BRIGANTINE OR PINK OF NO GREAT TONNAGE	468	3 DON JUAN	15	27	7
PINNACE					
THE OTHER BOATS THE YAWL AND PINNACE HAD	181	2 DON JUAN	2	48	1
PINNACLE					
WITHIN A NICHE NIGH TO ITS PINNACLE	386	3 DON JUAN	13	60	1
PINNED					
PINNED LIKE A FLOCK AND FLEECED TOO IN THEIR FOLD	468	3 DON JUAN	15	26	3
PINS					
PRICKING HER FINGERS WITH THOSE CURSED PINS	36	3 DON JUAN	6	61	7
THE PINS WERE PLACED SUFFICIENTLY BUT NOT	37	3 DON JUAN	6	62	7
PINT					
HERE TAVERNS WOOING TO A PINT OF PURL	278	3 DON JUAN	11	22	3
PIOUS					
OF PIOUS MEN HAVE PUBLISHED ON HIS ACTS	138	2 DON JUAN	1	203	V4
AND MADE A LOUD AND PIOUS LAMENTATION	175	2 DON JUAN	2	37	2
LEARN'D PIOUS TEMPERATE IN LOVE AND WINE	328	2 DON JUAN	3	91	4
AND PRAYERS AND OTHER PIOUS EVOLUTIONS	52	3 DON JUAN	6	92	3
THE PIOUS METALS MOST IN REQUISITION	152	3 DON JUAN	8	81	5
JUST PONDER WHAT A PIOUS PASTIME WAR IS	174	3 DON JUAN	8	124	8
WHEN SHE NO MORE COULD READ THE PIOUS PRINT	241	3 DON JUAN	10	34	8
FLUSHED WITH A PIOUS FURY TO SURVEY	262	3 DON JUAN	10	75	V7
BUT ERE THEY COULD PERFORM THIS PIOUS DUTY	276	3 DON JUAN	11	16	1
DAUGHTERS ADMIRED HIS DRESS AND PIOUS MOTHERS	293	3 DON JUAN	11	48	7
ALSO THERE BIN ANOTHER PIOUS REASON	370	3 DON JUAN	13	26	1
ALL PURGED AND PIOUS FROM THEIR NATIVE CLOUDS	396	3 DON JUAN	13	80	4
FOR WHEN HIS PIOUS CONSORT GAVE HIM STONES	410	3 DON JUAN	14	1	7
IN PIOUS LIBELS BY NO MEANS A FEW	414	3 DON JUAN	14	10	4
PIOUS AND PURE BEYOND WHAT I CAN TERM ANY	472	3 DON JUAN	15	36	5
PIPE					
A PIPE TOO AND A DRUM AND SHORTLY AFTER	290	2 DON JUAN	3	28	7
A TURK WITH BEADS IN HAND AND PIPE IN MOUTH	387	2 DON JUAN	4	78	6
SPOILT AS A PIPE OF CLARET IS WHEN PRICK'D	502	2 DON JUAN	5	158	5
SMOKING HIS PIPE QUITE CALMLY 'MIDST THE DIN	160	3 DON JUAN	8	98	4
PIPE'S					
HIS BEARD HE PUFFED HIS PIPE'S AMBROSIAL GALES	172	3 DON JUAN	8	121	7
PIPES					
TO FIND THREE PERFECT PIPES OF THE THIRD SEX	391	2 DON JUAN	4	86	8
AND DIVERS SMOKED SUPERB PIPES DECORATED	441	2 DON JUAN	5	53	5
PIPKINS					
THAT URNS AND PIPKINS ARE BUT FRAGILE BROTHERS	491	2 DON JUAN	5	138	4
PIPPIN					
A MOST PRODIGIOUS PIPPIN--BUT IT HUNG	44	3 DON JUAN	6	76	2
PIQUE					
WOULD PIQUE HIMSELF ON INTELLECTS WHOSE USE	428	2 DON JUAN	5	32	7
(I DON'T MUCH PIQUE MYSELF UPON ORTHOGRAPHY	149	3 DON JUAN	8	74	2
IF--BUT HERE ADELINE WHO SEEM'D TO PIQUE	478	3 DON JUAN	15	50	5
WILL PIQUE A GENTLEMAN FOR HIS OWN CREDIT	491	3 DON JUAN	15	79	5
SMILE OF AURORA'S THERE WAS NOUGHT TO PIQUE	544	3 DON JUAN	16	92	6
PIQUED					
BEING PIQUED BY CRITICS WHO HAVE DONE ME WRONG	410	2 DON JUAN	4	117	V5
PIQUES					
THEIR PLACE OF REST AND LEFT TO BOTH THEIR PIQUES	31	3 DON JUAN	6	50	6
WHICH PIQUES A PREUX CHEVALIER--AS IT OUGHT	490	3 DON JUAN	15	77	2
PIRACY					
A LITTLE SMUGGLING AND SOME PIRACY	222	2 DON JUAN	2	125	6
PIRATE					
HE SHOW'D THE ROYAL PENCHANTS OF A PIRATE	296	2 DON JUAN	3	40	8
IN SAILING FROM LIVORNO BY THE PIRATE	388	2 DON JUAN	4	80	7
WAS INTERRUPTED BY THE PIRATE CREW	393	2 DON JUAN	4	90	2
PIRATES					
THE FILE OF PIRATES SAVE THE FOREMOST WHO	370	2 DON JUAN	4	48	7
PIRATICAL					
WHILST HER PIRATICAL PAPA WAS CRUISING	282	2 DON JUAN	3	13	8
PISH					
TO SIGH INSTEAD OF COUGHING--AND CRYING-- PISH	228	3 DON JUAN	10	6	V8
PISTACHIO					
LAMB AND PISTACHIO NUTS--IN SHORT ALL MEATS	307	2 DON JUAN	3	62	2
PISTOL					
AND DRAWING FROM HIS BELT A PISTOL HE	365	2 DON JUAN	4	40	4
THAT COCKING OF A PISTOL WHEN YOU KNOW	366	2 DON JUAN	4	41	2
(AS PISTOL CALLS IT) BUT A YOUNG LIVONIAN	140	3 DON JUAN	8	56	8
WAS FROM A PISTOL SHOT THAT LAID HIM DEAD	152	3 DON JUAN	8	81	2
A MODERN ANCIENT PISTOL--BY THE HILTS	297	3 DON JUAN	11	57	8
PISTOLS					
IT WITH A PAIR OF PISTOLS AND THEIR FEARS	174	2 DON JUAN	2	35	4
OMITTING TURBAN SLIPPERS PISTOLS DIRK--	240	2 DON JUAN	2	160	6
PIT-A-PAT					
SO LIKE A SPIRITUAL PIT-A-PAT	556	3 DON JUAN	16	112	5
PITCH					
AND CARRY PRECEPT TO THE HIGHEST PITCH	138	2 DON JUAN	1	204	6
ALL NECK OR NOTHING AS LIKE PITCH OR ROSIN	135	3 DON JUAN	8	45	3
BUT THERE HIS PROJECT REACHED ITS UTMOST PITCH	147	3 DON JUAN	8	71	5
SHE WAS A PITCH BEYOND A COXCOMB'S FLIGHT	435	3 DON JUAN	14	57	4
(I STATE THIS FOR I AM CAUTIOUS TO A PITCH	507	3 DON JUAN	16	16	3
PITCHED					
HER ANGER PITCHED INTO A LOWER TUNE	490	2 DON JUAN	5	136	5

	PAGE	VOL	CANTO	STANZA	LN

PITCHER
WHICH SERVED THEM AS A SORT OF SPONGY PITCHER . . . . . 201 2 DON JUAN 2 85 3
PITCHES
OH JULIA--(THIS CURST VESSEL PITCHES SO)-- . . . . . . 167 2 DON JUAN 2 20 6
PITEOUS
(SHE ADDED IN A SOFT AND PITEOUS TONE) . . . . . . 47 3 DON JUAN 6 82 6
AND GENTLEMEN ARE IN A PITEOUS PLIGHT . . . . 198 3 DON JUAN 9 32 5
PITEOUSLY
OR SAUNTERED THROUGH THE GARDENS PITEOUSLY . . . . . 406 3 DON JUAN 13 102 3
PITH
'MONGST THEM WERE SEVERAL ENGLISHMEN OF PITH . . . . 75 3 DON JUAN 7 18 7
OUT OF THOSE NINETEEN WHO LATE RHYMED TO PITH . . . . 79 3 DON JUAN 7 25 6
WHICH LENT HIS LEARNED LUCUBRATIONS PITH . . . . . 294 3 DON JUAN 11 52 3
THOUGH MANY THOUSANDS BOTH OF PITH AND PLUCK TOO . . . 348 3 DON JUAN 12 70 V5
THE VERY POWERFUL PARSON PETER PITH . . . . . . 539 3 DON JUAN 16 81 7
PITHY
BY HIS DISPATCHES COUCHED IN PITHY PHRASE . . . . . 85 3 DON JUAN 7 39 6
PITIED
AS IF SHE PITIED HER FOR BEING THERE . . . . . . 28 3 DON JUAN 6 45 4
AND SEVERAL PITIED WITH SINCERE REGRET . . . . . 429 3 DON JUAN 14 44 7
THE WEALTHIEST ORPHANS ARE TO BE MORE PITIED . . . . 563 3 DON JUAN 17 3 8
PITIES
A THOUSAND PITIES ALSO WITH RESPECT . . . . . 38 2 DON JUAN 1 33 6
PITILESS
EVEN TIME THE PITILESS IN SORROW CLEFT . . . . . . 348 2 DON JUAN 4 8 3
PITT
THAN ANY OF THE PARODIES OF PITT . . . . . 283 2 DON JUAN 3 14 V8
TO FREE HIS COUNTRY PITT TOO HAD HIS PRIDE . . . . 186 3 DON JUAN 9 8 6
PITTANCE
THE PEASANTS GAVE THE POOR DUMB THING A PITTANCE . . . 285 3 DON JUAN 3 18 6
PITY
WHO HAS NOT SEEN IT WILL BE MUCH TO PITY . . . . . . 25 2 DON JUAN 1 8 3
'TIS PITY LEARNED VIRGINS EVER WED . . . . . 33 2 DON JUAN 1 22 1
'TIS PITY THOUGH IN THIS SUBLIME WORLD THAT . . . . 93 2 DON JUAN 1 133 3
SMALL PITY HAD HE FOR THE YOUNG AND FAIR . . . . 109 2 DON JUAN 1 160 6
BUT PITY HIM I NEITHER MUST NOR MAY . . . . . 112 2 DON JUAN 1 166 5
AND SECONDLY I PITY NOT BECAUSE . . . . . . 113 2 DON JUAN 1 167 1
TIS PITY THAT THEY HAD NO BROUGHAM IN SPAIN-- . . . 150 2 DON JUAN 1 V 1 2
YET DEEM'D HERSELF IN COMMON PITY BOUND . . . . 224 2 DON JUAN 2 129 6
PITY HE LOVED ADVENTUROUS LIFE'S VARIETY . . . . 296 2 DON JUAN 3 41 7
'TIS PITY WINE SHOULD BE SO DELETERIOUS . . . . 372 2 DON JUAN 4 52 7
THE MORE'S THE PITY WITH HER FACE AND FIGURE . . . 390 2 DON JUAN 4 85 8
OF GOOD EXAMPLES PITY THAT SO FEW BY . . . . . 486 2 DON JUAN 5 131 4
I SEE YOU'VE BOUGHT ANOTHER GIRL 'TIS PITY . . . . 500 2 DON JUAN 5 155 7
AND PITY LOVERS RATHER MORE THAN SEAMEN . . . . 32 3 DON JUAN 6 53 8
'TIS PITY THAT SUCH MEANING SHOULD PAVE HELL . . . 123 3 DON JUAN 8 25 8
BETWEEN YOUR FAME AND FEELINGS PRIDE AND PITY-- . . . 162 3 DON JUAN 8 101 4
NOW MOVED WITH PITY EVEN AS SOMETIMES NODS . . . 164 3 DON JUAN 8 106 6
IF HERE AND THERE SOME TRANSIENT TRAIT OF PITY . . . 174 3 DON JUAN 8 124 1
MUCH FLATTERY--EVEN VOLTAIRE'S AND THAT'S A PITY . . . 194 3 DON JUAN 9 23 6
'TIS NOT ADDRESSED TO YOU--THE MORE'S THE PITY . . . 233 3 DON JUAN 10 17 2
AND LOOK DOWN ON THE UNIVERSE WITH PITY-- . . . . 290 3 DON JUAN 11 45 6
TRUE 'TIS A PITY PITY 'TIS 'TIS TRUE) . . . . 334 3 DON JUAN 12 38 2
TRUE 'TIS A PITY PITY 'TIS 'TIS TRUE) . . . . 334 3 DON JUAN 12 38 2
THEN SHE WAS GIVEN TO CHARITY AND PITY . . . . 338 3 DON JUAN 12 47 6
AND BETWEEN PITY FOR HER CASE AND YOURS . . . . 343 3 DON JUAN 12 60 7
BESIDES (ALAS HIS TASTE--FORGIVE AND PITY) . . . . 347 3 DON JUAN 12 68 7
HALF HER ATTRACTIONS--PROBABLY FROM PITY-- . . . . 350 3 DON JUAN 12 74 4
WERE WELL NIGH OVER 'TIS PERHAPS A PITY . . . . 380 3 DON JUAN 13 48 2
'TIS PITY THAT IT TAKES NO FURTHER HOLD . . . . 382 3 DON JUAN 13 51 3
BUT MIX'D WITH PITY PURE AS E'ER WAS PENN'D . . . . 432 3 DON JUAN 14 51 6
INDICATIVE OF SOME SURPRISE AND PITY . . . . 545 3 DON JUAN 16 93 2
A THEME FOR PITY OR SOME WORSE EMOTION . . . . 563 3 DON JUAN 17 3 6
PITYING
AND PITYING SORE HIS MUTILATED CASE . . . . . 46 2 DON JUAN 1 44 6
RADIANT AND GRAVE--AS PITYING MAN'S DECLINE . . . . 476 3 DON JUAN 15 45 5
PITY'S
MAN'S PITY'S FOR HIMSELF OR FOR HIS SON . . . . . 377 3 DON JUAN 13 42 6
PIVOT
LIKE DERVISES WHO TURN AS ON A PIVOT HE . . . . . 290 2 DON JUAN 3 29 6
EXCEPT THE CREAK OF WHEELS WHICH ON THEIR PIVOT HE . . 272 3 DON JUAN 11 8 6
PLACE
WITH ALL THE LAKERS IN AND OUT OF PLACE . . . . . 9 2 DON JUAN D 1 6
AND WORDSWORTH HAS HIS PLACE IN THE EXCISE . . . . 12 2 DON JUAN D 6 6
EXPURGATED BY LEARNED MEN WHO PLACE . . . . 46 2 DON JUAN 1 44 2
I SAY THAT THERE'S THE PLACE--BUT VERBUM SAT . . . . 50 2 DON JUAN 1 53 4
BUT STILL NO LESS SUSPECTS IN THE WRONG PLACE . . . 74 2 DON JUAN 1 99 2
HOW THIS SAME INTERVIEW HAD TAKEN PLACE . . . . 77 2 DON JUAN 1 105 2
YOU'LL LOSE YOUR LIFE AND I SHALL LOSE MY PLACE . . . 115 2 DON JUAN 1 171 7
THE VERY PLACE WHERE WICKED PEOPLE GO . . . . 140 2 DON JUAN 1 207 8
CONTRIVED TO HELP PEDRILLO TO A PLACE . . . . 186 2 DON JUAN 2 56 2
WHILE T'OTHER HALF WERE LAID DOWN IN THEIR PLACE . . . 189 2 DON JUAN 2 63 5
BUT FINDING NO PLACE FOR THEIR LANDING BETTER . . . 211 2 DON JUAN 2 104 7
TO PLACE HIM IN THE CAVE FOR PRESENT REST . . . . 225 2 DON JUAN 2 131 3
UNLESS HE WISH'D TO DIE UPON THE PLACE-- . . . . 240 2 DON JUAN 2 159 6
AND PLACE THEM ON THEIR BREAST--BUT PLACE TO DIE-- . . 275 2 DON JUAN 3 2 6
AND PLACE THEM ON THEIR BREAST--BUT PLACE TO DIE-- . . 275 2 DON JUAN 3 2 6
ABOUT THE TIME AND PLACE WHERE HE HAD BEEN . . . . 286 2 DON JUAN 3 20 4
AND STILL MORE NEARLY TO THE PLACE ADVANCING . . . 290 2 DON JUAN 3 29 1

609

PLACE   (CONTINUED)

	PAGE	VOL	CANTO	STANZA	LN
WHICH TURN'D THE ISLE INTO A PLACE OF PLEASURE	295	2 DON JUAN	3	39	2
THEIR PLACE OF BIRTH ALONE IS MUTE	321	2 DON JUAN	3	L 2	4
PLACE ME ON SUNIUM'S MARBLED STEEP	326	2 DON JUAN	3	L 16	1
AVAILED FOR EITHER NEITHER CHANGE OF PLACE	381	2 DON JUAN	4	68	6
HIS SINGING I NO FURTHER TRUST CAN PLACE IN	391	2 DON JUAN	4	86	6
LIKE A BACKGAMMON BOARD THE PLACE WAS DOTTED	416	2 DON JUAN	5	10	1
SUCH AS I TOO WOULD SHED IF IN YOUR PLACE	420	2 DON JUAN	5	19	6
SOME BY A PLACE--AS TEND THEIR YEARS OR NATURES	425	2 DON JUAN	5	27	6
WE MUST BE NEAR SOME PLACE OF MAN'S ABODE--	436	2 DON JUAN	5	45	1
OF THOSE FORGETTING THE GREAT PLACE OF REST	448	2 DON JUAN	5	63	3
NO DOUBT IN PROPER PLACE AND TIME AND SEASON	454	2 DON JUAN	5	74	7
AND SO IT WAS IN PROPER TIME AND PLACE	478	2 DON JUAN	5	117	1
AND I SHALL PLACE JUANNA WITH DUDU	30	3 DON JUAN	6	49	4
THEIR PLACE OF REST AND LEFT TO BOTH THEIR PIQUES	31	3 DON JUAN	6	50	6
RETIRED INTO HER BOUDOIR A SWEET PLACE	54	3 DON JUAN	6	97	2
WHO HELD THE PLACE AND TO ASSIST THE FOE'S	71	3 DON JUAN	7	10	8
WITHIN A CANNON-SHOT LENGTH OF THE PLACE	89	3 DON JUAN	7	47	5
OF HEROISM AND TOOK HIS PLACE WITH SOLEMN	130	3 DON JUAN	8	34	6
THE LOFTIEST HURRIED BY THE TIME AND PLACE	139	3 DON JUAN	8	54	7
HER VERY PLACE OF BIRTH WAS BUT A SPECTRE	182	3 DON JUAN	8	141	5
'TWAS A HIGH PLACE THE HIGHEST IN THE NATION	208	3 DON JUAN	9	52	4
WHO WAS GONE TO HIS PLACE) AND PASSED FOR MUCH	209	3 DON JUAN	9	54	2
KEPT THE PLACE OPEN FOR THEIR EMULATION	248	3 DON JUAN	10	48	8
IN PLACE OF WHAT HER HOME AND FRIENDS ONCE WERE	252	3 DON JUAN	10	57	3
AS SOME HAVE QUALIFIED THAT WONDROUS PLACE	265	3 DON JUAN	10	81	4
SUNSET THE TIME THE PLACE THE SAME DECLIVITY	272	3 DON JUAN	11	8	2
IN SAFETY TO THE PLACE FOR WHICH YOU START	284	3 DON JUAN	11	34	7
JUAN PRESENTED IN THE PROPER PLACE	285	3 DON JUAN	11	35	1
HE DEEMS IT IS HIS PROPER PLACE TO BE	303	3 DON JUAN	11	70	5
EXCEPT THE WHIGS NOT GETTING INTO PLACE	309	3 DON JUAN	11	82	8
THOU ART IN LONDON--IN THAT PLEASANT PLACE	326	3 DON JUAN	12	23	2
THE NEXT OF PERILS THOUGH I PLACE IT STERNEST	345	3 DON JUAN	12	64	2
TO THAT IMPRACTICABLE PLACE TIMBUCTOO	348	3 DON JUAN	12	70	3
HINT THAT 'TIS TIME TO GIVE THE YOUNGER PLACE	360	3 DON JUAN	13	4	8
A PLACE WHERE PECCADILLOS ARE UNKNOWN	370	3 DON JUAN	13	27	2
THEREFORE I NAME NOT SQUARE STREET PLACE UNTIL I	370	3 DON JUAN	13	27	5
WHO COULD NOT GET THE PLACE FOR WHICH HE SUED	391	3 DON JUAN	13	70	8
HER PLACE WAS FAR BEYOND IT AND HER MIND	479	3 DON JUAN	15	54	2
OR EARTH BENEATH OR HEAVEN OR T'OTHER PLACE	510	3 DON JUAN	16	23	2
READY FOR JAIL THEIR PLACE OF CONVALESCENCE	530	3 DON JUAN	16	61	2
'TWIXT PLACE AND PATRIOTISM--ALBEIT COMPELLED	535	3 DON JUAN	16	72	4
AS FOR HIS PLACE HE COULD BUT SAY THIS OF IT	536	3 DON JUAN	16	73	7
SOONER COME PLACE INTO THE CIVIL LIST	536	3 DON JUAN	16	75	1
BUT SHOULD THE DAY COME WHEN PLACE CEASED TO EXIST	537	3 DON JUAN	16	75	5
AND JUAN TOOK HIS PLACE HE KNEW NOT WHERE	542	3 DON JUAN	16	87	2
YES SHE WAS TRULY WORTHY HER HIGH PLACE	550	3 DON JUAN	16	102	5

PLACED

	PAGE	VOL	CANTO	STANZA	LN
WHICH TREMBLED LIKE THE BOSOM WHERE 'TWAS PLACED	83	2 DON JUAN	1	115	3
HAD HE BUT BEEN PLACED AT A PUBLIC SCHOOL	158	2 DON JUAN	2	2	1
THE HAND FROM BURNING UNDERNEATH THEM PLACED	307	2 DON JUAN	3	63	6
UNTIL THEY REACH'D SOME GALLIOTS PLACED IN LINE	371	2 DON JUAN	4	50	6
THEY PLACED HIM O'ER THE WOMEN AS A SCOUT)	394	2 DON JUAN	4	92	5
WHEN SEEING HIM PLACED BY HER SIDE AT LAST	478	2 DON JUAN	5	116	V4
THE PINS WERE PLACED SUFFICIENTLY BUT NOT	37	3 DON JUAN	6	62	7
THE FORTRESS IS CALLED ISMAIL AND IS PLACED	70	3 DON JUAN	7	9	1
SO PLACED AS TO IMPEDE THE FIRE OF THOSE	71	3 DON JUAN	7	10	7
BEHOLD HIM PLACED AS IF UPON A PILLAR HE	204	3 DON JUAN	9	44	7
BEHOLD HIM PLACED IN YOUTH AND GLORY'S PILLORY	204	3 DON JUAN	9	44	V7
OF CANDIDATES REQUESTING TO BE PLACED	248	3 DON JUAN	10	48	3
THE GUESTS WERE PLACED ACCORDING TO THEIR ROLL	488	3 DON JUAN	15	74	3
BY SOME ODD CHANCE TOO HE WAS PLACED BETWEEN	489	3 DON JUAN	15	75	1

PLACEMAN

	PAGE	VOL	CANTO	STANZA	LN
ALWAYS A PATRIOT AND SOMETIMES A PLACEMAN	368	3 DON JUAN	13	21	8

PLACEMEN

	PAGE	VOL	CANTO	STANZA	LN
TO PROPER PLACEMEN EVERY RUSS CREDENTIAL	285	3 DON JUAN	11	35	2
RELUCTANT AS ALL PLACEMEN TO RESIGN	360	3 DON JUAN	13	5	2

PLACES

	PAGE	VOL	CANTO	STANZA	LN
AND PLACES ONE KEEPS LOOKING AT THE STEEPLE	164	2 DON JUAN	2	14	8
WHICH WELCOMES HAPLESS STRANGERS IN ALL PLACES	28	3 DON JUAN	6	45	7
WHICH FABLE PLACES IN HER BREAST OF WAIL	49	3 DON JUAN	6	87	6
ESPECIALLY WHEN SUCH LEAD TO HIGH PLACES	223	3 DON JUAN	9	82	8
ALL PEOPLE AT ALL TIMES AND IN MOST PLACES	334	3 DON JUAN	12	39	7
CONSTANTINOPLE AND SUCH DISTANT PLACES	368	3 DON JUAN	13	23	2
TO BUILD UP COMMON THINGS WITH COMMON PLACES	413	3 DON JUAN	14	7	8
HOW OFT WOULD VICE AND VIRTUE PLACES CHANGE	455	3 DON JUAN	14	101	5
FROM THEIR HIGH PLACES BY THE SIDEBOARD'S STAND--	539	3 DON JUAN	16	79	5
MIGHT COST BOTH MEN AND MASTER TOO--THEIR PLACES	539	3 DON JUAN	16	79	8
THE RIDICULES OF PEOPLE IN ALL PLACES--	548	3 DON JUAN	16	100	5

PLACID

	PAGE	VOL	CANTO	STANZA	LN
COLD-BLOODED SMOOTH-FACED PLACID MISCREANT	16	2 DON JUAN	D	12	1
THROUGH THE SERENE AND PLACID GLASSY DEEP	447	3 DON JUAN	14	87	7
AURORA WITH HER PURE AND PLACID MIEN	552	3 DON JUAN	16	105	3

PLAGUE

	PAGE	VOL	CANTO	STANZA	LN
TO PLAGUE THEMSELVES WITHAL THEY KNOW NOT WHY	71	2 DON JUAN	1	93	4
WITH WAR OR PLAGUE OR FAMINE ANY WAY	92	2 DON JUAN	1	131	5
UNLESS TO PLAGUE THE GRANTORS--YET SO TRUE IT IS	190	2 DON JUAN	2	65	3
HER CARGO FROM THE PLAGUE BEING SAFE AND SOUND	407	2 DON JUAN	4	113	5
A DAILY PLAGUE WHICH IN THE AGGREGATE	420	3 DON JUAN	14	24	1

610

	PAGE	VOL	CANTO	STANZA	LV

PLAGUED
WHEN PATIENTS NEITHER PLAGUED WITH FRIENDS NOR WIFE . . . . 190 2 DON JUAN 2 64 3
PLAGUES
THY PLAGUES THY FAMINES THY PHYSICIANS YET TICK . . . . 117 3 DON JUAN 8 12 5
ONE OF THOSE PRETTY PRECIOUS PLAGUES WHICH HAUNT . . . . 438 3 DON JUAN 14 63 3
PLAIDS
SCOTCH PLAIDS SCOTCH SNOODS THE BLUE HILLS AND CLEAR STREAMS 233 3 DON JUAN 10 18 2
PLAIN
I'M A PLAIN MAN AND IN A SINGLE STATION . . . . . . 33 2 DON JUAN 1 22 6
THE SONS NO MORE WERE SHORT THE DAUGHTERS PLAIN . . . . 53 2 DON JUAN 1 58 5
IF HE MUST FAIN SWEEP O'ER THE ETHERIAL PLAIN . . . . . 333 2 DON JUAN 3 99 1
A VAST UNTILL'D AND MOUNTAIN-SKIRTED PLAIN . . . . . . 386 2 DON JUAN 4 77 2
PLAIN--SIMPLE--SHORT AND BY NO MEANS INVITING . . . . . 412 2 DON JUAN 5 2 3
(PLAIN TRUTH DEAR MURRAY NEEDS FEW FLOWERS OF SPEECH) . 470 2 DON JUAN 5 101 2
'TIS TIME WE SHOULD RETURN TO PLAIN NARRATION . . . . 34 3 DON JUAN 6 57 1
IN THIS PLAIN PAIR SUWARROW AND HIS GUIDE . . . . . . 87 3 DON JUAN 7 43 8
NEITHER--BUT A GOOD PLAIN OLD TEMPERATE MAN . . . . . 164 3 DON JUAN 8 105 7
WHICH THEY RESISTED LIKE A SANDY PLAIN . . . . . . 166 3 DON JUAN 8 109 8
AND EPIC IF PLAIN TRUTH SHOULD PROVE NO BAR . . . . . 181 3 DON JUAN 8 138 5
THERE'S NO SUCH THING AS CERTAINTY THAT'S PLAIN . . . . 191 3 DON JUAN 9 17 5
TO THIS MY PLAIN SWORN DOWNRIGHT DETESTATION . . . . . 194 3 DON JUAN 9 24 7
PLAIN SIMPLE FORNICATION--NOR BEHOLD . . . . 314 3 DON JUAN 11 V 76 7
AND THIS REFLECTION BRINGS ME TO PLAIN PHYSICS . . . . 349 3 DON JUAN 12 72 5
TILL THIRTY SHOULD PERCEIVE THERE'S A PLAIN WOMAN . . . 359 3 DON JUAN 13 3 8
WHICH PROVE PLAIN ENGLISH TRUER OF THE TWO . . . . . 488 3 DON JUAN 15 72 6
PLAINLY
FOR SPEAKING OUT SO PLAINLY IN HIS SONG . . . . . . 45 2 DON JUAN 1 43 5
WHICH FORTUNE PLAINLY SEEMED TO RECOMMEND . . . . . 451 2 DON JUAN 5 69 5
IN ASPECT PLAINLY CLAD BESMEARED WITH DUST . . . . . 104 3 DON JUAN 7 73 6
HAVE PLAINLY MADE IT OUT THAT FOUR ARE THREE . . . . 548 3 DON JUAN 16 99 4
PLAINS
EVEN AS THE SIMOOM SWEEPS THE BLASTED PLAINS . . . . 375 2 DON JUAN 4 57 8
EVEN NIMROD'S SELF MIGHT LEAVE THE PLAINS OF DURA . . . 395 3 DON JUAN 13 78 5
PLAINTIVELY
AS TOUCHED AND PLAINTIVELY BEGAN TO PLAY . . . . . . 517 3 DON JUAN 16 38 7
PLAN
HER PLAN SHE DEEM'D BOTH INNOCENT AND FEASIBLE . . . . 66 2 DON JUAN 1 83 1
SO THAT THEIR PLAN AND PROSODY ARE ELIGIBLE . . . . . 70 2 DON JUAN 1 90 7
THE PLAN OF TWENTY YEARS AND ALL IS OVER . . . . . 75 2 DON JUAN 1 100 6
I'VE GOT A PLAN TO FORM A TREATISE WHICH . . . . . 138 2 DON JUAN 1 204 V2
BUT THE OLD MARCHIONESS SOME PLAN HAS HATCHED . . . . 332 3 DON JUAN 12 35 5
AN END TO ANSWER OR A PLAN TO LAY-- . . . . . . 342 3 DON JUAN 12 58 6
THE PLAN AT PRESENT'S SIMPLY IN CONCOCTION . . . . . 356 3 DON JUAN 12 87 5
MY PLAN (BUT I IF BUT FOR SINGULARITY . . . . . . 357 3 DON JUAN 12 89 5
AND THIN PRODUCED A PLAN WHEREBY TO ERECT . . . . . 529 3 DON JUAN 16 58 6
TO SOME SMALL PLAN OF INTEREST OR AMBITION-- . . . . 541 3 DON JUAN 16 85 7
PLANCO
CONSULE PLANCO HORACE SAID AND SO . . . . 143 2 DON JUAN 1 212 2
PLANET
ALTHOUGH ('TWILL HAPPEN AS OUR PLANET GUIDES) . . . . 251 3 DON JUAN 10 54 5
PLANET'S
THE MOORISH BLOOD PARTAKES THE PLANET'S HOUR . . . . 374 2 DON JUAN 4 56 4
PLANETS
WHOSE SMILE MAKES ALL THE PLANETS DANCE WITH MIRTH . . 494 2 DON JUAN 5 144 4
PLANKS
SOME BROKEN PLANKS AND OARS THAT TO THE TOUCH . . . . 226 2 DON JUAN 2 132 4
PLANN'D
TO--SAY MY PRAYERS--BUT NEVER WAS THERE PLANN'D . . . 160 2 DON JUAN 2 7 6
NONE IN PARTICULAR HAD SOUGHT OR PLANN'D IT . . . . 195 2 DON JUAN 2 75 5
WORK'D BY THE STORMS YET WORK'D AS IT WERE PLANN'D . . 253 2 DON JUAN 2 184 5
BUT THE FACT IS THAT I HAVE NOTHING PLANN'D . . . . . 346 2 DON JUAN 4 5 6
PLANNED
I'VE KNOWN SOME ODD ONES WHICH SEEMED REALLY PLANNED . . . 45 3 DON JUAN 6 78 5
PLANS
AND WATCH AND WARD WHOSE PLANS A WORD TOO MUCH . . . . 305 3 DON JUAN 11 73 3
LORD HENRY HEARD HER PLANS OF ARTLESS ART . . . . . 438 3 DON JUAN 14 65 5
PLANT
AND PLANT AND REAP AND SPIN AND GRIND AND SOW . . . . . 202 3 DON JUAN 9 40 4
PLANTED
BUT ONE THING'S PRETTY SURE A WOMAN PLANTED-- . . . . . 276 2 DON JUAN 3 4 2
PLANTS
OF ORIENTAL PLANTS ET CETERA . . . . 434 2 DON JUAN 5 42 5
HE FELT LIKE OTHER PLANTS CALLED SENSITIVE . . . . . 243 3 DON JUAN 10 37 2
PLAT
I MUST ALTHOUGH A FAVOURITE PLAT OF MINE . . . . . . 488 3 DON JUAN 15 73 3
PLATE
ENGRAVE UPON THE PLATE YOU ROSE AT FOUR . . . . . 230 2 DON JUAN 2 140 8
THE SEA-SHORE AT THIS HOUR MUST LEAVE HIS PLATE . . . . 240 2 DON JUAN 2 159 5
CERES PRESENTS A PLATE OF VERMICELLI-- . . . . . 246 2 DON JUAN 2 170 3
CRYSTAL AND MARBLE PLATE AND PORCELAIN . . . . . 310 2 DON JUAN 3 68 1
I'VE DONE NOW GO AND DINE FROM OFF THE PLATE . . . . 185 3 DON JUAN 9 6 1
ON A BRASS PLATE WAS GIVEN TO KNOCKS AND FAME . . . . 283 3 DON JUAN 11 31 V8
I SPARE YOU THEN THE FURNITURE AND PLATE . . . . . 393 3 DON JUAN 13 74 8
WITH MASSY PLATE FOR ARMOUR KNIVES AND FORKS . . . . 482 3 DON JUAN 15 62 2
A DIFFERENCE BETWEEN CROCKERY WARE AND PLATE . . . . 541 3 DON JUAN 16 84 6
PLATES
THEIR PLATES--WITHOUT IT MIGHT BE TOO MUCH BENDING . . . 538 3 DON JUAN 16 79 4
PLATO
OH PLATO PLATO YOU HAVE PAVED THE WAY . . . . . . 84 2 DON JUAN 1 116 1

		PAGE	VOL		CANTO	STANZA	LV

PLATO   (CONTINUED)
OH PLATO PLATO YOU HAVE PAVED THE WAY	84	2	DON JUAN	1	116	1
BY FENELON BY LUTHER AND BY PLATO	68	3	DON JUAN	7	4	2
WHICH PLATO IN HIS DIALOGUES DRAMATIC	494	3	DON JUAN	15	86	5

PLATONIC
PLATONIC PERFECT JUST SUCH LOVE AS MINE	64	2	DON JUAN	1	79	5
HIS FINGERS WITH A PURE PLATONIC SQUEEZE	81	2	DON JUAN	1	111	5
PLATONIC UNIVERSAL WONDERFUL	269	2	DON JUAN	2	212	3
IS THE PLATONIC PIMP OF ALL POSTERITY	411	2	DON JUAN	5	1	8
BESIDES PLATONIC LOVE BESIDES THE LOVE	219	3	DON JUAN	9	74	1
PLATONIC BLASPHEMY THE SOUL OF SWEARING	289	3	DON JUAN	11	43	8

PLATONICAL
| THE NOBLEST KIND OF LOVE IS LOVE PLATONICAL | 220 | 3 | DON JUAN | 9 | 76 | 1 |

PLATONISM
| THERE WAS THE PUREST PLATONISM AT BOTTOM | 251 | 3 | DON JUAN | 10 | 54 | 7 |
| OF PLATONISM WHICH LEADS SO OFT AMISS | 450 | 3 | DON JUAN | 14 | 92 | 3 |

PLATO'S
| TRAMPLING ON PLATO'S PRIDE WITH GREATER PRIDE | 522 | 3 | DON JUAN | 16 | 43 | 3 |

PLAY
EXCEPT TO BULL-FIGHTS MASS PLAY ROUT AND REVEL	102	2	DON JUAN	1	148	4
BUT NO DEVICE COULD BE BROUGHT INTO PLAY--	114	2	DON JUAN	1	169	4
FOR NAUGHTY CHILDREN WHO WOULD RATHER PLAY	162	2	DON JUAN	2	10	3
SOME PLAY THE DEVIL AND THEN WRITE A NOVEL	263	2	DON JUAN	2	201	8
BEGAN TO SING DANCE CHATTER SMILE AND PLAY	23	3	DON JUAN	6	34	8
IN RHYMES OR DREAMT (FOR FANCY WILL PLAY TRICKS)	230	3	DON JUAN	10	10	5
RECEIVED INSTRUCTIONS HOW TO PLAY HIS CARD	247	3	DON JUAN	10	46	6
WHO LIKE TO PLAY THE FOOL WITH CIRCUMSPECTION	304	3	DON JUAN	11	71	8
LIFE'S A POOR PLAYER --THEN PLAY OUT THE PLAY	310	3	DON JUAN	11	86	4
LIFE'S A POOR PLAYER --THEN PLAY OUT THE PLAY	310	3	DON JUAN	11	86	4
WHEN TIRED OF PLAY HE FLIRTED WITHOUT SIN	327	3	DON JUAN	12	25	5
AND FORTUNE HAS AN AWKWARD PART TO PLAY	342	3	DON JUAN	12	58	2
THUS GENTLEMEN MAY SOMETIMES PLAY THE FOOL	376	3	DON JUAN	13	39	V6
THE FIRST THING BOYS LIKE AFTER PLAY AND FRUIT	405	3	DON JUAN	13	101	3
BUT JUST TO PLAY WITH AS AN INFANT PLAYS	414	3	DON JUAN	14	8	8
I ASK IN TURN--WHY DO YOU PLAY AT CARDS	415	3	DON JUAN	14	11	3
IN PLAY THERE ARE TWO PLEASURES FOR YOUR CHOOSING--	415	3	DON JUAN	14	12	7
TO PLAY UPON THE SURFACE OF HUMANITY	482	3	DON JUAN	15	60	2
AS TOUCHED AND PLAINTIVELY BEGAN TO PLAY	517	3	DON JUAN	16	38	7
AND OPENING HER PIANO GAN TO PLAY	517	3	DON JUAN	16	38	V7
BUT I'M TOO LATE AND THEREFORE MUST MAKE PLAY	538	3	DON JUAN	16	78	1

PLAY'D
WHICH PLAY'D WITHIN THE TANGLES OF HER HAIR	80	2	DON JUAN	1	110	2
OF HAVING PLAY'D THE FOOL THOUGH BOTH I SPURN HE	103	2	DON JUAN	1	151	5
A PURPLE HECTIC PLAY'D LIKE DYING DAY	234	2	DON JUAN	2	147	2
AMIDST THE COURT A GOTHIC FOUNTAIN PLAY'D	389	3	DON JUAN	13	65	1

PLAYED
FORTUNE HAS PLAYED YOU HERE A PRETTY FREAK	418	2	DON JUAN	5	14	4
AS SUITS A MATRON WHO HAS PLAYED A PRANK	500	2	DON JUAN	5	154	4
FOR THIS GREAT CONQUEROR PLAYED THE CORPORAL	95	3	DON JUAN	7	56	2
HE PLAYED AND PAID MADE LOVE WITHOUT MUCH SIN	327	3	DON JUAN	12	25	V5
THE DUCHESS OF FITZ-FULKE PLAYED WITH HER VEIL	514	3	DON JUAN	16	31	5
OF EROS BUT THOUGH THOU HAST PLAYED US MANY TRICKS	554	3	DON JUAN	16	109	7

PLAYER
| LIFE'S A POOR PLAYER --THEN PLAY OUT THE PLAY | 310 | 3 | DON JUAN | 11 | 86 | 4 |

PLAYFUL
OR EATS FROM OUT THE PALM OR PLAYFUL LOWERS	292	2	DON JUAN	3	32	6
SWEET PLAYFUL PHRASES WHICH WOULD SEEM ABSURD	351	2	DON JUAN	4	14	7
UPON AN OBJECT WHETHER SAD OR PLAYFUL	463	3	DON JUAN	15	16	7

PLAYING
| JUANNA PLAYING WITH HER VEIL OR HAIR | 28 | 3 | DON JUAN | 6 | 45 | 2 |
| ON ADELINE WHILE PLAYING HER GRAND ROLE | 546 | 3 | DON JUAN | 16 | 96 | 3 |

PLAYS
TO PLAYS IN FIVE AND OPERAS IN THREE ACTS	138	2	DON JUAN	1	203	4
THE MOUTH OF SOME ONE IN HIS PLAYS SO DOATING	77	3	DON JUAN	7	21	7
SAVE IN THE CLUBS NO MAN OF HONOUR PLAYS--	407	3	DON JUAN	13	106	2
BUT JUST TO PLAY WITH AS AN INFANT PLAYS	414	3	DON JUAN	14	8	8
WHICH SOMETIMES PLAYS THE DEUCE WITH WOMANKIND	480	3	DON JUAN	15	57	2
MOST PEOPLE AS IT PLAYS ALONG THE ARRAS	509	3	DON JUAN	16	20	8

PLEAD
| LEAVING DON JUAN AND HAIDEE TO PLEAD | 271 | 2 | DON JUAN | 2 | 216 | 7 |
| THAT SUIT IN CHANCERY--WHICH SOME PERSONS PLEAD | 324 | 3 | DON JUAN | 12 | 18 | 1 |

PLEADED
IF LOVE PATERNAL IN HIS BOSOM PLEADED	300	2	DON JUAN	3	49	5
I CANNOT TELL THE WAY IN WHICH HE PLEADED	85	3	DON JUAN	7	38	4
CARED MOST ABOUT IT NEED NOT NOW BE PLEADED--	324	3	DON JUAN	12	17	5

PLEADERS
| BESIDES THOSE SOOTHING SPEECHES OF THE PLEADERS | 346 | 3 | DON JUAN | 12 | 65 | 7 |

PLEADING
| OF WHICH HE SPECIFIED IN THIS HIS PLEADING | 116 | 2 | DON JUAN | 1 | 174 | 6 |
| CANTOS WOULD DO BUT AT APOLLO'S PLEADING | 341 | 3 | DON JUAN | 12 | 55 | 6 |

PLEADINGS
| THE NAMES OF ALL THE WITNESSES THE PLEADINGS | 127 | 2 | DON JUAN | 1 | 189 | 3 |

PLEADS
| BY ALL THE LAWS THE STRICTEST LAWYER PLEADS | 352 | 3 | DON JUAN | 12 | 80 | 6 |
| THE OSTLER PLEADS FOR A SMALL REMINISCENCE | 379 | 3 | DON JUAN | 13 | 46 | 8 |

PLEASANT
IN SEVILLE WAS HE BORN A PLEASANT CITY	25	2	DON JUAN	1	8	1
'TIS ALSO PLEASANT TO BE DEEM'D MAGNANIMOUS	37	2	DON JUAN	1	30	3
OH PLEASURE YOU'RE INDEED A PLEASANT THING	85	2	DON JUAN	1	119	1

PLEASANT   (CONTINUED)

	PAGE	VOL	CANTO		STANZA	LN
THE PLEASANT SCANDAL WHICH AROSE NEXT DAY	126	2	DON JUAN	1	188	5
'TIS NOT SO PLEASANT IN THE GULF OF LYONS	176	2	DON JUAN	2	39	8
IS PLEASANT BESIDES BEING TRUE LOVE'S ESSENCE	245	2	DON JUAN	2	169	4
HOW PLEASANT WERE THE MAXIM (NOT QUITE NEW)	267	2	DON JUAN	2	207	6
HOW PLEASANT FOR THE HEART AS WELL AS LIVER	270	2	DON JUAN	2	213	8
IN COMPANY A VERY PLEASANT FELLOW	318	2	DON JUAN	3	82	2
'TIS PLEASANT PURCHASING OUR FELLOW CREATURES	425	2	DON JUAN	5	27	2
BECAUSE 'TIS PLEASANT SO THAT IT BE PURE	35	3	DON JUAN	6	59	4
AND THAT THIS WOOD WAS FULL OF PLEASANT FRUITS	43	3	DON JUAN	6	75	7
TO KNOW THAT NOTHING COULD BE KNOWN A PLEASANT	69	3	DON JUAN	7	5	2
A PLEASANT THING TO YOUNG MEN AT THEIR YEARS	75	3	DON JUAN	7	18	6
BUT FLEW TO WHERE THE PLEASANT NOISE GREW LOUDER	129	3	DON JUAN	8	33	V8
THE PLEASANT RIDDLES OF FUTURITY--	180	3	DON JUAN	8	137	6
IT IS A PLEASANT VOYAGE PERHAPS TO FLOAT	191	3	DON JUAN	9	18	1
THAT PLEASANT CAPITAL OF PAINTED SNOWS	203	3	DON JUAN	9	42	8
MOUNT PLEASANT AS CONTAINING NOUGHT TO PLEASE	278	3	DON JUAN	11	21	3
THOU ART IN LONDON--IN THAT PLEASANT PLACE	326	3	DON JUAN	12	23	2
WHICH ARE MORE PURE THAN PLEASANT TO BE SURE	335	3	DON JUAN	12	41	4
ALTHOUGH IT SEEMS BOTH PROMINENT AND PLEASANT	416	3	DON JUAN	14	15	5
'TIS PLEASANT IF THEN ANYTHING IS PLEASANT	422	3	DON JUAN	14	28	7
'TIS PLEASANT IF THEN ANYTHING IS PLEASANT	422	3	DON JUAN	14	28	7
SOME PLEASANT JESTING AT THE AWKWARD STRANGER	424	3	DON JUAN	14	32	4

PLEASANTER

	PAGE	VOL	CANTO		STANZA	LN
FOR PEOPLE WHO ARE PLEASANTER THAN OTHERS	63	2	DON JUAN	1	77	7

PLEASE

	PAGE	VOL	CANTO		STANZA	LN
AND THEN YOUR HERO TELLS WHENE'ER YOU PLEASE	24	2	DON JUAN	1	6	3
BY LAYING WHATE'ER SUM IN MULCT THEY PLEASE ON	57	2	DON JUAN	1	64	6
MIGHT PLEASE PERHAPS A VIRTUOUS WIFE CAN QUELL	64	2	DON JUAN	1	78	5
AS IF IT SAID DETAIN ME IF YOU PLEASE	81	2	DON JUAN	1	111	3
THE CHIMNEY--WOULD IT PLEASE YOU RING THE BELL	104	2	DON JUAN	1	153	V4
LOOK WHERE YOU PLEASE--WE'VE NOTHING SIR TO HIDE	106	2	DON JUAN	1	156	4
EXACTLY AS YOU PLEASE OR NOT THE ROD	140	2	DON JUAN	1	206	7
MEANTIME THEY'LL DOUBTLESS PLEASE TO RECOLLECT	141	2	DON JUAN	1	209	5
YET IF MY GENTLE MUSE HE PLEASE TO ROAST	142	2	DON JUAN	1	210	4
A SAD OLD FELLOW WAS HE IF YOU PLEASE	223	2	DON JUAN	2	127	6
WHO PLEASE--THE MORE BECAUSE THEY PREACH IN VAIN--	250	2	DON JUAN	2	178	6
AND YOUTH STILL WEEPS THE TENDER TEARS THAT PLEASE--	273	2	DON JUAN	2	V 2	4
THEN IF YOU'D HAVE THEM WEDDED PLEASE TO SHUT	282	2	DON JUAN	3	12	5
OF VERSE (THE NAME WITH WHICH WE CANTABS PLEASE	341	2	DON JUAN	3	110	7
GREAT WISH TO PLEASE--A MOST ATTRACTIVE DOWER	395	2	DON JUAN	4	94	7
WHILK WHICH (OR WHAT YOU PLEASE) WAS OWING TO	456	2	DON JUAN	5	78	1
WILL PLEASE TO ACCOMPANY THOSE GENTLEMEN	458	2	DON JUAN	5	81	2
WHICH DOTH YOUR TRUE BELIEVER SO MUCH PLEASE	17	3	DON JUAN	6	23	3
YOU PLEASE--WE WILL NOT QUARREL ABOUT THAT	25	3	DON JUAN	6	38	8
A LIBEL OR WHATE'ER YOU PLEASE TO RHYME ON	53	3	DON JUAN	6	94	4
WHERE WILL YOU SERVE--WHERE'ER YOU PLEASE--I KNOW	98	3	DON JUAN	7	62	1
MAY IT PLEASE YOUR EXCELLENCY THUS REPLIED	103	3	DON JUAN	7	71	1
IS THAT YOU NEITHER CAN BE PLEASED NOR PLEASE	144	3	DON JUAN	8	64	6
THE KOZAKS OR IF SO YOU PLEASE COSSACQUES--	149	3	DON JUAN	8	74	1
DO JUST WHATE'ER THEY PLEASE BY DINT OF FEATURES	167	3	DON JUAN	8	111	8
YOU PLEASE (IT CAUSES ALL THE THINGS WHICH BE	211	3	DON JUAN	9	57	3
TO PAIN THE MOMENT WHEN YOU CEASE TO PLEASE	231	3	DON JUAN	10	13	8
BUT WHAT THEY PLEASE AND IF THAT THINGS BE DEAR	273	3	DON JUAN	11	10	2
MOUNT PLEASANT AS CONTAINING NOUGHT TO PLEASE	278	3	DON JUAN	11	21	3
PERMITS WHATE'ER THEY PLEASE OR DID NOT LONG SINCE	305	3	DON JUAN	11	73	8
THAT NOVELTIES PLEASE LESS THAN THEY IMPRESS	347	3	DON JUAN	12	69	8
THAT ANYTHING HE VIEWS CAN GREATLY PLEASE	373	3	DON JUAN	13	34	7
BECAUSE--SUCH WAS HIS MAGIC POWER TO PLEASE--	399	3	DON JUAN	13	86	7
WOULD RISK TO PLEASE IT MY LAST RAG OF BREECHES	421	3	DON JUAN	14	26	V8
BARDS MAY SING WHAT THEY PLEASE ABOUT CONTENT	444	3	DON JUAN	14	79	6
SHOW OFF--TO PLEASE THEIR COMPANY OR MOTHER	522	3	DON JUAN	16	44	8

PLEASED

	PAGE	VOL	CANTO		STANZA	LN
WHEREAS IF ONE SOLE LADY PLEASED FOREVER	270	2	DON JUAN	2	213	7
THERE WAS NO MIGHTY REASON TO BE PLEASED	296	2	DON JUAN	3	40	3
SOME KINDER CASUISTS ARE PLEASED TO SAY	336	2	DON JUAN	3	104	1
BUT NOW WAS NOT MUCH PLEASED WITH CAPE SIGAEUM	384	2	DON JUAN	4	75	8
AMMON'S (ILL PLEASED WITH ONE WORLD AND ONE FATHER)	427	2	DON JUAN	5	31	8
IS THAT YOU NEITHER CAN BE PLEASED NOR PLEASE	144	3	DON JUAN	8	64	6
AND WHAT THEY PLEASED TO DO WITH THE YOUNG KHAN	167	3	DON JUAN	8	112	1
WHEN WROTH WHILE PLEASED SHE WAS AS FINE A FIGURE	213	3	DON JUAN	9	62	2
THEY PLEASED TO MAKE OR TAKE HIM FOR AND THEIR	463	3	DON JUAN	15	16	2
WAS NOT EXACTLY PLEASED TO BE SO CAUGHT	490	3	DON JUAN	15	77	6

PLEASES

	PAGE	VOL	CANTO		STANZA	LN
RATHER TO HIDE WHAT PLEASES MOST UNKNOWN	13	3	DON JUAN	6	15	4
OF FORTRESSES BUT FIGHTING WHERE IT PLEASES	149	3	DON JUAN	8	74	7
AND TAKE AS MANY HEROES AS HEAVEN PLEASES	459	3	DON JUAN	15	9	8

PLEASING

	PAGE	VOL	CANTO		STANZA	LN
'TIS PLEASING TO BE SCHOOL'D IN A STRANGE TONGUE	242	2	DON JUAN	2	164	1
WITH NO GREAT VOICE IS PLEASING TO BEHOLD	389	2	DON JUAN	4	83	5
AND PLEASING OR UNPLEASING STILL ARE LIKE	32	3	DON JUAN	6	52	8
FOR LOVE OR BREAKFAST PRIVATE PLEASING LONE	54	3	DON JUAN	6	97	3

PLEASURE

	PAGE	VOL	CANTO		STANZA	LN
TO THOSE WHO COULD INVENT HIM A NEW PLEASURE	85	2	DON JUAN	1	118	2
OH PLEASURE YOU'RE INDEED A PLEASANT THING	85	2	DON JUAN	1	119	1
PLEASURE'S A SIN AND SOMETIMES SIN'S A PLEASURE	93	2	DON JUAN	1	133	4
AND WHEN 'TIS FOUND LET ME TOO HAVE THAT PLEASURE	104	2	DON JUAN	1	153	8
YOU WILL PROCEED IN PLEASURE AND IN PRIDE	132	2	DON JUAN	1	195	1
BEFORE THE SHRINES OF SORROW AND OF PLEASURE	145	2	DON JUAN	1	217	2

	PAGE	VOL	CANTO	STANZA	LN

PLEASURE   (CONTINUED)
HAD FURTHER SLEEP A FURTHER PLEASURE MADE	235	2 DON JUAN	2	149	4
A PLEASURE--LIKE ALL PLEASURES--RATHER DEAR	238	2 DON JUAN	2	156	6
IT WAS SUCH PLEASURE TO BEHOLD HIM SUCH	247	2 DON JUAN	2	173	1
A PLEASURE WORTHY XERXES THE GREAT KING	251	2 DON JUAN	2	180	3
A PLEASURE NAUGHT BUT DRUNKENNESS CAN BRING	251	2 DON JUAN	2	180	V3
AND MIXED UNTIL THE VERY PLEASURE STUNG	254	2 DON JUAN	2	187	V8
PLEASURE OR PAIN TO ONE ANOTHER LIVING	258	2 DON JUAN	2	192	8
PLEASURE (WHENE'ER SHE SINGS AT LEAST) 'S A SIREN	294	2 DON JUAN	3	36	5
WHICH TURN'D THE ISLE INTO A PLACE OF PLEASURE	295	2 DON JUAN	3	39	2
WITH TEMPERANCE IN PLEASURE AS IN FOOD	302	2 DON JUAN	3	53	4
A PLEASURE IN THE GENTLE STREAM THAT FLOW'D	304	2 DON JUAN	3	56	6
THERE IS NO STERNER MORALIST THAN PLEASURE	308	2 DON JUAN	3	65	8
BUT IF IT GIVES THEM PLEASURE BE IT SO	347	2 DON JUAN	4	7	5
OF PLEASURE AND OF PAIN--EVEN WHILE I KISS	364	2 DON JUAN	4	38	5
'TWOULD GIVE ME PLEASURE--PRAY WHAT IS YOUR NATION	417	2 DON JUAN	5	13	8
CAN GIVE US EITHER PAIN OR PLEASURE WHO	428	2 DON JUAN	5	32	6
IN WHICH A PRINCESS WITH GREAT PLEASURE WOULD	453	2 DON JUAN	5	73	3
HAD BEEN HER SLAVES' CHIEF PLEASURE AS HER WILL	475	2 DON JUAN	5	112	4
TO BATTLES SIEGES AND THAT KIND OF PLEASURE	123	3 DON JUAN	8	24	7
IN JUAN'S LOOK PAIN PLEASURE HOPE FEAR MIXED	159	3 DON JUAN	8	96	3
YOUR HOURIS ALSO HAVE A NATURAL PLEASURE	168	3 DON JUAN	8	113	1
THE GREATER IS THE PLEASURE IN ARRIVING	260	3 DON JUAN	10	72	7
ALTHOUGH HE HAD KNOWN PLEASURE IN EXCESS	314	3 DON JUAN	11	V 75	V2
THEIRS IS THE PLEASURE THAT CAN NEVER PALL	316	3 DON JUAN	12	3	2
OR PLEASURE WHO MAKE POLITICS RUN GLIBBER ALL	318	3 DON JUAN	12	5	6
NOW HATRED IS BY FAR THE LONGEST PLEASURE	361	3 DON JUAN	13	6	7
BECAUSE ITS OWN GOOD PLEASURE HATH DECIDED	366	3 DON JUAN	13	16	8
THE ONLY SORT OF PLEASURE WHICH REQUITES	405	3 DON JUAN	13	100	4
TO THE GREAT PLEASURE OF OUR FRIENDS MANKIND	414	3 DON JUAN	14	9	5
THIS PARADISE OF PLEASURE AND ENNUI	417	3 DON JUAN	14	17	8
A PLEASURE BEFORE WHICH ALL OTHERS VANISH	453	3 DON JUAN	14	98	3
FOR YOU HAVE GOT THAT PLEASURE STILL TO COME	498	3 DON JUAN	15	95	4
SUCH WAS HIS SOVEREIGN'S PLEASURE (THOUGH UNFIT	535	3 DON JUAN	16	72	5

PLEASURE'S
| PLEASURE'S A SIN AND SOMETIMES SIN'S A PLEASURE | 93 | 2 DON JUAN | 1 | 133 | 4 |

PLEASURES
I CARE NOT FOR NEW PLEASURES AS THE OLD	85	2 DON JUAN	1	118	7
A PLEASURE--LIKE ALL PLEASURES--RATHER DEAR	238	2 DON JUAN	2	156	6
BY AGE IN EARTH HER DAYS AND PLEASURES WERE	382	2 DON JUAN	4	71	5
THROUGH PLEASURES THICK AND THIN TO FAME OR SHAME	189	3 DON JUAN	9	14	V7
THOSE PLEASURES AFTER WHICH WILD YOUTH WILL HANKER	240	3 DON JUAN	10	31	6
THE GHOST OF VANISHED PLEASURES ONCE IN VOGUE ILL	304	3 DON JUAN	11	72	6
WHICH HOLD FAST OTHER PLEASURES GREAT AND SMALL	316	3 DON JUAN	12	3	4
IN PLAY THERE ARE TWO PLEASURES FOR YOUR CHOOSING--	415	3 DON JUAN	14	12	7
A RACK OF PLEASURES WHERE WE MUST INVENT	444	3 DON JUAN	14	79	2

PLEDGED
| HE FOUND--BUT SOUGHT NOT I HAVE PLEDGED MY FAITH | 366 | 2 DON JUAN | 4 | 42 | 6 |

PLENIPO
| WITHOUT THE AID OF PRINCE OR PLENIPO | 53 | 3 DON JUAN | 6 | 95 | 6 |

PLENTIFUL
| SUCH PLENTIFUL PRECAUTIONS THAT STILL HE | 248 | 2 DON JUAN | 2 | 174 | 3 |
| AS PLENTIFUL AS IN A COURT OR FAIR | 310 | 2 DON JUAN | 3 | 68 | 8 |

PLENTY
OF FIFTY AND SUCH HUSBANDS ARE IN PLENTY	56	2 DON JUAN	1	62	2
BUT BY GOD'S GRACE HERE WRECKS WERE IN SUCH PLENTY	226	2 DON JUAN	2	132	7
REMEMBER WHEN THOUGH I HAD NO GREAT PLENTY	9	3 DON JUAN	6	5	4
AND YOU WILL FIND HER SUM OF YEARS IN PLENTY	433	3 DON JUAN	14	54	8
GREAT PLENTY MUCH FORMALITY SMALL CHEER	538	3 DON JUAN	16	78	7

PLIABLE
| LOCKLESS--SO PLIABLE FROM THE PURE GOLD | 312 | 2 DON JUAN | 3 | 71 | 2 |
| HIMSELF FROM BEING AS PLIABLE AS PINDAR | 319 | 2 DON JUAN | 3 | 85 | 8 |

PLIANT
| SNATCH WHEN DESPAIR MAKES HUMAN HEARTS LESS PLIANT | 138 | 3 DON JUAN | 8 | 51 | 4 |
| TO LIFE'S SMALL RUBS SHOULD SURELY BE MORE PLIANT | 566 | 3 DON JUAN | 17 | 10 | 3 |

PLIED
| THEY LAID HIM IN A BOAT AND PLIED THE OAR | 371 | 2 DON JUAN | 4 | 50 | 5 |

PLIGHT
IS THIS A TIME FOR GIGGLING THIS A PLIGHT	115	2 DON JUAN	1	171	5
AND REACH'D HIS HOME IN AN UNSEEMLY PLIGHT	126	2 DON JUAN	1	138	4
OF PLIGHT AND PROMISES TO BE A SPOUSE	257	2 DON JUAN	2	190	3
AND GENTLEMEN ARE IN A PITEOUS PLIGHT	198	3 DON JUAN	9	32	5
IN HAPPIER PLIGHT THAN IF THEY FORMED A PAIR	344	3 DON JUAN	12	61	8
IF HE HAD KNOWN EXACTLY HIS OWN PLIGHT	506	3 DON JUAN	16	12	5

PLIGHTED
| AND NOW 'TWAS DONE--ON THE LONE SHORE WERE PLIGHTED | 265 | 2 DON JUAN | 2 | 204 | 1 |
| IF SINGLE PROBABLY HIS PLIGHTED FAIR | 288 | 2 DON JUAN | 3 | 24 | 1 |

PLODDING
| AS THEY WERE PLODDING ON THEIR WINDING WAY | 434 | 2 DON JUAN | 5 | 42 | 1 |
| THAN THE MERE PLODDING THROUGH EACH VULGAR FRACTION | 321 | 3 DON JUAN | 12 | 11 | 6 |

PLOTTERY
| HER WAY BACK TO THE WORLD BY DINT OF PLOTTERY | 397 | 3 DON JUAN | 13 | 82 | 6 |

PLOUGH
TO SEVERAL SAINTS THAT SHORTLY PLOUGH OR HARROW	99	3 DON JUAN	7	63	6
FROM SOME FRESH PARADISE AND SET TO PLOUGH	202	3 DON JUAN	9	40	2
FROM MUCH IMPROVEMENT WITH THAT VIRTUOUS PLOUGH	335	3 DON JUAN	12	40	5

PLOUGHING
| ADAM EXCHANGED HIS PARADISE FOR PLOUGHING | 444 | 3 DON JUAN | 14 | 78 | 1 |

PLOUGHMAN
| THERE WAS A PRIZE OX A PRIZE PIG AND PLOUGHMAN | 530 | 3 DON JUAN | 16 | 60 | 7 |
| THE PRIZE PIG PLOUGHMAN POACHERS THE MEN SENT | 533 | 3 DON JUAN | 16 | 66 | 4 |

	PAGE	VOL	CANTO	STANZA	LN

PLOUGHS
NO MORE IT DOTH--ITS PLOUGHS BUT CHANGE THEIR BOYS . . . 228 3 DON JUAN 10 7 7
THAT OX OF VERSE WHO PLOUGHS FOR EVERY LINE-- . . . . . 297 3 DON JUAN 11 58 6
FOR EUROPE PLOUGHS IN AFRIC LIKE BOS PIGER . . . . . . 348 3 DON JUAN 12 70 6

PLUCK
AS THOSE WHO DOTE ON ODOURS PLUCK THE FLOWERS . . . . . 275 2 DON JUAN 3 2 5
THOUGH MANY THOUSANDS BOTH OF PITH AND PLUCK TOO . . . 348 3 DON JUAN 12 70 V5

PLUCK'D
THE TREE OF KNOWLEDGE HAS BEEN PLUCK'D--ALL'S KNOWN-- . . 90 2 DON JUAN 1 127 4
DROPP'D IN THEIR LAPS SCARCE PLUCK'D THEIR MELLOW STORE . 291 2 DON JUAN 3 31 8

PLUCKED
FAIR AS THE ROSE JUST PLUCKED TO CROWN THE WREATH . . . 235 2 DON JUAN 2 148 V5

PLUCKING
WENT PLUCKING VARIOUS FRUIT WITHOUT HER LEAVE . . . . . 30 2 DON JUAN 1 18 8

PLUCKS
MEANTIME APOLLO PLUCKS ME BY THE EAR . . . . 347 2 DON JUAN 4 7 7

PLUMAGE
AND PLUMAGE (PROBABLY IT MIGHT HAVE ERR'D . . . . . 206 2 DON JUAN 2 94 3
THE HANDSOME HERALD ON WHOSE PLUMAGE SAT . . . . . . 211 3 DON JUAN 9 57 6

PLUME
A SCARLET COAT BLACK FACINGS A LONG PLUME . . . . . 204 3 DON JUAN 9 43 2

PLUMED
PLUMED BY LONGINUS OR THE STAGYRITE . . . . 467 3 DON JUAN 15 25 4

PLUMES
OF GEMS AND PLUMES AND PEARLS AND SILKS TO WHERE . . . 303 3 DON JUAN 11 70 4

PLUMPNESS
HER PLUMPNESS HER IMPERIAL CONDESCENSION . . . . . . 218 3 DON JUAN 9 72 2

PLUNDER
WILL SERVE WHEN THERE IS PLUNDER IN A CITY-- . . . 162 3 DON JUAN 8 101 6
AND ALL ALLOWANCES BESIDES OF PLUNDER . . . . . . 163 3 DON JUAN 8 103 1
MUCH DID THEY SLAY MORE PLUNDER AND NO LESS . . . 176 3 DON JUAN 8 129 1
BUT WHILE THE THIRST FOR GORE AND PLUNDER RAGED . . . 178 3 DON JUAN 8 132 5

PLUNDER'D
SOME PLUNDER'D SOME DRANK SPIRITS SOME SUNG PSALMS . . . 174 2 DON JUAN 2 34 3

PLUNDERED
AND NATURALLY THOUGHT THEY COULD HAVE PLUNDERED . . . . 149 3 DON JUAN 8 75 3

PLUNDERERS
THOSE CORNISH PLUNDERERS OF PARNASSIAN WRECKS . . . . . 403 2 DON JUAN 4 108 6

PLUNDERING
PRAYING INSTRUCTING DESOLATING PLUNDERING . . . . . . 95 3 DON JUAN 7 55 6

PLUNGE
MOST EPIC POETS PLUNGE IN MEDIAS RES . . . . 24 2 DON JUAN 1 6 1
(UNLESS AT ONCE SHE PLUNGE FOR LIFE IN PRAYERS)-- . . . 276 2 DON JUAN 3 4 3
AS A RESERVE A PLUNGE INTO REMORSE . . . . 349 3 DON JUAN 12 73 8
WITHOUT AN AWFUL WISH TO PLUNGE WITHIN IT . . . . . 412 3 DON JUAN 14 5 8
TO PLUNGE WITH ALL YOUR FEARS--BUT WHERE YOU KNOW NOT . 413 3 DON JUAN 14 6 7

PLUNGED
HIS LIKE ALL DEEP GRIEF PLUNGED IN SOLITUDE . . . . . . 68 2 DON JUAN 1 87 4
OR PLUNGED A PROVINCE OR A REALM IN GRIEF . . . . . 101 3 DON JUAN 7 68 4
HER HIDDEN FACE WAS PLUNGED AMIDST THE DEAD . . . . . 158 3 DON JUAN 8 93 3

PLURAL
SHE THEN PREFERS HIM IN THE PLURAL NUMBER . . . . . 276 2 DON JUAN 3 3 7

PLUTARCH'S
EVEN PLUTARCH'S LIVES HAVE BUT PICKED OUT A FEW . . . 324 3 DON JUAN 12 19 5

PLY
HE BUOY'D HIS BOYISH LIMBS AND STROVE TO PLY . . . . 212 2 DON JUAN 2 106 2

POACHER
HAD BAGGED THIS POACHER UPON NATURE'S MANOR . . . . . 531 3 DON JUAN 16 62 8

POACHERS
AND AH YE POACHERS--'TIS NO SPORT FOR PEASANTS . . . 394 3 DON JUAN 13 75 8
THERE WERE TWO POACHERS CAUGHT IN A STEEL TRAP . . . 530 3 DON JUAN 16 61 1
THE PRIZE PIG PLOUGHMAN POACHERS THE MEN SENT . . . 533 3 DON JUAN 16 66 4

POCKET
BUT KEEP YOUR HANDS OUT OF HIS BREECHES' POCKET . . . 264 3 DON JUAN 10 79 8

POCKET-HANDKERCHIEF
ANTONIA WHERE'S MY POCKET-HANDKERCHIEF . . . . . . 107 2 DON JUAN 1 157 8

POCKET-PISTOL
DREW FORTH A POCKET-PISTOL FROM HIS VESTURE . . . . . 274 3 DON JUAN 11 13 3

POCKETS
(SIGNS OF TRUE GENIUS AND OF EMPTY POCKETS) . . . . . 91 2 DON JUAN 1 129 2
HIS POCKETS FIRST AND THEN HIS BODY RIDDLED . . . . . 276 3 DON JUAN 11 17 8

POEM
FIT FOR MY POEM (THAT IS FOR MY NEW ONE) . . . . . 24 2 DON JUAN 1 5 7
CATULLUS SCARCELY HAS A DECENT POEM . . . . . . 45 2 DON JUAN 1 42 3
A DROWSY FROWZY POEM CALL'D THE EXCURSION . . . . . 330 2 DON JUAN 3 94 7
BUT WORDSWORTH'S POEM AND HIS FOLLOWERS LIKE . . . . 330 2 DON JUAN 3 95 3
AND TRACE IT IN THIS POEM EVERY LINE . . . . . 346 2 DON JUAN 4 5 3
BUT SPOIL (I THINK) A VERY PRETTY POEM . . . . . 403 2 DON JUAN 4 107 8
THIS POEM WILL BECOME A MORAL MODEL . . . . . . 412 2 DON JUAN 5 2 8
I'LL MAKE THIS POEM QUITE A MORAL MODEL . . . . . 412 2 DON JUAN 5 2 V8
THE PRESENT POEM--OF--I KNOW NOT WHAT-- . . . . . 67 3 DON JUAN 7 3 2
'TIS TIME WE SHOULD PROCEED WITH OUR GOOD POEM . . . . 193 3 DON JUAN 9 22 1
BUT NOW I WILL BEGIN MY POEM--'TIS . . . . . 341 3 DON JUAN 12 54 1
I MEANT TO MAKE THIS POEM VERY SHORT . . . . . 466 3 DON JUAN 15 22 3

POEM'S
MY POEM'S EPIC AND IS MEANT TO BE . . . . . . 135 2 DON JUAN 1 200 1
I QUITE FORGET THIS POEM'S MERELY QUIZZICAL . . . . . 203 3 DON JUAN 9 41 3
A POEM'S PROGRESS SHOULD BE PERPENDICULAR . . . . . 290 3 DON JUAN 11 44 V8

POEMS
SEASON'D HIS PEDLAR POEMS WITH DEMOCRACY . . . . . . 329 2 DON JUAN 3 93 4

615

		PAGE	VOL	CANTO	STANZA	LN

POEMS   (CONTINUED)

| WHO ADVERTISE NEW POEMS BY YOUR LOOKS | 403 | 2 DON JUAN | 4 | 108 | 3 |
| ON GENERAL TOPICS POEMS MUST CONFINE | 290 | 3 DON JUAN | 11 | 44 | 7 |

POESY

THAT POESY HAS WREATHS FOR YOU ALONE	12	2 DON JUAN	D	5	6
SO BY THE POESY OF HIS OWN MIND	72	2 DON JUAN	1	95	4
A THING WHICH POESY BUT SELDOM MENTIONS	221	2 DON JUAN	2	123	6
IN POESY UNLESS PERHAPS THE END	344	2 DON JUAN	4	1	2
MAKE EPIC POESY SO RARE AND RICH	156	2 DON JUAN	8	90	8
I WISH TO DO AS MUCH BY POESY	226	3 DON JUAN	10	3	8
UP ANNALS REVELATIONS POESY	286	3 DON JUAN	11	37	6
IS POESY ACCORDING AS THE MIND GLOWS	414	3 DON JUAN	14	8	4
APOLOGUE FABLE POESY AND PARABLE	495	3 DON JUAN	15	89	1

POET

BOB SOUTHEY YOU'RE A POET--POET-LAUREATE	9	2 DON JUAN	D	1	1
AND RECOLLECT A POET NOTHING LOSES	14	2 DON JUAN	D	8	5
THE POET MEANT NO DOUBT AND THUS APPEALS	69	2 DON JUAN	1	89	1
OR EVERY POET HIS OWN ARISTOTLE	138	2 DON JUAN	1	204	8
DWARFS DANCING GIRLS BLACK EUNUCHS AND A POET	316	2 DON JUAN	3	78	6
THEIR POET A SAD TRIMMER BUT NO LESS	318	2 DON JUAN	3	82	1
THEIR POET--A DAMNED RASCAL--BUT NO LESS	318	2 DON JUAN	3	82	V1
FOR WHAT IS LEFT THE POET HERE	323	2 DON JUAN	3	L 6	5
AND FEELING IN A POET IS THE SOURCE	326	2 DON JUAN	3	87	6
WHY THEN I'LL SWEAR AS POET WORDY SWORE	404	2 DON JUAN	4	109	5
BECAUSE ONE POET TRAVELLED 'MONGST THE TURKS)	434	2 DON JUAN	5	42	8
ALL THAT A POET DRAGS INTO DETAIL	60	3 DON JUAN	6	109	6
BY SAINT BY SAGE BY PREACHER AND BY POET	69	3 DON JUAN	7	6	6
AND OTHERS OF THEMSELVES AS POET SAMUEL IS	94	3 DON JUAN	7	54	V8
OF A TRUE POET TO ESCAPE FROM FICTION	154	3 DON JUAN	8	86	2
IN TWICE FIVE YEARS THE GREATEST LIVING POET	296	3 DON JUAN	11	55	1
WITHOUT THE AID OF TOO SINCERE A POET	311	3 DON JUAN	11	87	8
HE IS YOUR ONLY POET--PASSION PURE	319	3 DON JUAN	12	8	1
NOR WORN THE MOTLEY MANTLE OF A POET	467	3 DON JUAN	15	24	7
BUT STILL I AM OR WAS A PRETTY POET	482	3 DON JUAN	15	60	8
BUT LOVER POET OR ASTRONOMER	506	3 DON JUAN	16	14	1
WAS WEAK ENOUGH TO DEEM POPE A GREAT POET	524	3 DON JUAN	16	47	7

POETESS

| FOR ADELINE IS HALF A POETESS | 517 | 3 DON JUAN | 16 | 39 | 2 |

POETIC

THIS LIBERTY IS A POETIC LICENCE	86	2 DON JUAN	1	120	4
WITHOUT WHOSE EPOCH MY POETIC SKILL	86	2 DON JUAN	1	121	3
MY PEN AND LIKED POETIC WAR TO WAGE	397	2 DON JUAN	4	98	6
THIS IS A FACT AND NO POETIC FABLE--	428	2 DON JUAN	5	33	2
BY MERELY WIELDING WITH POETIC ARM	106	3 DON JUAN	7	79	3
FOR WHAT IS SOMETIMES CALLED POETIC DICTION	154	3 DON JUAN	8	86	6
THE HERO OF THIS GRAND POETIC RIDDLE	181	3 DON JUAN	8	139	3
OF NO GREAT PROMISE FOR POETIC PAGES	416	3 DON JUAN	14	15	8
I HAVE NOT HEARD SHE WAS AT ALL POETIC	525	3 DON JUAN	16	50	1

POETICAL

I'LL WRITE POETICAL COMMANDMENTS WHICH	138	2 DON JUAN	1	204	2
AND WORDSWORTH--BOTH POETICAL BUFFOONS	341	2 DON JUAN	3	110	V2
MUCH TOO POETICAL MEN SHOULD KNOW WHY	203	3 DON JUAN	9	41	6
AND IN-DOOR LIFE IS LESS POETICAL	423	3 DON JUAN	14	30	1

POET-LAUREATE

| BOB SOUTHEY YOU'RE A POET--POET-LAUREATE | 9 | 2 DON JUAN | D | 1 | 1 |

POETRY

'TIS POETRY--AT LEAST BY HIS ASSERTION	11	2 DON JUAN	D	4	5
DASH INTO POETRY WHICH IS BUT PASSION	402	2 DON JUAN	4	106	7
IF NOT IN POETRY AT LEAST IN FACT	107	3 DON JUAN	7	81	1
TALK ABOUT POETRY AND RACK AND MANGER	305	3 DON JUAN	11	74	6
(A THING WITH POETRY IN GENERAL HARD)	322	3 DON JUAN	12	13	4

POET'S

BUT THEN THEY SHONE NOT ON THE POET'S PAGE	24	2 DON JUAN	1	5	4
NOR GLOWING REVERIE NOR POET'S LAY	73	2 DON JUAN	1	96	3
THE ARAB LORE AND POET'S SONG WERE DONE	334	2 DON JUAN	3	101	3
THE CHIEFTAIN'S TROPHY AND THE POET'S VOLUME	400	2 DON JUAN	4	104	6
TRICKED OUT BUT MODEST MORE THAN POET'S PEN	380	2 DON JUAN	13	47	4
SAITH HORACE THE GREAT LITTLE POET'S WRONG	443	3 DON JUAN	14	77	2

POETS

YOU'RE SHABBY FELLOWS--TRUE--BUT POETS STILL	12	2 DON JUAN	D	6	7
MOST EPIC POETS PLUNGE IN MEDIAS RES	24	2 DON JUAN	1	6	1
THERE POETS FIND MATERIALS FOR THEIR BOOKS	70	2 DON JUAN	1	90	5
WHEN POETS SAY I'VE WRITTEN FIFTY RHYMES	79	2 DON JUAN	1	108	3
OF POETS AND ROMANCERS--YOU'RE A BORE	84	2 DON JUAN	1	116	6
WHICH MAKES SO MANY POETS AND SOME FOOLS	136	2 DON JUAN	1	201	4
PROSE POETS LIKE BLANK-VERSE I'M FOND OF RHYME	136	2 DON JUAN	1	201	5
OF CLAP-TRAP WHICH YOUR RECENT POETS PRIZE	222	2 DON JUAN	2	124	4
I HATE YOUR POETS SO READ NONE OF THOSE	243	2 DON JUAN	2	165	8
'TIS STRANGE THAT POETS NEVER TRY TO WREATHE	280	2 DON JUAN	3	9	V5
'TIS STRANGE THAT POETS OF THE CATHOLIC FAITH	280	2 DON JUAN	3	9	V5
(THE LEAST OF WHICH WOULD SET TEN POETS RAVING)	291	2 DON JUAN	3	30	6
FROM POETS OR THE MORALISTS THEIR BETTERS	308	2 DON JUAN	3	64	8
MILTON'S THE PRINCE OF POETS--SO WE SAY	328	2 DON JUAN	3	91	1
OF POETS WHO COME DOWN TO US THROUGH DISTANCE	398	2 DON JUAN	4	100	1
WHEN AMATORY POETS SING THEIR LOVES	411	2 DON JUAN	5	1	1
POETS AND PRIVATE TUTORS ARE EXPOSED	486	2 DON JUAN	5	131	5
ALSO THE EIGHTY GREATEST LIVING POETS	295	3 DON JUAN	11	54	7
WITH POETS ALMOST CLERGYMEN OR WHOLLY	297	3 DON JUAN	11	57	4
AMONGST LIVE POETS AND BLUE LADIES PAST	300	3 DON JUAN	11	64	2

```
                                                                    PAGE VOL      CANTO    STANZA LV
POETS    (CONTINUED)
      I HAVE SEEN SMALL POETS AND GREAT PROSERS AND   . . . . .  310   3 DON JUAN 11        85    1
      THAT POETS WERE SO FROM THEIR EARLIEST DATE . . . . . . .  393   3 DON JUAN 13        74    5
      THE POETS OF ARITHMETIC ARE THEY  . . . . . . . . . . .    548   3 DON JUAN 16        99    1
POIETIKES
      FROM ARISTOTLE PASSIM--SEE POIETIKES  . . . . . . . . .    342   2 DON JUAN  3       111    8
POINT
      IN THAT POINT SO PRECISE IN EACH DEGREE  . . . . . . .      52   2 DON JUAN  1        57    5
      HE GAIN'D NO POINT EXCEPT SOME SELF-REBUKES . . . . . .    110   2 DON JUAN  1       161    5
      SO THESE POINT THE EPIGRAM OF HUMAN BREATH  . . . . .      280   2 DON JUAN  3         9   V3
      BY SETTING THINGS IN THEIR RIGHT POINT OF VIEW  . . . .    422   2 DON JUAN  5        23    5
      WAS ON THE POINT OF BEING SET ASIDE   . . . . . . . .      440   2 DON JUAN  5        51    4
      HE CHOSE HIMSELF TO POINT OUT WHAT HE THOUGHT  . . . .     450   2 DON JUAN  5        67    7
      BUT TO THE MAIN POINT WHERE WE HAVE BEEN TENDING--  . .    478   2 DON JUAN  5       116    1
      IN CITIES CAGED THE PRESENT CASE IN POINT I  . . . . .     143   3 DON JUAN  8        62    7
      HER LIFE TO CHANCE BUT POINT ME OUT SOME NOOK  . . . .     161   3 DON JUAN  8        99    3
      TO TAKE HIM WAS THE POINT THE TRULY BRAVE  . . . . . .     164   3 DON JUAN  8       106    1
      THE SOLDIERS WHO BEHELD HIM DROP HIS POINT  . . . . .      170   3 DON JUAN  8       117    1
      SHOULD SO CONTINUE--'TIS A POINT OF HONOUR  . . . . .      231   3 DON JUAN 10        12    2
      NO TITLE TO POINT OUT WITH DUE PRECISION . . . . . . .     283   3 DON JUAN 11        32    3
      IN ONE POINT ONLY WERE YOU SETTLED--AND  . . . . . .       329   3 DON JUAN 12        29    1
      THE WIND IS WINGED FROM ONE POINT OF HEAVEN  . . . . .     388   3 DON JUAN 13        63    2
      THAT IS UP TO A CERTAIN POINT WHICH POINT  . . . . .       396   3 DON JUAN 13        81    1
      THAT IS UP TO A CERTAIN POINT WHICH POINT  . . . . .       396   3 DON JUAN 13        81    1
      OR (TO THE POINT WITH HORACE AND WITH PULCI)  . . . .      396   3 DON JUAN 13        81    7
      BUT TILL THAT POINT D'APPUI IS FOUND ALAS  . . . . . .     446   3 DON JUAN 14        84    7
      AND THEN HE HAD GOOD LOOKS--THAT POINT WAS CARRIED  . .    493   3 DON JUAN 15        84    1
POINTED
      AS DRESS YOURSELF-- AND POINTED OUT A SUIT  . . . . .      453   2 DON JUAN  5        73    2
      POINTED TO JUAN WHO REMAINED BELOW . . . . . . . . . .     466   2 DON JUAN  5        96    8
      WERE POINTED OUT AS USUAL BY THE BEDRAL  . . . . . .       261   3 DON JUAN 10        73    3
POINTER
      THE POINTER RANGES AND THE SPORTSMAN BEATS  . . . . .      394   3 DON JUAN 13        75    4
POINTS
      (AND OTHER CHIEF POINTS OF A BELLA DONNA)  . . . . .       395   2 DON JUAN  4        94    4
      AT LEAST THE SHARP POINTS OF THAT BURNING MARLE  . . .     124   3 DON JUAN  8        26   V7
      WHICH ROUSSEAU POINTS OUT TO THE DUBIOUS FAIR  . . . .     139   3 DON JUAN  8        53    6
      AND ALL HER POINTS AS THOROUGH-BRED TO SHOW . . . . .      330   3 DON JUAN 12        31    6
      TO SHOW IT--(POINTS WE NEED NOT NOW DISCUSS)--  . . .      460   3 DON JUAN 15        10    5
      UPON ALL POINTS-- NO MATTER WHAT OR WHOSE--  . . . . .     564   3 DON JUAN 17         6    2
POISON
      AND OFFER POISON LONG ALREADY MIX'D  . . . . . . . . .      16   2 DON JUAN  D        12    8
      TO FEEL THE POISON THROUGH HER SPIRIT CREEPING  . . .      274   2 DON JUAN  3         1    5
      IT WAS AS IF THEIR LITTLE LOOKS COULD POISON  . . . .      463   2 DON JUAN  5        90    7
      AND WITHOUT THAT THEIR POISON AND THEIR CLAWS  . . . .     196   3 DON JUAN  9        28    2
POISONED
      SOME SAID HE HAD BEEN POISONED BY POTEMKIN  . . . . .      244   3 DON JUAN 10        40    2
POISON-TREE
      BUT THERE TOO MANY A POISON-TREE HAS ROOT  . . . . .       373   2 DON JUAN  4        55    4
POKE
      AND MORE MIGHT BE FOUND OUT IF I COULD POKE ENOUGH   . .    74   3 DON JUAN  7        15    6
POLAND
      THEY JOURNEYED ON THROUGH POLAND AND THROUGH WARSAW  . .   253   3 DON JUAN 10        58    1
      THROUGH POLAND THERE IS KOSCIUSKO'S NAME  . . . . . .      254   3 DON JUAN 10        59    7
      FROM POLAND THEY CAME ON THROUGH PRUSSIA PROPER  . . .     254   3 DON JUAN 10        60    1
POLAR
      HIS POLAR STAR BEING ONE WHICH RATHER RANGES  . . . .      317   2 DON JUAN  3        80    3
      THE SUN WHICH YEARLY MELTS THE POLAR ICE . . . . . . .     501   2 DON JUAN  5       157    7
      THERE'S NOT A METEOR IN THE POLAR SKY . . . . . . . .       66   3 DON JUAN  7         1    3
      HE WROTE THIS POLAR MELODY AND SET IT . . . . . . . .      179   3 DON JUAN  8       135    1
      THOSE POLAR SUMMERS ALL SUN AND SOME ICE . . . . . .       349   3 DON JUAN 12        72    8
POLE
      SO SHAKES THE NEEDLE AND SO STANDS THE POLE  . . . . .     133   2 DON JUAN  1       196    7
      AS TURNS THE NEEDLE TREMBLING TO THE POLE  . . . . .       133   2 DON JUAN  1       196   V7
      BY THE NORTH POLE--THEY SOUGHT HER CAUSE OF CARE  . . .     42   3 DON JUAN  6        72    6
      THEIR GOODS AND EDICTS OUT FROM POLE TO POLE  . . . .      257   3 DON JUAN 10        65    7
      THEIR GOODS AND EDICTS OUT FROM POLE TO POLE  . . . .      257   3 DON JUAN 10        65    7
      WHERE'S BRUMMELL DISHED WHERE'S LONG POLE WELLESLEY DIDDLED 307   3 DON JUAN 11        78    1
      HAVE NOT EXACTLY ASCERTAINED THE POLE . . . . . . . .      376   3 DON JUAN 13        39    4
      PROPORTION'D AS A POPLAR OR A POLE . . . . . . . . .       441   3 DON JUAN 14        71    5
      WITH SELF-LOVE IN THE CENTRE AS THEIR POLE  . . . . .      455   3 DON JUAN 14       102    4
POLE'S
      FOR IF THE POLE'S NOT OPEN BUT ALL FROST . . . . . . .     376   3 DON JUAN 13        39    7
POLES
      TOMBUCTOO TRAVELS VOYAGES TO THE POLES   . . . . . . .      93   2 DON JUAN  1       132    6
POLICY
      BUT POLITICS AND POLICY AND PIETY . . . . . . . . . .      497   3 DON JUAN 15        93    1
POLISH
      (HERE HE CALLED UP A POLISH ORDERLY)  . . . . . . . .      100   3 DON JUAN  7        66    4
      THAT CALM PATRICIAN POLISH IN THE ADDRESS  . . . . . .     373   3 DON JUAN 13        34    2
      THAT POLISH OF INDIFFERENCE--IN THE MANNER  . . . . .      373   3 DON JUAN 13        34   V2
      IF BUT TO SET ITS EDGE TO A FRESH POLISH . . . . . . .     433   3 DON JUAN 14        53   V7
POLISH'D
      BUT STRONGBOW'S WIT WAS OF MORE POLISH'D BREED  . . . .    401   3 DON JUAN 13        92    4
      SOCIETY IS NOW ONE POLISH'D HORDE  . . . . . . . . .       402   3 DON JUAN 13        95    7
      IN THIS OUR PARTY POLISH'D SMOOTH AND COLD  . . . . .      409   3 DON JUAN 13       110    2
POLISHED
      THE POLISHED CHIEF WHO DEIGNED TO SMILE  . . . . . .       321   2 DON JUAN  3    L   2   V1
      OF ALL THE CUSTOMS OF THIS POLISHED NATION  . . . . .      452   2 DON JUAN  5        70    8
```

	PAGE	VOL	CANTO	STANZA	LN
POLISHED (CONTINUED)					
THAN THOUSANDS OF THIS NEW AND POLISHED NATION	73	3	DON JUAN 7	14	7
HAS FEELINGS PURE AND POLISHED AS A GEM--	157	3	DON JUAN 8	92	4
OF THE IMMORTAL PETER'S POLISHED BOORS	194	3	DON JUAN 9	23	3
AND AVARICE--DISGUST A POLISHED NATION	223	3	DON JUAN 9	81	V8
DON JUAN GREW A VERY POLISHED RUSSIAN--	235	3	DON JUAN 10	21	1
POLITE					
E'ER SAW HER MOST POLITE OF SONS EXCEEDING	299	2	DON JUAN 3	46	4
HIS MAJESTY WAS ALWAYS SO POLITE	495	2	DON JUAN 5	146	4
BECAUSE IT MIGHT NOT SOLACE EARS POLITE	158	3	DON JUAN 8	93	6
TO ALL SHE WAS POLITE WITHOUT PARADE	372	3	DON JUAN 13	32	1
THE WORLD (AS SINCE THAT HISTORY LESS POLITE	420	3	DON JUAN 14	23	2
POLITELY					
THE MOMENT AFTER HE POLITELY ENDS	200	2	DON JUAN 2	83	4
POLITENESS					
FOR TRUE OR FALSE POLITENESS (AND SCARCE THAT	290	3	DON JUAN 11	44	2
IF THAT POLITENESS SET IT NOT APART	326	3	DON JUAN 12	22	5
NOR LESS APPLAUDS AS IN POLITENESS BOUND	521	3	DON JUAN 16	41	6
THE WARMTH OF HER POLITENESS WHOSE SINCERITY	550	3	DON JUAN 16	102	2
POLITESSE					
THOUGH BY THIS POLITESSE SHE RATHER SUFFERED	36	3	DON JUAN 6	61	6
IN POLITESSE AND HAVE A SOUND AFFRONTING IN'T--	289	3	DON JUAN 11	43	6
POLITICAL					
WILL TURN UPON POLITICAL ECONOMY	356	3	DON JUAN 12	88	8
POLITICIAN					
(NO MATTER WHICH) TURN POLITICIAN STUPIDER	309	3	DON JUAN 11	83	3
CONVINCES ALL MEN EVEN A POLITICIAN	478	3	DON JUAN 15	51	6
POLITICIANS					
OF POLITICIANS AND THEIR DOUBLE FRONT	285	3	DON JUAN 11	36	4
THE POLITICIANS IN A NOOK APART	408	3	DON JUAN 13	109	1
POLITICS					
MY POLITICS AS YET ARE ALL TO EDUCATE	20	2	DON JUAN D	17	5
AND FIGHT LIKE FIENDS FOR PAY OR POLITICS	122	3	DON JUAN 8	22	8
STATISTICS TACTICS POLITICS AND GEOGRAPHY)--	149	3	DON JUAN 8	74	4
OR PLEASURE WHO MAKE POLITICS RUN GLIBBER ALL	318	3	DON JUAN 12	5	6
BUT I AM SICK OF POLITICS BEGIN	327	3	DON JUAN 12	25	1
ESPECIALLY WITH POLITICS ON HAND	435	3	DON JUAN 14	58	4
IN POLITICS MY DUTY IS TO SHOW JOHN	497	3	DON JUAN 15	92	5
BUT POLITICS AND POLICY AND PIETY	497	3	DON JUAN 15	93	1
POLL					
TO HEAD THE POLL I WONDER WHO WOULD BUY IT	154	2	DON JUAN 1	V 5	4
POLLUTION					
LIKE THE PROMETHEAN VULTURE THIS POLLUTION	195	2	DON JUAN 2	75	4
ALONE CAN SAVE THE EARTH FROM HELL'S POLLUTION	138	3	DON JUAN 8	51	8
POLOUZKI					
MARCHED WITH THE BRAVE BATTALION OF POLOUZKI--	150	3	DON JUAN 8	76	8
POLYCRATES					
HE SERVED--BUT SERVED POLYCRATES--	324	2	DON JUAN 3	L 11	4
POLYGAMY					
POLYGAMY MAY WELL BE HELD IN DREAD	12	3	DON JUAN 6	12	3
BUT FLANKED BY FIVE BRAVE SONS (SUCH IS POLYGAMY	164	3	DON JUAN 8	105	1
POLYGAMY'S					
BUT THEN THEIR OWN POLYGAMY'S TO BLAME	502	2	DON JUAN 5	158	6
POMEGRANATE					
THE ORANGE AND POMEGRANATE NODDING O'ER	291	2	DON JUAN 3	31	7
OF RAISIN ORANGE AND POMEGRANATE JUICE	307	2	DON JUAN 3	62	7
POMEGRANATES					
CRIMSON AS CLEFT POMEGRANATES THEIR LONG TRESSES	292	2	DON JUAN 3	33	3
POMMELL'D					
ALFONSO POMMELL'D TO HIS HEART'S DESIRE	122	2	DON JUAN 1	184	4
POMP					
THE ASIAN POMP OF OTTOMAN PARADE	440	2	DON JUAN 5	51	8
WITH ALL THE POMP OF POWER IT WAS A DOUBT	104	3	DON JUAN 7	74	7
ANNOUNCED WITH NO LESS POMP THAN VICTORY'S WINNER	383	3	DON JUAN 13	54	3
POMPEY					
CAESAR AND POMPEY MAHOMET BELISARIUS	266	2	DON JUAN 2	206	3
POMPILIUS					
AS NUMA'S (WHO WAS ALSO NAMED POMPILIUS)	40	2	DON JUAN 1	35	7
PONDER					
WE PONDER DEEPLY ON EACH PAST EMOTION	345	2	DON JUAN 4	2	8
JUST PONDER WHAT A PIOUS PASTIME WAR IS	174	3	DON JUAN 8	124	8
DEATH LAUGHS--GO PONDER O'ER THE SKELETON	188	3	DON JUAN 9	11	1
SHE 'GAN TO PONDER HOW TO SAVE HIS SOUL	468	3	DON JUAN 15	28	8
PONDER'D					
AND WHILE SHE PONDER'D THIS BESIDES MUCH MORE	80	2	DON JUAN 1	109	6
BUT OTHERS PONDER'D ON A NEW DISSECTION	199	2	DON JUAN 2	80	5
ON WHAT I'VE SEEN OR PONDER'D SAD OR CHEERY	415	3	DON JUAN 14	11	6
PONDERED					
BUT JUAN WAS NO CASUIST NOR HAD PONDERED	353	3	DON JUAN 12	81	1
PONDERED UPON HIS VISITANT OR VISION	512	3	DON JUAN 16	28	2
PONDERING					
SURVEYING DRILLING ORDERING JESTING PONDERING	95	3	DON JUAN 7	55	2
AND PONDERING ON THE PRESENT AND THE PAST	142	3	DON JUAN 8	60	7
PONDERING ON GLORY CHIVALRY AND KINGS	197	3	DON JUAN 9	30	4
NOW PONDERING--IT IS TIME WE SHOULD NARRATE	203	3	DON JUAN 9	42	2
MAY PAUSE IN PONDERING HOW ALL SOULS ARE DIPT	210	3	DON JUAN 9	55	4
PONIARD					
A PONIARD DECKED HER GIRDLE AS THE SIGN	475	2	DON JUAN 5	111	7
SO THAT A PONIARD PIERCES IF 'TIS STUCK HARD	492	2	DON JUAN 5	140	4

618

PONTIC
   WHERE ALL THE PONTIC SPOILS MADE SUCH A SHOW 485   3 DON JUAN 15   67 V3
POOH
   OUR MISTRESS QUOTH A THIRD OUR MISTRESS--POOH-- 297   2 DON JUAN 3   43   7
   OR A HA HA OR BAH--A YAWN OR POOH 456   3 DON JUAN 15   1   7
   YE POWERS IT IS THE--THE--THE--POOH THE CAT 556   3 DON JUAN 16   112   3
POOR
   AND HEARTLESS DAUGHTERS--WORN--AND PALE--AND POOR 15   2 DON JUAN 0   11   6
   POOR FELLOW HE HAD MANY THINGS TO WOUND HIM 41   2 DON JUAN 1   36   2
   POOR JULIA'S HEART WAS IN AN AWKWARD STATE 62   2 DON JUAN 1   75   1
   POOR LITTLE FELLOW HE HAD NO IDEA 68   2 DON JUAN 1   86   2
   POOR DONNA JULIA STARTING AS FROM SLEEP 97   2 DON JUAN 1   140   1
   APPEAR'D LIKE TWO POOR HARMLESS WOMEN WHO 98   2 DON JUAN 1   141   2
   POOR FELLOW HE HAD BETTER FAR BEEN BLIND 155   2 DON JUAN 1 V 7   4
   BUT HE POOR FELLOW HAD A WIFE AND CHILDREN 179   2 DON JUAN 2   43   7
   WHICH COURAGE GIVES WHILE POOR PEDRILLO'S PAIR 186   2 DON JUAN 2   56   5
   AND THE POOR LITTLE CUTTER QUICKLY SWAMP'D 188   2 DON JUAN 2   60   8
   THE SAILORS ATE THE REST OF POOR PEDRILLO 197   2 DON JUAN 2   77   8
   OF POOR PEDRILLO SOMETHING STILL REMAIN'D 200   2 DON JUAN 2   82   1
   HAVE SUCH A CHARM FOR US POOR HUMAN CREATURES 267   2 DON JUAN 2   208   8
   THE PEASANTS GAVE THE POOR DUMB THING A PITTANCE 285   2 DON JUAN 3   18   6
   NOT SOUND POOR FELLOW BUT SEVERELY WOUNDED 373   2 DON JUAN 4   54   2
   POOR CREATURES THEIR GOOD LOOKS WERE SADLY CHANGED 414   2 DON JUAN 5   7   4
   POOR FELLOW FOR SOME REASON SURELY BAD 429   2 DON JUAN 5   34   1
   SHE THOUGHT OF KILLING JUAN--BUT POOR LAD 492   2 DON JUAN 5   140   5
   TO POOR KATINKA SPAIN'S AN ISLAND NEAR 28   3 DON JUAN 6   44   7
   AND CHAFED AT POOR DUDU WHO ONLY SIGHED 45   3 DON JUAN 6   79   7
   AND POOR JUANNA TOO THE CHILD'S FIRST NIGHT 46   3 DON JUAN 6   81   1
   BUT POOR DUDU WITH LARGE DROPS IN HER OWN 47   3 DON JUAN 6   82   2
   INTO THEIR ANNALS AND PERSUADE POOR FAME 74   3 DON JUAN 7   15 V7
   NO MATTER WHAT POOR SOULS MIGHT BE UNDONE 78   3 DON JUAN 7   23   5
   TO THEM POOR THINGS IT IS AN AWKWARD STEP 103   3 DON JUAN 7   72   6
   MEANTIME THESE TWO POOR GIRLS WITH SWIMMING EYES 104   3 DON JUAN 7   73   1
   WHEN MY POOR GREECE WAS ONCE AS NOW SURROUNDED 108   3 DON JUAN 7   82   4
   POOR THING WHAT'S TO BE DONE I'M PUZZLED QUITE 161   3 DON JUAN 8   99   8
   HOWEVER THE POOR JACKALLS ARE LESS FOUL 196   3 DON JUAN 9   27   6
   CORRUPTION FOR ITS CROP) WITH THE POOR DEVILS 237   3 DON JUAN 10   25   6
   SHE WAS NO HYPOCRITE AT LEAST POOR SOUL 242   3 DON JUAN 10   35   1
   POOR LITTLE THING SHE WAS AS FAIR AS DOCILE 250   3 DON JUAN 10   52   1
   THE POOR MAN'S SPARKLING SUBSTITUTE FOR RICHES 256   3 DON JUAN 10   63   4
   IS THE POOR PRIVILEGE TO TURN THE KEY 258   3 DON JUAN 10   68   5
   PREACH TO POOR ROUGES AND WHEREFORE NOT BEGIN 266   3 DON JUAN 10   85   2
   POOR TOM WAS ONCE A KIDDY UPON TOWN 276   3 DON JUAN 11   17   5
   POOR FELLOW HIS WAS AN UNTOWARD FATE-- 298   3 DON JUAN 11   60   6
   LIFE'S A POOR PLAYER --THEN PLAY OUT THE PLAY 310   3 DON JUAN 11   86   4
   WHILE THE POOR RICH WRETCH OBJECT OF THESE CARES 331   3 DON JUAN 12   33   7
   POOR FREDERICK WHY DID SHE ACCORD PERUSALS 332   3 DON JUAN 12   34   6
   AND AFTER ALL POOR FREDERICK MAY DO BETTER-- 332   3 DON JUAN 12   35   7
   POOR THING EVE'S WAS A TRIFLING CASE TO HER'S 345   3 DON JUAN 12   64   8
   POOR THING HOW FREQUENTLY BY ME AND OTHERS 374   3 DON JUAN 13   36   7
   ALAS POOR GHOST--WHAT UNEXPECTED WOES 403   3 DON JUAN 13   97   7
   WHEN HE ALLURED POOR DOLON--YOU HAD BETTER 407   3 DON JUAN 13   105   7
   POOR THING OF USAGES COERC'D COMPELL'D 420   3 DON JUAN 14   23   5
   POOR LORD AUGUSTUS FITZ-PLANTAGENET 429   3 DON JUAN 14   44   8
   WHATE'ER THOU TAKEST SPARE AWHILE POOR BEAUTY 459   3 DON JUAN 15   9   1
   POOR SOUL FOR SHE WAS COUNTRY BORN AND BRED 532   3 DON JUAN 16   64   6
   WHICH THE POOR THING AT TIMES ESSAYED TO DRY 532   3 DON JUAN 16   65   3
   BUT THIS POOR GIRL WAS LEFT IN THE GREAT HALL 533   3 DON JUAN 16   67   1
   OF THE POOR PARTRIDGE THROUGH HIS STUBBLE SCREEN 539   3 DON JUAN 16   80   5
   THE POOR PRIEST WAS REDUCED TO COMMON SENSE 540   3 DON JUAN 16   83   6
POPE
   THOU SHALT BELIEVE IN MILTON DRYDEN POPE 139   2 DON JUAN 1   205   1
   OF POPE AND DRYDEN ARE WE COME TO THIS 334   2 DON JUAN 3   100   2
   OH POPE WOULD THAT THOU WERT LIVING FOR THEIR SAKES . . 334   2 DON JUAN 3   100 V7
   FROM ALL THE POPE MAKES YEARLY 'TWOULD PERPLEX 391   2 DON JUAN 4   86   7
   AND THUS POPE QUOTES THE PRECEPT TO RE-TEACH 470   2 DON JUAN 5   101   6
   WOULD POPE HAVE SUNG OR HORACE BEEN INSPIRED 470   2 DON JUAN 5   101   8
   TO ANY SHOE UNLESS IT SHOD THE POPE 470   2 DON JUAN 5   102   8
   WITH THOSE WHO POPE SAYS GREATLY DARING DINE 383   3 DON JUAN 13   53   6
   AND THE POPE THUNDER EXCOMMUNICATION 478   3 DON JUAN 15   50   4
   WAS WEAK ENOUGH TO DEEM POPE A GREAT POET 524   3 DON JUAN 16   47   7
POPE'S
   ('TIS POPE'S PHRASE) A GREAT LONGING THO' A RASH ONE . . 216   3 DON JUAN 9   68   6
POPLAR
   PROPORTION'D AS A POPLAR OR A POLE 441   3 DON JUAN 14   71   5
POPLARS
   LIKE POPLARS WITH GOOD PRINCIPLES FOR ROOTS 343   3 DON JUAN 12   59   4
POPPIES
   RATHER THAN REST INSTEAD OF POPPIES WILLOWS 555   3 DON JUAN 16   110   5
POPPING
   OF NIGHT WHICH ROBE THE CHAMBER OR WHERE POPPING 442   2 DON JUAN 5   55   5
POPULAR
   BECAUSE THE ARMY'S GROWN MORE POPULAR 23   2 DON JUAN 1   4   5
   THE GLORIOUS MEED OF POPULAR APPLAUSE 318   2 DON JUAN 3   82   7
   WITH CLOWNISH HEEL YOUR POPULAR CIRCULATION 200   3 DON JUAN 9   35   7
POPULARITY
   THAT IS YOUR PRESENT THEME FOR POPULARITY 357   3 DON JUAN 12   89   1
POPULATION
   THE POPULATION THERE SO SPREADS THEY SAY 92   2 DON JUAN 1   131   3

PORCELAIN
CRYSTAL AND MARBLE PLATE AND PORCELAIN . . . . 310 2 DON JUAN 3 68 1
THE PRECIOUS PORCELAIN OF HUMAN CLAY . . . . 350 2 DON JUAN 4 11 3
OF PORCELAIN HELD IN THE FETTERED FLOWERS . . . . . . 54 3 DON JUAN 6 97 7
PORCH
FOR HE'S SEEN IN THE PORCH AND HE'S SEEN IN THE CHURCH . . 518 3 DON JUAN 16 L 2 7
PORCO
SAYING OUR PORCO OF AN IMPRESARIO . . . . 389 2 DON JUAN 4 82 V2
PORCUPINE
MAKING A WOMAN LIKE A PORCUPINE . . . . 37 3 DON JUAN 6 62 1
PORED
HE PORED UPON THE LEAVES AND ON THE FLOWERS . . . . . 72 2 DON JUAN 1 94 1
PORK
AND WITH A PIECE OF PORK MOREOVER MET . . . . 181 2 DON JUAN 2 47 6
RELIEVED ITSELF BY PORK FOR GREATER GLORY . . . . . . 483 3 DON JUAN 15 63 8
POROUS
AND SHERBET COOLING IN THE POROUS VASE . . . . . . 291 2 DON JUAN 3 31 5
PORPHYRY
MOTHER OF PEARL AND PORPHYRY AND MARBLE . . . . . . 55 3 DON JUAN 6 98 1
PORT
WAS STEERING DULY FOR THE PORT LEGHORN . . . . . . 169 2 DON JUAN 2 24 2
BY NAME--WAS DESTINED FOR THE PORT LEGHORN . . . . . 169 2 DON JUAN 2 24 V2
SHE GAVE A HEEL AND THEN A LURCH TO PORT . . . . . . 183 2 DON JUAN 2 51 7
HIS PORT LAY ON THE OTHER SIDE O' THE ISLE . . . . . 285 2 DON JUAN 3 19 8
HIS HIGHNESS WAS A MAN OF SOLEMN PORT . . . . . . 495 2 DON JUAN 5 147 1
ENOUGH TO MAKE FOR PORT ERE TIME SHALL SUMMON . . . . 376 3 DON JUAN 13 40 4
PORTAL
TILL A GIGANTIC PORTAL THROUGH THE GLOOM . . . . . . 460 2 DON JUAN 5 85 4
THIS MASSY PORTAL STOOD AT THE WIDE CLOSE . . . . . 462 2 DON JUAN 5 87 1
TO HEAVING BACK THE PORTAL FOLDS IT SCARED . . . . . 463 2 DON JUAN 5 90 4
THAT WHICH A PORTAL TO THEIR EYES DID SEEM-- . . . . . 148 3 DON JUAN 8 72 6
PORTAL'S
BE READY BY THE SECRET PORTAL'S SIDE . . . . 62 3 DON JUAN 6 113 3
PORTENTOUS
IS THAT PORTENTOUS PHRASE I TOLD YOU SO . . . . . . 432 3 DON JUAN 14 50 3
PORTER
ALTHOUGH THEIR PORTER AFTERWARDS CONFESS'D . . . . . 34 2 DON JUAN 1 24 5
AS A FULL POT OF PORTER TO THEIR THINKING . . . . . 201 2 DON JUAN 2 85 7
THE PORTER SOME SLIGHT SCANDALS STRANGE AND QUAINT . . 418 3 DON JUAN 14 19 5
PORT-HOLE
AND THE WAVES OOZING THROUGH THE PORT-HOLE MADE . . . 169 2 DON JUAN 2 25 7
PORTINGALE
WITH TU MI CHAMAS'S FROM PORTINGALE . . . . 523 3 DON JUAN 16 45 7
PORTION
A CERTAIN PORTION OF UNCERTAIN PAPER . . . . 146 2 DON JUAN 1 218 2
A PORTION OF THEIR BEEF UP FROM BELOW . . . . . . 181 2 DON JUAN 2 47 5
LIFE SEEMS THE SMALLEST PORTION OF EXISTENCE . . . . 398 2 DON JUAN 4 100 3
THE YOUNGER PORTION STOOD--A LUCKLESS VICTIM . . . . 409 2 DON JUAN 4 116 V7
A PORTION OF YOUR FADING TWILIGHT HUES . . . . . . 108 3 DON JUAN 7 82 7
BUT OF THE PORTION WHICH ATTACKED BY WATER . . . . . 116 3 DON JUAN 8 9 2
FOR I HAVE SEEN A PORTION OF THAT SAME . . . . . . 414 3 DON JUAN 14 9 2
THE PORTION OF THIS WORLD WHICH I AT PRESENT . . . . 416 3 DON JUAN 14 15 1
PORTION'D
WAS KILL'D AND PORTION'D OUT FOR PRESENT EATING . . . 193 2 DON JUAN 2 70 8
PORTIONED
THESE AT SOME CERTAIN PORTIONED HOURS WERE SPREAD . . 310 2 DON JUAN 3 69 V6
PORTIONS
EXCEPT SOME CERTAIN PORTIONS OF THE PREY . . . . . 284 2 DON JUAN 3 17 3
OF CARE OR GAIN THE GREEN WOODS WERE THEIR PORTIONS . . 145 3 DON JUAN 8 66 4
WHICH PORTIONS OUT UPON THE JUDGMENT DAY . . . . . . 242 3 DON JUAN 10 35 4
PORTMANTEAU
BEHIND THEIR CARRIAGES THEIR NEW PORTMANTEAU . . . . 165 2 DON JUAN 2 16 7
PORTMANTEAUS
AND THOUGH THESE LINES SHOULD ONLY LINE PORTMANTEAUS . . 416 3 DON JUAN 14 14 7
PORTRAIT
TO THE TRUE PORTRAIT OF ONE BATTLE-FIELD . . . . . 117 3 DON JUAN 8 12 8
THE REAL PORTRAIT OF THE HIGHEST TRIBE . . . . . . 418 3 DON JUAN 14 20 7
PORTRAITS
TO THE SWEET PORTRAITS OF THE VIRGIN MARY . . . . . 235 2 DON JUAN 2 149 8
OLD PORTRAITS FROM OLD WALLS UPON ME SCOWL-- . . . . 499 3 DON JUAN 15 97 5
BUT BY DIM LIGHTS THE PORTRAITS OF THE DEAD . . . . 508 3 DON JUAN 16 17 7
PORTUGAL
THE LAST WAR--MUCH THE SAME IN PORTUGAL . . . . . . 320 2 DON JUAN 3 86 4
POSE
WHICH IF IT DOES NOT SILENCE STILL MUST POSE . . . . 117 2 DON JUAN 1 175 5
HER EYES WERE ELOQUENT HER WORDS WOULD POSE . . . . 236 2 DON JUAN 2 150 5
TWO WEEDS WHICH POSE OUR ECONOMIC CATOS . . . . . 472 3 DON JUAN 15 37 8
POSED
THE LETTER OPEN WITH AN AIR WHICH POSED . . . . . 211 3 DON JUAN 9 58 4
THE MORE HE THOUGHT THE MORE HIS MIND WAS POSED . . . 512 3 DON JUAN 16 28 5
POSITION
OF HIS POSITION I CAN GIVE NO NOTION . . . . 113 2 DON JUAN 1 168 1
PERHAPS THIS NEW POSITION--BUT I'M RIGHT . . . . . 348 3 DON JUAN 12 71 5
POSITIONS
WAS ONE OF THEIR MOST FAVOURITE POSITIONS . . . . . 191 3 DON JUAN 9 17 4
POSITIVE
'TIS SO SENTENTIOUS POSITIVE AND TERSE . . . . . . 17 3 DON JUAN 6 23 6
POSITIVELY
AND POSITIVELY HENCEFORTH NO TEMPTATION . . . . . . 498 3 DON JUAN 15 94 2

620

	PAGE	VOL	CANTO	STANZA	LV
POSSE					
WITH HIM RETIRED HIS POSSE COMITATUS	111	2 DON JUAN	1	164	1
POSSESS					
OH TO POSSESS SUCH LUSTRE--AND THEN LACK	381	2 DON JUAN	4	69	8
POSSESS'D					
I THINK THE FOOLISH PEOPLE WERE POSSESS'D	34	2 DON JUAN	1	24	3
POSSESS'D AN AIR AND GRACE BY NO MEANS COMMON	55	2 DON JUAN	1	61	7
POSSESS'D THE ORE OF WHICH MERE HOPES ALLURE	319	3 DON JUAN	12	8	3
BUT NONE OF THESE POSSESS'D A STING TO WOUND HER--	435	3 DON JUAN	14	57	3
POSSESSION					
ALL THESE ARE LITTLE PRELUDES TO POSSESSION	62	2 DON JUAN	1	74	5
MOST LOVE POSSESSION UNTO THEM APPEAR'D	352	2 DON JUAN	4	16	7
UPON ALL LEGAL OBJECTS OF POSSESSION	11	3 DON JUAN	6	10	2
A KING IN CONSTITUTIONAL POSSESSION	354	3 DON JUAN	12	83	3
WAS FAINT AS OF AN EVERY-DAY POSSESSION	372	3 DON JUAN	13	31	8
WHAT HOPE REMAINS OF HOPE THE FULL POSSESSION	379	3 DON JUAN	13	45	4
POSSESSOR					
THOUGH PRINCES THE POSSESSOR WERE BESIEGING ALL	528	3 DON JUAN	16	56	4
POSSESSORS					
BY THEIR POSSESSORS THROWN INTO THE SHADE	485	2 DON JUAN	5	129	6
UNKNOWN TO THOSE POSSESSORS--OR UNDISPLAYED	485	2 DON JUAN	5	129	V6
POSSIBLE					
ALL THE ATTENTION POSSIBLE AND SEEN	102	3 DON JUAN	7	70	4
FOR I WILL TEACH IF POSSIBLE THE STONES	179	3 DON JUAN	8	135	4
IF POSSIBLE AND THIRDLY NEVER FLINCH	404	3 DON JUAN	13	98	6
POSSIBLY					
HOW COULD HE POSSIBLY SHOW THINGS EXISTENT	494	3 DON JUAN	15	87	8
POSSIDETIS					
WHICH BRITONS DEEM THEIR UTI POSSIDETIS	246	3 DON JUAN	10	45	8
POST					
WHO THANK'D ME DULY BY RETURN OF POST--	142	2 DON JUAN	1	210	2
LIKE BRUTES--AND THUS HIS DANGEROUS POST KEPT HE	175	2 DON JUAN	2	36	5
LET TO THE MORNING POST ITS ARISTOCRACY	329	2 DON JUAN	3	93	6
HIS POST I MEAN THE REGIMENT NIKOLAIEW	100	3 DON JUAN	7	66	5
OR DOUBLE POST AND RAIL WHERE THE EXISTENCE	140	3 DON JUAN	8	55	3
WHERE THE CHIEF PACHA CALMLY HELD HIS POST	171	3 DON JUAN	8	120	2
AND WISHING THAT POST HORSES HAD THE WINGS	197	3 DON JUAN	9	30	6
OF PEGASUS--OR AT THE LEAST POST CHAISES	197	3 DON JUAN	9	30	7
HE OWED TO AN OLD WOMAN AND HIS POST	239	3 DON JUAN	10	29	8
WHILE THIS HIGH POST OF HONOUR'S IN ABEYANCE	248	3 DON JUAN	10	49	1
HURRAH HOW SWIFTLY SPEEDS THE POST SO MERRY	260	3 DON JUAN	10	71	3
THOU MORNING POST SOLE RECORD OF THE PANNELS	308	3 DON JUAN	11	80	4
THEIR POST BUT THEIR'S IS MERELY A CHIMERA	360	3 DON JUAN	13	5	3
BUT FOR POST HORSES WHO FINDS SYMPATHY	377	3 DON JUAN	13	42	5
THE MORNING POST WAS FOREMOST TO PROCLAIM--	382	3 DON JUAN	13	51	6
AND THUS WE SEE--WHO DOUBTS THE MORNING POST	383	3 DON JUAN	13	53	1
HE CLEAR'D HEDGE DITCH AND DOUBLE POST AND RAIL	424	3 DON JUAN	14	33	2
WILL HAVE A FIRM POST OBIT ON POSTERITY	566	3 DON JUAN	17	9	8
POSTBOYS					
BY GERMAN POSTBOYS DRIVEN A GERMAN MILE	260	3 DON JUAN	10	71	V8
BUT--I WON'T WEEP--COME POSTBOYS WHIRL ALONG	263	3 DON JUAN	10	77	V2
SIGH--AS THE POSTBOYS FASTEN ON THE TRACES	378	3 DON JUAN	13	44	8
THE POSTBOYS HAVE NO REASON TO DISPARAGE	379	3 DON JUAN	13	46	6
POSTED					
BUT JUAN POSTED ON THROUGH MANHEIM BONN	255	3 DON JUAN	10	62	1
POSTERITY					
'GAINST YOU THE QUESTION WITH POSTERITY	13	2 DON JUAN	D	7	8
HE THAT RESERVES HIS LAURELS FOR POSTERITY	14	2 DON JUAN	D	9	1
IS THE PLATONIC PIMP OF ALL POSTERITY	411	2 DON JUAN	5	1	8
BAPTIZE POSTERITY OR FUTURE CLAY--	324	3 DON JUAN	12	18	4
SINCE ODDS ARE THAT POSTERITY WILL KNOW	324	3 DON JUAN	12	18	7
WHY I'M POSTERITY--AND SO ARE YOU	324	3 DON JUAN	12	19	1
WHOSE FAME SHE RATHER DOUBTED WITH POSTERITY	432	3 DON JUAN	14	51	3
A LINE AND LEAVE POSTERITY UNDONE	470	3 DON JUAN	15	33	5
WILL HAVE A FIRM POST OBIT ON POSTERITY	566	3 DON JUAN	17	9	8
POST-HORSES					
LIFE'S SAD POST-HORSES O'ER THE DREARY FRONTIER	238	3 DON JUAN	10	27	7
POST-HOUSE					
THEY ARE A SORT OF POST-HOUSE WHERE THE FATES	76	2 DON JUAN	1	103	4
POSTILLION'S					
'TIS THE POSTILLION'S PARADISE WHEELS FLY	377	3 DON JUAN	13	42	3
POSTILLIONS					
HAVE PRINCES WHO SPUR MORE THAN THEIR POSTILLIONS	254	3 DON JUAN	10	60	8
BUT I WON'T WEEP--AND SO DRIVE ON POSTILLIONS	263	3 DON JUAN	10	77	2
A BLEST HOUR FOR POSTILLIONS--CHARIOTS FLY	377	3 DON JUAN	13	42	V3
POSTING					
BEYOND THE RULES OF POSTING--AND THE MOB	137	3 DON JUAN	8	50	7
POST-OBITS					
EXCEPTING THE POST-OBITS OF THEOLOGY	76	2 DON JUAN	1	103	8
NEXT OWNER FOR THEIR DOUBLE-DAMN'D POST-OBITS	89	2 DON JUAN	1	125	8
POSTPONE					
I KNOW THAT SOME WOULD FAIN POSTPONE THIS ERA	360	3 DON JUAN	13	5	1
AND PRUDENTLY POSTPONE UNTIL MID-DAY	500	3 DON JUAN	15	98	5
POSTPONED					
MUST BE POSTPONED DISCREETLY FOR THE PRESENT	410	2 DON JUAN	4	117	4
POSTS					
A PHANTOM UPON EACH OF THE FOUR POSTS	30	3 DON JUAN	6	48	4
EXPLICITLY OUR SEVERAL POSTS MY FRIEND	100	3 DON JUAN	7	65	7
POSTURE					
MOST THINGS WERE IN THIS POSTURE ON THE EVE	94	3 DON JUAN	7	54	1

621

POT
  AS A FULL POT OF PORTER TO THEIR THINKING . . . . . . 201 2 DON JUAN 2   85   7
  AND WHEN I THINK UPON A POT OF BEER-- . . . . 263 3 DON JUAN 10   77   1
POTASSAE
  BOLUS POTASSAE SULPHURET SUMENDUS . . . . 244 3 DON JUAN 10   41   7
POTATIONS
  EXCHANGED FOR THIN POTATIONS BY JOHN BULL-- . . . . . 310 3 DON JUAN 11   85   7
POTATO
  WHO KNEW THIS LIFE WAS NOT WORTH A POTATO . . . . . 68 3 DON JUAN 7   4   4
POTATOE
  BUT SOMETIMES STUMBLING OVER A POTATOE-- . . . . . . 401 3 DON JUAN 13   92   7
POTATOES
  BREAD HAS BEEN MADE (INDIFFERENT) FROM POTATOES . . . . 92 2 DON JUAN 1   130   1
  THOUGH AS AN IRISHMAN YOU LOVE POTATOES . . . . . . 186 2 DON JUAN 9   7   5
  THAT SAD RESULT OF PASSIONS AND POTATOES-- . . . . . 472 3 DON JUAN 15   37   7
POTEMKIN
  THIS WAS POTEMKIN--A GREAT THING IN DAYS . . . . . 84 3 DON JUAN 7   37   1
  SOME SAID HE HAD BEEN POISONED BY POTEMKIN . . . . . 244 3 DON JUAN 10   40   2
POTENTIAL
  BY THOSE WHO GOVERN IN THE MOOD POTENTIAL . . . . . 285 3 DON JUAN 11   35   4
  ARE GROWN OF THE BEAU MONDE A PART POTENTIAL . . . . 418 3 DON JUAN 14   20   2
POTION
  HOW THE PHYSICIANS LEAVING PILL AND POTION . . . . . 113 2 DON JUAN 1   168   3
POTIPHAR
  THE SPOUSE OF POTIPHAR THE LADY BOOBY . . . . . . 486 2 DON JUAN 5   131   2
POTTERY
  AND WORKS OF THE SAME POTTERY BAD OR GOOD . . . . . 491 2 DON JUAN 5   138   5
POTTLEDEEP
  AND SIR JOHN POTTLEDEEP THE MIGHTY DRINKER . . . . . 398 3 DON JUAN 13   84   8
POUNCE
  AS HAWKS MAY POUNCE UPON A WOODLAND SONGSTER . . . . 285 3 DON JUAN 11   35   8
POUNDS
  TO VIRGIN MARY SEVERAL POUNDS OF CANDLES . . . . . 128 2 DON JUAN 1   190   6
  SOME POUNDS OF BREAD THOUGH INJURED BY THE WET . . . . 181 2 DON JUAN 2   47   2
POUR
  THOUGH SAGES MAY POUR OUT THEIR WISDOM'S TREASURE . . . 308 2 DON JUAN 3   65   7
  AND O'ER HER UPPER LIP THEY SEEM'D TO POUR . . . . . 361 2 DON JUAN 4   31   5
  THEY NATURALLY POUR THE WINE AND OIL . . . . . . 480 2 DON JUAN 5   120   5
  AS IF HIS VEINS WOULD POUR OUT HIS EXISTENCE . . . . 275 3 DON JUAN 11   14   6
  AND NOT TO POUR THEIR OCEAN IN A SIEVE . . . . . 431 3 DON JUAN 14   49   8
POUR'D
  HAD POUR'D UPON HIM FOR THE LAST HALF-HOUR . . . . . 110 2 DON JUAN 1   161   7
  IT POUR'D DOWN TORRENTS BUT THEY WERE NO RICHER . . . . 201 2 DON JUAN 2   85   1
  THEN WAS THE CORDIAL POUR'D AND MANTLE FLUNG . . . . 216 2 DON JUAN 2   114   1
  THEIR INTENSE SOULS INTO EACH OTHER POUR'D . . . . . 257 2 DON JUAN 2   191   3
  WHEN TWO PURE HEARTS ARE POUR'D IN ONE ANOTHER . . . . 357 2 DON JUAN 4   26   5
POURED
  WHICH REALLY POURED AS IF ALL HELL WERE RAINING . . . 121 3 DON JUAN 8   20   6
  AND HUMAN BREATH IS POURED UPON THE AIR . . . . . 155 3 DON JUAN 8   88 V2
  AND POURED UPON HIM AND HIS SONS LIKE RAIN . . . . . 166 3 DON JUAN 8   109   7
  IN ONE WIDE WOUND POURED FORTH HIS SOUL AT ONCE . . . 170 3 DON JUAN 8   118   8
  FROM WHENCE POURED FORTH A TRIBE OF WELL-CLAD WAITERS . . 313 3 DON JUAN 11 V 29   2
POURS
  'TIS AS THE SNAKE LATE COIL'D WHO POURS HIS LENGTH . . . 218 2 DON JUAN 2   117   7
  WHILE BACCHUS POURS OUT WINE OR HANDS A JELLY . . . . 246 2 DON JUAN 2   170   5
  POURS FORTH AT LAST THE HEART'S-BLOOD TURN'D TO TEARS . . 270 2 DON JUAN 2   214   7
  ON HIM THE DIAMOND POURS ITS BRILLIANT BLAZE . . . . 319 3 DON JUAN 12   8   6
POUSKIN
  KOCLOBSKI KOURAKIN AND MOUSKIN POUSKIN . . . . . . 75 3 DON JUAN 7   17   2
POUTING
  THERE MIGHT ARISE SOME POUTING PETTY CARE . . . . . 480 2 DON JUAN 5   119   6
  AUGHT SAVE SOME LITTLE POUTING PETTY CARE . . . . . 480 2 DON JUAN 5   119 V5
  THE OTHERS POUTING AT THE MATRON'S PREFERENCE . . . . 31 3 DON JUAN 6   50   7
POWER
  TO OPEN ALL ITSELF WITHOUT THE POWER . . . . . . 82 2 DON JUAN 1   114   3
  BUT WHETHER GLORY POWER OR LOVE OR TREASURE . . . . . 93 2 DON JUAN 1   133   6
  THAT I SHOULD FALL INTO A MONSTER'S POWER . . . . . 106 2 DON JUAN 1   155   8
  ALAS 'TWAS NOT IN THEM BUT IN THY POWER . . . . . 144 2 DON JUAN 1   214   7
  GROPING ALL PATHS TO POWER AND ALL IN VAIN . . . . . 150 2 DON JUAN 1 V   1   6
  THE PRINCE'S TYRANT--THROUGH LUST OF POWER . . . . . 151 2 DON JUAN 1 V   2 V8
  WITH ALL THE ARROGANCE OF ENDLESS POWER . . . . . 152 2 DON JUAN 1 V   3   7
  RAILING AT POWER--BUT ENVYING ALL IT'S TOOLS . . . . 152 2 DON JUAN 1 V   3 V7
  IN GROVELING ON TO POWER SUCH STAINS NOW DYE IT . . . 154 2 DON JUAN 1 V   5   6
  PANTING FOR POWER AS HARTS FOR COOLING STREAMS . . . . 155 2 DON JUAN 1 V   6   1
  PANTING FOR POWER AS TANTALUS FOR WATER . . . . . 155 2 DON JUAN 1 V   6 V1
  LOVE'S A CAPRICIOUS POWER I'VE KNOWN IT HOLD . . . . 168 2 DON JUAN 2   22   1
  A GUST--WHICH ALL DESCRIPTIVE POWER TRANSCENDS-- . . . 172 2 DON JUAN 2   30   7
  AND HAVING O'ER ITSELF NO FURTHER POWER . . . . . 258 2 DON JUAN 2   192   4
  O'ERFLOW'D HER SOUL WITH THEIR UNITED POWER . . . . 262 2 DON JUAN 2   198   3
  THE LOVE OF POWER AND RAPID GAIN OF GOLD . . . . . 303 2 DON JUAN 3   54   1
  ITS POWER UNCONSCIOUSLY FULL MANY A TIME-- . . . . . 304 2 DON JUAN 3   56   3
  THE POWER OF ART WAS TURN'D TO NOTHING FOR . . . . . 314 2 DON JUAN 3   75   7
  HAVE FELT THAT MOMENT IN ITS FULLEST POWER . . . . . 335 2 DON JUAN 3   102   3
  OF FEELING FOR SOME KINDNESS DONE WHEN POWER . . . . 339 2 DON JUAN 3   109   7
  FOR IT HAD MADE THEM WHAT THEY WERE THE POWER . . . . 354 2 DON JUAN 4   20   3
  BY THE IMMORTAL WISH AND POWER TO BLESS . . . . . 357 2 DON JUAN 4   26   8
  HER HUMAN CLAY IS KINDLED FULL OF POWER . . . . . 374 2 DON JUAN 4   56   2
  SENSES TO SLEEP--THE POWER SEEM'D GONE FOREVER . . . . 381 2 DON JUAN 4   68   8
  ESPECIALLY WHEN ADDED TO THE POWER . . . . . . 395 2 DON JUAN 4   94   8

POWER   (CONTINUED)

	PAGE	VOL	CANTO	STANZA	LN
BUT ALL THAT POWER WAS WASTED UPON HIM	396	2 DON JUAN	4	95	1
ACQUIRE THE DEEP AND BITTER POWER TO GIVE	402	2 DON JUAN	4	107	4
IN THIS OUR WORLD--AND HAVE THE POWER TO GIVE	403	2 DON JUAN	4	107	V4
I GRANT THE POWER OF PATHOS AND OF GOLD	439	2 DON JUAN	5	49	2
PASSION AND POWER A GLANCE ON HIM SHE CAST	478	2 DON JUAN	5	116	6
BUT NATURE TEACHES MORE THAN POWER CAN SPOIL	480	2 DON JUAN	5	120	1
WHATE'ER THY POWER AND GREAT IT SEEMS TO BE	484	2 DON JUAN	5	127	6
HER THRONE AND POWER AND EVERYTHING BESIDE	24	3 DON JUAN	6	36	8
AT HUMAN POWER AND VIRTUE AND ALL THAT	67	3 DON JUAN	7	3	4
BUT AS IT WAS MERE LUST OF POWER TO O'ER-ARCH ALL	86	3 DON JUAN	7	40	5
WITH ALL THE POMP OF POWER IT WAS A DOUBT	104	3 DON JUAN	7	74	7
HOW POWER COULD CONDESCEND TO DO WITHOUT	104	3 DON JUAN	7	74	8
AS HELL--MERE MORTALS WHO THEIR POWER ABUSE--	173	3 DON JUAN	8	123	7
BY WHICH THEIR POWER OF MISCHIEF IS ENCREASED	342	3 DON JUAN	12	56	4
WHICH MOURN'D THE POWER OF TIME'S OR TEMPEST'S MARCH	386	3 DON JUAN	13	59	7
SHAPED BY DECAY PERCHANCE HATH GIVEN THE POWER	388	3 DON JUAN	13	64	2
BECAUSE--SUCH WAS HIS MAGIC POWER TO PLEASE--	399	3 DON JUAN	13	86	7
TO NOVEL POWER AND AS SHE WAS THE LAST	476	3 DON JUAN	15	46	7

POWERFUL

	PAGE	VOL	CANTO	STANZA	LN
THE VERY POWERFUL PARSON PETER PITH	539	3 DON JUAN	16	81	7

POWERLESS

	PAGE	VOL	CANTO	STANZA	LN
AN AGE--EXPECTANT POWERLESS WITH HIS EYES	511	3 DON JUAN	16	25	2

POWER'S

	PAGE	VOL	CANTO	STANZA	LN
POWER'S BASE PURVEYORS WHO FOR PICKINGS PROWL	196	3 DON JUAN	9	27	4

POWERS

	PAGE	VOL	CANTO	STANZA	LN
SO FAR ABOVE THE CUNNING POWERS OF HELL	30	2 DON JUAN	1	17	3
BY ALL THE VOWS BELOW TO POWERS ABOVE	80	2 DON JUAN	1	109	3
OH POWERS OF HEAVEN WHAT DARK EYE MEETS SHE THERE	363	2 DON JUAN	4	35	7
OH POWERS OF FORM--WHAT ASPECT SEES SHE THERE	363	2 DON JUAN	4	35	V7
GLORY TO GOD AND TO THE EMPRESS (POWERS	178	3 DON JUAN	8	133	7
ALL THE AMBASSADORS OF ALL THE POWERS	222	3 DON JUAN	9	79	1
YE POWERS IT IS THE--THE--THE--POOH THE CAT	556	3 DON JUAN	16	112	3
JUAN PUT FORTH ONE ARM--ETERNAL POWERS	559	3 DON JUAN	16	120	1

POWLEY

	PAGE	VOL	CANTO	STANZA	LN
BENEATH THE VERY REVEREND ROWLEY POWLEY	297	3 DON JUAN	11	57	6

POX

	PAGE	VOL	CANTO	STANZA	LN
WITH WHICH THE DOCTOR PAID OFF AN OLD POX	91	2 DON JUAN	1	129	7

PRACTICABLE

	PAGE	VOL	CANTO	STANZA	LN
BY THEORIES QUITE PRACTICABLE TOO	267	2 DON JUAN	2	207	4

PRACTICE

	PAGE	VOL	CANTO	STANZA	LN
HAS NOT YET GIVEN UP THE PRACTICE QUITE	420	3 DON JUAN	14	23	4
REDUCED TO PRACTICE AND PERFORM'D LIKE DANCES	444	3 DON JUAN	14	79	8

PRACTISE

	PAGE	VOL	CANTO	STANZA	LN
NOT PRACTISE OH FOR TRUMPS OF CHERUBIM	241	3 DON JUAN	10	34	4

PRACTISED

	PAGE	VOL	CANTO	STANZA	LN
AND MERELY PRACTISED AS A SEA-ATTORNEY	283	2 DON JUAN	3	14	8
A GOOD DEAL PRACTISED HERE UPON OCCASION	464	2 DON JUAN	5	92	8
AND WHEN WELL PRACTISED IN THESE MIMIC SCENES	93	3 DON JUAN	7	53	5

PRACTISING

	PAGE	VOL	CANTO	STANZA	LN
AN ASS WAS PRACTISING RECITATIVE	391	2 DON JUAN	4	87	8

PRAETORIAN

	PAGE	VOL	CANTO	STANZA	LN
WHERE THE PRAETORIAN BANDS TAKE UP THE MATTER--	299	3 DON JUAN	11	62	2

PRAISE

	PAGE	VOL	CANTO	STANZA	LN
IS NOT THE CERTAIN PATH TO FUTURE PRAISE	14	2 DON JUAN	D	8	8
THAT EVEN ITS GROSSEST FLATTERERS DARE NOT PRAISE	17	2 DON JUAN	D	13	3
I PRAISE YOUR VAST FORBEARANCE NOT TO BEAT	103	2 DON JUAN	1	150	5
I CAN'T HELP PUTTING IN MY CLAIM TO PRAISE--	149	2 DON JUAN	1	222	6
ALAS HIS COUNTRY SHOW'D NO PATH TO PRAISE	303	2 DON JUAN	3	55	6
HE TURN'D PREFERRING PUDDING TO NO PRAISE--	316	2 DON JUAN	3	79	4
WHERE STILL WE FLUTTER ON FOR PENCE OR PRAISE	422	2 DON JUAN	5	22	8
AND SPAWNS HIS QUARTO AND DEMANDS YOUR PRAISE--	440	2 DON JUAN	5	52	4
MARVEL AND PRAISE FOR BOTH OR NONE THINGS WIN	469	2 DON JUAN	5	100	6
IN ALL HER LIFE WITH AUGHT SAVE PRAYERS AND PRAISE	482	2 DON JUAN	5	122	3
PRAISE) IF A MAN'S NAME IN A BULLETIN	77	3 DON JUAN	7	21	2
IF STARS AND TITLES COULD ENTAIL LONG PRAISE	84	3 DON JUAN	7	37	3
INTO ALL PANTERS FOR NEWSPAPER PRAISE	85	3 DON JUAN	7	39	4
INTO ALL ASPIRANTS FOR MARTIAL PRAISE	85	3 DON JUAN	7	39	V4
GOES WHEN SOME PERSON CONDESCENDS TO PRAISE	156	3 DON JUAN	8	90	V4
GOES WHEN SOME PERT PRETENDER DEALS HIS PRAISE	156	3 DON JUAN	8	90	V4
IN ONE THING NE'ERTHELESS 'TIS FIT TO PRAISE	176	3 DON JUAN	8	128	1
YOU HAVE OBTAINED GREAT PENSIONS AND MUCH PRAISE	183	3 DON JUAN	9	1	6
THY PRAISE HYPOCRISY OH FOR A HYMN	241	3 DON JUAN	10	34	2
BUT SINCE STEAM ENGINES PRAISE AND HONOUR VAPOUR	317	3 DON JUAN	12	4	V8
THE THEME OF PRAISE A HERMIT WOULD NOT MISS	319	3 DON JUAN	12	7	4
NEW VESTALS CLAIM MEN'S EYES WITH THE SAME PRAISE	340	3 DON JUAN	12	53	6
WE MAY PRESUME TO CRITICISE OR PRAISE	360	3 DON JUAN	13	4	4
WHO WERE OR ARE THE PUPPET-SHOWS OF PRAISE	373	3 DON JUAN	13	33	4
THE PRAISE OF PERSECUTION GAZE AGAIN	373	3 DON JUAN	13	33	5
FLIRTATION--BUT DECOROUS THE MERE PRAISE	408	3 DON JUAN	13	108	5
AND MINE'S A BUBBLE NOT BLOWN UP FOR PRAISE	414	3 DON JUAN	14	8	7
BUT OF ALL VERSE WHAT MOST INSURED HER PRAISE	525	3 DON JUAN	16	50	7
HE WOULD NOT TREAD A FACTIOUS PATH TO PRAISE	536	3 DON JUAN	16	73	5
AND NOT A JOKE HE CUT BUT EARNED ITS PRAISE	540	3 DON JUAN	16	82	3
LIKE ADDISON'S FAINT PRAISE SO WONT TO DAMN	552	3 DON JUAN	16	104	4
MORE JOY THAN FROM ALL FUTURE PRIDE OR PRAISE	554	3 DON JUAN	16	108	5

PRAISED

	PAGE	VOL	CANTO	STANZA	LN
TO SCHOOL (AS GOD BE PRAISED THAT I HAVE NONE)	50	2 DON JUAN	1	52	4
THREE OR FOUR THINGS FOR WHICH THE LORD HE PRAISED	239	2 DON JUAN	2	157	5
HE PRAISED THE PRESENT AND ABUSED THE PAST	316	2 DON JUAN	3	79	1

PRAISED   (CONTINUED)
  MAY LIKE BEING PRAISED FOR EVERY LUCKY BLUNDER 185   3 DON JUAN 9   5   6
  ALL PRAISED THE EMPRESS'S MATERNAL LOVE 240   3 DON JUAN 10   32   8
  PRAISED BE ALL LIARS AND ALL LIES WHO NOW 286   3 DON JUAN 11   38   1
  SOME PRAISED HER BEAUTY OTHERS HER GREAT GRACE 550   3 DON JUAN 16 102   1
PRAISES
  WITH ALL THE PRAISES EVER SAID OR SUNG 199   3 DON JUAN 9   34   6
  SWORE PRAISES AND RECALL'D THEIR FORMER FIRES 425   3 DON JUAN 14   34   6
  MEANWHILE SWEET ADELINE DESERVED THEIR PRAISES 550   3 DON JUAN 16 103   1
PRANCE
  IN GERMANY THE PEGASUS HE'D PRANCE ON 320   2 DON JUAN 3   86   5
PRANCING
  OR PROUDLIER PRANCING WITH MERCURIAL SKILL 303   3 DON JUAN 11   70   7
PRANK
  AS SUITS A MATRON WHO HAS PLAYED A PRANK 500   2 DON JUAN 5 154   4
  WHICH WITH YOUR CONQUERORS IS A COMMON PRANK 71   3 DON JUAN 7   9   6
PRANKS
  LIKE CROMWELL'S PRANKS--BUT ALTHOUGH TRUTH EXACTS . . 329   2 DON JUAN 3   92   5
  TOWNS NATIONS WORLDS IN HER REVOLVING PRANKS   135   3 DON JUAN 8   44   5
PRATE
  YE GODS I GROW A TALKER LET US PRATE 345   3 DON JUAN 12   64   1
PRATED
  HE PRATED TO THE WORLD OF PANTISOCRASY   329   2 DON JUAN 3   93   2
  AND TELL THEM--BUT YOU WON'T AND I HAVE PRATED 267   3 DON JUAN 10   87   6
PRATTLE
  JUST NOW ENOUGH BUT BY-AND-BY I'LL PRATTLE 267   3 DON JUAN 10   87   7
  MY LADY'S PRATTLE FILTER'D THROUGH HER WOMAN 418   3 DON JUAN 14   19   8
PRAY
  COULD TURN THEIR OPTICS TO THE TEXT AND PRAY 47   2 DON JUAN 1   46   6
  THAT HOWSOEVER PEOPLE FAST AND PRAY 56   2 DON JUAN 1   63   5
  DO PRAY UNDO THE BOLT A LITTLE FASTER-- 96   2 DON JUAN 1 137   5
  BUT AS MY MAID'S UNDREST PRAY TURN YOUR SPIES OUT . . 104   2 DON JUAN 1 152   7
  PRAY HAVE THE COURTESY TO MAKE IT KNOWN 105   2 DON JUAN 1 154   3
  WITH PRAY SIR LEAVE THE ROOM AND SAY NO MORE 111   2 DON JUAN 1 163   4
  PRAY KEEP YOUR NONSENSE FOR SOME LUCKIER NIGHT-- . . . 115   2 DON JUAN 1 171   1
  AND BEAR WITH LIFE TO LOVE AND PRAY FOR YOU 134   2 DON JUAN 1 197   8
  THIS STORY IS NOT MORAL FIRST I PRAY 140   2 DON JUAN 1 207   2
  I PRAY YE FLOG THEM UPON ALL OCCASIONS 157   2 DON JUAN 2   1   3
  (FOR THAT'S THE NAME THEY LIKE TO PRAY BENEATH)-- . . 309   2 DON JUAN 3   66   4
  OR PRAY MEDEA FOR A SINGLE DRAGON 333   2 DON JUAN 3   99   4
  BUT SET THOSE PERSONS DOWN WITH ME TO PRAY 336   2 DON JUAN 3 104   3
  'TWOULD GIVE ME PLEASURE--PRAY WHAT IS YOUR NATION . . 417   2 DON JUAN 5   13   8
  PRAY SIR SAID JUAN IF I MAY PRESUME 418   2 DON JUAN 5   15   1
  CUT OFF A THOUSAND HEADS BEFORE-- --NOW PRAY 453   2 DON JUAN 5   72   1
  SAID BABA BUT PRAY DO AS I DESIRE 454   2 DON JUAN 5   74   2
  REJOINED THE NEGRO PRAY BE NOT PROVOKING 454   2 DON JUAN 5   75   2
  TO JUAN WHO THOUGH NOT MUCH USED TO PRAY 466   2 DON JUAN 5   95   5
  BUT PRAY GIVE BACK A LITTLE TO THE NATION 185   3 DON JUAN 9   6   8
  NO MORE OF THIS THEN--LET US PRAY WE HAVE 192   3 DON JUAN 9   19   2
  AND SHOULD YOU DOUBT PRAY ASK OF YOUR NEXT NEIGHBOUR . 288   3 DON JUAN 11   41   4
  TO HIS BILLETS WHY WALTZ WITH HIM WHY I PRAY 332   3 DON JUAN 12   34   7
  PRAY DID YOU SEE HER ANSWER TO HIS LETTER 332   3 DON JUAN 12   35   8
  IS DIFFICULT PRAY TELL ME CAN YOU MAKE FAST 411   3 DON JUAN 14   2   3
  YOU HAVE FREED THE BLACKS--NOW PRAY SHUT UP THE WHITES 445   3 DON JUAN 14   82   8
  THE LAST TIME WAS--I PRAY SAID ADELINE--   516   3 DON JUAN 16   37   1
PRAY'D
  SHE PRAY'D THE VIRGIN MARY FOR HER GRACE 62   2 DON JUAN 1   75   7
  THAT NIGHT THE VIRGIN WAS NO FURTHER PRAY'D 63   2 DON JUAN 1   76   8
  WHILE A FEW PRAY'D--(THE FIRST TIME FOR SOME YEARS)-- 208   2 DON JUAN 2   98   5
  FOR JUAN SO THAT EVEN WHEN HE PRAY'D 235   2 DON JUAN 2 149   6
PRAYER
  SHE KNEW THE LATIN--THAT IS THE LORD'S PRAYER 28   2 DON JUAN 1   13   1
  AND YET THE FOREST LEAVES SEEM'D STIRR'D WITH PRAYER . 335   2 DON JUAN 3 102   8
  AVE MARIA 'TIS THE HOUR OF PRAYER 336   2 DON JUAN 3 103   1
  AND DECORATES THE BOOK OF COMMON PRAYER 17   3 DON JUAN 6   23   7
  IN LIKE CHURCH BELLS WITH SIGH HOWL GROAN YELL PRAYER 141   3 DON JUAN 8   58   7
  TO PRAYER WAS HEARD NO MORE--AND JUAN WEPT 182   3 DON JUAN 8 141   7
  FOR HE MUTTERS HIS PRAYER IN THE MIDNIGHT AIR 518   3 DON JUAN 16 L 1   3
  AND WHATSOE'ER MAY BE HIS PRAYER 520   3 DON JUAN 16 L 6   7
  HE HAD PAID HIS NEIGHBOUR'S PRAYER WITH HALF A TURBOT 543   3 DON JUAN 16   88   8
PRAYER-BOOK
  SO LEAVING EACH THEIR PRIEST AND PRAYER-BOOK READY . . 280   2 DON JUAN 3   9   7
PRAYERS
  TO--SAY MY PRAYERS--BUT NEVER WAS THERE PLANN'D . . . 160   2 DON JUAN 2   7   6
  SOME WENT TO PRAYERS AGAIN AND MADE A VOW 179   2 DON JUAN 2   44   3
  SOME TAKE A LOVER SOME TAKE DRAMS OR PRAYERS 263   2 DON JUAN 2 201   1
  (UNLESS AT ONCE SHE PLUNGE FOR LIFE IN PRAYERS)-- . . 276   2 DON JUAN 3   4   3
  IN ALL HER LIFE WITH AUGHT SAVE PRAYERS AND PRAISE . . 482   2 DON JUAN 5 122   3
  HE WENT TO MOSQUE IN STATE AND SAID HIS PRAYERS . . . 496   2 DON JUAN 5 148   1
  AND PRAYERS AND OTHER PIOUS EVOLUTIONS 52   3 DON JUAN 6   92   3
PRAYING
  THEN DRESSING NURSING PRAYING AND ALL'S OVER 263   2 DON JUAN 2 200   8
  PRAYING INSTRUCTING DESOLATING PLUNDERING 95   3 DON JUAN 7   55   6
PREACH
  FOR THIS MEN WRITE SPEAK PREACH AND HEROES KILL . . . 146   2 DON JUAN 2 218   5
  FEW THINGS SURPASS OLD WINE AND THEY MAY PREACH . . . 250   2 DON JUAN 2 178   5
  WHO PLEASE--THE MORE BECAUSE THEY PREACH IN VAIN-- . . 250   2 DON JUAN 2 178   6
  PREACH TO POOR ROUGES AND WHEREFORE NOT BEGIN 266   3 DON JUAN 10   85   2
PREACHER
  BY SAINT BY SAGE BY PREACHER AND BY POET 69   3 DON JUAN 7   6   6

PREACHER   (CONTINUED)
    A PREACHER HAD HELD FORTH (WHO NOBLY SPURNED . . . . . .   99 3 DON JUAN 7   64   5
    NOW HERE I HAVE GOT THE PREACHER AT A DEAD LOCK   . . . . . 471 3 DON JUAN 15   35   8
PREACHERS
    LEARNING THAT LANGUAGE CHIEFLY FROM ITS PREACHERS . . . . 243 2 DON JUAN 2   165   4
    MOST MODERN PREACHERS SAY THE SAME OR SHOW IT . . . . .   69 3 DON JUAN 7   6   2
PRECARIOUS
    THOU MAK'ST THE CHASTE CONNUBIAL STATE PRECARIOUS . . . . 266 2 DON JUAN 2   206   1
    WHICH IS BUT A PRECARIOUS BOND IN SOUTH . . . .   14 3 DON JUAN 6   16   5
    PERHAPS PRECARIOUS HAD THEY BUT THOUGHT GOOD   . . . . .   53 3 DON JUAN 6   95   5
PRECAUTION
    BUT THEN THERE WAS A GREAT WANT OF PRECAUTION . . . . .   72 3 DON JUAN 7   11   5
PRECAUTIONARY
    BUT THESE PRECAUTIONARY HINTS CAN TOUCH . . . . 305 3 DON JUAN 11   73   1
PRECAUTIONS
    SUCH PLENTIFUL PRECAUTIONS THAT STILL HE . . . . 248 2 DON JUAN 2   174   3
PRECAUTIOUS
    ARE PUZZLES TO THE MOST PRECAUTIOUS BENCHES . . . . . . 531 3 DON JUAN 16   63   8
PRECEDENCE
    FOR SUCH PRECEDENCE UPON SUCH OCCASIONS . . . . 136 3 DON JUAN 8   48   2
PRECEDENT
    SUPPOSE THE CONVERSE OF THIS PRECEDENT . . . . 564 3 DON JUAN 17   5   5
PRECEDES
    THAT FEVER WHICH PRECEDES THE LANGUID ROUT . . . . . . 220 3 DON JUAN 9   75   6
PRECEPT
    AND CARRY PRECEPT TO THE HIGHEST PITCH   . . . . 138 2 DON JUAN 1   204   6
    AND THUS POPE QUOTES THE PRECEPT TO RE-TEACH   . . . . . 470 2 DON JUAN 5   101   6
PRECEPTS
    THE ONLY HIGH SOUND PRECEPTS OF THE TRUE SUBLIME . . . . 136 2 DON JUAN 1   201 V3
PRECINCTS
    AND ROUND ITS ONCE WARM PRECINCTS PALELY LYING . . . . . 301 2 DON JUAN 3   51   6
    IF ONCE BEYOND HER BOUDOIR'S PRECINCTS IN YE WENT . . . . 214 3 DON JUAN 9   63   5
PRECIOUS
    IS THAT SAME TIME SO COMMON YET SO PRECIOUS . . . . . . 145 2 DON JUAN 1   217 V7
    LOST THAT MOST PRECIOUS STONE OF STONES--HIS MODESTY . . . 157 2 DON JUAN 2   1 V8
    FLOW'D IN HER VEIL AND MANY A PRECIOUS STONE   . . . . . 220 2 DON JUAN 2   121   6
    THAT E'ER BY PRECIOUS METAL WAS HELD IN . . . . 312 2 DON JUAN 3   71   8
    THE PRECIOUS PORCELAIN OF HUMAN CLAY . . . . 350 2 DON JUAN 4   11   3
    THOSE GAY RECESSES--MANY A PRECIOUS STONE . . . . . .   54 3 DON JUAN 6   97   5
    ONE OF THOSE PRETTY PRECIOUS PLAGUES WHICH HAUNT . . . . 438 3 DON JUAN 14   63   3
    NOT THE LESS PRECIOUS THAT WE SELDOM HEAR IT   . . . . . 518 3 DON JUAN 16   40   8
    SO PRECIOUS THAT IT WAS NOT TO BE BOUGHT . . . . 528 3 DON JUAN 16   56   3
PRECIPICE
    THE PRECIPICE SHE STOOD ON WAS IMMENSE   . . . .   78 2 DON JUAN 1   106   7
    YOU LOOK DOWN O'ER THE PRECIPICE AND DREAR . . . . . . 412 3 DON JUAN 14   5   6
PRECIPICES
    WHICH MIXES UP VINES OLIVES PRECIPICES   . . . . 262 3 DON JUAN 10   76   7
PRECIPITATE
    'TWILL BUT PRECIPITATE A SITUATION . . . . 429 3 DON JUAN 14   43   6
PRECIPITATION
    BUT SUCH PRECIPITATION MAY END ILL . . . .   62 3 DON JUAN 6   114   5
PRECISE
    IN THAT POINT SO PRECISE IN EACH DEGREE . . . .   52 2 DON JUAN 1   57   5
PRECISIAN
    THERE WAS THE REVEREND RODOMONT PRECISIAN   . . . . . . 399 3 DON JUAN 13   87   5
PRECISION
    LET EVERYTHING BE NOTED WITH PRECISION   . . . . 104 2 DON JUAN 1   152   5
    INSTEAD OF HOARDING IT WITH DUE PRECISION   . . . . . . 192 2 DON JUAN 2   68   8
    SAVE ZOE WHO ALTHOUGH WITH DUE PRECISION . . . . 252 2 DON JUAN 2   182   4
    AS WE MAY ASCERTAIN WITH DUE PRECISION   . . . . 477 2 DON JUAN 5   115   7
    IF 'TIS SUMMED UP WITH FEMININE PRECISION   . . . . . .   10 3 DON JUAN 6   9   3
    LAND BATTERIES WORKED THEIR GUNS WITH GREAT PRECISION . .   81 3 DON JUAN 7   30   3
    NO TITLE TO POINT OUT WITH DUE PRECISION . . . . 283 3 DON JUAN 11   32   3
    IN THE MEANTIME HIS VALET WHOSE PRECISION   . . . . . . 512 3 DON JUAN 16   28   6
PRECOCIOUS
    IF ANY SAID SO FOR TO BE PRECOCIOUS   . . . .   51 2 DON JUAN 1   54   7
    WHICH IN THE NORTH PREVENTS PRECOCIOUS CRIMES . . . . . 501 2 DON JUAN 5   157   5
PREDECESSORS
    HIS PREDECESSORS IN THE COLCHIAN DAYS . . . . 303 2 DON JUAN 3   55   4
PREDICAMENT
    JUAN WHO DID NOT STAND IN THE PREDICAMENT   . . . . . . 346 3 DON JUAN 12   67   1
PREDICATE
    AND IF IN FLATTERING STRAINS I DO NOT PREDICATE   . . . .   20 2 DON JUAN D   17   3
PREDICTIONS
    THOUGHT HER PREDICTIONS WENT NOT MUCH AMISS . . . . . . 492 3 DON JUAN 15   81   3
PREDILECTION
    HE HAD A PREDILECTION FOR THAT TIE . . . . 469 3 DON JUAN 15   30   2
PREDOMINANCE
    AN INNOCENT PREDOMINANCE ANNEX . . . . 451 3 DON JUAN 14   93   3
PREFACE
    WITHOUT MORE PREFACE IN HER BLUE EYES BLENDING . . . . . 478 2 DON JUAN 5   116   5
PREFER
    PREFER A SPOUSE WHOSE AGE IS SHORT OF THIRTY   . . . . .   56 2 DON JUAN 1   62   8
    SOME PEOPLE PREFER WINE--'TIS NOT AMISS . . . . 356 2 DON JUAN 4   24   6
    THEY WOULD PREFER TO PADISHA OR PACHA . . . .   25 3 DON JUAN 6   39   8
    BUT DOUBTLESS THEY PREFER A FINE YOUNG MAN . . . . . . 167 3 DON JUAN 8   112   3
    MAKE SOME PREFER THE CIRCULATING MEDIUM . . . . 235 3 DON JUAN 10   22   8
    OH GOLD I STILL PREFER THEE UNTO PAPER   . . . . 317 3 DON JUAN 12   4   7
PREFERENCE
    PREFERENCE THAT WE MUST FEEL UPON OCCASION . . . . . .   63 2 DON JUAN 1   77   6

PREFERENCE   (CONTINUED)
    IN PREFERENCE SURE TO CLARENCE' MALMSEY BUTT . . . . . 112 2 DON JUAN 1   166 V8
    THE OTHERS POUTING AT THE MATRON'S PREFERENCE . .   31 3 DON JUAN 6   50 7
    HER PREFERENCE OF A BOY TO MEN MUCH BIGGER . . . . . 218 3 DON JUAN 9   72 3
    SOME DIFFICULTIES AS IN HIS OWN PREFERENCE   . . . . . 469 3 DON JUAN 15   30 5
    OF WHICH THE LATTER MERITS EVERY PREFERENCE . . . . . 541 3 DON JUAN 16   85 4
PREFERMENT
    AND AS A SERVANT SOME PREFERMENT GET . . . .   391 2 DON JUAN 4   86 5
    UNTIL PREFERMENT COMING AT A SURE RATE   . . . . . .   540 3 DON JUAN 16   82 4
PREFERR'D
    PREFERR'D A DRAUGHT FROM THE FAST-FLOWING VEINS . . . 197 2 DON JUAN 2   77 4
PREFERRED
    HE STILL PREFERRED HIS OWN NECK TO ANOTHER'S . . . .   63 3 DON JUAN 6   116 8
    UNTO AN EMPRESS WHO PREFERRED YOUNG MEN . .   241 3 DON JUAN 10   33 2
    AGAINST HIS HEART PREFERRED THEIR USUAL CLAIMS . . . 293 3 DON JUAN 11   48 5
    BECAUSE THE MONKS PREFERRED A HILL BEHIND . . . . .   384 3 DON JUAN 13   55 7
PREFERRING
    HE TURN'D PREFERRING PUDDING TO NO PRAISE-- . . .   316 2 DON JUAN 3   79 4
PREFERS
    SHE THEN PREFERS HIM IN THE PLURAL NUMBER   . . . . . 276 2 DON JUAN 3   3 7
PREJUDICE
    WHY ADELINE HAD THIS SLIGHT PREJUDICE-- . . . . .   478 3 DON JUAN 15   52 1
    FOR PREJUDICE IT WAS--AGAINST A CREATURE . . . . .   478 3 DON JUAN 15   52 2
PREJUDICES
    FOR BOTH OUR PREJUDICES HE MUST BACK . . . .   349 3 DON JUAN 12   71 V6
PRELUDES
    ALL THESE ARE LITTLE PRELUDES TO POSSESSION . . . . .   62 2 DON JUAN 1   74 5
PRELUDIOS
    PRELUDIOS TRYING JUST A STRING OR TWO . . . .   341 3 DON JUAN 12   54 6
PREMATURE
    IN CASE OF ANY PREMATURE DISCLOSURE   . . . . . .   62 3 DON JUAN 6   114 8
PREMISES
    CONCEAL'D AMONGST HIS PREMISES 'TIS TRUE . . . . . . 118 2 DON JUAN 1   177 5
PREMISING
    ALWAYS PREMISING THAT SAID SON AT COLLEGE   . . . . . 377 3 DON JUAN 13   42 7
PREPARATION
    AND HERE I LEAVE THEM AT THEIR PREPARATION . . . .   65 3 DON JUAN 6   119 1
    BUT SO IT WAS AND EVERY PREPARATION . . . . . .   91 3 DON JUAN 7   50 1
    BOTH IN PERFORMANCE AND IN PREPARATION . . . . .   416 3 DON JUAN 14   14 6
    THERE WAS MUCH BUSTLE TOO AND PREPARATION   . . . .   534 3 DON JUAN 16   68 3
PREPARATIONS
    IN PREPARATIONS FOR A CANNONADE . . . .   106 3 DON JUAN 7   78 2
PREPARATIVES
    BUT ALL HIS GREAT PREPARATIVES FOR DYING . . . . .   492 2 DON JUAN 5   141 7
PREPARED
    AT LENGTH THE LOTS WERE TORN UP AND PREPARED   . . . 195 2 DON JUAN 2   74 5
    AND THE FIRST BREAKFAST SPOILT PREPARED A NEW ONE . . 234 2 DON JUAN 2   146 6
    OF HELL-FIRE--ALL PREPARED FOR PEOPLE GIVING . . . . 258 2 DON JUAN 2   192 7
    OF LACQUEYS USHER TO THE FEAST PREPARED . . . . .   439 2 DON JUAN 5   50 4
    PREPARED FOR SUPPER WITH A GLASS OF RUM . . . . .   441 2 DON JUAN 5   53 8
    IN FORMER WORKS MADE NEW PREPARED FASCINES . . . .   89 3 DON JUAN 7   47 7
    ALL WAS PREPARED--THE FIRE THE SWORD THE MEN . . .   113 3 DON JUAN 8   2 1
    SEVERAL PREPARED THEMSELVES FOR EMIGRATIONS . . . .   239 3 DON JUAN 10   30 5
    AT LEAST IT RHYMES TO LOVE BUT I'M PREPARED . . .   322 3 DON JUAN 12   13 6
    PREPARED EACH MORN FOR EVENINGS LIST OH LIST-- . . . 403 3 DON JUAN 13   97 6
    THE COMPANY PREPARED TO SEPARATE . . . .   527 3 DON JUAN 16   55 2
PREPOSSESSION
    TO THE UNKNOWN A SECRET PREPOSSESSION . . . . . .   413 3 DON JUAN 14   6 6
PREPOSSESSIONS
    HIS PREPOSSESSIONS LIKE THE LAWS OF PERSIANS . . . . 366 3 DON JUAN 13   17 3
PRESAGE
    (THOUGH PARRY'S EFFORTS LOOK A LUCKY PRESAGE) . . . . 376 3 DON JUAN 13   39 5
PRESAGED
    AND ALL PRESAGED GOOD FORTUNE TO THEIR CAUSE . . . .   89 3 DON JUAN 7   47 4
PRESAGING
    PRESAGING A MOST LUMINOUS ATTACK . . . .   89 3 DON JUAN 7   46 4
PRESBYTERIAN
    FOR I WAS BRED A MODERATE PRESBYTERIAN   . . . . . . 496 3 DON JUAN 15   91 8
PRESCIENCE
    HAVE SUCH A PRESCIENCE IT SHOULD BE NO BAR . . . . . 194 3 DON JUAN 9   24 6
PRESCRIBED
    PRESCRIBED BY WAY OF BLISTER A YOUNG BELLE . . . . . 113 2 DON JUAN 1   168 4
PRESCRIPTION
    BUT HERE IS ONE PRESCRIPTION OUT OF MANY . . . . . . 244 3 DON JUAN 10   41 1
PRESENCE
    HER OVERPOWERING PRESENCE MADE YOU FEEL   . . . . .   313 2 DON JUAN 3   74 7
    I KNOW NOT HOW--HER PRESENCE MADE YE FEEL . . . . . 313 2 DON JUAN 3   74 V7
    HER PRESENCE WAS AS LOFTY AS HER STATE . . . . . .   467 2 DON JUAN 5   97 1
    FOR THE IMPERIAL PRESENCE WHERIN WHETHER . . . . .   65 3 DON JUAN 6   119 2
    A HIDDEN NECTAR UNDER A COLD PRESENCE . . . . . .   375 3 DON JUAN 13   38 3
PRESENT
    OF MERIT AND COMPLAINT OF PRESENT DAYS . . . . . .   14 2 DON JUAN D   8 7
    BUT CAN'T FIND ANY IN THE PRESENT AGE . . . . . .   24 2 DON JUAN 1   5 6
    THERE FOR THE PRESENT AT THE LEAST HE'S FAST . . . . 115 2 DON JUAN 1   172 6
    HOWEVER PRESENT REMEDY WAS NONE . . . .   116 2 DON JUAN 1   173 5
    BUT FOR THE PRESENT GENTLE READER AND . . . . . .   147 2 DON JUAN 1   221 1
    REFLECTED ON HIS PRESENT SITUATION . . . .   165 2 DON JUAN 2   17 7
    HERSELF FROM OUT HER PRESENT JEOPARDY . . . . . .   170 2 DON JUAN 2   27 6
    AND YET THEIR PRESENT HOPE WAS HARDLY MORE . . . . . 185 2 DON JUAN 2   54 3

PRESENT (CONTINUED)

		PAGE	VOL	CANTO	STANZA	LN
AND PRESENT PERIL ALL BEFORE SURPASS'D	. . . . . .	188	2	DON JUAN	2	61	6
WAS ALL THAT FOR THE PRESENT COULD BE DONE	. . . .	189	2	DON JUAN	2	62	4
WAS KILL'D AND PORTION'D OUT FOR PRESENT EATING	. . .	193	2	DON JUAN	2	70	8
WAS A SMALL PRESENT MADE TO HIM AT CADIZ	. . . . .	199	2	DON JUAN	2	81	7
A PRESENT LIBERALLY MADE BY LADIES	. . . . . .	199	2	DON JUAN	2	81	V8
TO PLACE HIM IN THE CAVE FOR PRESENT REST	. . . . .	225	2	DON JUAN	2	131	3
JUST FOR THE PRESENT AND IN HIS LULL'D HEAD	. . . .	227	2	DON JUAN	2	134	4
AND DRESS'D HIM FOR THE PRESENT LIKE A TURK	. . . .	240	2	DON JUAN	2	160	4
BETWEEN THEIR PRESENT AND THEIR FUTURE STATE	. . . .	278	2	DON JUAN	3	6	2
THE PRESENT WEATHER WOULD BE MUCH MORE RAINY--	. . .	301	2	DON JUAN	3	50	6
HE PRAISED THE PRESENT AND ABUSED THE PAST	. . . .	316	2	DON JUAN	3	79	1
OH THAT THE PRESENT HOUR WOULD LEND	. . . . . .	325	2	DON JUAN	3	L 12	4
THE PRESENT CENTURY WAS GROWING BLIND	. . . . .	328	2	DON JUAN	3	90	6
SUCH NAMES AT PRESENT CUT A CONVICT FIGURE	. . . .	330	2	DON JUAN	3	94	1
THE PAST STILL WELCOME AS THE PRESENT THOUGHT	. . .	354	2	DON JUAN	4	20	8
DONE THINE THE PRESENT VOUCHES FOR THE PAST	. . . .	368	2	DON JUAN	4	46	8
HANDSOME AND YOUNG ENJOYING ALL THE PRESENT	. . . .	371	2	DON JUAN	4	51	4
I LEAVE DON JUAN FOR THE PRESENT SAFE--	. . . .	373	2	DON JUAN	4	54	1
ABOUT HIS PAST OR PRESENT SITUATION	. . . . .	387	2	DON JUAN	4	79	8
MUST BE POSTPONED DISCREETLY FOR THE PRESENT	. . . .	410	2	DON JUAN	4	117	4
FAR LESS DESCRIBE PRESENT THE VERY VIEW	. . . . .	412	2	DON JUAN	5	3	7
AT PRESENT WEIGHED DOWN BY A DOOM WHICH HAD	. . .	417	2	DON JUAN	5	12	3
'TIS NOT SAID JUAN FOR MY PRESENT DOOM	. . . . .	420	2	DON JUAN	5	18	1
'TIS NOT MY PRESENT LOT AS I HAVE SAID	. . . . .	420	2	DON JUAN	5	18	6
NO--ONLY TWO AT PRESENT ABOVE GROUND	. . . . .	421	2	DON JUAN	5	20	3
IT BETTERS PRESENT TIMES WITH ME OR YOU	. . . . .	422	2	DON JUAN	5	23	3
THEIR PRESENT LESSONS ON OUR PAGAN FRIENDS HERE	. . .	423	2	DON JUAN	5	24	2
BUT AFTER ALL WHAT IS OUR PRESENT STATE	. . . . .	423	2	DON JUAN	5	25	1
FOR WHICH HE OWNED A PRESENT APPETITE	. . . . .	452	2	DON JUAN	5	71	4
MUST MAKE A PRESENT TO HIS SIRE IN LAW	. . . . .	498	2	DON JUAN	5	152	8
OUR ULTIMATE EXISTENCE WHAT'S OUR PRESENT	. . . . .	37	3	DON JUAN	6	63	7
IMPLORED THAT PRESENT PARDON MIGHT BE SHOWN	. . . .	47	3	DON JUAN	6	32	4
I LEAVE THEM FOR THE PRESENT WITH GOOD WISHES	. . .	65	3	DON JUAN	6	120	1
AND SUCH AS THEY ARE SUCH MY PRESENT TALE IS	. . .	67	3	DON JUAN	7	2	1
THEY ACCUSE ME--ME--THE PRESENT WRITER OF	. . . .	67	3	DON JUAN	7	3	1
THE PRESENT POEM--OF--I KNOW NOT WHAT--	. . . .	67	3	DON JUAN	7	3	2
EACH MAN OF WISDOM FUTURE PAST OR PRESENT	. . . .	69	3	DON JUAN	7	5	4
THEY PARTED FOR THE PRESENT THESE TO AWAIT	. . . .	105	3	DON JUAN	7	76	2
HERE PAUSE WE FOR THE PRESENT--AS EVEN THEN	. . .	111	3	DON JUAN	7	87	1
AT PRESENT SUCH THINGS SINCE THEY ARE HER THEME	. . .	112	3	DON JUAN	8	1	6
PAST PRESENT AND TO COME--BUT ALL MAY YIELD	. . .	117	3	DON JUAN	8	12	7
AND PONDERING ON THE PRESENT AND THE PAST	. . . .	142	3	DON JUAN	8	60	7
IN CITIES CAGED THE PRESENT CASE IN POINT I	. . .	143	3	DON JUAN	8	62	7
A LITTLE SCORCHED AT PRESENT WITH THE BLAZE	. . . .	156	3	DON JUAN	8	90	6
ON CITIES AS HATH BEEN THE PRESENT CASE)	. . . . .	160	3	DON JUAN	8	97	4
OF PRESENT LIFE A GOOD DEAL MORE THAN WE--	. . . .	161	3	DON JUAN	8	100	3
READ YOUR OWN HEARTS AND IRELAND'S PRESENT STORY	. . .	174	3	DON JUAN	8	125	7
BETWEEN THE PRESENT AND PAST WORLDS AND HOVER	. . .	255	3	DON JUAN	10	61	7
THEY KNOW NOT HOW) THE ONE HALF THE PRESENT CASE	. . .	314	3	DON JUAN	11	V 75	7
THAT IS YOUR PRESENT THEME FOR POPULARITY	. . . .	357	3	DON JUAN	12	89	1
OF BRITAIN'S PRESENT WEALTH AND HAPPINESS--	. . .	371	3	DON JUAN	13	29	8
PRESENT LORDS A B C--EARLS DUKES BY NAME	. . . .	383	3	DON JUAN	13	54	2
THE PORTION OF THIS WORLD WHICH I AT PRESENT	. . . .	416	3	DON JUAN	14	15	1
BUT THIS IS NOT AT PRESENT MY CONCERN	. . . . .	436	3	DON JUAN	14	59	7
AT PRESENT I AM GLAD OF A PRETENCE	. . . . .	453	3	DON JUAN	14	97	4
ALL PRESENT LIFE IS BUT AN INTERJECTION	. . . . .	456	3	DON JUAN	15	1	5
THE PRESENT WITH THEIR COMMON-PLACE COSTUME	. . . .	468	3	DON JUAN	15	26	8
BUT THAT AT PRESENT WITH IMMEDIATE REFERENCE	. . . .	469	3	DON JUAN	15	30	3
SOME OLD--SOME PAST--SOME PRESENT--SOME TO BE	. . .	495	3	DON JUAN	15	89	V7
ABOUT THE PRESENT PAST OR FUTURE STATE	. . . . .	496	3	DON JUAN	15	91	6
DYED PURPLE NONE AT PRESENT CAN TELL HOW	. . . .	505	3	DON JUAN	16	10	6
AND BEING PRESENT NOW BEGAN TO EXPRESS	. . . . .	514	3	DON JUAN	16	32	6
BECAUSE THE PRESENT TALE HAS OFT BEEN TOLD	. . . .	516	3	DON JUAN	16	37	7
SO MUCH THE PRESENT DYE SHE WAS REMOTE	. . . . .	524	3	DON JUAN	16	47	6
ABOUT THE PRESENT FAMILY'S DEATHS AND WOOINGS	. . .	527	3	DON JUAN	16	53	8
THEREFORE THE PRESENT PIECE OF NATURAL HISTORY	. . .	531	3	DON JUAN	16	62	3
THE PRESENT CULPRIT WAS EXTREMELY PALE	. . . . .	532	3	DON JUAN	16	64	1
AND THIS AT PRESENT WAS HER KIND EMPLOYMENT	. . . .	548	3	DON JUAN	16	100	8
WHEN ANY DARE A NEW LIGHT TO PRESENT	. . . . .	564	3	DON JUAN	17	5	3

PRESENTED

WAS THE DISEASE PRESENTED HIM AT CADIZ	. . . . .	199	2	DON JUAN	2	81	V7
PRESENTED THE O'ERFLOWING CUP AND SAID	. . . . .	297	2	DON JUAN	3	43	3
LAMBRO PRESENTED AND ONE INSTANT MORE	. . . . .	366	2	DON JUAN	4	42	1
PRESENTED A FINE MARK TO THROW A SHELL IN	. . . .	78	3	DON JUAN	7	23	8
PRESENTED BY THE PRINCE OF THE BRAZILS	. . . . .	185	3	DON JUAN	9	6	2
JUAN PRESENTED IN THE PROPER PLACE	. . . . .	285	3	DON JUAN	11	35	1
DON JUAN WAS PRESENTED AND HIS DRESS	. . . . .	287	3	DON JUAN	11	39	1
AT SIXTEEN SHE CAME OUT PRESENTED VAUNTED	. . . .	434	3	DON JUAN	14	55	1

PRESENT'S

THE PLAN AT PRESENT'S SIMPLY IN CONCOCTION	. . . .	356	3	DON JUAN	12	87	5

PRESENTS

CERES PRESENTS A PLATE OF VERMICELLI--	. . .	246	2	DON JUAN	2	170	3
WHICH GOT HIM A FEW PRESENTS AND SOME THANKS	. . .	319	2	DON JUAN	3	84	5
UPON HIS CABINET BESIDES THE PRESENTS	. . . . .	222	2	DON JUAN	9	79	7
A CITY WHICH PRESENTS TO THE INSPECTOR	. . . . .	255	3	DON JUAN	10	62	6
PRESENTS THE PROBLEM OF A DOUBLE FIGURE	. . . . .	530	3	DON JUAN	16	61	8

PRESERVATION

THEIR PRESERVATION WOULD HAVE BEEN A MIRACLE	. . . .	183	2	DON JUAN	2	50	8
GLANCED FROM THE WALLS IN GOODLY PRESERVATION	. . .	390	3	DON JUAN	13	68	3

	PAGE	VOL	CANTO	STANZA	LV
PRESERVE					
PRESERVE YOUR STATE--THOUGH EVE EARTH'S MOTHER FELL	460	2 DON JUAN	5	84	V6
PRESERVE OF BORES WHO OUGHT TO BE MADE GAME	395	3 DON JUAN	13	78	8
PRESERVED					
WHOM HE PRESERVED--A PURE AND LIVING PEARL	249	3 DON JUAN	10	51	8
ELSEWHERE PRESERVED THE CLOISTERS STILL WERE STABLE	389	3 DON JUAN	13	66	3
HAD STILL PRESERVED HIS PERPENDICULAR	441	3 DON JUAN	14	71	8
PRESERVING					
PRESERVING PARTRIDGES AND PRETTY WENCHES	531	3 DON JUAN	16	63	7
PRESIDE					
SNATCHED FROM A PRISON TO PRESIDE AT COURT	495	2 DON JUAN	5	147	3
PRESS					
AROUND THEM MADE THEM TO EACH OTHER PRESS	255	2 DON JUAN	2	188	6
A CERTAIN PRESS OR CUPBOARD NICHED IN YONDER	450	2 DON JUAN	5	66	6
NO SCANDALS MADE THE DAILY PRESS A CURSE--	496	2 DON JUAN	5	149	7
NOT ONLY IN MERE TALKING BUT THE PRESS MAN	288	2 DON JUAN	11	42	5
GIVE GENTLY WAY WHEN THERE'S TOO GREAT A PRESS	366	3 DON JUAN	13	18	5
PRESS'D					
BUT PRESS'D HER BLOODLESS LIP TO JUAN'S CHEEK	114	2 DON JUAN	1	169	8
JUAN WOULD QUESTION FURTHER BUT SHE PRESS'D	356	2 DON JUAN	4	24	1
PRESSED					
BENEATH HIS ART THE DAME PRESSED TO DISCLOSE THEM	208	2 DON JUAN	9	51	7
IT PRESSED UPON A HARD BUT GLOWING BUST	560	3 DON JUAN	16	122	3
PRESSING					
I HAVE ANSWERED ALL YOUR QUESTIONS WITHOUT PRESSING	419	2 DON JUAN	5	16	3
PRESSURE					
A LITTLE PRESSURE THRILLING AND SO BLAND	60	2 DON JUAN	1	71	4
PRESSURE OF HANDS PERHAPS EVEN A CHASTE KISS--	242	2 DON JUAN	2	164	7
THE GENTLE PRESSURE AND THE THRILLING TOUCH	351	2 DON JUAN	4	14	1
PREST					
THE GENERAL LASCY WHO HAD BEEN HARD PREST	140	3 DON JUAN	8	56	1
HERE LET US PAUSE--WE ARE NOT PREST FOR TIME	455	3 DON JUAN	14	102	V1
PRESUME					
IF ANY PERSON SHOULD PRESUME TO ASSERT	140	2 DON JUAN	1	207	1
PRAY SIR SAID JUAN IF I MAY PRESUME	418	2 DON JUAN	5	15	1
HAD SETTLED ALL NOR COULD HE THEN PRESUME	57	3 DON JUAN	6	103	5
OF YELLOW CASSIMERE WE MAY PRESUME	204	3 DON JUAN	9	43	6
AND FAR BE IT FROM MY MUSES TO PRESUME	227	3 DON JUAN	10	5	3
WE MAY PRESUME TO CRITICISE OR PRAISE	360	3 DON JUAN	13	4	4
WHEN ONCE DECANTED--I PRESUME TO GUESS SO	458	3 DON JUAN	15	6	6
PRESUMED					
AND ALSO AS MAY BE PRESUMED SHE LAID	485	2 DON JUAN	5	129	4
HE NE'ER PRESUMED TO MAKE AN ERROR CLEARER--	426	3 DON JUAN	14	37	7
BUT ADELINE WHO PROBABLY PRESUMED	473	3 DON JUAN	15	39	1
PRESUMES					
SOME FEMALE HEAD MOST CURIOUSLY PRESUMES	442	2 DON JUAN	5	55	6
PRETENCE					
UNDER PRETENCE OF BUSINESS INDISPENSIBLE	103	2 DON JUAN	1	151	2
WITH SOME PRETENCE ABOUT THE SUN THAT MAKES	230	2 DON JUAN	2	139	2
FOOD SHE REFUSED AND RAIMENT NO PRETENCE	381	2 DON JUAN	4	68	5
HE DANCED WITHOUT THEATRICAL PRETENCE	427	3 DON JUAN	14	38	6
AT PRESENT I AM GLAD OF A PRETENCE	453	3 DON JUAN	14	97	4
NOW JUAN THOUGH NO COXCOMB IN PRETENCE	490	3 DON JUAN	15	77	5
PRETENCES					
THE SOUND THAN SENSE)--BESIDES ALL THESE PRETENCES	219	3 DON JUAN	9	74	7
TO SET UP VAIN PRETENCES OF BEING GREAT	267	3 DON JUAN	10	87	3
PRETEND					
HE HAD BEEN HID--I DON'T PRETEND TO SAY	112	2 DON JUAN	1	166	1
MUCH ENGLISH I CANNOT PRETEND TO SPEAK	243	2 DON JUAN	2	165	3
I DON'T PRETEND THAT I QUITE UNDERSTAND	346	2 DON JUAN	4	5	4
FOR MY PART I PRETEND NOT TO BE CATO	68	3 DON JUAN	7	4	6
IN HEAVEN I KNOW NOT NOR PRETEND TO GUESS	167	3 DON JUAN	8	112	2
BUT DON'T PRETEND TO SETTLE WHICH WAS BEST	309	3 DON JUAN	11	83	8
WHICH SOME PRETEND TO TRACE IN LADIES' SMILES	544	3 DON JUAN	16	92	8
PRETENDED					
THE TURKS AT FIRST PRETENDED TO HAVE SCAMPERED	149	3 DON JUAN	8	75	6
PRETENDER					
GOES WHEN SOME PERT PRETENDER DEALS HIS PRAISE	156	3 DON JUAN	8	90	V4
PRETENDERS					
THE LIST GROWS LONG OF LIVE AND DEAD PRETENDERS	299	3 DON JUAN	11	61	1
PRETENSION					
LIKE VIRTUE AND THE ABSENCE OF PRETENSION	462	3 DON JUAN	15	14	7
PRETENSIONS					
MY EPICAL PRETENSIONS TO THE LAUREL	141	2 DON JUAN	1	209	6
PRETENSIONS WHICH THEY NEVER DREAMED TO HAVE SHOWN--	344	3 DON JUAN	12	61	4
PRETTIEST					
I SAW THE PRETTIEST CREATURE FRESH FROM MILAN	268	2 DON JUAN	2	209	7
ABOUT THE PRETTIEST ANKLE IN THE WORLD	312	2 DON JUAN	3	72	8
PRETTILY					
AND HAVE OR HAD AN EAR THAT SERVED ME PRETTILY)--	350	3 DON JUAN	12	75	8
PRETTY					
OF ALL THE SPANISH TOWNS IS NONE MORE PRETTY	25	2 DON JUAN	1	8	5
PRETTY WERE BUT TO GIVE A FEEBLE NOTION	51	2 DON JUAN	1	55	4
JUAN SHE SAW AND AS A PRETTY CHILD	59	2 DON JUAN	1	69	1
WHEN JULIA SATE WITHIN AS PRETTY A BOWER	77	2 DON JUAN	1	104	3
NOW TELL ME DON'T YOU CUT A PRETTY FIGURE	103	2 DON JUAN	1	150	8
HIS SUFFOCATION BY THAT PRETTY PAIR	112	2 DON JUAN	1	166	6
THIS PRETTY GENTLEMAN WITHIN THE CLOSET	114	2 DON JUAN	1	170	8
A PRETTY WOMAN--(THAT'S QUITE NATURAL	158	2 DON JUAN	2	3	5

PRETTY   (CONTINUED)
    A PRETTY TOWN I RECOLLECT IT WELL-- . . . . 159 2 DON JUAN 2   5   2
    IN SHORT HE WAS A VERY PRETTY FELLOW . . . . 235 2 DON JUAN 2   148   7
    BESIDES HER MAID'S AS PRETTY FOR THEIR SIZE . . . . . 246 2 DON JUAN 2   171   4
    BUT ONE THING'S PRETTY SURE A WOMAN PLANTED-- . . . . 276 2 DON JUAN 3   4   2
    ALL PRETTY PASTIMES IN WHICH NO OFFENCE IS . . . . . 293 2 DON JUAN 3   35   4
    OH--THE THIRD CANTO--AND THE PRETTY PAIR-- . . . . . 317 2 DON JUAN 3   81   6
    ARE NOT THESE PRETTY STANZAS--SOME FOLKS SAY-- . . . 336 2 DON JUAN 3   104 V1
    A PRETTY PERSON WHICH PERHAPS MAY STRIKE . . . . . . 390 2 DON JUAN 4   85   3
    A PRETTY LAD BUT BURSTING WITH CONCEIT . . . . 392 2 DON JUAN 4   89   2
    BUT SPOIL (I THINK) A VERY PRETTY POEM . . . . 403 2 DON JUAN 4   107   8
    FORTUNE HAS PLAYED YOU HERE A PRETTY FREAK . . . . . 418 2 DON JUAN 5   14   4
    NEW PAINTED OR A PRETTY OPERA-SCENE . . . . 436 2 DON JUAN 5   46   8
    THAT A MERE CHRISTIAN SHOULD BE HALF SO PRETTY . . . 500 2 DON JUAN 5   155   8
    JUANNA--WELL A PRETTY NAME ENOUGH . . . . 28 3 DON JUAN 6   44   2
    A PRETTY STRANGER WITHOUT FRIEND OR GUIDE . . . . . 28 3 DON JUAN 6   45   5
    HOWEVER THIS MAY BE 'TIS PRETTY SURE . . . . 154 3 DON JUAN 8   85   1
    WITH ALL THEIR PRETTY MILK-AND-WATER WAYS . . . . . 156 3 DON JUAN 8   90   4
    THE CHILD'S A PRETTY CHILD--A VERY PRETTY-- . . . . 162 3 DON JUAN 8   101   2
    THE CHILD'S A PRETTY CHILD--A VERY PRETTY-- . . . . 162 3 DON JUAN 8   101   2
    THOSE HOURIS LIKE ALL OTHER PRETTY CREATURES . . . 167 3 DON JUAN 8   111   7
    ITS BLOODY BOND AND SAVED PERHAPS SOME PRETTY . . . 174 3 DON JUAN 8   124   3
    SOME PRETTY SHELL IS BEST FOR MODERATE BATHERS . . 191 3 DON JUAN 9   18   8
    OR PRETTY IS A THING TO RECOLLECT . . . . 199 3 DON JUAN 9   34   3
    AND AS ROMANTIC HEADS ARE PRETTY PAINTERS . . . . 284 3 DON JUAN 11   33   3
    HOWEVER HE DID PRETTY WELL AND WAS . . . . 295 3 DON JUAN 11   54   1
    AND WHEN AT LAST THE PRETTY CREATURE GETS . . . . 333 3 DON JUAN 12   36   5
    AS WHO HAS NOT IF FEMALE YOUNG AND PRETTY . . . . 338 3 DON JUAN 12   47   2
    AT FIRST HE DID NOT THINK THE WOMEN PRETTY . . . 347 3 DON JUAN 12   68   8
    I SAID THAT JUAN DID NOT THINK THEM PRETTY . . . 350 3 DON JUAN 12   74   2
    THERE WERE THE SIX MISS RAWBOLDS--PRETTY DEARS . . 398 3 DON JUAN 13   85   6
    TO CATCH A GLIMPSE EVEN OF A PRETTY PEASANT . . . 422 3 DON JUAN 14   28   8
    ONE OF THOSE PRETTY PRECIOUS PLAGUES WHICH HAUNT . 438 3 DON JUAN 14   63   3
    WHICH PRETTY WOMEN--THE SWEET SOULS--CALL SOUL . . 441 3 DON JUAN 14   71   3
    A PRETTY NAME AS ONE WOULD WISH TO READ . . . . . 458 3 DON JUAN 15   5   3
    BUT STILL I AM OR WAS A PRETTY POET . . . . 482 3 DON JUAN 15   60   8
    THERE'S PRETTY PICKING IN THOSE PETITS PUITS . . . 486 3 DON JUAN 15   68   8
    (WHEN SEATED WITH HIM) OF SOME PRETTY LISPER . . . 487 3 DON JUAN 15   70   8
    ARE SOMEHOW ECHOED TO THE PRETTY DEARS . . . . . 489 3 DON JUAN 15   76   3
    SOME MILLIONS MUST BE WRONG THAT'S PRETTY CLEAR . 496 3 DON JUAN 15   90   1
    PRESERVING PARTRIDGES AND PRETTY WENCHES . . . . 531 3 DON JUAN 16   63   7
PREUX
    FOR OUT OF THESE THREE PREUX CHEVALIERS HOW . . . 82 3 DON JUAN 7   33   2
    THERE WAS THE PREUX CHEVALIER DE LA RUSE . . . . 398 3 DON JUAN 13   86   3
    WHICH PIQUES A PREUX CHEVALIER--AS IT OUGHT . . . 490 3 DON JUAN 15   77   2
PREVAIL
    AT ALL SUCH AUCTIONS KNEW HOW TO PREVAIL . . . . 477 2 DON JUAN 5   114   6
    (SO THAT THEIR EFFORTS SHOULD AT LENGTH PREVAIL) . 105 3 DON JUAN 7   77   6
    DISCUSSED THE FASHION WHICH MIGHT NEXT PREVAIL . . 406 3 DON JUAN 13   104   5
PREVAILED
    THAT STRANGER TO MOST COUNCILS HERE PREVAILED . . . 92 3 DON JUAN 7   51   3
PREVAILING
    THE SUN NO DOUBT IS THE PREVAILING REASON . . . . . 76 2 DON JUAN 1   102   4
PREVARICATION
    MAINTAINED WITH ALL THE DUE PREVARICATION . . . . 246 3 DON JUAN 10   45   4
PREVENTATIVE
    CERTES BUT A PREVENTATIVE AND THEREFORE . . . . . 470 3 DON JUAN 15   31   7
PREVENTED
    BUT AGGRAVATE THE CRIME YOU HAVE NOT PREVENTED . . 353 3 DON JUAN 12   80   7
PREVENTS
    WHICH IN THE NORTH PREVENTS PRECOCIOUS CRIMES . . 501 2 DON JUAN 5   157   5
PREVIOUS
    WITHOUT A WORD OF PREVIOUS ADMONITION . . . . . . 97 2 DON JUAN 1   139   5
PREVIOUSLY
    THAT THEREFORE DO I PREVIOUSLY DECLARE . . . . . 369 3 DON JUAN 13   25   7
PREY
    BUT LIKE THE SHARK AND TIGER MUST HAVE PREY . . . 191 2 DON JUAN 2   67   4
    EXCEPT SOME CERTAIN PORTIONS OF THE PREY . . . . 284 2 DON JUAN 3   17   3
    UPON THEIR PREY AS DARTS AN ANGRY ASP . . . . . 370 2 DON JUAN 4   48   6
    OR ANY INTERESTING BEAST OF PREY . . . . 487 2 DON JUAN 5   132   2
    OF COSSACQUES AND THEIR PREY TURNED ROUND AND CAST . . 97 3 DON JUAN 7   59   2
    BECAUSE THEIR THOUGHTS HAD NEVER BEEN THE PREY . 145 3 DON JUAN 8   66   3
    SUCH AS HE THOUGHT THE LEAST GIVEN UP TO PREY . 162 3 DON JUAN 8   102   4
    AND SCENT THE PREY THEIR MASTERS WOULD ATTACK ALL . 196 3 DON JUAN 9   27   5
    THAT SAD INEXPLICABLE BEAST OF PREY-- . . . . . 207 3 DON JUAN 9   50   2
    SHE IS SO RARE AND THOU HAST SO MUCH PREY . . . 459 3 DON JUAN 15   9   2
    MADE NORMAN CHURCH HIS PREY . . . . 518 3 DON JUAN 16 L   1   6
PRIAM'S
    BUT NOW INSTEAD OF SLAYING PRIAM'S SON . . . . . 106 3 DON JUAN 7   78   5
    DESCRIBING PRIAM'S PELEUS' OR JOVE'S SON . . . . 164 3 DON JUAN 8   105   6
PRICE
    SINCE GOLD ALONE SHOULD NOT HAVE BEEN ITS PRICE . . 12 2 DON JUAN D   6   4
    THE LOVER WHO MUST PAY A HANDSOME PRICE . . . . . 57 2 DON JUAN 1   66   7
    OF ALL EXPERIENCE 'TIS THE USUAL PRICE . . . . . 122 2 DON JUAN 1   183   3
    BESIDES THY PRICE IS SOMETHING DEARER STILL . . . 372 2 DON JUAN 4   53 V4
    A HEAVY PRICE MUST ALL PAY WHO THUS ERR . . . . 383 2 DON JUAN 4   73   6
    TWELVE NEGRESSES FROM NUBIA BROUGHT A PRICE . . . 408 2 DON JUAN 4   115   1
    WITH AMBER MOUTHS OF GREATER PRICE OR LESS . . . 441 2 DON JUAN 5   53   6
    JUST AS ONE VIEWS A HORSE TO GUESS HIS PRICE . . 441 2 DON JUAN 5   54   6

PRICE   (CONTINUED)

YOU WILL TAKE ISMAIL AT WHATEVER PRICE	86	3 DON JUAN 7	40	8
DEFENDED AT A PRICE EXTREMELY DEAR	151	3 DON JUAN 8	79	8
ALTHOUGH NO DOUBT IT WAS BEYOND ALL PRICE	200	3 DON JUAN 9	36	8
ONLY TO KEEP ITS CORN AT THE OLD PRICE	335	3 DON JUAN 12	40	8
COMPARED WITH THOSE OF OUR PURE PEARLS OF PRICE	349	3 DON JUAN 12	72	7
YET IN THE VERY CENTRE PAST ALL PRICE	375	3 DON JUAN 13	37	5
AND YOUR COLD PEOPLE ARE BEYOND ALL PRICE	375	3 DON JUAN 13	38	7
AND LOWER THE PRICE OF ROUGE--AT LEAST SOME WINTERS	409	3 DON JUAN 13	111	8
AND WHATNOT THOUGH HE RODE BEYOND ALL PRICE	425	3 DON JUAN 14	35	7
FOR WHICH SMALL THANKS ARE STILL THE MARKET PRICE	469	3 DON JUAN 15	29	3
THE PRICE WOULD SPEEDILY REPAY ITS WORTH IN	529	3 DON JUAN 16	59	4

PRICES
| THE MOST BY READY CASH--BUT ALL HAVE PRICES | 425 | 2 DON JUAN 5 | 27 | 7 |

PRICK'D
| ARRAS THEY PRICK'D AND CURTAINS WITH THEIR SWORDS | 99 | 2 DON JUAN 1 | 143 | 7 |
| SPOILT AS A PIPE OF CLARET IS WHEN PRICK'D | 502 | 2 DON JUAN 5 | 158 | 5 |

PRICKING
| PRICKING HER FINGERS WITH THOSE CURSED PINS | 36 | 3 DON JUAN 6 | 61 | 7 |

PRICKS
| WHO KICK AGAINST THE PRICKS JUST AT THIS JUNCTURE | 263 | 3 DON JUAN 10 | 77 | 7 |
| HEEDLESS OF PRICKS BECAUSE IT WAS OBTUSE | 565 | 3 DON JUAN 17 | 6 | 6 |

PRIDE
NO CHOICE WAS LEFT HIS FEELINGS OR HIS PRIDE	41	2 DON JUAN 1	36	7
FLASH'D AN EXPRESSION MORE OF PRIDE THAN IRE	54	2 DON JUAN 1	60	4
PRIDE FAME AMBITION TO FILL UP HIS HEART	131	2 DON JUAN 1	194	5
YOU WILL PROCEED IN PLEASURE AND IN PRIDE	132	2 DON JUAN 1	195	1
YOU WILL RETURN IN BEAUTY AND IN PRIDE	132	2 DON JUAN 1	195	V1
AT WASSAIL IN THEIR BEAUTY AND THEIR PRIDE	306	2 DON JUAN 3	61	4
BEING PRIDE WHICH LEADS THE MIND TO SOAR TOO FAR	344	2 DON JUAN 4	1	7
AND MASTER'D BY HER WISDOM OR HER PRIDE	356	2 DON JUAN 4	23	4
O'ER THEM IN ALMOST PYRAMIDIC PRIDE	462	2 DON JUAN 5	87	6
O'ER THEM LIKE DEATH UPON A MONARCH'S PRIDE	462	2 DON JUAN 5	87	V6
BABA INDIGNANT AT THIS ILL-TIMED PRIDE	471	2 DON JUAN 5	103	1
BUT HE WAS STEELED BY SORROW WRATH AND PRIDE	484	2 DON JUAN 5	126	2
THOUGH PALE WITH CONFLICTS BETWEEN LOVE AND PRIDE--	50	3 DON JUAN 6	89	6
DESPITE HER INJURED LOVE AND FIERY PRIDE	62	3 DON JUAN 6	113	5
THEIR OBSTINACY PRIDE AND INDECISION	64	3 DON JUAN 6	117	5
BETWEEN YOUR FAME AND FEELINGS PRIDE AND PITY--	162	3 DON JUAN 8	101	4
TO FREE HIS COUNTRY PITT TOO HAD HIS PRIDE	186	3 DON JUAN 9	8	6
HIS PRIDE TOO FELT THAT SHE WAS NOT ENSLAVED	251	3 DON JUAN 10	55	4
A KIND OF PRIDE THAT HE SHOULD BE AMONG	257	3 DON JUAN 10	65	5
O'ER THE HIGH HILL WHICH LOOKS WITH PRIDE OR SCORN	264	3 DON JUAN 10	80	4
AND (SHOULD SHE NOT HOLD FAST BY LOVE OR PRIDE)	292	3 DON JUAN 11	46	4
THE PRIDE OF A MERE CHILD WITH A NEW SASH ON	351	3 DON JUAN 12	77	5
RESERVE AND PRIDE COULD MAKE HIM AND FULL SLOW	366	3 DON JUAN 13	16	2
HAD ALL THE PERTINACITY PRIDE HAS	366	3 DON JUAN 13	16	5
HIS COUNTRY'S PRIDE HE CAME DOWN TO THE COUNTRY	401	3 DON JUAN 13	91	8
AND WHETHER COLDNESS PRIDE OR VIRTUE DIGNIFY	435	3 DON JUAN 14	57	7
AND PRIDE MY FEEBLE--LET US RAMBLE ON	466	3 DON JUAN 15	22	2
WHO NOW ARE BASKING IN THEIR FULL-BLOWN PRIDE	466	3 DON JUAN 15	23	3
THE DEVIL WAS IN THE GIRL COULD IT BE PRIDE	490	3 DON JUAN 15	78	5
NOR THOUGHT HE HAD PRIDE ENOUGH--FOR SHE WAS PROUD	493	3 DON JUAN 15	83	V6
TRAMPLING ON PLATO'S PRIDE WITH GREATER PRIDE	522	3 DON JUAN 16	43	3
TRAMPLING ON PLATO'S PRIDE WITH GREATER PRIDE	522	3 DON JUAN 16	43	3
TO PROVE THEIR PRIDE AS FOOTMEN TO A BEGGAR	537	3 DON JUAN 16	76	8
MORE JOY THAN FROM ALL FUTURE PRIDE OR PRAISE	554	3 DON JUAN 16	108	5

PRIDED
| AS ONCE (A FEAT ON WHICH OURSELVES WE PRIDED) | 211 | 2 DON JUAN 2 | 105 | 7 |
| WITH SOME OF THOSE FAIR CREATURES WHO HAVE PRIDED | 327 | 3 DON JUAN 12 | 25 | 6 |

PRIDE'S
| FOR HONOUR'S PRIDE'S RELIGION'S VIRTUE'S SAKE | 62 | 2 DON JUAN 1 | 75 | 4 |
| THAN SOLITARY PRIDE'S OPPRESSIVE WEIGHT | 367 | 3 DON JUAN 13 | 19 | 6 |

PRIEST
A PRIEST THE OTHER--AT LEAST SO THEY SAY	39	2 DON JUAN 1	34	5
THE PRIEST INSTRUCTS AND SO OUR LIFE EXHALES	159	2 DON JUAN 2	4	6
A PRIEST A SHARK AN ALDERMAN OR PIKE	239	2 DON JUAN 2	157	8
THEIR PRIEST WAS SOLITUDE AND THEY WERE WED	265	2 DON JUAN 2	204	6
SO LEAVING EACH THEIR PRIEST AND PRAYER-BOOK READY	280	2 DON JUAN 3	9	7
WE'RE TOLD THIS GREAT HIGH PRIEST OF ALL THE NINE	328	2 DON JUAN 3	91	6
THE HOWLING HEBREWS OF CYBELE'S PRIEST--	297	3 DON JUAN 11	58	8
A RIGID GUARDIAN OR A ZEALOUS PRIEST	334	3 DON JUAN 12	39	5
THE POOR PRIEST WAS REDUCED TO COMMON SENSE	540	3 DON JUAN 16	83	6

PRIESTS
| THOUGH PRIESTS AND SLAVES MAY JOIN IN THE SERVILE CRY | 195 | 3 DON JUAN 9 | 26 | V8 |
| HISTORIANS HEROES LAWYERS PRIESTS TO PUT | 286 | 3 DON JUAN 11 | 37 | 3 |

PRIM
| MORALITY'S PRIM PERSONIFICATION | 29 | 2 DON JUAN 1 | 16 | 5 |
| AS THAT PRIM SILENT COLD AURORA RABY | 477 | 3 DON JUAN 15 | 49 | 8 |

PRIMA-DONNA
| THAN DID THE PRIMA-DONNA AND THE TENOR | 388 | 2 DON JUAN 4 | 81 | 8 |
| THE PRIMA-DONNA THOUGH A LITTLE OLD | 389 | 2 DON JUAN 4 | 83 | 1 |

PRIMA-DONNA'S
| BUT BEING THE PRIMA-DONNA'S NEAR RELATION | 391 | 2 DON JUAN 4 | 87 | 5 |

PRIMATE
| I COULD SEND FORTH MY MANDATE LIKE A PRIMATE | 327 | 3 DON JUAN 12 | 24 | 3 |

PRIME
| FOR INTO A PRIME MINISTER BUT CHANGE | 283 | 2 DON JUAN 3 | 14 | 3 |
| HER PRIME OF LIFE JUST NOW IN JUICY VIGOUR | 218 | 3 DON JUAN 9 | 72 | 5 |

630

PRIME   (CONTINUED)
  SO PRIME SO SWELL SO NUTTY AND SO KNOWING . . . . . . 277 3 DON JUAN 11   19   8
  AND FULL OF PROMISE AS THE SPRING OF PRIME . . . . 354 3 DON JUAN 12   84   4
PRIMLY
  JUST NAMED THESE PALISADES WERE PRIMLY SET . . . . . 136 3 DON JUAN 8   46   8
PRIMROSE
  THEIR WAY THROUGH VIRTUE'S PRIMROSE PATHS OF SNOWS . . 328 3 DON JUAN 12   26   4
PRINCE
  PRINCE FERDINAND GRANBY BURGOYNE KEPPEL HOWE . . . . 22 2 DON JUAN 1   2   2
  BESIDES THE PRINCE IS ALL FOR THE LAND-SERVICE . . . . 23 2 DON JUAN 1   4   7
  MILTON'S THE PRINCE OF POETS--SO WE SAY . . . . . 328 3 DON JUAN 3   91   1
  WITHOUT THE AID OF PRINCE OR PLENIPO . . . . 53 3 DON JUAN 6   95   6
  THE PRINCE DELIGNE AND LANGERON AND DAMAS . . . . 82 3 DON JUAN 7   32   7
  'TIS TRUE THE MEMOIRS OF THE PRINCE DELIGNE . . . . 82 3 DON JUAN 7   33   7
  A COURIER TO THE PRINCE AND HE SUCCEEDED . . . . 85 3 DON JUAN 7   38   2
  THE LETTER OF THE PRINCE TO THE SAME MARSHAL . . . . 86 3 DON JUAN 7   40   1
  THE PRINCE DELIGNE WAS WOUNDED IN THE KNEE . . . . 116 3 DON JUAN 8   10   1
  INSISTING ON REMOVAL OF THE PRINCE . . . . . . 117 3 DON JUAN 8   11   2
  PRESENTED BY THE PRINCE OF THE BRAZILS . . . . . 185 3 DON JUAN 9   6   2
  A PRINCE THE PRINCE OF PRINCES AT THE TIME . . . . 354 3 DON JUAN 12   84   2
  A PRINCE THE PRINCE OF PRINCES AT THE TIME . . . . 354 3 DON JUAN 12   84   2
PRINCELY
  WAS PRINCELY AS THE PROOFS HAVE ALWAYS SHOWN . . . . 499 2 DON JUAN 5   153   6
PRINCE'S
  THE PEOPLE'S SYCOPHANT THE PRINCE'S FOE . . . . 151 2 DON JUAN 1 V 2   7
  THE PRINCE'S TYRANT--TILL HE HEARS THE DRUMS . . . 151 2 DON JUAN 1 V 2 V8
  THE PRINCE'S TYRANT--THROUGH LUST OF POWER . . . . 151 2 DON JUAN 1 V 2 V8
PRINCES
  HAVE PRINCES WHO SPUR MORE THAN THEIR POSTILLIONS . . . 254 3 DON JUAN 10   60   8
  A PRINCE THE PRINCE OF PRINCES AT THE TIME . . . . 354 3 DON JUAN 12   84   2
  THOUGH PRINCES THE POSSESSOR WERE BESIEGING ALL . . . 528 3 DON JUAN 16   56   4
PRINCESS
  AROUND AS PRINCESS OF HER FATHER'S LAND . . . . . 312 2 DON JUAN 3   72   1
  FROM AN OLD ROMAN PRINCESS AT BOLOGNA . . . . . 389 2 DON JUAN 4   83   8
  IN WHICH A PRINCESS WITH GREAT PLEASURE WOULD . . . 453 2 DON JUAN 5   73   3
  OR DUTCHESS PRINCESS EMPRESS DEIGNS TO PROVE . . . . 216 3 DON JUAN 9   68   5
PRINCESSES
  LEST THEY SHOULD SEEM PRINCESSES IN DISGUISE . . . . 222 2 DON JUAN 2   124   2
PRINCIPAL
  HAVE SPENT MY LIFE BOTH INTEREST AND PRINCIPAL . . . 143 2 DON JUAN 1   213   7
PRINCIPLE
  WHILE LIFE'S STRANGE PRINCIPLE WILL OFTEN LIE . . . . 350 2 DON JUAN 4   11   7
  A SECOND PRINCIPLE OF LIFE WHICH MIGHT . . . . . 382 2 DON JUAN 4   70   2
  MAY BE THE HOARDER'S PRINCIPLE OF ACTION . . . . . 321 3 DON JUAN 12   11   2
PRINCIPLES
  LIKE POPLARS WITH GOOD PRINCIPLES FOR ROOTS . . . . 343 3 DON JUAN 12   59   4
  OF THE TWO PRINCIPLES BUT LEAVES BEHIND . . . . . 377 3 DON JUAN 13   41   6
PRINT
  IN NAMELESS PRINT--THAT I HAVE NO DEVOTION . . . . 336 2 DON JUAN 3   104   2
  AS THEY WHO PRINT THEM THINK IS NECESSARY . . . . 79 3 DON JUAN 7   26   6
  AND SEE HIS STATUE RAISED--AND PRINT ENGRAVED . . . 185 3 DON JUAN 9   5 V8
  WHEN SHE NO MORE COULD READ THE PIOUS PRINT . . . . 241 3 DON JUAN 10   34   8
  A PAGE WHERE TIME SHOULD HESITATE TO PRINT AGE . . . 458 3 DON JUAN 15   7   5
PRINTED
  WAS PRINTED GROVE ALTHOUGH HIS NAME WAS GROSE . . . . 120 3 DON JUAN 8   18   8
  A PERIOD SOMETHING LIKE A PRINTED PAGE . . . . . 315 3 DON JUAN 12   1   6
  ESPECIALLY UPON A PRINTED PAGE . . . . 494 3 DON JUAN 15   85   4
PRINTING
  FEEDS YOU BY PRINTING HALF THE REALM'S STARVATION-- . . . 200 3 DON JUAN 9   35   8
PRIOR
  OF SMOLLET PRIOR ARIOSTO FIELDING . . . . 397 2 DON JUAN 4   98   3
PRIORITY
  AND THEIRS--WITHOUT A STRUGGLE FOR PRIORITY . . . . 462 3 DON JUAN 15   15   7
  BUT SAINT AUGUSTINE HAS THE GREAT PRIORITY . . . . 503 3 DON JUAN 16   5   5
PRISCIAN
  NOR BROKEN MY OWN HEAD NOR THAT OF PRISCIAN . . . . 467 3 DON JUAN 15   24   6
PRISM
  BUT WHICH I DOUBT EXTREMELY--THOU SOLE PRISM . . . . 269 3 DON JUAN 11   2   6
PRISON
  SNATCHED FROM A PRISON TO PRESIDE AT COURT . . . . 495 2 DON JUAN 5   147   3
  HIS SONS WERE KEPT IN PRISON TILL THEY GREW . . . . 499 2 DON JUAN 5   153   1
  IN PRISON--BUT THE JAILOR WHAT IS HE . . . . . 258 3 DON JUAN 10   68   3
  SO FAR RELAX'D HER THOUGHTS FROM THEIR SWEET PRISON . . 491 3 DON JUAN 15   80   7
PRISONED
  THE PRISONED EAGLE WILL NOT PAIR NOR I . . . . . 484 2 DON JUAN 5   126   7
PRISONER
  AND I BECAME A PRISONER TO THE FOE-- . . . . . 98 3 DON JUAN 7   61   6
  TO MAKE HIM PRISONER WAS ALSO DISHED . . . . . 152 3 DON JUAN 8   80   8
PRISONERS
  HIS PRISONERS DIVIDING THEM LIKE CHAPTERS . . . . 283 2 DON JUAN 3   15   6
PRISONS
  RACKS PRISONS INQUISITIONS RESURRECTION . . . . . 272 3 DON JUAN 11   9   7
PRITHEE
  (PRITHEE EXCUSE THIS ENGINEERING SLANG) . . . . . 72 3 DON JUAN 7   11   6
  BUT ONCE THERE (IF YOU DOUBT THIS PRITHEE TRY) . . . 350 3 DON JUAN 12   74   7
PRIVATE
  FOR MALICE STILL IMPUTES SOME PRIVATE END) . . . . 58 2 DON JUAN 1   66   6
  ON TO THE HOUSE BUT BY A PRIVATE WAY . . . . . 300 2 DON JUAN 3   49   2
  OLD LAMBRO PASS'D UNSEEN A PRIVATE GATE . . . . . 306 2 DON JUAN 3   61   1

```
                                                          PAGE VOL        CANTO    STANZA LN
PRIVATE   (CONTINUED)
     POETS AND PRIVATE TUTORS ARE EXPOSED  . . . . . . .  486  2 DON JUAN    5      131    5
     FOR LOVE OR BREAKFAST PRIVATE PLEASING LONE  . . . .   54  3 DON JUAN    6       97    3
     THE PUBLIC BUILDINGS AND THE PRIVATE TOO . . . . . .   78  3 DON JUAN    7       23    4
     ALL PRIVATE FAVOURITES OF DON JUAN FOR  . . . . . .   249  3 DON JUAN   10       50    2
     PRIVATE THOUGH PUBLICLY IMPORTANT BORE  . . . . . .   283  3 DON JUAN   11       32    2
     REAPING ALLUSIONS PRIVATE AND INGLORIOUS . . . . .    369  3 DON JUAN   13       25    4
     HEAVEN AND HIS FRIENDS KNEW THAT A PRIVATE LIFE  . . . 536  3 DON JUAN   16       74    1
PRIVATEER
     LIKE THE FIRST OLD GREEK PRIVATEER THE ARGO . . . . . 191  2 DON JUAN    2       66    8
PRIVILEGE
     IS THE POOR PRIVILEGE TO TURN THE KEY . . . . . . .   258  3 DON JUAN   10       68    5
     UPON THE GUIDE-BOOK'S PRIVILEGE THE SUN . . . . . .   279  3 DON JUAN   11       23    6
PRIVILEGES
     THE COMMON PRIVILEGES OF MY SEX . . . . . . . . .    101  2 DON JUAN    1      147    2
PRIVY
     AND BEING OF THE COUNCIL CALLED THE PRIVY  . . . . .  440  3 DON JUAN   14       68    1
PRIZE
     IN CASE HE THOUGHT HIS WIFE TOO GREAT A PRIZE  . . . . 75  2 DON JUAN    1      101    8
     OF CLAP-TRAP WHICH YOUR RECENT POETS PRIZE  . . . .   222  2 DON JUAN    2      124    4
     A SAILOR WHEN THE PRIZE HAS STRUCK IN FIGHT . . . .   261  2 DON JUAN    2      196    5
     IS TO THE DEVIL NOW NO FURTHER PRIZE  . . . . . .     88  3 DON JUAN    7       45    3
     TO DRAW A HIGH PRIZE NOW HOWE'ER HE GOT HER I  . . .  333  3 DON JUAN   12       37    7
     THERE WAS A PRIZE OX A PRIZE PIG AND PLOUGHMAN . . .  530  3 DON JUAN   16       60    7
     THERE WAS A PRIZE OX A PRIZE PIG AND PLOUGHMAN . . .  530  3 DON JUAN   16       60    7
     THE PRIZE PIG PLOUGHMAN POACHERS THE MEN SENT . . .   533  3 DON JUAN   16       66    4
PRIZE-MONEY
     PILLAGE TO SOLDIERS PRIZE-MONEY TO SEAMEN  . . . . .   88  2 DON JUAN    1      124    8
PRIZES
     BY SWAMPING ONE OF THE PRIZES HE HAD CHAIN'D  . . .   283  2 DON JUAN    3       15    5
PRO
     WOULD YOU DO LESS PRO FOCIS ET PRO ARIS . . . . . .   174  3 DON JUAN    8      124   V8
     WOULD YOU DO LESS PRO FOCIS ET PRO ARIS . . . . . .   174  3 DON JUAN    8      124   V8
PROBABLY
     SLEEPING MOST PROBABLY--WHEN AT HER DOOR . . . . . .   95  2 DON JUAN    1      136    2
     AND PLUMAGE (PROBABLY IT MIGHT HAVE ERR'D  . . . .   206  2 DON JUAN    2       94    3
     IF SINGLE PROBABLY HIS PLIGHTED FAIR  . . . . . . .  288  2 DON JUAN    3       24    1
     WOULD SHARE MOST PROBABLY ITS RESURRECTION  . . . .  301  2 DON JUAN    3       50    8
     THIS MONSTROUS TALE HAD PROBABLY ITS SOURCE . . . .  446  2 DON JUAN    5       61    5
     MIGHT PROBABLY OBTAIN BOTH IN THE END . . . . . . .  451  2 DON JUAN    5       69    3
     BUT A THIRD MOTIVE WAS AS PROBABLY  . . . . . . .     78  3 DON JUAN    7       24    5
     OFFENCE WE KNOW NOT PROBABLY IT PERCHED  . . . . .   192  3 DON JUAN    9       19    7
     HALF HER ATTRACTIONS--PROBABLY FROM PITY--  . . . .  350  3 DON JUAN   12       74    4
     BUT ADELINE WHO PROBABLY PRESUMED . . . . . . . .    473  3 DON JUAN   15       39    1
     THOUGH PROBABLY MUCH LESS A FACT THAN GUESS)  . . .  491  3 DON JUAN   15       80    6
     HE PROBABLY WOULD HAVE PHILOSOPHISED  . . . . . .    506  3 DON JUAN   16       12    6
PROBE
     I'M SORRY THUS TO PROBE A WOUND SO RAW  . . . . . .  155  2 DON JUAN    1    V  7    5
PROBLEM
     HER THOUGHTS WERE THEOREMS HER WORDS A PROBLEM . . . . 28  2 DON JUAN    1       13    7
     PRESENTS THE PROBLEM OF A DOUBLE FIGURE  . . . . .   530  3 DON JUAN   16       61    8
     I LEAVE THE THING A PROBLEM LIKE ALL THINGS--  . . .  568  3 DON JUAN   17       13    1
PROCEED
     MEANTIME--SIR LAUREATE--I PROCEED TO DEDICATE  . . .   20  2 DON JUAN    D       17    1
     BY ALL MEANS LET THE GENTLEMAN PROCEED  . . . . .    104  2 DON JUAN    1      152    2
     BUT TO PROCEED--FOR THERE IS MORE BEHIND  . . . . .  112  2 DON JUAN    1      165    6
     YOU WILL PROCEED IN PLEASURE AND IN PRIDE . . . . .  132  2 DON JUAN    1      195    1
     I SHALL PROCEED WITH HIS ADVENTURES IS  . . . . .    135  2 DON JUAN    1      199    2
     LEAVING MY PEOPLE TO PROCEED ALONE . . . . . . . .   331  2 DON JUAN    3       96    3
     'TIS TIME WE SHOULD PROCEED WITH OUR GOOD POEM . . .  193  3 DON JUAN    9       22    1
     AND NOW I WILL PROCEED UPON THE PAIR  . . . . . .    365  3 DON JUAN   13       13    3
     THAT CLAUSE IS HARD) AND SECONDLY PROCEED . . . . .  393  3 DON JUAN   13       73    6
     AND AS FOR LOVE--OH LOVE--WE WILL PROCEED  . . . .   458  3 DON JUAN   15        5    1
     METHINKS WE MAY PROCEED UPON OUR NARRATIVE  . . . .  481  3 DON JUAN   15       59    2
     I SAY IN MY SLIGHT WAY I MAY PROCEED  . . . . . .    482  3 DON JUAN   15       60    1
PROCEEDED
     HE ASK'D NO FURTHER QUESTIONS AND PROCEEDED . . . .  300  2 DON JUAN    3       49    1
     AND NEXT PROCEEDED QUIETLY TO COCK . . . . . . . .   365  2 DON JUAN    4       40    8
     IN THE MEANTIME THE BATTERIES PROCEEDED  . . . . .    85  3 DON JUAN    7       38    6
     THESE FREEBORN SOUNDS PROCEEDED FROM FOUR PADS  . .  273  3 DON JUAN   11       11    1
PROCEEDING
     SOME STRANGE EXCUSES FOR HIS LATE PROCEEDING  . . .  116  2 DON JUAN    1      174    2
     IN THE MEANTIME WITHOUT PROCEEDING MORE  . . . . .   271  2 DON JUAN    2      216    1
     AND THAT PROCEEDING AT A VERY HIGH RATE  . . . . .   296  2 DON JUAN    3       40    7
PROCEEDINGS
     IF YOU WOULD LIKE TO SEE THE WHOLE PROCEEDINGS . . .  127  2 DON JUAN    1      189    1
PROCEEDS
     AND THUS MY NARRATIVE PROCEEDS--DUDU . . . . . . .    34  3 DON JUAN    6       57    2
PROCESS
     AFTER THE USUAL PROCESS MIGHT BE FOUND  . . . . .    407  2 DON JUAN    4      113    3
     NO PROCESS PROVED CONNUBIAL ANIMOSITY . . . . . . .  496  2 DON JUAN    5      148    6
     AND WITH IT ALL THE PROCESS OF DIGESTION . . . . .   232  3 DON JUAN   10       14    8
     SOLE CREDITOR WHOSE PROCESS DOTH INVOLVE IN'T . . .  458  3 DON JUAN   15        7    7
PROCLAIM
     TO CALL MEN LOVE-BEGOTTEN OR PROCLAIM . . . . . .     53  3 DON JUAN    6       94    1
     THE MORNING POST WAS FOREMOST TO PROCLAIM--  . . .   382  3 DON JUAN   13       51    6
PROCLAIM'D
     NO HIDEOUS SIGN PROCLAIM'D HER SURELY DEAD  . . . .  377  2 DON JUAN    4       60    4
PROCLAIMED
     WITH TO BE LET UPON THEIR DOORS PROCLAIMED  . . . .  278  3 DON JUAN   11       21    6
```

632

		PAGE	VOL	CANTO	STANZA	LN
PROCREATION						
WHILE SAGES WRITE AGAINST ALL PROCREATION	. . . . . .	325	3 DON JUAN	12	21	6
PROCREATIVE						
IN THE FAITH OF THEIR PROCREATIVE CREED	. . . .	324	3 DON JUAN	12	18	3
PROCUL						
BEATUS ILLE PROCUL FROM NEGOTIIS	. . . .	443	3 DON JUAN	14	77	1
PRODIGALLY						
THE MOVEABLES WERE PRODIGALLY RICH	. . . .	449	2 DON JUAN	5	65	4
PRODIGIOUS						
A MOST PRODIGIOUS APPETITE THE STEAM	. . . . . .	237	2 DON JUAN	2	153	3
A MOST PRODIGIOUS PIPPIN--BUT IT HUNG	. . . . . .	44	3 DON JUAN	6	76	2
PRODIGY						
A PRODIGY--HER MORNING DRESS WAS DIMITY	. . . .	27	2 DON JUAN	1	12	6
THAT PRODIGY MISS ARAMINTA SMITH	. . . .	294	3 DON JUAN	11	52	5
PRODUCE						
AND LIKES PARTICULARLY TO PRODUCE	. . . . . .	91	2 DON JUAN	1	128	3
BY NO MEANS WOULD PRODUCE THE TOWN'S SUBMISSION	. . .	81	3 DON JUAN	7	30	5
YET AS THEY FOUNDED CHURCHES WITH THE PRODUCE	. . . .	242	3 DON JUAN	10	36	7
FOR HIM THE FRAGRANT PRODUCE OF EACH TRIP	. . . . .	320	3 DON JUAN	12	9	3
INDIFFERENCE CERTES DON'T PRODUCE DISTRESS	. . . .	374	3 DON JUAN	13	35	6
THAT HALF ITS PRODUCE TENDS TO EMIGRATION	. . . . .	472	3 DON JUAN	15	37	6
PRODUCED						
PRODUCED HER DON MORE HEIRS AT LOVE THAN LAW	. . . .	53	2 DON JUAN	1	58	8
THE HARDNESS BY LONG HABITUDE PRODUCED	. . . .	303	2 DON JUAN	3	54	2
WHO HATH PRODUCED AND WILL RECEIVE THE SOUL	. . . .	336	2 DON JUAN	3	104	8
OF HERBS AND CORDIALS THEY PRODUCED THEIR STORE	. . .	376	2 DON JUAN	4	59	6
TO BE PRODUCED WHEN BROUGHT UP TO THE TEST	. . . .	123	3 DON JUAN	8	25	4
FROM THEIR FEROCITIES PRODUCED BY VANITY	. . . .	182	3 DON JUAN	8	140	4
AND MY SUCCESS PRODUCED WHAT I IN SOUTH	. . . .	324	3 DON JUAN	12	17	4
AND THIN PRODUCED A PLAN WHEREBY TO ERECT	. . . . .	529	3 DON JUAN	16	58	6
PRODUCES						
FALLING LIKE DEW UPON A THOUGHT PRODUCES	. . . . . .	327	2 DON JUAN	3	88	2
PRODUCTION						
BUT MAN IS A CARNIVOROUS PRODUCTION	. . . . .	191	2 DON JUAN	2	67	1
A PARADISE OF HOPS AND HIGH PRODUCTION	. . . . .	262	3 DON JUAN	10	76	2
PROEM						
NOT ONLY IN THE BODY BUT THE PROEM	. . . .	193	3 DON JUAN	9	22	3
PROFANELY						
THUS HE PROFANELY TERMED THE FINEST LACE	. . . .	455	2 DON JUAN	5	76	7
I DO NOT SPEAK PROFANELY TO RECALL	. . . .	503	3 DON JUAN	16	6	5
PROFESSED						
ROUGH JOHNSON THE GREAT MORALIST PROFESSED	. . . . .	361	3 DON JUAN	13	7	1
PROFESSION						
WITH MORE THAN ONE PROFESSION GAINS BY ALL	. . . . .	390	2 DON JUAN	4	84	2
THEIR SORT OF HALF PROFESSION FOR IT GROWS	. . . .	522	3 DON JUAN	16	44	4
PROFESSIONAL						
PROFESSIONAL AND THERE IS NOUGHT TO CULL	. . . .	402	3 DON JUAN	13	95	4
PROFESSIONAL--ALL CLASSES MOSTLY PULL	. . . . .	403	3 DON JUAN	13	95	V4
WHO DO NOT GIVE PROFESSIONAL ATTENDANCE	. . . . .	537	3 DON JUAN	16	76	6
PROFESSIONS						
PROFESSIONS TOO ARE NO MORE TO BE FOUND	. . . . .	402	3 DON JUAN	13	95	3
PROFESSOR						
HAS LATELY BEEN THE GREAT PROFESSOR KANT	. . . . .	254	3 DON JUAN	10	60	4
PROFESSORS						
PROFESSORS OF THAT GENIAL ART AND PATRONS	. . . . .	472	3 DON JUAN	15	37	3
PROFFERED						
OF MODESTY DECLINED THE ASSISTANCE PROFFERED	. . . .	36	3 DON JUAN	6	61	4
PROFILES						
THEIR CLASSICAL PROFILES AND GLITTERING DRESSES	. . .	292	2 DON JUAN	3	33	1
PROFIT						
THE SECOND OBJECT WAS TO PROFIT BY	. . . .	78	3 DON JUAN	7	24	1
IN BALANCING THE PROFIT AND THE LOSS	. . . . . .	113	3 DON JUAN	8	3	3
WITH SOME SMALL PROFIT THROUGH THAT FIELD SO STERILE	. . .	300	3 DON JUAN	11	64	3
WHO MIGHT NOT PROFIT MUCH BY BEING AT LARGE	. . .	335	3 DON JUAN	12	41	8
OF FAME OR PROFIT WHEN THE WORLD GROWS WEARY	. . .	415	3 DON JUAN	14	11	2
THAT THE FATIGUE WAS GREATER THAN THE PROFIT	. . . .	536	3 DON JUAN	16	73	8
PROFIT HE CARED NOT FOR LET OTHERS REAP IT	. . . .	536	3 DON JUAN	16	75	4
PROFITS						
AND SCIENCE PROFITS BY THIS RESURRECTION--	. . . .	37	2 DON JUAN	1	31	7
HOW FAR IT PROFITS IS ANOTHER MATTER--	. . . . .	339	3 DON JUAN	12	51	1
PROFOUND						
SOME LOOK'D PERPLEX'D AND OTHERS LOOK'D PROFOUND	. . .	429	3 DON JUAN	14	44	6
PROFOUNDER						
PERHAPS SHE WISH'D AN ASPIRANT PROFOUNDER	. . . . .	435	3 DON JUAN	14	57	5
PROFUSE						
FOR THEN THEIR ELOQUENCE GROWS QUITE PROFUSE	. . . .	119	2 DON JUAN	1	179	4
PROFUSELY						
BUT THROUGH THEM GOLD AND GEMS PROFUSELY SHONE	. . . .	220	2 DON JUAN	2	121	4
THE FURNITURE WAS MOST PROFUSELY RICH	. . . . . .	449	2 DON JUAN	5	65	V4
PROFUSION						
IN BACCHANAL PROFUSION REEL TO EARTH	. . . . .	88	2 DON JUAN	1	124	2
PROFUSION WITH YOUNG BEAUTY COVERS O'ER	. . . .	269	2 DON JUAN	2	211	4
THERE BEING NO SUCH PROFUSION IN THE NORTH	. . . .	434	2 DON JUAN	5	42	4
PROGENIES						
AND FOUND HIM NOT AMIDST THE VARIOUS PROGENIES	. . . .	281	3 DON JUAN	11	28	3
PROGENY						
MUCH AS OLD SATURN ATE HIS PROGENY	. . . .	410	3 DON JUAN	14	1	6
OF WHOM HALF MY PHILOSOPHY THE PROGENY IS	. . . . .	488	3 DON JUAN	15	73	8
PROGRESS						
AND NOW DELAY THE PROGRESS OF DON JUAN	. . . . . .	410	2 DON JUAN	4	117	7

		PAGE	VOL		CANTO	STANZA	LN

PROGRESS   (CONTINUED)
TO WATCH THE PROGRESS OF THOSE ROLLING SEAS . . . . 413 2 DON JUAN 5   5   4
THE USUAL PROGRESS OF INTRIGUES BETWEEN . . . . 236 3 DON JUAN 10   24   2
A POEM'S PROGRESS SHOULD BE PERPENDICULAR . . . . . . 290 3 DON JUAN 11   44   V8.
TO GENTLY SMOOTHE THE PROGRESS OF DECLINE . . . . . 360 3 DON JUAN 13   5   V6
THE FURTHER PROGRESS OF THIS SAD MISTAKE . . . . 437 3 DON JUAN 14   61   3
HAD MADE MORE PROGRESS THAN FOR THE LAST CENTURY . . . . 536 3 DON JUAN 16   73   4
PROGRESSION
THOUGH DESPOTS KNOW IT NOT--TILL THE PROGRESSION . . . . 354 3 DON JUAN 12   83   5
PROHIBITED
IS NOT ALL LOVE PROHIBITED WHATEVER . . . . . . 323 3 DON JUAN 12   15   1
PROJECT
BUT THERE HIS PROJECT REACHED ITS UTMOST PITCH . . . . . 147 3 DON JUAN 8   71   5
PERHAPS SHE MERELY HAD THE SIMPLE PROJECT . . . . . . 526 3 DON JUAN 16   51   5
PROJECTS
PERHAPS HE HATH GREAT PROJECTS IN HIS MIND . . . . . . 320 3 DON JUAN 12   10   1
PROLIFIC
WITH GOOD AND BAD AND WORSE ALIKE PROLIFIC . . . . . . 156 3 DON JUAN 8   89   4
PROLOGUE
PROLOGUE IS ALWAYS CERTAIN THROES AND THROBS . . . . 110 2 DON JUAN 1   162   4
A PROLOGUE WHICH BUT SLIGHTLY HARMONISED . . . . 543 3 DON JUAN 16   90   3
PROLONG'D
NOW SHE PROLONG'D HER VISITS AND HER TALK . . . . . 249 2 DON JUAN 2   176   1
PROLONGS
PROLONGS IT THIS IS OBVIOUS TO PHYSICIANS . . . . . . 190 2 DON JUAN 2   64   2
PROMETHEAN
LIKE THE PROMETHEAN VULTURE THIS POLLUTION . . . . . 195 2 DON JUAN 2   75   4
PROMETHEUS
FIRE WHICH PROMETHEUS FILCH'D FOR US FROM HEAVEN . . . . 90 2 DON JUAN 1   127   8
PROMINENT
ALTHOUGH IT SEEMS BOTH PROMINENT AND PLEASANT . . . . 416 3 DON JUAN 14   15   5
PROMISE
WITH ALL THE PROMISE OF AS FINE A FACE . . . . . . 48 2 DON JUAN 1   49   3
AND BREAK A PROMISE AFTER HAVING MADE IT HER . . . . . 142 2 DON JUAN 1   210   5
AND SEND HIM LIKE A DOVE OF PROMISE FORTH . . . . . . 161 2 DON JUAN 2   8   8
'TWAS WELL THIS BIRD OF PROMISE DID NOT PERCH . . . . . 206 2 DON JUAN 2   95   2
AND FULL OF PROMISE AS THE SPRING OF PRIME . . . . . 354 3 DON JUAN 12   84   4
OF NO GREAT PROMISE FOR POETIC PAGES . . . . . . 416 3 DON JUAN 14   15   8
PROMISED
PROMISED TO TURN OUT WELL IN PROPER HANDS . . . . . 42 2 DON JUAN 1   37   4
SHE AND HER MAID AND PROMISED BY DAY-BREAK . . . . . . 226 2 DON JUAN 2   133   6
SHE PROMISED NEVER MORE TO HAVE A DREAM . . . . . . 47 3 DON JUAN 6   83   1
AS THE FIRST CANTO PROMISED YOU HAVE NOW . . . . . 181 3 DON JUAN 8   138   2
WHO PROMISED TO BE GREAT IN SOME FEW HOURS . . . . . 222 3 DON JUAN 9   79   3
JUST AS HE REALLY PROMISED SOMETHING GREAT . . . . . 298 3 DON JUAN 11   60   2
THE PROMISED PARTY TO ENJOY ITS SWEETS . . . . . . 394 3 DON JUAN 13   75   2
PROMISES
OF PLIGHT AND PROMISES TO BE A SPOUSE . . . . . 257 2 DON JUAN 2   190   3
UNLESS HIS HIGHNESS PROMISES TO MARRY ME . . . . . 460 2 DON JUAN 5   84   8
FOR T'OTHER ONE WHO PROMISES MUCH DUTY . . . . . 471 2 DON JUAN 15   34   4
AND PROMISES TO ALL--WHICH LAST COMMENCED . . . . . 535 3 DON JUAN 16   71   4
PROMONTORY
AND THE SEA DASHES ROUND THE PROMONTORY . . . . . 94 2 DON JUAN 1   134   6
MAKING A SIGNAL OFF SOME PROMONTORY . . . . . . 389 3 DON JUAN 4   82   3
I PERCH UPON AN HUMBLER PROMONTORY . . . . . . 464 3 DON JUAN 15   19   1
PROMOTED
THAT PASIPHAE PROMOTED BREEDING CATTLE . . . . . 238 2 DON JUAN 2   155   7
O'ER THE PROMOTED COUPLE OF BRAVE MEN . . . . . 101 3 DON JUAN 7   68   1
PROMOTING
USEFUL LIKE MALTHUS IN PROMOTING MARRIAGE-- . . . . . 282 3 DON JUAN 11   30   7
PROMOTION
TO ONE OF SEVENTY SUITORS HIS PROMOTION . . . . . . 434 3 DON JUAN 14   55   V6
PROMPT
ALL HEROES WHEN ALIVE QUITE PROMPT TO SLAY US . . . . 385 2 DON JUAN 4   76   V8
PROMPTER'S
SHE COULD HAVE SERVED HIM FOR THE PROMPTER'S COPY . . . . 27 2 DON JUAN 1   11   4
PROMPTS
PROMPTS DEEDS ETERNITY CAN NOT ANNUL . . . . . . 258 2 DON JUAN 2   192   5
PRONE
AND YET HE SHUDDERED AND SEEMED RATHER PRONE . . . . 62 3 DON JUAN 6   112   4
PRONOUNCE
TASTE OR THE GOUT--PRONOUNCE IT AS INCLINES . . . . . 488 3 DON JUAN 15   72   3
PRONOUNCED
HE HAD PRONOUNCED HER NAME--BUT SHE FORGOT . . . . . 228 2 DON JUAN 2   135   7
BUT IN A HUSBAND IS PRONOUNCED UXORIOUS . . . . . 278 2 DON JUAN 3   6   8
PRONOUNCES
PRONOUNCES THAT AN ONLY 'S A SPOILT CHILD-- . . . . . 563 3 DON JUAN 17   2   3
PRONUNCIATION
WHOSE NAMES WANT NOTHING BUT--PRONUNCIATION . . . . . 73 3 DON JUAN 7   14   8
PROOF
IN MAIL OF PROOF--HER PURITY OF SOUL . . . . . 66 2 DON JUAN 1   82   2
LAST NIGHT I HAD ANOTHER PROOF HOW TRULY IT . . . . . 272 2 DON JUAN 2 V 1   6
THOU ASK'ST IF I CAN LOVE BE THIS THE PROOF . . . . . 484 2 DON JUAN 5   127   1
BUT WHAT IS STRANGE--AND A STRONG PROOF HOW GREAT . . . . 42 2 DON JUAN 6   73   1
A FURTHER PROOF WE SHOULD NOT JUDGE IN HASTE . . . . . 347 3 DON JUAN 12   69   5
INDEED WE SEE THE DAILY PROOF DISPLAYED . . . . . 371 3 DON JUAN 13   29   4
PROOFS
BUT I MUST LEAVE THE PROOFS TO THOSE WHO'VE SEEN 'EM . . . 28 2 DON JUAN 1   14   4
WE WILL OMIT THE PROOFS SAVE ONE OR TWO . . . . . 396 2 DON JUAN 4   96   4
WAS PRINCELY AS THE PROOFS HAVE ALWAYS SHOWN . . . . . 499 2 DON JUAN 5   153   6

```
                                                        PAGE VOL     CANTO  STANZA LN
PROP
   A PROP NOT QUITE SO CERTAIN AS BEFORE . . . . . . . . 184  3 DON JUAN  9      3   4
PROPAGATE
   OF OURS ALTHOUGH THEY PROPAGATE MORE BROADLY  . . . . . 472  3 DON JUAN 15     36   6
PROPAGATED
   ALL PROPAGATED WITH THE BEST INTENTIONS . . . . . . .  93  2 DON JUAN  1    132   3
PROPAGATION
   COULD STOP THAT WORST OF VICES--PROPAGATION . . . . . . 15  3 DON JUAN  6     19   8
   COULD STOP THE TENDENCY TO PROPAGATION . . . . . . . .  15  3 DON JUAN  6     19  V8
   OF ALL THE MODEST PART OF PROPAGATION . . . . . . . . 472  3 DON JUAN 15     37   4
PROPENSITIES
   ALL BAD PROPENSITIES IN FIFTEEN HUNDRED . . . . . . .  21  3 DON JUAN  6     31   7
PROPENSITY
   WITHOUT THE LEAST PROPENSITY TO JEER . . . . . . . . . 245  3 DON JUAN 10     42   4
PROPER
   PROMISED TO TURN OUT WELL IN PROPER HANDS   . . . . . . 42  2 DON JUAN  1     37   4
   AND THEN WHAT 'PROPER PERSON CAN BE PARTIAL . . . . . . 45  2 DON JUAN  1     43   7
   LOVE THEN BUT LOVE WITHIN ITS PROPER LIMITS . . . . . . 65  2 DON JUAN  1     81   1
   MOST PROPER FOR THE CHRISTIANS HE HAD BOUGHT . . . . . 450  2 DON JUAN  5     67   8
   IF THEY WOULD BUT PURSUE THE PROPER WAY . . . . . . . 451  2 DON JUAN  5     69   4
   NO DOUBT IN PROPER PLACE AND TIME AND SEASON  . . . . . 454  2 DON JUAN  5     74   7
   TO USE ALL FIT AND PROPER COURTESIES . . . . . . . . . 472  2 DON JUAN  5    105   5
   AND SO IT WAS IN PROPER TIME AND PLACE . . . . . . . . 478  2 DON JUAN  5    117   1
   IT NE'ER CAN BE REPLACED IN PROPER FRAME . . . . . . . 502  2 DON JUAN  5    158   4
   STUCK ALL EXACTLY IN THE PROPER SPOT . . . . . . . . .  37  3 DON JUAN  6     62   8
   WHOSE HEADLONG PASSIONS FORM THEIR PROPER WOES . . . . . 49 3 DON JUAN  6     87   8
   ALL PROPER MEN OF WEAPONS AS E'ER SCOFFED HIGH . . . . . 75 3 DON JUAN  7     17   3
   IN CHIEF IN PROPER PERSON DEIGNED TO DRILL . . . . . .  93  3 DON JUAN  7     52   2
   HE JUDGED THEM PROPER TO ASSAIL THE WORKS . . . . . . . 93 3 DON JUAN  7     53   6
   AND SET UP IN THEIR STEAD SOME PROPER STUFF . . . . . . 195 3 DON JUAN  9     25   4
   FROM POLAND THEY CAME ON THROUGH PRUSSIA PROPER   . . . 254 3 DON JUAN 10     60   1
   JUAN PRESENTED IN THE PROPER PLACE . . . . . . . . . . 285 3 DON JUAN 11     35   1
   TO PROPER PLACEMEN EVERY RUSS CREDENTIAL . . . . . . . 285 3 DON JUAN 11     35   2
   JUST AT THE PROPER TIME AND THOUGH A LAD . . . . . . . 292 3 DON JUAN 11     47   6
   HE DEEMS IT IS HIS PROPER PLACE TO BE . . . . . . . . 303 3 DON JUAN 11     70   5
   WHICH IS REQUIRED BY PROPER COURTESY . . . . . . . . . 311 3 DON JUAN 11     88   3
   TO VIRTUE PROPER OR GOOD EDUCATION . . . . . . . . . . 372 3 DON JUAN 13     31   3
   YET EACH WAS RADIANT IN HER PROPER SPHERE  . . . . . . 481 3 DON JUAN 15     58   3
   AND JUAN'S MIND WAS IN THE PROPER TONE  . . . . . . . 506 3 DON JUAN 16     13   5
   ITS KIND ATTENTIONS TO THEIR PROPER PALE . . . . . . . 533 3 DON JUAN 16     67   6
PROPEREST
   AND YOU SHALL SEE WHO HAS THE PROPEREST NOTION . . . . . 336 2 DON JUAN  3   104   4
PROPERLY
   BE SUCH AS I CAN PROPERLY ACCEPT  . . . . . . . . . . 453 2 DON JUAN  5     72   6
PROPERTIES
   HIS KNIGHTS WITH LOTTING OTHERS' PROPERTIES . . . . . . 242 3 DON JUAN 10     35   7
PROPERTY
   WHEN BEING MADE HER PROPERTY AT LAST . . . . . . . . . 478 2 DON JUAN  5    116   4
   SOME HEIR TO A LARGE PROPERTY SOME FRIEND  . . . . . . 470 3 DON JUAN 15     33   2
PROPHECIES
   THE BLOOD OF MONARCHS WITH HIS PROPHECIES  . . . . . .  15 3 DON JUAN  0     11   3
   SPARKLED WITH HER SUCCESSFUL PROPHECIES . . . . . . . 490 3 DON JUAN 15     78   8
PROPHECY
   AND PROPHECY--EXCEPT IT SHOULD BE DATED . . . . . . . 286 3 DON JUAN 11     37   7
PROPHESY
   PERHAPS YOU PROPHESY SOME SUDDEN ACT . . . . . . . . . 296 2 DON JUAN  3     40   4
   FOR ALL MEN PROPHESY WHAT IS OR WAS  . . . . . . . . . 491 3 DON JUAN 15     79   7
PROPHET
   THAT LARGE BLACK PROPHET EYE SEEM'D TO DILATE  . . . . 355 2 DON JUAN  4     22   1
   SEVERE SUBLIME THE PROPHET WROTE NO FARCE ON . . . . . 179 3 DON JUAN  8    134   6
   SHE STILL HELD OUT THAT MAHOMET WAS A PROPHET  . . . . 252 3 DON JUAN 10     56   8
   AND ANSWER'D LIKE A STATESMAN OR A PROPHET . . . . . . 438 3 DON JUAN 14     65   7
   'TIS TIME THAT SOME NEW PROPHET SHOULD APPEAR  . . . . 496 3 DON JUAN 15     90   5
PROPHETIC
   THAN WHOM CASSANDRA WAS NOT MORE PROPHETIC . . . . . . 372 2 DON JUAN  4     52   3
   WITH THE PROPHETIC EYE OF APPETITE . . . . . . . . . . 439 2 DON JUAN  5     50   8
   SO MUCH THE BARD HAD REALLY BEEN PROPHETIC . . . . . . 525 3 DON JUAN 16     50   5
PROPHETICALLY
   PROPHETICALLY OR THAT WHICH ONE DEEMS . . . . . . . .  45 3 DON JUAN  6     78   6
PROPHET'S
   ANTICIPATE THE PROPHET'S PARADISE . . . . . . . . . . 458 2 DON JUAN  5     81   8
PROPHETS
   WITH PROPHETS HOURIS ANGELS SAINTS DESCRIED . . . . . . 169 3 DON JUAN  8   115   7
   UTTER'D BY FRIENDS THOSE PROPHETS OF THE PAST . . . . . 432 3 DON JUAN 14     50   4
PROPORTION
   IN SUCH PROPORTION--BUT MY MUSE WITHSTANDS . . . . . .  20 3 DON JUAN  6     28   3
   AGAINST PROPORTION--THE WILD STROKES OF NATURE . . . . . 32 3 DON JUAN  6     52   5
   IN FAIR PROPORTION WITH THEIR COMRADES--THEN  . . . . . 163 3 DON JUAN  8   103   2
PROPORTIONATE
   A KIND OF PHANTASY PROPORTIONATE  . . . . . . . . . .  84 3 DON JUAN  7     37   6
PROPORTION'D
   PROPORTION'D AS A POPLAR OR A POLE . . . . . . . . . . 441 3 DON JUAN 14     71   5
PROPORTIONS
   (KEEPING THE DUE PROPORTIONS STILL IN SIGHT)  . . . . . 467 3 DON JUAN 15     25   6
PROPOS
   AND A PROPOS OF MONKS THEIR PIETY . . . . . . . . . . 445 3 DON JUAN 14     81   5
PROPOSAL
   I SHALL PERPEND IF YOUR PROPOSAL MAY . . . . . . . . . 453 2 DON JUAN  5     72   5
PROPOSE
   SO MUCH AS TO PROPOSE TO TAKE A WALK-- . . . . . . . . 249 2 DON JUAN  2    176   3
```

635

PROPOSED
  BABA PROPOSED THAT HE SHOULD KISS THE HAND . . . . . . 471 2 DON JUAN 5   104   8
  AS PHILIP'S SON PROPOSED TO DO WITH ATHOS . . . . . . 355 3 DON JUAN 12   86   8
PROPOSITION
  WOULD LEAVE HIS PROPOSITION TO THEIR CHOICE . . . . . . 452 2 DON JUAN 5   70   3
  LOLAH'S EYES SPARKLED AT THE PROPOSITION . . . . 47 3 DON JUAN 6   82   1
  FOR ALL THE ANSWER TO HIS PROPOSITION . . . . 152 3 DON JUAN 8   81   1
PROPOSITIONS
  TO ALL THE PROPOSITIONS OF SURRENDER . . . . 165 3 DON JUAN 8   107   2
PROPRIETY
  WAS TO RESTORE HIM TO HIS SELF PROPRIETY . . . . 526 3 DON JUAN 16   52   2
PROSCRIBED
  PROSCRIBED FROM TASTING YOUR CASTALIAN TEA . . . . . . 403 2 DON JUAN 4   108   8
PROSE
  PROSE POETS LIKE BLANK-VERSE I'M FOND OF RHYME . . . . . 136 2 DON JUAN 1   201   5
  IF EVER I SHOULD CONDESCEND TO PROSE . . . . 138 2 DON JUAN 1   204   1
  OF ELOQUENCE IN PIETY AND PROSE-- . . . . 243 2 DON JUAN 2   165   7
  OF TRUTH THAN PROSE UNLESS TO SUIT THE MART . . . . . . 154 3 DON JUAN 8   86   5
  IN PROSE I BEND MY HUMBLE VERSE) DOTH CALL . . . . . . 163 3 DON JUAN 8   104   7
PROSECUTED
  ARE PROSECUTED FOR THAT FALSE CRIME BIGAMY) . . . . . . 164 3 DON JUAN 8   105   3
PROSECUTIONS
  WITH SUITS AND PROSECUTIONS THEY BESIEGE US . . . . . . 11 3 DON JUAN 6   10   5
PROSERS
  I HAVE SEEN SMALL POETS AND GREAT PROSERS AND . . . . . 310 3 DON JUAN 11   85   1
  OF BARDS AND PROSERS WORDS ARE VOID OF COLOUR . . . . . 428 3 DON JUAN 14   40   8
PROSODY
  SO THAT THEIR PLAN AND PROSODY ARE ELIGIBLE . . . . . . 70 2 DON JUAN 1   90   7
  I OWN NO PROSODY CAN EVER RATE IT . . . . 15 3 DON JUAN 6   18   7
PROSPECT
  THE PROSPECT AND THEIR MORALS AND BESIDES . . . . . . 471 3 DON JUAN 15   33   7
PROSPECTS
  COMMENCE WITH FEELINGS WARM AND PROSPECTS HIGH . . . . . 421 2 DON JUAN 5   21   5
  (LIKE LUCUS FROM NO LIGHT) THROUGH PROSPECTS NAMED . . . 278 3 DON JUAN 11   21   2
PROSPERITY
  NO ONE COULD ENVY HER DESERVED PROSPERITY . . . . . . 550 3 DON JUAN 16   102   6
PROSPEROUS
  ARE GENERALLY PROSPEROUS IN REIGNING . . . . 247 3 DON JUAN 10   47   2
PROSTITUTION
  SAY CONSTITUTION STEAD OF PROSTITUTION . . . . 537 3 DON JUAN 16   76 V7
PROSTRATE
  HIS MAN WAS PROSTRATE BLEEDING AT HIS FOOT . . . . . . 370 2 DON JUAN 4   49 V5
PROTASOFF
  AS ALSO DID MISS PROTASOFF THEN THERE . . . . 224 3 DON JUAN 9   84   6
PROTECT
  WHATE'ER OUR HOUSEHOLD GODS PROTECT OF DEAR . . . . . . 338 2 DON JUAN 3   107   6
PROTECTED
  HE NATURALLY LOVED WHAT HE PROTECTED . . . . 252 3 DON JUAN 10   57   4
PROTECTION
  SHE FLATTER'D JULIA WITH HER SAGE PROTECTION . . . . . 58 2 DON JUAN 1   67   5
  OR ROAMS THE HERD BENEATH THE BULL'S PROTECTION . . . . 90 3 DON JUAN 7   48   4
PROTECTOR
  THE MOSLEM ORPHAN WENT WITH HER PROTECTOR . . . . . . 182 3 DON JUAN 8   141   1
PROTECTORS
  THEIR OWN PROTECTORS--NOR WAS THEIR SURPRISE . . . . . 104 3 DON JUAN 7   73   3
PROTECTS
  PROTECTS HIS DUST BUT REVERENCE HERE IS PAID . . . . . 400 2 DON JUAN 4   104   3
  PROTECTS HIS TOMB BUT GREATER CARE IS PAID . . . . . . 400 2 DON JUAN 4   104 V3
PROTEGE
  HER SPEECH OUT TO HER PROTEGE AND FRIEND . . . . 241 2 DON JUAN 2   161   6
PROTEGEE
  UNTO HIS PROTEGEE WHILE HER'S TRANSFIXED . . . . 159 3 DON JUAN 8   96   5
PROTESILAUS
  PATROCLUS AJAX OR PROTESILAUS . . . . 385 2 DON JUAN 4   76   7
PROTEST
  BUT SCANDAL'S MY AVERSION--I PROTEST . . . . 49 2 DON JUAN 1   51   7
PROTESTED
  TO PAY UNPAID PROTESTED OR DISCOUNTED . . . . 16 3 DON JUAN 6   21   2
PROUD
  WHEN PROUD GRENADA FELL AND FORCED TO FLY . . . . . . 52 2 DON JUAN 1   56   5
  THAT BEING THE LAST THING A PROUD WOMAN TRIES . . . . . 483 2 DON JUAN 5   125   6
  AND HER PROUD BROW'S BLUE VEINS TO SWELL AND DARKLE . . . 56 3 DON JUAN 6   101   8
  WITH ITS PROUD BROW IT MERITS SLIGHT APPLAUSE . . . . . 86 3 DON JUAN 7   40   6
  WITH YOU THAN AUGHT (SAVE SCOTT) IN YOUR PROUD CITY . . . 233 3 DON JUAN 10   17   4
  WOULD SHE BE PROUD OR BOAST HERSELF THE FREE . . . . . 258 3 DON JUAN 10   68   1
  PROUD OF HIMSELF AND HER THE WORLD COULD TELL . . . . . 365 3 DON JUAN 13   14   6
  OR CONTRADICTED BUT WITH PROUD HUMILITY . . . . 368 3 DON JUAN 13   22   4
  PROUD OF HIS HEAR HIMS PROUD TOO OF HIS VOTE . . . . . 401 3 DON JUAN 13   91   1
  PROUD OF HIS HEAR HIMS PROUD TOO OF HIS VOTE . . . . . 401 3 DON JUAN 13   91   1
  PROUD OF HIS LEARNING (JUST ENOUGH TO QUOTE) . . . . . 401 3 DON JUAN 13   91   3
  PROUD OF HIS BIRTH AND PROUD OF EVERYTHING . . . . . . 440 3 DON JUAN 14   70   2
  PROUD OF HIS BIRTH AND PROUD OF EVERYTHING . . . . . . 440 3 DON JUAN 14   70   2
  PROUD WITH THE PROUD YET COURTEOUSLY PROUD . . . . . . 462 3 DON JUAN 15   15   5
  PROUD WITH THE PROUD YET COURTEOUSLY PROUD . . . . . . 462 3 DON JUAN 15   15   5
  PROUD WITH THE PROUD YET COURTEOUSLY PROUD . . . . . . 462 3 DON JUAN 15   15   5
  PERHAPS BECAUSE 'TWAS FALLEN HER SIRES WERE PROUD . . . . 476 3 DON JUAN 15   46   4
  THE DASHING AND PROUD AIR OF ADELINE . . . . 480 3 DON JUAN 15   56   1
  A PROUD HUMILITY IF SUCH THERE BE . . . . 492 3 DON JUAN 15   82   2
  TO FEEL THAT FLATTERY WHICH ATTRACTS THE PROUD . . . . 493 3 DON JUAN 15   83   6
  NOR THOUGHT HE HAD PRIDE ENOUGH--FOR SHE WAS PROUD . . . 493 3 DON JUAN 15   83 V6

		PAGE	VOL	CANTO	STANZA	LN

PROUDER
PROUDER OF SUCH A TOY THAN OF THEIR BREED . . . . . . 391 3 DON JUAN 13 70 V6
PROUDEST
BE UNIMPEDED BY THE PROUDEST MOSQUE . . . . . . 99 3 DON JUAN 7 63 8
PROUDEST OF PARIAN PATRICIAN (BRED . . . . 314 3 DON JUAN 11 V 75 6
AMONG THE PROUDEST OF OUR ARISTOCRACY . . . . . . 346 3 DON JUAN 12 66 6
OF SUCH A THRONE AS IS THE PROUDEST STATION . . . . . 354 3 DON JUAN 12 83 4
PROUDLIER
OR PROUDLIER PRANCING WITH MERCURIAL SKILL . . . . . 303 3 DON JUAN 11 70 7
PROUDLY
THOSE SERVILE DOGS ARE NOT SO PROUDLY EYED . . . . . 418 2 DON JUAN 5 14 3
MY LORDS AND LADIES PROUDLY CONDESCENDING . . . . . 538 3 DON JUAN 16 79 2
PROVE
AND TRIED TO PROVE HER LOVING LORD WAS MAD . . . . . 35 2 DON JUAN 1 27 2
FOR EARLY STOMACHS TO PROVE WHOLESOME FOOD . . . . . 45 2 DON JUAN 1 43 2
UNLESS LIKE WORDSWORTH THEY PROVE UNINTELLIGIBLE . . . . 70 2 DON JUAN 1 90 8
TO PROVE HIMSELF THE THING HE MOST ABHORR'D . . . . . 97 2 DON JUAN 1 139 8
TO PROVE HER MISTRESS HAD BEEN SLEEPING DOUBLE . . . . 97 2 DON JUAN 1 140 8
AND NOT AT ALL DISPOSED TO PROVE A MARTYR . . . . . 122 2 DON JUAN 1 184 8
SPAIN MAY PROVE AN EXCEPTION TO THE RULE . . . . . 158 2 DON JUAN 2 2 5
BUT THEN EXCEPTIONS ALWAYS PROVE ITS WORTH-- . . . . 158 2 DON JUAN 2 2 6
MEN WILL PROVE HUNGRY EVEN WHEN NEXT PERDITION . . . . 180 2 DON JUAN 2 46 V5
AS YOU MAY FIND WHENE'ER YOU LIKE TO PROVE HER . . . . 276 2 DON JUAN 3 3 5
TO PROVE ITS GRAND INGREDIENT IS ENNUI . . . . . 332 2 DON JUAN 3 97 8
I'LL PROVE THAT SUCH THE OPINION OF THE CRITIC IS . . . 342 2 DON JUAN 3 111 7
WHAT CAN I PROVE A LION THEN NO MORE . . . . . 404 2 DON JUAN 4 109 1
TO PROVE RELUCTANT AND BEGGED LEAVE TO CRAVE . . . . 62 3 DON JUAN 6 112 5
AND EPIC IF PLAIN TRUTH SHOULD PROVE NO BAR . . . . 181 3 DON JUAN 8 138 5
TO PROVE THE PUBLIC DEBT IS NOT CONSUMING US-- . . . . 200 3 DON JUAN 9 35 5
OR DUTCHESS PRINCESS EMPRESS DEIGNS TO PROVE . . . . 216 3 DON JUAN 9 68 5
HE WAS NOT YET QUITE OLD ENOUGH TO PROVE . . . . . 250 3 DON JUAN 10 53 4
UPON THE ROAD UNLESS HE PROVE A FIGHTER . . . . . 273 3 DON JUAN 11 11 6
OF PEERS TO PROVE THEIR TITLE NO DISGRACE . . . . . 314 3 DON JUAN 11 V 75 8
WHICH IT WERE RATHER DIFFICULT TO PROVE . . . . . 322 3 DON JUAN 12 13 3
THIS I COULD PROVE BEYOND A SINGLE DOUBT . . . . . 446 3 DON JUAN 14 84 5
BUT TRUE--AS IF EXPEDIENT I COULD PROVE) . . . . . 452 3 DON JUAN 14 96 2
WHICH PROVE PLAIN ENGLISH TRUER OF THE TWO . . . . . 488 3 DON JUAN 15 72 6
TO PROVE THEIR PRIDE AS FOOTMEN TO A BEGGAR . . . . 537 3 DON JUAN 16 76 8
WHO THOUGH THEY PROVE NOT TWO AND TWO TO BE . . . . 548 3 DON JUAN 16 99 2
PROVED
SHE PROVED IT SOMEHOW OUT OF SACRED SONG . . . . . 28 2 DON JUAN 1 14 3
WERE PROVED BY COMPETENT FALSE WITNESSES . . . . . 109 2 DON JUAN 1 160 8
AND THAT WHICH CHIEFLY PROVED HIS SAVING CLAUSE . . . . 199 2 DON JUAN 2 81 6
PROVED EVEN STILL A MORE NUTRITIOUS MATTER . . . . . 208 2 DON JUAN 2 99 5
ALL IT HATH FELT INFLICTED PASS'D AND PROVED . . . . 261 2 DON JUAN 2 197 5
HAVE PROVED BUT DROPSIES TAKEN FOR DIVINITIES . . . . 330 2 DON JUAN 3 95 8
BOIL'D UP AND PROVED HER TRULY OF HIS RACE . . . . . 367 2 DON JUAN 4 44 8
NO PROCESS PROVED CONNUBIAL ANIMOSITY . . . . . 496 2 DON JUAN 5 148 6
GULBEYAZ PROVED IN THAT BRIEF AGONY . . . . . 59 3 DON JUAN 6 106 7
PROVED DEATH IN BATTLE EQUAL TO A PENSION-- . . . . . 96 3 DON JUAN 7 58 8
AND PROVED IT--'TWAS NO MATTER WHAT HE SAID . . . . 268 3 DON JUAN 11 1 2
THE FIRST ATTACK AT ONCE PROVED THE DIVINITY . . . . 271 3 DON JUAN 11 6 1
HE WHO HATH PROVED WAR STORM OR WOMAN'S RAGE . . . . 339 3 DON JUAN 12 50 6
'TWILL MAKE IF PROVED VAST EFFORTS WITHOUT PAINING . . . 366 3 DON JUAN 13 18 8
OF PASSIONS TOO I HAVE PROVED ENOUGH TO BLAME . . . . 414 3 DON JUAN 14 9 4
UNLESS LIKE WISE TIRESIAS WE HAD PROVED . . . . . 442 3 DON JUAN 14 73 2
IF I HAD NEVER PROVED THE SOFT CONDITION . . . . . 467 3 DON JUAN 15 24 2
PROVERB
SO SAYS THE PROVERB--AND I QUITE AGREE . . . . . 25 2 DON JUAN 1 8 4
NEWTON (THAT PROVERB OF THE MIND) ALAS . . . . . 69 3 DON JUAN 7 5 5
PROVES
THE GREATER THEIR SUCCESS THE WORSE IT PROVES . . . . 411 2 DON JUAN 5 1 5
HIS CAP AND HEAD WHICH PROVES THE HEAD TO BE . . . . 116 3 DON JUAN 8 10 3
PROVIDED
(PROVIDED THEY DON'T COME IN AFTER DINNER) . . . . . 306 2 DON JUAN 3 60 2
PROVIDED ALWAYS YOUR GREAT GOODNESS STILL . . . . . 453 2 DON JUAN 5 72 7
PROVIDENCE
BY SPECIAL PROVIDENCE TO LEAD TO-MORROW . . . . . 99 3 DON JUAN 7 63 4
WHAT SAGES CALL CHANCE PROVIDENCE OR FATE-- . . . . 105 3 DON JUAN 7 76 4
IS SPECIAL PROVIDENCE THOUGH HOW IT GAVE . . . . . 192 3 DON JUAN 9 19 6
AND WONDER PROVIDENCE IS NOT MORE SAGE . . . . . 339 3 DON JUAN 12 50 4
(OH PROVIDENCE HOW WONDROUS ARE THY WAYS . . . . . 540 3 DON JUAN 16 82 5
PROVIDENTIALLY
WHICH PROVIDENTIALLY FOR HIM WAS WASH'D . . . . . 212 2 DON JUAN 2 107 2
PROVIDERS
(AS BEING THE BRAVE LIONS' KEEN PROVIDERS) . . . . . 196 3 DON JUAN 9 27 7
PROVINCE
THE SOIL OF THE GREEN PROVINCE HE HAD WASTED . . . . 84 3 DON JUAN 7 36 7
OR PLUNGED A PROVINCE OR A REALM IN GRIEF . . . . . 101 3 DON JUAN 7 68 4
PROVING
PROVING THAT TRITE OLD TRUTH THAT LIFE'S AS FRAIL . . . 134 3 DON JUAN 8 43 3
A MODE OF PROVING THAT THE EARTH TURNED ROUND . . . . 225 3 DON JUAN 10 1 5
PROVISION
'TWAS DIFFICULT TO GET OUT SUCH PROVISION . . . . . 180 2 DON JUAN 2 46 3
AND FELL ALL RAVENOUSLY ON THEIR PROVISION . . . . . 192 2 DON JUAN 2 68 7
SHE DREW OUT HER PROVISION FROM THE BASKET . . . . . 233 2 DON JUAN 2 144 8
PROVOCATIONS
APT TO WEAR OUT ON TRIFLING PROVOCATIONS . . . . . 165 3 DON JUAN 8 107 8
PROVOKE
PROVOKE MY THIRST--WHAT--HO OF WINE A STOUP . . . . . 392 3 DON JUAN 13 72 V8

PROVOKED
      WOULD HAVE PROVOKED REMARKS WHICH NOW IT SHAN'T   397   2 DON JUAN   4   98   8
PROVOKING
      REJOINED THE NEGRO PRAY BE NOT PROVOKING 454   2 DON JUAN   5   75   2
      BUT ALWAYS AT A MOST PROVOKING HEIGHT-- 44   3 DON JUAN   6   76   8
PROWL
      POWER'S BASE PURVEYORS WHO FOR PICKINGS PROWL   196   3 DON JUAN   9   27   4
PROWS
      AT LAST HER FATHER'S PROWS PUT OUT TO SEA   248   2 DON JUAN   2   174   5
PRUDE
      TO BEAR THESE CROSSES) FOR EACH WANING PRUDE   177   3 DON JUAN   8   131   6
      WHILE THE HARSH PRUDE INDEMNIFIES HER VIRTUE   337   3 DON JUAN 12   45   1
PRUDENCE
      SHE HAD NO PRUDENCE BUT HE HAD AND THIS   477   2 DON JUAN   5   114   7
PRUDENT
      FORGOT WITH HIM HER VERY PRUDENT CARRIAGE   58   2 DON JUAN   1   66   8
      A FEELING DANGEROUS TO A PRUDENT SPOUSE 81   2 DON JUAN   1   111   8
PRUDENTLY
      AND PRUDENTLY POSTPONE UNTIL MID-DAY   500   3 DON JUAN 15   98   5
PRUDES
      THAN THOSE BRED UP BY PRUDES WITHOUT A HEART   337   3 DON JUAN 12   46   8
PRUDISH
      AND OF THE FOLLY OF ALL PRUDISH FEARS 78   2 DON JUAN   1   107   2
      FOR FEAR SOME PRUDISH READERS SHOULD GROW SKITTISH   . . 141   2 DON JUAN   1   209   7
PRUSSIA
      FROM POLAND THEY CAME ON THROUGH PRUSSIA PROPER   . . . 254   3 DON JUAN 10   60   1
PRUSSIANS
      WAS BEATEN--THOUGH THE PRUSSIANS SAY SO TOO--   136   3 DON JUAN   8   48   8
PRYING
      WITH PRYING SNUB-NOSE AND SMALL EYES HE STOOD   109   2 DON JUAN   1   160   1
      SEEM'D ALMOST PRYING INTO HIS FOR BREATH 215   2 DON JUAN   2   113   2
PSALM
      AS THE PSALM SAYS INDITING A GOOD MATTER 316   2 DON JUAN   3   78   8
PSALMIST
      OH SAITH THE PSALMIST THAT I HAD A DOVE'S   228   3 DON JUAN 10   6   2
PSALMODIC
      AND PEGASUS HATH A PSALMODIC AMBLE 297   3 DON JUAN 11   57   5
PSALMS
      SOME PLUNDER'D SOME DRANK SPIRITS SOME SUNG PSALMS   . . 174   2 DON JUAN   2   34   3
      AND SEVERAL WHO SUNG FEWER PSALMS THAN CATCHES   539   3 DON JUAN 16   80   8
PSEUDO-SYPHILIS
      THEIR REAL LUES OR OUR PSEUDO-SYPHILIS   92   2 DON JUAN   1   131   8
PSYCHE
      AND PURE AS PSYCHE ERE SHE GREW A WIFE-- 313   2 DON JUAN   3   74   5
      BUT STILL SO LIKE THAT PSYCHE WERE MORE CLEVER 205   3 DON JUAN   9   45   6
PUBERTY
      I CAN'T HELP THINKING PUBERTY ASSISTED   71   2 DON JUAN   1   93   8
PUBLIC
      TO PUBLIC FEELING WHICH ON THIS OCCASION 38   2 DON JUAN   1   33   7
      THE PUBLIC FEELING AND THE LAWYERS' FEES 39   2 DON JUAN   1   34   2
      DEPENDENT ON THE PUBLIC ALTOGETHER 135   2 DON JUAN   1   199   3
      THE PUBLIC APPROBATION I EXPECT 141   2 DON JUAN   1   209   1
      I MAY ENSURE THE PUBLIC AND DEFY   142   2 DON JUAN   1   211   2
      HAD HE BUT BEEN PLACED AT A PUBLIC SCHOOL   158   2 DON JUAN   2   2   1
      EVEN GOOD MEN LIKE TO MAKE THE PUBLIC STARE--   317   2 DON JUAN   3   81   4
      THE PUBLIC MIND SO FEW ARE THE ELECT   330   2 DON JUAN   3   95   6
      THE PUBLIC KNEW NO MORE THAN DOES THIS RHYME   496   2 DON JUAN   5   149   6
      THE PUBLIC BUILDINGS AND THE PRIVATE TOO   78   3 DON JUAN   7   23   4
      TO PROVE THE PUBLIC DEBT IS NOT CONSUMING US--   200   3 DON JUAN   9   35   5
      BESTOWED UPON HIM AS THE PUBLIC LEARNED   287   3 DON JUAN 11   39   7
      NOW THAT THE PUBLIC HEDGE HATH SCARCE A STAKE   357   3 DON JUAN 12   89   2
      AND--THOUGH NO DOUBT 'TIS FOR THE PUBLIC WEAL   357   3 DON JUAN 12   V 18   6
      HAVE PUBLIC DAYS WHEN ALL MEN MAY CAROUSE   534   3 DON JUAN 16   68   7
      THOUGH FOR THE PUBLIC WEAL DISPOSED TO VENTURE HIGH   . . 536   3 DON JUAN 16   73   6
      BUT 'TWAS A PUBLIC FEAST AND PUBLIC DAY--   538   3 DON JUAN 16   78   5
      BUT 'TWAS A PUBLIC FEAST AND PUBLIC DAY--   538   3 DON JUAN 16   78   5
PUBLICATIONS
      LIKE MANY PUBLICATIONS OF JOHN MURRAY 237   3 DON JUAN 10   26   V3
PUBLICLY
      PRIVATE THOUGH PUBLICLY IMPORTANT BORE   283   3 DON JUAN 11   32   2
PUBLIC'S
      I'LL NOT GAINSAY THE GENEROUS PUBLIC'S VOICE   334   3 DON JUAN 12   38   7
PUBLISH
      BUT WHY THEN PUBLISH--THERE ARE NO REWARDS   415   3 DON JUAN 14   11   1
PUBLISHED
      OF PIOUS MEN HAVE PUBLISHED ON HIS ACTS   138   2 DON JUAN   1   203   V4
PUBLISHER
      BECAUSE THE PUBLISHER DECLARES IN SOOTH 397   2 DON JUAN   4   97   6
      DEATH TO HIS PUBLISHER TO HIM 'TIS SPORT 440   2 DON JUAN   5   52   5
PUDDING
      HE TURN'D PREFERRING PUDDING TO NO PRAISE--   316   2 DON JUAN   3   79   4
      AND FIRED IT INTO ONE ASSAILANT'S PUDDING--   274   3 DON JUAN 11   13   4
PUDDLE
      WHOSE BLOOD THE PUDDLE GREATLY DID ENRICH   147   3 DON JUAN   8   71   3
      TRAMP TRAMP O'ER PEBBLE AND SPLASH SPLASH THRO PUDDLE   . 260   3 DON JUAN 10   71   2
PUFFED
      HIS BEARD HE PUFFED HIS PIPE'S AMBROSIAL GALES   172   3 DON JUAN   8   121   7
PUITS
      FOLLOW'D BY PETITS PUITS D'AMOUR--A DISH 486   3 DON JUAN 15   68   2
      THERE'S PRETTY PICKING IN THOSE PETITS PUITS   486   3 DON JUAN 15   68   8

		PAGE	VOL		CANTO	STANZA	LN

PUKES
THERE'S NOT A SEA THE PASSENGER E'ER PUKES IN . . . . . 413 2 DON JUAN 5 5 7
PULCI
PULCI WAS SIRE OF THE HALF-SERIOUS RHYME . . . . 347 2 DON JUAN 4 6 3
OR (TO THE POINT WITH HORACE AND WITH PULCI) . . . . . 396 3 DON JUAN 13 81 7
PULL
PERHAPS HIS RECENT LOSS OF BLOOD MIGHT PULL . . . . . 415 2 DON JUAN 5 8 5
AS FAST AS OARS COULD PULL AND WATER FLOAT . . . . . . 432 2 DON JUAN 5 40 4
TO TAKE US FROM OUR NATURAL REST AND PULL . . . . . . 46 3 DON JUAN 6 80 3
WHEN ALL THE HEART-STRINGS LIKE WILD HORSES PULL . . . 59 3 DON JUAN 6 107 4
AND INFIDELS TO PULL DOWN EVERY STEEPLE . . . . 195 3 DON JUAN 9 25 3
SAVE THAT THE PUPPETS PULL AT THEIR OWN STRINGS . . . . 400 3 DON JUAN 13 89 3
THEY'RE BARREN AND NOT WORTH THE PAINS TO PULL . . . . 402 3 DON JUAN 13 95 6
PROFESSIONAL--ALL CLASSES MOSTLY PULL . . . . . . 403 3 DON JUAN 13 95 V4
SHOULD HAVE A HOOK AND A SMALL TROUT TO PULL IT . . . . 407 3 DON JUAN 13 106 8
PULL'D
THAT EACH PULL'D DIFFERENT WAYS WITH MANY AN OATH . . . 394 2 DON JUAN 4 93 7
PULLED
THE BOATS PULLED OFF WITH THEIR HALF NAKED CREWS . . . 183 2 DON JUAN 2 51 V6
THAT EACH PULLED DIFFERENT WAYS--AND WAXING ROUGH . . . 395 2 DON JUAN 4 93 V7
I SAY UNLOCKING THE RECESS PULLED FORTH . . . . . . 450 2 DON JUAN 5 67 2
UNTIL THE TREE OF KNOWLEDGE WAS PULLED DOWN . . . . . . 476 2 DON JUAN 5 113 V8
PULLING
AND PULLING OUT RELUCTANT PURSES AND . . . . 426 2 DON JUAN 5 29 2
PULSE
STIFF ON HIS HEART AND PULSE AND HOPE WERE PAST . . . 204 2 DON JUAN 2 90 4
HE KNEW NOT TILL EACH PAINFUL PULSE AND LIMB . . . . . 214 2 DON JUAN 2 111 6
EACH PULSE TO ANIMATION TILL BENEATH . . . . 215 2 DON JUAN 2 113 6
AND THE BLOOD'S LAVA AND THE PULSE A BLAZE . . . . . . 254 2 DON JUAN 2 186 6
SHE HAD NO PULSE BUT DEATH SEEM'D ABSENT STILL . . . . 377 2 DON JUAN 4 60 3
COULD STIR HIS PULSE OR MAKE HIS FAITH FEEL BRITTLE . . 396 2 DON JUAN 4 95 7
OF HIS FIERCE PULSE BETOKEN A CONDITION . . . . . . 244 3 DON JUAN 10 39 4
HIS READINESS TO FEEL HIS PULSE AND TELL . . . . 514 3 DON JUAN 16 32 7
PULV
R PULV COM THREE GRAINS IPECACUANHAE . . . . 244 3 DON JUAN 10 41 5
PUMP'D
THE STRONGER PUMP'D THE WEAKER THRUMM'D A SAIL . . . . 176 2 DON JUAN 2 38 8
PUMPS
THE PUMPS AND THERE WERE FOUR FEET WATER FOUND . . . . 170 2 DON JUAN 2 27 8
UPON THE PUMPS AND THE REMAINDER SET . . . . 171 2 DON JUAN 2 28 2
BUT FOR THE PUMPS I'M GLAD TO MAKE THEM KNOWN . . . . . 171 2 DON JUAN 2 29 4
THEY TRIED THE PUMPS AGAIN AND THOUGH BEFORE . . . . . 176 2 DON JUAN 2 38 5
OF ALL OUR PUMPS--A WRECK COMPLETE SHE ROLL'D . . . . . 178 2 DON JUAN 2 42 6
PUN
WITH WIT TO HATCH A PUN OR TELL A STORY . . . . 401 3 DON JUAN 13 91 6
PUNCH
I WOULD TAKE REFUGE IN WEAK PUNCH BUT RACK . . . . . . 372 2 DON JUAN 4 53 5
METHINKS GAY PUNCH HATH SOMETHING OF THE SAME . . . . . 400 3 DON JUAN 13 89 4
PUNCHEON
THEN THERE WAS RUM EIGHT GALLONS IN A PUNCHEON . . . . 181 2 DON JUAN 2 47 8
PUNCHEONS
IN RIDING ROUND THOSE VEGETABLE PUNCHEONS . . . . . . 301 3 DON JUAN 11 66 3
PUNCTUATION
FORMS THE MOST DIFFICULT IN PUNCTUATION . . . . 396 3 DON JUAN 13 81 2
PUNCTUM
OMNE TULIT PUNCTUM QUAE MISCUIT UTILE DULCI . . . . . . 396 3 DON JUAN 13 81 8
PUNCTURATIONS
AND FOR THEIR PAINS GET SMARTER PUNCTURATIONS . . . . . 263 3 DON JUAN 10 77 V8
PUNCTURE
AND FOR THEIR PAINS GET ONLY A FRESH PUNCTURE . . . . . 263 3 DON JUAN 10 77 8
PUNIC
OLD ERSE OR IRISH OR IT MAY BE PUNIC-- . . . . 122 3 DON JUAN 8 23 2
PUNISH
AND THEN BOTH WORLDS WOULD PUNISH THEIR MISCARRIAGE . . 280 2 DON JUAN 3 9 6
MEN'S WRONGS AND RATHER CHECK THAN PUNISH CRIMES . . . 361 3 DON JUAN 13 8 6
PUNISH'D
WERE ONE NOT PUNISH'D ALL WOULD BE OUTRAGEOUS . . . . . 96 2 DON JUAN 1 138 8
PUNNED
BUT PUNNED IT DOWN TO THIS FACETIOUS PHRASE-- . . . . . 183 3 DON JUAN 9 1 4
PUNY
'TIS TIME TO STRIKE SUCH PUNY DOUBTERS DUMB AS . . . . 502 3 DON JUAN 16 4 7
PUP
EVEN WORLDS MISCARRY WHEN TOO OFT THEY PUP . . . . . . 202 3 DON JUAN 9 39 5
PUPPETS
TO MAKE SUCH PUPPETS OF US THINGS BELOW) . . . . . . 232 3 DON JUAN 10 16 4
SAVE THAT THE PUPPETS PULL AT THEIR OWN STRINGS . . . 400 3 DON JUAN 13 89 3
PUPPET-SHOWS
WHO WERE OR ARE THE PUPPET-SHOWS OF PRAISE . . . . . . 373 3 DON JUAN 13 33 4
PURBLIND
BUT THE OLD WAY IS BEST FOR THE PURBLIND . . . . 281 3 DON JUAN 11 27 4
PURCHASE
LORD HENRY WISHED TO RAISE FOR A NEW PURCHASE . . . . . 530 3 DON JUAN 16 60 2
PURCHASED
OF PURCHASED INFIDELS SOME RAISED THEIR EYES . . . . . 441 2 DON JUAN 5 54 2
ARE PURCHASED BY ALL AGONIES AND CRIMES . . . . . . 174 3 DON JUAN 8 125 2
WAS DEARLY PURCHASED BY HIS LAND'S PERDITION . . . . . 364 3 DON JUAN 13 11 8
HATH YET A PURCHASED CHOICE OF CHOICEST WINES . . . . . 394 3 DON JUAN 13 76 5
PURCHASER
STILL GENTLER PURCHASER THE BARD--THAT'S I-- . . . . . 147 2 DON JUAN 1 221 2
THE PURCHASER OF JUAN AND ACQUAINTANCE . . . . . . 432 2 DON JUAN 5 40 1

PURCHASING
    'TIS PLEASANT PURCHASING OUR FELLOW CREATURES . . . . . 425 2 DON JUAN 5   27   2
PURE
    ALTHOUGH HER MODE OF SPEAKING WAS NOT PURE . . . . . . 28 2 DON JUAN 1   13   4
    BUT VIRGIL'S SONGS ARE PURE EXCEPT THAT HORRID ONE . . . 45 2 DON JUAN 1   42   7
    BRIGHT AND IMMACULATE UNMIX'D AND PURE . . . . 64 2 DON JUAN 1   79   2
    AND LIGHTED AT TOO PURE A SHRINE TO DIM ITS . . . . . 65 2 DON JUAN 1   81   5
    HIS FINGERS WITH A PURE PLATONIC SQUEEZE . . . . . . 81 2 DON JUAN 1   111   5
    AND HER TRANSPARENT CHEEK ALL PURE AND WARM . . . . . 216 2 DON JUAN 2   114   4
    HER BROW WAS WHITE AND LOW HER CHEEK'S PURE DYE . . . 218 2 DON JUAN 2   118   1
    SHE WAS ALL WHICH PURE IGNORANCE ALLOWS . . . . . . 257 2 DON JUAN 2   190   5
    AND TURN'D HER PURE HEART'S PUREST BLOOD TO TEARS . . . 274 2 DON JUAN 3   1   8
    A LONELY PURE AFFECTION UNOPPOSED . . . . 304 2 DON JUAN 3   57   5
    AND MOCHA'S BERRY FROM ARABIA PURE . . . . 307 2 DON JUAN 3   63   3
    LOCKLESS--SO PLIABLE FROM THE PURE GOLD . . . . . . 312 2 DON JUAN 3   71   2
    AND PURE AS PSYCHE ERE SHE GREW A WIFE-- . . . . . . 313 2 DON JUAN 3   74   5
    TOO PURE EVEN FOR THE PUREST HUMAN TIES . . . . . . 313 2 DON JUAN 3   74   6
    PURE BLOOD TO STAGNATE THEIR GREAT HEARTS TO FAIL . . . 348 2 DON JUAN 4   9   2
    WHEN TWO PURE HEARTS ARE POUR'D IN ONE ANOTHER . . . . 357 2 DON JUAN 4   26   5
    FOR IF MY PURE LIBATIONS EXCEED THREE . . . . 372 2 DON JUAN 4   52   4
    A VEIN HAD BURST AND HER SWEET LIPS' PURE DYES . . . . 376 2 DON JUAN 4   59   1
    AND MAKES OUR SNOW LESS PURE THAN OUR MORALITY . . . . 501 2 DON JUAN 5   157   6
    RESTORE ME THOSE PURE FEELINGS GONE FOREVER . . . . .   9 3 DON JUAN 6   5   8
    EXTREMELY PURE WHICH MADE THEM ALL CONCUR . . . . . 25 3 DON JUAN 6   39   4
    BECAUSE 'TIS PLEASANT SO THAT IT BE PURE . . . . . . 35 3 DON JUAN 6   59   4
    WHITE COLD AND PURE AS LOOKS A FROZEN RILL . . . . . 40 3 DON JUAN 6   68   3
    'TWAS CERTAIN THAT HIS CONDUCT HAD BEEN PURE . . . . . 58 3 DON JUAN 6   104   3
    HAS FEELINGS PURE AND POLISHED AS A GEM-- . . . . . 157 3 DON JUAN 8   92   4
    A PURE TRANSPARENT PALE YET RADIANT FACE . . . . . . 159 3 DON JUAN 8   96   7
    O'ERSPREADS THE CHEEK WHICH SEEMS TOO PURE FOR CLAY . . . 229 3 DON JUAN 10   8   7
    WHOM HE PRESERVED--A PURE AND LIVING PEARL . . . . . 249 3 DON JUAN 10   51   8
    HERE ARE CHASTE WIVES PURE LIVES HERE PEOPLE PAY . . . 273 3 DON JUAN 11   10   1
    AND MONEY THAT MOST PURE IMAGINATION . . . . 316 3 DON JUAN 12   2   7
    HE IS YOUR ONLY POET--PASSION PURE . . . . 319 3 DON JUAN 12   8   1
    SUCH PURE DISINTERESTEDNESS OF PASSION . . . . 331 3 DON JUAN 12   33   3
    FOR LIKE A DAY-DAWN SHE WAS YOUNG AND PURE . . . . . 335 3 DON JUAN 12   41   2
    WHICH ARE MORE PURE THAN PLEASANT TO BE SURE . . . . . 335 3 DON JUAN 12   41   4
    COMPARED WITH THOSE OF OUR PURE PEARLS OF PRICE . . . . 349 3 DON JUAN 12   72   7
    FOR LETTING THAT PURE SANCTUARY ALONE . . . . 370 3 DON JUAN 13   27   4
    BUT MIX'D WITH PITY PURE AS E'ER WAS PENN'D . . . . . 432 3 DON JUAN 14   51   6
    AND THY PURE CREED MADE SANCTION OF ALL ILL . . . . . 464 3 DON JUAN 15   18   4
    PIOUS AND PURE BEYOND WHAT I CAN TERM ANY . . . . . 472 3 DON JUAN 15   36   5
    AS PURE AS SANCTITY ITSELF FROM VICE . . . . 478 3 DON JUAN 15   52   3
    WITH MOTIVES THE MOST CLASSICAL AND PURE . . . . . . 528 3 DON JUAN 16   57   3
    AURORA WITH HER PURE AND PLACID MIEN . . . . 552 3 DON JUAN 16   105   3
PUREE
    THE SALMI THE CONSOMME THE PUREE . . . . 487 3 DON JUAN 15   71   2
PURELY
    OR GERMANY WHERE PEOPLE PURELY KISS . . . . 450 3 DON JUAN 14   92   5
PURER
    AND THEREFORE LEAVE THEM TO THE PURER PAGE . . . . . 397 2 DON JUAN 4   98   2
    NO WONDER THEN A PURER SOUL SHOULD DREAD . . . . . . 438 3 DON JUAN 14   64   3
    OF RANK AND YOUTH THOUGH PURER THAN THE REST . . . . 480 3 DON JUAN 15   55   4
PUREST
    AND TURN'D HER PURE HEART'S PUREST BLOOD TO TEARS . . . 274 2 DON JUAN 3   1   8
    THE PUREST ORE INCLOSED THE WHITEST SKIN . . . . . . 312 2 DON JUAN 3   71   7
    TOO PURE EVEN FOR THE PUREST HUMAN TIES . . . . . . 313 2 DON JUAN 3   74   6
    THERE WAS THE PUREST PLATONISM AT BOTTOM . . . . . . 251 3 DON JUAN 10   54   7
    THAT EVEN THE PUREST PEOPLE MAY MISTAKE . . . . . . 328 3 DON JUAN 12   26   3
    BUT ADELINE WAS OF THE PUREST VINTAGE . . . . 458 3 DON JUAN 15   7   1
PURGATIVES
    AND PURGATIVES ARE DANGEROUS TO HIS REIGN . . . . . 168 2 DON JUAN 2   23   5
PURGATORIAL
    TAKES OFF ONE PECK OF PURGATORIAL COALS . . . . . . 185 2 DON JUAN 2   55   5
PURGATORY
    AND HELL AND PURGATORY--BUT FORGOT . . . . 258 2 DON JUAN 2   193   7
PURGED
    ALL PURGED AND PIOUS FROM THEIR NATIVE CLOUDS . . . . 396 3 DON JUAN 13   80   4
PURITY
    IN MAIL OF PROOF--HER PURITY OF SOUL . . . . 66 2 DON JUAN 1   82   2
PURL
    HERE TAVERNS WOOING TO A PINT OF PURL . . . . 278 3 DON JUAN 11   22   3
PURPLE
    HER CHEEK ALL PURPLE WITH THE BEAM OF YOUTH . . . . . 55 2 DON JUAN 1   61   4
    PURPLE AND GUSHING SWEET ARE OUR ESCAPES . . . . . . 88 2 DON JUAN 1   124   3
    BROUGHT FORTH IN PURPLE CRADLED IN VERMILLION . . . . 205 2 DON JUAN 2   92   3
    ✓ AND THE SEA SHINES WITH PURPLE--WHITE--AND GOLD . . . 230 2 DON JUAN 2   139   V7
    A PURPLE HECTIC PLAY'D LIKE DYING DAY . . . . 234 2 DON JUAN 2   147   2
    THE PALE CONTENDED WITH THE PURPLE ROSE . . . . . . 236 2 DON JUAN 2   150   3
    NOR WINE IN ALL THE PURPLE OF ITS GLOW . . . . . . 251 2 DON JUAN 2   180   V6
    YIELDED TO THE DEEP TWILIGHT'S PURPLE CHARM . . . . . 253 2 DON JUAN 2   184   8
    I KNOW ONE WOMAN OF THAT PURPLE SCHOOL . . . . . . 405 2 DON JUAN 4   111   7
    AS PURPLE TO THE BABYLONIAN HARLOT . . . . 108 3 DON JUAN 7   84   3
    THROUGH ALL THE PURPLE AND FINE LINEN FITTER . . . . 237 3 DON JUAN 10   26   6
    ✓ AS PURPLE CLOUDS BEFRINGE THE SUN BUT MOST . . . . . 239 3 DON JUAN 10   29   7
    AS MACHIAVEL SHOWS THOSE IN PURPLE RAIMENT . . . . . 264 3 DON JUAN 10   79   3
    DYED PURPLE NONE AT PRESENT CAN TELL HOW . . . . . . 505 3 DON JUAN 16   10   6
PURPOSE
    WHO TO MADRID ON PURPOSE MADE A JOURNEY . . . . . . 127 2 DON JUAN 1   189   8

PURPOSE   (CONTINUED)
```
  WHENE2R IT SUITS HIS PURPOSE TO ADVANCE  . . . . . . .  152   2 DON JUAN  1   V 3    3
  I HAVE SAT UP ON PURPOSE ALL THE NIGHT   . . . . . . .  230   2 DON JUAN  2   140    3
  AS THE REAL PURPOSE OF A PYRAMID  . .  . . . . . . . .  180   3 DON JUAN  8.  137    8
  LITTLE BUT TO THE PURPOSE AND HIS MANNER . . . . . . .  223   3 DON JUAN  9   83     7
  ON PURPOSE TO BELIEVE SO MUCH THE MORE  . . . . . . .   271   3 DON JUAN 11   6      8
  BUT WHAT'S THIS TO THE PURPOSE YOU WILL SAY . . . . . . 413   3 DON JUAN 14   7      1
  IS MUCH MORE TO THE PURPOSE OF HIS SONG  . . . . . . .  443   3 DON JUAN 14   77     4
  SAY SOMETHING TO THE PURPOSE AND DISPLAY  . . . . . . . 453   3 DON JUAN 14   98     7
  'TIS NOT MY PURPOSE ON HIS VIEWS TO DWELL  . . . . . .  472   3 DON JUAN 15   38     5
  BUT THEN 'TWAS TO THE PURPOSE WHAT SHE SPOKE  . . . . . 552   3 DON JUAN 16   104    3
PURPOSED
  IF THEY WERE FITTED FOR THE PURPOSED CAGE  . . . . . .  424   2 DON JUAN  5   26     5
PURPOSES
  BOUGHT UP FOR DIFFERENT PURPOSES AND PASSIONS . . . . . 407   2 DON JUAN  4   113    8
PURSE
  AND READ YOUR BIBLE SIR AND MIND YOUR PURSE . . . . . . 147   2 DON JUAN  1   220    8
  IN HEALTH AND PURSE BEGIN YOUR DAY TO DATE  . . . . . . 230   2 DON JUAN  2   140    6
  HIS PURSE HIS SOUL HIS SENSE AND EVEN HIS NONSENSE . .  88    3 DON JUAN  7   44     7
PURSES
  AND PULLING OUT RELUCTANT PURSES AND  . . . . . . . .   426   2 DON JUAN  5   29     2
  TAKE LIVES TAKE WIVES TAKE AUGHT EXCEPT MEN'S PURSES . . 264   3 DON JUAN 10   79     2
PURSUE
  AND IN THE INTERIM (TO PURSUE THIS VISION)  . . . . .   67    2 DON JUAN  1   85     5
  WHICH SHE MUST STILL PURSUE HOWE'ER AFRAID  . . . . . . 361   2 DON JUAN  4   32     5
  IF THEY WOULD BUT PURSUE THE PROPER WAY . . . . . . .   451   2 DON JUAN  5   69     4
  ONLY THE COMMON RUN WHO MUST PURSUE  . . . . . . . .    305   3 DON JUAN 11   73     2
  ALL THINGS PURSUE EXACTLY THE SAME ROUTE . . . . . . .  446   3 DON JUAN 14   84     3
PURSUED
  HE JUAN (AND NOT WORDSWORTH) SO PURSUED  . . . . . . .  70    2 DON JUAN  1   91     1
  PURSUED O'ER THE HIGH SEAS HIS WATERY JOURNEY  . . . .  283   2 DON JUAN  3   14     7
  TWO VILLAINOUS COSSACQUES PURSUED THE CHILD  . . . . .  157   3 DON JUAN  8   92     1
  ABOUT PHILOSOPHY PURSUED HIS JAUNT . .  . . . . . . .   254   3 DON JUAN 10   60     6
  AS SOON AS CROWNER'S QUEST ALLOWED PURSUED  . . . . . . 277   3 DON JUAN 11   18     3
  PURSUED HIS PATH AND DROVE PAST SOME HOTELS . . . . . . 282   3 DON JUAN 11   29     7
  TO BE PURSUED AS FOOD FOR INANITION) . . . . . . . .    328   3 DON JUAN 12   27     6
  TO THE LOT OF HIM WHO SCARCE PURSUED AT ALL . . . . . . 333   3 DON JUAN 12   37     4
  PURSUED ITS COURSE NOW GLEAMING AND NOW HIDING . . . .  385   3 DON JUAN 13   58     6
  PURSUED AN INSTANT FOR HER OWN CONTENT  . . . . . . .   521   3 DON JUAN 16   42     4
PURSUER
  FOR SOMETIMES THEY ACCEPT SOME LONG PURSUER . . . . . . 333   3 DON JUAN 12   37     1
PURSUES
  A PASSION WHICH PURSUES THOUGH IN DESPAIR  . . . . . .  114   2 DON JUAN  1   170    V4
  LET HIM TAKE CARE THAT THAT WHICH HE  PURSUES . . . . . 304   3 DON JUAN 11   71     3
  AND STILL PURSUES THE RIGHT--TO CURB THE BAD  . . . .   363   3 DON JUAN 13   9      3
PURSUITS
  EXAMPLES MAY BE FOUND OF SUCH PURSUITS  . . . . . . .   343   3 DON JUAN 12   59     2
PURVEY
  WHILE BACCHUS WILL PURVEY WITH WINES AND JELLIES  . . . 246   2 DON JUAN  2   170    V5
PURVEYOR
  BUT WHO IS THEIR PURVEYOR FROM ABOVE  . . . . . . . .   246   2 DON JUAN  2   170    7
PURVEYORS
  POWER'S BASE PURVEYORS WHO FOR PICKINGS PROWL  . . . .  196   3 DON JUAN  9   27     4
PUSH
  ALL EARTHLY GOODS SAVE TITHES) AND BADE THEM PUSH ON . . 99   3 DON JUAN  7   64     6
  (FOR I HAVE MORE THAN ONE MUSE AT A PUSH)  . . . . . .  227   3 DON JUAN 10   5      4
  WITH WHICH GREAT STATES SUCH THINGS ARE APT TO PUSH ON  246   3 DON JUAN 10   45     5
  BECAUSE AS AGES UPON AGES PUSH ON . . . . . . . . .     564   3 DON JUAN 17   6      3
PUSH'D
  WHICH KEEPS WHEN PUSH'D BY QUESTIONS RATHER ROUGH  . .  119   2 DON JUAN  1   178    5
PUSHED
  THE TROOPS ALREADY DISEMBARKED PUSHED ON  . . . . . .   119   3 DON JUAN  8   15     1
PUSHING
  KEPT ALWAYS PUSHING ONWARDS TO THE GLACIS  . . . . . .  130   3 DON JUAN  8   34     V8
PUT
  AND PUT THE BUSINESS PAST ALL KIND OF DOUBT . . . . . . 35    2 DON JUAN  1   26     8
  BUT NEVER PUT ON PANTALOONS OR BODDICES . . . . . . .   44    2 DON JUAN  1   41     4
  THAT IF I HAD AN ONLY SON TO PUT  . . . . . . . . .     50    2 DON JUAN  1   52     3
  BY BLOOD OR INK 'TIS SWEET TO PUT AN END . . . . . . .  90    2 DON JUAN  1   126    2
  THE COUNT STRONGSTROGANOFF I PUT IN PAIN  . . . . . .   102   2 DON JUAN  1   149    6
  IF DEAD HIS MODE OF DYING MIGHT BE PUT  . . . . . . .   112   2 DON JUAN  1   166    V7
  ANTONIA'S SKILL WAS PUT UPON THE RACK  . . . . . . . .  114   2 DON JUAN  1   169    3
  WHO CAN HAVE PUT MY MASTER IN THIS MOOD  . . . . . . .  115   2 DON JUAN  1   171    2
  ONE GANG OF PEOPLE INSTANTLY WAS PUT . . . . . . . .    171   2 DON JUAN  2   28     1
  SOME LASH'D THEM IN THEIR HAMMOCKS SOME PUT ON . . . .  180   2 DON JUAN  2   45     1
  THE BOATS PUT OFF O'ERCROWDED WITH THEIR CREWS . . . .  183   2 DON JUAN  2   51     6
  A JOINT UPON THEIR BARBAROUS SPITS THEY PUT ON . . . .  238   2 DON JUAN  2   154    4
  AT LAST HER FATHER'S PROWS PUT OUT TO SEA . . . . . .   248   2 DON JUAN  2   174    5
  OUR DAYS AND PUT ONE'S SERVANTS INTO MOURNING . . . .   278   2 DON JUAN  3   7      8
  CHASTE READER THEN IN ANY WAY TO PUT  . . . . . . . .   282   2 DON JUAN  3   12     3
  AND PUT HIS HOUSE IN MOURNING SEVERAL WEEKS . . . . .   295   2 DON JUAN  3   38     6
  WHICH PUT OFF BUSINESS TO THE ENSUING SESSION  . . . .  331   2 DON JUAN  3   96     6
  PUT UP YOUNG MAN PUT UP YOUR SILLY SWORD . . . . . . .  364   2 DON JUAN  4   37     8
  PUT UP YOUNG MAN PUT UP YOUR SILLY SWORD . . . . . . .  364   2 DON JUAN  4   37     8
  THE BLOWS UPON HIS CUTLASS AND THEN PUT . . . . . . .   370   2 DON JUAN  4   49     3
  WE'LL PUT ABOUT AND TRY ANOTHER TACK . . . . . . . .    384   2 DON JUAN  4   74     7
  BUT COULD NOT FOR THE MUSE OF ME PUT LESS IN'T . . . .  410   2 DON JUAN  4   117    6
  TO BE PUT UP FOR AUCTION AMONGST TARTARS . . . . . . .  415   2 DON JUAN  5   8      8
  AND PUT HIMSELF UPON HIS GOOD BEHAVIOUR  . . . . . . .  437   2 DON JUAN  5   47     5
```

641

		PAGE	VOL		CANTO	STANZA	LN

PUT   (CONTINUED)

YOU PUT ME OUT IN WHAT I HAD TO SAY	453	2 DON JUAN	5	72	3
OF EYES WHICH PUT OUT EACH SURROUNDING GEM	466	2 DON JUAN	5	96	4
WHEN HE PUT ON THE CHERUB TO PERPLEX	474	2 DON JUAN	5	109	3
WHOSE FROWN WOULD PUT THE SPHERES ALL OUT OF TUNE	494	2 DON JUAN	5	144	3
THEY ARE PUT ON AS EASILY AS A HAT	13	3 DON JUAN	6	14	4
LOOKED MORE ADAPTED TO BE PUT TO BED	26	3 DON JUAN	6	41	6
THEY PUT BEHOLDERS IN A TENDER TAKING	27	3 DON JUAN	6	43	4
MY FAULTS EVEN WITH YOUR OWN WHICH MEANETH PUT	34	3 DON JUAN	6	56	6
MAY LIKEWISE PUT OFF FOR A TIME WHAT STORY	79	3 DON JUAN	7	26	7
PUT TO SUCH TRIAL JOHN BULL'S PARTIAL PATIENCE	136	3 DON JUAN	8	48	6
BUT LET ME PUT AN END UNTO MY THEME	175	3 DON JUAN	8	127	1
BECAUSE SHE PUT A FAVOURITE TO DEATH	222	3 DON JUAN	9	81	6
YOU'LL DEEM NO DOUBT THEY PUT IT TO A GOOD USE	242	3 DON JUAN	10	36	8
ARE BOWED AND PUT THE SUN OUT LIKE A TAPER	266	3 DON JUAN	10	83	6
HISTORIANS HEROES LAWYERS PRIESTS TO PUT	286	3 DON JUAN	11	37	3
OR WHAT'S STILL WORSE TO PUT YOU OUT OF FASHION--	337	3 DON JUAN	12	45	4
IS NOT TO BE PUT HASTILY TOGETHER	355	3 DON JUAN	12	86	2
BECAUSE MY CASES PUT HIS LORDSHIP TO'T--	357	3 DON JUAN	12	V 18	5
I'VE SEEN A VIRTUOUS WOMAN PUT DOWN QUITE	397	3 DON JUAN	13	82	3
AND RATHER HELD IN THAN PUT FORTH HIS VIGOUR	427	3 DON JUAN	14	39	4
SHE PUT ALL CORONETS INTO COMMOTION	434	3 DON JUAN	14	55	2
TO SHIELD HIMSELF'THAN PUT YOU ON YOUR GUARD	462	3 DON JUAN	15	14	4
ASIDE HIS VERY MIRROR SOON WAS PUT	513	3 DON JUAN	16	29	4
TO PUT THE QUESTION WITH AN AIR SEDATE	515	3 DON JUAN	16	35	6
JUAN PUT FORTH ONE ARM--ETERNAL POWERS	559	3 DON JUAN	16	120	1

PUTS

WE NEEDS MUST FOLLOW WHEN FATE PUTS FROM SHORE	460	2 DON JUAN	5	84	5
I THINK ONE SHAKESPEAR PUTS THE SAME THOUGHT IN	77	3 DON JUAN	7	21	6
WHICH PUTS MY PEGASUS TO THESE GRAVE PACES	334	3 DON JUAN	12	39	8
WHEN SOME SMART TALKER PUTS THEM TO THE TEST	404	3 DON JUAN	13	98	7

PUTTING

| I CAN'T HELP PUTTING IN MY CLAIM TO PRAISE-- | 149 | 2 DON JUAN | 1 | 222 | 6 |
| PUTTING THE VERY BRAVEST WHO WERE KNOCKED | 134 | 3 DON JUAN | 8 | 43 | 7 |

PUZZLE

HIS CLASSIC STUDIES MADE A LITTLE PUZZLE	44	2 DON JUAN	1	41	1
YET AFTER ALL 'TWOULD PUZZLE TO SAY WHERE	27	3 DON JUAN	6	42	7
ALIKE MIGHT PUZZLE EITHER WIT OR DUNCE	43	3 DON JUAN	6	74	4

PUZZLED

I'M REALLY PUZZLED WHAT TO THINK OR SAY	59	2 DON JUAN	1	68	7
HE PUZZLED OVER WHAT HE FOUND A NEW ONE	68	2 DON JUAN	1	86	5
ANTONIA PUZZLED JULIA DID NOT SPEAK	114	2 DON JUAN	1	169	7
PUZZLED HIS TUTORS VERY MUCH OF COURSE	158	2 DON JUAN	2	2	8
BUT BE MUCH PUZZLED BY A COUGH AND COLD	168	2 DON JUAN	2	22	3
WHICH PUZZLED NATURE MUCH TO KNOW WHAT ART MEANT	448	2 DON JUAN	5	64	8
I'M PUZZLED WHAT TO DO WITH YOU MY DEAR	29	3 DON JUAN	6	46	3
IN HIS REPLIES SHE PUZZLED HIM FOR FRESH ONES	56	3 DON JUAN	6	101	5
WAS ON A SUDDEN RATHER PUZZLED HERE	125	3 DON JUAN	8	27	6
POOR THING WHAT'S TO BE DONE I'M PUZZLED QUITE	161	3 DON JUAN	8	99	8
HAS EVER PUZZLED FAITH WITHAL OR YOKED HER IN	377	3 DON JUAN	13	41	8
THAT SHE HAD PUZZLED ALL THE ACUTEST HINTERS	434	3 DON JUAN	14	56	3
AND JUAN PUZZLED BUT STILL CURIOUS THRUST	560	3 DON JUAN	16	122	1

PUZZLES

I CAN'T SAY THAT IT PUZZLES ME AT ALL	158	2 DON JUAN	2	3	1
WHICH PUZZLES US TO KNOW WHAT FORTUNE MEANS	247	3 DON JUAN	10	47	3
ARE PUZZLES TO THE MOST PRECAUTIOUS BENCHES	531	3 DON JUAN	16	63	8

PUZZLING

AND OTHER STUFFS WITH WHICH I WON'T STAY PUZZLING	27	2 DON JUAN	1	12	8
THE WATER RUSH'D THROUGH IN A WAY QUITE PUZZLING	171	2 DON JUAN	2	28	7
AND YET 'TIS VERY PUZZLING ON THE BRINK	234	3 DON JUAN	10	20	6
THE VERY SERVANTS PUZZLING HOW TO HAND	538	3 DON JUAN	16	79	3

PYE

| LIKE FOUR AND TWENTY BLACKBIRDS IN A PYE | 9 | 2 DON JUAN | D | 1 | 8 |
| WHICH PYE BEING OPEN'D THEY BEGAN TO SING | 10 | 2 DON JUAN | D | 2 | 1 |

PYGMALION

| CALLED CAVALIER SERVENTE--A PYGMALION | 208 | 3 DON JUAN | 9 | 51 | 5 |

PYGMALION'S

| FROM MARBLE LIKE PYGMALION'S STATUE WAKING | 27 | 3 DON JUAN | 6 | 43 | 6 |

PYRAMID

| CHEOPS ERECTED THE FIRST PYRAMID | 146 | 2 DON JUAN | 1 | 219 | 2 |
| AS THE REAL PURPOSE OF A PYRAMID | 180 | 3 DON JUAN | 8 | 137 | 8 |

PYRAMIDIC

| O'ER THEM IN ALMOST PYRAMIDIC PRIDE | 462 | 2 DON JUAN | 5 | 87 | 6 |

PYRAMUS

| 'TWAS FAMOUS TOO FOR THISBE AND FOR PYRAMUS | 445 | 2 DON JUAN | 5 | 60 | 7 |

PYRRHIC

PERCEIVED IT WAS THE PYRRHIC DANCE SO MARTIAL	290	2 DON JUAN	3	29	7
YOU HAVE THE PYRRHIC DANCE AS YET	324	2 DON JUAN	3	L 10	1
WHERE IS THE PYRRHIC PHALANX GONE	324	2 DON JUAN	3	L 10	2

PYRRHO

| LIKE PYRRHO ON A SEA OF SPECULATION | 191 | 3 DON JUAN | 9 | 18 | 2 |
| THERE WAS LORD PYRRHO TOO THE GREAT FREETHINKER | 398 | 3 DON JUAN | 13 | 84 | 7 |

PYTHAGORAS

| PYTHAGORAS LOCKE SOCRATES--BUT PAGES | 566 | 3 DON JUAN | 17 | 9 | 1 |

PYTHONESS

| SHE STOOD A MOMENT AS A PYTHONESS | 59 | 3 DON JUAN | 6 | 107 | 1 |

QUA

| OBSERVE FOR THAT WITH ME'S A SINE QUA | 494 | 3 DON JUAN | 15 | 86 | 8 |

QUACKS

| THE KING COMMANDS US AND THE DOCTOR QUACKS US | 159 | 2 DON JUAN | 2 | 4 | 5 |

QUADRILLE
    WHERE SCIENCE MARSHALS FORTH HER OWN QUADRILLE . . . . . 303 3 DON JUAN 11   70   8
QUADRUPLE
    AND AS FOUR WIVES MUST HAVE QUADRUPLE CLAIMS   . . . . . 11 3 DON JUAN 6   11   7
QUAE
    OMNE TULIT PUNCTUM QUAE MISCUIT UTILE DULCI . . . . 396 3 DON JUAN 13   81   8
QUAFF
    TO QUAFF A BROOK WHICH MURMURED LIKE A BIRD . . . . 384 3 DON JUAN 13   56   8
QUAFF'D
    UNLESS WITH PEOPLE WHO TOO MUCH HAVE QUAFF'D . . . . . . 183 2 DON JUAN 2   50   5
QUAINT
    THE SECOND DRUNK THE THIRD SO QUAINT AND MOUTHEY . . . . 139 2 DON JUAN 1   205   4
    IN THE SAME QUAINT UNINTERESTED TONE-- . . . . 261 3 DON JUAN 10   73   4
    SYMMETRICAL BUT DECK'D WITH CARVINGS QUAINT-- . . . . . . 389 3 DON JUAN 13   65   2
    THE QUAINT OLD CRUEL COXCOMB IN HIS GULLET . . . . 407 3 DON JUAN 13   106   7
    THE PORTER SOME SLIGHT SCANDALS STRANGE AND QUAINT . . . 418 3 DON JUAN 14   19   5
    APPEAR TO WAKE AND SHADOWS WILD AND QUAINT . . . . 508 3 DON JUAN 16   18   5
QUAKE
    AND ALMOST MIGHT HAVE MADE A TARQUIN QUAKE . . . . 62 2 DON JUAN 1   75   6
    AND THERE IS NO GREAT CAUSE TO QUAKE . . . .   86 2 DON JUAN 1   120   3
    BUT THEN THE THOUGHT OF PARTING MADE HER QUAKE . . . . . 247 2 DON JUAN 2   173   6
    TO TOSS TO TUMBLE DOZE REVIVE AND QUAKE . . . .   18 3 DON JUAN 6   24   7
QUAKING
    WITHIN HIM AND TO QUELL HIS CORPORAL QUAKING-- . . . . . 558 3 DON JUAN 16   118   6
QUALIFIED
    UNLESS WHEN QUALIFIED WITH THEE COGNIAC . . . . 372 2 DON JUAN 4   53   1
    BUT BEING QUALIFIED IN ONE WAY YET . . . . 391 2 DON JUAN 4   86   3
    AND NOT OUR OWN I AM TOO QUALIFIED . . . . 103 3 DON JUAN 7   71   3
    AS SOME HAVE QUALIFIED THAT WONDROUS PLACE . . . . 265 3 DON JUAN 10   81   4
QUALITIES
    A GREAT OPINION OF HER OWN GOOD QUALITIES   . . . . . .   32 2 DON JUAN 1   20   2
    BESIDES HE HAD SOME QUALITIES WHICH FIX . . . .   230 2 DON JUAN 10   10   1
    HIS QUALITIES (WITH THEM) INTO SUBLIME . . . .   295 3 DON JUAN 11   53   6
    AND RECONCILED ALL QUALITIES WHICH GRACE MAN . . . . . 368 3 DON JUAN 13   21   7
QUALITY
    THE NAME AND QUALITY OF HIS NEW PATRON . . . .   298 2 DON JUAN 3   44   7
    IS NOT A THING OF THAT ASTRINGENT QUALITY . . . . . .   501 2 DON JUAN 5   157   4
    LET NOT THE LATTER QUALITY OFFEND . . . .   52 3 DON JUAN 6   93   V2
    TO HIM WHOSE BREEDING MARCHES WITH HIS QUALITY . . . .   369 3 DON JUAN 13   24   8
    ITS QUANTITY IS BUT CONDENSED TO QUALITY . . . .   381 3 DON JUAN 13   49   8
    HE ALSO HAD A QUALITY UNCOMMON . . . .   426 3 DON JUAN 14   36   1
    A QUALITY AGREEABLE TO WOMAN . . . .   426 3 DON JUAN 14   36   5
    TO FIX THE DUE BOUNDS OF THIS DANGEROUS QUALITY . . . . 448 3 DON JUAN 14   89   8
    THAN TO WAX WHITE--FOR BLUSHES ARE FOR QUALITY . . . .   532 3 DON JUAN 16   64   8
QUALM
    OF OCEAN WHEN THEY WOKE THEY FELT A QUALM . . . . . .   192 2 DON JUAN 2   68   6
QUALMS
    THE HOARSE HARSH WAVES KEPT TIME FRIGHT CURED THE QUALMS . 174 2 DON JUAN 2   34   5
    IN SHORT UPON THAT SUBJECT I'VE SOME QUALMS VERY . . . 499 3 DON JUAN 15   96   7
QUANTITY
    A QUANTITY OF CLOTHES FIT FOR THE BACK   . . . .   450 2 DON JUAN 5   67   3
    A QUANTITY OF PALISADES UPRIGHT . . . .   71 3 DON JUAN 7   10   6
    NOR DID SHE FIND THE QUANTITY ENCUMBER . . . .   248 3 DON JUAN 10   48   6
    AGAINST THE SAME GIVEN QUANTITY OF RHYME . . . .   312 3 DON JUAN 11   90   3
    THE QUANTITY OF GOOD SHE DID'S UNKNOWN . . . .   338 3 DON JUAN 12   48   5
    NOT THAT THERE'S NOT A QUANTITY OF THOSE . . . .   349 3 DON JUAN 12   73   3
    ITS QUANTITY IS BUT CONDENSED TO QUALITY . . . .   381 3 DON JUAN 13   49   8
QUANTUM
    A CERTAIN QUANTUM OF ACCOMPLISHMENT . . . .   340 3 DON JUAN 12   52   V2
QUARANTINE
    HAVING NO CUSTOM-HOUSE NOR QUARANTINE . . . .   286 2 DON JUAN 3   20   2
QUARREL
    GOOD WORKMEN NEVER QUARREL WITH THEIR TOOLS . . . . . . 136 2 DON JUAN 1   201   6
    MAY QUARREL AND THE LADY GROWING WISER   . . . .   288 2 DON JUAN 3   24   4
    THE MAN WAS GONE IN SOME ITALIAN QUARREL . . . .   429 2 DON JUAN 5   34   7
    YOU PLEASE--WE WILL NOT QUARREL ABOUT THAT . . . . . .   25 3 DON JUAN 6   38   8
    WHEN MAN IN BATTLE OR IN QUARREL TILTS . . . .   342 3 DON JUAN 12   56   5
    AND NEXT A QUARREL (AS HE SEEMED TO FRET) . . . . . .   437 3 DON JUAN 14   62   7
    THAT LIKE TO MAKE A QUARREL WHEN THEY CAN'T . . . . .   438 3 DON JUAN 14   63   5
QUARREL'D
    DON JOSE AND HIS LADY QUARRELL'D--WHY . . . .   33 2 DON JUAN 1   23   1
QUARRELLING
    INSTEAD OF QUARRELLING HAD THEY BEEN BUT BOTH IN . . .   34 2 DON JUAN 1   25   5
QUARRELS
    BUT FOR DOMESTIC QUARRELS ONE WILL DO . . . .   31 2 DON JUAN 1   19   8
    AND IF OUR QUARRELS SHOULD RIP UP OLD STORIES . . . .   37 2 DON JUAN 1   31   1
    TO STRIFE 'TIS SOMETIMES SWEET TO HAVE OUR QUARRELS . .   90 2 DON JUAN 1   126   3
    SO THERE WERE QUARRELS CARED NOT FOR THE CAUSE . . . .   109 2 DON JUAN 1   159   7
    WILL OFTENTIMES MAKE DEADLY QUARRELS BURST . . . . . .   136 3 DON JUAN 8   48   3
QUARTER
    I WONDER IN WHAT QUARTER NOW THE MOON IS . . . .   103 2 DON JUAN 1   150   4
    AT LAST THEY REACHED A QUARTER MOST RETIRED . . . . .   448 2 DON JUAN 5   64   1
    AND THEY HAD WASTED NOW ALMOST A QUARTER . . . .   482 2 DON JUAN 5   122   8
    THE TRAIN MIGHT REACH A QUARTER OF A MILE . . . . . .   495 2 DON JUAN 5   146   3
    AMONG THE FOREMOST OFFERED HIM GOOD QUARTER . . . . .   152 3 DON JUAN 8   80   2
    WHO MAKE THE BEDS OF THOSE WHO WON'T TAKE QUARTER . .   167 3 DON JUAN 8   111   5
    QUARTER IN CASE HE BADE THEM NOT AROINT . . . .   170 3 DON JUAN 8   117   3
QUARTERED
    TO BE IMPALED OR QUARTERED AS A DISH . . . .   492 2 DON JUAN 5   141   2

QUARTERLY
```
    AND THAT THE EDINBURGH REVIEW AND QUARTERLY . . . . . .  142  2 DON JUAN  1   211   7
QUARTERS
    A MISTRESS AND SUCH COMFORTABLE QUARTERS . . . . . . .  415  2 DON JUAN  5     8   7
    WAS HE SINCE SO RENOWNED IN COUNTRY QUARTERS  . . . .  76  3 DON JUAN  7    19   7
QUARTO
    (I THINK THE QUARTO HOLDS FIVE HUNDRED PAGES)  . . . .  11  2 DON JUAN  D     4   2
    IN ENGLAND A SIX CANTO QUARTO TALE . . . . . . .  320  2 DON JUAN  3    86   2
    WORDSWORTH'S LAST QUARTO BY THE WAY IS BIGGER  . . . .  330  2 DON JUAN  3    94   5
    AND SPAWNS HIS QUARTO AND DEMANDS YOUR PRAISE--  . . .  440  2 DON JUAN  5    52   4
QUARUM
    HAUD IGNARA LOQUOR THESE ARE NUGAE QUARUM  . . . . .  419  3 DON JUAN 14    21   1
QUAVERING
    THE LASCIAMI'S AND QUAVERING ADDIO'S . . . . . . .  523  3 DON JUAN 16    45   5
QUE
    QUE SCAIS-JE WAS THE MOTTO OF MONTAIGNE . . . . . .  191  3 DON JUAN  9    17   1
QUEAN
    PERHAPS AS WRETCHED IF A PEASANT'S QUEAN . . . . . .  18  3 DON JUAN  6    25   8
QUEANS
    THIS MODERN AMAZON AND QUEEN OF QUEANS  . . . . . .  54  3 DON JUAN  6    96   4
QUEEN
    THE QUEEN OF DENMARK FOR OPHELIA BROUGHT . . . . . .  165  2 DON JUAN  2    17   5
    AND THE CALUMNIATED QUEEN SEMIRAMIS--  . . . . . .  445  2 DON JUAN  5    60   8
    THAT INJURED QUEEN BY CHRONICLERS SO COARSE . . . . .  446  2 DON JUAN  5    61   1
    SUCH AS WAS MARY'S QUEEN OF SCOTS TRUE--TEARS  . . . .  468  2 DON JUAN  5    98   5
    WERE RULED AS CALMLY AS A CHRISTIAN QUEEN  . . . . .  496  2 DON JUAN  5   148   8
    HE DIED AT FIFTY FOR A QUEEN OF FORTY . . . . . .  9  3 DON JUAN  6     5   1
    THIS MODERN AMAZON AND QUEEN OF QUEANS  . . . . . .  54  3 DON JUAN  6    96   4
    NAPOLEON'S MARY'S (QUEEN OF SCOTLAND) SHOULD  . . . .  218  3 DON JUAN  9    71   5
    A YOUNG LIEUTENANT'S WITH A NOT OLD QUEEN  . . . . .  236  3 DON JUAN 10    24   4
    WHERE IS THE UNHAPPY QUEEN WITH ALL HER WOES  . . . .  307  3 DON JUAN 11    77   5
    I HAVE SEEN THAT SAD AFFAIR OF THE LATE QUEEN--  . . .  310  3 DON JUAN 11    84   4
    FEMALE OR MALE A SCHOOL-BOY OR A QUEEN  . . . . . .  421  3 DON JUAN 14    25   8
    A BEGGAR AND A QUEEN OR WAS (OF LATE . . . . . .  541  3 DON JUAN 16    84   2
QUEEN-BEE
    WAS THE QUEEN-BEE THE GLASS OF ALL THAT'S FAIR . . . .  365  3 DON JUAN 13    13   5
QUEENLY
    QUITE IN A CONFIDENTIAL QUEENLY WAY  . . . . . . .  466  2 DON JUAN  5    95   3
QUEENS
    EARTH BEING ONLY MADE FOR QUEENS AND KINGS  . . . . .  485  2 DON JUAN  5   128   4
    BUT SHE WAS LUCKY AND LUCK'S ALL  YOUR QUEENS  . . . .  247  3 DON JUAN 10    47   1
    STATESMEN CHIEFS ORATORS QUEENS PATRIOTS KINGS . . . .  306  3 DON JUAN 11    76   7
    QUEENS BISHOPS KNIGHTS ROOKS PAWNS THE WORLD'S A GAME  .  400  3 DON JUAN 13    89   2
QUEER
    WITH HIS TWO CAPTIVES BY SO QUEER A ROAD . . . . . .  436  2 DON JUAN  5    45   3
    PERHAPS YOU MAY PICK OUT SOME QUEER NO-MEANING . . . .  207  3 DON JUAN  9    49   7
    WHO QUEER A FLAT WHO (SPITE OF BOW-STREET'S BAN)  . . .  277  3 DON JUAN 11    19   5
QUELL
    MIGHT PLEASE PERHAPS A VIRTUOUS WIFE CAN QUELL . . . .  64  2 DON JUAN  1    78   5
    PASS'D BUT HE STROVE QUITE COURTEOUSLY TO QUELL  . . .  298  3 DON JUAN  3    44   4
    'TIS STRANGE THE MIND SHOULD LET SUCH PHRASES QUELL IT'S  298  3 DON JUAN 11    60  V7
    WITHIN HIM AND TO QUELL HIS CORPORAL QUAKING--  . . . .  558  3 DON JUAN 16   118   6
QUENCH
    THEY CANNOT QUENCH YOUNG FEELINGS FRESH AND EARLY . . .  234  3 DON JUAN 10    19   6
QUENCH'D
    OF HIS QUENCH'D HEART AND THE SEA DIRGES LOW  . . . .  362  2 DON JUAN  4    34   6
    LIE WITH THEIR HALLELUJAHS QUENCH'D LIKE FIRE  . . . .  387  3 DON JUAN 13    62   8
QUENCHED
    AND THEN HER THIRST OF BLOOD WAS QUENCHED IN TEARS . . .  490  2 DON JUAN  5   136   8
    THESE QUENCHED A MOMENT HER AMBITION'S THIRST--  . . .  212  3 DON JUAN  9    59   5
    QUENCHED IN THE LAP OF THE SALT SEA OR THETIS . . . .  217  3 DON JJAN  9    69   8
QUENCHLESS
    IN VAIN--AS FALL THE DEWS ON QUENCHLESS SANDS  . . . .  212  3 DON JUAN  9    59   7
QUEST
    OR COELEBS' WIFE SET OUT IN QUEST OF LOVERS . . . . .  29  2 DON JUAN  1    16   4
    OFF EACH ATTACK WHEN PEOPLE ARE IN QUEST . . . . . .  123  3 DON JUAN  8    25   6
    AS SOON AS CROWNER'S QUEST ALLOWED PURSUED  . . . . .  277  3 DON JUAN 11    18   3
QUESTION
    'GAINST YOU THE QUESTION WITH POSTERITY  . . . . . .  13  2 DON JUAN  D     7   8
    HER ONLY SON WITH QUESTION OR SURMISE . . . . . . .  73  2 DON JUAN  1    97   6
    YOUR LABOURING PEOPLE THINK BEYOND ALL QUESTION  . . .  191  2 DON JUAN  2    67   7
    PERPLEXING QUESTION BUT NO DOUBT THE MOON  . . . . .  267  2 DON JUAN  2   208   4
    HIS QUESTION MUCH TOO MERRY TO DIVINE  . . . . . .  297  2 DON JUAN  3    42   7
    JUAN WOULD QUESTION FURTHER BUT SHE PRESS'D  . . . . .  356  2 DON JUAN  4    24   1
    AND CONSCIENCE ASK A CURIOUS SORT OF QUESTION  . . . .  426  2 DON JUAN  5    30   4
    COULD YOU ASK SUCH A QUESTION--BUT WE WILL . . . . .  22  3 DON JUAN  6    33   2
    I HOPE THIS LITTLE QUESTION IS NO SIN . . . . . . .  77  3 DON JUAN  7    21   4
    NOT THAT HIS MANHOOD COULD BE CALLED IN QUESTION . . .  84  3 DON JUAN  7    36   2
    TO BE OR NOT TO BE THAT IS THE QUESTION  . . . . . .  189  3 DON JUAN  9    14   1
    DISSECTING THE WHOLE INSIDE OF A QUESTION  . . . . .  232  3 DON JUAN 10    14   7
    OUR SOARINGS WITH ANOTHER SORT OF QUESTION . . . . .  269  3 DON JUAN 11     3   3
    AFTER DUE SEARCH YOUR FAITH TO ANY QUESTION . . . . .  411  3 DON JUAN 14     2   4
    FOR MORALS MARRIAGE AND THIS QUESTION CARRIED  . . . .  469  3 DON JUAN 15    29   7
    FOR ME APPEARS A QUESTION FAR TOO NICE . . . . . .  478  3 DON JUAN 15    52   5
    FROM ANSWERING SHE BEGAN TO QUESTION THIS  . . . . .  492  3 DON JUAN 15    81   1
    TO PUT THE QUESTION WITH AN AIR SEDATE . . . . . .  515  3 DON JUAN 16    35   6
    TO QUESTION THAT FRIAR'S RIGHT . . . . . . . .  520  3 DON JUAN 16  L  5   8
    OF TWO THINGS--HOW (THE QUESTION RATHER ODD IS)  . . .  543  3 DON JUAN 16    90   7
QUESTIONER
    THE QUESTIONER FILL'D UP A GLASS OF WINE . . . . . .  297  2 DON JUAN  3    42   8
```

644

QUESTION'S
   BUT WHAT CONDUCTED IF THE QUESTION'S FAIR . . . . . . 418 2 DON JUAN 5   15   4
QUESTIONS
   WHICH KEEPS WHEN PUSH'D BY QUESTIONS RATHER ROUGH . . . . 119 2 DON JUAN 1 178   5
   TO ASK HIM AWKWARD QUESTIONS ON THE WAY . . . . . . 286 2 DON JUAN 3   20   3
   DIRECT YOUR QUESTIONS TO MY NEIGHBOUR THERE . . . . . 298 2 DON JUAN 3   45   6
   HE ASK'D NO FURTHER QUESTIONS AND PROCEEDED . . . . . 300 2 DON JUAN 3   49   1
   A FEW BRIEF QUESTIONS AND THE ANSWERS GAVE . . . . . 387 2 DON JUAN 4   79   6
   I HAVE ANSWERED ALL YOUR QUESTIONS WITHOUT PRESSING . . . 419 2 DON JUAN 5   16   3
   ARE QUESTIONS ANSWERLESS AND YET INCESSANT . . . . . 37 3 DON JUAN 6   63   8
   TO THIS LONG CATECHISM OF QUESTIONS ASKED . . . . . 56 3 DON JUAN 6 100   2
QUI
   VETABO CERERIS SACRUM QUI VULGARET-- . . . . . . 419 3 DON JUAN 14   21   7
QUIA
   QUIETS AT ONCE WITH QUIA IMPOSSIBILE . . . . . . 503 3 DON JUAN 16   5   8
QUIBBLE
   BECAUSE 'TIS SO WHO NIBBLE SCRIBBLE QUIBBLE HE . . . . 503 3 DON JUAN 16   5   7
QUIBUSDAM
   DE REBUS CUNCTIS ET QUIBUSDAM ALIIS . . . . . . 502 3 DON JUAN 16   3   8
QUICK
   IN FEELINGS QUICK AS OVID'S MISS MEDEA . . . . . 68 2 DON JUAN 1   86   4
   QUICK THICK AND HEAVY--AS A THUNDER-SHOWER . . . . . 110 2 DON JUAN 1 161   8
   QUICK WITHOUT WIT AND VIOLENT WITHOUT STRENGTH . . . . 155 2 DON JUAN 1 V 6   7
   WITH THE QUICK WAVE AND GAIN ERE IT WAS DARK . . . . 212 2 DON JUAN 2 106   3
   AND NEAR THE CAVE HER QUICK LIGHT FOOTSTEPS DREW . . . 232 2 DON JUAN 2 142   2
   BUT HAIDEE STOPP'D HER WITH HER QUICK SMALL HAND . . . 234 2 DON JUAN 2 146   3
   AND DARTS IN ONE QUICK GLANCE A LONG REPLY . . . . 241 2 DON JUAN 2 162   6
   DEADLY AND QUICK AND CRUSHING YET AS REAL . . . . 262 2 DON JUAN 2 199   7
   QUICK TO PERCEIVE AND STRONG TO BEAR AND MEANT . . . 302 2 DON JUAN 3   53   5
   IT HAS A STRANGE QUICK JAR UPON THE EAR . . . . 366 2 DON JUAN 4   41   1
   RELIEVED HER THOUGHTS DULL SILENCE AND QUICK CHAT . . . 378 2 DON JUAN 4   63   6
   SHORT SOLACE VAIN RELIEF--THOUGHT CAME TOO QUICK . . . 380 2 DON JUAN 4   67   1
   UNCONSCIOUS ALBEIT TURNED OF QUICK SEVENTEEN . . . . 33 3 DON JUAN 6   54   6
   SHE LIKED QUICK ANSWERS IN ALL CONVERSATIONS . . . . 56 3 DON JUAN 6 101   3
   WHICH AUGURED OF THE DEAD HOWEVER QUICK . . . . 244 3 DON JUAN 10   39   5
   QUICK SILVER SMALL TALK ENDING (IF YOU NOTE IT) . . . 328 3 DON JUAN 12   26   7
QUICKENING
   AND OH THAT QUICKENING OF THE HEART THAT BEAT . . . 264 2 DON JUAN 2 203   1
QUICKER
   JULIA MY LOVE--(YOU RASCAL PEDRO QUICKER)-- . . . . 167 2 DON JUAN 2   20   5
   AS BLACK BUT QUICKER AND OF SMALLER SIZE . . . . 221 2 DON JUAN 2 122   8
   BUT MAKING MONEY SLOWLY FIRST THEN QUICKER . . . . 317 3 DON JUAN 12   4   3
QUICKLY
   AND THE POOR LITTLE CUTTER QUICKLY SWAMP'D . . . . 188 2 DON JUAN 2   60   8
   RING FOR YOUR VALET--BID HIM QUICKLY BRING . . . . 251 2 DON JUAN 2 180   1
   DESCENDING RATHER QUICKLY THE DECLIVITY . . . . 290 2 DON JUAN 3   29   2
   AS I WILL MAKE YOU QUICKLY UNDERSTAND . . . . 411 2 DON JUAN 5   1 V6
   CAME MOUNTING QUICKLY UP FOR IT WAS NOW . . . . 135 3 DON JUAN 8   45   2
   JUAN YET QUICKLY UNDERSTOOD THEIR GESTURE . . . . 274 3 DON JUAN 11   13   1
   AND CHANGED AS QUICKLY AS HEARTS AFTER MARRIAGE . . . 379 3 DON JUAN 13   46   4
   THAT VIOLENT THINGS MORE QUICKLY FIND A TERM . . . 451 3 DON JUAN 14   94   3
QUICKNESS
   THE UNUSUAL QUICKNESS OF THESE COMMON CHANGES . . . . 309 3 DON JUAN 11   81   8
QUICKSILVER
   OF SUCH QUICKSILVER CLAY THAT IN HIS BREAST . . . . 268 2 DON JUAN 2 209   3
QUICKSILVER'S
   WHEN ITS QUICKSILVER'S DOWN AT ZERO--LO . . . . 378 3 DON JUAN 13   44   1
QUIESCENT
   HOW CLAY SHRINKS BACK FROM MORE QUIESCENT CLAY . . . . 412 3 DON JUAN 14   4   3
QUIET
   AT TWELVE HE WAS A FINE BUT QUIET BOY . . . . 49 2 DON JUAN 1   50   2
   A QUIET CONSCIENCE MAKES ONE SO SERENE . . . . 66 2 DON JUAN 1   83   6
   AND NEVER HAD AS YET A QUIET DAY . . . . 177 2 DON JUAN 2   40   4
   LAY AT THIS PERIOD QUIET AS THE SKY . . . . 251 2 DON JUAN 2 181   3
   THE QUIET SHEEP FEEDS AND THE TORTOISE CRAWLS . . . 386 2 DON JUAN 4   77   8
   BECAUSE HE KEPT THEM QUIET IN HIS CLOSET HE . . . 496 2 DON JUAN 5 148 V6
   WHO'S QUIET INOFFENSIVE SILENT SHY . . . . 30 3 DON JUAN 6   49   5
   WHERE ALL WAS HARMONY AND CALM AND QUIET . . . 32 3 DON JUAN 6   53   2
   TO TAKE A QUIET RIDE IN SOME GREEN LANE . . . 224 3 DON JUAN 9   85   8
   DREW QUIET CONSOLATION THROUGH ITS HINT . . . 241 3 DON JUAN 10   34   7
   MADE CATHERINE TASTE NEXT NIGHT A QUIET SLUMBER-- . . 248 3 DON JUAN 10   48   4
   MORE QUIET WHEN OUR MOON'S NO MORE AT FULL . . . 360 3 DON JUAN 13   4   3
   WITH QUIET CRUIZING O'ER THE OCEAN WOMAN . . . 376 3 DON JUAN 13   40   2
   QUIET--SANK INTO SOFTER RIPPLES GLIDING . . . 385 3 DON JUAN 13   58   4
   LOVE'S RIOTOUS BUT MARRIAGE SHOULD HAVE QUIET . . . 474 3 DON JUAN 15   41   7
   PERHAPS SHE DID NOT LIKE THE QUIET WAY . . . 479 3 DON JUAN 15   53   1
   'TWAS A MERE QUIET SMILE OF CONTEMPLATION . . . 545 3 DON JUAN 16   93   1
QUIETEST
   AND AS THE QUIETEST OF ALL SHE MIGHT . . . . 46 3 DON JUAN 6   81   5
QUIETLY
   'TIS WITH OUR HERO QUIETLY INURN'D . . . . 23 2 DON JUAN 1   4   4
   AND NEXT PROCEEDED QUIETLY TO COCK . . . . 365 2 DON JUAN 4   40   8
   MAN QUITE AS QUIETLY AS BLOWS THE MONSOON . . . 132 3 DON JUAN 8   39   5
   AS GROWS A FLOWER THUS QUIETLY SHE GREW . . . 476 3 DON JUAN 15   47   3
QUIETS
   QUIETS AT ONCE WITH QUIA IMPOSSIBILE . . . . 503 3 DON JUAN 16   5   8
QUILL
   BECAUSE BOLD BRITONS HAVE A TONGUE AND FREE QUILL . . 367 3 DON JUAN 13   20   5
   MUST PERCH HARMONIOUS ON MY TUNEFUL QUILL . . . 458 3 DON JUAN 15   5   4

```
                                                        PAGE VOL    CANTO STANZA LN
QUINSY
     AND FIND A QUINSY VERY HARD TO TREAT . . . . . . .  168  2 DON JUAN  2    22    4
QUINTESSENCE
     'TIS THE WHOLE SPIRIT BROUGHT TO A QUINTESSENCE  . . . .  375  3 DON JUAN 13    38    1
QUINTESSENTIAL
     A QUINTESSENTIAL LAUDANUM OR BLACK DROP . . . . . .  216  3 DON JUAN  9    67    5
QUIRE
     THE OWL HIS ANTHEM WHERE THE SILENCED QUIRE . . . . .  387  3 DON JUAN 13    62    7
QUIT
     AT QUITTING EVEN THOSE WE QUIT IN STRIFE . . . . . .  164  2 DON JUAN  2    15    6
     TO QUIT HIS ACADEMIC OCCUPATION . . . . . . . .  175  2 DON JUAN  2    37    6
     HAD MADE HER MISTRESS QUIT HER BED TO TRACE . . . . .  240  2 DON JUAN  2   159    4
     BUT LET ME QUIT THE THEME AS SUCH THINGS CLAIM . . . .  431  2 DON JUAN  5    38    4
     TO QUIT HER GENTLE PARTNER AND TO DWELL  . . . . .   48  3 DON JUAN  6    84    6
     DONE I'LL NOT QUIT HER TILL SHE SEEMS SECURE  . . . .  161  3 DON JUAN  8   100    2
     QUIT AND THOUGH DEATH HAD THREATENED AN EJECTION . . .  245  3 DON JUAN 10    43    2
     WHICH EVE MIGHT QUIT WITHOUT MUCH SACRIFICE-- . . . .  278  3 DON JUAN 11    21    8
     WHO DID NOT QUIT ME WHEN OPPRESSION TROD . . . . . .  452  3 DON JUAN 14    96    5
     BUT COULD HE QUIT HIS KING IN TIMES OF STRIFE . . . .  536  3 DON JUAN 16    74    3
     EARLIEST TO RISE AND LAST TO QUIT THE SEARCH . . . .  539  3 DON JUAN 16    80    4
QUITE
     AND FALL FOR LACK OF MOISTURE QUITE A-DRY BOB . . . .   10  2 DON JUAN  D     3    8
     TO KEEP ONE CREED'S A TASK GROWN QUITE HERCULEAN . . .   20  2 DON JUAN  D    17    7
     A GOOD DEAL LIKE HIM TOO THOUGH QUITE THE SAME NONE . .   24  2 DON JUAN  1     5    3
     SO SAYS THE PROVERB--AND I QUITE AGREE . . . . . .   25  2 DON JUAN  1     8    4
     SHE MADE THE CLEVEREST PEOPLE QUITE ASHAMED . . . . .   26  2 DON JUAN  1    10    5
     RESOLVED THAT JUAN SHOULD BE QUITE A PARAGON . . . .   42  2 DON JUAN  1    38    2
     WITH DONNA INEZ QUITE A FAVOURITE FRIEND . . . . . .   58  2 DON JUAN  1    66    2
     QUITE INNOCENTLY DONE AND HARMLESS STYLED . . . . .   59  2 DON JUAN  1    69    3
     IF PEOPLE GO BEYOND 'TIS QUITE A CRIME . . . . . .   65  2 DON JUAN  1    80    7
     CHRISTIANS HAVE BURNT EACH OTHER QUITE PERSUADED . . .   66  2 DON JUAN  1    83    7
     THING QUITE IN COURSE AND NOT AT ALL ALARMING . . . .   68  2 DON JUAN  1    86    7
     QUITE BY MISTAKE--SHE THOUGHT IT WAS HER OWN . . . .   80  2 DON JUAN  1   109    8
     ARE QUITE ENOUGH FOR ME SO THEY BUT HOLD . . . . .   85  2 DON JUAN  1   118    8
     AND MEAN NEXT WINTER TO BE QUITE RECLAIM'D . . . . .   85  2 DON JUAN  1   119    8
     FOR THEN THEIR ELOQUENCE GROWS QUITE PROFUSE . . . .  119  2 DON JUAN  1   179    4
     AND THEN HIS ONLY GARMENT QUITE GAVE WAY . . . . .  124  2 DON JUAN  1   186    6
     THEY SO EMBELLISH THAT 'TIS QUITE A BORE . . . . .  137  2 DON JUAN  1   202    6
     A PRETTY WOMAN--(THAT'S QUITE NATURAL . . . . . . .  158  2 DON JUAN  2     3    5
     THANK HEAVEN I'VE GOT NO METAPHOR QUITE READY . . . .  160  2 DON JUAN  2     6    7
     THE GROWING WATERS IT UNMANS ONE QUITE . . . . . .  163  2 DON JUAN  2    12    3
     THE WATER RUSH'D THROUGH IN A WAY QUITE PUZZLING . . .  171  2 DON JUAN  2    28    7
     THE GOOD OLD GENTLEMAN WAS QUITE AGHAST . . . . . .  175  2 DON JUAN  2    37    1
     TWO THINGS FOR DYING PEOPLE QUITE BEWILDERING . . . .  179  2 DON JUAN  2    43    8
     WHO WERE NOT QUITE SO FOND OF ANIMAL FOOD . . . . .  198  2 DON JUAN  2    78    2
     QUITE A CELESTIAL KALEIDOSCOPE . . . . . . . . .  205  2 DON JUAN  2    93    8
     ALTHOUGH THE MORTAL QUITE AS FRESH AND FAIR . . . . .  232  2 DON JUAN  2   142    7
     TO STIR HER VIANDS MADE HIM QUITE AWAKE . . . . . .  237  2 DON JUAN  2   153    7
     AS ALL HIS LATTER MEALS HAD BEEN QUITE RAW . . . . .  239  2 DON JUAN  2   157    4
     LOVE THOUGH GOOD ALWAYS IS NOT QUITE SO GOOD) . . . .  246  2 DON JUAN  2   170    2
     WHILE VENUS FILLS THE HEART (WHICH QUITE AS WELL IS . .  246  2 DON JUAN  2   170   V1
     FOR WITHOUT HEART LOVE'S NOT QUITE SO GOOD) . . . .  246  2 DON JUAN  2   170   V2
     AND THUS THEY FORM A GROUP THAT'S QUITE ANTIQUE . . .  259  2 DON JUAN  2   194    7
     BY THEORIES QUITE PRACTICABLE TOO . . . . . . . .  267  2 DON JUAN  2   207    4
     HOW PLEASANT WERE THE MAXIM (NOT QUITE NEW) . . . .  267  2 DON JUAN  2   207    6
     BUT JUAN HAD HE QUITE FORGOTTEN JULIA . . . . . . .  267  2 DON JUAN  2   208    1
     IN THE SAME OBJECT GRACES QUITE AS KILLING . . . . .  270  2 DON JUAN  2   213    3
     MADE QUITE A PICTURE OF THESE LITTLE GREEKS . . . . .  292  2 DON JUAN  3    33    6
     PASS'D BUT HE STROVE QUITE COURTEOUSLY TO QUELL . . .  298  2 DON JUAN  3    44    4
     THEY  KINDLY LEAVE US THOUGH NOT QUITE ALONE . . . .  305  2 DON JUAN  3    59    7
     QUITE COMMON IN THOSE COUNTIES ARE A KIND . . . . .  308  2 DON JUAN  3    65    2
     OF THE APARTMENT--AND APPEAR'D QUITE NEW . . . . . .  309  2 DON JUAN  3    67    4
     IF NOT LIKE ORPHEUS QUITE WHEN GREECE WAS YOUNG . . .  326  2 DON JUAN  3    87    3
     THE WORLD NOT QUITE SO GREAT AS ARIOSTO  . . . . .  331  2 DON JUAN  3    96    8
     I DON'T PRETEND THAT I QUITE UNDERSTAND . . . . . .  346  2 DON JUAN  4     5    4
     ALL HEROES WHEN ALIVE QUITE PROMPT TO SLAY US . . . .  385  2 DON JUAN  4    76   V8
     THE LITTLE FELLOW REALLY LOOK'D QUITE HEARTY . . . .  388  2 DON JUAN  4    81    5
     THE LOVELIEST CHASTEST BEST BUT--QUITE A FOOL . . . .  405  2 DON JUAN  4   111    8
     I'LL MAKE THIS POEM QUITE A MORAL MODEL . . . . . .  412  2 DON JUAN  5     2   V8
     A SPELL FROM WHICH EVEN YET I AM NOT QUITE FREE . . .  413  2 DON JUAN  5     4    6
     EUROPE AND ASIA YOU BEING QUITE AT EASE . . . . . .  413  2 DON JUAN  5     5    6
     WOULD RECONCILE HIM TO THE BUSINESS QUITE . . . . .  452  2 DON JUAN  5    71    6
     WHICH IS NOT QUITE SO LIGHT AS YOU MAY DEEM . . . .  459  2 DON JUAN  5    82    4
     QUITE IN A CONFIDENTIAL QUEENLY WAY . . . . . . .  466  2 DON JUAN  5    95    3
     ABOUT A BOW-STRING--QUITE IN VAIN NOT YET . . . . .  471  2 DON JUAN  5   103    4
     AS THOUGH THEY WERE QUITE CONSCIOUS OF HER STATION-- .  475  2 DON JUAN  5   111    4
     CONCEIVED THAT PHRASE WAS QUITE ENOUGH TO MOVE . . .  478  2 DON JUAN  5   116    8
     BUT JUAN WHO HAD STILL HIS HEART QUITE FULL . . . .  478  2 DON JUAN  5   117   V2
     TO LOSE THE HOUR WOULD MAKE HER QUITE A MARTYR . . .  482  2 DON JUAN  5   122    7
     ALTHOUGH OF CLAY ARE YET NOT QUITE OF MUD . . . . .  491  2 DON JUAN  5   138    3
     HAS QUITE THE CONTRARY EFFECT ON VICE . . . . . .  501  2 DON JUAN  5   157    8
     HIS HIGHNESS QUITE CONNUBIALLY INCLINED . . . . . .   12  3 DON JUAN  6    13   V5
     ITS TWINKLE THROUGH THE LATTICE DUSKY QUITE . . . . .   18  3 DON JUAN  6    24    6
     MY WISH IS QUITE AS WIDE BUT NOT SO BAD . . . . . .   19  3 DON JUAN  6    27    4
     WHILE OTHERS WISHED THAT SHE HAD BEEN SO QUITE . . .   23  3 DON JUAN  6    35    8
     SHE LOOKED (THIS SIMILE'S QUITE NEW) JUST CUT . . . .   27  3 DON JUAN  6    43    5
     BUT THERE SHE SLEPT HIS HEART QUITE FULL . . . . .   41  3 DON JUAN  6    69    5
     YOUR FATHER'S SON 'TIS QUITE ENOUGH FOR ME . . . . .   52  3 DON JUAN  6    93    8
     BUT FROM THE RIVER THE TOWN'S OPEN QUITE . . . . . .   73  3 DON JUAN  7    13    1
```

QUITE   (CONTINUED)
QUITE ORDERLY AS IF UPON PARADE . . . . 119 3 DON JUAN 8   15   8
BUT JUAN WAS QUITE A BROTH OF A BOY . . . . 123 3 DON JUAN 8   24   1
MUST NOT HAVE LATTERLY BEEN QUITE WORN OUT . . . . . . 124 3 DON JUAN 8   26   3
QUITE DISAPPEARED--THE GODS KNOW HOW (I CAN'T . . . . . 127 3 DON JUAN 8   31   3
MAN QUITE AS QUIETLY AS BLOWS THE MONSOON . . . . . . 132 3 DON JUAN 8   39   5
THE FIRST TIME THOUGHT QUITE TERRIBLE ENOUGH . . . . . 134 3 DON JUAN 8   42   2
SO MUCH INTO THE RAW AS QUITE TO WRONG HER . . . . . . 137 3 DON JUAN 8   50   6
AMIDST SUCH SCENES--THOUGH THIS WAS QUITE A NEW ONE . . . 138 3 DON JUAN 8   52   4
NAMED AFTER THEE ACHILLES) AND QUITE THROUGH'T . . . . . 153 3 DON JUAN 8   84   5
IS QUITE REFRESHING IN THE AFFECTED PHRASE . . . . . . 156 3 DON JUAN 8   90   2
SMOKING HIS PIPE QUITE CALMLY 'MIDST THE DIN . . . . . 160 3 DON JUAN 8   98   4
POOR THING WHAT'S TO BE DONE I'M PUZZLED QUITE . . . . 161 3 DON JUAN 8   99   8
QUOTH JOHNSON--NEITHER WILL I QUITE ENSURE . . . . . . 161 3 DON JUAN 8   100   4
I DON'T THINK THAT YOU USED KINNAIRD QUITE WELL . . . . 184 3 DON JUAN 9   2   1
A PROP NOT QUITE SO CERTAIN AS BEFORE . . . . 184 3 DON JUAN 9   3   4
GENTLEMEN FARMERS--A RACE WORN OUT QUITE . . . . 198 3 DON JUAN 9   32   3
I QUITE FORGET THIS POEM'S MERELY QUIZZICAL . . . . . . 203 3 DON JUAN 9   41   3
I QUITE FORGET WHICH OF THEM WAS IN HAND . . . . 205 3 DON JUAN 9   46   3
FORGETTING QUITE THE WOMAN (WHICH COMPOSED . . . . . . 211 3 DON JUAN 9   58   2
FIRST ISMAIL'S CAPTURE CAUGHT YOUR FANCY QUITE . . . . . 215 3 DON JUAN 9   65   6
WHOSE TEMPORARY PASSION WAS QUITE FLATTERING . . . . . 217 3 DON JUAN 9   70   3
(THE LAST IF THEY HAVE SOUL ARE QUITE AS GOOD . . . . . 218 3 DON JUAN 9   71   3
HE WAS NOT YET QUITE OLD ENOUGH TO PROVE . . . . 250 3 DON JUAN 10   53   4
I AM QUITE OF THEIR OPINION--AND AM HOARDING . . . . . 270 3 DON JUAN 11   4   V5
BEING QUITE PERSPICUOUS AND EXTREMELY FAIR . . . . . . 270 3 DON JUAN 11   5   4
I DON'T MEAN THAT THEY ARE PASSIONLESS BUT QUITE . . . . 284 3 DON JUAN 11   34   1
BUT DAMME'S QUITE ETHEREAL THOUGH TOO DARING . . . . . 289 3 DON JUAN 11   43   7
SUCH AS NO GENTLEMAN CAN QUITE REFUSE . . . . 293 3 DON JUAN 11   48   6
I HAVE SEEN NAPOLEON WHO SEEMED QUITE A JUPITER . . . . 309 3 DON JUAN 11   83   1
IF COURTS AND CAMPS BE QUITE SO SENTIMENTAL . . . . . . 322 3 DON JUAN 12   13   8
AND OUGHT TO GO BY QUITE ANOTHER NAME . . . . 323 3 DON JUAN 12   15   8
(NOW HERE'S A WORD QUITE AFTER MY OWN HEART . . . . . . 326 3 DON JUAN 12   22   3
PERHAPS A LITTLE STRANGE IF NOT QUITE NEW . . . . 341 3 DON JUAN 12   54   2
SUCH THOUGHTS ARE QUITE BELOW THE STRAIN THEY HAVE CHOSEN . . 341 3 DON JUAN 12   55   3
NOT QUITE ADULTERY BUT ADULTERATION . . . . 345 3 DON JUAN 12   63   8
NOR IS SHE QUITE SO READY WITH HER SMILE . . . . 351 3 DON JUAN 12   76   4
COOL AND QUITE ENGLISH IMPERTURBABLE . . . . 365 3 DON JUAN 13   14   4
IT HATH BEEN STIRRED UP TILL ITS SMOKE QUITE SMOTHERS . . . 374 3 DON JUAN 13   36   8
MIDST WHOM WE HAVE HEARD FROM SOURCES QUITE CORRECT . . . 382 3 DON JUAN 13   52   4
BY NO QUITE LAWFUL MARRIAGE OF THE ARTS . . . . 390 3 DON JUAN 13   67   2
HIS BELL-MOUTHED GOBLET MAKES ME FEEL QUITE DANISH . . . 392 3 DON JUAN 13   72   7
I'VE SEEN A VIRTUOUS WOMAN PUT DOWN QUITE . . . . . . 397 3 DON JUAN 13   82   3
I MUST NOT QUITE OMIT THE TALKING SAGE . . . . 403 3 DON JUAN 13   97   3
AND QUITE ENOUGH FOR ME TO KEEP IN MIND-- . . . . 414 3 DON JUAN 14   9   3
HAS NOT YET GIVEN UP THE PRACTICE QUITE . . . . 420 3 DON JUAN 14   23   4
QUITE INDEPENDENT OF THE ZODIAC'S SIGNS . . . . 423 3 DON JUAN 14   29   3
A LITTLE SPOILT BUT BY NO MEANS SO QUITE . . . . 428 3 DON JUAN 14   41   3
OH JOB YOU HAD TWO FRIENDS ONE'S QUITE ENOUGH . . . . . 431 3 DON JUAN 14   48   1
IN ENGLAND RANKS QUITE ON A DIFFERENT LIST . . . . . . 436 3 DON JUAN 14   60   6
NEITHER CAN SHOW QUITE HOW THEY WOULD BE LOVED . . . . . 442 3 DON JUAN 14   73   4
PERHAPS 'TWAS HARDLY QUITE ASSURED ENOUGH . . . . . . 462 3 DON JUAN 15   14   5
IMAGINATION'S QUITE ENOUGH FOR THAT . . . . 463 3 DON JUAN 15   16   3
WHOSE SOLE ACCOMPLISHMENTS WERE QUITE A BOOTY . . . . . 471 3 DON JUAN 15   34   6
BUT IF A WRITER SHOULD BE QUITE CONSISTENT . . . . . . 494 3 DON JUAN 15   87   7
THOUGHTS QUITE AS YELLOW BUT LESS CLEAR THAN AMBER . . . 505 3 DON JUAN 16   11   4
THE CAUSE BUT JUAN SAID HE WAS QUITE WELL . . . . . . 514 3 DON JUAN 16   32   8
QUITE WELL YES NO--THESE ANSWERS WERE MYSTERIOUS . . . . 514 3 DON JUAN 16   33   1
FOR FEAR WE SHOULD SUPPOSE US QUITE IN HEAVEN . . . . . 525 3 DON JUAN 16   49   8
A THING QUITE NECESSARY TO THE ELECT . . . . 526 3 DON JUAN 16   52   3
QUITE FULL RIGHT DULL GUESTS HOT AND DISHES COLD . . . . 538 3 DON JUAN 16   78   6
NOR SEEM EMBARRASSED--QUITE THE CONTRARY . . . . 545 3 DON JUAN 16   94   2
AND GROW QUITE FIGURATIVE WITH THEIR FIGURES . . . . . 547 3 DON JUAN 16   98   8
WAS EVER EVERYBODY YET SO QUITE . . . . 564 3 DON JUAN 17   5   8
TO PAINT A SOLE SENSATION--THOUGH QUITE COMMON-- . . . . 569 3 DON JUAN 17   V 13   4
QUITTING
AT QUITTING EVEN THOSE WE QUIT IN STRIFE . . . . 164 2 DON JUAN 2   15   6
QUIVER
HIS WINGS SUBDUED TO EPAULETTES HIS QUIVER . . . . . . 205 3 DON JUAN 9   45   2
QUIVERING
AND GAVE NO SIGN OF LIFE SAVE HIS LIMBS QUIVERING . . . 204 2 DON JUAN 2   90   8
RESTING ITS BRIGHT BASE ON THE QUIVERING BLUE . . . . . 204 2 DON JUAN 2   91   3
AND QUIVERING HAND AND THEN HE LOOK'D FOR THOSE . . . . 213 2 DON JUAN 2   109   3
QUIVER'S
THE DEVIL HATH NOT IN ALL HIS QUIVER'S CHOICE . . . . . 461 3 DON JUAN 15   13   7
QUIXOTE
OF QUIXOTE SHOWN HOW ALL SUCH EFFORTS FAIL . . . . . . 361 3 DON JUAN 13   8   8
AND SOCRATES HIMSELF BUT WISDOM'S QUIXOTE . . . . . . 363 3 DON JUAN 13   10   8
TO READ DON QUIXOTE IN THE ORIGINAL . . . . 453 3 DON JUAN 14   98   2
QUIXOTIC
WHO SANG WHEN CHIVALRY WAS MORE QUIXOTIC . . . . 347 2 DON JUAN 4   6   4
QUIZ
THE MANSION HOUSE TOO (THOUGH SOME PEOPLE QUIZ IT) . . . 280 3 DON JUAN 11   25   6
THOUGH TOO WELL BRED TO QUIZ MEN TO THEIR FACES . . . 548 3 DON JUAN 16   100   3
QUIZZED
AT RISK OF BEING QUIZZED FOR SUPERSTITION . . . . . . 512 3 DON JUAN 16   28   4
QUIZZICAL
I QUITE FORGET THIS POEM'S MERELY QUIZZICAL . . . . . . 203 3 DON JUAN 9   41   3
QUOI
THAT UNDEFINABLE JE NE SCAIS QUOI . . . . 441 3 DON JUAN 14   72   2

647

```
                                                      PAGE VOL      CANTO STANZA LN
QUOTATION
   SAY I BY WHICH QUOTATION THERE IS MEANT A    . . . . . . 143  2 DON JUAN  1    212   3
QUOTE
   THE BARD I QUOTE FROM DOES NOT SING AMISS     . . . . . .  69  2 DON JUAN  1     88   5
   SHOULD RASHLY QUOTE FOR FEAR OF A MISTAKE)    . . . . . .  74  2 DON JUAN  1     98   6
   SWEETS TO THE SWEET (I LIKE SO MUCH TO QUOTE  . . . . . . 165  2 DON JUAN  2     17   3
   OF MELANCHOLY MERRIMENT TO QUOTE   . . . . . . . . . . . 156  3 DON JUAN  8     89   5
   OF HORRIBLE OR LUDICROUS TO QUOTE  . . . . . . . . . . . 156  3 DON JUAN  8     89   V5
   THIS SUBJECT QUOTE AS IT WOULD BE SCHISMATIC  . . . . . . 289  3 DON JUAN 11     43   5
   UNLESS IT TEACHES ONE TO QUOTE AND CAVIL)     . . . . . . 380  3 DON JUAN 13     47   8
   PROUD OF HIS LEARNING (JUST ENOUGH TO QUOTE)  . . . . . . 401  3 DON JUAN 13     91   3
   FURTHER I'D QUOTE BUT SCRIPTURE INTERVENING . . . . . . . 403  3 DON JUAN 13     96   5
   (I MERELY QUOTE WHAT I HAVE HEARD FROM MANY)  . . . . . . 452  3 DON JUAN 14     95   2
QUOTED
   ALL WHICH MIGHT IF OCCASION SERVED BE QUOTED  . . . . . .  36  2 DON JUAN  1     28   3
QUOTES
   AND THUS POPE QUOTES THE PRECEPT TO RE-TEACH  . . . . . . 470  2 DON JUAN  5    101   6
QUOTH
   OUR MISTRESS QUOTH A THIRD OUR MISTRESS--POOH--  . . . . 297  2 DON JUAN  3     43   7
   I KNOW NOT QUOTH THE FELLOW WHO OR WHAT  . . . . . . . . 298  2 DON JUAN  3     45   1
   AY QUOTH HIS FRIEND I THOUGHT IT WOULD APPEAR  . . . . . 420  2 DON JUAN  5     19   3
   MY THIRD-- --YOUR THIRD QUOTH JUAN TURNING ROUND  . . . . 421  2 DON JUAN  5     20   1
   NO QUOTH THE OTHER YET YOU WILL ALLOW  . . . . . . . . . 422  2 DON JUAN  5     23   4
   BLOCKHEAD COME ON AND SEE QUOTH BABA WHILE  . . . . . . . 459  2 DON JUAN  5     83   1
   NAY QUOTH THE MAID THE SULTAN'S SELF SHAN'T CARRY ME . . 460  2 DON JUAN  5     84   7
   BESIDES I HATE TO SLEEP ALONE QUOTH SHE  . . . . . . . .  30  3 DON JUAN  6     48   1
   QUOTH JOHNSON--NEITHER WILL I QUITE ENSURE   . . . . . . 161  3 DON JUAN  8    100   4
   YOU LOOK QUOTH HE AS IF YOU HAD HAD YOUR REST  . . . . . 515  3 DON JUAN 16     35   3
   JEST QUOTH MILOR WHY ADELINE YOU KNOW . . . . . . . . . 517  3 DON JUAN 16     38   1
QUOTING
   WHICH MANY PEOPLE PASS FOR WITS BY QUOTING  . . . . . . .  77  3 DON JUAN  7     21   8
R
   R PULV COM THREE GRAINS IPECACUANHAE  . . . . . . . . . 244  3 DON JUAN 10     41   5
RABBI
   AND MRS RABBI THE RICH BANKER'S SQUAW  . . . . . . . . . 396  3 DON JUAN 13     79   6
RABBIT
   BURROWING FOR BOROUGHS LIKE A RAT OR RABBIT  . . . . . . 534  3 DON JUAN 16     70   2
RABBLE
   LEAVING SUCH TO THE LITERARY RABBLE  . . . . . . . . . . 398  2 DON JUAN  4     99   3
RABBLE'S
   NOW--THAT THE RABBLE'S FIRST VAIN SHOUTS ARE O'ER  . . . 187  3 DON JUAN  9      9   6
RABY
   AURORA RABY A YOUNG STAR WHO SHONE  . . . . . . . . . . 475  3 DON JUAN 15     43   5
   AS THAT PRIM SILENT COLD AURORA RABY  . . . . . . . . . 477  3 DON JUAN 15     49   8
   AURORA RABY WITH HER LARGE DARK EYES  . . . . . . . . . 514  3 DON JUAN 16     31   7
RABY'S
   HE THOUGHT AURORA RABY'S EYES MORE BRIGHT  . . . . . . . 506  3 DON JUAN 16     12   3
RACE
   AND REPRESENTATIVE OF ALL THE RACE . . . . . . . . . . .   9  2 DON JUAN  D      1   2
   HOWEVER THIS MIGHT BE THE RACE WENT ON  . . . . . . . .  54  2 DON JUAN  1     59   1
   (A RACE OF MERE IMPOSTORS WHEN ALL'S DONE--  . . . . . . 218  2 DON JUAN  2    118   6
   HAD DYED IT WITH THE HEADLONG BLOOD WHOSE RACE  . . . . 231  2 DON JUAN  2    141   3
   THOUGH LINK'D AMONG A FETTER'D RACE  . . . . . . . . . . 323  2 DON JUAN  3   L  6   2
   THE RACE HE SPRAINS A WING AND DOWN WE TEND  . . . . . . 344  2 DON JUAN  4      1   4
   BOIL'D UP AND PROVED HER TRULY OF HIS RACE  . . . . . . 367  2 DON JUAN  4     44   8
   AS ALSO AT THE RACE AND COUNTY BALLS  . . . . . . . . . 471  2 DON JUAN  5    103   8
   HER FATE HAD BEEN TO THAT OF ALL HER RACE  . . . . . . . 139  3 DON JUAN  8     54   8
   HOURIS OR AUGHT EXCEPT HIS FLORID RACE  . . . . . . . . 169  3 DON JUAN  8    116   3
   GENTLEMEN FARMERS--A RACE WORN OUT QUITE  . . . . . . . 198  3 DON JUAN  9     32   3
   AS ONE WHO THOUGH HE WERE NOT OF THE RACE  . . . . . . . 265  3 DON JUAN 10     81   6
   NOUGHT'S PERMANENT AMONG THE HUMAN RACE  . . . . . . . . 309  3 DON JUAN 11     82   7
   TO-MORROW SEES ANOTHER RACE AS GAY . . . . . . . . . . 310  3 DON JUAN 11     86   2
   TO BUILD A COLLEGE OR TO FOUND A RACE . . . . . . . . . 320  3 DON JUAN 12     10   2
   WHICH CAN AWAIT WARM YOUTH IN ITS WILD RACE  . . . . . . 326  3 DON JUAN 12     23   4
   AND FAR AWAY THE LAST BUD OF HER RACE . . . . . . . . . 329  3 DON JUAN 12     29   4
   SAINT FROM HIS BEADS TO JOIN THE JOCUND RACE  . . . . . 395  3 DON JUAN 13     78   4
   DECEMBER'S DROWSY DAY TO HIS DULL RACE--  . . . . . . . 426  3 DON JUAN 14     36   4
RACE-HORSE
   LIKE A RACE-HORSE MUCH TO EACH DRESS HE SPORTED  . . . . 239  3 DON JUAN 10     29   5
   AND A YOUNG RACE-HORSE OF OLD PEDIGREE   . . . . . . . . 527  3 DON JUAN 16     55   7
RACER
   FOR LIKE A RACER OR A BOXER TRAINING . . . . . . . . . . 366  3 DON JUAN 13     18   7
RACES
   WELL LIKE MOST ENGLISHMEN AND LOVED THE RACES  . . . . . 368  3 DON JUAN 13     23   6
RACE-WINNER
   SIR HENRY SILVERCUP THE GREAT RACE-WINNER  . . . . . . . 399  3 DON JUAN 13     87   4
RACK
   ANTONIA'S SKILL WAS PUT UPON THE RACK . . . . . . . . . 114  2 DON JUAN  1    169   3
   THE WHIP THE RACK OR DUNGEON AT THE LEAST  . . . . . . . 296  2 DON JUAN  3     40   5
   I WOULD TAKE REFUGE IN WEAK PUNCH BUT RACK  . . . . . . 372  2 DON JUAN  4     53   5
   LET THIS ONE TOIL FOR BREAD--THAT RACK FOR RENT  . . . . 190  3 DON JUAN  9     15   7
   TALK ABOUT POETRY AND RACK AND MANGER . . . . . . . . . 305  3 DON JUAN 11     74   6
   A RACK OF PLEASURES WHERE WE MUST INVENT  . . . . . . . 444  3 DON JUAN 14     79   2
RACK'D
   AND FOAM AND ROLL WITH STRANGE CONVULSIONS RACK'D . . . 198  2 DON JUAN  2     79   5
RACKRHYME
   THERE WAS THE YOUNG BARD RACKRHYME WHO HAD NEWLY  . . . 398  3 DON JUAN 13     84   5
RACKS
   RACKS PRISONS INQUISITIONS RESURRECTION  . . . . . . . . 272  3 DON JUAN 11      9   7
```

RADIANT
    A PURE TRANSPARENT PALE YET RADIANT FACE . . . . 159 3 DON JUAN 8   96   7
    RADIANT AND GRAVE--AS PITYING MAN'S DECLINE . . . . . . 476 3 DON JUAN 15   45   5
    YET EACH WAS RADIANT IN HER PROPER SPHERE . . . . . . 481 3 DON JUAN 15   58   3
    WHOSE TRAITS WERE RADIANT WITH THE RAYS OF VERITY . . . 550 3 DON JUAN 16   102   4
RADICALS
    LET RADICALS ITS OTHER ACTS ATTACK . . . . 378 3 DON JUAN 13   43   7
RADULPHUS
    ERNEIS RADULPHUS--EIGHT-AND-FORTY MANORS . . . . 242 3 DON JUAN 10   36   2
RAFT
    SOME TRIAL HAD BEEN MAKING AT A RAFT . . . . 183 2 DON JUAN 2   50   1
RAG
    SENDS SIN WITHOUT A RAG ON SHIVERING FORTH . . . . . . 57 2 DON JUAN 1   64   3
    NOR RAG OF CANVAS WHAT COULD THEY EXPECT . . . . 176 2 DON JUAN 2   39   4
    HE SQUEEZED FROM OUT A RAG SOME DROPS OF RAIN . . . . . 203 2 DON JUAN 2   89   7
    FRAIL MAN WHEN PAPER--EVEN A RAG LIKE THIS . . . . . . 327 2 DON JUAN 3   88   7
    WOULD RISK TO PLEASE IT MY LAST RAG OF BREECHES . . . 421 3 DON JUAN 14   26   V8
RAGAMUFFINS
    ALL RAGAMUFFINS DIFFERING BUT IN HUE . . . . 417 2 DON JUAN 5   13   3
RAGE
    HIM ALMOST MAN BUT SHE FLEW IN A RAGE . . . . 51 2 DON JUAN 1   54   5
    WHAT COULD THEY DO AND HUNGER'S RAGE GREW WILD . . . . 193 2 DON JUAN 2   70   6
    RAGE FEAR HATE JEALOUSY REVENGE COMPUNCTION . . . . . 271 2 DON JUAN 2   215   6
    MY PEN AND EASILY FLEW IN A RAGE . . . . 397 2 DON JUAN 4   98   V6
    HER RAGE WAS BUT A MINUTE'S AND 'TWAS WELL-- . . . . . 489 2 DON JUAN 5   135   1
    TO MATCH A COMMON FURY WITH HER RAGE . . . . 490 2 DON JUAN 5   136   2
    THEIR BAFFLED RAGE AND PAIN WHILE WAXING COLDER . . . 158 3 DON JUAN 8   94   5
    HE WHO HATH PROVED WAR STORM OR WOMAN'S RAGE . . . . 339 3 DON JUAN 12   50   6
    THE WIND SHIFTS AND I FLY INTO A RAGE . . . . 566 3 DON JUAN 17   10   8
RAGED
    A STORM IT RAGED AND LIKE THE STORM IT PASSED . . . . 490 2 DON JUAN 5   137   1
    BUT WHILE THE THIRST FOR GORE AND PLUNDER RAGED . . . 178 3 DON JUAN 8   132   5
RAGES
    AND MAY APPEAR SO WHEN THE DOG-STAR RAGES-- . . . . . 11 2 DON JUAN D   4   6
    THE PASSION WHICH STILL RAGES AS BEFORE . . . . 132 2 DON JUAN 1   195   6
RAGGED
    UNTIL THEY FOUND A RAGGED PIECE OF SHEET . . . . 201 2 DON JUAN 2   85   2
RAGING
    WENT RAGING MAD--LORD HOW THEY DID BLASPHEME . . . . . 198 2 DON JUAN 2   79   4
    THE CUBLESS TIGRESS IN HER JUNGLE RAGING . . . . 305 2 DON JUAN 3   58   1
    BY YOUR REFUSAL RECOLLECT HER RAGING . . . . 486 2 DON JUAN 5   130   5
RAGOUT
    REDOUBLED WHEN A ROAST AND A RAGOUT . . . . 428 2 DON JUAN 5   32   4
    IN SOUPS OR SAUCES OR A SOLE RAGOUT . . . . 482 3 DON JUAN 15   62   7
RAGOUTS
    I WILL NOT DWELL UPON RAGOUTS OR ROASTS . . . . 404 3 DON JUAN 13   99   5
RAGS
    AND MOST OF THEM HAD LITTLE CLOTHES BUT RAGS . . . . 189 2 DON JUAN 2   62   8
    AND IN THE FIRE HIS RECENT RAGS THEY SCATTER'D . . . . 240 2 DON JUAN 2   160   3
    TO THESE THEY ARE RAGS OR DUST WHERE IS THE ARCH . . 485 3 DON JUAN 15   67   2
RAGUSAN
    BUT THREE RAGUSAN VESSELS BOUND FOR SCIO . . . . 248 2 DON JUAN 2   174   8
RAIL
    THREW IN BY GOOD LUCK OVER THE SHIP'S RAIL . . . . . . 181 2 DON JUAN 2   48   6
    ONE SHOULD NOT RAIL WITHOUT A DECENT CAUSE . . . . . . 219 2 DON JUAN 2   119   2
    OR DOUBLE POST AND RAIL WHERE THE EXISTENCE . . . . . 140 3 DON JUAN 8   55   3
    HE CLEAR'D HEDGE DITCH AND DOUBLE POST AND RAIL . . . 424 3 DON JUAN 14   33   2
    IN VAIN HE HEARD THE OTHERS RAIL OR RALLY . . . . . 552 3 DON JUAN 16   105   7
RAILED
    I RAILED AT SCOTS TO SHEW MY WRATH AND WIT . . . . . . 234 3 DON JUAN 10   19   3
    HE ADDED MODESTLY WHEN REBELS RAILED) . . . . 535 3 DON JUAN 16   72   6
RAILING
    RAILING AT POWER--BUT ENVYING ALL IT'S TOOLS . . . . 152 2 DON JUAN 1 V 3 V7
    BY RAILING AT THE UNKNOWN AND ENVIED PASSION . . . . 337 3 DON JUAN 12   45   2
RAIMENT
    WITH FOOD AND RAIMENT AND THOSE SOFT ATTENTIONS . . . 221 2 DON JUAN 2   123   2
    FOOD SHE REFUSED AND RAIMENT NO PRETENCE . . . . . . 381 2 DON JUAN 4   68   5
    WHEN SOME UNTOWARD PART OF RAIMENT STUCK HARD . . . . 456 2 DON JUAN 5   78   6
    AS MACHIAVEL SHOWS THOSE IN PURPLE RAIMENT . . . . . 264 3 DON JUAN 10   79   3
RAIN
    LIKE SKIES THAT RAIN AND LIGHTEN AS A VEIL . . . . . . 108 2 DON JUAN 1   158   3
    AND THE SAME NIGHT THERE FELL A SHOWER OF RAIN . . . . 201 2 DON JUAN 2   84   1
    TO BEG THE BEGGAR WHO COULD NOT RAIN BACK . . . . . . 202 2 DON JUAN 2   86   5
    HE SQUEEZED FROM OUT A RAG SOME DROPS OF RAIN . . . . 203 2 DON JUAN 2   89   7
    THAT SPRING-DEW OF THE SPIRIT THE HEART'S RAIN . . . . 250 2 DON JUAN 2   178   4
    WHICH RAIN DOWN ON THE DUST OF OUR YEARS . . . . . . 270 2 DON JUAN 2   214   V8
    O'ERCHARGED WITH RAIN HER SUMMON'D HANDMAIDS BORE . . 376 2 DON JUAN 4   59   4
    LIKE MOUNTAIN MISTS AT LENGTH DISSOLVED IN RAIN . . . 380 2 DON JUAN 4   66   8
    AND POURED UPON HIM AND HIS SONS LIKE RAIN . . . . . 166 3 DON JUAN 8   109   7
    SO ARAB DESERTS DRINK IN SUMMER'S RAIN . . . . 212 3 DON JUAN 9   59   6
    OF RUBLES RAIN AS FAST AS SPECIE CAN . . . . 222 3 DON JUAN 9   79   6
    WHICH LEAVES FEW DROPS OF THAT IMMORTAL RAIN . . . . 375 3 DON JUAN 13   37   4
RAINBOW
    THE RAINBOW BASED ON OCEAN SPAN THE SKY . . . . 87 2 DON JUAN 1   122   8
    NOW OVERHEAD A RAINBOW BURSTING THROUGH . . . . . . 204 2 DON JUAN 2   91   1
    THAN THESE AND SO THIS RAINBOW LOOK'D LIKE HOPE-- . . 205 2 DON JUAN 2   93   7
    AS DOTH A RAINBOW THE JUST CLEARING AIR . . . . 17 3 DON JUAN 6   23   8
RAINBOWS
    THERE STILL ARE MANY RAINBOWS IN YOUR SKY . . . . . . 421 2 DON JUAN 5   21   3

		PAGE	VOL		CANTO	STANZA	LN
RAINED							
	WHICH RAINED FROM BASTION BATTERY PARAPET	131	3 DON JUAN	8	37	2
	AT WHICH HE MARVELLED SINCE IT HAD NOT RAINED	515	3 DON JUAN	16	34	4
RAINING							
	WHICH REALLY POURED AS IF ALL HELL WERE RAINING	121	3 DON JUAN	8	20	6
RAINS							
	THERE THE LARGE OLIVE RAINS ITS AMBER STORE	373	2 DON JUAN	4	55	1
RAINY							
	THE PRESENT WEATHER WOULD BE MUCH MORE RAINY--	301	2 DON JUAN	3	50	6
RAISE							
	OF SEAMEN'S FATES AND THE LOUD TEMPESTS RAISE	414	2 DON JUAN	5	6	4
	THIS FELLOW BEING SIX FOOT HIGH COULD RAISE	84	3 DON JUAN	7	37	5
	OF THE TROOPS WERE EMBARKED THE SIEGE TO RAISE	85	3 DON JUAN	7	39	2
	RAISE BUT AN ARM 'TWILL BRUSH THEIR WEB AWAY	196	3 DON JUAN	9	28	1
	AND FARMERS CAN'T RAISE CERES FROM HER FALL	198	3 DON JUAN	9	32	6
	NOR WINE NOR WASSAIL COULD RAISE A VASSAL	520	3 DON JUAN	16	L 5	7
	LORD HENRY WISHED TO RAISE FOR A NEW PURCHASE	530	3 DON JUAN	16	60	2
RAISED							
	WHO IN THE EARLIER AGES RAISED A BUSTLE	44	2 DON JUAN	1	41	3
	AND O'ER HIM BENT HIS SIRE AND NEVER RAISED	203	2 DON JUAN	2	89	1
	RAISED HIGHER THE FAINT HEAD WHICH O'ER IT HUNG	216	2 DON JUAN	2	114	3
	BUT TO RESUME THE LANGUID JUAN RAISED	239	2 DON JUAN	2	157	1
	HE RAISED HIS WHISTLE AS THE WORD HE SAID	369	2 DON JUAN	4	47	3
	OF PURCHASED INFIDELS SOME RAISED THEIR EYES	441	2 DON JUAN	5	54	2
	SHE STOPT AND RAISED HER HEAD TO SPEAK--BUT PAUSED	61	3 DON JUAN	6	111	1
	A GREEK HAD RAISED AROUND THIS ELEVATION	71	3 DON JUAN	7	10	5
	PASSIVE OBEDIENCE--NOW RAISED UP THE HEAD	101	3 DON JUAN	7	67	6
	DON JUAN RAISED HIS LITTLE CAPTIVE FROM	158	3 DON JUAN	8	94	7
	AND SEE HIS STATUE RAISED--AND PRINT ENGRAVED	185	3 DON JUAN	9	5	V8
	AND ASKED WHY SUCH A STRUCTURE HAD BEEN RAISED	261	3 DON JUAN	10	74	8
	HAD RAISED AN INTEREST IN HER WHICH ENCREASED	338	3 DON JUAN	12	48	8
RAISIN							
	OF RAISIN ORANGE AND POMEGRANATE JUICE	307	2 DON JUAN	3	62	7
RAISING							
	LET NOT HIS MODE OF RAISING CASH SEEM STRANGE	283	2 DON JUAN	3	14	1
	THE PEOPLE'S AWE AND ADMIRATION RAISING	445	2 DON JUAN	5	60	6
	AND RAISING UP AN ARM AS MOONLIGHT FAIR	466	2 DON JUAN	5	96	5
RAKE							
	OVID'S A RAKE AS HALF HIS VERSES SHOW HIM	45	2 DON JUAN	1	42	1
	A RAKE TURN'D METHODISTIC OR ECLECTIC--	309	2 DON JUAN	3	66	3
RAKES							
	SAD RAKES TO SADDER HUSBANDS CHASTELY TAMING	418	3 DON JUAN	14	18	5
RALLY							
	HER FOURTH TO RALLY HIM INTO REPENTANCE	491	2 DON JUAN	5	139	4
	AND RALLY BACK HIS ROMANS TO THE FIELD	125	3 DON JUAN	8	28	8
	JOHNSON RETIRED A LITTLE JUST TO RALLY	131	3 DON JUAN	8	36	7
	STOOD LIKE CARACTACUS IN ACT TO RALLY	384	3 DON JUAN	13	56	3
	AND THEREFORE JUAN NOW BEGAN TO RALLY	526	3 DON JUAN	16	53	1
	IN VAIN HE HEARD THE OTHERS RAIL OR RALLY	552	3 DON JUAN	16	105	7
RAM							
	A BAND OF CHILDREN ROUND A SNOW-WHITE RAM	292	2 DON JUAN	3	32	1
RAMBLE							
	SO ON I RAMBLE NOW AND THEN NARRATING	203	3 DON JUAN	9	42	1
	THE MUSES UPON SION'S HILL MUST RAMBLE	297	3 DON JUAN	11	57	3
	AND PRIDE MY FEEBLE--LET US RAMBLE ON	466	3 DON JUAN	15	22	2
RAMPART							
	THE RAMPART HIGHER THAN YOU'D WISH TO HANG	72	3 DON JUAN	7	11	4
	WHILE THE WHOLE RAMPART BLAZED LIKE ETNA WHEN	115	3 DON JUAN	8	7	7
	RAMPART WALL CASEMENT HOUSE--FOR THERE WAS NOT	131	3 DON JUAN	8	37	3
	REACHED THE INTERIOR TALUS OF THE RAMPART	135	3 DON JUAN	8	44	8
	AND SCRAMBLING ROUND THE RAMPART THESE SAME TROOPS	148	3 DON JUAN	8	73	1
	UPON THEM NE'ERTHELESS HAD REACHED THE RAMPART	149	3 DON JUAN	8	75	2
	THE DEATH-DISGORGING RAMPART ONCE AGAIN	151	3 DON JUAN	8	79	5
RAN							
	AS IF HER VEINS RAN LIGHTNING SHE IN SOOTH	55	2 DON JUAN	1	61	6
	ON WHOM HER REVERIES CELESTIAL RAN	64	2 DON JUAN	1	79	8
	BECAUSE THE SEA RAN HIGHER EVERY MINUTE	186	2 DON JUAN	2	57	7
	WERE MAD FOR LAND AND THUS THEIR COURSE THEY RAN	211	2 DON JUAN	2	104	3
	THEY RAN THE BOAT FOR SHORE AND OVERSET HER	211	2 DON JUAN	2	104	8
	AND ROUGH WITH REEFS WHICH RAN OUT MANY A MILE	285	2 DON JUAN	3	19	7
	AND ROUND THEM RAN A YELLOW BORDER TOO	308	2 DON JUAN	3	64	4
	AND RAN BUT IT ESCAPED HER AS SHE CLASP'D	361	2 DON JUAN	4	32	8
	WERE DABBLED WITH THE DEEP BLOOD WHICH RAN O'ER	376	2 DON JUAN	4	59	2
	AND ALSO WHEN MY SECOND RAN AWAY	420	2 DON JUAN	5	19	8
	NO FAITH--WHAT THEN--I RAN AWAY FROM HER	421	2 DON JUAN	5	20	8
	AND THOUGH HE CERTAINLY RAN MANY RISKS	20	3 DON JUAN	6	29	3
	THEIR TALK OF COURSE RAN MOST ON THE NEW COMER	23	3 DON JUAN	6	35	1
	THE WIND WAS DOWN BUT STILL THE SEA RAN HIGH	61	3 DON JUAN	6	110	8
	AGAINST A FOE OR RAN A SABRE THROUGH SKIN	75	3 DON JUAN	7	17	4
	AND NEVER RAN AWAY EXCEPT WHEN RUNNING	130	3 DON JUAN	8	35	7
	AND THEREFORE WHEN HE RAN AWAY HE DID SO	133	3 DON JUAN	8	40	1
	BUT JOHNSON ONLY RAN OFF TO RETURN	133	3 DON JUAN	8	41	1
	AND REDLY RAN HIS BLUSHING WATERS DOWN	175	3 DON JUAN	8	127	4
	THE TWO FIRST FEELINGS RAN THEIR COURSE COMPLETE	213	3 DON JUAN	9	61	1
	AND HONOUR'D RAN A RISK OF GROWING LESS SO	458	3 DON JUAN	15	6	2
	OR STEP RAN SADLY THROUGH THAT ANTIQUE HOUSE	509	3 DON JUAN	16	20	4
RANG							
	RANG IN HER SAD EARS LIKE A MERMAID'S SONG	362	2 DON JUAN	4	34	7
	WHEN ALL AROUND RANG LIKE A TOCSIN BELL	48	3 DON JUAN	6	84	4

RANGE
    'TIS WOMAN'S WHOLE EXISTENCE MAN MAY RANGE . . . . . . 131 2 DON JUAN 1 194 2
    BUT HE MORE MODEST TOOK AN HUMBLER RANGE . . . . . . 283 2 DON JUAN 3 14 5
    ON THROUGH A FARTHER RANGE OF GOODLY ROOMS . . . . . 442 2 DON JUAN 5 55 2
    A RANGE OR SUITE OF FURTHER CHAMBERS WHICH . . . . . 449 2 DON JUAN 5 65 2
    BLOOD-RED AS SUNSET SUMMER CLOUDS WHICH RANGE . . . . 473 2 DON JUAN 5 108 5
    BUT JUAN HAD BEEN EARLY TAUGHT TO RANGE . . . . . . 424 3 DON JUAN 14 32 5
RANGED
    THESE WERE RANGED ROUND EACH IN ITS CRYSTAL EWER . . . . 307 2 DON JUAN 3 63 1
    AND AGE AND SEX WERE IN THE MARKET RANGED . . . . . 414 2 DON JUAN 5 7 2
    THE TURKISH TITLE) AND RANGED ROUND THE WALL . . . . 31 3 DON JUAN 6 51 2
RANGER
    OF ALL O'ER WHICH SUCH LOVE MAY BE A RANGER . . . . . 65 2 DON JUAN 1 80 6
RANGES
    HIS POLAR STAR BEING ONE WHICH RATHER RANGES . . . . . 317 2 DON JUAN 3 80 3
    THE POINTER RANGES AND THE SPORTSMAN BEATS . . . . . 394 3 DON JUAN 13 75 4
RANK
    ANNOUNCED HER RANK TWELVE RINGS WERE ON HER HAND . . . . 312 2 DON JUAN 3 72 3
    BECOME A THING OR NOTHING SAVE TO RANK . . . . . . 327 2 DON JUAN 3 89 3
    SOME TWENTY OF HIS TRAIN CAME RANK ON RANK . . . . . 369 2 DON JUAN 4 47 7
    SOME TWENTY OF HIS TRAIN CAME RANK ON RANK . . . . . 369 2 DON JUAN 4 47 7
    THAT HE A MAN OF RANK AND BIRTH HAD BEEN . . . . . . 415 2 DON JUAN 5 9 V6
    WITH ALL THE CEREMONIES OF HIS RANK . . . . . . 500 2 DON JUAN 5 154 2
    BUT STILL A FORTRESS OF THE FOREMOST RANK . . . . . 70 3 DON JUAN 7 9 4
    THE HUM OF ARMIES GATHERING RANK ON RANK . . . . . 110 3 DON JUAN 7 86 2
    THE HUM OF ARMIES GATHERING RANK ON RANK . . . . . 110 3 DON JUAN 7 86 2
    HIS SYMPATHY FOR RANK BY THE SAME TOKEN . . . . . 117 3 DON JUAN 8 11 7
    YOUR RANK AND FILE BY THOUSANDS WHILE THE REST . . . . 118 3 DON JUAN 8 13 7
    HE RECOGNIZED AN OFFICER OF RANK . . . . . 141 3 DON JUAN 8 57 8
    IN FACT IF NOT IN RANK AND THE SUSPICION . . . . . 208 3 DON JUAN 9 52 5
    A FOREIGNER OF RANK HAD GRACED OUR SHORE . . . . . 283 3 DON JUAN 11 32 6
    OF RANK ENOUGH TO SET IN STONE OR LEAD . . . . 314 3 DON JUAN 11 V 75 2
    IN BIRTH IN RANK IN FORTUNE LIKEWISE EQUAL . . . . 367 3 DON JUAN 13 20 1
    WITH MANY MORE BY RANK AND FASHION DECKED . . . . 382 3 DON JUAN 13 52 6
    WITH OTHER COUNTESSES OF BLANK--BUT RANK . . . 396 3 DON JUAN 13 80 1
    OF RANK AND YOUTH THOUGH PURER THAN THE REST . . . . 480 3 DON JUAN 15 55 4
    BECAUSE AS SUITS THEIR RANK AND SITUATION . . . . . 534 3 DON JUAN 16 68 5
RANK'D
    AND RANK'D WITH WHAT IS EVERY DAY DISPLAY'D-- . . . . . 400 3 DON JUAN 13 90 7
RANKLE
    WHILE WEEDS AND ORDURE RANKLE ROUND THE BASE . . . . . 400 2 DON JUAN 4 103 8
    A CURE FOR GRIEF--FOR WHAT CAN EVER RANKLE . . . . . 422 3 DON JUAN 14 27 7
RANKS
    AND HAVING LIVED WITH PEOPLE OF ALL RANKS . . . . . 319 2 DON JUAN 3 84 3
    IN NATIVE SWORDS AND NATIVE RANKS . . . . . 325 2 DON JUAN 3 L 14 3
    THE FEMALE RANKS SO THAT NONE STIRRED OR TALKED . . . . 21 3 DON JUAN 6 30 6
    MEDALS RANKS RIBBONS LACE EMBROIDERY SCARLET . . . . 108 3 DON JUAN 7 84 1
    AND SWEPT AS GALES SWEEP FOAM AWAY WHOLE RANKS . . . . 134 3 DON JUAN 8 44 3
    WHICH THINNED AT EVERY STEP THEIR RANKS OF MEN . . . . 163 3 DON JUAN 8 103 4
    THEY BREAK THEIR RANKS AND GLADLY LEAVE THE DRILL . . . . 417 3 DON JUAN 14 17 2
    IN ENGLAND RANKS QUITE ON A DIFFERENT LIST . . . . . 436 3 DON JUAN 14 60 6
RANSACK'D
    ANTONIA BUSTLED ROUND THE RANSACK'D ROOM . . . . . 109 2 DON JUAN 1 159 2
RANSOM
    RESERVED FOR FUTURE RANSOM IN THE HOLD-- . . . . . 284 2 DON JUAN 3 16 6
    AND THEN--THEY CALCULATED ON HIS RANSOM . . . . . 415 2 DON JUAN 5 9 8
    LIKE OTHER SLAVES OF COURSE MUST PAY HIS RANSOM . . . 305 3 DON JUAN 11 74 3
    ON READY MONEY OR A DRAFT ON RANSOM . . . . . 459 3 DON JUAN 15 8 8
RAP
    I HAVE SEEN THE LANDHOLDERS WITHOUT A RAP-- . . . . . 310 3 DON JUAN 11 84 1
    ADVANCES WITH EXASPERATED RAP . . . . 459 3 DON JUAN 15 8 6
RAPACIOUS
    OF WHICH WE ARE LAVISH FIRST AND THEN RAPACIOUS . . . . 145 2 DON JUAN 1 217 V8
RAPE
    ANTONIA CRIED OUT RAPE AND JULIA FIRE . . . . 122 2 DON JUAN 1 184 2
RAPHAEL
    THEY CAN TRANSFIGURE BRIGHTER THAN A RAPHAEL . . . . 463 3 DON JUAN 15 16 8
RAPID
    THE LOVE OF POWER AND RAPID GAIN OF GOLD . . . . . 303 2 DON JUAN 3 54 1
    AND THEN MOVED ON AGAIN WITH RAPID PACE . . . . . 61 3 DON JUAN 6 111 2
RAPIDLY
    ALL TIMIDLY YET RAPIDLY SHE SAW . . . . 232 2 DON JUAN 2 143 2
RAPP
    WHEN RAPP THE HARMONIST EMBARGOED MARRIAGE . . . . . 471 3 DON JUAN 15 35 1
    BUT WHETHER REVEREND RAPP LEARN'D THIS IN GERMANY . . . 472 3 DON JUAN 15 36 3
    BUT RAPP IS THE REVERSE OF ZEALOUS MATRONS . . . . . 472 3 DON JUAN 15 37 1
RAPS
    FOR WARNING TO THE REST COMPELS THESE RAPS . . . . . 155 2 DON JUAN 1 V 7 7
RAPTURE
    FEEL RAPTURE BUT NOT SUCH TRUE JOY ARE REAPING . . . . 261 2 DON JUAN 2 196 7
    BUT WITH A HEAVENLY RAPTURE ON HIS FACE . . . . . 169 3 DON JUAN 8 116 1
RAPTURE'S
    AND RAPTURE'S SELF WILL SEEM ALMOST A PAIN . . . . . 474 2 DON JUAN 5 110 4
RAPTURES
    ALTHOUGH A SQUALL OR TWO HAD DAMP'D HIS RAPTURES . . . . 283 2 DON JUAN 3 15 4
    FULL OF DEEP RAPTURES AND OF BUMPERS THEY-- . . . . . 343 2 DON JUAN 3 V 98 7
RARE
    AT FIFTY LOVE FOR LOVE IS RARE 'TIS TRUE . . . . . . 79 2 DON JUAN 1 108 6
    BUT BEEF IS RARE WITHIN THESE OXLESS ISLES . . . . . 238 2 DON JUAN 2 154 1

RARE   (CONTINUED)
```
    I SAY THAT BEEF IS RARE AND CAN'T HELP THINKING    . . . . 238  2 DON JUAN  2   155   1
    (BUT THAT OF COURSE IS RARE) AND THEN DESPOND      . . . . 278  2 DON JUAN  3     7   3
    OR WERE OF TORTOISE-SHELL OR RARE WOODS MADE       . . . . 310  2 DON JUAN  3    69   4
    MAY TURN HIS NAME UP AS A RARE DEPOSIT    . . . . . . 327  2 DON JUAN  3    89   8
    OH BEAUTIFUL AND RARE AS BEAUTIFUL . . . .          . . . . 353  2 DON JUAN  4    17   1
    WHAT BROUGHT YOU HERE--OH NOTHING VERY RARE--      . . . . 418  2 DON JUAN  5    15   2
    OF WORKMANSHIP SO RARE THEY MADE YOU WISH          . . . . 449  2 DON JUAN  5    65   7
    MAKE EPIC POESY SO RARE AND RICH . . . . .          . . . . 156  3 DON JUAN  8    90   8
    AS RARE IN LIVING BEINGS AS A FOSSILE . . .        . . . . 250  3 DON JUAN 10    52   3
    HE HAD THEN THE GRACE TOO RARE IN EVERY CLIME      . . . . 354  3 DON JUAN 12    84   6
    STILL OLDER MANSION OF A RICH AND RARE    . . . . . . 384  3 DON JUAN 13    55   3
    SHE IS SO RARE AND THOU HAST SO MUCH PREY          . . . . 459  3 DON JUAN 15     9   2
    BUT WHETHER ENGLISH DUKES GREW RARE OF LATE . . . . . . 474  3 DON JUAN 15    42   4
    WITH HER WAS RARE AND ADELINE WHO AS YET  . . . . . . 492  3 DON JUAN 15    81   2
    A WILDERNESS OF THE MOST RARE CONCEITS    . . . . . . 502  3 DON JUAN 16     3   3
RARELY
    BECAUSE THAT NUMBER RARELY MUCH ENDEARS   . . . . . .  78  2 DON JUAN  1   107   6
    BUT AT SIXTEEN THE CONSCIENCE RARELY GNAWS        . . . . 113  2 DON JUAN  1   167   5
    AND RARELY CEASED THE HAUGHTY BILLOW'S ROAR       . . . . 249  2 DON JUAN  2   177   6
    BUT VERY RARELY EXECUTES ITS FUNCTION . . .        . . . . 271  2 DON JUAN  2   215   2
    THAT LOVE AND MARRIAGE RARELY CAN COMBINE         . . . . 277  2 DON JUAN  3     5   3
    HIS VERSES RARELY WANTED THEIR DUE FEET--          . . . . 316  2 DON JUAN  3    78   5
    AND THOUGH HIS MEANING THEY COULD RARELY GUESS    . . . . 318  2 DON JUAN  3    82   5
    AS RARELY THEY BEHELD THROUGHOUT THEIR ROUND      . . . . 352  2 DON JUAN  4    16   3
    I'VE RARELY SEEN THE MAN THEY DID NOT FRET        . . . .  16  3 DON JUAN  6    21   8
    THEIR OWN TRUE INTERESTS WHICH KINGS RARELY KNOW  . . . .  53  3 DON JUAN  6    95   2
    AROUND US EVER RARELY TO ALIGHT . . . . .          . . . .  66  3 DON JUAN  7     1   2
    THEIR NAMES ARE RARELY FOUND NOR OFTEN SOUGHT     . . . .  83  3 DON JUAN  7    34   4
    SPARE OR SMITE RARELY--MAN'S MAKE MILLIONS ASHES  . . . . 115  3 DON JUAN  8     6   8
    OCCUR THOUGH RARELY WHEN THERE IS A SPARK         . . . . 177  3 DON JUAN  8   130   5
    A THING WHICH HAPPENS RARELY THIS HE OWED         . . . . 239  3 DON JUAN 10    29   2
    EXTREMELY WHOLESOME THOUGH BUT RARELY CLEAR       . . . . 266  3 DON JUAN 10    83   8
    AND EVEN THAT HE HAD SO RARELY HEARD      . . . . . . 274  3 DON JUAN 11    12   3
    THE FIRST THE EMBLEM (RARELY THOUGH) OF WHAT      . . . . 290  3 DON JUAN 11    44   4
    ALIGHTING RARELY--WERE SHE BUT A HORNET   . . . . . . 400  3 DON JUAN 13    89   7
    SOMETIMES A DANCE (THOUGH RARELY ON FIELD DAYS    . . . . 408  3 DON JUAN 13   108   1
    THAT GOOD BUT RARELY CAME FROM GOOD ADVICE . . . . . . 439  3 DON JUAN 14    66   8
    THAT YOUNG MEN RARELY MADE MONASTIC VOWS  . . . . . . 439  3 DON JUAN 14    67   6
    'TIS RARELY FOUND BUT WOULD REPAY ALL CHECKS      . . . . 451  3 DON JUAN 14    93  V5
    BUT RARELY SEEN LIKE GOLD COMPARED WITH PAPER     . . . . 510  3 DON JUAN 16    22   7
    FOR LAUGHTER RARELY SHAKES THESE AGUISH FOLKS     . . . . 540  3 DON JUAN 16    83  V3
    IN THOSE WHO RARELY SMILE THEIR SMILES BESPEAK    . . . . 544  3 DON JUAN 16    92   4
RARELY-TRODDEN
    HER HOME IS IN THE RARELY-TRODDEN WILD    . . . . . . 143  3 DON JUAN  8    62   3
RARITY
    AND ALTHOUGH HERE AND THERE SOME GLORIOUS RARITY  . . . .  14  2 DON JUAN  D     9   5
    ARE SAVING--VICE SPARES NOTHING FOR A RARITY      . . . . 408  2 DON JUAN  4   115   8
RASCAL
    JULIA MY LOVE--(YOU RASCAL PEDRO QUICKER)--  . . . . . 167  2 DON JUAN  2    20   5
    THEIR POET--A DAMNED RASCAL--BUT NO LESS .         . . . . 318  2 DON JUAN  3    82  V1
RASCALS
    WITH THAT SUBLIME OF RASCALS YOUR ATTORNEY        . . . . 103  2 DON JUAN  1   151   3
    (A SET OF HUMBUG RASCALS WHEN ALL'S DONE)         . . . . 219  2 DON JUAN  2   118  V6
    THESE RASCALS BEING NEW COMERS KNEW NOT WHOM      . . . . 298  2 DON JUAN  3    44   1
RASH
    NOT THAT HE WAS NOT SOMETIMES RASH OR SO . . . . . . 300  2 DON JUAN  3    48   1
    OR AT THE LEAST FORGIVE THE LOVING RASH ONE . . . .   8  3 DON JUAN  6     4   4
    ('TIS POPE'S PHRASE) A GREAT LONGING THO' A RASH ONE . . 216  3 DON JUAN  9    68   6
    AND RASH ENTHUSIASM IN GOOD SOCIETY   . . . . . . 374  3 DON JUAN 13    35   7
RASHLY
    SHOULD RASHLY QUOTE FOR FEAR OF A MISTAKE)        . . . .  74  2 DON JUAN  1    98   6
    IF SHE LOVED RASHLY HER LIFE PAID FOR WRONG--     . . . . 383  2 DON JUAN  4    73   5
    NOT TO BE RASHLY TOUCHED BUT STILL MORE DREAD     . . . .  37  3 DON JUAN  6    62   2
RAT
    BURROWING FOR BOROUGHS LIKE A RAT OR RABBIT . . . . . . 534  3 DON JUAN 16    70   2
RATE
    THE SAME THINGS CHANGE THEIR NAMES AT SUCH A RATE . . . . 278  2 DON JUAN  3     6   6
    AND THAT PROCEEDING AT A VERY HIGH RATE   . . . . . . 296  2 DON JUAN  3    40   7
    BUT SOLD BY THE IMPRESARIO AT NO HIGH RATE        . . . . 388  2 DON JUAN  4    80   8
    I OWN NO PROSODY CAN EVER RATE IT    . . . . . . .  15  3 DON JUAN  6    18   7
    NOW WE'LL GET O'ER THE GROUND AT A GREAT RATE     . . . . 203  3 DON JUAN  9    42   4
    IF I MIGHT AUGUR I SHOULD RATE BUT LOW    . . . . . . 299  3 DON JUAN 11    61   4
    OF BEING APT TO TALK AT A GREAT RATE      . . . . . . 329  3 DON JUAN 12    28   6
    HAVE BUILT AND LAID OUT GROUND AT SUCH A RATE     . . . . 393  3 DON JUAN 13    74   3
    EVEN WHERE THE ARTICLE AT HIGHEST RATE IS  . . . . . . 469  3 DON JUAN 15    29   4
    WHICH AFTER ALL AT SUCH A DESPERATE RATE RUNS     . . . . 472  3 DON JUAN 15    37   5
    UNTIL PREFERMENT COMING AT A SURE RATE    . . . . . . 540  3 DON JUAN 16    82   4
RATED
    AND RATED HIM ALMOST A WHIPPER-IN . . . . .        . . . . 425  3 DON JUAN 14    34   8
    AS IF SHE RATED SUCH ACCOMPLISHMENT  . . . . . . . 521  3 DON JUAN 16    42   2
RATHER
    YOU BOB ARE RATHER INSOLENT YOU KNOW      . . . . . .  10  2 DON JUAN  D     3   1
    AND WORDSWORTH IN A RATHER LONG EXCURSION         . . . .  11  2 DON JUAN  D     4   1
    AND ALSO OF HIS MOTHER IF YOU'D RATHER    . . . . . .  25  2 DON JUAN  1     7   8
    SHOULD RATHER FACE AND OVERCOME TEMPTATION        . . . .  63  2 DON JUAN  1    77   2
    METHINKS THE REQUISITION'S RATHER HARD    . . . . . .  85  2 DON JUAN  1   118   3
    HE STOOD IN ACT TO SPEAK OR RATHER STAMMER        . . . . 111  2 DON JUAN  1   163   1
    AT LEAST 'TWAS RATHER EARLY TO BEGIN . . . . .      . . . . 113  2 DON JUAN  1   167   4
```

	PAGE	VOL	CANTO		STANZA	LN
WHICH KEEPS WHEN PUSH'D BY QUESTIONS RATHER ROUGH	119	2	DON	JUAN 1	178	5
SINCE IN A WAY THAT'S RATHER OF THE ODDEST HE	157	2	DON	JUAN 2	1	7
A HUSBAND RATHER OLD NOT MUCH IN UNITY	158	2	DON	JUAN 2	3	7
FOR NAUGHTY CHILDREN WHO WOULD RATHER PLAY	162	2	DON	JUAN 2	10	3
ESPECIALLY WHEN LIFE IS RATHER NEW	163	2	DON	JUAN 2	12	4
OR RATHER STOMACH WHICH ALAS ATTENDS	167	2	DON	JUAN 2	21	2
THE WIND IN FACT PERHAPS WAS RATHER LESS	178	2	DON	JUAN 2	41	1
HE HAD BEEN RATHER INDISPOSED OF LATE	199	2	DON	JUAN 2	81	5
ALTHOUGH HIS WOES HAD TURN'D HIM RATHER YELLOW	235	2	DON	JUAN 2	148	8
A PLEASURE--LIKE ALL PLEASURES--RATHER DEAR	238	2	DON	JUAN 2	156	6
RATHER BY DEEDS THAN WORDS BECAUSE THE CASE	240	2	DON	JUAN 2	159	2
AND EVERY DAY BY DAY-BREAK--RATHER EARLY	245	2	DON	JUAN 2	168	1
ALL THOSE MAY LEAP WHO RATHER WOULD BE NEUTER--	266	2	DON	JUAN 2	205	5
DESCENDING RATHER QUICKLY THE DECLIVITY	290	2	DON	JUAN 3	29	2
HIS POLAR STAR BEING ONE WHICH RATHER RANGES	317	2	DON	JUAN 3	80	3
RATHER THE DEAD FOR LIFE SEEM'D SOMETHING NEW	378	2	DON	JUAN 4	62	2
FOR FEAR OF SEEMING RATHER TOUCH'D MYSELF--	384	2	DON	JUAN 4	74	4
AND HAVING LED A RATHER LOOSISH LIFE	389	2	DON	JUAN 4	83	V2
FORMED RATHER FOR INSTRUCTING THAN DELIGHTING	412	2	DON	JUAN 5	2	5
THOUGH RATHER MORE IRREGULARLY SPOTTED	416	2	DON	JUAN 5	10	3
A MAN OF THIRTY RATHER STOUT AND HALE	416	2	DON	JUAN 5	10	6
GOOD TEETH WITH CURLING RATHER DARK BROWN HAIR	416	2	DON	JUAN 5	11	3
ONE ARM HAD ON A BANDAGE RATHER BLOODY	416	2	DON	JUAN 5	11	6
REPLETION RATHER ADDS TO WHAT HE FEELS	427	2	DON	JUAN 5	31	4
OF FOOD I THINK WITH PHILIP'S SON OR RATHER	427	2	DON	JUAN 5	31	7
I'D RATHER LEAVE IT MUCH TO YOUR OWN MIND	467	2	DON	JUAN 5	97	4
BOILED IN HIS VEINS AND RATHER THAN DESCEND	471	2	DON	JUAN 5	104	4
AS IF SHE RATHER ORDERED THAN WAS GRANTING--	474	2	DON	JUAN 5	109	8
RATHER THAN SIN--EXCEPT TO HIS OWN WISH	492	2	DON	JUAN 5	141	6
FURTHER OLD BABA RATHER BRISKLY ENTERED	493	2	DON	JUAN 5	143	8
BELOVED IN HER OWN WAY AND RATHER WHISK	7	3	DON	JUAN 6	3	4
OR RATHER BONNET WHICH THE FAIR SEX WEAR	13	3	DON	JUAN 6	14	5
RATHER TO HIDE WHAT PLEASES MOST UNKNOWN	13	3	DON	JUAN 6	15	4
OR RATHER LAKE--FOR RILLS DO NOT RUN SLOWLY--	22	3	DON	JUAN 6	33	7
SOME THOUGHT HER RATHER MASCULINE IN HEIGHT	23	3	DON	JUAN 6	35	7
BUT RATHER SKIM THE EARTH WHILE DUDU'S FORM	26	3	DON	JUAN 6	41	5
SAID LOLAH WITH AN ACCENT RATHER ROUGH	28	3	DON	JUAN 6	44	6
AND PITY LOVERS RATHER MORE THAN SEAMEN	32	3	DON	JUAN 6	53	8
THOUGH BY THIS POLITESSE SHE RATHER SUFFERED	36	3	DON	JUAN 6	61	6
RATHER TOO HIGH AND DISTANT THAT SHE THREW	44	3	DON	JUAN 6	76	3
WITH THE FIRST RAY OR RATHER GREY OF MORN	49	3	DON	JUAN 6	87	1
UNTIL 'TIS TAUGHT BY LESSONS RATHER RUDE	53	3	DON	JUAN 6	95	3
OR RATHER SOFA (FOR IT WAS ALL PILLOW	60	3	DON	JUAN 6	108	4
AND YET HE SHUDDERED AND SEEMED RATHER PRONE	62	3	DON	JUAN 6	112	4
AND THIS THEY SAY IN LANGUAGE RATHER ROUGH	67	3	DON	JUAN 7	3	5
WHEN IT GREW RATHER LATE TO SET THINGS RIGHT	73	3	DON	JUAN 7	13	5
NOW I SHOULD LIKE TO KNOW BEING RATHER CURIOUS	77	3	DON	JUAN 7	21	V1
I'D RATHER TELL TEN LIES THAN SAY A WORD	77	3	DON	JUAN 7	22	4
A HABIT RATHER BLAMEABLE WHICH IS	79	3	DON	JUAN 7	25	1
TO SEE AN OLD MAN RATHER WILD THAN WISE	104	3	DON	JUAN 7	73	5
WAS ON A SUDDEN RATHER PUZZLED HERE	125	3	DON	JUAN 8	27	6
MEN RUN AWAY MUCH RATHER THAN GO THROUGH	130	3	DON	JUAN 8	35	3
UNTO THAT RATHER SOMEWHAT MISTY BOURN	133	3	DON	JUAN 8	41	3
I RATHER DOUBT AND I WOULD FAIN SAY FIE ON'T	138	3	DON	JUAN 8	51	6
(I WISH YOUR BARDS WOULD SING IT RATHER BETTER)	184	3	DON	JUAN 9	3	8
IS RATHER DEAR--I'M SURE I MEAN NO HARM	186	3	DON	JUAN 9	7	8
BUT WOULD MUCH RATHER HAVE A SOUND DIGESTION	189	3	DON	JUAN 9	14	5
RATHER THAN LIFE A MERE AFFAIR OF BREATH	190	3	DON	JUAN 9	16	8
AS IS THE CHRISTIAN DOGMA RATHER ROUGH	195	3	DON	JUAN 9	25	6
(OR RATHER PEOPLES)--GO ON WITHOUT PAUSE	196	3	DON	JUAN 9	28	4
AND DEVIATE INTO MATTERS RATHER DRY	203	3	DON	JUAN 9	41	4
JUST THEN AS THEY ARE RATHER NUMEROUS FOUND	205	3	DON	JUAN 9	46	4
IF RATHER BROAD MADE STOCKS RISE AND THEIR HOLDERS	208	3	DON	JUAN 9	52	8
FAIR WEATHER FOR THE DAY THOUGH RATHER SPACIOUS	211	3	DON	JUAN 9	58	7
GREAT JOY WAS HER'S OR RATHER JOYS THE FIRST	212	3	DON	JUAN 9	59	1
INTO A RUSSIAN COUPLET RATHER DULL	212	3	DON	JUAN 9	60	3
'TIS VERY TRUE THE HILL SEEMED RATHER HIGH	215	3	DON	JUAN 9	66	5
BEYOND ITS DIMMED EYE'S SPHERE--BUT WOULD MUCH RATHER	228	3	DON	JUAN 10	6	7
OR LADIES' FANCIES--RATHER TRANSITORY	229	3	DON	JUAN 10	9	4
MUST COME MUCH RATHER SHOULD HE COURT THE RAY	229	3	BON	JUAN 10	9	7
I RATHER THINK THE MOON SHOULD DATE THE DEARS	230	3	DON	JUAN 10	10	8
FOR ME FOR I WOULD RATHER TAKE MY WINE	233	3	DON	JUAN 10	17	3
WHERE HIS ASSETS WERE WAXING RATHER FEW	240	3	DON	JUAN 10	31	3
AND THUS THEY FORMED A RATHER CUROUS PAIR	252	3	DON	JUAN 10	57	5
THE TRUTH IS I'VE GROWN LATELY RATHER PHTHISICAL	270	3	DON	JUAN 11	5	5
THAT'S RATHER FINE THE GENTLE SOUND OF THAMIS--	279	3	DON	JUAN 11	24	1
WHOSE SHAMROCK NOW SEEMS RATHER WORSE FOR WEARING	286	3	DON	JUAN 11	38	8
DIPLOMATISTS OF RATHER WAVERING KINGS	287	3	DON	JUAN 11	40	3
AND YET THE BRITISH DAMME'S RATHER ATTIC	289	3	DON	JUAN 11	43	1
HE'LL FIND IT RATHER DIFFICULT SOME DAY	298	3	DON	JUAN 11	59	3
WHICH IT WERE RATHER DIFFICULT TO PROVE	322	3	DON	JUAN 12	13	3
AND RATHER WISHED IN SUCH THINGS TO STAND NEUTER	336	3	DON	JUAN 12	42	3
THE WORLD BY EXPERIENCE RATHER THAN BY LECTURE	337	3	DON	JUAN 12	46	5
AND RATHER CALMLY INTO THE HEART GLIDES	350	3	DON	JUAN 12	74	5
MEN'S WRONGS AND RATHER CHECK THAN PUNISH CRIMES	361	3	DON	JUAN 13	8	6
THE SEASON RATHER THAN TO WINTER DREAR--	395	3	DON	JUAN 13	77	4
BUT THE CLUBS FOUND IT RATHER SERIOUS LAUGHTER	398	3	DON	JUAN 13	86	6
FOR THEN THE GENTLEMEN WERE RATHER TIRED)	408	3	DON	JUAN 13	108	2

	PAGE	VOL	CANTO	STANZA	LN

RATHER (CONTINUED)

	PAGE	VOL	CANTO	STANZA	LN
FOR I WAS RATHER FAMOUS IN MY TIME	414	3	DON JUAN 14	9	7
AND RATHER HELD IN THAN PUT FORTH HIS VIGOUR	427	3	DON JUAN 14	39	4
I'D RATHER NOT SAY WHAT MIGHT BE RELATED	428	3	DON JUAN 14	42	4
WHOSE FAME SHE RATHER DOUBTED WITH POSTERITY	432	3	DON JUAN 14	51	3
'TWAS RATHER HER EXPERIENCE MADE HER SAGE	433	3	DON JUAN 14	54	3
AH WHO CAN TELL OR RATHER WHO CAN NOT	457	3	DON JUAN 15	4	1
WAS SUCH AS RATHER SEEM'D TO KEEP ALOOF	462	3	DON JUAN 15	14	3
THE FIRST IS RATHER MORE THAN MORTAL CAN DO	465	3	DON JUAN 15	21	3
ADELINE AND DON JUAN RATHER BLENDED	482	3	DON JUAN 15	61	3
OF WHICH PERHAPS THE COOKERY RATHER VARIES	486	3	DON JUAN 15	68	3
THAT HE WOULD RATHER·MAKE THEM MORE THAN LESS	491	3	DON JUAN 15	80	4
RATHER BY DEFERENCE THAN COMPLIMENT	493	3	DON JUAN 15	83	7
BECAUSE I'D RATHER IT SHOULD BE FORGOT	499	3	DON JUAN 15	96	5
SOMETIMES UNLESS MY FEELINGS RATHER ERR)	506	3	DON JUAN 16	14	5
FOR CONTEMPLATION RATHER THAN HIS PILLOW	507	3	DON JUAN 16	15	2
UNDREST AND RATHER SLOWLY WENT TO BED	512	3	DON JUAN 16	27	4
THIS MORNING RATHER SPENT LESS TIME UPON'T	513	3	DON JUAN 16	29	3
HE STARTED AND SAID YES--NO--RATHER--YES	514	3	DON JUAN 16	32	4
HER GRACE REPLIED HIS GRACE WAS RATHER PAINED	515	3	DON JUAN 16	34	6
HAD CAUSED HIS NERVES--MADE ANSWERS RATHER CLOUDED	527	3	DON JUAN 16	54	V8
RATHER THAN SELLER HAD HIS WANTS BEEN FEWER	528	3	DON JUAN 16	57	5
TO NAME A THING IN NOMENCLATURE RATHER	533	3	DON JUAN 16	67	7
BUT COUNTRY CONTESTS COST HIM RATHER DEARER	534	3	DON JUAN 16	70	3
OF TWO THINGS--HOW (THE QUESTION RATHER ODD IS)	543	3	DON JUAN 16	90	7
NOW THIS HE REALLY RATHER TOOK AMISS	544	3	DON JUAN 16	92	3
RATHER THAN REST INSTEAD OF POPPIES WILLOWS	555	3	DON JUAN 16	110	5
AND RATHER VARIABLY FOR STONY DEATH	560	3	DON JUAN 16	121	2
YET ONE THING RATHER GOOD THE GRAVE HAD SPARED	560	3	DON JUAN 16	121	3
CHEERFUL--BUT SOMETIMES RATHER APT TO WHIMPER	567	3	DON JUAN 17	11	5
A VIGIL OR DREAMT RATHER MORE THAN SLEPT	568	3	DON JUAN 17	14	8

RATION

	PAGE	VOL	CANTO	STANZA	LN
THE MILLIONS SLAIN BY SOLDIERS FOR THEIR RATION	146	3	DON JUAN 8	68	6
THERE IS NO DOUBT THAT YOU DESERVE YOUR RATION	185	3	DON JUAN 9	6	7
WHO WOULD SUPPOSE FROM ADAM'S SIMPLE RATION	486	3	DON JUAN 15	69	5

RATIONAL

	PAGE	VOL	CANTO	STANZA	LN
FROM THE HIGH LYRIC DOWN TO THE LOW RATIONAL	319	2	DON JUAN 3	85	6
OF DIDO'S ALPHABET AND THIS IS RATIONAL	122	3	DON JUAN 8	23	7

RATTLE

	PAGE	VOL	CANTO	STANZA	LN
I RATTLE ON EXACTLY AS I'D TALK	464	3	DON JUAN 15	19	7

RATTLES

	PAGE	VOL	CANTO	STANZA	LN
ARE NOTHING BUT A CHILD OF MURDER'S RATTLES	114	3	DON JUAN 8	4	8
AND IF MY THUNDERBOLT NOT ALWAYS RATTLES	356	3	DON JUAN 12	88	1
DESPITE THE SNAKE SOCIETY'S LOUD RATTLES	452	3	DON JUAN 14	96	8
RATTLES AROUND ME HER DISCORDANT HYMN	499	3	DON JUAN 15	97	4

RATTLING

	PAGE	VOL	CANTO	STANZA	LN
OVER THE STONES STILL RATTLING UP PALL MALL	282	3	DON JUAN 11	29	1

RAUCOCANTI

	PAGE	VOL	CANTO	STANZA	LN
YOU'VE HEARD OF RAUCOCANTI--I'M THE MAN	392	2	DON JUAN 4	88	5
WITH RAUCOCANTI LUCKLESSLY WAS CHAIN'D	394	2	DON JUAN 4	93	1

RAUCOCANTI'S

	PAGE	VOL	CANTO	STANZA	LN
HERE RAUCOCANTI'S ELOQUENT RECITAL	393	2	DON JUAN 4	90	1

RAVAGE

	PAGE	VOL	CANTO	STANZA	LN
AND WHICH IN RAVAGE THE MORE LOATHSOME EVIL IS--	92	2	DON JUAN 1	131	7

RAVE

	PAGE	VOL	CANTO	STANZA	LN
SHE WAS NOT ONE TO WEEP AND RAVE AND CHAFE	373	2	DON JUAN 4	54	5
HERS WAS A PHRENSY WHICH DISDAIN'D TO RAVE	380	2	DON JUAN 4	67	7

RAVEN

	PAGE	VOL	CANTO	STANZA	LN
FORTH FROM ITS RAVEN FRINGE THE FULL GLANCE FLIES	218	2	DON JUAN 2	117	5
AND RAVEN RINGLETS GATHERED IN DARK CROWD	39	3	DON JUAN 6	66	2

RAVENNA'S

	PAGE	VOL	CANTO	STANZA	LN
WHICH BOUNDS RAVENNA'S IMMEMORIAL WOOD	337	2	DON JUAN 3	105	3
RECORDS RAVENNA'S CARNAGE ON ITS FACE	400	2	DON JUAN 4	103	7

RAVENOUS

	PAGE	VOL	CANTO	STANZA	LN
FOR THEY WHO WERE MOST RAVENOUS IN THE ACT	198	2	DON JUAN 2	79	3

RAVENOUSLY

	PAGE	VOL	CANTO	STANZA	LN
AND FELL ALL RAVENOUSLY ON THEIR PROVISION	192	2	DON JUAN 2	68	7

RAVING

	PAGE	VOL	CANTO	STANZA	LN
(THE LEAST OF WHICH WOULD SET TEN POETS RAVING)	291	2	DON JUAN 3	30	6
THAT WOULD HAVE SET TOM MOORE THOUGH MARRIED RAVING	291	2	DON JUAN 3	30	V6

RAVISHED

	PAGE	VOL	CANTO	STANZA	LN
HAD MADE THEM CHASTE--THEY RAVISHED VERY LITTLE	176	3	DON JUAN 8	128	8

RAVISHING

	PAGE	VOL	CANTO	STANZA	LN
WHEREFORE THE RAVISHING DID NOT BEGIN	178	3	DON JUAN 8	132	4

RAW

	PAGE	VOL	CANTO	STANZA	LN
I'M SORRY THUS TO PROBE A WOUND SO RAW	155	2	DON JUAN 1	V 7	5
AND WRAPT HIM CLOSER LEST THE AIR TOO RAW	232	2	DON JUAN 2	143	6
AS ALL HIS LATTER MEALS HAD BEEN QUITE RAW	239	2	DON JUAN 2	157	4
'TWAS A RAW DAY OF AUTUMN'S BLEAK BEGINNING	414	2	DON JUAN 5	6	1
SO MUCH INTO THE RAW AS QUITE TO WRONG HER	137	3	DON JUAN 8	50	6
BUT THEY WHO BLUNDER THUS ARE RAW BEGINNERS	346	3	DON JUAN 12	66	1
MISS RAW MISS FLAW MISS SHOWMAN AND MISS KNOWMAN	473	3	DON JUAN 15	40	4

RAWBOLDS

	PAGE	VOL	CANTO	STANZA	LN
THERE WERE THE SIX MISS RAWBOLDS--PRETTY DEARS	398	3	DON JUAN 13	85	6
THE FOUR MISS,RAWBOLDS IN A GLEE WOULD SHINE	408	3	DON JUAN 13	107	5

RAY

	PAGE	VOL	CANTO	STANZA	LN
IF 'TWAS NOT LAND THAT ROSE WITH THE SUN'S RAY	207	2	DON JUAN 2	97	3
HER DAUGHTER TEMPER'D WITH A MILDER RAY	375	2	DON JUAN 4	57	1
THE SUN HIMSELF HAS SENT ME LIKE A RAY	494	2	DON JUAN 5	144	7

654

RAY   (CONTINUED)

WITH THE FIRST RAY OR RATHER GREY OF MORN 49   3 DON JUAN 6   87   1
VARIED EACH RAY--BUT ALL DESCRIPTIONS GARBLE 55   3 DON JUAN 6   98   5
OF WOLVES WILL THE BRIGHT MUSE WITHDRAW ONE RAY 70   3 DON JUAN 7   7   6
LEND TO THAT COLOUR A TRANSCENDANT RAY 218   3 DON JUAN 9   71   6
MUST COME MUCH RATHER SHOULD HE COURT THE RAY 229   3 DON JUAN 10   9   7
THE SUN'S TRUE SON NO VAPOUR BUT A RAY 300   3 DON JUAN 11   64   8
RAY FADES ON RAY AS YEARS ON YEARS DEPART 554   3 DON JUAN 16   109   4
RAY FADES ON RAY AS YEARS ON YEARS DEPART 554   3 DON JUAN 16   109   4

RAYS

AND BEAUTY ALL CONCENTRATING LIKE RAYS 254   2 DON JUAN 2   186   2
FLASH'D O'ER HIS SOUL A FEW HEROIC RAYS 303   2 DON JUAN 3   55   2
A SUN EMBOSS'D IN GOLD WHOSE RAYS OF TISSUE 309   2 DON JUAN 3   67   7
WHOSE RAYS SHONE EVER TREMBLING BUT INCESSANT 315   2 DON JUAN 3   77   8
TO COLOUR UP HIS RAYS FROM YOUR DESPATCHES 107   3 DON JUAN 7   81   8
SUNS AS RAYS--WORLDS LIKE ATOMS--YEARS LIKE HOURS . . 189   3 DON JUAN 9   13   8
OF THE TRUTH'S RAYS SPOIL NOT MY DRAUGHT OF SPIRIT . . 269   3 DON JUAN 11   2   7
NATIONS ATHWART THE DEEP THE GOLDEN RAYS 319   3 DON JUAN 12   8   4
DECKED BY THE RAYS REFLECTED FROM HIS HOST 383   3 DON JUAN 13   53   5
IN EGYPT'S RAYS TO HARP AT A FIXED HOUR) 388   3 DON JUAN 13   64   4
THEN TURN'D UNTO THE STARS FOR LOFTIER RAYS 480   3 DON JUAN 15   56   4
WHOSE TRAITS WERE RADIANT WITH THE RAYS OF VERITY . . 550   3 DON JUAN 16   102   4

REACH

IT NE'ER CAN REACH SO TURNS TO YOU MY SOUL 133   2 DON JUAN 1   196   V8
HER SMALL WHITE HAND COULD HARDLY REACH THE TAPER . . 134   2 DON JUAN 1   198   3
HER SMALL WHITE FINGERS SCARCE COULD REACH THE TAPER . 134   2 DON JUAN 1   198   V3
SHOULD REACH HIS BLOOD THEN O'ER HIM STILL AS DEATH . 232   2 DON JUAN 2   143   7
WHEN O'ER THE BRIM THE SPARKLING BUMPERS REACH . . . 250   2 DON JUAN 2   178   3
A CANDIOTE CLOAK WHICH TO THE KNEE MIGHT REACH . . . 451   2 DON JUAN 5   68   3
AND YET SHE DID NOT WANT TO REACH THE MOON 490   2 DON JUAN 5   136   3
THE TRAIN MIGHT REACH A QUARTER OF A MILE 495   2 DON JUAN 5   146   3
THINE EAR IF IT SHOULD REACH--AND NOW RHYMES WANDER . 52   3 DON JUAN 6   93   3
OF LIFE REACH TEN O'CLOCK AND WHILE A GLOW 229   3 DON JUAN 10   8   5
COULD REACH WITH HERE AND THERE A SAIL JUST SKIPPING . 265   3 DON JUAN 10   82   3

REACH'D

JUAN HAD REACH'D THE ROOM-DOOR IN A TRICE 122   2 DON JUAN 1   183   5
AND REACH'D HIS HOME IN AN UNSEEMLY PLIGHT 126   2 DON JUAN 1   188   4
THEY NEARLY REACH'D HER HEEL AND IN HER AIR 217   2 DON JUAN 2   116   6
UNTIL THEY REACH'D SOME GALLIOTS PLACED IN LINE . . 371   2 DON JUAN 4   50   6
WHO BADE ON TILL THE HUNDREDS REACH'D ELEVEN 407   2 DON JUAN 4   114   6

REACHED

AT LAST THEY REACHED A QUARTER MOST RETIRED 448   2 DON JUAN 5   64   1
BUT WHEN THEY REACHED THEIR OWN APARTMENTS THERE . . 23   3 DON JUAN 6   34   1
BEFORE THEY REACHED A SPOT TO TAKE EFFECT 80   3 DON JUAN 7   28   4
REACHED THE INTERIOR TALUS OF THE RAMPART 135   3 DON JUAN 8   44   8
BUT THERE HIS PROJECT REACHED ITS UTMOST PITCH . . . 147   3 DON JUAN 8   71   5
UNTIL THEY REACHED AS DAY-BREAK WAS EXPANDING . . . 148   3 DON JUAN 8   72   5
UPON THEM NE'ERTHELESS HAD REACHED THE RAMPART . . . 149   3 DON JUAN 8   75   2
UNTIL HE REACHED THE CASTELLATED RHINE-- 255   3 DON JUAN 10   61   2
THEY REACHED THE HOTEL FORTH STREAMED FROM THE FRONT DOOR . 282   3 DON JUAN 11   30   1
HE REACHED THE ANCIENT WALL THEN STOOD STONE STILL . . 559   3 DON JUAN 16   119   8

REACHERS

I STUDY ALSO BLAIR THE HIGHEST REACHERS 243   2 DON JUAN 2   165   6

REACHES

BUT SOMETIMES IT MAY MEND AND OFTEN REACHES 491   2 DON JUAN 5   138   8

REACHING

THERE WAS SLIGHT CHANCE OF REACHING ANY SHORE . . . 185   2 DON JUAN 2   54   5
WITH A FAR REACHING GLANCE--A PAPHIAN PAIR 466   2 DON JUAN 5   96   V3

READ

SHE READ SOME FRENCH ROMANCES HERE AND THERE 28   2 DON JUAN 1   13   3
IN ALL THESE HE WAS MUCH AND DEEPLY READ 44   2 DON JUAN 1   40   5
SERMONS HE READ AND LECTURES HE ENDURED 47   2 DON JUAN 1   47   1
AND EVERY NOW AND THEN WE READ THEM THROUGH 70   2 DON JUAN 1   90   6
AND THAT THEY HAVE BEEN SO WE ALL HAVE READ 95   2 DON JUAN 1   136   5
THEN THAT THEY'LL READ IT O'ER AGAIN AND SAY . . . 140   2 DON JUAN 1   207   4
AND READ YOUR BIBLE SIR AND MIND YOUR PURSE 147   2 DON JUAN 1   220   8
WHEN SOUTHEY'S READ AND WORDSWORTH UNDERSTOOD . . . 149   2 DON JUAN 1   222   5
A LETTER TOO SHE GAVE (HE NEVER READ IT) 161   2 DON JUAN 2   9   7
HER LETTER OUT AGAIN AND READ IT THROUGH) 166   2 DON JUAN 2   18   8
KNEW (BY TRADITION FOR SHE NE'ER HAD READ) 239   2 DON JUAN 2   158   6
AND READ (THE ONLY BOOK SHE COULD) THE LINES . . . 241   2 DON JUAN 2   162   3
I HATE YOUR POETS SO READ NONE OF THOSE 243   2 DON JUAN 2   165   8
SOME FLIRT SOME READ AND SOME IN VICES GROVEL . . . 263   2 DON JUAN 2   201   V7
FOR THEM AND THEIRS WITH ALL WHO DEIGN TO READ . . 271   2 DON JUAN 2   216   8
'TIS DANGEROUS TO READ OF LOVES UNLAWFUL 282   2 DON JUAN 3   12   8
EACH WAS THE OTHER'S MIRROR AND BUT READ 351   2 DON JUAN 4   13   5
WHERE ARE THE EPITAPHS OUR FATHERS READ 399   2 DON JUAN 4   102   5
READ--WERE IT BUT YOUR GRANDMOTHERS TO VEX 403   2 DON JUAN 4   108   V6
(BECAUSE THE WORLD WON'T READ HIM ALWAYS SNARLING) . 404   2 DON JUAN 4   109   6
YOU READ MY STANZAS AND I READ YOUR FEATURES . . . 405   2 DON JUAN 4   111   3
YOU READ MY STANZAS AND I READ YOUR FEATURES . . . 405   2 DON JUAN 4   111   3
READ OR READ NOT WHAT I AM NOW ESSAYING 70   3 DON JUAN 7   7   3
READ OR READ NOT WHAT I AM NOW ESSAYING 70   3 DON JUAN 7   7   3
AS THEY COULD READ IN ALL EYES NOW TO THEM 104   3 DON JUAN 7   74   2
ALL THAT WE READ HEAR DREAM OF MAN'S DISTRESSES . . 173   3 DON JUAN 8   123   3
READ YOUR OWN HEARTS AND IRELAND'S PRESENT STORY . . 174   3 DON JUAN 8   125   7
WHAT DANIEL READ WAS SHORT-HAND OF THE LORD'S . . . 179   3 DON JUAN 8   134   5
TRUTHS THAT YOU WILL NOT READ IN THE GAZETTES . . . 187   3 DON JUAN 9   10   3
THOU RIDDLE--WHICH ALL READ--NONE UNDERSTAND . . . 210   3 DON JUAN 9   56   V7

```
                                                            PAGE VOL        CANTO STANZA LN
READ   (CONTINUED)
    I WON'T PHILOSOPHIZE AND WILL BE READ  . . . . . . .  238   3 DON JUAN  10    28    8
    WHEN SHE NO MORE COULD READ THE PIOUS PRINT . . . . .  241   3 DON JUAN  10    34    8
    BEFORE HIM SUMMED THE AWFUL SCROLL AND READ IT) . . .  259   3 DON JUAN  10    70    6
    MOST WILLINGLY ALL EVER SEEN OR READ MATTERS  . . . .  268   3 DON JUAN  11     1   V6
    UNTIL THEIR ROYAL RIDDLE'S FULLY READ . . . . . . . .  287   3 DON JUAN  11    40    4
    I CAN'T OBLIGE YOU READER TO READ ON . . . . . . . .   356   3 DON JUAN  12    87    6
    MEANTIME READ ALL THE NATIONAL DEBT SINKERS . . . . .  357   3 DON JUAN  12    89    7
    OH READER   IF THAT THOU CANST READ--AND KNOW  . . .   393   3 DON JUAN  13    73    1
    'TIS NOT ENOUGH TO SPELL OR EVEN TO READ . . . . . .   393   3 DON JUAN  13    73    2
    OR ON THE MORNING PAPERS READ THEIR LECTURES  . . . .  406   3 DON JUAN  13   102    6
    OR WALKED IF FOUL THEY READ OR TOLD A TALE  . . . . .  406   3 DON JUAN  13   104    3
    WHY DRINK WHY READ--TO MAKE SOME HOUR LESS DREARY . .  415   3 DON JUAN  14    11    4
    ROMANCES I NE'ER READ LIKE THOSE I HAVE SEEN  . . . .  444   3 DON JUAN  14    80    2
    TO READ DON QUIXOTE IN THE ORIGINAL  . . . . . . . .   453   3 DON JUAN  14    98    2
    A PRETTY NAME AS ONE WOULD WISH TO READ . . . . . . .  458   3 DON JUAN  15     5    3
    HAD ADELINE READ MALTHUS  I CAN'T TELL  . . . . . . .  472   3 DON JUAN  15    38    1
    I WRITE THE WORLD NOR CARE IF THE WORLD READ  . . . .  482   3 DON JUAN  15    60    3
    BECAUSE IT SOMETIMES AS I'VE SEEN OR READ IT  . . . .  491   3 DON JUAN  15    79    3
    HE READ AN ARTICLE THE KING ATTACKING . . . . . . . .  512   3 DON JUAN  16    26    7
    HE SHUT HIS DOOR AND AFTER HAVING READ  . . . . . . .  512   3 DON JUAN  16    27    2
    FOR ALL OF US HAVE EITHER HEARD OR READ--  . . . . .   538   3 DON JUAN  16    77    3
READER
    WHICH MAKE THE READER ENVY HIS TRANSGRESSIONS . . . .   47   2 DON JUAN   1    47    8
    START NOT STILL CHASTER READER--SHE'LL BE NICE HENCEFORWARD  86  2 DON JUAN  1  120  2
    THIS LICENCE IS TO HOPE THE READER WILL  . . . . . .    86   2 DON JUAN   1   121    1
    BUT FOR THE PRESENT GENTLE READER AND . . . . . . . .  147   2 DON JUAN   1   221    1
    FOR GOD'S SAKE READER TAKE THEM NOT FOR MINE  . . . .  149   2 DON JUAN   1   222    8
    BUT WHY--WE LEAVE THE READER IN THE DARK--  . . . . .  161   2 DON JUAN   2     8    4
    CHASTE READER THEN IN ANY WAY TO PUT . . . . . . . .   282   2 DON JUAN   3    12    3
    THE READER BUT 'TWOULD NOT BE HARD TO BRING . . . . .  332   2 DON JUAN   3    97    6
    THE READER--BUT THE RULE IS --AND I'LL BRING  . . . .  332   2 DON JUAN   3    97   V6
    TO THE KIND READER OF OUR SOBER CLIME . . . . . . . .  347   2 DON JUAN   4     6    1
    THE BRAZEN UPPERMOST) KIND READER PASS  . . . . . . .   34   3 DON JUAN   6    56    3
    TOO GENTLE READER AND MOST SHOCKING SOUNDS  . . . . .  112   3 DON JUAN   8     1    3
    (START NOT KIND READER SINCE GREAT HOMER THOUGHT  . .  126   3 DON JUAN   8    29    6
    READER I HAVE KEPT MY WORD--AT LEAST SO FAR . . . . .  181   3 DON JUAN   8   138    1
    OUR HERO (AND I TRUST KIND READER YOUR'S) --  . . . .  194   3 DON JUAN   9    23    1
    FOR ONE OR TWO DAYS READER WE REQUEST . . . . . . . .  248   3 DON JUAN  10    49    2
    THERE'S GLORY AGAIN FOR YOU GENTLE READER  ALL  . . .  261   3 DON JUAN  10    73    5
    I CAN'T OBLIGE YOU READER TO READ ON . . . . . . . .   356   3 DON JUAN  12    87    6
    REMEMBER READER YOU HAVE HAD BEFORE  . . . . . . . .   356   3 DON JUAN  12    88    2
    OH READER   IF THAT THOU CANST READ--AND KNOW  . . .   393   3 DON JUAN  13    73    1
    TO CONSTITUTE A READER THERE MUST GO  . . . . . . . .  393   3 DON JUAN  13    73    3
    BUT READER THOU HAST PATIENT BEEN OF LATE . . . . . .  393   3 DON JUAN  13    74    1
    AND GENTLE READER WHEN YOU GATHER MEANING . . . . . .  403   3 DON JUAN  13    96    3
    GENT READER NOTHING A MERE SPECULATION  . . . . . . .  413   3 DON JUAN  14     7    2
    AND KEEPS THE ATROCIOUS READER IN SUSPENSE  . . . . .  453   3 DON JUAN  14    97    6
    BUT I MAY HAVE AND YOU TOO READER DREAD IT  . . . . .  488   3 DON JUAN  15    72    8
    GRIM READER DID YOU EVER SEE A GHOST  . . . . . . . .  498   3 DON JUAN  15    95    1
READER'S
    A LIVELY READER'S FANCY DOES THE REST . . . . . . . .   55   3 DON JUAN   6    98    8
    I'LL LEAVE A SINGLE READER'S EYELID DRY . . . . . . .  355   3 DON JUAN  12    86    5
READERS
    FOR FEAR SOME PRUDISH READERS SHOULD GROW SKITTISH . .  141   2 DON JUAN   1   209    7
    BECAUSE ALL GENTLE READERS HAVE THE GIFT  . . . . . .   50   3 DON JUAN   6    88    4
    MANY OF COMMON READERS GIVE A GUESS  . . . . . . . .    82   3 DON JUAN   7    33    3
    I DOUBT FEW READERS E'ER WOULD MOUNT THE BREACH . . .   83   3 DON JUAN   7    35    8
    YE GENTLE READERS AND UNGENTLE WRITERS  . . . . . . .  325   3 DON JUAN  12    20    2
    AND EVIDENCES WHICH REGALE ALL READERS  . . . . . . .  346   3 DON JUAN  12    65    8
    TIRING OLD READERS NOR DISCOVERING NEW  . . . . . . .  414   3 DON JUAN  14    10    6
READIEST
    THE READIEST WAY OF REASONING WITH COSSACQUES . . . .  158   3 DON JUAN   8    93    8
READILY
    O'ERTHROWS THE SAME WE READILY FORGET . . . . . . . .    8   3 DON JUAN   6     4    3
    WHICH WITH THE BLOOD TOO READILY WILL CLAIM KIN . . .  244   3 DON JUAN  10    40    6
    WAS NOT AT FIRST TOO READILY IMPRESS'D  . . . . . . .  448   3 DON JUAN  14    88    8
    TO LIKE TOO READILY OR TOO HIGH BRED . . . . . . . .   460   3 DON JUAN  15    10    4
READINESS
    HIS READINESS TO FEEL HIS PULSE AND TELL  . . . . . .  514   3 DON JUAN  16    32    7
READING
    AN OPIUM DREAM OF TOO MUCH YOUTH AND READING  . . . .  354   2 DON JUAN   4    19    2
    AS AFTER READING ATHANASIUS' CURSE . . . . . . . . .    17   3 DON JUAN   6    23    2
    IF THIS BE THE RIGHT READING--'TIS NO MATTER  . . . .   70   3 DON JUAN   7     8    2
    THINK HOW THE JOYS OF READING A GAZETTE . . . . . . .  174   3 DON JUAN   8   125    1
    'TIS A GREAT MORAL LESSON THEY ARE READING  . . . . .  341   3 DON JUAN  12    55    4
    BUT THEN WITH WHOM   THERE WAS THE SAGE MISS READING .  473   3 DON JUAN  15    40    3
    THOUGH ONCE SHE WAS SEEN READING THE BATH GUIDE . . .  525   3 DON JUAN  16    50    2
READINGS
    THERE'S MORE THAN ONE EDITION AND THE READINGS . . . .  127   2 DON JUAN   1   189    5
READY
    A READY ANSWER WHICH AT ONCE ENABLES . . . . . . . .   117   2 DON JUAN   1   175    2
    I WAS MOST READY TO RETURN A BLOW . . . . . . . . . .  143   2 DON JUAN   1   212    6
    THANK HEAVEN I'VE GOT NO METAPHOR QUITE READY . . . .  160   2 DON JUAN   2     6    7
    AND ZOE WHEN THE EGGS WERE READY AND . . . . . . . .   234   2 DON JUAN   2   146    1
    WHEN JUAN WOKE HE FOUND SOME GOOD THINGS READY . . . .  246   2 DON JUAN   2   171    4
    SO LEAVING EACH THEIR PRIEST AND PRAYER-BOOK READY . .  280   2 DON JUAN   3     9    7
    THE GREATER PART OF THESE WERE READY SPREAD . . . . .  310   2 DON JUAN   3    69    6
    HAD SOMETHING READY UPON MOST OCCASIONS--  . . . . .   319   2 DON JUAN   3    84    4
```

656

READY   (CONTINUED)

	PAGE	VOL	CANTO	STANZA	LN
THE MOST BY READY CASH--BUT ALL HAVE PRICES	425	2 DON JUAN	5	27	7
AND WHEN THE OLD NEGRO TOLD HIM TO GET READY	453	2 DON JUAN	5	73	7
BE READY BY THE SECRET PORTAL'S SIDE	62	3 DON JUAN	6	113	3
THE RUSSIANS NOW WERE READY TO ATTACK	73	3 DON JUAN	7	14	1
IF HOMER HAD FOUND MORTARS READY MADE	106	3 DON JUAN	7	78	4
DAMSELS AND DANCES REVELS READY MONEY	235	3 DON JUAN	10	21	7
OTHERS AGAIN WERE READY TO MAINTAIN	244	3 DON JUAN	10	40	7
YES READY MONEY IS ALADDIN'S LAMP	321	3 DON JUAN	12	12	8
AND YOU MAY GET THE WEDDING DRESSES READY	343	3 DON JUAN	12	59	8
NOR IS SHE QUITE SO READY WITH HER SMILE	351	3 DON JUAN	12	76	4
ALAS TO THEM OF READY CASH BEREFT	379	3 DON JUAN	13	45	3
THEN THERE WAS SMALL-TALK READY WHEN REQUIRED	408	3 DON JUAN	13	108	4
ON READY MONEY OR A DRAFT ON RANSOM	459	3 DON JUAN	15	8	8
THE SILVERY BELL RUNG NOT FOR DINNER READY	482	3 DON JUAN	15	61	6
READY FOR JAIL THEIR PLACE OF CONVALESCENCE	530	3 DON JUAN	16	61	2
NO LONGER READY EARS AND SHORT-HAND PENS	540	3 DON JUAN	16	83	4

REAL

	PAGE	VOL	CANTO	STANZA	LN
ALTHOUGH NO DOUBT HIS REAL INTENT WAS GOOD	45	2 DON JUAN	1	43	4
A REAL HUSBAND ALWAYS IS SUSPICIOUS	74	2 DON JUAN	1	99	1
THEIR REAL LUES OR OUR PSEUDO-SYPHILIS	92	2 DON JUAN	1	131	8
I'VE SEEN MUCH FINER WOMEN RIPE AND REAL	218	2 DON JUAN	2	118	7
DEADLY AND QUICK AND CRUSHING YET AS REAL	262	2 DON JUAN	2	199	7
THIS SORT OF ADORATION OF THE REAL	269	2 DON JUAN	2	211	7
THE REAL NAME OF THE FAIR VERONESE--	273	2 DON JUAN	2	V 2	2
YOU NEVER COULD DIVINE HIS REAL THOUGHT	296	2 DON JUAN	3	41	4
BUT NEVER IN HIS REAL AND SERIOUS MOOD	300	2 DON JUAN	3	48	2
THEY WERE NOT MADE IN THE REAL WORLD TO FILL	352	2 DON JUAN	4	15	3
WAS MORE TRIUMPHANT AND NOT MUCH LESS REAL	396	2 DON JUAN	4	96	8
IF PEOPLE WOULD BUT SEE ITS REAL DRIFT--	50	3 DON JUAN	6	88	2
AS THE REAL PURPOSE OF A PYRAMID	180	3 DON JUAN	8	137	8
DON JUAN WHO WAS REAL OR IDEAL--	234	3 DON JUAN	10	20	1
EXISTS WHEN THE ONCE THINKERS ARE LESS REAL	234	3 DON JUAN	10	20	3
A THOROUGH VARMINT AND A REAL SWELL	276	3 DON JUAN	11	17	6
THAT'S YOUR AFFAIR NOT MINE A REAL SPIRIT	356	3 DON JUAN	12	87	7
BY THAT REAL EPIC UNTO ALL WHO HAVE THOUGHT	363	3 DON JUAN	13	9	8
THE REAL PORTRAIT OF THE HIGHEST TRIBE	418	3 DON JUAN	14	20	7
WHICH BEARS THE SAME RELATION TO THE REAL	419	3 DON JUAN	14	22	3
THE REAL SUFFERINGS OF THEIR SHE CONDITION	420	3 DON JUAN	14	24	4
NO REAL LIKENESS--LIKE THE OLD TYRIAN VEST	505	3 DON JUAN	16	10	5
SOME DOUBT HOW MUCH OF ADELINE WAS REAL	546	3 DON JUAN	16	96	8
ARE SO DIVINE THAT I MUST DEEM THEM REAL--	553	3 DON JUAN	16	107	8

REALITIES

	PAGE	VOL	CANTO	STANZA	LN
AND SOMETIMES MIX'D UP FANCIES WITH REALITIES	32	2 DON JUAN	1	20	6

REALITY

	PAGE	VOL	CANTO	STANZA	LN
BY THE WATCHMAN OR SOME SUCH REALITY	237	2 DON JUAN	2	152	4
THE WOMEN UP--BECAUSE IN SAD REALITY	501	2 DON JUAN	5	157	2
AND ALMOST EVERY DAY IN SAD REALITY	108	3 DON JUAN	7	83	3
'TIS SAID IT MAKES REALITY MORE BEARABLE	495	3 DON JUAN	15	89	5
BUT WHAT'S REALITY WHO HAS ITS CLUE	495	3 DON JUAN	15	89	6

REALLY

	PAGE	VOL	CANTO	STANZA	LN
I'M REALLY PUZZLED WHAT TO THINK OR SAY	59	2 DON JUAN	1	68	7
I REALLY DON'T KNOW WHAT NOR JULIA EITHER	65	2 DON JUAN	1	81	8
THE CHIMNEY--WHICH WOULD REALLY HOLD A LOVER	104	2 DON JUAN	1	153	4
(I REALLY MADAM WONDER AT YOUR TASTE--	115	2 DON JUAN	1	172	4
AT LAST THEY DID GET AT IT REALLY BUT	171	2 DON JUAN	2	28	5
THAT SOME I REALLY THINK DO NEVER DIE	190	2 DON JUAN	2	65	4
MEN REALLY KNOW NOT WHAT GOOD WATER'S WORTH	201	2 DON JUAN	2	84	4
AND SO IN SHORT THE GIRLS THEY REALLY WERE	222	2 DON JUAN	2	124	5
WHILE VENUS FILLS THE HEART (WITHOUT HEART REALLY	246	2 DON JUAN	2	170	1
AND REALLY LONGED TO KISS HER--LIKE A VILLAIN	268	2 DON JUAN	2	209	V8
ARE THINGS THAT REALLY TAKE AWAY THE BREATH	309	2 DON JUAN	3	66	6
BUT WHICH TO CHOOSE I REALLY HARDLY KNOW	357	2 DON JUAN	4	25	4
THE LITTLE FELLOW REALLY LOOK'D QUITE HEARTY	388	2 DON JUAN	4	81	5
I REALLY THINK YET JUAN'S THEN ORDEAL	396	2 DON JUAN	4	96	7
AND LONG BESIDES -- OH IF 'TIS REALLY SO	419	2 DON JUAN	5	16	6
SAID JUAN BUT I REALLY DON'T SEE HOW	422	2 DON JUAN	5	23	2
FOR HIS OWN PART HE REALLY SHOULD REJOICE	452	2 DON JUAN	5	70	1
TO OPE THIS DOOR WHICH THEY COULD REALLY DO	463	2 DON JUAN	5	89	3
I'VE KNOWN SOME ODD ONES WHICH SEEMED REALLY PLANNED	45	3 DON JUAN	6	78	5
I DID--WHAT NEXT--I REALLY HARDLY KNOW	98	3 DON JUAN	7	61	2
WHICH REALLY POURED AS IF ALL HELL WERE RAINING	121	3 DON JUAN	8	20	6
THE BRITON MUST BE BOLD WHO REALLY DURST	136	3 DON JUAN	8	48	5
JOHNSON WHO REALLY LOVED HIM IN HIS WAY	162	3 DON JUAN	8	102	2
FOR I MAINTAIN THAT IT IS REALLY GOOD	193	3 DON JUAN	9	22	2
JUST AS HE REALLY PROMISED SOMETHING GREAT	298	3 DON JUAN	11	60	2
MY NATURAL TEMPER'S REALLY AUGHT BUT STERN	300	3 DON JUAN	11	63	5
OF MAN IT IS--I REALLY SCARCE KNOW WHAT	315	3 DON JUAN	12	1	3
WHY--WHY--BESIDES FRED REALLY WAS ATTACHED	332	3 DON JUAN	12	35	1
I MEAN TO SHOW THINGS REALLY AS THEY ARE	335	3 DON JUAN	12	40	2
THAT NOBLE SIGHT WHEN REALLY FREE THE NATION	354	3 DON JUAN	12	83	2
IF THAT A BONNE FORTUNE BE REALLY BONNE	438	3 DON JUAN	14	64	8
WHICH REALLY KNEW OR THOUGHT IT KNEW NO GUILE	438	3 DON JUAN	14	65	2
AND REALLY IF THE SAGE SUBLIME AND ATTIC	494	3 DON JUAN	15	86	3
SO MUCH THE BARD HAD REALLY BEEN PROPHETIC	525	3 DON JUAN	16	50	5
NOW THIS HE REALLY RATHER TOOK AMISS	544	3 DON JUAN	16	92	3

REALM

	PAGE	VOL	CANTO	STANZA	LN
OR PLUNGED A PROVINCE OR A REALM IN GRIEF	101	3 DON JUAN	7	68	4

REALM'S

	PAGE	VOL	CANTO	STANZA	LN
FEEDS YOU BY PRINTING HALF THE REALM'S STARVATION--	200	3 DON JUAN	9	35	8

657

		PAGE	VOL	CANTO	STANZA	LN

REALMS
AND STILL IT HALF CALLS UP THE REALMS OF FAIRY . . . . . 413 2 DON JUAN 5 4 3
THE SPOTS WHICH WERE HER REALMS FOR EVERMORE . . . . . 443 2 DON JUAN 5 57 4
THE GRAND NAPOLEON OF THE REALMS OF RHYME . . . . . . 296 3 DON JUAN 11 55 8
NOR WISHED OF SUCH FRAIL REALMS TO BE THE KING . . . . 296 3 DON JUAN 11 55 V6

REAP
WHETHER THEY MAY SOW SCEPTICISM TO REAP HELL . . . . . 195 3 DON JUAN 9 25 5
AND PLANT AND REAP AND SPIN AND GRIND AND SOW . . . . . 202 3 DON JUAN 9 40 4
PROFIT HE CARED NOT FOR LET OTHERS REAP IT . . . . . . 536 3 DON JUAN 16 75 4

REAPERS
YE RIGID GUTS OF REAPERS--I TRANSLATE . . . . 190 3 DON JUAN 9 15 2

REAPING
FEEL RAPTURE BUT NOT SUCH TRUE JOY ARE REAPING . . . . 261 2 DON JUAN 2 196 7
REAPING ALLUSIONS PRIVATE AND INGLORIOUS . . . . 369 3 DON JUAN 13 25 4

REAR
THEIR WHILE TO REAR WHOLE HOTBEDS IN THEIR WORKS . . . 434 2 DON JUAN 5 42 7
SOME SUCKING HERO IS COMPELLED TO REAR . . . . 108 3 DON JUAN 7 83 4
THE WORST TO KNOW IT--WHEN THE MOUNTAINS REAR . . . . 412 3 DON JUAN 14 5 4

REAR'D
IN SICILY--ALL SINGERS DULY REAR'D . . . . 388 2 DON JUAN 4 80 5

REARED
THEIR NAMES WHO REARED IT BUT HUGE HOUSES FIT ILL-- . . 444 2 DON JUAN 5 59 5
IS LIKE--A DUCKLING BY DAME PARTLETT REARED . . . . . 564 3 DON JUAN 17 4 6

REARS
IS THAT WHATEVER BAR THE REASON REARS . . . . 504 3 DON JUAN 16 7 6

REASON
('TWAS SNOW THAT BROUGHT SAINT ANTHONY TO REASON) . . . 57 2 DON JUAN 1 64 4
THAT DONNA JULIA KNEW THE REASON WHY . . . . 60 2 DON JUAN 1 70 6
THE SUN NO DOUBT IS THE PREVAILING REASON . . . . . 76 2 DON JUAN 1 102 4
'TWAS NOT WITHOUT SOME REASON FOR THE WIND . . . . . 170 2 DON JUAN 2 26 1
DECIDED THUS AND SHOW'D GOOD REASON WHY . . . . . . 281 2 DON JUAN 3 11 6
OF THE TRUE REASON OF HIS NOT BEING SAD . . . . . . 289 2 DON JUAN 3 26 5
THERE WAS NO MIGHTY REASON TO BE PLEASED . . . . . . 296 2 DON JUAN 3 40 3
IS THIS A FANCY WHICH OUR REASON SCORNS . . . . . . 338 2 DON JUAN 3 108 7
SO THAT THERE WAS NO REASON FOR THEIR LOVES . . . . . 354 2 DON JUAN 4 19 7
POOR FELLOW FOR SOME REASON SURELY BAD . . . . . . 429 2 DON JUAN 5 34 1
SOME TO MEN'S FEELINGS OTHERS TO THEIR REASON . . . . 437 2 DON JUAN 5 48 2
FOR REASON THINKS ALL REASONING OUT OF SEASON . . . . 437 2 DON JUAN 5 48 4
AND THAT'S THE REASON I'M SO MELANCHOLY . . . . . . 444 2 DON JUAN 5 58 8
I HAVE NO AUTHORITY TO TELL THE REASON . . . . . . 454 2 DON JUAN 5 74 8
'TIS TRUE THE REASON IS THAT THE BASHAW . . . . . . 498 2 DON JUAN 5 152 7
HER REASON BEING WEAK HER PASSIONS STRONG . . . . . 10 3 DON JUAN 6 8 5
'GAINST REASON--REASON NE'ER WAS HAND-AND-GLOVE . . . 219 3 DON JUAN 9 74 5
'GAINST REASON--REASON NE'ER WAS HAND-AND-GLOVE . . . 219 3 DON JUAN 9 74 5
I KNOW NO OTHER REASON WHATSOE'ER . . . . 230 3 DON JUAN 10 11 2
AND THAT'S THE REASON HE HIMSELF'S SO DIRTY . . . . . 232 3 DON JUAN 10 15 2
I DON'T KNOW WHAT THE REASON IS--THE AIR . . . . . . 270 3 DON JUAN 11 5 6
OF SOBER REASON WHERESOE'ER IT MOVES . . . . 284 3 DON JUAN 11 33 6
YOU HAD REASON--'TWAS THAT A YOUNG CHILD OF GRACE . . 329 3 DON JUAN 12 29 2
ALSO THERE BIN ANOTHER PIOUS REASON . . . . 370 3 DON JUAN 13 26 1
THE POSTBOYS HAVE NO REASON TO DISPARAGE . . . . . . 379 3 DON JUAN 13 46 6
AND THAT'S THE REASON WHY YOU DO--OR DO NOT . . . . . 413 3 DON JUAN 14 6 8
THE REASON WHY IS EASY TO DETERMINE . . . . 416 3 DON JUAN 14 15 4
WITHOUT STRONG REASON OF THOSE SORTS OF THINGS . . . . 439 3 DON JUAN 14 66 4
HAD LOVERS NOT SOME REASON TO REGRET . . . . 452 3 DON JUAN 14 95 3
WHOM I HAD NOT SOME REASON TO REGRET . . . . 452 3 DON JUAN 14 95 V3
THE MORE'S THE REASON WHY YOU OUGHT TO STAY . . . . . 459 3 DON JUAN 15 9 4
THAT IS NO DOUBT THE ONLY REASON WHEREFORE . . . . . 470 3 DON JUAN 15 31 8
AS USUAL--THE SAME REASON WHICH SHE LATE DID . . . . 478 3 DON JUAN 15 50 8
AND WHEREFORE NOT A REASONABLE REASON . . . . . . 478 3 DON JUAN 15 51 1
IS THAT WHATEVER BAR THE REASON REARS . . . . 504 3 DON JUAN 16 7 6

REASONABLE
MAN BEING REASONABLE MUST GET DRUNK . . . . 250 2 DON JUAN 2 179 1
AND WHEREFORE NOT A REASONABLE REASON . . . . . . 478 3 DON JUAN 15 51 1

REASONING
FOR REASON THINKS ALL REASONING OUT OF SEASON . . . . 437 2 DON JUAN 5 48 4
THE READIEST WAY OF REASONING WITH COSSACQUES . . . . 158 3 DON JUAN 8 93 8

REASON'S
THE REASON'S OBVIOUS IF THERE'S AN ECLAT . . . . . . 352 3 DON JUAN 12 78 1

REASONS
THIS I WILL SAY--MY REASONS ARE MY OWN-- . . . . . . 50 2 DON JUAN 1 52 2
BUT THERE WERE AMPLE REASONS FOR IT NONE . . . . . . 116 2 DON JUAN 1 174 5
THERE WERE SOME OTHER REASONS THE FIRST WAS . . . . . 199 2 DON JUAN 2 81 4
FOR BOTH SIDES I COULD MANY REASONS SHOW . . . . . . 357 2 DON JUAN 4 25 6
ALONE FOR REASONS WHICH DON'T MATTER YOU . . . . . . 30 3 DON JUAN 6 49 2
THEIR REASONS WERE UNCERTAINTY OR SHAME . . . . . . 132 3 DON JUAN 8 38 5
FOR REASONS WHICH I CHOOSE TO KEEP APART . . . . . . 419 3 DON JUAN 14 21 6
FOR CERTAIN REASONS MY BELIEF IS SERIOUS . . . . . . 498 3 DON JUAN 15 95 8

RE-ASSURE
AND LONG HE PAUSED TO RE-ASSURE HIS EYES . . . . . . 294 2 DON JUAN 3 37 6

REBEL
(OR WAS BEFORE PERU LEARN'D TO REBEL) . . . . 159 2 DON JUAN 2 5 4
TO GIVE SOME REBEL PACHA A CRAVAT . . . . 463 2 DON JUAN 5 89 7
BY REBEL PACHAS AND ENCROACHING GIAOURS . . . . . . 497 2 DON JUAN 5 150 7

REBELS
THE GLOSSY REBELS MOCK'D THE JETTY STAIN . . . . . . 314 2 DON JUAN 3 75 4
HE ADDED MODESTLY WHEN REBELS RAILED) . . . . 535 3 DON JUAN 16 72 6

REBUILT
FOR FAME'S A CARTHAGE NOT SO SOON REBUILT . . . . . 352 3 DON JUAN 12 78 8

	PAGE	VOL	CANTO	STANZA	LN
REBUKE					
WOE TO THE MAN WHO VENTURES A REBUKE	429	3 DON JUAN 14	43	5
REBUKED					
THAN FINDING THUS THEIR GENIUS STAND REBUKED	479	3 DON JUAN 15	53	6
HER GRACE TOO HAD A SORT OF AIR REBUKED--	568	3 DON JUAN 17	14	6
REBUS					
DE REBUS CUNCTIS ET QUIBUSDAM ALIIS	502	3 DON JUAN 16	3	8
RECALL					
AND LIFE YIELDS NOTHING FURTHER TO RECALL	90	2 DON JUAN 1	127	5
OF MONITORS ADAPTED TO RECALL	308	2 DON JUAN 3	65	3
(IF 'TIS NOT VAIN EXAMPLES TO RECALL)	333	3 DON JUAN 12	37	6
EXISTS--AND WHERE THAT SHALL I NOT RECALL	499	3 DON JUAN 15	96	4
I DO NOT SPEAK PROFANELY TO RECALL	503	3 DON JUAN 16	6	5
MAY SIT LIKE THAT OF NESSUS AND RECALL	505	3 DON JUAN 16	11	3
SITS LIKE A SEDATIVE WHILE WE RECALL	505	3 DON JUAN 16	11	V3
SHE WAITED UNTIL JUSTICE COULD RECALL	533	3 DON JUAN 16	67	5
RECALL'D					
RECALL'D HIS ANSWERING SPIRITS BACK FROM DEATH	215	2 DON JUAN 2	113	4
SWORE PRAISES AND RECALL'D THEIR FORMER FIRES	425	3 DON JUAN 14	34	6
RECALLED					
THEN BY DEGREES RECALLED HIS ENERGIES	511	3 DON JUAN 16	25	4
RECEDING					
TO SEE ONE'S NATIVE LAND RECEDING THROUGH	163	2 DON JUAN 2	12	2
BEHELD HIS NATIVE SPAIN RECEDING FAR	164	2 DON JUAN 2	14	2
RECEIPT					
DENYING THE RECEIPT OF WHAT IT COST	142	2 DON JUAN 1	210	6
RECEIPTS					
RECEIPTS IN FULL BEGAN TO THINK OF DINING	426	2 DON JUAN 5	29	8
RECEIVE					
DREST TO RECEIVE SO MUCH GOOD COMPANY	106	2 DON JUAN 1	156	8
(SO CHILDREN CUTTING TEETH RECEIVE A CORAL)	141	2 DON JUAN 1	209	4
WHO HATH PRODUCED AND WILL RECEIVE THE SOUL	336	2 DON JUAN 3	104	8
ITS FARTHER COURSE BUT MUST RECEIVE ITS WRECK	60	3 DON JUAN 6	108	8
HIS ORDERS ALSO TO RECEIVE HIS PENSIONS	137	3 DON JUAN 8	49	7
THAT--BUT MY CHASTER EAR WILL NOT RECEIVE	336	3 DON JUAN 12	43	4
LIKE ALL WHO GIVE AND EKE RECEIVE IT GRATIS	469	3 DON JUAN 15	29	2
RECEIVE AS GOSPEL AND WHICH GROW MORE ROOTED	503	3 DON JUAN 16	6	7
RECEIVED					
THE ANVIL OF HIS SPEECH RECEIVED THE HAMMER	111	2 DON JUAN 1	163	3
ACCORDING TO DIRECTION THEN RECEIVED	161	2 DON JUAN 2	9	2
WITH SOME REMORSE RECEIVED (THOUGH FIRST DENIED)	193	2 DON JUAN 2	71	5
RECEIVED A CUT WHICH CLOVE HIS TURBAN THROUGH	370	2 DON JUAN 4	48	V8
AS IF SHE HAD RECEIVED A SUDDEN BLOW	58	3 DON JUAN 6	105	6
BECAUSE IT THEN RECEIVED NO INJURY	117	3 DON JUAN 8	10	5
RECEIVED INSTRUCTIONS HOW TO PLAY HIS CARD	247	3 DON JUAN 10	46	6
AND WAS RECEIVED WITH ALL THE DUE GRIMACE	285	3 DON JUAN 11	35	3
BUT JUAN WAS RECEIVED WITH MUCH EMPRESSEMENT --	288	3 DON JUAN 11	42	1
WAS WELL RECEIVED BY PERSONS OF CONDITION	290	3 DON JUAN 11	45	8
AND JUAN WAS RECEIVED AS HATH BEEN SAID	355	3 DON JUAN 12	85	1
RECEIVES					
THE FAMILY VAULT RECEIVES ANOTHER LORD	306	3 DON JUAN 11	75	8
AS FAR AS I KNOW THAT THE CHURCH RECEIVES	444	3 DON JUAN 14	78	4
THE DEBT UNSUNK YET SINKS ALL IT RECEIVES	548	3 DON JUAN 16	99	8
RECEIVING					
RECEIVING SPRITES WITH SYMPATHETIC VAPOUR	512	3 DON JUAN 16	26	3
RECENT					
JUST LIKE A BLACK EYE IN A RECENT SCUFFLE	205	2 DON JUAN 2	92	7
OF CLAP-TRAP WHICH YOUR RECENT POETS PRIZE	222	2 DON JUAN 2	124	4
AND IN THE FIRE HIS RECENT RAGS THEY SCATTER'D	240	2 DON JUAN 2	160	3
PERHAPS HIS RECENT WOUNDS MIGHT HELP A LITTLE	396	2 DON JUAN 4	95	8
PERHAPS HIS RECENT LOSS OF BLOOD MIGHT PULL	415	2 DON JUAN 5	8	5
DECLARED WITH ALL HIS GRAND DISCOVERIES RECENT	69	3 DON JUAN 7	5	6
IS ONE OF WHICH THERE'S NO DESCRIPTION RECENT	416	3 DON JUAN 14	15	3
RECENTLY					
WHOSE VICTORIES HAD RECENTLY INCREASED	52	3 DON JUAN 6	92	6
RECEPTACLES					
AND IN THE WORN AND WILD RECEPTACLES	253	2 DON JUAN 2	184	4
RECEPTION					
LAMBRO'S RECEPTION AT HIS PEOPLE'S BANQUET	294	2 DON JUAN 3	36	7
RECESS					
IN THAT REMOTE RECESS WHICH YOU MAY SEE--	450	2 DON JUAN 5	66	7
I SAY UNLOCKING THE RECESS PULLED FORTH	450	2 DON JUAN 5	67	2
RECESSES					
THOSE GAY RECESSES--MANY A PRECIOUS STONE	54	3 DON JUAN 6	97	5
RECHERCHE					
WAS JUAN A RECHERCHE WELCOME GUEST	370	3 DON JUAN 13	28	2
RECITAL					
HERE RAUCOCANTI'S ELOQUENT RECITAL	393	2 DON JUAN 4	90	1
RECITATIVE					
AN ASS WAS PRACTISING RECITATIVE	391	2 DON JUAN 4	87	8
RECITE					
THEY MAKE YOU DREAD THAT THEY'LL RECITE THEM TOO	79	2 DON JUAN 1	108	4
RECITED					
MUST BE RECITED AND--WITHOUT A BRIBE	187	3 DON JUAN 9	10	6
RECK					
I RECK NOT IF AN ACORN GAVE IT BIRTH	436	3 DON JUAN 14	59	4
RECK'D					
AND RECK'D NOT WHO AROUND HER PILLOW SAT	378	2 DON JUAN 4	63	4
RECKON					
SOME RECKON WOMEN BY THEIR SUNS OR YEARS	230	3 DON JUAN 10	10	7

659

RECKON'D
AND THEN THE LEAK THEY RECKON'D TO REDUCE . . . . . . 172 2 DON JUAN 2 30 2
I THINK IT MUST BE RECKON'D BY ITS LENGTH . . . . 254 2 DON JUAN 2 186 8
HEAVEN KNOWS HOW LONG--NO DOUBT THEY NEVER RECKON'D . . . 254 2 DON JUAN 2 187 2
RECKONED
WAS RECKONED A CONSIDERABLE TIME . . . . 296 3 DON JUAN 11 55 7
THE LAST'S A MIRACLE AND SUCH WAS RECKONED . . . . . 365 3 DON JUAN 13 13 7
RECKONING
NOT RECKONING HIM TO BE A BASE BEZONIAN . . . . . . 140 3 DON JUAN 8 56 7
RECLAIM'D
AND MEAN NEXT WINTER TO BE QUITE RECLAIM'D . . . . . 85 2 DON JUAN 1 119 8
RECLINED
UNDER A CANOPY AND THERE RECLINED . . . . 466 2 DON JUAN 5 95 2
RECOGNISED
SHE RECOGNISED NO BEING AND NO SPOT . . . . . . 379 2 DON JUAN 4 64 3
RECOGNIZE
WHAT CAN YE RECOGNIZE--A GILDED CLOUD . . . . . . 373 3 DON JUAN 13 33 8
RECOGNIZED
HE RECOGNIZED AN OFFICER OF RANK . . . . 141 3 DON JUAN 8 57 8
RECOLLECT
AND RECOLLECT A POET NOTHING LOSES . . . . 14 2 DON JUAN D 8 5
MEANTIME THEY'LL DOUBTLESS PLEASE TO RECOLLECT . . . . 141 2 DON JUAN 1 209 5
A PRETTY TOWN I RECOLLECT IT WELL-- . . . . . . 159 2 DON JUAN 2 5 2
I RECOLLECT GREAT BRITAIN'S COAST LOOKS WHITE . . . . 163 2 DON JUAN 2 12 5
AND RECOLLECT THE TIME WHEN ALL THIS CANT . . . . 397 2 DON JUAN 4 98 7
SO RECOLLECT THAT THE EXTREMEST GRACE . . . . . . 482 2 DON JUAN 5 123 6
BY YOUR REFUSAL RECOLLECT HER RAGING . . . . . . 486 2 DON JUAN 5 130 5
OR RECOLLECT ALL THAT WAS SAID OR SUNG . . . . . 486 2 DON JUAN 5 130 6
OR PRETTY IS A THING TO RECOLLECT . . . . 199 3 DON JUAN 9 34 5
I RECOLLECT SOME INNKEEPERS WHO DON'T . . . . . . 275 3 DON JUAN 11 15 3
AND RECOLLECT THE WORK IS ONLY FICTION . . . . . 311 3 DON JUAN 11 88 4
OF ALL THE MUSES THAT I RECOLLECT . . . . 502 3 DON JUAN 16 2 5
RECOLLECTING
THEN RECOLLECTING THE WHOLE EMPRESS NOR . . . . . 211 3 DON JUAN 9 58 1
RECOLLECTION
LIKE ADAM'S RECOLLECTION OF HIS FALL . . . . . . 90 2 DON JUAN 1 127 3
AND SOME OF THEM HAD LOST THEIR RECOLLECTION . . . . 199 2 DON JUAN 2 80 3
THE ONLY TWO THAT IN MY RECOLLECTION . . . . . . 281 2 DON JUAN 3 10 1
HER RECOLLECTION ON HER FLASH'D THE DREAM . . . . . 380 2 DON JUAN 4 66 4
PERHAPS FROM HEARSAY OR FROM RECOLLECTION . . . . . 238 3 DON JUAN 10 27 2
RECOLLECTS
AND WHO THAT RECOLLECTS YOUNG YEARS AND LOVES-- . . . 228 3 DON JUAN 10 6 4
RECOMMENCE
COULD RECOMMENCE TO HUNT HIS HONEST MAN . . . . . 281 3 DON JUAN 11 28 2
TO RECOMMENCE IN AUGUST--NOW WAS DONE . . . . . . 377 3 DON JUAN 13 42 2
RECOMMEND
I RECOMMEND AS MUCH TO EVERY WIFE . . . . 48 2 DON JUAN 1 48 8
I RECOMMEND YOUNG LADIES TO MAKE TRIAL . . . . . 64 2 DON JUAN 1 78 8
WHICH FORTUNE PLAINLY SEEMED TO RECOMMEND . . . . 451 2 DON JUAN 5 69 5
A KIND OF TRIUMPH I'LL NOT RECOMMEND . . . . . . 491 3 DON JUAN 15 79 2
RECOMMENDATION
RECOMMENDATION--AND TO BE WELL DREST . . . . . . 371 3 DON JUAN 13 28 7
RECOMMENDED
MOST STRONGLY RECOMMENDED AN ASSAULT . . . . . . 83 3 DON JUAN 7 35 4
SHE ALSO RECOMMENDED HIM TO GOD . . . . 240 3 DON JUAN 10 32 1
RECOMPENSES
GREAT MEN HAVE ALWAYS SCORNED GREAT RECOMPENSES . . . 186 3 DON JUAN 9 8 1
RECONCIL'D
SHOWING A MUCH MORE RECONCIL'D DEMEANOUR . . . . . 388 2 DON JUAN 4 81 7
RECONCILE
WOULD RECONCILE HIM TO THE BUSINESS QUITE . . . . 452 2 DON JUAN 5 71 6
RECONCILED
AND RECONCILED ALL QUALITIES WHICH GRACE MAN . . . . 368 3 DON JUAN 13 21 7
RECONCILIATION
THEIR FRIENDS HAD TRIED AT RECONCILIATION . . . . 38 2 DON JUAN 1 32 1
RECONNOITRE
HAD SEIZED THE LUCKY HOUR TO RECONNOITRE . . . . . 273 3 DON JUAN 11 11 4
RECORD
STILL I'LL RECORD A FEW IF BUT TO ENCREASE . . . . 74 3 DON JUAN 7 15 1
BUT I'M TOO GREAT A PATRIOT TO RECORD . . . . . 77 3 DON JUAN 7 22 2
CALLS ILION'S THE FIRST DAMAGES ON RECORD . . . . 209 3 DON JUAN 9 53 8
THE OLDEST THING ON RECORD AND YET NEW . . . . . 214 3 DON JUAN 9 64 8
THOU MORNING POST SOLE RECORD OF THE PANNELS . . . . 308 3 DON JUAN 11 80 4
RECORDED
RECORDED IN THE MONITEUR AND COURIER . . . . . . 22 2 DON JUAN 1 2 8
RECORDS
RECORDS RAVENNA'S CARNAGE ON ITS FACE . . . . . . 400 2 DON JUAN 4 103 7
RECOURSE
TO WHOM IT MAY BE BEST TO HAVE RECOURSE-- . . . . 38 2 DON JUAN 1 32 4
AND THEN SHE HAD RECOURSE TO NODS AND SIGNS . . . . 241 2 DON JUAN 2 162 1
THAT I MUST HAVE RECOURSE TO BLACK BOHEA . . . . . 372 2 DON JUAN 4 52 6
TO WHICH EMBARRASSED PEOPLE HAVE RECOURSE . . . . 56 3 DON JUAN 6 100 8
WHICH MADE HIM HAVE RECOURSE UNTO HIS SPOON . . . . 513 3 DON JUAN 16 30 5
RECOVER
THIS WEAKNESS IN A FEW HOURS AND RECOVER . . . . . 47 3 DON JUAN 6 83 8
RECOVERY
DESPAIR OF ALL RECOVERY SPOILS LONGEVITY . . . . . 190 2 DON JUAN 2 64 7
RECREATIONS
OF GENTLE DAMES AMONG WHOSE RECREATIONS . . . . . 223 3 DON JUAN 9 82 6

RECRUITED
    RECRUITED ALL WITH CONSTANT MARRIED MEN 323   3 DON JUAN 12   16   2
RECRUITS
    WAS TEACHING HIS RECRUITS TO USE THE BAYONET   92   3 DON JUAN 7   51   8
    SAVE WED A YEAR I HATE RECRUITS WITH WIVES 102   3 DON JUAN 7   70   8
RED
    THE SUN ROSE RED AND FIERY A SURE SIGN   189   2 DON JUAN 2   62   1
    OR THE RED SEA--BUT THE SEA IS NOT RED   231   2 DON JUAN 2   141   8
    OR THE RED SEA--BUT THE SEA IS NOT RED   231   2 DON JUAN 2   141   8
    RED SUN SINKS DOWN BEHIND THE AZURE HILL 252   2 DON JUAN 2   183   2
    WHILE YOUTH'S HOT WISHES IN OUR RED VEINS REVEL 345   2 DON JUAN 4   2   5
    FROM TWO SMART SABRE GASHES DEEP AND RED-- 370   2 DON JUAN 4   49   7
    WITH NOTHING LIVID STILL HER LIPS WERE RED 377   2 DON JUAN 4   60   2
    KATINKA WAS A GEORGIAN WHITE AND RED 26   3 DON JUAN 6   41   2
    AT LEAST AS RED AS THE FLAMINGO'S CREST 48   3 DON JUAN 6   85 V4
    THE FIRE WAS THAT WERE RED VESUVIUS LOADED 119   3 DON JUAN 8   16   2
    FLOWED FROM THEIR BLOOD-SHOT EYES ALL RED WITH STRIFE . 171   3 DON JUAN 8   119   7
    BUT RED WITH NO REDEEMING GORE THE GLOW 172   3 DON JUAN 8   122   6
    THE RED GRAPE IN THE SUNNY LANDS OF SONG 394   3 DON JUAN 13   76   4
    PALE AS IF PAINTED SO HER CHEEK BEING RED 532   3 DON JUAN 16   64   2
    A RED LIP WITH TWO ROWS OF PEARLS BENEATH 560   3 DON JUAN 16   121   6
REDDEN
    NOR INFLAMMATIONS REDDEN HIS BLIND EYE   168   2 DON JUAN 2   22   8
REDEEM
    THAT HIRED HUZZAS REDEEM NO LAND'S DISTRESSES 267   3 DON JUAN 10   86   4
REDEEMING
    BUT RED WITH NO REDEEMING GORE THE GLOW 172   3 DON JUAN 8   122   6
    REDEEMING WORLDS TO BE BY BIGOTS SHAKEN 464   3 DON JUAN 15   18   5
REDLY
    AND REDLY RAN HIS BLUSHING WATERS DOWN   175   3 DON JUAN 8   127   4
REDOUBLED
    REDOUBLED WHEN A ROAST AND A RAGOUT   428   2 DON JUAN 5   32   4
REDOUBTED
    DEAR JEFFREY ONCE MY MOST REDOUBTED FOE 232   3 DON JUAN 10   16   2
REDRESS
    I SHOULD BE VERY WILLING TO REDRESS   361   3 DON JUAN 13   8   5
REDRESSING
    REDRESSING INJURY REVENGING WRONG 363   3 DON JUAN 13   10   1
REDUCE
    AND THEN THE LEAK THEY RECKON'D TO REDUCE 172   2 DON JUAN 2   30   2
    IS LEARNING TO REDUCE HIS PAST EXPENSES 240   3 DON JUAN 10   31   8
REDUCED
    THEIR LIVING FREIGHT WAS NOW REDUCED TO FOUR   209   2 DON JUAN 2   101   4
    THEY DIED AWAY TILL THUS REDUCED TO FEW 210   2 DON JUAN 2   102 V6
    BUT NOW REDUCED AS IS A BULKY VOLUME 130   3 DON JUAN 8   34   4
    TO TELL HOW HE REDUCED THE NATION'S DEBT 440   3 DON JUAN 14   68   4
    REDUCED TO PRACTICE AND PERFORM'D LIKE DANCES 444   3 DON JUAN 14   79   8
    THE POOR PRIEST WAS REDUCED TO COMMON SENSE 540   3 DON JUAN 16   83   6
    THE SACRAMENTS HAVE BEEN REDUCED TO TWO 565   3 DON JUAN 17   7   1
REDUCES
    OF AGES TO WHAT STRAITS OLD TIME REDUCES 327   2 DON JUAN 3   88   6
REDUNDANCY
    I'M SENSIBLE REDUNDANCY IS WRONG   410   2 DON JUAN 4   117   5
REED
    A ROD TO WEAKNESS TO THE BRAVE A REED 151   2 DON JUAN 1   V 2   6
    AND SHOOK (TILL NOW UNSHAKEN) LIKE A REED 170   3 DON JUAN 8   117   6
    TO ME SEEMS BUT A DUBIOUS KIND OF REED   324   3 DON JUAN 12   18   5
    THERE'S MUSIC IN THE SIGHING OF A REED   458   3 DON JUAN 15   5   5
REEF
    A REEF BETWEEN THEM ALSO NOW BEGAN 211   2 DON JUAN 2   104   5
REEFS
    AND ROUGH WITH REEFS WHICH RAN OUT MANY A MILE 285   2 DON JUAN 3   19   7
REEKING
    THE REEKING BAYONET AND THE FLASHING BLADE 146   3 DON JUAN 8   69   3
REEL
    IN BACCHANAL PROFUSION REEL TO EARTH 88   2 DON JUAN 1   124   2
    A REEL WITHIN A BOTTLE IS A MYSTERY   531   3 DON JUAN 16   62   1
RE-ELECTIONS
    SAFE CONDUCT THROUGH THE ROCKS OF RE-ELECTIONS 546   3 DON JUAN 16   95   8
REELING
    AND FOR THE FUTURE--(BUT I WRITE THIS REELING 156   2 DON JUAN 1   V 8   4
REELS
    FROM HIS OWN BRAIN'S OPPRESSION WHILE IT REELS 427   2 DON JUAN 5   31   6
RE-EMBARK'D
    THUS RE-EMBARK'D HIS TUTOR AND HIS SPANIEL 187   2 DON JUAN 2   59   8
RE-ENTERED
    AS SOON AS THEY RE-ENTERED THEIR OWN ROOM 57   3 DON JUAN 6   103   3
REFECTION
    AND AFTER SWALLOWING DOWN A SLIGHT REFECTION   452   2 DON JUAN 5   71   3
    HOWEVER DOTH REQUIRE SOME SLIGHT REFECTION 483   3 DON JUAN 15   64   7
REFECTORY
    THE CELLS TOO AND REFECTORY I WEEN 389   3 DON JUAN 13   66   4
REFER
    AND I REFER YOU TO WISE OXENSTIERN 436   3 DON JUAN 14   59   8
REFERENCE
    MY MUSE DESPISES REFERENCE AS YOU HAVE GUESS'D 433   3 DON JUAN 14   54   6
    BUT THAT AT PRESENT WITH IMMEDIATE REFERENCE   469   3 DON JUAN 15   30   3
    AND ONLY THINK OR ACT OR FEEL WITH REFERENCE   541   3 DON JUAN 16   85   6
REFERRING
    BOLDLY REFERRING TO THE LIST OF PEERS 432   3 DON JUAN 14   52   3

REFINED
   TO GILD REFINED GOLD OR PAINT THE LILY . . . . . . 314 2 DON JUAN 3   76   8
   FOR DOGS OR TO BE SLAIN WITH PANGS REFINED . . . . . 492 2 DON JUAN 5   141   3
   IN MOTION BUT SHE HERE TOO MUCH REFINED-- . . . . . 492 3 DON JUAN 15   81   7
REFINEMENT
   THESE PHRASES OF REFINEMENT I MUST BORROW . . . . . 288 3 DON JUAN 11   42   2
REFINES
   AND FRUITS AND ICE AND ALL THAT ART REFINES . . . . 488 3 DON JUAN 15   72   1
REFLECT
   MEN WITH THEIR HEADS REFLECT ON THIS AND THAT-- . . . 7 3 DON JUAN 6   2   7
   I DON'T MEAN TO REFLECT--A MAN SO GREAT AS . . . . 186 3 DON JUAN 9   7   1
   OH YE OR WE OR HE OR SHE REFLECT . . . . . . 199 3 DON JUAN 9   34   1
   DESCRIPTION AND I WON'T REFLECT--THAT IS . . . . . 238 3 DON JUAN 10   28   2
REFLECTED
   REFLECTED ON HIS PRESENT SITUATION . . . . . . 165 2 DON JUAN 2   17   7
   DECKED BY THE RAYS REFLECTED FROM HIS HOST . . . . 383 3 DON JUAN 13   53   5
REFLECTION
   O'ER WHICH REFLECTION MAY BE MADE AT LEISURE . . . 145 2 DON JUAN 1   217   4
   AND KNEW SUCH BRIGHTNESS WAS BUT THE REFLECTION . . 351 2 DON JUAN 4   13   7
   HE DOUBTED NOT A FEW HOURS OF REFLECTION . . . . . 452 2 DON JUAN 5   71   5
   UPON REFLECTION KNOWING THAT BEHIND . . . . . 133 3 DON JUAN 8   40   2
   YOU MY LORD DUKE IS FAR ABOVE REFLECTION . . . . 186 3 DON JUAN 9   7   2
   HUT WHERE WE TRAVELLERS BAIT WITH DIM REFLECTION . . 238 3 DON JUAN 10   27 V6
   OF HEALTH BUT FLICKERED WITH A FAINT REFLECTION . . 245 3 DON JUAN 10   43   6
   AMONGST A PEOPLE FAMOUS FOR REFLECTION . . . . 304 3 DON JUAN 11   71   7
   AND THIS REFLECTION BRINGS ME TO PLAIN PHYSICS . . 349 3 DON JUAN 12   72   5
   AH--WHAT SHOULD FOLLOW SLIPS FROM MY REFLECTION . . 456 3 DON JUAN 15   1   1
REFLECTS
   MAN WITH HIS HEAD REFLECTS--(AS SPURZHEIM TELLS) . . 7 3 DON JUAN 6   2 V7
REFORM
   AND IS THERE NOT RELIGION AND REFORM . . . . . 360 3 DON JUAN 13   6   1
REFORMADOES
   WOULD SCARCELY JOIN AGAIN THE REFORMADOES . . . . 231 3 DON JUAN 10   13   3
REFORMATION
   OF REFORMATION ERE THE YEAR RUN OUT . . . . . 85 2 DON JUAN 1   119   4
   AND SERIOUSLY RESOLVED ON REFORMATION . . . . . 165 2 DON JUAN 2   17   8
   IRREVOCABLE VOW OF REFORMATION . . . . . . 175 2 DON JUAN 2   37   4
   YES I'LL BEGIN A THOROUGH REFORMATION . . . . . 498 3 DON JUAN 15   94   4
RE-FORM'D
   OUR LITTLE SELVES RE-FORM'D IN FINER CLAY . . . 305 2 DON JUAN 3   59   4
   THE REST HAD BEEN REFORM'D REPLACED OR SUNK . . . 389 3 DON JUAN 13   66   7
REFORMED
   BUT THOUGH I ALSO HAD REFORMED BEFORE . . . . . 334 3 DON JUAN 12   38   5
REFORMER
   DEATH'S A REFORMER ALL MEN MUST ALLOW . . . . . 237 3 DON JUAN 10   25   8
REFRESHING
   IS QUITE REFRESHING IN THE AFFECTED PHRASE . . . 156 3 DON JUAN 8   90   2
REFRESHMENT
   WITHOUT A SMALL REFRESHMENT FROM THE SPHERES . . . 496 3 DON JUAN 15   90   8
REFUGE
   I WOULD TAKE REFUGE IN WEAK PUNCH BUT RACK . . . 372 2 DON JUAN 4   53   5
   TO THIS VAIN REFUGE MADE THE GOOD HEART DROOP . . 157 3 DON JUAN 8   91   4
REFUSAL
   BY YOUR REFUSAL RECOLLECT HER RAGING . . . . . 486 2 DON JUAN 5   130   5
REFUSALS
   'TIS FINE TO SEE THEM SCATTERING REFUSALS . . . 332 3 DON JUAN 12   34   2
REFUSE
   BESEECHING SHE NO FURTHER WOULD REFUSE . . . . 120 2 DON JUAN 1   180   7
   HAVE FOUND THE FAME YOUR SHORES REFUSE . . . . 321 2 DON JUAN 3 L 2   3
   SUCH AS NO GENTLEMAN CAN QUITE REFUSE . . . . 293 3 DON JUAN 11   48   6
   HE RUBBED HIS EYES AND THEY DID NOT REFUSE . . . 512 3 DON JUAN 16   26   4
REFUSED
   AND JUAN WHO HAD STILL REFUSED BECAUSE . . . . 193 2 DON JUAN 2   71   2
   SHE SNATCH'D IT AND REFUSED ANOTHER MORSEL . . . 240 2 DON JUAN 2   159   7
   FOOD SHE REFUSED AND RAIMENT NO PRETENCE . . . 381 2 DON JUAN 4   68   5
   AND FIRST HE WONDERED WHY HE HAD REFUSED . . . 493 2 DON JUAN 5   142   3
   THE LITTLE TURK REFUSED TO BE CONVERTED . . . . 251 3 DON JUAN 10   55   8
REFUSING
   REFUSING HIS OWN SPANIEL HARDLY COULD . . . . 198 2 DON JUAN 2   78   4
REGAL
   WHEREAS THE OTHERS HUNT FOR REGAL SPIDERS . . . 196 3 DON JUAN 9   27 V8
REGALE
   AND EVIDENCES WHICH REGALE ALL READERS . . . . 346 3 DON JUAN 12   65   8
   BUT MERELY AS A CRITICAL REGALE . . . . . 528 3 DON JUAN 16   57 V8
REGALED
   REGALED TWO SHARKS WHO FOLLOW'D O'ER THE BILLOW-- . 197 2 DON JUAN 2   77   3
REGARD
   WITH STRICT REGARD TO ARISTOTLE'S RULES . . . . 136 2 DON JUAN 1   201   2
   SUWARROW WHO HAD SMALL REGARD FOR TEARS . . . 102 3 DON JUAN 7   69   1
   WHICH MEET THE GAZE WHAT'ER IT MAY REGARD-- . . 118 3 DON JUAN 8   13   4
   TO COME OFF HANDSOMELY IN THAT REGARD . . . . 235 3 DON JUAN 10   22   4
   IS WHEN WITHOUT REGARD TO CHURCH OR STATE . . . 345 3 DON JUAN 12   64   3
   OF MEN'S REGARD THE FEVER OR THE CHILL . . . . 366 3 DON JUAN 13   17   8
   SUSPICION THOUGH NOT TIMID HIS REGARD . . . . 462 3 DON JUAN 15   14   2
REGARDING
   REGARDING BOTH WITH SLOW AND SIDELONG VIEW . . . 116 2 DON JUAN 1   173   7
REGARDS
   IT OCCUPIES ME TO TURN BACK REGARDS . . . . . 415 3 DON JUAN 14   11   5
REGENT
   OR REGENT WHO ADMIRES SUCH KIND OF FOOD-- . . . 10 2 DON JUAN D   2   4

```
                                                          PAGE VOL      CANTO STANZA LN
REGIMENT
    IN THE NIKOLAIEW REGIMENT--THE SAME  . . . . . . .  97   3 DON JUAN   7    60    8
    WILL JOIN YOUR FORMER REGIMENT WHICH SHOULD BE . . . 100   3 DON JUAN   7    66    2
    HIS POST I MEAN THE REGIMENT NIKOLAIEW  . . . . . . 100   3 DON JUAN   7    66    5
    WHICH FILLS A REGIMENT (BESIDES THEIR PAY  . . . . . 134   3 DON JUAN   8    42    5
    THE SLAP-DASH REGIMENT SO WELL KNOWN TO FAME . . . . 383   3 DON JUAN  13    54    6
REGIMENTAL
    THE REGIMENTAL SURGEON COULD NOT CURE . . . . . . . 154   3 DON JUAN   8    85    5
REGIMENT'S
    CONTINUED YOUR OLD REGIMENT'S ALLOWED . . . . . . .  99   3 DON JUAN   7    63    3
REGION
    ABOUT THE LOWER REGION OF THE BOWELS  . . . . . . . 168   2 DON JUAN   2    23    2
REGRET
    AND YET CAN NOT REGRET WHAT IT HATH COST . . . . . . 130   2 DON JUAN   1   193    3
    OR ANY OTHER THING THAT BRINGS REGRET . . . . . . . 172   2 DON JUAN   2    31    5
    I FEEL A MIXED REGRET AND VENERATION  . . . . . . . 257   3 DON JUAN  10    66    4
    WHOSE LOSS IN THE LATE ACTION WE REGRET  . . . . . . 383   3 DON JUAN  13    54    7
    OF PAYING DEBTS WHICH CREDITORS REGRET)  . . . . . . 412   3 DON JUAN  14     4    6
    AND SEVERAL PITIED WITH SINCERE REGRET  . . . . . . 429   3 DON JUAN  14    44    7
    HAD LOVERS NOT SOME REASON TO REGRET  . . . . . . . 452   3 DON JUAN  14    95    3
    WHOM I HAD NOT SOME REASON TO REGRET  . . . . . . . 452   3 DON JUAN  14    95   V3
    AND DON'T REGRET THE TIME YOU MAY HAVE LOST . . . . . 498   3 DON JUAN  15    95    3
REGRETTED
    WAS MUCH REGRETTED) FOR THE MOSLEM MEN  . . . . . . 147   3 DON JUAN   8    71    7
    WHO STILL REGRETTED THAT HE DID NOT RHYME . . . . . 295   3 DON JUAN  11    53    4
REGRETTING
    ALL THOSE THAT WOULD--REGRETTING THOSE I MISSED  . . . 232   2 DON JUAN   2   142   V8
    REGRETTING MUCH THAT SHE HAD CHOSEN SO BAD A LINE . . . 430   3 DON JUAN  14    46    5
REGULAR
    THE LAMPS OF WESTMINSTER'S MORE REGULAR GLEAM  . . . 279   3 DON JUAN  11    24    4
    WITH REGULAR DESCENT IN THESE OUR DAYS  . . . . . . 340   3 DON JUAN  12    53    4
    JUST AS A REGULAR COMMON SOLDIER OR A WHORE . . . . . 537   3 DON JUAN  16    76   V3
    WITH AWFUL FOOTSTEPS REGULAR AS RHYME . . . . . . . 556   3 DON JUAN  16   113    3
REGULARITY
    THE REGULARITY OF MY DESIGN . . . . . . . . . . . .  25   2 DON JUAN   1     7    3
REGULARLY
    HE TOOK TO REGULARLY PEOPLING EARTH  . . . . . . . . 312   3 DON JUAN  11    89    5
REGULATED
    WITH THE MOST REGULATED CHARMS OF FEATURE  . . . . .  32   3 DON JUAN   6    52    3
REHEARSED
    SUNG OR REHEARSED THE LAST DANCE FROM ABROAD  . . . . 406   3 DON JUAN  13   104    4
REIGN
    AND PURGATIVES ARE DANGEROUS TO HIS REIGN  . . . . . 168   2 DON JUAN   2    23    5
    IN CATHERINE'S REIGN WHOM GLORY STILL ADORES  . . . .  52   3 DON JUAN   6    92    7
    NOR REIGN AT ALL OR AS A MONARCH REIGN  . . . . . . 296   3 DON JUAN  11    56    6
    NOR REIGN AT ALL OR AS A MONARCH REIGN  . . . . . . 296   3 DON JUAN  11    56    6
    WHO HOLD THE BALANCE OF THE WORLD WHO REIGN . . . . . 318   3 DON JUAN  12     5    1
    FOR THOSE WHO KNEW NOT TO RESIGN OR REIGN . . . . . . 386   3 DON JUAN  13    60    8
    AND SUCH I MEAN TO MAKE HIM WHEN I REIGN . . . . . . 440   3 DON JUAN  14    70    8
REIGN'D
    REIGN'D TILL ONE SUMMER'S DAY HE TOOK TO GRAZING . . . 445   2 DON JUAN   5    60    4
REIGNED
    SIR WALTER REIGNED BEFORE ME MOORE AND CAMPBELL  . . . 297   3 DON JUAN  11    57    1
REIGNING
    A LIST OF SHIPS AND CAPTAINS AND KINGS REIGNING  . . . 135   2 DON JUAN   1   200    4
    THE EMPRESS SMILED THE REIGNING FAVOURITE FROWNED-- . . 205   3 DON JUAN   9    46    2
    ARE GENERALLY PROSPEROUS IN REIGNING  . . . . . . . 247   3 DON JUAN  10    47    2
    OF MODERN REIGNING STERLING STUPID STAMP--  . . . . . 321   3 DON JUAN  12    12    7
REJECT
    SOME ARE SOON BAGGED BUT SOME REJECT THREE DOZEN . . . 332   3 DON JUAN  12    34    1
    ADMIT REJECT CONTEMN AND WHAT KNOW YOU  . . . . . . 411   3 DON JUAN  14     3    2
    FOR THIS A LADY NO ONE CAN REJECT  . . . . . . . . . 471   3 DON JUAN  15    34    5
REJECTED
    REJECTED SEVERAL SUITORS JUST TO LEARN  . . . . . . 224   2 DON JUAN   2   128    7
    IT SOOTHES THE AWKWARD SQUAD OF THE REJECTED  . . . . 333   3 DON JUAN  12    36    7
REJECTS
    PHILOSOPHY  NO SHE TOO MUCH REJECTS  . . . . . . . . 495   3 DON JUAN  15    89    7
REJOICE
    FOR HIS OWN PART HE REALLY SHOULD REJOICE  . . . . . 452   2 DON JUAN   5    70    1
REJOINED
    REJOINED THE OTHER WHEN OUR BAD LUCK MENDS HERE  . . . 423   2 DON JUAN   5    24    6
    REJOINED THE NEGRO PRAY BE NOT PROVOKING  . . . . . 454   2 DON JUAN   5    75    2
    JUAN REJOINED--SHE WAS A CATHOLIC  . . . . . . . . . 478   3 DON JUAN  15    50    1
RELAPSING
    BUT I'M RELAPSING INTO METAPHYSICS . . . . . . . . . 349   3 DON JUAN  12    72    1
RELATE
    THAN LESSEN IT BY WHAT I COULD RELATE . . . . . . . 467   2 DON JUAN   5    97    5
    GREAT DEEDS ARE DOING--HOW SHALL I RELATE 'EM . . . . 107   3 DON JUAN   7    81    6
    WHATEVER DEED BE DONE I WILL RELATE 'EM  . . . . . . 107   3 DON JUAN   7    81   V6
    AND HERE I MUST AN ANECDOTE RELATE . . . . . . . . . 207   3 DON JUAN   9    50    7
    CAN TENDER SOULS RELATE THE RISE AND FALL  . . . . . 304   3 DON JUAN  11    72    7
    BUT HOW SHALL I RELATE IN OTHER CANTOS  . . . . . . 311   3 DON JUAN  11    87    1
RELATED
    TO THOSE RELATED IN MY GRAND-DAD'S NARRATIVE  . . . . 229   2 DON JUAN   2   137    8
    HE COULD NOT HELP THE THINGS WHICH HE RELATED  . . . .  57   3 DON JUAN   6   102    4
    AND THEREFORE ALL WE HAVE RELATED IN  . . . . . . . 142   3 DON JUAN   8    59    1
    SOME YEARS BEFORE THE INCIDENTS RELATED  . . . . . . 286   3 DON JUAN  11    37    8
    I'D RATHER NOT SAY WHAT MIGHT BE RELATED . . . . . . 428   3 DON JUAN  14    42    4
RELATION
    I CAN'T SAY MUCH FOR FRIEND OR YET RELATION)  . . . .  38   2 DON JUAN   1    32    5
```

		PAGE	VOL		CANTO	STANZA	LN
RELATION (CONTINUED)							
BUT BEING THE PRIMA-DONNA'S NEAR RELATION		391	2	DON JUAN	4	87	5
WHICH BEARS THE SAME RELATION TO THE REAL		419	3	DON JUAN	14	22	3
AND FAMILIES EVEN TO THE LAST RELATION		550	3	DON JUAN	16	103	6
RELATIONS							
THEN THEIR RELATIONS WHO MADE MATTERS WORSE		38	2	DON JUAN	1	32	2
HE SAW TOO IN PERSPECTIVE HER RELATIONS		110	2	DON JUAN	1	162	7
THEY WERE RELATIONS AND FOR THEM HE HAD A		169	2	DON JUAN	2	24	5
HE BORE THESE SNEERS AGAINST HIS NEAR RELATIONS		299	2	DON JJAN	3	46	5
OR NEAR RELATIONS WHO ARE MUCH THE SAME		139	3	DON JUAN	8	54	2
HE WROTE TO SPAIN--AND ALL HIS NEAR RELATIONS		239	3	DON JUAN	10	30	1
IT CHANCED SOME DIPLOMATICAL RELATIONS		365	3	DON JUAN	13	15	1
RELATIVES							
THAN THEIR HE RELATIVES) LIKE FLIES O'ER CANDY		331	3	DON JUAN	12	32	6
RELAX'D							
SO FAR RELAX'D HER THOUGHTS FROM THEIR SWEET PRISON		491	3	DON JUAN	15	80	7
RELEASED							
ANON--SHE WAS RELEASED AND THEN SHE STRAY'D		361	2	DON JUAN	4	32	1
RELENT							
YET WITH DISPLAY IN FACT AT TIMES RELENT		521	3	DON JUAN	16	42	6
RELENTED							
THE HUNTSMAN'S SELF RELENTED TO A GRIN		425	3	DON JUAN	14	34	7
RELICS							
WITH OTHER RELICS OF A FORMER WORLD		201	3	DON JUAN	9	37	2
I SAY WILL THESE GREAT RELICS WHEN THEY SEE 'EM		202	3	DON JUAN	9	40	7
BUT EVEN THE FAINTEST RELICS OF A SHRINE		387	3	DON JUAN	13	61	7
RELIEF							
SHORT SOLACE VAIN RELIEF--THOUGHT CAME TOO QUICK		380	2	DON JUAN	4	67	1
TO THEM 'TIS A RELIEF TO US A TORTURE		479	2	DON JUAN	5	118	8
A TURBOT FOR RELIEF OF THOSE WHO CRAM		483	3	DON JUAN	15	63	3
SOUPE A LA BEAUVEAU WHOSE RELIEF WAS DORY		483	3	DON JUAN	15	63	7
RELIES							
(A VIRGIN ALWAYS ON HER MAID RELIES)		225	2	DON JJAN	2	131	2
RELIEVE							
JUST TO RELIEVE HER SPIRITS FROM DEJECTION		483	3	DON JUAN	15	64	8
RELIEVED							
THE SKIN RELIEVED APPEAR MORE FAIRLY FAIR		314	2	DON JJAN	3	76	2
RELIEVED HER THOUGHTS DULL SILENCE AND QUICK CHAT		378	2	DON JUAN	4	63	6
RELIEVED WITH DINDON A LA PERIGUEUX		483	3	DON JUAN	15	63	4
RELIEVED ITSELF BY PORK FOR GREATER GLORY		483	3	DON JUAN	15	63	8
RELIGION							
AS RUM AND TRUE RELIGION THUS IT WAS		174	2	DON JUAN	2	34	2
EXTREMELY TAKEN WITH HIS OWN RELIGION		387	2	DON JUAN	4	78	7
(LOVE LIKE RELIGION SOMETIMES RUNS TO HERESY)		446	2	DON JUAN	5	61	4
I THOUGHT YOU HAD MORE RELIGION MRS FRY		267	3	DON JUAN	10	85	8
AND IS THERE NOT RELIGION AND REFORM		360	3	DON JUAN	13	6	1
RELIGION YES BUT WHICH OF ALL HER SECTS		495	3	DON JUAN	15	89	8
KINDLING RELIGION TILL SHE THROWS DOWN HER GAGE		530	3	DON JUAN	16	60	5
RELIGION'S							
FOR HONOUR'S PRIDE'S RELIGION'S VIRTUE'S SAKE		62	2	DON JUAN	1	75	4
RELIGIOUS							
AND NOT THE LEAST SO WHEN THEY ARE RELIGIOUS		11	3	DON JUAN	6	10	3
RELINQUISH'D							
HE LEFT THE ROOM FOR HIS RELINQUISH'D SWORD		121	2	DON JUAN	1	182	1
RELINQUISHED							
HE MADE THE TEETH MEET NOR RELINQUISHED IT		153	3	DON JUAN	8	84	6
RELUCTANCE							
WITH MUCH HEART-FELT RELUCTANCE BE IT SAID		112	2	DON JUAN	1	165	7
RELUCTANT							
RELUCTANT PAST HER BRIGHT EYES ROLLED--AS A VEIL		108	2	DON JUAN	1	158	V3
FROM WHOSE RELUCTANT ROAR HIS LIFE HE WRUNG		213	2	DON JUAN	2	108	3
AND PULLING OUT RELUCTANT PURSES AND		426	2	DON JUAN	5	29	2
TO PROVE RELUCTANT AND BEGGED LEAVE TO CRAVE		62	3	DON JUAN	6	112	5
RELUCTANT AS ALL PLACEMEN TO RESIGN		360	3	DON JUAN	13	5	2
RELUCTANTLY							
RELUCTANTLY STILL TARRYING THERE AS LATE AS		111	2	DON JUAN	1	164	3
RELYING							
ITS VOTARIES LIKE INNOCENCE RELYING		131	3	DON JUAN	8	36	5
REMAIN							
HER GREAT GREAT GRANDMAMMA CHOSE TO REMAIN		52	2	DON JUAN	1	56	8
BUT NOW I'LL BEAR NO MORE NOR HERE REMAIN		100	2	DON JUAN	1	145	7
AND OLD SCAMANDER (IF 'TIS HE) REMAIN		386	2	DON JUAN	4	77	4
THE STRANGER STRIPLING MAY REMAIN WITH ME		100	3	DON JUAN	7	66	6
WHERE THREE PARTS OF HIS COLUMN YET REMAIN		148	3	DON JUAN	8	72	8
ABOUT A LIQUID GLASSFUL WILL REMAIN		375	3	DON JUAN	13	37	6
REMAIN'D							
SOME LEATHERN CAPS AND WHAT REMAIN'D OF SHOES		195	2	DON JUAN	2	74	2
OF POOR PEDRILLO SOMETHING STILL REMAIN'D		200	2	DON JUAN	2	82	1
REMAIN'D UNKNOWN WITHIN HIS CRAGGY NOOK		248	2	DON JUAN	2	174	4
AND IN THE HOPE OF MORE AT SEA REMAIN'D		283	2	DON JUAN	3	15	3
REMAINDER							
UPON THE PUMPS AND THE REMAINDER SET		171	2	DON JUAN	2	28	2
REMAINED							
ONE DIFFICULTY STILL REMAINED--HIS HAIR		457	2	DON JUAN	5	79	1
POINTED TO JUAN WHO REMAINED BELOW		466	2	DON JUAN	5	96	8
WHERE MANY A GOTHIC ORNAMENT REMAINED		507	3	DON JUAN	16	16	6
A MONK REMAINED UNCHASED UNCHAINED		518	3	DON JUAN	16	L 2	5
BUT STILL THE SHADE REMAINED THE BLUE EYES GLARED		560	3	DON JUAN	16	121	1
REMAINING							
AND THERE ARE OTHER INCIDENTS REMAINING		135	2	DON JUAN	1	200	V6

<pre>
                                                          PAGE VOL   CANTO STANZA LN
RENDER   (CONTINUED)
    WELL CULTIVATED IT WILL RENDER DOUBLE . . . . 351 3 DON JUAN 12   76   8
    NOW THIS AT ALL EVENTS MUST RENDER COLD . . . . . . 468 3 DON JUAN 15   26   5
RENDER'D
    WHICH TIME HAD LATELY RENDER'D MUCH MORE CHASTE . . 58 2 DON JUAN 1   67   2
    ARE FALSE BUT MAY BE RENDER'D ALSO TRUE . . . . .   495 3 DON JUAN 15   89   2
RENDERED
    THE CITY'S TAKEN BUT NOT RENDERED--NO . . . . 155 3 DON JUAN 8   87   1
RENDERING
    BY RENDERING DESPERATE THOSE WHO HAD ELSE REPENTED . . 353 3 DON JUAN 12 80   8
RENDERS
    THE CONQUEROR AT LEAST WHO ERE TIME RENDERS . . . . . 299 3 DON JUAN 11   61   3
RENDEZVOUS
    GLIDING THE FIRST TIME TO A RENDEZVOUS . . . . . . 556 3 DON JUAN 16   112   7
REND'RING
    AND REND'RING GENERAL THAT WHICH IS ESPECIAL . . . 467 3 DON JUAN 15   25   8
RENDS
    AMBITION RENDS AND GAMING GAINS A LOSS . . . . . . 317 3 DON JUAN 12   4   2
RENEGADE
    AND NOW MY EPIC RENEGADE WHAT ARE YE AT . . . . . .   9 2 DON JUAN 0   1   5
RENEGADO
    THEIR LOYAL TREASON RENEGADO RIGOUR . . . .   330 2 DON JUAN 3   94   3
    THEIR LOYAL ZEAL AND RENEGADO VIGOUR . . . . 330 2 DON JUAN 3   94 V3
RENEGADOES
    AS RENEGADOES WHILE IN HAPLESS GROUP . . . .   409 2 DON JUAN 4   115   5
    THIS WERE THE WORST DESERTION--RENEGADOES . . . . . 231 3 DON JUAN 10   13   1
RENEW
    BEGOT--BUT THAT'S TO COME--WELL TO RENEW . . . . .   26 2 DON JUAN 1   9   8
    AND THOUGH AT FIRST THEIR STRENGTH IT MIGHT RENEW . 192 2 DON JUAN 2   68   3
    LAY JUAN NOR COULD AUGHT RENEW THE BEAT . . . . .   362 2 DON JUAN 4   34   5
    MY GENTLE COUNTRYMEN WE WILL RENEW . . . .   266 3 DON JUAN 10   84   3
RENEW'D
    AND HOW TO PARRY THE RENEW'D ATTACK . . . .   114 2 DON JUAN 1   169   5
    AS EVERY RISING WAVE HIS DREAD RENEW'D . . . . . .   187 2 DON JUAN 2   59   5
RENEWED
    AND CERTAINLY AURORA HAD RENEWED . . . .   553 3 DON JUAN 16   107   5
RENOVATE
    SUMMERS COULD RENOVATE THOUGH THEY SHOULD BE . . .   86 3 DON JUAN 7   41   6
RENOWN
    THEN THERE WERE FOREIGNERS OF MUCH RENOWN . . . .   75 3 DON JUAN 7   18   1
    OH WILBERFORCE THOU MAN OF BLACK RENOWN . . . . .   445 3 DON JUAN 14   82   1
RENOWNED
    WAS HE SINCE SO RENOWNED IN COUNTRY QUARTERS . . .   76 3 DON JUAN 7   19   7
    RENOWNED FOR RUINING GREAT BRITAIN GRATIS . . . .   186 3 DON JUAN 9   8   8
    ESPECIALLY AS HE HAD BEEN RENOWNED . . . .   544 3 DON JUAN 16   91   4
RENOWN'S
    FOR AUGHT WE KNOW) RENOWN'S ALL HIT OR MISS . . .   82 3 DON JUAN 7   33   5
RENT
    LET THIS ONE TOIL FOR BREAD--THAT RACK FOR RENT . . 190 3 DON JUAN 9   15   7
    AT LEAST HE PAYS NO RENT AND HAS BEST RIGHT . . . . 198 3 DON JUAN 9   32   1
RENTAL
    TO DOUBT (NO LESS THAN LANDLORDS OF THEIR RENTAL) . . 322 3 DON JUAN 12   13   7
RENTS
    SINCE LATELY THERE HAVE BEEN NO RENTS AT ALL . . . 198 3 DON JUAN 9   32   4
    AND WHERE--OH WHERE THE DEVIL ARE THE RENTS . . . . 307 3 DON JUAN 11   77   8
REPAIRED
    THEY DREW CONSTRUCTED LADDERS REPAIRED FLAWS . . .   89 3 DON JUAN 7   47   6
    YOU HAVE REPAIRED LEGITIMACY'S CRUTCH-- . . . . .   184 3 DON JUAN 9   3   3
REPAIRS
    HIS VESSEL HAVING NEED OF SOME REPAIRS . . . . . . 285 2 DON JUAN 3   19   3
REPARTEE
    LOST FOR HIS REPARTEE WAS TAKING CITIES . . . . . .   93 3 DON JUAN 7   53 V8
    WAS MUCH CONSOLED BY HIS OWN REPARTEE . . . . 522 3 DON JUAN 16   43   8
REPARTEES
    THE DICE SEEM'D CHARM'D TOO WITH HIS REPARTEES . . . 399 3 DON JUAN 13   86   8
REPASSED
    ONCE TWICE THRICE PASSED REPASSED--THE THING OF AIR . 510 3 DON JUAN 16   23   1
REPAST
    AND FRUITS AND DATE-BREAD LOAVES CLOSED THE REPAST . 307 2 DON JUAN 3   63   2
    WHEN WHERE AND HOW HE CHOSE FOR THAT REPAST . . . . 406 3 DON JUAN 13   103   8
    A SLIGHT REPAST MAKES PEOPLE LOVE MUCH MORE . . . . 542 3 DON JUAN 16   86   3
REPAY
    SHE COULD REPAY EACH AMATORY LOOK YOU LENT . . . . 213 3 DON JUAN 9   62   5
    SUCH AS THE CONQUEROR WILLIAM DID REPAY . . . . .   242 3 DON JUAN 10   35   6
    'TIS RARELY FOUND BUT WOULD REPAY ALL CHECKS . . . 451 3 DON JUAN 14   93 V5
    THE PRICE WOULD SPEEDILY REPAY ITS WORTH IN . . . . 529 3 DON JUAN 16   59   4
REPEAT
    TO HEAR NEW WORDS AND TO REPEAT THEM BUT . . . . .   244 2 DON JUAN 2   167   2
    JOY OF ITS ALCHYMY AND TO REPEAT . . . .   264 2 DON JUAN 2   203   5
    JOY OF ITS GLITTERING TREASURE AND REPEAT . . . .   264 2 DON JUAN 2   203 V5
    YOU CAN'T REPEAT NINE NAMES FROM EACH GAZETTE . . .   83 3 DON JUAN 7   34   8
REPEATED
    AND WORDS REPEATED AFTER HER HE TOOK . . . .   242 2 DON JUAN 2   163   2
    HE HEARD REPEATED JUAN WITH A FROWN . . . .   470 2 DON JUAN 5   102   5
REPEATERS
    THE HEARERS OF HER CASE BECAME REPEATERS . . . . .   36 2 DON JUAN 1   28   6
REPENT
    OR THAT THE RUSSIAN ARMY SHOULD REPENT ALL . . . . 105 3 DON JUAN 7   75   6
REPENTANCE
    HAD COST HIS ENEMIES A LONG REPENTANCE . . . . . . 303 2 DON JUAN 3   54   7
</pre>

666

		PAGE	VOL	CANTO	STANZA	LN

REPENTANCE   (CONTINUED)
  THE WATERS AND REPENTANCE FOR PAST SINNING . . . . . . 414 2 DON JUAN 5   6   5
  HER FOURTH TO RALLY HIM INTO REPENTANCE . . . . 491 2 DON JUAN 5 139   4
  OR DULL REPENTANCE HATH HAD DREARY LEISURE . . . . . . 168 3 DON JUAN 8 113   5
REPENTED
  A LITTLE STILL SHE STROVE AND MUCH REPENTED . . . . . 84 2 DON JUAN 1 117   7
  REPENTED ALL HIS SINS AND MADE A LAST . . . . 175 2 DON JUAN 2   37   3
  BY RENDERING DESPERATE THOSE WHO HAD ELSE REPENTED . . 353 3 DON JUAN 12   80   8
REPENTS
  OR AS A DAME REPENTS HER OF HER OATH . . . . 493 2 DON JUAN 5 142   7
REPERTORY
  SHE GATHERS A REPERTORY OF FACTS . . . . 416 3 DON JUAN 14   13   2
REPETITION
  IF GOOD IS NONE THE WORSE FOR REPETITION . . . . . . 478 3 DON JUAN 15   51   2
REPETITION'S
  AND REPETITION'S TIRESOME AND UNWISE-- . . . . 246 2 DON JUAN 2 171   6
REPLACED
  HIS WEAPON AND REPLACED IT BUT STOOD STILL . . . . . 368 2 DON JUAN 4   46   2
  IT NE'ER CAN BE REPLACED IN PROPER FRAME . . . . . . 502 2 DON JUAN 5 158   4
  THE REST HAD BEEN REFORM'D REPLACED OR SUNK . . . . . 389 3 DON JUAN 13   66   7
REPLENISH
  THOU DOST REPLENISH WORLDS BOTH GREAT AND SMALL . . . 210 3 DON JUAN 9   56   6
REPLETION
  REPLETION RATHER ADDS TO WHAT HE FEELS . . . . 427 2 DON JUAN 5   31   4
REPLIED
  OF THIS THEIR MUTUAL FEELING SHE REPLIED-- . . . . . 356 2 DON JUAN 4   23   6
  JUAN REPLIED NOT WHILE THIS ARM IS FREE . . . . . . 365 2 DON JUAN 4   40   2
  REPLIED YOUR BLOOD BE THEN ON YOUR OWN HEAD . . . . . 365 2 DON JUAN 4   40   5
  JUAN REPLIED IT MUST BE WON NOT GIVEN . . . . 365 2 DON JUAN 4   40   V2
  WHEN JUAN ANSWERED SPANISH HE REPLIED . . . . 418 2 DON JUAN 5   14   1
  REPLIED THE OTHER WHAT CAN A MAN DO . . . . 421 2 DON JUAN 5   21   2
  REPLIED THE OTHER DO NOT INTERRUPT . . . . 453 2 DON JUAN 5   72   2
  REPLIED OLD GENTLEMAN I'M NOT A LADY . . . . 453 2 DON JUAN 5   73   8
  REPLIED THE OTHER THOUGH IT GRIEVES ME SORE . . . . . 460 2 DON JUAN 5   84   3
  REPLIED KATINKA I AM SURE I SEE . . . . 30 3 DON JUAN 6   48   3
  THE DAME REPLIED BETWEEN YOUR DREAMS AND YOU . . . . 30 3 DON JUAN 6   48   7
  BABA WITH SOME EMBARRASSMENT REPLIED . . . . 56 3 DON JUAN 6 100   1
  THE GEORGIAN AND HER PARAMOUR REPLIED . . . . 62 3 DON JUAN 6 113   1
  MAY IT PLEASE YOUR EXCELLENCY THUS REPLIED . . . . . 103 3 DON JUAN 7   71   1
  AND BLACK SILK NECKCLOTH--AND REPLIED YOU'RE RIGHT . . 161 3 DON JUAN 8   99   7
  JUAN REPLIED--AT LEAST I WILL ENDURE . . . . 161 3 DON JUAN 8 100   6
  BUT HE WOULD NOT BE TAKEN AND REPLIED . . . . 165 3 DON JUAN 8 107   1
  REPLIED THAT SHE WAS GLAD TO SEE HIM THROUGH . . . . 240 3 DON JUAN 10   31   5
  HOWEVER HE REPLIED AT HAZARD WITH . . . . 294 3 DON JUAN 11   52   1
  JUAN REPLIED WITH ALL BECOMING DEFERENCE . . . . . . 469 3 DON JUAN 15   30   1
  WHEN ADELINE REPLIED WITH SOME DISGUST . . . . . . 477 3 DON JUAN 15   49   5
  TO HIS GAY NOTHINGS NOTHING WAS REPLIED . . . . . . 490 3 DON JUAN 15   78   1
  HER GRACE REPLIED HIS GRACE WAS RATHER PAINED . . . . 515 3 DON JUAN 16   34   6
REPLIES
  OF WONDERFUL REPLIES FROM ARAB JOKERS . . . . 293 2 DON JUAN 3   34   4
  LOOKED INTO HIS FOR LOVE WHERE NONE REPLIES . . . . . 483 2 DON JUAN 5 125   4
  IN HIS REPLIES SHE PUZZLED HIM FOR FRESH ONES . . . . 56 3 DON JUAN 6 101   5
REPLY
  TO WHICH THE SOLE REPLY WERE TEARS AND SOBS . . . . . 110 2 DON JUAN 1 162   2
  IN ANY CASE ATTEMPTING A REPLY . . . . 119 2 DON JUAN 1 179   3
  TO THESE KIND EFFORTS MADE A LOW REPLY . . . . . . 215 2 DON JUAN 2 113   8
  AND DARTS IN ONE QUICK GLANCE A LONG REPLY . . . . . 241 2 DON JUAN 2 162   6
  HE LOOK'D UPON HER BUT GAVE NO REPLY . . . . 365 2 DON JUAN 4   39   4
  CAPTIVES JUST NOW ESCAPED WAS THE REPLY . . . . . . 97 2 DON JUAN 7   59   5
  A SNEER OR SHORT REPLY UNTO THEIR NEIGHBOUR . . . . . 288 3 DON JUAN 11   41   V4
  TAKE CARE WHAT YOU REPLY TO SUCH A LETTER . . . . . 407 3 DON JUAN 13 105   8
REPORT
  THAT A REPORT (ESPECIALLY THE GREEKS) . . . . 295 2 DON JUAN 3   38   2
  WERE THEY ACCORDING TO THE BEST REPORT . . . . . . 26 3 DON JUAN 6   40   5
  IF (SAYS THE HISTORIAN HERE) I COULD REPORT . . . . . 82 3 DON JUAN 7   32   1
REPORTED
  MUCH TO HIS YOUTH AND MUCH TO HIS REPORTED . . . . . 239 3 DON JUAN 10   29   3
REPOSE
  A LOVING LANGUOR WHICH IS NOT REPOSE . . . . 82 2 DON JUAN 1 114   8
  ON WHICH THEY MIGHT REPOSE OR EVEN COMMENCE . . . . . 177 2 DON JUAN 2   40   5
  AND THUS THEY LEFT HIM TO HIS LONE REPOSE . . . . . 227 2 DON JUAN 2 134   1
  WE LEAVE THIS ROYAL COUPLE TO REPOSE . . . . 16 3 DON JUAN 6   20   1
  A STERN REPOSE WHICH YOU WOULD SCARCE CONCEIVE . . . . 94 3 DON JUAN 7   54   3
REPOSED
  AND WISH'D IT DEATH IN WHICH HE HAD REPOSED . . . . . 215 2 DON JUAN 2 112   5
  BUT WHATSOE'ER HE HAD OF LOVE REPOSED . . . . 304 2 DON JUAN 3   57   1
REPOSES
  FOR ON SUCH THINGS THE MEMORY REPOSES . . . . 187 2 DON JUAN 2   58   3
REPOSING
  TO SEE HER BIRD REPOSING IN HIS NEST . . . . 245 2 DON JUAN 2 168   4
REPRESENTATIVE
  AND REPRESENTATIVE OF ALL THE RACE . . . .   9 2 DON JUAN D   1   2
REPROACH
  SUSPECTS WITH ONE DO YOU REPROACH WITH THREE . . . . 117 2 DON JUAN 1 175   8
  I'VE NOTHING TO REPROACH OR TO REQUEST . . . . . . 130 2 DON JUAN 1 193   8
  PETTICOAT INFLUENCE IS A GREAT REPROACH . . . . . . 421 3 DON JUAN 14   26   1
REPROOF'S
  AND EVEN MY MUSE'S WORST REPROOF'S A SMILE . . . . . 300 3 DON JUAN 11   63   6
REPROVE
  NOR LEAVE A WISH WHICH WISDOM MIGHT REPROVE . . . . . 80 2 DON JUAN 1 109   5
  SHE HAD NOTHING TO COMPLAIN OF OR REPROVE . . . . . 447 3 DON JUAN 14   86   5

667

	PAGE	VOL		CANTO	STANZA	LN
REPROVED						
BRIGHT WITH THE VERY WEAKNESS HE REPROVED	481	2	DON JUAN	5	121	6
REPROVER						
SHE WAS THE MILD REPROVER OF THE YOUNG	338	3	DON JUAN	12	48	2
REPUBLICS						
REPUBLICS ALSO GET INVOLVED A BIT	318	3	DON JUAN	12	6	5
REPULSE						
ROUSED BY REPULSE--THROUGH A TOLERABLE LEAK	490	2	DON JUAN	5	137	V6
REPULSED						
AT OTHER TIMES REPULSED BY THE CLOSE FIRE	121	3	DON JUAN	8	20	5
REPULSES						
ADVANCES OR REPULSES THEY BEHOLD	366	3	DON JUAN	13	17	V8
REPUTATION						
A MOMENT MORE WOULD HURT YOUR REPUTATION	482	2	DON JUAN	5	123	8
AND HATE ALL VICE EXCEPT ITS REPUTATION	327	3	DON JUAN	12	25	8
REPUTATIONS						
FOR REPUTATIONS HE HAD LITTLE CARE	109	2	DON JUAN	1	160	4
REQUEST						
I'VE NOTHING TO REPROACH OR TO REQUEST	130	2	DON JUAN	1	193	8
WHEREON IMMEDIATELY AT HIS REQUEST	96	3	DON JUAN	7	57	1
REQUEST THAT THEY MAY BOTH BE USED GENTEELLY	103	3	DON JUAN	7	72	8
FOR ONE OR TWO DAYS READER WE REQUEST	248	3	DON JUAN	10	49	2
IS NO GREAT MATTER SO 'TIS IN REQUEST	359	3	DON JUAN	13	3	4
REQUESTED						
HE BUT REQUESTED TO BE BLED TO DEATH	197	2	DON JUAN	2	76	1
HIS SMILE REQUESTED ONE OF THEM TO TELL	298	2	DON JUAN	3	44	6
REQUESTING						
OF CANDIDATES REQUESTING TO BE PLACED	248	3	DON JUAN	10	48	3
REQUIRE						
ALTHOUGH MY OPINION MAY REQUIRE APOLOGY	281	2	DON JUAN	3	11	3
HOWEVER DOTH REQUIRE SOME SLIGHT REFECTION	483	3	DON JUAN	15	64	7
REQUIRED						
REQUIRED THIS CONDUCT--WHICH SEEM'D VERY ODD	35	2	DON JUAN	1	27	8
OF ARTICLES WHICH NOBODY REQUIRED	448	2	DON JUAN	5	64	5
AND HERE SHE SUMMONED BABA AND REQUIRED	55	3	DON JUAN	6	99	1
WHICH IS REQUIRED BY PROPER COURTESY	311	3	DON JUAN	11	88	3
THEN THERE WAS SMALL-TALK READY WHEN REQUIRED	408	3	DON JUAN	13	108	4
REQUIRED AURORA SCARCELY LOOK'D ASIDE	490	3	DON JUAN	15	78	3
REQUIRES						
NEGLECT INDEED REQUIRES A SAINT TO BEAR IT	32	2	DON JUAN	1	20	3
REQUIRES IT THAT'S TO SAY THE ENGLISH RHYME	14	3	DON JUAN	6	18	2
REQUIRES DECORUM AND IS APT TO DOUBLE	292	3	DON JUAN	11	46	7
REQUIRES ARITHMETIC BEYOND MY FORCES	486	3	DON JUAN	15	69	4
REQUISITE						
THERE WANTED BUT THIS REQUISITE TO SWELL	295	3	DON JUAN	11	53	5
REQUISITION						
THE PIOUS METALS MOST IN REQUISITION	152	3	DON JUAN	8	81	5
REQUISITION'S						
METHINKS THE REQUISITION'S RATHER HARD	85	2	DON JUAN	1	118	3
REQUITES						
THE ONLY SORT OF PLEASURE WHICH REQUITES	405	3	DON JUAN	13	100	4
RES						
MOST EPIC POETS PLUNGE IN MEDIAS RES	24	2	DON JUAN	1	6	1
RESCUE						
THEY COULD NOT RESCUE HIM ALTHOUGH SO CLOSE	186	2	DON JUAN	2	57	6
RESEARCH						
WE SURELY SHALL FIND SOMETHING WORTH RESEARCH	468	3	DON JUAN	15	27	5
FURTHER I SHALL NOT FOLLOW THE RESEARCH	485	3	DON JUAN	15	67	6
RESEMBLANCE						
THERE WAS RESEMBLANCE SUCH AS TRUE BLOOD WEARS	368	2	DON JUAN	4	45	4
RESEMBLING						
HIGH YET RESEMBLING NOT HIS LOST HAIDEE	481	3	DON JUAN	15	58	2
RE-SENT						
HER THOUGHTS FROM SORROW THROUGH HER HEART RE-SENT	379	2	DON JUAN	4	65	6
RESENTFULLY						
AND STILL THEY SEEM RESENTFULLY TO FEEL	313	2	DON JUAN	3	73	5
RESENTMENTS						
OF ABSENCE LAY ONE'S OLD RESENTMENTS LEVEL	257	3	DON JUAN	10	66	7
RESERVE						
AS A RESERVE A PLUNGE INTO REMORSE	349	3	DON JUAN	12	73	8
RESERVE IT) WILL BE VERY SURE TO TAKE	357	3	DON JUAN	12	89	6
RESERVE AND PRIDE COULD MAKE HIM AND FULL SLOW	366	3	DON JUAN	13	16	2
OF COURSE WITH SOME RESERVE AND SLIGHT RESTRICTION	416	3	DON JUAN	14	13	3
FOR WHICH MOST FRIENDS RESERVE THEIR SENSIBILITY	430	3	DON JUAN	14	46	8
RESERVED						
RESERVED FOR FUTURE RANSOM IN THE HOLD--	284	2	DON JUAN	3	16	6
THOSE SUFFERINGS ONCE RESERVED FOR HELL ALONE	401	2	DON JUAN	4	105	V8
ALL THIS MUST BE RESERVED FOR FURTHER SONG	410	2	DON JUAN	4	117	1
INTO CLOSE CONTACT THOUGH RESERVED NOR CAUGHT	365	3	DON JUAN	13	15	4
THOUGH THIS WE HOPE--HAS BEEN RESERVED FOR THIS AGE	376	3	DON JUAN	13	39	V5
AND TAUGHT HIM WHEN TO BE RESERVED OR FREE	492	3	DON JUAN	15	82	6
RESERVES						
HE THAT RESERVES HIS LAURELS FOR POSTERITY	14	2	DON JUAN	D	9	1
RESET						
RESET IT SHAVE MORE SMOOTHLY ALSO SLOWER	433	3	DON JUAN	14	53	7
RESIDENT						
A SPECTRAL RESIDENT--WHOSE PALLID BEAM	279	3	DON JUAN	11	24	6
RESIGN						
THAN I RESIGN THINE IMAGE OH MY FAIR	166	2	DON JUAN	2	19	5

		PAGE	VOL	CANTO	STANZA	LN

RESIGN (CONTINUED)
WHATE'ER IS TO BE BORNE--BUT NOT RESIGN . . . . 161 3 DON JUAN 8 100 7
WAS BENT WITH GRIEF THAT MAHOMET SHOULD RESIGN . . . . 262 3 DON JUAN 10 75 7
RELUCTANT AS ALL PLACEMEN TO RESIGN . . . . 360 3 DON JUAN 13 5 2
FOR THOSE WHO KNEW NOT TO RESIGN OR REIGN . . . . . 386 3 DON JUAN 13 60 8
AS IF 'TWOULD TO A SECOND SPRING RESIGN . . . . . . 395 3 DON JUAN 13 77 3
RESIGNED
AND THUS HEROICALLY STOOD RESIGNED . . . . 492 3 DON JUAN 5 141 5
MORE IN THE EYELIDS THAN THE EYES RESIGNED . . . . . 13 3 DON JUAN 6 15 3
RESIGNS
RESIGNS HERSELF WITH EXEMPLARY PATIENCE . . . . . . 440 2 DON JUAN 5 52 7
RESIST
RESIST HIS STOMACH NE'ER AT SEA BEFORE . . . . . 168 2 DON JUAN 2 23 8
NO LONGER NOW RESIST THE ATTRACTION OF GUNPOWDER . . . 129 3 DON JUAN 8 33 V7
THAT JUAN WAS UNLIKELY TO RESIST-- . . . . 436 3 DON JUAN 14 60 4
AND SEEM TO SAY RESIST US IF YOU CAN-- . . . . . 461 3 DON JUAN 15 12 7
RESISTANCE
AND GIVING UP ALL NOTIONS OF RESISTANCE . . . . . . 440 2 DON JUAN 5 51 1
AND THOUGH AS YET THE TURKS MADE NO RESISTANCE . . . 80 3 DON JUAN 7 28 V5
BY THE RESISTANCE OF THE CHASE THEY BATTERED . . . 131 3 DON JUAN 8 37 8
SO WAS HIS BLOOD STIRRED WHILE HE FOUND RESISTANCE . . 140 3 DON JUAN 8 55 1
WITHOUT RESISTANCE SEE THEIR CITY BURN . . . . . 150 3 DON JUAN 8 77 4
AND THOUGH THE TURK'S RESISTANCE WAS SUBLIME . . . 151 3 DON JUAN 8 79 6
RESISTED
TO SLAY THE PAGANS WHO RESISTED BATTERING . . . . . 99 3 DON JUAN 7 64 7
WHICH THEY RESISTED LIKE A SANDY PLAIN . . . . . 166 3 DON JUAN 8 109 8
RESOLUTION
I MAKE A RESOLUTION EVERY SPRING . . . . 85 2 DON JUAN 1 119 3
'TWAS NATURE GNAW'D THEM TO THIS RESOLUTION . . . . 195 2 DON JUAN 2 75 6
WITH RESOLUTION IN HIS DARK GRAY EYE . . . . 416 2 DON JUAN 5 10 7
RESOLUTIONS
HER RESOLUTIONS WERE MOST TRULY GREAT . . . . . . 62 2 DON JUAN 1 75 5
RESOLVE
BUT--GOD KNOWS HOW--THIS WISE RESOLVE TAKES WING . . . 85 2 DON JUAN 1 119 V5
SOONER SHALL EARTH RESOLVE ITSELF TO SEA . . . . . 166 2 DON JUAN 2 19 4
RESOLVED
RESOLVED THAT JUAN SHOULD BE QUITE A PARAGON . . . . 42 2 DON JUAN 1 38 2
SHE FELT IT GOING AND RESOLVED TO MAKE . . . . 62 2 DON JUAN 1 75 2
SHE HAD RESOLVED THAT HE SHOULD TRAVEL THROUGH . . . 129 2 DON JUAN 1 191 1
AND SERIOUSLY RESOLVED ON REFORMATION . . . . . 165 2 DON JUAN 2 17 8
OFT CAME AND WENT AS THERE RESOLVED TO DIE . . . 365 2 DON JUAN 4 39 6
YET MEN RESOLVED TO DASH THROUGH THICK AND THIN . . 94 3 DON JUAN 7 54 4
SHE THEN RESOLVED TO SEND HIM ON A MISSION . . . 246 3 DON JUAN 10 44 7
BUT I'M RESOLVED TO SAY NOUGHT THAT'S AMISS)-- . . . 326 3 DON JUAN 12 22 6
THE LADY ADELINE RESOLVED TO TAKE . . . . . 437 3 DON JUAN 14 61 1
RESOLVED TO THRUST THE MYSTERY CARTE AND TIERCE . . . 559 3 DON JUAN 16 119 5
RESOLVES
IN THEIR RESOLVES--ALAS THAT I SHOULD SAY SO . . . . 458 3 DON JUAN 15 6 4
RESORT
ARMS TO WHICH MEN WILL NEVER MORE RESORT . . . . . 106 3 DON JUAN 7 79 4
RESOUNDED
RESOUNDED ALLAH AND THE CLOUDS WHICH CLOSE . . . . . 116 3 DON JUAN 8 8 5
RESOURCE
THE LASH TO BABA--BUT HER GRAND RESOURCE . . . . 491 2 DON JUAN 5 139 7
HE SCRATCHED HIS EAR THE INFALLIBLE RESOURCE . . . 56 3 DON JUAN 6 100 7
HER CHIEF RESOURCE WAS IN HER OWN HIGH SPIRIT . . . 372 3 DON JUAN 13 31 4
A GREAT RESOURCE TO ALL AND NE'ER DENIED . . . . 506 3 DON JUAN 16 12 7
HE SIGHED--THE NEXT RESOURCE IS THE FULL MOON . . . 506 3 DON JUAN 16 13 1
RESOURCES
MEN HAVE ALL THESE RESOURCES WE BUT ONE . . . . . 131 2 DON JUAN 1 194 7
THAT COOKERY COULD HAVE CALL'D FORTH SUCH RESOURCES . . 486 3 DON JUAN 15 69 6
THOSE WHO IN COUNTIES HAVE GREAT LAND RESOURCES . . . 534 3 DON JUAN 16 68 6
FROM THOSE WHO HAVE FEW RESOURCES OF THEIR OWN . . . 541 3 DON JUAN 16 85 5
RESPECT
A THOUSAND PITIES ALSO WITH RESPECT . . . . . 38 2 DON JUAN 1 33 6
WHO HAVE A DUE RESPECT FOR THEIR OWN WISHES . . . 349 3 DON JUAN 12 73 4
MUCH I RESPECT AND MUCH I HAVE ADORED . . . . 422 3 DON JUAN 14 27 1
JUAN--IN THIS RESPECT AT LEAST LIKE SAINTS-- . . . 424 3 DON JUAN 14 31 1
STILL WE RESPECT THEE ALMA VENUS GENETRIX . . . . 554 3 DON JUAN 16 109 8
RESPECTABLE
PERHAPS NOT SO RESPECTABLE IN TRUTH . . . . . . 222 2 DON JUAN 2 125 5
TO SO RESPECTABLE AN ANCIENT RITE . . . . 452 2 DON JUAN 5 71 2
RESPECTABLY
THEY LIVED RESPECTABLY AS MAN AND WIFE . . . . . 35 2 DON JUAN 1 26 4
RESPECTS
HE LOOKED IN ALMOST ALL RESPECTS A MAID . . . . . 458 2 DON JUAN 5 80 3
WHICH IS IN ALL RESPECTS SAVE NOW AND THEN . . . . 373 3 DON JUAN 13 33 1
RESPIRATION'S
IS FREE THE RESPIRATION'S WORTH THE MONEY . . . . . 259 3 DON JUAN 10 70 8
REST
I TRACE THIS SCRAWL BECAUSE I CANNOT REST-- . . . . 130 2 DON JUAN 1 193 7
FOR WARNING TO THE REST COMPELS THESE RAPS . . . . 155 2 DON JUAN 1 V 7 7
ALL THE REST PERISH'D NEAR TWO HUNDRED SOULS . . . 185 2 DON JUAN 2 55 1
THE SAILORS ATE THE REST OF POOR PEDRILLO . . . 197 2 DON JUAN 2 77 8
AND ALL THE REST WERE THIN ENOUGH HEAVEN KNOWS . . . 199 2 DON JUAN 2 80 2
AND THE REST RUBB'D THEIR EYES AND SAW A BAY . . . 207 2 DON JUAN 2 97 5
TO PLACE HIM IN THE CAVE FOR PRESENT REST . . . 225 2 DON JUAN 2 131 3
HIS REST THE RUSHING OF THE NEIGHBOURING RILL . . . 229 2 DON JUAN 2 137 3
LULL'D LIKE THE DEPTH OF OCEAN WHEN AT REST . . . 235 2 DON JUAN 2 148 4

```
                                                           PAGE VOL      CANTO STANZA LN
REST   (CONTINUED)
   FOR JUAN WHO WAS SOMEWHAT FOND OF REST--  .  .  .  .  .  . 245  2 DON JUAN  2   168   2
   THEY TURN'D TO REST AND EACH CLASP'D BY AN ARM  .  .  .  . 253  2 DON JUAN  2   184   7
   EAT DRINK AND LOVE WHAT CAN THE REST AVAIL US  .  .  .  .  267  2 DON JUAN  2   207   7
   THAT ALL THE REST CREEP IN AND FORM A JUNCTION  .  .  .  . 271  2 DON JUAN  2   215   4
   OR KNOW WHO RESTED THERE A FOE TO REST  .  .  .  .  .  .   274  2 DON JUAN  3     1   6
   THE REST--SAVE HERE AND THERE SOME RICHER ONE  .  .  .  .  284  2 DON JUAN  3    16   5
   ARE GATHER'D ROUND US BY THY LOOK OF REST  .  .  .  .  .   338  2 DON JUAN  3   107   7
   WHICH PERISH IN THE REST BUT IN THEM WERE  .  .  .  .  .   353  2 DON JUAN  4    18   6
   THE REST OF ALL THAT TRIBE WITH HERE AND THERE  .  .  .  . 390  2 DON JUAN  4    85   2
   THE REST ARE HARDLY FITTED FOR A FAIR  .  .  .  .  .  .  . 390  2 DON JUAN  4    85   4
   OF THOSE FORGETTING THE GREAT PLACE OF REST  .  .  .  .  . 448  2 DON JUAN  5    63   3
   A HALF-WAY HOUSE OF DIPLOMATIC REST  .  .  .  .  .  .  .   472  2 DON JUAN  5   105   2
   WHICH TAKEN AT THE FLOOD--YOU KNOW THE REST  .  .  .  .  .   6  3 DON JUAN  6     1   2
   WHO SAW HIS VIRTUES AS THEY SAW THE REST  .  .  .  .  .  .  12  3 DON JUAN  6    13  V4
   ALONG THE REST CONTRIVED TO KEEP THIS DEN  .  .  .  .  .    22  3 DON JUAN  6    32   6
   LIKE ALL THE REST BUT UPON THIS OCCASION  .  .  .  .  .  .  25  3 DON JUAN  6    38   2
   WITH LADIES IT IS TIME TO GO TO REST  .  .  .  .  .  .  .   29  3 DON JUAN  6    46   2
   THEIR PLACE OF REST AND LEFT TO BOTH THEIR PIQUES  .  .  .  31  3 DON JUAN  6    50   6
   TO TAKE US FROM OUR NATURAL REST AND PULL  .  .  .  .  .    46  3 DON JUAN  6    80   3
   WITH YOU DUDU A GOOD NIGHT'S REST HAVE KNOWN  .  .  .  .    46  3 DON JUAN  6    81   6
   THE MYSTERY OF THIS RUPTURE OF THEIR REST  .  .  .  .  .    48  3 DON JUAN  6    85   6
   A LIVELY READER'S FANCY DOES THE REST  .  .  .  .  .  .  .  55  3 DON JUAN  6    98   8
   YOU KNOW THE REST THE WORDS STUCK IN HER THROAT  .  .  .    62  3 DON JUAN  6   113   4
   BUT YOUR OWN FEELINGS EVEN SHOULD ALL THE REST  .  .  .  .  63  3 DON JUAN  6   115   1
   JACK THOMSON AND BILL THOMSON--ALL THE REST  .  .  .  .  .  76  3 DON JUAN  7    19   1
   THE REST WERE JACKS AND GILLS AND WILLS AND BILLS  .  .  .  76  3 DON JUAN  7    20   1
   YOUR RANK AND FILE BY THOUSANDS WHILE THE REST  .  .  .  . 118  3 DON JUAN  8    13   7
   AND THAT THE REST HAD FACED UNTO THE RIGHT  .  .  .  .  .  125  3 DON JUAN  8    28   3
   AIR 'MIDST THE REST WHO KEPT THEIR VALIANT FACES  .  .  .  130  3 DON JUAN  8    34   7
   AIR MIDST THE REST WHOSE SHORT BREATH AND LONG FACES  .  . 130  3 DON JUAN  8    34  V7
   THE MAN IN ALL THE REST MIGHT BE CONFEST  .  .  .  .  .  . 139  3 DON JUAN  8    53   3
   MOTION WAS IN THEIR DAYS REST IN THEIR SLUMBERS  .  .  .   145  3 DON JUAN  8    67   1
   ON WHICH THE REST WITHOUT MORE INTERMISSION  .  .  .  .  . 152  3 DON JUAN  8    81   3
   AMIDST THE BODIES LULLED IN BLOODY REST  .  .  .  .  .  .  157  3 DON JUAN  8    91   8
   AND YET THE REST RUSHED EAGERLY--NO WONDER  .  .  .  .  .  163  3 DON JUAN  8   103   5
   IF YET THE CITY'S REST WERE WON OR LOST  .  .  .  .  .  .  171  3 DON JUAN  8   120   6
   SOME HUNDREDS BREATHED--THE REST WERE SILENT ALL  .  .  .  175  3 DON JUAN  8   127   8
   IN WINTER'S DEPTH OR WANT OF REST AND VICTUAL  .  .  .  .  176  3 DON JUAN  8   128   7
   UPON THE REST 'TIS NOT WORTH WHILE TO DWELL  .  .  .  .  . 184  3 DON JUAN  9     2   5
   IS ALL THE REST ABOUT HER WHETHER WED  .  .  .  .  .  .  . 214  3 DON JUAN  9    64   4
   PINIONS TO FLEE AWAY AND BE AT REST  .  .  .  .  .  .  .   228  3 DON JUAN 10     6   3
   IS THAT I FIND NO SPOT WHERE MAN CAN REST EYE ON  .  .  .  269  3 DON JUAN 11     3   5
   UPON THE REST OF EUROPE'S SOCIAL STATE  .  .  .  .  .  .   327  3 DON JUAN 12    24   4
   WILL VERY OFTEN SUPERSEDE THE REST  .  .  .  .  .  .  .  . 371  3 DON JUAN 13    28   8
   DEPARTED LIKE THE REST OF THEIR COMPEERS  .  .  .  .  .  . 381  3 DON JUAN 13    50   2
   THE REST HAD BEEN REFORM'D REPLACED OR SUNK  .  .  .  .  . 389  3 DON JUAN 13    66   7
   SMALL IS THE REST OF THOSE WHO WOULD BE SMART  .  .  .  .  408  3 DON JUAN 13   109   5
   MAKING THE COUNTENANCE A MASQUE OF REST  .  .  .  .  .  .  457  3 DON JUAN 15     3   3
   WHILE ALL WITHOUT'S INDICATIVE OF REST  .  .  .  .  .  .   457  3 DON JUAN 15     3  V3
   OF RANK AND YOUTH THOUGH PURER THAN THE REST  .  .  .  .   480  3 DON JUAN 15    55   4
   OR LIKE AN OPIATE WHICH BRINGS TROUBLED REST  .  .  .  .   505  3 DON JUAN 16    10   1
   BUT FOR THE REST AS HE HIMSELF SEEMED LOTH  .  .  .  .  .  514  3 DON JUAN 16    33   6
   YOU LOOK QUOTH HE AS IF YOU HAD HAD YOUR REST  .  .  .  .  515  3 DON JUAN 16    35   3
   TURNING ROUND TO THE REST HE SMILING SAID  .  .  .  .  .   517  3 DON JUAN 16    39   3
   TRUE SHE SAID LITTLE--'TWAS THE REST THAT BROKE  .  .  .   552  3 DON JUAN 16   104   1
   RATHER THAN REST INSTEAD OF POPPIES WILLOWS  .  .  .  .  . 555  3 DON JUAN 16   110   5
RESTED
   OR KNOW WHO RESTED THERE A FOE TO REST  .  .  .  .  .  .   274  2 DON JUAN  3     1   6
RESTING
   RESTING ITS BRIGHT BASE ON THE QUIVERING BLUE  .  .  .  .  204  2 DON JUAN  2    91   3
   FOR EVERYTHING SEEMED RESTING ON HIS NOD  .  .  .  .  .  . 104  3 DON JUAN  7    74   1
RESTIVE
   TO FIND OUR CHILDREN RUNNING RESTIVE--THEY  .  .  .  .  .  305  2 DON JUAN  3    59   2
   AND PEGASUS RUNS RESTIVE IN HIS WAGGON  .  .  .  .  .  .   333  2 DON JUAN  3    99   2
RESTLESS
   SILENT AND PENSIVE IDLE RESTLESS SLOW  .  .  .  .  .  .  .  68  2 DON JUAN  1    87   1
   THE RESTLESS TITAN HICCUPS IN HIS DEN  .  .  .  .  .  .  . 115  3 DON JUAN  8     7   8
   FELT RESTLESS AND PERPLEXED AND COMPROMISED  .  .  .  .  . 506  3 DON JUAN 16    12   2
RESTLESSNESS
   TREMBLINGS WHEN MET AND RESTLESSNESS WHEN LEFT  .  .  .  .  62  2 DON JUAN  1    74   4
   GULBEYAZ ROSE FROM RESTLESSNESS AND PALE  .  .  .  .  .  .  49  3 DON JUAN  6    87   2
RESTORATION
   AND THROW DOWN OLD WHICH HE CALLED RESTORATION  .  .  .  . 529  3 DON JUAN 16    58   8
RESTORE
   RESTORE ME THOSE PURE FEELINGS GONE FOREVER  .  .  .  .  .   9  3 DON JUAN  6     5   8
   HAVE SEEN AND FELT HOW STRONGLY YOU RESTORE  .  .  .  .  . 184  3 DON JUAN  9     3   6
   WAS TO RESTORE HIM TO HIS SELF PROPRIETY  .  .  .  .  .  . 526  3 DON JUAN 16    52   2
RESTORED
   THIS HEATHENISH CROSS RESTORED THE BREED AGAIN  .  .  .  .  53  2 DON JUAN  1    58   1
   BUT BY DEGREES THEIR SENSES WERE RESTORED  .  .  .  .  .   257  2 DON JUAN  2   191   5
   THE OBSEQUIOUS LANDLORD HATH THE CHANGE RESTORED  .  .  .  379  3 DON JUAN 13    46   5
RESTORES
   RESTORES ALL HUMAN FEELINGS TO BURLESQUE  .  .  .  .  .  . 345  2 DON JUAN  4     3  V8
RESTRAIN
   MUST I RESTRAIN ME THROUGH THE FEAR OF STRIFE  .  .  .  .   69  3 DON JUAN  7     6   7
RESTRAINT
   THE SILKEN FILLET'S SLIGHT RESTRAINT AND SHUN  .  .  .  .  313  2 DON JUAN  3    73  V6
RESTRAINTS
   HE DID NOT TAKE SUCH STUDIES FOR RESTRAINTS  .  .  .  .  .  47  2 DON JUAN  1    47   4
```

670

RESTRICTION
	PAGE	VOL	CANTO	STANZA	LN
IN LEAVING VERSE MORE FREE FROM THE RESTRICTION	154	3	DON JUAN 8	86	4
MY TOPIC WITH OF COURSE THE DUE RESTRICTION	311	3	DON JUAN 11	88	2
OF COURSE WITH SOME RESERVE AND SLIGHT RESTRICTION	416	3	DON JUAN 14	13	3

RESTS
BUYS THEM IN MARRIAGE--AND WHAT RESTS BEYOND	263	2	DON JUAN 2	200	6
BUT) OF FINE UNCLIPT GOLD WHERE DULLY RESTS	321	3	DON JUAN 12	12	5
AND THE WHOLE MATTER RESTS UPON EYE-SIGHT	348	3	DON JUAN 12	71	3

RESULT
THAT SAD RESULT OF PASSIONS AND POTATOES--	472	3	DON JUAN 15	37	7

RESULTING
RESULTING FROM THE SCOLDING OR THE VISION	47	3	DON JUAN 6	82	3

RESUME
BUT TO RESUME THE LANGUID JUAN RAISED	239	2	DON JUAN 2	157	1
HE MAY RESUME HIS AMATORY CARE	288	2	DON JUAN 3	24	5
THE EXPRESSION AND ENDEAVOURING TO RESUME	298	2	DON JUAN 3	44	5
AND TELLS ME TO RESUME MY STORY HERE	347	2	DON JUAN 4	7	8
A MOMENT AND THEN DROPPED BUT TO RESUME	420	2	DON JUAN 5	18	5
BUT TO RESUME--SHOULD THERE BE (WHAT MAY NOT	447	2	DON JUAN 5	62	1

RESUMED
IN HIS RESUMED AMUSEMENT I CONFESS	100	3	DON JUAN 7	65	4

RESURRECTION
BESIDES THEIR RESURRECTION AIDS OUR GLORIES	37	2	DON JUAN 1	31	5
AND SCIENCE PROFITS BY THIS RESURRECTION--	37	2	DON JUAN 1	31	7
THERE'S MERIT IN THIS SORT OF RESURRECTION	37	2	DON JUAN 1	31	V7
WOULD SHARE MOST PROBABLY ITS RESURRECTION	301	2	DON JUAN 3	50	8
RACKS PRISONS INQUISITIONS RESURRECTION	272	3	DON JUAN 11	9	7

RETAIN
'TIS THAT I STILL RETAIN MY BUFF AND BLUE	20	2	DON JUAN 0	17	4
'TWAS STRANGE ENOUGH SHE SHOULD RETAIN THE IMPRESSION	252	3	DON JUAN 10	56	1

RETAINED
AND HAD RETAINED HIS BOYISH LOOK BEYOND	209	3	DON JUAN 9	53	2

RETAINS
RETAINS THE SABLE STAINS OF THE DARK CREEPER	232	3	DON JUAN 10	15	5
HE STILL RETAINS HIS SWAY	520	3	DON JUAN 16	L 5	2

RETCHING
(HERE HE GREW INARTICULATE WITH RETCHING)	167	2	DON JUAN 2	20	8

RE-TEACH
AND THUS POPE QUOTES THE PRECEPT TO RE-TEACH	470	2	DON JUAN 5	101	6

RETICULAR
YET MANY HAVE A METHOD MORE RETICULAR--	343	3	DON JUAN 12	59	5

RETIRE
BABA RETIRE WHICH HE OBEYED IN STYLE	473	2	DON JUAN 5	107	2
BUT WHEN THEY SAW THE ENEMY RETIRE	82	3	DON JUAN 7	31	2
RETIRE A LITTLE MERELY TO TAKE BREATH	133	3	DON JUAN 8	40	8
SOME TWENTY TIMES HE MADE THE RUSS RETIRE	171	3	DON JUAN 8	120	3
RETIRE BUT LOOK INTO YOUR PAST IMPRESSION	413	3	DON JUAN 14	6	2

RETIRED
WITH HIM RETIRED HIS POSSE COMITATUS	111	2	DON JUAN 1	164	1
FOR DEATH THOUGH VANQUISH'D STILL RETIRED WITH STRIFE	214	2	DON JUAN 2	111	8
THE DWARFS AND DANCING GIRLS HAD ALL RETIRED	334	2	DON JUAN 3	101	2
AT LAST THEY REACHED A QUARTER MOST RETIRED	448	2	DON JUAN 5	64	1
RETIRED INTO HER BOUDOIR A SWEET PLACE	54	3	DON JUAN 6	97	2
OF WHAT HAD PAST SINCE ALL THE SLAVES RETIRED	55	3	DON JUAN 6	99	3
JOHNSON RETIRED A LITTLE JUST TO RALLY	131	3	DON JUAN 8	36	7
JUAN RETIRED--AND SO WILL I UNTIL	224	3	DON JUAN 9	85	2
AT LEAST HE KEPT HIS VANITY RETIRED	428	3	DON JUAN 14	41	4
RETIRED AND AS HE WENT OUT CALMLY KISSED HER	440	3	DON JUAN 14	69	7
LIKE FLEECY CLOUDS INTO THE SKY RETIRED	504	3	DON JUAN 16	8	6
RETIRED WITH MOST UNFASHIONABLE BOWS	549	3	DON JUAN 16	101	5
ARRIVED RETIRED TO HIS BUT TO DESPOND	555	3	DON JUAN 16	110	4
THE GHOST STOPPED MENACED THEN RETIRED UNTIL	559	3	DON JUAN 16	119	7

RETIREMENT
AT LEAST SINCE THE RETIREMENT OF THE VANDALS	128	2	DON JUAN 1	190	4

RETIRING
AND HALF RETIRING FROM THE GLOWING ARM	83	2	DON JUAN 1	115	2
THEY BOWED OBEISANCE AND WITHDREW RETIRING	469	2	DON JUAN 5	100	1
HE FOUND HIMSELF ALONE AND FRIENDS RETIRING	125	3	DON JUAN 8	27	8
AND JUAN ON RETIRING FOR THE NIGHT	506	3	DON JUAN 16	12	1

RETORT
'TIS TO RETORT WITH FIRMNESS AND WHEN HE	117	2	DON JUAN 1	175	7
AND FEEL NO MORE THE SPIRIT TO RETORT I	143	2	DON JUAN 1	213	6
THOUGH NAMELESS IN OUR LANGUAGE--WE RETORT	405	3	DON JUAN 13	101	6

RETORTS
TO FIND RETORTS FOR INNOCENT BLOOD SHED	314	3	DON JUAN 11	V 75	4

RETRACE
IN WHOM OUR BRIGHTEST DAYS WE WOULD RETRACE	305	2	DON JUAN 3	59	3
SHE GAZED BUT NONE SHE EVER COULD RETRACE	381	2	DON JUAN 4	68	4

RETREAT
AND MADE A SIGNAL TO RETREAT AT ONE	81	3	DON JUAN 7	30	6
BEGAN TO SIGNALIZE THE RUSS RETREAT	87	3	DON JUAN 7	42	2
FOR ONE WOULD NOT RETREAT NOR T'OTHER FLINCH	150	3	DON JUAN 8	77	8

RETREATED
WHO HAD RETREATED AS THE PHRASE IS WHEN	130	3	DON JUAN 8	35	2
AND THEN RETREATED SOBERLY--AT TEN	408	3	DON JUAN 13	108	8
AND HE AROSE ADVANCED--THE SHADE RETREATED	559	3	DON JUAN 16	119	2

RETREATING
AS IF WELL-USED TO THE RETREATING TRADE	473	2	DON JUAN 5	107	3

RETREATS
AND AS SHE TREATS ALL THINGS AND NE'ER RETREATS	502	3	DON JUAN 16	3	1

                                                        PAGE VOL   CANTO STANZA LN
RETROGRADE
     MAY RETROGRADE A LITTLE IN THE DANCE . . . . 473 3 DON JUAN 15   39   6
RETROSPECTION
     AS APROPOS OF HOPE OR RETROSPECTION . . . . 456 3 DON JUAN 15   1   3
RETURN
     PERHAPS IT MAY SET OUT ON ITS RETURN-- . . . . .   92 2 DON JUAN 1   131   2
     AND SO GOOD NIGHT--RETURN WE TO OUR STORY . . . .   94 2 DON JUAN 1   134   2
     AND TRUANT HUSBAND SHOULD RETURN AND SAY . . . . .   98 2 DON JUAN 1   141   7
     YOU WILL RETURN IN BEAUTY AND IN PRIDE . . . . .   132 2 DON JUAN 1   195   V1
     WHO THANK'D ME DULY BY RETURN OF POST-- . . . . .   142 2 DON JUAN 1   210   2
     I WAS MOST READY TO RETURN A BLOW . . . .   143 2 DON JUAN 1   212   6
     RETURN WE TO DON JUAN HE BEGUN . . . .   244 2 DON JUAN 2   167   1
     BUT TO RETURN--GET VERY DRUNK AND WHEN . . . . .   250 2 DON JUAN 2   179   7
     STOP SO I STOPP'D--BUT TO RETURN THAT WHICH . . .   269 2 DON JUAN 2   211   1
     AN HONEST GENTLEMAN AT HIS RETURN . . . . . .   287 2 DON JUAN 3   23   1
     IF ALL THE DEAD COULD NOW RETURN TO LIFE . . . .   301 2 DON JUAN 3   50   1
     'TIS TIME WE SHOULD RETURN TO PLAIN NARRATION . .   34 3 DON JUAN 6   57   1
     BUT JOHNSON ONLY RAN OFF TO RETURN . . . . . .   133 3 DON JUAN 8   41   1
     THEY FOUND ON THEIR RETURN THE SELF-SAME WELCOME . 134 3 DON JUAN 8   42   7
     FOR A RETURN TO HATRED I WOULD SHUN HER . . . .   231 3 DON JUAN 10   12   4
     FOR HER RETURN TO VIRTUE--AS THEY CALL . . . . .   352 3 DON JUAN 12   79   7
     AND GRIEVED FOR THOSE WHO COULD RETURN NO MORE . . 476 3 DON JUAN 15   45   8
     BUT TO RETURN UNTO THE STRICTER RULE-- . . . . .   563 3 DON JUAN 17   3   1
RETURN'D
     THE BLOOM TOO HAD RETURN'D TO HAIDEE'S CHEEKS . .   295 2 DON JUAN 3   38   6
     HER TEARS TOO BEING RETURN'D INTO THEIR FOUNT . .   295 2 DON JUAN 3   38   7
RETURNED
     WHICH WAS RETURNED WITH INTEREST I MAY SAY . . .   81 3 DON JUAN 7   29   6
     WAKING ALREADY AND RETURNED AT LENGTH . . . . .   511 3 DON JUAN 16   25   7
RETURNING
     RETURNING THERE FROM HER SUCCESSFUL SEARCH . . .   206 2 DON JUAN 2   95   6
     FAST TO THE SAND LEST THE RETURNING WAVE . . . .   213 2 DON JUAN 2   108   2
     BUT CERTAINLY TO ONE DEEM'D DEAD RETURNING . . .   300 2 DON JUAN 3   49   7
     OR ANDALUSIAN GIRL FROM MASS RETURNING . . . . .   350 3 DON JUAN 12   75   2
RETURNS
     WHEN FIRST SHE STARTS AND THEN RETURNS TO PEEP . .   36 3 DON JUAN 6   60   7
     TELL THEM THAT YOUTH ONCE GONE RETURNS NO MORE . .   267 3 DON JUAN 10   86   3
REVEALED
     AND THEY REVEALED--ALAS THAT ERE THEY SHOULD . .   561 3 DON JUAN 16   123   6
REVEL
     EXCEPT TO BULL-FIGHTS MASS PLAY ROUT AND REVEL . . 102 2 DON JUAN 1   148   4
     THIS REVEL SEEM'D A CURIOUS MODE OF MOURNING . .   300 2 DON JUAN 3   49   8
     WHILE YOUTH'S HOT WISHES IN OUR RED VEINS REVEL .   345 2 DON JUAN 4   2   5
     OR REVEL IN THE JOYS OF CALCULATION . . . . .   320 3 DON JUAN 12   10   8
     YOUR EYES TO REVEL IN A LIVELIER SIGHT . . . . .   392 3 DON JUAN 13   72   6
REVELATIONS
     UP ANNALS REVELATIONS POESY . . . .   286 3 DON JUAN 11   37   6
REVEL'D
     HE REVEL'D IN HIS CICERONIAN GLORY . . . .   401 3 DON JUAN 13   91   4
REVELL'D
     AND REVELL'D IN THE FANCIES OF THE TIME . . . . .   347 2 DON JUAN 4   6   5
REVELRY
     FROM CIVIC REVELRY TO RURAL MIRTH . . . .   88 2 DON JUAN 1   124   4
     AND EVERY SOUND OF REVELRY EXPIRED . . . .   334 2 DON JUAN 3   101   4
REVELS
     SO ORDERED IT AMIDST THESE SULPHURY REVELS . . .   135 3 DON JUAN 8   44   6
     DAMSELS AND DANCES REVELS READY MONEY . . . . .   235 3 DON JUAN 10   21   7
     OF HIM WHO FEASTS AND FIGHTS AND ROARS AND REVELS . 237 3 DON JUAN 10   25   4
     WARS REVELS LOVES--DO THESE BRING MEN MORE EASE .   321 3 DON JUAN 12   11   5
REVENGE
     REVENGE IN PERSON'S CERTAINLY NO VIRTUE . . . .   37 2 DON JUAN 1   30   7
     SWEET IS REVENGE--ESPECIALLY TO WOMEN . . . . .   88 2 DON JUAN 1   124   7
     AND THEIR REVENGE IS AS THE TIGER'S SPRING . . .   262 2 DON JUAN 2   199   6
     RAGE FEAR HATE JEALOUSY REVENGE COMPUNCTION . . .   271 2 DON JUAN 2   215   6
     WELL YOU SHALL HAVE REVENGE AND THAT UNBOUNDED . .   98 3 DON JUAN 7   61   V7
REVENGED
     SWORE LUSTILY HE'D BE REVENGED THIS NIGHT . . .   122 2 DON JUAN 1   184   5
REVENGING
     REDRESSING INJURY REVENGING WRONG . . . .   363 3 DON JUAN 13   10   1
REVERED
     REVERED THE SOIL OF THOSE TRUE SONS THE MOTHER . .   265 3 DON JUAN 10   81   7
REVERENCE
     PROTECTS HIS DUST BUT REVERENCE HERE IS PAID . .   400 2 DON JUAN 4   104   3
REVEREND
     HIS REVEREND TUTORS HAD AT TIMES A TUSSLE . . .   44 2 DON JUAN 1   41   5
     AND EVEN PEDRILLO HIS MOST REVEREND TUTOR . . .   175 2 DON JUAN 2   36   7
     BENEATH THE VERY REVEREND ROWLEY POWLEY . . . .   297 3 DON JUAN 11   57   6
     THERE WAS THE REVEREND RODOMONT PRECISIAN . . .   399 3 DON JUAN 13   87   5
     BUT WHETHER REVEREND RAPP LEARN'D THIS IN GERMANY . 472 3 DON JUAN 15   36   3
     TO ASK THE REVEREND PERSON WHAT HE WANTED . . .   511 3 DON JUAN 16   23   8
REVERIE
     NOR GLOWING REVERIE NOR POET'S LAY . . . . . .   73 2 DON JUAN 1   96   3
     OBSERVING LITTLE IN HIS REVERIE . . . .   553 3 DON JUAN 16   106   7
REVERIES
     ON WHOM HER REVERIES CELESTIAL RAN . . . . . .   64 2 DON JUAN 1   79   8
     THOSE LONELY WALKS AND LENGTHENING REVERIES . . .   73 2 DON JUAN 1   97   1
     NOT ALL THE REVERIES OF JACOB BEHMEN . . . . .   7 3 DON JUAN 6   2   5
REVERSE
     I LOVE THE SEX AND SOMETIMES WOULD REVERSE . . .   19 3 DON JUAN 6   27   1
```

672
```

REVERSE   (CONTINUED)
    BUT SYSTEM DOTH REVERSE THE TITAN'S BREAKFAST 411   3 DON JUAN 14   2   1
    BUT RAPP IS THE REVERSE OF ZEALOUS MATRONS 472   3 DON JUAN 15   37   1
REVERSING
    REVERSING THE GOOD CUSTOM OF OLD DAYS 316   2 DON JUAN 3   79   2
REVERSION
    (WHO DOES NOT OFTEN CLAIM THE BRIGHT REVERSION) 14   2 DON JUAN D   9   2
REVERT
    THE LAW AT LEAST UNTIL THE BENCH REVERT TO TRUE 314   3 DON JUAN 11   V 76   6
REVIEW
    I'VE BRIBED MY GRANDMOTHER'S REVIEW--THE BRITISH 141   2 DON JUAN 1   209   8
    AND THAT THE EDINBURGH REVIEW AND QUARTERLY 142   2 DON JUAN 1   211   7
    AND WITH THE PAGES OF THE LAST REVIEW 294   3 DON JUAN 11   50   2
REVISIT
    PERHAPS I MAY REVISIT THEE NO MORE 166   2 DON JUAN 2   18   2
REVIVE
    WE WILL REVIVE OUR FORTUNES BEFORE LONG 389   2 DON JUAN 4   82   8
    TO TOSS TO TUMBLE DOZE REVIVE AND QUAKE 18   3 DON JUAN 6   24   7
    ALL THAT I WRITE OR WROTE CAN NE'ER REVIVE 569   3 DON JUAN 17   V 13   3
REVIVING
    THY LATE REVIVING ROMAN SOUL DESPONDS 19   2 DON JUAN D   16   3
REVOKE
    SHE WOULD REVOKE THE ORDER HE HAD HEARD 62   3 DON JUAN 6   113   8
    AND MEDES WOULD NE'ER REVOKE WHAT WENT BEFORE 366   3 DON JUAN 13   17   4
REVOLUTION
    IF I HAD NOT PERCEIVED THAT REVOLUTION 138   3 DON JUAN 8   51   7
REVOLVED
    AN AWKWARD LOOK AS HE REVOLVED THE CASE 111   2 DON JUAN 1   164   7
REVOLVING
    TOWNS NATIONS WORLDS IN HER REVOLVING PRANKS 135   3 DON JUAN 8   44   5
REWARD
    'TIS SAID THAT XERXES OFFER'D A REWARD 85   2 DON JUAN 1   118   1
    TURNED BACK WITHIN ITS SOCKET--THESE REWARD 118   3 DON JUAN 8   13   6
    FOR LOVE WAR OR AMBITION WHICH REWARD 235   3 DON JUAN 10   22   6
    WERE THEIR REWARD FOR FOLLOWING BILLY'S BANNERS 242   3 DON JUAN 10   36   4
    AT ONCE HER ROYAL SPLENDOUR AND REWARD 247   3 DON JUAN 10   46   4
    YIELDS HIM BUT VINEGAR FOR HIS REWARD-- 297   3 DON JUAN 11   58   3
    BUT MODESTY'S AT TIMES ITS OWN REWARD 462   3 DON JUAN 15   14   6
REWARDED
    HOW WAS THY TOIL REWARDED WE MIGHT FILL 464   3 DON JUAN 15   18   6
REWARDS
    BUT WHY THEN PUBLISH--THERE ARE NO REWARDS 415   3 DON JUAN 14   11   1
RHENISH
    OR DUTCH WITH THIRST--WHAT HO A FLASK OF RHENISH . . . 392   3 DON JUAN 13   72   8
RHETORIC
    OF RHETORIC WHICH THE LEARN'D CALL RIGMAROLE 116   2 DON JUAN 1   174   8
RHIMA
    DREADFUL AS DANTE'S RHIMA OR THIS STANZA 557   3 DON JUAN 16   116   4
RHINE
    UNTIL HE REACHED THE CASTELLATED RHINE-- 255   3 DON JUAN 10   61   2
RHODES
    OF CANDIA CYPRUS RHODES OR OTHER ISLANDS 209   2 DON JUAN 2   100   8
RHONE
    OR LIKE THE RHONE BY LEMAN'S WATERS WASH'D 447   3 DON JUAN 14   87   4
RHYME
    IN FRENCH BUT THEN THE RHYME WOULD GO FOR NOUGHT) . . . 67   2 DON JUAN 1   84   8
    WITH GOOD DISCRETION AND IN CURRENT RHYME 135   2 DON JUAN 1   200 V8
    PROSE POETS LIKE BLANK-VERSE I'M FOND OF RHYME 136   2 DON JUAN 1   201   5
    SOME PEOPLE LIKE BLANK VERSE I'M FOND OF RHYME 136   2 DON JUAN 1   201 V5
    PULCI WAS SIRE OF THE HALF-SERIOUS RHYME 347   2 DON JUAN 4   6   3
    (THE RHYME OBLIGES ME TO THIS SOMETIMES 456   2 DON JUAN 5   77   7
    THE PUBLIC KNEW NO MORE THAN DOES THIS RHYME 496   2 DON JUAN 5   149   6
    TO SLACKEN SAIL AND ANCHOR WITH OUR RHYME 503   2 DON JUAN 5   159   4
    REQUIRES IT THAT'S TO SAY THE ENGLISH RHYME 14   3 DON JUAN 6   18   2
    A LIBEL OR WHATE'ER YOU PLEASE TO RHYME ON 53   3 DON JUAN 6   94   4
    A NON-DESCRIPT AND EVER VARYING RHYME 67   3 DON JUAN 7   2   2
    WHICH MAY BE NAMES AT MOSCOW INTO RHYME 74   3 DON JUAN 7   16   2
    COULD RHYME LIKE NERO O'ER A BURNING CITY 179   3 DON JUAN 8   134   8
    OF FAITHFUL PAIRS--(I NEEDS MUST RHYME WITH DOVE . . . 219   3 DON JUAN 9   74   3
    WITH RHYME BUT ALWAYS LEANT LESS TO IMPROVING 219   3 DON JUAN 9   74   6
    (AS FAR AS RHYME AND CRITICISM COMBINE 232   3 DON JUAN 10   16   3
    OF WRATH AND RHYME WHEN JUVENILE AND CURLY 234   3 DON JUAN 10   19   2
    WHO STILL REGRETTED THAT HE DID NOT RHYME 295   3 DON JUAN 11   53   4
    THE GRAND NAPOLEON OF THE REALMS OF RHYME 296   3 DON JUAN 11   55   8
    AGAINST THE SAME GIVEN QUANTITY OF RHYME 312   3 DON JUAN 11   90   3
    BUT THOU ART THE MOST DIFFICULT TO RHYME AT 327   3 DON JUAN 12   24   5
    WHILE I WITHOUT REMORSE OF RHYME OR FEAR 393   3 DON JUAN 13   74   2
    BUT TA'EN AT HAZARD AS THE RHYME MAY RUN 397   3 DON JUAN 13   83   6
    UNTIL I FAIRLY KNOCK'D IT UP WITH RHYME 414   3 DON JUAN 14   9   8
    THOUGH CERTAINLY MORE DIFFICULT TO RHYME AT 423   3 DON JUAN 14   29   4
    SHOWN IN THIS SORT OF DESULTORY RHYME 465   3 DON JUAN 15   20   2
    'GAINST RHYME I NEVER SHOULD HAVE KNOCK'D MY BROWS . . 467   3 DON JUAN 15   24   5
    TO RHYME AT NOON--WHEN I HAVE OTHER THINGS 500   3 DON JUAN 15   98   2
    WITH AWFUL FOOTSTEPS REGULAR AS RHYME 556   3 DON JUAN 16   113   3
RHYMED
    OUT OF THOSE NINETEEN WHO LATE RHYMED TO PITH 79   3 DON JUAN 7   25   6
RHYME'S
    IF IN MY EXTREMITY OF RHYME'S DISTRESS 442   3 DON JUAN 14   75   5
RHYMES
    BUT NOT AT ALL ADAPTED TO MY RHYMES 22   2 DON JUAN 1   3   8

```
                                                            PAGE VOL        CANTO   STANZA LN

RHYMES   (CONTINUED)
    WHEN POETS SAY I'VE WRITTEN FIFTY RHYMES . . . . . .  .  .  79  2 DON JUAN   1     108    3
    MY HEART IN PASSION AND MY HEAD ON RHYMES . . . . . .  .  . 145  2 DON JUAN   1     217    8
    THE FOUR FIRST RHYMES ARE SOUTHEY'S EVERY LINE . . . .  .  . 149  2 DON JUAN   1     222    7
    AND PAIR THEIR RHYMES AS VENUS YOKES HER DOVES . . . .  .  . 411  2 DON JUAN   5       1    3
    TO GUIDE-BOOKS RHYMES TOURS SKETCHES ILLUSTRATIONS .  .  .  . 440  2 DON JUAN   5      52    8
    MONARCHS ARE LESS IMPERATIVE THAN RHYMES)-- . . . . .  .  . 456  2 DON JUAN   5      77    8
    THE HINGES BEING AS SMOOTH AS ROGERS' RHYMES . . . . .  .  . 463  2 DON JUAN   5      89    4
    KISS RHYMES TO BLISS IN FACT AS WELL AS VERSE-- . . .  .  .  35  3 DON JUAN   6      59    7
    THINE EAR IF IT SHOULD REACH--AND NOW RHYMES WANDER .  .  .  52  3 DON JUAN   6      93    3
    THINE EAR IMPERIAL AND JUST NOW RHYMES WANDER . . . .  .  .  52  3 DON JUAN   6      93   V3
    AND MAY SERVE THEREFORE TO BEDEW THESE RHYMES . . . .  .  . 156  3 DON JUAN   8      90    5
    ARE HINTS AS GOOD AS SERMONS OR AS RHYMES . . . . . .  .  . 174  3 DON JUAN   8     125    6
    SHE SMILED AT MAD SUWARROW'S RHYMES WHO THREW . . . .  .  . 212  3 DON JUAN   9      60    2
    IN RHYMES OR DREAMT (FOR FANCY WILL PLAY TRICKS) . . .  .  . 230  3 DON JUAN  10      10    5
    WHICH SHRINK FROM TOUCH AS MONARCHS DO FROM RHYMES . .  .  . 243  3 DON JUAN  10      37    3
    AT LEAST IT RHYMES TO LOVE BUT I'M PREPARED . . . . .  .  . 322  3 DON JUAN  12      13    6
    AND NOW AND THEN IT ALSO SUITS MY RHYMES . . . . . . .  .  . 361  3 DON JUAN  13       8    4
    ALL WHICH I USE TO MAKE MY RHYMES RUN GLIBBER . . . .  .  . 487  3 DON JUAN  15      71    3
    COULD WRITE RHYMES AND COMPOSE MORE THAN SHE WROTE . .  .  . 524  3 DON JUAN  16      47    2
    OR (AS RHYMES MAY BE IN THESE DAYS) MUCH MORE . . . .  .  . 556  3 DON JUAN  16     113    4
RHYMING
    BUT TIMES ARE ALTER'D SINCE A RHYMING LOVER . . . . .  .  . 405  2 DON JUAN   4     111    2
RIB
    I MUST NOT INTRODUCE EVEN A SPARE RIB HERE . . . . . .  .  . 487  3 DON JUAN  15      71    5
RIBAS
    AND ADMIRAL RIBAS (KNOWN IN RUSSIAN STORY) . . . . . .  .  .  83  3 DON JUAN   7      35    3
    WHILE THINGS WERE IN ABEYANCE RIBAS SENT . . . . . . .  .  .  85  3 DON JUAN   7      38    1
RIBAS'
    TO ANSWER RIBAS' SUMMONS TO GIVE WAY . . . . . . . . .  .  . 171  3 DON JUAN   8     120    8
RIBAUPIERRE'S
    ('MONGST OTHER DEATHS THE GENERAL RIBAUPIERRE'S . . .  .  . 147  3 DON JUAN   8      71    6
RIBBON
    MAY WIN PERHAPS A RIBBON AT THE BREAST . . . . . . . .  .  . 118  3 DON JUAN   8      13    8
RIBBONS
    MEDALS RANKS RIBBONS LACE EMBROIDERY SCARLET . . . . .  .  . 108  3 DON JUAN   7      84    1
    FOR SEEING ONE WITH RIBBONS BLACK AND BLUE . . . . . .  .  . 141  3 DON JUAN   8      57    5
    OF SEVERAL RIBBONS AND SOME THOUSAND PEASANTS . . . .  .  . 222  3 DON JUAN   9      79    8
    SCOTCH WITH BLUE GREEN RIBBONS--IRISH WITH A BLUE . .  .  . 314  3 DON JUAN  11   V 76    2
RIB'S
    A RIB'S A THORN IN A WED GALLANT'S SIDE . . . . . . .  .  . 292  3 DON JUAN  11      46    6
RICCHI
    CAN PAINT COSI VIAGGINO I RICCHI . . . . . . . . . . .  .  . 380  3 DON JUAN  13      47    5
RICE
    HENCE ALL THIS RICE MEAT DANCING WINE AND FIDDLING . .  .  . 295  2 DON JUAN   3      39    1
RICH
    AS THE RICH MAN'S IN HELL WHO VAINLY SCREAM'D . . . .  .  . 202  2 DON JUAN   2      86    4
    THIS THOUGH NOT LARGE WAS ONE OF THE MOST RICH . . . .  .  . 238  2 DON JUAN   2     154    8
    LIKE A RICH WRECK--HER FIRST LOVE AND HER LAST . . . .  .  . 247  2 DON JUAN   2     173    8
    THAN ADMIRATION DUE WHERE NATURE'S RICH . . . . . . .  .  . 269  2 DON JUAN   2     211    3
    HAS IN HIS ABSENCE WEDDED SOME RICH MISER . . . . . .  .  . 288  2 DON JUAN   3      24    2
    A GENTLEMAN SO RICH IN THE WORLD'S GOODS . . . . . . .  .  . 371  2 DON JUAN   4      51    3
    WHO SWORE HIS VOICE WAS VERY RICH AND MELLOW . . . . .  .  . 391  2 DON JUAN   4      87    6
    (THOUGH CLAUDIUS RICH ESQUIRE SOME BRICKS HAS GOT . .  .  . 447  2 DON JUAN   5      62    5
    THE MOVEABLES WERE PRODIGALLY RICH . . . . . . . . . .  .  . 449  2 DON JUAN   5      65    4
    THE FURNITURE WAS MOST PROFUSELY RICH . . . . . . . .  .  . 449  2 DON JUAN   5      65   V4
    SLIPPERS OF SAFFRON DAGGER RICH AND HANDY . . . . . .  .  . 451  2 DON JUAN   5      68    7
    AND WAFTED FAR AROSE A RICH PERFUME . . . . . . . . .  .  . 460  2 DON JUAN   5      85    6
    A RICH CONFUSION FORMED A DISARRAY . . . . . . . . . .  .  . 465  2 DON JUAN   5      93    3
    FOR RICH MEN AND THEIR BRIDES TO LAY THEIR HEADS . . .  .  .  18  3 DON JUAN   6      25    4
    AND RICH WITH ALL CONTRIVANCES WHICH GRACE . . . . . .  .  .  54  3 DON JUAN   6      97    4
    IN SHORT THIS LAST ATTACK THOUGH RICH IN GLORY . . . .  .  .  83  3 DON JUAN   7      35    1
    TO SEE THE SULTAN RICH IN MANY A GEM . . . . . . . . .  .  . 104  3 DON JUAN   7      74    4
    MAKE EPIC POESY SO RARE AND RICH . . . . . . . . . . .  .  . 156  3 DON JUAN   8      90    8
    GRIEF A RICH FIELD WHICH NEVER WOULD LIE FALLOW . . .  .  . 228  3 DON JUAN  10       7    6
    AND RICH IN RUBLES DIAMONDS CASH AND CREDIT . . . . .  .  . 259  3 DON JUAN  10      70    2
    OF A RICH FOREIGNER'S INITIATION . . . . . . . . . . .  .  . 293  3 DON JUAN  11      49    6
    NOBLE RICH CELEBRATED AND A STRANGER . . . . . . . . .  .  . 305  3 DON JUAN  11      74    2
    HANDSOME BUT WASTED RICH WITHOUT A SOU . . . . . . . .  .  . 306  3 DON JUAN  11      75    2
    WHILE THE POOR RICH WRETCH OBJECT OF THESE CARES . . .  .  . 331  3 DON JUAN  12      33    7
    STILL OLDER MANSION OF A RICH AND RARE . . . . . . . .  .  . 384  3 DON JUAN  13      55    3
    AND MRS RABBI THE RICH BANKER'S SQUAW . . . . . . . .  .  . 396  3 DON JUAN  13      79    6
    LONGBOW WAS RICH IN AN IMAGINATION . . . . . . . . . .  .  . 401  3 DON JUAN  13      92    5
    OR NO 'TIS SAID HIS SECT IS RICH AND GODLY . . . . . .  .  . 472  3 DON JUAN  15      36    4
    RICH NOBLE BUT AN ORPHAN LEFT AN ONLY . . . . . . . .  .  . 475  3 DON JUAN  15      44    1
RICHARD
    SHADOWS THE SOUL OF RICHARD MAY APPAL . . . . . . . .  .  . 499  3 DON JUAN  15      96    6
RICHELIEU
    THE DUKE OF RICHELIEU HAD A BALL BETWEEN . . . . . . .  .  . 117  3 DON JUAN   8      10   V2
RICHER
    IT POUR'D DOWN TORRENTS BUT THEY WERE NO RICHER . . .  .  . 201  2 DON JUAN   2      85    1
    THE REST--SAVE HERE AND THERE SOME RICHER ONE . . . .  .  . 284  2 DON JUAN   3      16    5
RICHES
    BORN TO SOME FRIEND WHO HOLDS HIS WIFE AND RICHES . .  .  . 287  2 DON JUAN   3      23    7
    THE POOR MAN'S SPARKLING SUBSTITUTE FOR RICHES . . . .  .  . 256  3 DON JUAN  10      63    4
    MAY FIND HIMSELF WITHIN THAT ISLE OF RICHES . . . . .  .  . 273  3 DON JUAN  11      11    7
    IF HE FOUND NOT THIS SPAWN OF TAX-BORN RICHES . . . .  .  . 288  3 DON JUAN  11      41    7
    AND THOUGH--BY NO MEANS OVERPOWERED WITH RICHES . . .  .  . 421  3 DON JUAN  14      26   V7
RICHEST
    HER GIRDLE SPARKLED AND THE RICHEST LACE . . . . . . .  .  . 220  2 DON JUAN   2     121    5
```

674

	PAGE	VOL		CANTO	STANZA	LN
RICHLY						
THE UPPER BORDER RICHLY WROUGHT DISPLAY'D	308	2 DON JUAN	3	64	5
THE WOUNDS THEY RICHLY MERITED AND SHRIEK	158	3 DON JUAN	8	94	4
OR GLORIOUS AS A DIAMOND RICHLY SET	458	3 DON JUAN	15	7	4
RID						
OR GOT RID OF THE PARTIES ALTOGETHER	65	3 DON JUAN	6	119	4
HE WOULD FIND OTHERS WHO WOULD FAIN BE RID SO	133	3 DON JUAN	8	40	3
OF COURSERS ALSO SPAKE THEY HENRY RID	368	3 DON JUAN	13	23	5
RIDDEN						
I'VE SEEN THE PEOPLE RIDDEN O'ER LIKE SAND	310	3 DON JUAN	11	85	5
AND WHATNOT--THOUGH HE HAD RIDDEN LIKE A CENTAUR	425	3 DON JUAN	14	35	V7
RIDDLE						
THE HERO OF THIS GRAND POETIC RIDDLE	181	3 DON JUAN	8	139	3
THOU RIDDLE--WHICH ALL READ--NONE UNDERSTAND	210	3 DON JUAN	9	56	V7
THOU RIDDLE WITHOUT WHOM EARTH'S ASHES END	210	3 DON JUAN	9	56	V7
DARK RIDDLE OF ALL LIFE EARTH'S LIFELESS END	210	3 DON JUAN	9	56	V7
EXPOUNDING AND ILLUSTRATING THE RIDDLE	337	3 DON JUAN	12	45	7
A JEST A RIDDLE FAME THROUGH THIN AND THICK SOUGHT	363	3 DON JUAN	13	10	7
RIDDLED						
HIS POCKETS FIRST AND THEN HIS BODY RIDDLED	276	3 DON JUAN	11	17	8
RIDDLE'S						
UNTIL THEIR ROYAL RIDDLE'S FULLY READ	287	3 DON JUAN	11	40	4
RIDDLES						
THE PLEASANT RIDDLES OF FUTURITY--	180	3 DON JUAN	8	137	6
RIDE						
TO TAKE A QUIET RIDE IN SOME GREEN LANE	224	3 DON JUAN	9	85	8
BY BIDDING OTHERS CARRY WHILE THEY RIDE	367	3 DON JUAN	13	19	8
COULD BACK A HORSE AS DESPOTS RIDE A RUSSIAN	368	3 DON JUAN	13	23	8
WITH ANYBODY IN A RIDE OR WALK	464	3 DON JUAN	15	19	8
TO DRAW THE BOW TO RIDE AND SPEAK THE TRUTH	501	3 DON JUAN	16	1	2
HORSES THEY RIDE WITHOUT REMORSE OR RUTH	501	3 DON JUAN	16	1	6
RIDER						
KNEW THAT HE HAD A RIDER ON HIS BACK	424	3 DON JUAN	14	32	8
RIDGE						
HAD SET SOME TIME AND NIGHT WAS ON THE RIDGE	279	3 DON JUAN	11	23	7
RIDICULE						
OF THESE THINGS OR BY RIDICULE BENUMB	498	3 DON JUAN	15	95	6
RIDICULES						
OUR RIDICULES ARE KEPT IN THE BACK-GROUND--	402	3 DON JUAN	13	95	1
THE RIDICULES OF PEOPLE IN ALL PLACES--	548	3 DON JUAN	16	100	5
RIDICULOUS						
RIDICULOUS ENOUGH BUT ALSO DULL	402	3 DON JUAN	13	95	2
RIDING						
HE LEARN'D THE ARTS OF RIDING FENCING GUNNERY	42	2 DON JUAN	1	38	7
IN RIDING ROUND THOSE VEGETABLE PUNCHEONS	301	3 DON JUAN	11	66	3
HAD MUSIC--WALKING--RIDING--BOOKS--AND TALK	407	3 DON JUAN	13	104	V2
RIFE						
THEY WERE SO SOFT AND BEAUTIFUL AND RIFE	313	2 DON JUAN	3	74	3
RIFE WITH MORE HORNS THAN HOUNDS--SHE HATH THE CHASE	395	3 DON JUAN	13	78	2
RIFLES						
SIMPLE THEY WERE NOT SAVAGE AND THEIR RIFLES	145	3 DON JUAN	8	66	7
RIFT						
WHICH STRUCK HER AFT AND MADE AN AWKWARD RIFT	170	2 DON JUAN	2	27	3
RIGHT						
I CAN'T BUT SAY THAT HIS MAMMA WAS RIGHT	48	2 DON JUAN	1	48	2
AND SEEM'D AT LEAST IN THE RIGHT ROAD TO HEAVEN	48	2 DON JUAN	1	49	6
THREW THE SHIP RIGHT INTO THE TROUGH OF THE SEA	170	2 DON JUAN	2	27	2
THOUGH RIGHT AHEAD THE ROARING BREAKERS LAY	211	2 DON JUAN	2	104	4
AND SO ALL YE WHO WOULD BE IN THE RIGHT	230	2 DON JUAN	2	140	5
THEY SMILE SO WHEN ONE'S RIGHT AND WHEN ONE'S WRONG	242	2 DON JUAN	2	164	5
THEY ARE RIGHT FOR MAN TO MAN SO OFT UNJUST	263	2 DON JUAN	2	200	1
HIS STRAIN DISPLAY'D SOME FEELING--RIGHT OR WRONG	326	2 DON JUAN	3	87	5
HAD FALLEN WITH HIS RIGHT SHOULDER HALF CUT THROUGH	370	2 DON JUAN	4	48	8
WHILE THE RIGHT HAND WHICH WROTE IT STILL IS ABLE	398	2 DON JUAN	4	99	5
YOU MAY DO RIGHT FORBIDDING THEM TO SHOW 'EM	403	2 DON JUAN	4	107	7
YOU'RE RIGHT ON BOTH ACCOUNTS TO HOLD YOUR TONGUE	419	2 DON JUAN	5	16	7
BY SETTING THINGS IN THEIR RIGHT POINT OF VIEW	422	2 DON JUAN	5	23	5
ABOUT THE RIGHT DIVINE HOW FAR WE SHOULD	426	2 DON JUAN	5	30	5
AND GAZED AROUND THEM TO THE LEFT AND RIGHT	439	2 DON JUAN	5	50	7
IF HEARTS LAY ON THE LEFT SIDE OR THE RIGHT	485	2 DON JUAN	5	128	5
SHE THOUGHT HERS GAVE A DOUBLE RIGHT DIVINE	485	2 DON JUAN	5	129	7
FULL OF EXPRESSION RIGHT OR WRONG THAT STRIKE	32	3 DON JUAN	6	52	7
WITH SUCH A CLAMOUR--I HAD THOUGHT IT RIGHT	46	3 DON JUAN	6	81	3
IF THIS BE THE RIGHT READING--'TIS NO MATTER	70	3 DON JUAN	7	8	2
ROSE OVER THE TOWN'S RIGHT SIDE IN BRISTLING TIER	72	3 DON JUAN	7	12	7
WHEN IT GREW RATHER LATE TO SET THINGS RIGHT	73	3 DON JUAN	7	13	5
WHICH ALL WHO SAW IT FOLLOWED WRONG OR RIGHT	89	3 DON JUAN	7	46	8
RIGHT I WAS BUSY AND FORGOT WHY YOU	100	3 DON JUAN	7	66	1
NO HARM UNTO A RIGHT LEGITIMATE HEAD	117	3 DON JUAN	8	10	7
TO TAKE A BATTERY ON THE RIGHT THE OTHERS	119	3 DON JUAN	8	15	2
AND THAT THE REST HAD FACED UNTO THE RIGHT	125	3 DON JUAN	8	28	3
RIGHT IN THE MIDDLE OF THE PARAPET	136	3 DON JUAN	8	46	7
AND BLACK SILK NECKCLOTH--AND REPLIED YOU'RE RIGHT	161	3 DON JUAN	8	99	7
UNLESS HER CAUSE BY RIGHT BE SANCTIFIED	184	3 DON JUAN	9	4	4
AT LEAST HE PAYS NO RENT AND HAS BEST RIGHT	198	3 DON JUAN	9	32	1
TO THEE BOTH OH AND AH BELONG OF RIGHT	215	3 DON JUAN	9	65	2
THEY'RE RIGHT OUR DAYS ARE TOO BRIEF FOR AFFORDING	270	3 DON JUAN	11	4	5
PERHAPS THIS NEW POSITION--BUT I'M RIGHT	348	3 DON JUAN	12	71	5
IN RIGHT GOOD EARNEST--ALSO AN APPEAL	357	3 DON JUAN	12	V 18	2

675

RIGHT   (CONTINUED)
```
     RIGHT HONESTLY HE LIKED AN HONEST HATER--        .   .   .   .   .   . 361   3 DON JUAN 13       7    2
     BECAUSE IT MAKES US SMILE HIS HERO'S RIGHT       .   .   .   .   .   . 363   3 DON JUAN 13       9    2
     AND STILL PURSUES THE RIGHT--TO CURB THE BAD     .   .   .   .   .   . 363   3 DON JUAN 13       9    3
     A SINGLE LAUGH DEMOLISHED THE RIGHT ARM   .   .   .   .   .   .   .   . 364   3 DON JUAN 13      11    2
     DETERMINED RIGHT OR WRONG ON FRIEND OR FOE       .   .   .   .   .   . 366   3 DON JUAN 13      16    4
     HIS CAUSE BY LEANING MUCH FROM MIGHT TO RIGHT    .   .   .   .   .   . 391   3 DON JUAN 13      69    4
     I CAN'T EXACTLY TRACE THEIR RULE OF RIGHT        .   .   .   .   .   . 397   3 DON JUAN 13      82    1
     VICTIM WHEN WRONG AND MARTYR OFT WHEN RIGHT      .   .   .   .   .   . 420   3 DON JUAN 14      23    6
     OF PANTOMIME--HE DANCED I SAY RIGHT WELL  .   .   .   .   .   .   .   . 427   3 DON JUAN 14      38    3
     HER GAIETIES NONE HAD A RIGHT TO STARE    .   .   .   .   .   .   .   . 430   3 DON JUAN 14      45    6
     GAVE HER A RIGHT TO HAVE MATERNAL FEARS   .   .   .   .   .   .   .   . 432   3 DON JUAN 14      52    5
     BUT WHATSOE'ER SHE WISHED SHE ACTED RIGHT .   .   .   .   .   .   .   . 435   3 DON JUAN 14      57    6
     WERE THINGS BUT ONLY CALL'D BY THEIR RIGHT NAME  .   .   .   .   .   . 455   3 DON JUAN 14     102    7
     THE LADY ADELINE RIGHT HONOURABLE         .   .   .   .   .   .   .   . 458   3 DON JUAN 15       6    1
     BUT RIGHT OR WRONG DON JUAN WAS WITHOUT IT   .   .   .   .   .   .   . 461   3 DON JUAN 15      13    3
     PERHAPS IT MAY TURN OUT THAT ALL WERE RIGHT  .   .   .   .   .   .   . 496   3 DON JUAN 15      90    2
     THE PAPER WAS RIGHT EASY TO PERUSE  .   .   .   .   .   .   .   .   .   . 512   3 DON JUAN 16      26    6
     THOUGH HE CAME IN HIS MIGHT WITH KING HENRY'S RIGHT   .   .   .   .   . 518   3 DON JUAN 16   L  2    1
     TO QUESTION THAT FRIAR'S RIGHT            .   .   .   .   .   .   .   . 520   3 DON JUAN 16   L  5    8
     QUITE FULL RIGHT DULL GUESTS HOT AND DISHES COLD .   .   .   .   .   . 538   3 DON JUAN 16      78    6
     IF YOU ARE RIGHT THEN EVERYBODY'S WRONG   .   .   .   .   .   .   .   . 564   3 DON JUAN 17       5    4
     IF YOU ARE WRONG THEN EVERYBODY'S RIGHT   .   .   .   .   .   .   .   . 564   3 DON JUAN 17       5    7
     BUT NOW IT SEEMS HE'S RIGHT--HIS NOTION JUST     .   .   .   .   .   . 565   3 DON JUAN 17       8    7
RIGHTED
     AND THEN WITH VIOLENCE THE OLD SHIP RIGHTED  .   .   .   .   .   .   . 173   2 DON JUAN  2      32    8
RIGHTEOUSNESS
     WHO DIE IN RIGHTEOUSNESS SHE LEAN'D AND THERE    .   .   .   .   .   . 233   2 DON JUAN  2     144    2
RIGHTLY
     A YEAR OR TWO'S AN AGE WHEN RIGHTLY SPENT .   .   .   .   .   .   .   . 228   2 DON JUAN  2     136    5
     FROM WHICH OUR MODERN MORALS RIGHTLY SHRINKING   .   .   .   .   .   . 238   2 DON JUAN  2     155    3
RIGHTS
     LEAVE TO O'ERSTEP THE WRITTEN RIGHTS OF WOMAN    .   .   .   .   .   .  74   2 DON JUAN  1      98    3
     AWARE OF THEIR DUE ROYAL RIGHTS O'ER MEN  .   .   .   .   .   .   .   . 485   3 DON JUAN  5     128    8
     AND FOR THEIR RIGHTS CONNUBIAL MAKE A STAND  .   .   .   .   .   .   .  11   3 DON JUAN  6      11    5
     HIDES TRAIN-OIL TALLOW AND THE RIGHTS OF THETIS  .   .   .   .   .   . 246   3 DON JUAN 10      45    7
     AND SET THE OTHER HALF OF EARTH TO RIGHTS .   .   .   .   .   .   .   . 445   3 DON JUAN 14      82    7
RIGHT-WELL
     THE SCANTY BUT RIGHT-WELL THRASHED EARS OF TRUTH .   .   .   .   .   . 403   3 DON JUAN 13      96    2
RIGID
     TILL SOME LESS RIGID EDITOR SHALL STOOP   .   .   .   .   .   .   .   .  46   3 DON JUAN  1      45    5
     YE RIGID GUTS OF REAPERS--I TRANSLATE     .   .   .   .   .   .   .   . 190   3 DON JUAN  9      15    2
     A RIGID GUARDIAN OR A ZEALOUS PRIEST      .   .   .   .   .   .   .   . 334   3 DON JUAN 12      39    5
RIGMAROLE
     OF RHETORIC WHICH THE LEARN'D CALL RIGMAROLE     .   .   .   .   .   . 116   2 DON JUAN  1     174    8
RIGOUR
     AND TREATING A YOUNG WIFE WITH SO MUCH RIGOUR    .   .   .   .   .   . 110   2 DON JUAN  1     161    4
     THEIR LOYAL TREASON RENEGADO RIGOUR       .   .   .   .   .   .   .   . 330   2 DON JUAN  3      94    3
     WITH INTEREST AND IN TURN WAS WONT WITH RIGOUR   .   .   .   .   .   . 213   3 DON JUAN  9      62    6
     WHICH MIGHT DEFY A CROTCHET CRITIC'S RIGOUR  .   .   .   .   .   .   . 427   3 DON JUAN 14      39    6
     SUCH ABERRATIONS THAN WE MEN OF RIGOUR    .   .   .   .   .   .   .   . 460   3 DON JUAN 15      11    4
     THAT SCARLET CLOAK ALAS UNCLOSED WITH RIGOUR     .   .   .   .   .   . 530   3 DON JUAN 16      61    7
RIGOURS
     OF LATE YEARS TO DISPENSE WITH COCKER'S RIGOURS  .   .   .   .   .   . 547   3 DON JUAN 16      98    7
RILL
     HIS REST THE RUSHING OF THE NEIGHBOURING RILL    .   .   .   .   .   . 229   2 DON JUAN  2     137    3
     BUT LIKE TWO BEINGS BORN FROM OUT A RILL  .   .   .   .   .   .   .   . 352   2 DON JUAN  4      15    5
     SWEET NAIAD OF THE PHLEGETHONTIC RILL .   .   .   .   .   .   .   .   . 372   2 DON JUAN  4      53    2
     BUT THOU--OH SWEET FURY OF THE FIERY RILL .   .   .   .   .   .   .   . 372   2 DON JUAN  4      53   V2
     LIKE WATER-LILIES FLOATING DOWN A RILL    .   .   .   .   .   .   .   .  22   3 DON JUAN  6      33    6
     WHITE COLD AND PURE AS LOOKS A FROZEN RILL   .   .   .   .   .   .   .  40   3 DON JUAN  6      68    3
     THERE'S MUSIC IN THE GUSHING OF A RILL    .   .   .   .   .   .   .   . 458   3 DON JUAN 15       5    6
RILLS
     OR RATHER LAKE--FOR RILLS DO NOT RUN SLOWLY--    .   .   .   .   .   .  22   3 DON JUAN  6      33    7
RIMES
     WERE SONNETS TO HERSELF OR BOUTS RIMES    .   .   .   .   .   .   .   . 525   3 DON JUAN 16      50    8
RIND
     SQUEEZED THROUGH THE RIND WHICH MAKES IT BEST FOR USE   .   .   . 307   2 DON JUAN  3      62    8
     AT THAT HIS HEART HAD GOT A TOUGHER RIND  .   .   .   .   .   .   .   . 353   3 DON JUAN 12      81    6
RING
     SHE NEVER WOULD DISGRACE THE RING SHE WORE   .   .   .   .   .   .   .  80   2 DON JUAN  1     109    4
     THE CHIMNEY--WOULD IT PLEASE YOU RING THE BELL   .   .   .   .   .   . 104   2 DON JUAN  1     153   V4
     RING FOR YOUR VALET--BID HIM QUICKLY BRING   .   .   .   .   .   .   . 251   2 DON JUAN  2     180    1
     OR WONDERED AT HER EARS WITHOUT A RING    .   .   .   .   .   .   .   .  23   3 DON JUAN  6      35    4
     THE NEXT SHALL RING A PEAL TO SHAKE ALL PEOPLE   .   .   .   .   .   . 109   3 DON JUAN  7      85    7
     A ROYAL HUSBAND IN ALL SAVE THE RING--    .   .   .   .   .   .   .   . 217   3 DON JUAN  9      70    6
     A FOOL WHOSE BELLS HAVE CEASED TO RING AT ALL--  .   .   .   .   .   . 267   3 DON JUAN 10      86    8
     LIKE TO THE CHAMPION IN THE FISTY RING    .   .   .   .   .   .   .   . 296   3 DON JUAN 11      55    2
RINGLETS
     AND RAVEN RINGLETS GATHERED IN DARK CROWD .   .   .   .   .   .   .   .  39   3 DON JUAN  6      66    2
RINGS
     ANNOUNCED HER RANK TWELVE RINGS WERE ON HER HAND .   .   .   .   .   . 312   2 DON JUAN  3      72    3
     RINGS O'ER THE DIALOGUE AND MANY A CRIME  .   .   .   .   .   .   .   . 141   3 DON JUAN  8      58    4
     SHE RINGS THE WORLD'S TE DEUM AND HER BROW   .   .   .   .   .   .   . 286   3 DON JUAN 11      38    3
     WHICH RINGS WHAT'S UPPERMOST OF NEW OR HOARY     .   .   .   .   .   . 465   3 DON JUAN 15      20    7
     WHICH NO ONE HEARS SO LOUDLY THOUGH IT RINGS     .   .   .   .   .   . 489   3 DON JUAN 15      76    6
RIOT
     HOW GRAND HIS SENTIMENTS WHICH NEER RUN RIOT     .   .   .   .   .   . 154   2 DON JUAN  1   V  5    2
     DAYS NEARLY O'ER MIGHT BE DISPOSED TO RIOT   .   .   .   .   .   .   . 173   2 DON JUAN  2      33    6
```

		PAGE	VOL	CANTO	STANZA	LN

RIOT (CONTINUED)
THAT WITHOUT ANY DANGER OF A RIOT HE . . . . 318 2 DON JUAN 3 83 5
WITH NOTHING VERY GRAND TO MAKE A RIOT . . . . 32 3 DON JUAN 6 53 V4
RIOTOUS
LOVE'S RIOTOUS BUT MARRIAGE SHOULD HAVE QUIET . . . . 474 3 DON JUAN 15 41 7
RIP
AND IF OUR QUARRELS SHOULD RIP UP OLD STORIES . . . . 37 2 DON JUAN 1 31 1
FROM WHICH THE SECRET NOBODY COULD RIP . . . . . . 496 2 DON JUAN 5 149 5
RIPE
I'VE SEEN MUCH FINER WOMEN RIPE AND REAL . . . . . . 218 2 DON JUAN 2 118 7
WERE RIPE THEY MIGHT MAKE SIX AND TWENTY SPRINGS . . . 468 2 DON JUAN 5 98 2
AS THOSE WHO LIKE THINGS ROSY RIPE AND SUCCULENT . . . 213 3 DON JUAN 9 62 3
BUT ADELINE WAS FAR FROM THAT RIPE AGE . . . . . . 433 3 DON JUAN 14 54 1
CAN'T LIKE RIPE AGE IN GOURMANDISE EXCEL . . . . . . 487 3 DON JUAN 15 70 6
RIPENED
LOVELY AS THOSE WHICH RIPENED EDEN'S FRUIT . . . . . 86 3 DON JUAN 7 41 7
RIPENESS
WHOSE RIPENESS IS BUT BITTER AT THE BEST . . . . . . 433 3 DON JUAN 14 54 2
RIPER
FOR WHEN THEY HAPPEN AT A RIPER AGE . . . . . . 339 3 DON JUAN 12 50 2
RIPPLE
AND THE SMALL RIPPLE SPLIT UPON THE BEACH . . . . . 250 2 DON JUAN 2 178 1
A BEAUTEOUS RIPPLE OF THE BRILLIANT STREAM . . . . . 480 3 DON JUAN 15 55 3
RIPPLE'S
AND SULKILY THE RIVER'S RIPPLE'S FLOWING . . . . . . 422 3 DON JUAN 14 28 4
RIPPLES
QUIET--SANK INTO SOFTER RIPPLES GLIDING . . . . . . 385 3 DON JUAN 13 58 4
RIPPLING
LET IN THE RIPPLING SOUND OF THE LAKE'S BILLOW . . . . 507 3 DON JUAN 16 15 4
RISE
THEY HOPED THE WIND WOULD RISE THESE FOOLISH MEN . . . 192 2 DON JUAN 2 69 5
I'VE SEEN HIM RISE FULL OFT INDEED OF LATE . . . . . 230 2 DON JUAN 2 140 2
THOSE THEIR BRIGHT RISE HAD LIGHTED TO SUCH JOYS . . . 352 2 DON JUAN 4 16 2
AND YOU AND I MAY CHANCE ERE MORNING RISE . . . . . 464 2 DON JUAN 5 92 5
SO SUPERNATURAL WAS HER PASSION'S RISE . . . . . . 489 2 DON JUAN 5 134 5
HIS LATELY BOWSTRUNG BROTHER CAUSED HIS RISE . . . . 495 2 DON JUAN 5 147 4
TO RISE AGAINST EARTH'S TYRANTS NEVER LET IT . . . . 179 3 DON JUAN 8 135 5
HUMANITY WOULD RISE AND THUNDER NAY . . . . . . 183 3 DON JUAN 9 1 8
IF RATHER BROAD MADE STOCKS RISE AND THEIR HOLDERS . . 208 3 DON JUAN 9 52 8
NOW THAT THE LION'S FALL'N MAY RISE AGAIN . . . . . 296 3 DON JUAN 11 56 4
CAN TENDER SOULS RELATE THE RISE AND FALL . . . . . 304 3 DON JUAN 11 72 7
'TIS WHITE AT LEAST WHEN THEY JUST RISE FROM BED . . . 532 3 DON JUAN 16 64 4
EARLIEST TO RISE AND LAST TO QUIT THE SEARCH . . . . 539 3 DON JUAN 16 80 4
AND RISE AT NINE IN LIEU OF LONG ELEVEN . . . . . . 539 3 DON JUAN 16 81 4
RISEN
THE OCEAN-BURIED RISEN FROM DEATH TO BE . . . . . . 363 2 DON JUAN 4 36 4
RISERS
TO EARLY RISERS AFTER A LONG CHASE . . . . 426 3 DON JUAN 14 36 2
RISES
SWEET SKIES JUST WHEN HE RISES OR IS SET . . . . . 230 2 DON JUAN 2 139 3
STRONG PALPITATION RISES 'TIS HER BOON . . . . . . 267 2 DON JUAN 2 208 6
AS PASSION RISES WITH ITS BOSOM WORN . . . . . . 49 3 DON JUAN 6 87 3
WHICH RISES FOAMS AND BREAKS BUT NOT IN VAIN . . . . 60 3 DON JUAN 6 108 V7
OF HER FIRST FRUIT BUT HOW HE FALLS AND RISES . . . . 210 3 DON JUAN 9 55 7
THE VERY SEASON RISES AND SUBSIDES . . . . 378 3 DON JUAN 13 43 V7
RISING
AS EVERY RISING WAVE HIS DREAD RENEW'D . . . . . . 187 2 DON JUAN 2 59 5
MEANTIME THE CURRENT WITH A RISING GALE . . . . . . 209 2 DON JUAN 2 101 1
HOW MUCH IT COSTS US YET EACH RISING THROB . . . . . 264 2 DON JUAN 2 203 2
HARK RISING TO THE IGNOBLE CALL-- . . . . 324 2 DON JUAN 3 L 9 5
THE LADY RISING UP WITH SUCH AN AIR . . . . 466 2 DON JUAN 5 96 1
THEN RISING HAUGHTILY HE GLANCED AROUND . . . . . . 484 2 DON JUAN 5 126 5
UNTO THE NEW CREATION RISING OUT . . . . 201 3 DON JUAN 9 38 2
RISK
HAD RUN THE RISK OF BEING DAMN'D FOR EVER . . . . . 258 2 DON JUAN 2 193 4
COULD RISK OR COMPASS SUCH STRANGE PHANTASIES . . . . 477 2 DON JUAN 5 115 3
THEIR LIES YCLEPED DESPATCHES WITHOUT RISK OR . . . . 498 2 DON JUAN 5 151 7
YOUNG BEAUTIFUL AND DARING--WHO WOULD RISK . . . . . 7 3 DON JUAN 6 3 2
FOR GENTLEMEN MUST SOMETIMES RISK THEIR SKIN . . . . 10 3 DON JUAN 6 7 3
RUN MUCH LESS RISK OF LOVERS TURNING RUDE . . . . . 43 3 DON JUAN 6 75 6
WOULD RISK TO PLEASE IT MY LAST RAG OF BREECHES . . . 421 3 DON JUAN 14 26 V8
AND HONOUR'D RAN A RISK OF GROWING LESS SO . . . . . 458 3 DON JUAN 15 6 2
AT RISK OF BEING QUIZZED FOR SUPERSTITION . . . . . 512 3 DON JUAN 16 28 4
AT WHATSOEVER RISK OF BEING DEFEATED . . . . 559 3 DON JUAN 16 119 6
RISKED
AND AS SHE ALSO RISKED HER LIFE TO GET . . . . . . 482 2 DON JUAN 5 122 4
WHERE LIVES NOT LAW-SUITS MUST BE RISKED FOR PASSION . . 347 3 DON JUAN 12 68 2
RISKS
AND THOUGH HE CERTAINLY RAN MANY RISKS . . . . . . 20 3 DON JUAN 6 29 3
RITE
TO SO RESPECTABLE AN ANCIENT RITE . . . . 452 2 DON JUAN 5 71 2
RITUAL
MY OBJECTION'S TO HIS TITLE NOT HIS RITUAL . . . . . 472 3 DON JUAN 15 36 7
RIVAL
THIS BY HIS HEART--HIS RIVAL BY HIS HEAD . . . . . 402 3 DON JUAN 13 93 8
RIVAL'S
OR WISH TO MAKE A RIVAL'S BOSOM BLEED . . . . . . 351 3 DON JUAN 12 77 6
RIVALSHIP
OF RIVALSHIP ROSE IN EACH CLOUDED EYE . . . . . . 221 3 DON JUAN 9 78 7

```
                                                                PAGE VOL       CANTO STANZA LN
RIVEN
    BUT WHEN IT HATH BEEN SCORCH'D AND PIERCED AND RIVEN . . .   270  2 DON JUAN  2   214    5
RIVER
    DON JUAN'S PARENTS LIVED BESIDE THE RIVER . . . . . .         25  2 DON JUAN  1     8    7
    AND HAVING LEARNT TO SWIM IN THAT SWEET RIVER . . . . .      211  2 DON JUAN  2   105    3
    HAD DOUBTLESS HEARD ABOUT THE STYGIAN RIVER . . . . . .      258  2 DON JUAN  2   193    6
    CUT FROM ITS FOREST ROOT OF YEARS--THE RIVER . . . . .       349  2 DON JUAN  4    10    4
    (AS HE BLED INWARDLY NO HIDEOUS RIVER . . . . . . . .        430  2 DON JUAN  5    35    6
    BUT FROM THE RIVER THE TOWN'S OPEN QUITE . . . . . . .        73  3 DON JUAN  7    13    1
    THEY BLEW UP IN THE MIDDLE OF THE RIVER . . . . . .           80  3 DON JUAN  7    28    7
    OF THE ARMED RIVER WHILE WITH STRAGGLING LIGHT . . . .       110  3 DON JUAN  7    86    5
    BELIEVE THAT VIRTUE THAWED BEFORE THE RIVER . . . . .        241  3 DON JUAN 10    33    8
    BY A RIVER WHICH ITS SOFTEN'D WAY DID TAKE . . . . .         385  3 DON JUAN 13    57    3
    THE RIVER FROM THE LAKE ALL BLUELY DASH'D . . . . .          447  3 DON JUAN 14    87    6
RIVER-CHILD
    WHICH FAIN WOULD LULL ITS RIVER-CHILD TO SLEEP . . . .       447  3 DON JUAN 14    87    8
RIVER'S
    THAT OVERPOWERS SOME ALPINE RIVER'S RUSH . . . . . . .       231  2 DON JUAN  2   141    6
    AND SULKILY THE RIVER'S RIPPLE'S FLOWING . . . . . .         422  3 DON JUAN 14    28    4
RIVULET
    INTO A RIVULET AND THUS ALLAY'D . . . . . . . . .            385  3 DON JUAN 13    58    5
RIVULET'S
    HE HEARD HIS RIVULET'S LIGHT BUBBLING RUN . . . . . .        289  2 DON JUAN  3    27    3
ROACH
    TO FLY FROM AS FROM HUNGRY PIKES A ROACH . . . . . .         421  3 DON JUAN 14    26    3
ROAD
    (HORACE MAKES THIS THE HEROIC TURNPIKE ROAD) . . . . .        24  2 DON JUAN  1     6    2
    AND SEEM'D AT LEAST IN THE RIGHT ROAD TO HEAVEN . . . .       48  2 DON JUAN  1    49    6
    WITH HIS TWO CAPTIVES BY SO QUEER A ROAD . . . . . .         436  2 DON JUAN  5    45    3
    EVE AND PAVED (GOD KNOWS HOW) THE ROAD TO EVIL . . . .       474  2 DON JUAN  5   109    4
    THROUGH THE THEN UNPAVED STARS THE TURNPIKE ROAD . . .       226  3 DON JUAN 10     2    4
    ALONG THE ROAD AS IF THEY WENT TO BURY . . . . . .          260  3 DON JUAN 10    71    5
    WHAT A DELIGHTFUL THING'S A TURNPIKE ROAD . . . . .          263  3 DON JUAN 10    78    1
    UPON THE ROAD UNLESS HE PROVE A FIGHTER . . . . . .          273  3 DON JUAN 11    11    6
    THE FELLOW TO LIE GROANING ON THE ROAD . . . . . . .        275  3 DON JUAN 11    15    7
    WHAT MATTERS IF THE ROAD BE HEAD OR HEART . . . . .          284  3 DON JUAN 11    34    8
ROADS
    WHICH ON ROUGH ROADS LEAVES SCARCELY A WHOLE BONE) . . .     197  3 DON JUAN  9    30    3
    BENEATH HIS CARS OF CERES GROAN THE ROADS . . . . .          320  3 DON JUAN 12     9    4
    ON ROADS EAST SOUTH NORTH WEST THERE IS A RUN . . . .        377  3 DON JUAN 13    42    4
ROAM
    BRIGHTEN'D AND FOR A MOMENT SEEM'D TO ROAM . . . . .         203  2 DON JUAN  2    89    6
    THEIR BOSOMS WHO HAVE BEEN INDUCED TO ROAM . . . . .         286  2 DON JUAN  3    21    4
    THAT BRINGS LOCHABER BACK TO EYES THAT ROAM . . . . .        523  3 DON JUAN 16    46    3
ROAMS
    OR ROAMS THE HERD BENEATH THE BULL'S PROTECTION . . . .       90  3 DON JUAN  7    48    4
    THE RUDEST BRUTE THAT ROAMS SIBERIA'S WILD . . . . . .       157  3 DON JUAN  8    92    3
ROAR
    COULD JUAN'S PASSION WHILE THE BILLOWS ROAR . . . . .        168  2 DON JUAN  2    23    7
    FROM WHOSE RELUCTANT ROAR HIS LIFE HE WRUNG . . . . .        213  2 DON JUAN  2   108    3
    AND RARELY CEASED THE HAUGHTY BILLOW'S ROAR . . . . .        249  2 DON JUAN  2   177    6
    A MOST UNORIENTAL ROAR OF LAUGHTER . . . . . . . .          290  2 DON JUAN  3    28    8
    AMIDST THE ROAR OF LIBERATED ROME . . . . . . . . .         339  2 DON JUAN  3   109    3
    SHE COULD NOT FROM THE SPOT AND THE LOUD ROAR . . . .        361  2 DON JUAN  4    31    3
    AND MIDNIGHT LISTENS TO THE LION'S ROAR . . . . . .          373  2 DON JUAN  4    55    5
    THEY TOOK HER WORD THAT HIS DULL ROAR WAS MELLOW . . .       391  2 DON JUAN  4    87   V6
    THEIR ROAR EVEN WITH THE BALTIC'S--SO YOU BE . . . . .        52  3 DON JUAN  6    93    7
    THE DEATH-CRY DROWNING IN THE BATTLE'S ROAR . . . . .        111  3 DON JUAN  7    87    8
    A MIRRORED HELL THE VOLLEYING ROAR AND LOUD . . . . .        115  3 DON JUAN  8     6    5
    IN THE SAME MOMENT LOUD AS EVEN THE ROAR . . . . .          116  3 DON JUAN  8     8    2
    HARK HOW THE ROAR INCREASES--NO EXCUSE . . . . . .          162  3 DON JUAN  8   101    5
    BLAZED AND THE CANNON'S ROAR WAS SCARCE ALLAYED . . . .      178  3 DON JUAN  8   133    4
    THE OCEAN OF ETERNITY THE ROAR . . . . . . . . . .          227  3 DON JUAN 10     4    5
    OF WHEELS AND ROAR OF VOICES AND CONFUSION . . . . .        278  3 DON JUAN 11    22    2
    THEN GLARE THE LAMPS THEN WHIRL THE WHEELS THEN ROAR . .     302  3 DON JUAN 11    67    2
ROARED
    IN VAIN THE YELL OF VICTORY IS ROARED . . . . . . .         155  3 DON JUAN  8    87    6
    AND ROARED OUT AS HE WRITHED HIS NATIVE MUD IN . . . .       274  3 DON JUAN 11    13    6
ROARING
    CLAMOUR'D IN CHORUS TO THE ROARING OCEAN . . . . . .         174  2 DON JUAN  2    34    8
    THOUGH RIGHT AHEAD THE ROARING BREAKERS LAY . . . . .        211  2 DON JUAN  2   104    4
    CAMBYSES' ROARING ROMANS BEAT AT LEAST . . . . . .          297  3 DON JUAN 11    58    7
ROARS
    OF HIM WHO FEASTS AND FIGHTS AND ROARS AND REVELS . . .      237  3 DON JUAN 10    25    4
ROAST
    YET IF MY GENTLE MUSE HE PLEASE TO ROAST . . . . . .        142  2 DON JUAN  1   210    4
    BUT THIS I KNOW THAT THIS ROAST CAPON'S FAT . . . . .        298  2 DON JUAN  3    45    3
    REDOUBLED WHEN A ROAST AND A RAGOUT . . . . . . . .         428  2 DON JUAN  5    32    4
    THAN COULD ROAST BEEF IN OUR ROUGH JOHN BULL WAY . . .       487  3 DON JUAN 15    71    4
ROAST-MEAT
    YET SMELT ROAST-MEAT BEHELD A HUGE FIRE SHINE . . . .        439  2 DON JUAN  5    50    5
ROAST-MEATS
    OF CERTAIN STEWS AND ROAST-MEATS AND PILAUS . . . . .        437  2 DON JUAN  5    47    2
ROASTS
    I WILL NOT DWELL UPON RAGOUTS OR ROASTS . . . . . .         404  3 DON JUAN 13    99    5
ROB
    THAT WISDOM EVER ON THE WATCH TO ROB . . . . . . .          264  2 DON JUAN  2   203    4
ROBBED
    ROBBED FOR HIS DAUGHTER BY THE BEST OF FATHERS . . . .       284  2 DON JUAN  3    17    8
    A TIGRESS ROBBED OF YOUNG A LIONESS . . . . . . .           487  2 DON JUAN  5   132    1
```

ROBBING
  DIFFER EXCEPT IN ROBBING WITH A BOW 275   3 DON JUAN 11   15   4
ROBE
  OF NIGHT WHICH ROBE THE CHAMBER OR WHERE POPPING 442   2 DON JUAN 5   55   5
  OF HER DEEP-PURPLE ROBE AND SPEAKING LOW 466   2 DON JUAN 5   96   7
  AS CAESAR WORE HIS ROBE YOU WEAR YOUR GOWN 232   3 DON JUAN 10   15   8
  WHILE GREAT LUCULLUS' ROBE TRIUMPHAL MUFFLES-- 484   3 DON JUAN 15   66   7
  SO PERISH EVERY TYRANT'S ROBE PIECE-MEAL 505   3 DON JUAN 16   10   8
  UNDRESSING IS A WOE OUR ROBE DE CHAMBRE 505   3 DON JUAN 16   11   2
ROBES
  AND COUNTESSES MATURE IN ROBES AND PEARLS 390   3 DON JUAN 13   68   6
  AND ROBES SWEET FRIENDSHIP IN A BRUSSELS LACE 430   3 DON JUAN 14   47   4
  THOUGH LADIES' ROBES SEEM SCANT ENOUGH FOR LESS . . . 482   3 DON JUAN 15   61   8
ROBUST
  WAS MORE ROBUST AND HARDY TO THE VIEW 202   2 DON JUAN 2   87   3
  AND MORE ROBUST OF FIGURE--THEN BEGUN 216   2 DON JUAN 2   115   4
ROCHEFOUCAULT
  BY SWIFT BY MACHIAVEL BY ROCHEFOUCAULT 68   3 DON JUAN 7   4   1
ROCK
  AND THAT HER HONOUR WAS A ROCK OR MOLE 66   2 DON JUAN 1   82   4
  AND THE LOUD BREAKER BOILS AGAINST THE ROCK 94   2 DON JUAN 1   134   7
  BY SOME LOW ROCK OR SHELVE THAT MADE IT FRET 251   2 DON JUAN 2   181   7
  (LEUCADIA'S ROCK STILL OVERLOOKS THE WAVE) 266   2 DON JUAN 2   205   6
  IS AWFUL TO THE VESSEL NEAR THE ROCK 305   2 DON JUAN 3   58   4
  ON SULI'S ROCK AND PARGA'S SHORE 325   2 DON JUAN 3   L 13   2
  CHAIN'D TO A ROCK SHE KNEW NOT HOW BUT STIR 361   2 DON JUAN 4   31   2
  HOLDS BY THE ROCK OR AS A LOVER'S KISS 238   3 DON JUAN 10   28   6
  THE GULF OF ROCK YAWNS--YOU CAN'T GAZE A MINUTE . . . 412   3 DON JUAN 14   5   7
  'TIS ODD OR ODDS IT MAY TURN OUT A ROCK 442   3 DON JUAN 14   74   8
ROCKED
  WHICH ROCKED AS 'TWERE BENEATH THE MIGHTY NOISES . . . 115   3 DON JUAN 8   7   6
ROCKETS
  A KIND ANTITHESIS TO CONGREVE'S ROCKETS 91   2 DON JUAN 1   129   6
ROCKING
  AND ROCKING IN HIS HAMMOCK LONG'D FOR LAND 169   2 DON JUAN 2   25   5
ROCKS
  AND STAND LIKE ROCKS THE TEMPEST'S WEAR AND TEAR . . . 191   2 DON JUAN 2   66   4
  LIGHT TO THE ROCKS THAT ROOF'D THEM WHICH THE SUN . . . 216   2 DON JUAN 2   115   6
  FOR SOME OF THESE ARE ROCKS WITH SCARCE A HUT ON . . . 238   2 DON JUAN 2   154   6
  GUARDED BY SHOALS AND ROCKS AS BY AN HOST 249   2 DON JUAN 2   177   3
  AMIDST THE BARREN SAND AND ROCKS SO RUDE 262   2 DON JUAN 2   198   4
  OF ROCKS BEWITCH'D THAT OPEN TO THE KNOCKERS 293   2 DON JUAN 3   34   6
  THE SHARP ROCKS LOOK'D BELOW EACH DROP THEY CAUGHT . . 362   2 DON JUAN 4   33   7
  WHEREIN SHE LIKED HER OWN TO STAND LIKE ROCKS 197   3 DON JUAN 9   29   8
  'MIDST MANY ROCKS WE GUARD MORE AGAINST WRECKS 371   3 DON JUAN 13   30   6
  SAFE CONDUCT THROUGH THE ROCKS OF RE-ELECTIONS 546   3 DON JUAN 16   95   8
ROCKY
  THE LAND APPEAR'D A HIGH AND ROCKY COAST 209   2 DON JUAN 2   100   1
  A KING SATE ON THE ROCKY BROW 322   2 DON JUAN 3   L 4   1
  LIKE OCEAN WARRING 'GAINST A ROCKY ISLE 489   2 DON JUAN 5   135   6
ROD
  EXACTLY AS YOU PLEASE OR NOT THE ROD 140   2 DON JUAN 1   206   7
  A ROD TO WEAKNESS TO THE BRAVE A REED 151   2 DON JUAN 1   V 2   6
  THAT YOU WERE LIVING--OR I HAD YOUR ROD 334   2 DON JUAN 3   100 V7
RODE
  BUT ON THEY RODE UPON TWO UKRAINE HACKS 87   3 DON JUAN 7   43   6
  OR RODE A NAG WHICH TROTTED NOT TOO HIGH 406   3 DON JUAN 13   102   5
  MET THE MORN AS THEY MIGHT IF FINE THEY RODE 406   3 DON JUAN 13   104   2
  RODE O'ER THE HOUNDS IT MAY BE NOW AND THEN 424   3 DON JUAN 14   33   7
  AND WHATNOT THOUGH HE RODE BEYOND ALL PRICE 425   3 DON JUAN 14   35   7
  WHETHER THEY RODE OR WALK'D OR STUDIED SPANISH 453   3 DON JUAN 14   98   1
RODERIC'S
  SINCE RODERIC'S GOTH'S OR OLDER GENSERIC'S VANDALS . . 129   2 DON JUAN 1   190 V4
RODOMONT
  THERE WAS THE REVEREND RODOMONT PRECISIAN 399   3 DON JUAN 13   87   5
ROD'S
  THAT GREAT ENCHANTER AT WHOSE ROD'S COMMAND 204   3 DON JUAN 9   44   3
ROE
  WITH THAT SHE ROSE AS GRACEFUL AS A ROE 517   3 DON JUAN 16   38 V5
ROGERS
  SCOTT ROGERS CAMPBELL MOORE AND CRABBE WILL TRY . . . 13   2 DON JUAN D   7   7
  THOU SHALT NOT STEAL FROM SAMUEL ROGERS NOR 139   2 DON JUAN 1   205   7
ROGERS'
  THE HINGES BEING AS SMOOTH AS ROGERS' RHYMES 463   2 DON JUAN 5   89   4
ROGUE
  HAS TAKEN FOR A SWAN ROGUE SOUTHEY'S GANDER 298   3 DON JUAN 11   59   8
  AND SMILING BUT IN SECRET--CUNNING ROGUE 426   3 DON JUAN 14   37   6
ROGUENOFF
  AND TSCHITSSHAKOFF AND ROGUENOFF AND CHOKENOFF 74   3 DON JUAN 7   15   4
ROGUES
  (LIKE TRUANT ROGUES) THE DEVIL OR THE FOOL 162   2 DON JUAN 2   10   4
ROLAND'S
  LIKE ROLAND'S HORN IN RONCEVALLES' BATTLE 267   3 DON JUAN 10   87   8
ROLE
  ON ADELINE WHILE PLAYING HER GRAND ROLE 546   3 DON JUAN 16   96   3
ROLL
  AS ROLL THE WAVES BEFORE THE SETTLED WIND 133   2 DON JUAN 1   196   4
  AND FOAM AND ROLL WITH STRANGE CONVULSIONS RACK'D . . . 198   2 DON JUAN 2   79   5
  HIS OWN SHALL ROLL BEFORE YOU LIKE A BALL 369   2 DON JUAN 4   47   2

		PAGE	VOL	CANTO	STANZA	LN

ROLL   (CONTINUED)

	PAGE	VOL		CANTO	STANZA	LN
NAMES GREAT AS ANY THAT THE ROLL OF FAME HAS	82	3 DON JUAN	7	32	8
AS ROLL THE WATERS TO THE BREATHING WIND	90	3 DON JUAN	7	48	3
THE GROAN THE ROLL IN DUST THE ALL-WHITE EYE	118	3 DON JUAN	8	13	5
AS ANYBODY ON THE ELECTED ROLL	242	3 DON JUAN	10	35	3
WITH THE YORK MAIL--BUT ONWARD AS WE ROLL	263	3 DON JUAN	10	78	7
THEN ROLL THE BRAZEN THUNDERS OF THE DOOR	302	3 DON JUAN	11	67	6
THE GUESTS WERE PLACED ACCORDING TO THEIR ROLL	488	3 DON JUAN	15	74	3

ROLL-CALL

BUT THEN THE ROLL-CALL DRAWS THEM BACK AFRAID	417	3 DON JUAN	14	17	3

ROLL'D

OF ALL OUR PUMPS--A WRECK COMPLETE SHE ROLL'D	178	2 DON JUAN	2	42	6
THOUGH EVERY WAVE ROLL'D MENACING TO FILL	188	2 DON JUAN	2	61	5
ROLL'D ON THE BEACH HALF SENSELESS FROM THE SEA	212	2 DON JUAN	2	107	8
HER CLUSTERING HAIR WHOSE LONGER LOCKS WERE ROLL'D	217	2 DON JUAN	2	116	3
AND THUS A MOON ROLL'D ON AND FAIR HAIDEE	248	2 DON JUAN	2	174	1
MOONS CHANGING HAD ROLL'D ON AND CHANGELESS FOUND	352	2 DON JUAN	4	16	1
AND SOMETHING ROLL'D BEFORE HER IN A SHEET	361	2 DON JUAN	4	32	4

ROLLED

RELUCTANT PAST HER BRIGHT EYES ROLLED--AS A VEIL	108	2 DON JUAN	1	158	V3
AND NIGHT IS BACKWARD LIKE A MANTLE ROLLED	230	2 DON JUAN	2	139	V8
A LIKE GOLD BAR ABOVE HER INSTEP ROLLED	312	2 DON JUAN	3	72	2
AND THERE IN A KIBITKA HE ROLLED ON	197	3 DON JUAN	9	30	1

ROLLING

WITH LITTLE HOPE IN SUCH A ROLLING SEA	183	2 DON JUAN	2	50	2
TO WATCH THE PROGRESS OF THOSE ROLLING SEAS	413	2 DON JUAN	5	5	4
BE HIDDEN BY THE ROLLING WAVES WHICH HIDE	63	3 DON JUAN	6	115	2
THAT JUAN'S CHARIOT ROLLING LIKE A DRUM	277	3 DON JUAN	11	20	5
DEEP SECRETS TO HER ROLLING LIGHT ARE TOLD	506	3 DON JUAN	16	14	6

ROLLS

A DEVIL OF A SEA ROLLS IN THAT BAY	162	2 DON JUAN	2	11	3
WHEN OVER CATHOLICS THE OCEAN ROLLS	185	2 DON JUAN	2	55	3
FROM EVERY FLAKE AND YET ROLLS ON THE SAME	398	2 DON JUAN	4	100	6
ROLLS BY THE CITY WALL BUT DEED NOR WORD	155	3 DON JUAN	8	87	4
WHO FELL AS ROLLS AN OX O'ER IN HIS PASTURE	274	3 DON JUAN	11	13	5
OF TIME AND TIDE ROLLS ON AND BEARS AFAR	500	3 DON JUAN	15	99	5

ROMAGNOLE

JUAN'S COMPANION WAS A ROMAGNOLE	395	2 DON JUAN	4	94	1

ROMAIC

SHE SAW HE DID NOT UNDERSTAND ROMAIC	241	2 DON JUAN	2	161	8

ROMAN

THY LATE REVIVING ROMAN SOUL DESPONDS	19	2 DON JUAN	D	16	3
'TWAS AN OLD CUSTOM OF THE GREEK AND ROMAN	205	2 DON JUAN	2	93	3
FROM AN OLD ROMAN PRINCESS AT BOLOGNA	389	2 DON JUAN	4	83	8
AND DON'T AGREE AT ALL WITH THE WISE ROMAN	10	3 DON JUAN	6	7	6
WHICH SETTLES ALL THINGS ROMAN GREEK OR RUNIC	122	3 DON JUAN	8	23	4
TO MAKE A ROMAN SORT OF SABINE WEDDING	177	3 DON JUAN	8	131	7
THE HIGH ROMAN FASHION TOO OF CINCINNATUS	186	3 DON JUAN	9	7	3
LIKE TO A ROMAN TRUMPET ERE A BATTLE	267	3 DON JUAN	10	87	V8

ROMANCE

IN SPAIN HE'D MAKE A BALLAD OR ROMANCE ON	320	2 DON JUAN	3	86	3
HAS SPAIN HAD HEROES WHILE ROMANCE COULD CHARM	364	3 DON JUAN	13	11	4
WITHOUT THE FARCE OF FRIENDSHIP OR ROMANCE	450	3 DON JUAN	14	92	2

ROMANCERS

OF POETS AND ROMANCERS--YOU'RE A BORE	84	2 DON JUAN	1	116	6
THIS MAKES YOUR ACTORS ARTISTS AND ROMANCERS	547	3 DON JUAN	16	98	1

ROMANCES

SHE READ SOME FRENCH ROMANCES HERE AND THERE	28	2 DON JUAN	1	13	3
ROMANCES PAINT AT FULL LENGTH PEOPLE'S WOOINGS	279	2 DON JUAN	3	8	3
BLUE DEVILS AND BLUE-STOCKINGS AND ROMANCES	444	3 DON JUAN	14	79	7
ROMANCES I NE'ER READ LIKE THOSE I HAVE SEEN	444	3 DON JUAN	14	80	2

ROMANS

TO DO AT ROME AS ROMANS DO A PIECE	319	2 DON JUAN	3	84	7
AND RALLY BACK HIS ROMANS TO THE FIELD	125	3 DON JUAN	8	28	8
CAMBYSES' ROARING ROMANS BEAT AT LEAST	297	3 DON JUAN	11	58	7

ROMANTIC

TURNS WHAT WAS ONCE ROMANTIC TO BURLESQUE	345	2 DON JUAN	4	3	8
INHERENT WHAT WE MORTALS CALL ROMANTIC	353	2 DON JUAN	4	18	7
AND AS ROMANTIC HEADS ARE PRETTY PAINTERS	284	3 DON JUAN	11	33	3
THAT'S NOBLE THAT'S ROMANTIC FOR MY PART	326	3 DON JUAN	12	22	1
HER CHARMING FIGURE AND ROMANTIC HISTORY	328	3 DON JUAN	12	27	7
FORMS A SAD CLIMAX TO ROMANTIC HOMAGES	346	3 DON JUAN	12	65	6
BUT COMING YOUNG FROM LANDS AND SCENES ROMANTIC	347	3 DON JUAN	12	68	1

ROME

TO DO AT ROME AS ROMANS DO A PIECE	319	2 DON JUAN	3	84	7
AMIDST THE ROAR OF LIBERATED ROME	339	2 DON JUAN	3	109	3
AND HEARD TROY DOUBTED TIME WILL DOUBT OF ROME	399	2 DON JUAN	4	101	8
OF ROME TRANSPLANTED FELL WITH CONSTANTINE	461	2 DON JUAN	5	86	8
ROME BABYLON TYRE CARTHAGE NINEVEH	142	3 DON JUAN	8	60	5
OR ROME ON TIBER--NAPLES ON THE SEA	271	3 DON JUAN	11	7	V6
IS WORTH A TOUR TO ROME ALTHOUGH NO MORE A	428	3 DON JUAN	14	40	3

ROME'S

MOCK TYRANTS WHEN ROME'S ANNALS WAXED BUT DIRTY	299	3 DON JUAN	11	61	8
(WHILE YET THE CHURCH WAS ROME'S) STOOD HALF APART	386	3 DON JUAN	13	59	2

ROMILLY

LIKE THE LAMENTED LATE SIR SAMUEL ROMILLY	29	2 DON JUAN	1	15	4
WHERE'S WHITBREAD ROMILLY WHERE'S GEORGE THE THIRD	307	3 DON JUAN	11	78	2

RONCEVALLES'

LIKE ROLAND'S HORN IN RONCEVALLES' BATTLE	267	3 DON JUAN	10	87	8

ROOF
 I AM NOT DAZZLED BY THIS SPLENDID ROOF . . . . 484 2 DON JUAN 5 127 5
 SPARKLED ALONG ITS ROOF AND MANY A VASE . . . . 54 3 DON JUAN 6 97 6
ROOF'D
 LIGHT TO THE ROCKS THAT ROOF'D THEM WHICH THE SUN . . . 216 2 DON JUAN 2 115 6
ROOFS
 IN HOLLOW HALLS WITH SPARRY ROOFS AND CELLS . . . . . 253 2 DON JUAN 2 184 6
ROOKS
 QUEENS BISHOPS KNIGHTS ROOKS PAWNS THE WORLD'S A GAME . . 400 3 DON JUAN 13 89 2
ROOM
 A STILLNESS WHICH LEAVES ROOM FOR THE FULL SOUL . . . . 82 2 DON JUAN 1 114 2
 SEARCH THEN THE ROOM ALFONSO SAID I WILL . . . . 98 2 DON JUAN 1 142 8
 ANTONIA BUSTLED ROUND THE RANSACK'D ROOM . . . . 109 2 DON JUAN 1 159 2
 WITH PRAY SIR LEAVE THE ROOM AND SAY NO MORE . . . . . 111 2 DON JUAN 1 163 4
 HE LEFT THE ROOM FOR HIS RELINQUISH'D SWORD . . . . . . 121 2 DON JUAN 1 182 1
 WHICH LEFT SCARCE ROOM FOR MOTION OR EXERTION . . . . . 189 2 DON JUAN 2 63 2
 THE HANGINGS OF THE ROOM WERE TAPESTRY MADE . . . . . . 308 2 DON JUAN 3 64 1
 THEY CHANGED FROM ROOM TO ROOM BUT ALL FORGOT . . . . . 379 2 DON JUAN 4 64 5
 THEY CHANGED FROM ROOM TO ROOM BUT ALL FORGOT . . . . . 379 2 DON JUAN 4 64 5
 THAN AN ENORMOUS ROOM WITHOUT A SOUL . . . . 442 2 DON JUAN 5 56 7
 BABA LED JUAN ONWARD ROOM BY ROOM . . . . 460 2 DON JUAN 5 85 2
 BABA LED JUAN ONWARD ROOM BY ROOM . . . . 460 2 DON JUAN 5 85 2
 INTO A ROOM STILL NOBLER THAN THE LAST . . . . 465 2 DON JUAN 5 93 2
 THE GALLERIES FROM ROOM TO ROOM THEY WALKED . . . . . 21 3 DON JUAN 6 30 2
 THE GALLERIES FROM ROOM TO ROOM THEY WALKED . . . . . 21 3 DON JUAN 6 30 2
 AS SOON AS THEY RE-ENTERED THEIR OWN ROOM . . . . . . 57 3 DON JUAN 6 103 3
 SLOWLY ALONG THE ROOM BUT SILENT STILL . . . . . . 61 3 DON JUAN 6 110 6
 OVER A COCKED HAT IN A CROWDED ROOM . . . . 204 3 DON JUAN 9 43 4
 OR ON MIGHT DREAD HER MAJESTY HAD NOT ROOM ENOUGH . . . 206 3 DON JUAN 9 48 3
 SALOON ROOM HALL O'ERFLOW BEYOND THEIR BRINK . . . . 302 3 DON JUAN 11 68 5
ROOM-DOOR
 JUAN HAD REACH'D THE ROOM-DOOR IN A TRICE . . . . . 122 2 DON JUAN 1 183 5
ROOMS
 ON THROUGH A FARTHER RANGE OF GOODLY ROOMS . . . . . 442 2 DON JUAN 5 55 2
ROOSTING
 WAS NOT SO SAFE FOR ROOSTING AS A CHURCH . . . . . . 206 2 DON JUAN 2 95 4
ROOT
 FOR FROM A ROOT THE UGLIEST IN OLD SPAIN . . . . . . 53 2 DON JUAN 1 58 3
 CUT FROM ITS FOREST ROOT OF YEARS--THE RIVER . . . . . 349 2 DON JUAN 4 10 4
 BUT THERE TOO MANY A POISON-TREE HAS ROOT . . . . . . 373 2 DON JUAN 4 55 4
 LIKE FLOWERS OF DIFFERENT HUE AND CLIME AND ROOT . . . 38 3 DON JUAN 6 65 2
 FOR WAR CUTS UP NOT ONLY BRANCH BUT ROOT . . . . . . 86 3 DON JUAN 7 41 8
 FOR ENNUI IS A GROWTH OF ENGLISH ROOT . . . . 405 3 DON JUAN 13 101 5
ROOTED
 ROOTED WHERE ONCE THE ADRIAN WAVE FLOW'D O'ER . . . . 337 2 DON JUAN 3 105 4
 RECEIVE AS GOSPEL AND WHICH GROW MORE ROOTED . . . . 503 3 DON JUAN 16 6 7
ROOTS
 AND TREES OF GOODLY GROWTH AND SPREADING ROOTS . . . . 43 3 DON JUAN 6 75 8
 LIKE POPLARS WITH GOOD PRINCIPLES FOR ROOTS . . . . . 343 3 DON JUAN 12 59 4
 'TIS SAD TO HACK INTO THE ROOTS OF THINGS . . . . . 436 3 DON JUAN 14 59 1
ROSE
 CALMLY SHE HEARD EACH CALUMNY THAT ROSE . . . . . . 36 2 DON JUAN 1 29 6
 THE SUN SET AND UP ROSE THE YELLOW MOON . . . . 82 2 DON JUAN 1 113 1
 JULIA SAID NOUGHT THOUGH ALL THE WHILE THERE ROSE . . . 117 2 DON JUAN 1 175 1
 THEN ROSE FROM SEA TO SKY THE WILD FAREWELL . . . . . 184 2 DON JUAN 2 52 1
 THE SUN ROSE RED AND FIERY A SURE SIGN . . . . 189 2 DON JUAN 2 62 1
 IF 'TWAS NOT LAND THAT ROSE WITH THE SUN'S RAY . . . . 207 2 DON JUAN 2 97 3
 ENGRAVE UPON THE PLATE YOU ROSE AT FOUR . . . . 230 2 DON JUAN 2 140 8
 FAIR AS THE CROWNING ROSE OF THE WHOLE WREATH . . . . 235 2 DON JUAN 2 148 5
 FAIR AS THE ROSE JUST PLUCKED TO CROWN THE WREATH . . . 235 2 DON JUAN 2 148 V5
 THE PALE CONTENDED WITH THE PURPLE ROSE . . . . . . 236 2 DON JUAN 2 150 3
 WHENCE THE BROAD MOON ROSE CIRCLING INTO SIGHT . . . . 253 2 DON JUAN 2 185 4
 AS WHEN SHE ROSE UPON US LIKE AN EVE . . . . 270 2 DON JUAN 2 213 4
 WHERE DELOS ROSE AND PHOEBUS SPRUNG . . . . 320 2 DON JUAN 3 L 1 4
 AND VESPER BELL'S THAT ROSE THE BOUGHS ALONG . . . . . 337 2 DON JUAN 3 106 4
 GREW AND EACH WAVE ROSE ROUGHLY THREATENING HER . . . . 361 2 DON JUAN 4 31 4
 AND OTHERS ROSE TO THE COMMAND OF CREWS . . . . . . 409 2 DON JUAN 4 116 4
 IN MOCKERY TO THE ENORMOUS GATE WHICH ROSE . . . . . 462 2 DON JUAN 5 87 5
 AS VENUS ROSE WITH FROM THE WAVE ON THEM . . . . . . 466 2 DON JUAN 5 96 2
 SHE ROSE AND PAUSING ONE CHASTE MOMENT THREW . . . . . 483 2 DON JUAN 5 125 7
 BUT SHE ROSE UP AND KISSED THE MATRON'S BROW . . . . . 31 3 DON JUAN 6 50 1
 GULBEYAZ ROSE FROM RESTLESSNESS AND PALE . . . . . . 49 3 DON JUAN 6 87 2
 ROSE THE SULTANA FROM A BED OF SPLENDOUR . . . . . . 50 3 DON JUAN 6 89 1
 AND NOW HE ROSE AND AFTER DUE ABLUTIONS . . . . . . 52 3 DON JUAN 6 92 1
 AT LENGTH SHE ROSE UP AND BEGAN TO WALK . . . . . . 61 3 DON JUAN 6 110 5
 ROSE OVER THE TOWN'S RIGHT SIDE IN BRISTLING TIER . . . 72 3 DON JUAN 7 12 7
 AT SEVEN THEY ROSE HOWEVER AND SURVEYED . . . . . . 81 3 DON JUAN 7 29 1
 WHEN UP THE BRISTLING MOSLEM ROSE AT LAST . . . . . . 115 3 DON JUAN 8 7 3
 AND ONE ENORMOUS SHOUT OF ALLAH ROSE . . . . 116 3 DON JUAN 8 8 1
 WHICH SCARCELY ROSE MUCH HIGHER THAN GRASS BLADES . . . 136 3 DON JUAN 8 47 8
 WHENCE HER HAIR HAIR ROSE TWINING WITH AFFRIGHT . . . . 158 3 DON JUAN 8 93 2
 ROSE STILL BUT FAINTER WERE THE THUNDERS GROWN . . . . 175 3 DON JUAN 8 127 6
 OF RIVALSHIP ROSE IN EACH CLOUDED EYE . . . . 221 3 DON JUAN 9 78 7
 BUT WHEN THE LEVEE ROSE AND ALL WAS BUSTLE . . . . . 223 3 DON JUAN 9 82 1
 MAN FELL WITH APPLES AND WITH APPLES ROSE . . . . . . 226 3 DON JUAN 10 2 1
 AT LENGTH THEY ROSE LIKE A WHITE WALL ALONG . . . . . 257 3 DON JUAN 10 65 1
 THE SUN WENT DOWN THE SMOKE ROSE UP AS FROM . . . . . 265 3 DON JUAN 10 81 1
 COULEUR DE ROSE WHO'S NEITHER WHITE NOR SCARLET . . . . 344 3 DON JUAN 12 62 8
 THERE ROSE A CARLO DOLCE OR A TITIAN . . . . 392 3 DON JUAN 13 71 3

```
                                                         PAGE VOL       CANTO STANZA LN

ROSE    (CONTINUED)
    EACH ROSE UP AT HIS OWN AND HAD TO SPARE  . . . . . .  406   3 DON JUAN 13    103    6
    A SORT OF ROSE ENTWINING WITH A THISTLE . . . . . .    407   3 DON JUAN 13    105    V6
    MAY THE ROSE CALL BACK ITS TRUE COLOURS SOON  . . . .  409   3 DON JUAN 13    111    6
    OF RUIN ROSE FROM SUCH A SLIGHT OCCASION  . . . . .    454   3 DON JUAN 14    100    4
    A ROSE WITH ALL ITS SWEETEST LEAVES YET FOLDED . . .   475   3 DON JUAN 15     43    8
    WITH THAT SHE ROSE AS GRACEFUL AS A ROE . . . . . .    517   3 DON JUAN 16     38    V5
    WITH THAT SHE ROSE AND GLIDED OFF AS SNOW . . . . .    517   3 DON JUAN 16     38    V5
    EACH CARRIAGE WAS ANNOUNCED AND LADIES ROSE . . . .    549   3 DON JUAN 16    101    3
ROSE-LEAF
    TO BROOK A RUFFLED ROSE-LEAF BY HIS SIDE . . . . . .    50   3 DON JUAN  6     89    4
ROSE-LEAVES
    STIRR'D WITH HER DREAM AS ROSE-LEAVES WITH THE AIR  . . 359   2 DON JUAN  4     29    8
ROSE'S
    THE COLOUR OF A BUDDING ROSE'S CREST  . . . . . .       48   3 DON JUAN  6     85    4
ROSES
    AS O'ER A BED OF ROSES THE SWEET SOUTH  . . . . .      245   2 DON JUAN  2    168    8
ROSIN
    ALL NECK OR NOTHING AS LIKE PITCH OR ROSIN . . . . .   135   3 DON JUAN  8     45    3
    MY MUSES DO NOT CARE A PINCH OF ROSIN . . . . . .      341   3 DON JUAN 12     55    1
ROSS
    OF NATURE OR THE MAN OF ROSS RUN WILD . . . . . .      144   3 DON JUAN  8     63    8
ROSY
    LIKE TWILIGHT ROSY STILL WITH THE SET SUN  . . . .     218   2 DON JUAN  2    118    2
    UPON THE OTHER AND THE ROSY SKY . . . . . . .          252   2 DON JUAN  2    183    7
    SPREAD LIKE A ROSY OCEAN VAST AND BRIGHT . . . . .     253   2 DON JUAN  2    185    2
    THEY COULD NOT LOOK MORE ROSY THAN BEFORE  . . . .     314   2 DON JUAN  3     75    8
    THE ROSY FLOOD OF TWILIGHT'S SKY ADMIRED--  . . . .    334   2 DON JUAN  3    101    6
    THE ROSY SKY WITH THE LAST SUNLIGHT FIRED . . . . .    335   2 DON JUAN  3    101    V6
    AND NOT A BREATH CREPT THROUGH THE ROSY AIR . . . .    335   2 DON JUAN  3    102    7
    THAT WOMANKIND HAD BUT ONE ROSY MOUTH . . . . . .       19   3 DON JUAN  6     27    7
    AS THOSE WHO LIKE THINGS ROSY RIPE AND SUCCULENT  . .  213   3 DON JUAN  9     62    3
ROTE
    WITH MEMORY EXCELLENT TO GET BY ROTE . . . . . .       401   3 DON JUAN 13     91    5
ROTHSCHILD
    JEW ROTHSCHILD AND HIS FELLOW CHRISTIAN BARING . . .   318   3 DON JUAN 12      5    8
ROTTEN
    THE TURNPIKES GLOW WITH DUST AND ROTTEN ROW . . . .    378   3 DON JUAN 13     44    5
ROUBLES
    THEY SHOULD AT LEAST HAVE FIFTY ROUBLES ROUND  . . .   162   3 DON JUAN  8    102    8
ROUGE
    BLUSHED TOO BUT IT WAS HIDDEN BY THEIR ROUGE  . . .    293   3 DON JUAN 11     48    V2
    AND LOWER THE PRICE OF ROUGE--AT LEAST SOME WINTERS  . 409   3 DON JUAN 13    111    8
ROUGED
    THE LADIES--SOME ROUGED SOME A LITTLE PALE--  . . .    406   3 DON JUAN 13    104    1
ROUGES
    PREACH TO POOR ROUGES AND WHEREFORE NOT BEGIN . . .    266   3 DON JUAN 10     85    2
ROUGH
    WHICH KEEPS WHEN PUSH'D BY QUESTIONS RATHER ROUGH . .  119   2 DON JUAN  1    178    5
    THE WIND WAS FAIR THE WATER PASSING ROUGH  . . . .     162   2 DON JUAN  2     11    2
    IN HIS ROUGH EYES AND TOLD THE CAPTAIN HE  . . . .     179   2 DON JUAN  2     43    2
    THAT A TIGHT BOAT WILL LIVE IN A ROUGH SEA . . . .     180   2 DON JUAN  2     45    7
    'TWAS A ROUGH NIGHT AND BLEW SO STIFFLY YET . . . .    188   2 DON JUAN  2     60    1
    AND ROUGH WITH REEFS WHICH RAN OUT MANY A MILE . . .   285   2 DON JUAN  3     19    7
    THAT EACH PULLED DIFFERENT WAYS--AND WAXING ROUGH  . . 395   2 DON JUAN  4     93    V7
    ON THE ROUGH DEEP BUT THIS LAST BLOW--AND HERE . . .   420   2 DON JUAN  5     19    1
    WITH THEIR ROUGH FACES THRONGED ABOUT THE BED  . . .   431   2 DON JUAN  5     37    2
    SAID LOLAH WITH AN ACCENT RATHER ROUGH  . . . . .       28   3 DON JUAN  6     44    6
    AND THIS THEY SAY IN LANGUAGE RATHER ROUGH . . . .      67   3 DON JUAN  7      3    5
    FOR ONE ROUGH WEATHER-BEATEN VETERAN BODY  . . . .     167   3 DON JUAN  8    112    7
    'TIS STRANGE ENOUGH--THE ROUGH TOUGH SOLDIERS WHO  . . 171   3 DON JUAN  8    119    1
    AS IS THE CHRISTIAN DOGMA RATHER ROUGH  . . . . .      195   3 DON JUAN  9     25    6
    WHICH ON ROUGH ROADS LEAVES SCARCELY A WHOLE BONE) . . 197   3 DON JUAN  9     30    3
    ALONG THE ASPECT WHETHER SMOOTH OR ROUGH . . . . .     206   3 DON JUAN  9     48    6
    ROUGH JOHNSON THE GREAT MORALIST PROFESSED . . . .     361   3 DON JUAN 13      7    1
    A SLEEP WITHOUT DREAMS AFTER A ROUGH DAY . . . . .     412   3 DON JUAN 14      4    1
    WHEN CALLED NEXT DAY DECLINED THE ROUGH ADVENTURE  . . 425   3 DON JUAN 14     35    V8
    THEY ARE BUT BAD PILOTS WHEN THE WEATHER'S ROUGH  . .  431   3 DON JUAN 14     48    3
    THAN COULD ROAST BEEF IN OUR ROUGH JOHN BULL WAY  . .  487   3 DON JUAN 15     71    4
ROUGHEST
    AND KINDLED FEELINGS IN THE ROUGHEST HEART . . . .     386   3 DON JUAN 13     59    6
ROUGHING
    BUT THOSE WHO HAVE BEEN A LITTLE USED TO ROUGHING  . . 345   3 DON JUAN 12     63    V6
ROUGHLY
    GREW AND EACH WAVE ROSE ROUGHLY THREATENING HER . . .  361   2 DON JUAN  4     31    4
    OR ROUGHLY TREADING ON THE COURTIER'S KIBES  . . .     200   3 DON JUAN  9     35    6
ROULEAUS
    HOW BEAUTEOUS ARE ROULEAUS HOW CHARMING CHESTS . . .   321   3 DON JUAN 12     12    1
    YE BEAUTIFUL ROULEAUS YE IRON CASKETS . . . . .        321   3 DON JUAN 12     12    V1
ROUND
    WHERE ALL HIS HOUSEHOLD GODS LAY SHIVER'D ROUND HIM  . 41   2 DON JUAN  1     36    6
    AND THE SEA DASHES ROUND THE PROMONTORY . . . . .       94   2 DON JUAN  1    134    6
    WITH THE PILED WOOD ROUND WHICH THE FAMILY CROWD  . .   94   2 DON JUAN  1    135    4
    TO HOLD A LEVEE ROUND HIS LADY'S BED . . . . . .        97   2 DON JUAN  1    139    6
    AND THEN THEY STARED EACH OTHERS' FACES ROUND  . . .   100   2 DON JUAN  1    144    5
    ANTONIA BUSTLED ROUND THE RANSACK'D ROOM . . . . .     109   2 DON JUAN  1    159    2
    NO DOUBT IN LITTLE COMPASS ROUND OR SQUARE . . . .     112   2 DON JUAN  1    166    4
    THE LEAK INCREASED SHOALS ROUND HER BUT NO SHORE  . .  176   2 DON JUAN  2     38    3
    WHISPER'D ANOTHER AND THUS IT WENT ROUND . . . . .     194   2 DON JUAN  2     73    2
```

```
                                                              PAGE VOL   CANTO STANZA LN
ROUND   (CONTINUED)
    IT CAME AND WENT AND FLUTTER'D ROUND THEM TILL . . . . .  206  2 DON JUAN   2    94   7
    SWAM ROUND AND ROUND AND ALL HIS SENSES PASS'D . . . . .  214  2 DON JUAN   2   110   3
    SWAM ROUND AND ROUND AND ALL HIS SENSES PASS'D . . . . .  214  2 DON JUAN   2   110   3
    HER LOCKS CURL'D NEGLIGENTLY ROUND HER FACE . . . . . .   220  2 DON JUAN   2   121   3
    MATERIALS AS WERE CAST UP ROUND THE BAY . . . . . . .     226  2 DON JUAN   2   132   3
    ROUND JUAN'S HEAD AND HIS AROUND HERS LIES . . . . . .    259  2 DON JUAN   2   194   3
    AND HERE ASSEMBLED CROSS-LEGG'D ROUND THEIR TRAYS . . .   291  2 DON JUAN   3    31   1
    A BAND OF CHILDREN ROUND A SNOW-WHITE RAM . . . . . .     292  2 DON JUAN   3    32   1
    AND ROUND ITS ONCE WARM PRECINCTS PALELY LYING . . . .    301  2 DON JUAN   3    51   6
    LIKE CHERUBS ROUND AN ALTAR-PIECE THEY CLING . . . . .    306  2 DON JUAN   3    60   5
    THESE WERE RANGED ROUND EACH IN ITS CRYSTAL EWER . . .    307  2 DON JUAN   3    63   1
    AND ROUND THEM RAN A YELLOW BORDER TOO . . . . . . .      308  2 DON JUAN   3    64   4
    LIKE FLEECY CLOUDS ABOUT THE MOON FLOW'D ROUND HER . .    311  2 DON JUAN   3    70   8
    ROUND HER SHE MADE AN ATMOSPHERE OF LIFE . . . . . .      313  2 DON JUAN   3    74   1
    ARE GATHER'D ROUND US BY THY LOOK OF REST . . . . . .     338  2 DON JUAN   3   107   7
    AS RARELY THEY BEHELD THROUGHOUT THEIR ROUND . . . .      352  2 DON JUAN   4    16   3
    WHILE WEEDS AND ORDURE RANKLE ROUND THE BASE . . . .      400  2 DON JUAN   4   103   8
    ROUND THE PATRICIAN LEFT-LEGS WHICH ADORN . . . . .       404  2 DON JUAN   4   110   7
    MY THIRD-- --YOUR THIRD QUOTH JUAN TURNING ROUND . . .    421  2 DON JUAN   5    20   1
    HE SAW WITH HIS OWN EYES THE MOON WAS ROUND . . . .       497  2 DON JUAN   5   150   1
    THE TURKISH TITLE) AND RANGED ROUND THE WALL . . . .       31  3 DON JUAN   6    51   2
    BUT WIDE AWAKE SHE WAS AND ROUND HER BED . . . . . .       42  3 DON JUAN   6    72   1
    AS THUS JUANNA SPOKE DUDU TURNED ROUND . . . . . . .       48  3 DON JUAN   6    85   1
    OF DEWY DAWN WOUND SLOWLY ROUND EACH HEIGHT . . . . .      49  3 DON JUAN   6    86   6
    HER CHEEK TURNED ASHES EARS RUNG BRAIN WHIRLED ROUND . .   58  3 DON JUAN   6   105   5
    AND MEASURES ROUND OF TOISES THOUSANDS THREE . . . .       71  3 DON JUAN   7     9   8
    SOME COSSACQUES HOVERING LIKE HAWKS ROUND A HILL . . .     95  3 DON JUAN   7    56   3
    OF COSSACQUES AND THEIR PREY TURNED ROUND AND CAST . .     97  3 DON JUAN   7    59   2
    AND SCRAMBLING ROUND THE RAMPART THESE SAME TROOPS . .    148  3 DON JUAN   8    73   1
    LIE ROUND THE BATTERY BUT STILL IT BATTERS . . . . .      160  3 DON JUAN   8    98   7
    THEY SHOULD AT LEAST HAVE FIFTY ROUBLES ROUND . . . .     162  3 DON JUAN   8   102   8
    WHO GREW LIKE CEDARS ROUND HIM GLORIOUSLY-- . . . . .     169  3 DON JUAN   8   116   4
    WITH GARLANDS ROUND BY EVERY NATION HUNG . . . . . .      199  3 DON JUAN   9    34  V6
    ROUND THE YOUNG MAN WITH THEIR CONGRATULATIONS . . . .    223  3 DON JUAN   9    82   4
    SO LOFTY THAT I FEEL MY BRAIN TURN ROUND . . . . . .      224  3 DON JUAN   9    85   1
    A MODE OF PROVING THAT THE EARTH TURNED ROUND . . . .     225  3 DON JUAN  10     1   5
    SHOULD NOT VEER ROUND WITH EVERY BREATH NOR SEIZE . .     231  3 DON JUAN  10    13   7
    IN RIDING ROUND THOSE VEGETABLE PUNCHEONS . . . . .       301  3 DON JUAN  11    66   3
    AND LET THE BABEL ROUND RUN AS IT MAY . . . . . . .       303  3 DON JUAN  11    69   5
    BUZZ ROUND THE FORTUNE WITH THEIR BUSY BATTERY . . .      331  3 DON JUAN  12    32   7
    THOSE BRIGHT MOTHS FLUTTERING ROUND A DYING FLAME . .     349  3 DON JUAN  12    72   4
    WITH HER SON IN HER BLESSED ARMS LOOK'D ROUND . . . .     387  3 DON JUAN  13    61   3
    'TIS ROUND HIM NEAR HIM HERE THERE EVERYWHERE . . . .     412  3 DON JUAN  14     5   1
    WHEN YOUR AFFAIRS COME ROUND ONE WAY OR T'OTHER . . .     431  3 DON JUAN  14    48   7
    WHICH MAY ROUND OFF AN HOUR UPON A TIME . . . . . .       465  3 DON JUAN  15    20   4
    TURNING ROUND TO THE REST HE SMILING SAID . . . . .       517  3 DON JUAN  16    39   3
    PERVADES A MOMENT THOSE WHO LISTEN ROUND . . . . . .      521  3 DON JUAN  16    41   4
    THOUGH KNIVES AND FORKS CLANGED ROUND AS IN A FRAY . .    542  3 DON JUAN  16    87   5
    UNWITHERING MYRTLE ROUND THE UNBLUNTED DART . . . . .     554  3 DON JUAN  16   109   6
    THE STARRY DARKNESS ROUND HER LIKE A GIRDLE . . . . .     556  3 DON JUAN  16   113   7
    HOW EARTH COULD ROUND THE SOLAR ORBIT RUN . . . . .       565  3 DON JUAN  17     8   3
ROUNDED
    IT WAS THE COOLING HOUR JUST WHEN THE ROUNDED . . . .     252  2 DON JUAN   2   183   1
ROUSAMOUSKI
    OF WHOM WE CAN INSERT BUT ROUSAMOUSKI . . . . . . .        74  3 DON JUAN   7    16   8
ROUSE
    HAD SHE IMAGINED SUCH A THING COULD ROUSE . . . . .        81  2 DON JUAN   1   111   7
    WHICH STILL ELSEWHERE MAY ROUSE A BRIGHTER SPRING-- . .   188  3 DON JUAN   9    11   4
    AS ACIDS ROUSE A DORMANT ALKALI) . . . . . . . .         251  3 DON JUAN  10    54   4
    WHO ROUSE THE SHIRTLESS PATRIOTS OF SPAIN . . . . .       318  3 DON JUAN  12     5   3
    A TOPIC SCANDAL DOTH DELIGHT TO ROUSE . . . . . . .       370  3 DON JUAN  13    26   6
ROUSED
    ROUSED BY REPULSE--THROUGH A TOLERABLE LEAK . . . . .     490  2 DON JUAN   5   137  V6
    TO HEAR DEBATES WHOSE THUNDER ROUSED (NOT ROUSES) . . .   353  3 DON JUAN  12    82   4
ROUSES
    TO HEAR DEBATES WHOSE THUNDER ROUSED (NOT ROUSES) . . .   353  3 DON JUAN  12    82   4
ROUSSEAU
    BY TILLOTSON AND WESLEY AND ROUSSEAU . . . . . . .         68  3 DON JUAN   7     4   3
    WHICH ROUSSEAU POINTS OUT TO THE DUBIOUS FAIR . . . .     139  3 DON JUAN   8    53   6
    OR SWISS ROUSSEAU CRY VOILA LA PERVENCHE . . . . . .      442  3 DON JUAN  14    75   8
ROUSSEAU'S
    IS ROUSSEAU'S JULIETTA--I NEER KNEW . . . . . . .        273  2 DON JUAN   2  V  2   7
ROUT
    EXCEPT TO BULL-FIGHTS MASS PLAY ROUT AND REVEL . . . .    102  2 DON JUAN   1   148   4
    THE ORNAMENTS OF LEVEES AND A ROUT . . . . . . . .       404  2 DON JUAN   4   110  V8
    THAT FEVER WHICH PRECEDES THE LANGUID ROUT . . . . .     220  3 DON JUAN   9    75   6
    MEANING A VIRGIN'S FIRST BLUSH AT A ROUT . . . . . .     330  3 DON JUAN  12    31   5
    AS I'LL TELL AUREA AT TO-MORROW'S ROUT . . . . . .       332  3 DON JUAN  12    35   6
    BUT NEXT TO DRESSING FOR A ROUT OR BALL . . . . . .      505  3 DON JUAN  16    11   1
ROUTE
    ALL THINGS PURSUE EXACTLY THE SAME ROUTE . . . . . .     446  3 DON JUAN  14    84   3
    SO THE END'S GAIN'D WHAT SIGNIFIES THE ROUTE . . . .     478  3 DON JUAN  15    51   8
ROUTS
    SO BRILLIANT WHERE THE LIST OF ROUTS AND DANCES IS-- . .  308  3 DON JUAN  11    80   3
    AND THUS ACQUAINTANCE GREW AT NOBLE ROUTS . . . . .      369  3 DON JUAN  13    24   1
ROVES
    AND PALSIED FANCY WHICH NO LONGER ROVES . . . . . .      228  3 DON JUAN  10     6   6
    AND ABOVE ALL AN ENGLISHWOMAN'S ROVES . . . . . . .      284  3 DON JUAN  11    33   4
```

ROW
	PAGE	VOL	CANTO	STANZA	LN
WERE STRUNG TOGETHER LIKE A ROW OF PEARLS	291	2 DON JUAN	3	30	3
AND THEN I'M WITH YOU IF YOU'RE FOR A ROW	437	2 DON JJAN	5	47	8
CONTINUE AS I SAID THIS GOODLY ROW	22	3 DON JUAN	6	33	3
OF THAT ODD STRING OF WORDS ALL IN A ROW	207	3 DON JUAN	9	49	5
WHO IN A ROW LIKE TOM COULD LEAD THE VAN	277	3 DON JUAN 11		19	3
A ROW OF GENTLEMEN ALONG THE STREETS	281	3 DON JUAN 11		27	1
THE TURNPIKES GLOW WITH DUST AND ROTTEN ROW	378	3 DON JUAN 13		44	5

ROWED
WHO ROWED OFF LEAVING THEM WITHOUT A WORD	433	2 DON JJAN	5	41	8

ROWLEY
BENEATH THE VERY REVEREND ROWLEY POWLEY	297	3 DON JUAN 11		57	6

ROWS
AS BOYS LOVE ROWS MY BOYHOOD LIKED A SQUABBLE	398	2 DON JUAN	4	99	1
THROUGH ROWS MOST MODESTLY CALLED PARADISE	278	3 DON JUAN 11		21	7
TO SILKEN ROWS OF GAY AND GARTER'D EARLS	390	3 DON JUAN 13		68	2
A RED LIP WITH TWO ROWS OF PEARLS BENEATH	560	3 DON JUAN 16		121	6

ROYAL
CONDEMN THE ROYAL LADY'S TASTE WHO WORE	238	2 DON JUAN	2	155	4
SO SAID THE ROYAL SAGE SARDANAPALUS	267	2 DON JUAN	2	207	8
HE SHOW'D THE ROYAL PENCHANTS OF A PIRATE	296	2 DON JUAN	3	40	8
AWARE OF THEIR DUE ROYAL RIGHTS O'ER MEN	485	2 DON JUAN	5	128	8
AND SHOWED BUT LITTLE ROYAL CURIOSITY	496	2 DON JUAN	5	148	4
WE LEAVE THIS ROYAL COUPLE TO REPOSE	16	3 DON JUAN	6	20	1
(THAT ROYAL BIRD WHOSE TAIL'S A DIADEM)	104	3 DON JUAN	7	74	6
UNTIL A ROYAL SMILE AT LENGTH DISCLOSED	211	3 DON JUAN	9	58	6
A ROYAL HUSBAND IN ALL SAVE THE RING--	217	3 DON JUAN	9	70	6
FOR BABYLON'S THAN RUSSIA'S ROYAL HARLOT--	237	3 DON JUAN 10		26	7
AT ONCE HER ROYAL SPLENDOUR AND REWARD	247	3 DON JUAN 10		46	4
UNTIL THEIR ROYAL RIDDLE'S FULLY READ	287	3 DON JUAN 11		40	4
'MIDST ROYAL DUKES AND DAMES CONDEMNED TO CLIMB	302	3 DON JUAN 11		68	7
AND WHERE IS FUM THE FOURTH OUR ROYAL BIRD	307	3 DON JUAN 11		78	4
THIS SCENE OF ROYAL ITCH AND LOYAL SCRATCHING	307	3 DON JUAN 11		78	8
THE ROYAL GAME OF GOOSE AS I MAY SAY	342	3 DON JUAN 12		58	4

ROYALIST
O'ER CONGRESS WHETHER ROYALIST OR LIBERAL	318	3 DON JUAN 12		5	2

ROYALTY
IN ALL THE ROYALTY OF SWEET SEVENTEEN	236	3 DON JUAN 10		24	6
THOUGH ROYALTY WAS WRITTEN ON HIS BROW	354	3 DON JUAN 12		84	5
BECAUSE I HATE EVEN DEMOCRATIC ROYALTY	466	3 DON JUAN 15		23	8

ROYALTY'S
IN ROYALTY'S VAST ARMS HE SIGHED FOR BEAUTY	243	3 DON JUAN 10		37	8

RUB
THERE LIES THE RUB--AND THIS THEY ARE BUT WEAK IN	442	3 DON JUAN 14		74	4

RUBB'D
AND THE REST RUBB'D THEIR EYES AND SAW A BAY	207	2 DON JUAN	2	97	5

RUBBED
HE RUBBED HIS EYES AND THEY DID NOT REFUSE	512	3 DON JJAN 16		26	4

RUBLES
OF RUBLES RAIN AS FAST AS SPECIE CAN	222	3 DON JUAN	9	79	6
DAMSELS AND RUBLES AND CHIVALRIC ORDERS	235	3 DON JUAN 10		21	V7
AND RICH IN RUBLES DIAMONDS CASH AND CREDIT	259	3 DON JUAN 10		70	2

RUBS
TO LIFE'S SMALL RUBS SHOULD SURELY BE MORE PLIANT	566	3 DON JUAN 17		10	3

RUBY
THE RUBY GLASS THAT SHAKES WITHIN HIS HAND	457	3 DON JUAN 15		4	7

RUDDER
THE RUDDER TORE AWAY 'TWAS TIME TO SOUND	170	2 DON JUAN	2	27	7
A JURYMAST OR RUDDER OR COULD SAY	177	2 DON JUAN	2	40	6

RUDDY
IN MAKE OF A COMPLEXION WHITE AND RUDDY	416	2 DON JUAV	5	11	2

RUDE
SO MUCH INDEED AS TO BE DOWNRIGHT RUDE	45	2 DON JUAN	1	43	6
'TWAS BORNE BY THE RUDE WAVE WHEREIN 'TWAS CAST	204	2 DON JUAN	2	90	6
AMIDST THE BARREN SAND AND ROCKS SO RUDE	262	2 DON JUAN	2	198	4
WITH HIS RUDE SCYTHE SUCH GENTLE BOSOMS HE	348	2 DON JUAN	4	8	4
RUN MUCH LESS RISK OF LOVERS TURNING RUDE	43	3 DON JUAN	6	75	4
UNTIL 'TIS TAUGHT BY LESSONS RATHER RUDE	53	3 DON JUAN	6	95	3
WITH THOUGHT--AND OF THOUGHT'S FOES BY FAR MOST RUDE	194	3 DON JUAV	9	24	3
OF HUMAN YEARS THAT HALF-WAY HOUSE THAT RUDE	238	3 DON JUAN 10		27	5
AS SEVERAL PEOPLE THINK SUCH HAZARDS RUDE	270	3 DON JUAN 11		4	4
WERE HARDLY RUDE ENOUGH TO EARN THEIR PAY	287	3 DON JUAN 11		40	8

RUDENESS
FOR DOWNRIGHT RUDENESS YE MAY STAY AT HOME	290	3 DON JUAN 11		44	1

RUDEST
THE RUDEST BRUTE THAT ROAMS SIBERIA'S WILD	157	3 DON JUAN	8	92	3

RUDIMENTS
FOR HE WOULD LEARN THE RUDIMENTS OF LOVE	67	2 DON JUAN	1	85	7

RUE
BUT IN HIS SILENCE THERE WAS MUCH TO RUE	300	2 DON JUAN	3	48	7

RUEFUL
HE CAST A RUEFUL LOOK OR TWO AND DID	111	2 DON JUAN	1	163	7
A RUEFUL GLANCE UPON THE WAVES (WHICH BRIGHT ALL	393	2 DON JUAN	4	90	5

RUES
FULL MANY AN EAGER GENTLEMAN OFT RUES	304	3 DON JUAN 11		71	5

RUFFLED
TO BROOK A RUFFLED ROSE-LEAF BY HIS SIDE	50	3 DON JUAN	6	89	4
IS RUFFLED BY A WRINKLE OR THE SUN	229	3 DON JUAN 10		8	4

RUFFLES
TEMPERANCE DELIGHTS HER BUT LONG FASTING RUFFLES	542	3 DON JUAN 16		86	8

RUGGED
    BUT MANY A FISHER IN HIS RUGGED SONG 383   2 DON JUAN   4   73 V1
    THE RUGGED TREE UNTO THE SUMMER WIND 164   3 DON JUAN   8   106   7
RUIN
    HAD SOWN THE RUIN OF HER FEW FAIR YEARS 275   2 DON JUAN   3   1 V7
    THAN HAUNTING SOME OLD RUIN OR WILD WASTE 38   3 DON JUAN   6   64   8
    A GREY WALL A GREEN RUIN RUSTY PIKE 255   3 DON JUAN 10   61   5
    THOUGH THIS MIGHT RUIN OTHERS IT DID NOT HIM . . . 338   3 DON JUAN 12   49   6
    TO THIS GREY RUIN WITH A VOICE TO CHARM 388   3 DON JUAN 13   64   5
    ITS INNER CRASH IS LIKE AN EARTHQUAKE'S RUIN . . . 446   3 DON JUAN 14   85   8
    WILL FALL BUT IF THEY DO 'TWILL BE THEIR RUIN . . 454   3 DON JUAN 14   99   8
    OF RUIN ROSE FROM SUCH A SLIGHT OCCASION 454   3 DON JUAN 14   100   4
RUIN'D
    RUIN'D ITS BLOOD BUT MUCH IMPROVED ITS FLESH . . . 53   2 DON JUAN   1   58   2
    OF FAULT OR TEMPER RUIN'D THE CONNEXION 281   2 DON JUAN   3   10   5
RUINING
    RENOWNED FOR RUINING GREAT BRITAIN GRATIS   . . . 186   3 DON JUAN   9   8   8
RUINS
    AMONG THE SCORCHING RUINS HE SAT SMOKING 172   3 DON JUAN   8   121   2
    I'VE HEARD THEM IN THE EPHESIAN RUINS HOWL 196   3 DON JUAN   9   27   2
    TO SIT AMIDST THE RUINS OF THEIR GUILT 352   3 DON JUAN 12   78   7
RULE
    SPAIN MAY PROVE AN EXCEPTION TO THE RULE 158   2 DON JUAN   2   2   5
    THE READER--BUT THE RULE IS --AND I'LL BRING . . . 332   3 DON JUAN   3   97 V6
    AS A RULE BUT TRUTH MAY IF YOU TRANSLATE IT . . . 15   3 DON JUAN   6   18   8
    I CAN'T EXACTLY TRACE THEIR RULE OF RIGHT 397   3 DON JUAN 13   82   1
    BUT TO RETURN UNTO THE STRICTER RULE-- 563   3 DON JUAN 17   3   1
RULED
    WERE RULED AS CALMLY AS A CHRISTIAN QUEEN   . . . 496   2 DON JUAN   5   148   8
RULER
    SO CASH RULES LOVE THE RULER ON HIS OWN 322   3 DON JUAN 12   14   5
RULES
    OF ARISTOTLE AND THE RULES 'TIS FIT   86   2 DON JUAN   1   120   7
    WITH STRICT REGARD TO ARISTOTLE'S RULES 136   2 DON JUAN   1   201   2
    TO BREAK THE RULES BY BRINGING ONE'S OWN BRIDE . 103   3 DON JUAN   7   71   5
    BEYOND THE RULES OF POSTING--AND THE MOB 137   3 DON JUAN   8   50   7
    LOVE RULES THE CAMP THE COURT THE GROVE--FOR LOVE . 322   3 DON JUAN 12   13   1
    CASH RULES THE GROVE AND FELLS IT TOO BESIDES . . 322   3 DON JUAN 12   14   2
    SO CASH RULES LOVE THE RULER ON HIS OWN 322   3 DON JUAN 12   14   5
    AS FAR AS WORDS MAKE RULES--OUR COMMON NOTION . . 563   3 DON JUAN 17   3   2
RULING
    THE RULING PASSION SUCH AS MARBLE SHOWS 377   2 DON JUAN   4   61   1
RUM
    FOR GROG AND SOMETIMES DRINK RUM FROM THE CASK . . 173   2 DON JUAN   2   33   8
    AS RUM AND TRUE RELIGION THUS IT WAS 174   2 DON JUAN   2   34   2
    WAS FOR SOME RUM -A DISAPPOINTED SUITOR 175   2 DON JUAN   2   36   8
    THEN THERE WAS RUM EIGHT GALLONS IN A PUNCHEON . . 181   2 DON JUAN   2   47   8
    A FEW TEA-SPOONFULS OF THEIR RUM AND WINE . . . 189   2 DON JUAN   2   62   5
    PREPARED FOR SUPPER WITH A GLASS OF RUM 441   2 DON JUAN   5   53   8
RUMMAGED
    HE SEARCH'D THEY SEARCH'D AND RUMMAGED EVERYWHERE . . 99   2 DON JUAN   1   143   1
RUMMAGING
    BUT SOMEBODY OR OTHER RUMMAGING 146   2 DON JUAN   1   219   5
    WHO AFTER RUMMAGING THE ABBEY THROUGH THICK . . . 529   3 DON JUAN 16   58   5
RUMOUR
    BUT THERE'S A RUMOUR WHICH I FAIN WOULD HUSH   . . 53   2 DON JUAN   1   58   6
    SOME RUMOUR ALSO OF SOME STRANGE ADVENTURES . . . 284   3 DON JUAN 11   33   1
    SOME PARTS OF JUAN'S HISTORY WHICH RUMOUR 460   3 DON JUAN 15   11   1
    BEYOND THE RUMOUR WHICH SUCH SPOTS UNFOLD 510   3 DON JUAN 16   22   4
RUMOUR'D
    TRUE HE WAS ABSENT AND 'TWAS RUMOUR'D TOOK 430   3 DON JUAN 14   45   3
RUMOURS
    LOW WERE THE WHISPERS MANIFOLD THE RUMOURS . . . 244   3 DON JUAN 10   40   1
RUN
    OF REFORMATION ERE THE YEAR RUN OUT   85   2 DON JUAN   1   119   4
    UNTIL THE HOURS OF ABSENCE SHOULD RUN THROUGH . . 98   2 DON JUAN   1   141   6
    HOW GRAND HIS SENTIMENTS WHICH NEER RUN RIOT . . 154   2 DON JUAN   1   V 5   2
    OF THE CONTINUANCE OF THE GALE TO RUN 189   2 DON JUAN   2   62   2
    HAD RUN THE RISK OF BEING DAMN'D FOR EVER 258   2 DON JUAN   2   193   4
    SOME RUN AWAY AND BUT EXCHANGE THEIR CARES . . . 263   2 DON JUAN   2   201   3
    AND DAUGHTERS SOMETIMES RUN OFF WITH THE BUTLER . 287   2 DON JUAN   3   22   8
    HE HEARD HIS RIVULET'S LIGHT BUBBLING RUN   . . . 289   2 DON JUAN   3   27   3
    HER PERSON IF ALLOW'D AT LARGE TO RUN 313   2 DON JUAN   3   73   4
    SHE DID NOT RUN AWAY TOO DID SHE SIR 421   2 DON JUAN   5   20   7
    OR RATHER LAKE--FOR RILLS DO NOT RUN SLOWLY-- . . 22   3 DON JUAN   6   33   7
    RUN MUCH LESS RISK OF LOVERS TURNING RUDE 43   3 DON JUAN   6   75   6
    YET FOR ALL THIS HE DID NOT RUN AWAY 121   3 DON JUAN   8   21   8
    FREDERICK THE GREAT FROM MOLWITZ DEIGNED TO RUN . 122   3 DON JUAN   8   22   4
    MEN RUN AWAY MUCH RATHER THAN GO THROUGH 130   3 DON JUAN   8   35   3
    OF NATURE OR THE MAN OF ROSS RUN WILD 144   3 DON JUAN   8   63   8
    ALL THAT THE DEVIL WOULD DO IF RUN STARK MAD . . 173   3 DON JUAN   8   123   4
    THEY MUST BE PAID THOUGH SIX DAYS SMOOTHLY RUN . 243   3 DON JUAN 10   38   7
    AND LET THE BABEL ROUND RUN AS IT MAY 303   3 DON JUAN 11   69   5
    ONLY THE COMMON RUN WHO MUST PURSUE 305   3 DON JUAN 11   73   2
    OR PLEASURE WHO MAKE POLITICS RUN GLIBBER ALL . . 318   3 DON JUAN 12   5   6
    OF PEERESSES WHOSE FOLLIES HAD RUN DRY 329   3 DON JUAN 12   29   8
    THUS GENTLEMEN MAY RUN UPON A SHOAL 376   3 DON JUAN 13   39   6
    ON ROADS EAST SOUTH NORTH WEST THERE IS A RUN . . 377   3 DON JUAN 13   42   4
    BUT TA'EN AT HAZARD AS THE RHYME MAY RUN 397   3 DON JUAN 13   83   6

685

		PAGE	VOL	CANTO	STANZA	LN
RUN	(CONTINUED)					
	WHEN HER SOFT LIQUID WORDS RUN ON APACE	426	3	DON JUAN 14	36	6
	THEY RUN BEFORE THE WIND THROUGH HIGH SEAS BREAKING	442	3	DON JUAN 14	74	6
	ARE APT EXCEEDINGLY TO RUN TO SEED	445	3	DON JUAN 14	81	8
	AND GATHER'D AS THEY RUN LIKE GROWING WATER	448	3	DON JUAN 14	88	6
	BUT NOW I CAN'T TELL WHERE IT MAY NOT RUN	466	3	DON JUAN 15	22	4
	MY MUSE WOULD RUN MUCH MORE INTO EXCESS	483	3	DON JUAN 15	64	3
	ALL WHICH I USE TO MAKE MY RHYMES RUN GLIBBER	487	3	DON JUAN 15	71	3
	THERE WAS A GOODLY MATCH TOO TO BE RUN	527	3	DON JUAN 16	55	5
	HOW EARTH COULD ROUND THE SOLAR ORBIT RUN	565	3	DON JUAN 17	8	3
RUNG						
	HER CHEEK TURNED ASHES EARS RUNG BRAIN WHIRLED ROUND	58	3	DON JUAN 6	105	5
	THE WHOLE CAMP RUNG WITH JOY YOU WOULD HAVE THOUGHT	90	3	DON JUAN 7	49	1
	WAS RUNG BY DINNER'S KNELL TILL THEN ALL WERE	406	3	DON JUAN 13	103	2
	THE SILVERY BELL RUNG NOT FOR DINNER READY	482	3	DON JUAN 15	61	6
	NO MORE ON THIS--THE DINNER BELL HATH RUNG	538	3	DON JUAN 16	77	7
RUNIC						
	WHICH SETTLES ALL THINGS ROMAN GREEK OR RUNIC	122	3	DON JUAN 8	23	4
RUNNING						
	TO FIND OUR CHILDREN RUNNING RESTIVE--THEY	305	2	DON JUAN 3	59	2
	WITH THE BLOOD RUNNING LIKE A LITTLE BROOK	370	2	DON JUAN 4	49	6
	HIS BLOOD WAS RUNNING ON THE VERY FLOOR	375	2	DON JUAN 4	58	3
	AND RUNNING OUT AS FAST AS I WAS ABLE	428	2	DON JUAN 5	33	6
	RUNNING AGROUND WAS TAKEN BY THE TURKS	81	3	DON JUAN 7	30	8
	AND NEVER RAN AWAY EXCEPT WHEN RUNNING	130	3	DON JUAN 8	35	7
	THY WAITERS RUNNING MUCKS AT EVERY BELL	259	3	DON JUAN 10	69	4
	THE OLD HEN--BY RUNNING HEADLONG TO THE WATER	564	3	DON JUAN 17	4	8
RUNS						
	AND PEGASUS RUNS RESTIVE IN HIS WAGGON	333	2	DON JUAN 3	99	2
	GUSH FROM THE EARTH UNTIL THE LAND RUNS O'ER	373	2	DON JUAN 4	55	3
	(LOVE LIKE RELIGION SOMETIMES RUNS TO HERESY)	446	2	DON JUAN 5	61	4
	BECAUSE HE RUNS BEFORE IT LIKE A PIG	109	3	DON JUAN 7	85	2
	THE SHUDDER WHICH RUNS NATURALLY THROUGH	212	3	DON JUAN 9	60	6
	WHICH AFTER ALL AT SUCH A DESPERATE RATE RUNS	472	3	DON JUAN 15	37	5
RUPTURE						
	THE MYSTERY OF THIS RUPTURE OF THEIR REST	48	3	DON JUAN 6	85	6
RURAL						
	FROM CIVIC REVELRY TO RURAL MIRTH	88	2	DON JUAN 1	124	4
RUSE						
	THERE WAS THE PREUX CHEVALIER DE LA RUSE	398	3	DON JUAN 13	86	3
RUSH						
	THAT OVERPOWERS SOME ALPINE RIVER'S RUSH	231	2	DON JUAN 2	141	6
	RUSH BACK UPON HIS HEART WHICH FILLED APACE	478	3	DON JUAN 15	117	5
	'TIS BEST TO PAUSE AND THINK ERE YOU RUSH ON	438	3	DON JUAN 14	64	7
RUSH'D						
	THE WATER RUSH'D THROUGH IN A WAY QUITE PUZZLING	171	2	DON JUAN 2	28	7
	AND FIRST ONE UNIVERSAL SHRIEK THERE RUSH'D	184	2	DON JUAN 2	53	1
	THE TEARS RUSH'D FORTH FROM HER O'ERCLOUDED BRAIN	380	2	DON JUAN 4	66	7
RUSHED						
	RUSHED WHERE THE THICKEST FIRE ANNOUNCED MOST FOES	127	3	DON JUAN 8	32	8
	HE RUSHED WHILE EARTH AND AIR WERE SADLY SHAKEN	129	3	DON JUAN 8	33	7
	AND AS HE RUSHED ALONG IT CAME TO PASS HE	130	3	DON JUAN 8	34	1
	AND YET THE REST RUSHED EAGERLY--NO WONDER	163	3	DON JUAN 8	103	5
	BUT BRAVELY RUSHED ON HIS FIRST HEAVENLY NIGHT	168	3	DON JUAN 8	114	3
RUSHES						
	MY BLOOD STILL RUSHES WHERE MY SPIRIT'S SET	133	2	DON JUAN 1	196	3
	WHICH RUSHES TO SOME SHORE WHOSE SHINGLES CHECK	60	3	DON JUAN 6	108	7
RUSHING						
	HIS REST THE RUSHING OF THE NEIGHBOURING RILL	229	2	DON JUAN 2	137	3
	AND RUSHING IN DISORDERLY THOUGH LED	369	2	DON JUAN 4	47	5
	LIKE RUSSIANS RUSHING FROM HOT BATHS TO SNOWS	349	3	DON JUAN 12	73	5
	LETS OUT IMPATIENTLY HIS RUSHING BREATH	412	3	DON JUAN 14	4	7
RUSS						
	THE RUSS FLOTILLA GETTING UNDER WAY	81	3	DON JUAN 7	29	2
	BEGAN TO SIGNALIZE THE RUSS RETREAT	87	3	DON JUAN 7	42	2
	SOME TWENTY TIMES HE MADE THE RUSS RETIRE	171	3	DON JUAN 8	120	3
	THE FATE OF NATIONS--BUT THIS RUSS SO WITTY	179	3	DON JUAN 8	134	7
	TO PROPER PLACEMEN EVERY RUSS CREDENTIAL	285	3	DON JUAN 11	35	2
	OUR GAY RUSS SPANIARD WAS ORDAINED TO SHINE	383	3	DON JUAN 13	53	4
	A RUSS OR TURK--THE ONE'S AS GOOD AS T'OTHER	474	3	DON JUAN 15	42	8
RUSSET						
	IN RUSSET JACKET--LYNX-LIKE IS HIS AIM	394	3	DON JUAN 13	75	5
	NO MATTER WHETHER RUSSET SILK OR DIMITY	421	3	DON JUAN 14	26	8
RUSSIAN						
	MONTHS WITH THE RUSSIAN ARMY HERE AND THERE	418	2	DON JUAN 5	15	6
	A RUSSIAN VESSEL E'ER WOULD HEAVE IN SIGHT	73	3	DON JUAN 7	13	3
	THE RUSSIAN BATTERIES WERE INCOMPLETE	79	3	DON JUAN 7	26	1
	AND ADMIRAL RIBAS (KNOWN IN RUSSIAN STORY)	83	3	DON JUAN 7	35	3
	IN THE THEN SOVEREIGN OF THE RUSSIAN PEOPLE	84	3	DON JUAN 7	37	7
	TO RUSSIAN TARTAR ENGLISH FRENCH COSSACQUE	89	3	DON JUAN 7	46	2
	AND DRILLED AWAY IN THE MOST CLASSIC RUSSIAN	99	3	DON JUAN 7	64	2
	OR THAT THE RUSSIAN ARMY SHOULD REPENT ALL	105	3	DON JUAN 7	75	6
	BEYOND THE RUSSIAN BATTERIES A FEW TOISES	115	3	DON JUAN 8	7	2
	A RUSSIAN OFFICER IN MARTIAL TREAD	153	3	DON JUAN 8	83	1
	THE RUSSIAN OFFICER FOR LIFE WAS LAMED	154	3	DON JUAN 8	85	2
	WHEREON THE RUSSIAN PATHOS GREW LESS TENDER	165	3	DON JUAN 8	107	6
	UPON THE RUSSIAN STEEL HIS BREAST HE FLUNG	170	3	DON JUAN 8	118	2
	THE RUSSIAN ARMY UPON THIS OCCASION	176	3	DON JUAN 8	128	2
	BETWEEN YOUR TURK AND RUSSIAN AS A MAIN	197	3	DON JUAN 9	29	V7

686

	PAGE	VOL		CANTO	STANZA	LV
RUSSIAN (CONTINUED)						
INTO A RUSSIAN COUPLET RATHER DULL	212	3	DON JUAN	9	60	3
DON JUAN GREW A VERY POLISHED RUSSIAN--	235	3	DON JUAN	10	21	1
BETWEEN THE BRITISH CABINET AND RUSSIAN	246	3	DON JUAN	10	45	3
AND WHICH WAS SOFTEST RUSSIAN OR CASTILIAN	294	3	DON JUAN	11	50	7
COULD BACK A HORSE AS DESPOTS RIDE A RUSSIAN	368	3	DON JUAN	13	23	8
THE ENVOY OF THE SECRET RUSSIAN MISSION	382	3	DON JUAN	13	52	8
RUSSIANS						
WERE THERE NOT ALSO RUSSIANS ENGLISH MANY	102	2	DON JUAN	1	149	5
AND THERE WITH GEORGIANS RUSSIANS AND CIRCASSIANS	407	2	DON JUAN	4	113	7
OF GEORGIANS RUSSIANS NUBIANS AND WHATNOT	417	2	DON JUAN	5	13	2
AND THEN WITHDREW TO HEAR ABOUT THE RUSSIANS	52	3	DON JUAN	6	92	5
THE RUSSIANS NOW WERE READY TO ATTACK	73	3	DON JUAN	7	14	1
THE RUSSIANS HAVING BUILT TWO BATTERIES ON	78	3	DON JUAN	7	23	1
AND GALLED THE RUSSIANS WITH A HEAVY FIRE	82	3	DON JUAN	7	31	4
ALL THAT THE RUSSIANS DID UPON THIS DAY	82	3	DON JUAN	7	32	2
LIKE RUSSIANS RUSHING FROM HOT BATHS TO SNOWS	349	3	DON JUAN	12	73	5
RUSSIA'S						
BUT IN SUCH MATTERS RUSSIA'S MIGHTY EMPRESS	221	3	DON JUAN	9	77	7
FOR BABYLON'S THAN RUSSIA'S ROYAL HARLOT--	237	3	DON JUAN	10	26	7
RUST						
WITH RUST SHOULD SURELY CEASE TO HACK AND HEW	433	3	DON JUAN	14	53	6
RUSTLE						
ALSO THE SOFTER SILKS WERE HEARD TO RUSTLE	223	3	DON JUAN	9	82	5
WHOSE LITTLE NIBBLING RUSTLE WILL EMBARRASS	509	3	DON JUAN	16	20	7
RUSTLED						
EVEN AS THE PAGE IS RUSTLED WHILE WE LOOK	72	2	DON JUAN	1	95	3
RUSTS						
OF GOUT WHICH RUSTS ARISTOCRATIC HINGES	515	3	DON JUAN	16	34	8
RUSTY						
A GREY WALL A GREEN RUIN RUSTY PIKE	255	3	DON JUAN	10	61	5
ENDS IN A RUSTY CASQUE AND DUBIOUS BONE	261	3	DON JUAN	10	73	6
RUTH						
YOU MAY BE BOAZ AND I--MODEST RUTH	403	3	DON JUAN	13	96	4
HIS INEXPERIENCE MOVED HER GENTLE RUTH	432	3	DON JUAN	14	51	7
HORSES THEY RIDE WITHOUT REMORSE OR RUTH	501	3	DON JUAN	16	1	6
RUTS						
TO RUTS AND FLINTS AND LOVELY NATURE'S SKILL	198	3	DON JUAN	9	31	5
SABINE						
TO MAKE A ROMAN SORT OF SABINE WEDDING	177	3	DON JUAN	8	131	7
AND HALF A MILLION FOR YOUR SABINE FARM	186	3	DON JUAN	9	7	7
FOR HENRY WAS A SORT OF SABINE SHOWMAN	530	3	DON JUAN	16	60	8
SABLE						
THEY FOLLOWED CLOSE BEHIND THEIR SABLE GUIDE	440	2	DON JUAN	5	51	2
RETAINS THE SABLE STAINS OF THE DARK CREEPER	232	3	DON JUAN	10	15	5
IT IS THE SABLE FRIAR AS BEFORE	556	3	DON JUAN	16	113	2
THE SABLE FRIAR IN HIS SOLEMN HOOD	558	3	DON JUAN	16	117	8
BACK FELL THE SABLE FROCK AND DREARY COWL	561	3	DON JUAN	16	123	5
SABLES						
FOR HAIDEE STRIPP'D HER SABLES OFF TO MAKE	226	2	DON JUAN	2	133	2
SABRE						
SNATCH'D DOWN HIS SABRE IN HOT HASTE TO WREAK	364	2	DON JUAN	4	37	3
FROM TWO SMART SABRE GASHES DEEP AND RED--	370	2	DON JUAN	4	49	7
AGAINST A FOE OR RAN A SABRE THROUGH SKIN	75	3	DON JUAN	7	17	4
THE BAYONET PIERCES AND THE SABRE CLEAVES	155	3	DON JUAN	8	88	1
SABRED						
HIS THIRD WAS SABRED AND THE FOURTH MOST CHERISHED	166	3	DON JUAN	8	110	3
SABRES						
A THOUSAND SHARPER SABRES WAIT THE WORD	364	2	DON JUAN	4	37	V7
THEIR SABRES GLITTERED O'ER HER LITTLE HEAD	158	3	DON JUAN	8	93	1
HE MADE 'GAINST COSSAQUE SABRES IN THE WIDE	249	3	DON JUAN	10	51	5
SACK						
THE SACK AND SEA HAD SETTLED ALL IN TIME	496	2	DON JUAN	5	149	4
SACKED						
BUT ENDED IN HIS BEING FOUND OUT AND SACKED	58	3	DON JUAN	6	104	6
SACKING						
ALSO TO HAVE THE SACKING OF A TOWN	75	3	DON JUAN	7	18	5
SACKS						
STITCHED UP IN SACKS--A MODE OF NAVIGATION	464	2	DON JUAN	5	92	7
SACRAMENTS						
THE SACRAMENTS HAVE BEEN REDUCED TO TWO	565	3	DON JUAN	17	7	1
SACRED						
SHE PROVED IT SOMEHOW OUT OF SACRED SONG	28	2	DON JUAN	1	14	3
AND WHISPER'D THINK OF EVERY SACRED TIE	268	2	DON JUAN	2	210	2
WHILE SWUNG THE SIGNAL FROM THE SACRED TOWER	335	2	DON JUAN	3	102	V5
MAKE THIS A SACRED PART OF ALBION'S ISLE	279	3	DON JUAN	11	24	8
SACRIFICE						
AND NONE TO BE THE SACRIFICE WOULD CHOOSE	195	2	DON JUAN	2	74	4
WHICH EVE MIGHT QUIT WITHOUT MUCH SACRIFICE--	278	3	DON JUAN	11	21	8
SACRUM						
VETABO CERERIS SACRUM QUI VULGARET--	419	3	DON JUAN	14	21	7
SAD						
ONE SAD EXAMPLE MORE THAT ALL IS VANITY	29	2	DON JUAN	1	15	7
'TIS A SAD THING I CANNOT CHOOSE BUT SAY	56	2	DON JUAN	1	63	1
(THAT MODERN PHRASE APPEARS TO ME SAD STUFF	119	2	DON JUAN	1	178	3
A SAD OLD FELLOW WAS HE IF YOU PLEASE	223	2	DON JUAN	2	127	6
THESE ARE SOME SAD EXAMPLES TO ALLURE US	267	2	DON JUAN	2	207	V5
OER WHOSE SAD TALE LOVE ECHOS STILL ALAS--	273	2	DON JUAN	2	V 2	3
A SAD SOUR SOBER BEVERAGE--BY TIME	277	2	DON JUAN	3	5	6

687

		PAGE	VOL	CANTO	STANZA	LN

SAD   (CONTINUED)

SAD THOUGHT TO LOSE THE SPOUSE THAT WAS ADORNING	278	2 DON JUAN	3	7	7
OF THE TRUE REASON OF HIS NOT BEING SAD	289	2 DON JUAN	3	26	5
THEIR POET A SAD TRIMMER BUT NO LESS	318	2 DON JUAN	3	82	1
AND THE SAD TRUTH WHICH HOVERS O'ER MY DESK	345	2 DON JUAN	4	3	7
RANG IN HER SAD EARS LIKE A MERMAID'S SONG	362	2 DON JUAN	4	34	7
BUT LET ME CHANGE THIS THEME WHICH GROWS TOO SAD	384	2 DON JUAN	4	74	1
THE CAPTIVES BACK TO THEIR SAD BERTHS EACH THREW	393	2 DON JUAN	4	90	4
SAD STRIFE AROSE FOR THEY WERE SO CROSS-GRAIN'D	394	2 DON JUAN	4	93	5
BUT I GROW SAD--AND LET A TALE GROW COLD	413	2 DON JUAN	5	4	7
A KIND OF BLUNT COMPASSION FOR THE SAD	417	2 DON JUAN	5	12	5
A SAD TALE SADDENS DOUBLY WHEN 'TIS LONG	419	2 DON JUAN	5	16	8
WHICH TURNS UP OUT OF THE SAD TWENTY-FOUR	426	2 DON JUAN	5	30	8
THE WOMEN UP--BECAUSE IN SAD REALITY	501	2 DON JUAN	5	157	2
FOR THAT SAD TEMPTER A FORBIDDEN WOMAN	10	3 DON JUAN	6	7	4
TO THOSE SAD HUNGRY JACOBINS THE WORMS	12	3 DON JUAN	6	13	4
AT A SAD DISCOUNT WHILE YOUR OVER-CHILLY	14	3 DON JUAN	6	16	7
A SAD MISCALCULATION ABOUT DISTANCE	80	3 DON JUAN	7	28	1
THUS EVEN GOOD FAME MAY SUFFER SAD CONTRACTIONS	83	3 DON JUAN	7	34	5
AND ALMOST EVERY DAY IN SAD REALITY	108	3 DON JUAN	7	83	3
OR A GOOD BOXER INTO A SAD PICKLE	134	3 DON JUAN	8	43	6
WHEN JUAN CAUGHT A GLIMPSE OF THIS SAD SIGHT	158	3 DON JUAN	8	93	4
AND THE SAD SECOND MOON GROWS DIM AGAIN	168	3 DON JUAN	8	113	4
ALL BY WHICH HELL IS PEOPLED OR AS SAD	173	3 DON JUAN	8	123	6
HER FRIENDS LIKE THE SAD FAMILY OF HECTOR	182	3 DON JUAN	8	141	3
AND THUS DEATH LAUGHS--IT IS SAD MERRIMENT	189	3 DON JUAN	9	13	1
THAN HE IN THESE SAD HIGHWAYS LEFT AT LARGE	198	3 DON JUAN	9	31	4
THAT SAD INEXPLICABLE BEAST OF PREY--	207	3 DON JUAN	9	50	2
WHICH IS A SAD THING AND NOT ONLY TRAMPLES	236	3 DON JUAN	10	23	4
LIFE'S SAD POST-HORSES O'ER THE DREARY FRONTIER	238	3 DON JUAN	10	27	7
OF THEIR SALT VEINS AND THEIR SAD SHALLOW SEAS	251	3 DON JUAN	10	54	V4
WITH SCHNAPPS--SAD DOGS WHOM HUNDSFOT OR FERFLUCTER	260	3 DON JUAN	10	71	7
WILL KISS NOT IN SAD METAPHOR--BUT EARNEST--	286	3 DON JUAN	11	38	V7
SOFTEST OF MELODIES AND COULD BE SAD	292	3 DON JUAN	11	47	4
I HAVE SEEN THAT SAD AFFAIR OF THE LATE QUEEN--	310	3 DON JUAN	11	84	4
AND ONE OR TWO SEPARATE WIVES WITHOUT	330	3 DON JUAN	12	31	1
OF THE SAD CONSEQUENCE OF GOING ASTRAY	336	3 DON JUAN	12	44	6
FORMS A SAD CLIMAX TO ROMANTIC HOMAGES	346	3 DON JUAN	12	65	6
OF ALL TALES 'TIS THE SADDEST--AND MORE SAD	363	3 DON JUAN	13	9	1
JUST TO CONSOLE SAD GLORY FOR BEING GLORIOUS	372	3 DON JUAN	13	32	8
SAD BUT SERENE IT SWEEPS O'ER TREE OR TOWER	388	3 DON JUAN	13	64	6
ON WHAT I'VE SEEN OR PONDER'D SAD OR CHEERY	415	3 DON JUAN	14	11	6
SAD RAKES TO SADDER HUSBANDS CHASTELY TAMING	418	3 DON JUAN	14	18	5
THE SOBER SAD ANTITHESIS TO GLOWING--	422	3 DON JUAN	14	28	6
BUT OH THAT I SHOULD EVER PEN SO SAD A LINE	430	3 DON JUAN	14	46	1
'TIS SAD TO HACK INTO THE ROOTS OF THINGS	436	3 DON JUAN	14	59	1
THE FURTHER PROGRESS OF THIS SAD MISTAKE	437	3 DON JUAN	14	61	3
COST HER AN EFFORT WHICH IS A SAD TOIL	447	3 DON JUAN	14	86	2
LEAVES A SAD SEDIMENT OF TIME'S WORST SAND	457	3 DON JUAN	15	4	8
UPON AN OBJECT WHETHER SAD OR PLAYFUL	463	3 DON JUAN	15	16	7
VOLUMES WITH SIMILAR SAD ILLUSTRATIONS	464	3 DON JUAN	15	18	7
WHICH IS FOR INNOCENCE A SAD TEMPTATION--	468	3 DON JUAN	15	28	6
WITHOUT THOSE SAD EXPENSES WHICH DISPARGE	471	3 DON JUAN	15	35	5
THAT SAD RESULT OF PASSIONS AND POTATOES--	472	3 DON JUAN	15	37	7
SINCE--SINCE--IN YOUTH I HAD THE SAD MISHAP--	530	3 DON JUAN	16	61	5
WITH THE SAD USAGE OF ALL SORTS OF SAGES	566	3 DON JUAN	17	9	3

SADDENS

| A SAD TALE SADDENS DOUBLY WHEN 'TIS LONG | 419 | 2 DON JUAN | 5 | 16 | 8 |
| BUT SADDENS MORE BY NIGHT AS WELL AS DAY | 442 | 2 DON JUAN | 5 | 56 | 6 |

SADDER

| SAD RAKES TO SADDER HUSBANDS CHASTELY TAMING | 418 | 3 DON JUAN | 14 | 18 | 5 |
| SADDER THAN OWL-SONGS OR THE MIDNIGHT BLAST | 432 | 3 DON JUAN | 14 | 50 | 2 |

SADDEST

| OF ALL TALES 'TIS THE SADDEST--AND MORE SAD | 363 | 3 DON JUAN | 13 | 9 | 1 |
| BUT SADDEST WHEN HIS SCIENCE IS WELL KNOWN | 463 | 3 DON JUAN | 15 | 17 | 6 |

SADLY

FOR HAVING USED THEIR APPETITES SO SADLY	199	2 DON JUAN	2	80	8
NOT SO HAIDEE SHE SADLY TOSS'D AND TUMBLED	229	2 DON JUAN	2	138	1
POOR CREATURES THEIR GOOD LOOKS WERE SADLY CHANGED	414	2 DON JUAN	5	7	4
HE RUSHED WHILE EARTH AND AIR WERE SADLY SHAKEN	129	3 DON JUAN	8	33	7
THE SECOND MAY BE SADLY DONE OR GAILY	465	3 DON JUAN	15	21	4
IN EYES WHICH SADLY SHONE AS SERAPHS' SHINE	476	3 DON JUAN	15	45	3
OR STEP RAN SADLY THROUGH THAT ANTIQUE HOUSE	509	3 DON JUAN	16	20	4

SADNESS

| SHE LOOK'D A SADNESS SWEETER THAN HER SMILE | 61 | 2 DON JUAN | 1 | 72 | 2 |

SAD'S

| BESIDES THE SAD'S A SOURCE OF THE SUBLIME | 358 | 3 DON JUAN | 13 | 1 | 5 |

SAFE

WAS NOT SO SAFE FOR ROOSTING AS A CHURCH	206	2 DON JUAN	2	95	4
I LEAVE DON JUAN FOR THE PRESENT SAFE--	373	2 DON JUAN	4	54	1
HER CARGO FROM THE PLAGUE BEING SAFE AND SOUND	407	2 DON JUAN	4	113	5
IN FACT THEY CAN BE SAFE YOU SHOULD HAVE BEEN	102	3 DON JUAN	7	70	6
BUT IF SHE WERE DELIVERED SAFE AND SOUND	162	3 DON JUAN	8	102	7
SAFE WITH A LADY WHOSE LAST GROWN-UP DAUGHTER	339	3 DON JUAN	12	51	3
SAFE CONDUCT THROUGH THE ROCKS OF RE-ELECTIONS	546	3 DON JUAN	16	95	8

SAFEGUARD

| OF A MERE NOVICE HAD ONE SAFEGUARD MORE | 346 | 3 DON JUAN | 12 | 67 | 2 |

SAFELY

| ARE SAFELY MINED FOR IN THE MODE HE MENTIONS | 93 | 2 DON JUAN | 1 | 132 | 5 |

SAFELY   (CONTINUED)
    THEIR SPLEEN IN MAKING STRIFE AND SAFELY WORDING . . . . 498 2 DON JUAN 5   151 6
    FOR THE MAN WAS WE SAFELY MAY ASSERT . . . . 95 3 DON JUAN 7   55 3
    WITH SUCH A CHART AS MAY BE SAFELY STUCK TO-- . . . . 348 3 DON JUAN 12   70 5
SAFEST
    THE LIGHTEST BEING THE SAFEST AT A DISTANCE . . . . . 140 3 DON JUAN 8   55 5
SAFETY
    IN SAFETY TO THE WAGGONS WHERE ALONE . . . . 102 3 DON JUAN 7   70 5
    OF SAFETY WHERE SHE LESS MAY SHRINK AND GRIEVE . . . 161 3 DON JUAN 8   99 4
    SAFETY THAN HIS NEW ORDER OF SAINT VLADIMIR . . . . 182 3 DON JUAN 8   140 8
    IN SAFETY TO THE PLACE FOR WHICH YOU START . . . . . 284 3 DON JUAN 11   34 7
    AND SINCE THERE'S SAFETY IN A MULTITUDE . . . . . . 371 3 DON JUAN 13   29 1
    BUT AS THERE'S SAFETY GRAFTED IN THE NUMBER . . . . 371 3 DON JUAN 13   30 1
    SELF-LOVE THERE'S SAFETY IN A CROWD OF COXCOMBS . . 371 3 DON JUAN 13   30 8
SAFFRON
    AND SAFFRON SOUPS AND SWEETBREADS AND THE FISHES . . 307 2 DON JUAN 3   62 3
    CLOVES CINNAMON AND SAFFRON TOO WERE BOIL'D . . . . 307 2 DON JUAN 3   63 7
    SLIPPERS OF SAFFRON DAGGER RICH AND HANDY . . . . . 451 2 DON JUAN 5   68 7
SAGACITY
    I LEAVE IT TO YOUR PEOPLE OF SAGACITY . . . . 449 3 DON JUAN 14   90 4
SAGE
    AND SINCE EXCEEDING VALOROUS AND SAGE . . . . 24 2 DON JUAN 1   5 2
    WAS TO DECLARE HOW SAGE AND STILL AND STEADY . . . . 49 2 DON JUAN 1   50 7
    SHE FLATTER'D JULIA WITH HER SAGE PROTECTION . . . . 58 2 DON JUAN 1   67 5
    BUT SAGE ANTONIA CUT HIM SHORT BEFORE . . . . 111 2 DON JUAN 1   163 2
    SAPPHO THE SAGE BLUE-STOCKING IN WHOSE GRAVE . . . . 266 2 DON JUAN 2   205 4
    SO SAID THE ROYAL SAGE SARDANAPALUS . . . . 267 2 DON JUAN 2   207 8
    BY SAINT BY SAGE BY PREACHER AND BY POET . . . . . . 69 3 DON JUAN 7   6 6
    THAT SAGE (SAID JOHN) SURRENDERS AT DISCRETION . . . 88 3 DON JUAN 7   44 6
    A MODERATE PENSION SHAKES FULL MANY A SAGE . . . . . 118 3 DON JUAN 8   14 4
    BUT BEDLAM STILL EXISTS WITH ITS SAGE FETTER . . . . 280 3 DON JUAN 11   25 3
    OFFSPRING OF SOME SAGE HUSBAND--HUNTING COUNTESS . . 312 3 DON JUAN 11   89 2
    BUT WHEN WE HOVER BETWEEN FOOL AND SAGE . . . . . . 315 3 DON JUAN 12   1 4
    AND WONDER PROVIDENCE IS NOT MORE SAGE . . . . 339 3 DON JUAN 12   50 4
    OR SOMEONE FOR HIM IN SOME SAGE GRAVE MOOD . . . . . 371 3 DON JUAN 13   29 3
    I MUST NOT QUITE OMIT THE TALKING SAGE . . . . 403 3 DON JUAN 13   97 3
    'TWAS RATHER HER EXPERIENCE MADE HER SAGE . . . . . 433 3 DON JUAN 14   54 3
    BUT THEN WITH WHOM THERE WAS THE SAGE MISS READING . 473 3 DON JUAN 15   40 3
    WAS VERY YOUNG ALTHOUGH SO VERY SAGE . . . . 494 3 DON JUAN 15   85 2
    AND REALLY IF THE SAGE SUBLIME AND ATTIC . . . . . . 494 3 DON JUAN 15   86 3
    AND STUFF WITH SAGE THAT VERY VERDANT GOOSE . . . . 497 3 DON JUAN 15   93 6
    AND THE LOUD SHRIEK OF SAGE MINERVA'S FOWL . . . . . 499 3 DON JUAN 15   97 3
    DEEMING THE SAGE WOULD BE MUCH MORTIFIED . . . . . . 522 3 DON JUAN 16   43 5
    TO BE A TOTUS TERES STOIC SAGE . . . . 566 3 DON JUAN 17   10 7
SAGELY
    EXCEEDING SAGELY FROM THAT HOUR DISPENSED . . . . . 66 2 DON JUAN 1   82 5
SAGE'S
    FOR ANY SAGE'S CREED OR CALCULATION)-- . . . . . . 225 3 DON JUAN 10   1 4
SAGES
    OF HIS NEW SYSTEM TO PERPLEX THE SAGES . . . . 11 2 DON JUAN D   4 4
    THOUGH SAGES MAY POUR OUT THEIR WISDOM'S TREASURE . . 308 2 DON JUAN 3   65 7
    AND GLORY LONG HAS MADE THE SAGES SMILE . . . . . . 328 2 DON JUAN 3   90 1
    AND GLORY MAKES THE SAGES OFTEN SMILE . . . . 328 2 DON JUAN 3   90 V1
    WHAT SAGES CALL CHANCE PROVIDENCE OR FATE-- . . . . 105 3 DON JUAN 7   76 4
    (LET DEEPER SAGES THE TRUE CAUSE DETERMINE) . . . . 249 3 DON JUAN 10   50 3
    SENATES AND SAGES HAVE CONDEMNED ITS USE-- . . . . . 256 3 DON JUAN 10   63 5
    WHILE SAGES WRITE AGAINST ALL PROCREATION . . . . . 325 3 DON JUAN 12   21 6
    BUT SIXTEEN DOWAGERS TEN UNWED SHE SAGES . . . . . . 330 3 DON JUAN 12   30 7
    AND PERSECUTED SAGES TEACH THE SCHOOLS . . . . . . 463 3 DON JUAN 15   17 7
    HEROES SOMETIMES THOUGH SELDOM--SAGES NEVER . . . . 547 3 DON JUAN 16   98 2
    WITH THE SAD USAGE OF ALL SORTS OF SAGES . . . . . 566 3 DON JUAN 17   9 3
SAGES'
    AS SOMETIMES HAVE BEEN GREATER SAGES' LOTS-- . . . . 200 3 DON JUAN 9   36 3
SAGEST
    SAGEST OF WOMEN EVEN OF WIDOWS SHE . . . . 42 2 DON JUAN 1   38 1
    HOW SELF-DECEITFUL IS THE SAGEST PART . . . . 78 2 DON JUAN 1   106 5
    OF HUNTING--FOR THE SAGEST YOUTH IS FRAIL . . . . . 424 3 DON JUAN 14   33 6
SAIL
    AT SUNSET THEY BEGAN TO TAKE IN SAIL . . . . 170 2 DON JUAN 2   26 6
    THE STRONGER PUMP'D THE WEAKER THRUMM'D A SAIL . . . 176 2 DON JUAN 2   38 8
    UNDER THE VESSEL'S KEEL THE SAIL WAS PAST . . . . . 176 2 DON JUAN 2   39 1
    WAS USED--NOR SAIL NOR SHORE APPEAR'D IN SIGHT . . . 178 2 DON JUAN 2   41 7
    AS THERE WERE BUT TWO BLANKETS FOR A SAIL . . . . . 181 2 DON JUAN 2   48 4
    THAT THE SAIL WAS BECALM'D BETWEEN THE SEAS . . . . 188 2 DON JUAN 2   60 2
    INSTEAD OF SAIL WERE TO THE OAR MADE FAST . . . . . 188 2 DON JUAN 2   61 4
    HE WISHES FOR A BOAT TO SAIL THE DEEPS-- . . . . . 333 2 DON JUAN 3   98 5
    OF THOSE WHO SAIL THE SEAS ON THE FIRST DAY . . . . 338 2 DON JUAN 3   108 2
    WHERE LAY SOME SHIPS WHICH WERE TO SAIL AT NINE . . 371 2 DON JUAN 4   50 4
    TO SLACKEN SAIL AND ANCHOR WITH OUR RHYME . . . . . 503 2 DON JUAN 5   159 4
    BUT WHAT IF CARRYING SAIL CAPSIZE THE BOAT . . . . . 191 3 DON JUAN 9   18 3
    THAN IF I SOUGHT TO SAIL BEFORE THE WIND . . . . . 195 3 DON JUAN 9   26 4
    DISCOVER STARS AND SAIL IN THE WIND'S EYE . . . . . 226 3 DON JUAN 10   3 7
    IN THE WIND'S EYE I HAVE SAILED AND SAIL BUT FOR . . 227 3 DON JUAN 10   4 1
    HERE HE EMBARKED AND WITH A FLOWING SAIL . . . . . 256 3 DON JUAN 10   64 1
    COULD REACH WITH HERE AND THERE A SAIL JUST SKIPPING . 265 3 DON JUAN 10   82 3
    AND SAIL FOR A NEW THEME--I HAVE SEEN--AND SHOOK . . 309 3 DON JUAN 11   83 6
SAILED
    THEIR DELHIS MANNED SOME BOATS AND SAILED AGAIN . . . 82 3 DON JUAN 7   31 3
    IN THE WIND'S EYE I HAVE SAILED AND SAIL BUT FOR . . 227 3 DON JUAN 10   4 1
    WHO HAS SAILED WHERE PICTURESQUE CONSTANTINOPLE IS . . 271 3 DON JUAN 11   7 3

```
                                                              PAGE VOL       CANTO STANZA LN
SAILING
    SAILING SIX KNOTS AN HOUR BEFORE THE WIND    . . . . .  . 384  2 DON JUAN  4   75   5
    IN SAILING FROM LIVORNO BY THE PIRATE . . . . . . . .   . 388  2 DON JUAN  4   80   7
SAILOR
    A SAILOR WHEN THE PRIZE HAS STRUCK IN FIGHT . . . . .   . 261  2 DON JUAN  2  196   5
SAILOR'S
    AND HARDSHIP STILL HAS BEEN THE SAILOR'S LOT   . . . .  . 191  2 DON JUAN  2   66   5
SAILORS
    THE WIND SUNG CORDAGE STRAIN'D AND SAILORS SWORE  . . . . 163  2 DON JUAN  2   13   2
    FOR SAILORS ARE IN FACT A DIFFERENT KIND . . . .   . . . 170  2 DON JUAN  2   26   5
    THE SAILORS ATE THE REST OF POOR PEDRILLO  . . . .  . . 197  2 DON JUAN  2   77   8
    THE SAILORS ATE HIM ALL SAVE THREE OR FOUR  . . . .  . . 198  2 DON JUAN  2   78   1
    AN IGNIS FATUUS OR AS SAILORS STRANDED   . . . . .   . . 127  3 DON JUAN  8   32   5
SAILS
    AND AS THE VEERING WIND SHIFTS SHIFT OUR SAILS . . . . . 159  2 DON JUAN  2    4   4
    WAVING LIKE SAILS NEW SHIVERED IN A STORM   . . . .  . . 204  3 DON JUAN  9   43   3
SAIN
    HEAVEN SAIN HIM FAIR OR FOUL . . . . . . . . . .   . . . 520  3 DON JUAN 16  L  6   6
SAINT
    NEGLECT INDEED REQUIRES A SAINT TO BEAR IT . . . . .  .   32  2 DON JUAN  1   20   3
    AS SAINT AUGUSTINE IN HIS FINE CONFESSIONS . . . . .  .   47  2 DON JUAN  1   47   7
    ('TWAS SNOW THAT BROUGHT SAINT ANTHONY TO REASON) . . .   57  2 DON JUAN  1   64   4
    (SAINT PAUL SAYS 'TIS THE TOLL WHICH MUST BE GIVEN) . . 225  2 DON JUAN  2  131   8
    FROM SAINT BARTHOLOMEW WE HAVE SAVED OUR SKIN  . . . . . 435  2 DON JUAN  5   44   4
    EVEN WERE SAINT FRANCIS' PARAMOUR THEIR GUEST  . . . .    14  3 DON JUAN  6   17   5
    BY SAINT BY SAGE BY PREACHER AND BY POET . . . . .  . .   69  3 DON JUAN  7    6   6
    TWO BATTERIES CAP-A-PIE AS OUR SAINT GEORGE  . . . .  .   72  3 DON JUAN  7   12   3
    THAT YOU AND I WILL WIN SAINT GEORGE'S COLLAR  . . . . . 160  3 DON JUAN  8   97   8
    SAFETY THAN HIS NEW ORDER OF SAINT VLADIMIR .  . . . . . 182  3 DON JUAN  8  140   8
    SAINT JAMES'S PALACE AND SAINT JAMES'S HELLS   . . . . . 282  3 DON JUAN 11   29   8
    SAINT JAMES'S PALACE AND SAINT JAMES'S HELLS   . . . . . 282  3 DON JUAN 11   29   8
    MY LEIPSIC AND MY MONT SAINT JEAN SEEMS CAIN   . . . . . 296  3 DON JUAN 11   56   2
    WHICH IN A SAINT OR CYNIC EVER WAS . . . . . . .  . . . 319  3 DON JUAN 12    7   3
    AND HERE PERHAPS A MONSTER THERE A SAINT . . . . .  . . 389  3 DON JUAN 13   65   4
    SAINT FROM HIS BEADS TO JOIN THE JOCUND RACE   . . . . . 395  3 DON JUAN 13   78   4
    WHO LIKES A LISTENER WHETHER SAINT OR SINNER--  . . . . 426  3 DON JUAN 14   36   7
    BUT SAINT AUGUSTINE HAS THE GREAT PRIORITY . . . . .  . 503  3 DON JUAN 16    5   5
    THE FORMS OF THE GRIM KNIGHT AND PICTURED SAINT  . . . 508  3 DON JUAN 16   18   1
SAINTED
    HIS BRUSH WITH ALL THE BLOOD OF ALL THE SAINTED  . . . 392  3 DON JUAN 13   71   8
SAINTLY
    AND JUAN WAS A BOY OF SAINTLY BREEDING  . . . . . .  . 354  2 DON JUAN  4   19   6
SAINT'S
    OF ANY MODERN FEMALE SAINT'S COMPARISON . . . . . .  .   30  2 DON JUAN  1   17   2
SAINTS
    AND HOMILIES AND LIVES OF ALL THE SAINTS . . . . .  . .   47  2 DON JUAN  1   47   2
    OF CANDLES TO THEIR SAINTS--BUT THERE WERE NONE  . . . 179  2 DON JUAN  2   44   4
    HE TURN'D FROM GRISLY SAINTS AND MARTYRS HAIRY   . . . 235  2 DON JUAN  2  149   7
    TO SEVERAL SAINTS THAT SHORTLY PLOUGH OR HARROW  . . .   99  3 DON JUAN  7   63   6
    WITH PROPHETS HOURIS ANGELS SAINTS DESCRIED  . . . . . 169  3 DON JUAN  8  115   7
    WHERE ARE THOSE MARTYRED SAINTS THE FIVE PER CENTS   . 307  3 DON JUAN 11   77   7
    I LEAVE THE SAINTS TO SETTLE THEIR OWN SCORE   . . . . 352  3 DON JUAN 12   79   4
    TWELVE SAINTS HAD ONCE STOOD SANCTIFIED IN STONE  . . 386  3 DON JUAN 13   60   2
    JUAN--IN THIS RESPECT AT LEAST LIKE SAINTS--   . . . . 424  3 DON JUAN 14   31   1
SAITH
    IN AWE HE SAID AS THE CENTURION SAITH  . . . . . . . . 430  2 DON JUAN  5   36   5
    IF HISTORY THE GRAND LIAR EVER SAITH . . . . . . .  . 222  3 DON JUAN  9   81   4
    OH SAITH THE PSALMIST THAT I HAD A DOVE'S  . . . . . . 228  3 DON JUAN 10    6   2
    YOU KNOW OR DON'T KNOW THAT GREAT BACON SAITH  . . . . 414  3 DON JUAN 14    8   1
    SAITH HORACE THE GREAT LITTLE POET'S WRONG . . . . .  443  3 DON JUAN 14   77   2
SAKE
    FOR HONOUR'S PRIDE'S RELIGION'S VIRTUE'S SAKE  . . . .   62  2 DON JUAN  1   75   4
    FOR GOD'S SAKE MADAM--MADAM--HERE'S MY MASTER  . . . .   96  2 DON JUAN  1  137   1
    OR FOR THE SAKE OF DECENCY ABIDE . . . . . . . . .  . 106  2 DON JUAN  1  156   6
    FLY JUAN FLY FOR HEAVEN'S SAKE--NOT A WORD--   . . . . 121  2 DON JUAN  1  182   3
    FOR GOD'S SAKE READER TAKE THEM NOT FOR MINE   . . . . 149  2 DON JUAN  1  222   8
    (FOR GOD'S SAKE LET ME HAVE A GLASS OF LIQUOR  . . . . 167  2 DON JUAN  2   20   3
    FOR HAIDEE'S SAKE IS MORE THAN I CAN SAY . . . . .  . 300  2 DON JUAN  3   49   6
    SO THAT I TRUST FOR EVERYBODY'S SAKE . . . . . . . .  459  2 DON JUAN  5   82   7
    IN BEGGING HIM FOR GOD'S SAKE JUST TO SHOW   . . . . . 165  3 DON JUAN  8  108   3
    AND MERELY FOR THE SAKE OF ITS OWN MERITS  . . . . . . 260  3 DON JUAN 10   72   5
    NOT ONLY FOR THE SAKE OF THEIR VARIETY . . . . . .  . 497  3 DON JUAN 15   93   3
SAKES
    SIGH'D FOR THEIR SAKES--THAT THEY SHOULD E'ER GROW OLDER . 292  2 DON JUAN  3   33   8
    WISHED FOR THEIR SAKES--THEY NEVER MIGHT GROW OLDER  . . 292  2 DON JUAN  3   33  V8
    OH POPE WOULD THAT THOU WERT LIVING FOR THEIR SAKES  . . 334  2 DON JUAN  3  100  V7
SAL
    A KERCHIEF CRYING GIVE SAL THAT--AND DIED  . . . . . . 276  3 DON JUAN 11   16   8
    WHO ON A LARK WITH BLACK-EYED SAL (HIS BLOWING)  . . . 277  3 DON JUAN 11   19   7
SALAD
    A LOBSTER SALAD AND CHAMPAIGNE AND CHAT  . . . . . . .  94  2 DON JUAN  1  135   8
SALAM
    HE SOMETIMES THOUGHT 'TWAS ONLY THEIR SALAM  . . . . . 274  3 DON JUAN 11   12   4
SALAMANCA
    IN CLOISTERS OF THE CLASSIC SALAMANCA  . . . . . . . . 175  2 DON JUAN  2   37   7
SALAMANDER
    JUST AS YOU'D BREAK A SUCKING SALAMANDER . . . . . .    93  3 DON JUAN  7   52   5
    SHUT UP EACH HIGH HEROIC SALAMANDER  . . . . . . . . . 446  3 DON JUAN 14   83   5
SALAMIS
    WHICH LOOKS O'ER SEA-BORN SALAMIS  . . . . . . . . .  322  2 DON JUAN  3  L  4   2

                              690
```

	PAGE	VOL	CANTO		STANZA	LN
SALARIO						
WITHOUT A SINGLE SCUDO OF SALARIO	389	2 DON JUAN	4	82	6
SALARY						
YOU HAVE YOUR SALARY WAS'T FOR THAT YOU WROUGHT	12	2 DON JUAN	D	6	5
SALE						
HER SALE SENT HOME SOME DISAPPOINTED BAWLERS	407	2 DON JUAN	4	114	5
WITH WHITES AND BLACKS IN GROUPS ON SHOW FOR SALE	416	2 DON JUAN	5	10	2
HER EYE IN PASSING ON HIS WAY TO SALE	477	2 DON JUAN	5	114	2
WHEN THE SALE OF NEW BOOKS IS NOT SO FLEET	79	3 DON JUAN	7	26	5
HAD BROUGHT THE CAPO D'OPERA NOT FOR SALE	528	3 DON JUAN	16	57	7
SALLIED						
FROM WHENCE THEY SALLIED ON THOSE CHRISTIAN SCORNERS	149	3 DON JUAN	8	75	8
SALLIES						
YET 'TIS IN VAIN SUCH SALLIES TO PERMIT	234	3 DON JUAN	10	19	5
SALLUST						
BY SALLUST IN HIS CATILINE WHO CHASED	61	3 DON JUAN	6	111	6
SALLY						
THE FOREMOST IN THE CHARGE OR IN THE SALLY	431	2 DON JUAN	5	37	7
AND FROM BENEATH HIS BOUGHS WERE SEEN TO SALLY	384	3 DON JUAN	13	56	5
TO JEST UPON SUCH THEMES IN MANY A SALLY	526	3 DON JUAN	16	53	3
HE WOULD NOT JOIN THEM IN A SINGLE SALLY	552	3 DON JUAN	16	105	8
SALMI						
THE SALMI THE CONSOMME THE PUREE	487	3 DON JUAN	15	71	2
SALMON						
FOWLS A LA CONDE SLICES EKE OF SALMON	484	3 DON JUAN	15	65	1
SALOON						
THIS STRANGE SALOON MUCH FITTED FOR INSPIRING	469	2 DON JUAN	5	100	5
SALOON ROOM HALL O'ERFLOW BEYOND THEIR BRINK	302	3 DON JUAN	11	68	5
AND NOTHING BRIGHTER GLEAMED THROUGH THE SALOON	504	3 DON JUAN	16	8	7
AND WHEN HE WALKED DOWN INTO THE SALOON	513	3 DON JUAN	16	30	1
NOT NIGH THE GAY SALOON OF LADIES GENT	533	3 DON JUAN	16	66	2
SALPICON						
A L'ESPAGNOLE TIMBALLE AND SALPICON--	484	3 DON JUAN	15	66	2
SALT						
AS SWEETNESS TO THE FLOWER OR SALT TO OCEAN	51	2 DON JUAN	1	55	6
WHILE HIS SALT TEARS DROPP'D INTO THE SALT SEA	165	2 DON JUAN	2	17	2
WHILE HIS SALT TEARS DROPP'D INTO THE SALT SEA	165	2 DON JUAN	2	17	2
IN WASHING DOWN PEDRILLO WITH SALT WATER	210	2 DON JUAN	2	102	8
AWAY THE VAST SALT DREAD ETERNAL DEEP	210	2 DON JUAN	2	103	8
WHICH WEIGH'D UPON THEM YET ALL DAMP AND SALT	234	2 DON JUAN	2	147	7
OR LOT'S WIFE DONE IN SALT--OR WHAT YOU WILL	40	3 DON JUAN	6	68	5
QUENCHED IN THE LAP OF THE SALT SEA OR THETIS	217	3 DON JUAN	9	69	8
(WHO LIKE SOUR FRUIT TO STIR THEIR VEINS' SALT TIDES	251	3 DON JUAN	10	54	3
OF THEIR SALT VEINS AND THEIR SAD SHALLOW SEAS	251	3 DON JUAN	10	54	V4
FAMOUS FOR MINES OF SALT AND YOKES OF IRON	253	3 DON JUAN	10	58	2
FACTITIOUS PASSIONS WIT WITHOUT MUCH SALT	417	3 DON JUAN	14	16	5
SALT-WATER						
DRINKING SALT-WATER LIKE A MOUNTAIN-STREAM	198	2 DON JUAN	2	79	6
SALUTED						
HIS MAJESTY SALUTED HIS FOURTH SPOUSE	500	2 DON JUAN	5	154	1
THE FLEET AND CAMP SALUTED WITH GREAT GRACE	89	3 DON JUAN	7	47	3
SALVATION						
STILL THEIR SALVATION WAS AN EVEN BET	171	2 DON JUAN	2	28	6
OWING TO HIM--AS ALSO HER SALVATION	251	3 DON JUAN	10	55	5
SALVATORE'S						
OR WILDER GROUPE OF SAVAGE SALVATORE'S	392	3 DON JUAN	13	71	4
SAMARITANS						
SAMARITANS IN EVERY SITUATION	480	2 DON JUAN	5	120	6
SAME						
A GOOD DEAL LIKE HIM TOO THOUGH QUITE THE SAME NONE	24	2 DON JUAN	1	5	3
ITSELF 'TIS STILL THE SAME HYPOCRISY	61	2 DON JUAN	1	73	6
FOR THAT SAME TWINING TRANSPORT AND SECURITY	69	2 DON JUAN	1	88	7
I SAY WHEN THESE SAME GENTLEMEN ARE JEALOUS	74	2 DON JUAN	1	98	7
HOW THIS SAME INTERVIEW HAD TAKEN PLACE	77	2 DON JUAN	1	105	2
FIFTY OR SIXTY--IT IS ALL THE SAME--	101	2 DON JUAN	1	146	4
IS THAT SAME TIME SO COMMON YET SO PRECIOUS	145	2 DON JUAN	1	217	V7
IS THAT SAME TIME WHICH I HAVE SPENT BETIMES	145	2 DON JUAN	1	217	V7
BUT THE SAME CAUSE CONDUCIVE TO HIS LOSS	186	2 DON JUAN	2	57	2
AND THE SAME NIGHT THERE FELL A SHOWER OF RAIN	201	2 DON JUAN	2	84	1
WERE BLACK AS DEATH THEIR LASHES THE SAME HUE	218	2 DON JUAN	2	117	2
SEEM AT THE SAME TIME MYSTICAL AND GAY	220	2 DON JUAN	2	120	8
TAKING HER FOR A SISTER JUST THE SAME	232	2 DON JUAN	2	142	5
YET TO THESE FOUR IN THREE THINGS THE SAME LUCK HOLDS	266	2 DON JUAN	2	206	7
IN THE SAME OBJECT GRACES QUITE AS KILLING	270	2 DON JUAN	2	213	3
CAN CALM--FOR WHAT IT MADE ME ON THAT SAME	272	2 DON JUAN	2	V 1	7
ALTHOUGH THEY BOTH ARE BORN IN THE SAME CLIME	277	2 DON JUAN	3	5	4
THE SAME THINGS CHANGE THEIR NAMES AT SUCH A RATE	278	2 DON JUAN	3	6	6
THE SAME THINGS CANNOT ALWAYS BE ADMIRED	278	2 DON JUAN	3	7	4
THE MERCHANDISE WAS SERVED IN THE SAME WAY	284	2 DON JUAN	3	17	1
OR SHOW THE SAME DISLIKE TO SUITORS' KISSES	287	2 DON JUAN	3	23	4
WAS MUCH THE SAME AS FIRE GIVES A WET BLANKET	294	2 DON JUAN	3	36	V8
'TWAS ALL THE SAME TO HIM--GOD SAVE THE KING	319	2 DON JUAN	3	85	3
THE LAST WAR--MUCH THE SAME IN PORTUGAL	320	2 DON JUAN	3	86	4
WHEN HE AND SOUTHEY FOLLOWING THE SAME PATH	329	2 DON JUAN	3	93	7
OUR SIN THE SAME AND HARD AS HIS TO MEND	344	2 DON JUAN	4	1	6
AND WISH'D THAT OTHERS HELD THE SAME OPINION	345	2 DON JUAN	4	3	2
HOW LIKE THEY LOOKED THE EXPRESSION WAS THE SAME	367	2 DON JUAN	4	44	2
YET LOOKS NOT LIFE FOR THEY ARE STILL THE SAME	377	2 DON JUAN	4	61	8
THESE SMILE AND WRITHE AND PERISH STILL THE SAME	377	2 DON JUAN	4	61	V7

691

```
                                                          PAGE VOL   CANTO STANZA LV
SAME   (CONTINUED)
    AND IDA IN THE DISTANCE STILL THE SAME  . . . . . .  386  2 DON JUAN  4    77   3
    'TIS ALL THE SAME TO ME I'M FOND OF YIELDING  . . . .  397  2 DON JUAN  4    98   1
    FROM EVERY FLAKE AND YET ROLLS ON THE SAME  . . . .  398  2 DON JUAN  4   100   6
    SHE HAS SERVED ME ALSO MUCH THE SAME AS YOU . . . .  418  2 DON JUAN  5    14   7
    FROM ME I GAZED (AS OFT I HAVE GAZED THE SAME) . . .  431  2 DON JUAN  5    38   6
    WHISPERED TO HIS COMPANION--'TWAS THE SAME  . . . .  434  2 DON JUAN  5    43   3
    OF THAT SAME BABEL OR BECAUSE THEY WON'T . . . . .  447  2 DON JUAN  5    62   4
    BUT NOT BY THE SAME DOOR THROUGH WHICH CAME IN . . .  469  2 DON JUAN  5   100   2
    AND WORKS OF THE SAME POTTERY BAD OR GOOD  . . . .  491  2 DON JUAN  5   138   5
    THOUGH NOT ALL BORN OF THE SAME SIRES AND MOTHERS .  491  2 DON JUAN  5   138   6
    AND WEDLOCK AND A PADLOCK MEAN THE SAME  . . . . .  502  2 DON JUAN  5   158   2
    O'ERTHROWS THE SAME WE READILY FORGET . . . . . .    8  3 DON JUAN  6     4   3
    THE SAME KATINKA UNTIL BY-AND-BY  . . . . . . .     30  3 DON JUAN  6    49   3
    MOST MODERN PREACHERS SAY THE SAME OR SHOW IT . . .   69  3 DON JUAN  7     6   2
    THE FACT'S ABOUT THE SAME I AM SECURE . . . . . .    70  3 DON JUAN  7     8   3
    I THINK ONE SHAKESPEAR PUTS THE SAME THOUGHT IN . .   77  3 DON JUAN  7    21   6
    THUS THE SAME CAUSE WHICH MAKES A VERSE WANT FEET .   79  3 DON JUAN  7    26   3
    THE LETTER OF THE PRINCE TO THE SAME MARSHAL  . . .   86  3 DON JUAN  7    40   1
    IN THE NIKOLAIEW REGIMENT--THE SAME  . . . . . .     97  3 DON JUAN  7    60   8
    AND IN THE DANUBE'S WATERS SHONE THE SAME-- . . . .  115  3 DON JUAN  8     6   4
    IN THE SAME MOMENT LOUD AS EVEN THE ROAR . . . . .  116  3 DON JUAN  8     8   2
    HIS SYMPATHY FOR RANK BY THE SAME TOKEN  . . . . .  117  3 DON JUAN  8    11   7
    SWEAR THAT PAT'S LANGUAGE SPRUNG FROM THE SAME CLIME  122  3 DON JUAN  8    23   5
    HER STEADY BREATH (WHICH SOME MONTHS THE SAME STILL IS)  132  3 DON JUAN  8    39   6
    OR NEAR RELATIONS WHO ARE MUCH THE SAME  . . . . .  139  3 DON JUAN  8    54   2
    BUT IN THE SAME SMALL MINUTE EVERY SIN . . . . . .  142  3 DON JUAN  8    59   3
    AND SCRAMBLING ROUND THE RAMPART THESE SAME TROOPS .  148  3 DON JUAN  8    73   1
    FOR THE SAME BLOW WHICH LAID HER MOTHER HERE  . . .  159  3 DON JUAN  8    95   4
    BEATING OR BEATEN SHE WILL LAUGH THE SAME)-- . . .  183  3 DON JUAN  9     1   5
    AND PALLAS ALSO SANCTIONS THE SAME HUE . . . . . .  218  3 DON JUAN  9    71   7
    FOR BOTH ARE MUCH THE SAME SINCE WHAT MEN THINK . .  234  3 DON JUAN 10    20   2
    AND THIS SAME STATE WE WON'T DESCRIBE WE COULD . .  238  3 DON JUAN 10    27   1
    FOR COUSINS ALSO ANSWERED THE SAME DAY . . . . . .  239  3 DON JUAN 10    30   4
    AND HUMBLY HOPE THAT THE SAME GOD WHICH HATH GIVEN .  242  3 DON JUAN 10    36  V7
    (THE SAME WHO PHYSICKED PETER) FOUND THE TICK  . .  244  3 DON JUAN 10    39   3
    EXHAUSTION OR DISORDERS OF THE SAME KIN  . . . . .  244  3 DON JUAN 10    40   4
    'TIS THE SAME LANDSCAPE WHICH THE MODERN MARS SAW .  253  3 DON JUAN 10    58   5
    IN THE SAME QUAINT UNINTERESTED TONE-- . . . . . .  261  3 DON JUAN 10    73   4
    SUNSET THE TIME THE PLACE THE SAME DECLIVITY  . . .  272  3 DON JUAN 11     8   2
    I'VE DONE TO FIND THE SAME THROUGHOUT LIFE'S JOURNEY  281  3 DON JUAN 11    28   7
    LABOURER IN THE SAME VINEYARD THOUGH THE VINE  . .  297  3 DON JUAN 11    58   2
    WITH THE SAME FEELINGS AS YOU'D COAX A VAMPIRE . .  299  3 DON JUAN 11    62   5
    AND TRANSIENT AND DEVOURED BY THE SAME HARPY  . . .  310  3 DON JUAN 11    86   3
    AGAINST THE SAME GIVEN QUANTITY OF RHYME . . . . .  312  3 DON JUAN 11    90   3
    THAT IS IF SAME LORDSHIP HAS AN ANCESTOR . . . . .  314  3 DON JUAN 11  V 75   1
    WITH THE SAME THOUGHT THE TWO WORDS HAVE HELPED OUT  323  3 DON JUAN 12    15   4
    (I WISH THAT OTHERS WOULD FIND OUT THE SAME) . . .  336  3 DON JUAN 12    42   2
    NEW VESTALS CLAIM MEN'S EYES WITH THE SAME PRAISE .  340  3 DON JUAN 12    53   6
    FOR TALK SIX TIMES WITH THE SAME SINGLE LADY  . . .  343  3 DON JUAN 12    59   7
    COUNTRY WHERE A YOUNG COUPLE OF THE SAME AGES  . .  346  3 DON JUAN 12    65   2
    THAT LABYRINTH WHOSE CLUE IS OF THE SAME  . . . . .  349  3 DON JUAN 12    72   2
    AND AS HE THOUGHT IN COUNTRY MUCH THE SAME-- . . .  367  3 DON JUAN 13    20   4
    AND THAT SAME DEVILISH DOCTRINE OF THE PERSIAN . .  377  3 DON JUAN 13    41   5
    THAN AN ADVERTISEMENT OR MUCH THE SAME . . . . . .  382  3 DON JUAN 13    51   4
    THEN UNDERNEATH AND IN THE VERY SAME . . . . . . .  383  3 DON JUAN 13    54   4
    METHINKS GAY PUNCH HATH SOMETHING OF THE SAME  . .  400  3 DON JUAN 13    89   4
    FOR I HAVE SEEN A PORTION OF THAT SAME . . . . . .  414  3 DON JUAN 14     9   2
    WHICH BEARS THE SAME RELATION TO THE REAL  . . . .  419  3 DON JUAN 14    22   3
    BUT HOW TO FILL UP THAT SAME VACANT PART . . . . .  442  3 DON JUAN 14    74   3
    ALL THINGS PURSUE EXACTLY THE SAME ROUTE . . . . .  446  3 DON JUAN 14    84   3
    ARRANGING THEM LIKE BOOKS ON THE SAME SHELF  . . .  470  3 DON JUAN 15    31   3
    LIKE HOLBEIN'S DANCE OF DEATH--BUT 'TIS THE SAME)--  473  3 DON JUAN 15    39   8
    AS USUAL--THE SAME REASON WHICH SHE LATE DID . . .  478  3 DON JUAN 15    50   8
    OR--WHAT IS JUST THE SAME--IT WEARIES OUT  . . . .  478  3 DON JUAN 15    51   7
    MORE FOES BY THIS SAME SCROLL WHEN I BEGAN IT I . .  482  3 DON JUAN 15    60   6
    LIKE THAT SAME MYSTIC MUSIC OF THE SPHERES . . . .  489  3 DON JUAN 15    76   5
    BE GILT WHO SATE HATH CEASED TO BE THE SAME  . . .  509  3 DON JUAN 16    19   8
    WITH THIS SAME LEGEND)--IF YOU BUT DESIGN  . . . .  516  3 DON JUAN 16    37   5
    OF ADELINE IN BRINGING THIS SAME LAY . . . . . . .  526  3 DON JUAN 16    51   2
    HER GRACE TOO ALSO SEIZED THE SAME OCCASION  . . .  526  3 DON JUAN 16    53   4
    OF THIS SAME MYSTIC FRIAR'S CURIOUS DOINGS . . . .  527  3 DON JUAN 16    53   7
    OF THAT SAME TUNE WHEN PEOPLE HUM IT LONG)-- . . .  529  3 DON JUAN 16    59   3
    OF THOSE WHO HAVE NOT A LICENCE FOR THE SAME . . .  531  3 DON JUAN 16    63   4
    THE SAME SELF-INTEREST WITH A DIFFERENT LEANING) .  535  3 DON JUAN 16    70   8
    HIS WORD HAD THE SAME VALUE AS ANOTHER'S . . . . .  535  3 DON JUAN 16    71   8
    THEIR DOCILE ESQUIRES ALSO DID THE SAME  . . . . .  549  3 DON JUAN 16   101   6
    AND CURTSIED OFF THE STAGE--THEIR LORDS THE SAME .  549  3 DON JUAN 16   101  V4
    SO THAT I ALMOST THINK THAT THE SAME SKIN  . . . .  567  3 DON JUAN 17    11   7
SAMENESS
    THERE IS A SAMENESS IN ITS GEMS AND ERMINE . . . .  416  3 DON JUAN 14    15   6
SAMIAN
    AND FLASKS OF SAMIAN AND OF CHIAN WINE  . . . . .   291  2 DON JUAN  3    31   4
    FILL HIGH THE CUP WITH SAMIAN WINE . . . . . . .    324  2 DON JUAN  3  L  9   2
    FILL HIGH THE BOWL WITH SAMIAN WINE  . . . . . .    324  2 DON JUAN  3  L 11   1
    FILL HIGH THE BOWL WITH SAMIAN WINE  . . . . . .    325  2 DON JUAN  3  L 13   1
    FILL HIGH THE BOWL WITH SAMIAN WINE  . . . . . .    326  2 DON JUAN  3  L 15   1
    DASH DOWN YON CUP OF SAMIAN WINE  . . . . . . .     326  2 DON JUAN  3  L 16   6
SAMPHIRE
    A DREADFUL TRADE LIKE HIS WHO GATHERS SAMPHIRE . . .  299  3 DON JUAN 11    62   3
```

	PAGE	VOL	CANTO	STANZA	LN
SAMPLE					
HAS GIVEN A SAMPLE FROM THE VASTY VERSION	11	2 DON JUAN	D	4	3
ANACREON'S MORALS ARE A STILL WORSE SAMPLE	45	2 DON JUAN	1	42	2
HIS SPEECH WAS A FINE SAMPLE ON THE WHOLE	116	2 DON JUAN	1	174	7
YOUR PATIENCE FURTHER THAN BY THIS SHORT SAMPLE--	147	2 DON JUAN	1	221	7
TO ME--OF WHICH THESE MORALS ARE A SAMPLE	323	3 DON JUAN	12	16	8
SAMPLES					
WITH ALL KINDS OF INCORRIGIBLE SAMPLES	236	3 DON JUAN	10	23	6
SAMSON					
AND SEND HIM FORTH LIKE SAMSON--STRONG IN BLINDNESS	304	2 DON JUAN	3	57	V8
SAMSONLIKE					
AND MAKE HIM SAMSONLIKE--MORE FIERCE WITH BLINDNESS	304	2 DON JUAN	3	57	V8
SAMUEL					
LIKE SAMUEL FROM THE GRAVE TO FREEZE ONCE MORE	15	2 DON JUAN	D	11	2
LIKE THE LAMENTED LATE SIR SAMUEL ROMILLY	29	2 DON JUAN	1	15	4
THOU SHALT NOT STEAL FROM SAMUEL ROGERS NOR	139	2 DON JUAN	1	205	1
AND OTHERS OF THEMSELVES AS POET SAMUEL IS	94	3 DON JUAN	7	54	V8
SANCHO					
TO FOLLOW JUAN'S WAKE LIKE SANCHO PANCA	175	2 DON JUAN	2	37	8
SANCTIFIED					
UNLESS HER CAUSE BY RIGHT BE SANCTIFIED	184	3 DON JUAN	9	4	4
TWELVE SAINTS HAD ONCE STOOD SANCTIFIED IN STONE	386	3 DON JUAN	13	60	2
SANCTIFY					
BUT ALMOST SANCTIFY THE SWEET EXCESS	357	2 DON JUAN	4	26	7
SANCTION					
WITHOUT HER SANCTION ON THEIR SHE-PARADES	21	3 DON JUAN	6	30	7
AND THY PURE CREED MADE SANCTION OF ALL ILL	464	3 DON JUAN	15	18	4
AND YET HIS LOOKS APPEARED TO SANCTION BOTH	514	3 DON JUAN	16	33	2
SANCTIONS					
AND PALLAS ALSO SANCTIONS THE SAME HUE	218	3 DON JUAN	9	71	7
SANCTITY					
AS PURE AS SANCTITY ITSELF FROM VICE	478	3 DON JUAN	15	52	3
SANCTUARY					
FOR LETTING THAT PURE SANCTUARY ALONE	370	3 DON JUAN	13	27	4
SAND					
FAST TO THE SAND LEST THE RETURNING WAVE	213	2 DON JUAN	2	108	2
AND DOWN HE SUNK AND AS HE SUNK THE SAND	214	2 DON JUAN	2	110	2
GLIDED ALONG THE SMOOTH AND HARDEN'D SAND	253	2 DON JUAN	2	184	3
AMIDST THE BARREN SAND AND ROCKS SO RUDE	262	2 DON JUAN	2	198	4
ARE OR WOULD BE THOU SEA WHICH LAVEST LIFE'S SAND	210	3 DON JUAN	9	56	V8
I'VE SEEN THE PEOPLE RIDDEN O'ER LIKE SAND	310	3 DON JUAN	11	85	5
WHO WHIRL THE DUST AS SIMOOMS WHIRL THE SAND	435	3 DON JUAN	14	58	6
LEAVES A SAD SEDIMENT OF TIME'S WORST SAND	457	3 DON JUAN	15	4	8
SAND-PITS					
OF THEIR OWN SAND-PITS TO MIX WITH A GODDESS	220	3 DON JUAN	9	75	3
SANDS					
THE SANDS UNTUMBLED THE BLUE WAVES UNTOST	251	2 DON JUAN	2	181	4
THE VOICELESS SANDS AND DROPPING CAVES THAT LAY	255	2 DON JUAN	2	188	5
THUS TO THEIR LAST SANDS ARE THE PASSIONS BROUGHT	402	2 DON JUAN	4	106	V6
IN VAIN--AS FALL THE DEWS ON QUENCHLESS SANDS	212	3 DON JUAN	9	59	7
SANDWICH					
OF CLARET SANDWICH AND AN APPETITE	444	2 DON JUAN	5	58	3
SANDY					
WITH CLIFFS ABOVE AND A BROAD SANDY SHORE	249	2 DON JUAN	2	177	2
WHICH THEY RESISTED LIKE A SANDY PLAIN	166	3 DON JUAN	8	109	8
SANG					
THEIR LEADER SANG--AND BOUNDED TO HER SONG	291	2 DON JUAN	3	30	7
IF PINDAR SANG HORSE-RACES WHAT SHOULD HINDER	319	2 DON JUAN	3	85	7
WHO SANG WHEN CHIVALRY WAS MORE QUIXOTIC	347	2 DON JUAN	4	6	4
IN THE MEANTIME CROSS-LEGGED WITH GREAT SANG FROID	172	3 DON JUAN	8	121	1
AND SANG WITH MUCH SIMPLICITY--A MERIT	518	3 DON JUAN	16	40	7
SANG-FROID					
AND THERE HE STOOD WITH SUCH SANG-FROID THAT GREATER	416	2 DON JUAN	5	11	7
SANGUINARY					
ITS SANGUINARY WAY GOOD--THEN ANOTHER	146	3 DON JUAN	8	69	2
SANK					
SOME DULL MS OBLIVION LONG HAS SANK	327	2 DON JUAN	3	89	5
QUIET--SANK INTO SOFTER RIPPLES GLIDING	385	3 DON JUAN	13	58	4
SANS					
PERHAPS--BUT SANS PERHAPS WE NEED NOT SEEK	243	3 DON JUAN	10	38	1
BUT LOVE SANS BANNS IS BOTH A SIN AND SHAME	323	3 DON JUAN	12	15	7
SUCH CLASSIC PAS--SANS FLAWS--SET OFF OUR HERO	427	3 DON JUAN	14	39	7
WHY CALL'D HE HARMONY A STATE SANS WEDLOCK	471	3 DON JUAN	15	35	7
BUT EVEN SANS CONFITURES IT NO LESS TRUE IS	486	3 DON JUAN	15	68	7
COMPLETELY SANS CULOTTE AND WITHOUT VEST	555	3 DON JUAN	16	111	3
SANSCRIT					
AS MUCH OF GERMAN AS OF SANSCRIT AND	141	3 DON JUAN	8	57	2
SAP					
WITHOUT THEIR SAP HOW BRANCHLESS WERE THE TRUNK	250	2 DON JUAN	2	179	5
SOME SPLENDID DEBTOR HE WOULD TAKE BY SAP	459	3 DON JUAN	15	8	4
SAPLESS					
ABOVE HIS BURNT-OUT BRAIN AND SAPLESS CINDERS	299	3 DON JUAN	11	61	5
SAPPHO					
SAPPHO THE SAGE BLUE-STOCKING IN WHOSE GRAVE	266	2 DON JUAN	2	205	4
WHERE BURNING SAPPHO LOVED AND SUNG	320	2 DON JUAN	3	L 1	1
THE LESBIAN SAPPHO AND THE BLIND OLD MAN	320	2 DON JUAN	3	L 1	V2
SAPPHO'S					
I DON'T THINK SAPPHO'S ODE A GOOD EXAMPLE	45	2 DON JUAN	1	42	4
FOR BEINGS PASSIONATE AS SAPPHO'S SONG	358	2 DON JUAN	4	27	6

		PAGE	VOL	CANTO		STANZA	LV
SAPPING							
AND LOVE DESTROY AND SAPPING SORROW WRINGS		468	2	DON JUAN	5	98	6
SARACEN							
SCOTT WHO CAN PAINT YOUR CHRISTIAN KNIGHT OR SARACEN		481	3	DON JUAN	15	59	5
SARDANAPALUS							
SO SAID THE ROYAL SAGE SARDANAPALUS		267	2	DON JUAN	2	207	8
SASH							
THE PRIDE OF A MERE CHILD WITH A NEW SASH ON		351	3	DON JUAN	12	77	5
SAT							
I SAY THAT THERE'S THE PLACE--BUT VERBUM SAT		50	2	DON JUAN	1	53	4
I HAVE SAT UP ON PURPOSE ALL THE NIGHT		230	2	DON JUAN	2	140	3
AND RECK'D NOT WHO AROUND HER PILLOW SAT		378	2	DON JUAN	4	63	4
DUDU SAID NOTHING BUT SAT DOWN BESIDE		28	3	DON JUAN	6	45	1
AMONG THE SCORCHING RUINS HE SAT SMOKING		172	3	DON JUAN	8	121	2
THE HANDSOME HERALD ON WHOSE PLUMAGE SAT		211	3	DON JUAN	9	57	6
SAT LITTLE LEILA WHO SURVIVED THE PARRIES		249	3	DON JUAN	10	51	4
OR SAT AMIDST THE BRICKS OF NINEVEH		271	3	DON JUAN	11	7	6
THEY FILL THE CANVASS UP--AND VERBUM SAT		463	3	DON JUAN	15	16	5
SHE LOOK'D AS IF SHE SAT BY EDEN'S DOOR		476	3	DON JUAN	15	45	7
DON JUAN SAT NEXT AN A L'ESPAGNOLE--		488	3	DON JUAN	15	74	5
AURORA SAT WITH THAT INDIFFERENCE		490	3	DON JUAN	15	77	1
SATAN							
WHICH SATAN ANGLES WITH FOR SOULS LIKE FLIES		154	3	DON JUAN	8	86	8
THE TWIGS WHICH SATAN LIMES FOR HUMAN FLIES		154	3	DON JUAN	8	86	V8
SATE							
WHEN JULIA SATE WITHIN AS PRETTY A BOWER		77	2	DON JUAN	1	104	3
SHE SATE BUT NOT ALONE I KNOW NOT WELL		77	2	DON JUAN	1	105	1
AND JULIA SATE WITH JUAN HALF EMBRACED		83	2	DON JUAN	1	115	1
ONE HALF SATE UP THOUGH NUMB'D WITH THE IMMERSION		189	2	DON JUAN	2	63	4
MEANTIME THE LADY AND HER LOVER SATE		306	2	DON JUAN	3	61	3
A KING SATE ON THE ROCKY BROW		322	2	DON JUAN	3	L 4	1
BUT THOSE WHO SATE NE'ER STIRRED IN ANY WISE		441	2	DON JUAN	5	54	4
WERE SATE LIKE UGLY IMPS AS IF ALLIED		462	2	DON JUAN	5	87	4
AND THOSE THAT SATE UPON THEM LET IT BE		180	3	DON JUAN	8	137	2
HAD SATE BENEATH THE GALLERY AT NIGHTS		353	3	DON JUAN	12	82	3
I THINK TOO THAT I HAVE SATE UP TOO LATE		499	3	DON JUAN	15	97	8
BE GILT WHO SATE HATH CEASED TO BE THE SAME		509	3	DON JUAN	16	19	8
HE SATE HIM PENSIVE O'ER A DISH OF TEA		513	3	DON JUAN	16	30	2
I SATE NEXT THAT O'ERWHELMING SON OF HEAVEN		539	3	DON JUAN	16	81	6
SATE SILENT NOW HIS USUAL SPIRITS GONE		552	3	DON JUAN	16	105	6
HE SATE WITH FEELINGS AWKWARD TO EXPRESS		555	3	DON JUAN	16	111	6
SATED							
ON LIFE'S WORN CONFINE JADED BLOATED SATED		267	3	DON JUAN	10	87	2
SATIETY							
IF YOU HAVE NOUGHT ELSE HERE'S AT LEAST SATIETY		416	3	DON JUAN	14	14	5
SATIN							
ON CRIMSON SATIN BORDER'D WITH PALE BLUE		309	2	DON JUAN	3	67	2
A PAIR OF DRAWERS--OF FINE CRIMSON SATIN		456	2	DON JUAN	5	77	V2
SATIRE							
AND SWALLOWING EULOGY MUCH MORE THAN SATIRE HE		185	3	DON JUAN	9	5	5
NOW WERE I ONCE AT HOME AND IN GOOD SATIRE		299	3	DON JUAN	11	62	6
THAN I HAVE YET DONE IN THIS EPIC SATIRE		454	3	DON JUAN	14	99	6
SATIRISE							
HE BEING PAID TO SATIRISE OR FLATTER		316	2	DON JUAN	3	78	7
SATISFACTION							
TOOK LEAVE WITH SUCH A FACE OF SATISFACTION		473	2	DON JUAN	5	107	7
SATISFACTORY							
NO VERY SATISFACTORY INFORMATION		387	2	DON JUAN	4	79	7
SATISFIED							
OR IF THEY DID SO SATISFIED TO MEAN		66	2	DON JUAN	1	83	4
AND IF YOU ARE NOT SATISFIED WITH THAT		298	2	DON JUAN	3	45	5
SATISFY							
HAD TOLD HIS SON TO SATISFY HIS CRAVING		263	3	DON JUAN	10	78	6
SATURN							
SHRINK TO A SATURN I HAVE SEEN A DUKE		309	3	DON JUAN	11	83	2
MUCH AS OLD SATURN ATE HIS PROGENY		410	3	DON JUAN	14	1	6
SAUCE							
TEACH THEM THAT SAUCE FOR GOOSE IS SAUCE FOR GANDER		446	3	DON JUAN	14	83	3
TEACH THEM THAT SAUCE FOR GOOSE IS SAUCE FOR GANDER		446	3	DON JUAN	14	83	3
SAUCES							
IN SOUPS OR SAUCES OR A SOLE RAGOUT		482	3	DON JUAN	15	62	7
WITH SAUCES GENEVOISES AND HAUNCH OF VENISON		484	3	DON JUAN	15	65	2
SAUNTERED							
OR SAUNTERED THROUGH THE GARDENS PITEOUSLY		406	3	DON JUAN	13	102	3
SAVAGE							
LULL'D EVEN THE SAVAGE HUNGER WHICH DEMANDED		195	2	DON JUAN	2	75	3
OF MILD DEMEANOUR THOUGH OF SAVAGE MOOD		302	2	DON JUAN	3	53	2
AMIDST THE SAVAGE DEEDS HE HAD DONE AND SEEN		304	2	DON JUAN	3	57	4
SERENELY SAVAGE WITH A LITTLE CHANGE		367	2	DON JUAN	4	44	3
AND NEXT HIS SAVAGE VIRTUE HE ACCUSED		493	2	DON JUAN	5	142	5
SIMPLE THEY WERE NOT SAVAGE AND THEIR RIFLES		145	3	DON JUAN	8	66	7
A SAVAGE SORT OF MILITARY MARTYR		152	3	DON JUAN	8	80	6
COMPASSION BREATHES ALONG THE SAVAGE MIND		164	3	DON JUAN	8	106	8
AND THAT DEEP-MOUTHED BOEOTIAN SAVAGE LANDOR		298	3	DON JUAN	11	59	4
OR WILDER GROUPE OF SAVAGE SALVATORE'S		392	3	DON JUAN	13	71	4
SAVAGELY							
SAVE IN THE BREEZE THAT CAME NOT SAVAGELY		194	2	DON JUAN	2	72	4
SAVAGES							
MORE THAN YOU SCORN THE SAVAGES OF YORE		180	3	DON JUAN	8	136	7

SAVE

	PAGE	VOL	CANTO	STANZA	LN
SAVE THINE INCOMPARABLE OIL MACASSAR	30	2 DON JUAN 1	17	8
SAVE THAT HER DUTY BOTH TO MAN AND GOD	35	2 DON JUAN 1	27	7
SAVE DEATH OR DOCTORS' COMMONS--SO HE DIED	41	2 DON JUAN 1	36	8
TO SAVE ONE HALF THE PEOPLE THEN ON BOARD	181	2 DON JUAN 2	48	8
SAVE THE WILD WIND AND THE REMORSELESS DASH	184	2 DON JUAN 2	53	4
PEDRO HIS VALET TOO HE TRIED TO SAVE	186	2 DON JUAN 2	57	1
IT WOULD HAVE BEEN MORE WISE TO SAVE THEIR VICTUAL	192	2 DON JUAN 2	69	8
SAVE IN THE BREEZE THAT CAME NOT SAVAGELY	194	2 DON JUAN 2	72	4
THE SAILORS ATE HIM ALL SAVE THREE OR FOUR	198	2 DON JUAN 2	78	1
AND GAVE NO SIGN OF LIFE SAVE HIS LIMBS QUIVERING	204	2 DON JUAN 2	90	8
SAVE ONE A CORPSE FROM OUT THE FAMISH'D THREE	213	2 DON JUAN 2	109	6
WAS NOT EXACTLY THE BEST WAY TO SAVE	225	2 DON JUAN 2	130	2
NEXT THEY--HE BEING NAKED SAVE A TATTER'D	240	2 DON JUAN 2	160	1
SAVE ON THE DEAD LONG SUMMER DAYS WHICH MAKE	249	2 DON JUAN 2	177	7
AND ALL WAS STILLNESS SAVE THE SEA-BIRD'S CRY	251	2 DON JUAN 2	181	5
SAVE ZOE WHO ALTHOUGH WITH DUE PRECISION	252	2 DON JUAN 2	182	4
SAVE THEIRS AND THAT THEIR LIFE COULD NEVER DIE	255	2 DON JUAN 2	188	8
'TWOULD SAVE US MANY A HEART-ACHE MANY A SHILLING	270	2 DON JUAN 2	213	5
TO HIS TUNIS CORRESPONDENTS SAVE ONE MAN	284	2 DON JUAN 3	16	3
THE REST--SAVE HERE AND THERE SOME RICHER ONE	284	2 DON JUAN 3	16	5
HIS COUNTRY'S WRONGS AND HIS DESPAIR TO SAVE HER	302	2 DON JUAN 3	53	7
AND BEING FLUENT (SAVE INDEED WHEN FEE'D ILL)	317	2 DON JUAN 3	80	6
'TWAS ALL THE SAME TO HIM--GOD SAVE THE KING	319	2 DON JUAN 3	85	3
WHERE NOTHING SAVE THE WAVES AND I	326	2 DON JUAN 3	L 16	2
BECOME A THING OR NOTHING SAVE TO RANK	327	2 DON JUAN 3	89	3
WERE THE SOLE ECHOS SAVE MY STEED'S AND MINE	337	2 DON JUAN 3	106	3
BUT ALL THESE SAVE THE LAST BEING OBSOLETE	347	2 DON JUAN 4	6	7
WHICH MEN WEEP OVER MAY BE MEANT TO SAVE	350	2 DON JUAN 4	12	8
THEY FOUND NO FAULT WITH TIME SAVE THAT HE FLED	351	2 DON JUAN 4	13	3
THE FILE OF PIRATES SAVE THE FOREMOST WHO	370	2 DON JUAN 4	48	7
NO SIGN SAVE BREATH OF HAVING LEFT THE GRAVE	378	2 DON JUAN 4	63	8
EVEN WHEN THEY SMOTE HER IN THE HOPE TO SAVE	380	2 DON JUAN 4	67	8
NO DIRGE SAVE WHEN ARISE THE STORMY SEAS	383	2 DON JUAN 4	72	V7
WE WILL OMIT THE PROOFS SAVE ONE OR TWO	396	2 DON JUAN 4	96	4
SAVE CHANGE I'VE STOOD UPON ACHILLES' TOMB	399	2 DON JUAN 4	101	7
SAVE A FEW GLEAN'D FROM THE SEPULCHRAL GLOOM	399	2 DON JUAN 4	102	6
ALL SAVE THE BLACKS SEEM'D JADED WITH VEXATION	414	2 DON JUAN 5	7	5
SPLENDID BUT SILENT SAVE IN ONE WHERE DROPPING	442	2 DON JUAN 5	55	3
HE LOOKED--IN ALL SAVE MODESTY--A MAID	458	2 DON JUAN 5	80	V3
AUGHT SAVE SOME LITTLE POUTING PETTY CARE	480	2 DON JUAN 5	119	V5
IN ALL HER LIFE WITH AUGHT SAVE PRAYERS AND PRAISE	482	2 DON JUAN 5	122	3
SAVE SOLYMAN THE GLORY OF THEIR LINE	495	2 DON JUAN 5	147	8
TO SAVE THE CREDIT OF THEIR BREAKING BANK	500	2 DON JUAN 5	154	6
FOR NO ONE SAVE IN VERY EARLY YOUTH	14	3 DON JUAN 6	16	3
AND NOTHING EVER HEARD OF SAVE STARVATION	15	3 DON JUAN 6	19	V7
IN WISHING HER THEIR SISTER SAVE A FEW	25	3 DON JUAN 6	39	5
(TO SAVE DESCRIPTION) FAIR AS FAIR CAN BE	26	3 DON JUAN 6	40	4
WITH ALL THINGS LADIES WANT SAVE ONE OR TWO	31	3 DON JUAN 6	51	7
SAVE THAT OF DREAMING ONCE MAL-A-PROPOS	48	3 DON JUAN 6	84	8
OF ALL SAVE DUDU'S DREAM WHICH WAS NO JOKE	58	3 DON JUAN 6	104	8
WHO NAME THE FRENCH IN ENGLISH SAVE TO SHEW	77	3 DON JUAN 7	22	7
SAVE FOR ITS STYLE WHICH SAID ALL IN A TRICE	86	3 DON JUAN 7	40	7
WHO HATING HOGS YET WISHED TO SAVE THEIR BACON	87	3 DON JUAN 7	42	8
ALL EARTHLY GOODS SAVE TITHES) AND BADE THEM PUSH ON	99	3 DON JUAN 7	64	6
SAVE WED A YEAR I HATE RECRUITS WITH WIVES	102	3 DON JUAN 7	70	8
NOUGHT TO BE SEEN SAVE THE ARTILLERY'S FLAME	115	3 DON JUAN 8	6	2
BUT NEVER MIND--GOD SAVE THE KING AND KINGS	137	3 DON JUAN 8	50	1
ALONE CAN SAVE THE EARTH FROM HELL'S POLLUTION	138	3 DON JUAN 8	51	8
WITH JOY TO SAVE AND DREAD OF SOME MISCHANCE	159	3 DON JUAN 8	96	4
ARE TOUCHED WITH A DESIRE TO SHIELD AND SAVE--	164	3 DON JUAN 8	106	3
TO SAVE A SIRE WHO BLUSHED THAT HE BEGOT HIM	166	3 DON JUAN 8	110	8
BUT ALL THE LADIES SAVE SOME TWENTY SCORE	176	3 DON JUAN 8	129	7
OF LIGHT TO SAVE THE VENERABLY CHASTE--	177	3 DON JUAN 8	130	6
SAVE YOU AND YOURS HAVE GAINED BY WATERLOO	184	3 DON JUAN 9	4	8
SOULS TO SAVE SINCE EVE'S SLIP AND ADAM'S FALL	192	3 DON JUAN 9	19	3
NONE SAVE THE SPANISH FLY AND ATTIC BEE	196	3 DON JUAN 9	28	7
AND CATHERINE WHO LOVED ALL THINGS (SAVE HER LORD	209	3 DON JUAN 9	54	1
IN LOVE DRINKS ALL LIFE'S FOUNTAINS (SAVE TEARS) DRY	216	3 DON JUAN 9	67	8
A ROYAL HUSBAND IN ALL SAVE THE RING--	217	3 DON JUAN 9	70	6
WITH YOU THAN AUGHT (SAVE SCOTT) IN YOUR PROUD CITY	233	3 DON JUAN 10	17	4
SAVE SUCH AS SOUTHEY CAN AFFORD TO GIVE	243	3 DON JUAN 10	37	4
TO FOREIGNER OR NATIVE SAVE SOME SILLY ONES	263	3 DON JUAN 10	77	6
OF ENGLISH SAVE THEIR SHIBBOLETH GOD DAMN	274	3 DON JUAN 11	12	2
I HEARD THEM WISH GOD WITH YOU SAVE THAT WAY--	274	3 DON JUAN 11	12	8
TO SAVE HIS FAME WITH EACH ACCOMPLISHED BELLE	295	3 DON JUAN 11	53	3
ALL KINDS OF TOIL SAVE FOR OUR COUNTRY'S GOOD--	301	3 DON JUAN 11	65	7
BUT THIS WON'T DO SAVE BY AND BY AND HE	303	3 DON JUAN 11	70	1
FIRST SAVE IN CASE OF PIGEONS--HOW THE GROVE	322	3 DON JUAN 12	13	V5
SEEKING FAR LESS TO SAVE YOU THAN TO HURT YOU	337	3 DON JUAN 12	45	3
THE MARRIED ONES TO SAVE THE VIRGINS TROUBLE	342	3 DON JUAN 12	58	8
BUT MY BEST CANTO SAVE ONE ON ASTRONOMY	356	3 DON JUAN 12	88	7
WHICH IS IN ALL RESPECTS SAVE NOW AND THEN	373	3 DON JUAN 13	33	1
BUT THERE'S NO SHOOTING (SAVE GROUSE) TILL SEPTEMBER	380	3 DON JUAN 13	48	8
SAVE THAT THE PUPPETS PULL AT THEIR OWN STRINGS	400	3 DON JUAN 13	89	3
SAVE IN THE CLUBS NO MAN OF HONOUR PLAYS--	407	3 DON JUAN 13	106	2
SHE 'GAN TO PONDER HOW TO SAVE HIS SOUL	468	3 DON JUAN 15	28	8
ALL THIS (SAVE THE LAST STANZA) HENRY SAID	538	3 DON JUAN 16	77	1
SINCE BURNING AGED WOMEN (SAVE A FEW--	565	3 DON JUAN 17	7	3

SAVED
```
        AS FATTEST BUT HE SAVED HIMSELF BECAUSE    . . . . .    199   2 DON JUAN  2    81    2
        AND DEEM THAT IT WAS SAVED PERHAPS IN VAIN   . . . . .   213   2 DON JUAN  2   108    8
        FROM SAINT BARTHOLOMEW WE HAVE SAVED OUR SKIN  . . . .   435   2 DON JUAN  5    44    4
        WHICH BREATHES OF NATIONS SAVED NOT WORLDS UNDONE . . .  114   3 DON JUAN  8     5    4
        NOT BY THE NUMBERS GOOD INTENT HATH SAVED   . . . . .    124   3 DON JUAN  8    26    4
        UPON THIS CHILD--I SAVED HER--MUST NOT LEAVE   . . . .   161   3 DON JUAN  8    99    2
        ITS BLOODY BOND AND SAVED PERHAPS SOME PRETTY  . . . .   174   3 DON JUAN  8   124    3
        CALLED SAVIOUR OF THE NATIONS--NOT YET SAVED   . . . .   185   3 DON JUAN  9     5    7
        EPAMINONDAS SAVED HIS THEBES AND DIED  . . . . .        186   3 DON JUAN  9     8    2
        WHOM HE HAD SAVED FROM SLAUGHTER--WHAT A TROPHY  . . .   199   3 DON JUAN  9    33    2
        THAT ONE LIFE SAVED ESPECIALLY IF YOUNG   . . . . .     199   3 DON JUAN  9    34    2
        HE LOVED THE INFANT ORPHAN HE HAD SAVED   . . . . .     251   3 DON JUAN 10    55    2
        HAS SAVED THE FAME OF THOUSAND SPLENDID SINNERS  . . .   346   3 DON JUAN 12    66    3
```
SAVES
```
        WHICH SAVES IN FACT THE TROUBLE OF AN INDEX   . . . .     46   2 DON JUAN  1    44    8
```
SAVING
```
        FOR KILLING BODIES AND FOR SAVING SOULS   . . . . .      93   2 DON JUAN  1   132    2
        AND THAT WHICH CHIEFLY PROVED HIS SAVING CLAUSE  . . .   199   2 DON JUAN  2    81    6
        ARE SAVING--VICE SPARES NOTHING FOR A RARITY   . . . .   408   2 DON JUAN  4   115    8
        HIS FRIEND TOO ADDING A NEW SAVING CLAUSE   . . . . .    437   2 DON JUAN  5    47    6
        IN OUTWARD SHOW WHICH IS A SAVING CLAUSE)   . . . . .     35   3 DON JUAN  6    58    3
        SAVING HIS SOUL BY CHEATING IN THE WARE   . . . . .      80   3 DON JUAN  7    27    4
        OF ALL MEN SAVING SYLLA THE MAN-SLAYER   . . . . .      143   3 DON JUAN  8    61    1
        FOR THEM IN SAVING SUCH A DESPERATE FOE--   . . . . .    165   3 DON JUAN  8   108    5
        FOR SAVING HER AMIDST THE WILD INSANITY   . . . . .     182   3 DON JUAN  8   140    6
        YE WHO BUT SEE THE SAVING MAN AT TABLE   . . . . .      316   3 DON JUAN 12     3    5
        (A THING APPROVED AS SAVING TIME AND TOIL)--   . . . .   351   3 DON JUAN 12    76    6
        WITH THE KIND VIEW OF SAVING AN ECLAT . . . . .         436   3 DON JUAN 14    60    1
        SAVING HIS NIGHT GOWN WHICH IS AN UNDRESS   . . . . .    555   3 DON JUAN 16   111    2
```
SAVIOUR
```
        CALLED SAVIOUR OF THE NATIONS--NOT YET SAVED   . . . .   185   3 DON JUAN  9     5    7
```
SAVOUR
```
        DOWN TO A VERY HOMELY HOUSEHOLD SAVOUR   . . . . .      277   2 DON JUAN  3     5    8
        AND NEARER AS THEY CAME A GENIAL SAVOUR   . . . . .     437   2 DON JUAN  5    47    1
        HOWEVER THEY MIGHT SAVOUR OF DELIRIOUS   . . . . .      514   3 DON JUAN 16    33    3
```
SAVOURED
```
        THIS SAVOURED OF THIS WORLD BUT HIS HAND SHOOK--   . . .  512   3 DON JUAN 16    27    1
```
SAW
```
        WHO SAW THEIR SPOUSES KILL'D AND NOBLY CHOSE   . . . .    36   2 DON JUAN  1    29    4
        AND SAW HIS AGONIES WITH SUCH SUBLIMITY . . . . .        36   2 DON JUAN  1    29    7
        AND SAW INTO HERSELF EACH DAY BEFORE ALL . . . . .       43   2 DON JUAN  1    39    2
        WHO SAW THOSE FIGURES ON THE MARGIN KISS ALL   . . . .    47   2 DON JUAN  1    46    5
        I CAN'T TELL WHETHER JULIA SAW THE AFFAIR   . . . . .     59   2 DON JUAN  1    68    1
        JUAN SHE SAW AND AS A PRETTY CHILD . . . . .             59   2 DON JUAN  1    69    1
        THAN HE WHO NEVER SAW THE SEA OF OCEAN   . . . . .       60   2 DON JUAN  1    70    8
        SHE SAW THAT JUAN WAS NOT AT HIS EASE . . . . .          73   2 DON JUAN  1    97    3
        YOU NEVER YET TO ANY SAW ME CIVIL . . . . .            102   2 DON JUAN  1   148   V6
        YOU SAW THAT SHE WAS SLEEPING BY MY SIDE   . . . . .    106   2 DON JUAN  1   156    2
        ALFONSO SAW HIS WIFE AND THOUGHT OF JOB'S   . . . . .   110   2 DON JUAN  1   162    6
        HE SAW TOO IN PERSPECTIVE HER RELATIONS   . . . . .     110   2 DON JUAN  1   162    7
        FOR JUAN VERY LUCKILY NE'ER SAW IT . . . . .           123   2 DON JUAN  1   185    3
        SAW JUAN'S LAST ELOPEMENT WITH THE DEVIL   . . . . .    138   2 DON JUAN  1   203    8
        ARE THESE THE DREAMS HIS YOUNG AMBITION SAW . . . . .   155   2 DON JUAN  1  V  7    3
        NOR LIKEN IT--I NEVER SAW THE LIKE . . . . .           159   2 DON JUAN  2     5    8
        BUT DAMN ME--IF I EVER SAW THE LIKE . . . . .          159   2 DON JUAN  2     5   V8
        SOME CURSED THE DAY ON WHICH THEY SAW THE SUN   . . .   180   2 DON JUAN  2    45    3
        I CAN DO NOTHING AND HE SAW HIM THROWN   . . . . .      202   2 DON JUAN  2    87    7
        HE SAW INCREASING ON HIS FATHER'S HEART   . . . . .     203   2 DON JUAN  2    88    7
        AND TRIED TO BEAR ALTHOUGH IT SAW AND HEARD   . . . .   206   2 DON JUAN  2    94    5
        SOME FANCIED THEY SAW LAND AND SOME SAID NO . . . . .   207   2 DON JUAN  2    96    5
        AND THE REST RUBB'D THEIR EYES AND SAW A BAY   . . . .  207   2 DON JUAN  2    97    5
        OR THOUGHT THEY SAW AND SHAPED THEIR COURSE FOR SHORE . 207   2 DON JUAN  2    97    6
        I NE'ER SAW JUSTICE DONE AND YET SHE WAS   . . . . .    219   2 DON JUAN  2   119    4
        ALL TIMIDLY YET RAPIDLY SHE SAW . . . . .              232   2 DON JUAN  2   143    2
        HIS HEAD UPON HIS ELBOW AND HE SAW . . . . .           239   2 DON JUAN  2   157    2
        SHE SAW HE DID NOT UNDERSTAND ROMAIC   . . . . .        241   2 DON JUAN  2   161    8
        AND THUS IN EVERY LOOK SHE SAW EXPREST   . . . . .      241   2 DON JUAN  2   162    7
        AND SAW THE SUN SET OPPOSITE THE MOON . . . . .         249   2 DON JUAN  2   176    8
        AND SAW EACH OTHER'S DARK EYES DARTING LIGHT   . . . .  253   2 DON JUAN  2   185    6
        SAW NOTHING HAPPIER THAN HER GLOWING FACE   . . . . .   262   2 DON JUAN  2   198    8
        I SAW THE PRETTIEST CREATURE FRESH FROM MILAN   . . .   268   2 DON JUAN  2   209    7
        HE CHOSE FROM SEVERAL ANIMALS HE SAW--   . . . . .      285   2 DON JUAN  3    18    3
        HE SAW HIS WHITE WALLS SHINING IN THE SUN   . . . . .   289   2 DON JUAN  3    27    1
        BUT LAMBRO SAW ALL THESE THINGS WITH AVERSION   . . .   293   2 DON JUAN  3    35    5
        E'ER SAW HER MOST POLITE OF SONS EXCEEDING   . . . . .  299   2 DON JUAN  3    46    4
        NOT WHAT THEY SAW BUT WHAT THEY WISH'D TO SEE   . . .   347   2 DON JUAN  4     7    4
        THEY SAW NOT IN THEMSELVES AUGHT TO CONDEMN . . . . .   351   2 DON JUAN  4    13    4
        AND TWILIGHT SAW THEM LINK'D IN PASSION'S TIES   . . .  354   2 DON JUAN  4    20    6
        THE LAST SIGHT WHICH SHE SAW WAS JUAN'S GORE   . . . .  375   2 DON JUAN  4    58    1
        SHE SAW THEM WATCH HER WITHOUT ASKING WHY   . . . . .   378   2 DON JUAN  4    63    3
        HE SAW SOME FELLOW CAPTIVES WHO APPEAR'D   . . . . .    388   2 DON JUAN  4    80    1
        THOSE SUFFERINGS DANTE SAW IN HELL ALONE   . . . . .    401   2 DON JUAN  4   105    8
        SAW ONE WHOM SUCH AN ACCIDENT BEFELL . . . . .         430   2 DON JUAN  5    35    3
        NO CHRISTIAN KNOLL TO TABLE SAW NO LINE   . . . . .     439   2 DON JUAN  5    50    3
        FOR HIS OWN SHARE--HE SAW BUT SMALL OBJECTION   . . .   452   2 DON JUAN  5    71    1
        AT SOME SMALL DISTANCE ALL HE SAW WITHIN   . . . . .    469   2 DON JUAN  5   100    4
        WHATE'ER SHE SAW AND COVETED WAS BROUGHT   . . . . .    476   2 DON JUAN  5   113    1
        AND ALL WHO HAVE SEEN A HUMAN NURSERY SAW   . . . . .   488   2 DON JUAN  5   133    5
```

SAW   (CONTINUED)
```
HE SAW WITH HIS OWN EYES THE MOON WAS ROUND . . . . . . 497   2 DON JUAN  5   150    1
WHO SAW HIS VIRTUES AS THEY SAW THE REST . . . . . . .  12   3 DON JUAN  6    13   V4
WHO SAW HIS VIRTUES AS THEY SAW THE REST . . . . . . .  12   3 DON JUAN  6    13   V4
AND WHEN SHE SAW HIM STUMBLING LIKE A STEED . . . . .   56   3 DON JUAN  6   101    4
WHEN BABA SAW THESE SYMPTOMS WHICH HE KNEW . . . . .    57   3 DON JUAN  6   102    1
BUT WHEN THEY SAW THE ENEMY RETIRE . . . . . . . . .    82   3 DON JUAN  7    31    2
(FOR DAY NE'ER SAW HIS MERITS) COULD DECREE . . . . .   86   3 DON JUAN  7    41    4
WHICH ALL WHO SAW IT FOLLOWED WRONG OR RIGHT . . . . .  89   3 DON JUAN  7    46    8
SUWARROW WHEN HE SAW THIS COMPANY . . . . . . . . . .   97   3 DON JUAN  7    59    1
SUWARROW--WHO BUT SAW THINGS IN THE GROSS . . . . . . 105   3 DON JUAN  7    77    1
THE LIVELIEST FIRE AND SAW THE FIERCEST FLOOD . . . . 129   3 DON JUAN  8    33   V4
I NEVER SAW SUCH EYES--BUT HARK NOW CHOOSE . . . . . . 162   3 DON JUAN  8   101    3
WHO ONLY SAW THE BLACK-EYED GIRLS IN GREEN . . . . . . 167   3 DON JUAN  8   111    4
HE SHOUTED ALLAH AND SAW PARADISE . . . . . . . . . . 169   3 DON JUAN  8   115    3
SAW NOTHING LIKE THE SCENE AROUND--YET LOOKING . . . . 172   3 DON JUAN  8   121    4
KNOW NOT SINCE KNOWLEDGE SAW HER BRANCHES STRIPT . . . 210   3 DON JUAN  9    55    6
VICTORY AND PAUSING AS SHE SAW HIM KNEEL . . . . . . . 211   3 DON JUAN  9    57    7
WHEN NEWTON SAW AN APPLE FALL HE FOUND . . . . . . . . 225   3 DON JUAN 10     1    1
BUT WHEN SHE SAW HIS DAZZLING EYE WAX DIM . . . . . . 246   3 DON JUAN 10    44    5
THROUGH COURLAND ALSO WHICH THAT FAMOUS FARCE SAW . . 253   3 DON JUAN 10    58    3
'TIS THE SAME LANDSCAPE WHICH THE MODERN MARS SAW . . 253   3 DON JUAN 10    58    5
DON JUAN NOW SAW ALBION'S EARLIEST BEAUTIES-- . . . . 259   3 DON JUAN 10    69    1
THEY SAW AT CANTERBURY THE CATHEDRAL . . . . . . . . . 261   3 DON JUAN 10    73    1
HE BREATHED A THOUSAND CRESSYS AS HE SAW . . . . . . . 261   3 DON JUAN 10    74    2
BUT JUAN SAW NOT THIS EACH WREATH OF SMOKE . . . . . . 266   3 DON JUAN 10    83    1
JUAN WHO SAW THE MOON'S LATE MINION BLEED . . . . . . 275   3 DON JUAN 11    14    5
AND WHETHER IN HIS TRAVELS HE SAW ILION . . . . . . . 294   3 DON JUAN 11    50    8
HE SAW TEN THOUSAND LIVING AUTHORS PASS . . . . . . . 295   3 DON JUAN 11    54    5
WHAT JUAN SAW AND UNDERWENT SHALL BE . . . . . . . . . 311   3 DON JUAN 11    88    1
(WHICH SAW ALL WESTERN THINGS WITH SMALL SURPRISE . . 328   3 DON JUAN 12    27    3
SO WHEN HE SAW EACH ANCIENT DAME A SUITOR . . . . . . 336   3 DON JUAN 12    42    5
OUR HERO GLADLY SAW HIS LITTLE CHARGE . . . . . . . . 339   3 DON JUAN 12    51    2
DON JUAN SAW THAT MICROCOSM ON STILTS . . . . . . . . 342   3 DON JUAN 12    56    1
HE SAW HOWEVER AT THE CLOSING SESSION . . . . . . . . 354   3 DON JUAN 12    83    1
THERE TOO HE SAW (WHATE'ER HE MAY BE NOW) . . . . . . 354   3 DON JUAN 12    84    1
THE LADY ADELINE AS SOON'S SHE SAW . . . . . . . . . . 436   3 DON JUAN 14    60    3
SHE MARVELL'D WHAT HE SAW IN SUCH A BABY . . . . . . . 477   3 DON JUAN 15    49    7
IMPOSED NOT UPON HER SHE SAW HER BLAZE . . . . . . . . 480   3 DON JUAN 15    56    2
SHE LOOKED AND SAW HIM PALE AND TURNED AS PALE . . . . 514   3 DON JUAN 16    31    1
SAW--WELL NO MATTER 'TWAS SO LONG AGO . . . . . . . . 517   3 DON JUAN 16    38    3
'TIS TRUE HE SAW AURORA LOOK AS THOUGH . . . . . . . . 553   3 DON JUAN 16   106    1
YET SAW THIS MUCH WHICH HE WAS GLAD TO SEE . . . . . . 553   3 DON JUAN 16   106    8
WHO GROW UP CHILDREN ONLY SINCE THE OLD SAW . . . . . 563   3 DON JUAN 17     2    2
```
SAWNEY'S
```
UNTO BY SAWNEY'S VIOLIN WE HAVE HEARD . . . . . . . . 307   3 DON JUAN 11    78    6
```
SAXONS
```
TO STRIP THE SAXONS OF THEIR HYDES LIKE TANNERS . . . 242   3 DON JUAN 10    36    6
```
SAYING
```
SAYING HE HAD GORGED ENOUGH TO MAKE A HORSE ILL . . . 240   2 DON JUAN  2   159    8
SAYING OUR MACHIAVELIAN IMPRESARIO . . . . . . . . . . 389   2 DON JUAN  4    82    2
SAYING OUR PORCO OF AN IMPRESARIO . . . . . . . . . . 389   2 DON JUAN  4    82   V2
AND MERELY SAYING CHRISTIAN CANST THOU LOVE . . . . . 478   2 DON JUAN  5   116    7
DOGS OR MEN (FOR I FLATTER YOU IN SAYING . . . . . . .  70   3 DON JUAN  7     7    1
OF THEIR DESIGNS BY SAYING THEY MEANT WELL . . . . . . 123   3 DON JUAN  8    25    7
FOR THERE'S NO SAYING WHAT THEY WILL OR MAY DO . . . . 351   3 DON JUAN 12    77    8
WHO 'STEAD OF SAYING WHAT YOU NOW SHOULD DO . . . . . 432   3 DON JUAN 14    50    5
```
SAYINGS
```
HER SERIOUS SAYINGS DARKEN'D TO SUBLIMITY . . . . . .  27   2 DON JUAN  1    12    4
SET DOWN HIS SAYINGS IN HER COMMON-PLACE BOOK . . . . 294   3 DON JUAN 11    52    8
```
SCABBARD
```
SHRUNK TO A SCABBARD WITH HIS ARROWS AT . . . . . . . 205   3 DON JUAN  9    45    3
A GOLDEN SCABBARD ON A DAMASQUE SWORD . . . . . . . . 422   3 DON JUAN 14    27    5
```
SCAIS
```
THAT UNDEFINABLE JE NE SCAIS QUOI . . . . . . . . . . 441   3 DON JUAN 14    72    2
```
SCAIS-JE
```
QUE SCAIS-JE WAS THE MOTTO OF MONTAIGNE . . . . . . . 191   3 DON JUAN  9    17    1
```
SCALDING
```
HAD IT NOT HAPPENED SCALDING HOT TO BE . . . . . . . . 513   3 DON JUAN 16    30    4
```
SCALE
```
AND HOW TO SCALE A FORTRESS--OR A NUNNERY . . . . . .  42   2 DON JUAN  1    38    8
I'VE SEEN THEM BALANCE EVEN THE SCALE WITH FIGHTERS . 418   3 DON JUAN 14    20    3
```
SCALED
```
BUT THOSE WHO SCALED FOUND OUT THAT THEIR ADVANCE . . 136   3 DON JUAN  8    46    1
```
SCAMANDER
```
AND OLD SCAMANDER (IF 'TIS HE) REMAIN . . . . . . . . 386   2 DON JUAN  4    77    4
```
SCAMPERED
```
THAT JOHNSON AND SOME FEW WHO HAD NOT SCAMPERED . . . 135   3 DON JUAN  8    44    7
THE TURKS AT FIRST PRETENDED TO HAVE SCAMPERED . . . . 149   3 DON JUAN  8    75    6
```
SCAN
```
THEREFORE HIS FRAILTIES I'LL NO FURTHER SCAN . . . . .  40   2 DON JUAN  1    35    3
MAY HAVE ANOTHER NAME FOR HALF WE SCAN . . . . . . . . 163   3 DON JUAN  8   104    3
AND THAT'S THE CAUSE NO DOUBT WHY IF WE SCAN . . . . . 167   3 DON JUAN  8   112    5
```
SCANDAL
```
AND IF SHE COULD NOT (WHO CAN) SILENCE SCANDAL . . . .  58   2 DON JUAN  1    67    7
THE PLEASANT SCANDAL WHICH AROSE NEXT DAY . . . . . . 126   2 DON JUAN  1   188    5
AND CLIMATE STOPPED ALL SCANDAL (NOW AND THEN)-- . . . 241   3 DON JUAN 10    33    4
BUT NOW NO MORE THE GHOST OF SCANDAL STALKED ABOUT . . 338   3 DON JUAN 12    47    3
A TOPIC SCANDAL DOTH DELIGHT TO ROUSE . . . . . . . . 370   3 DON JUAN 13    26    6
UPON ME WHOM NO SCANDAL COULD REMOVE . . . . . . . . . 452   3 DON JUAN 14    96    6
```

		PAGE	VOL		CANTO	STANZA	LN

SCANDAL'S
BUT SCANDAL'S MY AVERSION--I PROTEST . . . . 49 2 DON JUAN 1 51 7
NOT SCANDAL'S FANGS COULD FIX ON MUCH THAT'S SEIZABLE . . 66 2 DON JUAN 1 83 3
AND CLIMATE--STOPPED THE LION SCANDAL'S DEN . . . . . 241 3 DON JUAN 10 33 V4

SCANDALS
DEAD SCANDALS FORM GOOD SUBJECTS FOR DISSECTION . . . . 37 2 DON JJAN 1 31 8
OF ONE OF THE MOST CIRCULATING SCANDALS . . . . . . 128 2 DON JJAN 1 190 2
NO SCANDALS MADE THE DAILY PRESS A CURSE-- . . . . . 496 2 DON JUAN 5 149 7
THE PORTER SOME SLIGHT SCANDALS STRANGE AND QUAINT . . 418 3 DON JUAN 14 19 5

SCANN'D
A FAIRER MARK AND WITH A FIX'D EYE SCANN'D . . . . . 367 2 DON JUAN 4 43 7

SCANNED
TO GOD KNOWS WHAT--BUT NEVER YET I SCANNED . . . . . 161 2 DON JUAN 2 7 V6
UNTIL THE SUM WAS ACCURATELY SCANNED . . . . 426 2 DON JUAN 5 29 6
A MIXTURE OF SENSATIONS MIGHT BE SCANNED . . . . . . 473 2 DON JUAN 5 108 7

SCANT
WAS SCANT ENOUGH IN VAIN THE TELESCOPE . . . . . . 178 2 DON JUAN 2 41 6
THOUGH LADIES' ROBES SEEM SCANT ENOUGH FOR LESS . . . 482 3 DON JUAN 15 61 8

SCANTY
WHEN SHIPWRECK'S SHORT ALLOWANCE GROWS TOO SCANTY . . . 200 2 DON JUAN 2 83 7
MIGHT NOT HAVE THOUGHT THE SCANTY DRAUGHT SO SWEET . . 201 2 DON JUAN 2 85 6
THE SCANTY BUT RIGHT-WELL THRASHED EARS OF TRUTH . . . 403 3 DON JUAN 13 96 2
TOO SCANTY IN THESE TIMES OF LOW TAXATION . . . . . 528 3 DON JUAN 16 56 8

'SCAPED
SO VILE HE 'SCAPED THE DOOM WHICH OFT AVENGES . . . . 317 2 DON JUAN 3 80 5

SCAR
WHICH SKIMS THE SURFACE LEAVING SCARCE A SCAR . . . . 335 3 DON JJAN 12 40 6

SCARCE
AND THERE WERE OTHERS SCARCE FORGOTTEN YET . . . . . 22 2 DON JUAN 1 3 4
BUT SCARCE A FEE WAS PAID ON EITHER SIDE . . . . . . 38 2 DON JUAN 1 32 7
IS IT FOR THIS I SCARCE WENT ANYWHERE . . . . 102 2 DON JUAN 1 148 3
MY MISERY CAN SCARCE BE MORE COMPLETE . . . . 134 2 DON JUAN 1 197 4
HER SMALL WHITE FINGERS SCARCE COULD REACH THE TAPER . . 134 2 DJN JUAN 1 198 V3
BUT THE SHIP LABOUR'D SO THEY SCARCE COULD HOPE . . . 178 2 DON JUAN 2 41 2
BUT SCARCE ENOUGH TO SERVE THEM FOR A LUNCHEON-- . . . 181 2 DON JUAN 2 47 7
WHICH LEFT SCARCE ROOM FOR MOTION OR EXERTION . . . . 189 2 DON JUAN 2 63 2
A BETTER SWIMMER YOU COULD SCARCE SEE EVER . . . . . 211 2 DJN JUAN 2 105 5
FOR SOME OF THESE ARE ROCKS WITH SCARCE A HUT ON . . . 238 2 DON JUAN 2 154 6
PAIR OF SCARCE DECENT TROWSERS--WENT TO WORK . . . . 240 2 DON JUAN 2 160 2
DROPP'D IN THEIR LAPS SCARCE PLUCK'D THEIR MELLOW STORE . 291 2 DON JUAN 3 31 8
WHICH SCARCE EVEN FRANCE THE PARAGON OF NATIONS . . . 299 2 DON JJAN 3 46 3
OF LAVISH PEARLS WHOSE WORTH COULD SCARCE BE TOLD . . 312 2 DON JUAN 3 72 6
ON HER SIRE'S ARM WHICH UNTIL NOW SCARCE HELD . . . . 375 2 DJN JUAN 4 58 7
WEAK STILL WITH LOSS OF BLOOD HE SCARCE COULD URGE . . 387 2 DJN JUAN 4 79 5
FORSOOTH SCARCE FIT FOR BALLADS IN THE STREET . . . . 392 2 DON JUAN 4 89 6
WHICH THE WEST INDIAN MARKET SCARCE WOULD BRING . . . 408 2 DON JUAN 4 115 2
COULD SCARCE BE SHOWN EVEN BY A MERE SPECTATOR . . . . 416 2 DON JUAN 5 11 8
I HEARD A SHOT--'TWAS EIGHT O'CLOCK SCARCE PAST-- . . . 428 2 DON JUAN 5 33 5
STRETCHED IN THE STREET AND ABLE SCARCE TO PANT . . . 428 2 DON JUAN 5 33 8
TRAMPLED WHAT THEY SCARCE TROD FOR FEAR OF STAINING . . 450 2 DON JJAN 5 66 3
THOUGH SOMEWHAT GRIEVED COULD SCARCE FORBEAR A SMILE . 459 2 DON JUAN 5 83 3
THE SUN HIMSELF WAS SCARCE MORE FREE FROM SPECKS . . . 474 2 DON JUAN 5 109 5
HER BLOOD WAS HIGH HER BEAUTY SCARCE OF EARTH . . . . 475 2 DON JUAN 5 112 5
SUCH NOTICE OF A GIAOUR WHILE SCARCE TO ONE . . . . . 501 2 DON JUAN 5 156 5
WAS SCARCE ENOUGH FOR HE HAD FIFTY-NINE . . . . . . 10 3 DON JJAN 6 8 7
AND FEET SO SMALL THEY SCARCE SEEMED MADE TO TREAD . . 26 3 DON JJAN 6 41 4
THINNER SHE MIGHT HAVE BEEN AND YET SCARCE LOSE . . . 27 3 DON JUAN 6 42 6
AND SCARCE SECURE AS SUCH DIGRESSIONS ARE FAIR . . . . 65 3 DON JUAN 6 120 7
A STERN REPOSE WHICH YOU WOULD SCARCE CONCEIVE . . . . 94 3 DON JUAN 7 54 3
TO WOMEN THERE IS SCARCE A CRIMSON VARLET . . . . . 108 3 DON JUAN 7 84 5
THE COLUMN ORDERED ON THE ASSAULT SCARCE PASSED . . . 115 3 DON JUAN 8 7 1
SO THAT YOU SCARCE COULD SAY WHO BEST HAD CHOSEN . . . 135 3 DON JUAN 8 45 5
WHICH WAS CUT OFF AND SCARCE EVEN THEN LET GO . . . . 154 3 DON JUAN 8 85 8
INDEED THE SMOKE WAS SUCH THEY SCARCE COULD MARK . . . 177 3 DON JUAN 8 130 3
BLAZED AND THE CANNON'S ROAR WAS SCARCE ALLAYED . . . 178 3 DJN JUAN 8 133 4
AND SCARCE TO THE MOGUL A CUP OF COFFEE . . . . . . 199 3 DON JUAN 9 33 6
AND THOUGH I CAN'T HELP THINKING 'TWAS SCARCE FAIR . . 242 3 DON JUAN 10 36 5
THE EARTH AS SCARCE THE EAGLE IN THE BROAD . . . . . 263 3 DON JUAN 10 78 3
FOR TRUE OR FALSE POLITENESS (AND SCARCE THAT . . . . 290 3 DON JUAN 11 44 2
JURY OF MATRONS SCARCE KNEW WHAT TO ANSWER . . . . . 294 3 DON JUAN 11 51 4
OF MAN IT IS--I REALLY SCARCE KNOW WHAT . . . . . . 315 3 DON JUAN 12 1 3
TO THE LOT OF HIM WHO SCARCE PURSUED AT ALL . . . . . 333 3 DON JUAN 12 37 4
WHICH SKIMS THE SURFACE LEAVING SCARCE A SCAR . . . . 335 3 DON JUAN 12 40 6
AND HOW HE HAD BEEN TOSSED HE SCARCE KNEW WHITHER . . 338 3 DON JUAN 12 49 5
FOR THE FIRST SEASON SUCH A LIFE SCARCE PALLS . . . . 342 3 DON JUAN 12 57 8
AN USURER COULD SCARCE EXPECT MUCH MORE-- . . . . . 356 3 DJN JUAN 12 88 6
NOW THAT THE PUBLIC HEDGE HATH SCARCE A STAKE . . . . 357 3 DON JUAN 12 89 2
WHICH IS THAT THERE IS SCARCE A SINGLE SEASON . . . . 370 3 DON JUAN 13 26 3
NIMRODS WHOSE CANVAS SCARCE CONTAIN'D THE STEED . . . 391 3 DON JUAN 13 70 6
LIKE SWIFT CAMILLA HE SCARCE SKIMM'D THE GROUND . . . 427 3 DON JUAN 14 39 3
BUT OTHERS WHO WERE LEFT WITH SCARCE A THIRD . . . . 543 3 DON JUAN 16 89 3
THAT ONE SCARCE KNEW AT WHAT TO MARVEL MOST . . . . 543 3 DON JUAN 16 90 6
BY A LOOK SCARCE PERCEPTIBLY ASKANCE . . . . 546 3 DON JUAN 16 96 6

SCARCE-CLAD
AROUND HIS SCARCE-CLAD LIMBS AND THE FAIR ARM . . . . 216 2 DON JUAN 2 114 2

SCARCE-DRAWN
BENT WITH HUSH'D LIPS THAT DRANK HIS SCARCE-DRAWN BREATH . 232 2 DON JUAN 2 143 8

SCARCELY
CATULLUS SCARCELY HAS A DECENT POEM . . . . 45 2 DON JUAN 1 42 3

SCARCELY   (CONTINUED)
    SHE SCARCELY TRUSTED HIM FROM OUT HER SIGHT . .   . . . 48 2 DON JUAN 1   48   4
    SCARCELY O'ERPASS'D THE CREAM OF YOUR CHAMPAIGNE . . . 250 2 DON JUAN 2   178   2
    AGAINST THE BOUNDARY IT SCARCELY WET . . . . 251 2 DON JUAN 2   181   8
    NO COURTIER COULD AND SCARCELY WOMAN CAN . . . . . . 296 2 DON JUAN 3   41   5
    YOU SCARCELY CAN BE THIRTY HAVE YOU THREE . . . . . 421 2 DON JUAN 5   20   2
    JUST KILLED AND SCARCELY COMPETENT TO PANT . . . . . 429 2 DON JUAN 5   33   V8
    HE SEEMED TO SLEEP FOR YOU COULD SCARCELY TELL . . . . 430 2 DON JUAN 5   35   5
    I SCARCELY COULD BELIEVE THAT HE WAS DEAD . . . . . 432 2 DON JUAN 5   39   V4
    IN SUCH A TRIFLE SCARCELY COULD EXPRESS . . . . . . 452 2 DON JUAN 5   70   6
    THE STORY SCARCELY PASSED A SINGLE LIP-- . . . . . . 496 2 DON JUAN 5   149   3
    WILL SCARCELY FIND PHILOSOPHY FOR MORE . . . . . . 12 3 DON JUAN 6   12   6
    WHICH SCARCELY ROSE MUCH HIGHER THAN GRASS BLADES . . . 136 3 DON JUAN 8   47   8
    WHICH ON ROUGH ROADS LEAVES SCARCELY A WHOLE BONE) . . . 197 3 DON JUAN 9   30   3
    WOULD SCARCELY JOIN AGAIN THE REFORMADOES . . . . . 231 3 DON JUAN 10   13   3
    CRACKED SHIVERED VANISHED SCARCELY GAZED ON ERE . . . 306 3 DON JUAN 11   76   5
    A LOVELY BEING SCARCELY FORM'D OR MOULDED . . . . . 475 3 DON JUAN 15   43   7
    SHE GAZED UPON A WORLD SHE SCARCELY KNEW . . . . . . 476 3 DON JUAN 15   47   1
    REQUIRED AURORA SCARCELY LOOK'D ASIDE . . . . . . 490 3 DON JUAN 15   78   3
SCARED
    TO HEAVING BACK THE PORTAL FOLDS IT SCARED . . . . . 463 2 DON JUAN 5   90   4
SCARLESS
    ESCAPING WITH A FEW SLIGHT SCARLESS SNEERS . . . . . 397 3 DON JUAN 13   82   8
SCARLET
    WERE SCARLET FROM WHOSE GLOWING CENTER GREW . . . . . 309 2 DON JUAN 3   67   6
    MEDALS RANKS RIBBONS LACE EMBROIDERY SCARLET . . . . 108 3 DON JUAN 7   84   1
    AS THE YEAR CLOSING WHIRLS THE SCARLET LEAVES . . . . 155 3 DON JUAN 8   88   3
    A SCARLET COAT BLACK FACINGS A LONG PLUME . . . . . 204 3 DON JUAN 9   43   2
    AND NEUTRALIZE HER OUTWARD SHOW OF SCARLET . . . . . 237 3 DON JUAN 10   26   8
    COULEUR DE ROSE WHO'S NEITHER WHITE NOR SCARLET . . . 344 3 DON JUAN 12   62   8
    AND SCARLET CLOAK (I HATE THE SIGHT TO SEE SINCE-- . . . 530 3 DON JUAN 16   61   4
    THAT SCARLET CLOAK ALAS UNCLOSED WITH RIGOUR . . . . 530 3 DON JUAN 16   61   7
    THAT SCARLET CLOAK--GOD HELP US--WHEN CLOSE WRAPPED . . 530 3 DON JUAN 16   61   V7
SCARRED
    HAD SCARRED HER BROW AND LEFT ITS CRIMSON TRACE . . . 159 3 DON JUAN 8   95   5
SCARS
    THE SCARS OF HIS OLD WOUNDS WERE NEAR HIS NEW . . . . 431 2 DON JUAN 5   38   1
    THOSE HONOURABLE SCARS WHICH BROUGHT HIM FAME . . . . 431 2 DON JUAN 5   38   2
SCATTER
    MIGHT SCATTER FIRE THROUGH ICE LIKE HECLA'S FLAME . . . 254 3 DON JUAN 10   59   8
SCATTER'D
    INSTEAD OF BEING SCATTER'D THROUGH THE PAGES . . . . 46 2 DON JUAN 1   45   2
    SOME HALF-TORN DRAPERY SCATTER'D ON THE GROUND . . . . 125 2 DON JUAN 1   187   5
    AND IN THE FIRE HIS RECENT RAGS THEY SCATTER'D . . . . 240 2 DON JUAN 2   160   3
    BY WAY OF SPRINKLING SCATTER'D AMONGST THESE . . . . 397 3 DON JUAN 13   83   7
    THAT LIVE GAZETTE HAD SCATTER'D TO DISFIGURE . . . . 460 3 DON JUAN 15   11   2
SCATTERED
    HE FOUND A NUMBER OF CHASSEURS ALL SCATTERED . . . . 131 3 DON JUAN 8   37   7
    AND JUAN'S SUITE LATE SCATTERED AT A DISTANCE . . . . 275 3 DON JUAN 11   14   2
    OF COURSE THESE GROUPS WERE SCATTERED HERE AND THERE . . 533 3 DON JUAN 16   66   1
SCATTERING
    THE SCATTERING CLOUDS SHONE SPANNING THE DARK SEA . . . 204 2 DON JUAN 2   91   2
    O'ER WHOM AN EMPRESS HER CROWN JEWELS SCATTERING . . . 217 3 DON JUAN 9   70   V5
    'TIS FINE TO SEE THEM SCATTERING REFUSALS . . . . . 332 3 DON JUAN 12   34   2
SCATTERS
    AND GRAPE IN VOLLEYS LIKE A VINEYARD SCATTERS . . . . 160 3 DON JUAN 8   98   8
SCENE
    AND MADE A SCENE MEN DO NOT SOON FORGET . . . . . . 172 2 DON JUAN 2   31   3
    A BUSY CHARACTER IN THE DULL SCENE . . . . 352 2 DON JUAN 4   15   4
    AND IN THIS SCENE OF ALL-CONFESSED INANITY . . . . . 69 3 DON JUAN 7   6   5
    BUT HERE A SORT OF SCENE BEGAN TO ENSUE . . . . . . 101 3 DON JUAN 7   67   1
    SAW NOTHING LIKE THE SCENE AROUND--YET LOOKING . . . . 172 3 DON JUAN 8   121   4
    THRO' SUCH A SCENE OF CHANGE AND DREAD AND SLAUGHTER . . 252 3 DON JUAN 10   56   2
    THIS SCENE OF ROYAL ITCH AND LOYAL SCRATCHING . . . . 307 3 DON JUAN 11   78   8
    STILL UNIMPAIR'D TO DECORATE THE SCENE . . . . . . 389 3 DON JUAN 13   66   6
    INTO A SCENE AND SWELL THE CLIENTS' CLAN . . . . . . 437 3 DON JUAN 14   62   4
SCENERY
    AND VERY HANDSOME SUPERNATURAL SCENERY . . . . . . 136 2 DON JUAN 1   201   8
    AND DEVILS FOR MY SUPERNATURAL SCENERY . . . . . . 136 2 DON JUAN 1   201   V8
SCENES
    A LOVE OF MUSIC AND OF SCENES SUBLIME . . . . 304 2 DON JUAN 3   56   5
    AND WHEN WELL PRACTISED IN THESE MIMIC SCENES . . . . 93 3 DON JUAN 7   53   5
    AMIDST SUCH SCENES--THOUGH THIS WAS QUITE A NEW ONE . . 138 3 DON JUAN 8   52   4
    THE SCENES LIKE CATHERINE'S BOUDOIR AT THREE-SCORE . . 146 3 DON JUAN 8   68   7
    YE GLORIOUS GOTHIC SCENES HOW MUCH YE STRIKE . . . . 255 3 DON JUAN 10   61   3
    BUT COMING YOUNG FROM LANDS AND SCENES ROMANTIC . . . 347 3 DON JUAN 12   68   1
SCENT
    AND SCENT THE PREY THEIR MASTERS WOULD ATTACK ALL . . . 196 3 DON JUAN 9   27   5
    AND ONLY FRETTED WHEN THE SCENT 'GAN FAIL . . . . . 424 3 DON JUAN 14   33   4
SCENTING
    AND THE HARD FROST DESTROY'D THE SCENTING DAYS . . . . 407 3 DON JUAN 13   106   4
SCEPTICISM
    WHETHER THEY MAY SOW SCEPTICISM TO REAP HELL . . . . 195 3 DON JUAN 9   25   5
SCEPTICS
    WHEN THEY DISPUTE WITH SCEPTICS AND WITH CURSES . . . 165 3 DON JUAN 8   108   7
    THE SCEPTICS WHO WOULD NOT BELIEVE COLUMBUS . . . . . 502 3 DON JUAN 16   4   8
SCHERBATOFF
    OR SCHERBATOFF OR ANY OTHER OFF . . . . 206 3 DON JUAN 9   48   2
SCHEREMATOFF
    SCHEREMATOFF AND CHREMATOFF KOKLOPHTI . . . . 75 3 DON JUAN 7   17   1

	PAGE	VOL	CANTO	STANZA	LN
SCHISM					
WORLD (BE IT WHAT YOU WILL) THAT THAT'S NO SCHISM	269	3 DON JUAN 11	2	4
SCHISMATIC					
THIS SUBJECT QUOTE AS IT WOULD BE SCHISMATIC	289	3 DON JUAN 11	43	5
SCHMACKSMITH					
THREE LINES OF THE DISPATCH IN TAKING SCHMACKSMITH	76	3 DON JUAN 7	20	6
SCHNAPPS					
WITH SCHNAPPS--SAD DOGS WHOM HUNDSFOT OR FERFLUCTER	260	3 DON JUAN 10	71	7
WITH SCHNAPPS--DEMOCRITUS WOULD CEASE TO SMILE	260	3 DON JUAN 10	71	V7
SCHOLAR					
HEAVEN HELP THE SCHOLAR WHOM HIS FORTUNE SENDS HERE	423	2 DON JUAN 5	24	4
SCHOLARS					
HORACE CATULLUS SCHOLARS OVID TUTOR	266	2 DON JUAN 2	205	3
SCHOOL					
TO SCHOOL OR HAD HIM SOUNDLY WHIPP'D AT HOME	34	2 DON JUAN 1	25	7
TO SCHOOL (AS GOD BE PRAISED THAT I HAVE NONE)	50	2 DON JUAN 1	52	4
HAD HE BUT BEEN PLACED AT A PUBLIC SCHOOL	158	2 DON JUAN 2	2	1
BRAVE INEZ NOW SET UP A SUNDAY SCHOOL	162	2 DON JUAN 2	10	2
INTRIGUES ADVENTURES OF THE COMMON SCHOOL	353	2 DON JUAN 4	17	5
I KNOW ONE WOMAN OF THAT PURPLE SCHOOL	405	2 DON JUAN 4	111	7
OF ORPHANS PAINTS AT ONCE A PARISH SCHOOL	563	3 DON JUAN 17	3	3
SCHOOLBOY					
AGAINST THE WORLD AND DEAR THE SCHOOLBOY SPOT	90	2 DON JUAN 1	126	7
WHOM TO THE SPOT THEIR SCHOOL-BOY FEELINGS BEAR	387	2 DON JUAN 4	78	5
FEMALE OR MALE A SCHOOL-BOY OR A QUEEN	421	3 DON JUAN 14	25	8
SCHOOLBOY'S					
JUDICIOUSLY FROM OUT THE SCHOOLBOY'S VISION	46	2 DON JUAN 1	44	3
BUT SOMEHOW--IT MAY SEEM A SCHOOLBOY'S WHINE	233	3 DON JUAN 10	17	5
SCHOOL'D					
'TIS PLEASING TO BE SCHOOL'D IN A STRANGE TONGUE	242	2 DON JUAN 2	164	1
SCHOOLS					
AND PERSECUTED SAGES TEACH THE SCHOOLS	463	3 DON JUAN 15	17	7
SCHOONER					
A SCHOONER OR--BUT IT IS TIME TO EASE	109	3 DON JUAN 7	85	5
SCIAN					
THE SCIAN AND THE TEIAN MUSE	321	2 DON JUAN 3	L 2	1
SCIENCE					
FOR EVERY BRANCH OF EVERY SCIENCE KNOWN--	26	2 DON JUAN 1	10	2
HER FAVOURITE SCIENCE WAS THE MATHEMATICAL	27	2 DON JUAN 1	12	1
AND SCIENCE PROFITS BY THIS RESURRECTION--	37	2 DON JUAN 1	31	7
ALL OTHER MAGAZINES OF ART OR SCIENCE	142	2 DON JUAN 1	211	3
WITH GRACEFUL ACTION SCIENCE NOT A JOT	392	2 DON JUAN 4	89	3
I HAVE GAINED SCIENCE IN THE THINGS WHICH PASS	403	2 DON JUAN 4	107	V3
SO GOODLY WAS HER THIRST FOR SCIENCE GROWN	476	2 DON JUAN 5	113	V7
SCIENCE ENOUGH WHICH LEVELS TO AN ASS	69	3 DON JUAN 7	5	3
WHERE SCIENCE MARSHALS FORTH HER OWN QUADRILLE	303	3 DON JUAN 11	70	8
BUT SADDEST WHEN HIS SCIENCE IS WELL KNOWN	463	3 DON JUAN 15	17	6
AS FORM A SCIENCE AND A NOMENCLATURE	486	3 DON JUAN 15	69	7
SCIENCES					
ARTS SCIENCES NO BRANCH WAS MADE A MYSTERY	43	2 DON JUAN 1	39	7
THE SCIENCES AND MOST OF ALL THE ABSTRUSE	44	2 DON JUAN 1	40	2
SCIENTIFIC					
GROW TIRED OF SCIENTIFIC CONVERSATION	33	2 DON JUAN 1	22	4
SCILLY					
THE LADIES SCILLY BUSEY--MISS ECLAT	396	3 DON JUAN 13	79	4
SCIMITARS					
A THOUSAND SCIMITARS AWAIT THE WORD	364	2 DON JUAN 4	37	7
SCIO					
WITH SCIO WINE--AND ALL FOR LOVE NOT MONEY	233	2 DON JUAN 2	145	8
BUT THREE RAGUSAN VESSELS BOUND FOR SCIO	248	2 DON JUAN 2	174	8
SCIONS					
AS MANY OTHER NOBLE SCIONS WERE	370	3 DON JUAN 13	28	3
SCIO'S					
THE TEIAN BARD OF SCIO'S ISLE	321	2 DON JUAN 3	L 2	V1
AND SHED THE BLOOD OF SCIO'S VINE	324	2 DON JUAN 3	L 9	4
SCISSORS					
WITH SOME SMALL AID FROM SCISSORS PAINT AND TWEEZERS	458	2 DON JUAN 5	80	2
SCOFF					
A TENDENCY TO UNDER-RATE AND SCOFF	67	3 DON JUAN 7	3	3
SCOFFED					
ALL PROPER MEN OF WEAPONS AS E'ER SCOFFED HIGH	75	3 DON JUAN 7	17	3
SCOFFING					
THEN SEES YOUR HEART WRECKED WITH AN INWARD SCOFFING	345	3 DON JUAN 12	63	4
SCOLD					
THEY MEAN TO SCOLD AND VERY OFTEN DO	79	2 DON JUAN 1	108	5
AND NEVER ONCE HE HAS HAD CAUSE TO SCOLD	101	2 DON JUAN 1	147	5
TO SCOLD A LITTLE AT THE FALSE ALARM	45	3 DON JUAN 6	79	3
HOW TO ENCOUNTER WITH THIS MARTIAL SCOLD	54	3 DON JUAN 6	96	3
SCOLDING					
A SCOLDING WIFE A SULLEN SON A BILL	16	3 DON JUAN 6	21	1
RESULTING FROM THE SCOLDING OR THE VISION	47	3 DON JUAN 6	82	3
SCOPE					
SCOPE TO ALL SUCH AS FEEL THE INHERENT GLOW	13	2 DON JUAN D	7	6
SCORCH					
AND LONG LONG DESERTS SCORCH THE CAMEL'S FOOT	373	2 DON JUAN 4	55	6
SCORCH'D					
BLISTER'D AND SCORCH'D AND STAGNANT ON THE SEA	194	2 DON JUAN 2	72	2
BY NIGHT CHILL'D BY DAY SCORCH'D THUS ONE BY ONE	210	2 DON JUAN 2	102	5
BUT WHEN IT HATH BEEN SCORCH'D AND PIERCED AND RIVEN	270	2 DON JUAN 2	214	5

700

	PAGE	VOL	CANTO	STANZA	LN
SCORCHED					
A LITTLE SCORCHED AT PRESENT WITH THE BLAZE	156	3 DON JUAN	8	90	6
SCORCHES					
SHOWERS TRIPLE LIGHT AND SCORCHES EVEN THE KISS	264	2 DON JUAN	2	202	3
SCORCHING					
AMONG THE SCORCHING RUINS HE SAT SMOKING	172	3 DON JUAN	8	121	2
SCORE					
THAT SHE SPAWNS WARRIORS BY THE SCORE WHERE NONE	164	3 DON JUAN	8	125	2
BUT ALL THE LADIES SAVE SOME TWENTY SCORE	176	3 DON JUAN	8	129	7
THE MOB STOOD AND AS USUAL SEVERAL SCORE	282	3 DON JUAN	11	30	3
WAS CHOSEN FROM OUT AN AMATORY SCORE	334	3 DON JUAN	12	38	3
I LEAVE THE SAINTS TO SETTLE THEIR OWN SCORE	352	3 DON JUAN	12	79	4
SEEN BEAUTIES BROUGHT TO MARKET BY THE SCORE	418	3 DON JUAN	14	18	4
BELOW STAIRS ON THE SCORE OF SECOND COURSES	534	3 DON JUAN	16	68	4
O'ER THE VOLUNTEERS--ON EITHER SCORE	537	3 DON JUAN	16	76	V5
SCORN					
THE DOUBLE BOBADIL TAKES SCORN FOR AWE	153	2 DON JUAN	1	V 4	8
AS IF THE PEASANT'S SCORN THIS MODE INVENTED	401	2 DON JUAN	4	105	V3
AND SCORN TO ADD A SYLLABLE UNTRUE	41	3 DON JUAN	6	70	3
THEY HONOURED SUCH DETERMINED SCORN OF LIFE	171	3 DON JUAN	8	119	8
MORE THAN YOU SCORN THE SAVAGES OF YORE	180	3 DON JUAN	8	136	7
PERHAPS BUT WHO WOULD SCORN THE MONTH OF JUNE	229	3 DON JUAN	10	9	5
CONVERTED FOES SHOULD SCORN TO JOIN WITH THOSE	231	3 DON JUAN	10	12	8
O'ER THE HIGH HILL WHICH LOOKS WITH PRIDE OR SCORN	264	3 DON JUAN	10	80	4
AND SCORN HIS TEMPERATE BOARD AS NONE AT ALL	316	3 DON JUAN	12	3	6
IT WAS NOT SCORN--WHICH COULD NOT LIGHT ON ONE	479	3 DON JUAN	15	54	3
NOR INSOLENT ENOUGH TO SCORN THE SCORNER	532	3 DON JUAN	16	65	6
OF WEARINESS OR SCORN) BEGAN TO FEEL	546	3 DON JUAN	16	96	7
SCORNED					
A SCRIBBLING SELF-SOLD SOUL-HIRED SCORNED ISCARIOT	15	2 DON JUAN	D	11	V8
GREAT MEN HAVE ALWAYS SCORNED GREAT RECOMPENSES	186	3 DON JUAN	9	8	1
SCORNER					
AS GREAT A SCORNER OF THE NAZARENE	167	3 DON JUAN	8	111	2
AND LOOK ON AS A MOURNER OR A SCORNER	303	3 DON JUAN	11	69	6
NOR INSOLENT ENOUGH TO SCORN THE SCORNER	532	3 DON JUAN	16	65	6
SCORNERS					
FROM WHENCE THEY SALLIED ON THOSE CHRISTIAN SCORNERS	149	3 DON JUAN	8	75	8
SCORNFULLY					
SMILED SCORNFULLY AND SAID WITHIN MY CALL	364	2 DON JUAN	4	37	6
SCORNING					
AND AS YOU'D HAVE ME PARDON YOUR PAST SCORNING--	494	2 DON JUAN	5	145	6
SCORNS					
IS THIS A FANCY WHICH OUR REASON SCORNS	338	2 DON JUAN	3	108	7
MARK HOW IT LAUGHS AND SCORNS AT ALL YOU ARE	188	3 DON JUAN	9	12	1
SCORPION					
HE LAY DARK AS THE SCORPION IN YOUR PATH	300	2 DON JUAN	3	48	V4
SCOT					
BUT I AM HALF A SCOT BY BIRTH AND BRED	233	3 DON JUAN	10	17	7
SCOTCH					
WHICH--AS WE SAY--OR AS THE SCOTCH SAY WHILK	456	2 DON JUAN	5	77	6
SCOTCH PLAIDS SCOTCH SNOODS THE BLUE HILLS AND CLEAR STREAMS	233	3 DON JUAN	10	18	2
SCOTCH PLAIDS SCOTCH SNOODS THE BLUE HILLS AND CLEAR STREAMS	233	3 DON JUAN	10	18	2
SCOTCH WITH BLUE GREEN RIBBONS--IRISH WITH A BLUE	314	3 DON JUAN	11	V 76	2
BECAUSE THE NEIGHBOURING SCOTCH EARL OF GIFTGABBIT	534	3 DON JUAN	16	70	4
SCOTCHED					
I SCOTCHED NOT KILLED THE SCOTCHMAN IN MY BLOOD	234	3 DON JUAN	10	19	7
SCOTCHMAN					
I SCOTCHED NOT KILLED THE SCOTCHMAN IN MY BLOOD	234	3 DON JUAN	10	19	7
SCOTLAND					
NAPOLEON'S MARY'S (QUEEN OF SCOTLAND) SHOULD	218	3 DON JUAN	9	71	5
AS AULD LANG SYNE BRINGS SCOTLAND ONE AND ALL	233	3 DON JUAN	10	18	1
GONE DOWN IT SEEMS TO SCOTLAND TO BE FIDDLED	307	3 DON JUAN	11	78	5
SCOTS					
SUCH AS WAS MARY'S QUEEN OF SCOTS TRUE--TEARS	468	2 DON JUAN	5	98	5
I RAILED AT SCOTS TO SHEW MY WRATH AND WIT	234	3 DON JUAN	10	19	3
SCOTT					
SCOTT ROGERS CAMPBELL MOORE AND CRABBE WILL TRY	13	2 DON JUAN	D	7	7
WITH YOU THAN AUGHT (SAVE SCOTT) IN YOUR PROUD CITY	233	3 DON JUAN	10	17	4
STRANGE TOO IN MY BUON CAMERADO SCOTT	323	3 DON JUAN	12	16	5
AND AS MY FRIEND SCOTT SAYS I SOUND MY WARISON	481	3 DON JUAN	15	59	3
SCOTT THE SUPERLATIVE OF MY COMPARATIVE--	481	3 DON JUAN	15	59	4
SCOTT WHO CAN PAINT YOUR CHRISTIAN KNIGHT OR SARACEN	481	3 DON JUAN	15	59	5
SCOTT--OF SUCH TALENT--I COULD HARDLY HAVE	481	3 DON JUAN	15	59	V6
SCOUNDREL					
BUT HE HAD GENIUS--MANY A SCOUNDREL HAS IT--	317	2 DON JUAN	3	81	V1
AND WHEN A SCOUNDREL HAS IT--HE TAKES CARE	317	2 DON JUAN	3	81	V2
A SCOUNDREL AND YOU'LL HAVE GOOD COMPANY	310	3 DON JUAN	11	86	V8
TO SEE MEN LET THESE SCOUNDREL SOVEREIGNS BREAK LAW	497	3 DON JUAN	15	92	8
SCOUNDRELS					
THOSE SCOUNDRELS WHO HAVE NEVER HAD A SWORD IN	498	2 DON JUAN	5	151	4
SCOUR					
BY THOSE WHO SCOUR THOSE DOUBLE VALES OF STRIFE	232	3 DON JUAN	10	14	4
SCOURGE					
THE KINGLY SCOURGE THE LUST OF NOTORIETY	146	3 DON JUAN	8	68	5
SCOUT					
THEY PLACED HIM O'ER THE WOMEN AS A SCOUT)	394	2 DON JUAN	4	92	5
THEY LEFT THIS BEING FREE AND NEUTRAL AS A SCOUT	394	2 DON JUAN	4	92	V5
LORD HENRY WAS A JUSTICE AND THAT SCOUT	531	3 DON JUAN	16	62	6
WHILE SCOUT THE PARISH GUARDIAN OF THE FRAIL	533	3 DON JUAN	16	67	2

701

		PAGE	VOL		CANTO	STANZA	LN

SCOWL
OLD PORTRAITS FROM OLD WALLS UPON ME SCOWL-- . . . . . . 499 3 DON JUAN 15 97 5
SCRAMBLING
AT LAST WITH SWIMMING WADING SCRAMBLING HE . . . . . 212 2 DON JUAN 2 107 7
AND SCRAMBLING ROUND THE RAMPART THESE SAME TROOPS . . 148 3 DON JUAN 8 73 1
SCRAPE
OF GETTING HER LIEGE LORD INTO A SCRAPE . . . . . . 32 2 DON JUAN 1 20 8
THIS WAS DON JUAN'S EARLIEST SCRAPE BUT WHETHER . . 135 2 DON JUAN 1 199 1
THAN ANY OTHER SCRAPE A THING OF COURSE . . . . . 417 2 DON JUAN 5 12 8
THEY WARM INTO A SCRAPE BUT KEEP OF COURSE . . . . . 349 3 DON JUAN 12 73 7
SCRATCHED
HE SCRATCHED HIS EAR THE INFALLIBLE RESOURCE . . . . . 56 3 DON JUAN 6 100 7
SCRATCHING
THIS SCENE OF ROYAL ITCH AND LOYAL SCRATCHING . . . . 307 3 DON JUAN 11 78 8
SCRAWL
I TRACE THIS SCRAWL BECAUSE I CANNOT REST-- . . . . . . 130 2 DON JUAN 1 193 7
SCREAM
BEGAN AT ONCE TO SCREAM AND YAWN AND WEEP . . . . . 97 2 DON JUAN 1 140 3
AND SO--SHE WOKE WITH A GREAT SCREAM AND START . . . 44 3 DON JUAN 6 77 8
SHE WONDERED AT HERSELF HOW SHE COULD SCREAM-- . . . . 47 3 DON JUAN 6 83 3
THE HORRID WAR-WHOOP AND THE SHRILLER SCREAM . . . . 175 3 DON JUAN 8 127 5
SCREAM'D
AND BIT HER LIPS (FOR ELSE SHE MIGHT HAVE SCREAM'D) . . 51 2 DON JUAN 1 54 6
AS THE RICH MAN'S IN HELL WHO VAINLY SCREAM'D . . . . 202 2 DON JUAN 2 86 4
SCREAMED
THE APARTMENT ON A SUDDEN SHE SCREAMED OUT . . . . . 41 3 DON JUAN 6 70 8
SCREECHING
TEARING AND GRINNING HOWLING SCREECHING SWEARING . . . . 198 2 DON JUAN 2 79 7
SCREEN
AND FELL UPON THEIR GLAZED EYES LIKE A SCREEN . . . . 210 2 DON JUAN 2 103 5
AND THE TRUE HYMEN (THE FIRST'S BUT A SCREEN)-- . . . 288 2 DON JUAN 3 25 6
EACH VILLA ON THE BOSPHORUS LOOKS A SCREEN . . . . 436 2 DON JUAN 5 46 7
HAVE HALF WITHDRAWN FROM HIM OBLIVION'S SCREEN . . . 82 3 DON JUAN 7 33 8
I WOULD NOT BE A TORTOISE IN HIS SCREEN . . . . . 431 3 DON JUAN 14 49 3
SOME TRUTHS ARE BETTER KEPT BEHIND A SCREEN . . . 444 3 DON JUAN 14 80 6
OF THE POOR PARTRIDGE THROUGH HIS STUBBLE SCREEN . . 539 3 DON JUAN 16 80 5
SCREENED
IN A GRAND ARCH WHICH ONCE SCREENED MANY AN AISLE . . . 386 3 DON JUAN 13 59 3
SCRIBBLE
BECAUSE 'TIS SO WHO NIBBLE SCRIBBLE QUIBBLE HE . . . 503 3 DON JUAN 16 5 7
SCRIBBLERS
BUT THAT OF LATE YOUR SCRIBBLERS THINK IT WORTH . . . 434 2 DON JUAN 5 42 6
SCRIBBLING
A SCRIBBLING SELF-SOLD SOUL-HIRED SCORNED ISCARIOT . . 15 2 DON JUAN D 11 V8
AND YET I CAN'T HELP SCRIBBLING ONCE A WEEK . . . . . 414 3 DON JUAN 14 10 5
SCRIBE
THOUGH EVERY SCRIBE IN SOME SLIGHT TURN OF DICTION . . 311 3 DON JUAN 11 88 6
SCRIBES
THESE AMIABLE DESCRIPTIONS FROM THE SCRIBES . . . . . 329 2 DON JUAN 3 92 6
YE TWICE TEN HUNDRED THOUSAND DAILY SCRIBES . . . . . 200 3 DON JUAN 9 35 2
SCRIPTURE
FURTHER I'D QUOTE BUT SCRIPTURE INTERVENING . . . . . 403 3 DON JUAN 13 96 5
SCRIPTURES
THAT SCRIPTURES OUT OF CHURCH ARE BLASPHEMIES . . . . 403 3 DON JUAN 13 96 8
SCROLL
HEAVEN'S FREEHOLDS IN A SORT OF DOOMSDAY SCROLL . . . . 242 3 DON JUAN 10 35 5
BEFORE HIM SUMMED THE AWFUL SCROLL AND READ IT) . . . 259 3 DON JUAN 10 70 6
MORE FOES BY THIS SAME SCROLL WHEN I BEGAN IT I . . . 482 3 DON JUAN 15 60 6
SCRUPLES
HAIDEE SPOKE NOT OF SCRUPLES ASK'D NO VOWS . . . . . 257 2 DON JUAN 2 190 1
SCRUPULOSITY
WITH MORE THAN ORIENTAL SCRUPULOSITY . . . . 496 2 DON JUAN 5 148 2
SCUDO
WITHOUT A SINGLE SCUDO OF SALARIO . . . . 389 2 DON JUAN 4 82 6
SCUDS
SAY THAT HE SCUDS BEFORE IT LIKE A BRIG . . . . . 109 3 DON JUAN 7 85 4
SCUFFLE
DIRE WAS THE SCUFFLE AND OUT WENT THE LIGHT . . . . 122 2 DON JUAN 1 184 1
JUST LIKE A BLACK EYE IN A RECENT SCUFFLE . . . . 205 2 DON JUAN 2 92 7
SCUM
OF CITIES THAT BOILS OVER WITH THEIR SCUM-- . . . . . 272 3 DON JUAN 11 8 8
SCUMLIKE
FLOATS SCUMLIKE UPPERMOST AND THESE JACK CADES . . . 334 2 DON JUAN 3 100 5
SCUTTLED
THAT EVER SCUTTLED SHIP OR CUT A THROAT . . . . . . 296 2 DON JUAN 3 41 2
SCYMITAR
CLASHED 'GAINST THE SCYMITAR AND BABE AND MOTHER . . . 146 3 DON JUAN 8 69 4
SCYMITARS
LIKE MEN WITH TURBANS SCYMITARS AND DIRKS . . . . 93 3 DON JUAN 7 53 2
SCYTHE
WITH HIS RUDE SCYTHE SUCH GENTLE BOSOMS HE . . . . 348 2 DON JUAN 4 8 4
AND TURNS ASIDE HIS SCYTHE TO VULGAR THINGS . . . 468 2 DON JUAN 5 98 4
OH TIME WHY DOST NOT PAUSE THY SCYTHE SO DIRTY . . . 433 3 DON JUAN 14 53 5
SCYTHES
GRASS BEFORE SCYTHES OR CORN BELOW THE SICKLE . . . . 134 3 DON JUAN 8 43 2
SEA
THAN HE WHO NEVER SAW THE SEA OF OCEAN . . . . . . 60 2 DON JUAN 1 70 8
AND THE SEA DASHES ROUND THE PROMONTORY . . . . . . 94 2 DON JUAN 1 134 6
ALL EUROPEAN CLIMES BY LAND OR SEA . . . . 129 2 DON JUAN 1 191 2

SEA   (CONTINUED)

WITH LOVE AND WAR A HEAVY GALE AT SEA 135   2 DON JUAN 1   200   3
A DEVIL OF A SEA ROLLS IN THAT BAY 162   2 DON JUAN 2   11   3
WHILE HIS SALT TEARS DROPP'D INTO THE SALT SEA 165   2 DON JUAN 2   17   2
SOONER SHALL EARTH RESOLVE ITSELF TO SEA 166   2 DON JUAN 2   19   4
BUT THE SEA ACTED AS A STRONG EMETIC 167   2 DON JUAN 2   21   8
RESIST HIS STOMACH NE'ER AT SEA BEFORE 168   2 DON JUAN 2   23   8
THREW THE SHIP RIGHT INTO THE TROUGH OF THE SEA . . . 170   2 DON JUAN 2   27   2
NOUGHT BUT THE HEAVY SEA AND COMING NIGHT 178   2 DON JUAN 2   41   8
AND LONG HAD VOYAGED THROUGH MANY A STORMY SEA 179   2 DON JUAN 2   43   4
THAT A TIGHT BOAT WILL LIVE IN A ROUGH SEA 180   2 DON JUAN 2   45   7
WITH LITTLE HOPE IN SUCH A ROLLING SEA 183   2 DON JUAN 2   50   2
BUT E'ER TWAS WELL BEGUN--A HEAVY SEA 183   2 DON JUAN 2   50   V2
THEN ROSE FROM SEA TO SKY THE WILD FAREWELL 184   2 DON JUAN 2   52   1
AND THE SEA YAWN'D AROUND HER LIKE A HELL 184   2 DON JUAN 2   52   5
BECAUSE THE SEA RAN HIGHER EVERY MINUTE 186   2 DON JUAN 2   57   7
EACH SEA CURL'D O'ER THE STERN AND KEPT THEM WET . . . 188   2 DON JUAN 2   60   5
BEFORE THE SEA UNTIL IT SHOULD GROW FINE 189   2 DON JUAN 2   62   3
THE SEA AND SKY WERE BLUE AND CLEAR AND MILD-- 193   2 DON JUAN 2   70   4
BLISTER'D AND SCORCH'D AND STAGNANT ON THE SEA 194   2 DON JUAN 2   72   2
PART WAS DIVIDED PART THROWN IN THE SEA 197   2 DON JUAN 2   77   5
HIS TALE IF FOES BE FOOD IN HELL AT SEA 200   2 DON JUAN 2   83   5
THE SCATTERING CLOUDS SHONE SPANNING THE DARK SEA . . 204   2 DON JUAN 2   91   2
ROLL'D ON THE BEACH HALF SENSELESS FROM THE SEA . . . 212   2 DON JUAN 2   107   8
WHO LONG HAD BEEN HIS MATES UPON THE SEA 213   2 DON JUAN 2   109   4
ADDED TO HIS CONNEXION WITH THE SEA 222   2 DON JUAN 2   125   4
AND THE SEA SHINES WITH PURPLE--WHITE--AND GOLD . . . 230   2 DON JUAN 2   139   V7
OR THE RED SEA--BUT THE SEA IS NOT RED 231   2 DON JUAN 2   141   8
OR THE RED SEA--BUT THE SEA IS NOT RED 231   2 DON JUAN 2   141   8
AND FELT HER VEINS CHILL'D BY THE NEIGHBOURING SEA . . 233   2 DON JUAN 2   145   4
WELL--JUAN AFTER BATHING IN THE SEA 246   2 DON JUAN 2   171   7
AT LAST HER FATHER'S PROWS PUT OUT TO SEA 248   2 DON JUAN 2   174   5
AT LAST HER FATHER TOOK A VOYAGE TO SEA 248   2 DON JUAN 2   174   V5
SO THAT HER FATHER BEING AT SEA SHE WAS 248   2 DON JUAN 2   175   2
ON ONE SIDE AND THE DEEP SEA CALM AND CHILL 252   2 DON JUAN 2   183   6
THEY GAZED UPON THE GLITTERING SEA BELOW 253   2 DON JUAN 2   185   3
AND IN THE HOPE OF MORE AT SEA REMAIN'D 283   2 DON JUAN 3   15   3
AND MARATHON LOOKS ON THE SEA 321   2 DON JUAN 3   L 3   2
AVE MARIA O'ER THE EARTH AND SEA 334   2 DON JUAN 3   101   7
OF HIS QUENCH'D HEART AND THE SEA DIRGES LOW 362   2 DON JUAN 4   34   6
ON SUCH A THING IS SUDDENLY TO SEA SENT 371   2 DON JUAN 4   51   6
BY THE SEA SHORE WHEREON SHE LOVED TO DWELL 382   2 DON JUAN 4   71   8
AND WHEN HE DID HE FOUND HIMSELF AT SEA 384   2 DON JUAN 4   75   4
(FLANK'D BY THE HELLESPONT AND BY THE SEA) 385   2 DON JUAN 4   76   2
THERE'S NOT A SEA THE PASSENGER E'ER PUKES IN 413   2 DON JUAN 5   5   7
THE SACK AND SEA HAD SETTLED ALL IN TIME 496   2 DON JUAN 5   149   4
AND THROWN INTO THE SEA--THUS BABA SPOKE 58   3 DON JUAN 6   104   7
THE WIND WAS DOWN BUT STILL THE SEA RAN HIGH 61   3 DON JUAN 6   110   8
IT STANDS SOME EIGHTY VERSTS FROM THE HIGH SEA . . . 71   3 DON JUAN 7   9   7
LET THERE BE BLOOD SAYS MAN AND THERE'S A SEA 86   3 DON JUAN 7   41   2
FOR GLORY GAPING O'ER A SEA OF SLAUGHTER 91   3 DON JUAN 7   50   7
OF BLOOD AND TEARS MUST FLOW THE UNEBBING SEA . . . 101   3 DON JUAN 7   68   8
WAS IMAGED BACK IN BLOOD THE SEA OF SLAUGHTER . . . 172   3 DON JUAN 8   122   8
LIKE PYRRHO ON A SEA OF SPECULATION 191   3 DON JUAN 9   18   2
ON HER CANALS WHERE GOD TAKES SEA AND LAND 198   3 DON JUAN 9   31   7
ARE OR WOULD BE THOU SEA OF LIFE'S DRY LAND 210   3 DON JUAN 9   56   8
ARE OR WOULD BE THOU SEA WHICH LAVEST LIFE'S SAND . . 210   3 DON JUAN 9   56   V8
QUENCHED IN THE LAP OF THE SALT SEA OR THETIS . . . 217   3 DON JUAN 9   69   8
HIGH DASHED THE SPRAY THE BOWS DIPPED IN THE SEA . . 256   3 DON JUAN 10   64   4
OR ROME ON TIBER--NAPLES ON THE SEA 271   3 DON JUAN 11   7   V6
MORE THAN ON CONTINENTS--AS IF THE SEA 288   3 DON JUAN 11   42   7
MUST STEER WITH CARE THROUGH ALL THAT GLITTERING SEA . 303   3 DON JUAN 11   70   3
HERE DANCED ALBANO'S BOYS AND HERE THE SEA SHONE . . 392   3 DON JUAN 13   71   5
WHEN EVEN THE SEA LOOKS DIM WITH ALL ITS SPRAY . . . 422   3 DON JUAN 14   28   3
THERE WAS MISS MILLPOND SMOOTH AS SUMMER'S SEA . . . 474   3 DON JUAN 15   41   1
THE ISLAND GIRL BRED UP BY THE LONE SEA 481   3 DON JUAN 15   58   4
THE SINKING FUND'S UNFATHOMABLE SEA 548   3 DON JUAN 16   99   6
SEA-ATTORNEY
AND MERELY PRACTISED AS A SEA-ATTORNEY 283   2 DON JUAN 3   14   8
SEA-BIRD'S
AND ALL WAS STILLNESS SAVE THE SEA-BIRD'S CRY 251   2 DON JUAN 2   181   5
SEA-BORN
WHICH LOOKS O'ER SEA-BORN SALAMIS 322   2 DON JUAN 3   L 4   2
SEA-COAL
ON TIPTOE THROUGH THEIR SEA-COAL CANOPY 265   3 DON JUAN 10   82   6
THE SEA-COAL FIRES THE EARLIEST OF THE YEAR 395   3 DON JUAN 13   77   6
SEA-GULLS
THE SEA-GULLS WITH A STEADY SOBER FLIGHT-- 558   3 DON JUAN 16   117   2
SEAL
AND DARE NOT SET MY SEAL UPON THIS SHEET 134   2 DON JUAN 1   197   2
THE SEAL A SUNFLOWER ELLE VOUS SUIT PARTOUT 134   2 DON JUAN 1   198   6
WITH HIS DISPATCH FORGOT TO BREAK THE SEAL 211   3 DON JUAN 9   57   8
A LOVING LETTER WITH A MYSTIC SEAL 422   3 DON JUAN 14   27   6
SEAL'D
THIS TOO WAS A SEAL'D BOOK TO LITTLE JUAN-- 48   2 DON JUAN 1   48   1
SENSELESS TO FEEL AND WITH SEAL'D EYES TO SEE . . . 360   2 DON JUAN 4   30   8
SEALED
THEIR WAY THROUGH HER SEALED EYELIDS' GLOSSY FRINGES . . . 40   3 DON JUAN 6   67   V7
SEALS
WHERE WAVES MIGHT WASH AND SEALS MIGHT BREED AND LURK . 362   2 DON JUAN 4   33   4
THESE SEALS UPON HER WAX MADE NO IMPRESSION 480   3 DON JUAN 15   57   7

SEAMAN
THAT EVEN THE ABLE SEAMAN DEEMING HIS . . . . 173 2 DON JUAN 2 33 5
SEAMEN
PILLAGE TO SOLDIERS PRIZE-MONEY TO SEAMEN . . . . . 88 2 DON JUAN 1 124 8
OUR SHIPWRECK'D SEAMEN THOUGHT IT A GOOD OMEN-- . . . 205 2 DON JUAN 2 93 1
THOSE NAVIGATORS MUST BE ABLE SEAMEN . . . . . . 7 3 DON JUAN 6 2 3
AND PITY LOVERS RATHER MORE THAN SEAMEN . . . . . 32 3 DON JUAN 6 53 8
FIRMNESS YCLEPT IN HEROES KINGS AND SEAMEN . . . . 448 3 DON JUAN 14 89 3
SEAMEN'S
OF SEAMEN'S FATES AND THE LOUD TEMPESTS RAISE . . . . 414 2 DON JUAN 5 6 4
SEARCH
SEARCH THEN THE ROOM ALFONSO SAID I WILL . . . . . 98 2 DON JUAN 1 142 8
WAS NOT ASLEEP--YES SEARCH AND SEARCH SHE CRIED . . . 100 2 DON JUAN 1 145 2
WAS NOT ASLEEP--YES SEARCH AND SEARCH SHE CRIED . . . 100 2 DON JUAN 1 145 2
THE ANTI-CHAMBER--SEARCH THEM UNDER OVER . . . . 104 2 DON JUAN 1 153 2
WHO IS THE MAN YOU SEARCH FOR HOW D'YE CALL . . . . 105 2 DON JUAN 1 154 4
RETURNING THERE FROM HER SUCCESSFUL SEARCH . . . . 206 2 DON JUAN 2 95 6
OUR EYES IN SEARCH OF EITHER LOVELY LIGHT . . . . . 66 3 DON JUAN 7 1 6
IN SEARCH OF GLORY SHOULD LOOK ON BEFORE . . . . . 127 3 DON JUAN 8 31 7
AFTER DUE SEARCH YOUR FAITH TO ANY QUESTION . . . . 411 3 DON JUAN 14 2 4
EARLIEST TO RISE AND LAST TO QUIT THE SEARCH . . . . 539 3 DON JUAN 16 80 4
SEARCH'D
HE SEARCH'D THEY SEARCH'D AND RUMMAGED EVERYWHERE . . . 99 2 DON JUAN 1 143 1
HE SEARCH'D THEY SEARCH'D AND RUMMAGED EVERYWHERE . . . 99 2 DON JUAN 1 143 1
UNDER THE BED THEY SEARCH'D AND THERE THEY FOUND-- . . 100 2 DON JUAN 1 144 1
SEARCHED
UPON THE TREE WHICH EVE SO FONDLY SEARCHED . . . . 192 3 DON JUAN 9 19 8
I HAVE SEARCHED THE WORLD AND MIDST SUCCESS OR CHECKS . 451 3 DON JUAN 14 93 V5
SEARCHING
WHEN AFTER SEARCHING IN FIVE HUNDRED NOOKS . . . . 110 2 DON JUAN 1 161 3
SEARS
A WOMAN'S TEAR-DROP MELTS A MAN'S HALF SEARS . . . . 479 2 DON JUAN 5 118 5
OF FEELING FOR HOWEVER HABIT SEARS . . . . 102 3 DON JUAN 7 69 5
SEA'S
ARISE LIKE TITAN FROM THE SEA'S IMMERSION . . . . . 14 2 DON JUAN D 9 6
WHAT WAS NO DIRGE EXCEPT THE HOLLOW SEA'S . . . . . 383 2 DON JUAN 4 72 7
THE BLUE SEA'S BORDER AND DON JUAN FELT-- . . . . . 257 3 DON JUAN 10 65 2
SEAS
THAT THE SAIL WAS BECALM'D BETWEEN THE SEAS . . . . 188 2 DON JUAN 2 60 2
PURSUED O'ER THE HIGH SEAS HIS WATERY JOURNEY . . . . 283 2 DON JUAN 3 14 7
THE WILD SEAS AND WILD MEN WITH WHOM HE CRUISED . . . 303 2 DON JUAN 3 54 6
AND DRIVELS SEAS TO SET IT WELL AFLOAT . . . . . 333 2 DON JUAN 3 98 8
OF THOSE WHO SAIL THE SEAS ON THE FIRST DAY . . . . 338 2 DON JUAN 3 108 2
NO DIRGE SAVE WHEN ARISE THE STORMY SEAS . . . . . 383 2 DON JUAN 4 72 V7
TO WATCH THE PROGRESS OF THOSE ROLLING SEAS . . . . 413 2 DON JUAN 5 5 4
I'VE SEEN YOUR STORMY SEAS AND STORMY WOMEN . . . . 32 3 DON JUAN 6 53 7
OF HONEST FAME THAN SHEDDING SEAS OF GORE . . . . . 113 3 DON JUAN 8 3 8
OF THEIR SALT VEINS AND THEIR SAD SHALLOW SEAS . . . 251 3 DON JUAN 10 54 V4
THEY RUN BEFORE THE WIND THROUGH HIGH SEAS BREAKING . . 442 3 DON JUAN 14 74 6
IF SOME COLUMBUS OF THE MORAL SEAS . . . . 455 3 DON JUAN 14 101 7
AS DEEP SEAS IN A SUNNY ATMOSPHERE . . . . 545 3 DON JUAN 16 94 8
SEA-SHORE
THE SEA-SHORE AT THIS HOUR MUST LEAVE HIS PLATE . . . 240 2 DON JUAN 2 159 5
SHE DREAM'D OF BEING ALONE ON THE SEA-SHORE . . . . 361 2 DON JUAN 4 31 1
SEA-SICK
(HERE THE SHIP GAVE A LURCH AND HE GREW SEA-SICK) . . 166 2 DON JUAN 2 19 8
OF ALL THE LUCKLESS LANDSMEN'S SEA-SICK MAWS . . . . 174 2 DON JUAN 2 34 6
AND SEA-SICK PASSENGERS TURNED SOMEWHAT PALE . . . . 256 3 DON JUAN 10 64 5
SEA-SICKNESS
AGAINST SEA-SICKNESS TRY IT SIR BEFORE . . . . . 163 2 DON JUAN 2 13 6
SEA-SICKNESS DEATH HIS LOVE WAS PERFECT HOW ELSE . . . 168 2 DON JUAN 2 23 6
SEA-SOLICITOR
LAMBRO OUR SEA-SOLICITOR WHO HAD . . . . 289 2 DON JUAN 3 26 1
SEASON
WHERE ALL IS VIRTUE AND THE WINTER SEASON . . . . . 57 2 DON JUAN 1 64 2
SUMMER'S INDEED A VERY DANGEROUS SEASON . . . . . 76 2 DON JUAN 1 102 2
FOR REASON THINKS ALL REASONING OUT OF SEASON . . . . 437 2 DON JUAN 5 48 4
PERHAPS BECAUSE OUR APPELLANTS MADE OUT OF SEASON . . 437 2 DON JUAN 5 48 V4
NO DOUBT IN PROPER PLACE AND TIME AND SEASON . . . . 454 2 DON JUAN 5 74 7
THROUGHOUT THE SEASON UPON SPECULATION . . . . . 293 3 DON JUAN 11 49 2
TASTES THEIR FIRST SEASON (MOSTLY IF THEY HAVE MONEY) . 330 3 DON JUAN 12 31 8
FOR THE FIRST SEASON SUCH A LIFE SCARCE PALLS . . . . 342 3 DON JUAN 12 57 8
WHICH IS THAT THERE IS SCARCE A SINGLE SEASON . . . . 370 3 DON JUAN 13 26 3
THE VERY SEASON RISES AND SUBSIDES . . . . 378 3 DON JUAN 13 43 V7
THE DUKE OF D-- THE SHOOTING SEASON SPENDS . . . . 382 3 DON JUAN 13 52 5
THE SEASON RATHER THAN TO WINTER DREAR-- . . . . . 395 3 DON JUAN 13 77 4
WHEREAS INSISTING IN OR OUT OF SEASON . . . . . . 478 3 DON JUAN 15 51 5
SEASON'D
SEASON'D HIS PEDLAR POEMS WITH DEMOCRACY . . . . . 329 2 DON JUAN 3 93 4
SEASONED
BUT JUAN SEASONED AS WELL MIGHT BE . . . . 256 3 DON JUAN 10 64 6
SEASONING
ALSO A SEASONING SLIGHT OF LUCUBRATION . . . . . 416 3 DON JUAN 14 14 2
SEASON'S
A BEAUTY AT THE SEASON'S CLOSE GROWN HECTIC . . . . 309 2 DON JUAN 3 66 1
PERHAPS THE SEASON'S CHILL AND THEIR LONG STATION . . 176 3 DON JUAN 8 128 6
SEASONS
THE USUAL HIRSUTE SEASONS WHICH DESTROY . . . . . 209 3 DON JUAN 9 53 3
SEAT
SHE SUNK DOWN ON HER SEAT BY SLOW DEGREES . . . . . 59 3 DON JUAN 6 107 7

```
                                                                   PAGE VOL      CANTO STANZA LN
SEAT    (CONTINUED)
      SMOOTHED FOR A MONARCH'S SEAT OF HONOUR GAY . . . . . . . 235  3 DON JUAN 10     21    6
      DEPARTURE FOR HIS COUNTRY SEAT TO-DAY . . . . . . . . . . 382  3 DON JUAN 13     51    7
      TO BE ASSEMBLED AT A COUNTRY SEAT . . . . . . . . . . . . 402  3 DON JUAN 13     94    2
SEATED
      AND DULY SEATED ON THE IMMORTAL HILL . . . . . . . . . .  12   2 DON JUAN  D      6    8
      WHILE SEATED AFTER DINNER AT HIS EASE . . . . . . . . . . 24   2 DON JUAN  1      6    5
      AND SEATED HER ALL DROOPING BY HIS SIDE . . . . . . . . . 484  2 DON JUAN  5    126    4
      OF LOVE WHEN SEATED ON HIS LOVELIEST THRONE . . . . . . . 13   3 DON JUAN  6     15    6
      HER SPIRIT SEEM'D AS SEATED ON A THRONE . . . . . . . . . 477  3 DON JUAN 15     47    6
      (WHEN SEATED NEXT HIM) OF SOME PRETTY LISPER  . . . . . . 487  3 DON JUAN 15     70    8
SEATS
      THE BENCH TOO SEATS OR SUITS FULL MANY A DEBTOR  . . . .  280  3 DON JUAN 11     25    5
      AS ALSO BONFIRES MADE OF COUNTRY SEATS . . . . . . . . .  281  3 DON JUAN 11     27    3
      BUT SEATS A NATION OR UPSETS A THRONE . . . . . . . . . . 318  3 DON JUAN 12      6    4
SEA-WORTHY
      BUT STILL SEA-WORTHY SKIFF AND SHE MAY FLOAT . . . . . .  227  3 DON JUAN 10      4    7
SECLUSION
      YOU--GENTLEMEN BY DINT OF LONG SECLUSION . . . . . . . .  12   2 DON JUAN  D      5    1
SECOND
      WITH THE EXCEPTION OF THE SECOND LINE . . . . . . . . .   69   2 DON JUAN  1     88    6
      THE SECOND DRUNK THE THIRD SO QUAINT AND MOUTHEY . . . .  139  2 DON JUAN  1    205    4
      THE SUM OF THEIR SENSATIONS TO A SECOND . . . . . . . .   254  2 DON JUAN  2    187    4
      A SECOND HICCUP'D OUR OLD MASTER'S DEAD . . . . . . . .   297  2 DON JUAN  3     43    5
      OF WHICH THE FIRST NE'ER KNOWS THE SECOND CAUSE . . . .   318  2 DON JUAN  3     82    8
      THE SECOND HAD HIS CHEEK LAID OPEN BUT  . . . . . . . .   370  2 DON JUAN  4     49    1
      A SECOND PRINCIPLE OF LIFE WHICH MIGHT  . . . . . . . .   382  2 DON JUAN  4     70    2
      BENIGN CERULEANS OF THE SECOND SEX . . . . . . . . . . .  403  2 DON JUAN  4    108    2
      AND ALSO WHEN MY SECOND RAN AWAY . . . . . . . . . . . .  420  2 DON JUAN  5     19    8
      A SECOND TIME DESIRED HIM TO KNEEL DOWN . . . . . . . .   470  2 DON JUAN  5    102    3
      AND THIS STRONG SECOND CAUSE (TO TIRE NO LONGER . . . .   488  2 DON JUAN  5    133   V7
      HER SECOND TO CUT ONLY HIS--ACQUAINTANCE . . . . . . . .  491  2 DON JUAN  5    139    2
      THE SECOND OBJECT WAS TO PROFIT BY . . . . . . . . . . .  78   3 DON JUAN  7     24    1
      ONE BARK BLEW UP A SECOND NEAR THE WORKS . . . . . . . .  81   3 DON JUAN  7     30    7
      YOUR NAME BEFORE THE SECOND IS A NEW ONE . . . . . . . .  97   3 DON JUAN  7     60    5
      FELL IN WITH WHAT WAS LATE THE SECOND COLUMN . . . . . .  130  3 DON JUAN  8     34    2
      EGAD THEY FOUND THE SECOND TIME WHAT THEY . . . . . . .   134  3 DON JUAN  8     42    1
      THE FIRST WITH SIGHS THE SECOND WITH AN OATH . . . . . .  166  3 DON JUAN  8    109    3
      HIS SECOND SON WAS LEVELLED BY A SHOT . . . . . . . . .   166  3 DON JUAN  8    110    2
      AND THE SAD SECOND MOON GROWS DIM AGAIN . . . . . . . .   168  3 DON JUAN  8    113    4
      AFTER WHICH SHADOWS THE--SAY--SECOND YEAR . . . . . . .   220  3 DON JUAN  9     75   V8
      BORN IN A SECOND WEDLOCK AND ABOVE . . . . . . . . . . .  240  3 DON JUAN 10     32    7
      AND SINCE THAT TIME THERE HAS NOT BEEN A SECOND . . . .   365  3 DON JUAN 13     13    8
      AS IF 'TWOULD TO A SECOND SPRING RESIGN . . . . . . . .   395  3 DON JUAN 13     77    3
      THE SECOND MAY BE SADLY DONE OR GAILY . . . . . . . . .   465  3 DON JUAN 15     21    4
      A SECOND FOR HER EXCELLENT CONNEXIONS . . . . . . . . .   471  3 DON JUAN 15     34    7
      TWIN OPPOSITES THE SECOND IS THE BEST . . . . . . . . .   494  3 DON JUAN 15     87    4
      OR OLD INDULGE MAN WITH A SECOND SIGHT . . . . . . . . .  496  3 DON JUAN 15     90    6
      BELOW STAIRS ON THE SCORE OF SECOND COURSES . . . . . .   534  3 DON JUAN 16     68    4
SECONDED
      BEFORE BEING BADLY SECONDED JUST THEN) . . . . . . . . .  151  3 DON JUAN  8     79    3
SECONDLY
      AND SECONDLY I PITY NOT BECAUSE . . . . . . . . . . . .   113  2 DON JUAN  1    167    1
      THAT CLAUSE IS HARD) AND SECONDLY PROCEED . . . . . . .   393  3 DON JUAN 13     73    6
      AND SECONDLY MUST LET SLIP NO OCCASION  . . . . . . . .   404  3 DON JUAN 13     98    3
SECOND'S
      UPON THE FOE THE SECOND'S ORDINATION . . . . . . . . . .  91   3 DON JUAN  7     50    5
SECRET
      THE SECRET CAVERN OF THIS LURKING TREASURE--  . . . . .   104  2 DON JUAN  1    153    7
      OF SECRET TREASURES FOUND IN HIDDEN VALES . . . . . . .   293  2 DON JUAN  3     34    3
      FROM WHICH THE SECRET NOBODY COULD RIP . . . . . . . . .  496  2 DON JUAN  5    149    5
      BE READY BY THE SECRET PORTAL'S SIDE . . . . . . . . . .  62   3 DON JUAN  6    113    3
      THIS SECRET CHARGE ON JUAN TO DISPLAY . . . . . . . . .   247  3 DON JUAN 10     46    3
      'TWAS MERELY KNOWN THAT ON A SECRET MISSION . . . . . .   283  3 DON JUAN 11     32    5
      THE ENVOY OF THE SECRET RUSSIAN MISSION . . . . . . . .   382  3 DON JUAN 13     52    8
      TO THE UNKNOWN A SECRET PREPOSSESSION . . . . . . . . .   413  3 DON JUAN 14      6    6
      AND SMILING BUT IN SECRET--CUNNING ROGUE . . . . . . . .  426  3 DON JUAN 14     37    6
      TO TRACE ALL ACTIONS TO THEIR SECRET SPRINGS . . . . . . 436  3 DON JUAN 14     59    5
      NO DOUBT THE SECRET INFLUENCE OF THE SEX . . . . . . . . 451  3 DON JUAN 14     93    1
SECRETARIES
      THEIR STATION THERE WERE VALETS SECRETARIES . . . . . .   249  3 DON JUAN 10     51    2
SECRETARY
      A SECRETARY--LAP DOG AND A BULL DOG--AND . . . . . . . .  249  3 DON JUAN 10     50   V1
SECRETS
      DEEP SECRETS TO HER ROLLING LIGHT ARE TOLD . . . . . . .  506  3 DON JUAN 16     14    6
SECT
      JOANNA SOUTHCOTE'S SHILOH AND HER SECT . . . . . . . . .  330  2 DON JUAN  3     95    4
      OR NO 'TIS SAID HIS SECT IS RICH AND GODLY . . . . . . .  472  3 DON JUAN 15     36    4
SECTION
      THAT HORRID EQUINOX THAT HATEFUL SECTION . . . . . . . .  238  3 DON JUAN 10     27    4
SECTIONS
      JUST NOW YOUR'S WERE CUT OUT IN DIFFERENT SECTIONS  . . . 215  3 DON JUAN  9     65    5
SECTS
      RELIGION  YES BUT WHICH OF ALL HER SECTS . . . . . . . . 495  3 DON JUAN 15     89    8
SECUNDUM
      SECUNDUM ARTEM BUT ALTHOUGH WE SNEER . . . . . . . . . .  245  3 DON JUAN 10     42    2
SECURE
      AND MATRONS WHO WOULD BE NO LESS SECURE . . . . . . . .   64   2 DON JUAN  1     79    4
      THESE TO SECURE IN THIS STRONG BLOWING WEATHER . . . . .  285  2 DON JUAN  3     18    7
```

705

SECURE   (CONTINUED)
        GOLD CUPS OF FILIGREE MADE TO SECURE   307   2 DON JUAN   3   63   5
        MORE TO SECURE THEM IN THEIR NAVAL CELLS   393   2 DON JUAN   4   91   5
        AND SCARCE SECURE AS SUCH DIGRESSIONS ARE FAIR   65   2 DON JUAN   6   120   7
        THE FACT'S ABOUT THE SAME I AM SECURE   70   3 DON JUAN   7   8   3
        DONE I'LL NOT QUIT HER TILL SHE SEEMS SECURE   161   3 DON JUAN   8   100   2
        DON JUAN WAS DELIGHTED TO SECURE   335   3 DON JUAN 12   41   6
        NOUGHT AGAINST EITHER AND BOTH SEEMED SECURE--   365   3 DON JUAN 13   14   7
        SECURE OF ADMIRATION ITS IMPRESSION   372   3 DON JUAN 13   31   7
SECURED
        AND IF THEY HAD THEY COULD NOT HAVE SECURED   254   2 DON JUAN   2   187   3
        WE FOR SOME MOMENTS HAD SECURED OUR SKIN   435   2 DON JUAN   5   44   V4
SECURITY
        WHERE TRANSPORT AND SECURITY ENTWINE   69   2 DON JUAN   1   88   2
        FOR THAT SAME TWINING TRANSPORT AND SECURITY   69   2 DON JUAN   1   88   7
        BUT BEG SECURITY WILL BOLT THE DOOR   69   2 DON JUAN   1   89   8
SEDATE
        TO A SEDATE GREY CIRCLE OF OLD SMOKERS   293   2 DON JUAN   3   34   2
        BUT JUST REMARKED WITH AIR SEDATE AND WISE   500   2 DON JUAN   5   155   5
        OF HOT OR COLD MERCURIAL OR SEDATE   327   3 DON JUAN 12   24   2
        TO PUT THE QUESTION WITH AN AIR SEDATE   515   3 DON JUAN 16   35   6
SEDATIVE
        SITS LIKE A SEDATIVE WHILE WE RECALL   505   3 DON JUAN 16   11   V3
SEDGES
        AND SEDGES BROODING IN THEIR LIQUID BED   385   3 DON JUAN 13   57   6
SEDIMENT
        LEAVES A SAD SEDIMENT OF TIME'S WORST SAND   457   3 DON JUAN 15   4   8
SEDUCE
        BECAUSE HE NE'ER SEEM'D ANXIOUS TO SEDUCE   461   3 DON JUAN 15   12   2
SEDUCED
        SEDUCED BY YOUTH AND DANGEROUS EXAMPLES   236   3 DON JUAN 10   23   2
SEDUCTIVE
        HIS MANNER WAS PERHAPS THE MORE SEDUCTIVE   461   3 DON JUAN 15   12   1
SEE
        CADIZ PERHAPS--BUT THAT YOU SOON MAY SEE--   25   2 DON JUAN   1   8   6
        TO SEE A KINGDOM OR A HOUSE O'ERTURN'D   31   2 DON JUAN   1   19   6
        JULIA WAS--YET I NEVER COULD SEE WHY--   58   2 DON JUAN   1   66   1
        SHE VOW'D SHE NEVER WOULD SEE JUAN MORE   63   2 DON JUAN   1   76   1
        WHETHER IT WAS SHE DID NOT SEE OR WOULD NOT   73   2 DON JUAN   1   97   7
        'TIS SWEET TO SEE THE EVENING STAR APPEAR   87   2 DON JUAN   1   122   5
        WHOM I SEE STANDING THERE AND LOOKING SENSIBLE   103   2 DON JUAN   1   151   4
        WERE MASCULINE TO SEE THEM AND TO SEIZE   121   2 DON JUAN   1   181   4
        IF YOU WOULD LIKE TO SEE THE WHOLE PROCEEDINGS   127   2 DON JUAN   1   189   1
        WE'LL SEE HOWEVER WHAT THEY SAY TO THIS   135   2 DON JUAN   1   199   4
        WHICH OUT OF ALL THE LOVELY THINGS WE SEE   144   2 DON JUAN   1   214   3
        TO SEE ONE'S NATIVE LAND RECEDING THROUGH   163   2 DON JUAN   2   12   2
        OF ITS OWN THIRST TO SEE AGAIN THY SHORE   166   2 DON JUAN   2   18   4
        WATER AND WINE AND FOOD--AND YOU MIGHT SEE   194   2 DON JUAN   2   72   6
        HE WISH'D THAT LAND HE NEVER MIGHT SEE MORE   207   2 DON JUAN   2   97   4
        A BETTER SWIMMER YOU COULD SCARCE SEE EVER   211   2 DON JUAN   2   105   5
        AND 'TIS NO DOUBT A SIGHT TO SEE WHEN BREAKS   230   2 DON JUAN   2   139   4
        HIM PAST ALL BOUNDS BECAUSE SHE SMILED TO SEE   239   2 DON JUAN   2   158   3
        JUST IN THE WAY WE VERY OFTEN SEE   244   2 DON JUAN   2   167   8
        TO SEE HER BIRD REPOSING IN HIS NEST   245   2 DON JUAN   2   168   4
        TO WATCH HIM SLUMBERING AND TO SEE HIM WAKE   247   2 DON JUAN   2   173   4
        YOU WAKE WITH HEAD-ACHE YOU SHALL SEE WHAT THEN . . .   250   2 DON JUAN   2   179   8
        SUCH WORTHIES TIME WILL NEVER SEE AGAIN   266   2 DON JUAN   2   206   6
        TO SEE HIS ORDERS DONE TOO OUT OF HAND--   299   2 DON JUAN   3   47   3
        'TIS BEAUTIFUL TO SEE A MATRON BRING   306   2 DON JUAN   3   60   3
        BUT TO MY SUBJECT--LET ME SEE--WHAT WAS IT--   317   2 DON JUAN   3   81   5
        WOULD BE OLD GOETHE'S--(SEE WHAT SAYS DESTAEL)   320   2 DON JUAN   3   86   6
        I SEE THEIR GLORIOUS BLACK EYES SHINE   326   2 DON JUAN   3 L 15   3
        AND YOU SHALL SEE WHO HAS THE PROPEREST NOTION   336   2 DON JUAN   3   104   4
        FROM ARISTOTLE PASSIM--SEE POIETIKES   342   2 DON JUAN   3   111   8
        NOT WHAT THEY SAW BUT WHAT THEY WISH'D TO SEE   347   2 DON JUAN   4   7   4
        THE CHILD DIVIDED IT WERE LESS TO SEE   349   2 DON JUAN   4   10   V5
        OR I AT LEAST SHALL NOT SURVIVE TO SEE   356   2 DON JUAN   4   23   8
        SENSELESS TO FEEL AND WITH SEAL'D EYES TO SEE   360   2 DON JUAN   4   30   8
        AND WHO CAN KNOW ALL FALSE WHAT THEN WE SEE   360   2 DON JUAN   4   30   V8
        WITH JOY AND SORROW HOPE AND FEAR TO SEE   363   2 DON JUAN   4   36   2
        THEN LOOK'D CLOSE AT THE FLINT AS IF TO SEE   365   2 DON JUAN   4   40   6
        AND NOW TO SEE THEM THUS DIVIDED STAND   368   2 DON JUAN   4   45   5
        ANOTHER TIME HE MIGHT HAVE LIKED TO SEE 'EM   384   2 DON JUAN   4   75   7
        MY OWN MERITS AND THOUGH YOUNG--I SEE SIR--YOU   392   2 DON JUAN   4   88   2
        SURELY 'TIS NOTHING WONDERFUL TO SEE   421   2 DON JUAN   5   20   4
        SAID JUAN BUT I REALLY DON'T SEE HOW   422   2 DON JUAN   5   23   2
        TO-MORROW'D SEE US IN SOME OTHER DEN   435   2 DON JUAN   5   44   5
        AND THERE YOU SEE THIS TURN HAS BROUGHT US THROUGH . .   436   2 DON JUAN   5   45   7
        (FOR SUCH EXAGGERATIONS HERE AND THERE I SEE)   446   2 DON JUAN   5   61   6
        IN THAT REMOTE RECESS WHICH YOU MAY SEE--   450   2 DON JUAN   5   66   7
        TO SEE THEM TRUE BELIEVERS BUT NO LESS   452   2 DON JUAN   5   70   2
        AND BABA SMILINGLY EXCLAIMED YOU SEE SIRS   458   2 DON JUAN   5   80   4
        BLOCKHEAD COME ON AND SEE QUOTH BABA WHILE   459   2 DON JUAN   5   83   1
        AND I MUST SAY I NE'ER COULD SEE THE VERY   469   2 DON JUAN   5   100   7
        AS YOU WILL SEE IF SHE YOU LOVE SHALL BRING HERS . . .   472   2 DON JUAN   5   106   6
        WHATE'ER SHE DID NOT SEE IF SHE SUPPOSED   476   2 DON JUAN   5   113   2
        THOUGH HORRIBLE TO SEE YET GRAND TO TELL   489   2 DON JUAN   5   135   5
        I SEE YOU'VE BOUGHT ANOTHER GIRL 'TIS PITY   500   2 DON JUAN   5   155   7
        AND SEE A SENTIMENTAL PASSION GLOW   14   3 DON JUAN   6   17   4

SEE (CONTINUED)

	PAGE	VOL	CANTO	STANZA	LN
ALTHOUGH THEY COULD NOT SEE THROUGH HIS DISGUISE	25	3	DON JUAN 6	38	5
REPLIED KATINKA I AM SURE I SEE	30	3	DON JUAN 6	48	3
BUT THERE SHE SLEPT NOT QUITE SO FAIR TO SEE	41	3	DON JUAN 6	69	5
YOU SURELY ARE UNWELL CHILD WE MUST SEE	46	3	DON JUAN 6	80	6
IF PEOPLE WOULD BUT SEE ITS REAL DRIFT--	50	3	DON JUAN 6	88	2
WHAT ARE YE--WHAT YOU SEE US BRIEFLY PAST	97	3	DON JUAN 7	59	6
TO SEE AN OLD MAN RATHER WILD THAN WISE	104	3	DON JUAN 7	73	5
TO SEE THE SULTAN RICH IN MANY A GEM	104	3	DON JUAN 7	74	4
SWORE THEY SHOULD SEE HIM BY THE DAWN OF DAY	105	3	DON JUAN 7	75	5
BEING MUCH TOO GROSS TO SEE THEM IN DETAIL	105	3	DON JUAN 7	77	2
WE SHALL NOT SEE HIS LIKENESS HE COULD KILL HIS	132	3	DON JUAN 8	39	4
TO SEE IN FORTS OF NETHERLANDS OR FRANCE--	136	3	DON JUAN 8	46	5
OF HIS OPINION WHEN I SEE CAST DOWN	142	3	DON JUAN 8	60	4
WITHOUT RESISTANCE SEE THEIR CITY BURN	150	3	DON JUAN 8	77	4
THE GOOD OLD KHAN WHO LONG HAD CEASED TO SEE	169	3	DON JUAN 8	116	2
AND WONDER WHAT OLD WORLD SUCH THINGS COULD SEE	180	3	DON JUAN 8	137	4
AND SEE HIS STATUE RAISED--AND PRINT ENGRAVED	185	3	DON JUAN 9	5	V8
AND DEEM BECAUSE WE SEE WE ARE ALL-SEEING	190	3	DON JUAN 9	16	4
UNTIL I SEE BOTH SIDES FOR ONCE AGREEING	190	3	DON JUAN 9	16	6
ARISE WHEN WE SEE EMPERORS FALL WITH OATS	198	3	DON JUAN 9	32	8
I SAY WILL THESE GREAT RELICS WHEN THEY SEE 'EM	202	3	DON JUAN 9	40	7
CATHERINE I SAY WAS VERY GLAD TO SEE	211	3	DON JUAN 9	57	5
REPLIED THAT SHE WAS GLAD TO SEE HIM THROUGH	240	3	DON JUAN 10	31	5
BUT SEE THE WORLD IS ONLY ONE ATTORNEY	281	3	DON JUAN 11	28	8
(SEE BILLINGSGATE) MADE EVEN THE TONGUE MORE FREE	288	3	DON JUAN 11	42	8
BOTH SENATES SEE THEIR NIGHTLY VOTES PARTICIPATED	306	3	DON JUAN 11	75	5
TO SEE IT--THE KING HISSED AND THEN CAREST	309	3	DON JUAN 11	83	7
NOT WHAT YOU SEEM BUT ALWAYS WHAT YOU SEE	310	3	DON JUAN 11	86	8
YE WHO BUT SEE THE SAVING MAN AT TABLE	316	3	DON JUAN 12	3	5
'TIS FINE TO SEE THEM SCATTERING REFUSALS	332	3	DON JUAN 12	34	2
PRAY DID YOU SEE HER ANSWER TO HIS LETTER	332	3	DON JUAN 12	35	8
SEE NOUGHT MORE STRANGE IN THIS THAN T'OTHER LOTTERY	333	3	DON JUAN 12	37	8
THAT TILL WE SEE WHAT'S WHAT IN FACT WE'RE FAR	335	3	DON JUAN 12	40	4
YOU MAY SEE SUCH AT ALL THE BALLS AND DINNERS	346	3	DON JUAN 12	66	5
HE KNEW THE WORLD AND WOULD NOT SEE DEPRAVITY	368	3	DON JUAN 13	22	5
INDEED WE SEE THE DAILY PROOF DISPLAYED	371	3	DON JUAN 13	29	4
AND THUS WE SEE--WHO DOUBTS THE MORNING POST	383	3	DON JUAN 13	53	1
THE VACANCIES ARE FILLED UP--SEE GAZETTE	383	3	DON JUAN 13	54	8
I HAVE SEEN MORE THAN I'LL SAY--BUT WE WILL SEE	397	3	DON JUAN 13	83	1
THE GRAND ARCANUM'S NOT FOR MEN TO SEE ALL	419	3	DON JUAN 14	22	5
LOOKED GRAVE AND PALE TO SEE HER FRIEND'S FRAGILITY	430	3	DON JUAN 14	46	7
THEN BROKE HIS PACKET TO SEE WHAT WAS IN'T	440	3	DON JUAN 14	69	5
FOR WHICH SEE SHAKSPEARE'S EVER BLOOMING GARDEN--	442	3	DON JUAN 14	75	2
THE FOURTH WE HEAR AND SEE AND SAY TOO DAILY	465	3	DON JUAN 15	21	6
A MAN LIKE WHOM I HOPE WE SHAN'T SEE MANY SOON	484	3	DON JUAN 15	65	4
(SEE LITTLETON) WHENE'ER I HAVE EXPRESSED	494	3	DON JUAN 15	87	2
TO SEE MEN LET THESE SCOUNDREL SOVEREIGNS BREAK LAW	497	3	DON JUAN 15	92	8
GRIM READER DID YOU EVER SEE A GHOST	498	3	DON JUAN 15	95	1
AND DID HE SEE THIS OR WAS IT A VAPOUR	510	3	DON JUAN 16	22	8
SO MUCH DISTRAIT HE WAS THAT ALL COULD SEE	513	3	DON JUAN 16	30	6
IN COURTESY THEIR WISH TO SEE DISPLAYED	517	3	DON JUAN 16	39	5
MATCHED FOR THE SPRING WHOM SEVERAL WENT TO SEE	527	3	DON JUAN 16	55	8
AND SCARLET CLOAK (I HATE THE SIGHT TO SEE SINCE--	530	3	DON JUAN 16	61	4
YOU SEE HERE WAS ENOUGH OF OCCUPATION	534	3	DON JUAN 16	68	1
YET SAW THIS MUCH WHICH HE WAS GLAD TO SEE	553	3	DON JUAN 16	106	8
I SEE--I SEE--AH NO--'TIS NOT--YET 'TIS--	556	3	DON JUAN 16	112	2
I SEE--I SEE--AH NO--'TIS NOT--YET 'TIS--	556	3	DON JUAN 16	112	2

SEED

	PAGE	VOL	CANTO	STANZA	LN
AND THERE PERHAPS SOME SEED IS SOWN	325	2	DON JUAN 3	L 13	5
WHOSE FANGS EVE TAUGHT HER HUMAN SEED TO FEEL	153	3	DON JUAN 8	83	4
ARE APT EXCEEDINGLY TO RUN TO SEED	445	3	DON JUAN 14	81	8

SEEING

	PAGE	VOL	CANTO	STANZA	LN
MISTAKE YOU WOULD HAVE MADE ON SEEING THE TWO	232	2	DON JUAN 2	142	6
ON SEEING HIS OWN CHIMNEY-SMOKE FELT GLAD	289	2	DON JUAN 3	26	3
SEEING A TROOP OF HIS DOMESTICS DANCING	290	2	DON JUAN 3	29	5
BUT SEEING AT HIS ELBOW A MERE LAD	417	2	DON JUAN 5	12	1
SEEING WHAT'S MEANT FOR MANY WITH BUT ONE	443	2	DON JUAN 5	57	8
WHEN SEEING HIM PLACED BY HER SIDE AT LAST	478	2	DON JUAN 5	116	V4
JOHN JOHNSON SEEING THEIR EXTREME DISMAY	105	3	DON JUAN 7	75	1
BUT SEEING FLASHING FORWARD LIKE THE DAY	126	3	DON JUAN 8	30	3
SEEING ARRIVE AN AID SO OPPORTUNE	140	3	DON JUAN 8	56	2
FOR SEEING ONE WITH RIBBONS BLACK AND BLUE	141	3	DON JUAN 8	57	5
SEEING HOW ART CAN MAKE HER WORK MORE GRAND	204	3	DON JUAN 9	44	5
WHO SEEING A HANDSOME STRIPLING WITH SMOOTH FACE	285	3	DON JUAN 11	35	5
UPON MY FIDDLE--SEEING IF ALL'S SURE	341	3	DON JUAN 12	54	V7
HE ALSO HAD BEEN BUSY SEEING SIGHTS--	353	3	DON JUAN 12	82	1
IN SEEING MATTERS WHICH ARE OUT OF SIGHT	457	3	DON JUAN 15	2	8
WITHOUT THEIR SEEING WHAT HE WAS ABOUT	492	3	DON JUAN 15	82	8
BUT SEEING HIM ALL COLD AND SILENT STILL	514	3	DON JUAN 16	32	1

SEEK

	PAGE	VOL	CANTO	STANZA	LN
SONG IN THE WORLD WILL SEEK WHAT THEN THEY SOUGHT	402	2	DON JUAN 4	106	4
WHERE IF MEN SEEK HER NOT AND DEATH BE MORE	143	3	DON JUAN 8	62	4
AND DROVE THEM WITH THEIR BRUTAL YELLS TO SEEK	158	3	DON JUAN 8	94	2
OH GENTLE LADIES SHOULD YOU SEEK TO KNOW	207	3	DON JUAN 9	49	1
AND YET I SEEK NOT TO BE GRAND NOR WITTY--	233	3	DON JUAN 10	17	6
PERHAPS--BUT SANS PERHAPS WE NEED NOT SEEK	243	3	DON JUAN 10	38	1
BUT IN THE COUNTRY LADIES SEEK THEIR BOWER	409	3	DON JUAN 13	111	3

SEEKERS

	PAGE	VOL	CANTO	STANZA	LN
'TIS ODD NOT ONE OF ALL THESE SEEKERS THOUGHT	100	2	DON JUAN 1	144	6

SEEKING

	PAGE	VOL	CANTO	STANZA	LN
SEEKING FAR LESS TO SAVE YOU THAN TO HURT YOU	337	3	DON JUAN 12	45	3
IS THAT FOR WHICH THE SEX ARE ALWAYS SEEKING	442	3	DON JUAN 14	74	2
AS SEEKING NOT TO KNOW IT SILENT LONE	476	3	DON JUAN 15	47	2

SEEM

	PAGE	VOL	CANTO	STANZA	LN
BUT THEN THEY ONLY SEEM SO MANY BROTHERS	63	2	DON JUAN 1	77	8
THIS MAY SEEM STRANGE BUT YET 'TIS VERY COMMON	74	2	DON JUAN 1	98	1
SO THAT I SEEM TO STAND UPON THE CEILING)	156	2	DON JUAN 1	V 8	6
SEEM AT THE SAME TIME MYSTICAL AND GAY	220	2	DON JUAN 2	120	8
LEST THEY SHOULD SEEM PRINCESSES IN DISGUISE	222	2	DON JUAN 2	124	2
BUT SEEM THE GROWTH OF A MOST DIFFERENT CLIME	277	2	DON JUAN 3	5	V4
LET NOT HIS MODE OF RAISING CASH SEEM STRANGE	283	2	DON JUAN 3	14	1
IT MAY SEEM STRANGE TO FIND HIS MANNERS BLAND	299	2	DON JUAN 3	47	5
AND STILL THEY SEEM RESENTFULLY TO FEEL	313	2	DON JUAN 3	73	5
SWEET PLAYFUL PHRASES WHICH WOULD SEEM ABSURD	351	2	DON JUAN 4	14	7
O'ERPOWERING US TO BE WHATE'ER MAY SEEM	360	2	DON JUAN 4	30	5
AND IN SUCH COLOURS THAT THEY SEEM TO LIVE	402	2	DON JUAN 4	107	6
NEED NOT SEEM VERY WONDERFUL FOR VICE	408	2	DON JUAN 4	115	5
THE ONLY GENTLEMEN SEEM I AND YOU	417	2	DON JUAN 5	13	5
THE CIRCUMSTANCES SEEM THE SPORT OF MEN	419	2	DON JUAN 5	17	8
TWO OR THREE SEEM SO LITTLE ONE SEEMS NOTHING	443	2	DON JUAN 5	57	1
IF ANY TAKE ME FOR THAT WHICH I SEEM	459	2	DON JUAN 5	82	6
AND RAPTURE'S SELF WILL SEEM ALMOST A PAIN	474	2	DON JUAN 5	110	4
WHICH MADE HIM SEEM EXCEEDINGLY ILL-BRED	483	2	DON JUAN 5	124	4
THESE MUST SEEM DOUBLY MINDFUL OF THEIR VOWS	500	2	DON JUAN 5	154	5
WOMEN ON T'OTHER HAND SEEM SOMEWHAT SILLY	14	3	DON JUAN 6	16	8
AND PHANTOMS HOVERED OR MIGHT SEEM TO HOVER	41	3	DON JUAN 6	70	6
OR THE SENSATION (IF THAT PHRASE SEEM WRONG)	123	3	DON JUAN 8	24	4
THAT WHICH A PORTAL TO THEIR EYES DID SEEM--	148	3	DON JUAN 8	72	6
BUT SOMEHOW--IT MAY SEEM A SCHOOLBOY'S WHINE	233	3	DON JUAN 10	17	5
MADE ICE SEEM PARADISE AND WINTER SUNNY	235	3	DON JUAN 10	21	8
LET NOT THIS SEEM AN ANTI-CLIMAX--OH	254	3	DON JUAN 10	59	1
WITH SLIGHT EXCEPTIONS ALL THE WAYS SEEM ONE	279	3	DON JUAN 11	23	4
NOT WHAT YOU SEEM BUT ALWAYS WHAT YOU SEE	310	3	DON JUAN 11	86	8
MANKIND JUST NOW SEEM WRAPT IN MEDITATION	325	3	DON JUAN 12	21	4
SHE MADE THE EARTH BELOW SEEM HOLY GROUND	387	3	DON JUAN 13	61	5
IF ALL THESE SEEM AN HETEROGENEOUS MASS	402	3	DON JUAN 13	94	1
AND THEY MUST BE OR SEEM WHAT THEY WERE STILL	417	3	DON JUAN 14	17	4
OR IF THE OATH SEEM STRONG--I SWEAR BY JOVE	452	3	DON JUAN 14	96	V2
WHAT THOUGH ON LETHE'S STREAM HE SEEM TO FLOAT	457	3	DON JUAN 15	4	5
AND SEEM TO SAY RESIST US IF YOU CAN--	461	3	DON JUAN 15	12	7
THOUGH LADIES' ROBES SEEM SCANT ENOUGH FOR LESS	482	3	DON JUAN 15	61	8
THE CHARMING OF THESE CHARMERS WHO SEEM BOUND	518	3	DON JUAN 16	40	2
AND HE DID NOT SEEM FORMED OF CLAY	518	3	DON JUAN 16	L 2	6
AND THEY SEEM OF A PARTED SOUL	519	3	DON JUAN 16	L 4	8
NOR SEEM EMBARRASSED--QUITE THE CONTRARY	545	3	DON JUAN 16	94	2

SEEM'D

	PAGE	VOL	CANTO	STANZA	LN
REQUIRED THIS CONDUCT--WHICH SEEM'D VERY ODD	35	2	DON JUAN 1	27	8
AND SEEM'D AT LEAST IN THE RIGHT ROAD TO HEAVEN	48	2	DON JUAN 1	49	6
AT LEAST IT SEEM'D SO AND HIS MOTHER'S JOY	49	2	DON JUAN 1	50	6
TALL HANDSOME SLENDER BUT WELL KNIT HE SEEM'D	51	2	DON JUAN 1	54	2
SHE SEEM'D BY THE DISTRACTION OF HER AIR	80	2	DON JUAN 1	110	4
AND NO GREAT GOOD SEEM'D ANSWER'D IF SHE STAID	116	2	DON JUAN 1	173	6
AS DAY ADVANCED THE WEATHER SEEM'D TO ABATE	172	2	DON JUAN 2	30	1
THERE SHE LAY MOTIONLESS AND SEEM'D UPSET	172	2	DON JUAN 2	31	1
THEIR DESPERATE EFFORTS SEEM'D ALL USELESS GROWN	176	2	DON JUAN 2	38	6
IT SEEM'D AS IF THEY HAD EXCHANGED THEIR CARE	186	2	DON JUAN 2	56	3
A DROP OF DEW WHEN EVERY DROP HAD SEEM'D	202	2	DON JUAN 2	86	6
BRIGHTEN'D AND FOR A MOMENT SEEM'D TO ROAM	203	2	DON JUAN 2	89	6
NIGHT FELL--THIS SEEM'D A BETTER OMEN STILL	206	2	DON JUAN 2	94	8
AND SEEM'D AS IF THEY HAD NO FURTHER CARE	208	2	DON JUAN 2	98	4
LOVELY SEEM'D ANY OBJECT THAT SHOULD SWEEP	210	2	DON JUAN 2	103	7
AND TINGLING VEIN SEEM'D THROBBING BACK TO LIFE	214	2	DON JUAN 2	111	7
SEEM'D ALMOST PRYING INTO HIS FOR BREATH	215	2	DON JUAN 2	113	2
THAT SLEEP WHICH SEEM'D AS IT WOULD NE'ER AWAKE	234	2	DON JUAN 2	146	8
THAT BATHING PASS'D FOR NOTHING JUAN SEEM'D	247	2	DON JUAN 2	172	2
HER FATHER'S HOSPITALITY SEEM'D MIDDLING	295	2	DON JUAN 3	39	5
WHO SEEM'D TO HAVE TURN'D HAIDEE INTO A MATRON	298	2	DON JUAN 3	44	8
THIS REVEL SEEM'D A CURIOUS MODE OF MOURNING	300	2	DON JUAN 3	49	8
THE VERY AIR SEEM'D LIGHTER FROM HER EYES	313	2	DON JUAN 3	74	2
AND YET THE FOREST LEAVES SEEM'D STIRR'D WITH PRAYER	335	2	DON JUAN 3	102	8
THE HEAVENS AND EARTH AND AIR SEEM'D MADE FOR THEM	351	2	DON JUAN 4	13	2
THAT LARGE BLACK PROPHET EYE SEEM'D TO DILATE	355	2	DON JUAN 4	22	1
WHATEVER FEELING SHOOK HER IT SEEM'D SHORT	356	2	DON JUAN 4	23	3
AND O'ER HER UPPER LIP THEY SEEM'D TO POUR	361	2	DON JUAN 4	31	5
OF HER BLACK EYES SEEM'D TURN'D TO TEARS AND MURK	362	2	DON JUAN 4	33	6
WERE ONCE HER CARES HOW IDLE SEEM'D THEY NOW)	362	2	DON JUAN 4	34	4
SHE HAD NO PULSE BUT DEATH SEEM'D ABSENT STILL	377	2	DON JUAN 4	60	3
NEW THOUGHTS OF LIFE FOR IT SEEM'D FULL OF SOUL	377	2	DON JUAN 4	60	7
RATHER THE DEAD FOR LIFE SEEM'D SOMETHING NEW	378	2	DON JUAN 4	62	2
SENSES TO SLEEP--THE POWER SEEM'D GONE FOREVER	381	2	DON JUAN 4	68	8
ALL SAVE THE BLACKS SEEM'D JADED WITH VEXATION	414	2	DON JUAN 5	7	5
WHICH FOR HIMSELF HE SEEM'D TO DEEM NO WORSE	417	2	DON JUAN 5	12	7
THE DICE SEEM'D CHARM'D TOO WITH HIS REPARTEES	399	3	DON JUAN 13	86	8
UNTO SUCH FEELINGS AS SEEM'D INNOCENT	460	3	DON JUAN 15	10	7
BECAUSE HE NE'ER SEEM'D ANXIOUS TO SEDUCE	461	3	DON JUAN 15	12	2
WAS SUCH AS RATHER SEEM'D TO KEEP ALOOF	462	3	DON JUAN 15	14	3
WHO SEEM'D THE CREAM OF EQUANIMITY	474	3	DON JUAN 15	41	3
HER SPIRIT SEEM'D AS SEATED ON A THRONE	477	3	DON JUAN 15	47	6

```
                                                        PAGE VOL    CANTO  STANZA LN
SEEM'D   (CONTINUED)
     HER BEAUTY ALSO SEEM'D TO FORM NO CLOG  . . . . . .  477  3 DON JUAN 15    48    5
     IF--BUT HERE ADELINE WHO SEEM'D TO PIQUE . . . . . .  478  3 DON JUAN 15    50    5
SEEMED
     THE CAPTIVES SEEMED TO MARK THEIR LOOKS AND AGE  . . . .  424  2 DON JUAN  5    26    3
     HE SEEMED TO SLEEP FOR YOU COULD SCARCELY TELL . . . . .  430  2 DON JUAN  5    35    5
     THERE SEEMED TO BE BESPRENT A DEAL OF GILDING  . . . .  436  2 DON JUAN  5    46    3
     AND SOME SEEMED MUCH IN LOVE WITH THEIR OWN DRESS  . . .  441  2 DON JUAN  5    53    4
     IT SEEMED HOWEVER BUT TO OPEN ON  . . . . . . .  449  2 DON JUAN  5    65    1
     WHICH FORTUNE PLAINLY SEEMED TO RECOMMEND  . . . . .  451  2 DON JUAN  5    69    5
     IT SEEMED AS THOUGH THEY CAME UPON A SHRINE . . . . .  460  2 DON JUAN  5    85    7
     AT WHICH HE SEEMED NO WHIT SURPRISED NOR GRIEVED  . . .  500  2 DON JUAN  5   155    4
     AND FEET SO SMALL THEY SCARCE SEEMED MADE TO TREAD  . .   26  3 DON JUAN  6    41    4
     A KIND OF SLEEPY VENUS SEEMED DUDU . . . . . . .   27  3 DON JUAN  6    42    1
     FOR SHE SEEMED AGITATED FLUSHED AND FRIGHTENED . . . .   42  3 DON JUAN  6    72    7
     I'VE KNOWN SOME ODD ONES WHICH SEEMED REALLY PLANNED . .   45  3 DON JUAN  6    78    5
     BUT THERE SEEMED SOMETHING THAT HE WISHED TO HIDE  . . .   56  3 DON JUAN  6   100    5
     AND YET HE SHUDDERED AND SEEMED RATHER PRONE  . . . .   62  3 DON JUAN  6   112    4
     FOR EVERYTHING SEEMED RESTING ON HIS NOD . . . . .  104  3 DON JUAN  7    74    1
     ADDRESSING HIM IN TONES WHICH SEEMED TO THANK  . . . .  141  3 DON JUAN  8    57    7
     BUT HERE IT SEEMED HIS JOKES HAD CEASED TO TAKE  . . .  147  3 DON JUAN  8    70    8
     WITH MARTIAL STOICISM NOUGHT SEEMED TO ANNOY . . . . .  172  3 DON JUAN  8   121    5
     AND STILL MORE IN HIS EYE WHICH SEEMED TO EXPRESS  . . .  206  3 DON JUAN  9    47    4
     'TIS VERY TRUE THE HILL SEEMED RATHER HIGH . . . . .  215  3 DON JUAN  9    66    5
     SEEMED TAKING OUT THE STING TO LEAVE THE HONEY . . . .  217  3 DON JUAN  9    70    8
     ALONG HIS WASTED CHEEK AND SEEMED TO GRAVEL  . . . .  245  3 DON JUAN 10    43    7
     WAS JUAN WHOM SHE SEEMED TO HAVE SELECTED  . . . .  252  3 DON JUAN 10    57    2
     I HAVE SEEN NAPOLEON WHO SEEMED QUITE A JUPITER  . . .  309  3 DON JUAN 11    83    1
     SEEMED TO HIM HALF COMMERCIAL HALF PEDANTIC . . . . .  347  3 DON JUAN 12    68    5
     NOUGHT AGAINST EITHER AND BOTH SEEMED SECURE-- . . . .  365  3 DON JUAN 13    14    7
     AND NEXT A QUARREL (AS HE SEEMED TO FRET) . . . . .  437  3 DON JUAN 14    62    7
     WITH TWO TRANSCENDANT EYES SEEMED TO LOOK THROUGH HIM . .  489  3 DON JUAN 15    75    8
     THROUGH WHICH THE SPECTRE SEEMED TO EVAPORATE  . . . .  511  3 DON JUAN 16    24    8
     HE STOOD--HOW LONG HE KNEW NOT BUT IT SEEMED . . . . .  511  3 DON JUAN 16    25    1
     BUT FOR THE REST AS HE HIMSELF SEEMED LOTH . . . . .  514  3 DON JUAN 16    33    6
     HE SEEMED UNCONSCIOUS OF ALL PASSING THERE . . . . .  542  3 DON JUAN 16    87    6
     THE FAIR FITZ-FULKE SEEMED VERY MUCH AT EASE . . . .  548  3 DON JUAN 16   100    2
     VOI CHE ENTRATE THE HINGE SEEMED TO SPEAK  . . . .  557  3 DON JUAN 16   116    3
     THE GHOST IF GHOST IT WERE SEEMED A SWEET SOUL . . . .  561  3 DON JUAN 16   123    1
     SEEMED PALE AND SHIVERED AS IF SHE HAD KEPT  . . . .  568  3 DON JUAN 17    14    7
     OF THOSE IN WHICH THE BODY SEEMED TO DRIVE . . . . .  569  3 DON JUAN 17  V 13    5
SEEMING
     BY HIS SEEMING INDEPENDENT IN HIS LAYS  . . . . .  316  2 DON JUAN  3    79    6
     SEEMING TO WEEP THE DYING DAY'S DECAY .  . . . . .  338  2 DON JUAN  3   108    6
     FOR FEAR OF SEEMING RATHER TOUCH'D MYSELF-- . . . . .  384  2 DON JUAN  4    74    4
     BY SPECIOUS SEEMING JUAN'S YOUTH AND PATIENCE  . . . .  365  3 DON JUAN 13    15    5
     PERHAPS SHE WAS ASHAMED OF SEEMING FRAIL . . . . .  532  3 DON JUAN 16    64    5
     THOUGH SEEMING SO FROM ITS SUPPOSED FACILITY . . . .  547  3 DON JUAN 16    97    6
SEEMS
     AND SEEMS TO ME ALMOST A SORT OF BLUNDER . . . . . .  100  2 DON JUAN  1   144    7
     AND CAMPBELL'S SPRING SEEMS SOMEWHAT DRY AND DROUTHY . . .  139  2 DON JUAN  1   205  V6
     NOW SHRINKING BACK NOW MIDST THE FIRST HE SEEMS  . . .  155  2 DON JUAN  1  V  6    5
     WHICH THEN SEEMS AS IF THE WHOLE EARTH IT BOUNDED  . . .  252  2 DON JUAN  2   183    3
     I CAN'T BUT SAY IT SEEMS TO ME MOST TRULY A . . . .  267  2 DON JUAN  2   208    3
     FOR OFTENTIMES WHEN PEGASUS SEEMS WINNING  . . . .  344  2 DON JUAN  4     1    3
     THE SITUATION SEEMS STILL FORM'D FOR FAME-- . . . . .  386  2 DON JUAN  4    77    5
     IT SEEMS WHEN THIS ALLOTMENT WAS MADE OUT  . . . .  394  2 DON JUAN  4    92    1
     LIFE SEEMS THE SMALLEST PORTION OF EXISTENCE . . . .  398  2 DON JUAN  4   100    3
     MEANTIME (YON OLD BLACK EUNUCH SEEMS TO EYE US)  . . .  423  2 DON JUAN  5    24    7
     TWO OR THREE SEEM SO LITTLE ONE SEEMS NOTHING  . . . .  443  2 DON JUAN  5    57    1
     SEEMS FERTILE IN ADVENTURES STRANGE AND NEW  . . . .  459  2 DON JUAN  5    83    6
     IT SEEMS THE WORK OF TIMES BEFORE THE LINE . . . . .  461  2 DON JUAN  5    86    7
     WHATE'ER THY POWER AND GREAT IT SEEMS TO BE . . . . .  484  2 DON JUAN  5   127    6
     SOMETIMES AT SIX YEARS OLD--THOUGH THIS SEEMS ODD  . .  498  2 DON JUAN  5   152    6
     FOR SO IT SEEMS TO LOVERS SWIFT OR SLOW  . . . . .   14  3 DON JUAN  6    17    2
     ALTHOUGH HIS SITUATION NOW SEEMS STRANGE . . . . .   65  3 DON JUAN  6   120    6
     IT SEEMS HAS GOT AN EAR AS WELL AS TRUMPET . . . . .   74  3 DON JUAN  7    15    8
     DONE I'LL NOT QUIT HER TILL SHE SEEMS SECURE . . . .  161  3 DON JUAN  8   100    2
     SEEMS LOVE TURNED A LIEUTENANT OF ARTILLERY  . . . .  204  3 DON JUAN  9    44    8
     ON WHICH THE PASSION'S SELF SEEMS TO DEPEND  . . . .  219  3 DON JUAN  9    73    6
     O'ERSPREADS THE CHEEK WHICH SEEMS TOO PURE FOR CLAY  . .  229  3 DON JUAN 10     8    7
     LIKE BANQUO'S OFFSPRING--FLOATING PAST ME SEEMS  . . .  233  3 DON JUAN 10    18    6
     GOOD GOVERNMENT HAS LEFT THEM SEEMS BUT CRUEL  . . . .  256  3 DON JUAN 10    63    8
     SO WELL THE VERY TRUTH SEEMS FALSEHOOD TO IT  . . . .  285  3 DON JUAN 11    36    8
     WHOSE SHAMROCK NOW SEEMS RATHER WORSE FOR WEARING  . . .  286  3 DON JUAN 11    38    8
     IN ISLANDS IS IT SEEMS DOWNRIGHT AND THOROUGH  . . . .  288  3 DON JUAN 11    42    6
     MY LEIPSIC AND MY MONT SAINT JEAN SEEMS CAIN . . . .  296  3 DON JUAN 11    56    2
     GONE DOWN IT SEEMS TO SCOTLAND TO BE FIDDLED . . . .  307  3 DON JUAN 11    78    5
     TO ME SEEMS BUT A DUBIOUS KIND OF REED . . . . . .  324  3 DON JUAN 12    18    5
     WHATE'ER ASTONISHMENT THIS SEEMS TO CALL . . . . .  333  3 DON JUAN 12    37   V6
     IT SEEMS THE VIRGIN'S HEART EXPECTS YOUR HAND  . . . .  343  3 DON JUAN 12    60    6
     HIS LORDSHIP'S JUSTICE--SEEMS NOT THAT OF SOLOMON-- . . .  357  3 DON JUAN 12  V 18    7
     ALTHOUGH IT SEEMS BOTH PROMINENT AND PLEASANT  . . . .  416  3 DON JUAN 14    15    5
     WHICH SEEMS AT FIRST TO NEED NO LOFTY WING . . . . .  467  3 DON JUAN 15    25    3
     OF ONE OR BOTH OF WHOM HE SEEMS THE HEIR . . . . .  481  3 DON JUAN 15    59    8
     WHICH SEEMS TO HINT YOU ARE NOT WORTH A THOUGHT  . . . .  490  3 DON JUAN 15    77    4
     OR NONE AT ALL--WHICH SEEMS A SORRY JEST . . . . .  494  3 DON JUAN 15    87    6
     BUT NOW IT SEEMS HE'S RIGHT--HIS NOTION JUST . . . .  565  3 DON JUAN 17     8    7
SEEN
     WE ALL HAVE SEEN HIM IN THE PANTOMIME. . . . . . . .   21  2 DON JUAN  1     1    7
```

SEEN   (CONTINUED)

		PAGE	VOL	CANTO	STANZA	LN
WHO HAS NOT SEEN IT WILL BE MUCH TO PITY		25	2	DON JUAN	1	8	3
BUT I MUST LEAVE THE PROOFS TO THOSE WHO'VE SEEN 'EM		28	2	DON JUAN	1	14	4
WHAT OPPOSITE DISCOVERIES WE HAVE SEEN		91	2	DON JUAN	1	129	1
BUT THIS WILL MORE PECULIARLY BE SEEN)		137	2	DON JUAN	1	202	5
AS THEY DREW NIGH THE LAND WHICH NOW WAS SEEN		210	2	DON JUAN	2	103	1
AND SLOWLY BY HIS SWIMMING EYES WAS SEEN		215	2	DON JUAN	2	112	7
AND BY HIS EYES--THOUGH SLOWLY--THERE WAS SEEN		215	2	DON JUAN	2	112	V7
HAD NEVER SEEN THE MAID OR WHATSOE'ER		216	2	DON JUAN	2	115	7
EVER TO HAVE SEEN SUCH FOR SHE WAS ONE		218	2	DON JUAN	2	118	4
I'VE SEEN MUCH FINER WOMEN RIPE AND REAL		218	2	DON JUAN	2	118	7
I'VE SEEN HIM RISE FULL OFT INDEED OF LATE		230	2	DON JUAN	2	140	2
THE ONLY THING OF THIS SORT EVER SEEN		288	2	DON JUAN	3	25	4
I'VE SEEN A FRIEND BETRAYED FOUR TIMES A DAY		288	2	DON JUAN	3	25	V8
A TASTE SEEN IN THE CHOICE OF HIS ABODE		304	2	DON JUAN	3	56	4
AMIDST THE SAVAGE DEEDS HE HAD DONE AND SEEN		304	2	DON JUAN	3	57	4
MERIDIAN-LIKE WERE SEEN ALL LIGHT TO ISSUE		309	2	DON JUAN	3	67	8
WITH GREAT MAGNIFICENCE WERE SEEN TO ISSUE		309	2	DON JUAN	3	67	V8
HE WAS A MAN WHO HAD SEEN MANY CHANGES		317	2	DON JUAN	3	80	1
I HAVE SEEN SUCH--BUT MUST NOT CALL TO MIND		363	2	DON JUAN	4	36	8
I HAVE SEEN SOME SUCH--BUT THEY UNHINGED MY MIND		363	2	DON JUAN	4	36	V8
OF WHICH SOME GILDED REMNANTS STILL WERE SEEN		415	2	DON JUAN	5	9	4
AND THOUGH I HAVE SEEN MANY CORPSES NEVER		430	2	DON JUAN	5	35	2
(OF WHICH I HAVE ALSO SEEN SOME SIX OR SEVEN)		465	2	DON JUAN	5	94	4
IT MIGHT BE SEEN WITH DILIGENCE WAS SOUGHT		476	2	DON JUAN	5	113	3
AND ALL WHO HAVE SEEN A HUMAN NURSERY SAW		488	2	DON JUAN	5	133	5
I'VE RARELY SEEN THE MAN THEY DID NOT FRET		16	3	DON JUAN	6	21	8
I MIGHT DESCRIBE AS I HAVE SEEN IT ALL		31	3	DON JUAN	6	51	4
I'VE SEEN YOUR STORMY SEAS AND STORMY WOMEN		32	3	DON JUAN	6	53	7
HER NECK ALONE WAS SEEN BUT THAT WAS FOUND		48	3	DON JUAN	6	85	3
ALL THE ATTENTION POSSIBLE AND SEEN		102	3	DON JUAN	7	70	4
MORE FEARED THAN ALL THE SULTANS EVER SEEN		104	3	DON JUAN	7	73	8
NOUGHT TO BE SEEN SAVE THE ARTILLERY'S FLAME		115	3	DON JUAN	8	6	2
ARISTOCRATIC AS WAS EVER SEEN		116	3	DON JUAN	8	10	4
AND WHERE THE HOTTEST FIRE WAS SEEN AND HEARD		129	3	DON JUAN	8	33	5
FOR CHECQUERED AS IS SEEN OUR HUMAN LOT		156	3	DON JUAN	8	89	3
ON EARTH IN PARADISE AND WHEN ONCE SEEN		167	3	DON JUAN	8	111	6
HAVE SEEN AND FELT HOW STRONGLY YOU RESTORE		184	3	DON JUAN	9	3	6
MOST WILLINGLY ALL EVER SEEN OR READ MATTERS		268	3	DON JUAN	11	1	V6
OR SEEN TOMBUCTOO OR HATH TAKEN TEA		271	3	DON JUAN	11	7	4
HAD SEEN THE WORLD--WHICH IS A CURIOUS SIGHT		292	3	DON JUAN	11	47	7
I HAVE SEEN MORE CHANGES DOWN FROM MONARCHS TO		309	3	DON JUAN	11	82	2
I HAVE SEEN NAPOLEON WHO SEEMED QUITE A JUPITER		309	3	DON JUAN	11	83	1
SHRINK TO A SATURN I HAVE SEEN A DUKE		309	3	DON JUAN	11	83	2
AND SAIL FOR A NEW THEME--I HAVE SEEN--AND SHOOK		309	3	DON JUAN	11	83	6
I HAVE SEEN THE LANDHOLDERS WITHOUT A RAP--		310	3	DON JUAN	11	84	1
I HAVE SEEN JOHANNA SOUTHCOTE--I HAVE SEEN		310	3	DON JUAN	11	84	2
I HAVE SEEN JOHANNA SOUTHCOTE--I HAVE SEEN		310	3	DON JUAN	11	84	2
I HAVE SEEN THAT SAD AFFAIR OF THE LATE QUEEN--		310	3	DON JUAN	11	84	4
I HAVE SEEN CROWNS WORN INSTEAD OF A FOOL'S CAP--		310	3	DON JUAN	11	84	5
I HAVE SEEN A CONGRESS DOING ALL THAT'S MEAN--		310	3	DON JUAN	11	84	6
I HAVE SEEN SOME NATIONS LIKE O'ERLOADED ASSES		310	3	DON JUAN	11	84	7
I HAVE SEEN SMALL POETS AND GREAT PROSERS AND		310	3	DON JUAN	11	85	1
I HAVE SEEN THE FUNDS AT WAR WITH HOUSE AND LAND--		310	3	DON JUAN	11	85	3
I'VE SEEN THE COUNTRY GENTLEMEN TURN SQUEAKERS--		310	3	DON JUAN	11	85	4
I'VE SEEN THE PEOPLE RIDDEN O'ER LIKE SAND		310	3	DON JUAN	11	85	5
BY SLAVES ON HORSEBACK--I HAVE SEEN MALT LIQUORS		310	3	DON JUAN	11	85	6
I HAVE SEEN JOHN HALF DETECT HIMSELF A FOOL--		310	3	DON JUAN	11	85	8
AT LEAST ENTIRELY FOR HE HAD SEEN TOO MANY		338	3	DON JUAN	12	49	7
BUT HE HAD SEEN SO MUCH GOOD LOVE BEFORE		346	3	DON JUAN	12	67	4
BESIDES HE HAD NOT SEEN OF SEVERAL HUNDRED		353	3	DON JUAN	12	81	3
AND FROM BENEATH HIS BOUGHS WERE SEEN TO SALLY		384	3	DON JUAN	13	56	5
I'VE SEEN A VIRTUOUS WOMAN PUT DOWN QUITE		397	3	DON JUAN	13	82	3
I HAVE SEEN MORE THAN I'LL SAY--BUT WE WILL SEE		397	3	DON JUAN	13	83	1
FOR I HAVE SEEN A PORTION OF THAT SAME		414	3	DON JUAN	14	9	2
ON WHAT I'VE SEEN OR PONDER'D SAD OR CHEERY		415	3	DON JUAN	14	11	6
SEEN BEAUTIES BROUGHT TO MARKET BY THE SCORE		418	3	DON JUAN	14	18	4
I'VE SEEN THEM BALANCE EVEN THE SCALE WITH FIGHTERS		418	3	DON JUAN	14	20	3
'TIS BETTER ON THE WHOLE TO HAVE FELT AND SEEN		431	3	DON JUAN	14	49	5
FOR SHE HAD SEEN THE WORLD AND STOOD ITS TEST		433	3	DON JUAN	14	54	4
ROMANCES I NE'ER READ LIKE THOSE I HAVE SEEN		444	3	DON JUAN	14	80	2
AS SHE HAD SEEN NOUGHT CLAIMING ITS EXPANSION		446	3	DON JUAN	14	85	4
I'VE ALSO SEEN SOME WIVES (NOT TO FORGET)		452	3	DON JUAN	14	95	5
I'VE ALSO SEEN SOME FEMALE FRIENDS ('TIS ODD		452	3	DON JUAN	14	96	1
MUCH AS SHE WOULD HAVE SEEN A GLOWWORM SHINE		480	3	DON JUAN	15	56	3
ALSO THE CONFERENCE WHICH WE HAVE SEEN		489	3	DON JUAN	15	75	5
BECAUSE IT SOMETIMES AS I'VE SEEN OR READ IT		491	3	DON JUAN	15	79	3
BUT RARELY SEEN LIKE GOLD COMPARED WITH PAPER		510	3	DON JUAN	16	22	7
WITH WHAT HE HAD SEEN HIS PHANTASY HE FED		512	3	DON JUAN	16	27	6
FOR HE'S SEEN IN THE PORCH AND HE'S SEEN IN THE CHURCH		518	3	DON JUAN	16	L 2	7
FOR HE'S SEEN IN THE PORCH AND HE'S SEEN IN THE CHURCH		518	3	DON JUAN	16	L 2	7
THOUGH HE IS NOT SEEN BY DAY		518	3	DON JUAN	16	L 2	8
BUT HIS EYES MAY BE SEEN FROM THE FOLDS BETWEEN		519	3	DON JUAN	16	L 4	7
THOUGH ONCE SHE WAS SEEN READING THE BATH GUIDE		525	3	DON JUAN	16	50	2
SOME DEADLY SHOTS TOO SEPTEMBRIZERS SEEN		539	3	DON JUAN	16	80	3
THE LATTER WORSE USED OF THE TWO WE'VE SEEN--		541	3	DON JUAN	16	84	3
THAT HE THE NIGHT BEFORE HAD SEEN A GHOST		543	3	DON JUAN	16	90	2
IN GAY REMARK ON WHAT HE HAD HEARD OR SEEN		552	3	DON JUAN	16	105	5

SEES

| SEES HALF THE BUSINESS IN A WICKED WAY | | 82 | 2 | DON JUAN | 1 | 113 | 6 |

SEES   (CONTINUED)
      OH POWERS OF FORM--WHAT ASPECT SEES SHE THERE . . . . . 363 2 DON JUAN 4   35 V7
      WHAT THAT IS--ASK THE PIG WHO SEES THE WIND . . . . . . 108 3 DON JUAN 7   84 8
      AT LEAST HE FEELS IT AND SOME SAY HE SEES . . . . 109 3 DON JUAN 7   85 1
      TO-MORROW SEES ANOTHER RACE AS GAY . . . . 310 3 DON JUAN 11   86 2
      THEN SEES YOUR HEART WRECKED WITH AN INWARD SCOFFING . . . 345 3 DON JUAN 12   63 4
      AND EVERYBODY SEES THAT WHAT THEY LACK . . . . . . 348 3 DON JUAN 12   71 V4
SEES'T
      WITHIN AND WHAT SEES'T THOU A DUBIOUS SPARK . . . . . 348 3 DON JUAN 12   71 8
SEIZABLE
      NOT SCANDAL'S FANGS COULD FIX ON MUCH THAT'S SEIZABLE . . 66 2 DON JUAN 1   83 3
SEIZE
      WERE MASCULINE TO SEE THEM AND TO SEIZE . . . . . . 121 2 DON JUAN 1   181 4
      SHOULD NOT VEER ROUND WITH EVERY BREATH NOR SEIZE . . . . 231 3 DON JUAN 10   13 7
      BUT SEIZE THE LAST WORD WHICH NO DOUBT'S THE BEST . . . 404 3 DON JUAN 13   98 8
      HER LAUGHING BLUE EYES WITH A GLANCE COULD SEIZE . . . . 548 3 DON JUAN 16   100 4
SEIZED
      HAS MADNESS SEIZED YOU WOULD THAT I HAD DIED . . . . . 98 2 DON JUAN 1   142 3
      HER BEAUTIES SEIZED THE UNCONSCIOUS HOUR OF NIGHT . . . 39 3 DON JUAN 6   66 7
      SEIZED FAST AS IF 'TWERE BY THE SERPENT'S HEAD . . . . 153 3 DON JUAN 8   83 3
      HAD SEIZED THE LUCKY HOUR TO RECONNOITRE . . . . . . 273 3 DON JUAN 11   11 4
      SHE SEIZED HER HARP WHOSE STRINGS WERE KINDLED SOON . . 517 3 DON JUAN 16   38 6
      HER GRACE TOO ALSO SEIZED THE SAME OCCASION . . . . . 526 3 DON JUAN 16   53 4
SEIZES
      A PHANTASY WHICH SOMETIMES SEIZES WARRIORS . . . . . . 78 3 DON JUAN 7   24 7
SELDOM
      A THING WHICH POESY BUT SELDOM MENTIONS . . . . . . 221 2 DON JUAN 2   123 6
      BUT THIS OCCURS BUT SELDOM BETWEEN WHILES . . . . . 238 2 DON JUAN 2   154 5
      WHERE WIVES AT LEAST ARE SELDOM KEPT IN GARRISON . . . 248 2 DON JUAN 2   175 8
      HE--BEING A MAN WHO SELDOM USED A WORD . . . . . . 294 2 DON JUAN 3   37 1
      AND FOR HIS THEME--HE SELDOM SUNG BELOW IT . . . . . 316 2 DON JUAN 3   78 6
      SOME STRESS ON CHARMS WHICH SELDOM ARE IF E'ER . . . . 485 2 DON JUAN 5   129 5
      SELDOM HE VARIED FEATURE HUE OR MUSCLE . . . . . . 132 3 DON JUAN 8   39 7
      BUT DOUBTLESS AS THE AIR THOUGH SELDOM SUNNY . . . . 259 3 DON JUAN 10   70 7
      THEMSELVES ON SELDOM YIELDING TO TEMPTATION . . . . . 327 3 DON JUAN 12   25 V7
      OF HIS OWN COUNTRY--SELDOM SINCE THAT DAY . . . . . 364 3 DON JUAN 13   11 3
      BORN WITH THAT HAPPY SOUL WHICH SELDOM FAINTS . . . . 424 3 DON JUAN 14   31 5
      GRACE OF THE SOFT IDEAL SELDOM SHOWN . . . . 428 3 DON JUAN 14   40 6
      ALAS BY ALL EXPERIENCE SELDOM YET . . . . 452 3 DON JUAN 14   95 1
      NOT THE LESS PRECIOUS THAT WE SELDOM HEAR IT . . . . 518 3 DON JUAN 16   40 8
      HEROES SOMETIMES THOUGH SELDOM--SAGES NEVER . . . . 547 3 DON JUAN 16   98 2
      BUT SELDOM PAY THE ABSENT NOR WOULD LOOK . . . . . 553 3 DON JUAN 16   106 4
SELECT
      OF ALL THE DRESSES I SELECT HAIDEE'S . . . . 311 2 DON JUAN 3   70 1
      TO ENTERTAIN THIS AUTUMN A SELECT . . . . 382 3 DON JUAN 13   52 2
      FROM THESE THEY WILL BE CAREFUL TO SELECT . . . . . 471 3 DON JUAN 15   34 1
      SLIGHT BUT SELECT AND JUST ENOUGH TO EXPRESS . . . . 491 3 DON JUAN 15   80 2
SELECTED
      SELECTED FOR DISCRETION AND DEVOTION . . . . 51 2 DON JUAN 1   55 2
      ALL WHICH SELECTED FROM THE SPOIL HE GATHERS . . . . 284 2 DON JUAN 3   17 7
      WAS JUAN WHOM SHE SEEMED TO HAVE SELECTED . . . . . 252 3 DON JUAN 10   57 2
      TO FIND HOW VERY BADLY SHE SELECTED . . . . 333 3 DON JUAN 12   36 8
SELF
      IN WHICH NOT ENVY'S SELF A FLAW DISCOVERS . . . . . 29 2 DON JUAN 1   16 6
      EVEN PETRARCH'S SELF IF JUDGED WITH DUE SEVERITY . . . 411 2 DON JUAN 5   1 7
      NAY QUOTH THE MAID THE SULTAN'S SELF SHAN'T CARRY ME . . 460 2 DON JUAN 5   84 7
      AND RAPTURE'S SELF WILL SEEM ALMOST A PAIN . . . . . 474 2 DON JUAN 5   110 4
      TO MEDITATE UPON THEIR SINS AND SELF . . . . 41 3 DON JUAN 6   69 8
      ACHILLES' SELF WAS NOT MORE GRIM AND GORY . . . . . 73 3 DON JUAN 7   14 6
      AND SELF WOULD KNOW WHAT DUTY TO ATTEND . . . . . 100 3 DON JUAN 7   65 8
      BEAUTY SPRINGS FORTH AND NATURE'S SELF TURNS PALER . . 204 3 DON JUAN 9   44 4
      (FELLOWS WHOM MESSALINA'S SELF WOULD PENSION) . . . . 218 3 DON JUAN 9   72 4
      ON WHICH THE PASSION'S SELF SEEMS TO DEPEND . . . . 219 3 DON JUAN 9   73 6
      AND PASSION'S SELF MUST HAVE A SPICE OF FRANTIC . . . 347 3 DON JUAN 12   68 4
      THE MANSION'S SELF WAS VAST AND VENERABLE . . . . . 389 3 DON JUAN 13   66 1
      EVEN NIMROD'S SELF MIGHT LEAVE THE PLAINS OF DURA . . 395 3 DON JUAN 13   78 5
      OF YOUR OWN THOUGHTS IN ALL THEIR SELF CONFESSION . . 413 3 DON JUAN 14   6 4
      THE HUNTSMAN'S SELF RELENTED TO A GRIN . . . . . 425 3 DON JUAN 14   34 7
      BUT VIRTUE'S SELF WITH ALL HER TIGHTEST LACES . . . 494 3 DON JUAN 15   85 5
      EVEN MY VERACIOUS SELF--BUT THAT'S A LIE . . . . . 495 3 DON JUAN 15   88 3
      WAS TO RESTORE HIM TO HIS SELF PROPRIETY . . . . . 526 3 DON JUAN 16   52 2
SELF-APPROBATION
      AND WHY BECAUSE IT BRINGS SELF-APPROBATION . . . . . 114 3 DON JUAN 8   4 1
SELF-COMMUNION
      HIS SELF-COMMUNION WITH HIS OWN HIGH SOUL . . . . . 70 2 DON JUAN 1   91 2
SELF-CONTROL
      OF CALLING WHOLLY BACK ITS SELF-CONTROL . . . . . 82 2 DON JUAN 1   114 4
SELF-DECEITFUL
      HOW SELF-DECEITFUL IS THE SAGEST PART . . . . . . 78 2 DON JUAN 1   106 5
SELF-DEFENCE
      IN SELF-DEFENCE--THIS MADE HIM MEDITATIVE . . . . . 277 3 DON JUAN 11   18 8
SELF-DENIAL
      THEN THERE'S MORE MERIT IN HIS SELF-DENIAL . . . . . 319 3 DON JUAN 12   7 8
SELF-DIRECTOR
      AN ALL-IN-ALL-SUFFICIENT SELF-DIRECTOR . . . . . . 29 2 DON JUAN 1   15 3
SELF-INTEREST
      THE SAME SELF-INTEREST WITH A DIFFERENT LEANING) . . . 535 3 DON JUAN 16   70 8
SELFISH
      SELFISH IN ITS BEGINNING AS ITS END . . . . 219 3 DON JUAN 9   73 2
      OF FRAIL HUMANITY--MUST MAKE US SELFISH . . . . . . 236 3 DON JUAN 10   23 7

		PAGE	VOL	CANTO	STANZA	LN
SELFISHNESS						
HAS MUCH OF SELFISHNESS AND MORE SUSPICION		420	3	DON JUAN 14	24	6
SELF-LOVE						
NOR COIN MY SELF-LOVE TO SO BASE A VICE		12	2	DON JUAN D	6	2
SELF-LOVE IN MAN TOO BEATS ALL FEMALE ART		15	3	DON JUAN 6	19	5
SELF-LOVE THAT WHETSTONE OF DAN CUPID'S DART		15	3	DON JUAN 6	19	V5
SELF-LOVE--WHICH WHEN SOME SORT OF THING ABOVE		216	3	DON JUAN 9	68	3
SELF-LOVE THERE'S SAFETY IN A CROWD OF COXCOMBS		371	3	DON JUAN 13	30	8
WITH SELF-LOVE IN THE CENTRE AS THEIR POLE		455	3	DON JUAN 14	102	4
SELF-LOVES						
AND KNEW THE SELF-LOVES OF THE DIFFERENT NATIONS		319	2	DON JUAN 3	84	2
SELF-POSSESSION						
SUCH WAS HER COLDNESS OR HER SELF-POSSESSION		480	3	DON JUAN 15	57	8
SELF-REBUKES						
HE GAIN'D NO POINT EXCEPT SOME SELF-REBUKES		110	2	DON JUAN 1	161	5
SELF-SAME						
ALSO AROSE ABOUT THE SELF-SAME TIME		51	3	DON JUAN 6	90	1
THEY FOUND ON THEIR RETURN THE SELF-SAME WELCOME		134	3	DON JUAN 8	42	7
CANONIZATION FOR THE SELF-SAME CAUSE		319	3	DON JUAN 12	7	5
HAD ENGLISH INFLUENCE IN THE SELF-SAME SPHERE HERE		534	3	DON JUAN 16	70	5
SELF-SLAUGHTER						
BUT CHIEFLY BY A SPECIES OF SELF-SLAUGHTER		210	2	DON JUAN 2	102	7
SELF-SOLD						
A SCRIBBLING SELF-SOLD SOUL-HIRED SCORNED ISCARIOT		15	2	DON JUAN D	11	V8
SELF-WILL						
THERE WAS A SELF-WILL EVEN IN HER SMALL FEET		475	2	DON JUAN 5	111	3
SELL						
AS WHEN HE SWORE BY GOD HE'D SELL HIS SHIRT		154	2	DON JUAN 1	V 5	3
WITH SLAVES TO SELL OFF IN THE CAPITAL		407	2	DON JUAN 4	113	2
SELL FLESH AND BLOOD WHEN DINNER HAS OPPREST ONE		426	2	DON JUAN 5	30	6
SELLER						
RATHER THAN SELLER HAD HIS WANTS BEEN FEWER		528	3	DON JUAN 16	57	5
SELLS						
THEY HAVE A KING WHO BUYS AND SELLS		325	2	DON JUAN 3	L 14	2
SELVES						
OUR LITTLE SELVES RE-FORM'D IN FINER CLAY		305	2	DON JUAN 3	59	4
TO THEIR TWO SELVES ONE WHOLE BRIGHT BULLETIN		121	3	DON JUAN 8	19	8
THEIR HIDEOUS WIVES THEIR HORRID SELVES AND DRESSES		550	3	DON JUAN 16	103	7
SEMIRAMIS						
AND THE CALUMNIATED QUEEN SEMIRAMIS--		445	2	DON JUAN 5	60	8
SEMPER						
A FOOLISH CLEVER FELLOW IDEM SEMPER		150	2	DON JUAN 1	V 1	8
CHANGEABLE TOO--YET SOMEHOW IDEM SEMPER		567	3	DON JUAN 17	11	3
SEMPRONIUS						
BUT DO YOU MORE SEMPRONIUS--DON'T DESERVE IT		366	3	DON JUAN 13	18	2
SEMPSTRESS						
BEHAVED NO BETTER THAN A COMMON SEMPSTRESS		221	3	DON JUAN 9	77	8
SENATE						
WHO BOUND THE BAR OR SENATE IN THEIR SPELL		307	3	DON JUAN 11	77	4
THE SENATE WHICH TIBERIUS MET OF OLD--		314	3	DON JUAN 11	V 76	8
AND SENATE WHEN INVITED ELSEWHERE TRULY		398	3	DON JUAN 13	84	3
SENATES						
BULLY IN SENATES SKULKER IN THE FIELD		151	2	DON JUAN 1	V 2	1
SENATES AND SAGES HAVE CONDEMNED ITS USE--		256	3	DON JUAN 10	63	5
BOTH SENATES SEE THEIR NIGHTLY VOTES PARTICIPATED		306	3	DON JUAN 11	75	5
IN SENATES AT THE BAR IN WORDY FEUD		371	3	DON JUAN 13	29	5
SENATORS						
WITH DANDIES DINED HEARD SENATORS DECLAIMING		418	3	DON JUAN 14	18	3
SEND						
NO--NO--I'D SEND HIM OUT BETIMES TO COLLEGE		50	2	DON JUAN 1	52	7
AND SEND HIM LIKE A DOVE OF PROMISE FORTH		161	2	DON JUAN 2	8	8
AND SEND HIM FORTH LIKE SAMSON--STRONG IN BLINDNESS		304	2	DON JUAN 3	57	V8
OR THREE OR TWO OR ONE SEND VERY FAR		432	2	DON JUAN 5	39	3
AND SEND THE SENTINEL BEFORE YOUR GATE		185	3	DON JUAN 9	6	3
SHE THEN RESOLVED TO SEND HIM ON A MISSION		246	3	DON JUAN 10	44	7
I COULD SEND FORTH MY MANDATE LIKE A PRIMATE		327	3	DON JUAN 12	24	3
SENDS						
WHEN EVERY YEAR AND MONTH SENDS FORTH A NEW ONE		21	2	DON JUAN 1	1	2
SENDS SIN WITHOUT A RAG ON SHIVERING FORTH		57	2	DON JUAN 1	64	3
HEAVEN HELP THE SCHOLAR WHOM HIS FORTUNE SENDS HERE		423	2	DON JUAN 5	24	4
AND SENDS NEW WERTERS YEARLY TO THEIR COFFIN		345	3	DON JUAN 12	63	6
SENEGAL						
SHIP OFF THE HOLY THREE TO SENEGAL		446	3	DON JUAN 14	83	2
SENHOR						
THE SENHOR DON ALFONSO STOOD CONFUSED		109	2	DON JUAN 1	159	1
SENNAE						
AQ FERVENT OUNCE AND A HALF TWO DRAMS TINCT SENNAE		244	3	DON JUAN 10	41	3
SENSATION						
WAS MANIFESTED IN A GREAT SENSATION		38	2	DON JUAN 1	33	8
SHOULD EVER GIVE HER HEART THE LEAST SENSATION		63	2	DON JUAN 1	77	4
A STRANGE SENSATION WHICH SHE MUST PARTAKE		378	2	DON JUAN 4	62	3
AND WHEN A STRONG ALTHOUGH A STRANGE SENSATION		480	2	DON JUAN 5	120	2
OR THE SENSATION (IF THAT PHRASE SEEM WRONG)		123	3	DON JUAN 8	24	4
AND NOW THERE WAS A GENERAL SENSATION		329	3	DON JUAN 12	28	7
BUT TAKE AN ELL--AND MAKE A GREAT SENSATION		404	3	DON JUAN 13	98	5
THE WILD SENSATION UNTO HER A NEW ONE		449	3	DON JUAN 14	91	4
PARTLY PERHAPS BECAUSE A FRESH SENSATION		468	3	DON JUAN 15	28	4
TO PAINT A SOLE SENSATION--THOUGH QUITE COMMON--		569	3	DON JUAN 17	V 13	4
EXPIRING IN THE HOPE OF SENSATION--		569	3	DON JUAN 17	V 13	7

SENSATIONS
    THE SUM OF THEIR SENSATIONS TO A SECOND . . . . . . 254 2 DON JUAN 2   187   4
    WHICH GAVE ME SOME SENSATIONS LIKE A VILLAIN . . . . 268 2 DON JUAN 2   209   8
    AND SWEET SENSATIONS SHOULD HAVE WELCOMED BOTH . . . 368 2 DON JUAN 4   45   7
    A MIXTURE OF SENSATIONS MIGHT BE SCANNED . . . . . . 473 2 DON JUAN 5   108   7
    OF OUR SENSATIONS WHAT A CURIOUS WAY . . . . 220 3 DON JUAN 9   75   7
    OF SUCH SENSATIONS IN THE DROWSY DREAR . . . . . . 220 3 DON JUAN 9   75 V7
SENSE
    TO THE GOOD SENSE AND SENSES OF MANKIND . . . . . . 69 2 DON JUAN 1   89   2
    IN THE DESIGN AND AS I HAVE A HIGH SENSE . . . . . . 86 2 DON JUAN 1   120   6
    WITHOUT THE SENSE TO KEEP IT FOR AN HOUR . . . . . . 152 2 DON JUAN 1 V 3   8
    WIT WITHOUT SENSE--AND VIOLENCE WITHOUT FORCE . . . . 155 2 DON JUAN 1 V 6 V7
    OUR JUAN WHO WITH SENSE BEYOND HIS YEARS . . . . . . 174 2 DON JUAN 2   35   2
    WHERE HEART AND SOUL AND SENSE IN CONCERT MOVE . . . 254 2 DON JUAN 2   186   5
    OF SENSE AND SONG ABOVE YOUR GRAVES MAY HISS-- . . . 334 2 DON JUAN 3   100   6
    AS BUT TO LOVERS A TRUE SENSE AFFORDS . . . . 351 2 DON JUAN 4   14   6
    IT WAS THEIR VERY SPIRIT--NOT A SENSE . . . . 358 2 DON JUAN 4   27   8
    (IN EACH SENSE OF THE WORD) WHENE'ER I FILL . . . . 372 2 DON JUAN 4   53   6
    BROUGHT BACK THE SENSE OF PAIN WITHOUT THE CAUSE . . 378 2 DON JUAN 4   62   7
    YET SHE BETRAY'D AT TIMES A GLEAM OF SENSE . . . . . 381 2 DON JUAN 4   68   1
    FOR SORROW O'ER EACH SENSE HELD STERN COMMAND . . . 396 2 DON JUAN 4   95   2
    DUDU HAD NEVER PASSED FOR WANTING SENSE . . . . . . 43 3 DON JUAN 6   74   6
    YOUR ORDERS EVEN IN THEIR SEVEREST SENSE . . . . . . 62 3 DON JUAN 6   114   4
    HIS PURSE HIS SOUL HIS SENSE AND EVEN HIS NONSENSE . 88 3 DON JUAN 7   44   7
    TO GRATIFY LIKE A HUGE MOTH THIS ONE SENSE . . . . . 88 3 DON JUAN 7   44   8
    THE SOUND THAN SENSE)--BESIDES ALL THESE PRETENCES . 219 3 DON JUAN 9   74   7
    OR FAME OR NAME FOR WIT WAR SENSE OR NONSENSE . . . 305 3 DON JUAN 11   73   7
    BESIDES THEIR KNOWLEDGE OF THE WORLD AND SENSE . . . 336 3 DON JUAN 12   44   5
    WHILE THOSE WHO ARE NOT BEGINNERS SHOULD HAVE SENSE . 376 3 DON JUAN 13   40   3
    WITH EMPHASIS AND ALSO WITH GOOD SENSE-- . . . . . . 427 3 DON JUAN 14   38   4
    WERE THERE A JOT OF SENSE AMONG MANKIND . . . . . . 446 3 DON JUAN 14   84   6
    GREW FRIENDS IN THIS OR ANY OTHER SENSE . . . . . . 453 3 DON JUAN 14   97   2
    WHEN ADELINE IN ALL HER GROWING SENSE . . . . 468 3 DON JUAN 15   28   1
    HE DAZZLED BUT ASTONISHED NOT HER SENSE . . . . . . 480 3 DON JUAN 15   56 V7
    OF FLUTTERERS THOUGH SHE DEEM'D HE HAD MORE SENSE . 493 3 DON JUAN 15   83   3
    THE POOR PRIEST WAS REDUCED TO COMMON SENSE . . . . 540 3 DON JUAN 16   83   6
    WHO ARE SO IN THE STRICT SENSE OF THE PHRASE . . . 562 3 DON JUAN 17   1   2
SENSELESS
    ROLL'D ON THE BEACH HALF SENSELESS FROM THE SEA . . 212 2 DON JUAN 2   107   8
    SENSELESS TO FEEL AND WITH SEAL'D EYES TO SEE . . . 360 2 DON JUAN 4   30   8
SENSES
    THEIR SENSES THEY'D HAVE SENT YOUNG MASTER FORTH . . 34 2 DON JUAN 1   25   6
    TO THE GOOD SENSE AND SENSES OF MANKIND . . . . . . 69 2 DON JUAN 1   89   2
    SWAM ROUND AND ROUND AND ALL HIS SENSES PASS'D . . . 214 2 DON JUAN 2   110   3
    FOR HIS CONGEALING BLOOD AND SENSES DIM . . . . . . 214 2 DON JUAN 2   111   4
    UPON HIS SENSES AND THE KINDLING BEAM . . . . 237 2 DON JUAN 2   153   5
    BUT BY DEGREES THEIR SENSES WERE RESTORED . . . . . 257 2 DON JUAN 2   191   5
    WITH ONE OR TWO SMALL SENSES ADDED JUST . . . . . . 269 2 DON JUAN 2   212   7
    FOR THE IMAGINATION OR THE SENSES . . . . 293 2 DON JUAN 3   35   2
    BY THE MERE SENSES AND THAT WHICH DESTROYS . . . . 352 2 DON JUAN 4   16   6
    SENSES TO SLEEP--THE POWER SEEM'D GONE FOREVER . . . 381 2 DON JUAN 4   68   8
    TO LOVE THERE ARE THOSE THINGS WHICH WORDS NAME SENSES-- 219 3 DON JUAN 9   74   8
    AS THE SOLE SIGN OF MAN'S BEING IN HIS SENSES . . . 240 3 DON JUAN 10   31   7
    A COUNTRY IN ALL SENSES THE MOST DEAR . . . . 263 3 DON JUAN 10   77   5
    NOTHING MORE TRUE THAN NOT TO TRUST YOUR SENSES . . 411 3 DON JUAN 14   2   7
    AS JUAN SHOULD HAVE KNOWN HAD NOT HIS SENSES . . . . 545 3 DON JUAN 16   93   7
SENSIBILITIES
    NO DOUBT HIS SENSIBILITIES WERE LESS . . . . 353 3 DON JUAN 12   81   8
SENSIBILITY
    FOR WHICH MOST FRIENDS RESERVE THEIR SENSIBILITY . . 430 3 DON JUAN 14   46   8
    PARADING ALL HER SENSIBILITY . . . . 532 3 DON JUAN 16   65   5
SENSIBLE
    WHOM I SEE STANDING THERE AND LOOKING SENSIBLE . . . 103 2 DON JUAN 1   151   4
    I'M SENSIBLE REDUNDANCY IS WRONG . . . . 410 2 DON JUAN 4   117   5
SENSITIVE
    AND ALTHOUGH SENSITIVE TO BEAUTY HE . . . . 481 2 DON JUAN 5   121   7
    WHICH MUST BE OWNED WAS SENSITIVE AND SURLY . . . . 234 3 DON JUAN 10   19   4
    HE FELT LIKE OTHER PLANTS CALLED SENSITIVE . . . . . 243 3 DON JUAN 10   37   2
    'TWILL TEACH DISCERNMENT TO THE SENSITIVE . . . . . 431 3 DON JUAN 14   49   7
SENSUAL
    SERVE A SULTANA'S SENSUAL PHANTASY . . . . 484 2 DON JUAN 5   126   8
    AND STILL LESS WAS IT SENSUAL FOR BESIDES . . . . . 251 3 DON JUAN 10   54   1
    WHILE HE DESPISING EVERY SENSUAL CALL . . . . 320 3 DON JUAN 12   9   7
    THE SENSUAL FOR A SHORT TIME BUT CONNECTS US-- . . . 442 3 DON JUAN 14   73   5
SENT
    SENT TO THE DEVIL SOMEWHAT ERE HIS TIME . . . . . . 21 2 DON JUAN 1   1   8
    THEIR SENSES THEY'D HAVE SENT YOUNG MASTER FORTH . . 34 2 DON JUAN 1   25   6
    HIS HOUSE WAS SOLD HIS SERVANTS SENT AWAY . . . . . 39 2 DON JUAN 1   34   3
    THE MOMENT HE HAS SENT HIS FOOLS AWAY . . . . 114 2 DON JUAN 1   169   2
    SHE SENT HER SON TO BE SHIPP'D OFF FROM CADIZ . . . 128 2 DON JUAN 1   190   8
    JULIA WAS SENT INTO A CONVENT SHE . . . . 129 2 DON JUAN 1   191   6
    JULIA WAS SENT INTO A NUNNERY . . . . 129 2 DON JUAN 1   191 V6
    I SENT IT IN A LETTER TO THE EDITOR . . . . 142 2 DON JUAN 1   210   1
    I SAID THAT JUAN HAD BEEN SENT TO CADIZ-- . . . . . 159 2 DON JUAN 2   5   1
    BUT TO OUR TALE THE DONNA INEZ SENT . . . . 161 2 DON JUAN 2   8   1
    OF HIS DEPARTURE HAD BEEN SENT HIM BY . . . . 169 2 DON JUAN 2   24   7
    HAD SENT THEM THIS FOR THEIR DELIVERANCE . . . . . . 208 2 DON JUAN 2   99   8
    TO HER AS 'TWERE THE KIND OF BEING SENT . . . . . . 247 2 DON JUAN 2   172   3
    HIS DAUGHTER--HAD NOT SENT BEFORE TO ADVISE . . . . 294 2 DON JUAN 3   37   4

			PAGE	VOL		CANTO	STANZA	LN

SENT   (CONTINUED)
    ON SUCH A THING IS SUDDENLY TO SEA SENT . . . . 371 2 DON JUAN 4   51 6
    HER FEELINGS SUDDEN THROUGH HER BOSOM SENT . . . . . . 379 2 DON JUAN 4   65 V6
    HER SALE SENT HOME SOME DISAPPOINTED BAWLERS . . . . . 407 2 DON JUAN 4 114 5
    THE SUN HIMSELF HAS SENT ME LIKE A RAY . . . . 494 2 DON JUAN 5 144 7
    EXCEPT IN SHAPE OF ENVOYS WHO WERE SENT . . . . 498 2 DON JUAN 5 151 1
    THEY LIVED TILL SOME BASHAW WAS SENT ABROAD . . . . . 498 2 DON JUAN 5 152 4
    AND SENT ONE ON A SUMMONS TO THE PAIR . . . . 64 3 DON JUAN 6 118 2
    WHILE THINGS WERE IN ABEYANCE RIBAS SENT . . . . 85 3 DON JUAN 7   38 1
    HE'S A FINE BOY THE WOMEN MAY BE SENT . . . . 100 3 DON JUAN 7   66 7
    AND BEING TOLD THE LATTER SENT A BEY . . . . 171 3 DON JUAN 8 120 7
    WHILE JUAN IS SENT OFF WITH THE DISPATCH . . . . 181 3 DON JUAN 8 139 7
    AND SENT THE DOCTORS IN A NEW DIRECTION . . . . 245 3 DON JUAN 10   43 4
    THE EXACT AFFAIR ON WHICH HE WAS SENT O'ER . . . . . . 283 3 DON JUAN 11   32 4
    AND DRAW THEM NIGHTLY WHEN A TICKET'S SENT . . . . . . 342 3 DON JUAN 12   57 6
    AND DEBT AND WHATNOT FOR THEIR SOLACE SENT . . . . . . 360 3 DON JUAN 13   5 8
    AND AS THE GOOD SHIPS SENT UPON THAT MESSAGE . . . . . 376 3 DON JUAN 13   39 3
    THE PRIZE PIG PLOUGHMAN POACHERS THE MEN SENT . . . . 533 3 DON JUAN 16   66 4
SENTENCE
    THEY LOOKED LIKE PERSONS BEING LED TO SENTENCE . . . . 432 2 DON JUAN 5   40 5
    HER SIXTH TO STAB HERSELF HER SEVENTH TO SENTENCE . . . 491 2 DON JUAN 5 139 6
    OR IF THAT SIMPLE SENTENCE SHOULD DISPLEASE . . . . . 109 3 DON JUAN 7   85 3
SENTENCES
    SOFT PERSIAN SENTENCES IN LILAC LETTERS . . . . 308 2 DON JUAN 3   64 7
SENTENTIOUS
    HEROIC STOIC CATO THE SENTENTIOUS . . . . 10 3 DON JUAN 6   7 7
    'TIS SO SENTENTIOUS POSITIVE AND TERSE . . . . 17 3 DON JUAN 6   23 6
SENTIMENT
    A SENTIMENT TILL THEN IN HER BUT WEAK . . . . 490 2 DON JUAN 5 137 4
    NOW SWIMMING IN THE SENTIMENT OF JOY . . . . 123 3 DON JUAN 8   24 2
    OF SENTIMENT AND HE SHE MOST ADORED . . . . 209 3 DON JUAN 9   54 5
    OF GOD THE LOVE OF SENTIMENT THE LOVING . . . . 219 3 DON JUAN 9   74 2
    ALL SONG AND SENTIMENT WHOSE HEARTS WERE SET . . . . . 398 3 DON JUAN 13   85 7
    AND HENCE ARISE THE WOES OF SENTIMENT . . . . 444 3 DON JUAN 14   79 6
    FOR OBJECTS WORTHY OF THE SENTIMENT . . . . 460 3 DON JUAN 15   10 8
SENTIMENTAL
    YET HAS A SENTIMENTAL KIND OF AIR . . . . 390 2 DON JUAN 4   85 6
    AND SEE A SENTIMENTAL PASSION GLOW . . . . 14 3 DON JUAN 6   17 4
    A SENTIMENTAL FRIENDSHIP THROUGH AND THROUGH . . . . . 25 3 DON JUAN 6   39 3
    OF SENTIMENTAL FRIENDSHIP THERE WERE THREE . . . . . . 26 3 DON JUAN 6   40 2
    DON JUAN WHO WAS MUCH MORE SENTIMENTAL . . . . 105 3 DON JUAN 7   75 4
    AN AIR AS SENTIMENTAL AS MOZART'S . . . . 292 3 DON JUAN 11   47 3
    IN MIND A SORT OF SENTIMENTAL BOGLE . . . . 304 3 DON JUAN 11   72 4
    IF COURTS AND CAMPS BE QUITE SO SENTIMENTAL . . . . . 322 3 DON JUAN 12   13 8
    THIS WORKS A WORLD OF SENTIMENTAL WOE . . . . 345 3 DON JUAN 12   63 5
    THE SENTIMENTAL BOASTS TO BE UNMOVED . . . . 442 3 DON JUAN 14   73 6
    OF SUCH A SENTIMENTAL SITUATION . . . . 454 3 DON JUAN 14 100 6
    FOR SHE WAS NOT A SENTIMENTAL MOURNER . . . . 532 3 DON JUAN 16   65 4
SENTIMENTS
    HOW GRAND HIS SENTIMENTS WHICH NEER RUN RIOT . . . . . 154 2 DON JUAN 1 V 5 2
    AND FULL OF SENTIMENTS SUBLIME AS BILLOWS . . . . . . 555 3 DON JUAN 16 110 1
SENTINEL
    AND SEND THE SENTINEL BEFORE YOUR GATE . . . . 185 3 DON JUAN 9   6 3
SEPARATE
    TO CALL THEM BACK INTO THEIR SEPARATE CAGES . . . . . 46 2 DON JUAN 1   45 6
    COULD NOT YET SEPARATE THEIR HOPES FROM FEARS . . . . 208 2 DON JUAN 2   98 3
    WEARY UNLESS WHEN SEPARATE THE TREE . . . . 349 2 DON JUAN 4   10 3
    AND THUS THEY PARTED EACH BY SEPARATE DOORS . . . . . 460 2 DON JUAN 5   85 1
    IT WOULD NOT SPOIL SOME SEPARATE CHARM TO PARE . . . . 27 3 DON JUAN 6   42 8
    AND ONE OR TWO SAD SEPARATE WIVES WITHOUT . . . . . . 330 3 DON JUAN 12   31 1
    WHERE EVERYBODY HAS SOME SEPARATE AIM . . . . 342 3 DON JUAN 12   58 5
    WHERE MINGLED AND YET SEPARATE APPEARS . . . . 447 3 DON JUAN 14   87 5
    OR SEPARATE MAINTENANCE IN CASE 'TWAS DOOM'D-- . . . . 473 3 DON JUAN 15   39 3
    THE COMPANY PREPARED TO SEPARATE . . . . 527 3 DON JUAN 16   55 2
SEPARATED
    THEY SEPARATED AT AN EARLY HOUR . . . . 409 3 DON JUAN 13 111 1
SEPARATELY
    HE MUST HIS LAURELS SEPARATELY EARN . . . . 120 3 DON JUAN 8   17 3
SEPTEMBER
    BUT THERE'S NO SHOOTING (SAVE GROUSE) TILL SEPTEMBER . . 380 3 DON JUAN 13   48 8
SEPTEMBRIZERS
    SOME DEADLY SHOTS TOO SEPTEMBRIZERS SEEN . . . . 539 3 DON JUAN 16   80 3
SEPULCHRAL
    SAVE A FEW GLEAN'D FROM THE SEPULCHRAL GLOOM . . . . . 399 2 DON JUAN 4 102 6
    BY WAY OF CHANGE FROM THEIR SEPULCHRAL SITES . . . . . 38 3 DON JUAN 6   64 6
SEPULCHRI
    AND ET SEPULCHRI IMMEMOR STRUIS DOMOS . . . . 448 2 DON JUAN 5   63 7
SEQUEL
    IS THAT WHICH MUST BE MENTION'D IN THE SEQUEL . . . . 66 2 DON JUAN 1   82 8
    IN YEARS HE HAD THE ADVANTAGE OF TIME'S SEQUEL . . . . 367 3 DON JUAN 13   20 3
SEQUINS
    AND BY MISTAKE SEQUINS WITH PARAS JUMBLING . . . . . . 426 2 DON JUAN 5   29 5
SERAGLIO
    MAY THE SERAGLIO DO TO SET HIS FACE IN . . . . 391 2 DON JUAN 4   86 4
    AT ANCHOR UNDER THE SERAGLIO WALL . . . . 407 2 DON JUAN 4 113 4
    IN THE SERAGLIO WHERE THE LADIES LAY . . . . 19 3 DON JUAN 6   26 6
    BUT THIS IS HER SERAGLIO TITLE GOT . . . . 21 3 DON JUAN 6   31 3
    YOU LOVE THIS BOYISH NEW SERAGLIO GUEST . . . . 63 3 DON JUAN 6 115 5
SERAPH
    I MEAN THE SERAPH WAY OF THOSE ABOVE . . . . 67 2 DON JUAN 1   85 8

714

	PAGE	VOL		CANTO	STANZA	LN

SERAPHIC
    THEIR LARGE BLACK EYES AND SOFT SERAPHIC CHEEKS . . . . . 292 2 DON JUAN 3 33 2
    YET SOME OF YOU ARE MOST SERAPHIC CREATURES-- . . . . . 405 2 DON JUAN 4 111 1
SERAPHIM
    THAT THOUGH HE LOOKED ONE OF THE SERAPHIM . . . . . . 206 3 DON JUAN 9 47 5
SERAPH'S
    STREAMING FROM OFF THE SUN LIKE SERAPH'S WINGS . . . . . 387 3 DON JUAN 13 62 4
SERAPHS'
    IN EYES WHICH SADLY SHONE AS SERAPHS' SHINE . . . . . . 476 3 DON JUAN 15 45 3
SERASKIER
    THEY TOOK THE BASTION WHICH THE SERASKIER . . . . . . 151 3 DON JUAN 8 79 7
    AND SIXTEEN BAYONETS PIERCED THE SERASKIER . . . . . . 152 3 DON JUAN 8 81 8
    THE SERASKIER IS KNOCKED UPON THE HEAD . . . . . . 160 3 DON JUAN 8 98 1
SERASKIERS
    A WORD WHICH LITTLE SUITS WITH SERASKIERS . . . . . . 152 3 DON JUAN 8 80 3
SERE
    NOW MY SERE FANCY FALLS INTO THE YELLOW . . . . . . 345 2 DON JUAN 4 3 5
SERENE
    A QUIET CONSCIENCE MAKES ONE SO SERENE . . . . . . 66 2 DON JUAN 1 83 6
    UPON THE WHOLE HIS CARRIAGE WAS SERENE . . . . . . 415 2 DON JUAN 5 9 2
    AND SERIOUS MORE THAN PENSIVE AND SERENE . . . . . . 33 3 DON JUAN 6 54 2
    SIMPLE SERENE THE ANTIPODES OF SHAME . . . . . . 144 3 DON JUAN 8 63 5
    SERENE NOT SULLEN WERE THE SOLITUDES . . . . . . 145 3 DON JUAN 8 67 7
    AND AFTER THAT SERENE AND SOMEWHAT DULL . . . . . . 360 3 DON JUAN 13 4 1
    SAD BUT SERENE IT SWEEPS O'ER TREE OR TOWER . . . . . 388 3 DON JUAN 13 64 6
    THEN IF SHE HATH NOT THAT SERENE DECLINE . . . . . . 395 3 DON JUAN 13 77 1
    THE LADY ADELINE'S SERENE SEVERITY . . . . . . 432 3 DON JUAN 14 51 1
    SERENE AND NOBLE--CONJUGAL BUT COLD . . . . . . 447 3 DON JUAN 14 86 8
    THROUGH THE SERENE AND PLACID GLASSY DEEP . . . . . . 447 3 DON JUAN 14 87 7
    SERENE ACCOMPLISH'D CHEERFUL BUT NOT LOUD . . . . . . 462 3 DON JUAN 15 15 1
    AND KEPT HER HEART SERENE WITHIN ITS ZONE . . . . . . 476 3 DON JUAN 15 47 4
SERENELY
    SERENELY SAVAGE WITH A LITTLE CHANGE . . . . . . 367 2 DON JUAN 4 44 3
    BLUE AS THE GARTERS WHICH SERENELY LIE . . . . . . 404 2 DON JUAN 4 110 6
SERENITY
    WITH SUCH SERENITY HER HUSBAND'S WOES . . . . 36 2 DON JUAN 1 29 2
SERF
    SERF LORD MAN WITH SUCH SKILL AS NONE WOULD SHARE IT IF . 481 3 DON JUAN 15 59 6
SERGE
    MEKNOP SERGE LWOW ARSENIEW OF MODERN GREECE . . . . . 74 3 DON JUAN 7 15 3
SERIOUS
    HER SERIOUS SAYINGS DARKEN'D TO SUBLIMITY . . . . . . 27 2 DON JUAN 1 12 4
    I SAY--THE FUTURE IS A SERIOUS MATTER-- . . . . . . 156 2 DON JUAN 1 V 8 7
    A FEMALE FAMILY'S A SERIOUS MATTER . . . . . . 287 2 DON JUAN 3 22 4
    BUT NEVER IN HIS REAL AND SERIOUS MOOD . . . . . . 300 2 DON JUAN 3 48 2
    FOR TEA AND COFFEE LEAVE US MUCH MORE SERIOUS . . . . 372 2 DON JUAN 4 52 8
    AUGHT OF A SERIOUS SORROWING KIND ALTHOUGH . . . . . 480 2 DON JUAN 5 119 5
    AND SERIOUS MORE THAN PENSIVE AND SERENE . . . . . . 33 3 DON JUAN 6 54 2
    AND WITH THAT GENTLE SERIOUS CHARACTER . . . . . . 250 3 DON JUAN 10 52 2
    AS SERIOUS AS IF I HAD FOR INDITERS . . . . . . 325 3 DON JUAN 12 20 4
    I'M SERIOUS--SO ARE ALL MEN UPON PAPER . . . . . . 325 3 DON JUAN 12 21 1
    IT IS A VERY SERIOUS THING INDEED . . . . 351 3 DON JUAN 12 77 2
    I NOW MEAN TO BE SERIOUS--IT IS TIME . . . . . . 358 3 DON JUAN 13 1 1
    SINCE LAUGHTER NOW-A-DAYS IS DEEMED TOO SERIOUS . . . . 358 3 DON JUAN 13 1 2
    BUT THE CLUBS FOUND IT RATHER SERIOUS LAUGHTER . . . . 398 3 DON JUAN 13 86 6
    THE SERIOUS ANGLES IN THE ELOQUENCE . . . . . . 427 3 DON JUAN 14 38 2
    OR SERIOUS ARE THE TOPICS I MUST BANISH . . . . . . 453 3 DON JUAN 14 98 5
    AND I SHALL TAKE A MUCH MORE SERIOUS AIR . . . . . . 454 3 DON JUAN 14 99 5
    THIS HE EXPRESS'D HALF SMILING AND HALF SERIOUS . . . 477 3 DON JUAN 15 49 4
    TO BRING WHAT WAS A JEST TO A SERIOUS END . . . . . 491 3 DON JUAN 15 79 6
    FOR CERTAIN REASONS MY BELIEF IS SERIOUS . . . . . . 498 3 DON JUAN 15 95 8
    SERIOUS YOU LAUGH--YOU MAY THAT WILL I NOT . . . . . 499 3 DON JUAN 15 96 1
    WEIGHED ON HIS SPIRIT THOUGH BY NO MEANS SERIOUS . . . 514 3 DON JUAN 16 33 5
    FOR IMMATERIALISM'S A SERIOUS MATTER . . . . . . 556 3 DON JUAN 16 114 6
SERIOUSLY
    AND SERIOUSLY RESOLVED ON REFORMATION . . . . . . 165 2 DON JUAN 2 17 8
    SHE SERIOUSLY ADVISED HIM TO GET MARRIED . . . . . . 469 3 DON JUAN 15 29 8
SERMON
    EACH EYE A SERMON AND HER BROW A HOMILY . . . . . . 29 2 DON JUAN 1 15 2
    BISHOPS WHO HAD NOT LEFT A SINGLE SERMON . . . . . . 391 3 DON JUAN 13 69 5
    HAVE TAKEN UP TO FILL THE FOLLOWING SERMON . . . . . 416 3 DON JUAN 14 15 2
SERMONS
    SERMONS HE READ AND LECTURES HE ENDURED . . . . . . 47 2 DON JUAN 1 47 1
    TO NEWSPAPERS--SERMONS WHICH THE ZEAL . . . . . . 138 2 DON JUAN 1 203 V3
    SERMONS AND SODA WATER THE DAY AFTER . . . . . . 250 2 DON JUAN 2 178 8
    ARE HINTS AS GOOD AS SERMONS OR AS RHYMES . . . . . 174 3 DON JUAN 8 125 6
    HIS JOKES WERE SERMONS AND HIS SERMONS JOKES . . . . 540 3 DON JUAN 16 83 1
    HIS JOKES WERE SERMONS AND HIS SERMONS JOKES . . . . 540 3 DON JUAN 16 83 1
SERPENT
    WITH SHRINKING SERPENT OPTICS ON HIM STARED . . . . . 463 2 DON JUAN 5 90 6
SERPENT'S
    HIS ARMS WERE LIKE A SERPENT'S COIL THEN FLEW . . . . 370 2 DON JUAN 4 48 5
    SEIZED FAST AS IF 'TWERE BY THE SERPENT'S HEAD . . . . 153 3 DON JUAN 8 83 3
SERPENTS
    THEY TWINED LIKE SERPENTS AND THEY KISSED LIKE DOVES . . 257 2 DON JUAN 2 191 V7
SERVANT
    BUT NOT A SERVANT STIRR'D TO AID THE FIGHT . . . . . 122 2 DON JUAN 1 184 3
    AND SO YOUR HUMBLE SERVANT AND GOOD BYE . . . . . . 147 2 DON JUAN 1 221 4
    AND AS A SERVANT SOME PREFERMENT GET . . . . . . 391 2 DON JUAN 4 86 5

	PAGE	VOL	CANTO	STANZA	LN

SERVANTS
HIS HOUSE WAS SOLD HIS SERVANTS SENT AWAY	39	2 DON JUAN	1	34	3
WITH TORCHES FRIENDS AND SERVANTS IN GREAT NUMBER	96	2 DON JUAN	1	138	2
THEMSELVES AND THE NEXT TIME THEIR SERVANTS TIE ON	165	2 DON JUAN	2	16	6
HIS SUITE CONSISTED OF THREE SERVANTS AND	169	2 DON JUAN	2	25	1
OUR DAYS AND PUT ONE'S SERVANTS INTO MOURNING	278	2 DON JUAN	3	7	8
THE SERVANTS ALL WERE GETTING DRUNK OR IDLING	295	2 DON JUAN	3	39	3
THAT IS WITH THIRTY SERVANTS FOR PARADE	381	3 DON JUAN	13	49	4
THE VERY SERVANTS PUZZLING HOW TO HAND	538	3 DON JUAN	16	79	3

SERVE
HATH BUT TWO OBJECTS HOW TO SERVE AND BIND	18	2 DON JUAN	D	15	3
THE LITTLE I HAVE SAID MAY SERVE TO SHOW	107	2 DON JUAN	1	157	2
BUT IT WILL SERVE TO KEEP MY VERSE COMPACT)	119	2 DON JUAN	1	178	4
BUT SCARCE ENOUGH TO SERVE THEM FOR A LUNCHEON--	181	2 DON JUAN	2	47	7
SERVE A SULTANA'S SENSUAL PHANTASY	484	2 DON JUAN	5	126	8
MAY SERVE PERHAPS AS OUTLINES OR SLIGHT HINTS	60	3 DON JUAN	6	109	8
THIS CIRCUMSTANCE MAY SERVE TO GIVE A NOTION	72	3 DON JUAN	7	11	1
WHERE WILL YOU SERVE--WHERE'ER YOU PLEASE--I KNOW	98	3 DON JUAN	7	62	1
HAVING BEEN USED TO SERVE ON HORSES' BACKS	149	3 DON JUAN	8	74	5
AND MAY SERVE THEREFORE TO BEDEW THESE RHYMES	156	3 DON JUAN	8	90	5
WILL SERVE WHEN THERE IS PLUNDER IN A CITY--	162	3 DON JUAN	8	101	6
BE WARY WATCH THE TIME AND ALWAYS SERVE IT	366	3 DON JUAN	13	18	4
TO SERVE IN THIS CONUNDRUM OF A DISH	465	3 DON JUAN	15	21	8

SERVED
SHE COULD HAVE SERVED HIM FOR THE PROMPTER'S COPY	27	2 DON JUAN	1	11	4
ALL WHICH MIGHT IF OCCASION SERVED BE QUOTED	36	2 DON JUAN	1	28	3
WAS SERVED OUT TO THE PEOPLE WHO BEGUN	189	2 DON JUAN	2	62	6
WHICH SERVED THEM AS A SORT OF SPONGY PITCHER	201	2 DON JUAN	2	85	3
LAY DROOPING OER THE OAR WHICH SERVED FOR MAST	214	2 DON JUAN	2	110	V5
THE MERCHANDISE WAS SERVED IN THE SAME WAY	284	2 DON JUAN	3	17	1
EVER SINCE JUAN SERVED HER FOR A SPOUSE	295	2 DON JUAN	3	39	V8
HE SERVED--BUT SERVED POLYCRATES--	324	2 DON JUAN	3	L 11	4
HE SERVED--BUT SERVED POLYCRATES--	324	2 DON JUAN	3	L 11	4
WERE TRIED IN VAIN BY THOSE WHO SERVED SHE GAVE	378	2 DON JUAN	4	63	7
SHE HAS SERVED ME ALSO MUCH THE SAME AS YOU	418	2 DON JUAN	5	14	7
IS THAT WHICH I WOULD LEARN -- I SERVED FOR SOME	418	2 DON JUAN	5	15	5
BUT THOUGH MY TURN WILL NOT BE SERVED WITH LESS	487	2 DON JUAN	5	132	5
AT HALIFAX BUT NOW HE SERVED THE TARTARS	76	3 DON JUAN	7	19	8
YOU SERVED AT WIDIN--YES--YOU LED THE ATTACK	98	3 DON JUAN	7	61	1
O'ER SILENCED CITIES MERELY SERVED TO FLATTER	197	3 DON JUAN	9	29	5
AND HAVE OR HAD AN EAR THAT SERVED ME PRETTILY)--	350	3 DON JUAN	12	75	8
HER OWN BUT SERVED TO SET OFF EVERY JOKE	552	3 DON JUAN	16	104	5

SERVENTE
| AS CAVALIER SERVENTE OR DESPISE HER | 288 | 2 DON JUAN | 3 | 24 | 6 |
| CALLED CAVALIER SERVENTE--A PYGMALION | 208 | 3 DON JUAN | 9 | 51 | 5 |

SERVES
WHICH SERVES THE HAPPY COUPLE FOR A TAVERN	24	2 DON JUAN	1	6	8
BLOOD ONLY SERVES TO WASH AMBITION'S HANDS	212	3 DON JUAN	9	59	8
WHICH SERVES OUR THINKING PEOPLE FOR A PASSION	284	3 DON JUAN	11	33	8

SERVICE
THOUGHT DAILY SERVICE WAS HER ONLY MISSION	252	2 DON JUAN	2	182	6
GEMS GOLD AND SILVER FORM'D THE SERVICE MOSTLY	306	2 DON JUAN	3	61	7
BY SERVICE WITH MY MILITARY BROTHERS	103	3 DON JUAN	7	71	4
FROM NATURE FOR THE SERVICE OF THE GOUT--	488	3 DON JUAN	15	72	2

SERVICES
| HIS SERVICES HE KISSED HANDS THE NEXT DAY | 247 | 3 DON JUAN | 10 | 46 | 5 |

SERVILE
THE INSULTS TOO OF EVERY SERVILE GLUTTON	299	2 DON JUAN	3	46	7
THOSE SERVILE DOGS ARE NOT SO PROUDLY EYED	418	2 DON JUAN	5	14	3
THE SERVILE AND THE VAIN SUCH NAMES WILL BE	114	3 DON JUAN	8	5	7
THOUGH PRIESTS AND SLAVES MAY JOIN IN THE SERVILE CRY	195	3 DON JUAN	9	26	V8
A LAUREATE'S ODE OR SERVILE PEER'S CONTENT	435	3 DON JUAN	14	58	8

SERVILITY
| OF THIS I'M SURE AT LEAST THERE'S NO SERVILITY | 465 | 3 DON JUAN | 15 | 20 | 5 |

SERVING
| AND SERVING HIM THE MORE BY BEING SO | 151 | 2 DON JUAN | 1 | V 2 | 8 |

SESSION
WHICH PUT OFF BUSINESS TO THE ENSUING SESSION	331	2 DON JUAN	3	96	6
AS THE TRIBUNALS SHOW THROUGH MANY A SESSION	11	3 DON JUAN	6	10	6
HE SAW HOWEVER AT THE CLOSING SESSION	354	3 DON JUAN	12	83	1
TO THE GREEK KALENDS OF ANOTHER SESSION	379	3 DON JUAN	13	45	2
AN ORATOR THE LATEST OF THE SESSION	400	3 DON JUAN	13	90	2

SESSIONS
| ITS SESSIONS FORM OUR ONLY ALMANACK | 378 | 3 DON JUAN | 13 | 43 | 8 |

SET
A DAINTY DISH TO SET BEFORE THE KING	10	2 DON JUAN	D	2	3
AN ORATOR OF SUCH SET TRASH OF PHRASE	17	2 DON JUAN	D	13	1
WITH MANY OF THE MILITARY SET	22	2 DON JUAN	1	3	6
OR COELEBS' WIFE SET OUT IN QUEST OF LOVERS	29	2 DON JUAN	1	16	4
THE SUN SET AND UP ROSE THE YELLOW MOON	82	2 DON JUAN	1	113	1
AND GALVANISM HAS SET SOME CORPSES GRINNING	92	2 DON JUAN	1	130	2
PERHAPS IT MAY SET OUT ON ITS RETURN--	92	2 DON JUAN	1	131	2
AND SOBER SUNS MUST SET AT FIVE O'CLOCK	94	2 DON JUAN	1	134	8
MY BLOOD STILL RUSHES WHERE MY SPIRIT'S SET	133	2 DON JUAN	1	196	3
AND DARE NOT SET MY SEAL UPON THIS SHEET	134	2 DON JUAN	1	197	2
THOU SHALT NOT SET UP WORDSWORTH COLERIDGE SOUTHEY	139	2 DON JUAN	1	205	2
BRAVE INEZ NOW SET UP A SUNDAY SCHOOL	162	2 DON JUAN	2	10	2
DUNCES WERE WHIPT OR SET UPON A STOOL	162	2 DON JUAN	2	10	6
UPON THE PUMPS AND THE REMAINDER SET	171	2 DON JUAN	2	28	2

SET   (CONTINUED)

	PAGE	VOL	CANTO		STANZA	LN
A GLIMPSE OF SUNSHINE SET SOME HANDS TO BALE--	176	2	DON JUAN	2	38	7
THOUGH ON THE WAVE'S HIGH TOP TOO MUCH TO SET	188	2	DON JUAN	2	60	3
SET BY A CURRENT TOWARD IT THEY WERE LOST	209	2	DON JUAN	2	100	3
STILL SET THEM ONWARDS TO THE WELCOME SHORE	209	2	DON JUAN	2	101	2
LIKE TWILIGHT ROSY STILL WITH THE SET SUN	218	2	DON JUAN	2	118	2
(A SET OF HUMBUG RASCALS WHEN ALL'S DONE)	219	2	DON JUAN	2	118	V6
SWEET SKIES JUST WHEN HE RISES OR IS SET	230	2	DON JUAN	2	139	3
AND SAW THE SUN SET OPPOSITE THE MOON	249	2	DON JUAN	2	176	8
(THE LEAST OF WHICH WOULD SET TEN POETS RAVING)	291	2	DON JUAN	3	30	6
THAT WOULD HAVE SET TOM MOORE THOUGH MARRIED RAVING	291	2	DON JUAN	3	30	V6
BUT ALL EXCEPT THEIR SUN IS SET	320	2	DON JUAN	3	L 1	6
AND WHEN THE SUN SET WHERE WERE THEY	322	2	DON JUAN	3	L 4	6
AND DRIVELS SEAS TO SET IT WELL AFLOAT	333	2	DON JUAN	3	98	8
BUT SET THOSE PERSONS DOWN WITH ME TO PRAY	336	2	DON JUAN	3	104	3
NO NOVELS E'ER HAD SET THEIR YOUNG HEARTS BLEEDING	354	2	DON JUAN	4	19	4
AS FOR THE MEN THEY ARE A MIDDLING SET	391	2	DON JUAN	4	86	1
MAY THE SERAGLIO DO TO SET HIS FACE IN	391	2	DON JUAN	4	86	4
IF WE SHOULD STRIKE A STROKE TO SET US FREE	434	2	DON JUAN	5	43	6
WAS ON THE POINT OF BEING SET ASIDE	440	2	DON JUAN	5	51	4
WHICH E'ER SET OFF A MARRIAGE-MORNING FACE	455	2	DON JUAN	5	76	8
WHILE TWO AND TWENTY CANNON DULY SET	72	3	DON JUAN	7	12	6
WHEN IT GREW RATHER LATE TO SET THINGS RIGHT	73	3	DON JUAN	7	13	5
HAD SET TO WORK AS BRISKLY AS THEIR BROTHERS	119	3	DON JUAN	8	15	4
JUST NAMED THESE PALISADES WERE PRIMLY SET	136	3	DON JUAN	8	46	8
HE WROTE THIS POLAR MELODY AND SET IT	179	3	DON JUAN	8	135	1
THAT HIDES THE PAST WORLD LIKE TO A SET SUN	188	3	DON JUAN	9	11	3
AND SET UP IN THEIR STEAD SOME PROPER STUFF	195	3	DON JUAN	9	25	4
FROM SOME FRESH PARADISE AND SET TO PLOUGH	202	3	DON JUAN	9	40	2
O'ER LIMBS WHOSE SYMMETRY SET OFF THE SILK	204	3	DON JUAN	9	43	8
OF THE STRANGE THING SOME WOMEN SET A VALUE ON	208	3	DON JUAN	9	51	3
WHICH SET THE BEAUTY OFF IN WHICH HE GLOWED	239	3	DON JUAN	10	29	6
TO SET UP VAIN PRETENCES OF BEING GREAT	267	3	DON JUAN	10	87	3
ON WHICH JACK AND HIS TRAIN SET OFF AT SPEED	275	3	DON JUAN	11	14	1
HAD SET SOME TIME AND NIGHT WAS ON THE RIDGE	279	3	DON JUAN	11	23	7
THERE IS A MOVE SET DOWN FOR JOY OR SORROW	288	3	DON JUAN	11	42	4
SET DOWN HIS SAYINGS IN HER COMMON-PLACE BOOK	294	3	DON JUAN	11	52	8
SOME WHO ONCE SET THEIR CAPS AT CAUTIOUS DUKES	308	3	DON JUAN	11	81	1
OF RANK ENOUGH TO SET IN STONE OR LEAD	314	3	DON JUAN	11	V 75	2
MALTHUS AND WILBERFORCE--THE LAST SET FREE	325	3	DON JUAN	12	20	5
IF THAT POLITENESS SET IT NOT APART	326	3	DON JUAN	12	22	5
BEING LONG MARRIED AND THUS SET AT LARGE	339	3	DON JUAN	12	51	4
ALL SONG AND SENTIMENT WHOSE HEARTS WERE SET	398	3	DON JUAN	13	85	7
WHO HAD DELIVER'D WELL A VERY SET	400	3	DON JUAN	13	90	3
BUT THE TWO YOUNGEST LOVED MORE TO BE SET	408	3	DON JUAN	13	107	6
SUCH CLASSIC PAS--SANS FLAWS--SET OFF OUR HERO	427	3	DON JUAN	14	39	7
HER LATE PERFORMANCE HAD BEEN A DEAD SET	428	3	DON JUAN	14	42	7
IF BUT TO SET ITS EDGE TO A FRESH POLISH	433	3	DON JUAN	14	53	V7
AND SET THE OTHER HALF OF EARTH TO RIGHTS	445	3	DON JUAN	14	82	7
OR GLORIOUS AS A DIAMOND RICHLY SET	458	3	DON JUAN	15	7	4
THEY ARE WRONG--THAT'S NOT THE WAY TO SET ABOUT IT	461	3	DON JUAN	15	13	1
THEY ALSO SET A GLAZED WESTPHALIAN HAM ON	484	3	DON JUAN	15	65	5
TO KEEP EXTREMES FROM MEETING WHEN ONCE SET	492	3	DON JUAN	15	81	6
BUT COME I'LL SET YOUR STORY TO A TUNE	517	3	DON JUAN	16	38	4
SET TO SOME THOUSANDS ('TIS THE USUAL BURTHEN	529	3	DON JUAN	16	59	2
HER OWN BUT SERVED TO SET OFF EVERY JOKE	552	3	DON JUAN	16	104	5

SETS

	PAGE	VOL	CANTO		STANZA	LN
ONE BREAKS YOUR BONES ONE SETS THEM IN THEIR SOCKETS	91	2	DON JUAN	1	129	4
A KIND OF SHOCK THAT SETS ONE'S HEART AJAR	164	2	DON JUAN	2	14	6
SETS UP FOR BEING A SORT OF MORAL ME	298	3	DON JUAN	11	59	2
SETS TO SOFT MUSIC THE HARMONIOUS SIGH	430	3	DON JUAN	14	47	3
DISSIMULATION ALWAYS SETS APART	457	3	DON JUAN	15	3	6
WHICH SETS THE TEETH ON EDGE AND A SLIGHT CLATTER	556	3	DON JUAN	16	114	2

SETTING

	PAGE	VOL	CANTO		STANZA	LN
BY SETTING THINGS IN THEIR RIGHT POINT OF VIEW	422	2	DON JUAN	5	23	5
SO MUCH DID JUAN'S SETTING OFF DISTRESS HER	247	3	DON JUAN	10	47	7
I THOUGHT AT SETTING OFF ABOUT TWO DOZEN	341	3	DON JUAN	12	55	5
TO CRITICS OR TO HAIL THE SETTING SUN	466	3	DON JUAN	15	22	6

SETTLE

	PAGE	VOL	CANTO		STANZA	LN
THE DEVIL MAY DECOMPOSE BUT NEVER SETTLE	33	3	DON JUAN	6	55	8
MAY SETTLE BUT FAR BE'T FROM ME TO ANTICIPATE	65	3	DON JUAN	6	119	7
(THE ANTIQUARIANS WHO CAN SETTLE TIME	122	3	DON JUAN	8	23	3
BUT DON'T PRETEND TO SETTLE WHICH WAS BEST	309	3	DON JUAN	11	83	8
I LEAVE THE SAINTS TO SETTLE THEIR OWN SCORE	352	3	DON JUAN	12	79	4

SETTLED

	PAGE	VOL	CANTO		STANZA	LN
KNOWING THEY MUST BE SETTLED BY THE LAWS	109	2	DON JUAN	1	159	8
AS ROLL THE WAVES BEFORE THE SETTLED WIND	133	2	DON JUAN	1	196	4
WERE SETTLED LONG ERE JUAN'S SIRE WAS BORN	169	2	DON JUAN	2	24	4
THEN HAVING SETTLED HIS MARINE AFFAIRS	285	2	DON JUAN	3	19	1
AT LAST THEY SETTLED INTO SIMPLE GRUMBLING	426	2	DON JUAN	5	29	1
THE SACK AND SEA HAD SETTLED ALL IN TIME	496	2	DON JUAN	5	149	4
WE WILL HAVE ALL THINGS SETTLED FOR YOU FAIRLY	29	3	DON JUAN	6	46	8
BY WHICH SUCH THINGS ARE SETTLED NOW-A-DAYS	45	3	DON JUAN	6	78	8
HAD SETTLED ALL NOR COULD HE THEN PRESUME	57	3	DON JUAN	6	103	5
THAT ALL IS SETTLED--THERE WAS LITTLE DIN	94	3	DON JUAN	7	54	6
SINCE THOU HAST SETTLED BEYOND ALL SURMISES	210	3	DON JUAN	9	55	8
IN ONE POINT ONLY WERE YOU SETTLED--AND	329	3	DON JUAN	12	29	1
AND SETTLED BONNETS BY THE NEWEST CODE	406	3	DON JUAN	13	104	6
DISCUSS'D THE WORLD AND SETTLED ALL THE SPHERES	408	3	DON JUAN	13	109	2

SETTLEMENT
SO DRAMAS CLOSE WITH DEATH OR SETTLEMENT FOR LIFE . . . 280 2 DON JUAN 3 9 V7
IN HIS HARMONIOUS SETTLEMENT--(WHICH FLOURISHES . . . 471 3 DON JUAN 15 35 2
SETTLES
WHICH SETTLES ALL THINGS ROMAN GREEK OR RUNIC . . . 122 3 DON JUAN 8 23 4
FOR THAT'S THE PHRASE THAT SETTLES ALL THINGS NOW . . . 330 3 DON JUAN 12 31 4
NOR SETTLES ALL THINGS IN ONE INTERVIEW . . . . . . 351 3 DON JUAN 12 76 5
SETTLING
THE SHIP WAS EVIDENTLY SETTLING NOW . . . . . . 179 2 DON JUAN 2 44 1
SEVEN
EVEN SEVEN YEARS HENCE IT WOULD NOT BE TOO LATE . . . 67 2 DON JUAN 1 85 4
OF HALF-PAST SIX--PERHAPS STILL NEARER SEVEN . . . 77 2 DON JUAN 1 104 2
HINT THAT SOME SIX OR SEVEN GOOD YEARS AGO . . . 143 2 DON JUAN 1 212 4
SHINE LIKE A GUINEA AND SEVEN SHILLING PIECES . . . 306 2 DON JUAN 3 60 8
WHO HAD BID HIGH AS HUNDREDS SIX OR SEVEN . . . 407 2 DON JUAN 4 114 V6
(OF WHICH I HAVE ALSO SEEN SOME SIX OR SEVEN) . . . 465 2 DON JUAN 5 94 4
BUT THEN THEY NEVER CAME TO THE SEVEN TOWERS . . . 497 2 DON JUAN 5 150 8
AT SEVEN THEY ROSE HOWEVER AND SURVEYED . . . . . 81 3 DON JUAN 7 29 1
AND HELL THERE MUST AT LEAST BE SIX OR SEVEN . . . 168 3 DON JUAN 8 114 8
OR SEVEN AND TWENTY--BUT IT DOES NOT MATTER . . . 236 3 DON JUAN 10 24 V7
SEVEN YEARS (THE USUAL TERM OF TRANSPORTATION) . . . 257 3 DON JUAN 10 66 6
TALK NOT OF SEVENTY YEARS AS AGE IN SEVEN . . . 309 3 DON JUAN 11 82 1
TO LIKE THOUGH I HAVE BEEN SEVEN YEARS IN ITALY . . . 350 3 DON JUAN 12 75 7
SEVEN-AND-TWENTY
SAY SEVEN-AND-TWENTY FOR I NEVER KNEW . . . . . 433 3 DON JUAN 14 53 2
BY THIS TIME--BUT STRIKE SIX FROM SEVEN-AND-TWENTY . . . 433 3 DON JUAN 14 54 7
SEVENTEEN
A LOVELY FEMALE FACE OF SEVENTEEN . . . . . . 215 2 DON JUAN 2 112 8
UNCONSCIOUS ALBEIT TURNED OF QUICK SEVENTEEN . . . 33 3 DON JUAN 6 54 6
IN ALL THE ROYALTY OF SWEET SEVENTEEN . . . . . 236 3 DON JUAN 10 24 6
AT SEVENTEEN TOO THE WORLD WAS STILL ENCHANTED . . . 434 3 DON JUAN 14 55 3
SEVENTH
THE SEVENTH DAY AND NO WIND--THE BURNING SUN . . . 194 2 DON JUAN 2 72 1
HER SIXTH TO STAB HERSELF HER SEVENTH TO SENTENCE . . . 491 2 DON JUAN 5 139 6
THE SEVENTH WILL BRING BLUE DEVILS OR A DUN . . . 243 3 DON JUAN 10 38 8
SEVENTY
OR GENTLEMAN OF SEVENTY YEARS COMPLETE . . . . . 89 2 DON JUAN 1 125 3
BUT SIX OLD DAMSELS EACH OF SEVENTY YEARS . . . 177 3 DON JUAN 8 130 7
TALK NOT OF SEVENTY YEARS AS AGE IN SEVEN . . . 309 3 DON JUAN 11 82 1
TO ONE OF SEVENTY SUITORS HIS PROMOTION . . . . 434 3 DON JUAN 14 55 V6
AT SEVENTY YEARS HAD PHANTASIES LIKE THESE . . . 494 3 DON JUAN 15 86 4
SEVENTY-FOUR
HERE AND THERE STUDDED WITH A SEVENTY-FOUR . . . 412 2 DON JUAN 5 3 3
SEVERAL
THOUGH SEVERAL THOUSAND PEOPLE CHOSE TO TRY . . . 33 2 DON JUAN 1 23 3
WITH--SEVERAL OTHER THINGS WHICH I FORGET . . . 73 2 DON JUAN 1 96 7
IN SIGHT THAT SEVERAL MONTHS HAVE PASS'D WE'LL SAY . . . 86 2 DON JUAN 1 121 6
AND FOUND MUCH LINEN LACE AND SEVERAL PAIR . . . 99 2 DON JUAN 1 143 3
AND WOUNDED SEVERAL SHUTTERS AND SOME BOARDS . . . 99 2 DON JUAN 1 143 8
DENYING SEVERAL LITTLE THINGS HE WANTED . . . . 120 2 DON JUAN 1 160 4
SOME BLOOD AND SEVERAL FOOTSTEPS BUT NO MORE . . . 125 2 DON JUAN 1 187 6
TO VIRGIN MARY SEVERAL POUNDS OF CANDLES . . . 128 2 DON JUAN 1 190 6
(NOT THAT I HAVE NOT SEVERAL MERITS MORE . . . 137 2 DON JUAN 1 202 4
IS THAT MYSELF AND SEVERAL NOW IN SEVILLE . . . 138 2 DON JUAN 1 203 7
WHO SEVERAL LANGUAGES DID UNDERSTAND . . . . 169 2 DON JUAN 2 25 3
HAVING BEEN SEVERAL DAYS IN GREAT DISTRESS . . . 180 2 DON JUAN 2 46 2
AND IN THEM CROWDED SEVERAL OF THE CREW . . . 185 2 DON JUAN 2 54 2
THEY MUST WAIT SEVERAL WEEKS BEFORE A MASS . . . 185 2 DON JUAN 2 55 4
REJECTED SEVERAL SUITORS JUST TO LEARN . . . . 224 2 DON JUAN 2 128 7
IN SEVERAL OATHS--ARMENIAN TURK AND GREEK-- . . . 229 2 DON JUAN 2 138 7
HE CHOSE FROM SEVERAL ANIMALS HE SAW-- . . . 285 2 DON JUAN 3 18 3
AND PUT HIS HOUSE IN MOURNING SEVERAL WEEKS . . . 295 2 DON JUAN 3 38 4
AND HAVING PICKED UP SEVERAL ODDS AND ENDS . . . 318 2 DON JUAN 3 83 2
BUT HEAR THAT SEVERAL PEOPLE TAKE EXCEPTION . . . 397 2 DON JUAN 4 97 3
AND SEVERAL STRUTTED OTHERS SLEPT AND SOME . . . 441 2 DON JUAN 5 53 7
IN WHICH WE LEFT HIM SEVERAL LINES ABOVE . . . 20 3 DON JUAN 6 28 8
YET THERE WERE SEVERAL WORTH COMMEMORATION . . . 74 3 DON JUAN 7 16 3
'MONGST THEM WERE SEVERAL ENGLISHMEN OF PITH . . . 75 3 DON JUAN 7 18 7
I THINK THAT SEVERAL VOLUMES WOULD FALL SHORT . . . 82 3 DON JUAN 7 32 3
TO SEVERAL SAINTS THAT SHORTLY PLOUGH OR HARROW . . . 99 3 DON JUAN 7 63 6
EXPLICITLY OUR SEVERAL POSTS MY FRIEND . . . . 100 3 DON JUAN 7 65 7
OF SEVERAL RIBBONS AND SOME THOUSAND PEASANTS . . . 222 3 DON JUAN 9 79 8
SEVERAL PREPARED THEMSELVES FOR EMIGRATIONS . . . 239 3 DON JUAN 10 30 5
AS SEVERAL PEOPLE THINK SUCH HAZARDS RUDE . . . 270 3 DON JUAN 11 4 4
THE MOB STOOD AND AS USUAL SEVERAL SCORE . . . 282 3 DON JUAN 11 30 3
JUAN KNEW SEVERAL LANGUAGES--AS WELL . . . . 295 3 DON JUAN 11 53 1
AND SEVERAL OF HER BEST BON-MOTS WERE HAWKED ABOUT . . . 338 3 DON JUAN 12 47 5
THOUGH SEVERAL ALSO KEEP THEIR PERPENDICULAR . . . 343 3 DON JUAN 12 59 3
BESIDES HE HAD NOT SEEN OF SEVERAL HUNDRED . . . 353 3 DON JUAN 12 81 3
AND MADE UPON THE HOT-HOUSE SEVERAL STRICTURES . . . 406 3 DON JUAN 13 102 4
AND ONCE O'ER SEVERAL COUNTRY GENTLEMEN . . . 424 3 DON JUAN 14 33 8
FOR SEVERAL WINTERS IN THE GRAND GRAND MONDE . . . 428 3 DON JUAN 14 42 3
AND SEVERAL PITIED WITH SINCERE REGRET . . . 429 3 DON JUAN 14 44 7
BY TURNS THE DIFFERENCE OF THE SEVERAL SEXES . . . 442 3 DON JUAN 14 73 3
SOME TO THEIR SEVERAL PASTIMES OR TO NONE . . . 527 3 DON JUAN 16 55 3
MATCHED FOR THE SPRING WHOM SEVERAL WENT TO SEE . . . 527 3 DON JUAN 16 55 8
WRITING DISPATCHES) IN THEIR SEVERAL STATIONS . . . 533 3 DON JUAN 16 66 7
HAVE IN THEIR SEVERAL ARTS OR PARTS ASCENDENCE . . . 537 3 DON JUAN 16 76 4
AND SEVERAL WHO SUNG FEWER PSALMS THAN CATCHES . . . 539 3 DON JUAN 16 80 8
MY TREMBLING LYRE ALREADY SEVERAL STRINGS . . . 568 3 DON JUAN 17 13 5

SEVERE
  SEVERE SUBLIME THE PROPHET WROTE NO FARCE ON . . . . . 179 3 DON JUAN 8 134 6
SEVERED
  TO THE LIVE LEG STILL CLUNG THE SEVERED HEAD . . . . . 153 3 DON JUAN 8 84 8
SEVERELY
  NOT SOUND POOR FELLOW BUT SEVERELY WOUNDED . . . . . 373 2 DON JUAN 4 54 2
SEVEREST
  YOUR ORDERS EVEN IN THEIR SEVEREST SENSE . . . . . 62 3 DON JUAN 6 114 4
SEVERITY
  EVEN PETRARCH'S SELF IF JUDGED WITH DUE SEVERITY . . . . 411 2 DON JUAN 5 1 7
  THE LADY ADELINE'S SERENE SEVERITY . . . . 432 3 DON JUAN 14 51 1
SEVILLE
  IN SEVILLE WAS HE BORN A PLEASANT CITY . . . . . 25 2 DON JUAN 1 8 1
  AND THEN SHE HAD ALL SEVILLE FOR ABETTORS . . . . . 36 2 DON JUAN 1 28 4
  I YET HAVE CHOSEN FROM OUT THE YOUTH OF SEVILLE . . . 102 2 DON JUAN 1 148 2
  IS THAT MYSELF AND SEVERAL NOW IN SEVILLE . . . . . 138 2 DON JUAN 1 203 7
SEX
  THE COMMON PRIVILEGES OF MY SEX . . . . . 101 2 DON JUAN 1 147 2
  (NONE TRUSTS THE SEX MORE OR SO MUCH ADMIRES-- . . . 287 2 DON JUAN 3 22 5
  AND TALL BEYOND HER SEX AND THEIR COMPEERS . . . . 367 2 DON JUAN 4 43 5
  THEIR STATURE DIFFERING BUT IN SEX AND YEARS . . . . 368 2 DON JUAN 4 45 2
  TO FIND THREE PERFECT PIPES OF THE THIRD SEX . . . . 391 2 DON JUAN 4 86 8
  AND WITH HIS FELLOWS OF THE THIRD SEX GET . . . . 391 2 DON JUAN 4 86 V5
  BENIGN CERULEANS OF THE SECOND SEX . . . . . 403 2 DON JUAN 4 108 2
  AND AGE AND SEX WERE IN THE MARKET RANGED . . . . 414 2 DON JUAN 5 7 2
  OF THE THIRD SEX STEPT UP AND PEERING OVER . . . . 424 2 DON JUAN 5 26 2
  THOSE WHO WILL LEAVE YOU OF NO SEX AT ALL . . . . 454 2 DON JUAN 5 75 8
  HER FORM HAD ALL THE SOFTNESS OF HER SEX . . . . 474 2 DON JUAN 5 109 1
  PERHAPS THE FAULT OF HER SOFT SEX AND AGE-- . . . . 490 2 DON JUAN 5 136 6
  OR RATHER BONNET WHICH THE FAIR SEX WEAR . . . . 13 3 DON JUAN 6 14 5
  I LOVE THE SEX AND SOMETIMES WOULD REVERSE . . . . 19 3 DON JUAN 6 27 1
  THAN IS THE CUSTOM OF THE GENTLE SEX . . . . . 24 3 DON JUAN 6 37 6
  SPARED NEITHER SEX NOR AGE IN THEIR CAREER . . . . 171 3 DON JUAN 8 119 2
  AND STINGINESS DISGRACE HER SEX AND STATION . . . . 222 3 DON JUAN 9 81 8
  AMONGST THE SEX IN LITTLE THINGS OR GREAT . . . . 329 3 DON JUAN 12 28 2
  THE FAIR SEX SHOULD BE ALWAYS FAIR AND NO MAN . . . 359 3 DON JUAN 13 3 7
  OF COUNSELLORS FOR MEN--THUS FOR THE SEX . . . . 371 3 DON JUAN 13 30 2
  CONSISTED OF--WE GIVE THE SEX THE PAS-- . . . . 396 3 DON JUAN 13 79 2
  IS THAT FOR WHICH THE SEX ARE ALWAYS SEEKING . . . . 442 3 DON JUAN 14 74 2
  NO DOUBT THE SECRET INFLUENCE OF THE SEX . . . . 451 3 DON JUAN 14 93 1
  FOR FEW OF THE SOFT SEX ARE VERY STABLE . . . . 458 3 DON JUAN 15 6 3
  'TIS WONDERFUL HOW OFT THE SEX HAVE HEARD . . . . 489 3 DON JUAN 15 76 7
SEXES
  WITHOUT CONFUSION OF THE SORTS AND SEXES . . . . . 269 3 DON JUAN 11 3 6
  BY TURNS THE DIFFERENCE OF THE SEVERAL SEXES . . . . 442 3 DON JUAN 14 73 3
SEX'S
  AND THEN HER SEX'S SHAME BROKE IN AT LAST . . . . 490 2 DON JUAN 5 137 3
SHABBY
  YOU'RE SHABBY FELLOWS--TRUE--BUT POETS STILL . . . . 12 2 DON JUAN D 6 7
  IN MARINET'S AFFAIR--IN FACT 'TWAS SHABBY . . . . 184 3 DON JUAN 9 2 2
SHADE
  OUR VIRGINS DANCE BENEATH THE SHADE-- . . . . 326 2 DON JUAN 3 L 15 2
  BY THEIR POSSESSORS THROWN INTO THE SHADE . . . . 485 2 DON JUAN 5 129 6
  A SLIGHT EXAMPLE JUST TO CAST A SHADE . . . . . 22 3 DON JUAN 6 32 5
  AND NATURAL AGONIES WITH A SLIGHT SHADE . . . . . 102 3 DON JUAN 7 69 4
  SHADE OF LEONIDAS WHO FOUGHT SO HEARTY . . . . . 108 3 DON JUAN 7 82 3
  THE SHADE OF BONAPARTE'S NOBLE DARING-- . . . . . 318 3 DON JUAN 12 5 7
  WITH A SLIGHT SHADE OF BLUE TOO IT MIGHT BE . . . . 474 3 DON JUAN 15 41 5
  THAT FLASHED AND AFTER DARKENED IN THE SHADE . . . . 507 3 DON JUAN 16 15 8
  NOW IN THE MOONLIGHT AND NOW LAPSED IN SHADE . . . . 510 3 DON JUAN 16 21 3
  THUS ADELINE WOULD THROW INTO THE SHADE . . . . 522 3 DON JUAN 16 44 1
  AND HE AROSE ADVANCED--THE SHADE RETREATED . . . . 559 3 DON JUAN 16 119 2
  BUT STILL THE SHADE REMAINED THE BLUE EYES GLARED . . . 560 3 DON JUAN 16 121 1
SHADE'S
  A SINGLE SHADE'S SUFFICIENT TO ENTRANCE A . . . . . 557 3 DON JUAN 16 116 6
SHADES
  PEDLARS AND BOATS AND WAGGONS OH YE SHADES . . . . . 334 2 DON JUAN 3 100 1
  WHILE THE MILD EMERALD'S BEAM SHADES DOWN THE DYES . . . 319 3 DON JUAN 12 8 7
  UPON THE SHADES OF THOSE DISTINGUISHED MEN . . . . 373 3 DON JUAN 13 33 3
SHADOW
  OF DOWNCAST LENGTH IN WHOSE SILK SHADOW LIES . . . . 218 2 DON JUAN 2 117 3
  HER SWEET FACE INTO SHADOW DULL AND SLOW . . . . 381 2 DON JUAN 4 69 6
  THE VERY SHADOW OF TRUE TRUTH WOULD SHUT . . . . 286 3 DON JUAN 11 37 5
  A SHADOW WHICH THE ONWARD SOUL BEHIND THROWS . . . . 414 3 DON JUAN 14 8 6
  THE SHADOW PASSED AWAY--BUT WHERE THE HALL . . . . 511 3 DON JUAN 16 24 2
SHADOW'D
  FROM A TRUE LOVER SHADOW'D MY MIND'S EYE . . . . . 337 2 DON JUAN 3 106 8
SHADOWED
  'TIS SHADOWED BY HIS COWL . . . . . 519 3 DON JUAN 16 L 4 6
SHADOWS
  SHADOWS OF GLORY (LEST I BE CONFOUNDED) . . . . 108 3 DON JUAN 7 82 6
  THOSE WHO CATCH COLD IN SHADOWS OF DEATH'S VALLEY . . . 131 3 DON JUAN 8 36 8
  AFTER WHICH SHADOWS THE--SAY--SECOND YEAR . . . . 220 3 DON JUAN 9 75 V8
  ACCORDING AS THE SKIES THEIR SHADOWS THREW . . . . 385 3 DON JUAN 13 58 8
  SHADOWS THE SOUL OF RICHARD MAY APPAL . . . . 499 3 DON JUAN 15 96 6
  SHADOWS--BUT YOU MUST BE IN MY CONDITION . . . . 500 3 DON JUAN 15 98 7
  APPEAR TO WAKE AND SHADOWS WILD AND QUAINT . . . . 508 3 DON JUAN 16 18 5
  AGAIN THROUGH SHADOWS OF THE NIGHT SUBLIME . . . . 556 3 DON JUAN 16 113 5
  HALF LETTING IN LONG SHADOWS ON THE LIGHT . . . . 558 3 DON JUAN 16 117 4

		PAGE	VOL		CANTO	STANZA	LN

SHADOWY
WHERE THE BLUE VEINS LOOK'D SHADOWY SHRUNK AND WEAK . . . 234 2 DON JUAN 2 147 5
HIS GARDEN TREES ALL SHADOWY AND GREEN . . . . . . 289 2 DON JUAN 3 27 2
BEHOLDS HER OWN SHY SHADOWY IMAGE PASS . . . . . 36 3 DON JUAN 6 60 6
BUT DEATH IS IMAGED IN THEIR SHADOWY BEAMS . . . . . 509 3 DON JUAN 16 19 6
HE MOVED AS SHADOWY AS THE SISTERS WEIRD . . . . . . 510 3 DON JUAN 16 21 6

SHAFTS
THE OLD ARCHER'S SHAFTS PERHAPS THE EARLY GRAVE . . . 350 2 DON JUAN 4 12 7

SHAH
WITH GORE LIKE NADIR SHAH THAT COSTIVE SOPHY . . . . 199 3 DON JUAN 9 33 4

SHAKE
MUST WITH PERMISSION SHAKE YOU BY THE HAND . . . . 147 2 DON JUAN 1 221 3
WHICH SHAKE SO MUCH THE HUMAN BRAIN AND BREAST-- . . 343 2 DON JUAN 3 V 98 3
WERE THINGS TO SHAKE A STOIC NE'ERTHELESS . . . . 415 2 DON JUAN 5 9 1
WHICH SHOULD CONFIRM OR SHAKE OR MAKE A FAITH . . . . 431 2 DON JUAN 5 38 8
THE NEW-BOUGHT VIRGIN MADE HER BLUSH AND SHAKE . . . 501 2 DON JUAN 5 156 2
THE NEXT SHALL RING A PEAL TO SHAKE ALL PEOPLE . . . 109 3 DON JUAN 7 85 7
OF HOPES AND FEARS WHICH SHAKE A SINGLE BALL . . . 304 3 DON JUAN 11 72 8
WHICH DOTH NOT SHAKE SOME VERY SPLENDID HOUSE . . . 370 3 DON JUAN 13 26 4
OR SHOULD IT SHAKE THE CHOICE WILL MORE PERPLEX-- . . 371 3 DON JUAN 13 30 4

SHAKEN
WALKS O'ER IT WAS SHE SHAKEN BY THE DREAM . . . . 360 2 DON JUAN 4 30 3
HE RUSHED WHILE EARTH AND AIR WERE SADLY SHAKEN . . . 129 3 DON JUAN 8 33 7
REDEEMING WORLDS TO BE BY BIGOTS SHAKEN . . . . . 464 3 DON JUAN 15 18 5
WERE SHAKEN DOWN AND DOGS HAD HAD THEIR DAY . . . . 466 3 DON JUAN 15 23 4
DON JUAN SHOOK AS ERST HE HAD BEEN SHAKEN . . . . . 558 3 DON JUAN 16 118 1

SHAKES
SO SHAKES THE NEEDLE AND SO STANDS THE POLE . . . . 133 2 DON JUAN 1 196 7
A MODERATE PENSION SHAKES FULL MANY A SAGE . . . . 118 3 DON JUAN 8 14 4
THE RUBY GLASS THAT SHAKES WITHIN HIS HAND . . . . 457 3 DON JUAN 15 4 7
FOR LAUGHTER RARELY SHAKES THESE AGUISH FOLKS . . . 540 3 DON JUAN 16 83 V3

SHAKESPEAR
I THINK ONE SHAKESPEAR PUTS THE SAME THOUGHT IN . . . 77 3 DON JUAN 7 21 6

SHAKESPEARE
SHAKESPEARE EXCLAIMS--HANG UP PHILOSOPHY . . . . . 272 2 DON JUAN 2 V 1 1
LIKE NATURAL SHAKESPEARE ON THE IMMORTAL PAGE . . . 490 2 DON JUAN 5 136 V4
SAYS SHAKESPEARE WHO JUST NOW IS MUCH IN FASHION . . 189 3 DON JUAN 9 14 2
THERE HAD NOT BEEN ONE SHAKESPEARE AND VOLTAIRE . . . 481 3 DON JUAN 15 59 7

SHAKESPEARIAN
WAS MORE SHAKESPEARIAN IF I DO NOT ERR . . . . . 524 3 DON JUAN 16 48 4

SHAKING
BUT PERISHED WITHOUT SHIVERING OR SHAKING . . . . 150 3 DON JUAN 8 76 5
THE NIGHT BEFORE BUT BEING SICK OF SHAKING . . . . 558 3 DON JUAN 16 118 2

SHAKSPEARE
BUT SHAKSPEARE ALSO SAY 'TIS VERY SILLY . . . . . 314 2 DON JUAN 3 76 7
SHAKSPEARE TALKS OF THE HERALD MERCURY . . . . . 215 3 DON JUAN 9 66 1

SHAKSPEARE'S
LIKE SHAKSPEARE'S STEALING DEER LORD BACON'S BRIBES . . 329 2 DON JUAN 3 92 2
THE PHRASE IS SHAKSPEARE'S AND NOT MISAPPLIED-- . . 184 3 DON JUAN 9 4 2
FOR WHICH SEE SHAKSPEARE'S EVER BLOOMING GARDEN-- . . 442 3 DON JUAN 14 75 2

SHALLOW
IS APT TO TIRE A CALM AND SHALLOW STATION . . . . 191 3 DON JUAN 9 18 6
LIKE ARNO IN THE SUMMER TO A SHALLOW . . . . . 228 3 DON JUAN 10 7 2
OF THEIR SALT VEINS AND THEIR SAD SHALLOW SEAS . . . 251 3 DON JUAN 10 54 V4

SHAME
NO SOONER WAS IT BOLTED THAN--OH SHAME . . . . . 112 2 DON JUAN 1 165 1
MY SHAME AND SORROW DEEP IN MY HEART'S CORE . . . 132 2 DON JUAN 1 195 4
TO FEEL AT LEAST A PATRIOT'S SHAME . . . . . . 323 2 DON JUAN 3 L 6 3
SHALL SORROW LIGHT OR SHAME SHE WAS NOT MADE . . . 382 2 DON JUAN 4 71 2
METHINKS--SAID HE--IT WOULD BE NO GREAT SHAME . . . 434 2 DON JUAN 5 43 5
AND THEN HER SEX'S SHAME BROKE IN AT LAST . . . . 490 2 DON JUAN 5 137 3
NOR SHOW YOUR GEORGIAN IGNORANCE--FOR SHAME . . . 28 3 DON JUAN 6 44 5
THAT HATER OF MANKIND WOULD BE A SHAME . . . . . 53 3 DON JUAN 6 94 3
THEIR REASONS WERE UNCERTAINTY OR SHAME . . . . . 132 3 DON JUAN 8 38 5
SIMPLE SERENE THE ANTIPODES OF SHAME . . . . . 144 3 DON JUAN 8 63 5
THROUGH FIFTY VICTORIES TO SHAME OR FAME . . . . 189 3 DON JUAN 9 14 7
THROUGH PLEASURES THICK AND THIN TO FAME OR SHAME . . 189 3 DON JUAN 9 14 V7
SO NARROW AS TO SHAME THEIR WINTRY BRINK . . . . 228 3 DON JUAN 10 7 3
BUT LOVE SANS BANNS IS BOTH A SIN AND SHAME . . . 323 3 DON JUAN 12 15 7

SHAMROCK
WHOSE SHAMROCK NOW SEEMS RATHER WORSE FOR WEARING . . . 286 3 DON JUAN 11 38 8

SHA'N'T
BUT WHAT THAT MOTIVE WAS I SHA'N'T SAY HERE . . . 75 2 DON JUAN 1 101 5
WOULD HAVE PROVOKED REMARKS WHICH NOW IT SHAN'T . . 397 2 DON JUAN 4 98 8
NAY QUOTH THE MAID THE SULTAN'S SELF SHAN'T CARRY ME . . 460 2 DON JUAN 5 84 7
A MAN LIKE WHOM I HOPE WE SHAN'T SEE MANY SOON . . . 484 3 DON JUAN 15 65 4

SHAPE
HER EYEBROW'S SHAPE WAS LIKE THE AERIAL BOW . . . 55 2 DON JUAN 1 61 3
A COW'S SHAPE FOR A MASK--WAS ONLY (SINKING . . . 238 2 DON JUAN 2 155 5
SO BEAUTIFUL--ITS VERY SHAPE WOULD CHARM . . . . 312 2 DON JUAN 3 71 5
IN SOME SHAPE LET NONE THINK TO FLY THE DANGER . . . 383 2 DON JUAN 4 73 7
EXCEPT IN SHAPE OF ENVOYS WHO WERE SENT . . . . 498 2 DON JUAN 5 151 1
HER SHAPE HER HAIR HER AIR HER EVERYTHING . . . . 23 3 DON JUAN 6 35 2
THE CITY'S SHAPE SUGGESTED THIS 'TIS TRUE . . . . 78 3 DON JUAN 7 23 6
AND SHELLS AND SHOT OF EVERY SIZE AND SHAPE . . . 81 3 DON JUAN 7 29 8
A THOUSAND PERILS IN THIS DUBIOUS SHAPE . . . . . 103 3 DON JUAN 7 72 4
IN SHAPE OF MOONSHINE HOVERS O'ER THE PILE-- . . . 279 3 DON JUAN 11 24 7
COULD E'ER EXPRESS IN ITS EXPANDED SHAPE . . . . 375 3 DON JUAN 13 37 8
OTHERS THAT SOME ORIGINAL SHAPE OR FORM . . . . . 388 3 DON JUAN 13 64 1

SHAPED
    OR THOUGHT THEY SAW AND SHAPED THEIR COURSE FOR SHORE . . 207 2 DON JUAN 2   97   6
    HE SHAPED HIS COURSE TO WHERE HIS DAUGHTER FAIR . . . . 285 2 DON JUAN 3   19   4
    SHAPED BY DECAY PERCHANCE HATH GIVEN THE POWER . . . . 388 3 DON JUAN 13   64   2
SHAPES
    ENGENDERED MONSTROUS SHAPES OF EVERY CRIME . . . . . 152 3 DON JUAN 8   82   8
SHARE
    TO OTHERS' SHARE LET FEMALE ERRORS FALL . . . . . . 29 2 DON JUAN 1   16   7
    BUT NONE OF THEM APPEAR'D TO SHARE HIS WOES . . . . . 213 2 DON JUAN 2 109   5
    MUST SHARE IT--HAPPINESS WAS BORN A TWIN . . . . . . 247 2 DON JUAN 2 172   8
    WOULD SHARE MOST PROBABLY ITS RESURRECTION . . . . . 301 2 DON JUAN 3   50   8
    FOR HIS OWN SHARE--HE SAW BUT SMALL OBJECTION . . . . 452 2 DON JUAN 5   71   1
    SO SILLY AS TO BUY SLAVES WHO MIGHT SHARE . . . . . . 24 3 DON JUAN 6   36   6
    AND FOR THEIR OTHER MATTERS MEET AND SHARE 'EM . . . . 53 3 DON JUAN 6   95   8
    TO SHARE HER BEAUTY AND HER BANISHMENT . . . . . . 193 3 DON JUAN 9   22   8
    WHO LIKE DON JUAN TAKES AN ACTIVE SHARE . . . . . . 303 3 DON JUAN 11   70   2
    WHICH MEANS THAT VULGAR PEOPLE MUST NOT SHARE IT . . . 419 3 DON JUAN 14   21   8
    SERF LORD MAN WITH SUCH SKILL AS NONE WOULD SHARE IT IF . 481 3 DON JUAN 15   59   6
    THE WISE MAN'S SURE WHEN HE NO MORE CAN SHARE IT HE . . 566 3 DON JUAN 17   9   7
SHARED
    BUT ERE THEY CAME TO THIS THEY THAT DAY SHARED . . . . 195 2 DON JUAN 2   74   1
    FILLED AS WITH LIGHTNING--FOR HIS SPIRIT SHARED . . . 129 3 DON JUAN 8   33   3
    OF FRIAR BACON'S BRIGHT INVENTION--SHARED . . . . . 129 3 DON JUAN 8   33 V5
    BUT JUAN ALSO SHARED IN HER AUSTERITY . . . . 432 3 DON JUAN 14   51   5
SHARES
    WHEN THEY SUSPECT THAT ANYONE GOES SHARES . . . . . 11 3 DON JUAN 6   10   7
SHARK
    BUT LIKE THE SHARK AND TIGER MUST HAVE PREY . . . . . 191 2 DON JUAN 2   67   4
    THE GREATEST DANGER HERE WAS FROM A SHARK . . . . . 212 2 DON JUAN 2 106   5
    A PRIEST A SHARK AN ALDERMAN OR PIKE . . . . 239 2 DON JUAN 2 157   8
SHARKS
    REGALED TWO SHARKS WHO FOLLOW'D O'ER THE BILLOW-- . . 197 2 DON JUAN 2   77   7
    THOUGH THE TWO SHARKS STILL FOLLOW'D THEM AND DASH'D . 209 2 DON JUAN 2 101   7
SHARP
    AND SHARP ADVERSITY WILL TEACH AT LAST . . . . . . 345 2 DON JUAN 4   2   2
    O'ER THE SHARP SHINGLES WITH HER BLEEDING FEET . . . 361 2 DON JUAN 4   32   2
    THE SHARP ROCKS LOOK'D BELOW EACH DROP THEY CAUGHT . . 362 2 DON JUAN 4   33   7
    AT THE FIRST NOTES IRREGULAR AND SHARP . . . . . . 379 2 DON JUAN 4   65   3
    AT LEAST THE SHARP POINTS OF THAT BURNING MARLE . . . 124 3 DON JUAN 8   26 V7
    HIS SIDE AS A SMALL SWORD BUT SHARP AS EVER . . . . . 205 3 DON JUAN 9   45   4
    YE VILLAINS AND ABOVE ALL KEEP A SHARP EYE . . . . . 310 3 DON JUAN 11   86   5
    AND MAKE A MUSIC WHETHER FLAT OR SHARP . . . . . . 402 3 DON JUAN 13   93   4
SHARPEN'D
    IS SHARPEN'D FROM ITS HIGH CELESTIAL FLAVOUR . . . . 277 2 DON JUAN 3   5   7
SHARPER
    A THOUSAND SHARPER SABRES WAIT THE WORD . . . . . . 364 2 DON JUAN 4   37 V7
SHARPERS'
    SOME HEIRESSES HAVE BIT AT SHARPERS' HOOKS . . . . . 308 3 DON JUAN 11   81   3
SHARPLY
    WILL IT SAID JUAN SHARPLY STRIKE ME DEAD . . . . . . 452 2 DON JUAN 5   71   7
SHATTER
    AND YET WHO CAN BELIEVE IT I WOULD SHATTER . . . . . 268 3 DON JUAN 11   1   5
SHATTER'D
    STARTED THE STERN-POST ALSO SHATTER'D THE . . . . . 170 2 DON JUAN 2   27   4
    BECAUSE THE TACKLE OF OUR SHATTER'D BARK . . . . . . 206 2 DON JUAN 2   95   3
SHAVE
    RESET IT SHAVE MORE SMOOTHLY ALSO SLOWER . . . . . . 433 3 DON JUAN 14   53   7
SHAVED
    THOSE ANTIENT GOOD INTENTIONS WHICH ONCE SHAVED . . . 124 3 DON JUAN 8   26   6
SHAVING
    SO SMOOTH SO LEVEL SUCH A MODE OF SHAVING . . . . . 263 3 DON JUAN 10   78   2
    HAVE SHAVING TOO ENTAILED UPON THEIR CHINS-- . . . . 420 3 DON JUAN 14   23   8
SHAWL
    JUAN HAD ON A SHAWL OF BLACK AND GOLD . . . . 315 2 DON JUAN 3   77   1
    A SHAWL WHOSE FOLDS IN CASHMIRE HAD BEEN NURST . . . 451 2 DON JUAN 5   68   6
SHAWLED
    SHAWLED TO THE NOSE AND BEARDED TO THE EYES . . . . . 495 2 DON JUAN 5 147   2
SHEARS
    NOR SHEARS OF ATROPOS BEFORE THEIR VISIONS . . . . . 190 2 DON JUAN 2   64   6
SHEATH
    TURNS LIFE TO TERROR EVEN THOUGH IN ITS SHEATH . . . 188 3 DON JUAN 9   11   7
    STINGS IN LIFE WITH APPREHENSION IN ITS SHEATH . . . 188 3 DON JUAN 9   11 V7
SHE'D
    AND BEGGED THEY WOULD EXCUSE HER SHE'D GET OVER . . . 47 3 DON JUAN 6   83   7
    HER ANGER AND BESEECH'D SHE'D HEAR HIM THROUGH-- . . 57 3 DON JUAN 6 102   3
    WITH MORE EASE TOO SHE'D TELL A DIFFERENT STORY . . . 416 3 DON JUAN 14   13   8
    THAT--BUT ASK ANY WOMAN IF SHE'D CHOOSE . . . . . . 421 3 DON JUAN 14   25   6
    BEGAN TO DREAD SHE'D THAW TO A COQUETTE-- . . . . . 492 3 DON JUAN 15   81   4
SHED
    I AM ASHAMED OF HAVING SHED THESE TEARS . . . . . . 106 2 DON JUAN 1 155   5
    BUT BEAUTIFUL SHE LAY--HER EYES SHED TEARS . . . . . 108 2 DON JUAN 1 158 V2
    THEIR HEARTS THE STARS THEIR NUPTIAL TORCHES SHED . . 265 2 DON JUAN 2 204   2
    HIS ANGRY WORD ONCE O'ER HE SHED NO BLOOD . . . . . 300 2 DON JUAN 3   48   6
    TEARS SHED INTO THE GRAVE OF THE CONNEXION . . . . . 301 2 DON JUAN 3   50   7
    SHED ITS IONIAN ELEGANCE WHICH SHOW'D . . . . 304 2 DON JUAN 3   56   2
    AND SHED THE BLOOD OF SCIO'S VINE . . . . 324 2 DON JUAN 3 L 9   4
    SUCH AS I TOO WOULD SHED IF IN YOUR PLACE . . . . . 420 2 DON JUAN 5   19   6
    AND IS THIS BLOOD THEN FORMED BUT TO BE SHED . . . . 432 2 DON JUAN 5   39   4
    FOR WOMEN SHED AND USE THEM AT THEIR LIKING . . . . 479 2 DON JUAN 5 118   2

SHED   (CONTINUED)
     HER EYES ANOTHER'S EYE COULD SHED A TEAR . . . . 480 2 DON JUAN 5   119   8
     TO FIND RETORTS FOR INNOCENT BLOOD SHED . . . . 314 3 DON JUAN 11 V 75   4
SHEDDING
     OF HONEST FAME THAN SHEDDING SEAS OF GORE . . . . 113 3 DON JUAN 8   3   8
SHEDS
     SHEDS BEAUTY AND DEEP SOFTNESS O'ER THE WHOLE . . . . . 82 2 DON JUAN 1   114   6
     TIME SHEDS A MOMENT O'ER EACH SPARKLING CREST . . . . . 480 3 DON JUAN 15   55   6
SHEEN
     THE MOVING FIGURES AND THE SPARKLING SHEEN . . . . 289 2 DON JUAN 3   27   6
SHEEP
     THE QUIET SHEEP FEEDS AND THE TORTOISE CRAWLS . . . . . 386 2 DON JUAN 4   77   8
     WHO LOOK'D A WHITE LAMB YET WAS A BLACK SHEEP . . . . . . 396 3 DON JUAN 13   79   8
SHEET
     BE ON THIS SHEET 'TIS NOT WHAT IT APPEARS . . . . 130 2 DON JUAN 1   192   7
     AND DARE NOT SET MY SEAL UPON THIS SHEET . . . . 134 2 DON JUAN 1   197   2
     UNTIL THEY FOUND A RAGGED PIECE OF SHEET . . . . 201 2 DON JUAN 2   85   2
     AND SOMETHING ROLL'D BEFORE HER IN A SHEET . . . . 361 2 DON JUAN 4   32   4
     AND LAY THIS SHEET OF SORROWS ON THE SHELF . . . . 384 2 DON JUAN 4   74   2
     IN TAKING UP THIS PALTRY SHEET OF PAPER . . . . 226 3 DON JUAN 10   3   2
SHEETS
     WHILE THEY THRUST SHEETS SHIRTS JACKETS BALES OF MUSLIN . 171 2 DON JUAN 2   28   8
     UPON IN SHEETS WHITE AS WHAT BARDS CALL DRIVEN . . . . . 18 3 DON JUAN 6   25   5
     THE OTHER LOOKS LIKE PHOSPHORUS ON SHEETS . . . . 281 3 DON JUAN 11   27   5
     OR CRAMM'D TWELVE SHEETS INTO ONE LITTLE LETTER . . . . 406 3 DON JUAN 13   104   7
SHELF
     AND LAY THIS SHEET OF SORROWS ON THE SHELF . . . . 384 2 DON JUAN 4   74   2
     WHICH LAYS BOTH MEN AND WOMEN ON THE SHELF . . . . 41 3 DON JUAN 6   69   7
     ARRANGING THEM LIKE BOOKS ON THE SAME SHELF . . . . . . 470 3 DON JUAN 15   31   3
SHE'LL
     START NOT STILL CHASTER READER--SHE'LL BE NICE HENCEFORWARD 86 2 DON JUAN 1   120   2
     BUT NEVER MIND--SHE'LL TURN PERHAPS NEXT WEEK . . . . . 418 2 DON JUAN 5   14   6
     OR DONE IS LIGHT TO WHAT SHE'LL SAY OR DO-- . . . . . . 214 3 DON JUAN 9   64   7
     THE TIME WILL COME SHE'LL WISH THAT SHE HAD SNATCHED . . 332 3 DON JUAN 12   35   3
SHELL
     PRESENTED A FINE MARK TO THROW A SHELL IN . . . . 78 3 DON JUAN 7   23   8
     SOME PRETTY SHELL IS BEST FOR MODERATE BATHERS . . . . . 191 3 DON JUAN 9   18   8
     MORE MUSE-LIKE--SAY LIKE CYTHEREA'S SHELL . . . . 339 3 DON JUAN 12   51   8
     OF STUBBORN SHELL WHICH WAVES AND WEATHER WEAR NOT . . . 431 3 DON JUAN 14   49   4
     BECAUSE HE MOPETH IDLY IN HIS SHELL . . . . 445 3 DON JUAN 14   81   2
SHELL-FISH
     AND SHUT OUR SOULS UP IN US LIKE A SHELL-FISH . . . . . 236 3 DON JUAN 10   23   8
     IF FROM A SHELL-FISH OR FROM COCHINEAL . . . . 505 3 DON JUAN 16   10   7
SHELLS
     OVER THE SHINING PEBBLES AND THE SHELLS . . . . 253 2 DON JUAN 2   184   2
     PICKING UP SHELLS BY THE GREAT OCEAN--TRUTH . . . . . . 69 3 DON JUAN 7   5   8
     AND SHELLS AND SHOT OF EVERY SIZE AND SHAPE . . . . . . 81 3 DON JUAN 7   29   8
     AND SHELLS OR HELLS IT COULD NOT MORE HAVE GOADED . . . 119 3 DON JUAN 8   16   4
SHELTER
     TO SHELTER THEIR DEVOTION FROM THE WIND . . . . 384 3 DON JUAN 13   55   8
SHELTERED
     AND THERE A LITTLE SHELTERED FROM THE SHOT . . . . 131 3 DON JUAN 8   37   1
SHELVE
     BY SOME LOW ROCK OR SHELVE THAT MADE IT FRET . . . . . . 251 2 DON JUAN 2   181   7
SHE-PARADES
     WITHOUT HER SANCTION ON THEIR SHE-PARADES . . . . 21 3 DON JUAN 6   30   7
SHEPHERD
     IS DREADFUL TO THE SHEPHERD AND THE FLOCK . . . . 305 3 DON JUAN 3   58   2
     SHEPHERD OR SWAIN WHOEVER MAY BEHOLD . . . . 506 3 DON JUAN 16   14   2
SHEPHERDS
     SOME SHEPHERDS (UNLIKE PARIS) LED TO STARE . . . . 387 2 DON JUAN 4   78   3
SHERBET
     FOR NOT THE BLEST SHERBET SUBLIMED WITH SNOW . . . . . . 251 2 DON JUAN 2   180   4
     AND SHERBET COOLING IN THE POROUS VASE . . . . 291 2 DON JUAN 3   31   5
SHERBETS
     THE BEVERAGE WAS VARIOUS SHERBETS . . . . 307 2 DON JUAN 3   62   6
     WITH VIANDS AND SHERBETS IN ICE--AND WINE-- . . . . . . 310 2 DON JUAN 3   69   7
SHERIDAN
     WHERE GRATTAN CURRAN SHERIDAN ALL THOSE . . . . 307 3 DON JUAN 11   77   3
SHE'S
     WILL HARDLY LEAVE YOU (AS SHE'S NOT YOUR WIFE) . . . . . 419 2 DON JUAN 5   17   3
     THOUGH SUCH A SHE'S A DEVIL (IF THAT THERE BE ONE) . . .   7 3 DON JUAN 6   3   7
     AND WHY BECAUSE SHE'S CHANGEABLE AND CHASTE . . . . . . 230 3 DON JUAN 10   11   1
     A WOMAN SO SHE'S GOOD WHAT DOES IT SIGNIFY . . . . 435 3 DON JUAN 14   57   8
SHEW
     WHO NAME THE FRENCH IN ENGLISH SAVE TO SHEW . . . . . . 77 3 DON JUAN 7   22   7
     I RAILED AT SCOTS TO SHEW MY WRATH AND WIT . . . . 234 3 DON JUAN 10   19   3
SHEWED
     SHEWED JUAN OR JUANNA THROUGH AND THROUGH . . . . 34 3 DON JUAN 6   57   4
     GULBEYAZ SHEWED THEM BOTH COMMISERATION . . . . 65 3 DON JUAN 6   119   3
     SHEWED THAT SOMEWHERE SOMEHOW THERE WAS A FAULT . . . . 83 3 DON JUAN 7   35   2
     HE SHEWED HIMSELF AS KIND AS MORTAL CAN . . . . 144 3 DON JUAN 8   64   8
SHIBBOLETH
     OF ENGLISH SAVE THEIR SHIBBOLETH GOD DAMN . . . . 274 3 DON JUAN 11   12   2
SHIELD
     THE LIBELLER'S GRATIS COUNSEL DIRTY SHIELD . . . . 151 2 DON JUAN 1 V 2   3
     A BLOTTED SHIELD NO SHIRE'S TRUE KNIGHT WOULD WEAR . . . 153 2 DON JUAN 1 V 4   6
     A SORT OF BLOTTED SHIELD FEW KNIGHTS WOULD WEAR . . . . 153 2 DON JUAN 1 V 4   V6
     WOULD BREAK YOUR SHIELD HOWEVER BROAD . . . . 325 2 DON JUAN 3 L 14   6

SHIELD   (CONTINUED)
    IN COURAGE WAS OBLIGED TO SNATCH A SHIELD 125   3 DON JUAN   8   28   7
    JUAN WHO HAD NO SHIELD TO SNATCH AND WAS 126   3 DON JUAN   8   29   1
    ARE TOUCHED WITH A DESIRE TO SHIELD AND SAVE-- 164   3 DON JUAN   8   106   3
    BECAUSE A HUNCHBACK--MADE HIS BREAST THE SHIELD 166   3 DON JUAN   8   110   V7
    HIS STUBBORN VALOUR WAS NO FUTURE SHIELD 172   3 DON JUAN   8   122   3
    AND MADE A VOW TO SHIELD HER WHICH HE KEPT 182   3 DON JUAN   8   141   8
    FOR SUCH A SHIELD WHICH LEAVES BUT LITTLE MERIT 372   3 DON JUAN 13   31   2
    SUCH WERE HIS TROPHIES--NOT OF SPEAR AND SHIELD 425   3 DON JUAN 14   35   1
    TO SHIELD HIMSELF THAN PUT YOU ON YOUR GUARD 462   3 DON JUAN 15   14   4
    HOW SWEET THE TASK TO SHIELD AN ABSENT FRIEND 552   3 DON JUAN 16   104   7
SHIFT
    AND AS THE VEERING WIND SHIFTS SHIFT OUR SAILS 159   2 DON JUAN   2   4   4
    AT ONE O'CLOCK THE WIND WITH SUDDEN SHIFT 170   2 DON JUAN   2   27   1
SHIFTS
    AND AS THE VEERING WIND SHIFTS SHIFT OUR SAILS 159   2 DON JUAN   2   4   4
    THE WIND SHIFTS AND I FLY INTO A RAGE 566   3 DON JUAN 17   10   8
SHILLING
    'TWOULD SAVE US MANY A HEART-ACHE MANY A SHILLING 270   2 DON JUAN   2   213   5
    SHINE LIKE A GUINEA AND SEVEN SHILLING PIECES 306   2 DON JUAN   3   60   8
    OF BEAUTY FLATTERY THREATS A SHILLING--NO 439   2 DON JUAN   5   49   3
    THAT DAILY SHILLING WHICH MAKES WARRIORS TOUGH)-- 134   3 DON JUAN   8   42   6
SHILOH
    JOANNA SOUTHCOTE'S SHILOH AND HER SECT   330   2 DON JUAN   3   95   4
SHINE
    BUT IF THERE'S ANY THING IN WHICH I SHINE 33   2 DON JUAN   1   23   6
    SHINE LIKE A GUINEA AND SEVEN SHILLING PIECES 306   2 DON JUAN   3   60   8
    I SEE THEIR GLORIOUS BLACK EYES SHINE 326   2 DON JUAN   3 L 15   3
    YET SMELT ROAST-MEAT BEHELD A HUGE FIRE SHINE 439   2 DON JUAN   5   50   5
    I WISH TO HEAVEN HE WOULD NOT SHINE TILL MORNING 494   2 DON JUAN   5   145   2
    OF CANTEMIR OR KNOLLES WHERE FEW SHINE 495   2 DON JUAN   5   147   7
    I DID MY VERY BOYISH BEST TO SHINE 37   3 DON JUAN   6   62   5
    WITH MUSIC THE MOST MODERATE SHINE AS WITS 340   3 DON JUAN 12   52   7
    OUR GAY RUSS SPANIARD WAS ORDAINED TO SHINE 383   3 DON JUAN 13   53   4
    AND SHINE THE VERY SIRIA OF THE SPHERES 397   3 DON JUAN 13   82   7
    THE FOUR MISS RAWBOLDS IN A GLEE WOULD SHINE 408   3 DON JUAN 13   107   5
    IN EYES WHICH SADLY SHONE AS SERAPHS' SHINE 476   3 DON JUAN 15   45   3
    MUCH AS SHE WOULD HAVE SEEN A GLOWWORM SHINE 480   3 DON JUAN 15   56   3
    WAS NOT SUCH AS TO ENCOURAGE HIM TO SHINE 489   3 DON JUAN 15   75   6
SHINES
    BECAUSE THEY STILL CAN HOPE NOR SHINES THE KNIFE 190   2 DON JUAN   2   64   5
    AND THE SEA SHINES WITH PURPLE--WHITE--AND GOLD 230   2 DON JUAN   2   139   V7
    THE ANSWER ELOQUENT WHERE THE SOUL SHINES 241   2 DON JUAN   2   162   5
    WEIGH NOT THE THIN ORE WHERE THEIR VISAGE SHINES 321   3 DON JUAN 12   12   4
    BECAUSE THE SUN AND STARS AND AUGHT THAT SHINES . . . 423   3 DON JUAN 14   29   5
SHINGLES
    O'ER THE SHARP SHINGLES WITH HER BLEEDING FEET 361   3 DON JUAN   4   32   2
    WHICH RUSHES TO SOME SHORE WHOSE SHINGLES CHECK . . . 60   3 DON JUAN   6   108   7
SHINING
    AND LOSE IN SHINING SNOW THEIR SUMMITS BLUE 94   2 DON JUAN   1   134   V5
    OVER THE SHINING PEBBLES AND THE SHELLS 253   2 DON JUAN   2   184   2
    HE SAW HIS WHITE WALLS SHINING IN THE SUN 289   2 DON JUAN   3   27   1
    ITS GLORY THROUGH ALL AGES SHINING SUNNY 529   3 DON JUAN 16   59   7
SHIP
    AS IF A SPANISH SHIP WERE NOAH'S ARK 161   2 DON JUAN   2   8   6
    JUAN EMBARK'D--THE SHIP GOT UNDER WAY 162   2 DON JUAN   2   11   1
    AND THE SHIP CREAK'D THE TOWN BECAME A SPECK 163   2 DON JUAN   2   13   3
    (HERE THE SHIP GAVE A LURCH AND HE GREW SEA-SICK) . . . 166   2 DON JUAN   2   19   8
    THE SHIP CALL'D THE MOST HOLY TRINIDADA 169   2 DON JUAN   2   24   1
    THREW THE SHIP RIGHT INTO THE TROUGH OF THE SEA 170   2 DON JUAN   2   27   2
    AND KEEP THE SHIP AFLOAT THOUGH THREE FEET YET 172   2 DON JUAN   2   30   3
    LAID WITH ONE BLAST THE SHIP ON HER BEAM ENDS 172   2 DON JUAN   2   30   8
    THE MAINMAST FOLLOW'D BUT THE SHIP STILL LAY 173   2 DON JUAN   2   32   3
    AND THEN WITH VIOLENCE THE OLD SHIP RIGHTED 173   2 DON JUAN   2   32   8
    THE SHIP WOULD SWIM AN HOUR WHICH BY GOOD LUCK 177   2 DON JUAN   2   40   7
    BUT THE SHIP LABOUR'D SO THEY SCARCE COULD HOPE 178   2 DON JUAN   2   41   2
    THE SHIP WAS EVIDENTLY SETTLING NOW 179   2 DON JUAN   2   44   1
    HE LEFT HIS SHIP TO BE HOVE DOWN NEXT DAY 286   2 DON JUAN   3   20   5
    THAT EVER SCUTTLED SHIP OR CUT A THROAT 296   2 DON JUAN   3   41   2
    THEREFORE I'LL MAKE DON JUAN LEAVE THE SHIP SOON 397   2 DON JUAN   4   97   5
    THE LANDS ON EITHER SIDE ARE HIS THE SHIP 320   3 DON JUAN 12   9   1
    SHIP OFF THE HOLY THREE TO SENEGAL 446   3 DON JUAN 14   83   2
    LIKE A GOOD SHIP ENTANGLED AMONG ICE 490   3 DON JUAN 15   77   7
SHIPP'D
    SHE SENT HER SON TO BE SHIPP'D OFF FROM CADIZ 128   2 DON JUAN   1   190   8
SHIPPING
    A MIGHTY MASS OF BRICK AND SMOKE AND SHIPPING 265   3 DON JUAN 10   82   1
SHIP'S
    THREW IN BY GOOD LUCK OVER THE SHIP'S RAIL 181   2 DON JUAN   2   48   6
SHIPS
    A LIST OF SHIPS AND CAPTAINS AND KINGS REIGNING 135   2 DON JUAN   1   200   4
    AND SHIPS BY THOUSANDS LAY BELOW 322   2 DON JUAN   3 L 4   3
    WHERE LAY SOME SHIPS WHICH WERE TO SAIL AT NINE 371   2 DON JUAN   4   50   4
    THE MOSLEM TOO HAD LOST BOTH SHIPS AND MEN 82   3 DON JUAN   7   31   1
    WHERE SHIPS HAVE FOUNDERED AS DOTH MANY A BOAT 227   3 DON JUAN 10   4   8
    AND AS THE GOOD SHIPS SENT UPON THAT MESSAGE 376   3 DON JUAN 13   39   3
    BY HOMER'S CATALOGUE OF SHIPS IS CLEAR   393   3 DON JUAN 13   74   6
    IN CAMPS IN SHIPS IN COTTAGES OR COURTS-- 424   3 DON JUAN 14   31   4
SHIPWRECK'D
    FORSOOK THE DIM EYES OF THESE SHIPWRECK'D MEN 204   2 DON JUAN   2   91   8

                                      723

	PAGE	VOL		CANTO	STANZA	LN
SHIPWRECK'D (CONTINUED)						
OUR SHIPWRECK'D SEAMEN THOUGHT IT A GOOD OMEN--	205	2 DON JUAN	2	93	1
ALL TRANQUILLY THE SHIPWRECK'D BOY WAS LYING	233	2 DON JUAN	2	144	3
AND THAT A SHIPWRECK'D YOUTH WOULD HUNGRY BE	233	2 DON JUAN	2	145	2
SHIPWRECK'S						
WHEN SHIPWRECK'S SHORT ALLOWANCE GROWS TOO SCANTY	200	2 DON JUAN	2	83	7
SHIRE'S						
A BLOTTED SHIELD NO SHIRE'S TRUE KNIGHT WOULD WEAR	153	2 DON JUAN	1	V 4	6
SHIRT						
AS WHEN HE SWORE BY GOD HE'D SELL HIS SHIRT	154	2 DON JUAN	1	V 5	3
WITH A CLEAN SHIRT AND VERY SPACIOUS BREECHES	240	2 DON JUAN	2	160	8
STRIPT TO HIS SHIRT WAS COME TO LEAD THE VAN	90	3 DON JUAN	7	49	8
SUWARROW WHO WAS STANDING IN HIS SHIRT	96	3 DON JUAN	7	58	1
THAN CAN BE HID BY ALTERING HIS SHIRT HE	232	3 DON JUAN	10	15	4
SHIRTLESS						
WHO ROUSE THE SHIRTLESS PATRIOTS OF SPAIN	318	3 DON JUAN	12	5	3
SHIRTS						
WHILE THEY THRUST SHEETS SHIRTS JACKETS BALES OF MUSLIN	171	2 DON JUAN	2	28	8
FOR THERE WERE BUT THREE SHIRTS BETWEEN THE TWO	87	3 DON JUAN	7	43	5
SHIVER						
AND SHIVER THEM TO ASHES BUT TO TRAIL	348	2 DON JUAN	4	9	6
PERHAPS MIGHT MAKE HIM SHIVER YAWN OR THROW	121	3 DON JUAN	8	21	5
SHIVER'D						
WHERE ALL HIS HOUSEHOLD GODS LAY SHIVER'D ROUND HIM	41	2 DON JUAN	1	36	6
SHIVERED						
WAVING LIKE SAILS NEW SHIVERED IN A STORM	204	3 DON JUAN	9	43	3
CRACKED SHIVERED VANISHED SCARCELY GAZED ON ERE	306	3 DON JUAN	11	76	5
SEEMED PALE AND SHIVERED AS IF SHE HAD KEPT	568	3 DON JUAN	17	14	7
SHIVERING						
SENDS SIN WITHOUT A RAG ON SHIVERING FORTH	57	2 DON JUAN	1	64	3
AT WATCH AND WATCH THUS SHIVERING LIKE THE TERTIAN	189	2 DON JUAN	2	63	6
THEN HE HIMSELF SUNK DOWN ALL DUMB AND SHIVERING	204	2 DON JUAN	2	90	7
A CROWD OF SHIVERING SLAVES OF EVERY NATION	414	2 DON JUAN	5	7	1
BUT PERISHED WITHOUT SHIVERING OR SHAKING	150	3 DON JUAN	8	76	5
SHOAL						
AS GEOGRAPHERS LAY DOWN A SHOAL IN MAPS	155	2 DON JUAN	1	V 7	8
BUT THAT PART OF THE COAST BEING SHOAL AND BARE	285	2 DON JUAN	3	19	6
THUS GENTLEMEN MAY RUN UPON A SHOAL	376	3 DON JUAN	13	39	6
SHOALS						
THE LEAK INCREASED SHOALS ROUND HER BUT NO SHORE	176	2 DON JUAN	2	38	3
GUARDED BY SHOALS AND ROCKS AS BY AN HOST	249	2 DON JUAN	2	177	3
SHOCK						
A KIND OF SHOCK THAT SETS ONE'S HEART AJAR	164	2 DON JUAN	2	14	6
BUT OF MATERIALS THAT MUCH SHOCK THE MUSE--	195	2 DON JUAN	2	74	6
THEIR FURY BEING SPENT BY ITS OWN SHOCK	305	2 DON JUAN	3	58	6
AND THUS WITH WOMEN HOWSOE'ER IT SHOCK SOME'S	371	3 DON JUAN	13	30	7
MIGHT SHOCK A CONNOISSEUR BUT WHEN COMBINED	390	3 DON JUAN	13	67	3
AND WHEN THEY HAVE MADE THE SHORE THROUGH EV'RY SHOCK	442	3 DON JUAN	14	74	7
SHOCK'D						
BUT BEING NAKED SHE WAS SHOCK'D YOU KNOW	224	2 DON JUAN	2	129	5
SHOCKED						
SHE WAS A GOOD DEAL SHOCKED NOT SHOCKED AT TEARS	479	2 DON JUAN	5	118	1
SHE WAS A GOOD DEAL SHOCKED NOT SHOCKED AT TEARS	479	2 DON JUAN	5	118	1
THE SOVEREIGN SHOCKED AND ALL HIS MEDICINES DOUBLED	244	3 DON JUAN	10	39	8
SHOCKING						
AND IF PEDRILLO'S FATE SHOULD SHOCKING BE	200	2 DON JUAN	2	83	1
FLASH'D ON HER LITTLE HAND BUT WHAT WAS SHOCKING	220	2 DON JUAN	2	121	1
TOO GENTLE READER AND MOST SHOCKING SOUNDS	112	3 DON JUAN	8	1	3
SHOCKS						
PERHAPS BUT AS I SUFFER FROM THE SHOCKS	270	3 DON JUAN	11	5	7
SHOD						
NOW IF MY PEGASUS SHOULD NOT BE SHOD ILL	412	2 DON JUAN	5	2	7
TO ANY SHOE UNLESS IT SHOD THE POPE	470	2 DON JUAN	5	102	8
SHOE						
TO ANY SHOE UNLESS IT SHOD THE POPE	470	2 DON JUAN	5	102	8
AND DREADING THE CHASTE ECHOES OF HER SHOE	556	3 DON JUAN	16	112	8
SHOES						
WHEN LO HE STUMBLED O'ER A PAIR OF SHOES	120	2 DON JUAN	1	180	8
A PAIR OF SHOES--WHAT THEN NOT MUCH IF THEY	121	2 DON JUAN	1	181	1
SOME LEATHERN CAPS AND WHAT REMAIN'D OF SHOES	195	2 DON JUAN	2	74	2
AND ATAGHAN OF GOLD AND SHOES OF YELLOW	451	2 DON JUAN	5	68	V7
WHO SHOES THE GLORIOUS ANIMAL WITH STILTS	297	3 DON JUAN	11	57	7
SHOESTRING						
AND THEN THERE WAS THE MISS AUDACIA SHOESTRING	474	3 DON JUAN	15	42	1
SHONE						
BUT THEN THEY SHONE NOT ON THE POET'S PAGE	24	2 DON JUAN	1	5	4
THE SCATTERING CLOUDS SHONE SPANNING THE DARK SEA	204	2 DON JUAN	2	91	2
BUT NOT WITH VIOLENCE THE STARS SHONE OUT	207	2 DON JUAN	2	96	2
BUT THROUGH THEM GOLD AND GEMS PROFUSELY SHONE	220	2 DON JUAN	2	121	4
ALL GOLD AND CRIMSON SHONE HER JELICK'S FELLOW	311	2 DON JUAN	3	70	6
WHOSE RAYS SHONE EVER TREMBLING BUT INCESSANT	315	2 DON JUAN	3	77	8
AND THROUGH HER CLEAR BRUNETTE COMPLEXION SHONE A	395	2 DON JUAN	4	94	6
CALLED BACK THE STOIC TO HIS EYES WHICH SHONE	481	2 DON JUAN	5	121	5
O'ER WHOM SUWARROW SHONE LIKE A GAS LAMP	89	3 DON JUAN	7	46	3
AND IN THE DANUBE'S WATERS SHONE THE SAME--	115	3 DON JUAN	8	6	4
DON JUAN WHO HAD SHONE IN THE LATE SLAUGHTER	197	3 DON JUAN	9	29	1
AND GREATLY SHONE WHENEVER THERE HAD BEEN A STIR	368	3 DON JUAN	13	21	6
HERE DANCED ALBANO'S BOYS AND HERE THE SEA SHONE	392	3 DON JUAN	13	71	5
DREST VOTED SHONE AND MAYBE SOMETHING MORE	418	3 DON JUAN	14	18	2

724

SHONE   (CONTINUED)
    AND SHONE IN THE BEST PART OF DIALOGUE   426   3 DON JUAN 14   37   2
    AURORA RABY A YOUNG STAR WHO SHONE 475   3 DON JUAN 15   43   5
    IN EYES WHICH SADLY SHONE AS SERAPHS' SHINE 476   3 DON JUAN 15   45   3
    IT HAPPENED LUCKILY THE CHASTE ORB SHONE   506   3 DON JUAN 16   13   3
    THE LIGHT THAT THROUGH THE GOTHIC WINDOWS SHONE   . . . 568   3 DON JUAN 17   14   5
SHOOK
    OVER THE MYSTIC LEAF HIS SOUL WAS SHOOK   72   2 DON JUAN 1   95   5
    ASLEEP THEY SHOOK THEM BY THE HAND AND HEAD   208   2 DON JUAN 2   98   7
    THE WORDS WHICH SHOOK BELSHAZZAR IN HIS HALL   308   2 DON JUAN 3   65   5
    WHEN ONE IS SHOOK IN SOUND AND ONE IN SIGHT   355   2 DON JUAN 4   21   5
    WHATEVER FEELING SHOOK HER IT SEEM'D SHORT   356   2 DON JUAN 4   23   3
    FOREVER AND ANON A SOMETHING SHOOK   359   2 DON JUAN 4   29   4
    OF SLUMBER ERE THEY SHOOK HER--SO THEY SAY   42   3 DON JUAN 6   73   6
    BELLONA SHOOK HER SPEAR WITH SUCH SUBLIMITY   92   3 DON JUAN 7   51 V6
    AND SHOOK (TILL NOW UNSHAKEN) LIKE A REED   170   3 DON JUAN 8   117   6
    AND SAIL FOR A NEW THEME--I HAVE SEEN--AND SHOOK   . . 309   3 DON JUAN 11   83   6
    THIS SAVOURED OF THIS WORLD BUT HIS HAND SHOOK--   . . 512   3 DON JUAN 16   27   1
    DON JUAN SHOOK AS ERST HE HAD BEEN SHAKEN   558   3 DON JUAN 16   118   1
SHOOT
    WITH COST AND CARE AND WARMTH INDUCED TO SHOOT   38   3 DON JUAN 6   65   4
    THE GENTLEMEN GOT UP BETIMES TO SHOOT 405   3 DON JUAN 13   101   1
SHOOTER'S
    BOLD BRITONS WE ARE NOW ON SHOOTER'S HILL   264   3 DON JUAN 10   80   8
    DON JUAN HAD GOT OUT ON SHOOTER'S HILL   272   3 DON JUAN 11   8   1
SHOOTING
    PERHAPS AS SHOOTING THEM AT WATERLOO   93   2 DON JUAN 1   132   8
    BUT THERE'S NO SHOOTING (SAVE GROUSE) TILL SEPTEMBER . . 380 3 DON JUAN 13   48   8
    THE DUKE OF D-- THE SHOOTING SEASON SPENDS   382   3 DON JUAN 13   52   5
SHOP
    AND HE HIMSELF OBLIGED TO SHUT UP SHOP--HE   27   2 DON JUAN 1   11   6
SHOP-KEEPERS
    THOSE HAUGHTY SHOP-KEEPERS WHO STERNLY DEALT   257   3 DON JUAN 10   65   6
SHORE
    TRANSFERR'D TO GORGE UPON A SISTER SHORE   16   2 DON JUAN D   12   4
    OF ITS OWN THIRST TO SEE AGAIN THY SHORE   166   2 DON JUAN 2   18   4
    THE LEAK INCREASED SHOALS ROUND HER BUT NO SHORE   . . 176   2 DON JUAN 2   38   3
    WAS USED--NOR SAIL NOR SHORE APPEAR'D IN SIGHT 178   2 DON JUAN 2   41   7
    THERE WAS SLIGHT CHANCE OF REACHING ANY SHORE 185   2 DON JUAN 2   54   5
    AND CARRY THEM TO SHORE THESE HOPES WERE FINE 192   2 DON JUAN 2   69   6
    OR THOUGHT THEY SAW AND SHAPED THEIR COURSE FOR SHORE . 207 2 DON JUAN 2   97   6
    FOR SHORE IT WAS AND GRADUALLY GREW 207   2 DON JUAN 2   97   7
    STILL SET THEM ONWARDS TO THE WELCOME SHORE 209   2 DON JUAN 2   101   2
    THE SHORE LOOK'D WILD WITHOUT A TRACE OF MAN 211   2 DON JUAN 2   104   1
    THEY RAN THE BOAT FOR SHORE AND OVERSET HER 211   2 DON JUAN 2   104   8
    SO NOBODY ARRIVED ON SHORE BUT HIM   212   2 DON JUAN 2   106   8
    AND HANDSOME CORPSES STREW'D UPON THE SHORE 229   2 DON JUAN 2   138   4
    WITH CLIFFS ABOVE AND A BROAD SANDY SHORE   249   2 DON JUAN 2   177   2
    AND NOW 'TWAS DONE--ON THE LONE SHORE WERE PLIGHTED . 265 2 DON JUAN 2   204   1
    MY COUNTRY ON THY VOICELESS SHORE   322   2 DON JUAN 3 L 5   2
    ON SULI'S ROCK AND PARGA'S SHORE   325   2 DON JUAN 3 L 13   2
    OF THE PINE FOREST AND THE SILENT SHORE   337   2 DON JUAN 3   105   2
    EXCEPT MERE BREATH AND SINCE THE SILENT SHORE 350   2 DON JUAN 4   12   5
    DESCEND--THE FAULT IS MINE THIS FATAL SHORE 366   2 DON JUAN 4   42   5
    OLD LAMBRO BADE THEM TAKE HIM TO THE SHORE   371   2 DON JUAN 4   50   3
    BY THE SEA SHORE WHEREON SHE LOVED TO DWELL 382   2 DON JUAN 4   71   8
    THE EUROPEAN WITH THE ASIAN SHORE   412   2 DON JUAN 5   3   1
    IN DESERTS FORESTS CROWDS OR BY THE SHORE   443   2 DON JUAN 5   57   2
    WE NEEDS MUST FOLLOW WHEN FATE PUTS FROM SHORE 460   2 DON JUAN 5   84   5
    THROUGH THE HEAVED BREAST THE DREAM OF SOME FAR SHORE . 40 3 DON JUAN 6   67   5
    WHICH RUSHES TO SOME SHORE WHOSE SHINGLES CHECK . . . 60   3 DON JUAN 6   108   7
    HURLING DEFIANCE CITY STREAM AND SHORE   116   3 DON JUAN 8   4   4
    OF TYRANTS AND BEEN BLEST FROM SHORE TO SHORE 187   3 DON JUAN 9   9   4
    OF TYRANTS AND BEEN BLEST FROM SHORE TO SHORE 187   3 DON JUAN 9   9   4
    WELL NIGH THE SHORE WHERE ONE STOOPS DOWN AND GATHERS . 191 3 DON JUAN 9   18   7
    BUT AT THE LEAST I HAVE SHUNNED THE COMMON SHORE   . . 227   3 DON JUAN 10   4   3
    A FOREIGNER OF RANK HAD GRACED OUR SHORE 283   3 DON JUAN 11   32   6
    ON A LEE SHORE TILL IT BEGINS TO BLOW--   345   3 DON JUAN 12   63   3
    BUT THUS MUCH AND NO SNEER AGAINST THE SHORE   346   3 DON JUAN 12   67   6
    AND WHEN THEY HAVE MADE THE SHORE THROUGH EV'RY SHOCK . 442 3 DON JUAN 14   74   7
    AS COMMON SOLDIERS OR A COMMON--SHORE   537   3 DON JUAN 16   76   3
SHORES
    HAVE FOUND THE FAME YOUR SHORES REFUSE   321   2 DON JUAN 3 L 2   3
    THE SHORES OF ILION LAY BENEATH THEIR LEE-- 384   2 DON JUAN 4   75   6
SHORN
    SHORN OF ITS BEST AND LOVELIEST AND LEFT BARE 155   3 DON JUAN 8   88   6
    SHORN OF ITS GLASS OF THOUSAND COLOURINGS   387   3 DON JUAN 13   62   2
    BACK TO HIS CHAMBER SHORN OF HALF HIS STRENGTH 511   3 DON JUAN 16   25   8
SHORT
    IN SHORT IN ALL THINGS SHE WAS FAIRLY WHAT I CALL . . 27   2 DON JUAN 1   12   5
    IN SHORT SHE WAS A WALKING CALCULATION   29   2 DON JUAN 1   16   1
    THE SONS NO MORE WERE SHORT THE DAUGHTERS PLAIN . . . 53   2 DON JUAN 1   58   5
    PREFER A SPOUSE WHOSE AGE IS SHORT OF THIRTY   56   2 DON JUAN 1   62   8
    THESE FEW SHORT YEARS MAKE WOND'ROUS ALTERATIONS   . . 59   2 DON JUAN 1   69   7
    BUT SAGE ANTONIA CUT HIM SHORT BEFORE   111   2 DON JUAN 1   163   2
    THOU SHALT NOT WRITE IN SHORT BUT WHAT I CHOOSE   . . 140   2 DON JUAN 1   206   5
    MY HEART IS NOT MUCH GREENER AND IN SHORT I   143   2 DON JUAN 1   213   4
    IN SHORT I MUST NOT LEAD THE LIFE I DID DO   144   2 DON JUAN 1   216   4
    YOUR PATIENCE FURTHER THAN BY THIS SHORT SAMPLE-- . . 147   2 DON JUAN 1   221   7

SHORT (CONTINUED)

	PAGE	VOL	CANTO		STANZA	LN
AND GOING DOWN HEAD FOREMOST--SUNK IN SHORT	183	2	DON JUAN	2	51	8
WHEN SHIPWRECK'S SHORT ALLOWANCE GROWS TOO SCANTY	200	2	DON JUAN	2	83	7
SHORT UPPER LIP--SWEET LIPS THAT MAKE US SIGH	218	2	DON JUAN	2	118	3
AND SO IN SHORT THE GIRLS THEY REALLY WERE	222	2	DON JUAN	2	124	5
IN SHORT HE WAS A VERY PRETTY FELLOW	235	2	DON JUAN	2	148	7
IN SHORT IT IS THE USE OF OUR OWN EYES	269	2	DON JUAN	2	212	6
LAMB AND PISTACHIO NUTS--IN SHORT ALL MEATS	307	2	DON JUAN	3	62	2
AGREE TO A SHORT ARMISTICE WITH TRUTH	318	2	DON JUAN	3	83	8
WHATEVER FEELING SHOOK HER IT SEEM'D SHORT	356	2	DON JUAN	4	23	3
SHORT SOLACE VAIN RELIEF--THOUGHT CAME TOO QUICK	380	2	DON JUAN	4	67	1
PLAIN--SIMPLE--SHORT AND BY NO MEANS INVITING	412	2	DON JUAN	5	2	3
THE PARCAE THEN CUT SHORT THE FURTHER SPINNING	414	2	DON JUAN	5	6	3
BUT NO ONE EVER DREAMS OF BEING SHORT--	437	2	DON JUAN	5	48	8
IN SHORT ALL THINGS WHICH FORM A TURKISH DANDY	451	2	DON JUAN	5	68	8
THE EFFEMINATE GARB--THUS AFTER A SHORT PAUSE	455	2	DON JUAN	5	76	4
TO CUTTING SHORT THEIR HOPES OF HAVING ANY	487	2	DON JUAN	5	132	8
(ENOUGH GOD KNOWS) WOULD MUCH FALL SHORT OF THIS	489	2	DON JUAN	5	134	8
IT LASTED 'TWAS LIKE A SHORT GLIMPSE OF HELL	489	2	DON JUAN	5	135	3
YOU'LL PARDON TO MY MUSE A FEW SHORT NAPS	503	2	DON JUAN	5	159	8
IN SHORT THE MAXIM FOR THE AMOROUS TRIBE IS	14	3	DON JUAN	6	17	7
LOLAH KATINKA AND DUDU IN SHORT	26	3	DON JUAN	6	40	3
THAT SHE WAS FAIR OR DARK OR SHORT OR TALL	33	3	DON JUAN	6	54	7
WITH EVERY KINDNESS SHORT OF OSTENTATION	34	3	DON JUAN	6	57	3
FOR BABA'S FUNCTION STOPT SHORT AT THE DOOR	57	3	DON JUAN	6	103	4
IT WAS BUT A CONVULSION WHICH THOUGH SHORT	59	3	DON JUAN	6	106	3
IN SHORT ALL KNOW OR VERY SOON MAY KNOW IT	69	3	DON JUAN	7	6	4
BUT HERE THE EFFECT FELL SHORT OF THEIR DESIRE	82	3	DON JUAN	7	31	6
I THINK THAT SEVERAL VOLUMES WOULD FALL SHORT	82	3	DON JUAN	7	32	3
IN SHORT THIS LAST ATTACK THOUGH RICH IN GLORY	83	3	DON JUAN	7	35	1
HAD BEEN AS SHORT IN YOUTH AS INDIGESTION	84	3	DON JUAN	7	36	4
ALL EARS THOUGH LONG ALL AGES THOUGH SO SHORT	106	3	DON JUAN	7	79	2
AIR MIDST THE REST WHOSE SHORT BREATH AND LONG FACES	130	3	DON JUAN	8	34	V7
SHORT SPEECHES PASS BETWEEN TWO MEN WHO SPEAK	141	3	DON JUAN	8	58	1
AND FOUND THEIR LIVES WERE LET AT A SHORT LEASE--	150	3	DON JUAN	8	76	4
IN SHORT HOWE'ER OUR BETTER FAITH DERIDES	168	3	DON JUAN	8	114	4
A SNEER OR SHORT REPLY UNTO THEIR NEIGHBOUR	288	3	DON JUAN	11	41	V4
IN SHORT THE LIST OF ALTERATIONS BOTHERS	308	3	DON JUAN	11	81	6
THE MIDDLE-AGED TO MAKE THE DAY MORE SHORT	405	3	DON JUAN	13	101	4
IN SHORT THERE NEVER WAS A BETTER HEARER	426	3	DON JUAN	14	37	8
THE SENSUAL FOR A SHORT TIME BUT CONNECTS US--	442	3	DON JUAN	14	73	5
I MEANT TO MAKE THIS POEM VERY SHORT	466	3	DON JUAN	15	22	3
IN SHORT UPON THAT SUBJECT I'VE SOME QUALMS VERY	499	3	DON JUAN	15	96	7
OF PHYSICS BODIES WHETHER SHORT OR TALL	511	3	DON JUAN	16	24	6
IN SHORT HE HARDLY COULD BE CLOTHED WITH LESS	555	3	DON JUAN	16	111	4

SHORTEN

	PAGE	VOL	CANTO		STANZA	LN
THE TRUTH AND THOUGH GRIEF HER OLD AGE MIGHT SHORTEN	222	3	DON JUAN	9	81	5

SHORTER

	PAGE	VOL	CANTO		STANZA	LN
HIS HEART TO FORCE IT OUT FOR (TO BE SHORTER)	479	3	DON JUAN	5	118	7
THOUGH THERE'S A SHORTER A GOOD DEAL THAN THIS	326	3	DON JUAN	12	22	4

SHORTEST

	PAGE	VOL	CANTO		STANZA	LN
'TIS STRANGE THE SHORTEST LETTER WHICH MAN USES	327	2	DON JUAN	3	88	4
OF GETTING INTO HEAVEN THE SHORTEST WAY	336	2	DON JUAN	3	104	5
SUCH IS THE SHORTEST WAY TO GENERAL CURSES	264	3	DON JUAN	10	79	4

SHORTHAND

	PAGE	VOL	CANTO		STANZA	LN
THE BEST IS THAT IN SHORTHAND TA'EN BY GURNEY	127	2	DON JUAN	1	189	7
WHAT DANIEL READ WAS SHORT-HAND OF THE LORD'S	179	3	DON JUAN	8	134	5
NO LONGER READY EARS AND SHORT-HAND PENS	540	3	DON JUAN	16	83	4

SHORTLY

	PAGE	VOL	CANTO		STANZA	LN
BATTISTA THOUGH (A NAME CALL'D SHORTLY TITA)	186	2	DON JUAN	2	56	7
A PIPE TOO AND A DRUM AND SHORTLY AFTER	290	2	DON JUAN	3	28	7
SHORTLY AND SWEETLY THE MASONIC FOLLY	448	2	DON JUAN	5	63	2
BUT SHORTLY HE HAD CAUSE TO BE CONTENT	85	3	DON JUAN	7	38	5
TO SEVERAL SAINTS THAT SHORTLY PLOUGH OR HARROW	99	3	DON JUAN	7	63	6

SHORT-SIGHTED

	PAGE	VOL	CANTO		STANZA	LN
THUS PARENTS ALSO ARE AT TIMES SHORT-SIGHTED	75	2	DON JUAN	1	100	1

SHOT

	PAGE	VOL	CANTO		STANZA	LN
I HEARD A SHOT--'TWAS EIGHT O'CLOCK SCARCE PAST--	428	2	DON JUAN	5	33	5
AND SHELLS AND SHOT OF EVERY SIZE AND SHAPE	81	3	DON JUAN	7	29	8
WHAT FOLLOWED--A SHOT LAID ME ON MY BACK	98	3	DON JUAN	7	61	5
BESIDES ITS LAVA WITH ALL SORTS OF SHOT	119	3	DON JUAN	8	16	3
AND THERE A LITTLE SHELTERED FROM THE SHOT	131	3	DON JUAN	8	37	1
WAS FROM A PISTOL SHOT THAT LAID HIM DEAD	152	3	DON-JUAN	8	81	2
THAT THEY SHOULD ALL BE SHOT ON THE NEXT DAY	162	3	DON JUAN	8	102	6
HIS SECOND SON WAS LEVELLED BY A SHOT	166	3	DON JUAN	8	110	2

SHOTS

	PAGE	VOL	CANTO		STANZA	LN
SOME DEADLY SHOTS TOO SEPTEMBRIZERS SEEN	539	3	DON JUAN	16	80	3

SHOULDER

	PAGE	VOL	CANTO		STANZA	LN
TO HIDE THE GLOSSY SHOULDER WHICH UPREARS	108	2	DON JUAN	1	158	6
TAPPING THE SHOULDER OF THE NIGHEST GUEST	297	2	DON JUAN	3	42	2
OVER HIS SHOULDER WITH A BACCHANT AIR	297	2	DON JUAN	3	43	2
HAD FALLEN WITH HIS RIGHT SHOULDER HALF CUT THROUGH	370	2	DON JUAN	4	48	8
ONE'S HIP HE SLASHED AND SPLIT THE OTHER'S SHOULDER	158	3	DON JUAN	8	94	1

SHOULDERS

	PAGE	VOL	CANTO		STANZA	LN
NO DOUBT GAVE PAIN WHERE EACH NEW PAIR OF SHOULDERS	208	3	DON JUAN	9	52	7
UPON MY SHOULDERS HERE I MUST AVER	378	3	DON JUAN	13	43	4

SHOUT

	PAGE	VOL	CANTO		STANZA	LN
AND ONE ENORMOUS SHOUT OF ALLAH ROSE	116	3	DON JUAN	8	8	1

SHOUTED

	PAGE	VOL	CANTO		STANZA	LN
AND ONLY SHOUTED ALLA AND BIS MILLAH	73	3	DON JUAN	7	13	8
HE SHOUTED ALLAH AND SAW PARADISE	169	3	DON JUAN	8	115	3

SHOUTS
    THE MARCH THE CHARGE THE SHOUTS OF EITHER FAITH . . . . 111 3 DON JUAN 7   87 6
    SHOUTS BRIDGES ARCHES PENSIONS FROM A NATION . . . . 114 3 DON JUAN 8   4 3
    NOW--THAT THE RABBLE'S FIRST VAIN SHOUTS ARE O'ER . . . 187 3 DON JUAN 9   9 6
    WHERE ARE THE DUBLIN SHOUTS--AND LONDON HISSES . . . . 308 3 DON JUAN 11   79 6
SHOW
    OVID'S A RAKE AS HALF HIS VERSES SHOW HIM . . . . . . 45 2 DON JUAN 1   42 1
    YET HE WAS JEALOUS THOUGH HE DID NOT SHOW IT . . . . 57 2 DON JUAN 1   65 7
    AND MERELY TEND TO SHOW HOW GREATLY LOVE IS . . . . . 62 2 DON JUAN 1   74 7
    SOME NEW EXPERIMENT TO SHOW HIS PARTS . . . . . . 91 2 DON JUAN 1 128 4
    THE LITTLE I HAVE SAID MAY SERVE TO SHOW . . . . . 107 2 DON JUAN 1 157 2
    BESIDES IN CANTO TWELFTH I MEAN TO SHOW . . . . . 140 2 DON JUAN 1 207 7
    TO SHOW ITS BOILING SURF AND BOUNDING SPRAY . . . . 211 2 DON JUAN 2 104 6
    OR SHOW THE SAME DISLIKE TO SUITORS' KISSES . . . . 287 2 DON JUAN 3   23 4
    AND SHOW THAT LATE HOURS WINE AND LOVE ARE ABLE . . 309 2 DON JUAN 3   66 7
    THE LAST WAS OF GREAT FAME AND LIKED TO SHOW IT . . 316 2 DON JUAN 3   78 4
    TO SHOW HOW ESSENTIAL TO IT IS ENNUI . . . . . . 332 2 DON JUAN 3   97 V8
    TO SHOW WITH WHAT COMPLACENCY HE CREEPS . . . . . 333 2 DON JUAN 3   98 3
    WHO HAVE IMPUTED SUCH DESIGNS AS SHOW . . . . . 347 2 DON JUAN 4   7 3
    FOR BOTH SIDES I COULD MANY REASONS SHOW . . . . 357 2 DON JUAN 4   25 6
    SHE DREW UP TO HER HEIGHT AS IF TO SHOW . . . . 367 2 DON JUAN 4   43 6
    SHOW WHAT THE PASSIONS ARE IN THEIR FULL GROWTH . 368 2 DON JUAN 4   45 8
    WITHOUT A GROAN OR SIGH OR GLANCE TO SHOW . . . 381 2 DON JUAN 4   69 2
    NO STONE IS THERE TO SHOW NO TONGUE TO SAY . . 383 2 DON JUAN 4   72 6
    HAVING NO HEART TO SHOW HE SHOWS HIS TEETH . . 392 2 DON JUAN 4   89 8
    TO SHOW HIS LOATHING OF THE SPOT HE SOIL'D . . . 401 2 DON JUAN 4 105 4
    YOU MAY DO RIGHT FORBIDDING THEM TO SHOW 'EM . . 403 2 DON JUAN 4 107 7
    WITH WHITES AND BLACKS IN GROUPS ON SHOW FOR SALE . 416 2 DON JUAN 5   10 2
    O'ERTHROWN EVEN MEN HE SOON BEGAN TO SHOW . . . 417 2 DON JUAN 5   12 4
    AND YOU AN EQUAL COURTESY SHOULD SHOW-- . . . . 419 2 DON JUAN 5   16 4
    BUT NOT ENOUGH TO SHOW THE IMPERIAL HALLS . . . 442 2 DON JUAN 5   56 3
    AS FAR AS OUTWARD SHOW MAY CORRESPOND . . . . 469 2 DON JUAN 5   99 7
    AS THE TRIBUNALS SHOW THROUGH MANY A SESSION . . 11 3 DON JUAN 6   10 6
    NOR SHOW YOUR GEORGIAN IGNORANCE--FOR SHAME . . 28 3 DON JUAN 6   44 5
    SHE TOOK JUANNA BY THE HAND TO SHOW . . . . . 31 3 DON JUAN 6   50 5
    IN OUTWARD SHOW WHICH IS A SAVING CLAUSE) . . . 35 3 DON JUAN 6   58 3
    APART FROM ONE WHO HAD NO SIN TO SHOW . . . . 48 3 DON JUAN 6   84 7
    WHAT PEDIGREE THE BEST WOULD HAVE TO SHOW . . . 53 3 DON JUAN 6   94 8
    WHAT AFTER ALL ARE ALL THINGS--BUT A SHOW . . . 67 3 DON JUAN 7   2 8
    MOST MODERN PREACHERS SAY THE SAME OR SHOW IT . . 69 3 DON JUAN 7   6 2
    TO SHOW YE WHAT YE ARE IN EVERY WAY . . . . . 70 3 DON JUAN 7   7 4
    THIS BEING THE CASE MAY SHOW US WHAT FAME IS . . 82 3 DON JUAN 7   33 1
    HER INWARD GRACE FOR OUTWARD SHOW AND MAKES . . 96 3 DON JUAN 7   57 7
    THE GENTLEMEN THAT WERE THE FIRST TO SHOW . . . 135 3 DON JUAN 8   45 6
    THE DUKE OF WELLINGTON HAD CEASED TO SHOW . . . 137 3 DON JUAN 8   49 6
    IN BEGGING HIM FOR GOD'S SAKE JUST TO SHOW . . 165 3 DON JUAN 8 108 3
    JUST NOW--BUT BY AND BY THE TRUTH WILL SHOW 'EM . 193 3 DON JUAN 9   22 5
    BID IRELAND'S LONDONDERRY'S MARQUESS SHOW . . . 207 3 DON JUAN 9   49 3
    AND NEUTRALIZE HER OUTWARD SHOW OF SCARLET . . . 237 3 DON JUAN 10   26 8
    THEIR CASH TO SHOW HOW MUCH THEY HAVE A YEAR . . 273 3 DON JUAN 11   10 4
    AS EVERY PALTRY MAGAZINE CAN SHOW IT'S . . . . 295 3 DON JUAN 11   54 8
    IS CALLED ON TO SUPPORT HIS CLAIM OR SHOW IT . . 296 3 DON JUAN 11   55 3
    AND SHOW THEM WHAT AN INTELLECTUAL WAR IS . . . 299 3 DON JUAN 11   62 8
    AND ALL HER POINTS AS THOROUGH-BRED TO SHOW . . 330 3 DON JUAN 12   31 6
    I MEAN TO SHOW THINGS REALLY AS THEY ARE . . . 335 3 DON JUAN 12   40 2
    TURN OUT MUCH BETTER FOR THE SMITHFIELD SHOW . . 337 3 DON JUAN 12   46 6
    THE SHOW OF VIRTUE EVEN IN THE VITIATED-- . . . 344 3 DON JUAN 12   62 5
    'TIS NOT MERE SPLENDOUR MAKES THE SHOW AUGUST . . 354 3 DON JUAN 12   83 7
    TO SHOW THE PEOPLE THE BEST WAY TO BREAK . . . 357 3 DON JUAN 12   89 4
    IN FAULTS WHICH SOMETIMES SHOW THE SOIL'S FERTILITY . 368 3 DON JUAN 13   22 6
    AND ALL MEN LIKE TO SHOW THEIR HOSPITALITY . . . 369 3 DON JUAN 13   24 7
    IF BUT TO SHOW I'VE TRAVELL'D AND WHAT'S TRAVEL . 380 3 DON JUAN 13   47 7
    FLING UP A STRAW 'TWILL SHOW THE WAY THE WIND BLOWS . 414 3 DON JUAN 14   8 2
    NEITHER CAN SHOW QUITE HOW THEY WOULD BE LOVED . . 442 3 DON JUAN 14   73 4
    WOULD SHOW MANKIND THEIR SOUL'S ANTIPODES . . . 455 3 DON JUAN 14 101 8
    FEW MEN DARE SHOW THEIR THOUGHTS OF WORST OR BEST . 457 3 DON JUAN 15   3 5
    TO SHOW IT--(POINTS WE NEED NOT NOW DISCUSS)-- . 460 3 DON JUAN 15   10 5
    WHICH DID NOT SHOW BUT YET CONCEALED A STORM . . 474 3 DON JUAN 15   41 V2
    WHERE ALL THE PONTIC SPOILS MADE SUCH A SHOW . . 485 3 DON JUAN 15   67 V3
    HOW COULD HE POSSIBLY SHOW THINGS EXISTENT . . . 494 3 DON JUAN 15   87 8
    IN POLITICS MY DUTY IS TO SHOW JOHN . . . . . 497 3 DON JUAN 15   92 5
    A THING OF WHICH SIMILITUDES CAN SHOW . . . . 505 3 DON JUAN 16   10 4
    TO SHOW SHE COULD IF IT WERE WORTH HER WHILE . . 521 3 DON JUAN 16   42 8
    SHOW OFF--TO PLEASE THEIR COMPANY OR MOTHER . . 522 3 DON JUAN 16   44 8
    AND WHAT WAS WORSE WAS NOT ASHAMED TO SHOW IT . . 524 3 DON JUAN 16   47 8
    SUCH AS ENABLES MAN TO SHOW HIS STRENGTH . . . 567 3 DON JUAN 17   12 3
SHOW'D
    FOR THE SKY SHOW'D IT WOULD COME ON TO BLOW . . . 170 2 DON JUAN 2   26 7
    DECIDED THUS AND SHOW'D GOOD REASON WHY . . . . 281 2 DON JUAN 3   11 6
    HE SHOW'D THE ROYAL PENCHANTS OF A PIRATE . . . 296 2 DON JUAN 3   40 8
    AND CERTAINLY HE SHOW'D THE BEST OF BREEDING . . 299 2 DON JUAN 3   46 2
    ALAS HIS COUNTRY SHOW'D NO PATH TO PRAISE . . . 303 2 DON JUAN 3   55 6
    SHED ITS IONIAN ELEGANCE WHICH SHOW'D . . . . 304 2 DON JUAN 3   56 2
    BUT HER LARGE DARK EYE SHOW'D DEEP PASSION'S FORCE . 374 2 DON JUAN 4   56 7
    WHICH SHOW'D SUCH DEFERENCE TO WHAT FEMALES SAY . . 492 3 DON JUAN 15   82 3
SHOWED
    AND SHOWED BUT LITTLE ROYAL CURIOSITY . . . . 496 2 DON JUAN 5 148 4
    AND LIPS APART WHICH SHOWED THE PEARLS BENEATH . . 38 3 DON JUAN 6   65 8
    BY ALL THE DEMONS OF ALL PASSIONS SHOWED . . . 61 3 DON JUAN 6 111 7

SHOWED   (CONTINUED)
HE SHOWED THEM HOW TO MOUNT A LADDER (WHICH . . . . . . 93 3 DON JUAN 7   52 7
WHICH SHOWED A WANT OF LANTHORNS OR OF TASTE-- . . . . 177 3 DON JUAN 8 130 2
SHOWED WHAT THINGS WERE BEFORE THE WORLD WAS FREE . . . 179 3 DON JUAN 8 135 8
VALOUR MUCH ALSO TO THE BLOOD HE SHOWED . . . . 239 3 DON JUAN 10   29 4
ITSELF AND SHOWED A FEVERISH DISPOSITION . . . . 244 3 DON JUAN 10   39 6
WHICH SHOWED WHAT GREAT DISCERNMENT WAS THE DONOR'S . . 247 3 DON JUAN 10   46 8
SHE SHOWED A GREAT DISLIKE TO HOLY WATER . . . . 252 3 DON JUAN 10   56 4
HIS MANNER SHEWED HIM SPRUNG FROM A HIGH MOTHER . . . . 369 3 DON JUAN 13   24 6
TO SOME SHE SHOWED ATTENTION OF THAT KIND . . . . . . 372 3 DON JUAN 13   32 2
A STRAGGLING CURL SHOWED HE HAD BEEN FAIR-HAIRED . . . 560 3 DON JUAN 16 121 5
SHOWER
AND THE SAME NIGHT THERE FELL A SHOWER OF RAIN . . . . 201 2 DON JUAN 2   84 1
AND WHEN THE WISH'D-FOR SHOWER AT LENGTH WAS COME . . . 203 2 DON JUAN 2   89 4
BUT PAYS OFF MOMENTS IN AN ENDLESS SHOWER . . . . . . 258 2 DON JUAN 2 192 6
SHOWERED
FLAME WAS SHOWERED FORTH ABOVE AS WELL'S BELOW . . . . 135 3 DON JUAN 8   45 4
SHOWERING
SWEET IS THE VINTAGE WHEN THE SHOWERING GRAPES . . . . 88 2 DON JUAN 1 124 1
SHOWERS
SHOWERS TRIPLE LIGHT AND SCORCHES EVEN THE KISS . . . 264 2 DON JUAN 2 202 3
ALREADY THEY BEHELD THE SILVER SHOWERS . . . . 222 3 DON JUAN 9   79 5
AND OUT OF DOOR HATH SHOWERS AND MISTS AND SLEET . . . 423 3 DON JUAN 14   30 2
LIKE SHOWERS WHICH ON THE MIDNIGHT GUSTS WILL PASS . . 556 3 DON JUAN 16 114 3
ON WHICH THE MOONBEAMS FELL IN SILVERY SHOWERS . . . . 559 3 DON JUAN 16 120 3
SHOWING
SHOWING A MUCH MORE RECONCIL'D DEMEANOUR . . . . 388 3 DON JUAN 4   81 7
AND SINCE THAT TIME IT NEED NOT COST MUCH SHOWING . . . 444 3 DON JUAN 14   78 5
SHOWMAN
MISS RAW MISS FLAW MISS SHOWMAN AND MISS KNOWMAN . . . 473 3 DON JUAN 15   40 4
FOR HENRY WAS A SORT OF SABINE SHOWMAN . . . . 530 3 DON JUAN 16   60 8
SHOWN
THAT THEY BRED IN AND IN AS MIGHT BE SHOWN . . . . . . 52 2 DON JUAN 1   57 6
OF THIS AT LEAST NO SYMPTOM E'ER WAS SHOWN . . . . . . 59 2 DON JUAN 1   68 4
WORTHY OF THIS AMBROSIAL SIN SO SHOWN . . . . 90 2 DON JUAN 1 127 6
HIM WHAT'S HIS LINEAGE LET HIM BUT BE SHOWN-- . . . . 105 2 DON JUAN 1 154 5
BUT THAT CAN'T BE AS HAS BEEN OFTEN SHOWN . . . . . . 118 2 DON JUAN 1 176 4
SHOWN IN THE FOLLOWING COPY OF HER LETTER . . . . . . 129 2 DON JUAN 1 191 8
THUS TO THEIR HOPELESS EYES THE NIGHT WAS SHOWN . . . 182 2 DON JUAN 2   49 5
AND THEN AS AN IMPROVEMENT 'TWILL BE SHOWN . . . . . . 342 2 DON JUAN 3 111 6
COULD SCARCE BE SHOWN EVEN BY A MERE SPECTATOR . . . . 416 2 DON JUAN 5   11 8
HAD PARADISE ITSELF TO HER BEEN SHOWN . . . . 476 2 DON JUAN 5 113 V7
WAS PRINCELY AS THE PROOFS HAVE ALWAYS SHOWN . . . . . 499 2 DON JUAN 5 153 6
OF GENTLE FEMININE DELIGHT AND SHOWN . . . . 13 3 DON JUAN 6   15 2
THUS MOST APPROPRIATELY HAS BEEN SHOWN . . . . 33 3 DON JUAN 6   55 4
AND SHOWN THEMSELVES AS GHOSTS OF BETTER TASTE . . . . 38 3 DON JUAN 6   64 7
IMPLORED THAT PRESENT PARDON MIGHT BE SHOWN . . . . . 47 3 DON JUAN 6   82 4
(THOUGH HE WELL KNEW THE MEANING) TO BE SHOWN . . . . 62 3 DON JUAN 6 112 6
BY BRINGING WOMEN HERE THEY SHALL BE SHOWN . . . . . . 102 3 DON JUAN 7   70 3
WAS SHOWN AND SOME MORE NOBLE HEART BROKE THROUGH . . . 174 3 DON JUAN 8 124 2
WHO STILL HAVE SHOWN THEMSELVES MORE BRAVE THAN WITTY . 194 3 DON JUAN 9   23 4
WHENEVER--WHICH MEANS EVERY DAY--THEY'D SHOWN . . . . 338 3 DON JUAN 12   48 3
PRETENSIONS WHICH THEY NEVER DREAMED TO HAVE SHOWN-- . 344 3 DON JUAN 12   61 4
OF QUIXOTE SHOWN HOW ALL SUCH EFFORTS FAIL . . . . . . 361 3 DON JUAN 13   8 8
FIND ONE WHERE NOTHING NAUGHTY CAN BE SHOWN . . . . . 370 3 DON JUAN 13   27 6
GRACE OF THE SOFT IDEAL SELDOM SHOWN . . . . 428 3 DON JUAN 14   40 6
IS SHOWN THROUGH NATURE'S WHOLE ANALOGIES . . . . . . 451 3 DON JUAN 14   94 4
AS IF THEY TOLD THE TRUTH COULD WELL BE SHOWN . . . . 461 3 DON JUAN 15   13 2
AND EKE THE WISE AS HAS BEEN OFTEN SHOWN . . . . 463 3 DON JUAN 15   17 4
SHOWN IN THIS SORT OF DESULTORY RHYME . . . . 465 3 DON JUAN 15   20 2
HAS SHOWN I KNOW NOT WHY THEY SHOULD DISPLEASE . . . . 494 3 DON JUAN 15   86 6
FOR GOTHIC DARING SHOWN IN ENGLISH MONEY . . . . 529 3 DON JUAN 16   59 8
SHOWS
SHOWS STARS AND WOMEN IN A BETTER LIGHT . . . . 237 2 DON JUAN 2 152 8
TILL OUR OWN WEAKNESS SHOWS US WHAT WE ARE . . . . . . 344 2 DON JUAN 4   1 8
THE RULING PASSION SUCH AS MARBLE SHOWS . . . . 377 2 DON JUAN 4   61 1
HAVE GOT A TRAVELL'D AIR WHICH SHOWS YOU ONE . . . . . 392 2 DON JUAN 4   88 3
HAVING NO HEART TO SHOW HE SHOWS HIS TEETH . . . . . . 392 2 DON JUAN 4   89 8
SHOWS THAT HE THINKS HIS FRIENDS HAVE NOT BEEN SLEEPING 436 2 DON JUAN 5   45 4
SHOWS THAT WE BUILD WHEN WE SHOULD BUT ENTOMB US . . . 448 2 DON JUAN 5   63 8
YOUR PATIENCE) SHOWS THE CAUSE MUST STILL BE STRONGER . 488 2 DON JUAN 5 133 8
AS MACHIAVEL SHOWS THOSE IN PURPLE RAIMENT . . . . . . 264 3 DON JUAN 10   79 3
SOME DEVILISH ESCAPADE OR STIR WHICH SHOWS . . . . . . 328 3 DON JUAN 12   26 2
WHICH SHOWS HOW VERY USEFUL GOOD ADVICE IS . . . . . . 333 3 DON JUAN 12   37 V8
HE SHOWS MORE APPETITE FOR WORDS THAN WAR . . . . . . 398 3 DON JUAN 13   84 4
WHATE'ER IT SHOWS WITH TRUTH A SMOOTH MONOTONY . . . . 417 3 DON JUAN 14   16 7
AND THE SKY SHOWS THAT VERY ANCIENT GRAY . . . . 422 3 DON JUAN 14   28 5
SHRANK
OF SOLITUDE HEALTH SHRANK NOT FROM HIM--FOR . . . . . 143 3 DON JUAN 8   62 2
'TIS TRUE HE SHRANK FROM MEN EVEN OF HIS NATION . . . 144 3 DON JUAN 8   64 1
SHRIEK
AND FIRST ONE UNIVERSAL SHRIEK THERE RUSH'D . . . . . 184 2 DON JUAN 2   53 1
A SOLITARY SHRIEK THE BUBBLING CRY . . . . 184 2 DON JUAN 2   53 7
UP JUAN SPRUNG TO HAIDEE'S BITTER SHRIEK . . . . 364 2 DON JUAN 4   37 1
BUT NO ONE EVER HEARD HER SPEAK OR SHRIEK . . . . . . 380 2 DON JUAN 4   67 5
AND SHRIEK FOR WATER INTO A DEAF EAR-- . . . . 117 3 DON JUAN 8   11 5
OF WAR AND TAKING TOWNS WHEN MANY A SHRIEK . . . . . . 141 3 DON JUAN 8   58 3
THE WOUNDS THEY RICHLY MERITED AND SHRIEK . . . . . . 158 3 DON JUAN 8   94 4
AND THE LOUD SHRIEK OF SAGE MINERVA'S FOWL . . . . . . 499 3 DON JUAN 15   97 3

	PAGE	VOL		CANTO	STANZA	LV

SHRIEK'D
THEN SHRIEK'D THE TIMID AND STOOD STILL THE BRAVE . . . . . 184 2 DON JUAN 2 52 2
SHRIEKING
THEN SHRIEKING SHE AROSE AND SHRIEKING FELL . . . . 363 2 DON JUAN 4 36 1
THEN SHRIEKING SHE AROSE AND SHRIEKING FELL . . . . 363 2 DON JUAN 4 36 1
SHRIEKS
WITH DISTANT SHRIEKS WERE HEARD HEAVEN TO UPBRAID-- . . . 146 3 DON JUAN 8 69 5
DULY ACCOMPANIED BY SHRIEKS AND GROANS . . . . 179 3 DON JUAN 8 135 2
SHRILL
THE SHRILL CICALAS PEOPLE OF THE PINE . . . . 337 2 DON JUAN 3 106 1
SHRILLER
THE HORRID WAR-WHOOP AND THE SHRILLER SCREAM . . . . . . 175 3 DON JUAN 8 127 5
ITS SHRILLER ECHOES--LIKE AN INFANT MADE . . . . 385 3 DON JUAN 13 58 3
SHRINE
AND LIGHTED AT TOO PURE A SHRINE TO DIM ITS . . . . . . 65 2 DON JUAN 1 81 5
HIS ONLY SHRINE OF FEELINGS UNDEFILED . . . . 302 2 DON JUAN 3 52 8
WHERE HYMEN'S SHRINE BUT STAMPS ONE STRUMPET MORE . . . 353 2 DON JUAN 4 17 V7
IT SEEMED AS THOUGH THEY CAME UPON A SHRINE . . . . . . 460 2 DON JUAN 5 85 7
THE BREADTH OF PAVEMENT AND YON SHRINE WHERE FAME IS . . 279 3 DON JUAN 11 24 5
A VESTAL SHRINE OF INNOCENCE OF HEART . . . . 370 3 DON JUAN 13 27 7
BUT EVEN THE FAINTEST RELICS OF A SHRINE . . . . 387 3 DON JUAN 13 61 7
SHRINES
BEFORE THE SHRINES OF SORROW AND OF PLEASURE . . . . . 145 2 DON JUAN 1 217 2
SHRINK
OF SAFETY WHERE SHE LESS MAY SHRINK AND GRIEVE . . . . 161 3 DON JUAN 8 99 4
ALL THAT THE MIND WOULD SHRINK FROM OF EXCESSES . . . . 173 3 DON JUAN 8 123 1
BUT SIGHS SUBSIDE AND TEARS (EVEN WIDOWS') SHRINK . . . 228 3 DON JUAN 10 7 1
WHICH SHRINK FROM TOUCH AS MONARCHS DO FROM RHYMES . . 243 3 DON JUAN 10 37 3
SHRINK TO A SATURN I HAVE SEEN A DUKE . . . . 309 3 DON JUAN 11 83 2
SHRINKING
NOW SHRINKING BACK NOW MIDST THE FIRST HE SEEMS . . . 155 2 DON JUAN 1 V 6 5
FROM WHICH OUR MODERN MORALS RIGHTLY SHRINKING . . . . 238 2 DON JUAN 2 155 3
WITH SHRINKING SERPENT OPTICS ON HIM STARED . . . . . 463 2 DON JUAN 5 90 6
AT SHRINKING FROM A BULLET OR A BOMB . . . . 132 3 DON JUAN 8 38 6
SHRINKS
SHRINKS FROM THE APPLICATION OF HOT TOWELS . . . . . 168 2 DON JUAN 2 23 4
HOW CLAY SHRINKS BACK FROM MORE QUIESCENT CLAY . . . 412 3 DON JUAN 14 4 3
SHROUD
AS SLIGHTLY STIRRING IN HER SNOWY SHROUD . . . . . . 39 3 DON JUAN 6 66 6
GLEAMED FORTH AS THROUGH THE CASEMENT'S IVY SHROUD . . 560 3 DON JUAN 16 121 7
SHROUDS
NO MATTER HOW OR WHY THE PASSPORT SHROUDS . . . . . 396 3 DON JUAN 13 80 6
SHRUGGED
A GLANCE AROUND--AND SHRUGGED--AND TWITCHED HIS SLEEVE . 161 3 DON JUAN 8 99 6
SHRUNK
SHE WOULD HAVE SHRUNK AS FROM A TOAD OR ASP . . . . . 81 2 DON JUAN 1 111 6
I'M SURE SHE WOULD HAVE SHRUNK AS FROM AN ASP . . . . 81 2 DON JUAN 1 111 V6
WHERE THE BLUE VEINS LOOK'D SHADOWY SHRUNK AND WEAK . 234 2 DON JUAN 2 147 5
SHRUNK TO A SCABBARD WITH HIS ARROWS AT . . . . . . 205 3 DON JUAN 9 45 3
OF LIFE SHRUNK IN HIS HEART AND THICK AND SOOTY . . 276 3 DON JUAN 11 16 5
SHUDDER
AND SHUDDER--WHILE AS BEAUTIFUL AS MAY . . . . . . 157 3 DON JUAN 8 91 5
THE SHUDDER WHICH RUNS NATURALLY THROUGH . . . . . 212 3 DON JUAN 9 60 6
SHUDDERED
AND YET HE SHUDDERED AND SEEMED RATHER PRONE . . . 62 3 DON JUAN 6 112 4
HE SHUDDERED AS NO DOUBT THE BRAVEST COWERS . . . . 559 3 DON JUAN 16 120 5
SHUDDERING
JUAN AND SHUDDERING O'ER HIS FRAME WOULD CREEP . . 359 2 DON JUAN 4 29 5
AND YOU WILL FIND THOUGH SHUDDERING AT THE MIRROR . . 413 3 DON JUAN 14 6 3
SHUDDERINGS
I FEEL SOME CHILLY MIDNIGHT SHUDDERINGS . . . . . 500 3 DON JUAN 15 98 4
SHUFFLING
EVEN SHUFFLING SOUTHEY THAT INCARNATE LIE . . . . 231 3 DON JUAN 10 13 2
TRACE UP THOSE SHUFFLING NEGROES NILE OR NIGER . . . 348 3 DON JUAN 12 70 2
SHUN
THE SILKEN FILLET'S CURB AND SOUGHT TO SHUN . . . . 313 2 DON JUAN 3 73 6
THE SILKEN FILLET'S SLIGHT RESTRAINT AND SHUN . . . 313 2 DON JUAN 3 73 V6
IT DIFFICULT TO SHUN SOME STRANGE MISTAKES . . . . 96 3 DON JUAN 7 57 8
FOR A RETURN TO HATRED I WOULD SHUN HER . . . . . 231 3 DON JUAN 10 12 4
IT WAS NOT JEALOUSY I THINK BUT SHUN . . . . . . 479 3 DON JUAN 15 54 5
IN SOULS IMMORTAL SHUN THEM TETE A TETE . . . . . 556 3 DON JUAN 16 114 8
SHUNNED
I SHUNNED THEM AS I WOULD DO THE DEVIL . . . . . 102 2 DON JUAN 1 148 V6
I SHUNNED THEM TO LEAVE NO CAUSE FOR CAVIL . . . . 102 2 DON JUAN 1 148 V6
BUT AT THE LEAST I HAVE SHUNNED THE COMMON SHORE . . 227 3 DON JUAN 10 4 3
SHUNS
DEATH SHUNS THE WRETCH WHO FAIN THE BLOW WOULD MEET . 134 2 DON JUAN 1 197 6
SHUT
AND HE HIMSELF OBLIGED TO SHUT UP SHOP--HE . . . . 27 2 DON JUAN 1 11 6
'TIS NOT WITH DONNA INEZ I WOULD SHUT . . . . . . 50 2 DON JUAN 1 52 5
BUT VERY DIFFICULT TO SHUT THEIR EYES . . . . . . 77 2 DON JUAN 1 105 8
'TWERE BETTER SURE TO DIE SO THAN BE SHUT . . . . 112 2 DON JUAN 1 166 7
HIS EYES HE OPEN'D SHUT AGAIN UNCLOSED . . . . . 215 2 DON JUAN 2 112 1
WERE SUCH AS COULD NOT IN HIS BREAST BE SHUT . . . 244 2 DON JUAN 2 167 4
WHO SHUT IN CHAMBERS THINK IT LONELINESS . . . . 255 2 DON JUAN 2 188 2
THEN IF YOU'D HAVE THEM WEDDED PLEASE TO SHUT . . . 282 2 DON JUAN 3 12 5
THAT THE HAND STRETCH'D AND SHUT IT WITHOUT HARM . . 312 2 DON JUAN 3 71 3
THE TURKS DO WELL TO SHUT--AT LEAST SOMETIMES-- . . 501 2 DON JUAN 5 157 1
THIS LONG PARENTHESIS I COULD NOT SHUT . . . . . 34 3 DON JUAN 6 56 4

		PAGE	VOL	CANTO	STANZA	LN

SHUT   (CONTINUED)
AND SHUT OUR SOULS UP IN US LIKE A SHELL-FISH . . . . . 236 3 DON JUAN 10   23 8
THE VERY SHADOW OF TRUE TRUTH WOULD SHUT . . . . . . 286 3 DON JUAN 11   37 5
YOU HAVE FREED THE BLACKS--NOW PRAY SHUT UP THE WHITES . 445 3 DON JUAN 14   82 8
SHUT UP THE BALD-COOT BULLY ALEXANDER . . . . 446 3 DON JUAN 14   83 1
SHUT UP EACH HIGH HEROIC SALAMANDER . . . . 446 3 DON JUAN 14   83 5
SHUT UP--NO NOT THE KING BUT THE PAVILION . . . . . 446 3 DON JUAN 14   83 7
SHUT UP THE WORLD AT LARGE LET BEDLAM OUT . . . . . 446 3 DON JUAN 14   84 1
HE SHUT HIS DOOR AND AFTER HAVING READ . . . . . . 512 3 DON JUAN 16   27 2

SHUTTERS
AND WOUNDED SEVERAL SHUTTERS AND SOME BOARDS . . . . . 99 2 DON JUAN 1 143 8

SHY
CHANGED FOR THE DAME GREW DISTANT THE YOUTH SHY . . . 60 2 DON JUAN 1   70 2
WHO'S QUIET INOFFENSIVE SILENT SHY . . . . 30 3 DON JUAN 6   49 5
BEHOLDS HER OWN SHY SHADOWY IMAGE PASS . . . . . . 36 3 DON JUAN 6   60 6

SHYER
WHETHER WITH TIME THE SPECTRE HAS GROWN SHYER . . . . 516 3 DON JUAN 16   36 5

SHYLY
OF BAFFLED HEROES WHO STOOD SHYLY NEAR . . . . . . 148 3 DON JUAN 8   73 6

SIBERIA'S
THE RUDEST BRUTE THAT ROAMS SIBERIA'S WILD . . . . . 157 3 DON JUAN 8   92 3

SIBYL
BEING NO SIBYL IN THE NEW WORLD'S WAYS . . . . . . 480 3 DON JUAN 15   56 6

SICILY
IN SICILY--ALL SINGERS DULY REAR'D . . . . 388 2 DON JUAN 4   80 5

SICK
BUT NOW LAY SICK AND SPEECHLESS ON HIS PILLOW . . . . 169 2 DON JUAN 2   25 4
ARE SOMEWHAT SICK AND SORRY THE NEXT DAY . . . . . . 343 2 DON JUAN 3 V 98 8
AND WE ARE SICK OF ITS HACK SOUNDS AND SIGHTS . . . . 353 2 DON JUAN 4   17 4
AS ONE WHO NE'ER HAD DWELT AMONG THE SICK . . . . . 380 2 DON JUAN 4   67 3
TO THE OTHER BAGGAGE OR TO THE SICK TENT . . . . . . 100 3 DON JUAN 7   66 8
AT LAST FALL SICK OF IMITATING JOB . . . . 137 3 DON JUAN 8   50 8
I DON'T KNOW HOW IT WAS BUT HE GREW SICK . . . . . . 244 3 DON JUAN 10   39 1
LOVE OR LUST MAKES MAN SICK AND WINE MUCH SICKER . . . 317 3 DON JUAN 12   4 1
BUT I AM SICK OF POLITICS BEGIN . . . . 327 3 DON JUAN 12   25 1
FOR HE WAS SICK--NO 'TWAS NOT THE WORD SICK I MEANT-- . 346 3 DON JUAN 12   67 3
FOR HE WAS SICK--NO 'TWAS NOT THE WORD SICK I MEANT-- . 346 3 DON JUAN 12   67 3
SINCE HE WAS SURE HIS MOTHER WOULD FALL SICK . . . . 478 3 DON JUAN 15   50 3
THE NIGHT BEFORE BUT BEING SICK OF SHAKING . . . . . 558 3 DON JUAN 16 118 2

SICKER
SOONER SHALL HEAVEN KISS EARTH--(HERE HE FELL SICKER) . 167 2 DON JUAN 2   20 1
LOVE OR LUST MAKES MAN SICK AND WINE MUCH SICKER . . . 317 3 DON JUAN 12   4 1

SICKLE
AS IF THE CORN-SHEAF SHOULD OPPOSE THE SICKLE . . . . 419 2 DON JUAN 5   17 6
GRASS BEFORE SCYTHES OR CORN BELOW THE SICKLE . . . . 134 3 DON JUAN 8   43 2

SIDE
BUT SCARCE A FEE WAS PAID ON EITHER SIDE . . . . . . 38 2 DON JUAN 1   32 7
AND THEREFORE SIDE BY SIDE WERE GENTLY LAID . . . . . 98 2 DON JUAN 1 141 5
AND THEREFORE SIDE BY SIDE WERE GENTLY LAID . . . . . 98 2 DON JUAN 1 141 5
A HUSBAND LIKE ALFONSO AT MY SIDE . . . . 100 2 DON JUAN 1 145 6
YOU SAW THAT SHE WAS SLEEPING BY MY SIDE . . . . . . 106 2 DON JUAN 1 156 2
HE FELL UPON HIS SIDE AND HIS STRETCH'D HAND . . . . 214 2 DON JUAN 2 110 4
ON ONE SIDE AND THE DEEP SEA CALM AND CHILL . . . . 252 2 DON JUAN 2 183 6
HIS PORT LAY ON THE OTHER SIDE O' THE ISLE . . . . . 285 2 DON JUAN 3   19 8
BEFORE THEM AND FAIR SLAVES ON EVERY SIDE . . . . . 306 2 DON JUAN 3   61 6
AND FISH AND SOUP BY SOME SIDE DISHES BACKED . . . . 428 2 DON JUAN 5   32 5
OF A HUGE HALL AND ON ITS EITHER SIDE . . . . 462 2 DON JUAN 5   87 2
TO SWING A LITTLE LESS FROM SIDE TO SIDE . . . . . . 464 2 DON JUAN 5   91 6
TO SWING A LITTLE LESS FROM SIDE TO SIDE . . . . . . 464 2 DON JUAN 5   91 6
WHEN SEEING HIM PLACED BY HER SIDE AT LAST . . . . . 478 2 DON JUAN 5 116 V4
AND SEATED HER ALL DROOPING BY HIS SIDE . . . . . . 484 2 DON JUAN 5 126 4
IF HEARTS LAY ON THE LEFT SIDE OR THE RIGHT . . . . 485 2 DON JUAN 5 128 5
TO BROOK A RUFFLED ROSE-LEAF BY HIS SIDE . . . . . . 50 3 DON JUAN 6   89 4
BE READY BY THE SECRET PORTAL'S SIDE . . . . 62 3 DON JUAN 6 113 3
ROSE OVER THE TOWN'S RIGHT SIDE IN BRISTLING TIER . . 72 3 DON JUAN 7   12 7
SO THAT ON EITHER SIDE SOME NINE OR TEN . . . . . . 136 3 DON JUAN 8   47 1
BY MOWING CHRISTIANS DOWN ON EVERY SIDE . . . . . . 165 3 DON JUAN 8 107 3
FOR MY PART I'LL ENLIST ON NEITHER SIDE . . . . . . 190 3 DON JUAN 9   16 5
SUPPOSE HIM SWORD BY SIDE AND HAT IN HAND . . . . . 204 3 DON JUAN 9   44 1
HIS SIDE AS A SMALL SWORD BUT SHARP AS EVER . . . . 205 3 DON JUAN 9   45 4
IN OTHER VEHICLES BUT AT HIS SIDE . . . . 249 3 DON JUAN 10   51 3
A RIB'S A THORN IN A WED GALLANT'S SIDE . . . . . . 292 3 DON JUAN 11   46 6
THE LANDS ON EITHER SIDE ARE HIS THE SHIP . . . . . 320 3 DON JUAN 12   9 1
BUT THEN 'TIS MOSTLY ON THE WEAKER SIDE . . . . . . 466 3 DON JUAN 15   23 1
ALMOST AN HAIR'S BREADTH TOO MUCH ON ONE SIDE . . . . 513 3 DON JUAN 16   29 8

SIDEBOARD'S
FROM THEIR HIGH PLACES BY THE SIDEBOARD'S STAND-- . . 539 3 DON JUAN 16   79 5

SIDELONG
REGARDING BOTH WITH SLOW AND SIDELONG VIEW . . . . . 116 2 DON JUAN 1 173 7

SIDES
FOR BOTH SIDES I COULD MANY REASONS SHOW . . . . . 357 2 DON JUAN 4   25 6
LIKE CHASTEST WIVES FROM CONSTANT HUSBANDS' SIDES . . 125 3 DON JUAN 8   27 3
UNTIL I SEE BOTH SIDES FOR ONCE AGREEING . . . . . . 190 3 DON JUAN 9   16 6
THE BASER SIDES OF LITERATURE AND LIFE . . . . . . 232 3 DON JUAN 10   14 2
AND MUCH WAS TALKED ON ALL SIDES ON THAT HEAD . . . . 527 3 DON JUAN 16   54 5

SIEGE
A TOWN WHICH DID A FAMOUS SIEGE ENDURE . . . . . . 70 3 DON JUAN 7   8 5
OF THE TROOPS WERE EMBARKED THE SIEGE TO RAISE . . . 85 3 DON JUAN 7   39 2
TO PAINT A SIEGE WHEREIN MORE MEN WERE SLAIN . . . . 106 3 DON JUAN 7   80 2

		PAGE	VOL	CANTO	STANZA	LN

SIEGES
TO BATTLES SIEGES AND THAT KIND OF PLEASURE . . . . . . 123 3 DON JUAN 8 24 7
SIESTA
HAIDEE AND JUAN THEIR SIESTA TOOK . . . . 359 2 DON JUAN 4 29 2
SIEVE
AND NOT TO POUR THEIR OCEAN IN A SIEVE . . . . . . 431 3 DON JJAN 14 49 8
SIGAEUM
BUT NOW WAS NOT MUCH PLEASED WITH CAPE SIGAEUM . . . . 384 2 DON JUAN 4 75 8
SIGH
AND WHEN AT LENGTH THEY'RE OUT OF BREATH THEY SIGH . . 119 2 DON JUAN 1 179 5
AND IF WE NOW AND THEN A SIGH MUST HEAVE . . . . . 164 2 DON JUAN 2 15 5
NOR THAT A SNEEZE SHOULD INTERRUPT HIS SIGH . . . . . 168 2 DON JUAN 2 22 7
ITS GENTLE TOUCH AND TREMBLING CARE A SIGH . . . . . 215 2 DON JUAN 2 113 7
A SIGH FROM HIS HEAVED BOSOM--AND HERS TOO . . . . . 216 2 DON JUAN 2 114 8
SHORT UPPER LIP--SWEET LIPS THAT MAKE US SIGH . . . . 218 2 DON JUAN 2 118 3
FOUND IN ONE SIGH THE BEST INTERPRETER . . . . . 256 2 DON JUAN 2 189 6
AND MADE THY BEST INTERPRETER A SIGH . . . . . . 275 2 DON JUAN 3 2 4
AND CALLED FROM JUAN'S BREAST A FAINT LOW SIGH . . . 355 2 DON JUAN 4 21 7
NOT SPEECHLESS THOUGH SHE SPOKE NOT NOT A SIGH . . . 378 2 DON JUAN 4 63 5
WITHOUT A GROAN OR SIGH OR GLANCE TO SHOW . . . . 381 2 DON JUAN 4 69 2
AND SIGH TO MIDNIGHT WINDS BUT NOT TO SONG . . . . 398 2 DON JUAN 4 99 8
AND SIGH I CAN'T GET OUT LIKE YORICK'S STARLING . . . 404 2 DON JUAN 4 109 4
SAID JUAN--SWALLOWING A HEART-BURNING SIGH . . . . 423 2 DON JUAN 5 24 3
WHILE STILL A FLUTTERING SIGH GULBEYAZ HEAVED . . . 500 2 DON JUAN 5 155 6
LIE DOWN IN DUDGEON TO SIGH FOR THE LIGHT . . . . 18 3 DON JUAN 6 24 4
IN LIKE CHURCH BELLS WITH SIGH HOWL GROAN YELL PRAYER . 141 3 DON JUAN 8 58 7
SIGH LIKE HIS SON THAN COUGH LIKE HIS GRANDFATHER . . 228 3 DON JUAN 10 6 8
TO SIGH INSTEAD OF COUGHING--AND CRYING-- PISH . . . 228 3 DON JUAN 10 6 V8
BLUSHES FOR THOSE WHO WILL NOT--BUT TO SIGH . . . . 286 3 DON JUAN 11 38 4
THE BLUES THAT TENDER TRIBE WHO SIGH O'ER SONNETS . . 294 3 DON JUAN 11 50 1
SIGH--AS THE POSTBOYS FASTEN ON THE TRACES . . . . 378 3 DON JUAN 13 44 8
SETS TO SOFT MUSIC THE HARMONIOUS SIGH . . . . . 430 3 DON JUAN 14 47 3
AND HEAVES A LONELY SUBTERRAQUEOUS SIGH . . . . . 445 3 DON JUAN 14 81 3
BUT ALL ARE BETTER THAN THE SIGH SUPPREST . . . . 457 3 DON JUAN 15 3 1
NO SOUND EXCEPT THE ECHO OF HIS SIGH . . . . . . 509 3 DON JUAN 16 20 3
WHO WOULD NOT SIGH AI AI TAN KUTHEREIAN . . . . . 554 3 DON JUAN 16 109 1
SIGH'D
HER BRAIN THOUGH IN A DREAM (AND THEN SHE SIGH'D) . . . 67 2 DON JUAN 1 84 3
AND JUAN WEPT AND MUCH HE SIGH'D AND THOUGHT . . . 165 2 DON JUAN 2 17 1
SIGH'D FOR THEIR SAKES--THAT THEY SHOULD E'ER GROW OLDER . 292 2 DON JUAN 3 33 8
SIGH'D TO BEHOLD THEM OF THEIR HOURS BEREFT . . . . 348 2 DON JUAN 4 8 5
SIGHED
SIGHED JUAN MUTTERING ALSO SOME SLIGHT OATHS . . . . 455 2 DON JUAN 5 76 5
AND LOOKING AT HER STEADFASTLY SHE SIGHED . . . . 28 3 DON JUAN 6 45 3
AND CHAFED AT POOR DUDU WHO ONLY SIGHED . . . . . 45 3 DON JUAN 6 79 7
IN ROYALTY'S VAST ARMS HE SIGHED FOR BEAUTY . . . . 243 3 DON JUAN 10 37 8
THAT FUTURE BRIDEGROOMS SWORE AND SIGHED AND PAID IT . . 293 3 DON JUAN 11 49 8
TILL WANTED THEREFORE JUAN ONLY SIGHED . . . . . 506 3 DON JUAN 16 12 8
HE SIGHED--THE NEXT RESOURCE IS THE FULL MOON . . . 506 3 DON JUAN 16 13 1
SIGHING
AND THEN HE SWORE AND SIGHING ON HE SLIPPED . . . . 456 2 DON JUAN 5 77 1
THERE'S MUSIC IN THE SIGHING OF A REED . . . . . 458 3 DON JUAN 15 5 5
SIGHS
THEN THERE WERE SIGHS THE DEEPER FOR SUPPRESSION . . . 62 2 DON JUAN 1 74 1
AND JULIA'S VOICE WAS LOST EXCEPT IN SIGHS . . . . 84 2 DON JUAN 1 117 1
SHE SITS UPON HIS KNEE AND DRINKS HIS SIGHS . . . . 259 2 DON JUAN 2 194 5
SIGHS O'ER HER NAME AND MANY AN ISLANDER . . . . 383 2 DON JUAN 4 73 2
AND THEN WITH TEARS AND SIGHS AND SOME SLIGHT KISSES . . 105 3 DON JUAN 7 76 1
THE FIRST WITH SIGHS THE SECOND WITH AN OATH . . . 166 3 DON JUAN 8 109 3
BUT SIGHS SUBSIDE AND TEARS (EVEN WIDOWS') SHRINK . . 228 3 DON JJAN 10 7 1
BUT COUGHS WILL COME WHEN SIGHS DEPART--AND NOW . . 229 3 DON JUAN 10 8 1
AND THEN BEFORE SIGHS CEASE FOR OFT THE ONE . . . 229 3 DON JUAN 10 8 2
WHERE ALL SIGHS ARE DEPOSITED AND NOW . . . . . . 506 3 DON JUAN 16 13 2
SIGHT
SHE SCARCELY TRUSTED HIM FROM OUT HER SIGHT . . . . 48 2 DON JUAN 1 48 4
OF SIGHT THAT I MUST THINK ON THIS OCCASION . . . . 75 2 DON JUAN 1 101 2
IN SIGHT THAT SEVERAL MONTHS HAVE PASS'D WE'LL SAY . . 86 2 DON JUAN 1 121 6
I CAN'T BUT SAY IT IS AN AWKWARD SIGHT . . . . . 163 2 DON JUAN 2 12 1
WAS USED--NOR SAIL NOR SHORE APPEAR'D IN SIGHT . . . 178 2 DON JUAN 2 41 7
AND 'TIS NO DOUBT A SIGHT TO SEE WHEN BREAKS . . . 230 2 DON JUAN 2 139 4
I SAY THE SUN IS A MOST GLORIOUS SIGHT . . . . . 230 2 DON JUAN 2 140 1
A SIGHT ON WHICH HE HAD NOT LATELY GAZED . . . . 239 2 DON JUAN 2 157 3
WHENCE THE BROAD MOON ROSE CIRCLING INTO SIGHT . . . 253 2 DON JUAN 2 185 4
A DEVOTEE WHEN SOARS THE HOST IN SIGHT . . . . . 261 2 DON JUAN 2 196 3
TO THE FIRE-SIDE (A SIGHT TO TOUCH A SINNER) . . . 306 2 DON JUAN 3 60 6
WHEN ONE IS SHOOK IN SOUND AND ONE IN SIGHT . . . 355 2 DON JUAN 4 21 5
A MOMENT MORE WILL BRING THE SIGHT TO BEAR . . . . 366 2 DON JUAN 4 41 3
THE LAST SIGHT WHICH SHE SAW WAS JUAN'S GORE . . . 375 2 DON JUAN 4 58 1
'TIS A GRAND SIGHT FROM OFF THE GIANT'S GRAVE . . . 413 2 DON JUAN 5 5 3
THOUGH CERTES BY NO MEANS SO GRAND A SIGHT . . . 444 2 DON JUAN 5 58 5
TO ITS OWN BOUGH AND DANGLED YET IN SIGHT . . . . 44 3 DON JUAN 6 76 7
AND THE MOSQUE CRESCENT STRUGGLED INTO SIGHT . . . 49 3 DON JUAN 6 86 4
A RUSSIAN VESSEL E'ER WOULD HEAVE IN SIGHT . . . . 73 3 DON JUAN 7 13 3
IN SIGHT TWO HORSEMEN WHO WERE DEEMED COSSACQUES . . 87 3 DON JUAN 7 43 2
LO DUSKY MASSES STEAL IN DUBIOUS SIGHT . . . . . 110 3 DON JUAN 7 86 3
CAESAR HIMSELF WHO IN THE VERY SIGHT . . . . . 125 3 DON JUAN 8 28 5
WHEN JUAN CAUGHT A GLIMPSE OF THIS SAD SIGHT . . . 158 3 DON JUAN 8 93 4
THUS THE YOUNG KHAN WITH HOURIS IN HIS SIGHT . . . 168 3 DON JUAN 8 114 1
AT SIGHT NOR WOULD PERMIT YOU TO DISCOUNT . . . . 213 3 DON JUAN 9 62 8

731

SIGHT   (CONTINUED)

	PAGE	VOL	CANTO	STANZA	LN
AND LEAVING LAND FAR OUT OF SIGHT WOULD SKIM	227	3 DON JUAN 10	4	4
AT THE FIRST SIGHT OF ALBION'S CHALKY BELT--	257	3 DON JUAN 10	65	4
A GREEN FIELD IS A SIGHT WHICH MAKES HIM PARDON	262	3 DON JUAN 10	76	5
IN SIGHT THEN LOST AMIDST THE FORESTRY	265	3 DON JUAN 10	82	4
HAD SEEN THE WORLD--WHICH IS A CURIOUS SIGHT	292	3 DON JUAN 11	47	7
THAT NOBLE SIGHT WHEN REALLY FREE THE NATION	354	3 DON JUAN 12	83	2
BUT HIS ADVENTURES FORM A SORRY SIGHT--	363	3 DON JUAN 13	9	6
ATTORNIES-GENERAL AWFUL TO THE SIGHT	391	3 DON JUAN 13	69	6
YOUR EYES TO REVEL IN A LIVELIER SIGHT	392	3 DON JUAN 13	72	6
FOR TOO MUCH TRUTH AT FIRST SIGHT NE'ER ATTRACTS	416	3 DON JUAN 14	13	6
BUT WHEN OF THE FIRST SIGHT YOU HAVE HAD YOUR FILL	417	3 DON JUAN 14	17	6
IN SEEING MATTERS WHICH ARE OUT OF SIGHT	457	3 DON JUAN 15	2	8
(KEEPING THE DUE PROPORTIONS STILL IN SIGHT)	467	3 DON JUAN 15	25	6
OPINIONS TWO WHICH AT FIRST SIGHT MAY LOOK	494	3 DON JUAN 15	87	3
OR OLD INDULGE MAN WITH A SECOND SIGHT	496	3 DON JUAN 15	90	6
AND THESE DISSENTIONS MAKE A SORRY SIGHT	496	3 DON JUAN 15	90	V4
AND SCARLET CLOAK (I HATE THE SIGHT TO SEE SINCE--	530	3 DON JUAN 16	61	4

SIGHTS

THE SIGHTS HE WAS ACCUSTOM'D TO BEHOLD	303	2 DON JUAN 3	54	5
AND WE ARE SICK OF ITS HACK SOUNDS AND SIGHTS	353	2 DON JUAN 4	17	4
HE ALSO HAD BEEN BUSY SEEING SIGHTS--	353	3 DON JUAN 12	82	1
FOR SUCH SIGHTS THOUGH THE TALE IS HALF BELIEVED	516	3 DON JUAN 16	36	7

SIGN

THE SUN ROSE RED AND FIERY A SURE SIGN	189	2 DON JUAN 2	62	1
AND GAVE NO SIGN OF LIFE SAVE HIS LIMBS QUIVERING	204	2 DON JUAN 2	90	8
AND WITHOUT WORD A SIGN HER FINGER DREW ON	234	2 DON JUAN 2	146	4
'TIS MELANCHOLY AND A FEARFUL SIGN	277	2 DON JUAN 3	5	1
JUAN FROM THE APARTMENT WITH A SIGN	371	2 DON JUAN 4	50	2
NO HIDEOUS SIGN PROCLAIM'D HER SURELY DEAD	377	2 DON JUAN 4	60	4
NO SIGN SAVE BREATH OF HAVING LEFT THE GRAVE	378	2 DON JUAN 4	63	8
THE EUNUCH MADE A SIGN TO THOSE ON BOARD	433	2 DON JUAN 5	41	7
A PONIARD DECKED HER GIRDLE AS THE SIGN	475	2 DON JUAN 5	111	7
NO SIGN THAT IT WAS CIRCULAR ANYWHERE	497	2 DON JUAN 5	150	4
OF WHICH THE SUREST SIGN IS IN THE END	6	3 DON JUAN 6	1	7
AS THE SOLE SIGN OF MAN'S BEING IN HIS SENSES	240	3 DON JUAN 10	31	7

SIGNAL

WHILE SWUNG THE SIGNAL FROM THE SACRED TOWER	335	2 DON JUAN 3	102	V5
MAKING A SIGNAL OFF SOME PROMONTORY	389	2 DON JUAN 4	82	3
AND AT THE USUAL SIGNAL TA'EN THEIR WAY	19	3 DON JUAN 6	26	4
AT THE GIVEN SIGNAL JOINED TO THEIR ARRAY	20	3 DON JUAN 6	29	2
AND MADE A SIGNAL TO RETREAT AT ONE	81	3 DON JUAN 7	30	6
WHICH IS A SIGNAL TO MY NERVES AND BRAIN	224	3 DON JUAN 9	85	7
WITH HIS GREY SIGNAL FLAG AND THE PAST TENSE	376	3 DON JUAN 13	40	5

SIGNALIZE

BEGAN TO SIGNALIZE THE RUSS RETREAT	87	3 DON JUAN 7	42	2

SIGNAL'S

AND WAITED BUT THE SIGNAL'S VOICE TO BURST	91	3 DON JUAN 7	50	4

SIGNED

A LADY BABA STOPPED AND KNEELING SIGNED	466	2 DON JUAN 5	95	4
SHE SIGNED TO BABA WHO FIRST KISSED THE HEM	466	2 DON JUAN 5	96	6

SIGNIFIES

SO THE END'S GAIN'D WHAT SIGNIFIES THE ROUTE	478	3 DON JUAN 15	51	8

SIGNIFY

WHAT AFTER ALL CAN SIGNIFY THE SITE	284	3 DON JUAN 11	34	5
A WOMAN SO SHE'S GOOD WHAT DOES IT SIGNIFY	435	3 DON JUAN 14	57	8

SIGNING

AND THEN THE MERCHANT GIVING CHANGE AND SIGNING	426	2 DON JUAN 5	29	7

SIGN-POSTS

AND FILL'D THEIR SIGN-POSTS THEN LIKE WELLESLEY NOW	22	2 DON JUAN 1	2	4

SIGNS

AND GAVE NO OUTWARD SIGNS OF INWARD STRIFE	35	2 DON JUAN 1	26	6
(SIGNS OF TRUE GENIUS AND OF EMPTY POCKETS)	91	2 DON JUAN 1	129	2
HAD SIGNS OR FOOTMARKS BUT THE EARTH SAID NOUGHT	100	2 DON JUAN 1	144	4
AND THEN SHE HAD RECOURSE TO NODS AND SIGNS	241	2 DON JUAN 2	162	1
SURPRISED AT THESE UNWONTED SIGNS OF IDLING	290	2 DON JUAN 3	28	2
NOT ALWAYS SIGNS WITH HIM OF CALMEST MOOD	365	2 DON JUAN 4	39	3
THEY SPOKE BY SIGNS--THAT IS NOT SPOKE AT ALL	463	2 DON JUAN 5	90	1
THEIR PAUSE NOR SIGNS HIS HEART WAS OUT OF JOINT	170	3 DON JUAN 8	117	5
QUITE INDEPENDENT OF THE ZODIAC'S SIGNS	423	3 DON JUAN 14	29	3
BUT AFTER THERE ARE SOMETIMES CERTAIN SIGNS	488	3 DON JUAN 15	72	5

SIKTUM

TO THE SOFT OATH OF ANA-SEING SIKTUM	409	2 DON JUAN 4	116	V8

SILENCE

AND IF SHE COULD NOT (WHO CAN) SILENCE SCANDAL	58	2 DON JUAN 1	67	7
THERE IS A DANGEROUS SILENCE IN THAT HOUR	82	2 DON JUAN 1	114	1
FOR THIS IN SILENCE I HAVE SUFFER'D LONG	100	2 DON JUAN 1	145	5
THE GUILELESS HEART IN SILENCE MAY GRIEVE O'ER	107	2 DON JUAN 1	157	3
WHICH IF IT DOES NOT SILENCE STILL MUST POSE	117	2 DON JUAN 1	175	5
IT MIGHT BE THAT HER SILENCE SPRANG ALONE	118	2 DON JUAN 1	176	6
SILENCE IS BEST BESIDES THERE IS A TACT	119	2 DON JUAN 1	178	2
ENJOINING SILENCE STRICT TO ZOE WHO	228	2 DON JUAN 2	136	2
BUT IN HIS SILENCE THERE WAS MUCH TO RUE	300	2 DON JUAN 3	48	7
RELIEVED HER THOUGHTS DULL SILENCE AND QUICK CHAT	378	2 DON JUAN 4	63	6
OF SILENCE WOULD NOT LONG BE BORNE BY THOUGHT	402	2 DON JUAN 4	106	V4
FOR WOMAN'S SILENCE STARTLES MORE THAN THUNDER	34	3 DON JUAN 6	57	V8
THERE WAS DEEP SILENCE IN THE CHAMBER DIM	38	3 DON JUAN 6	64	1
HARK THROUGH THE SILENCE OF THE COLD DULL NIGHT	110	3 DON JUAN 7	86	1
SHE APPROVED HIS SILENCE SHE PERHAPS MISTOOK	553	3 DON JUAN 16	106	2

SILENCED
HIS LIP TO HERS AND SILENCED HIM WITH THIS . . . . . . 356 2 DON JUAN 4   24   2
O'ER SILENCED CITIES MERELY SERVED TO FLATTER . . . . . 197 3 DON JUAN 9   29   5
THE OWL HIS ANTHEM WHERE THE SILENCED QUIRE . . . . . . 387 3 DON JUAN 13   62   7
SILENT
SILENT AND PENSIVE IDLE RESTLESS SLOW . . . . 68 2 DON JUAN 1   87   1
IN SILENT HORROR AND THEIR DISTRIBUTION . . . . 195 2 DON JUAN 2   75   2
THE SILENT OCEAN AND THE STARLIGHT BAY . . . . 255 2 DON JUAN 2   188   3
WHAT SILENT STILL AND SILENT ALL . . . . 323 2 DON JUAN 3 L 8   1
WHAT SILENT STILL AND SILENT ALL . . . . 323 2 DON JUAN 3 L 8   1
OF THE PINE FOREST AND THE SILENT SHORE . . . . 337 2 DON JUAN 3   105   2
EXCEPT MERE BREATH AND SINCE THE SILENT SHORE . . . . . 350 2 DON JUAN 4   12   5
AND NOW AS SILENT AS AN UNSTRUNG DRUM . . . . 430 2 DON JUAN 5   36 V7
SPLENDID BUT SILENT SAVE IN ONE WHERE DROPPING . . . . . 442 2 DON JUAN 5   55   3
WHO'S QUIET INOFFENSIVE SILENT SHY . . . . 30 3 DON JUAN 6   49   5
HER TALENTS WERE OF THE MORE SILENT CLASS . . . . . . 30 3 DON JUAN 6   49   8
FOR WORDLESS WOMAN WHICH IS SILENT THUNDER . . . . . . 34 3 DON JUAN 6   57   8
SLOWLY ALONG THE ROOM BUT SILENT STILL . . . . 61 3 DON JUAN 6   110   6
ARE VERY SILENT WHEN THEY ONCE BELIEVE . . . . 94 3 DON JUAN 7   54   5
THE NIGHTLY MUSTER AND THE SILENT MARCH . . . . 121 3 DON JUAN 8   21   2
SOME HUNDREDS BREATHED--THE REST WERE SILENT ALL . . . . 175 3 DON JUAN 8   127   8
A SILENT CHANGE DISSOLVES THE GLITTERING MASS . . . . . 306 3 DON JUAN 11   76   6
AND WHEN UPON A SILENT SULLEN DAY . . . . 422 3 DON JUAN 14   28   1
AS SEEKING NOT TO KNOW IT SILENT LONE . . . . 476 3 DON JUAN 15   47   2
AS THAT PRIM SILENT COLD AURORA RABY . . . . 477 3 DON JUAN 15   49   8
THE SONG WAS SILENT AND THE DANCE EXPIRED . . . . . . 504 3 DON JUAN 16   8   4
BUT SEEING HIM ALL COLD AND SILENT STILL . . . . 514 3 DON JUAN 16   32   1
THOUGHTS BOUNDLESS DEEP BUT SILENT TOO AS SPACE . . . . 524 3 DON JUAN 16   48   8
SATE SILENT NOW HIS USUAL SPIRITS GONE . . . . 552 3 DON JUAN 16   105   6
BUT JUAN SITTING SILENT IN HIS NOOK . . . . 553 3 DON JUAN 16   106   6
IN MAKING HIM AS SILENT AS A GHOST . . . . 553 3 DON JUAN 16   107   2
SILK
HER EVENING SILK OR IN THE SUMMER MUSLIN . . . . . . 27 2 DON JUAN 1   12   7
OF DOWNCAST LENGTH IN WHOSE SILK SHADOW LIES . . . . . 218 2 DON JUAN 2   117   3
AND THICK WITH DAMASK FLOWERS OF SILK INLAID . . . . . 308 2 DON JUAN 3   64   3
HER ORANGE SILK FULL TURKISH TROWSERS FURL'D . . . . . 312 2 DON JUAN 3   72   7
A PAIR OF TROWSERS OF FLESH-COLOURED SILK . . . . . . 456 2 DON JUAN 5   77   2
FOUR-POSTED AND SILK CURTAINED WHICH ARE GIVEN . . . . 18 3 DON JUAN 6   25   3
AND BLACK SILK NECKCLOTH--AND REPLIED YOU'RE RIGHT . . . 161 3 DON JUAN 8   99   7
O'ER LIMBS WHOSE SYMMETRY SET OFF THE SILK . . . . . . 204 3 DON JUAN 9   43   8
NO MATTER WHETHER RUSSET SILK OR DIMITY . . . . 421 3 DON JUAN 14   26   8
SILKEN
THE SILKEN FILLET'S CURB AND SOUGHT TO SHUN . . . . . 313 2 DON JUAN 3   73   6
THE SILKEN FILLET'S SLIGHT RESTRAINT AND SHUN . . . . . 313 2 DON JUAN 3   73 V6
TO SILKEN ROWS OF GAY AND GARTER'D EARLS . . . . . . 390 3 DON JUAN 13   68   2
SILKS
ALSO THE SOFTER SILKS WERE HEARD TO RUSTLE . . . . . 223 3 DON JUAN 9   82   5
OF GEMS AND PLUMES AND PEARLS AND SILKS TO WHERE . . . 303 3 DON JUAN 11   70   4
SILLY
BUT SHAKSPEARE ALSO SAY 'TIS VERY SILLY . . . . . . 314 2 DON JUAN 3   76   7
PUT UP YOUNG MAN PUT UP YOUR SILLY SWORD . . . . . . 364 2 DON JUAN 4   37   8
YET HAS A KIND OF SOFT AND SILLY AIR . . . . 390 2 DON JUAN 4   85 V6
WOMEN ON T'OTHER HAND SEEM SOMEWHAT SILLY . . . . . . 14 3 DON JUAN 6   16   8
SO SILLY AS TO BUY SLAVES WHO MIGHT SHARE . . . . . . 24 3 DON JUAN 6   36   6
AT WHICH DUDU LOOKED STRANGE AND JUAN SILLY . . . . . 64 3 DON JUAN 6   118   7
TO FOREIGNER OR NATIVE SAVE SOME SILLY ONES . . . . . 263 3 DON JUAN 10   77   6
FOR SILLY WARDS WILL BRING THEIR GUARDIANS BLAME . . . . 336 3 DON JUAN 12   42   4
BUT I HAVE MOTIVES WHETHER WISE OR SILLY . . . . . . 370 3 DON JUAN 13   27   3
THAT HE HAD MADE AT FIRST A SILLY BLUNDER . . . . . . 560 3 DON JUAN 16   122   6
SILVER
THE SILVER LIGHT WHICH HALLOWING TREE AND TOWER . . . . 82 2 DON JUAN 1   114   5
HER HAIR HAD SILVER ONLY BOUND TO BE . . . . 221 2 DON JUAN 2   122   4
GEMS GOLD AND SILVER FORM'D THE SERVICE MOSTLY . . . . 306 2 DON JUAN 3   61   7
AND GEMS--AND GOLD--AND SILVER--GLITTERED MOSTLY . . . . 306 2 DON JUAN 3   61 V7
FRETTED WITH GOLD OR SILVER--BY COMMAND . . . . . . 310 2 DON JUAN 3   69   5
TURNING EACH PIECE OF SILVER O'ER AND TUMBLING . . . . 426 2 DON JUAN 5   29   3
ISMAIL'S NO MORE THE CRESCENT'S SILVER BOW . . . . . 172 3 DON JUAN 8   122   4
ALREADY THEY BEHELD THE SILVER SHOWERS . . . . 222 3 DON JUAN 9   79   5
ON 'CHANGE AND EVEN THY SILVER SOIL PERU . . . . . . 318 3 DON JUAN 12   6   7
QUICK SILVER SMALL TALK ENDING (IF YOU NOTE IT) . . . . 328 3 DON JUAN 12   26   7
SILVERCUP
SIR HENRY SILVERCUP THE GREAT RACE-WINNER . . . . . 399 3 DON JUAN 13   87   4
SILVERS
WHILE SHE STILL SILVERS O'ER YOUR GLOOMY PATH . . . . . 70 3 DON JUAN 7   7   8
SILVERY
LIKE SUMMER CLOUDS ALL SILVERY SMOOTH AND FAIR . . . . 375 2 DON JUAN 4   57   2
THE SILVERY BELL RUNG NOT FOR DINNER READY . . . . . 482 3 DON JUAN 15   61   6
ON WHICH THE MOONBEAMS FELL IN SILVERY SHOWERS . . . . 559 3 DON JUAN 16   120   3
SIMILAR
VOLUMES WITH SIMILAR SAD ILLUSTRATIONS . . . . 464 3 DON JUAN 15   18   7
WITH VARIOUS SIMILAR REMARKS TO TALLY . . . . 526 3 DON JUAN 16   53   5
AT THEIR LORD'S SON'S OR SIMILAR CONNECTION'S . . . . . 546 3 DON JUAN 16   95   7
SIMILE
(THIS OLD SONG AND NEW SIMILE HOLDS GOOD) . . . . . . 10 2 DON JUAN D   2   2
(BUT THIS LAST SIMILE IS TRITE AND STUPID) . . . . . . 51 2 DON JUAN 1   55   8
I HAVE BUT ONE SIMILE AND THAT'S A BLUNDER . . . . . . 34 3 DON JUAN 6   57   7
THIS SIMILE ENOUGH FOR AJAX JUAN . . . . 126 3 DON JUAN 8   29   7
THAT'S AN APPROPRIATE SIMILE THAT JACKALL-- . . . . . 196 3 DON JUAN 9   27   1
SIMILE'S
SHE LOOKED (THIS SIMILE'S QUITE NEW) JUST CUT . . . . . 27 3 DON JUAN 6   43   5

733

	PAGE	VOL	CANTO	STANZA	LN

SIMILES
    ARE SIMILES AT HAND FOR THE DISTRESS . . . . 487 2 DON JUAN 5 132 3
    MY SIMILES ARE GATHERED IN A HEAP . . . . 40 3 DON JUAN 6 68 6
SIMILIE
    I'VE GOT A BETTER SIMILIE THAN THAT . . . . 375 3 DON JUAN 13 37 V1
SIMILITUDES
    A THING OF WHICH SIMILITUDES CAN SHOW . . . . 505 3 DON JUAN 16 10 4
SIMOOM
    EVEN AS THE SIMOOM SWEEPS THE BLASTED PLAINS . . . 375 2 DON JUAN 4 57 8
SIMOOMS
    WHO WHIRL THE DUST AS SIMOOMS WHIRL THE SAND . . . . 435 3 DON JUAN 14 58 6
SIMPLE
    IN HONEST SIMPLE VERSE THIS SONG TO YOU . . . . . 20 2 DON JUAN D 17 2
    HER TALE IS TOLD WITH SO MUCH SIMPLE EASE-- . . . . 273 2 DON JUAN 2 V 2 6
    PLAIN--SIMPLE--SHORT AND BY NO MEANS INVITING . . . 412 2 DON JUAN 5 2 3
    AT LAST THEY SETTLED INTO SIMPLE GRUMBLING . . . . 426 2 DON JUAN 5 29 1
    BECAUSE THOUGH I AM BUT A SIMPLE NODDY . . . . . 77 3 DON JUAN 7 21 5
    OR IF THAT SIMPLE SENTENCE SHOULD DISPLEASE . . . . 109 3 DON JUAN 7 85 3
    SIMPLE SERENE THE ANTIPODES OF SHAME . . . . . 144 3 DON JUAN 8 63 5
    SIMPLE THEY WERE NOT SAVAGE AND THEIR RIFLES . . . 145 3 DON JUAN 8 66 7
    PLAIN SIMPLE FORNICATION--NOR BEHOLD . . . . . 314 3 DON JUAN 11 V 76 7
    AND SIMPLE IN THE WORLD AND DOTH NOT NEED . . . . 437 3 DON JUAN 14 61 6
    WHO WOULD SUPPOSE FROM ADAM'S SIMPLE RATION . . . 486 3 DON JUAN 15 69 5
    THE SIMPLE OLIVES BEST ALLIES OF WINE . . . . . 488 3 DON JUAN 15 73 1
    PERHAPS SHE MERELY HAD THE SIMPLE PROJECT . . . . 526 3 DON JUAN 16 51 5
SIMPLER
    SIMPLER AND YET OF COLOURS NOT SO GRAVE . . . . 220 2 DON JUAN 2 120 3
    THAT FINER SIMPLER MUSIC NE'ER WAS HEARD . . . . . 236 2 DON JUAN 2 151 5
SIMPLICITY
    SHE THOUGHT WITH SOME SIMPLICITY INDEED . . . . . 437 3 DON JUAN 14 61 4
    AND SANG WITH MUCH SIMPLICITY--A MERIT . . . . . 518 3 DON JUAN 16 40 7
    AND THEN HER DRESS--WHAT BEAUTIFUL SIMPLICITY . . . 550 3 DON JUAN 16 102 7
SIMPLON'S
    SMOOTHED EVEN THE SIMPLON'S STEEP AND BY GOD'S BLESSING . 215 3 DON JUAN 9 66 7
SIMPLY
    THE PLAN AT PRESENT'S SIMPLY IN CONCOCTION . . . . . 356 3 DON JUAN 12 87 5
SIN
    IN SPAIN YOU KNOW THIS IS A SORT OF SIN) . . . . 52 2 DON JUAN 1 56 4
    SENDS SIN WITHOUT A RAG ON SHIVERING FORTH . . . . 57 2 DON JUAN 1 64 3
    WORTHY OF THIS AMBROSIAL SIN SO SHOWN . . . . . 90 2 DON JUAN 1 127 6
    PLEASURE'S A SIN AND SOMETIMES SIN'S A PLEASURE . . 93 2 DON JUAN 1 133 4
    OH SIN OH SORROW AND OH WOMANKIND . . . . 112 2 DON JUAN 1 165 2
    HE HAD NO BUSINESS TO COMMIT A SIN . . . . . . 113 2 DON JUAN 1 167 2
    OUR SIN THE SAME AND HARD AS HIS TO MEND . . . . 344 2 DON JUAN 4 1 6
    HAVE DAWN'D A FAIR AND SINLESS CHILD OF SIN . . . 382 2 DON JUAN 4 70 3
    SOFAS 'TWAS HALF A SIN TO SIT UPON . . . . . . 449 2 DON JUAN 5 65 5
    RATHER THAN SIN--EXCEPT TO HIS OWN WISH . . . . . 492 2 DON JUAN 5 141 1
    SULTANS TOO MUCH ABHOR THIS SORT OF SIN . . . . 10 3 DON JUAN 6 7 5
    NOT ONLY AS SIN BUT AS A BORE-- . . . . 12 3 DON JUAN 6 12 4
    APART FROM ONE WHO HAD NO SIN TO SHOW . . . . . 48 3 DON JUAN 6 84 7
    I HOPE THIS LITTLE QUESTION IS NO SIN . . . . . . 77 3 DON JUAN 7 21 4
    BUT IN THE SAME SMALL MINUTE EVERY SIN . . . . . 142 3 DON JUAN 8 59 3
    THERE WAS SMALL LEISURE FOR SUPERFLUOUS SIN . . . 178 3 DON JUAN 8 132 6
    YOUR HAND AT HARDENED AND IMPERIAL SIN . . . . . 266 3 DON JUAN 10 85 4
    THE HORRID SIN--AND WHAT'S STILL WORSE THE TROUBLE . 292 3 DON JUAN 11 46 8
    BUT LOVE SANS BANNS IS BOTH A SIN AND SHAME . . . 323 3 DON JUAN 12 15 7
    WHEN TIRED OF PLAY HE FLIRTED WITHOUT SIN . . . . 327 3 DON JUAN 12 25 5
    HE PLAYED AND PAID MADE LOVE WITHOUT MUCH SIN . . 327 3 DON JUAN 12 25 V5
    A COMMENT ON THE GOSPEL'S SIN NO MORE . . . . . 352 3 DON JUAN 12 79 2
    WHO DID NOT HATE SO MUCH THE SIN AS SINNER . . . . 399 3 DON JUAN 13 87 6
    WHOSE VERDICT FOR SUCH SIN A CERTAIN CURE IS)-- . . 436 3 DON JUAN 14 60 8
    THAN MATCH-MAKING IN GENERAL 'TIS NO SIN . . . . 470 3 DON JUAN 15 31 6
SINCE
    SINCE GOLD ALONE SHOULD NOT HAVE BEEN ITS PRICE . . 12 2 DON JUAN D 6 4
    AND SINCE EXCEEDING VALOROUS AND SAGE . . . . 24 2 DON JUAN 1 5 2
    LET'S OWN SINCE IT CAN DO NO GOOD ON EARTH . . . . 41 2 DON JUAN 1 36 3
    AS WELL AS ALL THE GREEK I SINCE HAVE LOST . . . 50 2 DON JUAN 1 53 3
    ME ALSO SINCE THE TIME SO OPPORTUNE IS-- . . . . 103 2 DON JUAN 1 150 6
    TELL ME--AND BE ASSURED THAT SINCE YOU STAIN . . . 105 2 DON JUAN 1 154 7
    AT LEAST SINCE THE RETIREMENT OF THE VANDALS . . . 128 2 DON JUAN 1 190 4
    SINCE RODERIC'S GOTH'S OR OLDER GENSERIC'S VANDALS . 129 2 DON JUAN 1 190 V4
    SINCE AFTER ALL THE CONSEQUENCE IS VAPOUR . . . . 146 2 DON JUAN 1 218 V4
    SINCE NOT A PINCH OF DUST REMAINS OF CHEOPS . . . 146 2 DON JUAN 1 219 8
    SINCE IN A WAY THAT'S RATHER OF THE ODDEST HE . . 157 2 DON JUAN 2 1 7
    FAREWELL MY MOTHER AND SINCE ALL IS O'ER . . . . 166 2 DON JUAN 2 18 6
    SINCE NOAH'S ARK WENT CRUISING HERE AND THERE . . 191 2 DON JUAN 2 66 6
    BUT THE BEST DISH THAT E'ER WAS COOK'D SINCE HOMER'S . 221 2 DON JUAN 2 123 7
    WERE NEARLY TINDER SINCE SO LONG THEY LAY . . . 226 2 DON JUAN 2 132 5
    SINCE AFTER ALL NO DOUBT THE YOUTHFUL PAIR . . . . 233 2 DON JUAN 2 144 6
    FOR LITTLE HAD HE WANDER'D SINCE THE DAY . . . . 249 2 DON JUAN 2 176 4
    WHICH EVE HAS LEFT HER DAUGHTERS SINCE HER FALL . . 256 2 DON JUAN 2 189 8
    EVER SINCE JUAN SERVED HER FOR A SPOUSE . . . . 295 2 DON JUAN 3 39 V8
    THAN ANY SINCE THE BIRTHDAY OF TYPOGRAPHY . . . . 330 2 DON JUAN 3 94 6
    EXCEPT MERE BREATH AND SINCE THE SILENT SHORE . . 350 2 DON JUAN 4 12 5
    PERFORCE SINCE WHATSOEVER MET HER VIEW . . . . 378 2 DON JUAN 4 62 4
    BUT TIMES ARE ALTER'D SINCE A RHYMING LOVER . . . 405 2 DON JUAN 4 111 2
    AND HUGE TOMBS WORSE--MANKIND SINCE ADAM FELL . . 444 2 DON JUAN 5 59 6
    OF WHAT HAD PAST SINCE ALL THE SLAVES RETIRED . . 55 3 DON JUAN 6 99 3
    OR WAS AT LEAST UNLESS 'TIS SINCE DEFACED . . . . 71 3 DON JUAN 7 9 5

SINCE　(CONTINUED)

	PAGE	VOL		CANTO	STANZA	LN
WAS HE SINCE SO RENOWNED IN COUNTRY QUARTERS	76	3	DON JUAN	7	19	7
SINCE JOHN HAS LATELY LOST THE USE OF BOTH	88	3	DON JUAN	7	45	4
SINCE THERE IS DISCORD AFTER BOTH AT LEAST)	90	3	DON JUAN	7	49	4
OH GLORIOUS LAUREL SINCE FOR ONE SOLE LEAF	101	3	DON JUAN	7	68	6
AT PRESENT SUCH THINGS SINCE THEY ARE HER THEME	112	3	DON JUAN	8	1	6
(START NOT KIND READER SINCE GREAT HOMER THOUGHT	126	3	DON JUAN	8	29	6
WAS HERE (AS HERETOFORE AND SINCE) LET LOOSE	173	3	DON JUAN	8	123	8
(SINCE IT WAS NOT THEIR FAULT BUT ONLY FATE	177	3	DON JUAN	8	131	5
SINCE MENE MENE TEKEL AND UPHARSIN	179	3	DON JUAN	8	134	2
SOULS TO SAVE SINCE EVE'S SLIP AND ADAM'S FALL	192	3	DON JUAN	9	19	3
SINCE LATELY THERE HAVE BEEN NO RENTS AT ALL	198	3	DON JUAN	9	32	4
SINCE FIRST HER MAJESTY WAS SINGLY CROWNED	205	3	DON JUAN	9	46	6
KNOW NOT SINCE KNOWLEDGE SAW HER BRANCHES STRIPT	210	3	DON JUAN	9	55	6
SINCE THOU HAST SETTLED BEYOND ALL SURMISES	210	3	DON JUAN	9	55	8
OR WASTE A WORLD SINCE NO ONE CAN DENY	210	3	DON JUAN	9	56	5
SINCE ADAM WITH A FALL OR WITH AN APPLE	225	3	DON JUAN	10	1	8
FOR EVER SINCE IMMORTAL MAN HATH GLOWED	226	3	DON JUAN	10	2	6
FOR BOTH ARE MUCH THE SAME SINCE WHAT MEN THINK	234	3	DON JUAN	10	20	2
GAVE WAY TO'T SINCE HE COULD NOT OVERCOME IT	272	3	DON JUAN	11	9	4
EMPLOYED FOR SINCE IT IS THEIR DAILY LABOUR	288	3	DON JUAN	11	41	2
PERMITS WHATE'ER THEY PLEASE OR DID NOT LONG SINCE	305	3	DON JUAN	11	73	8
AND FRAILER SINCE WITHOUT A BREATH OF AIR	306	3	DON JUAN	11	76	V5
BUT SINCE THEY ARE THAT EPOCH IS A BORE	316	3	DON JUAN	12	2	4
BUT SINCE STEAM ENGINES PRAISE AND HONOUR VAPOUR	317	3	DON JUAN	12	4	V8
SINCE ODDS ARE THAT POSTERITY WILL KNOW	324	3	DON JUAN	12	18	7
SINCE I'VE GROWN MORAL STILL I MUST ACCUSE YOU ALL	329	3	DON JUAN	12	28	5
SINCE LAUGHTER NOW-A-DAYS IS DEEMED TOO SERIOUS	358	3	DON JUAN	13	1	2
OF HIS OWN COUNTRY--SELDOM SINCE THAT DAY	364	3	DON JUAN	13	11	3
AND SINCE THAT TIME THERE HAS NOT BEEN A SECOND	365	3	DON JUAN	13	13	8
BY NAMING STREETS SINCE MEN ARE SO CENSORIOUS	369	3	DON JUAN	13	25	2
AND SINCE THERE'S SAFETY IN A MULTITUDE	371	3	DON JUAN	13	29	1
SINCE EVE ATE APPLES MUCH DEPENDS ON DINNER	404	3	DON JUAN	13	99	8
TO THIS WE HAVE ADDED SINCE THE LOVE OF MONEY	405	3	DON JUAN	13	100	3
ALAS WORLDS FALL--AND WOMAN SINCE SHE FELL'D	420	3	DON JUAN	14	23	1
THE WORLD (AS SINCE THAT HISTORY LESS POLITE	420	3	DON JUAN	14	23	2
BUT SINCE BENEATH IT UPON EARTH WE ARE BROUGHT	421	3	DON JUAN	14	26	4
SINCE THEN SHE HAD SPARKLED THROUGH THREE GLOWING WINTERS	434	3	DON JUAN	14	56	1
SHE HAD ALSO SNATCH'D A MOMENT SINCE HER MARRIAGE	434	3	DON JUAN	14	56	7
TO HOMER'S ILIAD SINCE IT DREW TO TROY	441	3	DON JUAN	14	72	4
MUCH PASSION SINCE THE MERCHANT-SHIP THE ARGO	443	3	DON JUAN	14	76	7
AND SINCE THAT TIME IT NEED NOT COST MUCH SHOWING	444	3	DON JUAN	14	78	5
WHO EATS FIRE GRATIS (SINCE THE PAY'S BUT SMALL)	446	3	DON JUAN	14	83	6
BESIDES HIS CONDUCT SINCE IN ENGLAND GREW MORE	460	3	DON JUAN	15	11	5
SINCE HE WAS SURE HIS MOTHER WOULD FALL SICK	478	3	DON JUAN	15	50	3
SINCE ADELINE WAS LIBERAL BY NATURE	478	3	DON JUAN	15	52	6
FOR WEAPONS BUT WHAT MUSE SINCE HOMER'S ABLE	482	3	DON JUAN	15	62	3
SINCE WITH DIGRESSIONS WE TOO LONG HAVE TARRIED	493	3	DON JUAN	15	84	5
GOD HELP US SINCE WE HAVE NEED ON OUR CAREER	496	3	DON JUAN	15	90	3
A MODE ADOPTED SINCE BY MODERN YOUTH	501	3	DON JUAN	16	1	4
BUT WONDER THEY SO FEW ARE SINCE MY TALE IS	502	3	DON JUAN	16	3	7
AT WHICH HE MARVELLED SINCE HE HAD NOT RAINED	515	3	DON JUAN	16	34	4
AURORA--SINCE WE ARE TOUCHING UPON TASTE	524	3	DON JUAN	16	48	1
OF WHAT SHE HAD GONE THROUGH WITH--SINCE A BRIDE	525	3	DON JUAN	16	50	6
AND SCARLET CLOAK (I HATE THE SIGHT TO SEE SINCE--	530	3	DON JUAN	16	61	4
SINCE--SINCE--IN YOUTH I HAD THE SAD MISHAP--	530	3	DON JUAN	16	61	5
SINCE--SINCE--IN YOUTH I HAD THE SAD MISHAP--	530	3	DON JUAN	16	61	5
BUT LUCKILY I HAVE PAID FEW PARISH FEES SINCE)	530	3	DON JUAN	16	61	6
SINCE HE HAD GAINED AT LEAST HER OBSERVATION	545	3	DON JUAN	16	93	5
WHO GROW UP CHILDREN ONLY SINCE THE OLD SAW	563	3	DON JUAN	17	2	2
SINCE BURNING AGED WOMEN (SAVE A FEW--	565	3	DON JUAN	17	7	3

SINCERE

	PAGE	VOL		CANTO	STANZA	LN
A SINCERE WOMAN'S BREAST--FOR OVER-WARM	13	3	DON JUAN	6	15	7
MY WORDS AT LEAST ARE MORE SINCERE AND HEARTY	195	3	DON JUAN	9	26	3
BUT WENT TO HEAVEN IN AS SINCERE A WAY	242	3	DON JUAN	10	35	2
WITHOUT THE AID OF TOO SINCERE A POET	311	3	DON JUAN	11	87	8
AND SEVERAL PITIED WITH SINCERE REGRET	429	3	DON JUAN	14	44	7
SINCERE HE WAS--AT LEAST YOU COULD NOT DOUBT IT	461	3	DON JUAN	15	13	5
SHE WAS A CATHOLIC TOO SINCERE AUSTERE	476	3	DON JUAN	15	46	1
MORE WARM AS LOVELY AND NOT LESS SINCERE	481	3	DON JUAN	15	58	5
MY SMILES MUST BE SINCERE OR NOT AT ALL	499	3	DON JUAN	15	96	2
THE MOST SINCERE THAT EVER DEALT IN FICTION	502	3	DON JUAN	16	2	8

SINCEREST

	PAGE	VOL		CANTO	STANZA	LN
AND FALSE--THOUGH TRUE FOR SURELY THEY'RE SINCEREST	547	3	DON JUAN	16	97	7

SINCERITY

	PAGE	VOL		CANTO	STANZA	LN
THE WARMTH OF HER POLITENESS WHOSE SINCERITY	550	3	DON JUAN	16	02	2

SINE

	PAGE	VOL		CANTO	STANZA	LN
OBSERVE FOR THAT WITH ME'S A SINE QUA	494	3	DON JUAN	15	86	8

SINECURE

	PAGE	VOL		CANTO	STANZA	LN
A GOODLY SINECURE NO DOUBT BUT MADE	22	3	DON JUAN	6	32	1

SINECURES

	PAGE	VOL		CANTO	STANZA	LN
TO HOLD SOME SINECURES HE WISHED ABOLISHED	535	3	DON JUAN	16	72	7

SINEWS

	PAGE	VOL		CANTO	STANZA	LN
MARCHED FORTH WITH NERVE AND SINEWS BENT TO SLAY--	113	3	DON JUAN	8	2	4

SING

	PAGE	VOL		CANTO	STANZA	LN
WHICH PYE BEING OPEN'D THEY BEGAN TO SING	10	2	DON JUAN	D	2	1
AND SOUTHEY LIVES TO SING THEM VERY ILL	19	2	DON JUAN	D	16	8
THE BARD I QUOTE FROM DOES NOT SING AMISS	69	2	DON JUAN	1	88	5
SING AT MY HEART SIX MONTHS AT LEAST IN VAIN	102	2	DON JUAN	1	149	2

		PAGE	VOL	CANTO	STANZA	LN

SING   (CONTINUED)
```
    HERE ENDS THIS CANTO--NEED I SING OR SAY . . . . . . . . 126  2 DON JUAN  1   188   1
    THUS USUALLY WHEN HE WAS ASK'D TO SING . . . . . . . . . 319  2 DON JUAN  3    85   1
    IN GREECE HE'D SING SOME SORT OF HYMN LIKE THIS T'YE . . 320  2 DON JUAN  3    86   8
    EVEN AS I SING SUFFUSE MY FACE . . . . . . . . . . . . . 323  2 DON JUAN  3  L  6   4
    THERE SWAN-LIKE LET ME SING AND DIE . . . . . . . . . . 326  2 DON JUAN  3  L 16   4
    BUT NEXT WHEN I'M ENGAGED TO SING THERE--DO GO . . . . . 392  2 DON JUAN  4    88   8
    WHEN AMATORY POETS SING THEIR LOVES . . . . . . . . . . 411  2 DON JUAN  5     1   1
    BEGAN TO SING DANCE CHATTER SMILE AND PLAY . . . . . . .  23  3 DON JUAN  6    34   8
    I SING THEM BOTH AND AM ABOUT TO BATTER . . . . . . . .   70  3 DON JUAN  7     8   4
    AND HEROES ARE BUT MADE FOR BARDS TO SING . . . . . . . 118  3 DON JUAN  8    14   5
    WHICH FEW WILL SING I TRUST BUT NONE FORGET IT-- . . . . 179  3 DON JUAN  8   135   3
    THAN MY FORERUNNERS  CARELESSLY I SING . . . . . . . . . 181  3 DON JUAN  8   138   7
    (I WISH YOUR BARDS WOULD SING IT RATHER BETTER) . . . . 184  3 DON JUAN  9     3   8
    AND THAT I SING OF NEITHER MINE NOR ME . . . . . . . . . 311  3 DON JJAN 11    88   5
    BARDS MAY SING WHAT THEY PLEASE ABOUT CONTENT . . . . . 444  3 DON JUAN 14    79   4
    WHOSE MERIT NONE ENOUGH CAN SING OR SAY . . . . . . . . 445  3 DON JUAN 14    82   2
    BUT LAISSEZ ALLER--KNIGHTS AND DAMES I SING . . . . . . 467  3 DON JUAN 15    25   1
    THE NIGHT (I SING BY NIGHT--SOMETIMES AN OWL . . . . . . 499  3 DON JUAN 15    97   1
SINGED
    SHOULD STILL BE SINGED BUT SLIGHTLY LET ME STATE) . . . 565  3 DON JUAN 17     7   6
SINGEING
    THE SINGEING OF A SINGLE INKY WHISKER . . . . . . . . . 498  2 DON JUAN  5   151   8
SINGER
    OURSELVES A SINGER DANCER MUCH IN FASHION . . . . . . . 216  3 DON JUAN  9    68   4
SINGERS
    IN SICILY--ALL SINGERS DULY REAR'D . . . . . . . . . . . 388  2 DON JUAN  4    80   5
SINGING
    AND SINGING AS HE SUNG IN HIS WARM YOUTH . . . . . . . . 318  2 DON JUAN  3    83   7
    HIS SINGING I NO FURTHER TRUST CAN PLACE IN . . . . . . 391  2 DON JUAN  4    86   6
    IN FACT HE HAD NO SINGING EDUCATION . . . . . . . . . . 391  2 DON JUAN  4    87   3
    AND SINGING BIRDS WITHOUT WERE HEARD TO WARBLE . . . . .  55  3 DON JUAN  6    98   3
SINGLE
    I'M A PLAIN MAN AND IN A SINGLE STATION . . . . . . . .   33  2 DON JUAN  1    22   6
    MAY HAVE SUGGESTED THAT THIS SINGLE ONE . . . . . . . .   54  2 DON JUAN  1    59   5
    ON WHICH THREE SINGLE HOURS OF MOONSHINE SMILE-- . . . .  82  2 DON JUAN  1   113   7
    WITH BUT THE SINGLE OBJECT--TO ADVANCE . . . . . . . . . 152  2 DON JUAN  1  V  3  V3
    ABOVE HIM HANGING BY A SINGLE HAIR . . . . . . . . . . . 153  2 DON JUAN  1  V  4   2
    DESPATCHING SINGLE CRUISERS HERE AND THERE . . . . . . . 285  2 DON JUAN  3    19   2
    IF SINGLE PROBABLY HIS PLIGHTED FAIR . . . . . . . . . . 288  2 DON JUAN  3    24   1
    BEYOND A SINGLE GENTLEMAN'S BELIEF . . . . . . . . . . . 301  2 DON JUAN  3    51   8
    THAN THE STERN SINGLE DEEP AND WORDLESS IRE . . . . . . 305  2 DON JUAN  3    58   7
    OR PRAY MEDEA FOR A SINGLE DRAGON . . . . . . . . . . . 333  2 DON JUAN  3    99   4
    WHO NEVER FOUND A SINGLE HOUR TOO SLOW . . . . . . . . . 353  2 DON JUAN  4    18   3
    WITHOUT A SINGLE SCUDO OF SALARIO . . . . . . . . . . . 389  2 DON JUAN  4    82   6
    A SINGLE TEAR UPON HIS EYELASH STAID . . . . . . . . . . 420  2 DON JUAN  5    18   4
    A SINGLE CRY WOULD BRING THEM ALL ABROAD . . . . . . . . 436  2 DON JUAN  5    45   5
    A BOOK FRIEND SINGLE LADY OR A GLASS . . . . . . . . . . 444  2 DON JUAN  5    58   2
    THE STORY SCARCELY PASSED A SINGLE LIP-- . . . . . . . . 496  2 DON JUAN  5   149   3
    THE SINGEING OF A SINGLE INKY WHISKER . . . . . . . . . 498  2 DON JUAN  5   151   8
    'TIS THUS THE SPIRIT OF A SINGLE MIND . . . . . . . . .   90  3 DON JUAN  7    48   1
    IS BUTCHERY SOMETIMES A SINGLE SORROW . . . . . . . . . 102  3 DON JUAN  7    69   7
    THE DRYING UP A SINGLE TEAR HAS MORE . . . . . . . . . . 113  3 DON JUAN  8     3   7
    NOR CARE A SINGLE DAMN ABOUT HIS CORPS . . . . . . . . . 127  3 DON JJAN  8    31  V8
    HIS WAY TO--WHERE HE KNEW NOT--SINGLE HANDED . . . . . . 127  3 DON JUAN  8    32   3
    BY CHRISTIAN SOLDIERY A SINGLE SPOT . . . . . . . . . . 131  3 DON JUAN  8    37   5
    ON SUCH OCCASIONS NOT A SINGLE HEAD . . . . . . . . . . 152  3 DON JUAN  8    81   6
    WHILE COURAGE CLUNG BUT TO A SINGLE TWIG--AM I . . . . . 164  3 DON JUAN  8   105   5
    OF SINGLE BLESSEDNESS AND THOUGHT IT GOOD . . . . . . . 177  3 DON JUAN  8   131   4
    OF HOPES AND FEARS WHICH SHAKE A SINGLE BALL . . . . . . 304  3 DON JUAN 11    72   8
    THE SINGLE LADIES WISHING TO BE DOUBLE . . . . . . . . . 342  3 DON JUAN 12    58   7
    FOR TALK SIX TIMES WITH THE SAME SINGLE LADY . . . . . . 343  3 DON JUAN 12    59   7
    I'LL LEAVE A SINGLE READER'S EYELID DRY . . . . . . . . 355  3 DON JUAN 12    86   5
    A SINGLE LAUGH DEMOLISHED THE RIGHT ARM . . . . . . . . 364  3 DON JUAN 13    11   2
    WHICH IS THAT THERE IS SCARCE A SINGLE SEASON . . . . . 370  3 DON JUAN 13    26   3
    BISHOPS WHO HAD NOT LEFT A SINGLE SERMON . . . . . . . . 391  3 DON JUAN 13    69   5
    I TOUCH A SINGLE LEAF WHERE HE IS WARDEN-- . . . . . . . 442  3 DON JUAN 14    75   6
    THIS I COULD PROVE BEYOND A SINGLE DOUBT . . . . . . . . 446  3 DON JUAN 14    84   5
    OF SINGLE GENTLEMEN WHO WOULD BE DOUBLE . . . . . . . . 477  3 DON JUAN 15    48   8
    TO DRAW UP IN ARRAY A SINGLE DAY-BILL . . . . . . . . . 482  3 DON JUAN 15    62   5
    HE WOULD NOT JOIN THEM IN A SINGLE SALLY . . . . . . . . 552  3 DON JUAN 16   105   8
    A SINGLE SHADE'S SUFFICIENT TO ENTRANCE A . . . . . . . 557  3 DON JUAN 16   116   6
    HOW ODD A SINGLE HOBGOBLIN'S NON-ENTITY . . . . . . . . 559  3 DON JUAN 16   120   7
    MY SOUL FROM OUT ME AT THY SINGLE SUMMON . . . . . . . . 569  3 DON JUAN 17  V 13   6
SINGLY
    SINCE FIRST HER MAJESTY WAS SINGLY CROWNED . . . . . . . 205  3 DON JUAN  9    46   6
    OPPOSING SINGLY THE UNITED STRONG . . . . . . . . . . . 363  3 DON JUAN 13    10   3
SINGS
    PLEASURE (WHENE'ER SHE SINGS AT LEAST) 'S A SIREN . . . 294  2 DON JUAN  3    36   5
    UNSEEN AS SINGS THE NIGHTINGALE THEY WERE . . . . . . . 358  2 DON JUAN  4    28   2
    AS SOMEONE SOMEWHERE SINGS ABOUT THE SKY . . . . . . . . 404  2 DON JUAN  4   110   2
    THE NIGHTINGLE THAT SINGS WITH THE DEEP THORN . . . . .  49  3 DON JUAN  6    87   5
    I THINK I HEAR A LITTLE BIRD WHO SINGS . . . . . . . . . 137  3 DON JUAN  8    50   3
    IS HEAVEN AND HEAVEN IS LOVE--SO SINGS THE BARD . . . . 322  3 DON JUAN 12    13   2
    THE GALE SWEEPS THROUGH ITS FRETWORK AND OFT SINGS . . . 387  3 DON JUAN 13    62   6
    WHATEVER ISAAC WALTON SINGS OR SAYS . . . . . . . . . . 407  3 DON JUAN 13   106   6
    BUT MOSTLY SINGS OF HUMAN THINGS AND ACTS-- . . . . . . 416  3 DON JUAN 14    13   4
    OF WHICH MOST MEN PARTAKE BUT NO ONE SINGS . . . . . . . 568  3 DON JUAN 17    13   3
SINGULAR
    HE STOPP'D--WHAT SINGULAR EMOTIONS FILL . . . . . . . . 286  2 DON JUAN  3    21   3
```

736

		PAGE	VOL		CANTO	STANZA	LN

SINGULARITY
MY PLAN (BUT I IF BUT FOR SINGULARITY . . . . 357 3 DON JUAN 12   89   5
SINGULTUS
OR A SINGULTUS--EMBLEMS OF EMOTION . . . . 457 3 DON JUAN 15   2   2
SINISTER
IT WAS HIS FOIBLE BUT BY NO MEANS SINISTER-- . . . . . 368 3 DON JUAN 13   21   2
SINK
BUT LET US DIE LIKE MEN NOT SINK BELOW . . . . 175 2 DON JUAN 2   36   4
NO DOUBT THE VESSEL WAS ABOUT TO SINK . . . . 187 2 DON JUAN 2   58   6
SINK O'ER THE EARTH SO BEAUTIFUL AND SOFT . . . . . . 335 2 DON JUAN 3 102   4
MUST SINK AT LAST INTO A SWOON DIVINE-- . . . . 343 2 DON JUAN 3 V 98 6
WILL SINK WHERE LIE THE SONGS AND WARS OF EARTH . . . 400 2 DON JUAN 4 104   7
SHE ONLY WISHED TO SINK BURN AND DESTROY . . . . . . 490 2 DON JUAN 5 136 V7
THAN WHAT THEY THOUGHT FOR MIND CAN NEVER SINK . . . 234 3 DON JUAN 10   20   4
THERE STANDS THE NOBLE HOSTESS NOR SHALL SINK . . . . 302 3 DON JUAN 11   68   1
TO SWIM OR SINK--I HAVE HAD AT LEAST MY DREAM . . . . 415 3 DON JUAN 14   11   8
HE CANNOT SINK HIS TREMORS OR HIS TERRORS . . . . . . 457 3 DON JUAN 15   4   6
SINKERS
MEANTIME READ ALL THE NATIONAL DEBT SINKERS . . . . . 357 3 DON JUAN 12   89   7
SINKING
A COW'S SHAPE FOR A MASK--WAS ONLY (SINKING . . . . . 238 2 DON JUAN 2 155   5
NO SINKING SPIRITS TOLD THEM THEY GREW GREY . . . . . 145 3 DON JUAN 8   66   5
BY DRIVING THE YORK MAIL--BUT AH MY SINKING SOUL . . 263 3 DON JUAN 10   78 V7
THE SINKING FUND'S UNFATHOMABLE SEA . . . . 548 3 DON JUAN 16   99   6
SINKS
RED SUN SINKS DOWN BEHIND THE AZURE HILL . . . . . . 252 2 DON JUAN 2 183   2
AND BURIED SINKS BENEATH ITS OFFSPRING'S DOOM . . . . 399 2 DON JUAN 4 102   4
THROUGH THE HUGE ARCH WHICH SOARS AND SINKS AGAIN . . 388 3 DON JUAN 13   63   5
THE DEBT UNSUNK YET SINKS ALL IT RECEIVES . . . . . . 548 3 DON JUAN 16   99   8
SINLESS
HAD SOIL'D THE CURRENT OF HER SINLESS YEARS . . . . . 274 2 DON JUAN 3   1   7
HAVE DAWN'D A FAIR AND SINLESS CHILD OF SIN . . . . . 382 2 DON JUAN 4   70   3
SINNER
IS ALL THAT LIFE ALLOWS THE LUCKIEST SINNER . . . . . 294 2 DON JUAN 3   36   4
TO THE FIRE-SIDE (A SIGHT TO TOUCH A SINNER) . . . . 306 2 DON JUAN 3   60   6
TO SOOTHE HIS WOES WITHAL WAS SLAIN--THE SINNER . . . 199 3 DON JUAN 9   33   7
DON JUAN OUR YOUNG DIPLOMATIC SINNER . . . . 282 3 DON JUAN 11   29   6
WHO DID NOT HATE SO MUCH THE SIN AS SINNER . . . . . 399 3 DON JUAN 13   87   6
THAT HAPPINESS FOR MAN--THE HUNGRY SINNER-- . . . . . 404 3 DON JUAN 13   99   7
WHO LIKES A LISTENER WHETHER SAINT OR SINNER-- . . . 426 3 DON JUAN 14   36   7
THERE ALSO WAS--THE SINNER THAT I AM . . . . 483 3 DON JUAN 15   63   5
SINNERS
HAS SAVED THE FAME OF THOUSAND SPLENDID SINNERS . . . 346 3 DON JUAN 12   66   3
SINNING
FORBIDS ALL WANDERING AS THE WORST OF SINNING . . . . 25 2 DON JUAN 1   7   4
LIKE LUCIFER WHEN HURL'D FROM HEAVEN FOR SINNING . . 344 2 DON JUAN 4   1   5
THE WATERS AND REPENTANCE FOR PAST SINNING . . . . . 414 2 DON JUAN 5   6   5
WHICH PAINTERS CANNOT CATCH LIKE FACES SINNING . . . 32 3 DON JUAN 6   52   4
THIRDLY COMMENCE NOT WITH THE END--OR SINNING . . . . 393 3 DON JUAN 13   73   7
SIN'S
PLEASURE'S A SIN AND SOMETIMES SIN'S A PLEASURE . . . 93 2 DON JUAN 1 133   4
SINS
REPENTED ALL HIS SINS AND MADE A LAST . . . . 175 2 DON JUAN 2   37   3
OF EARTH WAS WRINKLED BY THE SINS AND TEARS . . . . .   9 3 DON JUAN 6   6   7
WHICH SURELY WERE INVENTED FOR OUR SINS-- . . . . . . 36 3 DON JUAN 6   61   8
TO MEDITATE UPON THEIR SINS AND SELF . . . . 41 3 DON JUAN 6   69   8
AND BE THY SINS FORGIVEN--BUT UPON THIS . . . . 352 3 DON JUAN 12   79   3
CONDEMN'D TO CHILD-BED AS MEN FOR THEIR SINS . . . . 420 3 DON JUAN 14   23   7
SION
BY BABEL'S WATERS STILL REMEMBERING SION . . . . . . 165 2 DON JUAN 2   16   2
SION'S
THE MUSES UPON SION'S HILL MUST RAMBLE . . . . 297 3 DON JUAN 11   57   3
SIR
MEANTIME--SIR LAUREATE--I PROCEED TO DEDICATE . . . . 20 2 DON JUAN D   17   1
LIKE THE LAMENTED LATE SIR SAMUEL ROMILLY . . . . . . 29 2 DON JUAN 1   15   4
SIR HUMPHREY DAVY'S LANTERN BY WHICH COALS . . . . . 93 2 DON JUAN 1 132   4
THERE'S PEN AND INK FOR YOU SIR WHEN YOU NEED-- . . . 104 2 DON JUAN 1 152   4
LOOK WHERE YOU PLEASE--WE'VE NOTHING SIR TO HIDE . . 106 2 DON JUAN 1 156   4
AND NOW SIR I HAVE DONE AND SAY NO MORE . . . . 107 2 DON JUAN 1 157   1
WITH PRAY SIR LEAVE THE ROOM AND SAY NO MORE . . . . 111 2 DON JUAN 1 163   4
COME SIR GET IN)--MY MASTER MUST BE NEAR . . . . . . 115 2 DON JUAN 1 172   5
AND READ YOUR BIBLE SIR AND MIND YOUR PURSE . . . . . 147 2 DON JUAN 1 220   8
AGAINST SEA-SICKNESS TRY IT SIR BEFORE . . . . 163 2 DON JUAN 2   13   6
MY OWN MERITS AND THOUGH YOUNG--I SEE SIR--YOU . . . 392 2 DON JUAN 4   88   2
PRAY SIR SAID JUAN IF I MAY PRESUME . . . . 418 2 DON JUAN 5   15   1
SHE DID NOT RUN AWAY TOO DID SHE SIR . . . . 421 2 DON JUAN 5   20   7
YOU TAKE THINGS COOLLY SIR SAID JUAN WHY . . . . . . 421 2 DON JUAN 5   21   1
SIR--AS I SAID AS SOON AS I HAVE SUPT . . . . 453 2 DON JUAN 5   72   4
WHAT SIR SAID JUAN SHALL IT E'ER BE TOLD . . . . . . 454 2 DON JUAN 5   75   5
YOU SIR SAID BABA NODDING TO THE ONE . . . . 458 2 DON JUAN 5   81   1
WILL FOLLOW ME NO TRIFLING SIR FOR WHEN . . . . 458 2 DON JUAN 5   81   4
BUT 'TIS A NAME SO SPREAD O'ER SIR AND MADAM . . . . 79 3 DON JUAN 7   25   7
IN WHICH SIR ISAAC NEWTON COULD DISCLOSE . . . . . . 226 3 DON JUAN 10   2   3
TELL THEM SIR WILLIAM CURTIS IS A BORE . . . . 267 3 DON JUAN 10   86   5
SIR WALTER REIGNED BEFORE ME MOORE AND CAMPBELL . . . 297 3 DON JUAN 11   57   1
ALSO SOME BEAUTIES OF SIR PETER LELY . . . . 390 3 DON JUAN 13   68   7
AND SIR JOHN POTTLEDEEP THE MIGHTY DRINKER . . . . . 398 3 DON JUAN 13   84   8
SIR HENRY SILVERCUP THE GREAT RACE-WINNER . . . . . . 399 3 DON JUAN 13   87   4
OF AN OLD FAMILY SOME GAY SIR JOHN . . . . 470 3 DON JUAN 15   33   3
MALGRE SIR MATTHEW HALES'S GREAT HUMANITY . . . . . . 565 3 DON JUAN 17   7   8

737

	PAGE	VOL			CANTO	STANZA	LN

SIRE
HE DID NOT LOATHE THE SIRE TO LAUD THE SON . . . . 15 2 DON JUAN D 10 7
(HIS SIRE WAS OF CASTILE HIS DAM FROM ARRAGON) . . . . . 42 2 DON JUAN 1 38 4
FROM SIRE TO SON TO AUGUR GOOD OR ILL . . . . 49 2 DON JUAN 1 51 5
WERE SETTLED LONG ERE JUAN'S SIRE WAS BORN . . . . . . 169 2 DON JUAN 2 24 4
HIS NEAREST MESSMATE TOLD HIS SIRE WHO THREW . . . . . 202 2 DON JUAN 2 87 5
AND O'ER HIM BENT HIS SIRE AND NEVER RAISED . . . . . . 203 2 DON JUAN 2 89 1
AND FORTH THEY WANDER'D HER SIRE BEING GONE . . . . . . 252 2 DON JUAN 2 182 1
OF A STRONG HUMAN HEART AND IN A SIRE . . . . 305 2 DON JUAN 3 58 8
WAS WHIPT AT COLLEGE--A HARSH SIRE--ODD SPOUSE . . . . . 328 2 DON JUAN 3 91 7
PULCI WAS SIRE OF THE HALF-SERIOUS RHYME . . . . . . 347 2 DON JUAN 4 6 3
STERN AS HER SIRE ON ME SHE CRIED LET DEATH . . . . . . 366 2 DON JUAN 4 42 4
MUST MAKE A PRESENT TO HIS SIRE IN LAW . . . . . . 498 2 DON JUAN 5 152 8
TO SAVE A SIRE WHO BLUSHED THAT HE BEGOT HIM . . . . . 166 3 DON JUAN 8 110 8
HAS CAUSE TO WISH HER SIRE HAD HAD MALE HEIRS . . . . . 331 3 DON JUAN 12 33 8
SIREN
PLEASURE (WHENE'ER SHE SINGS AT LEAST) 'S A SIREN . . . 294 2 DON JUAN 3 36 5
SIREN'S
TO WEAN DON JUAN FROM THE SIREN'S WILE . . . . . . 438 3 DON JUAN 14 65 6
SIRENS
FISHERS FOR MEN LIKE SIRENS WITH SOFT LUTES . . . . . 343 3 DON JUAN 12 59 6
BY WHICH SUCH SIRENS CAN ATTRACT OUR GREAT . . . . . 474 3 DON JUAN 15 42 6
SIRE'S
HAIDEE FORGOT THE ISLAND WAS HER SIRE'S . . . . . 282 2 DON JUAN 3 13 4
ON HER SIRE'S ARM WHICH UNTIL NOW SCARCE HELD . . . . 375 2 DON JUAN 4 58 7
WITH HER SIRE'S STORY MAKES THE NIGHT LESS LONG . . . . 383 2 DON JUAN 4 73 3
SIRES
AT SUCH ALLIANCES HIS SIRES WOULD FROWN . . . . . 52 2 DON JUAN 1 57 4
THE APPROACH OF HOME TO HUSBANDS AND TO SIRES . . . . 287 2 DON JUAN 3 22 1
THOUGH NOT ALL BORN OF THE SAME SIRES AND MOTHERS . . . . 491 2 DON JUAN 5 138 6
TOLD OF THEIR SIRES A TOMB IN EVERY TREE . . . . . 381 3 DON JUAN 13 50 9
THE BOORS CRIED DANG IT WHO'D HAVE THOUGHT IT--SIRES . . . 425 3 DON JUAN 14 34 4
PERHAPS BECAUSE 'TWAS FALLEN HER SIRES WERE PROUD . . . . 476 3 DON JUAN 15 46 4
OR THAT OUR SIRES HAD A MORE GIFTED EYE . . . . . . 516 3 DON JUAN 16 36 6
SIRES'
THAN YOUR SIRES' ISLANDS OF THE BLEST . . . . . . 321 2 DON JUAN 3 L 2 6
SIRIA
AND SHINE THE VERY SIRIA OF THE SPHERES . . . . . 397 3 DON JUAN 13 82 7
SIROCCO
WITH A SIROCCO FOR EXAMPLE BLOWING . . . . 422 3 DON JUAN 14 28 2
SIRS
AND BABA SMILINGLY EXCLAIMED YOU SEE SIRS . . . . 458 2 DON JUAN 5 80 4
AND NOW THEN YOU MUST COME ALONG WITH ME SIRS . . . . 458 2 DON JUAN 5 80 6
SISTER
TRANSFERR'D TO GORGE UPON A SISTER SHORE . . . . . 16 2 DON JUAN D 12 4
TAKING HER FOR A SISTER JUST THE SAME . . . . . 232 2 DON JUAN 2 142 5
BRIDE OF THE SUN AND SISTER OF THE MOON . . . . . 494 2 DON JUAN 5 144 1
IN WISHING HER THEIR SISTER SAVE A FEW . . . . . 25 3 DON JUAN 6 39 5
IF HE SPEAK TRUTH SHE IS CHRIST'S SISTER AND . . . . 116 3 DON JUAN 8 9 7
NOR BROTHER FATHER SISTER DAUGHTER LOVE . . . . . 250 3 DON JUAN 10 53 2
HIS BOSOM--FOR HE NEVER HAD A SISTER . . . . . 250 3 DON JUAN 10 53 7
LESS LIKE A YOUNG WIFE THAN AN AGED SISTER . . . . . 440 3 DON JUAN 14 69 8
SISTERS
THE WATCHFUL MOTHERS AND THE CAREFUL SISTERS . . . . 331 3 DON JUAN 12 32 3
AND DAUGHTERS BROTHERS SISTERS KITH OR KIN . . . . 470 3 DON JUAN 15 31 2
HE MOVED AS SHADOWY AS THE SISTERS WEIRD . . . . . 510 3 DON JUAN 16 21 6
SIT
AND THEN--AND THEN--SIT DOWN AND SUP . . . . . 119 2 DON JUAN 1 179 8
SOFAS 'TWAS HALF A SIN TO SIT UPON . . . . . . 449 2 DON JUAN 5 65 5
WAS TO SIT DOWN AGAIN AND CRY OF COURSE . . . . . 491 2 DON JUAN 5 139 8
BUT TO SIT UP WHILE OTHERS LIE IN BED . . . . . . 290 3 DON JUAN 11 45 5
TO SIT AMIDST THE RUINS OF THEIR GUILT . . . . . 352 3 DON JUAN 12 78 7
MAY SIT LIKE THAT OF NESSUS AND RECALL . . . . . 505 3 DON JUAN 16 11 3
AT THE FULL BOARD AND SIT ALIKE DELIGHTED . . . . . 534 3 DON JUAN 16 69 5
SITE
COMMANDS THE CITY AND UPON ITS SITE . . . . . 71 3 DON JUAN 7 10 4
WHAT AFTER ALL CAN SIGNIFY THE SITE . . . . . 284 3 DON JUAN 11 34 5
SITES
BY WAY OF CHANGE FROM THEIR SEPULCHRAL SITES . . . . 38 3 DON JUAN 6 64 6
SITS
SHE SITS UPON HIS KNEE AND DRINKS HIS SIGHS . . . . 259 2 DON JUAN 2 194 5
THE OLD PACHA SITS AMONG SOME HUNDREDS DEAD . . . . 160 3 DON JUAN 8 98 3
WHICH SITS FOREVER UPON MEMORY'S CRUPPER . . . . . 304 3 DON JUAN 11 72 5
SITS LIKE A SEDATIVE WHILE WE RECALL . . . . . 505 3 DON JUAN 16 11 V3
SITTETH
WHO SITTETH BY NORMAN STONE . . . . . . 518 3 DON JUAN 16 L 1 2
SITTING
AND SITTING AS IF NAILED UPON HIS CHAIR . . . . 542 3 DON JUAN 16 87 4
BUT JUAN SITTING SILENT IN HIS NOOK . . . . . 553 3 DON JUAN 16 106 6
SITUATION
BUT THEN THE SITUATION HAD ITS CHARM . . . . . 83 2 DON JUAN 1 115 6
REFLECTED ON HIS PRESENT SITUATION . . . . . 165 2 DON JUAN 2 17 7
THEIRS BEING AN UNNATURAL SITUATION . . . . . 263 2 DON JUAN 2 201 6
THE SITUATION SEEMS STILL FORM'D FOR FAME-- . . . . 386 2 DON JUAN 4 77 5
ABOUT HIS PAST OR PRESENT SITUATION . . . . . 387 2 DON JUAN 4 79 8
SAMARITANS IN EVERY SITUATION . . . . . 480 2 DON JUAN 5 120 6
ALTHOUGH HIS SITUATION NOW SEEMS STRANGE . . . . . 65 3 DON JUAN 6 120 6
THEN HELD THAT HIGH OFFICIAL SITUATION . . . . . 206 3 DON JUAN 9 48 8
'TWILL BUT PRECIPITATE A SITUATION . . . . . 429 3 DON JUAN 14 43 6

	PAGE	VOL	CANTO	STANZA	LN
SITUATION (CONTINUED)					
OF SUCH A SENTIMENTAL SITUATION	454	3 DON JUAN 14	100	6
OF JUAN'S MERITS AND HIS SITUATION	468	3 DON JUAN 15	28	2
A SITUATION DIFFICULT I WEEN	489	3 DON JUAN 15	75	3
BECAUSE AS SUITS THEIR RANK AND SITUATION	534	3 DON JUAN 16	68	5
LEFT IN A TENDER MOONLIGHT SITUATION	567	3 DON JUAN 17	12	2
SIX					
AT SIX A CHARMING CHILD AND AT ELEVEN	48	2 DON JUAN 1	49	2
AT SIX I SAID HE WAS A CHARMING CHILD	49	2 DON JUAN 1	50	1
OF HALF-PAST SIX--PERHAPS STILL NEARER SEVEN	77	2 DON JUAN 1	104	2
SING AT MY HEART SIX MONTHS AT LEAST IN VAIN	102	2 DON JUAN 1	149	2
HINT THAT SOME SIX OR SEVEN GOOD YEARS AGO	143	2 DON JJAN 1	212	4
SIX FLASKS OR WINE AND THEY CONTRIVED TO GET	181	2 DON JUAN 2	47	4
IN ENGLAND A SIX CANTO QUARTO TALE	320	2 DON JUAN 3	86	2
SAILING SIX KNOTS AN HOUR BEFORE THE WIND	384	2 DON JUAN 4	75	5
WHO HAD BID HIGH AS HUNDREDS SIX OR SEVEN	407	2 DON JUAN 4	114	V6
SIX TARTARS AND A DRAG-CHAIN-- --TO THIS DOOM	418	2 DON JUAN 5	15	3
(OF WHICH I HAVE ALSO SEEN SOME SIX OR SEVEN)	465	2 DON JUAN 5	94	4
WERE RIPE THEY MIGHT MAKE SIX AND TWENTY SPRINGS	468	2 DON JUAN 5	98	2
SOMETIMES AT SIX YEARS OLD--THOUGH THIS SEEMS ODD	498	2 DON JUAN 5	152	6
HE DRANK SIX CUPS OF COFFEE AT THE LEAST	52	3 DON JUAN 6	92	4
FOR SIX HOURS BORE THEY WITHOUT INTERMISSION	81	3 DON JUAN 7	30	1
THIS FELLOW BEING SIX FOOT HIGH COULD RAISE	84	3 DON JUAN 7	37	5
FIRST ONE OR TWO THEN FIVE SIX AND A DOZEN	135	3 DON JUAN 8	45	1
AND HELL THERE MUST AT LEAST BE SIX OR SEVEN	168	3 DON JUAN 8	114	8
FOR SIX AND THIRTY THOUSAND BRAVE DEFENDERS	175	3 DON JUAN 8	127	V7
BUT SIX OLD DAMSELS EACH OF SEVENTY YEARS	177	3 DON JUAN 8	130	7
THEY MUST BE PAID THOUGH SIX DAYS SMOOTHLY RUN	243	3 DON JUAN 10	38	7
SODAE-SULPHAT SIX DRAMS HALF DRAM MANNAE OPTIM	244	3 DON JUAN 10	41	2
CAW ME CAW THEE--FOR SIX MONTHS HATH BEEN HATCHING	307	3 DON JUAN 11	78	7
FOR TALK SIX TIMES WITH THE SAME SINGLE LADY	343	3 DON JUAN 12	59	7
THERE WERE THE SIX MISS RAWBOLDS--PRETTY DEARS	398	3 DON JUAN 13	85	6
LONGING AT SIXTY FOR THE HOUR OF SIX	406	3 DON JUAN 13	102	8
AND (AS HER JUNIOR BY SIX WEEKS) HIS YOUTH	432	3 DON JUAN 14	51	8
BY THIS TIME--BUT STRIKE SIX FROM SEVEN-AND-TWENTY	433	3 DON JUAN 14	54	7
THAT IN THE COURSE OF SOME SIX THOUSAND YEARS	504	3 DON JUAN 16	7	2
SIX-FOOT					
BUT THEY WERE MOSTLY NERVOUS SIX-FOOT FELLOWS	205	3 DON JUAN 9	46	7
SIXTEEN					
YOUNG JUAN NOW WAS SIXTEEN YEARS OF AGE	51	2 DON JUAN 1	54	1
WHEN HE WAS SIXTEEN JULIA TWENTY-THREE	59	2 DON JUAN 1	69	6
AND SURELY WITH A STRIPLING OF SIXTEEN	66	2 DON JUAN 1	83	2
BUT AT SIXTEEN THE CONSCIENCE RARELY GNAWS	113	2 DON JUAN 1	167	5
A LAD OF SIXTEEN CAUSING A DIVORCE	158	2 DON JUAN 2	2	7
SIXTEEN CALLED THOMSON AND NINETEEN NAMED SMITH	75	3 DON JUAN 7	18	8
AND SIXTEEN BAYONETS PIERCED THE SERASKIER	152	3 DON JUAN 8	81	8
(WHO AT SIXTEEN TRANSLATED HERCULES FURENS	294	3 DON JUAN 11	52	6
BUT SIXTEEN DOWAGERS TEN UNWED SHE SAGES	330	3 DON JUAN 12	30	7
AT SIXTEEN SHE CAME OUT PRESENTED VAUNTED	434	3 DON JUAN 14	55	1
AND GIRLS OF SIXTEEN ARE THUS FAR SOCRATIC	494	3 DON JUAN 15	86	1
SIXTEENTH					
FOR ON THE SIXTEENTH AT FULL GALLOP DREW	87	3 DON JUAN 7	43	1
OUR HERO WAS IN CANTO THE SIXTEENTH	567	3 DON JUAN 17	12	1
SIXTH					
'TWAS ON A SUMMER'S DAY--THE SIXTH OF JUNE--	76	2 DON JUAN 1	103	1
'TWAS ON THE SIXTH OF JUNE ABOUT THE HOUR	77	2 DON JUAN 1	104	1
SUPPOSE FROM JUNE THE SIXTH (THE FATAL DAY	86	2 DON JUAN 1	121	2
ON THE SIXTH DAY THEY FED UPON HIS HIDE	193	2 DON JUAN 2	71	1
HER SIXTH TO STAB HERSELF HER SEVENTH TO SENTENCE	491	2 DON JUAN 5	139	6
THE SIXTH SHALL HAVE A TOUCH OF THE SUBLIME	503	2 DON JUAN 5	159	6
(ESPECIALLY AS THE SIXTH YEAR IS ENDING)	546	3 DON JUAN 16	95	6
SIXTY					
FIFTY OR SIXTY--IT IS ALL THE SAME--	101	2 DON JUAN 1	146	4
AT LEAST PERHAPS HE HAS NOT SIXTY YEARS	106	2 DON JUAN 1	155	1
AT SIXTY YEARS AND DRAW THE ACCOMPTS OF EVIL	113	2 DON JUAN 1	167	7
INTO SOME SIXTY THOUSAND NEW KNIGHTS' FEES	242	3 DON JUAN 10	35	8
LONGING AT SIXTY FOR THE HOUR OF SIX	406	3 DON JUAN 13	102	8
SIX-WEEKS'					
COME OUT AND GLIMMER'D AS A SIX-WEEKS' STAR	398	3 DON JUAN 13	84	6
SIZE					
WEBFOOTED NOT UNLIKE A DOVE IN SIZE	206	2 DON JUAN 2	94	2
AS BLACK BUT QUICKER AND OF SMALLER SIZE	221	2 DON JUAN 2	122	8
AND THEIR COMPASSION GREW TO SUCH A SIZE	225	2 DON JUAN 2	131	6
BESIDES HER MAID'S AS PRETTY FOR THEIR SIZE	246	2 DON JUAN 2	171	4
ACCORDING TO THEIR SIZE AND AGE AND LENGTH	283	2 DON JUAN 3	15	V7
AND SHELLS AND SHOT OF EVERY SIZE AND SHAPE	81	3 DON JUAN 7	29	8
IN SIZE FROM OVERWORKING THE MATERIAL--	202	3 DON JUAN 9	39	7
SKAITER					
ABOVE THE ICE HAD LIKE A SKAITER GLIDED	327	3 DON JUAN 12	25	4
SKAITING					
BOATS WHEN 'TWAS WATER SKAITING WHEN 'TWAS ICE	407	3 DON JUAN 13	106	3
SKELETON					
DEATH LAUGHS--GO PONDER O'ER THE SKELETON	188	3 DON JUAN 9	11	1
OLD SKELETON WITH AGES FOR YOUR BOOTY	459	3 DON JUAN 15	9	V5
SKELETONS					
AMIDST THE SKELETONS OF THAT GAUNT CREW	210	2 DON JUAN 2	102	4
SKETCH					
I SKETCH YOUR WORLD EXACTLY AS IT GOES	156	3 DON JUAN 8	89	8
NOW I COULD MUCH MORE EASILY SKETCH A HAREM	419	3 DON JUAN 14	21	3

739

	PAGE	VOL	CANTO		STANZA	LN
SKETCHES						
TO GUIDE-BOOKS RHYMES TOURS SKETCHES ILLUSTRATIONS	440	2	DON JUAN	5	52	8
HAD SKETCHES OF LOVE TEMPEST TRAVEL WAR--	181	3	DON JUAN	8	138	3
WHY DO THEIR SKETCHES FAIL THEM AS INDITERS	418	3	DON JUAN	14	20	5
SKEWER						
FOR THE TURK'S TEETH STUCK FASTER THAN A SKEWER	154	3	DON JUAN	8	85	3
SKIES						
TO PERFECT KNOWLEDGE OF THE BOUNDLESS SKIES	71	2	DON JUAN	1	92	7
LIKE SKIES THAT RAIN AND LIGHTEN AS A VEIL	108	2	DON JUAN	1	158	3
FROM GLISTENING WAVES AND SKIES SO HOT AND BARE--	210	2	DON JUAN	2	103	6
SWEET SKIES JUST WHEN HE RISES OR IS SET	230	2	DON JUAN	2	139	3
AS HE WHO STUDIES FERVENTLY THE SKIES	242	2	DON JUAN	2	163	5
DRAWN FROM THE STARS AND FILTER'D THROUGH THE SKIES	269	2	DON JUAN	2	212	4
WITH ALL WE CAN IMAGINE OF THE SKIES	313	2	DON JUAN	3	74	4
OF LOVE HAD FIRST O'ERWHELM'D THEM FROM SUCH SKIES	354	2	DON JUAN	4	20	4
FROM THE BLUE SKIES DERIVED A DOUBLE BLUE	393	2	DON JUAN	4	90	6
FROM OUT HER SKIES--THEN HOWL YOUR IDLE WRATH	70	3	DON JUAN	7	7	7
IN VISIONS OF THOSE SKIES FROM WHENCE LOVE SPRUNG	230	3	DON JUAN	10	10	6
ACCORDING AS THE SKIES THEIR SHADOWS THREW	385	3	DON JUAN	13	58	8
WOULD YOU HAVE ENDLESS LIGHTNING IN THE SKIES	451	3	DON JUAN	14	94	6
SKIFF						
BUT STILL SEA-WORTHY SKIFF AND SHE MAY FLOAT	227	3	DON JUAN	10	4	7
SKIFFS						
BY FORMER VOYAGES STOOD TO WATCH THE SKIFFS	256	3	DON JUAN	10	64	7
SKILL						
THE FAME YOU ENVY AND THE SKILL YOU NEED	14	2	DON JUAN	D	8	4
I KNEW HIS FATHER WELL AND HAVE SOME SKILL	49	2	DON JUAN	1	51	3
WITHOUT WHOSE EPOCH MY POETIC SKILL	86	2	DON JUAN	1	121	3
ANTONIA'S SKILL WAS PUT UPON THE RACK	114	2	DON JUAN	1	169	3
HE VARIED WITH SOME SKILL HIS ADULATIONS	319	2	DON JUAN	3	84	6
TO THE GREAT MARLBOROUGH'S SKILL IN GIVING KNOCKS	328	2	DON JUAN	3	90	7
NOR TIME NOR SKILL NOR REMEDY COULD GIVE HER	381	2	DON JUAN	4	68	7
PICKED OUT AMONGST HIS FOLLOWERS WITH SOME SKILL	162	3	DON JUAN	8	102	3
TO RUTS AND FLINTS AND LOVELY NATURE'S SKILL	198	3	DON JUAN	9	31	5
FOR A LIEUTENANT TO CLIMB UP BUT SKILL	215	3	DON JUAN	9	66	6
HE MIGHT--AND BROUGHT THEM UP WITH SKILL IN TIME	295	3	DON JUAN	11	53	2
OR PROUDLIER PRANCING WITH MERCURIAL SKILL	303	3	DON JUAN	11	70	7
SERF LORD MAN WITH SUCH SKILL AS NONE WOULD SHARE IT IF	481	3	DON JUAN	15	59	6
THE FAMILY PHYSICIAN HAD GREAT SKILL	514	3	DON JUAN	16	32	5
THE VOICE THE WORDS THE HARPER'S SKILL AT ONCE	517	3	DON JUAN	16	39	7
SKILL'D						
IN HIS GRAVE OFFICE SO COMPLETELY SKILL'D	399	3	DON JUAN	13	88	6
SKILLED						
A GAUDY TASTE FOR THEY ARE LITTLE SKILLED IN	436	2	DON JUAN	5	46	5
SKIM						
BUT RATHER SKIM THE EARTH WHILE DUDU'S FORM	26	3	DON JUAN	6	41	5
AND LEAVING LAND FAR OUT OF SIGHT WOULD SKIM	227	3	DON JUAN	10	4	4
SKIMM'D						
LIKE SWIFT CAMILLA HE SCARCE SKIMM'D THE GROUND	427	3	DON JUAN	14	39	3
TILL SKIMM'D--AND THEN THERE WAS SOME MILK AND WATER	474	3	DON JUAN	15	41	4
SKIMS						
WHICH SKIMS THE SURFACE LEAVING SCARCE A SCAR	335	3	DON JUAN	12	40	6
SKIN						
THE SKIN HAS PASSED THROUGH SUCH A DEAL OF DIRT	154	2	DON JUAN	1	V 5	5
A STRANGER DYING WITH SO WHITE A SKIN	224	2	DON JUAN	2	129	8
THE PUREST ORE INCLOSED THE WHITEST SKIN	312	2	DON JUAN	3	71	7
THE SKIN RELIEVED APPEAR MORE FAIRLY FAIR	314	2	DON JUAN	3	76	2
CASTS OFF ITS BRIGHT SKIN YEARLY LIKE THE SNAKE	421	2	DON JUAN	5	21	4
THIS SKIN MUST GO THE WAY TOO OF ALL FLESH	422	2	DON JUAN	5	22	3
FROM SAINT BARTHOLOMEW WE HAVE SAVED OUR SKIN	435	2	DON JUAN	5	44	4
WE FOR SOME MOMENTS HAD SECURED OUR SKIN	435	2	DON JUAN	5	44	V4
WE FROM IMPALEMENT HAD ENSURED OUR SKIN	435	2	DON JUAN	5	44	V4
FOR GENTLEMEN MUST SOMETIMES RISK THEIR SKIN	10	3	DON JUAN	6	7	3
AGAINST A FOE OR RAN A SABRE THROUGH SKIN	75	3	DON JUAN	7	17	4
UNLESS TO MAKE THEIR KETTLE DRUMS A NEW SKIN	75	3	DON JUAN	7	17	6
THAN EVEN THE TAILOR'S) HIS INCARNATE SKIN	188	3	DON JUAN	9	12	7
THOUGH BEAUTIFUL IN YOUTH HIS CARNAL SKIN--	188	3	DON JUAN	9	12	V7
SO THAT I ALMOST THINK THAT THE SAME SKIN	567	3	DON JUAN	17	11	7
SKIPPING						
COULD REACH WITH HERE AND THERE A SAIL JUST SKIPPING	265	3	DON JUAN	10	82	3
SKIRMISH						
SKIRMISH OF WITS O'ER THE DEPARTED ONE	552	3	DON JUAN	16	105	2
SKITTISH						
FOR FEAR SOME PRUDISH READERS SHOULD GROW SKITTISH	141	2	DON JUAN	1	209	7
SKULKER						
BULLY IN SENATES SKULKER IN THE FIELD	151	2	DON JUAN	1	V 2	1
SKULL						
TO THINK HIS SKULL HAD NOT SOME NEED OF CAULKING	565	3	DON JUAN	17	8	6
SKULLS						
LIKE SKULLS AT MEMPHIAN BANQUETS TO THE MIND	308	2	DON JUAN	3	65	4
AND WALLS AS THICK AS MOST SKULLS BORN AS YET	72	3	DON JUAN	7	12	2
SKY						
EVEN BY ITS DARKNESS AS THE BLACKEST SKY	61	2	DON JUAN	1	73	2
HIS BRAIN ABOUT THE ACTION OF THE SKY	71	2	DON JUAN	1	93	6
THE RAINBOW BASED ON OCEAN SPAN THE SKY	87	2	DON JUAN	1	122	8
FOR THE SKY SHOW'D IT WOULD COME ON TO BLOW	170	2	DON JUAN	2	26	7
THEN ROSE FROM SEA TO SKY THE WILD FAREWELL	184	2	DON JUAN	2	52	1
WITH NOTHING BUT THE SKY FOR A GREAT COAT	189	2	DON JUAN	2	63	5
THE SEA AND SKY WERE BLUE AND CLEAR AND MILD--	193	2	DON JUAN	2	70	4

```
                                                                PAGE  VOL       CANTO  STANZA  LN
SKY   (CONTINUED)
      LAY AT THIS PERIOD QUIET AS THE SKY  . . . . .  . . . 251   2 DON JUAN   2      181     3
      UPON THE OTHER AND THE ROSY SKY .  . . .  .  . . . . . 252   2 DON JUAN   2      183     7
      THEY LOOK'D UP TO THE SKY WHOSE FLOATING GLOW  . . . . 253   2 DON JUAN   2      185     1
      AS IF THERE WERE NO LIFE BENEATH THE SKY . . . . . .   255   2 DON JUAN   2      188     7
      THE HEART IS LIKE THE SKY A PART OF HEAVEN  . . . . .  270   2 DON JUAN   2      214     1
      BUT CHANGES NIGHT AND DAY TOO LIKE THE SKY  . . . . .  270   2 DON JUAN   2      214     2
      THE ROSY FLOOD OF TWILIGHT'S SKY ADMIRED--  . . . . .  334   2 DON JUAN   3      101     6
      THE ROSY SKY WITH THE LAST SUNLIGHT FIRED  . . . . .   335   2 DON JUAN   3      101     V6
      AS SOMEONE SOMEWHERE SINGS ABOUT THE SKY .  . . . . .  404   2 DON JUAN   4      110     2
      A LONDON BAS WILL BEAT THY SKY PERU  . . . . . . . .   406   2 DON JUAN   4      112     V8
      THERE STILL ARE MANY RAINBOWS IN YOUR SKY  . . . . .   421   2 DON JUAN   5      21      3
      THE STARS FROM OUT THE SKY THAN NOT BE FREE . . . . .  7     3 DON JUAN   6      3       5
      THERE'S NOT A METEOR IN THE POLAR SKY .  . . . . . .   66    3 DON JUAN   7      1       3
      AND THE SKY SHOWS THAT VERY ANCIENT GRAY . . . . . .   422   3 DON JUAN   14     28      5
      LIKE FLEECY CLOUDS INTO THE SKY RETIRED  . . . . . .   504   3 DON JUAN   16     8       6
SKY-BLUE
      BENT AN ITALIAN SKY-BLUE PAPHIAN PAIR . . . . . .  .   467   2 DON JUAN   5      96      V3
SKY'S
      EVEN AS A SUMMER SKY'S WITHOUT A CLOUD  . . . . .      94    2 DON JUAN   1      135     6
      WHETHER A SKY'S OR TRADESMAN'S IS ALL ONE  . . . . .   423   3 DON JUAN   14     29      8
SLACK
      YOU WERE THE FIRST I' THE BREACH  I WAS NOT SLACK . .  98    3 DON JUAN   7      61      3
SLACKEN
      TO SLACKEN SAIL AND ANCHOR WITH OUR RHYME   . . . . .  503   2 DON JUAN   5      159     4
SLACKENED
      THEN SLACKENED IT WHICH IS THE MARCH MOST CAUSED  . .  61    3 DON JUAN   6      111     3
SLACKENING
      A MOMENT WITHOUT SLACKENING FROM THEIR PACE .  . . .   441   2 DON JUAN   5      54      3
SLAIN
      THEY HAD SLAIN HIM WITH FIVE SLUGS AND LEFT HIM THERE  . 429  2 DON JUAN   5      34      2
      A MOMENT'S MORE HAD SLAIN HER BUT THE WHILE . . . .   489   2 DON JUAN   5      135     2
      FOR DOGS OR TO BE SLAIN WITH PANGS REFINED . . . . .  492   2 DON JUAN   5      141     3
      THAT EVER PEOPLED HELL WITH HEROES SLAIN . . . . . .  101   3 DON JUAN   7      68      3
      TO PAINT A SIEGE WHEREIN MORE MEN WERE SLAIN . . . .  106   3 DON JUAN   7      80      2
      THE MILLIONS SLAIN BY SOLDIERS FOR THEIR RATION  . .  146   3 DON JUAN   8      68      6
      SLAIN BY SOME MUSSULMANS WHO WOULD NOT YET . . . . .  150   3 DON JUAN   8      77      3
      A GLANCE ON THAT SLAIN SON HIS FIRST AND LAST  . . .  169   3 DON JUAN   8      116     8
      TO SOOTHE HIS WOES WITHAL WAS SLAIN--THE SINNER  . .  199   3 DON JUAN   9      33      7
      WAS A TA'EN CITY--THIRTY THOUSAND SLAIN  .  . . . .   212   3 DON JUAN   9      59      2
      WINES TOO WHICH MIGHT AGAIN HAVE SLAIN YOUNG AMMON--  . 484  3 DON JUAN   15     65      3
SLANG
      (PRITHEE EXCUSE THIS ENGINEERING SLANG)  . . . . . .  72    3 DON JUAN   7      11      6
SLAP-DASH
      THE SLAP-DASH REGIMENT SO WELL KNOWN TO FAME  . . . . 383   3 DON JUAN   13     54      6
SLASHED
      ONE'S HIP HE SLASHED AND SPLIT THE OTHER'S SHOULDER  .  158  3 DON JUAN   8      94      1
SLASHING
      FIRING AND THRUSTING SLASHING SWEATING GLOWING . . . . 120  3 DON JUAN   8      19      6
SLAUGHTER
      AT THAT AGE HE WOULD BE TOO OLD FOR SLAUGHTER  . . .  106   2 DON JUAN   1      155     2
      AFTER LONG TRAVEL ENNUI LOVE OR SLAUGHTER   . . . .   251   2 DON JUAN   2      180     7
      PELL-MELL AND WITH A WHOLE GAZETTE OF SLAUGHTER  . .  82    3 DON JUAN   7      31      8
      FOR GLORY GAPING O'ER A SEA OF SLAUGHTER .  . . . .   91    3 DON JUAN   7      50      7
      THOUGH LED BY ARSENIEW THAT GREAT SON OF SLAUGHTER  .  116  3 DON JUAN   8      9       4
      WAS IMAGED BACK IN BLOOD THE SEA OF SLAUGHTER  . . .  172   3 DON JUAN   8      122     8
      OF BURNING CITIES THOSE FULL MOONS OF SLAUGHTER  . .  173   3 DON JUAN   8      122     V7
      DON JUAN WHO HAD SHONE IN THE LATE SLAUGHTER  . . .   197   3 DON JUAN   9      29      1
      WHOM HE HAD SAVED FROM SLAUGHTER--WHAT A TROPHY  . .  199   3 DON JUAN   9      33      2
      SLAUGHTER OF ISMAIL  THOUGH MY WILD MUSE VARIES  . .  249   3 DON JUAN   10     51      6
      THRO' SUCH A SCENE OF CHANGE AND DREAD AND SLAUGHTER  . 252  3 DON JUAN   10     56      2
SLAUGHTERED
      THOUSANDS OF SLAUGHTERED MEN A YET WARM GROUP  . . .  157   3 DON JUAN   8      91      2
SLAVE
      TITUS THE MASTER ANTONY THE SLAVE . . . . . . .  .    266   2 DON JUAN   2      205     2
      HAD STUNG HIM FROM A SLAVE TO AN ENSLAVER .  . . . .  302   2 DON JUAN   3      53      8
      I COULD NOT DEEM MYSELF A SLAVE . . . . . . . . .     321   2 DON JUAN   3 L    3       6
      THINK YE HE MEANT THEM FOR A SLAVE . . . . . . . .    324   2 DON JUAN   3 L    10      6
      AND THEN A SLAVE BETHOUGHT HER OF A HARP  . . . . .   379   2 DON JUAN   4      65      1
      FROM HIS DULL CABIN FOUND HIMSELF A SLAVE  . . . . .  387   2 DON JUAN   4      79      2
      FOR THE SLAVE MARKET OF CONSTANTINOPLE  . . . . . .   393   2 DON JUAN   4      91      8
      AS IS A SLAVE BY HIS INTENDED BIDDER . . . . . . .    425   2 DON JUAN   5      27      1
      YOUR SLAVE BRINGS TIDINGS--HE HOPES NOT TOO SOON--  .  494  2 DON JUAN   5      144     5
      GULBEYAZ STOPPED AND BECKONED BABA--SLAVE  . . . . .  62    3 DON JUAN   6      112     1
SLAVE-MAKER
      A TINKERING SLAVE-MAKER WHO MENDS OLD CHAINS  . . . . 18    2 DON JUAN   D      14      7
SLAVE-MARKET
      HE SOUGHT IN THE SLAVE-MARKET TOO AND DISH'D  . . .   223   2 DON JUAN   2      126     6
SLAVERY
      WE KNOW WHAT SLAVERY IS AND OUR DISASTERS  . . . . .  422   2 DON JUAN   5      23      7
SLAVERY'S
      NOR GIVE MY VOICE TO SLAVERY'S JACKALL CRY  . . . .   195   3 DON JUAN   9      26      8
SLAVES
      EUROPE HAS SLAVES--ALLIES--KINGS--ARMIES STILL . . .  19    2 DON JUAN   D      16      7
      AND CALL'D HER FATHER'S OLD SLAVES UP WHO SWORE  . .  229   2 DON JUAN   2      138     6
      BEFORE THEM AND FAIR SLAVES ON EVERY SIDE  . . . . .  306   2 DON JUAN   3      61      6
      TO THINK SUCH BREASTS MUST SUCKLE SLAVES . . . . . .  326   2 DON JUAN   3 L    15      6
      A LAND OF SLAVES SHALL NE'ER BE MINE--  . . . . . .   326   2 DON JUAN   3 L    16      5
      T' OUR TALE--THE FEAST WAS OVER THE SLAVES GONE  . .  334   2 DON JUAN   3      101     1
```

```
                                                          PAGE VOL      CANTO STANZA LN
SLAVES   (CONTINUED)
    WITH SLAVES TO SELL OFF IN THE CAPITAL  . . . . . .  407  2 DON JUAN  4    113   2
    A CROWD OF SHIVERING SLAVES OF EVERY NATION . . . .  414  2 DON JUAN  5      7   1
    MOST MEN ARE SLAVES NONE MORE SO THAN THE GREAT  . .  423  2 DON JUAN  5     25   3
    A GLANCE AT THAT WHICH WRAPT THE SLAVES IN WONDER . .  450  2 DON JUAN  5     66   2
    SO SILLY AS TO BUY SLAVES WHO MIGHT SHARE  . . . . .   24  3 DON JUAN  6     36   6
    OF WHAT HAD PAST SINCE ALL THE SLAVES RETIRED  . . .   55  3 DON JUAN  6     99   3
    BRING THE TWO SLAVES SHE SAID IN A LOW TONE  . . . .   62  3 DON JUAN  6    112   2
    WHAT SLAVES HER HIGHNESS WISHED TO INDICATE  . . . .   62  3 DON JUAN  6    112   7
    THOUGH PRIESTS AND SLAVES MAY JOIN IN THE SERVILE CRY 195  3 DON JUAN  9     26  V8
    WHO IS BUT FIRST OF SLAVES THE NATIONS ARE  . . . .  258  3 DON JUAN 10     68   2
    LIKE OTHER SLAVES OF COURSE MUST PAY HIS RANSOM  . .  305  3 DON JUAN 11     74   3
    BY SLAVES ON HORSEBACK--I HAVE SEEN MALT LIQUORS . .  310  3 DON JUAN 11     85   6
SLAVES'
    HAD BEEN HER SLAVES' CHIEF PLEASURE AS HER WILL  . .  475  2 DON JUAN  5    112   4
SLAY
    HE GAVE THE WORD ARREST OR SLAY THE FRANK  . . . . .  369  2 DON JUAN  4     47   8
    ALL HEROES WHO IF LIVING STILL WOULD SLAY US  . . .  385  2 DON JUAN  4     76   8
    ALL HEROES WHEN ALIVE QUITE PROMPT TO SLAY US  . . .  385  2 DON JUAN  4     76  V8
    TO SLAY THE PAGANS WHO RESISTED BATTERING  . . . . .   99  3 DON JUAN  7     64   7
    MARCHED FORTH WITH NERVE AND SINEWS BENT TO SLAY--  . 113  3 DON JUAN  8      2   4
    MUCH DID THEY SLAY MORE PLUNDER AND NO LESS . . . . . 176  3 DON JUAN  8    129   1
    HAVE BEEN OBLIGED TO SLAY A FREEBORN NATIVE . . . . . 277  3 DON JUAN 11     18   7
SLAYING
    BUT NOW INSTEAD OF SLAYING PRIAM'S SON  . . . . . .  106  3 DON JUAN  7     78   5
SLAYS
    THE DEATH OF FRIENDS AND THAT WHICH SLAYS EVEN MORE--  350  2 DON JUAN  4     12   3
SLEEK
    DABBLING ITS SLEEK YOUNG HANDS IN ERIN'S GORE . . .   16  2 DON JUAN  D     12   2
SLEEP
    POOR DONNA JULIA STARTING AS FROM SLEEP  . . . . . .   97  2 DON JUAN  1    140   1
    I WISH TO SLEEP AND BEG YOU WILL TAKE CARE  . . . .  104  2 DON JUAN  1    153   5
    OUR COUNSEL--(JUAN MIND YOU MUST NOT SLEEP)  . . . .  115  2 DON JUAN  1    172   8
    WHO SLEEP AT LAST PERHAPS (GOD ONLY KNOWS)  . . . .  227  2 DON JUAN  2    134   3
    TROUBLED HIM NOT AND HE MIGHT SLEEP HIS FILL  . . .  229  2 DON JUAN  2    137   5
    AND THOSE WHO ARE NOT DROWNED AT LEAST MAY SLEEP  . .  229  2 DON JUAN  2    137  V8
    AND STARTED FROM HER SLEEP AND TURNING O'ER . . . .  229  2 DON JUAN  2    138   2
    (FOR SLEEP IS AWFUL) AND ON TIPTOE CREPT  . . . . .  232  2 DON JUAN  2    143   5
    THAT SLEEP WHICH SEEM'D AS IT WOULD NE'ER AWAKE . .  234  2 DON JUAN  2    146   8
    HAD FURTHER SLEEP A FURTHER PLEASURE MADE  . . . . .  235  2 DON JUAN  2    149   4
    OR SLEEP OR WHATSOE'ER IT WAS BY FEELING . . . . . .  237  2 DON JUAN  2    153   2
    AND JUAN SUNK TO SLEEP WITHIN HER ARMS . . . . . . .  260  2 DON JUAN  2    195   2
    MUST END IN LANGUOR--MEN WON'T SLEEP LIKE SWINE--  .  343  2 DON JUAN  3  V 98   1
    ERE WHAT WE LEAST WISH TO BEHOLD WILL SLEEP . . . .  346  2 DON JUAN  4      4   6
    NOW PILLOW'D CHEEK TO CHEEK IN LOVING SLEEP . . . .  359  2 DON JUAN  4     29   1
    SENSES TO SLEEP--THE POWER SEEM'D GONE FOREVER  . .  381  2 DON JUAN  4     68   8
    HE SEEMED TO SLEEP FOR YOU COULD SCARCELY TELL  . .  430  2 DON JUAN  5     35   5
    A BED IS NOT A THRONE AND THEY MAY SLEEP . . . . . .   16  3 DON JUAN  6     20   2
    YET VERY FIT TO MURDER SLEEP IN THOSE  . . . . . . .   27  3 DON JUAN  6     42   2
    YOU DON'T SLEEP SOUNDLY AND I CANNOT BEAR  . . . . .   29  3 DON JUAN  6     47   2
    BESIDES I HATE TO SLEEP ALONE QUOTH SHE  . . . . . .   30  3 DON JUAN  6     48   1
    LAY IN A BREATHLESS HUSHED AND STONY SLEEP  . . . .   40  3 DON JUAN  6     68   2
    A BLESSING IS SOUND SLEEP--JUANNA LAY  . . . . . . .   42  3 DON JUAN  6     73   2
    WHERE SHE THEN WAS AS HER SOUND SLEEP DISCLOSED . .   48  3 DON JUAN  6     84   3
    ALSO THE HONOURABLE MRS SLEEP  . . . . . . . . . .  396  3 DON JUAN 13     79   7
    THAT AWFUL YAWN WHICH SLEEP CAN NOT ABATE  . . . . .  405  3 DON JUAN 13    101   8
    AND YET A THIRD OF LIFE IS PASS'D IN SLEEP  . . . .  411  3 DON JUAN 14      3   8
    A SLEEP WITHOUT DREAMS AFTER A ROUGH DAY . . . . . .  412  3 DON JUAN 14      4   1
    WHICH FAIN WOULD LULL ITS RIVER-CHILD TO SLEEP  . .  447  3 DON JUAN 14     87   8
    A VIGIL THERE WHERE ALL BUT DEATH SHOULD SLEEP  . .  508  3 DON JUAN 16     18   8
    OF THOSE SWEET BITTER THOUGHTS WHICH BANISH SLEEP .  555  3 DON JUAN 16    110   7
    WHEN DEEP SLEEP FELL ON MEN AND THE WORLD WORE . . .  556  3 DON JUAN 16    113   6
SLEEPERS
    SHE WOKE AT LENGTH BUT NOT AS SLEEPERS WAKE . . . .  378  2 DON JUAN  4     62   1
SLEEPING
    SLEEPING MOST PROBABLY--WHEN AT HER DOOR . . . . . .   95  2 DON JUAN  1    136   2
    TO PROVE HER MISTRESS HAD BEEN SLEEPING DOUBLE . . .   97  2 DON JUAN  1    140   8
    YOU SAW THAT SHE WAS SLEEPING BY MY SIDE . . . . . .  106  2 DON JUAN  1    156   2
    LULL'D THEM LIKE TURTLES SLEEPING ON THE BLUE . . .  192  2 DON JUAN  2     68   5
    THE DAY BEFORE FAST SLEEPING ON THE WATER  . . . . .  208  2 DON JUAN  2     99   1
    AS THEY WHO WATCH O'ER WHAT THEY LOVE WHILE SLEEPING  261  2 DON JUAN  2    196   8
    HAIL MUSE ET CETERA--WE LEFT JUAN SLEEPING  . . . .  274  2 DON JUAN  3      1   1
    THOUGH SLEEPING LIKE A LION NEAR A SOURCE  . . . . .  374  2 DON JUAN  4     56   8
    SHOWS THAT HE THINKS HIS FRIENDS HAVE NOT BEEN SLEEPING 436 2 DON JUAN  5     45   4
    GULBEYAZ AND HER LORD WERE SLEEPING OR  . . . . . .   18  3 DON JUAN  6     24   1
    THE TRAITS OF SLEEPING SORROW AND BETRAYED . . . . .   40  3 DON JUAN  6     67   4
    THAT BROKE FOR NOTHING ON THEIR SLEEPING EAR . . . .   45  3 DON JUAN  6     79   4
SLEEPS
    WE LEARN FROM HORACE HOMER SOMETIMES SLEEPS . . . .  333  2 DON JUAN  3     98   1
    LONG WITH HER DESTINY BUT SHE SLEEPS WELL  . . . . .  382  2 DON JUAN  4     71   7
    MEANWHILE AS HOMER SOMETIMES SLEEPS PERHAPS  . . . .  503  2 DON JUAN  5    159   7
    HE WHO SLEEPS BEST MAY BE THE MOST CONTENT  . . . .  190  3 DON JUAN  9     15   8
    SLEEPS FROM THE CHIVALRY OF THIS BRIGHT AGE . . . .  378  3 DON JUAN 13     44   6
SLEEPY
    A KIND OF SLEEPY VENUS SEEMED DUDU . . . . . . . . .   27  3 DON JUAN  6     42   1
SLEET
    AND OUT OF DOOR HATH SHOWERS AND MISTS AND SLEET  . .  423  3 DON JUAN 14     30   2
SLEEVE
    A GLANCE AROUND--AND SHRUGGED--AND TWITCHED HIS SLEEVE  161  3 DON JUAN  8     99   6
```

		PAGE	VOL	CANTO	STANZA	LN
SLENDER						
TALL HANDSOME SLENDER BUT WELL KNIT HE SEEM'D		51	2	DON JUAN 1	54	2
AT LEAST SHE LEFT IT A MORE SLENDER HANDLE		58	2	DON JUAN 1	67	8
YOUNG SLENDER AND PACK'D EASILY HE LAY		112	2	DON JUAN 1	166	3
HIS SLENDER FRAME AND PALLID ASPECT LAY		214	2	DON JUAN 2	110	7
A SLENDER STREAK OF BLOOD ANNOUNCED HOW NEAR		159	3	DON JUAN 8	95	2
SLENDERER						
I'LL TAKE JUANNA WE'RE A SLENDERER PAIR		29	3	DON JUAN 6	47	4
SLEPT						
(MIND--THAT I DO NOT SAY--SHE HAD NOT SLEPT)		97	2	DON JUAN 1	140	2
JUAN SLEPT LIKE A TOP OR LIKE THE DEAD		227	2	DON JUAN 2	134	2
YOUNG JUAN SLEPT ALL DREAMLESS--BUT THE MAID		228	2	DON JUAN 2	135	1
THAT LIKE AN INFANT JUAN SWEETLY SLEPT		232	2	DON JUAN 2	143	3
HE WOKE AND GAZED AND WOULD HAVE SLEPT AGAIN		235	2	DON JUAN 2	149	1
SHE SLEPT NOT BUT ALL TENDERLY THOUGH FAST		260	2	DON JUAN 2	195	3
SPEAK BUT HE SPOKE NOT WAKE BUT STILL HE SLEPT--		430	2	DON JUAN 5	36	2
AND SEVERAL STRUTTED OTHERS SLEPT AND SOME		441	2	DON JUAN 5	53	7
BUT THERE SHE SLEPT NOT QUITE SO FAIR TO SEE		41	3	DON JUAN 6	69	5
BUT ALL THIS TIME HOW SLEPT OR DREAMED DUDU		41	3	DON JUAN 6	70	1
WHILE THOUGH 'TWAS DAWN THE TURKS SLEPT FAST AS EVER		80	3	DON JUAN 7	28	8
UPON HIM BY DEGREES AND SO HE SLEPT		512	3	DON JUAN 16	27	8
A VIGIL OR DREAMT RATHER MORE THAN SLEPT		568	3	DON JUAN 17	14	8
SLEW						
TOUCHED BY THE HEROISM OF HIM THEY SLEW		171	3	DON JUAN 8	119	5
THE WHOLE GAZETTE OF THOUSANDS WHOM HE SLEW		212	3	DON JUAN 9	60	4
SLICE						
A SLICE OR TWO FROM YOUR LUXURIOUS MEALS		185	3	DON JUAN 9	6	4
SLICES						
FOWLS A LA CONDE SLICES EKE OF SALMON		484	3	DON JUAN 15	65	1
SLIDING						
SLIDING KNEE-DEEP IN LATELY FROZEN MUD		148	3	DON JUAN 8	73	7
SLIGHT						
AND SLIGHT SO VERY SLIGHT THAT TO THE MIND		60	2	DON JUAN 1	71	5
AND SLIGHT SO VERY SLIGHT THAT TO THE MIND		60	2	DON JUAN 1	71	5
WITH A NEAT LITTLE CROW-QUILL SLIGHT AND NEW		134	2	DON JUAN 1	198	2
THERE'S ONLY ONE SLIGHT DIFFERENCE BETWEEN		137	2	DON JUAN 1	202	1
THERE WAS SLIGHT CHANCE OF REACHING ANY SHORE		185	2	DON JUAN 2	54	5
THE SILKEN FILLET'S SLIGHT RESTRAINT AND SHUN		313	2	DON JUAN 3	73	V6
AND AFTER SWALLOWING DOWN A SLIGHT REFECTION		452	2	DON JUAN 5	71	3
GAVE IT A SLIGHT KICK WITH HIS CHRISTIAN FOOT		453	2	DON JUAN 5	73	6
SIGHED JUAN MUTTERING ALSO SOME SLIGHT OATHS		455	2	DON JUAN 5	76	5
WHICH GIRT A SLIGHT CHEMISE AS WHITE AS MILK		456	2	DON JUAN 5	77	4
TO JUAN SOME SLIGHT LESSONS AS HIS GUIDE		464	2	DON JUAN 5	91	2
IF NOW AND THEN THERE HAPPENED A SLIGHT SLIP		496	2	DON JUAN 5	149	1
A SLIGHT BLUSH A SOFT TREMOR A CALM KIND		13	3	DON JUAN 6	15	1
A SLIGHT EXAMPLE JUST TO CAST A SHADE		22	3	DON JUAN 6	32	5
MAY SERVE PERHAPS AS OUTLINES OR SLIGHT HINTS		60	3	DON JUAN 6	109	8
WITH ITS PROUD BROW IT MERITS SLIGHT APPLAUSE		86	3	DON JUAN 7	40	6
THE PARTY A SLIGHT GLANCE THEN SAID I HAVE HEARD		97	3	DON JUAN 7	60	4
AND NATURAL AGONIES WITH A SLIGHT SHADE		102	3	DON JUAN 7	69	4
SUGGESTED SOME SLIGHT COMFORT IN HIS WAY		105	3	DON JUAN 7	75	3
AND THEN WITH TEARS AND SIGHS AND SOME SLIGHT KISSES		105	3	DON JUAN 7	76	1
THERE SHOULD BE NE'ERTHELESS A SLIGHT SUBSTRATUM		107	3	DON JUAN 7	81	4
A PATH TO ADD HIS OWN SLIGHT ARM AND FORCES		126	3	DON JUAN 8	30	7
TO JACK HOWE'ER THIS GAVE BUT SLIGHT CONCERN		133	3	DON JUAN 8	41	5
TOOK LIKE CAMELIONS SOME SLIGHT TINGE OF FEAR		148	3	DON JUAN 8	73	4
MEN BECOME WOLVES ON ANY SLIGHT OCCASION		192	3	DON JUAN 9	20	8
JUAN WAS NONE OF THESE BUT SLIGHT AND SLIM		206	3	DON JUAN 9	47	1
IN THAT SLIGHT STARTLE FROM HIS CONTEMPLATION--		225	3	DON JUAN 10	1	2
OF BREAKERS HAS NOT DAUNTED MY SLIGHT TRIM		227	3	DON JUAN 10	4	6
OF ANY SLIGHT TEMPTATION IN THEIR WAY		235	3	DON JUAN 10	21	4
THAT WITH THE ADDITION OF A SLIGHT PELISSE		239	3	DON JUAN 10	30	7
WITH SLIGHT EXCEPTIONS ALL THE WAYS SEEM ONE		279	3	DON JUAN 11	23	4
ENOUGH TO GRATIFY A BEE'S SLIGHT MUNCHINGS		301	3	DON JUAN 11	66	5
CAN FORM A SLIGHT ACQUAINTANCE WITH FRESH AIR		301	3	DON JUAN 11	66	8
THOUGH EVERY SCRIBE IN SOME SLIGHT TURN OF DICTION		311	3	DON JUAN 11	88	6
A SLIGHT OBSERVER IN A MODEST WAY)		336	3	DON JUAN 12	44	2
WITH SOME SLIGHT HEART-QUAKE OF DOMESTIC TREASON--		370	3	DON JUAN 13	26	5
ESCAPING WITH A FEW SLIGHT SCARLESS SNEERS		397	3	DON JUAN 13	82	8
WHO LIKE TO MIX SOME SLIGHT ALLOY WITH FAME		414	3	DON JUAN 14	9	6
OF COURSE WITH SOME RESERVE AND SLIGHT RESTRICTION		416	3	DON JUAN 14	13	3
ALSO A SEASONING SLIGHT OF LUCUBRATION		416	3	DON JUAN 14	14	2
A SLIGHT GLANCE THROWN ON MEN OF EVERY STATION		416	3	DON JUAN 14	14	4
THE PORTER SOME SLIGHT SCANDALS STRANGE AND QUAINT		418	3	DON JUAN 14	19	5
AND SOLACE YOUR SLIGHT LAPSE 'GAINST BONOS MORES		432	3	DON JUAN 14	50	7
BUT ERE HE WENT HE ADDED A SLIGHT HINT		440	3	DON JUAN 14	69	1
OF RUIN ROSE FROM SUCH A SLIGHT OCCASION		454	3	DON JUAN 14	100	4
SUPPRESS THEN SOME SLIGHT FEMININE DISEASES		459	3	DON JUAN 15	9	7
WITH A SLIGHT SHADE OF BLUE TOO IT MIGHT BE		474	3	DON JUAN 15	41	5
WHY ADELINE HAD THIS SLIGHT PREJUDICE--		478	3	DON JUAN 15	52	1
I SAY IN MY SLIGHT WAY I MAY PROCEED		482	3	DON JUAN 15	60	1
HOWEVER DOTH REQUIRE SOME SLIGHT REFECTION		483	3	DON JUAN 15	64	7
SLIGHT BUT SELECT AND JUST ENOUGH TO EXPRESS		491	3	DON JUAN 15	80	2
COMMENCED (FROM SUCH SLIGHT THINGS WILL GREAT COMMENCE)		493	3	DON JUAN 15	83	5
HIS GARMENTS ONLY A SLIGHT MURMUR MADE		510	3	DON JUAN 16	21	5
WITH SOME SLIGHT LIGHT HEREDITARY TWINGES		515	3	DON JUAN 16	34	7
MIGHT HAVE FROM TIME ACQUIRED SOME SLIGHT DEFECT		529	3	DON JUAN 16	58	4
OFF--OR UPON THE HUSTINGS--SOME SLIGHT SUCH		538	3	DON JUAN 16	77	4
A SLIGHT REPAST MAKES PEOPLE LOVE MUCH MORE		542	3	DON JUAN 16	86	3

743

		PAGE	VOL	CANTO	STANZA	LN
SLIGHT (CONTINUED)						
WHICH SETS THE TEETH ON EDGE AND A SLIGHT CLATTER	. . . .	556	3 DON JUAN	16	114	2
MODEST I AM--YET WITH SOME SLIGHT ASSURANCE	. . . .	567	3 DON JUAN	17	11	2
SLIGHTEST						
THE SLIGHTEST OBSTACLE WHICH MAY ENCUMBER	. . . .	371	3 DON JUAN	13	30	V5
THEY COULD NOT EVEN GLEAN THE SLIGHTEST SPLINTERS	. . .	434	3 DON JUAN	14	56	5
SLIGHTLY						
AS SLIGHTLY STIRRING IN HER SNOWY SHROUD	. . . . .	39	3 DON JUAN	6	66	6
NAY HE HAD WOUNDED THOUGH BUT SLIGHTLY BOTH	. . . .	166	3 DON JUAN	8	109	1
YET MIXED SO SLIGHTLY THAT YOU CAN'T COMPLAIN	. . . .	502	3 DON JUAN	16	3	6
A PROLOGUE WHICH BUT SLIGHTLY HARMONISED	. . . .	543	3 DON JUAN	16	90	3
SHOULD STILL BE SINGED BUT SLIGHTLY LET ME STATE)	. . .	565	3 DON JUAN	17	7	6
SLIM						
JUAN WAS NONE OF THESE BUT SLIGHT AND SLIM	. . . . .	206	3 DON JUAN	9	47	1
SLIME						
OF CARNAGE LIKE THE NILE'S SUN-SODDEN SLIME	. . . . .	152	3 DON JUAN	8	82	7
SLIP						
THE DOOR IS OPEN--YOU MAY YET SLIP THROUGH	. . .	121	2 DON JUAN	1	182	4
(THE HEART WILL SLIP EVEN AS THE TONGUE AND PEN)	. . .	228	2 DON JUAN	2	135	6
IF NOW AND THEN THERE HAPPENED A SLIGHT SLIP	. . . .	496	3 DON JUAN	15	149	1
AND IF ONE LADY'S SLIP COULD LEAVE A CRIME ON	. . . .	53	3 DON JUAN	6	94	6
SOULS TO SAVE SINCE EVE'S SLIP AND ADAM'S FALL	. . . .	192	3 DON JUAN	9	19	3
AND SECONDLY MUST LET SLIP NO OCCASION	. . . . .	404	3 DON JUAN	13	98	3
WHAT THOUGH SHE NOW AND THEN MAY SLIP FROM DUTY	. . .	459	3 DON JUAN	15	9	3
SLIPP'D						
YOUNG JUAN SLIPP'D HALF-SMOTHER'D FROM THE BED	. . . .	112	2 DON JUAN	1	165	8
SLIPPED						
AND THEN HE SWORE AND SIGHING ON HE SLIPPED	. . . .	456	2 DON JUAN	5	77	1
HIS BANDAGE SLIPPED DOWN INTO A CRAVAT	. . . . .	205	3 DON JUAN	9	45	1
SLIPPERS						
OF STOCKINGS SLIPPERS BRUSHES COMBS COMPLETE	. . . .	99	2 DON JUAN	1	143	4
HER SMALL SNOW FEET HAD SLIPPERS BUT NO STOCKING	. . .	220	2 DON JUAN	2	121	8
OMITTING TURBAN SLIPPERS PISTOLS DIRK--	. . . .	240	2 DON JUAN	2	160	6
SLIPPERS OF SAFFRON DAGGER RICH AND HANDY	. . . .	451	2 DON JUAN	5	68	7
SLIPS						
AH--WHAT SHOULD FOLLOW SLIPS FROM MY REFLECTION	. . .	456	3 DON JUAN	15	1	1
SLIPS FROM THE MOUNTAIN IN THE MONTH OF JUNE	. . .	517	3 DON JUAN	16	38	V6
YET LEAVE THE GATE WHICH ELOQUENCE SLIPS THROUGH	. . .	557	3 DON JUAN	16	115	3
SLIPSLOP						
(EXCUSE A FOREIGN SLIPSLOP NOW AND THEN	. . . . .	380	3 DON JUAN	13	47	6
SLOPED						
THE WOODS SLOPED DOWNWARDS TO ITS BRINK AND STOOD	. . .	385	3 DON JUAN	13	57	7
SLOTH						
WITH SLOTH HATH FOUND IT DIFFICULT TO DWELL	. . . .	445	3 DON JUAN	14	81	6
SLOW						
HE DIED OF THE SLOW FEVER CALL'D THE TERTIAN	. . . .	39	2 DON JUAN	1	34	7
SILENT AND PENSIVE IDLE RESTLESS SLOW	. . . . .	68	2 DON JUAN	1	87	1
THE WRONGS TO WHOSE EXPOSURE IT IS SLOW--	. . .	107	2 DON JUAN	1	157	4
REGARDING BOTH WITH SLOW AND SIDELONG VIEW	. . . .	116	2 DON JUAN	1	173	7
WITH SLOW AND STAGGERING EFFORT HE AROSE	. . . .	213	2 DON JUAN	2	109	1
THEN CALM CONCENTRATED AND STILL AND SLOW	. . . .	300	2 DON JUAN	3	48	3
WHO NEVER FOUND A SINGLE HOUR TOO SLOW	. . . .	353	2 DON JUAN	4	18	3
HER SWEET FACE INTO SHADOW DULL AND SLOW	. . . .	381	2 DON JUAN	4	69	6
FOR SO IT SEEMS TO LOVERS SWIFT OR SLOW	. . . .	14	3 DON JUAN	6	17	2
OF ONE GOOD MAN WITH STATELY MARCH AND SLOW	. . . .	22	3 DON JUAN	6	33	5
SHE SUNK DOWN ON HER SEAT BY SLOW DEGREES	. . . .	59	3 DON JUAN	6	107	7
WERE DAMNABLY MISTAKEN FEW ARE SLOW	. . . .	87	3 DON JUAN	7	42	3
UPON THEM HIS SLOW BROW AND PIERCING EYE--	. . . .	97	3 DON JUAN	7	59	3
NOT LIKE SLOW GERMANY WHERIN THEY MUDDLE	. . . .	260	3 DON JUAN	10	71	4
RESERVE AND PRIDE COULD MAKE HIM AND FULL SLOW	. . . .	366	3 DON JUAN	13	16	2
SLOWER						
RESET IT SHAVE MORE SMOOTHLY ALSO SLOWER	. . . . .	433	3 DON JUAN	14	53	7
SLOWLY						
AND SLOWLY BY HIS SWIMMING EYES WAS SEEN	. . . . .	215	2 DON JUAN	2	112	7
AND BY HIS EYES--THOUGH SLOWLY--THERE WAS SEEN	. . . .	215	2 DON JUAN	2	112	V7
THAT FAMISH'D PEOPLE MUST BE SLOWLY NURST	. . . .	239	2 DON JUAN	2	158	7
TILL SLOWLY CHARGED WITH THUNDER THEY DISPLAY	. . .	375	2 DON JUAN	4	57	3
OR RATHER LAKE--FOR RILLS DO NOT RUN SLOWLY--	. . . .	22	3 DON JUAN	6	33	7
BELOVED AND DEPLORED WHILE SLOWLY STRAYED	. . . .	40	3 DON JUAN	6	67	6
OF DEWY DAWN WOUND SLOWLY ROUND EACH HEIGHT	. . . .	49	3 DON JUAN	6	86	6
SLOWLY ALONG THE ROOM BUT SILENT STILL	. . . .	61	3 DON JUAN	6	110	6
SLOWLY DISTILLED INTO THE GLIMMERING GLASS	. . . .	278	3 DON JUAN	11	22	7
BUT MAKING MONEY SLOWLY FIRST THEN QUICKER	. . . .	317	3 DON JUAN	12	4	3
BUT SLOWLY AND AS HE PASSED JUAN BY	. . . . .	510	3 DON JUAN	16	21	7
UNDREST AND RATHER SLOWLY WENT TO BED	. . . . .	512	3 DON JUAN	16	27	4
SLUGS						
THEY HAD SLAIN HIM WITH FIVE SLUGS AND LEFT HIM THERE	.	429	2 DON JUAN	5	34	2
SLUMBER						
AND THEREFORE PAUSED NOT TO DISTURB THE SLUMBER	. . .	96	2 DON JUAN	1	138	4
AND NEED HE HAD OF SLUMBER YET FOR NONE	. . . .	229	2 DON JUAN	2	137	6
WHO LIKE A MORNING SLUMBER--FOR THE NIGHT	. . . .	237	2 DON JUAN	2	152	7
A GENTLE SLUMBER BUT IT WAS NOT DEEP	. . . .	359	2 DON JUAN	4	29	3
WHERE ECHO WOKE AS IF FROM A LONG SLUMBER	. . . .	448	2 DON JUAN	5	64	2
AND SLUMBER HOVERED O'ER EACH LOVELY LIMB	. . . .	38	3 DON JUAN	6	64	3
OF SLUMBER ERE THEY SHOOK HER--SO THEY SAY	. . . .	42	3 DON JUAN	6	73	6
AT LENGTH SHE SAID THAT IN A SLUMBER SOUND	. . . .	43	3 DON JUAN	6	75	1
BY THE DECEASED WHO LIE IN FAMOUS SLUMBER	. . . .	120	3 DON JUAN	8	18	3
MADE CATHERINE TASTE NEXT NIGHT A QUIET SLUMBER--	. . .	248	3 DON JUAN	10	48	4
A LARGE ACQUAINTANCE LETS NOT VIRTUE SLUMBER	. . . .	371	3 DON JUAN	13	30	3
AND THOUGH IT WAS NO OPIATE SLUMBER CREPT	. . . .	512	3 DON JUAN	16	27	7

744

```
                                                        PAGE VOL     CANTO STANZA LN
SLUMBER'D
   AND OCEAN SLUMBER'D LIKE AN UNWEAN'D CHILD  . . . . .  193  2 DON JUAN   2    70   2
   HE SLUMBER'D YET SHE THOUGHT AT LEAST SHE SAID . . . .  228  2 DON JUAN   2   135   5
SLUMBERING
   THE MORN BROKE AND FOUND JUAN SLUMBERING STILL . . . .  229  2 DON JUAN   2   137   1
   WITHOUT DISTURBING HER YET SLUMBERING GUEST  . . . . .  245  2 DON JUAN   2   168   6
   TO WATCH HIM SLUMBERING AND TO SEE HIM WAKE  . . . . .  247  2 DON JUAN   2   173   4
   NODS FROM THE TREE WAS SLUMBERING WITH SOFT BREATH . .   38  3 DON JUAN   6    65   7
SLUMBERS
   MOTION WAS IN THEIR DAYS REST IN THEIR SLUMBERS  . . .  145  3 DON JUAN   8    67   1
   PEACE TO THE SLUMBERS OF EACH FOLDED FLOWER--  . . . .  409  3 DON JUAN  13   111   5
SLUT
   THEN THERE'S THAT LAUGHING SLUT THE PELEGRINI  . . . .  390  2 DON JUAN   4    84   3
SLY
   THE DEVIL'S SO VERY SLY--SHE SHOULD DISCOVER  . . . .   64  2 DON JUAN   1    78   2
SMALL
   BETWEEN THEIR TASTES THERE WAS SMALL SYMPATHY  . . . .   58  2 DON JUAN   1    66   3
   AND TREMULOUSLY GENTLE HER SMALL HAND . . . . . . . .   60  2 DON JUAN   1    71   2
   WITH PRYING SNUB-NOSE AND SMALL EYES HE STOOD  . . . .  109  2 DON JUAN   1   160   1
   SMALL PITY HAD HE FOR THE YOUNG AND FAIR . . . . . . .  109  2 DON JUAN   1   160   6
   HER SMALL WHITE HAND COULD HARDLY REACH THE TAPER  . .  134  2 DON JUAN   1   198   3
   HER SMALL WHITE FINGERS SCARCE COULD REACH THE TAPER .  134  2 DON JUAN   1   198  V3
   A SMALL OLD SPANIEL--WHICH HAD BEEN DON JOSE'S . . . .  187  2 DON JUAN   2    58   1
   WAS A SMALL PRESENT MADE TO HIM AT CADIZ . . . . . . .  199  2 DON JUAN   2    81   7
   'TWAS BENDING CLOSE O'ER HIS AND THE SMALL MOUTH . . .  215  2 DON JUAN   2   113   1
   HER SMALL SNOW FEET HAD SLIPPERS BUT NO STOCKING . . .  220  2 DON JUAN   2   121   8
   BUT HAIDEE STOPP'D HER WITH HER QUICK SMALL HAND . . .  234  2 DON JUAN   2   146   3
   AND THE SMALL RIPPLE SPLIT UPON THE BEACH  . . . . . .  250  2 DON JUAN   2   178   1
   WITH ONE OR TWO SMALL SENSES ADDED JUST  . . . . . . .  269  2 DON JUAN   2   212   7
   MOST NATURALLY SOME SMALL DOUBT INSPIRES--  . . . . .  287  2 DON JUAN   3    22   3
   SMALL SOCIAL PARTIES JUST BEGUN TO DINE  . . . . . . .  291  2 DON JUAN   3    31   2
   YIELDING TO THEIR SMALL HANDS DRAWS BACK AGAIN . . . .  292  2 DON JUAN   3    32   8
   IN SMALL FINE CHINA CUPS CAME IN AT LAST . . . . . . .  307  2 DON JUAN   3    63   4
   LIKE SMALL STARS THROUGH THE MILKY WAY APPARENT  . . .  315  2 DON JUAN   3    77   4
   BUT WORDS ARE THINGS AND A SMALL DROP OF INK . . . . .  327  2 DON JUAN   3    88   1
   OF A SMALL IRON DOOR 'TWAS OPENED AND  . . . . . . . .  433  2 DON JUAN   5    41   2
   HE MOTIONED THEM TO STOP AT SOME SMALL DISTANCE  . . .  440  2 DON JUAN   5    51   5
   FOR HIS OWN SHARE--HE SAW BUT SMALL OBJECTION  . . . .  452  2 DON JUAN   5    71   1
   WITH SOME SMALL AID FROM SCISSORS PAINT AND TWEEZERS .  458  2 DON JUAN   5    80   2
   THE WOND'ROUS HIDEOUSNESS OF THOSE SMALL MEN . . . . .  462  2 DON JUAN   5    88   3
   JUAN A MOMENT AS THIS PAIR SO SMALL  . . . . . . . . .  463  2 DON JUAN   5    90   5
   AT SOME SMALL DISTANCE ALL HE SAW WITHIN . . . . . . .  469  2 DON JUAN   5   100   4
   THERE WAS A SELF-WILL EVEN IN HER SMALL FEET . . . . .  475  2 DON JUAN   5   111   3
   BUT HERE A SMALL DELAY FORMS A GREAT CRIME . . . . . .  482  2 DON JUAN   5   123   5
   OR MINCED IN PIECES AS SMALL BAITS FOR FISH  . . . . .  492  2 DON JUAN   5   141  V4
   WHICH MOSTLY ENDS IN SOME SMALL BREACH OF BOTH . . . .  493  2 DON JUAN   5   142   8
   AND FEET SO SMALL THEY SCARCE SEEMED MADE TO TREAD . .   26  3 DON JUAN   6    41   4
   SUWARROW WHO HAD SMALL REGARD FOR TEARS  . . . . . . .  102  3 DON JUAN   7    69   1
   AS LEAVING A SMALL FAMILY AT LARGE . . . . . . . . . .  103  3 DON JUAN   7    71   8
   WITH SOME SMALL VARIATIONS IN THE LIST . . . . . . . .  107  3 DON JUAN   7    81  V7
   BUT IN THE SAME SMALL MINUTE EVERY SIN . . . . . . . .  142  3 DON JUAN   8    59   3
   THERE WAS SMALL LEISURE FOR SUPERFLUOUS SIN  . . . . .  178  3 DON JUAN   8   132   6
   WITH MODERN HISTORY HAS BUT SMALL CONNECTION . . . . .  186  3 DON JUAN   9     7   4
   WHICH MAKES ALL STYX THROUGH ONE SMALL LIVER FLOW  . .  190  3 DON JUAN   9    15   5
   HE WHO HAS NOUGHT TO GAIN CAN HAVE SMALL ART HE  . . .  195  3 DON JUAN   9    26   5
   HIS SIDE AS A SMALL SWORD BUT SHARP AS EVER  . . . . .  205  3 DON JUAN   9    45   4
   THOU DOST REPLENISH WORLDS BOTH GREAT AND SMALL  . . .  210  3 DON JUAN   9    56   6
   ABOVE BELOW BY TURNPIKES GREAT OR SMALL--  . . . . . .  222  3 DON JUAN   9    80   4
   TO ONE SMALL GRASS-GROWN PATCH (WHICH MUST AWAIT . . .  237  3 DON JUAN  10    25   5
   ADMITTED A SMALL PARTY AS NIGHT FELL--  . . . . . . .  282  3 DON JUAN  11    29   5
   AND CANNOT FIND A BILL'S SMALL ITEMS COSTLY  . . . . .  283  3 DON JUAN  11    31   4
   AT GREAT ASSEMBLIES OR IN PARTIES SMALL  . . . . . . .  295  3 DON JUAN  11    54   4
   WITH SUCH SMALL GEAR TO GIVE MYSELF CONCERN  . . . . .  300  3 DON JUAN  11    63   3
   WITH SOME SMALL PROFIT THROUGH THAT FIELD SO STERILE .  300  3 DON JUAN  11    64   3
   WHERE HE MAY FIX HIMSELF LIKE SMALL JACK HORNER  . . .  303  3 DON JUAN  11    69   4
   I HAVE SEEN SMALL POETS AND GREAT PROSERS AND  . . . .  310  3 DON JUAN  11    85   1
   WHICH HOLD FAST OTHER PLEASURES GREAT AND SMALL  . . .  316  3 DON JUAN  12     3   4
   WHAT WITH A SMALL DIVERSITY OF CLIMATE . . . . . . . .  327  3 DON JUAN  12    24   1
   QUICK SILVER SMALL TALK ENDING (IF YOU NOTE IT)  . . .  328  3 DON JUAN  12    26   7
   (WHICH SAW ALL WESTERN THINGS WITH SMALL SURPRISE  . .  328  3 DON JUAN  12    27   3
   HAWKED ABOUT AT A DISCOUNT SMALL OR LARGE--  . . . . .  379  3 DON JUAN  13    45   7
   THE OSTLER PLEADS FOR A SMALL REMINISCENCE . . . . . .  379  3 DON JUAN  13    46   8
   AN EXQUISITE SMALL CHAPEL HAD BEEN ABLE  . . . . . . .  389  3 DON JUAN  13    66   5
   SHOULD HAVE A HOOK AND A SMALL TROUT TO PULL IT . . . .  407  3 DON JUAN  13   106   8
   SMALL IS THE REST OF THOSE WHO WOULD BE SMART  . . . .  408  3 DON JUAN  13   109   5
   SUCH SMALL DISTINCTION BETWEEN FRIENDS AND FOES . . . .  421  3 DON JUAN  14    25   4
   ALL DIFFICULTIES WHETHER GREAT OR SMALL  . . . . . . .  423  3 DON JUAN  14    30   5
   BEGAN TO TREAT HIM WITH SOME SMALL AGACERIE  . . . . .  428  3 DON JUAN  14    41   8
   BUT SUCH SMALL LICENCES MUST LOVERS BROOK  . . . . . .  429  3 DON JUAN  14    43   3
   BUT SMALL CONCERN ABOUT THE WHEN OR WHERE  . . . . . .  430  3 DON JUAN  14    45   4
   WHO EATS FIRE GRATIS (SINCE THE PAY'S BUT SMALL) . . .  446  3 DON JUAN  14    83   6
   WHETHER THEIR TALK WAS OF THE KIND CALL'D SMALL  . . .  453  3 DON JUAN  14    98   4
   HAD NOT THE FLESH MADE SOME SMALL OPTION . . . . . . .  467  3 DON JUAN  15    24  V4
   FOR WHICH SMALL THANKS ARE STILL THE MARKET PRICE  . .  469  3 DON JUAN  15    29   3
   WITHOUT A SMALL REFRESHMENT FROM THE SPHERES . . . . .  496  3 DON JUAN  15    90   8
   DISCUSSED (HE HATED BEER YCLEPT THE SMALL) . . . . . .  533  3 DON JUAN  16    67   3
   GREAT PLENTY MUCH FORMALITY SMALL CHEER  . . . . . . .  538  3 DON JUAN  16    78   7
   TO SOME SMALL PLAN OF INTEREST OR AMBITION--  . . . .  541  3 DON JUAN  16    85   7
   TO LIFE'S SMALL RUBS SHOULD SURELY BE MORE PLIANT  . .  566  3 DON JUAN  17    10   3
```

745

			PAGE	VOL	CANTO	STANZA	LN

SMALLER
AS BLACK BUT QUICKER AND OF SMALLER SIZE . . . . 221 2 DON JUAN 2 122 8
(ONE OF THE WILD AND SMALLER CYCLADES) . . . . 223 2 DON JUAN 2 127 2
ALTHOUGH NO FAIRER--SMALLER--SOFTER HAND . . . . . 472 2 DON JUAN 5 106 V2
SMALLEST
LIFE SEEMS THE SMALLEST PORTION OF EXISTENCE . . . . . 398 2 DON JUAN 4 100 3
SMALL-EYED
IN SMALL-EYED CHINA'S CROCKERY-WARE METROPOLIS . . . . . 271 3 DON JUAN 11 7 5
SMALL-POX
I SAID THE SMALL-POX HAS GONE OUT OF LATE . . . . . . 92 2 DON JUAN 1 130 7
SMALL-TALK
THEN THERE WAS SMALL-TALK READY WHEN REQUIRED . . . . 408 3 DON JUAN 13 108 4
WERE GOOD SMALL-TALK FOR OTHERS STILL LESS GREAT)-- . . 544 3 DON JUAN 16 91 8
SMART
FROM TWO SMART SABRE GASHES DEEP AND RED-- . . . . 370 2 DON JUAN 4 49 7
(HIS MAGGIOR DUOMO A SMART SUBTLE GREEK . . . . . 259 3 DON JUAN 10 70 5
AS THE SMART BOYS SPURRED FAST IN THEIR CAREER . . . . 263 3 DON JUAN 10 77 3
SMART UNIFORMS AND SPARKLING CORONETS . . . . . 333 3 DON JUAN 12 36 1
WHEN SOME SMART TALKER PUTS THEM TO THE TEST . . . . 404 3 DON JUAN 13 98 7
SMALL IS THE REST OF THOSE WHO WOULD BE SMART . . . . 408 3 DON JUAN 13 109 5
SMARTER
AND FOR THEIR PAINS GET SMARTER PUNCTURATIONS . . . . . 263 3 DON JUAN 10 77 V8
SMEAR
AND SMEAR HIS PAGE WITH GALL INSTEAD OF HONEY . . . . . 142 2 DON JUAN 1 210 7
SMELT
YET SMELT ROAST-MEAT BEHELD A HUGE FIRE SHINE . . . . . 439 2 DON JUAN 5 50 5
SMIL'D
THE CIRCLE SMIL'D THEN WHISPER'D AND THEN SNEER'D . . . 429 3 DON JUAN 14 44 1
SMILE
NOR FOES--ALL NATIONS--CONDESCEND TO SMILE-- . . . . . 17 2 DON JUAN D 13 4
SHE LOOK'D A SADNESS SWEETER THAN HER SMILE . . . . . 61 2 DON JUAN 1 72 2
ON WHICH THREE SINGLE HOURS OF MOONSHINE SMILE-- . . . 82 2 DON JUAN 1 113 7
THEY SMILE SO WHEN ONE'S RIGHT AND WHEN ONE'S WRONG . . 242 2 DON JUAN 2 164 5
THEY SMILE STILL MORE AND THEN THERE INTERVENE . . . . 242 2 DON JUAN 2 164 6
WITH A PECULIAR SMILE WHICH BY THE WAY . . . . . 297 2 DON JUAN 3 42 3
HIS SMILE REQUESTED ONE OF THEM TO TELL . . . . . 298 2 DON JUAN 3 44 6
THE POLISHED CHIEF WHO DEIGNED TO SMILE . . . . . 321 2 DON JUAN 3 L 2 V1
AND GLORY LONG HAS MADE THE SAGES SMILE . . . . . 328 2 DON JUAN 3 90 1
AND GLORY MAKES THE SAGES OFTEN SMILE . . . . . 328 2 DON JUAN 3 90 V1
WHICH MAKES NOT OTHERS SMILE THEN TURN'D ASIDE . . . . 356 2 DON JUAN 4 23 2
THESE SMILE AND WRITHE AND PERISH STILL THE SAME . . . 377 2 DON JUAN 4 61 V7
THOUGH SOMEWHAT GRIEVED COULD SCARCE FORBEAR A SMILE . . 459 2 DON JUAN 5 83 3
AND LOOKING ON HIM WITH A SORT OF SMILE . . . . . 473 2 DON JUAN 5 107 6
HER VERY SMILE WAS HAUGHTY THOUGH SO SWEET . . . . . 475 2 DON JUAN 5 111 1
JUST AS A LANGUID SMILE BEGAN TO FLATTER . . . . . 493 2 DON JUAN 5 143 6
WHOSE SMILE MAKES ALL THE PLANETS DANCE WITH MIRTH . . 494 2 DON JUAN 5 144 4
BEGAN TO SING DANCE CHATTER SMILE AND PLAY . . . . . 23 3 DON JUAN 6 34 8
WITH HIS SUPERIOR IN A SMILE TO TRAMPLE . . . . . 189 3 DON JUAN 9 13 4
UNTIL A ROYAL SMILE AT LENGTH DISCLOSED . . . . . 211 3 DON JUAN 9 58 6
HER SWEET SMILE AND HER THEN MAJESTIC FIGURE . . . . . 218 3 DON JUAN 9 72 1
WITH SCHNAPPS--DEMOCRITUS WOULD CEASE TO SMILE . . . . 260 3 DON JUAN 10 71 V7
YOUR VEINS OF COCKNEY SPIRIT SMILE OR MOURN . . . . . 264 3 DON JUAN 10 80 6
AND EVEN MY MUSE'S WORST REPROOF'S A SMILE . . . . . 300 3 DON JUAN 11 63 6
NOR IS SHE QUITE SO READY WITH HER SMILE . . . . . 351 3 DON JUAN 12 76 4
BECAUSE IT MAKES US SMILE HIS HERO'S RIGHT . . . . . 363 3 DON JUAN 13 9 2
AND BADE HIM COUNSEL JUAN WITH A SMILE . . . . . 438 3 DON JUAN 14 65 4
AS ONCE OR TWICE TO SMILE IF NOT TO LISTEN . . . . . 491 3 DON JUAN 15 80 8
AND THE PALE SMILE OF BEAUTIES IN THE GRAVE . . . . . 509 3 DON JUAN 16 19 1
TO SUCH PERFORMANCES WITH HAUGHTY SMILE . . . . . 521 3 DON JUAN 16 42 7
BUT WHAT CONFUSED HIM MORE THAN SMILE OR STARE . . . . 544 3 DON JUAN 16 91 1
AND SOMETHING LIKE A SMILE UPON HER CHEEK . . . . . 544 3 DON JUAN 16 92 2
IN THOSE WHO RARELY SMILE THEIR SMILES BESPEAK . . . . 544 3 DON JUAN 16 92 4
SMILE OF AURORA'S THERE WAS NOUGHT TO PIQUE . . . . . 544 3 DON JUAN 16 92 6
'TWAS A MERE QUIET SMILE OF CONTEMPLATION . . . . . 545 3 DON JUAN 16 93 1
SMILED
BUT I AM NOT SO SURE I SHOULD HAVE SMILED . . . . . 59 2 DON JUAN 1 69 5
AND IF SHE MET HIM THOUGH SHE SMILED NO MORE . . . . 61 2 DON JUAN 1 72 1
LITTLE HE SAID AND NOW AND THEN HE SMILED . . . . . 203 2 DON JUAN 2 88 5
WHILE THE SUN SMILED ON HER WITH HIS FIRST FLAME . . . 232 2 DON JUAN 2 142 3
HIM PAST ALL BOUNDS BECAUSE SHE SMILED TO SEE . . . . 239 2 DON JUAN 2 158 3
SHE TURN'D TO HIM AND SMILED BUT IN THAT SORT . . . . 356 2 DON JUAN 4 23 1
SMILED SCORNFULLY AND SAID WITHIN MY CALL . . . . . 364 2 DON JUAN 4 37 6
THE EMPRESS SMILED THE REIGNING FAVOURITE FROWNED-- . . 205 3 DON JUAN 9 46 2
SHE SMILED AT MAD SUWARROW'S RHYMES WHO THREW . . . . 212 3 DON JUAN 9 60 2
SMILED AS SHE TALKED THE MATTER O'ER BUT TEARS . . . . 221 3 DON JUAN 9 78 6
CERVANTES SMILED SPAIN'S CHIVALRY AWAY . . . . . 364 3 DON JUAN 13 11 1
HAD SHE KNOWN THIS SHE WOULD HAVE CALMLY SMILED-- . . 480 3 DON JUAN 15 55 7
NOR EVEN SMILED ENOUGH FOR ANY VANITY . . . . . . 490 3 DON JUAN 15 78 4
SMILES
HER DOWRY WAS AS NOTHING TO HER SMILES . . . . . 224 2 DON JUAN 2 128 4
AND WHEN A HOLIDAY UPON THEM SMILES . . . . . 238 2 DON JUAN 2 154 3
AND SMILES AND SPARKLES OF THE SPEAKING EYE . . . . . 241 2 DON JUAN 2 162 2
BUT STILL HE SMILES AND WHETHER NEAR OR FAR . . . . . 188 3 DON JUAN 9 12 5
MY SMILES MUST BE SINCERE OR NOT AT ALL . . . . . 499 3 DON JUAN 15 96 2
HE STARTED AND PERCEIVING SMILES AROUND . . . . . 542 3 DON JUAN 16 88 2
IN THOSE WHO RARELY SMILE THEIR SMILES BESPEAK . . . . 544 3 DON JUAN 16 92 4
WHICH SOME PRETEND TO TRACE IN LADIES' SMILES . . . . 544 3 DON JUAN 16 92 8\
SMILING
AND SMILING THROUGH HER DREAM AS THROUGH A CLOUD . . . 39 3 DON JUAN 6 66 4

SMILING   (CONTINUED)
  AND SMILING BUT IN SECRET--CUNNING ROGUE 426   3 DON JUAN 14   37   6
  THIS HE EXPRESS'D HALF SMILING AND HALF SERIOUS   477   3 DON JUAN 15   49   4
  TURNING ROUND TO THE REST HE SMILING SAID   517   3 DON JUAN 16   39   3
SMILINGLY
  AND BABA SMILINGLY EXCLAIMED YOU SEE SIRS   458   2 DON JUAN 5   80   4
SMITE
  SPARE OR SMITE RARELY--MAN'S MAKE MILLIONS ASHES   115   3 DON JUAN 8   6   8
SMITH
  SIXTEEN CALLED THOMSON AND NINETEEN NAMED SMITH   75   3 DON JUAN 7   18   8
  BUT WHEN I'VE ADDED THAT THE ELDER JACK SMITH   76   3 DON JUAN 7   20   2
  THE CAUSE OF KILLING TCHITCHITZKOFF AND SMITH   79   3 DON JUAN 7   25   4
  THAT PRODIGY MISS ARAMINTA SMITH 294   3 DON JUAN 11   52   5
SMITHFIELD
  TURN OUT MUCH BETTER FOR THE SMITHFIELD SHOW   337   3 DON JUAN 12   46   6
SMITHS
  THREE OF THE SMITHS WERE PETERS BUT THE BEST   76   3 DON JUAN 7   19   5
  ONE OF THE VALOUROUS SMITHS WHOM WE SHALL MISS 79   3 DON JUAN 7   25   5
SMITTEN
  TELL FOR ITSELF THE SOVEREIGN WAS SMITTEN   221   3 DON JUAN 9   77   2
SMOKE
  YET THERE WILL STILL BE BARDS THOUGH FAME IS SMOKE   . . . 402   2 DON JUAN 4   106   1
  WHICH CURL IN CURIOUS WREATHS--HOW SOON THE SMOKE . . . 110   3 DON JUAN 7   86   7
  INDEED THE SMOKE WAS SUCH THEY SCARCE COULD MARK . . . 177   3 DON JUAN 8   130   3
  THE SUN WENT DOWN THE SMOKE ROSE UP AS FROM 265   3 DON JUAN 10   81   1
  A MIGHTY MASS OF BRICK AND SMOKE AND SHIPPING 265   3 DON JUAN 10   82   1
  BUT JUAN SAW NOT THIS EACH WREATH OF SMOKE 266   3 DON JUAN 10   83   1
  IT HATH BEEN STIRRED UP TILL ITS SMOKE QUITE SMOTHERS   . . 374   3 DON JUAN 13   36   8
SMOKED
  AND DIVERS SMOKED SUPERB PIPES DECORATED 441   2 DON JUAN 5   53   5
SMOKERS
  TO A SEDATE GREY CIRCLE OF OLD SMOKERS   293   2 DON JUAN 3   34   2
SMOKING
  SMOKING HIS PIPE QUITE CALMLY 'MIDST THE DIN   160   3 DON JUAN 8   98   4
  AMONG THE SCORCHING RUINS HE SAT SMOKING 172   3 DON JUAN 8   121   2
SMOLLET
  OF SMOLLET PRIOR ARIOSTO FIELDING 397   2 DON JUAN 4   98   3
SMOOTH
  BRIGHT WITH INTELLIGENCE AND FAIR AND SMOOTH   55   2 DON JUAN 1   61   2
  GLIDED ALONG THE SMOOTH AND HARDEN'D SAND 253   2 DON JUAN 2   184   3
  LIKE SUMMER CLOUDS ALL SILVERY SMOOTH AND FAIR 375   2 DON JUAN 4   57   2
  THE HINGES BEING AS SMOOTH AS ROGERS' RHYMES   463   2 DON JUAN 5   89   4
  LIKE DAVID FLINGS SMOOTH PEBBLES 'GAINST A GIANT 138   3 DON JUAN 8   51   2
  ALONG THE ASPECT WHETHER SMOOTH OR ROUGH 206   3 DON JUAN 9   48   6
  SO SMOOTH SO LEVEL SUCH A MODE OF SHAVING   263   3 DON JUAN 10   78   2
  WHO SEEING A HANDSOME STRIPLING WITH SMOOTH FACE . . . 285   3 DON JUAN 11   35   5
  SMOOTH SPEECH HIS FIRST AND MAIDENLY TRANSGRESSION . . . 400   3 DON JUAN 13   90   4
  IN THIS OUR PARTY POLISH'D SMOOTH AND COLD 409   3 DON JUAN 13   110   2
  WHATE'ER IT SHOWS WITH TRUTH A SMOOTH MONOTONY 417   3 DON JUAN 14   16   7
  THERE WAS MISS MILLPOND SMOOTH AS SUMMER'S SEA 474   3 DON JUAN 15   41   1
SMOOTH'D
  THAT WAVED IN FOREST-TOPS AND SMOOTH'D THE AIR 210   2 DON JUAN 2   103   4
  WHO SMOOTH'D HIS PILLOW AS SHE LEFT THE DEN 228   2 DON JUAN 2   135   2
  SOCIETY IS SMOOTH'D TO THAT EXCESS 402   3 DON JUAN 13   94   7
SMOOTHE
  TO GENTLY SMOOTHE THE PROGRESS OF DECLINE   360   3 DON JUAN 13   5 V6
SMOOTHED
  WHO CLEARED HER SPARKLING EYES AND SMOOTHED HER BROWS   . . 500   2 DON JUAN 5   154   3
  AND SMOOTHED THE BRIMSTONE OF THAT STREET OF HELL . . . 124   3 DON JUAN 8   26   7
  SMOOTHED EVEN THE SIMPLON'S STEEP AND BY GOD'S BLESSING . . 215   3 DON JUAN 9   66   7
  SMOOTHED FOR A MONARCH'S SEAT OF HONOUR GAY 235   3 DON JUAN 10   21   6
SMOOTH-FACED
  COLD-BLOODED SMOOTH-FACED PLACID MISCREANT   16   2 DON JUAN 0   12   1
SMOOTHLY
  THEY MUST BE PAID THOUGH SIX DAYS SMOOTHLY RUN 243   3 DON JUAN 10   38   7
  RESET IT SHAVE MORE SMOOTHLY ALSO SLOWER 433   3 DON JUAN 14   53   7
SMOTE
  EVEN WHEN THEY SMOTE HER IN THE HOPE TO SAVE   380   2 DON JUAN 4   67   8
SMOTHER
  AND TO CONTEND WITH THOUGHTS SHE COULD NOT SMOTHER   . . 80   2 DON JUAN 1   110   3
  HER OFFICE WAS TO KEEP ALOOF OR SMOTHER 21   3 DON JUAN 6   31   6
  STILL CLOSER SULPHURY CLOUDS BEGAN TO SMOTHER 146   3 DON JUAN 8   69   6
  IN CATHOLIC EYES BUT TOLD HIM TOO TO SMOTHER   240   3 DON JUAN 10   32   4
SMOTHER'D
  UNTIL AT LENGTH THE SMOTHER'D FIRE BROKE OUT   35   2 DON JUAN 1   26   7
SMOTHERS
  IT HATH BEEN STIRRED UP TILL ITS SMOKE QUITE SMOTHERS   . . 374   3 DON JUAN 13   36   8
SMUGGLING
  A LITTLE SMUGGLING AND SOME PIRACY 222   2 DON JUAN 2   125   6
SNAKE
  'TIS AS THE SNAKE LATE COIL'D WHO POURS HIS LENGTH   . . . 218   2 DON JUAN 2   117   7
  CASTS OFF ITS BRIGHT SKIN YEARLY LIKE THE SNAKE   421   2 DON JUAN 5   21   8
  DESPITE THE SNAKE SOCIETY'S LOUD RATTLES 452   3 DON JUAN 14   96   8
SNAKE-LIKE
  A LONG AND SNAKE-LIKE LIFE OF DULL DECAY 348   2 DON JUAN 4   9   7
SNAKES
  AS DO THE SUBTLE SNAKES DESCRIBED OF OLD 153   3 DON JUAN 8   83   8
  TWINE LIKE A KNOT OF SNAKES AROUND HIS FACE 510   3 DON JUAN 16   23   6
SNAPP'D
  ON WHICH LIKE A YOUNG FLOWER SNAPP'D FROM THE STALK . . . 249   2 DON JUAN 2   176   5

		PAGE	VOL	CANTO	STANZA	LN
SNARLING						
(BECAUSE THE WORLD WON'T READ HIM ALWAYS SNARLING)	. . .	404	2 DON JUAN	4	109	6
SNATCH						
IN COURAGE WAS OBLIGED TO SNATCH A SHIELD	. . . . .	125	3 DON JUAN	8	28	7
JUAN WHO HAD NO SHIELD TO SNATCH AND WAS	. . .	126	3 DON JUAN	8	29	1
SNATCH WHEN DESPAIR MAKES HUMAN HEARTS LESS PLIANT	. .	138	3 DON JUAN	8	51	4
OF THOUGHT WE COULD BUT SNATCH A CERTAINTY	. . . .	410	3 DON JUAN	14	1	2
SOME SAY THAT AUTHORS ONLY SNATCH BY BRIBING	. . . .	418	3 DON JUAN	14	19	4
SNATCH'D						
SHE SNATCH'D IT AND REFUSED ANOTHER MORSEL	. . . . .	240	2 DON JUAN	2	159	7
SNATCH'D DOWN HIS SABRE IN HOT HASTE TO WREAK	. . .	364	3 DON JUAN	4	37	3
SHE HAD ALSO SNATCH'D A MOMENT SINCE HER MARRIAGE	. . .	434	3 DON JUAN	14	56	7
SNATCHED						
SNATCHED FROM A PRISON TO PRESIDE AT COURT	. . . . .	495	2 DON JUAN	5	147	3
OF FOE O'ER HIM SNATCHED AT IT AND BIT	. . . . . .	153	3 DON JUAN	8	84	2
THE TIME WILL COME SHE'LL WISH THAT SHE HAD SNATCHED	. .	332	3 DON JUAN	12	35	3
SNEER						
YOU SNEER AND I ASSURE YOU THIS IS TRUE	. . . . . .	163	2 DON JUAN	2	13	7
CAN SNEER AT HIM WHO DREW ACHITOPHEL	. . . .	334	2 DON JUAN	3	100	8
SECUNDUM ARTEM BUT ALTHOUGH WE SNEER	. . . . . .	245	3 DON JUAN	10	42	2
A SNEER OR SHORT REPLY UNTO THEIR NEIGHBOUR	. . . .	288	3 DON JUAN	11	41	V4
BUT THUS MUCH AND NO SNEER AGAINST THE SHORE	. . .	346	3 DON JUAN	12	67	6
THOUGH 'TWAS NOT ONCE SO IF I SNEER SOMETIMES	. . . .	361	3 DON JUAN	13	8	2
BECAUSE HE EITHER MEANT TO SNEER AT HARMONY	. . . .	472	3 DON JUAN	15	36	1
AND DO NOT THINK I MEAN TO SNEER AT MOST	. . . . .	498	3 DON JUAN	15	95	5
AND MAKE THE WORLDING SNEER THE YOUNGLING WEEP	. . . .	555	3 DON JUAN	16	110	8
SNEER'D						
THE CIRCLE SMIL'D THEN WHISPER'D AND THEN SNEER'D	. . .	429	3 DON JUAN	14	44	1
SNEERED						
AT WHICH YOUR WISE MEN SNEERED IN PHRASES WITTY	. . . .	93	3 DON JUAN	7	53	7
SNEERS						
HE BORE THESE SNEERS AGAINST HIS NEAR RELATIONS	. . .	299	2 DON JUAN	3	46	5
ESCAPING WITH A FEW SLIGHT SCARLESS SNEERS	. . . . .	397	3 DON JUAN	13	82	8
SNEEZE						
NOR THAT A SNEEZE SHOULD INTERRUPT HIS SIGH	. . . . .	168	2 DON JUAN	2	22	7
SNOODS						
SCOTCH PLAIDS SCOTCH SNOODS THE BLUE HILLS AND CLEAR STREAMS	233	3 DON JUAN	10	18	2
SNORE						
MY MODERN MUSE MAY BE ALLOWED TO SNORE	. . . . . .	503	2 DON JUAN	5	159	V8
SNORES						
IN HOLY MATRIMONY SNORES AWAY	. . . .	42	3 DON JUAN	6	73	4
SNOW						
('TWAS SNOW THAT BROUGHT SAINT ANTHONY TO REASON)	. . .	57	2 DON JUAN	1	64	4
AND LOSE IN SHINING SNOW THEIR SUMMITS BLUE	. . . . .	94	2 DON JUAN	1	134	V5
ITS SNOW THROUGH ALL--HER SOFT LIPS LIE APART	. . .	108	2 DON JUAN	1	158	7
HER SMALL SNOW FEET HAD SLIPPERS BUT NO STOCKING	. . .	220	2 DON JUAN	2	121	8
FOR NOT THE BLEST SHERBET SUBLIMED WITH SNOW	. . . .	251	2 DON JUAN	2	180	4
BUT LIKE THE CLIMES THAT KNOW NOR SNOW NOR HAIL	. . . .	348	2 DON JUAN	4	9	4
BUT AFTER ALL 'TIS NOTHING BUT COLD SNOW	. . . . . .	398	2 DON JUAN	4	100	8
DISSOLVED LIKE SNOW BEFORE A WOMAN CRYING	. . . . .	492	2 DON JUAN	5	141	8
AND MAKES OUR SNOW LESS PURE THAN OUR MORALITY	. . . .	501	2 DON JUAN	5	157	6
IN HIS MONASTIC CONCUBINE OF SNOW--	. . . .	14	3 DON JUAN	6	17	6
SNOW WELL 'TIS ALL HAP-HAZARD WHEN ONE WEDS	. . . .	18	3 DON JUAN	6	25	6
OR THE SNOW MINARET ON AN ALPINE STEEP	. . . . . .	40	3 DON JUAN	6	68	4
(WITH SOME ASSISTANCE FROM THE FROST AND SNOW)	. . . .	147	3 DON JUAN	8	70	2
ALAS THAT GLORY SHOULD BE CHILLED BY SNOW	. . . . .	254	3 DON JUAN	10	59	5
(NOW FOR A COMMONPLACE) BENEATH THE SNOW	. . . . . .	374	3 DON JUAN	13	36	2
WITH THAT SHE ROSE AND GLIDED OFF AS SNOW	. . . . .	517	3 DON JUAN	16	38	V5
SNOWBALL						
'TIS AS A SNOWBALL WHICH DERIVES ASSISTANCE	. . . . .	398	2 DON JUAN	4	100	5
SNOWDROPS						
AND LEFT HIS CHEEKS AS PALE AS SNOWDROPS BLOWING	. . . .	478	2 DON JUAN	5	117	6
SNOWS						
THAT PLEASANT CAPITAL OF PAINTED SNOWS	. . . . . .	203	3 DON JUAN	9	42	8
THEIR WAY THROUGH VIRTUE'S PRIMROSE PATHS OF SNOWS	. . .	328	3 DON JUAN	12	26	4
OR LIKE THE OLD COMPARISON OF SNOWS	. . . .	335	3 DON JUAN	12	41	3
LIKE RUSSIANS RUSHING FROM HOT BATHS TO SNOWS	. . . .	349	3 DON JUAN	12	73	5
SNOW-TOPS						
ON THE SNOW-TOPS OF DISTANT HILLS THE STREAK	. . . .	234	2 DON JUAN	2	147	3
SNOW-WHITE						
A BAND OF CHILDREN ROUND A SNOW-WHITE RAM	. . . . .	292	2 DON JUAN	3	32	1
SNOWY						
AND THROUGH ALL CLIMES THE SNOWY AND THE SUNNY	. . . .	78	2 DON JUAN	1	107	7
AS SLIGHTLY STIRRING IN HER SNOWY SHROUD	. . . . . .	39	3 DON JUAN	6	66	6
SNUB-NOSE						
WITH PRYING SNUB-NOSE AND SMALL EYES HE STOOD	. . . .	109	2 DON JUAN	1	160	1
SNUFF						
NOR CARE A PINCH OF SNUFF ABOUT HIS CORPS)--	. . . .	127	3 DON JUAN	8	31	8
SNUFF'D						
SHE SNUFF'D THE CANDLE CURTSIED AND WITHDREW	. . . .	116	2 DON JUAN	1	173	8
SNUFFED						
SHOULD LET ITSELF BE SNUFFED OUT BY AN ARTICLE	. . . .	298	3 DON JUAN	11	60	8
SNUG						
A NEAT SNUG STUDY ON A WINTER'S NIGHT	. . . .	444	2 DON JUAN	5	58	1
SNUGLY						
THERE COUCHED ALL SNUGLY ON HIS PILLOW'S NOOK	. . . .	512	3 DON JUAN	16	27	5
SOAR						
GASPING ON DECK BECAUSE YOU SOAR TOO HIGH BOB	. . . .	10	2 DON JUAN	D	3	7
BEING PRIDE WHICH LEADS THE MIND TO SOAR TOO FAR	. . .	344	2 DON JUAN	4	1	7
AND THEREFORE SHALL MY LAY SOAR HIGH AND SOLEMN	. . .	358	3 DON JUAN	13	1	7

```
                                                          PAGE VOL      CANTO STANZA LN
SOARINGS
    OUR SOARINGS WITH ANOTHER SORT OF QUESTION  . . . . .  . 269   3 DON JUAN 11      3    3
SOARS
    WHERE THE SUBLIME SOARS FORTH ON WINGS MORE AMPLE . . .  . 45   2 DON JUAN  1     42    6
    A DEVOTEE WHEN SOARS THE HOST IN SIGHT   . . . . . . .  . 261  2 DON JUAN  2    196    3
    THE EAGLE SOARS ALONE THE GULL AND CROW  . . . . . . .  . 358  2 DON JUAN  4     28    7
    THROUGH THE HUGE ARCH WHICH SOARS AND SINKS AGAIN . . .  . 388  3 DON JUAN 13     63    5
SOB
    WHAT WAS'T TO HIM TO HEAR TWO WOMEN SOB  . . . . . . .  . 105   3 DON JUAN  7     77    8
SOBB'D
    OH SOBB'D ANTONIA I COULD TEAR THEIR EYES OUT  . . . .  . 104   2 DON JUAN  1    152    8
    UNTIL SHE SOBB'D FOR BREATH AND SOON THEY WERE  . . . .  . 361  2 DON JUAN  4     31    6
SOBBING
    FLOWERS TO THE GRAVE) AND SOBBING OFTEN HE  . . . . . .  . 165  2 DON JUAN  2     17    6
SOBER
    AND SOBER SUNS MUST SET AT FIVE O'CLOCK  . . . . . . .  .  94   2 DON JUAN  1    134    8
    (AND SO MY SOBER MUSE--COME LET'S BE STEADY--  . . . .  . 160  2 DON JUAN  2      6    8
    A SAD SOUR SOBER BEVERAGE--BY TIME . . . . . . . . . .  . 277  2 DON JUAN  3      5    6
    HIS SOBER HEAD MAJESTICALLY TAME . . . . . . . . . . .  . 292  2 DON JUAN  3     32    5
    TO THE KIND READER OF OUR SOBER CLIME  . . . . . . . .  . 347  2 DON JUAN  4      6    1
    OF SOBER REASON WHERESOE'ER IT MOVES . . . . . . . . .  . 284  3 DON JUAN 11     33    6
    THE SOBER SAD ANTITHESIS TO GLOWING--  . . . . . . . .  . 422  3 DON JUAN 14     28    6
    THE SEA-GULLS WITH A STEADY SOBER FLIGHT--  . . . . . .  . 558  3 DON JUAN 16    117    2
SOBERLY
    AND THEN RETREATED SOBERLY--AT TEN . . . . . . . . . .  . 408  3 DON JUAN 13    108    8
SOBS
    TO WHICH THE SOLE REPLY WERE TEARS AND SOBS  . . . . .  . 110  2 DON JUAN  1    162    2
SOCIAL
    SMALL SOCIAL PARTIES JUST BEGUN TO DINE  . . . . . . .  . 291  2 DON JUAN  3     31    2
    CALL'D SOCIAL HAUNTS OF HATE AND VICE AND CARE . . . .  . 358  2 DON JUAN  4     28    4
    TO FEEL FOR NONE IS THE TRUE SOCIAL ART  . . . . . . .  . 423  2 DON JUAN  5     25    7
    UPON THE REST OF EUROPE'S SOCIAL STATE   . . . . . . .  . 327  3 DON JUAN 12     24    4
SOCIETY
    HE WAS SO GREAT A LOSS TO GOOD SOCIETY   . . . . . . .  . 296  2 DON JUAN  3     41    8
    BUT NOW BEING LIFTED INTO HIGH SOCIETY   . . . . . . .  . 318  2 DON JUAN  3     83    1
    TO THEIR OWN HEARTS' MOST SWEET SOCIETY  . . . . . . .  . 348  2 DON JUAN  4      8    2
    SOCIETY ITSELF WHICH SHOULD CREATE . . . . . . . . . .  . 423  2 DON JUAN  5     25    5
    WHICH KNITS SOCIETY--THE DINNER BELL . . . . . . . . .  . 439  2 DON JUAN  5     49   V8
    AND THE SWEET CONSEQUENCE OF LARGE SOCIETY . . . . . .  . 146  3 DON JUAN  8     68    3
    CONSULTING THE SOCIETY FOR VICE  . . . . . . . . . . .  . 336  3 DON JUAN 12     42    7
    FOR GOOD SOCIETY IS BUT A GAME . . . . . . . . . . . .  . 342  3 DON JUAN 12     58    3
    SOCIETY THAT CHINA WITHOUT FLAW  . . . . . . . . . . .  . 352  3 DON JUAN 12     78    5
    INTO THE BEST SOCIETY AND THERE  . . . . . . . . . . .  . 355  3 DON JUAN 12     85    2
    AND RASH ENTHUSIASM IN GOOD SOCIETY  . . . . . . . . .  . 374  3 DON JUAN 13     35    7
    THE PASSEE AND THE PASSED FOR GOOD SOCIETY . . . . . .  . 396  3 DON JUAN 13     80    7
    SOCIETY IS SMOOTH'D TO THAT EXCESS . . . . . . . . . .  . 402  3 DON JUAN 13     94    7
    SOCIETY IS NOW ONE POLISH'D HORDE  . . . . . . . . . .  . 402  3 DON JUAN 13     95    7
    A BIRD'S-EYE VIEW TOO OF THAT WILD SOCIETY . . . . . .  . 416  3 DON JUAN 14     14    3
    BECAUSE MY BUSINESS IS TO DRESS SOCIETY  . . . . . . .  . 497  3 DON JUAN 15     93    5
    WHO WISH TO TAKE THE TONE OF THEIR SOCIETY . . . . . .  . 526  3 DON JUAN 16     52    4
SOCIETY'S
    OF THE HUMANE SOCIETY'S BEGINNING  . . . . . . . . . .  .  92   2 DON JUAN  1    130    4
    DESPITE THE SNAKE SOCIETY'S LOUD RATTLES . . . . . . .  . 452  3 DON JUAN 14     96    8
SOCIIS
    HIS OTHER MAXIM NOSCITUR A SOCIIS  . . . . . . . . . .  . 443  3 DON JUAN 14     77    3
SOCKET
    TURNED BACK WITHIN ITS SOCKET--THESE REWARD  . . . . .  . 118  3 DON JUAN  8     13    6
SOCKETS
    ONE BREAKS YOUR BONES ONE SETS THEM IN THEIR SOCKETS . .  . 91   2 DON JUAN  1    129    4
SOCRATES
    SOCRATES SAID OUR ONLY KNOWLEDGE WAS . . . . . . . . .  .  69   3 DON JUAN  7      5    1
    AND SOCRATES HIMSELF BUT WISDOM'S QUIXOTE  . . . . . .  . 363  3 DON JUAN 13     10    8
    GREAT SOCRATES AND THOU DIVINER STILL . . . . . . . .  . 464  3 DON JUAN 15     18    2
    AND SOCRATES THAT MODEL OF ALL DUTY  . . . . . . . . .  . 494  3 DON JUAN 15     85    7
    BUT INNOCENTLY SO AS SOCRATES  . . . . . . . . . . . .  . 494  3 DON JUAN 15     86    2
    PYTHAGORAS LOCKE SOCRATES--BUT PAGES . . . . . . . . .  . 566  3 DON JUAN 17      9    1
SOCRATIC
    AND GIRLS OF SIXTEEN ARE THUS FAR SOCRATIC . . . . . .  . 494  3 DON JUAN 15     86    1
SODA
    AND SO--FOR GODSAKE--HOCK AND SODA WATER . . . . . . .  . 156  2 DON JUAN  1   V  8    8
    SERMONS AND SODA WATER THE DAY AFTER . . . . . . . . .  . 250  2 DON JUAN  2    178    8
    OR LIKE A SODA BOTTLE WHEN ITS SPRAY . . . . . . . . .  . 504  3 DON JUAN 16      9    5
SODAE-SULPHAT
    SODAE-SULPHAT  SIX DRAMS  HALF DRAM MANNAE OPTIM . . .  . 244  3 DON JUAN 10     41    2
SODAS
    HALF-SOLVED INTO THOSE SODAS OR MAGNESIAS  . . . . . .  . 261  3 DON JUAN 10     73    7
SODA-WATER
    SOME HOCK AND SODA-WATER THEN YOU'LL KNOW  . . . . . .  . 251  2 DON JUAN  2    180    2
    VIE WITH THAT DRAUGHT OF HOCK AND SODA-WATER . . . . .  . 251  2 DON JUAN  2    180    8
SOFA
    THERE IS THE SOFA THERE THE GREAT ARM-CHAIR  . . . . .  . 104  2 DON JUAN  1    153    3
    A SOFA LIKE A BED MAY COME BY WRONG  . . . . . . . . .  . 288  2 DON JUAN  3     25   V8
    THEIR SOFA OCCUPIED THREE PARTS COMPLETE . . . . . . .  . 309  2 DON JUAN  3     67    3
    OR RATHER SOFA (FOR IT WAS ALL PILLOW  . . . . . . . .  .  60   3 DON JUAN  6    108    4
SOFAS
    SOFAS 'TWAS HALF A SIN TO SIT UPON . . . . . . . . . .  . 449  2 DON JUAN  5     65    5
SOFT
    BESIDE HIS MISTRESS IN SOME SOFT ABODE   . . . . . . .  .  24   2 DON JUAN  1      6    6
    UNTIL SHE SPOKE THEN THROUGH ITS SOFT DISGUISE . . . .  .  54   2 DON JUAN  1     60    3
```

749

SOFT (CONTINUED)
ITS SNOW THROUGH ALL--HER SOFT LIPS LIE APART . . . . . . 108 2 DON JUAN 1   158   7
OF A SOFT CHEEK AND ASPECT DELICATE . . . . 203 2 DON JUAN 2   88   2
AND CHAFING HIM THE SOFT WARM HAND OF YOUTH . . . . . . 215 2 DON JUAN 2   113   3
WITH FOOD AND RAIMENT AND THOSE SOFT ATTENTIONS . . . . 221 2 DON JUAN 2   123   2
SOFT AS THE CALLOW CYGNET IN ITS NEST . . . . 235 2 DON JUAN 2   148   6
SO SOFT SO SWEET SO DELICATELY CLEAR . . . . 236 2 DON JUAN 2   151   4
THEIR LARGE BLACK EYES AND SOFT SERAPHIC CHEEKS . . . . 292 2 DON JUAN 3   33   2
SOFT PERSIAN SENTENCES IN LILAC LETTERS . . . . . . 308 2 DON JUAN 3   64   7
THEY WERE SO SOFT AND BEAUTIFUL AND RIFE . . . . . . 313 2 DON JUAN 3   74   3
SINK O'ER THE EARTH SO BEAUTIFUL AND SOFT . . . . . . 335 2 DON JUAN 3   102   4
SOFT HOUR WHICH WAKES THE WISH AND MELTS THE HEART . . . 338 2 DON JUAN 3   108   1
HAD HELD TILL NOW HER SOFT AND MILKY WAY . . . . . . 375 2 DON JUAN 4   57   5
YET HAS A KIND OF SOFT AND SILLY AIR . . . . 390 2 DON JUAN 4   85   V6
TO THE SOFT OATH OF ANA-SEING SIKTUM . . . . 409 2 DON JUAN 4   116   V8
WITH HAIDEE'S ISLE AND SOFT IONIAN FACE . . . . . . 478 2 DON JUAN 5   117   3
PERHAPS THE FAULT OF HER SOFT SEX AND AGE-- . . . . . 490 2 DON JUAN 5   136   6
A SLIGHT BLUSH A SOFT TREMOR A CALM KIND . . . . . . 13 3 DON JUAN 6   15   1
ALL FELT A SOFT KIND OF CONCATENATION . . . . 25 3 DON JUAN 6   38   6
BUT SHE WAS A SOFT LANDSCAPE OF MILD EARTH . . . . . 32 3 DON JUAN 6   53   1
NODS FROM THE TREE WAS SLUMBERING WITH SOFT BREATH . . . 38 3 DON JUAN 6   65   7
ABOVE HER BROW LAY DREAMING SOFT AND WARM . . . . . . 39 3 DON JUAN 6   66   3
(SHE ADDED IN A SOFT AND PITEOUS TONE) . . . . . . 47 3 DON JUAN 6   82   6
SOFTER THAN THE SOFT SYBARITE'S WHO CRIED . . . . . . 50 3 DON JUAN 6   89   2
A LOW SOFT OTTOMAN) AND BLACK DESPAIR . . . . 60 3 DON JUAN 6   108   5
SOFT WORDS TOO FITTED FOR THE PERORATION . . . . . . 74 3 DON JUAN 7   16   5
HARD WORDS WHICH STICK IN THE SOFT MUSES' GULLETS . . . 106 3 DON JUAN 7   78   8
WE TEASE MILD BAILLIE OR SOFT ABERNETHY . . . . . . 245 3 DON JUAN 10   42   8
WITH A SOFT BESOM WILL I SWEEP YOUR HALLS . . . . . . 266 3 DON JUAN 10   84   7
DISSOLVING IN THE WALTZ TO SOME SOFT AIR . . . . . . 303 3 DON JUAN 11   70   6
FISHERS FOR MEN LIKE SIRENS WITH SOFT LUTES . . . . . 343 3 DON JUAN 12   59   6
WHEN HER SOFT LIQUID WORDS RUN ON APACE . . . . . . 426 3 DON JUAN 14   36   6
GRACE OF THE SOFT IDEAL SELDOM SHOWN . . . . 428 3 DON JUAN 14   40   6
SETS TO SOFT MUSIC THE HARMONIOUS SIGH . . . . . . 430 3 DON JUAN 14   47   3
A LOVER WITH CAPRICES SOFT AND DEAR . . . . 438 3 DON JUAN 14   63   4
FOR FEW OF THE SOFT SEX ARE VERY STABLE . . . . . . 458 3 DON JUAN 15   6   3
BY NATURE SOFT HIS WHOLE ADDRESS HELD OFF . . . . . . 462 3 DON JUAN 15   14   1
IF I HAD NEVER PROVED THE SOFT CONDITION . . . . . . 467 3 DON JUAN 15   24   2
FOR ALL HER PAST EXERTION AND SOFT PHRASES . . . . . 550 3 DON JUAN 16   103   3
SOFTEN
WITH ISMAIL'S STORM TO SOFTEN IT THE MORE . . . . . 146 3 DON JUAN 8   68   8
SOFTEN'D
BY A RIVER WHICH ITS SOFTEN'D WAY DID TAKE . . . . . 385 3 DON JUAN 13   57   3
SOFTER
ALTHOUGH NO FAIRER--SMALLER--SOFTER HAND . . . . . . 472 2 DON JUAN 5   106   V2
SOFTER THAN THE SOFT SYBARITE'S WHO CRIED . . . . . . 50 3 DON JUAN 6   89   2
ALSO THE SOFTER SILKS WERE HEARD TO RUSTLE . . . . . 223 3 DON JUAN 9   82   5
QUIET--SANK INTO SOFTER RIPPLES GLIDING . . . . . . 385 3 DON JUAN 13   58   4
SOFTEST
SOFTEST OF MELODIES AND COULD BE SAD . . . . 292 3 DON JUAN 11   47   4
AND WHICH WAS SOFTEST RUSSIAN OR CASTILIAN . . . . . 294 3 DON JUAN 11   50   7
SOFTLY
AND BY GOOD FORTUNE GLIDING SOFTLY CAUGHT HER . . . . 208 2 DON JUAN 2   99   3
AND SHE WOULD SOFTLY STIR HIS LOCKS SO CURLY . . . . 245 2 DON JUAN 2   168   5
SOFTNESS
SHEDS BEAUTY AND DEEP SOFTNESS O'ER THE WHOLE . . . . 82 2 DON JUAN 1   114   6
HER FORM HAD ALL THE SOFTNESS OF HER SEX . . . . . . 474 2 DON JUAN 5   109   1
SOHO
WHEELS WHIRL FROM CARLTON PALACE TO SOHO . . . . . . 378 3 DON JUAN 13   44   3
SOI-DISANT
ANGLE THE SOI-DISANT MATHEMATICIAN . . . . 399 3 DON JUAN 13   87   3
AS NOW WITH THOSE OF SOI-DISANT SOUND MIND . . . . . 446 3 DON JUAN 14   84   4
SOIL
LIKE KNOTS OF VIPERS ON A DUNGHILL'S SOIL . . . . . 271 2 DON JUAN 2   215   5
AND AS THE SOIL IS SO THE HEART OF MAN . . . . . . 373 2 DON JUAN 4   55   8
AND LIKE THE SOIL BENEATH IT WILL BRING FORTH . . . . 374 2 DON JUAN 4   56   5
FAREWELL THEY MUTUALLY EXCLAIMED THIS SOIL . . . . . 459 2 DON JUAN 5   83   5
MOVES--FEMALE HEARTS ARE SUCH A GENIAL SOIL . . . . . 480 2 DON JUAN 5   120   3
THE SOIL OF THE GREEN PROVINCE HE HAD WASTED . . . . 84 3 DON JUAN 7   36   7
CORRUPTION COULD NOT MAKE THEIR HEARTS HER SOIL . . . . 145 3 DON JUAN 8   67   4
WHO FURROW SOME NEW SOIL TO SOW FOR JOYS . . . . . . 228 3 DON JUAN 10   7   8
REVERED THE SOIL OF THOSE TRUE SONS THE MOTHER . . . . 265 3 DON JUAN 10   81   7
ON *CHANGE AND EVEN THY SILVER SOIL PERU . . . . . . 318 3 DON JUAN 12   6   7
BUT THOUGH THE SOIL MAY GIVE YOU TIME AND TROUBLE . . . 351 3 DON JUAN 12   76   7
THE GOODLIEST SOIL OF BODY AND OF MIND . . . . . . 359 3 DON JUAN 13   2   8
THE FIRST YET FROWNED SUPERBLY O'ER THE SOIL . . . . 386 3 DON JUAN 13   59   5
OUR FEELINGS 'GAINST THE NATURE OF THE SOIL . . . . . 447 3 DON JUAN 14   86   4
SOIL'D
HAD SOIL'D THE CURRENT OF HER SINLESS YEARS . . . . . 274 2 DON JUAN 3   1   7
TO SHOW HIS LOATHING OF THE SPOT HE SOIL'D . . . . . 401 2 DON JUAN 4   105   4
SOIL'S
IN FAULTS WHICH SOMETIMES SHOW THE SOIL'S FERTILITY . . 368 3 DON JUAN 13   22   6
SOIREE
THE DINNER AND THE SOIREE TOO WERE DONE . . . . . . 504 3 DON JUAN 16   8   1
SOLACE
SHORT SOLACE VAIN RELIEF--THOUGHT CAME TOO QUICK . . . 380 2 DON JUAN 4   67   1
BECAUSE IT MIGHT NOT SOLACE EARS POLITE . . . . . . 158 3 DON JUAN 8   93   6
AND DEBT AND WHATNOT FOR THEIR SOLACE SENT . . . . . 360 3 DON JUAN 13   5   8
ALSO THE SOLACE OF AN OVERCHARGE . . . . 379 3 DON JUAN 13   45   8
AND SOLACE YOUR SLIGHT LAPSE 'GAINST BONOS MORES . . . 432 3 DON JUAN 14   50   7

SOLAR
      HOW EARTH COULD ROUND THE SOLAR ORBIT RUN 565   3 DON JUAN 17   8   3
SOLD
      HIS HOUSE WAS SOLD HIS SERVANTS SENT AWAY 39   2 DON JUAN 1   34   3
      AND SOLD HIM INSTANTLY WHEN OUT OF DANGER 225   2 DON JUAN 2   130   8
      AMONG HIS FRIENDS THE MAINOTS SOME HE SOLD 284   2 DON JUAN 3   16   2
      BUT SOLD BY THE IMPRESARIO AT NO HIGH RATE 388   2 DON JUAN 4   80   8
      AND ALL ARE TO BE SOLD IF YOU CONSIDER 425   2 DON JUAN 5   27   3
SOLDER
      IF THERE MIGHT BE CHIRURGEONS WHO COULD SOLDER 158   3 DON JUAN 8   94   3
SOLDIER
      JUST AS A REGULAR COMMON SOLDIER OR A WHORE 537   3 DON JUAN 16   76   V3
SOLDIERS
      PILLAGE TO SOLDIERS PRIZE-MONEY TO SEAMEN 88   2 DON JUAN 1   124   8
      THE MILLIONS SLAIN BY SOLDIERS FOR THEIR RATION . . . 146   3 DON JUAN 8   68   6
      FATAL TO BISHOPS AS TO SOLDIERS--THESE 150   3 DON JUAN 8   76   2
      THE SOLDIERS WHO BEHELD HIM DROP HIS POINT 170   3 DON JUAN 8   117   1
      'TIS STRANGE ENOUGH--THE ROUGH TOUGH SOLDIERS WHO . . 171   3 DON JUAN 8   119   1
      SOMETIMES INDEED LIKE SOLDIERS OFF PARADE 417   3 DON JUAN 14   17   1
      AS COMMON SOLDIERS OR A COMMON--SHORE 537   3 DON JUAN 16   76   3
SOLDIERY
      BY CHRISTIAN SOLDIERY A SINGLE SPOT 131   3 DON JUAN 8   37   5
      THE INSOLENT SOLDIERY TO SOOTHE AND FLATTER 299   3 DON JUAN 11   62   4
SOLE
      DYING INTESTATE JUAN WAS SOLE HEIR 42   2 DON JUAN 1   37   1
      INEZ BECAME SOLE GUARDIAN WHICH WAS FAIR 42   2 DON JUAN 1   37   5
      TO WHICH THE SOLE REPLY WERE TEARS AND SOBS 110   2 DON JUAN 1   162   2
      CANST THOU BE MY SOLE WORLD MY UNIVERSE 144   2 DON JUAN 1   215   2
      LEFT HIM AT LAST THE SOLE OF MANY MASTERS 222   2 DON JUAN 2   125   7
      IS ALWAYS SO TO WOMEN ONE SOLE BOND 263   2 DON JUAN 2   200   2
      WHEREAS IF ONE SOLE LADY PLEASED FOREVER 270   2 DON JUAN 2   213   7
      OF MAGIC LADIES WHO BY ONE SOLE ACT 293   2 DON JUAN 3   34   7
      WERE THE SOLE ECHOS SAVE MY STEED'S AND MINE 337   2 DON JUAN 3   106   3
      IN THAT TO WHICH THE LAW MAKES THEM SOLE HEIRS 11   3 DON JUAN 6   10   8
      OH GLORIOUS LAUREL SINCE FOR ONE SOLE LEAF 101   3 DON JUAN 7   68   6
      OF THAT WEAK WORDY HARVEST THE SOLE GLEANING 207   3 DON JUAN 9   49   8
      AND THIS IS THE SOLE MORTAL WHO COULD GRAPPLE 225   3 DON JUAN 10   1   7
      AS THE SOLE SIGN OF MAN'S BEING IN HIS SENSES 240   3 DON JUAN 10   31   7
      BUT WHICH I DOUBT EXTREMELY--THOU SOLE PRISM 269   3 DON JUAN 11   2   6
      THOU MORNING POST SOLE RECORD OF THE PANNELS 308   3 DON JUAN 11   80   4
      FOR WHICH MY SOLE EXCUSE IS--'TIS MY WAY 413   3 DON JUAN 14   7   3
      REMNANT WERE THERE OF THE OLD WORLD'S SOLE THRONE . . 428   3 DON JUAN 14   40   4
      SOLE CREDITOR WHOSE PROCESS DOTH INVOLVE IN'T 458   3 DON JUAN 15   7   7
      WHOSE SOLE ACCOMPLISHMENTS WERE QUITE A BOOTY 471   3 DON JUAN 15   34   6
      IN SOUPS OR SAUCES OR A SOLE RAGOUT 482   3 DON JUAN 15   62   7
      HAD EVER BEEN HIS SOLE AND WHOLE AMBITION 536   3 DON JUAN 16   74   2
      TO PAINT A SOLE SENSATION--THOUGH QUITE COMMON-- . . . 569   3 DON JUAN 17   V 13   4
SOLELY
      I PASS MY EVENINGS IN LONG GALLERIES SOLELY 444   2 DON JUAN 5   58   7
SOLEMN
      A LITTLE CUPOLA MORE NEAT THAN SOLEMN 400   2 DON JUAN 4   104   2
      HIS HIGHNESS WAS A MAN OF SOLEMN PORT 495   2 DON JUAN 5   147   1
      OF HEROISM AND TOOK HIS PLACE WITH SOLEMN 130   3 DON JUAN 8   34   6
      AND THEREFORE SHALL MY LAY SOAR HIGH AND SOLEMN . . . 358   3 DON JUAN 13   1   7
      THE SABLE FRIAR IN HIS SOLEMN HOOD 558   3 DON JUAN 16   117   8
SOLICIT
      THEREFORE I WOULD SOLICIT FREE DISCUSSION 564   3 DON JUAN 17   6   1
SOLID
      FOR WANT OF WATER AND THEIR SOLID MESS 178   2 DON JUAN 2   41   5
SOLIDITY
      OF HOMICIDE BUT THERE WAS NO SOLIDITY 80   3 DON JUAN 7   27   5
SOLILOQUIZE
      WHILE I SOLILOQUIZE BEYOND EXPRESSION 331   2 DON JUAN 3   96   4
SOLITARY
      FOUND--GOD KNOWS HOW--HIS SOLITARY WAY 126   2 DON JUAN 1   188   V3
      A SOLITARY SHRIEK THE BUBBLING CRY 184   2 DON JUAN 2   53   7
      THAN SOLITARY PRIDE'S OPPRESSIVE WEIGHT 367   3 DON JUAN 13   19   6
      OR SOLITARY AS THEY CHOSE TO BEAR 406   3 DON JUAN 13   103   4
      AND ANGLING TOO THAT SOLITARY VICE 407   3 DON JUAN 13   106   5
SOLITUDE
      HIS LIKE ALL DEEP GRIEF PLUNGED IN SOLITUDE 68   2 DON JUAN 1   87   4
      I'M FOND MYSELF OF SOLITUDE OR SO 68   2 DON JUAN 1   87   5
      BY SOLITUDE I MEAN A SULTAN'S NOT 68   2 DON JUAN 1   87   7
      GO LITTLE BOOK FROM THIS MY SOLITUDE 149   2 DON JUAN 1   222   1
      OF LOVE'S AND NIGHT'S AND OCEAN'S SOLITUDE 262   2 DON JUAN 2   198   2
      THEIR PRIEST WAS SOLITUDE AND THEY WERE WED 265   2 DON JUAN 2   204   6
      THE SOLITUDE OF PASSING HIS OWN DOOR 302   2 DON JUAN 3   52   3
      SWEET HOUR OF TWILIGHT--IN THE SOLITUDE 337   2 DON JUAN 3   105   1
      THERE SOLITUDE WE KNOW HAS HER FULL GROWTH IN 443   2 DON JUAN 5   57   3
      OF SOLITUDE HEALTH SHRANK NOT FROM HIM--FOR 143   3 DON JUAN 8   62   2
SOLITUDES
      UNFIT TO MIX IN THESE THICK SOLITUDES 358   2 DON JUAN 4   28   3
      SERENE NOT SULLEN WERE THE SOLITUDES 145   3 DON JUAN 8   67   7
SOLMS
      TO MAKE A TWILIGHT IN JUST AS SOLMS HEAT IS 217   3 DON JUAN 9   69   7
SOLOMON
      VERSE AND BY SOLOMON AND BY CERVANTES 67   3 DON JUAN 7   3   8
      HIS LORDSHIP'S JUSTICE--SEEMS NOT THAT OF SOLOMON-- . . 357   3 DON JUAN 12   V 18   7
      OF COUNSELLORS AS SOLOMON HAS SAID 371   3 DON JUAN 13   29   2
      THE PASSION WHICH MADE SOLOMON A ZANY 452   3 DON JUAN 14   95   4

```
                                                    PAGE VOL      CANTO    STANZA LN
SOLUTION
    TO VENTURE A SOLUTION DAVUS SUM . . . . . . . . .  365  3 DON JUAN 13      13    2
SOLVE
    THE CAUSE I KNOW NOT NOR CAN SOLVE BUT SUCH . . . . .  388  3 DON JUAN 13      64    7
SOLVENT
    THE LUCK OF FINDING EVERYBODY SOLVENT . . . . . . .  458  3 DON JUAN 15       7    8
SOLVING
    I LEAVE TO THOSE WHO ARE FOND OF SOLVING DOUBT . . . .  531  3 DON JUAN 16      62    4
SOLYMAN
    SAVE SOLYMAN THE GLORY OF THEIR LINE . . . . . . .  495  2 DON JUAN  5     147    8
SOMBRE
    'TWAS MIDNIGHT--DARK AND SOMBRE WAS THE NIGHT . . . .   94  2 DON JUAN  1     135   V1
    INTO A GALLERY OF A SOMBRE HUE . . . . . . . .  508  3 DON JUAN 16      17    3
SOMEBODY
    BUT SOMEBODY OR OTHER RUMMAGING . . . . . . . .  146  2 DON JUAN  1     219 . 5
    I WISH TO GOD THAT SOMEBODY WOULD BUY US . . . . .  423  2 DON JUAN  5      24    8
SOMEHOW
    SHE PROVED IT SOMEHOW OUT OF SACRED SONG . . . . . .   28  2 DON JUAN  1      14    3
    BUT SOMEHOW THIS MY VESTAL VOW TAKES WING . . . . .   85  2 DON JUAN  1     119    5
    ALL HEAPED TOGETHER SOMEHOW IN A LITTER . . . . . .  465  2 DON JUAN  5      93   V8
    YET SOMEHOW THERE WAS SOMETHING SOMEWHERE WANTING . . .  474  2 DON JUAN  5     109    7
    SHEWED THAT SOMEWHERE SOMEHOW THERE WAS A FAULT . . .   83  3 DON JUAN  7      35    2
    THIS CHIEFTAIN--SOMEHOW WOULD NOT YIELD AT ALL . . .  163  3 DON JUAN  8     104    8
    BUT SOMEHOW--IT MAY SEEM A SCHOOLBOY'S WHINE . . . .  233  3 DON JUAN 10      17    5
    AFTER A SORT BUT SOMEHOW PEOPLE NEVER . . . . . .  323  3 DON JUAN 12      15    3
    ARE SOMEHOW ECHOED TO THE PRETTY DEARS . . . . . .  489  3 DON JUAN 15      76    3
    AND ALWAYS HAVE DONE SOMEHOW THESE GOOD LOOKS . . . .  493  3 DON JUAN 15      84    7
    CHANGEABLE TOO--YET SOMEHOW IDEM SEMPER . . . . . .  567  3 DON JUAN 17      11    3
SOMEONE
    AS SOMEONE SOMEWHERE SINGS ABOUT THE SKY . . . . .  404  2 DON JUAN  4     110    2
    OR SOMEONE FOR HIM IN SOME SAGE GRAVE MOOD . . . . .  371  3 DON JUAN 13      29    3
    IF SOMEONE HAD NOT TOLD ME TO FOREGO IT . . . . .  467  3 DON JUAN 15      24    8
    TILL SOMEONE WITH A GROAN EXPREST A WISH . . . . .  542  3 DON JUAN 16      87    7
SOME'S
    AND THUS WITH WOMEN HOWSOE'ER IT SHOCK SOME'S . . . .  371  3 DON JUAN 13      30    7
SOMETHING
    SOMETHING OF WHICH ITS MASTERS ARE AFRAID . . . . .   18  2 DON JUAN  D      14    3
    A SOMETHING IN THEM WHICH WAS NOT DESIRE . . . . .   54  2 DON JUAN  1      60    6
    THERE'S SOMETHING CHEERFUL IN THAT SORT OF LIGHT . . .   94  2 DON JUAN  1     135    5
    OF POOR PEDRILLO SOMETHING STILL REMAIN'D . . . . .  200  2 DON JUAN  2      82    1
    THERE WAS A SOMETHING WHICH BESPOKE COMMAND . . . .  217  2 DON JUAN  2     116    7
    A SOMETHING TO BE LOVED A CREATURE MEANT . . . . .  247  2 DON JUAN  2     172    5
    THERE'S SOMETHING OF ANTIPATHY AS 'TWERE . . . . .  278  2 DON JUAN  3       6    1
    THERE'S DOUBTLESS SOMETHING IN DOMESTIC DOINGS . . .  279  2 DON JUAN  3       8    1
    FOR SOMETHING BETTER IF NOT WHOLLY GOOD . . . . .  302  2 DON JUAN  3      53    6
    BUT SOMETHING OF THE SPIRIT OF OLD GREECE . . . . .  303  2 DON JUAN  3      55    1
    HAD SOMETHING READY UPON MOST OCCASIONS-- . . . . .  319  2 DON JUAN  3      84.   4
    HE GAVE THE DIFFERENT NATIONS SOMETHING NATIONAL . . .  319  2 DON JUAN  3      85    2
    'TIS SOMETHING IN THE DEARTH OF FAME . . . . . .  323  2 DON JUAN  3    L  6    1
    'TIS SOMETHING NOTHING WORDS ILLUSION WIND-- . . . .  328  2 DON JUAN  3      90    2
    AH SURELY NOTHING DIES BUT SOMETHING MOURNS . . . .  338  2 DON JUAN  3     108    8
    FOREVER AND ANON A SOMETHING SHOOK . . . . . . .  359  2 DON JUAN  4      29    4
    AND SOMETHING ROLL'D BEFORE HER IN A SHEET . . . .  361  2 DON JUAN  4      32    4
    FADED OR ALTER'D INTO SOMETHING NEW-- . . . . . .  363  2 DON JUAN  4      35    2
    BESIDES THY PRICE IS SOMETHING DEARER STILL . . . .  372  2 DON JUAN  4      53   V4
    RATHER THE DEAD FOR LIFE SEEM'D SOMETHING NEW . . .  378  2 DON JUAN  4      62    2
    YET SOMEHOW THERE WAS SOMETHING SOMEWHERE WANTING . .  474  2 DON JUAN  5     109    7
    SOMETHING IMPERIAL OR IMPERIOUS THREW . . . . . .  474  2 DON JUAN  5     110    1
    BUT THERE IS SOMETHING WHEN MAN'S EYE APPEARS . . .  479  2 DON JUAN  5     118    3
    BUT WOMAN WITH THE HEART--OR SOMETHING ELSE . . . .    7  3 DON JUAN  6       2   V8
    COMPANION SOMETHING NEWER STILL AS 'TWERE . . . .   25  3 DON JUAN  6      39    2
    I WISH IT NEVER LED TO SOMETHING WORSE . . . . .   35  3 DON JUAN  6      59    8
    BUT THERE SEEMED SOMETHING THAT HE WISHED TO HIDE . .   56  3 DON JUAN  6     100    5
    WITH SOMETHING NOT MUCH BETTER OR AS BAD . . . . .  122  3 DON JUAN  8      22    3
    'TWAS SOMETHING CALCULATED TO ALLAY . . . . . .  200  3 DON JUAN  9      36    4
    THERE WAS A SOMETHING IN HIS TURN OF LIMB . . . .  206  3 DON JUAN  9      47    3
    SOMETHING ABOUT THE BALTIC'S NAVIGATION . . . . .  246  3 DON JUAN 10      45    6
    JUST AS HE REALLY PROMISED SOMETHING GREAT . . . .  298  3 DON JUAN 11      60    2
    THERE'S LITTLE STRANGE IN THIS BUT SOMETHING STRANGE IS .  309  3 DON JUAN 11      81    7
    A PERIOD SOMETHING LIKE A PRINTED PAGE . . . . .  315  3 DON JUAN 12       1    6
    PERHAPS THERE MAY BE SOMETHING IN THE GROVE . . . .  322  3 DON JUAN 12      13    5
    METHINKS GAY PUNCH HATH SOMETHING OF THE SAME . . .  400  3 DON JUAN 13      89    4
    DREST VOTED SHONE AND MAYBE SOMETHING MORE . . . .  418  3 DON JUAN 14      18    2
    WHO ONE MIGHT THINK WAS SOMETHING IN THE AFFAIR . . .  430  3 DON JUAN 14      45    2
    BUT THERE WAS SOMETHING WANTING ON THE WHOLE-- . . .  441  3 DON JUAN 14      71    1
    STILL THERE WAS SOMETHING WANTING AS I'VE SAID-- . .  441  3 DON JUAN 14      72    1
    A SOMETHING ALL-SUFFICIENT FOR THE HEART . . . . .  442  3 DON JUAN 14      74    1
    A SOMETHING WHEREWITHAL TO BE ANNOY'D . . . . . .  444  3 DON JUAN 14      79    3
    SAY SOMETHING TO THE PURPOSE AND DISPLAY . . . . .  453  3 DON JUAN 14      98    7
    WE SURELY SHALL FIND SOMETHING WORTH RESEARCH . . .  468  3 DON JUAN 15      27    5
    SHE DEEMED HIS MERITS SOMETHING MORE THAN COMMON . .  473  3 DON JUAN 15      40    6
    IN LOVE THERE'S SOMETHING OF INTOXICATION . . . .  474  3 DON JUAN 15      41   V7
    IN FIGURE SHE HAD SOMETHING OF SUBLIME . . . . .  476  3 DON JUAN 15      45    2
    JUAN WAS SOMETHING SHE COULD NOT DIVINE . . . . .  480  3 DON JUAN 15      56    5
    OR SOMETHING WHICH WAS NOTHING AS URBANITY . . . .  490  3 DON JUAN 15      78    2
    BULL SOMETHING OF THE LOWER WORLD'S CONDITION . . .  497  3 DON JUAN 15      92    6
    'GAINST SUCH BELIEF THERE'S SOMETHING STRONGER STILL .  504  3 DON JUAN 16       7    7
    HAVE SOMETHING GHASTLY DESOLATE AND DREAD . . . .  508  3 DON JUAN 16      17    8
    THAT SOMETHING WAS THE MATTER--ADELINE . . . . .  513  3 DON JUAN 16      30    7
```

SOMETHING   (CONTINUED)
    SOMETHING BUT WHAT'S NOT STATED IN MY TALE 514   3 DON JUAN 16   31   3
    SOMETHING LIKE ILLNESS OF A SUDDEN GROWTH 514   3 DON JUAN 16   33   4
    TO SOMETHING LIKE THIS WHEN TOO OFT DISPLAYED 522   3 DON JUAN 16   44   5
    WERE SOMETHING VERY GLORIOUS TO BEHOLD 538   3 DON JUAN 16   78   4
    AND SOMETHING LIKE A SMILE UPON HER CHEEK 544   3 DON JUAN 16   92   2
    A SOMETHING MUCH MIRTH-MOVING--AND IN THIS 544   3 DON JUAN 16   92   V5
    FORTH INTO SOMETHING MUCH LIKE FLESH AND BLOOD 561   3 DON JUAN 16   123   4
    A SOMETHING LIKE IT--AS BEAR WITNESS LUTHER 565   3 DON JUAN 17   6   8
SOMETIMES
    HER WIT (SHE SOMETIMES TRIED AT WIT) WAS ATTIC ALL . . . 27   2 DON JUAN 1   12   3
    AND SOMETIMES MIX'D UP FANCIES WITH REALITIES 32   2 DON JUAN 1   20   6
    AND SOMETIMES LADIES HIT EXCEEDING HARD 33   2 DON JUAN 1   21   6
    SOMETIMES HE TURN'D TO GAZE UPON HIS BOOK 72   2 DON JUAN 1   95   1
    TO STRIFE 'TIS SOMETIMES SWEET TO HAVE OUR QUARRELS . . 90   2 DON JUAN 1   126   3
    PLEASURE'S A SIN AND SOMETIMES SIN'S A PLEASURE 93   2 DON JUAN 1   133   4
    FOR GROG AND SOMETIMES DRINK RUM FROM THE CASK 173   2 DON JUAN 2   33   8
    (FOR SOMETIMES WE MUST BOX WITHOUT THE MUFFLE) 205   2 DON JUAN 2   92   8
    AND SOMETIMES CAUGHT AS MANY AS HE WISH'D 223   2 DON JUAN 2   126   4
    THROBB'D IN ACCURSED DREAMS WHICH SOMETIMES SPREAD . . 227   2 DON JUAN 2   134   6
    WITH SOMETIMES MORE WITHIN THEM THAN ONE TONGUE 254   2 DON JUAN 2   187   V8
    THEY SOMETIMES ALSO GET A LITTLE TIRED 278   2 DON JUAN 3   7   2
    AND DAUGHTERS SOMETIMES RUN OFF WITH THE BUTLER 287   2 DON JUAN 3   22   8
    NOT THAT HE WAS NOT SOMETIMES RASH OR SO 300   2 DON JUAN 3   48   1
    NOT THAT HIS ANGER DID NOT SOMETIMES GLOW 300   2 DON JUAN 3   48   V1
    WE LEARN FROM HORACE HOMER SOMETIMES SLEEPS 333   2 DON JUAN 3   98   1
    WE FEEL WITHOUT HIM WORDSWORTH SOMETIMES WAKES 333   2 DON JUAN 3   98   2
    FOR SOMETIMES SUCH A WORLD OF VIRTUES COVER 405   2 DON JUAN 4   111   6
    OR SOMETIMES ONLY WEAR A WEEK OR TWO-- 422   2 DON JUAN 5   22   4
    (LOVE LIKE RELIGION SOMETIMES RUNS TO HERESY) 446   2 DON JUAN 5   61   4
    (THE RHYME OBLIGES ME TO THIS SOMETIMES 456   2 DON JUAN 5   77   7
    IN CONTACT AND SOMETIMES EVEN A FAIR STRANGER'S 472   2 DON JUAN 5   106   7
    IS SOMETIMES GOOD FOR PEOPLE IN HER STATION 490   2 DON JUAN 5   137   8
    BUT SOMETIMES IT MAY MEND AND OFTEN REACHES 491   2 DON JUAN 5   138   8
    SOMETIMES AT SIX YEARS OLD--THOUGH THIS SEEMS ODD . . . 498   2 DON JUAN 5   152   6
    THE TURKS DO WELL TO SHUT--AT LEAST SOMETIMES-- 501   2 DON JUAN 5   157   1
    MEANWHILE AS HOMER SOMETIMES SLEEPS PERHAPS 503   2 DON JUAN 5   159   7
    WHEN THINGS ARE AT THE WORST THEY SOMETIMES MEND   6   3 DON JUAN 6   1   8
    FOR GENTLEMEN MUST SOMETIMES RISK THEIR SKIN 10   3 DON JUAN 6   7   3
    I LOVE THE SEX AND SOMETIMES WOULD REVERSE 19   3 DON JUAN 6   27   1
    IN SOME EXOTIC GARDEN SOMETIMES FOUND 38   3 DON JUAN 6   65   3
    SOMETIMES A LITTLE HEAVY ON THE BACKS 54   3 DON JUAN 6   96   7
    BY DEEP EMOTION--YOU MAY SOMETIMES TRACE 61   3 DON JUAN 6   111   4
    OF THIS OUR BANQUET WE MUST SOMETIMES CHANGE 65   3 DON JUAN 6   120   4
    A PHANTASY WHICH SOMETIMES SEIZES WARRIORS 78   3 DON JUAN 7   24   7
    SOMETIMES CALLS MURDER AND AT OTHERS GLORY 79   3 DON JUAN 7   26   8
    AS SOMETIMES HAPPENS IN A GREAT EXTREMITY 92   3 DON JUAN 7   51   4
    LURKED CHRISTIANITY WHICH SOMETIMES BARTERS 96   3 DON JUAN 7   57   6
    IS BUTCHERY SOMETIMES A SINGLE SORROW 102   3 DON JUAN 7   69   7
    OF DEAD AND DYING THOUSANDS--SOMETIMES GAINING 121   3 DON JUAN 8   20   2
    THEY SOMETIMES WITH A HANKERING FOR EXISTENCE 151   3 DON JUAN 8   78   7
    FOR WHAT IS SOMETIMES CALLED POETIC DICTION 154   3 DON JUAN 8   86   6
    NOW MOVED WITH PITY EVEN AS SOMETIMES NODS 164   3 DON JUAN 8   106   6
    FOR ME I SOMETIMES THINK THAT LIFE IS DEATH 190   3 DON JUAN 9   16   7
    AS SOMETIMES HAVE BEEN GREATER SAGES' LOTS-- 200   3 DON JUAN 9   36   3
    BESIDES THE EMPRESS SOMETIMES LIKED A BOY 206   3 DON JUAN 9   47   7
    (AS IT WILL LOOK SOMETIMES WITH THE FIRST STARE 224   3 DON JUAN 9   84   4
    PEEP OUT SOMETIMES WHEN THINGS ARE IN A FLURRY 237   3 DON JUAN 10   26   5
    HE SOMETIMES THOUGHT 'TWAS ONLY THEIR SALAM 274   3 DON JUAN 11   12   4
    OR MANY (FOR THE NUMBER'S SOMETIMES SUCH) 305   3 DON JUAN 11   73   5
    FOR SOMETIMES THEY ACCEPT SOME LONG PURSUER 333   3 DON JUAN 12   37   1
    THOUGH 'TWAS NOT ONCE SO   IF I SNEER SOMETIMES 361   3 DON JUAN 13   8   2
    ALWAYS A PATRIOT AND SOMETIMES A PLACEMAN 368   3 DON JUAN 13   21   8
    IN FAULTS WHICH SOMETIMES SHOW THE SOIL'S FERTILITY . . 368   3 DON JUAN 13   22   6
    THUS GENTLEMEN MAY SOMETIMES PLAY THE FOOL 376   3 DON JUAN 13   39   V6
    IS SOMETIMES TRUCULENT--BUT NEVER MIND 377   3 DON JUAN 13   41   2
    SOMETIMES A LITTLE LATER   I DON'T ERR 378   3 DON JUAN 13   43   2
    BUT SOMETIMES STUMBLING OVER A POTATOE-- 401   3 DON JUAN 13   92   7
    AT LONGBOW'S PHRASES YOU MIGHT SOMETIMES CARP 402   3 DON JUAN 13   93   6
    SOMETIMES A DANCE (THOUGH RARELY ON FIELD DAYS 408   3 DON JUAN 13   108   1
    SOMETIMES WITH AND SOMETIMES WITHOUT OCCASION 413   3 DON JUAN 14   7   4
    SOMETIMES WITH AND SOMETIMES WITHOUT OCCASION 413   3 DON JUAN 14   7   4
    SOMETIMES INDEED LIKE SOLDIERS OFF PARADE 417   3 DON JUAN 14   17   1
    BUT LEAPS AND BURSTS AND SOMETIMES FOX'S BRUSHES . . . 425   3 DON JUAN 14   35   2
    THOUGH EVEN THAT WERE SOMETIMES TOO FEROCIOUS 443   3 DON JUAN 14   77   5
    AS THOSE OF ARISTOTLE THOUGH SOMETIMES 470   3 DON JUAN 15   32   7
    WHICH SOMETIMES PLAYS THE DEUCE WITH WOMANKIND 480   3 DON JUAN 15   57   2
    BUT AFTER THERE ARE SOMETIMES CERTAIN SIGNS 488   3 DON JUAN 15   72   5
    I SOMETIMES ALMOST THINK THAT EYES HAVE EARS 489   3 DON JUAN 15   76   1
    BECAUSE IT SOMETIMES AS I'VE SEEN OR READ IT 491   3 DON JUAN 15   79   3
    ARE TOPICS WHICH I SOMETIMES INTRODUCE 497   3 DON JUAN 15   93   2
    THE NIGHT (I SING BY NIGHT--SOMETIMES AN OWL 499   3 DON JUAN 15   97   1
    SOMETIMES UNLESS MY FEELINGS RATHER ERR) 506   3 DON JUAN 16   14   5
    WHY FAME--BUT FAME YOU KNOW'S SOMETIMES A LIAR-- . . . 516   3 DON JUAN 16   36   3
    WHO WOULD SUPPOSE THY GIFTS SOMETIMES OBDURATE) 540   3 DON JUAN 16   82   6
    THOUGH SOMETIMES FAINTLY FLUSHED--AND ALWAYS CLEAR . . 545   3 DON JUAN 16   94   7
    HEROES SOMETIMES THOUGH SELDOM--SAGES NEVER 547   3 DON JUAN 16   98   2
    CHEERFUL--BUT SOMETIMES RATHER APT TO WHIMPER 567   3 DON JUAN 17   11   5
SOMEWHAT
    SENT TO THE DEVIL SOMEWHAT ERE HIS TIME 21   2 DON JUAN 1   1   8

SOMEWHAT   (CONTINUED)

	PAGE	VOL		CANTO	STANZA	LN
NARRATING SOMEWHAT OF DON JUAN'S FATHER	25	2 DON JUAN	1	7	7
AN ORDER SOMEWHAT SULLENLY OBEY'D	116	2 DON JUAN	1	173	4
AND CAMPBELL'S HIPPOCRENE IS SOMEWHAT DROUTHY	139	2 DON JUAN	1	205	6
AND CAMPBELL'S SPRING SEEMS SOMEWHAT DRY AND DROUTHY	139	2 DON JUAN	1	205	V6
FOR JUAN WHO WAS SOMEWHAT FOND OF REST--	245	2 DON JUAN	2	168	2
ARE SOMEWHAT SICK AND SORRY THE NEXT DAY	343	2 DON JUAN	3	V 98	8
THOUGH SOMEWHAT GRIEVED COULD SCARCE FORBEAR A SMILE	459	2 DON JUAN	5	83	3
THAT SOMEWHAT MANLY MAJESTY OF STRIDE	464	2 DON JUAN	5	91	4
WOMEN ON T'OTHER HAND SEEM SOMEWHAT SILLY	14	3 DON JUAN	6	16	8
BEING SOMEWHAT LARGE AND LANGUISHING AND LAZY	26	3 DON JUAN	6	41	7
UNTO THAT RATHER SOMEWHAT MISTY BOURN	133	3 DON JUAN	8	41	3
THOUGH SOMEWHAT LARGE EXUBERANT AND TRUCULENT	213	3 DON JUAN	9	62	1
TO GERMANY WHOSE SOMEWHAT TARDY MILLIONS	254	3 DON JUAN	10	60	7
AND SEA-SICK PASSENGERS TURNED SOMEWHAT PALE	256	3 DON JUAN	10	64	5
AND BEING SOMEWHAT CHOLERIC AND SUDDEN	274	3 DON JUAN	11	13	2
THE VERY CLERKS--THOSE SOMEWHAT DIRTY SPRINGS	287	3 DON JUAN	11	40	5
AND AFTER THAT SERENE AND SOMEWHAT DULL	360	3 DON JUAN	13	4	1
EMBARRASS'D SOMEWHAT BOTH WITH FIRE AND WATER	423	3 DON JUAN	14	30	8
SHE WAS A FINE AND SOMEWHAT FULL-BLOWN BLONDE	428	3 DON JUAN	14	42	1
AND SOMEWHAT MECHANTE IN HER AMOROUS SPHERE	438	3 DON JUAN	14	63	2
JUAN FELT SOMEWHAT PENSIVE AND DISPOSED	507	3 DON JUAN	16	15	1
TO GATHER TO A SOMEWHAT LARGE AMOUNT HE	535	3 DON JUAN	16	71	5
AND WITCHES UNTO NONE THOUGH SOMEWHAT LATE	565	3 DON JUAN	17	7	2

SOMEWHERE

	PAGE	VOL		CANTO	STANZA	LN
AS SOMEONE SOMEWHERE SINGS ABOUT THE SKY	404	2 DON JUAN	4	110	2
YET SOMEHOW THERE WAS SOMETHING SOMEWHERE WANTING	474	2 DON JUAN	5	109	7
SHEWED THAT SOMEWHERE SOMEHOW THERE WAS A FAULT	83	3 DON JUAN	7	35	2
THIS MAY BE FIXED AT SOMEWHERE BEFORE THIRTY--	433	3 DON JUAN	14	53	1

SON

	PAGE	VOL		CANTO	STANZA	LN
HE DID NOT LOATHE THE SIRE TO LAUD THE SON	15	2 DON JUAN	D	10	7
DON JOSE LIKE A LINEAL SON OF EVE	30	2 DON JUAN	1	18	7
AN ONLY SON LEFT WITH AN ONLY MOTHER	42	2 DON JUAN	1	37	7
KEPT THIS HERSELF AND GAVE HER SON ANOTHER	47	2 DON JUAN	1	46	8
FROM SIRE TO SON TO AUGUR GOOD OR ILL	49	2 DON JUAN	1	51	5
THAT IF I HAD AN ONLY SON TO PUT	50	2 DON JUAN	1	52	3
UNTIL IT CENTER'D IN AN ONLY SON	54	2 DON JUAN	1	59	3
HER ONLY SON WITH QUESTION OR SURMISE	73	2 DON JUAN	1	97	6
SHE WHO FOR MANY YEARS HAD WATCH'D HER SON SO--	80	2 DON JUAN	1	110	7
SHE SENT HER SON TO BE SHIPP'D OFF FROM CADIZ	128	2 DON JUAN	1	190	8
HER SON TO CADIZ ONLY TO EMBARK	161	2 DON JUAN	2	8	2
SUCH THINGS A MOTHER HAD NOT KNOWN HER SON	210	2 DON JUAN	2	102	3
THETIS BAPTIZED HER MORTAL SON IN STYX	346	2 DON JUAN	4	4	7
OF FOOD I THINK WITH PHILIP'S SON OR RATHER	427	2 DON JUAN	5	31	7
A SCOLDING WIFE A SULLEN SON A BILL	16	3 DON JUAN	6	21	1
HER SON'S SON LET NOT THIS LAST PHRASE OFFEND	52	3 DON JUAN	6	93	2
YOUR FATHER'S SON 'TIS QUITE ENOUGH FOR ME	52	3 DON JUAN	6	93	8
BUT NOW INSTEAD OF SLAYING PRIAM'S SON	106	3 DON JUAN	7	78	5
THOUGH LED BY ARSENIEW THAT GREAT SON OF SLAUGHTER	116	3 DON JUAN	8	9	4
DESCRIBING PRIAM'S PELEUS' OR JOVE'S SON	164	3 DON JUAN	8	105	6
HIS SECOND SON WAS LEVELLED BY A SHOT	166	3 DON JUAN	8	110	2
A GLANCE ON THAT SLAIN SON HIS FIRST AND LAST	169	3 DON JUAN	8	116	8
SIGH LIKE HIS SON THAN COUGH LIKE HIS GRANDFATHER	228	3 DON JUAN	10	6	8
AND NO LESS TO GOD'S SON AS WELL AS MOTHER	240	3 DON JUAN	10	32	2
HAD TOLD HIS SON TO SATISFY HIS CRAVING	263	3 DON JUAN	10	78	6
THE SUN'S TRUE SON NO VAPOUR BUT A RAY	300	3 DON JUAN	11	64	8
AS PHILIP'S SON PROPOSED TO DO WITH ATHOS	355	3 DON JUAN	12	86	8
MAN'S PITY'S FOR HIMSELF OR FOR HIS SON	377	3 DON JUAN	13	42	6
ALWAYS PROMISING THAT SAID SON AT COLLEGE	377	3 DON JUAN	13	42	7
WITH HER SON IN HER BLESSED ARMS LOOK'D ROUND	387	3 DON JUAN	13	61	3
TO BEAR A SON AND HEIR--AND ONE MISCARRIAGE	434	3 DON JUAN	14	56	8
THEY GENERALLY HAVE SOME ONLY SON	470	3 DON JUAN	15	33	1
HIS SON THE HONOURABLE DICK DICEDRABBIT	534	3 DON JUAN	16	70	6
I SATE NEXT THAT O'ERWHELMING SON OF HEAVEN	539	3 DON JUAN	16	81	6

SONG

	PAGE	VOL		CANTO	STANZA	LN
(THIS OLD SONG AND NEW SIMILE HOLDS GOOD)	10	2 DON JUAN	D	2	2
IN HONEST SIMPLE VERSE THIS SONG TO YOU	20	2 DON JUAN	D	17	2
SHE PROVED IT SOMEHOW OUT OF SACRED SONG	28	2 DON JUAN	1	14	3
FOR SPEAKING OUT SO PLAINLY IN HIS SONG	45	2 DON JUAN	1	43	5
WITH ALL THE TROPHIES OF TRIUMPHANT SONG--	77	2 DON JUAN	1	104	7
THE SONG AND OAR OF ADRIA'S GONDOLIER	87	2 DON JUAN	1	122	3
OF BEES THE VOICE OF GIRLS THE SONG OF BIRDS	88	2 DON JUAN	1	123	7
THEIR LEADER SANG--AND BOUNDED TO HER SONG	291	2 DON JUAN	3	30	7
SONG DANCE WINE MUSIC STORIES FROM THE PERSIAN	293	2 DON JUAN	3	35	3
IT MADE ANACREON'S SONG DIVINE	324	2 DON JUAN	3	L 11	3
OF SENSE AND SONG ABOVE YOUR GRAVES MAY HISS--	334	2 DON JUAN	3	100	6
THE ARAB LORE AND POET'S SONG WERE DONE	334	2 DON JUAN	3	101	3
MAKING THEIR SUMMER LIVES ONE CEASELESS SONG	337	2 DON JUAN	3	106	2
FOR BEINGS PASSIONATE AS SAPPHO'S SONG	358	2 DON JUAN	4	27	6
RANG IN HER SAD EARS LIKE A MERMAID'S SONG	362	2 DON JUAN	4	34	7
AND HE BEGUN A LONG LOW ISLAND SONG	379	2 DON JUAN	4	65	7
BUT MANY A GREEK MAID IN A LOVING SONG	383	2 DON JUAN	4	73	1
BUT MANY A FISHER IN HIS RUGGED SONG	383	2 DON JUAN	4	73	V1
BUT IF THE SULTAN HAS A TASTE FOR SONG	389	2 DON JUAN	4	82	7
AND SIGH TO MIDNIGHT WINDS BUT NOT TO SONG	398	2 DON JUAN	4	99	8
SONG IN THE WORLD WILL SEEK WHAT THEN THEY SOUGHT	402	2 DON JUAN	4	106	4
ALL THIS MUST BE RESERVED FOR FURTHER SONG	410	2 DON JUAN	4	117	1
BUT I DETEST ALL FICTION EVEN IN SONG	10	3 DON JUAN	6	8	3
A THING OF IMPULSE AND A CHILD OF SONG	123	3 DON JUAN	8	24	2

SONG   (CONTINUED)
```
    WITHOUT WHICH GLORY'S BUT A TAVERN SONG--      . . . . .   144  3 DON JUAN  8    63   4
    OR AT THE LEAST WOULD LENGTHEN OUT MY SONG--   . . . . .   338  3 DON JUAN 12    48   6
    ALAS  MUST NOBLEST VIEWS LIKE AN OLD SONG      . . . . .   363  3 DON JUAN 13    10   5
    THE RED GRAPE IN THE SUNNY LANDS OF SONG .     . . . . .   394  3 DON JUAN 13    76   4
    ALL SONG AND SENTIMENT WHOSE HEARTS WERE SET   . . . . .   398  3 DON JUAN 13    85   7
    IS MUCH MORE TO THE PURPOSE OF HIS SONG        . . . . .   443  3 DON JUAN 14    77   4
    THE SONG WAS SILENT AND THE DANCE EXPIRED      . . . . .   504  3 DON JUAN 16     8   4
    AND THE PAUSE FOLLOWED WHICH WHEN SONG EXPIRES . . . . .   521  3 DON JUAN 16    41   3
    THE COST WOULD BE A TRIFLE--AN OLD SONG        . . . . .   529  3 DON JUAN 16    59   1
    THERE IS A DIFFERENCE SAYS THE SONG BETWEEN .  . . . . .   541  3 DON JUAN 16    84   1
SONG-BIRDS
    THE SWEETEST SONG-BIRDS NESTLE IN A PAIR .     . . . . .   358  2 DON JUAN  4    28   6
SONGS
    HE DEIGN'D NOT TO BELIE HIS SOUL IN SONGS      . . . . .    15  2 DON JUAN  D    10   5
    BUT VIRGIL'S SONGS ARE PURE EXCEPT THAT HORRID ONE . . .    45  2 DON JUAN  1    42   7
    WILL SINK WHERE LIE THE SONGS AND WARS OF EARTH  . . . .   400  2 DON JUAN  4   104   7
SONGSTER
    AS HAWKS MAY POUNCE UPON A WOODLAND SONGSTER   . . . . .   285  3 DON JUAN 11    35   8
SONGSTRESS
    FOR ONE A SONGSTRESS WHO HATH NO DEFECT .      . . . . .   471  3 DON JUAN 15    34   8
SONNETS
    HE WOULD HAVE WRITTEN SONNETS ALL HIS LIFE     . . . . .   279  2 DON JUAN  3     8   8
    HOW MANY SONNETS HAD ENSUED THE BEDDING .      . . . . .   279  2 DON JUAN  3     8   V8
    THE BLUES THAT TENDER TRIBE WHO SIGH O'ER SONNETS . . . .  294  3 DON JUAN 11    50   1
    WERE SONNETS TO HERSELF OR BOUTS RIMES         . . . . .   525  3 DON JUAN 16    50   8
SON'S
    LOOK UP TO THINE AND TO THY SON'S ABOVE .      . . . . .   336  2 DON JUAN  3   103   4
    HER SON'S SON LET NOT THIS LAST PHRASE OFFEND  . . . . .    52  3 DON JUAN  6    93   2
    AT THEIR LORD'S SON'S OR SIMILAR CONNECTION'S  . . . . .   546  3 DON JUAN 16    95   7
SONS
    THAT SONS SHOULD NOT BE EDUCATED SO .          . . . . .    50  2 DON JUAN  1    53   8
    THE SONS NO MORE WERE SHORT THE DAUGHTERS PLAIN  . . . .    53  2 DON JUAN  1    58   5
    AND WITH THEM THEIR TWO SONS OF WHOM THE ONE   . . . . .   202  2 DON JUAN  2    87   2
    E'ER SAW HER MOST POLITE OF SONS EXCEEDING     . . . . .   299  2 DON JUAN  3    46   4
    HE HAD FIFTY DAUGHTERS AND FOUR DOZEN SONS     . . . . .   498  2 DON JUAN  5   152   1
    HIS SONS WERE KEPT IN PRISON TILL THEY GREW .  . . . . .   499  2 DON JUAN  5   153   1
    BUT FLANKED BY FIVE BRAVE SONS (SUCH IS POLYGAMY  . . . .  164  3 DON JUAN  8   105   1
    AND POURED UPON HIM AND HIS SONS LIKE RAIN     . . . . .   166  3 DON JUAN  8   109   7
    AND THROWING BACK A DIM LOOK ON HIS SONS .     . . . . .   170  3 DON JUAN  8   118   7
    REVERED THE SOIL OF THOSE TRUE SONS THE MOTHER . . . . .   265  3 DON JUAN 10    81   7
    LIKE LAP-DOGS THE LEAST CIVIL SONS OF BITCHES  . . . . .   288  3 DON JUAN 11    41   8
    IN LIEU OF SONS OF THESE HE MADE NO BONES      . . . . .   410  3 DON JUAN 14     1   8
SOON
    CADIZ PERHAPS--BUT THAT YOU SOON MAY SEE--     . . . . .    25  2 DON JUAN  1     8   6
    WHO CALL'D HER CHASTE METHINKS BEGAN TOO SOON  . . . . .    82  2 DON JUAN  1   113   3
    AND MADE A SCENE MEN DO NOT SOON FORGET        . . . . .   172  2 DON JUAN  2    31   3
    AND SHOULD HE HAVE FORGOTTEN HER SO SOON       . . . . .   267  2 DON JUAN  2   208   2
    BUT SOON PHILOSOPHY CAME TO MY AID .  .        . . . . .   268  2 DON JUAN  2   210   1
    UNTIL SHE SOBB'D FOR BREATH AND SOON THEY WERE . . . . .   361  2 DON JUAN  4    31   6
    FOR SOON OR LATE LOVE IS HIS OWN AVENGER .     . . . . .   383  2 DON JUAN  4    73   8
    THEREFORE I'LL MAKE DON JUAN LEAVE THE SHIP SOON . . . .   397  2 DON JUAN  4    97   5
    WHO LIVED TOO LONG FOR MEN BUT DIED TOO SOON   . . . . .   400  2 DON JUAN  4   103   3
    O'ERTHROWN EVEN MEN HE SOON BEGAN TO SHOW      . . . . .   417  2 DON JUAN  5    12   4
    BUT THEY AS SOON SHALL CIRCUMCISE MY HEAD      . . . . .   452  2 DON JUAN  5    71   8
    SIR--AS I SAID AS SOON AS I HAVE SUPT .        . . . . .   453  2 DON JUAN  5    72   4
    THAT SOON HIS HEAD WAS MOST COMPLETELY CROWNED . . . . .   457  2 DON JUAN  5    79   4
    I YIELD THUS FAR BUT SOON WILL BREAK THE CHARM . . . . .   459  2 DON JUAN  5    82   5
    BUT TEARS MUST STOP LIKE ALL THINGS ELSE AND SOON  . . .   481  2 DON JUAN  5   121   1
    YOUR SLAVE BRINGS TIDINGS--HE HOPES NOT TOO SOON--  . . .  494  2 DON JUAN  5   144   5
    AS SOON AS THEY RE-ENTERED THEIR OWN ROOM  .   . . . . .    57  3 DON JUAN  6   103   3
    IN SHORT ALL KNOW OR VERY SOON MAY KNOW IT  .  . . . . .    69  3 DON JUAN  7     6   4
    THE MATCH WAS LIT TOO SOON AND NO ASSISTANCE   . . . . .    80  3 DON JUAN  7    28   5
    WHICH CURL IN CURIOUS WREATHS--HOW SOON THE SMOKE  . . .   110  3 DON JUAN  7    86   7
    SOUNDS LESS HARMONIOUS UNDERNEATH THE SUN SOON . . . . .   132  3 DON JUAN  8    39   3
    OFT ARE SOON CLOSED ALL HEROES ARE NOT BLIND . . . . . .   133  3 DON JUAN  8    40   6
    HIS THANKS AND HOPES TO TAKE THE CITY SOON .   . . . . .   140  3 DON JUAN  8    56   6
    AS SOON AS THUNDER 'MIDST THE GENERAL NOISE .  . . . . .   142  3 DON JUAN  8    59   7
    FOR THOSE FOR WHOM IT SOON SHALL CEASE TO BEAT . . . . .   152  3 DON JUAN  8    82   4
    WHICH IS FULL SOON (THOUGH LIFE IS BUT A SPAN) . . . . .   222  3 DON JUAN  9    79   4
    WITH ALL KINDS OF MECHANICS AND FULL SOON  .   . . . . .   226  3 DON JUAN 10     2   7
    BUT SOON THEY GROW AGAIN AND LEAVE THEIR NEST  . . . . .   228  3 DON JUAN 10     6   1
    BUT JUAN WAS NOT MEANT TO DIE SO SOON .  .     . . . . .   229  3 DON JUAN 10     9   1
    AS SOON AS CROWNER'S QUEST ALLOWED PURSUED     . . . . .   277  3 DON JUAN 11    18   3
    WHERE IS HIS WILL  (THAT'S NOT SO SOON UNRIDDLED)  . . .   307  3 DON JUAN 11    78   3
    SOME ARE SOON BAGGED BUT SOME REJECT THREE DOZEN  . . . .  332  3 DON JUAN 12    34   1
    THOSE BECAME ONE WHO SOON WERE TO BE TWO .     . . . . .   334  3 DON JUAN 12    38   6
    FOR FAME'S A CARTHAGE NOT SO SOON REBUILT .    . . . . .   352  3 DON JUAN 12    78   8
    MAY THE ROSE CALL BACK ITS TRUE COLOURS SOON   . . . . .   409  3 DON JUAN 13   111   6
    THE GILDING WEARS SO SOON FROM OFF HER FETTER  . . . . .   421  3 DON JUAN 14    25   5
    A MAN LIKE WHOM I HOPE WE SHAN'T SEE MANY SOON . . . . .   484  3 DON JUAN 15    65   4
    ASIDE HIS VERY MIRROR SOON WAS PUT .  .        . . . . .   513  3 DON JUAN 16    29   4
    WHICH HE PERHAPS HAD NOT DISCOVERED SOON .     . . . . .   513  3 DON JUAN 16    30   3
    SHE SEIZED HER HARP WHOSE STRINGS WERE KINDLED SOON  . .   517  3 DON JUAN 16    38   6
    TOO SOON THEY ARE PARENTS TO THEMSELVES FOR WHAT  . . . .  564  3 DON JUAN 17     4   1
SOONER
    NO SOONER WAS IT BOLTED THAN--OH SHAME .       . . . . .   112  2 DON JUAN  1   165   1
    SOONER SHALL THIS BLUE OCEAN MELT TO AIR .     . . . . .   166  2 DON JUAN  2    19   3
    SOONER SHALL EARTH RESOLVE ITSELF TO SEA .     . . . . .   166  2 DON JUAN  2    19   4
```

PAGE VOL   CANTO STANZA LN

SOONER (CONTINUED)
    SOONER SHALL HEAVEN KISS EARTH--(HERE HE FELL SICKER) . . 167 2 DON JUAN 2   20   1
    BUT VIOLENT THINGS WILL SOONER BEAR ASSUAGING . . . . 305 2 DON JUAN 3   58   5
    IT SOONER FOR THE SOUL OF ME AND CLASS . . . . . 34 3 DON JUAN 6   56   5
    AND IS EXTINGUISHED SOONER THAN SHE OUGHT . . . . 83 3 DON JUAN 7   34   6
    SOONER COME PLACE INTO THE CIVIL LIST . . . . . 536 3 DON JUAN 16   75   1
SOON'S
    THE LADY ADELINE AS SOON'S SHE SAW . . . . 436 3 DON JUAN 14   60   3
SOOT
    THE ENDLESS SOOT BESTOWS A TINT FAR DEEPER . . . . 232 3 DON JUAN 10   15   3
SOOTH
    AS IF HER VEINS RAN LIGHTNING SHE IN SOOTH . . . 55 2 DON JUAN 1   61   6
    I WISH THESE LAST HAD NOT OCCURR'D IN SOOTH . . . 78 2 DON JUAN 1   107   5
    BUT OTHER SPECULATIONS WERE IN SOOTH . . . . . 222 2 DON JUAN 2   125   3
    BECAUSE THE PUBLISHER DECLARES IN SOOTH . . . . 397 2 DON JUAN 4   97   6
    WHICH IS BUT A PRECARIOUS BOND IN SOOTH . . . . 14 3 DON JUAN 6   16   5
    AND MY SUCCESS PRODUCED WHAT I IN SOOTH . . . . 324 3 DON JUAN 12   17   4
SOOTHE
    AND BATHING HIS CHILL TEMPLES TRIED TO SOOTHE . . . 215 2 DON JUAN 2   113   5
    NO DOUBT CAN SOOTHE THEM WITH A LULLABY-- . . . 272 2 DON JUAN 2 V 1   5
    TO SOOTHE HIS WOES WITHAL WAS SLAIN--THE SINNER . . 199 3 DON JUAN 9   33   7
    THE INSOLENT SOLDIERY TO SOOTHE AND FLATTER . . 299 3 DON JUAN 11   62   4
    OF OTHER STONES TO SOOTHE THE MISER'S EYES . . . 319 3 DON JUAN 12   8   8
    BUT EVER AND ANON TO SOOTHE YOUR VISION . . . 392 3 DON JUAN 13   71   1
    TO SOOTHE OUR EARS LEST ITALY SHOULD FAIL . . . 523 3 DON JUAN 16   45   8
SOOTHERS
    THOSE CAPTIVE SOOTHERS OF A CAPTIVE'S HOURS . . . 54 3 DON JUAN 6   97   8
SOOTHES
    IT SOOTHES THE AWKWARD SQUAD OF THE REJECTED . . 333 3 DON JUAN 12   36   7
SOOTHING
    BESIDES THOSE SOOTHING SPEECHES OF THE PLEADERS . . 346 3 DON JUAN 12   65   7
SOOTY
    OF LIFE SHRUNK IN HIS HEART AND THICK AND SOOTY . . 276 3 DON JUAN 11   16   5
SOPHAS
    AND ON OUR SOPHAS MAKES US LIE DEJECTED . . . 301 3 DON JUAN 11   65   5
SOPHIA'S
    SOPHIA'S CUPOLA WITH GOLDEN GLEAM . . . . . . 412 2 DON JUAN 5   3   4
SOPHIAS
    AND OUR SOPHIAS ARE NOT SO EMPHATIC . . . . . 409 3 DON JUAN 13   110   5
SOPHISTRY
    FLOURISHED ITS SOPHISTRY FOR ARISTOCRACY . . . 329 2 DON JUAN 3   93 V6
SOPHY
    WITH GORE LIKE NADIR SHAH THAT COSTIVE SOPHY . . 199 3 DON JUAN 9   33   4
SOPORIFIC
    TOO MUCH OF ONE SORT WOULD BE SOPORIFIC-- . . . 156 3 DON JUAN 8   89   6
SOPRANO
    IF THE SOPRANO MIGHT BE DEEM'D TO BE MALE . . . 394 2 DON JUAN 4   92   4
SORE
    AND PITYING SORE HIS MUTILATED CASE . . . . . 46 2 DON JUAN 1   44   6
    GRATEFUL SHE WAS AND YET A LITTLE SORE-- . . . 63 2 DON JUAN 1   76   5
    ANTONIA LET HIM--NOT A LITTLE SORE . . . . . 111 2 DON JUAN 1   164   4
    WITHIN HIS GRASP HE CLUNG TO IT AND SORE . . . 212 2 DON JUAN 2   107   5
    REPLIED THE OTHER THOUGH IT GRIEVES ME SORE . . 460 2 DON JUAN 5   84   3
    IN THIS EXTENSIVE CITY SORE BESET . . . . . 131 3 DON JUAN 8   37   4
SORRIER
    A SORRIER STILL IS THE GREAT MORAL TAUGHT . . . 363 3 DON JUAN 13   9   7
SORROW
    OH SIN OH SORROW AND OH WOMANKIND . . . . . 112 2 DON JUAN 1   165   2
    MY SHAME AND SORROW DEEP IN MY HEART'S CORE . . 132 2 DON JUAN 1   195   4
    I HAD NOT LIVED TILL NOW COULD SORROW KILL . . 134 2 DON JUAN 1   197   5
    BEFORE THE SHRINES OF SORROW AND OF PLEASURE . . 145 2 DON JUAN 1   217   2
    AND THAT HIS SORROW MAY NOT BE A DUMB ONE . . . 288 2 DON JUAN 3   24   7
    EVEN TIME THE PITILESS IN SORROW CLEFT . . . 348 2 DON JUAN 4   8   3
    WITH JOY AND SORROW HOPE AND FEAR TO SEE . . . 363 2 DON JUAN 4   36   2
    HER THOUGHTS FROM SORROW THROUGH HER HEART RE-SENT . 379 2 DON JUAN 4   65   6
    SHALL SORROW LIGHT OR SHAME SHE WAS NOT MADE . . 382 2 DON JUAN 4   71   2
    FOR SORROW O'ER EACH SENSE HELD STERN COMMAND . . 396 2 DON JUAN 4   95   2
    AND LOVE DESTROY AND SAPPING SORROW WRINGS . . 468 2 DON JUAN 5   98   6
    TO SUCH A SORROW BY THE INTRUSIVE TONE . . . 481 2 DON JUAN 5   121   3
    BUT HE WAS STEELED BY SORROW WRATH AND PRIDE . . 484 2 DON JUAN 5   126   2
    THE TRAITS OF SLEEPING SORROW AND BETRAYED . . 40 3 DON JUAN 6   67   4
    IS BUTCHERY SOMETIMES A SINGLE SORROW . . . 102 3 DON JUAN 7   69   7
    NOR SWORD NOR SORROW YET HAD LEFT A TRACE . . . 145 3 DON JUAN 8   65   4
    THERE IS A MOVE SET DOWN FOR JOY OR SORROW . . 288 3 DON JUAN 11   42   4
SORROWING
    AUGHT OF A SERIOUS SORROWING KIND ALTHOUGH . . 480 2 DON JUAN 5   119   5
SORROWS
    AND LAY THIS SHEET OF SORROWS ON THE SHELF . . 384 2 DON JUAN 4   74   2
    OUR LEAST OF SORROWS ARE SUCH AS WE WEEP . . . 16 3 DON JUAN 6   20   6
SORRY
    I'M ALMOST SORRY THAT I E'ER BEGUN . . . . . 83 2 DON JUAN 1   115   8
    I'M VERY SORRY VERY MUCH ASHAMED . . . . . 85 2 DON JUAN 1   119   7
    HOW SORRY YOU WILL BE WHEN I'VE MISCARRIED . . 101 2 DON JUAN 1   147   8
    I'M SORRY THUS TO PROBE A WOUND SO RAW . . . 155 2 DON JUAN 1 V 7   5
    ARE SOMEWHAT SICK AND SORRY THE NEXT DAY . . . 343 3 DON JUAN 3 V 98   8
    AND SAID THAT SHE WAS SORRY SHE HAD CRIED . . . 45 3 DON JUAN 6   79   8
    BUT HIS ADVENTURES FORM A SORRY SIGHT-- . . . 363 3 DON JUAN 13   9   6
    OR NONE AT ALL--WHICH SEEMS A SORRY JEST . . . 494 3 DON JUAN 15   87   6
    AND THESE DISSENTIONS MAKE A SORRY SIGHT . . . 496 3 DON JUAN 15   90 V4

	PAGE	VOL		CANTO	STANZA	LV
SORT						
WITH PERSONS OF NO SORT OF EDUCATION	33	2	DON JUAN	1	22	2
FOR SOME TIME AN UNHAPPY SORT OF LIFE	35	2	DON JUAN	1	26	2
NO SORT OF EXPLANATION COULD BE HAD	35	2	DON JUAN	1	27	6
THERE'S MERIT IN THIS SORT OF RESURRECTION	37	2	DON JUAN	1	31	V7
WERE FORCED TO MAKE AN ODD SORT OF APOLOGY	44	2	DON JUAN	1	41	7
WAS ORNAMENTED IN A SORT OF WAY	47	2	DON JUAN	1	46	2
IN SPAIN YOU KNOW THIS IS A SORT OF SIN)	52	2	DON JUAN	1	56	4
THEY ARE A SORT OF POST-HOUSE WHERE THE FATES	76	2	DON JUAN	1	103	4
THERE'S SOMETHING CHEERFUL IN THAT SORT OF LIGHT	94	2	DON JUAN	1	135	5
AND SEEMS TO ME ALMOST A SORT OF BLUNDER	100	2	DON JUAN	1	144	7
A SORT OF INCOME-TAX LAID ON BY FATE	122	2	DON JUAN	1	183	4
AND WOULD NOT BROOK AT ALL THIS SORT OF THING	143	2	DON JUAN	1	212	7
A SORT OF ORATOR BY SUFFERANCE	152	2	DON JUAN	1	V 3	5
A SORT OF BLOTTED SHIELD FEW KNIGHTS WOULD WEAR	153	2	DON JUAN	1	V 4	V6
THERE IS A SORT OF UNEXPREST CONCERN	164	2	DON JUAN	2	14	5
A SORT OF THING AT WHICH ONE WOULD HAVE LAUGH'D	183	2	DON JUAN	2	50	3
WHICH SERVED THEM AS A SORT OF SPONGY PITCHER	201	2	DON JUAN	2	85	3
AND STILL A SORT OF FISHERMAN WAS HE	222	2	DON JUAN	2	125	2
IN GAINING ALL THAT USEFUL SORT OF KNOWLEDGE	228	2	DON JUAN	2	136	7
THE SORT OF SOUND WE ECHO WITH A TEAR	236	2	DON JUAN	2	151	6
THIS SORT OF ADORATION OF THE REAL	269	2	DON JUAN	2	211	7
THE ONLY THING OF THIS SORT EVER SEEN	288	2	DON JUAN	3	25	4
IN GREECE HE'D SING SOME SORT OF HYMN LIKE THIS T'YE	320	2	DON JUAN	3	86	8
THAT TRASH OF SUCH SORT NOT ALONE EVADES	334	2	DON JUAN	3	100	3
SHE TURN'D TO HIM AND SMILED BUT IN THAT SORT	356	2	DON JUAN	4	23	1
AND CONSCIENCE ASK A CURIOUS SORT OF QUESTION	426	2	DON JUAN	5	30	4
IN SUCH SORT THAT THE EYE ALONG IT CAST	465	2	DON JUAN	5	93	4
AND LOOKING ON HIM WITH A SORT OF SMILE	473	2	DON JUAN	5	107	6
HE WAS AS GOOD A SOVEREIGN OF THE SORT	495	2	DON JUAN	5	147	5
SULTANS TOO MUCH ABHOR THIS SORT OF SIN	10	3	DON JUAN	6	7	5
OF THOSE WHO HAD MOST GENIUS FOR THIS SORT	26	3	DON JUAN	6	40	1
BUT WHAT WAS NOT A SORT OF STYLE THAT'S GROWN	33	3	DON JUAN	6	55	6
ALTHOUGH SHE WAS NOT OF THE FAINTING SORT	59	3	DON JUAN	6	106	1
FOR ONCE BY SOME ODD SORT OF MAGNANIMITY	92	3	DON JUAN	7	51	V4
BUT HERE A SORT OF SCENE BEGAN TO ENSUE	101	3	DON JUAN	7	67	1
WHO WERE ACCUSTOMED AS A SORT OF GOD	104	3	DON JUAN	7	74	3
AFFLICTING YOUNG FOLKS WITH A SORT OF DIZZINESS	108	3	DON JUAN	7	83	8
A SAVAGE SORT OF MILITARY MARTYR	152	3	DON JUAN	8	80	6
TOO MUCH OF ONE SORT WOULD BE SOPORIFIC--	156	3	DON JUAN	8	89	6
TO MAKE A ROMAN SORT OF SABINE WEDDING	177	3	DON JUAN	8	131	7
(A CURSED SORT OF CARRIAGE WITHOUT SPRINGS	197	3	DON JUAN	9	30	2
SELF-LOVE--WHICH WHEN SOME SORT OF THING ABOVE	216	3	DON JUAN	9	68	3
BECAUSE EACH LOVER LOOKED A SORT OF KING	217	3	DON JUAN	9	70	4
THE THIRD SORT TO BE NOTED IN OUR CHRONICLE	220	3	DON JUAN	9	76	5
HEAVEN'S FREEHOLDS IN A SORT OF DOOMSDAY SCROLL	242	3	DON JUAN	10	35	5
A SORT OF TREATY OR NEGOCIATION	246	3	DON JUAN	10	45	2
OUR SOARINGS WITH ANOTHER SORT OF QUESTION	269	3	DON JUAN	11	3	3
A SORT OF IGNIS-FATUUS TO THE MIND	281	3	DON JUAN	11	27	6
SETS UP FOR BEING A SORT OF MORAL ME	298	3	DON JUAN	11	59	2
IN MIND A SORT OF SENTIMENTAL BOGLE	304	3	DON JUAN	11	72	4
AFTER A SORT BUT SOMEHOW PEOPLE NEVER	323	3	DON JUAN	12	15	3
JUAN TOO WAS A SORT OF FAVOURITE WITH HER	338	3	DON JUAN	12	49	1
BUT TO DENOUNCE THE AMPHIBIOUS SORT OF HARLOT	344	3	DON JUAN	12	62	7
IN SUCH A SORT AS CANNOT LEAVE BEHIND	372	3	DON JUAN	13	32	4
IN THIS SORT END AT LEAST WITH THE BEGINNING	393	3	DON JUAN	13	73	8
THE ONLY SORT OF PLEASURE WHICH REQUITES	405	3	DON JUAN	13	100	4
A SORT OF ROSE ENTWINING WITH A THISTLE	407	3	DON JUAN	13	105	V6
A SORT OF VARNISH OVER EVERY FAULT	417	3	DON JUAN	14	16	3
THE SORT OF THING TO TURN A YOUNG MAN'S HEAD	438	3	DON JUAN	14	64	1
THIS SORT OF CHASTE LIAISON FOR A FRIEND	438	3	DON JUAN	14	64	6
SHOWN IN THIS SORT OF DESULTORY RHYME	465	3	DON JUAN	15	20	2
BUT JUAN HAD A SORT OF WINNING WAY	492	3	DON JUAN	15	82	1
THEIR SORT OF HALF PROFESSION FOR IT GROWS	522	3	DON JUAN	16	44	4
FOR HENRY WAS A SORT OF SABINE SHOWMAN	530	3	DON JUAN	16	60	8
MILD--BUT AT TIMES A SORT OF HERCULES FURENS	567	3	DON JUAN	17	11	6
HER GRACE TOO HAD A SORT OF AIR REBUKED--	568	3	DON JUAN	17	14	6
SORTS						
PILAUS AND MEATS OF ALL SORTS MET THE GAZE	291	2	DON JUAN	3	31	3
BESIDES ITS LAVA WITH ALL SORTS OF SHOT	119	3	DON JUAN	8	16	3
WITHOUT CONFUSION OF THE SORTS AND SEXES	269	3	DON JUAN	11	3	6
WAS ALL THINGS UNTO PEOPLE OF ALL SORTS	424	3	DON JUAN	14	31	2
WITHOUT STRONG REASON OF THOSE SORTS OF THINGS	439	3	DON JUAN	14	66	4
WITH THE SAD USAGE OF ALL SORTS OF SAGES	566	3	DON JUAN	17	9	3
SO-SO						
ALSO A SO-SO MATRON BOLDLY FIGHT	397	3	DON JUAN	13	82	5
SOT						
THE DRAINER OF OBLIVION EVEN THE SOT	457	3	DON JUAN	15	4	3
SOTHEBY'S						
THOU SHALT NOT COVET MR SOTHEBY'S MUSE	140	2	DON JUAN	1	206	1
SOU						
HANDSOME BUT WASTED RICH WITHOUT A SOU	306	3	DON JUAN	11	75	2
SOUGHT						
NO MATTER WHAT--IT WAS NOT THAT THEY SOUGHT	100	2	DON JUAN	1	144	2
NONE IN PARTICULAR HAD SOUGHT OR PLANN'D IT	195	2	DON JUAN	2	75	5
HE SOUGHT IN THE SLAVE-MARKET TOO AND DISH'D	223	2	DON JUAN	2	126	6
THE SILKEN FILLET'S CURB AND SOUGHT TO SHUN	313	2	DON JUAN	3	73	6
HE FOUND--BUT SOUGHT NOT I HAVE PLEDGED MY FAITH	366	2	DON JUAN	4	42	6
NOT I HE SAID HAVE SOUGHT THIS STRANGER'S ILL	368	2	DON JUAN	4	46	4

757

	PAGE	VOL	CANTO	STANZA	LN

SOUGHT (CONTINUED)

WITH EASE BUT WHERE I SOUGHT FOR ILION'S WALLS	386	2	DON JUAN	4	77	7
SONG IN THE WORLD WILL SEEK WHAT THEN THEY SOUGHT	402	2	DON JUAN	4	106	4
AN AIRY INSTRUMENT WITH WHICH HE SOUGHT	406	2	DON JUAN	4	112	5
IT MIGHT BE SEEN WITH DILIGENCE WAS SOUGHT	476	2	DON JUAN	5	113	3
BY THE NORTH POLE--THEY SOUGHT HER CAUSE OF CARE	42	3	DON JUAN	6	72	6
THEIR NAMES ARE RARELY FOUND NOR OFTEN SOUGHT	83	3	DON JUAN	7	34	4
THERE WAS NOT NOW A LUGGAGE BOY BUT SOUGHT	90	3	DON JUAN	7	49	5
THAN IF I SOUGHT TO SAIL BEFORE THE WIND	195	3	DON JUAN	9	26	4
NOR SOUGHT OF FOOLSCAP SUBJECTS TO BE KING--	296	3	DON JUAN	11	55	6
A JEST A RIDDLE FAME THROUGH THIN AND THICK SOUGHT	363	3	DON JUAN	13	10	7
ON WHICH THE MUSE HAS ALWAYS SOUGHT TO ENTER--	375	3	DON JUAN	13	38	6
ONLY THE WALL INSTEAD OF WHAT HE SOUGHT	560	3	DON JUAN	16	122	8

SOUL

HE DEIGN'D NOT TO BELIE HIS SOUL IN SONGS	15	2	DON JUAN	D	10	5
THY LATE REVIVING ROMAN SOUL DESPONDS	19	2	DON JUAN	D	16	3
BUT WOULD HAVE BEEN PERHAPS BUT FOR THE SOUL	54	2	DON JUAN	1	60	7
THE FLESH IS FRAIL AND SO THE SOUL UNDONE	56	2	DON JUAN	1	63	6
IN MAIL OF PROOF--HER PURITY OF SOUL	66	2	DON JUAN	1	82	2
HIS SELF-COMMUNION WITH HIS OWN HIGH SOUL	70	2	DON JUAN	1	91	2
OVER THE MYSTIC LEAF HIS SOUL WAS SHOOK	72	2	DON JUAN	1	95	5
A STILLNESS WHICH LEAVES ROOM FOR THE FULL SOUL	82	2	DON JUAN	1	114	2
AS VIBRATES MY FOND HEART TO MY FIX'D SOUL	133	2	DON JUAN	1	196	8
IT NE'ER CAN REACH SO TURNS TO YOU MY SOUL	133	2	DON JUAN	1	196	V8
AND DEEM NOT WHAT I DEEM'D MY SOUL INVINCIBLE	143	2	DON JUAN	1	213	8
THE ANSWER ELOQUENT WHERE THE SOUL SHINES	241	2	DON JUAN	2	162	5
WHERE HEART AND SOUL AND SENSE IN CONCERT MOVE	254	2	DON JUAN	2	186	5
O'ERFLOW'D HER SOUL WITH THEIR UNITED POWER	262	2	DON JUAN	2	198	3
FLASH'D O'ER HIS SOUL A FEW HEROIC RAYS	303	2	DON JUAN	3	55	2
WHO HATH PRODUCED AND WILL RECEIVE THE SOUL	336	2	DON JUAN	3	104	8
GOOD TO THE SOUL WHICH WE NO MORE CAN BIND	360	2	DON JUAN	4	30	6
NEW THOUGHTS OF LIFE FOR IT SEEM'D FULL OF SOUL	377	2	DON JUAN	4	60	7
WITH EYES THAT LOOK'D INTO THE VERY SOUL	395	2	DON JUAN	4	94	3
THE TOCSIN OF THE SOUL--THE DINNER BELL	439	2	DON JUAN	5	49	8
THAN AN ENORMOUS ROOM WITHOUT A SOUL	442	2	DON JUAN	5	56	7
WHY YOU SHOULD WEAR THEM--WHAT THOUGH MY SOUL LOATHES	455	2	DON JUAN	5	76	3
THESE WORDS WENT THROUGH HIS SOUL LIKE ARAB-SPEARS	478	2	DON JUAN	5	117	1
THE SOUL OUT (LIKE THE STONE) WITH PETTY CARES	16	3	DON JUAN	6	20	8
AND I CAN GIVE MY WHOLE SOUL UP TO MIND	17	3	DON JUAN	6	22	6
THOUGH WHAT IS SOUL OR MIND THEIR BIRTH OR GROWTH	17	3	DON JUAN	6	22	7
IT SOONER FOR THE SOUL OF ME AND CLASS	34	3	DON JUAN	6	56	5
SAVING HIS SOUL BY CHEATING IN THE WARE	80	3	DON JUAN	7	27	4
HIS PURSE HIS SOUL HIS SENSE AND EVEN HIS NONSENSE	88	3	DON JUAN	7	44	7
HIS SOUL (LIKE GALVANISM UPON THE DEAD)	133	3	DON JUAN	8	41	6
ON HIS SOUL LIKE A CEASELESS SUNRISE DART--	169	3	DON JUAN	8	115	6
IN ONE WIDE WOUND POURED FORTH HIS SOUL AT ONCE	170	3	DON JUAN	8	118	8
(THE LAST IF THEY HAVE SOUL ARE QUITE AS GOOD	218	3	DON JUAN	9	71	3
MOST NOBLY AND I OWN IT FROM MY SOUL	232	3	DON JUAN	10	16	8
SHE WAS NO HYPOCRITE AT LEAST POOR SOUL	242	3	DON JUAN	10	35	1
MAKE MY SOUL PASS THE EQUINOCTIAL LINE	255	3	DON JUAN	10	61	6
BY DRIVING THE YORK MAIL--BUT AH MY SINKING·SOUL	263	3	DON JUAN	10	78	V7
PLATONIC BLASPHEMY THE SOUL OF SWEARING	289	3	DON JUAN	11	43	8
UNTO THE GLOWING INDIA OF THE SOUL	376	3	DON JUAN	13	39	2
A SHADOW WHICH THE ONWARD SOUL BEHIND THROWS	414	3	DON JUAN	14	8	6
BORN WITH THAT HAPPY SOUL WHICH SELDOM FAINTS	424	3	DON JUAN	14	31	5
'TIS SO BECOMING TO THE SOUL AND FACE	430	3	DON JUAN	14	47	2
NO WONDER THEN A PURER SOUL SHOULD DREAD	438	3	DON JUAN	14	64	3
WHICH PRETTY WOMEN--THE SWEET SOULS--CALL SOUL	441	3	DON JUAN	14	71	3
WOULD BE DISCOVER'D IN THE HUMAN SOUL	455	3	DON JUAN	14	102	2
SHE 'GAN TO PONDER HOW TO SAVE HIS SOUL	468	3	DON JUAN	15	28	8
GENTLY TO LULL DOWN THE SUBSIDING SOUL	484	3	DON JUAN	15	66	6
SWEET SOUL--SHE WAS SO VERY INNOCENT	493	3	DON JUAN	15	83	V8
SHADOWS THE SOUL OF RICHARD MAY APPAL	499	3	DON JUAN	15	96	6
AND THEY SEEM OF A PARTED SOUL	519	3	DON JUAN	16	L 4	8
LET OURS BE FOR HIS SOUL	520	3	DON JUAN	16	L 6	8
POOR SOUL FOR SHE WAS COUNTRY BORN AND BRED	532	3	DON JUAN	16	64	5
(BETRAYING ONLY NOW AND THEN HER SOUL	546	3	DON JUAN	16	96	5
ANACREON ONLY HAD THE SOUL TO TIE AN	554	3	DON JUAN	16	109	5
HINTING THAT SOUL AND BODY ON THE WHOLE	558	3	DON JUAN	16	118	7
WERE ODDS AGAINST A DISEMBODIED SOUL	558	3	DON JUAN	16	118	8
IT TOUCHED NO SOUL NOR BODY BUT THE WALL	559	3	DON JUAN	16	120	2
THE GHOST IF GHOST IT WERE SEEMED A SWEET SOUL	561	3	DON JUAN	16	123	1
MY SOUL FROM OUT ME AT THY SINGLE SUMMON	569	3	DON·JUAN	17	V 13	6

SOUL-HIRED

| A SCRIBBLING SELF-SOLD SOUL-HIRED SCORNED ISCARIOT | 15 | 2 | DON JUAN | D | 11 | V8 |

SOUL'S

TO BE HER SOUL'S FIRST IDOL AND ITS LAST	247	2	DON JUAN	2	173	V8
WOULD SHOW MANKIND THEIR SOUL'S ANTIPODES	455	3	DON JUAN	14	101	8
WHICH MINISTERS UNTO THE SOUL'S DELIGHT	457	3	DON JUAN	15	2	7

SOULS

FOR KILLING BODIES AND FOR SAVING SOULS	93	2	DON JUAN	1	132	2
ALL THE REST PERISH'D NEAR TWO HUNDRED SOULS	185	2	DON JUAN	2	55	1
NINE SOULS MORE WENT IN HER THE LONG-BOAT STILL	188	2	DON JUAN	2	61	1
AS IF THEIR SOULS AND LIPS EACH OTHER BECKON'D	254	2	DON JUAN	2	187	6
THEIR INTENSE SOULS INTO EACH OTHER POUR'D	257	2	DON JUAN	2	191	3
IF SOULS COULD DIE HAD PERISH'D IN THAT PASSION	257	2	DON JUAN	2	191	4
WHERE MEN HAVE SOULS OR BODIES SHE MUST ANSWER	390	2	DON JUAN	4	84	8
OUR SOULS AT LEAST ARE FREE AND 'TIS IN VAIN	474	2	DON JUAN	5	110	6
WHY DON'T THEY KNEAD TWO VIRTUOUS SOULS FOR LIFE	502	2	DON JUAN	5	158	7

SOULS   (CONTINUED)
    NO MATTER WHAT POOR SOULS MIGHT BE UNDONE   . . . . . .   78 3 DON JUAN   7   23   5
    SOULS OF IMMORTAL GENERALS PHOEBUS WATCHES   . . . . . .   107 3 DON JUAN   7   81   7
    THEIR CLAY FOR THE LAST TIME THEIR SOULS ENCUMBER-- . . . 120 3 DON JUAN   8   18   5
    WHICH SATAN ANGLES WITH FOR SOULS LIKE FLIES   . . . . .   154 3 DON JUAN   8   86   8
    SOULS TO SAVE SINCE EVE'S SLIP AND ADAM'S FALL . . . . .   192 3 DON JUAN   9   19   3
    MAY PAUSE IN PONDERING HOW ALL SOULS ARE DIPT   . . . . .   210 3 DON JUAN   9   55   4
    THE WHOLE THING IS OF CLOTHING SOULS IN CLAY   . . . . .   220 3 DON JJAN   9   75   8
    AND SHUT OUR SOULS UP IN US LIKE A SHELL-FISH   . . . . .   236 3 DON JUAN 10   23   8
    OF WORLDS AND SPECIES--MATTERS--SOULS AND BODY . . . . .   269 3 DON JUAN 11   3   V7
    CAN TENDER SOULS RELATE THE RISE AND FALL   . . . . . .   304 3 DON JUAN 11   72   7
    WHICH PRETTY WOMEN--THE SWEET SOULS--CALL SOUL . . . . .   441 3 DON JUAN 14   71   3
    SUCH BODIES COULD HAVE SOULS OR SOULS SUCH BODIES . . . .   543 3 DON JUAN 16   90   8
    SUCH BODIES COULD HAVE SOULS OR SOULS SUCH BODIES . . . .   543 3 DON JUAN 16   90   8
    IN SOULS IMMORTAL SHUN THEM TETE A TETE   . . . .   556 3 DON JUAN 16   114   8
SOUND
    THE ONLY HIGH SOUND PRECEPTS OF THE TRUE SUBLIME . . . .   136 2 DON JUAN   1   201   V3
    THE RUDDER TORE AWAY 'TWAS TIME TO SOUND . . . .   170 2 DON JUAN   2   27   7
    AN OMINOUS AND WILD AND DESPERATE SOUND   . . . . . .   194 2 DON JUAN   2   73   4
    THE SORT OF SOUND WE ECHO WITH A TEAR . . . .   236 2 DON JUAN   2   151   6
    AT LEAST IT IS A HEAVY SOUND TO ME . . . .   237 2 DON JUAN   2   152   6
    BUT AN UNHALLOW'D EARTHLY SOUND OF FIDDLING . . . . . .   290 2 DON JUAN   3   28   4
    SOUND LIKE A DISTANT TORRENT'S FALL   . . . .   323 2 DON JUAN   3 L 8   3
    AND EVERY SOUND OF REVELRY EXPIRED . . . .   334 2 DON JUAN   3   101   4
    WHEN ONE IS SHOOK IN SOUND AND ONE IN SIGHT . . . . . .   355 2 DON JUAN   4   21   5
    NOT SOUND POOR FELLOW BUT SEVERELY WOUNDED   . . . . .   373 2 DON JUAN   4   54   2
    HER CARGO FROM THE PLAGUE BEING SAFE AND SOUND . . . . .   407 2 DON JJAN   4   113   5
    FOR ONCE IT WAS A MAGIC SOUND TO ME   . . . .   413 2 DON JJAN   5   4   2
    SOUND AND THEN BY A CRY THE SULTAN'S COMING . . . . . .   494 2 DON JUAN   5   145   8
    A BLESSING IS SOUND SLEEP--JUANNA LAY . . . .   42 3 DON JJAN   6   73   2
    AT LENGTH SHE SAID THAT IN A SLUMBER SOUND   . . . . .   43 3 DON JUAN   6   75   1
    WHERE SHE THEN WAS AS HER SOUND SLEEP DISCLOSED   . . . .   48 3 DON JUAN   6   84   3
    HOW SWEETLY ON THE EAR SUCH ECHOES SOUND . . . .   114 3 DON JUAN   8   5   5
    BUT IF SHE WERE DELIVERED SAFE AND SOUND . . . .   162 3 DON JUAN   8   102   7
    BUT WOULD MUCH RATHER HAVE A SOUND DIGESTION   . . . . .   189 3 DON JUAN   9   14   5
    THE SOUND THAN SENSE)--BESIDES ALL THESE PRETENCES . . .   219 3 DON JUAN   9   74   7
    THAT'S RATHER FINE THE GENTLE SOUND OF THAMIS--   . . . .   279 3 DON JUAN 11   24   1
    IN POLITESSE AND HAVE A SOUND AFFRONTING IN'T--   . . . .   289 3 DON JUAN 11   43   6
    WHEN ERE THE INK BE DRY THE SOUND GROWS COLD   . . . . .   382 3 DON JUAN 13   51   5
    THERE MOANS A STRANGE UNEARTHLY SOUND WHICH THEN . . . .   388 3 DON JUAN 13   63   3
    AND THEN HE HAD AN EAR FOR MUSIC'S SOUND . . . .   427 3 DON JUAN 14   39   5
    AS NOW WITH THOSE OF SOI-DISANT SOUND MIND   . . . . .   446 3 DON JUAN 14   84   4
    AND AS MY FRIEND SCOTT SAYS I SOUND MY WARISON . . . . .   481 3 DON JUAN 15   59   3
    LET IN THE RIPPLING SOUND OF THE LAKE'S BILLOW . . . . .   507 3 DON JUAN 16   15   4
    NO SOUND EXCEPT THE ECHO OF HIS SIGH . . . .   509 3 DON JUAN 16   20   3
    ADDED HER SWEET VOICE TO THE LYRIC SOUND . . . .   518 3 DON JUAN 16   40   6
    DIED FROM THE TOUCH THAT KINDLED THEM TO SOUND . . . . .   521 3 DON JUAN 16   41   2
SOUNDED
    SO THAT THEIR BARGAIN SOUNDED LIKE A BATTLE . . . . . .   425 2 DON JUAN   5   28   7
SOUNDING
    SOUNDING LIKE VERY SUPERNATURAL WATER . . . .   556 3 DON JUAN 16   114   4
SOUNDLY
    TO SCHOOL OR HAD HIM SOUNDLY WHIPP'D AT HOME   . . . . .   34 2 DON JUAN   1   25   7
    YOU DON'T SLEEP SOUNDLY AND I CANNOT BEAR   . . . . .   29 3 DON JUAN   6   47   2
SOUNDS
    SOUNDS ILL IN LOVE WHATE'ER IT MAY IN MONEY . . . . . .   78 2 DON JUAN   1   107   8
    STRANGE SOUNDS OF WAILING BLASPHEMY DEVOTION   . . . . .   174 2 DON JUAN   2   34   7
    TO SOUNDS WHICH ECHO FURTHER WEST   . . . .   321 2 DON JUAN   3 L 2   5
    AND WE ARE SICK OF ITS HACK SOUNDS AND SIGHTS   . . . . .   353 2 DON JUAN   4   17   4
    THIS IS NO BULL ALTHOUGH IT SOUNDS SO FOR   . . . . .   40 3 DON JUAN   6   67   1
    BY TINKLING SOUNDS WHEN THEY GO FORTH TO VICTUAL . . . .   90 3 DON JUAN   7   48   7
    TOO GENTLE READER AND MOST SHOCKING SOUNDS   . . . . .   112 3 DON JUAN   8   1   3
    ALL SOUNDS IT PIERCETH ALLAH ALLAH HU . . . .   116 3 DON JUAN   8   8   8
    SOUNDS LESS HARMONIOUS UNDERNEATH THE SUN SOON . . . . .   132 3 DON JUAN   8   39   3
    UPON THE EAR AND SOUNDS OF HORROR CHIME   . . . . . .   141 3 DON JUAN   8   58   6
    SOUNDS THE HEROIC SYLLABLES BOTH WAYS . . . .   183 3 DON JUAN   9   1   2
    THESE FREEBORN SOUNDS PROCEEDED FROM FOUR PADS . . . . .   273 3 DON JUAN 11   11   1
SOUP
    AND FISH AND SOUP BY SOME SIDE DISHES BACKED   . . . . .   428 2 DON JUAN   5   32   5
SOUPE
    THERE WAS A GOODLY SOUPE A LA BONNE FEMME   . . . . .   483 3 DON JUAN 15   63   1
    SOUPE A LA BEAUVEAU WHOSE RELIEF WAS DORY   . . . . .   483 3 DON JUAN 15   63   7
SOUPS
    AND SAFFRON SOUPS AND SWEETBREADS AND THE FISHES . . . .   307 2 DON JUAN   3   62   3
    IN SOUPS OR SAUCES OR A SOLE RAGOUT   . . . .   482 3 DON JUAN 15   62   7
SOUR
    A SAD SOUR SOBER BEVERAGE--BY TIME . . . .   277 2 DON JUAN   3   5   6
    (WHO LIKE SOUR FRUIT TO STIR THEIR VEINS' SALT TIDES . . .   251 3 DON JUAN 10   54   3
SOURCE
    OF MOOR OR HEBREW BLOOD HE TRACED HIS SOURCE   . . . . .   26 2 DON JUAN   1   9   3
    AND FEELING IN A POET IS THE SOURCE . . . .   326 2 DON JUAN   3   87   6
    THOUGH SLEEPING LIKE A LION NEAR A SOURCE   . . . . .   374 2 DON JUAN   4   56   8
    THIS MONSTROUS TALE HAD PROBABLY ITS SOURCE . . . . . .   446 2 DON JUAN   5   61   5
    BESIDES THE SAD'S A SOURCE OF THE SUBLIME   . . . . .   358 3 DON JUAN 13   1   5
    THAT SOURCE OF THE SUBLIME AND THE MYSTERIOUS--   . . . .   498 3 DON JUAN 15   95   7
SOURCES
    MIDST WHOM WE HAVE HEARD FROM SOURCES QUITE CORRECT . . .   382 3 DON JUAN 13   52   4
SOUTH
    BARROW SOUTH TILLOTSON WHOM EVERY WEEK   . . . . . .   243 2 DON JUAN   2   165   5

		PAGE	VOL		CANTO	STANZA	LN

SOUTH   (CONTINUED)
```
    AS O'ER A BED OF ROSES THE SWEET SOUTH  . . . . . . 245  2 DON JUAN  2    168   8
    FOR THROUGH THE SOUTH THE CUSTOM STILL COMMANDS  . . . . 472  2 DON JUAN  5    105   7
    TO KISS THEM ALL AT ONCE FROM NORTH TO SOUTH  . . . .  19  3 DON JUAN  6     27   8
    THUS THE LOW WORLD NORTH SOUTH OR WEST OR EAST  . . . . 342  3 DON JUAN 12     56   6
    ON ROADS EAST SOUTH NORTH WEST THERE IS A RUN  . . . . 377  3 DON JUAN 13     42   4
SOUTHCOTE
    I HAVE SEEN JOHANNA SOUTHCOTE--I HAVE SEEN  . . . . . 310  3 DON JUAN 11     84   2
SOUTHCOTE'S
    JOANNA SOUTHCOTE'S SHILOH AND HER SECT  . . . . . . 330  2 DON JUAN  3     95   4
SOUTHERN
    WHICH MAKES THE SOUTHERN AUTUMN'S DAY APPEAR  . . . . 395  3 DON JUAN 13     77   2
SOUTHEY
    BOB SOUTHEY YOU'RE A POET--POET-LAUREATE . . . . . .   9  2 DON JUAN  D      1   1
    AND SOUTHEY LIVES TO SING THEM VERY ILL  . . . . . .  19  2 DON JUAN  D     16   8
    THOU SHALT NOT SET UP WORDSWORTH COLERIDGE SOUTHEY  . . 139  2 DON JUAN  1    205   2
    WITH TRUTH LIKE SOUTHEY AND WITH VERSE LIKE CRASHAW  . . 316  2 DON JUAN  3     79   8
    BELIEVED LIKE SOUTHEY--AND PERUSED LIKE CRASHAW  . . . 316  2 DON JUAN  3     79  V8
    ALL ARE NOT MORALISTS LIKE SOUTHEY WHEN . . . . . . 329  2 DON JUAN  3     93   1
    WHEN HE AND SOUTHEY FOLLOWING THE SAME PATH . . . . . 329  2 DON JUAN  3     93   7
    AN EPIC FROM BOB SOUTHEY EVERY SPRING--)  . . . . . 332  2 DON JUAN  3     97   4
    EVEN SHUFFLING SOUTHEY THAT INCARNATE LIE  . . . . . 231  3 DON JUAN 10     13   2
    SAVE SUCH AS SOUTHEY CAN AFFORD TO GIVE  . . . . . . 243  3 DON JUAN 10     37   4
    WITH TURNCOAT SOUTHEY FOR MY TURNKEY LOWE  . . . . . 296  3 DON JUAN 11     56   8
SOUTHEY'S
    WHEN SOUTHEY'S READ AND WORDSWORTH UNDERSTOOD  . . . . 149  2 DON JUAN  1    222   5
    THE FOUR FIRST RHYMES ARE SOUTHEY'S EVERY LINE . . . . 149  2 DON JUAN  1    222   7
    HAS TAKEN FOR A SWAN ROGUE SOUTHEY'S GANDER . . . . . 298  3 DON JUAN 11     59   8
SOUVAROFF
    BATTLES TO THE COMMAND FIELD MARSHAL SOUVAROFF . . . .  85  3 DON JUAN  7     39   8
    WHILE SOUVAROFF DETERMINED TO OBTAIN IT . . . . . .  92  3 DON JUAN  7     51   7
SOVEREIGN
    OR ANY SUCH LIKE SOVEREIGN BUFFOONS  . . . . . . . 341  2 DON JUAN  3    110   2
    THE MOST IMPERATIVE OF SOVEREIGN SPELLS  . . . . . . 393  2 DON JUAN  4     91   3
    HE WAS AS GOOD A SOVEREIGN OF THE SORT  . . . . . . 495  2 DON JUAN  5    147   5
    IN THE THEN SOVEREIGN OF THE RUSSIAN PEOPLE . . . . .  84  3 DON JUAN  7     37   7
    TELL FOR ITSELF THE SOVEREIGN WAS SMITTEN  . . . . . 221  3 DON JUAN  9     77   2
    AND DEATH THE SOVEREIGN'S SOVEREIGN THOUGH THE GREAT  . . 237  3 DON JUAN 10     25   1
    THE SOVEREIGN SHOCKED AND ALL HIS MEDICINES DOUBLED  . . 244  3 DON JUAN 10     39   8
SOVEREIGN'S
    AND DEATH THE SOVEREIGN'S SOVEREIGN THOUGH THE GREAT  . . 237  3 DON JUAN 10     25   1
    (IN WHISPERS) TO HAVE TURNED HIS SOVEREIGN'S HEAD  . . . 283  3 DON JUAN 11     32   8
    SUCH WAS HIS SOVEREIGN'S PLEASURE (THOUGH UNFIT  . . . 535  3 DON JUAN 16     72   5
SOVEREIGNS
    AS GREATEST OF ALL SOVEREIGNS AND WHORES . . . . . .  52  3 DON JUAN  6     92   8
    THEIR NATURES OR THEIR SOVEREIGNS WHO EMPLOY  . . . . 157  3 DON JUAN  8     92   7
    OUR VEINS WHEN THINGS CALLED SOVEREIGNS THINK IT BEST  . . 212  3 DON JUAN  9     60   7
    SOVEREIGNS MAY SWAY MATERIALS BUT NOT MATTER  . . . . 236  3 DON JUAN 10     24   7
    TO SEE MEN LET THESE SCOUNDREL SOVEREIGNS BREAK LAW  . . 497  3 DON JUAN 15     92   8
SOW
    FOLLOWERS OF FAME NINE FARROW OF THAT SOW  . . . . .  22  2 DON JUAN  1      2   6
    WHETHER THEY MAY SOW SCEPTICISM TO REAP HELL . . . . . 195  2 DON JUAN  9     25   5
    AND PLANT AND REAP AND SPIN AND GRIND AND SOW  . . . . 202  3 DON JUAN  9     40   4
    WHO FURROW SOME NEW SOIL TO SOW FOR JOYS . . . . . . 228  3 DON JUAN 10      7   6
    AND APT TO SOW AN AUTHOR'S WHEAT WITH TARES . . . . . 369  3 DON JUAN 13     25   3
    BY THOSE WHO SOW THEM IN A LAND THAT'S ARABLE  . . . . 495  3 DON JUAN 15     89   3
SOWN
    HAD SOWN THE RUIN OF HER FEW FAIR YEARS  . . . . . . 275  2 DON JUAN  3      1  V7
    AND THERE PERHAPS SOME SEED IS SOWN  . . . . . . . 325  2 DON JUAN  3  L 13   5
SPACE
    THEY COUNTED THIRTY CROWDED IN A SPACE  . . . . . . 189  2 DON JUAN  2     63   1
    AND ALL THE STARS THAT CROWDED THE BLUE SPACE  . . . . 262  2 DON JUAN  2    198   7
    A HALF-UNQUENCHED VOLCANO O'ER A SPACE  . . . . . . 265  3 DON JUAN 10     81   2
    SPACE TO DISPUTE WHAT NO ONE EVER COULD  . . . . . . 270  3 DON JUAN 11      4   6
    IN TWELVE HOURS' TIME AND VERY LITTLE SPACE . . . . . 277  3 DON JUAN 11     18   6
    HIMSELF FOR FIVE FOUR THREE OR TWO YEAR'S SPACE  . . . 329  3 DON JUAN 12     29   6
    AND WEAR THE MELTON JACKET FOR A SPACE-- . . . . . . 395  3 DON JUAN 13     78   6
    THOUGHTS BOUNDLESS DEEP BUT SILENT TOO AS SPACE  . . . 524  3 DON JUAN 16     48   8
SPACIOUS
    BUT THIS I KNOW IT WAS A SPACIOUS BUILDING  . . . . . 223  2 DON JUAN  2    127   7
    WITH A CLEAN SHIRT AND VERY SPACIOUS BREECHES  . . . . 240  2 DON JUAN  2    160   8
    IT WAS A SPACIOUS CHAMBER (ODA IS  . . . . . . . .  31  3 DON JUAN  6     51   1
    FAIR WEATHER FOR THE DAY THOUGH RATHER SPACIOUS  . . . 211  3 DON JUAN  9     58   7
    HUGE HALLS LONG GALLERIES SPACIOUS CHAMBERS JOIN'D  . . 390  3 DON JUAN 13     67   1
SPADE
    TO BE FILLED UP BY SPADE OR MATTOCK'S NEAR  . . . . . 245  3 DON JUAN 10     42   6
SPAGNOLETTO
    OF MARTYRS AWED AS SPAGNOLETTO TAINTED  . . . . . . 392  3 DON JUAN 13     71   7
SPAIN
    THROUGH THE MOST GOTHIC GENTLEMEN OF SPAIN  . . . . .  26  2 DON JUAN  1      9   4
    FROM THE MOST GOTHIC GOTHS OF GOTHIC SPAIN  . . . . .  26  2 DON JUAN  1      9  V4
    IN SPAIN YOU KNOW THIS IS A SORT OF SIN) . . . . . .  52  2 DON JUAN  1     56   4
    SOME WENT TO AFRICA SOME STAID IN SPAIN  . . . . . .  52  2 DON JUAN  1     56   7
    FOR FROM A ROOT THE UGLIEST IN OLD SPAIN . . . . . .  53  2 DON JUAN  1     58   3
    IF THERE BE LAW OR LAWYERS IN ALL SPAIN  . . . . . . 100  2 DON JUAN  1    145   8
    CALL ME THE ONLY VIRTUOUS WIFE IN SPAIN  . . . . . . 102  2 DON JUAN  1    149   4
    THAT HAD FOR CENTURIES BEEN KNOWN IN SPAIN  . . . . . 128  2 DON JUAN  1    190   3
    TIS PITY THAT THEY HAD NO BROUGHAM IN SPAIN--  . . . . 150  2 DON JUAN  1  V  1   2
    HOLLAND FRANCE ENGLAND GERMANY OR SPAIN  . . . . . . 157  2 DON JUAN  2      1   2
```

SPAIN   (CONTINUED)

	PAGE	VOL	CANTO	STANZA	LN
SPAIN MAY PROVE AN EXCEPTION TO THE RULE	158	2 DON JUAN	2	2	5
HIS FIRST--PERHAPS HIS LAST--FAREWELL OF SPAIN	162	2 DON JUAN	2	11	8
BEHELD HIS NATIVE SPAIN RECEDING FAR	164	2 DON JUAN	2	14	2
FAREWELL MY SPAIN A LONG FAREWELL HE CRIED	166	2 DON JUAN	2	18	1
IF YOU HAD BEEN IN TURKEY OR IN SPAIN	201	2 DON JUAN	2	84	5
IN SPAIN HE'D MAKE A BALLAD OR ROMANCE ON	320	2 DON JUAN	3	86	3
FROM SPAIN--BUT WHERE IS SPAIN--DON'T ASK SUCH STUFF	28	3 DON JUAN	6	44	4
FROM SPAIN--BUT WHERE IS SPAIN--DON'T ASK SUCH STUFF	28	3 DON JUAN	6	44	4
HE WROTE TO SPAIN--AND ALL HIS NEAR RELATIONS	239	3 DON JUAN	10	30	1
WHO ROUSE THE SHIRTLESS PATRIOTS OF SPAIN	318	3 DON JUAN	12	5	3
HAS SPAIN HAD HEROES WHILE ROMANCE COULD CHARM	364	3 DON JUAN	13	11	4
IN SPAIN AND LUCCA ATHENS EVERYWHERE	488	3 DON JUAN	15	73	4

SPAIN'S

| TO POOR KATINKA SPAIN'S AN ISLAND NEAR | 28 | 3 DON JUAN | 6 | 44 | 7 |
| CERVANTES SMILED SPAIN'S CHIVALRY AWAY | 364 | 3 DON JUAN | 13 | 11 | 1 |

SPAKE

THE TRUMP AND BUGLE TILL HE SPAKE WERE DUMB--	430	2 DON JUAN	5	36	7
SHE SPAKE SOME WORDS TO HER ATTENDANTS WHO	469	2 DON JUAN	5	99	1
('TWAS THUS HE SPAKE) AND EMPRESS OF THE EARTH	494	2 DON JUAN	5	144	2
OF THEM HIS LIPS IMPERIAL EVER SPAKE	501	2 DON JUAN	5	156	6
AND THEN MEN STARE AS IF A NEW ASS SPAKE	328	3 DON JUAN	12	26	5
OF COURSERS ALSO SPAKE THEY HENRY RID	368	3 DON JUAN	13	23	5

SPAN

THE RAINBOW BASED ON OCEAN SPAN THE SKY	87	2 DON JUAN	1	122	8
FOR HAD HE NOT BEEN HERCULES HIS SPAN	84	3 DON JUAN	7	36	3
WHICH IS FULL SOON (THOUGH LIFE IS BUT A SPAN)	222	3 DON JUAN	9	79	4

SPANGLED

| SPANGLED WITH GEMS--THE MONK MADE HIS BLOOD CURDLE | 556 | 3 DON JUAN | 16 | 113 | 8 |

SPANIARD

| HE LIKED THE GENTLE SPANIARD FOR HIS GRAVITY | 368 | 3 DON JUAN | 13 | 22 | 1 |
| OUR GAY RUSS SPANIARD WAS ORDAINED TO SHINE | 383 | 3 DON JUAN | 13 | 53 | 4 |

SPANIEL

A SMALL OLD SPANIEL--WHICH HAD BEEN DON JOSE'S	187	2 DON JUAN	2	58	1
THUS RE-EMBARK'D HIS TUTOR AND HIS SPANIEL	187	2 DON JUAN	2	59	8
SO JUAN'S SPANIEL SPITE OF HIS ENTREATING	193	2 DON JUAN	2	70	7
REFUSING HIS OWN SPANIEL HARDLY COULD	198	2 DON JUAN	2	78	4

SPANISH

OF ALL THE SPANISH TOWNS IS NONE MORE PRETTY	25	2 DON JUAN	1	8	5
FOR NATIVE SPANISH SHE HAD NO GREAT CARE	28	2 DON JUAN	1	13	5
(HER BLOOD WAS NOT ALL SPANISH BY THE BY	52	2 DON JUAN	1	56	3
AS IF A SPANISH SHIP WERE NOAH'S ARK	161	2 DON JUAN	2	8	6
FOR THERE THE SPANISH FAMILY MONCADA	169	2 DON JUAN	2	24	3
HIS SPANISH FRIENDS FOR THOSE IN ITALY	169	2 DON JUAN	2	24	8
HER DRESS WAS VERY DIFFERENT FROM THE SPANISH	220	2 DON JUAN	2	120	2
FOR AS YOU KNOW THE SPANISH WOMEN BANISH	220	2 DON JUAN	2	120	4
THAT IS SOME WORDS OF SPANISH TURK AND GREEK	243	2 DON JUAN	2	165	1
WHEN JUAN ANSWERED SPANISH HE REPLIED	418	2 DON JUAN	5	14	1
THE SPANISH AND THE FRENCH AS WELL AS DUTCH	184	3 DON JUAN	9	3	5
NONE SAVE THE SPANISH FLY AND ATTIC BEE	196	3 DON JUAN	9	28	7
THEY TALKED BAD FRENCH OF SPANISH AND UPON ITS	294	3 DON JUAN	11	50	5
BOTH LONGED EXTREMELY TO BE SUNG IN SPANISH	295	3 DON JUAN	11	53	8
WHETHER THEY RODE OR WALK'D OR STUDIED SPANISH	453	3 DON JUAN	14	98	1

SPANNING

| THE SCATTERING CLOUDS SHONE SPANNING THE DARK SEA | 204 | 2 DON JUAN | 2 | 91 | 2 |

SPARE

HAS GENERALLY NO GREAT CROP TO SPARE IT HE	14	2 DON JUAN	D	9	3
WHILE SHE HAD NOT ONE HOUR TO SPARE FROM LOVING	295	2 DON JUAN	3	39	8
TALKING'S DRY WORK I HAVE NO TIME TO SPARE	297	2 DON JUAN	3	43	4
DEAL WITH ME AS THOU WILT BUT SPARE THIS BOY	364	2 DON JUAN	4	38	8
I HAVE NO MORE TIME NOR MANY WORDS TO SPARE	454	2 DON JUAN	5	74	3
SO MANY FALSE LONG TRESSES ALL TO SPARE	457	2 DON JUAN	5	79	3
WHICH (IT MAY BE) HAS NOT MUCH LEFT TO SPARE	114	3 DON JUAN	8	4	4
SPARE OR SMITE RARELY--MAN'S MAKE MILLIONS ASHES	115	3 DON JUAN	8	6	8
HAVE ALWAYS HAD A TENDENCY TO SPARE--	193	3 DON JUAN	9	21	6
I SPARE YOU THEN THE FURNITURE AND PLATE	393	3 DON JUAN	13	74	8
EACH ROSE UP AT HIS OWN AND HAD TO SPARE	406	3 DON JUAN	13	103	6
THAN THESE THINGS AND BESIDES I WISH TO SPARE 'EM	419	3 DON JUAN	14	21	5
WHATE'ER THOU TAKEST SPARE AWHILE POOR BEAUTY	459	3 DON JUAN	15	9	1
AT LEAST FOR THIS I CANNOT SPARE ITS VANITY	482	3 DON JUAN	15	60	4
I MUST NOT INTRODUCE EVEN A SPARE RIB HERE	487	3 DON JUAN	15	71	5

SPARED

BECAUSE IF DROWN'D THEY CAN'T--IF SPARED THEY WON'T	414	2 DON JUAN	5	6	8
WAS SPARED--THREE THOUSAND MOSLEMS PERISHED HERE	152	3 DON JUAN	8	81	7
SPARED NEITHER SEX NOR AGE IN THEIR CAREER	171	3 DON JUAN	8	119	2
SPARED BY SOME CHANCE WHEN ALL BESIDE WAS SPOIL'D	387	3 DON JUAN	13	61	4
SOME HEART-ACHES HAD BEEN SPARED ME YET I CARE NOT--	431	3 DON JUAN	14	49	2
YET ONE THING RATHER GOOD THE GRAVE HAD SPARED	560	3 DON JUAN	16	121	3

SPARES

| ARE SAVING--VICE SPARES NOTHING FOR A RARITY | 408 | 2 DON JUAN | 4 | 115 | 8 |

SPARING

| AND WONDER HOW THE WEALTHY CAN BE SPARING | 316 | 3 DON JUAN | 12 | 3 | 7 |

SPARINGLY

| BUT WAS USED SPARINGLY--SOME WERE AFRAID | 200 | 2 DON JUAN | 2 | 82 | 2 |

SPARK

NOT EVEN A SPRIGHTLY BLUNDER'S SPARK CAN BLAZE	17	2 DON JUAN	D	13	5
OCCUR THOUGH RARELY WHEN THERE IS A SPARK	177	3 DON JUAN	8	130	5
TOWARD THE GREAT CITY--YE WHO HAVE A SPARK IN	264	3 DON JUAN	10	80	5
WITHIN AND WHAT SEES'T THOU A DUBIOUS SPARK	348	3 DON JUAN	12	71	8

761

```
                                              PAGE VOL      CANTO STANZA LN

SPARKLE
  NOR THE FIRST SPARKLE OF THE DESERT-SPRING  . . . . .  251  2 DON JUAN  2    180    5
  HER CHEEK BEGAN TO FLUSH HER EYES TO SPARKLE  . . . .   56  3 DON JUAN  6    101    7
SPARKLED
  THAT SPARKLED O'ER THE AUBURN OF HER HAIR  . . . . .   217  2 DON JUAN  2    116    2
  HER GIRDLE SPARKLED AND THE RICHEST LACE . . . . . .   220  2 DON JUAN  2    121    5
  LOLAH'S EYES SPARKLED AT THE PROPOSITION . . . . . .    47  3 DON JUAN  6     82    1
  SPARKLED ALONG ITS ROOF AND MANY A VASE  . . . . . .    54  3 DON JUAN  6     97    6
  AND SPARKLED INTO BASINS WHERE IT SPENT  . . . . . .   389  3 DON JUAN 13     65    6
  SINCE THEN SHE HAD SPARKLED THROUGH THREE GLOWING WINTERS . 434  3 DON JUAN 14     56    1
  SPARKLED WITH HER SUCCESSFUL PROPHECIES  . . . . . .   490  3 DON JUAN 15     78    8
  HAS SPARKLED AND LET HALF ITS SPIRIT OUT . . . . . .   504  3 DON JUAN 16      9    6
SPARKLES
  AND SMILES AND SPARKLES OF THE SPEAKING EYE  . . . .   241  2 DON JUAN  2    162    2
SPARKLING
  BY GUSTS AND MANY A SPARKLING HEARTH WAS BRIGHT  . . .   94  2 DON JUAN  1    135    3
  WHEN O'ER THE BRIM THE SPARKLING BUMPERS REACH . . .   250  2 DON JUAN  2    178    3
  WITH ONE STAR SPARKLING THROUGH IT LIKE AN EYE . . .   252  2 DON JUAN  2    183    8
  THE MOVING FIGURES AND THE SPARKLING SHEEN . . . . .   289  2 DON JUAN  3     27    6
  THE SPARKLING GEMS BENEATH YOU MIGHT BEHOLD  . . . .   315  2 DON JUAN  3     77    3
  JOY SPARKLING IN THEIR DARK EYES LIKE A GEM  . . . .   351  2 DON JUAN  4     13    6
  WHO CLEARED HER SPARKLING EYES AND SMOOTHED HER BROWS . 500  2 DON JUAN  5    154    3
  HER EYES WERE NOT TOO SPARKLING YET HALF-SHUT  . . .    27  3 DON JUAN  6     43    3
  THE POOR MAN'S SPARKLING SUBSTITUTE FOR RICHES . . .   256  3 DON JUAN 10     63    4
  AND SPARKLING ON FROM HEAP TO HEAP DISPLAYS  . . . .   319  3 DON JUAN 12      8    2
  SMART UNIFORMS AND SPARKLING CORONETS  . . . . . . .   333  3 DON JUAN 12     36    1
  SPARKLING WITH FOAM UNTIL AGAIN SUBSIDING  . . . . .   385  3 DON JUAN 13     58    2
  TIME SHEDS A MOMENT O'ER EACH SPARKLING CREST  . . .   480  3 DON JUAN 15     55    6
SPARROW'S
  BESIDES FISH BEASTS AND BIRDS THE SPARROW'S FALL . . .  192  3 DON JUAN  9     19    5
SPARRY
  IN HOLLOW HALLS WITH SPARRY ROOFS AND CELLS  . . . .   253  2 DON JUAN  2    184    6
SPARS
  AT HALF-PAST EIGHT O'CLOCK BOOMS HENCOOPS SPARS  . .   183  2 DON JUAN  2     51    1
  ON OURS OR SPARS WITHIN SOME DUSKY CAVE  . . . . . .   509  3 DON JUAN 16     19    5
SPARTAN
  JUST AS THE SPARTAN LADIES DID OF YORE . . . . . . .    36  2 DON JUAN  1     29    3
  A REMNANT OF OUR SPARTAN DEAD  . . . . . . . . . . .   323  2 DON JUAN  3  L  7    4
  WAS WORTHY OF A SPARTAN HAD THE CAUSE  . . . . . . .    86  3 DON JUAN  7     40    2
  AS BETWEEN ENGLISH BEEF AND SPARTAN BROTH--  . . . .   541  3 DON JUAN 16     84    7
SPARTAN'S
  THE GREEK EVE HELEN FROM THE SPARTAN'S BED . . . . .   441  3 DON JUAN 14     72    5
SPAWN
  OF THIS ENORMOUS CITY'S SPREADING SPAWN  . . . . . .   281  3 DON JUAN 11     28    4
  IF HE FOUND NOT THIS SPAWN OF TAX-BORN RICHES  . . .   288  3 DON JUAN 11     41    7
SPAWNS
  AND SPAWNS HIS QUARTO AND DEMANDS YOUR PRAISE--  . .   440  2 DON JUAN  5     52    4
  THAT SHE SPAWNS WARRIORS BY THE SCORE WHERE NONE . .   164  3 DON JUAN  8    105    2
SPEAK
  I SHALL HAVE MUCH TO SPEAK ABOUT) AND SHE  . . . . .    54  2 DON JUAN  1     59    7
  SHE BLUSH'D AND FROWN'D NOT BUT SHE STROVE TO SPEAK .    81  2 DON JUAN  1    112    7
  HE STOOD IN ACT TO SPEAK OR RATHER STAMMER . . . . .   111  2 DON JUAN  1    163    1
  ANTONIA PUZZLED JULIA DID NOT SPEAK  . . . . . . . .   114  2 DON JUAN  1    169    7
  TO SPEAK OF INEZ NOW WERE ONE MAY SAY  . . . . . . .   118  2 DON JUAN  1    177    7
  FOR THIS MEN WRITE SPEAK PREACH AND HEROES KILL  . .   146  2 DON JUAN  1    218    5
  AS WITH AN EFFORT SHE BEGAN TO SPEAK . . . . . . . .   236  2 DON JUAN  2    150    4
  MUCH ENGLISH I CANNOT PRETEND TO SPEAK . . . . . . .   243  2 DON JUAN  2    165    3
  I SPEAK OF CHRISTIAN LANDS IN THIS COMPARISON  . . .   248  2 DON JUAN  2    175    7
  THEN LAMBRO WHO TILL NOW FORBORE TO SPEAK  . . . . .   364  2 DON JUAN  4     37    5
  BUT NO ONE EVER HEARD HER SPEAK OR SHRIEK  . . . . .   380  2 DON JUAN  4     67    5
  SPEAK BUT HE SPOKE NOT WAKE BUT STILL HE SLEPT--  .    430  2 DON JUAN  5     36    2
  PASSED WITHOUT WORDS--IN FACT SHE COULD NOT SPEAK  .   490  2 DON JUAN  5    137    2
  SHE STOPT AND RAISED HER HEAD TO SPEAK--BUT PAUSED .    61  3 DON JUAN  6    111    1
  IF HE SPEAK TRUTH SHE IS CHRIST'S SISTER AND . . . .   116  3 DON JUAN  8      9    7
  SHORT SPEECHES PASS BETWEEN TWO MEN WHO SPEAK  . . .   141  3 DON JUAN  8     58    1
  MUCH AS THEY MIGHT HAVE BEEN SUPPOSED TO SPEAK . . .   298  3 DON JUAN 11     60    5
  THIS--WHEN I SPEAK I DON'T HINT BUT SPEAK OUT  . . .   311  3 DON JUAN 11     88    8
  THIS--WHEN I SPEAK I DON'T HINT BUT SPEAK OUT  . . .   311  3 DON JUAN 11     88    8
  WHOSE CHARMS MADE ALL MEN SPEAK AND WOMEN DUMB . . .   365  3 DON JUAN 13     13    6
  TO DRAW THE BOW TO RIDE AND SPEAK THE TRUTH  . . . .   501  3 DON JUAN 16      1    2
  I DO NOT SPEAK PROFANELY TO RECALL . . . . . . . . .   503  3 DON JUAN 16      6    5
  YET COULD NOT SPEAK OR MOVE BUT ON ITS BASE  . . . .   510  3 DON JUAN 16     23    4
  VOI CHE ENTRATE THE HINGE SEEMED TO SPEAK  . . . . .   557  3 DON JUAN 16    116    3
SPEAKERS
  SOME SPEAKERS WHINE AND OTHERS LAY THE LASH ON . . .   437  2 DON JUAN  5     48    5
  INTERMINABLE--NOT ETERNAL--SPEAKERS--  . . . . . . .   310  3 DON JUAN 11     85    2
  BUT SPEAKERS BARDS DIPLOMATISTS AND DANCERS  . . . .   547  3 DON JUAN 16     98    3
SPEAKING
  ALTHOUGH HER MODE OF SPEAKING WAS NOT PURE . . . . .    28  2 DON JUAN  1     13    4
  FOR SPEAKING OUT SO PLAINLY IN HIS SONG  . . . . . .    45  2 DON JUAN  1     43    5
  AGAINST ALL EVIL SPEAKING EVEN IN JEST . . . . . . .    49  2 DON JUAN  1     51    8
  AND THEN FAIR HAIDEE TRIED HER TONGUE AT SPEAKING  .   241  2 DON JUAN  2    161    1
  AND SMILES AND SPARKLES OF THE SPEAKING EYE  . . . .   241  2 DON JUAN  2    162    2
  OF HER DEEP-PURPLE ROBE AND SPEAKING LOW . . . . . .   466  2 DON JUAN  5     96    7
  GULBEYAZ' TACITURN OR SPEAKING WILL  . . . . . . . .    61  3 DON JUAN  6    110    4
  AT SPEAKING TRUTH PERHAPS THEY ARE LESS CLEVER . . .   501  3 DON JUAN 16      1    7
SPEAKS
  THE GESTURE WHICH ENCHANTS THE EYE THAT SPEAKS . . .   292  2 DON JUAN  3     33    4
  WHAT SPEAKS OF HEAVEN SHOULD BY NO MEANS BE BRITTLE .   444  2 DON JUAN  5     59    3
  NOTHING THAT SPEAKS TO ALL MEN AND ALL TIMES . . . .   417  3 DON JUAN 14     16    2
```

762

SPEAR
BELLONA SHOOK HER SPEAR WITH SUCH SUBLIMITY	92	3 DON JUAN	7	51	V6
SUCH WERE HIS TROPHIES--NOT OF SPEAR AND SHIELD	425	3 DON JUAN	14	35	1

SPECIAL
BY SPECIAL PROVIDENCE TO LEAD TO-MORROW	99	3 DON JUAN	7	63	4
THIS SPECIAL HONOUR WAS CONFERRED BECAUSE	182	3 DON JUAN	8	140	1
IS SPECIAL PROVIDENCE THOUGH HOW IT GAVE	192	3 DON JUAN	9	19	6
A SPECIAL TITIAN WARRANTED ORIGINAL	528	3 DON JUAN	16	56	2

SPECIE
OF RUBLES RAIN AS FAST AS SPECIE CAN	222	3 DON JUAN	9	79	6

SPECIES
OR HINTS CONTINUATION OF THE SPECIES	44	2 DON JUAN	1	40	7
BUT CHIEFLY BY A SPECIES OF SELF-SLAUGHTER	210	2 DON JUAN	2	102	7
WHICH FORM THAT BITTER DRAUGHT THE HUMAN SPECIES . . .	261	3 DON JUAN	10	73	8
OF WORLDS AND .SPECIES--MATTERS--SOULS AND BODY	269	3 DON JUAN	11	3	V7

SPECIFIED
OF WHICH HE SPECIFIED IN THIS HIS PLEADING	116	2 DON JUAN	1	174	6
WHICH SHALL BE SPECIFIED IN FITTING TIME	135	2 DON JUAN	1	200	V7
ALL THESE THINGS WILL BE SPECIFIED IN TIME	136	2 DON JUAN	1	201	1

SPECIMEN
YET THINK A SPECIMEN OF EVERY CLASS	402	3 DON JUAN	13	94	3

SPECIMENS
FEW SPECIMENS YET LEFT US CAN COMPARE	384	3 DON JUAN	13	55	5

SPECIOUS
BY SPECIOUS SEEMING JUAN'S YOUTH AND PATIENCE	365	3 DON JUAN	13	15	5

SPECK
AND THE SHIP CREAK'D THE TOWN BECAME A SPECK	163	2 DON JUAN	2	13	3

SPECKS
THE SUN HIMSELF WAS SCARCE MORE FREE FROM SPECKS . . .	474	2 DON JUAN	5	109	5
THEY ALL FOUND OUT AS FEW OR FEWER SPECKS	24	3 DON JUAN	6	37	4

SPECTACLE
AN AWKWARD SPECTACLE THEIR EYES BEFORE	125	2 DON JUAN	1	187	2

SPECTACLES
WHO THOUGH HER SPECTACLES AT LAST GREW DIM	241	3 DON JUAN	10	34	6

SPECTATOR
COULD SCARCE BE SHOWN EVEN BY A MERE SPECTATOR . . .	416	3 DON JUAN	5	11	8
OR AN APPROVER OR A MERE SPECTATOR	303	3 DON JUAN	11	69	7
FOR MY PART I AM BUT A MERE SPECTATOR	361	3 DON JUAN	13	7	6

SPECTATORS
STOOD AS THE UNPACKING GATHERED MORE SPECTATORS) . . .	313	3 DON JUAN	11	V 29	6

SPECTRAL
A SPECTRAL RESIDENT--WHOSE PALLID BEAM	279	3 DON JUAN	11	24	6
BUT APPREHENSIVE OF HIS SPECTRAL GUEST	555	3 DON JUAN	16	111	5

SPECTRE
THE SPECTRE HUNTSMAN OF ONESTI'S LINE	337	2 DON JUAN	3	106	5
HER VERY PLACE OF BIRTH WAS BUT A SPECTRE	182	3 DON JUAN	8	141	4
WHICH DRACHENFELS FROWNS OVER LIKE A SPECTRE	255	3 DON JUAN	10	62	2
THROUGH WHICH THE SPECTRE SEEMED TO EVAPORATE	511	3 DON JUAN	16	24	8
WHETHER WITH TIME THE SPECTRE HAS GROWN SHYER	516	3 DON JUAN	16	36	5

SPECTRES
LIKE CHARON'S BARK OF SPECTRES DULL AND PALE	209	2 DON JUAN	2	101	3

SPECULATE
'TIS TRUE WE SPECULATE BOTH FAR AND WIDE	190	3 DON JUAN	9	16	3
IT IS TO SPECULATE ON HANDSOME FACES	223	3 DON JUAN	9	82	7

SPECULATING
BUT SPECULATING AS I CAST MINE EYE	464	3 DON JUAN	15	19	4

SPECULATION
LIKE PYRRHO ON A SEA OF SPECULATION	191	3 DON JUAN	9	18	2
THROUGHOUT THE SEASON UPON SPECULATION	293	3 DON JUAN	11	49	2
AND WHY SHOULD I NOT FORM MY SPECULATION	325	3 DON JUAN	12	21	2
EACH AUNT EACH COUSIN HATH HER SPECULATION	331	3 DON JUAN	12	33	1
THE LANDED AND THE MONIED SPECULATION	360	3 DON JUAN	13	6	4
GENT READER NOTHING A MERE SPECULATION	413	3 DON JUAN	14	7	2

SPECULATIONS
BUT OTHER SPECULATIONS WERE IN SOOTH	222	2 DON JUAN	2	125	3
THE ADMIRATIONS AND THE SPECULATIONS	523	3 DON JUAN	16	45	2

SPECULATIVE
IS NOT A MERELY SPECULATIVE HIT	318	3 DON JUAN	12	6	3

SPEECH
THE ANVIL OF HIS SPEECH RECEIVED THE HAMMER	111	2 DON JUAN	1	163	3
HIS SPEECH WAS A FINE SAMPLE ON THE WHOLE	116	2 DON JUAN	1	174	7
ALFONSO CLOSED HIS SPEECH AND BEGG'D HER PARDON . . .	120	2 DON JUAN	1	180	1
HER SPEECH OUT TO HER PROTEGE AND FRIEND	241	2 DON JUAN	2	161	6
ALL IN ALL TO EACH OTHER THOUGH THEIR SPEECH	256	2 DON JUAN	2	189	3
INSTEAD OF SPEECH MAY FORM A LASTING LINK	327	2 DON JUAN	3	88	5
(PLAIN TRUTH DEAR MURRAY NEEDS FEW FLOWERS OF SPEECH) .	470	2 DON JUAN	5	101	2
AND AS HIS SPEECH GREW STILL MORE BROKEN-KNEED . . .	56	3 DON JUAN	6	101	6
FOR IF I WROTE DOWN EVERY WARRIOR'S SPEECH	83	3 DON JUAN	7	35	7
BUT WHETHER FROM HIS VOICE OR SPEECH OR MANNER . . .	95	3 DON JUAN	7	56	7
HIS PARTS OF SPEECH AND IN THE STRANGE DISPLAYS . . .	207	3 DON JUAN	9	49	4
SMOOTH SPEECH HIS FIRST AND MAIDENLY TRANSGRESSION . .	400	3 DON JUAN	13	90	4
THE BEST FIRST SPEECH THAT EVER YET WAS MADE	400	3 DON JUAN	13	90	8
AS WIDE AS IF A LONG SPEECH WERE TO COME	557	3 DON JUAN	16	115	4

SPEECHES
OF MEN AND MADE THEM SPEECHES WHEN HALF MELLOW	318	2 DON JUAN	3	82	4
SHORT SPEECHES PASS BETWEEN TWO MEN WHO SPEAK	141	3 DON JUAN	8	58	1
BESIDES THOSE SOOTHING SPEECHES OF THE PLEADERS . . .	346	3 DON JUAN	12	65	7

SPEECHLESS
BUT NOW LAY SICK AND SPEECHLESS ON HIS PILLOW	169	2 DON JUAN	2	25	4

		PAGE	VOL		CANTO	STANZA	LN

SPEECHLESS   (CONTINUED)
| WITH SWIMMING LOOKS OF SPEECHLESS TENDERNESS | 357 | 2 DON JUAN | 4 | 26 | 2 |
| NOT SPEECHLESS THOUGH SHE SPOKE NOT NOT A SIGH | 378 | 2 DON JUAN | 4 | 63 | 5 |
SPEED
AND AS HE FLOUNDERED ON WITHOUT DUE SPEED	56	3 DON JUAN	6	101	V6
THEIR SPEED ABATED OR THEIR STRENGTH GREW DULL	59	3 DON JUAN	6	107	6
AS GOING AT FULL SPEED--NO MATTER WHERE ITS	260	3 DON JUAN	10	72	3
ON WHICH JACK AND HIS TRAIN SET OFF AT SPEED	275	3 DON JUAN	11	14	1
SPEEDIER
WITH DEADLIER ENGINES AND A SPEEDIER BLOW	106	3 DON JUAN	7	80	3
SPEEDILY
THINGS SPEEDILY WERE WAXING TO EXTREMITY	92	3 DON JUAN	7	51	V6
THE PRICE WOULD SPEEDILY REPAY ITS WORTH IN	529	3 DON JUAN	16	59	4
SPEEDS
HURRAH HOW SWIFTLY SPEEDS THE POST SO MERRY	260	3 DON JUAN	10	71	3
SPELL
NOT YET A DREAMER TILL THE SPELL IS BROKE	237	2 DON JUAN	2	152	3
A SPELL FROM WHICH EVEN YET I AM NOT QUITE FREE	413	2 DON JUAN	5	4	6
HOW SHALL I SPELL THE NAME OF EACH COSSACQUE	73	3 DON JUAN	7	14	3
AS THUNDERED KNOCKERS BROKE THE LONG-SEALED SPELL	282	3 DON JUAN	11	29	3
WHO BOUND THE BAR OR SENATE IN THEIR SPELL	307	3 DON JUAN	11	77	4
'TIS NOT ENOUGH TO SPELL OR EVEN TO READ	393	3 DON JUAN	13	73	2
SPELLKEN
BOOZE IN THE KEN OR AT THE SPELLKEN HUSTLE	277	3 DON JUAN	11	19	4
SPELLS
THEIR SPELLS AND GIVE THEM TO THE PASSING GALE	72	2 DON JUAN	1	95	7
THE MOST IMPERATIVE OF SOVEREIGN SPELLS	393	2 DON JUAN	4	91	3
SPELT
THRICE HAPPY HE WHOSE NAME HAS BEEN WELL SPELT	120	3 DON JUAN	8	18	6
SPENDING
HE HAD BROUGHT HIS SPENDING TO A HANDSOME ANCHOR--	240	3 DON JUAN	10	31	4
SPENDS
BUT SPENDS SO FAST SHE HAS NOT NOW A PAUL	390	2 DON JUAN	4	84	6
THE DUKE OF D-- THE SHOOTING SEASON SPENDS	382	3 DON JUAN	13	52	5
SPENDTHRIFTS'
LET SPENDTHRIFTS' HEIRS ENQUIRE OF YOURS--WHO'S WISER	321	3 DON JUAN	12	11	8
SPENT
HAVE SPENT MY LIFE BOTH INTEREST AND PRINCIPAL	143	2 DON JUAN	1	213	7
IS GLITTERING YOUTH WHICH I HAVE SPENT BETIMES--	145	2 DON JUAN	1	217	7
IS THAT SAME TIME WHICH I HAVE SPENT BETIMES	145	2 DON JUAN	1	217	V7
A YEAR OR TWO'S AN AGE WHEN RIGHTLY SPENT	228	2 DON JUAN	2	136	5
AND ZOE SPENT HERS AS MOST WOMEN DO	228	2 DON JUAN	2	136	6
THEIR FURY BEING SPENT BY ITS OWN SHOCK	305	2 DON JUAN	3	58	6
UPON THE NOTHINGS WHICH ARE DAILY SPENT	189	3 DON JUAN	9	13	5
AND SPARKLED INTO BASINS WHERE IT SPENT	389	3 DON JUAN	13	65	6
THIS MORNING RATHER SPENT LESS TIME UPON'T	513	3 DON JUAN	16	29	3
SPERANZA
LIKE THAT OF HELL LASCIATE OGNI SPERANZA	557	3 DON JUAN	16	116	2
SPHERE
BEYOND ITS DIMMED EYE'S SPHERE--BUT WOULD MUCH RATHER	228	3 DON JUAN	10	6	7
AND SOMEWHAT MECHANTE IN HER AMOROUS SPHERE	438	3 DON JUAN	14	63	2
YET EACH WAS RADIANT IN HER PROPER SPHERE	481	3 DON JUAN	15	58	3
HAD ENGLISH INFLUENCE IN THE SELF-SAME SPHERE HERE	534	3 DON JUAN	16	70	5
AND EVERYBODY OUT OF THEIR OWN SPHERE	538	3 DON JUAN	16	78	8
SPHERES
HE HEARS--ALAS NO MUSIC OF THE SPHERES	290	2 DON JUAN	3	28	3
WHOSE FROWN WOULD PUT THE SPHERES ALL OUT OF TUNE	494	2 DON JUAN	5	144	3
AND SHINE THE VERY SIRIA OF THE SPHERES	397	3 DON JUAN	13	82	7
DISCUSS'D THE WORLD AND SETTLED ALL THE SPHERES	408	3 DON JUAN	13	109	2
THEY MOVED LIKE STARS UNITED IN THEIR SPHERES	447	3 DON JUAN	14	87	3
THEIR EARTH IS BUT AN ECHO OF THE SPHERES	458	3 DON JUAN	15	5	8
LIKE THAT SAME MYSTIC MUSIC OF THE SPHERES	489	3 DON JUAN	15	76	5
WITHOUT A SMALL REFRESHMENT FROM THE SPHERES	496	3 DON JUAN	15	90	8
SPHINX
THAT SPHINX WHOSE WORDS WOULD EVER BE A DOUBT	207	3 DON JUAN	9	50	3
BUT I'M NOT OEDIPUS AND LIFE'S A SPHINX	364	3 DON JUAN	13	12	8
SPICE
AND LADIES LIKE A LITTLE SPICE OF MARS	284	3 DON JUAN	11	33	V4
AND PASSION'S SELF MUST HAVE A SPICE OF FRANTIC	347	3 DON JUAN	12	68	3
SPIDERS
THAN HUMAN INSECTS CATERING FOR SPIDERS	196	3 DON JUAN	9	27	8
WHEREAS THE OTHERS HUNT FOR REGAL SPIDERS	196	3 DON JUAN	9	27	V8
WHEREAS YOUR MODERN MONARCHS ARE MERE SPIDERS	196	3 DON JUAN	9	27	V8
SPIES
BUT AS MY MAID'S UNDREST PRAY TURN YOUR SPIES OUT	104	2 DON JUAN	1	152	7
SPILL
TO SWALLOW FLAME AND NEITHER SWERVE NOR SPILL	93	3 DON JUAN	7	52	V6
SPILT
HEAVEN KNOWS WHAT CASH HE GOT OR BLOOD HE SPILT	223	2 DON JUAN	2	127	5
SPIN
AND PLANT AND REAP AND SPIN AND GRIND AND SOW	202	3 DON JUAN	9	40	4
SPINNING
(ALTHOUGH IT COST ME HALF AN HOUR IN SPINNING)	25	2 DON JUAN	1	7	6
WHAT WONDROUS NEW MACHINES HAVE LATE BEEN SPINNING	92	2 DON JUAN	1	130	6
THE PARCAE THEN CUT SHORT THE FURTHER SPINNING	414	2 DON JUAN	5	6	3
SPIRIT
BUT THEN SHE HAD A DEVIL OF A SPIRIT	32	2 DON JUAN	1	20	5
HIS NATURAL SPIRIT NOT IN VAIN THEY TOIL'D	49	2 DON JUAN	1	50	5
COULD YIELD HIS SPIRIT THAT FOR WHICH IT PANTED	73	2 DON JUAN	1	96	4

SPIRIT   (CONTINUED)
    AND FEEL NO MORE THE SPIRIT TO RETORT I . . . . . . 143 2 DON JUAN 1   213   6
    THERE'S NOUGHT NO DOUBT SO MUCH THE SPIRIT CALMS . . . . 174 2 DON JUAN 2   34   1
    AND PATIENT SPIRIT HELD ALOOF HIS FATE . . . . . . 203 2 DON JUAN 2   88   4
    THAT SPRING-DEW OF THE SPIRIT THE HEART'S RAIN . . . . . 250 2 DON JUAN 2   178   4
    TO FEEL THE POISON THROUGH HER SPIRIT CREEPING . . . . . 274 2 DON JUAN 3   1   5
    BUT SOMETHING OF THE SPIRIT OF OLD GREECE . . . . . 303 2 DON JUAN 3   55   1
    BEDEW'D HIS SPIRIT IN HIS CALMER HOURS . . . . . . 304 2 DON JUAN 3   56   8
    IT WAS THEIR VERY SPIRIT--NOT A SENSE . . . . . . 358 2 DON JUAN 4   27   8
    A PARTING PANG THE SPIRIT FROM HER PAST . . . . . . 381 2 DON JUAN 4   69   3
    HIS SPIRIT DOWN AND THEN THE LOSS OF WEALTH . . . . . 415 2 DON JUAN 5   8   6
    OF A HIGH SPIRIT EVIDENTLY THOUGH . . . . 417 2 DON JUAN 5   12   2
    THE SPIRIT IN THE END WILL HAVE ITS WAY . . . . . . 474 2 DON JUAN 5   110   8
    STOLE ON YOUR SPIRIT LIKE A MAY-DAY BREAKING . . . . . 27 3 DON JUAN 6   43   2
    'TIS THUS THE SPIRIT OF A SINGLE MIND . . . . 90 3 DON JUAN 7   48   1
    FILLED AS WITH LIGHTNING--FOR HIS SPIRIT SHARED . . . . 129 3 DON JUAN 8   33   3
    A MADDENING SPIRIT WHICH WOULD STRIVE TO BLEND . . . . 219 3 DON JUAN 9   73   4
    AND MY INTERNAL SPIRIT CUT A CAPER . . . . 226 3 DON JUAN 10   3   4
    YOUR VEINS OF COCKNEY SPIRIT SMILE OR MOURN . . . . . 264 3 DON JUAN 10   80   6
    OR ADAMANT TO FIND THE WORLD A SPIRIT . . . . . . 268 3 DON JUAN 11   1   7
    TO KNOW MYSELF AND ALL BESIDES MERE SPIRIT . . . . . 268 3 DON JUAN 11   1 V7
    OF THE TRUTH'S RAYS SPOIL NOT MY DRAUGHT OF SPIRIT . . . 269 3 DON JUAN 11   2   7
    AND THAT WHICH AFTER ALL MY SPIRIT VEXES . . . . . . 269 3 DON JUAN 11   3   4
    SPIRIT WOULD NAME AND THEREFORE EVEN I WON'T ANENT . . . 289 3 DON JUAN 11   43   4
    THAT'S YOUR AFFAIR NOT MINE A REAL SPIRIT . . . . . 356 3 DON JUAN 12   87   7
    AND TALENT ON HIS HAUGHTY SPIRIT WROUGHT . . . . . . 365 3 DON JUAN 13   15   6
    HER CHIEF RESOURCE WAS IN HER OWN HIGH SPIRIT . . . . . 372 3 DON JUAN 13   31   4
    'TIS THE WHOLE SPIRIT BROUGHT TO A QUINTESSENCE . . . . 375 3 DON JUAN 13   38   1
    AND WORK AWAY LIKE SPIRIT UPON MATTER . . . . . . 423 3 DON JUAN 14   30   7
    A GOODLY SPIRIT FOR A STATE DIVAN . . . . 440 3 DON JUAN 14   70   3
    A WAVERING SPIRIT MAY BE EASIER WRECK'D . . . . . . 446 3 DON JUAN 14   85   5
    HER SPIRIT SEEM'D AS SEATED ON A THRONE . . . . . . 477 3 DON JUAN 15   47   6
    AURORA'S SPIRIT WAS NOT OF THAT KIND . . . . . . 492 3 DON JUAN 15   81   8
    HAS SPARKLED AND LET HALF ITS SPIRIT OUT . . . . . . 504 3 DON JUAN 16   9   6
    OF SUCH A SPIRIT IN THESE HALLS OF OLD . . . . . . 510 3 DON JUAN 16   22   2
    WEIGHED ON HIS SPIRIT THOUGH BY NO MEANS SERIOUS . . . . 514 3 DON JUAN 16   33   5
    THE SPIRIT OF THESE WALLS--IN TRUTH NOT I . . . . . 516 3 DON JUAN 16   36   2
    THAT INNOVATION'S SPIRIT NOW-A-DAYS . . . . 536 3 DON JUAN 16   73   3
    HERO--FOR WHAT IS SUBSTANCE TO A SPIRIT . . . . . . 557 3 DON JUAN 16   116   7
SPIRIT-ROOM
    GOT TO THE SPIRIT-ROOM AND STOOD BEFORE . . . . . . 174 2 DON JUAN 2   35   3
SPIRIT'S
    MY BLOOD STILL RUSHES WHERE MY SPIRIT'S SET . . . . . 133 2 DON JUAN 1   196   3
    THIS SPIRIT'S WELL BUT IT MAY WAX TOO BOLD . . . . . 454 2 DON JUAN 5   75   3
    THERE LURKED A MAN BENEATH THE SPIRIT'S DRESS . . . . . 206 3 DON JUAN 9   47   6
SPIRITS
    SOME PLUNDER'D SOME DRANK SPIRITS SOME SUNG PSALMS . . . 174 2 DON JUAN 2   34   3
    RECALL'D HIS ANSWERING SPIRITS BACK FROM DEATH . . . . . 215 2 DON JUAN 2   113   4
    AVE MARIA MAY OUR SPIRITS DARE . . . . 336 2 DON JUAN 3   103   3
    FOR THEIRS WERE BUOYANT SPIRITS NEVER BOUND . . . . . 352 2 DON JUAN 4   16   5
    STILL KEPT HIS SPIRITS UP--AT LEAST HIS FACE . . . . . 388 2 DON JUAN 4   81   4
    FOR LAUGHTER--BUT SHE FELT HER SPIRITS LOW . . . . . 47 3 DON JUAN 6   83   6
    UNTO HIS CALL UNLIKE THE SPIRITS FROM . . . . . . 132 3 DON JUAN 8   38   2
    NO SINKING SPIRITS TOLD THEM THEY GREW GREY . . . . . 145 3 DON JUAN 8   66   5
    NOW THERE IS NOTHING GIVES A MAN SUCH SPIRITS . . . . . 260 3 DON JUAN 10   72   1
    AMONGST THE HIGHER SPIRITS OF THE DAY . . . . . . 300 3 DON JUAN 11   64   7
    JUST TO RELIEVE HER SPIRITS FROM DEJECTION . . . . . 483 3 DON JUAN 15   64   8
    HIS SPIRITS AND WITHOUT MORE EXPLANATION . . . . . . 526 3 DON JUAN 16   53   2
    SATE SILENT NOW HIS USUAL SPIRITS GONE . . . . . . 552 3 DON JUAN 16   105   6
SPIRITUAL
    WHICH LAST I LEAVE UNTO THE LORD'S SPIRITUAL . . . . . 472 3 DON JUAN 15   36 V8
    SO LIKE A SPIRITUAL PIT-A-PAT . . . . 556 3 DON JUAN 16   112   5
SPITE
    OF FIRE THAN WATER SPITE OF OATHS AND TEARS . . . . . 174 2 DON JUAN 2   35   6
    IN SPITE OF ALL REMONSTRANCES AND THEN . . . . . . 192 2 DON JUAN 2   69   3
    SO JUAN'S SPANIEL SPITE OF HIS ENTREATING . . . . . 193 2 DON JUAN 2   70   7
    AND SPITE OF JOHNSON AND OF JUAN WHO . . . . . . 165 3 DON JUAN 8   108   1
    WHO QUEER A FLAT WHO (SPITE OF BOW-STREET'S BAN) . . . . 277 3 DON JUAN 11   19   5
SPITS
    A JOINT UPON THEIR BARBAROUS SPITS THEY PUT ON . . . . . 238 2 DON JUAN 2   154   4
SPLASH
    ACCOMPANIED WITH A CONVULSIVE SPLASH . . . . . . 184 2 DON JUAN 2   53   6
    THEY HEARD THE WAVE'S SPLASH AND THE WIND SO LOW . . . . 253 2 DON JUAN 2   185   5
    TRAMP TRAMP O'ER PEBBLE AND SPLASH SPLASH THRO PUDDLE . . 260 3 DON JUAN 10   71   2
    TRAMP TRAMP O'ER PEBBLE AND SPLASH SPLASH THRO PUDDLE . . 260 3 DON JUAN 10   71   2
SPLASH'D
    THE SPRAY INTO THEIR FACES AS THEY SPLASH'D . . . . . 209 2 DON JUAN 2   101   8
SPLEEN
    A SUDDEN FIT OF DRUNKENNESS OR SPLEEN . . . . . . 98 2 DON JUAN 1   142   6
    THEIR SPLEEN IN MAKING STRIFE AND SAFELY WORDING . . . . 498 2 DON JUAN 5   151   6
SPLENDID
    IS ALWAYS MUCH MORE SPLENDID THAN A KING . . . . . 408 2 DON JUAN 4   115   6
    SPLENDID BUT SILENT SAVE IN ONE WHERE DROPPING . . . . . 442 2 DON JUAN 5   55   3
    THE GATE SO SPLENDID WAS IN ALL ITS FEATURES . . . . . 462 2 DON JUAN 5   87   7
    I AM NOT DAZZLED BY THIS SPLENDID ROOF . . . . . . 484 2 DON JUAN 5   127   5
    HAS SAVED THE FAME OF THOUSAND SPLENDID SINNERS . . . . 346 3 DON JUAN 12   66   3
    WHICH DOTH NOT SHAKE SOME VERY SPLENDID HOUSE . . . . . 370 3 DON JUAN 13   26   4
    WE UNDERSTAND THE SPLENDID HOST INTENDS . . . . . . 382 3 DON JUAN 13   52   1
    HER HEART WAS VACANT THOUGH A SPLENDID MANSION . . . . . 446 3 DON JUAN 14   85   2
    SOME SPLENDID DEBTOR HE WOULD TAKE BY SAP . . . . . 459 3 DON JUAN 15   8   4

	PAGE	VOL		CANTO	STANZA	LV
SPLENDOR						
TO BREAK THE LIFELESS SPLENDOR OF THE WHOLE	442	2	DON JUAN	5	56	8
SPLENDOUR						
HAD DONE THEIR WORK OF SPLENDOUR INDIAN MATS	310	2	DON JUAN	3	68	2
HIS FIGURE AND THE SPLENDOUR OF HIS DRESS	415	2	DON JUAN	5	9	3
ROSE THE SULTANA FROM A BED OF SPLENDOUR	50	3	DON JUAN	6	89	1
THE LUST WHICH STINGS THE SPLENDOUR WHICH ENCUMBERS	145	3	DON JUAN	8	67	5
AT ONCE HER ROYAL SPLENDOUR AND REWARD	247	3	DON JUAN	10	46	4
'TIS NOT MERE SPLENDOUR MAKES THE SHOW AUGUST	354	3	DON JUAN	12	83	7
SPLINTERS						
BUT STILL IT FALLS WITH VAST AND AWFUL SPLINTERS	155	3	DON JUAN	8	88	7
THEY COULD NOT EVEN GLEAN THE SLIGHTEST SPLINTERS	434	3	DON JUAN	14	56	5
SPLIT						
AND THE SMALL RIPPLE SPLIT UPON THE BEACH	250	2	DON JUAN	2	178	1
ONE'S HIP HE SLASHED AND SPLIT THE OTHER'S SHOULDER	158	3	DON JUAN	8	94	1
SPOIL						
HIS DEATH CONTRIVED TO SPOIL A CHARMING CAUSE	38	2	DON JUAN	1	33	5
TO LOSE THEIR LIVES AS WELL AS SPOIL THEIR DIET	173	2	DON JUAN	2	33	4
ALL WHICH SELECTED FROM THE SPOIL HE GATHERS	284	2	DON JUAN	3	17	7
BUT SPOIL (I THINK) A VERY PRETTY POEM	403	2	DON JUAN	4	107	8
BUT NATURE TEACHES MORE THAN POWER CAN SPOIL	480	2	DON JUAN	5	120	1
IT WOULD NOT SPOIL SOME SEPARATE CHARM TO PARE	27	3	DON JUAN	6	42	8
DANGER AND SPOIL WITH ARDOUR MUCH ENCREASED	90	3	DON JUAN	7	49	6
WITH THE FREE FORESTERS DIVIDE NO SPOIL	145	3	DON JUAN	8	67	6
OF THE TRUTH'S RAYS SPOIL NOT MY DRAUGHT OF SPIRIT	269	3	DON JUAN	11	2	7
BUT THEN 'TWOULD SPOIL MUCH GOOD PHILOSOPHY	410	3	DON JUAN	14	1	4
TO SPOIL HIS UNDERTAKING OR COMPLETE	423	3	DON JUAN	14	30	6
BUBBLE AND SQUEAK WOULD SPOIL MY LIQUID LAY	487	3	DON JUAN	15	71	6
SPOIL'D						
UP WITH THE COFFEE WHICH (I THINK) THEY SPOIL'D	307	2	DON JUAN	3	63	8
SPARED BY SOME CHANCE WHEN ALL BESIDE WAS SPOIL'D	387	3	DON JUAN	13	61	4
SPOILED						
THE FIAT OF THIS SPOILED CHILD OF THE NIGHT	86	3	DON JUAN	7	41	3
A LITTLE SPOILED BUT NOT SO ALTOGETHER	338	3	DON JUAN	12	49	3
SPOILS						
WHICH ALWAYS SPOILS THE BREED IF IT INCREASES	52	2	DON JUAN	1	57	8
DESPAIR OF ALL RECOVERY SPOILS LONGEVITY	190	2	DON JUAN	2	64	7
WHICH MAKES A DANDY WHILE IT SPOILS A MAN	461	3	DON JUAN	15	12	8
WHICH NODDED TO THE NATION'S SPOILS BELOW	485	3	DON JUAN	15	67	3
WHERE ALL THE PONTIC SPOILS MADE SUCH A SHOW	485	3	DON JUAN	15	67	V3
SPOILT						
AND THE FIRST BREAKFAST SPOILT PREPARED A NEW ONE	234	2	DON JUAN	2	146	6
THE TENOR'S VOICE IS SPOILT BY AFFECTATION	391	2	DON JUAN	4	87	1
SPOILT AS A PIPE OF CLARET IS WHEN PRICK'D	502	2	DON JUAN	5	158	5
A LITTLE SPOILT BUT BY NO MEANS SO QUITE	428	3	DON JUAN	14	41	3
FOR A SPOILT CARPET--BUT THE ATTIC BEE	522	3	DON JUAN	16	43	7
PRONOUNCES THAT AN ONLY 'S A SPOILT CHILD--	563	3	DON JUAN	17	2	3
SPOKE						
UNTIL SHE SPOKE THEN THROUGH ITS SOFT DISGUISE	54	2	DON JUAN	1	60	3
(ALTHOUGH THEY SPOKE NOT) IN THEIR WOLFISH EYES	194	2	DON JUAN	2	72	8
AND OUT THEY SPOKE OF LOTS FOR FLESH AND BLOOD	194	2	DON JUAN	2	73	7
HAIDEE SPOKE NOT OF SCRUPLES ASK'D NO VOWS	257	2	DON JUAN	2	190	1
WHEN JUAN SPOKE TOO--IT MIGHT BE IN SPORT--	356	2	DON JUAN	4	23	5
NOT SPEECHLESS THOUGH SHE SPOKE NOT NOT A SIGH	378	2	DON JUAN	4	63	5
SPEAK BUT HE SPOKE NOT WAKE BUT STILL HE SLEPT--	430	2	DON JUAN	5	36	2
THEY SPOKE BY SIGNS--THAT IS NOT SPOKE AT ALL	463	2	DON JUAN	5	90	1
THEY SPOKE BY SIGNS--THAT IS NOT SPOKE AT ALL	463	2	DON JUAN	5	90	1
SO THAT HE SPOKE NOT BUT BURST INTO TEARS	478	2	DON JUAN	5	117	8
WHICH AS ALL SPOKE AT ONCE AND MORE THAN ONCE	43	3	DON JUAN	6	74	2
AS THUS JUANNA SPOKE DUDU TURNED ROUND	48	3	DON JUAN	6	85	1
AND THROWN INTO THE SEA--THUS BABA SPOKE	58	3	DON JUAN	6	104	7
ONE OF WHOM SPOKE THEIR TONGUE OR WELL OR ILL	95	3	DON JUAN	7	56	5
TO WHOM HE SPOKE AND MADE HIS WORDS BUT FEW	97	3	DON JUAN	7	59	8
JUAN TO WHOM HE SPOKE IN GERMAN KNEW	141	3	DON JUAN	8	57	1
PERHAPS THE FINE OLD FELLOW SPOKE IN JEST--	361	3	DON JUAN	13	7	5
AND SPOKE MORE OF THE BARON THAN THE MONK	389	3	DON JUAN	13	66	8
BUT THEN 'TWAS TO THE PURPOSE WHAT SHE SPOKE	552	3	DON JUAN	16	104	3
SPOKEN						
NOW LIKE FRIAR BACON'S BRAZEN HEAD I'VE SPOKEN	145	2	DON JUAN	1	217	5
BUT I HAVE SPOKEN OF ALL THIS ALREADY--	246	2	DON JUAN	2	171	5
THEY HAD NOT SPOKEN BUT THEY FELT ALLURED	254	2	DON JUAN	2	187	5
SPONGY						
WHICH SERVED THEM AS A SORT OF SPONGY PITCHER	201	2	DON JUAN	2	85	3
SPOON						
WHICH MADE HIM HAVE RECOURSE UNTO HIS SPOON	513	3	DON JUAN	16	30	5
SPOONFULS						
AND FED BY SPOONFULS ELSE THEY ALWAYS BURST	239	2	DON JUAN	2	158	8
SPOONS						
AND I GROWN ONE OF MANY WOODEN SPOONS	341	2	DON JUAN	3	110	6
SPORT						
WHEN JUAN SPOKE TOO--IT MIGHT BE IN SPORT--	356	2	DON JUAN	4	23	5
MEN ARE THE SPORT OF CIRCUMSTANCES WHEN	419	2	DON JUAN	5	17	7
THE CIRCUMSTANCES SEEM THE SPORT OF MEN	419	2	DON JUAN	5	17	8
DEATH TO HIS PUBLISHER TO HIM 'TIS SPORT	440	2	DON JUAN	5	52	5
FOR THEN WEALTH KINGDOMS WORLDS ARE BUT A SPORT--I	9	3	DON JUAN	6	5	3
BE FOR MERE FANCY'S SPORT A THEME CREATIVE	363	3	DON JUAN	13	10	6
AND AH YE POACHERS--'TIS NO SPORT FOR PEASANTS	394	3	DON JUAN	13	75	8
OR HUNT THE YOUNG BECAUSE THEY LIKED THE SPORT--	405	3	DON JUAN	13	101	2
SPORTED						
LIKE A RACE-HORSE MUCH TO EACH DRESS HE SPORTED	239	3	DON JUAN	10	29	5

	PAGE	VOL		CANTO	STANZA	LN
SPORTING						
THE NESTORS OF THE SPORTING GENERATION	425	3	DON JUAN	14	34	5
SPORTS						
AND MINGLING MODESTLY IN TOILS OR SPORTS	424	3	DON JUAN	14	31	6
SPORTSMAN						
THE POINTER RANGES AND THE SPORTSMAN BEATS	394	3	DON JUAN	13	75	4
SPORUS						
THAT SWARTHY SPORUS NEITHER MAN NOR BARD	297	3	DON JUAN	11	58	5
SPOT						
AGAINST THE WORLD AND DEAR THE SCHOOLBOY SPOT	90	2	DON JUAN	1	126	7
AND AS THE SPOT WHERE THEY APPEAR HE NEARS	290	2	DON JUAN	3	28	1
THE TIME THE CLIME THE SPOT WHERE I SO OFT	335	2	DON JUAN	3	102	2
SHE COULD NOT FROM THE SPOT AND THE LOUD ROAR	361	2	DON JUAN	4	31	3
SHE RECOGNISED NO BEING AND NO SPOT	379	2	DON JUAN	4	64	3
WHOM TO THE SPOT THEIR SCHOOL-BOY FEELINGS BEAR	387	2	DON JUAN	4	78	5
I CANTER BY THE SPOT EACH AFTERNOON	400	2	DON JUAN	4	103	1
TO SHOW HIS LOATHING OF THE SPOT HE SOIL'D	401	2	DON JUAN	4	105	4
BECAUSE THEY CAN'T FIND OUT THE VERY SPOT	447	2	DON JUAN	5	62	3
STUCK ALL EXACTLY IN THE PROPER SPOT	37	3	DON JUAN	6	62	8
VIED WITH EACH OTHER ON THIS COSTLY SPOT	55	3	DON JUAN	6	98	2
BEFORE THEY REACHED A SPOT TO TAKE EFFECT	80	3	DON JUAN	7	28	4
OF OFFICERS A THIRD FELL ON THE SPOT	119	3	DON JUAN	8	16	5
BY CHRISTIAN SOLDIERY A SINGLE SPOT	131	3	DON JUAN	8	37	5
TO SOME SPOT WHERE THEY LOST THEIR UNDERSTANDING	148	3	DON JUAN	8	72	3
I HAVE NO GREAT CAUSE TO LOVE THAT SPOT OF EARTH	257	3	DON JUAN	10	66	1
IS THAT I FIND NO SPOT WHERE MAN CAN REST EYE ON	269	3	DON JUAN	11	3	5
I SAY I DO BELIEVE A HAUNTED SPOT	499	3	DON JUAN	15	96	3
STRAINED ON THE SPOT WHERE FIRST THE FIGURE GLEAMED	511	3	DON JUAN	16	25	3
SPOTS						
THE SPOTS WHICH WERE HER REALMS FOR EVERMORE	443	2	DON JUAN	5	57	4
BEYOND THE RUMOUR WHICH SUCH SPOTS UNFOLD	510	3	DON JUAN	16	22	4
SPOTTED						
THOUGH RATHER MORE IRREGULARLY SPOTTED	416	2	DON JUAN	5	10	3
SPOUSE						
PREFER A SPOUSE WHOSE AGE IS SHORT OF THIRTY	56	2	DON JUAN	1	62	8
AND WHEN THE SPOUSE AND FRIEND ARE GONE OFF WHOLLY	74	2	DON JUAN	1	99	7
A FEELING DANGEROUS TO A PRUDENT SPOUSE	81	2	DON JUAN	1	111	8
OF PLIGHT AND PROMISES TO BE A SPOUSE	257	2	DON JUAN	2	190	3
SAD THOUGHT TO LOSE THE SPOUSE THAT WAS ADORNING	278	2	DON JUAN	3	7	7
EVER SINCE JUAN SERVED HER FOR A SPOUSE	295	2	DON JUAN	3	39	V8
WAS WHIPT AT COLLEGE--A HARSH SIRE--ODD SPOUSE	328	2	DON JUAN	3	91	7
THE SPOUSE OF POTIPHAR THE LADY BOOBY	486	2	DON JUAN	5	131	2
HIS MAJESTY SALUTED HIS FOURTH SPOUSE	500	2	DON JUAN	5	154	1
OF THE LAST AXIOM HE ADVISED HIS SPOUSE	439	3	DON JUAN	14	67	2
I THINK I SHOULD HAVE MADE A DECENT SPOUSE	467	3	DON JUAN	15	24	1
SPOUSELESS						
BUT STILL THE SPOUSELESS VIRGIN KNOWLEDGE FLIES	37	3	DON JUAN	6	63	5
SPOUSES						
WHO SAW THEIR SPOUSES KILL'D AND NOBLY CHOSE	36	2	DON JUAN	1	29	4
WERE NOT DRAWN FROM THEIR SPOUSES YOU CONCEIVE	281	2	DON JUAN	3	10	8
SPOUT						
THAT MONSTROUS HIEROGLYPHIC--THAT LONG SPOUT	207	3	DON JUAN	9	50	5
THAT MONSTROUS MYSTAGOGUE--THAT MERE SPOUT	207	3	DON JUAN	9	50	V5
SPOUTING						
THE SPOUTING BLOOD GUSHED THROUGH HER MOUTH HER EYES	376	2	DON JUAN	4	59	V1
SPRAINS						
THE RACE HE SPRAINS A WING AND DOWN WE TEND	344	2	DON JUAN	4	1	4
SPRANG						
IT MIGHT BE THAT HER SILENCE SPRANG ALONE	118	2	DON JUAN	1	176	6
AND THE HEART'S DEW OF PAIN SPRANG FAST AND CHILLY	58	3	DON JUAN	6	105	7
SPRAWLING						
A WOUNDED COMRADE SPRAWLING IN HIS GORE	121	3	DON JUAN	8	20	8
SPRAY						
AND STANDING UPON DECK THE DASHING SPRAY	162	2	DON JUAN	2	11	5
THE SPRAY INTO THEIR FACES AS THEY SPLASH'D	209	2	DON JUAN	2	101	8
TO SHOW ITS BOILING SURF AND BOUNDING SPRAY	211	2	DON JUAN	2	104	6
AND HIS BLACK CURLS WERE DEWY WITH THE SPRAY	234	2	DON JUAN	2	147	6
HIGH DASHED THE SPRAY THE BOWS DIPPED IN THE SEA	256	3	DON JUAN	10	64	4
WHEN EVEN THE SEA LOOKS DIM WITH ALL ITS SPRAY	422	3	DON JUAN	14	28	3
OR LIKE A SODA BOTTLE WHEN ITS SPRAY	504	3	DON JUAN	16	9	5
SPREAD						
THROBB'D IN ACCURSED DREAMS WHICH SOMETIMES SPREAD	227	2	DON JUAN	2	134	6
CHECKS TO A LAKE WHOSE WAVES IN CIRCLES SPREAD	231	2	DON JUAN	2	141	7
SPREAD LIKE A ROSY OCEAN VAST AND BRIGHT	253	2	DON JUAN	2	185	2
AN IVORY INLAID TABLE SPREAD WITH STATE	306	2	DON JUAN	3	61	5
OVER THE FLOORS WERE SPREAD GAZELLES AND CATS	310	2	DON JUAN	3	68	4
THE GREATER PART OF THESE WERE READY SPREAD	310	2	DON JUAN	3	69	6
THESE AT SOME CERTAIN PORTIONED HOURS WERE SPREAD	310	2	DON JUAN	3	69	V6
BUT 'TIS A NAME SO SPREAD O'ER SIR AND MADAM	79	3	DON JUAN	7	25	7
BUT HIS JUST NOW WERE SPREAD AS IS A CUSHION	235	3	DON JUAN	10	21	5
BUT DESTINY AND PASSION SPREAD THE NET	364	3	DON JUAN	13	12	5
IN CURRENTS THROUGH THE CALMER WATER SPREAD	385	3	DON JUAN	13	57	4
HERE SWEETLY SPREAD A LANDSCAPE OF LORRAINE	392	3	DON JUAN	13	72	1
SPREADING						
AND TREES OF GOODLY GROWTH AND SPREADING ROOTS	43	3	DON JUAN	6	75	8
OF THIS ENORMOUS CITY'S SPREADING SPAWN	281	3	DON JUAN	11	28	4
SPREADS						
THE POPULATION THERE SO SPREADS THEY SAY	92	2	DON JUAN	1	131	3
LOVE'S THE FIRST NET WHICH SPREADS ITS DEADLY MESH	422	2	DON JUAN	5	22	5

	PAGE	VOL	CANTO	STANZA	LN
SPRIGHTLY					
NOT EVEN A SPRIGHTLY BLUNDER'S SPARK CAN BLAZE	17	2 DON JUAN	D	13	5
ACTIVE THOUGH NOT SO SPRIGHTLY AS A PAGE	51	2 DON JUAN	1	54	3
SPRING					
AND SO IS SPRING ABOUT THE END OF MAY	76	2 DON JUAN	1	102	3
I MAKE A RESOLUTION EVERY SPRING	85	2 DON JUAN	1	119	3
AND CAMPBELL'S SPRING SEEMS SOMEWHAT DRY AND DROUTHY	139	2 DON JUAN	1	205	V6
AND THEIR REVENGE IS AS THE TIGER'S SPRING	262	2 DON JUAN	2	199	6
SO THAT ALL MISCHIEFS SPRING UP FROM THIS ENTRAIL	271	2 DON JUAN	2	215	7
AN EPIC FROM BOB SOUTHEY EVERY SPRING--)	332	2 DON JUAN	3	97	4
OUR HEARTS FIRST IN THE DEPTHS OF LETHE'S SPRING	346	2 DON JUAN	4	4	5
MEANT TO GROW OLD BUT DIE IN HAPPY SPRING	348	2 DON JUAN	4	8	7
IN ARMS AT LEAST HE STOOD IN ACT TO SPRING	365	2 DON JUAN	4	39	7
OTHERS CONTENDED THEY WERE BUT IN SPRING	23	3 DON JUAN	6	35	6
BUT 'TWAS A TRANSIENT TREMOR--WITH A SPRING	170	3 DON JUAN	8	118	1
WHICH STILL ELSEWHERE MAY ROUSE A BRIGHTER SPRING--	188	3 DON JUAN	9	11	4
MAKE LOVE THE MAIN SPRING OF THE UNIVERSE	219	3 DON JUAN	9	73	8
KNOW NOT WHAT VISIONS SPRING FROM EACH CHEESE-PARING	316	3 DON JUAN	12	3	8
AND FULL OF PROMISE AS THE SPRING OF PRIME	354	3 DON JUAN	12	84	4
THE SPRING GUSH'D THROUGH GRIM MOUTHS OF GRANITE MADE	389	3 DON JUAN	13	65	5
AS IF 'TWOULD TO A SECOND SPRING RESIGN	395	3 DON JUAN	13	77	3
AND STILL MORE WOMEN SPRING FROM NOT EMPLOYING	444	3 DON JUAN	14	78	7
BUT GREAT THINGS SPRING FROM LITTLE--WOULD YOU THINK	454	3 DON JUAN	14	100	1
MATCHED FOR THE SPRING WHOM SEVERAL WENT TO SEE	527	3 DON JUAN	16	55	8
SPRINGALD					
ALSO THE YOUNGER MEN TOO FOR A SPRINGALD	487	3 DON JUAN	15	70	5
SPRING-DEW					
THAT SPRING-DEW OF THE SPIRIT THE HEART'S RAIN	250	2 DON JUAN	2	178	4
SPRINGS					
A LECTURE AND SOME MONEY FOR FOUR SPRINGS	161	2 DON JUAN	2	9	3
FROM WHENCE SPRINGS UP ABUNDANCE OF ABUSES	327	2 DON JUAN	3	88	V4
EARTH AIR STARS--ALL THAT SPRINGS FROM THE GREAT WHOLE	336	2 DON JUAN	3	104	7
WERE RIPE THEY MIGHT MAKE SIX AND TWENTY SPRINGS	468	3 DON JUAN	5	98	2
(A CURSED SORT OF CARRIAGE WITHOUT SPRINGS	197	3 DON JUAN	9	30	2
BEAUTY SPRINGS FORTH AND NATURE'S SELF TURNS PALER	204	3 DON JUAN	9	44	4
THE VERY CLERKS--THOSE SOMEWHAT DIRTY SPRINGS	287	3 DON JUAN	11	40	5
TO TRACE ALL ACTIONS TO THEIR SECRET SPRINGS	436	3 DON JUAN	14	59	5
OF WHICH I CAN'T TELL WHENCE THEIR KNOWLEDGE SPRINGS	489	3 DON JUAN	15	76	4
IT MAKES MY BLOOD BOIL LIKE THE SPRINGS OF HECLA	497	3 DON JUAN	15	92	7
SPRING-TIDE					
WAVES AT SPRING-TIDE OR WOMEN ANYWHERE	23	3 DON JUAN	6	34	3
SPRINKLED					
SPRINKLED WITH PALACES THE OCEAN STREAM	412	2 DON JUAN	5	3	2
AND ELEGANCE WAS SPRINKLED O'ER HIS FIGURE	427	3 DON JUAN	14	39	2
SPRINKLING					
A LITTLE GENIAL SPRINKLING OF HYPOCRISY	346	3 DON JUAN	12	66	2
BY WAY OF SPRINKLING SCATTER'D AMONGST THESE	397	3 DON JUAN	13	83	7
SPRITELIEST					
THEY SHOULD HAVE WALKED THERE IN THEIR SPRITELIEST TRIM	38	3 DON JUAN	6	64	5
SPRITES					
OF THE FAIR OCCUPANTS IF THERE BE SPRITES	38	3 DON JUAN	6	64	4
RECEIVING SPRITES WITH SYMPATHETIC VAPOUR	512	3 DON JUAN	16	26	3
SPRUNG					
SPRUNG UP A BRANCH AS BEAUTIFUL AS FRESH	53	2 DON JUAN	1	58	4
THEIR HEARTS THE FLOWER FROM WHENCE THE HONEY SPRUNG	254	2 DON JUAN	2	187	8
WHERE DELOS ROSE AND PHOEBUS SPRUNG	320	2 DON JUAN	3	L 1	4
UP JUAN SPRUNG TO HAIDEE'S BITTER SHRIEK	364	2 DON JUAN	4	37	1
SWEAR THAT PAT'S LANGUAGE SPRUNG FROM THE SAME CLIME	122	3 DON JUAN	8	23	5
FAR SWEETER THAN THE GREENEST LAURELS SPRUNG	199	3 DON JUAN	9	34	4
IN VISIONS OF THOSE SKIES FROM WHENCE LOVE SPRUNG	230	3 DON JUAN	10	10	6
HIS MANNER SHOWED HIM SPRUNG FROM A HIGH MOTHER	369	3 DON JUAN	13	24	6
IT ALL SPRUNG FROM A HARMLESS GAME AT BILLIARDS	454	3 DON JUAN	14	100	8
SPUN					
AND AS HE GAZED HIS DIZZY BRAIN SPUN FAST	214	2 DON JUAN	2	110	1
HER DRESS WAS MANY-COLOUR'D FINELY SPUN	220	2 DON JUAN	2	121	2
MUST BE DECLINED WHILE LIFE'S THIN THREAD'S SPUN OUT	376	3 DON JUAN	13	40	7
SPUR					
THEN SPUR AWAY O'ER EMPIRES AND O'ER STATES	76	2 DON JUAN	1	103	6
A COURIER ON THE SPUR INSPIRED NEW HEART	85	3 DON JUAN	7	39	3
HAVE PRINCES WHO SPUR MORE THAN THEIR POSTILLIONS	254	3 DON JUAN	10	60	8
SPURN					
OF HAVING PLAY'D THE FOOL THOUGH BOTH I SPURN HE	103	2 DON JUAN	1	151	5
SPURNED					
A PREACHER HAD HELD FORTH (WHO NOBLY SPURNED	99	3 DON JUAN	7	64	5
ARE SPURNED IN TURN UNTIL HER TURN ARRIVES	333	3 DON JUAN	12	36	2
SPURR'D					
SPURR'D HER TO TEACH ANOTHER GENERATION	162	2 DON JUAN	2	10	8
SPURRED					
DASHED ON LIKE A SPURRED BLOOD-HORSE IN A RACE	139	3 DON JUAN	8	54	8
AS THE SMART BOYS SPURRED FAST IN THEIR CAREER	263	3 DON JUAN	10	77	3
SPURZHEIM					
MAN WITH HIS HEAD REFLECTS--(AS SPURZHEIM TELLS)	7	3 DON JUAN	6	2	V7
SQUABBLE					
AS BOYS LOVE ROWS MY BOYHOOD LIKED A SQUABBLE	398	2 DON JUAN	4	99	1
SQUAD					
THE AWKWARD SQUAD AND COULD AFFORD TO SQUANDER	93	3 DON JUAN	7	52	3
IT SOOTHES THE AWKWARD SQUAD OF THE REJECTED	333	3 DON JUAN	12	36	7
SQUADRON					
AND IN PERSPECTIVE MANY A SQUADRON FLIES	461	2 DON JUAN	5	86	6

768

	PAGE	VOL	CANTO	STANZA	LN

SQUALL
A SQUALL CAME ON AND WHILE SOME GUNS BROKE LOOSE . . . . . 172 2 DON JUAN 2 30 6
ALTHOUGH A SQUALL OR TWO HAD DAMP'D HIS RAPTURES . . . . 283 2 DON JUAN 3 15 4
SQUALLS
HOW MOTHERS LOVE THEIR CHILDREN'S SQUALLS AND CHUCKLINGS . 488 2 DON JUAN 5 133 6
SQUANDER
THE AWKWARD SQUAD AND COULD AFFORD TO SQUANDER . . . . . 93 3 DON JUAN 7 52 3
SQUANDER'D
HAVE SQUANDER'D MY WHOLE SUMMER WHILE 'TWAS MAY . . . . 143 2 DON JUAN 1 213 5
SQUARE
NO DOUBT IN LITTLE COMPASS ROUND OR SQUARE . . . . . . 112 2 DON JUAN 1 166 4
HE HAD AN ENGLISH LOOK THAT IS WAS SQUARE . . . . . . 416 2 DON JUAN 5 11 1
WAS ALSO CERTAIN THAT THE EARTH WAS SQUARE . . . . . 497 2 DON JUAN 5 150 2
UNTIL TO SOME CONSPICUOUS SQUARE THEY PASS . . . . . 283 3 DON JUAN 11 31 7
THROUGH STREET AND SQUARE FAST FLASHING CHARIOTS HURLED . 302 3 DON JUAN 11 67 3
AT BLANK-BLANK SQUARE--FOR WE WILL BREAK NO SQUARES . . . 369 3 DON JUAN 13 25 1
LORD HENRY'S MANSION WAS IN BLANK-BLANK SQUARE . . . . . 369 3 DON JUAN 13 25 8
THEREFORE I NAME NOT SQUARE STREET PLACE UNTIL I . . . . 370 3 DON JUAN 13 27 5
AT HENRY'S MANSION THEN IN BLANK-BLANK SQUARE . . . . . 370 3 DON JUAN 13 28 1
SQUARES
AT BLANK-BLANK SQUARE--FOR WE WILL BREAK NO SQUARES . . 369 3 DON JUAN 13 25 1
FOR MAKING SQUARES AND STREETS ANONYMOUS . . . . 370 3 DON JUAN 13 26 2
UNLESS I KNEW THE VERY CHASTEST SQUARES . . . . 370 3 DON JUAN 13 26 8
SQUATTED
ALONG THIS HALL AND UP AND DOWN SOME SQUATTED . . . . . 441 2 DON JUAN 5 53 1
SQUAW
AND MRS RABBI THE RICH BANKER'S SQUAW . . . . 396 3 DON JUAN 13 79 6
SQUEAK
(THAT MAKE OLD EUROPE'S JOURNALS SQUEAK AND GIBBER ALL) . 318 3 DON JUAN 12 5 4
BUBBLE AND SQUEAK WOULD SPOIL MY LIQUID LAY . . . . . 487 3 DON JUAN 15 71 6
SQUEAKERS
I'VE SEEN THE COUNTRY GENTLEMEN TURN SQUEAKERS-- . . . . 310 3 DON JUAN 11 85 4
SQUEAMISH
THAN WHEN SOME SQUEAMISH PEOPLE DEEM HER FRAIL . . . . 483 3 DON JUAN 15 64 4
SQUEEZE
HIS FINGERS WITH A PURE PLATONIC SQUEEZE . . . . 81 2 DON JUAN 1 111 5
SQUEEZED
HE SQUEEZED FROM OUT A RAG SOME DROPS OF RAIN . . . . 203 2 DON JUAN 2 89 7
SQUEEZED THROUGH THE RIND WHICH MAKES IT BEST FOR USE . 307 2 DON JUAN 3 62 8
'SQUIRE
THERE NOW ARE NO 'SQUIRE WESTERNS AS OF OLD . . . . . 409 3 DON JUAN 13 110 4
'SQUIRES
HE ACQUITTED BOTH HIMSELF AND HORSE THE 'SQUIRES . . . 425 3 DON JUAN 14 34 2
FROM ALL THE 'SQUIRES AND 'SQUIRESSES AROUND . . . . 544 3 DON JUAN 16 91 2
SQUIRES
UNTYING SQUIRES TO FIGHT AGAINST THE CHURCHES . . . . . 530 3 DON JUAN 16 60 6
THE SQUIRES FAMILIARLY FORMAL AND . . . . 538 3 DON JUAN 16 79 1
'SQUIRESSES
FROM ALL THE 'SQUIRES AND 'SQUIRESSES AROUND . . . . 544 3 DON JUAN 16 91 2
STAB
HER SIXTH TO STAB HERSELF HER SEVENTH TO SENTENCE . . . 491 2 DON JUAN 5 139 6
SHE THOUGHT TO STAB HERSELF BUT THEN SHE HAD . . . . 492 2 DON JUAN 5 140 1
STABLE
ELSEWHERE PRESERVED THE CLOISTERS STILL WERE STABLE . . 389 3 DON JUAN 13 66 3
FOR FEW OF THE SOFT SEX ARE VERY STABLE . . . . . . 458 3 DON JUAN 15 6 3
STAG
AN ARAB HORSE A STATELY STAG A BARB . . . . 160 2 DON JUAN 2 6 1
THE BRANCHING STAG SWEPT DOWN WITH ALL HIS HERD . . . 384 3 DON JUAN 13 56 7
STAGE
FOUND ONLY ON THE STAGE AND EACH MORE PAIN'D . . . . 394 2 DON JUAN 4 93 3
AND CURTSIED OFF THE STAGE--THEIR LORDS THE SAME . . . 549 3 DON JUAN 16 101 V4
STAGGERING
WITH SLOW AND STAGGERING EFFORT HE AROSE . . . . . . 213 2 DON JUAN 2 109 1
STAGNANT
BLISTER'D AND SCORCH'D AND STAGNANT ON THE SEA . . . . 194 2 DON JUAN 2 72 2
STAGNATE
PURE BLOOD TO STAGNATE THEIR GREAT HEARTS TO FAIL . . . 348 2 DON JUAN 4 9 2
STAGNATES
ITS VERY COURAGE STAGNATES TO A VICE . . . . 18 2 DON JUAN D 15 8
STAGYRITE
PLUMED BY LONGINUS OR THE STAGYRITE . . . . 467 3 DON JUAN 15 25 4
STAID
SOME WENT TO AFRICA SOME STAID IN SPAIN . . . . . 52 2 DON JUAN 1 56 7
AND NO GREAT GOOD SEEM'D ANSWER'D IF SHE STAID . . . . 116 2 DON JUAN 1 173 6
LOOK'D BACK UPON HIM AND A MOMENT STAID . . . . . 228 2 DON JUAN 2 135 3
BRIEF BUT DELIGHTFUL--SUCH AS HAD NOT STAID . . . . 382 2 DON JUAN 4 71 6
A SINGLE TEAR UPON HIS EYELASH STAID . . . . . . 420 2 DON JUAN 5 18 4
STAIN
A TRUE HIDALGO FREE FROM EVERY STAIN . . . . 26 2 DON JUAN 1 9 2
TELL ME--AND BE ASSURED THAT SINCE YOU STAIN . . . . 105 2 DON JUAN 1 154 7
I USED--I WRITE IN HASTE AND IF A STAIN . . . . . 130 2 DON JUAN 1 192 6
AND PERSIAN CARPETS WHICH THE HEART BLED TO STAIN . . 310 2 DON JUAN 3 60 3
THE GLOSSY REBELS MOCK'D THE JETTY STAIN . . . . . 314 2 DON JUAN 3 75 4
TO STAIN HIS PEDIGREE A THOUSAND SWORDS . . . . . 471 2 DON JUAN 5 104 5
OR GLOOMY CARAVAGGIO'S GLOOMIER STAIN . . . . . . 392 3 DON JUAN 13 72 3
STAINED
AND THE STAINED GLASS WHICH LIGHTED THIS FAIR GROT . . 55 3 DON JUAN 6 98 4
THE CRAVAT STAINED WITH BLOODY DROPS FELL DOWN . . . 276 3 DON JUAN 11 17 1
STAINING
TRAMPLED WHAT THEY SCARCE TROD FOR FEAR OF STAINING . . 450 2 DON JUAN 5 66 3

769

```
                                                        PAGE VOL      CANTO STANZA LN
STAINS
     IN GROVELING ON TO POWER SUCH STAINS NOW DYE IT    . . . 154  2 DON JUAN  1   V  5    6
     RETAINS THE SABLE STAINS OF THE DARK CREEPER   . . . . . 232  3 DON JUAN 10      15    5
STAIR
     THEY'RE ON THE STAIR JUST NOW AND IN A CRACK   . . . .    96  2 DON JUAN  1     137    6
     HIM BORNE INTO THE HOUSE AND UP THE STAIR   . . . . .    429  2 DON JUAN  5      34    4
STAIRCASE
     AND GAIN AN INCH OF STAIRCASE AT A TIME  . . . . . .     302  3 DON JUAN 11      68    8
STAIRS
     FOR LITTLE JUAN O'ER ME THREW DOWN STAIRS   . . . . .     34  2 DON JUAN  1      24    7
     BELOW STAIRS ON THE SCORE OF SECOND COURSES . . . . .    534  3 DON JUAN 16      68    4
STAKE
     THOUGH LIFE AND DEATH AND VICTORY WERE AT STAKE   . . .  147  2 DON JUAN  8      70    7
     THAT ALL'S IDEAL--ALL OURSELVES I'LL STAKE THE  . . .    269  3 DON JUAN 11       2    3
     NOW THAT THE PUBLIC HEDGE HATH SCARCE A STAKE  . . .     357  3 DON JUAN 12      89    2
     LOOK BACK O'ER AGES ERE UNTO THE STAKE FAST . . . .      411  3 DON JUAN 14       2    5
     BUT INNOCENCE IS BOLD EVEN AT THE STAKE  . . . . .       437  3 DON JUAN 14      61    5
STALE
     AND THE NEW BIRTHS OF BOTH THEIR STALE VIRGINITIES   . . 330  2 DON JUAN  3      95    7
STALK
     EACH IN THEIR TURN LIKE BANQUO'S MONARCHS STALK  . . .    22  2 DON JUAN  1       2    5
     ON WHICH LIKE A YOUNG FLOWER SNAPP'D FROM THE STALK  . . 249  2 DON JUAN  2     176    5
     LIKE AN IMPERIAL PEACOCK STALK ABROAD . . . . . . .      104  3 DON JUAN  7      74    5
STALKED
     BY EUNUCHS FLANKED WHILE AT THEIR HEAD THERE STALKED  .   21  3 DON JUAN  6      30    4
     BUT NOW NO MORE THE GHOST OF SCANDAL STALKED ABOUT   . . 338  3 DON JUAN 12      47    3
STALKS
     HERE STALKS THE VICTOR THERE THE VANQUISHED LIES  . . .  461  2 DON JUAN  5      86    4
STALL
     THE WELCOME STALL TO THE O'ERLABOUR'D STEER . . . . .    338  2 DON JUAN  3     107    4
STAMINA
     STILL BREAKING BUT WITH STAMINA SO STEADY   . . . . .     89  2 DON JUAN  1     125    6
STAMMER
     HE STOOD IN ACT TO SPEAK OR RATHER STAMMER  . . . . .    111  2 DON JUAN  1     163    1
     SO HE BEGAN TO STAMMER SOME EXCUSES   . . . . . .        493  2 DON JUAN  5     143    1
STAMP
     OF MODERN REIGNING STERLING STUPID STAMP--  . . . . .    321  3 DON JUAN 12      12    7
STAMPS
     WHERE HYMEN'S SHRINE BUT STAMPS ONE STRUMPET MORE . . .  353  2 DON JUAN  4      17   V7
STANCH
     BECAUSE 'TIS FRAILER DOUBTLESS THAN A STANCH ONE   . . . 446  3 DON JUAN 14      85    6
STAND
     THEY STAND FORTH MARSHALL'D IN A HANDSOME TROOP   . . .   46  2 DON JUAN  1      45    3
     AND STAND CONVICTED OF MORE TRUTH THAN TREASON . . .      76  2 DON JUAN  1     102    6
     ANTONIA'S PATIENCE NOW WAS AT A STAND--  . . . . .       114  2 DON JUAN  1     170    5
     SO THAT I SEEM TO STAND UPON THE CEILING)   . . . .      156  2 DON JUAN  1   V  8    6
     AND STAND LIKE ROCKS THE TEMPEST'S WEAR AND TEAR  . .    191  2 DON JUAN  2      66    4
     AND NOW TO SEE THEM THUS DIVIDED STAND   . . . . .       368  2 DON JUAN  4      45    5
     AT LENGTH PERCEIVING THE FOOT COULD NOT STAND  . . .     471  2 DON JUAN  5     104    7
     AND FOR THEIR RIGHTS CONNUBIAL MAKE A STAND . . . .       11  3 DON JUAN  6      11    5
     THE TU'S TOO MUCH--BUT LET IT STAND--THE VERSE  . . .     14  3 DON JUAN  6      18    1
     WHEREIN SHE LIKED HER OWN TO STAND LIKE ROCKS  . . .     197  3 DON JUAN  9      29    8
     WITH OR WITHOUT THEE ALL THINGS AT A STAND  . . . .      210  3 DON JUAN  9      56    7
     FEW YOUTHFUL MINDS CAN STAND THE STRONG CONCUSSION . .   235  3 DON JUAN 10      21    3
     SO MUCH THE BETTER--I MAY STAND ALONE . . . . . .        312  3 DON JUAN 11      90    7
     AND RATHER WISHED IN SUCH THINGS TO STAND NEUTER  . .    336  3 DON JUAN 12      42    3
     JUAN WHO DID NOT STAND IN THE PREDICAMENT   . . . .      346  3 DON JUAN 12      67    1
     WHICH WITH THE LANDLORD MAKES TOO LONG A STAND  . . .    435  3 DON JUAN 14      58    2
     THE THIRD IS STILL MORE DIFFICULT TO STAND TO  . . .     465  3 DON JUAN 15      21    5
     THAN FINDING THUS THEIR GENIUS STAND REBUKED  . . . .    479  3 DON JUAN 15      53    6
     FROM THEIR HIGH PLACES BY THE SIDEBOARD'S STAND--  . .   539  3 DON JUAN 16      79    5
STANDING
     STANDING ALONE BESIDE HIS DESOLATE HEARTH   . . . .       41  2 DON JUAN  1      36    5
     INSTEAD OF STANDING STARING ALTOGETHER   . . . . .        46  2 DON JUAN  1      45    7
     WHOM I SEE STANDING THERE AND LOOKING SENSIBLE  . . .    103  2 DON JUAN  1     151    4
     AND STANDING UPON DECK THE DASHING SPRAY . . . . .       162  2 DON JUAN  2      11    5
     FOR STANDING ON THE PERSIAN'S GRAVE   . . . . . .        321  2 DON JUAN  3   L  3    4
     ARRAY HER LIMBS BUT JUAN STANDING MUTE   . . . . .       453  2 DON JUAN  5      73    4
     SUWARROW WHO WAS STANDING IN HIS SHIRT   . . . . .        96  3 DON JUAN  7      58    1
     OF ALL THE STANDING ARMY WHO STOOD BY . . . . . .       221  3 DON JUAN  9      78    8
STANDS
     IS FIRST AND PASSIONATE LOVE--IT STANDS ALONE  . . .      90  2 DON JUAN  1     127    2
     SO SHAKES THE NEEDLE AND SO STANDS THE POLE . . . .      133  2 DON JUAN  1     196    7
     STANDS ON HER TRIPOD AGONIZED AND FULL  . . . . .         59  3 DON JUAN  6     107    2
     IT STANDS SOME EIGHTY VERSTS FROM THE HIGH SEA  . .       71  3 DON JUAN  7       9    7
     THERE STANDS THE NOBLE HOSTESS NOR SHALL SINK  . . .     302  3 DON JUAN 11      68    1
     AS STANDS A STATUE STOOD HE FELT HIS HAIR   . . . .      510  3 DON JUAN 16      23    5
STANZA
     HOW SHALL I GET THIS GOURMAND STANZA THROUGH   . . .     483  3 DON JUAN 15      63    6
     ALL THIS (SAVE THE LAST STANZA) HENRY SAID  . . . .      538  3 DON JUAN 16      77    1
     DREADFUL AS DANTE'S RHIMA OR THIS STANZA  . . . . .      557  3 DON JUAN 16     116    4
STANZAS
     TWO HUNDRED AND ODD STANZAS AS BEFORE . . . . . .        271  2 DON JUAN  2     216    3
     ARE NOT THESE PRETTY STANZAS--SOME FOLKS SAY--  . . .    336  2 DON JUAN  3     104   V1
     WITH JUAN LEFT HALF-KILL'D SOME STANZAS BACK  . . .      384  2 DON JUAN  4      74    8
     YOU READ MY STANZAS AND I READ YOUR FEATURES  . . .      405  2 DON JUAN  4     111    3
STAR
     'TIS SWEET TO SEE THE EVENING STAR APPEAR   . . . .       87  2 DON JUAN  1     122    5
     WITH ONE STAR SPARKLING THROUGH IT LIKE AN EYE . . . .   252  2 DON JUAN  2     183    8
```

STAR   (CONTINUED)
	PAGE	VOL	CANTO	STANZA	LN
HIS POLAR STAR BEING ONE WHICH RATHER RANGES	317	2 DON JUAN	3	80	3
BENEATH THE INFLUENCE OF THE EASTERN STAR	347	3 DON JUAN	12	69	4
OF THE STAR CHAMBER THAN OF HABEAS CORPUS	391	3 DON JUAN	13	69	8
COME OUT AND GLIMMER'D AS A SIX-WEEKS' STAR	398	3 DON JUAN	13	84	6
ON BIRTH-DAYS GLORIOUS WITH A STAR AND STRING	440	3 DON JUAN	14	70	6
WHENE'ER THEIR TRIUMPH PALES OR STAR IS TAMED--	448	3 DON JUAN	14	89	6
WHOSE HEART WAS FIX'D UPON A STAR OR BLUESTRING	474	3 DON JUAN	15	42	3
AURORA RABY A YOUNG STAR WHO SHONE	475	3 DON JUAN	15	43	5
BETWEEN TWO WORLDS LIFE HOVERS LIKE A STAR	500	3 DON JUAN	15	99	1
ALAS HER STAR MUST WANE LIKE THAT OF DIAN	554	3 DON JUAN	16	109	3

STARCH
	PAGE	VOL	CANTO	STANZA	LN
A GLANCE ON THE DULL CLOUDS (AS THICK AS STARCH	121	3 DON JUAN	8	21	6
OR STARCH AS ARE THE EDICTS STATESMEN UTTER	468	3 DON JUAN	15	27	4

STAR-CHAMBER
	PAGE	VOL	CANTO	STANZA	LN
A CHILD OF CHANCERY THAT STAR-CHAMBER WARD	564	3 DON JUAN	17	4	4

STARE
	PAGE	VOL	CANTO	STANZA	LN
AND OTHERS LOOKING WITH A STUPID STARE	208	2 DON JUAN	2	98	2
EVEN GOOD MEN LIKE TO MAKE THE PUBLIC STARE--	317	2 DON JUAN	3	81	4
SOME SHEPHERDS (UNLIKE PARIS) LED TO STARE	387	3 DON JUAN	4	78	3
AND ALL ABASHED TOO AT THE GENERAL STARE	28	3 DON JUAN	6	45	6
WHICH STARE HIM IN THE FACE HE WON'T EXAMINE	88	3 DON JUAN	7	45	7
THOUGH THEY MAY MAKE CORRUPTION GAPE OR STARE	114	3 DON JUAN	8	4	6
OF THE GREAT NAMES WHICH IN OUR FACES STARE	143	3 DON JUAN	8	61	3
(AS IT WILL LOOK SOMETIMES WITH THE FIRST STARE	224	3 DON JUAN	9	84	4
OF WHAT IS CALLED ETERNITY TO STARE	234	3 DON JUAN	10	20	7
AND THEN MEN STARE AS IF A NEW ASS SPAKE	328	3 DON JUAN	12	26	5
HER GAIETIES NONE HAD A RIGHT TO STARE	430	3 DON JUAN	14	45	6
AND JUAN GAZED UPON IT WITH A STARE	510	3 DON JUAN	16	23	3
BUT WHAT CONFUSED HIM MORE THAN SMILE OR STARE	544	3 DON JUAN	16	91	1

STARED
	PAGE	VOL	CANTO	STANZA	LN
AND THEN THEY STARED EACH OTHERS' FACES ROUND	100	2 DON JUAN	1	144	5
ONE OR TWO STARED THE CAPTIVES IN THE FACE	441	2 DON JUAN	5	54	5
WITH SHRINKING SERPENT OPTICS ON HIM STARED	463	2 DON JUAN	5	90	6
THE COURTIERS STARED THE LADIES WHISPERED AND	205	3 DON JUAN	9	46	1
YET STARED AT THIS A LITTLE THOUGH HE PAID IT--	259	3 DON JUAN	10	70	4

STARING
	PAGE	VOL	CANTO	STANZA	LN
INSTEAD OF STANDING STARING ALTOGETHER	46	2 DON JUAN	1	45	7

STARK
	PAGE	VOL	CANTO	STANZA	LN
SO HERE THOUGH FAINT EMACIATED AND STARK	212	2 DON JUAN	2	106	1
ALL THAT THE DEVIL WOULD DO IF RUN STARK MAD	173	3 DON JUAN	8	123	4

STARLIGHT
	PAGE	VOL	CANTO	STANZA	LN
THE SILENT OCEAN AND THE STARLIGHT BAY	255	2 DON JUAN	2	188	3
THE CHARMS OF OTHER DAYS IN STARLIGHT GLEAMS	509	3 DON JUAN	16	19	2

STARLING
	PAGE	VOL	CANTO	STANZA	LN
AND SIGH I CAN'T GET OUT LIKE YORICK'S STARLING	404	2 DON JUAN	4	109	4

STARR'D
	PAGE	VOL	CANTO	STANZA	LN
HER HAIR WAS STARR'D WITH GEMS HER VEIL'S FINE FOLD	312	2 DON JUAN	3	72	4

STARRY
	PAGE	VOL	CANTO	STANZA	LN
THE STARRY DARKNESS ROUND HER LIKE A GIRDLE	556	3 DON JUAN	16	113	7

STARS
	PAGE	VOL	CANTO	STANZA	LN
OF MAN THE WONDERFUL AND OF THE STARS	71	2 DON JUAN	1	92	2
NO MOON NO STARS THE WIND WAS LOW OR LOUD	94	2 DON JUAN	1	135	2
SO THANK YOUR STARS THAT MATTERS ARE NO WORSE	147	2 DON JUAN	1	220	7
THERE WAS NO LIGHT IN HEAVEN BUT A FEW STARS	183	2 DON JUAN	2	51	5
BUT NOT WITH VIOLENCE THE STARS SHONE OUT	207	2 DON JUAN	2	96	2
SHOWS STARS AND WOMEN IN A BETTER LIGHT	237	2 DON JUAN	2	152	8
TURNS OFTENER TO THE STARS THAN TO HIS BOOK	242	2 DON JUAN	2	163	6
AND ALL THE STARS THAT CROWDED THE BLUE SPACE	262	2 DON JUAN	2	198	7
THEIR HEARTS THE STARS THEIR NUPTIAL TORCHES SHED	265	2 DON JUAN	2	204	2
DRAWN FROM THE STARS AND FILTER'D THROUGH THE SKIES	269	2 DON JUAN	2	212	4
LIKE SMALL STARS THROUGH THE MILKY WAY APPARENT	315	2 DON JUAN	3	77	4
EARTH AIR STARS--ALL THAT SPRINGS FROM THE GREAT WHOLE	336	2 DON JUAN	3	104	7
WITH ALL ITS STARS AND WITH A STRETCH ATTAINING	450	2 DON JUAN	5	66	5
HENCE MY OLD COMET GIVE THE STARS DUE WARNING--	494	2 DON JUAN	5	145	4
THE STARS FROM OUT THE SKY THAN NOT BE FREE	7	3 DON JUAN	6	3	5
IF STARS AND TITLES COULD ENTAIL LONG PRAISE	84	3 DON JUAN	7	37	3
WHEN STARS AND WHORES AND DESPOTS COULD MAKE GREAT	84	3 DON JUAN	7	37	V2
THE STARS PEEP THROUGH THE VAPOURS DIM AND DANK	110	3 DON JUAN	7	86	6
STARS MEDALS AND A BLOODY SWORD IN HAND	141	3 DON JUAN	8	57	6
THROUGH THE THEN UNPAVED STARS THE TURNPIKE ROAD	226	3 DON JUAN	10	2	4
DISCOVER STARS AND SAIL IN THE WIND'S EYE	226	3 DON JUAN	10	3	7
THE STARS I OWN MY TELESCOPE IS DIM	227	3 DON JUAN	10	4	2
OF BEING STARS AND THIS UNRIDDLED WONDER	269	3 DON JUAN	11	3	7
BECAUSE THE SUN AND STARS AND AUGHT THAT SHINES	423	3 DON JUAN	14	29	5
THEY MOVED LIKE STARS UNITED IN THEIR SPHERES	447	3 DON JUAN	14	87	3
THEN TURN'D UNTO THE STARS FOR LOFTIER RAYS	480	3 DON JUAN	15	56	4

START
	PAGE	VOL	CANTO	STANZA	LN
START NOT STILL CHASTER READER--SHE'LL BE NICE HENCEFORWARD	86	2 DON JUAN	1	120	2
AS THE FAR BELL OF VESPER MAKES HIM START	338	2 DON JUAN	3	108	5
AND SO--SHE WOKE WITH A GREAT SCREAM AND START	44	3 DON JUAN	6	77	8
(START NOT KIND READER SINCE GREAT HOMER THOUGHT	126	3 DON JUAN	8	29	6
YOU ARE THE BEST OF CUT-THROATS--DO NOT START	184	3 DON JUAN	9	4	1
IN SAFETY TO THE PLACE FOR WHICH YOU START	284	3 DON JUAN	11	34	7
START FROM THE FRAMES WHICH FENCE THEIR ASPECTS STERN	508	3 DON JUAN	16	18	6

STARTED
	PAGE	VOL	CANTO	STANZA	LN
STARTED THE STERN-POST ALSO SHATTER'D THE	170	2 DON JUAN	2	27	4
AND STARTED FROM HER SLEEP AND TURNING O'ER	229	2 DON JUAN	2	138	2
YOU STARTED BACK IN HORROR TO SURVEY	462	2 DON JUAN	5	88	2

		PAGE	VOL		CANTO	STANZA	LN

STARTED   (CONTINUED)
```
    HE STARTED AND SAID YES--NO--RATHER--YES  . . . . . .  514   3 DON JUAN 16    32    4
    HE STARTED AND PERCEIVING SMILES AROUND   . . . . . .  542   3 DON JUAN 16    88    2
STARTING
    EMBARRASS'D AT FIRST STARTING WITH A NOVICE  . . . . .   62   2 DON JUAN  1    74    8
    POOR DONNA JULIA STARTING AS FROM SLEEP  . . . . . . .   97   2 DON JUAN  1   140    1
    AND STARTING SHE AWOKE AND WHAT TO VIEW  . . . . . . .  363   2 DON JUAN  4    35    6
    WITH FLASHING EYES AND STARTING TEARS AND FLUNG  . . .  101   3 DON JUAN  7    67    7
STARTING-POST
    AND BRING OUR HEARTS BACK TO THEIR STARTING-POST  . . .  286   2 DON JUAN  3    21    8
STARTLE
    IN THAT SLIGHT STARTLE FROM HIS CONTEMPLATION--  . . .  225   3 DON JUAN 10     1    2
STARTLES
    FOR WOMAN'S SILENCE STARTLES MORE THAN THUNDER  . . . .   34   3 DON JUAN  6    57   V8
STARTS
    WHEN FIRST SHE STARTS AND THEN RETURNS TO PEEP  . . . .   36   3 DON JUAN  6    60    7
    OR CHEERFUL WITHOUT ANY FLAWS OR STARTS  . . . . . . .  292   3 DON JUAN 11    47    5
STARVATION
    AND NO ONE VIRTUE YET EXCEPT STARVATION  . . . . . . .   15   3 DON JUAN  6    19    7
    AND NOTHING EVER HEARD OF SAVE STARVATION  . . . . . .   15   3 DON JUAN  6    19   V7
    FEEDS YOU BY PRINTING HALF THE REALM'S STARVATION--  . .  200   3 DON JUAN  9    35    8
STARVE
    THOUGH IRELAND STARVE GREAT GEORGE WEIGHS TWENTY STONE  . .  175   3 DON JUAN  8   126    8
STATE
    BENEATH THE LIE THIS STATE THING BREATHED O'ER THEE  . . .   19   2 DON JUAN  D    16    4
    POOR JULIA'S HEART WAS IN AN AWKWARD STATE  . . . . . .   62   2 DON JUAN  1    75    1
    STATE STATION HEAVEN MANKIND'S MY OWN ESTEEM  . . . . .  130   2 DON JUAN  1   193    2
    AND SO SHE TOOK THE LIBERTY TO STATE  . . . . . . . . .  240   2 DON JUAN  2   159    1
    THOU MAK'ST THE CHASTE CONNUBIAL STATE PRECARIOUS  . . .  266   2 DON JUAN  2   206    1
    BETWEEN THEIR PRESENT AND THEIR FUTURE STATE  . . . . .  278   2 DON JUAN  3     6    2
    THAT HOLY STATE--BUT CERTAINLY BENEATH  . . . . . . . .  280   2 DON JUAN  3     9   V5
    AN IVORY INLAID TABLE SPREAD WITH STATE  . . . . . . .  306   2 DON JUAN  3    61    5
    THIS IS IN OTHERS A FACTITIOUS STATE  . . . . . . . . .  354   2 DON JUAN  4    19    1
    STRANGE STATE OF BEING (FOR 'TIS STILL TO BE)  . . . .  360   2 DON JUAN  4    30    7
    DAYS LAY SHE IN THAT STATE UNCHANGED THOUGH CHILL  . . .  377   2 DON JUAN  4    60    1
    TO ASCERTAIN THE ATMOSPHERIC STATE  . . . . . . . . . .  406   2 DON JUAN  4   112    6
    BUT AFTER ALL WHAT IS OUR PRESENT STATE  . . . . . . .  423   2 DON JUAN  5    25    1
    PRESERVE YOUR STATE--THOUGH EVE EARTH'S MOTHER FELL  . .  460   2 DON JUAN  5    84   V6
    HER PRESENCE WAS AS LOFTY AS HER STATE  . . . . . . . .  467   2 DON JUAN  5    97    1
    HER STATE (IT IS THE CUSTOM OF HER NATION)  . . . . . .  475   2 DON JUAN  5   111    6
    BEING A TRUE WOMAN IN A STATE OF NATURE  . . . . . . .  476   2 DON JUAN  5   113   V7
    HE WENT TO MOSQUE IN STATE AND SAID HIS PRAYERS  . . . .  496   2 DON JUAN  5   148    1
    HE LEFT TO HIS VIZIER ALL STATE AFFAIRS  . . . . . . .  496   2 DON JUAN  5   148    3
    A KIND OF STATE MORE AWKWARD THAN UNCOMMON  . . . . . .   10   3 DON JUAN  6     7    2
    NOT ALL THE CLAMOUR BROKE HER HAPPY STATE  . . . . . .   42   3 DON JUAN  6    73    5
    ALL THAT I KNOW IS THAT THE FACTS I STATE  . . . . . .   48   3 DON JUAN  6    85    7
    OF ALL THE PILLARS OF THE STATE WHICH LEANS  . . . . .   54   3 DON JUAN  6    96    6
    TO THOSE WHO HAD FELT THE INCONVENIENT STATE  . . . . .  177   3 DON JUAN  8   131    3
    AND AS A HIGH-SOUL'D MINISTER OF STATE IS  . . . . . .  186   3 DON JUAN  9     8    7
    AND THIS SAME STATE WE WON'T DESCRIBE WE COULD  . . . .  238   3 DON JUAN 10    27    1
    BUT STILL HIS STATE WAS DELICATE THE HUE  . . . . . . .  245   3 DON JUAN 10    43    5
    THE WORTHIEST KINGS HAVE EVER LOVED LEAST STATE  . . . .  267   3 DON JUAN 10    87    5
    THOUGHT (WHAT IN STATE AFFAIRS IS MOST ESSENTIAL)  . . .  285   3 DON JUAN 11    35    6
    UPON THE REST OF EUROPE'S SOCIAL STATE  . . . . . . . .  327   3 DON JUAN 12    24    4
    I HAVE ALWAYS LIKED YOU BETTER THAN I STATE  . . . . .  329   3 DON JUAN 12    28    4
    IS WHEN WITHOUT REGARD TO CHURCH OR STATE  . . . . . .  345   3 DON JUAN 12    64    3
    AT LEAST THEY THINK SO TO EXERT THEIR STATE  . . . . .  367   3 DON JUAN 13    19    4
    A GOODLY SPIRIT FOR A STATE DIVAN  . . . . . . . . . .  440   3 DON JUAN 14    70    3
    BUT IN HIS TEETH WHATE'ER THEIR STATE OR STATION  . . .  443   3 DON JUAN 14    77    7
    THE MARRIAGE STATE THE BEST OR WORST OF ANY)  . . . . .  452   3 DON JUAN 14    95    6
    AND MORALLY DECIDED THE BEST STATE IS  . . . . . . . .  469   3 DON JUAN 15    29    6
    WHY CALL'D HE HARMONY A STATE SANS WEDLOCK  . . . . . .  471   3 DON JUAN 15    35    7
    ABOUT THE PRESENT PAST OR FUTURE STATE  . . . . . . . .  496   3 DON JUAN 15    91    6
    I WISH THEY'D STATE HOW MANY THEY HAVE GAINED  . . . .  505   3 DON JUAN 16    11    8
    (I STATE THIS FOR I AM CAUTIOUS TO A PITCH  . . . . . .  507   3 DON JUAN 16    16    3
    MIGHT COME OR GO BUT JUAN COULD NOT STATE  . . . . . .  511   3 DON JUAN 16    24    7
    TO STATE THE CASE IT MIGHT BE TA'EN FOR GRANTED  . . . .  514   3 DON JUAN 16    33    7
    A FEW WORDS OF CONDOLENCE ON HIS STATE  . . . . . . . .  515   3 DON JUAN 16    35    2
    AND MERELY STATE THOUGH NOT FOR THE CONSISTORY  . . . .  531   3 DON JUAN 16    62    5
    BUT WE'LL SAY NOTHING OF AFFAIRS OF STATE)  . . . . . .  541   3 DON JUAN 16    84    4
    SHOULD STILL BE SINGED BUT SLIGHTLY LET ME STATE)  . . .  565   3 DON JUAN 17     7    6
STATED
    THE BOATS AS STATED HAD GOT OFF BEFORE  . . . . . . . .  185   2 DON JUAN  2    54    1
    WHO CAME AT STATED MOMENTS TO INVITE ALL  . . . . . . .  393   2 DON JUAN  4    90    3
    JUAN WAS GIVEN IN CHARGE AS HATH BEEN STATED  . . . . .   57   3 DON JUAN  6   102    6
    'TIS NOT SO TO BE GOOD AND BE IT STATED  . . . . . . .  267   3 DON JUAN 10    87    4
    BESIDES THERE MIGHT BE FALSEHOOD IN WHAT'S STATED  . . .  428   3 DON JUAN 14    42    6
    OF OTHERS WITH HER OWN OPINIONS STATED--  . . . . . . .  478   3 DON JUAN 15    50    7
    SOMETHING BUT WHAT'S NOT STATED IN MY TALE  . . . . . .  514   3 DON JUAN 16    31    3
    STATED) HIS MOUTH WHAT OPENED NEXT--THE DOOR  . . . . .  557   3 DON JUAN 16   115    8
STATELY
    AN ARAB HORSE A STATELY STAG A BARB  . . . . . . . . .  160   2 DON JUAN  2     6    1
    OF ONE GOOD MAN WITH STATELY MARCH AND SLOW  . . . . .   22   3 DON JUAN  6    33    5
    TALL STATELY FORM'D TO LEAD THE COURTLY VAN  . . . . .  440   3 DON JUAN 14    70    5
STATEMENT
    ALL THESE CONFIRM MY STATEMENT A GOOD DEAL  . . . . . .  138   2 DON JUAN  1   203    5
STATE'S
    THE LAW'S EXPOUNDER AND THE STATE'S CORRECTOR  . . . . .   29   2 DON JUAN  1    15    5
STATES
    STATES TO BE CURB'D AND THOUGHTS TO BE CONFINED  . . . .   18   2 DON JUAN  D    14    4
```

772

	PAGE	VOL		CANTO	STANZA	LN
STATES (CONTINUED)						
THEN SPUR AWAY O'ER EMPIRES AND O'ER STATES	76	2	DON JUAN	1	103	6
THE FUTURE STATES OF BOTH ARE LEFT TO FAITH	280	2	DON JUAN	3	9	3
LEAVING THE FUTURE STATES OF LOVE AND LIFE	280	2	DON JUAN	3	9	V7
WITH WHICH GREAT STATES SUCH THINGS ARE APT TO PUSH ON	246	3	DON JUAN	10	45	5
STATESMAN						
THE STATESMAN HERO HARLOT LAWYER--WARD	123	2	DON JUAN	8	25	5
AND ANSWER'D LIKE A STATESMAN OR A PROPHET	438	3	DON JUAN	14	65	7
STATESMAN'S						
THE GAMESTER'S COUNTER OR THE STATESMAN'S DROSS	317	3	DON JUAN	12	4	6
STATESMEN						
STATESMEN CHIEFS ORATORS QUEENS PATRIOTS KINGS	306	3	DON JUAN	11	76	7
OR STARCH AS ARE THE EDICTS STATESMEN UTTER	468	3	DON JUAN	15	27	4
THUS ON THE MOB ALL STATESMEN ARE AS EAGER	537	3	DON JUAN	16	76	7
STATING						
I SHALL NOT BE PARTICULAR IN STATING	203	3	DON JUAN	9	42	5
STATION						
I'M A PLAIN MAN AND IN A SINGLE STATION	33	2	DON JUAN	1	22	6
STATE STATION HEAVEN MANKIND'S MY OWN ESTEEM	130	2	DON JUAN	1	193	2
LOSING THE ADVANTAGE OF A VIRTUOUS STATION	263	2	DON JUAN	2	201	4
HIS STATION GENERATION EVEN HIS NATION	327	2	DON JUAN	3	89	2
OR GRAVEN STONE FOUND IN A BARRACK'S STATION	327	2	DON JUAN	3	89	6
EACH BEVY WITH THE MERCHANT IN HIS STATION	414	2	DON JUAN	5	7	3
SOME NODDED TO THE NEGRO FROM THEIR STATION	441	2	DON JUAN	5	54	7
AS THOUGH THEY WERE QUITE CONSCIOUS OF HER STATION--	475	2	DON JUAN	5	111	4
IS SOMETIMES GOOD FOR PEOPLE IN HER STATION	490	2	DON JUAN	5	137	8
THIS LABYRINTH OF FEMALES AND EACH STATION	34	3	DON JUAN	6	57	5
AND WHETHER HE HAD OCCUPIED THEIR STATION	55	3	DON JUAN	6	99	4
UPON THE LEFT WHICH FROM ITS LOFTIER STATION	71	3	DON JUAN	7	10	3
EXTREMELY TRANQUIL ANCHORED AT ITS STATION	78	3	DON JUAN	7	24	4
DETACHMENT OF THREE COLUMNS TOOK ITS STATION	91	3	DON JUAN	7	50	3
A HIGHER TITLE OR A LOFTIER STATION	114	3	DON JUAN	8	4	5
HE MOVED SOME HUNDRED MILES OFF FOR A STATION	144	3	DON JUAN	8	64	3
PERHAPS THE SEASON'S CHILL AND THEIR LONG STATION	176	3	DON JUAN	8	128	6
IS APT TO TIRE A CALM AND SHALLOW STATION	191	3	DON JUAN	9	18	6
OF HIM WHO IN THE LANGUAGE OF HIS STATION	206	3	DON JUAN	9	48	7
OF ANYONE'S ATTAINING TO HIS STATION	208	3	DON JUAN	9	52	6
AND STINGINESS DISGRACE HER SEX AND STATION	222	3	DON JUAN	9	81	8
THEIR STATION THERE WERE VALETS SECRETARIES	249	3	DON JUAN	10	51	2
AND HERE HE CRIED IS FREEDOM'S CHOSEN STATION	272	3	DON JUAN	11	9	5
TANTAENE SUCH THE VIRTUES OF HIGH STATION	331	3	DON JUAN	12	33	5
OF SUCH A THRONE AS IS THE PROUDEST STATION	354	3	DON JUAN	12	83	4
WITH FAIR LONG LOCKS HAD ALSO KEPT THEIR STATION	390	3	DON JUAN	13	68	5
ON WHICH IT HINGES IN A HIGHER STATION	396	3	DON JUAN	13	81	4
A SLIGHT GLANCE THROWN ON MEN OF EVERY STATION	416	3	DON JUAN	14	14	4
BUT IN HIS TEETH WHATE'ER THEIR STATE OR STATION	443	3	DON JUAN	14	77	7
SO AS TO MAKE THEM FEEL HE KNEW HIS STATION	462	3	DON JUAN	15	15	6
MAY DROP IN WITHOUT CARDS AND TAKE THEIR STATION	534	3	DON JUAN	16	69	4
STATIONS						
OF GETTING ON HIMSELF AND FINDING STATIONS	239	3	DON JUAN	10	30	3
HIMSELF AND JUAN IN THEIR MUTUAL STATIONS	365	3	DON JUAN	13	15	3
WRITING DISPATCHES) IN THEIR SEVERAL STATIONS	533	3	DON JUAN	16	66	7
STATISTICS						
STATISTICS TACTICS POLITICS AND GEOGRAPHY)--	149	3	DON JUAN	8	74	4
STATUARY						
FIT FOR THE MODEL OF A STATUARY	218	2	DON JUAN	2	118	5
STATUE						
A LOVELY STATUE WE ALMOST ADORE	269	2	DON JUAN	2	211	6
FROM MARBLE LIKE PYGMALION'S STATUE WAKING	27	3	DON JUAN	6	43	6
AND SEE HIS STATUE RAISED--AND PRINT ENGRAVED	185	3	DON JUAN	9	5	V8
(THOUGH LESS THAN THAT OF MEMNON'S STATUE WARM	388	3	DON JUAN	13	64	3
AS STANDS A STATUE STOOD HE FELT HIS HAIR	510	3	DON JUAN	16	23	5
STATUE-LIKE						
PALE STATUE-LIKE AND STERN SHE WOO'D THE BLOW	367	2	DON JUAN	4	43	4
A FOURTH AS MARBLE STATUE-LIKE AND STILL	40	3	DON JUAN	6	68	1
STATUES						
GROUPS OF BAD STATUES TABLES CHAIRS AND PICTURES	465	3	DON JUAN	5	94	7
WHOSE STATUES WARM (I FEAR ALAS TOO TRUE 'TIS)	208	3	DON JUAN	9	51	6
STATURE						
HER STATURE TALL--I HATE A DUMPY WOMAN	55	2	DON JUAN	1	61	8
IN BRAIDS BEHIND AND THOUGH HER STATURE WERE	217	2	DON JUAN	2	116	4
MAKING HER STATURE TALL EVEN TALLER--NEAR	367	2	DON JUAN	4	43	V5
THEIR STATURE DIFFERING BUT IN SEX AND YEARS	368	2	DON JUAN	4	45	2
THOUGH DIFFERING IN STATURE AND DEGREE	26	3	DON JUAN	6	40	6
WE GAZE UPON A GIANT FOR HIS STATURE	390	3	DON JUAN	13	67	7
STATUTES						
HE BROKE 'TIS TRUE SOME STATUTES OF THE LAWS	424	3	DON JUAN	14	33	5
STAUNCHEST						
BY BUTCHERS IN HER STREETS THAN FOR THE STAUNCHEST OR	314	3	DON JUAN	11	V 75	5
STAVE						
IF I CAN STAVE OFF THOUGHT WHICH AS A WHELP	238	3	DON JUAN	10	28	3
STAVES						
LORDLINGS WITH STAVES OF WHITE OR KEYS OF GOLD	391	3	DON JUAN	13	70	5
STAY						
AND OTHER STUFFS WITH WHICH I WON'T STAY PUZZLING	27	2	DON JUAN	1	12	8
TO STAY THERE HAD NOT ANSWER'D HER INTENT	161	2	DON JUAN	2	8	3
FOR DOWNRIGHT RUDENESS YE MAY STAY AT HOME	290	3	DON JUAN	11	44	1
THE MORE'S THE REASON WHY YOU OUGHT TO STAY	459	3	DON JUAN	15	9	4
STAYS						
FOR THE FIRST PASSION STAYS THERE SUCH A WHILE	271	2	DON JUAN	2	215	3

773

```
                                                              PAGE VOL        CANTO STANZA LN
STAYS    (CONTINUED)
     FOR EASTERN STAYS ARE LITTLE MADE TO PAD  . . . . . . .  492  2 DON JUAN   5    140   3
     THEOLOGY FINE ARTS OR FINER STAYS  . . . . . . . . .     340  3 DON JUAN  12     53   2
     ALL STRUT AND STAYS AND WHISKERS TO DEMAND  . . . . .    343  3 DON JUAN  12     60   4
     BUT GENTLEMEN IN STAYS AS STIFF AS STONES  . . . . . .   409  3 DON JUAN  13    110   8
     HAS NOT THE NATURAL STAYS OF STRICT OLD AGE . . . . .    494  3 DON JUAN  15     85   6
'STEAD
     WHO 'STEAD OF SAYING WHAT YOU NOW SHOULD DO  . . . . .   432  3 DON JUAN  14     50   5
STEAD
     AND IN THY STEAD I'VE GOT A DEAL OF JUDGMENT  . . . .    144  2 DON JUAN   1    215   7
     AND SET UP IN THEIR STEAD SOME PROPER STUFF . . . . .    195  2 DON JUAN   9     25   4
     SAY CONSTITUTION STEAD OF PROSTITUTION  . . . . . .      537  3 DON JUAN  16     76  V7
STEADFASTLY
     AND LOOKING AT HER STEADFASTLY SHE SIGHED  . . . . .      28  3 DON JUAN   6     45   3
STEADILY
     HE STUDIED STEADILY AND GREW APACE . . . . . . . . .      48  2 DON JUAN   1     49   5
STEADY
     WAS TO DECLARE HOW SAGE AND STILL AND STEADY  . . . .     49  2 DON JUAN   1     50   7
     STILL BREAKING BUT WITH STAMINA SO STEADY  . . . . .      89  2 DON JUAN   1    125   6
     (AND SO MY SOBER MUSE--COME LET'S BE STEADY--  . . .     160  2 DON JUAN   2      6   8
     THAT EVER MADE A YOUTHFUL HEART LESS STEADY . . . . .    246  2 DON JUAN   2    171   3
     TO LAST--OF ALL CONNEXIONS THE MOST STEADY  . . . . .    288  2 DON JUAN   3     25   5
     HER STEADY BREATH (WHICH SOME MONTHS THE SAME STILL IS)  132  3 DON JUAN   8     39   6
     HIS STEADY APPLICATION AS A DANCER . . . . . . . . .     294  3 DON JUAN  11     51   6
     THE SEA-GULLS WITH A STEADY SOBER FLIGHT--  . . . . .    558  3 DON JUAN  16    117   2
STEAL
     THOU SHALT NOT STEAL FROM SAMUEL ROGERS NOR . . . . .    139  2 DON JUAN   1    205   7
     LO DUSKY MASSES STEAL IN DUBIOUS SIGHT  . . . . . .      110  3 DON JUAN   7     86   3
     STEAL FROM THE WALLS TILL YOU ALMOST DISCERN  . . . .    508  3 DON JUAN  16     18  V6
STEALING
     OF ZOE'S COOKERY NO DOUBT WAS STEALING  . . . . . .      237  2 DON JUAN   2    153   4
     LIKE SHAKSPEARE'S STEALING DEER LORD BACON'S BRIBES  .   329  2 DON JUAN   3     92   2
     FOR WHAT IS STEALING YOUNG ONES FEW OR MANY . . . .      487  2 DON JUAN   5    132   7
STEALTH
     BY STEALTH HER HUSBAND'S TEMPLES TO ENCUMBER  . . . .     96  2 DON JUAN   1    138   6
     AND NOW AND THEN A TEAR STOLE DOWN BY STEALTH . . . .    415  2 DON JUAN   5      8   4
STEALTHY
     THE DEVIL MAY TAKE THAT STEALTHY PACE OF HIS  . . . .    556  3 DON JUAN  16    112   4
STEAM
     A MOST PRODIGIOUS APPETITE THE STEAM  . . . . . . .      237  2 DON JUAN   2    153   3
     BUT SINCE STEAM ENGINES PRAISE AND HONOUR VAPOUR  . .    317  3 DON JUAN  12      4  V8
STEAM-BOAT
     THAT GOOD OLD STEAM-BOAT WHICH KEEPS VERSES MOVING  .    219  3 DON JUAN   9     74   4
STEAM-BOATS
     ON CONSTITUTIONS AND STEAM-BOATS OF VAPOUR  . . . . .    325  3 DON JUAN  12     21   5
STEAM-ENGINES
     STEAM-ENGINES WILL CONDUCT HIM TO THE MOON  . . . . .    226  3 DON JUAN  10      2   8
STEED
     CONTEND NOT WITH YOU ON THE WINGED STEED  . . . . .       14  2 DON JUAN   D      8   2
     AND WHEN SHE SAW HIM STUMBLING LIKE A STEED . . . . .     56  3 DON JUAN   6    101   4
     NIMRODS WHOSE CANVAS SCARCE CONTAIN'D THE STEED . . .    391  3 DON JUAN  13     70   6
     AS BEAUTIFUL AND BOUNDING AS A STEED . . . . . . .       401  3 DON JUAN  13     92   6
STEED'S
     WERE THE SOLE ECHOS SAVE MY STEED'S AND MINE  . . . .    337  2 DON JUAN   3    106   3
STEEL
     HUMANITY MUST YIELD TO STEEL AND FLAME  . . . . . .      139  3 DON JUAN   8     54   4
     BEGAN TO LAY ABOUT WITH STEEL AND LEAD--  . . . . .      152  3 DON JUAN   8     81   4
     UPON THE RUSSIAN STEEL HIS BREAST HE FLUNG  . . . . .    170  3 DON JUAN   8    118   2
     STEEL BARONS MOLTEN THE NEXT GENERATION . . . . . .      390  3 DON JUAN  13     68   1
     THERE WERE TWO POACHERS CAUGHT IN A STEEL TRAP  . . .    530  3 DON JUAN  16     61   1
STEELED
     BUT HE WAS STEELED BY SORROW WRATH AND PRIDE  . . . .    484  2 DON JUAN   5    126   2
STEEP
     PLACE ME ON SUNIUM'S MARBLED STEEP . . . . . . . .       326  2 DON JUAN   3   L 16   1
     ITSELF TO APATHY FOR WE MUST STEEP  . . . . . . . .      346  2 DON JUAN   4      4   4
     OR THE SNOW MINARET ON AN ALPINE STEEP  . . . . . .       40  3 DON JUAN   6     68   4
     SMOOTHED EVEN THE SIMPLON'S STEEP AND BY GOD'S BLESSING  215  3 DON JUAN   9     66   7
     ITS OUTLET DASH'D INTO A STEEP CASCADE  . . . . . .      385  3 DON JUAN  13     58   1
STEEPLE
     AND PLACES ONE KEEPS LOOKING AT THE STEEPLE  . . . .     164  2 DON JUAN   2     14   8
     WHO MEASURED MEN AS YOU WOULD DO A STEEPLE . . . . .      84  3 DON JUAN   7     37   8
     LIKE A BOB-MAJOR FROM A VILLAGE STEEPLE  . . . . . .     109  3 DON JUAN   7     85   8
     AND INFIDELS TO PULL DOWN EVERY STEEPLE  . . . . . .     195  3 DON JUAN   9     25   3
STEEPLES
     OF MASTS A WILDERNESS OF STEEPLES PEEPING  . . . . .     265  3 DON JUAN  10     82   5
STEER
     THE WELCOME STALL TO THE O'ERLABOUR'D STEER . . . . .    338  2 DON JUAN   3    107   4
     MUST STEER WITH CARE THROUGH ALL THAT GLITTERING SEA .   303  3 DON JUAN  11     70   3
STEERING
     WAS STEERING DULY FOR THE PORT LEGHORN  . . . . . .      169  2 DON JUAN   2     24   2
     FOR THEY WERE FORCED WITH STEERING TO DISPENSE  . . .    177  2 DON JUAN   2     40   3
STEERS
     WHERE TIME THROUGH HEROES AND THROUGH BEAUTIES STEERS    381  3 DON JUAN  13     50   6
STEM
     WITNESS THOSE CI-DEVANT JEUNES HOMMES WHO STEM  . . .    418  3 DON JUAN  14     18   7
STEP
     WITH CHORAL STEP AND VOICE THE VIRGIN THRONG  . . . .    291  2 DON JUAN   3     30   8
     AND STUMBLED ALMOST EVERY STEP SHE MADE  . . . . . .     361  2 DON JUAN   4     32   3
     TO THEM POOR THINGS IT IS AN AWKWARD STEP  . . . . .     103  3 DON JUAN   7     72   6
```

STEP   (CONTINUED)
    WHICH THINNED AT EVERY STEP THEIR RANKS OF MEN 163   3 DON JUAN 8   103   4
    SHE CANNOT STEP AS DOES AN ARAB BARB 350   3 DON JUAN 12   75   1
    OR STEP RAN SADLY THROUGH THAT ANTIQUE HOUSE 509   3 DON JUAN 16   20   4
STEPP'D
    AND JUAN CAUGHT HIM UP AND ERE HE STEPP'D 187   2 DON JUAN 2   58   7
    AND WHEN INTO THE CAVERN HAIDEE STEPP'D 232   2 DON JUAN 2   143   1
    GO AND HE GOETH COME AND FORTH HE STEPP'D 430   2 DON JUAN 5   36   6
STEPPING
    MISS EDGEWORTH'S NOVELS STEPPING FROM THEIR COVERS . . . 29   2 DON JUAN 1   16   2
    BUT JUAN NOW IS STEPPING FROM HIS CARRIAGE 282   3 DON JUAN 11   30   8
STEPS
    WHOSE ACCENTS ARE THE STEPS OF MUSIC'S THRONE 237   2 DON JUAN 2   151   V8
    CHASTE WERE HIS STEPS EACH KEPT WITHIN DUE BOUND . . . 427   2 DON JUAN 14   39   1
    WITH STEPS THAT TROD AS HEAVY YET UNHEARD 510   3 DON JUAN 16   21   4
STEPT
    OF THE THIRD SEX STEPT UP AND PEERING OVER 424   2 DON JUAN 5   26   2
STERILE
    WITH SOME SMALL PROFIT THROUGH THAT FIELD SO STERILE . . 300   3 DON JUAN 11   64   3
STERLING
    OF MODERN REIGNING STERLING STUPID STAMP-- 321   3 DON JUAN 12   12   7
STERN
    DON JUAN STOOD AND GAZING FROM THE STERN 164   2 DON JUAN 2   14   1
    EACH SEA CURL'D O'ER THE STERN AND KEPT THEM WET . . . 188   2 DON JUAN 2   60   5
    YIELD TO STERN TIME AND NATURE'S WRINKLING LAWS . . . 219   2 DON JUAN 2   119   6
    THAN THE STERN SINGLE DEEP AND WORDLESS IRE 305   2 DON JUAN 3   58   7
    STERN AS HER SIRE ON ME SHE CRIED LET DEATH 366   2 DON JUAN 4   42   4
    PALE STATUE-LIKE AND STERN SHE WOO'D THE BLOW 367   2 DON JUAN 4   43   4
    FOR SORROW O'ER EACH SENSE HELD STERN COMMAND 396   2 DON JUAN 4   95   2
    A STERN REPOSE WHICH YOU WOULD SCARCE CONCEIVE 94   3 DON JUAN 7   54   3
    HIS STERN PHILOSOPHY BUT GENTLY STROKING 172   3 DON JUAN 8   121   6
    MY NATURAL TEMPER'S REALLY AUGHT BUT STERN 300   3 DON JUAN 11   63   5
    AND HERE AND THERE SOME STERN HIGH PATRIOT STOOD . . . 391   3 DON JUAN 13   70   7
    START FROM THE FRAMES WHICH FENCE THEIR ASPECTS STERN . 508   3 DON JUAN 16   18   6
    HER ASPECT WAS AS USUAL STILL--NOT STERN-- 545   3 DON JUAN 16   94   3
STERNER
    THERE IS NO STERNER MORALIST THAN PLEASURE 308   2 DON JUAN 3   65   8
STERNEST
    UNLESS ON TYRANT'S STERNS--WE TURN THE STERNEST . . . 286   3 DON JUAN 11   38   V8
    THE NEXT OF PERILS THOUGH I PLACE IT STERNEST 345   3 DON JUAN 12   64   2
STERN-FRAME
    WHOLE OF HER STERN-FRAME AND ERE SHE COULD LIFT . . . 170   2 DON JUAN 2   27   5
STERNLY
    THOSE HAUGHTY SHOP-KEEPERS WHO STERNLY DEALT 257   3 DON JUAN 10   65   6
STERN-POST
    STARTED THE STERN-POST ALSO SHATTER'D THE 170   2 DON JUAN 2   27   4
STERNS
    UNLESS ON TYRANT'S STERNS--WE TURN THE STERNEST . . . 286   3 DON JUAN 11   38   V8
STEWS
    OF CERTAIN STEWS AND ROAST-MEATS AND PILAUS 437   2 DON JUAN 5   47   2
STICK
    BUT WITH A LEAK AND NOT A STICK OF MAST 176   2 DON JUAN 2   39   3
    HARD WORDS WHICH STICK IN THE SOFT MUSES' GULLETS . . . 106   3 DON JUAN 7   78   8
STICKLE
    AS ANY OTHER BOON FOR WHICH MEN STICKLE 134   3 DON JUAN 8   43   4
STICKS
    CLINGS TO ITS TEAT STICKS TO ME THROUGH THE ABYSS . . . 238   3 DON JUAN 10   28   4
STIFF
    STIFF ON HIS HEART AND PULSE AND HOPE WERE PAST . . . 204   2 DON JUAN 2   90   4
    TO ME APPEARS A STIFF YET GRAND ERECTION 280   3 DON JUAN 11   25   7
    BUT GENTLEMEN IN STAYS AS STIFF AS STONES 409   3 DON JUAN 13   110   8
STIFFENED
    WHICH STIFFENED HEAVEN) AS IF HE WISHED FOR DAY-- . . . 121   3 DON JUAN 8   21   7
STIFFER
    THERE'S ONE THOUGH TALL AND STIFFER THAN A PIKE . . . 390   2 DON JUAN 4   85   5
STIFFLY
    'TWAS A ROUGH NIGHT AND BLEW SO STIFFLY YET 188   2 DON JUAN 2   60   1
STILL
    AT KESWICK AND THROUGH STILL CONTINUED FUSION 12   2 DON JUAN D   5   3
    YOU'RE SHABBY FELLOWS--TRUE--BUT POETS STILL 12   2 DON JUAN D   6   7
    AND BOTCHING PATCHING LEAVING STILL BEHIND 18   2 DON JUAN D   14   2
    EUROPE HAS SLAVES--ALLIES--KINGS--ARMIES STILL 19   2 DON JUAN D   16   7
    'TIS THAT I STILL RETAIN MY BUFF AND BLUE 20   2 DON JUAN D   17   4
    AND STILL SHOULD BE SO BUT THE TIDE IS TURN'D 23   2 DON JUAN 1   4   2
    ANACREON'S MORALS ARE A STILL WORSE SAMPLE 45   2 DON JUAN 1   42   2
    WAS TO DECLARE HOW SAGE AND STILL AND STEADY 49   2 DON JUAN 1   50   7
    I HAD MY DOUBTS PERHAPS I HAVE THEM STILL 49   2 DON JUAN 1   51   1
    IMPROVING STILL THROUGH EVERY GENERATION 54   2 DON JUAN 1   59   2
    FOR MALICE STILL IMPUTES SOME PRIVATE END) 58   2 DON JUAN 1   66   6
    AND THAT STILL KEEPING UP THE OLD CONNEXION 58   2 DON JUAN 1   67   1
    YET JULIA'S VERY COLDNESS STILL WAS KIND 60   2 DON JUAN 1   71   1
    ITSELF 'TIS STILL THE SAME HYPOCRISY 61   2 DON JUAN 1   73   6
    ARE MASKS IT OFTEN WEARS AND STILL TOO LATE 61   2 DON JUAN 1   73   8
    AND IF STILL FREE THAT SUCH OR SUCH A LOVER 64   2 DON JUAN 1   78   4
    BUT STILL NO LESS SUSPECTS IN THE WRONG PLACE 74   2 DON JUAN 1   99   2
    OF HALF-PAST SIX--PERHAPS STILL NEARER SEVEN 77   2 DON JUAN 1   104   2
    THE HAND WHICH STILL HELD JUAN'S BY DEGREES 81   2 DON JUAN 1   111   1
    YET STILL SHE MUST HAVE THOUGHT THERE WAS NO HARM . . . 83   2 DON JUAN 1   115   4
    A LITTLE STILL SHE STROVE AND MUCH REPENTED 84   2 DON JUAN 1   117   7

STILL (CONTINUED)

	PAGE	VOL		CANTO	STANZA	LN
YET STILL I TRUST IT MAY BE KEPT THROUGHOUT	85	2 DON JUAN		1	119	6
START NOT STILL CHASTER READER--SHE'LL BE NICE HENCEFORWARD	86	2 DON JUAN		1	120	2
BUT KEEPING JULIA AND DON JUAN STILL	86	2 DON JUAN		1	121	5
STILL BREAKING BUT WITH STAMINA SO STEADY	89	2 DON JUAN		1	125	6
BUT SWEETER STILL THAN THIS THAN THESE THAN ALL	90	2 DON JUAN		1	127	1
OF GOBLINS BUT STILL MORE OF MEN AFRAID	98	2 DON JUAN		1	141	3
RELUCTANTLY STILL TARRYING THERE AS LATE AS	111	2 DON JUAN		1	164	3
WHICH IF IT DOES NOT SILENCE STILL MUST POSE	117	2 DON JUAN		1	175	5
SO DEAR IS STILL THE MEMORY OF THAT DREAM	130	2 DON JUAN		1	193	4
THE PASSION WHICH STILL RAGES AS BEFORE	132	2 DON JUAN		1	195	6
BUT STILL I THINK I CAN COLLECT MY MIND	133	2 DON JUAN		1	196	2
MY BLOOD STILL RUSHES WHERE MY SPIRIT'S SET	133	2 DON JUAN		1	196	3
I HAVE NO MORE TO SAY BUT LINGER STILL	134	2 DON JUAN		1	197	1
THE CHARMS OF MAID WIFE AND STILL LESS OF WIDOW	144	2 DON JUAN		1	216	2
STILL GENTLER PURCHASER THE BARD--THAT'S I--	147	2 DON JUAN		1	221	2
BY BABEL'S WATERS STILL REMEMBERING SION	165	2 DON JUAN		2	16	2
BELOVED JULIA HEAR ME STILL BESEECHING	167	2 DON JUAN		2	20	7
STILL THEIR SALVATION WAS AN EVEN BET	171	2 DON JUAN		2	28	6
KEPT TWO HAND AND ONE CHAIN-PUMP STILL IN USE	172	2 DON JUAN		2	30	4
THE MAINMAST FOLLOW'D BUT THE SHIP STILL LAY	173	2 DON JUAN		2	32	3
KEPT STILL ALOOF THE CREW WHO ERE THEY SUNK	174	2 DON JUAN		2	35	7
THE VESSEL SWAM YET STILL SHE HELD HER OWN	176	2 DON JUAN		2	38	4
BUT STILL 'TIS BEST TO STRUGGLE TO THE LAST	176	2 DON JUAN		2	39	5
STILL SWAM--THOUGH NOT EXACTLY LIKE A DUCK	177	2 DON JUAN		2	40	8
THAT STILL COULD KEEP AFLOAT THE STRUGGLING TARS	183	2 DON JUAN		2	51	3
THEN SHRIEK'D THE TIMID AND STOOD STILL THE BRAVE	184	2 DON JUAN		2	52	2
BUT JUAN TRUSTING THEY MIGHT STILL GET THROUGH	187	2 DON JUAN		2	59	6
NINE SOULS MORE WENT IN HER THE LONG-BOAT STILL	188	2 DON JUAN		2	61	1
BECAUSE THEY STILL CAN HOPE NOR SHINES THE KNIFE	190	2 DON JUAN		2	64	5
AND HARDSHIP STILL HAS BEEN THE SAILOR'S LOT	191	2 DON JUAN		2	66	5
AND JUAN WHO HAD STILL REFUSED BECAUSE	193	2 DON JUAN		2	71	2
HAPPIER THAN THEY WHO STILL PERCEIVED THEIR WOES	199	2 DON JUAN		2	80	4
OF POOR PEDRILLO SOMETHING STILL REMAIN'D	200	2 DON JUAN		2	82	1
AND OTHERS STILL THEIR APPETITES CONSTRAIN'D	200	2 DON JUAN		2	82	3
NIGHT FELL--THIS SEEM'D A BETTER OMEN STILL	206	2 DON JUAN		2	94	8
PROVED EVEN STILL A MORE NUTRITIOUS MATTER	208	2 DON JUAN		2	99	5
STILL SET THEM ONWARDS TO THE WELCOME SHORE	209	2 DON JUAN		2	101	2
THOUGH THE TWO SHARKS STILL FOLLOW'D THEM AND DASH'D	209	2 DON JUAN		2	101	7
FOR DEATH THOUGH VANQUISH'D STILL RETIRED WITH STRIFE	214	2 DON JUAN		2	111	8
HE STILL WAS IN THE BOAT AND HAD BUT DOZED	215	2 DON JUAN		2	112	3
LIKE TWILIGHT ROSY STILL WITH THE SET SUN	218	2 DON JUAN		2	118	2
AND STILL A SORT OF FISHERMAN WAS HE	222	2 DON JUAN		2	125	2
STILL IN HER TEENS AND LIKE A LOVELY TREE	224	2 DON JUAN		2	128	5
THE MORN BROKE AND FOUND JUAN SLUMBERING STILL	229	2 DON JUAN		2	137	1
BRIGHT PHOEBUS WHILE THE MOUNTAINS STILL ARE WET	230	2 DON JUAN		2	139	5
SHOULD REACH HIS BLOOD THEN O'ER HIM STILL AS DEATH	232	2 DON JUAN		2	143	7
FOR STILL HE LAY AND ON HIS THIN WORN CHEEK	234	2 DON JUAN		2	147	1
AND FEELING STILL THE FAMISH'D VULTURE GNAW	239	2 DON JUAN		2	157	6
THEY SMILE STILL MORE AND THEN THERE INTERVENE	242	2 DON JUAN		2	164	6
SUCH PLENTIFUL PRECAUTIONS THAT STILL HE	248	2 DON JUAN		2	174	3
CIRCLING ALL NATURE HUSH'D AND DIM AND STILL	252	2 DON JUAN		2	183	4
(LEUCADIA'S ROCK STILL OVERLOOKS THE WAVE)	266	2 DON JUAN		2	205	6
OER WHOSE SAD TALE LOVE ECHOS STILL ALAS--	273	2 DON JUAN		2 V	2	3
AND YOUTH STILL WEEPS THE TENDER TEARS THAT PLEASE--	273	2 DON JUAN		2 V	2	4
CONTINUED STILL HER HOSPITABLE CARES	285	2 DON JUAN		3	19	5
AND STILL MORE NEARLY TO THE PLACE ADVANCING	290	2 DON JUAN		3	29	7
WHILE PEACEFUL AS IF STILL AN UNWEAN'D LAMB	292	2 DON JUAN		3	32	3
AH WHAT IS MAN WHAT PERILS STILL ENVIRON	294	2 DON JUAN		3	36	1
THEN CALM CONCENTRATED AND STILL AND SLOW	300	2 DON JUAN		3	48	3
STILL O'ER HIS MIND THE INFLUENCE OF THE CLIME	304	2 DON JUAN		3	56	1
AND STILL THEY SEEM RESENTFULLY TO FEEL	313	2 DON JUAN		3	73	5
YET STILL THEY DEIGN'D TO HICCUP OR TO BELLOW	318	2 DON JUAN		3	82	6
I DREAM'D THAT GREECE MIGHT STILL BE FREE	321	2 DON JUAN		3 L	3	4
WHAT SILENT STILL AND SILENT ALL	323	2 DON JUAN		3 L	8	1
WERE STILL AT LEAST OUR COUNTRYMEN	324	2 DON JUAN		3 L	11	6
WHICH STILL SAID ALL AND NE'ER COULD SAY TOO MUCH	351	2 DON JUAN		4	14	3
ALL THESE WERE THEIRS FOR THEY WERE CHILDREN STILL	352	2 DON JUAN		4	15	1
AND CHILDREN STILL THEY SHOULD HAVE EVER BEEN	352	2 DON JUAN		4	15	2
THE PAST STILL WELCOME AS THE PRESENT THOUGHT	354	2 DON JUAN		4	20	8
STRANGE STATE OF BEING (FOR 'TIS STILL TO BE)	360	2 DON JUAN		4	30	7
WHICH SHE MUST STILL PURSUE HOWE'ER AFRAID	361	2 DON JUAN		4	32	5
HER GLANCE NOR GRASP FOR STILL SHE GAZED AND GRASP'D	361	2 DON JUAN		4	32	7
HIS WEAPON AND REPLACED IT BUT STOOD STILL	368	2 DON JUAN		4	46	2
BESIDES THY PRICE IS SOMETHING DEARER STILL	372	2 DON JUAN		4	53	V4
WITH NOTHING LIVID STILL HER LIPS WERE RED	377	2 DON JUAN		4	60	2
SHE HAD NO PULSE BUT DEATH SEEM'D ABSENT STILL	377	2 DON JUAN		4	60	3
WHEN EXQUISITELY CHISELL'D STILL LAY THERE	377	2 DON JUAN		4	61	2
YET LOOKS NOT LIFE FOR THEY ARE STILL THE SAME	377	2 DON JUAN		4	61	8
THESE SMILE AND WRITHE AND PERISH STILL THE SAME	377	2 DON JUAN		4	61	V7
LAY AT HER HEART WHOSE EARLIEST BEAT STILL TRUE	378	2 DON JUAN		4	62	6
AND FURTHER DOWNWARD TALL AND TOWERING STILL IS	385	2 DON JUAN		4	76	5
ALL HEROES WHO IF LIVING STILL WOULD SLAY US	385	2 DON JUAN		4	76	8
AND IDA IN THE DISTANCE STILL THE SAME	386	2 DON JUAN		4	77	3
THE SITUATION SEEMS STILL FORM'D FOR FAME--	386	2 DON JUAN		4	77	5
WEAK STILL WITH LOSS OF BLOOD HE SCARCE COULD URGE	387	2 DON JUAN		4	79	5
STILL KEPT HIS SPIRITS UP--AT LEAST HIS FACE	388	2 DON JUAN		4	81	4
WHILE THE RIGHT HAND WHICH WROTE IT STILL IS ABLE	398	2 DON JUAN		4	99	5
YET THERE WILL STILL BE BARDS THOUGH FAME IS SMOKE	402	2 DON JUAN		4	106	1

STILL   (CONTINUED)

	PAGE	VOL	CANTO	STANZA	LN
OF THIS DELUSION STILL THE CHILLING YOKE	402	2	DON JUAN 4	106	V3
STILL I HAVE NO DISLIKE TO LEARNED NATURES	405	2	DON JUAN 4	111	5
AND STILL IT HALF CALLS UP THE REALMS OF FAIRY	413	2	DON JUAN 5	4	3
OF WHICH SOME GILDED REMNANTS STILL WERE SEEN	415	2	DON JUAN 5	9	4
THERE STILL ARE MANY RAINBOWS IN YOUR SKY	421	2	DON JUAN 5	21	3
WHERE STILL WE FLUTTER ON FOR PENCE OR PRAISE	422	2	DON JUAN 5	22	8
MY HAT AND GLOVES STILL LYING ON THE TABLE	428	2	DON JUAN 5	33	4
SPEAK BUT HE SPOKE NOT WAKE BUT STILL HE SLEPT--	430	2	DON JUAN 5	36	2
BUT MORE OR LESS CONTINUE STILL TO TEASE ON	437	2	DON JUAN 5	48	6
PROVIDED ALWAYS YOUR GREAT GOODNESS STILL	453	2	DON JUAN 5	72	7
ONE DIFFICULTY STILL REMAINED--HIS HAIR	457	2	DON JUAN 5	79	1
FOR ALL WAS VAST STILL FRAGRANT AND DIVINE	460	2	DON JUAN 5	85	8
INTO A ROOM STILL NOBLER THAN THE LAST	465	2	DON JUAN 5	93	2
FOR THROUGH THE SOUTH THE CUSTOM STILL COMMANDS	472	2	DON JUAN 5	105	7
JUDGE THEN IF HER CAPRICES E'ER STOOD STILL	475	2	DON JUAN 5	112	6
BUT JUAN WHO HAD STILL HIS MIND O'ERFLOWING	478	2	DON JUAN 5	117	2
BUT JUAN WHO HAD STILL HIS HEART QUITE FULL	478	2	DON JUAN 5	117	V2
WET STILL MORE DISAGREEABLE AND STRIKING	479	2	DON JUAN 5	118	4
FELT MOST INDIGNANT STILL AT NOT BEING FREE	481	2	DON JUAN 5	121	8
JUAN'S WAS GOOD AND MIGHT HAVE BEEN STILL BETTER	483	2	DON JUAN 5	124	1
AND HANDS OBEY)--OUR HEARTS ARE STILL OUR OWN	484	2	DON JUAN 5	127	8
YOUR PATIENCE) SHOWS THE CAUSE MUST STILL BE STRONGER	488	2	DON JUAN 5	133	8
AND WHAT'S STILL BETTER--TEACHES THEM THAT OTHERS	491	2	DON JUAN 5	138	V2
SO THAT THE HEIR APPARENT STILL WAS FOUND	499	2	DON JUAN 5	153	7
WHILE STILL A FLUTTERING SIGH GULBEYAZ HEAVED	500	2	DON JUAN 5	155	6
OF WORLDS TO LOSE YET STILL TO PAY MY COURT I	9	3	DON JJAN 6	5	5
ALL WHO HAVE LOVED OR LOVE WILL STILL ALLOW	9	3	DON JUAN 6	6	4
STILL HE FORGOT NOT HIS DISGUISE--ALONG	21	3	DON JUAN 6	30	1
COMPANION SOMETHING NEWER STILL AS 'TWERE	25	3	DON JJAN 6	39	2
THE MORTAL AND THE MARBLE STILL AT STRIFE	27	3	DON JUAN 6	43	7
YOU LOLAH MUST CONTINUE STILL TO LIE	30	3	DON JUAN 6	49	1
AND PLEASING OR UNPLEASING STILL ARE LIKE	32	3	DON JUAN 6	52	8
THE GENDER STILL WAS EPICENE AT LEAST	35	3	DON JUAN 6	58	2
NOT TO BE RASHLY TOUCHED BUT STILL MORE DREAD	37	3	DON JUAN 6	62	2
BUT STILL THE SPOUSELESS VIRGIN KNOWLEDGE FLIES	37	3	DON JUAN 6	63	5
A FOURTH AS MARBLE STATUE-LIKE AND STILL	40	3	DON JUAN 6	68	1
BRING DOWN THE FRUIT WHICH STILL PERVERSELY CLUNG	44	3	DON JUAN 6	76	6
IN CATHERINE'S REIGN WHOM GLORY STILL ADORES	52	3	DON JUAN 6	92	7
AND AS HIS SPEECH GREW STILL MORE BROKEN-KNEED	56	3	DON JUAN 6	101	6
MIGHT MAKE THE MATTER STILL WORSE THAN IT WAS	57	3	DON JUAN 6	103	8
SLOWLY ALONG THE ROOM BUT SILENT STILL	61	3	DON JUAN 6	110	6
THE WIND WAS DOWN BUT STILL THE SEA RAN HIGH	61	3	DON JUAN 6	110	8
TO HEAR IS TO OBEY HE SAID BUT STILL	62	3	DON JUAN 6	114	1
HE STILL PREFERRED HIS OWN NECK TO ANOTHER'S	63	3	DON JUAN 6	116	8
WHILE SHE STILL SILVERS O'ER YOUR GLOOMY PATH	70	3	DON JUAN 7	7	8
BUT STILL A FORTRESS OF THE FOREMOST RANK	70	3	DON JUAN 7	9	4
STILL I'LL RECORD A FEW IF BUT TO ENCREASE	74	3	DON JUAN 7	15	1
'TWAS NINE WHEN STILL ADVANCING UNDISMAYED	81	3	DON JUAN 7	29	3
AND I SHOULD STILL HAVE MANY THINGS TO SAY	82	3	DON JUAN 7	32	4
NOTHING--THE WORK OF GLORY STILL WENT ON	106	3	DON JUAN 7	78	1
BUT STILL WE MODERNS EQUAL YOU IN BLOOD	106	3	DON JUAN 7	80	8
THERE THE STILL VARYING PANGS WHICH MULTIPLY	118	3	DON JUAN 8	13	1
WHICH IS STILL BETTER THUS IN VERSE TO WAGE	118	3	DON JUAN 8	14	6
AND WHAT IS WORSE STILL A MUCH LONGER STORY	120	3	DON JUAN 8	17	8
AND STILL LESS GUESSING WHERE THEY MIGHT BE GOING	120	3	DON JUAN 8	19	4
AND LEVELLED WEAPONS STILL AGAINST THE GLACIS	130	3	DON JUAN 8	34	8
HER STEADY BREATH (WHICH SOME MONTHS THE SAME STILL IS)	132	3	DON JUAN 8	39	6
AND WHAT'S STILL STRANGER LEFT BEHIND A NAME	144	3	DON JUAN 8	63	1
STILL CLOSER SULPHURY CLOUDS BEGAN TO SMOTHER	146	3	DON JUAN 8	69	6
THE TEETH STILL KEPT THEIR GRATIFYING HOLD	146	3	DON JUAN 8	69	8
TO THE LIVE LEG STILL CLUNG THE SEVERED HEAD	153	3	DON JUAN 8	83	7
BUT STILL IT FALLS WITH VAST AND AWFUL SPLINTERS	153	3	DON JUAN 8	84	8
BUT THE STONE BASTION STILL REMAINS WHEREIN	155	3	DON JUAN 8	88	7
LIE ROUND THE BATTERY BUT STILL IT BATTERS	160	3	DON JUAN 8	98	2
THAT DRINKS AND STILL IS DRY AT LAST THEY PERISHED--	160	3	DON JUAN 8	98	7
BUT THE STONE BASTION STILL KEPT UP ITS FIRE	166	3	DON JUAN 8	110	1
BUT STILL THERE IS UNTO A PATRIOT NATION	171	3	DON JUAN 8	120	1
ROSE STILL BUT FAINTER WERE THE THUNDERS GROWN	175	3	DON JUAN 8	126	1
BE SAID THAT WE STILL TRUCKLE UNTO THRONES--	175	3	DON JUAN 8	127	6
YET IF PERCHANCE REMEMBERED STILL DISDAIN YOU 'EM	179	3	DON JUAN 8	135	6
WITH WHICH I STILL CAN HARP AND CARP AND FIDDLE	180	3	DON JUAN 8	136	6
IN FACT YOUR GRACE IS STILL BUT A YOUNG HERO	181	3	DON JUAN 8	139	1
AND EUROPE'S LIBERATOR--STILL ENSLAVED	184	3	DON JUAN 9	2	8
WHICH STILL ELSEWHERE MAY ROUSE A BRIGHTER SPRING--	185	3	DON JUAN 9	5	8
BUT STILL HE SMILES AND WHETHER NEAR OR FAR	188	3	DON JUAN 9	11	4
BUT STILL IT IS SO AND WITH SUCH EXAMPLE	188	3	DON JUAN 9	12	5
WHO STILL HAVE SHOWN THEMSELVES MORE BRAVE THAN WITTY	189	3	DON JUAN 9	13	2
MAY STILL EXPATIATE FREELY AS WILL I	194	3	DON JUAN 9	23	4
AT EVERY JOLT--AND THEY WERE MANY--STILL	195	3	DON JUAN 9	26	7
BUT STILL SO LIKE THAT PSYCHE WERE MORE CLEVER	198	3	DON JUAN 9	31	1
AND STILL MORE IN HIS EYE WHICH SEEMED TO EXPRESS	205	3	DON JUAN 9	45	6
WHILE HER YOUNG HERALD KNELT BEFORE HER STILL	206	3	DON JUAN 9	47	4
BUT STILL SEA-WORTHY SKIFF AND SHE MAY FLOAT	215	3	DON JUAN 9	66	4
WHOSE AGE AND WHAT WAS BETTER STILL WHOSE NATION	227	3	DON JUAN 10	4	7
BUT STILL HIS STATE WAS DELICATE THE HUE	241	3	DON JUAN 10	33	3
AND STILL LESS WAS IT SENSUAL FOR BESIDES	245	3	DON JUAN 10	43	5
SHE STILL HELD OUT THAT MAHOMET WAS A PROPHET	251	3	DON JUAN 10	54	1
	252	3	DON JUAN 10	56	8

777

STILL (CONTINUED)

	PAGE	VOL	CANTO	STANZA	LN
TO THE OLD TEXT STILL BETTER--LEST IT SHOULD	270	3 DON JUAN 11		4	2
KNOW VERY CLEARLY--OR AT LEAST LIE STILL	270	3 DON JUAN 11		4	8
WHILE EVERYTHING AROUND WAS CALM AND STILL	272	3 DON JUAN 11		8	5
BUT BEDLAM STILL EXISTS WITH ITS SAGE FETTER	280	3 DON JUAN 11		25	3
OVER THE STONES STILL RATTLING UP PALL MALL	282	3 DON JUAN 11		29	1
THE HORRID SIN--AND WHAT'S STILL WORSE THE TROUBLE	292	3 DON JUAN 11		46	8
WHO STILL REGRETTED THAT HE DID NOT RHYME	295	3 DON JUAN 11		53	4
STILL HE EXCELS THAT ARTIFICIAL HARD	297	3 DON JUAN 11		58	1
LOVE LINGERS STILL ALTHOUGH 'TWERE LATE TO WIVE	316	3 DON JUAN 12		2	5
AND ADDING STILL A LITTLE THROUGH EACH CROSS	317	3 DON JUAN 12		4	4
OH GOLD I STILL PREFER THEE UNTO PAPER	317	3 DON JUAN 12		4	7
SINCE I'VE GROWN MORAL STILL I MUST ACCUSE YOU ALL	329	3 DON JUAN 12		28	5
OR WHAT'S STILL WORSE TO PUT YOU OUT OF FASHION--	337	3 DON JUAN 12		45	4
MUST STILL OBEY THE HIGH--WHICH IS THEIR HANDLE	342	3 DON JUAN 12		56	7
THOSE BRAVURAS (WHICH I STILL AM LEARNING	350	3 DON JUAN 12		75	6
IN PEDIGREES BY THOSE WHO WANDER STILL	359	3 DON JUAN 13		2	3
AND STILL PURSUES THE RIGHT--TO CURB THE BAD	363	3 DON JUAN 13		9	3
A SORRIER STILL IS THE GREAT MORAL TAUGHT	363	3 DON JUAN 13		9	7
WHAT THEY SHOULD LAUGH AT--THE MERE AGUE STILL	366	3 DON JUAN 13		17	7
(A CHANCE STILL) 'TIS A VOYAGE OR VESSEL LOST	376	3 DON JUAN 13		39	8
STILL OLDER MANSION OF A RICH AND RARE	384	3 DON JUAN 13		55	3
ELSEWHERE PRESERVED THE CLOISTERS STILL WERE STABLE	389	3 DON JUAN 13		66	3
STILL UNIMPAIR'D TO DECORATE THE SCENE	389	3 DON JUAN 13		66	6
OF IN-DOOR COMFORTS STILL SHE HATH A MINE--	395	3 DON JUAN 13		77	5
AND THEY MUST BE OR SEEM WHAT THEY WERE STILL	417	3 DON JUAN 14		17	4
PARS PARVA FUI BUT STILL ART AND PART	419	3 DON JUAN 14		21	2
AT SEVENTEEN TOO THE WORLD WAS STILL ENCHANTED	434	3 DON JUAN 14		55	3
AT EIGHTEEN THOUGH BELOW HER FEET STILL PANTED	434	3 DON JUAN 14		55	5
HAD STILL PRESERVED HIS PERPENDICULAR	441	3 DON JUAN 14		71	8
STILL THERE WAS SOMETHING WANTING AS I'VE SAID--	441	3 DON JUAN 14		72	1
AND STILL MORE WOMEN SPRING FROM NOT EMPLOYING	444	3 DON JUAN 14		78	7
GREAT SOCRATES AND THOU DIVINER STILL	464	3 DON JUAN 15		18	2
THE THIRD IS STILL MORE DIFFICULT TO STAND TO	465	3 DON JUAN 15		21	5
(KEEPING THE DUE PROPORTIONS STILL IN SIGHT)	467	3 DON JUAN 15		25	6
FOR WHICH SMALL THANKS ARE STILL THE MARKET PRICE	469	3 DON JUAN 15		29	3
THAT STILL HE'D WED WITH SUCH OR SUCH A LADY	469	3 DON JUAN 15		30	7
BUT STILL HER ASPECT HAD AN AIR SO LONELY	475	3 DON JUAN 15		44	3
MY MUSE HATH BRED AND STILL PERHAPS MAY BREED	482	3 DON JUAN 15		60	5
BUT STILL I AM OR WAS A PRETTY POET	482	3 DON JUAN 15		60	8
FOR YOU HAVE GOT THAT PLEASURE STILL TO COME	498	3 DON JUAN 15		95	4
'GAINST SUCH BELIEF THERE'S SOMETHING STRONGER STILL	504	3 DON JUAN 16		7	7
GLIMMER ON HIGH THEIR BURIED LOCKS STILL WAVE	509	3 DON JUAN 16		19	3
THE THIRD TIME AFTER A STILL LONGER PAUSE	511	3 DON JUAN 16		24	1
ALL THERE WAS AS HE LEFT IT STILL HIS TAPER	512	3 DON JUAN 16		26	1
BUT SEEING HIM ALL COLD AND SILENT STILL	514	3 DON JUAN 16		32	1
TO HINDER HIM FROM GROWING STILL MORE PALLID	515	3 DON JUAN 16		35	8
AND EXPELLED THE FRIARS ONE FRIAR STILL	518	3 DON JUAN 16	L	1	7
BUT STILL TO THE HOUSE OF AMUNDEVILLE	519	3 DON JUAN 16	L	3	3
HE STILL RETAINS HIS SWAY	520	3 DON JUAN 16	L	5	2
BUT STILL FROM THAT SUBLIMER AZURE HUE	524	3 DON JUAN 16		47	5
BUT WISHED FOR A STILL MORE DETAILED NARRATION	526	3 DON JUAN 16		53	6
WERE GOOD SMALL-TALK FOR OTHERS STILL LESS GREAT)--	544	3 DON JUAN 16		91	8
WHICH WAS NOT VERY WISE AND STILL LESS WITTY	545	3 DON JUAN 16		93	4
HER ASPECT WAS AS USUAL STILL--NOT STERN--	545	3 DON JUAN 16		94	7
STILL WE RESPECT THEE ALMA VENUS GENETRIX	554	3 DON JUAN 16		109	8
WHICH STILL IN JUAN'S CANDLESTICKS BURNED HIGH	558	3 DON JUAN 16		117	5
HE REACHED THE ANCIENT WALL THEN STOOD STONE STILL	559	3 DON JUAN 16		119	8
BUT STILL THE SHADE REMAINED THE BLUE EYES GLARED	560	3 DON JUAN 16		121	1
AND JUAN PUZZLED BUT STILL CURIOUS THRUST	560	3 DON JUAN 16		122	1
SHOULD STILL BE SINGED BUT SLIGHTLY LET ME STATE)	565	3 DON JUAN 17		7	6

STILLNESS

	PAGE	VOL	CANTO	STANZA	LN
A STILLNESS WHICH LEAVES ROOM FOR THE FULL SOUL	82	2 DON JUAN 1		114	2
AND ALL WAS STILLNESS SAVE THE SEA-BIRD'S CRY	251	2 DON JUAN 2		181	5

STILTS

	PAGE	VOL	CANTO	STANZA	LN
WHO SHOES THE GLORIOUS ANIMAL WITH STILTS	297	3 DON JUAN 11		57	7
DON JUAN SAW THAT MICROCOSM ON STILTS	342	3 DON JUAN 12		56	1

STING

	PAGE	VOL	CANTO	STANZA	LN
THIS HOURLY DREAD OF ALL WHOSE THREATENED STING	188	3 DON JUAN 9		11	6
SEEMED TAKING OUT THE STING TO LEAVE THE HONEY	217	3 DON JUAN 9		70	8
BUT NONE OF THESE POSSESS'D A STING TO WOUND HER--	435	3 DON JUAN 14		57	3

STINGINESS

	PAGE	VOL	CANTO	STANZA	LN
AND STINGINESS DISGRACE HER SEX AND STATION	222	3 DON JUAN 9		81	8

STINGING

	PAGE	VOL	CANTO	STANZA	LN
AS YET ARE STRONGLY STINGING TO BE FREE	196	3 DON JUAN 9		28	8

STINGS

	PAGE	VOL	CANTO	STANZA	LN
(AS EVERY KIND OF PARTING HAS ITS STINGS)	161	2 DON JUAN 2		9	5
THE LUST WHICH STINGS THE SPLENDOUR WHICH ENCUMBERS	145	3 DON JUAN 8		67	5
STINGS IN LIFE WITH APPREHENSION IN ITS SHEATH	188	3 DON JUAN 9		11	V7
NOT STINGS AND FLITS THROUGH ETHER WITHOUT AIM	400	3 DON JUAN 13		89	6

STINT

	PAGE	VOL	CANTO	STANZA	LN
IF YOU COULD JUST CONTRIVE HE SAID TO STINT	464	2 DON JUAN 5		91	3

STIR

	PAGE	VOL	CANTO	STANZA	LN
TO STIR HER VIANDS MADE HIM QUITE AWAKE	237	2 DON JUAN 2		153	7
AND SHE WOULD SOFTLY STIR HIS LOCKS SO CURLY	245	2 DON JUAN 2		168	5
CHAIN'D TO A ROCK SHE KNEW NOT HOW BUT STIR	361	2 DON JUAN 4		31	2
COULD STIR HIS PULSE OR MAKE HIS FAITH FEEL BRITTLE	396	2 DON JUAN 4		95	7
(WHO LIKE SOUR FRUIT TO STIR THEIR VEINS' SALT TIDES	251	3 DON JUAN 10		54	3
SOME DEVILISH ESCAPADE OR STIR WHICH SHOWS	328	3 DON JUAN 12		26	2
AND GREATLY SHONE WHENEVER THERE HAD BEEN A STIR	368	3 DON JUAN 13		21	6

```
                                                              PAGE VOL        CANTO  STANZA  LN
STIRLESS
    AS O'ER HIM LAY THE CALM AND STIRLESS AIR     . . . . . . . 233  2 DON JUAN  2     144   4
    SO GENTLE STIRLESS HELPLESS AND UNMOVED   . . . . . . . .   261  2 DON JUAN  2     197   3
STIRR'D
    BUT NOT A SERVANT STIRR'D TO AID THE FIGHT    . . . . .     122  2 DON JUAN  1     184   3
    AND YET THE FOREST LEAVES SEEM'D STIRR'D WITH PRAYER . . .  335  2 DON JUAN  3     102   8
    STIRR'D WITH HER DREAM AS ROSE-LEAVES WITH THE AIR   . . .  359  2 DON JUAN  4      29   8
STIRRED
    OF HIS ARRIVAL SO THAT NO ONE STIRRED .  . . . . . .        294  2 DON JUAN  3      37   5
    BUT THOSE WHO SATE NE'ER STIRRED IN ANY WISE  . . . . .     441  2 DON JUAN  5      54   4
    THE FEMALE RANKS SO THAT NONE STIRRED OR TALKED  . . . .     21  3 DON JUAN  6      30   6
    STIRRED UP AND DOWN HER BOSOM LIKE A BILLOW . . . . . .      60  3 DON JUAN  6     108   6
    SO WAS HIS BLOOD STIRRED WHILE HE FOUND RESISTANCE  . . .   140  3 DON JUAN  8      55   1
    IT HATH BEEN STIRRED UP TILL ITS SMOKE QUITE SMOTHERS  . .  374  3 DON JUAN 13      36   8
    HAD STIRRED HIM ANSWERED IN A WAY TO CLOUD IT   . . . . .   527  3 DON JUAN 16      54   8
STIRRING
    OR AS THE STIRRING OF A DEEP CLEAR STREAM   . . . . .       360  2 DON JUAN  4      30   1
    AS SLIGHTLY STIRRING IN HER SNOWY SHROUD . . . . . . . .     39  3 DON JUAN  6      66   6
STITCH
    SO COSTLY WERE THEY CARPETS EVERY STITCH . . . . . . .      449  2 DON JUAN  5      65   6
STITCH'D
    TWO BLANKETS STITCH'D TOGETHER ANSWERING ILL    . . . . .   188  2 DON JUAN  2      61   3
STITCHED
    STITCHED UP IN SACKS--A MODE OF NAVIGATION  . . . . .       464  2 DON JUAN  5      92   7
    AND STITCHED ITS LEAVES INTO A DRESSING GOWN    . . . . .   476  2 DON JUAN  5     113   V8
STITCHES
    THEY FURNISH'D HIM ENTIRE EXCEPT SOME STITCHES . . . . .    240  2 DON JUAN  2     160   7
STOCK
    I'VE LAID IN TOO A STOCK OF GOOD MACHINERY  . . . . .       136  2 DON JUAN  1     201   V7
    THEIR STOCK WAS DAMAGED BY THE WEATHER'S STRESS . . . . .   180  2 DON JUAN  2      46   6
    COLUMBIA'S STOCK HATH HOLDERS NOT UNKNOWN   . . . . . .     318  3 DON JUAN 12       6   6
STOCK-HOLDER
    MORE (LIKE A STOCK-HOLDER IN GROWING PELF) . . . . . .      470  3 DON JUAN 15      31   5
STOCKING
    HER SMALL SNOW FEET HAD SLIPPERS BUT NO STOCKING  . . . .   220  2 DON JUAN  2     121   8
STOCKINGS
    OF STOCKINGS SLIPPERS BRUSHES COMBS COMPLETE   . . . . .     99  2 DON JUAN  1     143   4
    THEY SAY YOUR STOCKINGS ARE SO (HEAVEN KNOWS WHY  . . . .   404  2 DON JUAN  4     110   4
    I'LL BET SOME PAIR OF STOCKINGS BEAT PERU   . . . . . .     406  2 DON JUAN  4     112   V8
    WHITE STOCKINGS DRAWN UNCURDLED AS NEW MILK . . . . . .     204  3 DON JUAN  9      43   7
    OF WHITE CLIFFS WHITE NECKS BLUE EYES BLUER STOCKINGS  . .  346  3 DON JUAN 12      67   7
    AND STOCKINGS VIRTUES LOVES AND CHASTITIES . . . . . .      347  3 DON JUAN 12      67   V8
STOCKS
    IF RATHER BROAD MADE STOCKS RISE AND THEIR HOLDERS  . .     208  3 DON JUAN  9      52   8
STOIC
    WERE THINGS TO SHAKE A STOIC NE'ERTHELESS   . . . . .       415  2 DON JUAN  5       9   1
    CALLED BACK THE STOIC TO HIS EYES WHICH SHONE . . . . .     481  2 DON JUAN  5     121   5
    HEROIC STOIC CATO THE SENTENTIOUS . . . . . . . . .          10  3 DON JUAN  6       7   7
    BRONZED O'ER SOME LEAN AND STOIC ANCHORITE-- . . . . .      392  3 DON JUAN 13      72   4
    TO BE A TOTUS TERES STOIC SAGE  . . . . . . . . . . .       566  3 DON JUAN 17      10   7
STOICISM
    AND THEN MY STOICISM LEAVES NOUGHT BEHIND   . . . . .        17  3 DON JUAN  6      22   4
    WITH MARTIAL STOICISM NOUGHT SEEMED TO ANNOY   . . . .      172  3 DON JUAN  8     121   5
STOICS
    OF THE WORLD'S STOICS--MEN WITHOUT A HEART  . . . . .       423  2 DON JUAN  5      25   8
STOLE
    OR THE FAINT DYING DAY-HYMN STOLE ALOFT  . . . . . .        335  2 DON JUAN  3     102   6
    AND NOW AND THEN A TEAR STOLE DOWN BY STEALTH   . . . .     415  2 DON JUAN  5       8   4
    STOLE ON YOUR SPIRIT LIKE A MAY-DAY BREAKING    . . . .      27  3 DON JUAN  6      43   2
    A DIMPLED CHIN A NECK OF IVORY STOLE . . . . . . . .        561  3 DON JUAN 16     123   3
STOLEN
    AND STOLEN GLANCES SWEETER FOR THE THEFT .  . . . . .        62  2 DON JUAN  1      74   2
STOMACH
    OR RATHER STOMACH WHICH ALAS ATTENDS  . . . . . . .        167  2 DON JUAN  2      21   2
    RESIST HIS STOMACH NE'ER AT SEA BEFORE  . . . . . . .       168  2 DON JUAN  2      23   8
    SO CALM THOUGH PIERCED THROUGH STOMACH HEART AND LIVER  .   430  2 DON JUAN  5      35   4
    WITHOUT A STOMACH--WHAT WERE A GOOD NAME .  . . . . .       189  3 DON JUAN  9      14   8
    YOUR STOMACH ERE YOU DINE THE FRENCH WILL DO    . . . .     488  3 DON JUAN 15      72   4
STOMACH'S
    HER STOMACH'S NOT HER PECCANT PART THIS TALE    . . . .     483  3 DON JUAN 15      64   6
STOMACHS
    FOR EARLY STOMACHS TO PROVE WHOLESOME FOOD  . . . . .        45  2 DON JUAN  1      43   2
    TROUBLE HEROIC STOMACHS THOUGH THEIR LIDS SO    . . . .     133  3 DON JUAN  8      40   5
STONE
    LOST THAT MOST PRECIOUS STONE OF STONES--HIS MODESTY . .    157  2 DON JUAN  2       1   V8
    THAN ALL THE NONSENSE OF THEIR STONE IDEAL) . . . . . .     218  2 DON JUAN  2     118   8
    FLOW'D IN HER VEIL AND MANY A PRECIOUS STONE    . . . .     220  2 DON JUAN  2     121   6
    BUT IN GOOD COMPANY--THE GOUT OR STONE  . . . . . . .       305  2 DON JUAN  3      59   8
    OR GRAVEN STONE FOUND IN A BARRACK'S STATION    . . . .     327  2 DON JUAN  3      89   6
    NO STONE IS THERE TO SHOW NO TONGUE TO SAY  . . . . .       383  2 DON JUAN  4      72   6
    THE SOUL OUT (LIKE THE STONE) WITH PETTY CARES  . . . .      16  3 DON JUAN  6      20   8
    THOSE GAY RECESSES--MANY A PRECIOUS STONE   . . . . .        54  3 DON JUAN  6      97   5
    BUT A STONE BASTION WITH A NARROW GORGE  . . . . . .         72  3 DON JUAN  7      12   1
    BUT THE STONE BASTION STILL REMAINS WHEREIN .  . . . .      160  3 DON JUAN  8      98   2
    BUT THE STONE BASTION STILL KEPT UP ITS FIRE    . . . .     171  3 DON JUAN  8     120   1
    THOUGH IRELAND STARVE GREAT GEORGE WEIGHS TWENTY STONE .    175  3 DON JUAN  8     126   8
    BLACK EDWARD'S HELM AND BECKET'S BLOODY STONE   . . . .     261  3 DON JUAN 10      73   2
    GLADLY ALL MATTERS DOWN TO STONE OR LEAD .  . . . . .       268  3 DON JUAN 11       1   6
    OF RANK ENOUGH TO SET IN STONE OR LEAD   . . . . . .        314  3 DON JUAN 11    V 75   2
```

779

	PAGE	VOL	CANTO	STANZA	LN

STONE (CONTINUED)
TWELVE SAINTS HAD ONCE STOOD SANCTIFIED IN STONE . . . . . 386 3 DON JUAN 13 60 2
THE STONE OF SYSIPHUS IF ONCE WE MOVE . . . . 447 3 DON JUAN 14 86 3
IN CHISELLED STONE AND PAINTED GLASS AND ALL . . . . . 507 3 DON JUAN 16 16 7
WHO SITTETH BY NORMAN STONE . . . . 518 3 DON JUAN 16 L 1 2
HE REACHED THE ANCIENT WALL THEN STOOD STONE STILL . . . 559 3 DON JUAN 16 119 8

STONE-HENGE
STONE-HENGE IS NOT--BUT WHAT THE DEVIL IS IT-- . . . . 280 3 DON JUAN 11 25 2

STONES
LOST THAT MOST PRECIOUS STONE OF STONES--HIS MODESTY . . . 157 2 DON JUAN 2 1 V8
STONES AND WHATEVER SHE COULD PICK UP TO . . . . . . 44 3 DON JUAN 6 76 5
FOR I WILL TEACH IF POSSIBLE THE STONES . . . . . . 179 3 DON JUAN 8 135 4
OR HIEROGLYPHICS ON EGYPTIAN STONES . . . . 180 3 DON JUAN 8 137 5
OVER THE STONES STILL RATTLING UP PALL MALL . . . . . 282 3 DON JUAN 11 29 1
OF OTHER STONES TO SOOTHE THE MISER'S EYES . . . . . 319 3 DON JUAN 12 8 8
BUT GENTLEMEN IN STAYS AS STIFF AS STONES . . . . . 409 3 DON JUAN 13 110 8
FOR WHEN HIS PIOUS CONSORT GAVE HIM STONES . . . . . 410 3 DON JUAN 14 1 7

STONY
MIX'D WITH THE STONY VAPOURS OF THE VAULT . . . . . 234 2 DON JUAN 2 147 8
LAY IN A BREATHLESS HUSHED AND STONY SLEEP . . . . . 40 3 DON JUAN 6 68 2
THAT STRETCHES TO THE STONY BELT WHICH GIRDS . . . . 49 3 DON JUAN 6 86 7
AND RATHER VARIABLY FOR STONY DEATH . . . . 560 3 DON JUAN 16 121 2

STOOD
THE PRECIPICE SHE STOOD ON WAS IMMENSE . . . . . . 78 2 DON JUAN 1 106 7
THE SENHOR DON ALFONSO STOOD CONFUSED . . . . . . 109 2 DON JUAN 1 159 1
WITH PRYING SNUB-NOSE AND SMALL EYES HE STOOD . . . . 109 2 DON JUAN 1 160 1
BUT DON ALFONSO STOOD WITH DOWNCAST LOOKS . . . . . 110 2 DON JUAN 1 161 1
HE STOOD IN ACT TO SPEAK OR RATHER STAMMER . . . . . 111 2 DON JUAN 1 163 1
HE STOOD LIKE ADAM LINGERING NEAR HIS GARDEN . . . . 120 2 DON JUAN 1 180 5
AND THERE HE STOOD TO TAKE AND TAKE AGAIN . . . . . 162 2 DON JUAN 2 11 7
SO JUAN STOOD BEWILDER'D ON THE DECK . . . . . . 163 2 DON JUAN 2 13 1
DON JUAN STOOD AND GAZING FROM THE STERN . . . . . 164 2 DON JUAN 2 14 1
GOT TO THE SPIRIT-ROOM AND STOOD BEFORE . . . . . 174 2 DON JUAN 2 35 3
THEN SHRIEK'D THE TIMID AND STOOD STILL THE BRAVE . . . 184 2 DON JUAN 2 52 2
WITH TENDERNESS--STOOD HOWLING ON THE BRINK . . . . 187 2 DON JUAN 2 58 4
AND THEN SHE STOPP'D AND STOOD AS IF IN AWE . . . . 232 2 DON JUAN 2 143 4
AFAR A DWARF BUFFOON STOOD TELLING TALES . . . . . 293 2 DON JUAN 3 34 1
AND STOOD WITHIN HIS HALL AT EVENTIDE . . . . . . 306 2 DON JUAN 3 61 2
WITH MOTHER OF PEARL OR IVORY STOOD AT HAND . . . . 310 2 DON JUAN 3 69 3
AND IN THEIR NATIVE BEAUTY STOOD AVENGED . . . . . 314 2 DON JUAN 3 75 5
TO WHERE THE LAST CESAREAN FORTRESS STOOD . . . . . 337 2 DON JUAN 3 105 5
THE DREAM CHANGED IN A CAVE SHE STOOD ITS WALLS . . . 362 2 DON JUAN 4 33 1
HIGH AND INSCRUTABLE THE OLD MAN STOOD . . . . . 365 2 DON JUAN 4 39 1
IN ARMS AT LEAST HE STOOD IN ACT TO SPRING . . . . 365 2 DON JUAN 4 39 7
SHE STOOD AS ONE WHO CHAMPION'D HUMAN FEARS-- . . . 367 2 DON JUAN 4 43 3
HIS WEAPON AND REPLACED IT BUT STOOD STILL . . . . 368 2 DON JUAN 4 46 2
SAVE CHANGE I'VE STOOD UPON ACHILLES' TOMB . . . . 399 2 DON JUAN 4 101 7
THE FEMALES STOOD AS ONE BY ONE THEY PICK'D 'EM . . . 409 2 DON JUAN 4 116 7
THE YOUNGER PORTION STOOD--A LUCKLESS VICTIM . . . . 409 2 DON JUAN 4 116 V7
THE FEMALES STOOD TILL CHOSEN EACH AS VICTIM . . . . 409 2 DON JUAN 4 116 V7
NEXT JUAN STOOD TILL SOME MIGHT CHOOSE TO BUY . . . 416 2 DON JUAN 5 10 8
AND THERE HE STOOD WITH SUCH SANG-FROID THAT GREATER . . 416 2 DON JUAN 5 11 7
THIS MASSY PORTAL STOOD AT THE WIDE CLOSE . . . . 462 2 DON JUAN 5 87 1
BABA AND JUAN WHICH LAST STOOD ADMIRING . . . . . 469 2 DON JUAN 5 100 3
HE STOOD LIKE ATLAS WITH A WORLD OF WORDS . . . . 471 2 DON JUAN 5 104 1
JUDGE THEN IF HER CAPRICES E'ER STOOD STILL . . . . 475 2 DON JUAN 5 112 6
AND THUS HEROICALLY STOOD RESIGNED . . . . . . 492 2 DON JUAN 5 141 5
SHE STOOD A MOMENT AS A PYTHONESS . . . . . . 59 3 DON JUAN 6 107 1
OF BAFFLED HEROES WHO STOOD SHYLY NEAR . . . . . 148 3 DON JUAN 8 73 6
OF ALL THE STANDING ARMY WHO STOOD BY . . . . . 221 3 DON JUAN 9 78 8
BY FORMER VOYAGES STOOD TO WATCH THE SKIFFS . . . . 256 3 DON JUAN 10 64 7
TO OUR THEME--THE MAN WHO HAS STOOD ON THE ACROPOLIS . . 271 3 DON JUAN 11 7 1
STOOD CALLING OUT FOR BANDAGES AND LINT . . . . . 275 3 DON JUAN 11 14 7
THE MOB STOOD AND AS USUAL SEVERAL SCORE . . . . . 282 3 DON JUAN 11 30 3
STOOD AS THE UNPACKING GATHERED MORE SPECTATORS) . . . 313 3 DON JUAN 11 V 29 6
HE HAD ALSO STOOD AT TIMES BEHIND THE THRONE-- . . . 353 3 DON JUAN 12 82 7
FOR JUAN STOOD WELL BOTH WITH INS AND OUTS . . . . 369 3 DON JUAN 13 24 3
IT STOOD EMBOSOM'D IN A HAPPY VALLEY . . . . . 384 3 DON JUAN 13 56 1
STOOD LIKE CARACTACUS IN ACT TO RALLY . . . . . 384 3 DON JUAN 13 56 3
THE WOODS SLOPED DOWNWARDS TO ITS BRINK AND STOOD . . . 385 3 DON JUAN 13 57 7
(WHILE YET THE CHURCH WAS ROME'S) STOOD HALF APART . . . 386 3 DON JUAN 13 59 2
TWELVE SAINTS HAD ONCE STOOD SANCTIFIED IN STONE . . . 386 3 DON JUAN 13 60 2
AND HERE AND THERE SOME STERN HIGH PATRIOT STOOD . . . 391 3 DON JUAN 13 70 7
BUT LIGHT AND AIRY STOOD ON THE ALERT . . . . . 426 3 DON JUAN 14 37 1
FOR SHE HAD SEEN THE WORLD AND STOOD ITS TEST . . . 433 3 DON JUAN 14 54 4
AND HE STOOD GAZING OUT ON THE CASCADE . . . . . 507 3 DON JUAN 16 15 7
AS STANDS A STATUE STOOD HE FELT HIS HAIR . . . . 510 3 DON JUAN 16 23 5
HE STOOD--HOW LONG HE KNEW NOT BUT IT SEEMED . . . 511 3 DON JUAN 16 25 1
BUT STOOD IN TREMBLING PATIENT TRIBULATION . . . . 532 3 DON JUAN 16 65 7
AND THEN SWUNG BACK NOR CLOSE--BUT STOOD AWRY . . . 558 3 DON JUAN 16 117 3
AND IN THE DOOR-WAY DARKENING DARKNESS STOOD . . . 558 3 DON JUAN 16 117 7
HE REACHED THE ANCIENT WALL THEN STOOD STONE STILL . . 559 3 DON JUAN 16 119 8

STOOL
DUNCES WERE WHIPT OR SET UPON A STOOL . . . . . 162 2 DON JUAN 2 10 6

STOOP
TILL SOME LESS RIGID EDITOR SHALL STOOP . . . . . 46 2 DON JUAN 1 45 5
HOW SOME TO BURDENS WERE OBLIGED TO STOOP . . . . 409 2 DON JUAN 4 116 3
AND SAID IT GRIEVED HIM BUT HE COULD NOT STOOP . . . 470 2 DON JUAN 5 102 7
HER FEET THAT HER FIRST MOVEMENT.WAS TO STOOP . . . 44 3 DON JUAN 6 77 3
A FEMALE CHILD OF TEN YEARS TRIED TO STOOP . . . 157 3 DON JUAN 8 91 6

STOOPED
```
    THE CASQUE WHICH NEVER STOOPED EXCEPT TO TIME  . . . . .  261  3 DON JUAN 10    74   3
STOOPING
    HER HEAD HUNG DOWN AND HER LONG HAIR IN STOOPING  . . . .   60  3 DON JUAN  6   109   1
STOOPS
    WELL NIGH THE SHORE WHERE ONE STOOPS DOWN AND GATHERS  .   191  3 DON JUAN  9    18   7
STOP
    STOP CRIED PHILOSOPHY WITH AIR SO GRECIAN  . . . . .      268  2 DON JUAN  2   210   7
    STOP SO I STOPP'D--BUT TO RETURN THAT WHICH . . . . .     269  2 DON JUAN  2   211   1
    HE MOTIONED THEM TO STOP AT SOME SMALL DISTANCE  . . .    440  2 DON JUAN  5    51   5
    BUT TEARS MUST STOP LIKE ALL THINGS ELSE AND SOON  . .    481  2 DON JUAN  5   121   1
    COULD STOP THAT WORST OF VICES--PROPAGATION . . . . .      15  3 DON JUAN  6    19   8
    COULD STOP THE TENDENCY TO PROPAGATION  . . . . . .        15  3 DON JUAN  6    19  V8
    I CANNOT STOP TO ALTER WORDS ONCE WRITTEN  . . . . .      221  3 DON JUAN  9    77   4
    FOR THEN THEY ARE VERY DIFFICULT TO STOP . . . . . .      368  3 DON JUAN 13    22   8
    BECAUSE HE FIXED IT AND TO STOP HIS TALKING . . . . .     565  3 DON JUAN 17     8   2
STOPP'D
    AND THEN SHE STOPP'D AND STOOD AS IF IN AWE . . . . .     232  2 DON JUAN  2   143   4
    BUT HAIDEE STOPP'D HER WITH HER QUICK SMALL HAND  . .     234  2 DON JUAN  2   146   3
    STOP SO I STOPP'D--BUT TO RETURN THAT WHICH . . . . .     269  2 DON JUAN  2   211   1
    HE STOPP'D--WHAT SINGULAR EMOTIONS FILL  . . . . .        286  2 DON JUAN  3    21   3
    'TWAS WHITE AND INDISTINCT NOR STOPP'D TO MEET . . .      361  2 DON JUAN  4    32   6
    HAD STOPP'D THIS CANTO AND DON JUAN'S BREATH  . . . .     366  2 DON JUAN  4    42   2
    HER FATHER'S FACE--BUT NEVER STOPP'D HIS HAND . . . .     367  2 DON JUAN  4    43   8
STOPPED
    AND SO I STOPPED TO TALK WITH A VENETIAN . . . . . .      268  2 DON JUAN  2   210  V8
    HE STOPPED AGAIN AND TURNED AWAY HIS FACE  . . . . .      420  2 DON JUAN  5    19   2
    A LADY BABA STOPPED AND KNEELING SIGNED  . . . . . .      466  2 DON JUAN  5    95   4
    GULBEYAZ STOPPED AND BECKONED BABA--SLAVE  . . . . .       62  3 DON JUAN  6   112   1
    STOPPED FOR A MINUTE AS PERHAPS HE OUGHT . . . . . .      126  3 DON JUAN  8    29   4
    STOPPED AS IF ONCE MORE WILLING TO CONCEDE  . . . .       170  3 DON JUAN  8   117   2
    AND CLIMATE STOPPED ALL SCANDAL (NOW AND THEN)-- . .      241  3 DON JUAN 10    33   4
    AND CLIMATE--STOPPED THE LION SCANDAL'S DEN . . . .       241  3 DON JUAN 10    33  V4
    THE GHOST STOPPED MENACED THEN RETIRED UNTIL  . . .       559  3 DON JUAN 16   119   7
STOPPED'EM
    (WITH MORE BESIDE IF JUAN HAD NOT STOPPED'EM)  . . . .    244  3 DON JUAN 10    41   6
STOPPING
    HE LEADS THEM THROUGH THE HALL AND WITHOUT STOPPING  .    442  2 DON JUAN  5    55   1
STOPS
    AS LITTLE AS THE MOON STOPS FOR THE BAYING  . . . . .      70  3 DON JUAN  7     7   5
STOPT
    FOR BABA'S FUNCTION STOPT SHORT AT THE DOOR . . . . .      57  3 DON JUAN  6   103   4
    SHE STOPT AND RAISED HER HEAD TO SPEAK--BUT PAUSED  . .    61  3 DON JUAN  6   111   1
STORE
    AS IF HER HEART HAD DEEPER THOUGHTS IN STORE . . . .       61  2 DON JUAN  1    72   3
    DROPP'D IN THEIR LAPS SCARCE PLUCK'D THEIR MELLOW STORE . 291  2 DON JUAN  3    31   8
    THERE THE LARGE OLIVE RAINS ITS AMBER STORE . . . . .     373  2 DON JUAN  4    55   1
    OF HERBS AND CORDIALS THEY PRODUCED THEIR STORE  . .      376  2 DON JUAN  4    59   6
    AND THEREFORE OF CIRCASSIANS HAD GOOD STORE . . . . .      51  3 DON JUAN  6    91   5
    AND STORE IT UP FOR MISCHIEVOUS ENJOYMENT  . . . . .      548  3 DON JUAN 16   100   7
STORED
    AND TWO BOATS COULD NOT HOLD FAR LESS BE STORED  . . .    181  2 DON JUAN  2    48   7
STORIES
    AND IF OUR QUARRELS SHOULD RIP UP OLD STORIES . . . .      37  2 DON JUAN  1    31   1
    SONG DANCE WINE MUSIC STORIES FROM THE PERSIAN  . . .     293  2 DON JUAN  3    35   3
    I'VE HEARD OF STORIES OF A COCK AND BULL . . . . . .       46  3 DON JUAN  6    80   1
    IN VERNET'S OCEAN LIGHTS AND THERE THE STORIES . . . .    392  3 DON JUAN 13    71   6
    WITH A LONG MEMORANDUM OF OLD STORIES  . . . . . . .      432  3 DON JUAN 14    50   8
STORM
    HIS DEWY CURLS LONG DRENCH'D BY EVERY STORM . . . . .     216  2 DON JUAN  2   114   6
    MADE HER A BEAUTIFUL EMBODIED STORM . . . . . . . .       489  2 DON JUAN  5   135   8
    A STORM IT RAGED AND LIKE THE STORM IT PASSED . . . .     490  2 DON JUAN  5   137   1
    A STORM IT RAGED AND LIKE THE STORM IT PASSED . . . .     490  2 DON JUAN  5   137   1
    NOW MARS NOW MOMUS AND WHEN BENT TO STORM  . . . . .       95  3 DON JUAN  7    55   7
    WITH ISMAIL'S STORM TO SOFTEN IT THE MORE  . . . . .      146  3 DON JUAN  8    68   8
    TAKE TOWNS BY STORM NO CAUSES CAN I GUESS  . . . . .      176  3 DON JUAN  8   129   5
    WAVING LIKE SAILS NEW SHIVERED IN A STORM  . . . . .      204  3 DON JUAN  9    43   3
    HIS BILLS IN AND HOWEVER WE MAY STORM  . . . . . . .      243  3 DON JUAN 10    38   6
    HE WHO HATH PROVED WAR STORM OR WOMAN'S RAGE . . . .      339  3 DON JUAN 12    50   6
    THE STRUGGLE TO BE PILOTS IN A STORM . . . . . . .        360  3 DON JUAN 13     6   3
    WHICH DID NOT SHOW BUT YET CONCEALED A STORM . . . .      474  3 DON JUAN 15    41  V2
STORMS
    WORK'D BY THE STORMS YET WORK'D AS IT WERE PLANN'D  . .   253  2 DON JUAN  2   184   5
    ITS STORMS EXPIRE IN WATER-DROPS THE EYE  . . . . .       270  2 DON JUAN  2   214   6
    THAN STORMS IT AS A FOE WOULD TAKE A CITY  . . . . .      350  2 DON JUAN 12    74   6
    OR LIKE A BILLOW LEFT BY STORMS BEHIND  . . . . . .       504  3 DON JUAN 16     9   7
STORMY
    AND LONG HAD VOYAGED THROUGH MANY A STORMY SEA  . . .     179  2 DON JUAN  2    43   4
    NO DIRGE SAVE WHEN ARISE THE STORMY SEAS . . . . .        383  2 DON JUAN  4    72  V7
    I'VE SEEN YOUR STORMY SEAS AND STORMY WOMEN . . . .        32  3 DON JUAN  6    53   7
    I'VE SEEN YOUR STORMY SEAS AND STORMY WOMEN . . . .        32  3 DON JUAN  6    53   7
STORY
    TO ADD A STORY TO THE TOWER OF BABEL  . . . . . .          11  2 DON JUAN  D     4   8
    AND SO GOOD NIGHT--RETURN WE TO OUR STORY  . . . . .       94  2 DON JUAN  1   134   2
    THIS STORY IS NOT MORAL FIRST I PRAY . . . . . . .        140  2 DON JUAN  1   207   2
    AS MOST ESSENTIAL TO THEIR HERO'S STORY  . . . . . .      329  2 DON JUAN  3    92   7
    BUT LET ME TO MY STORY I MUST OWN  . . . . . . . .        331  2 DON JUAN  3    96   1
    AND TELLS ME TO RESUME MY STORY HERE . . . . . . .        347  2 DON JUAN  4     7   8
    WITH HER SIRE'S STORY MAKES THE NIGHT LESS LONG . . .     383  2 DON JUAN  4    73   3
```

		PAGE	VOL		CANTO	STANZA	LN

STORY   (CONTINUED)
IN A FEW WORDS HE TOLD THEIR HAPLESS STORY . . . . . . 389 2 DON JUAN 4   82   1
BUT LET US TO THE STORY AS BEFORE . . . . 432 2 DON JUAN 5   39   8
METHINKS THE STORY OF THE TOWER OF BABEL . . . . 444 2 DON JUAN 5   59   7
PHEDRA AND ALL WHICH STORY HAS DISCLOSED . . . . 486 2 DON JUAN 5   131   3
THE STORY SCARCELY PASSED A SINGLE LIP-- . . . . 496 2 DON JUAN 5   149   3
WHO WERE IMMORTAL COULD ONE TELL THEIR STORY . . . . . 73 3 DON JUAN 7   14   4
MAY LIKEWISE PUT OFF FOR A TIME WHAT STORY . . . . . . 79 3 DON JUAN 7   26   7
AND ADMIRAL RIBAS (KNOWN IN RUSSIAN STORY) . . . . . . 83 3 DON JUAN 7   35   3
AND WHAT IS WORSE STILL A MUCH LONGER STORY . . . . . 120 3 DON JUAN 8   17   8
READ YOUR OWN HEARTS AND IRELAND'S PRESENT STORY . . . 174 3 DON JUAN 8   125   7
WELL WE WON'T ANALYZE--OUR STORY MUST . . . . 221 3 DON JUAN 9   77   1
WITH WIT TO HATCH A PUN OR TELL A STORY . . . . 401 3 DON JUAN 13   91   6
WITH MORE EASE TOO SHE'D TELL A DIFFERENT STORY . . . 416 3 DON JUAN 14   13   8
ON WHAT MAY SUIT OR MAY NOT SUIT MY STORY . . . . . . 464 3 DON JUAN 15   19   5
I SAID IT WAS A STORY OF A GHOST-- . . . . 502 3 DON JUAN 16   4   3
TELLS AN ODD STORY OF WHICH BY THE BYE . . . . 516 3 DON JUAN 16   36   4
BUT COME I'LL SET YOUR STORY TO A TUNE . . . . 517 3 DON JUAN 16   38   4
STORY'S
WHEREAS THIS STORY'S ACTUALLY TRUE . . . . 137 2 DON JUAN 1   202   8
A DULL STORY'S DOUBLY GRIEVOUS WHEN 'TIS LONG . . . . 419 2 DON JUAN 5   16 V8
STOUP
PROVOKE MY THIRST--WHAT--HO OF WINE A STOUP . . . . . 392 3 DON JUAN 13   72 V8
STOUT
HAD IT BUT BEEN FOR A STOUT CAVALIER . . . . 115 2 DON JUAN 1   172   1
A MAN OF THIRTY RATHER STOUT AND HALE . . . . 416 2 DON JUAN 5   10   6
STOUTER
WAS FOR THE ELDER AND THE STOUTER FIRST . . . . 451 2 DON JUAN 5   68   2
STOVE
BEEN STOVE IN THE BEGINNING OF THE GALE . . . . 181 2 DON JUAN 2   48   2
STOW
BUT IN THE LONG-BOAT THEY CONTRIVED TO STOW . . . . . 181 2 DON JUAN 2   47   1
STOWED
THEY STOWED HIM WITH STRICT ORDERS TO THE WATCHES . . 371 2 DON JUAN 4   50   8
OF WHOM ALL SUCH AS CAME OF AGE WERE STOWED . . . . . 498 2 DON JUAN 5   152   2
STRAGGLING
OF THE ARMED RIVER WHILE WITH STRAGGLING LIGHT . . . . 110 3 DON JUAN 7   86   5
A STRAGGLING CURL SHOWED HE HAD BEEN FAIR-HAIRED . . . 560 3 DON JUAN 16   121   5
STRAIGHTWAY
AND WHEN 'TWAS FOUND STRAIGHTWAY THE BARGAIN CLOSED . 476 2 DON JUAN 5   113   4
STRAIN
HIS STRAIN DISPLAY'D SOME FEELING--RIGHT OR WRONG . . 326 2 DON JUAN 3   87   5
FROM OUR OLD CRASH SOME MYSTIC ANCIENT STRAIN . . . . 201 3 DON JUAN 9   38   3
SUCH THOUGHTS ARE QUITE BELOW THE STRAIN THEY HAVE CHOSEN . 341 3 DON JUAN 12   55   3
STRAIN'D
THE WIND SUNG CORDAGE STRAIN'D AND SAILORS SWORE . . . 163 2 DON JUAN 2   13   2
STRAINED
STRAINED ON THE SPOT WHERE FIRST THE FIGURE GLEAMED . 511 3 DON JUAN 16   25   3
STRAINING
TO SOME ODD ANGLE FOR WHICH ALL WERE STRAINING . . . . 121 3 DON JUAN 8   20   4
AND NEVER STRAINING HARD TO VERSIFY . . . . 464 3 DON JUAN 15   19   6
STRAINS
AND IF IN FLATTERING STRAINS I DO NOT PREDICATE . . . 20 2 DON JUAN D   17   3
AND THE LOUD CANNON PEALED HIS HOARSEST STRAINS . . . 129 3 DON JUAN 8   33   6
WHOSE STRAINS--WHATE'ER THEY BE--SURPASS AT LEAST . . 297 3 DON JUAN 11   57 V7
STRAITS
OF AGES TO WHAT STRAITS OLD TIME REDUCES . . . . 327 2 DON JUAN 3   88   6
STRANDED
AN IGNIS FATUUS OR AS SAILORS STRANDED . . . . 127 3 DON JUAN 8   32   5
STRANGE
'TIS STRANGE--THE HEBREW NOUN WHICH MEANS I AM . . . . 28 2 DON JUAN 1   14   7
'TWAS STRANGE THAT ONE SO YOUNG SHOULD THUS CONCERN . . 71 2 DON JUAN 1   93   5
THIS MAY SEEM STRANGE BUT YET 'TIS VERY COMMON . . . . 74 2 DON JUAN 1   98   1
'TIS STRANGE OLD PEOPLE DONT LIKE TO BE BURIED . . . . 89 2 DON JUAN 1   125 V8
MAN'S A STRANGE ANIMAL AND MAKES STRANGE USE . . . . . 91 2 DON JUAN 1   128   1
MAN'S A STRANGE ANIMAL AND MAKES STRANGE USE . . . . . 91 2 DON JUAN 1   128   1
AT THIS MOST STRANGE AND UNEXPLAIN'D HIATUS . . . . . 111 2 DON JUAN 1   164   5
SOME STRANGE EXCUSES FOR HIS LATE PROCEEDING . . . . . 116 2 DON JUAN 1   174   2
A STRANGE EXAMPLE OF THE FORCE OF LAW . . . . 155 2 DON JUAN 1 V 7   1
STRANGE SOUNDS OF WAILING BLASPHEMY DEVOTION . . . . . 174 2 DON JUAN 2   34   7
AND FOAM AND ROLL WITH STRANGE CONVULSIONS RACK'D . . 198 2 DON JUAN 2   79   5
'TIS PLEASING TO BE SCHOOL'D IN A STRANGE TONGUE . . . 242 2 DON JUAN 2   164   1
OF LIFE'S STRANGE TREE SO FRUITFUL ON OCCASION . . . . 250 2 DON JUAN 2   179   6
'TIS STRANGE THAT POETS NEVER TRY TO WREATHE . . . . . 280 2 DON JUAN 3   9 V5
'TIS STRANGE THAT POETS OF THE CATHOLIC FAITH . . . . 280 2 DON JUAN 3   9 V5
LET NOT HIS MODE OF RAISING CASH SEEM STRANGE . . . . 283 2 DON JUAN 3   14   1
IT MAY SEEM STRANGE TO FIND HIS MANNERS BLAND . . . . 299 2 DON JUAN 3   47   5
HE WAS A MAN OF A STRANGE TEMPERAMENT . . . . 302 2 DON JUAN 3   53   1
'TIS STRANGE THE SHORTEST LETTER WHICH MAN USES . . . 327 2 DON JUAN 3   88   4
SOME HAVE ACCUSED ME OF A STRANGE DESIGN . . . . 346 2 DON JUAN 4   5   1
WHILE LIFE'S STRANGE PRINCIPLE WILL OFTEN LIE . . . . 350 2 DON JUAN 4   11   7
STRANGE STATE OF BEING (FOR 'TIS STILL TO BE) . . . . 360 2 DON JUAN 4   30   7
IT HAS A STRANGE QUICK JAR UPON THE EAR . . . . 366 2 DON JUAN 4   41   1
HE GAZED ON HER AND SHE ON HIM 'TWAS STRANGE . . . . . 367 2 DON JUAN 4   44   1
THE WORLD IS FULL OF STRANGE VICISSITUDES . . . . . . 371 2 DON JUAN 4   51   1
A STRANGE SENSATION WHICH SHE MUST PARTAKE . . . . . . 378 2 DON JUAN 4   62   3
HAIL'D A STRANGE BRIG CORPO DI CAIO MARIO . . . . . . 389 2 DON JUAN 4   82   4
WHO SAY STRANGE THINGS FOR SO CORRECT AN AGE . . . . . 397 2 DON JUAN 4   98   4
SEEMS FERTILE IN ADVENTURES STRANGE AND NEW . . . . . 459 2 DON JUAN 5   83   6

STRANGE   (CONTINUED)

	PAGE	VOL		CANTO	STANZA	LN
THIS STRANGE SALOON MUCH FITTED FOR INSPIRING	469	2	DON JUAN	5	100	5
BUT O'ER HER BRIGHT BROW FLASHED A TUMULT STRANGE	473	2	DON JUAN	5	108	3
COULD RISK OR COMPASS SUCH STRANGE PHANTASIES	477	2	DON JUAN	5	115	3
AND WHEN A STRONG ALTHOUGH A STRANGE SENSATION	480	2	DON JUAN	5	120	2
HOWEVER STRANGE HE COULD NOT YET FORGET HER	483	2	DON JUAN	5	124	3
WITH ITS STRANGE WHIRLS AND EDDIES CAN COMPARE--	7	3	DON JUAN	6	2	6
DESCRIBED--WHAT'S STRANGE--IN WORDS EXTREMELY FEW	34	3	DON JUAN	6	57	6
BUT WHAT IS STRANGE--AND A STRONG PROOF HOW GREAT	42	3	DON JUAN	6	73	1
A STRANGE COINCIDENCE TO USE A PHRASE	45	3	DON JUAN	6	78	7
AT WHICH DUDU LOOKED STRANGE AND JUAN SILLY	64	3	DON JUAN	6	118	7
ALTHOUGH HIS SITUATION NOW SEEMS STRANGE	65	3	DON JUAN	6	120	6
'TIS STRANGE THAT HE SHOULD FURTHER DAMN HIS EYES	88	3	DON JUAN	7	45	1
IT DIFFICULT TO SHUN SOME STRANGE MISTAKES	96	3	DON JUAN	7	57	8
AND STRANGE TO SAY THEY FOUND SOME CONSOLATION	105	3	DON JUAN	7	75	7
JUAN BY SOME STRANGE CHANCE WHICH OFT DIVIDES	125	3	DON JUAN	8	27	1
AND THESE HE CALLED ON AND WHAT'S STRANGE THEY CAME	132	3	DON JUAN	8	38	1
'TIS STRANGE ENOUGH--THE ROUGH TOUGH SOLDIERS WHO	171	3	DON JUAN	8	119	1
SHE FELL WITH BUONAPARTE--WHAT STRANGE THOUGHTS	198	3	DON JUAN	9	32	7
HIS PARTS OF SPEECH AND IN THE STRANGE DISPLAYS	207	3	DON JUAN	9	49	4
OF THE STRANGE THING SOME WOMEN SET A VALUE ON	208	3	DON JUAN	9	51	3
WHAT A STRANGE THING IS MAN AND WHAT A STRANGER	214	3	DON JUAN	9	64	1
'TWAS STRANGE ENOUGH SHE SHOULD RETAIN THE IMPRESSION	252	3	DON JUAN	10	56	1
SOME RUMOUR ALSO OF SOME STRANGE ADVENTURES	284	3	DON JUAN	11	33	1
'TIS STRANGE THE MIND THAT VERY FIERY PARTICLE	298	3	DON JUAN	11	60	7
'TIS STRANGE THE MIND SHOULD LET SUCH PHRASES QUELL IT'S	298	3	DON JUAN	11	60	V7
THERE'S LITTLE STRANGE IN THIS BUT SOMETHING STRANGE IS	309	3	DON JUAN	11	81	7
THERE'S LITTLE STRANGE IN THIS BUT SOMETHING STRANGE IS	309	3	DON JUAN	11	81	7
STRANGE TOO IN MY BUON CAMERADO SCOTT	323	3	DON JUAN	12	16	5
SEE NOUGHT MORE STRANGE IN THIS THAN T'OTHER LOTTERY	333	3	DON JUAN	12	37	8
PERHAPS A LITTLE STRANGE IF NOT QUITE NEW	341	3	DON JUAN	12	54	2
HIS FEELINGS HAD NOT THOSE STRANGE FITS LIKE TERTIANS	366	3	DON JUAN	13	17	5
THERE MOANS A STRANGE UNEARTHLY SOUND WHICH THEN	388	3	DON JUAN	13	63	3
STRANGE FACES LIKE TO MEN IN MASQUERADE	389	3	DON JUAN	13	65	3
THE PORTER SOME SLIGHT SCANDALS STRANGE AND QUAINT	418	3	DON JUAN	14	19	5
A FOX-HUNT TO A FOREIGNER IS STRANGE	424	3	DON JUAN	14	32	1
'TIS STRANGE--BUT TRUE FOR TRUTH IS ALWAYS STRANGE	455	3	DON JUAN	14	101	1
'TIS STRANGE--BUT TRUE FOR TRUTH IS ALWAYS STRANGE	455	3	DON JUAN	14	101	1
IN ITS OWN STRENGTH--MOST STRANGE IN ONE SO YOUNG	477	3	DON JUAN	15	47	8
AND WHAT IS STRANGEST UPON THIS STRANGE HEAD	504	3	DON JUAN	16	7	5
THE THEME HALF CREDITED THE STRANGE TRADITION	527	3	DON JUAN	16	54	4

STRANGELY

	PAGE	VOL		CANTO	STANZA	LN
STRANGELY ENOUGH AS YET WITHOUT MISCARRIAGE	471	3	DON JUAN	15	35	3

STRANGER

	PAGE	VOL		CANTO	STANZA	LN
FOR MY PART TO SUCH DOINGS I'M A STRANGER	65	2	DON JUAN	1	80	4
A STRANGER DYING WITH SO WHITE A SKIN	224	2	DON JUAN	2	129	8
HE WOULD HAVE HOSPITABLY CURED THE STRANGER	225	2	DON JUAN	2	130	7
AN ARAB WITH A STRANGER FOR A GUEST	261	2	DON JUAN	2	196	4
A PRETTY STRANGER WITHOUT FRIEND OR GUIDE	28	3	DON JUAN	6	45	5
THAT THE YOUNG STRANGER SHOULD NOT LIE ALONE	46	3	DON JUAN	6	81	4
THAT STRANGER TO MOST COUNCILS HERE PREVAILED	92	3	DON JUAN	7	51	3
THE STRANGER STRIPLING MAY REMAIN WITH ME	100	3	DON JUAN	7	66	6
AND WHAT WAS STRANGER NEVER LOOKED BEHIND	126	3	DON JUAN	8	30	2
AND WHAT'S STILL STRANGER LEFT BEHIND A NAME	144	3	DON JUAN	8	63	1
WHAT A STRANGE THING IS MAN AND WHAT A STRANGER	214	3	DON JUAN	9	64	1
NOBLE RICH CELEBRATED AND A STRANGER	305	3	DON JUAN	11	74	2
SOME PLEASANT JESTING AT THE AWKWARD STRANGER	424	3	DON JUAN	14	32	4
HER HUSBAND'S FRIEND HER OWN YOUNG AND A STRANGER	449	3	DON JUAN	14	91	8
STRANGER THAN FICTION IF IT COULD BE TOLD	455	3	DON JUAN	14	101	2

STRANGER'S

	PAGE	VOL		CANTO	STANZA	LN
NOT I HE SAID HAVE SOUGHT THIS STRANGER'S ILL	368	2	DON JUAN	4	46	4
IN CONTACT AND SOMETIMES EVEN A FAIR STRANGER'S	472	2	DON JUAN	5	106	7

STRANGERS

	PAGE	VOL		CANTO	STANZA	LN
WHICH WELCOMES HAPLESS STRANGERS IN ALL PLACES	28	3	DON JUAN	6	45	7
TO SOME DISTINGUISHED STRANGERS IN THAT FRAY	82	3	DON JUAN	7	32	6
WHAT EVEN YOUNG STRANGERS FEEL A LITTLE STRONG	257	3	DON JUAN	10	65	3
AND LAST NOT LEAST TO STRANGERS UNINSTRUCTED	259	3	DON JUAN	10	69	7

STRANGEST

	PAGE	VOL		CANTO	STANZA	LN
BUT WHAT WAS STRANGEST IN THIS VIRGIN CREW	24	3	DON JUAN	6	37	1
THE STRANGEST THING WAS BEAUTEOUS SHE WAS WHOLLY	33	3	DON JUAN	6	54	5
AND WHAT IS STRANGEST UPON THIS STRANGE HEAD	504	3	DON JUAN	16	7	5

STRANGLE

	PAGE	VOL		CANTO	STANZA	LN
AND STRIVES TO STRANGLE HIM BEFORE HE DIE	184	2	DON JUAN	2	52	8

STRAW

	PAGE	VOL		CANTO	STANZA	LN
FLING UP A STRAW 'TWILL SHOW THE WAY THE WIND BLOWS	414	3	DON JUAN	14	8	2
AND SUCH A STRAW BORNE ON BY HUMAN BREATH	414	3	DON JUAN	14	8	3

STRAY

	PAGE	VOL		CANTO	STANZA	LN
AND HAD IT NOT BEEN FOR SOME STRAY TROOPS LANDING	148	3	DON JUAN	8	72	1

STRAY'D

	PAGE	VOL		CANTO	STANZA	LN
ANON--SHE WAS RELEASED AND THEN SHE STRAY'D	361	2	DON JUAN	4	32	1

STRAYED

	PAGE	VOL		CANTO	STANZA	LN
BELOVED AND DEPLORED WHILE SLOWLY STRAYED	40	3	DON JUAN	6	67	6

STREAK

	PAGE	VOL		CANTO	STANZA	LN
ON THE SNOW-TOPS OF DISTANT HILLS THE STREAK	234	2	DON JUAN	2	147	3
A SLENDER STREAK OF BLOOD ANNOUNCED HOW NEAR	159	3	DON JUAN	8	95	2

STREAM

	PAGE	VOL		CANTO	STANZA	LN
A NOBLE STREAM AND CALL'D THE GUADALQUIVIR	25	2	DON JUAN	1	8	8
BUT IN HIS NATIVE STREAM THE GUADALQUIVIR	211	2	DON JUAN	2	105	1
A PLEASURE IN THE GENTLE STREAM THAT FLOW'D	304	2	DON JUAN	3	56	6

STREAM   (CONTINUED)
    OR AS THE STIRRING OF A DEEP CLEAR STREAM . . . . . . 360 2 DON JUAN 4   30   1
    TO BE SO BEING IN A GUSHING STREAM . . . . 380 2 DON JUAN 4   66   6
    SPRINKLED WITH PALACES THE OCEAN STREAM . . . . . . 412 2 DON JUAN 5   3   2
    THEN ONE VAST FIRE AIR EARTH AND STREAM EMBRACED . . . 115 3 DON JUAN 8   7   5
    HURLING DEFIANCE CITY STREAM AND SHORE . . . . . . 116 3 DON JUAN 8   8   4
    THEY KNEW NOT WHERE BEING CARRIED BY THE STREAM . . . 148 3 DON JUAN 8   72   2
    FAR FLASHED HER BURNING TOWERS O'ER DANUBE'S STREAM . 175 3 DON JUAN 8   127   3
    WHO VINDICATES A MOMENT TOO HIS STREAM-- . . . . . 279 3 DON JUAN 11   24   2
    AND WHAT I WRITE I CAST UPON THE STREAM . . . . . . 415 3 DON JUAN 14   11   7
    THE STREAM NOR LEAVE THE WORLD WHICH LEAVETH THEM . . 418 3 DON JUAN 14   18   8
    WHAT THOUGH ON LETHE'S STREAM HE SEEM TO FLOAT . . . 457 3 DON JUAN 15   4   5
    A BEAUTEOUS RIPPLE OF THE BRILLIANT STREAM . . . . . 480 3 DON JUAN 15   55   3
STREAM'D
    SUCK'D IN THE MOISTURE WHICH LIKE NECTAR STREAM'D . . . 202 2 DON JUAN 2   86   2
STREAMED
    THEY REACHED THE HOTEL FORTH STREAMED FROM THE FRONT DOOR . 282 3 DON JUAN 11   30   1
STREAMING
    HER STREAMING HAIR THE BLACK CURLS STRIVE BUT FAIL . . . 108 2 DON JUAN 1   158   5
    STREAMING FROM OFF THE SUN LIKE SERAPH'S WINGS . . . . 387 3 DON JUAN 13   62   4
STREAMS
    PANTING FOR POWER AS HARTS FOR COOLING STREAMS . . . . 155 2 DON JUAN 1   V 6   1
    SCOTCH PLAIDS SCOTCH SNOODS THE BLUE HILLS AND CLEAR STREAMS 233 3 DON JUAN 10   18   2
    BY FOUL CORRUPTION INTO STREAMS--EVEN THEY . . . . . 287 3 DON JUAN 11   40   7
    OF FASHION--SAY WHAT STREAMS NOW FILL THOSE CHANNELS . . 308 3 DON JUAN 11   80   6
    TRUTH'S FOUNTAINS MAY BE CLEAR--HER STREAMS ARE MUDDY . 495 3 DON JUAN 15   88   6
STREET
    DAY HAS NOT BROKE--THERE'S NO ONE IN THE STREET . . . 121 2 DON JUAN 1   182   8
    FORSOOTH SCARCE FIT FOR BALLADS IN THE STREET . . . . 392 2 DON JUAN 4   89   6
    STRETCHED IN THE STREET AND ABLE SCARCE TO PANT . . . 428 2 DON JUAN 5   33   8
    AND SMOOTHED THE BRIMSTONE OF THAT STREET OF HELL . . . 124 3 DON JUAN 8   26   7
    AND DEATH IS DRUNK WITH GORE THERE'S NOT A STREET . . . 152 3 DON JUAN 8   82   2
    THROUGH STREET AND SQUARE FAST FLASHING CHARIOTS HURLED . 302 3 DON JUAN 11   67   3
    THEREFORE I NAME NOT SQUARE STREET PLACE UNTIL I . . . 370 3 DON JUAN 13   27   5
STREETS
    SO THAT THE STREETS OF COLOURED LAMPS ARE FULL . . . . 88 3 DON JUAN 7   44   5
    OF BURNING STREETS LIKE MOONLIGHT ON THE WATER . . . . 172 3 DON JUAN 8   122   7
    WHILE MOSQUES AND STREETS BENEATH HIS EYES LIKE THATCH . 178 3 DON JUAN 8   133   3
    WHERE LONDON STREETS FERMENT IN FULL ACTIVITY . . . . 272 3 DON JUAN 11   8   4
    A ROW OF GENTLEMEN ALONG THE STREETS . . . . 281 3 DON JUAN 11   27   1
    BY BUTCHERS IN HER STREETS THAN FOR THE STAUNCHEST OR . 314 3 DON JUAN 11   V 75   5
    BY NAMING STREETS SINCE MEN ARE SO CENSORIOUS . . . . 369 3 DON JUAN 13   25   2
    FOR MAKING SQUARES AND STREETS ANONYMOUS . . . . . . 370 3 DON JUAN 13   26   2
STRENGTH
    SHE FOR THE FUTURE OF HER STRENGTH CONVINCED . . . . 66 2 DON JUAN 1   82   3
    SHE THOUGHT OF HER OWN STRENGTH AND JUAN'S YOUTH . . . 78 2 DON JUAN 1   107   1
    QUICK WITHOUT WIT AND VIOLENT WITHOUT STRENGTH . . . . 155 2 DON JUAN 1   V 6   7
    AND THOUGH AT FIRST THEIR STRENGTH IT MIGHT RENEW . . . 192 2 DON JUAN 2   68   3
    AND THREE DEAD WHOM THEIR STRENGTH COULD NOT AVAIL . . 209 2 DON JUAN 2   101   5
    AND HURLS AT ONCE HIS VENOM AND HIS STRENGTH . . . . 218 2 DON JUAN 2   117   8
    EACH KISS A HEART-QUAKE--FOR A KISS'S STRENGTH . . . . 254 2 DON JUAN 2   186   7
    THEIR SPEED ABATED OR THEIR STRENGTH GREW DULL . . . . 59 3 DON JUAN 6   107   6
    OF DANUBE--WITH SOME STRENGTH BUT LITTLE TASTE . . . . 71 3 DON JUAN 7   9   V3
    ON ITS OWN STRENGTH WITH CARELESS NERVES AND THEWS-- . 131 3 DON JUAN 8   36   6
    IF SO SHE WOULD HAVE HAD THE STRENGTH TO FLY . . . . 449 3 DON JUAN 14   91   3
    IN ITS OWN STRENGTH--MOST STRANGE IN ONE SO YOUNG . . . 477 3 DON JUAN 15   47   8
    BACK TO HIS CHAMBER SHORN OF HALF HIS STRENGTH . . . . 511 3 DON JUAN 16   25   8
    SUCH AS ENABLES MAN TO SHOW HIS STRENGTH . . . . . . 567 3 DON JUAN 17   12   3
STRENGTHENING
    STRENGTHENING THE WEAK AND TRAMPLING ON THE STRONG . . . 78 2 DON JUAN 1   106   4
STRESS
    THEIR STOCK WAS DAMAGED BY THE WEATHER'S STRESS . . . . 180 2 DON JUAN 2   46   6
    SOME STRESS ON CHARMS WHICH SELDOM ARE IF E'ER . . . . 485 2 DON JUAN 5   129   5
STRETCH
    WITH ALL ITS STARS AND WITH A STRETCH ATTAINING . . . . 450 2 DON JUAN 5   66   5
    MY BIDDING BABA VANISHED FOR TO STRETCH . . . . . . 63 3 DON JUAN 6   116   3
    OR MASS FOR SHOULD I STRETCH INTO DETAIL . . . . . . 483 3 DON JUAN 15   64   2
STRETCH'D
    HE FELL UPON HIS SIDE AND HIS STRETCH'D HAND . . . . 214 2 DON JUAN 2   110   4
    THAT THE HAND STRETCH'D AND SHUT IT WITHOUT HARM . . . 312 2 DON JUAN 3   71   3
STRETCHED
    STRETCHED IN THE STREET AND ABLE SCARCE TO PANT . . . 428 2 DON JUAN 5   33   8
STRETCHES
    THAT STRETCHES TO THE STONY BELT WHICH GIRDS . . . . 49 3 DON JUAN 6   86   7
STREW'D
    AND HANDSOME CORPSES STREW'D UPON THE SHORE . . . . . 229 2 DON JUAN 2   138   4
    SOME HANDS UNSEEN STREW'D FLOWERS UPON HIS TOMB . . . . 339 2 DON JUAN 3   109   5
STRICT
    WITH STRICT REGARD TO ARISTOTLE'S RULES . . . . . . 136 2 DON JUAN 1   201   2
    ENJOINING SILENCE STRICT TO ZOE WHO . . . . 228 2 DON JUAN 2   136   2
    THEY STOWED HIM WITH STRICT ORDERS TO THE WATCHES . . . 371 2 DON JUAN 4   50   8
    THUS IN THE EAST THEY ARE EXTREMELY STRICT . . . . . 502 2 DON JUAN 5   158   1
    WITH STRICT ENQUIRY I COULD N'ER DISCOVER . . . . . 41 3 DON JUAN 6   70   2
    AND NOW COMMENCED A STRICT INVESTIGATION . . . . . . 43 3 DON JUAN 6   74   1
    STRICT AND HIS MIND ASSUMED A MANLIER VIGOUR . . . . 460 3 DON JUAN 15   11   6
    HAS NOT THE NATURAL STAYS OF STRICT OLD AGE . . . . 494 3 DON JUAN 15   85   6
    WHO ARE SO IN THE STRICT SENSE OF THE PHRASE . . . . 562 3 DON JUAN 17   1   2
STRICTER
    THE STRICTER DOUBTLESS GROW THE VESTAL DUTIES . . . . . 35 3 DON JUAN 6   58   7

```
                                                         PAGE VOL      CANTO  STANZA  LN
STRICTER  (CONTINUED)
    NOW WHETHER IT BE THUS OR THAT THEY ARE STRICTER . . . .  337  3 DON JUAN 12     46    1
    BUT TO RETURN UNTO THE STRICTER RULE--  . . . . . .      563  3 DON JUAN 17      3    1
STRICTEST
    BY ALL THE LAWS THE STRICTEST LAWYER PLEADS . . . . .    352  3 DON JUAN 12     80    6
    THE STRICTEST IN CHRONOLOGY AND VIRTUE  . . . . . . .    433  3 DON JUAN 14     53    3
STRICTLY
    WAS THAT HIS BREEDING SHOULD BE STRICTLY MORAL . . . .    43  2 DON JUAN  1     39    4
    THAN TRUE HATH BEEN A CREED SO STRICTLY HELD) . . . .    420  3 DON JUAN 14     23    3
    OBSERVED AS STRICTLY BOTH AT BOARD AND BED . . . . .     470  3 DON JUAN 15     32    6
STRICTURES
    ON WHICH I CANNOT PAUSE TO MAKE MY STRICTURES . . . .    465  2 DON JUAN  5     94    8
    AND MADE UPON THE HOT-HOUSE SEVERAL STRICTURES . . . .   406  3 DON JUAN 13    102    4
STRIDE
    THAT SOMEWHAT MANLY MAJESTY OF STRIDE . . . . . . .      464  2 DON JUAN  5     91    4
STRIFE
    AND GAVE NO OUTWARD SIGNS OF INWARD STRIFE . . . . .      35  2 DON JUAN  1     26    6
    TO STRIFE 'TIS SOMETIMES SWEET TO HAVE OUR QUARRELS . .   90  2 DON JUAN  1    126    5
    AT QUITTING EVEN THOSE WE QUIT IN STRIFE . . . . .      164  2 DON JUAN  2     15    6
    FOR DEATH THOUGH VANQUISH'D STILL RETIRED WITH STRIFE .  214  2 DON JUAN  2    111    8
    NO DOUBT WHATE'ER MIGHT BE THEIR FORMER STRIFE . . . .   301  2 DON JUAN  3     50    5
    I CAN'T HELP THINKING THAT ALL FORMER STRIFE . . . .    301  2 DON JUAN  3     50   V5
    LAST CARNIVAL SHE MADE A DEAL OF STRIFE . . . . . .     389  2 DON JUAN  4     83    6
    SAD STRIFE AROSE FOR THEY WERE SO CROSS-GRAIN'D . . .   394  2 DON JUAN  4     93    5
    TO STRIVE TOO WITH OUR FATE WERE SUCH A STRIFE . . .    419  2 DON JUAN  5     17    5
    THEIR SPLEEN IN MAKING STRIFE AND SAFELY WORDING . . .  498  2 DON JUAN  5    151    6
    THE MORTAL AND THE MARBLE STILL AT STRIFE . . . . .      27  3 DON JUAN  6     43    7
    THERE WAS A WAY TO END THEIR STRIFE ALTHOUGH . . . .     53  3 DON JUAN  6     95    4
    MUST I RESTRAIN ME THROUGH THE FEAR OF STRIFE . . . .    69  3 DON JUAN  7      6    7
    FLOWED FROM THEIR BLOOD-SHOT EYES ALL RED WITH STRIFE .  171  3 DON JUAN  8    119    7
    BY THOSE WHO SCOUR THOSE DOUBLE VALES OF STRIFE . . .   232  3 DON JUAN 10     14    4
    BUT COULD HE QUIT HIS KING IN TIMES OF STRIFE . . .     536  3 DON JUAN 16     74    3
STRIKE
    I CAN'T DESCRIBE IT THOUGH SO MUCH IT STRIKE . . . .    159  2 DON JUAN  2      5    7
    JUST AS HIS FEEBLE ARMS COULD STRIKE NO MORE . . . .    212  2 DON JUAN  2    107    3
    HAD NOT SO MANY ORNAMENTS TO STRIKE . . . . . . .       221  2 DON JUAN  2    122    3
    IN VAIN--IN VAIN STRIKE OTHER CHORDS . . . . . . .      324  2 DON JUAN  3  L  9    1
    ARE THINGS WHICH IN THIS CENTURY DON'T STRIKE . . . .   330  2 DON JUAN  3     95    5
    WHAT THOUGH 'TIS BUT A PICTURED IMAGE STRIKE-- . . .    336  2 DON JUAN  3    103    7
    A PRETTY PERSON WHICH PERHAPS MAY STRIKE . . . . . .    390  2 DON JUAN  4     85    3
    IF WE SHOULD STRIKE A STROKE TO SET US FREE . . . .     434  2 DON JUAN  5     43    6
    WILL IT SAID JUAN SHARPLY STRIKE ME DEAD . . . . . .    452  2 DON JUAN  5     71    7
    OF FORMS AND FEATURES IT WOULD STRIKE YOU BLIND . . .   467  2 DON JUAN  5     97    6
    FULL OF EXPRESSION RIGHT OR WRONG THAT STRIKE . . . .    32  3 DON JUAN  6     52    7
    YE GLORIOUS GOTHIC SCENES HOW MUCH YE STRIKE . . . .    255  3 DON JUAN 10     61    3
    BY THIS TIME--BUT STRIKE SIX FROM SEVEN-AND-TWENTY . .  433  3 DON JUAN 14     54    7
    'TIS TIME TO STRIKE SUCH PUNY DOUBTERS DUMB AS . . .    502  3 DON JUAN 16      4    7
STRIKES
    IN FEMALE DATES STRIKES TIME ALL OF A HEAP . . . . .    433  3 DON JUAN 14     52    8
STRIKING
    WET STILL MORE DISAGREEABLE AND STRIKING . . . . . .    479  2 DON JUAN  5    118    4
STRING
    BUT PHOEBUS LENDS ME NOW AND THEN A STRING . . . . .    181  3 DON JUAN  8    138    8
    OF THAT ODD STRING OF WORDS ALL IN A ROW . . . . . .    207  3 DON JUAN  9     49    5
    PRELUDIOS TRYING JUST A STRING OR TWO . . . . . . .     341  3 DON JUAN 12     54    6
    ON BIRTH-DAYS GLORIOUS WITH A STAR AND STRING . . . .   440  3 DON JUAN 14     70    6
    OR THAT SHE HAD NOT HARP'D UPON THE TRUE STRING . . .   474  3 DON JUAN 15     42    5
STRINGS
    AND NOW AND THEN WITH TOUGH STRINGS OF THE BOW . . . .  463  2 DON JUAN  5     89    5
    SAVE THAT THE PUPPETS PULL AT THEIR OWN STRINGS . . .   400  3 DON JUAN 13     89    3
    AND WAS NOT TO BE HELD IN LEADING STRINGS . . . . .     439  3 DON JUAN 14     66    6
    BOWS HAVE THEY GENERALLY WITH TWO STRINGS . . . . .     501  3 DON JUAN 16      1    5
    SHE SEIZED HER HARP WHOSE STRINGS WERE KINDLED SOON . . 517  3 DON JUAN 16     38    6
    THE GORDIAN OR THE GEORDI-AN KNOT WHOSE STRINGS . . .   536  3 DON JUAN 16     74    7
    THE THREE STRINGS OF OUR HAPPY CONSTITUTION . . . . .   536  3 DON JUAN 16     74   V8
    MY TREMBLING LYRE ALREADY SEVERAL STRINGS . . . . .     568  3 DON JUAN 17     13    5
STRIP
    STRIP YOUR GREEN FIELDS AND TO YOUR HARVESTS CLING . .  175  3 DON JUAN  8    126    6
    TO STRIP THE SAXONS OF THEIR HYDES LIKE TANNERS . . .   242  3 DON JUAN 10     36    6
STRIPED
    AND THE STRIPED WHITE GAUZE BARACAN THAT BOUND HER . .  311  2 DON JUAN  3     70    7
STRIPLING
    AND SURELY WITH A STRIPLING OF SIXTEEN . . . . . .       66  2 DON JUAN  1     83    2
    THE STRANGER STRIPLING MAY REMAIN WITH ME . . . . .     100  3 DON JUAN  7     66    6
    ENOUGH TO MAKE A STRIPLING VERY VAIN . . . . . . .      218  3 DON JUAN  9     72    8
    WHO SEEING A HANDSOME STRIPLING WITH SMOOTH FACE . . .  285  3 DON JUAN 11     35    5
STRIPP'D
    FOR HAIDEE STRIPP'D HER SABLES OFF TO MAKE . . . . .    226  2 DON JUAN  2    133    2
STRIPPED
    AND STRIPPED AND LOOKED TO--BUT WHY SHOULD I ADD . . .  429  2 DON JUAN  5     34    5
    AND THEN HIS TATTERED JACKET OFF HE STRIPPED . . . .    456  2 DON JUAN  5     77   V3
STRIPS
    BUT TIME STRIPS OUR ILLUSIONS OF THEIR HUE . . . . .    421  2 DON JUAN  5     21    6
    HE STRIPS FROM MAN THAT MANTLE (FAR MORE DEAR . . . .   188  3 DON JUAN  9     12    6
STRIPT
    STRIPT TO HIS SHIRT WAS COME TO LEAD THE VAN . . . .     90  3 DON JUAN  7     49    8
    STRIPT TO HIS WAISTCOAT AND THAT NOT TOO CLEAN . . . .  104  3 DON JUAN  7     73    7
    WHEN THE STRIPT FOREST BOWS TO THE BLEAK AIR . . . .    155  3 DON JUAN  8     88    4
    KNOW NOT SINCE KNOWLEDGE SAW HER BRANCHES STRIPT . . .  210  3 DON JUAN  9     55    6
```

785

STRIVE
   HER STREAMING HAIR THE BLACK CURLS STRIVE BUT FAIL . . . . 108 2 DON JUAN 1   158 5
   TO STRIVE TOO WITH OUR FATE WERE SUCH A STRIFE . . . . . 419 2 DON JUAN 5   17 5
   AND THAT WHICH FURTHER AIDED THEM TO STRIVE . . . . . . 136 3 DON JUAN 8   47 6
   A MADDENING SPIRIT WHICH WOULD STRIVE TO BLEND . . . . . 219 3 DON JUAN 9   73 4
STRIVES
   AND STRIVES TO STRANGLE HIM BEFORE HE DIE . . . . . . 184 2 DON JUAN 2   52 8
STROKE
   IF WE SHOULD STRIKE A STROKE TO SET US FREE . . . . . 434 2 DON JUAN 5   43 6
   ONE NECK WHICH HE WITH ONE FELL STROKE MIGHT PIERCE . . . 19 3 DON JUAN 6   27 3
STROKES
   AGAINST PROPORTION--THE WILD STROKES OF NATURE . . . . . 32 3 DON JUAN 6   52 5
STROKING
   THAT I UNSEXED MY DRESS BUT BABA STROKING . . . . . 454 2 DON JUAN 5   75 6
   HIS STERN PHILOSOPHY BUT GENTLY STROKING . . . . . . 172 3 DON JUAN 8   121 6
STROKONOFF
   OUR EUPHONY--THERE WAS STRONGENOFF AND STROKONOFF . . . . 74 3 DON JUAN 7   15 2
STRONG
   LUCRETIUS' IRRELIGION IS TOO STRONG . . . . 45 2 DON JUAN 1   43 1
   STRENGTHENING THE WEAK AND TRAMPLING ON THE STRONG . . . 78 2 DON JUAN 1   106 4
   BUT THE SEA ACTED AS A STRONG EMETIC . . . . . . 167 2 DON JUAN 2   21 8
   OF SOME STRONG SWIMMER IN HIS AGONY . . . . . . 184 2 DON JUAN 2   53 8
   THAN WHAT IT HAD BEEN FOR SO STRONG IT BLEW . . . . . 185 2 DON JUAN 2   54 4
   STRONG PALPITATION RISES 'TIS HER BOON . . . . . 267 2 DON JUAN 2   208 6
   THESE TO SECURE IN THIS STRONG BLOWING WEATHER . . . . 285 2 DON JUAN 3   18 7
   OR THAT OF ANY OTHER STRONG EMOTION . . . . . . 289 2 DON JUAN 3   26 6
   QUICK TO PERCEIVE AND STRONG TO BEAR AND MEANT . . . . 302 2 DON JUAN 3   53 5
   AND SEND HIM FORTH LIKE SAMSON--STRONG IN BLINDNESS . . . 304 2 DON JUAN 3   57 V8
   OF A STRONG HUMAN HEART AND IN A SIRE . . . . . . 305 2 DON JUAN 3   58 8
   OF ANCIENT DAYS ERE TYRANNY GREW STRONG . . . . . 379 2 DON JUAN 4   65 8
   BUT STRONG AND LASTING TILL NO TONGUE CAN TELL . . . . 444 2 DON JUAN 5   59 4
   THEIR DUTY WAS--FOR THEY WERE STRONG AND THOUGH . . . . 463 2 DON JUAN 5   89 1
   THEY LOOKED SO LITTLE DID STRONG THINGS AT TIMES-- . . . 463 2 DON JUAN 5   89 2
   AND WHEN A STRONG ALTHOUGH A STRANGE SENSATION . . . . 480 2 DON JUAN 5   120 2
   AND THIS STRONG SECOND CAUSE (TO TIRE NO LONGER . . . . 488 2 DON JUAN 5   133 V7
   HER REASON BEING WEAK HER PASSIONS STRONG . . . . . 10 3 DON JUAN 6   8 5
   BUT WHAT IS STRANGE--AND A STRONG PROOF HOW GREAT . . . 42 3 DON JUAN 6   73 1
   IS TWICE AS STRONG AS THAT WHERE YOU WERE WOUNDED . . . 98 3 DON JUAN 7   61 8
   AND TALL AND STRONG AND SWIFT OF FOOT WERE THEY . . . 145 3 DON JUAN 8   66 1
   AND 'GAINST THE BODY MAKES A STRONG APPEAL . . . . 234 3 DON JUAN 10   20 5
   FEW YOUTHFUL MINDS CAN STAND THE STRONG CONCUSSION . . . 235 3 DON JUAN 10   21 3
   WHAT EVEN YOUNG STRANGERS FEEL A LITTLE STRONG . . . . 257 3 DON JUAN 10   65 3
   OPPOSING SINGLY THE UNITED STRONG . . . . . . 363 3 DON JUAN 13   10 3
   THE CLARET LIGHT AND THE MADEIRA STRONG . . . . 394 3 DON JUAN 13   76 6
   WITH THIS DEBUT WHICH MADE A STRONG IMPRESSION . . . . 400 3 DON JUAN 13   90 6
   WITHOUT STRONG REASON OF THOSE SORTS OF THINGS . . . . 439 3 DON JUAN 14   66 4
   OR IF THE OATH SEEM STRONG--I SWEAR BY JOVE . . . . 452 3 DON JUAN 14   96 V2
   APART FROM THE SURROUNDING WORLD AND STRONG . . . . 477 3 DON JUAN 15   47 7
   AN EDIFICE NO LESS SUBLIME THAN STRONG . . . . . 529 3 DON JUAN 16   59 5
   A STRONG EXTERNAL MOTIVE AND IN THIS . . . . . 544 3 DON JUAN 16   92 5
STRONGBOW
   LONGBOW FROM IRELAND STRONGBOW FROM THE TWEED . . . . 401 3 DON JUAN 13   92 2
   STRONGBOW WAS LIKE A NEW-TUNED HARPSICHORD . . . . 402 3 DON JUAN 13   93 1
STRONGBOW'S
   BUT STRONGBOW'S WIT WAS OF MORE POLISH'D BREED . . . . 401 3 DON JUAN 13   92 4
   WHILE STRONGBOW'S BEST THINGS MIGHT HAVE COME FROM CATO . 401 3 DON JUAN 13   92 8
   OF STRONGBOW'S TALK YOU WOULD NOT CHANGE A WORD . . . 402 3 DON JUAN 13   93 5
STRONGENOFF
   OUR EUPHONY--THERE WAS STRONGENOFF AND STROKONOFF . . . 74 3 DON JUAN 7   15 2
STRONGER
   THE STRONGER PUMP'D THE WEAKER THRUMM'D A SAIL . . . . 176 2 DON JUAN 2   38 8
   YOUR PATIENCE) SHOWS THE CAUSE MUST STILL BE STRONGER . 488 2 DON JUAN 5   133 8
   THE PEOPLE BY-AND-BY WILL BE THE STRONGER . . . . 137 3 DON JUAN 8   50 4
   AND THIS IS STRONGER THAN THE STRONGEST GRAPE . . . 375 3 DON JUAN 13   37 7
   IMPRESSIONS WERE MUCH STRONGER THAN SHE GUESS'D . . . 448 3 DON JUAN 14   88 5
   'GAINST SUCH BELIEF THERE'S SOMETHING STRONGER STILL . . 504 3 DON JUAN 16   7 7
   CONNECTIONS STRONGER THAN HE CHOSE TO AVOW . . . . 516 3 DON JUAN 16   37 4
STRONGEST
   AND THIS IS STRONGER THAN THE STRONGEST GRAPE . . . . 375 3 DON JUAN 13   37 7
STRONGLY
   MOST STRONGLY RECOMMENDED AN ASSAULT . . . . . 83 3 DON JUAN 7   35 4
   HAVE SEEN AND FELT HOW STRONGLY YOU RESTORE . . . . 184 3 DON JUAN 9   3 6
   AS YET ARE STRONGLY STINGING TO BE FREE . . . . 196 3 DON JUAN 9   28 8
   WHO ARE STRONGLY ACTED ON BY WHAT IS NEAREST . . . 547 3 DON JUAN 16   97 8
STRONGSTROGANOFF
   THE COUNT STRONGSTROGANOFF I PUT IN PAIN . . . . 102 2 DON JUAN 1   149 6
STROVE
   SHE BLUSH'D AND FROWN'D NOT BUT SHE STROVE TO SPEAK . . 81 2 DON JUAN 1   112 7
   A LITTLE STILL SHE STROVE AND MUCH REPENTED . . . . 84 2 DON JUAN 1   117 7
   FOR YET THEY STROVE ALTHOUGH OF NO GREAT USE . . . 183 2 DON JUAN 2   51 4
   HE BUOY'D HIS BOYISH LIMBS AND STROVE TO PLY . . . 212 2 DON JUAN 2   106 2
   PASS'D BUT HE STROVE QUITE COURTEOUSLY TO QUELL . . 298 2 DON JUAN 3   44 4
STRUCK
   WHICH STRUCK HER AFT AND MADE AN AWKWARD RIFT . . . 170 2 DON JUAN 2   27 3
   A SAILOR WHEN THE PRIZE HAS STRUCK IN FIGHT . . . . 261 2 DON JUAN 2   196 5
   BUT MOST AN ALDERMAN STRUCK APOPLECTIC . . . . 309 2 DON JUAN 3   66 5
   STRUCK NOT ON MEMORY THOUGH A HEAVY ACHE . . . . 378 2 DON JUAN 4   62 5
   AND SUNG OF LOVE THE FIERCE NAME STRUCK THROUGH ALL . . 380 2 DON JUAN 4   66 3
   STRUCK FOR AN INSTANT ON THE HEARTS OF MEN . . . . 111 3 DON JUAN 7   87 3

STRUCK   (CONTINUED)
    STRUCK AT HIS FRIENDS AS BABIES BEAT THEIR NURSES 165   3 DON JUAN   8   108   8
    BUT IN THE WAR WHICH STRUCK CHARLES FROM HIS THRONE . . . 386   3 DON JUAN 13   60   4
    'TIS TRUE YOU DON'T--BUT PALE AND STRUCK WITH TERROR . . . 413   3 DON JUAN 14   6   1
    THOU HAST STRUCK ONE IMMENSE COLOSSUS DOWN 445   3 DON JUAN 14   82   3
STRUCTURE
    AND ASKED WHY SUCH A STRUCTURE HAD BEEN RAISED 261   3 DON JUAN 10   74   8
STRUGGLE
    I STRUGGLE BUT CAN NOT COLLECT MY MIND   133   2 DON JUAN   1   196   V2
    BUT STILL 'TIS BEST TO STRUGGLE TO THE LAST 176   2 DON JUAN   2   39   5
    ALL BASHFULLY TO STRUGGLE INTO LIGHT   39   3 DON JUAN   6   66   8
    THE STRUGGLE TO BE PILOTS IN A STORM 360   3 DON JUAN 13   6   3
    AND THEIRS--WITHOUT A STRUGGLE FOR PRIORITY 462   3 DON JUAN 15   15   7
STRUGGLED
    WHICH STRUGGLED THROUGH AND CHASTEN'D DOWN THE WHOLE . . 54   2 DON JUAN   1   60   8
    IN VAIN SHE STRUGGLED IN HER FATHER'S GRASP-- 370   2 DON JUAN   4   48   4
    AND THE MOSQUE CRESCENT STRUGGLED INTO SIGHT   49   3 DON JUAN   6   86   4
STRUGGLES
    HER STRUGGLES CEASED WITH ONE CONVULSIVE GROAN 375   2 DON JUAN   4   58   6
STRUGGLING
    THAT STILL COULD KEEP AFLOAT THE STRUGGLING TARS 183   2 DON JUAN   2   51   3
STRUIS
    AND ET SEPULCHRI IMMEMOR STRUIS DOMOS 448   2 DON JUAN   5   63   7
STRUMPET
    WHERE HYMEN'S TORCH BUT BRANDS ONE STRUMPET MORE 353   2 DON JUAN   4   17   7
    WHERE HYMEN'S SHRINE BUT STAMPS ONE STRUMPET MORE 353   2 DON JUAN   4   17   V7
    INTO GAZETTES BUT FAME (CAPRICIOUS STRUMPET)   74   3 DON JUAN   7   15   7
STRUNG
    WERE STRUNG TOGETHER LIKE A ROW OF PEARLS   291   2 DON JUAN   3   30   3
STRUT
    ALL STRUT AND STAYS AND WHISKERS TO DEMAND 343   3 DON JUAN 12   60   4
STRUTTED
    AND SEVERAL STRUTTED OTHERS SLEPT AND SOME   441   2 DON JUAN   5   53   7
STUBBLE
    OF THE POOR PARTRIDGE THROUGH HIS STUBBLE SCREEN 539   3 DON JUAN 16   80   5
STUBBORN
    HIS STUBBORN VALOUR WAS NO FUTURE SHIELD 172   3 DON JUAN   8   122   3
    WORN OUT WITH BATTERING ISMAIL'S STUBBORN WALL 181   3 DON JUAN   8   139   6
    OF STUBBORN SHELL WHICH WAVES AND WEATHER WEAR NOT . . . 431   3 DON JUAN 14   49   4
STUCK
    WHEN SOME UNTOWARD PART OF RAIMENT STUCK HARD   456   2 DON JUAN   5   78   6
    SO THAT A PONIARD PIERCES IF 'TIS STUCK HARD 492   2 DON JUAN   5   140   4
    STUCK ALL EXACTLY IN THE PROPER SPOT 37   3 DON JUAN   6   62   8
    YOU KNOW THE REST THE WORDS STUCK IN HER THROAT   62   3 DON JUAN   6   113   4
    FOR THE TURK'S TEETH STUCK FASTER THAN A SKEWER   . . . 154   3 DON JUAN   8   85   3
    WITH SUCH A CHART AS MAY BE SAFELY STUCK TO-- 348   3 DON JUAN 12   70   5
STUDDED
    HERE AND THERE STUDDED WITH A SEVENTY-FOUR 412   2 DON JUAN   5   3   3
STUDIED
    HE STUDIED STEADILY AND GREW APACE 48   2 DON JUAN   1   49   5
    AWAIT THOSE WHO HAVE STUDIED THEIR BON MOTS 403   3 DON JUAN 13   97   8
    LADIES WHO HAVE STUDIED FRIENDSHIP BUT IN FRANCE 450   3 DON JUAN 14   92   4
    WHETHER THEY RODE OR WALK'D OR STUDIED SPANISH 453   3 DON JUAN 14   98   1
    NOTHING AFFECTED STUDIED OR CONSTRUCTIVE 461   3 DON JUAN 15   12   3
STUDIES
    MUCH INTO ALL HIS STUDIES SHE INQUIRED   43   2 DON JUAN   1   39   5
    HIS CLASSIC STUDIES MADE A LITTLE PUZZLE 44   2 DON JUAN   1   41   1
    HE DID NOT TAKE SUCH STUDIES FOR RESTRAINTS 47   2 DON JUAN   1   47   4
    AS HE WHO STUDIES FERVENTLY THE SKIES 242   2 DON JUAN   2   163   5
STUDY
    I STUDY ALSO BLAIR THE HIGHEST REACHERS 243   2 DON JUAN   2   165   6
    AND IT MIGHT BE FROM THOUGHT OR TOIL OR STUDY 416   2 DON JUAN   5   11   4
    A NEAT SNUG STUDY ON A WINTER'S NIGHT 444   2 DON JUAN   5   58   1
    THE LAWYERS IN THE STUDY AND IN AIR 533   3 DON JUAN 16   66   3
STUFF
    (THAT MODERN PHRASE APPEARS TO ME SAD STUFF 119   2 DON JUAN   1   178   3
    OR ALL THE STUFF WHICH UTTERED BY THE BLUES IS 493   2 DON JUAN   5   143   V5
    FROM SPAIN--BUT WHERE IS SPAIN--DON'T ASK SUCH STUFF . . . 28   3 DON JUAN   6   44   4
    OF GLORY AND ALL THAT IMMORTAL STUFF 134   3 DON JUAN   8   42   4
    AND SET UP IN THEIR STEAD SOME PROPER STUFF 195   3 DON JUAN   9   25   4
    AND STUFF WITH SAGE THAT VERY VERDANT GOOSE 497   3 DON JUAN 15   93   6
STUFF'D
    HE ALSO STUFF'D HIS MONEY WHERE HE COULD 187   2 DON JUAN   2   59   1
STUFFS
    AND OTHER STUFFS WITH WHICH I WON'T STAY PUZZLING 27   2 DON JUAN   1   12   8
    FRENCH STUFFS LACE TWEEZERS TOOTHPICKS TEAPOT TRAY   . . 284   2 DON JUAN   3   17   5
    FRENCH STUFFS LACE TWEEZERS TOOTHPICKS A BIDET 284   2 DON JUAN   3   17   V5
STUMBLE
    SUCH I MIGHT STUMBLE OVER UNAWARES 370   3 DON JUAN 13   26   7
STUMBLED
    WHEN LO HE STUMBLED O'ER A PAIR OF SHOES 120   2 DON JUAN   1   180   8
    DREAM'D OF A THOUSAND WRECKS O'ER WHICH SHE STUMBLED . . 229   2 DON JUAN   2   138   3
    AND STUMBLED ALMOST EVERY STEP SHE MADE   361   2 DON JUAN   4   32   3
    INSTEAD OF HEAVEN THEY STUMBLED BACKWARDS O'ER 121   3 DON JUAN   8   20   7
    HE STUMBLED ON TO TRY IF HE COULD FIND   126   3 DON JUAN   8   30   6
STUMBLING
    PERHAPS YOU THINK IN STUMBLING ON THIS FEAST   296   2 DON JUAN   3   40   1
    AND WHEN SHE SAW HIM STUMBLING LIKE A STEED 56   3 DON JUAN   6   101   4
    BUT SOMETIMES STUMBLING OVER A POTATOE-- 401   3 DON JUAN 13   92   7

		PAGE	VOL		CANTO	STANZA	LN

STUN
WHILE THE MERE VICTOR'S MAY APPAL OR STUN . . . . . . 114 3 DON JUAN 8 5 6

STUNG
AND MIXED UNTIL THE VERY PLEASURE STUNG . . . . . . 254 2 DON JUAN 2 187 V8
HAD STUNG HIM FROM A SLAVE TO AN ENSLAVER . . . . . 302 2 DON JUAN 3 53 8
LOVE WITH YOU AND BEEN IN THE DOG-DAYS STUNG . . . . 486 2 DON JUAN 5 130 4
A BEE FLEW OUT AND STUNG HER TO THE HEART . . . . . 44 3 DON JUAN 6 77 7

STUPID
(BUT THIS LAST SIMILE IS TRITE AND STUPID) . . . . . 51 2 DON JUAN 1 55 8
AND OTHERS LOOKING WITH A STUPID STARE . . . . . . 208 2 DON JUAN 2 98 2
THAN SOME WIVES (WHO MAKE BLUNDERS NO LESS STUPID) . . 205 3 DON JUAN 9 45 7
HE WAS YOUR MASTER OF YOUR STUPID COLLEGE . . . . . 264 3 DON JUAN 10 80 V2
OF MODERN REIGNING STERLING STUPID STAMP-- . . . . . 321 3 DON JUAN 12 12 7

STUPIDER
(NO MATTER WHICH) TURN POLITICIAN STUPIDER . . . . . 309 3 DON JUAN 11 83 3

STUPIDITY
WHETHER IT WAS THEIR ENGINEER'S STUPIDITY . . . . . 80 3 DON JUAN 7 27 1

STY
WHOM HE FORSOOK TO FILL THE LAUREATE'S STY . . . . . 231 3 DON JUAN 10 13 4

STYGIAN
HAD DOUBTLESS HEARD ABOUT THE STYGIAN RIVER . . . . 258 2 DON JUAN 2 193 6

STYLE
AFTER THE STYLE OF VIRGIL AND OF HOMER . . . . . 135 2 DON JUAN 1 200 7
DEPENDING MORE UPON THE HISTORIAN'S STYLE . . . . . 328 2 DON JUAN 3 90 3
BABA RETIRE WHICH HE OBEYED IN STYLE . . . . . . 473 2 DON JUAN 5 107 2
BUT WHAT WAS NOT A SORT OF STYLE THAT'S GROWN . . . . 33 3 DON JUAN 6 55 6
SAVE FOR ITS STYLE WHICH SAID ALL IN A TRICE . . . . 86 3 DON JUAN 7 40 7
BUT IN A STYLE BECOMING HIS CONDITION . . . . . . 246 3 DON JUAN 10 44 8
OTHERS IN THAT OFF-HAND AND DASHING STYLE . . . . . 351 3 DON JUAN 12 76 2
AND THAT THEIR BOOKS HAVE BUT ONE STYLE IN COMMON-- . . 418 3 DON JUAN 14 19 7

STYLED
QUITE INNOCENTLY DONE AND HARMLESS STYLED . . . . . 59 2 DON JUAN 1 69 3
SO STYLED ACCORDING TO THE USUAL FORMS . . . . . 12 3 DON JUAN 6 13 2
THE NEXT ARE ONLY CHILDREN AS THEY ARE STYLED . . . . 563 3 DON JUAN 17 2 1

STYX
THETIS BAPTIZED HER MORTAL SON IN STYX . . . . . 346 2 DON JUAN 4 4 7
WHICH MAKES ALL STYX THROUGH ONE SMALL LIVER FLOW . . 190 3 DON JUAN 9 15 5
TO PASS THE STYX FOR MORE SUBSTANTIAL FEASTS . . . . 404 3 DON JUAN 13 99 4

SUAVITY
BECAUSE THOUGH YOUNG HE ACQUIESCED WITH SUAVITY . . . 368 3 DON JUAN 13 22 3

SUBDUED
AND THEN GIVE WAY SUBDUED BECAUSE SURROUNDED . . . . 373 2 DON JUAN 4 54 6
HIS WINGS SUBDUED TO EPAULETTES HIS QUIVER . . . . . 205 3 DON JUAN 9 45 2

SUBJECT
WITH THINGS NOT VERY SUBJECT TO CONTROL . . . . . 70 2 DON JUAN 1 91 6
FROM THIS MY SUBJECT HAS NO BUSINESS HERE . . . . . 238 2 DON JUAN 2 156 4
BUT TO MY SUBJECT--LET ME SEE--WHAT WAS IT-- . . . . 317 2 DON JUAN 3 81 5
I CHOSE A MODERN SUBJECT AS MORE MEET . . . . . 347 2 DON JUAN 4 6 8
AND SUBJECT WHEN THE HOUSE IS THIN TO COLD . . . . . 389 2 DON JUAN 4 83 3
ON SUCH A SUBJECT THEN SUPPOSE THE FACE . . . . . 486 2 DON JUAN 5 130 7
BUT TO OUR SUBJECT A BRAVE TARTAR KHAN-- . . . . . 163 3 DON JUAN 8 104 5
A SUBJECT OF SUBLIMEST EXULTATION-- . . . . . . 175 3 DON JUAN 8 126 3
THIS SUBJECT QUOTE AS IT WOULD BE SCHISMATIC . . . . 289 3 DON JUAN 11 43 5
FOR BEING AS MUCH THE SUBJECT OF ATTACK . . . . . 312 3 DON JUAN 11 90 4
'TIS ALSO SUBJECT TO THE DOUBLE DANGER . . . . . 424 3 DON JUAN 14 32 2
SHE THOUGHT UPON THE SUBJECT TWICE OR THRICE . . . . 469 3 DON JUAN 15 29 5
IN SHORT UPON THAT SUBJECT I'VE SOME QUALMS VERY . . . 499 3 DON JUAN 15 96 7
TO BEAR ON WHAT APPEARED TO HER THE SUBJECT . . . . 526 3 DON JUAN 16 51 3

SUBJECTS
DEAD SCANDALS FORM GOOD SUBJECTS FOR DISSECTION . . . 37 2 DON JUAN 1 31 8
ALL ARTS TO TEACH THEIR SUBJECTS TO DESTROY . . . . 157 3 DON JUAN 8 92 8
NOR SOUGHT OF FOOLSCAP SUBJECTS TO BE KING-- . . . . 296 3 DON JUAN 11 55 6
HIS SUBJECTS BY HIS GRACIOUS ACCEPTATION) . . . . . 528 3 DON JUAN 16 56 7

SUBLIME
AND MAKES THE WORD MILTONIC MEAN SUBLIME . . . . . 15 2 DON JUAN D 10 4
WHERE THE SUBLIME SOARS FORTH ON WINGS MORE AMPLE . . 45 2 DON JUAN 1 42 6
LONGINGS SUBLIME AND ASPIRATIONS HIGH . . . . . 71 2 DON JUAN 1 93 2
'TIS PITY THOUGH IN THIS SUBLIME WORLD THAT . . . . . 93 2 DON JUAN 1 133 3
WITH THAT SUBLIME OF RASCALS YOUR ATTORNEY . . . . . 103 2 DON JUAN 1 151 3
THE VADE MECUM OF THE TRUE SUBLIME . . . . . . 136 2 DON JUAN 1 201 3
THE ONLY HIGH SOUND PRECEPTS OF THE TRUE SUBLIME . . . 136 2 DON JUAN 1 201 V3
A LOVE OF MUSIC AND OF SCENES SUBLIME . . . . . 304 2 DON JUAN 3 56 5
AS WELL AS THE SUBLIME DISCOVERY'S DATE . . . . . 406 2 DON JUAN 4 112 4
NOUGHT'S MORE SUBLIME THAN ENERGETIC BILE . . . . . 489 2 DON JUAN 5 135 4
WHICH YOUR SUBLIME ATTENTION MAY BE WORTH . . . . . 494 2 DON JUAN 5 144 6
THE SIXTH SHALL HAVE A TOUCH OF THE SUBLIME . . . . 503 2 DON JUAN 5 159 6
WHICH SOME CALL THE SUBLIME I WISH THEY'D TRY IT . . . 32 3 DON JUAN 6 53 6
IS THE SUBLIME--I WISH THAT THEY WOULD TRY IT . . . . 32 3 DON JUAN 6 53 V6
MASTER OF THIRTY KINGDOMS SO SUBLIME . . . . . . 51 3 DON JUAN 6 90 3
HE WAS WHAT ERIN CALLS IN HER SUBLIME . . . . . 122 3 DON JUAN 8 23 1
AND THOUGH THE TURK'S RESISTANCE WAS SUBLIME . . . . 151 3 DON JUAN 8 79 6
SEVERE SUBLIME THE PROPHET WROTE NO FARCE ON . . . . 179 3 DON JUAN 8 134 6
THE EFFECT ON JUAN WAS OF COURSE SUBLIME . . . . . 261 3 DON JUAN 10 74 1
THE ABSENCE OF THAT MORE SUBLIME CONSTRUCTION . . . . 262 3 DON JUAN 10 76 6
WHAT A SUBLIME DISCOVERY 'TWAS TO MAKE THE . . . . . 269 3 DON JUAN 11 2 1
HIS QUALITIES (WITH THEM) INTO SUBLIME . . . . . 295 3 DON JUAN 11 53 6
AS EVER YET WAS ANY WORK SUBLIME . . . . . . 312 3 DON JUAN 11 90 6
BESIDES THE MOST SUBLIME OF--HEAVEN KNOWS WHAT ELSE-- . 356 3 DON JUAN 12 88 5
BESIDES THE SAD'S A SOURCE OF THE SUBLIME . . . . . 358 3 DON JUAN 13 1 5

SUBLIME (CONTINUED)

	PAGE	VOL	CANTO	STANZA	LN
MOUNTAINS AND ALL WE CAN BE MOST SUBLIME AT	423	3 DON JUAN 14		29	6
AND WHEN YOU MAY NOT BE SUBLIME BE ARCH	468	3 DON JUAN 15		27	3
IN FIGURE SHE HAD SOMETHING OF SUBLIME	476	3 DON JUAN 15		45	2
HAVING WOUND UP WITH THIS SUBLIME COMPARISON	481	3 DON JUAN 15		59	1
AND REALLY IF THE SAGE SUBLIME AND ATTIC	494	3 DON JUAN 15		86	3
THAT SOURCE OF THE SUBLIME AND THE MYSTERIOUS--	498	3 DON JUAN 15		95	7
AN EDIFICE NO LESS SUBLIME THAN STRONG	529	3 DON JUAN 16		59	5
AND FULL OF SENTIMENTS SUBLIME AS BILLOWS	555	3 DON JUAN 16		110	1
AGAIN THROUGH SHADOWS OF THE NIGHT SUBLIME	556	3 DON JUAN 16		113	5

SUBLIMED

FOR NOT THE BLEST SHERBET SUBLIMED WITH SNOW	251	2 DON JUAN 2		180	4

SUBLIMER

| BUT STILL FROM THAT SUBLIMER AZURE HUE | 524 | 3 DON JUAN 16 | | 47 | 5 |

SUBLIMES

| A WANT OF THAT TRUE NATURE WHICH SUBLIMES | 417 | 3 DON JUAN 14 | | 16 | 6 |

SUBLIMEST

HIS HIGHNESS THE SUBLIMEST OF MANKIND--	12	3 DON JUAN 6		13	1
A SUBJECT OF SUBLIMEST EXULTATION--	175	3 DON JUAN 8		126	3
HERSELF IN HER SUBLIMEST ATTITUDE	193	3 DON JUAN 9		22	6

SUBLIMITY

HER SERIOUS SAYINGS DARKEN'D TO SUBLIMITY	27	2 DON JUAN 1		12	4
AND SAW HIS AGONIES WITH SUCH SUBLIMITY	36	2 DON JUAN 1		29	7
GLORY BEGAN TO DAWN WITH DUE SUBLIMITY	92	3 DON JUAN 7		51	6
BELLONA SHOOK HER SPEAR WITH SUCH SUBLIMITY	92	3 DON JUAN 7		51	V6
A GARMENT OF A MYSTICAL SUBLIMITY	421	3 DON JUAN 14		26	7

SUBLIMITY'S

| WAITING FOR HIS SUBLIMITY'S FIRMAN | 393 | 2 DON JUAN 4 | | 91 | 2 |

SUBMISSION

| BY NO MEANS WOULD PRODUCE THE TOWN'S SUBMISSION | 81 | 3 DON JUAN 7 | | 30 | 5 |

SUBMITTED

| AND SO THEY WERE SUBMITTED FIRST TO HER ALL | 43 | 2 DON JUAN 1 | | 39 | 6 |

SUBSCRIPTION

| BY GENERAL SUBSCRIPTION OF THE LADIES | 199 | 2 DON JUAN 2 | | 81 | 8 |
| TO TALK OF A SUBSCRIPTION OR PETITION | 330 | 3 DON JUAN 12 | | 30 | 6 |

SUBSERVIENT

| BUT AS SUBSERVIENT TO A MORAL USE | 497 | 3 DON JUAN 15 | | 93 | 4 |

SUBSIDE

| WOULD HE SUBSIDE INTO A HACKNEY LAUREAT | 15 | 2 DON JUAN 0 | | 11 | V7 |
| BUT SIGHS SUBSIDE AND TEARS (EVEN WIDOWS') SHRINK | 228 | 3 DON JUAN 10 | | 7 | 1 |

SUBSIDES

| THE VERY SEASON RISES AND SUBSIDES | 378 | 3 DON JUAN 13 | | 43 | V7 |

SUBSIDING

| SPARKLING WITH FOAM UNTIL AGAIN SUBSIDING | 385 | 3 DON JUAN 13 | | 58 | 2 |
| GENTLY TO LULL DOWN THE SUBSIDING SOUL | 484 | 3 DON JUAN 15 | | 66 | 6 |

SUBSTANCE

| HERO--FOR WHAT IS SUBSTANCE TO A SPIRIT | 557 | 3 DON JUAN 16 | | 116 | 7 |

SUBSTANTIAL

UPON THE SWEEPSTAKES FOR SUBSTANTIAL WIVES	333	3 DON JUAN 12		36	4
TO PASS THE STYX FOR MORE SUBSTANTIAL FEASTS	404	3 DON JUAN 13		99	4
WITH THE SUBSTANTIAL COMPANY ENGROSSED	543	3 DON JUAN 16		90	4

SUBSTITUTE

| AND NO MORE HANDY SUBSTITUTE BEEN NEAR | 75 | 3 DON JUAN 7 | | 17 | 8 |
| THE POOR MAN'S SPARKLING SUBSTITUTE FOR RICHES | 256 | 3 DON JUAN 10 | | 63 | 4 |

SUBSTRATUM

| THERE SHOULD BE NE'ERTHELESS A SLIGHT SUBSTRATUM | 107 | 3 DON JUAN 7 | | 81 | 4 |

SUBTERRAQUEOUS

| AND HEAVES A LONELY SUBTERRAQUEOUS SIGH | 445 | 3 DON JUAN 14 | | 81 | 3 |

SUBTLE

AS DO THE SUBTLE SNAKES DESCRIBED OF OLD	153	3 DON JUAN 8		83	8
(HIS MAGGIOR DUOMO A SMART SUBTLE GREEK	259	3 DON JUAN 10		70	5
TOO SUBTLE FOR THE AIRIEST HUMAN HEAD	268	3 DON JUAN 11		1	4

SUBTLER

| WIVES IN THEIR HUSBANDS' ABSENCES GROW SUBTLER | 287 | 2 DON JUAN 3 | | 22 | 7 |

SUCCEED

| WELL IF I DON'T SUCCEED I HAVE SUCCEEDED | 324 | 3 DON JUAN 12 | | 17 | 1 |
| THAT IS WHEN THEY SUCCEED BUT GREATLY BLAMED | 448 | 3 DON JUAN 14 | | 89 | 4 |

SUCCEEDED

I KNOW NOT--IT SUCCEEDED AND SUCCESS	15	3 DON JUAN 6		19	2
A COURIER TO THE PRINCE AND HE SUCCEEDED	85	3 DON JUAN 7		38	2
WELL IF I DON'T SUCCEED I HAVE SUCCEEDED	324	3 DON JUAN 12		17	1
AND THAT'S ENOUGH SUCCEEDED IN MY YOUTH	324	3 DON JUAN 12		17	2
THAT NO ONE HAS SUCCEEDED IN DESCRIBING	418	3 DON JUAN 14		19	2

SUCCEEDING

| ABOUT WHAT'S CALLED SUCCESS OR NOT SUCCEEDING | 341 | 3 DON JUAN 12 | | 55 | 2 |

SUCCESS

THE GREAT SUCCESS OF JUAN'S EDUCATION	162	2 DON JUAN 2		10	7
THE GREATER THEIR SUCCESS THE WORSE IT PROVES	411	2 DON JUAN 5		1	5
I KNOW NOT--IT SUCCEEDED AND SUCCESS	15	3 DON JUAN 6		19	2
THE ONLY TIME WHEN MUCH SUCCESS IS NEEDED	324	3 DON JUAN 12		17	3
AND MY SUCCESS PRODUCED WHAT I IN SOOTH	324	3 DON JUAN 12		17	4
OF LATE THE PENALTY OF SUCH SUCCESS	324	3 DON JUAN 12		17	7
ABOUT WHAT'S CALLED SUCCESS OR NOT SUCCEEDING	341	3 DON JUAN 12		55	2
AND THOUGH NOT VAINER FROM HIS PAST SUCCESS	353	3 DON JUAN 12		81	7
'TIS NOT IN MORTALS TO COMMAND SUCCESS	366	3 DON JUAN 13		18	1
AND HAVE NOT YET ATTAINED TO MUCH SUCCESS	374	3 DON JUAN 13		35	4
I THINK THAT WERE I CERTAIN OF SUCCESS	415	3 DON JUAN 14		12	1
I HAVE SEARCHED THE WORLD AND MIDST SUCCESS OR CHECKS	451	3 DON JUAN 14		93	V5

SUCCESSFUL

| RETURNING THERE FROM HER SUCCESSFUL SEARCH | 206 | 2 DON JUAN 2 | | 95 | 6 |
| SPARKLED WITH HER SUCCESSFUL PROPHECIES | 490 | 3 DON JUAN 15 | | 78 | 8 |

```
                                                         PAGE VOL    CANTO  STANZA LN
SUCCESSOR
    SHE COULD NOT FIND AT FIRST A FIT SUCCESSOR . . . . . . 247  3 DON JUAN 10      47   8
SUCCULENT
    AS THOSE WHO LIKE THINGS ROSY RIPE AND SUCCULENT  . . . . 213  3 DON JUAN  9      62   3
SUCK
    SHOULD SUCK HIM BACK TO HER INSATIATE GRAVE . . . . . . 213  2 DON JUAN  2     108   4
SUCK'D
    AND DOWN SHE SUCK'D WITH HER THE WHIRLING WAVE . . . . . 184  2 DON JUAN  2      52   6
    SUCK'D IN THE MOISTURE WHICH LIKE NECTAR STREAM'D . . . . 202  2 DON JUAN  2      86   2
SUCKING
    JUST AS YOU'D BREAK A SUCKING SALAMANDER . . . . . . .  93  3 DON JUAN  7      52   5
    SOME SUCKING HERO IS COMPELLED TO REAR . . . . . . . 108  3 DON JUAN  7      83   4
SUCKLE
    TO THINK SUCH BREASTS MUST SUCKLE SLAVES . . . . . . . 326  2 DON JUAN  3    L 15   6
SUCKLINGS
    LIKE AN INVASION OF THEIR BABES AND SUCKLINGS . . . . . 488  2 DON JUAN  5     133   4
SUCKS
    A CHILD THE FIRST TIME THAT IT SUCKS THE BREAST . . . . 261  2 DON JUAN  2     196  V2
SUCTION
    HE CANNOT LIVE LIKE WOODCOCKS UPON SUCTION . . . . . . 191  2 DON JUAN  2      67   3
    COUNTRIES OF GREATER HEAT BUT LESSER SUCTION  . . . . . 262  3 DON JUAN 10      76   4
SUDDEN
    A SUDDEN FIT OF DRUNKENNESS OR SPLEEN . . . . . . .  98  2 DON JUAN  1     142   6
    WAS IT FOR THIS YOU TOOK YOUR SUDDEN JOURNEY  . . . . . 103  2 DON JUAN  1     151   1
    AT ONE O'CLOCK THE WIND WITH SUDDEN SHIFT  . . . . . . 170  2 DON JUAN  2      27   1
    PERHAPS YOU PROPHESY SOME SUDDEN ACT  . . . . . . . 296  2 DON JUAN  3      40   4
    EVEN AS THEY GAZED A SUDDEN TREMOR CAME  . . . . . . . 355  2 DON JUAN  4      21   2
    THEN WITH A SUDDEN MOVEMENT HE WITHDREW . . . . . . . 370  2 DON JUAN  4      48   1
    HER FEELINGS SUDDEN THROUGH HER BOSOM SENT  . . . . . . 379  2 DON JUAN  4      65  V6
    WHEN HE WAS GONE THERE WAS A SUDDEN CHANGE . . . . . . 473  2 DON JUAN  5     108   1
    THE APARTMENT ON A SUDDEN SHE SCREAMED OUT  . . . . . .  41  3 DON JUAN  6      70   8
    THAT ON A SUDDEN WHEN SHE LEAST HAD HOPE . . . . . . .  44  3 DON JUAN  6      77   1
    AS IF SHE HAD RECEIVED A SUDDEN BLOW  . . . . . . . .  58  3 DON JUAN  6     105   6
    WAS ON A SUDDEN RATHER PUZZLED HERE  . . . . . . . . 125  3 DON JUAN  8      27   6
    AND BEING SOMEWHAT CHOLERIC AND SUDDEN  . . . . . . . 274  3 DON JUAN 11      13   2
    SOMETHING LIKE ILLNESS OF A SUDDEN GROWTH  . . . . . . 514  3 DON JUAN 16      33   4
SUDDENLY
    ON SUCH A THING IS SUDDENLY TO SEA SENT  . . . . . . . 371  2 DON JUAN  4      51   6
    WHEN SUDDENLY HE HEARD OR THOUGHT SO NIGH  . . . . . . 509  3 DON JUAN 16      20   5
SUED
    AND HOW ALFONSO SUED FOR A DIVORCE . . . . . . . . 126  2 DON JUAN  1     188   7
    WHO COULD NOT GET THE PLACE FOR WHICH HE SUED  . . . . . 391  3 DON JUAN 13      70   8
SUFFER
    THUS EVEN GOOD FAME MAY SUFFER SAD CONTRACTIONS  . . . .  83  3 DON JUAN  7      34   5
    WOULD THIS DAMNED HEADACHE SUFFER ME TO BEAR IT  . . . . 268  3 DON JUAN 11       1  V8
    PERHAPS BUT AS I SUFFER FROM THE SHOCKS  . . . . . . . 270  3 DON JUAN 11       5   7
SUFFERANCE
    A SORT OF ORATOR BY SUFFERANCE . . . . . . . . . 152  2 DON JUAN  1    V 3   5
    OF SUFFERANCE YET UPON HIS FOREHEAD LAY  . . . . . . . 234  2 DON JUAN  2     147   4
SUFFER'D
    WAS EVER SUFFER'D LEST HE SHOULD GROW VICIOUS  . . . . .  44  2 DON JUAN  1      40   8
    FOR THIS IN SILENCE I HAVE SUFFER'D LONG . . . . . . . 100  2 DON JUAN  1     145   5
    HAD SUFFER'D MORE--HIS HARDSHIPS WERE COMPARATIVE . . . . 229  2 DON JUAN  2     137   7
SUFFERED
    THOUGH BY THIS POLITESSE SHE RATHER SUFFERED  . . . . .  36  3 DON JUAN  6      61   6
    ANOTHER COLUMN ALSO SUFFERED MUCH--  . . . . . . . . 151  3 DON JUAN  8      78   1
    HE SUFFERED INFIDELS IN HIS HOMESTEAD  . . . . . . . 262  3 DON JUAN 10      75   3
SUFFERER
    AND WHEN HIS COMRADE'S THOUGHT EACH SUFFERER KNEW . . . . 194  2 DON JUAN  2      73   5
SUFFERERS
    THE SUFFERERS--BE'T IN HEART OR INTELLECT--  . . . . . 563  3 DON JUAN 17       2   7
SUFFERING
    SUFFERING EACH OTHER'S FOIBLES BY ACCORD . . . . . .  57  2 DON JUAN  1      65   5
    AS NOW MIGHT RENDER THEIR LONG SUFFERING LESS  . . . . . 180  2 DON JUAN  2      46   4
    WHO HAD ALREADY PERISH'D SUFFERING MADLY . . . . . . . 199  2 DON JUAN  2      80   7
SUFFERINGS
    THOSE SUFFERINGS DANTE SAW IN HELL ALONE . . . . . . 401  2 DON JUAN  4     105   8
    THOSE SUFFERINGS ONCE RESERVED FOR HELL ALONE  . . . . . 401  2 DON JUAN  4     105  V8
    THE REAL SUFFERINGS OF THEIR SHE CONDITION  . . . . . . 420  3 DON JUAN 14      24   4
SUFFERS
    AT LEAST HIS MANNER SUFFERS NOT TO GUESS . . . . . . 373  3 DON JUAN 13      34   6
SUFFICE
    THAN MIGHT SUFFICE A MODERATE CENTURY THROUGH  . . . . . 309  3 DON JUAN 11      82   4
SUFFICES
    BUT IT SUFFICES--LITTLE WAS AMISS  . . . . . . . . .  31  3 DON JUAN  6      51   5
SUFFICIENT
    A SINGLE SHADE'S SUFFICIENT TO ENTRANCE A  . . . . . . 557  3 DON JUAN 16     116   6
SUFFICIENTLY
    AS IF NOT WARN'D SUFFICIENTLY BY THOSE  . . . . . . . 199  2 DON JUAN  2      80   6
    SUFFICIENTLY (HE SAID) HIS APPROBATION  . . . . . . . 452  2 DON JUAN  5      70   7
    THE PINS WERE PLACED SUFFICIENTLY BUT NOT  . . . . . .  37  3 DON JUAN  6      62   7
SUFFOCATION
    HIS SUFFOCATION BY THAT PRETTY PAIR  . . . . . . . . 112  2 DON JUAN  1     166   6
SUFFUSE
    EVEN AS I SING SUFFUSE MY FACE . . . . . . . . . 323  2 DON JUAN  3    L 6   4
SUGGEST
    I ALSO WOULD SUGGEST THE FITTING TIME . . . . . . . 482  2 DON JUAN  5     123   1
SUGGESTED
    MAY HAVE SUGGESTED THAT THIS SINGLE ONE . . . . . . .  54  2 DON JUAN  1      59   5
```

SUGGESTED   (CONTINUED)
    THE CITY'S SHAPE SUGGESTED THIS 'TIS TRUE   78   3 DON JUAN   7   23   6
    SUGGESTED SOME SLIGHT COMFORT IN HIS WAY 105   3 DON JUAN   7   75   3
SUICIDE
    WHOSE SUICIDE WAS ALMOST AN ANOMALY--   29   2 DON JUAN   1   15   6
    THE VERY SUICIDE THAT PAYS HIS DEBT   412   3 DON JUAN 14   4   4
SUIT
    TO A CHANCERY SUIT AND MESSUAGES AND LANDS   42   2 DON JUAN   1   37   2
    WOULD FULLY SUIT A WIDOW OF CONDITION   67   2 DON JUAN   1   85   3
    SO THAT A SUIT OR ACTION WERE MADE GOOD 109   2 DON JUAN   1   160   5
    THE SEAL A SUNFLOWER ELLE VOUS SUIT PARTOUT 134   2 DON JUAN   1   198   6
    AND NIGHT IS FLUNG OFF LIKE A MOURNING SUIT   230   2 DON JUAN   2   139   7
    THE SUIT HE THOUGHT MOST SUITABLE TO EACH   451   2 DON JUAN   5   68   1
    AS DRESS YOURSELF-- AND POINTED OUT A SUIT   453   2 DON JUAN   5   73   2
    I OFFER YOU A HANDSOME SUIT OF CLOTHES   455   2 DON JUAN   5   76   1
    OF TRUTH THAN PROSE UNLESS TO SUIT THE MART   154   3 DON JUAN   8   86   5
    THAT SUIT IN CHANCERY--WHICH SOME PERSONS PLEAD   . . . 324   3 DON JUAN 12   18   1
    THAT SUIT IN CHANCERY--(I HAVE A CHANCERY SUIT   . . .   357   3 DON JUAN 12   V 18   1
    THAT SUIT IN CHANCERY--(I HAVE A CHANCERY SUIT   . . .   357   3 DON JUAN 12   V 18   1
    ON WHAT MAY SUIT OR MAY NOT SUIT MY STORY   464   3 DON JUAN 15   19   5
    ON WHAT MAY SUIT OR MAY NOT SUIT MY STORY   464   3 DON JUAN 15   19   5
SUITABLE
    THE SUIT HE THOUGHT MOST SUITABLE TO EACH   451   2 DON JUAN   5   68   1
SUITE
    HIS SUITE CONSISTED OF THREE SERVANTS AND   169   2 DON JUAN   2   25   1
    AND NOW THEY WERE DIVERTED BY THEIR SUITE   316   2 DON JUAN   3   78   1
    A RANGE OR SUITE OF FURTHER CHAMBERS WHICH   449   2 DON JUAN   5   65   2
    AND JUAN'S SUITE LATE SCATTERED AT A DISTANCE   275   3 DON JUAN 11   14   2
SUITED
    AS SUITED THE ENSEMBLE OF HIS TOILET   457   2 DON JUAN   5   79   7
    OR AT LEAST SUITED NOT THIS VALIANT TARTAR   152   3 DON JUAN   8   80   4
SUITOR
    WAS FOR SOME RUM A DISAPPOINTED SUITOR   175   2 DON JUAN   2   36   8
    OH LOVE OF WHOM GREAT CAESAR WAS THE SUITOR   266   2 DON JUAN   2   205   1
    SO WHEN HE SAW EACH ANCIENT DAME A SUITOR   336   3 DON JUAN 12   42   5
SUITORS
    IS IT FOR THIS WHATE'ER MY SUITORS WERE   102   2 DON JUAN   1   148   5
    REJECTED SEVERAL SUITORS JUST TO LEARN   224   2 DON JUAN   2   128   7
    A HECATOMB OF SUITORS WITH DEVOTION   434   3 DON JUAN 14   55   6
    TO ONE OF SEVENTY SUITORS HIS PROMOTION   434   3 DON JUAN 14   55   V6
SUITORS'
    OR SHOW THE SAME DISLIKE TO SUITORS' KISSES   287   2 DON JUAN   3   23   4
SUITS
    WHENEER IT SUITS HIS PURPOSE TO ADVANCE   152   2 DON JUAN   1   V 3   3
    AS SUITS A MATRON WHO HAS PLAYED A PRANK   500   2 DON JUAN   5   154   4
    WITH SUITS AND PROSECUTIONS THEY BESIEGE US   11   3 DON JUAN   6   10   5
    A WORD WHICH LITTLE SUITS WITH SERASKIERS   152   3 DON JUAN   8   80   3
    THE BENCH TOO SEATS OR SUITS FULL MANY A DEBTOR   . . . 280   3 DON JUAN 11   25   5
    AND NOW AND THEN IT ALSO SUITS MY RHYMES   361   3 DON JUAN 13   8   4
    BECAUSE AS SUITS THEIR RANK AND SITUATION   534   3 DON JUAN 16   68   5
SULI'S
    ON SULI'S ROCK AND PARGA'S SHORE   325   2 DON JUAN   3   L 13   2
SULKILY
    AND SULKILY THE RIVER'S RIPPLE'S FLOWING   422   3 DON JUAN 14   28   4
SULKY
    THE SULKY HUNTSMAN GRIMLY SAID THE FRENCHMAN   425   3 DON JUAN 14   34   V7
SULLEN
    A SCOLDING WIFE A SULLEN SON A BILL   16   3 DON JUAN   6   21   1
    SERENE NOT SULLEN WERE THE SOLITUDES   145   3 DON JUAN   8   67   7
    AND WHEN UPON A SILENT SULLEN DAY   422   3 DON JUAN 14   28   1
SULLENLY
    AN ORDER SOMEWHAT SULLENLY OBEY'D   116   2 DON JUAN   1   173   4
SULLIES
    DUKES--FOOLS BY BIRTH WHILE CLOGHER'S BISHOP SULLIES .   . . 314   3 DON JUAN 11   V 76   5
SULPHURET
    BOLUS POTASSAE SULPHURET SUMENDUS   244   3 DON JUAN 10   41   7
SULPHURY
    SO ORDERED IT AMIDST THESE SULPHURY REVELS   135   3 DON JUAN   8   44   6
    STILL CLOSER SULPHURY CLOUDS BEGAN TO SMOTHER   . . .   146   3 DON JUAN   8   69   6
SULTAN
    WOULD HE ADORE A SULTAN HE OBEY   15   2 DON JUAN   D   11   7
    BUT NOW HE SUNG THE SULTAN AND THE PACHA   316   2 DON JUAN   3   79   7
    BUT IF THE SULTAN HAS A TASTE FOR SONG   389   2 DON JUAN   4   82   7
    'TWAS FOR THE SULTAN AND AT ONCE WITHDREW   407   2 DON JUAN   4   114   8
    FOR WERE THE SULTAN JUST TO ALL HIS DEARS   10   3 DON JUAN   6   9   6
    HAD CATHERINE AND THE SULTAN UNDERSTOOD   53   3 DON JUAN   6   95   1
    TO SEE THE SULTAN RICH IN MANY A GEM   104   3 DON JUAN   7   74   4
    OR SULTAN AS THE AUTHOR (TO WHOSE NOD   163   3 DON JUAN   8   104   6
SULTANA
    THE FAIR SULTANA ERRED FROM INANITION   10   3 DON JUAN   6   9   5
    ROSE THE SULTANA FROM A BED OF SPLENDOUR   50   3 DON JUAN   6   89   1
    SULTANA THINK UPON THE CONSEQUENCE   62   3 DON JUAN   6   114   2
SULTANA'S
    SERVE A SULTANA'S SENSUAL PHANTASY   484   2 DON JUAN   5   126   8
    THUS ENDED MANY A FAIR SULTANA'S TRIP   496   2 DON JUAN   5   149   V5
SULTANAS
    THIS I MUST LEAVE SULTANAS TO DECIDE   477   2 DON JUAN   5   115   4
    ESPECIALLY SULTANAS AND THEIR WAYS   64   3 DON JUAN   6   117   4
SULTAN'S
    BY SOLITUDE I MEAN A SULTAN'S NOT   68   2 DON JUAN   1   87   7

SULTAN'S   (CONTINUED)
    NAY QUOTH THE MAID THE SULTAN'S SELF SHAN'T CARRY ME 460   2 DON JUAN   5   84   7
    SHE WAS A SULTAN'S BRIDE (THANK HEAVEN NOT MINE) 475   2 DON JUAN   5   111   8
    AND SHOULD YOU ASK HOW SHE A SULTAN'S BRIDE 477   2 DON JUAN   5   115   2
    SOUND AND THEN BY A CRY THE SULTAN'S COMING 494   2 DON JUAN   5   145   8
SULTANS
    SULTANS TOO MUCH ABHOR THIS SORT OF SIN 10   3 DON JUAN   6   7   5
    MORE FEARED THAN ALL THE SULTANS EVER SEEN 104   3 DON JUAN   7   73   8
SULTANSHIP
    UPON HIS ANGRY SULTANSHIP PELL-MELL 166   3 DON JUAN   8   109   4
SULTRY
    IS MUCH MORE COMMON WHERE THE CLIMATE'S SULTRY 56   2 DON JUAN   1   63   8
SUM
    BY LAYING WHATE'ER SUM IN MULCT THEY PLEASE ON 57   2 DON JUAN   1   64   6
    THE SUM OF THEIR SENSATIONS TO A SECOND 254   2 DON JUAN   2   187   4
    UNTIL THE SUM WAS ACCURATELY SCANNED 426   2 DON JUAN   5   29   6
    MONSTERS WHO COST A NO LESS MONSTROUS SUM 462   2 DON JUAN   5   88   8
    WHO WHEN WE COME TO SUM UP THE TOTALITY 108   3 DON JUAN   7   83   5
    TO VENTURE A SOLUTION DAVUS SUM 365   3 DON JUAN 13   13   2
    AND YOU WILL FIND HER SUM OF YEARS IN PLENTY 433   3 DON JUAN 14   54   8
SUMENDUS
    BOLUS POTASSAE SULPHURET SUMENDUS 244   3 DON JUAN 10   41   7
SUMMED
    IF 'TIS SUMMED UP WITH FEMININE PRECISION 10   3 DON JUAN   6   9   3
    BEFORE HIM SUMMED THE AWFUL SCROLL AND READ IT) . . . 259   3 DON JUAN 10   70   6
SUMMER
    HER EVENING SILK OR IN THE SUMMER MUSLIN 27   2 DON JUAN   1   12   7
    EVEN AS A SUMMER SKY'S WITHOUT A CLOUD 94   2 DON JUAN   1   135   6
    HAVE SQUANDER'D MY WHOLE SUMMER WHILE 'TWAS MAY . . . 143   2 DON JUAN   1   213   5
    WHEN DRIED TO SUMMER DUST TILL TAUGHT BY PAIN 201   2 DON JUAN   2   84   3
    SAVE ON THE DEAD LONG SUMMER DAYS WHICH MAKE 249   2 DON JUAN   2   177   7
    ETERNAL SUMMER GILDS THEM YET 320   2 DON JUAN   3 L 1   5
    MAKING THEIR SUMMER LIVES ONE CEASELESS SONG 337   2 DON JUAN   3   106   2
    THEY WERE ALL SUMMER LIGHTNING MIGHT ASSAIL 348   2 DON JUAN   4   9   5
    LIKE SUMMER CLOUDS ALL SILVERY SMOOTH AND FAIR . . . 375   2 DON JUAN   4   57   2
    BLOOD-RED AS SUNSET SUMMER CLOUDS WHICH RANGE . . . 473   2 DON JUAN   5   108   5
    SOME SAID HER YEARS WERE GETTING NIGH THEIR SUMMER . . 23   3 DON JUAN   6   35   5
    THE RUGGED TREE UNTO THE SUMMER WIND 164   3 DON JUAN   8   106   7
    LIKE ARNO IN THE SUMMER TO A SHALLOW 228   3 DON JUAN 10   7   2
    THE LONDON WINTER AND THE COUNTRY SUMMER 380   3 DON JUAN 13   48   1
SUMMER'S
    IT WAS UPON A DAY A SUMMER'S DAY-- 76   2 DON JUAN   1   102   1
    SUMMER'S INDEED A VERY DANGEROUS SEASON 76   2 DON JUAN   1   102   2
    'TWAS ON A SUMMER'S DAY--THE SIXTH OF JUNE-- 76   2 DON JUAN   1   103   1
    REIGN'D TILL ONE SUMMER'S DAY HE TOOK TO GRAZING . . 445   2 DON JUAN   5   60   4
    SO ARAB DESERTS DRINK IN SUMMER'S RAIN 212   3 DON JUAN   9   59   6
    HECTIC AND BRIEF AS SUMMER'S DAY NIGH DONE 229   3 DON JUAN 10   8   6
    WHICH YOU SHOULD PERPETRATE SOME SUMMER'S DAY . . . 445   3 DON JUAN 14   82   6
    THERE WAS MISS MILLPOND SMOOTH AS SUMMER'S SEA . . . 474   3 DON JUAN 15   41   1
SUMMERS
    SUMMERS COULD RENOVATE THOUGH THEY SHOULD BE 86   3 DON JUAN   7   41   6
    THOSE POLAR SUMMERS ALL SUN AND SOME ICE 349   3 DON JUAN 12   72   8
SUMMIT
    WHOSE SUMMIT LIKE ALL HILLS IS LOST IN VAPOUR . . . 146   2 DON JUAN   1   218   4
    ARRIVING AT THE SUMMIT OF A HILL 286   2 DON JUAN   3   21   1
    WALKED ON BEHIND HIS CARRIAGE O'ER THE SUMMIT . . . 272   3 DON JUAN 11   9   2
SUMMITS
    AND LOSE IN SHINING SNOW THEIR SUMMITS BLUE 94   2 DON JUAN   1   134   V5
SUMMON
    AND SUMMON LACKEYS ARM'D WITH FIRE AND SWORD 97   2 DON JUAN   1   139   7
    ENOUGH TO MAKE FOR PORT ERE TIME SHALL SUMMON . . . 376   3 DON JUAN 13   40   4
    WHO WAKE IN WINTER ERE THE COCK CAN SUMMON 426   3 DON JUAN 14   36   3
    MY SOUL FROM OUT ME AT THY SINGLE SUMMON 569   3 DON JUAN 17   V 13   6
SUMMON'D
    O'ERCHARGED WITH RAIN HER SUMMON'D HANDMAIDS BORE . . 376   2 DON JUAN   4   59   4
SUMMONED
    AND HERE SHE SUMMONED BABA AND REQUIRED 55   3 DON JUAN   6   99   1
SUMMONS
    AND SENT ONE ON A SUMMONS TO THE PAIR 64   3 DON JUAN   6   118   2
    TO ANSWER RIBAS' SUMMONS TO GIVE WAY 171   3 DON JUAN   8   120   8
SUN
    ESPECIALLY IN COUNTRIES NEAR THE SUN 56   2 DON JUAN   1   62   5
    AND ALL THE FAULT OF THAT INDECENT SUN 56   2 DON JUAN   1   63   2
    THE SUN NO DOUBT IS THE PREVAILING REASON 76   2 DON JUAN   1   102   4
    THE SUN SET AND UP ROSE THE YELLOW MOON 82   2 DON JUAN   1   113   1
    SOME CURSED THE DAY ON WHICH THEY SAW THE SUN . . . 180   2 DON JUAN   2   45   3
    THE SUN ROSE RED AND FIERY A SURE SIGN 189   2 DON JUAN   2   62   1
    THE SEVENTH DAY AND NO WIND--THE BURNING SUN . . . 194   2 DON JUAN   2   72   1
    THE AIRY CHILD OF VAPOUR AND THE SUN 205   2 DON JUAN   2   92   2
    CHILLED BY THE NIGHT--AND BLACKENED BY THE SUN . . 210   2 DON JUAN   2   102   V5
    LIGHT TO THE ROCKS THAT ROOF'D THEM WHICH THE SUN . 216   2 DON JUAN   2   115   6
    LIKE TWILIGHT ROSY STILL WITH THE SET SUN 218   2 DON JUAN   2   118   2
    AND THE YOUNG BEAMS OF THE EXCLUDED SUN 229   2 DON JUAN   2   137   4
    WITH SOME PRETENCE ABOUT THE SUN THAT MAKES . . . 230   2 DON JUAN   2   139   2
    I SAY THE SUN IS A MOST GLORIOUS SIGHT 230   2 DON JUAN   2   140   1
    WHILE THE SUN SMILED ON HER WITH HIS FIRST FLAME . 232   2 DON JUAN   2   142   5
    SOME FEELINGS UNIVERSAL AS THE SUN 244   2 DON JUAN   2   167   3
    AND SAW THE SUN SET OPPOSITE THE MOON 249   2 DON JUAN   2   176   8
    SHE WAITED ON HER LADY WITH THE SUN 252   2 DON JUAN   2   182   5

SUN   (CONTINUED)

	PAGE	VOL		CANTO	STANZA	LN
RED SUN SINKS DOWN BEHIND THE AZURE HILL	252	2	DON JUAN	2	183	2
HAIDEE WAS PASSION'S CHILD BORN WHERE THE SUN	264	2	DON JUAN	2	202	2
HE SAW HIS WHITE WALLS SHINING IN THE SUN	289	2	DON JUAN	3	27	1
A SUN EMBOSS'D IN GOLD WHOSE RAYS OF TISSUE	309	2	DON JUAN	3	67	7
FLOW'D LIKE AN ALPINE TORRENT WHICH THE SUN	313	2	DON JUAN	3	73	2
BUT ALL EXCEPT THEIR SUN IS SET	320	2	DON JUAN	3	L 1	6
AND WHEN THE SUN SET WHERE WERE THEY	322	2	DON JUAN	3	L 4	6
AND FOLLOW FAR THE DISAPPEARING SUN	355	2	DON JUAN	4	22	2
BORN OF THE SUN AS AFRIC'S CLIMATE IS	373	2	DON JUAN	4	54	V8
DANCING ALL FREE AND HAPPY IN THE SUN)	393	2	DON JUAN	4	90	7
THE SUN HIMSELF WAS SCARCE MORE FREE FROM SPECKS	474	2	DON JUAN	5	109	5
BRIDE OF THE SUN AND SISTER OF THE MOON	494	2	DON JUAN	5	144	1
THE SUN HIMSELF HAS SENT ME LIKE A RAY	494	2	DON JUAN	5	144	7
THE SUN WHICH YEARLY MELTS THE POLAR ICE	501	2	DON JUAN	5	157	7
SOUNDS LESS HARMONIOUS UNDERNEATH THE SUN SOON	132	3	DON JUAN	8	39	3
THAT HIDES THE PAST WORLD LIKE TO A SET SUN	188	3	DON JUAN	9	11	3
SO THAT WE CAN OUR NATIVE SUN ASSUAGE	217	3	DON JUAN	9	69	5
IS RUFFLED BY A WRINKLE OR THE SUN	229	3	DON JUAN	10	8	4
AS PURPLE CLOUDS BEFRINGE THE SUN BUT MOST	239	3	DON JUAN	10	29	7
THE SUN WENT DOWN THE SMOKE ROSE UP AS FROM	265	3	DON JUAN	10	81	1
ARE BOWED AND PUT THE SUN OUT LIKE A TAPER	266	3	DON JUAN	10	83	6
UPON THE GUIDE-BOOK'S PRIVILEGE THE SUN	279	3	DON JUAN	11	23	6
AND HOLD UP TO THE SUN MY LITTLE TAPER	325	3	DON JUAN	12	21	3
THEIR MOON THEIR SUN THEIR GAS THEIR FARTHING CANDLE	342	3	DON JUAN	12	56	8
THOSE POLAR SUMMERS ALL SUN AND SOME ICE	349	3	DON JUAN	12	72	8
STREAMING FROM OFF THE SUN LIKE SERAPH'S WINGS	387	3	DON JUAN	13	62	4
BECAUSE THE SUN AND STARS AND AUGHT THAT SHINES	423	3	DON JUAN	14	29	5
TO CRITICS OR TO HAIL THE SETTING SUN	466	3	DON JUAN	15	22	6
GREAT GALILEO WAS DEBARRED THE SUN	565	3	DON JUAN	17	8	1

SUN-BURNT

	PAGE	VOL		CANTO	STANZA	LN
PARTICULARLY AMONGST SUN-BURNT NATIONS	59	2	DON JUAN	1	69	8

SUNDAY

	PAGE	VOL		CANTO	STANZA	LN
BRAVE INEZ NOW SET UP A SUNDAY SCHOOL	162	2	DON JUAN	2	10	2

SUNFLOWER

	PAGE	VOL		CANTO	STANZA	LN
THE SEAL A SUNFLOWER ELLE VOUS SUIT PARTOUT	134	2	DON JUAN	1	198	6

SUNG

	PAGE	VOL		CANTO	STANZA	LN
THE WIND SUNG CORDAGE STRAIN'D AND SAILORS SWORE	163	2	DON JUAN	2	13	2
SOME PLUNDER'D SOME DRANK SPIRITS SOME SUNG PSALMS	174	2	DON JUAN	2	34	3
WHEN HE WHO HAD THE WATCH SUNG OUT AND SWORE	207	2	DON JUAN	2	97	2
HAVE SUNG OF HEAVEN AND HELL OR MARRIAGE ARE	281	2	DON JUAN	3	10	2
AND FOR HIS THEME--HE SELDOM SUNG BELOW IT	316	2	DON JUAN	3	78	6
BUT NOW HE SUNG THE SULTAN AND THE PACHA	316	2	DON JUAN	3	79	7
AND SINGING AS HE SUNG IN HIS WARM YOUTH	318	2	DON JUAN	3	83	7
THUS SUNG HE AND SUCH IS THE INHERENT FIRE	319	2	DON JUAN	3	84	V1
WHERE BURNING SAPPHO LOVED AND SUNG	320	2	DON JUAN	3	L 1	2
THUS SUNG OR WOULD OR COULD OR SHOULD HAVE SUNG	326	2	DON JUAN	3	87	1
THUS SUNG OR WOULD OR COULD OR SHOULD HAVE SUNG	326	2	DON JUAN	3	87	1
AND SUNG OF LOVE THE FIERCE NAME STRUCK THROUGH ALL	380	2	DON JUAN	4	66	3
WOULD POPE HAVE SUNG OR HORACE BEEN INSPIRED	470	2	DON JUAN	5	101	8
OR RECOLLECT ALL THAT WAS SAID OR SUNG	486	2	DON JUAN	5	130	6
HAVE SUNG OR EVEN A DANDY'S DANDIEST CHATTER	493	2	DON JUAN	5	143	4
WITH ALL THE PRAISES EVER SAID OR SUNG	199	3	DON JUAN	9	34	6
KNOW LITTLE MORE OF LOVE THAN WHAT IS SUNG	230	3	DON JUAN	10	10	4
AND PARTS AND HEARTS HE DANCED AND SUNG AND HAD	292	3	DON JUAN	11	47	2
BOTH LONGED EXTREMELY TO BE SUNG IN SPANISH	295	3	DON JUAN	11	53	8
SUNG OR REHEARSED THE LAST DANCE FROM ABROAD	406	3	DON JUAN	13	104	4
AND GRACE IS SAID THE GRACE I SHOULD HAVE SUNG--	538	3	DON JUAN	16	77	8
AND SEVERAL WHO SUNG FEWER PSALMS THAN CATCHES	539	3	DON JUAN	16	80	8

SUNIUM

	PAGE	VOL		CANTO	STANZA	LN
ON SUNIUM OR HYMETTUS LIKE DIOGENES	488	3	DON JUAN	15	73	7

SUNIUM'S

	PAGE	VOL		CANTO	STANZA	LN
PLACE ME ON SUNIUM'S MARBLED STEEP	326	2	DON JUAN	3	L 16	1

SUNK

	PAGE	VOL		CANTO	STANZA	LN
KEPT STILL ALOOF THE CREW WHO ERE THEY SUNK	174	2	DON JUAN	2	35	7
AND GOING DOWN HEAD FOREMOST--SUNK IN SHORT	183	2	DON JUAN	2	51	8
THEN HE HIMSELF SUNK DOWN ALL DUMB AND SHIVERING	204	2	DON JUAN	2	90	7
BUT SUNK AGAIN UPON HIS BLEEDING KNEE	213	2	DON JUAN	2	109	2
AND DOWN HE SUNK AND AS HE SUNK THE SAND	214	2	DON JUAN	2	110	2
AND DOWN HE SUNK AND AS HE SUNK THE SAND	214	2	DON JUAN	2	110	2
GLORY THE GRAPE LOVE GOLD IN THESE ARE SUNK	250	2	DON JUAN	2	179	3
AND JUAN SUNK TO SLEEP WITHIN HER ARMS	260	2	DON JUAN	2	195	2
SHE SUNK DOWN ON HER SEAT BY SLOW DEGREES	59	3	DON JUAN	6	107	7
SUNK AND THE CRIMSON CROSS GLARED O'ER THE FIELD	172	3	DON JUAN	8	122	5
BUT WHERE THERMOMETERS SUNK DOWN TO TEN	241	3	DON JUAN	10	33	6
THE REST HAD BEEN REFORM'D REPLACED OR SUNK	389	3	DON JUAN	13	66	7

SUNLESS

	PAGE	VOL		CANTO	STANZA	LN
'TWAS TWILIGHT AND THE SUNLESS DAY WENT DOWN	182	2	DON JUAN	2	49	1

SUNLIGHT

	PAGE	VOL		CANTO	STANZA	LN
THE ROSY SKY WITH THE LAST SUNLIGHT FIRED	335	2	DON JUAN	3	101	V6

SUNLIKE

	PAGE	VOL		CANTO	STANZA	LN
WHICH KINDLES SUNLIKE O'ER THE LAUREL-BROWED	373	3	DON JUAN	13	33	V7

SUNNY

	PAGE	VOL		CANTO	STANZA	LN
AND THROUGH ALL CLIMES THE SNOWY AND THE SUNNY	78	2	DON JUAN	1	107	7
FLASHES INTO THE HEART--ALL SUNNY LAND	160	2	DON JUAN	2	7	4
MADE ICE SEEM PARADISE AND WINTER SUNNY	235	3	DON JUAN	10	21	8
BUT DOUBTLESS AS THE AIR THOUGH SELDOM SUNNY	259	3	DON JUAN	10	70	7
THE RED GRAPE IN THE SUNNY LANDS OF SONG	394	3	DON JUAN	13	76	4
YOUTH FADES AND LEAVES OUR DAYS NO LONGER SUNNY	405	3	DON JUAN	13	100	5

SUNNY   (CONTINUED)
ITS GLORY THROUGH ALL AGES SHINING SUNNY . . . . . . 529 3 DON JUAN 16 59 7
AS DEEP SEAS IN A SUNNY ATMOSPHERE . . . . 545 3 DON JUAN 16 94 8
SUNRISE
ON HIS SOUL LIKE A CEASELESS SUNRISE DART-- . . . . . 169 3 DON JUAN 8 115 6
AS AN EAST INDIAN SUNRISE ON THE MAIN . . . . 212 3 DON JUAN 9 59 4
SUN'S
IF 'TWAS NOT LAND THAT ROSE WITH THE SUN'S RAY . . . . 207 2 DON JUAN 2 97 3
AFRIC IS ALL THE SUN'S AND AS HER EARTH . . . . . . 374 2 DON JUAN 4 56 1
THE SUN'S TRUE SON NO VAPOUR BUT A RAY . . . . . . 300 3 DON JUAN 11 64 8
SUNS
AND SOBER SUNS MUST SET AT FIVE O'CLOCK . . . . . . 94 2 DON JUAN 1 134 8
SUNS AS RAYS--WORLDS LIKE ATOMS--YEARS LIKE HOURS . . . 189 3 DON JUAN 9 13 8
SOME RECKON WOMEN BY THEIR SUNS OR YEARS . . . . . . 230 3 DON JUAN 10 10 7
SUNSET
AT SUNSET THEY BEGAN TO TAKE IN SAIL . . . . 170 2 DON JUAN 2 26 6
THE CLIFF TOWARDS SUNSET ON THAT DAY SHE FOUND . . . 224 2 DON JUAN 2 129 2
NOR BURGUNDY IN ALL ITS SUNSET GLOW . . . . 251 2 DON JUAN 2 180 6
AND CLOUDS COME O'ER THE SUNSET OF OUR DAY . . . . . 305 2 DON JUAN 3 59 6
THEY GAZED UPON THE SUNSET 'TIS AN HOUR . . . . . . 354 2 DON JUAN 4 20 1
BLOOD-RED AS SUNSET SUMMER CLOUDS WHICH RANGE . . . . 473 2 DON JUAN 5 108 5
SUNSET THE TIME THE PLACE THE SAME DECLIVITY . . . . 272 3 DON JUAN 11 8 2
OF SUNSET HALOS O'ER THE LAUREL-BROWED . . . . . . 373 3 DON JUAN 13 33 7
SUNSHINE
A GLIMPSE OF SUNSHINE SET SOME HANDS TO BALE-- . . . . 176 2 DON JUAN 2 38 7
SUN-SODDEN
OF CARNAGE LIKE THE NILE'S SUN-SODDEN SLIME . . . . . 152 3 DON JUAN 8 82 7
SUP
AND THEN--AND THEN--AND THEN--SIT DOWN AND SUP . . . . 119 2 DON JUAN 1 179 8
WILL WONDER WHERE SUCH ANIMALS COULD SUP . . . . . . 202 3 DON JUAN 9 39 3
SUPERB
AND DIVERS SMOKED SUPERB PIPES DECORATED . . . . . . 441 2 DON JUAN 5 53 5
THERE IS BUT ONE SUPERB MENAGERIE . . . . 327 3 DON JUAN 12 24 8
SUPERBLY
THE FIRST YET FROWNED SUPERBLY O'ER THE SOIL . . . . 386 3 DON JUAN 13 59 5
SUPERBLY AND CONTAINED A WORLD OF ZEST . . . . . . 488 3 DON JUAN 15 74 8
SUPERCARGO
CONVEY'D MEDEA AS HER SUPERCARGO . . . . 443 3 DON JUAN 14 76 8
SUPERFICIAL
JUAN WHO WAS A LITTLE SUPERFICIAL . . . . 294 3 DON JUAN 11 51 1
SUPERFINE
THE WAX WAS SUPERFINE ITS HUE VERMILLION . . . . . . 134 2 DON JUAN 1 198 8
SUPERFLUOUS
THERE WAS SMALL LEISURE FOR SUPERFLUOUS SIN . . . . . 178 3 DON JUAN 8 132 6
SUPERIOR
THEY MADE A MOST SUPERIOR MESS OF BROTH . . . . . . 221 2 DON JUAN 2 123 5
FOR THIS SUPERIOR YOKE OF HUMAN CATTLE . . . . . . 425 2 DON JUAN 5 28 8
WITH HIS SUPERIOR IN A SMILE TO TRAMPLE . . . . . . 189 3 DON JUAN 9 13 4
LORD HENRY ALSO LIKED TO BE SUPERIOR . . . . 367 3 DON JUAN 13 19 1
SUPERIORITY
HE NEITHER BROOK'D NOR CLAIM'D SUPERIORITY . . . . . 462 3 DON JUAN 15 15 8
MEN WHOSE HISTORICAL SUPERIORITY . . . . 503 3 DON JUAN 16 5 3
SUPERLATIVE
SCOTT THE SUPERLATIVE OF MY COMPARATIVE-- . . . . . 481 3 DON JUAN 15 59 4
SUPERNATURAL
AND VERY HANDSOME SUPERNATURAL SCENERY . . . . . . 136 2 DON JUAN 1 201 8
AND DEVILS FOR MY SUPERNATURAL SCENERY . . . . . . 136 2 DON JUAN 1 201 V8
SO SUPERNATURAL WAS HER PASSION'S RISE . . . . . . 489 2 DON JUAN 5 134 5
TASTES WE ARE GOING TO TRY THE SUPERNATURAL . . . . . 497 3 DON JUAN 15 93 8
A SUPERNATURAL AGENT--OR A MOUSE . . . . 509 3 DON JUAN 16 20 6
SOUNDING LIKE VERY SUPERNATURAL WATER . . . . 556 3 DON JUAN 16 114 4
SUPERNUMERARY
OF ANY SUPERNUMERARY BEAUTIES . . . . 35 3 DON JUAN 6 58 8
SUPERSEDE
TO SUPERSEDE ALL WARBLERS HERE BELOW . . . . 10 2 DON JUAN D 3 3
SHALL SUPERSEDE BEYOND ALL DOUBT ALL THOSE . . . . . 138 2 DON JUAN 1 204 3
WILL VERY OFTEN SUPERSEDE THE REST . . . . 371 3 DON JUAN 13 28 8
SUPERSTITION
THIS MAY BE SUPERSTITION WEAK OR WILD . . . . 387 3 DON JUAN 13 61 6
BUT FOR MY OWN PECULIAR SUPERSTITION . . . . 467 3 DON JUAN 15 24 4
HAD SUPERSTITION LOST HER TALISMAN . . . . 467 3 DON JUAN 15 24 V4
BEFORE YOU LEARN TO CALL THIS SUPERSTITION . . . . . 500 3 DON JUAN 15 98 8
AT RISK OF BEING QUIZZED FOR SUPERSTITION . . . . . 512 3 DON JUAN 16 28 4
THEY PASSED AS SUCH THINGS DO FOR SUPERSTITION . . . 527 3 DON JUAN 16 54 2
SUPERSTITION'S
COINED FROM SURVIVING SUPERSTITION'S MINT . . . . . 510 3 DON JUAN 16 22 5
SUPERSTRATUM
THE SUPERSTRATUM WHICH WILL OVERLAY US . . . . . . 201 3 DON JUAN 9 37 8
SUPPED
I AM NO FLATTERER--YOU'VE SUPPED FULL OF FLATTERY . . . 185 3 DON JUAN 9 5 1
SUPPER
OR BUT AT TIMES A LITTLE SUPPER MADE . . . . 200 2 DON JUAN 2 82 4
SAID IN HEAVEN'S NAME LET'S GET SOME SUPPER NOW . . . 437 2 DON JUAN 5 47 7
PREPARED FOR SUPPER WITH A GLASS OF RUM . . . . . . 441 2 DON JUAN 5 53 8
TO SUPPER BUT YOU WORTHY CHRISTIAN NUN . . . . . . 458 2 DON JUAN 5 81 3
BUT IF YOU CAN CONTRIVE GET NEXT AT SUPPER . . . . . 304 3 DON JUAN 11 72 1
THE SUPPER TOO DISCUSSED THE DAMES ADMIRED . . . . . 504 3 DON JUAN 16 8 2
SUPPLICATE
AND THUS I SUPPLICATE YOUR SUPPOSITION . . . . 208 3 DON JUAN 9 52 1

794

SUPPLICATOR
	PAGE	VOL	CANTO	STANZA	LN
THE SUPPLICATOR BEING AN AMATEUR	543	3 DON JUAN	16	89	2

SUPPLIED
HE ATE AND HE WAS WELL SUPPLIED AND SHE	239	2 DON JUAN	2	158	1

SUPPLY
AND THAT'S THEIR MODE OF FURNISHING SUPPLY	190	2 DON JUAN	2	65	6

SUPPORT
IS CALLED ON TO SUPPORT HIS CLAIM OR SHOW IT	296	3 DON JUAN	11	55	3
TO LEAN ON FOR SUPPORT IN ANY WAY	324	3 DON JUAN	12	18	6

SUPPORTERS
AND WORDSWORTH HAS SUPPORTERS TWO OR THREE	298	3 DON JUAN	11	59	6

SUPPOSE
BUT JUST SUPPOSE THAT MOMENT SHOULD BETIDE	67	2 DON JUAN	1	84	5
I ONLY SAY SUPPOSE IT--INTER NOS	67	2 DON JUAN	1	84	6
I ONLY SAY SUPPOSE THIS SUPPOSITION	67	2 DON JUAN	1	85	1
SUPPOSE FROM JUNE THE SIXTH (THE FATAL DAY	86	2 DON JUAN	1	121	2
TWO LITTLE DWARFS THE LEAST YOU COULD SUPPOSE	462	2 DON JUAN	5	87	3
ON SUCH A SUBJECT THEN SUPPOSE THE FACE	486	2 DON JUAN	5	130	7
SUPPOSE BUT YOU ALREADY HAVE SUPPOSED	486	2 DON JUAN	5	131	1
YOU CAN'T SUPPOSE GULBEYAZ' ANGRY BROW	486	2 DON JUAN	5	131	8
SUPPOSE HIM THEN AT PETERSBURGH SUPPOSE	203	3 DON JUAN	9	42	7
SUPPOSE HIM THEN AT PETERSBURGH SUPPOSE	203	3 DON JUAN	9	42	7
SUPPOSE HIM IN A HANDSOME UNIFORM	204	3 DON JUAN	9	43	1
SUPPOSE HIM SWORD BY SIDE AND HAT IN HAND	204	3 DON JUAN	9	44	1
SAID--LADY I BESEECH YOU TO SUPPOSE THEM	208	3 DON JUAN	9	51	8
WHO WOULD SUPPOSE FROM ADAM'S SIMPLE RATION	486	3 DON JUAN	15	69	5
FOR FEAR WE SHOULD SUPPOSE US QUITE IN HEAVEN	525	3 DON JUAN	16	49	8
WHO WOULD SUPPOSE THY GIFTS SOMETIMES OBDURATE)	540	3 DON JUAN	16	82	6
SUPPOSE THE CONVERSE OF THIS PRECEDENT	564	3 DON JUAN	17	5	5

SUPPOSED
IT MAY BE EASILY SUPPOSED WHILE THIS	173	2 DON JUAN	2	33	1
WHATE'ER SHE DID NOT SEE IF SHE SUPPOSED	476	2 DON JUAN	5	113	2
SUPPOSE BUT YOU ALREADY HAVE SUPPOSED	486	2 DON JUAN	5	131	1
BUT WHEN YOU HAVE SUPPOSED THE FEW WE KNOW	486	2 DON JUAN	5	131	7
MUCH AS THEY MIGHT HAVE BEEN SUPPOSED TO SPEAK	298	3 DON JUAN	11	60	5
HE WOKE BETIMES AND AS MAY BE SUPPOSED	512	3 DON JUAN	16	28	1
TO LAUGH HIM OUT OF HIS SUPPOSED DISMAY	526	3 DON JUAN	16	51	6
WHICH SOME SUPPOSED (THOUGH HE HAD NOT AVOWED IT)	527	3 DON JUAN	16	54	7
THOUGH SEEMING SO FROM ITS SUPPOSED FACILITY	547	3 DON JUAN	16	97	6

SUPPOSITION
I ONLY SAY SUPPOSE THIS SUPPOSITION	67	2 DON JUAN	1	85	1
AND THUS I SUPPLICATE YOUR SUPPOSITION	208	3 DON JUAN	9	52	1

SUPPRESS
SHE TAUGHT THEM TO SUPPRESS THEIR VICE AND URINE	162	2 DON JUAN	2	10	V8
SUPPRESS THEN SOME SLIGHT FEMININE DISEASES	459	3 DON JUAN	15	9	7

SUPPRESS'D
'TWAS BUT HIS OWN SUPPRESS'D TILL NOW HE FOUND	194	2 DON JUAN	2	73	6

SUPPRESSING
WAS LARGE AND DARK SUPPRESSING HALF ITS FIRE	54	2 DON JUAN	1	60	2

SUPPRESSION
THEN THERE WERE SIGHS THE DEEPER FOR SUPPRESSION	62	2 DON JUAN	1	74	1
SUPPRESSION LADY PINCHBECK WAS HIS CHOICE	336	3 DON JUAN	12	42	8

SUPPREST
BUT ALL ARE BETTER THAN THE SIGH SUPPREST	457	3 DON JUAN	15	3	1

SUPT
SIR--AS I SAID AS SOON AS I HAVE SUPT	453	2 DON JUAN	5	72	4

SURE
AND GREEK--THE ALPHABET--I'M NEARLY SURE	28	2 DON JUAN	1	13	2
YOU MIGHT BE SURE SHE WAS A PERFECT FRIGHT	48	2 DON JUAN	1	48	6
BUT I AM NOT SO SURE I SHOULD HAVE SMILED	59	2 DON JUAN	1	69	5
THUS JULIA SAID--AND THOUGHT SO TO BE SURE	64	2 DON JUAN	1	79	6
I'M SURE SHE WOULD HAVE SHRUNK AS FROM AN ASP	81	2 DON JUAN	1	111	V6
'TWAS IN NOVEMBER BUT I'M NOT SO SURE	86	2 DON JUAN	1	121	7
LABOUR THERE'S A SURE MARKET FOR IMPOSTURE	91	2 DON JUAN	1	128	8
'TWERE BETTER SURE TO DIE SO THAN BE SHUT	112	2 DON JUAN	1	166	7
IN PREFERENCE SURE TO CLARENCE' MALMSEY BUTT	112	2 DON JUAN	1	166	V8
THE SUN ROSE RED AND FIERY A SURE SIGN	189	2 DON JUAN	2	62	1
BUT ONE THING'S PRETTY SURE A WOMAN PLANTED--	276	2 DON JUAN	3	4	2
SUCH CHAINS AS HIS WERE SURE TO BIND	325	2 DON JUAN	3	L 12	6
SURE MY INVENTION MUST BE DOWN AT ZERO	341	2 DON JUAN	3	110	5
METHOD'S MORE SURE AT MOMENTS TO TAKE HOLD	439	2 DON JUAN	5	49	4
AT LEAST SAID JUAN SURE I MAY INQUIRE	454	2 DON JUAN	5	74	4
REPLIED KATINKA I AM SURE I SEE	30	3 DON JUAN	6	48	3
DUDU WAS FOND OF KISSING--WHICH I'M SURE	35	3 DON JUAN	6	59	2
HE HOPED INDEED HE THOUGHT HE COULD BE SURE	58	3 DON JUAN	6	104	1
FIERCE LOVES AND FAITHLESS WARS--I AM NOT SURE	70	3 DON JUAN	7	8	1
HOWEVER THIS MAY BE 'TIS PRETTY SURE	154	3 DON JUAN	8	85	1
IS RATHER DEAR--I'M SURE I MEAN NO HARM	186	3 DON JUAN	9	7	8
EVEN I--ALBEIT I'M SURE I DID NOT KNOW IT	296	3 DON JUAN	11	55	5
A HAZY WIDOWER TURNED OF FORTY'S SURE	333	3 DON JUAN	12	37	5
A DRUNKEN GENTLEMAN OF FORTY'S SURE	333	3 DON JUAN	12	37	V5
WHICH ARE MORE PURE THAN PLEASANT TO BE SURE	335	3 DON JUAN	12	41	4
UPON MY LYRE OR MAKING THE PEGS SURE	341	3 DON JUAN	12	54	7
UPON MY FIDDLE--SEEING IF ALL'S SURE	341	3 DON JUAN	12	54	V7
RESERVE IT) WILL BE VERY SURE TO TAKE	357	3 DON JUAN	12	89	6
OF THIS I'M SURE AT LEAST THERE'S NO SERVILITY	465	3 DON JUAN	15	20	5
SINCE HE WAS SURE HIS MOTHER WOULD FALL SICK	478	3 DON JUAN	15	50	3
THIS MUCH IS SURE THAT OUT OF EARSHOT THINGS	489	3 DON JUAN	15	76	2
AND ONE ON TITHES WHICH SURE ARE DISCORD'S TORCHES	530	3 DON JUAN	16	60	4

SURE (CONTINUED)

	PAGE	VOL	CANTO	STANZA	LN
UNTIL PREFERMENT COMING AT A SURE RATE	540	3 DON JUAN 16	82	4
WERE ANGRY--AS THEY WELL MIGHT TO BE SURE	543	3 DON JUAN 16	89	4
THE WISE MAN'S SURE WHEN HE NO MORE CAN SHARE IT HE	566	3 DON JUAN 17	9	7

SURELY

	PAGE	VOL	CANTO	STANZA	LN
'TWAS SURELY NO CONCERN OF THEIRS NOR MINE	33	2 DON JUAN 1	23	4
THERE SURELY WILL BE LITTLE DOUBT WITH SOME	60	2 DON JUAN 1	70	5
'TIS SURELY JUAN NOW--NO I'M AFRAID	63	2 DON JUAN 1	76	7
AND SURELY WITH A STRIPLING OF SIXTEEN	66	2 DON JUAN 1	83	2
'TWAS SURELY VERY WRONG IN JUAN'S MOTHER	80	2 DON JUAN 1	110	5
SURELY THE WINDOW'S NOT SO VERY HIGH	96	2 DON JUAN 1	137	8
IT SURELY WAS EXCEEDINGLY ILL-BRED	97	2 DON JUAN 1	139	4
'TIS SURELY FAIR TO DINE UPON OUR FRIENDS	200	2 DON JUAN 2	83	6
FOLKS ARE DISCOURAGED AND MOST SURELY NO MEN	205	2 DON JUAN 2	93	5
FOR SURELY IF WE ALWAYS COULD PERCEIVE	270	2 DON JUAN 2	213	2
AH SURELY NOTHING DIES BUT SOMETHING MOURNS	338	2 DON JUAN 3	108	8
NO HIDEOUS SIGN PROCLAIM'D HER SURELY DEAD	377	2 DON JUAN 4	60	4
SURELY 'TIS NOTHING WONDERFUL TO SEE	421	2 DON JUAN 5	20	4
POOR FELLOW FOR SOME REASON SURELY BAD	429	2 DON JUAN 5	34	1
WHICH SURELY WERE INVENTED FOR OUR SINS--	36	3 DON JUAN 6	61	8
YOU SURELY ARE UNWELL CHILD WE MUST SEE	46	3 DON JUAN 6	80	6
LOVE WAR A TEMPEST--SURELY THERE'S VARIETY	416	3 DON JUAN 14	14	1
WITH RUST SHOULD SURELY CEASE TO HACK AND HEW	433	3 DON JUAN 14	53	6
WE SURELY SHALL FIND SOMETHING WORTH RESEARCH	468	3 DON JUAN 15	27	5
AND FALSE--THOUGH TRUE FOR SURELY THEY'RE SINCEREST	547	3 DON JUAN 16	97	7
TO LIFE'S SMALL RUBS SHOULD SURELY BE MORE PLIANT	566	3 DON JUAN 17	10	3

SUREST

	PAGE	VOL	CANTO	STANZA	LN
OF WHICH THE SUREST SIGN IS IN THE END	6	3 DON JUAN 6	1	7
THE SUREST WAY FOR LADIES AND FOR BOOKS	453	3 DON JUAN 14	97	7

SURF

	PAGE	VOL	CANTO	STANZA	LN
TO SHOW ITS BOILING SURF AND BOUNDING SPRAY	211	2 DON JUAN 2	104	6

SURFACE

	PAGE	VOL	CANTO	STANZA	LN
WHICH SKIMS THE SURFACE LEAVING SCARCE A SCAR	335	3 DON JUAN 12	40	6
BENEATH THE SURFACE BUT WHAT DID IT MATTER	474	3 DON JUAN 15	41	6
TO PLAY UPON THE SURFACE OF HUMANITY	482	3 DON JUAN 15	60	2

SURGE

	PAGE	VOL	CANTO	STANZA	LN
FORLORN AND GAZING ON THE DEEP BLUE SURGE	387	2 DON JUAN 4	79	3
HOW LESS WHAT WE MAY BE THE ETERNAL SURGE	500	3 DON JUAN 15	99	4

SURGEON

	PAGE	VOL	CANTO	STANZA	LN
THE SURGEON HAD HIS INSTRUMENTS AND BLED	197	2 DON JUAN 2	76	2
THE SURGEON AS THERE WAS NO OTHER FEE	197	2 DON JUAN 2	77	1
THE REGIMENTAL SURGEON COULD NOT CURE	154	3 DON JUAN 8	85	5
HAUSTUS (AND HERE THE SURGEON CAME AND CUPPED HIM)	244	3 DON JUAN 10	41	4

SURGEON'S

	PAGE	VOL	CANTO	STANZA	LN
THE LAWYER'S BRIEF IS LIKE THE SURGEON'S KNIFE	232	3 DON JUAN 10	14	6

SURGIT

	PAGE	VOL	CANTO	STANZA	LN
(SURGIT AMARI ALIQUID)--THE TOLL	263	3 DON JUAN 10	78	8

SURLY

	PAGE	VOL	CANTO	STANZA	LN
WHICH MUST BE OWNED WAS SENSITIVE AND SURLY	234	3 DON JUAN 10	19	4

SURMISE

	PAGE	VOL	CANTO	STANZA	LN
HER ONLY SON WITH QUESTION OR SURMISE	73	2 DON JUAN 1	97	6
A LESSON IN HER TONGUE BUT BY SURMISE	242	2 DON JUAN 2	163	3
BUT COULD NOT WAKE HE WAS HE DID SURMISE	511	3 DON JUAN 16	25	6

SURMISES

	PAGE	VOL	CANTO	STANZA	LN
SINCE THOU HAST SETTLED BEYOND ALL SURMISES	210	3 DON JUAN 9	55	8

SURMOUNTED

	PAGE	VOL	CANTO	STANZA	LN
SURMOUNTED AS ITS CLASP--A GLOWING CRESCENT	315	2 DON JUAN 3	77	7
SOME DOME SURMOUNTED BY HIS MEAGRE FACE	320	3 DON JUAN 12	10	4

SURPASS

	PAGE	VOL	CANTO	STANZA	LN
IN VIRTUES NOTHING EARTHLY COULD SURPASS HER	30	2 DON JUAN 1	17	7
FEW THINGS SURPASS OLD WINE AND THEY MAY PREACH	250	2 DON JUAN 2	178	5
WHOSE STRAINS--WHATE'ER THEY BE--SURPASS AT LEAST	297	3 DON JUAN 11	57	V7

SURPASS'D

	PAGE	VOL	CANTO	STANZA	LN
AND PRESENT PERIL ALL BEFORE SURPASS'D	188	2 DON JUAN 2	61	6

SURPRISE

	PAGE	VOL	CANTO	STANZA	LN
BUT THAT WHICH CHIEFLY MAY AND MUST SURPRISE	73	2 DON JUAN 1	97	4
TOO MUCH AND WISHING GLADLY TO SURPRISE	294	2 DON JUAN 3	37	2
THEIR OWN PROTECTORS--NOR WAS THEIR SURPRISE	104	3 DON JUAN 7	73	3
AND GAZED ON JUAN WITH A WILD SURPRISE	159	3 DON JUAN 8	95	8
(WHICH SAW ALL WESTERN THINGS WITH SMALL SURPRISE	328	3 DON JUAN 12	27	3
TO THE SURPRISE OF PEOPLE OF CONDITION	328	3 DON JUAN 12	27	4
SURVEYED HIM WITH A KIND OF CALM SURPRISE	514	3 DON JUAN 16	31	8
INDICATIVE OF SOME SURPRISE AND PITY	545	3 DON JUAN 16	93	2
SURPRISE HAS THIS EFFECT--TO MAKE ONE DUMB	557	3 DON JUAN 16	115	2

SURPRISED

	PAGE	VOL	CANTO	STANZA	LN
SURPRISED AT THESE UNWONTED SIGNS OF IDLING	290	2 DON JUAN 3	28	2
(IN GENERAL HE SURPRISED MEN WITH THE SWORD)	294	2 DON JUAN 3	37	3
AT WHICH HE SEEMED NO WHIT SURPRISED NOR GRIEVED	500	2 DON JUAN 5	155	4
CHANGES IN YOUTH TO BE SURPRISED AT ANY	338	3 DON JUAN 12	49	8
AND YOU WILL BE PERHAPS SURPRISED TO FIND	446	3 DON JUAN 14	84	2

SURPRIZE

	PAGE	VOL	CANTO	STANZA	LN
AND YAWNED A GOOD DEAL WITH DISCREET SURPRIZE	42	3 DON JUAN 6	73	8

SURRENDER

	PAGE	VOL	CANTO	STANZA	LN
TO ALL THE PROPOSITIONS OF SURRENDER	165	3 DON JUAN 8	107	2

SURRENDERS

	PAGE	VOL	CANTO	STANZA	LN
THAT SAGE (SAID JOHN) SURRENDERS AT DISCRETION	88	3 DON JUAN 7	44	6

SURROUNDED

	PAGE	VOL	CANTO	STANZA	LN
WITH THE FAR MOUNTAIN-CRESCENT HALF SURROUNDED	252	2 DON JUAN 2	183	5
AND THEN GIVE WAY SUBDUED BECAUSE SURROUNDED	373	2 DON JUAN 4	54	6

SURROUNDED (CONTINUED)
    YOU SHALL HAVE VENGEANCE FOR THE TOWN SURROUNDED . . . . 98 3 DON JUAN 7 61 7
    WHEN MY POOR GREECE WAS ONCE AS NOW SURROUNDED . . . . . 108 3 DON JUAN 7 82 4
SURROUNDING
    OF EYES WHICH PUT OUT EACH SURROUNDING GEM . . . . . . 466 2 DON JUAN 5 96 4
    APART FROM THE SURROUNDING WORLD AND STRONG . . . . . . 477 3 DON JUAN 15 47 7
SURVEY
    HE PAUSED AND TOOK A SURVEY UP AND DOWN . . . . 456 2 DON JUAN 5 78 8
    YOU STARTED BACK IN HORROR TO SURVEY . . . . 462 2 DON JUAN 5 88 2
    WHEN THEY SURVEY WITH CHRISTIAN EYES OR HEATHEN . . . . 24 3 DON JUAN 6 37 7
    FLUSHED WITH A PIOUS FURY TO SURVEY . . . . 262 3 DON JUAN 10 75 V7
    THRICE HAPPY HE WHO AFTER A SURVEY . . . . 303 3 DON JUAN 11 69 1
    BROUGHT TO SURVEY THESE GREY WALLS WHICH THOUGH SO THICK . 529 3 DON JUAN 16 58 3
SURVEYED
    AT SEVEN THEY ROSE HOWEVER AND SURVEYED . . . . . . 81 3 DON JUAN 7 29 1
    AND NOT MUCH SYMPATHY FOR BLOOD SURVEYED . . . . . . 102 3 DON JUAN 7 69 2
    SURVEYED HIM WITH A KIND OF CALM SURPRISE . . . . . . 514 3 DON JUAN 16 31 8
SURVEYING
    SURVEYING DRILLING ORDERING JESTING PONDERING . . . . . 95 3 DON JUAN 7 55 2
SURVIVE
    NEVER COULD SHE SURVIVE THAT COMMON LOSS . . . . 67 2 DON JUAN 1 84 4
    AND I MUST EVEN SURVIVE THIS LAST ADIEU . . . . 134 2 DON JUAN 1 197 7
    SURVIVE THROUGH VERY DESPERATE CONDITIONS . . . . . . 190 2 DON JUAN 2 64 4
    OR I AT LEAST SHALL NOT SURVIVE TO SEE . . . . 356 2 DON JUAN 4 23 8
SURVIVED
    SAT LITTLE LEILA WHO SURVIVED THE PARRIES . . . . . . 249 3 DON JUAN 10 51 4
SURVIVES
    SURVIVES HIMSELF HIS TOMB AND ALL THAT'S HIS . . . . . 327 2 DON JUAN 3 88 8
SURVIVING
    COINED FROM SURVIVING SUPERSTITION'S MINT . . . . . . 510 3 DON JUAN 16 22 5
SURVIVORS
    AND SWIMMERS WHO MAY CHANCE TO BE SURVIVORS . . . . . . 172 2 DON JUAN 2 31 8
SUSPECT
    DARE YOU SUSPECT ME WHOM THE THOUGHT WOULD KILL . . . . 98 2 DON JUAN 1 142 7
    WHEN THEY SUSPECT THAT ANYONE GOES SHARES . . . . . . 11 3 DON JUAN 6 10 7
    BUT I SUSPECT IN FACT THAT WHITE IS BLACK . . . . . 348 3 DON JUAN 12 71 2
SUSPECTS
    BUT STILL NO LESS SUSPECTS IN THE WRONG PLACE . . . . 74 2 DON JUAN 1 99 2
    SUSPECTS WITH ONE DO YOU REPROACH WITH THREE . . . . . 117 2 DON JUAN 1 175 8
SUSPENDED
    SUSPENDED MAY ILLUMINATE MANKIND . . . . 281 3 DON JUAN 11 27 2
SUSPENSE
    WITHOUT THE EXPENSE AND THE SUSPENSE OF BEDDING . . . . 177 3 DON JUAN 8 131 8
    AND KEEPS THE ATROCIOUS READER IN SUSPENSE . . . . . . 453 3 DON JUAN 14 97 6
SUSPICION
    I CAN'T TELL HOW OR WHY OR WHAT SUSPICION . . . . . 97 2 DON JUAN 1 139 1
    WITH MUCH SUSPICION IN HIS ATTITUDE . . . . . . 109 2 DON JUAN 1 160 3
    WITH BASE SUSPICION NOW NO LONGER HAUNTED . . . . . 120 2 DON JUAN 1 180 V6
    BUT THAT THEY WILL NOT DO WITHOUT SUSPICION . . . . . 50 3 DON JUAN 6 88 3
    WITHOUT EXCITING SUCH SUSPICION AS . . . . 57 3 DON JUAN 6 103 7
    IN FACT IF NOT IN RANK AND THE SUSPICION . . . . . . 208 3 DON JUAN 9 52 5
    HAS MUCH OF SELFISHNESS AND MORE SUSPICION . . . . . . 420 3 DON JUAN 14 24 6
    SUSPICION THOUGH NOT TIMID HIS REGARD . . . . 462 3 DON JUAN 15 14 2
SUSPICIOUS
    A REAL HUSBAND ALWAYS IS SUSPICIOUS . . . . 74 2 DON JUAN 1 99 1
    SUSPICIOUS PEOPLE WHO FIND FAULT IN HASTE . . . . . . 230 3 DON JUAN 10 11 3
SUSTAIN'D
    FOR LOVE MUST BE SUSTAIN'D LIKE FLESH AND BLOOD-- . . . 246 2 DON JUAN 2 170 4
    SUSTAIN'D HIS HEAD UPON HER BOSOM'S CHARMS . . . . . 260 2 DON JUAN 2 195 4
SUVAROFF
    BY SUVAROFF OR ANGLICE SUWARROW . . . . 70 3 DON JUAN 7 8 7
SUWARROW
    BY SUVAROFF OR ANGLICE SUWARROW . . . . 70 3 DON JUAN 7 8 7
    IN THIS PLAIN PAIR SUWARROW AND HIS GUIDE . . . . . . 87 3 DON JUAN 7 43 8
    O'ER WHOM SUWARROW SHONE LIKE A GAS LAMP . . . . . . 89 3 DON JUAN 7 46 5
    SUWARROW CHIEFLY WAS ON THE ALERT . . . . 95 3 DON JUAN 7 55 1
    SUWARROW WHO WAS STANDING IN HIS SHIRT . . . . . . 96 3 DON JUAN 7 58 1
    SUWARROW WHEN HE SAW THIS COMPANY . . . . 97 3 DON JUAN 7 59 1
    LOW AS THE COMPLIMENT DESERVED SUWARROW . . . . . . 99 3 DON JUAN 7 63 2
    SUWARROW THOUGH ENGAGED WITH ACCENTS HIGH . . . . . . 100 3 DON JUAN 7 65 3
    SUWARROW WHO HAD SMALL REGARD FOR TEARS . . . . . . 102 3 DON JUAN 7 69 1
    WILL TOUCH EVEN HEROES AND SUCH WAS SUWARROW . . . . . 102 3 DON JUAN 7 69 8
    SUWARROW--WHO BUT SAW THINGS IN THE GROSS . . . . . . 105 3 DON JUAN 7 77 1
    SUWARROW NOW WAS CONQUEROR--A MATCH . . . . 178 3 DON JUAN 8 133 1
SUWARROW'S
    AND TAKING LATELY BY SUWARROW'S BIDDING . . . . . . 418 2 DON JUAN 5 15 7
    SHE SMILED AT MAD SUWARROW'S RHYMES WHO THREW . . . . 212 3 DON JUAN 9 60 2
SWAIN
    SHEPHERD OR SWAIN WHOEVER MAY BEHOLD . . . . 506 3 DON JUAN 16 14 2
SWALLOW
    TO SWALLOW FLAME AND NEVER TAKE IT ILL . . . . . . 93 3 DON JUAN 7 52 6
    TO SWALLOW FLAME AND NEITHER SWERVE NOR SPILL . . . . . 93 3 DON JUAN 7 52 V6
SWALLOW'D
    THOUGH SWALLOW'D WITH MUCH ZEST UPON THE WHOLE . . . . 484 3 DON JUAN 15 66 4
SWALLOWED
    KILLED BECAUSE WHAT HE SWALLOWED WOULD NOT PASS . . . . 199 3 DON JUAN 9 33 V8
SWALLOWING
    SAID JUAN--SWALLOWING A HEART-BURNING SIGH . . . . . 423 2 DON JUAN 5 24 3
    AND AFTER SWALLOWING DOWN A SLIGHT REFECTION . . . . . 452 2 DON JUAN 5 71 3
    AND SWALLOWING EULOGY MUCH MORE THAN SATIRE HE . . . . 185 3 DON JUAN 9 5 5

```
                                                          PAGE VOL      CANTO STANZA LN
SWAM
    THE VESSEL SWAM YET STILL SHE HELD HER OWN  . . . . . .  176  2 DON JUAN   2    38   4
    STILL SWAM--THOUGH NOT EXACTLY LIKE A DUCK . . . . . .   177  2 DON JUAN   2    40   8
    SWAM ROUND AND ROUND AND ALL HIS SENSES PASS'D . . . .   214  2 DON JUAN   2   110   3
SWAMP'D
    AND THE POOR LITTLE CUTTER QUICKLY SWAMP'D . . . . . .   188  2 DON JUAN   2    60   8
SWAMPING
    BY SWAMPING ONE OF THE PRIZES HE HAD CHAIN'D  . . . .    283  2 DON JUAN   3    15   5
SWAN
    HAS TAKEN FOR A SWAN ROGUE SOUTHEY'S GANDER . . . . .    298  3 DON JUAN  11    59   8
SWAN-LIKE
    THERE SWAN-LIKE LET ME SING AND DIE  . . . . . . .      326  2 DON JUAN   3  L 16   4
SWARMING
    WHICH BEING JOIN'D LIKE SWARMING BEES THEY CLUNG-- . . . 254  2 DON JUAN   2   187   7
SWARTHY
    THAT SWARTHY SPORUS NEITHER MAN NOR BARD . . . . . .    297  3 DON JUAN  11    58   5
SWATHED
    BAPTIZED IN MOLTEN GOLD AND SWATHED IN DUN . . . . .    205  2 DON JUAN   2    92   4
SWAY
    IMMORAL CONDUCT BY THE FANCIED SWAY . . . . . . .        84  2 DON JUAN   1   116   3
    SUCH IS THE SWAY OF YOUR GREAT MEN O'ER LITTLE . . . .    90  3 DON JUAN   7    48   8
    SOVEREIGNS MAY SWAY MATERIALS BUT NOT MATTER . . . .     236  3 DON JUAN  10    24   7
    SOME PERSONS THINK THAT COLERIDGE HATH THE SWAY . . .    298  3 DON JUAN  11    59   5
    HE STILL RETAINS HIS SWAY . . . . . . . . .             520  3 DON JUAN  16  L  5   2
SWAYS
    HIGH GROUND AS VIRGIN CYNTHIA SWAYS THE TIDES . . . .    322  3 DON JUAN  17    14   6
    THE OCEAN'S TIDES AND MORTAL'S BRAINS SHE SWAYS . . .    506  3 DON JUAN  16    14   7
SWEAR
    YOU'DE SWEAR HIS VERY HEART HAD SWEATED THROUGH  . . .   154  2 DON JUAN   1  V  5   8
    AND OH IF E'ER I SHOULD FORGET I SWEAR-- . . . . . .    166  2 DON JUAN   2    19   1
    WHY THEN I'LL SWEAR AS POET WORDY SWORE . . . . . .     404  2 DON JUAN   4   109   5
    I'LL SWEAR--AS MOTHER WORDSWORTH SWORE  . . . . . .     404  2 DON JUAN   4   109  V5
    SWEAR THAT PAT'S LANGUAGE SPRUNG FROM THE SAME CLIME . . 122  3 DON JUAN   8    23   5
    IT IS  I WILL NOT SWEAR THAT BLACK IS WHITE . . . .     348  3 DON JUAN  12    71   1
    BUT BY THE GODS I SWEAR THAT WHITE IS BLACK . . . .     348  3 DON JUAN  12    71  V2
    WHICH THOSE MOST SWEAR TO WHO BELIEVE THEM MOST)-- . .   383  3 DON JUAN  13    53   3
    OR IF THE OATH SEEM STRONG--I SWEAR BY JOVE . . . .     452  3 DON JUAN  14    96  V2
    BUT WILL NOT SWEAR YET BOTH UPON OCCASION . . . . .     458  3 DON JUAN  15     6   7
SWEARING
    TEARING AND GRINNING HOWLING SCREECHING SWEARING . . .   198  2 DON JUAN   2    79   7
    AND THEN HE SWORE AGAIN BUT SWEARING DREW . . . . .     455  2 DON JUAN   5    76  V7
    EXCLAIMING FOOLING SWEARING AT THE INERT . . . . .      96  3 DON JUAN   7    58   3
    AND SWEARING IF THE INFANT CAME TO ILL . . . . . .     162  3 DON JUAN   8   102   5
    PLATONIC BLASPHEMY THE SOUL OF SWEARING . . . . . .    289  3 DON JUAN  11    43   8
SWEARS
    AND THEN THE MOTHER CRIES THE FATHER SWEARS . . . .     75  2 DON JUAN   1   100   7
    OR SWEARS THAT CERES HATH BEGOTTEN FAMINE . . . . .     88  3 DON JUAN   7    45   8
    AT FIRST IT GRUMBLES THEN IT SWEARS AND THEN . . . .   138  3 DON JUAN   8    51   1
SWEAT
    A PEASANT'S SWEAT IS WORTH HIS LORD'S ESTATE . . . .    190  3 DON JUAN   9    15   6
    AND DIG AND SWEAT AND TURN THEMSELVES ABOUT . . . .     202  3 DON JUAN   9    40   3
SWEATED
    YOU'DE SWEAR HIS VERY HEART HAD SWEATED THROUGH  . . .   154  2 DON JUAN   1  V  5   8
SWEATING
    FIRING AND THRUSTING SLASHING SWEATING GLOWING . . .    120  3 DON JUAN   8    19   6
SWEATY
    TO LOSE THOSE BEST MONTHS IN A SWEATY CITY . . . . .    380  3 DON JUAN  13    48   4
SWEDISH
    AS OBSTINATE AS SWEDISH CHARLES AT BENDER . . . . .     165  3 DON JUAN   8   107   4
SWEEP
    BY DISTANCE MELLOW'D O'ER THE WATERS SWEEP . . . . .     87  2 DON JUAN   1   122   4
    LOVELY SEEM'D ANY OBJECT THAT SHOULD SWEEP . . . . .    210  2 DON JUAN   2   103   7
    MAY HEAR OUR MUTUAL MURMURS SWEEP  . . . . . . .       326  2 DON JUAN   3  L 16   3
    IF HE MUST FAIN SWEEP O'ER THE ETHERIAL PLAIN . . . .   333  3 DON JUAN   3    99   1
    AND SWEPT AS GALES SWEEP FOAM AWAY WHOLE RANKS . . .    134  3 DON JUAN   8    44   3
    WITH A SOFT BESOM WILL I SWEEP YOUR HALLS . . . . .     266  3 DON JUAN  10    84   7
SWEEPING
    SWEEPING THE MARBLE UNDERNEATH HER CHAIR . . . . .     60  3 DON JUAN   6   108   3
    ARE THEY--NOW FURIOUS AS THE SWEEPING WAVE . . . . .    164  3 DON JUAN   8   106   5
SWEEPS
    EVEN AS THE SIMOOM SWEEPS THE BLASTED PLAINS  . . .     375  2 DON JUAN   4    57   8
    THE GALE SWEEPS THROUGH ITS FRETWORK AND OFT SINGS . .   387  3 DON JUAN  13    62   6
    SAD BUT SERENE IT SWEEPS O'ER TREE OR TOWER . . . .     388  3 DON JUAN  13    64   6
    HE SWEEPS ALONG IN HIS DUSKY PALL  . . . . . . .       520  3 DON JUAN  16  L  6   3
SWEEPSTAKES
    UPON THE SWEEPSTAKES FOR SUBSTANTIAL WIVES . . . . .    333  3 DON JUAN  12    36   4
SWEET
    ETHERIAL LUSTRE WITH WHAT SWEET PERSUASION . . . .     65  2 DON JUAN   1    81   6
    WE'LL TALK OF THAT ANON--'TIS SWEET TO HEAR . . . .     87  2 DON JUAN   1   122   1
    'TIS SWEET TO SEE THE EVENING STAR APPEAR . . . . .     87  2 DON JUAN   1   122   5
    'TIS SWEET TO LISTEN AS THE NIGHTWINDS CREEP . . . .    87  2 DON JUAN   1   122   6
    FROM LEAF TO LEAF 'TIS SWEET TO VIEW ON HIGH . . . .    87  2 DON JUAN   1   122   7
    'TIS SWEET TO HEAR THE WATCHDOG'S HONEST BARK . . . .   88  2 DON JUAN   1   123   1
    'TIS SWEET TO KNOW THERE IS AN EYE WILL MARK . . . .    88  2 DON JUAN   1   123   3
    'TIS SWEET TO BE AWAKEN'D BY THE LARK  . . . . . .      88  2 DON JUAN   1   123   5
    OR LULL'D BY FALLING WATERS SWEET THE HUM . . . . .     88  2 DON JUAN   1   123   6
    SWEET IS THE VINTAGE WHEN THE SHOWERING GRAPES . . .    88  2 DON JUAN   1   124   1
    PURPLE AND GUSHING SWEET ARE OUR ESCAPES . . . . .     88  2 DON JUAN   1   124   3
    SWEET TO THE MISER ARE HIS GLITTERING HEAPS . . . .    88  2 DON JUAN   1   124   5
```

SWEET (CONTINUED)
```
SWEET TO THE FATHER IS HIS FIRST-BORN'S BIRTH . . . . .  88  2 DON JUAN  1   124   6
SWEET IS REVENGE--ESPECIALLY TO WOMEN . . . . . . . . .  88  2 DON JUAN  1   124   7
SWEET IS A LEGACY AND PASSING SWEET . . . . . . . . . .  89  2 DON JUAN  1   125   1
SWEET IS A LEGACY AND PASSING SWEET . . . . . . . . . .  89  2 DON JUAN  1   125   1
'TIS SWEET TO WIN NO MATTER HOW ONE'S LAURELS . . . . .  90  2 DON JUAN  1   126   1
BY BLOOD OR INK 'TIS SWEET TO PUT AN END . . . . . . .   90  2 DON JUAN  1   126   2
TO STRIFE 'TIS SOMETIMES SWEET TO HAVE OUR QUARRELS . .  90  2 DON JUAN  1   126   3
SWEET IS OLD WINE IN BOTTLES ALE IN BARRELS . . . . . .  90  2 DON JUAN  1   126   5
AND SUCH SWEET GIRLS--I MEAN SUCH GRACEFUL LADIES . . . 159  2 DON JUAN  2     5   5
SWEETS TO THE SWEET (I LIKE SO MUCH TO QUOTE . . . . . 165  2 DON JUAN  2    17   3
MIGHT NOT HAVE THOUGHT THE SCANTY DRAUGHT SO SWEET . . . 201  2 DON JUAN  2    85   6
AND HAVING LEARNT TO SWIM IN THAT SWEET RIVER . . . . . 211  2 DON JUAN  2   105   3
SHORT UPPER LIP--SWEET LIPS THAT MAKE US SIGH . . . . . 218  2 DON JUAN  2   118   3
SWEET SKIES JUST WHEN HE RISES OR IS SET . . . . . . . 230  2 DON JUAN  2   139   3
TO THE SWEET PORTRAITS OF THE VIRGIN MARY . . . . . . . 235  2 DON JUAN  2   149   8
WITH AN IONIAN ACCENT LOW AND SWEET . . . . . . . . . . 236  2 DON JUAN  2   150   7
SO SOFT SO SWEET SO DELICATELY CLEAR . . . . . . . . . 236  2 DON JUAN  2   151   4
AS O'ER A BED OF ROSES THE SWEET SOUTH . . . . . . . . 245  2 DON JUAN  2   168   8
IS IN ITS CAUSE AS ITS EFFECT SO SWEET . . . . . . . . 264  2 DON JUAN  2   203   3
OVER THE INNOCENCE OF THAT SWEET CHILD . . . . . . . . 302  2 DON JUAN  3    52   7
SWEET HOUR OF TWILIGHT--IN THE SOLITUDE . . . . . . . . 337  2 DON JUAN  3   105   1
WHEN THEY FROM THEIR SWEET FRIENDS ARE TORN APART . . . 338  2 DON JUAN  3   108   3
TO THEIR OWN HEARTS' MOST SWEET SOCIETY . . . . . . . . 348  2 DON JUAN  4     8   2
SWEET PLAYFUL PHRASES WHICH WOULD SEEM ABSURD . . . . . 351  2 DON JUAN  4    14   7
BUT ALMOST SANCTIFY THE SWEET EXCESS . . . . . . . . . 357  2 DON JUAN  4    26   7
AND HAIDEE'S SWEET LIPS MURMUR'D LIKE A BROOK . . . . . 359  2 DON JUAN  4    29   6
WHICH SHE ESSAY'D IN VAIN TO CLEAR (HOW SWEET . . . . . 362  2 DON JUAN  4    34   3
AND SWEET SENSATIONS SHOULD HAVE WELCOMED BOTH . . . . 368  2 DON JUAN  4    45   7
SWEET NAIAD OF THE PHLEGETHONTIC RILL . . . . . . . . . 372  2 DON JUAN  4    53   2
BUT THOU--OH SWEET FURY OF THE FIERY RILL . . . . . . . 372  2 DON JUAN  4    53  V2
A VEIN HAD BURST AND HER SWEET LIPS' PURE DYES . . . . 376  2 DON JUAN  4    59   1
ALL HOPE TO LOOK UPON HER SWEET FACE BRED . . . . . . . 377  2 DON JUAN  4    60   6
HER SWEET FACE INTO SHADOW DULL AND SLOW . . . . . . . 381  2 DON JUAN  4    69   6
A VOICE OF NO GREAT COMPASS AND NOT SWEET . . . . . . . 392  2 DON JUAN  4    89   4
FOR ONE CIRCASSIAN A SWEET GIRL WERE GIVEN . . . . . . 407  2 DON JUAN  4   114   2
HER VERY SMILE WAS HAUGHTY THOUGH SO SWEET . . . . . . 475  2 DON JUAN  5   111   1
KISSES SWEET WORDS EMBRACES AND ALL THAT . . . . . . .  13  3 DON JUAN  6    14   2
WHOM IF THEY WERE AT HOME IN SWEET CIRCASSIA . . . . .  25  3 DON JUAN  6    39   7
DUDU AS HAS BEEN SAID WAS A SWEET CREATURE . . . . . .  32  3 DON JUAN  6    52   1
RETIRED INTO HER BOUDOIR A SWEET PLACE . . . . . . . .  54  3 DON JUAN  6    97   2
AND THE SWEET CONSEQUENCE OF LARGE SOCIETY . . . . . . 146  3 DON JUAN  8    68   3
BUT JUAN TURNED HIS EYES ON THE SWEET CHILD . . . . . . 199  3 DON JUAN  9    33   1
THE WHOLE COURT LOOKED IMMEDIATELY MOST SWEET . . . . . 213  3 DON JUAN  9    61   3
HER SWEET SMILE AND HER THEN MAJESTIC FIGURE . . . . . 218  3 DON JUAN  9    72   1
IN ALL THE ROYALTY OF SWEET SEVENTEEN . . . . . . . . . 236  3 DON JUAN 10    24   6
ON THAT SWEET ORE WHICH EVERYBODY NURSES . . . . . . . 264  3 DON JUAN 10    79   6
HER VOICE THOUGH SWEET IS NOT SO FIT TO WARBLE . . . . 350  3 DON JUAN 12    75   5
SWEET ADELINE AMIDST THE GAY WORLD'S HUM . . . . . . . 365  3 DON JUAN 13    13   4
AND ROBES SWEET FRIENDSHIP IN A BRUSSELS LACE . . . . . 430  3 DON JUAN 14    47   4
WHICH PRETTY WOMEN--THE SWEET SOULS--CALL SOUL . . . . 441  3 DON JUAN 14    71   3
AN ARROW FOR THE HEART LIKE A SWEET VOICE . . . . . . . 461  3 DON JUAN 15    13   8
O'ER LIFE TOO SWEET AN IMAGE FOR SUCH GLASS . . . . . . 475  3 DON JUAN 15    43   6
SO FAR RELAX'D HER THOUGHTS FROM THEIR SWEET PRISON . . 491  3 DON JUAN 15    80   7
SWEET SOUL--SHE WAS SO VERY INNOCENT . . . . . . . . . 493  3 DON JUAN 15    83  V8
ADDED HER SWEET VOICE TO THE LYRIC SOUND . . . . . . . 518  3 DON JUAN 16    40   6
MEANWHILE SWEET ADELINE DESERVED THEIR PRAISES . . . . 550  3 DON JUAN 16   103   1
HOW SWEET THE TASK TO SHIELD AN ABSENT FRIEND . . . . . 552  3 DON JUAN 16   104   7
OF THOSE SWEET BITTER THOUGHTS WHICH BANISH SLEEP . . . 555  3 DON JUAN 16   110   7
THE GHOST HAD A REMARKABLY SWEET BREATH . . . . . . . . 560  3 DON JUAN 16   121   4
THE GHOST IF GHOST IT WERE SEEMED A SWEET SOUL . . . . 561  3 DON JUAN 16   123   1
```
SWEETBREADS
```
AND SAFFRON SOUPS AND SWEETBREADS AND THE FISHES . . . . 307  2 DON JUAN  3    62   3
```
SWEETER
```
SHE LOOK'D A SADNESS SWEETER THAN HER SMILE . . . . . .  61  2 DON JUAN  1    72   2
AND STOLEN GLANCES SWEETER FOR THE THEFT . . . . . . .  62  2 DON JUAN  1    74   2
BUT SWEETER STILL THAN THIS THAN THESE THAN ALL . . . .  90  2 DON JUAN  1   127   1
FAR SWEETER THAN THE GREENEST LAURELS SPRUNG . . . . . 199  3 DON JUAN  9    34   4
```
SWEETEST
```
THE SWEETEST SONG-BIRDS NESTLE IN A PAIR . . . . . . . 358  2 DON JUAN  4    28   6
INTO ONE OF THE SWEETEST OF HOTELS . . . . . . . . . . 283  3 DON JUAN 11    31   1
A ROSE WITH ALL ITS SWEETEST LEAVES YET FOLDED . . . . 475  3 DON JUAN 15    43   8
```
SWEETLY
```
THAT LIKE AN INFANT JUAN SWEETLY SLEPT . . . . . . . . 232  2 DON JUAN  2   143   3
SHORTLY AND SWEETLY THE MASONIC FOLLY . . . . . . . . . 448  2 DON JUAN  5    63   2
HOW SWEETLY ON THE EAR SUCH ECHOES SOUND . . . . . . . 114  3 DON JUAN  8     5   5
HERE SWEETLY SPREAD A LANDSCAPE OF LORRAINE . . . . . . 392  3 DON JUAN 13    72   1
```
SWEETNESS
```
AS SWEETNESS TO THE FLOWER OR SALT TO OCEAN . . . . . .  51  2 DON JUAN  1    55   6
TO DOUBLE EVEN THE SWEETNESS OF A FLOWER . . . . . . . 144  2 DON JUAN  1   214   8
HER FEATURES ALL THE SWEETNESS OF THE DEVIL . . . . . . 474  2 DON JUAN  5   109   2
```
SWEETS
```
SWEETS TO THE SWEET (I LIKE SO MUCH TO QUOTE . . . . . 165  2 DON JUAN  2    17   3
THE PROMISED PARTY TO ENJOY ITS SWEETS . . . . . . . . 394  3 DON JUAN 13    75   2
SOME ACIDS WITH THE SWEETS--FOR SHE WAS HEADY . . . . . 482  3 DON JUAN 15    61   4
'TIS TRUE THERE BE SOME BITTERS WITH THE SWEETS . . . . 502  3 DON JUAN 16     3   5
```
SWELL
```
THEIR VERY WALK WOULD MAKE YOUR BOSOM SWELL . . . . . . 159  2 DON JUAN  2     5   6
AND HER PROUD BROW'S BLUE VEINS TO SWELL AND DARKLE . .  56  3 DON JUAN  6   101   8
```

		PAGE	VOL	CANTO	STANZA	LN

SWELL   (CONTINUED)
YOUR FORTUNE WAS IN A FAIR WAY TO SWELL . . . . 214 3 DON JUAN 9   63 6
A THOROUGH VARMINT AND A REAL SWELL . . . . 276 3 DON JUAN 11   17 6
SO PRIME SO SWELL SO NUTTY AND SO KNOWING . . . . . . 277 3 DON JUAN 11   19 8
THERE WANTED BUT THIS REQUISITE TO SWELL . . . . 295 3 DON JUAN 11   53 5
INTO A SCENE AND SWELL THE CLIENTS' CLAN . . . . 437 3 DON JUAN 14   62 4
SWELLING
HIS BREATH--HE FROM HIS SWELLING THROAT UNTIED . . . . 276 3 DON JUAN 11   16 7
SWELLS
FOR THOSE WHOM FAVOUR OR WHOM FORTUNE SWELLS . . . . . 283 3 DON JUAN 11   31 3
SWEPT
THERE HIS FEW PEACEFUL DAYS TIME HAD SWEPT O'ER . . . . 302 2 DON JUAN 3   52 5
AND SWEPT AS 'TWERE ACROSS THEIR HEART'S DELIGHT . . . 355 2 DON JUAN 4   21 3
ARE SWEPT AWAY AND TOMB INHERITS TOMB . . . . 399 2 DON JUAN 4 102 2
THE WIND SWEPT DOWN THE EUXINE AND THE WAVE . . . . . 413 2 DON JUAN 5   5 1
AND SWEPT AS GALES SWEEP FOAM AWAY WHOLE RANKS . . . . 134 3 DON JUAN 8   44 3
THE BRANCHING STAG SWEPT DOWN WITH ALL HIS HERD . . . 384 3 DON JUAN 13   56 7
SWERVE
TO SWALLOW FLAME AND NEITHER SWERVE NOR SPILL . . . . 93 3 DON JUAN 7   52 V6
SWIFT
FOR SO IT SEEMS TO LOVERS SWIFT OR SLOW . . . . 14 3 DON JUAN 6   17 2
BY SWIFT BY MACHIAVEL BY ROCHEFOUCAULT . . . . 68 3 DON JUAN 7   4 1
AND TALL AND STRONG AND SWIFT OF FOOT WERE THEY . . . 145 3 DON JUAN 8   66 1
LIKE SWIFT CAMILLA HE SCARCE SKIMM'D THE GROUND . . . 427 3 DON JUAN 14   39 3
SWIFTEST
NE'ER WITH SUCH FORCE THE SWIFTEST ARROW FLEW . . . . 218 2 DON JUAN 2 117 6
SWIFTLY
HURRAH HOW SWIFTLY SPEEDS THE POST SO MERRY . . . . . 260 3 DON JUAN 10   71 3
THE DOOR FLEW WIDE NOT SWIFTLY--BUT AS FLY . . . . . . 558 3 DON JUAN 16 117 1
SWIM
THE SHIP WOULD SWIM AN HOUR WHICH BY GOOD LUCK . . . . 177 2 DON JUAN 2   40 7
AND HAVING LEARNT TO SWIM IN THAT SWEET RIVER . . . . 211 2 DON JUAN 2 105 3
AS FOR THE OTHER TWO THEY COULD NOT SWIM . . . . 212 2 DON JUAN 2 106 7
TO SWIM OR SINK--I HAVE HAD AT LEAST MY DREAM . . . . 415 3 DON JUAN 14   11 8
SWIMMER
OF SOME STRONG SWIMMER IN HIS AGONY . . . . 184 2 DON JUAN 2   53 8
A BETTER SWIMMER YOU COULD SCARCE SEE EVER . . . . . . 211 2 DON JUAN 2 105 5
SWIMMERS
AND SWIMMERS WHO MAY CHANCE TO BE SURVIVORS . . . . . 172 2 DON JUAN 2   31 8
SWIMMING
AT LAST WITH SWIMMING WADING SCRAMBLING HE . . . . . . 212 2 DON JUAN 2 107 7
AND SLOWLY BY HIS SWIMMING EYES WAS SEEN . . . . 215 2 DON JUAN 2 112 7
WITH SWIMMING LOOKS OF SPEECHLESS TENDERNESS . . . . . 357 2 DON JUAN 4   26 2
MEANTIME THESE TWO POOR GIRLS WITH SWIMMING EYES . . . 104 3 DON JUAN 7   73 1
NOW SWIMMING IN THE SENTIMENT OF JOY . . . . 123 3 DON JUAN 8   24 3
AND SWIMMING LONG IN THE ABYSS OF THOUGHT . . . . . . 191 3 DON JUAN 9   18 5
SWINE
MUST END IN LANGUOR--MEN WON'T SLEEP LIKE SWINE-- . . 343 2 DON JUAN 3 V 98 4
A MOSQUE SO NOBLE FLUNG LIKE PEARLS TO SWINE . . . . . 262 3 DON JUAN 10   75 8
SWING
TO SWING A LITTLE LESS FROM SIDE TO SIDE . . . . 464 2 DON JUAN 5   91 6
SWISS
OR SWISS ROUSSEAU CRY VOILA LA PERVENCHE . . . . 442 3 DON JUAN 14   75 8
SWOLN
THEIR THROATS WERE OVENS THEIR SWOLN TONGUES WERE BLACK . 202 2 DON JUAN 2   86 3
SWOON
MUST SINK AT LAST INTO A SWOON DIVINE-- . . . . 343 2 DON JUAN 3 V 98 6
SWOON'D
ANTONIA IN HYSTERICS JULIA SWOON'D . . . . 125 2 DON JUAN 1 187 3
SWOOP
FOR THERE WE HAVE THEM ALL AT ONE FELL SWOOP . . . . . 46 2 DON JUAN 1   45 1
SWORD
AND SUMMON LACKEYS ARM'D WITH FIRE AND SWORD . . . . . 97 2 DON JUAN 1 139 7
OH VALIANT MAN WITH SWORD DRAWN AND COCK'D TRIGGER . . 103 2 DON JUAN 1 150 7
HE LEFT THE ROOM FOR HIS RELINQUISH'D SWORD . . . . . 121 2 DON JUAN 1 182 1
ALFONSO'S SWORD HAD DROPP'D ERE HE COULD DRAW IT . . . 123 2 DON JUAN 1 185 1
SWORD GOWN GAIN GLORY OFFER IN EXCHANGE . . . . 131 2 DON JUAN 1 194 4
(IN GENERAL HE SURPRISED MEN WITH THE SWORD) . . . . . 294 2 DON JUAN 3   37 3
PUT UP YOUNG MAN PUT UP YOUR SILLY SWORD . . . . 364 2 DON JUAN 4   37 8
YOUNG MAN YOUR SWORD SO LAMBRO ONCE MORE SAID . . . . 365 2 DON JUAN 4   40 1
THOSE SCOUNDRELS WHO HAVE NEVER HAD A SWORD IN . . . . 498 2 DON JUAN 5 151 4
ALL WAS PREPARED--THE FIRE THE SWORD THE MEN . . . . . 113 3 DON JUAN 8   2 1
STARS MEDALS AND A BLOODY SWORD IN HAND . . . . 141 3 DON JUAN 8   57 6
NOR SWORD NOR SORROW YET HAD LEFT A TRACE . . . . . . 145 3 DON JUAN 8   65 4
THERE'S NOT A MOSLEM THAT HATH YIELDED SWORD . . . . . 155 3 DON JUAN 8   87 2
SUPPOSE HIM SWORD BY SIDE AND HAT IN HAND . . . . . . 204 3 DON JUAN 9   44 1
HIS SIDE AS A SMALL SWORD BUT SHARP AS EVER . . . . . 205 3 DON JUAN 9   45 4
WHICH SHALL LAY BARE HER BOSOM TO THE SWORD . . . . . 258 3 DON JUAN 10   67 4
A GOLDEN SCABBARD ON A DAMASQUE SWORD . . . . 422 3 DON JUAN 14   27 5
WITH SWORD IN HAND AND TORCH TO LIGHT . . . . 518 3 DON JUAN 16 L 2 3
SWORDER
THE THIRD A WARY COOL OLD SWORDER TOOK . . . . 370 2 DON JUAN 4   49 2
SWORDS
ARRAS THEY PRICK'D AND CURTAINS WITH THEIR SWORDS . . . 99 2 DON JUAN 1 143 7
ON EACH HARANGUE DEPENDS SOME HOSTILE SWORDS . . . . . 153 2 DON JUAN 1 V 4 3
IN NATIVE SWORDS AND NATIVE RANKS . . . . 325 2 DON JUAN 3 L 14 3
TO STAIN HIS PEDIGREE A THOUSAND SWORDS . . . . 471 2 DON JUAN 5 104 5
WHICH HANDS OR PENS HAVE EVER TRACED OF SWORDS . . . . 179 3 DON JUAN 8 134 3
ALTHOUGH THE HIGHEST BUT AS SWORDS HAVE HILTS . . . . 342 3 DON JUAN 12   56 3

SWORDSMAN
    A GREAT TACTICIAN AND NO LESS A SWORDSMAN 399   3 DON JUAN 13   88   3
SWORE
    FOR DON ALFONSO AND SHE INLY SWORE 80   2 DON JUAN 1   109   2
    SWORE LUSTILY HE'D BE REVENGED THIS NIGHT 122   2 DON JUAN 1   184   5
    AS WHEN HE SWORE BY GOD HE'D SELL HIS SHIRT 154   2 DON JUAN 1   V 5   3
    THE WIND SUNG CORDAGE STRAIN'D AND SAILORS SWORE . . . 163   2 DON JUAN 2   13   2
    SOME SWORE THAT THEY HEARD BREAKERS OTHERS GUNS . . . 207   2 DON JUAN 2   96   7
    WHEN HE WHO HAD THE WATCH SUNG OUT AND SWORE 207   2 DON JUAN 2   97   2
    AND CALL'D HER FATHER'S OLD SLAVES UP WHO SWORE . . . 229   2 DON JUAN 2   138   6
    WHO SWORE HIS VOICE WAS VERY RICH AND MELLOW 391   2 DON JUAN 4   87   6
    WHY THEN I'LL SWEAR AS POET WORDY SWORE 404   2 DON JUAN 4   109   5
    I'LL SWEAR--AS MOTHER WORDSWORTH SWORE 404   2 DON JUAN 4   109   V5
    THEY HAGGLED WRANGLED SWORE TOO--SO THEY DID 425   2 DON JUAN 5   28   4
    AND THEN HE SWORE AGAIN BUT SWEARING DREW 455   2 DON JUAN 5   76   V7
    AND THEN HE SWORE AND SIGHING ON HE SLIPPED 456   2 DON JUAN 5   77   1
    BUT NOT BY BABA'S FAULT HE SAID AND SWORE ON 57   3 DON JUAN 6   102   7
    SWORE THEY SHOULD SEE HIM BY THE DAWN OF DAY 105   3 DON JUAN 7   75   5
    IN VAIN HE KICKED AND SWORE AND WRITHED AND BLED . . . 153   3 DON JUAN 8   83   5
    THAT FUTURE BRIDEGROOMS SWORE AND SIGHED AND PAID IT . . 293   3 DON JUAN 11   49   8
    SWORE PRAISES AND RECALL'D THEIR FORMER FIRES 425   3 DON JUAN 14   34   6
SWORN
    TO THIS MY PLAIN SWORN DOWNRIGHT DETESTATION 194   3 DON JUAN 9   24   7
SWUNG
    WHILE SWUNG THE DEEP BELL IN THE DISTANT TOWER 335   2 DON JUAN 3   102   5
    WHILE SWUNG THE SIGNAL FROM THE SACRED TOWER 335   2 DON JUAN 3   102   V5
    AND THEN SWUNG BACK NOR CLOSE--BUT STOOD AWRY 558   3 DON JUAN 16   117   3
SYBARITE'S
    DREST TO A SYBARITE'S MOST PAMPER'D WISHES 307   2 DON JUAN 3   62   5
    SOFTER WHEN THE SOFT SYBARITE'S WHO CRIED 50   3 DON JUAN 6   89   2
SYCOPHANT
    THE PEOPLE'S SYCOPHANT THE PRINCE'S FOE 151   2 DON JUAN 1   V 2   7
    THE PEOPLE'S SYCOPHANT--TILL DANGER COMES 151   2 DON JUAN 1   V 2   V7
    THE PEOPLE'S SYCOPHANT--IN JUSTICE'S HOUR 151   2 DON JUAN 1   V 2   V7
SYCOPHANTS
    TYRANTS AND SYCOPHANTS HAVE BEEN AND ARE 194   3 DON JUAN 9   24   4
SYLLA
    OF ALL MEN SAVING SYLLA THE MAN-SLAYER 143   3 DON JUAN 8   61   1
SYLLABLE
    AND SCORN TO ADD A SYLLABLE UNTRUE 41   3 DON JUAN 6   70   3
    AN ECHO OF A SYLLABLE THAT'S WRONG 336   3 DON JUAN 12   43   5
SYLLABLES
    SOUNDS THE HEROIC SYLLABLES BOTH WAYS 183   3 DON JUAN 9   1   2
SYLPH-LIKE
    DISPLAY'D SOME SYLPH-LIKE FIGURES IN ITS MAZE 408   3 DON JUAN 13   108   3
SYLVAN
    A SYLVAN TRIBE OF CHILDREN OF THE CHACE 145   3 DON JUAN 8   65   2
SYMMETRICAL
    SYMMETRICAL BUT DECK'D WITH CARVINGS QUAINT-- 389   3 DON JUAN 13   65   2
SYMMETRY
    O'ER LIMBS WHOSE SYMMETRY SET OFF THE SILK 204   3 DON JUAN 9   43   8
SYMPATHETIC
    I FEEL MY HEART BECOME SO SYMPATHETIC 372   2 DON JUAN 4   52   5
    RECEIVING SPRITES WITH SYMPATHETIC VAPOUR 512   3 DON JUAN 16   26   3
SYMPATHIES
    WHETHER THERE ARE SUCH THINGS AS SYMPATHIES 25   3 DON JUAN 6   38   3
SYMPATHISED
    THEY LITTLE KNEW OR MIGHT HAVE SYMPATHISED 543   3 DON JUAN 16   90   1
SYMPATHY
    BETWEEN THEIR TASTES THERE WAS SMALL SYMPATHY 58   2 DON JUAN 1   66   3
    OF HIS FAIR FACE AND FOUND BY SYMPATHY 241   2 DON JUAN 2   162   4
    INFECTED HER WITH SYMPATHY TILL NOW 480   2 DON JUAN 5   119   3
    AND NOT MUCH SYMPATHY FOR BLOOD SURVEYED 102   3 DON JUAN 7   69   2
    HIS SYMPATHY FOR RANK BY THE SAME TOKEN 117   3 DON JUAN 8   11   7
    BUT FOR POST HORSES WHO FINDS SYMPATHY 377   3 DON JUAN 13   42   5
    MAN'S VERY SYMPATHY WITH THEIR ESTATE 420   3 DON JUAN 14   24   5
    TO PATRIOT SYMPATHY A BRITON'S BLUSHES-- 425   3 DON JUAN 14   35   4
    THERE'S NOUGHT IN THIS BAD WORLD LIKE SYMPATHY 430   3 DON JUAN 14   47   1
    SHE MERELY FELT A COMMON SYMPATHY 449   3 DON JUAN 14   91   5
SYMPLEGADES
    BROKE FOAMING O'ER THE BLUE SYMPLEGADES 413   2 DON JUAN 5   5   2
SYMPTOM
    OF THIS AT LEAST NO SYMPTOM E'ER WAS SHOWN 59   2 DON JUAN 1   68   4
SYMPTOMS
    WHEN BABA SAW THESE SYMPTOMS WHICH HE KNEW 57   3 DON JUAN 6   102   1
SYNCOPE
    BUT MORE OR LESS THE WHOLE'S A SYNCOPE 457   3 DON JUAN 15   2   1
SYNE
    ARE OVER HERE'S A HEALTH TO AULD LANG SYNE 232   3 DON JUAN 10   16   5
    AND WHEN I USE THE PHRASE OF AULD LANG SYNE 233   3 DON JUAN 10   17   1
    AS AULD LANG SYNE BRINGS SCOTLAND ONE AND ALL 233   3 DON JUAN 10   18   1
    I CARE NOT--'TIS A GLIMPSE OF AULD LANG SYNE 233   3 DON JUAN 10   18   8
SYNONIMOUS
    OR ON HIS MISTRESS--TERMS SYNONIMOUS-- 509   3 DON JUAN 16   20   2
SYNONYM
    WAKES ME NEXT MORNING WITH ITS SYNONYM 372   2 DON JUAN 4   53   8
SYREN
    WHO MARCHED TO MOSCOW LED BY FAME THE SYREN 253   3 DON JUAN 10   58   6
SYSIPHUS
    THE STONE OF SYSIPHUS IF ONCE WE MOVE . . . . 447 3 DON JUAN 14   86   3

	PAGE	VOL	CANTO	STANZA	LN
SYSTEM					
OF HIS NEW SYSTEM TO PERPLEX THE SAGES	11	2 DON JUAN	D	4	4
YOUR SYSTEM FEIGNS O'ER THE CONTROLLESS CORE	84	2 DON JUAN	1	116	4
THEY SAY HIS SYSTEM 'TIS IN VAIN TO BATTER	268	3 DON JUAN	11	1	3
ONE SYSTEM EATS ANOTHER UP AND THIS	410	3 DON JUAN	14	1	5
BUT SYSTEM DOTH REVERSE THE TITAN'S BREAKFAST	411	3 DON JUAN	14	2	1
OR LIKE A SYSTEM COUPLED WITH A DOUBT	504	3 DON JUAN	16	9	4
TABBY					
SUCH TALES BEING FOR THE TEA HOURS OF SOME TABBY	184	3 DON JUAN	9	2	6
TABLE					
AN IVORY INLAID TABLE SPREAD WITH STATE	306	2 DON JUAN	3	61	5
TO DO NOT MUCH LESS DAMAGE THAN THE TABLE	309	2 DON JUAN	3	66	8
MY HAT AND GLOVES STILL LYING ON THE TABLE	428	2 DON JUAN	5	33	4
NO CHRISTIAN KNOLL TO TABLE SAW NO LINE	439	2 DON JUAN	5	50	3
YE WHO BUT SEE THE SAVING MAN AT TABLE	316	3 DON JUAN	12	3	5
THEIR TABLE WAS A BOARD TO TEMPT EVEN GHOSTS	404	3 DON JUAN	13	99	3
GREAT THINGS WERE NOW TO BE ACHIEVED AT TABLE	482	3 DON JUAN	15	62	1
UPON HIS TABLE OR HIS TOILET--WHICH	507	3 DON JUAN	16	16	1
LORD HENRY AT HIS TABLE SHOULD ENDURE	543	3 DON JUAN	16	89	6
TABLE-CLOTH					
THE GRASS MY TABLE-CLOTH IN OPEN AIR	488	3 DON JUAN	15	73	6
TABLES					
BY A FEW TIMELY WORDS TO TURN THE TABLES	117	2 DON JUAN	1	175	4
THE TABLES MOST OF EBONY INLAID	310	2 DON JUAN	3	69	2
GROUPS OF BAD STATUES TABLES CHAIRS AND PICTURES	465	2 DON JUAN	5	94	7
TACITURN					
GULBEYAZ' TACITURN OR SPEAKING WILL	61	3 DON JUAN	6	110	4
AND TACITURN ASIATIC DISPOSITION	328	3 DON JUAN	12	27	2
TACK					
WE'LL PUT ABOUT AND TRY ANOTHER TACK	384	2 DON JUAN	4	74	7
TACKED					
BUT WITH A MORAL TO EACH ERROR TACKED	412	2 DON JUAN	5	2	4
TACKLE					
BECAUSE THE TACKLE OF OUR SHATTER'D BARK	206	2 DON JUAN	2	95	3
TACT					
SILENCE IS BEST BESIDES THERE IS A TACT	119	2 DON JUAN	1	178	2
AND ALL BY HAVING TACT AS WELL AS TASTE	346	3 DON JUAN	12	66	8
SUCH WAS HIS TACT HE COULD ALIKE DELIGHT	428	3 DON JUAN	14	41	5
HIS TACT TOO TEMPER'D HIM FROM GRAVE TO GAY	492	3 DON JUAN	15	82	5
TACTICIAN					
A GREAT TACTICIAN AND NO LESS A SWORDSMAN)	399	3 DON JUAN	13	88	3
TACTICS					
STATISTICS TACTICS POLITICS AND GEOGRAPHY)--	149	3 DON JUAN	8	74	4
TA'EN					
THE BEST IS THAT IN SHORTHAND TA'EN BY GURNEY	127	2 DON JUAN	1	189	7
A TOWN WAS TA'EN MYSELF INSTEAD OF WIDIN	418	2 DON JUAN	5	15	8
AND AT THE USUAL SIGNAL TA'EN THEIR WAY	19	3 DON JUAN	6	26	4
WAS A TA'EN CITY--THIRTY THOUSAND SLAIN	212	3 DON JUAN	9	59	2
OR IF I'M WRONG I'LL NOT BE TA'EN ABACK--	348	3 DON JUAN	12	71	6
AND IRON TIME ERE LEAD HAD TA'EN THE LEAD	391	3 DON JUAN	13	70	2
BUT TA'EN AT HAZARD AS THE RHYME MAY RUN	397	3 DON JUAN	13	83	6
NOW WHEN SHE ONCE HAD TA'EN AN INTEREST	448	3 DON JUAN	14	88	1
TO STATE THE CASE IT MIGHT BE TA'EN FOR GRANTED	514	3 DON JUAN	16	33	7
TAIL					
THEN BEING TAKEN BY THE TAIL--A TAKING	150	3 DON JUAN	8	76	1
THEN BEING TAKEN BY THE TAIL--A-MODE	150	3 DON JUAN	8	76	V1
TAILOR					
HORSE BY A BLACKLEG BROADCLOTH BY A TAILOR	424	2 DON JUAN	5	26	7
MADE UP BY YOUTH FAME AND AN ARMY TAILOR--	204	3 DON JUAN	9	44	2
TAILOR'S					
THAN EVEN THE TAILOR'S) HIS INCARNATE SKIN	188	3 DON JUAN	9	12	7
TAIL'S					
(THAT ROYAL BIRD WHOSE TAIL'S A DIADEM)	104	3 DON JUAN	7	74	6
TAILS					
AND ALL MANKIND TURN WITH IT HEADS OR TAILS	159	2 DON JUAN	2	4	2
AS IF HE HAD THREE LIVES AS WELL AS TAILS	172	3 DON JUAN	8	121	8
TAINTED					
OF MARTYRS AWED AS SPAGNOLETTO TAINTED	392	3 DON JUAN	13	71	7
TAKE					
I'LL THEREFORE TAKE OUR ANCIENT FRIEND DON JUAN	21	2 DON JUAN	1	1	6
SO AS I SAID I'LL TAKE MY FRIEND DON JUAN	24	2 DON JUAN	1	5	8
HE DID NOT TAKE SUCH STUDIES FOR RESTRAINTS	47	2 DON JUAN	1	47	4
FOR INSTANCE--GENTLEMEN WHOSE LADIES TAKE	74	2 DON JUAN	1	98	2
HERE MY CHASTE MUSE A LIBERTY MUST TAKE--	86	2 DON JUAN	1	120	1
I CAN'T TELL WHY SHE SHOULD TAKE ALL THIS TROUBLE	97	2 DON JUAN	1	140	7
IF HE COMES HERE TO TAKE A DEPOSITION	104	2 DON JUAN	1	152	1
I WISH TO SLEEP AND BEG YOU WILL TAKE CARE	104	2 DON JUAN	1	153	5
A NAME THE LADIES MUST NOT TAKE AMISS	140	2 DON JUAN	1	206	V4
AND BEG THEY'LL TAKE MY WORD ABOUT THE MORAL	141	2 DON JUAN	1	209	2
I THINK I MUST TAKE UP WITH AVARICE	144	2 DON JUAN	1	216	8
FOR GOD'S SAKE READER TAKE THEM NOT FOR MINE	149	2 DON JUAN	1	222	8
AND THERE HE STOOD TO TAKE AND TAKE AGAIN	162	2 DON JUAN	2	11	7
AND THERE HE STOOD TO TAKE AND TAKE AGAIN	162	2 DON JUAN	2	11	7
AT SUNSET THEY BEGAN TO TAKE IN SAIL	170	2 DON JUAN	2	26	6
THEY DARED NOT TAKE IT IN FOR ALL THE BREEZE	188	2 DON JUAN	2	60	4
AS FAR AS IN HER LAY TO TAKE HIM IN	224	2 DON JUAN	2	129	7
TILL PAUSING AT THE LAST HER BREATH TO TAKE	241	2 DON JUAN	2	161	7
SO MUCH AS TO PROPOSE TO TAKE A WALK--	249	2 DON JUAN	2	176	3
SOME TAKE A LOVER SOME TAKE DRAMS OR PRAYERS	263	2 DON JUAN	2	201	1

TAKE   (CONTINUED)

	PAGE	VOL	CANTO	STANZA	LN
SOME TAKE A LOVER SOME TAKE DRAMS OR PRAYERS	263	2 DON JUAN	2	201	1
ARE THINGS THAT REALLY TAKE AWAY THE BREATH	309	2 DON JUAN	3	66	6
AND TAKE ALL COLOURS--LIKE THE HANDS OF DYERS	326	2 DON JUAN	3	87	8
I HAVE TRIED BOTH SO THOSE WHO WOULD A PART TAKE	356	2 DON JUAN	4	24	7
OLD LAMBRO BADE THEM TAKE HIM TO THE SHORE	371	2 DON JUAN	4	50	3
I WOULD TAKE REFUGE IN WEAK PUNCH BUT RACK	372	2 DON JUAN	4	53	5
BUT HEAR THAT SEVERAL PEOPLE TAKE EXCEPTION	397	2 DON JUAN	4	97	3
OR OF SOME CENTURIES TO TAKE A LEASE	398	2 DON JUAN	4	99	6
IN ALL WHO O'ER THE GREAT DEEP TAKE THEIR WAYS	414	2 DON JUAN	5	6	6
YOU TAKE THINGS COOLLY SIR SAID JUAN WHY	421	2 DON JUAN	5	21	1
BESIDES I'M HUNGRY AND JUST NOW WOULD TAKE	435	2 DON JUAN	5	44	7
METHOD'S MORE SURE AT MOMENTS TO TAKE HOLD	439	2 DON JUAN	5	49	4
IF ANY TAKE ME FOR THAT WHICH I SEEM	459	2 DON JUAN	5	82	6
(SO TAKE IT IN THE VERY WORDS OF CREECH)	470	2 DON JUAN	5	101	4
OH MAHOMET THAT HIS MAJESTY SHOULD TAKE	501	2 DON JUAN	5	156	4
AND TAKE WHAT KINGS CALL AN IMPOSING ATTITUDE	11	3 DON JUAN	6	11	4
IS MORE THAN I KNOW--THE DEUCE TAKE THEM BOTH	17	3 DON JUAN	6	22	8
I'LL TAKE JUANNA WE'RE A SLENDERER PAIR	29	3 DON JUAN	6	47	4
AND I OF YOUR YOUNG CHARGE WILL TAKE DUE CARE	29	3 DON JUAN	6	47	6
THAT NOBODY CAN EVER TAKE AMISS	35	3 DON JUAN	6	59	3
TO TAKE US FROM OUR NATURAL REST AND PULL	46	3 DON JUAN	6	80	3
THE MUSE WILL TAKE A LITTLE TOUCH AT WARFARE	65	3 DON JUAN	6	120	8
BEFORE THEY REACHED A SPOT TO TAKE EFFECT	80	3 DON JUAN	7	28	4
YOU WILL TAKE ISMAIL AT WHATEVER PRICE	86	3 DON JUAN	7	40	8
MAKES THAT OF MULTITUDES TAKE ONE DIRECTION	90	3 DON JUAN	7	48	2
TO SWALLOW FLAME AND NEVER TAKE IT ILL	93	3 DON JUAN	7	52	6
NOW UNDER ARMS HO KATSKOFF TAKE HIM TO--	100	3 DON JUAN	7	66	3
HISTORY CAN ONLY TAKE THINGS IN THE GROSS	113	3 DON JUAN	8	3	1
TO TAKE A BATTERY ON THE RIGHT THE OTHERS	119	3 DON JUAN	8	15	2
RETIRE A LITTLE MERELY TO TAKE BREATH	133	3 DON JUAN	8	40	8
HIS THANKS AND HOPES TO TAKE THE CITY SOON	140	3 DON JUAN	8	56	6
BUT HERE IT SEEMED HIS JOKES HAD CEASED TO TAKE	147	3 DON JUAN	8	70	8
TO TAKE HIM WAS THE POINT THE TRULY BRAVE	164	3 DON JUAN	8	106	1
WHO MAKE THE BEDS OF THOSE WHO WON'T TAKE QUARTER	167	3 DON JUAN	8	111	5
TAKE TOWNS BY STORM NO CAUSES CAN I GUESS	176	3 DON JUAN	8	129	5
YOU NEED NOT TAKE THEM UNDER YOUR DIRECTION	186	3 DON JUAN	9	7	6
SO YOU MAY TAKE YOUR CHOICE OF THIS OR THAT)--	211	3 DON JUAN	9	57	4
BECAUSE THE CLERGY TAKE THE THING IN HAND	220	3 DON JUAN	9	76	4
TO TAKE A QUIET RIDE IN SOME GREEN LANE	224	3 DON JUAN	9	85	8
FOR ME FOR I WOULD RATHER TAKE MY WINE	233	3 DON JUAN	10	17	3
TAKE LIVES TAKE WIVES TAKE AUGHT EXCEPT MEN'S PURSES	264	3 DON JUAN	10	79	2
TAKE LIVES TAKE WIVES TAKE AUGHT EXCEPT MEN'S PURSES	264	3 DON JUAN	10	79	2
TAKE LIVES TAKE WIVES TAKE AUGHT EXCEPT MEN'S PURSES	264	3 DON JUAN	10	79	2
ACCORDING AS YOU TAKE THINGS WELL OR ILL--	264	3 DON JUAN	10	80	7
TO TELL YOU TRUTHS YOU WILL NOT TAKE AS TRUE	266	3 DON JUAN	10	84	5
OH DOUBT--IF THOU BE'ST DOUBT FOR WHICH SOME TAKE THEE	269	3 DON JUAN	11	2	5
SO TAKE HIM UP I'LL HELP YOU WITH THE LOAD	275	3 DON JUAN	11	15	8
WHERE THE PRAETORIAN BANDS TAKE UP THE MATTER--	299	3 DON JUAN	11	62	2
LET HIM TAKE CARE THAT THAT WHICH HE PURSUES	304	3 DON JUAN	11	71	3
WITHOUT CASH MALTHUS TELLS YOU TAKE NO BRIDES	322	3 DON JUAN	12	14	4
THAN STORMS IT AS A FOE WOULD TAKE A CITY	350	3 DON JUAN	12	74	6
COQUETRY OR A WISH TO TAKE THE LEAD	351	3 DON JUAN	12	77	4
RESERVE IT) WILL BE VERY SURE TO TAKE	357	3 DON JUAN	12	89	6
AND TAKE MY WORD YOU WON'T HAVE ANY LESS	366	3 DON JUAN	13	18	3
BY A RIVER WHICH ITS SOFTEN'D WAY DID TAKE	385	3 DON JUAN	13	57	3
BUT TAKE AN ELL--AND MAKE A GREAT SENSATION	404	3 DON JUAN	13	98	5
TAKE CARE WHAT YOU REPLY TO SUCH A LETTER	407	3 DON JUAN	13	105	8
(TAKE HER AT THIRTY THAT IS) TO HAVE BEEN	421	3 DON JUAN	14	25	7
GO TO THE COFFEE-HOUSE AND TAKE ANOTHER	431	3 DON JUAN	14	48	8
THE LADY ADELINE RESOLVED TO TAKE	437	3 DON JUAN	14	61	1
AND I SHALL TAKE A MUCH MORE SERIOUS AIR	454	3 DON JUAN	14	99	5
SOME SPLENDID DEBTOR HE WOULD TAKE BY SAP	459	3 DON JUAN	15	8	4
AND TAKE AS MANY HEROES AS HEAVEN PLEASES	459	3 DON JUAN	15	9	8
THEY PLEASED TO MAKE OR TAKE HIM FOR AND THEIR	463	3 DON JUAN	15	16	2
THAN I HAVE TIME OR WILL TO TAKE TO PIECES	478	3 DON JUAN	15	52	8
'TIS ALWAYS BEST TO TAKE THINGS UPON TRUST	503	3 DON JUAN	16	6	4
TO TAKE SOME TROUBLE WITH HIS TOILET BUT	513	3 DON JUAN	16	29	2
WHO WISH TO TAKE THE TONE OF THEIR SOCIETY	526	3 DON JUAN	16	52	4
MAY DROP IN WITHOUT CARDS AND TAKE THEIR STATION	534	3 DON JUAN	16	69	4
WHICH MANY PEOPLE TAKE FOR WANT OF HEART	547	3 DON JUAN	16	97	3
JUDGING BY WHAT THEY TAKE AND WHAT THEY PAY	548	3 DON JUAN	16	99	5
THE DEVIL MAY TAKE THAT STEALTHY PACE OF HIS	556	3 DON JUAN	16	112	4
(I'LL TAKE THE LIKENESS I CAN FIRST COME AT)	564	3 DON JUAN	17	4	5

TAKEN

	PAGE	VOL	CANTO	STANZA	LN
AND COLERIDGE TOO HAS LATELY TAKEN WING	10	2 DON JUAN	D	2	5
HOW THIS SAME INTERVIEW HAD TAKEN PLACE	77	2 DON JUAN	1	105	2
HAVE PROVED BUT DROPSIES TAKEN FOR DIVINITIES	330	2 DON JUAN	3	95	8
BEFORE ONE CHARM OR HOPE HAD TAKEN WING	348	2 DON JUAN	4	8	8
EXTREMELY TAKEN WITH HIS OWN RELIGION	387	2 DON JUAN	4	78	7
WHICH TAKEN AT THE FLOOD--YOU KNOW THE REST	6	3 DON JUAN	6	1	2
WHICH TAKEN AT THE FLOOD LEADS--GOD KNOWS WHERE	7	3 DON JUAN	6	2	2
JUANNA SHOULD BE TAKEN FROM HER AND	47	3 DON JUAN	6	82	7
RUNNING AGROUND WAS TAKEN BY THE TURKS	81	3 DON JUAN	7	30	8
THEN BEING TAKEN BY THE TAIL--A TAKING	150	3 DON JUAN	8	76	1
THEN BEING TAKEN BY THE TAIL--A-MODE	150	3 DON JUAN	8	76	V1
THE CITY'S TAKEN--ONLY PART BY PART--	152	3 DON JUAN	8	82	1
THE CITY'S TAKEN BUT NOT RENDERED--NO	155	3 DON JUAN	8	87	1
UPON A TAKEN BASTION WHERE THERE LAY	157	3 DON JUAN	8	91	1

	PAGE VOL		CANTO STANZA LN		

TAKEN   (CONTINUED)

	PAGE	VOL	CANTO	STANZA	LN
BUT HE WOULD NOT BE TAKEN AND REPLIED	165	3 DON JUAN	8	107	1
THE TOWN WAS TAKEN--WHETHER HE MIGHT YIELD	172	3 DON JUAN	8	122	1
OR SEEN TOMBUCTOO OR HATH TAKEN TEA	271	3 DON JUAN	11	7	4
HAS TAKEN FOR A SWAN ROGUE SOUTHEY'S GANDER	298	3 DON JUAN	11	59	8
HAVE TAKEN UP AT LENGTH WITH YOUNGER BROTHERS	308	3 DON JUAN	11	81	2
OR WHETHER HE WAS TAKEN IN FOR DAMAGES	312	3 DON JUAN	11	89	7
AMONGST THE PATHS OF BEING TAKEN IN	327	3 DON JUAN	12	25	3
MOST YOUNG BEGINNERS MAY BE TAKEN SO	345	3 DON JUAN	12	63	V5
THE KINDEST MAY BE TAKEN AS A TEST	359	3 DON JUAN	13	3	6
HAVE TAKEN UP TO FILL THE FOLLOWING SERMON	416	3 DON JUAN	14	15	2

TAKERS

TAKERS OF TITHES AND MAKERS OF GOOD MATCHES	539	3 DON JUAN	16	80	7

TAKES

BUT SOMEHOW THIS MY VESTAL VOW TAKES WING	85	2 DON JUAN	1	119	5
BUT--GOD KNOWS HOW--THIS WISE RESOLVE TAKES WING	85	2 DON JUAN	1	119	V5
THE DOUBLE BOBADIL TAKES SCORN FOR AWE	153	2 DON JUAN	1	V 4	8
THE BRAGGADOCIO TAKES CONTEMPT FOR AWE	153	2 DON JUAN	1	V 4	V8
TAKES OFF ONE PECK OF PURGATORIAL COALS	185	2 DON JUAN	2	55	5
THE VATES IRRITABILIS TAKES CARE	317	2 DON JUAN	3	81	2
AND WHEN A SCOUNDREL HAS IT--HE TAKES CARE	317	2 DON JUAN	3	81	V2
AT LAST IT TAKES TO WEAPONS SUCH AS MEN	138	3 DON JUAN	8	51	3
ON HER CANALS WHERE GOD TAKES SEA AND LAND	198	3 DON JUAN	9	31	7
WHO LIKE DON JUAN TAKES AN ACTIVE SHARE	303	3 DON JUAN	11	70	2
A WIFE MAKES OR TAKES LOVE IN UPRIGHT EARNEST	345	3 DON JUAN	12	64	4
WHICH TAKES SO MUCH--TO GIVE THE DEVIL HIS DUE--	351	3 DON JUAN	12	76	3
AND IF IN FACT SHE TAKES TO A GRANDE PASSION	351	3 DON JUAN	12	77	1
'TIS PITY THAT IT TAKES NO FURTHER HOLD	382	3 DON JUAN	13	51	3
DAN PHOEBUS TAKES ME FOR AN AUCTIONEER	393	3 DON JUAN	13	74	4

TAKEST

WHATE'ER THOU TAKEST SPARE AWHILE POOR BEAUTY	459	3 DON JUAN	15	9	1

TAKING

FOR CALLING NAMES AND TAKING THEM AGAIN	150	2 DON JUAN	1	V 1	4
BUT TAKING HIM INTO HER FATHER'S HOUSE	225	2 DON JUAN	2	130	1
TAKING HER FOR A SISTER JUST THE SAME	232	2 DON JUAN	2	142	5
AND TAKING LATELY BY SUWARROW'S BIDDING	418	2 DON JUAN	5	15	7
AND TAKING HINTS IN GOOD PART ALL THE WHILE	473	2 DON JUAN	5	107	4
THEY PUT BEHOLDERS IN A TENDER TAKING	27	3 DON JUAN	6	43	4
THREE LINES OF THE DISPATCH IN TAKING SCHMACKSMITH	76	3 DON JUAN	7	20	6
LOST FOR HIS REPARTEE WAS TAKING CITIES	93	3 DON JUAN	7	53	V8
OF WAR AND TAKING TOWNS WHEN MANY A SHRIEK	141	3 DON JUAN	8	58	3
AFTER THE TAKING OF THE CAVALIER	148	3 DON JUAN	8	73	2
THEN BEING TAKEN BY THE TAIL--A TAKING	150	3 DON JUAN	8	76	1
SEEMED TAKING OUT THE STING TO LEAVE THE HONEY	217	3 DON JUAN	9	70	8
IN TAKING UP THIS PALTRY SHEET OF PAPER	226	3 DON JUAN	10	3	2

TALE

ACCORDING TO SOME GOOD OLD WOMAN'S TALE	72	2 DON JUAN	1	95	8
THAT THIS IS NOT A MORAL TALE THOUGH GAY	140	2 DON JUAN	1	207	6
BUT TO OUR TALE THE DONNA INEZ SENT	161	2 DON JUAN	2	8	1
HIS TALE IF FOES BE FOOD IN HELL AT SEA	200	2 DON JUAN	2	83	5
OER WHOSE SAD TALE LOVE ECHOS STILL ALAS--	273	2 DON JUAN	2	V 2	3
HER TALE IS TOLD WITH SO MUCH SIMPLE EASE--	273	2 DON JUAN	2	V 2	6
IN ENGLAND A SIX CANTO QUARTO TALE	320	2 DON JUAN	3	86	2
T' OUR TALE--THE FEAST WAS OVER THE SLAVES GONE	334	2 DON JUAN	3	101	1
BUT I GROW SAD--AND LET A TALE GROW COLD	413	2 DON JUAN	5	4	7
ALAS SAID JUAN 'TWERE A TALE DISTRESSING	419	2 DON JUAN	5	16	5
A SAD TALE SADDENS DOUBLY WHEN 'TIS LONG	419	2 DON JUAN	5	16	8
THIS MONSTROUS TALE HAD PROBABLY ITS SOURCE	446	2 DON JUAN	5	61	5
WHEN WE NEXT MEET WE'LL HAVE A TALE TO TELL	460	2 DON JUAN	5	84	4
AND SUCH AS THEY ARE SUCH MY PRESENT TALE IS	67	3 DON JUAN	7	2	1
BUT TO THE TALE--GREAT JOY UNTO THE CAMP	89	3 DON JUAN	7	46	1
WHOSE TALE BELONGS TO HALLAM'S MIDDLE AGES	330	3 DON JUAN	12	30	8
HAD NOT CERVANTES IN THAT TOO TRUE TALE	361	3 DON JUAN	13	8	7
I TELL THE TALE AS IT IS TOLD NOR DARE	365	3 DON JUAN	13	13	1
OR WALKED IF FOUL THEY READ OR TOLD A TALE	406	3 DON JUAN	13	104	3
WOULD SOME BELIEVE THAT SUCH A TALE HAD BEEN	444	3 DON JUAN	14	80	4
HER STOMACH'S NOT HER PECCANT PART THIS TALE	483	3 DON JUAN	15	64	6
BUT WONDER THEY SO FEW ARE SINCE MY TALE IS	502	3 DON JUAN	16	3	7
SOMETHING BUT WHAT'S NOT STATED IN MY TALE	514	3 DON JUAN	16	31	3
FOR SUCH SIGHTS THOUGH THE TALE IS HALF BELIEVED	516	3 DON JUAN	16	36	7
BECAUSE THE PRESENT TALE HAS OFT BEEN TOLD	516	3 DON JUAN	16	37	7

TALENT

NOR TURN HIS VERY TALENT TO A CRIME	15	2 DON JUAN	D	10	6
WITH JUST ENOUGH OF TALENT AND NO MORE	16	2 DON JUAN	D	12	6
THE TALENT AND GOOD HUMOUR HE DISPLAYED	355	3 DON JUAN	12	85	5
AND TALENT ON HIS HAUGHTY SPIRIT WROUGHT	365	3 DON JUAN	13	15	6
UPON HIS TALENT HENRY HAD NO DOUBTS	369	3 DON JUAN	13	24	5
AND SOME WHO HAD BUT TALENT FOR THEIR CREST	370	3 DON JUAN	13	28	4
WHOSE CHIEFLY HARMLESS TALENT WAS TO AMUSE	398	3 DON JUAN	13	86	5
CONSIDERABLE TALENT IN MY WAY	453	3 DON JUAN	14	98	8
HIS TALENT I WILL NOT DENY NOR DWELL	473	3 DON JUAN	15	38	V5
SCOTT--OF SUCH TALENT--I COULD HARDLY HAVE	481	3 DON JUAN	15	59	V6

TALENTS

WHERE DIFFERENT TALENTS FIND THEIR DIFFERENT MARTS	91	2 DON JUAN	1	128	6
HER TALENTS WERE OF THE MORE SILENT CLASS	30	3 DON JUAN	6	49	8
OF THE HIGH TALENTS OF THIS NEW VAUBAN	72	3 DON JUAN	7	11	2
BY ONE THREE TALENTS FOR THERE WERE NO LESS--	517	3 DON JUAN	16	39	6

TALES

AFAR A DWARF BUFFOON STOOD TELLING TALES	293	2 DON JUAN	3	34	1

TALES   (CONTINUED)
   SUCH TALES BEING FOR THE TEA HOURS OF SOME TABBY . . . . 184 3 DON JUAN 9   2   6
   OF ALL TALES 'TIS THE SADDEST--AND MORE SAD . . . . . . 363 3 DON JUAN 13   9   1
TALISMAN
   THE MAGIC OF HER GRACE'S TALISMAN . . . . 437 3 DON JUAN 14   62   6
   HAD SUPERSTITION LOST HER TALISMAN . . . . 467 3 DON JUAN 15   24   V4
TALK
   EVIL AND GOOD HAVE HAD THEIR TITHE OF TALK 22   2 DON JUAN 1   2   3
   WE'LL TALK OF THAT ANON--'TIS SWEET TO HEAR 87   2 DON JUAN 1   122   1
   THAT HE WAS FAINT AND MUST NOT TALK BUT EAT . . . . . . 236 2 DON JUAN 2   150   8
   NOW SHE PROLONG'D HER VISITS AND HER TALK . . . . . . 249 2 DON JUAN 2   176   1
   (FOR THEY MUST TALK) AND HE HAD LEARNT TO SAY . . . . . 249 2 DON JUAN 2   176   2
   AND SO I STOPPED TO TALK WITH A VENETIAN . . . . 268 2 DON JUAN 2   210   V8
   SOME TALK OF AN APPEAL UNTO SOME PASSION . . . . 437 2 DON JUAN 5   48   1
   OTHERS IN MONOSYLLABLE TALK CHATTED . . . . 441 2 DON JUAN 5   53   3
   THEIR TALK OF COURSE RAN MOST ON THE NEW COMER 23   3 DON JUAN 6   35   1
   BABA WHO KNEW BY EXPERIENCE WHEN TO TALK 61   3 DON JUAN 6   110   1
   WE ONLY CAN BUT TALK OF ESCALADE . . . . 106 3 DON JUAN 7   78   6
   AND WHEN YOU HEAR HISTORIANS TALK OF THRONES . . . . . 180 3 DON JUAN 8   137   1
   O'ER KINGS WHO NOW AT LEAST MUST TALK OF LAW . . . . . 261 3 DON JUAN 10   74   6
   AND BY WE'LL TALK OF THAT AND IF WE DON'T . . . . . . 285 3 DON JUAN 11   36   2
   CONTRIVED TO TALK ABOUT THE GODS OF LATE . . . . . . 298 3 DON JUAN 11   60   4
   AND TALK IN TENDER HORRORS OF OUR LOATHING . . . . . . 301 3 DON JUAN 11   65   5
   TALK ABOUT POETRY AND RACK AND MANGER . . . . 305 3 DON JUAN 11   74   6
   TALK NOT OF SEVENTY YEARS AS AGE IN SEVEN . . . . . . 309 3 DON JUAN 11   82   1
   QUICK SILVER SMALL TALK ENDING (IF YOU NOTE IT) . . . . 328 3 DON JUAN 12   26   7
   OF BEING APT TO TALK AT A GREAT RATE . . . . 329 3 DON JUAN 12   28   6
   TO TALK OF A SUBSCRIPTION OR PETITION . . . . 330 3 DON JUAN 12   30   6
   FOR TALK SIX TIMES WITH THE SAME SINGLE LADY . . . . . 343 3 DON JUAN 12   59   7
   OF STRONGBOW'S TALK YOU WOULD NOT CHANGE A WORD . . . . 402 3 DON JUAN 13   93   5
   HAD MUSIC--WALKING--RIDING--BOOKS--AND TALK . . . . . 407 3 DON JUAN 13   104   V2
   WHETHER THEIR TALK WAS OF THE KIND CALL'D SMALL . . . . 453 3 DON JUAN 14   98   4
   I RATTLE ON EXACTLY AS I'D TALK . . . . 464 3 DON JUAN 15   19   7
   TALK O'ER THEMSELVES THE PAST AND NEXT ELECTION . . . . 534 3 DON JUAN 16   69   8
TALK'D
   THUS DROWNINGS ARE MUCH TALK'D OF BY THE DIVERS . . . . 172 2 DON JUAN 2   31   7
TALKED
   THE FEMALE RANKS SO THAT NONE STIRRED OR TALKED 21   3 DON JUAN 6   30   6
   AND TALKED AWAY AND MIGHT HAVE TALKED TILL NOW 58   3 DON JUAN 6   105   2
   AND TALKED AWAY AND MIGHT HAVE TALKED TILL NOW 58   3 DON JUAN 6   105   2
   WHERE BLOOD WAS TALKED OF AS WE WOULD OF WATER . . . . 197 3 DON JUAN 9   29   3
   SMILED AS SHE TALKED THE MATTER O'ER BUT TEARS . . . . 221 3 DON JUAN 9   78   6
   OTHERS TALKED LEARNEDLY OF CERTAIN TUMOURS . . . . . . 244 3 DON JUAN 10   40   3
   THEY TALKED BAD FRENCH OF SPANISH AND UPON ITS . . . . 294 3 DON JUAN 11   50   5
   I SAID THAT LADY PINCHBECK HAD BEEN TALKED ABOUT-- . . . 338 3 DON JUAN 12   47   1
   AND THEN HE TALKED WITH HIM ABOUT MADRID . . . . . . 368 3 DON JUAN 13   23   1
   AND MUCH WAS TALKED ON ALL SIDES ON THAT HEAD . . . . 527 3 DON JUAN 16   54   5
TALKER
   YE GODS I GROW A TALKER LET US PRATE . . . . 345 3 DON JUAN 12   64   1
   WHEN SOME SMART TALKER PUTS THEM TO THE TEST . . . . . 404 3 DON JUAN 13   98   7
TALKING
   FAMOUS FOR ALWAYS TALKING AND NEER FIGHTING . . . . . 150 2 DON JUAN 1 V 1   3
   NOT ONLY IN MERE TALKING BUT THE PRESS MAN . . . . . 288 3 DON JUAN 11   42   5
   I MUST NOT QUITE OMIT THE TALKING SAGE . . . . . . 403 3 DON JUAN 13   97   3
   BECAUSE HE FIXED IT AND TO STOP HIS TALKING . . . . . 565 3 DON JUAN 17   8   2
TALKING'S
   TALKING'S DRY WORK I HAVE NO TIME TO SPARE . . . . . 297 2 DON JUAN 3   43   4
TALK'S
   (ALTHOUGH THEIR TALK'S OBSCURE AND CIRCUMSPECT) 38   2 DON JUAN 1   33   4
TALKS
   SHAKSPEARE TALKS OF THE HERALD MERCURY . . . . . . 215 3 DON JUAN 9   66   1
TALL
   TALL HANDSOME SLENDER BUT WELL KNIT HE SEEM'D 51   2 DON JUAN 1   54   2
   HER STATURE TALL--I HATE A DUMPY WOMAN 55   2 DON JUAN 1   61   8
   I HOPE HE'S YOUNG AND HANDSOME--IS HE TALL . . . . . . 105 2 DON JUAN 1   154   6
   SHE WAS APPEAR'D DISTINCT AND TALL AND FAIR . . . . . 216 2 DON JUAN 2   115   8
   AND TALL BEYOND HER SEX AND THEIR COMPEERS . . . . . 367 2 DON JUAN 4   43   5
   MAKING HER STATURE TALL EVEN TALLER--NEAR . . . . . . 367 2 DON JUAN 4   43   V5
   AND FURTHER DOWNWARD TALL AND TOWERING STILL IS . . . . 385 2 DON JUAN 4   76   5
   THERE'S ONE THOUGH TALL AND STIFFER THAN A PIKE . . . . 390 2 DON JUAN 4   85   5
   O'ERTOPPED WITH CYPRESSES DARK-GREEN AND TALL . . . . . 432 2 DON JUAN 5   40   8
   THAT SHE WAS FAIR OR DARK OR SHORT OR TALL 33   3 DON JUAN 6   54   7
   AND TALL AND STRONG AND SWIFT OF FOOT WERE THEY . . . . 145 3 DON JUAN 8   66   1
   TALL STATELY FORM'D TO LEAD THE COURTLY VAN . . . . . 440 3 DON JUAN 14   70   5
   OF PHYSICS BODIES WHETHER SHORT OR TALL . . . . . . 511 3 DON JUAN 16   24   6
TALLER
   MAKING HER STATURE TALL EVEN TALLER--NEAR . . . . . . 367 2 DON JUAN 4   43   V5
TALLEST
   THE FIRST AND TALLEST HER WHITE KERCHIEF WAVING . . . . 291 2 DON JUAN 3   30   2
TALLOW
   HIDES TRAIN-OIL TALLOW AND THE RIGHTS OF THETIS . . . . 246 3 DON JUAN 10   45   7
TALLY
   WITH VARIOUS SIMILAR REMARKS TO TALLY . . . . 526 3 DON JUAN 16   53   5
TALUS
   REACHED THE INTERIOR TALUS OF THE RAMPART . . . . . . 135 3 DON JUAN 8   44   8
TAME
   HIS SOBER HEAD MAJESTICALLY TAME . . . . 292 2 DON JUAN 3   32   5
   IF CAUSE SHOULD BE--A LIONESS THOUGH TAME . . . . . . 367 2 DON JUAN 4   44   6
   FLUNG HERE BY FATE OR CIRCUMSTANCE WHICH TAME . . . . . 139 3 DON JUAN 8   54   6

TAME   (CONTINUED)

	PAGE	VOL	CANTO		STANZA	LN
TO MAKE HIS LITTLE WILD ASIATIC TAME	336	3 DON JUAN	12		42	6
IF SHE HATH NO WILD BOARS SHE HATH A TAME	395	3 DON JUAN	13		78	7
FAULTS WHICH ATTRACT BECAUSE THEY ARE NOT TAME	480	3 DON JUAN	15		57	5
PERHAPS THESE ARE MOST DIFFICULT TO TAME	531	3 DON JUAN	16		63	6

TAMED

	PAGE	VOL	CANTO		STANZA	LN
THEY TAMED HIM DOWN AMONGST THEM TO DESTROY	49	2 DON JUAN	1		50	4
AND DANIEL TAMED THE LIONS IN THEIR DEN	445	3 DON JUAN	5		60	5
WHENE'ER THEIR TRIUMPH PALES OR STAR IS TAMED--	448	3 DON JUAN	14		89	6

TAMELESS

	PAGE	VOL	CANTO		STANZA	LN
THE ELDEST WAS A TRUE AND TAMELESS TARTAR	167	3 DON JUAN	8		111	1

TAMING

	PAGE	VOL	CANTO		STANZA	LN
SAD RAKES TO SADDER HUSBANDS CHASTELY TAMING	418	3 DON JUAN	14		18	5

TAN

	PAGE	VOL	CANTO		STANZA	LN
WHO WOULD NOT SIGH AI AI TAN KUTHEREIAN	554	3 DON JUAN	16		109	1

TANGIER

	PAGE	VOL	CANTO		STANZA	LN
MOROCCO BETWIXT EGYPT AND TANGIER	28	3 DON JUAN	6		44	8

TANGLES

	PAGE	VOL	CANTO		STANZA	LN
WHICH PLAY'D WITHIN THE TANGLES OF HER HAIR	80	2 DON JUAN	1		110	2
CALL'D BACK THE TANGLES OF HER WANDERING HAIR	114	2 DON JUAN	1		170	2

TANK

	PAGE	VOL	CANTO		STANZA	LN
WHO PASS LIKE WATER FILTERED IN A TANK	396	3 DON JUAN	13		80	3

TANNERS

	PAGE	VOL	CANTO		STANZA	LN
TO STRIP THE SAXONS OF THEIR HYDES LIKE TANNERS	242	3 DON JUAN	10		36	6

TANTAENE

	PAGE	VOL	CANTO		STANZA	LN
TANTAENE SUCH THE VIRTUES OF HIGH STATION	331	3 DON JUAN	12		33	5

TANTALIZATION

	PAGE	VOL	CANTO		STANZA	LN
THEMSELVES ON INNOCENT TANTALIZATION	327	3 DON JUAN	12		25	7

TANTALUS

	PAGE	VOL	CANTO		STANZA	LN
PANTING FOR POWER AS TANTALUS FOR WATER	155	2 DON JUAN	1	V 6	V1

TANTI

	PAGE	VOL	CANTO		STANZA	LN
THE TANTI PALPITI'S ON SUCH OCCASIONS	523	3 DON JUAN	16		45	4

TAP

	PAGE	VOL	CANTO		STANZA	LN
KNOCKEST AT DOORS AT FIRST WITH MODEST TAP	459	3 DON JUAN	15		8	2

TAPER

	PAGE	VOL	CANTO		STANZA	LN
HER SMALL WHITE HAND COULD HARDLY REACH THE TAPER	134	2 DON JUAN	1		198	3
HER SMALL WHITE FINGERS SCARCE COULD REACH THE TAPER	134	2 DON JUAN	1		198	V3
AND BARDS BURN WHAT THEY CALL THEIR MIDNIGHT TAPER	146	2 DON JUAN	1		218	6
ARE BOWED AND PUT THE SUN OUT LIKE A TAPER	266	3 DON JUAN	10		83	6
AND HOLD UP TO THE SUN MY LITTLE TAPER	325	3 DON JUAN	12		21	3
ALL THERE WAS AS HE LEFT IT STILL HIS TAPER	512	3 DON JUAN	16		26	1

TAPERS

	PAGE	VOL	CANTO		STANZA	LN
THAN DYING TAPERS--AND THE PEEPING MOON	504	3 DON JUAN	16		8	8
BURNT AND NOT BLUE AS MODEST TAPERS USE	512	3 DON JUAN	16		26	2

TAPESTRY

	PAGE	VOL	CANTO		STANZA	LN
THE HANGINGS OF THE ROOM WERE TAPESTRY MADE	308	2 DON JUAN	3		64	1

TAPPING

	PAGE	VOL	CANTO		STANZA	LN
TAPPING THE SHOULDER OF THE NIGHEST GUEST	297	2 DON JUAN	3		42	2
HERE THEIR CONDUCTOR TAPPING AT THE WICKET	433	2 DON JUAN	5		41	1

TARANTULAS

	PAGE	VOL	CANTO		STANZA	LN
THE WEB OF THESE TARANTULAS EACH DAY	196	3 DON JUAN	9		28	5

TARDY

	PAGE	VOL	CANTO		STANZA	LN
TO GERMANY WHOSE SOMEWHAT TARDY MILLIONS	254	3 DON JUAN	10		60	7
THE LOFTIEST MINDS OUTRUN THEIR TARDY AGES	566	3 DON JUAN	17		9	5

TARES

	PAGE	VOL	CANTO		STANZA	LN
AND APT TO SOW AN AUTHOR'S WHEAT WITH TARES	369	3 DON JUAN	13		25	3

TARQUIN

	PAGE	VOL	CANTO		STANZA	LN
AND ALMOST MIGHT HAVE MADE A TARQUIN QUAKE	62	2 DON JUAN	1		75	6

TARRIED

	PAGE	VOL	CANTO		STANZA	LN
SINCE WITH DIGRESSIONS WE TOO LONG HAVE TARRIED	493	3 DON JUAN	15		84	5

TARRYING

	PAGE	VOL	CANTO		STANZA	LN
RELUCTANTLY STILL TARRYING THERE AS LATE AS	111	2 DON JUAN	1		164	3

TARS

	PAGE	VOL	CANTO		STANZA	LN
TO ALL THE BROTHER TARS WHO MAY HAVE NEED HENCE	171	2 DON JUAN	2		29	5
AS UPON SUCH OCCASIONS TARS WILL ASK	173	2 DON JUAN	2		33	7
THAT STILL COULD KEEP AFLOAT THE STRUGGLING TARS	183	2 DON JUAN	2		51	3

TARTAR

	PAGE	VOL	CANTO		STANZA	LN
HIS BLOOD WAS UP THOUGH YOUNG HE WAS A TARTAR	122	2 DON JUAN	1		184	7
TO RUSSIAN TARTAR ENGLISH FRENCH COSSACQUE	89	3 DON JUAN	7		46	2
OR AT LEAST SUITED NOT THIS VALIANT TARTAR	152	3 DON JUAN	8		80	4
BUT TO OUR SUBJECT A BRAVE TARTAR KHAN--	163	3 DON JUAN	8		104	5
THE ELDEST WAS A TRUE AND TAMELESS TARTAR	167	3 DON JUAN	8		111	1

TARTARS

	PAGE	VOL	CANTO		STANZA	LN
TO BE PUT UP FOR AUCTION AMONGST TARTARS	415	2 DON JUAN	5		8	8
SIX TARTARS AND A DRAG-CHAIN-- --TO THIS DOOM	418	2 DON JUAN	5		15	3
AT HALIFAX BUT NOW HE SERVED THE TARTARS	76	3 DON JUAN	7		19	8
THAT THESE WERE MERELY MASQUERADING TARTARS	96	3 DON JUAN	7		57	4

TASK

	PAGE	VOL	CANTO		STANZA	LN
TO KEEP ONE CREED'S A TASK GROWN QUITE HERCULEAN	20	2 DON JUAN	0		17	7
BUT WHETHER JULIA TO THE TASK WAS EQUAL	66	2 DON JUAN	1		82	7
AND YET I MAY AS WELL THE TASK FULFIL	134	2 DON JUAN	1		197	3
HIS DAILY TASK HAD KEPT HIS FANCY COOL	158	2 DON JUAN	2		2	3
HOW SWEET THE TASK TO SHIELD AN ABSENT FRIEND	552	3 DON JUAN	16		104	7

TASKED

	PAGE	VOL	CANTO		STANZA	LN
HIS BEST TO OBEY IN WHAT HE HAD BEEN TASKED	56	3 DON JUAN	6		100	4

TASTE

	PAGE	VOL	CANTO		STANZA	LN
AND COMPLIMENTED DON ALFONSO'S TASTE	58	2 DON JUAN	1		67	6
(I REALLY MADAM WONDER AT YOUR TASTE--	115	2 DON JUAN	1		172	4
TO TASTE OF HEAVEN--IF THIS BE TRUE INDEED	202	2 DON JUAN	2		86	7

	PAGE	VOL	CANTO	STANZA	LN
TASTE (CONTINUED)					
CONDEMN THE ROYAL LADY'S TASTE WHO WORE	238	2 DON JUAN	2	155	4
A TASTE SEEN IN THE CHOICE OF HIS ABODE	304	2 DON JUAN	3	56	4
TO HELP THE TASTE OF MORTALS FOR ENNUI	332	2 DON JUAN	3	97	V8
BUT IF THE SULTAN HAS A TASTE FOR SONG	389	2 DON JUAN	4	82	7
THAT TASTE IS GONE THAT FAME IS BUT A LOTTERY . . .	404	2 DON JUAN	4	109	7
A GAUDY TASTE FOR THEY ARE LITTLE SKILLED IN . . .	436	2 DON JUAN	5	46	5
WEALTH HAD DONE WONDERS--TASTE NOT MUCH SUCH THINGS . .	465	2 DON JUAN	5	94	1
THAT IS WE CANNOT PARDON THEIR BAD TASTE	14	3 DON JUAN	6	17	1
AND SHOWN THEMSELVES AS GHOSTS OF BETTER TASTE . . .	38	3 DON JUAN	6	64	7
WITH BUILDINGS IN THE ORIENTAL TASTE	70	3 DON JUAN	7	9	3
OF DANUBE--WITH SOME STRENGTH BUT LITTLE TASTE . . .	71	3 DON JUAN	7	9	V3
WHICH SHOWED A WANT OF LANTHORNS OR OF TASTE-- . . .	177	3 DON JUAN	8	130	2
LOVE--(THOUGH SHE HAD A CURSED TASTE FOR WAR . . .	222	3 DON JUAN	9	80	5
NOR FLATTERING .TO THEIR TEMPER OR THEIR TASTE . . .	230	3 DON JUAN	10	11	5
MADE CATHERINE TASTE NEXT NIGHT A QUIET SLUMBER-- . .	248	3 DON JUAN	10	48	4
AND ALL BY HAVING TACT AS WELL AS TASTE	346	3 DON JUAN	12	66	8
BESIDES (ALAS HIS TASTE--FORGIVE AND PITY)	347	3 DON JUAN	12	68	7
TO TASTE--THE TRUTH IS IF MEN WOULD CONFESS . . .	347	3 DON JUAN	12	69	7
I LEAVE THEM TO THEIR TASTE NO DOUBT THE BEST . . .	359	3 DON JUAN	13	3	2
TASTE OR THE GOUT--PRONOUNCE IT AS INCLINES . . .	488	3 DON JUAN	15	72	3
AURORA--SINCE WE ARE TOUCHING UPON TASTE	524	3 DON JUAN	16	48	1
BY WHICH LORD HENRY'S GOOD TASTE WOULD GO FORTH IN .	529	3 DON JUAN	16	59	6
TASTES					
BETWEEN THEIR TASTES THERE WAS SMALL SYMPATHY . . .	58	2 DON JUAN	1	66	3
TASTES THEIR FIRST SEASON (MOSTLY IF THEY HAVE MONEY) .	330	3 DON JUAN	12	31	8
TASTES WE ARE GOING TO TRY THE SUPERNATURAL	497	3 DON JUAN	15	93	8
TASTING					
PROSCRIBED FROM TASTING YOUR CASTALIAN TEA	403	2 DON JUAN	4	108	8
TATTER'D					
NEXT THEY--HE BEING NAKED SAVE A TATTER'D	240	2 DON JUAN	2	160	1
TATTERED					
AND THEN HIS TATTERED JACKET OFF HE STRIPPED . . .	456	2 DON JUAN	5	77	V3
TATTLE					
AS THAT ABOMINABLE TITTLE TATTLE	336	3 DON JUAN	12	43	7
TAUGHT					
AND THUS FOR WIDER CARNAGE TAUGHT TO PANT	16	2 DON JUAN	0	12	3
JUAN WAS TAUGHT FROM OUT THE BEST EDITION	46	2 DON JUAN	1	44	1
AND LOVE IS TAUGHT HYPOCRISY FROM YOUTH	61	2 DON JUAN	1	72	8
HE MIGHT BE TAUGHT BY LOVE AND THEM TOGETHER-- . . .	65	2 DON JUAN	1	81	7
INFANTS OF THREE YEARS OLD WERE TAUGHT THAT DAY . .	162	2 DON JUAN	2	10	5
SHE TAUGHT THEM TO SUPPRESS THEIR VICE AND URINE . .	162	2 DON JUAN	2	10	V8
WHEN DRIED TO SUMMER DUST TILL TAUGHT BY PAIN . . .	201	2 DON JUAN	2	84	3
WHEN BOTH THE TEACHER AND THE TAUGHT ARE YOUNG . . .	242	2 DON JUAN	2	164	3
TAUGHT TO CONCEAL THEIR BURSTING HEARTS DESPOND . .	263	2 DON JUAN	2	200	4
UNTIL 'TIS TAUGHT BY LESSONS RATHER RUDE	53	3 DON JUAN	6	95	3
OH FOOLISH MORTALS ALWAYS TAUGHT IN VAIN	101	3 DON JUAN	7	68	5
WHOSE FANGS EVE TAUGHT HER HUMAN SEED TO FEEL . . .	153	3 DON JUAN	8	83	4
WOULD BE MUCH BETTER TAUGHT BENEATH THE EYE . . .	329	3 DON JUAN	12	29	7
HAD LEFT ALL THE ACCOMPLISHMENTS SHE TAUGHT HER . .	339	3 DON JUAN	12	51	5
A SORRIER STILL IS THE GREAT MORAL TAUGHT	363	3 DON JUAN	13	9	7
HE LIKED TO TEACH THAT WHICH HE HAD BEEN TAUGHT . .	368	3 DON JUAN	13	21	5
BUT JUAN HAD BEEN EARLY TAUGHT TO RANGE	424	3 DON JUAN	14	32	5
AND TAUGHT HIM WHEN TO BE RESERVED OR FREE . . .	492	3 DON JUAN	15	82	6
THE ANTIQUE PERSIANS TAUGHT THREE USEFUL THINGS . .	501	3 DON JUAN	16	1	1
TAURIS					
(WHEN A NEW IPHIGENE SHE WENT TO TAURIS)	248	3 DON JUAN	10	49	7
TAVERN					
WHICH SERVES THE HAPPY COUPLE FOR A TAVERN	24	2 DON JUAN	1	6	8
WITHOUT WHICH GLORY'S BUT A TAVERN SONG--	144	3 DON JUAN	8	63	4
TAVERNS					
HERE TAVERNS WOOING TO A PINT OF PURL	278	3 DON JUAN	11	22	3
TAX					
SO GOOD--I WONDER CASTLEREAGH DON'T TAX 'EM	264	2 DON JUAN	2	203	8
IN MORAL ENGLAND WHERE THE THING'S A TAX)	20	3 DON JUAN	6	29	7
OF THOSE WHO CANNOT LAY ON A NEW TAX	54	3 DON JUAN	6	96	8
MAY CHOOSE TO TAX ME WITH WHICH IS NOT FAIR . . .	230	3 DON JUAN	10	11	4
THE WEALTH OF WORLDS (A WEALTH OF TAX AND PAPER) . .	266	3 DON JUAN	10	83	4
CAN TAX MY MILD MUSE WITH MISANTHROPY	286	3 DON JUAN	11	38	2
TAXATION					
HIS TITLE AND 'TIS NOTHING BUT TAXATION	283	2 DON JUAN	3	14	4
TOO SCANTY IN THESE TIMES OF LOW TAXATION	528	3 DON JUAN	16	56	8
TAX-BORN					
IF HE FOUND NOT THIS SPAWN OF TAX-BORN RICHES . . .	288	3 DON JUAN	11	41	7
TAXED					
HE TAXED HIS TONGUE FOR WORDS WHICH WERE NOT GRANTED . .	511	3 DON JUAN	16	23	7
TAXES					
AND LIVE AND DIE MAKE LOVE AND PAY OUR TAXES . . .	159	2 DON JUAN	2	4	3
BOTH MALADIES ARE TAXES ON OUR JOYS	357	2 DON JUAN	4	25	3
DEBT HE CALLS WEALTH AND TAXES PARADISE	88	3 DON JUAN	7	45	5
MEANTIME THE TAXES CASTLEREAGH AND DEBT	174	3 DON JUAN	8	125	5
TITHES TAXES DUNS AND DOORS WITH DOUBLE KNOCKINGS . .	346	3 DON JUAN	12	67	8
PEACE WAR THE TAXES AND WHAT'S CALLED THE NATION . .	360	3 DON JUAN	13	6	2
TAXING					
ESPECIALLY OF WAR AND TAXING--HOW	202	3 DON JUAN	9	40	6
TAX-TRAP					
THE HOUSE OF COMMONS TURNED TO A TAX-TRAP--	310	3 DON JUAN	11	84	3
TCHITCHITZKOFF					
THE CAUSE OF KILLING TCHITCHITZKOFF AND SMITH . . .	79	3 DON JUAN	7	25	4

```
                                                       PAGE VOL    CANTO  STANZA LN
TE
   SHE RINGS THE WORLD'S TE DEUM AND HER BROW  . . . . .  286  3 DON JUAN 11    38   3
TEA
   I CAN'T SAY THAT SHE GAVE THEM ANY TEA  . . . . . . .  233  2 DON JUAN  2   145   6
   MOVED BY THE CHINESE NYMPH OF TEARS GREEN TEA . . . .  372  2 DON JUAN  4    52   2
   FOR TEA AND COFFEE LEAVE US MUCH MORE SERIOUS . . . .  372  2 DON JUAN  4    52   8
   PROSCRIBED FROM TASTING YOUR CASTALIAN TEA . . . . .   403  2 DON JUAN  4   108   8
   SUCH TALES BEING FOR THE TEA HOURS OF SOME TABBY . . . 184  3 DON JUAN  9     2   6
   OR SEEN TOMBUCTOO OR HATH TAKEN TEA  . . . . . . . .   271  3 DON JUAN 11     7   4
   HE SATE HIM PENSIVE O'ER A DISH OF TEA  . . . . . . .  513  3 DON JUAN 16    30   2
   THE MORNING CAME--AND BREAKFAST TEA AND TOAST . . . .  568  3 DON JUAN 17    13   2
TEACH
   TO TEACH HIM MANNERS FOR THE TIME TO COME  . . . . .    34  2 DON JUAN  1    25   8
   OH YE WHO TEACH THE INGENUOUS YOUTH OF NATIONS . . . . 157  2 DON JUAN  2     1   1
   SPURR'D HER TO TEACH ANOTHER GENERATION . . . . . .    162  2 DON JUAN  2    10   8
   AND ALL THE BURNING TONGUES THE PASSION TEACH . . . .  256  2 DON JUAN  2   189   5
   TO TEACH HIS PEOPLE TO BE MORE EXACT . . . . . . .     296  2 DON JUAN  3    40   6
   AND SHARP ADVERSITY WILL TEACH AT LAST . . . . . .     345  2 DON JUAN  4     2   2
   MAY TEACH US BETTER TO BEHAVE WHEN MASTERS . . . . .   422  2 DON JUAN  5    23   8
   MIGHT TEACH THEM THIS MUCH BETTER THAN I'M ABLE . . .  444  2 DON JUAN  5    59   8
   TO TEACH HIM GREATER HAD HIS OWN LEG BROKEN . . . .    117  3 DON JUAN  8    11   8
   ALL ARTS TO TEACH THEIR SUBJECTS TO DESTROY . . . .    157  3 DON JUAN  8    92   8
   FOR I WILL TEACH IF POSSIBLE THE STONES . . . . . .    179  3 DON JUAN  8   135   4
   BUT WHICH 'TIS TIME TO TEACH THE HIRELING TRIBE . . .  187  3 DON JUAN  9    10   4
   TEACH THEM THE DECENCIES OF GOOD THREESCORE . . . .    267  3 DON JUAN 10    86   1
   HE LIKED TO TEACH THAT WHICH HE HAD BEEN TAUGHT . . .  368  3 DON JUAN 13    21   5
   'TWILL TEACH DISCERNMENT TO THE SENSITIVE . . . . .    431  3 DON JUAN 14    49   7
   TEACH THEM THAT SAUCE FOR GOOSE IS SAUCE FOR GANDER . . 446  3 DON JUAN 14    83   3
   AND PERSECUTED SAGES TEACH THE SCHOOLS  . . . . . .    463  3 DON JUAN 15    17   7
TEACHER
   WHEN BOTH THE TEACHER AND THE TAUGHT ARE YOUNG . . . . 242  2 DON JUAN  2   164   3
TEACHERS
   ITALIAN NOT AT ALL HAVING NO TEACHERS . . . . . . .    243  2 DON JUAN  2   165   2
TEACHES
   BUT NATURE TEACHES MORE THAN POWER CAN SPOIL  . . . .  480  2 DON JUAN  5   120   1
   IT TEACHES THEM THAT THEY ARE FLESH AND BLOOD . . . .  491  2 DON JUAN  5   138   1
   IT TEACHES--HEAVEN KNOWS ONLY WHAT IT TEACHES . . . .  491  2 DON JUAN  5   138   7
   IT TEACHES--HEAVEN KNOWS ONLY WHAT IT TEACHES . . . .  491  2 DON JUAN  5   138   7
   AND WHAT'S STILL BETTER--TEACHES THEM THAT OTHERS . .  491  2 DON JUAN  5   138  V2
   THE ONLY DANCE WHICH TEACHES GIRLS TO THINK . . . .    302  3 DON JUAN 11    68   3
   UNLESS IT TEACHES ONE TO QUOTE AND CAVIL) . . . . .    380  3 DON JUAN 13    47   8
TEACHING
   WAS TEACHING HIS RECRUITS TO USE THE BAYONET  . . . .   92  3 DON JUAN  7    51   8
TEAPOT
   FRENCH STUFFS LACE TWEEZERS TOOTHPICKS TEAPOT TRAY . . 284  2 DON JUAN  3    17   5
TEAR
   OH SOBB'D ANTONIA I COULD TEAR THEIR EYES OUT . . . .  104  2 DON JUAN  1   152   8
   A TEAR OR TWO AND THEN WE MAKE IT UP . . . . . . .     119  2 DON JUAN  1   179   7
   AND YET SHE DID NOT LET ONE TEAR ESCAPE HER . . . .    134  2 DON JUAN  1   198   5
   AND STAND LIKE ROCKS THE TEMPEST'S WEAR AND TEAR . . . 191  2 DON JUAN  2    66   4
   INTO THE DEEP WITHOUT A TEAR OR GROAN . . . . . . .    202  2 DON JUAN  2    87   8
   THE SORT OF SOUND WE ECHO WITH A TEAR . . . . . . .    236  2 DON JUAN  2   151   6
   FOR GREEKS A BLUSH--FOR GREECE A TEAR . . . . . . .    323  2 DON JUAN  3  L 6   6
   WHILE ONE NEW TEAR AROSE IN HAIDEE'S EYE  . . . . .    355  2 DON JUAN  4    21   8
   AND NOW AND THEN A TEAR STOLE DOWN BY STEALTH . . . .  415  2 DON JUAN  5     8   4
   A SINGLE TEAR UPON HIS EYELASH STAID . . . . . . .     420  2 DON JUAN  5    18   4
   AND THESE ARE THINGS WHICH ASK A TENDER TEAR . . . .   420  2 DON JUAN  5    19   5
   HER EYES ANOTHER'S EYE COULD SHED A TEAR . . . . .     480  2 DON JUAN  5   119   8
   THE DRYING UP A SINGLE TEAR HAS MORE . . . . . . .     113  3 DON JUAN  8     3   7
   WERE MELTED FOR A MOMENT THOUGH NO TEAR . . . . . .    171  3 DON JUAN  8   119   6
   A LOVER AS HAD COST HER MANY A TEAR . . . . . . .      209  3 DON JUAN  9    54   7
   OF AGE AND LOOKING BACK TO YOUTH GIVE ONE TEAR-- . . . 238  3 DON JUAN 10    27   8
   HAD GATHERED A LARGE TEAR INTO ITS CORNER . . . . .    532  3 DON JUAN 16    65   2
TEAR-DROP
   MY OWN THE BURNING TEAR-DROP LAVES . . . . . . . .     326  2 DON JUAN  3  L 15   5
   A WOMAN'S TEAR-DROP MELTS A MAN'S HALF SEARS . . . .   479  2 DON JUAN  5   118   5
TEAR-DROPS
   THE BLACK BOUGH) TEAR-DROPS THROUGH HER EYES' DARK FRINGES . 40  3 DON JUAN  6    67   8
TEARING
   TEARING AND GRINNING HOWLING SCREECHING SWEARING . . . 198  2 DON JUAN  2    79   7
TEARS
   THE TEARS WERE GUSHING FROM HER GENTLE EYES . . . . .   84  2 DON JUAN  1   117   3
   I AM ASHAMED OF HAVING SHED THESE TEARS . . . . . .    106  2 DON JUAN  1   155   5
   SHE LAY HER DARK EYES FLASHING THROUGH THEIR TEARS . . 108  2 DON JUAN  1   158   2
   BUT BEAUTIFUL SHE LAY--HER EYES SHED TEARS . . . . .   108  2 DON JUAN  1   158  V2
   TO WHICH THE SOLE REPLY WERE TEARS AND SOBS . . . .    110  2 DON JUAN  1   162   2
   MY EYEBALLS BURN AND THROB BUT HAVE NO TEARS . . . .   130  2 DON JUAN  1   192   8
   THAT IS TILL DEEPER GRIEFS CONGEAL OUR TEARS . . . .   164  2 DON JUAN  2    15   8
   WHILE HIS SALT TEARS DROPP'D INTO THE SALT SEA . . . . 165  2 DON JUAN  2    17   2
   OF FIRE THAN WATER SPITE OF OATHS AND TEARS . . . .    174  2 DON JUAN  2    35   6
   THEN CAME THE CARPENTER AT LAST WITH TEARS . . . .     179  2 DON JUAN  2    43   1
   AND THEN OF THESE SOME PART BURST INTO TEARS . . . .   208  2 DON JUAN  2    98   1
   TILL THE EYE CHEATED OPENS THICK WITH TEARS . . . .    227  2 DON JUAN  2   134   8
   POURS FORTH AT LAST THE HEART'S-BLOOD TURN'D TO TEARS . 270  2 DON JUAN  2   214   7
   AND YOUTH STILL WEEPS THE TENDER TEARS THAT PLEASE-- . 273  2 DON JUAN  2  V 2   4
   AND TURN'D HER PURE HEART'S PUREST BLOOD TO TEARS . .  274  2 DON JUAN  3     1   8
   AND CLOG THE FOUNTAIN OF ETERNAL TEARS . . . . . .     275  2 DON JUAN  3     1  V8
   HER TEARS TOO BEING RETURN'D INTO THEIR FOUNT . . . .  295  2 DON JUAN  3    38   7
   TEARS SHED INTO THE GRAVE OF THE CONNEXION . . . . .   301  2 DON JUAN  3    50   7
```

808

TEARS   (CONTINUED)
```
    OF HER BLACK EYES SEEM'D TURN'D TO TEARS AND MURK . . . . 362  2 DON JUAN  4    33    6
    A MINUTE PAST AND SHE HAD BEEN ALL TEARS . . . . . . . 367  2 DON JUAN  4    43    1
    IN FIX'D FEROCITY WHEN JOYOUS TEARS . . . . . . . . 368  2 DON JUAN  4    45    6
    MOVED BY THE CHINESE NYMPH OF TEARS GREEN TEA . . . . . 372  2 DON JUAN  4    52    2
    THE TEARS RUSH'D FORTH FROM HER O'ERCLOUDED BRAIN . . . . 380  2 DON JUAN  4    66    7
    SUCH AS WAS MARY'S QUEEN OF SCOTS TRUE--TEARS . . . . . 468  2 DON JUAN  5    98    5
    SO THAT HE SPOKE NOT BUT BURST INTO TEARS . . . . . 478  2 DON JUAN  5   117    8
    SHE WAS A GOOD DEAL SHOCKED NOT SHOCKED AT TEARS . . . . 479  2 DON JUAN  5   118    1
    BUT TEARS MUST STOP LIKE ALL THINGS ELSE AND SOON . . . 481  2 DON JUAN  5   121    1
    AND THEN HER THIRST OF BLOOD WAS QUENCHED IN TEARS . . . 490  2 DON JUAN  5   136    8
    OF EARTH WAS WRINKLED BY THE SINS AND TEARS . . . . . . 9  3 DON JUAN  6     6    7
    WITH FLASHING EYES AND STARTING TEARS AND FLUNG . . . . 101  3 DON JUAN  7    67    7
    OF BLOOD AND TEARS MUST FLOW THE UNEBBING SEA . . . . . 101  3 DON JUAN  7    68    8
    SUWARROW WHO HAD SMALL REGARD FOR TEARS . . . . . . 102  3 DON JUAN  7    69    1
    AND THEN WITH TEARS AND SIGHS AND SOME SLIGHT KISSES . . . 105  3 DON JUAN  7    76    1
    HE DIED DESERVING WELL HIS COUNTRY'S TEARS . . . . . . 152  3 DON JUAN  8    80    5
    IN LOVE DRINKS ALL LIFE'S FOUNTAINS (SAVE TEARS) DRY . . . 216  3 DON JUAN  9    67    8
    SMILED AS SHE TALKED THE MATTER O'ER BUT TEARS . . . . 221  3 DON JUAN  9    78    6
    BUT SIGHS SUBSIDE AND TEARS (EVEN WIDOWS') SHRINK . . . . 228  3 DON JUAN 10     7    1
```
TEASE
```
    IS THAT THE DONNA INEZ DID NOT TEASE . . . . . . . . 73  2 DON JUAN  1    97    5
    BUT MORE OR LESS CONTINUE STILL TO TEASE ON . . . . . 437  2 DON JUAN  5    48    6
    WE TEASE MILD BAILLIE OR SOFT ABERNETHY . . . . . . 245  3 DON JUAN 10    42    8
```
TEASED
```
    HER CLIMACTERIC TEASED HER LIKE HER TEENS . . . . . . 247  3 DON JUAN 10    47    5
```
TEA-SPOONFULS
```
    A FEW TEA-SPOONFULS OF THEIR RUM AND WINE . . . . . . 189  2 DON JUAN  2    62    5
```
TEAT
```
    CLINGS TO ITS TEAT STICKS TO ME THROUGH THE ABYSS . . . . 238  3 DON JUAN 10    28    4
```
TEAZE
```
    IF BAD THE BEST WAY'S CERTAINLY TO TEAZE ON . . . . . 478  3 DON JUAN 15    51    3
```
TEDIOUSNESS
```
    I FEEL THIS TEDIOUSNESS WILL NEVER DO-- . . . . . . 342  2 DON JUAN  3   111    1
```
TEDIUM
```
    THEIR LUCKIER VOTARIES TILL OLD AGE'S TEDIUM . . . . . 235  3 DON JUAN 10    22    7
```
TEENS
```
    STILL IN HER TEENS AND LIKE A LOVELY TREE . . . . . . 224  2 DON JUAN  2   128    5
    I KNOW NOT NEVER COUNTING PAST THEIR TEENS . . . . . . 41  3 DON JUAN  6    69    4
    HER CLIMACTERIC TEASED HER LIKE HER TEENS . . . . . . 247  3 DON JUAN 10    47    5
```
TEETH
```
    MY TEETH BEGIN TO CHATTER MY VEINS FREEZE-- . . . . . 121  2 DON JUAN  1   181    6
    (SO CHILDREN CUTTING TEETH RECEIVE A CORAL) . . . . . 141  2 DON JUAN  1   209    4
    AND GNASH'D THEIR TEETH AND HOWLING TORE THEIR HAIR . . . 180  2 DON JUAN  2    45    4
    BUT THEN HER TEETH AND THEN OH HEAVEN HER EYES . . . . . 268  2 DON JUAN  2   210    4
    HAVING NO HEART TO SHOW HE SHOWS HIS TEETH . . . . . . 392  2 DON JUAN  4    89    8
    GOOD TEETH WITH CURLING RATHER DARK BROWN HAIR . . . . . 416  2 DON JUAN  5    11    3
    THE TEETH STILL KEPT THEIR GRATIFYING HOLD . . . . . 153  3 DON JUAN  8    83    7
    HE MADE THE TEETH MEET NOR RELINQUISHED IT . . . . . . 153  3 DON JUAN  8    84    6
    FOR THE TURK'S TEETH STUCK FASTER THAN A SKEWER . . . . 154  3 DON JUAN  8    85    3
    BUT IN HIS TEETH WHATE'ER THEIR STATE OR STATION . . . . 443  3 DON JUAN 14    77    7
    WHICH SETS THE TEETH ON EDGE AND A SLIGHT CLATTER . . . . 556  3 DON JUAN 16   114    2
```
TEIAN
```
    THE SCIAN AND THE TEIAN MUSE . . . . . . . . . 321  2 DON JUAN  3  L 2    1
    THE TEIAN BARD OF SCIO'S ISLE . . . . . . . . . 321  2 DON JUAN  3  L 2   V1
```
TEKEL
```
    SINCE MENE MENE TEKEL AND UPHARSIN . . . . . . . . 179  3 DON JUAN  8   134    2
```
TELESCOPE
```
    WAS SCANT ENOUGH IN VAIN THE TELESCOPE . . . . . . 178  2 DON JUAN  2    41    6
    THE STARS I OWN MY TELESCOPE IS DIM . . . . . . . 227  3 DON JUAN 10     4    2
```
TELL
```
    ('TWERE HARD TO TELL UPON A LIKE OCCASION . . . . . . 38  2 DON JUAN  1    32    3
    INDEED THERE WERE NOT MANY MORE TO TELL . . . . . . 40  2 DON JUAN  1    35    4
    I CAN'T TELL WHETHER JULIA SAW THE AFFAIR . . . . . . 59  2 DON JUAN  1    68    1
    AND EVEN IF BY CHANCE--AND WHO CAN TELL . . . . . . 64  2 DON JUAN  1    78    1
    BUT NOT MY FAULT--I TELL THEM ALL IN TIME . . . . . 65  2 DON JUAN  1    80    8
    THEY MAKE SOME BLUNDER WHICH THEIR LADIES TELL US . . . . 74  2 DON JUAN  1    98    8
    AND EVEN IF I KNEW I SHOULD NOT TELL-- . . . . . . 77  2 DON JUAN  1   105    3
    I CAN'T TELL HOW OR WHY OR WHAT SUSPICION . . . . . . 97  2 DON JUAN  1   139    1
    I CAN'T TELL WHY SHE SHOULD TAKE ALL THIS TROUBLE . . . . 97  2 DON JUAN  1   140    7
    NOW TELL ME DON'T YOU CUT A PRETTY FIGURE . . . . . . 103  2 DON JUAN  1   150    8
    TELL ME--AND BE ASSURED THAT SINCE YOU STAIN . . . . . 105  2 DON JUAN  1   154    7
    ONLY ANOTHER TIME I TRUST YOU'LL TELL US . . . . . . 106  2 DON JUAN  1   156    5
    (NO ONE CAN TELL HOW MUCH I GRIEVE TO SAY) . . . . . 121  2 DON JUAN  1   181    3
    THEY TELL ME 'TIS DECIDED YOU DEPART . . . . . . . 130  2 DON JUAN  1   192    1
    I TELL HIM IF A CLERGYMAN HE LIES . . . . . . . 141  2 DON JUAN  1   208    6
    BECAUSE THEY TELL ME 'TWERE IN VAIN TO TRY . . . . . 142  2 DON JUAN  1   211    6
    I'LL TELL YOU WHY I SAY SO FOR 'TIS JUST . . . . . 219  2 DON JUAN  2   119    1
    I'LL TELL YOU WHO THEY WERE THIS FEMALE PAIR . . . . . 222  2 DON JUAN  2   124    1
    HIS SMILE REQUESTED ONE OF THEM TO TELL . . . . . . 298  2 DON JUAN  3    44    6
    HE SEEMED TO SLEEP FOR YOU COULD SCARCELY TELL . . . . 430  2 DON JUAN  5    35    5
    BUT STRONG AND LASTING TILL NO TONGUE CAN TELL . . . . 444  2 DON JUAN  5    59    4
    I HAVE NO AUTHORITY TO TELL THE REASON . . . . . . 454  2 DON JUAN  5    74    8
    YOU FOOL I TELL YOU NO ONE MEANS YOU HARM . . . . . 459  2 DON JUAN  5    82    1
    WHEN WE NEXT MEET WE'LL HAVE A TALE TO TELL . . . . . 460  2 DON JUAN  5    84    4
    THOUGH HORRIBLE TO SEE YET GRAND TO TELL . . . . . . 489  2 DON JUAN  5   135    5
    AND SO MUST TELL THE TRUTH HOWE'ER YOU BLAME IT . . . . 10  3 DON JUAN  6     8    4
    SO CANTEMIR CAN TELL YOU OR DETOTT . . . . . . . 21  3 DON JUAN  6    31    5
    I CAN'T TELL WHY SHE BLUSHED NOR CAN EXPOUND . . . . . 48  3 DON JUAN  6    85    5
```

TELL   (CONTINUED)
	PAGE	VOL		CANTO	STANZA	LN
WHO WERE IMMORTAL COULD ONE TELL THEIR STORY	73	3 DON JUAN		7	14	4
I'D RATHER TELL TEN LIES THAN SAY A WORD	77	3 DON JUAN		7	22	4
I CANNOT TELL THE WAY IN WHICH HE PLEADED	85	3 DON JUAN		7	38	4
I BY-AND-BY MAY TELL YOU IF AT ALL	181	3 DON JUAN		8	139	4
AND LIKE SOME OTHER THINGS WON'T DO TO TELL	184	3 DON JUAN		9	2	3
WAS NOT SO NECESSARY FOR THEY TELL	214	3 DON JUAN		9	63	2
TELL FOR ITSELF THE SOVEREIGN WAS SMITTEN	221	3 DON JUAN		9	77	2
I CANNOT TELL EXACTLY WHAT IT WAS	250	3 DON JUAN		10	53	3
TO TELL YOU TRUTHS YOU WILL NOT TAKE AS TRUE	266	3 DON JUAN		10	84	5
TELL THEM THAT YOUTH ONCE GONE RETURNS NO MORE	267	3 DON JUAN		10	86	3
TELL THEM SIR WILLIAM CURTIS IS A BORE	267	3 DON JUAN		10	86	5
TELL THEM THOUGH IT MAY BE PERHAPS TOO LATE	267	3 DON JUAN		10	87	1
AND TELL THEM--BUT YOU WON'T AND I HAVE PRATED	267	3 DON JUAN		10	87	6
BEFORE DON JUAN'S FEET HE COULD NOT TELL	276	3 DON JUAN		11	17	2
WHERE LITTLE CASTLEREAGH THE DEVIL CAN TELL	307	3 DON JUAN		11	77	2
AS I'LL TELL AUREA AT TO-MORROW'S ROUT	332	3 DON JUAN		12	35	6
AND THESE VICISSITUDES TELL BEST IN YOUTH	339	3 DON JUAN		12	50	1
TO THE NEXT COMER OR--AS IT WILL TELL	339	3 DON JUAN		12	51	7
ALL CARVED AND GILDED OR--AS IT WILL TELL	339	3 DON JUAN		12	51	V7
AND TELL ME WHAT YOU THINK OF YOUR GREAT THINKERS	357	3 DON JUAN		12	89	8
I TELL THE TALE AS IT IS TOLD NOR DARE	365	3 DON JUAN		13	13	1
PROUD OF HIMSELF AND HER THE WORLD COULD TELL	365	3 DON JUAN		13	14	6
WHEN EACH HOUSE WAS A FORTALICE--AS TELL	386	3 DON JUAN		13	60	5
IF BRITAIN MOURN HER BLEAKNESS WE CAN TELL HER	394	3 DON JUAN		13	76	7
WITH WIT TO HATCH A PUN OR TELL A STORY	401	3 DON JUAN		13	91	6
IS DIFFICULT PRAY TELL ME CAN YOU MAKE FAST	411	3 DON JUAN		14	2	3
WITH MORE EASE TOO SHE'D TELL A DIFFERENT STORY	416	3 DON JUAN		14	13	8
TO TELL HOW HE REDUCED THE NATION'S DEBT	440	3 DON JUAN		14	68	4
I DON'T KNOW WHAT AND THEREFORE CANNOT TELL--	441	3 DON JUAN		14	71	2
AH WHO CAN TELL OR RATHER WHO CAN NOT	457	3 DON JUAN		15	4	1
BUT NOW I CAN'T TELL WHERE IT MAY NOT RUN	466	3 DON JUAN		15	22	4
HAD ADELINE READ MALTHUS I CAN'T TELL	472	3 DON JUAN		15	38	1
IN THE FEAST PECKING LESS THAN I CAN TELL	487	3 DON JUAN		15	70	4
OF WHICH I CAN'T TELL WHENCE THEIR KNOWLEDGE SPRINGS	489	3 DON JUAN		15	76	4
TRUE IS THAT WHICH SHE IS ABOUT TO TELL	502	3 DON JUAN		16	4	2
DYED PURPLE NONE AT PRESENT CAN TELL HOW	505	3 DON JUAN		16	10	6
HIS READINESS TO FEEL HIS PULSE AND TELL	514	3 DON JUAN		16	32	7
I CAN'T TELL WHY TO THIS DISSIMULATION--	518	3 DON JUAN		16	40	1
ONE CAN'T TELL HOW IT E'ER GOT IN OR OUT	531	3 DON JUAN		16	62	2
WHEN HE CAN'T TELL WHAT 'TIS THAT DOTH APPAL	559	3 DON JUAN		16	120	6

TELLING
	PAGE	VOL		CANTO	STANZA	LN
AFAR A DWARF BUFFOON STOOD TELLING TALES	293	2 DON JUAN		3	34	1
REMEMBER WITHOUT TELLING PASSION'S ERRORS	457	3 DON JUAN		15	4	2

TELLS
	PAGE	VOL		CANTO	STANZA	LN
AND THEN YOUR HERO TELLS WHENE'ER YOU PLEASE	24	2 DON JUAN		1	6	3
ALTHOUGH LONGINUS TELLS US THERE IS NO HYMN	45	2 DON JUAN		1	42	5
AND TELLS ME TO RESUME MY STORY HERE	347	2 DON JUAN		4	7	8
AND NOTHING OUTWARD TELLS OF HUMAN CLAY	383	2 DON JUAN		4	72	4
VOLTAIRE SAYS NO HE TELLS YOU THAT CANDIDE	427	2 DON JUAN		5	31	1
MAN WITH HIS HEAD REFLECTS--(AS SPURZHEIM TELLS)	7	3 DON JUAN		6	2	V7
CARNAGE (SO WORDSWORTH TELLS YOU) IS GOD'S DAUGHTER	116	3 DON JUAN		8	9	6
WHICH HAMLET TELLS US IS A PASS OF DREAD	133	3 DON JUAN		8	41	4
WITHOUT CASH MALTHUS TELLS YOU TAKE NO BRIDES	322	3 DON JUAN		12	14	4
TELLS AN ODD STORY OF WHICH BY THE BYE	516	3 DON JUAN		16	36	4

TEMPER
	PAGE	VOL		CANTO	STANZA	LN
HIS TEMPER NOT BEING UNDER GREAT COMMAND	123	2 DON JUAN		1	185	4
LOSING ELECTIONS CHARACTER AND TEMPER	150	2 DON JUAN		1	V 1	7
AND HASTY TEMPER ON A KINDLING MIND	155	2 DON JUAN		1	V 7	2
OF FAULT OR TEMPER RUIN'D THE CONNEXION	281	2 DON JUAN		3	10	5
NOR FLATTERING TO THEIR TEMPER OR THEIR TASTE	230	3 DON JUAN		10	11	5
THAT TIME WOULD TEMPER JUAN'S FAULTS OF YOUTH	439	3 DON JUAN		14	67	5
THOUGH MUCH IN TEMPER BUT THEY NEVER CLASH'D	447	3 DON JUAN		14	87	2
BECAUSE SHE SAID HER TEMPER HAD BEEN TRIED	525	3 DON JUAN		16	50	4
TEMPERATE I AM--YET NEVER HAD A TEMPER	567	3 DON JUAN		17	11	1

TEMPERAMENT
	PAGE	VOL		CANTO	STANZA	LN
HE WAS A MAN OF A STRANGE TEMPERAMENT	302	2 DON JUAN		3	53	1
A THING OF TEMPERAMENT AND NOT OF ART	547	3 DON JUAN		16	97	5

TEMPERANCE
	PAGE	VOL		CANTO	STANZA	LN
WITH TEMPERANCE IN PLEASURE AS IN FOOD	302	2 DON JUAN		3	53	4
TEMPERANCE DELIGHTS HER BUT LONG FASTING RUFFLES	542	3 DON JUAN		16	86	8

TEMPERATE
	PAGE	VOL		CANTO	STANZA	LN
LEARN'D PIOUS TEMPERATE IN LOVE AND WINE	328	2 DON JUAN		3	91	4
NEITHER--BUT A GOOD PLAIN OLD TEMPERATE MAN	164	3 DON JUAN		8	105	7
AND SCORN HIS TEMPERATE BOARD AS NONE AT ALL	316	3 DON JUAN		12	3	6
BUT THOUGH I AM A TEMPERATE THEOLOGIAN	497	3 DON JUAN		15	92	1
TEMPERATE I AM--YET NEVER HAD A TEMPER	567	3 DON JUAN		17	11	1

TEMPER'D
	PAGE	VOL		CANTO	STANZA	LN
HER DAUGHTER TEMPER'D WITH A MILDER RAY	375	2 DON JUAN		4	57	1
HIS TACT TOO TEMPER'D HIM FROM GRAVE TO GAY	492	3 DON JUAN		15	82	5

TEMPER'S
	PAGE	VOL		CANTO	STANZA	LN
MY NATURAL TEMPER'S REALLY AUGHT BUT STERN	300	3 DON JUAN		11	63	5

TEMPEST
	PAGE	VOL		CANTO	STANZA	LN
FORETELLS THE HEAVIEST TEMPEST IT DISPLAYS	61	2 DON JUAN		1	73	3
TERROR TO EARTH AND TEMPEST TO THE AIR	375	2 DON JUAN		4	57	4
A VULGAR TEMPEST 'TWERE TO A TYPHOON	490	2 DON JUAN		5	136	1
HAD SKETCHES OF LOVE TEMPEST TRAVEL WAR--	181	3 DON JUAN		8	138	3
LOVE WAR A TEMPEST--SURELY THERE'S VARIETY	416	3 DON JUAN		14	14	1

TEMPEST'S
	PAGE	VOL		CANTO	STANZA	LN
AND STAND LIKE ROCKS THE TEMPEST'S WEAR AND TEAR	191	2 DON JUAN		2	66	4
WHICH MOURN'D THE POWER OF TIME'S OR TEMPEST'S MARCH	386	3 DON JUAN		13	59	7

		PAGE	VOL		CANTO	STANZA	LN

TEMPESTS
OF SEAMEN'S FATES AND THE LOUD TEMPESTS RAISE . . . . . 414 2 DON JUAN 5 6 4
THE WORST OF TEMPESTS AND THE BEST OF BATTLES . . . . . 356 3 DON JUAN 12 88 3
TEMPEST-TOST
A BETTER WELCOME TO THE TEMPEST-TOST . . . . 249 2 DON JUAN 2 177 5
TEMPLE
AS AN OLD TEMPLE DWINDLED TO A COLUMN . . . . 358 3 DON JUAN 13 1 8
TEMPLES
BY STEALTH HER HUSBAND'S TEMPLES TO ENCUMBER . . . . 96 2 DON JUAN 1 138 6
AND BATHING HIS CHILL TEMPLES TRIED TO SOOTHE . . . . . 215 2 DON JUAN 2 113 5
HIS HOLY TEMPLES IN THE LANDS WHICH BRED . . . . . . 262 3 DON JUAN 10 75 5
TEMPORARY
WHOSE TEMPORARY PASSION WAS QUITE FLATTERING . . . . . 217 3 DON JUAN 9 70 3
TEMPT
NOTHING SHOULD TEMPT HIM MORE (THIS PERIL PAST) . . . . 175 2 DON JUAN 2 37 5
THEIR TABLE WAS A BOARD TO TEMPT EVEN GHOSTS . . . . . 404 3 DON JUAN 13 99 3
TEMPTATION
SHOULD RATHER FACE AND OVERCOME TEMPTATION . . . . . 63 2 DON JUAN 1 77 2
FOR LEAVING JUAN TO THIS NEW TEMPTATION . . . . 75 2 DON JUAN 1 101 4
NOT THAT REMORSE DID NOT OPPOSE TEMPTATION . . . . . 84 2 DON JUAN 1 117 6
FORM NOT THE TRUE TEMPTATION WHICH ALLURES . . . . . 332 2 DON JUAN 3 97 5
HAVING WITHSTOOD TEMPTATION IN MY YOUTH . . . . 397 2 DON JUAN 4 97 2
OF ANY SLIGHT TEMPTATION IN THEIR WAY . . . . 235 3 DON JUAN 10 21 4
JUST NOW THERE WAS NO PERIL OF TEMPTATION . . . . . . 251 3 DON JUAN 10 55 1
THEMSELVES ON SELDOM YIELDING TO TEMPTATION . . . . . 327 3 DON JUAN 12 25 V7
EXPOSED HIM AS WAS NATURAL TO TEMPTATION . . . . . . 355 3 DON JUAN 12 85 7
WHICH IS FOR INNOCENCE A SAD TEMPTATION-- . . . . . . 468 3 DON JUAN 15 28 6
AND POSITIVELY HENCEFORTH NO TEMPTATION . . . . . . 498 3 DON JUAN 15 94 2
TEMPTER
FOR THAT SAD TEMPTER A FORBIDDEN WOMAN . . . . . . 10 3 DON JUAN 6 7 4
TEN
AND HAVE TEN THOUSAND DELICATE INVENTIONS . . . . . . 221 2 DON JUAN 2 123 4
AND AVERAGED EACH FROM TEN TO A HUNDRED DOLLARS . . . 283 2 DON JUAN 3 15 8
(THE LEAST OF WHICH WOULD SET TEN POETS RAVING) . . . 291 2 DON JUAN 3 30 6
COMPOSED A CHOIR OF GIRLS TEN OR A DOZEN . . . . . . 469 2 DON JUAN 5 99 2
I'D RATHER TELL TEN LIES THAN SAY A WORD . . . . . . 77 2 DON JUAN 7 22 4
SO THAT ON EITHER SIDE SOME NINE OR TEN . . . . . . 136 3 DON JUAN 8 47 1
A FEMALE CHILD OF TEN YEARS TRIED TO STOOP . . . . . 157 3 DON JUAN 8 91 6
YOU'LL FIND TEN THOUSAND HANDSOME COXCOMBS BLOODY . . . . 167 3 DON JUAN 8 112 8
YE TWICE TEN HUNDRED THOUSAND DAILY SCRIBES . . . . . 200 3 DON JUAN 9 35 2
OF LIFE REACH TEN O'CLOCK AND WHILE A GLOW . . . . . 229 3 DON JUAN 10 8 5
BUT WHERE THERMOMETERS SUNK DOWN TO TEN . . . . . . 241 3 DON JUAN 10 33 6
BUT SHE WAS YET BUT TEN YEARS OLD AND THEREFORE . . . 250 3 DON JUAN 10 52 7
HE SAW TEN THOUSAND LIVING AUTHORS PASS . . . . . . 295 3 DON JUAN 11 54 5
WHERE ARE TEN THOUSAND LOVELY INNOCENTS . . . . . . 307 3 DON JUAN 11 77 V7
BUT SIXTEEN DOWAGERS TEN UNWED SHE SAGES . . . . . . 330 3 DON JUAN 12 30 7
NINE TIMES IN TEN 'TIS BUT CAPRICE OR FASHION . . . . 351 3 DON JUAN 12 77 3
PEOPLE SOME TEN TIMES LESS IN FACT TO MIND IT . . . . 352 3 DON JUAN 12 80 3
AND THEN RETREATED SOBERLY--AT TEN . . . . 408 3 DON JUAN 13 108 8
WHAT ANTHROPOPHAGI IN NINE OF TEN . . . . 455 3 DON JUAN 14 102 5
AT LEAST NINE AND A NINTH BESIDE OF TEN . . . . . . 468 3 DON JUAN 15 26 4
TENANT
BECAUSE THE TIMES HAVE HARDLY LEFT THEM ONE TENANT . . . 308 3 DON JUAN 11 80 8
TENANTS
ITS DWELLINGS DOWN ITS TENANTS PAST AWAY . . . . . . 383 2 DON JUAN 4 72 2
TEND
AND MERELY TEND TO SHOW HOW GREATLY LOVE IS . . . . . 62 2 DON JUAN 1 74 7
THE RACE HE SPRAINS A WING AND DOWN WE TEND . . . . . 344 2 DON JUAN 4 1 4
SOME BY A PLACE--AS TEND THEIR YEARS OR NATURES . . . . 425 2 DON JUAN 5 27 6
'TWOULD GREATLY TEND TO BETTER THEIR CONDITION . . . . 451 2 DON JUAN 5 69 7
BUT THOUGH YOUR YEARS AS MAN TEND FAST TO ZERO . . . . 184 3 DON JUAN 9 2 7
TENDED
AND THESE TWO TENDED HIM AND CHEER'D HIM BOTH . . . . 221 2 DON JUAN 2 123 1
HER HANDMAIDS TENDED BUT SHE HEEDED NOT . . . . . . 379 2 DON JUAN 4 64 1
TENDENCY
COULD STOP THE TENDENCY TO PROPAGATION . . . . 15 3 DON JUAN 6 19 V8
MY TENDENCY IS TO PHILOSOPHIZE . . . . 37 3 DON JUAN 6 63 3
A TENDENCY TO UNDER-RATE AND SCOFF . . . . 67 3 DON JUAN 7 3 3
HAVE ALWAYS HAD A TENDENCY TO SPARE-- . . . . 193 3 DON JUAN 9 21 6
TENDER
A HINT IN TENDER CASES IS ENOUGH . . . . 119 2 DON JUAN 1 178 1
AND YOUTH STILL WEEPS THE TENDER TEARS THAT PLEASE-- . . 273 2 DON JUAN 2 V 2 4
AND THESE ARE THINGS WHICH ASK A TENDER TEAR . . . . 420 2 DON JUAN 5 19 5
MORE TENDER AS WE EVERY DAY BEHOLD . . . . 439 2 DON JUAN 5 49 6
AND MUCH MORE TENDER ON THE WHOLE THAN FIERCE . . . . 19 3 DON JUAN 6 27 5
THEY PUT BEHOLDERS IN A TENDER TAKING . . . . . . 27 3 DON JUAN 6 43 4
ALOUD BECAUSE HIS FEELINGS WERE TOO TENDER . . . . . 50 3 DON JUAN 6 89 3
WHEREON THE RUSSIAN PATHOS GREW LESS TENDER . . . . . 165 3 DON JUAN 8 107 6
THE TOPIC'S TENDER SO SHALL BE MY PHRASE-- . . . . . 176 3 DON JUAN 8 128 5
AND YET THIS WANT OF TIES MADE THEIR'S MORE TENDER . . 252 3 DON JUAN 10 57 8
THE BLUES THAT TENDER TRIBE WHO SIGH O'ER SONNETS . . . 294 3 DON JUAN 11 50 1
AND TALK IN TENDER HORRORS OF OUR LOATHING . . . . . 301 3 DON JUAN 11 65 6
CAN TENDER SOULS RELATE THE RISE AND FALL . . . . . 304 3 DON JUAN 11 72 7
HOW SHOULD THE TENDER PASSION E'ER BE TOUGH . . . . . 451 3 DON JUAN 14 94 8
TO BAIT THEIR TENDER OR THEIR TENTER HOOKS . . . . . 453 3 DON JUAN 14 97 8
THEIR TENDER PARENTS IN THEIR BUDDING DAYS . . . . . 562 3 DON JUAN 17 1 6
LEFT IN A TENDER MOONLIGHT SITUATION . . . . 567 3 DON JUAN 17 12 2
TENDERLY
SHE SLEPT NOT BUT ALL TENDERLY THOUGH FAST . . . . . 260 2 DON JUAN 2 195 3

```
                                                           PAGE VOL      CANTO STANZA  LV
TENDERNESS
    WITH TENDERNESS--STOOD HOWLING ON THE BRINK . . . . .  187  2 DON JUAN  2    58    4
    WITH SWIMMING LOOKS OF SPEECHLESS TENDERNESS  . . . .  357  2 DON JUAN  4    26    2
    AND TENDERNESS AND INFANCY BUT NOW . . . . . . . . .   367  2 DON JUAN  4    43    2
    BUT MERELY THEIR PARENTAL TENDERNESS . . . . . . . .   562  3 DON JUAN 17     1    7
TENDING
    BUT TO THE MAIN POINT WHERE WE HAVE BEEN TENDING--  . .  478  2 DON JUAN  5   116    1
TENDON
    THE VERY TENDON WHICH IS MOST ACUTE-- . . . . . . . .  153  3 DON JUAN  8    84    3
TENDS
    THAT HALF ITS PRODUCE TENDS TO EMIGRATION  . . . . .   472  3 DON JUAN 15    37    6
TENIERS
    BUT LO A TENIERS WOOS AND NOT IN VAIN  . . . . . . .   392  3 DON JUAN 13    72    5
TENOR
    THAN DID THE PRIMA-DONNA AND THE TENOR . . . . . . .   388  2 DON JUAN  4    81    8
    THE TENOR THESE TWO HATED WITH A HATE . . . . . . .    394  2 DON JUAN  4    93    2
TENOR'S
    HAS SOME GOOD NOTES AND THEN THE TENOR'S WIFE  . . .   389  2 DON JUAN  4    83    4
    THE TENOR'S VOICE IS SPOILT BY AFFECTATION . . . . .   391  2 DON JUAN  4    87    1
TENSE
    WITH HIS GREY SIGNAL FLAG AND THE PAST TENSE  . . . .  376  3 DON JUAN 13    40    5
TENT
    TO THE OTHER BAGGAGE OR TO THE SICK TENT . . . . . .   100  3 DON JUAN  7    66    8
    BOTH BUSY (AS A GENERAL IN HIS TENT  . . . . . . . .   533  3 DON JUAN 16    66    6
TENTER
    TO BAIT THEIR TENDER OR THEIR TENTER HOOKS  . . . . .  453  3 DON JUAN 14    97    8
TENTH
    THE TENTH OR TWENTIETH NAME WOULD BE BUT BLUNDERED  . .  324  3 DON JUAN 12    19    4
    BUT THE TENTH INSTANCE WILL BE A TORNADO . . . . . .   351  3 DON JUAN 12    77    7
TENURES
    ALSO A LAWSUIT UPON TENURES BURGAGE  . . . . . . .     530  3 DON JUAN 16    60    3
TER
    ET HAUSTUS TER IN DIE CAPIENDUS . . . . . . . . .      244  3 DON JUAN 10    41    8
TERES
    TO BE A TOTUS TERES STOIC SAGE . . . . . . . . . .     566  3 DON JUAN 17    10    7
TERM
    A TERM INEXPLICABLE TO THE MUSE . . . . . . . . .      224  3 DON JUAN  9    84    8
    SEVEN YEARS (THE USUAL TERM OF TRANSPORTATION) . . .   257  3 DON JUAN 10    66    6
    THAT VIOLENT THINGS MORE QUICKLY FIND A TERM . . . .   451  3 DON JUAN 14    94    3
    PIOUS AND PURE BEYOND WHAT I CAN TERM ANY  . . . . .   472  3 DON JUAN 15    36    5
TERMED
    THUS HE PROFANELY TERMED THE FINEST LACE . . . . . .   455  2 DON JUAN  5    76    7
TERMS
    AND (IF LET IN) INSISTS IN TERMS UNHANDSOME . . . . .  459  3 DON JUAN 15     8    7
    OR ON HIS MISTRESS--TERMS SYNONIMOUS--  . . . . . .    509  3 DON JUAN 16    20    2
TERRESTRIAL
    AS BEING A VIRTUE LIKE TERRESTRIAL PATIENCE . . . . .  165  3 DON JUAN  8   107    7
TERRIBLE
    AS TERRIBLE AS THAT OF ILION . . . . . . . . . . .     106  3 DON JUAN  7    78    3
    TO WIELD THEM IN THEIR TERRIBLE ARRAY . . . . . . .    113  3 DON JUAN  8     2    2
    THE FIRST TIME THOUGHT QUITE TERRIBLE ENOUGH . . . .   134  3 DON JUAN  8    42    2
TERRIER
    A TERRIER TOO WHICH ONCE HAD BEEN A BRITON'S . . . .   285  2 DON JUAN  3    18    4
TERRIFIC
    MY CUE FOR ANY TIME TO BE TERRIFIC . . . . . . . .     156  3 DON JUAN  8    89    2
TERROR
    TERROR TO EARTH AND TEMPEST TO THE AIR . . . . . .     375  2 DON JUAN  4    57    4
    TURNS LIFE TO TERROR EVEN THOUGH IN ITS SHEATH . . .   188  3 DON JUAN  9    11    7
    'TIS TRUE YOU DON'T--BUT PALE AND STRUCK WITH TERROR .  413  3 DON JUAN 14     6    1
TERRORS
    THEY FELT NO TERRORS FROM THE NIGHT THEY WERE  . . .   256  2 DON JUAN  2   189    2
    AND ALL ITS CHARM LIKE DEATH WITHOUT ITS TERRORS . .   261  2 DON JUAN  2   197    8
    WITH INFANT TERRORS GLARED AS FROM A TRANCE . . . .    159  3 DON JUAN  8    96    6
    HE CANNOT SINK HIS TREMORS OR HIS TERRORS  . . . . .   457  3 DON JUAN 15     4    6
TERSE
    'TIS SO SENTENTIOUS POSITIVE AND TERSE  . . . . . .     17  3 DON JUAN  6    23    6
TERTIAN
    HE DIED OF THE SLOW FEVER CALL'D THE TERTIAN . . . .    39  2 DON JUAN  1    34    7
    AT WATCH AND WATCH THUS SHIVERING LIKE THE TERTIAN  . .  189  2 DON JUAN  2    63    6
TERTIANS
    HIS FEELINGS HAD NOT THOSE STRANGE FITS LIKE TERTIANS .  366  3 DON JUAN 13    17    5
TEST
    THIS WAS AN AWKWARD TEST AS JUAN FOUND . . . . . .     484  3 DON JUAN  5   126    1
    TO BE PRODUCED WHEN BROUGHT UP TO THE TEST . . . . .   123  3 DON JUAN  8    25    4
    AND HE COULD EVEN WITHSTAND THAT AWKWARD TEST  . . .   139  3 DON JUAN  8    53    5
    THE KINDEST MAY BE TAKEN AS A TEST . . . . . . . .     359  3 DON JUAN 13     3    6
    WHEN SOME SMART TALKER PUTS THEM TO THE TEST . . . .   404  3 DON JUAN 13    98    7
    FOR SHE HAD SEEN THE WORLD AND STOOD ITS TEST  . . .   433  3 DON JUAN 14    54    4
TETE
    IN SOULS IMMORTAL SHUN THEM TETE A TETE . . . . . .    556  3 DON JUAN 16   114    8
    IN SOULS IMMORTAL SHUN THEM TETE A TETE . . . . . .    556  3 DON JUAN 16   114    8
TETE-A-TETE
    INTO A COMFORTABLE TETE-A-TETE . . . . . . . . .      482  2 DON JUAN  5   122    6
    IS BETTER THAN AN HUMDRUM TETE-A-TETE . . . . . . .    402  3 DON JUAN 13    94    4
TETERRIMA
    OH THOU TETERRIMA CAUSA OF ALL BELLI--  . . . . . .    210  3 DON JUAN  9    55    1
TEXT
    COULD TURN THEIR OPTICS TO THE TEXT AND PRAY . . . .    47  2 DON JUAN  1    46    6
    MY TEXT WITH MANY THINGS THAT NO ONE KNOWS . . . . .   138  2 DON JUAN  1   204    5
```

TEXT   (CONTINUED)

TEXT	PAGE	VOL	CANTO		STANZA	LN
THEY WRITE AND FOR WHAT END BUT NOTE OR TEXT	203	3	DON JUAN	9	41	7
TO THE OLD TEXT STILL BETTER--LEST IT SHOULD	270	3	DON JUAN	11	4	2

THAMES

THE TIGRIS HATH ITS JEALOUSIES LIKE THAMES	11	3	DON JUAN	6	11	8
FOR BOTH COMMODITIES DWELL BY THE THAMES	293	3	DON JUAN	11	48	3

THAMIS

HAIL THAMIS HAIL UPON THY VERGE IT IS	277	3	DON JUAN	11	20	4
THAT'S RATHER FINE THE GENTLE SOUND OF THAMIS--	279	3	DON JUAN	11	24	1

THAN

THAN JOSE WHO BEGOT OUR HERO WHO	26	2	DON JUAN	1	9	7
IS BROUGHT UP MUCH MORE WISELY THAN ANOTHER	42	2	DON JUAN	1	37	8
IS MORE THAN I KNOW--BUT DON JUAN'S MOTHER	47	2	DON JUAN	1	46	7
HIS BLOOD LESS NOBLE THAN SUCH BLOOD SHOULD BE	52	2	DON JUAN	1	57	3
PRODUCED HER DON MORE HEIRS AT LOVE THAN LAW	53	2	DON JUAN	1	58	8
FLASH'D AN EXPRESSION MORE OF PRIDE THAN IRE	54	2	DON JUAN	1	60	4
AND LOVE THAN EITHER AND THERE WOULD ARISE	54	2	DON JUAN	1	60	5
THAN HE WHO NEVER SAW THE SEA OF OCEAN	60	2	DON JUAN	1	70	8
SHE LOOK'D A SADNESS SWEETER THAN HER SMILE	61	2	DON JUAN	1	72	2
FOR PEOPLE WHO ARE PLEASANTER THAN OTHERS	63	2	DON JUAN	1	77	7
AND STAND CONVICTED OF MORE TRUTH THAN TREASON	76	2	DON JUAN	1	102	6
OF HUMAN HEARTS THAN ALL THE LONG ARRAY	84	2	DON JUAN	1	116	5
AT BEST NO BETTER THAN A GO-BETWEEN	84	2	DON JUAN	1	116	8
BUT SWEETER STILL THAN THIS THAN THESE THAN ALL	90	2	DON JUAN	1	127	1
BUT SWEETER STILL THAN THIS THAN THESE THAN ALL	90	2	DON JUAN	1	127	1
BUT SWEETER STILL THAN THIS THAN THESE THAN ALL	90	2	DON JUAN	1	127	1
WITH MORE THAN HALF THE CITY AT HIS BACK--	96	2	DON JUAN	1	137	2
AND LOUDER THAN HER BREATHING BEATS HER HEART	108	2	DON JUAN	1	158	8
NO SOONER WAS IT BOLTED THAN--OH SHAME	112	2	DON JUAN	1	165	1
'TWERE BETTER SURE TO DIE SO THAN BE SHUT	112	2	DON JUAN	1	166	7
THERE'S MORE THAN ONE EDITION AND THE READINGS	127	2	DON JUAN	1	189	5
NONE CAN DEEM HARSHLIER OF ME THAN I DEEM	130	2	DON JUAN	1	193	6
YOUR PATIENCE FURTHER THAN BY THIS SHORT SAMPLE--	147	2	DON JUAN	1	221	7
LESS FOR THE COMPREHENSION THAN THE EAR	152	2	DON JUAN	1	V 3	6
THAN MANY PERSONS MORE ADVANCED IN LIFE	164	2	DON JUAN	2	15	4
THAN I RESIGN THINE IMAGE OH MY FAIR	166	2	DON JUAN	2	19	5
OF FIRE THAN WATER SPITE OF OATHS AND TEARS	174	2	DON JUAN	2	35	6
LOUDER THAN THE LOUD OCEAN LIKE A CRASH	184	2	DON JUAN	2	53	2
THAN WHAT IT HAD BEEN FOR SO STRONG IT BLEW	185	2	DON JUAN	2	54	4
ARE LONGER LIVED THAN OTHERS--GOD KNOWS WHY	190	2	DON JUAN	2	65	2
MORE THAN CAN BE BELIEVED OR EVEN THOUGHT	191	2	DON JUAN	2	66	3
HAPPIER THAN THEY WHO STILL PERCEIVED THEIR WOES	199	2	DON JUAN	2	80	4
WITHOUT BEING MUCH MORE HORRIBLE THAN DANTE	200	2	DON JUAN	2	83	8
CLEARER THAN THAT WITHOUT AND ITS WIDE HUE	204	2	DON JUAN	2	91	5
THAN THESE AND SO THIS RAINBOW LOOK'D LIKE HOPE--	205	2	DON JUAN	2	93	7
THEY THOUGHT THAT IN SUCH PERILS MORE THAN CHANCE	208	2	DON JUAN	2	99	7
THAN ALL THE NONSENSE OF THEIR STONE IDEAL)	218	2	DON JUAN	2	118	8
BETTER THAN HER KNEW WHAT IN FACT SHE MEANT	228	2	DON JUAN	2	136	3
BUT ZOE BEING OLDER THAN HAIDEE	239	2	DON JUAN	2	158	5
RATHER BY DEEDS THAN WORDS BECAUSE THE CASE	240	2	DON JUAN	2	159	2
NO DOUBT LESS OF HER LANGUAGE THAN HER LOOK	242	2	DON JUAN	2	163	4
TURNS OFTENER TO THE STARS THAN TO HIS BOOK	242	2	DON JUAN	2	163	6
FROM HAIDEE'S GLANCE THAN ANY GRAVEN LETTER	242	2	DON JUAN	2	163	8
AND THINKS HEAVEN BRIGHTER EVEN THAN NEWTON'S PAGE	242	2	DON JUAN	2	163	V7
MORE THAN WITHIN THE BOSOM OF A NUN	244	2	DON JUAN	2	167	5
WITH SOMETIMES MORE WITHIN THEM THAN ONE TONGUE	254	2	DON JUAN	2	187	V8
SAW NOTHING HAPPIER THAN HER GLOWING FACE	262	2	DON JUAN	2	198	8
THAN ADMIRATION DUE WHERE NATURE'S RICH	269	2	DON JUAN	2	211	3
THAN ANY OF THE PARODIES OF PITT	283	2	DON JUAN	3	14	V8
MUCH LESS EXPERIENCE OF DRY LAND THAN OCEAN	289	2	DON JUAN	3	26	2
BUT KNEW THE CAUSE NO MORE THAN A PHILOSOPHER	289	2	DON JUAN	3	26	8
IN FACT MUCH MORE ASTONISH'D THAN DELIGHTED	294	2	DON JUAN	3	37	7
FOR HAIDEE'S SAKE IS MORE THAN I CAN SAY	300	2	DON JUAN	3	49	6
PERHAPS THAN EVEN THE MENTAL PANGS OF DYING	301	2	DON JUAN	3	51	4
THAN THE STERN SINGLE DEEP AND WORDLESS IRE	305	2	DON JUAN	3	58	7
THERE IS NO STERNER MORALIST THAN PLEASURE	308	2	DON JUAN	3	65	8
TO DO NOT MUCH LESS DAMAGE THAN THE TABLE	309	2	DON JUAN	3	66	8
THEY COULD NOT LOOK MORE ROSY THAN BEFORE	314	2	DON JUAN	3	75	8
ON MOUNTAINS TOPS MORE HEAVENLY WHITE THAN HER	314	2	DON JUAN	3	76	4
THAN YOUR SIRES' ISLANDS OF THE BLEST	321	2	DON JUAN	3	L 2	6
THAN ON THE NAME A PERSON LEAVES BEHIND	328	2	DON JUAN	3	90	4
THAN ANY SINCE THE BIRTHDAY OF TYPOGRAPHY	330	2	DON JUAN	3	94	6
MORE THAN SUCH MADMEN'S FELLOW MAN--THE MOON'S	341	2	DON JUAN	3	110	4
PERHAPS NO BETTER THAN THEY HAVE TREATED ME	347	2	DON JUAN	4	7	2
WOULD WITHER LESS THAN THESE TWO TORN APART	349	2	DON JUAN	4	10	7
THE LEAST GLANCE BETTER UNDERSTOOD THAN WORDS	351	2	DON JUAN	4	14	2
MORE THAN FOR THOSE OF NIGHTINGALES OR DOVES	354	2	DON JUAN	4	19	8
IT WERE MUCH BETTER TO HAVE BOTH THAN NEITHER	357	2	DON JUAN	4	25	8
THAN WHOM CASSANDRA WAS NOT MORE PROPHETIC	372	2	DON JUAN	4	52	3
THAN DID THE PRIMA-DONNA AND THE TENOR	388	2	DON JUAN	4	81	8
WITH MORE THAN ONE PROFESSION GAINS BY ALL	390	2	DON JUAN	4	84	2
THERE'S ONE THOUGH TALL AND STIFFER THAN A PIKE	390	2	DON JUAN	4	85	5
WITH THIS HIS TUNEFUL NEIGHBOUR THAN HIS FATE	394	2	DON JUAN	4	93	4
TO PASS THAN THOSE TWO CANTOS INTO FAMILIES	397	2	DON JUAN	4	97	8
AND SO GREAT NAMES ARE NOTHING MORE THAN NOMINAL	399	2	DON JUAN	4	101	1
A LITTLE CUPOLA MORE NEAT THAN SOLEMN	400	2	DON JUAN	4	104	2
IS ALWAYS MUCH MORE SPLENDID THAN A KING	408	2	DON JUAN	4	115	6
FORMED RATHER FOR INSTRUCTING THAN DELIGHTING	412	2	DON JUAN	5	2	5
THE TWELVE ISLES AND THE MORE THAN I COULD DREAM	412	2	DON JUAN	5	3	6

THAN (CONTINUED)

	PAGE	VOL	CANTO	STANZA	LN
TURNS UP MORE DANGEROUS BREAKERS THAN THE EUXINE	413	2	DON JUAN	5	5	8
THAN ANY OTHER SCRAPE A THING OF COURSE	417	2	DON JUAN	5	12	8
MOST MEN ARE SLAVES NONE MORE SO THAN THE GREAT	423	2	DON JUAN	5	25	3
PERHAPS EVEN MORE ATTENTION THAN IS DUE	431	2	DON JUAN	5	38	5
AND MARCH AWAY--'TWERE EASIER DONE THAN SAID	434	2	DON JUAN	5	43	8
AND WORSE OFF THAN WE HITHERTO HAVE BEEN	435	2	DON JUAN	5	44	6
THAN THAT ALL-SOFTENING OVER-POWERING KNELL	439	2	DON JUAN	5	49	7
THAN AN ENORMOUS ROOM WITHOUT A SOUL	442	2	DON JUAN	5	56	7
MIGHT TEACH THEM THIS MUCH BETTER THAN I'M ABLE	444	2	DON JUAN	5	59	8
MONARCHS ARE LESS IMPERATIVE THAN RHYMES)--	456	2	DON JUAN	5	77	8
INTO A ROOM STILL NOBLER THAN THE LAST	465	2	DON JUAN	5	93	2
THAN LESSEN IT BY WHAT I COULD RELATE	467	2	DON JUAN	5	97	5
BOILED IN HIS VEINS AND RATHER THAN DESCEND	471	2	DON JUAN	5	104	4
THAN SHE FROM AUGHT AT WHICH THE EYE COULD CAVIL	474	2	DON JUAN	5	109	6
AS IF SHE RATHER ORDERED THAN WAS GRANTING--	474	2	DON JUAN	5	109	8
BUT NATURE TEACHES MORE THAN POWER CAN SPOIL	480	2	DON JUAN	5	120	1
NOUGHT'S MORE SUBLIME THAN ENERGETIC BILE	489	2	DON JUAN	5	135	4
RATHER THAN SIN--EXCEPT TO HIS OWN WISH	492	2	DON JUAN	5	141	6
WITH MORE THAN ORIENTAL SCRUPULOSITY	496	2	DON JUAN	5	148	2
THE PUBLIC KNEW NO MORE THAN DOES THIS RHYME	496	2	DON JUAN	5	149	6
NO LESS DESERVING TO BE HANGED THAN CROWNED	499	2	DON JUAN	5	153	8
AND MAKES OUR SNOW LESS PURE THAN OUR MORALITY	501	2	DON JUAN	5	157	6
THE STARS FROM OUT THE SKY THAN NOT BE FREE	7	3	DON JUAN	6	3	5
A KIND OF STATE MORE AWKWARD THAN UNCOMMON	10	3	DON JUAN	6	7	2
OF HEADS THAN THEIR CARESSES OF THE HEART	13	3	DON JUAN	6	14	8
MORE IN THE EYELIDS THAN THE EYES RESIGNED	13	3	DON JUAN	6	15	3
FOR OVER-WARMTH IF FALSE IS WORSE THAN TRUTH	14	3	DON JUAN	6	16	1
THAN OTHER ARTICLES OF FEMALE DRESS	15	3	DON JUAN	6	19	4
IS MORE THAN I KNOW--THE DEUCE TAKE THEM BOTH	17	3	DON JUAN	6	22	8
IS MORE THAN I KNOW AND SO DAMN THEM BOTH	17	3	DON JUAN	6	22	V8
AND MUCH MORE TENDER ON THE WHOLE THAN FIERCE	19	3	DON JUAN	6	27	5
ARE WORSE THAN THE WORST DAMAGES MEN PAY	20	3	DON JUAN	6	29	6
THAN IS THE CUSTOM OF THE GENTLE SEX	24	3	DON JUAN	6	37	6
THAN YOU WOULD MAKE THE HALF OF--DON'T SAY NO	29	3	DON JUAN	6	47	5
WERE COUCHES TOILETS--AND MUCH MORE THAN THIS	31	3	DON JUAN	6	51	3
AND EVEN THOSE WERE NEARER THAN THEY KNEW	31	3	DON JUAN	6	51	8
THAN ARE YOUR MIGHTY PASSIONS AND SO FORTH	32	3	DON JUAN	6	53	5
AND PITY LOVERS RATHER MORE THAN SEAMEN	32	3	DON JUAN	6	53	8
BUT SHE WAS PENSIVE MORE THAN MELANCHOLY	33	3	DON JUAN	6	54	1
AND SERIOUS MORE THAN PENSIVE AND SERENE	33	3	DON JUAN	6	54	2
IT MAY BE MORE THAN EITHER--NOT UNHOLY	33	3	DON JUAN	6	54	3
WHICH MADE HIM WONDER MORE THAN ANY WONDER	34	3	DON JUAN	6	57	V7
FOR WOMAN'S SILENCE STARTLES MORE THAN THUNDER	34	3	DON JUAN	6	57	V8
AND BETWEEN FEMALES MEANS NO MORE THAN THIS--	35	3	DON JUAN	6	59	5
AND I LOVE WISDOM MORE THAN SHE LOVES ME	37	3	DON JUAN	6	63	2
THAN HAUNTING SOME OLD RUIN OR WILD WASTE	38	3	DON JUAN	6	64	8
MORE THAN I HAVE MYSELF OF WHAT COULD MAKE	42	3	DON JUAN	6	71	7
WHICH AS ALL SPOKE AT ONCE AND MORE THAN ONCE	43	3	DON JUAN	6	74	2
IS LIGHTER FAR OF HEART AND VOICE THAN THOSE	49	3	DON JUAN	6	87	7
SOFTER THAN THE SOFT SYBARITE'S WHO CRIED	50	3	DON JUAN	6	89	2
THAN WHERE TWO WIVES ARE UNDER AN EMBARGO	51	3	DON JUAN	6	90	8
MORE EASILY THAN ANSWERED--THAT HE HAD TRIED	56	3	DON JUAN	6	100	3
WHICH HESITATION MORE BETRAYED THAN MASQUED--	56	3	DON JUAN	6	100	6
MIGHT MAKE THE MATTER STILL WORSE THAN IT WAS	57	3	DON JUAN	6	103	8
CONCEALED HER FEATURES BETTER THAN A VEIL	60	3	DON JUAN	6	109	2
I SAY NO MORE THAN HAS BEEN SAID IN DANTE'S	67	3	DON JUAN	7	3	7
BUT WHICH IS BEST YOU KNOW NO MORE THAN I	68	3	DON JUAN	7	4	8
THE RAMPART HIGHER THAN YOU'D WISH TO HANG	72	3	DON JUAN	7	11	4
THAN THOUSANDS OF THIS NEW AND POLISHED NATION	73	3	DON JUAN	7	14	7
I'D RATHER TELL TEN LIES THAN SAY A WORD	77	3	DON JUAN	7	22	4
AND IS EXTINGUISHED SOONER THAN SHE OUGHT	83	3	DON JUAN	7	34	6
MORE EVIL IN AN HOUR THAN THIRTY BRIGHT	86	3	DON JUAN	7	41	5
IN WAR THAN LOVE HE HAD BETTER LEAD THE ASSAULT	98	3	DON JUAN	7	62	8
LESS THAN THEIR GRIEF (AND TRULY NOT LESS JUST)	104	3	DON JUAN	7	73	4
TO SEE AN OLD MAN RATHER WILD THAN WISE	104	3	DON JUAN	7	73	5
MORE FEARED THAN ALL THE SULTANS EVER SEEN	104	3	DON JUAN	7	73	8
MUCH LESS THAN IS THE HOPE OF EVERY COURT	106	3	DON JUAN	7	79	6
THAN IN THY GREEK GAZETTE OF THAT CAMPAIGN	106	3	DON JUAN	7	80	4
OF HONEST FAME THAN SHEDDING SEAS OF GORE	113	3	DON JUAN	8	3	8
THE EAR FAR MORE THAN THUNDER FOR HEAVEN'S FLASHES	115	3	DON JUAN	8	6	7
THICKER THAN LEAVES THE LIVES BEGAN TO FALL	116	3	DON JUAN	8	9	3
MORE THAN THE CAP IN FACT THE BALL COULD MEAN	117	3	DON JUAN	8	10	8
PERHAPS MAY FIND IT BETTER THAN A NEW ONE)--	126	3	DON JUAN	8	29	8
MEN RUN AWAY MUCH RATHER THAN GO THROUGH	130	3	DON JUAN	8	35	3
AND THOUGH HIS NAME THAN AJAX OR ACHILLES	132	3	DON JUAN	8	39	2
WHICH SCARCELY ROSE MUCH HIGHER THAN GRASS BLADES	136	3	DON JUAN	8	47	8
THEIR CHOICE THAN LIFE FORGIVE THEM AS BEGUILED	143	3	DON JUAN	8	62	5
FOR THE TURK'S TEETH STUCK FASTER THAN A SKEWER	154	3	DON JUAN	8	85	3
MORE THAN THE HEAD OF THE INVETERATE FOE	154	3	DON JUAN	8	85	7
OF TRUTH THAN PROSE UNLESS TO SUIT THE MART	154	3	DON JUAN	8	86	5
OF PRESENT LIFE A GOOD DEAL MORE THAN WE--	161	3	DON JUAN	8	100	3
MORE THAN YOU SCORN THE SAVAGES OF YORE	180	3	DON JUAN	8	136	7
THAN MY FORERUNNERS CARELESSLY I SING	181	3	DON JUAN	8	138	7
SAFETY THAN HIS NEW ORDER OF SAINT VLADIMIR	182	3	DON JUAN	8	140	8
AND SWALLOWING EULOGY MUCH MORE THAN SATIRE HE	185	3	DON JUAN	9	5	5
THAN EVEN THE TAILOR'S) HIS INCARNATE SKIN	188	3	DON JUAN	9	12	7
THAN THE ETERNAL DELUGE WHICH DEVOURS	189	3	DON JUAN	9	13	7
THAN BUONAPARTE'S CANCER--COULD I DASH ON	189	3	DON JUAN	9	14	6

```
THAN   (CONTINUED)
     RATHER THAN LIFE A MERE AFFAIR OF BREATH  .  .  .  .  .  .  . 190  3 DON JUAN  9    16   8
     AND YET I KNOW NO MORE THAN THE MAHOGANY  .  .  .  .  .  .  . 192  3 DON JUAN  9    20   5
     WHO STILL HAVE SHOWN THEMSELVES MORE BRAVE THAN WITTY  .  .  . 194  3 DON JUAN  9    23   4
     NOT A BARBARIAN BUT MUCH WORSE THAN THAT  .  .  .  .  .  .  . 194  3 DON JUAN  9    23   8
     THAN IF I SOUGHT TO SAIL BEFORE THE WIND  .  .  .  .  .  .  . 195  3 DON JUAN  9    26   4
     THAN HUMAN INSECTS CATERING FOR SPIDERS  .  .  .  .  .  .  .  . 196  3 DON JUAN  9    27   8
     THAN HE IN THESE SAD HIGHWAYS LEFT AT LARGE  .  .  .  .  .  . 198  3 DON JUAN  9    31   4
     FAR SWEETER THAN THE GREENEST LAURELS SPRUNG  .  .  .  .  .  . 199  3 DON JUAN  9    34   4
     THAN SOME WIVES (WHO MAKE BLUNDERS NO LESS STUPID)  .  .  .  . 205  3 DON JUAN  9    45   7
     THE SOUND THAN SENSE)--BESIDES ALL THESE PRETENCES  .  .  .  . 219  3 DON JUAN  9    74   7
     BEHAVED NO BETTER THAN A COMMON SEMPSTRESS  .  .  .  .  .  .  . 221  3 DON JUAN  9    77   8
     THAT ONE SHOULD DIE THAN TWO DRAG ON THE FETTER)  .  .  .  .  . 222  3 DON JUAN  9    80   8
     (FOR I HAVE MORE THAN ONE MUSE AT A PUSH)  .  .  .  .  .  .  . 227  3 DON JUAN 10     5   4
     SIGH LIKE HIS SON COUGH LIKE HIS GRANDFATHER  .  .  .  .  .  . 228  3 DON JUAN 10     6   8
     MIDDLE-AGED LADIES EVEN MORE THAN YOUNG  .  .  .  .  .  .  .  . 230  3 DON JUAN 10    10   2
     KNOW LITTLE MORE OF LOVE THAN WHAT IS SUNG  .  .  .  .  .  .  . 230  3 DON JUAN 10    10   4
     THAN CAN BE HID BY ALTERING HIS SHIRT HE  .  .  .  .  .  .  . 232  3 DON JUAN 10    15   4
     WITH YOU THAN AUGHT (SAVE SCOTT) IN YOUR PROUD CITY  .  .  .  . 233  3 DON JUAN 10    17   4
     THAN WHAT THEY THOUGHT FOR MIND CAN NEVER SINK  .  .  .  .  .  . 234  3 DON JUAN 10    20   4
     AND KNOW NO MORE OF WHAT IS HERE THAN THERE--  .  .  .  .  .  . 234  3 DON JUAN 10    20   8
     FOR BABYLON'S THAN RUSSIA'S ROYAL HARLOT--  .  .  .  .  .  .  . 237  3 DON JUAN 10    26   7
     HAVE PRINCES WHO SPUR MORE THAN THEIR POSTILLIONS  .  .  .  . 254  3 DON JUAN 10    60   8
     THAT WORSE THAN WORST OF FOES THE ONCE ADORED  .  .  .  .  .  . 258  3 DON JUAN 10    67   6
     AFFECT NO MORE THAN LIGHTNING A CONDUCTOR  .  .  .  .  .  .  . 260  3 DON JUAN 10    71   8
     THEY HATE A MURDERER MUCH LESS THAN A CLAIMANT  .  .  .  .  .  . 264  3 DON JUAN 10    79   5
     OR CAN'T DO OTHERWISE THAN LIE BUT DO IT  .  .  .  .  .  .  . 285  3 DON JUAN 11    36   7
     MORE THAN ON CONTINENTS--AS IF THE SEA  .  .  .  .  .  .  .  . 288  3 DON JUAN 11    42   7
     THAN MIGHT SUFFICE A MODERATE CENTURY THROUGH  .  .  .  .  .  . 309  3 DON JUAN 11    82   4
     IF THAT CAN WELL BE THAN HIS WOODEN LOOK  .  .  .  .  .  .  . 309  3 DON JUAN 11    83   4
     MUCH LESS ON WHAT YOU DO THAN WHAT YOU SAY  .  .  .  .  .  .  . 310  3 DON JUAN 11    86   6
     BY BUTCHERS IN HER STREETS THAN FOR THE STAUNCHEST OR  .  .  . 314  3 DON JUAN 11  V 75   5
     THAN THE MERE PLODDING THROUGH EACH VULGAR FRACTION  .  .  .  . 321  3 DON JUAN 12    11   6
     TO DOUBT (NO LESS THAN LANDLORDS OF THEIR RENTAL)  .  .  .  . 322  3 DON JUAN 12    13   7
     NO MORE OF THEM THAN THEY OF HER I TROW  .  .  .  .  .  .  .  . 324  3 DON JUAN 12    18   8
     THOUGH THERE'S A SHORTER A GOOD DEAL THAN THIS  .  .  .  .  .  . 326  3 DON JUAN 12    22   4
     I HAVE ALWAYS LIKED YOU BETTER THAN I STATE  .  .  .  .  .  . 329  3 DON JUAN 12    28   4
     THAN THEIR HE RELATIVES) LIKE FLIES O'ER CANDY  .  .  .  .  .  . 331  3 DON JUAN 12    32   6
     SEE NOUGHT MORE STRANGE IN THIS THAN T'OTHER LOTTERY  .  .  .  . 333  3 DON JUAN 12    37   8
     ALBEIT MY YEARS WERE LESS DISCREET THAN FEW  .  .  .  .  .  . 334  3 DON JUAN 12    38   4
     WHICH ARE MORE PURE THAN PLEASANT TO BE SURE  .  .  .  .  .  . 335  3 DON JUAN 12    41   4
     SEEKING FAR LESS TO SAVE YOU THAN TO HURT YOU  .  .  .  .  .  . 337  3 DON JUAN 12    45   3
     THE WORLD BY EXPERIENCE RATHER THAN BY LECTURE  .  .  .  .  .  . 337  3 DON JUAN 12    46   5
     THAN THOSE BRED UP BY PRUDES WITHOUT A HEART  .  .  .  .  .  . 337  3 DON JUAN 12    46   8
     IN HAPPIER PLIGHT THAN IF THEY FORMED A PAIR  .  .  .  .  .  . 344  3 DON JUAN 12    61   8
     THAN THE MORE GLOWING DAMES WHOSE LOT IS CAST  .  .  .  .  .  . 347  3 DON JUAN 12    69   3
     THAT NOVELTIES PLEASE LESS THAN THEY IMPRESS  .  .  .  .  .  . 347  3 DON JUAN 12    69   8
     THAN STORMS IT AS A FOE WOULD TAKE A CITY  .  .  .  .  .  .  . 350  3 DON JUAN 12    74   6
     IN LAW THAN EQUITY--AS I CAN FEEL--  .  .  .  .  .  .  .  .  . 357  3 DON JUAN 12  V 18   4
     MEN'S WRONGS AND RATHER CHECK THAN PUNISH CRIMES  .  .  .  .  . 361  3 DON JUAN 13     8   6
     THAN SOLITARY PRIDE'S OPPRESSIVE WEIGHT  .  .  .  .  .  .  .  . 367  3 DON JUAN 13    19   6
     THAT FEW OR NONE MORE THAN HIMSELF HAD CAUGHT  .  .  .  .  .  . 368  3 DON JUAN 13    21   3
     AND THIS IS STRONGER THAN THE STRONGEST GRAPE  .  .  .  .  .  . 375  3 DON JUAN 13    37   7
     I'VE GOT A BETTER SIMILIE THAN THAT  .  .  .  .  .  .  .  .  . 375  3 DON JUAN 13    37  VI
     HAS NOT CONTRACTED MUCH MORE DEBT THAN KNOWLEDGE  .  .  .  .  . 377  3 DON JUAN 13    42   8
     TRICKED OUT BUT MODEST MORE THAN POET'S PEN  .  .  .  .  .  . 380  3 DON JUAN 13    47   4
     NONE THAN THEMSELVES COULD BOAST A LONGER LINE  .  .  .  .  .  . 381  3 DON JUAN 13    50   5
     THAN AN ADVERTISEMENT OR MUCH THE SAME  .  .  .  .  .  .  .  . 382  3 DON JUAN 13    51   4
     MORE WITH THESE DINNERS THAN THE KILLED OR WOUNDED--  .  .  .  . 383  3 DON JUAN 13    53   8
     ANNOUNCED WITH NO LESS POMP THAN VICTORY'S WINNER  .  .  .  . 383  3 DON JUAN 13    54   3
     (THOUGH LESS THAN THAT OF MEMNON'S STATUE WARM  .  .  .  .  .  . 388  3 DON JUAN 13    64   3
     WITH MORE OF THE MONASTIC THAN HAS BEEN  .  .  .  .  .  .  .  . 389  3 DON JUAN 13    66   2
     AND SPOKE MORE OF THE BARON THAN THE MONK  .  .  .  .  .  .  . 389  3 DON JUAN 13    66   8
     OF THE STAR CHAMBER THAN OF HABEAS CORPUS  .  .  .  .  .  .  . 391  3 DON JUAN 13    69   8
     HUGER THAN TWELVE OF OUR DEGENERATE BREED  .  .  .  .  .  .  . 391  3 DON JUAN 13    70   4
     PROUDER OF SUCH A TOY THAN OF THEIR BREED  .  .  .  .  .  .  . 391  3 DON JUAN 13    70  V6
     THE SEASON RATHER THAN TO WINTER DREAR--  .  .  .  .  .  .  . 395  3 DON JUAN 13    77   4
     RIFE WITH MORE HORNS THAN HOUNDS--SHE HATH THE CHASE  .  .  . 395  3 DON JUAN 13    78   2
     IS NO LESS FAMED FOR TOLERANCE THAN PIETY  .  .  .  .  .  .  . 396  3 DON JUAN 13    80   8
     I HAVE SEEN MORE THAN I'LL SAY--BUT WE WILL SEE  .  .  .  .  . 397  3 DON JUAN 13    83   1
     HE SHOWS MORE APPETITE FOR WORDS THAN WAR  .  .  .  .  .  .  . 398  3 DON JUAN 13    84   4
     LESS ON A CONVENT THAN A CORONET  .  .  .  .  .  .  .  .  .  . 398  3 DON JUAN 13    85   8
     HONOUR WAS MORE BEFORE THEIR NAMES THAN AFTER  .  .  .  .  .  . 398  3 DON JUAN 13    86   2
     WHO ATE LAST WAR MORE YANKEES THAN HE KILL'D  .  .  .  .  .  . 399  3 DON JUAN 13    88   4
     IS BETTER THAN AN HUMDRUM TETE-A-TETE  .  .  .  .  .  .  .  . 402  3 DON JUAN 13    94   4
     THAT MANNERS HARDLY DIFFER MORE THAN DRESS  .  .  .  .  .  .  . 402  3 DON JUAN 13    94   8
     A LITTLE EARLIER THAN THE WANING MOON  .  .  .  .  .  .  .  . 409  3 DON JUAN 13   111   4
     NOTHING MORE TRUE THAN NOT TO TRUST YOUR SENSES  .  .  .  .  . 411  3 DON JUAN 14     2   7
     LESS FROM DISGUST OF LIFE THAN DREAD OF DEATH  .  .  .  .  .  . 412  3 DON JUAN 14     4   8
     THAN THESE THINGS AND BESIDES I WISH TO SPARE 'EM  .  .  .  . 419  3 DON JUAN 14    21   5
     THAN TRUE HATH BEEN A CREED SO STRICTLY HELD)  .  .  .  .  .  . 420  3 DON JUAN 14    23   3
     AND RATHER HELD IN THAN PUT FORTH HIS VIGOUR  .  .  .  .  .  . 427  3 DON JUAN 14    39   4
     DOCTORS LESS FAMOUS FOR THEIR CURES THAN FEES  .  .  .  .  .  . 431  3 DON JUAN 14    48   4
     SADDER THAN OWL-SONGS OR THE MIDNIGHT BLAST  .  .  .  .  .  . 432  3 DON JUAN 14    50   2
     THAN WEAR A HEART A WOMAN LOVES TO REND  .  .  .  .  .  .  .  . 438  3 DON JUAN 14    64   6
     THIRDLY THAT JUAN HAD MORE BRAIN THAN BEARD  .  .  .  .  .  . 439  3 DON JUAN 14    66   5
     LESS LIKE A YOUNG WIFE THAN AN AGED SISTER  .  .  .  .  .  .  . 440  3 DON JUAN 14    69   8
     BECAUSE 'TIS FRAILER DOUBTLESS THAN A STANCH ONE  .  .  .  .  . 446  3 DON JUAN 14    85   6
     IMPRESSIONS WERE MUCH STRONGER THAN SHE GUESS'D  .  .  .  .  . 448  3 DON JUAN 14    88   5
```

815

THAN   (CONTINUED)

				PAGE	VOL		CANTO	STANZA	LN

AT HOME FAR MORE THAN EVER YET WAS LOVE-- . . . . . . 452 3 DON JUAN 14 96 4
THAN I HAVE YET DONE IN THIS EPIC SATIRE . . . . . . 454 3 DON JUAN 14 99 6
STRANGER THAN FICTION IF IT COULD BE TOLD . . . . . 455 3 DON JUAN 14 101 2
BUT ALL ARE BETTER THAN THE SIGH SUPPREST . . . . . 457 3 DON JUAN 15 3 1
SUCH ABERRATIONS THAN WE MEN OF RIGOUR . . . . . . 460 3 DON JUAN 15 11 4
TO SHIELD HIMSELF THAN PUT YOU ON YOUR GUARD . . . . 462 3 DON JUAN 15 14 4
WILL GO MUCH FURTHER THAN THERE'S NEED TO MENTION . . 462 3 DON JUAN 15 14 8
THEY CAN TRANSFIGURE BRIGHTER THAN A RAPHAEL . . . . 463 3 DON JUAN 15 16 8
THE FIRST IS RATHER MORE THAN MORTAL CAN DO . . . . 465 3 DON JUAN 15 21 3
THAN MATCH-MAKING IN GENERAL 'TIS NO SIN . . . . . 470 3 DON JUAN 15 31 6
BECAUSE IT BREEDS NO MORE MOUTHS THAN IT NOURISHES . 471 3 DON JUAN 15 35 4
SHE DEEMED HIS MERITS SOMETHING MORE THAN COMMON . . 473 3 DON JUAN 15 40 6
OF THE BEST CLASS AND BETTER THAN HER CLASS-- . . . 475 3 DON JUAN 15 43 4
THAN I HAVE TIME OR WILL TO TAKE TO PIECES . . . . 478 3 DON JUAN 15 52 8
THAN FINDING THUS THEIR GENIUS STAND REBUKED . . . . 479 3 DON JUAN 15 53 6
TO SAY WHAT IT WAS NOT THAN WHAT IT WAS . . . . . 479 3 DON JUAN 15 54 8
OF RANK AND YOUTH THOUGH PURER THAN THE REST . . . . 480 3 DON JUAN 15 55 4
THAN WITCHES BITCHES OR PHYSICIANS BREW . . . . . 482 3 DON JUAN 15 62 8
THAN WHEN SOME SQUEAMISH PEOPLE DEEM HER FRAIL . . . 483 3 DON JUAN 15 64 4
IN THE FEAST PECKING LESS THAN I CAN TELL . . . . 487 3 DON JUAN 15 70 4
BUT THINKS LESS OF GOOD EATING THAN THE WHISPER . . 487 3 DON JUAN 15 70 7
THAN COULD ROAST BEEF IN OUR ROUGH JOHN BULL WAY . . 487 3 DON JUAN 15 71 4
THAT HE WOULD RATHER MAKE THEM MORE THAN LESS . . . 491 3 DON JUAN 15 80 4
THOUGH PROBABLY MUCH LESS A FACT THAN GUESS) . . . . 491 3 DON JUAN 15 80 6
THAN WHISPERING FOPLINGS OR THAN WITLINGS LOUD . . . 493 3 DON JUAN 15 83 4
THAN WHISPERING FOPLINGS OR THAN WITLINGS LOUD . . . 493 3 DON JUAN 15 83 4
RATHER BY DEFERENCE THAN COMPLIMENT . . . . . . 493 3 DON JUAN 15 83 7
MAKE MORE IMPRESSION THAN THE BEST OF BOOKS . . . . 493 3 DON JUAN 15 84 8
AURORA WHO LOOK'D MORE ON BOOKS THAN FACES . . . . 494 3 DON JUAN 15 85 1
ADMIRING MORE MINERVA THAN THE GRACES . . . . . 494 3 DON JUAN 15 85 3
BUT DRAW THE LONG BOW BETTER NOW THAN EVER . . . . 501 3 DON JUAN 16 1 8
THAN DYING TAPERS--AND THE PEEPING MOON . . . . . 504 3 DON JUAN 16 8 8
THOUGHTS QUITE AS YELLOW BUT LESS CLEAR THAN AMBER . 505 3 DON JUAN 16 11 4
THAN ADELINE (SUCH IS ADVICE) ADVISED . . . . . 506 3 DON JUAN 16 12 4
FOR CONTEMPLATION RATHER THAN HIS PILLOW . . . . . 507 3 DON JUAN 16 15 2
CONNECTIONS STRONGER THAN HE CHOSE TO AVOW . . . . 516 3 DON JUAN 16 37 4
COULD WRITE RHYMES AND COMPOSE MORE THAN SHE WROTE . 524 3 DON JUAN 16 47 2
OF THESE FEW COULD SAY MORE THAN HAS BEEN SAID . . . 527 3 DON JUAN 16 54 1
RATHER THAN SELLER HAD HIS WANTS BEEN FEWER . . . . 528 3 DON JUAN 16 57 5
AN EDIFICE NO LESS SUBLIME THAN STRONG . . . . . 529 3 DON JUAN 16 59 5
THAN TO WAX WHITE--FOR BLUSHES ARE FOR QUALITY . . . 532 3 DON JUAN 16 64 8
HAD MADE MORE PROGRESS THAN FOR THE LAST CENTURY . . 536 3 DON JUAN 16 73 4
THAT THE FATIGUE WAS GREATER THAN THE PROFIT . . . . 536 3 DON JUAN 16 73 8
THAN THOSE WHO WERE NOT PAID FOR INDEPENDENCE . . . 537 3 DON JUAN 16 76 2
AND SEVERAL WHO SUNG FEWER PSALMS THAN CATCHES . . . 539 3 DON JUAN 16 80 8
UPON THE WHOLE IS GREATER THAN THE DIFFERENCE . . . 541 3 DON JUAN 16 85 2
BROADENING TO GRINS HE COLOURED MORE THAN ONCE . . . 542 3 DON JUAN 16 88 3
A WISE MAN MORE THAN LAUGHTER FROM A DUNCE-- . . . . 542 3 DON JUAN 16 88 5
BUT WHAT CONFUSED HIM MORE THAN SMILE OR STARE . . . 544 3 DON JUAN 16 91 1
MORE JOY THAN FROM ALL FUTURE PRIDE OR PRAISE . . . 554 3 DON JUAN 16 108 5
RATHER THAN REST INSTEAD OF POPPIES WILLOWS . . . . 555 3 DON JUAN 16 110 5
SHOULD CAUSE MORE FEAR THAN A WHOLE HOST'S IDENTITY . 559 3 DON JUAN 16 120 8
THAN OTHERS CROWDED IN THE FOREST'S MAZE-- . . . . 562 3 DON JUAN 17 1 4
IS MORE THAN I SHALL VENTURE TO DESCRIBE-- . . . . 567 3 DON JUAN 17 12 7
AS IF HE HAD COMBATED WITH MORE THAN ONE . . . . . 568 3 DON JUAN 17 14 3
A VIGIL OR DREAMT RATHER MORE THAN SLEPT . . . . . 568 3 DON JUAN 17 14 8

THANK
SO THANK YOUR STARS THAT MATTERS ARE NO WORSE . . . 147 2 DON JUAN 1 220 7
THANK HEAVEN I'VE GOT NO METAPHOR QUITE READY . . . 160 2 DON JUAN 2 6 7
SHE WAS A SULTAN'S BRIDE (THANK HEAVEN NOT MINE) . . 475 2 DON JUAN 5 111 8
ADDRESSING HIM IN TONES WHICH SEEMED TO THANK . . . 141 3 DON JUAN 8 57 7

THANK'D
HIS YOUNG LIP THANK'D IT WITH A GRATEFUL KISS . . . 81 2 DON JUAN 1 112 3
WHO THANK'D ME DULY BY RETURN OF POST-- . . . . . 142 2 DON JUAN 1 210 2

THANKING
THE OTHER THANKING HIM FOR THIS EXCESS . . . . . 452 2 DON JUAN 5 70 4

THANKLESS
A THANKLESS HUSBAND NEXT A FAITHLESS LOVER . . . . 263 2 DON JUAN 2 200 7

THANKS
WHICH GOT HIM A FEW PRESENTS AND SOME THANKS . . . 319 3 DON JUAN 3 84 5
HIS THANKS AND HOPES TO TAKE THE CITY SOON . . . . 140 3 DON JUAN 8 56 6
GEORGE WASHINGTON HAD THANKS AND NOUGHT BESIDE . . . 186 3 DON JUAN 9 8 4
FOR WHICH SMALL THANKS ARE STILL THE MARKET PRICE . 469 3 DON JUAN 15 29 3

THATCH
WHILE MOSQUES AND STREETS BENEATH HIS EYES LIKE THATCH . 178 3 DON JUAN 8 133 3
AND CARCASES THAT LAY AS THICK AS THATCH . . . . 197 3 DON JUAN 9 29 4

THAT'S
BEGOT--BUT THAT'S TO COME--WELL TO RENEW . . . . 26 2 DON JUAN 1 9 8
BUT THAT'S NO MATTER AND THE WORST'S BEHIND . . . . 34 2 DON JUAN 1 24 6
BUT NOT A PAGE OF ANY THING THAT'S LOOSE . . . . . 44 2 DON JUAN 1 40 6
NOT SCANDAL'S FANGS COULD FIX ON MUCH THAT'S SEIZABLE . 66 2 DON JUAN 1 83 3
HIS PEGASUS NOR ANYTHING THAT'S HIS . . . . . . 140 2 DON JUAN 1 206 2
HIS OX--HIS ASS--NOR ANYTHING THAT'S HIS . . . . . 140 2 DON JUAN 1 206 V2
STILL GENTLER PURCHASER THE BARD--THAT'S I-- . . . 147 2 DON JUAN 1 221 2
SINCE IN A WAY THAT'S RATHER OF THE ODDEST HE . . . 157 2 DON JUAN 2 1 7
A PRETTY WOMAN--(THAT'S QUITE NATURAL . . . . . 158 2 DON JUAN 2 3 5
BUT THAT'S IMPOSSIBLE AND CANNOT BE-- . . . . . 166 2 DON JUAN 2 19 2
IT COSTS THREE FRANCS FOR EVERY MASS THAT'S SAID . . 185 2 DON JUAN 2 55 8

THAT'S   (CONTINUED)
AND THAT'S THEIR MODE OF FURNISHING SUPPLY 190	2 DON JUAN	2	65	6
THEN CHANGED LIKE TO A BOW THAT'S BENT AND THEN 204	2 DON JUAN	2	91	7
AND THUS THEY FORM A GROUP THAT'S QUITE ANTIQUE 259	2 DON JUAN	2	194	7
A KIND OF FLATTERY THAT'S HARDLY FAIR 278	2 DON JUAN	3	6	3
TRANSFORM'D THEIR LORDS TO BEASTS (BUT THAT'S A FACT) . . 293	2 DON JUAN	3	34	8
(FOR THAT'S THE NAME THEY LIKE TO PRAY BENEATH)-- . . . 309	2 DON JUAN	3	66	4
THEIR BREAD AS MINISTERS AND FAVOURITES--(THAT'S . . . 310	2 DON JUAN	3	68	6
SURVIVES HIMSELF HIS TOMB AND ALL THAT'S HIS 327	2 DON JUAN	3	88	8
BUT THAT'S HER WAY WITH ALL MEN TILL THEY'RE TRIED . . 418	2 DON JUAN	5	14	5
AND THAT'S THE REASON I'M SO MELANCHOLY 444	2 DON JUAN	5	58	8
REQUIRES IT THAT'S TO SAY THE ENGLISH RHYME 14	3 DON JUAN	6	18	2
BUT WHAT WAS NOT A SORT OF STYLE THAT'S GROWN 33	3 DON JUAN	6	55	6
I HAVE BUT ONE SIMILE AND THAT'S A BLUNDER 34	3 DON JUAN	6	57	7
AND THAT'S THE MORAL OF THIS COMPOSITION 50	3 DON JUAN	6	88	1
AND THAT'S THE CAUSE NO DOUBT WHY IF WE SCAN 167	3 DON JUAN	8	112	5
THERE'S NO SUCH THING AS CERTAINTY THAT'S PLAIN . . . 191	3 DON JUAN	9	17	5
MUCH FLATTERY--EVEN VOLTAIRE'S AND THAT'S A PITY . . . 194	3 DON JUAN	9	23	6
THAT'S AN APPROPRIATE SIMILE THAT JACKALL-- 196	3 DON JUAN	9	27	1
AND THAT'S ONE COMFORT FOR MY LOST ADVICE 200	3 DON JUAN	9	36	7
AND THAT'S ENOUGH FOR LOVE IS VANITY 219	3 DON JUAN	9	73	1
AND THAT'S THE REASON HE HIMSELF'S SO DIRTY 232	3 DON JUAN	10	15	2
WHICH (THOUGH I HATE TO SAY A THING THAT'S BITTER) . . 237	3 DON JUAN	10	26	4
WORLD (BE IT WHAT YOU WILL) THAT THAT'S NO SCHISM . . 269	3 DON JUAN	11	2	4
THAT'S RATHER FINE THE GENTLE SOUND OF THAMIS-- . . . 279	3 DON JUAN	11	24	1
A DOOR THAT'S IN OR BOUDOIR OUT OF THE WAY 303	3 DON JUAN	11	69	3
WHERE IS HIS WILL (THAT'S NOT SO SOON UNRIDDLED) . . . 307	3 DON JUAN	11	78	3
WHERE'S CHARLOTTE (THAT'S NOT EASILY OWN'D) 307	3 DON JUAN	11	78	V3
I HAVE SEEN A CONGRESS DOING ALL THAT'S MEAN-- . . . 310	3 DON JUAN	11	84	6
AND THAT'S ENOUGH SUCCEEDED IN MY YOUTH 324	3 DON JUAN	12	17	2
THAT'S NOBLE THAT'S ROMANTIC FOR MY PART 326	3 DON JUAN	12	22	1
THAT'S NOBLE THAT'S ROMANTIC FOR MY PART 326	3 DON JUAN	12	22	1
BUT I'M RESOLVED TO SAY NOUGHT THAT'S AMISS)-- . . . 326	3 DON JUAN	12	22	6
FOR THAT'S THE PHRASE THAT SETTLES ALL THINGS NOW . . 330	3 DON JUAN	12	31	4
AN ECHO OF A SYLLABLE THAT'S WRONG 336	3 DON JUAN	12	43	5
THAT'S YOUR AFFAIR NOT MINE A REAL SPIRIT 356	3 DON JUAN	12	87	7
WAS THE QUEEN-BEE THE GLASS OF ALL THAT'S FAIR . . . 365	3 DON JUAN	13	13	5
AND THAT'S THE REASON WHY YOU DO--OR DO NOT 413	3 DON JUAN	14	6	8
THE OTHER THAT'S TO SAY THE CLERGY--WHO 414	3 DON JUAN	14	10	2
AND THAT'S ONE CAUSE SHE MEETS WITH CONTRADICTION . . 416	3 DON JUAN	14	13	5
ESPECIALLY WHEN YOUNG FOR THAT'S ESSENTIAL 418	3 DON JUAN	14	20	4
THEY ARE WRONG--THAT'S NOT THE WAY TO SET ABOUT IT . . 461	3 DON JUAN	15	13	1
IN HER OWN MIND AND THAT'S ENOUGH FOR WOMAN 473	3 DON JUAN	15	40	2
OF ALL OFFENCES THAT'S THE WORST OFFENCE 490	3 DON JUAN	15	77	3
EVEN MY VERACIOUS SELF--BUT THAT'S A LIE 495	3 DON JUAN	15	88	3
BY THOSE WHO SOW THEM IN A LAND THAT'S ARABLE . . . 495	3 DON JUAN	15	89	3
SOME MILLIONS MUST BE WRONG THAT'S PRETTY CLEAR . . . 496	3 DON JUAN	15	90	1
ALSO THEREON--BUT THAT'S NOT MUCH WE FIND 525	3 DON JUAN	16	49	6
LITTLE THAT'S GREAT BUT MUCH OF WHAT IS CLEVER . . . 547	3 DON JUAN	16	98	4

THAW
BEGAN TO DREAD SHE'D THAW TO A COQUETTE-- 492	3 DON JUAN	15	81	4

THAWED
NOW THAWED INTO A MARSH OF HUMAN BLOOD 148	3 DON JUAN	8	73	8
BELIEVE THAT VIRTUE THAWED BEFORE THE RIVER 241	3 DON JUAN	10	33	8

THEATRE
AS IS A THEATRE LIT UP BY GAS 444	2 DON JUAN	5	58	6

THEATRICAL
HE DANCED WITHOUT THEATRICAL PRETENCE 427	3 DON JUAN	14	38	6

THEBES
EPAMINONDAS SAVED HIS THEBES AND DIED 186	3 DON JUAN	9	8	2

THEFT
AND STOLEN GLANCES SWEETER FOR THE THEFT 62	2 DON JUAN	1	74	2

THEIR'S
AND YET THIS WANT OF TIES MADE THEIR'S MORE TENDER . . 252	3 DON JUAN	10	57	8
THEIR POST BUT THEIR'S IS MERELY A CHIMERA 360	3 DON JUAN	13	5	3

THEME
AND FOR HIS THEME--HE SELDOM SUNG BELOW IT 316	2 DON JUAN	3	78	6
IN TIME TO HIS OLD TUNE HE CHANGED THE THEME . . . 380	2 DON JUAN	4	66	2
BUT LET ME CHANGE THIS THEME WHICH GROWS TOO SAD . . 384	2 DON JUAN	4	74	1
BUT LET ME QUIT THE THEME AS SUCH THINGS CLAIM . . . 431	2 DON JUAN	5	38	4
A FOND HALLUCINATION AND A THEME 47	3 DON JUAN	6	83	5
AT PRESENT SUCH THINGS SINCE THEY ARE HER THEME . . 112	3 DON JUAN	8	1	6
BUT LET ME PUT AN END UNTO MY THEME 175	3 DON JUAN	8	127	1
TO OUR THEME--THE MAN WHO HAS STOOD ON THE ACROPOLIS . 271	3 DON JUAN	11	7	1
AND SAIL FOR A NEW THEME--I HAVE SEEN--AND SHOOK . . 309	3 DON JUAN	11	83	6
THE THEME OF PRAISE A HERMIT WOULD NOT MISS 319	3 DON JUAN	12	7	4
THAT IS YOUR PRESENT THEME FOR POPULARITY 357	3 DON JUAN	12	89	1
BE FOR MERE FANCY'S SPORT A THEME CREATIVE 363	3 DON JUAN	13	10	6
LITTLE AURORA DEEM'D SHE WAS THE THEME 480	3 DON JUAN	15	55	1
TO JEST YOU'LL CHOOSE SOME OTHER THEME JUST NOW . . 516	3 DON JUAN	16	37	6
THE THEME HALF CREDITED THE STRANGE TRADITION . . . 527	3 DON JUAN	16	54	4
A THEME FOR PITY OR SOME WORSE EMOTION 563	3 DON JUAN	17	3	6

THEMES
WE WILL NOT THINK OF THEMES LIKE THESE 324	2 DON JUAN	3 L 11		2
TO JEST UPON SUCH THEMES IN MANY A SALLY 526	3 DON JUAN	16	53	3
OR--BUT ALL WORDS UPON SUCH THEMES ARE WEAK . . . 557	3 DON JUAN	16	116	5

THENCE
THERE WINDS AND WAVES HAD HURL'D THEM AND FROM THENCE . 177	2 DON JUAN	2	40	1
EMBARKED HIMSELF AND THEM AND OFF THEY WENT THENCE . 432	2 DON JUAN	5	40	3

			PAGE	VOL	CANTO	STANZA	LN
THENCE (CONTINUED)							
AND THENCE THROUGH BERLIN DRESDEN AND THE LIKE	. . . . .	.	255	3	DON JUAN 10	61	1
FROM THENCE HE WAS DRAWN ONWARDS TO COLOGNE	. . .	.	255	3	DON JUAN 10	62	5
FROM THENCE TO HOLLAND'S HAGUE AND HELVOETSLUYS	. . .	.	256	3	DON JUAN 10	63	1
GREAT THOUGHTS WE CATCH FROM THENCE (BESIDES A COLD	. .	.	506	3	DON JUAN 16	14	4
THEOGONY							
OH YE IMMORTAL GODS WHAT IS THEOGONY	. . . . . .	.	192	3	DON JUAN 9	20	1
THEOLOGIAN							
BUT THOUGH I AM A TEMPERATE THEOLOGIAN	. . . . .	.	497	3	DON JUAN 15	92	1
THEOLOGY							
EXCEPTING THE POST-OBITS OF THEOLOGY	. . . .	.	76	2	DON JUAN 1	103	8
SOME PERSONS SAY THAT DANTE MEANT THEOLOGY	. . . .	.	281	2	DON JUAN 3	11	1
HE HEWED AWAY LIKE DOCTORS OF THEOLOGY	. . . . .	.	165	3	DON JUAN 8	108	6
THEOLOGY FINE ARTS OR FINER STAYS	. . . .	.	340	3	DON JUAN 12	53	2
THEOREMS							
HER THOUGHTS WERE THEOREMS HER WORDS A PROBLEM	. . . .	.	28	2	DON JUAN 1	13	7
THEORIC							
BUT BY THE BOOKISH THEORIC IT APPEARS	. . . . . .	.	10	3	DON JUAN 6	9	2
THEORIES							
BY THEORIES QUITE PRACTICABLE TOO	. . . .	.	267	2	DON JUAN 2	207	4
THEREANENT							
DIVORCED OR DOING THEREANENT YE ANNALS	. . . . . .	.	308	3	DON JUAN 11	80	2
THEREIN							
FOR MAN THEREIN WITH EYES AND HEART TO DINE	. . . .	.	489	3	DON JUAN 15	75	4
THEREON							
WARRIORS THEREON WERE BATTLING FURIOUSLY	. . . . .	.	461	2	DON JUAN 5	86	3
ALSO THEREON--BUT THAT'S NOT MUCH WE FIND	. . . .	.	525	3	DON JUAN 16	49	6
THERE'S							
THERE'S NO MORE TO BE SAID OF TRAFALGAR	. . . . .	.	23	2	DON JUAN 1	4	3
BUT IF THERE'S ANY THING IN WHICH I SHINE	. . . .	.	33	2	DON JUAN 1	23	6
THERE'S MERIT IN THIS SORT OF RESURRECTION	. . . .	.	37	2	DON JUAN 1	31	V7
I SAY THAT THERE'S THE PLACE--BUT VERBUM SAT	. . .	.	50	2	DON JUAN 1	53	4
BUT THERE'S A RUMOUR WHICH I FAIN WOULD HUSH	. . .	.	53	2	DON JUAN 1	58	6
YET THERE'S NO DOUBT SHE ONLY MEANT TO CLASP	. . .	.	81	2	DON JUAN 1	111	4
LABOUR THERE'S A SURE MARKET FOR IMPOSTURE	. . . .	.	91	2	DON JUAN 1	128	8
THERE'S SOMETHING CHEERFUL IN THAT SORT OF LIGHT	. .	.	94	2	DON JUAN 1	135	5
THERE'S PEN AND INK FOR YOU SIR WHEN YOU NEED--	. .	.	104	2	DON JUAN 1	152	4
THERE'S NOTHING SO BECOMING TO THE FACE	. . . .	.	119	2	DON JUAN 1	178	8
DAY HAS NOT BROKE--THERE'S NO ONE IN THE STREET	. .	.	121	2	DON JUAN 1	182	8
THERE'S MORE THAN ONE EDITION AND THE READINGS	. . .	.	127	2	DON JUAN 1	189	5
THERE'S ONLY ONE SLIGHT DIFFERENCE BETWEEN	. . . .	.	137	2	DON JUAN 1	202	1
(THERE'S ONE AT LEAST IS VERY FOND OF THIS)	. . . .	.	140	2	DON JUAN 1	206	4
THERE'S NOUGHT NO DOUBT SO MUCH THE SPIRIT CALMS	. .	.	174	2	DON JUAN 2	34	1
THOU MAK'ST PHILOSOPHERS THERE'S EPICURUS	. . . .	.	267	2	DON JUAN 2	207	1
THERE'S SOMETHING OF ANTIPATHY AS 'TWERE	. . . . .	.	278	2	DON JUAN 3	6	1
THERE'S DOUBTLESS SOMETHING IN DOMESTIC DOINGS	. . .	.	279	2	DON JUAN 3	8	1
THERE'S NOTHING WRONG IN A CONNUBIAL KISS	. . . .	.	279	2	DON JUAN 3	8	6
OF FRIENDS--AND OPIATE DRAUGHTS--THERE'S LOVE AND WINE	.	.	343	2	DON JUAN 3	V 98	2
AND THEN THERE ARE THE DANCERS THERE'S THE NINI	. .	.	390	2	DON JUAN 4	84	1
THEN THERE'S THAT LAUGHING SLUT THE PELEGRINI	. . .	.	390	2	DON JUAN 4	84	3
AND THEN THERE'S THE GROTESCA--SUCH A DANCER	. . .	.	390	2	DON JUAN 4	84	7
THERE'S ONE THOUGH TALL AND STIFFER THAN A PIKE	. .	.	390	2	DON JUAN 4	85	5
THERE'S NOT A SEA THE PASSENGER E'ER PUKES IN	. . .	.	413	2	DON JUAN 5	5	7
PERHAPS THERE'S NOTHING--I'LL NOT SAY APPALS	. . .	.	442	2	DON JUAN 5	56	5
'TWOULD BE AS WELL AND--(THOUGH THERE'S NOT MUCH IN'T)	.	.	464	2	DON JUAN 5	91	5
THERE'S NOTHING IN THE WORLD LIKE ETIQUETTE	. . . .	.	471	2	DON JUAN 5	103	6
THERE'S NOTHING WHETS THE BEAK OR ARMS THE CLAW	. .	.	488	2	DON JUAN 5	133	3
BUT AFTER ALL THERE'S NEITHER TUNE NOR TIME	. . . .	.	14	3	DON JUAN 6	18	4
THERE'S NOT A METEOR IN THE POLAR SKY	. . . . . .	.	66	3	DON JUAN 7	1	3
THERE'S FORTUNE EVEN IN FAME WE MUST ALLOW	. . . .	.	82	3	DON JUAN 7	33	6
LET THERE BE BLOOD SAYS MAN AND THERE'S A SEA	. . .	.	86	3	DON JUAN 7	41	2
AND DEATH IS DRUNK WITH GORE THERE'S NOT A STREET	. .	.	152	3	DON JUAN 8	82	2
THERE'S NOT A MOSLEM THAT HATH YIELDED SWORD	. . .	.	155	3	DON JUAN 8	87	2
THERE'S NO SUCH THING AS CERTAINTY THAT'S PLAIN	. .	.	191	3	DON JUAN 9	17	5
THERE'S GLORY AGAIN FOR YOU GENTLE READER ALL	. . .	.	261	3	DON JUAN 10	73	5
THEN THERE'S MY GENTLE EUPHUES WHO THEY SAY	. . . .	.	298	3	DON JUAN 11	59	1
THERE'S LITTLE STRANGE IN THIS BUT SOMETHING STRANGE IS	.	.	309	3	DON JUAN 11	81	7
THEN THERE'S MORE MERIT IN HIS SELF-DENIAL	. . . .	.	319	3	DON JUAN 12	7	8
THOUGH THERE'S A SHORTER A GOOD DEAL THAN THIS	. . .	.	326	3	DON JUAN 12	22	4
IN FACT THERE'S NOTHING MAKES ME SO MUCH GRIEVE	. .	.	336	3	DON JUAN 12	43	6
THERE'S ALSO NIGHTLY TO THE UNINITIATED	. . . .	.	344	3	DON JUAN 12	62	1
THEN THERE'S THE VULGAR TRICK OF THOSE DAMNED DAMAGES	.	.	346	3	DON JUAN 12	65	4
NOT THAT THERE'S NOT A QUANTITY OF THOSE	. . . . .	.	349	3	DON JUAN 12	73	3
FOR THERE'S NO SAYING WHAT THEY WILL OR MAY DO	. . .	.	351	3	DON JUAN 12	77	8
THE REASON'S OBVIOUS IF THERE'S AN ECLAT	. . . . .	.	352	3	DON JUAN 12	78	1
TILL THIRTY SHOULD PERCEIVE THERE'S A PLAIN WOMAN	. .	.	359	3	DON JUAN 13	3	8
GIVE GENTLY WAY WHEN THERE'S TOO GREAT A PRESS	. . .	.	366	3	DON JUAN 13	18	5
AND SINCE THERE'S SAFETY IN A MULTITUDE	. . . .	.	371	3	DON JUAN 13	29	1
BUT AS THERE'S SAFETY GRAFTED IN THE NUMBER	. . . .	.	371	3	DON JUAN 13	30	1
SELF-LOVE THERE'S SAFETY IN A CROWD OF COXCOMBS	. .	.	371	3	DON JUAN 13	30	8
BUT THERE'S NO SHOOTING (SAVE GROUSE) TILL SEPTEMBER	.	.	380	3	DON JUAN 13	48	8
AND THERE'S A COURAGE WHICH GROWS OUT OF FEAR	. . .	.	412	3	DON JUAN 14	5	2
LOVE WAR A TEMPEST--SURELY THERE'S VARIETY	. . . .	.	416	3	DON JUAN 14	14	1
IS ONE OF WHICH THERE'S NO DESCRIPTION RECENT	. . .	.	416	3	DON JUAN 14	15	3
WITH MUCH TO EXCITE THERE'S LITTLE TO EXALT	. . . .	.	417	3	DON JUAN 14	16	1
THERE'S LITTLE LEFT BUT TO BE BORED OR BORE	. . . .	.	418	3	DON JUAN 14	18	6
'TIS THAT IN FACT THERE'S LITTLE TO DESCRIBE	. . .	.	418	3	DON JUAN 14	20	8
THERE'S NOUGHT IN THIS BAD WORLD LIKE SYMPATHY	. . .	.	430	3	DON JUAN 14	47	1
BUT THERE'S ANOTHER LITTLE THING I OWN	. . . . .	.	445	3	DON JUAN 14	82	5

```
                                                                   PAGE VOL      CANTO STANZA LN
THERE'S  (CONTINUED)
    THERE'S MUSIC IN THE SIGHING OF A REED   . . . . . .  . . 458  3 DON JUAN 15      5    5
    THERE'S MUSIC IN THE GUSHING OF A RILL   . . . . .  . . . 458  3 DON JUAN 15      5    6
    THERE'S MUSIC IN ALL THINGS IF MEN HAD EARS . . . . . . . 458  3 DON JUAN 15      5    7
    WILL GO MUCH FURTHER THAN THERE'S NEED TO MENTION . . . . 462  3 DON JUAN 15     14    8
    BUT THERE'S A CONVERSATIONAL FACILITY . . . . . . . . . . 465  3 DON JUAN 15     20    3
    OF THIS I'M SURE AT LEAST THERE'S NO SERVILITY . . . . . 465  3 DON JUAN 15     20    5
    THERE'S NOTHING WOMEN LOVE TO DABBLE IN . . . . . . . . . 470  3 DON JUAN 15     31    4
    IN LOVE THERE'S SOMETHING OF INTOXICATION . . . . . . . . 474  3 DON JUAN 15     41   V7
    (THERE'S FAME) YOUNG PARTRIDGE' FILLETS DECK'D WITH TRUFFLES 484  3 DON JUAN 15  66    8
    THERE'S PRETTY PICKING IN THOSE PETITS PUITS  . . . . . . 486  3 DON JUAN 15     68    8
    'GAINST SUCH BELIEF THERE'S SOMETHING STRONGER STILL . . 504  3 DON JUAN 16      7    7
THERETO
    THE WATERS BEAT WHILE HE THERETO WAS LASH'D . . . . . . . 212  2 DON JUAN  2    107    6
THERMOMETER
    WHICH NOW-A-DAYS IS THE THERMOMETER  . . . . . . . . . . 524  3 DON JUAN 16     48    2
THERMOMETERS
    BUT WHERE THERMOMETERS SUNK DOWN TO TEN . . . . . . . . . 241  3 DON JUAN 10     33    6
THERMOPYLAE
    TO MAKE A NEW THERMOPYLAE . . . . . . . . . . . . . . . . 323  2 DON JUAN  3  L  7    6
THERSITES
    THERSITES OF THE HOUSE PAROLLES OF LAW  . . . . . . . . . 153  2 DON JUAN  1  V  4    7
THETIS
    THETIS BAPTIZED HER MORTAL SON IN STYX  . . . . . . . . . 346  2 DON JUAN  4      4    7
    QUENCHED IN THE LAP OF THE SALT SEA OR THETIS . . . . . . 217  3 DON JUAN  9     69    8
    HIDES TRAIN-OIL TALLOW AND THE RIGHTS OF THETIS  . . . . 246  3 DON JUAN 10     45    7
THEWS
    ON ITS OWN STRENGTH WITH CARELESS NERVES AND THEWS-- . . 131  3 DON JUAN  8     36    6
THEY'D
    THEIR SENSES THEY'D HAVE SENT YOUNG MASTER FORTH  . . . .  34  2 DON JUAN  1     25    6
    WHICH SOME CALL THE SUBLIME I WISH THEY'D TRY IT  . . . .  32  3 DON JUAN  6     53    6
    WHENEVER--WHICH MEANS EVERY DAY--THEY'D SHOWN  . . . . . 338  3 DON JUAN 12     48    3
    I WISH THEY'D STATE HOW MANY THEY HAVE GAINED  . . . . . 505  3 DON JUAN 16     11    8
THEY'LL
    THEY MAKE YOU DREAD THAT THEY'LL RECITE THEM TOO  . . . .  79  2 DON JUAN  1    108    4
    PERHAPS THEY'LL HAVE SOME MORE ABOUT A YEAR HENCE . . . . 135  2 DON JUAN  1    199    8
    THEN THAT THEY'LL READ IT O'ER AGAIN AND SAY  . . . . . . 140  2 DON JUAN  1    207    4
    AND BEG THEY'LL TAKE MY WORD ABOUT THE MORAL  . . . . . . 141  2 DON JUAN  1    209    2
    MEANTIME THEY'LL DOUBTLESS PLEASE TO RECOLLECT . . . . . 141  2 DON JUAN  1    209    5
    AND BEG THEY'LL WAIT WITH PATIENCE FOR THE MORAL  . . . . 141  2 DON JUAN  1    209   V2
    THEY'LL NEVER FIND IT OUT UNLESS I OWN  . . . . . . . . . 342  2 DON JUAN  3    111    4
    THEY'LL ONLY MAKE MISTAKES ABOUT THE FAIR  . . . . . . . 454  3 DON JUAN 14     99    3
THEY'RE
    SUCH THOUGHTS AND BE THE BETTER WHEN THEY'RE OVER . . . .  64  2 DON JUAN  1     78    6
    THEY'RE ON THE STAIR JUST NOW AND IN A CRACK  . . . . . .  96  2 DON JUAN  1    137    6
    AND WHEN AT LENGTH THEY'RE OUT OF BREATH THEY SIGH  . . . 119  2 DON JUAN  1    179    5
    THAT THEY WILL NOT CRY OUT BEFORE THEY'RE HURT . . . . . 140  2 DON JUAN  1    207    3
    LIKE MOST IN THE BELIEF IN WHICH THEY'RE BRED  . . . . . 197  2 DON JUAN  2     76    6
    BUT THAT'S HER WAY WITH ALL MEN TILL THEY'RE TRIED  . . . 418  2 DON JUAN  5     14    5
    THEY'RE RIGHT OUR DAYS ARE TOO BRIEF FOR AFFORDING  . . . 270  3 DON JUAN 11      4    5
    THEIR CHANCES--THEY'RE TOO NUMEROUS LIKE THE THIRTY  . . 299  3 DON JUAN 11     61    7
    THEY'RE BARREN AND NOT WORTH THE PAINS TO PULL  . . . . . 402  3 DON JUAN 13     95    6
    AND FALSE--THOUGH TRUE FOR SURELY THEY'RE SINCEREST  . . 547  3 DON JUAN 16     97    7
THICK
    QUICK THICK AND HEAVY--AS A THUNDER-SHOWER  . . . . . . . 110  2 DON JUAN  1    161    8
    TILL THE EYE CHEATED OPENS THICK WITH TEARS  . . . . . . 227  2 DON JUAN  2    134    8
    AND THICK WITH DAMASK FLOWERS OF SILK INLAID  . . . . . . 308  2 DON JUAN  3     64    3
    UNFIT TO MIX IN THESE THICK SOLITUDES  . . . . . . . . . 358  2 DON JUAN  4     28    3
    AND WALLS AS THICK AS MOST SKULLS BORN AS YET  . . . . .  72  3 DON JUAN  7     12    2
    YET MEN RESOLVED TO DASH THROUGH THICK AND THIN  . . . .  94  3 DON JUAN  7     54    4
    THE NIGHT WAS DARK AND THE THICK MIST ALLOWED  . . . . . 115  3 DON JUAN  8      6    1
    A GLANCE ON THE DULL CLOUDS (AS THICK AS STARCH  . . . . 121  3 DON JUAN  8     21    6
    THEY FELL AS THICK AS HARVESTS BENEATH HAIL  . . . . . . 134  3 DON JUAN  8     43    1
    THROUGH PLEASURES THICK AND THIN TO FAME OR SHAME . . . . 189  3 DON JUAN  9     14   V7
    AND CARCASES THAT LAY AS THICK AS THATCH . . . . . . . . 197  3 DON JUAN  9     29    4
    OF LIFE SHRUNK IN HIS HEART AND THICK AND SOOTY  . . . . 276  3 DON JUAN 11     16    5
    A JEST A RIDDLE FAME THROUGH THIN AND THICK SOUGHT  . . . 363  3 DON JUAN 13     10    7
    THAT FAITHFUL WERE THROUGH THICK AND THIN ABROAD  . . . . 452  3 DON JUAN 14     96    3
    BROUGHT TO SURVEY THESE GREY WALLS WHICH THOUGH SO THICK  529  3 DON JUAN 16     58    3
    WHO AFTER RUMMAGING THE ABBEY THROUGH THICK . . . . . . . 529  3 DON JUAN 16     58    5
    TO HAMMER A HOARSE LAUGH FROM THE THICK THRONG  . . . . . 540  3 DON JUAN 16     83    8
THICKER
    HER HAIR WAS THICKER BUT LESS LONG HER EYES . . . . . . . 221  2 DON JUAN  2    122    7
    THICKER THAN LEAVES THE LIVES BEGAN TO FALL  . . . . . . 116  3 DON JUAN  8      9    3
THICKEST
    RUSHED WHERE THE THICKEST FIRE ANNOUNCED MOST FOES  . . . 127  3 DON JUAN  8     32    8
THICKET
    HE LED THEM ONWARD FIRST THROUGH A LOW THICKET . . . . . 433  2 DON JUAN  5     41    3
THICK'NING
    WITH THICK'NING CANOPY THE CONFLICT O'ER . . . . . . . . 116  3 DON JUAN  8      8    6
THIEVES
    IN GANGS OF FIFTY THIEVES COMMIT THEIR CRIMES  . . . . .  79  2 DON JUAN  1    108    5
    UNLIKE THE HONEST ARAB THIEVES SO BRAVE . . . . . . . . . 225  2 DON JUAN  2    130    6
THIGH
    THAT CARRIED OFF HIS NEIGHBOUR BY THE THIGH . . . . . . . 212  2 DON JUAN  2    106    6
THIN
    'TIS GROWN HIGH TIME TO THIN IT IN ITS TURN . . . . . . .  92  2 DON JUAN  1    131    4
    AND ALL THE REST WERE THIN ENOUGH HEAVEN KNOWS . . . . . 199  2 DON JUAN  2     80    2
    FOR STILL HE LAY AND ON HIS THIN WORN CHEEK . . . . . . . 234  2 DON JUAN  2    147    1
```

THIN   (CONTINUED)

	PAGE	VOL		CANTO	STANZA	LN
HER CHILDREN UP (IF NURSING THEM DON'T THIN HER)	306	2	DON JUAN	3	60	4
ANON HER THIN WAN FINGERS BEAT THE WALL	380	2	DON JUAN	4	66	1
AND SUBJECT WHEN THE HOUSE IS THIN TO COLD	389	2	DON JUAN	4	83	3
YET MEN RESOLVED TO DASH THROUGH THICK AND THIN	94	3	DON JUAN	7	54	4
THROUGH PLEASURES THICK AND THIN TO FAME OR SHAME	189	3	DON JUAN	9	14	V7
EXCHANGED FOR THIN POTATIONS BY JOHN BULL--	310	3	DON JUAN	11	85	7
WEIGH NOT THE THIN ORE WHERE THEIR VISAGE SHINES	321	3	DON JUAN	12	12	4
WITHOUT CASH CAMPS WERE THIN AND COURTS WERE NONE	322	3	DON JUAN	12	14	3
A JEST A RIDDLE FAME THROUGH THIN AND THICK SOUGHT	363	3	DON JUAN	13	10	7
MUST BE DECLINED WHILE LIFE'S THIN THREAD'S SPUN OUT	376	3	DON JUAN	13	40	7
THAT FAITHFUL WERE THROUGH THICK AND THIN ABROAD	452	3	DON JUAN	14	96	3
THE LAST THIN PETTICOATS WERE VANISHED GONE	504	3	DON JUAN	16	8	5
AND THIN PRODUCED A PLAN WHEREBY TO ERECT	529	3	DON JUAN	16	58	6

THING

	PAGE	VOL		CANTO	STANZA	LN
BENEATH THE LIE THIS STATE THING BREATHED O'ER THEE	19	2	DON JUAN	D	16	4
BUT IF THERE'S ANY THING IN WHICH I SHINE	33	2	DON JUAN	1	23	6
BUT NOT A PAGE OF ANY THING THAT'S LOOSE	44	2	DON JUAN	1	40	6
WAS IN HER EYES A THING THE MOST ATROCIOUS	51	2	DON JUAN	1	54	8
'TIS A SAD THING I CANNOT CHOOSE BUT SAY	56	2	DON JUAN	1	63	1
CARESS'D HIM OFTEN SUCH A THING MIGHT BE	59	2	DON JUAN	1	69	2
THING QUITE IN COURSE AND NOT AT ALL ALARMING	68	2	DON JUAN	1	86	7
THE VERY THING WHICH EVERYBODY FEELS	69	2	DON JUAN	1	89	3
NO MATTER HOW OR WHY THE THING BEFELL	77	2	DON JUAN	1	105	5
HAD SHE IMAGINED SUCH A THING COULD ROUSE	81	2	DON JUAN	1	111	7
OH PLEASURE YOU'RE INDEED A PLEASANT THING	85	2	DON JUAN	1	119	1
TO PROVE HIMSELF THE THING HE MOST ABHORR'D	97	2	DON JUAN	1	139	8
(AT LEAST THIS IS THE THING MOST PEOPLE DO)	129	2	DON JUAN	1	191	5
MAN'S LOVE IS OF MAN'S LIFE A THING APART	131	2	DON JUAN	1	194	1
AND WOULD NOT BROOK AT ALL THIS SORT OF THING	143	2	DON JUAN	1	212	7
ONCE ALL IN ALL BUT NOW A THING APART	144	2	DON JUAN	1	215	3
AND LARGEST THINKING IT WAS JUST THE THING	146	2	DON JUAN	1	219	3
OR ELSE THE THING HAD HARDLY COME TO PASS)	158	2	DON JUAN	2	3	6
AND SUCH LIGHT GRIEFS ARE NOT A THING TO DIE ON	165	2	DON JUAN	2	16	4
OR ANY OTHER THING THAT BRINGS REGRET	172	2	DON JUAN	2	31	5
A SORT OF THING AT WHICH ONE WOULD HAVE LAUGH'D	183	2	DON JUAN	2	50	3
AS FAIR A THING AS E'ER WAS FORM'D OF CLAY	214	2	DON JUAN	2	110	8
A THING WHICH POESY BUT SELDOM MENTIONS	221	2	DON JUAN	2	123	6
THERE LIES THE THING WE LOVE WITH ALL ITS ERRORS	261	2	DON JUAN	2	197	7
TO BE A LOVELY AND A FEARFUL THING	262	2	DON JUAN	2	199	2
THE PEASANTS GAVE THE POOR DUMB THING A PITTANCE	285	2	DON JUAN	3	18	6
THE ONLY THING OF THIS SORT EVER SEEN	288	2	DON JUAN	3	25	4
A THING TO HUMAN FEELINGS THE MOST TRYING	301	2	DON JUAN	3	51	2
THE ONLY THING WHICH KEPT HIS HEART UNCLOSED	304	2	DON JUAN	3	57	3
YET A FINE FAMILY IS A FINE THING	306	2	DON JUAN	3	60	1
BECOME A THING OR NOTHING SAVE TO RANK	327	2	DON JUAN	3	89	3
(WE'VE NOT SO GOOD A WORD BUT HAVE THE THING	332	2	DON JUAN	3	97	2
AND IF I LAUGH AT ANY MORTAL THING	346	2	DON JUAN	4	4	1
A THING WHICH EACH ENDEARMENT MORE ENDEAR'D	352	2	DON JUAN	4	16	8
ON SUCH A THING IS SUDDENLY TO SEA SENT	371	2	DON JUAN	4	51	6
YE COULD NOT KNOW WHERE LIES A THING SO FAIR	383	2	DON JUAN	4	72	5
WAS JUAN WHO--AN AWKWARD THING AT HIS AGE	394	2	DON JUAN	4	92	7
WHAT 'TWAS ERE ABOLITION AND THE THING	408	2	DON JUAN	4	115	4
THAN ANY OTHER SCRAPE A THING OF COURSE	417	2	DON JUAN	5	12	8
I SAY A THING IT MUST AT ONCE BE DONE	458	2	DON JUAN	5	81	7
THAT BEING THE LAST THING A PROUD WOMAN TRIES	483	2	DON JUAN	5	125	6
IS NOT A THING OF THAT ASTRINGENT QUALITY	501	2	DON JUAN	5	157	4
THE STRANGEST THING WAS BEAUTEOUS SHE WAS WHOLLY	33	3	DON JUAN	6	54	5
A THING OF MUCH LESS IMPORT IN THAT CLIME--	51	3	DON JUAN	6	90	4
A PLEASANT THING TO YOUNG MEN AT THEIR YEARS	75	3	DON JUAN	7	18	6
THIS WAS POTEMKIN--A GREAT THING IN DAYS	84	3	DON JUAN	7	37	1
A THING TO WONDER AT BEYOND MOST WONDERING	95	3	DON JUAN	7	55	4
YET I LOVE GLORY--GLORY'S A GREAT THING--	118	3	DON JUAN	8	14	1
A THING WHICH VICTORY BY NO MEANS BODED	119	3	DON JUAN	8	16	6
A THING OF IMPULSE AND A CHILD OF SONG	123	3	DON JUAN	8	24	2
I DON'T KNOW HOW THE THING OCCURRED--IT MIGHT	125	3	DON JUAN	8	28	1
POOR THING WHAT'S TO BE DONE I'M PUZZLED QUITE	161	3	DON JUAN	8	99	8
A THING WHICH HAPPENS EVERYWHERE EACH DAY--	163	3	DON JUAN	8	103	7
IN ONE THING NE'ERTHELESS 'TIS FIT TO PRAISE	176	3	DON JUAN	8	128	1
WITH WHICH MEN IMAGE OUT THE UNKNOWN THING	188	3	DON JUAN	9	11	2
THERE'S NO SUCH THING AS CERTAINTY THAT'S PLAIN	191	3	DON JUAN	9	17	5
OR PRETTY IS A THING TO RECOLLECT	199	3	DON JUAN	9	34	3
OF THE STRANGE THING SOME WOMEN SET A VALUE ON	208	3	DON JUAN	9	51	3
WHAT A STRANGE THING IS MAN AND WHAT A STRANGER	214	3	DON JUAN	9	64	1
THE OLDEST THING ON RECORD AND YET NEW	214	3	DON JUAN	9	64	8
SELF-LOVE--WHICH WHEN SOME SORT OF THING ABOVE	216	3	DON JUAN	9	68	3
THOUGH BOLD AND BLOODY WAS THE KIND OF THING	217	3	DON JUAN	9	70	2
THE WHOLE THING IS OF CLOTHING SOULS IN CLAY	220	3	DON JUAN	9	75	8
BECAUSE THE CLERGY TAKE THE THING IN HAND	220	3	DON JUAN	9	76	4
A THING TO COUNTERBALANCE HUMAN WOES	226	3	DON JUAN	10	2	5
WHICH IS A SAD THING AND NOT ONLY TRAMPLES	236	3	DON JUAN	10	23	4
WHICH (THOUGH I HATE TO SAY A THING THAT'S BITTER)	237	3	DON JUAN	10	26	4
A THING WHICH HAPPENS RARELY THIS HE OWED	239	3	DON JUAN	10	29	2
POOR LITTLE THING SHE WAS AS FAIR AS DOCILE	250	3	DON JUAN	10	52	1
ALTHOUGH 'TIS AN IMAGINARY THING	296	3	DON JUAN	11	55	4
(A THING WITH POETRY IN GENERAL HARD)	322	3	DON JUAN	12	13	4
AND MALTHUS DOES THE THING 'GAINST WHICH HE WRITES	325	3	DON JUAN	12	20	8
POOR THING EVE'S WAS A TRIFLING CASE TO HER'S	345	3	DON JUAN	12	64	8
(A THING APPROVED AS SAVING TIME AND TOIL)--	351	3	DON JUAN	12	76	6

THING (CONTINUED)

	PAGE	VOL		CANTO	STANZA	LN
IT IS A VERY SERIOUS THING INDEED	351	3	DON JUAN	12	77	2
POOR THING HOW FREQUENTLY BY ME AND OTHERS	374	3	DON JUAN	13	36	7
THE FIRST THING BOYS LIKE AFTER PLAY AND FRUIT	405	3	DON JUAN	13	101	3
A MOMENT'S GOOD THING MAY HAVE COST THEM YEARS	408	3	DON JUAN	13	109	6
DEATH SO CALL'D IS A THING WHICH MAKES MEN WEEP	411	3	DON JUAN	14	3	7
POOR THING OF USAGES COERC'D COMPELL'D	420	3	DON JUAN	14	23	5
A THING IN FOOTING INDISPENSABLE	427	3	DON JUAN	14	38	5
THE SORT OF THING TO TURN A YOUNG MAN'S HEAD	438	3	DON JUAN	14	64	1
THERE IS AN AWKWARD THING WHICH MUCH PERPLEXES	442	3	DON JUAN	14	73	1
BUT THERE'S ANOTHER LITTLE THING I OWN	445	3	DON JUAN	14	82	5
A THING OF WHICH SIMILITUDES CAN SHOW	505	3	DON JUAN	16	10	4
ONCE TWICE THRICE PASSED REPASSED--THE THING OF AIR	510	3	DON JUAN	16	23	1
A THING QUITE NECESSARY TO THE ELECT	526	3	DON JUAN	16	52	3
WHICH THE POOR THING AT TIMES ESSAYED TO DRY	532	3	DON JUAN	16	65	3
TO NAME A THING IN NOMENCLATURE RATHER	533	3	DON JUAN	16	67	7
A THING OF TEMPERAMENT AND NOT OF ART	547	3	DON JUAN	16	97	5
YET ONE THING RATHER GOOD THE GRAVE HAD SPARED	560	3	DON JUAN	16	121	3
I LEAVE THE THING A PROBLEM LIKE ALL THINGS--	568	3	DON JUAN	17	13	1

THING'S

	PAGE	VOL		CANTO	STANZA	LN
BUT ONE THING'S PRETTY SURE A WOMAN PLANTED--	276	2	DON JUAN	3	4	2
IN MORAL ENGLAND WHERE THE THING'S A TAX)	20	3	DON JUAN	6	29	7
BUT ONE THING'S ODD WHICH HERE MUST BE INSERTED	251	3	DON JUAN	10	55	7
WHAT A DELIGHTFUL THING'S A TURNPIKE ROAD	263	3	DON JUAN	10	78	1

THINGS

	PAGE	VOL		CANTO	STANZA	LN
IN THEIR OWN WAY BY ALL THE THINGS THAT SHE DID	26	2	DON JUAN	1	10	8
IN SHORT IN ALL THINGS SHE WAS FAIRLY WHAT I CALL	27	2	DON JUAN	1	12	5
POOR FELLOW HE HAD MANY THINGS TO WOUND HIM	41	2	DON JUAN	1	36	2
AND THEN THERE ARE SUCH THINGS AS LOVE DIVINE	64	2	DON JUAN	1	79	1
THINKING UNUTTERABLE THINGS HE THREW	70	2	DON JUAN	1	90	2
WITH THINGS NOT VERY SUBJECT TO CONTROL	70	2	DON JUAN	1	91	6
WITH--SEVERAL OTHER THINGS WHICH I FORGET	73	2	DON JUAN	1	96	7
HOW CAN YOU DO SUCH THINGS AND KEEP YOUR FAME	112	2	DON JUAN	1	165	3
DENYING SEVERAL LITTLE THINGS HE WANTED	120	2	DON JUAN	1	180	4
ALL THESE THINGS WILL BE SPECIFIED IN TIME	136	2	DON JUAN	1	201	1
MY TEXT WITH MANY THINGS THAT NO ONE KNOWS	138	2	DON JUAN	1	204	5
WHICH OUT OF ALL THE LOVELY THINGS WE SEE	144	2	DON JUAN	1	214	3
ALL THINGS THAT HAVE BEEN BORN WERE BORN TO DIE	147	2	DON JUAN	1	220	3
IF ALL THINGS BE CONSIDER'D FIRST THERE WAS	158	2	DON JUAN	2	3	2
UPON SUCH THINGS WOULD VERY NEAR ABSORB	160	2	DON JUAN	2	6	5
DON JUAN BADE HIS VALET PACK HIS THINGS	161	2	DON JUAN	2	9	1
BUT JUAN HAD GOT MANY THINGS TO LEAVE	164	2	DON JUAN	2	15	1
TWO THINGS FOR DYING PEOPLE QUITE BEWILDERING	179	2	DON JUAN	2	43	8
AND ALL THINGS FOR A CHANCE HAD BEEN CAST LOOSE	183	2	DON JUAN	2	51	2
FOR ON SUCH THINGS THE MEMORY REPOSES	187	2	DON JUAN	2	58	3
AND SUCH THINGS AS THE ENTRAILS AND THE BRAINS	197	2	DON JUAN	2	77	6
SUCH THINGS A MOTHER HAD NOT KNOWN HER SON	210	2	DON JUAN	2	102	3
THREE OR FOUR THINGS FOR WHICH THE LORD HE PRAISED	239	2	DON JUAN	2	157	5
A WORLD OF WORDS AND THINGS AT WHICH SHE GUESS'D	241	2	DON JUAN	2	162	8
BUT THAT LIKE OTHER THINGS HAS PASS'D AWAY	244	2	DON JUAN	2	166	5
WHEN JUAN WOKE HE FOUND SOME GOOD THINGS READY	246	2	DON JUAN	2	171	1
FEW THINGS SURPASS OLD WINE AND THEY MAY PREACH	250	2	DON JUAN	2	178	5
YET TO THESE FOUR IN THREE THINGS THE SAME LUCK HOLDS	266	2	DON JUAN	2	206	7
DOES THESE THINGS FOR US AND WHENEVER NEWLY A	267	2	DON JUAN	2	208	5
THE SAME THINGS CHANGE THEIR NAMES AT SUCH A RATE	278	2	DON JUAN	3	6	6
THE SAME THINGS CANNOT ALWAYS BE ADMIRED	278	2	DON JUAN	3	7	4
(SUCH THINGS IN FACT IT DON'T ASK MUCH TO MAR)	281	2	DON JUAN	3	10	6
BUT LAMBRO SAW ALL THESE THINGS WITH AVERSION	293	2	DON JUAN	3	35	5
'TWAS WONDERFUL HOW THINGS WENT ON IMPROVING	295	2	DON JUAN	3	39	7
YET SUCH THINGS ARE WHICH I CAN NOT EXPLAIN	299	2	DON JUAN	3	47	6
BUT VIOLENT THINGS WILL SOONER BEAR ASSUAGING	305	2	DON JUAN	3	58	5
ARE THINGS THAT REALLY TAKE AWAY THE BREATH	309	2	DON JUAN	3	66	6
AND DWARFS AND BLACKS AND SUCH LIKE THINGS THAT GAIN	310	2	DON JUAN	3	68	5
BUT WORDS ARE THINGS AND A SMALL DROP OF INK	327	2	DON JUAN	3	88	1
ARE THINGS WHICH IN THIS CENTURY DON'T STRIKE	330	2	DON JUAN	3	95	5
OH HESPERUS THOU BRINGEST ALL GOOD THINGS--	338	2	DON JUAN	3	107	1
CHARM'D WITH EACH OTHER ALL THINGS CHARM'D THAT BROUGHT	354	2	DON JUAN	4	20	7
YEARS COULD BUT BRING THEM CRUEL THINGS OR WRONG	358	2	DON JUAN	4	27	4
THOUGH ON ALL OTHER THINGS WITH LOOKS INTENSE	381	2	DON JUAN	4	68	3
WHO SAY STRANGE THINGS FOR SO CORRECT AN AGE	397	2	DON JUAN	4	98	4
I HAVE GAINED SCIENCE IN THE THINGS WHICH PASS	403	2	DON JUAN	4	107	V3
AND--BUT NO MATTER ALL THOSE THINGS ARE OVER	405	2	DON JUAN	4	111	4
WERE THINGS TO SHAKE A STOIC NE'ERTHELESS	415	2	DON JUAN	5	9	1
AND THESE ARE THINGS WHICH ASK A TENDER TEAR	420	2	DON JUAN	5	19	5
YOU TAKE THINGS COOLLY SIR SAID JUAN WHY	421	2	DON JUAN	5	21	1
BY SETTING THINGS IN THEIR RIGHT POINT OF VIEW	422	2	DON JUAN	5	23	5
BUT LET ME QUIT THE THEME AS SUCH THINGS CLAIM	431	2	DON JUAN	5	38	4
WE WHOSE MINDS COMPREHEND ALL THINGS NO MORE	432	2	DON JUAN	5	39	7
THINGS WHICH IN HUNGRY MORTALS' EYES FIND FAVOUR	437	2	DON JUAN	5	47	3
ARE THINGS WHICH MAKE AN ENGLISH EVENING PASS	444	2	DON JUAN	5	58	4
WE KNOW WHERE THINGS AND MEN MUST END AT BEST	448	2	DON JUAN	5	63	5
THOUGH FULL OF ALL THINGS WHICH COULD BE DESIRED	448	2	DON JUAN	5	64	3
IN SHORT ALL THINGS WHICH FORM A TURKISH DANDY	451	2	DON JUAN	5	68	8
THE THINGS DOWN SAID--INCENSE ME AND I CALL	454	2	DON JUAN	5	75	7
THEY LOOKED SO LITTLE DID STRONG THINGS AT TIMES--	463	2	DON JUAN	5	89	2
WEALTH HAD DONE WONDERS--TASTE NOT MUCH SUCH THINGS	465	2	DON JUAN	5	94	1
AND TURNS ASIDE HIS SCYTHE TO VULGAR THINGS	468	2	DON JUAN	5	98	4
MARVEL AND PRAISE FOR BOTH OR NONE THINGS WIN	469	2	DON JUAN	5	100	6
THERE WAS NO END UNTO THE THINGS SHE BOUGHT	476	2	DON JUAN	5	113	5

THINGS (CONTINUED)

	PAGE	VOL	CANTO	STANZA	LN
BUT TEARS MUST STOP LIKE ALL THINGS ELSE AND SOON	481	2	DON JUAN 5	121	1
NOT SO TO HER WHO NE'ER HAD HEARD SUCH THINGS	485	2	DON JUAN 5	128	2
WHEN THINGS ARE AT THE WORST THEY SOMETIMES MEND	6	3	DON JUAN 6	1	8
BUT WHETHER SUCH THINGS DO OR DO NOT WEIGH	9	3	DON JUAN 6	6	3
ARE APT TO CARRY THINGS WITH A HIGH HAND	11	3	DON JUAN 6	11	3
IS MUCH IN MOST THINGS NOT LESS IN THE HEART	15	3	DON JUAN 6	19	3
AS CERTAIN--THESE ARE PALTRY THINGS AND YET	16	3	DON JUAN 6	21	7
SO NOW ALL THINGS ARE DAMN'D ONE FEELS AT EASE	17	3	DON JUAN 6	23	1
AND HEADS IF THOU HADST ALL THINGS MULTIPLIED	20	3	DON JUAN 6	28	2
WHETHER THERE ARE SUCH THINGS AS SYMPATHIES	25	3	DON JUAN 6	38	3
WE WILL HAVE ALL THINGS SETTLED FOR YOU FAIRLY	29	3	DON JUAN 6	46	8
WITH ALL THINGS LADIES WANT SAVE ONE OR TWO	31	3	DON JUAN 6	51	7
BUT THESE ARE FOOLISH THINGS TO ALL THE WISE	37	3	DON JUAN 6	63	1
ON MOST THINGS FROM A TYRANT TO A TREE	37	3	DON JUAN 6	63	4
BY WHICH SUCH THINGS ARE SETTLED NOW-A-DAYS	45	3	DON JUAN 6	78	8
HE COULD NOT HELP THE THINGS WHICH HE RELATED	57	3	DON JUAN 6	102	4
WHEN THINGS BEYOND THE COMMON HAVE OCCURRED--	59	3	DON JUAN 6	106	6
ARE THINGS THE TURNING OF A HAIR OR FEATHER	65	3	DON JUAN 6	119	6
TO LAUGH AT ALL THINGS--FOR I WISH TO KNOW	67	3	DON JUAN 7	2	7
WHAT AFTER ALL ARE ALL THINGS--BUT A SHOW	67	3	DON JUAN 7	2	8
WHEN IT GREW RATHER LATE TO SET THINGS RIGHT	73	3	DON JUAN 7	13	5
AND I SHOULD STILL HAVE MANY THINGS TO SAY	82	3	DON JUAN 7	32	4
WHILE THINGS WERE IN ABEYANCE RIBAS SENT	85	3	DON JUAN 7	38	1
THINGS SPEEDILY WERE WAXING TO EXTREMITY	92	3	DON JUAN 7	51	V6
MOST THINGS WERE IN THIS POSTURE ON THE EVE	94	3	DON JUAN 7	54	1
TO THEM POOR THINGS IT IS AN AWKWARD STEP	103	3	DON JUAN 7	72	6
SUWARROW--WHO BUT SAW THINGS IN THE GROSS	105	3	DON JUAN 7	77	1
ARE THINGS IMMORTAL TO IMMORTAL MAN	108	3	DON JUAN 7	84	2
AT PRESENT SUCH THINGS SINCE THEY ARE HER THEME	112	3	DON JUAN 8	1	6
HISTORY CAN ONLY TAKE THINGS IN THE GROSS	113	3	DON JUAN 8	3	1
WHICH SETTLES ALL THINGS ROMAN GREEK OR RUNIC	122	3	DON JUAN 8	23	4
THEIR FRIENDS FROM FOES--BESIDES SUCH THINGS FROM HASTE	177	3	DON JUAN 8	130	4
SHOWED WHAT THINGS WERE BEFORE THE WORLD WAS FREE	179	3	DON JUAN 8	135	8
YOU HARDLY WILL BELIEVE SUCH THINGS WERE TRUE	180	3	DON JUAN 8	136	3
AND WONDER WHAT OLD WORLD SUCH THINGS COULD SEE	180	3	DON JUAN 8	137	4
AND LIKE SOME OTHER THINGS WON'T DO TO TELL	184	3	DON JUAN 9	2	3
YOU DID GREAT THINGS BUT NOT BEING GREAT IN MIND	187	3	DON JUAN 9	10	7
OF THINGS DESTROYED AND LEFT IN AIRY DOUBT	201	3	DON JUAN 9	38	4
AND CATHERINE WHO LOVED ALL THINGS (SAVE HER LORD	209	3	DON JUAN 9	54	1
WITH OR WITHOUT THEE ALL THINGS AT A STAND	210	3	DON JUAN 9	56	7
YOU PLEASE (IT CAUSES ALL THE THINGS WHICH BE	211	3	DON JUAN 9	57	3
OUR VEINS WHEN THINGS CALLED SOVEREIGNS THINK IT BEST	212	3	DON JUAN 9	60	7
AS THOSE WHO LIKE THINGS ROSY RIPE AND SUCCULENT	213	3	DON JUAN 9	62	3
TO LOVE THERE ARE THOSE THINGS WHICH WORDS NAME SENSES--	219	3	DON JUAN 9	74	8
OF YOUTH AND VIGOUR BEAUTY AND THOSE THINGS	227	3	DON JUAN 10	5	7
TO MAKE SUCH PUPPETS OF US THINGS BELOW)	232	3	DON JUAN 10	16	4
PEEP OUT SOMETIMES WHEN THINGS ARE IN A FLURRY	237	3	DON JUAN 10	26	5
WITH WHICH GREAT STATES SUCH THINGS ARE APT TO PUSH ON	246	3	DON JUAN 10	45	5
ACCORDING AS YOU TAKE THINGS WELL OR ILL--	264	3	DON JUAN 10	80	7
BUT WHAT THEY PLEASE AND IF THAT THINGS BE DEAR	273	3	DON JUAN 11	10	2
AND TURN ON THINGS WHICH NO ARISTOCRATIC	289	3	DON JUAN 11	43	3
(WHICH WILL COME OVER THINGS) BEATS LOVE OR LIQUOR	317	3	DON JUAN 12	4	5
(WHICH SAW ALL WESTERN THINGS WITH SMALL SURPRISE	328	3	DON JUAN 12	27	3
AMONGST THE SEX IN LITTLE THINGS OR GREAT	329	3	DON JUAN 12	28	2
FOR THAT'S THE PHRASE THAT SETTLES ALL THINGS NOW	330	3	DON JUAN 12	31	4
I MEAN TO SHOW THINGS REALLY AS THEY ARE	335	3	DON JUAN 12	40	2
AND RATHER WISHED IN SUCH THINGS TO STAND NEUTER	336	3	DON JUAN 12	42	3
I CALL SUCH THINGS TRANSMISSION FOR THERE IS	340	3	DON JUAN 12	52	1
ABROAD SUCH THINGS DECIDE FEW WOMEN'S FATE--	345	3	DON JUAN 12	64	5
SHE CANNOT DO THESE THINGS NOR ONE OR TWO	351	3	DON JUAN 12	76	1
NOR SETTLES ALL THINGS IN ONE INTERVIEW	351	3	DON JUAN 12	76	5
UPON FOR THERE ARE VERY FEW THINGS WEARIER	367	3	DON JUAN 13	19	5
THE DREARY FUIMUS OF ALL THINGS HUMAN	376	3	DON JUAN 13	40	6
(IF BUT FOR COMFORT) THAT ALL THINGS ARE KIND	377	3	DON JUAN 13	41	4
GOOD AT ALL THINGS BUT BETTER AT A BET	399	3	DON JUAN 13	87	8
WHILE STRONGBOW'S BEST THINGS MIGHT HAVE COME FROM CATO	401	3	DON JUAN 13	92	8
TO BUILD UP COMMON THINGS WITH COMMON PLACES	413	3	DON JUAN 14	7	8
BUT MOSTLY SINGS OF HUMAN THINGS AND ACTS--	416	3	DON JUAN 14	13	4
THAN THESE THINGS AND BESIDES I WISH TO SPARE 'EM	419	3	DON JUAN 14	21	5
WAS ALL THINGS UNTO PEOPLE OF ALL SORTS	424	3	DON JUAN 14	31	2
HE LIKEWISE COULD BE MOST THINGS TO ALL WOMEN	424	3	DON JUAN 14	31	7
SOME HOPED THINGS MIGHT NOT TURN OUT AS THEY FEAR'D	429	3	DON JUAN 14	44	3
'TIS SAD TO HACK INTO THE ROOTS OF THINGS	436	3	DON JUAN 14	59	1
WITHOUT STRONG REASON OF THOSE SORTS OF THINGS	439	3	DON JUAN 14	66	4
ALL THINGS PURSUE EXACTLY THE SAME ROUTE	446	3	DON JUAN 14	84	3
THAT VIOLENT THINGS MORE QUICKLY FIND A TERM	451	3	DON JUAN 14	94	3
BUT GREAT THINGS SPRING FROM LITTLE--WOULD YOU THINK	454	3	DON JUAN 14	100	1
WERE THINGS BUT ONLY CALL'D BY THEIR RIGHT NAME	455	3	DON JUAN 14	102	7
THERE'S MUSIC IN ALL THINGS IF MEN HAD EARS	458	3	DON JUAN 15	5	7
FOR THERE ARE FEW THINGS BY MANKIND LESS BROOK'D	479	3	DON JUAN 15	53	4
GREAT THINGS WERE NOW TO BE ACHIEVED AT TABLE	482	3	DON JUAN 15	62	1
WITH THINGS I CAN'T WITHSTAND OR UNDERSTAND	484	3	DON JUAN 15	66	3
THIS MUCH IS SURE THAT OUT OF EARSHOT THINGS	489	3	DON JUAN 15	76	2
WHO HITHERTO HAD FOUND THINGS NOT AMISS	492	3	DON JUAN 15	81	V3
COMMENCED (FROM SUCH SLIGHT THINGS WILL GREAT COMMENCE)	493	3	DON JUAN 15	83	5
HOW COULD HE POSSIBLY SHOW THINGS EXISTENT	494	3	DON JUAN 15	87	8
HE WHO DOUBTS ALL THINGS NOTHING CAN DENY	495	3	DON JUAN 15	88	5
OF THESE THINGS OR BY RIDICULE BENUMB	498	3	DON JUAN 15	95	6

THINGS   (CONTINUED)
      TO RHYME AT NOON--WHEN I HAVE OTHER THINGS 500   3 DON JUAN 15   98   2
      THE ANTIQUE PERSIANS TAUGHT THREE USEFUL THINGS .   .   . 501   3 DON JUAN 16   1   1
      IN SOME THINGS MINE'S BEYOND ALL CONTRADICTION 502   3 DON JUAN 16   2   7
      AND AS SHE TREATS ALL THINGS AND NE'ER RETREATS .   .   . 502   3 DON JUAN 16   3   1
      'TIS ALWAYS BEST TO TAKE THINGS UPON TRUST 503   3 DON JUAN 16   6   4
      THEY PASSED AS SUCH THINGS DO FOR SUPERSTITION 527   3 DON JUAN 16   54   2
      AND OF ALL THINGS EXCEPTING TITHES AND LEASES 531   3 DON JUAN 16   63   5
      HE WAS ALL THINGS TO ALL MEN AND DISPENSED 535   3 DON JUAN 16   71   2
      OF TWO THINGS--HOW (THE QUESTION RATHER ODD IS) .   .   . 543   3 DON JUAN 16   90   7
      (FOR LITTLE THINGS UPON MY LORD'S ESTATE   544   3 DON JUAN 16   91   7
      THE LOVE OF HIGHER THINGS AND BETTER DAYS 554   3 DON JUAN 16   108   1
      I LEAVE THE THING A PROBLEM LIKE ALL THINGS-- 568   3 DON JUAN 17   13   1
THINK
      (I THINK THE QUARTO HOLDS FIVE HUNDRED PAGES)   11   2 DON JUAN D   4   2
      AND ALL MAY THINK WHICH WAY THEIR JUDGMENTS LEAN 'EM . .   28   2 DON JUAN 1   14   6
      I THINK THE FOOLISH PEOPLE WERE POSSESS'D   34   2 DON JUAN 1   24   3
      I DON'T THINK SAPPHO'S ODE A GOOD EXAMPLE   45   2 DON JUAN 1   42   4
      I THINK I PICK'D UP TOO AS WELL AS MOST 50   2 DON JUAN 1   53   5
      I NEVER MARRIED--BUT I THINK I KNOW 50   2 DON JUAN 1   53   7
      AND YET I THINK INSTEAD OF SUCH A ONE   56   2 DON JUAN 1   62   3
      AND NOW I THINK ON'T MI VIEN IN MENTE   56   2 DON JUAN 1   62   6
      I'M REALLY PUZZLED WHAT TO THINK OR SAY 59   2 DON JUAN 1   68   7
      SUCH AS THE ANGELS THINK SO VERY FINE   64   2 DON JUAN 1   79   3
      AND SO I'D HAVE HER THINK WERE I THE MAN 64   2 DON JUAN 1   79   7
      IF YOU THINK 'TWAS PHILOSOPHY THAT THIS DID 71   2 DON JUAN 1   93   7
      (I HAVE FORGOT THE NUMBER AND THINK NO MAN 74   2 DON JUAN 1   98   5
      OF SIGHT THAT I MUST THINK ON THIS OCCASION 75   2 DON JUAN 1   101   2
      HOW DARE YOU THINK YOUR LADY WOULD GO ON SO . .   .   .   . 101 2 DON JUAN 1   146   6
      MUCH LONGER--THINK OF HUSBANDS' LOVERS' LIVES .   .   .   . 123 2 DON JUAN 1   185   7
      BUT STILL I THINK I CAN COLLECT MY MIND . .   .   .   .   . 133 2 DON JUAN 1   196   2
      I THINK THAT WITH THIS HOLY NEW ALLIANCE . .   .   .   .   . 142 2 DON JUAN 1   211   1
      I THINK I MUST TAKE UP WITH AVARICE   . .   .   . 144 2 DON JUAN 1   216   8
      OR THINK OF ANYTHING EXCEPTING THEE   . .   .   . 166 2 DON JUAN 2   19   6
      HIS FATHER'S WHOM HE LOVED AS YE MAY THINK . .   .   .   . 187 2 DON JUAN 2   58   2
      THAT SOME I REALLY THINK DO NEVER DIE . .   .   . 190 2 DON JUAN 2   65   4
      YOUR LABOURING PEOPLE THINK BEYOND ALL QUESTION .   .   .   191 2 DON JUAN 2   67   7
      IT IS AS WELL TO THINK SO NOW AND THEN . .   .   .   .   . 205 2 DON JUAN 2   93   2
      THEY KNEW NOT WHAT TO THINK OF SUCH A FREAK . .   .   .   . 229 2 DON JUAN 2   138   8
      THE COAST--I THINK IT WAS THE COAST THAT I . .   .   .   . 251 2 DON JUAN 2   181   1
      I THINK IT MUST BE RECKON'D BY ITS LENGTH . .   .   .   .   254 2 DON JUAN 2   186   8
      WHO SHUT IN CHAMBERS THINK IT LONELINESS . .   .   .   .   . 255 2 DON JUAN 2   188   2
      AND WHISPER'D THINK OF EVERY SACRED TIE . .   .   .   .   . 268 2 DON JUAN 2   210   2
      THINK YOU IF LAURA HAD BEEN PETRARCH'S WIFE . .   .   .   . 279 2 DON JUAN 3   8   7
      I THINK THAT DANTE'S MORE ABSTRUSE ECSTATICS . .   .   .   281 2 DON JUAN 3   11   7
      PERHAPS YOU THINK IN STUMBLING ON THIS FEAST .   .   .   . 296 2 DON JUAN 3   40   1
      UP WITH THE COFFEE WHICH (I THINK) THEY SPOIL'D . .   .   . 307 2 DON JUAN 3   63   8
      THINK YE HE MEANT THEM FOR A SLAVE . .   .   . 324 2 DON JUAN 3 L 10   6
      WE WILL NOT THINK OF THEMES LIKE THESE   . .   .   .   .   . 324 2 DON JUAN 3 L 11   7
      TO THINK SUCH BREASTS MUST SUCKLE SLAVES . .   .   .   .   . 326 2 DON JUAN 3 L 15   6
      THAT WHICH MAKES THOUSANDS PERHAPS MILLIONS THINK .   .   . 327 2 DON JUAN 3   88   3
      IN SOME SHAPE LET NONE THINK TO FLY THE DANGER . .   .   . 383 2 DON JUAN 4   73   7
      I REALLY THINK YET JUAN'S THEN ORDEAL . .   .   . 396 2 DON JUAN 4   96   7
      BUT SPOIL (I THINK) A VERY PRETTY POEM   . .   .   .   .   . 403 2 DON JUAN 4   107   8
      THEY LITTLE THINK WHAT MISCHIEF IS IN HAND . .   .   .   . 411 2 DON JUAN 5   1   4
      RECEIPTS IN FULL BEGAN TO THINK OF DINING . .   .   .   .   426 2 DON JUAN 5   29   8
      I THINK IT IS PERHAPS THE GLOOMIEST HOUR . .   .   .   .   . 426 2 DON JUAN 5   30   7
      OF FOOD I THINK WITH PHILIP'S SON OR RATHER . .   .   .   . 427 2 DON JUAN 5   31   7
      I THINK WITH ALEXANDER THAT THE ACT   . .   .   . 428 2 DON JUAN 5   32   1
      BUT THAT OF LATE YOUR SCRIBBLERS THINK IT WORTH   .   .   . 434 2 DON JUAN 5   42   6
      YET LET THEM THINK THAT HORACE HAS EXPREST . .   .   .   . 448 2 DON JUAN 5   63   1
      WHAT FEAR YOU THINK YOU THIS A LION'S DEN . .   .   .   .   458 2 DON JUAN 5   81   6
      AT LEAST WE THINK SO THOUGH BUT FEW HAVE GUESS'D .   .   .   6   3 DON JUAN 6   1   4
      WHICH DOUBLES WHAT THEY THINK OF THE TRANSGRESSION   .   .   11   3 DON JUAN 6   10   4
      WOULD LIKE (I THINK) TO TRUST ALL TO DESIRE 14   3 DON JUAN 6   16   4
      I THINK IT MAY BE OF CORINTHIAN BRASS 34   3 DON JUAN 6   56   1
      WOULD MAKE US THINK THE MOON IS AT ITS FULL 46   3 DON JUAN 6   80   5
      HE DID NOT THINK MUCH ON THE MATTER NOR 51   3 DON JUAN 6   91   1
      SULTANA THINK UPON THE CONSEQUENCE   62   3 DON JUAN 6   114   2
      I THINK ONE SHAKESPEAR PUTS THE SAME THOUGHT IN . .   .   77   3 DON JUAN 7   21   6
      THAT ONE WOULD THINK THE FIRST WHO BORE IT ADAM .   .   .   79   3 DON JUAN 7   25   8
      AS THEY WHO PRINT THEM THINK IS NECESSARY   79   3 DON JUAN 7   26   6
      I THINK THAT SEVERAL VOLUMES WOULD FALL SHORT 82   3 DON JUAN 7   32   3
      I NEVER THINK ABOUT IT IN A HEAT) 87   3 DON JUAN 7   42   6
      (THIS METAPHOR I THINK HOLDS GOOD AS AUGHT   90   3 DON JUAN 7   49   3
      BUT LET THAT PASS--I THINK I HAVE HEARD YOUR NAME .   .   .   97   3 DON JUAN 7   60   7
      THINK WHAT IT IS TO BE IN YOUR OLD AGE   118   3 DON JUAN 8   14   2
      WHICH MADE SOME THINK AND OTHERS KNOW A HELL COME   .   .   . 134   3 DON JUAN 8   42   8
      I THINK I HEAR A LITTLE BIRD WHO SINGS   137   3 DON JUAN 8   50   3
      THINK HOW THE JOYS OF READING A GAZETTE 174   3 DON JUAN 8   125   1
      BUT YE--OUR CHILDREN'S CHILDREN THINK HOW WE 179   3 DON JUAN 8   135   7
      OF CARNAGE--AND I THINK HE WAS MORE GLAD IN HER .   .   .   182   3 DON JUAN 8   140   7
      I DON'T THINK THAT YOU USED KINNAIRD QUITE WELL .   .   .   184   3 DON JUAN 9   2   1
      FOR ME I SOMETIMES THINK THAT LIFE IS DEATH 190   3 DON JUAN 9   16   7
      THINK IF THEN GEORGE THE FOURTH SHOULD BE DUG UP   .   .   . 202   3 DON JUAN 9   39   1
      I THINK I CAN EXPLAIN MYSELF WITHOUT 207   3 DON JUAN 9   50   1
      OUR VEINS WHEN THINGS CALLED SOVEREIGNS THINK IT BEST   .   . 212   3 DON JUAN 9   60   7
      SUCH DIFFERENCE DOTH A FEW MONTHS MAKE YOU'D THINK . .   . 228   3 DON JUAN 10   7   5
      I RATHER THINK THE MOON SHOULD DATE THE DEARS 230   3 DON JUAN 10   10   8

	PAGE	VOL		CANTO	STANZA	LN
THINK (CONTINUED)						
FOR BOTH ARE MUCH THE SAME SINCE WHAT MEN THINK	234	3	DON JUAN	10	20	2
THINK OF THE THUNDERER'S FALLING DOWN BELOW	254	3	DON JUAN	10	59	3
AND WHEN I THINK UPON A POT OF BEER--	263	3	DON JUAN	10	77	1
AS SEVERAL PEOPLE THINK SUCH HAZARDS RUDE	270	3	DON JUAN	11	4	4
MAY NOT THINK MUCH OF LONDON'S FIRST APPEARANCE--	271	3	DON JUAN	11	7	7
TO THINK SO FOR HALF ENGLISH AS I AM	274	3	DON JUAN	11	12	6
SOME PERSONS THINK THAT COLERIDGE HATH THE SWAY	298	3	DON JUAN	11	59	5
I THINK I KNOW A TRICK OR TWO WOULD TURN	300	3	DON JUAN	11	63	1
THE ONLY DANCE WHICH TEACHES GIRLS TO THINK	302	3	DON JUAN	11	68	3
I THINK THAT PHILO-GENITIVENESS IS--	326	3	DON JUAN	12	22	2
WHO THINK THAT NOVELTIES ARE BUTTERFLIES	328	3	DON JUAN	12	27	5
THINK NOT FAIR CREATURES THAT I MEAN TO ABUSE YOU ALL--	329	3	DON JUAN	12	28	3
I THINK YOU'LL FIND FROM MANY A FAMILY PICTURE	337	3	DON JUAN	12	46	3
WHICH WAS A WONDER IF YOU THINK WHO GOT HIM	338	3	DON JUAN	12	49	4
I THINK TO CANTER GENTLY THROUGH A HUNDRED	341	3	DON JUAN	12	55	8
AT FIRST HE DID NOT THINK THE WOMEN PRETTY	347	3	DON JUAN	12	68	8
I SAID THAT JUAN DID NOT THINK THEM PRETTY	350	3	DON JUAN	12	74	2
AND TELL ME WHAT YOU THINK OF YOUR GREAT THINKERS	357	3	DON JUAN	12	89	8
AT LEAST THEY THINK SO TO EXERT THEIR STATE	367	3	DON JUAN	13	19	4
THE ACCUSED TO THINK THEIR LORDSHIPS WOULD DETERMINE	391	3	DON JUAN	13	69	3
YET THINK A SPECIMEN OF EVERY CLASS	402	3	DON JUAN	13	94	3
I THINK THAT WERE I CERTAIN OF SUCCESS	415	3	DON JUAN	14	12	1
WHO ONE MIGHT THINK WAS SOMETHING IN THE AFFAIR	430	3	DON JUAN	14	45	2
BEGAN TO THINK THE DUCHESS' CONDUCT FREE	430	3	DON JUAN	14	46	4
'TIS BEST TO PAUSE AND THINK ERE YOU RUSH ON	438	3	DON JUAN	14	64	7
I THINK NOT SHE WAS THEN IN LOVE WITH JUAN	449	3	DON JUAN	14	91	2
BUT GREAT THINGS SPRING FROM LITTLE--WOULD YOU THINK	454	3	DON JUAN	14	100	1
I THINK I SHOULD HAVE MADE A DECENT SPOUSE	467	3	DON JUAN	15	24	1
I THINK I SHOULD HAVE MADE MONASTIC VOWS	467	3	DON JUAN	15	24	3
IT WAS NOT JEALOUSY I THINK BUT SHUN	479	3	DON JUAN	15	54	5
I SOMETIMES ALMOST THINK THAT EYES HAVE EARS	489	3	DON JUAN	15	76	1
WAS DANGEROUS--I THINK SHE IS AS HARMLESS	498	3	DON JUAN	15	94	7
AND DO NOT THINK I MEAN TO SNEER AT MOST	498	3	DON JUAN	15	95	5
I THINK TOO THAT I HAVE SATE UP TOO LATE	499	3	DON JUAN	15	97	8
TO THINK OF IF I EVER THINK--I SAY	500	3	DON JUAN	15	98	3
TO THINK OF IF I EVER THINK--I SAY	500	3	DON JUAN	15	98	3
TO THINK HIS VANISHING UNNATURAL	511	3	DON JUAN	16	24	4
A PARAGRAPH I THINK ABOUT HORNE TOOKE	512	3	DON JUAN	16	27	3
A FAT FEN VICARAGE AND NOUGHT TO THINK ON	540	3	DON JUAN	16	82	8
AND ONLY THINK OR ACT OR FEEL WITH REFERENCE	541	3	DON JUAN	16	85	6
HE FIRST INCLINED TO THINK HE HAD BEEN MISTAKEN	558	3	DON JUAN	16	118	3
TO THINK HIS SKULL HAD NOT SOME NEED OF CAULKING	565	3	DON JUAN	17	8	6
SO THAT I ALMOST THINK THAT THE SAME SKIN	567	3	DON JUAN	17	11	7
THINKERS						
EXISTS WHEN THE ONCE THINKERS ARE LESS REAL	234	3	DON JUAN	10	20	3
AND TELL ME WHAT YOU THINK OF YOUR GREAT THINKERS	357	3	DON JUAN	12	89	8
THINKING						
I CAN'T HELP THINKING JUVENAL WAS WRONG	45	2	DON JUAN	1	43	3
THINKING GOD MIGHT NOT UNDERSTAND HER CASE	62	2	DON JUAN	1	75	V8
THINKING UNUTTERABLE THINGS HE THREW	70	2	DON JUAN	1	90	2
I CAN'T HELP THINKING PUBERTY ASSISTED	71	2	DON JUAN	1	93	8
AND LARGEST THINKING IT WAS JUST THE THING	146	2	DON JUAN	1	219	3
AS A FULL POT OF PORTER TO THEIR THINKING	201	2	DON JUAN	2	85	7
I SAY THAT BEEF IS RARE AND CAN'T HELP THINKING	238	2	DON JUAN	2	155	1
I CAN'T HELP THINKING THAT ALL FORMER STRIFE	301	2	DON JUAN	3	50	V5
IN THINKING THAT THEIR ENEMY IS BEAT	87	3	DON JUAN	7	42	4
FOR SOME WERE THINKING OF THEIR HOME AND FRIENDS	94	3	DON JUAN	7	54	7
FOR SOME WERE THINKING OF THEIR WIVES AND FAMILIES	94	3	DON JUAN	7	54	V7
AND THOUGH I CAN'T HELP THINKING 'TWAS SCARCE FAIR	242	3	DON JUAN	10	36	5
WHICH SERVES OUR THINKING PEOPLE FOR A PASSION	284	3	DON JUAN	11	33	8
THINKS						
AND THINKS HEAVEN BRIGHTER EVEN THAN NEWTON'S PAGE	242	2	DON JUAN	2	163	V7
SHOWS THAT HE THINKS HIS FRIENDS HAVE NOT BEEN SLEEPING	436	2	DON JUAN	5	45	4
FOR REASON THINKS ALL REASONING OUT OF SEASON	437	2	DON JUAN	5	48	4
BUT ASK HIM WHAT HE THINKS OF IT A YEAR HENCE	271	3	DON JUAN	11	7	8
BUT THINKS LESS OF GOOD EATING THAN THE WHISPER	487	3	DON JUAN	15	70	7
THINK'ST						
THINK'ST THOU COULD HE--THE BLIND OLD MAN--ARISE	15	2	DON JUAN	D	11	1
THINK'ST THOU THE HONEY WITH THOSE OBJECTS GREW	144	2	DON JUAN	1	214	6
THINN'D						
THEIR NUMBERS WERE MUCH THINN'D BY THIS INFLICTION	199	2	DON JUAN	2	80	1
THEIR WORK ON THEM BY TURNS AND THINN'D THEM TO	210	2	DON JUAN	2	102	2
THINNED						
WHICH THINNED AT EVERY STEP THEIR RANKS OF MEN	163	3	DON JUAN	8	103	4
THINNER						
THINNER SHE MIGHT HAVE BEEN AND YET SCARCE LOSE	27	3	DON JUAN	6	42	6
THROUGH CROWDS AND CARRIAGES BUT WAXING THINNER	282	3	DON JUAN	11	29	2
THIRD						
THE SECOND DRUNK THE THIRD SO QUAINT AND MOUTHEY	139	2	DON JUAN	1	205	4
IN MY HOT YOUTH--WHEN GEORGE THE THIRD WAS KING	143	2	DON JUAN	1	212	8
IN THE THIRD FORM OR EVEN IN THE FOURTH	158	2	DON JUAN	2	2	2
FOR ON THE THIRD DAY THERE CAME ON A CALM	192	2	DON JUAN	2	68	2
OUR MISTRESS QUOTH A THIRD OUR MISTRESS--POOH--	297	2	DON JUAN	3	43	7
OH--THE THIRD CANTO--AND THE PRETTY PAIR--	317	2	DON JUAN	3	81	6
THE THIRD A WARY COOL OLD SWORDER TOOK	370	2	DON JUAN	4	49	2
TO FIND THREE PERFECT PIPES OF THE THIRD SEX	391	2	DON JUAN	4	86	8
AND WITH HIS FELLOWS OF THE THIRD SEX GET	391	2	DON JUAN	4	86	V5
MY THIRD-- --YOUR THIRD QUOTH JUAN TURNING ROUND	421	2	DON JUAN	5	20	1

```
                                                        PAGE  VOL        CANTO  STANZA  LN
THIRD   (CONTINUED)
    MY THIRD-- --YOUR THIRD QUOTH JUAN TURNING ROUND  .  .  .  .  421  2 DON JUAN   5    20    1
    WELL THEN YOUR THIRD SAID JUAN WHAT DID SHE  .  .  .  .  .  .  421  2 DON JUAN   5    20    6
    OF THE THIRD SEX STEPT UP AND PEERING OVER  .  .  .  .  .  .  424  2 DON JUAN   5    26    2
    HER THIRD TO ASK HIM WHERE HE HAD BEEN BRED  .  .  .  .  .  491  2 DON JUAN   5   139    3
    WE LEFT OUR HERO AND THIRD HEROINE IN  .  .  .  .  .  .  .  10  3 DON JUAN   6     7    1
    BUT A THIRD MOTIVE WAS AS PROBABLY  .  .  .  .  .  .  .  .  .  78  3 DON JUAN   7    24    5
    THE THIRD IN COLUMNS TWO ATTACKED BY WATER  .  .  .  .  .  91  3 DON JUAN   7    50    8
    THE OTHER TWO ARE WOMEN AND THE THIRD  .  .  .  .  .  .  97  3 DON JUAN   7    60    2
    OF OFFICERS A THIRD FELL ON THE SPOT  .  .  .  .  .  .  .  119  3 DON JUAN   8    16    5
    HIS THIRD WAS SABRED AND THE FOURTH MOST CHERISHED  .  .  .  166  3 DON JUAN   8   110    3
    HER THIRD WAS FEMININE ENOUGH TO ANNUL  .  .  .  .  .  .  212  3 DON JUAN   9    60    5
    THE THIRD SORT TO BE NOTED IN OUR CHRONICLE  .  .  .  .  .  220  3 DON JUAN   9    76    5
    THE THIRD THE USUAL ORIGIN OF EVIL  .  .  .  .  .  .  .  271  3 DON JUAN  11     6    4
    WHERE'S WHITBREAD ROMILLY  WHERE'S GEORGE THE THIRD  .  .  .  307  3 DON JUAN  11    78    2
    WHETHER HE MARRIED WITH THE THIRD OR FOURTH  .  .  .  .  .  312  3 DON JUAN  11    89    1
    AND YET A THIRD OF LIFE IS PASS'D IN SLEEP  .  .  .  .  .  .  411  3 DON JUAN  14     3    8
    THE THIRD IS STILL MORE DIFFICULT TO STAND TO  .  .  .  .  465  3 DON JUAN  15    21    5
    A THIRD BECAUSE THERE CAN BE NO OBJECTIONS  .  .  .  .  .  471  3 DON JUAN  15    34    8
    AND ADDS A THIRD TO WHAT WAS LATE A PAIR  .  .  .  .  .  .  481  3 DON JUAN  15    59   V8
    PERHAPS I HAVE A THIRD TOO IN A NOOK  .  .  .  .  .  .  .  494  3 DON JUAN  15    87    5
    THE THIRD TIME AFTER A STILL LONGER PAUSE  .  .  .  .  .  511  3 DON JUAN  16    24    1
    ON WHICH AT THE THIRD ASKING OF THE BANNS  .  .  .  .  .  542  3 DON JUAN  16    88    1
    BUT OTHERS WHO WERE LEFT WITH SCARCE A THIRD  .  .  .  .  543  3 DON JUAN  16    89    3
THIRDLY
    AND THIRDLY HE WHO BROUGHT YOU THE DISPATCH  .  .  .  .  .  215  3 DON JUAN   9    65    8
    THIRDLY COMMENCE NOT WITH THE END--OR SINNING  .  .  .  .  393  3 DON JUAN  13    73    7
    IF POSSIBLE AND THIRDLY NEVER FLINCH  .  .  .  .  .  .  .  404  3 DON JUAN  13    98    6
    THIRDLY THAT JUAN HAD MORE BRAIN THAN BEARD  .  .  .  .  .  439  3 DON JUAN  14    66    5
THIRD'S
    A THIRD'S ALL PALLID ASPECT OFFERED MORE  .  .  .  .  .  .  40  3 DON JUAN   6    67    3
THIRST
    OF ITS OWN THIRST TO SEE AGAIN THY SHORE  .  .  .  .  .  .  166  2 DON JUAN   2    18    4
    FAMINE DESPAIR COLD THIRST AND HEAT HAD DONE  .  .  .  .  210  2 DON JUAN   2   102    1
    SO GOODLY WAS HER THIRST FOR SCIENCE GROWN  .  .  .  .  .  476  2 DON JUAN   5   113   V7
    AND THEN HER THIRST OF BLOOD WAS QUENCHED IN TEARS  .  .  .  490  2 DON JUAN   5   136    8
    WAS ALSO IN THREE COLUMNS WITH A THIRST  .  .  .  .  .  .  91  3 DON JUAN   7    50    6
    TO HIM AND I SHOULD HOPE TO MOST THE THIRST  .  .  .  .  .  138  3 DON JUAN   8    52    5
    BUT WHILE THE THIRST FOR GORE AND PLUNDER RAGED  .  .  .  178  3 DON JUAN   8   132    5
    THESE QUENCHED A MOMENT HER AMBITION'S THIRST--  .  .  .  .  212  3 DON JUAN   9    59    5
    OR DUTCH WITH THIRST--WHAT HO A FLASK OF RHENISH  .  .  .  392  3 DON JUAN  13    72    8
    PROVOKE MY THIRST--WHAT--HO OF WINE A STOUP  .  .  .  .  .  392  3 DON JUAN  13    72   V8
THIRSTIEST
    BUT BEING THIRSTIEST AT THE MOMENT HE  .  .  .  .  .  .  197  2 DON JUAN   2    77    3
THIRSTY
    THEY WRUNG IT OUT AND THOUGH A THIRSTY DITCHER  .  .  .  .  201  2 DON JUAN   2    85    5
THIRTEEN
    WHEN SHE HAD TWENTY YEARS AND THIRTEEN HE  .  .  .  .  .  59  2 DON JUAN   1    69    4
THIRTEENTH
    BUT ON THE THIRTEENTH WHEN ALREADY PART  .  .  .  .  .  .  85  3 DON JUAN   7    39    1
THIRTY
    PREFER A SPOUSE WHOSE AGE IS SHORT OF THIRTY  .  .  .  .  56  2 DON JUAN   1    62    8
    OF TWENTY-FIVE OR THIRTY--(COME MAKE HASTE)  .  .  .  .  .  115  2 DON JUAN   1   172    2
    BUT NOW AT THIRTY YEARS MY HAIR IS GRAY--  .  .  .  .  .  143  2 DON JUAN   1   213    1
    NINE IN THE CUTTER THIRTY IN THE BOAT  .  .  .  .  .  .  .  185  2 DON JUAN   2    54    7
    THEY COUNTED THIRTY CROWDED IN A SPACE  .  .  .  .  .  .  189  2 DON JUAN   2    63    1
    A MAN OF THIRTY RATHER STOUT AND HALE  .  .  .  .  .  .  416  2 DON JUAN   5    10    6
    YOU SCARCELY CAN BE THIRTY HAVE YOU THREE  .  .  .  .  .  421  2 DON JUAN   5    20    2
    MASTER OF THIRTY KINGDOMS SO SUBLIME  .  .  .  .  .  .  .  51  3 DON JUAN   6    90    3
    MORE EVIL IN AN HOUR THAN THIRTY BRIGHT  .  .  .  .  .  .  86  3 DON JUAN   7    41    5
    AND THIRTY THOUSAND MUSQUETS FLUNG THEIR PILLS  .  .  .  .  117  3 DON JUAN   8    12    2
    FOR SIX AND THIRTY THOUSAND BRAVE DEFENDERS  .  .  .  .  .  175  3 DON JUAN   8   127   V7
    WAS A TA'EN CITY--THIRTY THOUSAND SLAIN  .  .  .  .  .  .  212  3 DON JUAN   9    59    2
    AT LEAST SOME TWENTY-NINE DO OUT OF THIRTY  .  .  .  .  .  232  3 DON JUAN  10    15    6
    SOME THIRTY YEARS BEFORE AT FAIR EIGHTEEN  .  .  .  .  .  236  3 DON JUAN  10    24   V6
    THEIR CHANCES--THEY'RE TOO NUMEROUS LIKE THE THIRTY  .  .  .  299  3 DON JUAN  11    61    7
    TILL THIRTY SHOULD PERCEIVE THERE'S A PLAIN WOMAN  .  .  .  359  3 DON JUAN  13     3    8
    THAT IS WITH THIRTY SERVANTS FOR PARADE  .  .  .  .  .  .  381  3 DON JUAN  13    49    4
    (WHOSE ARTICLES ARE LIKE THE THIRTY NINE  .  .  .  .  .  .  383  3 DON JUAN  13    53    2
    (TAKE HER AT THIRTY THAT IS) TO HAVE BEEN  .  .  .  .  .  .  421  3 DON JUAN  14    25    7
    THIS MAY BE FIXED AT SOMEWHERE BEFORE THIRTY--  .  .  .  .  433  3 DON JUAN  14    53    1
THIRTY-FIVE
    TOO OLD FOR YOUTH--TOO YOUNG AT THIRTY-FIVE  .  .  .  .  .  316  3 DON JUAN  12     2    1
THIRTY-THREE
    THE PARTY MIGHT CONSIST OF THIRTY-THREE  .  .  .  .  .  .  397  3 DON JUAN  13    83    3
THISBE
    'TWAS FAMOUS TOO FOR THISBE AND FOR PYRAMUS  .  .  .  .  .  445  2 DON JUAN   5    60    7
THISTLE
    A SORT OF ROSE ENTWINING WITH A THISTLE  .  .  .  .  .  .  407  3 DON JUAN  13   105   V6
THO'
    ('TIS POPE'S PHRASE) A GREAT LONGING THO' A RASH ONE  .  .  216  3 DON JUAN   9    68    6
THOMAS
    COMMIT ADULTERY WITH THOMAS MOORE  .  .  .  .  .  .  .  139  2 DON JUAN   1   205   V8
THOMSON
    SIXTEEN CALLED THOMSON AND NINETEEN NAMED SMITH  .  .  .  75  3 DON JUAN   7    18    8
    JACK THOMSON AND BILL THOMSON--ALL THE REST  .  .  .  .  76  3 DON JUAN   7    19    1
    JACK THOMSON AND BILL THOMSON--ALL THE REST  .  .  .  .  76  3 DON JUAN   7    19    1
THORN
    THE NIGHTINGLE THAT SINGS WITH THE DEEP THORN  .  .  .  .  49  3 DON JUAN   6    87    5
    A RIB'S A THORN IN A WED GALLANT'S SIDE  .  .  .  .  .  .  292  3 DON JUAN  11    46    6
```

THOROUGH
	PAGE	VOL	CANTO	STANZA	LN
A THOROUGH VARMINT AND A REAL SWELL	276	3	DON JUAN 11	17	6
IN ISLANDS IS IT SEEMS DOWNRIGHT AND THOROUGH	288	3	DON JUAN 11	42	6
YES I'LL BEGIN A THOROUGH REFORMATION	498	3	DON JUAN 15	94	4

THOROUGH-BRED
	PAGE	VOL	CANTO	STANZA	LN
THOUGH ON MORE THOROUGH-BRED OR FAIRER FINGERS	472	2	DON JUAN 5	106	2
AND ALL HER POINTS AS THOROUGH-BRED TO SHOW	330	3	DON JUAN 12	31	6

THOROUGHFARE
	PAGE	VOL	CANTO	STANZA	LN
TO HINT AT LEAST HERE IS NO THOROUGHFARE	72	3	DON JUAN 7	11	8

THOUGHT
	PAGE	VOL	CANTO	STANZA	LN
I WOULD NOT IMITATE THE PETTY THOUGHT	12	2	DON JUAN D	6	1
THAT IS TO SAY A THOUGHT BEYOND THE COMMON	63	2	DON JUAN 1	77	5
THUS JULIA SAID--AND THOUGHT SO TO BE SURE	64	2	DON JUAN 1	79	6
BUT HEAVEN FORBID THAT SUCH A THOUGHT SHOULD CROSS	67	2	DON JUAN 1	84	2
(THIS SHOULD BE ENTRE NOUS FOR JULIA THOUGHT	67	2	DON JUAN 1	84	7
HE THOUGHT ABOUT HIMSELF AND THE WHOLE EARTH	71	2	DON JUAN 1	92	1
AND THEN HE THOUGHT OF EARTHQUAKES AND OF WARS	71	2	DON JUAN 1	92	4
AND THEN HE THOUGHT OF DONNA JULIA'S EYES	71	2	DON JUAN 1	92	8
HE THOUGHT OF WOOD NYMPHS AND IMMORTAL BOWERS	72	2	DON JUAN 1	94	3
IN CASE HE THOUGHT HIS WIFE TOO GREAT A PRIZE	75	2	DON JUAN 1	101	8
SHE THOUGHT OF HER OWN STRENGTH AND JUAN'S YOUTH	78	2	DON JUAN 1	107	1
QUITE BY MISTAKE--SHE THOUGHT IT WAS HER OWN	80	2	DON JUAN 1	109	8
I CANNOT KNOW WHAT JUAN THOUGHT OF THIS	81	2	DON JUAN 1	112	1
YET STILL SHE MUST HAVE THOUGHT THERE WAS NO HARM	83	2	DON JUAN 1	115	4
HAD THOUGHT ONE MAN MIGHT BE DETERR'D BY TWO	98	2	DON JUAN 1	141	4
DARE YOU SUSPECT ME WHOM THE THOUGHT WOULD KILL	98	2	DON JUAN 1	142	7
'TIS ODD NOT ONE OF ALL THESE SEEKERS THOUGHT	100	2	DON JUAN 1	144	6
ALFONSO SAW HIS WIFE AND THOUGHT OF JOB'S	110	2	DON JUAN 1	162	6
AND LAID CONDITIONS HE THOUGHT VERY HARD ON	120	2	DON JUAN 1	180	3
I THOUGHT OF A PERUKE THE OTHER DAY)	143	2	DON JUAN 1	213	3
I THOUGHT OF DYEING IT THE OTHER DAY	143	2	DON JUAN 1	213	V3
AND JUAN WEPT AND MUCH HE SIGH'D AND THOUGHT	165	2	DON JUAN 2	17	1
THOUGHT IT WOULD BE BECOMING TO DIE DRUNK	174	2	DON JUAN 2	35	8
MORE THAN CAN BE BELIEVED OR EVEN THOUGHT	191	2	DON JUAN 2	66	3
AND WHEN HIS COMRADE'S THOUGHT EACH SUFFERER KNEW	194	2	DON JUAN 2	73	5
AND NEXT THEY THOUGHT UPON THE MASTER'S MATE	199	2	DON JUAN 2	81	1
MIGHT NOT HAVE THOUGHT THE SCANTY DRAUGHT SO SWEET	201	2	DON JUAN 2	85	6
WITH THE DEEP DEADLY THOUGHT THAT THEY MUST PART	203	2	DON JUAN 2	88	8
OUR SHIPWRECK'D SEAMEN THOUGHT IT A GOOD OMEN--	205	2	DON JUAN 2	93	1
OR THOUGHT THEY SAW AND SHAPED THEIR COURSE FOR SHORE	207	2	DON JUAN 2	97	6
THEY THOUGHT THAT IN SUCH PERILS MORE THAN CHANCE	208	2	DON JUAN 2	99	7
SOME THOUGHT IT WAS MOUNT AETNA SOME THE HIGHLANDS	209	2	DON JUAN 2	100	7
FOR ALL WAS DOUBT AND DIZZINESS HE THOUGHT	215	2	DON JUAN 2	112	2
THEY WILL DESTROY A FACE WHICH MORTAL THOUGHT	219	2	DON JUAN 2	119	7
AND THEREFORE WITH HER MAID SHE THOUGHT IT BEST	225	2	DON JUAN 2	131	1
HE SLUMBER'D YET SHE THOUGHT AT LEAST SHE SAID	228	2	DON JUAN 2	135	5
BUT THEN THE THOUGHT OF PARTING MADE HER QUAKE	247	2	DON JUAN 2	173	6
THOUGHT DAILY SERVICE WAS HER ONLY MISSION	252	2	DON JUAN 2	182	6
WAS BROKEN WORDS THEY THOUGHT A LANGUAGE THERE--	256	2	DON JUAN 2	189	4
TO SAY A WORD ABOUT THEM--IF SHE THOUGHT	258	2	DON JUAN 2	193	V8
SAD THOUGHT TO LOSE THE SPOUSE THAT WAS ADORNING	278	2	DON JUAN 3	7	7
A HORRID THOUGHT--FOR WHO WOULD BE A WIDOWER	278	2	DON JUAN 3	7	V7
YOU NEVER COULD DIVINE HIS REAL THOUGHT	296	2	DON JUAN 3	41	4
BUT THOUGHT HOW WORTHY ALTHOUGH NATURE'S WORK	315	2	DON JUAN 3	76	V7
FALLING LIKE DEW UPON A THOUGHT PRODUCES	327	2	DON JUAN 3	88	2
AS BOY I THOUGHT MYSELF A CLEVER FELLOW	345	2	DON JUAN 4	3	1
HAIDEE AND JUAN THOUGHT NOT OF THE DEAD	351	2	DON JUAN 4	13	1
THE PAST STILL WELCOME AS THE PRESENT THOUGHT	354	2	DON JUAN 4	20	8
WHICH FROZE TO MARBLE AS IT FELL SHE THOUGHT	362	2	DON JUAN 4	33	8
AND GAZING ON THE DEAD SHE THOUGHT HIS FACE	363	2	DON JUAN 4	35	1
SHORT SOLACE VAIN RELIEF--THOUGHT CAME TOO QUICK	380	2	DON JUAN 4	67	1
BY THOUGHT OF FROSTY CAUCASUS BUT FEW	396	2	DON JUAN 4	96	6
ITS FUMES ARE FRANKINCENSE TO HUMAN THOUGHT	402	2	DON JUAN 4	106	2
OF SILENCE WOULD NOT LONG BE BORNE BY THOUGHT	402	2	DON JUAN 4	106	V4
AND IT MIGHT BE FROM THOUGHT OR TOIL OR STUDY	416	2	DON JUAN 5	11	4
I THOUGHT IN FACT YOU COULD NOT BE A GREEK	418	2	DON JUAN 5	14	2
AY QUOTH HIS FRIEND I THOUGHT IT WOULD APPEAR	420	2	DON JUAN 5	19	3
SO AS I GAZED ON HIM I THOUGHT OR SAID--	430	2	DON JUAN 5	35	8
INTO DON JUAN'S HEAD A THOUGHT WHICH HE	434	2	DON JUAN 5	43	2
WHO LITTLE THOUGHT THAT HIS OWN CRACKED EXISTENCE	440	2	DON JUAN 5	51	3
HE CHOSE HIMSELF TO POINT OUT WHAT HE THOUGHT	450	2	DON JUAN 5	67	7
THE SUIT HE THOUGHT MOST SUITABLE TO EACH	451	2	DON JUAN 5	68	1
YOU NEVER THOUGHT ABOUT THOSE LITTLE CREATURES	462	2	DON JUAN 5	87	8
I KNOW NOT WHAT MIGHT BE THE LADY'S THOUGHT	473	2	DON JUAN 5	108	2
SHE THOUGHT HERS GAVE A DOUBLE RIGHT DIVINE	485	2	DON JUAN 5	129	7
HER FIRST THOUGHT WAS TO CUT OFF JUAN'S HEAD	491	2	DON JUAN 5	139	1
SHE THOUGHT TO STAB HERSELF BUT THEN SHE HAD	492	2	DON JUAN 5	140	1
SHE THOUGHT OF KILLING JUAN--BUT POOR LAD	492	2	DON JUAN 5	140	5
HER COMRADES ALSO THOUGHT THEMSELVES UNDONE	501	2	DON JUAN 5	156	3
SHE THOUGHT THAT HER LORD'S HEART (EVEN COULD SHE CLAIM IT)	10	3	DON JUAN 6	8	6
THE GIANT THOUGHT OF BEING A TITAN'S BRIDE	20	3	DON JUAN 6	28	4
SOME THOUGHT HER DRESS DID NOT SO MUCH BECOME HER	23	3	DON JUAN 6	35	3
SOME THOUGHT HER RATHER MASCULINE IN HEIGHT	23	3	DON JUAN 6	35	7
SHE NEVER THOUGHT ABOUT HERSELF AT ALL	33	3	DON JUAN 6	54	8
WITH SUCH A CLAMOUR--I HAD THOUGHT IT RIGHT	46	3	DON JUAN 6	81	3
PERHAPS PRECARIOUS HAD THEY BUT THOUGHT GOOD	53	3	DON JUAN 6	95	5
HE HOPED INDEED HE THOUGHT HE COULD BE SURE	58	3	DON JUAN 6	104	1
BABA THOUGHT SHE WOULD FAINT BUT THERE HE ERRED--	59	3	DON JUAN 6	106	2
I THINK ONE SHAKESPEAR PUTS THE SAME THOUGHT IN	77	3	DON JUAN 7	21	6

THOUGHT   (CONTINUED)

		PAGE	VOL	CANTO		STANZA	LN
THE WHOLE CAMP RUNG WITH JOY YOU WOULD HAVE THOUGHT	. .	90	3	DON JUAN	7	49	1
(START NOT KIND READER SINCE GREAT HOMER THOUGHT	. . .	126	3	DON JUAN	8	29	6
THE FIRST TIME THOUGHT QUITE TERRIBLE ENOUGH	. . .	134	3	DON JUAN	8	42	2
OR THOSE WHO THOUGHT IT BRAVE TO WAIT AS YET	. . . .	135	3	DON JUAN	8	45	8
AND NATURALLY THOUGHT THEY COULD HAVE PLUNDERED	. . .	149	3	DON JUAN	8	75	3
SUCH AS HE THOUGHT THE LEAST GIVEN UP TO PREY	. . .	162	3	DON JUAN	8	102	4
THOUGHT NOT UPON THE CHARMS OF FOUR YOUNG BRIDES	. . .	168	3	DON JUAN	8	114	2
OF SINGLE BLESSEDNESS AND THOUGHT IT GOOD	. . .	177	3	DON JUAN	8	131	4
AS NOW OCCUR I THOUGHT THAT I WOULD PEN YOU 'EM	. . .	180	3	DON JUAN	8	136	4
AND SWIMMING LONG IN THE ABYSS OF THOUGHT	. . .	191	3	DON JUAN	9	18	5
WITH THOUGHT--AND OF THOUGHT'S FOES BY FAR MOST RUDE	. . .	194	3	DON JUAN	9	24	3
FOR A NEW FLAME A THOUGHT TO CAST OF GLOOM ENOUGH	. . .	206	3	DON JUAN	9	48	5
THAN WHAT THEY THOUGHT FOR MIND CAN NEVER SINK	. . .	234	3	DON JUAN	10	20	4
IF I CAN STAVE OFF THOUGHT WHICH AS A WHELP	. . . .	238	3	DON JUAN	10	28	3
I THOUGHT YOU HAD MORE RELIGION MRS FRY	. . . . .	267	3	DON JUAN	10	85	8
HE SOMETIMES THOUGHT 'TWAS ONLY THEIR SALAM	. . . .	274	3	DON JUAN	11	12	4
PERHAPS THOUGHT HE IT IS THE COUNTRY'S WONT	. . . .	275	3	DON JUAN	11	15	1
THOUGHT (WHAT IN STATE AFFAIRS IS MOST ESSENTIAL)	. . .	285	3	DON JUAN	11	35	6
THOUGHT SUCH AN OPPORTUNITY AS THIS IS	. . . .	293	3	DON JUAN	11	49	5
WITH THE SAME THOUGHT THE TWO WORDS HAVE HELPED OUT	. . .	323	3	DON JUAN	12	15	4
WITH THE KIND WORLD'S AMEN--WHO WOULD HAVE THOUGHT IT	. . .	328	3	DON JUAN	12	26	8
BECAUSE SHE THOUGHT HIM A GOOD HEART AT BOTTOM	. . .	338	3	DON JUAN	12	49	2
I THOUGHT AT SETTING OFF ABOUT TWO DOZEN	. . . .	341	3	DON JUAN	12	55	5
BY THAT REAL EPIC UNTO ALL WHO HAVE THOUGHT	. . . .	363	3	DON JUAN	13	9	8
AND AS HE THOUGHT IN COUNTRY MUCH THE SAME--	. . .	367	3	DON JUAN	13	20	4
THESE WERE ADVANTAGES AND THEN HE THOUGHT--	. . . .	368	3	DON JUAN	13	21	1
OF THOUGHT WE COULD BUT SNATCH A CERTAINTY	. . . .	410	3	DON JUAN	14	1	2
WHICH EVEN THOSE WHO OBEY WOULD FAIN BE THOUGHT	. . .	421	3	DON JUAN	14	26	2
THE BOORS CRIED DANG IT WHO'D HAVE THOUGHT IT--SIRES	. .	425	3	DON JUAN	14	34	4
HE THOUGHT AT HEART LIKE COURTLY CHESTERFIELD	. . .	425	3	DON JUAN	14	35	5
CONSOLING US WITH--WOULD YOU HAD THOUGHT TWICE	. . .	430	3	DON JUAN	14	47	7
SUCH MEASURES AS SHE THOUGHT MIGHT BEST IMPEDE	. . .	437	3	DON JUAN	14	61	2
SHE THOUGHT WITH SOME SIMPLICITY INDEED	. . . . .	437	3	DON JUAN	14	61	4
WHICH REALLY KNEW OR THOUGHT IT KNEW NO GUILE	. . .	438	3	DON JUAN	14	65	2
SHE LOVED HER LORD OR THOUGHT SO BUT THAT LOVE	. . .	447	3	DON JUAN	14	86	1
IN HIM BECAUSE SHE THOUGHT HE WAS IN DANGER--	. . .	449	3	DON JUAN	14	91	7
SHE WAS OR THOUGHT SHE WAS HIS FRIEND--AND THIS	. . .	450	3	DON JUAN	14	92	1
AS THOUGH THE LURKING THOUGHT HAD FOLLOW'D FREE	. . .	456	3	DON JUAN	15	1	4
SHE THOUGHT UPON THE SUBJECT TWICE OR THRICE	. . .	469	3	DON JUAN	15	29	5
THOUGHT THAT IT MIGHT TURN OUT SO--NOW I KNOW IT	. . .	482	3	DON JUAN	15	60	7
WHICH SEEMS TO HINT YOU ARE NOT WORTH A THOUGHT	. . .	490	3	DON JUAN	15	77	4
THOUGHT HER PREDICTIONS WENT NOT MUCH AMISS	. . . .	492	3	DON JUAN	15	81	3
NOR THOUGHT HE HAD PRIDE ENOUGH--FOR SHE WAS PROUD	. . .	493	3	DON JUAN	15	83	V6
HE THOUGHT AURORA RABY'S EYES MORE BRIGHT	. . .	506	3	DON JUAN	16	12	3
WHEN SUDDENLY HE HEARD OR THOUGHT SO NIGH	. . .	509	3	DON JUAN	16	20	5
BUT THOUGHT LIKE MOST MEN THERE WAS NOTHING IN'T	. . .	510	3	DON JUAN	16	22	3
THE MORE HE THOUGHT THE MORE HIS MIND WAS POSED	. . .	512	3	DON JUAN	16	28	5
AND FROM ITS CONTEXT THOUGHT SHE COULD DIVINE	. . .	516	3	DON JUAN	16	37	3
THE KING HIMSELF HAD CHEAPENED IT BUT THOUGHT	. . .	528	3	DON JUAN	16	56	5
AND THOUGHT I SAY NO MORE--I'VE SAID TOO MUCH	. . .	538	3	DON JUAN	16	77	2

THOUGHTLESSLY

BUT FIGHTING THOUGHTLESSLY ENOUGH TO WIN .	. . . .	121	3	DON JUAN	8	19	7

THOUGHT'S

WITH THOUGHT--AND OF THOUGHT'S FOES BY FAR MOST RUDE	. . .	194	3	DON JUAN	9	24	3

THOUGHTS

STATES TO BE CURB'D AND THOUGHTS TO BE CONFINED	. . .	18	2	DON JUAN	0	14	4
HER THOUGHTS WERE THEOREMS HER WORDS A PROBLEM	. . .	28	2	DON JUAN	1	13	7
AS IF HER HEART HAD DEEPER THOUGHTS IN STORE	. . .	61	2	DON JUAN	1	72	3
SUCH THOUGHTS AND BE THE BETTER WHEN THEY'RE OVER	. . .	64	2	DON JUAN	1	78	6
IN THOUGHTS LIKE THESE TRUE WISDOM MAY DISCERN	. . .	71	2	DON JUAN	1	93	1
AND TO CONTEND WITH THOUGHTS SHE COULD NOT SMOTHER	. . .	80	2	DON JUAN	1	110	3
HIS THOUGHTS HOW WELL APPLIED THE NAME OF GOD	. . .	154	2	DON JUAN	1	V 5	V2
OF FREE THOUGHTS IN HIS TRAVELS FOR VARIETY	. . .	318	2	DON JUAN	3	83	3
THIS IS A LIBERAL AGE AND THOUGHTS ARE FREE .	. . .	347	2	DON JUAN	4	7	6
NEW THOUGHTS OF LIFE FOR IT SEEM'D FULL OF SOUL	. . .	377	2	DON JUAN	4	60	7
RELIEVED HER THOUGHTS DULL SILENCE AND QUICK CHAT	. . .	378	2	DON JUAN	4	63	6
BACK TO OLD THOUGHTS WAX'D FULL OF FEARFUL MEANING	. . .	379	2	DON JUAN	4	64	8
HER THOUGHTS FROM SORROW THROUGH HER HEART RE-SENT	. . .	379	2	DON JUAN	4	65	6
METHINKS AT MEALS SOME ODD THOUGHTS MIGHT INTRUDE	. . .	426	2	DON JUAN	5	30	3
HER THOUGHTS AT LEAST TILL NOW APPEAR TO HAVE BEEN	. . .	33	3	DON JUAN	6	54	4
THE DAMSELS WHO HAD THOUGHTS OF SOME GREAT HARM	. . .	45	3	DON JUAN	6	79	1
BECAUSE THEIR THOUGHTS HAD NEVER BEEN THE PREY .	. . .	145	3	DON JUAN	8	66	3
SHE FELL WITH BUONAPARTE--WHAT STRANGE THOUGHTS	. . .	198	3	DON JUAN	9	32	7
OF HUMAN THOUGHTS WHICH JOSTLE IN THEIR FLIGHT .	. . .	215	3	DON JUAN	9	65	4
BUT WOULD NOT CHANGE MY FREE THOUGHTS FOR A THRONE	. . .	312	3	DON JUAN	11	90	8
SUCH THOUGHTS ARE QUITE BELOW THE STRAIN THEY HAVE CHOSEN	. .	341	3	DON JUAN	12	55	3
OF ANY WORSHIP WAKE SOME THOUGHTS DIVINE .	. . .	387	3	DON JUAN	13	61	8
OF YOUR OWN THOUGHTS IN ALL THEIR SELF CONFESSION	. . .	413	3	DON JUAN	14	6	4
FEW MEN DARE SHOW THEIR THOUGHTS OF WORST OR BEST	. . .	457	3	DON JUAN	15	3	5
SO FAR RELAX'D HER THOUGHTS FROM THEIR SWEET PRISON	. . .	491	3	DON JUAN	15	80	7
THOUGHTS QUITE AS YELLOW BUT LESS CLEAR THAN AMBER	. . .	505	3	DON JUAN	16	11	4
GREAT THOUGHTS WE CATCH FROM THENCE (BESIDES A COLD	. . .	506	3	DON JUAN	16	14	4
THOUGHTS BOUNDLESS DEEP BUT SILENT TOO AS SPACE	. . .	524	3	DON JUAN	16	48	8
OF THOSE SWEET BITTER THOUGHTS WHICH BANISH SLEEP	. . .	555	3	DON JUAN	16	110	7

THOUSAND

THOUGH SEVERAL THOUSAND PEOPLE CHOSE TO TRY .	. . . .	33	2	DON JUAN	1	23	3
A THOUSAND PITIES ALSO WITH RESPECT	. . . .	38	2	DON JUAN	1	33	6
AND HAVE TEN THOUSAND DELICATE INVENTIONS	. . . .	221	2	DON JUAN	2	123	4

	PAGE	VOL	CANTO	STANZA	LN
THOUSAND (CONTINUED)					
DREAM'D OF A THOUSAND WRECKS O'ER WHICH SHE STUMBLED	229	2	DON JUAN 2	138	3
A THOUSAND SCIMITARS AWAIT THE WORD	364	2	DON JUAN 4	37	7
A THOUSAND SHARPER SABRES WAIT THE WORD	364	2	DON JUAN 4	37	V7
A HUNDRED THOUSAND MEN MIGHT FIGHT AGAIN	386	2	DON JUAN 4	77	6
A THOUSAND WARRIORS BY HIS WORD WERE KEPT	430	2	DON JUAN 5	36	4
WHILE NATURE TORTURED TWENTY THOUSAND WAYS	440	2	DON JUAN 5	52	6
CUT OFF A THOUSAND HEADS BEFORE-- --NOW PRAY	453	2	DON JUAN 5	72	1
TO STAIN HIS PEDIGREE A THOUSAND SWORDS	471	2	DON JUAN 5	104	5
A THOUSAND TIMES OF HIM HAD MADE AN END	471	2	DON JUAN 5	104	6
THEIR DELICATE LIMBS A THOUSAND BOSOMS THERE	19	3	DON JUAN 6	26	7
A THOUSAND AND A THOUSAND COLOURS THEY	66	3	DON JUAN 7	1	7
A THOUSAND AND A THOUSAND COLOURS THEY	66	3	DON JUAN 7	1	7
A THOUSAND PERILS IN THIS DUBIOUS SHAPE	103	3	DON JUAN 7	72	4
AND THIRTY THOUSAND MUSQUETS FLUNG THEIR PILLS	117	3	DON JUAN 8	12	2
FOR FIFTY THOUSAND HEROES NAME BY NAME	120	3	DON JUAN 8	17	4
WAS SPARED--THREE THOUSAND MOSLEMS PERISHED HERE	152	3	DON JUAN 8	81	7
AS OAKS BLOWN DOWN WITH ALL THEIR THOUSAND WINTERS	155	3	DON JUAN 8	88	8
YOU'LL FIND TEN THOUSAND HANDSOME COXCOMBS BLOODY	167	3	DON JUAN 8	112	8
WHERE THOUSAND LOVES AND TIES AND DUTIES GROW	174	3	DON JUAN 8	124	6
OF FORTY THOUSAND WHO HAD MANNED THE WALL	175	3	DON JUAN 8	127	7
FOR SIX AND THIRTY THOUSAND BRAVE DEFENDERS	175	3	DON JUAN 8	127	V7
YE TWICE TEN HUNDRED THOUSAND DAILY SCRIBES	200	3	DON JUAN 9	35	2
WAS A TA'EN CITY--THIRTY THOUSAND SLAIN	212	3	DON JUAN 9	59	2
OF SEVERAL RIBBONS AND SOME THOUSAND PEASANTS	222	3	DON JUAN 9	79	8
INTO SOME SIXTY THOUSAND NEW KNIGHTS' FEES	242	3	DON JUAN 10	35	8
ELEVEN THOUSAND MAIDENHEADS OF BONE	255	3	DON JUAN 10	62	7
HE BREATHED A THOUSAND CRESSYS AS HE SAW	261	3	DON JUAN 10	74	2
AND ABOUT TWICE TWO THOUSAND PEOPLE BRED	290	3	DON JUAN 11	45	3
HE SAW TEN THOUSAND LIVING AUTHORS PASS	295	3	DON JUAN 11	54	5
WHICH OPENS TO THE THOUSAND HAPPY FEW	302	3	DON JUAN 11	67	7
THEIR VIGOUR IN A THOUSAND ARMS IS DISSIPATED	306	3	DON JUAN 11	75	3
WHERE ARE TEN THOUSAND LOVELY INNOCENTS	307	3	DON JUAN 11	77	V7
HAS SAVED THE FAME OF THOUSAND SPLENDID SINNERS	346	3	DON JUAN 12	66	3
WITHIN THESE LATEST THOUSAND YEARS OR LATER	361	3	DON JUAN 13	7	4
THE TWICE TWO THOUSAND FOR WHOM EARTH WAS MADE	381	3	DON JUAN 13	49	2
THE GOTHIC BABEL OF A THOUSAND YEARS	381	3	DON JUAN 13	50	4
SHORN OF ITS GLASS OF THOUSAND COLOURINGS	387	3	DON JUAN 13	62	2
ITS LITTLE TORRENT IN A THOUSAND BUBBLES	389	3	DON JUAN 13	65	7
OPINIONS WEAR OUT IN SOME THOUSAND YEARS	496	3	DON JUAN 15	90	7
THAT IN THE COURSE OF SOME SIX THOUSAND YEARS	504	3	DON JUAN 16	7	2
THOUSANDS					
AND SHIPS BY THOUSANDS LAY BELOW	322	2	DON JUAN 3	L 4	3
THAT WHICH MAKES THOUSANDS PERHAPS MILLIONS THINK	327	2	DON JUAN 3	88	3
AND MEASURES ROUND OF TOISES THOUSANDS THREE	71	3	DON JUAN 7	9	8
THAN THOUSANDS OF THIS NEW AND POLISHED NATION	73	3	DON JUAN 7	14	7
THOUSANDS OF WHOM WERE DRAWING THEIR LAST BREATH	111	3	DON JUAN 7	87	4
AMIDST SOME GROANING THOUSANDS DYING NEAR--	117	3	DON JUAN 8	11	3
YOUR RANK AND FILE BY THOUSANDS WHILE THE REST	118	3	DON JUAN 8	13	7
OF DEAD AND DYING THOUSANDS--SOMETIMES GAINING	121	3	DON JUAN 8	20	2
THOUSANDS OF SLAUGHTERED MEN A YET WARM GROUP	157	3	DON JUAN 8	91	2
THE WHOLE GAZETTE OF THOUSANDS WHOM HE SLEW	212	3	DON JUAN 9	60	4
THOUSANDS BLAZE LOVE HOPE DIE--HOW HAPPY THEY--	229	3	DON JUAN 10	8	8
THOUGH MANY THOUSANDS BOTH OF PITH AND PLUCK TOO	348	3	DON JUAN 12	70	V5
SET TO SOME THOUSANDS ('TIS THE USUAL BURTHEN	529	3	DON JUAN 16	59	2
THRALL					
AND ASK THEM HOW THEY LIKE TO BE IN THRALL	446	3	DON JUAN 14	83	4
THRASHED					
THE TURKISH BATTERIES THRASHED THEM LIKE A FLAIL	134	3	DON JUAN 8	43	5
THE SCANTY BUT RIGHT-WELL THRASHED EARS OF TRUTH	403	3	DON JUAN 13	96	2
THREAD					
THEIR LABYRINTH OF FABLES TO THREAD THROUGH	137	2	DON JUAN 1	202	7
THREADING					
AS THEY WERE THREADING ON THEIR WAY THERE CAME	434	2	DON JUAN 5	43	1
THREAD'S					
MUST BE DECLINED WHILE LIFE'S THIN THREAD'S SPUN OUT	376	3	DON JUAN 13	40	7
THREAT					
MADE FIERCE REMONSTRANCES AND THEN A THREAT	471	2	DON JUAN 5	103	2
THREATEN'D					
WHO THREATEN'D DEATH--SO JUAN KNOCK'D HIM DOWN	122	2	DON JUAN 1	183	8
AGAIN THE WEATHER THREATEN'D--AGAIN BLEW	178	2	DON JUAN 2	42	1
THREATENED					
THIS HOURLY DREAD OF ALL WHOSE THREATENED STING	188	3	DON JUAN 9	11	6
QUIT AND THOUGH DEATH HAD THREATENED AN EJECTION	245	3	DON JUAN 10	43	2
WHICH THREATENED THE WHOLE COUNTRY WITH PERDITION	536	3	DON JUAN 16	74	4
THREATENING					
GREW AND EACH WAVE ROSE ROUGHLY THREATENING HER	361	2	DON JUAN 4	31	4
THREATENS					
WHICH THREATENS INUNDATIONS DEEP AND YELLOW	228	3	DON JUAN 10	7	4
THREATS					
OF BEAUTY FLATTERY THREATS A SHILLING--NO	439	2	DON JUAN 5	49	3
THREE					
ON WHICH THREE SINGLE HOURS OF MOONSHINE SMILE--	82	2	DON JUAN 1	113	7
SUSPECTS WITH ONE DO YOU REPROACH WITH THREE	117	2	DON JUAN 1	175	8
NEW CHARACTERS THE EPISODES ARE THREE	135	2	DON JUAN 1	200	5
TO PLAYS IN FIVE AND OPERAS IN THREE ACTS	138	2	DON JUAN 1	203	4
DAILY OR MONTHLY OR THREE MONTHLY I	142	2	DON JUAN 1	211	4
OF GOOD ADVICE--AND TWO OR THREE OF CREDIT	161	2	DON JUAN 2	9	8
INFANTS OF THREE YEARS OLD WERE TAUGHT THAT DAY	162	2	DON JUAN 2	10	5

828

```
                                                        PAGE VOL    CANTO STANZA LN
THREE   (CONTINUED)
      HIS SUITE CONSISTED OF THREE SERVANTS AND    . . . . . . 169  2 DON JUAN  2     25    1
      AND KEEP THE SHIP AFLOAT THOUGH THREE FEET YET . . . . . 172  2 DON JUAN  2     30    3
      IT COSTS THREE FRANCS FOR EVERY MASS THAT'S SAID . . . . 185  2 DON JUAN  2     55    8
      THE SAILORS ATE HIM ALL SAVE THREE OR FOUR   . . . . . . 198  2 DON JUAN  2     78    1
      AND AT THE BOTTOM OF THE BOAT THREE WERE . . . . . . . . 208  2 DON JUAN  2     98    6
      AND THREE DEAD WHOM THEIR STRENGTH COULD NOT AVAIL . . . 209  2 DON JUAN  2    101    5
      SAVE ONE A CORPSE FROM OUT THE FAMISH'D THREE  . . . . . 213  2 DON JUAN  2    109    6
      THREE OR FOUR THINGS FOR WHICH THE LORD HE PRAISED  . . .239  2 DON JUAN  2    157    5
      BUT THOUGH RAGUSAN VESSELS BOUND FOR SCIO . . . . . . . 248  2 DON JUAN  2    174    8
      YET TO THESE FOUR IN THREE THINGS THE SAME LUCK HOLDS . .266  2 DON JUAN  2    206    7
      TO HIS MEMORY AND TWO OR THREE YOUNG MISSES . . . . . . 287  2 DON JUAN  3     23    6
      THEIR SOFA OCCUPIED THREE PARTS COMPLETE . . . . . . . . 309  2 DON JUAN  3     67    3
      OF THE THREE HUNDRED GRANT BUT THREE . . . . . . . . . . 323  2 DON JUAN  3   L  7    5
      OF THE THREE HUNDRED GRANT BUT THREE . . . . . . . . . . 323  2 DON JUAN  3   L  7    5
      FOR IF MY PURE LIBATIONS EXCEED THREE . . . . . . . . . .372  2 DON JUAN  4     52    4
      TO FIND THREE PERFECT PIPES OF THE THIRD SEX . . . . . . 391  2 DON JUAN  4     86    8
      YOU SCARCELY CAN BE THIRTY HAVE YOU THREE . . . . . . . 421  2 DON JUAN  5     20    2
      OR THREE OR TWO OR ONE SEND VERY FAR . . . . . . . . . . 432  2 DON JUAN  5     39    3
      TWO OR THREE SEEM SO LITTLE ONE SEEMS NOTHING . . . . . 443  2 DON JUAN  5     57    1
      OF SENTIMENTAL FRIENDSHIP THERE WERE THREE . . . . . . . 26  3 DON JUAN  6     40    2
      THE WHOLE ODA FROM THEIR BEDS AT HALF-PAST THREE  . . . .46  3 DON JUAN  6     80    4
      ONE TWO OR THREE--OR FOUR OR LESS OR MORE . . . . . . . .51  3 DON JUAN  6     91   V5
      AND MEASURES ROUND OF TOISES THOUSANDS THREE  . . . . . .71  3 DON JUAN  7      9    8
      THREE OF THE SMITHS WERE PETERS BUT THE BEST  . . . . . .76  3 DON JUAN  7     19    5
      THREE LINES OF THE DISPATCH IN TAKING SCHMACKSMITH . . . 76  3 DON JUAN  7     20    6
      THREE FIRESHIPS LOST THEIR AMIABLE EXISTENCE  . . . . . .80  3 DON JUAN  7     28    3
      FOR OUT OF THESE THREE PREUX CHEVALIERS HOW . . . . . . 82  3 DON JUAN  7     33    2
      FOR THERE WERE BUT THREE SHIRTS BETWEEN THE TWO . . . . 87  3 DON JUAN  7     43    5
      DETACHMENT OF THREE COLUMNS TOOK ITS STATION  . . . . . .91  3 DON JUAN  7     50    3
      WAS ALSO IN THREE COLUMNS WITH A THIRST . . . . . . . . 91  3 DON JUAN  7     50    6
      TO BRING THE OTHER THREE HERE WAS ABSURD . . . . . . . . 97  3 DON JUAN  7     60    6
      THREE HUNDRED CANNON THREW UP THEIR EMETIC . . . . . . . 117  3 DON JUAN  8     12    1
      WHERE THREE PARTS OF HIS COLUMN YET REMAIN . . . . . . . 148  3 DON JUAN  8     72    8
      WAS SPARED--THREE THOUSAND MOSLEMS PERISHED HERE  . . . .152  3 DON JUAN  8     81    7
      AS IF HE HAD THREE LIVES AS WELL AS TAILS . . . . . . . 172  3 DON JUAN  8    121    8
      AT LEAST THREE PARTS OF THIS GREAT WHOLE) SHE TORE  . . .211  3 DON JUAN  9     58    3
      R PULV COM THREE GRAINS IPECACUANHAE . . . . . . . . . . 244  3 DON JUAN 10     41    5
      BUT THOUGH THREE BISHOPS TOLD HER THE TRANSGRESSION . . .252  3 DON JUAN 10     56    3
      THAT I DEVOUTLY WISHED THE THREE WERE FOUR . . . . . . . 271  3 DON JUAN 11      6    7
      AND WORDSWORTH HAS SUPPORTERS TWO OR THREE . . . . . . . 298  3 DON JUAN 11     59    6
      HIMSELF FOR FIVE FOUR THREE OR TWO YEAR'S SPACE . . . . 329  3 DON JUAN 12     29    6
      SOME ARE SOON BAGGED BUT SOME REJECT THREE DOZEN  . . . .332  3 DON JUAN 12     34    1
      SINCE THEN SHE HAD SPARKLED THROUGH THREE GLOWING WINTERS 434  3 DON JUAN 14     56    1
      SHIP OFF THE HOLY THREE TO SENEGAL . . . . . . . . . . . 446  3 DON JUAN 14     83    2
      THE ANTIQUE PERSIANS TAUGHT THREE USEFUL THINGS . . . . 501  3 DON JUAN 16      1    1
      BY ONE THREE TALENTS FOR THERE WERE NO LESS-- . . . . . 517  3 DON JUAN 16     39    6
      THE THREE STRINGS OF OUR HAPPY CONSTITUTION . . . . . . 536  3 DON JUAN 16     74   V8
      HAD FALLEN LAST MARKET COST HIS HOST THREE VOTES  . . . .543  3 DON JUAN 16     89    8
      HAVE PLAINLY MADE IT OUT THAT FOUR ARE THREE  . . . . . .548  3 DON JUAN 16     99    4
      FOR ONE WITHOUT--HAS TWO OR THREE WITHIN . . . . . . . . 567  3 DON JUAN 17     11    8
THREESCORE
      IS'T WORTHY OF YOUR YEARS--YOU HAVE THREESCORE . . . . . 101  2 DON JUAN  1    146    3
      THE SCENES LIKE CATHERINE'S BOUDOIR AT THREE-SCORE . . . 146  3 DON JUAN  8     68    7
      LIVE ANIMALS AN OLD MAID OF THREESCORE . . . . . . . . . 249  3 DON JUAN 10     50    6
      TEACH THEM THE DECENCIES OF GOOD THREESCORE  . . . . . . 267  3 DON JUAN 10     86    1
      TO HERD WITH BOYS OR HOARD WITH GOOD THREESCORE-- . . . .316  3 DON JUAN 12      2    2
THREE-THOUSANDTH
      WITH THE THREE-THOUSANDTH CURTSEY THERE THE WALTZ . . . .302  3 DON JUAN 11     68    2
THREW
      FOR LITTLE JUAN O'ER ME THREW DOWN STAIRS . . . . . . . 34  2 DON JUAN  1     24    7
      THINKING UNUTTERABLE THINGS HE THREW . . . . . . . . . . 70  2 DON JUAN  1     90    2
      THREW THE SHIP RIGHT INTO THE TROUGH OF THE SEA . . . . 170  2 DON JUAN  2     27    2
      THREW IN BY GOOD LUCK OVER THE SHIP'S RAIL  . . . . . . .181  2 DON JUAN  2     48    6
      OFF THREW HIM IN THEN AFTER HIM HE LEAP'D  . . . . . . . 187  2 DON JUAN  2     58    8
      HIS NEAREST MESSMATE TOLD HIS SIRE WHO THREW . . . . . . 202  2 DON JUAN  2     87    5
      WHEN HAIDEE THREW HERSELF HER BOY BEFORE . . . . . . . . 366  2 DON JUAN  4     42    3
      THE CAPTIVES BACK TO THEIR SAD BERTHS EACH THREW  . . . .393  2 DON JUAN  4     90    4
      SOMETHING IMPERIAL OR IMPERIOUS THREW  . . . . . . . . . 474  2 DON JUAN  5    110    1
      SHE ROSE AND PAUSING ONE CHASTE MOMENT THREW  . . . . . .483  2 DON JUAN  5    125    7
      RATHER TOO HIGH AND DISTANT THAT SHE THREW . . . . . . . 44  3 DON JUAN  6     76    3
      IS NEITHER MAN NOR WOMAN THE CHIEF THREW ON . . . . . . 97  3 DON JUAN  7     60    3
      THREE HUNDRED CANNON THREW UP THEIR EMETIC . . . . . . . 117  3 DON JUAN  8     12    1
      THREW THEM ALL DOWN INTO THE DITCH AGAIN . . . . . . . . 147  3 DON JUAN  8     71    8
      SHE SMILED AT MAD SUWARROW'S RHYMES WHO THREW . . . . . 212  3 DON JUAN  9     60    2
      ACCORDING AS THE SKIES THEIR SHADOWS THREW . . . . . . . 385  3 DON JUAN 13     58    8
      THEN AS THE NIGHT WAS CLEAR THOUGH COLD HE THREW  . . . .508  3 DON JUAN 16     17    1
THRICE
      THRICE FORTUNATE WHO OF THAT FRAGILE MOULD . . . . . . . 350  2 DON JUAN  4     11    2
      ONE PERSON THRICE IN HOLY WEDLOCK BOUND . . . . . . . . 421  2 DON JUAN  5     20    5
      THRICE HAPPY HE WHOSE NAME HAS BEEN WELL SPELT  . . . . .120  3 DON JUAN  8     18    6
      THRICE HAPPY HE WHO AFTER A SURVEY  . . . . . . . . . . .303  3 DON JUAN 11     69    1
      THRICE HAPPY THEY WHO HAVE AN OCCUPATION . . . . . . . . 443  3 DON JUAN 14     77    8
      SHE THOUGHT UPON THE SUBJECT TWICE OR THRICE  . . . . . .469  3 DON JUAN 15     29    5
      ONCE TWICE THRICE PASSED REPASSED--THE THING OF AIR . . 510  3 DON JUAN 16     23    1
THRILL
      NATURE WITH HIM TO THRILL BENEATH HIS TOUCH . . . . . . 247  2 DON JUAN  2    173    3
THRILLING
      A LITTLE PRESSURE THRILLING AND SO BLAND . . . . . . . . 60  2 DON JUAN  1     71    4

                                   829
```

THRILLING   (CONTINUED)
    THE GENTLE PRESSURE AND THE THRILLING TOUCH . . . . .   351 2 DON JUAN 4   14   1
    THE LADY'S VOICE CEASED AND THE THRILLING WIRES   . . .   521 3 DON JUAN 16   41   1
THRIVES
    AWARE THIS KIND OF BAGGAGE NEVER THRIVES . . . . . .   102 3 DON JUAN 7   70   7
THRO'
    THRO' SUCH A SCENE OF CHANGE AND DREAD AND SLAUGHTER . . .   252 3 DON JUAN 10   56   2
THROAT
    THAT EVER SCUTTLED SHIP OR CUT A THROAT . . . . . .   296 2 DON JUAN 3   41   2
    YOU KNOW THE REST THE WORDS STUCK IN HER THROAT   . . .   62 3 DON JUAN 6   113   4
    THE LAST EXPIRED IN CUT THROAT CASTLEREAGH . . . . .   254 3 DON JUAN 10   59   V4
    HIS BREATH--HE FROM HIS SWELLING THROAT UNTIED . . . .   276 3 DON JUAN 11   16   7
THROATS
    THEIR THROATS WERE OVENS THEIR SWOLN TONGUES WERE BLACK . .   202 2 DON JUAN 2   86   3
THROB
    MY EYEBALLS BURN AND THROB BUT HAVE NO TEARS   . . . .   130 2 DON JUAN 1   192   8
    AND WATCH'D WITH EAGERNESS EACH THROB THAT DREW   . . .   216 2 DON JUAN 2   114   7
    HOW MUCH IT COSTS US YET EACH RISING THROB   . . . . .   264 2 DON JUAN 2   203   2
THROBB'D
    THROBB'D IN ACCURSED DREAMS WHICH SOMETIMES SPREAD   . . .   227 2 DON JUAN 2   134   6
THROBBED
    CAME OVER JUAN'S EAR WHICH THROBBED ALAS . . . . . .   556 3 DON JUAN 16   114   5
THROBBING
    AND TINGLING VEIN SEEM'D THROBBING BACK TO LIFE   . . .   214 2 DON JUAN 2   111   7
    AND BOWED HER THROBBING HEAD O'ER TREMBLING KNEES . . .   59 3 DON JUAN 6   107   8
THROBS
    PROLOGUE IS ALWAYS CERTAIN THROES AND THROBS   . . . .   110 2 DON JUAN 1   162   4
THROES
    PROLOGUE IS ALWAYS CERTAIN THROES AND THROBS   . . . .   110 2 DON JUAN 1   162   4
    O'ER THE LAOCOON'S ALL ETERNAL THROES . . . . . .   377 2 DON JUAN 4   61   5
THRONE
    WHENCE MELODY DESCENDS AS FROM A THRONE   . . . . .   236 2 DON JUAN 2   151   8
    WHOSE ACCENTS ARE THE STEPS OF MUSIC'S THRONE   . . . .   237 2 DON JUAN 2   151   V8
    THE VELVET CUSHIONS--(FOR A THRONE MORE MEET)--   . . .   309 2 DON JUAN 3   67   5
    BUT THESE ARE MY ADDRESSES FROM THE THRONE   . . . . .   331 2 DON JUAN 3   96   5
    HEADS BOW KNEES BEND EYES WATCH AROUND A THRONE   . . .   484 2 DON JUAN 5   127   7
    OF YEARS TO FILL A BOWSTRING OR THE THRONE   . . . . .   499 2 DON JUAN 5   153   2
    A THRONE THE WORLD THE UNIVERSE TO BE . . . . . .   7 3 DON JUAN 6   3   3
    OF LOVE WHEN SEATED ON HIS LOVELIEST THRONE . . . . .   13 3 DON JUAN 6   15   6
    A BED IS NOT A THRONE AND THEY MAY SLEEP . . . . .   16 3 DON JUAN 6   20   2
    HER THRONE AND POWER AND EVERYTHING BESIDE . . . . .   24 3 DON JUAN 6   36   8
    GAUNT FAMINE NEVER SHALL APPROACH THE THRONE--   . . .   175 3 DON JUAN 8   126   7
    BUT WOULD NOT CHANGE MY FREE THOUGHTS FOR A THRONE   . .   312 3 DON JUAN 11   90   8
    BUT SEATS A NATION OR UPSETS A THRONE . . . . . .   318 3 DON JUAN 12   6   4
    HE HAD ALSO STOOD AT TIMES BEHIND THE THRONE--   . . .   353 3 DON JUAN 12   82   7
    OF SUCH A THRONE AS IS THE PROUDEST STATION . . . . .   354 3 DON JUAN 12   83   4
    BUT IN THE WAR WHICH STRUCK CHARLES FROM HIS THRONE   . .   386 3 DON JUAN 13   60   4
    REMNANT WERE THERE OF THE OLD WORLD'S SOLE THRONE   . .   428 3 DON JUAN 14   40   4
    HER SPIRIT SEEM'D AS SEATED ON A THRONE   . . . . .   477 3 DON JUAN 15   47   6
THRONES
    THRONES WORLDS ET CETERA ARE SO OFT UPSET   . . . . .   8 3 DON JUAN 6   4   1
    BE SAID THAT WE STILL TRUCKLE UNTO THRONES--   . . . .   179 3 DON JUAN 8   135   6
    AND WHEN YOU HEAR HISTORIANS TALK OF THRONES   . . . .   180 3 DON JUAN 8   137   1
THRONG
    WITH CHORAL STEP AND VOICE THE VIRGIN THRONG   . . . .   291 2 DON JUAN 3   30   8
    HIS HELL-DOGS AND THEIR CHASE AND THE FAIR THRONG . . .   337 2 DON JUAN 3   106   6
    A VIRGIN-LIKE AND EDIFYING THRONG . . . .   21 3 DON JUAN 6   30   4
    IN SUCH GOOD COMPANY AS ALWAYS THRONG . . . . . .   123 3 DON JUAN 8   24   6
    FOR WHICH MEN VAINLY DECIMATE THE THRONG . . . . .   144 3 DON JUAN 8   63   2
    TO HAMMER A HOARSE LAUGH FROM THE THICK THRONG . . . .   540 3 DON JUAN 16   83   8
THRONGED
    WITH THEIR ROUGH FACES THRONGED ABOUT THE BED   . . . .   431 2 DON JUAN 5   37   2
THROTTLE
    LEAVING ALL CLARETLESS THE UNMOISTENED THROTTLE   . . .   435 3 DON JUAN 14   58   3
THROTTLED
    AND JUAN THROTTLED HIM TO GET AWAY . . . .   124 2 DON JUAN 1   186   2
THROUGHOUT
    YET STILL I TRUST IT MAY BE KEPT THROUGHOUT . . . . .   85 2 DON JUAN 1   119   6
    ALL EXCEPT JUAN WHO THROUGHOUT ABSTAIN'D   . . . . .   200 2 DON JUAN 2   82   5
    AS RARELY THEY BEHELD THROUGHOUT THEIR ROUND   . . . .   352 2 DON JUAN 4   16   3
    ONE ON THE OTHER THROUGHOUT THE WHOLE HALL   . . . . .   42 3 DON JUAN 6   71   4
    HOW HER GREAT NAME IS NOW THROUGHOUT ABHORRED   . . . .   258 3 DON JUAN 10   67   2
    I'VE DONE TO FIND THE SAME THROUGHOUT LIFE'S JOURNEY . .   281 3 DON JUAN 11   28   7
    THROUGHOUT THE SEASON UPON SPECULATION . . . . . .   293 3 DON JUAN 11   49   2
THROUGH'T
    NAMED AFTER THEE ACHILLES) AND QUITE THROUGH'T   . . .   153 3 DON JUAN 8   84   5
THROW
    PRESENTED A FINE MARK TO THROW A SHELL IN   . . . . .   78 3 DON JUAN 7   23   8
    PERHAPS MIGHT MAKE HIM SHIVER YAWN OR THROW . . . . .   121 3 DON JUAN 8   21   5
    'TIS ONLY THAT THEY LOVE TO THROW AWAY . . . . .   273 3 DON JUAN 11   10   3
    AND THEREFORE WHAT I THROW OFF IS IDEAL--   . . . . .   419 3 DON JUAN 14   22   1
    THUS ADELINE WOULD THROW INTO THE SHADE   . . . . .   522 3 DON JUAN 16   44   1
    AND THROW DOWN OLD WHICH HE CALLED RESTORATION . . . .   529 3 DON JUAN 16   58   8
THROWING
    LIKE THROWING JUAN IN ALFONSO'S WAY . . . .   118 2 DON JUAN 1   177   8
    AND THROWING BACK A DIM LOOK ON HIS SONS . . . . .   170 3 DON JUAN 8   118   7
THROWN
    ONE HAND ON JUAN'S CARLESSLY WAS THROWN   . . . . .   80 2 DON JUAN 1   109   7
    FOR WANT OF FACTS WOULD ALL BE THROWN AWAY)   . . . .   86 2 DON JUAN 1   121   4

```
                                                          PAGE VOL    CANTO  STANZA LN
THROWN   (CONTINUED)
    AND NOW HIDALGO NOW THAT YOU HAVE THROWN . . . . . . 105  2 DON JUAN  1    154    1
    THROWN BACK UPON ITS HAUNCHES--A GAZELLE . . . . . . 160  2 DON JUAN  2      6   V2
    THROWN BACK A MOMENT WITH THE GLANCING HAND . . . . . 160  2 DON JUAN  2      7    2
    WERE ALL THAT COULD BE THROWN INTO THE CUTTER . . . . 180  2 DON JUAN  2     46    8
    PART WAS DIVIDED PART THROWN IN THE SEA . . . . . . 197  2 DON JUAN  2     77    5
    I CAN DO NOTHING AND HE SAW HIM THROWN . . . . . . . 202  2 DON JUAN  2     87    7
    FOR ALL OF THEIRS UPON THAT DIE IS THROWN . . . . . 262  2 DON JUAN  2    199    3
    WAS THROWN AS 'TWERE ABOUT THE NECK OF YOU-- . . . . 474  2 DON JUAN  5    110    3
    BY THEIR POSSESSORS THROWN INTO THE SHADE . . . . . 485  2 DON JUAN  5    129    6
    OR THROWN TO LIONS OR MADE BAITS FOR FISH . . . . . 492  2 DON JUAN  5    141    4
    AND THROWN INTO THE SEA--THUS BABA SPOKE . . . . . . 58   3 DON JUAN  6    104    7
    FOR HAVING THROWN HIMSELF INTO A DITCH . . . . . . . 147  3 DON JUAN  8     71    1
    CERTES IT WOULD HAVE BEEN BUT THROWN AWAY . . . . . 200  3 DON JUAN  9     36    6
    THROWN TOPSY-TURVY TWISTED CRISPED AND CURLED . . . . 201  3 DON JUAN  9     37    4
    EXACTLY WHY IT WAS BEFORE HIM THROWN . . . . . . . . 276  3 DON JUAN 11     17    3
    A SLIGHT GLANCE THROWN ON MEN OF EVERY STATION . . . 416  3 DON JUAN 14     14    4
    OR THROWN INTO A PHILOSOPHIC PASSION . . . . . . . . 522  3 DON JUAN 16     43    6
    BUT BOTH WERE THROWN AWAY AMONGST THE FENS . . . . . 540  3 DON JUAN 16     83    2
THROWS
    BREATHES ALSO TO THE HEART AND O'ER IT THROWS . . . . 82   2 DON JUAN  1    114    7
    BUT FIX'D AS MARBLE'S UNCHANGED ASPECT THROWS . . . . 377  2 DON JUAN  4     61    3
    AND THROWS A CLOUD O'ER LONGMAN AND JOHN MURRAY . . . 79   3 DON JUAN  7     26    4
    A SHADOW WHICH THE ONWARD SOUL BEHIND THROWS . . . . 414  3 DON JUAN 14      8    6
    KINDLING RELIGION TILL SHE THROWS DOWN HER GAGE . . . 530  3 DON JUAN 16     60    5
THRUMM'D
    THE STRONGER PUMP'D THE WEAKER THRUMM'D A SAIL . . . 176  2 DON JUAN  2     38    8
THRUST
    WHILE THEY THRUST SHEETS SHIRTS JACKETS BALES OF MUSLIN . 171  2 DON JUAN  2     28    8
    TO THRUST ITS BLACK EYES THROUGH THE DOOR OR LATTICE . . 442  2 DON JUAN  5     55    7
    LIKE MOLTEN LEAD AS IF YOU THRUST A PIKE IN . . . . 479  2 DON JUAN  5    118    6
    AND WAS THRUST IN TO CLOSE THE OCTAVE'S CHIME . . . . 14   3 DON JUAN  6     18    6
    HOW WILL--TO THESE YOUNG PEOPLE JUST THRUST OUT . . . 202  3 DON JUAN  9     40    1
    RESOLVED TO THRUST THE MYSTERY CARTE AND TIERCE . . . 559  3 DON JUAN 16    119    5
    AND JUAN PUZZLED BUT STILL CURIOUS THRUST . . . . . 560  3 DON JUAN 16    122    1
THRUSTING
    FIRING AND THRUSTING SLASHING SWEATING GLOWING . . . . 120  3 DON JUAN  8     19    6
THUNDER
    OF ECHOING THUNDER AND THEN ALL WAS HUSH'D . . . . . 184  2 DON JUAN  2     53    3
    NOW O'ER IT CLOUDS AND THUNDER MUST BE DRIVEN . . . . 270  2 DON JUAN  2    214    3
    TILL SLOWLY CHARGED WITH THUNDER THEY DISPLAY . . . . 375  2 DON JUAN  4     57    3
    FOR WORDLESS WOMAN WHICH IS SILENT THUNDER . . . . . 34   3 DON JUAN  6     57    8
    FOR WOMAN'S SILENCE STARTLES MORE THAN THUNDER . . . 34   3 DON JUAN  6     57   V8
    OH BLOOD AND THUNDER AND OH BLOOD AND WOUNDS . . . . 112  3 DON JUAN  8      1    1
    THE EAR FAR MORE THAN THUNDER FOR HEAVEN'S FLASHES . . 115  3 DON JUAN  8      6    7
    AS SOON AS THUNDER 'MIDST THE GENERAL NOISE . . . . 142  3 DON JUAN  8     59    7
    JUAN CONSENTED TO MARCH ON THROUGH THUNDER . . . . . 163  3 DON JUAN  8    103    3
    HUMANITY WOULD RISE AND THUNDER NAY . . . . . . . . 183  3 DON JUAN  9      1    8
    AT LAST MAY GET A LITTLE TIRED OF THUNDER . . . . . 185  3 DON JUAN  9      5    4
    IN THUNDER HOLDS THE WAY IT CAN'T WELL MISS . . . . 277  3 DON JUAN 11     20    6
    TO HEAR DEBATES WHOSE THUNDER ROUSED (NOT ROUSES) . . 353  3 DON JUAN 12     82    4
    AND THE POPE THUNDER EXCOMMUNICATION . . . . . . . . 478  3 DON JUAN 15     50    4
THUNDERBOLT
    AND IF MY THUNDERBOLT NOT ALWAYS RATTLES . . . . . . 356  3 DON JUAN 12     88    1
THUNDERED
    THEIR COLUMN THOUGH THE TURKISH BATTERIES THUNDERED . . 149  3 DON JUAN  8     75    1
    AS THUNDERED KNOCKERS BROKE THE LONG-SEALED SPELL . . 282  3 DON JUAN 11     29    3
    AND 'GAINST THOSE FEW YOUR ANNALISTS HAVE THUNDERED . 324  3 DON JUAN 12     19    6
THUNDERER'S
    THINK OF THE THUNDERER'S FALLING DOWN BELOW . . . . 254  3 DON JUAN 10     59    3
THUNDERS
    ANSWERING THE CHRISTIAN THUNDERS WITH LIKE VOICES . . 115  3 DON JUAN  8      7    4
    ROSE STILL BUT FAINTER WERE THE THUNDERS GROWN . . . 175  3 DON JUAN  8    127    6
    THEN ROLL THE BRAZEN THUNDERS OF THE DOOR . . . . . 302  3 DON JUAN 11     67    6
    UPON MY HEAD HAVE BID THEIR THUNDERS BREAK . . . . . 414  3 DON JUAN 14     10    3
THUNDER-SHOWER
    QUICK THICK AND HEAVY--AS A THUNDER-SHOWER . . . . . 110  2 DON JUAN  1    161    8
THUNDER-STROKE
    HIS HOST WITH BROAD ARMS 'GAINST THE THUNDER-STROKE . . 384  3 DON JUAN 13     56    4
THURSDAY
    AS THUS ON THURSDAY THERE WAS A GRAND DINNER . . . . 383  3 DON JUAN 13     54    1
TIBER
    OR ROME ON TIBER--NAPLES ON THE SEA . . . . . . . . 271  3 DON JUAN 11      7   V6
TIBERIUS
    THE SENATE WHICH TIBERIUS MET OF OLD-- . . . . . . . 314  3 DON JUAN 11  V 76    8
    OF BRUTUS AT THE PAGEANT OF TIBERIUS . . . . . . . . 477  3 DON JUAN 15     49    2
TICK
    THY PLAGUES THY FAMINES THY PHYSICIANS YET TICK . . . 117  3 DON JUAN  8     12    5
    (THE SAME WHO PHYSICKED PETER) FOUND THE TICK . . . . 244  3 DON JUAN 10     39    3
TICKET'S
    AND DRAW THEM NIGHTLY WHEN A TICKET'S SENT . . . . . 342  3 DON JUAN 12     57    6
TICKLISH
    OF HER EXPLOITS FOR THIS WERE TICKLISH GROUND . . . . 428  3 DON JUAN 14     42    5
TIDE
    AND STILL SHOULD BE SO BUT THE TIDE IS TURN'D . . . . 23   2 DON JUAN  1      4    2
    THERE IS A TIDE IN THE AFFAIRS OF MEN . . . . . . . 6    3 DON JUAN  6      1    1
    THERE IS A TIDE IN THE AFFAIRS OF WOMEN . . . . . . 7    3 DON JUAN  6      2    1
    DEEP IN THE CAVERNS OF THE DEADLY TIDE-- . . . . . . 63   3 DON JUAN  6    115    4
    A TIDE OF WELL-CLAD WAITERS AND AROUND . . . . . . . 282  3 DON JUAN 11     30    2
    OF TIME AND TIDE ROLLS ON AND BEARS AFAR . . . . . . 500  3 DON JUAN 15     99    5
```

```
                                                              PAGE VOL    CANTO    STANZA LV
TIDES
    BY ONE OF THOSE ODD TURNS OF FORTUNE'S TIDES    . . . .    125  3 DON JUAN  8      27   5
    (WHO LIKE SOUR FRUIT TO STIR THEIR VEINS' SALT TIDES . .    251  3 DON JUAN 10      54   3
    HIGH GROUND AS VIRGIN CYNTHIA SWAYS THE TIDES   . . . .    322  3 DON JUAN 12      14   6
    THE OCEAN'S TIDES AND MORTAL'S BRAINS SHE SWAYS  . . .     506  3 DON JUAN 16      14   7
TIDINGS
    YOUR SLAVE BRINGS TIDINGS--HE HOPES NOT TOO SOON--  . . .   494  2 DON JUAN  5     144   5
TIE
    THEMSELVES AND THE NEXT TIME THEIR SERVANTS TIE ON  . . .   165  2 DON JUAN  2      16   6
    AND WHISPER'D THINK OF EVERY SACRED TIE  . . . . .         268  2 DON JUAN  2     210   2
    BUT HERE HE WAS--WHERE EACH TIE THAT CAN BIND   . . .      139  2 DON JUAN  8      54   3
    HE HAD A PREDILECTION FOR THAT TIE . . . . . .            469  3 DON JUAN 15      30   2
    ANACREON ONLY HAD THE SOUL TO TIE AN . . . . .           554  3 DON JUAN 16     109   5
TIED
    THAT BOTH ARE TIED TILL ONE SHALL HAVE EXPIRED  . . . .    278  2 DON JUAN  3       7   6
    HIS VERY NECKCLOTH'S GORDIAN KNOT WAS TIED  . . . .        513  3 DON JUAN 16      29   7
    HAVE TIED TOGETHER COMMONS LORDS AND KINGS  . . . .       536  3 DON JUAN 16      74   8
    WHICH TIED IN ONE FIRM KNOT WITHOUT CONFUSION   . . . .    536  3 DON JUAN 16      74  V7
TIER
    ROSE OVER THE TOWN'S RIGHT SIDE IN BRISTLING TIER  . . .    72  3 DON JUAN  7      12   7
TIERCE
    RESOLVED TO THRUST THE MYSTERY CARTE AND TIERCE  . . .     559  3 DON JUAN 16     119   5
TIES
    TOO PURE EVEN FOR THE PUREST HUMAN TIES  . . . . .        313  2 DON JUAN  3      74   6
    AND TWILIGHT SAW THEM LINK'D IN PASSION'S TIES  . . .      354  2 DON JUAN  4      20   6
    WHERE THOUSAND LOVES AND TIES AND DUTIES GROW   . . .      174  3 DON JUAN  8     124   6
    IS WHEN CHASTE MATRONS TO THEIR OTHER TIES  . . . .       220  3 DON JUAN  9      76   7
    AND YET THIS WANT OF TIES MADE THEIR'S MORE TENDER  . .    252  3 DON JUAN 10      57   8
    WILL THERE AS ALSO IN THE TIES OF BLOOD  . . . . .        451  3 DON JUAN 14      93   2
    IS WANTING AND OUR BEST TIES IN THE TOMB . . . .         475  3 DON JUAN 15      44   8
TIGER
    BUT LIKE THE SHARK AND TIGER MUST HAVE PREY . . . .       191  2 DON JUAN  2      67   4
    HAVE VENTURED PAST THE JAWS OF MOOR AND TIGER   . . .      348  3 DON JUAN 12      70  V6
TIGER'S
    AND THEIR REVENGE IS AS THE TIGER'S SPRING  . . . .       262  2 DON JUAN  2     199   6
TIGERS
    AS TIGERS COMBAT WITH AN EMPTY CRAW  . . . . . .          137  3 DON JUAN  8      49   5
TIGHT
    THAT A TIGHT BOAT WILL LIVE IN A ROUGH SEA  . . . .       180  2 DON JUAN  2      45   7
    AND TROWSERS NOT SO TIGHT THAT THEY WOULD BURST  . .      451  2 DON JUAN  5      68   4
TIGHTEST
    BUT VIRTUE'S SELF WITH ALL HER TIGHTEST LACES   . . .      494  3 DON JUAN 15      85   5
TIGRESS
    THE CUBLESS TIGRESS IN HER JUNGLE RAGING . . . .         305  2 DON JUAN  3      58   1
    A TIGRESS ROBBED OF YOUNG A LIONESS  . . . . .           487  2 DON JUAN  5     132   1
TIGRESSES
    FROM TIGRESSES AND CUBS TO DUCKS AND DUCKLINGS  . . .      488  2 DON JUAN  5     133   2
TIGRIS
    THE TIGRIS HATH ITS JEALOUSIES LIKE THAMES  . . . .        11  3 DON JUAN  6      11   8
TILLOTSON
    BARROW SOUTH TILLOTSON WHOM EVERY WEEK   . . . .          243  2 DON JUAN  2     165   5
    BY TILLOTSON AND WESLEY AND ROUSSEAU  . . . . .            68  3 DON JUAN  7       4   3
TILTS
    WHEN MAN IN BATTLE OR IN QUARREL TILTS   . . . . .        342  3 DON JUAN 12      56   5
TIMBALLE
    A L'ESPAGNOLE TIMBALLE AND SALPICON--  . . . . .          484  3 DON JUAN 15      66   2
TIMBUCTOO
    TO THAT IMPRACTICABLE PLACE TIMBUCTOO  . . . . . .        348  3 DON JUAN 12      70   3
    BUT IF I HAD BEEN AT TIMBUCTOO THERE  . . . . .           348  3 DON JUAN 12      70   7
TIME
    MILTON APPEAL'D TO THE AVENGER TIME  . . . . . .           15  2 DON JUAN  D      10   2
    IF TIME THE AVENGER EXECRATES HIS WRONGS . . . .          15  2 DON JUAN  D      10   3
    WITH TIME AND TRIALS AND THOSE HELPLESS EYES . . .        15  2 DON JUAN  D      11   5
    SENT TO THE DEVIL SOMEWHAT ERE HIS TIME  . . . . .         21  2 DON JUAN  1       1   8
    TO TEACH HIM MANNERS FOR THE TIME TO COME . . . .         34  2 DON JUAN  1      25   8
    FOR SOME TIME AN UNHAPPY SORT OF LIFE  . . . . .          35  2 DON JUAN  1      26   2
    WHICH TIME HAD LATELY RENDER'D MUCH MORE CHASTE  . .       58  2 DON JUAN  1      67   2
    BUT NOT MY FAULT--I TELL THEM ALL IN TIME . . . .         65  2 DON JUAN  1      80   8
    HE FOUND HOW OLD TIME HAD BEEN A WINNER--  . . . .         72  2 DON JUAN  1      94   7
    'TIS GROWN HIGH TIME TO THIN IT IN ITS TURN  . . .        92  2 DON JUAN  1     131   4
    BY THIS TIME DON ALFONSO WAS ARRIVED  . . . . .           96  2 DON JUAN  1     138   1
    ME ALSO SINCE THE TIME SO OPPORTUNE IS--  . . . .        103  2 DON JUAN  1     150   6
    ONLY ANOTHER TIME I TRUST YOU'LL TELL US . . . .        106  2 DON JUAN  1     156   5
    BUT NOTHING ELSE THE TIME OF WORDS WAS O'ER  . . .       111  2 DON JUAN  1     163   6
    COME COME 'TIS NO TIME NOW FOR FOOLING THERE . . .       114  2 DON JUAN  1     170   6
    IS THIS A TIME FOR GIGGLING THIS A PLIGHT   . . .        115  2 DON JUAN  1     171   5
    WHICH SHALL BE SPECIFIED IN FITTING TIME . . . .        135  2 DON JUAN  1     200  V7
    ALL THESE THINGS WILL BE SPECIFIED IN TIME  . . .        136  2 DON JUAN  1     201   1
    TIME IS TIME WAS TIME'S PAST A CHYMIC TREASURE  . .       145  2 DON JUAN  1     217   6
    TIME IS TIME WAS TIME'S PAST A CHYMIC TREASURE  . .       145  2 DON JUAN  1     217   6
    IS THAT SAME TIME SO COMMON YET SO PRECIOUS . . .        145  2 DON JUAN  1     217  V7
    IS THAT SAME TIME WHICH I HAVE SPENT BETIMES . . .       145  2 DON JUAN  1     217  V7
    WITH HIS YOUNG WIFE--A TIME AND OPPORTUNITY  . . .       158  2 DON JUAN  2       3   8
    THEMSELVES AND THE NEXT TIME THEIR SERVANTS TIE ON  . .    165  2 DON JUAN  2      16   6
    THE RUDDER TORE AWAY 'TWAS TIME TO SOUND . . . .        170  2 DON JUAN  2      27   7
    THE HOARSE HARSH WAVES KEPT TIME FRIGHT CURED THE QUALMS  174  2 DON JUAN  2      34   5
    ABOUT THIS TIME A BEAUTIFUL WHITE BIRD   . . . .         206  2 DON JUAN  2      94   1
    WHILE A FEW PRAY'D--(THE FIRST TIME FOR SOME YEARS)--  .   208  2 DON JUAN  2      98   5
    AND TIME HAD NOTHING MORE OF NIGHT NOR DAY . . .        214  2 DON JUAN  2     111   3
```

TIME   (CONTINUED)

	PAGE	VOL	CANTO	STANZA	LN
YIELD TO STERN TIME AND NATURE'S WRINKLING LAWS	219	2 DON JUAN	2	119	6
SEEM AT THE SAME TIME MYSTICAL AND GAY	220	2 DON JUAN	2	120	8
A CHILD THE FIRST TIME THAT IT SUCKS THE BREAST	261	2 DON JUAN	2	196	V2
SUCH WORTHIES TIME WILL NEVER SEE AGAIN	266	2 DON JUAN	2	206	6
AFTER A DECENT TIME MUST BE GALLANTED	276	2 DON JUAN	3	4	4
A SAD SOUR SOBER BEVERAGE--BY TIME	277	2 DON JUAN	3	5	6
ABOUT THE TIME AND PLACE WHERE HE HAD BEEN	286	2 DON JUAN	3	20	4
TALKING'S DRY WORK I HAVE NO TIME TO SPARE	297	2 DON JUAN	3	43	4
WHO ALL THE TIME WERE EATING UP HIS MUTTON	299	2 DON JUAN	3	46	8
THERE HIS FEW PEACEFUL DAYS TIME HAD SWEPT O'ER	302	2 DON JUAN	3	52	5
ITS POWER UNCONSCIOUSLY FULL MANY A TIME--	304	2 DON JUAN	3	56	3
BUT THEN THIS WRATH WILL PASS AND TIME ASSUAGING	305	2 DON JUAN	3	58	V5
OF AGES TO WHAT STRAITS OLD TIME REDUCES	327	2 DON JUAN	3	88	6
THE TIME THE CLIME THE SPOT WHERE I SO OFT	335	2 DON JUAN	3	102	2
TIME HAS APPROVED ENNUI TO BE THE BEST	343	2 DON JUAN	3	V 98	1
BUT TIME WHICH BRINGS ALL BEINGS TO THEIR LEVEL	345	2 DON JUAN	4	2	1
AND REVELL'D IN THE FANCIES OF THE TIME	347	2 DON JUAN	4	6	5
EVEN TIME THE PITILESS IN SORROW CLEFT	348	2 DON JUAN	4	8	3
THEY FOUND NO FAULT WITH TIME SAVE THAT HE FLED	351	2 DON JUAN	4	13	3
JUST AT THE VERY TIME WHEN HE LEAST BROODS	371	2 DON JUAN	4	51	5
IN TIME TO HIS OLD TUNE HE CHANGED THE THEME	380	2 DON JUAN	4	66	2
NOR TIME NOR SKILL NOR REMEDY COULD GIVE HER	381	2 DON JUAN	4	68	7
ANOTHER TIME HE MIGHT HAVE LIKED TO SEE 'EM	384	2 DON JUAN	4	75	7
THE TIME MAY COME WHEN YOU MAY HEAR ME TOO	392	2 DON JUAN	4	88	6
AND RECOLLECT THE TIME WHEN ALL THIS CANT	397	2 DON JUAN	4	98	7
OF TIME AND TONGUES THE FOSTER-BABES OF FAME	398	2 DON JUAN	4	100	2
AND HEARD TROY DOUBTED TIME WILL DOUBT OF ROME	399	2 DON JUAN	4	101	8
THE TIME MUST COME WHEN BOTH ALIKE DECAY'D	400	2 DON JUAN	4	104	5
BUT DROOP NOT FORTUNE AT YOUR TIME OF LIFE	419	2 DON JUAN	5	17	1
BUT TIME STRIPS OUR ILLUSIONS OF THEIR HUE	421	2 DON JUAN	5	21	6
WHICH FOR THE LAST THOUGH NOT THE FIRST TIME BLED	431	2 DON JUAN	5	37	4
I HAVE NO MORE TIME NOR MANY WORDS TO SPARE	454	2 DON JUAN	5	74/	3
NO DOUBT IN PROPER PLACE AND TIME AND SEASON	454	2 DON JUAN	5	74	7
BUT THERE ARE FORMS WHICH TIME TO TOUCH FORBEARS	468	2 DON JUAN	5	98	3
BUT THERE ARE FORMS WHICH TIME ADORNS NOT WEARS	468	2 DON JUAN	5	98	V3
A SECOND TIME DESIRED HIM TO KNEEL DOWN	470	2 DON JUAN	5	102	3
AND SO IT WAS IN PROPER TIME AND PLACE	478	2 DON JUAN	5	117	1
GULBEYAZ FOR THE FIRST TIME IN HER DAYS	482	2 DON JUAN	5	122	1
I ALSO WOULD SUGGEST THE FITTING TIME	482	2 DON JUAN	5	123	1
THE SACK AND SEA HAD SETTLED ALL IN TIME	496	2 DON JUAN	5	149	4
THOUGH NOT FOR WANT OF MATTER BUT 'TIS TIME	503	2 DON JUAN	5	159	2
BUT AFTER ALL THERE'S NEITHER TUNE NOR TIME	14	3 DON JUAN	6	18	4
AND CLIME AND TIME AND COUNTRY AND COMPLEXION	26	3 DON JUAN	6	40	7
WITH LADIES IT IS TIME TO GO TO REST	29	3 DON JUAN	6	46	2
'TIS TIME WE SHOULD RETURN TO PLAIN NARRATION	34	3 DON JUAN	6	57	1
BUT ALL THIS TIME HOW SLEPT OR DREAMED DUDU	41	3 DON JUAN	6	70	1
ALSO AROSE ABOUT THE SELF-SAME TIME	51	3 DON JUAN	6	90	1
OF LONDONDERRY DRAWLING AGAINST TIME	74	3 DON JUAN	7	16	6
MAY LIKEWISE PUT OFF FOR A TIME WHAT STORY	79	3 DON JUAN	7	26	7
FOR SOME TIME TILL THEY CAME IN NEARER VIEW	87	3 DON JUAN	7	43	3
HIS TIME A CORPORAL'S DUTY TO FULFIL	93	3 DON JUAN	7	52	4
A SCHOONER OR--BUT IT IS TIME TO EASE	109	3 DON JUAN	7	85	5
THEIR CLAY FOR THE LAST TIME THEIR SOULS ENCUMBER--	120	3 DON JUAN	8	18	5
FOR THE FIRST AND LAST TIME FOR LIKE A PAD	122	3 DON JUAN	8	22	5
(THE ANTIQUARIANS WHO CAN SETTLE TIME	122	3 DON JUAN	8	23	3
FOR A MUCH LONGER TIME THEN LIKE AN ASS--	126	3 DON JUAN	8	29	5
EGAD THEY FOUND THE SECOND TIME WHAT THEY	134	3 DON JUAN	8	42	1
THE FIRST TIME THOUGHT QUITE TERRIBLE ENOUGH	134	3 DON JUAN	8	42	2
HAD NOT COME UP IN TIME TO CAST AN AWE	137	3 DON JUAN	8	49	3
THE LOFTIEST HURRIED BY THE TIME AND PLACE	139	3 DON JUAN	8	54	7
NO COMMON LANGUAGE AND BESIDES IN TIME	141	3 DON JUAN	8	58	2
(WITHOUT THE GENERAL WHO HAD FALLEN SOME TIME	151	3 DON JUAN	8	79	2
MY CUE FOR ANY TIME TO BE TERRIFIC	156	3 DON JUAN	8	89	2
JOHNSON SAID--JUAN WE'VE NO TIME TO LOSE	162	3 DON JUAN	8	101	1
WHICH LAST MEN LIKE WHEN THEY HAVE TIME TO PAUSE	182	3 DON JUAN	8	140	3
BUT WHICH 'TIS TIME TO TEACH THE HIRELING TRIBE	187	3 DON JUAN	9	10	4
'TIS TIME WE SHOULD PROCEED WITH OUR GOOD POEM	193	3 DON JUAN	9	22	1
THE TIME IS OUT OF JOINT--AND SO AM I	203	3 DON JUAN	9	41	2
NOW PONDERING--IT IS TIME WE SHOULD NARRATE	203	3 DON JUAN	9	42	2
YOUNG PEOPLE AT HIS TIME OF LIFE SHOULD BE ABLE	235	3 DON JUAN	10	22	3
ABOUT THIS TIME AS MIGHT HAVE BEEN ANTICIPATED	236	3 DON JUAN	10	23	1
BUT TIME THE COMFORTER WILL COME AT LAST	248	3 DON JUAN	10	48	1
IN NEITHER CLIME TIME BLOOD WITH HER DEFENDER	252	3 DON JUAN	10	57	7
ON WHICH I HAVE NOT TIME JUST NOW TO LECTURE	255	3 DON JUAN	10	62	4
THE CASQUE WHICH NEVER STOOPED EXCEPT TO TIME	261	3 DON JUAN	10	74	3
HAD SUCH BEEN CUT IN PHAETON'S TIME THE GOD	263	3 DON JUAN	10	78	5
SUNSET THE TIME THE PLACE THE SAME DECLIVITY	272	3 DON JUAN	11	8	2
IN TWELVE HOURS' TIME AND VERY LITTLE SPACE	277	3 DON JUAN	11	18	6
WHO IN HIS TIME HAD MADE HEROIC BUSTLE	277	3 DON JUAN	11	19	2
HAD SET SOME TIME AND NIGHT WAS ON THE RIDGE	279	3 DON JUAN	11	23	7
TO MEET HOWEVER 'TIS NO TIME TO CHAT	290	3 DON JUAN	11	44	6
JUST AT THE PROPER TIME AND THOUGH A LAD	292	3 DON JUAN	11	47	6
HE MIGHT--AND BROUGHT THEM UP WITH SKILL IN TIME	295	3 DON JUAN	11	53	2
WAS RECKONED A CONSIDERABLE TIME	296	3 DON JUAN	11	55	7
THE CONQUEROR AT LEAST WHO ERE TIME RENDERS	299	3 DON JUAN	11	61	3
BEING TIRED IN TIME AND NEITHER LEAST NOR LAST	300	3 DON JUAN	11	64	4
WHICH GROWS NO BETTER THOUGH 'TIS TIME IT SHOULD	301	3 DON JUAN	11	65	8
AND GAIN AN INCH OF STAIRCASE AT A TIME	302	3 DON JUAN	11	68	8

TIME   (CONTINUED)

	PAGE	VOL	CANTO	STANZA	LN
BUT IT IS TIME THAT I SHOULD HOIST MY BLUE PETER	309	3	DON JUAN 11	83	5
IS YET WITHIN THE UNREAD EVENTS OF TIME	312	3	DON JUAN 11	90	1
THE ONLY TIME WHEN MUCH SUCCESS IS NEEDED	324	3	DON JUAN 12	17	3
THE TIME WILL COME SHE'LL WISH THAT SHE HAD SNATCHED	332	3	DON JUAN 12	35	3
AFTER MALE LOSS OF TIME AND HEARTS AND BETS	333	3	DON JUAN 12	36	3
(A THING APPROVED AS SAVING TIME AND TOIL)--	351	3	DON JUAN 12	76	6
BUT THOUGH THE SOIL MAY GIVE YOU TIME AND TROUBLE	351	3	DON JUAN 12	76	7
A PRINCE THE PRINCE OF PRINCES AT THE TIME	354	3	DON JUAN 12	84	2
I NOW MEAN TO BE SERIOUS--IT IS TIME	358	3	DON JUAN 13	1	1
HINT THAT 'TIS TIME TO GIVE THE YOUNGER PLACE	360	3	DON JUAN 13	4	8
AND SINCE THAT TIME THERE HAS NOT BEEN A SECOND	365	3	DON JUAN 13	13	8
BE WARY WATCH THE TIME AND ALWAYS SERVE IT	366	3	DON JUAN 13	18	4
ENOUGH TO MAKE FOR PORT ERE TIME SHALL SUMMON	376	3	DON JUAN 13	40	4
WHERE TIME THROUGH HEROES AND THROUGH BEAUTIES STEERS	381	3	DON JUAN 13	50	6
AND IRON TIME ERE LEAD HAD TA'EN THE LEAD	391	3	DON JUAN 13	70	2
MASTERS OF THEIR OWN TIME--OR IN COMMUNION	406	3	DON JUAN 13	103	3
WHAT TIME HE CHOSE FOR DRESS AND BROKE HIS FAST	406	3	DON JUAN 13	103	7
FOR I WAS RATHER FAMOUS IN MY TIME	414	3	DON JUAN 14	9	7
IN FEMALE DATES STRIKES TIME ALL OF A HEAP	433	3	DON JUAN 14	52	8
OH TIME WHY DOST NOT PAUSE THY SCYTHE SO DIRTY	433	3	DON JUAN 14	53	5
BY THIS TIME--BUT STRIKE SIX FROM SEVEN-AND-TWENTY	433	3	DON JUAN 14	54	7
THAT TIME WOULD TEMPER JUAN'S FAULTS OF YOUTH	439	3	DON JUAN 14	67	5
THE SENSUAL FOR A SHORT TIME BUT CONNECTS US--	442	3	DON JUAN 14	73	5
AND SINCE THAT TIME IT NEED NOT COST MUCH SHOWING	444	3	DON JUAN 14	78	5
HERE LET US PAUSE--WE ARE NOT PREST FOR TIME	455	3	DON JUAN 14	102	V1
A PAGE WHERE TIME SHOULD HESITATE TO PRINT AGE	458	3	DON JUAN 15	7	5
WHICH MAY ROUND OFF AN HOUR UPON A TIME	465	3	DON JUAN 15	20	4
ALL YOUTH--BUT WITH AN ASPECT BEYOND TIME	476	3	DON JUAN 15	45	4
THAN I HAVE TIME OR WILL TO TAKE TO PIECES	478	3	DON JUAN 15	52	8
TIME SHEDS A MOMENT O'ER EACH SPARKLING CREST	480	3	DON JUAN 15	55	6
'TIS TIME THAT SOME NEW PROPHET SHOULD APPEAR	496	3	DON JUAN 15	90	5
AND DON'T REGRET THE TIME YOU MAY HAVE LOST	498	3	DON JUAN 15	95	3
OF TIME AND TIDE ROLLS ON AND BEARS AFAR	500	3	DON JUAN 15	99	5
'TIS TIME TO STRIKE SUCH PUNY DOUBTERS DUMB AS	502	3	DON JUAN 16	4	7
THAT TIME HAS LEFT OUR FATHERS OF THEIR HALL	507	3	DON JUAN 16	16	8
THE THIRD TIME AFTER A STILL LONGER PAUSE	511	3	DON JUAN 16	24	1
KNOCKED TO INFORM HIM IT WAS TIME TO DRESS	512	3	DON JUAN 16	28	8
THIS MORNING RATHER SPENT LESS TIME UPON'T	513	3	DON JUAN 16	29	3
WHETHER WITH TIME THE SPECTRE HAS GROWN SHYER	516	3	DON JUAN 16	36	5
THE LAST TIME WAS--I PRAY SAID ADELINE--	516	3	DON JUAN 16	37	1
MIGHT HAVE FROM TIME ACQUIRED SOME SLIGHT DEFECT	529	3	DON JUAN 16	58	4
GLIDING THE FIRST TIME TO A RENDEZVOUS	556	3	DON JUAN 16	112	7
AGAIN--WHAT IS'T THE WIND NO NO--THIS TIME	556	3	DON JUAN 16	113	1

TIMELESS

	PAGE	VOL	CANTO	STANZA	LN
AN IGNORANT NOTELESS TIMELESS TUNELESS FELLOW	391	2	DON JUAN 4	87	4

TIMELY

	PAGE	VOL	CANTO	STANZA	LN
BY A FEW TIMELY WORDS TO TURN THE TABLES	117	2	DON JUAN 1	175	4

TIME-PIECE

	PAGE	VOL	CANTO	STANZA	LN
AS THOSE OF THE BEST TIME-PIECE MADE BY HARRISON	30	2	DON JUAN 1	17	6

TIME'S

	PAGE	VOL	CANTO	STANZA	LN
TIME IS TIME WAS TIME'S PAST A CHYMIC TREASURE	145	2	DON JUAN 1	217	6
IN YEARS HE HAD THE ADVANTAGE OF TIME'S SEQUEL	367	3	DON JUAN 13	20	3
WHICH MOURN'D THE POWER OF TIME'S OR TEMPEST'S MARCH	386	3	DON JUAN 13	59	7
LEAVES A SAD SEDIMENT OF TIME'S WORST SAND	457	3	DON JUAN 15	4	8

TIMES

	PAGE	VOL	CANTO	STANZA	LN
EXCEEDINGLY REMARKABLE AT TIMES	22	2	DON JUAN 1	3	7
HIS REVEREND TUTORS HAD AT TIMES A TUSSLE	44	2	DON JUAN 1	41	5
MOUNTING AT TIMES TO A TRANSPARENT GLOW	55	2	DON JUAN 1	61	5
THUS PARENTS ALSO ARE AT TIMES SHORT-SIGHTED	75	2	DON JUAN 1	100	1
WHEN PEOPLE SAY I'VE TOLD YOU FIFTY TIMES	79	2	DON JUAN 1	108	1
IF ANY LAUGHTER AT SUCH TIMES COULD BE	183	2	DON JUAN 2	50	4
OR BUT AT TIMES A LITTLE SUPPER MADE	200	2	DON JUAN 2	82	4
I'VE KNOWN THE ABSENT WRONG'D FOUR TIMES A DAY	288	2	DON JUAN 3	25	8
I'VE SEEN A FRIEND BETRAYED FOUR TIMES A DAY	288	2	DON JUAN 3	25	V8
YET IN THESE TIMES HE MIGHT HAVE DONE MUCH WORSE	326	2	DON JUAN 3	87	4
YET SHE BETRAY'D AT TIMES A GLEAM OF SENSE	381	2	DON JUAN 4	68	1
BUT TIMES ARE ALTER'D SINCE A RHYMING LOVER	405	2	DON JUAN 4	111	2
IT BETTERS PRESENT TIMES WITH ME OR YOU	422	2	DON JUAN 5	23	3
IT SEEMS THE WORK OF TIMES BEFORE THE LINE	461	2	DON JUAN 5	86	7
THEY LOOKED SO LITTLE DID STRONG THINGS AT TIMES--	463	2	DON JUAN 5	89	2
WHICH HAS AT TIMES AN ASPECT OF THE ODDEST	464	2	DON JUAN 5	91	7
A THOUSAND TIMES OF HIM HAD MADE AN END	471	2	DON JUAN 5	104	6
YET HE COULD NOT AT TIMES KEEP BY THE WAY	20	3	DON JUAN 6	29	4
AT OTHER TIMES REPULSED BY THE CLOSE FIRE	121	3	DON JUAN 8	20	5
AT TIMES WOULD CURDLE O'ER SOME HEAVY GROAN	140	3	DON JUAN 8	55	8
OF THESE AMBROSIAL PHARISAIC TIMES	156	3	DON JUAN 8	90	3
SOME TWENTY TIMES HE MADE THE RUSS RETIRE	171	3	DON JUAN 8	120	3
SUCH DOOM MAY BE YOUR OWN IN AFTER TIMES	174	3	DON JUAN 8	125	4
WITH HER THE LATTER THOUGH AT TIMES CONVENIENT	214	3	DON JUAN 9	63	1
THE GENTLE JUAN FLOURISHED THOUGH AT TIMES	243	3	DON JUAN 10	37	1
OF THE GOOD FEUDAL TIMES FOREVER GONE	255	3	DON JUAN 10	62	3
BECAUSE THE TIMES HAVE HARDLY LEFT THEM ONE TENANT	308	3	DON JUAN 11	80	8
ALL PEOPLE AT ALL TIMES AND IN MOST PLACES	334	3	DON JUAN 12	39	7
FOR TALK SIX TIMES WITH THE SAME SINGLE LADY	343	3	DON JUAN 12	59	7
NINE TIMES IN TEN 'TIS BUT CAPRICE OR FASHION	351	3	DON JUAN 12	77	3
PEOPLE SOME TEN TIMES LESS IN FACT TO MIND IT	352	3	DON JUAN 12	80	3
HE HAD ALSO STOOD AT TIMES BEHIND THE THRONE--	353	3	DON JUAN 12	82	7
NOTHING THAT SPEAKS TO ALL MEN AND ALL TIMES	417	3	DON JUAN 14	16	2

834

TIMES   (CONTINUED)
   BUT MODESTY'S AT TIMES ITS OWN REWARD . . . . 462 3 DON JUAN 15   14   6
   SUCH AS THE TIMES MAY FURNISH 'TIS A FLIGHT . . . . 467 3 DON JUAN 15   25   2
   YET WITH DISPLAY IN FACT AT TIMES RELENT . . . . . . 521 3 DON JUAN 16   42   6
   TOO SCANTY IN THESE TIMES OF LOW TAXATION . . . . . 528 3 DON JUAN 16   56   8
   WHICH THE POOR THING AT TIMES ESSAYED TO DRY . . . . 532 3 DON JUAN 16   65   3
   BUT COULD HE QUIT HIS KING IN TIMES OF STRIFE . . . 536 3 DON JUAN 16   74   3
   MILD--BUT AT TIMES A SORT OF HERCULES FURENS . . . . 567 3 DON JUAN 17   11   6
TIMID
   LOVE IS SO VERY TIMID WHEN 'TIS NEW . . . . 81 2 DON JUAN 1   112   6
   THEN SHRIEK'D THE TIMID AND STOOD STILL THE BRAVE . . 184 2 DON JUAN 2   52   2
   SUSPICION THOUGH NOT TIMID HIS REGARD . . . . 462 3 DON JUAN 15   14   2
TIMIDLY
   ALL TIMIDLY YET RAPIDLY SHE SAW . . . . 232 2 DON JUAN 2   143   2
   AND TIMIDLY EXPANDING INTO LIFE . . . . 27 3 DON JUAN 6   43   8
TIMON
   THEIR MOTHERS AS THE ANTIPODES OF TIMON . . . . . . 53 3 DON JUAN 6   94   2
TIMOUR
   FOR TIMOUR OR FOR ZINGHIS IN HIS TRADE . . . . . . 178 3 DON JUAN 8   133   2
TINCT
   AQ FERVENT OUNCE AND A HALF TWO DRAMS TINCT SENNAE . 244 3 DON JJAN 10   41   3
TINDER
   WERE NEARLY TINDER SINCE SO LONG THEY LAY . . . . . 226 2 DON JUAN 2   132   5
TINGE
   WHICH HATE NOR ENVY E'ER COULD TINGE WITH WRONG . . 144 3 DON JUAN 8   63   6
   TOOK LIKE CAMELIONS SOME SLIGHT TINGE OF FEAR . . . 148 3 DON JUAN 8   73   4
   SHE ALSO HAD A TWILIGHT TINGE OF BLUE . . . . 524 3 DON JUAN 16   47   1
TINGED
   HER EYELASHES THOUGH DARK AS NIGHT WERE TINGED . . . 314 2 DON JUAN 3   75   1
TINGES
   (AS NIGHT DEW ON A CYPRESS GLITTERING TINGES . . . . 40 3 DON JUAN 6   67   7
TINGLED
   THE GLASSES JINGLED AND THE PALATES TINGLED . . . . 487 3 DON JUAN 15   70   1
TINGLING
   AND TINGLING VEIN SEEM'D THROBBING BACK TO LIFE . . 214 2 DON JUAN 2   111   7
TINKERING
   A TINKERING SLAVE-MAKER WHO MENDS OLD CHAINS . . . . 18 2 DON JUAN D   14   7
TINKLING
   BY TINKLING SOUNDS WHEN THEY GO FORTH TO VICTUAL . . . 90 3 DJN JUAN 7   48   7
TINT
   THE ENDLESS SOOT BESTOWS A TINT FAR DEEPER . . . . . 232 3 DON JUAN 10   15   3
TINTERS
   GOOD HOURS OF FAIR CHEEKS ARE THE FAIREST TINTERS . . 409 3 DON JUAN 13   111   7
TINTS
   OH THAT MY WORDS WERE COLOURS BUT THEIR TINTS . . . . 60 3 DON JUAN 6   109   7
TIPTOE
   (FOR SLEEP IS AWFUL) AND ON TIPTOE CREPT . . . . . . 232 2 DON JUAN 2   143   5
   ON TIPTOE THROUGH THEIR SEA-COAL CANOPY . . . . . . 265 3 DJN JUAN 10   82   6
   OR TIPTOE OF AN AMATORY MISS . . . . 556 3 DON JUAN 16   112   6
TIRADE
   I'VE DONE WITH MY TIRADE THE WORLD WAS GONE . . . 381 3 DON JUAN 13   49   1
TIRE
   AND THIS EXTREME EFFECT (TO TIRE NO LONGER . . . . . 488 2 DON JUAN 5   133   7
   AND THIS STRONG SECOND CAUSE (TO TIRE NO LONGER . . 488 2 DON JUAN 5   133   V7
   IS APT TO TIRE A CALM AND SHALLOW STATION . . . . . 191 3 DON JUAN 9   18   6
   MY PEGASUS SHALL TIRE OF TOUCHING GROUND . . . . . . 224 3 DON JUAN 9   85   3
   WE TIRE OF MISTRESSES AND PARASITES . . . . 405 3 DON JUAN 13   100   6
TIRED
   GROW TIRED OF SCIENTIFIC CONVERSATION . . . . 33 2 DON JUAN 1   22   4
   THEY SOMETIMES ALSO GET A LITTLE TIRED . . . . . . 278 2 DON JUAN 3   7   2
   AT LAST MAY GET A LITTLE TIRED OF THUNDER . . . . . 185 3 DON JUAN 9   5   4
   BEING TIRED IN TIME AND NEITHER LEAST NOR LAST . . . 300 3 DON JUAN 11   64   4
   WHEN TIRED OF PLAY HE FLIRTED WITHOUT SIN . . . . . 327 3 DON JUAN 12   25   5
   I HATE TO HUNT DOWN A TIRED METAPHOR . . . . 374 3 DON JUAN 13   36   5
   ᶜOR THEN THE GENTLEMEN WERE RATHER TIRED) . . . . . 408 3 DON JUAN 13   108   2
TIRES
   AT LEAST IN THE BEGINNING ERE ONE TIRES . . . . . . 282 2 DON JUAN 3   13   6
TIRESIAS
   UNLESS LIKE WISE TIRESIAS WE HAD PROVED . . . . . . 442 3 DON JUAN 14   73   2
TIRESOME
   PARTICULARLY WITH A TIRESOME FRIEND . . . . 90 2 DON JUAN 1   126   4
   AND REPETITION'S TIRESOME AND UNWISE-- . . . . . . 246 2 DON JUAN 2   171   6
   FOR LIKE AN AGED AUNT OR TIRESOME FRIEND . . . . . . 334 3 DON JUAN 12   39   4
TIRING
   TIRING OLD READERS NOR DISCOVERING NEW . . . . . . 414 3 DON JUAN 14   10   6
'TIS
   ALTHOUGH 'TIS TRUE THAT YOU TURN'D OUT A TORY AT . . .   9 2 DON JUAN D   1   3
   'TIS POETRY--AT LEAST BY HIS ASSERTION . . . . 11 2 DON JUAN D   4   5
   'TIS THAT I STILL RETAIN MY BUFF AND BLUE . . . . . 20 2 DON JUAN D   17   4
   'TIS WITH OUR HERO QUIETLY INURN'D . . . . 23 2 DON JUAN 1   4   4
   'TIS STRANGE--THE HEBREW NOUN WHICH MEANS I AM . . . 28 2 DON JUAN 1   14   7
   'TIS PITY LEARNED VIRGINS EVER WED . . . . 33 2 DON JUAN 1   22   1
   'TIS IN ARRANGING ALL MY FRIENDS' AFFAIRS . . . . . 33 2 DON JUAN 1   23   7
   'TIS ALSO PLEASANT TO BE DEEM'D MAGNANIMOUS . . . . . 37 2 DON JUAN 1   30   3
   BUT THEN 'TIS NOT MY FAULT IF OTHERS HURT YOU . . . 37 2 DON JUAN 1   30   8
   'TIS NOT WITH DONNA INEZ I WOULD SHUT . . . . 50 2 DON JUAN 1   52   5
   FOR THERE ONE LEARNS--'TIS NOT FOR ME TO BOAST . . . 50 2 DON JUAN 1   53   1
   'TIS SAID THAT DONNA JULIA'S GRANDMAMMA . . . . 53 2 DON JUAN 1   58   7
   'TIS A SAD THING I CANNOT CHOOSE BUT SAY . . . . . 56 2 DON JUAN 1   63   1

'TIS   (CONTINUED)

	PAGE	VOL	CANTO		STANZA	LN
ITSELF 'TIS STILL THE SAME HYPOCRISY	61	2	DON JUAN	1	73	6
'TIS SURELY JUAN NOW--NO I'M AFRAID	63	2	DON JUAN	1	76	7
AND IF THE MAN SHOULD ASK 'TIS BUT DENIAL	64	2	DON JUAN	1	78	7
IF PEOPLE GO BEYOND 'TIS QUITE A CRIME	65	2	DON JUAN	1	80	7
THIS MAY SEEM STRANGE BUT YET 'TIS VERY COMMON	74	2	DON JUAN	1	98	1
AT FIFTY LOVE FOR LOVE IS RARE 'TIS TRUE	79	2	DON JUAN	1	108	6
LOVE IS SO VERY TIMID WHEN 'TIS NEW	81	2	DON JUAN	1	112	6
'TIS SAID THAT XERXES OFFER'D A REWARD	85	2	DON JUAN	1	118	1
OF ARISTOTLE AND THE RULES 'TIS FIT	86	2	DON JUAN	1	120	7
WE'LL TALK OF THAT ANON--'TIS SWEET TO HEAR	87	2	DON JUAN	1	122	1
'TIS SWEET TO SEE THE EVENING STAR APPEAR	87	2	DON JUAN	1	122	5
'TIS SWEET TO LISTEN AS THE NIGHTWINDS CREEP	87	2	DON JUAN	1	122	6
FROM LEAF TO LEAF 'TIS SWEET TO VIEW ON HIGH	87	2	DON JUAN	1	122	7
'TIS SWEET TO HEAR THE WATCHDOG'S HONEST BARK	88	2	DON JUAN	1	123	1
'TIS SWEET TO KNOW THERE IS AN EYE WILL MARK	88	2	DON JUAN	1	123	3
'TIS SWEET TO BE AWAKEN'D BY THE LARK	88	2	DON JUAN	1	123	5
'TIS STRANGE OLD PEOPLE DONT LIKE TO BE BURIED	89	2	DON JUAN	1	125	V8
'TIS SWEET TO WIN NO MATTER HOW ONE'S LAURELS	90	2	DON JUAN	1	126	1
BY BLOOD OR INK 'TIS SWEET TO PUT AN END	90	2	DON JUAN	1	126	2
TO STRIFE 'TIS SOMETIMES SWEET TO HAVE OUR QUARRELS	90	2	DON JUAN	1	126	3
'TIS SAID THE GREAT CAME FROM AMERICA	92	2	DON JUAN	1	131	1
'TIS GROWN HIGH TIME TO THIN IT IN ITS TURN	92	2	DON JUAN	1	131	4
'TIS PITY THOUGH IN THIS SUBLIME WORLD THAT	93	2	DON JUAN	1	133	3
'TIS NOT MY FAULT--I KEPT GOOD WATCH--ALACK	96	2	DON JUAN	1	137	4
'TIS ODD NOT ONE OF ALL THESE SEEKERS THOUGHT	100	2	DON JUAN	1	144	6
AND WHEN 'TIS FOUND LET ME TOO HAVE THAT PLEASURE	104	2	DON JUAN	1	153	8
PERHAPS 'TIS OF ANTONIA YOU ARE JEALOUS	106	2	DON JUAN	1	156	1
'TIS WRITTEN IN THE HEBREW CHRONICLE	113	2	DON JUAN	1	168	2
COME COME 'TIS NO TIME NOW FOR FOOLING THERE	114	2	DON JUAN	1	170	6
'TIS TO RETORT WITH FIRMNESS AND WHEN HE	117	2	DON JUAN	1	175	7
CONCEAL'D AMONGST HIS PREMISES 'TIS TRUE	118	2	DON JUAN	1	177	5
HAVE ALWAYS DONE SO 'TIS OF NO GREAT USE	119	2	DON JUAN	1	179	2
OF ALL EXPERIENCE 'TIS THE USUAL PRICE	122	2	DON JUAN	1	183	3
THEY TELL ME 'TIS DECIDED YOU DEPART	130	2	DON JUAN	1	192	1
'TIS WISE--'TIS WELL BUT NOT THE LESS A PAIN	130	2	DON JUAN	1	192	2
'TIS WISE--'TIS WELL BUT NOT THE LESS A PAIN	130	2	DON JUAN	1	192	2
BE ON THIS SHEET 'TIS NOT WHAT IT APPEARS	130	2	DON JUAN	1	192	7
YET IF I NAME MY GUILT 'TIS NOT TO BOAST	130	2	DON JUAN	1	193	5
'TIS WOMAN'S WHOLE EXISTENCE MAN MAY RANGE	131	2	DON JUAN	1	194	2
THEY SO EMBELLISH THAT 'TIS QUITE A BORE	137	2	DON JUAN	1	202	6
WHAT IS THE END OF FAME 'TIS BUT TO FILL	146	2	DON JUAN	1	218	1
'TIS THERE THE MART OF THE COLONIAL TRADE IS	159	2	DON JUAN	2	5	3
YOU MUST EXCUSE THIS EXTRACT 'TIS WHERE SHE	165	2	DON JUAN	2	17	4
'TIS TRUE THAT DEATH AWAITS BOTH YOU AND ME	175	2	DON JUAN	2	36	3
BUT STILL 'TIS BEST TO STRUGGLE TO THE LAST	176	2	DON JUAN	2	39	5
'TIS NEVER TOO LATE TO BE WHOLLY WRECK'D	176	2	DON JUAN	2	39	6
AND THOUGH 'TIS TRUE THAT MAN CAN ONLY DIE ONCE	176	2	DON JUAN	2	39	7
'TIS NOT SO PLEASANT IN THE GULF OF LYONS	176	2	DON JUAN	2	39	8
'TIS VERY CERTAIN THE DESIRE OF LIFE	190	2	DON JUAN	2	64	1
'TIS SAID THAT PERSONS LIVING ON ANNUITIES	190	2	DON JUAN	2	65	1
'TIS THUS WITH PEOPLE IN AN OPEN BOAT	191	2	DON JUAN	2	66	1
'TIS SURELY FAIR TO DINE UPON OUR FRIENDS	200	2	DON JUAN	2	83	6
'TIS AS THE SNAKE LATE COIL'D WHO POURS HIS LENGTH	218	2	DON JUAN	2	117	7
I'LL TELL YOU WHY I SAY SO FOR 'TIS JUST	219	2	DON JUAN	2	119	1
(SAINT PAUL SAYS 'TIS THE TOLL WHICH MUST BE GIVEN)	225	2	DON JUAN	2	131	8
AND 'TIS NO DOUBT A SIGHT TO SEE WHEN BREAKS	230	2	DON JUAN	2	139	4
BECAUSE 'TIS LIQUOR ONLY AND BEING FAR	238	2	DON JUAN	2	156	3
'TIS PLEASING TO BE SCHOOL'D IN A STRANGE TONGUE	242	2	DON JUAN	2	164	1
AND ALL UNCONSCIOUS OF THE JOY 'TIS GIVING	261	2	DON JUAN	2	197	4
AND IF 'TIS LOST LIFE HATH NO MORE TO BRING	262	2	DON JUAN	2	199	4
STRONG PALPITATION RISES 'TIS HER BOON	267	2	DON JUAN	2	208	6
'TIS BUT MY CURIOSITY THAT CRIES	268	2	DON JUAN	2	210	V6
'TIS THE PERCEPTION OF THE BEAUTIFUL	269	2	DON JUAN	2	212	1
YET 'TIS A PAINFUL FEELING AND UNWILLING	270	2	DON JUAN	2	213	1
'TIS MELANCHOLY AND A FEARFUL SIGN	277	2	DON JUAN	3	5	1
YET 'TIS SO NOMINATED IN THE BOND	278	2	DON JUAN	3	7	5
'TIS STRANGE THAT POETS NEVER TRY TO WREATHE	280	2	DON JUAN	3	9	V5
'TIS STRANGE THAT POETS OF THE CATHOLIC FAITH	280	2	DON JUAN	3	9	V5
'TIS DANGEROUS TO READ OF LOVES UNLAWFUL	282	2	DON JUAN	3	12	8
WHEN WE HAVE WHAT WE LIKE 'TIS HARD TO MISS IT	282	2	DON JUAN	3	13	5
HIS TITLE AND 'TIS NOTHING BUT TAXATION	283	2	DON JUAN	3	14	4
'TIS TRUE HE HAD NO ARDENT LOVE FOR PEACE--	303	2	DON JUAN	3	55	5
'TIS BEAUTIFUL TO SEE A MATRON BRING	306	2	DON JUAN	3	60	3
BUT SHAKSPEARE ALSO SAY 'TIS VERY SILLY	314	2	DON JUAN	3	76	7
'TIS SOMETHING IN THE DEARTH OF FAME	323	2	DON JUAN	3 L	6	1
'TIS BUT THE LIVING WHO ARE DUMB	323	2	DON JUAN	3 L	8	6
'TIS STRANGE THE SHORTEST LETTER WHICH MAN USES	327	2	DON JUAN	3	88	4
'TIS SOMETHING NOTHING WORDS ILLUSION WIND--	328	2	DON JUAN	3	90	2
AVE MARIA 'TIS THE HOUR OF PRAYER	336	2	DON JUAN	3	103	1
AVE MARIA 'TIS THE HOUR OF LOVE	336	2	DON JUAN	3	103	2
WHAT THOUGH 'TIS BUT A PICTURED IMAGE STRIKE--	336	2	DON JUAN	3	103	7
THAT PAINTING IS NO IDOL 'TIS TOO LIKE	336	2	DON JUAN	3	103	8
'TIS BEING TOO EPIC AND I MUST CUT DOWN	342	2	DON JUAN	3	111	2
'TIS THAT I MAY NOT WEEP AND IF I WEEP	346	2	DON JUAN	4	4	2
'TIS THAT OUR NATURE CANNOT ALWAYS BRING	346	2	DON JUAN	4	4	3
THEY GAZED UPON THE SUNSET 'TIS AN HOUR	354	2	DON JUAN	4	20	1
AND NO DOUBT OF ALL METHODS 'TIS THE BEST	356	2	DON JUAN	4	24	5
SOME PEOPLE PREFER WINE--'TIS NOT AMISS	356	2	DON JUAN	4	24	6

'TIS   (CONTINUED)

	PAGE	VOL	CANTO	STANZA	LN
STRANGE STATE OF BEING (FOR 'TIS STILL TO BE)	360	2	DON JUAN 4	30	7
'TIS--'TIS HER FATHER'S--FIX'D UPON THE PAIR	363	2	DON JUAN 4	35	8
'TIS--'TIS HER FATHER'S--FIX'D UPON THE PAIR	363	2	DON JUAN 4	35	8
AND HAIDEE CLUNG AROUND HIM JUAN 'TIS--	364	2	DON JUAN 4	38	1
'TIS LAMBRO--'TIS MY FATHER KNEEL WITH ME--	364	2	DON JUAN 4	38	2
'TIS LAMBRO--'TIS MY FATHER KNEEL WITH ME--	364	2	DON JUAN 4	38	2
'TIS PITY WINE SHOULD BE SO DELETERIOUS	372	2	DON JUAN 4	52	7
AND OLD SCAMANDER (IF 'TIS HE) REMAIN	386	2	DON JUAN 4	77	4
'TIS SAID NO ONE IN HAND CAN HOLD A FIRE	396	2	DON JUAN 4	96	5
'TIS ALL THE SAME TO ME I'M FOND OF YIELDING	397	2	DON JUAN 4	98	1
'TIS AS A SNOWBALL WHICH DERIVES ASSISTANCE	398	2	DON JUAN 4	100	5
BUT AFTER ALL 'TIS NOTHING BUT COLD SNOW	398	2	DON JUAN 4	100	8
'TIS A GRAND SIGHT FROM OFF THE GIANT'S GRAVE	413	2	DON JUAN 5	5	3
AND LONG BESIDES -- OH IF 'TIS REALLY SO	419	2	DON JUAN 5	16	6
A SAD TALE SADDENS DOUBLY WHEN 'TIS LONG	419	2	DON JUAN 5	16	8
A DULL STORY'S DOUBLY GRIEVOUS WHEN 'TIS LONG	419	2	DON JUAN 5	16	V8
'TIS NOT SAID JUAN FOR MY PRESENT LOT	420	2	DON JUAN 5	18	1
'TIS NOT MY PRESENT LOT AS I HAVE SAID	420	2	DON JUAN 5	18	6
SURELY 'TIS NOTHING WONDERFUL TO SEE	421	2	DON JUAN 5	20	4
'TIS TRUE IT GETS ANOTHER BRIGHT AND FRESH	422	2	DON JUAN 5	22	1
'TIS BAD AND MAY BE BETTER--ALL MEN'S LOT	423	2	DON JUAN 5	25	2
'TIS PLEASANT PURCHASING OUR FELLOW CREATURES	425	2	DON JUAN 5	27	2
'TIS THEREFORE BETTER LOOKING BEFORE LEAPING--	436	2	DON JUAN 5	45	6
DEATH TO HIS PUBLISHER TO HIM 'TIS SPORT	440	2	DON JUAN 5	52	5
I GRANT YOU IN A CHURCH 'TIS VERY WELL	444	2	DON JUAN 5	59	2
WHY 'TIS A PALACE WHERE THE TRULY WISE	458	2	DON JUAN 5	81	7
OUR SOULS AT LEAST ARE FREE AND 'TIS IN VAIN	474	2	DON JUAN 5	110	6
TO THEM 'TIS A RELIEF TO US A TORTURE	479	2	DON JUAN 5	118	8
SO THAT A PONIARD PIERCES IF 'TIS STUCK HARD	492	2	DON JUAN 5	140	4
'TIS TRUE A LITTLE TROUBLED HERE AND THERE	497	2	DON JUAN 5	150	6
'TIS TRUE THE REASON IS THAT THE BASHAW	498	2	DON JUAN 5	152	7
I SEE YOU'VE BOUGHT ANOTHER GIRL 'TIS PITY	500	2	DON JUAN 5	155	7
THOUGH NOT FOR WANT OF MATTER BUT 'TIS TIME	503	2	DON JUAN 5	159	2
'TIS NOT HIS CONQUESTS KEEP HIS NAME IN FASHION	8	3	DON JUAN 6	4	6
IF 'TIS SUMMED UP WITH FEMININE PRECISION	10	3	DON JUAN 6	9	3
IF TRUE 'TIS NO GREAT LEASE OF ITS OWN FIRE	14	3	DON JUAN 6	16	2
IN THE DAMNED LINE ('TIS WORTH AT LEAST A CURSE)	15	3	DON JUAN 6	18	V5
'TIS THE VILE DAILY DROP ON DROP WHICH WEARS	16	3	DON JUAN 6	20	7
'TIS SO SENTENTIOUS POSITIVE AND TERSE	17	3	DON JUAN 6	23	6
SNOW WELL 'TIS ALL HAP-HAZARD WHEN ONE WEDS	18	3	DON JUAN 6	25	6
BUT CERTAIN 'TIS THEY ALL FELT FOR THEIR NEW	25	3	DON JUAN 6	39	1
FEW ANGLES WERE THERE IN HER FORM 'TIS TRUE	27	3	DON JUAN 6	42	5
'TIS TIME WE SHOULD RETURN TO PLAIN NARRATION	34	3	DON JUAN 6	57	1
BECAUSE 'TIS PLEASANT SO THAT IT BE PURE	35	3	DON JUAN 6	59	4
YOUR FATHER'S SON 'TIS QUITE ENOUGH FOR ME	52	3	DON JUAN 6	93	8
UNTIL 'TIS TAUGHT BY LESSONS RATHER RUDE	53	3	DON JUAN 6	95	3
'TIS NOT THEIR FAULT NOR MINE IF THIS BE SO--	68	3	DON JUAN 7	4	5
IF THIS BE THE RIGHT READING--'TIS NO MATTER	70	3	DON JUAN 7	8	2
OR WAS AT LEAST UNLESS 'TIS SINCE DEFACED	71	3	DON JUAN 7	9	5
'TIS BUILT BEGIRT WITH BATTERY AND TRENCH	71	3	DON JUAN 7	9	V4
THE CITY'S SHAPE SUGGESTED THIS 'TIS TRUE	78	3	DON JUAN 7	23	6
BUT 'TIS A NAME SO SPREAD O'ER SIR AND MADAM	79	3	DON JUAN 7	25	7
'TIS TRUE THE MEMOIRS OF THE PRINCE DELIGNE	82	3	DON JUAN 7	33	7
'TIS STRANGE THAT HE SHOULD FURTHER DAMN HIS EYES	88	3	DON JUAN 7	45	1
'TIS THUS THE SPIRIT OF A SINGLE MIND	90	3	DON JUAN 7	48	1
'TIS PITY THAT SUCH MEANING SHOULD PAVE HELL	123	3	DON JUAN 8	25	8
'TIS TRUE HE SHRANK FROM MEN EVEN OF HIS NATION	144	3	DON JUAN 8	64	1
EVEN WITH HIS LIFE--FOR (BUT THEY LIE) 'TIS SAID	153	3	DON JUAN 8	84	7
HOWEVER THIS MAY BE 'TIS PRETTY SURE	154	3	DON JUAN 8	85	1
BUT THEN THE FACT'S A FACT--AND 'TIS THE PART	154	3	DON JUAN 8	86	1
IT IS AN AWFUL TOPIC--BUT 'TIS NOT	156	3	DON JUAN 8	89	1
OF OUR ARTILLERY AND HIS OWN 'TIS SAID	160	3	DON JUAN 8	98	5
'TIS STRANGE ENOUGH--THE ROUGH TOUGH SOLDIERS WHO	171	3	DON JUAN 8	119	1
IN ONE THING NE'ERTHELESS 'TIS FIT TO PRAISE	176	3	DON JUAN 8	128	1
THAT HOUR IS NOT FOR US BUT 'TIS FOR YOU	180	3	DON JUAN 8	136	1
UPON THE REST 'TIS NOT WORTH WHILE TO DWELL	184	3	DON JUAN 9	2	5
THEY SAY YOU LIKE IT TOO--'TIS NO GREAT WONDER	185	3	DON JUAN 9	5	2
BUT WHICH 'TIS TIME TO TEACH THE HIRELING TRIBE	187	3	DON JUAN 9	10	4
'TIS TRUE WE SPECULATE BOTH FAR AND WIDE	190	3	DON JUAN 9	16	3
'TIS TIME WE SHOULD PROCEED WITH OUR GOOD POEM	193	3	DON JUAN 9	22	1
WHOSE STATUES WARM (I FEAR ALAS TOO TRUE 'TIS)	208	3	DON JUAN 9	51	6
'TIS VERY TRUE THE HILL SEEMED RATHER HIGH	215	3	DON JUAN 9	66	5
('TIS POPE'S PHRASE) A GREAT LONGING THO' A RASH ONE	216	3	DON JUAN 9	68	6
EXCEPT WHERE 'TIS A MERE INSANITY	219	3	DON JUAN 9	73	3
SUCH CLYTEMNESTRA THOUGH PERHAPS 'TIS BETTER	222	3	DON JUAN 9	80	7
'TIS SAID (FOR I'LL NOT ANSWER ABOVE GROUND	225	3	DON JUAN 10	1	3
SHOULD SO CONTINUE--'TIS A POINT OF HONOUR	231	3	DON JUAN 10	12	2
'TIS NOT ADDRESSED TO YOU--THE MORE'S THE PITY	233	3	DON JUAN 10	17	2
I CARE NOT--'TIS A GLIMPSE OF AULD LANG SYNE	233	3	DON JUAN 10	18	8
YET 'TIS IN VAIN SUCH SALLIES TO PERMIT	234	3	DON JUAN 10	19	5
AND YET 'TIS VERY PUZZLING ON THE BRINK	234	3	DON JUAN 10	20	6
'TIS THE SAME LANDSCAPE WHICH THE MODERN MARS SAW	253	3	DON JUAN 10	58	5
DIRECTION BE SO 'TIS BUT IN A HURRY	260	3	DON JUAN 10	72	4
'TIS NOT SO TO BE GOOD AND BE IT STATED	267	3	DON JUAN 10	87	4
THEY SAY HIS SYSTEM 'TIS IN VAIN TO BATTER	268	3	DON JUAN 11	1	3
'TIS ONLY THAT THEIR LOVE TO THROW AWAY	273	3	DON JUAN 11	10	3
OR GOD BE WITH YOU--AND 'TIS NOT ABSURD	274	3	DON JUAN 11	12	5
HEROES MUST DIE AND BY GOD'S BLESSING 'TIS	277	3	DON JUAN 11	20	2

'TIS   (CONTINUED)

	PAGE	VOL	CANTO	STANZA	LN
WHICH THOUGH 'TIS CERTAIN TO PERPLEX AND FRIGHTEN	281	3	DON JUAN 11	27	7
THE CONTRARY BUT THEN 'TIS IN THE HEAD	284	3	DON JUAN 11	34	2
OF FAIR PHILOSOPHY OR WHERE 'TIS THEY TREAD	284	3	DON JUAN 11	34	V6
AND AFTER ALL WHAT IS A LIE 'TIS BUT	286	3	DON JUAN 11	37	1
TO MEET HOWEVER 'TIS NO TIME TO CHAT	290	3	DON JUAN 11	44	6
'TIS ALSO OF SOME MOMENT TO THE LATTER	292	3	DON JUAN 11	46	5
ALTHOUGH 'TIS AN IMAGINARY THING	296	3	DON JUAN 11	55	4
'TIS STRANGE THE MIND THAT VERY FIERY PARTICLE	298	3	DON JUAN 11	60	7
'TIS STRANGE THE MIND SHOULD LET SUCH PHRASES QUELL IT'S	298	3	DON JUAN 11	60	V7
WHICH GROWS NO BETTER THOUGH 'TIS TIME IT SHOULD	301	3	DON JUAN 11	65	8
I LOOK FOR IT--'TIS GONE A GLOBE OF GLASS	306	3	DON JUAN 11	76	4
WHICH 'TIS THE COMMON CRY AND LIE TO VAUNT AS	311	3	DON JUAN 11	87	3
BUT 'TIS AS WELL AT ONCE TO UNDERSTAND	311	3	DON JUAN 11	87	6
IS WAX HEAVEN IS NOT LOVE 'TIS MATRIMONY	322	3	DON JUAN 12	14	8
IN THIS TWELFTH CANTO 'TIS MY WISH TO BE	325	3	DON JUAN 12	20	3
'TIS TRUE THAT THY CAREER IS NOT A NEW ONE	326	3	DON JUAN 12	23	5
AT MAKING MATCHES WHERE 'TIS GOLD THAT GLISTERS	331	3	DON JUAN 12	32	5
'TIS FINE TO SEE THEM SCATTERING REFUSALS	332	3	DON JUAN 12	34	2
(IF 'TIS NOT VAIN EXAMPLES TO RECALL)	333	3	DON JUAN 12	37	6
TRUE 'TIS A PITY PITY 'TIS 'TIS TRUE)	334	3	DON JUAN 12	38	2
TRUE 'TIS A PITY PITY 'TIS 'TIS TRUE)	334	3	DON JUAN 12	38	2
TRUE 'TIS A PITY PITY 'TIS 'TIS TRUE)	334	3	DON JUAN 12	38	2
PERUSE 'TIS ALWAYS WITH A MORAL END	334	3	DON JUAN 12	39	2
BUT NOW I WILL BEGIN MY POEM--'TIS	341	3	DON JUAN 12	54	1
'TIS A GREAT MORAL LESSON THEY ARE READING	341	3	DON JUAN 12	55	4
FOR 'TIS A LOW NEWSPAPER HUMDRUM LAW-SUIT	346	3	DON JUAN 12	65	1
INTO A COUNTRY WHERE 'TIS HALF A FASHION	347	3	DON JUAN 12	68	4
NINE TIMES IN TEN 'TIS BUT CAPRICE OR FASHION	351	3	DON JUAN 12	77	3
A LITTLE BLASE--'TIS NOT TO BE WONDERED	353	3	DON JUAN 12	81	5
'TIS NOT MERE SPLENDOUR MAKES THE SHOW AUGUST	354	3	DON JUAN 12	83	7
AND--THOUGH NO DOUBT 'TIS FOR THE PUBLIC WEAL	357	3	DON JUAN 12	V 18	6
('TIS AN OLD NORMAN NAME AND TO BE FOUND	359	3	DON JUAN 13	2	2
IS NO GREAT MATTER SO 'TIS IN REQUEST	359	3	DON JUAN 13	3	4
'TIS NONSENSE TO DISPUTE ABOUT A HUE--	359	3	DON JUAN 13	3	5
HINT THAT 'TIS TIME TO GIVE THE YOUNGER PLACE	360	3	DON JUAN 13	4	8
OF ALL TALES 'TIS THE SADDEST--AND MORE SAD	363	3	DON JUAN 13	9	1
HIS GUERDON 'TIS HIS VIRTUE MAKES HIM MAD	363	3	DON JUAN 13	9	5
'TIS NOT IN MORTALS TO COMMAND SUCCESS	366	3	DON JUAN 13	18	1
'TIS TRUE I MIGHT HAVE CHOSEN PICCADILLY	370	3	DON JUAN 13	27	1
HOWEVER 'TIS EXPEDIENT TO BE WARY	374	3	DON JUAN 13	35	5
'TIS THE WHOLE SPIRIT BROUGHT TO A QUINTESSENCE	375	3	DON JUAN 13	38	1
(A CHANCE STILL) 'TIS A VOYAGE OR VESSEL LOST	376	3	DON JUAN 13	39	8
'TIS THE POSTILLION'S PARADISE WHEELS FLY	377	3	DON JUAN 13	42	3
'TIS GRANTED AND THE VALET MOUNTS THE DICKEY--	380	3	DON JUAN 13	47	1
WERE WELL NIGH OVER 'TIS PERHAPS A PITY	380	3	DON JUAN 13	48	2
'TIS PITY THAT IT TAKES NO FURTHER HOLD	382	3	DON JUAN 13	51	3
'TIS ODD BUT TRUE--LAST WAR THE NEWS ABOUNDED	383	3	DON JUAN 13	53	7
'TIS NOT ENOUGH TO SPELL OR EVEN TO READ	393	3	DON JUAN 13	73	2
AND AH YE POACHERS--'TIS NO SPORT FOR PEASANTS	394	3	DON JUAN 13	75	8
'TIS ROUND HIM NEAR HIM HERE THERE EVERYWHERE	412	3	DON JUAN 14	5	1
'TIS TRUE YOU DON'T--BUT PALE AND STRUCK WITH TERROR	413	3	DON JUAN 14	6	1
FOR WHICH MY SOLE EXCUSE IS--'TIS MY WAY	413	3	DON JUAN 14	7	3
THIS FEELING 'TIS NOT EASY TO EXPRESS	415	3	DON JUAN 14	12	5
AND YET 'TIS NOT AFFECTED I OPINE	415	3	DON JUAN 14	12	6
'TIS SAID--INDEED A GENERAL COMPLAINT--	418	3	DON JUAN 14	19	1
'TIS THAT IN FACT THERE'S LITTLE TO DESCRIBE	418	3	DON JUAN 14	20	8
'TIS PLEASANT IF THEN ANYTHING IS PLEASANT	422	3	DON JUAN 14	28	7
'TIS ALSO SUBJECT TO THE DOUBLE DANGER	424	3	DON JUAN 14	32	2
HE BROKE 'TIS TRUE SOME STATUTES OF THE LAWS	424	3	DON JUAN 14	33	5
'TIS SO BECOMING TO THE SOUL AND FACE	430	3	DON JUAN 14	47	2
'TIS BETTER ON THE WHOLE TO HAVE FELT AND SEEN	431	3	DON JUAN 14	49	5
'TIS SAD TO HACK INTO THE ROOTS OF THINGS	436	3	DON JUAN 14	59	1
'TIS BEST TO PAUSE AND THINK ERE YOU RUSH ON	438	3	DON JUAN 14	64	7
UPON WHOSE BACK 'TIS BETTER NOT TO VENTURE	442	3	DON JUAN 14	73	8
'TIS ODD OR ODDS IT MAY TURN OUT A ROCK	442	3	DON JUAN 14	74	8
BECAUSE 'TIS FRAILER DOUBTLESS THAN A STANCH ONE	446	3	DON JUAN 14	85	6
IT HAD BEEN FIRMNESS NOW 'TIS PERTINACITY	449	3	DON JUAN 14	90	2
'TIS RARELY FOUND BUT WOULD REPAY ALL CHECKS	451	3	DON JUAN 14	93	V5
I'VE ALSO SEEN SOME FEMALE FRIENDS ('TIS ODD	452	3	DON JUAN 14	96	1
'TIS STRANGE--BUT TRUE FOR TRUTH IS ALWAYS STRANGE	455	3	DON JUAN 14	101	1
'TIS THUS THE GOOD WILL AMIABLY ERR	463	3	DON JUAN 15	17	3
BUT THEN 'TIS MOSTLY ON THE WEAKER SIDE	466	3	DON JUAN 15	23	1
SUCH AS THE TIMES MAY FURNISH 'TIS A FLIGHT	467	3	DON JUAN 15	25	2
THAN MATCH-MAKING IN GENERAL 'TIS NO SIN	470	3	DON JUAN 15	31	6
OR NO 'TIS SAID HIS SECT IS RICH AND GODLY	472	3	DON JUAN 15	36	4
'TIS NOT MY PURPOSE ON HIS VIEWS TO DWELL	472	3	DON JUAN 15	38	5
LIKE HOLBEIN'S DANCE OF DEATH--BUT 'TIS THE SAME)--	473	3	DON JUAN 15	39	8
IT WAS NOT--BUT 'TIS EASIER FAR ALAS	479	3	DON JUAN 15	54	7
'TIS WONDERFUL HOW OFT THE SEX HAVE HEARD	489	3	DON JUAN 15	76	7
'TIS WONDERFUL WHAT FABLE WILL NOT DO	495	3	DON JUAN 15	89	4
'TIS SAID IT MAKES REALITY MORE BEARABLE	495	3	DON JUAN 15	89	5
'TIS TIME THAT SOME NEW PROPHET SHOULD APPEAR	496	3	DON JUAN 15	90	5
AND THEREFORE THOUGH 'TIS BY NO MEANS MY WAY	500	3	DON JUAN 15	98	1
'TIS TRUE THERE BE SOME BITTERS WITH THE SWEETS	502	3	DON JUAN 16	3	5
'TIS TIME TO STRIKE SUCH PUNY DOUBTERS DUMB AS	502	3	DON JUAN 16	4	7
BECAUSE 'TIS SO WHO NIBBLE SCRIBBLE QUIBBLE HE	503	3	DON JUAN 16	5	7
BELIEVE--IF 'TIS IMPROBABLE YOU MUST	503	3	DON JUAN 16	6	2
'TIS ALWAYS BEST TO TAKE THINGS UPON TRUST	503	3	DON JUAN 16	6	4

```
                                                         PAGE VOL      CANTO STANZA L\
'TIS   (CONTINUED)
    BY THE MARRIAGE BED OF THEIR LORDS 'TIS SAID      . . . . .  519  3 DON JUAN 16   L 3    5
    AND 'TIS HELD AS FAITH TO THEIR BED OF DEATH      . . . . .  519  3 DON JUAN 16   L 3    7
    'TIS SHADOWED BY HIS COWL . . . . . . . . .       . . . . .  519  3 DON JUAN 16   L 4    6
    SET TO SOME THOUSANDS ('TIS THE USUAL BURTHEN     . . . . .  529  3 DON JUAN 16     59   2
    'TIS WHITE AT LEAST WHEN THEY JUST RISE FROM BED  . . . . .  532  3 DON JUAN 16     64   4
    IS'T ENGLISH NO--'TIS ONLY PARLIAMENTARY)         . . . . .  536  3 DON JUAN 16     73   2
    THEY ERR--'TIS MERELY WHAT IS CALLED MOBILITY     . . . . .  547  3 DON JUAN 16     97   4
    'TIS TRUE HE SAW AURORA LOOK AS THOUGH   . . .    . . . . .  553  3 DON JUAN 16    106   1
    I SEE--I SEE--AH NO--'TIS NOT--YET 'TIS--         . . . . .  556  3 DON JUAN 16    112   2
    I SEE--I SEE--AH NO--'TIS NOT--YET 'TIS--         . . . . .  556  3 DON JUAN 16    112   2
    WHEN HE CAN'T TELL WHAT 'TIS THAT DOTH APPAL      . . . . .  559  3 DON JUAN 16    120   6
    AND FRIGHTS--ESPECIALLY IF 'TIS A DAUGHTER        . . . . .  564  3 DON JUAN 17      4   7
TIS
    TIS PITY THAT THEY HAD NO BROUGHAM IN SPAIN--     . . . . .  150  2 DON JUAN  1   V 1    2
TISSUE
    A SUN EMBOSS'D IN GOLD WHOSE RAYS OF TISSUE  . . . . . .     309  2 DON JUAN  3     67   7
TITA
    BATTISTA THOUGH (A NAME CALL'D SHORTLY TITA) . . . . . .     186  2 DON JUAN  2     56   7
TITAN
    ARISE LIKE TITAN FROM THE SEA'S IMMERSION    . . . . . .      14  2 DON JUAN  D      9   6
    THE RESTLESS TITAN HICCUPS IN HIS DEN . . . . . . . . .      115  3 DON JUAN  8      7   8
TITAN'S
    THE GIANT THOUGHT OF BEING A TITAN'S BRIDE   . . . . . .      20  3 DON JUAN  6     28   4
    BUT SYSTEM DOTH REVERSE THE TITAN'S BREAKFAST    . . . .     411  3 DON JUAN 14      2   1
TITANS
    OF TITANS GIANTS FELLOWS OF ABOUT . . . . . . . .           201  3 DON JUAN  9     38   6
TITHE
    EVIL AND GOOD HAVE HAD THEIR TITHE OF TALK   . . . . .       22  2 DON JUAN  1      2   3
TITHES
    ALL EARTHLY GOODS SAVE TITHES) AND BADE THEM PUSH ON . . .   99  3 DON JUAN  7     64   6
    TITHES TAXES DUNS AND DOORS WITH DOUBLE KNOCKINGS . . .     346  3 DON JUAN 12     67   8
    AND ONE ON TITHES WHICH SURE ARE DISCORD'S TORCHES . . .    530  3 DON JUAN 16     60   4
    AND OF ALL THINGS EXCEPTING TITHES AND LEASES . . . . .     531  3 DON JUAN 16     63   5
    TAKERS OF TITHES AND MAKERS OF GOOD MATCHES . . . . . .     539  3 DON JUAN 16     80   7
TITIAN
    THERE ROSE A CARLO DOLCE OR A TITIAN . . . . . . . .        392  3 DON JUAN 13     71   3
    A SPECIAL TITIAN WARRANTED ORIGINAL  . . . . . . . .        528  3 DON JUAN 16     56   2
TITLE
    HIS TITLE AND 'TIS NOTHING BUT TAXATION . . . . . .         283  2 DON JUAN  3     14   4
    HER TITLE WAS THE MOTHER OF THE MAIDS . . . . . .           21  3 DON JUAN  6     30   8
    BUT THIS IS HER SERAGLIO TITLE GOT . . . . . . .            21  3 DON JUAN  6     31   3
    THE TURKISH TITLE) AND RANGED ROUND THE WALL . . . .        31  3 DON JUAN  6     51   2
    A HIGHER TITLE OR A LOFTIER STATION . . . . . .            114  3 DON JUAN  8      4   5
    NO TITLE TO POINT OUT WITH DUE PRECISION . . . . .         283  3 DON JUAN 11     32   3
    OF PEERS TO PROVE THEIR TITLE NO DISGRACE . . . .          314  3 DON JUAN 11   V 75   8
    METHINKS LOVE'S VERY TITLE SAYS ENOUGH . . . . .           451  3 DON JUAN 14     94   7
    MY OBJECTION'S TO HIS TITLE NOT HIS RITUAL . . .           472  3 DON JUAN 15     36   7
TITLES
    IF STARS AND TITLES COULD ENTAIL LONG PRAISE . . . .        84  3 DON JUAN  7     37   3
TITTLE
    AND SO SHE COOK'D THEIR BREAKFAST TO A TITTLE . . . .      233  2 DON JUAN  2    145   5
    AS THAT ABOMINABLE TITTLE TATTLE  . . . . . . .           336  3 DON JUAN 12     43   7
TITUS
    TITUS THE MASTER ANTONY THE SLAVE . . . . . . .           266  2 DON JUAN  2    205   2
    TITUS EXCLAIMED I'VE LOST A DAY OF ALL  . . . . .         505  3 DON JUAN 16     11   5
TITUS'
    LIKE TITUS' YOUTH AND CAESAR'S EARLIEST ACTS . . . .      329  2 DON JUAN  3     92   3
TOAD
    SHE WOULD HAVE SHRUNK AS FROM A TOAD OR ASP . . . . .      81  2 DON JUAN  1    111   6
TOAST
    THE MORNING CAME--AND BREAKFAST TEA AND TOAST . . . .     568  3 DON JUAN 17     13   2
TOBACCO
    TOBACCO ON A LITTLE CARPET--TROY  . . . . . . .          172  3 DON JUAN  8    121   3
TOBACCO-STOPPER
    JUAN WHO CARED NOT A TOBACCO-STOPPER . . . . . .         254  3 DON JUAN 10     60   5
TOBY-SPICE
    ON THE HIGH TOBY-SPICE SO FLASH THE MUZZLE . . . .       277  3 DON JUAN 11     19   6
TOCSIN
    THE TOCSIN OF THE SOUL--THE DINNER BELL . . . . .        439  2 DON JUAN  5     49   8
    WHEN ALL AROUND RANG LIKE A TOCSIN BELL . . . .          48  3 DON JUAN  6     84   4
TODAY
    HAVING GOT DRUNK EXCEEDINGLY TODAY . . . . . . .         156  2 DON JUAN  1   V 8    5
    LOOK YES LAST NIGHT AND YET SAY NO TO-DAY . . . . .      332  3 DON JUAN 12     34   8
    DEPARTURE FOR HIS COUNTRY SEAT TO-DAY . . . . . .        382  3 DON JUAN 13     51   7
TOE
    A FINISHED GENTLEMAN FROM TOP TO TOE . . . . . .         354  3 DON JUAN 12     84   8
TOGETHER
    THEY LIVED TOGETHER AS MOST PEOPLE DO . . . . .          57  2 DON JUAN  1     65   4
    HE MIGHT BE TAUGHT BY LOVE AND HER TOGETHER--   . . .     65  2 DON JUAN  1     81   7
    TO LEAVE TOGETHER THIS IMPRUDENT PAIR . . . . .          80  2 DON JUAN  1    110   6
    TWO BLANKETS STITCH'D TOGETHER ANSWERING ILL  . . .     188  2 DON JUAN  2     61   3
    WERE STRUNG TOGETHER LIKE A ROW OF PEARLS . . . .       291  2 DON JUAN  3     30   3
    THEY SHOULD HAVE LIVED TOGETHER DEEP IN WOODS . . .     358  2 DON JUAN  4     28   1
    WERE LINK'D TOGETHER AND IT HAPPEN'D THE MALE . . .     394  2 DON JUAN  4     92   4
    ALL HEAPED TOGETHER SOMEHOW IN A LITTER . . . . .       465  2 DON JUAN  5     93  V8
    IS NOT TO BE PUT HASTILY TOGETHER . . . . . .           355  3 DON JUAN 12     86   2
    BUT BOTH TOGETHER FORM A KIND OF CENTAUR . . . .        442  3 DON JUAN 14     73   7
    THE WHOLE TOGETHER IS WHAT I COULD WISH . . . .         465  3 DON JUAN 15     21   7
    HAVE TIED TOGETHER COMMONS LORDS AND KINGS . . . .      536  3 DON JUAN 16     74   8
```

TOIL
   FROM THAT IXION GRINDSTONE'S CEASELESS TOIL . . . . . . 17 2 DON JUAN D 13 6
   AND IT MIGHT BE FROM THOUGHT OR TOIL OR STUDY . . . . . 416 2 DON JUAN 5 11 4
   AND CHEERFULNESS THE HANDMAID OF THEIR TOIL . . . . . 145 3 DON JUAN 8 67 2
   LET THIS ONE TOIL FOR BREAD--THAT RACK FOR RENT . . . . 190 3 DON JUAN 9 15 7
   ALL KINDS OF TOIL SAVE FOR OUR COUNTRY'S GOOD-- . . . . 301 3 DON JUAN 11 65 7
   AND UGLINESS DISEASE AS TOIL AND TROUBLE-- . . . . . 305 3 DON JUAN 11 74 7
   (A THING APPROVED AS SAVING TIME AND TOIL)-- . . . . . 351 3 DON JUAN 12 76 6
   OF TOIL IS WHAT WE COVET MOST AND YET . . . . 412 3 DON JUAN 14 4 2
   COST HER AN EFFORT WHICH IS A SAD TOIL . . . . . . 447 3 DON JUAN 14 86 2
   HOW WAS THY TOIL REWARDED WE MIGHT FILL . . . . . 464 3 DON JUAN 15 18 6
TOIL'D
   HIS NATURAL SPIRIT NOT IN VAIN THEY TOIL'D . . . . . . 49 2 DON JUAN 1 50 5
TOILET
   THERE IS THE CLOSET THERE THE TOILET THERE . . . . . 104 2 DON JUAN 1 153 1
   HIS TOILET THOUGH NO DOUBT A LITTLE BACKWARD . . . . . 456 2 DON JUAN 5 78 4
   AS SUITED THE ENSEMBLE OF HIS TOILET . . . . 457 2 DON JUAN 5 79 7
   HER TOILET WHICH COST LITTLE FOR SHE WAS . . . . . . 36 3 DON JUAN 6 60 2
   UPON HIS TABLE OR HIS TOILET--WHICH . . . . 507 3 DON JUAN 16 16 1
   TO TAKE SOME TROUBLE WITH HIS TOILET BUT . . . . . . 513 3 DON JUAN 16 29 2
TOILETS
   WERE COUCHES TOILETS--AND MUCH MORE THAN THIS . . . . 31 3 DON JUAN 6 51 3
TOILS
   AND MINGLING MODESTLY IN TOILS OR SPORTS . . . . . . 424 3 DON JUAN 14 31 6
TOISES
   AND MEASURES ROUND OF TOISES THOUSANDS THREE . . . . . 71 3 DON JUAN 7 9 8
   BEYOND THE RUSSIAN BATTERIES A FEW TOISES . . . . . . 115 3 DON JUAN 8 7 2
TOKEN
   AND THE TWO LAST HAVE LEFT ME MANY A TOKEN . . . . . 145 2 DON JUAN 1 217 3
   ON MANY A TOKEN WITHOUT KNOWING WHAT . . . . . . 378 2 DON JUAN 4 63 2
   HIS SYMPATHY FOR RANK BY THE SAME TOKEN . . . . . . 117 2 DON JUAN 8 11 7
TOKENS
   ARE THE BEST TOKENS (TO A MODEST MIND) . . . . . . 13 3 DON JUAN 6 15 5
TOLD
   WHEN PEOPLE SAY I'VE TOLD YOU FIFTY TIMES . . . . . 79 2 DON JUAN 1 108 1
   SHE LOITER'D AND HE TOLD HER TO BE GONE . . . . . . 116 2 DON JUAN 1 173 3
   IN HIS ROUGH EYES AND TOLD THE CAPTAIN HE . . . . . 179 2 DON JUAN 2 43 2
   WHO TOLD HIM TO BE DAMN'D--IN HIS CONFUSION . . . . . 179 2 DON JUAN 2 44 8
   HIS NEAREST MESSMATE TOLD HIS SIRE WHO THREW . . . . . 202 2 DON JUAN 2 87 5
   ALTHOUGH SHE TOLD HIM IN GOOD MODERN GREEK . . . . . 236 2 DON JUAN 2 150 6
   HER TALE IS TOLD WITH SO MUCH SIMPLE EASE-- . . . . . 273 2 DON JUAN 2 V 2 6
   OF LAVISH PEARLS WHOSE WORTH COULD SCARCE BE TOLD . . . 312 2 DON JUAN 3 72 6
   WE'RE TOLD THIS GREAT HIGH PRIEST OF ALL THE NINE . . . 328 2 DON JUAN 3 91 6
   AND ALL WHICH MUST BE BORNE AND NEVER TOLD . . . . . 350 2 DON JUAN 4 11 6
   JUAN WAS TOLD ABOUT THEIR CURIOUS CASE . . . . . . 388 2 DON JUAN 4 81 2
   IN A FEW WORDS HE TOLD THEIR HAPLESS STORY . . . . . 389 2 DON JUAN 4 82 1
   WHICH MUST NOT BE PATHETICALLY TOLD . . . . 413 2 DON JUAN 5 4 8
   AND WHEN THE OLD NEGRO TOLD HIM TO GET READY . . . . 453 2 DON JUAN 5 73 7
   WHAT SIR SAID JUAN SHALL IT E'ER BE TOLD . . . . . . 454 2 DON JUAN 5 75 5
   ALL THIS SHE TOLD WITH SOME CONFUSION AND . . . . . 45 3 DON JUAN 6 78 1
   AND THE PERPLEXITY COULD NOT BE TOLD . . . . . . 54 3 DON JUAN 6 96 5
   NO SINKING SPIRITS TOLD THEM THEY GREW GREY . . . . . 145 3 DON JUAN 8 66 5
   AND BEING TOLD THE LATTER SENT A BEY . . . . . . 171 3 DON JUAN 8 120 7
   IN CATHOLIC EYES BUT TOLD HIM TOO TO SMOTHER . . . . . 240 3 DON JUAN 10 32 4
   BUT THOUGH THREE BISHOPS TOLD HER THE TRANSGRESSION . . . 252 3 DON JUAN 10 56 3
   AND BEING TOLD IT WAS GOD'S HOUSE SHE SAID . . . . . 262 3 DON JUAN 10 75 1
   HAD TOLD HIS SON TO SATISFY HIS CRAVING . . . . . . 263 3 DON JUAN 10 78 6
   NO DOUBT I SHOULD BE TOLD THAT BLACK IS FAIR . . . . . 348 3 DON JUAN 12 70 8
   I TELL THE TALE AS IT IS TOLD NOR DARE . . . . . . 365 3 DON JUAN 13 13 1
   TOLD OF THEIR SIRES A TOMB IN EVERY TREE . . . . . . 381 3 DON JUAN 13 50 8
   A PARAGRAPH IN EVERY PAPER TOLD . . . . 382 3 DON JUAN 13 51 1
   OR WALKED IF FOUL THEY READ OR TOLD A TALE . . . . . 406 3 DON JUAN 13 104 3
   IS THAT PORTENTOUS PHRASE I TOLD YOU SO . . . . . . 432 3 DON JUAN 14 50 3
   STRANGER THAN FICTION IF IT COULD BE TOLD . . . . . 455 3 DON JUAN 14 101 2
   AS IF THEY TOLD THE TRUTH COULD WELL BE SHOWN . . . . 461 3 DON JUAN 15 13 2
   IF SOMEONE HAD NOT TOLD ME TO FOREGO IT . . . . . . 467 3 DON JUAN 15 24 8
   BUT OF ALL TRUTHS WHICH SHE HAS TOLD THE MOST . . . . 502 3 DON JUAN 16 4 1
   DEEP SECRETS TO HER ROLLING LIGHT ARE TOLD . . . . . 506 3 DON JUAN 16 14 6
   BECAUSE THE PRESENT TALE HAS OFT BEEN TOLD . . . . . 516 3 DON JUAN 16 37 7
TOLERABLE
   JULIA IN FACT HAD TOLERABLE GROUNDS . . . . 118 2 DON JUAN 1 176 1
   THE MODERN GREEK IN TOLERABLE VERSE . . . . 326 2 DON JUAN 3 87 2
   FOUND LIFE MOST TOLERABLE AFTER MEALS . . . . . . 427 2 DON JUAN 5 31 2
   ROUSED BY REPULSE--THROUGH A TOLERABLE LEAK . . . . . 490 2 DON JUAN 5 137 V6
TOLERABLY
   SO THAT THE OUTLINE'S TOLERABLY FAIR . . . . . . 463 3 DON JUAN 15 16 4
   FOR HE HAD TWO BOTH TOLERABLY BRIGHT . . . . . . 558 3 DON JUAN 16 117 6
TOLERANCE
   IS NO LESS FAMED FOR TOLERANCE THAN PIETY . . . . . 396 3 DON JUAN 13 80 8
TOLL
   (SAINT PAUL SAYS 'TIS THE TOLL WHICH MUST BE GIVEN) . . . 225 2 DON JUAN 2 131 8
   AND MADE THE VERY BILLOWS PAY THEM TOLL . . . . . . 257 3 DON JUAN 10 65 8
   (SURGIT AMARI ALIQUID)--THE TOLL . . . . 263 3 DON JUAN 10 78 8
TOM
   THAT WOULD HAVE SET TOM MOORE THOUGH MARRIED RAVING . . . 291 2 DON JUAN 3 30 V6
   POOR TOM WAS ONCE A KIDDY UPON TOWN . . . . . . 276 3 DON JUAN 11 17 5
   WHO IN A ROW LIKE TOM COULD LEAD THE VAN . . . . . 277 3 DON JUAN 11 19 3
   BUT TOM'S NO MORE--AND SO NO MORE OF TOM . . . . . 277 3 DON JUAN 11 20 1
   WE HAVE NO ACCOMPLISH'D BLACKGUARDS LIKE TOM JONES . . . 409 3 DON JUAN 13 110 7

TOMB
      HE LIKE ACHATES FAITHFUL TO THE TOMB 109   2 DON JUAN 1   159   6
      TO FIND OUR HEARTHSTONE TURN'D INTO A TOMB 301   2 DON JUAN 3   51   5
      SURVIVES HIMSELF HIS TOMB AND ALL THAT'S HIS 327   2 DON JUAN 3   88   8
      SOME HANDS UNSEEN STREW'D FLOWERS UPON HIS TOMB . . . 339   2 DON JUAN 3   109   5
      SAVE CHANGE I'VE STOOD UPON ACHILLES' TOMB 399   2 DON JUAN 4   101   7
      ARE SWEPT AWAY AND TOMB INHERITS TOMB 399   2 DON JUAN 4   102   2
      ARE SWEPT AWAY AND TOMB INHERITS TOMB 399   2 DON JUAN 4   102   2
      TO THE BARD'S TOMB AND NOT THE WARRIOR'S COLUMN . . . 400   2 DON JUAN 4   104   4
      PROTECTS HIS TOMB BUT GREATER CARE IS PAID 400   2 DON JUAN 4   104 V3
      THE HEAP A MOMENT MORE HAD MADE HER TOMB 158   3 DON JUAN 8   94   8
      UPON YOUR TOMB IN WESTMINSTER'S OLD ABBEY 184   3 DON JUAN 9   2   4
      EVEN THE BOLD CHURCHMAN'S TOMB EXCITED AWE 261   3 DON JUAN 10   74   4
      TOLD OF THEIR SIRES A TOMB IN EVERY TREE 381   3 DON JUAN 13   50   8
      IS WANTING AND OUR BEST TIES IN THE TOMB 475   3 DON JUAN 15   44   8
TOMBS
      AND HUGE TOMBS WORSE--MANKIND SINCE ADAM FELL 444   2 DON JUAN 5   59   6
TOMBUCTOO
      TOMBUCTOO TRAVELS VOYAGES TO THE POLES 93   2 DON JUAN 1   132   6
      OR SEEN TOMBUCTOO OR HATH TAKEN TEA 271   3 DON JUAN 11   7   4
TO-MORROW
      PARTAKE OF MINE BUT BY TO-MORROW EARLY 29   3 DON JUAN 6   46   7
      TO-MORROW WHAT HIS HIGHNESS'S PHYSICIAN 46   3 DON JUAN 6   80   7
      BY SPECIAL PROVIDENCE TO LEAD TO-MORROW 99   3 DON JUAN 7   63   4
      TO-MORROW SEES ANOTHER RACE AS GAY 310   3 DON JUAN 11   86   2
TO-MORROW'D
      TO-MORROW'D SEE US IN SOME OTHER DEN 435   2 DON JUAN 5   44   5
TO-MORROW'S
      AS I'LL TELL AUREA AT TO-MORROW'S ROUT 332   3 DON JUAN 12   35   6
TOM'S
      BUT TOM'S NO MORE--AND SO NO MORE OF TOM 277   3 DON JUAN 11   20   1
TON
      OF HIGHEST CASTE--THE BRAHMINS OF THE TON 397   3 DON JUAN 13   83   4
TONE
      WITHOUT KNOWING WHY--AN OVERPOWERING TONE 236   2 DON JUAN 2   151   7
      TO SUCH A SORROW BY THE INTRUSIVE TONE 481   3 DON JUAN 5   121   3
      (SHE ADDED IN A SOFT AND PITEOUS TONE) 47   3 DON JUAN 6   82   6
      BRING THE TWO SLAVES SHE SAID IN A LOW TONE 62   3 DON JUAN 6   112   2
      HE SAID--AND IN THE KINDEST CALMUCK TONE-- 102   3 DON JUAN 7   70   1
      IN THE SAME QUAINT UNINTERESTED TONE-- 261   3 DON JUAN 10   73   4
      IN LISTENING MERELY TO HIS VOICE'S TONE 461   3 DON JUAN 15   13   6
      AND JUAN'S MIND WAS IN THE PROPER TONE 506   3 DON JUAN 16   13   5
      WHO WISH TO TAKE THE TONE OF THEIR SOCIETY 526   3 DON JUAN 16   52   4
TONES
      ADDRESSING HIM IN TONES WHICH SEEMED TO THANK 141   3 DON JUAN 8   57   7
      THE TONES THE FEELING AND THE EXECUTION 521   3 DON JUAN 16   41   7
TONGUE
      SHE LIKED THE ENGLISH AND THE HEBREW TONGUE 28   2 DON JUAN 1   14   1
      AND HELD HER TONGUE HER VOICE WAS GROWN SO WEAK . . . 81   2 DON JUAN 1   112   8
      DURING THIS INQUISITION JULIA'S TONGUE 100   2 DON JUAN 1   145   1
      (THE HEART WILL SLIP EVEN AS THE TONGUE AND PEN) . . 228   2 DON JUAN 2   135   6
      AND THEN FAIR HAIDEE TRIED HER TONGUE AT SPEAKING . . 241   2 DON JUAN 2   161   1
      A LESSON IN HER TONGUE BUT BY SURMISE 242   2 DON JUAN 2   163   3
      'TIS PLEASING TO BE SCHOOL'D IN A STRANGE TONGUE . . 242   2 DON JUAN 2   164   1
      WITH SOMETIMES MORE WITHIN THEM THAN ONE TONGUE . . . 254   2 DON JUAN 2   187 V8
      NO STONE IS THERE TO SHOW NO TONGUE TO SAY 383   2 DON JUAN 4   72   6
      YOU'RE RIGHT ON BOTH ACCOUNTS TO HOLD YOUR TONGUE . . 419   2 DON JUAN 5   16   7
      BUT STRONG AND LASTING TILL NO TONGUE CAN TELL . . . 444   2 DON JUAN 5   59   4
      AND WHEN TO HOLD ITS TONGUE NOW HELD IT TILL 61   3 DON JUAN 6   110   2
      ONE OF WHOM SPOKE THEIR TONGUE OR WELL OR ILL 95   3 DON JUAN 7   56   5
      (SEE BILLINGSGATE) MADE EVEN THE TONGUE MORE FREE . . 288   3 DON JUAN 11   42   8
      TO BALAAM AND FROM TONGUE TO EAR O'ERFLOWS 328   3 DON JUAN 12   26   6
      ALTHOUGH THE WORLD HAS SUCH AN EVIL TONGUE 336   3 DON JUAN 12   43   3
      BECAUSE BOLD BRITONS HAVE A TONGUE AND FREE QUILL . . 367   3 DON JUAN 13   20   5
      HE TAXED HIS TONGUE FOR WORDS WHICH WERE NOT GRANTED . 511 3 DON JUAN 16   23   7
      WHICH GLIBLY GLIDES FROM EVERY VULGAR TONGUE 564   3 DON JUAN 17   5   2
TONGUES
      IF FALLEN IN EVIL DAYS ON EVIL TONGUES 15   2 DON JUAN D   10   1
      HAVE VOICES--TONGUES TO CRY ALOUD FOR ME 19   2 DON JUAN D   16   6
      SOME WOMEN USE THEIR TONGUES--SHE LOOK'D A LECTURE . . 29   2 DON JUAN 1   15   1
      PEOPLE SHOULD HOLD THEIR TONGUES IN ANY CASE 77   2 DON JUAN 1   105   4
      THEIR THROATS WERE OVENS THEIR SWOLN TONGUES WERE BLACK . 202 2 DON JUAN 2   86   3
      AND ALL THE BURNING TONGUES THE PASSION TEACH 256   2 DON JUAN 2   189   5
      OF TIME AND TONGUES THE FOSTER-BABES OF FAME 398   2 DON JUAN 4   100   2
      OF DUDU THOUGH THEY HELD THEIR TONGUES FROM DEFERENCE . 31 3 DON JUAN 6   50   8
TO-NIGHT
      I KNOW NOT WHY BUT IN THAT HOUR TO-NIGHT 355   2 DON JUAN 4   21   1
      OR IT MAY BE TO-NIGHT THE ASSAULT I HAVE VOWED . . . 99   3 DON JUAN 7   63   5
TONNAGE
      OR BRIGANTINE OR PINK OF NO GREAT TONNAGE 468   3 DON JUAN 15   27   7
TONS
      FOR FIFTY TONS OF WATER WERE UPTHROWN 171   2 DON JUAN 2   29   6
      THROUGH KENNINGTON AND ALL THE OTHER TONS 277   3 DON JUAN 11   20   7
TOOK
      A JEW TOOK ONE OF HIS TWO MISTRESSES 39   2 DON JUAN 1   34   4
      HER MAIDS WERE OLD AND IF SHE TOOK A NEW ONE 48   2 DON JUAN 1   48   5
      SHE TOOK HIS LADY ALSO IN AFFECTION 58   2 DON JUAN 1   67   3
      WHO TOOK ALGIERS DECLARES I USED HIM VILELY 102   2 DON JUAN 1   148   8
      WAS IT FOR THIS YOU TOOK YOUR SUDDEN JOURNEY 103   2 DON JUAN 1   151   1

TOOK   (CONTINUED)

	PAGE	VOL	CANTO		STANZA	LN
THEY TOOK BY FORCE FROM JUAN JULIA'S LETTER	195	2 DON JUAN	2		74	8
AND SO SHE TOOK THE LIBERTY TO STATE	240	2 DON JUAN	2		159	1
AND WORDS REPEATED AFTER HER HE TOOK	242	2 DON JUAN	2		163	2
PAID DAILY VISITS TO HER BOY AND TOOK	248	2 DON JUAN	2		174	2
AT LAST HER FATHER TOOK A VOYAGE TO SEA	248	2 DON JUAN	2		174	V5
BUT HE MORE MODEST TOOK AN HUMBLER RANGE	283	2 DON JUAN	3		14	5
AND TOOK HIS KINGDOM FROM HIM YOU WILL FIND	308	2 DON JUAN	3		65	6
THEY TOOK IT UP WHEN MY DAYS GREW MORE MELLOW	345	2 DON JUAN	4		3	3
HAIDEE AND JUAN THEIR SIESTA TOOK	359	2 DON JUAN	4		29	2
THE THIRD A WARY COOL OLD SWORDER TOOK	370	2 DON JUAN	4		49	2
SHE TOOK THEIR MEDICINES WITHOUT ASKING WHY	378	2 DON JUAN	4		63	V3
THEY TOOK HER WORD THAT HIS DULL ROAR WAS MELLOW	391	2 DON JUAN	4		87	V6
REIGN'D TILL ONE SUMMER'S DAY HE TOOK TO GRAZING	445	2 DON JUAN	5		60	4
HE PAUSED AND TOOK A SURVEY UP AND DOWN	456	2 DON JUAN	5		78	8
TOOK LEAVE WITH SUCH A FACE OF SATISFACTION	473	2 DON JUAN	5		107	7
EXPLAINS THE GARB WHICH JUAN TOOK AMISS	477	2 DON JUAN	5		114	8
SHE TOOK JUANNA BY THE HAND TO SHOW	31	3 DON JUAN	6		50	5
AND OF THIS BABA WILLINGLY TOOK NOTE	62	3 DON JUAN	6		113	6
OF DANUBE'S BANK TOOK FORMIDABLE CHARGE	72	3 DON JUAN	7		12	5
BUT CERTES MATTERS TOOK A DIFFERENT FACE	89	3 DON JUAN	7		47	1
DETACHMENT OF THREE COLUMNS TOOK ITS STATION	91	3 DON JUAN	7		50	3
HE MADE NO ANSWER BUT HE TOOK THE CITY	93	3 DON JUAN	7		53	8
OF HEROISM AND TOOK HIS PLACE WITH SOLEMN	130	3 DON JUAN	8		34	6
TOOK LIKE CAMELIONS SOME SLIGHT TINGE OF FEAR	148	3 DON JUAN	8		73	4
THEY TOOK THE BASTION WHICH THE SERASKIER	151	3 DON JUAN	8		79	7
AND I AM WITH YOU--WHEREON JOHNSON TOOK	161	3 DON JUAN	8		99	5
WHO TOOK BY TURNS THAT DIFFICULT COMMAND	205	3 DON JUAN	9		46	5
HE TOOK TO REGULARLY PEOPLING EARTH	312	3 DON JUAN	11		89	5
TRUE HE WAS ABSENT AND 'TWAS RUMOUR'D TOOK	430	3 DON JUAN	14		45	3
SHE TOOK UP WITH SOME FOREIGN YOUNGER BROTHER	474	3 DON JUAN	15		42	7
THEIR OFFICE HE TOOK UP AN OLD NEWSPAPER	512	3 DON JUAN	16		26	5
AND JUAN TOOK HIS PLACE HE KNEW NOT WHERE	542	3 DON JUAN	16		87	2
NOW THIS HE REALLY RATHER TOOK AMISS	544	3 DON JUAN	16		92	3

TOOKE

A PARAGRAPH I THINK ABOUT HORNE TOOKE	512	3 DON JUAN	16		27	3

TOOL

THE VULGAREST TOOL THAT TYRANNY COULD WANT	16	2 DON JUAN	D		12	5

TOOLS

GOOD WORKMEN NEVER QUARREL WITH THEIR TOOLS	136	2 DON JUAN	1		201	6
RAILING AT POWER--BUT ENVYING ALL IT'S TOOLS	152	2 DON JUAN	1	V	3	V7

TOOTHPICKS

FRENCH STUFFS LACE TWEEZERS TOOTHPICKS TEAPOT TRAY	284	2 DON JUAN	3		17	5
FRENCH STUFFS LACE TWEEZERS TOOTHPICKS A BIDET	284	2 DON JUAN	3		17	V5

TOP

THOUGH ON THE WAVE'S HIGH TOP TOO MUCH TO SET	188	2 DON JUAN	2		60	3
JUAN SLEPT LIKE A TOP OR LIKE THE DEAD	227	2 DON JUAN	2		134	2
A FINISHED GENTLEMAN FROM TOP TO TOE	354	3 DON JUAN	12		84	8
SHALL FOOL ME TO THE TOP UP OF MY BENT--	498	3 DON JUAN	15		94	3

TOPIC

IT IS AN AWFUL TOPIC--BUT 'TIS NOT	156	3 DON JUAN	8		89	1
MY TOPIC WITH OF COURSE THE DUE RESTRICTION	311	3 DON JUAN	11		88	2
A TOPIC SCANDAL DOTH DELIGHT TO ROUSE	370	3 DON JUAN	13		26	6
TREATING A TOPIC WHICH ALAS BUT BRINGS	500	3 DON JUAN	15		98	6

TOPIC'S

THE TOPIC'S TENDER SO SHALL BE MY PHRASE--	176	3 DON JUAN	8		128	5

TOPICS

ON GENERAL TOPICS POEMS MUST CONFINE	290	3 DON JUAN	11		44	7
AND LISTENING TO THE TOPICS MOST IN VOGUE	426	3 DON JUAN	14		37	4
OR SERIOUS ARE THE TOPICS I MUST BANISH	453	3 DON JUAN	14		98	5
ARE TOPICS WHICH I SOMETIMES INTRODUCE	497	3 DON JUAN	15		93	2

TOPOGRAPHY

AND NO GREAT DILETTANTI IN TOPOGRAPHY	149	3 DON JUAN	8		74	6

TOPS

ON MOUNTAINS TOPS MORE HEAVENLY WHITE THAN HER	314	2 DON JUAN	3		76	4

TOPSY-TURVY

THROWN TOPSY-TURVY TWISTED CRISPED AND CURLED	201	3 DON JUAN	9		37	4

TORCH

WHERE HYMEN'S TORCH BUT BRANDS ONE STRUMPET MORE	353	2 DON JUAN	4		17	7
WITH SWORD IN HAND AND TORCH TO LIGHT	518	3 DON JUAN	16	L	2	3

TORCHES

WITH TORCHES FRIENDS AND SERVANTS IN GREAT NUMBER	96	2 DON JUAN	1		138	2
THEIR HEARTS THE STARS THEIR NUPTIAL TORCHES SHED	265	2 DON JUAN	2		204	2
AND ONE ON TITHES WHICH SURE ARE DISCORD'S TORCHES	530	3 DON JUAN	16		60	4

TORE

THE RUDDER TORE AWAY 'TWAS TIME TO SOUND	170	2 DON JUAN	2		27	7
AND GNASH'D THEIR TEETH AND HOWLING TORE THEIR HAIR	180	2 DON JUAN	2		45	4
BUT ALWAYS DANGEROUS WHEN THE HIGH WINDS TORE	249	2 DON JUAN	2		177	V6
AT LEAST THREE PARTS OF THIS GREAT WHOLE) SHE TORE	211	3 DON JUAN	9		58	3

TORMENTED

TORMENTED WITH A WOUND HE COULD NOT KNOW	68	2 DON JUAN	1		87	3

TORMENTS

OF ENDLESS TORMENTS AND PERPETUAL MOTION	17	2 DON JUAN	D		13	8

TORN

AT LENGTH THE LOTS WERE TORN UP AND PREPARED	195	2 DON JUAN	2		74	5
WHEN THEY FROM THEIR SWEET FRIENDS ARE TORN APART	338	2 DON JUAN	3		108	3
WOULD WITHER LESS THAN THESE TWO TORN APART	349	2 DON JUAN	4		10	7
HE WITH THE BEARDLESS CHIN AND GARMENTS TORN	98	3 DON JUAN	7		62	6

TORNADO

BUT THE TENTH INSTANCE WILL BE A TORNADO	351	3 DON JUAN	12		77	7

TORRENT
    LIKE TO A TORRENT WHICH A MOUNTAIN'S BASE . . . . . . 231 2 DON JUAN 2   141   5
    FLOW'D LIKE AN ALPINE TORRENT WHICH THE SUN . . . . . . 313 2 DON JUAN 3   73   2
    BUT AS THE TORRENT WIDENS TOWARDS THE OCEAN . . . . . . 345 2 DON JUAN 4   2   7
    AND FRESH AS IS A TORRENT OR A TREE . . . . 145 3 DON JUAN 8   65   8
    ITS LITTLE TORRENT IN A THOUSAND BUBBLES . . . . 389 3 DON JUAN 13   65   7
TORRENT'S
    SOUND LIKE A DISTANT TORRENT'S FALL . . . . 323 2 DON JUAN 3 L 8   3
TORRENTS
    IT POUR'D DOWN TORRENTS BUT THEY WERE NO RICHER . . . . 201 2 DON JUAN 2   85   1
TORTOISE
    THE QUIET SHEEP FEEDS AND THE TORTOISE CRAWLS . . . . . 386 2 DON JUAN 4   77   8
    I WOULD NOT BE A TORTOISE IN HIS SCREEN . . . . 431 3 DON JUAN 14   49   3
TORTOISE-SHELL
    OR WERE OF TORTOISE-SHELL OR RARE WOODS MADE . . . . . 310 2 DON JUAN 3   69   4
TORTUOSITY
    LED BY SOME TORTUOSITY OF MIND . . . . 141 2 DON JUAN 1   208   3
TORTURE
    TORTURE IS THEIRS WHAT THEY INFLICT THEY FEEL . . . . . 262 2 DON JUAN 2   199   8
    TO THEM 'TIS A RELIEF TO US A TORTURE . . . . 479 2 DON JUAN 5   118   8
TORTURED
    WHILE NATURE TORTURED TWENTY THOUSAND WAYS . . . . . . 440 2 DON JUAN 5   52   6
TORTURING
    BEWITCHING TORTURING AS THEY FREEZE OR GLOW . . . . . . 438 3 DON JUAN 14   63   7
TORY
    ALTHOUGH 'TIS TRUE THAT YOU TURN'D OUT A TORY AT . . . .   9 2 DON JUAN D   1   3
    IS IT NOT SO MY TORY ULTRA-JULIAN . . . . 20 2 DON JUAN D   17   8
    TORY BY NURTURE WHIG BY CIRCUMSTANCE . . . . 152 2 DON JUAN 1 V 3   1
    WHICH NEVER FLATTERS EITHER WHIG OR TORY . . . . 465 3 DON JUAN 15   20 V7
TOSS
    THERE WAS A GENERAL WHISPER TOSS AND WRIGGLE . . . . . 501 2 DON JUAN 5   156   7
    TO TOSS TO TUMBLE DOZE REVIVE AND QUAKE . . . . 18 3 DON JUAN 6   24   7
    AND WILL NOT TOSS AND CHATTER THE NIGHT THROUGH . . . . 30 3 DON JUAN 6   49   6
TOSS'D
    NOT SO HAIDEE SHE SADLY TOSS'D AND TUMBLED . . . . . . 229 2 DON JUAN 2   138   1
TOSSED
    AND TOSSED ALONG THE VESSEL FORE AND AFT . . . . 155 2 DON JUAN 1 V 6   4
    TOSSED OVERBOARD UNSALEABLE (BEING OLD) . . . . 284 2 DON JUAN 3   16   4
    AND HOW HE HAD BEEN TOSSED HE SCARCE KNEW WHITHER . . . 338 3 DON JUAN 12   49   5
TOST
    TO WHAT PART OF THE EARTH THEY HAD BEEN TOST . . . . . 209 2 DON JUAN 2   100   5
TO'T
    GAVE WAY TO'T SINCE HE COULD NOT OVERCOME IT . . . . . 272 3 DON JUAN 11   9   4
    BECAUSE MY CASES PUT HIS LORDSHIP TO'T-- . . . . 357 3 DON JUAN 12 V 18   5
TOTALITY
    WHO WHEN WE COME TO SUM UP THE TOTALITY . . . . 108 3 DON JUAN 7   83   5
T'OTHER
    UNLESS THIS WORLD AND T'OTHER TOO BE BLIND . . . . . . 112 2 DON JUAN 1   165   4
    WHILE T'OTHER HALF WERE LAID DOWN IN THEIR PLACE . . . . 189 2 DON JUAN 2   63   5
    WOMEN ON T'OTHER HAND SEEM SOMEWHAT SILLY . . . . . . 14 3 DON JUAN 6   16   8
    CASE-MATED ONE AND T'OTHER A BARBETTE . . . . 72 3 DON JUAN 7   12   4
    FOR ONE WOULD NOT RETREAT NOR T'OTHER FLINCH . . . . . 150 3 DON JUAN 8   77   8
    WHO BUTCHERED HALF THE EARTH AND BULLIED T'OTHER . . . . 265 3 DON JUAN 10   81   8
    SEE NOUGHT MORE STRANGE IN THIS THAN T'OTHER LOTTERY . . 333 3 DON JUAN 12   37   8
    WHEN YOUR AFFAIRS COME ROUND ONE WAY OR T'OTHER . . . . 431 3 DON JUAN 14   48   7
    FOR T'OTHER ONE WHO PROMISES MUCH DUTY . . . . 471 3 DON JUAN 15   34   4
    A RUSS OR TURK--THE ONE'S AS GOOD AS T'OTHER . . . . . 474 3 DON JUAN 15   42   8
    OR EARTH BENEATH OR HEAVEN OR T'OTHER PLACE . . . . . 510 3 DON JUAN 16   23   2
    WHO HAVE HEARD MISS THAT OR THIS OR LADY T'OTHER . . . . 522 3 DON JUAN 16   44   7
TOTUS
    TO BE A TOTUS TERES STOIC SAGE . . . . 566 3 DON JUAN 17   10   7
TOUCH
    LIKE WHAT THIS LIGHT TOUCH LEFT ON JUAN'S HEART . . . . 60 2 DON JUAN 1   71   8
    ITS GENTLE TOUCH AND TREMBLING CARE A SIGH . . . . . . 215 2 DON JUAN 2   113   7
    SOME BROKEN PLANKS AND OARS THAT TO THE TOUCH . . . . . 226 2 DON JUAN 2   132   4
    NATURE WITH HIM TO THRILL BENEATH HIS TOUCH . . . . . . 247 2 DON JUAN 2   173   3
    TO THE FIRE-SIDE (A SIGHT TO TOUCH A SINNER) . . . . . 306 2 DON JUAN 3   60   6
    THE GENTLE PRESSURE AND THE THRILLING TOUCH . . . . . . 351 2 DON JUAN 4   14   1
    BUT THERE ARE FORMS WHICH TIME TO TOUCH FORBEARS . . . . 468 2 DON JUAN 5   98   3
    THE SIXTH SHALL HAVE A TOUCH OF THE SUBLIME . . . . . . 503 2 DON JUAN 5   159   6
    THE MUSE WILL TAKE A LITTLE TOUCH AT WARFARE . . . . . 65 3 DON JUAN 6   120   8
    WILL TOUCH EVEN HEROES AND SUCH WAS SUWARROW . . . . . 102 3 DON JUAN 7   69   8
    WHEN MATTERS MUST BE CARRIED BY THE TOUCH . . . . . . 151 3 DON JUAN 8   78   5
    AS THESE NEW CANTOS TOUCH ON WARLIKE FEATS . . . . . . 187 3 DON JUAN 9   10   1
    GIGANTIC GENTLEMEN YET HAD A TOUCH . . . . 209 3 DON JUAN 9   54   4
    WHICH SHRINK FROM TOUCH AS MONARCHS DO FROM RHYMES . . . 243 3 DON JUAN 10   37   3
    BUT THESE PRECAUTIONARY HINTS CAN TOUCH . . . . 305 3 DON JUAN 11   73   1
    I TOUCH A SINGLE LEAF WHERE HE IS WARDEN-- . . . . . . 442 3 DON JUAN 14   75   6
    DIED FROM THE TOUCH THAT KINDLED THEM TO SOUND . . . . . 521 3 DON JUAN 16   41   2
    OF THE OFFICIAL CANDIDATE I'LL TOUCH . . . . 538 3 DON JUAN 16   77   6
TOUCH'D
    HER NAILS WERE TOUCH'D WITH HENNA BUT AGAIN . . . . . . 314 2 DON JUAN 3   75   6
    FOR FEAR OF SEEMING RATHER TOUCH'D MYSELF-- . . . . . . 384 2 DON JUAN 4   74   4
    TOUCH'D HIS NOR THAT--NOR ANY HANDSOME LIMB . . . . . . 396 2 DON JUAN 4   95   5
    THE PARTY WE HAVE TOUCH'D ON WERE THE GUESTS . . . . . 404 3 DON JUAN 13   99   2
TOUCHED
    NOT TO BE RASHLY TOUCHED BUT STILL MORE DREAD . . . . . 37 3 DON JUAN 6   62   2
    ARE TOUCHED WITH A DESIRE TO SHIELD AND SAVE-- . . . . . 164 3 DON JUAN 8   106   3
    TOUCHED BY THE HEROISM OF HIM THEY SLEW . . . . 171 3 DON JUAN 8   119   5

TOUCHED   (CONTINUED)
    AS TOUCHED AND PLAINTIVELY BEGAN TO PLAY 517   3 DON JUAN 16   38   7
    IT TOUCHED NO SOUL NOR BODY BUT THE WALL 559   3 DON JUAN 16   120   2
TOUCHES
    BENEATH HIS CEASELESS TOUCHES THE HESPERIAN 208   3 DON JJAN 9   51   V7
TOUCHING
    MY PEGASUS SHALL TIRE OF TOUCHING GROUND 224   3 DON JUAN 9   85   3
    AURORA--SINCE WE ARE TOUCHING UPON TASTE 524   3 DON JUAN 16   48   1
TOUGH
    FINE TRUTHS EVEN CONSCIENCE TOO HAS A TOUGH JOB 264   2 DON JUAN 2   203   6
    AND NOW AND THEN WITH TOUGH STRINGS OF THE BOW 463   2 DON JUAN 5   89   5
    THAT DAILY SHILLING WHICH MAKES WARRIORS TOUGH)-- . . . 134   3 DON JUAN 8   42   6
    TO TOUGH OLD HEROES AND CAN DO NO LESS 167   3 DON JUAN 8   112   4
    'TIS STRANGE ENOUGH--THE ROUGH TOUGH SOLDIERS WHO . . . 171   3 DON JUAN 8   119   1
    WITHIN HER BOSOM (WHICH WAS NOT TOO TOUGH) 206   3 DON JUAN 9   48   4
    HOW SHOULD THE TENDER PASSION E'ER BE TOUGH 451   3 DON JUAN 14   94   8
TOUGHER
    AT THAT HIS HEART HAD GOT A TOUGHER RIND 353   3 DON JUAN 12   81   6
TOUR
    IS WORTH A TOUR TO ROME ALTHOUGH NO MORE A 428   3 DON JUAN 14   40   3
TOURS
    TO GUIDE-BOOKS RHYMES TOURS SKETCHES ILLUSTRATIONS . . 440   2 DON JUAN 5   52   8
    HIS JOURNEY WE'VE SO MANY TOURS OF LATE 203   3 DON JUAN 9   42   6
    CURE THEM OF TOURS HUSSAR AND HIGHLAND DRESSES 267   3 DON JUAN 10   86   2
TOUT
    THE TOUT ENSEMBLE OF HIS MOVEMENTS WORE A 428   3 DON JUAN 14   40   5
TOWELS
    SHRINKS FROM THE APPLICATION OF HOT TOWELS 168   2 DON JUAN 2   23   4
TOWER
    TO ADD A STORY TO THE TOWER OF BABEL 11   2 DON JUAN D   4   8
    THE SILVER LIGHT WHICH HALLOWING TREE AND TOWER 82   2 DON JUAN 1   114   5
    WHILE SWUNG THE DEEP BELL IN THE DISTANT TOWER 335   2 DON JUAN 3   102   5
    WHILE SWUNG THE SIGNAL FROM THE SACRED TOWER 335   2 DON JUAN 3   102   V5
    METHINKS THE STORY OF THE TOWER OF BABEL 444   2 DON JUAN 5   59   7
    SAD BUT SERENE IT SWEEPS O'ER TREE OR TOWER 388   3 DON JUAN 13   64   6
TOWER'D
    FLANK'D BY LARGE GROVES WHICH TOWER'D ON EITHER HAND . 433   2 DON JUAN 5   41   4
TOWERING
    AND FURTHER DOWNWARD TALL AND TOWERING STILL IS . . . 385   2 DON JUAN 4   76   5
TOWERS
    BUT THEN THEY NEVER CAME TO THE SEVEN TOWERS 497   2 DON JUAN 5   150   8
    FAR FLASHED HER BURNING TOWERS O'ER DANUBE'S STREAM . . 175   3 DON JUAN 8   127   3
TOWN
    A PRETTY TOWN I RECOLLECT IT WELL-- 159   2 DON JUAN 2   5   2
    AND THE SHIP CREAK'D THE TOWN BECAME A SPECK 163   2 DON JUAN 2   13   3
    A TOWN WAS TA'EN MYSELF INSTEAD OF WIDIN 418   2 DON JUAN 5   15   4
    A TOWN OF GARDENS WALLS AND WEALTH AMAZING 445   2 DON JUAN 5   60   2
    A TOWN WHICH DID A FAMOUS SIEGE ENDURE 70   3 DON JUAN 7   8   5
    BUT THE TOWN DITCH BELOW WAS DEEP AS OCEAN 72   3 DON JUAN 7   11   3
    ALSO TO HAVE THE SACKING OF A TOWN 75   3 DON JUAN 7   18   5
    YOU SHALL HAVE VENGEANCE FOR THE TOWN SURROUNDED . . . 98   3 DON JUAN 7   61   7
    TO BURN A TOWN WHICH NEVER DID THEM HARM 105   3 DON JUAN 7   76   8
    BUT NOW THE TOWN IS GOING TO BE ATTACKED 107   3 DON JUAN 7   81   5
    THE TOWN WAS ENTERED OH ETERNITY-- 142   3 DON JUAN 8   60   1
    GOD MADE THE COUNTRY AND MAN MADE THE TOWN 142   3 DON JUAN 8   60   2
    THE TOWN WAS ENTERED FIRST ONE COLUMN MADE 146   3 DON JUAN 8   69   1
    THE TOWN WAS TAKEN--WHETHER HE MIGHT YIELD 172   3 DON JUAN 8   122   1
    THERE WAS AN END OF ISMAIL--HAPLESS TOWN 175   3 DON JUAN 8   127   2
    ON A FOOL'S HEAD--AND THERE IS LONDON TOWN 265   3 DON JUAN 10   82   8
    POOR TOM WAS ONCE A KIDDY UPON TOWN 276   3 DON JUAN 11   17   5
    WHICH MAKE US WISH OURSELVES IN TOWN AT ONCE-- 277   3 DON JUAN 11   20   8
    FAR EASIER THOUGH FOR THE GOOD TOWN OF MANCHESTER . . . 314   3 DON JUAN 11 V 75   3
    FROM TOWN VIZ ARCHITECT AND DEALER WERE 533   3 DON JUAN 16   66   5
    SOME EXILES FROM THE TOWN WHO HAD BEEN DRIVEN 539   3 DON JUAN 16   81   2
    BEHELD BETWEEN THE COUNTRY AND THE TOWN 541   3 DON JUAN 16   85   3
TOWN'S
    ROSE OVER THE TOWN'S RIGHT SIDE IN BRISTLING TIER . . . 72   3 DON JUAN 7   12   7
    BUT FROM THE RIVER THE TOWN'S OPEN QUITE 73   3 DON JUAN 7   13   1
    BY NO MEANS WOULD PRODUCE THE TOWN'S SUBMISSION 81   3 DON JUAN 7   30   5
TOWNS
    OF ALL THE SPANISH TOWNS IS NONE MORE PRETTY 25   2 DON JUAN 1   8   5
    TOWNS NATIONS WORLDS IN HER REVOLVING PRANKS 135   3 DJN JUAN 8   44   5
    OF WAR AND TAKING TOWNS WHEN MANY A SHRIEK 141   3 DON JUAN 8   58   3
    TAKE TOWNS BY STORM NO CAUSES CAN I GUESS 176   3 DON JUAN 8   129   5
TOY
    PROUDER OF SUCH A TOY THAN OF THEIR BREED 391   3 DON JUAN 13   70   V6
TRACASSERIE
    THE DUCHESS OF FITZ-FULKE WHO LOVED TRACASSERIE 428   3 DON JUAN 14   41   7
TRACE
    I TRACE THIS SCRAWL BECAUSE I CANNOT REST-- 130   2 DON JUAN 1   193   7
    THE SHORE LOOK'D WILD WITHOUT A TRACE OF MAN 211   2 DON JUAN 2   104   1
    HAD MADE HER MISTRESS QUIT HER BED TO TRACE 240   2 DON JUAN 2   159   4
    AND TRACE IT IN THIS POEM EVERY LINE 346   2 DON JUAN 4   5   3
    LIKE TO HER FATHER'S FEATURES TILL EACH TRACE 363   2 DON JUAN 4   35   3
    CAN TRACE ALTHOUGH PERHAPS THE PENCIL MAY 462   2 DON JUAN 5   88   6
    NO LIPS E'ER LEFT THEIR TRANSITORY TRACE 472   2 DON JUAN 5   106   3
    BY DEEP EMOTION--YOU MAY SOMETIMES TRACE 61   3 DON JUAN 6   111   4
    NOR SWORD NOR SORROW YET HAD LEFT A TRACE 145   3 DON JUAN 8   65   4
    HAD SCARRED HER BROW AND LEFT ITS CRIMSON TRACE . . . 159   3 DON JUAN 8   95   5

```
                                                                PAGE VOL      CANTO STANZA LN
TRACE   (CONTINUED)
    TRACE UP THOSE SHUFFLING NEGROES NILE OR NIGER . . . . . 348  3 DON JUAN 12    70    2
    A TRACE UNWORTHY EITHER WIFE OR MAID-- . . . . . . . . . 372  3 DON JUAN 13    32   V5
    I CAN'T EXACTLY TRACE THEIR RULE OF RIGHT  . . . . . . . 397  3 DON JUAN 13    82    1
    TO TRACE ALL ACTIONS TO THEIR SECRET SPRINGS  . . . . . 436  3 DON JUAN 14    59    5
    HIS FORM YOU MAY TRACE BUT NOT HIS FACE . . . . . . . . 519  3 DON JUAN 16  L  4    5
    A LITTLE TURN FOR MISCHIEF YOU MIGHT TRACE . . . . . . . 525  3 DON JUAN 16    49    5
    WHICH SOME PRETEND TO TRACE IN LADIES' SMILES . . . . . 544  3 DON JUAN 16    92    8
TRACED
    OF MOOR OR HEBREW BLOOD HE TRACED HIS SOURCE . . . . . .  26  2 DON JUAN  1     9    3
    WHICH HANDS OR PENS HAVE EVER TRACED OF SWORDS . . . . . 179  3 DON JUAN  8   134    3
TRACERY
    CHECQUERED WITH ALL THE TRACERY OF THE HALL . . . . . . 559  3 DON JUAN 16   120    4
TRACES
    SIGH--AS THE POSTBOYS FASTEN ON THE TRACES  . . . . . . 378  3 DON JUAN 13    44    8
TRACK
    TO TRACK OUR HERO ON HIS PATH OF FAME . . . . . . . . . 120  3 DON JUAN  8    17    2
    NAPOLEON ON HIS BOLD AND BLOODY TRACK . . . . . . . . . 147  3 DON JUAN  8    70    3
TRADE
    A BUNGLER EVEN IN ITS DISGUSTING TRADE  . . . . . . .    18  2 DON JUAN  D    14    1
    LAWYER BY TRADE--AND ORATOR BY CHANCE . . . . . . . . . 152  2 DON JUAN  1  V  3   V5
    'TIS THERE THE MART OF THE COLONIAL TRADE IS  . . . . . 159  2 DON JUAN  2     5    3
    FULL MANY A MORSEL FOR THAT TURKISH TRADE . . . . . . . 223  2 DON JUAN  2   126    7
    AS IF WELL-USED TO THE RETREATING TRADE . . . . . . . . 473  2 DON JUAN  5   107    3
    MEN'S HEARTS AGAINST WHOLE MILLIONS WHEN THEIR TRADE . . 102  3 DON JUAN  7    69    6
    FOR TIMOUR OR FOR ZINGHIS IN HIS TRADE  . . . . . . . . 178  3 DON JUAN  8   133    2
    AS IF BORN FOR THE MINISTERIAL TRADE  . . . . . . . . . 223  3 DON JUAN  9    83    4
    A DREADFUL TRADE LIKE HIS WHO GATHERS SAMPHIRE . . . . . 299  3 DON JUAN 11    62    3
    TRADE WILL BE ALL THE BETTER FOR THESE CANTOS . . . . . 416  3 DON JUAN 14    14    8
TRADESMAN
    LIKE A MEEK TRADESMAN WHEN APPROACHING PALELY . . . . . 459  3 DON JUAN 15     8    3
TRADESMAN'S
    WHETHER A SKY'S OR TRADESMAN'S IS ALL ONE  . . . . . . . 423  3 DON JUAN 14    29    8
TRADESMEN
    AND TRADESMEN WITH LONG BILLS AND LONGER FACES . . . . . 378  3 DON JUAN 13    44    7
TRADITION
    TO HISTORY TRADITION AND TO FACTS . . . . . . . . . . . 138  2 DON JUAN  1   203    2
    KNEW (BY TRADITION FOR SHE NE'ER HAD READ) . . . . . . . 239  2 DON JUAN  2   158    6
    SOME BY EXPERIENCE OTHERS BY TRADITION . . . . . . . . . 477  2 DON JUAN  5   115    8
    THE THEME HALF CREDITED THE STRANGE TRADITION . . . . . 527  3 DON JUAN 16    54    4
TRADITIONAL
    ANY ONE ELSE--THEY WERE BECOME TRADITIONAL . . . . . . .  37  2 DON JUAN  1    31    4
TRAFALGAR
    THERE'S NO MORE TO BE SAID OF TRAFALGAR . . . . . . . .  23  2 DON JUAN  1     4    3
TRAGEDIES
    ALL TRAGEDIES ARE FINISH'D BY A DEATH . . . . . . . . . 280  2 DON JUAN  3     9    1
TRAIL
    AND SHIVER THEM TO ASHES BUT TO TRAIL . . . . . . . . . 348  2 DON JUAN  4     9    6
TRAIN
    BUT DONNA INEZ TO DIVERT THE TRAIN . . . . . . . . . . . 128  2 DON JUAN  1   190    1
    SOME TWENTY OF HIS TRAIN CAME RANK ON RANK . . . . . . . 369  2 DON JUAN  4    47    7
    THE TRAIN MIGHT REACH A QUARTER OF A MILE  . . . . . . . 495  2 DON JUAN  5   146    3
    ON WHICH JACK AND HIS TRAIN SET OFF AT SPEED . . . . . . 275  3 DON JUAN 11    14    1
TRAINING
    A PANORAMA VIEW OF HELL'S IN TRAINING . . . . . . . . . 135  2 DON JUAN  1   200    6
    FOR LIKE A RACER OR A BOXER TRAINING . . . . . . . . . . 366  3 DON JUAN 13    18    7
TRAIN-OIL
    HIDES TRAIN-OIL TALLOW AND THE RIGHTS OF THETIS  . . . . 246  3 DON JUAN 10    45    7
TRAIT
    IF HERE AND THERE SOME TRANSIENT TRAIT OF PITY . . . . . 174  3 DON JUAN  8   124    1
TRAITORS
    THEIR COUNTRY AND AS TRAITORS ARE ABHORRED  . . . . . .  77  3 DON JUAN  7    22    6
TRAITS
    THE TRAITS OF SLEEPING SORROW AND BETRAYED  . . . . . .  40  3 DON JUAN  6    67    4
    WHOSE TRAITS WERE RADIANT WITH THE RAYS OF VERITY . . . 550  3 DON JUAN 16   102    4
TRAMP
    TRAMP TRAMP O'ER PEBBLE AND SPLASH SPLASH THRO PUDDLE . 260  3 DON JUAN 10    71    2
    TRAMP TRAMP O'ER PEBBLE AND SPLASH SPLASH THRO PUDDLE . 260  3 DON JUAN 10    71    2
TRAMPLE
    WITH HIS SUPERIOR IN A SMILE TO TRAMPLE . . . . . . . . 189  3 DON JUAN  9    13    4
TRAMPLED
    TRAMPLED WHAT THEY SCARCE TROD FOR FEAR OF STAINING . . 450  2 DON JUAN  5    66    3
TRAMPLES
    WHICH IS A SAD THING AND NOT ONLY TRAMPLES . . . . . . . 236  3 DON JUAN 10    23    4
TRAMPLING
    STRENGTHENING THE WEAK AND TRAMPLING ON THE STRONG  . .  78  2 DON JUAN  1   106    4
    BUT ON THEY MARCHED DEAD BODIES TRAMPLING O'ER  . . . . 120  2 DON JUAN  8    19    5
    TRAMPLING ON PLATO'S PRIDE WITH GREATER PRIDE  . . . . . 522  3 DON JUAN 16    43    3
TRANCE
    HOW LONG IN HIS DAMP TRANCE YOUNG JUAN LAY  . . . . . . 214  2 DON JUAN  2   111    1
    OR PEOPLE IN A TRANCE INTO THEIR GRAVE . . . . . . . . . 225  2 DON JUAN  2   130    4
    WITH INFANT TERRORS GLARED AS FROM A TRANCE . . . . . . 159  3 DON JUAN  8    96    6
    TO THIS IMPRACTICABLE NOVEL-READING TRANCE  . . . . . . 450  3 DON JUAN 14    92   V6
TRANQUIL
    FOR THERE IT LIES SO TRANQUIL SO BELOVED . . . . . . . . 261  2 DON JUAN  2   197    1
    EXTREMELY TRANQUIL ANCHORED AT ITS STATION . . . . . . .  78  3 DON JUAN  7    24    4
    WAS TRANQUIL THOUGH SHE KNEW NOT WHY OR WHEREFORE . . . 250  3 DON JUAN 10    52    8
TRANQUILLY
    ALL TRANQUILLY THE SHIPWRECK'D BOY WAS LYING  . . . . . 233  2 DON JUAN  2   144    3
```

		PAGE	VOL	CANTO	STANZA	LN
TRANSACTION						
WHAT IS HIS OWN--GO LOOK AT EACH TRANSACTION	. . . .	321	3 DON JUAN	12	11	4
TRANSACTIONS						
TO DO WITH THE TRANSACTIONS OF MY HERO	. . . . .	341	2 DON JUAN	3	110	3
BUT BURIED IN THE HEAP OF SUCH TRANSACTIONS	. . . .	83	3 DON JUAN	7	34	3
TRANSCENDANT						
WHO GAZED UPON HER CHEEK'S TRANSCENDANT HUE	. . .	27	3 DON JUAN	6	42	3
OF SUCH TRANSCENDANT AND MORE FLEETING FLIGHT	. . . .	66	3 DON JUAN	7	1	4
LEND TO THAT COLOUR A TRANSCENDANT RAY	. . . . .	218	3 DON JUAN	9	71	6
WITH TWO TRANSCENDANT EYES SEEMED TO LOOK THROUGH HIM	.	489	3 DON JUAN	15	75	8
TRANSCENDS						
A GUST--WHICH ALL DESCRIPTIVE POWER TRANSCENDS--	. . .	172	2 DON JUAN	2	30	7
TRANSFER						
BUT NOW I MUST TRANSFER HER TO THE CHARGE	. . . .	46	3 DON JUAN	6	81	7
TRANSFERR'D						
TRANSFERR'D TO GORGE UPON A SISTER SHORE	. . . . .	16	2 DON JUAN	D	12	4
WE WERE TRANSFERR'D ON BOARD HER IN A HURRY	. . . .	389	2 DON JUAN	4	82	5
TRANSFERRED						
AND APT TO BE TRANSFERRED TO THE FIRST BUYER	. . .	14	3 DON JUAN	6	16	6
TRANSFERS						
THE LAST YEAR TO THE NEW TRANSFERS ITS HOARDS	. . . .	340	3 DON JUAN	12	53	5
TRANSFIGURE						
THEY CAN TRANSFIGURE BRIGHTER THAN A RAPHAEL	. . .	463	3 DON JUAN	15	16	8
TRANSFIXED						
UNTO HIS PROTEGEE WHILE HER'S TRANSFIXED	. . . . .	159	3 DON JUAN	8	96	5
TRANSFORMATION						
A PERFECT TRANSFORMATION HERE DISPLAYED	. . . . .	458	2 DON JUAN	5	80	5
I COMPREHEND FOR WITHOUT TRANSFORMATION	. . . . .	192	3 DON JUAN	9	20	7
TRANSFORM'D						
TRANSFORM'D THEIR LORDS TO BEASTS (BUT THAT'S A FACT)	.	293	2 DON JUAN	3	34	8
TRANSGRESSES						
TRANSGRESSES THE GREAT BOUNDS OF LOVE OR AWE	. . .	563	3 DON JUAN	17	2	6
TRANSGRESSION						
AND BURNING BLUSHES THOUGH FOR NO TRANSGRESSION	. .	62	2 DON JUAN	1	74	3
WHICH DOUBLES WHAT THEY THINK OF THE TRANSGRESSION	. .	11	3 DON JUAN	6	10	4
BUT THOUGH THREE BISHOPS TOLD HER THE TRANSGRESSION	. .	252	3 DON JUAN	10	56	3
SMOOTH SPEECH HIS FIRST AND MAIDENLY TRANSGRESSION	. .	400	3 DON JUAN	13	90	4
TRANSGRESSIONS						
WHICH MAKE THE READER ENVY HIS TRANSGRESSIONS	. . .	47	2 DON JUAN	1	47	8
TRANSIENT						
BUT 'TWAS A TRANSIENT TREMOR--WITH A SPRING	. . . .	170	3 DON JUAN	8	118	1
IF HERE AND THERE SOME TRANSIENT TRAIT OF PITY	. . .	174	3 DON JUAN	8	124	1
AND TRANSIENT AND DEVOURED BY THE SAME HARPY	. . .	310	3 DON JUAN	11	86	3
TRANSITORY						
NO LIPS E'ER LEFT THEIR TRANSITORY TRACE	. . . . .	472	2 DON JUAN	5	106	3
OR LADIES' FANCIES--RATHER TRANSITORY	. . . . .	229	3 DON JUAN	10	9	4
BLOOMED ALSO IN LESS TRANSITORY HUES	. . . . .	293	3 DON JUAN	11	48	2
TRANSLATE						
AS A RULE BUT TRUTH MAY IF YOU TRANSLATE IT	. . . .	15	3 DON JUAN	6	18	8
YE RIGID GUTS OF REAPERS--I TRANSLATE	. . . . .	190	3 DON JUAN	9	15	2
THE FACT FOR WORDS AND LET THE FRENCH TRANSLATE	. .	405	3 DON JUAN	13	101	7
(THUS WE TRANSLATE A GENERAL INVITATION)	. . . . .	534	3 DON JUAN	16	69	2
TRANSLATED						
(WHO AT SIXTEEN TRANSLATED HERCULES FURENS)	. . . .	294	3 DON JUAN	11	52	6
CONTENTED WHEN TRANSLATED MEANS BUT CLOYED	. . . .	444	3 DON JUAN	14	79	5
TRANSLATION						
FROM HIS TRANSLATION BUT HAD NONE ADMIRED	. . . .	470	2 DON JUAN	5	101	7
TRANSMISSION						
I CALL SUCH THINGS TRANSMISSION FOR THERE IS	. . .	340	3 DON JUAN	12	52	1
TRANSMITTED						
WITH AN HIDALGO WHO TRANSMITTED DOWN	. . . . .	52	2 DON JUAN	1	57	2
TO BE TRANSMITTED LIKE THE LORD MAYOR'S BARGE	. . .	339	3 DON JUAN	12	51	6
TRANSPARENT						
MOUNTING AT TIMES TO A TRANSPARENT GLOW	. . . .	55	2 DON JUAN	1	61	5
AND HER TRANSPARENT CHEEK ALL PURE AND WARM	. . .	216	2 DON JUAN	2	114	4
BUT A WHITE BARACAN AND SO TRANSPARENT	. . . . .	315	2 DON JUAN	3	77	2
A PURE TRANSPARENT PALE YET RADIANT FACE	. . . . .	159	3 DON JUAN	8	96	7
BROAD AS TRANSPARENT DEEP AND FRESHLY FED	. . . .	385	3 DON JUAN	13	57	2
TRANSPIRE						
SAID BABA TO BE CURIOUS 'TWILL TRANSPIRE	. . . . .	454	2 DON JUAN	5	74	6
TRANSPLANTED						
OF ROME TRANSPLANTED FELL WITH CONSTANTINE	. . . .	461	2 DON JUAN	5	86	8
TRANSPORT						
WHERE TRANSPORT AND SECURITY ENTWINE	. . . .	69	2 DON JUAN	1	88	2
FOR THAT SAME TWINING TRANSPORT AND SECURITY	. . .	69	2 DON JUAN	1	88	7
OR TRANSPORT AS WE KNEW ALL THAT BEFORE	. . . .	69	2 DON JUAN	1	89	7
WHO IN THEIR TRANSPORT NEVER DREAMED OF WOE	. . .	353	2 DON JUAN	4	18	V3
THY GARMENT'S HEM WITH TRANSPORT CAN IT BE	. . .	364	2 DON JUAN	4	38	6
TRANSPORTATION						
SEVEN YEARS (THE USUAL TERM OF TRANSPORTATION)	. . .	257	3 DON JUAN	10	66	6
TRAP						
THERE WERE TWO POACHERS CAUGHT IN A STEEL TRAP	. . .	530	3 DON JUAN	16	61	1
TRAPS						
TRAPS FOR THE TRAVELLER EVERY HIGHWAY'S CLEAR	. . .	273	3 DON JUAN	11	10	6
MAY BE THE TRAPS FOR THEIR CONNUBIAL LORDS	. . . .	340	3 DON JUAN	12	53	V3
TRASH						
AN ORATOR OF SUCH SET TRASH OF PHRASE	. . . . .	17	2 DON JUAN	D	13	1
THAT TRASH OF SUCH SORT NOT ALONE EVADES	. . . .	334	2 DON JUAN	3	100	3
TRAVEL						
SHE HAD RESOLVED THAT HE SHOULD TRAVEL THROUGH	. . .	129	2 DON JUAN	1	191	1

```
                                                                  PAGE VOL    CANTO STANZA LV
TRAVEL   (CONTINUED)
     HE WAS TO TRAVEL AND THOUGH INEZ GRIEVED . . . . .  . . 161  2 DON JUAN  2     9    4
     YOUNG MEN SHOULD TRAVEL IF BUT TO AMUSE  . . . . .  . . 165  2 DON JUAN  2    16    5
     AFTER LONG TRAVEL ENNUI LOVE OR SLAUGHTER  . . . .  . . 251  2 DON JUAN  2   180    7
     HAD SKETCHES OF LOVE TEMPEST TRAVEL WAR--   . . . .  . . 181  3 DON JUAN  8   138    3
     THE FACULTY--WHO SAID THAT HE MUST TRAVEL  . . . .  . . 245  3 DON JUAN 10    43    8
     AT THE GREAT END OF TRAVEL--WHICH IS DRIVING . . .  . . 260  3 DON JUAN 10    72    8
     FOR AFTER YEARS OF TRAVEL BY A BARD IN  . . . . .   . . 262  3 DON JUAN 10    76    3
     IF BUT TO SHOW I'VE TRAVELL'D AND WHAT'S TRAVEL  .  . . 380  3 DON JUAN 13    47    7
TRAVELL'D
     HE HAD TRAVELL'D 'MONGST THE ARABS TURKS AND FRANKS . . 319  2 DON JUAN  3    84    1
     HAVE GOT A TRAVELL'D AIR WHICH SHOWS YOU ONE  . . .  . . 392  2 DON JUAN  4    88    3
     IF BUT TO SHOW I'VE TRAVELL'D AND WHAT'S TRAVEL  .  . . 380  3 DON JUAN 13    47    7
TRAVELLED
     BECAUSE ONE POET TRAVELLED 'MONGST THE TURKS)  . .  . . 434  2 DON JUAN  5    42    8
     THOUGH TRAVELLED I HAVE NEVER HAD THE LUCK TO  . .  . . 348  3 DON JUAN 12    70    1
TRAVELLER
     HAD FEATHERS WHEN A TRAVELLER ON DEEP WAYS IS . . .  . . 197  3 DON JUAN  9    30    8
     TRAPS FOR THE TRAVELLER EVERY HIGHWAY'S CLEAR . . .  . . 273  3 DON JUAN 11    10    6
     (SUCH EARLY TRAVELLER IS THE TRUTH THOU LEARNEST)-- . . 345  3 DON JUAN 12    64    6
TRAVELLERS
     HUMBOLDT THE FIRST OF TRAVELLERS BUT NOT . . . . .  . . 406  2 DON JUAN  4   112    1
     AS TRAVELLERS FOLLOW OVER BOG AND BRAKE  . . . . .  . . 127  3 DON JUAN  8    32    4
     HUT WHENCE WISE TRAVELLERS DRIVE WITH CIRCUMSPECTION . . 238  3 DON JUAN 10    27    6
     HUT WHERE WE TRAVELLERS BAIT WITH DIM REFLECTION .  . . 238  3 DON JUAN 10    27   V6
     OF TRAVELLERS TO MIGHTY BABYLON . . . . . . . . .   . . 279  3 DON JUAN 11    23    2
TRAVELLING
     AFTER LONG TRAVELLING BY LAND OR WATER  . . . . .   . . 287  2 DON JUAN  3    22    2
     OR TRAVELLING IN PATAGONIAN LANDS . . . . . . . .   . .  20  3 DON JUAN  6    28    5
TRAVELS
     TOMBUCTOO TRAVELS VOYAGES TO THE POLES   . . . . .  . .  93  2 DON JUAN  1   132    6
     OF FREE THOUGHTS IN HIS TRAVELS FOR VARIETY . . .   . . 318  2 DON JUAN  3    83    3
     HIS TRAVELS TO THE CAPITAL APACE--  . . . . . . .   . . 277  3 DON JUAN 11    18    4
     AND WHETHER IN HIS TRAVELS HE SAW ILION  . . . . .  . . 294  3 DON JUAN 11    50    8
TRAVERSES
     THE TURKS BEHIND THE TRAVERSES AND FLANKS  . . . .  . . 134  3 DON JUAN  8    44    1
TRAVESTY
     THE CAUSE OF THIS ODD TRAVESTY--FORBEAR . . . . .   . . 454  2 DON JUAN  5    74    5
TRAY
     FRENCH STUFFS LACE TWEEZERS TOOTHPICKS TEAPOT TRAY  . . 284  2 DON JUAN  3    17    5
     ADVANCING TO THE NEAREST DINNER TRAY . . . . . .    . . 297  2 DON JUAN  3    42    1
     WAS WONT TO BOAST--AS IF A GLUTTON'S TRAY  . . . .  . . 538  3 DON JUAN 16    78    3
TRAYS
     AND HERE ASSEMBLED CROSS-LEGG'D ROUND THEIR TRAYS  . . 291  2 DON JUAN  3    31    1
TREACHERY
     THE LOSS OF LOVE THE TREACHERY OF FRIENDS  . . . .  . . 167  2 DON JUAN  2    21    4
     AWAITS THEM TREACHERY IS ALL THEIR TRUST . . . .   . . 263  2 DON JUAN  2   200    3
TREAD
     AND FEET SO SMALL THEY SCARCE SEEMED MADE TO TREAD  . .  26  3 DON JUAN  6    41    4
     WITH EAGER EYES AND LIGHT BUT HURRIED TREAD . . .   . .  42  3 DON JUAN  6    72    3
     A RUSSIAN OFFICER IN MARTIAL TREAD  . . . . . . .  . . 153  3 DON JUAN  8    83    1
     OF FAIR PHILOSOPHY OR WHERE 'TIS THEY TREAD  . . .  . . 284  3 DON JUAN 11    34   V6
     HE WOULD NOT TREAD A FACTIOUS PATH TO PRAISE  . .  . . 536  3 DON JUAN 16    73    5
TREADING
     OR ROUGHLY TREADING ON THE COURTIER'S KIBES . . .  . . 200  3 DON JUAN  9    35    6
TREASON
     AND STAND CONVICTED OF MORE TRUTH THAN TREASON . .  . .  76  2 DON JUAN  1   102    6
     'TWAS TREASON TO BEHOLD HER AND NOT KNEEL  . . .   . . 313  2 DON JUAN  3    74   V8
     THEIR LOYAL TREASON RENEGADO RIGOUR  . . . . . .   . . 330  2 DON JUAN  3    94    3
     OF TRUTH--SUCH TRUTHS ARE TREASON THEY BETRAY . .  . .  77  3 DON JUAN  7    22    5
     WITH SOME SLIGHT HEART-QUAKE OF DOMESTIC TREASON--  . . 370  3 DON JUAN 13    26    5
TREASURE
     AND MUST HAVE COST HIS MAJESTY A TREASURE  . . . .  . .  85  2 DON JUAN  1   118    4
     BUT WHETHER GLORY POWER OR LOVE OR TREASURE . . .   . .  93  2 DON JUAN  1   133    6
     THE SECRET CAVERN OF THIS LURKING TREASURE--  . .  . . 104  2 DON JUAN  1   153    7
     TIME IS TIME WAS TIME'S PAST A CHYMIC TREASURE . .  . . 145  2 DON JUAN  1   217    6
     JOY OF ITS GLITTERING TREASURE AND REPEAT  . . . .  . . 264  2 DON JUAN  2   203   V5
     IN GETTING OUT GOODS BALLAST GUNS AND TREASURE . .  . . 286  2 DON JUAN  3    20    8
     COMPARED WITH WHAT HAIDEE DID WITH HIS TREASURE .   . . 295  2 DON JUAN  3    39    6
     THOUGH SAGES MAY POUR OUT THEIR WISDOM'S TREASURE   . . 308  2 DON JUAN  3    65    7
     YET UNDISCOVERED TREASURE WHAT I CAN . . . . . .   . . 281  3 DON JUAN 11    28    6
     WHICH HOLDS A TREASURE LIKE A MISER'S HOARD . . .   . . 422  3 DON JUAN 14    27    3
TREASURES
     OF SECRET TREASURES FOUND IN HIDDEN VALES  . . . .  . . 293  2 DON JUAN  3    34    3
TREAT
     AND IS IT THUS A FAITHFUL WIFE YOU TREAT . . . . .  . . 103  2 DON JUAN  1   150    3
     TREAT A DISSENTING AUTHOR VERY MARTYRLY  . . . . .  . . 142  2 DON JUAN  1   211    8
     AND FIND A QUINSY VERY HARD TO TREAT . . . . . .   . . 168  2 DON JUAN  2    22    4
     WHEN THEIR LIEGE HUSBANDS TREAT THEM WITH INGRATITUDE . 11  3 DON JUAN  6    11    6
     BEGAN TO TREAT HIM WITH SOME SMALL AGACERIE . . .   . . 428  3 DON JUAN 14    41    8
TREATED
     HOW I HAVE TREATED IT I DO NOT KNOW  . . . . . .   . . 347  2 DON JUAN  4     7    1
     PERHAPS NO BETTER THAN THEY HAVE TREATED ME . . .   . . 347  2 DON JUAN  4     7    2
     LEFT IT BEFORE HE HAD BEEN TREATED VERY ILL . . .  . . 300  3 DON JUAN 11    64    5
TREATING
     AND TREATING A YOUNG WIFE WITH SO MUCH RIGOUR . .  . . 110  2 DON JUAN  1   161    4
     TREATING A TOPIC WHICH ALAS BUT BRINGS . . . . .   . . 500  3 DON JUAN 15    98    6
TREATISE
     I'VE GOT A PLAN TO FORM A TREATISE WHICH . . . .   . . 138  2 DON JUAN  1   204   V2
```

```
                                                         PAGE VOL      CANTO STANZA LN
TREATMENT
     INTENTIONS BUT THEIR TREATMENT WAS NOT KIND . . . . . .   34  2 DON JUAN  1    24   2
TREATS
     THE BOOK WHICH TREATS OF THIS ERRONEOUS PAIR . . . .    282  2 DON JUAN  3    12   6
     AND AS SHE TREATS ALL THINGS AND NE'ER RETREATS . . . .  502  3 DON JUAN 16     3   1
TREATY
     A SORT OF TREATY OR NEGOCIATION . . . . . . . . .        246  3 DON JUAN 10    45   2
TREBLE
     THE HIGH WIND MADE THE TREBLE AND AS BASS . . . . .      174  2 DON JUAN  2    34   4
TRECENTISTI
     IN ITALY HE'D APE THE TRECENTISTI . . . . . . .          320  2 DON JUAN  3    86   7
     IN ENGLAND HE WOULD APE THE TRECENTISTI . . . . . .      320  2 DON JUAN  3    86  V2
TREE
     THE SILVER LIGHT WHICH HALLOWING TREE AND TOWER . . .     82  2 DON JUAN  1   114   5
     THE TREE OF KNOWLEDGE HAS BEEN PLUCK'D--ALL'S KNOWN--     90  2 DON JUAN  1   127   4
     STILL IN HER TEENS AND LIKE A LOVELY TREE . . . .        224  2 DON JUAN  2   128   5
     OF LIFE'S STRANGE TREE SO FRUITFUL ON OCCASION . . .     250  2 DON JUAN  2   179   6
     WEARY UNLESS WHEN SEPARATE THE TREE . . . . . .          349  2 DON JUAN  4    10   3
     UNTIL THE TREE OF KNOWLEDGE WAS PULLED DOWN . . .        476  2 DON JUAN  5   113  V8
     SHE WOULD HAVE CUT THE TREE OF KNOWLEDGE DOWN . . .      476  2 DON JUAN  5   113  V7
     ON MOST THINGS FROM A TYRANT TO A TREE . . . . .          37  3 DON JUAN  6    63   4
     NODS FROM THE TREE WAS SLUMBERING WITH SOFT BREATH        38  3 DON JUAN  6    65   7
     HE DIED BENEATH A TREE AS MUCH UNBLEST ON . . . .         84  3 DON JUAN  7    36   6
     OF THINE IMAGINARY DEATHLESS TREE . . . . . .            101  3 DON JUAN  7    68   7
     AND FRESH AS IS A TORRENT OR A TREE . . . . . .          145  3 DON JUAN  8    65   8
     THE RUGGED TREE UNTO THE SUMMER WIND . . . . . .         164  3 DON JUAN  8   106   7
     THE EARTH WHICH HE BECAME LIKE A FELLED TREE . . .       169  3 DON JUAN  8   116   6
     UPON THE TREE WHICH EVE SO FONDLY SEARCHED . . . .       192  3 DON JUAN  9    19   8
     HE NOW WAS GROWING UP LIKE A GREEN TREE ABLE . . .       235  3 DON JUAN 10    22   5
     TOLD OF THEIR SIRES A TOMB IN EVERY TREE . . . .         381  3 DON JUAN 13    50   8
     SAD BUT SERENE IT SWEEPS O'ER TREE OR TOWER . . .        388  3 DON JUAN '13    64   6
     WITH ALL HIS LAURELS GROWING UPON ONE TREE . . . .       401  3 DON JUAN 13    91  V7
     THE EARLIEST KNOWLEDGE FROM THE TREE SO KNOWING . .      444  3 DON JUAN 14    78   3
     BUT MANY A LONELY TREE THE LOFTIER GROWS . . . . .       562  3 DON JUAN 17     1   3
TREES
     HIS GARDEN TREES ALL SHADOWY AND GREEN . . . . .         289  2 DON JUAN  3    27   2
     AND TREES OF GOODLY GROWTH AND SPREADING ROOTS . . .      43  3 DON JUAN  6    75   8
     WHEN THEY BUILT UP UNTO HIS DARLING TREES-- . . . .      144  3 DON JUAN  8    64   2
     THROUGH GROVES SO CALLED AS BEING VOID OF TREES . . .    278  3 DON JUAN 11    21   1
TREMBLED
     WHICH TREMBLED LIKE THE BOSOM WHERE 'TWAS PLACED . . .    83  2 DON JUAN  1   115   3
     IT TREMBLED AS MAGNETIC NEEDLES DO . . . . . . .         134  2 DON JUAN  1   198   4
TREMBLES
     OR HOW IS'T MATTER TREMBLES TO COME NEAR IT . . . .      557  3 DON JUAN 16   116   8
TREMBLING
     AS TURNS THE NEEDLE TREMBLING TO THE POLE . . . .        133  2 DON JUAN  1   196  V7
     ITS GENTLE TOUCH AND TREMBLING CARE A SIGH . . . .       215  2 DON JUAN  2   113   7
     WHOSE RAYS SHONE EVER TREMBLING BUT INCESSANT . . .      315  2 DON JUAN  3    77   8
     ALL TREMBLING WONDERING WITHOUT THE LEAST NOTION . .      42  3 DON JUAN  6    71   6
     AND BOWED HER THROBBING HEAD O'ER TREMBLING KNEES .       59  3 DON JUAN  6   107   8
     BUT STOOD IN TREMBLING PATIENT TRIBULATION . . . .       532  3 DON JUAN 16    65   7
     MY TREMBLING LYRE ALREADY SEVERAL STRINGS . . . .        568  3 DON JUAN 17    13   5
TREMBLINGS
     TREMBLINGS WHEN MET AND RESTLESSNESS WHEN LEFT . . . .    62  2 DON JUAN  1    74   4
TREMENDOUS
     METHINKS THESE ARE THE MOST TREMENDOUS WORDS . . . .     179  3 DON JUAN  8   134   1
     TREMENDOUS TO A MORTAL TYMPANUM . . . . . . .            557  3 DON JUAN 16   115   6
TREMOR
     EVEN AS THEY GAZED A SUDDEN TREMOR CAME . . . . .        355  2 DON JUAN  4    21   2
     A SLIGHT BLUSH A SOFT TREMOR A CALM KIND . . . .          13  3 DON JUAN  6    15   1
     BUT 'TWAS A TRANSIENT TREMOR--WITH A SPRING . . . .      170  3 DON JUAN  8   118   1
TREMORS
     HE CANNOT SINK HIS TREMORS OR HIS TERRORS . . . . .      457  3 DON JUAN 15     4   6
TREMULOUSLY
     AND TREMULOUSLY GENTLE HER SMALL HAND . . . . . .         60  2 DON JUAN  1    71   2
TRENCH
     'TIS BUILT BEGIRT WITH BATTERY AND TRENCH . . . . .       71  3 DON JUAN  7     9  V4
TREPANNED
     TO SAY HER DAUGHTER'S FEELINGS ARE TREPANNED . . . .     343  3 DON JUAN 12    60   2
TRESSES
     OF HER DISHEVELLED TRESSES DARK APPEARS . . . . .        108  2 DON JUAN  1   158  V4
     BRINGING WARM WATER WREATHING HER LONG TRESSES . . .     252  2 DON JUAN  2   182   7
     HALF BURIED IN THE TRESSES WHICH IT GRASPS . . . .       259  2 DON JUAN  2   194   4
     CRIMSON AS CLEFT POMEGRANATES THEIR LONG TRESSES . .     292  2 DON JUAN  3    33   3
     SO MANY FALSE LONG TRESSES ALL TO SPARE . . . . .        457  2 DON JUAN  5    79   3
     ONE WITH HER AUBURN TRESSES LIGHTLY BOUND . . . .         38  3 DON JUAN  6    65   5
     FELL IN LONG TRESSES LIKE THE WEEPING WILLOW . . . .      60  3 DON JUAN  6   108   2
     AND TRUCULENT DISTORTION OF THEIR TRESSES . . . .        550  3 DON JUAN 16   103   8
     AND HOTTENTOT ADJUSTMENT OF THEIR TRESSES . . . .        550  3 DON JUAN 16   103  V8
TRIAL
     I RECOMMEND YOUNG LADIES TO MAKE TRIAL . . . . .          64  2 DON JUAN  1    78   8
     AS ALL HAVE FOUND ON TRIAL OR MAY FIND . . . . .          69  2 DON JUAN  1    89   4
     SOME TRIAL HAD BEEN MAKING AT A RAFT . . . . . .         183  2 DON JUAN  2    50   1
     PUT TO SUCH TRIAL JOHN BULL'S PARTIAL PATIENCE . . .     136  3 DON JUAN  8    48   6
     BECAUSE YOU'LL SAY NOUGHT CALLS FOR SUCH A TRIAL--  . .  319  3 DON JUAN 12     7   7
TRIALS
     WITH TIME AND TRIALS AND THOSE HELPLESS EYES . . . .      15  2 DON JUAN  D    11   5
     HE FOUND AS PEOPLE ON MOST TRIALS MUST . . . . .         560  3 DON JUAN 16   122   5
TRIBE
     THE REST OF ALL THAT TRIBE WITH HERE AND THERE . . . .   390  2 DON JUAN  4    85   2
```

TRIBE   (CONTINUED)
	PAGE	VOL	CANTO	STANZA	LV
IN SHORT THE MAXIM FOR THE AMOROUS TRIBE IS	14	3 DON JUAN	6	17	7
A SYLVAN TRIBE OF CHILDREN OF THE CHACE	145	3 DON JUAN	8	65	2
BUT WHICH 'TIS TIME TO TEACH THE HIRELING TRIBE	187	3 DON JUAN	9	10	4
THE BLUES THAT TENDER TRIBE WHO SIGH O'ER SONNETS	294	3 DON JUAN	11	50	1
FROM WHENCE POURED FORTH A TRIBE OF WELL-CLAD WAITERS	313	3 DON JUAN	11	V 29	2
THE REAL PORTRAIT OF THE HIGHEST TRIBE	418	3 DON JUAN	14	20	7

TRIBES
	PAGE	VOL	CANTO	STANZA	LV
FORM'D OF TWO MIGHTY TRIBES THE BORES AND BORED	402	3 DON JUAN	13	95	8

TRIBULATION
BUT STOOD IN TREMBLING PATIENT TRIBULATION	532	3 DON JUAN	16	65	7

TRIBUNALS
AS THE TRIBUNALS SHOW THROUGH MANY A SESSION	11	3 DON JUAN	6	10	6

TRIBUNES'
BETWEEN THE TYRANT'S AND THE TRIBUNES' CREW	306	3 DON JUAN	11	75	6

TRICE
JUAN HAD REACH'D THE ROOM-DOOR IN A TRICE	122	2 DON JUAN	1	183	5
FOUR BLACKS WERE AT HIS ELBOW IN A TRICE	458	2 DON JUAN	5	80	8
SAVE FOR ITS STYLE WHICH SAID ALL IN A TRICE	86	3 DON JUAN	7	40	7
I'LL HAVE ANOTHER FIGURE IN A TRICE--	375	3 DON JUAN	13	37	1

TRICK
I THINK I KNOW A TRICK OR TWO WOULD TURN	300	3 DON JUAN	11	63	1
THEN THERE'S THE VULGAR TRICK OF THOSE DAMNED DAMAGES	346	3 DON JUAN	12	65	4

TRICK'D
FOLLIES TRICK'D OUT SO BRIGHTLY THAT THEY BLIND--	480	3 DON JUAN	15	57	6

TRICKED
TRICKED OUT BUT MODEST MORE THAN POET'S PEN	380	3 DON JUAN	13	47	4

TRICKING
IN TRICKING HER OUT FOR A MASQUERADE	37	3 DON JUAN	6	62	6

TRICKS
WARM BOUT ARE BROKEN INTO THEIR NEW TRICKS	122	3 DON JUAN	8	22	7
IN RHYMES OR DREAMT (FOR FANCY WILL PLAY TRICKS)	230	3 DON JUAN	10	10	5
OF EROS BUT THOUGH THOU HAST PLAYED US MANY TRICKS	554	3 DON JUAN	16	109	7

TRICKY
ALSO MY LADY'S GENTLEWOMAN TRICKY	380	3 DON JUAN	13	47	3

TRIED
HER WIT (SHE SOMETIMES TRIED AT WIT) WAS ATTIC ALL	27	2 DON JUAN	1	12	3
AND TRIED TO PROVE HER LOVING LORD WAS MAD	35	2 DON JUAN	1	27	2
THEIR FRIENDS HAD TRIED AT RECONCILIATION	38	2 DON JUAN	1	32	1
AT FIRST HE TRIED TO HAMMER AN EXCUSE	110	2 DON JUAN	1	162	1
AND THEN HE TRIED TO MUSTER ALL HIS PATIENCE	110	2 DON JUAN	1	162	8
FOR I HAVE TRIED IT WELL--AND SO MAY YOU	163	2 DON JUAN	2	13	V8
THEY TRIED THE PUMPS AGAIN AND THOUGH BEFORE	176	2 DON JUAN	2	38	5
PEDRO HIS VALET TOO HE TRIED TO SAVE	186	2 DON JUAN	2	57	1
AS O'ER THE CUTTER'S EDGE HE TRIED TO CROSS	186	2 DON JUAN	2	57	4
AND TRIED TO PERCH ALTHOUGH IT SAW AND HEARD	206	2 DON JUAN	2	94	5
AND TRIED TO AWAKEN THEM BUT FOUND THEM DEAD	208	2 DON JUAN	2	98	8
AND BATHING HIS CHILL TEMPLES TRIED TO SOOTHE	215	2 DON JUAN	2	113	5
AND THEN FAIR HAIDEE TRIED HER TONGUE AT SPEAKING	241	2 DON JUAN	2	161	1
I HAVE TRIED BOTH SO THOSE WHO WOULD A PART TAKE	356	2 DON JUAN	4	24	7
WERE TRIED IN VAIN BY THOSE WHO SERVED SHE GAVE	378	2 DON JUAN	4	63	7
BUT THAT'S HER WAY WITH ALL MEN TILL THEY'RE TRIED	418	2 DON JUAN	5	14	5
MORE EASILY THAN ANSWERED--THAT HE HAD TRIED	56	3 DON JUAN	6	100	3
AND IF THIS VIOLENT REMEDY BE TRIED--	63	3 DON JUAN	6	115	6
AND TRIED TO MAKE A LANDING ON THE MAIN	82	3 DON JUAN	7	31	5
A FEMALE CHILD OF TEN YEARS TRIED TO STOOP	157	3 DON JUAN	8	91	6
BECAUSE SHE SAID HER TEMPER HAD BEEN TRIED	525	3 DON JUAN	16	50	4

TRIES
THAT BEING THE LAST THING A PROUD WOMAN TRIES	483	2 DON JUAN	5	125	6

TRIFLE
IN SUCH A TRIFLE SCARCELY COULD EXPRESS	452	2 DON JUAN	5	70	6
THE COST WOULD BE A TRIFLE--AN OLD SONG	529	3 DON JUAN	16	59	1

TRIFLES
THOUGH VERY TRUE WERE NOT YET USED FOR TRIFLES	145	3 DON JUAN	8	66	8
BUT THESE ARE TRIFLES DOWNWARD FLIES MY LORD	379	3 DON JUAN	13	46	1

TRIFLING
WILL FOLLOW ME NO TRIFLING SIR FOR WHEN	458	3 DON JUAN	5	81	4
APT TO WEAR OUT ON TRIFLING PROVOCATIONS	165	3 DON JUAN	8	107	8
POOR THING EVE'S WAS A TRIFLING CASE TO HER'S	345	3 DON JUAN	12	64	8

TRIGGER
OH VALIANT MAN WITH SWORD DRAWN AND COCK'D TRIGGER	103	2 DON JUAN	1	150	7

TRIM
THEY SHOULD HAVE WALKED THERE IN THEIR SPRITELIEST TRIM	38	3 DON JUAN	6	64	5
OF BREAKERS HAS NOT DAUNTED MY SLIGHT TRIM	227	3 DON JUAN	10	4	6

TRIMMED
TRIMMED EITHER HEADS OR HEARTS TO DECORATE	13	3 DON JUAN	6	14	6

TRIMMER
THEIR POET A SAD TRIMMER BUT NO LESS	318	2 DON JUAN	3	82	1

TRIMMER'S
OR MRS TRIMMER'S BOOKS ON EDUCATION	29	2 DON JUAN	1	16	3

TRIMMING
FOR BLUSTERING BUNGLING TRIMMING WRANGLING WRITING	150	2 DON JUAN	1	V 1	5

TRINIDADA
THE SHIP CALL'D THE MOST HOLY TRINIDADA	169	2 DON JUAN	2	24	1

TRINITY
THE FOURTH AT ONCE ESTABLISHED THE WHOLE TRINITY	271	3 DON JUAN	11	6	5

TRIOS
OH THE LONG EVENINGS OF DUETS AND TRIOS	523	3 DON JUAN	16	45	1

TRIP
THUS ENDED MANY A FAIR SULTANA'S TRIP	496	2 DON JUAN	5	149	V5
FOR HIM THE FRAGRANT PRODUCE OF EACH TRIP	320	3 DON JUAN	12	9	3

	PAGE	VOL	CANTO	STANZA	LV
TRIPLE					
SHOWERS TRIPLE LIGHT AND SCORCHES EVEN THE KISS	264	2 DON JUAN	2	202	3
TRIPOD					
STANDS ON HER TRIPOD AGONIZED AND FULL	59	3 DON JUAN	6	107	2
TRIPOLI					
HAD A LARGE ORDER FROM THE DEY OF TRIPOLI	284	2 DON JUAN	3	16	8
TRIPPED					
BUT TUGGING ON HIS PETTICOAT HE TRIPPED	456	2 DON JUAN	5	77	5
TRITE					
(BUT THIS LAST SIMILE IS TRITE AND STUPID)	51	2 DON JUAN	1	55	8
THIS WAS A TRUTH TO US EXTREMELY TRITE	485	2 DON JUAN	5	128	1
PROVING THAT TRITE OLD TRUTH THAT LIFE'S AS FRAIL	134	3 DON JUAN	8	43	3
TRIUMPH					
THERE CAPTIVES LED IN TRIUMPH DROOP THE EYE	461	2 DON JUAN	5	86	5
GLORY AND TRIUMPH O'ER HER ASPECT BURST	212	3 DON JUAN	9	59	3
WHENE'ER THEIR TRIUMPH PALES OR STAR IS TAMED--	448	3 DON JUAN	14	89	6
A KIND OF TRIUMPH I'LL NOT RECOMMEND	491	3 DON JUAN	15	79	2
TRIUMPHAL					
SO MUCH AS UNDER A TRIUMPHAL ARCH	121	3 DON JUAN	8	21	4
WHILE GREAT LUCULLUS' ROBE TRIUMPHAL MUFFLES--	484	3 DON JUAN	15	66	7
WHERE THE TRIUMPHAL CHARIOTS' HAUGHTY MARCH	485	3 DON JUAN	15	67	4
TRIUMPHANT					
WITH ALL THE TROPHIES OF TRIUMPHANT SONG--	77	2 DON JUAN	1	104	7
WAS MORE TRIUMPHANT AND NOT MUCH LESS REAL	396	2 DON JUAN	4	96	8
TRIUMPHED					
WHETHER HIS VIRTUE TRIUMPHED--OR AT LENGTH	567	3 DON JUAN	17	12	5
TRIUMPHS					
AND HAYLEY'S TRIUMPHS WHICH SHE DEEMED PATHETIC	525	3 DON JUAN	16	50	3
TROD					
WHERE LATE HE TROD HER BEAUTIFUL HER OWN	375	2 DON JUAN	4	58	4
TRAMPLED WHAT THEY SCARCE TROD FOR FEAR OF STAINING	450	2 DON JUAN	5	66	3
UNTIL YOU NEARLY TROD ON THEM AND THEN	462	2 DON JUAN	5	88	1
THEY TROD AS UPON NECKS AND TO COMPLETE	475	2 DON JUAN	5	111	5
THE WAY WHICH THEY HAD NEVER TROD BEFORE	120	3 DON JUAN	8	19	3
WHO DID NOT QUIT ME WHEN OPPRESSION TROD	452	3 DON JUAN	14	96	5
WITH STEPS THAT TROD AS HEAVY YET UNHEARD	510	3 DON JUAN	16	21	4
TRODE					
THEIR WORK EVEN BY THE WAY IN WHICH HE TRODE	61	3 DON JUAN	6	111	8
TROJAN					
YET I WISH WELL TO TROJAN AND TO TYRIAN	496	3 DON JUAN	15	91	7
IMPARTIAL BETWEEN TYRIAN AND TROJAN	497	3 DON JUAN	15	92	3
TROOP					
THEY STAND FORTH MARSHALL'D IN A HANDSOME TROOP	46	2 DON JUAN	1	45	3
SEEING A TROOP OF HIS DOMESTICS DANCING	290	2 DON JUAN	3	29	5
WHICH WAS AN ODD ONE A TROOP GOING TO ACT	388	2 DON JUAN	4	80	4
BUT FOR THE DESTINY OF THIS YOUNG TROOP	409	2 DON JUAN	4	116	1
TROOPS					
TROOPS OF UNTENDED HORSES HERE AND THERE	387	2 DON JUAN	4	78	1
OF THE TROOPS WERE EMBARKED- THE SIEGE TO RAISE	85	3 DON JUAN	7	39	2
THE TROOPS ALREADY DISEMBARKED PUSHED ON	119	3 DON JUAN	8	15	1
AND HAD IT NOT BEEN FOR SOME STRAY TROOPS LANDING	148	3 DON JUAN	8	72	1
AND SCRAMBLING ROUND THE RAMPART THESE SAME TROOPS	148	3 DON JUAN	8	73	1
TROOPS AS ARE MEANT TO MARCH WITH GREATEST GLORY ON	151	3 DON JUAN	8	78	4
TROPHIES					
WITH ALL THE TROPHIES OF TRIUMPHANT SONG--	77	2 DON JUAN	1	104	7
SUCH WERE HIS TROPHIES--NOT OF SPEAR AND SHIELD	425	3 DON JUAN	14	35	1
TROPHY					
THE CHIEFTAIN'S TROPHY AND THE POET'S VOLUME	400	2 DON JUAN	4	104	6
THUS IS THE TROPHY USED AND THUS LAMENTED	401	2 DON JUAN	4	105	5
WHOM HE HAD SAVED FROM SLAUGHTER--WHAT A TROPHY	199	3 DON JUAN	9	33	2
TROTTED					
OR RODE A NAG WHICH TROTTED NOT TOO HIGH	406	3 DON JUAN	13	102	5
TROUBLE					
WHICH SAVES IN FACT THE TROUBLE OF AN INDEX	46	2 DON JUAN	1	44	8
I CAN'T TELL WHY SHE SHOULD TAKE ALL THIS TROUBLE	97	2 DON JUAN	1	140	7
NOR TO THE TROUBLE WHICH HER FANCIES CAUSED	476	2 DON JUAN	5	113	6
THE TROUBLE THAT THEY GAVE THEIR IMMORALITY	64	3 DON JUAN	6	117	7
TROUBLE HEROIC STOMACHS THOUGH THEIR LIDS SO	133	3 DON JUAN	8	40	5
THE HORRID SIN--AND WHAT'S STILL WORSE THE TROUBLE	292	3 DON JUAN	11	46	8
AND UGLINESS DISEASE AS TOIL AND TROUBLE--	305	3 DON JUAN	11	74	7
THE MARRIED ONES TO SAVE THE VIRGINS TROUBLE	342	3 DON JUAN	12	58	8
BUT THOUGH THE SOIL MAY GIVE YOU TIME AND TROUBLE	351	3 DON JUAN	12	76	7
BY MANY VIRTUES TO BE WORTH THE TROUBLE	477	3 DON JUAN	15	48	7
TO TAKE SOME TROUBLE WITH HIS TOILET BUT	513	3 DON JUAN	16	29	2
TROUBLED					
TROUBLED HIM NOT AND HE MIGHT SLEEP HIS FILL	229	2 DON JUAN	2	137	5
HAVE NOT BEEN TROUBLED WITH THEM LATELY NOW	419	2 DON JUAN	5	16	2
BUT NO ONE TROUBLED HIM WITH CONVERSATION	441	2 DON JUAN	5	54	8
'TIS TRUE A LITTLE TROUBLED HERE AND THERE	497	2 DON JUAN	5	150	6
AND HER BROW CLEARED BUT NOT HER TROUBLED EYE	61	3 DON JUAN	6	110	7
AT WHICH THE WHOLE COURT WAS EXTREMELY TROUBLED	244	3 DON JUAN	10	39	7
OR LIKE AN OPIATE WHICH BRINGS TROUBLED REST	505	3 DON JUAN	16	10	1
TROUBLES					
LIKE MAN'S VAIN GLORY AND HIS VAINER TROUBLES	389	3 DON JUAN	13	65	8
SO MANY TROUBLES FROM HER BIRTH BESET HER	421	3 DON JUAN	14	25	3
TROUBLESOME					
WITH ANY KIND OF TROUBLESOME CONTROL	66	2 DON JUAN	1	82	6
WHICH I FOUND VERY TROUBLESOME TO PAY	190	2 DON JUAN	2	65	8
TROUGH					
THREW THE SHIP RIGHT INTO THE TROUGH OF THE SEA	170	2 DON JUAN	2	27	2

TROUT
SHOULD HAVE A HOOK AND A SMALL TROUT TO PULL IT . . . . . 407 3 DON JUAN 13 106 8
TROW
NO MORE OF THEM THAN THEY OF HER I TROW . . . . 324 3 DON JUAN 12 18 8
TROWSERS
PAIR OF SCARCE DECENT TROWSERS--WENT TO WORK . . . . . 240 2 DON JUAN 2 160 2
HER ORANGE SILK FULL TURKISH TROWSERS FURL'D . . . . . 312 2 DON JUAN 3 72 7
AND TROWSERS NOT SO TIGHT THAT THEY WOULD BURST . . . . 451 2 DON JUAN 5 68 4
A PAIR OF TROWSERS OF FLESH-COLOURED SILK . . . . . . 456 2 DON JUAN 5 77 2
TROY
TROY OWES TO HOMER WHAT WHIST OWES TO HOYLE . . . . . . 328 2 DON JUAN 3 90 5
AND HEARD TROY DOUBTED TIME WILL DOUBT OF ROME . . . . . 399 2 DON JUAN 4 101 8
BUT THEY WILL NOT FIND LIBERTY A TROY-- . . . . 106 3 DON JUAN 7 79 8
TOBACCO ON A LITTLE CARPET--TROY . . . . 172 3 DON JUAN 8 121 3
PARISIAN ASPECT WHICH UPSET OLD TROY . . . . 209 3 DON JUAN 9 53 5
TO HOMER'S ILIAD SINCE IT DREW TO TROY . . . . . . 441 3 DON JUAN 14 72 4
TRUANT
AND TRUANT HUSBAND SHOULD RETURN AND SAY . . . . . . 98 2 DON JUAN 1 141 7
(LIKE TRUANT ROGUES) THE DEVIL OR THE FOOL . . . . . 162 2 DON JUAN 2 10 4
TRUCE
THEIR GUARDS BEING GONE AND AS IT WERE A TRUCE . . . . 23 3 DON JUAN 6 34 6
TRUCKLE
BE SAID THAT WE STILL TRUCKLE UNTO THRONES-- . . . . 179 3 DON JUAN 8 135 6
TRUCULENT
THOUGH SOMEWHAT LARGE EXUBERANT AND TRUCULENT . . . . 213 3 DON JUAN 9 62 1
IS SOMETIMES TRUCULENT--BUT NEVER MIND . . . . . 377 3 DON JUAN 13 41 2
AND TRUCULENT DISTORTION OF THEIR TRESSES . . . . . 550 3 DON JUAN 16 103 8
TRUE
ALTHOUGH 'TIS TRUE THAT YOU TURN'D OUT A TORY AT . . . . 9 2 DON JUAN D 1 3
YOU'RE SHABBY FELLOWS--TRUE--BUT POETS STILL . . . . 12 2 DON JUAN D 6 7
THE AGE DISCOVERS HE IS NOT THE TRUE ONE . . . . . 21 2 DON JUAN 1 1 4
A TRUE HIDALGO FREE FROM EVERY STAIN . . . . 26 2 DON JUAN 1 9 2
IF SUCH AN EDUCATION WAS THE TRUE ONE . . . . 48 2 DON JUAN 1 48 3
OF HIS OWN CASE AND NEVER HIT THE TRUE ONE . . . . . 68 2 DON JUAN 1 86 3
IN THOUGHTS LIKE THESE TRUE WISDOM MAY DISCERN . . . . 71 2 DON JUAN 1 93 1
AT FIFTY LOVE FOR LOVE IS RARE 'TIS TRUE . . . . . 79 2 DON JUAN 1 108 6
BUT THEN NO DOUBT IT EQUALLY AS TRUE IS . . . . . 79 2 DON JUAN 1 108 7
(SIGNS OF TRUE GENIUS AND OF EMPTY POCKETS) . . . . 91 2 DON JUAN 1 129 2
ARE WAYS TO BENEFIT MANKIND AS TRUE . . . . . . 93 2 DON JUAN 1 132 7
CONCEAL'D AMONGST HIS PREMISES 'TIS TRUE . . . . . 118 2 DON JUAN 1 177 5
THE VADE MECUM OF THE TRUE SUBLIME . . . . . . 136 2 DON JUAN 1 201 3
THE ONLY HIGH SOUND PRECEPTS OF THE TRUE SUBLIME . . . . 136 2 DON JUAN 1 201 V3
WHEREAS THIS STORY'S ACTUALLY TRUE . . . . 137 2 DON JUAN 1 202 8
THIS IS TRUE CRITICISM AND YOU MAY KISS-- . . . . . 140 2 DON JUAN 1 206 6
BUT I BEING FOND OF TRUE PHILOSOPHY . . . . 147 2 DON JUAN 1 220 1
A BLOTTED SHIELD NO SHIRE'S TRUE KNIGHT WOULD WEAR . . . . 153 2 DON JUAN 1 V 4 6
YOU SNEER AND I ASSURE YOU THIS IS TRUE . . . . . 163 2 DON JUAN 2 13 7
AS RUM AND TRUE RELIGION THUS IT WAS . . . . . . 174 2 DON JUAN 2 34 2
'TIS TRUE THAT DEATH AWAITS BOTH YOU AND ME . . . . 175 2 DON JUAN 2 36 3
AND THOUGH 'TIS TRUE THAT MAN CAN ONLY DIE ONCE . . . . 176 2 DON JUAN 2 39 7
UNLESS TO PLAGUE THE GRANTORS--YET SO TRUE IT IS . . . . 190 2 DON JUAN 2 65 3
TO TASTE OF HEAVEN--IF THIS BE TRUE INDEED . . . . . 202 2 DON JUAN 2 86 7
IS PLEASANT BESIDES BEING TRUE LOVE'S ESSENCE . . . . 245 2 DON JUAN 4 169 4
FEEL RAPTURE BUT NOT SUCH JOY ARE REAPING . . . . 261 2 DON JUAN 2 196 7
WHICH FORMS IN FACT TRUE LOVE'S ANTITHESIS . . . . 279 2 DON JUAN 3 8 2
AND THE TRUE HYMEN (THE FIRST'S BUT A SCREEN)-- . . . . 288 2 DON JUAN 3 25 6
OF THE TRUE REASON OF HIS NOT BEING SAD . . . . . 289 2 DON JUAN 3 26 5
WITH SUCH TRUE BREEDING OF A GENTLEMAN . . . . . 296 2 DON JUAN 3 41 3
'TIS TRUE HE HAD NO ARDENT LOVE FOR PEACE-- . . . . 303 2 DON JUAN 3 55 5
AND ALWAYS CHANGED AS TRUE AS ANY NEEDLE . . . . 317 2 DON JUAN 3 80 2
FORM NOT THE TRUE TEMPTATION WHICH ALLURES . . . . 332 2 DON JUAN 3 97 5
FROM A TRUE LOVER SHADOW'D MY MIND'S EYE . . . . 337 2 DON JUAN 3 106 8
TRUE KNIGHTS CHASTE DAMES HUGE GIANTS KINGS DESPOTIC . . . 347 2 DON JUAN 4 6 6
AS BUT TO LOVERS A TRUE SENSE AFFORDS . . . . . 351 2 DON JUAN 4 14 6
THERE WAS RESEMBLANCE SUCH AS TRUE BLOOD WEARS . . . . 368 2 DON JUAN 4 45 4
LAY AT HER HEART WHOSE EARLIEST BEAT STILL TRUE . . . . 378 2 DON JUAN 4 62 6
BUT FACTS ARE FACTS NO KNIGHT COULD BE MORE TRUE . . . . 396 2 DON JUAN 4 96 2
'TIS TRUE IT GETS ANOTHER BRIGHT AND FRESH . . . . 422 2 DON JUAN 5 22 1
ALL THIS IS VERY FINE AND MAY BE TRUE . . . . . 422 2 DON JUAN 5 23 1
TO FEEL FOR NONE IS THE TRUE SOCIAL ART . . . . 423 2 DON JUAN 5 25 7
TO SEE THEM TRUE BELIEVERS BUT NO LESS . . . . . 452 2 DON JUAN 5 70 2
A WOMAN'S TRUE BUT THEN THERE IS A CAUSE . . . . 455 2 DON JUAN 5 76 2
SUCH AS WAS MARY'S QUEEN OF SCOTS TRUE--TEARS . . . . 468 2 DON JUAN 5 98 5
BEING A TRUE WOMAN IN A STATE OF NATURE . . . . 476 2 DON JUAN 5 113 V7
'TIS TRUE A LITTLE TROUBLED HERE AND THERE . . . . 497 2 DON JUAN 5 150 6
TO THE TRUE LAW OF NATIONS WHICH NE'ER MEANT . . . . 498 2 DON JUAN 5 151 3
'TIS TRUE THE REASON IS THAT THE BASHAW . . . . 498 2 DON JUAN 5 152 7
IF TRUE 'TIS NO GREAT LEASE OF ITS OWN FIRE . . . . 14 3 DON JUAN 6 16 2
WHICH DOTH YOUR TRUE BELIEVER SO MUCH PLEASE . . . . 17 3 DON JUAN 6 23 3
FEW ANGLES WERE THERE IN HER FORM 'TIS TRUE . . . . 27 3 DON JUAN 6 42 5
ARE TRUE AS TRUTH HAS EVER BEEN OF LATE . . . . 48 3 DON JUAN 6 85 8
THEIR OWN TRUE INTERESTS WHICH KINGS RARELY KNOW . . . . 53 3 DON JUAN 6 95 2
THE TRUE EFFECT AND SO WE HAD BETTER NOT . . . . 55 3 DON JUAN 6 98 6
GULBEYAZ WAS NO MODEL OF TRUE PATIENCE . . . . 56 3 DON JUAN 6 101 1
BY THEIR EXAMPLES OF TRUE CHRISTIANITY . . . . 69 3 DON JUAN 7 6 3
THE CITY'S SHAPE SUGGESTED THIS 'TIS TRUE . . . . 78 3 DON JUAN 7 23 6
'TIS TRUE THE MEMOIRS OF THE PRINCE DELIGNE . . . . 82 3 DON JUAN 7 33 7
DOUBTLESS TO THAT OF DOCTRINES THE MOST TRUE . . . . 101 3 DON JUAN 7 67 5
UNRIDDLED AND AS MY TRUE MUSE EXPOUNDS . . . . . 112 3 DON JUAN 8 1 5

TRUE   (CONTINUED)
```
      TO THE TRUE PORTRAIT OF ONE BATTLE-FIELD . . . . . . 117  3 DON JUAN  8    12   8
      'TIS TRUE HE SHRANK FROM MEN EVEN OF HIS NATION . . . . 144  3 DON JUAN  8    64   1
      THOUGH VERY TRUE WERE NOT YET USED FOR TRIFLES . . . . 145  3 DON JUAN  8    66   8
      OF A TRUE POET TO ESCAPE FROM FICTION . . . . . . . 154  3 DON JUAN  8    86   2
      THE ELDEST WAS A TRUE AND TAMELESS TARTAR . . . . . . 167  3 DON JUAN  8   111   1
      WHEREAS IF ALL BE TRUE WE HEAR OF HEAVEN . . . . . . 168  3 DON JUAN  8   114   7
      YOU HARDLY WILL BELIEVE SUCH THINGS WERE TRUE . . . . 180  3 DON JUAN  8   136   3
      'TIS TRUE WE SPECULATE BOTH FAR AND WIDE . . . . . . 190  3 DON JUAN  9    16   3
      WHOSE STATUES WARM (I FEAR ALAS TOO TRUE 'TIS) . . . . 208  3 DON JUAN  9    51   6
      'TIS VERY TRUE THE HILL SEEMED RATHER HIGH . . . . . 215  3 DON JUAN  9    66   5
      IF THIS BE TRUE FOR WE MUST DEEM THE MODE . . . . . . 226  3 DON JUAN 10     2   2
      (LET DEEPER SAGES THE TRUE CAUSE DETERMINE) . . . . . 249  3 DON JUAN 10    50   3
      THE TRUE BELIEVERS--AND HER INFANT BROW . . . . . . 262  3 DON JUAN 10    75   6
      REVERED THE SOIL OF THOSE TRUE SONS THE MOTHER . . . . 265  3 DON JUAN 10    81   7
      TO TELL YOU TRUTHS YOU WILL NOT TAKE AS TRUE . . . . 266  3 DON JUAN 10    84   5
      THE VERY SHADOW OF TRUE TRUTH WOULD SHUT . . . . . . 286  3 DON JUAN 11    37   5
      FOR TRUE OR FALSE POLITENESS (AND SCARCE THAT . . . . 290  3 DON JUAN 11    44   2
      THE SUN'S TRUE SON NO VAPOUR BUT A RAY . . . . . . . 300  3 DON JUAN 11    64   8
      THE LAW AT LEAST UNTIL THE BENCH REVERT TO TRUE . . . 314  3 DON JUAN 11  V 76   6
      ARE THE TRUE LORDS OF EUROPE EVERY LOAN . . . . . . 318  3 DON JUAN 12     6   2
      WERE EVERY MEMORY WRITTEN DOWN ALL TRUE . . . . . . 324  3 DON JUAN 12    19   3
      'TIS TRUE THAT THY CAREER IS NOT A NEW ONE . . . . . 326  3 DON JUAN 12    23   5
      TRUE 'TIS A PITY PITY 'TIS 'TIS TRUE) . . . . . . . 334  3 DON JUAN 12    38   2
      TRUE 'TIS A PITY PITY 'TIS 'TIS TRUE) . . . . . . . 334  3 DON JUAN 12    38   2
      SHE KEEPS IT FOR YOU LIKE A TRUE ALLY . . . . . . . 350  3 DON JUAN 12    74   8
      IN BRITAIN--WHICH OF COURSE TRUE PATRIOTS FIND . . . . 359  3 DON JUAN 13     2   7
      HAD NOT CERVANTES IN THAT TOO TRUE TALE . . . . . . 361  3 DON JUAN 13     8   7
      'TIS TRUE I MIGHT HAVE CHOSEN PICCADILLY . . . . . . 370  3 DON JUAN 13    27   1
      ERE PATRIOTS THEIR TRUE COUNTRY CAN REMEMBER-- . . . . 380  3 DON JUAN 13    48   7
      'TIS ODD BUT TRUE--LAST WAR THE NEWS ABOUNDED . . . . 383  3 DON JUAN 13    53   7
      NOR JUDGE AT FIRST IF ALL BE TRUE TO NATURE . . . . . 390  3 DON JUAN 13    67   8
      MAY THE ROSE CALL BACK ITS TRUE COLOURS SOON . . . . 409  3 DON JUAN 13   111   6
      NOTHING MORE TRUE THAN NOT TO TRUST YOUR SENSES . . . 411  3 DON JUAN 14     2   7
      'TIS TRUE YOU DON'T--BUT PALE AND STRUCK WITH TERROR . . 413  3 DON JUAN 14     6   1
      A WANT OF THAT TRUE NATURE WHICH SUBLIMES . . . . . . 417  3 DON JUAN 14    16   8
      BUT THIS CAN'T WELL BE TRUE JUST NOW FOR WRITERS . . . 418  3 DON JUAN 14    20   1
      THAN TRUE HATH BEEN A CREED SO STRICTLY HELD) . . . . 420  3 DON JUAN 14    23   3
      HE BROKE 'TIS TRUE SOME STATUTES OF THE LAWS . . . . 424  3 DON JUAN 14    33   5
      TRUE HE WAS ABSENT AND 'TWAS RUMOUR'D TOOK . . . . . 430  3 DON JUAN 14    45   3
      TO DRAW THE LINE BETWEEN THE FALSE AND TRUE . . . . . 449  3 DON JUAN 14    90   5
      (I WILL NOT SAY IT WAS A FALSE OR TRUE ONE) . . . . . 449  3 DON JUAN 14    91   6
      AND YOUR TRUE FEELINGS FULLY UNDERSTOOD . . . . . . 451  3 DON JUAN 14    93   6
      BUT TRUE--AS IF EXPEDIENT I COULD PROVE) . . . . . . 452  3 DON JUAN 14    96   2
      'TIS STRANGE--BUT TRUE FOR TRUTH IS ALWAYS STRANGE . . 455  3 DON JUAN 14   101   1
      OF WHICH PERHAPS THE LATTER IS MOST TRUE . . . . . . 456  3 DON JUAN 15     1   8
      OR THAT SHE HAD NOT HARP'D UPON THE TRUE STRING . . . 474  3 DON JUAN 15    42   5
      BUT EVEN SANS CONFITURES IT NO LESS TRUE IS . . . . . 486  3 DON JUAN 15    68   7
      ARE FALSE BUT MAY BE RENDER'D ALSO TRUE . . . . . . 495  3 DON JUAN 15    89   2
      'TIS TRUE THERE BE SOME BITTERS WITH THE SWEETS . . . 502  3 DON JUAN 16     3   5
      TRUE IS THAT WHICH SHE IS ABOUT TO TELL . . . . . . 502  3 DON JUAN 16     4   2
      AND FALSE--THOUGH TRUE FOR SURELY THEY'RE SINCEREST . . 547  3 DON JUAN 16    97   7
      TRUE SHE SAID LITTLE--'TWAS THE REST THAT BROKE . . . 552  3 DON JUAN 16   104   1
      'TIS TRUE HE SAW AURORA LOOK AS THOUGH . . . . . . . 553  3 DON JUAN 16   106   1
TRUE-BORN
      AND JUAN LIKE A TRUE-BORN ANDALUSIAN . . . . . . . 368  3 DON JUAN 13    23   7
TRUER
      WHICH PROVE PLAIN ENGLISH TRUER OF THE TWO . . . . . 488  3 DON JUAN 15    72   6
TRUFFLES
      (THERE'S FAME) YOUNG PARTRIDGE' FILLETS DECK'D WITH TRUFFLES 484  3 DON JUAN 15    66   8
      THOSE TRUFFLES TOO ARE NO BAD ACCESSARIES . . . . . 486  3 DON JUAN 15    68   1
      TO THESE THE INVENTION OF CHAMPAGNE AND TRUFFLES . . . 542  3 DON JUAN 16    86   7
TRUISM
      WHICH FURTHER TO EXPLAIN WOULD BE A TRUISM . . . . . 506  3 DON JUAN 16    13   8
TRULY
      INFORM US TRULY HAVE THEY NOT HEN-PECK'D YOU ALL . . . 33  2 DON JUAN  1    22   8
      HER RESOLUTIONS WERE MOST TRULY GREAT . . . . . . . 62  2 DON JUAN  1    75   5
      I CAN'T BUT SAY IT SEEMS TO ME MOST TRULY A . . . . . 267  2 DON JUAN  2   208   3
      LAST NIGHT I HAD ANOTHER PROOF HOW TRULY IT . . . . . 272  2 DON JUAN  2  V  1   6
      BOIL'D UP AND PROVED HER TRULY OF HIS RACE . . . . . 367  2 DON JUAN  4    44   8
      WHY 'TIS A PALACE WHERE THE TRULY WISE . . . . . . . 458  2 DON JUAN  5    81   7
      LESS THAN THEIR GRIEF (AND TRULY NOT LESS JUST) . . . 104  3 DON JUAN  7    73   4
      TO TAKE HIM WAS THE POINT THE TRULY BRAVE . . . . . 164  3 DON JUAN  8   106   1
      ALAS COULD SHE BUT FULLY TRULY KNOW . . . . . . . . 258  3 DON JUAN 10    67   1
      THOSE AND THE TRULY LIBERAL LAFITTE . . . . . . . . 318  3 DON JUAN 12     6   1
      AND SENATE WHEN INVITED ELSEWHERE TRULY . . . . . . 398  3 DON JUAN 13    84   3
      YES SHE WAS TRULY WORTHY HER HIGH PLACE . . . . . . 550  3 DON JUAN 16   102   5
TRUMP
      THE TRUMP AND BUGLE TILL HE SPAKE WERE DUMB-- . . . . 430  2 DON JUAN  5    36   7
      INTENTIONS WHICH FORM ALL MANKIND'S TRUMP CARD . . . . 123  3 DON JUAN  8    25   3
TRUMPET
      IT SEEMS HAS GOT AN EAR AS WELL AS TRUMPET . . . . . 74  3 DON JUAN  7    15   8
      LIKE TO A ROMAN TRUMPET ERE A BATTLE . . . . . . . 267  3 DON JUAN 10    87  V8
TRUMPS
      NOT PRACTISE OH FOR TRUMPS OF CHERUBIM . . . . . . . 241  3 DON JUAN 10    34   4
TRUNK
      WITHOUT THEIR SAP HOW BRANCHLESS WERE THE TRUNK . . . 250  2 DON JUAN  2   179   5
TRUNKS
      AND OPEN'D CERTAIN TRUNKS OF BOOKS AND LETTERS . . . . 36  2 DON JUAN  1    28   2
```

TRUST   PAGE VOL CANTO STANZA LN

```
TRUST                                                            PAGE VOL        CANTO STANZA LN
    AND WILL NOT DARE TO TRUST ITSELF WITH TRUTH  . . . . . .  61  2 DON JUAN   1    72    7
    YET STILL I TRUST IT MAY BE KEPT THROUGHOUT  . . . . .     85  2 DON JUAN   1   119    6
    ONLY ANOTHER TIME I TRUST YOU'LL TELL US . . . . . .      106  2 DON JUAN   1   156    5
    INSENSIBLE I TRUST BUT NONE THE WORSE . . . . . . .       144  2 DON JUAN   1   215    6
    AWAITS THEM TREACHERY IS ALL THEIR TRUST . . . . .        263  2 DON JUAN   2   200    3
    TRUST NOT FOR FREEDOM TO THE FRANKS-- . . . . . .         325  2 DON JUAN   3 L 14    1
    HIS SINGING I NO FURTHER TRUST CAN PLACE IN . . . .       391  2 DON JUAN   4    86    6
    SO THAT I TRUST FOR EVERYBODY'S SAKE . . . . . .          459  2 DON JUAN   5    82    7
    WOULD LIKE (I THINK) TO TRUST ALL TO DESIRE . . . .        14  3 DON JUAN   6    16    4
    LOOKED ON AS IF IN DOUBT IF THEY COULD TRUST . . .        104  3 DON JUAN   7    73    2
    WHICH FEW WILL SING I TRUST BUT NONE FORGET IT-- . .      179  3 DON JUAN   8   135    3
    OUR HERO (AND I TRUST KIND READER YOUR'S) -- . . . .      194  3 DON JUAN   9    23    1
    HOWEVER I FORGIVE HIM AND I TRUST . . . . . . .           230  3 DON JUAN  10    11    7
    TO EYE OR HEART--IT IS THE PEOPLE'S TRUST . . . .         354  3 DON JUAN  12    83    8
    NOTHING MORE TRUE THAN NOT TO TRUST YOUR SENSES . . .     411  3 DON JUAN  14     2    7
    'TIS ALWAYS BEST TO TAKE THINGS UPON TRUST . . . .        503  3 DON JUAN  16     6    4
TRUSTED
    SHE SCARCELY TRUSTED HIM FROM OUT HER SIGHT . . . . .      48  2 DON JUAN   1    48    4
TRUSTETH
    NO HERO TRUSTETH WHOLLY TO HALF-PAY  . . . . . .         163  3 DON JUAN   8   103    8
TRUSTING
    BUT JUAN TRUSTING THEY MIGHT STILL GET THROUGH . . . .   187  2 DON JUAN   2    59    6
    AND TRUSTING JUAN MAY ESCAPE THE FISHES . . . . . .       65  3 DON JUAN   6   120    5
TRUSTS
    (NONE TRUSTS THE SEX MORE OR SO MUCH ADMIRES-- . . . .   287  2 DON JUAN   3    22    5
TRUSTY
    CLOSED THE ORATION OF THE TRUSTY MAID . . . . . .        116  2 DON JUAN   1   173    2
TRUTH
    AND WILL NOT DARE TO TRUST ITSELF WITH TRUTH  . . . .     61  2 DON JUAN   1    72    7
    AND STAND CONVICTED OF MORE TRUTH THAN TREASON . . .      76  2 DON JUAN   1   102    6
    VICTORIOUS VIRTUE AND DOMESTIC TRUTH . . . . . .          78  2 DON JUAN   1   107    3
    JULIA HAD HONOUR VIRTUE TRUTH AND LOVE . . . . .          80  2 DON JUAN   1   109    1
    YOU'D BEST BEGIN WITH TRUTH AND WHEN YOU'VE LOST YOUR     91  2 DON JUAN   1   128    7
    AND TRUTH TO SAY HE MADE A FOOLISH FIGURE . . . . .      110  2 DON JUAN   1   161    2
    TO NEWSPAPERS WHOSE TRUTH ALL KNOW AND FEEL . . . .      138  2 DON JUAN   1   203    3
    YOU'D WISH YOURSELF WHERE TRUTH IS--IN A WELL . . . .    201  2 DON JUAN   2    84    8
    PERHAPS NOT SO RESPECTABLE IN TRUTH . . . . . . .        222  2 DON JUAN   2   125    5
    IS USED UNTIL THE TRUTH ARRIVES TOO LATE-- . . . .      278  2 DON JUAN   3     6    4
    WITH TRUTH LIKE SOUTHEY AND WITH VERSE LIKE CRASHAW .    316  2 DON JUAN   3    79    8
    AGREE TO A SHORT ARMISTICE WITH TRUTH . . . . . .        318  2 DON JUAN   3    83    8
    LIKE CROMWELL'S PRANKS--BUT ALTHOUGH TRUTH EXACTS . .    329  2 DON JUAN   3    92    5
    AND THE SAD TRUTH WHICH HOVERS O'ER MY DESK . . . .      345  2 DON JUAN   4     3    7
    HARD WORDS HARSH TRUTH A TRUTH WHICH MANY KNOW . . .     353  2 DON JUAN   4    18    1
    HARD WORDS HARSH TRUTH A TRUTH WHICH MANY KNOW . . .     353  2 DON JUAN   4    18    1
    AT THE FIRST TWO BOOKS HAVING TOO MUCH TRUTH . . .       397  2 DON JUAN   4    97    4
    (PLAIN TRUTH DEAR MURRAY NEEDS FEW FLOWERS OF SPEECH)    470  2 DON JUAN   5   101    2
    THIS WAS A TRUTH TO US EXTREMELY TRITE . . . . .         485  2 DON JUAN   5   128    1
    AND SO MUST TELL THE TRUTH HOWE'ER YOU BLAME IT . .       10  3 DON JUAN   6     8    4
    FOR OVER-WARMTH IF FALSE IS WORSE THAN TRUTH . . .        14  3 DON JUAN   6    16    1
    AS A RULE BUT TRUTH MAY IF YOU TRANSLATE IT . . . .       15  3 DON JUAN   6    18    8
    ARE TRUE AS TRUTH HAS EVER BEEN OF LATE . . . . .         48  3 DON JUAN   6    85    8
    PICKING UP SHELLS BY THE GREAT OCEAN--TRUTH . . . .       69  3 DON JUAN   7     5    8
    FROM FOOLS WHO DREAD TO KNOW THE TRUTH OF LIFE . . .      69  3 DON JUAN   7     6   V8
    OF TRUTH--SUCH TRUTHS ARE TREASON THEY BETRAY . . .       77  3 DON JUAN   7    22    5
    AND FACT IS TRUTH THE GRAND DESIDERATUM . . . . .        107  3 DON JUAN   7    81    2
    IF HE SPEAK TRUTH SHE IS CHRIST'S SISTER AND . . . .     116  3 DON JUAN   8     9    7
    PROVING THAT TRITE OLD TRUTH THAT LIFE'S AS FRAIL .      134  3 DON JUAN   8    43    3
    OF TRUTH THAN PROSE UNLESS TO SUIT THE MART . . . .      154  3 DON JUAN   8    86    5
    AND EPIC IF PLAIN TRUTH SHOULD PROVE NO BAR . . . .      181  3 DON JUAN   8   138    5
    JUST NOW--BUT BY AND BY THE TRUTH WILL SHOW 'EM . .      193  3 DON JUAN   9    22    5
    THE TRUTH AND THOUGH GRIEF HER OLD AGE MIGHT SHORTEN     222  3 DON JUAN   9    81    5
    THE TRUTH IS I'VE GROWN LATELY RATHER PHTHISICAL . .     270  3 DON JUAN  11     5    5
    SO WELL THE VERY TRUTH SEEMS FALSEHOOD TO IT . . .       285  3 DON JUAN  11    36    8
    THE TRUTH IN MASQUERADE AND I DEFY . . . . . .          286  3 DON JUAN  11    37    2
    THE VERY SHADOW OF TRUE TRUTH WOULD SHUT . . . .         286  3 DON JUAN  11    37    5
    AND TO SAY TRUTH IT HAD BEEN FAIRLY EARNED . . . .       287  3 DON JUAN  11    39    8
    WHATE'ER IT WAS 'TWAS MINE I'VE PAID IN TRUTH . . .      324  3 DON JUAN  12    17    6
    GIVES WITH GREEK TRUTH THE GOOD OLD GREEK THE LIE .      325  3 DON JUAN  12    19    8
    ADVERSITY IS THE FIRST PATH TO TRUTH . . . . .          339  3 DON JUAN  12    50    5
    (SUCH EARLY TRAVELLER IS THE TRUTH THOU LEARNEST)--     345  3 DON JUAN  12    64    6
    TO TASTE--THE TRUTH IS IF MEN WOULD CONFESS . . .       347  3 DON JUAN  12    69    7
    THE ONLY TRUTH THAT YET HAS BEEN CONFEST . . . .        361  3 DON JUAN  13     7    3
    THE SCANTY BUT RIGHT-WELL THRASHED EARS OF TRUTH .      403  3 DON JUAN  13    96    2
    THE LURKING BIAS BE IT TRUTH OR ERROR . . . . .         413  3 DON JUAN  14     6    5
    FOR TOO MUCH TRUTH AT FIRST SIGHT NE'ER ATTRACTS .      416  3 DON JUAN  14    13    6
    WHATE'ER IT SHOWS WITH TRUTH A SMOOTH MONOTONY . .      417  3 DON JUAN  14    16    7
    AND THEREFORE DOUBTLESS TO APPROVE THE TRUTH . . .      439  3 DON JUAN  14    67    1
    'TIS STRANGE--BUT TRUE FOR TRUTH IS ALWAYS STRANGE      455  3 DON JUAN  14   101    1
    AS IF THEY TOLD THE TRUTH COULD WELL BE SHOWN . . .     461  3 DON JUAN  15    13    2
    TO DRAW THE BOW TO RIDE AND SPEAK THE TRUTH . . .       501  3 DON JUAN  16     1    2
    AT SPEAKING TRUTH PERHAPS THEY ARE LESS CLEVER . .      501  3 DON JUAN  16     1    7
    AND ALSO HEARTS IF THERE BE TRUTH IN LAYS . . . .       506  3 DON JUAN  16    14    8
    THE SPIRIT OF THESE WALLS--IN TRUTH NOT I  . . . .      516  3 DON JUAN  16    36    2
    BUT JUAN EAGER NOW THE TRUTH TO PIERCE . . . . .        559  3 DON JUAN  16   119    3
    WHAT WAS A PARADOX BECOMES A TRUTH OR . . . . .         565  3 DON JUAN  17     6    7
TRUTH'S
    OF THE TRUTH'S RAYS SPOIL NOT MY DRAUGHT OF SPIRIT  . .  269  3 DON JUAN  11     2    7
    TRUTH'S FOUNTAINS MAY BE CLEAR--HER STREAMS ARE MUDDY  .  495  3 DON JUAN  15    88    6
```

TRUTHS
  FINE TRUTHS EVEN CONSCIENCE TOO HAS A TOUGH JOB . . . . 264 2 DON JUAN 2   203 6
  OF TRUTH--SUCH TRUTHS ARE TREASON THEY BETRAY . . . . 77 3 DON JUAN 7   22 5
  TRUTHS THAT YOU WILL NOT READ IN THE GAZETTES . . . . 187 3 DON JUAN 9   10 3
  TO TELL YOU TRUTHS YOU WILL NOT TAKE AS TRUE . . . . . 266 3 DON JUAN 10   84 5
  SOME TRUTHS ARE BETTER KEPT BEHIND A SCREEN . . . . . 444 3 DON JUAN 14   80 6
  BUT OF ALL TRUTHS WHICH SHE HAS TOLD THE MOST . . . . 502 3 DON JUAN 16   4 1
  AS ALL TRUTHS MUST THE MORE THEY ARE DISPUTED . . . . 503 3 DON JUAN 16   6 8
TRY
  SCOTT ROGERS CAMPBELL MOORE AND CRABBE WILL TRY . . . 13 2 DON JUAN D   7 7
  THOUGH SEVERAL THOUSAND PEOPLE CHOSE TO TRY . . . . . 33 2 DON JUAN 1   23 3
  BECAUSE THEY TELL ME 'TWERE IN VAIN TO TRY . . . . . 142 2 DON JUAN 1   211 6
  EACH OTHER AND IF NOT I SHALL NOT TRY . . . . 147 2 DON JUAN 1   221 6
  AGAINST SEA-SICKNESS TRY IT SIR BEFORE . . . . . . 163 2 DON JUAN 2   13 6
  'TIS STRANGE THAT POETS NEVER TRY TO WREATHE . . . . 280 2 DON JUAN 3   9 V5
  WE'LL PUT ABOUT AND TRY ANOTHER TACK . . . . 384 2 DON JUAN 4   74 7
  WOULD WE WERE MASTERS NOW IF BUT TO TRY . . . . . . 423 2 DON JUAN 5   24 1
  TO TRY IF I COULD WRENCH AUGHT OUT OF DEATH . . . . 431 2 DON JUAN 5   38 7
  WHICH SOME CALL THE SUBLIME I WISH THEY'D TRY IT . . 32 3 DON JUAN 6   53 6
  IS THE SUBLIME--I WISH THAT THEY WOULD TRY IT . . . 32 3 DON JUAN 6   53 V6
  HE STUMBLED ON TO TRY IF HE COULD FIND . . . . . . 126 3 DON JUAN 8   30 6
  OUR OLD ACQUAINTANCE AND AT LEAST I'LL TRY . . . . 266 3 DON JUAN 10   84 4
  WITH CARLTON OR WITH OTHER HOUSES TRY . . . . . . 266 3 DON JUAN 10   85 3
  I'D TRY CONCLUSIONS WITH THOSE JANIZARIES . . . . 299 3 DON JUAN 11   62 7
  BUT ONCE THERE (IF YOU DOUBT THIS PRITHEE TRY) . . 350 3 DON JUAN 12   74 7
  TASTES WE ARE GOING TO TRY THE SUPERNATURAL . . . 497 3 DON JUAN 15   93 8
  THOSE WHO IN COUNTY INTEREST TRY THEIR FORCES . . 534 3 DON JUAN 16   68 V6
TRYING
  IT WAS A TRYING MOMENT THAT WHICH FOUND HIM . . . 41 2 DON JUAN 1   36 4
  A THING TO HUMAN FEELINGS THE MOST TRYING . . . . 301 2 DON JUAN 3   51 2
  PRELUDIOS TRYING JUST A STRING OR TWO . . . . . . 341 3 DON JUAN 12   54 6
TSCHITSSHAKOFF
  AND TSCHITSSHAKOFF AND ROGUENOFF AND CHOKENOFF . . 74 3 DON JUAN 7   15 4
TU
  HORATIAN MEDIO TU TUTISSIMUS IBIS . . . . 14 3 DON JUAN 6   17 8
  WITH TU MI CHAMAS'S FROM PORTINGALE . . . . 523 3 DON JUAN 16   45 7
TUG
  THEN COMES THE TUG OF WAR--'TWILL COME AGAIN . . . 138 3 DON JUAN 8   51 5
TUGGING
  BUT TUGGING ON HIS PETTICOAT HE TRIPPED . . . . . 456 2 DON JUAN 5   77 5
TUISM
  OF AMATORY EGOTISM THE TUISM . . . . 506 3 DON JUAN 16   13 7
TULIT
  OMNE TULIT PUNCTUM QUAE MISCUIT UTILE DULCI . . . 396 3 DON JUAN 13   81 8
TUMBLE
  AND TUMBLE DOWNWARD LIKE THE FLYING FISH . . . . 10 2 DON JUAN D   3 6
  TO TOSS TO TUMBLE DOZE REVIVE AND QUAKE . . . . . 18 3 DON JUAN 6   24 7
  THEIR TUMBLE I SHOULD TURN THE OTHER WAY . . . . 466 3 DON JUAN 15   23 6
TUMBLED
  NOT SO HAIDEE SHE SADLY TOSS'D AND TUMBLED . . . 229 2 DON JUAN 2   138 1
  WHICH TUMBLED ALL MANKIND INTO THE GRAVE . . . . 192 3 DON JUAN 9   19 4
  AND TUMBLED BOOKS OR CRITICISED THE PICTURES . . 406 3 DON JUAN 13   102 2
TUMBLES
  HOUNDS WHEN THE HUNTSMAN TUMBLES ARE AT FAULT . . 119 3 DON JUAN 8   16 8
TUMBLING
  TURNING EACH PIECE OF SILVER O'ER AND TUMBLING . 426 2 DON JUAN 5   29 3
  OF TUMBLING FIRST AND HAVING IN EXCHANGE . . . . 424 3 DON JUAN 14   32 3
TUMOURS
  OTHERS TALKED LEARNEDLY OF CERTAIN TUMOURS . . . 244 3 DON JUAN 10   40 3
TUMULT
  BUT O'ER HER BRIGHT BROW FLASHED A TUMULT STRANGE . 473 2 DON JUAN 5   108 3
  AMIDST THIS TUMULT OF FISH FLESH AND FOWL . . . 488 3 DON JUAN 15   74 1
TUMULUS
  THE TUMULUS--OF WHOM HEAVEN KNOWS 'T MAY BE . . 385 2 DON JUAN 4   76 6
TUNE
  CHANGE HORSES MAKING HISTORY CHANGE ITS TUNE . . 76 2 DON JUAN 1   103 5
  IN TIME TO HIS OLD TUNE HE CHANGED THE THEME . . 380 2 DON JUAN 4   66 2
  HER ANGER PITCHED INTO A LOWER TUNE . . . . . . 490 2 DON JUAN 5   136 5
  WHOSE FROWN WOULD PUT THE SPHERES ALL OUT OF TUNE . 494 2 DON JUAN 5   144 3
  BUT AFTER ALL THERE'S NEITHER TUNE NOR TIME . . 14 3 DON JUAN 6   18 4
  AND CANNOT TUNE THOSE DISCORDS OF NARRATION . . 74 3 DON JUAN 7   16 1
  AND CANNOT TUNE THOSE DISCORDS OF DAMNATION . . 74 3 DON JUAN 7   16 V1
  AND NOW--WHAT IS YOUR FAME SHALL THE MUSE TUNE IT YE . 187 3 DON-JUAN 9   9 5
  AND TUNE THE CONCORD TO A FINER MOOD . . . . . 451 3 DON JUAN 14   93 4
  BUT COME I'LL SET YOUR STORY TO A TUNE . . . . 517 3 DON JUAN 16   38 4
  OF THAT SAME TUNE WHEN PEOPLE HUM IT LONG)-- . . 529 3 DON JUAN 16   59 3
TUNED
  THE HARPER CAME AND TUNED HIS INSTRUMENT . . . 379 2 DON JUAN 4   65 2
TUNEFUL
  A NEST OF TUNEFUL PERSONS TO MY EYE . . . . . .   9 2 DON JUAN D   1 7
  WITH THIS HIS TUNEFUL NEIGHBOUR THAN HIS FATE . 394 2 DON JUAN 4   93 4
  MUST PERCH HARMONIOUS ON MY TUNEFUL QUILL . . . 458 3 DON JUAN 15   5 4
TUNELESS
  THE HEROIC LAY IS TUNELESS NOW-- . . . . 322 2 DON JUAN 3 L 5 3
  AN IGNORANT NOTELESS TIMELESS TUNELESS FELLOW . 391 2 DON JUAN 4   87 4
TUNIC
  WITH HANNIBAL AND WEARS THE TYRIAN TUNIC . . . 122 3 DON JUAN 8   23 6
TUNIS
  TO HIS TUNIS CORRESPONDENTS SAVE ONE MAN . . . 284 2 DON JUAN 3   16 3

TURBAN
    OMITTING TURBAN SLIPPERS PISTOLS DIRK-- 240   2 DON JUAN 2   160   6
    HIS TURBAN FURL'D IN MANY A GRACEFUL FOLD   315   2 DON JUAN 3   77   5
    AND ARM'D FROM BOOT TO TURBAN ONE AND ALL   369   2 DON JUAN 4   47   6
    RECEIVED A CUT WHICH CLOVE HIS TURBAN THROUGH 370   2 DON JUAN 4   48   V8
TURBANS
    LIKE MEN WITH TURBANS SCYMITARS AND DIRKS   93   3 DON JUAN 7   53   2
TURBID
    FOR WHEN THE TURBID PASSIONS ARE UNRULY IT   272   2 DON JUAN 2   V 1   4
TURBOT
    A TURBOT FOR RELIEF OF THOSE WHO CRAM 483   3 DON JUAN 15   63   3
    HE HAD PAID HIS NEIGHBOUR'S PRAYER WITH HALF A TURBOT   . 543   3 DON JUAN 16   88   8
TURBULENTLY
    THE CALM DUDU SO TURBULENTLY WAKE   42   3 DON JUAN 6   71   8
TURK
    IN SEVERAL OATHS--ARMENIAN TURK AND GREEK-- 229   2 DON JUAN 2   138   7
    AND DRESS'D HIM FOR THE PRESENT LIKE A TURK 240   2 DON JUAN 2   160   4
    THAT IS SOME WORDS OF SPANISH TURK AND GREEK 243   2 DON JUAN 2   165   1
    A TURK WITH BEADS IN HAND AND PIPE IN MOUTH 387   2 DON JUAN 4   78   6
    BY TURK AND CHRISTIAN EQUALLY HE COULD   129   3 DON JUAN 8   33   V6
    BETWEEN YOUR TURK AND RUSSIAN AS A MAIN   197   3 DON JUAN 9   29   V7
    THE LITTLE TURK REFUSED TO BE CONVERTED   251   3 DON JUAN 10   55   8
    A RUSS OR TURK--THE ONE'S AS GOOD AS T'OTHER 474   3 DON JUAN 15   42   8
TURKEY
    IF YOU HAD BEEN IN TURKEY OR IN SPAIN 201   2 DON JUAN 2   84   5
    TURKEY CONTAINS NO BELLS AND YET MEN DINE   439   2 DON JUAN 5   50   1
TURKISH
    FULL MANY A MORSEL FOR THAT TURKISH TRADE   223   2 DON JUAN 2   126   7
    HER ORANGE SILK FULL TURKISH TROWSERS FURL'D 312   2 DON JUAN 3   72   7
    LEAVE BATTLES TO THE TURKISH HORDES   324   2 DON JUAN 3   L 9   3
    BUT TURKISH FORCE AND LATIN FRAUD 325   2 DON JUAN 3   L 14   5
    FOR ALTHOUGH DESTINED TO THE TURKISH MART HE 388   2 DON JUAN 4   81   3
    AND VARIOUS HUES AS IS THE TURKISH WONT--   436   2 DON JUAN 5   46   4
    IN SHORT ALL THINGS WHICH FORM A TURKISH DANDY 451   2 DON JUAN 5   68   8
    THE TURKISH TITLE) AND RANGED ROUND THE WALL 31   3 DON JUAN 6   51   2
    GROWLING AND GRUMBLING IN GOOD TURKISH PHRASE 64   3 DON JUAN 6   117   2
    THE TURKISH FIRE AND AIDED BY THEIR OWN   81   3 DON JUAN 7   30   2
    BUT THESE ARE BUT TWO TURKISH LADIES WHO 103   3 DON JUAN 7   72   1
    THE TURKISH BATTERIES THRASHED THEM LIKE A FLAIL 134   3 DON JUAN 8   43   5
    THE GREEK OR TURKISH COHORN'S IGNORANCE   136   3 DON JUAN 8   46   3
    THEIR COLUMN THOUGH THE TURKISH BATTERIES THUNDERED . . 149   3 DON JUAN 8   75   1
TURKISH-FASHIONED
    AND THAT BENEATH EACH TURKISH-FASHIONED VEST 96   3 DON JUAN 7   57   5
TURK'S
    GLITTERING LIKE CRESCENTS O'ER A TURK'S PAVILION . . . 205   2 DON JUAN 2   92   5
    TO ATTACK THE TURK'S FLOTILLA WHICH LAY NIGH 78   3 DON JUAN 7   24   3
    AND THOUGH THE TURK'S RESISTANCE WAS SUBLIME 151   3 DON JUAN 8   79   6
    FOR THE TURK'S TEETH STUCK FASTER THAN A SKEWER 154   3 DON JUAN 8   85   3
TURKS
    HE HAD TRAVELL'D 'MONGST THE ARABS TURKS AND FRANKS . . 319   2 DON JUAN 3   84   1
    BECAUSE ONE POET TRAVELLED 'MONGST THE TURKS) 434   2 DON JUAN 5   42   8
    THE TURKS DO WELL TO SHUT--AT LEAST SOMETIMES-- 501   2 DON JUAN 5   157   1
    (CURTSIES ARE NEITHER USED BY TURKS NOR GREEKS) 31   3 DON JUAN 6   50   4
    BECAUSE THE TURKS COULD NEVER BE PERSUADED   73   3 DON JUAN 7   13   2
    WHILE THOUGH 'TWAS DAWN THE TURKS SLEPT FAST AS EVER . . 80   3 DON JUAN 7   28   8
    AND THOUGH AS YET THE TURKS MADE NO RESISTANCE 80   3 DON JUAN 7   28   V5
    RUNNING AGROUND WAS TAKEN BY THE TURKS   81   3 DON JUAN 7   30   8
    OUR FRIENDS THE TURKS WHO WITH LOUD ALLA'S NOW 87   3 DON JUAN 7   42   1
    BUT HERE I SAY THE TURKS WERE MUCH MISTAKEN 87   3 DON JUAN 7   42   7
    BY WAY OF LESSON AGAINST ACTUAL TURKS 93   3 DON JUAN 7   53   4
    THE TURKS BEHIND THE TRAVERSES AND FLANKS   134   3 DON JUAN 8   44   1
    THE MADDENED TURKS THEIR CITY STILL DISPUTE 146   3 DON JUAN 8   69   8
    THE TURKS AT FIRST PRETENDED TO HAVE SCAMPERED 149   3 DON JUAN 8   75   6
    THIS VALIANT MAN KILLED ALL THE TURKS HE MET 150   3 DON JUAN 8   77   1
TURMOIL
    NO BICKERINGS NO CONNUBIAL TURMOIL 447   3 DON JUAN 14   86   6
TURN
    NOR TURN HIS VERY TALENT TO A CRIME   15   2 DON JUAN D   10   6
    WHERE SHALL I TURN ME NOT TO VIEW ITS BONDS 19   2 DON JUAN D   16   1
    EACH IN THEIR TURN LIKE BANQUO'S MONARCHS STALK 22   2 DON JUAN 1   2   5
    AND FANS TURN INTO FALCHIONS IN FAIR HANDS   33   2 DON JUAN 1   21   7
    PROMISED TO TURN OUT WELL IN PROPER HANDS   42   2 DON JUAN 1   37   4
    COULD TURN THEIR OPTICS TO THE TEXT AND PRAY 47   2 DON JUAN 1   46   6
    SO MUCH FOR JULIA NOW WE'LL TURN TO JUAN 68   2 DON JUAN 1   86   1
    'TIS GROWN HIGH TIME TO THIN IT IN ITS TURN 92   2 DON JUAN 1   131   4
    BUT AS MY MAID'S UNDREST PRAY TURN YOUR SPIES OUT   . . . 104   2 DON JUAN 1   152   7
    BY A FEW TIMELY WORDS TO TURN THE TABLES   117   2 DON JUAN 1   175   4
    WELL--WELL THE WORLD MUST TURN UPON ITS AXIS 159   2 DON JUAN 2   4   1
    AND ALL MANKIND TURN WITH IT HEADS OR TAILS 159   2 DON JUAN 2   4   2
    HOW TO ACCEPT A BETTER IN HIS TURN 224   2 DON JUAN 2   128   8
    LIKE DERVISES WHO TURN AS ON A PIVOT HE   290   2 DON JUAN 3   29   6
    AND TURN HIM LIKE THE CYCLOPS MAD WITH BLINDNESS   . . . 304   2 DON JUAN 3   57   8
    MAY TURN HIS NAME UP AS A RARE DEPOSIT   327   2 DON JUAN 3   89   8
    AND WITH ALL PASSIONS IN THEIR TURN ATTACKED 412   2 DON JUAN 5   2   6
    BUT NEVER MIND--SHE'LL TURN PERHAPS NEXT WEEK 418   2 DON JUAN 5   14   6
    AND ONE BY ONE IN TURN SOME GRAND MISTAKE   421   2 DON JUAN 5   21   7
    AND THERE YOU SEE THIS TURN HAS BROUGHT US THROUGH . . . 436   2 DON JUAN 5   45   7
    BUT THOUGH MY TURN WILL NOT BE SERVED WITH LESS 487   2 DON JUAN 5   132   5
    WHEN SHE WHOSE TURN IT WAS WAS WED AT ONCE   498   2 DON JUAN 5   152   5

TURN (CONTINUED)

	PAGE	VOL	CANTO	STANZA	LN
IN EARLY YOUTH TO TURN A LADY'S MAID--	37	3	DON JUAN	6	62	4
THOUGH ALL DESERVING EQUALLY TO TURN	120	3	DON JUAN	8	17	5
BUT COULD NOT EAT THEM BEING IN HIS TURN	150	3	DON JUAN	8	77	2
AND DIG AND SWEAT AND TURN THEMSELVES ABOUT	202	3	DON JUAN	9	40	3
THERE WAS A SOMETHING IN HIS TURN OF LIMB	206	3	DON JUAN	9	47	3
TO KILL AND GENERALS TURN IT INTO JEST	212	3	DON JUAN	9	60	8
WITH INTEREST AND IN TURN WAS WONT WITH RIGOUR	213	3	DON JUAN	9	62	6
SO LOFTY THAT I FEEL MY BRAIN TURN ROUND	224	3	DON JUAN	9	85	5
IS THE POOR PRIVILEGE TO TURN THE KEY	258	3	DON JUAN	10	68	5
TURN OUT SO WE'LL SAY NOTHING 'GAINST THE WORDING	270	3	DON JUAN	11	4	3
INSTEAD OF WICKS THEY MADE A WICKED MAN TURN	280	3	DON JUAN	11	26	8
UNLESS ON TYRANT'S STERNS--WE TURN THE STERNEST	286	3	DON JUAN	11	38	V8
AND TURN ON THINGS WHICH NO ARISTOCRATIC	289	3	DON JUAN	11	43	3
TO TURN OUT BOTH OR EITHER IT MAY BE	298	3	DON JUAN	11	59	4
I THINK I KNOW A TRICK OR TWO WOULD TURN	300	3	DON JUAN	11	63	1
(NO MATTER WHICH) TURN POLITICIAN STUPIDER	309	3	DON JUAN	11	83	3
I'VE SEEN THE COUNTRY GENTLEMEN TURN SQUEAKERS--	310	3	DON JUAN	11	85	4
THOUGH EVERY SCRIBE IN SOME SLIGHT TURN OF DICTION	311	3	DON JUAN	11	88	6
TO TURN HER HEAD WITH WALTZING AND WITH FLATTERY	331	3	DON JUAN	12	32	8
ARE SPURNED IN TURN UNTIL HER TURN ARRIVES	333	3	DON JUAN	12	36	2
ARE SPURNED IN TURN UNTIL HER TURN ARRIVES	333	3	DON JUAN	12	36	2
TURN OUT MUCH BETTER FOR THE SMITHFIELD SHOW	337	3	DON JUAN	12	46	6
WILL TURN UPON POLITICAL ECONOMY	356	3	DON JUAN	12	88	8
BUT FROM BEING FARMERS WE TURN GLEANERS GLEANING	403	3	DON JUAN	13	96	1
AND BOTH MAY AFTER ALL TURN OUT UNTRUE	411	3	DON JUAN	14	3	4
I ASK IN TURN--WHY DO YOU PLAY AT CARDS	415	3	DON JUAN	14	11	3
IT OCCUPIES ME TO TURN BACK REGARDS	415	3	DON JUAN	14	11	5
SOME HOPED THINGS MIGHT NOT TURN OUT AS THEY FEAR'D	429	3	DON JUAN	14	44	3
THE SORT OF THING TO TURN A YOUNG MAN'S HEAD	438	3	DON JUAN	14	64	1
'TIS ODD OR ODDS IT MAY TURN OUT A ROCK	442	3	DON JUAN	14	74	8
THEIR TUMBLE I SHOULD TURN THE OTHER WAY	466	3	DON JUAN	15	23	6
THEY TURN OUT MELODRAMES OR PANTOMIMES	470	3	DON JUAN	15	32	8
THOUGHT THAT IT MIGHT TURN OUT SO--NOW I KNOW IT	482	3	DON JUAN	15	60	7
PERHAPS IT MAY TURN OUT THAT ALL WERE RIGHT	496	3	DON JUAN	15	90	2
LOOK LIVING IN THE MOON AND AS YOU TURN	508	3	DON JUAN	16	18	2
TO TURN CHURCH LANDS TO LAY	518	3	DON JUAN	16	L 2	2
A LITTLE TURN FOR MISCHIEF YOU MIGHT TRACE	525	3	DON JUAN	16	49	5
BUT WHAT WAS BAD SHE DID NOT BLUSH IN TURN	545	3	DON JUAN	16	94	1

TURNCOAT

| BUT HE HAD GENIUS--WHEN A TURNCOAT HAS IT | 317 | 2 | DON JUAN | 3 | 81 | 1 |
| WITH TURNCOAT SOUTHEY FOR MY TURNKEY LOWE | 296 | 3 | DON JUAN | 11 | 56 | 8 |

TURN'D

ALTHOUGH 'TIS TRUE THAT YOU TURN'D OUT A TORY AT	9	2	DON JUAN	D	1	3
AND STILL SHOULD BE SO BUT THE TIDE IS TURN'D	23	2	DON JUAN	1	4	2
AND TURN'D WITHOUT PERCEIVING HIS CONDITION	70	2	DON JUAN	1	91	7
SOMETIMES HE TURN'D TO GAZE UPON HIS BOOK	72	2	DON JUAN	1	95	1
SHE CEASED AND TURN'D UPON HER PILLOW PALE	108	2	DON JUAN	1	158	1
HE TURN'D HIS LIP TO HERS AND WITH HIS HAND	114	2	DON JUAN	1	170	1
JUAN THE GATE GAIN'D TURN'D THE KEY ABOUT	125	2	DON JUAN	1	187	7
HAD OFTEN TURN'D THE ART TO SOME ACCOUNT	211	2	DON JUAN	2	105	4
AND TURN'D BELIEVING THAT HE CALL'D AGAIN	228	2	DON JUAN	2	135	4
ALTHOUGH HIS WOES HAD TURN'D HIM RATHER YELLOW	235	2	DON JUAN	2	148	8
HE TURN'D FROM GRISLY SAINTS AND MARTYRS HAIRY	235	2	DON JUAN	2	149	7
THEY TURN'D TO REST AND EACH CLASP'D BY AN ARM	253	2	DON JUAN	2	184	1
POURS FORTH AT LAST THE HEART'S-BLOOD TURN'D TO TEARS	270	2	DON JUAN	2	214	7
AND TURN'D HER PURE HEART'S PUREST BLOOD TO TEARS	274	2	DON JUAN	3	1	8
WHICH TURN'D THE ISLE INTO A PLACE OF PLEASURE	295	2	DON JUAN	3	39	2
WHO SEEM'D TO HAVE TURN'D HAIDEE INTO A MATRON	298	2	DON JUAN	3	44	8
TO FIND OUR HEARTHSTONE TURN'D INTO A TOMB	301	2	DON JUAN	3	51	5
A RAKE TURN'D METHODISTIC OR ECLECTIC--	309	2	DON JUAN	3	66	3
THE POWER OF ART WAS TURN'D TO NOTHING FOR	314	2	DON JUAN	3	75	7
HE TURN'D PREFERRING PUDDING TO NO PRAISE--	316	2	DON JUAN	3	79	4
SHE TURN'D TO HIM AND SMILED BUT IN THAT SORT	356	2	DON JUAN	4	23	1
WHICH MAKES NOT OTHERS SMILE THEN TURN'D ASIDE	356	2	DON JUAN	4	23	2
OF HER BLACK EYES SEEM'D TURN'D TO TEARS AND MURK	362	2	DON JUAN	4	33	6
THEN TURN'D TO JUAN IN WHOSE CHEEK THE BLOOD	365	2	DON JUAN	4	39	5
HER FATHER WATCH'D SHE TURN'D HER EYES AWAY	379	2	DON JUAN	4	64	2
THEN TO THE WALL SHE TURN'D AS IF TO WARP	379	2	DON JUAN	4	65	5
TURN'D TO THE MERCHANT AND BEGUN TO BID	425	2	DON JUAN	5	28	2
THE WILDS AS DOTH AN ARAB TURN'D AVENGER	424	3	DON JUAN	14	32	6
THEN TURN'D UNTO THE STARS FOR LOFTIER RAYS	480	3	DON JUAN	15	56	4

TURNED

BOTH BLACK AS IF YOU HAD TURNED HIM INSIDE OUT	154	2	DON JUAN	1	V 5	V7
HE STOPPED AGAIN AND TURNED AWAY HIS FACE	420	2	DON JUAN	5	19	2
ONE'S TURNED HALF MUSSULMAN AND ONE A MAID	459	2	DON JUAN	5	83	7
UNCONSCIOUS ALBEIT TURNED OF QUICK SEVENTEEN	33	3	DON JUAN	6	54	6
AS THUS JUANNA SPOKE DUDU TURNED ROUND	48	3	DON JUAN	6	85	1
HER CHEEK TURNED ASHES EARS RUNG BRAIN WHIRLED ROUND	58	3	DON JUAN	6	105	5
OF COSSACQUES AND THEIR PREY TURNED ROUND AND CAST	97	3	DON JUAN	7	59	2
SO NOW MY LADS FOR GLORY--HERE HE TURNED	99	3	DON JUAN	7	64	1
TURNED BACK WITHIN ITS SOCKET--THESE REWARD	118	3	DON JUAN	8	13	6
AS HE TURNED O'ER EACH PALE AND GORY CHEEK	158	3	DON JUAN	8	94	6
HE TURNED HIS EYES UPON HIS LITTLE CHARGE	198	3	DON JUAN	9	31	4
BUT JUAN TURNED HIS EYES ON THE SWEET CHILD	199	3	DON JUAN	9	33	1
BAKED FRIED OR BURNT TURNED INSIDE-OUT OR DROWNED	201	3	DON JUAN	9	37	5
SEEMS LOVE TURNED A LIEUTENANT OF ARTILLERY	204	3	DON JUAN	9	44	8
A MODE OF PROVING THAT THE EARTH TURNED ROUND	225	3	DON JUAN	10	1	5
AND SEA-SICK PASSENGERS TURNED SOMEWHAT PALE	256	3	DON JUAN	10	64	5

856

TURNED   (CONTINUED)
(IN WHISPERS) TO HAVE TURNED HIS SOVEREIGN'S HEAD 283   3 DON JUAN 11   32   8
WHERE ARE THE GRENVILLES TURNED AS USUAL WHERE 308   3 DON JUAN 11   79   7
THE HOUSE OF COMMONS TURNED TO A TAX-TRAP-- 310   3 DON JUAN 11   84   3
SOME FOR HAVING TURNED CONVERTED CULLIES 314   3 DON JUAN 11   V 76   3
A HAZY WIDOWER TURNED OF FORTY'S SURE 333   3 DON JUAN 12   37   5
WHILE OTHERS HAVE A GENIUS TURNED FOR FITS 340   3 DON JUAN 12   52   8
EPOCH THAT AWKWARD CORNER TURNED FOR DAYS 360   3 DON JUAN 13   4   2
OR PAPER TURNED TO MONEY BY THE BANK 396   3 DON JUAN 13   80   5
SHE LOOKED AND SAW HIM PALE AND TURNED AS PALE 514   3 DON JUAN 16   31   1
THEN HENRY TURNED TO JUAN AND ADDRESSED 515   3 DON JUAN 16   35   1
WHICH TURNED UPON THEIR LATE GUESTS' MIENS AND FACES . . 550   3 DON JUAN 16   103   5
TURNING
AND TURNING UP HER NOSE WITH LOOKS ABUSED 109   2 DON JUAN 1   159   3
AND STARTED FROM HER SLEEP AND TURNING O'ER 229   2 DON JUAN 2   138   2
AND WITHOUT TURNING HIS FACETIOUS HEAD 297   2 DON JUAN 3   43   1
MY THIRD-- --YOUR THIRD QUOTH JUAN TURNING ROUND 421   2 DON JUAN 5   20   1
TURNING EACH PIECE OF SILVER O'ER AND TUMBLING 426   2 DON JUAN 5   29   3
DON JUAN TURNING TO HIS COMRADE WHO 459   2 DON JUAN 5   83   2
RUN MUCH LESS RISK OF LOVERS TURNING RUDE 43   3 DON JUAN 6   75   6
ARE THINGS THE TURNING OF A HAIR OR FEATHER 65   3 DON JUAN 6   119   6
AND TURNING HUMAN NATURE TO AN ART 457   3 DON JUAN 15   3   4
OR TURNING MARRIAGE INTO ARITHMETIC 472   3 DON JUAN 15   38   8
TURNING ROUND TO THE REST HE SMILING SAID 517   3 DON JUAN 16   39   3
TURNKEY
WITH TURNCOAT SOUTHEY FOR MY TURNKEY LOWE 296   3 DON JUAN 11   56   8
TURNPIKE
(HORACE MAKES THIS THE HEROIC TURNPIKE ROAD) 24   2 DON JUAN 1   6   2
THROUGH THE THEN UNPAVED STARS THE TURNPIKE ROAD . . . 226   3 DON JUAN 10   2   4
WHAT A DELIGHTFUL THING'S A TURNPIKE ROAD 263   3 DON JUAN 10   78   1
TURNPIKE-GATES
IT OPEN'D HALF THE TURNPIKE-GATES TO HEAVEN-- 225   2 DON JUAN 2   131   7
TURNPIKES
ABOVE BELOW BY TURNPIKES GREAT OR SMALL-- 222   3 DON JUAN 9   80   4
THROUGH COACHES DRAYS CHOKED TURNPIKES AND A WHIRL . . 278   3 DON JUAN 11   22   1
THE TURNPIKES GLOW WITH DUST AND ROTTEN ROW . . . 378   3 DON JUAN 13   44   5
TURNS
THAT TURNS AND TURNS TO GIVE THE WORLD A NOTION 17   2 DON JUAN D   13   7
THAT TURNS AND TURNS TO GIVE THE WORLD A NOTION 17   2 DON JUAN D   13   7
AS TURNS THE NEEDLE TREMBLING TO THE POLE 133   2 DON JUAN 1   196   V7
IT NE'ER CAN REACH SO TURNS TO YOU MY SOUL 133   2 DON JUAN 1   196   V8
WHILE THE O'ERPOWERING EYE THAT TURNS YOU PALE . . . 160   2 DON JUAN 2   7   3
THEIR WORK ON THEM BY TURNS AND THINN'D THEM TO . . 210   2 DON JUAN 2   102   2
TURNS OFTENER TO THE STARS THAN TO HIS BOOK 242   2 DON JUAN 2   163   6
TURNS WHAT WAS ONCE ROMANTIC TO BURLESQUE 345   2 DON JUAN 4   3   8
TURNS UP MORE DANGEROUS BREAKERS THAN THE EUXINE . . . 413   2 DON JUAN 5   5   8
WHICH TURNS UP OUT OF THE SAD TWENTY-FOUR 426   2 DON JUAN 5   30   8
AND TURNS ASIDE HIS SCYTHE TO VULGAR THINGS 468   2 DON JUAN 5   98   4
TURNS OUT TO BE A BUTCHER IN GREAT BUSINESS . . . 108   3 DON JUAN 7   83   7
BY ONE OF THOSE ODD TURNS OF FORTUNE'S TIDES . . . 125   3 DON JUAN 8   27   5
TURNS LIFE TO TERROR EVEN THOUGH IN ITS SHEATH . . . 188   3 DON JUAN 9   11   7
BEAUTY SPRINGS FORTH AND NATURE'S SELF TURNS PALER . . 204   3 DON JUAN 9   44   4
WHO TOOK BY TURNS THAT DIFFICULT COMMAND 205   3 DON JUAN 9   46   5
BY TURNS THE DIFFERENCE OF THE SEVERAL SEXES . . . 442   3 DON JUAN 14   73   3
BY TURNS--WITH THAT VIVACIOUS VERSATILITY 547   3 DON JUAN 16   97   2
TURPIN'S
TURPIN'S OR MONMOUTH GEOFFRY'S CHRONICLE 503   3 DON JUAN 16   5   2
TURTLE
THEY FOUND A TURTLE OF THE HAWK'S-BILL KIND 208   2 DON JUAN 2   99   2
TURTLES
LULL'D THEM LIKE TURTLES SLEEPING ON THE BLUE . . . 192   2 DON JUAN 2   68   5
TU'S
THE TU'S TOO MUCH--BUT LET IT STAND--THE VERSE . . . 14   3 DON JUAN 6   18   1
TUSK
SHALL PASS O'ER WHAT WAS ISMAIL AND ITS TUSK 99   3 DON JUAN 7   63   7
TUSSLE
HIS REVEREND TUTORS HAD AT TIMES A TUSSLE 44   2 DON JUAN 1   41   5
TUTISSIMUS
HORATIAN MEDIO TU TUTISSIMUS IBIS 14   3 DON JUAN 6   17   8
TUTOR
A--NEVER MIND HIS TUTOR AN OLD ASS 158   2 DON JUAN 2   3   4
A TUTOR THE LICENTIATE PEDRILLO 169   2 DON JUAN 2   25   2
AND EVEN PEDRILLO HIS MOST REVEREND TUTOR 175   2 DON JUAN 2   36   7
THUS RE-EMBARK'D HIS TUTOR AND HIS SPANIEL 187   2 DON JUAN 2   59   8
AND THE LOT FELL ON JUAN'S LUCKLESS TUTOR 195   2 DON JUAN 2   75   8
HORACE CATULLUS SCHOLARS OVID TUTOR 266   2 DON JUAN 2   205   3
HIM WHOM SHE MEANT TO TUTOR IN LOVE'S WAYS 482   2 DON JUAN 5   122   5
BESIDES HE HAD FOUND OUT THAT HE WAS NO TUTOR . . . 336   3 DON JUAN 12   42   1
TUTORS
THE LEARNED TUTORS WHOM FOR HIM SHE HIRED 43   2 DON JUAN 1   39   3
HIS REVEREND TUTORS HAD AT TIMES A TUSSLE 44   2 DON JUAN 1   41   5
BETWEEN HIS TUTORS CONFESSOR AND MOTHER 48   2 DON JUAN 1   49   8
PUZZLED HIS TUTORS VERY MUCH OF COURSE 158   2 DON JUAN 2   2   8
POETS AND PRIVATE TUTORS ARE EXPOSED 486   2 DON JUAN 5   131   5
ARE TUTORS GUARDIANS AND SO FORTH COMPARED . . . 564   3 DON JUAN 17   4   2
'TWAS
'TWAS SURELY NO CONCERN OF THEIRS NOR MINE . . . 33   2 DON JUAN 1   23   4
('TWAS SNOW THAT BROUGHT SAINT ANTHONY TO REASON) . . 57   2 DON JUAN 1   64   4
'TWAS BUT A DOUBT BUT NE'ER MAGICIAN'S WAND 60   2 DON JUAN 1   71   6

'TWAS   (CONTINUED)

	PAGE	VOL		CANTO	STANZA	LN
'TWAS STRANGE THAT ONE SO YOUNG SHOULD THUS CONCERN	71	2	DON JUAN	1	93	5
IF YOU THINK 'TWAS PHILOSOPHY THAT THIS DID	71	2	DON JUAN	1	93	7
'TWAS ON A SUMMER'S DAY--THE SIXTH OF JUNE--	76	2	DON JUAN	1	103	1
'TWAS ON THE SIXTH OF JUNE ABOUT THE HOUR	77	2	DON JUAN	1	104	1
'TWAS SURELY VERY WRONG IN JUAN'S MOTHER	80	2	DON JUAN	1	110	5
WHICH TREMBLED LIKE THE BOSOM WHERE 'TWAS PLACED	83	2	DON JUAN	1	115	3
'TWAS IN NOVEMBER BUT I'M NOT SO SURE	86	2	DON JUAN	1	121	7
'TWAS IN NOVEMBER WHEN FINE DAYS ARE FEW	94	2	DON JUAN	1	134	3
'TWAS AS THE WATCHMEN SAY A CLOUDY NIGHT	94	2	DON JUAN	1	135	1
'TWAS MIDNIGHT--DARK AND SOMBRE WAS THE NIGHT	94	2	DON JUAN	1	135	V1
'TWAS MIDNIGHT--DONNA JULIA WAS IN BED	95	2	DON JUAN	1	136	1
BECAUSE NO DOUBT 'TWAS FOR HIS DIRTY FEE	103	2	DON JUAN	1	151	7
AT LEAST 'TWAS RATHER EARLY TO BEGIN	113	2	DON JUAN	1	167	4
PERHAPS 'TWAS IN A DIFFERENT WAY APPLIED	113	2	DON JUAN	1	168	7
BUT WHETHER 'TWAS THAT ONE'S OWN GUILT CONFOUNDS	118	2	DON JUAN	1	176	3
AND BLOOD ('TWAS FROM THE NOSE) BEGAN TO FLOW	124	2	DON JUAN	1	186	3
HAVE SQUANDER'D MY WHOLE SUMMER WHILE 'TWAS MAY	143	2	DON JUAN	1	213	5
ALAS 'TWAS NOT IN THEM BUT IN THY POWER	144	2	DON JUAN	1	214	7
'TWAS A FINE CAUSE FOR THOSE IN LAW DELIGHTING	150	2	DON JUAN	1 V	1	1
'TWAS FOR A VOYAGE THAT THE YOUNG MAN WAS MEANT	161	2	DON JUAN	2	8	5
'TWAS NOT WITHOUT SOME REASON FOR THE WIND	170	2	DON JUAN	2	26	1
AND THOUGH 'TWAS NOT MUCH TO A NAVAL MIND	170	2	DON JUAN	2	26	3
THE RUDDER TORE AWAY 'TWAS TIME TO SOUND	170	2	DON JUAN	2	27	7
'TWAS DIFFICULT TO GET OUT SUCH PROVISION	180	2	DON JUAN	2	46	3
'TWAS TWILIGHT AND THE SUNLESS DAY WENT DOWN	182	2	DON JUAN	2	49	1
'TWAS A ROUGH NIGHT AND BLEW SO STIFFLY YET	188	2	DON JUAN	2	60	1
'TWAS BUT HIS OWN SUPPRESS'D TILL NOW HE FOUND	194	2	DON JUAN	2	73	6
'TWAS NATURE GNAW'D THEM TO THIS RESOLUTION	195	2	DON JUAN	2	75	6
'TWAS NOT TO BE EXPECTED THAT HE SHOULD	198	2	DON JUAN	2	78	6
'TWAS BETTER THAT HE DID NOT FOR IN FACT	198	2	DON JUAN	2	79	1
'TWAS BORNE BY THE RUDE WAVE WHEREIN 'TWAS CAST	204	2	DON JUAN	2	90	6
'TWAS BORNE BY THE RUDE WAVE WHEREIN 'TWAS CAST	204	2	DON JUAN	2	90	6
'TWAS AN OLD CUSTOM OF THE GREEK AND ROMAN	205	2	DON JUAN	2	93	3
'TWAS WELL THIS BIRD OF PROMISE DID NOT PERCH	206	2	DON JUAN	2	95	2
IF 'TWAS NOT LAND THAT ROSE WITH THE SUN'S RAY	207	2	DON JUAN	2	97	3
AND THE HARD WAVE O'ERWHELM'D HIM AS 'TWAS DASH'D	212	2	DON JUAN	2	107	4
'TWAS BENDING CLOSE O'ER HIS AND THE SMALL MOUTH	215	2	DON JUAN	2	113	1
'TWAS WELL BECAUSE HEALTH IN THE HUMAN FRAME	245	2	DON JUAN	2	169	3
AND NOW 'TWAS DONE--ON THE LONE SHORE WERE PLIGHTED	265	2	DON JUAN	2	204	1
'TWAS WONDERFUL HOW THINGS WENT ON IMPROVING	295	2	DON JUAN	3	39	7
'TWAS TREASON TO BEHOLD HER AND NOT KNEEL	313	2	DON JUAN	3	74	V8
'TWAS ALL THE SAME TO HIM--GOD SAVE THE KING	319	2	DON JUAN	3	85	3
'TWAS WHITE AND INDISTINCT NOR STOPP'D TO MEET	361	2	DON JUAN	4	32	6
'TWAS FRESH--FOR HE HAD LATELY USED THE LOCK--	365	2	DON JUAN	4	40	7
HE GAZED ON HER AND SHE ON HIM 'TWAS STRANGE	367	2	DON JUAN	4	44	1
'TWAS FOR THE SULTAN AND AT ONCE WITHDREW	407	2	DON JUAN	4	114	8
WHAT 'TWAS ERE ABOLITION AND THE THING	408	2	DON JUAN	4	115	4
'TWAS A RAW DAY OF AUTUMN'S BLEAK BEGINNING	414	2	DON JUAN	5	6	1
THE OTHER EVENING ('TWAS ON FRIDAY LAST)--	428	2	DON JUAN	5	33	1
I HEARD A SHOT--'TWAS EIGHT O'CLOCK SCARCE PAST--	428	2	DON JUAN	5	33	5
OF A SMALL IRON DOOR 'TWAS OPENED AND	433	2	DON JUAN	5	41	2
WHISPERED TO HIS COMPANION--'TWAS THE SAME	434	2	DON JUAN	5	43	3
AND KNOCKING AT THE GATE 'TWAS OPENED WIDE	440	2	DON JUAN	5	51	6
'TWAS FAMOUS TOO FOR THISBE AND FOR PYRAMUS	445	2	DON JUAN	5	60	7
SOFAS 'TWAS HALF A SIN TO SIT UPON	449	2	DON JUAN	5	65	5
AND WHEN 'TWAS FOUND STRAIGHTWAY THE BARGAIN CLOSED	476	2	DON JUAN	5	113	4
AND NEVER HAVING DREAMT WHAT 'TWAS TO BEAR	480	2	DON JUAN	5	119	4
HER RAGE WAS BUT A MINUTE'S AND 'TWAS WELL--	489	2	DON JUAN	5	135	1
IT LASTED 'TWAS LIKE A SHORT GLIMPSE OF HELL	489	2	DON JUAN	5	135	3
('TWAS THUS HE SPAKE) AND EMPRESS OF THE EARTH	494	2	DON JUAN	5	144	2
'TWAS THE BOY'S MITE AND LIKE THE WIDOW'S MAY	9	3	DON JUAN	6	1	1
'TWAS ON THE WHOLE A NOBLY FURNISHED HALL	31	3	DON JUAN	6	51	6
'TWAS LIKE THE FAWN WHICH IN THE LAKE DISPLAYED	36	3	DON JUAN	6	60	5
OH YE WHOSE FATE IT IS AS ONCE 'TWAS MINE	37	3	DON JUAN	6	62	3
'TWAS NIGHT BUT THERE WERE LAMPS AS HATH BEEN SAID	40	3	DON JUAN	6	67	2
'TWAS FOOLISH NERVOUS AS SHE MUST ALLOW	47	3	DON JUAN	6	83	4
'TWAS CERTAIN THAT HIS CONDUCT HAD BEEN PURE	58	3	DON JUAN	6	104	3
WHILE THOUGH 'TWAS DAWN THE TURKS SLEPT FAST AS EVER	80	3	DON JUAN	7	28	8
'TWAS NINE WHEN STILL ADVANCING UNDISMAYED	81	3	DON JUAN	7	29	3
'TWAS MUCH THAT HE WAS UNDERSTOOD AT ALL	95	3	DON JUAN	7	56	6
THOUGH 'TWAS DON JUAN'S FIRST OF FIELDS AND THOUGH	121	3	DON JUAN	8	21	1
THE WALLS WERE WON BUT 'TWAS AN EVEN BET	150	3	DON JUAN	8	77	5
'TWAS BLOW FOR BLOW DISPUTING INCH BY INCH	150	3	DON JUAN	8	77	7
BUT 'TWAS A TRANSIENT TREMOR--WITH A SPRING	170	3	DON JUAN	8	118	1
IN MARINET'S AFFAIR--IN FACT 'TWAS SHABBY	184	3	DON JUAN	9	2	2
'TWAS SOMETHING CALCULATED TO ALLAY	200	3	DON JUAN	9	36	4
'TWAS A HIGH PLACE THE HIGHEST IN THE NATION	208	3	DON JUAN	9	52	4
AND THOUGH I CAN'T HELP THINKING 'TWAS SCARCE FAIR	242	3	DON JUAN	10	36	5
SOME SAID 'TWAS A CONCOCTION OF THE HUMOURS	244	3	DON JUAN	10	40	5
'TWAS ONLY THE FATIGUE OF LAST CAMPAIGN	244	3	DON JUAN	10	40	8
'TWAS STRANGE ENOUGH SHE SHOULD RETAIN THE IMPRESSION	252	3	DON JUAN	10	56	7
'TWAS FIT THAT HERE AS IN THE HOLY LAND	262	3	DON JUAN	10	75	V2
AND PROVED IT--'TWAS NO MATTER WHAT HE SAID	268	3	DON JUAN	11	1	2
WHAT A SUBLIME DISCOVERY 'TWAS TO MAKE THE	269	3	DON JUAN	11	2	1
HE SOMETIMES THOUGHT 'TWAS ONLY THEIR SALAM	274	3	DON JUAN	11	12	4
'TWAS MERELY KNOWN THAT ON A SECRET MISSION	283	3	DON JUAN	11	32	5
WHERE IS THE WORLD OF EIGHT YEARS PAST 'TWAS THERE--	306	3	DON JUAN	11	76	3
WHATE'ER IT WAS 'TWAS MINE I'VE PAID IN TRUTH	324	3	DON JUAN	12	17	6

		PAGE	VOL		CANTO	STANZA	LN
'TWAS (CONTINUED)							
YOU HAD REASON--'TWAS THAT A YOUNG CHILD OF GRACE		329	3	DON JUAN	12	29	2
'TWAS NOT HER FORTUNE--HE HAS ENOUGH WITHOUT		332	3	DON JUAN	12	35	2
FOR HE WAS SICK--NO 'TWAS NOT THE WORD SICK I MEANT--		346	3	DON JUAN	12	67	3
THOUGH 'TWAS NOT ONCE SO IF I SNEER SOMETIMES		361	3	DON JUAN	13	8	2
BOATS WHEN 'TWAS WATER SKAITING WHEN 'TWAS ICE		407	3	DON JUAN	13	106	3
BOATS WHEN 'TWAS WATER SKAITING WHEN 'TWAS ICE		407	3	DON JUAN	13	106	3
TRUE HE WAS ABSENT AND 'TWAS RUMOUR'D TOOK		430	3	DON JUAN	14	45	3
'TWAS RATHER HER EXPERIENCE MADE HER SAGE		433	3	DON JUAN	14	54	3
LIKE ARCHIMEDES I LEAVE EARTH AS 'TWAS		446	3	DON JUAN	14	84	8
PERHAPS 'TWAS HARDLY QUITE ASSURED ENOUGH		462	3	DON JUAN	15	14	5
OR SEPARATE MAINTENANCE IN CASE 'TWAS DOOM'D--		473	3	DON JUAN	15	39	3
PERHAPS BECAUSE 'TWAS FALLEN HER SIRES WERE PROUD		476	3	DON JUAN	15	46	4
ON THEM AND BREAD 'TWAS OFT MY LUCK TO DINE		488	3	DON JUAN	15	73	5
BUT SO FAR LIKE A LADY THAT 'TWAS DREST		488	3	DON JUAN	15	74	7
THAT WE OURSELVES--'TWAS IN THE HONEY MOON--		517	3	DON JUAN	16	38	2
SAW--WELL NO MATTER 'TWAS SO LONG AGO		517	3	DON JUAN	16	38	3
THE AIR OF 'TWAS A FRIAR OF ORDERS GREY		517	3	DON JUAN	16	38	8
SOME WONDERING 'TWAS SO EARLY SOME SO LATE		527	3	DON JUAN	16	55	4
'TWAS A GREAT BANQUET SUCH AS ALBION OLD		538	3	DON JUAN	16	78	2
BUT 'TWAS A PUBLIC FEAST AND PUBLIC DAY--		538	3	DON JUAN	16	78	5
'TWAS A MERE QUIET SMILE OF CONTEMPLATION		545	3	DON JUAN	16	93	1
TRUE SHE SAID LITTLE--'TWAS THE REST THAT BROKE		552	3	DON JUAN	16	104	1
BUT THEN 'TWAS TO THE PURPOSE WHAT SHE SPOKE		552	3	DON JUAN	16	104	3
TWAS							
BUT E'ER TWAS WELL BEGUN--A HEAVY SEA		183	2	DON JUAN	2	50	V2
TWEED							
LONGBOW FROM IRELAND STRONGBOW FROM THE TWEED		401	3	DON JUAN	13	92	2
TWEEZERS							
FRENCH STUFFS LACE TWEEZERS TOOTHPICKS TEAPOT TRAY		284	2	DON JUAN	3	17	5
FRENCH STUFFS LACE TWEEZERS TOOTHPICKS A BIDET		284	2	DON JUAN	3	17	V5
WITH SOME SMALL AID FROM SCISSORS PAINT AND TWEEZERS		458	2	DON JUAN	5	80	2
TWELFTH							
BESIDES IN CANTO TWELFTH I MEAN TO SHOW		140	2	DON JUAN	1	207	7
IN THIS TWELFTH CANTO 'TIS MY WISH TO BE		325	3	DON JUAN	12	20	3
HERE THE TWELFTH CANTO OF OUR INTRODUCTION		356	3	DON JUAN	12	87	1
TWELVE							
(I WONDER HOW THEY GOT THROUGH THE TWELVE HOURS)		30	2	DON JUAN	1	18	6
AT TWELVE HE WAS A FINE BUT QUIET BOY		49	2	DON JUAN	1	50	2
DIVIDED IN TWELVE BOOKS EACH BOOK CONTAINING		135	2	DON JUAN	1	200	2
AND THE DIM DESOLATE DEEP TWELVE DAYS HAD FEAR		182	2	DON JUAN	2	49	7
GAZED DIM AND DESOLATE--TWELVE DAYS HAD FEAR		182	2	DON JUAN	2	49	V7
EACH CANTO OF THE TWELVE OR TWENTY-FOUR		271	2	DON JUAN	2	216	5
ANNOUNCED HER RANK TWELVE RINGS WERE ON HER HAND		312	2	DON JUAN	3	72	3
UPON YOUR PERSON TWELVE YARDS OFF OR SO		366	2	DON JUAN	4	41	4
TWELVE DAYS AND NIGHTS SHE WITHER'D THUS AT LAST		381	2	DON JUAN	4	69	1
TWELVE NEGRESSES FROM NUBIA BROUGHT A PRICE		408	2	DON JUAN	4	115	1
THE TWELVE ISLES AND THE MORE THAN I COULD DREAM		412	2	DON JUAN	5	3	6
AND OTHERS OF TWELVE CONSONANTS A-PIECE		74	3	DON JUAN	7	15	5
IN TWELVE HOURS' TIME AND VERY LITTLE SPACE		277	3	DON JUAN	11	18	6
THESE FIRST TWELVE BOOKS ARE MERELY FLOURISHES		341	3	DON JUAN	12	54	5
TWELVE SAINTS HAD ONCE STOOD SANCTIFIED IN STONE		386	3	DON JUAN	13	60	2
HUGER THAN TWELVE OF OUR DEGENERATE BREED		391	3	DON JUAN	13	70	4
AYE EVERY INCH A DUKE THERE WERE TWELVE PEERS		398	3	DON JUAN	13	85	2
OR CRAMM'D TWELVE SHEETS INTO ONE LITTLE LETTER		406	3	DON JUAN	13	104	7
TWELVEMONTH'S							
AN ALMOST TWELVEMONTH'S CONSTANCY ENDANGERS		472	2	DON JUAN	5	106	8
TWENTIETH							
THE TENTH OR TWENTIETH NAME WOULD BE BUT BLUNDERED		324	3	DON JUAN	12	19	4
TWENTY							
LIKE FOUR AND TWENTY BLACKBIRDS IN A PYE		9	2	DON JUAN	D	1	8
'TWERE BETTER TO HAVE TWO OF FIVE AND TWENTY		56	2	DON JUAN	1	62	4
WHEN SHE HAD TWENTY YEARS AND THIRTEEN HE		59	2	DON JUAN	1	69	4
THE PLAN OF TWENTY YEARS AND ALL IS OVER		75	2	DON JUAN	1	100	6
WATER A TWENTY GALLON CASK OR SO		181	2	DON JUAN	2	47	3
THAT THERE WAS FUEL TO HAVE FURNISH'D TWENTY		226	2	DON JUAN	2	132	8
SOME TWENTY OF HIS TRAIN CAME RANK ON RANK		369	2	DON JUAN	4	47	7
WHERE TWENTY AGES GATHER O'ER A NAME		398	2	DON JUAN	4	100	4
WHILE NATURE TORTURED TWENTY THOUSAND WAYS		440	2	DON JUAN	5	52	6
WERE RIPE THEY MIGHT MAKE SIX AND TWENTY SPRINGS		468	2	DON JUAN	5	98	2
I WISH THEIR YEARS HAD BEEN FIFTEEN AND TWENTY		9	3	DON JUAN	6	5	2
WHILE TWO AND TWENTY CANNON DULY SET		72	3	DON JUAN	7	12	6
SOME TWENTY TIMES HE MADE THE RUSS RETIRE		171	3	DON JUAN	8	120	3
THOUGH IRELAND STARVE GREAT GEORGE WEIGHS TWENTY STONE		175	3	DON JUAN	8	126	8
BUT ALL THE LADIES SAVE SOME TWENTY SCORE		176	3	DON JUAN	8	129	7
OR SEVEN AND TWENTY--BUT IT DOES NOT MATTER		236	3	DON JUAN	10	24	V7
TO LOSE BY ONE MONTH'S FROST SOME TWENTY YEARS		253	3	DON JUAN	10	58	7
TWENTY-FIRST							
THE LONGEST NOT THE TWENTY-FIRST OF JUNE		82	2	DON JUAN	1	113	5
TWENTY-FIVE							
OF TWENTY-FIVE OR THIRTY--(COME MAKE HASTE)		115	2	DON JUAN	1	172	2
TWENTY-FOUR							
EACH CANTO OF THE TWELVE OR TWENTY-FOUR		271	2	DON JUAN	2	216	5
WHICH TURNS UP OUT OF THE SAD TWENTY-FOUR		426	2	DON JUAN	5	30	8
TWENTY-NINE							
AT LEAST SOME TWENTY-NINE DO OUT OF THIRTY		232	3	DON JUAN	10	15	6
TWENTY-THREE							
WAS MARRIED CHARMING CHASTE AND TWENTY-THREE		54	2	DON JUAN	1	59	8
WHEN HE WAS SIXTEEN JULIA TWENTY-THREE		59	2	DON JUAN	1	69	6

'TWERE
  ('TWERE HARD TO TELL UPON A LIKE OCCASION . . . . . . 38 2 DON JUAN 1 32 3
  'TWERE BETTER TO HAVE TWO OF FIVE AND TWENTY . . . . 56 2 DON JUAN 1 62 4
  AS IF 'TWERE ONE WHEREON MAGICIANS BIND . . . . . . 72 2 DON JUAN 1 95 6
  OR ELSE 'TWERE EASY TO WITHDRAW HER WAIST . . . . . 83 2 DON JUAN 1 115 5
  'TWERE BETTER SURE TO DIE SO THAN BE SHUT . . . . . 112 2 DON JUAN 1 166 7
  BECAUSE THEY TELL ME 'TWERE IN VAIN TO TRY . . . . 142 2 DON JUAN 1 211 6
  'TWERE WELL IF OTHERS FOLLOW'D MY EXAMPLE . . . . . 147 2 DON JUAN 1 221 8
  TO HER AS 'TWERE THE KIND OF BEING SENT . . . . . . 247 2 DON JUAN 2 172 3
  THERE'S SOMETHING OF ANTIPATHY AS 'TWERE . . . . . 278 2 DON JUAN 3 6 1
  AND SWEPT AS 'TWERE ACROSS THEIR HEART'S DELIGHT . . 355 2 DON JUAN 4 21 3
  WHO WOULD AS 'TWERE IDENTIFY THEIR DUST . . . . . . 399 2 DON JUAN 4 101 4
  ALAS SAID JUAN 'TWERE A TALE DISTRESSING . . . . . 419 2 DON JUAN 5 16 5
  AND MARCH AWAY--'TWERE EASIER DONE THAN SAID . . . . 434 2 DON JUAN 5 43 8
  WOULD JUAN BEND THOUGH 'TWERE TO MAHOMET'S BRIDE . . 471 2 DON JUAN 5 103 5
  WAS THROWN AS 'TWERE ABOUT THE NECK OF YOU-- . . . . 474 2 DON JUAN 5 110 3
  'TWERE NOTHING--FOR HER EYES FLASHED ALWAYS FIRE . . 489 2 DON JUAN 5 134 2
  A VULGAR TEMPEST 'TWERE TO A TYPHOON . . . . 490 2 DON JUAN 5 136 1
  COMPANION SOMETHING NEWER STILL AS 'TWERE . . . . . 25 3 DON JUAN 6 39 2
  WHICH ROCKED AS 'TWERE BENEATH THE MIGHTY NOISES . . 115 3 DON JUAN 8 7 6
  SEIZED FAST AS IF 'TWERE BY THE SERPENT'S HEAD . . . 153 3 DON JUAN 8 83 3
  AMBASSADORS BEGAN AS 'TWERE TO HUSTLE . . . . 223 3 DON JUAN 9 82 3
  'TWERE NOT FOR WANT OF LAMPS TO AID HIS DODGING HIS . 281 3 DON JUAN 11 28 5
  LOVE LINGERS STILL ALTHOUGH 'TWERE LATE TO WIVE . . 316 3 DON JUAN 12 2 5
  WOULD NOW AND THEN AS 'TWERE WITHOUT DISPLAY . . . . 521 3 DON JUAN 16 42 5
  'TWERE DIFFICULT TO SAY WHAT WAS THE OBJECT . . . . 526 3 DON JUAN 16 51 1
  'TWERE DIFFICULT TO SAY--BUT JUAN LOOKED . . . . . . 568 3 DON JUAN 17 14 2
TWICE
  A DEMOCRAT SOME ONCE OR TWICE A YEAR . . . . 152 2 DON JUAN 1 V 3 2
  BUT AFTER BEING FIRED AT ONCE OR TWICE . . . . . . 366 2 DON JUAN 4 41 7
  THOUGH WILBERFORCE AT LAST HAS MADE IT TWICE . . . . 408 2 DON JUAN 4 115 3
  THAT IS--THE LADY CLAPPING HIS HANDS TWICE . . . . 458 2 DON JUAN 5 80 7
  FOUR WIVES AND TWICE FIVE HUNDRED MAIDS UNSEEN . . . 496 2 DON JUAN 5 148 7
  IS TWICE AS STRONG AS THAT WHERE YOU WERE WOUNDED . . 98 3 DON JUAN 7 61 8
  YE TWICE TEN HUNDRED THOUSAND DAILY SCRIBES . . . . 200 3 DON JUAN 9 35 2
  AND FOUR-AND-TWENTY HOURS AND TWICE THAT NUMBER . . 248 3 DON JUAN 10 48 2
  AND ABOUT TWICE TWO THOUSAND PEOPLE BRED . . . . . 290 3 DON JUAN 11 45 3
  IN TWICE FIVE YEARS THE GREATEST LIVING POET . . . 296 3 DON JUAN 11 55 1
  THE TWICE TWO THOUSAND FOR WHOM EARTH WAS MADE . . . 381 3 DON JUAN 13 49 2
  ASK'D NEXT DAY IF MEN EVER HUNTED TWICE . . . . . . 425 3 DON JUAN 14 35 3
  CONSOLING US WITH--WOULD YOU HAD THOUGHT TWICE . . . 430 3 DON JUAN 14 47 7
  AND FOURTHLY WHAT NEED HARDLY BE SAID TWICE . . . . 439 3 DON JUAN 14 66 7
  SHE THOUGHT UPON THE SUBJECT TWICE OR THRICE . . . . 469 3 DON JUAN 15 29 5
  AS ONCE OR TWICE TO SMILE IF NOT TO LISTEN . . . . 491 3 DON JUAN 15 80 8
  ONCE TWICE THRICE PASSED REPASSED--THE THING OF AIR . 510 3 DON JUAN 16 23 1
  (UNHEEDED TWICE) TO HAVE A FIN OF FISH . . . . . . 542 3 DON JUAN 16 87 8
TWIG
  WHILE COURAGE CLUNG BUT TO A SINGLE TWIG--AM I . . . 164 3 DON JUAN 8 105 5
TWIGS
  THE TWIGS WHICH SATAN LIMES FOR HUMAN FLIES . . . . 154 3 DON JUAN 8 86 V8
TWILIGHT
  'TWAS TWILIGHT AND THE SUNLESS DAY WENT DOWN . . . . 182 2 DON JUAN 2 49 1
  WITH TWILIGHT IT AGAIN CAME ON TO BLOW . . . . . . 207 2 DON JUAN 2 96 1
  LIKE TWILIGHT ROSY STILL WITH THE SET SUN . . . . . 218 2 DON JUAN 2 118 2
  THE TWILIGHT GLOW WHICH MOMENTLY GREW LESS . . . . 255 2 DON JUAN 2 188 4
  SWEET HOUR OF TWILIGHT--IN THE SOLITUDE . . . . . . 337 2 DON JUAN 3 105 1
  HOW HAVE I LOVED THE TWILIGHT HOUR AND THEE . . . . 337 2 DON JUAN 3 105 8
  AND TWILIGHT SAW THEM LINK'D IN PASSION'S TIES . . . 354 2 DON JUAN 4 20 6
  A PORTION OF YOUR FADING TWILIGHT HUES . . . . . . 108 3 DON JUAN 7 82 7
  TO MAKE A TWILIGHT IN JUST AS SOLMS HEAT IS . . . . 217 3 DON JUAN 9 69 7
  OF TWILIGHT AS THE PARTY CROSSED THE BRIDGE . . . . 279 3 DON JUAN 11 23 8
  LOUNGING AND BOXING AND THE TWILIGHT HOUR . . . . . 301 3 DON JUAN 11 66 2
  SHE ALSO HAD A TWILIGHT TINGE OF BLUE . . . . 524 3 DON JUAN 16 47 1
TWILIGHT'S
  YIELDED TO THE DEEP TWILIGHT'S PURPLE CHARM . . . . 253 2 DON JUAN 2 184 8
  THE ROSY FLOOD OF TWILIGHT'S SKY ADMIRED-- . . . . 334 2 DON JUAN 3 101 6
  HAD MET A PARTY TOWARDS THE TWILIGHT'S FALL . . . . 95 3 DON JUAN 7 56 4
'TWILL
  'TWILL ONE DAY ASK YOU WHY YOU USED ME SO . . . . . 107 2 DON JUAN 1 157 6
  AND THEN AS AN IMPROVEMENT 'TWILL BE SHOWN . . . . 342 2 DON JUAN 3 111 6
  SAID BABA TO BE CURIOUS 'TWILL TRANSPIRE . . . . . 454 2 DON JUAN 5 74 6
  THEN COMES THE TUG OF WAR--'TWILL COME AGAIN . . . . 138 3 DON JUAN 8 51 5
  RAISE BUT AN ARM 'TWILL BRUSH THEIR WEB AWAY . . . . 196 3 DON JUAN 9 28 1
  ALTHOUGH ('TWILL HAPPEN AS OUR PLANET GUIDES) . . . 251 3 DON JUAN 10 54 5
  'TWILL BE BECAUSE OUR NOTION IS NOT HIGH . . . . . 285 3 DON JUAN 11 36 3
  FROM WHAT SOME PEOPLE SAY 'TWILL BE WHEN DONE . . . 356 3 DON JUAN 12 87 4
  'TWILL MAKE IF PROVED VAST EFFORTS WITHOUT PAINING . 366 3 DON JUAN 13 18 8
  FLING UP A STRAW 'TWILL SHOW THE WAY THE WIND BLOWS . 414 3 DON JUAN 14 8 2
  'TWILL BUT PRECIPITATE A SITUATION . . . . 429 3 DON JUAN 14 43 6
  'TWILL TEACH DISCERNMENT TO THE SENSITIVE . . . . . 431 3 DON JUAN 14 49 7
  OR ELSE 'TWILL COST US ALL ANOTHER MILLION . . . . 446 3 DON JUAN 14 83 8
  AND 'TWILL PERPLEX THE CASUISTS IN MORALITY . . . . 448 3 DON JUAN 14 89 7
  WILL FALL BUT IF THEY DO 'TWILL BE THEIR RUIN . . . 454 3 DON JUAN 14 99 8
TWIN
  MUST SHARE IT--HAPPINESS WAS BORN A TWIN . . . . . 247 2 DON JUAN 2 172 8
  TWIN OPPOSITES THE SECOND IS THE BEST . . . . 494 3 DON JUAN 15 87 4
TWINE
  TWINE LIKE A KNOT OF SNAKES AROUND HIS FACE . . . . 510 3 DON JUAN 16 23 6
TWINED
  THEY TWINED LIKE SERPENTS AND THEY KISSED LIKE DOVES . . 257 2 DON JUAN 2 191 V7

```
                                                           PAGE VOL     CANTO STANZA LN
TWINGES
    WITH SOME SLIGHT LIGHT HEREDITARY TWINGES   . . . . . . 515  3 DON JUAN 16     34    7
TWINING
    FOR THAT SAME TWINING TRANSPORT AND SECURITY    . . . .  69  2 DON JUAN  1     88    7
    WHENCE HER FAIR HAIR ROSE TWINING WITH AFFRIGHT   . . . 158  3 DON JUAN  8     93    2
TWINKLE
    ITS TWINKLE THROUGH THE LATTICE DUSKY QUITE  . . . . .   18  3 DON JUAN  6     24    6
TWIRLED
    CHALK MIMICS PAINTING THEN FESTOONS ARE TWIRLED   . . . 302  3 DON JUAN 11     67    5
TWISTED
    ARE TWISTED TO A PHRASE OF SOME OBSCURITY  . . . . . .   69  2 DON JUAN  1     88    8
    THROWN TOPSY-TURVY TWISTED CRISPED AND CURLED   . . . . 201  3 DON JUAN  9     37    4
TWITCHED
    A GLANCE AROUND--AND SHRUGGED--AND TWITCHED HIS SLEEVE . 161  3 DON JUAN  8     99    6
'TWIXT
    'TWIXT HER AND JUAN INTERPOSED THE CREW  . . . . . . .  370  2 DON JUAN  4     48    3
    ONLY TO DRAW THEM 'TWIXT TWO BASTION CORNERS   . . . .  149  3 DON JUAN  8     75    7
    A 'PAPER KITE WHICH FLIES 'TWIXT LIFE AND DEATH   . . . 414  3 DON JUAN 14      8    5
    'TWIXT NIGHT AND MORN UPON THE HORIZON'S VERGE  . . . . 500  3 DON JUAN 15     99    2
    'TWIXT PLACE AND PATRIOTISM--ALBEIT COMPELLED   . . . . 535  3 DON JUAN 16     72    4
    A DIFFERENCE 'TWIXT A BISHOP AND A DEAN   . . . . . . . 541  3 DON JUAN 16     84    5
TWO
    HATH BUT TWO OBJECTS HOW TO SERVE AND BIND   . . . . .   18  2 DON JUAN  0     15    3
    WHISPER'D HE HAD A MISTRESS SOME SAID TWO   . . . . . .  31  2 DON JUAN  1     19    7
    AND HELP THEM WITH A LIE OR TWO ADDITIONAL   . . . . .   37  2 DON JUAN  1     31    2
    A JEW TOOK ONE OF HIS TWO MISTRESSES   . . . . . . . .   39  2 DON JUAN  1     34    4
    'TWERE BETTER TO HAVE TWO OF FIVE AND TWENTY   . . . .   56  2 DON JUAN  1     62    4
    AND NOT EXACTLY EITHER ONE OR TWO  . . . . . . .         57  2 DON JUAN  1     65    6
    WHEN TWO SUCH FACES ARE SO 'TWOULD BE WISE   . . . . .   77  2 DON JUAN  1    105    7
    APPEAR'D LIKE TWO POOR HARMLESS WOMEN WHO   . . . . .    98  2 DON JUAN  1    141    4
    HAD THOUGHT ONE MAN MIGHT BE DETERR'D BY TWO   . . . .   98  2 DON JUAN  1    141    4
    HAVE I NOT HAD TWO BISHOPS AT MY FEET  . . . . . . .    103  2 DON JUAN  1    150    1
    HE CAST A RUEFUL LOOK OR TWO AND DID   . . . . . . .    111  2 DON JUAN  1    163    7
    THERE MIGHT BE ONE MORE MOTIVE WHICH MAKES TWO   . . .  118  2 DON JUAN  1    177    1
    A TEAR OR TWO AND THEN WE MAKE IT UP   . . . . . . .    119  2 DON JUAN  1    179    7
    AND THE TWO LAST HAVE LEFT ME MANY A TOKEN   . . . . .  145  2 DON JUAN  1    217    3
    OF GOOD ADVICE--AND TWO OR THREE OF CREDIT   . . . . .  161  2 DON JUAN  2      9    8
    KEPT TWO HAND AND ONE CHAIN-PUMP STILL IN USE   . . . . 172  2 DON JUAN  2     30    4
    TWO THINGS FOR DYING PEOPLE QUITE BEWILDERING   . . . . 179  2 DON JUAN  2     43    8
    TWO CASKS OF BISCUIT AND A KEG OF BUTTER  . . . . . .   180  2 DON JUAN  2     46    7
    AS THERE WERE BUT TWO BLANKETS FOR A SAIL  . . . . . .  181  2 DON JUAN  2     48    4
    AND TWO BOATS COULD NOT HOLD FAR LESS BE STORED   . . . 181  2 DON JUAN  2     48    7
    ALL THE REST PERISH'D NEAR TWO HUNDRED SOULS   . . . .  185  2 DON JUAN  2     55    1
    TWO BLANKETS STITCH'D TOGETHER ANSWERING ILL   . . . .  188  2 DON JUAN  2     61    3
    REGALED TWO SHARKS WHO FOLLOW'D O'ER THE BILLOW--  . .  197  2 DON JUAN  2     77    7
    AT LENGTH THEY CAUGHT TWO BOOBIES AND A NODDY   . . . . 200  2 DON JUAN  2     82    7
    THERE WERE TWO FATHERS IN THIS GHASTLY CREW   . . . . . 202  2 DON JUAN  2     87    1
    AND WITH THEM THEIR TWO SONS OF WHOM THE ONE   . . . .  202  2 DON JUAN  2     87    2
    THOUGH THE TWO SHARKS STILL FOLLOW'D THEM AND DASH'D .  209  2 DON JUAN  2    101    7
    AS FOR THE OTHER TWO THEY COULD NOT SWIM   . . . . . .  212  2 DON JUAN  2    106    7
    WHO DIED TWO DAYS BEFORE AND NOW HAD FOUND   . . . . .  213  2 DON JUAN  2    109    7
    AND THESE TWO TENDED HIM AND CHEER'D HIM BOTH   . . . . 221  2 DON JUAN  2    123    1
    SHE BEING WISER BY A YEAR OR TWO   . . . . . . . .      228  2 DON JUAN  2    136    4
    MISTAKE YOU WOULD HAVE MADE ON SEEING THE TWO   . . . . 232  2 DON JUAN  2    142    6
    OF WHOM THESE TWO YEARS SHE HAD NIGHTLY DREAM'D  . . .  247  2 DON JUAN  2    172    4
    WITH ONE OR TWO SMALL SENSES ADDED JUST  . . . . . .    269  2 DON JUAN  2    212    7
    TWO HUNDRED AND ODD STANZAS AS BEFORE  . . . . . .      271  2 DON JUAN  2    216    3
    THESE TWO FORM THE LAST GASP OF PASSION'S BREATH  . . . 280  2 DON JUAN  3      9    V3
    THESE TWO ARE LEVELLERS AND HUMAN BREATH   . . . . . .  280  2 DON JUAN  3      9    V3
    THE ONLY TWO THAT IN MY RECOLLECTION   . . . . . . .    281  2 DON JUAN  3     10    1
    ALTHOUGH A SQUALL OR TWO HAD DAMP'D HIS RAPTURES  . . . 283  2 DON JUAN  3     15    4
    TWO PARROTS WITH A PERSIAN CAT AND KITTENS   . . . . .  285  2 DON JUAN  3     18    2
    TO HIS MEMORY AND TWO OR THREE YOUNG MISSES   . . . . . 287  2 DON JUAN  3     23    6
    AND HIS ONE BLOW LEFT LITTLE WORK FOR TWO  . . . . . .  300  2 DON JUAN  3     48    8
    SHE WORE TWO JELICKS--ONE WAS OF PALE YELLOW   . . . .  311  2 DON JUAN  3     70    2
    OF TWO SUCH LESSONS WHY FORGET  . . . . . . . .         324  2 DON JUAN  3  L 10    3
    ESPOUSED TWO PARTNERS (MILLINERS OF BATH)  . . . . . .  329  2 DON JUAN  3     93    8
    (IN COPYING) THIS LONG CANTO INTO TWO  . . . . . . .    342  2 DON JUAN  3    111    3
    WOULD WITHER LESS THAN THESE TWO TORN APART   . . . . . 349  2 DON JUAN  4     10    7
    BUT LIKE TWO BEINGS BORN FROM OUT A RILL   . . . . . .  352  2 DON JUAN  4     15    5
    ONE OF THE TWO ACCORDING TO YOUR CHOICE  . . . . . .    357  2 DON JUAN  4     25    1
    WHEN TWO PURE HEARTS ARE POUR'D IN ONE ANOTHER  . . . . 357  2 DON JUAN  4     26    5
    FROM TWO SMART SABRE GASHES DEEP AND RED--   . . . . .  370  2 DON JUAN  4     49    7
    THE TENOR THESE TWO HATED WITH A HATE  . . . . . . .    394  2 DON JUAN  4     93    2
    WE WILL OMIT THE PROOFS SAVE ONE OR TWO  . . . . . .    396  2 DON JUAN  4     94    4
    AT THE FIRST TWO BOOKS HAVING TOO MUCH TRUTH   . . . .  397  2 DON JUAN  4     97    4
    TO PASS THAN THOSE TWO CANTOS INTO FAMILIES   . . . . . 397  2 DON JUAN  4     97    8
    NO--ONLY TWO AT PRESENT ABOVE GROUND   . . . . . . .    421  2 DON JUAN  5     20    3
    OR SOMETIMES ONLY WEAR A WEEK OR TWO--   . . . . . . .  422  2 DON JUAN  5     22    4
    AFTER DISPOSING OF TWO FELLOW CREATURES  . . . . . .    426  2 DON JUAN  5     30    V2
    OR AMMON'S--FOR TWO FATHERS CLAIMED THIS ONE   . . . .  427  2 DON JUAN  5     31    V8
    OF EATING WITH ANOTHER ACT OR TWO  . . . . . . .        428  2 DON JUAN  5     32    2
    OR THREE OR TWO OR ONE SEND VERY FAR   . . . . . . .    432  2 DON JUAN  5     39    3
    WITH HIS TWO CAPTIVES BY SO QUEER A ROAD   . . . . . .  436  2 DON JUAN  5     45    3
    ONE OR TWO STARED THE CAPTIVES IN THE FACE   . . . . .  441  2 DON JUAN  5     54    5
    TWO OR THREE SEEM SO LITTLE ONE SEEMS NOTHING   . . . . 443  2 DON JUAN  5     57    1
    AND WRITTEN LATELY TWO MEMOIRS UPON'T)   . . . . . . .  447  2 DON JUAN  5     62    6
    FROM OUT THE HEAP A PETTICOAT OR TWO   . . . . . . .    455  2 DON JUAN  5     76    V8
    TWO LITTLE DWARFS THE LEAST YOU COULD SUPPOSE   . . . . 462  2 DON JUAN  5     87    3
```

TWO   (CONTINUED)

	PAGE	VOL	CANTO	STANZA	LN
AND LOOKING LIKE TWO INCUBI THEY GLARED	463	2 DON JUAN	5	90	2
IS JUST TWO MINUTES FOR YOUR DECLARATION--	482	2 DON JUAN	5	123	7
ONE OR THE OTHER BUT WHICH OF THE TWO	499	2 DON JUAN	5	153	3
WHY DON'T THEY KNEAD TWO VIRTUOUS SOULS FOR LIFE	502	2 DON JUAN	5	158	7
WITH ALL THINGS LADIES WANT SAVE ONE OR TWO	31	3 DON JUAN	6	51	7
THAN WHERE TWO WIVES ARE UNDER AN EMBARGO	51	3 DON JUAN	6	90	8
ONE TWO OR THREE--OR FOUR OR LESS OR MORE	51	3 DON JUAN	6	91	V5
BRING THE TWO SLAVES SHE SAID IN A LOW TONE	62	3 DON JUAN	6	112	2
THEIR NEVER KNOWING THEIR OWN MIND TWO DAYS	64	3 DON JUAN	6	117	6
TWO BATTERIES CAP-A-PIE AS OUR SAINT GEORGE	72	3 DON JUAN	7	12	3
WHILE TWO AND TWENTY CANNON DULY SET	72	3 DON JUAN	7	12	6
THE RUSSIANS HAVING BUILT TWO BATTERIES ON	78	3 DON JUAN	7	23	1
AN ISLE NEAR ISMAIL HAD TWO ENDS IN VIEW	78	3 DON JUAN	7	23	2
IN SIGHT TWO HORSEMEN WHO WERE DEEMED COSSACQUES	87	3 DON JUAN	7	43	2
FOR THERE WERE BUT THREE SHIRTS BETWEEN THE TWO	87	3 DON JUAN	7	43	5
BUT ON THEY RODE UPON TWO UKRAINE HACKS	87	3 DON JUAN	7	43	6
THE THIRD IN COLUMNS TWO ATTACKED BY WATER	91	3 DON JUAN	7	50	8
THE OTHER TWO ARE WOMEN AND THE THIRD	97	3 DON JUAN	7	60	2
BUT THESE ARE BUT TWO TURKISH LADIES WHO	103	3 DON JUAN	7	72	1
MEANTIME THESE TWO POOR GIRLS WITH SWIMMING EYES	104	3 DON JUAN	7	73	1
WHAT WAS'T TO HIM TO HEAR TWO WOMEN SOB	105	3 DON JUAN	7	77	8
TO THEIR TWO SELVES ONE WHOLE BRIGHT BULLETIN	121	3 DON JUAN	8	19	8
A YARD OR TWO OF GROUND WHICH BROUGHT THEM NIGHER	121	3 DON JUAN	8	20	3
FIRST ONE OR TWO THEN FIVE SIX AND A DOZEN	135	3 DON JUAN	8	45	1
SHORT SPEECHES PASS BETWEEN TWO MEN WHO SPEAK	141	3 DON JUAN	8	58	1
TWO LONG OCTAVES PASSED IN A LITTLE MINUTE	142	3 DON JUAN	8	59	2
ONLY TO DRAW THEM 'TWIXT TWO BASTION CORNERS	149	3 DON JUAN	8	75	7
TWO VILLAINOUS COSSACQUES PURSUED THE CHILD	157	3 DON JUAN	8	92	1
CHILD OR AN AGED HELPLESS MAN OR TWO--	174	3 DON JUAN	8	124	4
A SLICE OR TWO FROM YOUR LUXURIOUS MEALS	185	3 DON JUAN	9	6	4
THE TWO FIRST FEELINGS RAN THEIR COURSE COMPLETE	213	3 DON JUAN	9	61	1
AND THE TWO ARE SO MIXED WITH HUMAN DUST	221	3 DON JUAN	9	77	5
THAT ONE SHOULD DIE THAN TWO DRAG ON THE FETTER)	222	3 DON JUAN	9	80	8
AQ FERVENT OUNCE AND A HALF TWO DRAMS TINCT SENNAE	244	3 DON JUAN	10	41	3
FOR ONE OR TWO DAYS READER WE REQUEST	248	3 DON JUAN	10	49	2
AND BRUSH A WEB OR TWO FROM OFF THE WALLS	266	3 DON JUAN	10	84	8
AND ABOUT TWICE TWO THOUSAND PEOPLE BRED	290	3 DON JUAN	11	45	3
LATE AUTHORS ASKED HIM FOR A HINT OR TWO	294	3 DON JUAN	11	50	6
AND WORDSWORTH HAS SUPPORTERS TWO OR THREE	298	3 DON JUAN	11	59	6
I THINK I KNOW A TRICK OR TWO WOULD TURN	300	3 DON JUAN	11	63	1
WITH THE SAME THOUGHT THE TWO WORDS HAVE HELPED OUT	323	3 DON JUAN	12	15	4
HIMSELF FOR FIVE FOUR THREE OR TWO YEAR'S SPACE	329	3 DON JUAN	12	29	6
AND ONE OR TWO SAD SEPARATE WIVES WITHOUT	330	3 DON JUAN	12	31	1
THOSE BECAME ONE WHO SOON WERE TO BE TWO	334	3 DON JUAN	12	38	6
PRELUDIOS TRYING JUST A STRING OR TWO	341	3 DON JUAN	12	54	6
I THOUGHT AT SETTING OFF ABOUT TWO DOZEN	341	3 DON JUAN	12	55	5
SHE CANNOT DO THESE THINGS NOR ONE OR TWO	351	3 DON JUAN	12	76	1
OF THE TWO PRINCIPLES BUT LEAVES BEHIND	377	3 DON JUAN	13	41	6
THE TWICE TWO THOUSAND FOR WHOM EARTH WAS MADE	381	3 DON JUAN	13	49	2
THESE ALSO WERE TWO WITS BY ACCLAMATION	401	3 DON JUAN	13	92	1
FORM'D OF TWO MIGHTY TRIBES THE BORES AND BORED	402	3 DON JUAN	13	95	8
BUT THE TWO YOUNGEST LOVED MORE TO BE SET	408	3 DON JUAN	13	107	6
IN PLAY THERE ARE TWO PLEASURES FOR YOUR CHOOSING--	415	3 DON JUAN	14	12	7
OH JOB YOU HAD TWO FRIENDS ONE'S QUITE ENOUGH	431	3 DON JUAN	14	48	1
ANOTHER GENTLE COMMON-PLACE OR TWO	440	3 DON JUAN	14	69	2
MUST THE EVENT DECIDE BETWEEN THE TWO	449	3 DON JUAN	14	90	3
YET MADE THE MISERY OF AT LEAST TWO LIVES	452	3 DON JUAN	14	95	8
TWO WEEDS WHICH POSE OUR ECONOMIC CATOS	472	3 DON JUAN	15	37	8
AND THE TWO FAIR CO-HEIRESSES GILTBEDDING	473	3 DON JUAN	15	40	5
OF INTELLECT EXPENDED ON TWO COURSES	486	3 DON JUAN	15	69	2
WHICH PROVE PLAIN ENGLISH TRUER OF THE TWO	488	3 DON JUAN	15	72	6
WITH TWO TRANSCENDANT EYES SEEMED TO LOOK THROUGH HIM	489	3 DON JUAN	15	75	8
OPINIONS TWO WHICH AT FIRST SIGHT MAY LOOK	494	3 DON JUAN	15	87	3
BETWEEN TWO WORLDS LIFE HOVERS LIKE A STAR	500	3 DON JUAN	15	99	1
BOWS HAVE THEY GENERALLY WITH TWO STRINGS	501	3 DON JUAN	16	1	5
THERE WERE TWO LAWYERS BUSY ON A MORTGAGE	530	3 DON JUAN	16	60	1
THERE WERE TWO POACHERS CAUGHT IN A STEEL TRAP	530	3 DON JUAN	16	61	1
THE LATTER WORSE USED OF THE TWO WE'VE SEEN--	541	3 DON JUAN	16	84	3
OF TWO THINGS--HOW (THE QUESTION RATHER ODD IS)	543	3 DON JUAN	16	90	7
WHO THOUGH THEY PROVE NOT TWO AND TWO TO BE	548	3 DON JUAN	16	99	2
WHO THOUGH THEY PROVE NOT TWO AND TWO TO BE	548	3 DON JUAN	16	99	6
THERE WERE BUT TWO EXCEPTIONS TO THIS KEEN	552	3 DON JUAN	16	105	1
FOR HE HAD TWO BOTH TOLERABLY BRIGHT	558	3 DON JUAN	16	117	6
A RED LIP WITH TWO ROWS OF PEARLS BENEATH	560	3 DON JUAN	16	121	6
THE SACRAMENTS HAVE BEEN REDUCED TO TWO	565	3 DON JUAN	17	7	1
FOR ONE WITHOUT--HAS TWO OR THREE WITHIN	567	3 DON JUAN	17	11	8

TWO'S

	PAGE	VOL	CANTO	STANZA	LN
A YEAR OR TWO'S AN AGE WHEN RIGHTLY SPENT	228	2 DON JUAN	2	136	5

'TWOULD

	PAGE	VOL	CANTO	STANZA	LN
WHEN TWO SUCH FACES ARE SO 'TWOULD BE WISE	77	2 DON JUAN	1	105	7
AND IF YOU HAD IT O'ER AGAIN--'TWOULD PASS--	147	2 DON JUAN	1	220	6
'TWOULD SAVE US MANY A HEART-ACHE MANY A SHILLING	270	2 DON JUAN	2	213	5
THE READER BUT 'TWOULD NOT BE HARD TO BRING	332	2 DON JUAN	3	97	6
FROM ALL THE POPE MAKES YEARLY 'TWOULD PERPLEX	391	2 DON JUAN	4	86	7
'TWOULD NOT BECOME MYSELF TO DWELL UPON	392	2 DON JUAN	4	88	1
'TWOULD GIVE ME PLEASURE--PRAY WHAT IS YOUR NATION	417	2 DON JUAN	5	13	8
'TWOULD GREATLY TEND TO BETTER THEIR CONDITION	451	2 DON JUAN	5	69	7
'TWOULD BE AS WELL AND--(THOUGH THERE'S NOT MUCH IN'T)	464	2 DON JUAN	5	91	5

	PAGE	VOL	CANTO	STANZA	LN
'TWOULD (CONTINUED)					
'TWOULD BE CONVENIENT FOR THESE MUTES HAVE EYES	464	2 DON JUAN	5	92	1
YET AFTER ALL 'TWOULD PUZZLE TO SAY WHERE	27	3 DON JUAN	6	42	7
AS IF 'TWOULD TO A SECOND SPRING RESIGN	395	3 DON JUAN	13	77	3
BUT THEN 'TWOULD SPOIL MUCH GOOD PHILOSOPHY	410	3 DON JUAN	14	1	4
T'YE					
IN GREECE HE'D SING SOME SORT OF HYMN LIKE THIS T'YE	320	2 DON JUAN	3	86	8
TYMPANUM					
TREMENDOUS TO A MORTAL TYMPANUM	557	3 DON JUAN	16	115	6
TYPE					
THE ALLEGORY) A MERE TYPE NO MORE	238	2 DON JUAN	2	155	6
TYPHOON					
A VULGAR TEMPEST 'TWERE TO A TYPHOON	490	2 DON JUAN	5	136	1
TYPOGRAPHY					
THAN ANY SINCE THE BIRTHDAY OF TYPOGRAPHY	330	2 DON JUAN	3	94	6
TYRANNY					
THE VULGAREST TOOL THAT TYRANNY COULD WANT	16	2 DON JUAN	D	12	5
OF ANCIENT DAYS ERE TYRANNY GREW STRONG	379	2 DON JUAN	4	65	8
YET EVEN HER TYRANNY HAD SUCH A GRACE	476	2 DON JUAN	5	113	7
OF TYRANNY OF ALL KINDS MY CONCISION	466	3 DON JUAN	15	22	7
TYRANT					
THE PRINCE'S TYRANT--TILL HE HEARS THE DRUMS	151	2 DON JUAN	1 V	2	V8
THE PRINCE'S TYRANT--THROUGH LUST OF POWER	151	2 DON JUAN	1 V	2	V8
A TYRANT BUT OUR MASTERS THEN	324	2 DON JUAN	3 L	11	5
THE TYRANT OF THE CHERSONESE	325	2 DON JUAN	3 L	12	1
THAT TYRANT WAS MILTIADES	325	2 DON JUAN	3 L	12	3
ON MOST THINGS FROM A TYRANT TO A TREE	37	3 DON JUAN	6	63	4
TYRANT-HATER					
BUT CLOSED THE TYRANT-HATER HE BEGUN	15	2 DON JUAN	D	10	8
TYRANT'S					
THE TYRANT'S WISH THAT MANKIND ONLY HAD	19	3 DON JUAN	6	27	2
UNLESS ON TYRANT'S STERNS--WE TURN THE STERNEST	286	3 DON JUAN	11	38	V8
BETWEEN THE TYRANT'S AND THE TRIBUNES' CREW	306	3 DON JUAN	11	75	6
SO PERISH EVERY TYRANT'S ROBE PIECE-MEAL	505	3 DON JUAN	16	10	8
TYRANTS					
TO RISE AGAINST EARTH'S TYRANTS NEVER LET IT	179	3 DON JUAN	8	135	5
OF TYRANTS AND BEEN BLEST FROM SHORE TO SHORE	187	3 DON JUAN	9	9	4
TYRANTS AND SYCOPHANTS HAVE BEEN AND ARE	194	3 DON JUAN	9	24	4
MOCK TYRANTS WHEN ROME'S ANNALS WAXED BUT DIRTY	299	3 DON JUAN	11	61	8
TYRE					
ROME BABYLON TYRE CARTHAGE NINEVEH	142	3 DON JUAN	8	60	5
TYRIAN					
WITH HANNIBAL AND WEARS THE TYRIAN TUNIC	122	3 DON JUAN	8	23	6
YET I WISH WELL TO TROJAN AND TO TYRIAN	496	3 DON JUAN	15	91	7
IMPARTIAL BETWEEN TYRIAN AND TROJAN	497	3 DON JUAN	15	92	3
NO REAL LIKENESS--LIKE THE OLD TYRIAN VEST	505	3 DON JUAN	16	10	5
TYRTAEUS					
OF FREEDOM THAT THIS NOW INSPIRED TYRTAEUS	319	2 DON JUAN	3	84	V2
UGLIEST					
FOR FROM A ROOT THE UGLIEST IN OLD SPAIN	53	2 DON JUAN	1	58	3
IN A NEW FACE THE UGLIEST CREATURE BREATHING	24	3 DON JUAN	6	37	8
UGLINESS					
IN BATTLE TO OLD AGE AND UGLINESS	167	3 DON JUAN	8	112	V4
AND UGLINESS DISEASE AS TOIL AND TROUBLE--	305	3 DON JUAN	11	74	7
UGLY					
WERE SATE LIKE UGLY IMPS AS IF ALLIED	462	2 DON JUAN	5	87	4
UGLY FOR INSTANCE--NINON DEL'ENCLOS	468	2 DON JUAN	5	98	8
UGOLINO					
REMEMBER UGOLINO CONDESCENDS	200	2 DON JUAN	2	83	2
UKRAINE					
BUT ON THEY RODE UPON TWO UKRAINE HACKS	87	3 DON JUAN	7	43	6
ULTIMATE					
OUR ULTIMATE EXISTENCE WHAT'S OUR PRESENT	37	3 DON JUAN	6	63	7
ULTRA-JULIAN					
IS IT NOT SO MY TORY ULTRA-JULIAN	20	2 DON JUAN	D	17	8
ULTRA-ROYALIST					
AND WAX AN ULTRA-ROYALIST IN LOYALTY	466	3 DON JUAN	15	23	7
ULYSSES					
MAY NOT HAVE THE GOOD FORTUNE OF ULYSSES	287	2 DON JUAN	3	23	2
ULYSSES'					
BUT FULL OF CUNNING AS ULYSSES' WHISTLE	407	3 DON JUAN	13	105	6
UMBRAGE					
THE UMBRAGE OF THE WOOD SO COOL AND DUN	289	2 DON JUAN	3	27	5
UNANIMITY					
A GENERAL COUNCIL IN WHICH UNANIMITY	92	3 DON JUAN	7	51	2
UNAWARES					
A PAIL OF HOUSEMAID'S WATER UNAWARES	34	2 DON JUAN	1	24	8
SUCH I MIGHT STUMBLE OVER UNAWARES	370	3 DON JUAN	13	26	7
UNBELIEVERS					
BELIEVE THE JEWS THOSE UNBELIEVERS WHO	447	2 DON JUAN	5	62	7
UNBLEST					
HE DIED BENEATH A TREE AS MUCH UNBLEST ON	84	3 DON JUAN	7	36	6
FROM THOSE OF OTHER LANDS UNBLEST WITH JURIES	436	3 DON JUAN	14	60	7
UNBLUNTED					
UNWITHERING MYRTLE ROUND THE UNBLUNTED DART	554	3 DON JUAN	16	109	6
UNBORN					
AND WENT DOWN TO THE GRAVE UNBORN WHEREIN	382	2 DON JUAN	4	70	5
IN AN APPEAL TO THE UNBORN WHOM THEY	324	3 DON JUAN	12	18	2
UNBOUNDED					
WELL YOU SHALL HAVE REVENGE AND THAT UNBOUNDED	98	3 DON JUAN	7	61	VI
THE UNBOUNDED HOPE AND HEAVENLY IGNORANCE	554	3 DON JUAN	16	108	2

	PAGE	VOL	CANTO	STANZA	LN
UNCERTAIN					
A CERTAIN PORTION OF UNCERTAIN PAPER	146	2 DON JUAN	1	218	2
UNCERTAINTY					
UNCERTAINTY IS ONE OF MANY BLISSES	105	3 DON JUAN	7	76	5
THEIR REASONS WERE UNCERTAINTY OR SHAME	132	3 DON JUAN	8	38	5
UNCHAINED					
A MONK REMAINED UNCHASED UNCHAINED	518	3 DON JUAN	16 L	2	5
UNCHANGED					
DAYS LAY SHE IN THAT STATE UNCHANGED THOUGH CHILL . '. .	377	2 DON JUAN	4	60	1
BUT FIX'D AS MARBLE'S UNCHANGED ASPECT THROWS	377	2 DON JUAN	4	61	3
UNCHASED					
A MONK REMAINED UNCHASED UNCHAINED	518	3 DON JUAN	16 L	2	5
UNCIVIL					
I FAVOUR'D NONE--NAY WAS ALMOST UNCIVIL	102	2 DON JUAN	1	148	6
UNCLIPT					
BUT) OF FINE UNCLIPT GOLD WHERE DULLY RESTS	321	3 DON JUAN	12	12	5
UNCLOSED					
HIS EYES HE OPEN'D SHUT AGAIN UNCLOSED	215	2 DON JUAN	2	112	1
THE ONLY THING WHICH KEPT HIS HEART UNCLOSED	304	2 DON JUAN	3	57	3
AT LEAST--AND THEN SHE TOO UNCLOSED HER EYES	42	3 DON JUAN	6	73	7
THAT SCARLET CLOAK ALAS UNCLOSED WITH RIGOUR	530	3 DON JUAN	16	61	7
UNCOMMON					
I WANT A HERO AN UNCOMMON WANT	21	2 DON JUAN	1	1	1
A KIND OF STATE MORE AWKWARD THAN UNCOMMON	10	3 DON JUAN	6	7	2
HE ALSO HAD A QUALITY UNCOMMON	426	3 DON JUAN	14	36	1
UNCONSCIOUS					
AND ALL UNCONSCIOUS OF THE JOY 'TIS GIVING	261	2 DON JUAN	2	197	4
UNCONSCIOUS ALBEIT TURNED OF QUICK SEVENTEEN	33	3 DON JUAN	6	54	6
HER BEAUTIES SEIZED THE UNCONSCIOUS HOUR OF NIGHT . .	39	3 DON JUAN	6	66	7
HE SEEMED UNCONSCIOUS OF ALL PASSING THERE	542	3 DON JUAN	16	87	6
UNCONSCIOUSLY					
UNCONSCIOUSLY SHE LEAN'D UPON THE OTHER	80	2 DON JUAN	1	110	1
ITS POWER UNCONSCIOUSLY FULL MANY A TIME--	304	2 DON JUAN	3	56	3
UNCONTROVERTIBLE					
ON SO UNCONTROVERTIBLE A LEVEL	271	3 DON JUAN	11	6	6
UNCORRUPTED					
HAD LEFT THE WRETCH AN UNCORRUPTED HOUR	339	2 DON JUAN	3	109	8
UNCOUTH					
SOME LITTLE HAMLETS WITH NEW NAMES UNCOUTH	387	2 DON JUAN	4	78	2
UNCOUTHLY					
A BROKEN PILLAR NOT UNCOUTHLY HEWN	400	2 DON JUAN	4	103	5
UNCURDLED					
WHITE STOCKINGS DRAWN UNCURDLED AS NEW MILK	204	3 DON JUAN	9	43	7
UNDECIDED					
PAULO MAJORA JUAN UNDECIDED	327	3 DON JUAN	12	25	2
UNDEFILED					
HIS ONLY SHRINE OF FEELINGS UNDEFILED	302	2 DON JUAN	3	52	8
UNDEFINABLE					
THAT UNDEFINABLE JE NE SCAIS QUOI	441	3 DON JUAN	14	72	2
UNDER					
UNDER THE BED THEY SEARCH'D AND THERE THEY FOUND-- . .	100	2 DON JUAN	1	144	1
OF LOOKING IN THE BED AS WELL AS UNDER	100	2 DON JUAN	1	144	8
UNDER PRETENCE OF BUSINESS INDISPENSIBLE	103	2 DON JUAN	1	151	2
THE ANTI-CHAMBER--SEARCH THEM UNDER OVER	104	2 DON JUAN	1	153	2
HIS TEMPER NOT BEING UNDER GREAT COMMAND	123	2 DON JUAN	1	185	4
THEY ALSO LIE TOO--UNDER A MISTAKE	141	2 DON JUAN	1	208	8
JUAN EMBARK'D--THE SHIP GOT UNDER WAY	162	2 DON JUAN	2	11	1
UNDER THE VESSEL'S KEEL THE SAIL WAS PAST	176	2 DON JUAN	2	39	1
ON BOARD OF ONE OF THESE AND UNDER HATCHES	371	2 DON JUAN	4	50	7
AT ANCHOR UNDER THE SERAGLIO WALL	407	2 DON JUAN	4	113	4
AS IF THE MILKY WAY THEIR FEET WAS UNDER	450	2 DON JUAN	5	66	4
UNDER A CANOPY AND THERE RECLINED	466	2 DON JUAN	5	95	2
THAN WHERE TWO WIVES ARE UNDER AN EMBARGO	51	3 DON JUAN	6	90	8
THE RUSS FLOTILLA GETTING UNDER WAY	81	3 DON JUAN	7	29	2
NOW UNDER ARMS HO KATSKOFF TAKE HIM TO--	100	3 DON JUAN	7	66	3
SO MUCH AS UNDER A TRIUMPHAL ARCH	121	3 DON JUAN	8	21	4
UNDER THE ORDERS OF THE GENERAL LASCY	130	3 DON JUAN	8	34	3
(THOUGH THESE TO OUR GIBRALTAR MUST KNOCK UNDER)-- . .	136	3 DON JUAN	8	46	6
YOU NEED NOT TAKE THEM UNDER YOUR DIRECTION	186	3 DON JUAN	9	7	6
THE HUMBLEST INDIVIDUAL UNDER HEAVEN	309	3 DON JUAN	11	82	3
A HIDDEN NECTAR UNDER A COLD PRESENCE	375	3 DON JUAN	13	38	3
WHICH BEAT AS IF THERE WAS A WARM HEART UNDER	560	3 DON JUAN	16	122	4
UNDERGO					
WOMAN OR WINE YOU'LL HAVE TO UNDERGO	357	2 DON JUAN	4	25	2
TILL OLD MAY UNDERGO ADULTERATION	458	3 DON JUAN	15	6	8
UNDERGOES					
AS ANY MAN'S CLAY MIXTURE UNDERGOES	16	3 DON JUAN	6	20	5
UNDERGROUND					
WHEN THIS WORLD SHALL BE FORMER UNDERGROUND	201	3 DON JUAN	9	37	3
UNDERLINGS					
BESIDES THE MINISTERS AND UNDERLINGS	287	3 DON JUAN	11	40	1
UNDERNEATH					
THE HAND FROM BURNING UNDERNEATH THEM PLACED	307	2 DON JUAN	3	63	6
SWEEPING THE MARBLE UNDERNEATH HER CHAIR	60	3 DON JUAN	6	108	3
SOUNDS LESS HARMONIOUS UNDERNEATH THE SUN SOON	132	3 DON JUAN	8	39	4
THEN UNDERNEATH AND IN THE VERY SAME	383	3 DON JUAN	13	54	4
UNDER-RATE					
A TENDENCY TO UNDER-RATE AND SCOFF	67	3 DON JUAN	7	3	3
UNDERSTAND					
THINKING GOD MIGHT NOT UNDERSTAND HER CASE	62	2 DON JUAN	1	75	V8

864

PAGE VOL CANTO STANZA LN

UNDERSTAND   (CONTINUED)
  WE MEET AGAIN IF WE SHOULD UNDERSTAND . . . . 147 2 DON JUAN 1 221 5
  WHO SEVERAL LANGUAGES DID UNDERSTAND . . . . 169 2 DON JUAN 2   25 3
  HER LIP WHICH ZOE NEEDS MUST UNDERSTAND . . . . 234 2 DON JUAN 2 146 5
  NOW JUAN COULD NOT UNDERSTAND A WORD . . . . 236 2 DON JUAN 2 151 1
  SHE SAW HE DID NOT UNDERSTAND ROMAIC . . . . 241 2 DON JUAN 2 161 8
  TO MAKE US UNDERSTAND EACH GOOD OLD MAXIM . . . . . . 264 2 DON JUAN 2 203 7
  I DON'T PRETEND THAT I QUITE UNDERSTAND . . . . 346 2 DON JUAN 4   5 4
  AS OVID'S VERSE MAY GIVE TO UNDERSTAND . . . . 411 2 DON JUAN 5   1 6
  AS I WILL MAKE YOU QUICKLY UNDERSTAND . . . . 411 2 DON JUAN 5   1 V6
  THOU RIDDLE--WHICH ALL READ--NONE UNDERSTAND . . . . 210 3 DON JUAN 9   56 V7
  JUAN WHO DID NOT UNDERSTAND A WORD . . . . 274 3 DON JUAN 11   12 1
  BUT 'TIS AS WELL AT ONCE TO UNDERSTAND . . . . 311 3 DON JUAN 11   87 6
  WHICH FOREIGNERS CAN NEVER UNDERSTAND . . . . 326 3 DON JUAN 12   23 8
  WE UNDERSTAND THE SPLENDID HOST INTENDS . . . . 382 3 DON JUAN 13   52 1
  THIS HE (AS FAR AS I CAN UNDERSTAND) MEANT . . . . . 472 3 DON JUAN 15   38 4
  WITH THINGS I CAN'T WITHSTAND OR UNDERSTAND . . . . . 484 3 DON JUAN 15   66 3
  NO BUT YOU HAVE HEARD--I UNDERSTAND--BE DUMB . . . . 498 3 DON JUAN 15   95 2
UNDERSTANDING
  TO SOME SPOT WHERE THEY LOST THEIR UNDERSTANDING . . . 148 3 DON JUAN 8   72 3
UNDERSTANDS
  AND HE WHO UNDERSTANDS IT WOULD BE ABLE . . . . 11 2 DON JUAN D   4 7
  AND WHY AND WHEREFORE NO ONE UNDERSTANDS . . . . 33 2 DON JUAN 1   21 8
UNDERSTOOD
  BUT THEN I BEG IT MAY BE UNDERSTOOD . . . . 68 2 DON JUAN 1   87 6
  WHEN SOUTHEY'S READ AND WORDSWORTH UNDERSTOOD . . . . 149 2 DON JUAN 1 222 5
  THE LEAST GLANCE BETTER UNDERSTOOD THAN WORDS . . . . 351 2 DON JUAN 4   14 2
  HAD CATHERINE AND THE SULTAN UNDERSTOOD . . . . 53 3 DON JUAN 6   95 1
  'TWAS MUCH THAT HE WAS UNDERSTOOD AT ALL . . . . 95 3 DON JUAN 7   56 6
  HOWEVER LITTLE BOTH ARE UNDERSTOOD . . . . 193 3 DON JUAN 9   22 4
  JUAN YET QUICKLY UNDERSTOOD THEIR GESTURE . . . . . . 274 3 DON JUAN 11   13 1
  AND YOUR TRUE FEELINGS FULLY UNDERSTOOD . . . . 451 3 DON JUAN 14   93 6
UNDERTAKE
  TO UNDERTAKE THE ORPHAN'S EDUCATION   . . . . 330 3 DON JUAN 12   30 3
UNDERTAKING
  TO SPOIL HIS UNDERTAKING OR COMPLETE . . . . 423 3 DON JUAN 14   30 6
UNDERWENT
  MY BOSOM UNDERWENT A GLORIOUS GLOW . . . . 226 3 DON JUAN 10   3 3
  WHAT JUAN SAW AND UNDERWENT SHALL BE . . . . 311 3 DON JUAN 11   88 1
UNDESCRIBED
  ALAS I MUST LEAVE UNDESCRIBED THE GIBIER . . . . . . 487 3 DON JUAN 15   71 1
UNDISCOVERED
  YET UNDISCOVERED TREASURE WHAT I CAN . . . . 281 3 DON JUAN 11   28 6
UNDISMAYED
  'TWAS NINE WHEN STILL ADVANCING UNDISMAYED . . . . . . 81 3 DON JUAN 7   29 3
UNDISPLAYED
  UNKNOWN TO THOSE POSSESSORS--OR UNDISPLAYED . . . . . 485 2 DON JUAN 5 129 V6
UNDO
  DO PRAY UNDO THE BOLT A LITTLE FASTER-- . . . . 96 2 DON JUAN 1 137 5
  AND HIS BLOW DID WHAT WORDS COULD NOT UNDO . . . . . 300 2 DON JUAN 3   48 V8
UNDOING
  BUT WHEN THE LATTER WORKS ITS OWN UNDOING . . . . . . 446 3 DON JUAN 14   85 7
UNDONE
  THE FLESH IS FRAIL AND SO THE SOUL UNDONE . . . . . . 56 2 DON JUAN 1   63 6
  TO LOVE AGAIN AND BE AGAIN UNDONE . . . . 131 2 DON JUAN 1 194 8
  TO MOURN ALONE THE LOVE WHICH HAS UNDONE . . . . . . 131 2 DON JUAN 1 194 V8
  BY THEM PER HOUR AND THEY HAD ALL BEEN UNDONE . . . . 171 2 DON JUAN 2   29 7
  HER COMRADES ALSO THOUGHT THEMSELVES UNDONE . . . . . 501 2 DON JUAN 5 156 3
  NO MATTER WHAT POOR SOULS MIGHT BE UNDONE . . . . . . 78 3 DON JUAN 7   23 5
  WHICH BREATHES OF NATIONS SAVED NOT WORLDS UNDONE . . 114 3 DON JUAN 8   5 4
  HAVE LEFT UNDONE THE GREATEST--AND MANKIND . . . . . 187 3 DON JUAN 9   10 8
  THE ANNALS OF FULL MANY A LINE UNDONE-- . . . . . . 386 3 DON JUAN 13   60 6
  A LINE AND LEAVE POSTERITY UNDONE . . . . 470 3 DON JUAN 15   33 5
UNDRESS
  SAVING HIS NIGHT GOWN WHICH IS AN UNDRESS . . . . . . 555 3 DON JUAN 16 111 2
UNDRESSING
  UNDRESSING IS A WOE OUR ROBE DE CHAMBRE . . . . 505 3 DON JUAN 16   11 2
UNDREST
  BUT AS MY MAID'S UNDREST PRAY TURN YOUR SPIES OUT . . 104 2 DON JUAN 1 152 7
  UNDREST AND RATHER SLOWLY WENT TO BED . . . . 512 3 DON JUAN 16   27 4
  THE NIGHT WAS AS BEFORE HE WAS UNDREST . . . . 555 3 DON JUAN 16 111 1
UNEARTHLY
  THERE MOANS A STRANGE UNEARTHLY SOUND WHICH THEN . . . 388 3 DON JUAN 13   63 3
UNEASY
  LADIES EVEN OF THE MOST UNEASY VIRTUE . . . . 56 2 DON JUAN 1   62 7
  KNOWING THAT SUCH UNEASY VIRTUE LEADS . . . . 352 3 DON JUAN 12   80 2
UNEBBING
  OF BLOOD AND TEARS MUST FLOW THE UNEBBING SEA . . . . 101 3 DON JUAN 7   68 8
UNEMBARRASSED
  THOUGH MODEST ON HIS UNEMBARRASSED BROW . . . . 223 3 DON JUAN 9   83 5
UNEQUAL
  UNEQUAL IN ITS ASPECT HERE AND THERE . . . . 210 2 DON JUAN 2 103 2
  UNEQUAL MATCHES SUCH AS ARE ALAS   . . . . 236 3 DON JUAN 10   24 3
UNEXCISED
  OR WORDSWORTH UNEXCISED UNHIRED WHO THEN . . . . . . 329 2 DON JUAN 3   93 3
UNEXPECTED
  THE UNEXPECTED DEATH OF SOME OLD LADY . . . . 89 2 DON JUAN 1 125 2
  AS WATER THROUGH AN UNEXPECTED LEAK . . . . 490 2 DON JUAN 5 137 6
  YOUR COMING HAS BEEN UNEXPECTED HERE . . . . 29 3 DON JUAN 6   46 5
  ALAS POOR GHOST--WHAT UNEXPECTED WOES . . . . 403 3 DON JUAN 13   97 7

UNEXPLAIN'D
    AT THIS MOST STRANGE AND UNEXPLAIN'D HIATUS . . . . . . 111 2 DON JUAN 1   164   5
UNEXPREST
    THERE IS A SORT OF UNEXPREST CONCERN . . . . 164 2 DON JUAN 2   14   5
UNFASHIONABLE
    RETIRED WITH MOST UNFASHIONABLE BOWS . . . . 549 3 DON JUAN 16   101   5
UNFATHOMABLE
    THE SINKING FUND'S UNFATHOMABLE SEA . . . . 548 3 DON JUAN 16   99   6
UNFILCH'D
    NOTHING SO DEAR AS AN UNFILCH'D GOOD NAME . . . . . . 112 2 DON JUAN 1   165   5
UNFIT
    UNFIT TO MIX IN THESE THICK SOLITUDES . . . . 358 2 DON JUAN 4   28   3
    SUCH WAS HIS SOVEREIGN'S PLEASURE (THOUGH UNFIT . . . 535 3 DON JUAN 16   72   5
UNFLATTERING
    TO YOU THE UNFLATTERING MUSE DEIGNS TO INSCRIBE . . . 187 3 DON JUAN 9   10   2
UNFOLD
    BEYOND THE RUMOUR WHICH SUCH SPOTS UNFOLD . . . . . . 510 3 DON JUAN 16   22   4
UNFORGIVEN
    NO DOUBT IN FABLE AS THE UNFORGIVEN . . . . 90 2 DON JUAN 1   127   7
UNGENTLE
    YE GENTLE READERS AND UNGENTLE WRITERS . . . . 325 3 DON JUAN 12   20   2
UNGRATEFUL
    UNGRATEFUL PERJURED BARBAROUS DON ALFONSO . . . . . . 101 2 DON JUAN 1   146   7
UNHALLOW'D
    BUT AN UNHALLOW'D EARTHLY SOUND OF FIDDLING . . . . . 290 2 DON JUAN 3   28   4
UNHANDSOME
    AND (IF LET IN) INSISTS IN TERMS UNHANDSOME . . . . . 459 3 DON JUAN 15   8   7
UNHAPPY
    FOR SOME TIME AN UNHAPPY SORT OF LIFE . . . . 35 2 DON JUAN 1   26   2
    THEIR CHASTITY IN THESE UNHAPPY CLIMES . . . . 501 3 DON JUAN 5   157   3
    WHERE IS THE UNHAPPY QUEEN WITH ALL HER WOES . . . . 307 3 DON JUAN 11   77   5
UNHEARD
    WITH STEPS THAT TROD AS HEAVY YET UNHEARD . . . . . . 510 3 DON JUAN 16   21   4
UNHEEDED
    (UNHEEDED TWICE) TO HAVE A FIN OF FISH . . . . 542 3 DON JUAN 16   87   8
UNHINGED
    I HAVE SEEN SOME SUCH--BUT THEY UNHINGED MY MIND . . . 363 2 DON JUAN 4   36 V8
UNHIRED
    OR WORDSWORTH UNEXCISED UNHIRED WHO THEN . . . . . . 329 2 DON JUAN 3   93   3
UNHOLY
    A MODE SO BEAUTIFUL AND SO UNHOLY . . . . 161 2 DON JUAN 2   7 V7
    IT MAY BE MORE THAN EITHER--NOT UNHOLY . . . . 33 3 DON JUAN 6   54   3
UNHURT
    BUT ELSE UNHURT SHE OPENED HER LARGE EYES . . . . . . 159 3 DON JUAN 8   95   7
UNIFORM
    WHO WORE THEIR UNIFORM BY BABA CHOSEN . . . . 469 2 DON JUAN 5   99   4
    A FORTRESS HARLEQUIN IN UNIFORM . . . . 95 3 DON JUAN 7   55   8
    AN UNIFORM TO BOYS IS LIKE A FAN . . . . 108 3 DON JUAN 7   84   4
    SUPPOSE HIM IN A HANDSOME UNIFORM . . . . 204 3 DON JUAN 9   43   1
UNIFORMS
    SMART UNIFORMS AND SPARKLING CORONETS . . . . 333 3 DON JUAN 12   36   1
UNIMPAIR'D
    STILL UNIMPAIR'D TO DECORATE THE SCENE . . . . 389 3 DON JUAN 13   66   6
UNIMPEDED
    BE UNIMPEDED BY THE PROUDEST MOSQUE . . . . 99 3 DON JUAN 7   63   8
UNINITIATED
    THERE'S ALSO NIGHTLY TO THE UNINITIATED . . . . 344 3 DON JUAN 12   62   1
    IN ANY MANNER BY THE UNINITIATED . . . . 419 3 DON JUAN 14   22   8
UNINSTRUCTED
    AND LAST NOT LEAST TO STRANGERS UNINSTRUCTED . . . . 259 3 DON JUAN 10   69   7
UNINTELLIGIBLE
    UNLESS LIKE WORDSWORTH THEY PROVE UNINTELLIGIBLE . . . 70 2 DON JUAN 1   90   8
UNINTERESTED
    IN THE SAME QUAINT UNINTERESTED TONE-- . . . . 261 3 DON JUAN 10   73   4
UNINVITED
    BUT ONCE A WEEK OR FORTNIGHT UNINVITED . . . . 534 3 DON JUAN 16   69   1
UNION
    BUT NONE WERE GENE THE GREAT HOUR OF UNION . . . . . 406 3 DON JUAN 13   103   1
    THEIR UNION WAS A MODEL TO BEHOLD . . . . 447 3 DON JUAN 14   86   7
UNIONS
    THEIRS WAS THAT BEST OF UNIONS PAST ALL DOUBT . . . . 430 3 DON JUAN 14   45   7
UNITED
    O'ERFLOW'D HER SOUL WITH THEIR UNITED POWER . . . . . 262 2 DON JUAN 2   198   3
    BY THEIR OWN FEELINGS HALLOW'D AND UNITED . . . . . . 265 2 DON JUAN 2   204   5
    OPPOSING SINGLY THE UNITED STRONG . . . . 363 3 DON JUAN 13   10   3
    THEY MOVED LIKE STARS UNITED IN THEIR SPHERES . . . . 447 3 DON JUAN 14   87   3
    COULD HARDLY BE UNITED BY A DUNCE . . . . 517 3 DON JUAN 16   39   8
UNITIES
    SOME DRAMA OF THE MARRIAGE UNITIES . . . . 470 3 DON JUAN 15   32   5
UNITY
    A HUSBAND RATHER OLD NOT MUCH IN UNITY . . . . 158 2 DON JUAN 2   3   7
    YOU MIGHT HAVE FREED FALL'N EUROPE FROM THE UNITY . . . 187 3 DON JUAN 9   9   3
    THEMSELVES TO UNITY LIKE THIS OF MINE . . . . 290 3 DON JUAN 11   44   8
UNIVERSAL
    THE FIELD IS UNIVERSAL AND ALLOWS . . . . 13 2 DON JUAN D   7   5
    AND FIRST ONE UNIVERSAL SHRIEK THERE RUSH'D . . . . . 184 2 DON JUAN 2   53   1
    SOME FEELINGS UNIVERSAL AS THE SUN . . . . 244 2 DON JUAN 2   167   3
    PLATONIC UNIVERSAL WONDERFUL . . . . 269 2 DON JUAN 2   212   3
    AND LOSE THEIR OWN IN UNIVERSAL DEATH . . . . 399 2 DON JUAN 4   102   8

UNIVERSAL   (CONTINUED)
   UNIVERSE UNIVERSAL EGOTISM 269   3 DON JUAN 11   2   2
   FORTH INTO UNIVERSAL EPIGRAM 552   3 DON JUAN 16   104   2
UNIVERSE
   CANST THOU BE MY SOLE WORLD MY UNIVERSE 144   2 DON JUAN 1   215   2
   A THRONE THE WORLD THE UNIVERSE TO BE   7   3 DON JUAN 6   3   3
   MAKE LOVE THE MAIN SPRING OF THE UNIVERSE 219   3 DON JUAN 9   73   8
   UNIVERSE UNIVERSAL EGOTISM 269   3 DON JUAN 11   2   2
   AND LOOK DOWN ON THE UNIVERSE WITH PITY-- 290   3 DON JUAN 11   45   6
UNJUST
   THEY ARE RIGHT FOR MAN TO MAN SO OFT UNJUST . . . 263   2 DON JUAN 2   200   1
UNKIND
   DONE ANYTHING EXCEEDINGLY UNKIND 193   3 DON JUAN 9   21   3
UNKNOWN
   AN UNKNOWN BARREN BEACH FOR BURIAL GROUND 213   2 DON JUAN 2   109   8
   REMAIN'D UNKNOWN WITHIN HIS CRAGGY NOOK 248   2 DON JUAN 2   174   4
   UNKNOWN TO THOSE POSSESSORS--OR UNDISPLAYED . . . 485   2 DON JUAN 5   129   V6
   RATHER TO HIDE WHAT PLEASES MOST UNKNOWN   13   3 DON JUAN 6   15   4
   THE AGE OF GOLD (WHEN GOLD WAS YET UNKNOWN . . .   33   3 DON JUAN 6   55   2
   WITH WHICH MEN IMAGE OUT THE UNKNOWN THING . . . 188   3 DON JUAN 9   11   2
   COLUMBIA'S STOCK HATH HOLDERS NOT UNKNOWN 318   3 DON JUAN 12   6   6
   BY RAILING AT THE UNKNOWN AND ENVIED PASSION . . 337   3 DON JUAN 12   45   2
   THE QUANTITY OF GOOD SHE DID'S UNKNOWN 338   3 DON JUAN 12   48   5
   A PLACE WHERE PECCADILLOS ARE UNKNOWN 370   3 DON JUAN 13   27   2
   TO THE UNKNOWN A SECRET PREPOSSESSION 413   3 DON JUAN 14   6   6
UNLAWFUL
   'TIS DANGEROUS TO READ OF LOVES UNLAWFUL 282   2 DON JUAN 3   12   8
UNLESS
   UNLESS LIKE WORDSWORTH THEY PROVE UNINTELLIGIBLE . . .   70   2 DON JUAN 1   90   8
   UNLESS THIS WORLD AND T'OTHER TOO BE BLIND 112   2 DON JUAN 1   165   4
   UNLESS THE WORLD AND HEAVEN ITSELF BE BLIND . . . 112   2 DON JUAN 1   165   V4
   UNLESS WITH BREAKERS CLOSE BENEATH HER LEE 180   2 DON JUAN 2   45   8
   UNLESS WITH PEOPLE WHO TOO MUCH HAVE QUAFF'D . . 183   2 DON JUAN 2   50   5
   UNLESS TO PLAGUE THE GRANTORS--YET SO TRUE IT IS . 190   2 DON JUAN 2   65   3
   UNLESS HE WISH'D TO DIE UPON THE PLACE-- 240   2 DON JUAN 2   159   6
   UNLESS PHILOSOPHY CAN MAKE A JULIET 272   2 DON JUAN 2   V 1   2
   (UNLESS AT ONCE SHE PLUNGE FOR LIFE IN PRAYERS)-- . 276   2 DON JUAN 3   4   3
   UNLESS INDEED IT WAS FROM HIS OWN KNOWLEDGE HE . . 281   2 DON JUAN 3   11   5
   THE BLAME ON ME UNLESS YOU WISH THEY WERE 282   2 DON JUAN 3   12   4
   THEY'LL NEVER FIND IT OUT UNLESS I OWN 342   2 DON JUAN 3   111   4
   IN POESY UNLESS PERHAPS THE END 344   2 DON JUAN 4   1   2
   UNLESS IT WERE TO BE A MOMENT MERRY 346   2 DON JUAN 4   5   7
   WEARY UNLESS WHEN SEPARATE THE TREE 349   2 DON JUAN 4   10   3
   UNLESS WHEN QUALIFIED WITH THEE COGNIAC 372   2 DON JUAN 4   53   1
   HE'S WRONG--UNLESS MAN WERE A PIG INDEED 427   2 DON JUAN 5   31   3
   UNLESS HE'S DRUNK AND THEN NO DOUBT HE'S FREED . . 427   2 DON JUAN 5   31   5
   UNLESS HIS HIGHNESS PROMISES TO MARRY ME 460   2 DON JUAN 5   84   8
   TO ANY SHOE UNLESS IT SHOD THE POPE 470   2 DON JUAN 5   102   8
   OR WAS AT LEAST UNLESS 'TIS SINCE DEFACED   71   3 DON JUAN 7   9   5
   UNLESS TO MAKE THEIR KETTLE DRUMS A NEW SKIN . .   75   3 DON JUAN 7   17   6
   UNLESS THEY ARE GAME AS BULL-DOGS AND FOX-TERRIERS .   78   3 DON JUAN 7   24   8
   UNLESS GUN-POWDER SHOULD BE FOUND TO HARM 106   3 DON JUAN 7   79   5
   UNLESS COMPELLED BY FATE OR WAVE OR WIND . . . . : 139   3 DON JUAN 8   54   1
   OF TRUTH THAN PROSE UNLESS TO SUIT THE MART . . . 154   3 DON JUAN 8   86   5
   UNLESS HER CAUSE BY RIGHT BE SANCTIFIED 184   3 DON JUAN 9   4   4
   THOUGH HYMNED BY EVERY HARP UNLESS WITHIN 199   3 DON JUAN 9   34   7
   AND WAS NOT THE BEST WIFE UNLESS WE CALL 222   3 DON JUAN 9   80   6
   UNLESS YOU MAKE THEIR BETTERS BETTER--FIE 267   3 DON JUAN 10   85   7
   UPON THE ROAD UNLESS HE PROVE A FIGHTER 273   3 DON JUAN 11   11   6
   UNLESS ON TYRANT'S STERNS--WE TURN THE STERNEST . 286   3 DON JUAN 11   38   V8
   UNLESS A MAN CAN CALCULATE HIS MEANS 325   3 DON JUAN 12   21   7
   SUCH AS--UNLESS MISS (BLANK) MEANT TO HAVE CHOSEN . 332   3 DON JUAN 12   34   5
   UNLESS I KNEW THE VERY CHASTEST SQUARES 370   3 DON JUAN 13   26   8
   UNLESS IT TEACHES ONE TO QUOTE AND CAVIL) 380   3 DON JUAN 13   47   8
   AS HINTING MORE (UNLESS OUR JUDGMENTS WARP US) . 391   3 DON JUAN 13   69   7
   UNLESS HER HABITS SHOULD BEGIN TO MEND 432   3 DON JUAN 14   51   4
   UNLESS LIKE WISE TIRESIAS WE HAD PROVED 442   3 DON JUAN 14   73   2
   UNLESS GOOD COMPANY HE KEPT TOO LONG 443   3 DON JUAN 14   77   6
   UNLESS A MARRIAGE WAS APPLIED TO MEND 470   3 DON JUAN 15   33   6
   WHICH SAYS THOU SHALT NOT MARRY UNLESS WELL . . 472   3 DON JUAN 15   38   3
   UNLESS THE LADIES SHOULD GO OFF--THERE WAS . . . 475   3 DON JUAN 15   43   2
   SOMETIMES UNLESS MY FEELINGS RATHER ERR) 506   3 DON JUAN 16   14   5
   UNLESS SOME BEAUTY WITH A KISS SHOULD BRIBE . . . 567   3 DON JUAN 17   12   8
UNLIKE
   WEBFOOTED NOT UNLIKE A DOVE IN SIZE 206   2 DON JUAN 2   94   2
   THE OTHER FEMALE'S DRESS WAS NOT UNLIKE 221   2 DON JUAN 2   122   1
   UNLIKE THE HONEST ARAB THIEVES SO BRAVE 225   2 DON JUAN 2   130   6
   SOME SHEPHERDS (UNLIKE PARIS) LED TO STARE . . . 387   2 DON JUAN 4   78   3
   UNTO HIS CALL UNLIKE THE SPIRITS FROM 132   3 DON JUAN 8   38   2
   UNLIKE OUR OWN HALF-CHASTE ELIZABETH 222   3 DON JUAN 9   81   2
   AND VERY MUCH UNLIKE WHAT PEOPLE WRITE 292   3 DON JUAN 11   47   8
UNLIKELY
   THAT JUAN WAS UNLIKELY TO RESIST-- 436   3 DON JUAN 14   60   4
UNLIQUIDATING
   THAT MOST UNLIQUIDATING LIQUID LEAVES 548   3 DON JUAN 16   99   7
UNLOADS
   FROM CEYLON INDE OR FAR CATHAY UNLOADS 320   3 DON JUAN 12   9   2
UNLOCKING
   I SAY UNLOCKING THE RECESS PULLED FORTH 450   2 DON JUAN 5   67   2

		PAGE	VOL		CANTO	STANZA	LN

UNLUCKILY
    BEFORE UNLUCKILY DON JOSE DIED 38   2 DON JUAN   1   32   8
    HE DIED AND MOST UNLUCKILY BECAUSE 38   2 DON JUAN   1   33   1
UNMADE
    IN PERFECT INNOCENCE SHE THEN UNMADE 36   3 DON JUAN   6   60   1
UNMANS
    THE GROWING WATERS IT UNMANS ONE QUITE 163   2 DON JUAN   2   12   3
UNMARRIED
    MARRIED UNMARRIED AND REMARRIED (THIS IS 308   3 DON JUAN 11   79   4
    A YOUNG UNMARRIED MAN WITH A GOOD NAME 342   3 DON JUAN 12   58   1
UNMINGLED
    THE UNMINGLED ESSENCE OF THE GRAPE AND YET 458   3 DON JUAN 15   7   2
UNMIX'D
    BRIGHT AND IMMACULATE UNMIX'D AND PURE 64   2 DON JUAN   1   79   2
UNMOISTENED
    LEAVING ALL CLARETLESS THE UNMOISTENED THROTTLE 435   3 DON JUAN 14   58   3
UNMOVED
    SO GENTLE STIRLESS HELPLESS AND UNMOVED 261   2 DON JUAN   2   197   3
    THE SENTIMENTAL BOASTS TO BE UNMOVED 442   3 DON JUAN 14   73   6
UNNATURAL
    THEIRS BEING AN UNNATURAL SITUATION 263   2 DON JUAN   2   201   6
    TO THINK HIS VANISHING UNNATURAL 511   3 DON JUAN 16   24   4
UNOBJECTIONABLE
    ALL THESE WERE UNOBJECTIONABLE MATCHES 473   3 DON JUAN 15   40   7
UNOPPOSED
    A LONELY PURE AFFECTION UNOPPOSED 304   2 DON JUAN   3   57   5
UNORIENTAL
    A MOST UNORIENTAL ROAR OF LAUGHTER 290   2 DON JUAN   3   28   8
UNPACKING
    STOOD AS THE UNPACKING GATHERED MORE SPECTATORS) 313   3 DON JUAN 11 V 29   6
UNPAID
    TO PAY UNPAID PROTESTED OR DISCOUNTED 16   3 DON JUAN   6   21   2
UNPAVED
    THROUGH THE THEN UNPAVED STARS THE TURNPIKE ROAD 226   3 DON JUAN 10   2   4
UNPLEASANT
    AT LEAVING EVEN THE MOST UNPLEASANT PEOPLE 164   2 DON JUAN   2   14   7
    AND HERE WAS ONE EXCEEDINGLY UNPLEASANT 371   2 DON JUAN   4   51   2
    ALSO OUR HERO'S LOT HOWE'ER UNPLEASANT 410   2 DON JUAN   4   117   2
    OF THE UNPLEASANT KIND WITH NONE AT HAND 45   3 DON JUAN   6   78   3
UNPLEASANTLY
    YOU'VE PASS'D YOUR YOUTH NOT SO UNPLEASANTLY 147   2 DON JUAN   1   220   5
UNPLEASING
    AND PLEASING OR UNPLEASING STILL ARE LIKE 32   3 DON JUAN   6   52   8
UNPREPARED
    HAVE MOMENTS HOURS AND DAYS SO UNPREPARED 33   2 DON JUAN   1   21   4
UNQUIET
    UPON THE MOST UNQUIET IMP ON EARTH 34   2 DON JUAN   1   25   4
    WAS GOING ON SOME PEOPLE WERE UNQUIET 173   2 DON JUAN   2   33   2
    AND THE UNQUIET FEELINGS WHICH FIRST WOKE 402   2 DON JUAN   4   106   3
UNREAD
    IS YET WITHIN THE UNREAD EVENTS OF TIME 312   3 DON JUAN 11   90   1
UNRIDDLE
    DID NOT HIS DEEDS UNRIDDLE THEM EACH DAY-- 207   3 DON JUAN   9   50   4
UNRIDDLED
    UNRIDDLED AND AS MY TRUE MUSE EXPOUNDS 112   3 DON JUAN   8   1   5
    OF BEING STARS AND THIS UNRIDDLED WONDER 269   3 DON JUAN 11   3   7
    WHERE IS HIS WILL (THAT'S NOT SO SOON UNRIDDLED) . . . 307   3 DON JUAN 11   78   3
UNRIDDLING
    THE CAUSE BEING PAST HIS GUESSING OR UNRIDDLING 290   2 DON JUAN   3   28   6
UNRULY
    FOR WHEN THE TURBID PASSIONS ARE UNRULY IT 272   2 DON JUAN   2 V 1   4
UNSALEABLE
    TOSSED OVERBOARD UNSALEABLE (BEING OLD) 284   2 DON JUAN   3   16   4
UNSEEMLY
    AND REACH'D HIS HOME IN AN UNSEEMLY PLIGHT 126   2 DON JUAN   1   188   4
UNSEEN
    OLD LAMBRO PASS'D UNSEEN A PRIVATE GATE 306   2 DON JUAN   3   61   1
    SOME HANDS UNSEEN STREW'D FLOWERS UPON HIS TOMB . . . 339   2 DON JUAN   3   109   5
    A NYMPH AND HER BELOVED ALL UNSEEN 352   2 DON JUAN   4   15   6
    UNSEEN AS SINGS THE NIGHTINGALE THEY WERE 358   2 DON JUAN   4   28   2
    FOUR WIVES AND TWICE FIVE HUNDRED MAIDS UNSEEN . . . 496   2 DON JUAN   5   148   7
    HER FACE DECLINED AND WAS UNSEEN HER HAIR 60   3 DON JUAN   6   108   1
    AND NOUGHT REMAINS UNSEEN BUT MUCH UNTOLD 232   3 DON JUAN 10   14   3
UNSEXED
    THAT I UNSEXED MY DRESS BUT BABA STROKING 454   2 DON JUAN   5   75   6
UNSHAKEN
    AND SHOOK (TILL NOW UNSHAKEN) LIKE A REED 170   3 DON JUAN   8   117   6
UNSIGHING
    OF THIS UNSIGHING PEOPLE OF THE WOODS 145   3 DON JUAN   8   67   8
UNSOUGHT
    BY THIS OLD BLACK ENCHANTER'S UNSOUGHT AID 459   2 DON JUAN   5   83   8
UNSTRUNG
    AND NOW AS SILENT AS AN UNSTRUNG DRUM 430   2 DON JUAN   5   36   V7
UNSUFFOCATED
    BY WHICH MEN ARE UNSUFFOCATED GRATIS 92   2 DON JUAN   1   130   5
UNSUNK
    THE DEBT UNSUNK YET SINKS ALL IT RECEIVES 548   3 DON JUAN 16   99   8
UNTENDED
    TROOPS OF UNTENDED HORSES HERE AND THERE 387   2 DON JUAN   4   78   1

UNTIED
    HIS BREATH--HE FROM HIS SWELLING THROAT UNTIED 276   3 DON JUAN 11   16   7
UNTIL
    UNTIL AT LENGTH THE SMOTHER'D FIRE BROKE OUT 35   2 DON JUAN 1   26   7
    UNTIL IT CENTER'D IN AN ONLY SON 54   2 DON JUAN 1   59   3
    UNTIL SHE SPOKE THEN THROUGH ITS SOFT DISGUISE 54   2 DON JUAN 1   60   3
    UNTIL HIS MIGHTY HEART IN ITS GREAT MOOD 70   2 DON JUAN 1   91   3
    UNTIL TOO LATE FOR USEFUL CONVERSATION 84   2 DON JUAN 1   117   2
    UNTIL THE HOURS OF ABSENCE SHOULD RUN THROUGH 98   2 DON JUAN 1   141   6
    INCREASED AT NIGHT UNTIL IT BLEW A GALE 170   2 DON JUAN 2   26   2
    UNTIL THE CHAINS AND LEATHERS WERE WORN THROUGH 178   2 DON JUAN 2   42   5
    BEFORE THE SEA UNTIL IT SHOULD GROW FINE 189   2 DON JUAN 2   62   3
    UNTIL THEY FOUND A RAGGED PIECE OF SHEET 201   2 DON JUAN 2   85   2
    HE WATCH'D IT WISTFULLY UNTIL AWAY 204   2 DON JUAN 2   90   5
    THEY PERISH'D UNTIL WITHER'D TO THESE FEW 210   2 DON JUAN 2   102   6
    AND MIXED UNTIL THE VERY PLEASURE STUNG 254   2 DON JUAN 2   187   V8
    HE HERS UNTIL THEY END IN BROKEN GASPS 259   2 DON JUAN 2   194   6
    IS USED UNTIL THE TRUTH ARRIVES TOO LATE-- 278   2 DON JUAN 3   6   4
    UNTIL HIS LATE LIFE BY ARCHDEACON COXE 328   2 DON JUAN 3   90   8
    UNTIL SHE SOBB'D FOR BREATH AND SOON THEY WERE 361   2 DON JUAN 4   31   6
    UNTIL THEY REACH'D SOME GALLIOTS PLACED IN LINE 371   2 DON JUAN 4   50   6
    GUSH FROM THE EARTH UNTIL THE LAND RUNS O'ER 373   2 DON JUAN 4   55   3
    ON HER SIRE'S ARM WHICH UNTIL NOW SCARCE HELD 375   2 DON JUAN 4   58   7
    UNTIL THE MEMORY OF AN AGE IS FLED 399   2 DON JUAN 4   102   3
    UNTIL THE SUM WAS ACCURATELY SCANNED 426   2 DON JUAN 5   29   6
    HAD FACED NAPOLEON'S FOES UNTIL THEY FLED-- 431   2 DON JUAN 5   37   6
    UNTIL YOU NEARLY TROD ON THEM AND THEN 462   2 DON JUAN 5   88   1
    HIS HEAD UNTIL THE CEREMONY ENDED 466   2 DON JUAN 5   95   8
    UNTIL THE TREE OF KNOWLEDGE WAS PULLED DOWN 476   2 DON JUAN 5   113   V8
    THE SAME KATINKA UNTIL BY-AND-BY 30   3 DON JUAN 6   49   3
    UNTIL 'TIS TAUGHT BY LESSONS RATHER RUDE 53   3 DON JUAN 6   95   3
    UNTIL EACH HIGH HEROIC BOSOM BURNED 99   3 DON JUAN 7   64   3
    UNTIL THEIR VERY NUMBER MAKES MEN HARD 118   3 DON JUAN 8   13   2
    BLOOD UNTIL HEATED--AND EVEN THERE HIS OWN 140   3 DON JUAN 8   55   7
    UNTIL THEY REACHED AS DAY-BREAK WAS EXPANDING 148   3 DON JUAN 8   72   5
    BUT JUAN WAS IMMOVEABLE UNTIL 162   3 DON JUAN 8   102   1
    UNTIL I SEE BOTH SIDES FOR ONCE AGREEING 190   3 DON JUAN 9   16   6
    UNTIL A ROYAL SMILE AT LENGTH DISCLOSED 211   3 DON JUAN 9   58   6
    JUAN RETIRED--AND SO WILL I UNTIL 224   3 DON JUAN 9   85   2
    UNTIL HE REACHED THE CASTELLATED RHINE-- 255   3 DON JUAN 10   61   2
    FULL FLASH ALL FANCY UNTIL FAIRLY DIDDLED 276   3 DON JUAN 11   17   7
    UNTIL TO SOME CONSPICUOUS SQUARE THEY PASS 283   3 DON JUAN 11   31   7
    UNTIL THEIR ROYAL RIDDLE'S FULLY READ 287   3 DON JUAN 11   40   4
    THE LAW AT LEAST UNTIL THE BENCH REVERT TO TRUE 314   3 DON JUAN 11   V 76   6
    ARE SPURNED IN TURN UNTIL HER TURN ARRIVES 333   3 DON JUAN 12   36   2
    THEREFORE I NAME NOT SQUARE STREET PLACE UNTIL I 370   3 DON JUAN 13   27   5
    AND WAIT UNTIL THE NIGHTINGALE GROWS DUMBER 380   3 DON JUAN 13   48   5
    SPARKLING WITH FOAM UNTIL AGAIN SUBSIDING 385   3 DON JUAN 13   58   2
    UNTIL I FAIRLY KNOCK'D IT UP WITH RHYME 414   3 DON JUAN 14   9   8
    AND PRUDENTLY POSTPONE UNTIL MID-DAY 500   3 DON JUAN 15   98   5
    SHE WAITED UNTIL JUSTICE COULD RECALL 533   3 DON JUAN 16   67   5
    UNTIL PREFERMENT COMING AT A SURE RATE 540   3 DON JUAN 16   82   4
    THE GHOST STOPPED MENACED THEN RETIRED UNTIL 559   3 DON JUAN 16   119   7
UNTILL'D
    A VAST UNTILL'D AND MOUNTAIN-SKIRTED PLAIN 386   2 DON JUAN 4   77   2
UNTO
    MOST LOVE POSSESSION UNTO THEM APPEAR'D 352   2 DON JUAN 4   16   7
    DEAR UNTO ALL BUT DEAREST TO THEIR EYES 354   2 DON JUAN 4   20   2
    SOME TALK OF AN APPEAL UNTO SOME PASSION 437   2 DON JUAN 5   48   1
    THERE WAS NO END UNTO THE THINGS SHE BOUGHT 476   2 DON JUAN 5   113   5
    COULD YET BE KNOWN UNTO THE FATES ALONE 499   2 DON JUAN 5   153   4
    BUT TO THE TALE--GREAT JOY UNTO THE CAMP 89   3 DON JUAN 7   46   1
    NO HARM UNTO A RIGHT LEGITIMATE HEAD 117   3 DON JUAN 8   10   7
    AND THAT THE REST HAD FACED UNTO THE RIGHT 125   3 DON JUAN 8   28   3
    UNTO THE NEAREST HUT THEMSELVES BETAKE 127   3 DON JUAN 8   32   6
    UNTO HIS CALL UNLIKE THE SPIRITS FROM 132   3 DON JUAN 8   38   2
    UNTO THAT RATHER SOMEWHAT MISTY BOURN 133   3 DON JUAN 8   41   3
    WHEN THEY BUILT UP UNTO HIS DARLING TREES-- 144   3 DON JUAN 8   64   2
    UNTO HIS PROTEGEE WHILE HER'S TRANSFIXED 159   3 DON JUAN 8   96   5
    THE RUGGED TREE UNTO THE SUMMER WIND 164   3 DON JUAN 8   106   7
    UNTO THE BAYONETS WHICH HAD PIERCED HIS YOUNG 170   3 DON JUAN 8   118   6
    BUT STILL THERE IS UNTO A PATRIOT NATION 175   3 DON JUAN 8   126   1
    BUT LET ME PUT AN END UNTO MY THEME 175   3 DON JUAN 8   127   1
    BE SAID THAT WE STILL TRUCKLE UNTO THRONES-- 179   3 DON JUAN 8   135   6
    UNTO THE NEW CREATION RISING OUT 201   3 DON JUAN 9   38   2
    AND ALL LIPS WERE APPLIED UNTO ALL EARS 221   3 DON JUAN 9   78   2
    UNTO AN EMPRESS WHO PREFERRED YOUNG MEN 241   3 DON JUAN 10   33   2
    UNTO HIS NEAREST FOLLOWER OR HENCHMAN 274   3 DON JUAN 11   13   7
    A SNEER OR SHORT REPLY UNTO THEIR NEIGHBOUR 288   3 DON JUAN 11   41   V4
    UNTO BY SAWNEY'S VIOLIN WE HAVE HEARD 307   3 DON JUAN 11   78   6
    OH GOLD I STILL PREFER THEE UNTO PAPER 317   3 DON JUAN 12   4   7
    IT ADDS AN OUTWARD GRACE UNTO THEIR CARRIAGE-- 344   3 DON JUAN 12   62   6
    BY THAT REAL EPIC UNTO ALL WHO HAVE THOUGHT 363   3 DON JUAN 13   9   8
    AND WEDDED UNTO ONE SHE HAD LOVED WELL 365   3 DON JUAN 13   14   2
    WHERE NONE WERE DREAMT OF UNTO LOVE'S AFFAIRS 369   3 DON JUAN 13   25   5
    UNTO THE GLOWING INDIA OF THE SOUL 376   3 DON JUAN 13   39   2
    HELD OUT UNTO THE HUNGRY ISRAELITES 405   3 DON JUAN 13   100   2
    LOOK BACK O'ER AGES ERE UNTO THE STAKE FAST 411   3 DON JUAN 14   2   5
    WAS ALL THINGS UNTO PEOPLE OF ALL SORTS 424   3 DON JUAN 14   31   2

		PAGE VOL		CANTO	STANZA	LN

UNTO   (CONTINUED)
    NOR IF UNTO THE WORLD I EVER GAVE IT . . . . 444 3 DON JUAN 14 80 3
    THE WILD SENSATION UNTO HER A NEW ONE . . . . 449 3 DON JUAN 14 91 4
    WHICH MINISTERS UNTO THE SOUL'S DELIGHT . . . . 457 3 DON JUAN 15 2 7
    UNTO SUCH FEELINGS AS SEEM'D INNOCENT . . . . 460 3 DON JUAN 15 10 7
    WHICH LAST I LEAVE UNTO THE LORD'S SPIRITUAL . . . . . 472 3 DON JUAN 15 36 V8
    THEN TURN'D UNTO THE STARS FOR LOFTIER RAYS . . . . . 480 3 DON JUAN 15 56 4
    WHICH MADE HIM HAVE RECOURSE UNTO HIS SPOON . . . . . 513 3 DON JUAN 16 30 5
    BUT TO RETURN UNTO THE STRICTER RULE-- . . . . 563 3 DON JUAN 17 3 1
    AND WITCHES UNTO NONE THOUGH SOMEWHAT LATE . . . . . . 565 3 DON JUAN 17 7 2
UNTOLD
    AND NOUGHT REMAINS UNSEEN BUT MUCH UNTOLD . . . . . . 232 3 DON JUAN 10 14 3
UNTOST
    THE SANDS UNTUMBLED THE BLUE WAVES UNTOST . . . . . . 251 2 DON JUAN 2 181 4
UNTOWARD
    WHEN SOME UNTOWARD PART OF RAIMENT STUCK HARD . . . . 456 2 DON JUAN 5 78 6
    POOR FELLOW HIS WAS AN UNTOWARD FATE-- . . . . 298 3 DON JUAN 11 60 6
UNTRUE
    AND SCORN TO ADD A SYLLABLE UNTRUE . . . . 41 3 DON JUAN 6 70 3
    AND BOTH MAY AFTER ALL TURN OUT UNTRUE . . . . 411 3 DON JUAN 14 3 4
UNTUMBLED
    THE SANDS UNTUMBLED THE BLUE WAVES UNTOST . . . . . . 251 2 DON JUAN 2 181 4
UNTYING
    UNTYING SQUIRES TO FIGHT AGAINST THE CHURCHES . . . . 530 3 DON JUAN 16 60 6
UNUSUAL
    THOUGH AN UNUSUAL FIT OF LOVE OR DUTY . . . . 51 3 DON JUAN 6 91 7
    THE UNUSUAL QUICKNESS OF THESE COMMON CHANGES . . . . 309 3 DON JUAN 11 81 8
UNUTTERABLE
    THINKING UNUTTERABLE THINGS HE THREW . . . . 70 2 DON JUAN 1 90 2
UNVEILED
    THE MOON BREAKS HALF UNVEILED EACH FURTHER CHARM . . . 39 3 DON JUAN 6 66 5
UNWAKENED
    WHOSE YOUNG UNWAKENED WORLD WAS EVER NEW . . . . 145 3 DON JUAN 8 65 3
UNWEAN'D
    AND OCEAN SLUMBER'D LIKE AN UNWEAN'D CHILD . . . . . . 193 2 DON JUAN 2 70 2
    WHILE PEACEFUL AS IF STILL AN UNWEAN'D LAMB . . . . . 292 2 DON JUAN 3 32 3
UNWED
    BUT SIXTEEN DOWAGERS TEN UNWED SHE SAGES . . . . . . 330 3 DON JUAN 12 30 7
    UNWED OR MISTRESS NEVER TO BE WED . . . . 470 3 DON JUAN 15 32 2
UNWELCOME
    UNWELCOME VISIONS OF OUR FORMER YEARS . . . . 227 2 DON JUAN 2 134 7
UNWELL
    YOU SURELY ARE UNWELL CHILD WE MUST SEE . . . . 46 3 DON JUAN 6 80 6
UNWILLING
    YET 'TIS A PAINFUL FEELING AND UNWILLING . . . . . . 270 2 DON JUAN 2 213 1
UNWISE
    AND REPETITION'S TIRESOME AND UNWISE-- . . . . 246 2 DON JUAN 2 171 6
UNWITHERING
    UNWITHERING MYRTLE ROUND THE UNBLUNTED DART . . . . . 554 3 DON JUAN 16 109 6
UNWONTED
    SURPRISED AT THESE UNWONTED SIGNS OF IDLING . . . . . 290 2 DON JUAN 3 28 2
UNWORTHY
    THEY ARE UNWORTHY OF MY FATHER'S DAUGHTER . . . . . . 106 2 DON JUAN 1 155 6
    A TRACE UNWORTHY EITHER WIFE OR MAID-- . . . . 372 3 DON JUAN 13 32 5
UNWOUND
    WITH GENTLE FORCE HER WHITE ARMS HE UNWOUND . . . . . 484 2 DON JUAN 5 126 3
UNWRINKLED
    ON HER UNWRINKLED BROW NOR COULD YOU VIEW . . . . . . 145 3 DON JUAN 8 65 5
UPBRAID
    HER BROW GREW BLACK BUT SHE WOULD NOT UPBRAID . . . . 483 2 DON JUAN 5 125 5
    WITH DISTANT SHRIEKS WERE HEARD HEAVEN TO UPBRAID-- . . 146 3 DON JUAN 8 69 5
UPHARSIN
    SINCE MENE MENE TEKEL AND UPHARSIN . . . . 179 3 DON JUAN 8 134 2
UPHOLSTERER'S
    THE UPHOLSTERER'S FIAT LUX HAD BADE TO ISSUE . . . . . 309 2 DON JUAN 3 67 V8
UPON'T
    AND WRITTEN LATELY TWO MEMOIRS UPON'T) . . . . 447 2 DON JUAN 5 62 6
    THIS MORNING RATHER SPENT LESS TIME UPON'T . . . . . 513 3 DON JUAN 16 29 3
UPPER
    SHORT UPPER LIP--SWEET LIPS THAT MAKE US SIGH . . . . 218 2 DON JUAN 2 118 3
    THE UPPER BORDER RICHLY WROUGHT DISPLAY'D . . . . . . 308 2 DON JUAN 3 64 5
    AND O'ER HER UPPER LIP THEY SEEM'D TO POUR . . . . . 361 2 DON JUAN 4 31 5
    OH YE AMBROSIAL MOMENTS ALWAYS UPPER . . . . 304 3 DON JUAN 11 72 3
UPPERMOST
    FLOATS SCUMLIKE UPPERMOST AND THESE JACK CADES . . . . 334 2 DON JUAN 3 100 5
    THE BRAZEN UPPERMOST) KIND READER PASS . . . . 34 3 DON JUAN 6 56 3
    I WRITE WHAT'S UPPERMOST WITHOUT DELAY . . . . 413 3 DON JUAN 14 7 5
    WHICH RINGS WHAT'S UPPERMOST OF NEW OR HOARY . . . . . 465 3 DON JUAN 15 20 7
UPREARS
    TO HIDE THE GLOSSY SHOULDER WHICH UPREARS . . . . . . 108 2 DON JUAN 1 158 6
UPRIGHT
    A QUANTITY OF PALISADES UPRIGHT . . . . 71 3 DON JUAN 7 10 6
    A WIFE MAKES OR TAKES LOVE IN UPRIGHT EARNEST . . . . 345 3 DON JUAN 12 64 4
UPROOTED
    FOR HER MUST BE UPROOTED--OR BE BOUGHT . . . . 476 2 DON JUAN 5 113 V5
UPSET
    THERE SHE LAY MOTIONLESS AND SEEM'D UPSET . . . . . . 172 2 DON JUAN 2 31 1
    THRONES WORLDS ET CETERA ARE SO OFT UPSET . . . . . . 8 3 DON JUAN 6 4 1
    PARISIAN ASPECT WHICH UPSET OLD TROY . . . . 209 3 DON JUAN 9 53 5

UPSETS
   BUT SEATS A NATION OR UPSETS A THRONE . . . . 318 3 DON JUAN 12   6   4
UPSTARTED
   AND THAT SO LOUDLY THAT UPSTARTED ALL . . . . 42 3 DON JUAN 6   71   1
UPTHROWN
   FOR FIFTY TONS OF WATER WERE UPTHROWN . . . . 171 2 DON JUAN 2   29   6
UPWARDS
   EVEN FROM OUR GRAMMAR UPWARDS FRIENDS OF YORE . . . . . 542 3 DON JUAN 16   86   5
URBANITY
   OR SOMETHING WHICH WAS NOTHING AS URBANITY . . . . . . 490 3 DON JUAN 15   78   2
URCHIN
   THE DEVIL'S IN THE URCHIN AND NO GOOD-- . . . . 115 2 DON JUAN 1 171   4
URGE
   WEAK STILL WITH LOSS OF BLOOD HE SCARCE COULD URGE . . . 387 2 DON JUAN 4   79   5
URGED
   SO OFTEN URGED SO LOUDLY AND SO LONG . . . . 564 3 DON JUAN 17   5   6
URGENT
   WAS URGENT THAT THE GENTLEMAN WHOSE FATE . . . . 240 2 DON JUAN 2 159   3
URINE
   SHE TAUGHT THEM TO SUPPRESS THEIR VICE AND URINE . . . . 162 2 DON JUAN 2   10 V8
URN
   THE ODDS ARE THAT HE FINDS A HANDSOME URN . . . . . . 287 2 DON JUAN 3   23   5
   OF YOUR OWN FOOTSTEPS--VOICES FROM THE URN . . . . . . 508 3 DON JUAN 16   18   4
URNS
   THAT URNS AND PIPKINS ARE BUT FRAGILE BROTHERS . . . . 491 3 DON JUAN 5 138   4
US
   INFORM US TRULY HAVE THEY NOT HEN-PECK'D YOU ALL . . . . 33 2 DON JUAN 1   22   8
   NO DOUBT THIS PATIENCE WHEN THE WORLD IS DAMNING US . . . 37 2 DON JUAN 1   30   1
   ALTHOUGH LONGINUS TELLS US THERE IS NO HYMN . . . . . . 45 2 DON JUAN 1   42   5
   THEY MAKE SOME BLUNDER WHICH THEIR LADIES TELL US . . . . 74 2 DON JUAN 1   98   8
   WHO'VE MADE US YOUTH WAIT TOO--TOO LONG ALREADY . . . . 89 2 DON JUAN 1 125   4
   FIRE WHICH PROMETHEUS FILCH'D FOR US FROM HEAVEN . . . . 90 2 DON JUAN 1 127   8
   WHEN YOU BROKE IN UPON US WITH YOUR FELLOWS . . . . . . 106 2 DON JUAN 1 156   3
   ONLY ANOTHER TIME I TRUST YOU'LL TELL US . . . . 106 2 DON JUAN 1 156   5
   THE KING COMMANDS US AND THE DOCTOR QUACKS US . . . . . 159 2 DON JUAN 2   4   5
   THE KING COMMANDS US AND THE DOCTOR QUACKS US . . . . . 159 2 DON JUAN 2   4   5
   OF US DIES WITH THEM AS EACH FOND HOPE ENDS . . . . . . 167 2 DON JUAN 2   21   6
   GIVE US MORE GROG THEY CRIED FOR IT WILL BE . . . . . . 175 2 DON JUAN 2   36   1
   BUT LET US DIE LIKE MEN NOT SINK BELOW . . . . 175 2 DON JUAN 2   36   4
   SHORT UPPER LIP--SWEET LIPS THAT MAKE US SIGH . . . . . 218 2 DON JUAN 2 118   3
   WITHOUT WHOM VENUS WILL NOT LONG ATTACK US . . . . . . 245 2 DON JUAN 2 169   8
   LET US HAVE WINE AND WOMAN MIRTH AND LAUGHTER . . . . . 250 2 DON JUAN 2 178   7
   ALL THAT IT HATH OF LIFE WITH US IS LIVING . . . . . . 261 2 DON JUAN 2 197   2
   HOW MUCH IT COSTS US YET EACH RISING THROB . . . . . . 264 2 DON JUAN 2 203   2
   TO MAKE US UNDERSTAND EACH GOOD OLD MAXIM . . . . 264 2 DON JUAN 2 203   7
   WHO TO IMMORAL COURSES WOULD ALLURE US . . . . 267 2 DON JUAN 2 207   3
   IF ONLY FROM THE DEVIL THEY WOULD INSURE US . . . . . . 267 2 DON JUAN 2 207   5
   EAT DRINK AND LOVE WHAT CAN THE REST AVAIL US . . . . . 267 2 DON JUAN 2 207   7
   BESIDES THAT WOULD A HAPPY LOT INSURE US . . . . 267 2 DON JUAN 2 207 V3
   THESE ARE SOME SAD EXMAPLES TO ALLURE US . . . . 267 2 DON JUAN 2 207 V5
   DOES THESE THINGS FOR US AND WHENEVER NEWLY A . . . . . 267 2 DON JUAN 2 208   5
   HAVE SUCH A CHARM FOR US POOR HUMAN CREATURES . . . . . 267 2 DON JUAN 2 208   8
   AS WHEN SHE ROSE UPON US LIKE AN EVE . . . . 270 2 DON JUAN 2 213   4
   'TWOULD SAVE US MANY A HEART-ACHE MANY A SHILLING . . . . 270 2 DON JUAN 2 213   5
   THEY KINDLY LEAVE US THOUGH NOT QUITE ALONE . . . . . 305 2 DON JUAN 3   59   7
   ARE GATHER'D ROUND US BY THY LOOK OF REST . . . . 338 2 DON JUAN 3 107   7
   TILL OUR OWN WEAKNESS SHOWS US WHAT WE ARE . . . . . . 344 2 DON JUAN 4   1   8
   O'ERPOWERING US TO BE WHATE'ER MAY SEEM . . . . 360 2 DON JUAN 4   30   5
   HE WILL FORGIVE US--YES--IT MUST BE--YES . . . . 364 2 DON JUAN 4   38   3
   FOR TEA AND COFFEE LEAVE US MUCH MORE SERIOUS . . . . . 372 2 DON JUAN 4   52   8
   ALL HEROES WHO IF LIVING STILL WOULD SLAY US . . . . . 385 2 DON JUAN 4   76   8
   ALL HEROES WHEN ALIVE QUITE PROMPT TO SLAY US . . . . . 385 2 DON JUAN 4   76 V8
   OF POETS WHO COME DOWN TO US THROUGH DISTANCE . . . . . 398 2 DON JUAN 4 100   1
   SO LET US BE ACQUAINTED AS WE OUGHT . . . . 417 2 DON JUAN 5   13   6
   MAY TEACH US BETTER TO BEHAVE WHEN MASTERS . . . . . . 422 2 DON JUAN 5   23   8
   MEANTIME (YON OLD BLACK EUNUCH SEEMS TO EYE US) . . . . 423 2 DON JUAN 5   24   7
   I WISH TO GOD THAT SOMEBODY WOULD BUY US . . . . 423 2 DON JUAN 5   24   8
   MAKES US FEEL OUR MORTALITY IN FACT . . . . 428 2 DON JUAN 5   32   3
   CAN GIVE US EITHER PAIN OR PLEASURE WHO . . . . 428 2 DON JUAN 5   32   6
   BUT LET US TO THE STORY AS BEFORE . . . . 432 2 DON JUAN 5   39   8
   IF WE SHOULD STRIKE A STROKE TO SET US FREE . . . . . . 434 2 DON JUAN 5   43   6
   TO-MORROW'D SEE US IN SOME OTHER DEN . . . . 435 2 DON JUAN 5   44   5
   AND THERE YOU SEE THIS TURN HAS BROUGHT US THROUGH . . . 436 2 DON JUAN 5   45   7
   A KIND OF DEATH COMES O'ER US ALL ALONE . . . . 443 2 DON JUAN 5   57   7
   SHOWS THAT WE BUILD WHEN WE SHOULD BUT ENTOMB US . . . . 448 2 DON JUAN 5   63   8
   AND YOU WILL FIND US NOT TOO FOND OF JOKING . . . . . . 454 2 DON JUAN 5   75   4
   YOU KNOW HOW NEAR US THE DEEP BOSPHORUS FLOATS . . . . . 464 2 DON JUAN 5   92   4
   TO THEM 'TIS A RELIEF TO US A TORTURE . . . . 479 2 DON JUAN 5 118   8
   WITH US THERE IS MORE LAW GIVEN TO THE CHASE . . . . . 482 2 DON JUAN 5 123   4
   THIS WAS A TRUTH TO US EXTREMELY TRITE . . . . 485 2 DON JUAN 5 128   1
   AND MOST OF US HAVE FOUND IT NOW AND THEN . . . .   6 3 DON JUAN 6   1   3
   WITH SUITS AND PROSECUTIONS THEY BESIEGE US . . . . . . 11 3 DON JUAN 6   10   5
   SO LET US BACK TO LILLIPUT AND GUIDE . . . . 20 3 DON JUAN 6   28   6
   TO TAKE US FROM OUR NATURAL REST AND PULL . . . . 46 3 DON JUAN 6   80   3
   WOULD MAKE US THINK THE MOON IS AT ITS FULL . . . . . . 46 3 DON JUAN 6   80   5
   AND SOME OF US HAVE FELT THUS ALL AMORT . . . . 59 3 DON JUAN 6 106   5
   AROUND US EVER RARELY TO ALIGHT . . . . 66 3 DON JUAN 7   1   2
   ASSUME THEN LEAVE US ON OUR FREEZING WAY . . . . 66 3 DON JUAN 7   1   8
   WHEN WE KNOW WHAT ALL ARE WE MUST BEWAIL US . . . . . . 67 3 DON JUAN 7   2   5

US (CONTINUED)

	PAGE	VOL	CANTO	STANZA	LN
THIS BEING THE CASE MAY SHOW US WHAT FAME IS	82	3 DON JUAN	7	33	1
WHAT ARE YE--WHAT YOU SEE US BRIEFLY PAST	97	3 DON JUAN	7	59	6
AND AFTERWARDS ACCOMPANIED US THROUGH	103	3 DON JUAN	7	72	3
WHICH HAMLET TELLS US IS A PASS OF DREAD	133	3 DON JUAN	8	41	4
THAT HOUR IS NOT FOR US BUT 'TIS FOR YOU	180	3 DON JUAN	8	136	1
NO MORE OF THIS THEN--LET US PRAY WE HAVE	192	3 DON JUAN	9	19	2
WHOSE PAMPHLETS VOLUMES NEWSPAPERS ILLUMINE US	200	3 DON JUAN	9	35	3
TO PROVE THE PUBLIC DEBT IS NOT CONSUMING US--	200	3 DON JUAN	9	35	5
THE SUPERSTRATUM WHICH WILL OVERLAY US	201	3 DON JUAN	9	37	8
MAKES US BELIEVE OURSELVES AS GOOD AS ANY	216	3 DON JUAN	9	68	8
TO MAKE SUCH PUPPETS OF US THINGS BELOW)	232	3 DON JUAN	10	16	4
OF FRAIL HUMANITY--MUST MAKE US SELFISH	236	3 DON JUAN	10	23	7
AND SHUT OUR SOULS UP IN US LIKE A SHELL-FISH	236	3 DON JUAN	10	23	8
US LAND ON EARTH WILL DO NO LESS IN HEAVEN	242	3 DON JUAN	10	36	V8
THIS IS THE WAY PHYSICIANS MEND OR END US	245	3 DON JUAN	10	42	1
IN HEALTH--WHEN ILL WE CALL THEM TO ATTEND US	245	3 DON JUAN	10	42	3
WHICH PUZZLES US TO KNOW WHAT FORTUNE MEANS	247	3 DON JUAN	10	47	3
BUT SHOULD WE WISH TO WARM US ON OUR WAY	254	3 DON JUAN	10	59	6
WHICH MAKE US WISH OURSELVES IN TOWN AT ONCE--	277	3 DON JUAN	11	20	8
IS IDLE LET US LIKE MOST OTHERS BOW	286	3 DON JUAN	11	38	5
AND ON OUR SOPHAS MAKES US LIE DEJECTED	301	3 DON JUAN	11	65	5
YE GODS I GROW A TALKER LET US PRATE	345	3 DON JUAN	12	64	1
ALTHOUGH WHEN LONG A LITTLE APT TO WEARY US	358	3 DON JUAN	13	1	6
BECAUSE IT MAKES US SMILE HIS HERO'S RIGHT	363	3 DON JUAN	13	9	2
FEW SPECIMENS YET LEFT US CAN COMPARE	384	3 DON JUAN	13	55	5
AS HINTING MORE (UNLESS OUR JUDGMENTS WARP US)	391	3 DON JUAN	13	69	7
CONSOLING US WITH--WOULD YOU HAD THOUGHT TWICE	430	3 DON JUAN	14	47	7
BUT THUS IT IS SOME WOMEN WILL BETRAY US	441	3 DON JUAN	14	72	8
THE SENSUAL FOR A SHORT TIME BUT CONNECTS US--	442	3 DON JUAN	14	73	5
OR ELSE 'TWILL COST US ALL ANOTHER MILLION	446	3 DON JUAN	14	83	8
HERE LET US PAUSE--WE ARE NOT PREST FOR TIME	455	3 DON JUAN	14	102	V1
BECAUSE SHE WAS NOT APT LIKE SOME OF US	460	3 DON JUAN	15	10	3
AND SEEM TO SAY RESIST US IF YOU CAN--	461	3 DON JUAN	15	12	7
AND PRIDE MY FEEBLE--LET US RAMBLE ON	466	3 DON JUAN	15	22	2
I WISH TO GOD YOU'DE DRESS US SOME SUCH PARTRIDGES	485	3 DON JUAN	15	67	V8
GOD HELP US SINCE WE HAVE NEED ON OUR CAREER	496	3 DON JUAN	15	90	3
FOR FEAR WE SHOULD SUPPOSE US QUITE IN HEAVEN	525	3 DON JUAN	16	49	8
THAT SCARLET CLOAK--GOD HELP US--WHEN CLOSE WRAPPED	530	3 DON JUAN	16	61	V7
FOR ALL OF US HAVE EITHER HEARD OR READ--	538	3 DON JUAN	16	77	3
OF EROS BUT THOUGH THOU HAST PLAYED US MANY TRICKS	554	3 DON JUAN	16	109	7

USAGE

	PAGE	VOL	CANTO	STANZA	LN
WITH THE SAD USAGE OF ALL SORTS OF SAGES	566	3 DON JUAN	17	9	3

USAGES

	PAGE	VOL	CANTO	STANZA	LN
POOR THING OF USAGES COERC'D COMPELL'D	420	3 DON JUAN	14	23	5

USE

	PAGE	VOL	CANTO	STANZA	LN
THE ENGLISH ALWAYS USE TO GOVERN DAMN	28	2 DON JUAN	1	14	8
SOME WOMEN USE THEIR TONGUES--SHE LOOK'D A LECTURE	29	2 DON JUAN	1	15	1
TO BE THE MOST REMOTE FROM COMMON USE	44	2 DON JUAN	1	40	4
MAN'S A STRANGE ANIMAL AND MAKES STRANGE USE	91	2 DON JUAN	1	128	1
HAVE ALWAYS DONE SO 'TIS OF NO GREAT USE	119	2 DON JUAN	1	179	2
THE COPIOUS USE OF CLARET IS FORBID TOO	144	2 DON JUAN	1	216	6
KEPT TWO HAND AND ONE CHAIN-PUMP STILL IN USE	172	2 DON JUAN	2	30	4
FOR YET THEY STROVE ALTHOUGH OF NO GREAT USE	183	2 DON JUAN	2	51	4
IN SHORT IT IS THE USE OF OUR OWN EYES	269	2 DON JUAN	2	212	6
SQUEEZED THROUGH THE RIND WHICH MAKES IT BEST FOR USE	307	2 DON JUAN	3	62	8
WOULD PIQUE HIMSELF ON INTELLECTS WHOSE USE	428	2 DON JUAN	5	32	7
TO USE ALL FIT AND PROPER COURTESIES	472	2 DON JUAN	5	105	5
FOR WOMEN SHED AND USE THEM AT THEIR LIKING	479	2 DON JUAN	5	118	2
WHEN FREED FROM BONDS (WHICH ARE OF NO GREAT USE	23	3 DON JUAN	6	34	4
A STRANGE COINCIDENCE TO USE A PHRASE	45	3 DON JUAN	6	78	7
SINCE JOHN HAS LATELY LOST THE USE OF BOTH	88	3 DON JUAN	7	45	4
WAS TEACHING HIS RECRUITS TO USE THE BAYONET	92	3 DON JUAN	7	51	8
AND WHEN I USE THE PHRASE OF AULD LANG SYNE	233	3 DON JUAN	10	17	1
YOU'LL DEEM NO DOUBT THEY PUT IT TO A GOOD USE	242	3 DON JUAN	10	36	8
SENATES AND SAGES HAVE CONDEMNED ITS USE--	256	3 DON JUAN	10	63	5
HE WHO WILL COMBAT EVIL LONG IN USE	363	3 DON JUAN	13	10	V1
WHEN WE NO MORE CAN USE OR EVEN ABUSE THEE	405	3 DON JUAN	13	100	8
NOR USE THOSE PALISADES BY DAMES ERECTED	437	3 DON JUAN	14	61	7
ALL WHICH I USE TO MAKE MY RHYMES RUN GLIBBER	487	3 DON JUAN	15	71	3
BUT AS SUBSERVIENT TO A MORAL USE	497	3 DON JUAN	15	93	4
BURNT AND NOT BLUE AS MODEST TAPERS USE	512	3 DON JUAN	16	26	2

USED

	PAGE	VOL	CANTO	STANZA	LN
WHO TOOK ALGIERS DECLARES I USED HIM VILELY	102	2 DON JUAN	1	148	8
'TWILL ONE DAY ASK YOU WHY YOU USED ME SO	107	2 DON JUAN	1	157	6
I USED--I WRITE IN HASTE AND IF A STAIN	130	2 DON JUAN	1	192	6
WAS USED--NOR SAIL NOR SHORE APPEAR'D IN SIGHT	178	2 DON JUAN	2	41	7
FOR HAVING USED THEIR APPETITES SO SADLY	199	2 DON JUAN	2	80	8
BUT WAS USED SPARINGLY--SOME WERE AFRAID	200	2 DON JUAN	2	82	2
IS USED UNTIL THE TRUTH ARRIVES TOO LATE--	278	2 DON JUAN	3	6	4
HE--BEING A MAN WHO SELDOM USED A WORD	294	2 DON JUAN	3	37	1
NOW IN A PERSON USED TO MUCH COMMAND--	299	2 DON JUAN	3	47	1
'TWAS FRESH--FOR HE HAD LATELY USED THE LOCK--	365	2 DON JUAN	4	40	7
THUS IS THE TROPHY USED AND THUS LAMENTED	401	2 DON JUAN	4	105	5
USED TO IT NO DOUBT AS EELS ARE TO BE FLAY'D	414	2 DON JUAN	5	7	8
FOR MUTES ARE GENERALLY USED FOR THAT	463	2 DON JUAN	5	89	8
TO JUAN WHO THOUGH NOT MUCH USED TO PRAY--	466	2 DON JUAN	5	95	5
(CURTSIES ARE NEITHER USED BY TURKS NOR GREEKS)	31	3 DON JUAN	6	50	4
REQUEST THAT THEY MAY BOTH BE USED GENTEELLY	103	3 DON JUAN	7	72	8

USED (CONTINUED)

	PAGE	VOL	CANTO	STANZA	LN
THOUGH VERY TRUE WERE NOT YET USED FOR TRIFLES	145	3 DON JUAN	8	66	8
HAVING BEEN USED TO SERVE ON HORSES' BACKS	149	3 DON JUAN	8	74	5
I DON'T THINK THAT YOU USED KINNAIRD QUITE WELL	184	3 DON JUAN	9	2	1
TO BE THE FIRST OF WHAT WE USED TO CALL	198	3 DON JUAN	9	32	2
AND ALWAYS USED HER FAVOURITES TOO WELL	214	3 DON JUAN	9	63	4
BUT THOSE WHO HAVE BEEN A LITTLE USED TO ROUGHING	345	3 DON JUAN	12	63	V6
SO LET THE OFTEN USED VOLCANO GO	374	3 DON JUAN	13	36	6
THE LATTER WORSE USED OF THE TWO WE'VE SEEN--	541	3 DON JUAN	16	84	3

USEFUL

	PAGE	VOL	CANTO	STANZA	LN
EXERTION MIGHT BE USEFUL ON OCCASION	65	2 DON JUAN	1	81	4
UNTIL TOO LATE FOR USEFUL CONVERSATION	84	2 DON JUAN	1	117	2
IN GAINING ALL THAT USEFUL SORT OF KNOWLEDGE	228	2 DON JUAN	2	136	7
USEFUL LIKE MALTHUS IN PROMOTING MARRIAGE--	282	2 DON JUAN	11	30	7
WHICH SHOWS HOW VERY USEFUL GOOD ADVICE IS	333	3 DON JUAN	12	37	V8
THE ANTIQUE PERSIANS TAUGHT THREE USEFUL THINGS	501	3 DON JUAN	16	1	1

USELESS

	PAGE	VOL	CANTO	STANZA	LN
FOR HER FEINAGLE'S WERE AN USELESS ART	27	2 DON JUAN	1	11	5
WITH USELESS PENITENCE PERPLEX'D AND HAUNTED	120	2 DON JUAN	1	180	6
THEIR DESPERATE EFFORTS SEEM'D ALL USELESS GROWN	176	2 DON JUAN	2	38	6
ARE USELESS MIND GOOD PEOPLE WHAT I SAY--	196	3 DON JUAN	9	28	3

USES

	PAGE	VOL	CANTO	STANZA	LN
'TIS STRANGE THE SHORTEST LETTER WHICH MAN USES	327	2 DON JUAN	3	88	4

USHER

	PAGE	VOL	CANTO	STANZA	LN
OF LACQUEYS USHER TO THE FEAST PREPARED	439	2 DON JUAN	5	50	4

USUAL

	PAGE	VOL	CANTO	STANZA	LN
THAT IS THE USUAL METHOD BUT NOT MINE--	25	2 DON JUAN	1	7	1
THE WORLD AS USUAL WICKEDLY INCLINED	31	2 DON JUAN	1	19	5
OF ALL EXPERIENCE 'TIS THE USUAL PRICE	122	2 DON JUAN	1	183	3
AFTER THE USUAL PROCESS MIGHT BE FOUND	407	2 DON JUAN	4	113	3
SO STYLED ACCORDING TO THE USUAL FORMS	12	3 DON JUAN	6	13	2
AND AT THE USUAL SIGNAL TA'EN THEIR WAY	19	3 DON JUAN	6	26	4
DISMAY THE USUAL CONSEQUENCE OF DREAMS	45	3 DON JUAN	6	78	2
THE USUAL HIRSUTE SEASONS WHICH DESTROY	209	3 DON JUAN	9	53	3
THE USUAL PROGRESS OF INTRIGUES BETWEEN	236	3 DON JUAN	10	24	2
SEVEN YEARS (THE USUAL TERM OF TRANSPORTATION)	257	3 DON JUAN	10	66	6
WERE POINTED OUT AS USUAL BY THE BEDRAL	261	3 DON JUAN	10	73	3
THE THIRD THE USUAL ORIGIN OF EVIL	271	3 DON JUAN	11	6	4
AND OFFERING AS USUAL LATE ASSISTANCE	275	3 DON JUAN	11	14	4
THE MOB STOOD AND AS USUAL SEVERAL SCORE	282	3 DON JUAN	11	30	3
AGAINST HIS HEART PREFERRED THEIR USUAL CLAIMS	293	3 DON JUAN	11	48	5
WHERE ARE THE GRENVILLES TURNED AS USUAL WHERE	308	3 DON JUAN	11	79	7
THE WOMEN MUCH DIVIDED--AS IS USUAL	329	3 DON JUAN	12	28	1
THAT USUAL PARAGON AN ONLY DAUGHTER	474	3 DON JUAN	15	41	2
AS USUAL--THE SAME REASON WHICH SHE LATE DID	478	3 DON JUAN	15	50	8
HIS CLOTHES WERE NOT CURBED TO THEIR USUAL CUT	513	3 DON JUAN	16	29	6
SAID JUAN HAD NOT GOT HIS USUAL LOOK ELATE	515	3 DON JUAN	16	34	3
SET TO SOME THOUSANDS ('TIS THE USUAL BURTHEN	529	3 DON JUAN	16	59	2
HER ASPECT WAS AS USUAL STILL--NOT STERN--	545	3 DON JUAN	16	94	3
AND USUAL--JUAN WHEN HE CAST A GLANCE	546	3 DON JUAN	16	96	2
SATE SILENT NOW HIS USUAL SPIRITS GONE	552	3 DON JUAN	16	105	6

USUALLY

	PAGE	VOL	CANTO	STANZA	LN
THUS USUALLY WHEN HE WAS ASK'D TO SING	319	2 DON JUAN	3	85	1

USURER

	PAGE	VOL	CANTO	STANZA	LN
AN USURER COULD SCARCE EXPECT MUCH MORE--	356	3 DON JUAN	12	88	6

USURPER

	PAGE	VOL	CANTO	STANZA	LN
THE MYSTICAL USURPER OF THE MIND--	360	2 DON JUAN	4	30	4

UTI

	PAGE	VOL	CANTO	STANZA	LN
WHICH BRITONS DEEM THEIR UTI POSSIDETIS	246	3 DON JUAN	10	45	8

UTILE

	PAGE	VOL	CANTO	STANZA	LN
OMNE TULIT PUNCTUM QUAE MISCUIT UTILE DULCI	396	3 DON JUAN	13	81	8

UTMOST

	PAGE	VOL	CANTO	STANZA	LN
THE LAWYERS DID THEIR UTMOST FOR DIVORCE	38	2 DON JUAN	1	32	6
BUT HEAR THESE FREEDOMS FORM THE UTMOST LIST	65	2 DON JUAN	1	80	5
HERE WEALTH HAD DONE ITS UTMOST TO ENCUMBER	448	2 DON JUAN	5	64	6
BUT THERE HIS PROJECT REACHED ITS UTMOST PITCH	147	3 DON JUAN	8	71	5
AND CHAMPION HIM TO THE UTMOST--HE WOULD KEEP IT	536	3 DON JUAN	16	75	2

UTTER

	PAGE	VOL	CANTO	STANZA	LN
OR STARCH AS ARE THE EDICTS STATESMEN UTTER	468	3 DON JUAN	15	27	4

UTTER'D

	PAGE	VOL	CANTO	STANZA	LN
UTTER'D BY FRIENDS THOSE PROPHETS OF THE PAST	432	3 DON JUAN	14	50	4

UTTERED

	PAGE	VOL	CANTO	STANZA	LN
OR ALL THE STUFF WHICH UTTERED BY THE BLUES IS	493	2 DON JUAN	5	143	V5
AND LOOKED AT JUAN HARD BUT NOTHING UTTERED	514	3 DON JUAN	16	31	6

UXORIOUS

	PAGE	VOL	CANTO	STANZA	LN
BUT IN A HUSBAND IS PRONOUNCED UXORIOUS	278	2 DON JUAN	3	6	8

VACANCIES

	PAGE	VOL	CANTO	STANZA	LN
THE VACANCIES ARE FILLED UP--SEE GAZETTE	383	3 DON JUAN	13	54	8

VACANT

	PAGE	VOL	CANTO	STANZA	LN
SHE LOOK'D ON MANY A FACE WITH VACANT EYE	378	2 DON JUAN	4	63	1
BUT HOW TO FILL UP THAT SAME VACANT PART	442	3 DON JUAN	14	74	3
HER HEART WAS VACANT THOUGH A SPLENDID MANSION	446	3 DON JUAN	14	85	2

VACCINATION

	PAGE	VOL	CANTO	STANZA	LN
BUT VACCINATION CERTAINLY HAS BEEN	91	2 DON JUAN	1	129	5

VADE

	PAGE	VOL	CANTO	STANZA	LN
THE VADE MECUM OF THE TRUE SUBLIME	136	2 DON JUAN	1	201	3

VAGUE

	PAGE	VOL	CANTO	STANZA	LN
HIS VAIN AMBITION IN ITS VAGUE CAREER	152	2 DON JUAN	1	V 3	4

VAIN

	PAGE	VOL	CANTO	STANZA	LN
HIS NATURAL SPIRIT NOT IN VAIN THEY TOIL'D	49	2 DON JUAN	1	50	5

	PAGE	VOL		CANTO	STANZA	LN

VAIN   (CONTINUED)
```
    SING AT MY HEART SIX MONTHS AT LEAST IN VAIN  . . . . .   102  2 DON JUAN  1     149    2
    MY HONOUR THUS IT SHALL NOT BE IN VAIN  . . . . . . .     105  2 DON JUAN  1     154    8
    FIRST VOW'D (AND NEVER HAD SHE VOW'D IN VAIN)  . . . .    128  2 DON JUAN  1     190    5
    BECAUSE THEY TELL ME 'TWERE IN VAIN TO TRY  . . . . .     142  2 DON JUAN  1     211    6
    GROPING ALL PATHS TO POWER AND ALL IN VAIN  . . . . .     150  2 DON JUAN  1  V    1    6
    HIS VAIN AMBITION IN ITS VAGUE CAREER  . . . . . . . .    152  2 DON JUAN  1  V    3    4
    IN JUAN'S CASE WERE BUT EMPLOY'D IN VAIN  . . . . . .     157  2 DON JUAN  2       1    6
    WOULD HAVE BEEN VAIN AND THEY MUST HAVE GONE DOWN  . .    171  2 DON JUAN  2      29    2
    WAS SCANT ENOUGH IN VAIN THE TELESCOPE  . . . . . .       178  2 DON JUAN  2      41    6
    INTO HIS DYING CHILD'S MOUTH--BUT IN VAIN  . . . . .      203  2 DON JUAN  2      89    8
    AND DEEM THAT IT WAS SAVED PERHAPS IN VAIN  . . . . .     213  2 DON JUAN  2     108    8
    FOR WOMAN'S FACE WAS NEVER FORM'D IN VAIN  . . . .        235  2 DON JUAN  2     149    5
    WHO PLEASE--THE MORE BECAUSE THEY PREACH IN VAIN--        250  2 DON JUAN  2     178    6
    (IT IS THE COUNTRY'S CUSTOM) BUT IN VAIN  . . . . .       314  2 DON JUAN  3      75    2
    IN VAIN--IN VAIN STRIKE OTHER CHORDS  . . . . . . .       324  2 DON JUAN  3  L   9    1
    IN VAIN--IN VAIN STRIKE OTHER CHORDS  . . . . . . .       324  2 DON JUAN  3  L   9    1
    AND THESE WERE NOT OF THE VAIN KIND WHICH CLOYS  . .      352  2 DON JUAN  4      16    4
    WHICH SHE ESSAY'D IN VAIN TO CLEAR (HOW SWEET  . . .      362  2 DON JUAN  4      34    3
    IN VAIN SHE STRUGGLED IN HER FATHER'S GRASP--  . . .      370  2 DON JUAN  4      48    4
    WERE TRIED IN VAIN BY THOSE WHO SERVED SHE GAVE  . .      378  2 DON JUAN  4      63    7
    SHORT SOLACE VAIN RELIEF--THOUGHT CAME TOO QUICK  . .     380  2 DON JUAN  4      67    1
    IN VAIN THE DEWS OF HEAVEN DESCEND ABOVE  . . . . .       382  2 DON JUAN  4      70    7
    MORE CIRCUMSTANCES VAIN WAS EVERY CARE  . . . . . .       429  2 DON JUAN  5      34    6
    ABOUT A BOW-STRING--QUITE IN VAIN NOT YET  . . . . .      471  2 DON JUAN  5     103    4
    OUR SOULS AT LEAST ARE FREE AND 'TIS IN VAIN  . . .       474  2 DON JUAN  5     110    6
    TO EXPOUND THEIR VAIN AND VISIONARY GLEAMS  . . . .        45  3 DON JUAN  6      78    4
    WHICH RISES FOAMS AND BREAKS BUT NOT IN VAIN  . . .        60  3 DON JUAN  6     108  V7
    OH FOOLISH MORTALS ALWAYS TAUGHT IN VAIN  . . . . .       101  3 DON JUAN  7      68    5
    TO VIE WITH THEE WOULD BE ABOUT AS VAIN  . . . . .        106  3 DON JUAN  7      80    6
    WHOSE HEADS WERE HEROES WHICH CUT OFF IN VAIN  . . .      113  3 DON JUAN  8       2    7
    THE SERVILE AND THE VAIN SUCH NAMES WILL BE  . . . .      114  3 DON JUAN  8       5    7
    IN VAIN HE KICKED AND SWORE AND WRITHED AND BLED  . .     153  3 DON JUAN  8      83    5
    IN VAIN THE YELL OF VICTORY IS ROARED  . . . . . .       155  3 DON JUAN  8      87    6
    TO THIS VAIN REFUGE MADE THE GOOD HEART DROOP  . . .      157  3 DON JUAN  8      91    4
    NOW--THAT THE RABBLE'S FIRST VAIN SHOUTS ARE O'ER  .      187  3 DON JUAN  9       9    6
    IN VAIN--AS FALL THE DEWS ON QUENCHLESS SANDS  . . .      212  3 DON JUAN  9      59    7
    ENOUGH TO MAKE A STRIPLING VERY VAIN  . . . . . . .       218  3 DON JUAN  9      72    8
    YET 'TIS IN VAIN SUCH SALLIES TO PERMIT  . . . . .        234  3 DON JUAN 10      19    5
    TO SET UP VAIN PRETENCES OF BEING GREAT  . . . . .        267  3 DON JUAN 10      87    3
    THEY SAY HIS SYSTEM 'TIS IN VAIN TO BATTER  . . . .       268  3 DON JUAN 11       1    3
    (IF 'TIS NOT VAIN EXAMPLES TO RECALL)  . . . . . .        333  3 DON JUAN 12      37    6
    THE GALLANT CAVALIERS WHO FOUGHT IN VAIN  . . . . .       386  3 DON JUAN 13      60    7
    LIKE MAN'S VAIN GLORY AND HIS VAINER TROUBLES  . . .      389  3 DON JUAN 13      65    8
    BUT LO A TENIERS WOOS AND NOT IN VAIN  . . . . . .        392  3 DON JUAN 13      72    5
    WHICH YOU MIGHT ELSEWHERE HOPE TO FIND IN VAIN  . . .     502  3 DON JUAN 16       3    4
    IN VAIN HE HEARD THE OTHERS RAIL OR RALLY  . . . . .      552  3 DON JUAN 16     105    7
    AND NOT IN VAIN HE LISTENED--HUSH WHAT'S THAT  . . .      556  3 DON JUAN 16     112    1
VAINER
    AND THOUGH NOT VAINER FROM HIS PAST SUCCESS  . . . .      353  3 DON JUAN 12      81    7
    LIKE MAN'S VAIN GLORY AND HIS VAINER TROUBLES  . . .      389  3 DON JUAN 13      65    8
VAINLY
    ITS WORKINGS THROUGH THE VAINLY GUARDED EYE  . . . .       61  2 DON JUAN  1      73    4
    AS THE RICH MAN'S IN HELL WHO VAINLY SCREAM'D  . . .      202  2 DON JUAN  2      86    4
    OF THE GREY MORNING AND LOOK VAINLY FOR  . . . . .         18  3 DON JUAN  6      24    5
    FOR WHICH MEN VAINLY DECIMATE THE THRONG  . . . . .       144  3 DON JUAN  8      63    2
    AT WHICH ALL MODERN NATIONS VAINLY AIM  . . . . . .       367  3 DON JUAN 13      20    6
    MIGHT BE FILLED UP AS VAINLY AS BEFORE  . . . . . .       566  3 DON JUAN 17       9    2
VALE
    WHICH LOOKS ALONG THAT VALE OF GOOD AND ILL . . . .       272  3 DON JUAN 11       8    3
VALES
    OF SECRET TREASURES FOUND IN HIDDEN VALES  . . . .        293  2 DON JUAN  3      34    3
    BY THOSE WHO SCOUR THOSE DOUBLE VALES OF STRIFE  . .      232  2 DON JUAN 10      14    4
VALET
    DON JUAN BADE HIS VALET PACK HIS THINGS  . . . . .        161  2 DON JUAN  2       9    1
    PEDRO HIS VALET TOO HE TRIED TO SAVE  . . . . . .         186  2 DON JUAN  2      57    1
    RING FOR YOUR VALET--BID HIM QUICKLY BRING  . . . .       251  2 DON JUAN  2     180    1
    'TIS GRANTED AND THE VALET MOUNTS THE DICKEY--  . . .     380  3 DON JUAN 13      47    1
    IN THE MEANTIME HIS VALET WHOSE PRECISION  . . . .        512  3 DON JUAN 16      28    6
VALET'S
    OR BY ONE'S EARLY VALET'S CURSED KNOCK  . . . . . .       237  2 DON JUAN  2     152    5
VALETS
    THEIR STATION THERE WERE VALETS SECRETARIES . . . . .     249  3 DON JUAN 10      51    2
VALIANT
    OH VALIANT MAN WITH SWORD DRAWN AND COCK'D TRIGGER  . .   103  2 DON JUAN  1     150    7
    AIR 'MIDST THE REST WHO KEPT THEIR VALIANT FACES  . .     130  3 DON JUAN  8      34    7
    THIS VALIANT MAN KILLED ALL THE TURKS HE MET  . . .       150  3 DON JUAN  8      77    1
    OR AT LEAST SUITED NOT THIS VALIANT TARTAR  . . . .       152  3 DON JUAN  8      80    4
VALID
    OR CARELESS BUT THE EFFORT WAS NOT VALID . . . . . .      515  3 DON JUAN 16      35    7
VALLEY
    THOSE WHO CATCH COLD IN SHADOWS OF DEATH'S VALLEY . . .   131  3 DON JUAN  8      36    8
    IT STOOD EMBOSOM'D IN A HAPPY VALLEY . . . . . . .        384  3 DON JUAN 13      56    1
VALOROUS
    AND SINCE EXCEEDING VALOROUS AND SAGE . . . . . . .        24  2 DON JUAN  1       5    2
VALOUR
    VALOUR WAS HIS AND BEAUTY DWELT WITH HER . . . . .        383  2 DON JUAN  4      73    4
    AS THROUGH HIS PALMS BOB ACRES' VALOUR OOZED  . . .       493  2 DON JUAN  5     142    1
    MORE VIRGIN VALOUR NEVER DREAMT OF FLYING  . . . .        131  3 DON JUAN  8      36    3
```

874

```
                                                   PAGE VOL      CANTO  STANZA LN
VALOUR   (CONTINUED)
     HIS STUBBORN VALOUR WAS NO FUTURE SHIELD . . . . . . . 172  3 DON JUAN   8    122   3
     VALOUR MUCH ALSO TO THE BLOOD HE SHOWED . . . . . . .  239  3 DON JUAN  10     29   4
VALOUROUS
     ONE OF THE VALOUROUS SMITHS WHOM WE SHALL MISS . . . .  79  3 DON JUAN   7     25   5
     WAS NOTHING BUT A VALOUROUS KIND OF CUNNING . . . . . 130  3 DON JUAN   8     35   8
VALUE
     OF THE STRANGE THING SOME WOMEN SET A VALUE ON . . . . 208  3 DON JUAN   9     51   3
     HIS WORD HAD THE SAME VALUE AS ANOTHER'S . . . . . . . 535  3 DON JUAN  16     71   8
VAMPIRE
     WITH THE SAME FEELINGS AS YOU'D COAX A VAMPIRE . . . . 299  3 DON JUAN  11     62   5
VAN
     STRIPT TO HIS SHIRT WAS COME TO LEAD THE VAN . . . . .  90  3 DON JUAN   7     49   8
     BUT DEEMS HIMSELF THE FIRST IN GLORY'S VAN . . . . . . 108  3 DON JUAN   7     84   6
     WHO FOUGHT WITH HIS FIVE CHILDREN IN THE VAN . . . . . 164  3 DON JUAN   8    105   8
     WHO IN A ROW LIKE TOM COULD LEAD THE VAN . . . . . . . 277  3 DON JUAN  11     19   3
     NOT LIKE A BALLET-MASTER IN THE VAN  . . . . . . . . . 427  3 DON JUAN  14     38   7
     TALL STATELY FORM'D TO LEAD THE COURTLY VAN . . . . .  440  3 DON JUAN  14     70   5
VANDALS
     AT LEAST SINCE THE RETIREMENT OF THE VANDALS . . . .   128  2 DON JUAN   1    190   4
     SINCE RODERIC'S GOTH'S OR OLDER GENSERIC'S VANDALS . . 129  2 DON JUAN   1    190   V4
VANISH
     AROUND THEM (WHAT I HOPE WILL NEVER VANISH) . . . . .  220  2 DON JUAN   2    120   6
     A PLEASURE BEFORE WHICH ALL OTHERS VANISH . . . . . .  453  3 DON JUAN  14     98   3
VANISHED
     BUT MINE HAVE VANISHED ALL WHEN LIFE IS NEW . . . . .  421  2 DON JUAN   5     21   4
     MY BIDDING BABA VANISHED FOR TO STRETCH . . . . . . .   63  3 DON JUAN   6    116   3
     THE GHOST OF VANISHED PLEASURES ONCE IN VOGUE ILL . .  304  3 DON JUAN  11     72   6
     CRACKED SHIVERED VANISHED SCARCELY GAZED ON ERE . . .  306  3 DON JUAN  11     76   5
     WERE VANISHED TO BE WHAT THEY CALL ALONE-- . . . . . . 381  3 DON JUAN  13     49   3
     THE LAST THIN PETTICOATS WERE VANISHED GONE . . . . .  504  3 DON JUAN  16      8   5
VANISHING
     TO THINK HIS VANISHING UNNATURAL  . . . . . . . . . .  511  3 DON JUAN  16     24   4
VANITY
     ONE SAD EXAMPLE MORE THAT ALL IS VANITY . . . . . . .   29  2 DON JUAN   1     15   7
     FOR HUMAN VANITY THE YOUNG DEFOIX . . . . . . . . . .  400  2 DON JUAN   4    103   4
     ECCLESIASTES SAID THAT ALL IS VANITY-- . . . . . . . .  69  3 DON JUAN   7      6   1
     FROM THEIR FEROCITIES PRODUCED BY VANITY . . . . . . . 182  3 DON JUAN   8    140   4
     AND THAT'S ENOUGH FOR LOVE IS VANITY . . . . . . . . . 219  3 DON JUAN   9     73   1
     AT LEAST HE KEPT HIS VANITY RETIRED  . . . . . . . . . 428  3 DON JUAN  14     41   4
     AT LEAST FOR THIS I CANNOT SPARE ITS VANITY . . . . .  482  3 DON JUAN  15     60   4
     NOR EVEN SMILED ENOUGH FOR ANY VANITY . . . . . . . .  490  3 DON JUAN  15     78   4
VANQUISH'D
     FOR DEATH THOUGH VANQUISH'D STILL RETIRED WITH STRIFE . . 214  2 DON JUAN   2    111   8
VANQUISHED
     HERE STALKS THE VICTOR THERE THE VANQUISHED LIES . . . 461  2 DON JUAN   5     86   4
VAPOUR
     WHOSE SUMMIT LIKE ALL HILLS IS LOST IN VAPOUR . . . .  146  2 DON JUAN   1    218   4
     SINCE AFTER ALL THE CONSEQUENCE IS VAPOUR . . . . . .  146  2 DON JUAN   1    218   V4
     THE AIRY CHILD OF VAPOUR AND THE SUN . . . . . . . . . 205  2 DON JUAN   2     92   2
     TO THOSE WHO BY THE DINT OF GLASS AND VAPOUR . . . . . 226  3 DON JUAN  10      3   6
     APPEARED TO HIM BUT AS THE MAGIC VAPOUR . . . . . . .  266  3 DON JUAN  10     83   2
     THE SUN'S TRUE SON NO VAPOUR BUT A RAY . . . . . . . . 300  3 DON JUAN  11     64   8
     WHICH MAKES BANK CREDIT LIKE A BARK OF VAPOUR . . . .  317  3 DON JUAN  12      4   8
     BUT SINCE STEAM ENGINES PRAISE AND HONOUR VAPOUR . . . 317  3 DON JUAN  12      4   V8
     ON CONSTITUTIONS AND STEAM-BOATS OF VAPOUR . . . . . . 325  3 DON JUAN  12     21   5
     AND DID HE SEE THIS OR WAS IT A VAPOUR  . . . . . . .  510  3 DON JUAN  16     22   8
     RECEIVING SPRITES WITH SYMPATHETIC VAPOUR . . . - . .  512  3 DON JUAN  16     26   3
VAPOURS
     MIX'D WITH THE STONY VAPOURS OF THE VAULT . . . . . .  234  2 DON JUAN   2    147   8
     THE STARS PEEP THROUGH THE VAPOURS DIM AND DANK . . .  110  3 DON JUAN   7     86   6
VARIABLY
     AND RATHER VARIABLY FOR STONY DEATH  . . . . . . . . . 560  3 DON JUAN  16    121   2
VARIATIONS
     WITH SOME SMALL VARIATIONS IN THE LIST . . . . . . . . 107  3 DON JUAN   7     81   V7
VARIED
     HE VARIED WITH SOME SKILL HIS ADULATIONS . . . . . . . 319  2 DON JUAN   3     84   6
     VARIED EACH RAY--BUT ALL DESCRIPTIONS GARBLE . . . . .  55  3 DON JUAN   6     98   5
     SELDOM HE VARIED FEATURE HUE OR MUSCLE  . . . . . . .  132  3 DON JUAN   8     39   7
VARIES
     SLAUGHTER OF ISMAIL  THOUGH MY WILD MUSE VARIES . . .  249  3 DON JUAN  10     51   6
     OF WHICH PERHAPS THE COOKERY RATHER VARIES . . . . . . 486  3 DON JUAN  15     68   3
VARIETY
     BY LIKING A VARIETY OF LADIES  . . . . . . . . . . .   199  2 DON JUAN   2     81   V8
     PITY HE LOVED ADVENTUROUS LIFE'S VARIETY . . . . . . . 296  2 DON JUAN   3     41   7
     OF FREE THOUGHTS IN HIS TRAVELS FOR VARIETY . . . . .  318  2 DON JUAN   3     83   3
     AND OF VARIETY THERE WAS NO LACK-- . . . . . . . . . . 450  2 DON JUAN   5     67   5
     SO MUCH FOR NATURE--BY WAY OF VARIETY . . . . . . . .  146  3 DON JUAN   8     68   1
     VARIETY ITSELF WILL MORE ENCUMBER  . . . . . . . . . . 371  3 DON JUAN  13     30   5
     LOVE WAR A TEMPEST--SURELY THERE'S VARIETY . . . . . . 416  3 DON JUAN  14     14   1
     AMIDST LIFE'S INFINITE VARIETY . . . . . . . . . . . . 464  3 DON JUAN  15     19   2
     NOT ONLY FOR THE SAKE OF THEIR VARIETY  . . . . . . .  497  3 DON JUAN  15     93   3
VARIOUS
     WENT PLUCKING VARIOUS FRUIT WITHOUT HER LEAVE . . . .   30  2 DON JUAN   1     18   8
     OF HIS OWN NATURE AND THE VARIOUS ARTS . . . . . . . .  91  2 DON JUAN   1    128   2
     ARE VARIOUS BUT THEY NONE OF THEM ARE DULL . . . . .   127  2 DON JUAN   1    189   6
     IN VARIOUS CONJECTURES FOR NONE KNEW  . . . . . . . .  209  2 DON JUAN   2    100   4
     THEIR LIVES AND FORTUNES WERE EXTREMELY VARIOUS . . .  266  2 DON JUAN   2    206   5
     OF ARMS (IN THE EAST ALL ARM)--AND VARIOUS DYES . . .  289  2 DON JUAN   3     27   7
     THE BEVERAGE WAS VARIOUS SHERBETS . . . . . . . . . .  307  2 DON JUAN   3     62   6

                              875
```

VARIOUS   (CONTINUED)

	PAGE	VOL	CANTO	STANZA	LN
AND VARIOUS HUES AS IS THE TURKISH WONT--	436	2 DON JUAN	5	46	4
OF VARIOUS NATIONS AND ALL VOLUNTEERS	75	3 DON JUAN	7	18	2
FOLLOWED IN HASTE BY VARIOUS GRENADIERS	147	3 DON JUAN	8	71	2
AND FOUND HIM NOT AMIDST THE VARIOUS PROGENIES	281	3 DON JUAN	11	28	3
HAVE FILLED THEIR PAPERS WITH THEIR COMMENTS VARIOUS	352	3 DON JUAN	12	78	4
BY VARIOUS JOLTINGS OF LIFE'S HACKNEY COACH	421	3 DON JUAN	14	26	5
BUT VARIOUS AS THE VARIOUS MEATS DISPLAY'D	488	3 DON JUAN	15	74	4
BUT VARIOUS AS THE VARIOUS MEATS DISPLAY'D	488	3 DON JUAN	15	74	4
WITH VARIOUS SIMILAR REMARKS TO TALLY	526	3 DON JUAN	16	53	5

VARLET

	PAGE	VOL	CANTO	STANZA	LN
TO WOMEN THERE IS SCARCE A CRIMSON VARLET	108	3 DON JUAN	7	84	5

VARMINT

	PAGE	VOL	CANTO	STANZA	LN
A THOROUGH VARMINT AND A REAL SWELL	276	3 DON JUAN	11	17	6

VARNISH

	PAGE	VOL	CANTO	STANZA	LN
A SORT OF VARNISH OVER EVERY FAULT	417	3 DON JUAN	14	16	3

VARY

	PAGE	VOL	CANTO	STANZA	LN
ALL FEELINGS CHANGED BUT THIS WAS LAST TO VARY	413	2 DON JUAN	5	4	5
AN ART ON WHICH THE ARTISTS GREATLY VARY	374	3 DON JUAN	13	35	3

VARYING

	PAGE	VOL	CANTO	STANZA	LN
A NON-DESCRIPT AND EVER VARYING RHYME	67	3 DON JUAN	7	2	2
THERE THE STILL VARYING PANGS WHICH MULTIPLY	118	3 DON JUAN	8	13	1

VASE

	PAGE	VOL	CANTO	STANZA	LN
AND SHERBET COOLING IN THE POROUS VASE	291	3 DON JUAN	3	31	5
SPARKLED ALONG ITS ROOF AND MANY A VASE	54	3 DON JUAN	6	97	6
LIKE TO A LIGHTED ALABASTER VASE--	159	3 DON JUAN	8	96	8

VASSAL

	PAGE	VOL	CANTO	STANZA	LN
NOR WINE NOR WASSAIL COULD RAISE A VASSAL	520	3 DON JUAN	16	L 5	7

VAST

	PAGE	VOL	CANTO	STANZA	LN
I PRAISE YOUR VAST FORBEARANCE NOT TO BEAT	103	2 DON JUAN	1	150	5
AWAY THE VAST SALT DREAD ETERNAL DEEP	210	2 DON JUAN	2	103	8
SPREAD LIKE A ROSY OCEAN VAST AND BRIGHT	253	2 DON JUAN	2	185	2
CONTEMPT BUT FROM THE BATHOS' VAST ABYSS	334	2 DON JUAN	3	100	4
THAT NEITHER OF THEIR INTELLECTS ARE VAST	345	2 DON JUAN	4	2	4
A VAST UNTILL'D AND MOUNTAIN-SKIRTED PLAIN	386	2 DON JUAN	4	77	2
HINTED THE VAST ADVANTAGES WHICH THEY	451	2 DON JUAN	5	69	2
FOR ALL WAS VAST STILL FRAGRANT AND DIVINE	460	2 DON JUAN	5	85	8
THEN ONE VAST FIRE AIR EARTH AND STREAM EMBRACED	115	3 DON JUAN	8	7	5
BUT STILL IT FALLS WITH VAST AND AWFUL SPLINTERS	155	3 DON JUAN	8	88	7
IN ROYALTY'S VAST ARMS HE SIGHED FOR BEAUTY	243	3 DON JUAN	10	37	8
'TWILL MAKE IF PROVED VAST EFFORTS WITHOUT PAINING	366	3 DON JUAN	13	18	8
THE MANSION'S SELF WAS VAST AND VENERABLE	389	3 DON JUAN	13	66	1
WHAT ANTRES VAST AND DESARTS IDLE THEN	455	3 DON JUAN	14	102	1
WHAT DILETTANTI DO WITH VAST PARADE)	522	3 DON JUAN	16	44	3

VASTY

	PAGE	VOL	CANTO	STANZA	LN
HAS GIVEN A SAMPLE FROM THE VASTY VERSION	11	2 DON JUAN	D	4	3
THE VASTY DEEP TO WHOM YOU MAY EXCLAIM	132	3 DON JUAN	8	38	3

VATES

	PAGE	VOL	CANTO	STANZA	LN
THE VATES IRRITABILIS TAKES CARE	317	2 DON JUAN	3	81	2

VAUBAN

	PAGE	VOL	CANTO	STANZA	LN
OF THE HIGH TALENTS OF THIS NEW VAUBAN	72	3 DON JUAN	7	11	2

VAULT

	PAGE	VOL	CANTO	STANZA	LN
MIX'D WITH THE STONY VAPOURS OF THE VAULT	234	2 DON JUAN	2	147	8
THE FAMILY VAULT RECEIVES ANOTHER LORD	306	3 DON JUAN	11	75	8

VAUNT

	PAGE	VOL	CANTO	STANZA	LN
OF SUCH AS THESE I SHOULD NOT CARE TO VAUNT	21	2 DON JUAN	1	1	5
LOUD AS THE VIRTUES THOU DOST LOUDLY VAUNT	241	3 DON JUAN	10	34	3
AND KONINGSBERG THE CAPITAL WHOSE VAUNT	254	3 DON JUAN	10	60	2
WHICH 'TIS THE COMMON CRY AND LIE TO VAUNT AS	311	3 DON JUAN	11	87	3

VAUNTED

	PAGE	VOL	CANTO	STANZA	LN
HIS EVE WITH ALL THE INNOCENCE SHE VAUNTED	120	2 DON JUAN	1	180	V6
AT SIXTEEN SHE CAME OUT PRESENTED VAUNTED	434	3 DON JUAN	14	55	1

VEAL

	PAGE	VOL	CANTO	STANZA	LN
BEEF VEAL AND MUTTON BETTER FOR DIGESTION	191	2 DON JUAN	2	67	8

VEER

	PAGE	VOL	CANTO	STANZA	LN
SHOULD NOT VEER ROUND WITH EVERY BREATH NOR SEIZE	231	3 DON JUAN	10	13	7

VEERING

	PAGE	VOL	CANTO	STANZA	LN
AND AS THE VEERING WIND SHIFTS SHIFT OUR SAILS	159	2 DON JUAN	2	4	4

VEGETABLE

	PAGE	VOL	CANTO	STANZA	LN
IN RIDING ROUND THOSE VEGETABLE PUNCHEONS	301	3 DON JUAN	11	66	3

VEGETABLES

	PAGE	VOL	CANTO	STANZA	LN
BEARS VEGETABLES IN A GRUMBLING WAY	191	2 DON JUAN	2	67	6
THOSE VEGETABLES OF THE CATHOLIC CREED	445	3 DON JUAN	14	81	7
AND VEGETABLES ALL IN MASQUERADE	488	3 DON JUAN	15	74	2

VEHICLES

	PAGE	VOL	CANTO	STANZA	LN
IN OTHER VEHICLES BUT AT HIS SIDE	249	3 DON JUAN	10	51	3

VEIL

	PAGE	VOL	CANTO	STANZA	LN
LIKE SKIES THAT RAIN AND LIGHTEN AS A VEIL	108	2 DON JUAN	1	158	3
RELUCTANT PAST HER BRIGHT EYES ROLLED--AS A VEIL	108	2 DON JUAN	1	158	V3
THEIR VEIL AND PETTICOAT--ALAS TO DWELL	160	2 DON JUAN	2	6	4
CHASTE MUSE--(WELL IF YOU MUST YOU MUST)--THE VEIL	160	2 DON JUAN	2	7	1
OVER THE WASTE OF WATERS LIKE A VEIL	182	2 DON JUAN	2	49	2
FLOW'D IN HER VEIL AND MANY A PRECIOUS STONE	220	2 DON JUAN	2	121	6
HER DOWRY AND HER VEIL IN FORM ALIKE	221	2 DON JUAN	2	122	5
JUANNA PLAYING WITH HER VEIL OR HAIR	28	3 DON JUAN	6	45	2
ARRAYED HERSELF WITH MANTLE GEM AND VEIL	49	3 DON JUAN	6	87	4
CONCEALED HER FEATURES BETTER THAN A VEIL	60	3 DON JUAN	6	109	2
WITH ALL ITS VEIL OF MYSTERY DRAWN APART	169	3 DON JUAN	8	115	4
IN MY YOUNG DAYS THAT CHASTE AND GOODLY VEIL	422	3 DON JUAN	14	27	2
THE DUCHESS OF FITZ-FULKE PLAYED WITH HER VEIL	514	3 DON JUAN	16	31	5

```
                                                             PAGE VOL      CANTO STANZA LN
VEIL'S
     HER HAIR WAS STARR'D WITH GEMS HER VEIL'S FINE FOLD  .  .  . 312   2 DON JUAN  3     72    4
VEIN
     AND IF AS I BELIEVE THY VEIN BE GOOD  .  .  .  .  .  .  .  . 149   2 DON JUAN  1    222    3
     LOVE WHO HEROICALLY BREATHES A VEIN  .  .  .  .  .  .  .  . 168   2 DON JUAN  2     23    3
     AND TINGLING VEIN SEEM'D THROBBING BACK TO LIFE  .  .  .  . 214   2 DON JUAN  2    111    7
     A VEIN HAD BURST AND HER SWEET LIPS' PURE DYES  .  .  .  . 376   2 DON JUAN  4     59    1
VEINS
     AS IF HER VEINS RAN LIGHTNING SHE IN SOOTH  .  .  .  .  .  .  55   2 DON JUAN  1     61    6
     MY TEETH BEGIN TO CHATTER MY VEINS FREEZE--  .  .  .  .  . 121   2 DON JUAN  1    181    6
     PREFERR'D A DRAUGHT FROM THE FAST-FLOWING VEINS  .  .  .  . 197   2 DON JUAN  2     77    4
     AND FELT HER VEINS CHILL'D BY THE NEIGHBOURING SEA  .  .  . 233   2 DON JUAN  2    145    4
     WHERE THE BLUE VEINS LOOK'D SHADOWY SHRUNK AND WEAK  .  .  . 234   2 DON JUAN  2    147    5
     WHILE YOUTH'S HOT WISHES IN OUR RED VEINS REVEL  .  .  .  . 345   2 DON JUAN  4      2    5
     THE FIRE BURST FORTH FROM HER NUMIDIAN VEINS  .  .  .  .  . 375   2 DON JUAN  4     57    7
     BOILED IN HIS VEINS AND RATHER THAN DESCEND  .  .  .  .  . 471   2 DON JUAN  5    104    4
     AND HER PROUD BROW'S BLUE VEINS TO SWELL AND DARKLE  .  .  .  56   2 DON JUAN  6    101    8
     FOR HE WAS DIZZY BUSY AND HIS VEINS  .  .  .  .  .  .  .  . 129   3 DON JUAN  8     33    2
     LIGHTENING ALONG HIS VEINS AND WHERE HE HEARD  .  .  .  .  . 129   3 DON JUAN  8     33   V3
     OUR VEINS WHEN THINGS CALLED SOVEREIGNS THINK IT BEST  .  . 212   3 DON JUAN  9     60    7
     OF THEIR SALT VEINS AND THEIR SAD SHALLOW SEAS  .  .  .  . 251   3 DON JUAN 10     54   V4
     BESIDES SOME VEINS OF IRON LEAD OR COPPER  .  .  .  .  .  . 254   3 DON JUAN 10     60    3
     YOUR VEINS OF COCKNEY SPIRIT SMILE OR MOURN  .  .  .  .  . 264   3 DON JUAN 10     80    6
     AS IF HIS VEINS WOULD POUR OUT HIS EXISTENCE  .  .  .  .  . 275   3 DON JUAN 11     14    6
     FOLLOWED HIS VEINS NO LONGER COLD BUT HEATED  .  .  .  .  . 559   3 DON JUAN 16    119    4
VEINS'
     (WHO LIKE SOUR FRUIT TO STIR THEIR VEINS' SALT TIDES  .  . 251   3 DON JUAN 10     54    3
VELVET
     OF VELVET PANNELS EACH OF DIFFERENT HUE  .  .  .  .  .  .  . 308   2 DON JUAN  3     64    2
     THE VELVET CUSHIONS--(FOR A THRONE MORE MEET)--  .  .  .  . 309   2 DON JUAN  3     67    5
VENERABLE
     THERE WREATHE HIS VENERABLE HORNS WITH FLOWERS  .  .  .  . 292   2 DON JUAN  3     32    2
     IN GAZING ON THAT VENERABLE ARCH  .  .  .  .  .  .  .  .  . 386   3 DON JUAN 13     59    8
     THE MANSION'S SELF WAS VAST AND VENERABLE  .  .  .  .  .  . 389   3 DON JUAN 13     66    1
VENERABLY
     OF LIGHT TO SAVE THE VENERABLY CHASTE--  .  .  .  .  .  .  . 177   3 DON JUAN  8    130    6
VENERATE
     I FOR ONE VENERATE A PETTICOAT--  .  .  .  .  .  .  .  .  . 421   3 DON JUAN 14     26    6
VENERATION
     I FEEL A MIXED REGRET AND VENERATION  .  .  .  .  .  .  .  . 257   3 DON JUAN 10     66    4
VENETIAN
     EXCEPTING THE VENETIAN FAZZIOLI  .  .  .  .  .  .  .  .  . 160   2 DON JUAN  2      7    8
     (THOUGH SHE WAS MASQUED THEN AS A FAIR VENETIAN)  .  .  . 268   2 DON JUAN  2    210    8
     AND SO I STOPPED TO TALK WITH A VENETIAN  .  .  .  .  .  . 268   2 DON JUAN  2    210   V8
VENGEANCE
     HE WAGED IN VENGEANCE OF HER DEGRADATION  .  .  .  .  .  . 303   2 DON JUAN  3     55    8
     VENGEANCE ON HIM WHO WAS THE CAUSE OF ALL  .  .  .  .  .  . 364   2 DON JUAN  4     37    4
     AMBITION AVARICE VENGEANCE GLORY GLUE  .  .  .  .  .  .  . 422   2 DON JUAN  5     22    6
     YOU SHALL HAVE VENGEANCE FOR THE TOWN SURROUNDED  .  .  .  .  98   3 DON JUAN  7     61    7
VENISON
     WITH SAUCES GENEVOISES AND HAUNCH OF VENISON  .  .  .  .  . 484   3 DON JUAN 15     65    2
VENOM
     AND HURLS AT ONCE HIS VENOM AND HIS STRENGTH  .  .  .  .  . 218   2 DON JUAN  2    117    8
VENT
     THEIR DIRTY DIPLOMATIC HANDS TO VENT  .  .  .  .  .  .  .  . 498   2 DON JUAN  5    151    5
     WITH ONE GOOD HEARTY CURSE I VENT MY GALL  .  .  .  .  .  .  17   3 DON JUAN  6     22    3
     WHERE ALL THE PASSIONS HAVE ALAS BUT ONE VENT  .  .  .  .  22   3 DON JUAN  6     32    8
VENTED
     AS IF THE PEASANT'S COARSE CONTEMPT WERE VENTED  .  .  .  . 401   2 DON JUAN  4    105    3
VENTURE
     YET HALF AFRAID TO VENTURE FOR THE DRAUGHT  .  .  .  .  .  . 155   2 DON JUAN  1  V   6    2
     HE FEAR'D HIS NECK TO VENTURE SUCH A NAG ON  .  .  .  .  . 333   2 DON JUAN  3     99    6
     TO VENTURE A SOLUTION DAVUS SUM  .  .  .  .  .  .  .  .  . 365   3 DON JUAN 13     13    2
     UPON WHOSE BACK 'TIS BETTER NOT TO VENTURE  .  .  .  .  .  . 442   3 DON JUAN 14     73    8
     THOUGH FOR THE PUBLIC WEAL DISPOSED TO VENTURE HIGH  .  . 536   3 DON JUAN 16     73    6
     IS MORE THAN I SHALL VENTURE TO DESCRIBE--  .  .  .  .  .  . 567   3 DON JUAN 17     12    7
VENTURED
     HIS PEACE WAS MAKING BUT BEFORE HE VENTURED  .  .  .  .  . 493   2 DON JUAN  5    143    7
     HIMSELF A FAVOURITE VENTURED TO ADDRESS  .  .  .  .  .  . 100   3 DON JUAN  7     65    2
     HAVE VENTURED PAST THE JAWS OF MOOR AND TIGER  .  .  .  . 348   3 DON JUAN 12     70   V6
VENTURES
     WOE TO THE MAN WHO VENTURES A REBUKE  .  .  .  .  .  .  . 429   3 DON JUAN 14     43    5
VENUS
     HER ZONE TO VENUS OR HIS BOW TO CUPID  .  .  .  .  .  .  .  51   2 DON JUAN  1     55    7
     WITHOUT WHOM VENUS WILL NOT LONG ATTACK US  .  .  .  .  . 245   2 DON JUAN  2    169    8
     WHILE VENUS FILLS THE HEART (WITHOUT HEART REALLY  .  .  . 246   2 DON JUAN  2    170    1
     WHILE VENUS FILLS THE HEART (WHICH QUITE AS WELL IS  .  . 246   2 DON JUAN  2    170   V1
     O'ER THE FAIR VENUS BUT FOREVER FAIR  .  .  .  .  .  .  . 377   2 DON JUAN  4     61    4
     AND PAIR THEIR RHYMES AS VENUS YOKES HER DOVES  .  .  .  . 411   2 DON JUAN  5      1    3
     AS VENUS ROSE WITH FROM THE WAVE ON THEM  .  .  .  .  .  . 466   2 DON JUAN  5     96    2
     A KIND OF SLEEPY VENUS SEEMED DUDU  .  .  .  .  .  .  .  .  27   3 DON JUAN  6     42    1
     WITH THE NEW VENUS OF THEIR BRILLIANT OCEAN  .  .  .  .  . 434   3 DON JUAN 14     55    4
     WITH VIVIFYING VENUS WHO DOTH OWE  .  .  .  .  .  .  .  . 542   3 DON JUAN 16     86    6
     STILL WE RESPECT THEE ALMA VENUS GENETRIX  .  .  .  .  . 554   3 DON JUAN 16    109    8
VERACIOUS
     EVEN MY VERACIOUS SELF--BUT THAT'S A LIE  .  .  .  .  .  . 495   3 DON JUAN 15     88    3
VERBUM
     I SAY THAT THERE'S THE PLACE--BUT VERBUM SAT  .  .  .  .  .  50   2 DON JUAN  1     53    4
     THEY FILL THE CANVASS UP--AND VERBUM SAT  .  .  .  .  .  . 463   3 DON JUAN 15     16    5
```

VERDANT
AND STUFF WITH SAGE THAT VERY VERDANT GOOSE . . . . . . 497 3 DON JUAN 15 93 6
VERDICT
(THE JURY BROUGHT THEIR VERDICT IN INSANITY) . . . . . 29 2 DON JUAN 1 15 8
A VERDICT--GRIEVOUS FOE TO THOSE WHO CAUSE IT-- . . . 346 3 DON JUAN 12 65 5
WHOSE VERDICT FOR SUCH SIN A CERTAIN CURE IS)-- . . . 436 3 DON JUAN 14 60 8
VERDURE
SO THAT THE BRANCH A GOODLY VERDURE FLINGS . . . . . 436 3 DON JUAN 14 59 3
VERGE
THUS TO THEIR EXTREME VERGE THE PASSIONS BROUGHT . . . 402 2 DON JUAN 4 106 6
THE VERGE OF HEAVEN AND IN HER LARGE EYES WROUGHT . . . 473 2 DON JUAN 5 108 6
HAIL THAMIS HAIL UPON THY VERGE IT IS . . . . 277 3 DON JUAN 11 20 4
'TWIXT NIGHT AND MORN UPON THE HORIZON'S VERGE . . . 500 3 DON JUAN 15 99 2
VERIEST
THE VERIEST JADE WILL WINCE WHOSE HARNESS WRINGS . . . 137 3 DON JUAN 8 50 5
VERILY
SO THAT I VERILY BELIEVE IF THEY . . . . 466 3 DON JUAN 15 23 2
VERITY
WHOSE TRAITS WERE RADIANT WITH THE RAYS OF VERITY . . . 550 3 DON JUAN 16 102 4
VERMICELLI
CERES PRESENTS A PLATE OF VERMICELLI-- . . . . . . 246 2 DON JUAN 2 170 3
VERMILLION
THE WAX WAS SUPERFINE ITS HUE VERMILLION . . . . . 134 2 DON JUAN 1 198 8
BROUGHT FORTH IN PURPLE CRADLED IN VERMILLION . . . 205 2 DON JUAN 2 92 3
VERMIN
WEAKNESS FOR WHAT MOST PEOPLE DEEM MERE VERMIN-- . . . 249 3 DON JUAN 10 50 5
VERNET'S
IN VERNET'S OCEAN LIGHTS AND THERE THE STORIES . . . . 392 3 DON JUAN 13 71 6
VERNON
VERNON THE BUTCHER CUMBERLAND WOLFE HAWKE . . . . . 22 2 DON JUAN 1 2 1
VERONESE
THE REAL NAME OF THE FAIR VERONESE-- . . . . 273 2 DON JUAN 2 V 2 2
VERSATILITY
BY TURNS--WITH THAT VIVACIOUS VERSATILITY . . . . . 547 3 DON JUAN 16 97 2
VERSE
IN HONEST SIMPLE VERSE THIS SONG TO YOU . . . . . 20 2 DON JUAN D 17 2
BUT IT WILL SERVE TO KEEP MY VERSE COMPACT) . . . . 119 2 DON JUAN 1 178 4
SOME PEOPLE LIKE BLANK VERSE I'M FOND OF RHYME . . . 136 2 DON JUAN 1 201 V5
NOT TO BELIEVE MY VERSE AND THEIR OWN EYES . . . . 141 2 DON JUAN 1 208 4
WITH TRUTH LIKE SOUTHEY AND WITH VERSE LIKE CRASHAW . . 316 2 DON JUAN 3 79 8
THE MODERN GREEK IN TOLERABLE VERSE . . . . . 326 2 DON JUAN 3 87 2
OF VERSE (THE NAME WITH WHICH WE CANTABS PLEASE . . 341 2 DON JUAN 3 110 7
AS OVID'S VERSE MAY GIVE TO UNDERSTAND . . . . . 411 2 DON JUAN 5 1 6
THE TU'S TOO MUCH--BUT LET IT STAND--THE VERSE . . . 14 3 DON JUAN 6 18 1
KISS RHYMES TO BLISS IN FACT AS WELL AS VERSE-- . . . 35 3 DON JUAN 6 59 7
VERSE AND BY SOLOMON AND BY CERVANTES . . . . . 67 3 DON JUAN 7 3 8
THUS THE SAME CAUSE WHICH MAKES A VERSE WANT FEET . . 79 3 DON JUAN 7 26 3
WHICH IS STILL BETTER THUS IN VERSE TO WAGE . . . 118 3 DON JUAN 8 14 6
IN LEAVING VERSE MORE FREE FROM THE RESTRICTION . . 154 3 DON JUAN 8 86 4
IN PROSE I BEND MY HUMBLE VERSE) DOTH CALL . . . 163 3 DON JUAN 8 104 7
THAT OX OF VERSE WHO PLOUGHS FOR EVERY LINE-- . . . 297 3 DON JUAN 11 58 6
BUT OF ALL VERSE WHAT MOST INSURED HER PRAISE . . . 525 3 DON JUAN 16 50 7
VERSED
THOUGH LITTLE VERSED IN FEELINGS ORIENTAL . . . . 105 3 DON JUAN 7 75 2
WAS ADELINE WELL VERSED AS COMPOSITIONS . . . . . 523 3 DON JUAN 16 46 8
VERSE'S
WHETHER MY VERSE'S FAME BE DOOM'D TO CEASE . . . . 398 2 DON JUAN 4 99 4
VERSES
OVID'S A RAKE AS HALF HIS VERSES SHOW HIM . . . . 45 2 DON JUAN 1 42 1
HIS VERSES RARELY WANTED THEIR DUE FEET-- . . . . 316 2 DON JUAN 3 78 5
THAT GOOD OLD STEAM-BOAT WHICH KEEPS VERSES MOVING . . 219 3 DON JUAN 9 74 4
VERSIFIED
A VERSIFIED AURORA BOREALIS . . . . 67 3 DON JUAN 7 2 3
VERSIFY
AND NEVER STRAINING HARD TO VERSIFY . . . . . . 464 3 DON JUAN 15 19 6
VERSION
HAS GIVEN A SAMPLE FROM THE VASTY VERSION . . . . . 11 2 DON JUAN D 4 3
VERSTS
IT STANDS SOME EIGHTY VERSTS FROM THE HIGH SEA . . . . 71 3 DON JUAN 7 9 7
VESPER
AND VESPER BELL'S THAT ROSE THE BOUGHS ALONG . . . . 337 2 DON JUAN 3 106 4
AS THE FAR BELL OF VESPER MAKES HIM START . . . . 338 2 DON JUAN 3 108 5
VESSEL
THE COURT CAMP CHURCH THE VESSEL AND THE MART . . . 131 2 DON JUAN 1 194 3
AND TOSSED ALONG THE VESSEL FORE AND AFT . . . . 155 2 DON JUAN 1 V 6 4
OH JULIA--(THIS CURST VESSEL PITCHES SO)-- . . . . 167 2 DON JUAN 2 20 6
THE VESSEL SWAM YET STILL SHE HELD HER OWN . . . . 176 2 DON JUAN 2 38 4
NO DOUBT THE VESSEL WAS ABOUT TO SINK . . . . . 187 2 DON JUAN 2 58 6
HIS VESSEL HAVING NEED OF SOME REPAIRS . . . . . 285 2 DON JUAN 3 19 3
IS AWFUL TO THE VESSEL NEAR THE ROCK . . . . . 305 2 DON JUAN 3 58 4
BUT TO THE NARRATIVE THE VESSEL BOUND . . . . . 407 2 DON JUAN 4 113 1
A RUSSIAN VESSEL E'ER WOULD HEAVE IN SIGHT . . . . 73 3 DON JUAN 7 13 3
(A CHANCE STILL) 'TIS A VOYAGE OR VESSEL LOST . . . 376 3 DON JUAN 13 39 8
VESSEL'S
UNDER THE VESSEL'S KEEL THE SAIL WAS PAST . . . . 176 2 DON JUAN 2 39 1
VESSELS
FOR WANDERING MERCHANT VESSELS NOW AND THEN . . . . 223 2 DON JUAN 2 126 3
BUT THREE RAGUSAN VESSELS BOUND FOR SCIO . . . . 248 2 DON JUAN 2 174 8
WITHIN A CABLE'S LENGTH THEIR VESSELS LAY . . . . 81 3 DON JUAN 7 29 4

```
                                                          PAGE VOL    CANTO STANZA LN
VEST
   AND THAT BENEATH EACH TURKISH-FASHIONED VEST  . . . . .  96  3 DON JUAN  7     57   5
   NO REAL LIKENESS--LIKE THE OLD TYRIAN VEST . . . . . .  505  3 DON JUAN 16     10   5
   COMPLETELY SANS CULOTTE AND WITHOUT VEST . . . . . . .  555  3 DON JUAN 16    111   3
VESTAL
   BUT SOMEHOW THIS MY VESTAL VOW TAKES WING  . . . . . .   85  2 DON JUAN  1    119   5
   THE STRICTER DOUBTLESS GROW THE VESTAL DUTIES . . . . .  35  2 DON JUAN  6     58   7
   A VESTAL SHRINE OF INNOCENCE OF HEART . . . . . . . .   370  3 DON JUAN 13     27   7
VESTALS
   OF VESTALS BROUGHT INTO THE MARRIAGE MART  . . . . .    337  3 DON JUAN 12     46   7
   NEW VESTALS CLAIM MEN'S EYES WITH THE SAME PRAISE . . .  340  3 DON JUAN 12     53   6
VESTURE
   DREW FORTH A POCKET-PISTOL FROM HIS VESTURE . . . . .   274  3 DON JUAN 11     13   3
VESUVIUS
   THE FIRE WAS THAT WERE RED VESUVIUS LOADED . . . . .    119  3 DON JUAN  8     16   2
VETABO
   VETABO CERERIS SACRUM QUI VULGARET-- . . . . . . .      419  3 DON JUAN 14     21   7
VETERAN
   FOR ONE ROUGH WEATHER-BEATEN VETERAN BODY  . . . . .    167  3 DON JUAN  8    112   7
   THE KINDER VETERAN WITH CALM WORDS WILL COURT YOU . . .  337  3 DON JUAN 12     45   5
VEX
   AND DEAF THAT ANY OTHER IT WOULD VEX . . . . . . .      101  2 DON JUAN  1    147   4
   READ--WERE IT BUT YOUR GRANDMOTHERS TO VEX . . . . .    403  2 DON JUAN  4    108  V6
   ALTHOUGH HER BEAUTY WAS ENOUGH TO VEX . . . . . . .      24  3 DON JUAN  6     37   2
VEXATION
   ALL SAVE THE BLACKS SEEM'D JADED WITH VEXATION . . . .  414  2 DON JUAN  5      7   5
   AT HOME IT MIGHT HAVE GIVEN HER SOME VEXATION . . . .   241  3 DON JUAN 10     33   5
   AND JUAN GREW CARNATION WITH VEXATION . . . . . . .     545  3 DON JUAN 16     93   3
VEXES
   AND THAT WHICH AFTER ALL MY SPIRIT VEXES . . . . . .    269  3 DON JUAN 11      3   4
VIAGGINO
   CAN PAINT COSI VIAGGINO I RICCHI  . . . . . . . .       380  3 DON JUAN 13     47   5
VIANDS
   TO STIR HER VIANDS MADE HIM QUITE AWAKE . . . . . .     237  2 DON JUAN  2    153   7
   WITH VIANDS AND SHERBETS IN ICE--AND WINE-- . . . . .   310  2 DON JUAN  3     69   7
VIBRATE
   VIBRATE TO THE ETERNAL NAME  HARK THROUGH  . . . . .    116  3 DON JUAN  8      8   7
VIBRATES
   AS VIBRATES MY FOND HEART TO MY FIX'D SOUL . . . . .    133  2 DON JUAN  1    196   8
VICARAGE
   A FAT FEN VICARAGE AND NOUGHT TO THINK ON  . . . . .    540  3 DON JUAN 16     82   8
VICE
   NOR COIN MY SELF-LOVE TO SO BASE A VICE . . . . . .      12  2 DON JUAN  D      6   2
   ITS VERY COURAGE STAGNATES TO A VICE . . . . . . .       18  2 DON JUAN  D     15   8
   I LOATHE THAT LOW VICE CURIOSITY . . . . . . . .         33  2 DON JUAN  1     23   5
   BECAUSE IT IS A MARKETABLE VICE . . . . . . . .          57  2 DON JUAN  1     64   8
   HE WONDERS AT THEIR VICE AND NOT HIS FOLLY . . . . .     74  2 DON JUAN  1     99   8
   SO FOR A GOOD OLD-GENTLEMANLY VICE . . . . . . .        144  2 DON JUAN  1    216   7
   SHE TAUGHT THEM TO SUPPRESS THEIR VICE AND URINE . . .  162  2 DON JUAN  2     10  V8
   CALL'D SOCIAL HAUNTS OF HATE AND VICE AND CARE . . . .  358  2 DON JUAN  4     28   4
   NEED NOT SEEM VERY WONDERFUL FOR VICE . . . . . .       408  2 DON JUAN  4    115   5
   ARE SAVING--VICE SPARES NOTHING FOR A RARITY . . . .    408  2 DON JUAN  4    115   8
   HAS QUITE THE CONTRARY EFFECT ON VICE . . . . . .       501  2 DON JUAN  5    157   8
   AND HATE ALL VICE EXCEPT ITS REPUTATION . . . . . .     327  3 DON JUAN 12     25   8
   UPON THE BLACK LOAM LONG MANURED BY VICE . . . . .      335  3 DON JUAN 12     40   7
   CONSULTING THE SOCIETY FOR VICE . . . . . . . .         336  3 DON JUAN 12     42   7
   A JEST AT VICE BY VIRTUE'S CALLED A CRIME . . . . .     358  3 DON JUAN 13      1   3
   AND ANGLING TOO THAT SOLITARY VICE . . . . . . .        407  3 DON JUAN 13    106   5
   HOW OFT WOULD VICE AND VIRTUE PLACES CHANGE . . . . .   455  3 DON JUAN 14    101   5
   AS PURE AS SANCTITY ITSELF FROM VICE . . . . . .        478  3 DON JUAN 15     52   3
   HIS VICE--FOR HE WAS OF A KINDLING NATION-- . . . . .   567  3 DON JUAN 17     12   6
VICES
   SOME FLIRT SOME READ AND SOME IN VICES GROVEL . . . .   263  2 DON JUAN  2    201  V7
   FROM CROWNS TO KICKS ACCORDING TO THEIR VICES . . . .   425  2 DON JUAN  5     27   8
   COULD STOP THAT WORST OF VICES--PROPAGATION . . . . .    15  3 DON JUAN  6     19   8
   PERHAPS THERE MIGHT BE VICES WHICH WOULD MOURN IT . . . 400  3 DON JUAN 13     89   8
   HALF VIRTUES AND WHOLE VICES BEING COMBINED . . . . .   480  3 DON JUAN 15     57   4.
VICIOUS
   WAS EVER SUFFER'D LEST HE SHOULD GROW VICIOUS . . . .    44  2 DON JUAN  1     40   8
   BY HARBOURING SOME DEAR FRIEND EXTREMELY VICIOUS . . .   74  2 DON JUAN  1     99   5
   ARE THEY AT BOTTOM VIRTUOUS EVEN WHEN VICIOUS . . . .   349  3 DON JUAN 12     73   6
VICISSITUDES
   THE WORLD IS FULL OF STRANGE VICISSITUDES  . . . . .    371  2 DON JUAN  4     51   1
   AND THESE VICISSITUDES TELL BEST IN YOUTH . . . . .     339  3 DON JUAN 12     50   1
VICTIM
   ERE SUCH A MONSTER'S VICTIM I HAD BEEN . . . . . .       98  2 DON JUAN  1    142   4
   MINE IS THE VICTIM AND WOULD BE AGAIN . . . . . .       130  2 DON JUAN  1    192   4
   TO MAKE A MISTRESS OR FOURTH WIFE OR VICTIM . . . . .   409  2 DON JUAN  4    116   8
   THE YOUNGER PORTION STOOD--A LUCKLESS VICTIM . . . .    409  2 DON JUAN  4    116  V7
   THE FEMALES STOOD TILL CHOSEN EACH AS VICTIM . . . .    409  2 DON JUAN  4    116  V7
   NO LESS A VICTIM TO THE BOLT AND BAR . . . . . .        258  3 DON JUAN 10     68   4
   VICTIM WHEN WRONG AND MARTYR OFT WHEN RIGHT . . . .     420  3 DON JUAN 14     23   6
VICTOR
   HERE STALKS THE VICTOR THERE THE VANQUISHED LIES . . .  461  2 DON JUAN  5     86   4
VICTORIES
   OUTBALANCE ALL THE CAESAR'S VICTORIES . . . . . .        8  3 DON JUAN  6      4   8
   WHOSE VICTORIES HAD RECENTLY INCREASED  . . . . . .      52  3 DON JUAN  6     92   6
   BEHOLD THE WORLD AND CURSE YOUR VICTORIES  . . . . .    187  3 DON JUAN  9      9   8
   THROUGH FIFTY VICTORIES TO SHAME OR FAME . . . . . .    189  3 DON JUAN  9     14   7
   GONE TO WHERE VICTORIES MUST LIKE DINNERS GO . . . . .  485  3 DON JUAN 15     67   5
```

879

```
                                                      PAGE VOL      CANTO STANZA LN
VICTORIOUS
   VICTORIOUS VIRTUE AND DOMESTIC TRUTH . . . . . . . .  78  2 DON JUAN  1   107    3
VICTOR'S
   WHILE THE MERE VICTOR'S MAY APPAL OR STUN  . . . . . 114  3 DON JUAN  8     5    6
   WHAT ARE THE FILLETS ON THE VICTOR'S BROW  . . . . . 485  3 DON JUAN 15    67    1
VICTORS
   (NOT OF OLD VICTORS ALL WHOSE HEADS AND CRESTS . . . . 321  3 DON JUAN 12    12    3
VICTORY
   A THING WHICH VICTORY BY NO MEANS BODED  . . . . . . 119  2 DON JUAN  8    16    6
   THOUGH LIFE AND DEATH AND VICTORY WERE AT STAKE  . . . 147  2 DON JUAN  8    70    7
   IN VAIN THE YELL OF VICTORY IS ROARED . . . . . . . . 155  3 DON JUAN  8    87    6
   AND SUCH IS VICTORY AND SUCH IS MAN  . . . . . . . . 163  3 DON JUAN  8   104    1
   VICTORY AND PAUSING AS SHE SAW HIM KNEEL . . . . . . 211  3 DON JUAN  9    57    7
VICTORY'S
   ANNOUNCED WITH NO LESS POMP THAN VICTORY'S WINNER . . . 383  3 DON JUAN 13    54    3
VICTUAL
   IT WOULD HAVE BEEN MORE WISE TO SAVE THEIR VICTUAL  . . 192  2 DON JUAN  2    69    8
   SHE KNEW THAT THE BEST FEELINGS MUST HAVE VICTUAL  . . . 233  2 DON JUAN  2   145    1
   BY TINKLING SOUNDS WHEN THEY GO FORTH TO VICTUAL  . . .  90  3 DON JUAN  7    48    7
   IN WINTER'S DEPTH OR WANT OF REST AND VICTUAL . . . . 176  3 DON JUAN  8   128    7
VIE
   VIE WITH THAT DRAUGHT OF HOCK AND SODA-WATER  . . . . 251  2 DON JUAN  2   180    8
   TO VIE WITH THEE WOULD BE ABOUT AS VAIN . . . . . . . 106  3 DON JUAN  7    80    6
   WHEN CONGREVE'S FOOL COULD VIE WITH MOLIERE'S BETE . . . 402  3 DON JUAN 13    94    6
VIED
   VIED WITH EACH OTHER ON THIS COSTLY SPOT . . . . . . .  55  3 DON JUAN  6    98    2
VIEN
   AND NOW I THINK ON'T MI VIEN IN MENTE . . . . . . . .  56  2 DON JUAN  1    62    6
VIEW
   WHERE SHALL I TURN ME NOT TO VIEW ITS BONDS . . . . .  19  2 DON JUAN  D    16    1
   FROM LEAF TO LEAF 'TIS SWEET TO VIEW ON HIGH  . . . .  87  2 DON JUAN  1   122    7
   REGARDING BOTH WITH SLOW AND SIDELONG VIEW  . . . . . 116  2 DON JUAN  1   173    7
   A PANORAMA VIEW OF HELL'S IN TRAINING . . . . . . . . 135  2 DON JUAN  1   200    6
   WAS MORE ROBUST AND HARDY TO THE VIEW . . . . . . . . 202  2 DON JUAN  2    87    3
   DISTINCT AND HIGH AND PALPABLE TO VIEW  . . . . . . . 207  2 DON JUAN  2    97    8
   DEEPEST ATTRACTION FOR WHEN TO THE VIEW . . . . . . . 218  2 DON JUAN  2   117    4
   AND STARTING SHE AWOKE AND WHAT TO VIEW . . . . . . . 363  2 DON JUAN  4    35    6
   PERFORCE SINCE WHATSOEVER MET HER VIEW  . . . . . . . 378  2 DON JUAN  4    62    4
   FAR LESS DESCRIBE PRESENT THE VERY VIEW . . . . . . . 412  2 DON JUAN  5     3    7
   BY SETTING THINGS IN THEIR RIGHT POINT OF VIEW . . . . 422  2 DON JUAN  5    23    5
   AND HORRID WAS THE CONTRAST TO THE VIEW-- . . . . . . 431  2 DON JUAN  5    38    3
   WHICH OPENED ON THEIR VIEW AND O'ER THE FRONT . . . . 436  2 DON JUAN  5    46    2
   UPON THE METAMORPHOSIS IN VIEW  . . . . . . . . . . . 459  2 DON JUAN  5    83    4
   WITH AUGHT WHICH LOOKS LIKE DESPOTISM IN VIEW . . . . 474  2 DON JUAN  5   110    5
   AFTER THE FIRST INVESTIGATING VIEW  . . . . . . . . .  24  3 DON JUAN  6    37    3
   AN ISLE NEAR ISMAIL HAD TWO ENDS IN VIEW . . . . . . .  78  3 DON JUAN  7    23    2
   FOR SOME TIME TILL THEY CAME IN NEARER VIEW . . . . .  87  3 DON JUAN  7    43    3
   ON HER UNWRINKLED BROW NOR COULD YOU VIEW . . . . . . 145  3 DON JUAN  8    65    5
   A BIRD'S-EYE VIEW TOO OF THAT WILD SOCIETY . . . . . 416  3 DON JUAN 14    14    3
   WITH THE KIND VIEW OF SAVING AN ECLAT . . . . . . . . 436  3 DON JUAN 14    60    1
VIEW'D
   THUS MUCH SHE VIEW'D AN INSTANT AND NO MORE-- . . . . 375  2 DON JUAN  4    58    5
VIEWS
   JUST AS ONE VIEWS A HORSE TO GUESS HIS PRICE  . . . . 441  2 DON JUAN  5    54    6
   OR IF HE DANCE NOT BUT HATH HIGHER VIEWS . . . . . . 304  3 DON JUAN 11    71    1
   ALAS  MUST NOBLEST VIEWS LIKE AN OLD SONG  . . . . . 363  3 DON JUAN 13    10    5
   THAT ANYTHING HE VIEWS CAN GREATLY PLEASE  . . . . . 373  3 DON JUAN 13    34    7
   'TIS NOT MY PURPOSE ON HIS VIEWS TO DWELL  . . . . . 472  3 DON JUAN 15    38    5
VIGIL
   A VIGIL THERE WHERE ALL BUT DEATH SHOULD SLEEP  . . . 508  3 DON JUAN 16    18    8
   A VIGIL OR DREAMT RATHER MORE THAN SLEPT . . . . . . 568  3 DON JUAN 17    14    8
VIGOROUS
   ENJOYED THE LONELY VIGOROUS HARMLESS DAYS  . . . . . 143  3 DON JUAN  8    61    7
VIGOUR
   ADDED TO THOSE HIS LADY WITH SUCH VIGOUR . . . . . . 110  2 DON JUAN  1   161    6
   THEIR LOYAL ZEAL AND RENEGADO VIGOUR  . . . . . . . . 330  2 DON JUAN  3    94   V3
   WHICH MIGHT GO FAR BUT SHE DON'T DANCE WITH VIGOUR . . 390  2 DON JUAN  4    85    7
   WOULD WISH TO LOOK ON WHILE THEY ARE IN VIGOUR . . . 213  3 DON JUAN  9    62    4
   HER PRIME OF LIFE JUST NOW IN JUICY VIGOUR . . . . . 218  3 DON JUAN  9    72    5
   OF YOUTH AND VIGOUR BEAUTY AND THOSE THINGS . . . . . 227  3 DON JUAN 10     5    7
   THEIR VIGOUR IN A THOUSAND ARMS IS DISSIPATED . . . . 306  3 DON JUAN 11    75    3
   AND RATHER HELD IN THAN PUT FORTH HIS VIGOUR . . . . 427  3 DON JUAN 14    39    4
   STRICT AND HIS MIND ASSUMED A MANLIER VIGOUR  . . . . 460  3 DON JUAN 15    11    6
VILAINTON
   OH WELLINGTON (OR VILAINTON--FOR FAME . . . . . . . . 183  3 DON JUAN  9     1    1
VILE
   INEFFABLY--LEGITIMATELY VILE . . . . . . . . . . . .  17  2 DON JUAN  D    13    2
   SO VILE HE 'SCAPED THE DOOM WHICH OFT AVENGES . . . . 317  2 DON JUAN  3    80    5
   IN THIS VILE GARB THE DISTAFF WEB AND WOOF . . . . . 484  2 DON JUAN  5   127    3
   'TIS THE VILE DAILY DROP ON DROP WHICH WEARS  . . . .  16  3 DON JUAN  6    20    7
   HER VILE AMBIGUOUS METHOD OF FLIRTATION  . . . . . . 222  3 DON JUAN  9    81    7
   BUT WHAT WE CAN WE GLEAN IN THIS VILE AGE . . . . . . 403  3 DON JUAN 13    97    1
VILELY
   WHO TOOK ALGIERS DECLARES I USED HIM VILELY . . . . . 102  2 DON JUAN  1   148    8
VILLA
   EACH VILLA ON THE BOSPHORUS LOOKS A SCREEN . . . . . 436  2 DON JUAN  5    46    7
VILLAGE
   A VILLAGE OF MOLDAVIA'S WASTE WHEREIN . . . . . . . .  76  3 DON JUAN  7    20    7
   LIKE A BOB-MAJOR FROM A VILLAGE STEEPLE . . . . . . . 109  3 DON JUAN  7    85    8
```

	PAGE	VOL	CANTO	STANZA	LN

VILLAGE-COTTED
THERE ON THE GREEN AND VILLAGE-COTTED HILL IS . . . . . 385 2 DON JUAN 4 76 1
VILLAIN
WHICH GAVE ME SOME SENSATIONS LIKE A VILLAIN . . . . . 268 2 DON JUAN 2 209 8
AND REALLY LONGED TO KISS HER--LIKE A VILLAIN . . . . . 268 2 DON JUAN 2 209 V8
VILLAINOUS
TWO VILLAINOUS COSSACQUES PURSUED THE CHILD . . . . . 157 3 DON JUAN 8 92 1
VILLAINS
YE VILLAINS AND ABOVE ALL KEEP A SHARP EYE . . . . . 310 3 DON JUAN 11 86 5
VILLEGGIATURA
AND FOR THE EFFEMINATE VILLEGGIATURA-- . . . . . 395 3 DON JUAN 13 78 1
HOW OUR VILLEGGIATURA WILL GET ON . . . . 397 3 DON JUAN 13 83 2
VINDICATES
WHO VINDICATES A MOMENT TOO HIS STREAM-- . . . . . 279 3 DON JUAN 11 24 2
VINE
ABOVE THEM THEIR DESSERT GREW ON ITS VINE . . . . . 291 2 DON JUAN 3 31 6
AND SHED THE BLOOD OF SCIO'S VINE . . . . 324 2 DON JUAN 3 L 9 4
LABOURER IN THE SAME VINEYARD THOUGH THE VINE . . . . 297 3 DON JUAN 11 58 2
AND THE VINE BLUSHES LIKE AURORA'S LIP . . . . . . 320 3 DON JUAN 12 9 5
VINEGAR
MARRIAGE FROM LOVE LIKE VINEGAR FROM WINE-- . . . . . . 277 2 DON JUAN 3 5 5
YIELDS HIM BUT VINEGAR FOR HIS REWARD-- . . . . . . 297 3 DON JUAN 11 58 3
VINES
WHICH MIXES UP VINES OLIVES PRECIPICES . . . . . . 262 3 DON JUAN 10 76 7
AN ENGLISH AUTUMN THOUGH IT HATH NO VINES . . . . . 394 3 DON JUAN 13 76 1
VINEYARD
AND GRAPE IN VOLLEYS LIKE A VINEYARD SCATTERS . . . . 160 3 DON JUAN 8 98 8
LABOURER IN THE SAME VINEYARD THOUGH THE VINE . . . . 297 3 DON JUAN 11 58 2
VINEYARDS
THE VERY BEST OF VINEYARDS IS THE CELLAR . . . . . . 394 3 DON JUAN 13 76 8
VINOUS
THE VINOUS GREEK TO WHOM HE HAD ADDRESS'D . . . . . . 297 2 DON JUAN 3 42 6
FROZEN INTO A VERY VINOUS ICE . . . . 375 3 DON JUAN 13 37 3
VINTAGE
SWEET IS THE VINTAGE WHEN THE SHOWERING GRAPES . . . . . 88 2 DON JUAN 1 124 1
BUT ADELINE WAS OF THE PUREST VINTAGE . . . . 458 3 DON JUAN 15 7 1
VIOLATION
MIGHT HERE AND THERE OCCUR SOME VIOLATION . . . . . 176 3 DON JUAN 8 129 2
VIOLENCE
WHAT MAY THIS MIDNIGHT VIOLENCE BETIDE . . . . . 98 2 DON JUAN 1 142 5
WIT WITHOUT SENSE--AND VIOLENCE WITHOUT FORCE . . . . 155 2 DON JUAN 1 V 6 V7
AND THEN WITH VIOLENCE THE OLD SHIP RIGHTED . . . . 173 2 DON JUAN 2 32 8
BUT NOT WITH VIOLENCE THE STARS SHONE OUT . . . . 207 2 DON JUAN 2 96 2
VIOLENT
QUICK WITHOUT WIT AND VIOLENT WITHOUT STRENGTH . . . . 155 2 DON JUAN 1 V 6 7
BUT VIOLENT THINGS WILL SOONER BEAR ASSUAGING . . . . 305 2 DON JUAN 3 58 5
AND IF THIS VIOLENT REMEDY BE TRIED-- . . . . . . 63 3 DON JUAN 6 115 6
THAT VIOLENT THINGS MORE QUICKLY FIND A TERM . . . . 451 3 DON JUAN 14 94 3
VIOLENTLY
SHE WAS NOT VIOLENTLY LIVELY BUT . . . . 27 3 DON JUAN 6 43 1
VIOLIN
UNTO BY SAWNEY'S VIOLIN WE HAVE HEARD . . . . 307 3 DON JUAN 11 78 6
VIPERS
LIKE KNOTS OF VIPERS ON A DUNGHILL'S SOIL . . . . . 271 2 DON JUAN 2 215 5
VIRGIL
AFTER THE STYLE OF VIRGIL AND OF HOMER . . . . . 135 2 DON JUAN 1 200 7
VIRGIL'S
BUT VIRGIL'S SONGS ARE PURE EXCEPT THAT HORRID ONE . . 45 2 DON JUAN 1 42 7
VIRGIN
SHE PRAY'D THE VIRGIN MARY FOR HER GRACE . . . . 62 2 DON JUAN 1 75 7
THAT NIGHT THE VIRGIN WAS NO FURTHER PRAY'D . . . . . 63 2 DON JUAN 1 76 8
TO VIRGIN MARY SEVERAL POUNDS OF CANDLES . . . . . 128 2 DON JUAN 1 190 6
(A VIRGIN ALWAYS ON HER MAID RELIES) . . . . . 225 2 DON JUAN 2 131 2
AND DOWN THE CLIFF THE ISLAND VIRGIN CAME . . . . 232 2 DON JUAN 2 142 1
TO THE SWEET PORTRAITS OF THE VIRGIN MARY . . . . 235 2 DON JUAN 2 149 8
WITH CHORAL STEP AND VOICE THE VIRGIN THRONG . . . . 291 2 DON JUAN 3 30 8
WARRANTED VIRGIN BEAUTY'S BRIGHTEST COLOURS . . . . 407 2 DON JUAN 4 114 3
NEXT WITH A VIRGIN ZONE HE WAS EQUIPPED . . . . . 456 2 DON JUAN 5 77 3
THE NEW-BOUGHT VIRGIN MADE HER BLUSH AND SHAKE . . . . 501 2 DON JUAN 5 156 2
BUT WHAT WAS STRANGEST IN THIS VIRGIN CREW . . . . 24 3 DON JUAN 6 37 1
BUT STILL THE SPOUSELESS VIRGIN KNOWLEDGE FLIES . . . . 37 3 DON JUAN 6 63 5
AS ERE WAS VIRGIN OF A NUPTIAL CHIME . . . . . 74 3 DON JUAN 7 16 4
MORE VIRGIN VALOUR NEVER DREAMT OF FLYING . . . . 131 3 DON JUAN 8 36 3
OF IMPORT BOTH TO VIRGIN AND TO BRIDE . . . . . 292 3 DON JUAN 11 46 2
OR WHETHER WITH SOME VIRGIN OF MORE WORTH . . . . 312 3 DON JUAN 11 89 3
HIGH GROUND AS VIRGIN CYNTHIA SWAYS THE TIDES . . . . 322 3 DON JUAN 12 14 6
AND I ASSURE YOU THAT LIKE VIRGIN HONEY . . . . . 330 3 DON JUAN 12 31 7
THE VIRGIN MOTHER OF THE GOD-BORN CHILD . . . . . 387 3 DON JUAN 13 61 2
THE FOAM WHICH MADE ITS VIRGIN BUMPER GAY . . . . . 504 3 DON JUAN 16 9 3
THE LATEST JUAN WITH HIS VIRGIN FACE . . . . . 568 3 DON JUAN 17 13 8
VIRGINITIES
AND THE NEW BIRTHS OF BOTH THEIR STALE VIRGINITIES . . 330 2 DON JUAN 3 95 7
VIRGINITY
THE NEXT THE VIRGIN'S MYSTICAL VIRGINITY . . . . . 271 3 DON JUAN 11 6 3
AND LOST VIRGINITY OF ORATORY . . . . 401 3 DON JUAN 13 91 2
VIRGIN-LIKE
A VIRGIN-LIKE AND EDIFYING THRONG . . . . 21 3 DON JUAN 6 30 3
VIRGIN'S
WHICH BY THE VIRGIN'S GRACE LET IN ANOTHER . . . . . 63 2 DON JUAN 1 76 4

881

VIRGIN'S (CONTINUED)
THE NEXT THE VIRGIN'S MYSTICAL VIRGINITY . . . . . . 271 3 DON JUAN 11   6   3
MEANING A VIRGIN'S FIRST BLUSH AT A ROUT . . . . . . 330 3 DON JUAN 12   31   5
IT SEEMS THE VIRGIN'S HEART EXPECTS YOUR HAND . . . . 343 3 DON JUAN 12   60   6
VIRGINS
'TIS PITY LEARNED VIRGINS EVER WED . . . . 33 2 DON JUAN 1   22   1
OUR VIRGINS DANCE BENEATH THE SHADE-- . . . . . . 326 2 DON JUAN 3 L 15   2
THESE BLACK-EYED VIRGINS MAKE THE MOSLEMS FIGHT . . . 168 3 DON JUAN 8   114   5
WERE ALMOST AS MUCH VIRGINS AS BEFORE . . . . 176 3 DON JUAN 8   129   8
FAIR VIRGINS BLUSHED UPON HIM WEDDED DAMES . . . . . 293 3 DON JUAN 11   48   1
THE MARRIED ONES TO SAVE THE VIRGINS TROUBLE . . . . 342 3 DON JUAN 12   58   8
IN VIRGINS--ALWAYS IN A MODEST WAY . . . . 494 3 DON JUAN 15   86   7
PERPLEXING FOR MOST VIRGINS--A CHILD'S FATHER . . . . 533 3 DON JUAN 16   67   8
VIRTUE
HER NOBLEST VIRTUE WAS HER MAGNANIMITY . . . . . . 27 2 DON JUAN 1   12   2
REVENGE IN PERSON'S CERTAINLY NO VIRTUE . . . . . . 37 2 DON JUAN 1   30   7
LADIES EVEN OF THE MOST UNEASY VIRTUE . . . . 56 2 DON JUAN 1   62   7
WHERE ALL IS VIRTUE AND THE WINTER SEASON . . . . . 57 2 DON JUAN 1   64   2
VICTORIOUS VIRTUE AND DOMESTIC TRUTH . . . . 78 2 DON JUAN 1   107   3
JULIA HAD HONOUR VIRTUE TRUTH AND LOVE . . . . . . 80 2 DON JUAN 1   109   1
SO JUAN'S VIRTUE EBBED I KNOW NOT HOW . . . . . . 493 2 DON JUAN 5   142   2
AND NEXT HIS SAVAGE VIRTUE HE ACCUSED . . . . 493 2 DON JUAN 5   142   5
AND NO ONE VIRTUE YET EXCEPT STARVATION . . . . . . 15 3 DON JUAN 6   19   7
LIFE'S HALF-WAY HOUSE WHERE DAMES WITH VIRTUE CROWNED . . 43 3 DON JUAN 6   75   5
AT HUMAN POWER AND VIRTUE AND ALL THAT . . . . . . 67 3 DON JUAN 7   3   4
AS BEING A VIRTUE LIKE TERRESTRIAL PATIENCE . . . . . 165 3 DON JUAN 8   107   7
A VIRTUE MUCH IN FASHION NOW-A-DAYS . . . . 176 3 DON JUAN 8   128   3
BELIEVE THAT VIRTUE THAWED BEFORE THE RIVER . . . . . 241 3 DON JUAN 10   33   8
WHILE THE HARSH PRUDE INDEMNIFIES HER VIRTUE . . . . 337 3 DON JUAN 12   45   1
THE SHOW OF VIRTUE EVEN IN THE VITIATED-- . . . . . 344 3 DON JUAN 12   62   5
FOR HER RETURN TO VIRTUE--AS THEY CALL . . . . . . 352 3 DON JUAN 12   79   7
KNOWING THAT SUCH UNEASY VIRTUE LEADS . . . . 352 3 DON JUAN 12   80   2
HIS GUERDON 'TIS HIS VIRTUE MAKES HIM MAD . . . . . 363 3 DON JUAN 13   9   5
SHE IN HER VIRTUE HE IN HIS HAUTEUR . . . . 365 3 DON JUAN 13   14   8
A LARGE ACQUAINTANCE LETS NOT VIRTUE SLUMBER . . . . 371 3 DON JUAN 13   30   3
TO VIRTUE PROPER OR GOOD EDUCATION . . . . 372 3 DON JUAN 13   31   3
THEIR LOVE THEIR VIRTUE BEAUTY EDUCATION . . . . . . 420 3 DON JUAN 14   24   7
FIRED WITH AN ABSTRACT LOVE OF VIRTUE SHE . . . . . 430 3 DON JUAN 14   46   2
THE STRICTEST IN CHRONOLOGY AND VIRTUE . . . . . . 433 3 DON JUAN 14   53   3
AND WHETHER COLDNESS PRIDE OR VIRTUE DIGNIFY . . . . 435 3 DON JUAN 14   57   7
WHOSE VIRTUE LIES IN NEVER BEING DETECTED . . . . . 437 3 DON JUAN 14   61   8
HOW OFT WOULD VICE AND VIRTUE PLACES CHANGE . . . . . 455 3 DON JUAN 14   101   5
LIKE VIRTUE AND THE ABSENCE OF PRETENSION . . . . . 462 3 DON JUAN 15   14   7
WHETHER HIS VIRTUE TRIUMPHED--OR AT LENGTH . . . . . 567 3 DON JUAN 17   12   5
VIRTUE'S
FOR HONOUR'S PRIDE'S RELIGION'S VIRTUE'S SAKE . . . . 62 3 DON JUAN 1   75   4
THEIR WAY THROUGH VIRTUE'S PRIMROSE PATHS OF SNOWS . . 328 3 DON JUAN 12   26   4
A JEST AT VICE BY VIRTUE'S CALLED A CRIME . . . . . 358 3 DON JUAN 13   1   3
BUT VIRTUE'S SELF WITH ALL HER TIGHTEST LACES . . . . 494 3 DON JUAN 15   85   5
VIRTUES
WITH VIRTUES EQUALL'D BY HER WIT ALONE . . . . . . 26 2 DON JUAN 1   10   4
IN VIRTUES NOTHING EARTHLY COULD SURPASS HER . . . . 30 2 DON JUAN 1   17   7
FOR SOMETIMES SUCH A WORLD OF VIRTUES COVER . . . . . 405 2 DON JUAN 4   111   6
THE VIRTUES EVEN THE MOST EXALTED CHARITY . . . . . 408 2 DON JUAN 4   115   7
WHO SAW HIS VIRTUES AS THEY SAW THE REST . . . . . 12 3 DON JUAN 6   13   V4
LOUD AS THE VIRTUES THOU DOST LOUDLY VAUNT . . . . . 241 3 DON JUAN 10   34   3
TANTAENE SUCH THE VIRTUES OF HIGH STATION . . . . . 331 3 DON JUAN 12   33   5
AND STOCKINGS VIRTUES LOVES AND CHASTITIES . . . . . 347 3 DON JUAN 12   67   V8
VIRTUES OF WHICH BOTH YOU AND I HAVE NEED . . . . . 393 3 DON JUAN 13   73   4
BY MANY VIRTUES TO BE WORTH THE TROUBLE . . . . . . 477 3 DON JUAN 15   48   7
HALF VIRTUES AND WHOLE VICES BEING COMBINED . . . . . 480 3 DON JUAN 15   57   4
VIRTUOUS
PERHAPS SOME VIRTUOUS BLUSHES--LET THEM GO-- . . . . 13 2 DON JUAN D   7   2
SHE NOW DETERMINED THAT A VIRTUOUS WOMAN . . . . . . 63 2 DON JUAN 1   77   1
MIGHT PLEASE PERHAPS A VIRTUOUS WIFE CAN QUELL . . . . 64 2 DON JUAN 1   78   5
FOR FACTS AGAINST A VIRTUOUS WOMAN'S FAME . . . . . 101 2 DON JUAN 1   146   6
CALL ME THE ONLY VIRTUOUS WIFE IN SPAIN . . . . . . 102 2 DON JUAN 1   149   4
LOSING THE ADVANTAGE OF A VIRTUOUS STATION . . . . . 263 2 DON JUAN 2   201   4
AS GOOD MEN WEAR WHO HAVE DONE A VIRTUOUS ACTION . . . 473 2 DON JUAN 5   107   8
WHY DON'T THEY KNEAD TWO VIRTUOUS SOULS FOR LIFE . . . 502 2 DON JUAN 5   158   7
FROM MUCH IMPROVEMENT WITH THAT VIRTUOUS PLOUGH . . . 335 3 DON JUAN 12   40   5
VIRTUOUS SHE WAS--AND HAD BEEN I BELIEVE . . . . . 336 3 DON JUAN 12   43   2
OR SAY THEY ARE LIKE VIRTUOUS MERMAIDS WHOSE . . . . 349 3 DON JUAN 12   73   1
ARE THEY AT BOTTOM VIRTUOUS EVEN WHEN VICIOUS . . . . 349 3 DON JUAN 12   73   6
I'VE SEEN A VIRTUOUS WOMAN PUT DOWN QUITE . . . . . 397 3 DON JUAN 13   82   3
VISAGE
THEY THUS ADDRESS'D--AND LAMBRO'S VISAGE FELL-- . . . 298 2 DON JUAN 3   44   2
PAIR'D OFF WITH A BACCHANTE BLOOMING VISAGE . . . . . 394 2 DON JUAN 4   92   8
THE COURT THAT WATCHED EACH LOOK HER VISAGE WORE . . . 211 3 DON JUAN 9   58   5
WEIGH NOT THE THIN ORE WHERE THEIR VISAGE SHINES . . . 321 3 DON JUAN 12   12   4
VISION
JUDICIOUSLY FROM OUT THE SCHOOLBOY'S VISION . . . . . 46 2 DON JUAN 1   44   3
AND IN THE INTERIM (TO PURSUE THIS VISION) . . . . . 67 2 DON JUAN 1   85   5
NOT EVEN A VISION OF HIS FORMER WOES . . . . 227 2 DON JUAN 2   134   5
SHE WAS SO LIKE A VISION I MIGHT ERR . . . . 314 2 DON JUAN 3   76   6
UPON THE GOLDEN FRUIT THE VISION BORE . . . . 44 3 DON JUAN 6   77   6
WILL SAY TO THIS HYSTERIC OF A VISION . . . . 46 3 DON JUAN 6   80   8
RESULTING FROM THE SCOLDING OR THE VISION . . . . . 47 3 DON JUAN 6   82   3
OF CLOSING 'GAINST THE LIGHT THEIR ORBS OF VISION . . . 50 3 DON JUAN 6   88   5

```
                                                         PAGE VOL    CANTO  STANZA LN
VISION   (CONTINUED)
   BUT EVER AND ANON TO SOOTHE YOUR VISION . . . . . .  . 392  3 DON JUAN 13    71    1
   PONDERED UPON HIS VISITANT OR VISION . . .  . . . .  . 512  3 DON JUAN 16    28    2
   BUT JUAN WHEN CROSS-QUESTIONED ON THE VISION  . . . . . 527  3 DON JUAN 16    54    6
VISIONARY
   TO EXPOUND THEIR VAIN AND VISIONARY GLEAMS . . . . . . .  45  3 DON JUAN  6    78    4
VISIONS
   NOR SHEARS OF ATROPOS BEFORE THEIR VISIONS . . .  . . . 190  2 DON JUAN  2    64    6
   UNWELCOME VISIONS OF OUR FORMER YEARS . . . . .  . . . 227  2 DON JUAN  2   134    7
   BUT VISIONS OF AN APPLE AND A BEE . . .  . . . . . .  .  46  3 DON JUAN  6    80    2
   AND SOME SUCH VISIONS CROSSED HER MAJESTY  . . . . . . 215  3 DON JUAN  9    66    3
   IN VISIONS OF THOSE SKIES FROM WHENCE LOVE SPRUNG . . . 230  3 DON JUAN 10    10    6
   KNOW NOT WHAT VISIONS SPRING FROM EACH CHEESE-PARING . . 316  3 DON JUAN 12     3    8
   NO MORE TO BE BEHELD BUT IN SUCH VISIONS-- . . . . . . 523  3 DON JUAN 16    46    7
VISIT
   AND NEXT DAY PAID A VISIT TO HIS MOTHER . . . . . . .  .  63  2 DON JUAN  1    76    2
   TO PAY HIM A FRESH VISIT WITH A DISH . . . .  . . . . . 226  2 DON JUAN  2   133    7
   BUT MORE IMPRUDENT GROWN WITH EVERY VISIT  . . . . . . 282  2 DON JUAN  3    13    3
   THAT MADMEN MAY NOT BITE YOU ON A VISIT . . .  . . . . 280  3 DON JUAN 11    25    4
   PERHAPS YOU'LL HAVE A VISIT FROM THE BROTHER  . . . . . 343  3 DON JUAN 12    60    3
VISITANT
   A VISITANT AT INTERVALS APPEARS . . . . . . . . . . . . 504  3 DON JUAN 16     7    4
   PONDERED UPON HIS VISITANT OR VISION . . . . . . . . . 512  3 DON JUAN 16    28    2
VISITATIONS
   (BY THOSE WHO HAVE NOT HAD SUCH VISITATIONS) . . . . . 555  3 DON JUAN 16   111    7
VISITS
   PAID DAILY VISITS TO HER BOY AND TOOK . . .  . . . . . 248  2 DON JUAN  2   174    2
   NOW SHE PROLONG'D HER VISITS AND HER TALK  . . . . . . 249  2 DON JUAN  2   176    1
   AS TO ANNOUNCE HIS VISITS A LONG WHILE . .  . . . . . . 495  2 DON JUAN  5   146    5
   HIS AFTERNOONS HE PASSED IN VISITS LUNCHEONS . . . . . 301  3 DON JUAN 11    66    1
VITIATED
   THE SHOW OF VIRTUE EVEN IN THE VITIATED-- . . . . . .  . 344  3 DON JUAN 12    62    5
VIVACIOUS
   BY TURNS--WITH THAT VIVACIOUS VERSATILITY  . . . . .  . 547  3 DON JUAN 16    97    2
VIVACITY
   FOR SOME VIVACITY AMONG THE FAIR . . . . . . . . .  .  . 544  3 DON JUAN 16    91    5
VIVANTE
   BUT THOUGH A BONNE VIVANTE I MUST CONFESS  . . . . . . 483  3 DON JUAN 15    64    5
VIVIFYING
   WITH VIVIFYING VENUS WHO DOTH OWE . . . . . . . .  .  . 542  3 DON JUAN 16    86    6
VIZ
   FROM TOWN VIZ ARCHITECT AND DEALER WERE . . . . . . .  . 533  3 DON JUAN 16    66    5
VIZIER
   HOPING NO VERY OLD VIZIER MIGHT CHOOSE . . . . . . . . 409  2 DON JUAN  4   116    6
   HE LEFT TO HIS VIZIER ALL STATE AFFAIRS . . . . . . .  . 496  2 DON JUAN  5   148    3
VLADIMIR
   SAFETY THAN HIS NEW ORDER OF SAINT VLADIMIR . . . . .  . 182  3 DON JUAN  8   140    8
VOCABULARY
   A NOVEL WORD IN MY VOCABULARY . . . . . . . . . . . . . 346  2 DON JUAN  4     5    8
VOCATION
   OF LIFE AND IN AN HONESTER VOCATION  . . . . . . . . . 283  2 DON JUAN  3    14    6
   IN THEIR VOCATION HAD NOT BEEN ATTACK'D . . .  . . . . 388  2 DON JUAN  4    80    6
VOGUE
   THE GHOST OF VANISHED PLEASURES ONCE IN VOGUE ILL . . . 304  3 DON JUAN 11    72    6
   AND LISTENING TO THE TOPICS MOST IN VOGUE  . . .  . . . 426  3 DON JUAN 14    37    4
   ALTHOUGH HER BIRTH AND WEALTH HAD GIVEN HER VOGUE . . . 477  3 DON JUAN 15    48    3
VOI
   VOI CHE ENTRATE THE HINGE SEEMED TO SPEAK  . . . . . . 557  3 DON JUAN 16   116    3
VOICE
   AND HEARD A VOICE IN ALL THE WINDS AND THEN  . . . .  .  72  2 DON JUAN  1    94    2
   AND HELD HER TONGUE HER VOICE WAS GROWN SO WEAK . . . .  81  2 DON JUAN  1   112    8
   AND JULIA'S VOICE WAS LOST EXCEPT IN SIGHS . . .  . . .  84  2 DON JUAN  1   117    1
   OF BEES THE VOICE OF GIRLS THE SONG OF BIRDS . . . . .  88  2 DON JUAN  1   123    7
   THE DOOR WAS FASTEN'D BUT WITH VOICE AND FIST  . . . .  95  2 DON JUAN  1   136    7
   NOW JULIA FOUND AT LENGTH A VOICE AND CRIED  . . . . .  98  2 DON JUAN  1   142    1
   AND HER VOICE WAS THE WARBLE OF A BIRD . . .  . . . . . 236  2 DON JUAN  2   151    3
   WITH CHORAL STEP AND VOICE THE VIRGIN THRONG . . . . . 291  2 DON JUAN  3    30    8
   AND IF I HAD TO GIVE A CASTING VOICE . . . . . . . .  . 357  2 DON JUAN  4    25    5
   CALM IN HIS VOICE AND CALM WITHIN HIS EYE-- . . . . .  . 365  2 DON JUAN  4    39    2
   WITH NO GREAT VOICE IS PLEASING TO BEHOLD  . . . . . . 389  2 DON JUAN  4    83    5
   THE TENOR'S VOICE IS SPOILT BY AFFECTATION . . . . . . 391  2 DON JUAN  4    87    1
   WHO SWORE HIS VOICE WAS VERY RICH AND MELLOW . . . . . 391  2 DON JUAN  4    87    6
   A VOICE OF NO GREAT COMPASS AND NOT SWEET  . . . . . . 392  2 DON JUAN  4    89    4
   OF GOODNESS IN THUS LEAVING THEM A VOICE . .  . . . . . 452  2 DON JUAN  5    70    5
   IS LIGHTER FAR OF HEART AND VOICE THAN THOSE . . . . .  49  3 DON JUAN  6    87    7
   AND WAITED BUT THE SIGNAL'S VOICE TO BURST . . . . . .  91  3 DON JUAN  7    50    4
   BUT WHETHER FROM HIS VOICE OR SPEECH OR MANNER . . . .  95  3 DON JUAN  7    56    7
   OF HUMAN NATURE'S AGONIZING VOICE . . . . . . . . . . 142  3 DON JUAN  8    59    8
   NOR GIVE MY VOICE TO SLAVERY'S JACKALL CRY . . . . . . 195  3 DON JUAN  9    26    8
   HERE PEALS THE PEOPLE'S VOICE NOR CAN ENTOMB IT  . . . 272  3 DON JUAN 11     9    6
   I'LL NOT GAINSAY THE GENEROUS PUBLIC'S VOICE . . . . . 334  3 DON JUAN 12    38    7
   HER VOICE THOUGH SWEET IS NOT SO FIT TO WARBLE . . . . 350  3 DON JUAN 12    75    5
   TO THIS GREY RUIN WITH A VOICE TO CHARM . . .  . . . . 388  3 DON JUAN 13    64    5
   AN ARROW FOR THE HEART LIKE A SWEET VOICE  . . . . . . 461  3 DON JUAN 15    13    8
   THE VOICE THE WORDS THE HARPER'S SKILL AT ONCE . . . . 517  3 DON JUAN 16    39    7
   ADDED HER SWEET VOICE TO THE LYRIC SOUND . .  . . . . . 518  3 DON JUAN 16    40    6
   THE LADY'S VOICE CEASED AND THE THRILLING WIRES  . . . 521  3 DON JUAN 16    41    1
VOICELESS
   THE VOICELESS SANDS AND DROPPING CAVES THAT LAY  . . . 255  2 DON JUAN  2   188    5
   MY COUNTRY ON THY VOICELESS SHORE . . . . . . . . . . 322  2 DON JUAN  3  L  5    2
```

VOICE'S
IN LISTENING MERELY TO HIS VOICE'S TONE 461   3 DON JUAN 15   13   6
VOICES
HAVE VOICES--TONGUES TO CRY ALOUD FOR ME 19   2 DON JUAN D   16   6
AH NO--THE VOICES OF THE DEAD   323   2 DON JUAN 3   L 8   2
THEIR VOICES 'GAINST EACH OTHER WHICH IS NATURAL . . . 50   3 DON JUAN 6   88   7
ANSWERING THE CHRISTIAN THUNDERS WITH LIKE VOICES . . . 115   3 DON JUAN 8   7   4
SOME VOICES OF THE BUXOM MIDDLE-AGED   178   3 DON JUAN 8   132   1
OF WHEELS AND ROAR OF VOICES AND CONFUSION 278   3 DON JUAN 11   22   2
ATTUNED BY VOICES MORE OR LESS DIVINE 408   3 DON JUAN 13   107   3
OF YOUR OWN FOOTSTEPS--VOICES FROM THE URN 508   3 DON JUAN 16   18   4
VOID
PERHAPS THE WEAKNESS OF. A HEART NOT VOID 339   2 DON JUAN 3   109   6
THROUGH GROVES SO CALLED AS BEING VOID OF TREES . . . 278   3 DON JUAN 11   21   1
OF BARDS AND PROSERS WORDS ARE VOID OF COLOUR 428   3 DON JUAN 14   40   8
AND HENCE HIGH LIFE IS OFT A DREARY VOID 444   3 DON JUAN 14   79   1
VOILA
OR SWISS ROUSSEAU CRY VOILA LA PERVENCHE 442   3 DON JUAN 14   75   8
VOLCANO
A HALF-UNQUENCHED VOLCANO O'ER A SPACE   265   3 DON JUAN 10   81   2
AS A VOLCANO HOLDS THE LAVA MORE   374   3 DON JUAN 13   36   3
SO LET THE OFTEN USED VOLCANO GO   374   3 DON JUAN 13   36   6
VOLCANOS
GLACIERS VOLCANOS ORANGES AND ICES 262   3 DON JUAN 10   76   8
VOLLEY
A DRESS THROUGH WHICH THE EYES GIVE SUCH A VOLLEY . . . 160   2 DON JUAN 2   7   7
VOLLEYING
A MIRRORED HELL THE VOLLEYING ROAR AND LOUD 115   3 DON JUAN 8   6   5
VOLLEYS
AND GRAPE IN VOLLEYS LIKE A VINEYARD SCATTERS 160   3 DON JUAN 8   98   8
VOLTAIRE
VOLTAIRE SAYS NO HE TELLS YOU THAT CANDIDE 427   2 DON JUAN 5   31   1
THERE HAD NOT BEEN ONE SHAKESPEARE AND VOLTAIRE 481   3 DON JUAN 15   59   7
VOLTAIRE'S
MUCH FLATTERY--EVEN VOLTAIRE'S AND THAT'S A PITY . . . 194   3 DON JUAN 9   23   6
VOLUME
THE CHIEFTAIN'S TROPHY AND THE POET'S VOLUME 400   2 DON JUAN 4   104   6
BUT NOW REDUCED AS IS A BULKY VOLUME 130   3 DON JUAN 8   34   4
VOLUMES
I THINK THAT SEVERAL VOLUMES WOULD FALL SHORT 82   3 DON JUAN 7   32   3
WHOSE PAMPHLETS VOLUMES NEWSPAPERS ILLUMINE US 200   3 DON JUAN 9   35   3
AND THEREFORE HAVE HIS VOLUMES DONE SUCH HARM 364   3 DON JUAN 13   11   6
VOLUMES WITH SIMILAR SAD ILLUSTRATIONS 464   3 DON JUAN 15   18   7
VOLUMINOUS
OH YE GREAT AUTHORS LUMINOUS VOLUMINOUS 200   3 DON JUAN 9   35   1
VOLUNTEERS
OF VARIOUS NATIONS AND ALL VOLUNTEERS 75   3 DON JUAN 7   18   2
JUAN AND JOHNSON AND SOME VOLUNTEERS 152   3 DON JUAN 8   80   1
O'ER THE VOLUNTEERS--ON EITHER SCORE 537   3 DON JUAN 16   76   V5
VOLUPTUARY
JUAN AS A VOLUPTUARY WAS NEW 314   3 DON JUAN 11   V 75   V1
VOLUPTUOUS
IN ONE VOLUPTUOUS BLAZE--AND THEN HE DIED   169   3 DON JUAN 8   115   8
IN FULL VOLUPTUOUS BUT NOT O'ERGROWN BULK 561   3 DON JUAN 16   123   7
VOTARIES
LEGITIMACY ITS BORN VOTARIES WHEN 485   2 DON JUAN 5   128   7
ITS VOTARIES LIKE INNOCENCE RELYING 131   3 DON JUAN 8   36   5
THEIR LUCKIER VOTARIES TILL OLD AGE'S TEDIUM 235   3 DON JUAN 10   22   7
VOTE
PROUD OF HIS HEAR HIMS PROUD TOO OF HIS VOTE 401   3 DON JUAN 13   91   1
VOTED
AND HAVING VOTED DINED DRANK GAMED AND WHORED 306   3 DON JUAN 11   75   7
DREST VOTED SHONE AND MAYBE SOMETHING MORE 418   3 DON JUAN 14   18   2
VOTES
BOTH SENATES SEE THEIR NIGHTLY VOTES PARTICIPATED . . . 306   3 DON JUAN 11   75   5
HAD FALLEN LAST MARKET COST HIS HOST THREE VOTES . . . 543   3 DON JUAN 16   89   8
VOUCHES
DONE THINE THE PRESENT VOUCHES FOR THE PAST 368   2 DON JUAN 4   46   8
VOUS
THE SEAL A SUNFLOWER ELLE VOUS SUIT PARTOUT 134   2 DON JUAN 1   198   6
VOW
BUT SOMEHOW THIS MY VESTAL VOW TAKES WING   85   2 DON JUAN 1   119   5
IRREVOCABLE VOW OF REFORMATION 175   2 DON JUAN 2   37   4
SOME WENT TO PRAYERS AGAIN AND MADE A VOW 179   2 DON JUAN 2   44   3
THEY VOW TO AMEND THEIR LIVES AND YET THEY DON'T . . . 414   2 DON JUAN 5   6   7
JUST AS A FRIAR MAY ACCUSE HIS VOW 493   2 DON JUAN 5   142   6
AND MADE A VOW TO SHIELD HER WHICH HE KEPT 182   3 DON JUAN 8   141   8
VOW'D
SHE VOW'D SHE NEVER WOULD SEE JUAN MORE 63   2 DON JUAN 1   76   1
FIRST VOW'D (AND NEVER HAD SHE VOW'D IN VAIN) 128   2 DON JUAN 1   190   5
FIRST VOW'D (AND NEVER HAD SHE VOW'D IN VAIN) 128   2 DON JUAN 1   190   2
VOWED
OR IT MAY BE TO-NIGHT THE ASSAULT I HAVE VOWED 99   3 DON JUAN 7   63   5
VOWS
BY ALL THE VOWS BELOW TO POWERS ABOVE 80   2 DON JUAN 1   109   3
HAIDEE SPOKE NOT OF SCRUPLES ASK'D NO VOWS 257   2 DON JUAN 2   190   1
THESE MUST SEEM DOUBLY MINDFUL OF THEIR VOWS 500   2 DON JUAN 5   154   5
THAT YOUNG MEN RARELY MADE MONASTIC VOWS 439   3 DON JUAN 14   67   6
I THINK I SHOULD HAVE MADE MONASTIC VOWS 467   3 DON JUAN 15   24   3

		PAGE	VOL		CANTO	STANZA	LN

VOYAGE
'TWAS FOR A VOYAGE THAT THE YOUNG MAN WAS MEANT . . . . 161 2 DON JUAN 2 8 5
AT LAST HER FATHER TOOK A VOYAGE TO SEA . . . . . . 248 2 DON JUAN 2 174 V5
IT IS A PLEASANT VOYAGE PERHAPS TO FLOAT . . . . . . 191 3 DON JUAN 9 18 1
(A CHANCE STILL) 'TIS A VOYAGE OR VESSEL LOST . . . . 376 3 DON JUAN 13 39 8
AS CAPTAIN PARRY'S VOYAGE MAY DO TO JASON'S . . . . . 419 3 DON JUAN 14 22 4
VOYAGED
AND LONG HAD VOYAGED THROUGH MANY A STORMY SEA . . . . 179 2 DON JUAN 2 43 4
VOYAGES
TOMBUCTOO TRAVELS VOYAGES TO THE POLES . . . . . 93 2 DON JUAN 1 132 6
BY FORMER VOYAGES STOOD TO WATCH THE SKIFFS . . . . . 256 3 DON JUAN 10 64 7
VULGAR
BUT VULGAR ILLNESSES DON'T LIKE TO MEET . . . . . 168 2 DON JUAN 2 22 6
OR IF TOO CLASSIC FOR HIS VULGAR BRAIN . . . . . . 333 2 DON JUAN 3 99 5
HE WAS ABOVE THE VULGAR BY HIS MIEN . . . . . 415 2 DON JUAN 5 9 6
AND TURNS ASIDE HIS SCYTHE TO VULGAR THINGS . . . . . 468 2 DON JUAN 5 98 4
A VULGAR TEMPEST 'TWERE TO A TYPHOON . . . . . 490 2 DON JUAN 5 136 1
THESE ARE BUT VULGAR OATHS AS YOU MAY DEEM . . . . . 112 3 DON JUAN 8 1 2
FOR THAT WERE VULGAR COLD AND COMMONPLACE . . . . 160 3 DON JUAN 8 97 2
THAN THE MERE PLODDING THROUGH EACH VULGAR FRACTION . . 321 3 DON JUAN 12 11 6
THEN THERE'S THE VULGAR TRICK OF THOSE DAMNED DAMAGES . . 346 3 DON JUAN 12 65 4
WHICH MEANS THAT VULGAR PEOPLE MUST NOT SHARE IT . . . 419 3 DON JUAN 14 21 8
WHICH GLIBLY GLIDES FROM EVERY VULGAR TONGUE . . . . 564 3 DON JUAN 17 5 2
VULGAREST
THE VULGAREST TOOL THAT TYRANNY COULD WANT . . . . . 16 2 DON JUAN 0 12 5
VULGARET
VETABO CERERIS SACRUM QUI VULGARET-- . . . . . 419 3 DON JUAN 14 21 7
VULT
OMNIA VULT BELLE MATHO DICERE--DIC ALIQUANDO . . . . 465 3 DON JUAN 15 21 1
VULTURE
NOW FEELING ALL THE VULTURE IN HIS JAWS . . . . . 193 2 DON JUAN 2 71 4
LIKE THE PROMETHEAN VULTURE THIS POLLUTION . . . . 195 2 DON JUAN 2 75 4
AND FEELING STILL THE FAMISH'D VULTURE GNAW . . . . . 239 2 DON JUAN 2 157 6
WADED
BUT AS THE DANUBE COULD NOT WELL BE WADED . . . . . 73 3 DON JUAN 7 13 6
WADING
AT LAST WITH SWIMMING WADING SCRAMBLING HE . . . . . 212 2 DON JUAN 2 107 7
WAFT
WHOM FRANCE AND FORTUNE LATELY DEIGN'D TO WAFT HERE . . 398 3 DON JUAN 13 86 4
WAFTED
AND WAFTED FAR AROSE A RICH PERFUME . . . . 460 2 DON JUAN 5 85 6
WHICH WAFTED HIM FROM PETERSBURGH THE BEST . . . . . 248 3 DON JUAN 10 49 4
WAGE
MY PEN AND LIKED POETIC WAR TO WAGE . . . . 397 2 DON JUAN 4 98 6
WHICH IS STILL BETTER THUS IN VERSE TO WAGE . . . . 118 3 DON JUAN 8 14 6
FIRING THE COUNTIES TILL THEY IMPIOUS WAR WAGE . . . . 530 3 DON JUAN 16 60 V5
WAGED
HE WAGED IN VENGEANCE OF HER DEGRADATION . . . . . . 303 2 DON JUAN 3 55 8
WAGGISH
THERE WAS THE WAGGISH WELCH JUDGE JEFFERIES HARDSMAN . . 399 3 DON JUAN 13 88 5
WAGGON
AND PEGASUS RUNS RESTIVE IN HIS WAGGON . . . . 333 2 DON JUAN 3 99 2
WAGGONERS
WITH HIS DEAR WAGGONERS AROUND HIS LAKES . . . . . 333 2 DON JUAN 3 98 4
WAGGONS
PEDLARS AND BOATS AND WAGGONS OH YE SHADES . . . . 334 2 DON JUAN 3 100 1
IN SAFETY TO THE WAGGONS WHERE ALONE . . . . . 102 3 DON JUAN 7 70 5
WAGING
THE OCEAN WHEN ITS YEASTY WAR IS WAGING . . . . . 305 2 DON JUAN 3 58 3
WHILE SOME MORE DESPERATE DOWAGER HAS BEEN WAGING . . . 486 2 DON JUAN 5 130 3
WAGS
THERE WERE SOME COUNTRY WAGS TOO--AND ALAS . . . . . 539 3 DON JUAN 16 81 1
WAIL
WHICH FABLE PLACES IN HER BREAST OF WAIL . . . . . . 49 3 DON JUAN 6 87 6
AND AS THE WIND A WIDOWED NATION'S WAIL . . . . . . 105 3 DON JUAN 7 77 4
WAILING
STRANGE SOUNDS OF WAILING BLASPHEMY DEVOTION . . . . 174 2 DON JUAN 2 34 7
WAIN
COULD HE NOT BEG THE LOAN OF CHARLES WAIN . . . . . 333 2 DON JUAN 3 99 3
WAIST
OR ELSE 'TWERE EASY TO WITHDRAW HER WAIST . . . . . 83 2 DON JUAN 1 115 5
WAISTCOAT
STRIPT TO HIS WAISTCOAT AND THAT NOT TOO CLEAN . . . . 104 3 DON JUAN 7 73 7
WAIT
WHO'VE MADE US YOUTH WAIT TOO--TOO LONG ALREADY . . . 89 2 DON JUAN 1 125 4
AND BEG THEY'LL WAIT WITH PATIENCE FOR THE MORAL . . . 141 2 DON JUAN 1 209 V2
THEY MUST WAIT SEVERAL WEEKS BEFORE A MASS . . . . . 185 2 DON JUAN 2 55 4
A THOUSAND SHARPER SABRES WAIT THE WORD . . . . . 364 2 DON JUAN 4 37 V7
NOR MUCH DISPOSED TO WAIT IN WORD OR DEED . . . . . 56 3 DON JUAN 6 101 2
OR THOSE WHO THOUGHT IT BRAVE TO WAIT AS YET . . . . 135 3 DON JUAN 8 45 8
YET YOU'RE A NOBLE FELLOW AND BUT WAIT . . . . . 185 3 DON JUAN 9 6 V1
AND WAIT UNTIL THE NIGHTINGALE GROWS DUMBER . . . . . 380 3 DON JUAN 13 48 5
WAITED
SHE WAITED ON HER LADY WITH THE SUN . . . . . . 252 2 DON JUAN 2 182 5
AND THEY WHO WAITED ONCE AND WORSHIPPED--THEY . . . . 431 3 DON JUAN 5 37 1
AND WAITED BUT THE SIGNAL'S VOICE TO BURST . . . . . 91 3 DON JUAN 7 50 4
SHE WAITED UNTIL JUSTICE COULD RECALL . . . . . . 533 3 DON JUAN 16 67 5
WAITERS
THY WAITERS RUNNING MUCKS AT EVERY BELL . . . . . . 259 3 DON JUAN 10 69 4

	PAGE	VOL	CANTO		STANZA	LV
WAITERS (CONTINUED)						
A TIDE OF WELL-CLAD WAITERS AND AROUND	282	3 DON JUAN	11		30	2
FROM WHENCE POURED FORTH A TRIBE OF WELL-CLAD WAITERS .	313	3 DON JUAN	11	V	29	2
WAITING						
WAITING FOR HIS SUBLIMITY'S FIRMAN	393	2 DON JUAN	4		91	2
WAITS						
IF SUCH DOOM WAITS EACH INTELLECTUAL GIANT	566	3 DON JUAN	17		10	1
WAKE						
TO FOLLOW JUAN'S WAKE LIKE SANCHO PANCA	175	2 DON JUAN	2		37	8
TO WATCH HIM SLUMBERING AND TO SEE HIM WAKE	247	2 DON JUAN	2		173	4
YOU WAKE WITH HEAD-ACHE YOU SHALL SEE WHAT THEN . .	250	2 DON JUAN	2		179	8
SHE WOKE AT LENGTH BUT NOT AS SLEEPERS WAKE	378	2 DON JUAN	4		62	1
SPEAK BUT HE SPOKE NOT WAKE BUT STILL HE SLEPT-- .	430	2 DON JUAN	5		36	2
LEST THEIR TOO LAWFUL BED-FELLOW SHOULD WAKE . . .	18	3 DON JUAN	6		24	8
THE CALM DUDU SO TURBULENTLY WAKE	42	3 DON JUAN	6		71	8
OF ANY WORSHIP WAKE SOME THOUGHTS DIVINE	387	3 DON JUAN	13		61	8
WHO WAKE IN WINTER ERE THE COCK CAN SUMMON . . .	426	3 DON JUAN	14		36	3
APPEAR TO WAKE AND SHADOWS WILD AND QUAINT	508	3 DON JUAN	16		18	5
BUT COULD NOT WAKE HE WAS HE DID SURMISE	511	3 DON JUAN	16		25	6
WAKEN'D						
THE COFFEE MADE WOULD FAIN HAVE WAKEN'D JUAN . . .	234	2 DON JUAN	2		146	2
WAKES						
WE FEEL WITHOUT HIM WORDSWORTH SOMETIMES WAKES . . .	333	2 DON JUAN	3		98	2
SOFT HOUR WHICH WAKES THE WISH AND MELTS THE HEART .	338	2 DON JUAN	3		108	1
WAKES ME NEXT MORNING WITH ITS SYNONYM	372	2 DON JUAN	4		53	8
WAKING						
FROM MARBLE LIKE PYGMALION'S STATUE WAKING	27	3 DON JUAN	6		43	6
WAKING ALREADY AND RETURNED AT LENGTH	511	3 DON JUAN	16		25	7
WALK						
THEIR VERY WALK WOULD MAKE YOUR BOSOM SWELL	159	2 DON JUAN	2		5	6
SO MUCH AS TO PROPOSE TO TAKE A WALK--	249	2 DON JUAN	2		176	3
AT LENGTH SHE ROSE UP AND BEGAN TO WALK	61	3 DON JUAN	6		110	5
WHICH LEADS BEHOLDERS ON A BOGGY WALK	89	3 DON JUAN	7		46	6
OUR PASSIONS AND WE WALK IN WISDOM'S WAYS	360	3 DON JUAN	13		4	6
A FIGURE FIT TO WALK BEFORE A KING	440	3 DON JUAN	14		70	4
WITH ANYBODY IN A RIDE OR WALK	464	3 DON JUAN	15		19	8
WALK'D						
AND THUS THEY WALK'D OUT IN THE AFTERNOON	249	2 DON JUAN	2		176	7
LORD HENRY WALK'D INTO HIS CABINET	440	3 DON JUAN	14		68	2
WHETHER THEY RODE OR WALK'D OR STUDIED SPANISH . . .	453	3 DON JUAN	14		98	1
WALKED						
THE GALLERIES FROM ROOM TO ROOM THEY WALKED . . .	21	3 DON JUAN	6		30	2
THEY SHOULD HAVE WALKED THERE IN THEIR SPRITELIEST TRIM .	38	3 DON JUAN	6		64	5
WALKED O'ER THE WALLS OF ISMAIL AS IF NURST . . .	138	3 DON JUAN	8		52	5
WALKED ON BEHIND HIS CARRIAGE O'ER THE SUMMIT . . .	272	3 DON JUAN	11		9	2
THE ELDERLY WALKED THROUGH THE LIBRARY	406	3 DON JUAN	13		102	1
OR WALKED IF FOUL THEY READ OR TOLD A TALE . . .	406	3 DON JUAN	13		104	3
AND WHEN HE WALKED DOWN INTO THE SALOON	513	3 DON JUAN	16		30	1
WALKING						
IN SHORT SHE WAS A WALKING CALCULATION	29	2 DON JUAN	1		16	1
AND WALKING OUT UPON THE BEACH BELOW	224	2 DON JUAN	2		129	1
SHE DREAMED A DREAM OF WALKING IN A WOOD-- . . .	43	3 DON JUAN	6		75	2
HAD MUSIC--WALKING--RIDING--BOOKS--AND TALK . . .	407	3 DON JUAN	13		104	V2
FOUND HIS OWN LEGS EMBARGOED FROM MERE WALKING . .	565	3 DON JUAN	17		8	4
WALKS						
THOSE LONELY WALKS AND LENGTHENING REVERIES	73	2 DON JUAN	1		97	1
WALKS O'ER IT WAS SHE SHAKEN BY THE DREAM	360	2 DON JUAN	4		30	3
HE WALKS FROM HALL TO HALL	519	3 DON JUAN	16	L	4	4
SAY NOUGHT TO HIM AS HE WALKS THE HALL	520	3 DON JUAN	16	L	6	1
WALL						
THESE ORIENTAL WRITINGS ON THE WALL	308	2 DON JUAN	3		65	1
AND CAUGHT HER FALLING AND FROM OFF THE WALL . . .	364	2 DON JUAN	4		37	2
THEN TO THE WALL SHE TURN'D AS IF TO WARP . . .	379	2 DON JUAN	4		65	5
ANON HER THIN WAN FINGERS BEAT THE WALL	380	2 DON JUAN	4		66	1
AT ANCHOR UNDER THE SERAGLIO WALL	407	2 DON JUAN	4		113	4
UP IN A LITTLE CREEK BELOW A WALL	432	2 DON JUAN	5		40	7
THE TURKISH TITLE) AND RANGED ROUND THE WALL . . .	31	3 DON JUAN	6		51	2
ALONG THE LEAGUERED WALL AND BRISTLING BANK . . .	110	3 DON JUAN	7		86	4
RAMPART WALL CASEMENT HOUSE--FOR THERE WAS NOT . .	131	3 DON JUAN	8		37	3
ROLLS BY THE CITY WALL BUT DEED NOR WORD . . .	155	3 DON JUAN	8		87	4
OF FORTY THOUSAND WHO HAD MANNED THE WALL . . .	175	3 DON JUAN	8		127	7
WORN OUT WITH BATTERING ISMAIL'S STUBBORN WALL . .	181	3 DON JUAN	8		139	6
HAD PERISHED IN THE FIELD OR BY THE WALL . . .	182	3 DON JUAN	8		141	4
TO GET AT THEE NOT BATTER DOWN A WALL	210	3 DON JUAN	9		56	4
THE DEE THE DON BALGOUNIE'S BRIG'S BLACK WALL . .	233	3 DON JUAN	10		18	3
A GREY WALL A GREEN RUIN RUSTY PIKE	255	3 DON JUAN	10		61	5
AT LENGTH THEY ROSE LIKE A WHITE WALL ALONG . . .	257	3 DON JUAN	10		65	1
AND HARMONIZED BY THE OLD CHORAL WALL	388	3 DON JUAN	13		63	8
HE REACHED THE ANCIENT WALL THEN STOOD STONE STILL .	559	3 DON JUAN	16		119	8
IT TOUCHED NO SOUL NOR BODY BUT THE WALL	559	3 DON JUAN	16		120	2
ONLY THE WALL INSTEAD OF WHAT HE SOUGHT	560	3 DON JUAN	16		122	8
WALLOWED						
THUS ON THEY WALLOWED IN THE BLOODY MIRE	121	3 DON JUAN	8		20	1
WALLS						
WHICH OVERLOOK'D THE WHITE WALLS OF HIS HOME . . .	286	2 DON JUAN	3		21	1
HE SAW HIS WHITE WALLS SHINING IN THE SUN . . .	289	2 DON JUAN	3		27	1
THE DREAM CHANGED IN A CAVE SHE STOOD ITS WALLS .	362	2 DON JUAN	4		33	1
WITH EASE BUT WHERE I SOUGHT FOR ILION'S WALLS . .	386	2 DON JUAN	4		77	7
SOME FAINT LAMPS GLEAMING FROM THE LOFTY WALLS . . .	442	2 DON JUAN	5		56	1

886

```
                                                                      PAGE VOL      CANTO STANZA LN
WALLS   (CONTINUED)
      A TOWN OF GARDENS WALLS AND WEALTH AMAZING  .  .  .  .  .  . 445   2 DON JUAN  5       60    2
      AND GUARDS AND BOLTS AND WALLS AND NOW AND THEN  .  .  .  .  22   3 DON JUAN  6       32    4
      WITHIN THESE WALLS TO BE BROKE IN UPON  .  .  .  .  .  .  .  46   3 DON JUAN  6       81    2
      AND WALLS AS THICK AS MOST SKULLS BORN AS YET  .  .  .  .  .  72   3 DON JUAN  7       12    2
      WALKED O'ER THE WALLS OF ISMAIL AS IF NURST  .  .  .  .  . 138   3 DON JUAN  8       52    3
      ALL WALLS MEN KNOW AND MANY NEVER KNOWN  .  .  .  .  .  . 142   3 DON JUAN  8       60    6
      THE WALLS WERE WON BUT 'TWAS AN EVEN BET  .  .  .  .  .  . 150   3 DON JUAN  8       77    5
      AND BRUSH A WEB OR TWO FROM OFF THE WALLS  .  .  .  .  .  . 266   3 DON JUAN 10       84    8
      GLANCED FROM THE WALLS IN GOODLY PRESERVATION  .  .  .  . 390   3 DON JUAN 13       68    3
      OLD PORTRAITS FROM OLD WALLS UPON ME SCOWL--  .  .  .  .  . 499   3 DON JUAN 15       97    5
      STEAL FROM THE WALLS TILL YOU ALMOST DISCERN  .  .  .  .  . 508   3 DON JUAN 16       18   V6
      THE SPIRIT OF THESE WALLS--IN TRUTH NOT I  .  .  .  .  .  . 516   3 DON JUAN 16       36    2
      THEIR WALLS IF THEY SAID NAY .  .  .  .  .  .  .  .  .  .  . 518   3 DON JUAN 16   L   2    4
      BROUGHT TO SURVEY THESE GREY WALLS WHICH THOUGH SO THICK  . 529   3 DON JUAN 16       58    3
WALTER
      SIR WALTER REIGNED BEFORE ME MOORE AND CAMPBELL  .  .  .  . 297   3 DON JUAN 11       57    1
WALTON
      WHATEVER ISAAC WALTON SINGS OR SAYS  .  .  .  .  .  .  . 407   3 DON JUAN 13      106    6
WALTZ
      WITH THE THREE-THOUSANDTH CURTSEY THERE THE WALTZ  .  .  . 302   3 DON JUAN 11       68    2
      DISSOLVING IN THE WALTZ TO SOME SOFT AIR .  .  .  .  .  . 303   3 DON JUAN 11       70    6
      TO HIS BILLETS WHY WALTZ WITH HIM WHY I PRAY  .  .  .  . 332   3 DON JUAN 12       34    7
      SOME WALTZ SOME DRAW SOME FATHOM THE ABYSS  .  .  .  .  . 340   3 DON JUAN 12       52    5
WALTZING
      TO TURN HER HEAD WITH WALTZING AND WITH FLATTERY  .  .  . 331   3 DON JUAN 12       32    8
WAN
      WAVED AND O'ERSHADING HER WAN CHEEK APPEARS .  .  .  .  . 108   2 DON JUAN  1      158    4
      ANON HER THIN WAN FINGERS BEAT THE WALL  .  .  .  .  .  . 380   3 DON JUAN  4       66    1
      MADE HIS LAST ILLNESS WHEN ALL WORN AND WAN .  .  .  .  .  84   3 DON JUAN  7       36    5
      BEING WAN AND WORN WITH EYES THAT HARDLY BROOKED  .  .  . 568   3 DON JUAN 17       14    4
WAND
      'TWAS BUT A DOUBT BUT NE'ER MAGICIAN'S WAND .  .  .  .  .  60   2 DON JUAN  1       71    6
WANDER
      THINE EAR IF IT SHOULD REACH--AND NOW RHYMES WANDER  .  .  52   3 DON JUAN  6       93    3
      THINE EAR IMPERIAL AND JUST NOW RHYMES WANDER  .  .  .  .  52   3 DON JUAN  6       93   V3
      IN PEDIGREES BY THOSE WHO WANDER STILL  .  .  .  .  .  . 359   3 DON JUAN 13        2    3
WANDER'D
      YOUNG JUAN WANDER'D BY THE GLASSY BROOKS .  .  .  .  .  .  70   2 DON JUAN  1       90    1
      FOR LITTLE HAD HE WANDER'D SINCE THE DAY .  .  .  .  .  . 249   2 DON JUAN  2      176    4
      AND FORTH THEY WANDER'D HER SIRE BEING GONE .  .  .  .  . 252   2 DON JUAN  2      182    1
      AND THUS THEY WANDER'D FORTH AND HAND IN HAND  .  .  .  . 253   2 DON JUAN  2      184    1
WANDERED
      AND WANDERED UP AND DOWN AS IN A DREAM  .  .  .  .  .  . 148   3 DON JUAN  8       72    4
WANDERER
      A WANDERER FROM THE BRITISH WORLD OF FASHION  .  .  .  . 244   2 DON JUAN  2      166    2
WANDERING
      FOR ME WHO WANDERING WITH PEDESTRIAN MUSES .  .  .  .  .  14   2 DON JUAN  D        8    1
      FORBIDS ALL WANDERING AS THE WORST OF SINNING  .  .  .  .  25   2 DON JUAN  1        7    4
      CALL'D BACK THE TANGLES OF HER WANDERING HAIR  .  .  .  . 114   2 DON JUAN  1      170    2
      FOR WANDERING MERCHANT VESSELS NOW AND THEN .  .  .  .  . 223   2 DON JUAN  2      126    3
WANE
      JUST AS THE DAY BEGAN TO WANE AND DARKEN .  .  .  .  .  . 264   3 DON JUAN 10       80    3
      ALAS HER STAR MUST WANE LIKE THAT OF DIAN  .  .  .  .  . 554   3 DON JUAN 16      109    3
WANED
      JUST WHEN THE FADING LAMPS WANED DIM AND BLUE  .  .  .  .  41   3 DON JUAN  6       70    5
      HAVE WANED INTO A CRESCENT'S CORUSCATION .  .  .  .  .  . 293   3 DON JUAN 11       49    4
      THE EVENING ALSO WANED--AND COFFEE CAME  .  .  .  .  .  . 549   3 DON JUAN 16      101    2
WANING
      TO BEAR THESE CROSSES) FOR EACH WANING PRUDE  .  .  .  . 177   3 DON JUAN  8      131    6
      BUT TO CONTINUE THOUGH HER YEARS WERE WANING  .  .  .  . 247   3 DON JUAN 10       47    4
      A LITTLE EARLIER THAN THE WANING MOON .  .  .  .  .  .  . 409   3 DON JUAN 13      111    4
WANT
      THE VULGAREST TOOL THAT TYRANNY COULD WANT  .  .  .  .  .  16   2 DON JUAN  D       12    5
      I WANT A HERO AN UNCOMMON WANT  .  .  .  .  .  .  .  .  .  21   2 DON JUAN  1        1    1
      I WANT A HERO AN UNCOMMON WANT  .  .  .  .  .  .  .  .  .  21   2 DON JUAN  1        1    1
      FOR WANT OF FACTS WOULD ALL BE THROWN AWAY)  .  .  .  .  .  86   2 DON JUAN  1      121    4
      FOR WANT OF WATER AND THEIR SOLID MESS  .  .  .  .  .  . 178   2 DON JUAN  2       41    5
      HAVING NO PAPER FOR THE WANT OF BETTER  .  .  .  .  .  . 195   2 DON JUAN  2       74    7
      LIGHT CLASSIC ARTICLES OF FEMALE WANT .  .  .  .  .  .  . 284   2 DON JUAN  3       17    4
      THERE WAS NO WANT OF LOFTY MIRRORS AND  .  .  .  .  .  . 310   2 DON JUAN  3       69    1
      AND YET SHE DID NOT WANT TO REACH THE MOON .  .  .  .  . 490   2 DON JUAN  5      136    3
      THOUGH NOT FOR WANT OF MATTER BUT 'TIS TIME .  .  .  .  . 503   2 DON JUAN  5      159    2
      WITH ALL THINGS LADIES WANT SAVE ONE OR TWO .  .  .  .  .  31   3 DON JUAN  6       51    7
      BUT THEN THERE WAS A GREAT WANT OF PRECAUTION  .  .  .  .  72   3 DON JUAN  7       11    5
      WHOSE NAMES WANT NOTHING BUT--PRONUNCIATION  .  .  .  .  .  73   3 DON JUAN  7       14    8
      THUS THE SAME CAUSE WHICH MAKES A VERSE WANT FEET  .  .  .  79   3 DON JUAN  7       26    3
      IN WINTER'S DEPTH OR WANT OF REST AND VICTUAL  .  .  .  . 176   3 DON JUAN  8      128    7
      WHICH SHOWED A WANT OF LANTHORNS OR OF TASTE-- .  .  .  . 177   3 DON JUAN  8      130    2
      AND YET THIS WANT OF TIES MADE THEIR'S MORE TENDER  .  .  . 252   3 DON JUAN 10       57    8
      'TWERE NOT FOR WANT OF LAMPS TO AID HIS DODGING HIS  .  . 281   3 DON JUAN 11       28    5
      A WANT OF THAT TRUE NATURE WHICH SUBLIMES  .  .  .  .  . 417   3 DON JUAN 14       16    6
      AND PASS FOR WANT OF BETTER THOUGH NOT NEW .  .  .  .  . 440   3 DON JUAN 14       69    4
      WHICH MANY PEOPLE TAKE FOR WANT OF HEART .  .  .  .  .  . 547   3 DON JUAN 16       97    3
WANTED
      DISSATISFIED NOR KNOWING WHAT HE WANTED .  .  .  .  .  .  73   2 DON JUAN  1       96    2
      BESIDES IT WANTED BUT FEW HOURS OF DAY  .  .  .  .  .  . 114   2 DON JUAN  1      169    6
      DENYING SEVERAL LITTLE THINGS HE' WANTED .  .  .  .  .  . 120   2 DON JUAN  1      180    4
      THERE WANTED BUT THE LOSS OF THIS TO WEAN  .  .  .  .  . 304   2 DON JUAN  3       57    6
```

WANTED   (CONTINUED)
```
    HIS VERSES RARELY WANTED THEIR DUE FEET--  . . . . .  316   2 DON JUAN  3    78   5
    THERE WANTED BUT THIS REQUISITE TO SWELL . . . . . .  295   3 DON JUAN 11    53   5
    TILL WANTED THEREFORE JUAN ONLY SIGHED   . . . . . .  506   3 DON JUAN 16    12   8
    TO ASK THE REVEREND PERSON WHAT HE WANTED  . . . . .  511   3 DON JUAN 16    23   8
    IT WAS NOT THE PHYSICIAN THAT HE WANTED  . . . . . .  514   3 DON JUAN 16    33   8
WANTING
    YET SOMEHOW THERE WAS SOMETHING SOMEWHERE WANTING  . .  474   2 DON JUAN  5   109   7
    DUDU HAD NEVER PASSED FOR WANTING SENSE  . . . . . .   43   3 DON JUAN  6    74   6
    BUT THERE WAS SOMETHING WANTING ON THE WHOLE--  . . .  441   3 DON JUAN 14    71   1
    STILL THERE WAS SOMETHING WANTING AS I'VE SAID--  . .  441   3 DON JUAN 14    72   1
    IS WANTING AND OUR BEST TIES IN THE TOMB  . . . . .   475   3 DON JUAN 15    44   8
WANTS
    RATHER THAN SELLER HAD HIS WANTS BEEN FEWER  . . . .  528   3 DON JUAN 16    57   5
WAR
    NELSON WAS ONCE BRITANNIA'S GOD OF WAR  . . . . . .    23   2 DON JUAN  1     4   1
    IN CASE OUR LORD THE KING SHOULD GO TO WAR AGAIN  . .   42   2 DON JUAN  1    38   6
    WITH WAR OR PLAGUE OR FAMINE ANY WAY . . . . . . .     92   2 DON JUAN  1   131   5
    WITH LOVE AND WAR A HEAVY GALE AT SEA . . . . . . .   135   2 DON JUAN  1   200   3
    EVEN NATIONS FEEL THIS WHEN THEY GO TO WAR  . . . .   164   2 DON JUAN  2    14   4
    LIKE HUMAN BEINGS DURING CIVIL WAR . . . . . . . .   178   2 DON JUAN  2    42   8
    WE KNOW TOO THEY ARE VERY FOND OF WAR . . . . . . .   238   2 DON JUAN  2   156   5
    HATE TO THE WORLD AND WAR WITH EVERY NATION  . . . .  303   2 DON JUAN  3    55   7
    THE OCEAN WHEN ITS YEASTY WAR IS WAGING  . . . . . .  305   2 DON JUAN  3    58   3
    THE LAST WAR--MUCH THE SAME IN PORTUGAL  . . . . . .  320   2 DON JUAN  3    86   4
    WHERE GREW THE ARTS OF WAR AND PEACE--  . . . . . .   320   2 DON JUAN  3 L  1   3
    MY PEN AND LIKED POETIC WAR TO WAGE . . . . . . . .   397   2 DON JUAN  4    98   6
    TO LODGE THERE WHEN A WAR BROKE OUT ACCORDING  . . .  498   2 DON JUAN  5   151   2
    BUT OH YE GODDESSES OF WAR AND GLORY . . . . . . .    73   3 DON JUAN  7    14   2
    FOR WAR CUTS UP NOT ONLY BRANCH BUT ROOT . . . . .    86   3 DON JUAN  7    41   8
    IN WAR THEM LOVE HE HAD BETTER LEAD THE ASSAULT  . .   98   3 DON JUAN  7    62   8
    THEN COMES THE TUG OF WAR--'TWILL COME AGAIN  . . .   138   3 DON JUAN  8    51   5
    OF WAR AND TAKING TOWNS WHEN MANY A SHRIEK  . . . .   141   3 DON JUAN  8    58   3
    WAR PESTILENCE THE DESPOT'S DESOLATION  . . . . . .   146   3 DON JUAN  8    68   4
    HERE WAR FORGOT HIS OWN DESTRUCTIVE ART  . . . . . .  152   3 DON JUAN  8    82   5
    JUST PONDER WHAT A PIOUS PASTIME WAR IS  . . . . . .  174   3 DON JUAN  8   124   8
    HAD SKETCHES OF LOVE TEMPEST TRAVEL WAR--  . . . . .  181   3 DON JUAN  8   138   3
    AND I WILL WAR AT LEAST IN WORDS (AND--SHOULD  . . .  194   3 DON JUAN  9    24   1
    MY CHANCE SO HAPPEN--DEEDS) WITH ALL WHO WAR  . . .   194   3 DON JUAN  9    24   2
    ESPECIALLY OF WAR AND TAXING--HOW . . . . . . . .    202   3 DON JUAN  9    40   6
    SOME CALL THEE THE WORST CAUSE OF WAR BUT I  . . . .  210   3 DON JUAN  9    56   1
    OF THAT GREAT CAUSE OF WAR OR PEACE OR WHAT  . . . .  211   3 DON JUAN  9    57   2
    IN LOVE AND WAR) HOW ODD ARE THE CONNECTIONS  . . .   215   3 DON JUAN  9    65   3
    LOVE--(THOUGH SHE HAD A CURSED TASTE FOR WAR  . . .   222   3 DON JUAN  9    80   5
    FOR LOVE WAR OR AMBITION WHICH REWARD  . . . . . . .  235   3 DON JUAN 10    22   6
    IN THE DEAR OFFICES OF PEACE OR WAR . . . . . . .    288   3 DON JUAN 11    41   3
    AND SHOW THEM WHAT AN INTELLECTUAL WAR IS  . . . . .  299   3 DON JUAN 11    62   8
    OR FAME OR NAME FOR WIT WAR SENSE OR NONSENSE  . . .  305   3 DON JUAN 11    73   7
    I HAVE SEEN THE FUNDS AT WAR WITH HOUSE AND LAND--  .  310   3 DON JUAN 11    85   3
    HE WHO HATH PROVED WAR STORM OR WOMAN'S RAGE  . . .   339   3 DON JUAN 12    50   6
    PEACE WAR THE TAXES AND WHAT'S CALLED THE NATION  . .  360   3 DON JUAN 13     6   2
    'TIS ODD BUT TRUE--LAST WAR THE NEWS ABOUNDED  . . .  383   3 DON JUAN 13    53   7
    BUT IN THE WAR WHICH STRUCK CHARLES FROM HIS THRONE   386   3 DON JUAN 13    60   4
    HE SHOWS MORE APPETITE FOR WORDS THAN WAR  . . . . .  398   3 DON JUAN 13    84   4
    WHO ATE LAST WAR MORE YANKEES THAN HE KILL'D  . . .   399   3 DON JUAN 13    88   4
    LOVE WAR A TEMPEST--SURELY THERE'S VARIETY  . . . .   416   3 DON JUAN 14    14   1
    AND IN EACH CIRCUMSTANCE OF LOVE OR WAR  . . . . . .  441   3 DON JUAN 14    71   7
    FIRING THE COUNTIES TILL THEY IMPIOUS WAR WAGE  . . .  530   3 DON JUAN 16    60  V5
WARBLE
    AND HER VOICE WAS THE WARBLE OF A BIRD  . . . . . .   236   2 DON JUAN  2   151   3
    AND SINGING BIRDS WITHOUT WERE HEARD TO WARBLE  . . .   55   3 DON JUAN  6    98   3
    HER VOICE THOUGH SWEET IS NOT SO FIT TO WARBLE  . . .  350   3 DON JUAN 12    75   5
WARBLERS
    TO SUPERSEDE ALL WARBLERS HERE BELOW . . . . . . .    10   2 DON JUAN  D     3   3
WARD
    AMONGST THEM ALL HARD BLOWS TO INFLICT OR WARD  . . .   76   3 DON JUAN  7    19   6
    THE STATESMAN HERO HARLOT LAWYER--WARD  . . . . . .   123   3 DON JUAN  8    25   5
    A GUARDIAN GREEN IN YEARS A WARD CONNECTED  . . . .   252   3 DON JUAN 10    57   6
    AND WATCH AND WARD WHOSE PLANS A WORD TOO MUCH  . . .  305   3 DON JUAN 11    73   3
    A CHILD OF CHANCERY THAT STAR-CHAMBER WARD  . . . .   564   3 DON JUAN 17     4   4
WARDEN
    I TOUCH A SINGLE LEAF WHERE HE IS WARDEN--  . . . .   442   3 DON JUAN 14    75   6
WARDS
    FOR SILLY WARDS WILL BRING THEIR GUARDIANS BLAME  . .  336   3 DON JUAN 12    42   4
WARE
    TO MAKE THE NUPTIAL COUCH A BED OF WARE  . . . . . .   12   3 DON JUAN  6    12   8
    SAVING HIS SOUL BY CHEATING IN THE WARE  . . . . . .   80   3 DON JUAN  7    27   4
    A DIFFERENCE BETWEEN CROCKERY WARE AND PLATE  . . .   541   3 DON JUAN 16    84   6
WARFARE
    THE MUSE WILL TAKE A LITTLE TOUCH AT WARFARE  . . .    65   3 DON JUAN  6   120   8
WARISON
    AND AS MY FRIEND SCOTT SAYS I SOUND MY WARISON  . . .  481   3 DON JUAN 15    59   3
WARLIKE
    ARE BOUGHT UP OTHERS BY A WARLIKE LEADER  . . . . .   425   2 DON JUAN  5    27   5
    AS THESE NEW CANTOS TOUCH ON WARLIKE FEATS  . . . .   187   3 DON JUAN  9    10   1
    HIS DUTIES WARLIKE LOVING OR OFFICIAL . . . . . . .   294   3 DON JUAN 11    51   5
WARM
    AND CHAFING HIM THE SOFT WARM HAND OF YOUTH  . . . .  215   2 DON JUAN  2   113   3
    AND HER TRANSPARENT CHEEK ALL PURE AND WARM  . . . .  216   2 DON JUAN  2   114   4
```

WARM   (CONTINUED)

	PAGE	VOL	CANTO	STANZA	LN
AND WARM IN CASE BY CHANCE HE SHOULD AWAKE	226	2	DON JUAN 2	133	4
BRINGING WARM WATER WREATHING HER LONG TRESSES	252	2	DON JUAN 2	182	7
AND ROUND ITS ONCE WARM PRECINCTS PALELY LYING	301	2	DON JUAN 3	51	6
AND SINGING AS HE SUNG IN HIS WARM YOUTH	318	2	DON JUAN 3	83	7
COMMENCE WITH FEELINGS WARM AND PROSPECTS HIGH	421	2	DON JUAN 5	21	5
FELT THE WARM BLOOD WHICH IN HIS FACE WAS GLOWING	478	2	DON JUAN 5	117	4
LOLAH WAS DUSK AS INDIA AND AS WARM	26	3	DON JUAN 6	41	1
ABOVE HER BROW LAY DREAMING SOFT AND WARM	39	3	DON JUAN 6	66	3
THE MATRON TOO WAS WROTH TO LEAVE HER WARM	45	3	DON JUAN 6	79	5
WARM BOUT ARE BROKEN INTO THEIR NEW TRICKS	122	3	DON JUAN 8	22	7
AS WARM IN HEART AS FEMININE IN FEATURE	138	3	DON JUAN 8	52	8
THOUSANDS OF SLAUGHTERED MEN A YET WARM GROUP	157	3	DON JUAN 8	91	2
WHOSE STATUES WARM (I FEAR ALAS TOO TRUE 'TIS)	208	3	DON JUAN 9	51	6
BUT SHOULD WE WISH TO WARM US ON OUR WAY	254	3	DON JUAN 10	59	6
WHICH CAN AWAIT WARM YOUTH IN ITS WILD RACE	326	3	DON JUAN 12	23	4
THEY WARM INTO A SCRAPE BUT KEEP OF COURSE	349	3	DON JUAN 12	73	7
THE JOYS OF MUTUAL HATE TO KEEP THEM WARM	360	3	DON JUAN 13	6	5
(THOUGH LESS THAN THAT OF MEMNON'S STATUE WARM	388	3	DON JUAN 13	64	3
MORE WARM AS LOVELY AND NOT LESS SINCERE	481	3	DON JUAN 15	58	5
WHICH BEAT AS IF THERE WAS A WARM HEART UNDER	560	3	DON JUAN 16	122	4

WARMS

	PAGE	VOL	CANTO	STANZA	LN
AND THEN ON THE PALE CHEEK HER BREAST NOW WARMS	260	2	DON JUAN 2	195	6

WARMTH

	PAGE	VOL	CANTO	STANZA	LN
WITH COST AND CARE AND WARMTH INDUCED TO SHOOT	38	3	DON JUAN 6	65	4
TO HOARD UP WARMTH AGAINST A WINTRY DAY	229	3	DON JUAN 10	9	8
THE WARMTH OF HER POLITENESS WHOSE SINCERITY	550	3	DON JUAN 16	102	2

WARN'D

	PAGE	VOL	CANTO	STANZA	LN
AS IF NOT WARN'D SUFFICIENTLY BY THOSE	199	2	DON JUAN 2	80	6

WARNED

	PAGE	VOL	CANTO	STANZA	LN
WARNED HIM AGAINST GREEK-WORSHIP WHICH LOOKS ODD	240	3	DON JUAN 10	32	3

WARNING

	PAGE	VOL	CANTO	STANZA	LN
TO THEIR OWN GOOD THIS WARNING TO DESPISE	141	2	DON JUAN 1	208	2
FOR WARNING TO THE REST COMPELS THESE RAPS	155	2	DON JUAN 1	V 7	7
HENCE MY OLD COMET GIVE THE STARS DUE WARNING--	494	2	DON JUAN 5	145	4

WARNINGS

	PAGE	VOL	CANTO	STANZA	LN
ARE WISER IN THEIR WARNINGS 'GAINST THE WOE	336	3	DON JUAN 12	44	7

WARP

	PAGE	VOL	CANTO	STANZA	LN
THEN TO THE WALL SHE TURN'D AS IF TO WARP	379	2	DON JUAN 4	65	5
AS HINTING MORE (UNLESS OUR JUDGMENTS WARP US)	391	3	DON JUAN 13	69	7

WARRANTED

	PAGE	VOL	CANTO	STANZA	LN
WARRANTED VIRGIN BEAUTY'S BRIGHTEST COLOURS	407	2	DON JUAN 4	114	3
A SPECIAL TITIAN WARRANTED ORIGINAL	528	3	DON JUAN 16	56	2

WARRANT'S

	PAGE	VOL	CANTO	STANZA	LN
THE CONSTABLE BENEATH A WARRANT'S BANNER	531	3	DON JUAN 16	62	7

WARR'D

	PAGE	VOL	CANTO	STANZA	LN
BUT ALWAYS WITHOUT MALICE IF HE WARR'D	123	3	DON JUAN 8	25	1

WARRING

	PAGE	VOL	CANTO	STANZA	LN
LIKE OCEAN WARRING 'GAINST A ROCKY ISLE	489	2	DON JUAN 5	135	6

WARRIOR

	PAGE	VOL	CANTO	STANZA	LN
A WONDROUS WARRIOR AGAINST THOSE WHO YIELD	151	2	DON JUAN 1	V 2	5
WARRIOR FROM WARRIOR IN THEIR GRIM CAREER	125	3	DON JUAN 8	27	2
WARRIOR FROM WARRIOR IN THEIR GRIM CAREER	125	3	DON JUAN 8	27	2

WARRIOR'S

	PAGE	VOL	CANTO	STANZA	LN
TO THE BARD'S TOMB AND NOT THE WARRIOR'S COLUMN	400	2	DON JUAN 4	104	4
FOR IF I WROTE DOWN EVERY WARRIOR'S SPEECH	83	3	DON JUAN 7	35	7

WARRIORS

	PAGE	VOL	CANTO	STANZA	LN
A THOUSAND WARRIORS BY HIS WORD WERE KEPT	430	2	DON JUAN 5	36	4
WARRIORS THEREON WERE BATTLING FURIOUSLY	461	2	DON JUAN 5	86	3
A PHANTASY WHICH SOMETIMES SEIZES WARRIORS	78	3	DON JUAN 7	24	7
WITH MANY OTHER WARRIORS AS WE SAID	133	3	DON JUAN 8	41	2
THAT DAILY SHILLING WHICH MAKES WARRIORS TOUGH)--	134	3	DON JUAN 8	42	6
FATAL TO WARRIORS AS TO WOMEN--THESE	150	3	DON JUAN 8	76	V2
THAT SHE SPAWNS WARRIORS BY THE SCORE WHERE NONE	164	3	DON JUAN 8	105	2

WAR'S

	PAGE	VOL	CANTO	STANZA	LN
AS WELL AS DILETTANTI IN WAR'S ART	85	3	DON JUAN 7	39	5
WAR'S MERIT IT BY NO MEANS MIGHT ENHANCE	113	3	DON JUAN 8	3	4
OF WAR'S MOST MORTAL ENGINES TO THEIR FOES	116	3	DON JUAN 8	8	3
WAR'S A BRAIN-SPATTERING WINDPIPE-SLITTING ART	184	3	DON JUAN 9	4	3

WARS

	PAGE	VOL	CANTO	STANZA	LN
AND THEN HE THOUGHT OF EARTHQUAKES AND OF WARS	71	2	DON JUAN 1	92	4
WILL SINK WHERE LIE THE SONGS AND WARS OF EARTH	400	2	DON JUAN 4	104	7
FIERCE LOVES AND FAITHLESS WARS--I AM NOT SURE	70	3	DON JUAN 7	8	1
BELLONA WHAT YOU WILL--THEY MEAN BUT WARS	112	3	DON JUAN 8	1	8
YOUR WARS ETERNALLY BESIDES ENJOYING	118	3	DON JUAN 8	14	7
AND THAT ODD IMPULSE WHICH IN WARS OR CREEDS	132	3	DON JUAN 8	38	7
HAD GONE BEFORE HIM AND HIS WARS AND LOVES	284	3	DON JUAN 11	33	2
WARS REVELS LOVES--DO THESE BRING MEN MORE EASE	321	3	DON JUAN 12	11	5

WARSAW

	PAGE	VOL	CANTO	STANZA	LN
THEY JOURNEYED ON THROUGH POLAND AND THROUGH WARSAW	253	3	DON JUAN 10	58	1

WAR-WHOOP

	PAGE	VOL	CANTO	STANZA	LN
THE HORRID WAR-WHOOP AND THE SHRILLER SCREAM	175	3	DON JUAN 8	127	5

WARY

	PAGE	VOL	CANTO	STANZA	LN
THE THIRD A WARY COOL OLD SWORDER TOOK	370	2	DON JUAN 4	49	2
BE WARY WATCH THE TIME AND ALWAYS SERVE IT	366	3	DON JUAN 13	18	4
HOWEVER 'TIS EXPEDIENT TO BE WARY	374	3	DON JUAN 13	35	5

WASH

	PAGE	VOL	CANTO	STANZA	LN
WHERE WAVES MIGHT WASH AND SEALS MIGHT BREED AND LURK	362	2	DON JUAN 4	33	4
BLOOD ONLY SERVES TO WASH AMBITION'S HANDS	212	3	DON JUAN 9	59	8

WASH'D
THE WATER LEFT THE HOLD AND WASH'D THE DECKS . . . . . 172 2 DON JUAN 2   31   2
WHICH PROVIDENTIALLY FOR HIM WAS WASH'D . . . . 212 2 DON JUAN 2   107   2
AND THAT GOOD WINE NE'ER WASH'D DOWN BETTER FARE . . . 298 2 DON JUAN 3   45   4
OR LIKE THE RHONE BY LEMAN'S WATERS WASH'D . . . . . . 447 3 DON JUAN 14   87   4
WASHING
IN WASHING DOWN PEDRILLO WITH SALT WATER . . . . 210 2 DON JUAN 2   102   8
WASHINGTON
NOT SO LEONIDAS AND WASHINGTON . . . . 114 3 DON JUAN 8   5   2
GEORGE WASHINGTON HAD THANKS AND NOUGHT BESIDE . . . . 186 3 DON JUAN 9   8   4
THOU MORAL WASHINGTON OF AFRICA . . . . 445 3 DON JUAN 14   82   4
WASSAIL
AT WASSAIL IN THEIR BEAUTY AND THEIR PRIDE . . . . . . 306 2 DON JUAN 3   61   4
NOR WINE NOR WASSAIL COULD RAISE A VASSAL . . . . . . 520 3 DON JUAN 16 L 5   7
WAS'T
YOU HAVE YOUR SALARY WAS'T FOR THAT YOU WROUGHT . . . . 12 2 DON JUAN D   6   5
WHAT WAS'T TO HIM TO HEAR TWO WOMEN SOB . . . . 105 3 DON JUAN 7   77   8
WASTE
OVER THE WASTE OF WATERS LIKE A VEIL . . . . 182 2 DON JUAN 2   49   2
THAN HAUNTING SOME OLD RUIN OR WILD WASTE . . . . . . 38 3 DON JUAN 6   64   8
WHICH FLASHES O'ER A WASTE AND ICY CLIME . . . . 67 3 DON JUAN 7   2   4
A VILLAGE OF MOLDAVIA'S WASTE WHEREIN . . . . 76 3 DON JUAN 7   20   7
THEIR HASTE OR WASTE I NEITHER KNOW NOR CARE . . . . . 80 3 DON JUAN 7   27   2
TO WASTE SO MUCH GOLD FOR A LITTLE DROSS . . . . 113 3 DON JUAN 8   3   5
OR WASTE A WORLD SINCE NO ONE CAN DENY . . . . 210 3 DON JUAN 9   56   5
OF WASTE AND HASTE AND GLARE AND GLOSS AND GLITTER . . 237 3 DON JUAN 10   26   2
THE WORLDS BEYOND THIS WORLD'S PERPLEXING WASTE . . . 524 3 DON JUAN 16   48   5
WASTED
BUT ALL THAT POWER WAS WASTED UPON HIM . . . . 396 2 DON JUAN 4   95   1
AND THEY HAD WASTED NOW ALMOST A QUARTER . . . . 482 2 DON JUAN 5   122   8
THE SOIL OF THE GREEN PROVINCE HE HAD WASTED . . . . . 84 3 DON JUAN 7   36   7
WHOSE LEISURE HOURS ARE WASTED ON A HARLOT . . . . . . 109 3 DON JUAN 7   84 V3
ALONG HIS WASTED CHEEK AND SEEMED TO GRAVEL . . . . . 245 3 DON JUAN 10   43   7
HANDSOME BUT WASTED RICH WITHOUT A SOU . . . . 306 3 DON JUAN 11   75   2
WATCH
AND WHEN HE LOOK'D UPON HIS WATCH AGAIN . . . . 72 2 DON JUAN 1   94   6
'TIS NOT MY FAULT--I KEPT GOOD WATCH--ALACK . . . . . 96 2 DON JUAN 1   137   4
AT WATCH AND WATCH THUS SHIVERING LIKE THE TERTIAN . . 189 2 DON JUAN 2   63   6
AT WATCH AND WATCH THUS SHIVERING LIKE THE TERTIAN . . 189 2 DON JUAN 2   63   6
WHEN HE WHO HAD THE WATCH SUNG OUT AND SWORE . . . . . 207 2 DON JUAN 2   97   2
TO WATCH HIM SLUMBERING AND TO SEE HIM WAKE . . . . . 247 2 DON JUAN 2   173   4
AS THEY WHO WATCH O'ER WHAT THEY LOVE WHILE SLEEPING . 261 2 DON JUAN 2   196   8
THAT WISDOM EVER ON THE WATCH TO ROB . . . . 264 2 DON JUAN 2   203   4
SHE SAW THEM WATCH HER WITHOUT ASKING WHY . . . . . . 378 2 DON JUAN 4   63   3
TO WATCH THE PROGRESS OF THOSE ROLLING SEAS . . . . . 413 2 DON JUAN 5   5   4
HEADS BOW KNEES BEND EYES WATCH AROUND A THRONE . . . 484 2 DON JUAN 5   127   7
BUT ERE THE MIDDLE WATCH WAS HARDLY OVER . . . . 41 3 DON JUAN 6   70   4
FOR WHICH ALL PETERSBURGH IS ON THE WATCH . . . . . . 181 3 DON JUAN 8   139   8
GLANCED MILDLY ALL THE WORLD WAS ON THE WATCH . . . . 213 3 DON JUAN 9   61   8
BY FORMER VOYAGES STOOD TO WATCH THE SKIFFS . . . . . 256 3 DON JUAN 10   64   7
AND WATCH AND WARD WHOSE PLANS A WORD TOO MUCH . . . . 305 3 DON JUAN 11   73   3
BE WARY WATCH THE TIME AND ALWAYS SERVE IT . . . . . . 366 3 DON JUAN 13   18   4
OR ON THE WATCH THEIR LONGING EYES WOULD FIX . . . . . 406 3 DON JUAN 13   102   7
WATCH'D
SHE WHO FOR MANY YEARS HAD WATCH'D HER SON SO-- . . . 80 2 DON JUAN 1   110   7
HE WATCH'D IT WISTFULLY UNTIL AWAY . . . . 204 2 DON JUAN 2   90   5
AND WATCH'D WITH EAGERNESS EACH THROB THAT DREW . . . 216 2 DON JUAN 2   114   7
WHO WATCH'D HIM LIKE A MOTHER WOULD HAVE FED . . . . . 239 2 DON JUAN 2   158   2
THE LADY WATCH'D HER LOVER--AND THAT HOUR . . . . . . 262 2 DON JUAN 2   198   1
AND WATCH'D BY EYES THAT NEVER YET KNEW WEEPING . . . 274 2 DON JUAN 3   1   3
HER FATHER WATCH'D SHE TURN'D HER EYES AWAY . . . . . 379 2 DON JUAN 4   64   2
AND THEY WHO WATCH'D HER NEAREST COULD NOT KNOW . . . 381 2 DON JUAN 4   69   4
WATCHDOG'S
'TIS SWEET TO HEAR THE WATCHDOG'S HONEST BARK . . . . 88 2 DON JUAN 1   123   1
WATCHED
THE COURT THAT WATCHED EACH LOOK HER VISAGE WORE . . . 211 3 DON JUAN 9   58   5
THE WITS WATCHED EVERY LOOP-HOLE FOR THEIR ART . . . . 408 3 DON JUAN 13   109   3
(WHO WATCHED THE CHANGES OF DON JUAN'S BROW . . . . . 516 3 DON JUAN 16   37   2
WATCHER'S
HUSH'D INTO DEPTHS BEYOND THE WATCHER'S DIVING . . . . 261 2 DON JUAN 2   197   6
WATCHES
THEY STOWED HIM WITH STRICT ORDERS TO THE WATCHES . . 371 2 DON JUAN 4   50   8
SOULS OF IMMORTAL GENERALS PHOEBUS WATCHES . . . . . . 107 3 DON JUAN 7   81   7
WHO WATCHES O'ER THE CHAIN AS THEY WHO WEAR . . . . . 258 3 DON JUAN 10   68   8
AND MIGHT GO ON IF WELL WOUND UP LIKE WATCHES . . . . 473 3 DON JUAN 15   40   8
WATCHFUL
THOUGH WATCHFUL AS THE LYNX THEY NE'ER DISCOVER . . . 75 2 DON JUAN 1   100   2
THE WATCHFUL MOTHERS AND THE CAREFUL SISTERS . . . . . 331 3 DON JUAN 12   32   3
WATCHING
THIS DAY AND WATCHING WITCHING CONDESCENDING . . . . . 546 3 DON JUAN 16   95   2
WATCHMAN
BY THE WATCHMAN OR SOME SUCH REALITY . . . . 237 2 DON JUAN 2   152   4
WATCHMEN
'TWAS AS THE WATCHMEN SAY A CLOUDY NIGHT . . . . 94 2 DON JUAN 1   135   1
WATCHWORD
A WATCHWORD TILL THE FUTURE SHALL BE FREE . . . . . . 114 3 DON JUAN 8   5   8
WATER
A PAIL OF HOUSEMAID'S WATER UNAWARES . . . . 34 2 DON JUAN 1   24   8
(ANTONIA LET ME HAVE A GLASS OF WATER) . . . . 106 2 DON JUAN 1   155   4

890

		PAGE	VOL		CANTO	STANZA	LN
WATER	(CONTINUED)						
PANTING FOR POWER AS TANTALUS FOR WATER	. . . .	155	2	DON JUAN	1	V 6	V1
AND SO--FOR GODSAKE--HOCK AND SODA WATER	. . . . . .	156	2	DON JUAN	1	V 8	8
THE WIND WAS FAIR THE WATER PASSING ROUGH	. . . . .	162	2	DON JUAN	2	11	2
THE PUMPS AND THERE WERE FOUR FEET WATER FOUND	. . .	170	2	DON JUAN	2	27	8
THE WATER RUSH'D THROUGH IN A WAY QUITE PUZZLING	. .	171	2	DON JUAN	2	28	7
FOR FIFTY TONS OF WATER WERE UPTHROWN	171	2	DON JUAN	2	29	6
THE WATER LEFT THE HOLD AND WASH'D THE DECKS	172	2	DON JUAN	2	31	2
OF FIRE THAN WATER SPITE OF OATHS AND TEARS	174	2	DON JUAN	2	35	6
FOR WANT OF WATER AND THEIR SOLID MESS	178	2	DON JUAN	2	41	5
WATER APPEAR'D YET THOUGH THE PEOPLE KNEW	178	2	DON JUAN	2	42	3
WATER A TWENTY GALLON CASK OR SO	181	2	DON JUAN	2	47	3
KEPT ABOVE WATER WITH AN OAR FOR MAST	188	2	DON JUAN	2	61	2
WATER AND WINE AND FOOD--AND YOU MIGHT SEE	194	2	DON JUAN	2	72	6
THE DAY BEFORE FAST SLEEPING ON THE WATER	208	2	DON JUAN	2	99	1
IN WASHING DOWN PEDRILLO WITH SALT WATER	210	2	DON JUAN	2	102	8
OF AN OLD MAN WHO LIVED UPON THE WATER	222	2	DON JUAN	2	124	8
SERMONS AND SODA WATER THE DAY AFTER	250	2	DON JUAN	2	178	8
BRINGING WARM WATER WREATHING HER LONG TRESSES . . .	252	2	DON JUAN	2	182	7
AFTER LONG TRAVELLING BY LAND OR WATER	287	2	DON JUAN	3	22	2
IN DIGGING DRAINS FOR A NEW WATER CLOSET	327	2	DON JUAN	3	89	V7
AND AIR--EARTH--WATER--FIRE LIVE--AND WE DEAD	432	2	DON JUAN	5	39	6
AS FAST AS OARS COULD PULL AND WATER FLOAT	432	2	DON JUAN	5	40	4
AS WATER THROUGH AN UNEXPECTED LEAK	490	2	DON JUAN	5	137	6
AND WAS BELEAGUER'D BOTH BY LAND AND WATER	70	3	DON JUAN	7	8	6
COUNT DAMAS DROVE THEM BACK INTO THE WATER	82	3	DON JUAN	7	31	7
THE THIRD IN COLUMNS TWO ATTACKED BY WATER	91	3	DON JUAN	7	50	8
BUT OF THE PORTION WHICH ATTACKED BY WATER	116	3	DON JUAN	8	9	2
AND SHRIEK FOR WATER INTO A DEAF EAR--	117	3	DON JUAN	8	11	5
OF BURNING STREETS LIKE MOONLIGHT ON THE WATER	172	3	DON JUAN	8	122	7
MIRRORED THE CHRISTIAN FLAGS--AS MOONBEAMS ON THE WATER	.	173	3	DON JUAN	8	122	V8
WHERE BLOOD WAS TALKED OF AS WE WOULD OF WATER	197	3	DON JUAN	9	29	3
OF BLOOD AND WATER LEADEN CASTLEREAGH	207	3	DON JUAN	9	50	6
SHE SHOWED A GREAT DISLIKE TO HOLY WATER	252	3	DON JUAN	10	56	4
THAT WATER LAND OF DUTCHMEN AND OF DITCHES	256	3	DON JUAN	10	63	2
TO THOSE WHO UPON LAND OR WATER DWELL	259	3	DON JUAN	10	69	6
IN CURRENTS THROUGH THE CALMER WATER SPREAD	385	3	DON JUAN	13	57	4
WHO PASS LIKE WATER FILTERED IN A TANK	396	3	DON JUAN	13	80	3
BOATS WHEN 'TWAS WATER SKAITING WHEN 'TWAS ICE	407	3	DON JUAN	13	106	3
EMBARRASS'D SOMEWHAT BOTH WITH FIRE AND WATER	423	3	DON JUAN	14	30	8
AND GATHER'D AS THEY RUN LIKE GROWING WATER	448	3	DON JUAN	14	88	6
TILL SKIMM'D--AND THEN THERE WAS SOME MILK AND WATER . .	474	3	DON JUAN	15	41	4
BLOOD IS NOT WATER AND WHERE SHALL WE FIND	475	3	DON JUAN	15	44	4
SOUNDING LIKE VERY SUPERNATURAL WATER	556	3	DON JUAN	16	114	4
THE OLD HEN--BY RUNNING HEADLONG TO THE WATER	564	3	DON JUAN	17	4	8
WATER-DROPS							
ITS STORMS EXPIRE IN WATER-DROPS THE EYE	270	2	DON JUAN	2	214	6
WATERED							
LIKE FLOWERS WELL WATERED AFTER A LONG DROUTH-- . . .	213	3	DON JUAN	9	61	4
THEIR FEE BUT ERE THE WATERED WHEELS MAY HISS HENCE . .	379	3	DON JUAN	13	46	7
WATERFALL							
BACK TO THE NIGHT WIND BY THE WATERFALL	388	3	DON JUAN	13	63	7
WATER-FRETTED							
OF AGES ON ITS WATER-FRETTED HALLS	362	2	DON JUAN	4	33	3
WATER-LILIES							
LIKE WATER-LILIES FLOATING DOWN A RILL	22	3	DON JUAN	6	33	6
WATERLOO							
PERHAPS AS SHOOTING THEM AT WATERLOO	93	2	DON JUAN	1	132	8
AS SAY THAT WELLINGTON AT WATERLOO	136	3	DON JUAN	8	48	7
AND WATERLOO HAS MADE THE WORLD YOUR DEBTOR--	184	3	DON JUAN	9	3	7
SAVE YOU AND YOURS HAVE GAINED BY WATERLOO	184	3	DON JUAN	9	4	8
HAD BONAPARTE WON AT WATERLOO	449	3	DON JUAN	14	90	1
WATER'S							
MEN REALLY KNOW NOT WHAT GOOD WATER'S WORTH	201	2	DON JUAN	2	84	4
WATERS							
BY DISTANCE MELLOW'D O'ER THE WATERS SWEEP	87	2	DON JUAN	1	122	4
OR LULL'D BY FALLING WATERS SWEET THE HUM	88	2	DON JUAN	1	123	6
I CAST THEE ON THE WATERS GO THY WAYS	149	2	DON JUAN	1	222	1
THE GROWING WATERS IT UNMANS ONE QUITE	163	2	DON JUAN	2	12	3
BY BABEL'S WATERS STILL REMEMBERING SION	165	2	DON JUAN	2	16	2
FAREWELL WHERE GUADALQUIVIR'S WATERS GLIDE	166	2	DON JUAN	2	18	5
OVER THE WASTE OF WATERS LIKE A VEIL	182	2	DON JUAN	2	49	2
THE WATERS BEAT WHILE HE THERETO WAS LASH'D	212	2	DON JUAN	2	107	6
THE WATERS AND REPENTANCE FOR PAST SINNING	414	2	DON JUAN	5	6	5
AS ROLL THE WATERS TO THE BREATHING WIND	90	3	DON JUAN	7	48	3
AND IN THE DANUBE'S WATERS SHONE THE SAME--	115	3	DON JUAN	8	6	4
AND REDLY RAN HIS BLUSHING WATERS DOWN	175	3	DON JUAN	8	127	4
OR LIKE THE RHONE BY LEMAN'S WATERS WASH'D	447	3	DON JUAN	14	87	4
WATERY							
PURSUED O'ER THE HIGH SEAS HIS WATERY JOURNEY	283	2	DON JUAN	3	14	7
THAT WATERY OUTLINE OF ETERNITY	457	3	DON JUAN	15	2	5
WAVE							
AND DOWN SHE SUCK'D WITH HER THE WHIRLING WAVE	184	2	DON JUAN	2	52	6
LEFT HIM SO DRUNK HE JUMP'D INTO THE WAVE	186	2	DON JUAN	2	57	3
AS EVERY RISING WAVE HIS DREAD RENEW'D	187	2	DON JUAN	2	59	5
THOUGH EVERY WAVE ROLL'D MENACING TO FILL	188	2	DON JUAN	2	61	5
'TWAS BORNE BY THE RUDE WAVE WHEREIN 'TWAS CAST	204	2	DON JUAN	2	90	6
WITH THE QUICK WAVE AND GAIN ERE IT WAS DARK	212	2	DON JUAN	2	106	3
AND THE HARD WAVE O'ERWHELM'D HIM AS 'TWAS DASH'D . . .	212	2	DON JUAN	2	107	4

891

WAVE   (CONTINUED)

	PAGE	VOL	CANTO		STANZA	LN
FAST TO THE SAND LEST THE RETURNING WAVE	213	2	DON JUAN	2	108	2
BRIGHT HUES WHEN OUT OF DOORS AND YET WHILE WAVE	220	2	DON JUAN	2	120	5
(LEUCADIA'S ROCK STILL OVERLOOKS THE WAVE)	266	2	DON JUAN	2	205	6
ROOTED WHERE ONCE THE ADRIAN WAVE FLOW'D O'ER	337	2	DON JUAN	3	105	4
GREW AND EACH WAVE ROSE ROUGHLY THREATENING HER	361	2	DON JUAN	4	31	4
THE WIND SWEPT DOWN THE EUXINE AND THE WAVE	413	2	DON JUAN	5	5	1
AS VENUS ROSE WITH FROM THE WAVE ON THEM	466	2	DON JUAN	5	96	2
UNLESS COMPELLED BY FATE OR WAVE OR WIND	139	3	DON JUAN	8	54	1
ARE THEY--NOW FURIOUS AS THE SWEEPING WAVE	164	3	DON JUAN	8	106	5
GLIMMER ON HIGH THEIR BURIED LOCKS STILL WAVE	509	3	DON JUAN	16	19	3

WAVED

	PAGE	VOL	CANTO		STANZA	LN
WAVED AND O'ERSHADING HER WAN CHEEK APPEARS	108	2	DON JUAN	1	158	4
THAT WAVED IN FOREST-TOPS AND SMOOTH'D THE AIR	210	2	DON JUAN	2	103	4
THROUGH THE WAVED BRANCHES O'ER THE GREENSWARD GLANCING	290	2	DON JUAN	3	29	3
BELOW HIS WINDOW WAVED (OF COURSE) A WILLOW	507	3	DON JUAN	16	15	6
WAVED O'ER HIS COUCH HE MEDITATED FOND	555	3	DON JUAN	16	110	6

WAVERING

	PAGE	VOL	CANTO		STANZA	LN
DIPLOMATISTS OF RATHER WAVERING KINGS	287	3	DON JUAN	11	40	3
A WAVERING SPIRIT MAY BE EASIER WRECK'D	446	3	DON JUAN	14	85	5

WAVE'S

	PAGE	VOL	CANTO		STANZA	LN
THOUGH ON THE WAVE'S HIGH TOP TOO MUCH TO SET	188	2	DON JUAN	2	60	3
THEY HEARD THE WAVE'S SPLASH AND THE WIND SO LOW	253	2	DON JUAN	2	185	5

WAVES

	PAGE	VOL	CANTO		STANZA	LN
AS ROLL THE WAVES BEFORE THE SETTLED WIND	133	2	DON JUAN	1	196	4
AND THE WAVES OOZING THROUGH THE PORT-HOLE MADE	169	2	DON JUAN	2	25	7
THE HOARSE HARSH WAVES KEPT TIME FRIGHT CURED THE QUALMS	174	2	DON JUAN	2	34	5
THERE WINDS AND WAVES HAD HURL'D THEM AND FROM THENCE	177	2	DON JUAN	2	40	1
AT MERCY OF THE WAVES WHOSE MERCIES ARE	178	2	DON JUAN	2	42	7
FROM GLISTENING WAVES AND SKIES SO HOT AND BARE--	210	2	DON JUAN	2	103	6
AND GIRT BY FORMIDABLE WAVES BUT THEY	211	2	DON JUAN	2	104	2
CHECKS TO A LAKE WHOSE WAVES IN CIRCLES SPREAD	231	2	DON JUAN	2	141	7
THE SANDS UNTUMBLED THE BLUE WAVES UNTOST	251	2	DON JUAN	2	181	4
BY WINDS AND WAVES AND SOME IMPORTANT CAPTURES	283	2	DON JUAN	3	15	2
HER HAIR'S LONG AUBURN WAVES DOWN TO HER HEEL	313	2	DON JUAN	3	73	1
WHERE NOTHING SAVE THE WAVES AND I	326	2	DON JUAN	3	L 16	2
WHERE WAVES MIGHT WASH AND SEALS MIGHT BREED AND LURK	362	2	DON JUAN	4	33	4
A RUEFUL GLANCE UPON THE WAVES (WHICH BRIGHT ALL	393	2	DON JUAN	4	90	5
AS ON THE BEACH THE WAVES AT LAST ARE BROKE	402	2	DON JUAN	4	106	5
WAVES AT SPRING-TIDE OR WOMEN ANYWHERE	23	3	DON JUAN	6	34	3
NEITHER CAME CROWDING LIKE THE WAVES OF OCEAN	42	3	DON JUAN	6	71	4
OF MURMURING LIBERTY'S WIDE WAVES WHICH BLEND	52	3	DON JUAN	6	93	6
BE HIDDEN BY THE ROLLING WAVES WHICH HIDE	63	3	DON JUAN	6	115	2
OF STUBBORN SHELL WHICH WAVES AND WEATHER WEAR NOT	431	3	DON JUAN	14	49	4
OF EMPIRES HEAVE BUT LIKE SOME PASSING WAVES	500	3	DON JUAN	15	99	8

WAVE-WORN

	PAGE	VOL	CANTO		STANZA	LN
SHE AND HER WAVE-WORN LOVE HAD MADE THEIR BOWER	262	2	DON JUAN	2	198	5

WAVING

	PAGE	VOL	CANTO		STANZA	LN
WAX'D BROAD AND WAVING LIKE A BANNER FREE	204	2	DON JUAN	2	91	6
THE FIRST AND TALLEST HER WHITE KERCHIEF WAVING	291	2	DON JUAN	3	30	2
WAVING LIKE SAILS NEW SHIVERED IN A STORM	204	3	DON JUAN	9	43	3
AIR CAN ACCOMPLISH WITH HIS WIDE WINGS WAVING	263	3	DON JUAN	10	78	4

WAX

	PAGE	VOL	CANTO		STANZA	LN
AND THE FAR MOUNTAINS WAX A LITTLE HOARY	94	2	DON JUAN	1	134	4
THE WAX WAS SUPERFINE ITS HUE VERMILLION	134	2	DON JUAN	1	198	8
THIS SPIRIT'S WELL BUT IT MAY WAX TOO BOLD	454	2	DON JUAN	5	75	3
BUT WHEN SHE SAW HIS DAZZLING EYE WAX DIM	246	3	DON JUAN	10	44	5
IS WAX HEAVEN IS NOT LOVE 'TIS MATRIMONY	322	3	DON JUAN	12	14	8
AND WAX AN ULTRA-ROYALIST IN LOYALTY	466	3	DON JUAN	15	23	7
THESE SEALS UPON HER WAX MADE NO IMPRESSION	480	3	DON JUAN	15	57	7
THAN TO WAX WHITE--FOR BLUSHES ARE FOR QUALITY	532	3	DON JUAN	16	64	8

WAX'D

	PAGE	VOL	CANTO		STANZA	LN
YOUNG JUAN WAX'D IN GOODLINESS AND GRACE	48	2	DON JUAN	1	49	1
WAX'D BROAD AND WAVING LIKE A BANNER FREE	204	2	DON JUAN	2	91	6
BACK TO OLD THOUGHTS WAX'D FULL OF FEARFUL MEANING	379	2	DON JUAN	4	64	8

WAXED

	PAGE	VOL	CANTO		STANZA	LN
AND THOUGH THE DUTY WAXED A LITTLE HARD	235	3	DON JUAN	10	22	2
MOCK TYRANTS WHEN ROME'S ANNALS WAXED BUT DIRTY	299	3	DON JUAN	11	61	8

WAXEN

	PAGE	VOL	CANTO		STANZA	LN
WHITE WAXEN AND AS ALABASTER PALE	60	3	DON JUAN	6	109	4

WAXING

	PAGE	VOL	CANTO		STANZA	LN
THAT EACH PULLED DIFFERENT WAYS--AND WAXING ROUGH	395	2	DON JUAN	4	93	V7
THINGS SPEEDILY WERE WAXING TO EXTREMITY	92	3	DON JUAN	7	51	V6
THEIR BAFFLED RAGE AND PAIN WHILE WAXING COLDER	158	3	DON JUAN	8	94	5
WHERE HIS ASSETS WERE WAXING RATHER FEW	240	3	DON JUAN	10	31	3
THROUGH CROWDS AND CARRIAGES BUT WAXING THINNER	282	3	DON JUAN	11	29	2
AND WAXING CHILLER IN HER COURTESY	430	3	DON JUAN	14	46	6

WAY

	PAGE	VOL	CANTO		STANZA	LN
WHAT WENT BEFORE--BY WAY OF EPISODE	24	2	DON JUAN	1	6	4
MY WAY IS TO BEGIN WITH THE BEGINNING	25	2	DON JUAN	1	7	2
IN THEIR OWN WAY BY ALL THE THINGS THAT SHE DID	26	2	DON JUAN	1	10	8
AND ALL MAY THINK WHICH WAY THEIR JUDGMENTS LEAN 'EM	28	2	DON JUAN	1	14	6
WAS ORNAMENTED IN A SORT OF WAY	47	2	DON JUAN	1	46	2
SHE KEPT HER COUNSEL IN SO CLOSE A WAY	59	2	DON JUAN	1	68	8
I MEAN THE SERAPH WAY OF THOSE ABOVE	67	2	DON JUAN	1	85	8
SEES HALF THE BUSINESS IN A WICKED WAY	82	2	DON JUAN	1	113	6
OH PLATO PLATO YOU HAVE PAVED THE WAY	84	2	DON JUAN	1	116	1
WITH WAR OR PLAGUE OR FAMINE ANY WAY	92	2	DON JUAN	1	131	5
PRESCRIBED BY WAY OF BLISTER A YOUNG BELLE	113	2	DON JUAN	1	168	4

WAY   (CONTINUED)

PERHAPS 'TWAS IN A DIFFERENT WAY APPLIED 113   2 DON JUAN   1   168   7
LIKE THROWING JUAN IN ALFONSO'S WAY 118   2 DON JUAN   1   177   8
AND THEN HIS ONLY GARMENT QUITE GAVE WAY 124   2 DON JUAN   1   186   6
WHO FAVOURS WHAT SHE SHOULD NOT FOUND HIS WAY 126   2 DON JUAN   1   188   3
FOUND--GOD KNOWS HOW--HIS SOLITARY WAY 126   2 DON JUAN   1   188   V3
SINCE IN A WAY THAT'S RATHER OF THE ODDEST HE 157   2 DON JUAN   2   1   7
JUAN EMBARK'D--THE SHIP GOT UNDER WAY 162   2 DON JUAN   2   11   1
THE WATER RUSH'D THROUGH IN A WAY QUITE PUZZLING . . . 171   2 DON JUAN   2   28   7
IN MY YOUNG DAYS THEY LENT ME CASH THAT WAY 190   2 DON JUAN   2   65   7
BEARS VEGETABLES IN A GRUMBLING WAY 191   2 DON JUAN   2   67   6
WHICH IN THEIR WAY THAT MOMENT CHANCED TO FALL 206   2 DON JUAN   2   95   7
THE BOAT MADE WAY YET NOW THEY WERE SO LOW 207   2 DON JUAN   2   96   3
WAS NOT EXACTLY THE BEST WAY TO SAVE 225   2 DON JUAN   2   130   2
JUST IN THE WAY WE VERY OFTEN SEE 244   2 DON JUAN   2   167   8
CHASTE READER THEN IN ANY WAY TO PUT 282   2 DON JUAN   3   12   3
THE MERCHANDISE WAS SERVED IN THE SAME WAY 284   2 DON JUAN   3   17   1
TO ASK HIM AWKWARD QUESTIONS ON THE WAY 286   2 DON JUAN   3   20   3
WITH A PECULIAR SMILE WHICH BY THE WAY 297   2 DON JUAN   3   42   3
ON TO THE HOUSE BUT BY A PRIVATE WAY 300   2 DON JUAN   3   49   2
DREST IN THE WAY THAT ARISTIPPUS WISHES 307   2 DON JUAN   3   62   V5
LIKE SMALL STARS THROUGH THE MILKY WAY APPARENT . . . 315   2 DON JUAN   3   77   4
AND NOT THE FIX'D--HE KNEW THE WAY TO WHEEDLE 317   2 DON JUAN   3   80   4
BUT HIS LIFE FALLING INTO JOHNSON'S WAY 328   2 DON JUAN   3   91   5
WORDSWORTH'S LAST QUARTO BY THE WAY IS BIGGER 330   2 DON JUAN   3   94   5
OF GETTING INTO HEAVEN THE SHORTEST WAY 336   2 DON JUAN   3   104   5
OR FILLS WITH LOVE THE PILGRIM ON HIS WAY 338   2 DON JUAN   3   108   4
THIS WAY OF WRITING WILL APPEAR EXOTIC 347   2 DON JUAN   4   6   2
AND THEN GIVE WAY SUBDUED BECAUSE SURROUNDED 373   2 DON JUAN   4   54   6
HAD HELD TILL NOW HER SOFT AND MILKY WAY 375   2 DON JUAN   4   57   5
BUT BEING QUALIFIED IN ONE WAY YET 391   2 DON JUAN   4   86   3
EXCEPT IN SUCH A WAY AS NOT TO ATTRACT 412   2 DON JUAN   5   2   2
BUT THAT'S HER WAY WITH ALL MEN TILL THEY'RE TRIED . . 418   2 DON JUAN   5   14   5
THIS SKIN MUST GO THE WAY TOO OF ALL FLESH 422   2 DON JUAN   5   22   3
THEY ALMOST LOST THEIR WAY AND HAD TO PICK IT-- . . . 433   2 DON JUAN   5   41   5
AS THEY WERE PLODDING ON THEIR WINDING WAY 434   2 DON JUAN   5   42   1
AS THEY WERE THREADING ON THEIR WAY THERE CAME 434   2 DON JUAN   5   43   1
GAVE LIGHT ENOUGH TO HINT THEIR FARTHER WAY 442   2 DON JUAN   5   56   2
AS IF THE MILKY WAY THEIR FEET WAS UNDER 450   2 DON JUAN   5   66   4
IF THEY WOULD BUT PURSUE THE PROPER WAY 451   2 DON JUAN   5   69   4
TO FIND OUR WAY TO MARMORA WITHOUT BOATS 464   2 DON JUAN   5   92   6
WITH THIS ENCOURAGEMENT HE LED THE WAY 465   2 DON JUAN   5   93   1
QUITE IN A CONFIDENTIAL QUEENLY WAY 466   2 DON JUAN   5   95   3
THE SPIRIT IN THE END WILL HAVE ITS WAY 474   2 DON JUAN   5   110   8
HER EYE IN PASSING ON HIS WAY TO SALE 477   2 DON JUAN   5   114   2
AT LENGTH IN AN IMPERIAL WAY SHE LAID 483   2 DON JUAN   5   125   1
OF LADIES WHO CANNOT HAVE THEIR OWN WAY 487   2 DON JUAN   5   132   4
TO HINT THAT HE IS COMING UP THIS WAY 494   2 DON JUAN   5   144   8
BUT BID MY WOMEN FORM THE MILKY WAY 494   2 DON JUAN   5   145   3
BELOVED IN HER OWN WAY AND RATHER WHISK   7   3 DON JUAN   6   3   4
AND AT THE USUAL SIGNAL TA'EN THEIR WAY 19   3 DON JUAN   6   26   4
YET HE COULD NOT AT TIMES KEEP BY THE WAY 20   3 DON JUAN   6   29   4
BY WAY OF CHANGE FROM THEIR SEPULCHRAL SITES 38   3 DON JUAN   6   64   6
THEIR WAY THROUGH HER SEALED EYELIDS' GLOSSY FRINGES . 40   3 DON JUAN   6   67   V7
THERE WAS A WAY TO END THEIR STRIFE ALTHOUGH 53   3 DON JUAN   6   95   4
THEIR WORK EVEN BY THE WAY IN WHICH HE TRODE 61   3 DON JUAN   6   111   8
THAT KILLING HIM IS NOT THE WAY TO CURE YOU 63   3 DON JUAN   6   115   8
IN WHAT WAY FEMININE CAPRICE MAY DISSIPATE 65   3 DON JUAN   6   119   8
ASSUME THEN LEAVE US ON OUR FREEZING WAY 66   3 DON JUAN   7   1   8
TO SHOW YE WHAT YE ARE IN EVERY WAY 70   3 DON JUAN   7   7   4
NOR WORK ADVANCE NOR COVERED WAY WAS THERE 72   3 DON JUAN   7   11   7
THE RUSS FLOTILLA GETTING UNDER WAY 81   3 DON JUAN   7   29   2
I CANNOT TELL THE WAY IN WHICH HE PLEADED 85   3 DON JUAN   7   38   4
BY WAY OF LESSON AGAINST ACTUAL TURKS 93   3 DON JUAN   7   53   4
TO BE DISPOSED OF IN A WAY SO NEW 101   3 DON JUAN   7   67   3
SUGGESTED SOME SLIGHT COMFORT IN HIS WAY 105   3 DON JUAN   7   75   3
TO BREATHE DESTRUCTION ON ITS WINDING WAY 113   3 DON JUAN   8   2   6
THE WAY WHICH THEY HAD NEVER TROD BEFORE 120   3 DON JUAN   8   19   3
THEN LIKE AN ASS HE WENT UPON HIS WAY 126   3 DON JUAN   8   30   1
HIS WAY TO--WHERE HE KNEW NOT--SINGLE HANDED 127   3 DON JUAN   8   32   3
HAD PALISADOED IN A WAY YOU'D WONDER 136   3 DON JUAN   8   46   4
SO MUCH FOR NATURE--BY WAY OF VARIETY 146   3 DON JUAN   8   68   1
ITS SANGUINARY WAY GOOD--THEN ANOTHER 146   3 DON JUAN   8   69   2
OF MURDERED WOMEN WHO HAD FOUND THEIR WAY 157   3 DON JUAN   8   91   3
THE READIEST WAY OF REASONING WITH COSSACQUES 158   3 DON JUAN   8   93   8
JOHNSON WHO REALLY LOVED HIM IN HIS WAY 162   3 DON JUAN   8   102   2
TO ANSWER RIBAS' SUMMONS TO GIVE WAY 171   3 DON JUAN   8   120   8
WAS LEFT UPON HIS WAY TO THE CHIEF CITY 194   3 DON JUAN   9   23   2
WAS LEFT UPON HIS WAY WITH THE DISPATCH 197   3 DON JUAN   9   29   2
YOUR FORTUNE WAS IN A FAIR WAY TO SWELL 214   3 DON JUAN   9   63   6
OF OUR SENSATIONS WHAT A CURIOUS WAY 220   3 DON JUAN   9   75   7
OF ANY SLIGHT TEMPTATION IN THEIR WAY 235   3 DON JUAN 10   21   4
PERCEIVING HE WAS IN A HANDSOME WAY 239   3 DON JUAN 10   30   2
BUT WENT TO HEAVEN IN AS SINCERE A WAY 242   3 DON JUAN 10   35   2
THIS IS THE WAY PHYSICIANS MEND OR END US 245   3 DON JUAN 10   42   1
SO CATHERINE WHO HAD A HANDSOME WAY 247   3 DON JUAN 10   46   1
BUT SHOULD WE WISH TO WARM US ON OUR WAY 254   3 DON JUAN 10   59   6
SUCH IS THE SHORTEST WAY TO GENERAL CURSES 264   3 DON JUAN 10   79   4
GAVE WAY TO'T SINCE HE COULD NOT OVERCOME IT 272   3 DON JUAN 11   9   4

WAY   (CONTINUED)

	PAGE	VOL		CANTO	STANZA	LN
I HEARD THEM WISH GOD WITH YOU SAVE THAT WAY--	274	3	DON JUAN	11	12	8
TO WELCOME FOREIGNERS IN THIS WAY NOW	275	3	DON JUAN	11	15	2
IN THUNDER HOLDS THE WAY IT CAN'T WELL MISS	277	3	DON JUAN	11	20	6
BUT THE OLD WAY IS BEST FOR THE PURBLIND	281	3	DON JUAN	11	27	4
A DOOR THAT'S IN OR BOUDOIR OUT OF THE WAY	303	3	DON JUAN	11	69	3
TO LEAN ON FOR SUPPORT IN ANY WAY	324	3	DON JUAN	12	18	6
THEIR WAY THROUGH VIRTUE'S PRIMROSE PATHS OF SNOWS	328	3	DON JUAN	12	26	4
A SLIGHT OBSERVER IN A MODEST WAY)	336	3	DON JUAN	12	44	2
WHAT YOUR INTENTIONS ARE--ONE WAY OR OTHER	343	3	DON JUAN	12	60	5
TO SHOW THE PEOPLE THE BEST WAY TO BREAK	357	3	DON JUAN	12	89	4
GIVE GENTLY WAY WHEN THERE'S TOO GREAT A PRESS	366	3	DON JUAN	13	18	5
BY A RIVER WHICH ITS SOFTEN'D WAY DID TAKE	385	3	DON JUAN	13	57	3
HER WAY BACK TO THE WORLD BY DINT OF PLOTTERY	397	3	DON JUAN	13	82	6
BY WAY OF SPRINKLING SCATTER'D AMONGST THESE	397	3	DON JUAN	13	83	7
AT ONCE WITHOUT INSTALMENTS (AN OLD WAY	412	3	DON JUAN	14	4	5
FOR WHICH MY SOLE EXCUSE IS--'TIS MY WAY	413	3	DON JUAN	14	7	3
FLING UP A STRAW 'TWILL SHOW THE WAY THE WIND BLOWS	414	3	DON JUAN	14	8	2
WHEN YOUR AFFAIRS COME ROUND ONE WAY OR T'OTHER	431	3	DON JUAN	14	48	7
WHO IN HER WAY TOO WAS A HEROINE	449	3	DON JUAN	14	90	8
THE SUREST WAY FOR LADIES AND FOR BOOKS	453	3	DON JUAN	14	97	7
CONSIDERABLE TALENT IN MY WAY	453	3	DON JUAN	14	98	8
YOU SHOULD BE CIVIL IN A MODEST WAY	459	3	DON JUAN	15	9	6
THEY ARE WRONG--THAT'S NOT THE WAY TO SET ABOUT IT	461	3	DON JUAN	15	13	1
THEIR TUMBLE I SHOULD TURN THE OTHER WAY	466	3	DON JUAN	15	23	6
PERHAPS SHE DID NOT LIKE THE QUIET WAY	479	3	DON JUAN	15	53	1
I SAY IN MY SLIGHT WAY I MAY PROCEED	482	3	DON JUAN	15	60	1
THAN COULD ROAST BEEF IN OUR ROUGH JOHN BULL WAY	487	3	DON JUAN	15	71	4
BUT JUAN HAD A SORT OF WINNING WAY	492	3	DON JUAN	15	82	1
IN VIRGINS--ALWAYS IN A MODEST WAY	494	3	DON JUAN	15	86	7
AND THEREFORE THOUGH 'TIS BY NO MEANS MY WAY	500	3	DON JUAN	15	98	1
FAIR ADELINE THOUGH IN A CARELESS WAY	521	3	DON JUAN	16	42	1
HAD STIRRED HIM ANSWERED IN A WAY TO CLOUD IT	527	3	DON JUAN	16	54	8
FIVE AS THEY MIGHT DO IN A MODEST WAY	548	3	DON JUAN	16	99	3
WE LITTLE PEOPLE IN OUR LESSER WAY	566	3	DON JUAN	17	10	2

WAY'S

	PAGE	VOL		CANTO	STANZA	LN
IF BAD THE BEST WAY'S CERTAINLY TO TEAZE ON	478	3	DON JUAN	15	51	3

WAYS

	PAGE	VOL		CANTO	STANZA	LN
ARE WAYS TO BENEFIT MANKIND AS TRUE	93	2	DON JUAN	1	132	7
THE PATH IS THROUGH PERPLEXING WAYS AND WHEN	93	2	DON JUAN	1	133	7
I CAST THEE ON THE WATERS GO THY WAYS	149	2	DON JUAN	1	222	2
WAS MINGLED WITH HIS EVIL DEEDS AND WAYS	303	2	DON JUAN	3	55	V2
THAT EACH PULL'D DIFFERENT WAYS WITH MANY AN OATH	394	2	DON JUAN	4	93	7
THAT EACH PULLED DIFFERENT WAYS--AND WAXING ROUGH	395	2	DON JUAN	4	93	V7
IN ALL WHO O'ER THE GREAT DEEP TAKE THEIR WAYS	414	2	DON JUAN	5	6	6
WHILE NATURE TORTURED TWENTY THOUSAND WAYS	440	2	DON JUAN	5	52	6
HIM WHOM SHE MEANT TO TUTOR IN LOVE'S WAYS	482	2	DON JUAN	5	122	5
HIS DAILY COUNCIL UPON WAYS AND MEANS	54	3	DON JUAN	6	96	2
ESPECIALLY SULTANAS AND THEIR WAYS	64	3	DON JUAN	6	117	4
WITH ALL THEIR PRETTY MILK-AND-WATER WAYS	156	3	DON JUAN	8	90	4
AS HUMAN BEINGS OR HIS WAYS ARE ODD	163	3	DON JUAN	8	104	4
SOUNDS THE HEROIC SYLLABLES BOTH WAYS	183	3	DON JUAN	9	1	2
HAD FEATHERS WHEN A TRAVELLER ON DEEP WAYS IS	197	3	DON JUAN	9	30	8
THE WAYS THAT LEAD THERE BE THEY NEAR OR FAR	222	3	DON JUAN	9	80	3
WITH SLIGHT EXCEPTIONS ALL THE WAYS SEEM ONE	279	3	DON JUAN	11	23	4
OUR PASSIONS AND WE WALK IN WISDOM'S WAYS	360	3	DON JUAN	13	4	6
BEING NO SIBYL IN THE NEW WORLD'S WAYS	480	3	DON JUAN	15	56	6
(OH PROVIDENCE HOW WONDROUS ARE THY WAYS	540	3	DON JUAN	16	82	5
OF WHAT IS CALLED THE WORLD AND THE WORLD'S WAYS	554	3	DON JUAN	16	108	3

WE

	PAGE	VOL		CANTO	STANZA	LN
IF WE MAY JUDGE OF MATTER BY THE MIND	18	2	DON JUAN	D	15	1
WE ALL HAVE SEEN HIM IN THE PANTOMIME	21	2	DON JUAN	1	1	7
WERE FRENCH AND FAMOUS PEOPLE AS WE KNOW	22	2	DON JUAN	1	3	3
BY CONTRAST WHICH IS WHAT WE JUST WERE WISHING ALL	37	2	DON JUAN	1	31	6
FOR THERE WE HAVE THEM ALL AT ONE FELL SWOOP	46	2	DON JUAN	1	45	1
PREFERENCE THAT WE MUST FEEL UPON OCCASION	63	2	DON JUAN	1	77	6
OR TRANSPORT AS WE KNEW ALL THAT BEFORE	69	2	DON JUAN	1	89	7
AND EVERY NOW AND THEN WE READ THEM THROUGH	70	2	DON JUAN	1	90	6
EVEN AS THE PAGE IS RUSTLED WHILE WE LOOK	72	2	DON JUAN	1	95	3
BAY DEEP-MOUTH'D WELCOME AS WE DRAW NEAR HOME	88	2	DON JUAN	1	123	2
OUR COMING AND LOOK BRIGHTER WHEN WE COME	88	2	DON JUAN	1	123	4
DEAR IS THE HELPLESS CREATURE WE DEFEND	90	2	DON JUAN	1	126	6
WE NE'ER FORGET THOUGH THERE WE ARE FORGOT	90	2	DON JUAN	1	126	8
WE NE'ER FORGET THOUGH THERE WE ARE FORGOT	90	2	DON JUAN	1	126	8
WHAT OPPOSITE DISCOVERIES WE HAVE SEEN	91	2	DON JUAN	1	129	1
THE GOAL IS GAIN'D WE DIE YOU KNOW--AND THEN--	93	2	DON JUAN	1	133	8
AND SO GOOD NIGHT--RETURN WE TO OUR STORY	94	2	DON JUAN	1	134	2
AND THAT THEY HAVE BEEN SO WE ALL HAVE READ	95	2	DON JUAN	1	136	5
IS IT FOR THIS WE WERE THE ONLY PAIR	102	2	DON JUAN	1	148	V3
A MOMENT AT THE DOOR THAT WE MAY BE	106	2	DON JUAN	1	156	7
SO MUCH AS WHEN WE CALL OUR OLD DEBTS IN	113	2	DON JUAN	1	167	6
AND IF WE CAN BUT TILL THE MORNING KEEP	115	2	DON JUAN	1	172	7
THEY BLUSH AND WE BELIEVE THEM AT LEAST I	119	2	DON JUAN	1	179	1
A TEAR OR TWO AND THEN WE MAKE IT UP	119	2	DON JUAN	1	179	7
MEN HAVE ALL THESE RESOURCES WE BUT ONE	131	2	DON JUAN	1	194	7
AND IF THEIR APPROBATION WE EXPERIENCE	135	2	DON JUAN	1	199	7
WHICH OUT OF ALL THE LOVELY THINGS WE SEE	144	2	DON JUAN	1	214	3
OF WHICH WE ARE LAVISH FIRST AND THEN RAPACIOUS	145	2	DON JUAN	1	217	V8
WE MEET AGAIN IF WE SHOULD UNDERSTAND	147	2	DON JUAN	1	221	5

WE (CONTINUED)

	PAGE	VOL	CANTO	STANZA	LN
WE MEET AGAIN IF WE SHOULD UNDERSTAND	147	2 DON JUAN	1	221	5
AND DEEMS HE THAT WE ALWAYS WILL FORBEAR	153	2 DON JUAN	1	V 4	4
BUT WHY--WE LEAVE THE READER IN THE DARK--	161	2 DON JUAN	2	8	4
WE ENTER ON OUR NAUTICAL EXISTENCE	163	2 DON JUAN	2	12	8
AND IF WE NOW AND THEN A SIGH MUST HEAVE	164	2 DON JUAN	2	15	5
AT QUITTING EVEN THOSE WE QUIT IN STRIFE	164	2 DON JUAN	2	15	6
NO DOUBT WE WEEP FOR THOSE THE HEART ENDEARS--	164	2 DON JUAN	2	15	7
OR DEATH OF THOSE WE DOTE ON WHEN A PART	167	2 DON JUAN	2	21	5
EASED HER AT LAST (ALTHOUGH WE NEVER MEANT	173	2 DON JUAN	2	32	6
(FOR SOMETIMES WE MUST BOX WITHOUT THE MUFFLE)	205	2 DON JUAN	2	92	8
AS ONCE (A FEAT ON WHICH OURSELVES WE PRIDED)	211	2 DON JUAN	2	105	7
THE SORT OF SOUND WE ECHO WITH A TEAR	236	2 DON JUAN	2	151	6
FOR WE ALL KNOW THAT ENGLISH PEOPLE ARE	238	2 DON JUAN	2	156	1
WE KNOW TOO THEY ARE VERY FOND OF WAR	238	2 DON JUAN	2	156	5
RETURN WE TO DON JUAN HE BEGUN	244	2 DON JUAN	2	167	1
JUST IN THE WAY WE VERY OFTEN SEE	244	2 DON JUAN	2	167	8
THERE LIES THE THING WE LOVE WITH ALL ITS ERRORS	261	2 DON JUAN	2	197	7
FOR AFTER ALL WE CANNOT CALL THEE DEVIL	266	2 DON JUAN	2	205	8
A LOVELY STATUE WE ALMOST ADORE	269	2 DON JUAN	2	211	6
FOR SURELY IF WE ALWAYS COULD PERCEIVE	270	2 DON JUAN	2	213	2
(FOR WE MUST GET THEM ANYHOW OR GRIEVE)	270	2 DON JUAN	2	213	6
HAIL MUSE ET CETERA--WE LEFT JUAN SLEEPING	274	2 DON JUAN	3	1	1
THUS THE FRAIL BEINGS WE WOULD FONDLY CHERISH	275	2 DON JUAN	3	2	7
WHEN WE HAVE WHAT WE LIKE 'TIS HARD TO MISS IT	282	2 DON JUAN	3	13	5
WHEN WE HAVE WHAT WE LIKE 'TIS HARD TO MISS IT	282	2 DON JUAN	3	13	5
IN WHOM OUR BRIGHTEST DAYS WE WOULD RETRACE	305	2 DON JUAN	3	59	3
WITH ALL WE CAN IMAGINE OF THE SKIES	313	2 DON JUAN	3	74	4
MUST WE BUT WEEP O'ER DAYS MORE BLEST	323	2 DON JUAN	3	L 7	1
MUST WE BUT BLUSH--OUR FATHERS BLED	323	2 DON JUAN	3	L 7	2
BUT ONE ARISE--WE COME WE COME	323	2 DON JUAN	3	L 8	5
BUT ONE ARISE--WE COME WE COME	323	2 DON JUAN	3	L 8	5
WE WILL NOT THINK OF THEMES LIKE THESE	324	2 DON JUAN	3	L 11	2
MILTON'S THE PRINCE OF POETS--SO WE SAY	328	2 DON JUAN	3	91	1
WE LEARN FROM HORACE HOMER SOMETIMES SLEEPS	333	2 DON JUAN	3	98	1
WE FEEL WITHOUT HIM WORDSWORTH SOMETIMES WAKES	333	2 DON JUAN	3	98	2
OF POPE AND DRYDEN ARE WE COME TO THIS	334	2 DON JUAN	3	100	2
OF VERSE (THE NAME WITH WHICH WE CANTABS PLEASE	341	2 DON JUAN	3	110	7
THE RACE HE SPRAINS A WING AND DOWN WE TEND	344	2 DON JUAN	4	1	4
TILL OUR OWN WEAKNESS SHOWS US WHAT WE ARE	344	2 DON JUAN	4	1	8
MAN--AND AS WE WOULD HOPE--PERHAPS THE DEVIL	345	2 DON JUAN	4	2	3
WE KNOW NOT THIS--THE BLOOD FLOWS ON TOO FAST	345	2 DON JUAN	4	2	6
WE PONDER DEEPLY ON EACH PAST EMOTION	345	2 DON JUAN	4	2	8
ITSELF TO APATHY FOR WE MUST STEEP	346	2 DON JUAN	4	4	4
ERE WHAT WE LEAST WISH TO BEHOLD WILL SLEEP	346	2 DON JUAN	4	4	6
AND WE ARE SICK OF ITS HACK SOUNDS AND SIGHTS	353	2 DON JUAN	4	17	4
INHERENT WHAT WE MORTALS CALL ROMANTIC	353	2 DON JUAN	4	18	7
AND ALWAYS ENVY THOUGH WE DEEM IT FRANTIC	353	2 DON JUAN	4	18	8
GOOD TO THE SOUL WHICH WE NO MORE CAN BIND	360	2 DON JUAN	4	30	6
AND WHO CAN KNOW ALL FALSE WHAT THEN WE SEE	360	2 DON JUAN	4	30	V8
WE WERE TRANSFER'D ON BOARD HER IN A HURRY	389	2 DON JUAN	4	82	5
WE WILL REVIVE OUR FORTUNES BEFORE LONG	389	2 DON JUAN	4	82	8
NO MATTER WE SHOULD NE'ER TOO MUCH INQUIRE	396	2 DON JUAN	4	96	1
WE WILL OMIT THE PROOFS SAVE ONE OR TWO	396	2 DON JUAN	4	96	4
SO LET US BE ACQUAINTED AS WE OUGHT	417	2 DON JUAN	5	13	6
WHERE STILL WE FLUTTER ON FOR PENCE OR PRAISE	422	2 DON JUAN	5	22	8
WE KNOW WHAT SLAVERY IS AND OUR DISASTERS	422	2 DON JUAN	5	23	7
WOULD WE WERE MASTERS NOW IF BUT TO TRY	423	2 DON JUAN	5	24	1
PERHAPS WE SHALL BE ONE DAY BY AND BY	423	2 DON JUAN	5	24	5
KINDNESS DESTROYS WHAT LITTLE WE HAD GOT	423	2 DON JUAN	5	25	6
BENEVOLENCE DESTROYS WHAT WE HAD GOT	423	2 DON JUAN	5	25	V6
ABOUT THE RIGHT DIVINE HOW FAR WE SHOULD	426	2 DON JUAN	5	30	5
BUT IT WAS ALL A MYSTERY HERE WE ARE	432	2 DON JUAN	5	39	1
AND THERE WE GO--BUT WHERE FIVE BITS OF LEAD	432	2 DON JUAN	5	39	2
AND AIR--EARTH--WATER--FIRE LIVE--AND WE DEAD	432	2 DON JUAN	5	39	6
WE WHOSE MINDS COMPREHEND ALL THINGS NO MORE	432	2 DON JUAN	5	39	7
IF WE SHOULD STRIKE A STROKE TO SET US FREE	434	2 DON JUAN	5	43	6
HOW GET OUT HOW THE DEVIL GOT WE IN	435	2 DON JUAN	5	44	2
AND WHEN WE ONCE WERE FAIRLY OUT AND WHEN	435	2 DON JUAN	5	44	3
FROM SAINT BARTHOLOMEW WE HAVE SAVED OUR SKIN	435	2 DON JUAN	5	44	4
AND WORSE OFF THAN WE HITHERTO HAVE BEEN	435	2 DON JUAN	5	44	6
WE FOR SOME MOMENTS HAD SECURED OUR SKIN	435	2 DON JUAN	5	44	V4
WE FROM IMPALEMENT HAD ENSURED OUR SKIN	435	2 DON JUAN	5	44	V4
WE MUST BE NEAR SOME PLACE OF MAN'S ABODE--	436	2 DON JUAN	5	45	1
MORE TENDER AS WE EVERY DAY BEHOLD	439	2 DON JUAN	5	49	6
THERE SOLITUDE WE KNOW HAS HER FULL GROWTH IN	443	2 DON JUAN	5	57	3
WE KNOW WHERE THINGS AND MEN MUST END AT BEST	448	2 DON JUAN	5	63	1
SHOWS THAT WE BUILD WHEN WE SHOULD BUT ENTOMB US	448	2 DON JUAN	5	63	8
SHOWS THAT WE BUILD WHEN WE SHOULD BUT ENTOMB US	448	2 DON JUAN	5	63	8
WHICH--AS WE SAY--OR AS THE SCOTCH SAY WHILK	456	2 DON JUAN	5	77	6
FAREWELL SAID JUAN SHOULD WE MEET NO MORE	460	2 DON JUAN	5	84	1
WHEN WE NEXT MEET WE'LL HAVE A TALE TO TELL	460	2 DON JUAN	5	84	4
WE NEEDS MUST FOLLOW WHEN FATE PUTS FROM SHORE	460	2 DON JUAN	5	84	5
THUS HORACE WROTE WE ALL KNOW LONG AGO	470	2 DON JUAN	5	101	5
WE WOULD AGAINST THEM MAKE THE FLESH OBEY--	474	2 DON JUAN	5	110	7
WE SHOULD HAVE FOUND OUT THE PERPETUAL MOTION	475	2 DON JUAN	5	112	8
AS WE MAY ASCERTAIN WITH DUE PRECISION	477	2 DON JUAN	5	115	7
BUT TO THE MAIN POINT WHERE WE HAVE BEEN TENDING--	478	2 DON JUAN	5	116	1
BUT WHEN YOU HAVE SUPPOSED THE FEW WE KNOW	486	2 DON JUAN	5	131	7

WE   (CONTINUED)

	PAGE	VOL	CANTO	STANZA	LN
THUS FAR OUR CHRONICLE AND NOW WE PAUSE	503	2	DON JUAN 5	159	1
AT LEAST WE THINK SO THOUGH BUT FEW HAVE GUESS'D	6	3	DON JUAN 6	1	4
O'ERTHROWS THE SAME WE READILY FORGET	8	3	DON JUAN 6	4	3
WE LEFT OUR HERO AND THIRD HEROINE IN	10	3	DON JUAN 6	7	1
NOW HERE WE SHOULD DISTINGUISH FOR HOWE'ER	13	3	DON JUAN 6	14	1
THAT IS WE CANNOT PARDON THEIR BAD TASTE	14	3	DON JUAN 6	17	1
THEY LIE WE LIE ALL LIE BUT LOVE NO LESS	15	3	DON JUAN 6	19	6
WE LEAVE THIS ROYAL COUPLE TO REPOSE	16	3	DON JUAN 6	20	1
OUR LEAST OF SORROWS ARE SUCH AS WE WEEP	16	3	DON JUAN 6	20	6
IN WHICH WE LEFT HIM SEVERAL LINES ABOVE	20	3	DON JUAN 6	28	8
COULD YOU ASK SUCH A QUESTION--BUT WE WILL	22	3	DON JUAN 6	33	2
YOU PLEASE--WE WILL NOT QUARREL ABOUT THAT	25	3	DON JUAN 6	38	8
WE WILL HAVE ALL THINGS SETTLED FOR YOU FAIRLY	29	3	DON JUAN 6	46	8
'TIS TIME WE SHOULD RETURN TO PLAIN NARRATION	34	3	DON JUAN 6	57	1
WHAT ARE WE AND WHENCE CAME WE WHAT SHALL BE	37	3	DON JUAN 6	63	6
WHAT ARE WE AND WHENCE CAME WE WHAT SHALL BE	37	3	DON JUAN 6	63	6
YOU SURELY ARE UNWELL CHILD WE MUST SEE	46	3	DON JUAN 6	80	6
THE TRUE EFFECT AND SO WE HAD BETTER NOT	55	3	DON JUAN 6	98	6
CAN NEVER BE DESCRIBED WE ALL HAVE HEARD	59	3	DON JUAN 6	106	4
OF THIS OUR BANQUET WE MUST SOMETIMES CHANGE	65	3	DON JUAN 6	120	4
CHILL AND CHAINED TO COLD EARTH WE LIFT ON HIGH	66	3	DON JUAN 7	1	5
WHEN WE KNOW WHAT ALL ARE WE MUST BEWAIL US	67	3	DON JUAN 7	2	5
WHEN WE KNOW WHAT ALL ARE WE MUST BEWAIL US	67	3	DON JUAN 7	2	5
NOR EVEN DIOGENES--WE LIVE AND DIE	68	3	DON JUAN 7	4	7
OF WHOM WE CAN INSERT BUT ROUSAMOUSKI	74	3	DON JUAN 7	16	8
THAT OF DESPISING THOSE WE COMBAT WITH	79	3	DON JUAN 7	25	2
ONE OF THE VALOUROUS SMITHS WHOM WE SHALL MISS	79	3	DON JUAN 7	25	5
FOR AUGHT WE KNOW) RENOWN'S ALL HIT OR MISS	82	3	DON JUAN 7	33	5
THERE'S FORTUNE EVEN IN FAME WE MUST ALLOW	82	3	DON JUAN 7	33	6
FOR THE MAN WAS WE SAFELY MAY ASSERT	95	3	DON JUAN 7	55	3
WE ONLY CAN BUT TALK OF ESCALADE	106	3	DON JUAN 7	78	6
BUT STILL WE MODERNS EQUAL YOU IN BLOOD	106	3	DON JUAN 7	80	8
WHO WHEN WE COME TO SUM UP THE TOTALITY	108	3	DON JUAN 7	83	5
HERE PAUSE WE FOR THE PRESENT--AS EVEN THEN	111	3	DON JUAN 7	87	1
BUT COULD WE KNOW THEM IN DETAIL PERCHANCE	113	3	DON JUAN 8	3	2
AND THEREFORE WE MUST GIVE THE GREATER NUMBER	120	3	DON JUAN 8	18	1
OR LOVED IT WAS WITH WHAT WE CALL THE BEST	123	3	DON JUAN 8	25	2
IN HISTORY BUT WE AT LEAST MAY GRANT	127	3	DON JUAN 8	31	5
WE SHALL NOT SEE HIS LIKENESS HE COULD KILL HIS	132	3	DON JUAN 8	39	4
WITH MANY OTHER WARRIORS AS WE SAID	133	3	DON JUAN 8	41	2
AND THEREFORE ALL WE HAVE RELATED IN	142	3	DON JUAN 8	59	1
AND HERE WE MAY REMARK WITH THE HISTORIAN	151	3	DON JUAN 8	78	2
AND WHOM FOR THIS AT LAST MUST WE CONDEMN	157	3	DON JUAN 8	92	6
OF PRESENT LIFE A GOOD DEAL MORE THAN WE--	161	3	DON JUAN 8	100	3
AT LEAST NINE-TENTHS OF WHAT WE CALL SO--GOD	163	3	DON JUAN 8	104	3
MAY HAVE ANOTHER NAME FOR HALF WE SCAN	163	3	DON JUAN 8	104	3
AND THAT'S THE CAUSE NO DOUBT WHY IF WE SCAN	167	3	DON JUAN 8	112	5
WHEREAS IF ALL BE TRUE WE HEAR OF HEAVEN	168	3	DON JUAN 8	114	7
ALL THAT WE READ HEAR DREAM OF MAN'S DISTRESSES	173	3	DON JUAN 8	123	3
BE SAID THAT WE STILL TRUCKLE UNTO THRONES--	179	3	DON JUAN 8	135	6
BUT YE--OUR CHILDREN'S CHILDREN THINK HOW WE	179	3	DON JUAN 8	135	7
AS WE NOW GAZE UPON THE MAMMOTH'S BONES	180	3	DON JUAN 8	137	3
'TIS TRUE WE SPECULATE BOTH FAR AND WIDE	190	3	DON JUAN 9	16	3
AND DEEM BECAUSE WE SEE WE ARE ALL-SEEING	190	3	DON JUAN 9	16	4
AND DEEM BECAUSE WE SEE WE ARE ALL-SEEING	190	3	DON JUAN 9	16	4
SO LITTLE DO WE KNOW WHAT WE'RE ABOUT IN	191	3	DON JUAN 9	17	5
NO MORE OF THIS THEN--LET US PRAY WE HAVE	192	3	DON JUAN 9	19	2
OFFENCE WE KNOW NOT PROBABLY IT PERCHED	192	3	DON JUAN 9	19	7
'TIS TIME WE SHOULD PROCEED WITH OUR GOOD POEM	193	3	DON JUAN 9	22	1
WHERE BLOOD WAS TALKED OF AS WE WOULD OF WATER	197	3	DON JUAN 9	29	3
TO BE THE FIRST OF WHAT WE USED TO CALL	198	3	DON JUAN 9	32	2
ARISE WHEN WE SEE EMPERORS FALL WITH OATS	198	3	DON JUAN 9	32	8
OH YE OR WE OR HE OR SHE REFLECT	199	3	DON JUAN 9	34	1
LIKE TO THE NOTIONS WE NOW ENTERTAIN	201	3	DON JUAN 9	38	5
NOW PONDERING--IT IS TIME WE SHOULD NARRATE	203	3	DON JUAN 9	42	2
OF YELLOW CASSIMERE WE MAY PRESUME	204	3	DON JUAN 9	43	6
FROM THEE WE COME TO THEE WE GO AND WHY	210	3	DON JUAN 9	56	3
FROM THEE WE COME TO THEE WE GO AND WHY	210	3	DON JUAN 9	56	3
WE DON'T MUCH CARE WITH WHOM WE MAY ENGAGE	217	3	DON JUAN 9	69	3
WE DON'T MUCH CARE WITH WHOM WE MAY ENGAGE	217	3	DON JUAN 9	69	3
SO THAT WE CAN OUR NATIVE SUN ASSUAGE	217	3	DON JUAN 9	69	5
AND CATHERINE (WE MUST SAY THUS MUCH FOR CATHERINE)	217	3	DON JUAN 9	70	1
WITH OTHER EXTRAS WHICH WE NEED NOT MENTION--	218	3	DON JUAN 9	72	6
WELL WE WON'T ANALYZE--OUR STORY MUST	221	3	DON JUAN 9	77	1
AND WAS NOT THE BEST WIFE UNLESS WE CALL	222	3	DON JUAN 9	80	6
WE HAVE JUST LIT ON A HEAVEN-KISSING HILL	224	3	DON JUAN 9	85	4
IF THIS BE TRUE FOR WE MUST DEEM THE MODE	226	3	DON JUAN 10	2	2
WE LEFT OUR HERO JUAN IN THE BLOOM	227	3	DON JUAN 10	5	1
WE LEFT HIM IN THE FOCUS OF SUCH GLORY	229	3	DON JUAN 10	9	2
HOW WE WON'T MENTION WHY WE NEED NOT SAY	235	3	DON JUAN 10	21	2
HOW WE WON'T MENTION WHY WE NEED NOT SAY	235	3	DON JUAN 10	21	2
THIS WE PASS OVER WE WILL ALSO PASS	236	3	DON JUAN 10	24	1
THIS WE PASS OVER WE WILL ALSO PASS	236	3	DON JUAN 10	24	1
AND THIS SAME STATE WE WON'T DESCRIBE WE COULD	238	3	DON JUAN 10	27	1
AND THIS SAME STATE WE WON'T DESCRIBE WE COULD	238	3	DON JUAN 10	27	1
HUT WHERE WE TRAVELLERS BAIT WITH DIM REFLECTION	238	3	DON JUAN 10	27	V6
PERHAPS--BUT SANS PERHAPS WE NEED NOT SEEK	243	3	DON JUAN 10	38	5
HIS BILLS IN AND HOWEVER WE MAY STORM	243	3	DON JUAN 10	38	6

WE   (CONTINUED)

	PAGE	VOL	CANTO	STANZA	LN
SECUNDUM ARTEM BUT ALTHOUGH WE SNEER	245	3 DON JUAN	10	42	2
IN HEALTH--WHEN ILL WE CALL THEM TO ATTEND US	245	3 DON JUAN	10	42	3
WE TEASE MILD BAILLIE OR SOFT ABERNETHY	245	3 DON JUAN	10	42	8
FOR ONE OR TWO DAYS READER WE REQUEST	248	3 DON JUAN	10	49	2
BUT SHOULD WE WISH TO WARM US ON OUR WAY	254	3 DON JUAN	10	59	6
WITH THE YORK MAIL--BUT ONWARD AS WE ROLL	263	3 DON JUAN	10	78	7
BOLD BRITONS WE ARE NOW ON SHOOTER'S HILL	264	3 DON JUAN	10	80	8
MY GENTLE COUNTRYMEN WE WILL RENEW	266	3 DON JUAN	10	84	3
(FOR IN THOSE DAYS WE HAD NOT GOT TO GAS) --	278	3 DON JUAN	11	22	8
AND BY WE'LL TALK OF THAT AND IF WE DON'T	285	3 DON JUAN	11	36	2
UNLESS ON TYRANT'S STERNS--WE TURN THE STERNEST	286	3 DON JUAN	11	38	V8
UNTO BY SAWNEY'S VIOLIN WE HAVE HEARD	307	3 DON JUAN	11	78	6
BUT WHEN WE HOVER BETWEEN FOOL AND SAGE	315	3 DON JUAN	12	1	4
AND DON'T KNOW JUSTLY WHAT WE WOULD BE AT--	315	3 DON JUAN	12	1	5
GROWS GRIZZLED AND WE ARE NOT WHAT WE WERE--	315	3 DON JUAN	12	1	8
GROWS GRIZZLED AND WE ARE NOT WHAT WE WERE--	315	3 DON JUAN	12	1	8
OH GOLD WHY CALL WE MISERS MISERABLE	316	3 DON JUAN	12	3	1
AND WHOM DO WE REMEMBER NOT A HUNDRED	324	3 DON JUAN	12	19	2
THAT TILL WE SEE WHAT'S WHAT IN FACT WE'RE FAR	335	3 DON JUAN	12	40	4
I'VE NOT BEGUN WHAT WE HAVE TO GO THROUGH	341	3 DON JUAN	12	54	4
A FURTHER PROOF WE SHOULD NOT JUDGE IN HASTE	347	3 DON JUAN	12	69	5
WE MAY PRESUME TO CRITICISE OR PRAISE	360	3 DON JUAN	13	4	4
OUR PASSIONS AND WE WALK IN WISDOM'S WAYS	360	3 DON JUAN	13	4	6
AT BLANK-BLANK SQUARE--FOR WE WILL BREAK NO SQUARES	369	3 DON JUAN	13	25	1
INDEED WE SEE THE DAILY PROOF DISPLAYED	371	3 DON JUAN	13	29	4
WHICH IS THE ONLY CAUSE THAT WE CAN GUESS	371	3 DON JUAN	13	29	7
'MIDST MANY ROCKS WE GUARD MORE AGAINST WRECKS	371	3 DON JUAN	13	30	6
PERHAPS WE HAVE BORROWED THIS FROM THE CHINESE--	373	3 DON JUAN	13	34	8
THOUGH THIS WE HOPE--HAS BEEN RESERVED FOR THIS AGE	376	3 DON JUAN	13	39	V5
WE UNDERSTAND THE SPLENDID HOST INTENDS	382	3 DON JUAN	13	52	1
MIDST WHOM WE HAVE HEARD FROM SOURCES QUITE CORRECT	382	3 DON JUAN	13	52	4
AND THUS WE SEE--WHO DOUBTS THE MORNING POST	383	3 DON JUAN	13	53	1
WHOSE LOSS IN THE LATE ACTION WE REGRET	383	3 DON JUAN	13	54	7
WE GAZE UPON A GIANT FOR HIS STATURE	390	3 DON JUAN	13	67	7
WHOSE DRAPERY HINTS WE MAY ADMIRE THEM FREELY	390	3 DON JUAN	13	68	8
IF BRITAIN MOURN HER BLEAKNESS WE CAN TELL HER	394	3 DON JUAN	13	76	7
CONSISTED OF--WE GIVE THE SEX THE PAS--	396	3 DON JUAN	13	79	2
I HAVE SEEN MORE THAN I'LL SAY--BUT WE WILL SEE	397	3 DON JUAN	13	83	1
BUT FROM BEING FARMERS WE TURN GLEANERS GLEANING	403	3 DON JUAN	13	96	1
BUT WHAT WE CAN WE GLEAN IN THIS VILE AGE	403	3 DON JUAN	13	97	1
BUT WHAT WE CAN WE GLEAN IN THIS VILE AGE	403	3 DON JUAN	13	97	1
THE PARTY WE HAVE TOUCH'D ON WERE THE GUESTS	404	3 DON JUAN	13	99	2
TO THIS WE HAVE ADDED SINCE THE LOVE OF MONEY	405	3 DON JUAN	13	100	3
WE TIRE OF MISTRESSES AND PARASITES	405	3 DON JUAN	13	100	6
WHEN WE NO MORE CAN USE OR EVEN ABUSE THEE	405	3 DON JUAN	13	100	8
THOUGH NAMELESS IN OUR LANGUAGE--WE RETORT	405	3 DON JUAN	13	101	6
WE HAVE NO ACCOMPLISH'D BLACKGUARDS LIKE TOM JONES	409	3 DON JUAN	13	110	7
OF THOUGHT WE COULD BUT SNATCH A CERTAINTY	410	3 DON JUAN	14	1	2
OF TOIL IS WHAT WE COVET MOST AND YET	412	3 DON JUAN	14	4	2
WHEN WE HAVE MADE OUR LOVE AND GAMED OUR GAMING	418	3 DON JUAN	14	18	1
BUT SINCE BENEATH IT UPON EARTH WE ARE BROUGHT	421	3 DON JUAN	14	26	4
WE LEFT OUR HEROES AND OUR HEROINES	423	3 DON JUAN	14	29	1
MOUNTAINS AND ALL WE CAN BE MOST SUBLIME AT	423	3 DON JUAN	14	29	6
ESPECIALLY WHEN WE ARE ILL AT EASE	431	3 DON JUAN	14	48	2
UNLESS LIKE WISE TIRESIAS WE HAD PROVED	442	3 DON JUAN	14	73	2
A RACK OF PLEASURES WHERE WE MUST INVENT	444	3 DON JUAN	14	79	2
THE STONE OF SYSIPHUS IF ONCE WE MOVE	447	3 DON JUAN	14	86	3
HERE LET US PAUSE--WE ARE NOT PREST FOR TIME	455	3 DON JUAN	14	102	V1
WHEREWITH WE BREAK OUR BUBBLES ON THE OCEAN	457	3 DON JUAN	15	2	4
AND AS FOR LOVE--OH LOVE--WE WILL PROCEED	458	3 DON JUAN	15	5	1
TO SHOW IT--(POINTS WE NEED NOT NOW DISCUSS)--	460	3 DON JUAN	15	10	5
SUCH ABERRATIONS THAN WE MEN OF RIGOUR	460	3 DON JUAN	15	11	4
HOW WAS THY TOIL REWARDED WE MIGHT FILL	464	3 DON JUAN	15	18	6
THE FOURTH WE HEAR AND SEE AND SAY TOO DAILY	465	3 DON JUAN	15	21	6
WE SURELY SHALL FIND SOMETHING WORTH RESEARCH	468	3 DON JUAN	15	27	5
BLOOD IS NOT WATER AND WHERE SHALL WE FIND	475	3 DON JUAN	15	44	4
BY DEATH WHEN WE ARE LEFT ALAS BEHIND	475	3 DON JUAN	15	44	6
BEYOND THE CHARMERS WE HAVE ALREADY CITED	477	3 DON JUAN	15	48	4
AND WOMANKIND TOO IF WE SO MAY SAY	479	3 DON JUAN	15	53	5
METHINKS WE MAY PROCEED UPON OUR NARRATIVE	481	3 DON JUAN	15	59	2
A MAN LIKE WHOM I HOPE WE SHAN'T SEE MANY SOON	484	3 DON JUAN	15	65	4
ALSO THE CONFERENCE WHICH WE HAVE SEEN	489	3 DON JUAN	15	75	5
A CASE WHICH TO THE JURIES WE MAY LEAVE	493	3 DON JUAN	15	84	4
SINCE WITH DIGRESSIONS WE TOO LONG HAVE TARRIED	493	3 DON JUAN	15	84	5
NOW THOUGH WE KNOW OF OLD THAT LOOKS DECEIVE	493	3 DON JUAN	15	84	6
GOD HELP US SINCE WE HAVE NEED ON OUR CAREER	496	3 DON JUAN	15	90	3
AND NOW THAT WE MAY FURNISH WITH SOME MATTER ALL	497	3 DON JUAN	15	93	7
TASTES WE ARE GOING TO TRY THE SUPERNATURAL	497	3 DON JUAN	15	93	8
HOW LITTLE DO WE KNOW THAT WHICH WE ARE	500	3 DON JUAN	15	99	3
HOW LITTLE DO WE KNOW THAT WHICH WE ARE	500	3 DON JUAN	15	99	3
HOW LESS WHAT WE MAY BE THE ETERNAL SURGE	500	3 DON JUAN	15	99	4
SITS LIKE A SEDATIVE WHILE WE RECALL	505	3 DON JUAN	16	11	V3
GREAT THOUGHTS WE CATCH FROM THENCE (BESIDES A COLD	506	3 DON JUAN	16	14	4
THAT WE OURSELVES--'TWAS IN THE HONEY MOON--	517	3 DON JUAN	16	38	2
NOT THE LESS PRECIOUS THAT WE SELDOM HEAR IT	518	3 DON JUAN	16	40	8
NOW THIS (BUT WE WILL WHISPER IT ASIDE)	522	3 DON JUAN	16	43	1
AURORA--SINCE WE ARE TOUCHING UPON TASTE	524	3 DON JUAN	16	48	1
ALSO THEREON--BUT THAT'S NOT MUCH WE FIND	525	3 DON JUAN	16	49	6

WE (CONTINUED)

	PAGE	VOL	CANTO	STANZA	LN
FOR FEAR WE SHOULD SUPPOSE US QUITE IN HEAVEN	525	3 DON JUAN	16	49	8
(THUS WE TRANSLATE A GENERAL INVITATION)	534	3 DON JUAN	16	69	2
BACCHUS AND CERES BEING AS WE KNOW	542	3 DON JUAN	16	86	4
IF WE MAY JUDGE FROM EACH NEW YEAR'S DISPLAY	548	3 DON JUAN	16	99	V5
ITS MOTIVE FOR THAT CHARITY WE OWE	553	3 DON JUAN	16	106	3
THE MOMENTS WHEN WE GATHER FROM A GLANCE	554	3 DON JUAN	16	108	4
STILL WE RESPECT THEE ALMA VENUS GENETRIX	554	3 DON JUAN	16	109	8
WE LITTLE PEOPLE IN OUR LESSER WAY	566	3 DON JUAN	17	10	2

WEAK

	PAGE	VOL	CANTO	STANZA	LN
STRENGTHENING THE WEAK AND TRAMPLING ON THE STRONG	78	2 DON JUAN	1	106	4
AND HELD HER TONGUE HER VOICE WAS GROWN SO WEAK	81	2 DON JUAN	1	112	8
WHERE THE BLUE VEINS LOOK'D SHADOWY SHRUNK AND WEAK	234	2 DON JUAN	2	147	5
I WOULD TAKE REFUGE IN WEAK PUNCH BUT RACK	372	2 DON JUAN	4	53	5
WEAK STILL WITH LOSS OF BLOOD HE SCARCE COULD URGE	387	2 DON JUAN	4	79	5
A SENTIMENT TILL THEN IN HER BUT WEAK	490	2 DON JUAN	5	137	4
HER REASON BEING WEAK HER PASSIONS STRONG	10	3 DON JUAN	6	8	5
OF THAT WEAK WORDY HARVEST THE SOLE GLEANING	207	3 DON JUAN	9	49	8
THAT HE WAS NOT IN HEART SO VERY WEAK--I MEANT	346	3 DON JUAN	12	67	5
THIS MAY BE SUPERSTITION WEAK OR WILD	387	3 DON JUAN	13	61	6
THERE LIES THE RUB--AND THIS THEY ARE BUT WEAK IN	442	3 DON JUAN	14	74	4
WAS WEAK ENOUGH TO DEEM POPE A GREAT POET	524	3 DON JUAN	16	47	7
OR--BUT ALL WORDS UPON SUCH THEMES ARE WEAK	557	3 DON JUAN	16	116	5

WEAKER

	PAGE	VOL	CANTO	STANZA	LN
THE STRONGER PUMP'D THE WEAKER THRUMM'D A SAIL	176	2 DON JUAN	2	38	8
BUT THEN 'TIS MOSTLY ON THE WEAKER SIDE	466	3 DON JUAN	15	23	1

WEAKLIER

	PAGE	VOL	CANTO	STANZA	LN
THE OTHER FATHER HAD A WEAKLIER CHILD	203	2 DON JUAN	2	88	1

WEAKNESS

	PAGE	VOL	CANTO	STANZA	LN
MY BREAST HAS BEEN ALL WEAKNESS IS SO YET	133	2 DON JUAN	1	196	1
A ROD TO WEAKNESS TO THE BRAVE A REED	151	2 DON JUAN	1	V 2	6
PERHAPS THE WEAKNESS OF A HEART NOT VOID	339	2 DON JUAN	3	109	6
TILL OUR OWN WEAKNESS SHOWS US WHAT WE ARE	344	2 DON JUAN	4	1	8
BRIGHT WITH THE VERY WEAKNESS HE REPROVED	481	2 DON JUAN	5	121	6
THIS WEAKNESS IN A FEW HOURS AND RECOVER	47	3 DON JUAN	6	83	8
WEAKNESS FOR WHAT MOST PEOPLE DEEM MERE VERMIN--	249	3 DON JUAN	10	50	5

WEAL

	PAGE	VOL	CANTO	STANZA	LN
AND--THOUGH NO DOUBT 'TIS FOR THE PUBLIC WEAL	357	3 DON JUAN	12	V 18	6
THOUGH FOR THE PUBLIC WEAL DISPOSED TO VENTURE HIGH	536	3 DON JUAN	16	73	6

WEALTH

	PAGE	VOL	CANTO	STANZA	LN
HIS SPIRIT DOWN AND THEN THE LOSS OF WEALTH	415	2 DON JUAN	5	8	6
A TOWN OF GARDENS WALLS AND WEALTH AMAZING	445	2 DON JUAN	5	60	2
HERE WEALTH HAD DONE ITS UTMOST TO ENCUMBER	448	2 DON JUAN	5	64	6
WEALTH HAD DONE WONDERS--TASTE NOT MUCH SUCH THINGS	465	2 DON JUAN	5	94	1
FOR THEN WEALTH KINGDOMS WORLDS ARE BUT A SPORT--I	9	3 DON JUAN	6	5	3
DEBT HE CALLS WEALTH AND TAXES PARADISE	88	3 DON JUAN	7	45	5
DAMSELS GREAT WEALTH AND ILLUSTRIOUS ORDERS	235	3 DON JUAN	10	21	V7
THE WEALTH OF WORLDS (A WEALTH OF TAX AND PAPER)	266	3 DON JUAN	10	83	4
THE WEALTH OF WORLDS (A WEALTH OF TAX AND PAPER)	266	3 DON JUAN	10	83	4
THEIR CASH COMES FROM THEIR WEALTH GOES TO A JEW	306	3 DON JUAN	11	75	4
OR WEALTH WHICH IS A PASSPORT EVERYWHERE	370	3 DON JUAN	13	28	5
OF BRITAIN'S PRESENT WEALTH AND HAPPINESS--	371	3 DON JUAN	13	29	8
ALTHOUGH HER BIRTH AND WEALTH HAD GIVEN HER VOGUE	477	3 DON JUAN	15	48	3
THE COMPANY WHOSE BIRTH WEALTH WORTH HAVE COST	568	3 DON JUAN	17	13	4

WEALTHIER

	PAGE	VOL	CANTO	STANZA	LN
OVER THEIR IDOL TILL SOME WEALTHIER LUST	263	2 DON JUAN	2	200	5

WEALTHIEST

	PAGE	VOL	CANTO	STANZA	LN
PERHAPS HE WOULD BE WEALTHIEST OF HIS NATION	320	3 DON JUAN	12	10	7
THE WEALTHIEST ORPHANS ARE TO BE MORE PITIED	563	3 DON JUAN	17	3	8

WEALTH'S

	PAGE	VOL	CANTO	STANZA	LN
AND WHEREFORE BLAME GAUNT WEALTH'S AUSTERITIES	319	3 DON JUAN	12	7	6

WEALTHY

	PAGE	VOL	CANTO	STANZA	LN
AND WONDER HOW THE WEALTHY CAN BE SPARING	316	3 DON JUAN	12	3	7
WAS HIGH-BORN WEALTHY BY HER FATHER'S WILL	359	3 DON JUAN	13	2	5

WEAN

	PAGE	VOL	CANTO	STANZA	LN
TO WEAN HIM FROM THE WICKEDNESS OF EARTH	161	2 DON JUAN	2	8	7
THERE WANTED BUT THE LOSS OF THIS TO WEAN	304	2 DON JUAN	3	57	6
TO WEAN DON JUAN FROM THE SIREN'S WILE	438	3 DON JUAN	14	65	6

WEAN'D

	PAGE	VOL	CANTO	STANZA	LN
AND BREAST MATERNAL WEAN'D AT ONCE FOREVER	349	2 DON JUAN	4	10	6

WEANING

	PAGE	VOL	CANTO	STANZA	LN
WHEN IT'S LAST WEANING DRAUGHT IS DRAINED FOREVER	349	2 DON JUAN	4	10	V6
AT LENGTH THOSE EYES WHICH THEY WOULD FAIN BE WEANING	379	2 DON JUAN	4	64	7

WEANS

	PAGE	VOL	CANTO	STANZA	LN
OF FEEDING BRATS THE MOMENT HIS WIFE WEANS	325	3 DON JUAN	12	21	8

WEAPON

	PAGE	VOL	CANTO	STANZA	LN
HER BOSOM WAS THE WEAPON--AND EVEN SO	367	2 DON JUAN	4	43	V6
HIS WEAPON AND REPLACED IT BUT STOOD STILL	368	2 DON JUAN	4	46	2

WEAPONS

	PAGE	VOL	CANTO	STANZA	LN
ALL PROPER MEN OF WEAPONS AS E'ER SCOFFED HIGH	75	3 DON JUAN	7	17	3
AND LEVELLED WEAPONS STILL AGAINST THE GLACIS	130	3 DON JUAN	8	34	8
AT LAST IT TAKES TO WEAPONS SUCH AS MEN	138	3 DON JUAN	8	51	3
WITH FLASHING EYES AND WEAPONS MATCHED WITH THEM	157	3 DON JUAN	8	92	2
FOR WEAPONS BUT WHAT MUSE SINCE HOMER'S ABLE	482	3 DON JUAN	15	62	3

WEAR

	PAGE	VOL	CANTO	STANZA	LN
HE WON THEM WELL AND MAY HE WEAR THEM LONG	77	2 DON JUAN	1	104	8
A BLOTTED SHIELD NO SHIRE'S TRUE KNIGHT WOULD WEAR	153	2 DON JUAN	1	V 4	6
A SORT OF BLOTTED SHIELD FEW KNIGHTS WOULD WEAR	153	2 DON JUAN	1	V 4	V6
AND STAND LIKE ROCKS THE TEMPEST'S WEAR AND TEAR	191	2 DON JUAN	2	66	4

WEAR   (CONTINUED)
    OR SOMETIMES ONLY WEAR A WEEK OR TWO-- . . . . 422 2 DON JUAN 5   22   4
    WHY YOU SHOULD WEAR THEM--WHAT THOUGH MY SOUL LOATHES . . 455 2 DON JUAN 5   76   3
    AS GOOD MEN WEAR WHO HAVE DONE A VIRTUOUS ACTION . . . . 473 2 DON JUAN 5   107   8
    OR RATHER BONNET WHICH THE FAIR SEX WEAR . . . . 13 3 DON JUAN 6   14   5
    APT TO WEAR OUT ON TRIFLING PROVOCATIONS . . . . 165 3 DON JUAN 8   107   8
    AS CAESAR WORE HIS ROBE YOU WEAR YOUR GOWN . . . . . . 232 3 DON JUAN 10   15   8
    WHO WATCHES O'ER THE CHAIN AS THEY WHO WEAR . . . . . . 258 3 DON JUAN 10   68   8
    AND WEAR MY HEAD DENYING THAT I WEAR IT . . . . 268 3 DON JUAN 11   1   8
    AND WEAR MY HEAD DENYING THAT I WEAR IT . . . . 268 3 DON JUAN 11   1   8
    NOR WEAR AS GRACEFULLY AS GAULS HER GARB . . . . 350 3 DON JUAN 12   75   3
    AND FOR COQUETRY SHE DISDAINED TO WEAR IT . . . . . . 372 3 DON JUAN 13   31   6
    AND WEAR THE MELTON JACKET FOR A SPACE-- . . . . 395 3 DON JUAN 13   78   6
    OF STUBBORN SHELL WHICH WAVES AND WEATHER WEAR NOT . . . 431 3 DON JUAN 14   49   4
    THAN WEAR A HEART A WOMAN LOVES TO REND . . . . 438 3 DON JUAN 14   64   6
    OPINIONS WEAR OUT IN SOME THOUSAND YEARS . . . . 496 3 DON JUAN 15   90   7
    BUT WEAR THE NEWEST MANTLE OF HYPOCRISY . . . . 526 3 DON JUAN 16   52   7
WEARIED
    (IF THAT HIS HIGHNESS WEARIED OF HIS BRIDE) . . . . . . 24 3 DON JUAN 6   36   7
WEARIER
    UPON FOR THERE ARE VERY FEW THINGS WEARIER . . . . . . 367 3 DON JUAN 13   19   5
WEARIES
    OR--WHAT IS JUST THE SAME--IT WEARIES OUT . . . . . . 478 3 DON JUAN 15   51   7
WEARINESS
    AND LYING ON THEIR WEARINESS LIKE BALM . . . . 192 2 DON JUAN 2   68   4
    THOSE EYES TO CLOSE THOUGH WEARINESS AND PAIN . . . . . 235 2 DON JUAN 2   149   3
    OF WEARINESS OR SCORN) BEGAN TO FEEL . . . . 546 3 DON JUAN 16   96   7
WEARING
    WHOSE SHAMROCK NOW SEEMS RATHER WORSE FOR WEARING . . . 286 3 DON JUAN 11   38   8
WEARS
    DEEMING THE CHAIN IT WEARS EVEN MEN MAY FIT . . . . . . 18 3 DON JUAN D   15   4
    ARE MASKS IT OFTEN WEARS AND STILL TOO LATE . . . . . . 61 2 DON JUAN 1   73   8
    THERE WAS RESEMBLANCE SUCH AS TRUE BLOOD WEARS . . . . 368 2 DON JUAN 4   45   4
    BUT THERE ARE FORMS WHICH TIME ADORNS NOT WEARS . . . . 468 2 DON JUAN 5   98 V3
    'TIS THE VILE DAILY DROP ON DROP WHICH WEARS . . . . . 16 3 DON JUAN 6   20   7
    WITH HANNIBAL AND WEARS THE TYRIAN TUNIC . . . . 122 3 DON JUAN 8   23   6
    WHEN NATURE WEARS THE GOWN THAT DOTH BECOME HER . . . . 380 3 DON JUAN 13   48   3
    THE GILDING WEARS SO SOON FROM OFF HER FETTER . . . . . 421 3 DON JUAN 14   25   5
WEARY
    HOME TO THE WEARY TO THE HUNGRY CHEER . . . . 338 2 DON JUAN 3   107   2
    WEARY UNLESS WHEN SEPARATE THE TREE . . . . 349 2 DON JUAN 4   10   3
    ALTHOUGH WHEN LONG A LITTLE APT TO WEARY US . . . . . . 358 3 DON JUAN 13   1   6
    OF FAME OR PROFIT WHEN THE WORLD GROWS WEARY . . . . . 415 3 DON JUAN 14   11   2
WEATHER
    AS DAY ADVANCED THE WEATHER SEEM'D TO ABATE . . . . . . 172 2 DON JUAN 2   30   1
    TO WEATHER OUT MUCH LONGER THE DISTRESS . . . . 178 2 DON JUAN 2   41   3
    AGAIN THE WEATHER THREATEN'D--AGAIN BLEW . . . . 178 2 DON JUAN 2   42   1
    THESE TO SECURE IN THIS STRONG BLOWING WEATHER . . . . 285 2 DON JUAN 3   18   7
    THE PRESENT WEATHER WOULD BE MUCH MORE RAINY-- . . . . 301 2 DON JUAN 3   50   6
    EXCEPT COLD WEATHER AND COMMISERATION . . . . 176 3 DON JUAN 8   129   6
    FAIR WEATHER FOR THE DAY THOUGH RATHER SPACIOUS . . . . 211 3 DON JUAN 9   58   7
    OF STUBBORN SHELL WHICH WAVES AND WEATHER WEAR NOT . . . 431 3 DON JUAN 14   49   4
WEATHER-BEATEN
    FOR ONE ROUGH WEATHER-BEATEN VETERAN BODY . . . . . . 167 3 DON JUAN 8   112   7
WEATHEROLOGY
    MY MUSE A GLASS OF WEATHEROLOGY . . . . 378 3 DON JUAN 13   43   5
WEATHER'S
    THEIR STOCK WAS DAMAGED BY THE WEATHER'S STRESS . . . . 180 2 DON JUAN 2   46   6
    THEY ARE BUT BAD PILOTS WHEN THE WEATHER'S ROUGH . . . . 431 3 DON JUAN 14   48   3
WEATHER-TOUGH
    FLIES IN ONE'S FACE AND MAKES IT WEATHER-TOUGH . . . . 162 2 DON JUAN 2   11   6
WEB
    IN THIS VILE GARB THE DISTAFF WEB AND WOOF . . . . . . 484 2 DON JUAN 5   127   3
    RAISE BUT AN ARM 'TWILL BRUSH THEIR WEB AWAY . . . . . 196 3 DON JUAN 9   28   1
    THE WEB OF THESE TARANTULAS EACH DAY . . . . 196 3 DON JUAN 9   28   5
    AND BRUSH A WEB OR TWO FROM OFF THE WALLS . . . . . . 266 3 DON JUAN 10   84   8
WEBFOOTED
    WEBFOOTED NOT UNLIKE A DOVE IN SIZE . . . . 206 2 DON JUAN 2   94   2
WED
    'TIS PITY LEARNED VIRGINS EVER WED . . . . 33 2 DON JUAN 1   22   1
    THEIR PRIEST WAS SOLITUDE AND THEY WERE WED . . . . . . 265 2 DON JUAN 2   204   6
    WHEN SHE WHOSE TURN IT WAS WAS WED AT ONCE . . . . . . 498 2 DON JUAN 5   152   5
    MOST WISE MEN WITH ONE MODERATE WOMAN WED . . . . 12 3 DON JUAN 6   12   5
    SAVE WED A YEAR I HATE RECRUITS WITH WIVES . . . . . . 102 3 DON JUAN 7   70   8
    IS ALL THE REST ABOUT HER WHETHER WED . . . . 214 3 DON JUAN 9   64   4
    A RIB'S A THORN IN A WED GALLANT'S SIDE . . . . 292 3 DON JUAN 11   46   6
    IT WERE MUCH BETTER TO BE WED OR DEAD . . . . 438 3 DON JUAN 14   64   5
    THAT STILL HE'D WED WITH SUCH OR SUCH A LADY . . . . . 469 3 DON JUAN 15   30   7
    UNWED OR MISTRESS NEVER TO BE WED . . . . 470 3 DON JUAN 15   32   2
    OR WED ALREADY WHO OBJECT TO THIS . . . . 470 3 DON JUAN 15   32   3
WEDDED
    WEDDED SHE WAS SOME YEARS AND TO A MAN . . . . 56 2 DON JUAN 1   62   1
    THEN IF YOU'D HAVE THEM WEDDED PLEASE TO SHUT . . . . . 282 2 DON JUAN 3   12   5
    HAS IN HIS ABSENCE WEDDED SOME RICH MISER . . . . . . 288 2 DON JUAN 3   24   2
    FAIR VIRGINS BLUSHED UPON HIM WEDDED DAMES . . . . . . 293 3 DON JUAN 11   48   1
    AND WEDDED UNTO ONE SHE HAD LOVED WELL . . . . 365 3 DON JUAN 13   14   2
WEDDING
    HAD PETRARCH'S PASSION LED TO PETRARCH'S WEDDING . . . . 279 2 DON JUAN 3   8 V7
    TO MAKE A ROMAN SORT OF SABINE WEDDING . . . . 177 3 DON JUAN 8   131   7

```
                                                        PAGE VOL      CANTO STANZA LN
WEDDING   (CONTINUED)
        AND YOU MAY GET THE WEDDING DRESSES READY  . . . . . .  343  3 DON JUAN 12    59    8
        BUT ADELINE DETERMINED JUAN'S WEDDING . . . . . . . .   473  3 DON JUAN 15    40    1
WEDDINGS
        I'VE KNOWN A DOZEN WEDDINGS MADE EVEN THUS  . . . . .   344  3 DON JUAN 12    61    1
WEDLOCK
        ONE PERSON THRICE IN HOLY WEDLOCK BOUND  . . . . . .    421  2 DON JUAN  5    20    5
        AND WEDLOCK AND A PADLOCK MEAN THE SAME  . . . . . .    502  2 DON JUAN  5   158    2
        BORN IN A SECOND WEDLOCK AND ABOVE . . . . . . . .     240  3 DON JUAN 10    32    7
        OF WHICH YOUR LAWFUL AWFUL WEDLOCK FOUNT IS--  . . .    312  3 DON JUAN 11    89    6
        WHY CALL'D HE HARMONY A STATE SANS WEDLOCK . . . . .    471  3 DON JUAN 15    35    7
WEDS
        SNOW WELL 'TIS ALL HAP-HAZARD WHEN ONE WEDS  . . . .     18  3 DON JUAN  6    25    6
WEEDS
        WHILE WEEDS AND ORDURE RANKLE ROUND THE BASE  . . .    400  3 DON JUAN  4   103    8
        IF THAT THE WEEDS O'ERLIVE NOT THE FIRST CROP--  . .    368  3 DON JUAN 13    22    7
        TWO WEEDS WHICH POSE OUR ECONOMIC CATOS  . . . . .     472  3 DON JUAN 15    37    8
WEEK
        BARROW SOUTH TILLOTSON WHOM EVERY WEEK . . . . . .     243  2 DON JUAN  2   165    5
        BUT NEVER MIND--SHE'LL TURN PERHAPS NEXT WEEK  . . .    418  2 DON JUAN  5    14    6
        OR SOMETIMES ONLY WEAR A WEEK OR TWO--  . . . . . .    422  2 DON JUAN  5    22    4
        CARE LIKE A HOUSE-KEEPER BRINGS EVERY WEEK . . . . .    243  2 DON JUAN 10    38    5
        WHO DID NOT LIMIT MUCH HIS BILLS PER WEEK  . . . . .    259  3 DON JUAN 10    70    3
        AND YET I CAN'T HELP SCRIBBLING ONCE A WEEK  . . . .    414  3 DON JUAN 14    10    5
        BUT ONCE A WEEK OR FORTNIGHT UNINVITED . . . . . .     534  3 DON JUAN 16    69    1
WEEKLY
        THE INFLAMMATION OF HIS WEEKLY BILLS . . . . . . .     293  2 DON JUAN  3    35    8
WEEKS
        THEY MUST WAIT SEVERAL WEEKS BEFORE A MASS . . . . .    185  2 DON JUAN  2    55    4
        AND PUT HIS HOUSE IN MOURNING SEVERAL WEEKS  . . . .    295  2 DON JUAN  3    38    4
        AND (AS HER JUNIOR BY SIX WEEKS) HIS YOUTH . . . . .    432  3 DON JUAN 14    51    8
WEEN
        AND HERE THE ADVANTAGE IS MY OWN I WEEN  . . . . . .    137  2 DON JUAN  1   202    3
        THE CELLS TOO AND REFECTORY I WEEN . . . . . . . .     389  3 DON JUAN 13    66    4
        A SITUATION DIFFICULT I WEEN . . . . . . . . . .      489  3 DON JUAN 15    75    3
WEEP
        BEGAN AT ONCE TO SCREAM AND YAWN AND WEEP  . . . . .     97  2 DON JUAN  1   140    3
        NO DOUBT WE WEEP FOR THOSE THE HEART ENDEARS--  . .    164  2 DON JUAN  2    15    7
        I'D WEEP BUT MINE IS NOT A WEEPING MUSE  . . . . .     165  2 DON JUAN  2    16    3
        MUST WE BUT WEEP O'ER DAYS MORE BLEST . . . . . .     323  2 DON JUAN  3 L  7    1
        SEEMING TO WEEP THE DYING DAY'S DECAY  . . . . . .     338  2 DON JUAN  3   108    4
        'TIS THAT I MAY NOT WEEP AND IF I WEEP . . . . . .     346  2 DON JUAN  4     4    2
        'TIS THAT I MAY NOT WEEP AND IF I WEEP . . . . . .     346  2 DON JUAN  4     4    2
        WHICH MEN WEEP OVER MAY BE MEANT TO SAVE . . . . .     350  2 DON JUAN  4    12    8
        SHE WAS NOT ONE TO WEEP AND RAVE AND CHAFE . . . .     373  2 DON JUAN  4    54    4
        OUR LEAST OF SORROWS ARE SUCH AS WE WEEP . . . . .      16  3 DON JUAN  6    20    6
        DEATH LAUGHS AT ALL YOU WEEP FOR--LOOK UPON . . . .    188  3 DON JUAN  9    11    5
        BUT I WON'T WEEP--AND SO DRIVE ON POSTILLIONS  . . .    263  3 DON JUAN 10    77    2
        BUT--I WON'T WEEP--COME POSTBOYS WHIRL ALONG  . . .    263  3 DON JUAN 10    77   V2
        DEATH SO CALL'D IS A THING WHICH MAKES MEN WEEP  . .    411  3 DON JUAN 14     3    7
        THE COUNTRY WOULD HAVE FAR MORE CAUSE TO WEEP IT . .    537  3 DON JUAN 16    75    6
        AND MAKE THE WORLDING SNEER THE YOUNGLING WEEP . . .    555  3 DON JUAN 16   110    8
WEEPING
        I'D WEEP BUT MINE IS NOT A WEEPING MUSE  . . . . .     165  2 DON JUAN  2    16    3
        AND WATCH'D BY EYES THAT NEVER YET KNEW WEEPING  . .    274  2 DON JUAN  3     1    3
        FELL IN LONG TRESSES LIKE THE WEEPING WILLOW . . .      60  3 DON JUAN  6   108    2
WEEPS
        AND YOUTH STILL WEEPS THE TENDER TEARS THAT PLEASE--  .   273  2 DON JUAN  2 V  2    4
WEIGH
        BUT WHETHER SUCH THINGS DO OR DO NOT WEIGH . . . .       9  3 DON JUAN  6     6    3
        WEIGH NOT THE THIN ORE WHERE THEIR VISAGE SHINES . . .   321  3 DON JUAN 12    12    4
WEIGH'D
        WHICH WEIGH'D UPON THEM YET ALL DAMP AND SALT  . . .    234  2 DON JUAN  2   147    7
WEIGHED
        AT PRESENT WEIGHED DOWN BY A DOOM WHICH HAD  . . . .    417  2 DON JUAN  5    12    3
        PERHAPS BE WEIGHED HEREAFTER IF NOT NOW  . . . . .       9  3 DON JUAN  6     6    2
        WEIGHED ON HIS SPIRIT THOUGH BY NO MEANS SERIOUS  . .    514  3 DON JUAN 16    33    5
WEIGHING
        SOME DOWN AND WEIGHING OTHERS IN THEIR HAND  . . . .    426  2 DON JUAN  5    29    4
WEIGHS
        THOUGH IRELAND STARVE GREAT GEORGE WEIGHS TWENTY STONE  .   175  3 DON JUAN  8   126    8
WEIGHT
        AS IF TO WIN A PART FROM OFF THE WEIGHT  . . . . .     203  2 DON JUAN  2    88    6
        AND NEVER KNOW THE WEIGHT OF HUMAN HOURS . . . . .     352  2 DON JUAN  4    15    8
        THROUGH YEARS OR MOONS THE INNER WEIGHT TO BEAR  . .    382  2 DON JUAN  4    71    3
        ELSE THEY SHALL FEEL THE WEIGHT OF THIS MY ARM . . .    459  2 DON JUAN  5    82    3
        OF BRITAIN'S YOUTH DEPENDS UPON THEIR WEIGHT . . .     140  3 DON JUAN  8    55    4
        BUT LUCKILY OF NO GREAT LENGTH OR WEIGHT . . . . .     207  3 DON JUAN  9    50    8
        THAN SOLITARY PRIDE'S OPPRESSIVE WEIGHT  . . . . .     367  3 DON JUAN 13    19    6
WEIGHTY
        HATH WON THE EXPERIENCE WHICH IS DEEMED SO WEIGHTY  . .   339  3 DON JUAN 12    50    8
WEIRD
        HE MOVED AS SHADOWY AS THE SISTERS WEIRD . . . . .     510  3 DON JUAN 16    21    6
WELCH
        THERE WAS THE WAGGISH WELCH JUDGE JEFFERIES HARDSMAN  . .   399  3 DON JUAN 13    88    5
WELCOME
        BAY DEEP-MOUTH'D WELCOME AS WE DRAW NEAR HOME  . . .     88  2 DON JUAN  1   123    2
        STILL SET THEM ONWARDS TO THE WELCOME SHORE  . . . .    209  2 DON JUAN  2   101    2
        A BETTER WELCOME TO THE TEMPEST-TOST . . . . . . .     249  2 DON JUAN  2   177    5
```

900

WELCOME   (CONTINUED)   PAGE VOL   CANTO STANZA LN
      WITHOUT A WELCOME THERE HE LONG HAD DWELT   . . . . . . 302 2 DON JUAN 3   52   4
      THE WELCOME STALL TO THE O'ERLABOUR'D STEER   . . . . . . 338 2 DON JUAN 3   107   4
      A HAPPY LOVER AND A WELCOME GUEST--   . . . . . . 343 2 DON JUAN 3 V 98   5
      THE PAST STILL WELCOME AS THE PRESENT THOUGHT . . . . . . 354 2 DON JUAN 4   20   8
      EXPECTING ALL THE WELCOME OF A LOVER   . . . .   12 3 DON JUAN 6   13   7
      (A HIGHLAND WELCOME ALL THE WIDE WORLD OVER)   . . . . . . 12 3 DON JUAN 6   13   8
      THEY FOUND ON THEIR RETURN THE SELF-SAME WELCOME . . . . . 134 3 DON JUAN 8   42   7
      TO WELCOME FOREIGNERS IN THIS WAY NOW   . . . . 275 3 DON JUAN 11   15   2
      WAS JUAN A RECHERCHE WELCOME GUEST . . . . 370 3 DON JUAN 13   28   2
WELCOMED
      AND SWEET SENSATIONS SHOULD HAVE WELCOMED BOTH . . . . . . 368 2 DON JUAN 4   45   7
WELCOMES
      WHICH WELCOMES HAPLESS STRANGERS IN ALL PLACES . . . . . . 28 3 DON JUAN 6   45   7
WE'LL
      SO MUCH FOR JULIA NOW WE'LL TURN TO JUAN . . . . . .   68 2 DON JUAN 1   86   1
      IN SIGHT THAT SEVERAL MONTHS HAVE PASS'D WE'LL SAY   . . . 86 2 DON JUAN 1   121   6
      WE'LL TALK OF THAT ANON--'TIS SWEET TO HEAR   . . . . . .   87 2 DON JUAN 1   122   1
      WE'LL SEE HOWEVER WHAT THEY SAY TO THIS   . . . . 135 2 DON JUAN 1   199   4
      WE'LL PUT ABOUT AND TRY ANOTHER TACK   . . . . 384 2 DON JUAN 4   74   7
      WHEN WE NEXT MEET WE'LL HAVE A TALE TO TELL   . . . . . . 460 2 DON JUAN 5   84   4
      BY GOD WE'LL BE TOO LATE FOR THE FIRST CUT   . . . . . . 162 3 DON JUAN 8   101   8
      THEY HATE ME NOT I THEM--AND HERE WE'LL PAUSE   . . . . . 193 3 DON JUAN 9   21   8
      NOW WE'LL GET O'ER THE GROUND AT A GREAT RATE   . . . . . 203 3 DON JUAN 9   42   4
      TURN OUT SO WE'LL SAY NOTHING 'GAINST THE WORDING . . . . 270 3 DON JUAN 11   4   3
      AND BY WE'LL TALK OF THAT AND IF WE DON'T   . . . . . .   285 3 DON JUAN 11   36   2
      BUT FIRST OF LITTLE LEILA WE'LL DISPOSE   . . . . 285 3 DON JUAN 11   36   2
      WE'LL DO OUR BEST TO MAKE THE BEST ON'T--MARCH . . . . . 335 3 DON JUAN 12   41   1
      BUT WE'LL SAY NOTHING OF AFFAIRS OF STATE)   . . . . . . 468 3 DON JUAN 15   27   1
      BUT WE'LL SAY NOTHING OF AFFAIRS OF STATE)   . . . . . . 541 3 DON JUAN 16   84   4
WELL
      BEGOT--BUT THAT'S TO COME--WELL TO RENEW . . . .   26 2 DON JUAN 1   9   8
      EVEN HER MINUTEST MOTIONS WENT AS WELL   . . . .   30 2 DON JUAN 1   17   5
      I'M NOT TO BLAME AS YOU WELL KNOW NO MORE IS   . . . . .   37 2 DON JUAN 1   31   3
      THAT I MUST SAY WHO KNEW HIM VERY WELL   . . . .   40 2 DON JUAN 1   35   2
      PROMISED TO TURN OUT WELL IN PROPER HANDS   . . . . . .   42 2 DON JUAN 1   37   4
      SO WELL NOT ONE OF THE AFORESAID PAINTS   . . . .   47 2 DON JUAN 1   47   6
      I KNEW HIS FATHER WELL AND HAVE SOME SKILL   . . . . . .   49 2 DON JUAN 1   51   3
      AS WELL AS ALL THE GREEK I SINCE HAVE LOST   . . . . . .   50 2 DON JUAN 1   53   3
      I THINK I PICK'D UP TOO AS WELL AS MOST   . . . .   50 2 DON JUAN 1   53   5
      TALL HANDSOME SLENDER BUT WELL KNIT HE SEEM'D . . . . .   51 2 DON JUAN 1   54   2
      A MAN WELL LOOKING FOR HIS YEARS AND WHO . . . .   57 2 DON JUAN 1   65   2
      THAT ALL WITHIN WAS NOT SO VERY WELL   . . . .   64 2 DON JUAN 1   78   3
      FRAUGHT WITH THIS FINE INTENTION AND WELL FENCED . . . .   66 2 DON JUAN 1   82   1
      HE WON THEM WELL AND MAY HE WEAR THEM LONG   . . . . . .   77 2 DON JUAN 1   104   8
      SHE SATE BUT NOT ALONE I KNOW NOT WELL   . . . .   77 2 DON JUAN 1   105   1
      OF LOOKING IN THE BED AS WELL AS UNDER   . . . .   100 2 DON JUAN 1   144   8
      AND THAT THE MEDICINE ANSWER'D VERY WELL . . . . 113 2 DON JUAN 1   168   6
      ALFONSO'S LOVES WITH INEZ WERE WELL KNOWN   . . . . . . 118 2 DON JUAN 1   176   2
      ALFONSO FIRST EXAMINED WELL THEIR FASHION   . . . . . . 121 2 DON JUAN 1   181   7
      'TIS WISE--'TIS WELL BUT NOT THE LESS A PAIN   . . . . .   130 2 DON JUAN 1   192   2
      AND YET I MAY AS WELL THE TASK FULFIL . . . .   134 2 DON JUAN 1   197   3
      'TWERE WELL IF OTHERS FOLLOW'D MY EXAMPLE   . . . . . . 147 2 DON JUAN 1   221   8
      HIS THOUGHTS HOW WELL APPLIED THE NAME OF GOD . . . . .   154 2 DON JUAN 1 V 5   V2
      WELL--WELL THE WORLD MUST TURN UPON ITS AXIS   . . . . .   159 2 DON JUAN 2   4   1
      WELL--WELL THE WORLD MUST TURN UPON ITS AXIS   . . . . .   159 2 DON JUAN 2   4   1
      A PRETTY TOWN I RECOLLECT IT WELL--   . . . .   159 2 DON JUAN 2   5   2
      A CANTO--THEN THEIR FEET AND ANCLES--WELL   . . . . . . 160 2 DON JUAN 2   6   6
      CHASTE MUSE--(WELL IF YOU MUST YOU MUST)--THE VEIL . . . 160 2 DON JUAN 2   7   1
      AS I WHO'VE CROSS'D IT OFT KNOW WELL ENOUGH   . . . . . . 162 2 DON JUAN 2   11   4
      FOR I HAVE TRIED IT WELL--AND SO MAY YOU . . . . 163 2 DON JUAN 2   13   V8
      TO LOSE THEIR LIVES AS WELL AS SPOIL THEIR DIET . . . . . 173 2 DON JUAN 2   33   4
      GETTING THE BOATS OUT BEING WELL AWARE   . . . .   180 2 DON JUAN 2   45   6
      BUT E'ER TWAS WELL BEGUN--A HEAVY SEA . . . .   183 2 DON JUAN 2   50   V2
      SO THAT THEMSELVES AS WELL AS HOPES WERE DAMP'D . . . . . 188 2 DON JUAN 2   60   7
      SHE HAD A CURIOUS CREW AS WELL AS CARGO   . . . . 191 2 DON JUAN 2   66   7
      YOU'D WISH YOURSELF WHERE TRUTH IS--IN A WELL   . . . . . 201 2 DON JUAN 2   84   8
      IT IS AS WELL TO THINK SO NOW AND THEN   . . . .   205 2 DON JUAN 2   93   2
      'TWAS WELL THIS BIRD OF PROMISE DID NOT PERCH   . . . . . 206 2 DON JUAN 2   95   2
      HE ATE AND HE WAS WELL SUPPLIED AND SHE   . . . . 239 2 DON JUAN 2   158   1
      'TWAS WELL BECAUSE HEALTH IN THE HUMAN FRAME   . . . . .   245 2 DON JUAN 2   169   3
      WHILE VENUS FILLS THE HEART (WHICH QUITE AS WELL IS . . . 246 2 DON JUAN 2   170   V1
      WELL--JUAN AFTER BATHING IN THE SEA   . . . .   246 2 DON JUAN 2   171   7
      AND HAIDEE BEING DEVOUT AS WELL AS FAIR   . . . . 258 2 DON JUAN 2   193   5
      HOW PLEASANT FOR THE HEART AS WELL AS LIVER   . . . . . . 270 2 DON JUAN 2   213   8
      WITH FLUTTERING DOUBTS IF ALL BE WELL OR ILL-- . . . . . 286 2 DON JUAN 3   21   5
      THE EYE MIGHT DOUBT IF IT WERE WELL AWAKE   . . . . . . 314 2 DON JUAN 3   76   5
      LIKE BURNS (WHOM DOCTOR CURRIE WELL DESCRIBES) . . . . .   329 2 DON JUAN 3   92   4
      AND DRIVELS SEAS TO SET IT WELL AFLOAT   . . . .   333 2 DON JUAN 3   98   8
      PERCHANCE THE DEATH OF ONE SHE LOVED TOO WELL   . . . . . 363 2 DON JUAN 4   36   5
      HIS OWN WELL IN SO WELL ERE YOU COULD LOOK   . . . . . . 370 2 DON JUAN 4   49   4
      HIS OWN WELL IN SO WELL ERE YOU COULD LOOK   . . . . . . 370 2 DON JUAN 4   49   4
      LONG WITH HER DESTINY BUT SHE SLEEPS WELL   . . . . . . 382 2 DON JUAN 4   71   7
      LADY TO LADY WELL AS MAN TO MAN . . . .   393 2 DON JUAN 4   91   6
      AS WELL AS THE SUBLIME DISCOVERY'S DATE   . . . . 406 2 DON JUAN 4   112   4
      WELL THEN YOUR THIRD SAID JUAN WHAT DID SHE   . . . . . . 421 2 DON JUAN 5   20   6
      I GAZED UPON HIM FOR I KNEW HIM WELL   . . . .   430 2 DON JUAN 5   35   1
      BUT SADDENS MORE BY NIGHT AS WELL AS DAY . . . . 442 2 DON JUAN 5   56   6
      I GRANT YOU IN A CHURCH 'TIS VERY WELL   . . . .   444 2 DON JUAN 5   59   2
      THIS SPIRIT'S WELL BUT IT MAY WAX TOO BOLD   . . . . . . 454 2 DON JUAN 5   75   3

WELL   (CONTINUED)

	PAGE	VOL	CANTO	STANZA	LV
'TWOULD BE AS WELL AND--(THOUGH THERE'S NOT MUCH IN'T)	464	2 DON JUAN	5	91	5
HER RAGE WAS BUT A MINUTE'S AND 'TWAS WELL--	489	2 DON JUAN	5	135	1
THOUGH HE DESERVED IT WELL FOR BEING SO BACKWARD	492	2 DON JUAN	5	140	6
THE TURKS DO WELL TO SHUT--AT LEAST SOMETIMES--	501	2 DON JUAN	5	157	1
IF ANTHONY BE WELL REMEMBERED YET	8	3 DON JUAN	6	4	5
POLYGAMY MAY WELL BE HELD IN DREAD	12	3 DON JUAN	6	12	3
IN THE LAST LINE WHICH CANNOT WELL BE WORSE	14	3 DON JUAN	6	18	5
SNOW WELL 'TIS ALL HAP-HAZARD WHEN ONE WEDS	18	3 DON JUAN	6	25	6
JUANNA--WELL A PRETTY NAME ENOUGH	28	3 DON JUAN	6	44	2
KISS RHYMES TO BLISS IN FACT AS WELL AS VERSE--	35	3 DON JUAN	6	59	7
WHICH PAST WELL OFF--AS SHE COULD DO NO LESS	36	3 DON JUAN	6	61	5
AND SAID SHE FELT HERSELF EXTREMELY WELL	48	3 DON JUAN	6	84	2
(THOUGH HE WELL KNEW THE MEANING) TO BE SHOWN	62	3 DON JUAN	6	112	6
HIS OWN REMONSTRANCE FURTHER HE WELL KNEW	63	3 DON JUAN	6	116	4
THAT THEY MUST INSTANTLY BE WELL ARRAYED	64	3 DON JUAN	6	118	3
THOUGH DOUBTS OF THEIR WELL DOING TO ARRANGE	65	3 DON JUAN	6	120	2
BUT AS THE DANUBE COULD NOT WELL BE WADED	73	3 DON JUAN	7	13	6
IT SEEMS HAS GOT AN EAR AS WELL AS TRUMPET	74	3 DON JUAN	7	15	8
AS WELL AS DILETTANTI IN WAR'S ART	85	3 DON JUAN	7	39	5
AND WHEN WELL PRACTISED IN THESE MIMIC SCENES	93	3 DON JUAN	7	53	5
ONE OF WHOM SPOKE THEIR TONGUE OR WELL OR ILL	95	3 DON JUAN	7	56	5
WELL YOU SHALL HAVE REVENGE AND THAT UNBOUNDED	98	3 DON JUAN	7	61	V7
AS IN A GENERAL'S LETTER WHEN WELL WHACKED	107	3 DON JUAN	7	81	V5
THRICE HAPPY HE WHOSE NAME HAS BEEN WELL SPELT	120	3 DON JUAN	8	18	6
OF THEIR DESIGNS BY SAYING THEY MEANT WELL	123	3 DON JUAN	8	25	7
OUT BETWEEN FRIENDS AS WELL AS ALLIED NATIONS	136	3 DON JUAN	8	48	4
HE DIED DESERVING WELL HIS COUNTRY'S TEARS	152	3 DON JUAN	8	80	5
AS IF HE HAD THREE LIVES AS WELL AS TAILS	172	3 DON JUAN	8	121	8
WHICH LOVES SO WELL ITS COUNTRY AND ITS KING	175	3 DON JUAN	8	126	2
I DON'T THINK THAT YOU USED KINNAIRD QUITE WELL	184	3 DON JUAN	9	2	1
THE SPANISH AND THE FRENCH AS WELL AS DUTCH	184	3 DON JUAN	9	3	5
HE FOUGHT BUT HAS NOT FED SO WELL OF LATE	185	3 DON JUAN	9	6	5
WELL NIGH THE SHORE WHERE ONE STOOPS DOWN AND GATHERS	191	3 DON JUAN	9	18	7
WHENCE IS OUR EXIT AND OUR ENTRANCE--WELL I	210	3 DON JUAN	9	55	3
LIKE FLOWERS WELL WATERED AFTER A LONG DROUTH--	213	3 DON JUAN	9	61	4
AND ALWAYS USED HER FAVOURITES TOO WELL	214	3 DON JUAN	9	63	4
WELL WE WON'T ANALYZE--OUR STORY MUST	221	3 DON JUAN	9	77	1
AND NO LESS TO GOD'S SON AS WELL AS MOTHER	240	3 DON JUAN	10	32	2
OUTWARD DISLIKE WHICH DON'T LOOK WELL ABROAD	240	3 DON JUAN	10	32	5
AS WELL AS FURTHER DRAIN THE WITHERED FORM	243	3 DON JUAN	10	38	4
BUT JUAN SEASONED AS WELL MIGHT BE	256	3 DON JUAN	10	64	6
HE WAS WELL LODGED BUT ONLY WONDERED HOW	262	3 DON JUAN	10	75	2
ACCORDING AS YOU TAKE THINGS WELL OR ILL--	264	3 DON JUAN	10	80	7
WHICH WELL BESEEMED THE DEVIL'S DRAWING-ROOM	265	3 DON JUAN	10	81	3
EXPOSED TO LOSE HIS LIFE AS WELL AS BREECHES	273	3 DON JUAN	11	11	8
IN THUNDER HOLDS THE WAY IT CAN'T WELL MISS	277	3 DON JUAN	11	20	6
BUT LONDON'S SO WELL LIT THAT IF DIOGENES	281	3 DON JUAN	11	28	1
SO WELL THE VERY TRUTH SEEMS FALSEHOOD TO IT	285	3 DON JUAN	11	36	8
WAS WELL RECEIVED BY PERSONS OF CONDITION	290	3 DON JUAN	11	45	8
JUAN KNEW SEVERAL LANGUAGES--AS WELL	295	3 DON JUAN	11	53	1
HOWEVER HE DID PRETTY WELL AND WAS	295	3 DON JUAN	11	54	1
AND WHERE THE DAUGHTER WHOM THE ISLES LOVED WELL	307	3 DON JUAN	11	77	6
IF THAT CAN WELL BE THAN HIS WOODEN LOOK	309	3 DON JUAN	11	83	4
BUT 'TIS AS WELL AT ONCE TO UNDERSTAND	311	3 DON JUAN	11	87	6
WELL IF I DON'T SUCCEED I HAVE SUCCEEDED	324	3 DON JUAN	12	17	1
WELL LOOKED UPON BY BOTH TO THAT EXTENT	342	3 DON JUAN	12	57	2
AND ALL BY HAVING TACT AS WELL AS TASTE	346	3 DON JUAN	12	66	8
WELL CULTIVATED IT WILL RENDER DOUBLE	351	3 DON JUAN	12	76	8
IT IS BECAUSE I CANNOT WELL DO LESS	361	3 DON JUAN	13	8	3
AND WEDDED UNTO ONE SHE HAD LOVED WELL	365	3 DON JUAN	13	14	2
THOUGH OFT' WELL FOUNDED WHICH CONFIRMED BUT MORE	366	3 DON JUAN	13	17	2
WELL LIKE MOST ENGLISHMEN AND LOVED THE RACES	368	3 DON JUAN	13	23	6
FOR JUAN STOOD WELL BOTH WITH INS AND OUTS	369	3 DON JUAN	13	24	3
RECOMMENDATION--AND TO BE WELL DREST	371	3 DON JUAN	13	28	7
AND YOUNG BEGINNERS MAY AS WELL COMMENCE	376	3 DON JUAN	13	40	1
WERE WELL NIGH OVER 'TIS PERHAPS A PITY	380	3 DON JUAN	13	48	2
THE SLAP-DASH REGIMENT SO WELL KNOWN TO FAME	383	3 DON JUAN	13	54	6
WHO HAD DELIVER'D WELL A VERY SET	400	3 DON JUAN	13	90	3
BUT THIS CAN'T BE TRUE JUST NOW FOR WRITERS	418	3 DON JUAN	14	20	1
ALL THIS WERE VERY WELL AND CAN'T BE BETTER	421	3 DON JUAN	14	25	1
OF PANTOMIME--HE DANCED I SAY RIGHT WELL	427	3 DON JUAN	14	38	3
CERTES IT WAS NOT BODY HE WAS WELL	441	3 DON JUAN	14	71	4
AS IF THEY TOLD THE TRUTH COULD WELL BE SHOWN	461	3 DON JUAN	15	13	2
BUT SADDEST WHEN HIS SCIENCE IS WELL KNOWN	463	3 DON JUAN	15	17	6
WHICH SAYS THOU SHALT NOT MARRY UNLESS WELL	472	3 DON JUAN	15	38	3
AND MIGHT GO ON IF WELL WOUND UP LIKE WATCHES	473	3 DON JUAN	15	40	8
AGAINST HER BEING MENTION'D AS WELL FITTED	477	3 DON JUAN	15	48	6
THE DINERS OF CELEBRITY DINED WELL	487	3 DON JUAN	15	70	2
YET I WISH WELL TO TROJAN AND TO TYRIAN	496	3 DON JUAN	15	91	7
THE FIRST--BUT WHAT SHE COULD NOT WELL DIVINE	513	3 DON JUAN	16	30	8
THE CAUSE BUT JUAN SAID HE WAS QUITE WELL	514	3 DON JUAN	16	32	8
QUITE WELL YES NO--THESE ANSWERS WERE MYSTERIOUS	514	3 DON JUAN	16	33	1
SAW--WELL NO MATTER 'TWAS SO LONG AGO	517	3 DON JUAN	16	38	3
WAS ADELINE WELL VERSED AS COMPOSITIONS	523	3 DON JUAN	16	46	8
WERE ANGRY--AS THEY WELL MIGHT TO BE SURE	543	3 DON JUAN	16	89	4
SO WELL SHE ACTED ALL AND EVERY PART	547	3 DON JUAN	16	97	1
THOUGH TOO WELL BRED TO QUIZ MEN TO THEIR FACES	548	3 DON JUAN	16	100	3
AND SO FOR ONE WILL I--AS WELL I MAY--	566	3 DON JUAN	17	10	4

```
                                                      PAGE VOL    CANTO STANZA LN
WELL-A-DAY
     WAS BUT A MOMENT'S ACT--AH WELL-A-DAY  . . . . . . . 121  2 DON JUAN  1    181   5
WELL-BORN
     OR GENTLEMEN WHO THOUGH WELL-BORN AND BRED . . . . .  33  2 DON JUAN  1     22   3
WELL-BRED
     THEIR CONDUCT WAS EXCEEDINGLY WELL-BRED . . . . . .   35  2 DON JUAN  1     26   5
WELL-CLAD
     A TIDE OF WELL-CLAD WAITERS AND AROUND   . . . . . . 282  3 DON JUAN 11     30   2
     FROM WHENCE POURED FORTH A TRIBE OF WELL-CLAD WAITERS . . 313  3 DON JUAN 11  V 29   2
WELLESLEY
     AND FILL'D THEIR SIGN-POSTS THEN LIKE WELLESLEY NOW . .  22  2 DON JUAN  1      2   4
     WHERE'S BRUMMELL DISHED WHERE'S LONG POLE WELLESLEY DIDDLED 307  3 DON JUAN 11     78   1
WELLESLEY'S
     THEN FEED HER FAMINE FAT WITH WELLESLEY'S GLORY   . . . . 174  3 DON JUAN  8    125   8
WELLINGTON
     AS SAY THAT WELLINGTON AT WATERLOO . . . . . . . . . 136  3 DON JUAN  8     48   7
     THE DUKE OF WELLINGTON HAD CEASED TO SHOW    . . . . . 137  3 DON JUAN  8     49   6
     OH WELLINGTON (OR VILAINTON--FOR FAME . . . . . . . 183  3 DON JUAN  9      1   1
     WHILE WELLINGTON HAS BUT ENSLAVED THE WHITES   . . . . 325  3 DON JUAN 12     20   7
WELL-NIGH
     THE MAN WAS WELL-NIGH DEAD ERE MEN BEGUN . . . . . . 565  3 DON JUAN 17      8   5
WELL'S
     FLAME WAS SHOWERED FORTH ABOVE AS WELL'S BELOW . . . . 135  3 DON JUAN  8     45   4
WELL-USED
     AS IF WELL-USED TO THE RETREATING TRADE . . . . . . 473  2 DON JUAN  5    107   3
WENCHES
     PRESERVING PARTRIDGES AND PRETTY WENCHES . . . . . . 531  3 DON JUAN 16     63   7
WENT
     WHAT WENT BEFORE--BY WAY OF EPISODE   . . . . . . .   24  2 DON JUAN  1      6   4
     EVEN HER MINUTEST MOTIONS WENT AS WELL  . . . . . .   30  2 DON JUAN  1     17   5
     WENT PLUCKING VARIOUS FRUIT WITHOUT HER LEAVE   . . .  30  2 DON JUAN  1     18   8
     SOME WENT TO AFRICA SOME STAID IN SPAIN   . . . . .   52  2 DON JUAN  1     56   7
     HOWEVER THIS MIGHT BE THE RACE WENT ON  . . . . . .   54  2 DON JUAN  1     59   1
     IS IT FOR THIS I SCARCE WENT ANYWHERE . . . . . . . 102  2 DON JUAN  1    148   3
     DIRE WAS THE SCUFFLE AND OUT WENT THE LIGHT  . . . . 122  2 DON JUAN  1    184   1
     THAT WENT BEFORE IN THESE I SHALL ENRICH . . . . . . 138  2 DON JUAN  1    204   4
     BOTH MAIN AND MIZEN FIRST THE MIZEN WENT  . . . . . 173  2 DON JUAN  2     32   2
     SOME WENT TO PRAYERS AGAIN AND MADE A VOW   . . . . . 179  2 DON JUAN  2     44   3
     AND OTHERS WENT ON AS THEY HAD BEGUN  . . . . . . . 180  2 DON JUAN  2     45   5
     'TWAS TWILIGHT AND THE SUNLESS DAY WENT DOWN  . . . . 182  2 DON JUAN  2     49   1
     NINE SOULS MORE WENT IN HER THE LONG-BOAT STILL  . . 188  2 DON JUAN  2     61   1
     SINCE NOAH'S ARK WENT CRUISING HERE AND THERE  . . . 191  2 DON JUAN  2     66   6
     WHISPER'D ANOTHER AND THUS IT WENT ROUND  . . . . . 194  2 DON JUAN  2     73   2
     WENT RAGING MAD--LORD HOW THEY DID BLASPHEME  . . . . 198  2 DON JUAN  2     79   4
     IT CAME AND WENT AND FLUTTER'D ROUND THEM TILL  . . . 206  2 DON JUAN  2     94   7
     AND PENSIVE TO HER FATHER'S HOUSE SHE WENT  . . . . 228  2 DON JUAN  2    136   1
     PAIR OF SCARCE DECENT TROWSERS--WENT TO WORK  . . . . 240  2 DON JUAN  2    160   2
     AND AS HE INTERRUPTED NOT WENT EKING  . . . . . . . 241  2 DON JUAN  2    161   5
     AND THERE HE WENT ASHORE WITHOUT DELAY  . . . . . . 286  2 DON JUAN  3     20   1
     'TWAS WONDERFUL HOW THINGS WENT ON IMPROVING  . . . . 295  2 DON JUAN  3     39   7
     OFT CAME AND WENT AS THERE RESOLVED TO DIE  . . . . 365  2 DON JUAN  4     39   6
     AND WENT DOWN TO THE GRAVE UNBORN WHEREIN   . . . . . 382  2 DON JUAN  4     70   5
     AND THEN WENT DOWN THE HATCHWAY ONE BY ONE  . . . . 393  2 DON JUAN  4     90   8
     SOME WENT OFF DEARLY FIFTEEN HUNDRED DOLLARS  . . . . 407  2 DON JUAN  4    114   1
     BUT WHEN THE OFFER WENT BEYOND THEY KNEW . . . . . . 407  2 DON JUAN  4    114   7
     EMBARKED HIMSELF AND THEM AND OFF THEY WENT THENCE  . . 432  2 DON JUAN  5     40   3
     THESE WORDS WENT THROUGH HIS SOUL LIKE ARAB-SPEARS   . . 478  2 DON JUAN  5    117   7
     HE WENT TO MOSQUE IN STATE AND SAID HIS PRAYERS  . . 496  2 DON JUAN  5    148   1
     MEANTIME THE EDUCATION THEY WENT THROUGH . . . . . . 499  2 DON JUAN  5    153   5
     GAVE WHAT I HAD--A HEART--AS THE WORLD WENT I . . . .   9  3 DON JUAN  6      5   6
     HE WENT FORTH WITH THE LOVELY ODALISQUES  . . . . .   20  3 DON JUAN  6     29   1
     AWAY HE WENT THEN UPON HIS COMMISSION . . . . . . .   64  3 DON JUAN  6    117   1
     NOTHING--THE WORK OF GLORY STILL WENT ON . . . . . . 106  3 DON JUAN  7     78   1
     THEN LIKE AN ASS HE WENT UPON HIS WAY . . . . . . . 126  3 DON JUAN  8     30   1
     THE MOSLEM ORPHAN WENT WITH HER PROTECTOR   . . . . . 182  3 DON JUAN  8    141   1
     IF ONCE BEYOND HER BOUDOIR'S PRECINCTS IN YE WENT  . . 214  3 DON JUAN  9     63   5
     BUT WENT TO HEAVEN IN AS SINCERE A WAY  . . . . . . 242  3 DON JUAN 10     35   2
     (WHEN A NEW IPHIGENE SHE WENT TO TAURIS)  . . . . . 248  3 DON JUAN 10     49   7
     WENT BOUNDING FOR THE ISLAND OF THE FREE   . . . . . 256  3 DON JUAN 10     64   2
     ALONG THE ROAD AS IF THEY WENT TO BURY  . . . . . . 260  3 DON JUAN 10     71   5
     THE SUN WENT DOWN THE SMOKE ROSE UP AS FROM  . . . . 265  3 DON JUAN 10     81   1
     AND MEDES WOULD NE'ER REVOKE WHAT WENT BEFORE  . . . 366  3 DON JUAN 13     17   4
     BUT ERE HE WENT HE ADDED A SLIGHT HINT  . . . . . . 440  3 DON JUAN 14     69   1
     RETIRED AND AS HE WENT OUT CALMLY KISSED HER  . . . . 440  3 DON JUAN 14     69   7
     THOUGHT HER PREDICTIONS WENT NOT MUCH AMISS . . . . . 492  3 DON JUAN 15     81   3
     HIS CHAMBER DOOR WIDE OPEN--AND WENT FORTH  . . . . . 508  3 DON JUAN 16     17   2
     UNDREST AND RATHER SLOWLY WENT TO BED  . . . . . . . 512  3 DON JUAN 16     27   4
     MATCHED FOR THE SPRING WHOM SEVERAL WENT TO SEE  . . 527  3 DON JUAN 16     55   8
     WHICH SHE WENT THROUGH AS THOUGH IT WERE A DANCE  . . 546  3 DON JUAN 16     96   4
WEPT
     BOABDIL WEPT OF DONNA JULIA'S KIN . . . . . . . . .   52  2 DON JUAN  1     56   6
     SO JUAN WEPT AS WEPT THE CAPTIVE JEWS . . . . . . . 165  2 DON JUAN  2     16   1
     SO JUAN WEPT AS WEPT THE CAPTIVE JEWS . . . . . . . 165  2 DON JUAN  2     16   1
     AND JUAN WEPT AND MUCH HE SIGH'D AND THOUGHT   . . . 165  2 DON JUAN  2     17   1
     AND IF HE WEPT AT LENGTH THEY WERE NOT FEARS . . . . 179  2 DON JUAN  2     43   5
     HE LOVED HIS CHILD AND WOULD HAVE WEPT THE LOSS OF HER . 289  2 DON JUAN  3     26   7
     TO PRAYER WAS HEARD NO MORE--AND JUAN WEPT  . . . . 182  3 DON JUAN  8    141   7
WE'RE
     WE'RE TOLD THIS GREAT HIGH PRIEST OF ALL THE NINE . . . 328  2 DON JUAN  3     91   6
```

903

WE'RE (CONTINUED)

	PAGE	VOL	CANTO		STANZA	LN
I'LL TAKE JUANNA WE'RE A SLENDERER PAIR	29	3 DON JUAN	6		47	4
SO LITTLE DO WE KNOW WHAT WE'RE ABOUT IN	191	3 DON JUAN	9		17	7
THAT TILL WE SEE WHAT'S WHAT IN FACT WE'RE FAR	335	3 DON JUAN	12		40	4

WERTER

OR MAKE A WERTER OF HIM IN THE END	438	3 DON JUAN	14		64	2

WERTERS

AND SENDS NEW WERTERS YEARLY TO THEIR COFFIN	345	3 DON JUAN	12		63	6

WESLEY

BY TILLOTSON AND WESLEY AND ROUSSEAU	68	3 DON JUAN	7		4	3

WEST

TO SOUNDS WHICH ECHO FURTHER WEST	321	2 DON JUAN	3	L 2	5
WHICH THE WEST INDIAN MARKET SCARCE WOULD BRING	408	2 DON JUAN	4		115	2
MEANETH THE WEST OR WORST END OF A CITY	290	3 DON JUAN	11		45	2
THUS THE LOW WORLD NORTH SOUTH OR WEST OR EAST	342	3 DON JUAN	12		56	6
ON ROADS EAST SOUTH NORTH WEST THERE IS A RUN	377	3 DON JUAN	13		42	4

WESTERN

IN THE MORE CHASTENED DOMES OF WESTERN KINGS	465	2 DON JUAN	5		94	3
(WHICH SAW ALL WESTERN THINGS WITH SMALL SURPRISE	328	3 DON JUAN	12		27	3

WESTERNS

THERE NOW ARE NO 'SQUIRE WESTERNS AS OF OLD	409	3 DON JUAN	13		110	4

WESTMINSTER'S

UPON YOUR TOMB IN WESTMINSTER'S OLD ABBEY	184	3 DON JUAN	9		2	4
THE LAMPS OF WESTMINSTER'S MORE REGULAR GLEAM	279	3 DON JUAN	11		24	4

WESTPHALIAN

THEY ALSO SET A GLAZED WESTPHALIAN HAM ON	484	3 DON JUAN	15		65	5

WET

SOME POUNDS OF BREAD THOUGH INJURED BY THE WET	181	2 DON JUAN	2		47	2
EACH SEA CURL'D O'ER THE STERN AND KEPT THEM WET	188	2 DON JUAN	2		60	5
TO FAINT AND DAMAGED BREAD WET THROUGH THE BAGS	189	2 DON JUAN	2		62	7
BRIGHT PHOEBUS WHILE THE MOUNTAINS STILL ARE WET	230	2 DON JUAN	2		139	5
AGAINST THE BOUNDARY IT SCARCELY WET	251	2 DON JUAN	2		181	8
WAS SUCH AS FIRE ACCORDS TO A WET BLANKET	294	2 DON JUAN	3		36	8
WAS MUCH THE SAME AS FIRE GIVES A WET BLANKET	294	2 DON JUAN	3		36	V8
AND WET AND COLD AND LIFELESS AT HER FEET	362	2 DON JUAN	4		34	1
WET STILL MORE DISAGREEABLE AND STRIKING	479	2 DON JUAN	5		118	4
A NOISE LIKE TO WET FINGERS DRAWN ON GLASS	556	3 DON JUAN	16		114	1

WE'VE

LOOK WHERE YOU PLEASE--WE'VE NOTHING SIR TO HIDE	106	2 DON JUAN	1		156	4
(WE'VE NOT SO GOOD A WORD BUT HAVE THE THING	332	3 DON JUAN	3		97	2
JOHNSON SAID--JUAN WE'VE NO TIME TO LOSE	162	3 DON JUAN	8		101	1
HIS JOURNEY WE'VE SO MANY TOURS OF LATE	203	3 DON JUAN	9		42	6
OH FOR A GLASS OF MAX WE'VE MISS'D OUR BOOTY--	276	3 DON JUAN	11		16	3
THE LATTER WORSE USED OF THE TWO WE'VE SEEN--	541	3 DON JUAN	16		84	3

WHACKED

AS IN A GENERAL'S LETTER WHEN WELL WHACKED	107	3 DON JUAN	7		81	V5

WHATEER

WHATEER THE GARDEN BORE OR MART DISCLOSED	476	2 DON JUAN	5		113	V4

WHAT'ER

WHICH MEET THE GAZE WHAT'ER IT MAY REGARD--	118	3 DON JUAN	8		13	4

WHATNOT

OF GEORGIANS RUSSIANS NUBIANS AND WHATNOT	417	2 DON JUAN	5		13	2
TO THEIR OWN WHIMS AND PASSIONS AND WHATNOT	423	2 DON JUAN	5		25	4
AND DEBT AND WHATNOT FOR THEIR SOLACE SENT	360	3 DON JUAN	13		5	8
AND WHATNOT THOUGH HE RODE BEYOND ALL PRICE	425	3 DON JUAN	14		35	7
AND WHATNOT--THOUGH HE HAD RIDDEN LIKE A CENTAUR	425	3 DON JUAN	14		35	V7

WHAT'S

HIM WHAT'S HIS LINEAGE LET HIM BUT BE SHOWN--	105	2 DON JUAN	1		154	5
WHAT'S TO BE DONE ALFONSO WILL BE BACK	114	2 DON JUAN	1		169	1
HAD LEFT THEIR BODIES AND WHAT'S WORSE ALAS	185	2 DON JUAN	2		55	2
BECAUSE TILL PEOPLE KNOW WHAT'S COME TO PASS	185	2 DON JUAN	2		55	6
SEEING WHAT'S MEANT FOR MANY WITH BUT ONE	443	2 DON JUAN	5		57	8
AND WHAT'S STILL BETTER--TEACHES THEM THAT OTHERS	491	2 DON JUAN	5		138	V2
THE FAVOURITE BUT WHAT'S FAVOUR AMONGST FOUR	12	3 DON JUAN	6		12	2
DESCRIBED--WHAT'S STRANGE--IN WORDS EXTREMELY FEW	34	3 DON JUAN	6		57	6
OUR ULTIMATE EXISTENCE WHAT'S OUR PRESENT	37	3 DON JUAN	6		63	7
AND THESE HE CALLED ON AND WHAT'S STRANGE THEY CAME	132	3 DON JUAN	8		38	1
AND WHAT'S STILL STRANGER LEFT BEHIND A NAME	144	3 DON JUAN	8		63	1
POOR THING WHAT'S TO BE DONE I'M PUZZLED QUITE	161	3 DON JUAN	8		99	8
WHAT'S THIS IN ONE ANNIHILATED CITY	174	3 DON JUAN	8		124	5
THE FORMER KNOW WHAT'S WHAT WHILE NEW-FLEDGED CHICKS	230	3 DON JUAN	10		10	3
THE HORRID SIN--AND WHAT'S STILL WORSE THE TROUBLE	292	3 DON JUAN	11		46	8
THAT TILL WE SEE WHAT'S WHAT IN FACT WE'RE FAR	335	3 DON JUAN	12		40	4
OR WHAT'S STILL WORSE TO PUT YOU OUT OF FASHION--	337	3 DON JUAN	12		45	4
ABOUT WHAT'S CALLED SUCCESS OR NOT SUCCEEDING	341	3 DON JUAN	12		55	2
PEACE WAR THE TAXES AND WHAT'S CALLED THE NATION	360	3 DON JUAN	13		6	2
IF BUT TO SHOW I'VE TRAVELL'D AND WHAT'S TRAVEL	380	3 DON JUAN	13		47	7
BUT WHAT'S THIS TO THE PURPOSE YOU WILL SAY	413	3 DON JUAN	14		7	1
I WRITE WHAT'S UPPERMOST WITHOUT DELAY	413	3 DON JUAN	14		7	5
AND WERE HER OBJECT ONLY WHAT'S CALL'D GLORY	416	3 DON JUAN	14		13	7
BESIDES THERE MIGHT BE FALSEHOOD IN WHAT'S STATED	428	3 DON JUAN	14		42	6
WHICH RINGS WHAT'S UPPERMOST OF NEW OR HOARY	465	3 DON JUAN	15		20	7
BUT WHAT'S REALITY WHO HAS ITS CLUE	495	3 DON JUAN	15		89	6
SOMETHING BUT WHAT'S NOT STATED IN MY TALE	514	3 DON JUAN	16		31	3
THOUGH NOT EXACTLY WHAT'S CALLED OPEN HOUSE	534	3 DON JUAN	16		68	8
AND NOT IN VAIN HE LISTENED--HUSH WHAT'S THAT	556	3 DON JUAN	16		112	1

WHATSOE'ER

BUT WHATSOE'ER THE CAUSE IS ONE MAY SAY	76	2 DON JUAN	1		102	5
HAD NEVER SEEN THE MAID OR WHATSOE'ER	216	2 DON JUAN	2		115	7

	PAGE	VOL	CANTO	STANZA	LN
WHATSOE'ER (CONTINUED)					
OR SLEEP OR WHATSOE'ER IT WAS BY FEELING	237	2	DON JUAN 2	153	2
BUT WHATSOE'ER HE HAD OF LOVE REPOSED	304	2	DON JUAN 3	57	1
FOR KINDER FEELINGS WHATSOE'ER THEIR NATION	480	2	DON JUAN 5	120	4
I KNOW NO OTHER REASON WHATSOE'ER	230	3	DON JUAN 10	11	2
BUT WHATSOE'ER SHE WISHED SHE ACTED RIGHT	435	3	DON JUAN 14	57	6
AND WHATSOE'ER MAY BE HIS PRAYER	520	3	DON JUAN 16	L 6	7
WHATSOEVER					
PERFORCE SINCE WHATSOEVER MET HER VIEW	378	2	DON JUAN 4	62	4
SAID JUAN--WHATSOEVER IS TO BE	161	3	DON JUAN 8	100	1
AT WHATSOEVER RISK OF BEING DEFEATED	559	3	DON JUAN 16	119	6
WHEAT					
AND APT TO SOW AN AUTHOR'S WHEAT WITH TARES	369	3	DON JUAN 13	25	3
WHEEDLE					
AND NOT THE FIX'D--HE KNEW THE WAY TO WHEEDLE	317	2	DON JUAN 3	80	4
WHEELING					
FONDLY THE WHEELING FIRE-FLIES FLEW AROUND HER	435	3	DON JUAN 14	57	1
WHEELS					
EXCEPT THE CREAK OF WHEELS WHICH ON THEIR PIVOT HE	272	3	DON JUAN 11	8	6
OF WHEELS AND ROAR OF VOICES AND CONFUSION	278	3	DON JUAN 11	22	2
THEN GLARE THE LAMPS THEN WHIRL THE WHEELS THEN ROAR	302	3	DON JUAN 11	67	2
TO KEEP THE WHEELS GOING OF THE HIGHER CLASS	342	3	DON JUAN 12	57	5
'TIS THE POSTILLION'S PARADISE WHEELS FLY	377	3	DON JUAN 13	42	3
WHEELS WHIRL FROM CARLTON PALACE TO SOHO	378	3	DON JUAN 13	44	3
THEIR FEE BUT ERE THE WATERED WHEELS MAY HISS HENCE	379	3	DON JUAN 13	46	7
WHELM					
OR HEAVING WHELM THE HELPLESS CARAVAN	373	2	DON JUAN 4	55	7
WHELP					
IF I CAN STAVE OFF THOUGHT WHICH AS A WHELP	238	3	DON JUAN 10	28	3
WHENCE					
WHENCE MELODY DESCENDS AS FROM A THRONE	236	2	DON JUAN 2	151	8
WHENCE THE BROAD MOON ROSE CIRCLING INTO SIGHT	253	2	DON JUAN 2	185	4
THEIR HEARTS THE FLOWER FROM WHENCE THE HONEY SPRUNG	254	2	DON JUAN 2	187	8
HE IS NOR WHENCE HE CAME--AND LITTLE CARE	298	2	DON JUAN 3	45	2
FROM WHENCE SPRINGS UP ABUNDANCE OF ABUSES	327	2	DON JUAN 3	88	V4
KATINKA ASKED HER ALSO WHENCE SHE CAME--	28	3	DON JUAN 6	44	3
WHAT ARE WE AND WHENCE CAME WE WHAT SHALL BE	37	3	DON JUAN 6	63	6
WHENCE COME YE--FROM CONSTANTINOPLE LAST	97	3	DON JUAN 7	59	4
FROM WHENCE THEY SALLIED ON THOSE CHRISTIAN SCORNERS	149	3	DON JUAN 8	75	8
WHENCE HER FAIR HAIR ROSE TWINING WITH AFFRIGHT	158	3	DON JUAN 8	93	2
WHENCE IS OUR EXIT AND OUR ENTRANCE--WELL I	210	3	DON JUAN 9	55	3
IN VISIONS OF THOSE SKIES FROM WHENCE LOVE SPRUNG	230	3	DON JUAN 10	10	6
BUT WHENCE WISE TRAVELLERS DRIVE WITH CIRCUMSPECTION	238	3	DON JUAN 10	27	6
THY LONG LONG BILLS WHENCE NOTHING IS DEDUCTED	259	3	DON JUAN 10	69	8
OF SOME ALCHYMIC FURNACE FROM WHENCE BROKE	266	3	DON JUAN 10	83	3
FROM WHENCE POURED FORTH A TRIBE OF WELL-CLAD WAITERS	313	3	DON JUAN 11	V 29	2
THOUGH GOD KNOWS WHENCE IT CAME FROM THERE WAS TOO	483	3	DON JUAN 15	63	2
OF WHICH I CAN'T TELL WHENCE THEIR KNOWLEDGE SPRINGS	489	3	DON JUAN 15	76	4
HE WAS FREE TO CONFESS--(WHENCE COMES THIS PHRASE	536	3	DON JUAN 16	73	1
WHENE'ER					
WHENE'ER IT SUITS HIS PURPOSE TO ADVANCE	152	2	DON JUAN 1	V 3	3
WHEREAS					
WHEREAS THIS STORY'S ACTUALLY TRUE	137	2	DON JUAN 1	202	8
WHEREAS IF ONE SOLE LADY PLEASED FOREVER	270	2	DON JUAN 2	213	7
WHEREAS THE OTHER AFTER ALL ITS GLARE	114	3	DON JUAN 8	4	2
WHEREAS IF ALL BE TRUE WE HEAR OF HEAVEN	168	3	DON JUAN 8	114	7
WHEREAS THE OTHERS HUNT FOR REGAL SPIDERS	196	3	DON JUAN 9	27	V8
WHEREAS YOUR MODERN MONARCHS ARE MERE SPIDERS	196	3	DON JUAN 9	27	V8
WHEREAS INSISTING IN OR OUT OF SEASON	478	3	DON JUAN 15	51	5
WHEREBY					
AND THIN PRODUCED A PLAN WHEREBY TO ERECT	529	3	DON JUAN 16	58	6
WHEREFORE					
AND WHY AND WHEREFORE NO ONE UNDERSTANDS	33	2	DON JUAN 1	21	8
HE KNEW NOT WHEREFORE THAT WHICH HE WAS BID	111	2	DON JUAN 1	163	8
WHEREFORE THE RAVISHING DID NOT BEGIN	178	3	DON JUAN 8	132	4
AND WHEREFORE THIS EXORDIUM--WHY JUST NOW	226	3	DON JUAN 10	3	1
WAS TRANQUIL THOUGH SHE KNEW NOT WHY OR WHEREFORE	250	3	DON JUAN 10	52	8
PREACH TO POOR ROUGES AND WHEREFORE NOT BEGIN	266	3	DON JUAN 10	85	2
AND WHEREFORE BLAME GAUNT WEALTH'S AUSTERITIES	319	3	DON JUAN 12	7	6
THAT IS NO DOUBT THE ONLY REASON WHEREFORE	470	3	DON JUAN 15	31	8
AND WHEREFORE NOT A REASONABLE REASON	478	3	DON JUAN 15	51	1
WHEREIN					
'TWAS BORNE BY THE RUDE WAVE WHEREIN 'TWAS CAST	204	2	DON JUAN 2	90	6
AND WENT DOWN TO THE GRAVE UNBORN WHEREIN	382	2	DON JUAN 4	70	5
A VILLAGE OF MOLDAVIA'S WASTE WHEREIN	76	3	DON JUAN 7	20	7
TO PAINT A SIEGE WHEREIN MORE MEN WERE SLAIN	106	3	DON JUAN 7	80	2
BUT THE STONE BASTION STILL REMAINS WHEREIN	160	3	DON JUAN 8	98	2
AGAINST THE LIGHT WHEREIN SHE DIES HE CLUNG	170	3	DON JUAN 8	118	4
WHEREIN SHE LIKED HER OWN TO STAND LIKE ROCKS	197	3	DON JUAN 9	29	8
WHEREOF					
ALSO THE MUFFIN WHEREOF HE COMPLAINED	515	3	DON JUAN 16	34	2
WHEREON					
AS IF 'TWERE ONE WHEREON MAGICIANS BIND	72	2	DON JUAN 1	95	6
A BOSOM WHEREON HE HIS HEAD MIGHT LAY	73	2	DON JUAN 1	96	5
BY THE SEA SHORE WHEREON SHE LOVED TO DWELL	382	2	DON JUAN 4	71	8
WHEREON IMMEDIATELY AT HIS REQUEST	96	3	DON JUAN 7	57	1
PACES WERE LEFT WHEREON YOU COULD CONTRIVE	136	3	DON JUAN 8	47	2
AND I AM WITH YOU--WHEREON JOHNSON TOOK	161	3	DON JUAN 8	99	5
WHEREON THE RUSSIAN PATHOS GREW LESS TENDER	165	3	DON JUAN 8	107	6
WHEREON APICIUS WOULD BESTOW HIS BENISON	484	3	DON JUAN 15	65	6

905

```
                                                    PAGE VOL      CANTO STANZA LN
WHERE'S
    ANTONIA WHERE'S MY POCKET-HANDKERCHIEF  . . . . . .  107  2 DON JUAN  1    157   8
    WHERE'S BRUMMELL DISHED WHERE'S LONG POLE WELLESLEY DIDDLED  307  3 DON JUAN 11   78   1
    WHERE'S BRUMMELL DISHED WHERE'S LONG POLE WELLESLEY DIDDLED  307  3 DON JUAN 11   78   1
    WHERE'S WHITBREAD ROMILLY  WHERE'S GEORGE THE THIRD  . . .  307  3 DON JUAN 11   78   2
    WHERE'S WHITBREAD ROMILLY  WHERE'S GEORGE THE THIRD  . . .  307  3 DON JUAN 11   78   2
    WHERE'S CHARLOTTE (THAT'S NOT EASILY OWN'D) . . . . .  307  3 DON JUAN 11   78   V3
WHERESOE'ER
    IN DITCHES FIELDS OR WHERESOE'ER THEY FELT  . . . . .  120  3 DON JUAN  8   18   4
    OF SOBER REASON WHERESOE'ER IT MOVES  . . . . . .  284  3 DON JUAN 11   33   6
WHEREUPON
    JUAN AND JOHNSON WHEREUPON THEY FELL  . . . . . .  166  3 DON JUAN  8  109   2
WHEREWITH
    WHEREWITH WE BREAK OUR BUBBLES ON THE OCEAN . . . . .  457  3 DON JUAN 15    2   4
WHEREWITHAL
    A SOMETHING WHEREWITHAL TO BE ANNOY'D . . . . . . .  444  3 DON JUAN 14   79   3
WHERIN
    FOR THE IMPERIAL PRESENCE WHERIN WHETHER . . . . .   65  3 DON JUAN  6  119   2
    NOT LIKE SLOW GERMANY WHERIN THEY MUDDLE . . . . . .  260  3 DON JUAN 10   71   4
WHETS
    THERE'S NOTHING WHETS THE BEAK OR ARMS THE CLAW  . . .  488  2 DON JUAN  5  133   3
WHETSTONE
    SELF-LOVE THAT WHETSTONE OF DAN CUPID'S DART  . . . .   15  3 DON JUAN  6   19   V5
WHIG
    TORY BY NURTURE WHIG BY CIRCUMSTANCE  . . . . . .  152  2 DON JUAN  1  V 3   1
    WHICH NEVER FLATTERS EITHER WHIG OR TORY . . . . . .  465  3 DON JUAN 15   20   V7
WHIGS
    MY FRIENDS THE WHIGS EXACTLY WHERE THEY WERE  . . . .  308  3 DON JUAN 11   79   8
    EXCEPT THE WHIGS NOT GETTING INTO PLACE . . . . . .  309  3 DON JUAN 11   82   8
WHILE
    WHILE SEATED AFTER DINNER AT HIS EASE  . . . . . .   24  2 DON JUAN  1    6   5
    SHE MUST NOT OWN BUT CHERISH'D MORE THE WHILE  . . . .   61  2 DON JUAN  1   72   4
    EVEN AS THE PAGE IS RUSTLED WHILE WE LOOK  . . . . .   72  2 DON JUAN  1   95   3
    THUS WOULD HE WHILE HIS LONELY HOURS AWAY  . . . . .   73  2 DON JUAN  1   96   1
    THE WHILE THE WICKED WORLD BEHOLDS DELIGHTED  . . . .   75  2 DON JUAN  1  100   3
    AND WHILE SHE PONDER'D THIS BESIDES MUCH MORE  . . . .   80  2 DON JUAN  1  109   6
    AND THEN SHE LOOKS SO MODEST ALL THE WHILE  . . . . .   82  2 DON JUAN  1  113   8
    JULIA SAID NOUGHT THOUGH ALL THE WHILE THERE ROSE  . .  117  2 DON JUAN  1  175   1
    HAVE SQUANDER'D MY WHOLE SUMMER WHILE 'TWAS MAY  . . .  143  2 DON JUAN  1  213   5
    WHILE THE O'ERPOWERING EYE THAT TURNS YOU PALE . . . .  160  2 DON JUAN  2    7   3
    WHILE HIS SALT TEARS DROPP'D INTO THE SALT SEA . . . .  165  2 DON JUAN  2   17   2
    COULD JUAN'S PASSION WHILE THE BILLOWS ROAR . . . . .  168  2 DON JUAN  2   23   7
    WHILE THEY THRUST SHEETS SHIRTS JACKETS BALES OF MUSLIN .  171  2 DON JUAN  2   28   8
    A SQUALL CAME ON AND WHILE SOME GUNS BROKE LOOSE  . . .  172  2 DON JUAN  2   30   6
    IT MAY BE EASILY SUPPOSED WHILE THIS . . . . . . .  173  2 DON JUAN  2   33   1
    WHICH COURAGE GIVES WHILE POOR PEDRILLO'S PAIR . . . .  186  2 DON JUAN  2   56   5
    WHILE T'OTHER HALF WERE LAID DOWN IN THEIR PLACE . . .  189  2 DON JUAN  2   63   5
    WHILE A FEW PRAY'D--(THE FIRST TIME FOR SOME YEARS)--  .  208  2 DON JUAN  2   98   5
    THE WATERS BEAT WHILE HE THERETO WAS LASH'D . . . . .  212  2 DON JUAN  2  107   6
    BRIGHT HUES WHEN OUT OF DOORS AND YET WHILE WAVE . . .  220  2 DON JUAN  2  120   5
    BRIGHT PHOEBUS WHILE THE MOUNTAINS STILL ARE WET . . .  230  2 DON JUAN  2  139   5
    WHILE THE SUN SMILED ON HER WITH HIS FIRST FLAME . . .  232  2 DON JUAN  2  142   3
    WHILE VENUS FILLS THE HEART (WITHOUT HEART REALLY  . .  246  2 DON JUAN  2  170   1
    WHILE BACCHUS POURS OUT WINE OR HANDS A JELLY  . . . .  246  2 DON JUAN  2  170   5
    WHILE VENUS FILLS THE HEART (WHICH QUITE AS WELL IS  .  246  2 DON JUAN  2  170   V1
    WHILE BACCHUS WILL PURVEY WITH WINES AND JELLIES . . .  246  2 DON JUAN  2  170   V5
    AS THEY WHO WATCH O'ER WHAT THEY LOVE WHILE SLEEPING  .  261  2 DON JUAN  2  196   8
    FOR THE FIRST PASSION STAYS THERE SUCH A WHILE . . . .  271  2 DON JUAN  2  215   3
    WHILE PEACEFUL AS IF STILL AN UNWEAN'D LAMB  . . . . .  292  2 DON JUAN  3   32   3
    WHILE SHE HAD NOT ONE HOUR TO SPARE FROM LOVING  . . .  295  2 DON JUAN  3   39   8
    WHILE I SOLILOQUIZE BEYOND EXPRESSION  . . . . . .  331  2 DON JUAN  3   96   4
    WHILE I AM CHATTERING BEYOND ALL EXPRESSION . . . . .  331  2 DON JUAN  3   96   V4
    WHILE SWUNG THE DEEP BELL IN THE DISTANT TOWER . . . .  335  2 DON JUAN  3  102   5
    WHILE SWUNG THE SIGNAL FROM THE SACRED TOWER  . . . .  335  2 DON JUAN  3  102   V5
    WHILE YOUTH'S HOT WISHES IN OUR RED VEINS REVEL  . . .  345  2 DON JUAN  4    2   5
    WHILE LIFE'S STRANGE PRINCIPLE WILL OFTEN LIE  . . . .  350  2 DON JUAN  4   11   7
    WHILE ONE NEW TEAR AROSE IN HAIDEE'S EYE . . . . . .  355  2 DON JUAN  4   21   8
    OF PLEASURE AND OF PAIN--EVEN WHILE I KISS  . . . . .  364  2 DON JUAN  4   38   5
    JUAN REPLIED NOT WHILE THIS ARM IS FREE  . . . . . .  365  2 DON JUAN  4   40   2
    HIS DAUGHTER WHILE COMPRESS'D WITHIN HIS CLASP . . . .  370  2 DON JUAN  4   48   2
    FOR FOR A WHILE THE FURIES MADE A PAUSE  . . . . . .  378  2 DON JUAN  4   62   8
    WHILE THE RIGHT HAND WHICH WROTE IT STILL IS ABLE  . .  398  2 DON JUAN  4   99   5
    WHILE WEEDS AND ORDURE RANKLE ROUND THE BASE  . . . .  400  2 DON JUAN  4  103   8
    AS RENEGADOES WHILE IN HAPLESS GROUP . . . . . . .  409  2 DON JUAN  4  116   5
    SOME BOUGHT THE JET WHILE OTHERS CHOSE THE PALE  . . .  416  2 DON JUAN  5   10   4
    FROM HIS OWN BRAIN'S OPPRESSION WHILE IT REELS . . . .  427  2 DON JUAN  5   31   6
    THEIR WHILE TO REAR WHOLE HOTBEDS IN THEIR WORKS . . .  434  2 DON JUAN  5   42   7
    WHILE NATURE TORTURED TWENTY THOUSAND WAYS  . . . . .  440  2 DON JUAN  5   52   6
    WHILE HE WAS DRESSING BABA THEIR BLACK FRIEND  . . . .  451  2 DON JUAN  5   69   1
    WHILE BABA MADE HIM COMB HIS HEAD AND OIL IT  . . . .  457  2 DON JUAN  5   79   8
    BLOCKHEAD COME ON AND SEE QUOTH BABA WHILE  . . . . .  459  2 DON JUAN  5   83   1
    WHAT ALL THIS MEANT WHILE BABA BOWED AND BENDED  . . .  466  2 DON JUAN  5   95   7
    AND TAKING HINTS IN GOOD PART ALL THE WHILE . . . . .  473  2 DON JUAN  5  107   4
    WHILE SOME MORE DESPERATE DOWAGER HAS BEEN WAGING  . .  486  2 DON JUAN  5  130   3
    A MOMENT'S MORE HAD SLAIN HER BUT THE WHILE . . . . .  489  2 DON JUAN  5  135   2
    AS TO ANNOUNCE HIS VISITS A LONG WHILE  . . . . . .  495  2 DON JUAN  5  146   5
    WHILE STILL A FLUTTERING SIGH GULBEYAZ HEAVED  . . . .  500  2 DON JUAN  5  155   6
    SUCH NOTICE OF A GIAOUR WHILE SCARCE TO ONE . . . . .  501  2 DON JUAN  5  156   5
    AT A SAD DISCOUNT WHILE YOUR OVER-CHILLY . . . . . .   14  3 DON JUAN  6   16   7
```

WHILE   (CONTINUED)
IT BEING (NOT NOW BUT ONLY WHILE A LAD)	. .	. .	19	3 DON JUAN	6	27	6
BY EUNUCHS FLANKED WHILE AT THEIR HEAD THERE STALKED . . .		. .	21	3 DON JUAN	6	30	4
WHILE OTHERS WISHED THAT SHE HAD BEEN SO QUITE	. .	.	23	3 DON JUAN	6	35	8
BUT RATHER SKIM THE EARTH WHILE DUDU'S FORM	.	26	3 DON JUAN	6	41	5
BELOVED AND DEPLORED WHILE SLOWLY STRAYED	. .	40	3 DON JUAN	6	67	6
WHILE GENTLE WRITERS ALSO LOVE TO LIFT	. .	50	3 DON JUAN	6	88	6
WHILE SHE STILL SILVERS O'ER YOUR GLOOMY PATH	. .	70	3 DON JUAN	7	7	8
WHILE TWO AND TWENTY CANNON DULY SET	. .	72	3 DON JUAN	7	12	6
WHILE THOUGH 'TWAS DAWN THE TURKS SLEPT FAST AS EVER . . .		80	3 DON JUAN	7	28	8
WHILE THINGS WERE IN ABEYANCE RIBAS SENT	.	85	3 DON JUAN	7	38	1
WHILE SOUVAROFF DETERMINED TO OBTAIN IT	.	92	3 DON JUAN	7	51	7
THE DAY BEFORE THE ASSAULT WHILE UPON DRILL	.	95	3 DON JUAN	7	56	1
WHILE THEIR BELOVED FRIENDS BEGAN TO ARM	.	105	3 DON JUAN	7	76	7
OF THE ARMED RIVER WHILE WITH STRAGGLING LIGHT	.	110	3 DON JUAN	7	86	5
WHILE THE MERE VICTOR'S MAY APPAL OR STUN	. .	114	3 DON JUAN	8	5	6
WHILE THE WHOLE RAMPART BLAZED LIKE ETNA WHEN	.	115	3 DON JUAN	8	7	7
YOUR RANK AND FILE BY THOUSANDS WHILE THE REST	.	118	3 DON JUAN	8	13	7
HE RUSHED WHILE EARTH AND AIR WERE SADLY SHAKEN . . .	. .	129	3 DON JUAN	8	33	7
BUT JUAN NEVER LEFT THEM WHILE THEY HAD CHARMS . . .	. .	139	3 DON JUAN	8	53	8
SO WAS HIS BLOOD STIRRED WHILE HE FOUND RESISTANCE . . .	.	140	3 DON JUAN	8	55	1
AND SHUDDER--WHILE AS BEAUTIFUL AS MAY	. .	157	3 DON JUAN	8	91	5
THEIR BAFFLED RAGE AND PAIN WHILE WAXING COLDER	.	158	3 DON JUAN	8	94	5
JUST AT THIS INSTANT WHILE THEIR EYES WERE FIXED	.	159	3 DON JUAN	8	96	1
UNTO HIS PROTEGEE WHILE HER'S TRANSFIXED	.	159	3 DON JUAN	8	96	5
WHILE COURAGE CLUNG BUT TO A SINGLE TWIG--AM I	.	164	3 DON JUAN	8	105	5
BUT WHILE THE THIRST FOR GORE AND PLUNDER RAGED	.	178	3 DON JUAN	8	132	5
WHILE MOSQUES AND STREETS BENEATH HIS EYES LIKE THATCH . .	.	178	3 DON JUAN	8	133	3
WHILE JUAN IS SENT OFF WITH THE DISPATCH	. .	181	3 DON JUAN	8	139	7
UPON THE REST 'TIS NOT WORTH WHILE TO DWELL	.	184	3 DON JUAN	9	2	5
WHEN WROTH WHILE PLEASED SHE WAS AS FINE A FIGURE . . .	.	213	3 DON JUAN	9	62	2
WOULD WISH TO LOOK ON WHILE THEY ARE IN VIGOUR	.	213	3 DON JUAN	9	62	4
WHILE HER YOUNG HERALD KNELT BEFORE HER STILL	.	215	3 DON JUAN	9	66	4
OF LIFE REACH TEN O'CLOCK AND WHILE A GLOW	.	229	3 DON JUAN	10	8	5
THE FORMER KNOW WHAT'S WHAT WHILE NEW-FLEDGED CHICKS . . .		230	3 DON JUAN	10	10	3
WHILE COMMON MEN GROW IGNORANTLY OLD	. .	232	3 DON JUAN	10	14	5
WHILE THAT HIATUS MAXIME DEFLENDUS	. .	245	3 DON JUAN	10	42	5
WHILE THIS HIGH POST OF HONOUR'S IN ABEYANCE	.	248	3 DON JUAN	10	49	1
WHILE EVERYTHING AROUND WAS CALM AND STILL	.	272	3 DON JUAN	11	8	5
BUT TO SIT UP WHILE OTHERS LIE IN BED	. .	290	3 DON JUAN	11	45	5
THEIR FLANKS--BUT IT IS HARDLY WORTH MY WHILE	.	300	3 DON JUAN	11	63	2
(WHILE ON THE PAVEMENT MANY A HUNGRY WHORE	.	313	3 DON JUAN	11	V 29	3
DUKES--FOOLS BY BIRTH WHILE CLOGHER'S BISHOP SULLIES . . .		314	3 DON JUAN	11	V 76	5
BLACK LETTER UPON FOOLSCAP WHILE OUR HAIR	.	315	3 DON JUAN	12	1	7
WHILE THE MILD EMERALD'S BEAM SHADES DOWN THE DYES . . .	.	319	3 DON JUAN	12	8	7
WHILE HE DESPISING EVERY SENSUAL CALL	. .	320	3 DON JUAN	12	9	7
WHILE WELLINGTON HAS BUT ENSLAVED THE WHITES	.	325	3 DON JUAN	12	20	7
WHILE SAGES WRITE AGAINST ALL PROCREATION	.	325	3 DON JUAN	12	21	6
WHILE THE POOR RICH WRETCH OBJECT OF THESE CARES . . .	.	331	3 DON JUAN	12	33	7
WHILE THE HARSH PRUDE INDEMNIFIES HER VIRTUE	.	337	3 DON JUAN	12	45	1
WHILE OTHERS HAVE A GENIUS TURNED FOR FITS	.	340	3 DON JUAN	12	52	8
HAS SPAIN HAD HEROES WHILE ROMANCE COULD CHARM . . .	.	364	3 DON JUAN	13	11	4
BY BIDDING OTHERS CARRY WHILE THEY RIDE	. .	367	3 DON JUAN	13	19	8
WHILE THOSE WHO ARE NOT BEGINNERS SHOULD HAVE SENSE . . .		376	3 DON JUAN	13	40	3
MUST BE DECLINED WHILE LIFE'S THIN THREAD'S SPUN OUT . . .		376	3 DON JUAN	13	40	7
(WHILE YET THE CHURCH WAS ROME'S) STOOD HALF APART . . .	.	386	3 DON JUAN	13	59	2
WHILE I WITHOUT REMORSE OF RHYME OR FEAR	.	393	3 DON JUAN	13	74	2
WHILE STRONGBOW'S BEST THINGS MIGHT HAVE COME FROM CATO . .		401	3 DON JUAN	13	92	8
ADVANCE BEYOND WHILE THEY COULD PASS FOR NEW	.	433	3 DON JUAN	14	53	4
WHILE ALL WITHOUT'S INDICATIVE OF REST	. .	457	3 DON JUAN	15	3	V3
WHICH MAKES A DANDY WHILE IT SPOILS A MAN	.	461	3 DON JUAN	15	12	8
WHILE YET AMERICA WAS IN HER NON-AGE	. .	468	3 DON JUAN	15	27	8
WHILE GREAT LUCULLUS' ROBE TRIUMPHAL MUFFLES--	.	484	3 DON JUAN	15	66	7
LASH'D FROM THE FOAM OF AGES WHILE THE GRAVES	.	500	3 DON JUAN	15	99	7
SITS LIKE A SEDATIVE WHILE WE RECALL	. .	505	3 DON JUAN	16	11	V3
A LAMP BURNED HIGH WHILE HE LEANT FROM A NICHE	.	507	3 DON JUAN	16	16	5
TO SHOW SHE COULD IF IT WERE WORTH HER WHILE	.	521	3 DON JUAN	16	42	8
WITH SOME WHILE OTHERS WHO HAD MORE IN DREAD	.	527	3 DON JUAN	16	54	3
WHILE SCOUT THE PARISH GUARDIAN OF THE FRAIL	.	533	3 DON JUAN	16	67	2
ON ADELINE WHILE PLAYING HER GRAND ROLE	. .	546	3 DON JUAN	16	96	3
WHILE ADELINE DISPENSED HER AIRS AND GRACES	.	548	3 DON JUAN	16	100	1
BUT OH THAT I WERE DEAD--FOR WHILE ALIVE--	.	569	3 DON JUAN	17	V 13	1

WHILES
SHE GREW TO WOMANHOOD AND BETWEEN WHILES	.	224	2 DON JUAN	2	128	6
BUT THIS OCCURS BUT SELDOM BETWEEN WHILES	.	238	2 DON JUAN	2	154	5

WHILK
WHICH--AS WE SAY--OR AS THE SCOTCH SAY WHILK	.	456	2 DON JUAN	5	77	6
WHILK WHICH (OR WHAT YOU PLEASE) WAS OWING TO	.	456	2 DON JUAN	5	78	1

WHILST
WHILST HER PIRATICAL PAPA WAS CRUISING	.	282	2 DON JUAN	3	13	8

WHIMPER
CHEERFUL--BUT SOMETIMES RATHER APT TO WHIMPER	.	567	3 DON JUAN	17	11	5

WHIMS
TO THEIR OWN WHIMS AND PASSIONS AND WHATNOT	.	423	2 DON JUAN	5	25	4
JUAN THE LATEST OF HER WHIMS HAD CAUGHT	.	477	2 DON JUAN	5	114	1

WHINE
SOME SPEAKERS WHINE AND OTHERS LAY THE LASH ON	.	437	2 DON JUAN	5	48	5
BUT SOMEHOW--IT MAY SEEM A SCHOOLBOY'S WHINE	.	233	3 DON JUAN	10	17	5

WHIP
THE WHIP THE RACK OR DUNGEON AT THE LEAST	.	296	2 DON JUAN	3	40	5

907

WHIPP'D
  TO SCHOOL OR HAD HIM SOUNDLY WHIPP'D AT HOME . . . . .   34 2 DON JUAN 1   25   7
WHIPPER-IN
  AND RATED HIM ALMOST A WHIPPER-IN . . . . 425 3 DON JUAN 14   34   8
WHIPT
  DUNCES WERE WHIPT OR SET UPON A STOOL . . . . 162 2 DON JUAN 2   10   6
  WAS WHIPT AT COLLEGE--A HARSH SIRE--ODD SPOUSE . . . . 328 2 DON JUAN 3   91   7
WHIRL
  IN A MOST NATURAL WHIRL CALLED GRAVITATION . . . . . 225 3 DON JUAN 10   1   6
  BUT--I WON'T WEEP--COME POSTBOYS WHIRL ALONG . . . . 263 3 DON JUAN 10   77 V2
  THROUGH COACHES DRAYS CHOKED TURNPIKES AND A WHIRL . . 278 3 DON JUAN 11   22   1
  THEN GLARE THE LAMPS THEN WHIRL THE WHEELS THEN ROAR . 302 3 DON JUAN 11   67   2
  WHEELS WHIRL FROM CARLTON PALACE TO SOHO . . . . . 378 3 DON JUAN 13   44   3
  WHO WHIRL THE DUST AS SIMOOMS WHIRL THE SAND . . . . 435 3 DON JUAN 14   58   6
  WHO WHIRL THE DUST AS SIMOOMS WHIRL THE SAND . . . . 435 3 DON JUAN 14   58   6
WHIRL'D
  AND WHIRL'D HER BRAIN TO MADNESS SHE AROSE . . . . . 380 2 DON JUAN 4   67   2
WHIRLED
  HER CHEEK TURNED ASHES EARS RUNG BRAIN WHIRLED ROUND . .   58 3 DON JUAN 6   105   5
  TO NORMAN ABBEY WHIRLED THE NOBLE PAIR-- . . . . . . 384 3 DON JUAN 13   55   1
WHIRLING
  AND DOWN SHE SUCK'D WITH HER THE WHIRLING WAVE . . . . 184 2 DON JUAN 2   52   6
  AND ALL MY FANCIES WHIRLING LIKE A MILL . . . . . . 224 3 DON JUAN 9   85   6
WHIRLPOOL
  AND WHAT A WHIRLPOOL FULL OF DEPTH AND DANGER . . . . 214 2 DON JUAN 9   64   3
WHIRLS
  WITH ITS STRANGE WHIRLS AND EDDIES CAN COMPARE-- . . .   7 3 DON JUAN 6   2   6
  AS THE YEAR CLOSING WHIRLS THE SCARLET LEAVES . . . . 155 3 DON JUAN 8   88   3
  AND THEN THERE WAS CHAMPAGNE WITH FOAMING WHIRLS . . . 484 3 DON JUAN 15   65   7
WHIRLWIND
  IS WOMAN WHAT A WHIRLWIND IS HER HEAD . . . . 214 3 DON JUAN 9   64   2
WHISK
  BELOVED IN HER OWN WAY AND RATHER WHISK . . . . . .   7 3 DON JUAN 6   3   4
WHISKER
  THE SINGEING OF A SINGLE INKY WHISKER . . . . 498 2 DON JUAN 5   151   8
WHISKERS
  WITH BEARDS AND WHISKERS AND THE LIKE THE FOND . . . . 209 3 DON JUAN 9   53   4
  ALL STRUT AND STAYS AND WHISKERS TO DEMAND . . . . . 343 3 DON JUAN 12   60   4
WHISPER
  SOME PEOPLE WHISPER (BUT NO DOUBT THEY LIE . . . . .   58 2 DON JUAN 1   66   5
  THERE WAS A GENERAL WHISPER TOSS AND WRIGGLE . . . . 501 2 DON JUAN 5   156   7
  THE WHOLE COURT MELTED INTO ONE WIDE WHISPER . . . . 221 3 DON JUAN 9   78   1
  BUT THINKS LESS OF GOOD EATING THAN THE WHISPER . . . 487 3 DON JUAN 15   70   7
  NOW THIS (BUT WE WILL WHISPER IT ASIDE) . . . . . . 522 3 DON JUAN 16   43   1
WHISPER'D
  WHISPER'D HE HAD A MISTRESS SOME SAID TWO . . . . .   31 2 DON JUAN 1   19   7
  SHE WHISPER'D IN GREAT WRATH--I MUST DEPOSIT . . . . 114 2 DON JUAN 1   170   7
  AT LENGTH ONE WHISPER'D HIS COMPANION WHO . . . . . 194 2 DON JUAN 2   73   1
  WHISPER'D ANOTHER AND THUS IT WENT ROUND . . . . . . 194 2 DON JUAN 2   73   2
  AND WHISPER'D THINK OF EVERY SACRED TIE . . . . . . 268 2 DON JUAN 2   210   2
  THE CIRCLE SMIL'D THEN WHISPER'D AND THEN SNEER'D . . 429 3 DON JUAN 14   44   1
WHISPERED
  WHISPERED TO HIS COMPANION--'TWAS THE SAME . . . . . 434 2 DON JUAN 5   43   3
  HE WHISPERED JUAN NOT TO BE AFRAID . . . . 473 2 DON JUAN 5   107   5
  THEY BIT THEIR LIPS AND WHISPERED WITH A WRIGGLE . . . 501 2 DON JUAN 5   156 V7
  THE COURTIERS STARED THE LADIES WHISPERED AND . . . . 205 3 DON JUAN 9   46   1
WHISPERING
  AND WHISPERING I WILL NE'ER CONSENT--CONSENTED . . . .   84 2 DON JUAN 1   117   8
  AND NOT TO ENCOURAGE WHISPERING IN THE HOUSE . . . . 439 3 DON JUAN 14   67 V4
  THAN WHISPERING FOPLINGS OR THAN WITLINGS LOUD . . . . 493 3 DON JUAN 15   83   4
WHISPERS
  LOW WERE THE WHISPERS MANIFOLD THE RUMOURS . . . . . 244 3 DON JUAN 10   40   1
  (IN WHISPERS) TO HAVE TURNED HIS SOVEREIGN'S HEAD . . . 283 3 DON JUAN 11   32   8
WHIST
  TROY OWES TO HOMER WHAT WHIST OWES TO HOYLE . . . . . 328 2 DON JUAN 3   90   5
WHISTLE
  HE RAISED HIS WHISTLE AS THE WORD HE SAID . . . . . 369 2 DON JUAN 4   47   3
  BUT FULL OF CUNNING AS ULYSSES' WHISTLE . . . . . . 407 3 DON JUAN 13   105   6
WHIT
  AT WHICH HE SEEMED NO WHIT SURPRISED NOR GRIEVED . . . 500 2 DON JUAN 5   155   4
WHITBREAD
  WHERE'S WHITBREAD ROMILLY WHERE'S GEORGE THE THIRD . . 307 3 DON JUAN 11   78   2
WHITE
  AND CLAP A WHITE CAPE ON THEIR MANTLES BLUE . . . . .   94 2 DON JUAN 1   134   5
  HER SMALL WHITE HAND COULD HARDLY REACH THE TAPER . . . 134 2 DON JUAN 1   198   3
  THE MOTTO CUT UPON A WHITE CORNELIAN . . . . 134 2 DON JUAN 1   198   7
  HER SMALL WHITE FINGERS SCARCE COULD REACH THE TAPER . . 134 2 DON JUAN 1   198 V3
  I RECOLLECT GREAT BRITAIN'S COAST LOOKS WHITE . . . . 163 2 DON JUAN 2   12   5
  ABOUT THIS TIME A BEAUTIFUL WHITE BIRD . . . . . . 206 2 DON JUAN 2   94   1
  HER BROW WAS WHITE AND LOW HER CHEEK'S PURE DYE . . . 218 2 DON JUAN 2   118   1
  A STRANGER DYING WITH SO WHITE A SKIN . . . . 224 2 DON JUAN 2   129   8
  AND THE SEA SHINES WITH PURPLE--WHITE--AND GOLD . . . 230 2 DON JUAN 2   139 V7
  GLEAM IN THE MOONLIGHT AND HER WHITE ARM CLASPS . . . 259 2 DON JUAN 2   194   2
  YET LOVE MAY MAKE MARRIAGE AS GOOD WHITE WINE . . . . 277 2 DON JUAN 3   5 V5
  WHICH OVERLOOK'D THE WHITE WALLS OF HIS HOME . . . . 286 2 DON JUAN 3   21   2
  HE SAW HIS WHITE WALLS SHINING IN THE SUN . . . . . 289 2 DON JUAN 3   27   1
  THE FIRST AND TALLEST HER WHITE KERCHIEF WAVING . . . 291 2 DON JUAN 3   30   2
  DOWN HER WHITE NECK LONG FLOATING AUBURN CURLS-- . . . 291 2 DON JUAN 3   30   5
  OF AZURE PINK AND WHITE WAS HER CHEMISE-- . . . . . 311 2 DON JUAN 3   70   3

                                                           PAGE VOL   CANTO STANZA LN
WHITE   (CONTINUED)
    AND THE STRIPED WHITE GAUZE BARACAN THAT BOUND HER   .   . . . 311 2 DON JUAN 3   70   7
    ON MOUNTAINS TOPS MORE HEAVENLY WHITE THAN HER . .   . . . 314 2 DON JUAN 3   76   4
    BUT A WHITE BARACAN AND SO TRANSPARENT . . .   . . . 315 2 DON JUAN 3   77   2
    'TWAS WHITE AND INDISTINCT NOR STOPP'D TO MEET . .   . . . 361 2 DON JUAN 4   32   6
    IN MAKE OF A COMPLEXION WHITE AND RUDDY . .   . . . 416 2 DON JUAN 5   11   2
    WHICH GIRT A SLIGHT CHEMISE AS WHITE AS MILK   .   . . . 456 2 DON JUAN 5   77   4
    WHOSE COLOUR WAS NOT BLACK NOR WHITE NOR GRAY .   . . . 462 2 DON JUAN 5   88   4
    WITH GENTLE FORCE HER WHITE ARMS HE UNWOUND . .   . . . 484 2 DON JUAN 5   126   3
    AND THEN HIS HIGHNESS' EUNUCHS BLACK AND WHITE .   . . . 495 2 DON JUAN 5   146   2
    UPON IN SHEETS WHITE AS WHAT BARDS CALL DRIVEN .   . . . 18 3 DON JUAN 6   25   5
    KATINKA WAS A GEORGIAN WHITE AND RED . . .   . . . 26 3 DON JUAN 6   41   2
    ONE WITH HER FLUSHED CHEEK LAID ON HER WHITE ARM .   . . . 39 3 DON JUAN 6   66   1
    WHITE COLD AND PURE AS LOOKS A FROZEN RILL .   . . . 40 3 DON JUAN 6   68   3
    WHITE WAXEN AND AS ALABASTER PALE . . . . 60 3 DON JUAN 6   109   4
    WHITE BLACK OR COPPER--THE DEAD BONES WILL GRIN .   . . . 188 3 DON JUAN 9   12   8
    WHITE STOCKINGS DRAWN UNCURDLED AS NEW MILK .   . . . 204 3 DON JUAN 9   43   7
    AT LENGTH THEY ROSE LIKE A WHITE WALL ALONG .   . . . 257 3 DON JUAN 10   65   1
    NOW) YOU MAY CROSS THE BLUE DEEP AND WHITE FOAM--   . . . 290 3 DON JUAN 11   44   3
    BY THOSE WHO LOVE TO SAY THAT WHITE IS BLACK .   . . . 312 3 DON JUAN 11   90   6
    COULEUR DE ROSE WHO'S NEITHER WHITE NOR SCARLET   . . . 344 3 DON JUAN 12   62   8
    OF WHITE CLIFFS WHITE NECKS BLUE EYES BLUER STOCKINGS   . 346 3 DON JUAN 12   67   7
    OF WHITE CLIFFS WHITE NECKS BLUE EYES BLUER STOCKINGS   . 346 3 DON JUAN 12   67   7
    IT IS I WILL NOT SWEAR THAT BLACK IS WHITE .   . . . 348 3 DON JUAN 12   71   1
    BUT I SUSPECT IN FACT THAT WHITE IS BLACK .   . . . 348 3 DON JUAN 12   71   2
    BUT BY THE GODS I SWEAR THAT WHITE IS BLACK .   . . . 348 3 DON JUAN 12   71   V2
    LORDLINGS WITH STAVES OF WHITE OR KEYS OF GOLD .   . . . 391 3 DON JUAN 13   70   5
    WHO LOOK'D A WHITE LAMB YET WAS A BLACK SHEEP .   . . . 396 3 DON JUAN 13   79   8
    THEY ADDED GRACEFUL NECKS WHITE HANDS AND ARMS .   . . . 408 3 DON JUAN 13   107   8
    AS WHITE AS CLEOPATRA'S MELTED PEARLS . . .   . . . 484 3 DON JUAN 15   65   8
    'TIS WHITE AT LEAST WHEN THEY JUST RISE FROM BED .   . . 532 3 DON JUAN 16   64   4
    THAN TO WAX WHITE--FOR BLUSHES ARE FOR QUALITY .   . . . 532 3 DON JUAN 16   64   8
WHITES
    WITH WHITES AND BLACKS IN GROUPS ON SHOW FOR SALE .   . . 416 2 DON JUAN 5   10   2
    WHILE WELLINGTON HAS BUT ENSLAVED THE WHITES .   . . . 325 3 DON JUAN 12   20   7
    YOU HAVE FREED THE BLACKS--NOW PRAY SHUT UP THE WHITES . 445 3 DON JUAN 14   82   8
WHITEST
    THE PUREST ORE INCLOSED THE WHITEST SKIN . .   . . . 312 2 DON JUAN 3   71   7
WHITHER
    AND HOW HE HAD BEEN TOSSED HE SCARCE KNEW WHITHER .   . . 338 3 DON JUAN 12   49   5
WHO'D
    THE BOORS CRIED DANG IT WHO'D HAVE THOUGHT IT--SIRES . . 425 3 DON JUAN 14   34   4
WHOEVER
    SHEPHERD OR SWAIN WHOEVER MAY BEHOLD . . .   . . . 506 3 DON JUAN 16   14   2
    WHOEVER MAY BE THE LAY . . . . 520 3 DON JUAN 16 L 5   4
WHOLE
    WHICH STRUGGLED THROUGH AND CHASTEN'D DOWN THE WHOLE . . 54 2 DON JUAN 1   60   8
    HAD MITIGATED PART THOUGH NOT THE WHOLE . .   . . . 70 2 DON JUAN 1   91   4
    HE THOUGHT ABOUT HIMSELF AND THE WHOLE EARTH .   . . . 71 2 DON JUAN 1   92   1
    SHEDS BEAUTY AND DEEP SOFTNESS O'ER THE WHOLE .   . . . 82 2 DON JUAN 1   114   6
    HIS SPEECH WAS A FINE SAMPLE ON THE WHOLE .   . . . 116 2 DON JUAN 1   174   7
    IF YOU WOULD LIKE TO SEE THE WHOLE PROCEEDINGS .   . . . 127 2 DON JUAN 1   189   1
    'TIS WOMAN'S WHOLE EXISTENCE MAN MAY RANGE .   . . . 131 2 DON JUAN 1   194   2
    HAVE SQUANDER'D MY WHOLE SUMMER WHILE 'TWAS MAY   . . . 143 2 DON JUAN 1   213   5
    TO KEEP HIS MEMORY WHOLE AND MUMMY HID . .   . . . 146 2 DON JUAN 1   219   4
    WHOLE OF HER STERN-FRAME AND ERE SHE COULD LIFT   . . . 170 2 DON JUAN 2   27   4
    FAIR AS THE CROWNING ROSE OF THE WHOLE WREATH .   . . . 235 2 DON JUAN 2   148   5
    WHICH THEN SEEMS AS IF THE WHOLE EARTH IT BOUNDED .   . . 252 2 DON JUAN 2   183   3
    EARTH AIR STARS--ALL THAT SPRINGS FROM THE GREAT WHOLE . 336 2 DON JUAN 3   104   7
    SHE HAD SO MUCH EARTH COULD NOT CLAIM THE WHOLE   . . . 377 2 DON JUAN 4   60   8
    UPON THE WHOLE HIS CARRIAGE WAS SERENE . .   . . . 415 2 DON JUAN 5   9   2
    THEIR WHILE TO REAR WHOLE HOTBEDS IN THEIR WORKS .   . . 434 2 DON JUAN 5   42   7
    TO BREAK THE LIFELESS SPLENDOR OF THE WHOLE .   . . . 442 2 DON JUAN 5   56   8
    AND I CAN GIVE MY WHOLE SOUL UP TO MIND . .   . . . 17 3 DON JUAN 6   22   6
    AND MUCH MORE TENDER ON THE WHOLE THAN FIERCE .   . . . 19 3 DON JUAN 6   27   5
    BUT NO ONE DOUBTED ON THE WHOLE THAT SHE .   . . . 24 3 DON JUAN 6   36   1
    'TWAS ON THE WHOLE A NOBLY FURNISHED HALL .   . . . 31 3 DON JUAN 6   51   6
    ONE ON THE OTHER THROUGHOUT THE WHOLE HALL .   . . . 42 3 DON JUAN 6   71   5
    THE WHOLE ODA FROM THEIR BEDS AT HALF-PAST THREE .   . . 46 3 DON JUAN 6   80   4
    THE FILLING UP THEIR WHOLE CONNUBIAL CARGO-- .   . . . 51 3 DON JUAN 6   90   7
    THE DISCIPLINE OF THE WHOLE HAREM BORE . .   . . . 57 3 DON JUAN 6   103   2
    PELL-MELL AND WITH A WHOLE GAZETTE OF SLAUGHTER   . . . 82 3 DON JUAN 7   31   8
    THE WHOLE CAMP RUNG WITH JOY YOU WOULD HAVE THOUGHT .   . 90 3 DON JUAN 7   49   1
    MEN'S HEARTS AGAINST WHOLE MILLIONS WHEN THEIR TRADE . . 102 3 DON JUAN 7   69   6
    WHILE THE WHOLE RAMPART BLAZED LIKE ETNA WHEN .   . . . 115 3 DON JUAN 8   7   7
    TO THEIR TWO SELVES ONE WHOLE BRIGHT BULLETIN .   . . . 121 3 DON JUAN 8   19   8
    OF HIS WHOLE ARMY WHICH SO MUCH ABOUNDED .   . . . 125 3 DON JUAN 8   28   6
    AND SWEPT AS GALES SWEEP FOAM AWAY WHOLE RANKS .   . . 134 3 DON JUAN 8   44   3
    BUT ON THE WHOLE THEIR CONTINENCE WAS GREAT .   . . . 177 3 DON JUAN 8   131   1
    HE WHOSE WHOLE LIFE HAS BEEN ASSAULT AND BATTERY .   . . 185 3 DON JUAN 9   5   3
    BUT NOT AT THE EXPENCE OF A WHOLE NATION .   . . . 185 3 DON JUAN 9   6   V8
    WHICH ON ROUGH ROADS LEAVES SCARCELY A WHOLE BONE) .   . 197 3 DON JUAN 9   30   3
    THEN RECOLLECTING THE WHOLE EMPRESS NOR . .   . . . 211 3 DON JUAN 9   58   1
    AT LEAST THREE PARTS OF THIS GREAT WHOLE) SHE TORE .   . 211 3 DON JUAN 9   58   3
    THE WHOLE GAZETTE OF THOUSANDS WHOM HE SLEW .   . . . 212 3 DON JUAN 9   60   4
    THE WHOLE COURT LOOKED IMMEDIATELY MOST SWEET .   . . . 213 3 DON JUAN 9   61   3
    THE WHOLE THING IS OF CLOTHING SOULS IN CLAY .   . . . 220 3 DON JUAN 9   75   8
    THE WHOLE COURT MELTED INTO ONE WIDE WHISPER .   . . . 221 3 DON JUAN 9   78   1
    DISSECTING THE WHOLE INSIDE OF A QUESTION .   . . . 232 3 DON JUAN 10   14   7
```

909
```

```
                                                    PAGE VOL      CANTO STANZA LN
WHOLE   (CONTINUED)
    YOUR FACE--BUT YOU HAVE ACTED ON THE WHOLE  . . . . . .  232  3 DON JUAN 10    16    7
    A WHOLE ONE AND MY HEART FLIES TO MY HEAD-- . . .  . . . 233  3 DON JUAN 10    17    8
    AT WHICH THE WHOLE COURT WAS EXTREMELY TROUBLED . . . .  244  3 DON JUAN 10    39    7
    THE FOURTH AT ONCE ESTABLISHED THE WHOLE TRINITY . . .   271  3 DON JUAN 11     6    5
    BUT THEN THE ABBEY'S WORTH THE WHOLE COLLECTION . . . .  280  3 DON JUAN 11    25    8
    AND THE WHOLE MATTER RESTS UPON EYE-SIGHT   . . .  . .   348  3 DON JUAN 12    71    3
    'TIS THE WHOLE SPIRIT BROUGHT TO A QUINTESSENCE . . . .  375  3 DON JUAN 13    38    1
    THE WORLD UPON THE WHOLE IS WORTH THE ASSERTION . . . .  377  3 DON JUAN 13    41    3
    FORM'D A WHOLE WHICH IRREGULAR IN PARTS  . . . . . . .   390  3 DON JUAN 13    67    4
    MAY AVERAGE ON THE WHOLE WITH PARTURITION   . . . . .    420  3 DON JUAN 14    24    2
    BUT ON THE WHOLE TO GENERAL ADMIRATION  . . . . . .      425  3 DON JUAN 14    34    1
    'TIS BETTER ON THE WHOLE TO HAVE FELT AND SEEN  . . .    431  3 DON JUAN 14    49    5
    BUT THERE WAS SOMETHING WANTING ON THE WHOLE--  . . .    441  3 DON JUAN 14    71    1
    THOUGH ON THE WHOLE NO DOUBT THE DARDAN BOY . . . . .    441  3 DON JUAN 14    72    6
    IS SHOWN THROUGH NATURE'S WHOLE ANALOGIES   . . . . .    451  3 DON JUAN 14    94    4
    GAUNT GOURMAND WITH WHOLE NATIONS FOR YOUR BOOTY . . .   459  3 DON JUAN 15     9    5
    BY NATURE SOFT HIS WHOLE ADDRESS HELD OFF  . . . . .     462  3 DON JUAN 15    14    1
    THE WHOLE TOGETHER IS WHAT I COULD WISH  . . . . . .     465  3 DON JUAN 15    21    7
    FELT ON THE WHOLE AN INTEREST INTENSE--  . . . . . .     468  3 DON JUAN 15    28    3
    AS WOMEN HATE HALF MEASURES ON THE WHOLE  . . . . .      468  3 DON JUAN 15    28    7
    AS ON THE WHOLE IT IS AN EVEN CHANCE  . . . . . . .      473  3 DON JUAN 15    39    4
    HALF VIRTUES AND WHOLE VICES BEING COMBINED . . . . .    480  3 DON JUAN 15    57    4
    THOUGH SWALLOW'D WITH MUCH ZEST UPON THE WHOLE . . . .   484  3 DON JUAN 15    66    4
    AND WOULD HAVE PASSED THE WHOLE OFF AS A DREAM  . . .    511  3 DON JUAN 16    25    5
    HAD EVER BEEN HIS SOLE AND WHOLE AMBITION   . . . . .    536  3 DON JUAN 16    74    2
    WHICH THREATENED THE WHOLE COUNTRY WITH PERDITION  . .   536  3 DON JUAN 16    74    4
    UPON THE WHOLE IS GREATER THAN THE DIFFERENCE . . . .    541  3 DON JUAN 16    85    2
    THOUGH THIS WAS MOST EXPEDIENT ON THE WHOLE . . . . .    546  3 DON JUAN 16    96    1
    HINTING THAT SOUL AND BODY ON THE WHOLE  . . . . . .     558  3 DON JUAN 16   118    7
    SHOULD CAUSE MORE FEAR THAN A WHOLE HOST'S IDENTITY . .  559  3 DON JUAN 16   120    8
WHOLE'S
    BUT MORE OR LESS THE WHOLE'S A SYNCOPE   . . . . . .     457  3 DON JUAN 15     2    1
WHOLESOME
    FOR EARLY STOMACHS TO PROVE WHOLESOME FOOD  . . . . .     45  2 DON JUAN  1    43    2
    EXTREMELY WHOLESOME THOUGH BUT RARELY CLEAR . . . . .    266  3 DON JUAN 10    83    8
WHOLLY
    AND WHEN THE SPOUSE AND FRIEND ARE GONE OFF WHOLLY . .    74  2 DON JUAN  1    99    7
    OF CALLING WHOLLY BACK ITS SELF-CONTROL  . . . . . .     82  2 DON JUAN  1   114    4
    'TIS NEVER TOO LATE TO BE WHOLLY WRECK'D  . . . . . .    176  2 DON JUAN  2    39    6
    IS THAT TO WHICH HER HEART IS WHOLLY GRANTED  . . . .    276  2 DON JUAN  3     4    6
    FOR SOMETHING BETTER IF NOT WHOLLY GOOD  . . . . . .     302  2 DON JUAN  3    53    6
    WHO GIVE THEMSELVES TO ARCHITECTURE WHOLLY  . . . . .    448  2 DON JUAN  5    63    4
    THE STRANGEST THING WAS BEAUTEOUS SHE WAS WHOLLY  . .     33  3 DON JUAN  6    54    5
    NO HERO TRUSTETH WHOLLY TO HALF-PAY  . . . . . . .      163  3 DON JUAN  8   103    8
    WITH POETS ALMOST CLERGYMEN OR WHOLLY  . . . . . . .    297  3 DON JUAN 11    57    4
WHOME'ER
    OR FASCINATE WHOME'ER THEY FIXED THEIR EYES ON . . . .   463  2 DON JUAN  5    90    8
WHORE
    WHOSE HUSBAND ONLY KNOWS HER NOT A WHORE  . . . . .      353  2 DON JUAN  4    17    8
    (WHILE ON THE PAVEMENT MANY A HUNGRY WHORE  . . . . .    313  3 DON JUAN 11  V 29    3
    JUST AS A REGULAR COMMON SOLDIER OR A WHORE . . . . .    537  3 DON JUAN 16    76   V3
WHORED
    AND HAVING VOTED DINED DRANK GAMED AND WHORED . . . .    306  3 DON JUAN 11    75    7
WHORES
    AS GREATEST OF ALL SOVEREIGNS AND WHORES . . . . .       52  3 DON JUAN  6    92    8
    WHEN STARS AND WHORES AND DESPOTS COULD MAKE GREAT  . .   84  3 DON JUAN  7    37   V2
WHORESON
    TO CALL A MAN A WHORESON--OR TO SAY  . . . . . . .       53  3 DON JUAN  6    94   V1
WHO'S
    YOU'D BETTER ASK OUR MISTRESS WHO'S HIS HEIR  . . . .    297  2 DON JUAN  3    43    6
    WHO'S QUIET INOFFENSIVE SILENT SHY . . . . . . . .        30  3 DON JUAN  6    49    5
    LET SPENDTHRIFTS' HEIRS ENQUIRE OF YOURS--WHO'S WISER .  321  3 DON JUAN 12    11    8
    COULEUR DE ROSE WHO'S NEITHER WHITE NOR SCARLET  . . .   344  3 DON JUAN 12    62    8
WHO'VE
    BUT I MUST LEAVE THE PROOFS TO THOSE WHO'VE SEEN 'EM . .  28  2 DON JUAN  1    14    4
    WHO'VE MADE US YOUTH WAIT TOO--TOO LONG ALREADY  . . .    89  2 DON JUAN  1   125    4
    AS I WHO'VE CROSS'D IT OFT KNOW WELL ENOUGH . . . . .    162  2 DON JUAN  2    11    4
WICKED
    THE WHILE THE WICKED WORLD BEHOLDS DELIGHTED . . . .      75  2 DON JUAN  1   100    3
    SEES HALF THE BUSINESS IN A WICKED WAY  . . . . . .       82  2 DON JUAN  1   113    6
    OF ANY WICKED WOMAN WHO CONTRIVED  . . . . . . . .        96  2 DON JUAN  1   138    5
    THE VERY PLACE WHERE WICKED PEOPLE GO . . . . . . .      140  2 DON JUAN  1   207    8
    WHEN WICKED WIVES WHO LOVE SOME BACHELOR  . . . . .       18  3 DON JUAN  6    24    3
    INSTEAD OF WICKS THEY MADE A WICKED MAN TURN  . . . .    280  3 DON JUAN 11    26    8
WICKEDLY
    THE WORLD AS USUAL WICKEDLY INCLINED  . . . . . . .       31  2 DON JUAN  1    19    5
WICKEDNESS
    TO WEAN HIM FROM THE WICKEDNESS OF EARTH  . . . . .      161  2 DON JUAN  2     8    7
WICKET
    HERE THEIR CONDUCTOR TAPPING AT THE WICKET  . . . . .    433  2 DON JUAN  5    41    1
WICKS
    INSTEAD OF WICKS THEY MADE A WICKED MAN TURN  . . . .    280  3 DON JUAN 11    26    8
WIDE
    CLEARER THAN THAT WITHOUT AND ITS WIDE HUE  . . . . .    204  2 DON JUAN  2    91    5
    FROM OUT THE WIDE DESTRUCTION WHICH ENTOMBING ALL  . .   399  2 DON JUAN  4   101    5
    IT WAS INDEED A WIDE EXTENSIVE BUILDING  . . . . . .     436  2 DON JUAN  5    46    1
    AND KNOCKING AT THE GATE 'TWAS OPENED WIDE  . . . . .    440  2 DON JUAN  5    51    6
    THIS MASSY PORTAL STOOD AT THE WIDE CLOSE  . . . . .     462  2 DON JUAN  5    87    1
```

WIDE   (CONTINUED)

	PAGE	VOL		CANTO	STANZA	LN
(A HIGHLAND WELCOME ALL THE WIDE WORLD OVER)	12	3 DON JUAN	6	13	8
MY WISH IS QUITE AS WIDE BUT NOT SO BAD	19	3 DON JUAN	6	27	4
BUT WIDE AWAKE SHE WAS AND ROUND HER BED	42	3 DON JUAN	6	72	1
OF MURMURING LIBERTY'S WIDE WAVES WHICH BLEND	52	3 DON JUAN	6	93	6
IN ONE WIDE WOUND POURED FORTH HIS SOUL AT ONCE	170	3 DON JUAN	8	118	8
'TIS TRUE WE SPECULATE BOTH FAR AND WIDE	190	3 DON JUAN	9	16	3
THE WHOLE COURT MELTED INTO ONE WIDE WHISPER	221	3 DON JUAN	9	78	1
HE MADE 'GAINST COSSAQUE SABRES IN THE WIDE	249	3 DON JUAN	10	51	5
AIR CAN ACCOMPLISH WITH HIS WIDE WINGS WAVING	263	3 DON JUAN	10	78	4
DIRTY AND DUSKY BUT AS WIDE AS EYE	265	3 DON JUAN	10	82	2
HIS CHAMBER DOOR WIDE OPEN--AND WENT FORTH	508	3 DON JUAN	16	17	2
AS WIDE AS IF A LONG SPEECH WERE TO COME	557	3 DON JUAN	16	115	4
THE DOOR FLEW WIDE NOT SWIFTLY--BUT AS FLY	558	3 DON JUAN	16	117	1

WIDENS

BUT AS THE TORRENT WIDENS TOWARDS THE OCEAN	345	2 DON JUAN	4	2	7

WIDER

AND THUS FOR WIDER CARNAGE TAUGHT TO PANT	16	2 DON JUAN	D	12	3

WIDIN

A TOWN WAS TA'EN MYSELF INSTEAD OF WIDIN	418	3 DON JUAN	5	15	8
YOU SERVED AT WIDIN--YES--YOU LED THE ATTACK	98	3 DON JUAN	7	61	1

WIDOW

AND LEFT HIS WIDOW TO HER OWN AVERSION	39	2 DON JUAN	1	34	8
WOULD FULLY SUIT A WIDOW OF CONDITION	67	2 DON JUAN	1	85	3
THE CHARMS OF MAID WIFE AND STILL LESS OF WIDOW	144	2 DON JUAN	1	216	2
A MAN AS GILES SAYS FOR THOUGH SHE WOULD WIDOW ALL	214	3 DON JUAN	9	63	7
OR WIDOW MAID OR MOTHER SHE CAN CHANGE HER	214	3 DON JUAN	9	64	5

WIDOWED

AND AS THE WIND A WIDOWED NATION'S WAIL	105	3 DON JUAN	7	77	4

WIDOWER

A HORRID THOUGHT--FOR WHO WOULD BE A WIDOWER	278	2 DON JUAN	3	7	V7
A HAZY WIDOWER TURNED OF FORTY'S SURE	333	3 DON JUAN	12	37	5

WIDOW'S

'TWAS THE BOY'S MITE AND LIKE THE WIDOW'S MAY	9	3 DON JUAN	6	6	1

WIDOWS

SAGEST OF WOMEN EVEN OF WIDOWS SHE	42	2 DON JUAN	1	38	1
AND HOW YE MAY BE DOUBLY WIDOWS--WIVES	123	2 DON JUAN	1	185	8
(WIDOWS OF FORTY WERE THESE BIRDS LONG CAGED)	178	3 DON JUAN	8	132	3

WIDOWS'

BUT SIGHS SUBSIDE AND TEARS (EVEN WIDOWS') SHRINK	228	3 DON JUAN	10	7	1

WIELD

TO WIELD THEM IN THEIR TERRIBLE ARRAY	113	3 DON JUAN	8	2	2

WIELDING

I ONCE HAD A GREAT ALACRITY IN WIELDING	397	2 DON JUAN	4	98	5
BY MERELY WIELDING WITH POETIC ARM	106	3 DON JUAN	7	79	3

WIFE

OR COELEBS' WIFE SET OUT IN QUEST OF LOVERS	29	2 DON JUAN	1	16	4
THEY LIVED RESPECTABLY AS MAN AND WIFE	35	2 DON JUAN	1	26	4
I RECOMMEND AS MUCH TO EVERY WIFE	48	2 DON JUAN	1	48	8
HE AND HIS WIFE WERE AN ILL-SORTED PAIR--	49	2 DON JUAN	1	51	6
WHERE JURIES CAST UP WHAT A WIFE IS WORTH	57	2 DON JUAN	1	64	5
MIGHT PLEASE PERHAPS A VIRTUOUS WIFE CAN QUELL	64	2 DON JUAN	1	78	5
IN CASE HE THOUGHT HIS WIFE TOO GREAT A PRIZE	75	2 DON JUAN	1	101	8
ERE I THE WIFE OF SUCH A WRETCH HAD BEEN	98	2 DON JUAN	1	142	V4
CALL ME THE ONLY VIRTUOUS WIFE IN SPAIN	102	2 DON JUAN	1	149	4
AND IS IT THUS A FAITHFUL WIFE YOU TREAT	103	2 DON JUAN	1	150	3
AND TREATING A YOUNG WIFE WITH SO MUCH RIGOUR	110	2 DON JUAN	1	161	4
ALFONSO SAW HIS WIFE AND THOUGHT OF JOB'S	110	2 DON JUAN	1	162	6
THE CHARMS OF MAID WIFE AND STILL LESS OF WIDOW	144	2 DON JUAN	1	216	2
WITH HIS YOUNG WIFE--A TIME AND OPPORTUNITY	158	2 DON JUAN	2	3	8
HIS MOTHER AND A MISTRESS AND NO WIFE	164	2 DON JUAN	2	15	2
BUT HE POOR FELLOW HAD A WIFE AND CHILDREN	179	2 DON JUAN	2	43	7
WHEN PATIENTS NEITHER PLAGUED WITH FRIENDS NOR WIFE	190	2 DON JUAN	2	64	3
I'LL JUST INQUIRE IF SHE BE WIFE OR MAID	268	2 DON JUAN	2	210	5
THINK YOU IF LAURA HAD BEEN PETRARCH'S WIFE	279	2 DON JUAN	3	8	7
AND DON'T SAY MUCH OF PARADISE OR WIFE	280	2 DON JUAN	3	9	V8
BORN TO SOME FRIEND WHO HOLDS HIS WIFE AND RICHES	287	2 DON JUAN	3	23	7
FOR INSTANCE IF A HUSBAND OR HIS WIFE	301	2 DON JUAN	3	50	3
AND PURE AS PSYCHE ERE SHE GREW A WIFE--	313	2 DON JUAN	3	74	5
HAS SOME GOOD NOTES AND THEN THE TENOR'S WIFE	389	2 DON JUAN	4	83	4
TO MAKE A MISTRESS OR FOURTH WIFE OR VICTIM	409	2 DON JUAN	4	116	8
WILL HARDLY LEAVE YOU (AS SHE'S NOT YOUR WIFE)	419	2 DON JUAN	5	17	3
FOR BEING THE LAST WIFE OF THE EMPEROR	495	2 DON JUAN	5	146	7
INTO THAT MORAL CENTAUR MAN AND WIFE	502	2 DON JUAN	5	158	8
A SCOLDING WIFE A SULLEN SON A BILL	16	3 DON JUAN	6	21	1
OR LOT'S WIFE DONE IN SALT--OR WHAT YOU WILL	40	3 DON JUAN	6	68	5
AND OF A WIFE BY WHOM HE WAS ABHORRED	51	3 DON JUAN	6	90	4
AS WIFE AND FRIENDS DID FOR THE BOILS OF JOB--	105	3 DON JUAN	7	77	7
AND WAS NOT THE BEST WIFE UNLESS WE CALL	222	3 DON JUAN	9	80	6
OF FEEDING BRATS THE MOMENT HIS WIFE WEANS	325	3 DON JUAN	12	21	8
FOR BEING A MOST EXEMPLARY WIFE	338	3 DON JUAN	12	47	8
A WIFE MAKES OR TAKES LOVE IN UPRIGHT EARNEST	345	3 DON JUAN	12	64	4
A TRACE UNWORTHY EITHER WIFE OR MAID--	372	3 DON JUAN	13	32	5
LESS LIKE A YOUNG WIFE THAN AN AGED SISTER	440	3 DON JUAN	14	69	8

WIFE'S

I CRIED UPON MY FIRST WIFE'S DYING DAY	420	2 DON JUAN	5	19	7

WIGS

OTHERS IN WIGS OF MARLBOROUGH'S MARTIAL FOLD	391	3 DON JUAN	13	70	3

WILBERFORCE

THOUGH WILBERFORCE AT LAST HAS MADE IT TWICE	408	2 DON JUAN	4	115	3

911

WILBERFORCE   (CONTINUED)
    MALTHUS AND WILBERFORCE--THE LAST SET FREE . . . . . . 325 3 DON JUAN 12   20   5
    OH WILBERFORCE THOU MAN OF BLACK RENOWN . . . . . .   445 3 DON JUAN 14   82   1
WILD
    ALTHOUGH IN INFANCY A LITTLE WILD   49   2 DON JUAN 1   50   3
    WHERE THE WILD BRANCH OF THE CORK FOREST GREW 70   2 DON JUAN 1   90   4
    AND HAVE A KIND OF WILD AND HORRID GLEE . . . . .   183 2 DON JUAN 2   50   6
    THEN ROSE FROM SEA TO SKY THE WILD FAREWELL . . . . . 184 2 DON JUAN 2   52   1
    SAVE THE WILD WIND AND THE REMORSELESS DASH . . . . . 184 2 DON JUAN 2   53   4
    WHAT COULD THEY DO AND HUNGER'S RAGE GREW WILD . . . . 193 2 DON JUAN 2   70   6
    AN OMINOUS AND WILD AND DESPERATE SOUND . . . . .   194 2 DON JUAN 2   73   4
    THE SHORE LOOK'D WILD WITHOUT A TRACE OF MAN . . . . . 211 2 DON JUAN 2   104   1
    (ONE OF THE WILD AND SMALLER CYCLADES) . . . . .   223 2 DON JUAN 2   127   2
    IT WAS A WILD AND BREAKER-BEATEN COAST . . . . .   249 2 DON JUAN 2   177   1
    AND IN THE WORN AND WILD RECEPTACLES . . . . .   253 2 DON JUAN 2   184   4
    THE WILD SEAS AND WILD MEN WITH WHOM HE CRUISED . . . 303 2 DON JUAN 3   54   6
    THE WILD SEAS AND WILD MEN WITH WHOM HE CRUISED . . . 303 2 DON JUAN 3   54   6
    SHOULD EVER BE THOSE BLOOD-HOUNDS FROM WHOSE WILD . . . 401 3 DON JUAN 4   105   6
    AGAINST PROPORTION--THE WILD STROKES OF NATURE . . . . 32 3 DON JUAN 6   52   5
    THAN HAUNTING SOME OLD RUIN OR WILD WASTE   38   3 DON JUAN 6   64   8
    WHEN ALL THE HEART-STRINGS LIKE WILD HORSES PULL . . . 59 3 DON JUAN 6   107   4
    TO SEE AN OLD MAN RATHER WILD THAN WISE . . . . .   104 3 DON JUAN 7   73   5
    HER HOME IS IN THE RARELY-TRODDEN WILD . . . . .   143 3 DON JUAN 8   62   3
    OF NATURE OR THE MAN OF ROSS RUN WILD . . . . .   144 3 DON JUAN 8   63   8
    THE RUDEST BRUTE THAT ROAMS SIBERIA'S WILD . . . . .   157 3 DON JUAN 8   92   3
    AND GAZED ON JUAN WITH A WILD SURPRISE . . . . .   159 3 DON JUAN 8   95   8
    A MIXTURE OF WILD BEASTS AND DEMI-GODS . . . . .   164 3 DON JUAN 8   106   4
    FOR SAVING HER AMIDST THE WILD INSANITY . . . . .   182 3 DON JUAN 8   140   6
    WHO AFTER LEAVING HINDOSTAN A WILD . . . . .   199 3 DON JUAN 9   33   5
    THOSE PLEASURES AFTER WHICH WILD YOUTH WILL HANKER . . 240 3 DON JUAN 10   31   6
    SLAUGHTER OF ISMAIL THOUGH MY WILD MUSE VARIES . . . 249 3 DON JUAN 10   51   6
    WHICH CAN AWAIT WARM YOUTH IN ITS WILD RACE . . . .   326 3 DON JUAN 12   23   4
    AND WILD DISMAY O'ER EVERY ANGRY COUSIN . . . . .   332 3 DON JUAN 12   34   3
    TO MAKE HIS LITTLE WILD ASIATIC TAME . . . . .   336 3 DON JUAN 12   42   6
    AROUND THE WILD FOWL NESTLED IN THE BRAKE . . . . .   385 3 DON JUAN 13   57   5
    THIS MAY BE SUPERSTITION WEAK OR WILD . . . . .   387 3 DON JUAN 13   61   6
    IF SHE HATH NO WILD BOARS SHE HATH A TAME . . . . .   395 3 DON JUAN 13   78   7
    BUT LONGBOW WILD AS AN AEOLIAN HARP . . . . .   402 3 DON JUAN 13   93   2
    A BIRD'S-EYE VIEW TOO OF THAT WILD SOCIETY . . . . .   416 3 DON JUAN 14   14   3
    THE WILD SENSATION UNTO HER A NEW ONE . . . . .   449 3 DON JUAN 14   91   4
    APPEAR TO WAKE AND SHADOWS WILD AND QUAINT . . . . .   508 3 DON JUAN 16   18   5
WILDER
    OR WILDER GROUPE OF SAVAGE SALVATORE'S . . . . .   392 3 DON JUAN 13   71   4
WILDERNESS
    OH LOVE IN SUCH A WILDERNESS AS THIS   69   2 DON JUAN 1   88   1
    WHERE ALL IS EDEN OR A WILDERNESS . . . . .   373 2 DON JUAN 4   54   8
    A FIELD OF BATTLE'S GHASTLY WILDERNESS . . . . .   167 3 DON JUAN 8   112   6
    OF MASTS A WILDERNESS OF STEEPLES PEEPING . . . . .   265 3 DON JUAN 10   82   5
    A WILDERNESS OF THE MOST RARE CONCEITS . . . . .   502 3 DON JUAN 16   3   3
WILDS
    OF HIS OLD AGE IN WILDS OF DEEPEST MAZE . . . . .   143 3 DON JUAN 8   61   8
    THE WILDS AS DOTH AN ARAB TURN'D AVENGER . . . . .   424 3 DON JUAN 14   32   6
WILE
    EVEN INNOCENCE ITSELF HAS MANY A WILE   61   2 DON JUAN 1   72   6
    TO WEAN DON JUAN FROM THE SIREN'S WILE . . . . .   438 3 DON JUAN 14   65   6
WILES
    OR HOPE OR LOVE WITH ANY OF THE WILES . . . . .   544 3 DON JUAN 16   92   7
WILL
    WITHOUT THEIR WILL THEY CARRIED THEM AWAY . . . . .   177 2 DON JUAN 2   40   2
    ONE GLANCE ON HIM AND SAID HEAVEN'S WILL BE DONE . . . 202 2 DON JUAN 2   87   6
    HAD BEEN HER SLAVES' CHIEF PLEASURE AS HER WILL . . . 475 2 DON JUAN 5   112   4
    A BAD OLD WOMAN MAKING A WORSE WILL   16   3 DON JUAN 6   21   5
    OF LADIES OF ALL COUNTRIES AT THE WILL   22   3 DON JUAN 6   33   4
    GULBEYAZ' TACITURN OR SPEAKING WILL   61   3 DON JUAN 6   110   4
    WHERE IS HIS WILL (THAT'S NOT SO SOON UNRIDDLED) . . 307 3 DON JUAN 11   78   3
    WAS HIGH-BORN WEALTHY BY HER FATHER'S WILL . . . . .   359 3 DON JUAN 13   2   5
    (FATE IS A GOOD EXCUSE FOR OUR OWN WILL) . . . . .   364 3 DON JUAN 13   12   6
    THAN I HAVE TIME OR WILL TO TAKE TO PIECES . . . . .   478 3 DON JUAN 15   52   8
WILLIAM
    SUCH AS THE CONQUEROR WILLIAM DID REPAY . . . . .   242 3 DON JUAN 10   35   6
    TELL THEM SIR WILLIAM CURTIS IS A BORE . . . . .   267 3 DON JUAN 10   86   5
WILLING
    TO OFFER WILLING HOMAGE AS HER FAN . . . . .   313 2 DON JUAN 3   73 V8
    STOPPED AS IF ONCE MORE WILLING TO CONCEDE . . . . .   170 3 DON JUAN 8   117   2
    I SHOULD BE VERY WILLING TO REDRESS . . . . .   361 3 DON JUAN 13   8   5
WILLINGLY
    AND OF THIS BABA WILLINGLY TOOK NOTE   62   3 DON JUAN 6   113   6
    MOST WILLINGLY ALL EVER SEEN OR READ MATTERS . . . .   268 3 DON JUAN 11   1 V6
WILLINGNESS
    AND JUAN NOW HIS WILLINGNESS EXPREST . . . . .   472 2 DON JUAN 5   105   4
WILL-I-NILL-I
    BUT GO THEY MUST AT ONCE AND WILL-I-NILL-I   64   3 DON JUAN 6   118   8
WILLOW
    DROOP'D AS THE WILLOW WHEN NO WINDS CAN BREATHE . . . 235 2 DON JUAN 2   148   3
    FELL IN LONG TRESSES LIKE THE WEEPING WILLOW   60   3 DON JUAN 6   108   2
    BELOW HIS WINDOW WAVED (OF COURSE) A WILLOW . . . . . 507 3 DON JUAN 16   15   6
WILLOWS
    RATHER THAN REST INSTEAD OF POPPIES WILLOWS . . . . . 555 3 DON JUAN 16   110   5
WILLS
    THE REST WERE JACKS AND GILLS AND WILLS AND BILLS . . 76   3 DON JUAN 7   20   1

```
                                                        PAGE VOL    CANTO  STANZA LN
WIN
    'TIS SWEET TO WIN NO MATTER HOW ONE'S LAURELS  . . . . .    90   2 DON JUAN  1    126    1
    AS IF TO WIN A PART FROM OFF THE WEIGHT  . . . . . .   203   2 DON JUAN  2     88    6
    TO RENDER HAPPY ALL WHO JOY WOULD WIN . . . . . . .   247   2 DON JUAN  2    172    7
    MARVEL AND PRAISE FOR BOTH OR NONE THINGS WIN  . . . .   469   2 DON JUAN  5    100    6
    MAY WIN PERHAPS A RIBBON AT THE BREAST  . . . . . .   118   3 DON JUAN  8     13    8
    BUT FIGHTING THOUGHTLESSLY ENOUGH TO WIN . . . . . .   121   3 DON JUAN  8     19    7
    THAT YOU AND I WILL WIN SAINT GEORGE'S COLLAR  . . . .   160   3 DON JUAN  8     97    8
    OF THE GOOD COMPANY CAN WIN A CORNER . . . . . . .   303   3 DON JUAN 11     69    2
WINCE
    ALL COMMON FELLOWS WHO MIGHT WRITHE AND WINCE  . . . .   117   3 DON JUAN  8     11    4
    THE VERIEST JADE WILL WINCE WHOSE HARNESS WRINGS . . . .   137   3 DON JUAN  8     50    5
WIND
    BOSCAN OR GARCILASSO--BY THE WIND  . . . . . . . .    72   2 DON JUAN  1     95    2
    NO MOON NO STARS THE WIND WAS LOW OR LOUD  . . . . .    94   2 DON JUAN  1    135    2
    AS ROLL THE WAVES BEFORE THE SETTLED WIND  . . . . .   133   2 DON JUAN  1    196    4
    AND AS THE VEERING WIND SHIFTS SHIFT OUR SAILS . . . .   159   2 DON JUAN  2      4    4
    THE WIND WAS FAIR THE WATER PASSING ROUGH  . . . . .   162   2 DON JUAN  2     11    2
    THE WIND SUNG CORDAGE STRAIN'D AND SAILORS SWORE . . . .   163   2 DON JUAN  2     13    2
    'TWAS NOT WITHOUT SOME REASON FOR THE WIND . . . . .   170   2 DON JUAN  2     26    1
    AT ONE O'CLOCK THE WIND WITH SUDDEN SHIFT  . . . . .   170   2 DON JUAN  2     27    1
    THE WIND BLEW FRESH AGAIN AS IT GREW LATE  . . . . .   172   2 DON JUAN  2     30    5
    THE HIGH WIND MADE THE TREBLE AND AS BASS  . . . . .   174   2 DON JUAN  2     34    4
    DAY BROKE AND THE WIND LULL'D THE MASTS WERE GONE . . .   176   2 DON JUAN  2     38    2
    THE WIND IN FACT PERHAPS WAS RATHER LESS . . . . . .   178   2 DON JUAN  2     41    1
    SAVE THE WILD WIND AND THE REMORSELESS DASH  . . . . .   184   2 DON JUAN  2     53    4
    THEY HOPED THE WIND WOULD RISE THESE FOOLISH MEN . . . .   192   2 DON JUAN  2     69    5
    THE SEVENTH DAY AND NO WIND--THE BURNING SUN . . . .   194   2 DON JUAN  2     72    1
    AS MORNING BROKE THE LIGHT WIND DIED AWAY  . . . . .   207   2 DON JUAN  2     97    1
    THEY HEARD THE WAVE'S SPLASH AND THE WIND SO LOW . . .   253   2 DON JUAN  2    185    5
    'TIS SOMETHING NOTHING WORDS ILLUSION WIND-- . . . .   328   2 DON JUAN  3     90    2
    LIKE THE WIND O'ER A HARP-STRING OR A FLAME  . . . . .   355   2 DON JUAN  4     21    4
    WITHIN AN ALPINE HOLLOW WHEN THE WIND  . . . . . .   360   2 DON JUAN  4     30    2
    SAILING SIX KNOTS AN HOUR BEFORE THE WIND  . . . . .   384   2 DON JUAN  4     75    5
    THE WIND SWEPT DOWN THE EUXINE AND THE WAVE  . . . . .   413   2 DON JUAN  5      5    1
    THE WIND WAS DOWN BUT STILL THE SEA RAN HIGH . . . .    61   3 DON JUAN  6    110    8
    AS ROLL THE WATERS TO THE BREATHING WIND . . . . . .    90   3 DON JUAN  7     48    3
    AND AS THE WIND A WIDOWED NATION'S WAIL  . . . . . .   105   3 DON JUAN  7     77    4
    WHAT THAT IS--ASK THE PIG WHO SEES THE WIND  . . . . .   108   3 DON JUAN  7     84    8
    OF IDLE APPRENSIONS WHICH LIKE WIND  . . . . . .   133   3 DON JUAN  8     40    4
    UNLESS COMPELLED BY FATE OR WAVE OR WIND . . . . . .   139   3 DON JUAN  8     54    1
    THE RUGGED TREE UNTO THE SUMMER WIND . . . . . . .   164   3 DON JUAN  8    106    7
    THAN IF I SOUGHT TO SAIL BEFORE THE WIND . . . . . .   195   3 DON JUAN  9     26    4
    MIND LIKE THE WIND WHATEVER SHE HAS SAID . . . . . .   214   3 DON JUAN  9     64    6
    TOWARDS WHICH THE IMPATIENT WIND BLEW HALF A GALE  . . .   256   3 DON JUAN 10     64    3
    TO SHELTER THEIR DEVOTION FROM THE WIND  . . . . . .   384   3 DON JUAN 13     55    8
    THE WIND IS WINGED FROM ONE POINT OF HEAVEN  . . . . .   388   3 DON JUAN 13     63    2
    BACK TO THE NIGHT WIND BY THE WATERFALL  . . . . . .   388   3 DON JUAN 13     63    7
    FLING UP A STRAW 'TWILL SHOW THE WAY THE WIND BLOWS . . .   414   3 DON JUAN 14      8    2
    THEY RUN BEFORE THE WIND THROUGH HIGH SEAS BREAKING . . .   442   3 DON JUAN 14     74    6
    WITHOUT THE ANIMATION OF THE WIND  . . . . . . .   504   3 DON JUAN 16      9    8
    AGAIN--WHAT IS'T THE WIND NO NO--THIS TIME . . . . .   556   3 DON JUAN 16    113    1
    THE WIND SHIFTS AND I FLY INTO A RAGE  . . . . . .   566   3 DON JUAN 17     10    8
WINDING
    AS THEY WERE PLODDING ON THEIR WINDING WAY . . . . .   434   2 DON JUAN  5     42    1
    TO BREATHE DESTRUCTION ON ITS WINDING WAY  . . . . .   113   3 DON JUAN  8      2    6
WINDINGS
    ITS WINDINGS THROUGH THE WOODS NOW CLEAR NOW BLUE  . . .   385   3 DON JUAN 13     58    7
    BY MANY WINDINGS TO THEIR CLEVER CLINCH  . . . . . .   404   3 DON JUAN 13     98    2
WINDOW
    A MIGHTY WINDOW HOLLOW IN THE CENTRE . . . . . . .   387   3 DON JUAN 13     62    1
    BELOW HIS WINDOW WAVED (OF COURSE) A WILLOW  . . . . .   507   3 DON JUAN 16     15    6
WINDOW'S
    SURELY THE WINDOW'S NOT SO VERY HIGH . . . . . . .    96   2 DON JUAN  1    137    8
WINDOWS
    THEY OPEN'D WINDOWS GAZING IF THE GROUND . . . . . .   100   2 DON JUAN  1    144    3
    IN WINDOWS HERE THE LAMPLIGHTER'S INFUSION . . . . .   278   3 DON JUAN 11     22    6
    THE LIGHT THAT THROUGH THE GOTHIC WINDOWS SHONE . . . .   568   3 DON JUAN 17     14    5
WINDOW-SEAT
    CLOSET AND CLOTHES'-PRESS CHEST AND WINDOW-SEAT  . . . .    99   2 DON JUAN  1    143    2
WINDPIPE-SLITTING
    WAR'S A BRAIN-SPATTERING WINDPIPE-SLITTING ART . . . .   184   3 DON JUAN  9      4    3
WIND'S
    DISCOVER STARS AND SAIL IN THE WIND'S EYE  . . . . .   226   3 DON JUAN 10      3    7
    IN THE WIND'S EYE I HAVE SAILED AND SAIL BUT FOR . . . .   227   3 DON JUAN 10      4    1
    AND DANDIES ALL ARE GONE ON THE WIND'S WINGS . . . .   306   3 DON JUAN 11     76    8
WINDS
    AND HEARD A VOICE IN ALL THE WINDS AND THEN  . . . . .    72   2 DON JUAN  1     94    2
    THERE WINDS AND WAVES HAD HURL'D THEM AND FROM THENCE . .   177   2 DON JUAN  2     40    1
    SO CHANGEABLE HAD BEEN THE WINDS THAT BLEW . . . . .   209   2 DON JUAN  2    100    6
    DROOP'D AS THE WILLOW WHEN NO WINDS CAN BREATHE  . . . .   235   2 DON JUAN  2    148    3
    BUT ALWAYS DANGEROUS WHEN THE HIGH WINDS TORE  . . . .   249   2 DON JUAN  2    177   V6
    BY WINDS AND WAVES AND SOME IMPORTANT CAPTURES . . . .   283   2 DON JUAN  3     15    2
    AND SIGH TO MIDNIGHT WINDS BUT NOT TO SONG . . . . .   398   2 DON JUAN  4     99    8
    AS AUTUMN WINDS DISPERSE THE YELLOW LEAVES . . . . .   155   3 DON JUAN  8     88   V3
    WITH WHICH THE WINDS OF HEAVEN CAN CLAIM ACCORD  . . . .   402   3 DON JUAN 13     93    3
WINE
    SWEET IS OLD WINE IN BOTTLES ALE IN BARRELS  . . . . .    90   2 DON JUAN  1    126    5
    WHO KILL'D HIMSELF FOR LOVE (WITH WINE) LAST YEAR . . .   102   2 DON JUAN  1    149    8
```

WINE   (CONTINUED)

	PAGE	VOL	CANTO	STANZA	LN
I FIND THAT WINE OR BRANDY IS FORBID TOO	145	2 DON JUAN	1	216	V6
A LITTLE BREATH LOVE WINE AMBITION FAME	159	2 DON JUAN	2	4	7
SIX FLASKS OF WINE AND THEY CONTRIVED TO GET	181	2 DON JUAN	2	47	4
A FEW TEA-SPOONFULS OF THEIR RUM AND WINE	189	2 DON JUAN	2	62	5
THEY ATE UP ALL THEY HAD AND DRANK THEIR WINE	192	2 DON JUAN	2	69	2
WATER AND WINE AND FOOD--AND YOU MIGHT SEE	194	2 DON JUAN	2	72	6
WITH SCIO WINE--AND ALL FOR LOVE NOT MONEY	233	2 DON JUAN	2	145	8
WHILE BACCHUS POURS OUT WINE OR HANDS A JELLY	246	2 DON JUAN	2	170	5
FEW THINGS SURPASS OLD WINE AND THEY MAY PREACH	250	2 DON JUAN	2	178	5
LET US HAVE WINE AND WOMAN MIRTH AND LAUGHTER	250	2 DON JUAN	2	178	7
NOR WINE IN ALL THE PURPLE OF ITS GLOW	251	2 DON JUAN	2	180	V6
MARRIAGE FROM LOVE LIKE VINEGAR FROM WINE--	277	2 DON JUAN	3	5	5
YET LOVE MAY MAKE MARRIAGE AS GOOD WHITE WINE	277	2 DON JUAN	3	5	V5
AND FLASKS OF SAMIAN AND OF CHIAN WINE	291	2 DON JUAN	3	31	4
SONG DANCE WINE MUSIC STORIES FROM THE PERSIAN	293	2 DON JUAN	3	35	3
HENCE ALL THIS RICE MEAT DANCING WINE AND FIDDLING	295	2 DON JUAN	3	39	1
THE QUESTIONER FILL'D UP A GLASS OF WINE	297	2 DON JUAN	3	42	8
AND THAT GOOD WINE NE'ER WASH'D DOWN BETTER FARE	298	2 DON JUAN	3	45	4
AND SHOW THAT LATE HOURS WINE AND LOVE ARE ABLE	309	2 DON JUAN	3	66	7
WITH VIANDS AND SHERBETS IN ICE--AND WINE--	310	2 DON JUAN	3	69	7
FILL HIGH THE CUP WITH SAMIAN WINE	324	2 DON JUAN	3	L 9	2
FILL HIGH THE BOWL WITH SAMIAN WINE	324	2 DON JUAN	3	L 11	1
FILL HIGH THE BOWL WITH SAMIAN WINE	325	2 DON JUAN	3	L 13	1
FILL HIGH THE BOWL WITH SAMIAN WINE	326	2 DON JUAN	3	L 15	1
DASH DOWN YON CUP OF SAMIAN WINE	326	2 DON JUAN	3	L 16	6
LEARN'D PIOUS TEMPERATE IN LOVE AND WINE	328	2 DON JUAN	3	91	4
OF FRIENDS--AND OPIATE DRAUGHTS--THERE'S LOVE AND WINE	343	2 DON JUAN	3	V 98	1
SOME PEOPLE PREFER WINE--'TIS NOT AMISS	356	2 DON JUAN	4	24	6
WOMAN OR WINE YOU'LL HAVE TO UNDERGO	357	2 DON JUAN	4	25	2
'TIS PITY WINE SHOULD BE SO DELETERIOUS	372	2 DON JUAN	4	52	7
THEY NATURALLY POUR THE WINE AND OIL	480	2 DON JUAN	5	120	5
FOR ME FOR I WOULD RATHER TAKE MY WINE	233	3 DON JUAN	10	17	3
LOVE OR LUST MAKES MAN SICK AND WINE MUCH SICKER	317	3 DON JUAN	12	4	1
PROVOKE MY THIRST--WHAT--HO OF WINE A STOUP	392	3 DON JUAN	13	72	V8
WITH EVENING CAME THE BANQUET AND THE WINE	408	3 DON JUAN	13	107	1
THEY DIFFER AS WINE DIFFERS FROM ITS LABLE	458	3 DON JUAN	15	6	5
THE SIMPLE OLIVES BEST ALLIES OF WINE	488	3 DON JUAN	15	73	1
NOR WINE NOR WASSAIL COULD RAISE A VASSAL	520	3 DON JUAN	16	L 5	7

WINE-AND-WATERY

	PAGE	VOL	CANTO	STANZA	LN
AND SO HE FOUND A WINE-AND-WATERY GRAVE	186	2 DON JUAN	2	57	5

WINES

	PAGE	VOL	CANTO	STANZA	LN
WHILE BACCHUS WILL PURVEY WITH WINES AND JELLIES	246	2 DON JUAN	2	170	V5
HATH YET A PURCHASED CHOICE OF CHOICEST WINES	394	3 DON JUAN	13	76	5
WINES TOO WHICH MIGHT AGAIN HAVE SLAIN YOUNG AMMON--	484	3 DON JUAN	15	65	3
WITH FASHIONABLE WINES AND CONVERSATION	534	3 DON JUAN	16	69	6

WING

	PAGE	VOL	CANTO	STANZA	LN
AND COLERIDGE TOO HAS LATELY TAKEN WING	10	2 DON JUAN	D	2	5
BUT SOMEHOW THIS MY VESTAL VOW TAKES WING	85	2 DON JUAN	1	119	5
BUT--GOD KNOWS HOW--THIS WISE RESOLVE TAKES WING	85	2 DON JUAN	1	119	V5
THE RACE HE SPRAINS A WING AND DOWN WE TEND	344	2 DON JUAN	4	1	4
BEFORE ONE CHARM OR HOPE HAD TAKEN WING	348	2 DON JUAN	4	8	8
AS CARELESSLY AS HURLS THE MOTH HER WING	170	3 DON JUAN	8	118	3
BEAR IT YE MUSES ON YOUR BRIGHTEST WING	175	3 DON JUAN	8	126	4
WHICH SEEMS AT FIRST TO NEED NO LOFTY WING	467	3 DON JUAN	15	25	3

WINGED

	PAGE	VOL	CANTO	STANZA	LN
CONTEND NOT WITH YOU ON THE WINGED STEED	14	2 DON JUAN	D	8	2
AND MAMMOTHS AND YOUR WINGED CROCODILES	201	3 DON JUAN	9	38	8
THE WIND IS WINGED FROM ONE POINT OF HEAVEN	388	3 DON JUAN	13	63	2

WINGS

	PAGE	VOL	CANTO	STANZA	LN
WHERE THE SUBLIME SOARS FORTH ON WINGS MORE AMPLE	45	2 DON JUAN	1	42	6
TO THE YOUNG BIRD THE PARENT'S BROODING WINGS	338	2 DON JUAN	3	107	3
THEIR ARMS AS HENS THEIR YOUNG ABOUT THEIR YOUNG	101	3 DON JUAN	7	67	8
AND WISHING THAT POST HORSES HAD THE WINGS	197	3 DON JUAN	9	30	6
HIS WINGS SUBDUED TO EPAULETTES HIS QUIVER	205	3 DON JUAN	9	45	2
WHICH FOR AN INSTANT CLIP ENJOYMENT'S WINGS	227	3 DON JUAN	10	5	8
AIR CAN ACCOMPLISH WITH HIS WIDE WINGS WAVING	263	3 DON JUAN	10	78	4
AND DANDIES ALL ARE GONE ON THE WIND'S WINGS	306	3 DON JUAN	11	76	8
STREAMING FROM OFF THE SUN LIKE SERAPH'S WINGS	387	3 DON JUAN	13	62	4
MY MUSE THE BUTTERFLY HATH BUT HER WINGS	400	3 DON JUAN	13	89	5

WINNER

	PAGE	VOL	CANTO	STANZA	LN
HE FOUND HOW MUCH OLD TIME HAD BEEN A WINNER--	72	2 DON JUAN	1	94	7
ANNOUNCED WITH NO LESS POMP THAN VICTORY'S WINNER	383	3 DON JUAN	13	54	3

WINNING

	PAGE	VOL	CANTO	STANZA	LN
FOR OFTENTIMES WHEN PEGASUS SEEMS WINNING	344	2 DON JUAN	4	1	3
NOT VERY DASHING BUT EXTREMELY WINNING	32	3 DON JUAN	6	52	2
THE ONE IS WINNING AND THE OTHER LOSING	415	3 DON JUAN	14	12	8
BUT JUAN HAD A SORT OF WINNING WAY	492	3 DON JUAN	15	82	1

WINS

	PAGE	VOL	CANTO	STANZA	LN
AND WINS EVEN BY A DELICATE DISSENT	493	3 DON JUAN	15	83	8

WINTER

	PAGE	VOL	CANTO	STANZA	LN
WHERE ALL IS VIRTUE AND THE WINTER SEASON	57	2 DON JUAN	1	64	2
AND MEAN NEXT WINTER TO BE QUITE RECLAIM'D	85	2 DON JUAN	1	119	8
MADE ICE SEEM PARADISE AND WINTER SUNNY	235	3 DON JUAN	10	21	8
THE ENGLISH WINTER--ENDING IN JULY	377	3 DON JUAN	13	42	1
THE LONDON WINTER AND THE COUNTRY SUMMER	380	3 DON JUAN	13	48	1
THE SEASON RATHER THAN TO WINTER DREAR--	395	3 DON JUAN	13	77	4
WHO WAKE IN WINTER ERE THE COCK CAN SUMMON	426	3 DON JUAN	14	36	3

WINTER'S

	PAGE	VOL	CANTO	STANZA	LN
A NEAT SNUG STUDY ON A WINTER'S NIGHT	444	2 DON JUAN	5	58	1

WINTER'S   (CONTINUED)
    IN WINTER'S DEPTH OR WANT OF REST AND VICTUAL 176   3 DON JUAN 8   128   7
    THE LONDON WINTER'S ENDED IN JULY-- 378   3 DON JUAN 13   43   1
WINTERS
    AS OAKS BLOWN DOWN WITH ALL THEIR THOUSAND WINTERS . . . 155   3 DON JUAN 8   88   8
    WHETHER HIS WINTERS BE EIGHTEEN OR EIGHTY 339   3 DON JUAN 12   50   7
    AND LOWER THE PRICE OF ROUGE--AT LEAST SOME WINTERS . . . 409   3 DON JUAN 13   111   8
    FOR SEVERAL WINTERS IN THE GRAND GRAND MONDE 428   3 DON JUAN 14   42   3
    SINCE THEN SHE HAD SPARKLED THROUGH THREE GLOWING WINTERS . 434 3 DON JUAN 14   56   1
WINTRY
    SO NARROW AS TO SHAME THEIR WINTRY BRINK 228   3 DON JUAN 10   7   3
    TO HOARD UP WARMTH AGAINST A WINTRY DAY 229   3 DON JUAN 10   9   8
WIPED
    HIS EYES FROM OFF HIS FACE BUT WIPED THE FOAM 203   2 DON JUAN 2   89   2
WIRE
    ACTED UPON THE LIVING AS ON WIRE 133   3 DON JUAN 8   41   7
WIRES
    THE LADY'S VOICE CEASED AND THE THRILLING WIRES 521   3 DON JUAN 16   41   1
WISDOM
    TO WORTH AS FREEDOM WISDOM AS TO WIT   18   2 DON JUAN D   15   6
    IN THOUGHTS LIKE THESE TRUE WISDOM MAY DISCERN 71   2 DON JUAN 1   93   1
    NOR LEAVE A WISH WHICH WISDOM MIGHT REPROVE   80   2 DON JUAN 1   109   5
    THAT WISDOM EVER ON THE WATCH TO ROB   264   2 DON JUAN 2   203   4
    AND MASTER'D BY HER WISDOM OR HER PRIDE 356   2 DON JUAN 4   23   4
    AND I LOVE WISDOM MORE THAN SHE LOVES ME   37   3 DON JUAN 6   63   2
    EACH MAN OF WISDOM FUTURE PAST OR PRESENT   69   3 DON JUAN 7   5   4
    WHERE'ER COLLECTIVE WISDOM CAN PARADE 371   3 DON JUAN 13   29   6
WISDOM'S
    THOUGH SAGES MAY POUR OUT THEIR WISDOM'S TREASURE . . . 308   2 DON JUAN 3   65   7
    OUR PASSIONS AND WE WALK IN WISDOM'S WAYS   360   3 DON JUAN 13   4   6
    AND SOCRATES HIMSELF BUT WISDOM'S QUIXOTE   363   3 DON JUAN 13   10   8
WISE
    WHEN TWO SUCH FACES ARE SO 'TWOULD BE WISE   77   2 DON JUAN 1   105   7
    BUT WHO ALAS CAN LOVE AND THEN BE WISE   84   2 DON JUAN 1   117   5
    BUT--GOD KNOWS HOW--THIS WISE RESOLVE TAKES WING . . .   85   2 DON JUAN 1   119   V5
    IS'T WISE OR FITTING CAUSELESS TO EXPLORE   101   2 DON JUAN 1   146   5
    'TIS WISE--'TIS WELL BUT NOT THE LESS A PAIN   130   2 DON JUAN 1   192   2
    IT WOULD HAVE BEEN MORE WISE TO SAVE THEIR VICTUAL . .   192   2 DON JUAN 2   69   8
    BUT THOSE WHO SATE NE'ER STIRRED IN ANY WISE 441   2 DON JUAN 5   54   4
    WHY 'TIS A PALACE WHERE THE TRULY WISE   458   2 DON JUAN 5   81   7
    BUT JUST REMARKED WITH AIR SEDATE AND WISE   500   2 DON JUAN 5   155   5
    AND DON'T AGREE AT ALL WITH THE WISE ROMAN   10   3 DON JUAN 6   7   6
    MOST WISE MEN WITH ONE MODERATE WOMAN WED   12   3 DON JUAN 6   12   5
    BUT THESE ARE FOOLISH THINGS TO ALL THE WISE   37   3 DON JUAN 6   63   1
    AT WHICH WISE MEN SNEERED IN PHRASES WITTY   93   3 DON JUAN 7   53   7
    TO SEE AN OLD MAN RATHER WILD THAN WISE   104   3 DON JUAN 7   73   5
    YOUR WISE MEN DON'T KNOW MUCH OF NAVIGATION   191   3 DON JUAN 9   18   4
    TOO WISE TO LOOK THROUGH OPTICS BLACK OR BLUE)-- . . .   218   3 DON JUAN 9   71   8
    HUT WHENCE WISE TRAVELLERS DRIVE WITH CIRCUMSPECTION . . 238   3 DON JUAN 10   27   6
    BY NO MEANS TO BE VERY WISE OR WITTY   290   3 DON JUAN 11   45   4
    BUT I HAVE MOTIVES WHETHER WISE OR SILLY   370   3 DON JUAN 13   27   3
    LISTENING DEBATES NOT VERY WISE OR WITTY   380   3 DON JUAN 13   48   6
    AND I REFER YOU TO WISE OXENSTIERN   436   3 DON JUAN 14   59   8
    UNLESS LIKE WISE TIRESIAS WE HAD PROVED   442   3 DON JUAN 14   73   2
    AND EKE THE WISE AS HAS BEEN OFTEN SHOWN   463   3 DON JUAN 15   17   4
    THOSE HOLIER MYSTERIES WHICH THE WISE AND JUST   503   3 DON JUAN 16   6   6
    A WISE MAN MORE THAN LAUGHTER FROM A DUNCE--   542   3 DON JUAN 16   88   5
    WHICH WAS NOT VERY WISE AND STILL LESS WITTY   545   3 DON JUAN 16   93   4
    THE WISE MAN'S SURE WHEN HE NO MORE CAN SHARE IT HE . .   566   3 DON JUAN 17   9   7
WISELY
    IS BROUGHT UP MUCH MORE WISELY THAN ANOTHER   42   2 DON JUAN 1   37   8
WISER
    SHE BEING WISER BY A YEAR OR TWO   228   2 DON JUAN 2   136   4
    MAY QUARREL AND THE LADY GROWING WISER   288   2 DON JUAN 3   24   4
    LET SPENDTHRIFTS' HEIRS ENQUIRE OF YOURS--WHO'S WISER . 321   3 DON JUAN 12   11   8
    ARE WISER IN THEIR WARNINGS 'GAINST THE WOE   336   3 DON JUAN 12   44   7
WISEST
    AND EVEN THE WISEST DO THE BEST THEY CAN   33   2 DON JUAN 1   21   3
    THE GREATEST WISEST BRAVEST AS WAS BEST   12   3 DON JUAN 6   13   V2
WISH
    I WISH HE WOULD EXPLAIN HIS EXPLANATION   10   2 DON JUAN D   2   8
    AT BEING DISAPPOINTED IN YOUR WISH   10   2 DON JUAN D   3   2
    WHICH MAKES ME WISH YOU'D CHANGE YOUR LAKES FOR OCEAN . . 12   2 DON JUAN D   5   8
    I WISH YOUR FATE MAY YIELD YE WHEN SHE CHOOSES   14   2 DON JUAN D   8   3
    I WISH THESE LAST HAD NOT OCCURR'D IN SOOTH   78   2 DON JUAN 1   107   5
    NOR LEAVE A WISH WHICH WISDOM MIGHT REPROVE   80   2 DON JUAN 1   109   5
    I WISH INDEED THEY HAD NOT HAD OCCASION   84   2 DON JUAN 1   117   4
    I WISH TO SLEEP AND BEG YOU WILL TAKE CARE   104   2 DON JUAN 1   153   5
    WITH THEIR ONE OAR (I WISH THEY HAD HAD A PAIR) . . .   193   2 DON JUAN 2   70   5
    YOU'D WISH YOURSELF WHERE TRUTH IS--IN A WELL   201   2 DON JUAN 2   84   8
    THE BLAME ON ME UNLESS YOU WISH THEY WERE   282   2 DON JUAN 3   12   4
    BUT WISH THIS MASTERPIECE OF NATURE'S WORK   315   2 DON JUAN 3   76   V7
    SOFT HOUR WHICH WAKES THE WISH AND MELTS THE HEART . .   338   2 DON JUAN 3   108   1
    ERE WHAT WE LEAST WISH TO BEHOLD WILL SLEEP   346   2 DON JUAN 4   4   6
    BY THE IMMORTAL WISH AND POWER TO BLESS   357   2 DON JUAN 4   26   8
    GREAT WISH TO PLEASE--A MOST ATTRACTIVE DOWER   395   2 DON JUAN 4   94   7
    BUT AT THIS HOUR I WISH TO PART IN PEACE   398   2 DON JUAN 4   99   2
    I WISH TO GOD THAT SOMEBODY WOULD BUY US   423   2 DON JUAN 5   24   8
    I WISH THE CASE COULD COME BEFORE A JURY HERE   446   2 DON JUAN 5   61   8

		PAGE	VOL		CANTO	STANZA	LN
WISH	(CONTINUED)						
	OF WORKMANSHIP SO RARE THEY MADE YOU WISH	449	2 DON JUAN	5	65	7
	I WISH TO BE PERSPICUOUS AND THE BLACK	450	2 DON JUAN	5	67	1
	I WISH YOU A GOOD APPETITE--FAREWELL	460	2 DON JUAN	5	84	2
	HER WISH WAS BUT TO KILL KILL KILL LIKE LEAR'S	490	2 DON JUAN	5	136	7
	RATHER THAN SIN--EXCEPT TO HIS OWN WISH	492	2 DON JUAN	5	141	6
	I WISH TO HEAVEN HE WOULD NOT SHINE TILL MORNING	494	2 DON JUAN	5	145	2
	I WISH THEIR YEARS HAD BEEN FIFTEEN AND TWENTY	9	3 DON JUAN	6	5	2
	THE TYRANT'S WISH THAT MANKIND ONLY HAD	19	3 DON JUAN	6	27	2
	MY WISH IS QUITE AS WIDE BUT NOT SO BAD	19	3 DON JUAN	6	27	4
	WHICH SOME CALL THE SUBLIME I WISH THEY'D TRY IT	32	3 DON JUAN	6	53	6
	IS THE SUBLIME--I WISH THAT THEY WOULD TRY IT	32	3 DON JUAN	6	53	V6
	I WISH IT NEVER LED TO SOMETHING WORSE	35	3 DON JUAN	6	59	8
	TO LAUGH AT ALL THINGS--FOR I WISH TO KNOW	67	3 DON JUAN	7	2	7
	THE RAMPART HIGHER THAN YOU'D WISH TO HANG	72	3 DON JUAN	7	11	4
	I THEREFORE IF YOU WISH ME TO FIGHT FREELY	103	3 DON JUAN	7	72	7
	TO WISH HIM BACK A BACHELOR NOW AND THEN	168	3 DON JUAN	8	113	6
	(I WISH YOUR BARDS WOULD SING IT RATHER BETTER)	184	3 DON JUAN	9	3	8
	I DO NOT KNOW--I WISH MEN TO BE FREE	195	3 DON JUAN	9	25	7
	WOULD WISH TO LOOK ON WHILE THEY ARE IN VIGOUR	213	3 DON JUAN	9	62	4
	I WISH TO DO AS MUCH BY POESY	226	3 DON JUAN	10	3	8
	BUT SHOULD WE WISH TO WARM US ON OUR WAY	254	3 DON JUAN	10	59	6
	I HEARD THEM WISH GOD WITH YOU SAVE THAT WAY--	274	3 DON JUAN	11	12	8
	WHICH MAKE US WISH OURSELVES IN TOWN AT ONCE--	277	3 DON JUAN	11	20	8
	I WISH THEY KNEW THE LIFE OF A YOUNG NOBLE	305	3 DON JUAN	11	74	8
	BUT HAVE NOT LEARNED TO WISH IT ANY LESS	324	3 DON JUAN	12	17	8
	IN THIS TWELFTH CANTO 'TIS MY WISH TO BE	325	3 DON JUAN	12	20	3
	HAS CAUSE TO WISH HER SIRE HAD HAD MALE HEIRS	331	3 DON JUAN	12	33	8
	THE TIME WILL COME SHE'LL WISH THAT SHE HAD SNATCHED	332	3 DON JUAN	12	35	3
	(I WISH THAT OTHERS WOULD FIND OUT THE SAME)	336	3 DON JUAN	12	42	2
	COQUETRY OR A WISH TO TAKE THE LEAD	351	3 DON JUAN	12	77	4
	OR WISH TO MAKE A RIVAL'S BOSOM BLEED	351	3 DON JUAN	12	77	6
	WITHOUT AN AWFUL WISH TO PLUNGE WITHIN IT	412	3 DON JUAN	14	5	8
	THAN THESE THINGS AND BESIDES I WISH TO SPARE 'EM	419	3 DON JUAN	14	21	5
	A PRETTY NAME AS ONE WOULD WISH TO READ	458	3 DON JUAN	15	5	3
	THE WHOLE TOGETHER IS WHAT I COULD WISH	465	3 DON JUAN	15	21	7
	I WISH SHE HAD HIS BOOK'S THE ELEVENTH COMMANDMENT	472	3 DON JUAN	15	38	2
	I WISH TO GOD YOU'DE DRESS US SOME SUCH PARTRIDGES	485	3 DON JUAN	15	67	V8
	SO EVERYONE MAY DRESS IT TO HIS WISH	486	3 DON JUAN	15	68	4
	YET I WISH WELL TO TROJAN AND TO TYRIAN	496	3 DON JUAN	15	91	7
	I WISH TO HEAVEN THEY WOULD NOT LOOK SO GRIM	499	3 DON JUAN	15	97	6
	I WISH THEY'D STATE HOW MANY THEY HAVE GAINED	505	3 DON JUAN	16	11	8
	IN COURTESY THEIR WISH TO SEE DISPLAYED	517	3 DON JUAN	16	39	5
	PERHAPS SHE MIGHT WISH TO CONFIRM HIM IN IT	526	3 DON JUAN	16	51	7
	WHO WISH TO TAKE THE TONE OF THEIR SOCIETY	526	3 DON JUAN	16	52	4
	TILL SOMEONE WITH A GROAN EXPREST A WISH	542	3 DON JUAN	16	87	7
WISH'D							
	HE WISH'D THAT LAND HE NEVER MIGHT SEE MORE	207	2 DON JUAN	2	97	4
	AND WISH'D IT DEATH IN WHICH HE HAD REPOSED	215	2 DON JUAN	2	112	5
	AND SOMETIMES CAUGHT AS MANY AS HE WISH'D	223	2 DON JUAN	2	126	4
	UNLESS HE WISH'D TO DIE UPON THE PLACE--	240	2 DON JUAN	2	159	6
	AND WISH'D THAT OTHERS HELD THE SAME OPINION	345	2 DON JUAN	4	3	2
	NOT WHAT THEY SAW BUT WHAT THEY WISH'D TO SEE	347	2 DON JUAN	4	7	4
	PERHAPS SHE WISH'D AN ASPIRANT PROFOUNDER	435	3 DON JUAN	14	57	5
	NO DOUBT IF I HAD WISH'D TO PAY MY COURT	466	3 DON JUAN	15	22	5
WISH'D-FOR							
	AND WHEN THE WISH'D-FOR SHOWER AT LENGTH WAS COME	203	2 DON JUAN	2	89	4
WISHED							
	WISHED FOR THEIR SAKES--THEY NEVER MIGHT GROW OLDER	292	2 DON JUAN	3	33	V8
	SHE ONLY WISHED TO SINK BURN AND DESTROY	490	2 DON JUAN	5	136	V7
	WHILE OTHERS WISHED THAT SHE HAD BEEN SO QUITE	23	3 DON JUAN	6	35	8
	WHO WISHED THEY HAD A BROTHER JUST LIKE HER	25	3 DON JUAN	6	39	6
	HE HAD PASSED THE NIGHT WAS WHAT SHE WISHED TO KNOW	55	3 DON JUAN	6	99	8
	BUT THERE SEEMED SOMETHING THAT HE WISHED TO HIDE	56	3 DON JUAN	6	100	5
	WHAT SLAVES HER HIGHNESS WISHED TO INDICATE	62	3 DON JUAN	6	112	7
	AND THOUGH HE WISHED EXTREMELY TO GET THROUGH	63	3 DON JUAN	6	116	6
	WHO HATING HOGS YET WISHED TO SAVE THEIR BACON	87	3 DON JUAN	7	42	8
	WHICH STIFFENED HEAVEN) AS IF HE WISHED FOR DAY--	121	3 DON JUAN	8	21	7
	AN ENGLISH NAVAL OFFICER WHO WISHED	152	3 DON JUAN	8	80	7
	AS IF HE WISHED THAT SHE SHOULD FARE LESS ILL	198	3 DON JUAN	9	31	3
	THAT I DEVOUTLY WISHED THE THREE WERE FOUR	271	3 DON JUAN	11	6	7
	AND WISHED HE HAD BEEN LESS HASTY WITH HIS FLINT	275	3 DON JUAN	11	14	8
	NOR WISHED OF SUCH FRAIL REALMS TO BE THE KING	296	3 DON JUAN	11	55	V6
	AND RATHER WISHED IN SUCH THINGS TO STAND NEUTER	336	3 DON JUAN	12	42	3
	BUT WHATSOE'ER SHE WISHED SHE ACTED RIGHT	435	3 DON JUAN	14	57	6
	BUT WISHED FOR A STILL MORE DETAILED NARRATION	526	3 DON JUAN	16	53	6
	LORD HENRY WISHED TO RAISE FOR A NEW PURCHASE	530	3 DON JUAN	16	60	2
	TO HOLD SOME SINECURES HE WISHED ABOLISHED	535	3 DON JUAN	16	72	7
WISHES							
	JEALOUS OF SOME ONE WHO HAD NO SUCH WISHES	74	2 DON JUAN	1	99	3
	DREST TO A SYBARITE'S MOST PAMPER'D WISHES	307	2 DON JUAN	3	62	5
	DREST IN THE WAY THAT ARISTIPPUS WISHES	307	2 DON JUAN	3	62	V5
	HE WISHES FOR A BOAT TO SAIL THE DEEPS--	333	2 DON JUAN	3	98	5
	WHILE YOUTH'S HOT WISHES IN OUR RED VEINS REVEL	345	2 DON JUAN	4	2	5
	I LEAVE THEM FOR THE PRESENT WITH GOOD WISHES	65	3 DON JUAN	6	120	1
	WHO NEITHER WISHES TO BE BOUND NOR BIND	195	3 DON JUAN	9	26	6
	WHO HAVE A DUE RESPECT FOR THEIR OWN WISHES	349	3 DON JUAN	12	73	4
WISHING							
	WISHING EACH OTHER NOT DIVORCED BUT DEAD	35	2 DON JUAN	1	26	3

WISHING   (CONTINUED)

BY CONTRAST WHICH IS WHAT WE JUST WERE WISHING ALL	37	2 DON JUAN	1	31	6
WISHING THEM--NOT EXACTLY DAMNED BUT DEAD HE	89	2 DON JUAN	1	125	V6
TOO MUCH AND WISHING GLADLY TO SURPRISE	294	2 DON JUAN	3	37	2
IN WISHING HER THEIR SISTER SAVE A FEW	25	3 DON JUAN	6	39	5
BUT WISHING TO BE ONE DAY BRIGADIERS	75	3 DON JUAN	7	18	4
AND WISHING THAT POST HORSES HAD THE WINGS	197	3 DON JUAN	9	30	6
THE SINGLE LADIES WISHING TO BE DOUBLE	342	3 DON JUAN	12	58	7

WISP

OR LIKE A WISP ALONG THE MARSH SO DAMP	89	3 DON JUAN	7	46	5

WISTFULLY

HE WATCH'D IT WISTFULLY UNTIL AWAY	204	2 DON JUAN	2	90	5

WIT

TO WORTH AS FREEDOM WISDOM AS TO WIT	18	2 DON JUAN	D	15	6
WITH VIRTUES EQUALL'D BY HER WIT ALONE	26	2 DON JUAN	1	10	4
HER WIT (SHE SOMETIMES TRIED AT WIT) WAS ATTIC ALL	27	2 DON JUAN	1	12	3
HER WIT (SHE SOMETIMES TRIED AT WIT) WAS ATTIC ALL	27	2 DON JUAN	1	12	3
QUICK WITHOUT WIT AND VIOLENT WITHOUT STRENGTH	155	2 DON JUAN	1	V 6	7
WIT WITHOUT SENSE--AND VIOLENCE WITHOUT FORCE	155	2 DON JUAN	1	V 6	V7
DISPLAYED MUCH MORE OF NERVE PERHAPS OF WIT	283	2 DON JUAN	3	14	V7
ALIKE MIGHT PUZZLE EITHER WIT OR DUNCE	43	3 DON JUAN	6	74	4
(THAT WHICH SOME ANCIENT MUSE OR MODERN WIT	153	3 DON JUAN	8	84	4
I RAILED AT SCOTS TO SHEW MY WRATH AND WIT	234	3 DON JUAN	10	19	3
OR FAME OR NAME FOR WIT WAR SENSE OR NONSENSE	305	3 DON JUAN	11	73	7
WITH WIT TO HATCH A PUN OR TELL A STORY	401	3 DON JUAN	13	91	6
BUT STRONGBOW'S WIT WAS OF MORE POLISH'D BREED	401	3 DON JUAN	13	92	4
FACTITIOUS PASSIONS WIT WITHOUT MUCH SALT	417	3 DON JUAN	14	16	5
THE LOUDEST WIT I E'ER WAS DEAFENED WITH	539	3 DON JUAN	16	81	8
FOR WIT HATH NO GREAT FRIEND IN AGUISH FOLKS	540	3 DON JUAN	16	83	3

WITCH

THEE WITCH OR EACH MEDEA HAS HER JASON	396	3 DON JUAN	13	81	6

WITCHES

THAN WITCHES BITCHES OR PHYSICIANS BREW	482	3 DON JUAN	15	62	8
AND WITCHES UNTO NONE THOUGH SOMEWHAT LATE	565	3 DON JUAN	17	7	2
NOT WITCHES ONLY BITCHES--WHO CREATE	565	3 DON JUAN	17	7	4

WITCHING

THIS DAY AND WATCHING WITCHING CONDESCENDING	546	3 DON JUAN	16	95	2

WITHAL

TO PLAGUE THEMSELVES WITHAL THEY KNOW NOT WHY	71	2 DON JUAN	1	93	4
TO SOOTHE HIS WOES WITHAL WAS SLAIN--THE SINNER	199	3 DON JUAN	9	33	7
HAS EVER PUZZLED FAITH WITHAL OR YOKED HER IN	377	3 DON JUAN	13	41	8
WITHAL IT LIES PERHAPS A LITTLE LOW	384	3 DON JUAN	13	55	6

WITHDRAW

OR ELSE 'TWERE EASY TO WITHDRAW HER WAIST	83	2 DON JUAN	1	115	5
OF WOLVES WILL THE BRIGHT MUSE WITHDRAW ONE RAY	70	3 DON JUAN	7	7	6

WITHDRAWN

WHICH IF WITHDRAWN WOULD BUT DISCLOSE THE FROWN	182	2 DON JUAN	2	49	3
BABA WHEN ALL THE DAMSELS WERE WITHDRAWN	470	3 DON JUAN	5	102	1
HAVE HALF WITHDRAWN FROM HIM OBLIVION'S SCREEN	82	3 DON JUAN	7	33	8

WITHDREW

WITHDREW ITSELF FROM HIS BUT LEFT BEHIND	60	2 DON JUAN	1	71	3
AND THEN ABASH'D AT ITS OWN JOY WITHDREW	81	2 DON JUAN	1	112	4
SHE SNUFF'D THE CANDLE CURTSIED AND WITHDREW	116	2 DON JUAN	1	173	8
THE FATHER PAUSED A MOMENT THEN WITHDREW	368	2 DON JUAN	4	46	1
THEN WITH A SUDDEN MOVEMENT HE WITHDREW	370	2 DON JUAN	4	48	1
'TWAS FOR THE SULTAN AND AT ONCE WITHDREW	407	2 DON JUAN	4	114	8
THEY BOWED OBEISANCE AND WITHDREW RETIRING	469	2 DON JUAN	5	100	1
AND THEN WITHDREW TO HEAR ABOUT THE RUSSIANS	52	3 DON JUAN	6	92	5
AND SHE WITHDREW BUT CAST NOT DOWN HER EYE	545	3 DON JUAN	16	94	4

WITHER

WOULD WITHER LESS THAN THESE TWO TORN APART	349	2 DON JUAN	4	10	7
BUT HARROW UP HIS FEELINGS TILL THEY WITHER	355	3 DON JUAN	12	86	6

WITHER'D

THEY PERISH'D UNTIL WITHER'D TO THESE FEW	210	2 DON JUAN	2	102	6
AND LIKE A WITHER'D LILY ON THE LAND	214	2 DON JUAN	2	110	6
TWELVE DAYS AND NIGHTS SHE WITHER'D THUS AT LAST	381	2 DON JUAN	4	69	1
BLOSSOM AND BOUGH LIE WITHER'D WITH ONE BLIGHT	382	2 DON JUAN	4	70	6

WITHERED

AS WELL AS FURTHER DRAIN THE WITHERED FORM	243	3 DON JUAN	10	38	4

WITHERING

THOUGH HOARY NOW AND WITH A WITHERING BREAST	228	3 DON JUAN	10	6	5
A FRUIT TO BLOOM UPON THEIR WITHERING BOUGH	330	3 DON JUAN	12	31	2

WITHHELD

WHICH JULIA HALF WITHHELD AND THEN HALF GRANTED	120	2 DON JUAN	1	180	2

WITHOUT'S

WHILE ALL WITHOUT'S INDICATIVE OF REST	457	3 DON JUAN	15	3	V3

WITHSTAND

(AND SHE HAD SOME NOT EASY TO WITHSTAND)	396	2 DON JUAN	4	95	6
AND HE COULD EVEN WITHSTAND THAT AWKWARD TEST	139	3 DON JUAN	8	53	5
WITH THINGS I CAN'T WITHSTAND OR UNDERSTAND	484	3 DON JUAN	15	66	3

WITHSTANDS

IN SUCH PROPORTION--BUT MY MUSE WITHSTANDS	20	3 DON JUAN	6	28	3

WITHSTOOD

HAVING WITHSTOOD TEMPTATION IN MY YOUTH	397	2 DON JUAN	4	97	2

WITLESS

THE WITLESS FALSTAFF OF A HOARY HAL	267	3 DON JUAN	10	86	7

WITLINGS

THAN WHISPERING FOPLINGS OR THAN WITLINGS LOUD	493	3 DON JUAN	15	83	4

WITNESS

THOU SHALT NOT BEAR FALSE WITNESS LIKE THE BLUES	140	2 DON JUAN	1	206	3

WITNESS   (CONTINUED)
```
    OCEAN THEIR WITNESS AND THE CAVE THEIR BED . . . . .   265  2 DON JUAN  2   204   4
    WITNESS THE LANDS WHICH FLOW'D WITH MILK AND HONEY  . . .  405  3 DON JUAN 13   100   1
    WITNESS THOSE CI-DEVANT JEUNES HOMMES WHO STEM . . . .   418  3 DON JUAN 14    18   7
    A SOMETHING LIKE IT--AS BEAR WITNESS LUTHER . . . . .   565  3 DON JUAN 17     6   8
WITNESSES
    WERE PROVED BY COMPETENT FALSE WITNESSES . . . . . . .   109  2 DON JUAN  1   160   8
    THE NAMES OF ALL THE WITNESSES THE PLEADINGS  . . . .   127  2 DON JUAN  1   189   3
WITS
    WHICH MANY PEOPLE PASS FOR WITS BY QUOTING  . . . . .    77  3 DON JUAN  7    21   8
    WITH MUSIC THE MOST MODERATE SHINE AS WITS  . . . . .   340  3 DON JUAN 12    52   7
    BUT WHETHER FITS OR WITS OR HARPSICHORDS . . . . . .   340  3 DON JUAN 12    53   1
    THESE ALSO WERE TWO WITS BY ACCLAMATION . . . . . . .   401  3 DON JUAN 13    92   1
    BOTH WITS--ONE BORN SO AND THE OTHER BRED . . . . . .   402  3 DON JUAN 13    93   7
    THE WITS WATCHED EVERY LOOP-HOLE FOR THEIR ART  . . .   408  3 DON JUAN 13   109   3
    SKIRMISH OF WITS O'ER THE DEPARTED ONE  . . . . . . .   552  3 DON JUAN 16   105   2
WITTY
    AT WHICH YOUR WISE MEN SNEERED IN PHRASES WITTY  . . .    93  3 DON JUAN  7    53   7
    THE FATE OF NATIONS--BUT THIS RUSS SO WITTY . . . . .   179  3 DON JUAN  8   134   7
    WHO STILL HAVE SHOWN THEMSELVES MORE BRAVE THAN WITTY   194  3 DON JUAN  9    23   4
    AND YET I SEEK NOT TO BE GRAND NOR WITTY--  . . . . .   233  3 DON JUAN 10    17   6
    BY NO MEANS TO BE VERY WISE OR WITTY  . . . . . . . .   290  3 DON JUAN 11    45   4
    SHE MERELY WAS DEEMED AMIABLE AND WITTY . . . . . . .   338  3 DON JUAN 12    47   4
    LISTENING DEBATES NOT VERY WISE OR WITTY . . . . . .   380  3 DON JUAN 13    48   6
    WHICH WAS NOT VERY WISE AND STILL LESS WITTY  . . . .   545  3 DON JUAN 16    93   4
WIVE
    LOVE LINGERS STILL ALTHOUGH 'TWERE LATE TO WIVE  . . .   316  3 DON JUAN 12     2   5
WIVED
    THE MAJOR PART OF THEM HAD LONG BEEN WIVED  . . . . .    96  2 DON JUAN  1   138   3
WIVES
    AND HOW YE MAY BE DOUBLY WIDOWS--WIVES  . . . . . . .   123  2 DON JUAN  1   185   8
    WHERE WIVES AT LEAST ARE SELDOM KEPT IN GARRISON  . .   248  2 DON JUAN  2   175   8
    WIVES IN THEIR HUSBANDS' ABSENCES GROW SUBTLER  . . .   287  2 DON JUAN  3    22   7
    FOUR WIVES AND TWICE FIVE HUNDRED MAIDS UNSEEN  . . .   496  2 DON JUAN  5   148   7
    AS THOSE WHOSE WIVES HAVE MADE THEM FIT FOR HEAVEN  .   500  2 DON JUAN  5   154   8
    AND AS FOUR WIVES MUST HAVE QUADRUPLE CLAIMS  . . . .    11  3 DON JUAN  6    11   7
    BILLS--WOMEN--WIVES DOGS HORSES--AND MANKIND  . . . .    17  3 DON JUAN  6    22  V2
    WHEN WICKED WIVES WHO LOVE SOME BACHELOR . . . . . .    18  3 DON JUAN  6    24   3
    THAN WHERE TWO WIVES ARE UNDER AN EMBARGO . . . . . .    51  3 DON JUAN  6    90   8
    FOR SOME WERE THINKING OF THEIR WIVES AND FAMILIES  .    94  3 DON JUAN  7    54  V7
    SAVE WED A YEAR I HATE RECRUITS WITH WIVES  . . . . .   102  3 DON JUAN  7    70   8
    OUR BRITISH FRIEND THESE ARE THE WIVES OF OTHERS  . .   103  3 DON JUAN  7    71   2
    LIKE CHASTEST WIVES FROM CONSTANT HUSBANDS' SIDES  . .   125  3 DON JUAN  8    27   3
    THAN SOME WIVES (WHO MAKE BLUNDERS NO LESS STUPID)  .   205  3 DON JUAN  9    45   7
    OLD FLAMES NEW WIVES BECOME OUR BITTEREST FOES--  . .   231  3 DON JUAN 10    12   7
    TAKE LIVES TAKE WIVES TAKE AUGHT EXCEPT MEN'S PURSES   264  3 DON JUAN 10    79   2
    HERE ARE CHASTE WIVES PURE LIVES HERE PEOPLE PAY  . .   273  3 DON JUAN 11    10   1
    SOME MAIDS HAVE BEEN MADE WIVES SOME MERELY MOTHERS  .   308  3 DON JUAN 11    81   4
    AND ONE OR TWO SAD SEPARATE WIVES WITHOUT . . . . . .   330  3 DON JUAN 12    31   1
    UPON THE SWEEPSTAKES FOR SUBSTANTIAL WIVES  . . . . .   333  3 DON JUAN 12    36   4
    HE HAD MANY FRIENDS WHO HAD MANY WIVES AND WAS  . . .   342  3 DON JUAN 12    57   1
    I'VE ALSO SEEN SOME WIVES (NOT TO FORGET . . . . . .   452  3 DON JUAN 14    95   5
    WHO WERE THE VERY PARAGONS OF WIVES  . . . . . . . .   452  3 DON JUAN 14    95   7
    THEIR HIDEOUS WIVES THEIR HORRID SELVES AND DRESSES  .   550  3 DON JUAN 16   103   7
WIVES'
    EMPERORS ARE ONLY HUSBANDS IN WIVES' EYES  . . . . .   477  2 DON JUAN  5   115   5
WOE
    OH JULIA WHAT IS EVERY OTHER WOE--  . . . . . . . . .   167  2 DON JUAN  2    20   2
    WHO IN THEIR TRANSPORT NEVER DREAMED OF WOE . . . . .   353  2 DON JUAN  4    18  V3
    LOT OF SO YOUNG A PARTNER IN THE WOE  . . . . . . . .   417  2 DON JUAN  5    12   6
    ARE WISER IN THEIR WARNINGS 'GAINST THE WOE . . . . .   336  3 DON JUAN 12    44   7
    THIS WORKS A WORLD OF SENTIMENTAL WOE . . . . . . . .   345  3 DON JUAN 12    63   5
    WOE TO THE MAN WHO VENTURES A REBUKE  . . . . . . . .   429  3 DON JUAN 14    43   5
    OF ALL THE HORRID HIDEOUS NOTES OF WOE  . . . . . . .   432  3 DON JUAN 14    50   1
    UNDRESSING IS A WOE OUR ROBE DE CHAMBRE . . . . . . .   505  3 DON JUAN 16    11   2
WOES
    WITH SUCH SERENITY HER HUSBAND'S WOES . . . . . . . .    36  2 DON JUAN  1    29   2
    HAPPIER THAN THEY WHO STILL PERCEIVED THEIR WOES  . .   199  2 DON JUAN  2    80   4
    BUT NONE OF THEM APPEAR'D TO SHARE HIS WOES . . . . .   213  2 DON JUAN  2   109   5
    NOT EVEN A VISION OF HIS FORMER WOES  . . . . . . . .   227  2 DON JUAN  2   134   5
    ALTHOUGH HIS WOES HAD TURN'D HIM RATHER YELLOW  . . .   235  2 DON JUAN  2   148   8
    WHATE'ER THEIR DREAMS BE IF OF JOYS OR WOES . . . . .    16  3 DON JUAN  6    20   3
    YET DISAPPOINTED JOYS ARE WOES AS DEEP  . . . . . . .    16  3 DON JUAN  6    20   4
    WHOSE HEADLONG PASSIONS FORM THEIR PROPER WOES  . . .    49  3 DON JUAN  6    87   8
    TO SOOTHE HIS WOES WITHAL WAS SLAIN--THE SINNER . . .   199  3 DON JUAN  9    33   7
    A THING TO COUNTERBALANCE HUMAN WOES  . . . . . . . .   226  3 DON JUAN 10     2   5
    WHERE IS THE UNHAPPY QUEEN WITH ALL HER WOES  . . . .   307  3 DON JUAN 11    77   5
    ALAS POOR GHOST--WHAT UNEXPECTED WOES . . . . . . . .   403  3 DON JUAN 13    97   7
    AND HENCE ARISE THE WOES OF SENTIMENT . . . . . . . .   444  3 DON JUAN 14    79   6
WOKE
    OF OCEAN WHEN THEY WOKE THEY FELT A QUALM . . . . . .   192  2 DON JUAN  2    68   6
    AND WOKE HER MAID SO EARLY THAT SHE GRUMBLED  . . . .   229  2 DON JUAN  2   138   5
    HE WOKE AND GAZED AND WOULD HAVE SLEPT AGAIN  . . . .   235  2 DON JUAN  2   149   1
    WHEN JUAN WOKE HE FOUND SOME GOOD THINGS READY  . . .   246  2 DON JUAN  2   171   1
    SHE WOKE AT LENGTH BUT NOT AS SLEEPERS WAKE . . . . .   378  2 DON JUAN  4    62   1
    AND THE UNQUIET FEELINGS WHICH FIRST WOKE . . . . . .   402  2 DON JUAN  4   106   3
    WHERE ECHO WOKE AS IF FROM A LONG SLUMBER . . . . . .   448  2 DON JUAN  5    64   2
    AND SO--SHE WOKE WITH A GREAT SCREAM AND START  . . .    44  3 DON JUAN  6    77   8
    HE WOKE BETIMES AND AS MAY BE SUPPOSED  . . . . . . .   512  3 DON JUAN 16    28   1
```

```
                                                         PAGE VOL     CANTO STANZA  LV
WOLF
    THE BEAR IS CIVILIZED THE WOLF IS MILD    . . . . . . .  157   3 DON JUAN   8     92     5
WOLFE
    VERNON THE BUTCHER CUMBERLAND WOLFE HAWKE    . . . . . .   22   2 DON JUAN   1      2     1
WOLFISH
    (ALTHOUGH THEY SPOKE NOT) IN THEIR WOLFISH EYES   . . . .  194   2 DON JUAN   2     72     8
WOLVES
    OF WOLVES WILL THE BRIGHT MUSE WITHDRAW ONE RAY    . . . .   70   3 DON JUAN   7      7     6
    AND HOWLED FOR HELP AS WOLVES DO FOR A MEAL--    . . . .  153   3 DON JUAN   8     83     6
    MEN BECOME WOLVES ON ANY SLIGHT OCCASION .   . . . . .  192   3 DON JUAN   9     20     8
WOMAN
    AND THEN THIS BEST AND MEEKEST WOMAN BORE    . . . . .   36   2 DON JUAN   1     29     1
    HER STATURE TALL--I HATE A DUMPY WOMAN    . . . . .   55   2 DON JUAN   1     61     8
    SHE NOW DETERMINED THAT A VIRTUOUS WOMAN .   . . . .   63   2 DON JUAN   1     77     1
    LEAVE TO O'ERSTEP THE WRITTEN RIGHTS OF WOMAN    . . .   74   2 DON JUAN   1     98     3
    OF ANY WICKED WOMAN WHO CONTRIVED    . . . . . .   96   2 DON JUAN   1    138     5
    A PRETTY WOMAN--(THAT'S QUITE NATURAL .   . . . .  158   2 DON JUAN   2      3     5
    FREE AS A MARRIED WOMAN OR SUCH OTHER .   . . . .  248   2 DON JUAN   2    175     3
    LET US HAVE WINE AND WOMAN MIRTH AND LAUGHTER   . . .  250   2 DON JUAN   2    178     7
    IN HER FIRST PASSION WOMAN LOVES HER LOVER    . . . .  276   2 DON JUAN   3      3     1
    BUT ONE THING'S PRETTY SURE A WOMAN PLANTED--    . . .  276   2 DON JUAN   3      4     2
    WRITE ODES ON THE INCONSTANCY OF WOMAN    . . . .  288   2 DON JUAN   3     24     8
    NO COURTIER COULD AND SCARCELY WOMAN CAN .   . . .  296   2 DON JUAN   3     41     5
    WOMAN OR WINE YOU'LL HAVE TO UNDERGO   . . . . .  357   2 DON JUAN   4     25     2
    I KNOW ONE WOMAN OF THAT PURPLE SCHOOL    . . . .  405   2 DON JUAN   4    111     7
    BEING A TRUE WOMAN IN A STATE OF NATURE   . . . .  476   2 DON JUAN   5    113    V7
    THAT BEING THE LAST THING A PROUD WOMAN TRIES    . . .  483   2 DON JUAN   5    125     6
    EVEN YE WHO KNOW WHAT A CHECKED WOMAN IS .   . . .  489   2 DON JUAN   5    134     7
    DISSOLVED LIKE SNOW BEFORE A WOMAN CRYING .   . . .  492   2 DON JUAN   5    141     8
    BUT WOMAN WITH THE HEART--OR SOMETHING ELSE    . . . .    7   3 DON JUAN   6      2    V8
    FOR THAT SAD TEMPTER A FORBIDDEN WOMAN    . . . .   10   3 DON JUAN   6      7     4
    MOST WISE MEN WITH ONE MODERATE WOMAN WED    . . . .   12   3 DON JUAN   6     12     5
    A BAD OLD WOMAN MAKING A WORSE WILL    . . . . .   16   3 DON JUAN   6     21     5
    FOR WORDLESS WOMAN WHICH IS SILENT THUNDER    . . . .   34   3 DON JUAN   6     57     8
    MAKING A WOMAN LIKE A PORCUPINE .   . . . . .   37   3 DON JUAN   6     62     1
    IS NEITHER MAN NOR WOMAN THE CHIEF THREW ON .   . . .   97   3 DON JUAN   7     60     3
    FORGETTING QUITE THE WOMAN (WHICH COMPOSED    . . . .  211   3 DON JUAN   9     58     2
    IS WOMAN WHAT A WHIRLWIND IS HER HEAD .   . . . .  214   3 DON JUAN   9     64     2
    HE OWED TO AN OLD WOMAN AND HIS POST   . . . . .  239   3 DON JUAN  10     29     8
    AN ERRING WOMAN FINDS AN OPENER DOOR .   . . . . .  352   3 DON JUAN  12     79     6
    TILL THIRTY SHOULD PERCEIVE THERE'S A PLAIN WOMAN    . .  359   3 DON JUAN  13      3     8
    WITH QUIET CRUIZING O'ER THE OCEAN WOMAN .   . . .  376   3 DON JUAN  13     40     2
    I'VE SEEN A VIRTUOUS WOMAN PUT DOWN QUITE    . . . .  397   3 DON JUAN  13     82     3
    MY LADY'S PRATTLE FILTER'D THROUGH HER WOMAN    . . .  418   3 DON JUAN  14     19     8
    ALAS WORLDS FALL--AND WOMAN SINCE SHE FELL'D    . . .  420   3 DON JUAN  14     23     1
    THAT--BUT ASK ANY WOMAN IF SHE'D CHOOSE   . . . .  421   3 DON JUAN  14     25     6
    A QUALITY AGREEABLE TO WOMAN . .   . . . . .  426   3 DON JUAN  14     36     5
    TO CALCULATORS WHEN THEY COUNT ON WOMAN   . . . .  429   3 DON JUAN  14     43     8
    A WOMAN SO SHE'S GOOD WHAT DOES IT SIGNIFY    . . . .  435   3 DON JUAN  14     57     8
    THAN WEAR A HEART A WOMAN LOVES TO REND   . . . .  438   3 DON JUAN  14     64     6
    SHE WAS AS CAPABLE AS WOMAN CAN BE .   . . . .  450   3 DON JUAN  14     92     8
    NO FRIEND LIKE TO A WOMAN EARTH DISCOVERS    . . . .  451   3 DON JUAN  14     93     7
    AS E'ER BROUGHT MAN AND WOMAN TO THE BRINK    . . . .  454   3 DON JUAN  14    100     3
    IN HER OWN MIND AND THAT'S ENOUGH FOR WOMAN    . . . .  473   3 DON JUAN  15     40     2
    WOULD THAT I NEER HAD LOVED--OH WOMAN--WOMAN--   . . .  569   3 DON JUAN  17   V 13     2
    WOULD THAT I NEER HAD LOVED--OH WOMAN--WOMAN--   . . .  569   3 DON JUAN  17   V 13     2
WOMANHOOD
    SHE GREW TO WOMANHOOD AND BETWEEN WHILES .   . . . .  224   2 DON JUAN   2    128     6
    AND WHEN YOU ADD TO THIS HER WOMANHOOD    . . . .  218   2 DON JUAN   9     71     1
WOMANKIND
    OH SIN OH SORROW AND OH WOMANKIND    . . . . .  112   2 DON JUAN   1    165     2
    BILLS BEASTS AND MEN AND--NO NOT WOMANKIND    . . . .   17   3 DON JUAN   6     22     2
    THAT WOMANKIND HAD BUT ONE ROSY MOUTH .   . . . .   19   3 DON JUAN   6     27     7
    AND WOMANKIND TOO IF WE SO MAY SAY .   . . . . .  479   3 DON JUAN  15     53     5
    WHICH SOMETIMES PLAYS THE DEUCE WITH WOMANKIND   . . .  480   3 DON JUAN  15     57     2
WOMAN'S
    ACCORDING TO SOME GOOD OLD WOMAN'S TALE   . . . .   72   2 DON JUAN   1     95     8
    FOR FACTS AGAINST A VIRTUOUS WOMAN'S FAME    . . . .  101   2 DON JUAN   1    146     6
    'TIS WOMAN'S WHOLE EXISTENCE MAN MAY RANGE    . . . .  131   2 DON JUAN   1    194     2
    THAT MADE HIS EYELIDS AS A WOMAN'S BE .   . . . .  179   2 DON JUAN   2     43     6
    FOR WOMAN'S FACE WAS NEVER FORM'D IN VAIN    . . . .  235   2 DON JUAN   2    149     5
    A WOMAN'S TRUE BUT THEN THERE IS A CAUSE .   . . .  455   2 DON JUAN   5     76     2
    A WOMAN'S TEAR-DROP MELTS A MAN'S HALF SEARS    . . .  479   2 DON JUAN   5    118     5
    WOMAN'S THE HEART--OR ANYTHING INSTEAD    . . . .    7   3 DON JUAN   6      2    V8
    A SINCERE WOMAN'S BREAST--FOR OVER-WARM   . . . .   13   3 DON JUAN   6     15     7
    FOR WOMAN'S SILENCE STARTLES MORE THAN THUNDER   . . .   34   3 DON JUAN   6     57    V8
    AND HERE HE WAS--WHO UPON WOMAN'S BREAST    . . . .  139   3 DON JUAN   8     53     1
    HE WHO HATH PROVED WAR STORM OR WOMAN'S RAGE    . . .  339   3 DON JUAN  12     50     6
WOMEN
    FAMOUS FOR ORANGES AND WOMEN--HE   . . . . .   25   2 DON JUAN   1      8     2
    SOME WOMEN USE THEIR TONGUES--SHE LOOK'D A LECTURE   . .   29   2 DON JUAN   1     15     1
    SAGEST OF WOMEN EVEN OF WIDOWS SHE    . . . . .   42   2 DON JUAN   1     38     1
    SWEET IS REVENGE--ESPECIALLY TO WOMEN .   . . . .   88   2 DON JUAN   1    124     7
    APPEAR'D LIKE TWO POOR HARMLESS WOMEN WHO    . . . .   98   2 DON JUAN   1    141     2
    I'VE SEEN MUCH FINER WOMEN RIPE AND REAL .   . . .  218   2 DON JUAN   2    118     7
    FOR AS YOU KNOW THE SPANISH WOMEN BANISH .   . . .  220   2 DON JUAN   2    120     4
    AND ZOE SPENT HERS AS MOST WOMEN DO    . . . . .  228   2 DON JUAN   2    136     6
    SHOWS STARS AND WOMEN IN A BETTER LIGHT   . . . .  237   2 DON JUAN   2    152     8
    FOES FRIENDS MEN WOMEN NOW ARE NOUGHT TO ME .   . . .  244   2 DON JUAN   2    166     7
```

	PAGE	VOL		CANTO	STANZA	LN

WOMEN   (CONTINUED)

	PAGE	VOL		CANTO	STANZA	LN
ALAS THE LOVE OF WOMEN IT IS KNOWN	262	2 DON JUAN	2	199	1
IS ALWAYS SO TO WOMEN ONE SOLE BOND	263	2 DON JUAN	2	200	2
THEY PLACED HIM O'ER THE WOMEN AS A SCOUT)	394	2 DON JUAN	4	92	5
THE WOMEN PARDONED ALL EXCEPT HER FACE	476	2 DON JUAN	5	113	8
THE VERY WOMEN HALF-FORGAVE HER FACE	476	2 DON JUAN	5	113	V8
FOR WOMEN SHED AND USE THEM AT THEIR LIKING	479	2 DON JUAN	5	118	2
BUT BID MY WOMEN FORM THE MILKY WAY	494	2 DON JUAN	5	145	3
THE WOMEN UP--BECAUSE IN SAD REALITY	501	2 DON JUAN	5	157	2
THERE IS A TIDE IN THE AFFAIRS OF WOMEN	7	3 DON JUAN	6	2	1
BUT WOMEN WITH THEIR HEARTS OR HEAVEN KNOWS WHAT	7	3 DON JUAN	6	2	8
WOMEN ON T'OTHER HAND SEEM SOMEWHAT SILLY	14	3 DON JUAN	6	16	8
BILLS--WOMEN--WIVES DOGS HORSES--AND MANKIND	17	3 DON JUAN	6	22	V2
YOUNG WOMEN AND CORRECT THEM WHEN THEY BLUNDERED	21	3 DON JUAN	6	31	8
WAVES AT SPRING-TIDE OR WOMEN ANYWHERE	23	3 DON JUAN	6	34	3
I'VE SEEN YOUR ,STORMY SEAS AND STORMY WOMEN	32	3 DON JUAN	6	53	7
WHICH LAYS BOTH MEN AND WOMEN ON THE SHELF	41	3 DON JUAN	6	69	7
AGAINST ALL WOMEN OF WHATE'ER CONDITION	64	3 DON JUAN	6	117	3
THE OTHER TWO ARE WOMEN AND THE THIRD	97	3 DON JUAN	7	60	2
HE'S A FINE BOY THE WOMEN MAY BE SENT	100	3 DON JUAN	7	66	7
THE WOMEN WITH THEIR HAIR ABOUT THEIR EARS	102	3 DON JUAN	7	69	3
BY BRINGING WOMEN HERE THEY SHALL BE SHOWN	102	3 DON JUAN	7	70	3
WHAT WAS'T TO HIM TO HEAR TWO WOMEN SOB	105	3 DON JUAN	7	77	8
TO WOMEN THERE IS SCARCE A CRIMSON VARLET	108	3 DON JUAN	7	84	5
FATAL TO WARRIORS AS TO WOMEN--THESE	150	3 DON JUAN	8	76	V2
OF MURDERED WOMEN WHO HAD FOUND THEIR WAY	157	3 DON JUAN	8	91	3
OF THE STRANGE THING SOME WOMEN SET A VALUE ON	208	3 DON JUAN	9	51	3
FOR SUCH ALL WOMEN ARE AT FIRST NO DOUBT	220	3 DON JUAN	9	75	4
SOME RECKON WOMEN BY THEIR SUNS OR YEARS	230	3 DON JUAN	10	10	7
NOW WHAT I LOVE IN WOMEN IS THEY WON'T	285	3 DON JUAN	11	36	6
THE WOMEN MUCH DIVIDED--AS IS USUAL	329	3 DON JUAN	12	28	1
AT FIRST HE DID NOT THINK THE WOMEN PRETTY	347	3 DON JUAN	12	68	8
WHOSE CHARMS MADE ALL MEN SPEAK AND WOMEN DUMB	365	3 DON JUAN	13	13	6
AND THUS WITH WOMEN HOWSOE'ER IT SHOCK SOME'S	371	3 DON JUAN	13	30	7
BUT AS TO WOMEN WHO CAN PENETRATE	420	3 DON JUAN	14	24	3
HE LIKEWISE COULD BE MOST THINGS TO ALL WOMEN	424	3 DON JUAN	14	31	7
SOME WOULD NOT DEEM SUCH WOMEN COULD BE FOUND	429	3 DON JUAN	14	44	4
WHICH PRETTY WOMEN--THE SWEET SOULS--CALL SOUL	441	3 DON JUAN	14	71	3
BUT THUS IT IS SOME WOMEN WILL BETRAY US	441	3 DON JUAN	14	72	8
AND STILL MORE WOMEN SPRING FROM NOT EMPLOYING	444	3 DON JUAN	14	78	7
AS OBSTINACY BOTH IN MEN AND WOMEN	448	3 DON JUAN	14	89	5
SHE HAD HEARD BUT WOMEN HEAR WITH MORE GOOD HUMOUR	460	3 DON JUAN	15	11	3
THAT IS WITH MEN WITH WOMEN HE WAS WHAT	463	3 DON JUAN	15	16	1
AS WOMEN HATE HALF MEASURES ON THE WHOLE	468	3 DON JUAN	15	28	7
THERE'S NOTHING WOMEN LOVE TO DABBLE IN	470	3 DON JUAN	15	31	4
NEM CON AMONGST THE WOMEN WHICH I GRIEVE	493	3 DON JUAN	15	84	2
SINCE BURNING AGED WOMEN (SAVE A FEW--	565	3 DON JUAN	17	7	3

WOMEN'S

	PAGE	VOL		CANTO	STANZA	LN
ABROAD SUCH THINGS DECIDE FEW WOMEN'S FATE--	345	3 DON JUAN	12	64	5

WON

	PAGE	VOL		CANTO	STANZA	LN
HE WON THEM WELL AND MAY HE WEAR THEM LONG	77	2 DON JUAN	1	104	8
JUAN REPLIED IT MUST BE WON NOT GIVEN	365	2 DON JUAN	4	40	V2
THE WALLS WERE WON BUT 'TWAS AN EVEN BET	150	3 DON JUAN	8	77	5
HE NEVER WOULD BELIEVE THE CITY WON	164	3 DON JUAN	8	105	4
IF YET THE CITY'S REST WERE WON OR LOST	171	3 DON JUAN	8	120	6
AS MAY BE WON BY FAVOUR OF THE MOON	229	3 DON JUAN	10	9	3
HATH WON THE EXPERIENCE WHICH IS DEEMED SO WEIGHTY	339	3 DON JUAN	12	50	8
HAD BONAPARTE WON AT WATERLOO	449	3 DON JUAN	14	90	1

WONDER

	PAGE	VOL		CANTO	STANZA	LN
(I WONDER HOW THEY GOT THROUGH THE TWELVE HOURS)	30	2 DON JUAN	1	18	6
I WONDER IN WHAT QUARTER NOW THE MOON IS	103	2 DON JUAN	1	150	4
(I REALLY MADAM WONDER AT YOUR TASTE--	115	2 DON JUAN	1	172	4
THE NINE DAYS' WONDER WHICH WAS BROUGHT TO LIGHT	126	2 DON JUAN	1	188	6
(I WONDER WHAT IT WILL BE LIKE AT FORTY	143	2 DON JUAN	1	213	2
TO HEAD THE POLL I WONDER WHO WOULD BUY IT	154	2 DON JUAN	1	V 5	4
SO GOOD--I WONDER CASTLEREAGH DON'T TAX 'EM	264	2 DON JUAN	2	203	8
I WONDER IF HIS APPETITE WAS GOOD	426	2 DON JUAN	5	30	1
A GLANCE AT THAT WHICH WRAPT THE SLAVES IN WONDER	450	2 DON JUAN	5	66	2
WHICH MADE HIM WONDER MORE THAN ANY WONDER	34	3 DON JUAN	6	57	V7
WHICH MADE HIM WONDER MORE THAN ANY WONDER	34	3 DON JUAN	6	57	V7
GOOD GOD I WONDER WHAT THEY WOULD BE AT	67	3 DON JUAN	7	3	6
I WONDER (ALTHOUGH MARS NO DOUBT'S A GOD I	77	3 DON JUAN	7	21	1
A THING TO WONDER AT BEYOND MOST WONDERING	95	3 DON JUAN	7	55	4
HAD PALISADOED IN A WAY YOU'D WONDER	136	3 DON JUAN	8	46	4
AND YET THE REST RUSHED EAGERLY--NO WONDER	163	3 DON JUAN	8	103	5
WERE ALSO HEARD TO WONDER IN THE DIN	178	3 DON JUAN	8	132	2
AND WONDER WHAT OLD WORLD SUCH THINGS COULD SEE	180	3 DON JUAN	8	137	4
THEY SAY YOU LIKE IT TOO--'TIS NO GREAT WONDER	185	3 DON JUAN	9	5	2
WILL WONDER WHERE SUCH ANIMALS COULD SUP	202	3 DON JUAN	9	39	3
NO WONDER THEN THAT YERMOLOFF OR MOMONOFF	206	3 DON JUAN	9	48	1
OF BEING STARS AND THIS UNRIDDLED WONDER	269	3 DON JUAN	11	3	7
AND LOST IN WONDER OF SO GREAT A NATION	272	3 DON JUAN	11	9	3
I WONDER PEOPLE SHOULD BE LEFT ALIVE	316	3 DON JUAN	12	2	3
AND WONDER HOW THE WEALTHY CAN BE SPARING	316	3 DON JUAN	12	3	7
WHICH WAS A WONDER IF YOU THINK WHO GOT HIM	338	3 DON JUAN	12	49	4
AND WONDER PROVIDENCE IS NOT MORE SAGE	339	3 DON JUAN	12	50	4
NO WONDER THEN A PURER SOUL SHOULD DREAD	438	3 DON JUAN	14	64	3
ALTHOUGH I WONDER HOW IT GREW HABITUAL	472	3 DON JUAN	15	36	8
MADE JUAN WONDER AS NO DOUBT HE MUST	477	3 DON JUAN	15	49	3

```
                                                    PAGE VOL    CANTO   STANZA LN
WONDER   (CONTINUED)
    BUT WONDER THEY SO FEW ARE SINCE MY TALE IS  . . . . . .  502  3 DON JUAN 16      3    7
    HIS OTHER ARM FORTH--WONDER UPON WONDER  . . . . . . .    560  3 DON JUAN 16    122    2
    HIS OTHER ARM FORTH--WONDER UPON WONDER  . . . . . . .    560  3 DON JUAN 16    122    2
WONDERED
    ONE WONDERED WHAT TO DO WITH SUCH A NUMBER  . . . . .     448  2 DON JUAN  5     64    4
    TO CROSS HER BROW SHE WONDERED HOW SO NEAR  . . . . .     480  2 DON JUAN  5    119    7
    AND FIRST HE WONDERED WHY HE HAD REFUSED  . . . . . .     493  2 DON JUAN  5    142    3
    OR WONDERED AT HER EARS WITHOUT A RING  . . . . . .        23  3 DON JUAN  6     35    4
    THEY WONDERED HOW GULBEYAZ TOO COULD BE  . . . . . .       24  3 DON JUAN  6     36    5
    SHE WONDERED AT HERSELF HOW SHE COULD SCREAM--  . . .      47  3 DON JUAN  6     83    3
    HE WAS WELL LODGED BUT ONLY WONDERED HOW  . . . . .      262  3 DON JUAN 10     75    2
    A LITTLE BLASE--'TIS NOT TO BE WONDERED  . . . . . .     353  3 DON JUAN 12     81    5
    THEY WONDERED HOW A YOUNG MAN SO ABSURD  . . . . . .     543  3 DON JUAN 16     89    5
    WHO WONDERED AT THE ABSTRACTION OF HIS AIR  . . . . .    544  3 DON JUAN 16     91    3
WONDERFUL
    OF MAN THE WONDERFUL AND OF THE STARS  . . . .           71  2 DON JUAN  1     92    2
    AND WONDERFUL BEYOND ALL WONDROUS MEASURE  . . . . .     93  2 DON JUAN  1    133    2
    PLATONIC UNIVERSAL WONDERFUL  . . . . . . .              269  2 DON JUAN  2    212    3
    OF WONDERFUL REPLIES FROM ARAB JOKERS  . . . . . .      293  2 DON JUAN  3     34    4
    'TWAS WONDERFUL HOW THINGS WENT ON IMPROVING  . . .     295  2 DON JUAN  3     39    7
    NEED NOT SEEM VERY WONDERFUL FOR VICE  . . . . . .      408  2 DON JUAN  4    115    5
    SURELY 'TIS NOTHING WONDERFUL TO SEE  . . . .          421  2 DON JUAN  5     20    4
    FULL GROWS HIS BAG AND WONDERFUL HIS FEATS  . . . .    394  3 DON JUAN 13     75    6
    'TIS WONDERFUL HOW OFT THE SEX HAVE HEARD  . . . .     489  3 DON JUAN 15     76    7
    'TIS WONDERFUL WHAT FABLE WILL NOT DO  . . . . .       495  3 DON JUAN 15     89    4
WONDERING
    WONDERING WHAT NEXT TILL THE CAIQUE WAS BROUGHT  . . .  432  2 DON JUAN  5     40    6
    AS WONDERING WHAT THE DEVIL NOISE THAT IS  . . . .      442  2 DON JUAN  5     55    8
    KNELT DOWN BY INSTINCT WONDERING IN HIS MIND  . . .     466  2 DON JUAN  5     95    6
    ALL TREMBLING WONDERING WITHOUT THE LEAST NOTION  . .    42  3 DON JUAN  6     71    6
    CONJECTURING WONDERING ASKING A NARRATION  . . . .       43  3 DON JUAN  6     74    3
    A THING TO WONDER AT BEYOND MOST WONDERING  . . . .      95  3 DON JUAN  7     55    4
    AND EVERYBODY WONDERING MORE OR LESS  . . . .          514  3 DON JUAN 16     32    2
    SOME WONDERING 'TWAS SO EARLY SOME SO LATE  . . . .    527  3 DON JUAN 16     55    4
WONDERS
    HE WONDERS AT THEIR VICE AND NOT HIS FOLLY  . . . . .    74  2 DON JUAN  1     99    8
    AND WONDERS WHY THE DEVIL HE GOT HEIRS  . . . . . .      75  2 DON JUAN  1    100    8
    WEALTH HAD DONE WONDERS--TASTE NOT MUCH SUCH THINGS  .  465  2 DON JUAN  5     94    1
WOND'ROUS
    THESE FEW SHORT YEARS MAKE WOND'ROUS ALTERATIONS  . .    59  2 DON JUAN  1     69    7
    HIS WOND'ROUS JOURNEY TO SOME FOREIGN COURT  . . . .    440  2 DON JUAN  5     52    3
    THE WOND'ROUS HIDEOUSNESS OF THOSE SMALL MEN  . . .     462  2 DON JUAN  5     88    3
WONDROUS
    WHAT WONDROUS NEW MACHINES HAVE LATE BEEN SPINNING  .    92  2 DON JUAN  1    130    6
    AND WONDERFUL BEYOND ALL WONDROUS MEASURE  . . . .       93  2 DON JUAN  1    133    2
    A WONDROUS WARRIOR AGAINST THOSE WHO YIELD  . . . .     151  2 DON JUAN  1  V  2    5
    AS SOME HAVE QUALIFIED THAT WONDROUS PLACE  . . . .     265  3 DON JUAN 10     81    4
    (OH PROVIDENCE HOW WONDROUS ARE THY WAYS  . . . .      540  3 DON JUAN 16     82    5
WON'T
    AND OTHER STUFFS WITH WHICH I WON'T STAY PUZZLING  . .   27  2 DON JUAN  1     12    8
    OR LOVE--I WON'T SAY MORE ABOUT ENTWINED  . . . .       69  2 DON JUAN  1     89    6
    THEY WON'T LAY OUT THEIR MONEY ON THE DEAD--  . . .    185  2 DON JUAN  2     55    7
    FED UPON BEEF--I WON'T SAY MUCH OF BEER  . . . .       238  2 DON JUAN  2    156    2
    ALL FURTHER IS A BLANK--I WON'T DISPARAGE  . . . .     280  2 DON JUAN  3      9  V4
    MUST END IN LANGUOR--MEN WON'T SLEEP LIKE SWINE--  .   343  2 DON JUAN  3  V 98    1
    (BECAUSE THE WORLD WON'T READ HIM ALWAYS SNARLING)  .  404  2 DON JUAN  4    109    6
    BECAUSE IF DROWN'D THEY CAN'T--IF SPARED THEY WON'T  .  414  2 DON JUAN  5      6    8
    I WON'T DESCRIBE DESCRIPTION IS MY FORTE  . . . .      440  2 DON JUAN  5     52    1
    OF THAT SAME BABEL OR BECAUSE THEY WON'T  . . . .      447  2 DON JUAN  5     62    4
    I WON'T BE BAIL FOR ANYTHING BEYOND  . . . .          469  2 DON JUAN  5     99    8
    BUT THAT YOU WON'T--THEN DON'T--I AM NOT LESS FREE  .   34  3 DON JUAN  6     56    8
    WHICH STARE HIM IN THE FACE HE WON'T EXAMINE  . . .     88  3 DON JUAN  7     45    7
    WHO MAKE THE BEDS OF THOSE WHO WON'T TAKE QUARTER  .   167  3 DON JUAN  8    111    5
    AND LIKE SOME OTHER THINGS WON'T DO TO TELL  . . .     184  3 DON JUAN  9      2    3
    WELL WE WON'T ANALYZE--OUR STORY MUST  . . . .         221  3 DON JUAN  9     77    1
    HOW WE WON'T MENTION WHY WE NEED NOT SAY  . . . .      235  3 DON JUAN 10     21    2
    AND WRINKLES (THE DAMNED DEMOCRATS) WON'T FLATTER  .   236  3 DON JUAN 10     24    8
    AND THIS SAME STATE WE WON'T DESCRIBE WE COULD  . .    238  3 DON JUAN 10     27    1
    I WON'T DESCRIBE--THAT IS IF I CAN HELP  . . . .       238  3 DON JUAN 10     28    1
    DESCRIPTION AND I WON'T REFLECT--THAT IS  . . . .      238  3 DON JUAN 10     28    2
    I WON'T PHILOSOPHIZE AND WILL BE READ  . . . .         238  3 DON JUAN 10     28    8
    BUT I WON'T WEEP--AND SO DRIVE ON POSTILLIONS  . . .   263  3 DON JUAN 10     77    2
    BUT--I WON'T WEEP--COME POSTBOYS WHIRL ALONG  . . .    263  3 DON JUAN 10     77  V2
    AND TELL THEM--BUT YOU WON'T AND I HAVE PRATED  . .    267  3 DON JUAN 10     87    6
    NOW WHAT I LOVE IN WOMEN IS THEY WON'T  . . . .        285  3 DON JUAN 11     36    6
    SPIRIT WOULD NAME AND THEREFORE EVEN I WON'T ANENT  .  289  3 DON JUAN 11     43    4
    BUT THIS WON'T DO SAVE BY AND BY AND HE  . . . .       303  3 DON JUAN 11     70    1
    AND WON'T SAY YES AND KEEPS YOU ON AND OFF-ING  . .    345  3 DON JUAN 12     63    2
    AND TAKE MY WORD YOU WON'T HAVE ANY LESS  . . . .      366  3 DON JUAN 13     18    3
    AND--WHAT IS WORST OF ALL--WON'T LET YOU GO  . . .     438  3 DON JUAN 14     63    8
    AND HATE THOSE WHO WON'T LET THEM COME TO PASS  . .    491  3 DON JUAN 15     79    8
WONT
    JUAN TO LAVE HIS YOUTHFUL LIMBS WAS WONT  . . . .      211  2 DON JUAN  2    105    2
    AND VARIOUS HUES AS IS THE TURKISH WONT--  . . . .     436  3 DON JUAN  5     46    4
    WITH INTEREST AND IN TURN WAS WONT WITH RIGOUR  . .    213  3 DON JUAN  9     62    6
    PERHAPS THOUGHT HE IT IS THE COUNTRY'S WONT  . . .     275  3 DON JUAN 11     15    1
    HE DRESSED AND LIKE YOUNG PEOPLE HE WAS WONT  . .      513  3 DON JUAN 16     29    1
    WAS WONT TO BOAST--AS IF A GLUTTON'S TRAY  . . .       538  3 DON JUAN 16     78    3
    LIKE ADDISON'S FAINT PRAISE SO WONT TO DAMN  . . .     552  3 DON JUAN 16    104    4
```

```
                                                        PAGE VOL     CANTO  STANZA LV
WOO'D
    PALE STATUE-LIKE AND STERN SHE WOO'D THE BLOW  . . . . .  367  2 DON JUAN  4     43    4
WOOD
    HIS HOME DESERTED FOR THE LONELY WOOD . . . . . . . .  68  2 DON JUAN  1     87    2
    HE THOUGHT OF WOOD NYMPHS AND IMMORTAL BOWERS . . . . .  72  2 DON JUAN  1     94    3
    WITH THE PILED WOOD ROUND WHICH THE FAMILY CROWD . . . .  94  2 DON JUAN  1    135    4
    THE UMBRAGE OF THE WOOD SO COOL AND DUN . . . . . .  289  2 DON JUAN  3     27    5
    HE LAY COILED LIKE THE BOA IN THE WOOD . . . . . .  300  2 DON JUAN  3     48    4
    WHICH BOUNDS RAVENNA'S IMMEMORIAL WOOD . . . . . . .  337  2 DON JUAN  3    105    3
    SHE DREAMED A DREAM OF WALKING IN A WOOD-- . . . . .  43  3 DON JUAN  6     75    2
    A WOOD OBSCURE LIKE THAT WHERE DANTE FOUND . . . . .  43  3 DON JUAN  6     75    3
    AND THAT THIS WOOD WAS FULL OF PLEASANT FRUITS . . . .  43  3 DON JUAN  6     75    7
    BUT GETTING NIGH GRIM DANTE'S OBSCURE WOOD . . . . .  238  3 DON JUAN 10     27    3
WOODCOCKS
    HE CANNOT LIVE LIKE WOODCOCKS UPON SUCTION . . . . .  191  2 DON JUAN  2     67    3
WOODEN
    AND I GROWN ONE OF MANY WOODEN SPOONS . . . . . . .  341  2 DON JUAN  3    110    6
    IF THAT CAN WELL BE THAN HIS WOODEN LOOK . . . . . .  309  3 DON JUAN 11     83    4
WOODLAND
    AS HAWKS MAY POUNCE UPON A WOODLAND SONGSTER . . . . .  285  3 DON JUAN 11     35    8
WOODLANDS
    CROWN'D BY HIGH WOODLANDS WHERE THE DRUID OAK . . . . .  384  3 DON JUAN 13     56    2
WOODS
    OR WERE OF TORTOISE-SHELL OR RARE WOODS MADE . . . . .  310  2 DON JUAN  3     69    4
    THEY SHOULD HAVE LIVED TOGETHER DEEP IN WOODS . . . . .  358  2 DON JUAN  4     28    1
    TO DEEM THE WOODS SHALL BE OUR HOME AT LAST-- . . . . .  142  3 DON JUAN  8     60    8
    OF CARE OR GAIN THE GREEN WOODS WERE THEIR PORTIONS . . .  145  3 DON JUAN  8     66    4
    OF THIS UNSIGHING PEOPLE OF THE WOODS . . . . . . .  145  3 DON JUAN  8     67    6
    THE WOODS SLOPED DOWNWARDS TO ITS BRINK AND STOOD . . . .  385  3 DON JUAN 13     57    7
    ITS WINDINGS THROUGH THE WOODS NOW CLEAR NOW BLUE . . . .  385  3 DON JUAN 13     58    7
WOOF
    IN THIS VILE GARB THE DISTAFF WEB AND WOOF . . . . .  484  2 DON JUAN  5    127    3
WOOING
    HERE TAVERNS WOOING TO A PINT OF PURL . . . . . . .  278  3 DON JUAN 11     22    3
WOOINGS
    ROMANCES PAINT AT FULL LENGTH PEOPLE'S WOOINGS . . . . .  279  2 DON JUAN  3      8    3
    ABOUT THE PRESENT FAMILY'S DEATHS AND WOOINGS . . . . .  527  3 DON JUAN 16     53    8
WOOS
    BUT LO A TENIERS WOOS AND NOT IN VAIN . . . . . . .  392  3 DON JUAN 13     72    5
WORD
    AND MAKES THE WORD MILTONIC MEAN SUBLIME . . . . . .  15  2 DON JUAN  D     10    4
    NEVER TO SAY A WORD ABOUT THEM MORE-- . . . . . . .  36  2 DON JUAN  1     29    5
    WITHOUT A WORD OF PREVIOUS ADMONITION . . . . . . .  97  2 DON JUAN  1    139    5
    FLY JUAN FLY FOR HEAVEN'S SAKE--NOT A WORD-- . . . . .  121  2 DON JUAN  1    182    3
    THAT WORD IS IDLE NOW--BUT LET IT GO . . . . . . .  132  2 DON JUAN  1    195    8
    AND BEG THEY'LL TAKE MY WORD ABOUT THE MORAL . . . . .  141  2 DON JUAN  1    209    2
    AND WITHOUT WORD A SIGN HER FINGER DREW ON . . . . .  234  2 DON JUAN  2    146    4
    NOW JUAN COULD NOT UNDERSTAND A WORD . . . . . . .  236  2 DON JUAN  2    151    1
    BUT NOT A WORD COULD JUAN COMPREHEND . . . . . . .  241  2 DON JUAN  2    161    2
    HAD NOT ONE WORD TO SAY OF CONSTANCY . . . . . . .  257  2 DON JUAN  2    190    8
    TO SAY A WORD ABOUT THEM--IF SHE THOUGHT . . . . . .  258  2 DON JUAN  2    193   V8
    HE--BEING A MAN WHO SELDOM USED A WORD . . . . . .  294  2 DON JUAN  3     37    1
    WHETHER THE WORD WAS DEATH OR BUT THE CHAIN-- . . . . .  299  2 DON JUAN  3     47    4
    WITH HIM IT NEVER WAS A WORD AND BLOW . . . . . . .  300  2 DON JUAN  3     48    5
    HIS ANGRY WORD ONCE O'ER HE SHED NO BLOOD . . . . . .  300  2 DON JUAN  3     48    6
    (WE'VE NOT SO GOOD A WORD BUT HAVE THE THING . . . . .  332  2 DON JUAN  3     97    2
    A NOVEL WORD IN MY VOCABULARY . . . . . . . . .  346  2 DON JUAN  4      5    8
    A THOUSAND SCIMITARS AWAIT THE WORD . . . . . . .  364  2 DON JUAN  4     37    7
    A THOUSAND SHARPER SABRES WAIT THE WORD . . . . . .  364  2 DON JUAN  4     37   V7
    HE RAISED HIS WHISTLE AS THE WORD HE SAID . . . . . .  369  2 DON JUAN  4     47    3
    HE GAVE THE WORD ARREST OR SLAY THE FRANK . . . . . .  369  2 DON JUAN  4     47    8
    (IN EACH SENSE OF THE WORD) WHENE'ER I FILL . . . . .  372  2 DON JUAN  4     53    6
    THEY TOOK HER WORD THAT HIS DULL ROAR WAS MELLOW . . . .  391  2 DON JUAN  4     87   V6
    A THOUSAND WARRIORS BY HIS WORD WERE KEPT . . . . . .  430  2 DON JUAN  5     36    4
    WHO ROWED OFF LEAVING THEM WITHOUT A WORD . . . . . .  433  2 DON JUAN  5     41    8
    NOR MUCH DISPOSED TO WAIT IN WORD OR DEED . . . . . .  56  3 DON JUAN  6    101    2
    I'D RATHER TELL TEN LIES THAN SAY A WORD . . . . . .  77  3 DON JUAN  7     22    4
    IS PERPETRATED ERE A WORD CAN BREAK . . . . . . .  141  3 DON JUAN  8     58    5
    A WORD WHICH LITTLE SUITS WITH SERASKIERS . . . . . .  152  3 DON JUAN  8     80    3
    ROLLS BY THE CITY WALL BUT DEED NOR WORD . . . . . .  155  3 DON JUAN  8     87    4
    READER I HAVE KEPT MY WORD--AT LEAST SO FAR . . . . .  181  3 DON JUAN  8    138    1
    I NEVER KNOW THE WORD WHICH WILL COME NEXT . . . . .  203  3 DON JUAN  9     41    8
    JUAN WHO DID NOT UNDERSTAND A WORD . . . . . . . .  274  3 DON JUAN 11     12    1
    AND WATCH AND WARD WHOSE PLANS A WORD TOO MUCH . . . .  305  3 DON JUAN 11     73    6
    (NOW HERE'S A WORD QUITE AFTER MY OWN HEART . . . . .  326  3 DON JUAN 12     22    3
    FOR HE WAS SICK--NO 'TWAS NOT THE WORD SICK I MEANT-- . . .  346  3 DON JUAN 12     67    3
    AND TAKE MY WORD YOU WON'T HAVE ANY LESS . . . . . .  366  3 DON JUAN 13     18    3
    AWAY AWAY FRESH HORSES ARE THE WORD . . . . . . .  379  3 DON JUAN 13     46    3
    OF STRONGBOW'S TALK YOU WOULD NOT CHANGE A WORD . . . .  402  3 DON JUAN 13     93    5
    BUT SEIZE THE LAST WORD WHICH NO DOUBT'S THE BEST . . . .  404  3 DON JUAN 13     98    8
    LONG DIALOGUES WHICH PASS'D WITHOUT A WORD . . . . .  489  3 DON JUAN 15     76    8
    AS IF EACH CHARMING WORD WERE A DECREE . . . . . .  492  3 DON JUAN 15     82    4
    HIS WORD HAD THE SAME VALUE AS ANOTHER'S . . . . . .  535  3 DON JUAN 16     71    8
WORDING
    THEIR SPLEEN IN MAKING STRIFE AND SAFELY WORDING . . . .  498  2 DON JUAN  5    151    6
    TURN OUT SO WE'LL SAY NOTHING 'GAINST THE WORDING . . . .  270  3 DON JUAN 11      4    3
WORDLESS
    THAN THE STERN SINGLE DEEP AND WORDLESS IRE . . . . .  305  2 DON JUAN  3     58    7
    A WORDLESS MUSIC AND HER FACE SO FAIR . . . . . . .  359  2 DON JUAN  4     29    7
    FOR WORDLESS WOMAN WHICH IS SILENT THUNDER . . . . .  34  3 DON JUAN  6     57    8
```

922

WORDS
    HER THOUGHTS WERE THEOREMS HER WORDS A PROBLEM . . . . . 28 2 DON JUAN 1   13   7
    THE LISP OF CHILDREN AND THEIR EARLIEST WORDS . . . . . 88 2 DON JUAN 1   123   8
    BUT NOTHING ELSE THE TIME OF WORDS WAS O'ER . . . . . 111 2 DON JUAN 1   163   6
    BY A FEW TIMELY WORDS TO TURN THE TABLES . . . . . . 117 2 DON JUAN 1   175   4
    THE HOUSE OF COMMONS DAMOCLES OF WORDS . . . . . . 153 2 DON JUAN 1 V 4   1
    HER EYES WERE ELOQUENT HER WORDS WOULD POSE . . . . . 236 2 DON JUAN 2   150   5
    RATHER BY DEEDS THAN WORDS BECAUSE THE CASE . . . . . 240 2 DON JUAN 2   159   2
    A WORLD OF WORDS AND THINGS AT WHICH SHE GUESS'D . . . . 241 2 DON JUAN 2   162   8
    AND WORDS REPEATED AFTER HER HE TOOK . . . . . . 242 2 DON JUAN 2   163   2
    THAT IS SOME WORDS OF SPANISH TURK AND GREEK . . . . 243 2 DON JUAN 2   165   1
    TO HEAR NEW WORDS AND TO REPEAT THEM BUT . . . . . 244 2 DON JUAN 2   167   2
    WAS BROKEN WORDS THEY THOUGHT A LANGUAGE THERE-- . . . 256 2 DON JUAN 2   189   4
    AND HIS BLOW DID WHAT WORDS COULD NOT UNDO . . . . . 300 2 DON JUAN 3   48   V8
    THE WORDS WHICH SHOOK BELSHAZZAR IN HIS HALL . . . . 308 2 DON JUAN 3   65   5
    CANOVA'S MARBLE OR THE WORDS OF BURKE . . . . . . 315 2 DON JUAN 3   76   V8
    BUT WORDS ARE THINGS AND A SMALL DROP OF INK . . . . 327 2 DON JUAN 3   88   1
    'TIS SOMETHING NOTHING WORDS ILLUSION WIND-- . . . . 328 2 DON JUAN 3   90   2
    THE LEAST GLANCE BETTER UNDERSTOOD THAN WORDS . . . . 351 2 DON JUAN 4   14   2
    HARD WORDS HARSH TRUTH A TRUTH WHICH MANY KNOW . . . . 353 2 DON JUAN 4   18   1
    IN A FEW WORDS HE TOLD THEIR HAPLESS STORY . . . . . 389 2 DON JUAN 4   82   1
    I HAVE NO MORE TIME NOR MANY WORDS TO SPARE . . . . 454 2 DON JUAN 5   74   3
    SHE SPAKE SOME WORDS TO HER ATTENDANTS WHO . . . . . 469 2 DON JUAN 5   99   1
    (SO TAKE IT IN THE VERY WORDS OF CREECH) . . . . . 470 2 DON JUAN 5   101   4
    HE STOOD LIKE ATLAS WITH A WORLD OF WORDS . . . . . 471 2 DON JUAN 5   104   1
    THESE WORDS WENT THROUGH HIS SOUL LIKE ARAB-SPEARS . . . 478 2 DON JUAN 5   117   7
    PASSED WITHOUT WORDS--IN FACT SHE COULD NOT SPEAK . . . 490 2 DON JUAN 5   137   2
    BUT WORDS ARE NOT ENOUGH IN SUCH A MATTER . . . . . 493 2 DON JUAN 5   143   2
    KISSES SWEET WORDS EMBRACES AND ALL THAT . . . . . 13 3 DON JUAN 6   14   2
    DESCRIBED--WHAT'S STRANGE--IN WORDS EXTREMELY FEW . . . 34 3 DON JUAN 6   57   6
    OH THAT MY WORDS WERE COLOURS BUT THEIR TINTS . . . . 60 3 DON JUAN 6   109   7
    YOU KNOW THE REST THE WORDS STUCK IN HER THROAT . . . . 62 3 DON JUAN 6   113   4
    SOFT WORDS TOO FITTED FOR THE PERORATION . . . . . 74 3 DON JUAN 7   16   5
    TO WHOM HE SPOKE AND MADE HIS WORDS BUT FEW . . . . . 97 3 DON JUAN 7   59   8
    HARD WORDS WHICH STICK IN THE SOFT MUSES' GULLETS . . . 106 3 DON JUAN 7   78   8
    METHINKS THESE ARE THE MOST TREMENDOUS WORDS . . . . 179 3 DON JUAN 8   134   1
    AND I WILL WAR AT LEAST IN WORDS (AND--SHOULD . . . . 194 3 DON JUAN 9   24   1
    MY WORDS AT LEAST ARE MORE SINCERE AND HEARTY . . . . 195 3 DON JUAN 9   26   3
    OF THAT ODD STRING OF WORDS ALL IN A ROW . . . . . 207 3 DON JUAN 9   49   5
    THAT SPHINX WHOSE WORDS WOULD EVER BE A DOUBT . . . . 207 3 DON JUAN 9   50   3
    TO LOVE THERE ARE THOSE THINGS WHICH WORDS NAME SENSES-- . . 219 3 DON JUAN 9   74   8
    I CANNOT STOP TO ALTER WORDS ONCE WRITTEN . . . . . 221 3 DON JUAN 9   77   4
    WITH THE SAME THOUGHT THE TWO WORDS HAVE HELPED OUT . . . 323 3 DON JUAN 12   15   4
    THE KINDER VETERAN WITH CALM WORDS WILL COURT YOU . . . 337 3 DON JUAN 12   45   5
    HE SHOWS MORE APPETITE FOR WORDS THAN WAR . . . . . 398 3 DON JUAN 13   84   4
    THE FACT FOR WORDS AND LET THE FRENCH TRANSLATE . . . . 405 3 DON JUAN 13   101   7
    WHEN HER SOFT LIQUID WORDS RUN ON APACE . . . . . 426 3 DON JUAN 14   36   6
    OF BARDS AND PROSERS WORDS ARE VOID OF COLOUR . . . . 428 3 DON JUAN 14   40   8
    FOR ADELINE ADDRESSING FEW WORDS TO HIM . . . . . 489 3 DON JUAN 15   75   7
    HE TAXED HIS TONGUE FOR WORDS WHICH WERE NOT GRANTED . . 511 3 DON JUAN 16   23   7
    A FEW WORDS OF CONDOLENCE ON HIS STATE . . . . . 515 3 DON JUAN 16   35   2
    BUT ADD THE WORDS CRIED HENRY WHICH YOU MADE . . . . 517 3 DON JUAN 16   39   1
    THE VOICE THE WORDS THE HARPER'S SKILL AT ONCE . . . . 517 3 DON JUAN 16   39   7
    OR--BUT ALL WORDS UPON SUCH THEMES ARE WEAK . . . . 557 3 DON JUAN 16   116   5
    AS FAR AS WORDS MAKE RULES--OUR COMMON NOTION . . . . 563 3 DON JUAN 17   3   2
WORDSWORTH
    AND WORDSWORTH IN A RATHER LONG EXCURSION . . . . . 11 2 DON JUAN D   4   1
    AND WORDSWORTH HAS HIS PLACE IN THE EXCISE . . . . . 12 2 DON JUAN D   6   6
    UNLESS LIKE WORDSWORTH THEY PROVE UNINTELLIGIBLE . . . 70 2 DON JUAN 1   90   8
    HE JUAN (AND NOT WORDSWORTH) SO PURSUED . . . . . 70 2 DON JUAN 1   91   1
    THOU SHALT NOT SET UP WORDSWORTH COLERIDGE SOUTHEY . . . 139 2 DON JUAN 1   205   2
    WHEN SOUTHEY'S READ AND WORDSWORTH UNDERSTOOD . . . . 149 2 DON JUAN 1   222   5
    OR WORDSWORTH UNEXCISED UNHIRED WHO THEN . . . . . 329 2 DON JUAN 3   93   3
    WE FEEL WITHOUT HIM WORDSWORTH SOMETIMES WAKES . . . . 333 2 DON JUAN 3   98   2
    AND WORDSWORTH--BOTH POETICAL BUFFOONS . . . . . 341 2 DON JUAN 3   110   V2
    I'LL SWEAR--AS MOTHER WORDSWORTH SWORE . . . . . 404 2 DON JUAN 4   109   V5
    CARNAGE (SO WORDSWORTH TELLS YOU) IS GOD'S DAUGHTER . . . 116 3 DON JUAN 8   9   6
    AND WORDSWORTH HAS SUPPORTERS TWO OR THREE . . . . 298 3 DON JUAN 11   59   6
WORDSWORTH'S
    WORDSWORTH'S LAST QUARTO BY THE WAY IS BIGGER . . . . 330 2 DON JUAN 3   94   5
    BUT WORDSWORTH'S POEM AND HIS FOLLOWERS LIKE . . . . 330 2 DON JUAN 3   95   3
WORDY
    WHY THEN I'LL SWEAR AS POET WORDY SWORE . . . . . 404 2 DON JUAN 4   109   5
    OF THAT WEAK WORDY HARVEST THE SOLE GLEANING . . . . 207 3 DON JUAN 9   49   8
    IN SENATES AT THE BAR IN WORDY FEUD . . . . . . 371 3 DON JUAN 13   29   5
WORE
    SHE NEVER WOULD DISGRACE THE RING SHE WORE . . . . . 80 2 DON JUAN 1   109   4
    IN DON ALFONSO'S FACTS WHICH JUST NOW WORE . . . . . 111 2 DON JUAN 1   164   6
    FOR JUAN WORE THE MAGISTERIAL FACE . . . . . . 186 2 DON JUAN 2   56   4
    CONDEMN THE ROYAL LADY'S TASTE WHO WORE . . . . . 238 2 DON JUAN 2   155   4
    WITH HERE AND THERE A CREEK WHOSE ASPECT WORE . . . . 249 2 DON JUAN 2   177   4
    SHE WORE TWO JELICKS--ONE WAS OF PALE YELLOW . . . . 311 2 DON JUAN 3   70   2
    WHO WORE THEIR UNIFORM BY BABA CHOSEN . . . . . 469 2 DON JUAN 5   99   4
    THE COURT THAT WATCHED EACH LOOK HER VISAGE WORE . . . 211 3 DON JUAN 9   58   5
    AS CAESAR WORE HIS ROBE YOU WEAR YOUR GOWN . . . . 232 3 DON JUAN 10   15   8
    THE TOUT ENSEMBLE OF HIS MOVEMENTS WORE A . . . . . 428 3 DON JUAN 14   40   5
    WHEN DEEP SLEEP FELL ON MEN AND THE WORLD WORE . . . . 556 3 DON JUAN 16   113   6
WORK
    BUT FOR A CHILD WHAT PIECE OF WORK IS HERE . . . . . 115 2 DON JUAN 1   172   3

WORK (CONTINUED)

	PAGE	VOL	CANTO	STANZA	LN
I'LL CALL THE WORK LONGINUS O'ER A BOTTLE	138	2 DON JUAN	1	204	7
THEIR WORK ON THEM BY TURNS AND THINN'D THEM TO	210	2 DON JUAN	2	102	2
PAIR OF SCARCE DECENT TROWSERS--WENT TO WORK	240	2 DON JUAN	2	160	2
TALKING'S DRY WORK I HAVE NO TIME TO SPARE	297	2 DON JUAN	3	43	4
AND HIS ONE BLOW LEFT LITTLE WORK FOR TWO	300	2 DON JUAN	3	48	8
HAD DONE THEIR WORK OF SPLENDOUR INDIAN MATS	310	2 DON JUAN	3	68	2
BUT WISH THIS MASTERPIECE OF NATURE'S WORK	315	2 DON JUAN	3	76	V7
BUT THOUGHT HOW WORTHY ALTHOUGH NATURE'S WORK	315	2 DON JUAN	3	76	V7
WERE HUNG WITH MARBLE ICICLES THE WORK	362	2 DON JUAN	4	33	2
IT SEEMS THE WORK OF TIMES BEFORE THE LINE	461	2 DON JUAN	5	86	7
THEIR WORK EVEN BY THE WAY IN WHICH HE TRODE	61	3 DON JUAN	6	111	8
NOR WORK ADVANCE NOR COVERED WAY WAS THERE	72	3 DON JUAN	7	11	7
NOTHING--THE WORK OF GLORY STILL WENT ON	106	3 DON JUAN	7	78	1
HAD SET TO WORK AS BRISKLY AS THEIR BROTHERS	119	3 DON JUAN	8	15	4
SEEING HOW ART CAN MAKE HER WORK MORE GRAND	204	3 DON JUAN	9	44	5
AND RECOLLECT THE WORK IS ONLY FICTION	311	3 DON JUAN	11	88	4
AS EVER YET WAS ANY WORK SUBLIME	312	3 DON JUAN	11	90	5
OTHERS FOR OTHER DIRTY WORK GONE THROUGH	314	3 DON JUAN	11	V 76	4
AND WORK AWAY LIKE SPIRIT UPON MATTER	423	3 DON JUAN	14	30	7
WORK'D					
WORK'D BY THE STORMS YET WORK'D AS IT WERE PLANN'D	253	2 DON JUAN	2	184	5
WORK'D BY THE STORMS YET WORK'D AS IT WERE PLANN'D	253	2 DON JUAN	2	184	5
WORKED					
LAND BATTERIES WORKED THEIR GUNS WITH GREAT PRECISION	81	3 DON JUAN	7	30	3
WORKINGS					
ITS WORKINGS THROUGH THE VAINLY GUARDED EYE	61	2 DON JUAN	1	73	4
WORKMANSHIP					
OF WORKMANSHIP SO RARE THEY MADE YOU WISH	449	2 DON JUAN	5	65	7
WORKMEN					
GOOD WORKMEN NEVER QUARREL WITH THEIR TOOLS	136	2 DON JUAN	1	201	6
WORKS					
THEIR WHILE TO REAR WHOLE HOTBEDS IN THEIR WORKS	434	2 DON JUAN	5	42	7
AND WORKS OF THE SAME POTTERY BAD OR GOOD	491	2 DON JUAN	5	138	5
ONE BARK BLEW UP A SECOND NEAR THE WORKS	81	3 DON JUAN	7	30	7
IN FORMER WORKS MADE NEW PREPARED FASCINES	89	3 DON JUAN	7	47	7
HE JUDGED THEM PROPER TO ASSAIL THE WORKS	93	3 DON JUAN	7	53	6
THIS WORKS A WORLD OF SENTIMENTAL WOE	345	3 DON JUAN	12	63	5
BUT WHEN THE LATTER WORKS ITS OWN UNDOING	446	3 DON JUAN	14	85	7
(HIS FEASTS ARE NOT THE WORST PART OF HIS WORKS)	482	3 DON JUAN	15	62	4
WORLD					
THAT TURNS AND TURNS TO GIVE THE WORLD A NOTION	17	2 DON JUAN	D	13	7
INSIPID IN THIS NAUGHTY WORLD OF OURS	30	2 DON JUAN	1	18	2
THE WORLD AS USUAL WICKEDLY INCLINED	31	2 DON JUAN	1	19	5
THAT ALL THE WORLD EXCLAIM'D WHAT MAGNANIMITY	36	2 DON JUAN	1	29	8
NO DOUBT THIS PATIENCE WHEN THE WORLD IS DAMNING US	37	2 DON JUAN	1	30	1
FOR JEALOUSY DISLIKES THE WORLD TO KNOW IT	57	2 DON JUAN	1	65	8
THE WHILE THE WICKED WORLD BEHOLDS DELIGHTED	75	2 DON JUAN	1	100	3
AGAINST THE WORLD AND DEAR THE SCHOOLBOY SPOT	90	2 DON JUAN	1	126	7
'TIS PITY THOUGH IN THIS SUBLIME WORLD THAT	93	2 DON JUAN	1	133	3
UNLESS THIS WORLD AND T'OTHER TOO BE BLIND	112	2 DON JUAN	1	165	4
UNLESS THE WORLD AND HEAVEN ITSELF BE BLIND	112	2 DON JUAN	1	165	V4
CANST THOU BE MY SOLE WORLD MY UNIVERSE	144	2 DON JUAN	1	215	2
THE WORLD WILL FIND THEE AFTER MANY DAYS	149	2 DON JUAN	1	222	4
WELL--WELL THE WORLD MUST TURN UPON ITS AXIS	159	2 DON JUAN	2	4	1
A WORLD OF WORDS AND THINGS AT WHICH SHE GUESS'D	241	2 DON JUAN	2	162	8
A WANDERER FROM THE BRITISH WORLD OF FASHION	244	2 DON JUAN	2	166	2
OH LOVE WHAT IS IT IN THIS WORLD OF OURS	275	2 DON JUAN	3	2	1
HATE TO THE WORLD AND WAR WITH EVERY NATION	303	2 DON JUAN	3	55	7
ABOUT THE PRETTIEST ANKLE IN THE WORLD	312	2 DON JUAN	3	72	8
HE PRATED TO THE WORLD OF PANTISOCRASY	329	2 DON JUAN	3	93	2
THE WORLD NOT QUITE SO GREAT AS ARIOSTO	331	2 DON JUAN	3	96	8
OF NATIONS FREED AND THE WORLD OVERJOY'D	339	2 DON JUAN	3	109	4
THEY WERE NOT MADE IN THE REAL WORLD TO FILL	352	2 DON JUAN	4	15	3
TO LOSE ITSELF WHEN THE OLD WORLD GROWS DULL	353	2 DON JUAN	4	17	3
THE WORLD WAS NOT FOR THEM NOR THE WORLD'S ART	358	2 DON JUAN	4	27	5
THE WORLD IS FULL OF STRANGE VICISSITUDES	371	2 DON JUAN	4	51	1
SONG IN THE WORLD WILL SEEK WHAT THEN THEY SOUGHT	402	2 DON JUAN	4	106	4
IN THIS OUR WORLD--AND HAVE THE POWER TO GIVE	403	2 DON JUAN	4	107	V4
(BECAUSE THE WORLD WON'T READ HIM ALWAYS SNARLING)	404	2 DON JUAN	4	109	6
FOR SOMETIMES SUCH A WORLD OF VIRTUES COVER	405	2 DON JUAN	4	111	6
AMMON'S (ILL PLEASED WITH ONE WORLD AND ONE FATHER)	427	2 DON JUAN	5	31	8
THERE'S NOTHING IN THE WORLD LIKE ETIQUETTE	471	2 DON JUAN	5	103	5
HE STOOD LIKE ATLAS WITH A WORLD OF WORDS	471	2 DON JUAN	5	104	1
A THRONE THE WORLD THE UNIVERSE TO BE	7	3 DON JUAN	6	3	3
GAVE WHAT I HAD--A HEART--AS THE WORLD WENT I	9	3 DON JUAN	6	5	6
GAVE WHAT WAS WORTH A WORLD FOR WORLDS COULD NEVER	9	3 DON JUAN	6	5	7
(A HIGHLAND WELCOME ALL THE WIDE WORLD OVER)	12	3 DON JUAN	6	13	8
WHOSE YOUNG UNWAKENED WORLD WAS EVER NEW	145	3 DON JUAN	8	65	3
I SKETCH YOUR WORLD EXACTLY AS IT GOES	156	3 DON JUAN	8	89	8
SHOWED WHAT THINGS WERE BEFORE THE WORLD WAS FREE	179	3 DON JUAN	8	135	8
AND WONDER WHAT OLD WORLD SUCH THINGS COULD SEE	180	3 DON JUAN	8	137	4
AND WATERLOO HAS MADE THE WORLD YOUR DEBTOR--	184	3 DON JUAN	9	3	7
THE WORLD NOT THE WORLD'S MASTERS WILL DECIDE	184	3 DON JUAN	9	4	6
BEHOLD THE WORLD AND CURSE YOUR VICTORIES	187	3 DON JUAN	9	9	8
THAT HIDES THE PAST WORLD LIKE TO A SET SUN	188	3 DON JUAN	9	11	3
THIS WORLD I DOUBT IF DOUBT ITSELF BE DOUBTING	191	3 DON JUAN	9	17	3
OH WORLD WHICH WAS AND IS WHAT IS COSMOGONY	192	3 DON JUAN	9	20	3
WITH OTHER RELICS OF A FORMER WORLD	201	3 DON JUAN	9	37	2

WORLD   (CONTINUED)

	PAGE	VOL	CANTO	STANZA	LN
WHEN THIS WORLD SHALL BE FORMER UNDERGROUND	201	3 DON JUAN	9	37	3
OR WASTE A WORLD SINCE NO ONE CAN DENY	210	3 DON JUAN	9	56	5
GLANCED MILDLY ALL THE WORLD WAS ON THE WATCH	213	3 DON JUAN	9	61	8
OF THOSE IN OFFICE ALL THE WORLD LOOKED KIND	224	3 DON JUAN	9	84	3
WITH THIS O'ERWHELMING WORLD WHERE ALL MUST ERR	250	3 DON JUAN	10	52	6
OR ADAMANT TO FIND THE WORLD A SPIRIT	268	3 DON JUAN	11	1	7
WORLD (BE IT WHAT YOU WILL) THAT THAT'S NO SCHISM	269	3 DON JUAN	11	2	4
THE WORLD WHICH AT THE WORST'S A GLORIOUS BLUNDER--	269	3 DON JUAN	11	3	8
HE FROM THE WORLD HAD CUT OFF A GREAT MAN	277	3 DON JUAN	11	19	1
BUT SEE THE WORLD IS ONLY ONE ATTORNEY	281	3 DON JUAN	11	28	8
IN THE GREAT WORLD--WHICH BEING INTERPRETED	290	3 DON JUAN	11	45	1
HAD SEEN THE WORLD--WHICH IS A CURIOUS SIGHT	292	3 DON JUAN	11	47	7
THEN DRESS THEN DINNER THEN AWAKES THE WORLD	302	3 DON JUAN	11	67	1
WHERE IS THE WORLD CRIES YOUNG AT EIGHTY WHERE	306	3 DON JUAN	11	76	1
THE WORLD IN WHICH A MAN WAS BORN ALAS	306	3 DON JUAN	11	76	2
WHERE IS THE WORLD OF EIGHT YEARS PAST 'TWAS THERE--	306	3 DON JUAN	11	76	3
WHO HOLD THE BALANCE OF THE WORLD WHO REIGN	318	3 DON JUAN	12	5	1
WHO KEEP THE WORLD BOTH OLD AND NEW IN PAIN	318	3 DON JUAN	12	5	5
ALTHOUGH THE WORLD HAS SUCH AN EVIL TONGUE	336	3 DON JUAN	12	43	3
BESIDES THEIR KNOWLEDGE OF THE WORLD AND SENSE	336	3 DON JUAN	12	44	5
THE WORLD BY EXPERIENCE RATHER THAN BY LECTURE	337	3 DON JUAN	12	46	5
YCLEPT THE GREAT WORLD FOR IT IS THE LEAST	342	3 DON JUAN	12	56	2
THUS THE LOW WORLD NORTH SOUTH OR WEST OR EAST	342	3 DON JUAN	12	56	6
THIS WORKS A WORLD OF SENTIMENTAL WOE	345	3 DON JUAN	12	63	5
CAN'T FORM A FRIENDSHIP BUT THE WORLD O'ERAWES IT	346	3 DON JUAN	12	65	3
THE WORLD TO GAZE UPON THOSE NORTHERN LIGHTS	353	3 DON JUAN	12	82	5
THE WORLD GAVE GROUND BEFORE HER BRIGHT ARRAY	364	3 DON JUAN	13	11	5
PROUD OF HIMSELF AND HER THE WORLD COULD TELL	365	3 DON JUAN	13	14	6
HE KNEW THE WORLD AND WOULD NOT SEE DEPRAVITY	368	3 DON JUAN	13	22	5
THE WORLD UPON THE WHOLE IS WORTH THE ASSERTION	377	3 DON JUAN	13	41	3
I'VE DONE WITH MY TIRADE THE WORLD WAS GONE	381	3 DON JUAN	13	49	1
HER WAY BACK TO THE WORLD BY DINT OF PLOTTERY	397	3 DON JUAN	13	82	6
DISCUSS'D THE WORLD AND SETTLED ALL THE SPHERES	408	3 DON JUAN	13	109	2
THE WORLD IS ALL BEFORE ME OR BEHIND	414	3 DON JUAN	14	9	1
I HAVE BROUGHT THIS WORLD ABOUT MY EARS AND EKE	414	3 DON JUAN	14	10	1
OF FAME OR PROFIT WHEN THE WORLD GROWS WEARY	415	3 DON JUAN	14	11	2
THE PORTION OF THIS WORLD WHICH I AT PRESENT	416	3 DON JUAN	14	15	1
THE STREAM NOR LEAVE THE WORLD WHICH LEAVETH THEM	418	3 DON JUAN	14	18	8
THE WORLD (AS SINCE THAT HISTORY LESS POLITE	420	3 DON JUAN	14	23	2
THERE'S NOUGHT IN THIS BAD WORLD LIKE SYMPATHY	430	3 DON JUAN	14	47	1
FOR SHE HAD SEEN THE WORLD AND STOOD ITS TEST	433	3 DON JUAN	14	54	4
AT SEVENTEEN TOO THE WORLD WAS STILL ENCHANTED	434	3 DON JUAN	14	55	3
AND SIMPLE IN THE WORLD AND DOTH NOT NEED	437	3 DON JUAN	14	61	6
NOR IF UNTO THE WORLD I EVER GAVE IT	444	3 DON JUAN	14	80	3
SHUT UP THE WORLD AT LARGE LET BEDLAM OUT	446	3 DON JUAN	14	84	1
I HAVE SEARCHED THE WORLD AND MIDST SUCCESS OR CHECKS	451	3 DON JUAN	14	93	V5
HOW DIFFERENTLY THE WORLD WOULD MEN BEHOLD	455	3 DON JUAN	14	101	4
THE NEW WORLD WOULD BE NOTHING TO THE OLD	455	3 DON JUAN	14	101	6
COLUMBUS FOUND A NEW WORLD IN A CUTTER	468	3 DON JUAN	15	27	6
SHE GAZED UPON A WORLD SHE SCARCELY KNEW	476	3 DON JUAN	15	47	1
APART FROM THE SURROUNDING WORLD AND STRONG	477	3 DON JUAN	15	47	7
I WRITE THE WORLD NOR CARE IF THE WORLD READ	482	3 DON JUAN	15	60	3
I WRITE THE WORLD NOR CARE IF THE WORLD READ	482	3 DON JUAN	15	60	3
SUPERBLY AND CONTAINED A WORLD OF ZEST	488	3 DON JUAN	15	74	8
THIS SAVOURED OF THIS WORLD BUT HIS HAND SHOOK--	512	3 DON JUAN	16	27	1
OF WHAT IS CALLED THE WORLD AND THE WORLD'S WAYS	554	3 DON JUAN	16	108	3
HEAVING BETWEEN THIS WORLD AND WORLDS BEYOND	555	3 DON JUAN	16	110	2
WHEN DEEP SLEEP FELL ON MEN AND THE WORLD WORE	556	3 DON JUAN	16	113	6
THE WORLD IS FULL OF ORPHANS FIRSTLY THOSE	562	3 DON JUAN	17	1	1

WORLDING

	PAGE	VOL	CANTO	STANZA	LN
AND MAKE THE WORLDING SNEER THE YOUNGLING WEEP	555	3 DON JUAN	16	110	8

WORLDINGS

	PAGE	VOL	CANTO	STANZA	LN
HOW THE NEW WORLDINGS OF THE THEN NEW EAST	202	3 DON JUAN	9	39	2

WORLD'S

	PAGE	VOL	CANTO	STANZA	LN
THE WORLD WAS NOT FOR THEM NOR THE WORLD'S ART	358	2 DON JUAN	4	27	5
A GENTLEMAN SO RICH IN THE WORLD'S GOODS	371	2 DON JUAN	4	51	3
OF THE WORLD'S STOICS--MEN WITHOUT A HEART	423	2 DON JUAN	5	25	8
THE WORLD NOT THE WORLD'S MASTERS WILL DECIDE	184	3 DON JUAN	9	4	6
SHE RINGS THE WORLD'S TE DEUM AND HER BROW	286	3 DON JUAN	11	38	3
WITH THE KIND WORLD'S AMEN--WHO WOULD HAVE THOUGHT IT	328	3 DON JUAN	12	26	8
SWEET ADELINE AMIDST THE GAY WORLD'S HUM	365	3 DON JUAN	13	13	4
QUEENS BISHOPS KNIGHTS ROOKS PAWNS THE WORLD'S A GAME	400	3 DON JUAN	13	89	2
REMNANT WERE THERE OF THE OLD WORLD'S SOLE THRONE	428	3 DON JUAN	14	40	4
BEING NO SIBYL IN THE NEW WORLD'S WAYS	480	3 DON JUAN	15	56	6
BULL SOMETHING OF THE LOWER WORLD'S CONDITION	497	3 DON JUAN	15	92	6
THE WORLDS BEYOND THIS WORLD'S PERPLEXING WASTE	524	3 DON JUAN	16	48	5
OF WHAT IS CALLED THE WORLD AND THE WORLD'S WAYS	554	3 DON JUAN	16	108	3

WORLDS

	PAGE	VOL	CANTO	STANZA	LN
THE WORLDS TO COME OF BOTH OR FALL BENEATH	280	2 DON JUAN	3	9	5
AND THEN BOTH WORLDS WOULD PUNISH THEIR MISCARRIAGE	280	2 DON JUAN	3	9	6
THRONES WORLDS ET CETERA ARE SO OFT UPSET	8	3 DON JUAN	6	4	1
FOR THEN WEALTH KINGDOMS WORLDS ARE BUT A SPORT--I	9	3 DON JUAN	6	5	3
OF WORLDS TO LOSE YET STILL TO PAY MY COURT I	9	3 DON JUAN	6	5	5
GAVE WHAT WAS WORTH A WORLD FOR WORLDS COULD NEVER	9	3 DON JUAN	6	5	7
WHICH BREATHES OF NATIONS SAVED NOT WORLDS UNDONE	114	3 DON JUAN	8	5	4
TOWNS NATIONS WORLDS IN HER REVOLVING PRANKS	135	3 DON JUAN	8	44	5
SUNS AS RAYS--WORLDS LIKE ATOMS--YEARS LIKE HOURS	189	3 DON JUAN	9	13	8
LIKE ALL THE WORLDS BEFORE WHICH HAVE BEEN HURLED	201	3 DON JUAN	9	37	6

WORLDS   (CONTINUED)
    EVEN WORLDS MISCARRY WHEN TOO OFT THEY PUP . . . . . . 202 3 DON JUAN 9   39 5
    THOU DOST REPLENISH WORLDS BOTH GREAT AND SMALL . . . . 210 3 DON JUAN 9   56 6
    BETWEEN THE PRESENT AND PAST WORLDS AND HOVER . . . . . 255 3 DON JUAN 10   61 7
    THE WEALTH OF WORLDS (A WEALTH OF TAX AND PAPER) . . . 266 3 DON JUAN 10   83 4
    OF WORLDS AND SPECIES--MATTERS--SOULS AND BODY . . . . . 269 3 DON JUAN 11   3 V7
    ALAS WORLDS FALL--AND WOMAN SINCE SHE FELL'D . . . . . 420 3 DON JUAN 14   23 1
    REDEEMING WORLDS TO BE BY BIGOTS SHAKEN . . . . 464 3 DON JUAN 15   18 5
    BETWEEN TWO WORLDS LIFE HOVERS LIKE A STAR . . . . . . 500 3 DON JUAN 15   99 1
    THE WORLDS BEYOND THIS WORLD'S PERPLEXING WASTE . . . . 524 3 DON JUAN 16   48 5
    HEAVING BETWEEN THIS WORLD AND WORLDS BEYOND . . . . . 555 3 DON JUAN 16 110 2
WORMS
    TO THOSE SAD HUNGRY JACOBINS THE WORMS . . . . 12 3 DON JUAN 6   13 4
WORN
    AND HEARTLESS DAUGHTERS--WORN--AND PALE--AND POOR . . . 15 2 DON JUAN D   11 6
    SO BLACK THE LONG WORN LION'S HIDE IN HUE . . . . 154 2 DON JUAN 1 V 5 7
    UNTIL THE CHAINS AND LEATHERS WERE WORN THROUGH . . . . 178 2 DON JUAN 2   42 5
    WORN FOR A HUSBAND OR SOME OTHER BRUTE . . . . 230 2 DON JUAN 2 139 8
    FOR STILL HE LAY AND ON HIS THIN WORN CHEEK . . . . . . 234 2 DON JUAN 2 147 1
    AND IN THE WORN AND WILD RECEPTACLES . . . . 253 2 DON JUAN 2 184 4
    THERE HIS WORN BOSOM AND KEEN EYE WOULD MELT . . . . . 302 2 DON JUAN 3   52 5
    WITH ALL HIS KEEN WORN LOOK AND GRECIAN GRACE . . . . . 363 2 DON JUAN 4   35 5
    AS PASSION RISES WITH ITS BOSOM WORN . . . . 49 3 DON JUAN 6   87 3
    MADE HIS LAST ILLNESS WHEN ALL WORN AND WAN . . . . . . 84 3 DON JUAN 7   36 5
    MUST NOT HAVE LATTERLY BEEN QUITE WORN OUT . . . . . . 124 3 DON JUAN 8   26 3
    WORN OUT WITH BATTERING ISMAIL'S STUBBORN WALL . . . . 181 3 DON JUAN 8 139 6
    GENTLEMEN FARMERS--A RACE WORN OUT QUITE . . . . 198 3 DON JUAN 9   32 3
    ON LIFE'S WORN CONFINE JADED BLOATED SATED . . . . . . 267 3 DON JUAN 10   87 2
    I HAVE SEEN CROWNS WORN INSTEAD OF A FOOL'S CAP-- . . . 310 3 DON JUAN 11   84 5
    WORN OUT WITH IMPORTUNITY OR FALL . . . . 333 3 DON JUAN 12   37 2
    NOR WORN THE MOTLEY MANTLE OF A POET . . . . 467 3 DON JUAN 15   24 7
    AND THEN THE MID-DAY HAVING WORN TO ONE . . . . 527 3 DON JUAN 16   55 1
    BEING WAN AND WORN WITH EYES THAT HARDLY BROOKED . . . 568 3 DON JUAN 17   14 4
WORRIED
    KNOWS NOUGHT OF GRIEF WHO HAS NOT SO BEEN WORRIED . . . 89 2 DON JUAN 1 125 V7
WORSE
    THEN THEIR RELATIONS WHO MADE MATTERS WORSE . . . . . . 38 2 DON JUAN 1   32 2
    ANACREON'S MORALS ARE A STILL WORSE SAMPLE . . . . . . 45 2 DON JUAN 1   42 2
    INSENSIBLE I TRUST BUT NONE THE WORSE . . . . 144 2 DON JUAN 1 215 6
    A NAME A WRETCHED PICTURE AND WORSE BUST . . . . 146 2 DON JUAN 1 218 8
    A BOOK--A DAMNED BAD PICTURE AND WORSE BUST . . . . . . 146 2 DON JUAN 1 218 V8
    SO THANK YOUR STARS THAT MATTERS ARE NO WORSE . . . . . 147 2 DON JUAN 1 220 7
    HAD LEFT THEIR BODIES AND WHAT'S WORSE ALAS . . . . . . 185 2 DON JUAN 2   55 2
    HE'LL ANSWER ALL FOR BETTER OR FOR WORSE . . . . 298 2 DON JUAN 3   45 7
    YET IN THESE TIMES HE MIGHT HAVE DONE MUCH WORSE . . . 326 2 DON JUAN 3   87 4
    THE GREATER THEIR SUCCESS THE WORSE IT PROVES . . . . . 411 2 DON JUAN 5   1 5
    WHICH FOR HIMSELF HE SEEM'D TO DEEM NO WORSE . . . . . 417 2 DON JUAN 5   12 7
    AND WORSE OFF THAN WE HITHERTO HAVE BEEN . . . . 435 2 DON JUAN 5   44 6
    AND HUGE TOMBS WORSE--MANKIND SINCE ADAM FELL . . . . . 444 2 DON JUAN 5   59 6
    MORALS WERE BETTER AND THE FISH NO WORSE . . . . 496 2 DON JUAN 5 149 8
    FOR OVER-WARMTH IF FALSE IS WORSE THAN TRUTH . . . . . 14 3 DON JUAN 6   16 1
    IN THE LAST LINE WHICH CANNOT WELL BE WORSE . . . . . . 14 3 DON JUAN 6   18 7
    A BAD OLD WOMAN MAKING A WORSE WILL . . . . 16 3 DON JUAN 6   21 5
    I DOUBT IF ANY NOW COULD MAKE IT WORSE . . . . 17 3 DON JUAN 6   23 4
    ARE WORSE THAN THE WORST DAMAGES MEN PAY . . . . 20 3 DON JUAN 6   29 6
    I WISH IT NEVER LED TO SOMETHING WORSE . . . . 35 3 DON JUAN 6   59 8
    MIGHT MAKE THE MATTER STILL WORSE THAN IT WAS . . . . . 57 3 DON JUAN 6 103 8
    AND WHAT IS WORSE STILL A MUCH LONGER STORY . . . . . . 120 3 DON JUAN 8   17 8
    WITH GOOD AND BAD AND WORSE ALIKE PROLIFIC . . . . . . 156 3 DON JUAN 8   89 4
    NOT A BARBARIAN BUT MUCH WORSE THAN THAT . . . . 194 3 DON JUAN 9   23 8
    THAT WORSE THAN WORST OF FOES THE ONCE ADORED . . . . . 258 3 DON JUAN 10   67 6
    WHOSE SHAMROCK NOW SEEMS RATHER WORSE FOR WEARING . . . 286 3 DON JUAN 11   38 8
    THE HORRID SIN--AND WHAT'S STILL WORSE THE TROUBLE . . 292 3 DON JUAN 11   46 8
    FOR FAME IS DROSS OR WORSE--AND AT THE LAST . . . . . . 317 3 DON JUAN 12   4 V7
    OR WHAT'S STILL WORSE TO PUT YOU OUT OF FASHION-- . . . 337 3 DON JUAN 12   45 4
    IF GOOD IS NONE THE WORSE FOR REPETITION . . . . 478 3 DON JUAN 15   51 2
    AND WHAT WAS WORSE WAS NOT ASHAMED TO SHOW IT . . . . . 524 3 DON JUAN 16   47 8
    THE LATTER WORSE USED OF THE TWO WE'VE SEEN-- . . . . . 541 3 DON JUAN 16   84 3
    A THEME FOR PITY OR SOME WORSE EMOTION . . . . 563 3 DON JUAN 17   3 6
WORSHIP
    OF ANY WORSHIP WAKE SOME THOUGHTS DIVINE . . . . 387 3 DON JUAN 13   61 8
    AND DEEM'D THAT FALLEN WORSHIP FAR MORE DEAR . . . . . 476 3 DON JUAN 15   46 3
WORSHIPP'D
    AND SHE WAS WORSHIPP'D AFTER NATURE'S FASHION . . . . . 257 2 DON JUAN 2 191 2
WORSHIPPED
    AND THEY WHO WAITED ONCE AND WORSHIPPED--THEY . . . . . 431 2 DON JUAN 5   37 1
WORST
    FORBIDS ALL WANDERING AS THE WORST OF SINNING . . . . . 25 2 DON JUAN 1   7 4
    FOR SHE HAD NOT EVEN ONE--THE WORST OF ALL . . . . . . 29 2 DON JUAN 1   16 8
    DESERVES THE WORST HIS CONDUCT'S LESS DEFENSIBLE . . . . 103 2 DON JUAN 1 151 6
    BUT WORST OF ALL IS NAUSEA OR A PAIN . . . . 168 2 DON JUAN 2   23 1
    THE WORST OF ALL WAS THAT IN THEIR CONDITION . . . . . 180 2 DON JUAN 2   46 1
    OF ANY CREDITORS THE WORST A JEW IT IS . . . . 190 2 DON JUAN 2   65 5
    WHEN THINGS ARE AT THE WORST THEY SOMETIMES MEND . . .   6 3 DON JUAN 6   1 8
    COULD STOP THAT WORST OF VICES--PROPAGATION . . . . . . 15 3 DON JUAN 6   19 8
    O'ER HIS WORST ENEMY WHEN AT HIS KNEES . . . . 17 3 DON JUAN 6   23 5
    ARE WORSE THAN THE WORST DAMAGES MEN PAY . . . . 20 3 DON JUAN 6   29 5
    AND THEN I HAVE THE WORST DREAMS THAT CAN BE . . . . . 30 3 DON JUAN 6   48 5
    ALL THAT DEFIES THE WORST WHICH PEN EXPRESSES . . . . . 173 3 DON JUAN 8 123 5

WORST   (CONTINUED)
    SOME CALL THEE THE WORST CAUSE OF WAR BUT I 210   3 DON JUAN 9   56   1
    THIS WERE THE WORST DESERTION--RENEGADOES   231   3 DON JUAN 10   13   1
    HOW ALL THE NATIONS DEEM HER THEIR WORST FOE 258   3 DON JUAN 10   67   5
    THAT WORSE THAN WORST OF FOES THE ONCE ADORED 258   3 DON JUAN 10   67   6
    MEANETH THE WEST OR WORST END OF A CITY 290   3 DON JUAN 11   45   2
    AND EVEN MY MUSE'S WORST REPROOF'S A SMILE 300   3 DON JUAN 11   63   6
    THE WORST OF TEMPESTS AND THE BEST OF BATTLES 356   3 DON JUAN 12   88   3
    THE WORST TO KNOW IT--WHEN THE MOUNTAINS REAR 412   3 DON JUAN 14   5   4
    IT WAS NOT THAT SHE FEAR'D THE VERY WORST   437   3 DON JUAN 14   62   1
    AND--WHAT IS WORST OF ALL--WON'T LET YOU GO 438   3 DON JUAN 14   63   8
    THE MARRIAGE STATE THE BEST OR WORST OF ANY) 452   3 DON JUAN 14   95   6
    FEW MEN DARE SHOW THEIR THOUGHTS OF WORST OR BEST 457   3 DON JUAN 15   3   5
    LEAVES A SAD SEDIMENT OF TIME'S WORST WORTH 457   3 DON JUAN 15   4   8
    (HIS FEASTS ARE NOT THE WORST PART OF HIS WORKS) 482   3 DON JUAN 15   62   4
    OF ALL OFFENCES THAT'S THE WORST OFFENCE 490   3 DON JUAN 15   77   3
WORST'S
    BUT THAT'S NO MATTER AND THE WORST'S BEHIND 34   2 DON JUAN 1   24   6
    THE WORLD WHICH AT THE WORST'S A GLORIOUS BLUNDER-- . . . 269   3 DON JUAN 11   3   8
WORTH
    TO WORTH AS FREEDOM WISDOM AS TO WIT 18   2 DON JUAN D   15   6
    WHATE'ER MIGHT BE HIS WORTHLESSNESS OR WORTH 41   2 DON JUAN 1   36   1
    WHERE JURIES CAST UP WHAT A WIFE IS WORTH 57   2 DON JUAN 1   64   5
    BUT THEN EXCEPTIONS ALWAYS PROVE ITS WORTH-- 158   2 DON JUAN 2   2   6
    MEN REALLY KNOW NOT WHAT GOOD WATER'S WORTH 201   2 DON JUAN 2   84   4
    OF LAVISH PEARLS WHOSE WORTH COULD SCARCE BE TOLD 312   2 DON JUAN 3   72   6
    BUT THAT OF LATE YOUR SCRIBBLERS THINK IT WORTH 434   2 DON JUAN 5   42   6
    OF ANY MUSSULMAN WHATE'ER HIS WORTH 450   2 DON JUAN 5   67   4
    WHICH YOUR SUBLIME ATTENTION MAY BE WORTH 494   2 DON JUAN 5   144   6
    GAVE WHAT WAS WORTH A WORLD FOR WORLDS COULD NEVER . . .   9   3 DON JUAN 6   5   7
    IN THE DAMNED LINE ('TIS WORTH AT LEAST A CURSE) 15   3 DON JUAN 6   18   V5
    WHO KNEW THIS LIFE WAS NOT WORTH A POTATO   68   3 DON JUAN 7   4   4
    YET THERE WERE SEVERAL WORTH COMMEMORATION 74   3 DON JUAN 7   16   3
    HALF-PAY FOR LIFE MAKE MANKIND WORTH DESTROYING 118   3 DON JUAN 8   14   8
    UPON THE REST 'TIS NOT WORTH WHILE TO DWELL 184   3 DON JUAN 9   2   5
    A PEASANT'S SWEAT IS WORTH HIS LORD'S ESTATE 190   3 DON JUAN 9   15   6
    FOR ITS DECAYING FAME AND FORMER WORTH 257   3 DON JUAN 10   66   5
    IS FREE THE RESPIRATION'S WORTH THE MONEY 259   3 DON JUAN 10   70   8
    BUT THEN THE ABBEY'S WORTH THE WHOLE COLLECTION 280   3 DON JUAN 11   25   8
    THEIR FLANKS--BUT IT IS HARDLY WORTH MY WHILE 300   3 DON JUAN 11   63   2
    OR WHETHER WITH SOME VIRGIN OF MORE WORTH 312   3 DON JUAN 11   89   3
    THE NEGROES AND IS WORTH A MILLION FIGHTERS 325   3 DON JUAN 12   20   6
    THE WORLD UPON THE WHOLE IS WORTH THE ASSERTION 377   3 DON JUAN 13   41   3
    THEY'RE BARREN AND NOT WORTH THE PAINS TO PULL 402   3 DON JUAN 13   95   6
    IS WORTH A TOUR TO ROME ALTHOUGH NO MORE A 428   3 DON JUAN 14   40   3
    SOME HOURS TO MAKE THE REMNANT WORTH ENJOYING 444   3 DON JUAN 14   78   8
    WE SURELY SHALL FIND SOMETHING WORTH RESEARCH 468   3 DON JUAN 15   27   5
    BY MANY VIRTUES TO BE WORTH THE TROUBLE 477   3 DON JUAN 15   48   7
    WHICH SEEMS TO HINT YOU ARE NOT WORTH A THOUGHT 490   3 DON JUAN 15   77   4
    LONG FURNISHED WITH OLD PICTURES OF GREAT WORTH 508   3 DON JUAN 16   17   4
    TO SHOW SHE COULD IF IT WERE WORTH HER WHILE 521   3 DON JUAN 16   42   8
    THE PRICE WOULD SPEEDILY REPAY ITS WORTH IN 529   3 DON JUAN 16   59   4
    HE GAINED ESTEEM WHERE IT WAS WORTH THE MOST 553   3 DON JUAN 16   107   4
    THE COMPANY WHOSE BIRTH WEALTH WORTH HAVE COST 568   3 DON JUAN 17   13   4
WORTHIES
    SUCH WORTHIES TIME WILL NEVER SEE AGAIN 266   2 DON JUAN 2   206   6
WORTHIEST
    THAT HEAVENLIEST HOUR OF HEAVEN IS WORTHIEST THEE 334   2 DON JUAN 3   101   8
    THE WORTHIEST KINGS HAVE EVER LOVED LEAST STATE 267   3 DON JUAN 10   87   5
WORTHLESSNESS
    WHATE'ER MIGHT BE HIS WORTHLESSNESS OR WORTH 41   2 DON JUAN 1   36   1
WORTHY
    AND WORTHY OF THE NOBLEST PEDIGREE 42   2 DON JUAN 1   38   3
    WORTHY OF THIS AMBROSIAL SIN SO SHOWN 90   2 DON JUAN 1   127   6
    IS'T WORTHY OF YOUR YEARS--YOU HAVE THREESCORE 101   2 DON JUAN 1   146   3
    A PLEASURE WORTHY XERXES THE GREAT KING 251   2 DON JUAN 2   180   3
    BUT THOUGHT HOW WORTHY ALTHOUGH NATURE'S WORK 315   2 DON JUAN 3   76   V7
    TO SUPPER BUT YOU WORTHY CHRISTIAN NUN 458   2 DON JUAN 5   81   3
    WAS WORTHY OF A SPARTAN HAD THE CAUSE 86   3 DON JUAN 7   40   2
    AND THEREFORE WORTHY OF COMMEMORATION 176   3 DON JUAN 8   128   4
    WAS ALMOST WORTHY TO BECOME HIS HENCHMAN 425   3 DON JUAN 14   34   V8
    FOR OBJECTS WORTHY OF THE SENTIMENT 460   3 DON JUAN 15   10   8
    YES SHE WAS TRULY WORTHY HER HIGH PLACE 550   3 DON JUAN 16   102   5
WOUND
    POOR FELLOW HE HAD MANY THINGS TO WOUND HIM 41   2 DON JUAN 1   36   2
    TORMENTED WITH A WOUND HE COULD NOT KNOW 68   2 DON JUAN 1   87   3
    I'M SORRY THUS TO PROBE A WOUND SO RAW 155   2 DON JUAN 1 V 7   5
    OF DEWY DAWN WOUND SLOWLY ROUND EACH HEIGHT 49   3 DON JUAN 6   86   6
    IN ONE WIDE WOUND POURED FORTH HIS SOUL AT ONCE 170   3 DON JUAN 8   118   8
    BUT NONE OF THESE POSSESS'D A STING TO WOUND HER-- . . . 435   3 DON JUAN 14   57   3
    AND MIGHT GO ON IF WELL WOUND UP LIKE WATCHES 473   3 DON JUAN 15   40   8
    HAVING WOUND UP WITH THIS SUBLIME COMPARISON 481   3 DON JUAN 15   59   1
    INFLICTED ON THE DISH A DEADLY WOUND 542   3 DON JUAN 16   88   6
WOUNDED
    AND WOUNDED SEVERAL SHUTTERS AND SOME BOARDS 99   2 DON JUAN 1   143   8
    WOUNDED AND CHAIN'D SO THAT HE CANNOT MOVE 371   2 DON JUAN 4   51   7
    NOT SOUND POOR FELLOW BUT SEVERELY WOUNDED 373   2 DON JUAN 4   54   2
    WOUNDED AND FETTER'D CABIN'D CRIBB'D CONFINED 384   2 DON JUAN 4   75   1
    IS TWICE AS STRONG AS THAT WHERE YOU WERE WOUNDED 98   3 DON JUAN 7   61   8

WOUNDED (CONTINUED)

	PAGE	VOL	CANTO	STANZA	LN
OF KILLED AND WOUNDED WHO WILL NOT BE MISSED	107	3 DON JUAN	7	81	V8
OH YE LESS GRAND LONG LIST OF KILLED AND WOUNDED	108	3 DON JUAN	7	82	2
THE PRINCE DELIGNE WAS WOUNDED IN THE KNEE	116	3 DON JUAN	8	10	1
A WOUNDED COMRADE SPRAWLING IN HIS GORE	121	3 DON JUAN	8	20	8
BE THAT THE GREATER PART WERE KILLED OR WOUNDED	125	3 DON JUAN	8	28	2
NAY HE HAD WOUNDED THOUGH BUT SLIGHTLY BOTH	166	3 DON JUAN	8	109	1
MORE WITH THESE DINNERS THAN THE KILLED OR WOUNDED--	383	3 DON JUAN	13	53	8

WOUNDS

THY CLANKING CHAIN AND ERIN'S YET GREEN WOUNDS	19	2 DON JUAN	D	16	5
PERHAPS HIS RECENT WOUNDS MIGHT HELP A LITTLE	396	2 DON JUAN	4	95	8
THE SCARS OF HIS OLD WOUNDS WERE NEAR HIS NEW	431	2 DON JUAN	5	38	1
OH BLOOD AND THUNDER AND OH BLOOD AND WOUNDS	112	3 DON JUAN	8	1	1
THE WOUNDS THEY RICHLY MERITED AND SHRIEK	158	3 DON JUAN	8	94	4

WRANGLE

| SO MUCH AS I DO ANY KIND OF WRANGLE | 496 | 3 DON JUAN | 15 | 91 | 3 |

WRANGLED

| THEY HAGGLED WRANGLED SWORE TOO--SO THEY DID | 425 | 2 DON JUAN | 5 | 28 | 4 |

WRANGLING

| FOR BLUSTERING BUNGLING TRIMMING WRANGLING WRITING | 150 | 2 DON JUAN | 1 | V 1 | 5 |

WRAPPED

| THAT SCARLET CLOAK--GOD HELP US--WHEN CLOSE WRAPPED | 530 | 3 DON JUAN | 16 | 61 | V7 |

WRAPT

AND WRAPT HIM CLOSER LEST THE AIR TOO RAW	232	2 DON JUAN	2	143	6
A GLANCE AT THAT WHICH WRAPT THE SLAVES IN WONDER	450	2 DON JUAN	5	66	2
I SAY DON JUAN WRAPT IN CONTEMPLATION	272	3 DON JUAN	11	9	1
MANKIND JUST NOW SEEM WRAPT IN MEDITATION	325	3 DON JUAN	12	21	4

WRATH

SHE WHISPER'D IN GREAT WRATH--I MUST DEPOSIT	114	2 DON JUAN	1	170	7
BUT THEN THIS WRATH WILL PASS AND TIME ASSUAGING	305	2 DON JUAN	3	58	V5
BUT HE WAS STEELED BY SORROW WRATH AND PRIDE	484	2 DON JUAN	5	126	2
FROM OUT HER SKIES--THEN HOWL YOUR IDLE WRATH	70	3 DON JUAN	7	7	7
ALL WRATH IN BARRACKS PALACES OR COTS	200	3 DON JUAN	9	36	5
OF WRATH AND RHYME WHEN JUVENILE AND CURLY	234	3 DON JUAN	10	19	2
I RAILED AT SCOTS TO SHEW MY WRATH AND WIT	234	3 DON JUAN	10	19	3
AND THEN HIS DREAD GREW WRATH AND HIS WRATH FIERCE	559	3 DON JUAN	16	119	1
AND THEN HIS DREAD GREW WRATH AND HIS WRATH FIERCE	559	3 DON JUAN	16	119	1

WREAK

| SNATCH'D DOWN HIS SABRE IN HOT HASTE TO WREAK | 364 | 2 DON JUAN | 4 | 37 | 3 |

WREATH

FAIR AS THE CROWNING ROSE OF THE WHOLE WREATH	235	2 DON JUAN	2	148	5
FAIR AS THE ROSE JUST PLUCKED TO CROWN THE WREATH	235	2 DON JUAN	2	148	V5
BUT JUAN SAW NOT THIS EACH WREATH OF SMOKE	266	3 DON JUAN	10	83	1

WREATHE

| 'TIS STRANGE THAT POETS NEVER TRY TO WREATHE | 280 | 2 DON JUAN | 3 | 9 | V5 |
| THERE WREATHE HIS VENERABLE HORNS WITH FLOWERS | 292 | 2 DON JUAN | 3 | 32 | 2 |

WREATHED

| WITH CYPRESS BRANCHES HAST THOU WREATHED THY BOWERS | 275 | 2 DON JUAN | 3 | 2 | 3 |

WREATHING

| BRINGING WARM WATER WREATHING HER LONG TRESSES | 252 | 2 DON JUAN | 2 | 182 | 7 |

WREATHS

| THAT POESY HAS WREATHS FOR YOU ALONE | 12 | 2 DON JUAN | D | 5 | 6 |
| WHICH CURL IN CURIOUS WREATHS--HOW SOON THE SMOKE | 110 | 3 DON JUAN | 7 | 86 | 7 |

WRECK

OF ALL OUR PUMPS--A WRECK COMPLETE SHE ROLL'D	178	2 DON JUAN	2	42	6
NO BASELESS FABRIC BUT A WRECK BEHIND	227	2 DON JUAN	2	134	V8
LIKE A RICH WRECK--HER FIRST LOVE AND HER LAST	247	2 DON JUAN	2	173	8
ITS FARTHER COURSE BUT MUST RECEIVE ITS WRECK	60	3 DON JUAN	6	108	8
A BATTLE WRECK OR HISTORY OF THE HEART	419	3 DON JUAN	14	21	4
A HALF-STARVED BABE A WRECK UPON LIFE'S OCEAN	563	3 DON JUAN	17	3	4

WRECK'D

| 'TIS NEVER TOO LATE TO BE WHOLLY WRECK'D | 176 | 2 DON JUAN | 2 | 39 | 6 |
| A WAVERING SPIRIT MAY BE EASIER WRECK'D | 446 | 3 DON JUAN | 14 | 85 | 5 |

WRECKED

| THEN SEES YOUR HEART WRECKED WITH AN INWARD SCOFFING | 345 | 3 DON JUAN | 12 | 63 | 4 |

WRECKS

FOR THEY REMEMBER BATTLES FIRES AND WRECKS	172	2 DON JUAN	2	31	4
BUT BY GOD'S GRACE HERE WRECKS WERE IN SUCH PLENTY	226	2 DON JUAN	2	132	7
DREAM'D OF A THOUSAND WRECKS O'ER WHICH SHE STUMBLED	229	2 DON JUAN	2	138	3
THOSE CORNISH PLUNDERERS OF PARNASSIAN WRECKS	403	2 DON JUAN	4	108	6
'MIDST MANY ROCKS WE GUARD MORE AGAINST WRECKS	371	3 DON JUAN	13	30	6

WRENCH

| TO TRY IF I COULD WRENCH AUGHT OUT OF DEATH | 431 | 2 DON JUAN | 5 | 38 | 7 |

WRESTLING

| AT LAST AS THEY MORE FAINTLY WRESTLING LAY | 124 | 2 DON JUAN | 1 | 186 | 4 |
| AND WRESTLING BOTH HIS ARMS INTO A GOWN | 456 | 2 DON JUAN | 5 | 78 | 7 |

WRETCH

ERE I THE WIFE OF SUCH A WRETCH HAD BEEN	98	2 DON JUAN	1	142	V4
DEATH SHUNS THE WRETCH WHO FAIN THE BLOW WOULD MEET	134	2 DON JUAN	1	197	6
HAD LEFT THE WRETCH AN UNCORRUPTED HOUR	339	2 DON JUAN	3	109	8
WHAT DOST THOU KNOW OF LOVE OR FEELING--WRETCH	63	3 DON JUAN	6	116	1
WHILE THE POOR RICH WRETCH OBJECT OF THESE CARES	331	3 DON JUAN	12	33	7

WRETCHED

| A NAME A WRETCHED PICTURE AND WORSE BUST | 146 | 2 DON JUAN | 1 | 218 | 8 |
| PERHAPS AS WRETCHED IF A PEASANT'S QUEAN | 18 | 3 DON JUAN | 6 | 25 | 8 |

WRIGGLE

| THERE WAS A GENERAL WHISPER TOSS AND WRIGGLE | 501 | 2 DON JUAN | 5 | 156 | 7 |
| THEY BIT THEIR LIPS AND WHISPERED WITH A WRIGGLE | 501 | 2 DON JUAN | 5 | 156 | V7 |

WRING

| CLOSER THAT ALL THE DEADLIER THEY MIGHT WRING | 170 | 3 DON JUAN | 8 | 118 | 5 |

		PAGE	VOL		CANTO	STANZA	LN

WRINGS
AND LOVE DESTROY AND SAPPING SORROW WRINGS . . . . . . 468 2 DON JUAN 5 98 6
THE VERIEST JADE WILL WINCE WHOSE HARNESS WRINGS . . . . 137 3 DON JUAN 8 50 5
WRINKLE
IS RUFFLED BY A WRINKLE OR THE SUN . . . . 229 3 DON JUAN 10 8 4
WRINKLED
OF EARTH WAS WRINKLED BY THE SINS AND TEARS . . . . . . 9 3 DON JUAN 6 6 7
WRINKLES
THEIR FACES WERE NOT MADE FOR WRINKLES THEIR . . . . . 348 2 DON JUAN 4 9 1
THE ELDER LADIES' WRINKLES CURLED MUCH CRISPER . . . . 221 3 DON JUAN 9 78 3
AND WRINKLES (THE DAMNED DEMOCRATS) WON'T FLATTER . . . 236 3 DON JUAN 10 24 8
WRINKLING
YIELD TO STERN TIME AND NATURE'S WRINKLING LAWS . . . . 219 2 DON JUAN 2 119 6
WRIST
AND THEN HELD OUT HIS JUGULAR AND WRIST . . . . 197 2 DON JUAN 2 76 8
WRIT
WRIT IN A MANNER WHICH IS MY AVERSION . . . . 330 2 DON JUAN 3 94 8
WRITE
I USED--I WRITE IN HASTE AND IF A STAIN . . . . . . 130 2 DON JUAN 1 192 6
I'LL WRITE POETICAL COMMANDMENTS WHICH . . . . 138 2 DON JUAN 1 204 2
THOU SHALT NOT WRITE IN SHORT BUT WHAT I CHOOSE . . . . 140 2 DON JUAN 1 206 5
FOR THIS MEN WRITE SPEAK PREACH AND HEROES KILL . . . . 146 2 DON JUAN 1 218 5
AND FOR THE FUTURE--(BUT I WRITE THIS REELING . . . . . 156 2 DON JUAN 1 V 8 4
SOME PLAY THE DEVIL AND THEN WRITE A NOVEL . . . . . 263 2 DON JUAN 2 201 8
WRITE ODES ON THE INCONSTANCY OF WOMAN . . . . . . 288 2 DON JUAN 3 24 8
IN FRANCE FOR INSTANCE HE WOULD WRITE A CHANSON . . . . 320 2 DON JUAN 3 86 1
THEY WRITE AND FOR WHAT END BUT NOTE OR TEXT . . . . 203 3 DON JUAN 9 41 7
AND VERY MUCH UNLIKE WHAT PEOPLE WRITE . . . . . 292 3 DON JUAN 11 47 8
FOR I DISDAIN TO WRITE AN ATALANTIS . . . . 311 3 DON JUAN 11 87 5
WHILE SAGES WRITE AGAINST ALL PROCREATION . . . . . 325 3 DON JUAN 12 21 6
I WRITE WHAT'S UPPERMOST WITHOUT DELAY . . . . . . 413 3 DON JUAN 14 7 5
AND WHAT I WRITE I CAST UPON THE STREAM . . . . . 415 3 DON JUAN 14 11 7
I WRITE THE WORLD NOR CARE IF THE WORLD READ . . . . 482 3 DON JUAN 15 60 3
COULD WRITE RHYMES AND COMPOSE MORE THAN SHE WROTE . . 524 3 DON JUAN 16 47 2
ALL THAT I WRITE OR WROTE CAN NE'ER REVIVE . . . . . 569 3 DON JUAN 17 V 13 3
WRITER
THEY ACCUSE ME--ME--THE PRESENT WRITER OF . . . . . 67 3 DON JUAN 7 3 1
BUT IF A WRITER SHOULD BE QUITE CONSISTENT . . . . 494 3 DON JUAN 15 87 7
WRITERS
WHILE GENTLE WRITERS ALSO LOVE TO LIFT . . . . . 50 3 DON JUAN 6 88 6
YE GENTLE READERS AND UNGENTLE WRITERS . . . . . 325 3 DON JUAN 12 20 2
BUT THIS CAN'T WELL BE TRUE JUST NOW FOR WRITERS . . . 418 3 DON JUAN 14 20 1
YOUR WRITERS WHO MUST EITHER DRAW AGAIN . . . . 468 3 DON JUAN 15 26 6
WRITES
AS MY FRIEND JEFFREY WRITES WITH SUCH AN AIR . . . 230 3 DON JUAN 10 11 6
AND MALTHUS DOES THE THING 'GAINST WHICH HE WRITES . . 325 3 DON JUAN 12 20 8
SOME GENTLEMAN WHO FIGHTS OR WRITES OR DRIVES . . . 333 3 DON JUAN 12 36 6
WRITHE
THESE SMILE AND WRITHE AND PERISH STILL THE SAME . . 377 2 DON JUAN 4 61 V7
ALL COMMON FELLOWS WHO MIGHT WRITHE AND WINCE . . . . 117 3 DON JUAN 8 11 4
WRITHED
IN VAIN HE KICKED AND SWORE AND WRITHED AND BLED . . . 153 3 DON JUAN 8 83 5
AND ROARED OUT AS HE WRITHED HIS NATIVE MUD IN . . . 274 3 DON JUAN 11 13 6
WRITHING
HER WRITHING FELL SHE LIKE A CEDAR FELL'D . . . . . 375 2 DON JUAN 4 58 8
WRITING
FOR BLUSTERING BUNGLING TRIMMING WRANGLING WRITING . . 150 2 DON JUAN 1 V 1 5
THIS WAY OF WRITING WILL APPEAR EXOTIC . . . . 347 2 DON JUAN 4 6 2
I THEREFORE DO DENOUNCE ALL AMOROUS WRITING . . . 412 2 DON JUAN 5 2 1
IN WRITING COURSER BY MISTAKE FOR COURIER . . . 446 2 DON JUAN 5 61 7
WRITING DISPATCHES) IN THEIR SEVERAL STATIONS . . . 533 3 DON JUAN 16 66 7
WRITINGS
THESE ORIENTAL WRITINGS ON THE WALL . . . . . . 308 2 DON JUAN 3 65 1
WRITTEN
LEAVE TO O'ERSTEP THE WRITTEN RIGHTS OF WOMAN . . . 74 2 DON JUAN 1 98 3
WHEN POETS SAY I'VE WRITTEN FIFTY RHYMES . . . . 79 2 DON JUAN 1 108 3
'TIS WRITTEN IN THE HEBREW CHRONICLE . . . . . 113 2 DON JUAN 1 168 2
THIS NOTE WAS WRITTEN UPON GILT-EDGED PAPER . . . 134 2 DON JUAN 1 198 1
HE WOULD HAVE WRITTEN SONNETS ALL HIS LIFE . . . 279 2 DON JUAN 3 8 8
AND WRITTEN LATELY TWO MEMOIRS UPON'T) . . . . 447 2 DON JUAN 5 62 6
I CANNOT STOP TO ALTER WORDS ONCE WRITTEN . . . 221 3 DON JUAN 9 77 4
NATURE HAD WRITTEN GENTLEMAN HE SAID . . . . . 223 3 DON JUAN 9 83 6
WERE EVERY MEMORY WRITTEN DOWN ALL TRUE . . . . 324 3 DON JUAN 12 19 3
THOUGH ROYALTY WAS WRITTEN ON HIS BROW . . . . 354 3 DON JUAN 12 84 5
WRONG
BUT THIS I HEARD HER SAY AND CAN'T BE WRONG . . . 28 2 DON JUAN 1 14 5
OFT IN THE WRONG AND NEVER ON HIS GUARD . . . . 33 2 DON JUAN 1 21 2
I CAN'T HELP THINKING JUVENAL WAS WRONG . . . . 45 2 DON JUAN 1 43 3
BUT STILL NO LESS SUSPECTS IN THE WRONG PLACE . . 74 2 DON JUAN 1 99 2
GLOW'D IN HER CHEEK AND YET SHE FELT NO WRONG . . 78 2 DON JUAN 1 106 2
'TWAS SURELY VERY WRONG IN JUAN'S MOTHER . . . . 80 2 DON JUAN 1 110 5
INSULT ON INSULT HEAP AND WRONG ON WRONG . . . 100 2 DON JUAN 1 145 5
INSULT ON INSULT HEAP AND WRONG ON WRONG . . . 100 2 DON JUAN 1 145 3
THEY SMILE SO WHEN ONE'S RIGHT AND WHEN ONE'S WRONG . . 242 2 DON JUAN 2 164 5
THERE'S NOTHING WRONG IN A CONNUBIAL KISS . . . 279 2 DON JUAN 3 8 6
A SOFA LIKE A BED MAY COME BY WRONG . . . . 288 2 DON JUAN 3 25 V8
YOU'RE WRONG--HE WAS THE MILDEST MANNER'D MAN . . 296 2 DON JUAN 3 41 1
HIS STRAIN DISPLAY'D SOME FEELING--RIGHT OR WRONG . . 326 2 DON JUAN 3 87 5
AND THEN DECIDE WITHOUT GREAT WRONG TO EITHER . . 357 2 DON JUAN 4 25 7

WRONG (CONTINUED)
```
        YEARS COULD BUT BRING THEM CRUEL THINGS OR WRONG  . . .  358  2 DON JUAN  4    27   4
        IF SHE LOVED RASHLY HER LIFE PAID FOR WRONG--  . . . .  383  2 DON JUAN  4    73   5
        I'M SENSIBLE REDUNDANCY IS WRONG . . . . . . . . . .    410  2 DON JUAN  4   117   5
        BEING PIQUED BY CRITICS WHO HAVE DONE ME WRONG . . .    410  2 DON JUAN  4   117  V5
        HE'S WRONG--UNLESS MAN WERE A PIG INDEED . . . . . .    427  2 DON JUAN  5    31   3
        I KNOW GULBEYAZ WAS EXTREMELY WRONG  . . . . . . . .     10  3 DON JUAN  6     8   1
        FULL OF EXPRESSION RIGHT OR WRONG THAT STRIKE  . . .     32  3 DON JUAN  6    52   7
        WHICH ALL WHO SAW IT FOLLOWED WRONG OR RIGHT . . . .     89  3 DON JUAN  7    46   8
        OR THE SENSATION (IF THAT PHRASE SEEM WRONG) . . . .    123  3 DON JUAN  8    24   4
        SO MUCH INTO THE RAW AS QUITE TO WRONG HER . . . . .    137  3 DON JUAN  8    50   6
        WHICH HATE NOR ENVY E'ER COULD TINGE WITH WRONG  . .    144  3 DON JUAN  8    63   6
        AN ECHO OF A SYLLABLE THAT'S WRONG . . . . . . . . .    336  3 DON JUAN 12    43   5
        AN AWKWARD INCLINATION TO GO WRONG . . . . . . . . .    338  3 DON JUAN 12    48   4
        OR IF I'M WRONG I'LL NOT BE TA'EN ABACK--  . . . . .    348  3 DON JUAN 12    71   6
        REDRESSING INJURY REVENGING WRONG  . . . . . . . . .    363  3 DON JUAN 13    10   1
        DETERMINED RIGHT OR WRONG ON FRIEND OR FOE . . . . .    366  3 DON JUAN 13    16   4
        VICTIM WHEN WRONG AND MARTYR OFT WHEN RIGHT  . . . .    420  3 DON JUAN 14    23   6
        SAITH HORACE THE GREAT LITTLE POET'S WRONG . . . . .    443  3 DON JUAN 14    77   2
        THEY ARE WRONG--THAT'S NOT THE WAY TO SET ABOUT IT .    461  3 DON JUAN 15    13   1
        BUT RIGHT OR WRONG DON JUAN WAS WITHOUT IT . . . . .    461  3 DON JUAN 15    13   3
        SOME MILLIONS MUST BE WRONG THAT'S PRETTY CLEAR  . .    496  3 DON JUAN 15    90   1
        IF YOU ARE RIGHT THEN EVERYBODY'S WRONG . . . . . .     564  3 DON JUAN 17     5   4
        IF YOU ARE WRONG THEN EVERYBODY'S RIGHT  . . . . . .    564  3 DON JUAN 17     5   7
WRONG'D
        I'VE KNOWN THE ABSENT WRONG'D FOUR TIMES A DAY . . .    288  2 DON JUAN  3    25   8
WRONGS
        IF TIME THE AVENGER EXECRATES HIS WRONGS . . . . . .     15  2 DON JUAN  D    10   3
        THE WRONGS TO WHOSE EXPOSURE IT IS SLOW--  . . . . .    107  2 DON JUAN  1   157   4
        HIS COUNTRY'S WRONGS AND HIS DESPAIR TO SAVE HER . .    302  2 DON JUAN  3    53   7
        MEN'S WRONGS AND RATHER CHECK THAN PUNISH CRIMES . .    361  3 DON JUAN 13     8   6
WROTE
        WHILE THE RIGHT HAND WHICH WROTE IT STILL IS ABLE  .    398  2 DON JUAN  4    99   5
        THUS HORACE WROTE WE ALL KNOW LONG AGO . . . . . . .    470  2 DON JUAN  5   101   5
        FOR IF I WROTE DOWN EVERY WARRIOR'S SPEECH . . . . .     83  3 DON JUAN  7    35   7
        WITH BLOODY HANDS HE WROTE HIS FIRST DISPATCH  . . .    178  3 DON JUAN  8   133   5
        SEVERE SUBLIME THE PROPHET WROTE NO FARCE ON . . . .    179  3 DON JUAN  8   134   6
        HE WROTE THIS POLAR MELODY AND SET IT . . . . . . .     179  3 DON JUAN  8   135   1
        HE WROTE TO SPAIN--AND ALL HIS NEAR RELATIONS . . .     239  3 DON JUAN 10    30   1
        IN YOUTH I WROTE BECAUSE MY MIND WAS FULL  . . . . .    415  3 DON JUAN 14    10   7
        COULD WRITE RHYMES AND COMPOSE MORE THAN SHE WROTE .    524  3 DON JUAN 16    47   2
        ALL THAT I WRITE OR WROTE CAN NE'ER REVIVE . . . . .    569  3 DON JUAN 17  V 13   3
WROTH
        THE MATRON TOO WAS WROTH TO LEAVE HER WARM . . . . .     45  3 DON JUAN  6    79   5
        AND ALL AROUND WERE GROWN EXCEEDING WROTH  . . . . .    166  3 DON JUAN  8   109   5
        WHEN WROTH WHILE PLEASED SHE WAS AS FINE A FIGURE . .    213  3 DON JUAN  9    62   2
WROUGHT
        YOU HAVE YOUR SALARY WAS'T FOR THAT YOU WROUGHT . . .     12  2 DON JUAN  D     6   5
        WROUGHT CHANGE WITH ALL ARMIDA'S FAIRY ART . . . . .     60  2 DON JUAN  1    71   7
        NE'ER COMPASS'D NOR LESS MORTAL CHISEL WROUGHT . . .    219  2 DON JUAN  2   119   8
        THE UPPER BORDER RICHLY WROUGHT DISPLAY'D  . . . . .    308  2 DON JUAN  3    64   5
        THE VERGE OF HEAVEN AND IN HER LARGE EYES WROUGHT . .    473  2 DON JUAN  5   108   6
        IN ANY KIND OF MISCHIEF TO BE WROUGHT . . . . . . .     477  2 DON JUAN  5   114   5
        AND TALENT ON HIS HAUGHTY SPIRIT WROUGHT . . . . . .    365  3 DON JUAN 13    15   6
WRUNG
        THEY WRUNG IT OUT AND THOUGH A THIRSTY DITCHER . . .    201  2 DON JUAN  2    85   5
        FROM WHOSE RELUCTANT ROAR HIS LIFE HE WRUNG  . . . .    213  2 DON JUAN  2   108   3
        PILLOW'D HIS DEATH-LIKE FOREHEAD THEN SHE WRUNG . . .    216  2 DON JUAN  2   114   5
        SO DEEP AN ANGUISH WRUNG GULBEYAZM BROW . . . . . .      58  3 DON JUAN  6   105   4
XERXES
        'TIS SAID THAT XERXES OFFER'D A REWARD  . . . . . .      85  2 DON JUAN  1   118   1
        A PLEASURE WORTHY XERXES THE GREAT KING  . . . . . .    251  2 DON JUAN  2   180   3
YANKEES
        WHO ATE LAST WAR MORE YANKEES THAN HE KILL'D . . . .    399  3 DON JUAN 13    88   4
YARD
        A YARD OR TWO OF GROUND WHICH BROUGHT THEM NIGHER  .    121  3 DON JUAN  8    20   3
YARDS
        UPON YOUR PERSON TWELVE YARDS OFF OR SO  . . . . . .    366  2 DON JUAN  4    41   4
YAWL
        THE OTHER BOATS THE YAWL AND PINNACE HAD . . . . . .    181  2 DON JUAN  2    48   1
YAWN
        BEGAN AT ONCE TO SCREAM AND YAWN AND WEEP  . . . . .     97  2 DON JUAN  1   140   3
        PERHAPS MIGHT MAKE HIM SHIVER YAWN OR THROW  . . . .    121  3 DON JUAN  8    21   5
        THAT AWFUL YAWN WHICH SLEEP CAN NOT ABATE  . . . . .    405  3 DON JUAN 13   101   8
        OR A HA HA OR BAH--A YAWN OR POOH . . . . . . . . .     456  3 DON JUAN 15     1   7
YAWN'D
        AND THE SEA YAWN'D AROUND HER LIKE A HELL  . . . . .    184  2 DON JUAN  2    52   5
        BESIDES BEING LESS IN LOVE SHE YAWN'D A LITTLE . . .    233  2 DON JUAN  2   145   3
YAWNED
        AND YAWNED A GOOD DEAL WITH DISCREET SURPRIZE  . . .     42  3 DON JUAN  6    73   8
YAWNING
        YAWNING A LITTLE AS THE NIGHT GROWS LATER  . . . . .    303  3 DON JUAN 11    69   8
YAWNS
        NOW YAWNS ALL DESOLATE NOW LOUD NOW FAINTER  . . . .    387  3 DON JUAN 13    62   5
        THE GULF OF ROCK YAWNS--YOU CAN'T GAZE A MINUTE  . .    412  3 DON JUAN 14     5   7
YCLEPED
        THEIR LIES YCLEPED DESPATCHES WITHOUT RISK OR  . . .    498  2 DON JUAN  5   151   7
YCLEPT
        YCLEPT THE GREAT WORLD FOR IT IS THE LEAST . . . . .    342  3 DON JUAN 12    56   2
```

```
                                                      PAGE VOL    CANTO STANZA LN
YCLEPT   (CONTINUED)
   FIRMNESS YCLEPT IN HEROES KINGS AND SEAMEN . . . . . . 448   3 DON JUAN 14    89    3
   DISCUSSED (HE HATED BEER YCLEPT THE SMALL) . . . . . . 533   3 DON JUAN 16    67    3
YEAR
   WHEN EVERY YEAR AND MONTH SENDS FORTH A NEW ONE . . .   21   2 DON JUAN  1     1    2
   NOT ONLY OF THE AGE AND YEAR BUT MOON . . . . . . . .   76   2 DON JUAN  1   103    3
   OF REFORMATION ERE THE YEAR RUN OUT . . . . . . . . .   85   2 DON JUAN  1   119    4
   WHO KILL'D HIMSELF FOR LOVE (WITH WINE) LAST YEAR . .  102   2 DON JUAN  1   149    8
   PERHAPS THEY'LL HAVE SOME MORE ABOUT A YEAR HENCE . .  135   2 DON JUAN  1   199    8
   A DEMOCRAT SOME ONCE OR TWICE A YEAR . . . . . . . .   152   2 DON JUAN  1 V 3     2
   SHE BEING WISER BY A YEAR OR TWO . . . . . . . . . .   228   2 DON JUAN  2   136    4
   A YEAR OR TWO'S AN AGE WHEN RIGHTLY SPENT . . . . . .  228   2 DON JUAN  2   136    5
   THE LONG YEAR LINK'D WITH HEAVY DAY ON DAY . . . . .   350   2 DON JUAN  4    11    5
   YOU WAS NOT LAST YEAR AT THE FAIR OF LUGO . . . . . .  392   2 DON JUAN  4    88    7
   OR FRESHER BRIGHTER BUT THE YEAR GONE THROUGH . . . .  422   2 DON JUAN  5    22    2
   SAVE WED A YEAR I HATE RECRUITS WITH WIVES . . . . .   102   3 DON JUAN  7    70    8
   I MEAN THAT EVERY AGE AND EVERY YEAR . . . . . . . .   108   3 DON JUAN  7    83    2
   JUST AT THE CLOSE OF THE FIRST BRIDAL YEAR . . . . .   125   3 DON JUAN  8    27    4
   AS THE YEAR CLOSING WHIRLS THE SCARLET LEAVES . . . .  155   3 DON JUAN  8    88    3
   AFTER WHICH SHADOWS THE--SAY--SECOND YEAR . . . . . .  220   3 DON JUAN  9    75   V8
   BUT ASK HIM WHAT HE THINKS OF IT A YEAR HENCE . . . .  271   3 DON JUAN 11     7    8
   THEIR CASH TO SHOW HOW MUCH THEY HAVE A YEAR . . . .   273   3 DON JUAN 11    10    4
   THE LAST YEAR TO THE NEW TRANSFERS ITS HOARDS . . . .  340   3 DON JUAN 12    53    5
   THE SEA-COAL FIRES THE EARLIEST OF THE YEAR . . . . .  395   3 DON JUAN 13    77    6
   THOUGH SHE WAS FAR FROM THAT LEAP YEAR WHOSE LEAP . .  433   3 DON JUAN 14    52    7
   FIND ONE EACH DAY OF THE DELIGHTFUL YEAR . . . . . .   438   3 DON JUAN 14    63    6
   (ESPECIALLY AS THE SIXTH YEAR IS ENDING) . . . . . .   546   3 DON JUAN 16    95    6
YEARLY
   FROM ALL THE POPE MAKES YEARLY 'TWOULD PERPLEX . . .   391   2 DON JUAN  4    86    7
   CASTS OFF ITS BRIGHT SKIN YEARLY LIKE THE SNAKE . . .  421   2 DON JUAN  5    21    8
   THE SUN WHICH YEARLY MELTS THE POLAR ICE . . . . . .   501   2 DON JUAN  5   157    7
   AND SENDS NEW WERTERS YEARLY TO THEIR COFFIN . . . .   345   3 DON JUAN 12    63    6
YEAR'S
   HIMSELF FOR FIVE FOUR THREE OR TWO YEAR'S SPACE . . .  329   3 DON JUAN 12    29    6
   IF WE MAY JUDGE FROM EACH NEW YEAR'S DISPLAY . . . .   548   3 DON JUAN 16    99   V5
YEARS
   YOUNG JUAN NOW WAS SIXTEEN YEARS OF AGE . . . . . . .   51   2 DON JUAN  1    54    1
   WEDDED SHE WAS SOME YEARS AND TO A MAN . . . . . . .    56   2 DON JUAN  1    62    1
   A MAN WELL LOOKING FOR HIS YEARS AND WHO . . . . . .    57   2 DON JUAN  1    65    2
   WHEN SHE HAD TWENTY YEARS AND THIRTEEN HE . . . . .     59   2 DON JUAN  1    69    4
   THESE FEW SHORT YEARS MAKE WOND'ROUS ALTERATIONS . .    59   2 DON JUAN  1    69    7
   EVEN SEVEN YEARS HENCE IT WOULD NOT BE TOO LATE . . .   67   2 DON JUAN  1    85    4
   THE PLAN OF TWENTY YEARS AND ALL IS OVER . . . . . .    75   2 DON JUAN  1   100    6
   AND THEN OF DON ALFONSO'S FIFTY YEARS . . . . . . .     78   2 DON JUAN  1   107    4
   SHE WHO FOR MANY YEARS HAD WATCH'D HER SON SO-- . .     80   2 DON JUAN  1   110    7
   OR GENTLEMAN OF SEVENTY YEARS COMPLETE . . . . . . .    89   2 DON JUAN  1   125    3
   IS'T WORTHY OF YOUR YEARS--YOU HAVE THREESCORE . . .   101   2 DON JUAN  1   146    3
   AT LEAST PERHAPS HE HAS NOT SIXTY YEARS . . . . . .    106   2 DON JUAN  1   155    1
   AT SIXTY YEARS AND DRAW THE ACCOMPTS OF EVIL . . . .   113   2 DON JUAN  1   167    7
   FOR ME ON EARTH EXCEPT SOME YEARS TO HIDE . . . . .    132   2 DON JUAN  1   195    3
   HINT THAT SOME SIX OR SEVEN GOOD YEARS AGO . . . . .   143   2 DON JUAN  1   212    4
   BUT NOW AT THIRTY YEARS MY HAIR IS GRAY-- . . . . .    143   2 DON JUAN  1   213    1
   INFANTS OF THREE YEARS OLD WERE TAUGHT THAT DAY . . .  162   2 DON JUAN  2    10    5
   OUR JUAN WHO WITH SENSE BEYOND HIS YEARS . . . . . .   174   2 DON JUAN  2    35    2
   COULD DO NO MORE HE WAS A MAN IN YEARS . . . . . . .   179   2 DON JUAN  2    43    3
   WHILE A FEW PRAY'D--(THE FIRST TIME FOR SOME YEARS)-- 208   2 DON JUAN  2    98    5
   UNWELCOME VISIONS OF OUR FORMER YEARS . . . . . . .    227   2 DON JUAN  2   134    7
   I'VE CHANGED FOR SOME FEW YEARS THE DAY TO NIGHT . .   230   2 DON JUAN  2   140   V3
   OF WHOM THESE TWO YEARS SHE HAD NIGHTLY DREAM'D . . .  247   2 DON JUAN  2   172    4
   WHICH MAKE THE ENGLISH CLIMATE OF OUR YEARS . . . .    270   2 DON JUAN  2   214    8
   WHICH RAIN DOWN ON THE DUST OF OUR YEARS . . . . . .   270   2 DON JUAN  2   214   V8
   HAD SOIL'D THE CURRENT OF HER SINLESS YEARS . . . .    274   2 DON JUAN  3     1    7
   HAD SOWN THE RUIN OF HER FEW FAIR YEARS . . . . . .    275   2 DON JUAN  3     1   V7
   ALL FEELINGS WHICH O'ERLEAP THE YEARS LONG LOST . .    286   2 DON JUAN  3    21    7
   FOR SOME FEW YEARS HIS LOT HAD BEEN O'ERCAST . . . .   316   2 DON JUAN  3    79    5
   CUT FROM ITS FOREST ROOT OF YEARS--THE RIVER . . . .   349   2 DON JUAN  4    10    4
   YEARS COULD BUT BRING THEM CRUEL THINGS OR WRONG . .   358   2 DON JUAN  4    27    4
   THEIR STATURE DIFFERING BUT IN SEX AND YEARS . . . .   368   2 DON JUAN  4    45    2
   THROUGH YEARS OR MOONS THE INNER WEIGHT TO BEAR . . .  382   2 DON JUAN  4    71    3
   SOME BY A PLACE--AS TEND THEIR YEARS OR NATURES . .    425   2 DON JUAN  5    27    6
   THIS MUCH HOWEVER I MAY ADD--HER YEARS . . . . . .     468   2 DON JUAN  5    98    1
   SOMETIMES SIX YEARS OLD--THOUGH THIS SEEMS ODD . . .   498   2 DON JUAN  5   152    6
   OF YEARS TO FILL A BOWSTRING OR THE THRONE . . . .     499   2 DON JUAN  5   153    7
   I WISH THEIR YEARS HAD BEEN FIFTEEN AND TWENTY . . .     9   3 DON JUAN  6     5    2
   OF--BUT CHRONOLOGY BEST KNOWS THE YEARS . . . . . .      9   3 DON JUAN  6     6    8
   YEARS AND A FIFTEEN-HUNDREDTH CONCUBINE . . . . . .     10   3 DON JUAN  6     8    8
   THAT ADDING TO THE ACCOUNT HIS HIGHNESS' YEARS . . .    10   3 DON JUAN  6     9    4
   SOME SAID HER YEARS WERE GETTING NIGH THEIR SUMMER .    23   3 DON JUAN  6    35    5
   CERTAINLY AGED--WHAT HER YEARS MIGHT BE . . . . . .     41   3 DON JUAN  6    69    3
   A PLEASANT THING TO YOUNG MEN AT THEIR YEARS . . . .    75   3 DON JUAN  7    18    6
   A FEMALE CHILD OF TEN YEARS TRIED TO STOOP . . . . .  157   3 DON JUAN  8    91    6
   BUT SIX OLD DAMSELS EACH OF SEVENTY YEARS . . . . .   177   3 DON JUAN  8   130    7
   BUT THOUGH YOUR YEARS AS MAN TEND FAST TO ZERO . . .  184   3 DON JUAN  9     2    7
   SUNS AS RAYS--WORLDS LIKE ATOMS--YEARS LIKE HOURS . . 189   3 DON JUAN  9    13    8
   AND WHO THAT RECOLLECTS YOUNG YEARS AND LOVES-- . .   228   3 DON JUAN 10     6    4
   SOME RECKON WOMEN BY THEIR SUNS OR YEARS . . . . .    230   3 DON JUAN 10    10    7
   SOME THIRTY YEARS BEFORE AT FAIR EIGHTEEN . . . . .   236   3 DON JUAN 10    24   V6
   OF HUMAN YEARS THAT HALF-WAY HOUSE THAT RUDE . . . .  238   3 DON JUAN 10    27    5
   BUT TO CONTINUE THOUGH HER YEARS WERE WANING . . . .  247   3 DON JUAN 10    47    4
```

YEARS   (CONTINUED)

	PAGE	VOL	CANTO		STANZA	LN
BUT SHE WAS YET BUT TEN YEARS OLD AND THEREFORE	250	3	DON JUAN	10	52	7
A GUARDIAN GREEN IN YEARS A WARD CONNECTED	252	3	DON JUAN	10	57	6
TO LOSE BY ONE MONTH'S FROST SOME TWENTY YEARS	253	3	DON JUAN	10	58	7
SEVEN YEARS (THE USUAL TERM OF TRANSPORTATION)	257	3	DON JUAN	10	66	6
FOR AFTER YEARS OF TRAVEL BY A BARD IN	262	3	DON JUAN	10	76	3
SOME YEARS BEFORE THE INCIDENTS RELATED	286	3	DON JUAN	11	37	8
IN TWICE FIVE YEARS THE GREATEST LIVING POET	296	3	DON JUAN	11	55	1
WHERE IS THE WORLD OF EIGHT YEARS PAST 'TWAS THERE--	306	3	DON JUAN	11	76	3
TALK NOT OF SEVENTY YEARS AS AGE IN SEVEN	309	3	DON JUAN	11	82	1
ALBEIT MY YEARS WERE LESS DISCREET THAN FEW	334	3	DON JUAN	12	38	4
AND PASSED (AT LEAST THE LATTER YEARS OF LIFE)	338	3	DON JUAN	12	47	7
TO LIKE THOUGH I HAVE BEEN SEVEN YEARS IN ITALY	350	3	DON JUAN	12	75	7
WITHIN THESE LATEST THOUSAND YEARS OR LATER	361	3	DON JUAN	13	7	4
IN YEARS HE HAD THE ADVANTAGE OF TIME'S SEQUEL	367	3	DON JUAN	13	20	3
THE GOTHIC BABEL OF A THOUSAND YEARS	381	3	DON JUAN	13	50	4
A MOMENT'S GOOD THING MAY HAVE COST THEM YEARS	408	3	DON JUAN	13	109	6
THESE FORTY DAYS' ADVANTAGE OF HER YEARS--	432	3	DON JUAN	14	52	1
AND YOU WILL FIND HER SUM OF YEARS IN PLENTY	433	3	DON JUAN	14	54	8
THERE WAS NO GREAT DISPARITY OF YEARS	447	3	DON JUAN	14	87	1
EARLY IN YEARS AND YET MORE INFANTINE	476	3	DON JUAN	15	45	1
AT SEVENTY YEARS HAD PHANTASIES LIKE THESE	494	3	DON JUAN	15	86	4
OPINIONS WEAR OUT IN SOME THOUSAND YEARS	496	3	DON JUAN	15	90	7
THAT IN THE COURSE OF SOME SIX THOUSAND YEARS	504	3	DON JUAN	16	7	2
OF LATE YEARS TO DISPENSE WITH COCKER'S RIGOURS	547	3	DON JUAN	16	98	7
RAY FADES ON RAY AS YEARS ON YEARS DEPART	554	3	DON JUAN	16	109	4
RAY FADES ON RAY AS YEARS ON YEARS DEPART	554	3	DON JUAN	16	109	4

YEASTY

THE OCEAN WHEN ITS YEASTY WAR IS WAGING	305	2	DON JUAN	3	58	3

YELL

THEN SOME LEAP'D OVERBOARD WITH DREADFUL YELL	184	2	DON JUAN	2	52	3
IN LIKE CHURCH BELLS WITH SIGH HOWL GROAN YELL PRAYER	141	3	DON JUAN	8	58	7
IN VAIN THE YELL OF VICTORY IS ROARED	155	3	DON JUAN	8	87	6

YELLOW

THE SUN SET AND UP ROSE THE YELLOW MOON	82	2	DON JUAN	1	113	1
ALTHOUGH HIS WOES HAD TURN'D HIM RATHER YELLOW	235	2	DON JUAN	2	148	8
AND ROUND THEM RAN A YELLOW BORDER TOO	308	2	DON JUAN	3	64	4
SHE WORE TWO JELICKS--ONE WAS OF PALE YELLOW	311	2	DON JUAN	3	70	2
NOW MY SERE FANCY FALLS INTO THE YELLOW	345	2	DON JUAN	4	3	5
AND ATAGHAN OF GOLD AND SHOES OF YELLOW	451	2	DON JUAN	5	68	V7
AS AUTUMN WINDS DISPERSE THE YELLOW LEAVES	155	3	DON JUAN	8	88	V3
OF YELLOW CASSIMERE WE MAY PRESUME	204	3	DON JUAN	9	43	6
WHICH THREATENS INUNDATIONS DEEP AND YELLOW	228	3	DON JUAN	10	7	4
AS WHAT IS LOST IN GREEN IS GAINED IN YELLOW	395	3	DON JUAN	13	77	8
THOUGHTS QUITE AS YELLOW BUT LESS CLEAR THAN AMBER	505	3	DON JUAN	16	11	4

YELLS

AND DROVE THEM WITH THEIR BRUTAL YELLS TO SEEK	158	3	DON JUAN	8	94	2

YERMOLOFF

NO WONDER THEN THAT YERMOLOFF OR MOMONOFF	206	3	DON JUAN	9	48	1

YESOUSKOI

O'ER WHICH LIEUTENANT COLONEL YESOUSKOI	150	3	DON JUAN	8	76	7

YESTERDAY

BUT YESTERDAY AND WHO HAD MIGHTIER BREATH	430	2	DON JUAN	5	36	3

YIELD

I WISH YOUR FATE MAY YIELD YE WHEN SHE CHOOSES	14	2	DON JUAN	D	8	3
COULD YIELD HIS SPIRIT THAT FOR WHICH IT PANTED	73	2	DON JUAN	1	96	4
A WONDROUS WARRIOR AGAINST THOSE WHO YIELD	151	2	DON JUAN	1	V 2	5
YIELD TO STERN TIME AND NATURE'S WRINKLING LAWS	219	2	DON JUAN	2	119	6
IF I COULD YIELD YOU ANY CONSOLATION	417	2	DON JUAN	5	13	7
I YIELD THUS FAR BUT SOON WILL BREAK THE CHARM	459	2	DON JUAN	5	82	5
SHE DEEMED HER LEAST COMMAND MUST YIELD DELIGHT	485	2	DON JUAN	5	128	3
PAST PRESENT AND TO COME--BUT ALL MAY YIELD	117	3	DON JUAN	8	12	7
HUMANITY MUST YIELD TO STEEL AND FLAME	139	3	DON JUAN	8	54	4
THIS CHIEFTAIN--SOMEHOW WOULD NOT YIELD AT ALL	163	3	DON JUAN	8	104	8
THE TOWN WAS TAKEN--WHETHER HE MIGHT YIELD	172	3	DON JUAN	8	122	1
YET I MUST OWN--ALTHOUGH IN THIS I YIELD	425	3	DON JUAN	14	35	3

YIELDED

WHICH YIELDED A DAY'S LIFE AND TO THEIR MIND	208	2	DON JUAN	2	99	4
YIELDED TO THE DEEP TWILIGHT'S PURPLE CHARM	253	2	DON JUAN	2	184	8
ALL PHANTASIES WHICH YIELDED JOY OR MIRTH	475	2	DON JUAN	5	112	3
THERE'S NOT A MOSLEM THAT HATH YIELDED SWORD	155	3	DON JUAN	8	87	2

YIELDING

YIELDING TO THEIR SMALL HANDS DRAWS BACK AGAIN	292	2	DON JUAN	3	32	8
'TIS ALL THE SAME TO ME I'M FOND OF YIELDING	397	2	DON JUAN	4	98	1
THEMSELVES ON SELDOM YIELDING TO TEMPTATION	327	3	DON JUAN	12	25	V7

YIELDS

AND LIFE YIELDS NOTHING FURTHER TO RECALL	90	2	DON JUAN	1	127	5
YIELDS HIM BUT VINEGAR FOR HIS REWARD--	297	3	DON JUAN	11	58	3

YOKE

OF THIS DELUSION STILL THE CHILLING YOKE	402	2	DON JUAN	4	106	V3
FOR THIS SUPERIOR YOKE OF HUMAN CATTLE	425	2	DON JUAN	5	28	8
THE GLOOMY CLOUDS WHICH O'ER IT AS A YOKE	266	3	DON JUAN	10	83	5
FROM FOREIGN YOKE TO FREE THE HELPLESS NATIVE--	363	3	DON JUAN	13	10	4

YOKED

HAS EVER PUZZLED FAITH WITHAL OR YOKED HER IN	377	3	DON JUAN	13	41	8

YOKES

AND PAIR THEIR RHYMES AS VENUS YOKES HER DOVES	411	2	DON JUAN	5	1	3
FAMOUS FOR MINES OF SALT AND YOKES OF IRON	253	3	DON JUAN	10	58	2

YON

DASH DOWN YON CUP OF SAMIAN WINE	326	2	DON JUAN	3	L 16	6

		PAGE	VOL	CANTO	STANZA	LN
YON	**(CONTINUED)**					
MEANTIME (YON OLD BLACK EUNUCH SEEMS TO EYE US)	.	423	2 DON JUAN	5	24	7
THE BREADTH OF PAVEMENT AND YON SHRINE WHERE FAME IS . . .	.	279	3 DON JUAN	11	24	5
YONDER						
A CERTAIN PRESS OR CUPBOARD NICHED IN YONDER	.	450	2 DON JUAN	5	66	6
YORE						
JUST AS THE SPARTAN LADIES DID OF YORE	.	36	2 DON JUAN	1	29	3
NOT AS OF YORE TO CARRY OFF AN IO	.	248	2 DON JUAN	2	174	7
WHOM THE GODS LOVE DIE YOUNG WAS SAID OF YORE	.	350	2 DON JUAN	4	12	1
MORE MODERN BUILDINGS AND THOSE BUILT OF YORE	.	443	2 DON JUAN	5	57	6
MORE THAN YOU SCORN THE SAVAGES OF YORE	.	180	3 DON JUAN	8	136	7
WHICH FOR WHAT I KNOW MAY OF YORE HAVE LED	.	441	3 DON JUAN	14	72	3
EVEN FROM OUR GRAMMAR UPWARDS FRIENDS OF YORE	.	542	3 DON JUAN	16	86	5
YORICK'S						
AND SIGH I CAN'T GET OUT LIKE YORICK'S STARLING	.	404	2 DON JUAN	4	109	4
YORK						
WITH THE YORK' MAIL--BUT ONWARD AS WE ROLL	.	263	3 DON JUAN	10	78	7
BY DRIVING THE YORK MAIL--BUT AH MY SINKING SOUL	.	263	3 DON JUAN	10	78	V7
YOU'D						
WHICH MAKES ME WISH YOU'D CHANGE YOUR LAKES FOR OCEAN . .	.	12	2 DON JUAN	D	5	8
AND ALSO OF HIS MOTHER IF YOU'D RATHER	.	25	2 DON JUAN	1	7	8
YOU'D BEST BEGIN WITH TRUTH AND WHEN YOU'VE LOST YOUR . .	.	91	2 DON JUAN	1	128	7
YOU'D WISH YOURSELF WHERE TRUTH IS--IN A WELL	.	201	2 DON JUAN	2	84	8
THEN IF YOU'D HAVE THEM WEDDED PLEASE TO SHUT	.	282	2 DON JUAN	3	12	5
YOU'D BETTER ASK OUR MISTRESS WHO'S HIS HEIR	.	297	2 DON JUAN	3	43	6
THEY HIRED HIM THOUGH TO HEAR HIM YOU'D BELIEVE	.	391	2 DON JUAN	4	87	7
AND AS YOU'D HAVE ME PARDON YOUR PAST SCORNING--	.	494	2 DON JUAN	5	145	6
THE RAMPART HIGHER THAN YOU'D WISH TO HANG	.	72	3 DON JUAN	7	11	4
JUST AS YOU'D BREAK A SUCKING SALAMANDER	.	93	3 DON JUAN	7	52	5
AMONG THE FOREMOST BUT IF YOU'D EXPRESS	.	100	3 DON JUAN	7	65	6
HAD PALISADOED IN A WAY YOU'D WONDER	.	136	3 DON JUAN	8	46	4
SUCH DIFFERENCE DOTH A FEW MONTHS MAKE YOU'D THINK . .	.	228	3 DON JUAN	10	7	5
WITH THE SAME FEELINGS AS YOU'D COAX A VAMPIRE	.	299	3 DON JUAN	11	62	5
YOU'DE						
YOU'DE SWEAR HIS VERY HEART HAD SWEATED THROUGH	.	154	2 DON JUAN	1 V	5	8
I WISH TO GOD YOU'DE DRESS US SOME SUCH PARTRIDGES . . .	.	485	3 DON JUAN	15	67	V8
YOU'LL						
ONLY ANOTHER TIME I TRUST YOU'LL TELL US	.	106	2 DON JUAN	1	156	5
YOU'LL LOSE YOUR LIFE AND I SHALL LOSE MY PLACE . . .	.	115	2 DON JUAN	1	171	7
SOME HOCK AND SODA-WATER THEN YOU'LL KNOW	.	251	2 DON JUAN	2	180	2
WOMAN OR WINE YOU'LL HAVE TO UNDERGO	.	357	2 DON JUAN	4	25	2
YOU'LL PARDON TO MY MUSE A FEW SHORT NAPS	.	503	2 DON JUAN	5	159	8
SO PICK AND CHUSE--PERHAPS YOU'LL BE CONTENT	.	40	3 DON JUAN	6	68	7
YOU'LL FIND TEN THOUSAND HANDSOME COXCOMBS BLOODY . . .	.	167	3 DON JUAN	8	112	8
YOU'LL DEEM NO DOUBT THEY PUT IT TO A GOOD USE	.	242	3 DON JUAN	10	36	8
YOU'LL MOUNT WITH OUR YOUNG HERO THE CONVEYANCE . . .	.	248	3 DON JUAN	10	49	3
A SCOUNDREL AND YOU'LL HAVE GOOD COMPANY	.	310	3 DON JUAN	11	86	V8
BECAUSE YOU'LL SAY NOUGHT CALLS FOR SUCH A TRIAL-- . .	.	319	3 DON JUAN	12	7	7
I THINK YOU'LL FIND FROM MANY A FAMILY PICTURE	.	337	3 DON JUAN	12	46	3
PERHAPS YOU'LL HAVE A LETTER FROM THE MOTHER	.	343	3 DON JUAN	12	60	1
PERHAPS YOU'LL HAVE A VISIT FROM THE BROTHER	.	343	3 DON JUAN	12	60	3
YOU'LL ADD TO MATRIMONY'S LIST OF CURES	.	343	3 DON JUAN	12	60	8
ASK A BLIND MAN THE BEST JUDGE YOU'LL ATTACK . ; . .	.	348	3 DON JUAN	12	71	4
AND AS FOR CHASTITY YOU'LL NEVER BIND IT	.	352	3 DON JUAN	12	80	5
YOU'LL FIND IT OF A DIFFERENT CONSTRUCTION	.	356	3 DON JUAN	12	87	3
YOU'LL NEVER GUESS I'LL BET YOU MILLIONS MILLIARDS-- . .	.	454	3 DON JUAN	14	100	7
TO JEST YOU'LL CHOOSE SOME OTHER THEME JUST NOW	.	516	3 DON JUAN	16	37	6
YOUNG						
DABBLING ITS SLEEK YOUNG HANDS IN ERIN'S GORE	.	16	2 DON JUAN	D	12	2
THEIR SENSES THEY'D HAVE SENT YOUNG MASTER FORTH . . .	.	34	2 DON JUAN	1	25	6
YOUNG JUAN WAX'D IN GOODLINESS AND GRACE	.	48	2 DON JUAN	1	49	1
HER YOUNG PHILOSOPHER WAS GROWN ALREADY	.	49	2 DON JUAN	1	50	8
YOUNG JUAN NOW WAS SIXTEEN YEARS OF AGE	.	51	2 DON JUAN	1	54	1
OF WHICH YOUNG PASSION CANNOT BE BEREFT	.	62	2 DON JUAN	1	74	6
I RECOMMEND YOUNG LADIES TO MAKE TRIAL	.	64	2 DON JUAN	1	78	8
BETWEEN YOUNG PERSONS WITHOUT ANY DANGER	.	65	2 DON JUAN	1	80	2
IN YOUNG DON JUAN'S FAVOUR AND TO HIM ITS	.	65	2 DON JUAN	1	81	3
YOUNG JUAN WANDER'D BY THE GLASSY BROOKS	.	70	2 DON JUAN	1	90	1
'TWAS STRANGE THAT ONE SO YOUNG SHOULD THUS CONCERN . .	.	71	2 DON JUAN	1	93	5
YOUNG HOPEFUL'S MISTRESS OR MISS FANNY'S LOVER	.	75	2 DON JUAN	1	100	4
HIS YOUNG LIP THANK'D IT WITH A GRATEFUL KISS	.	81	2 DON JUAN	1	112	3
I HOPE HE'S YOUNG AND HANDSOME--IS HE TALL	.	105	2 DON JUAN	1	154	6
OR FOR SO YOUNG A HUSBAND'S JEALOUS FEARS--	.	106	2 DON JUAN	1	155	3
SMALL PITY HAD HE FOR THE YOUNG AND FAIR	.	109	2 DON JUAN	1	160	6
AND TREATING A YOUNG WIFE WITH SO MUCH RIGOUR	.	110	2 DON JUAN	1	161	4
YOUNG JUAN SLIPP'D HALF-SMOTHER'D FROM THE BED	.	112	2 DON JUAN	1	165	8
YOUNG SLENDER AND PACK'D EASILY HE LAY	.	112	2 DON JUAN	1	166	3
PRESCRIBED BY WAY OF BLISTER A YOUNG BELLE	.	113	2 DON JUAN	1	168	4
HIS BLOOD WAS UP THOUGH YOUNG HE WAS A TARTAR	.	122	2 DON JUAN	1	184	7
I HAVE NO FURTHER CLAIM ON YOUNG YOUNG HEART	.	130	2 DON JUAN	1	192	3
ARE THESE THE DREAMS HIS YOUNG AMBITION SAW	.	155	2 DON JUAN	1 V	7	3
WITH HIS YOUNG WIFE--A TIME AND OPPORTUNITY	.	158	2 DON JUAN	2	3	8
'TWAS FOR A VOYAGE THAT THE YOUNG MAN WAS MEANT . . .	.	161	2 DON JUAN	2	8	5
YOUNG MEN SHOULD TRAVEL IF BUT TO AMUSE	.	165	2 DON JUAN	2	16	5
AND ONE OAR FOR A MAST WHICH A YOUNG LAD	.	181	2 DON JUAN	2	48	5
IN MY YOUNG DAYS THEY LENT ME CASH THAT WAY	.	190	2 DON JUAN	2	65	7
HOW LONG IN HIS DAMP TRANCE YOUNG JUAN LAY	.	214	2 DON JUAN	2	111	1
YOUNG YET HER ELDER AND OF BROW LESS GRAVE	.	216	2 DON JUAN	2	115	3
YOUNG JUAN SLEPT ALL DREAMLESS--BUT THE MAID	.	228	2 DON JUAN	2	135	1

933

YOUNG   (CONTINUED)

	PAGE	VOL	CANTO	STANZA	LV
AND THE YOUNG BEAMS OF THE EXCLUDED SUN	229	2	DON JUAN 2	137	4
AND YOUNG AURORA KISS'D HER LIPS WITH DEW	232	2	DON JUAN 2	142	4
ALTHOUGH HE LISTEN'D SO THAT THE YOUNG GREEK IN	241	2	DON JUAN 2	161	3
WHEN BOTH THE TEACHER AND THE TAUGHT ARE YOUNG	242	2	DON JUAN 2	164	3
WITH A YOUNG BENEFACTRESS--SO WAS SHE	244	2	DON JUAN 2	167	7
BOTH WERE SO YOUNG AND ONE SO INNOCENT	247	2	DON JUAN 2	172	1
ON WHICH LIKE A YOUNG FLOWER SNAPP'D FROM THE STALK	249	2	DON JUAN 2	176	5
AND ONE WAS INNOCENT BUT BOTH TOO YOUNG	254	2	DON JUAN 2	187	V8
AND FLEW TO HER YOUNG MATE LIKE A YOUNG BIRD	257	2	DON JUAN 2	190	6
AND FLEW TO HER YOUNG MATE LIKE A YOUNG BIRD	257	2	DON JUAN 2	190	6
ALAS THEY WERE SO YOUNG SO BEAUTIFUL	258	2	DON JUAN 2	192	1
AND THEY WERE HAPPY FOR TO THEIR YOUNG EYES	265	2	DON JUAN 2	204	7
PROFUSION WITH YOUNG BEAUTY COVERS O'ER	269	2	DON JUAN 2	211	4
AND LOVED BY A YOUNG HEART TOO DEEPLY BLEST	274	2	DON JUAN 3	1	4
TO HIS MEMORY AND TWO OR THREE YOUNG MISSES	287	2	DON JUAN 3	23	6
THAT LURES TO FLAY ALIVE THE YOUNG BEGINNER	294	2	DON JUAN 3	36	6
TO OFFER HIS YOUNG PINION AS HER FAN	313	2	DON JUAN 3	73	8
IF NOT LIKE ORPHEUS QUITE WHEN GREECE WAS YOUNG	326	2	DON JUAN 3	87	3
TO THE YOUNG BIRD THE PARENT'S BROODING WINGS	338	2	DON JUAN 3	107	3
YOUNG JUAN AND HIS LADY-LOVE WERE LEFT	348	2	DON JUAN 4	8	1
WHOM THE GODS LOVE DIE YOUNG WAS SAID OF YORE	350	2	DON JUAN 4	12	1
YOUNG INNATE FEELINGS ALL HAVE FELT BELOW	353	2	DON JUAN 4	18	5
NO NOVELS E'ER HAD SET THEIR YOUNG HEARTS BLEEDING	354	2	DON JUAN 4	19	4
PUT UP YOUNG MAN PUT UP YOUR SILLY SWORD	364	2	DON JUAN 4	37	8
YOUNG MAN YOUR SWORD SO LAMBRO ONCE MORE SAID	365	2	DON JUAN 4	40	1
THIS HOUR WERE THINE--AND THY YOUNG MINION'S LAST	368	2	DON JUAN 4	46	V8
HANDSOME AND YOUNG ENJOYING ALL THE PRESENT	371	2	DON JUAN 4	51	4
FOR SHE GOT HOLD OF A YOUNG FOREIGN NINNY	390	2	DON JUAN 4	84	V5
MY OWN MERITS AND THOUGH YOUNG--I SEE SIR--YOU	392	2	DON JUAN 4	88	2
FOR HUMAN VANITY THE YOUNG DEFOIX	400	2	DON JUAN 4	103	4
BUT FOR THE DESTINY OF THIS YOUNG TROOP	409	2	DON JUAN 4	116	1
JUAN WAS YOUNG--HAD COURAGE--AND WAS FULL	415	2	DON JUAN 5	8	V1
LOT OF SO YOUNG A PARTNER IN THE WOE	417	2	DON JUAN 5	12	6
YE WHO HAVE KEPT YOUR CHASTITY WHEN YOUNG	486	2	DON JUAN 5	130	2
OF A YOUNG DOWNRIGHT BEAUTY IN THIS CASE	486	2	DON JUAN 5	130	8
A TIGRESS ROBBED OF YOUNG A LIONESS	487	2	DON JUAN 5	132	1
FOR WHAT IS STEALING YOUNG ONES FEW OR MANY	487	2	DON JUAN 5	132	7
YOUNG BEAUTIFUL AND DARING--WHO WOULD RISK	7	3	DON JUAN 6	3	2
YOUNG WOMEN AND CORRECT THEM WHEN THEY BLUNDERED	21	3	DON JUAN 6	31	8
AND I OF YOUR YOUNG CHARGE WILL TAKE DUE CARE	29	3	DON JUAN 6	47	5
THAT JUST AS HER YOUNG LIP BEGAN TO OPE	44	3	DON JUAN 6	77	5
THAT THE YOUNG STRANGER SHOULD NOT LIE ALONE	46	3	DON JUAN 6	81	4
A PLEASANT THING TO YOUNG MEN AT THEIR YEARS	75	3	DON JUAN 7	18	6
THEN THERE WERE FRENCHMEN GALLANT YOUNG AND GAY	77	3	DON JUAN 7	22	1
IN WHICH HE WAS OPPOSED BY YOUNG AND HOARY	83	3	DON JUAN 7	35	5
AND THIS YOUNG FELLOW SAY WHAT CAN HE DO	98	3	DON JUAN 7	62	5
THEIR ARMS AS HENS THEIR WINGS ABOUT THEIR YOUNG	101	3	DON JUAN 7	67	8
WHICH NOW IS LEAGUED YOUNG FREEDOM TO ANNOY	106	3	DON JUAN 7	79	7
AFFLICTING YOUNG FOLKS WITH A SORT OF DIZZINESS	108	3	DON JUAN 7	83	8
NO CAESAR BUT A FINE YOUNG LAD WHO FOUGHT	126	3	DON JUAN 8	29	2
AND LEFT AT LARGE LIKE A YOUNG HEIR TO MAKE	127	3	DON JUAN 8	32	2
(AS PISTOL CALLS IT) BUT A YOUNG LIVONIAN	140	3	DON JUAN 8	56	8
WHOSE YOUNG UNAWAKENED WORLD WAS EVER NEW	145	3	DON JUAN 8	65	3
AND WHAT THEY PLEASED TO DO WITH THE YOUNG KHAN	167	3	DON JUAN 8	112	1
BUT DOUBTLESS THEY PREFER A FINE YOUNG MAN	167	3	DON JUAN 8	112	3
THUS THE YOUNG KHAN WITH HOURIS IN HIS SIGHT	168	3	DON JUAN 8	114	1
THOUGHT NOT UPON THE CHARMS OF FOUR YOUNG BRIDES	168	3	DON JUAN 8	114	2
UNTO THE BAYONETS WHICH HAD PIERCED HIS YOUNG	170	3	DON JUAN 8	118	6
IN FACT YOUR GRACE IS STILL BUT A YOUNG HERO	184	3	DON JUAN 9	2	8
THAT ONE LIFE SAVED ESPECIALLY IF YOUNG	199	3	DON JUAN 9	34	2
HOW WILL--TO THESE YOUNG PEOPLE JUST THRUST OUT	202	3	DON JUAN 9	40	1
WHILE HER YOUNG HERALD KNELT BEFORE HER STILL	215	3	DON JUAN 9	66	4
INQUIRED WHO WAS THIS VERY NEW YOUNG MAN	222	3	DON JUAN 9	79	2
ROUND THE YOUNG MAN WITH THEIR CONGRATULATIONS	223	3	DON JUAN 9	82	4
OUR YOUNG LIEUTENANT TO THE GENIAL CARE	224	3	DON JUAN 9	84	2
AND WHO THAT RECOLLECTS YOUNG YEARS AND LOVES--	228	3	DON JUAN 10	6	4
MIDDLE-AGED LADIES EVEN MORE THAN YOUNG	230	3	DON JUAN 10	10	2
THEY CANNOT QUENCH YOUNG FEELINGS FRESH AND EARLY	234	3	DON JUAN 10	19	6
YOUNG PEOPLE AT HIS TIME OF LIFE SHOULD BE ABLE	235	3	DON JUAN 10	22	3
A YOUNG LIEUTENANT'S WITH A NOT OLD QUEEN	236	3	DON JUAN 10	24	4
UNTO AN EMPRESS WHO PREFERRED YOUNG MEN	241	3	DON JUAN 10	33	2
FOR CAUSES YOUNG OR OLD THE CANKER-WORM	243	3	DON JUAN 10	38	2
YOU'LL MOUNT WITH OUR YOUNG HERO THE CONVEYANCE	248	3	DON JUAN 10	49	6
WHAT EVEN YOUNG STRANGERS FEEL A LITTLE STRONG	257	3	DON JUAN 10	65	3
JUAN THOUGH CARELESS YOUNG AND MAGNIFIQUE	259	3	DON JUAN 10	70	1
DON JUAN OUR YOUNG DIPLOMATIC SINNER	282	3	DON JUAN 11	29	6
YOUNG HANDSOME AND ACCOMPLISHED WHO WAS SAID	283	3	DON JUAN 11	32	7
OUR HERO AS A HERO YOUNG AND HANDSOME	305	3	DON JUAN 11	74	1
I WISH THEY KNEW THE LIFE OF A YOUNG NOBLE	305	3	DON JUAN 11	74	8
THEY ARE YOUNG BUT KNOW NOT YOUTH--IT IS ANTICIPATED	306	3	DON JUAN 11	75	1
WHERE IS THE WORLD CRIES YOUNG AT EIGHTY WHERE	306	3	DON JUAN 11	76	1
TOO OLD FOR YOUTH--TOO YOUNG AT THIRTY-FIVE	316	3	DON JUAN 12	2	1
YOU HAD REASON--'TWAS THAT A YOUNG CHILD OF GRACE	329	3	DON JUAN 12	29	2
THAT THE YOUNG LADY MADE A MONSTROUS CHOICE	334	3	DON JUAN 12	38	8
FOR LIKE A DAY-DAWN SHE WAS YOUNG AND PURE	335	3	DON JUAN 12	41	2
OLDEN SHE WAS--BUT HAD BEEN VERY YOUNG	336	3	DON JUAN 12	43	1
AS WHO HAS NOT IF FEMALE YOUNG AND PRETTY	338	3	DON JUAN 12	47	2
SHE WAS THE MILD REPROVER OF THE YOUNG	338	3	DON JUAN 12	48	2
A YOUNG UNMARRIED MAN WITH A GOOD NAME	342	3	DON JUAN 12	58	1

		PAGE	VOL		CANTO	STANZA	LN
YOUNG	(CONTINUED)						
	YOUNG MEN WHO--THOUGH THEY HATED TO DISCUSS	344	3	DON JUAN	12	61	3
	MOST YOUNG BEGINNERS MAY BE TAKEN SO	345	3	DON JUAN	12	63	V5
	BUT IN OLD ENGLAND WHEN A YOUNG BRIDE ERRS	345	3	DON JUAN	12	64	7
	COUNTRY WHERE A YOUNG COUPLE OF THE SAME AGES	346	3	DON JUAN	12	65	2
	BUT COMING YOUNG FROM LANDS AND SCENES ROMANTIC	347	3	DON JUAN	12	68	1
	BECAUSE THOUGH YOUNG HE ACQUIESCED WITH SUAVITY	368	3	DON JUAN	13	22	3
	AND YOUNG BEGINNERS MAY AS WELL COMMENCE	376	3	DON JUAN	13	40	1
	THERE WAS THE YOUNG BARD RACKRHYME WHO HAD NEWLY	398	3	DON JUAN	13	84	5
	OR HUNT THE YOUNG BECAUSE THEY LIKED THE SPORT--	405	3	DON JUAN	13	101	2
	ESPECIALLY WHEN YOUNG FOR THAT'S ESSENTIAL	418	3	DON JUAN	14	20	4
	IN MY YOUNG DAYS THAT CHASTE AND GOODLY VEIL	422	3	DON JUAN	14	27	2
	FOR A YOUNG GENTLEMAN'S FIT EDUCATION	432	3	DON JUAN	14	52	6
	THE SORT OF THING TO TURN A YOUNG MAN'S HEAD	438	3	DON JUAN	14	64	1
	THAT YOUNG MEN RARELY MADE MONASTIC VOWS	439	3	DON JUAN	14	67	6
	LESS LIKE A YOUNG WIFE THAN AN AGED SISTER	440	3	DON JUAN	14	69	8
	HER HUSBAND'S FRIEND HER OWN YOUNG AND A STRANGER	449	3	DON JUAN	14	91	8
	AURORA RABY A YOUNG STAR WHO SHONE	475	3	DON JUAN	15	43	5
	IN ITS OWN STRENGTH--MOST STRANGE IN ONE SO YOUNG	477	3	DON JUAN	15	47	8
	WINES TOO WHICH MIGHT AGAIN HAVE SLAIN YOUNG AMMON--	484	3	DON JUAN	15	65	3
	(THERE'S FAME) YOUNG PARTRIDGE' FILLETS DECK'D WITH TRUFFLES	484	3	DON JUAN	15	66	8
	WAS VERY YOUNG ALTHOUGH SO VERY SAGE	494	3	DON JUAN	15	85	2
	HE DRESSED AND LIKE YOUNG PEOPLE HE WAS WONT	513	3	DON JUAN	16	29	1
	AND A YOUNG RACE-HORSE OF OLD PEDIGREE	527	3	DON JUAN	16	55	7
	THEY WONDERED HOW A YOUNG MAN SO ABSURD	543	3	DON JUAN	16	89	5
YOUNGER							
	THE YOUNGER PORTION STOOD--A LUCKLESS VICTIM	409	2	DON JUAN	4	116	V7
	AS THEY BEHELD THE YOUNGER CAST SOME LEERS	221	3	DON JUAN	9	78	4
	HAVE TAKEN UP AT LENGTH WITH YOUNGER BROTHERS	308	3	DON JUAN	11	81	2
	HINT THAT 'TIS TIME TO GIVE THE YOUNGER PLACE	360	3	DON JUAN	13	4	8
	SHE TOOK UP WITH SOME FOREIGN YOUNGER BROTHER	474	3	DON JUAN	15	42	7
	ALSO THE YOUNGER MEN TOO FOR A SPRINGALD	487	3	DON JUAN	15	70	5
YOUNGEST							
	BUT THE TWO YOUNGEST LOVED MORE TO BE SET	408	3	DON JUAN	13	107	6
YOUNGLING							
	AND MAKE THE WORLDING SNEER THE YOUNGLING WEEP	555	3	DON JUAN	16	110	8
YOUNGSTER							
	THAT THEY AS EASILY MIGHT DO THE YOUNGSTER	285	3	DON JUAN	11	35	7
YOUNGSTERS							
	AS WERE SOME HUNDRED YOUNGSTERS ALL ABREAST	140	3	DON JUAN	8	56	3
YOU'RE							
	BOB SOUTHEY YOU'RE A POET--POET-LAUREATE	9	2	DON JUAN	D	1	1
	YOU'RE SHABBY FELLOWS--TRUE--BUT POETS STILL	12	2	DON JUAN	D	6	7
	OF POETS AND ROMANCERS--YOU'RE A BORE	84	2	DON JUAN	1	116	6
	OH PLEASURE YOU'RE INDEED A PLEASANT THING	85	2	DON JUAN	1	119	1
	YOU'RE WRONG--HE WAS THE MILDEST MANNER'D MAN	296	3	DON JUAN	3	41	1
	YOU'RE RIGHT ON BOTH ACCOUNTS TO HOLD YOUR TONGUE	419	2	DON JUAN	5	16	7
	AND THEN I'M WITH YOU IF YOU'RE FOR A ROW	437	2	DON JUAN	5	47	8
	AND BLACK SILK NECKCLOTH--AND REPLIED YOU'RE RIGHT	161	3	DON JUAN	8	99	7
	YET YOU'RE A NOBLE FELLOW AND BUT WAIT	185	3	DON JUAN	9	6	V1
	WHETHER YOU'RE PAID BY GOVERNMENT IN BRIBES	200	3	DON JUAN	9	35	4
YOUR'S							
	OUR HERO (AND I TRUST KIND READER YOUR'S) --	194	3	DON JUAN	9	23	1
	JUST NOW YOUR'S WERE CUT OUT IN DIFFERENT SECTIONS	215	3	DON JUAN	9	65	5
YOUTH							
	TO MEET THE INGENUOUS YOUTH OF FUTURE AGES	46	2	DON JUAN	1	45	4
	HER CHEEK ALL PURPLE WITH THE BEAM OF YOUTH	55	2	DON JUAN	1	61	4
	CHANGED FOR THE DAME GREW DISTANT THE YOUTH SHY	60	2	DON JUAN	1	70	2
	AND LOVE IS TAUGHT HYPOCRISY FROM YOUTH	61	2	DON JUAN	1	72	8
	SHE THOUGHT OF HER OWN STRENGTH AND JUAN'S YOUTH	78	2	DON JUAN	1	107	1
	WHO'VE MADE US YOUTH WAIT TOO--TOO LONG ALREADY	89	2	DON JUAN	1	125	4
	I YET HAVE CHOSEN FROM OUT THE YOUTH OF SEVILLE	102	2	DON JUAN	1	148	2
	IN MY HOT YOUTH--WHEN GEORGE THE THIRD WAS KING	143	2	DON JUAN	1	212	8
	IS GLITTERING YOUTH WHICH I HAVE SPENT BETIMES--	145	2	DON JUAN	1	217	7
	YOU'VE PASS'D YOUR YOUTH NOT SO UNPLEASANTLY	147	2	DON JUAN	1	220	5
	OH YE WHO TEACH THE INGENUOUS YOUTH OF NATIONS	157	2	DON JUAN	2	1	1
	AND CHAFING HIM THE SOFT WARM HAND OF YOUTH	215	2	DON JUAN	2	113	3
	A FISHERMAN HE HAD BEEN IN HIS YOUTH	222	2	DON JUAN	2	125	1
	AND THAT A SHIPWRECK'D YOUTH WOULD HUNGRY BE	233	2	DON JUAN	2	145	2
	A LONG LONG KISS A KISS OF YOUTH AND LOVE	254	2	DON JUAN	2	186	1
	AND YOUTH STILL WEEPS THE TENDER TEARS THAT PLEASE--	273	2	DON JUAN	2	V 2	4
	AND SINGING AS HE SUNG IN HIS WARM YOUTH	318	2	DON JUAN	3	83	7
	LIKE TITUS' YOUTH AND CAESAR'S EARLIEST ACTS	329	2	DON JUAN	3	92	3
	THE DEATH OF FRIENDSHIP LOVE YOUTH ALL THAT IS	350	2	DON JUAN	4	12	4
	AN OPIUM DREAM OF TOO MUCH YOUTH AND READING	354	2	DON JUAN	4	19	2
	A MOMENT AT THE EUROPEAN YOUTH	387	2	DON JUAN	4	78	4
	HAVING WITHSTOOD TEMPTATION IN MY YOUTH	397	2	DON JUAN	4	97	2
	HIS YOUTH AND FEATURES FAVOURED THE DISGUISE	477	2	DON JUAN	5	115	1
	TO EDUCATE--YE YOUTH OF EUROPE--YOU BY	486	2	DON JUAN	5	131	6
	FOR NO ONE SAVE IN VERY EARLY YOUTH	14	3	DON JUAN	6	16	3
	IN EARLY YOUTH TO TURN A LADY'S MAID--	37	3	DON JUAN	6	62	4
	THAT HE HIMSELF FELT ONLY LIKE A YOUTH	69	3	DON JUAN	7	5	7
	HAD BEEN AS SHORT IN YOUTH AS INDIGESTION	84	3	DON JUAN	7	36	4
	OF BRITAIN'S YOUTH DEPENDS UPON THEIR WEIGHT	140	3	DON JUAN	8	55	4
	THOUGH BEAUTIFUL IN YOUTH HIS CARNAL SKIN--	188	3	DON JUAN	9	12	V7
	MADE UP BY YOUTH FAME AND AN ARMY TAILOR--	204	3	DON JUAN	9	44	2
	BEHOLD HIM PLACED IN YOUTH AND GLORY'S PILLORY	204	3	DON JUAN	9	44	V7
	HER MAJESTY WHO LIKED TO GAZE ON YOUTH	213	3	DON JUAN	9	61	6
	WITH YOUTH AND HEALTH ALL KISSES ARE HEAVEN-KISSING	215	3	DON JUAN	9	66	8
	HER MAJESTY LOOKED DOWN THE YOUTH LOOKED UP--	216	3	DON JUAN	9	67	1

YOUTH   (CONTINUED)
```
    WHICH YOUTH WOULD NOT ACT ILL TO KEEP IN MIND) . . .  .  .  224  3 DON JUAN  9    84   5
    OF YOUTH AND VIGOUR BEAUTY AND THOSE THINGS . . .  .  .  227  3 DON JUAN 10     5   7
    SEDUCED BY YOUTH AND DANGEROUS EXAMPLES . . .  .  .  .  236  3 DON JUAN 10    23   2
    OF AGE AND LOOKING BACK TO YOUTH GIVE ONE TEAR-- .  .  .  238  3 DON JUAN 10    27   8
    MUCH TO HIS YOUTH AND MUCH TO HIS REPORTED .  .  .  .  239  3 DON JUAN 10    29   3
    THOSE PLEASURES AFTER WHICH WILD YOUTH WILL HANKER  .  .  240  3 DON JUAN 10    31   6
    HIS YOUTH AND CONSTITUTION BORE HIM THROUGH .  .  .  .  245  3 DON JUAN 10    43   3
    HIS YOUTH WAS NOT THE CHASTEST THAT MIGHT BE  .  .  .  251  3 DON JUAN 10    54   6
    TELL THEM THAT YOUTH ONCE GONE RETURNS NO MORE .  .  .  267  3 DON JUAN 10    86   3
    THE PAINTING AND THE PAINTED YOUTH CERUSE .  .  .  .  293  3 DON JUAN 11    48   4
    THEY ARE YOUNG BUT KNOW NOT YOUTH--IT IS ANTICIPATED . .  306  3 DON JUAN 11    75   1
    TOO OLD FOR YOUTH--TOO YOUNG AT THIRTY-FIVE . .  .  .  316  3 DON JUAN 12     2   1
    AND THAT'S ENOUGH SUCCEEDED IN MY YOUTH . .  .  .  .  324  3 DON JUAN 12    17   2
    WHICH CAN AWAIT WARM YOUTH IN ITS WILD RACE . .  .  .  326  3 DON JUAN 12    23   4
    THAT LADIES IN THEIR YOUTH A LITTLE GAY .  .  .  .  .  336  3 DON JUAN 12    44   4
    CHANGES IN YOUTH TO BE SURPRISED AT ANY . .  .  .  .  338  3 DON JUAN 12    49   8
    AND THESE VICISSITUDES TELL BEST IN YOUTH .  .  .  .  339  3 DON JUAN 12    50   1
    BY SPECIOUS SEEMING JUAN'S YOUTH AND PATIENCE .  .  .  365  3 DON JUAN 13    15   5
    FORBIDS  A GREAT IMPRESSION IN MY YOUTH . .  .  .  .  403  3 DON JUAN 13    96   6
    YOUTH FADES AND LEAVES OUR DAYS NO LONGER SUNNY  .  .  405  3 DON JUAN 13   100   5
    IN YOUTH I WROTE BECAUSE MY MIND WAS FULL . .  .  .  415  3 DON JUAN 14    10   7
    OF HUNTING--FOR THE SAGEST YOUTH IS FRAIL . .  .  .  424  3 DON JUAN 14    33   6
    AND (AS HER JUNIOR BY SIX WEEKS) HIS YOUTH  .  .  .  432  3 DON JUAN 14    51   8
    THAT TIME WOULD TEMPER JUAN'S FAULTS OF YOUTH .  .  .  439  3 DON JUAN 14    67   5
    THAT IN OUR YOUTH AS DANGEROUS A PASSION . .  .  .  454  3 DON JUAN 14   100   2
    FEELINGS OF YOUTH LIKE THOSE WHICH OVERTHROWN LIE  .  .  475  3 DON JUAN 15    44   5
    ALL YOUTH--BUT WITH AN ASPECT BEYOND TIME . .  .  .  476  3 DON JUAN 15    45   4
    OF RANK AND YOUTH THOUGH PURER THAN THE REST  .  .  .  480  3 DON JUAN 15    55   4
    A MODE ADOPTED SINCE BY MODERN YOUTH . .  .  .  .  501  3 DON JUAN 16     1   4
    SINCE--SINCE--IN YOUTH I HAD THE SAD MISHAP--  .  .  .  530  3 DON JUAN 16    61   5
```
YOUTHFUL
```
    JUAN TO LAVE HIS YOUTHFUL LIMBS WAS WONT . .  .  .  .  211  2 DON JUAN  2   105   2
    SINCE AFTER ALL NO DOUBT THE YOUTHFUL PAIR .  .  .  .  233  2 DON JUAN  2   144   6
    THAT EVER MADE A YOUTHFUL HEART LESS STEADY .  .  .  246  2 DON JUAN  2   171   3
    FEW YOUTHFUL MINDS CAN STAND THE STRONG CONCUSSION  .  235  3 DON JUAN 10    21   3
    BUT ONE WHO IS NOT SO YOUTHFUL AS SHE WAS . .  .  .  236  3 DON JUAN 10    24   5
```
YOUTH'S
```
    HER PASSIONS HAD ARISEN AND HER YOUTH'S FLOWER .  .  .  262  2 DON JUAN  2   198  V5
    WHILE YOUTH'S HOT WISHES IN OUR RED VEINS REVEL  .  .  345  2 DON JUAN  4     2   5
```
YOU'VE
```
    YOU'D BEST BEGIN WITH TRUTH AND WHEN YOU'VE LOST YOUR . 91  2 DON JUAN  1   128   7
    YOU'VE MADE THE APARTMENT IN A FIT CONDITION--  .  .  104  2 DON JUAN  1   152   3
    YOU'VE PASS'D YOUR YOUTH NOT SO UNPLEASANTLY  .  .  .  147  2 DON JUAN  1   220   5
    YOU'VE HEARD OF RAUCOCANTI--I'M THE MAN  .  .  .  .  392  2 DON JUAN  4    88   5
    I SEE YOU'VE BOUGHT ANOTHER GIRL 'TIS PITY .  .  .  .  500  2 DON JUAN  5   155   7
    AFTER THE HARDSHIPS YOU'VE ALREADY BORNE .  .  .  .  98  3 DON JUAN  7    62   4
    I AM NO FLATTERER--YOU'VE SUPPED FULL OF FLATTERY  .  .  185  3 DON JUAN  9     5   1
```
ZANY
```
    THE PASSION WHICH MADE SOLOMON A ZANY .  .  .  .  .  452  3 DON JUAN 14    95   4
```
ZEAL
```
    TO NEWSPAPERS--SERMONS WHICH THE ZEAL .  .  .  .  .  138  2 DON JUAN  1   203  V3
    THEIR LOYAL ZEAL AND RENEGADO VIGOUR  .  .  .  .  .  330  2 DON JUAN  3    94  V3
```
ZEALOUS
```
    A RIGID GUARDIAN OR A ZEALOUS PRIEST . .  .  .  .  .  334  3 DON JUAN 12    39   5
    BUT RAPP IS THE REVERSE OF ZEALOUS MATRONS . .  .  .  472  3 DON JUAN 15    37   1
```
ZECCHINI
```
    AND MADE AT LEAST FIVE HUNDRED GOOD ZECCHINI  .  .  .  390  2 DON JUAN  4    84   5
```
ZEPHYR
```
    THEIR BONDS WHENE'ER SOME ZEPHYR CAUGHT BEGAN .  .  .  313  2 DON JUAN  3    73   7
```
ZERO
```
    SURE MY INVENTION MUST BE DOWN AT ZERO  .  .  .  .  341  2 DON JUAN  3   110   5
    BUT THOUGH YOUR YEARS AS MAN TEND FAST TO ZERO .  .  .  184  3 DON JUAN  9     2   7
    OR FIVE OR ONE OR ZERO SHE COULD NEVER  .  .  .  .  241  3 DON JUAN 10    33   7
    LA BELLE ALLIANCE OF DUNCES DOWN AT ZERO .  .  .  .  296  3 DON JUAN 11    56   3
    WHEN ITS QUICKSILVER'S DOWN AT ZERO--LO  .  .  .  .  378  3 DON JUAN 13    44   1
```
ZEST
```
    THOUGH SWALLOW'D WITH MUCH ZEST UPON THE WHOLE  .  .  .  484  3 DON JUAN 15    66   4
    SUPERBLY AND CONTAINED A WORLD OF ZEST  .  .  .  .  488  3 DON JUAN 15    74   8
```
ZINGHIS
```
    FOR TIMOUR OR FOR ZINGHIS IN HIS TRADE  .  .  .  .  178  3 DON JUAN  8   133   2
```
ZODIAC'S
```
    QUITE INDEPENDENT OF THE ZODIAC'S SIGNS  .  .  .  .  423  3 DON JUAN 14    29   3
```
ZOE
```
    ENJOINING SILENCE STRICT TO ZOE WHO . .  .  .  .  .  228  2 DON JUAN  2   136   2
    AND ZOE SPENT HERS AS MOST WOMEN DO  .  .  .  .  .  228  2 DON JUAN  2   136   6
    BUT ZOE THE MEANTIME SOME EGGS WAS FRYING .  .  .  .  233  2 DON JUAN  2   144   5
    AND ZOE WHEN THE EGGS WERE READY AND . .  .  .  .  234  2 DON JUAN  2   146   1
    HER LIP WHICH ZOE NEEDS MUST UNDERSTAND  .  .  .  .  234  2 DON JUAN  2   146   5
    OF THE NEW FIRE WHICH ZOE KEPT UP KNEELING .  .  .  237  2 DON JUAN  2   153   6
    BUT ZOE BEING OLDER THAN HAIDEE . .  .  .  .  .  .  239  2 DON JUAN  2   158   5
    SAVE ZOE WHO ALTHOUGH WITH DUE PRECISION .  .  .  .  252  2 DON JUAN  2   182   4
```
ZOE'S
```
    OF ZOE'S COOKERY NO DOUBT WAS STEALING  .  .  .  .  237  2 DON JUAN  2   153   4
```
ZONE
```
    HER ZONE TO VENUS OR HIS BOW TO CUPID . .  .  .  .  51  2 DON JUAN  1    55   7
    NEXT WITH A VIRGIN ZONE HE WAS EQUIPPED  .  .  .  .  456  2 DON JUAN  5    77   3
    AND KEPT HER HEART SERENE WITHIN ITS ZONE .  .  .  .  476  3 DON JUAN 15    47   4
    OF WHICH ANOTHER'S BOSOM IS THE ZONE . .  .  .  .  554  3 DON JUAN 16   108   8
```

APPENDIXES

1308	118	65	47
AS	THINK	COME	BLUE
1172	114	REST	CARE
I	TRUE	YOUTH	FACT
544	'TWAS	64	LORD
LIKE	112	DON'T	STATE
388	SEE	WISH	SUN
MY	111	63	WHITE
387	FAIR	ALWAYS	46
ONE	108	ENOUGH	FRIENDS
325	JUST	EYE	GLORY
MUCH	LIFE	LEAVE	HOPE
316	SAME	NE'ER	KEPT
JUAN	107	PLACE	LADIES
311	BEST	62	MERE
THAN	WORLD	DAYS	ROSE
301	106	LOOK	SEVERAL
WE	PEOPLE	SAD	WATER
289	104	61	45
'TIS	ONCE	BACK	COMMON
257	103	EARTH	GIVE
STILL	FOUND	FIND	I'LL
238	US	HEARD	PASSION
OUR	96	HUMAN	UNLESS
219	ANY	SOMETHING	WOMAN
LOVE	DOUBT	60	44
214	94	AIR	ALAS
GREAT	FEW	BESIDES	BENEATH
204	NOTHING	BLACK	FELL
GOOD	93	DONE	FORM
202	SAW	NEXT	FREE
MADE	TAKE	ROUND	FRIEND
192	92	TURN	SEEM'D
LITTLE	THING	59	43
176	88	CALL	EXCEPT
EVEN	SAVE	FAME	FELT
175	SEEN	LATE	FORTH
OLD	86	MAKES	GENTLE
171	HIGH	SLIGHT	HAVING
KNOW	LEFT	SOUL	LENGTH
MEN	SINCE	STOOD	PASS
166	81	THAT'S	POWER
OWN	BETTER	58	THOUSAND
164	80	I'VE	WAR
THINGS	KNEW	RIGHT	WORD
161	79	57	42
FIRST	DON	AWAY	CALLED
160	LAY	PART	CHILD
TIME	YEARS	THREE	END
154	78	TRUTH	FIRE
BEING	SOMETIMES	56	GET
ME	77	CAUSE	GOT
151	MIND	PAST	LAND
EYES	PRESENT	WOMEN	PAIR
148	76	55	PURE
MAN	BLOOD	GO	SIGHT
147	74	SCARCE	UNTO
WELL	HALF	54	41
144	73	GOD	BROUGHT
YOUNG	HEAD	GREW	CASE
143	LADY	I'M	FEEL
TWO	SMALL	SHORT	FURTHER
139	WHOLE	WORDS	MUSE
MAKE	72	53	SEEM
138	FAR	ADELINE	SINGLE
LEAST	NONE	POOR	SOON
137	SWEET	52	SPIRIT
LAST	THERE'S	CAN'T	40
LONG	71	FEELINGS	BRIGHT
136	CAME	HOUR	GONE
NEW	KIND	51	LIE
133	70	DEEP	SOFT
WAY	HEAVEN	MATTER	TIMES
132	SHOW	READ	WIND
QUITE	69	WENT	WINE
131	FULL	50	39
HEART	SEA	UNTIL	BEGAN
130	SET	49	DIE
WHILE	STRANGE	ALONE	GAVE
129	68	DEAD	MEANT
THOUGHT	DEATH	MOMENT	MOTHER
127	NIGHT	PUT	NATION
MANY	TELL	48	PLEASURE
125	67	AGE	SEEMS
PERHAPS	FACE	JUAN'S	38
RATHER	66	LIGHT	FINE
119	HAND	PRETTY	GENERAL
DAY	NAME	VAIN	GRACE
	SORT		

38 (CONTINUED)
NEAR
TOOK
WIFE
37
BABA
COUNTRY
KEEP
PALE
SEEMED
SHORE
TEARS
WILD
WRONG
36
ALMOST
GOLD
HELD
JULIA
LOVED
MEAN
MINE
NOUGHT
PLEASE
35
ART
CUT
ILL
LOST
OCEAN
REALLY
REASON
SMILE
SURE
TOLD
34
BEAUTIFUL
DEVIL
GRAND
KNOWN
MEANS
ODD
OFT
PRIDE
RUN
SON
SONG
SUBLIME
WORTH
33
BREAST
BREATH
FALL
HATE
HOUSE
LARGE
MORAL
NATURE
THIRD
WONDER
WORSE
32
BEAR
BEAUTY
CHASTE
COURSE
DULL
GROW
HEARTS
LOOKED
MAN'S
MISS
PITY
PRAISE
SLEEP
STRONG
WON'T
31
ALONG
AROUND
COLD
FAST
FELLOW
HAIR
HARDLY
HEAR
LOOK'D
MOON

SENT
SOUND
STATION
30
BROW
CAST
GRAVE
HAIDEE
HOLD
LINE
SHOWN
VIRTUE
29
DEAR
DOOR
DRESS
HANDSOME
HAPPY
KING
LOOKS
NATIONS
RHYME
RICH
SECOND
SENSE
SIDE
SIX
THOUGHTS
TURN'D
WHAT'S
28
BAD
BED
BROKE
CERTAIN
DIED
DUE
GENTLEMEN
HARD
MANKIND
MARRIAGE
MERELY
VOICE
27
ASK
BORE
BORN
DARK
DEEM
ENGLISH
EXTREMELY
GAZED
HOME
HOURS
KISS
MODERN
PRAY
READER
SIGH
SIR
TALK
TURNED
WISE
WORST
26
CHEEK
DREW
FEMALE
FOUR
GREEK
HERO
MAID
NOBLE
PROVE
RARELY
SILENT
STARS
'TWERE
USE
25
BRING
CHANGE
CHRISTIAN
CITY
FATE
FIT
GIVEN
HEROES

LOVER
LOW
OFTEN
PLEASANT
PROPER
SEX
SIN
TALE
TASTE
USUAL
24
FEAR
FOE
FRESH
GROWN
HANDS
INSTEAD
LAID
LEAD
LEAVES
NEED
OCCASION
READY
REAL
SOMEWHAT
SPEAK
STORY
TAKEN
USED
WIVES
23
ALFONSO
AWKWARD
BELIEVE
CLAY
DINNER
DREAM
DYING
EAR
ESPECIALLY
FEELING
FEET
FOND
GLANCE
PASSIONS
POETS
REPLIED
SAGE
SERIOUS
SOLE
SOULS
YEAR
22
ARM
ARMS
BEHOLD
BOSOM
DIFFERENT
DREAD
EXACTLY
FATHER'S
FAULT
GLASS
HELL
HELP
HENRY
HUNDRED
JOHNSON
JOY
LEAVING
NAMES
NATURE'S
PASSED
PHRASE
POET
RAN
SING
SKY
SPAIN
SUNG
TOWN
UNDER
WARM
21
AURORA
BIRTH
BREAK
BRED

CLOSE
CONDITION
DIFFICULT
EARLY
FASHION
'GAINST
GAY
GENTLEMAN
GROWS
LOSE
LOVES
PLAY
PROUD
RHYMES
ROUGH
RUSSIAN
SURELY
TREE
TRIED
VIEW
VIRGIN
WALL
WANT
WAVES
WAYS
20
ACCORDING
AMIDST
BRAVE
CALL'D
CHANCE
CLEAR
COURT
DIM
EARS
ELSE
FACES
FIVE
GREATER
GREEN
KINGS
LATELY
LED
LIES
LIPS
MARRIED
OPEN
PAIN
POINT
QUESTION
RACE
RANK
ROOM
SPRING
STONE
TEN
THIRTY
THROWN
WEAR
WISHED
WORK
WORLDS
YOU'LL
19
ACT
BLOW
BOUND
BOY
DIVINE
DONNA
FAITH
FILL
FLY
FORGET
FORTUNE
FUTURE
GLORIOUS
INEZ
LAW
LIFE'S
LIVING
MATTERS
PAUSE
PRICE
SAINT
SCARCELY
SHIP
SHONE

19 (CONTINUED)
SPOKE
SPOT
STAND
TAUGHT
TONGUE
VICE
WALLS
WHENCE
WORN

18
AGES
ALREADY
APT
ASPECT
AUGHT
BEAT
BLIND
BOAT
BOW
BURNING
CANTO
CASH
COST
DAILY
DEAL
DOUBLE
DOUBTLESS
DUDU
EASE
GROUND
HALL
HISTORY
KNOWLEDGE
LIKED
LIVED
LIVES
LONGER
LOUD
LOVELY
MEANTIME
MEET
MET
MISTRESS
MODE
MODEST
MORNING
MORTAL
NATURAL
PAY
POST
PUBLIC
RETURN
SAIL
SELF
SERVED
SLAVES
SOUGHT
SWORD
SWORE
THRONE
TOUCH
TRY
TURNS
TWELVE
TWICE
UNDERSTAND
WATCH
WIDE

17
ADDED
APART
BUSINESS
CALM
CAUGHT
CHILDREN
DUST
EDUCATION
'EM
EVIL
FATHER
FORGOT
FORMER
GULBEYAZ
HUE
LETTER
LIVE
LOSS

LOT
MAKING
MONEY
PAID
PARADISE
PLAIN
PROVED
QUIET
RARE
ROAR
SEEING
SOCIETY
SORROW
SUPPOSE
TEACH
TEAR
TENDER
THICK
THREW
TRACE
TWENTY
VEINS
VERSE
WAVE
WRITE

16
ANSWER
AWFUL
BEGUN
BENT
BODY
BRAIN
CHARM
CHOOSE
COMMAND
COMPANY
CRIED
DAUGHTER
DEEM'D
EVE
FAMOUS
FIGURE
FLESH
FOES
FRUIT
HEAVY
HILL
HOLY
IMMORTAL
JOHN
KNOWING
MARBLE
MEMORY
MIDNIGHT
MIGHTY
MUSIC
NATIVE
NINE
ONE'S
PASS'D
PHILOSOPHY
QUICK
ROYAL
SATE
SELDOM
SNOW
STRIFE
THEME
THIN
TRUST
VARIOUS
WEEP
WIT

15
AMISS
ATTACK
BECOME
BEGIN
BOOKS
BRIDE
CATHERINE
CHARMS
CHURCH
CLIME
CREW
DANCE
DREAMS
DUTY

ENDS
EPIC
EVERYBODY
FAIN
FIFTY
FOOD
FOOL
FRIAR
GHOST
GOING
HIGHER
HINT
HOPES
HUSBAND
LIST
LONDON
LOOKING
LOVING
MARCH
NOTION
OBJECT
PERSON
PIOUS
RED
SENSES
SILENCE
SKILL
SKIN
SLOW
SPANISH
SPARE
STRANGER
STREAM
TAKES
TURKS
'TWILL
VAST

14
BARD
BLOODY
BOLD
CRIME
CURIOUS
DANGEROUS
DARE
EMPRESS
EXPRESS
FAMILY
FAVOURITE
FORMS
FRENCH
GAZE
GLOW
GORE
GOTHIC
GREY
HASTE
HEADS
IMPERIAL
INNOCENT
JUANNA
LATTER
MYSELF
NIGH
PAGE
PAPER
PATIENCE
PLACED
PURPLE
RETIRED
RISE
SETTLED
SHAME
SHIELD
SHINE
SHOWS
SIRE
SITUATION
SOIL
SPEECH
STRENGTH
STRIKE
SUBJECT
SUDDEN
SUIT
SUMMER
THUNDER
TOMB

TURKISH
WEALTH
WE'LL
YOU'D

13
ADD
ANCIENT
ANYTHING
ARTS
BOOK
CHIEF
CHOSE
CLAIM
CLOUDS
CRY
DAMES
DANGER
DISTANCE
DRY
DWELL
EFFECT
FALSE
FAREWELL
FIELD
FIGHT
FISH
FLAME
FLEW
FLOWER
FOOT
FOURTH
FRAIL
FREEDOM
GLOWING
GREATEST
GROWING
GUEST
HAIDEE'S
HEROIC
HUGE
ICE
INNOCENCE
ISLE
LADY'S
LAWS
LIP
LORDS
MAJESTY
MILD
MORALS
MYSTERY
PEN
PRINCE
PUZZLED
QUEEN
RAISED
SAVED
SAVING
SEAS
SEASON
SERENE
SERVE
SEVEN
SHOWED
SICK
SIMPLE
SKIES
SLEPT
SMILED
SPARKLING
SPIRITS
STARE
STERN
TAKING
TALL
THINKING
THOUSANDS
'TWOULD
VEIL
VIRTUOUS
WATERS
WEAK
WOES
WORLD'S

12
ABLE
AID
ANTONIA

941

12   (CONTINUED)

APPEAR'D	AFFAIRS	SENSATION	MISCHIEF
APPEARS	ALFONSO'S	SIXTEEN	MORN
BAR	ALIKE	SLAIN	MOTHERS
BEGINNING	ALLOW	SLAUGHTER	MOVED
BLUSH	AMBITION	SOMEHOW	NAMED
CEASED	AROSE	SOUTHEY	OAR
CHARGE	BASE	SPOUSE	PARDON
CHARMING	BATTERIES	TEETH	PEARLS
CHOICE	BEAUTIES	TEMPTATION	PEGASUS
CHOSEN	BELL	TROUBLE	PLAN
COMPLETE	BELOVED	TUNE	PLEASED
DEEMED	BID	TURNING	POPE
DISGUISE	BILLS	UNKNOWN	PRIVATE
DISTANT	BIRD	VAPOUR	PURSUED
DRAW	BOATS	VENUS	QUOTE
DRAWN	BODIES	VIRTUES	REACHED
DUMB	BOUGHT	VISION	REFLECTION
ERR	BRIEF	VULGAR	REMEMBER
ETERNAL	BRINGS	WAKE	RESOLVED
EXISTENCE	BROKEN	WED	RISK
FAINT	BROTHER	WORE	ROAD
FLOWERS	BURST	WORTHY	ROCK
FOUGHT	CERTAINLY	YELLOW	ROCKS
FRIENDSHIP	CHANGED	10	ROLL
GAME	COLUMN	ADVICE	RUDE
GENTLY	CONDUCT	AFRAID	SAVAGE
GIRLS	CONFUSION	APPETITE	SEARCH
GLITTERING	CONTRIVED	ASIDE	SECURE
GOODLY	CREATURES	BATTLES	SEPARATE
GREATLY	DAME	BEG	SIGHS
GRIEF	DAMN	BEHELD	SIGNS
GUESS	DEBT	BESIDE	SILLY
HE'S	DEN	BLEW	SILVER
HORSE	DESPAIR	BOYS	SINCERE
HORSES	DESPERATE	BROAD	SINGS
LANDS	DINE	BUSY	SINK
LEARN	DIRTY	CAVE	SLAVE
LOVE'S	DRUNK	CONTENT	SOLITUDE
MASS	DUKE	CONVERSATION	SPRINGS
MASTER	FAIL	COUNTRY'S	STRUCK
MORTALS	FEATURES	CREATURE	SWEAR
MOUTH	FLUNG	CREED	SYMPATHY
NUMBER	FOREVER	CROSS	TALENT
OUGHT	GAIN	DAUGHTERS	TALKED
PARTY	GETTING	DEEDS	TELLS
PATH	GOD'S	DESTROY	THEY'RE
PEACE	GODS	DISH	THIRST
POEM	GREECE	DOGS	TOIL
PROBABLY	GROAN	EASILY	TRADE
PROCEED	HARM	ESTATE	TREASURE
RAIN	HENCE	ET	UNDONE
RAYS	HOLDS	EXAMPLE	VESSEL
RECOLLECT	HONOUR	EXAMPLES	WET
SAGES	HOT	EXCEEDINGLY	WILL
SALT	INFANT	EXCEPTING	WINGS
SAT	JEST	EXCUSE	WONDERED
SCORN	JOYS	EXPERIENCE	WONDERFUL
SENTIMENTAL	JUDGE	FACTS	WOOD
SHADE	JULIA'S	FEARS	WRITTEN
SHAPE	KILL	FIERCE	WROTE
SHARE	KILLED	FLATTER	YOU'RE
SHED	LANGUAGE	FLIES	9
SHOOK	LEARNED	FOLLOW	ABSENCE
SIGN	LONELY	FORCE	ANSWERED
SLEEPING	MEANING	FORM'D	ARISE
SLOWLY	MEN'S	GATE	AWE
SLUMBER	METHINKS	GEMS	BALL
SMOOTH	MISTAKE	GIRL	BARE
SONS	ORDERS	GROWTH	BASTION
SOUNDS	PARTS	HEAP	BECAME
SPOIL	PAUSED	HEIR	BLAME
SPREAD	PEOPLE'S	HELPLESS	BOARD
STAR	PERFECT	HIDE	BORNE
STORM	PERSONS	HONEST	BRILLIANT
SUCCESS	PLACES	HONEY	BROOK
SUNK	PREPARED	HONOURABLE	CARRIAGE
SUWARROW	PREY	HORACE	CARRY
TOGETHER	PURPOSE	HUNGRY	CHILL
T'OTHER	QUIT	I'D	CLEVER
TRULY	QUOTH	JACK	CLUNG
TWILIGHT	RATE	LEARN'D	COAST
WELCOME	RAY	LEST	COFFEE
WOMAN'S	REACH	LOVERS	COLOUR
WORDSWORTH	RECEIVED	MANNER	COMES
WOUNDED	RIVER	MARTIAL	CONCERN
YIELD	SAKE	MASTERS	CONSEQUENCE
11	SCIENCE	MEND	COURAGE
ADMIRED	SECRET	MERIT	DAMSELS

9   (CONTINUED)
DESCRIBE
DESCRIPTION
DESIRE
DIFFERENCE
DISPLAYED
DOOM
DRAUGHT
DROP
DULY
EARLIEST
EAST
EFFORTS
EQUAL
FAIRLY
FAVOUR
FIX'D
FLASHING
FOOLISH
FOREMOST
FORMED
FRANCE
GAINED
GALE
GRANTED
HAPPINESS
HARP
HEALTH
HIGHEST
HIGHNESS
HINTS
HORRID
HOST
INSTANT
INTEREST
KINDS
LAD
LAMBRO
LAUGH
LAUGHTER
LEADS
LIMBS
LONE
LUST
MAIDS
MINUTE
MODERATE
MOOD
MOSTLY
MOUNTAINS
MOVE
PAINT
PALACE
PASSION'S
PEDRILLO
PLATE
PLEASURES
POESY
POETIC
POLE
POSTERITY
PRAYER
PRECIOUS
PRIEST
PULL
QUALITY
RAGE
REGRET
ROSY
RUSSIANS
SAINTS
SCARLET
SCENE
SHADOWS
SHAKE
SILK
SNEER
SORRY
SPENT
SPLENDID
SPRUNG
SQUARE
STOP
STOPPED
STRICT
SUPPOSED
SURPRISE
TABLE

TA'EN
TEMPER
TITLE
TONE
TRAVEL
TRESSES
VARIETY
VIGOUR
WANTED
WASTE
WHEREFORE
WHOLLY
WINDS
WITHDREW
WOKE
WOUND
WRATH

8
ABROAD
ACQUAINTANCE
ACTED
AMATORY
ARAB
ARRAY
ASHAMED
ASS
ASSAULT
BADE
BARDS
BATTLE
BEACH
BEEF
BELIEVED
BIND
BIRDS
BLAZE
BLUNDER
BREAD
BREAKFAST
BREED
BULL
CALLS
CAMP
CARES
CASTLEREAGH
CEASE
CERTES
CHAIN
CITIES
CLIMATE
CLIMES
CLOSED
COMING
COMMONPLACE
COURTESY
DAMNED
DASH
DECENT
DECIDE
DEGREES
DELIGHTED
DISCOVER
DISPOSED
DOORS
DREAMT
DUBIOUS
EASY
ENNUI
ENVY
ESCAPE
EVERYTHING
EXCESS
FALLEN
FANCY
FED
FEMALES
FEMININE
FICTION
FINGERS
FLASHED
FLATTERY
FOAM
FOLLOW'D
FOLLOWING
FOOLS
GARDEN
GAZETTE
GAZING

GLAD
GRACEFUL
GRASS
GRIEVE
GRIM
HAIL
HEAVEN'S
HEIGHT
HOMER
HUMANITY
IDLE
IMPRESSION
INSTANCE
INTENTIONS
ISMAIL
KATINKA
LACE
LEISURE
LIGHTED
LOLAH
LOOSE
LORD'S
LUCK
MAD
MAIN
MALE
MARKET
MELLOW
MERITS
MIDDLE
'MIDST
MILLIONS
MODEL
MOMENTS
MONTHS
MOURN
MRS
MYSTIC
NEARLY
NECK
NORTH
OBEY
OPINION
OUTWARD
PARENTS
PETTICOAT
PHILOSOPHER
PIECE
POLITICS
PORTION
POWERS
PRECISION
PRESENTED
PRIZE
PRODUCED
PULSE
QUESTIONS
QUICKLY
RANKS
REASONS
RECALL
RECEIVE
REPLY
RING
ROMAN
RUIN
RULES
RUNNING
SAND
SAYING
SCORE
SERVANTS
SHARP
SHIPS
SHOT
SHOW'D
SHRIEK
SINNER
SISTER
SMILES
SOBER
SOONER
SPACE
SPARKLED
SPEAKING
SPHERES
SPORT
STANDING

STATED
STEADY
STONES
STREETS
STRINGS
STYLE
SULTAN
SUMMER'S
SUNNY
SUNSET
SUSPICION
TEA
THEY'LL
TONGUES
TURK
TUTOR
UNDERSTOOD
VANITY
VIRGINS
VOICES
WAIT
WARS
WATCH'D
WAX
WEARS
WEATHER
WHATSOE'ER
WHEREON
WIN
WING
WISDOM
WISH'D
WISHES
WISHING
WITTY
WOE
WON
WONDERING
WORKS
ZOE

7
ACTION
ADVANCE
AFFAIR
AIRY
ALBEIT
ALTOGETHER
AMUNDEVILLE
ANGRY
ANSWER'D
APPLAUSE
ARCH
ARMY
ASHES
ASKED
ATE
ATTIC
AWAKE
BABEL
BEINGS
BET
BILLOW
BITTER
BLED
BLEST
BRANCH
BREAKING
BRINK
BROTHERS
BURIED
CAESAR
CALMLY
CAPTIVES
CARED
CARNAGE
CERES
CHAMBER
CHANGES
CHARACTER
CHASE
CHIEFLY
CLASS
CLOSET
CLOUD
COLOURS
CONNUBIAL
CONSCIENCE
CORPS

7 (CONTINUED)
COUNSEL
COUNT
CREDIT
CRIMSON
CROWD
CUSTOM
DANCING
DARKNESS
DATE
DELICATE
DESOLATE
DEVOTION
DEW
DISPATCH
DISPLAY
DISTRESS
DOUBTS
DREARY
DRIVEN
ECHO
ENCUMBER
ENGLAND
ETERNITY
EUROPE
FASHIONABLE
FATAL
FEAST
FELLOWS
FINDING
FIX
FLOATING
FLOOD
FLOW'D
FORBEAR
FOREIGN
FOREST
FORGIVE
GARB
GENIAL
GENIUS
GEORGE
GIVING
GLORY'S
GOLDEN
GOUT
GRIEVED
GUARDIAN
GUESTS
GUIDE
HALLS
HAUGHTY
HE'D
HID
HIT
IDEAL
IN'T
IRISH
ITALY
JOSE
KILLING
KISSES
KNIGHTS
LA
LAMPS
LAWYERS
LESSONS
LIKENESS
LO
MADAM
MAHOMET
MANNERS
MANSION
MARK
MATRON
MATRONS
MELANCHOLY
MINDS
MIX'D
MONARCHS
MONSTROUS
MOSLEM
MOTION
MOTIVE
MOUNT
MUSES
NAY
NEAREST

NEEDS
OCCASIONS
ODDS
OFFICE
OPENED
ORDER
PALL
PARADE
PASSING
PEDIGREE
PENSIVE
PERCEIVED
PERCEIVING
PERISH'D
PERPLEX
PHRASES
PHYSICIANS
POLISHED
PRAISED
PRAYERS
PRESUME
PRETEND
PROFIT
PROGRESS
PROMISED
QUANTITY
QUARREL
QUARTER
RAISE
RAMPART
RAW
READERS
READING
RECENT
REDUCED
REGARD
REIGN
RELATIONS
RELIGION
REWARD
RILL
RISING
ROLL'D
ROMANTIC
ROME
ROW
RUSS
SADLY
SAFE
SAFETY
SCHOOL
SCOTT
SCREEN
SEEK
SEES
SEND
SENTIMENT
SHRINE
SIGHED
SIGNAL
SIRES
SIT
SIXTH
SIZE
SLAY
SLIP
SMOKE
SOLDIERS
SOOTHE
SOVEREIGN
SPRAY
STAIN
START
STIR
STIRRED
STOPP'D
STREET
STRONGER
SUITS
SUM
SWELL
TAME
TEACHES
THRICE
THROUGHOUT
THRUST
TIES
TIRED

TOUGH
TREMBLING
TRIBE
TROD
TROUBLED
TRUTHS
UNIVERSAL
UNLIKE
UNSEEN
VICTIM
VISIONS
WALK
WALKED
WARRIORS
WEAKNESS
WEEK
WEIGHT
WEPT
WHEELS
WHEREAS
WHEREIN
WHIRL
WINTER
WITS
WONT
WOODS
WROUGHT
YORE
YOU'VE

6
ABSENT
ADAM
ADVANTAGE
AGED
AIM
ALIVE
ALLAH
ALL'S
ANON
ANSWERS
APACE
APARTMENT
ARTICLES
ASK'D
AUTHORS
AVE
BACKS
BANK
BATTERY
BAY
BEAM
BETIMES
BIT
BLANK
BLEEDING
BLESSING
BLUSHES
BOB
BONES
BOSOMS
BOWED
BREEDING
BRIGHTER
BRITISH
BROWS
BUILT
BURN
BUST
CADIZ
CANTOS
CAREER
CARRIED
CATCH
CATHOLIC
CAUSED
CAVALIER
CHAIN'D
CHEEKS
CHEERFUL
CIRCUMSTANCES
CITY'S
CIVIL
CLASSIC
CLIMB
COLLEGE
COMMONS
COMPANION
CONDEMN

CONFOUNDED
CONTINUE
COUCH
CREST
CRIMES
CURE
CURSE
DANCED
DANTE'S
DANUBE'S
DEEMING
DEEPER
DEEPLY
DEFECT
DELIGHT
DENY
DESCRIBED
DEVILS
DIN
DIPLOMATIC
DISAPPOINTED
DISCLOSED
DISLIKE
DISPLAY'D
DIVIDED
DOMESTIC
DOUBTED
DOWNRIGHT
DOZEN
DREADFUL
DREAM'D
DRESSES
DREST
DROOPING
DROPS
DUKES
DUSKY
EAGER
EASTERN
EATING
ECHOES
EGGS
ENDED
EVENING
EVERYWHERE
EXPLAIN
EXPRESSION
FABLE
FAMINE
FATHERS
FAULTS
FEATURE
FIERY
FIFTH
FILLED
FIRED
FITTED
FITZ-FULKE
FIXED
FLIGHT
FLIRTATION
FLOW
FOLLOWED
FOLLY
FOREIGNERS
FORGOTTEN
FORTY
FRAME
FRONT
GEM
GENERATION
GENEROUS
GERMANY
GLANCED
GLIMPSE
GOES
GOWN
GRACES
GRAPE
GROVE
GUARD
GUNS
HAPLESS
HARMLESS
HARSH
HAT
HEART'S
HEAT

6 (CONTINUED)
HIDDEN
HILLS
HOARY
HURRY
HUSBAND'S
HUSBANDS
IGNORANCE
IMAGE
INCREASED
INTELLECTUAL
INTENSE
INTENT
IRON
ISLAND
ISLES
IS'T
ITALIAN
JEALOUS
JOG
JOIN
JOURNEY
JUNE
KEEPS
KINDLING
KISSED
LACK
LAKE
LATEST
LAURELS
LEAF
LEAK
LIGHTS
LINK'D
LIQUID
LOWER
LULL'D
MALTHUS
MANTLE
MARIA
MART
MASQUERADE
MAST
MATCHES
MAXIM
MEALS
MIDST
MILK
MINGLED
MIRTH
MISSED
MISSES
MIXED
MONK
MOORE
MOTHER'S
MUTUAL
NAPOLEON
NARRATION
NATURALLY
NE'ERTHELESS
NOBLEST
NONSENSE
NOOK
OATH
OBSCURE
OCCUPIED
OFFER
OPEN'D
ORIENTAL
OURSELVES
OX
PAINTED
PATIENT
PATRIOT
PERCHANCE
PERISH
PETER
PHANTASIES
PICTURE
PILLOW
PLATONIC
PLAYED
PLAYS
PLIGHT
POET'S
POINTS
PORT

POSSESSION
PREFER
PREFERENCE
PRETENCE
PRODUCE
PROMISE
PROOF
PUREST
QUAINT
RACK
RALLY
RANGE
RELATE
REMAIN
REQUIRED
RESERVED
RESIGN
RESISTANCE
RESUME
REVEREND
RIDDLE
RIDE
RIGOUR
RISES
ROBE
RODE
ROLLS
ROOT
ROUT
RUM
RUNS
SAMIAN
SANS
SCANDAL
SCENES
SEATED
SEEMING
SEIZED
SELF-LOVE
SENSATIONS
SERMONS
SETS
SHEET
SHOCK
SHUN
SINS
SMART
SOCRATES
SOOTH
SORE
SORTS
SOURCE
SOUTH
SOW
SPAKE
SPARED
SPECULATION
SPELL
SPLENDOUR
SPOILT
STANDS
STATURE
STAYS
STEP
STOCKINGS
STORE
STUCK
STUFF
SUPERNATURAL
SUPERSTITION
SUPPER
SURVEY
SWEEP
SWEPT
SWIMMING
SWORDS
SYSTEM
TAPER
TAX
TAXES
TEST
THENCE
THRONG
THROW
TIDE
TOILET
TOWER
TROOPS

TROY
TUTORS
'TWIXT
TYRANT
USEFUL
VAINLY
VAN
VANISHED
VENTURE
VILE
VOW
WASTED
WAXING
WE'VE
WHERE'S
WHISPER'D
WICKED
WRECK
YOUNGER
5
ABYSS
ACCEPT
ACCUSE
ACCUSED
ACTS
ADMIRATION
ADORED
ADVANCED
ADVENTURES
AFFECTION
AFLOAT
ALEXANDER
ALLOWED
ALLURE
AMBROSIAL
AMUSEMENT
ANNALS
ANNOUNCED
ANYWHERE
APPEAL
APPLIED
APPROBATION
ARRAYED
ARRIVED
ASKING
ASSISTANCE
ATTENTION
AUBURN
AWAIT
BAFFLED
BARK
BAYONET
BEARS
BEATS
BEAUTEOUS
BECOMING
BEE
BILLOWS
BISHOPS
BLACKS
BOAST
BOND
BOOTY
BOTTLE
BOTTOM
BRAVEST
BREAKERS
BREAKS
BREECHES
BRITAIN
BUSTLE
BY-AND-BY
CANNON
CANOPY
CAPTIVE
CARELESS
CATTLE
CAUTIOUS
CENTURY
CHAMBERS
CHANCED
CHANCERY
CHARITY
CHIVALRY
CHRISTIANS
CIRCUMSTANCE
CLARET
CLOAK

CLOTHES
COLERIDGE
COMMENCE
COMPARISON
CONFESS
CONNEXION
CONQUEST
CONSOLATION
CONSTRUCTION
CONTEMPLATION
COOL
CORRECT
CORRUPTION
COUPLE
COURIER
CRIES
CROWDED
CROWN
CUP
CURLS
CURSED
CUTTER
DANTE
DARING
DASHING
DAWN
DAZZLED
DEBTOR
DECIDED
DECLINED
DEED
DEIGNED
DEPENDS
DESERVED
DETAIL
DETERMINED
DEVIL'S
DIGESTION
DINED
DINNERS
DINT
DIRECTION
DISCUSSED
DISCUSSION
DISEASE
DISGRACE
DISPARAGE
DITCH
DOG
DOING
DOUBLY
DOVE
DRANK
DRIVE
DROSS
DUN
DUTIES
DYES
EARTH'S
EASIER
EAT
ELSEWHERE
EMOTION
EMPIRE
ENDLESS
ENTER
ENTERED
ERROR
ESCAPED
ESTEEM
EUNUCH
EXCEEDING
EXCLAIMED
EXPIRED
EXTREME
FAIRER
FAIRY
FAITHFUL
FALLING
FAMISH'D
FAN
FANCIES
FEARFUL
FEE
FEELS
FEWER
FIGHTING
FIGURES

4   (CONTINUED)

ANSWERING	CHAMPAGNE	DRINK	GRASP
ANTICIPATE	CHANGEABLE	DROPPED	GRAY
ANTITHESIS	CHASTEST	DROVE	GRECIAN
APPEARED	CHATTER	DRUM	GREEKS
APPLE	CHECKS	DUCHESS	GRENADIERS
APPROACH	CHILD'S	DUNCE	GROUP
ARISTOCRATIC	CHIME	DWARFS	GROUPS
ARISTOTLE	CHRONICLE	DWELT	GROVES
ARMIES	CIRCLE	EARLIER	GUESS'D
ARTICLE	CLAUSE	EARTHLY	GUILT
ARTISTS	CLIFFS	EATS	GUISE
ASIATIC	CLOSING	EFFORT	HABIT
ASSEMBLED	COCK	EIGHT	HACK
ATTACKED	COLDNESS	EIGHTEEN	HANDY
ATTORNEY	COLUMNS	EIGHTY	HAPPIER
AUGUSTUS	COMBAT	EKE	HAPPIEST
AULD	COMMANDS	ELBOW	HAREM
AURORA'S	COMMENCED	ELDER	HARMONIOUS
AUTUMN	COMMIT	ELEVEN	HATED
AVARICE	COMPARED	ELOQUENCE	HAUNTED
AVENGER	COMPASSION	ENCREASED	HEADACHE
AVERSION	COMPLETELY	ENDING	HEARTY
AWAITS	CONDESCEND	ENDURE	HEAVE
AWARE	CONDESCENDING	ENEMY	HEAVED
AWOKE	CONGRESS	ENORMOUS	HEBREW
BACCHUS	CONQUEROR	ENTRANCE	HECTIC
BACHELOR	CONSEQUENCES	EQUALLY	HEIRESS
BACKWARD	CONSTANT	ERECTED	HENRY'S
BACON	CONSTANTINOPLE	ERRED	HERCULES
BAGGAGE	CONSTITUTION	ERRORS	HERE'S
BALANCE	CONTINUED	ESSENTIAL	HER'S
BALLS	CONTRADICTION	EUROPE'S	HIDEOUS
BANISH	CONTRARY	EXAMINED	HIDES
BANNER	CONTRIVE	EXCHANGE	HOPED
BANQUET	CONVERTED	EXIST	HOUNDS
BARBAROUS	CORE	EXISTS	HOUSEHOLD
BAYONETS	CORNER	EXPEDIENT	HOUSES
BEASTS	COSTLY	EXPENSES	HOVERS
BEFELL	COUNTED	EXPREST	HOWLING
BEGGED	COUNTRIES	EXTREMITY	HUMBLE
BEGINNERS	COUNTY	EYED	HURT
BELIEF	COURTS	FACED	HUT
BELLE	CREPT	FAMILIES	HYMN
BEND	CROWNED	FARE	IDLENESS
BETRAYED	CRUEL	FATES	IDOL
BETTERS	CRYING	FAVOURITES	IMAGINATION
BEWARE	CUNNING	FEAR'D	IMMEDIATE
BLAND	CURIOSITY	FEASTS	IMMEDIATELY
BLOOM	CURRENT	FEES	IMMORAL
BLOOMING	DAMAGES	FEVER	IMPERIOUS
BLOWING	DAMN'D	FIELDS	IMPULSE
BLOWS	DAMP	FILL'D	INCLINATION
BLUSHED	DAMSEL	FIRING	INDIFFERENT
BONE	DARED	FIRM	INFERIOR
BONNE	DASH'D	FIRMNESS	INFIDELS
BOON	DAY-BREAK	FIRSTLY	INJURED
BORDER	DE	FITS	INK
BOUGH	DEARS	FITTING	INSPIRED
BOUNDS	DECKED	FITZ-PLANTAGENET	INTELLECT
BOWER	DECLINE	FLAWS	INTERRUPTED
BOWERS	DEEMS	FLED	INTRODUCE
BOWS	DEEPEST	FLOAT	ISLANDS
BOYISH	DEFERENCE	FLOCK	IT'S
BRANCHES	DEGREE	FLUSHED	JEALOUSY
BRAZEN	DEIGNS	FOLD	JOB
BREATHE	DELAY	FONDLY	JOINT
BREATHES	DEPTH	FOOLSCAP	JOKE
BREATHING	DESCRIBING	FOOTSTEPS	JOVE
BREEZE	DESIGN	FOREIGNER	JUDGED
BRIDES	DESIRED	FORMIDABLE	JUDGMENT
BRIGHTEST	DESPITE	FOUL	JULIET
BRINGING	DESTINY	FOWL	KEEPING
BUBBLES	DESTRUCTION	FREEBORN	KHAN
BUILD	DEWY	FREELY	KICK
BUILDINGS	DIAMOND	FROST	KILL'D
BURNED	DIES	FULFIL	KIN
BUY	DISCOVERIES	GAIN'D	KINDNESS
CAGED	DISCRETION	GAS	KNIFE
CALCULATION	DISHES	GATHER	KNIGHT
CAP	DISMAY	GATHERS	KNOT
CAPITAL	DISPUTE	GHOSTS	LAMB
CAPRICES	DISSIPATED	GLADLY	LAMBRO'S
CARGO	DISTINCTION	GLARE	LANDING
CAVERN	DOCTORS	GLAZED	LANG
CAVIL	DOWNCAST	GLEAM	LANGUID
CEASELESS	DRAWING	GLIDING	LASH
CETERA	DREAMED	GLOSSY	LAWFUL
	DRESSING	GOODS	LEAN

4   (CONTINUED)

LEAP	OUTLINE	REGULAR	SONNETS
LECTURE	OVERPOWERING	REIGNING	SPANIEL
LEGAL	OWES	RELATION	SPARK
LEILA	PAINS	RELIEF	SPARTAN
LEND	PALACES	RELIEVED	SPECIAL
LENT	PALISADES	REMAIN'D	SPECIES
LESSON	PALLID	REMAINS	SPEED
LET'S	PANGS	REMARK	SPLASH
LEVEL	PARAMOUR	RENEW	STANZAS
LIBERAL	PARAPET	REPAY	STARTING
LIBERTY	PARLIAMENT	REPEAT	STAY
LIEU	PARTIAL	REPENTANCE	STEED
LIFT	PARTRIDGES	REQUIRES	STEEPLE
LILY	PAS	RESIST	STINGS
LION	PATHS	RESOURCES	STOLE
LISTEN	PATRICIAN	RETIRING	STONY
LOFTIER	PAUSING	RETURNING	STORMS
LOSING	PAVED	REVELS	STORMY
LOVELIEST	PEARL	RIBBONS	STRANGERS
LOVER'S	PEASANT'S	RIOT	STRIPLING
LURKING	PEERS	ROAST	STRIPT
LUSTRE	PENSION	ROLLED	STRIVE
LYRE	PER	ROMANCES	STRONGLY
MARCHED	PERCEIVE	ROWS	STUDIES
MASSY	PERCH	RUMOUR	STUDY
MATE	PERISHED	RUSHING	STUNG
MAY	PERPLEXING	SABRE	SUBJECTS
MEDEA	PERT	SACRED	SUITE
MENTION	PERU	SAFELY	SUITORS
MENTIONS	PETERSBURGH	SALLY	SUMMON
MERCHANT	PETRARCH'S	SAMUEL	SUPERIOR
MERRY	PHYSICIAN	SANDS	SURGEON
MESS	PICK'D	SCANDALS	SURROUNDED
METAPHOR	PICKED	SCANTY	SURVIVE
MILES	PIKE	SCOLD	SWEEPS
MILITARY	PILLOW'D	SCOUNDREL	SWEETER
MILKY	PIPE	SCOUT	SWEETLY
MILLION	PLAINLY	SCRAPE	SWEETS
MILTON	PLANN'D	SCREAM	SWIFT
MIRACLE	PLATO	SEAL	SWIM
MIRROR	PLAY'D	SEAT	SYNE
MISSION	PLEASING	SEDATE	TACT
MOISTURE	PLUNDER	SEIZE	TALENTS
MOMENT'S	POETICAL	SELECT	TALKING
MONASTIC	POISON	SELECTED	TARTARS
'MONGST	POLISH	SELF-SAME	TENDENCY
MOONS	POLITENESS	SENATES	TENDERNESS
MOSCOW	PONDER	SENDS	TERM
MOSQUE	PORTAL	SENSITIVE	TERRORS
MOUNTED	POSSESS'D	SENSUAL	TEXT
MOURNING	POSTBOYS	SERVICE	THANK
MOUTHS	POURS	SETTING	THANKS
MYSTICAL	PRAY'D	SEVENTEEN	THEOLOGY
NEAT	PREACH	SEVILLE	THEY'D
NECESSARY	PREFERRED	SHAKES	THING'S
NECKS	PREPARATION	SHAKESPEARE	THIRDLY
NEER	PRIME	SHA'N'T	THROAT
NEGRO	PRINCESS	SHARED	THUNDERS
NEIGHBOUR'S	PRISON	SHEETS	TIDES
NERVOUS	PROCEEDED	SHE'LL	TIED
NEST	PROCESS	SHELLS	TIME'S
NEWSPAPERS	PROMISES	SHE'S	TOLERABLE
NICHE	PROUDEST	SHEWED	TO-MORROW
NOBLY	PULLED	SHILLING	TOP
NOMENCLATURE	PURCHASED	SHINING	TOPIC
NORMAN	PUSH	SHIPWRECK'D	TOPICS
NOVICE	PUTS	SHOUTS	TORE
NUMBERS	PUZZLING	SHRINKING	TORN
NUMEROUS	QUAKE	SIGH'D	TORY
NUPTIAL	QUALIFIED	SIGHTS	TOUCH'D
OBJECTS	QUALITIES	SINGING	TOWNS
OCCUR	QUARTO	SINKING	TRADITION
ODA	QUEENS	SINKS	TRAIN
OER	QUELL	SITS	TRANCE
O'ERFLOWING	QUIETLY	SLIPPERS	TRANSCENDANT
OFFENCE	RADIANT	SLUMBERING	TRANSGRESSION
OFFICER	RAIMENT	SMILING	TRANSLATE
OFFICIAL	RAINBOW	SMITH	TRAVELS
OIL	RANSOM	SMOOTHED	TREES
ONWARDS	RASH	SMOTHER	TRICE
OPENING	RATTLES	SNOWS	TRIUMPH
OPINIONS	READILY	SOARS	TROOP
OPPORTUNITY	REALMS	SOCIAL	TROWSERS
ORANGE	RECOMMEND	SOFA	TURBAN
ORDERED	REED	SOFTER	TURK'S
ORIGINAL	REFLECT	SOLOMON	TYRANNY
ORPHAN	REFORMATION	SOMEONE	TYRANT'S
	REFUSE	SOMEWHERE	TYRANTS

4 (CONTINUED)	AMOROUS	BOUDOIR	COMPARE
UNCLOSED	AMOUNT	BOUGHS	COMPASS
UNCONSCIOUS	AMPLE	BOUNDED	COMPELLED
UNDERNEATH	ANCHOR	BOUNDING	COMPLAIN
UNEXPECTED	ANGEL	BOWL	COMPLEXION
UNIFORM	ANGLE	BRACE	COMPLIMENT
UNPLEASANT	ANGLES	BRAINS	COMPREHEND
UPPER	ANIMAL	BRASS	COMRADES
UPPERMOST	ANIMATION	BREACH	CONCEAL
USELESS	ANNUL	BREASTS	CONDITIONS
VALIANT	ANTIPODES	BREATHED	CONFEST
VAUNT	ANTIQUE	BREATHLESS	CONFINE
VEIN	ANTONIA'S	BRETHREN	CONFINED
VENGEANCE	ANXIOUS	BRICKS	CONFIRM
VERGE	ANYBODY	BRIDAL	CONFUSED
VICTUAL	APOLOGY	BRISKLY	CONNECTION
VINE	APPAL	BRISTLING	CONSENTED
VIOLENCE	APPLES	BRITAIN'S	CONTAINING
VIOLENT	APPROACHING	BRITONS	CONTEMPT
VIRGIN'S	APPROVED	BRITTLE	CONVENT
VIRTUE'S	ARGUMENT	BROOKED	COOKERY
VISAGE	ARISTOCRACY	BROTH	COOLING
VISITS	ARITHMETIC	BRUSH	COPE
VOID	ARK	BUBBLING	CORDIAL
VOLUMES	ARRIVING	BUDDING	CORN
WAITED	ASLEEP	BULLETIN	CORPORAL
WALKS	ASP	BULLY	CORPSES
WALTZ	ASSAIL	BUMPERS	COUNCIL
WAN	ASSERT	BURNT	COUNTIES
WANDER'D	ASSERTION	BURSTING	COURSES
WANDERING	ASSUAGING	BUTCHER	COUSIN
WAR'S	ASSURE	BUTT	COVERS
WASH'D	ASSURED	CABINET	COWL
WATCHES	ATMOSPHERE	CAESAR'S	COXCOMB
WAVING	ATTENTIONS	CALCULATED	CRACK
WEARY	ATTITUDE	CALLING	CRASH
WEB	ATTRACT	CAMEL'S	CRAVAT
WEDDING	ATTRACTS	CAMPS	CREATE
WELLINGTON	AUNT	CANNONADE	CREATION
WE'RE	AZURE	CANVAS	CREEP
WHISPERED	BABE	CAPE	CREEPING
WHO'S	BACON'S	CAPRICE	CREWS
WINES	BAITS	CAPRICIOUS	CRITICS
WINNING	BANQUO'S	CARD	CROP
WISER	BARREN	CARDS	CROWDS
WITHAL	BATH	CARELESSLY	CROWN'D
WITHER'D	BATHING	CARPE	CRYSTAL
WRAPT	BATTER	CARRIAGES	CUPID
WRITERS	BEADS	CARVED	CUPID'S
WRONGS	BEARD	CASES	CUPOLA
WRUNG	BEAST	CAT	CUPS
YAWN	BEATEN	CATHERINE'S	CURB
YEARLY	BEATING	CATO	CURES
YIELDED	BEAU	CAUSES	CURL
YOKE	BEDS	CELEBRATED	CURST
ZONE	BEEF-STEAK	CELESTIAL	CUSTOMS
3	BEER	CELLS	CUTTING
ABHOR	BEES	CENTAUR	CYPRESS
ABOUND	BEGGAR	CENTRE	DAINTY
ABSTRUSE	BEGOT	CERVANTES	DAMME'S
ACCENT	BEHAVED	CHAINS	DANCER
ACCENTS	BELLS	CHARLES	DANCES
ACCOMPANIED	BELT	CHARM'D	DANDY
ACCOMPLISHMENT	BENDING	CHART	DANIEL
ACCOMPLISHMENTS	BENEFIT	CHASTITY	DART
ACTIVE	BEREFT	CHAT	DASHED
ACTUAL	BIDDING	CHIN	DEAF
ADAM'S	BILE	CHORUS	DEALT
ADAPTED	BILL	CHRONOLOGY	DEAREST
ADDRESS	BISHOP	CIRCUMSPECT	DEATHS
ADDRESSED	BITCHES	CLASP	DEBATE
ADDS	BLACK-EYED	CLASP'D	DEBTS
ADMIRES	BLANK-BLANK	CLEAN	DECAY
ADMITTED	BLAST	CLINGS	DECK
ADULTERY	BLASTED	CLOSER	DECK'D
ADVISED	BLEND	CLOTHING	DECLARE
AFFECTED	BLENDING	COACH	DEFY
AFFORD	BLINDNESS	COARSE	DEIGN'D
AFFORDS	BLISS	COAT	DELIGHTFUL
AFORESAID	BLUES	COCKED	DELIGNE
AGO	BLUNDERED	COLLECT	DEMANDS
AGONIES	BLUSHING	COLUMBUS	DENIED
AIDED	BOILS	COMERS	DENYING
AJAX	BOLDLY	COMFORT	DEPART
ALBION'S	BOLT	COMFORTABLE	DEPARTURE
ALDERMAN	BON	COMMEMORATION	DEPLORE
AMBER	BONDS	COMMISSION	DESCEND
AMIABLE	BOSPHORUS	COMMONEST	DESCRIBES

3   (CONTINUED)

DESERTS	EXCHANGED	GOVERN	JEFFREY
DESERVING	EXERTION	GOVERNMENT	JEWS
DESOLATION	EXPECT	GRACIOUS	JOKES
DESPOND	EXPENSE	GRIEVES	JUICE
DESPOTS	EXPLANATION	GROSS	JURIES
DESTROYS	EXPOSED	GRUMBLING	JURY
DETERMINE	EXPOUND	GUARDIANS	KINDER
DETEST	EXTENSIVE	GUARDS	KINDEST
DEUCE	EYE'S	GUESSING	KINGDOM
DIALOGUE	FADING	GUNPOWDER	KINGDOMS
DIAN	FALLS	HABITS	KNEES
DIC	FALSEHOOD	HALF-PAST	KNOCK'D
DIFFER	FARCE	HALF-WAY	KNOCKED
DIFFERING	FARMERS	HALLUCINATION	KNOCKS
DIFFICULTIES	FARTHER	HAMMER	LABOUR
DIFFICULTY	FASTEN'D	HAPPEN	LADS
DIGGING	FAT	HARDSHIPS	LAKES
DIGRESSION	FATIGUE	HARMONY	LAMENTED
DILETTANTI	FAVOUR'D	HASTILY	LAMP
DIOGENES	FAVOURED	HEARS	LANDED
DISCLOSE	FEEBLE	HEATED	LANDSCAPE
DISCOUNT	FEE'D	HEATHENISH	LANGUAGES
DISCOVERS	FETTER	HEAVEN-KISSING	LASH'D
DISCREET	FIE	HEAVIEST	LASTING
DISDAIN	FIFTEEN	HEAVING	LAVA
DISGUST	FIGHTS	HE'LL	LAYS
DISPATCHES	FILE	HELL'S	LEARNT
DISPENSED	FINEST	HERALD	LEASE
DISPLAYS	FIRES	HERD	LEE
DIVERS	FISHES	HEROINE	LESSER
DIVORCE	FLASHES	HIDALGO	LETTERS
DOCTOR	FLATTERING	HINGES	LEVEE
DOCTORS'	FLAW	HIRED	LEVELS
DOINGS	FLINGS	HO	LICENCE
DOLLARS	FLOTILLA	HOARD	LIFELESS
DOVES	FLUSH	HOCK	LIKEWISE
DOWER	FLUTTERING	HONOURED	LIKING
DOWNWARD	FOAMING	HOOD	LIMITS
DRAINS	FOLDS	HORRIBLE	LINK
DRAMS	FOLLIES	HORROR	LIONS
DRAPERY	FOLLOWERS	HOSPITALITY	LIQUOR
DRAWS	FORCED	HOVER	LISTENING
DREAR	FORCES	HOVERING	LIVELY
DRILL	FOREGO	HOWL	LOATHE
DRINKS	FOREHEAD	HOWSOEVER	LOFTIEST
DROOP	FORLORN	HUMBLER	LONDON'S
DROOP'D	FORSOOTH	HUMOUR	LONG-BOAT
DROPP'D	FORTE	HUNTING	LONGBOW
DROPPING	FORTUNES	HUNTSMAN	LONGED
DROWSY	FOUNDED	HUSBANDS'	LONGEST
DRUMS	FOUNTAINS	ILION	LONGINUS
DUNS	FRAY	ILLNESS	LOTH
DURING	FREDERICK	ILLS	LOTTERY
DUTCH	FREEDOM'S	IMPERATIVE	LOUDER
DWELLS	FREEZE	IMPORT	LOYAL
DYE	FRET	IMPORTANT	LUCKLESS
DYED	FRIGHT	IMPOSSIBLE	LUCUBRATIONS
EAGLE	FROWNED	IMPRESARIO	LULL
EARNEST	FROZEN	IMPROVING	LURCH
ECHOED	FRY	IMPRUDENT	LURKED
ECLAT	FUEL	INANITION	LYRIC
EDGE	FURNITURE	INANITY	MACHINES
EDICTS	GAINS	INCLINED	MAGNANIMITY
ELEMENTS	GAINSAY	INCONSTANCY	MAIL
ELOQUENT	GALLANT	INCREASES	MAINTAIN
EMBARKED	GALLERY	INDIAN	MALGRE
EMBARRASSED	GAMING	INDIGESTION	MALL
EMPLOY	GAZETTES	INDIVIDUAL	MAMMA
ENGAGED	GENERALS	INGENUOUS	MANAGED
ENGINES	GEOGRAPHY	INHERENT	MARROW
ENJOYING	GEORGIAN	INLAID	MARVEL
ENSLAVED	GEORGIANS	INQUIRE	MASTS
ENSUED	GHASTLY	INQUIRED	MATCHED
EPOCH	GIGANTIC	INSANITY	MATERNAL
EQUINOCTIAL	GILDING	INSIDE	MATRIMONY
ERIN	GIRDLE	INSOLENT	MAZE
ERMINE	GLANCES	INSTANTLY	MEASURES
ESPECIAL	GLANCING	INSTINCT	MEATS
EUNUCHS	GLEAMED	INTERFERED	MEETS
EUROPEAN	GLEAMS	INTERPOSED	MELODY
EVENINGS	GLIDED	INVENTED	MELTED
EVERYBODY'S	GLIDES	INVENTION	MELTS
EVERYONE	GLITTER	IONIAN	MENDS
EXACT	GLOOMY	ISSUE	MENTION'D
EXCELLENT	GLORIES	IVORY	METAPHYSICIAN
EXCEPTION	GO-BETWEEN	JACKET	METEOR
EXCEPTIONS	GODDESSES	JAILOR	METHOD
	GOOSE	JAWS	MIDDLE-AGED

3   (CONTINUED)
MIGHT
MILDEST
MILE
MINE'S
MINGLE
MINISTER
MINISTERS
MISCARRIAGE
MISERY
MISSAL
MISS'D
MIST
MISTAKES
MISTOOK
MISTRESSES
MIX
MODESTLY
MOLTEN
MONDE
MONTH
MONTHLY
MONUMENT
MOON'S
MOONSHINE
MOORISH
MORALITY
MORE'S
MORTALITY
MOULD
MOUNTAIN
MOUSE
MOVEMENT
MR
MUD
MURRAY
MUSIC'S
MUTTON
MYSTERIES
NAMELESS
NARROW
NATIONAL
NATION'S
NATURES
NAUGHTY
NAVIGATION
NEEDLE
NEGLECT
NEGROES
NEIGHBOURING
NERO
NERVES
NEUTER
NEWSPAPER
NEWTON
NICE
NIGHTINGALE
NIGHT'S
NOAH'S
NOD
NODDING
NODS
NOTED
NOTES
NOTICE
NOVEL
NOVELS
NURST
NYMPHS
OBLIGE
OBSERVE
OBSERVED
OBVIOUS
OCCUPATION
OCEAN'S
OFFEND
OFFER'D
OFFERED
OFFSPRING
OMEN
OMISSION
OPENS
OPIATE
OPPOSITE
OPTICS
OTTOMAN
OVERCOME
OVID'S

OWE
OWED
OWING
PACE
PACK
PAINFUL
PAINTING
PALTRY
PANT
PAPERS
PAPHIAN
PARAGON
PARISH
PARTED
PARTICULARLY
PARTING
PASSENGERS
PASSES
PASSPORT
PASTIME
PATHETIC
PATHOS
PEACEFUL
PEAL
PEASANTS
PEDRILLO'S
PEDRO
PEEP
PEEPING
PENSIONS
PEOPLED
PERDITION
PERFECTION
PERIOD
PERPENDICULAR
PERSPECTIVE
PERSPICUOUS
PHANTOM
PICTURES
PIERCE
PIERCES
PINCH
PINION
PINK
PIRATE
PITIED
PLACID
PLAYFUL
PLEADED
PLEASES
PLOUGH
PLOUGHS
PLUNGED
POACHERS
POEM'S
POEMS
POINTED
POLAND
POLISH'D
POMP
PONDER'D
POOH
POPULAR
PORCELAIN
PORTER
PORTIONS
PORTRAITS
POSE
POSSIBLE
POSTILLIONS
POTATOES
POUTING
PRACTISED
PRAISES
PREACHER
PRECARIOUS
PRESERVED
PRESSURE
PRESUMED
PREUX
PREVAIL
PRINCE'S
PRINCES
PRINCIPLE
PRINTED
PROBLEM
PROCEEDING
PROFESSIONAL

PROFUSION
PROMONTORY
PROOFS
PROPAGATION
PROPHETIC
PROPORTION
PROPOSITION
PROVISION
PURER
PURSE
PURSUES
PUZZLE
PUZZLES
PYRRHIC
QUEER
QUENCHED
QUEST
QUICKER
QUIVERING
QUIXOTE
RABY
RAGING
RAGS
RAISING
RAMBLE
RANGED
RAPP
RASCALS
RASHLY
RATION
REAP
REAR
REBEL
RECEIVES
RECKON'D
REFERENCE
REFINED
REJECT
REJOINED
RELICS
REMARKS
REMOTE
RENOWNED
REPAST
REPENTED
REPLACED
REPLIES
REPORT
REPROACH
RESOLUTION
RESTLESS
RESTORE
RESTORED
RESTRICTION
RESTS
RETORT
RETREAT
RETREATED
REVERIES
REVERSE
REVIEW
REVIVE
RICHLY
RID
RIDING
RIGID
ROADS
ROAM
ROARING
ROBES
ROCKY
ROD
ROMANCE
ROMANS
ROOTS
ROUSSEAU
ROYALTY
RUBLES
RUINS
RUSH
RUSH'D
RUTH
SABINE
SABRES
SAFFRON
SAGEST
SAILED
SAKES

SANCTION
SAPPHO
SATIRE
SAVOUR
SCAN
SCANDAL'S
SCANNED
SCATTERED
SCATTERING
SCHOOLBOY
SCORCH'D
SCORNER
SCOTLAND
SCROLL
SCYTHE
SEARCH'D
SEA'S
SEA-SICK
SEATS
SECONDLY
SECURITY
SEED
SEEKING
SELL
SELVES
SENATE
SENTENCE
SERASKIER
SERMON
SERVANT
SERVES
SETTLES
SEVENTH
SHADES
SHAKSPEARE'S
SHALLOW
SHAPED
SHARK
SHELF
SHIVERED
SHOAL
SHOCKED
SHOCKING
SHOOTING
SHORN
SHORTEST
SHORTHAND
SHOWER
SHUNNED
SHY
SIEGE
SILENCED
SILKEN
SILVERY
SIMILAR
SIMPLICITY
SIRE'S
SISTERS
SKETCHES
SLIPS
SMALLER
SMOOTH'D
SNAKE
SNATCH'D
SNATCHED
SOAR
SODA
SONGS
SON'S
SOUL'S
SOUTHEY'S
SOVEREIGN'S
SPAN
SPEAKERS
SPEAKS
SPECIFIED
SPECTATOR
SPEECHES
SPEECHLESS
SPIDERS
SPINNING
SPIRIT'S
SPOKEN
SPUN
SPUR
SQUARES
STALK
STANZA

3 (CONTINUED)

STATELY	TRANQUIL	WINDOWS	ANCESTORS
STATESMEN	TRANSIENT	WIND'S	ANCLES
STATIONS	TRANSITORY	WINGED	ANDALUSIAN
STEAD	TRAVELL'D	WINTER'S	ANGELS
STEAL	TRAVELLER	WISDOM'S	ANNEX
STEALING	TRAY	WITCHES	ANNOY
STEPP'D	TREATED	WITHDRAWN	ANTHONY
STEPS	TREMOR	WITHSTAND	ANTICIPATED
STIFF	TRICKS	WOLVES	APE
STING	TRIFLING	WONDERS	APIECE
STIRR'D	TRITE	WOND'ROUS	APPARENT
STOCK	TRIUMPHAL	WORDLESS	APPEALS
STRAIN	TROPHY	WORDY	APPELLANTS
STRAINS	TRUCULENT	WREATH	APPENDIX
STRANGEST	TRUFFLES	WRINKLES	APPETITES
STRETCH	TRYING	WRITES	APPLICATION
STRICTER	TUMBLE	WROTH	APROPOS
STRICTLY	TUMBLED	YCLEPT	ARCHITECT
STRONGBOW'S	TUNEFUL	YELL	ARGO
STRUGGLED	TURNPIKE	YIELDING	ARGUMENTS
STRUMPET	TURNPIKES	YON	ARIOSTO
STUBBORN	TWEEZERS		ARISTIPPUS
STUFFS	TWELFTH	2	ARM'D
STUMBLING	TWILIGHT'S	A	ARMOUR
STYLED	UNCOMMON	ABEYANCE	ARMY'S
STYX	UNDREST	ABHORR'D	AROINT
SUBLIMEST	UNHAPPY	ABOUNDED	ARRAGON
SUBSTANTIAL	UNITY	ABSTRACT	ARRANGING
SUBTLE	UNQUIET	ABSTRACTION	ARRAS
SUFFER	UNRIDDLED	ABUSES	ARRIVES
SUFFER'D	UPSET	ACCIDENT	ARROW
SUFFERED	VACANT	ACCOMPLISH'D	ARSENIEW
SUFFERING	VARIED	ACCOMPLISHED	ARTIFICIAL
SUFFERINGS	VASE	ACCOUNTS	ARTILLERY
SUFFICIENTLY	VEGETABLES	ACCURATE	ARTILLERY'S
SUGGESTED	VENERABLE	ACHILLES'	ASCERTAIN
SUITOR	VENETIAN	ACIDS	ASCERTAINED
SULLEN	VENT	ACTIONS	ASIA
SULTANA	VENTURED	ACUTE	ASIAN
SUMMIT	VERDICT	ADDITION	ASPECTS
SUN'S	VERSES	ADDRESS'D	ASPIRANT
SUNS	VESSELS	ADDRESSING	ASSUME
SUPERSEDE	VEST	ADELINE'S	ASSUMED
SURFACE	VESTAL	ADIEU	ASSURANCE
SURMISE	VEX	ADMIRARI	ATROCIOUS
SURPASS	VEXATION	ADMIRE	ATTAIN
SURVEYED	VICIOUS	ADORE	ATTAINING
SUSPECT	VIE	ADORN'D	ATTEND
SWALLOWING	VOGUE	ADULTERATION	ATTENDANT
SWAM	VOLCANO	ADVANCES	ATTRACTION
SWEARS	VOLUNTEERS	ADVANTAGES	ATTRACTIONS
SWEETEST	VOTARIES	ADVENTUROUS	AUGUR
SWEETNESS	VOW'D	ADVERSITY	AUGUST
SWUNG	VULTURE	AFAR	AUGUSTINE
SYCOPHANT	WAGE	AFRIC	AUTHOR
TABLES	WAITERS	AFRICA	AUTHORITY
TALES	WAKES	AFT	AUTHOR'S
TAMED	WALK'D	AFTERNOON	AUTUMN'S
TARS	WANDER	AGITATED	AVAIL
TASTES	WANED	AGREEABLE	AVERAGE
TEASE	WANING	AGUE	AVOW
TEENS	WARBLE	AGUISH	AWAKEN
TEMPLES	WARE	AI	AWAKES
TERRIBLE	WARLIKE	ALABASTER	AWARD
TERROR	WARMTH	ALACRITY	AYE
THEMES	WARNING	ALARMING	BABA'S
THETIS	WARRIOR	ALE	BABYLON
THOMSON	WARY	ALERT	BABYLON'S
THOROUGH	WASHINGTON	ALIQUANDO	BACCHANAL
THREATENED	WATCHED	ALLIANCE	BACCHANT
THRILLING	WAX'D	ALLIED	BACKGROUND
THROB	WEAN	ALLIES	BADLY
THRONES	WEARINESS	ALLOW'D	BAG
THUNDERED	WEEDS	ALLOY	BAGGED
TIMID	WEEKS	ALLURED	BAGS
TINGE	WEEN	ALLURES	BAIT
TIPTOE	WEEPING	ALLUSIONS	BAKED
TIRESOME	WEIGHED	ALOUD	BALE
TODAY	WHATSOEVER	ALPHABET	BALTIC'S
TOKEN	WHIRLS	ALTERATIONS	BAND
TOLL	WHISPERING	ALTER'D	BANDAGE
TORCHES	WHITES	AMBASSADORS	BANNS
TOSS	WHORE	AMBITION'S	BANQUETS
TOSSED	WHO'VE	AMENDS	BAPTIZED
TOURS	WIDOWS	AMERICA	BARACAN
TOWN'S	WILBERFORCE	AMMON'S	BARB
TRAMPLING	WILLING	AMUSE	BARGAIN
	WILLOW	ANACREON	BARGE
		ANACREON'S	

952

2   (CONTINUED)

BASIS	BROOK'D	CHILLY	CONQUER
BASS	BRUSHES	CHIMNEY	CONQUERORS
BATTERING	BRUTE	CHINA	CONSCIOUS
BATTISTA	BRUTUS	CHINESE	CONSIDERABLE
BATTLE-FIELD	BUBBLE	CHOOSING	CONSIGNED
BATTLE'S	BUFFOON	CHORAL	CONSISTED
BATTLING	BUFFOONS	CHRISTIANITY	CONSOLED
BEAMS	BUILDING	CHURCHES	CONSORT
BEARDLESS	BULLET	CHURCH'S	CONSPICUOUS
BEATRICE	BULLETS	CIRCASSIANS	CONSPIRACY
BEAUTY'S	BULLIED	CIRCLES	CONSTANCY
BECOMES	BULL'S	CIRCLING	CONSTRUCTED
BEDDING	BUONAPARTE	CIRCULATING	CONTACT
BEDLAM	BURIAL	CIRCUMSPECTION	CONTEND
BEFALL	BURKE	CIVIC	CONTENDED
BEGG'D	BURLESQUE	CIVILIZATION	CONTINENTS
BEGINS	BURTHEN	CLAD	CONTRAST
BEHOLDERS	BUTCHERED	CLAIMS	CONTROL
BEHOLDS	BUTTER	CLAMOUR	CONVALESCENCE
BELIEVERS	BUTTERFLIES	CLASH'D	CONVENIENT
BELLONA	BUYS	CLASSED	CONVERSE
BELLOW	BYE	CLASSES	CONVULSIVE
BELONG	CALMER	CLASSICAL	COOK'D
BENCH	CAMPAIGN	CLATTER	COOKS
BESEECHING	CAMPBELL	CLAW	COPPER
BESET	CAMPBELL'S	CLEARED	COPY
BESPOKE	CANALS	CLEARER	COQUETRY
BE'T	CANDLE	CLEFT	COQUETTE
BETIDE	CANDLES	CLEOPATRA'S	CORAL
BETRAY	CANT	CLERGY	CORONETS
BETRAYING	CANTEMIR	CLIFF	CORUSCATION
BEVERAGE	CANTER	CLIMAX	COSSACQUE
BIGGER	CANTERBURY	CLING	COSTS
BILIOUS	CANVASS	CLOG	COTERIE
BILLIARDS	CAPS	CLOISTERS	COUCHED
BIRTHS	CAPTAIN	CLOTHED	COUGH
BISCUIT	CAPTAINS	CLOUDED	COUNCILS
BITE	CARAVAN	CLUBS	COUNSELLORS
BITTEREST	CARCASES	CLUE	COUNTESS
BLACKGUARDS	CAREFUL	COALS	COUNTESSES
BLADE	CARLTON	COFFEEHOUSE	COUNTRYMEN
BLAMED	CARNIVAL	COINED	COUPLET
BLANKET	CARP	COINS	COURSERS
BLANKETS	CARPET	COLDER	COURTEOUS
BLASPHEMY	CARPETS	COLOURED	COURTEOUSLY
BLAZED	CARRYING	COLOURING	COURTLY
BLEAK	CARTHAGE	COMBINE	COUSINS
BLEED	CARTRIDGES	COMBINED	COVET
BLESS	CASCADE	COMER	COVETED
BLESSED	CASK	COMMANDANT	COWERS
BLIGHTED	CASKS	COMMANDER	COXCOMBRY
BLOCKHEAD	CASQUE	COMMANDMENT	COXCOMBS
BLOTTED	CASSIO	COMMISERATION	CRABBE
BLOWN	CASTE	COMMOTION	CRACKED
BLUNDERING	CASTILIAN	COMPARATIVE	CRASHAW
BLUNDERS	CASUISTS	COMPEERS	CREAK
BODED	CATALOGUE	COMPETENT	CREAM
BOIL	CATECHISM	COMPLAINING	CREDITOR
BOIL'D	CATS	COMPLAINT	CREDITORS
BOMB	CATULLUS	COMPOSE	CREEK
BONAPARTE	CAUSELESS	COMPOSED	CRESCENT
BONNETS	CAW	COMPOSITION	CRESCENT'S
BOOK'S	CENTURIES	COMPREHENSION	CRETANS
BOORS	CERTAINTY	COMPRISED	CRISIS
BORED	CHAIR	COMRADE	CRITIC
BORES	CHAMPAIGNE	COMRADE'S	CRITICISM
BOROUGH	CHAMPION	CON	CROSS'D
BORROWED	CHARACTERS	CONCEALED	CROSSED
BOTHERS	CHARIOT	CONCEIVE	CROWDING
BOUNDLESS	CHARIOTS	CONCEIVED	CROWNS
BOW-STRING	CHARMERS	CONCERN'D	CRUISING
BOXER	CHASTER	CONCISION	CRUTCH
BOY'S	CHECK	CONCOCTION	CUE
BRAKE	CHECKED	CONCUBINE	CUFFS
BRANDY	CHECQUERED	CONDEMNED	CULPRIT
BRAVURAS	CHEEK'S	CONDENSED	CUMBERLAND
BREADTH	CHEER	CONDESCENDS	CURB'D
BREW	CHEMISE	CONDUCTOR	CURDLE
BRIBE	CHEOPS	CONFERENCE	CURED
BRIBES	CHERISH'D	CONFERRED	CURL'D
BRIDEGROOMS	CHEST	CONFESSION	CURLED
BRIG	CHEVALIER	CONFESSOR	CURLY
BRIM	CHIEFS	CONFIDENCE	CURRENTS
BRITON	CHILDHOOD	CONFOUND	CURSES
BRITON'S	CHILDREN'S	CONGREVE'S	CURTSIED
BROODING	CHILL'D	CONNECTIONS	CURTSIES
BROODS	CHILLED	CONNEXIONS	CUSHION
	CHILLING	CONNOISSEUR	CUSTOM-HOUSE

953

2 (CONTINUED)

CYNIC	DISCOUNTED	ENABLES	FENELON
DAGGER	DISCOVERY	ENCOUNTER	FERTILE
DAMAGED	DISCREETLY	ENCOURAGE	FERVENT
DAMAS	DISCUSS	ENCOURAGEMENT	FETTER'D
DAMP'D	DISCUSS'D	ENDEARS	FETTERS
DAN	DISDAIN'D	ENDURANCE	FEVERISH
DANCERS	DISDAINED	ENDURED	FIAT
DANDIES	DISHED	ENEMIES	FIDDLE
DANUBE	DISPENSE	ENGAGE	FIDDLING
DARLING	DISPLEASE	ENGLISHMEN	FIGHTERS
DARTS	DISPOSITION	ENJOYMENT	FILLET'S
DATES	DISSECTION	ENQUIRE	FILLETS
DAUGHTER'S	DISSIMULATION	ENQUIRED	FILLING
DAVID	DISSOLVED	ENRICH	FILTER'D
DAY'S	DISSOLVING	ENSEMBLE	FINISH'D
DAYS'	DISTINCT	ENSURE	FINISHED
DAZZLING	DISTINGUISHED	ENTER'D	FISHER
DEADLIER	DISTRAIT	ENTERTAIN	FISHERMAN
DEAFENED	DISTRESSES	ENTHUSIASM	FITTER
DEALER	DISTURB	ENTOMB	FLAGS
DEALS	DITCHES	ENTREATING	FLAMES
DEARER	DIVAN	ENVIRON	FLANK'D
DEARLY	DIVERSION	ENVOY	FLANKED
DEARTH	DIVERTED	EPIGRAM	FLANKS
DEATH'S	DIVIDE	EPIGRAMS	FLASKS
DEBATES	DIVIDING	ERIN'S	FLAT
DECLARED	DIVORCED	ESCAPADE	FLATTERS
DECLARES	DIZZINESS	ESSAY'D	FLEECED
DECLIVITY	DIZZY	ESSENCE	FLEECY
DECORATE	DOCILE	ESTABLISHED	FLEET
DECOROUS	DOCTRINE	ETHERIAL	FLEETING
DECREE	DOOM'D	ETIQUETTE	FLINCH
DEFEND	DOTE	EULOGY	FLING
DEFIANCE	DOUBTING	EUXINE	FLINT
DEFIED	DOUBT'S	EVENTS	FLITS
DEFILED	DOVER	EVE'S	FLOATS
DEGENERATE	DOWRY	EVIDENCES	FLOOR
DEGRADATION	DRAFT	EVIDENTLY	FLOORS
DELETERIOUS	DRAWING-ROOM	EXACTS	FLOURISHED
DELICACY	DREADED	EXCEL	FLOURISHES
DELICATELY	DREADING	EXCESSES	FLOWED
DELIGHTING	DREAMING	EXCITED	FLOWING
DELIGHTS	DRESSED	EXCLAIMING	FLURRY
DELUSION	DRILLING	EXCURSION	FLUTTER
DEMAGOGUES	DRINKING	EXCURSIVE	FOCUS
DEMANDED	DRIPPING	EXCUSES	FOIBLE
DEMEANOUR	DRIVING	EXEMPLARY	FOIBLES
DEMOLISHED	DROUTHY	EXILED	FOLDED
DENOUNCE	DROWN'D	EXOTIC	FOLLOWS
DEPARTED	DROWNED	EXPANDING	FONT
DEPEND	DRUNKENNESS	EXPECTANT	FOOLING
DEPOSIT	DRYDEN	EXPECTED	FOOL'S
DEPOSITIONS	DUDU'S	EXPENDED	FORBADE
DEPTHS	DULLY	EXPLORED	FORBIDDEN
DESCRIPTIONS	DUNCES	EXPOSURE	FORBIDS
DESERVE	DURA	EXPRESS'D	FORE
DESIGNS	D'YE	EXPRESSES	FORESTERS
DESK	EARLS	EXQUISITE	FORGIVEN
DESPATCHES	EARN	EXTENT	FORKS
DESPISE	EARNED	EXTRACT	FORMER'S
DESPISING	EARTHQUAKES	EXTREMES	FORSOOK
DESPOTISM	ECHOS	EYELIDS	FORTUNATE
DESTINED	EDEN	FABLES	FORTUNE'S
DESTROY'D	EDEN'S	FACETIOUS	FORTY'S
DESTROYING	EDIFYING	FACILITY	FORWARD
DETAIN	EDITION	FACTITIOUS	FOUNDATION
DEVILISH	EDITOR	FACT'S	FOUNDERED
DEWS	EDUCATE	FADES	FOUNT
DIALOGUES	EFFEMINATE	FAINTER	FOURSCORE
DICE	EGOTISM	FAINTLY	FOX-HUNT
DICK	EGYPT'S	FAIREST	FRAGILE
DICTION	ELECT	FAITHLESS	FRAGRANT
DIDDLED	ELECTION	FALL'N	FRAILER
DIET	ELEGANCE	FAMED	FRANKS
DIGNITY	ELEGANT	FAMILY'S	FRANTIC
DIGRESSIONS	EMBARGO	FANCIED	FREAK
DILATED	EMBARGOED	FANGS	FREEDOMS
DIMITY	EMBARRASS'D	FARM	FRENCHMAN
DIPLOMATISTS	EMBARRASSMENT	FASCINATING	FREQUENT
DIRGE	EMBRACED	FASCINES	FRESHEST
DIRT	EMERGE	FASTER	FRESHNESS
DISAGREEABLE	EMETIC	FAUX	FRETTED
DISASTER	EMOTIONS	FEATHER	FRIAR'S
DISCERN	EMPERORS	FEATS	FRIARS
DISCERNMENT	EMPIRES	FEED	FRIGHTEN
DISCIPLINE	EMPLOY'D	FEEDS	FRIGHTENED
DISCORDS	EMPTY	FELL'D	FRINGES
	EMULATION	FEN	FROWN'D

955

2 (CONTINUED)
LITERARY
LITERATURE
LITTER
LIVELIER
LOAN
LOATHING
LOATHSOME
LOCK
LOCKE
LOCUST
LONGINGS
LORDSHIP
LORE
LOTTED
LOVERS'
LOWERS
LOYALTY
LUCID
LUCKIER
LUCUS
LUGGAGE
LUMINOUS
LUTE
LUTHER
MACHIAVEL
MACHINERY
MADEIRA
MADLY
MADNESS
MADRID
MAHOMET'S
MAID'S
MAINTAINED
MAINTENANCE
MAJOR
MAK'ST
MALADIES
MALICE
MALMSEY
MAMMOTHS
MANHOOD
MANKIND'S
MANLIER
MANNED
MANOR
MANURE
MAR
MARATHON
MARKED
MARKOW
MARLBOROUGH'S
MARR'D
MARRIAGES
MARRY
MARSH
MARSHAL
MARTS
MARTYRS
MARVELL'D
MARY'S
MASCULINE
MASQUED
MASQUERADING
MASTER'S
MATERIAL
MATHEMATICAL
MATRIMONIAL
MATRON'S
MAY-DAY
MEAL
MEANETH
MEANWHILE
MEAT
MEDALS
MEDICINES
MEDIUM
MEED
MEEK
MEEKEST
MEETING
MELT
MEMBERS
MEMOIRS
MENE
MERCURIAL
MERCY
MERIDIAN

MERIDIAN-BORN
MERRIMENT
METAL
METALS
METAPHYSICAL
MI
MID-DAY
MILDLY
MILLINERS
MILTON'S
MINION
MINT
MIRRORED
MIRRORS
MISANTHROPY
MISCHIEF'S
MISERABLE
MISER'S
MISTERS
MISTS
MIZEN
MODERNS
MODESTY'S
MONARCH
MONARCH'S
MONKEY
MONKS
MONSTER'S
MONSTERS
MOONBEAMS
MOOR
MORALIST
MORALISTS
MOREOVER
MORSEL
MORTGAGE
MOSES
MOSLEMS
MOT
MOTH
MOTIONED
MOTIONS
MOTIVES
MOTLEY
MOTTO
MOUNTING
MOURNER
MOURNFUL
MOURNS
MOVEMENTS
MOVES
MOVING
MUFFIN
MULTIPLY
MURDER
MURMUR
MUSCOVITE
MUSE'S
MUSICAL
MUSICO
MUSLIN
MUSSULMAN
MUSTER
MUTE
MUTES
MUTTERED
MYSTERIOUS
MYSTIFIED
NAG
NAILS
NAPOLEON'S
NARRATING
NECTAR
NEEDED
NEEDLES
NEGLIGENTLY
NELSON
NET
NEUTRAL
NEWER
NEWEST
NEWLY
NEWS
NIECES
NIKOLAIEW
NIL
NIMROD'S
NINETEEN

NINEVEH
NOBLER
NODDED
NODDY
NON
NON-DESCRIPT
NOOKS
NOON
NOSES
NOTHINGS
NOTIONS
NOUGHT'S
NOUS
NOVELTIES
NOVEMBER
NUN
NUNNERY
NURSES
NURSING
NYMPH
OAKS
OARS
OATS
OBLIVION
OBSCURITY
OBSERVATION
OBSTINACY
OBTAIN
ODDEST
ODE
O'ERCOME
O'ERPOWERING
O'ERWHELM'D
O'ERWHELMING
OFFSPRING'S
OFTENTIMES
OGLE
OLDEN
OLIVES
OMIT
OPE
OPENER
OPERA
OPINE
OPPORTUNE
OPPOSE
OPPOSED
OPPOSITION
OPPRESSION
ORANGES
ORATION
ORATORS
ORB
ORDERING
ORDERLY
ORIENT
ORIGIN
ORNAMENT
ORNAMENTS
OTHERWISE
OUTRAGEOUS
OUTRUN
OVERBOARD
OWL
OWN'D
OWNED
OWNER
OYSTERS
PACES
PACHAS
PAD
PAINTERS
PAINTS
PALELY
PALLS
PALPABLY
PANNELS
PANTED
PANTING
PANTOMIME
PARAGRAPH
PARENTAL
PARIS
PAROLLES
PARRY'S
PARSON
PARTICIPATED
PARTNER

PASSAGE
PASSIONATE
PASSIONLESS
PASTIMES
PASTOR
PATAGONIAN
PATENT
PAUL
PAVILION
PAYMENT
PEACEABLE
PEBBLES
PECULIAR
PEDANTIC
PEDESTRIAN
PEER
PELISSE
PELL-MELL
PENCHANT
PENETRATE
PENN'D
PENS
PERFORMANCE
PERMANENT
PERMIT
PERMITTED
PERPETUAL
PERPLEX'D
PERPLEXES
PERSIANS
PERSONAGE
PERSUADE
PERSUADED
PERSUASION
PERTINACITY
PERUSE
PETITS
PETTICOATS
PHIDIAN
PHILIP'S
PHILO-GENITIVENESS
PHILOSOPHERS
PHILOSOPHIC
PHILOSOPHIZE
PHYSICS
PICKING
PICKLE
PICTURED
PILAUS
PILE
PILED
PILLAR
PILOTS
PIN
PINCHBECK
PINDAR
PINE
PINS
PIPES
PIQUES
PISTOLS
PITEOUS
PITT
PITYING
PIVOT
PLACEMEN
PLAGUES
PLAINS
PLANS
PLANTS
PLATONISM
PLAYING
PLEAD
PLEADING
PLEADS
PLENTIFUL
PLIABLE
PLIANT
PLIGHTED
PLODDING
PLOUGHMAN
PLUCK
PLUCK'D
PLUMAGE
POCKETS
POLITESSE
POLITICIAN
POLITICIANS

2   (CONTINUED)

POLYGAMY	PUBLISHER	REQUIRE	SCENT
POMEGRANATE	PUDDING	RESEARCH	SCEPTICS
PONDERED	PUDDLE	RESIGNED	SCHNAPPS
PONIARD	PUITS	RESISTED	SCHOOLBOY'S
PORK	PULCI	RESOLVE	SCIENCES
PORTRAIT	PUNCH	RESPECTABLE	SCIO
POSED	PUNISH	RESPECTS	SCIO'S
POSITION	PUPPETS	RESTING	SCOLDING
POSSESSORS	PURCHASER	RESTIVE	SCORNED
POST-OBITS	PURSES	RESTLESSNESS	SCORNS
POSTPONE	PUTTING	RETAIN	SCOTS
POSTS	PYE	RETAINS	SCRAMBLING
POT	PYRAMID	RETRACE	SCREAM'D
POTEMKIN	PYRRHO	RETURN'D	SCRIBBLING
POTENTIAL	QUALMS	RETURNED	SCRIBES
POUNDS	QUARTERS	RETURNS	SCUFFLE
PRACTICE	QUENCH'D	REVELRY	SEA-COAL
PRANK	QUILL	REVERIE	SEAL'D
PRANKS	QUIZ	REVOKE	SEALS
PRATED	RACE-HORSE	RIBAS	SEARCHED
PRATTLE	RAGED	RICHER	SEARS
PRAYING	RAGES	RIDDEN	SEA-SHORE
PREACHERS	RAGOUT	RIDICULES	SEA-SICKNESS
PRECEPT	RAILED	RIFE	SEASON'S
PRECINCTS	RAILING	RIGHTLY	SECT
PRECIPICE	RAINED	RIND	SECURED
PRECOCIOUS	RAKE	RIP	SELFISH
PREFERMENT	RANG	RIPPLE	SEMPER
PREJUDICE	RANGES	RISKED	SENSELESS
PRESERVATION	RANKLE	RIVER'S	SENSIBILITY
PRESERVE	RAP	ROAMS	SENSIBLE
PRESS'D	RAPID	ROARED	SENTENTIOUS
PRESSED	RAPTURE	ROBBED	SENTIMENTS
PREST	RAPTURES	ROBUST	SEPULCHRAL
PRETENCES	RARITY	ROGERS	SEQUEL
PRETENSIONS	RASCAL	ROGUE	SERAPHIC
PRETTIEST	RATED	ROMANCERS	SERENELY
PRIAM'S	RATIONAL	ROME'S	SERIOUSLY
PRICK'D	RAUCOCANTI	ROMILLY	SERPENT'S
PRICKS	RAVE	ROOF	SERVENTE
PRIDED	RAVEN	ROOTED	SETTLEMENT
PRIDE'S	RAVENNA'S	ROSIN	SEVEN-AND-TWENTY
PRIESTS	RAVING	ROUGE	SEVERITY
PRIM	RAWBOLDS	ROUGHLY	SEXES
PRIMA-DONNA	REACHING	ROULEAUS	SHABBY
PRINCIPLES	READER'S	ROUSED	SHAKING
PRIORITY	REAPING	ROUTE	SHAKSPEARE
PRISONER	REARED	ROUTS	SHARKS
PRITHEE	REASONABLE	ROVES	SHATTER'D
PRIVILEGE	REASONING	RUDDER	SHAVING
PRO	REBELS	RUEFUL	SHAWL
PROCLAIM	REBUKED	RUFFLED	SHEATH
PRODIGIOUS	RECALL'D	RUGGED	SHEDS
PRODIGY	RECEDING	RUIN'D	SHEEP
PRODUCTION	RECESS	RUMMAGING	SHELL-FISH
PROFANELY	RECKONED	RUSHES	SHEPHERD
PROFESSION	RECOMMENCE	RUSSET	SHERBET
PROFITS	RECOMMENDED	RUSSIA'S	SHERBETS
PROFUSELY	RECRUITS	RUSTLE	SHEW
PROGENY	REDEEMING	RUSTY	SHIFT
PROJECT	REDUCE	SACRIFICE	SHIFTS
PROLOGUE	REEL	SADDENS	SHINGLES
PROMOTED	REFECTION	SADDER	SHIRTS
PRONOUNCED	REFLECTED	SADDEST	SHIVER
PROPERTY	RE-FORM'D	SAILING	SHOALS
PROPHECIES	REFUGE	SAILS	SHOD
PROPHESY	REGALE	SAL	SHOE
PROPHETS	REGRETTED	SALAMANDER	SHOOT
PROPOSED	REGRETTING	SALUTED	SHOOTER'S
PROSERS	REJECTED	SALVATION	SHORES
PROSODY	REMARKED	SANCTIFIED	SHORTER
PROSPECTS	REMEDIES	SANDY	SHOULDERS
PROTECTION	REMEMBERED	SANK	SHOUTED
PROTECTS	REMONSTRANCES	SAP	SHOWING
PROUDLY	RENDER'D	SAPPHO'S	SHOWMAN
PROVERB	RENEGADO	SATAN	SHRANK
PROVES	RENEGADOES	SATIN	SHRIEKING
PROVIDED	RENEW'D	SATISFIED	SHRIEKS
PROVINCE	RENOWN	SATURN	SHRILLER
PROVING	RENT	SAUCE	SHRINKS
PROVOKING	RENTS	SAUCES	SHROUD
PRUDE	REPAIRED	SAYINGS	SHUDDER
PRUDENT	REPARTEE	SCABBARD	SHUDDERED
PRUDISH	REPEATED	SCALE	SHUDDERING
PRYING	REPOSED	SCAMPERED	SHUFFLING
PSALMS	REPROVE	SCANT	SICKER
PSYCHE	REPUTATIÓN	SCARS	SICKLE
	REQUESTED	SCENERY	SIGHING

957

2   (CONTINUED)
SIGNIFY
SILKS
SIMILES
SIMPLER
SINGLY
SINLESS
SIRENS
SIRS
SITE
SITTING
SIXTEENTH
SKELETON
SKETCH
SKIM
SKIMM'D
SKULLS
SKY'S
SLEW
SLIGHTEST
SLIPPED
SLUMBER'D
SLUMBERS
SMALL-TALK
SMITHS
SMOKING
SMOOTHLY
SNAKES
SNEERS
SNOWY
SOBB'D
SOCIETY'S
SODA-WATER
SOFTEST
SOFTLY
SOFTNESS
SOI-DISANT
SOIL'D
SOLDIERY
SOLITUDES
SOMBRE
SOMEBODY
SORROWS
SOUNDLY
SOUPE
SOUPS
SOUR
SOUVAROFF
SOWN
SPAIN'S
SPANIARD
SPARKLE
SPARS
SPAWN
SPAWNS
SPEAR
SPECKS
SPECTRAL
SPECULATE
SPECULATIONS
SPEEDILY
SPELLS
SPENDS
SPHINX
SPICE
SPIRITUAL
SPLEEN
SPLINTERS
SPLIT
SPOIL'D
SPOILED
SPOTS
SPOUSES
SPOUT
SPRANG
SPREADING
SPREADS
SPRIGHTLY
SPRINKLED
SPRINKLING
SPRITES
SPURNED
SPURRED
SQUAD
SQUALL
SQUEAK
SQUEEZED
'SQUIRES

SQUIRES
STAB
STABLE
STAG
STAGE
STAINED
STAINS
STAIR
STAIRS
STALKED
STAMMER
STARCH
STARK
STARLIGHT
STARTS
STATESMAN
STATUE-LIKE
STATUES
STEALTH
STEAM
STEER
STEERING
STEPPING
STERNEST
STICK
STILLNESS
STILTS
STIRLESS
STIRRING
STITCHED
STOICISM
STOMACHS
STOPT
STORY'S
STOUT
STOWED
STRAGGLING
STRAINING
STRANGER'S
STRAW
STREAK
STREAMING
STRESS
STRETCH'D
STREW'D
STRICTEST
STRICTURES
STRIP
STRIPPED
STRIPS
STROKE
STROKING
STRONGBOW
SUBDUED
SUBSCRIPTION
SUBSIDE
SUBSIDING
SUBSTITUTE
SUCCEED
SUCCESSFUL
SUCK'D
SUCKING
SUCTION
SUDDENLY
SUED
SUFFERANCE
SUICIDE
SUITED
SULPHURY
SULTANA'S
SULTANAS
SULTANS
SUMMED
SUMMERS
SUMMONS
SUNRISE
SUP
SUPERB
SUPERBLY
SUPERIORITY
SUPPORT
SUPPOSITION
SUPPRESS
SUPPRESSION
SUREST
SURGE
SURMOUNTED
SURROUNDING

SUSPECTS
SUSPENSE
SUSPICIOUS
SUSTAIN'D
SUWARROW'S
SWALLOW
SWAYS
SWEAT
SWEEPING
SWIFTLY
SWIMMER
SWINE
SYBARITE'S
SYLLABLE
SYMPATHETIC
TACITURN
TAIL
TAILOR
TAILS
TALISMAN
TALKER
TANGLES
TAPERS
TAPPING
TARDY
TAVERN
TAXATION
TEAR-DROP
TEIAN
TELESCOPE
TELLING
TEMPERAMENT
TEMPERANCE
TEMPER'D
TEMPEST'S
TEMPESTS
TEMPT
TENDED
TENOR
TENOR'S
TENT
TENTH
TERMS
TERTIAN
TETE
TETE-A-TETE
THAMES
THAMIS
THANK'D
THATCH
THAWED
THEIR'S
THEREON
THICKER
THIEVES
THINKERS
THINK'ST
THINN'D
THINNER
THORN
THOROUGH-BRED
THRASHED
THREATEN'D
THROBBING
THROES
THROWING
TIBERIUS
TICK
TIGER
TIGHT
TIGRESS
TILLOTSON
TIMBUCTOO
TIMIDLY
TITAN
TITAN'S
TITIAN
TITTLE
TITUS
TOCSIN
TOISES
TOLERABLY
TOMBUCTOO
TONES
TO-NIGHT
TONS
TOOLS
TOOTHPICKS

TORCH
TORTOISE
TORTURE
TO'T
TOUCHING
TOWERS
TRACED
TRACK
TRAINING
TRAITS
TRAMP
TRANSACTIONS
TRANSFERR'D
TRANSFORMATION
TRANSLATED
TRANSMITTED
TRAPS
TRASH
TRAVELLED
TRAVELLING
TREACHERY
TREATING
TREATS
TRECENTISTI
TREMBLED
TREMENDOUS
TRIALS
TRICK
TRIFLE
TRIFLES
TRIM
TRIP
TRIUMPHANT
TROJAN
TROPHIES
TROUBLES
TROUBLESOME
TRUANT
TRUMP
TRUMPET
TRUSTING
TRUTH'S
TU
TUMBLING
TUMULT
TUNELESS
TURBOT
TURKEY
TURNCOAT
TWENTY-FOUR
TWENTY-THREE
TWIN
TWINING
TWISTED
UGLIEST
UGLINESS
UGLY
UNAWARES
UNBLEST
UNBORN
UNBOUNDED
UNCERTAINTY
UNCHANGED
UNCONSCIOUSLY
UNDERGO
UNDERSTANDS
UNDERWENT
UNDO
UNEASY
UNEQUAL
UNFIT
UNHOLY
UNINITIATED
UNION
UNLUCKILY
UNMARRIED
UNMOVED
UNNATURAL
UNTOWARD
UNTRUE
UNUSUAL
UNWEAN'D
UNWED
UNWORTHY
UPBRAID
UPON'T
UPRIGHT
URN

1   (CONTINUED)
ANCHORITE
ANCLE
ANCONA
ANECDOTE
ANENT
ANGLICE
ANGLING
ANGUISH
ANIMATED
ANIMOSITY
ANIMUS
ANKLE
ANNALISTS
ANNIHILATED
ANNIHILATES
ANNOUNCE
ANNOUNCING
ANNOY'D
ANNUITIES
ANOMALY
ANONYMOUS
ANSWERLESS
ANTELOPE
ANTHEM
ANTHONY'S
ANTHROPOPHAGI
ANTIC
ANTI-CHAMBER
ANTICIPATING
ANTI-CLIMAX
ANTIENT
ANTIENTS
ANTIJACOBIN
ANTIPATHY
ANTIQUARIANS
ANTONY
ANTRES
ANVIL
ANXIETY
ANYBODY'S
ANYHOW
ANYONE
ANYONE'S
APARTMENTS
APATHY
APES
APICIUS
APOLLO
APOLLO'S
APOLOGIES
APOLOGUE
APOPLECTIC
APOSTASY'S
APOSTLE
APOSTLES
APOSTROPHE
APOTHECARY'S
APPALS
APPARATUS
APPAREL
APPEAL'D
APPEARANCE
APPEARANCES
APPEARING
APPENDAGE
APPLAUDS
APPLY
APPOINTMENT
APPRECIATED
APPREHENSION
APPREHENSIVE
APPRENSIONS
APPROPRIATE
APPROPRIATELY
APPROVE
APPROVER
AQ
AQUA-VITA
ARABIA
ARABLE
ARABS
ARAB-SPEARS
ARAMINTA
ARCADES
ARCADIANS
ARCANUM'S
ARCHDEACON

ARCHED
ARCH-ENEMY
ARCHER'S
ARCHES
ARCHIMEDES
ARCHITECTURE
ARDENT
ARDOUR
ARGUS
ARIEL
ARIS
ARISEN
ARISING
ARISTOTLE'S
ARITHMETICIAN
ARM-CHAIR
ARMED
ARMENIAN
ARMIDA'S
ARMISTICE
ARNO
ARRANGE
ARRAYS
ARREST
ARRIVAL
ARRIVALS
ARRIVE
ARROGANCE
ARROWS
ARTEM
ARTLESS
ARTLESSLY
ASCENDENCE
ASCETIC
ASHORE
ASKANCE
ASK'ST
ASPIRANTS
ASPIRATIONS
ASSAILANT'S
ASSAULTS
ASSEMBLIES
ASSES
ASSETS
ASSIGN
ASSIST
ASSISTED
ASSUAGE
ASTONISH'D
ASTONISHED
ASTONISHMENT
ASTRAY
ASTRINGENT
ASTRONOMER
ASTRONOMY
ASUNDER
ASYOUR
ATAGHAN
ATALANTIS
ATHANASIUS'
ATHENS
ATHOS
ATHWART
ATLANTIC
ATLAS
ATMOSPHERIC
ATOMS
ATROPOS
ATTACHED
ATTACHES
ATTACK'D
ATTACKING
ATTAINED
ATTEMPT
ATTEMPTING
ATTENDANCE
ATTENDANTS
ATTENDS
ATTESTS
ATTICA
ATTORNIES-GENERAL
ATTRACTIVE
ATTUNED
AU
AUCTION
AUCTIONEER
AUCTIONS
AUDACIA

AUGURED
AUGURY
AUNTS
AUREA
AUSONIA'S
AUSTERE
AUSTERITIES
AUSTERITY
AUTOCRAT
AUTOCRATIC
AVAILED
AVANT
AVENGE
AVENGED
AVENGES
AVER
AVERAGED
AVERSE
AVERSIONS
AVOIDED
AVOUCH'D
AVOWED
AWAKEN'D
AWED
AWHILE
AWRY
AXIOM
AXIS
AY
AZURE'S
B
BABEL'S
BABES
BABIES
BABY
BABYLONIAN
BACCHANTE
BACKED
BACKGAMMON
BACKWARDS
BACK-WOODSMAN
BAH
BAIL
BAILLIE
BAITING
BAKING
BALAAM
BALANCING
BALD-COOT
BALDNESS
BALES
BALGOUNIE'S
BALK
BALLAD
BALLADS
BALLAST
BALLET-MASTER
BALLOON
BALL-ROOM
BALM
BAMBOO
BAN
BANDAGES
BANDS
BANISHMENT
BANKER
BANKER'S
BANKERS
BANNERS
BANQUETEERS
BAPTIZE
BARBADOES
BARBARIAN
BARBARIC
BARBER'S
BARBETTE
BARD'S
BARED
BARGAINS
BARING
BARITONE
BARNAVE
BAROMETER
BARON
BARONS
BAROUCHE
BARRACK'S
BARRACKS

BARRELS
BARROW
BARROWS
BARS
BARTERS
BARTHOLOMEW
BAS
BASED
BASELESS
BASER
BASHFULLY
BASIN
BASINS
BASK
BASKET
BASKING
BASQUINA
BASTIONS
BATCHES
BATE
BATHERS
BATHOS'
BATHS
BATTALION
BATTERED
BATTERS
BATTLED
BAUBLES
BAWLERS
BAYING
BAYS
BEACONS
BEAK
BEAKERS
BEARABLE
BEARDED
BEARDS
BEARING
BEAR-SKINS
BEATUS
BEAUTIFULLY
BEAUVEAU
BECALM'D
BECASSE
BECKET'S
BECKON'D
BECKONED
BED-CLOTHES
BEDEW
BEDEW'D
BED-FELLOW
BEDLAMITES
BEDRAL
BEE-LIKE
BEE'S
BEFALLEN
BEFRINGE
BEGGING
BEGINNER
BEGINNINGS
BEGIRT
BEGONE
BEGOTTEN
BEGUILED
BEHALF
BEHAVE
BEHAVIOUR
BEHMEN
BEHOLDER
BEHOLDING
BELEAGUER'D
BELIE
BELIEVER
BELIEVING
BELISARIUS
BELLA
BELLI
BELLIES
BELL-MOUTHED
BELL'S
BELL-WETHER
BELONGS
BELSHAZZAR
BENCHES
BENDED
BENDER
BENE
BENEFACTRESS

1   (CONTINUED)

BENEVOLENT	BLISTER	BOURN	BULKY
BENIGN	BLISTER'D	BOUT	BULL-DOG
BENISON	BLOATED	BOUTS	BULL-DOGS
BENUMB	BLOCKS	BOW'D	BULLETINS
BERKELEY	BLONDE	BOWELS	BULL-FIGHTS
BERLIN	BLOOD-HORSE	BOWER-ANCHOR	BULL-FINCH
BERRY	BLOOD-HOUNDS	BOWSPRIT	BULLIES
BERTH	BLOODIER	BOW-STREET'S	BULOW
BERTHS	BLOODLESS	BOWSTRUNG	BUMPER
BESEECH	BLOOD-RED	BOX	BUNGLER
BESEECH'D	BLOOD'S	BOXES	BUNGLING
BESEEMED	BLOOD-SHOT	BOXING	BUON
BESIEGE	BLOOMED	BOYHOOD	BUONAPARTE'S
BESIEGING	BLOSSOM	BRACELET	BUOYANT
BESMEARED	BLOSSOMS	BRAGGADOCIO	BUOY'D
BESOM	BLUCHER	BRAHMINS	BURDENS
BESPEAK	BLUE-COAT	BRAIDS	BURGAGE
BESPRENT	BLUELY	BRAIN'S	BURGLARIOUSLY
BE'ST	BLUER	BRAIN-SPATTERING	BURGOYNE
BESTOW	BLUE-STOCKING	BRANCHING	BURGUNDY
BESTOWED	BLUE-STOCKINGS	BRANCHLESS	BURNS
BESTOWS	BLUESTRING	BRANDS	BURNT-OUT
BETA	BLUNDER'S	BRANDY'S	BURROWING
BETAKE	BLUNT	BRATS	BURSTS
BETE	BLUSH'D	BRAVELY	BURTHENS
BETHOUGHT	BLUSTERING	BRAZILS	BURY
BETOKEN	BOA	BREAKER	BUSEY
BETRAY'D	BOABDIL	BREAKER-BEATEN	BUSHES
BETRAYS	BOARDS	BREECH	BUSTLED
BETS	BOARS	BREECHES'	BUTCHER'S
BEVY	BOASTS	BREEDS	BUTCHERS
BEWAIL	BOATMAN	BRENTA	BUTCHERY
BEWILDER'D	BOAT'S-CREW	BREVITY	BUTLER
BEWILDERING	BOAZ	BREWED	BUTTERED
BEWITCH'D	BOBADIL	BREWING	BUTTERFLY
BEWITCHING	BOB-MAJOR	BRIAREUS	BUTTONS
BEY	BOCCACIO'S	BRIBED	BUXOM
BEZONIAN	BODDICES	BRIBING	BUYER
BIAS	BODE	BRICK	BUZZ
BIBLE	BODING	BRICKLAYER	C
BICKERINGS	BOEOTIAN	BRIDE'S	CA
BIDDER	BOG	BRIDGE	CABIN
BIDET	BOGGY	BRIDGES	CABIN'D
BIDS	BOGLE	BRIDLED	CABLE
BIENSEANCE	BOHEA	BRIEFLY	CABLE'S
BIGAMY	BOILED	BRIGADIER	CADES
BIGOTS	BOILING	BRIGADIERS	CADMUS
BILLETS	BOLERO	BRIGANTINE	CAETERA
BILLINGSGATE	BOLOGNA	BRIGHTEN'D	CAGE
BILLOW'S	BOLTED	BRIGHTLY	CAGES
BILL'S	BOLTS	BRIGHTNESS	CAIN
BILLY'S	BOLUS	BRIG'S	CAIO
BIN	BOMBARD	BRIMSTONE	CAIQUE
BIOGRAPHY	BOMBAZEEN	BRINGEST	CAIRN
BIRD'S-EYE	BOMBS	BRING'ST	CAITIFF
BIRON	BONAPARTE'S	BRISK	CALCULATE
BIRTHDAY	BONDAGE	BRISSOT	CALCULATING
BIRTH-DAYS	BONFIRES	BRITANNIA'S	CALCULATORS
BIRTHRIGHT	BON-MOTS	BROADCLOTH	CALDERON
BIS	BONN	BROADENING	CALEDON
BITES	BONNET	BROADLY	CALENTURES
BITS	BONOS	BROADSIDE	CALIDA
BITTERS	BONY	BROILING	CALLOUS
BLACKBIRD	BOOBIES	BROKEN-HEARTED	CALLOW
BLACKBIRDS	BOOBY	BROKEN-KNEED	CALMEST
BLACKENED	BOOKISH	BRONZE	CALMS
BLACKEST	BOOMING	BRONZED	CALMUCK
BLACKING	BOOMS	BROODED	CALMUCKS
BLACKLEG	BOOT	BROOKS	CALUMNIATED
BLACKLY	BOOTIES	BROOM'S	CALUMNY
BLACKSMITH	BOOZE	BROTHERLY	CALVIN
BLADES	BORDER'D	BROUGHAM	CAMBYSES'
BLAIR	BOREALIS	BROWN	CAMEL
BLAMEABLE	BOROUGHS	BROW'S	CAMELEON
BLANK-VERSE	BORROW	BROWSES	CAMELIONS
BLASE	BORROWING	BRUMMELL	CAMELOPARD
BLASPHEME	BOS	BRUNETTE	CAMERADO
BLASPHEMED	BOSCAN	BRUSSELS	CAMILLA
BLASPHEMIES	BOSOM'S	BRUTAL	CANCER
BLAZON	BOTANY	BRUTES	CANDIA
BLEAKNESS	BOTCHING	BRYANT	CANDIDATE
BLENDED	BOTTES	BUCK	CANDIDATES
BLESSEDNESS	BOTTLE-CONJURER	BUD	CANDIDE
BLESSES	BOTTLES	BUFF	CANDIOTE
BLIGHT	BOUDOIR'S	BUFFO	CANDLESTICKS
BLINDLY	BOUNDARY	BUGLE	CANDY
BLISSES	BOUNTIES	BUILDS	CANKER-WORM
	BOUNTY	BULK	CANNIBAL

1 (CONTINUED)	CENTAUR-NESSUS	CHICKS	CLIMBED
CANNON-SHOT	CENTER	CHIEFTAIN	CLIMBING
CANONICAL	CENTER'D	CHIEFTAIN'S	CLINCH
CANONIZATION	CENTRAL	CHILD-BED	CLINGING
CANOVA	CENTS	CHILDISHNESS	CLIP
CANOVA'S	CENTURION	CHILLER	CLIPT
CANTABS	CEREMONIES	CHILLIEST	CLOGHER'S
CAPABILITIES	CEREMONY	CHIMERA	CLOOTZ
CAPABLE	CERERIS	CHIMES	CLOTHE
CAPACITY	CERULEANS	CHIMNEY-SMOKE	CLOTHES'-PRESS
CAP-A-PIE	CERUSE	CHIMNEY-SWEEPER	CLOUDY
CAPER	CESARE	CHINA'S	CLOVE
CAPIENDUS	CESAREAN	CHINS	CLOVES
CAPITULATION	CEYLON	CHIRURGEONS	CLOWNISH
CAPO	CHACE	CHISEL	CLOYED
CAPON'S	CHAFE	CHISELL'D	CLOYING
CAP'S	CHAFED	CHISELLED	CLOYS
CAPSIZE	CHAFF	CHIVALRIC	CLUSTER'D
CAPTIVE'S	CHAFING	CHOCOLATE	CLUSTERING
CAPTURE	CHAINED	CHOICEST	CLYTEMNESTRA
CAPTURES	CHAIN-PUMP	CHOIR	COACHES
CARACTACUS	CHAIRS	CHOKED	COAL
CARAVAGGIO'S	CHAISE	CHOKENOFF	COARSER
CARCASSES	CHAISES	CHOLERIC	COAX
CAREEN	CHALK	CHOOSES	COBBETT
CARESS'D	CHALKY	CHORDS	COBBLING
CARESSES	CHAMAS'S	CHREMATOFF	COCHINEAL
CAREST	CHAMBERLAIN	CHRIST	COCK'D
CARGOES	CHAMBRE	CHRISTENED	COCKER'S
CARLESSLY	CHAMPION'D	CHRIST'S	COCKING
CARLO	CHANCELLOR'S	CHRONICLERS	COCKNEY
CARNAL	CHANCELLORS	CHRONOLOGICAL	COCKNEYS
CARNATION	CHANCES	CHRYSOSTOM	COCKS
CARNIVOROUS	'CHANGE	CHUCKLINGS	CODE
CAROLINES	CHANGELESS	CHURCHMAN'S	COELEBS'
CAROTID-ARTERY-CUTTING	CHANGING	CHUSE	COERC'D
CAROUSE	CHANNELS	CHYMIC	COFFIN
CARPENTER	CHANSON	CICALAS	COFFIN'D
CARPETED	CHAOS	CICERONIAN	COFFIN'S
CARRION	CHAPEAU-BRAS	CICOGNA	COGNIAC
CARS	CHAPEL	CI-DEVANT	CO-HEIRESSES
CARTE	CHAPTERS	CINCINNATUS	COHORN'S
CARVING	CHARGED	CINDERS	COIL
CARVINGS	CHARGER	CINNAMON	COIL'D
CASE-MATED	CHARING	CIRCASSIA	COILED
CASEMENT	CHARIOTS'	CIRCASSIAN	COIN
CASEMENT'S	CHARITABLE	CIRCLE'S	COINCIDENCE
CASHMIRE	CHARLATAN	CIRCULAR	COKE
CASKETS	CHARLEMAGNE'S	CIRCULATION	COLCHIAN
CASSANDRA	CHARLOTTE	CIRCUMCISE	COLCHIS
CASSIMERE	CHARMED	CIRCUMCISION	COLD-BLOODED
CASTALIAN	CHARMER	CIRQUE	COLDLY
CASTANETS	CHARON'S	CITE	COLLAR
CASTELLATED	CHARTS	CITED	COLLARS
CASTILE	CHASED	CIVILISATION	COLLECTION
CASTING	CHASSEURS	CIVILITY	COLLECTIVE
CAST-OFF	CHASTELY	CIVILIZED	COLLOQUY
CASTS	CHASTEN'D	CLAIMANT	COLOGNE
CASUALLY	CHASTENED	CLAIM'D	COLONEL
CASUIST	CHASTITIES	CLAIMED	COLONIAL
CATCHES	CHATHAM	CLAIMING	COLOSSUS
CATERING	CHATTED	CLAMOUR'D	COLOUR'D
CATERS	CHATTERING	CLAN	COLOURINGS
CATHAY	CHAUNT	CLANGED	COLUMBIA'S
CATHEDRAL	CHE	CLANKING	COM
CATHOLICS	CHEAPENED	CLAP	COMB
CATILINE	CHEAPENING	CLAPPING	COMBATED
CATOS	CHEATED	CLAP-TRAP	COMBED
CAUCASUS	CHEATING	CLARENCE	COMBINATION
CAULKING	CHEER'D	CLARENCE'	COMBS
CAUSA	CHEERFULNESS	CLARETLESS	COMEDIES
CAUSING	CHEERY	CLASHED	COMEDY
CAUTION	CHEESE-PARING	CLASPS	COMET
CAVALIERE	CHEQUERED	CLAUDIUS	COMFORTER
CAVALIERS	CHERISH	CLAWS	COMFORTS
CAVERNS	CHERISHED	CLEAR'D	COMITATUS
CAVES	CHERSONESE	CLEARING	COMMANDED
CAYENNE	CHERUB	CLEARLY	COMMANDING
CAZZANI	CHERUBIM	CLEAVES	COMMANDMENTS
CEDAR	CHERUBS	CLERGYMAN	COMMENT
CEDARS	CHESS	CLERGYMEN	COMMENTARIES
CEILING	CHESS-BOARD	CLERKS	COMMENTATOR'S
CELEBRITY	CHESSMAN	CLEVEREST	COMMENTS
CELL	CHESTERFIELD	CLIENTS	COMMERCIAL
CELLAR	CHESTS	CLIENTS'	COMMISSARY
CELLARS	CHEVALIERS	CLIFF-WORN	COMMODIOUS
CEMENTED	CHEWING	CLIMACTERIC	COMMODITIES
CENSORIOUS	CHIAN	CLIMATE'S	COMMONERS

1   (CONTINUED)
COMPACT
COMPANY'S
COMPASS'D
COMPELL'D
COMPELS
COMPETE
COMPETITION
COMPLACENCY
COMPLAINED
COMPLAINTS
COMPLIMENTED
COMPLIMENTS
COMPOSITIONS
COMPREHENDS
COMPREHENSIONS
COMPRESS'D
COMPRESSION
COMPRISE
COMPROMISE
COMPROMISED
COMPUNCTION
CONCATENATION
CONCEAL'D
CONCEDE
CONCEDED
CONCEIT
CONCEITS
CONCENTRATED
CONCENTRATING
CONCENTRE
CONCERT
CONCLUDED
CONCLUSION
CONCLUSIONS
CONCORD
CONCUR
CONCUSSION
CONDE
CONDEMNATION
CONDEMN'D
CONDESCENDED
CONDESCENSION
CONDOLENCE
CONDORCET
CONDUCIVE
CONDUCTED
CONDUCT'S
CONDUCTS
CONFESS'D
CONFESSIONS
CONFIDENTIAL
CONFINES
CONFIRM'D
CONFIRMED
CONFISCATED
CONFITURES
CONFLICT
CONFLICTS
CONFORMATION
CONFOUNDS
CONGEAL
CONGEALING
CONGRATULATIONS
CONGRESSES
CONJECTURES
CONJECTURING
CONJUGAL
CONNECT
CONNECTED
CONNECTION'S
CONNECTS
CONNED
CONNUBIALLY
CONQUESTS
CONSENT
CONSEQUENTIAL
CONSIDER
CONSIDERATION
CONSIDER'D
CONSIST
CONSISTENT
CONSISTORY
CONSOLE
CONSOLING
CONSOMME
CONSONANTS
CONSORTS

CONSTABLE
CONSTANTINE
CONSTERNATION
CONSTITUTE
CONSTITUTIONAL
CONSTITUTIONS
CONSTRAIN'D
CONSTRUCTIVE
CONSULE
CONSULTING
CONSUMERS
CONSUMING
CONSUMPTIVE
CONTAGIOUS
CONTAIN
CONTAIN'D
CONTAINED
CONTAINS
CONTEMN
CONTEMPLATIVE
CONTENTED
CONTENTEDLY
CONTENTS
CONTESTS
CONTEXT
CONTINENCE
CONTINENT
CONTINENTAL
CONTINENT'S
CONTINUANCE
CONTINUATION
CONTRACTED
CONTRACTIONS
CONTRACTOR'S
CONTRACTORS
CONTRADICT
CONTRADICTED
CONTRADICTING
CONTRIBUTE
CONTRIVANCES
CONTROLLESS
CONTROUL
CONUNDRUM
CONVENIENCE
CONVERSATIONAL
CONVERSATIONIST
CONVERSATION'S
CONVERSATIONS
CONVERSAZIONE
CONVERSION
CONVEYANCE
CONVEY'D
CONVEYED
CONVEYING
CONVICT
CONVICTED
CONVINCED
CONVINCES
CONVULSION
CONVULSIONS
COOINGS
COOLLY
COPIOUS
COPYING
CORDAGE
CORDIALS
CORINTHIAN
CORK
CORNELIAN
CORNERS
CORNIANI
CORNISH
CORN-SHEAF
CORONALS
CORONET
CORPO
CORPORAL'S
CORPORATION
CORPSE
CORPUS
CORRECTEST
CORRECTOR
CORRESPOND
CORRESPONDENT
CORRESPONDENTS
CORRODING
CORSES
CORTEJO

CORYDON
COSI
COSMOGONY
COSSAQUE
COSTIVE
COSTUME
COTERIES
COTS
COTTAGES
COUCHES
COUGHING
COUGHS
COULEUR
COUNTENANCE
COUNTER
COUNTERBALANCE
COUNTING
COUNTRYMAN
COUNTRY-SEAT
COUPLED
COURLAND
COURSER
COURTED
COURTESIES
COURTIER
COURTIER'S
COURTIERS
COURTING
COURTISAN
COVER
COVERED
COWPER
COW'S
COXCOMB'S
COXE
CRABBEY
CRACK'D
CRACKS
CRADLED
CRAFT
CRAGGY
CRAM
CRAMM'D
CRANED
CRAVE
CRAVING
CRAW
CRAWLS
CRAZED
CRAZY
CREAK'D
CREATIVE
CREDENTIAL
CREDITED
CREDULOUS
CREECH
CREED'S
CREEDS
CREEPER
CREEPS
CRESCENTS
CRESSYS
CRESTS
CRIBB'D
CRICKETS
CRIM
CRIMINAL
CRISPED
CRISPER
CRITICAL
CRITICALLY
CRITICISE
CRITICISED
CRITIC'S
CRITIQUE
CROCKERY
CROCKERY-WARE
CROCODILES
CROMWELL'S
CROSSES
CROSS-GRAIN'D
CROSS-LEGG'D
CROSS-LEGGED
CROSS-QUESTIONED
CROST
CROTCHET
CROW
CROWNER'S

CROWNING
CROW-QUILL
CRUCIFIX
CRUELTY
CRUISED
CRUISERS
CRUIZING
CRUMBLED
CRUPPER
CRUSHING
CUBLESS
CUBS
CUCKOLDS
CUD
CUFFED
CULL
CULLIES
CULOTTE
CULTIVATED
CULVIER
CUNCTIS
CUPBOARD
CUPIDITY
CUPIDON
CUPPED
CURATE
CURBED
CURING
CURIOUSLY
CURLING
CURLY-HEADED
CUROUS
CURRAN
CURRENCY
CURRIE
CURRY
CURTAINED
CURTAINS
CURTIS
CURTSEY
CURTSEYING
CURTSY
CUSHIONS
CUTLASS
CUTS
CUTTER'S
CUT-THROATS
CUVIER
CYBELE'S
CYCLOPS
CYGNET
CYNTHIA
CYPRESSES
CYPRUS
CYRUS
CYTHEREA'S
CZARINA'S
D
DABBLE
DABBLED
DABBLING
DALES
DAM
DAMAGE
DAMASK
DAMASQUE
DAMM'D
DAMNABLE
DAMNABLY
DAMNATION
DAMN'DEST
DAMNING
DAMOCLES
D'AMOUR
DAMSEL'S
DANDIEST
DANDY'S
DANG
DANGERS
DANGLED
DANISH
DANK
DANTON
DAPHNE
DAPPLED
D'APPUI
DARDAN
DARDANELLES

1   (CONTINUED)
DARKEN'D
DARKENED
DARKENING
DARK-GREEN
DARKLE
DARKLED
DARKLY
DARTING
DASHES
DASTARDLY
DATE-BREAD
DATED
DATING
DAUNTED
DAVID'S
DAVUS
DAVY'S
DAWN'D
DAY-BILL
DAY-DAWN
DAY-HYMN
DAYLIGHT'S
DEAN
DEATH-CRY
DEATH-DISGORGING
DEATHLESS
DEATH-LIKE
DEATH-WATCH
DEATH-WOUND
DEBARRED
DEBATER
DEBAUCHEE
DEBONNAIRE
DEBUT
DECANTED
DECAY'D
DECAYING
DECEASED
DECEIT
DECEIVE
DECEMBER
DECEMBER'S
DECENCIES
DECENCY
DECIMATE
DECKS
DECLAIMING
DECLARATION
DECOMPOSE
DECORATED
DECORATES
DECORUM
DECREASED
DEDICATE
DEDUCE
DEDUCTED
DEE
DEEPEN'D
DEEP-MOUTH'D
DEEP-MOUTHED
DEEP-PURPLE
DEEPS
DEER
DEFACE
DEFACED
DEFEAT
DEFEATED
DEFECTIVE
DEFENCE
DEFENCES
DEFENDED
DEFENDER
DEFENDERS
DEFENSIBLE
DEFIES
DEFLENDUS
DEFLOWERED
DEFOIX
DEFORMED
DEFYING
DEIGN
DEIGNING
DEJECTED
DEJECTION
DEL'ENCLOS
DELHIS
DELIBERATION

DELICACIES
DELIRIOUS
DELIVERANCE
DELIVER'D
DELIVERED
DELOS
DELPHIAN
DELUGE
DEMAND
DEMI-GODS
DEMOCRACY
DEMOCRAT
DEMOCRATIC
DEMOCRATS
DEMOCRITUS
DEMOISELLE
DEMON
DEMONS
DEMOURIER
DEMUR
DEMURRED
DENIAL
DENMARK
DEPENDENT
DEPENDING
DEPLORED
DEPOSITED
DEPOSITION
DEPRAVITY
DEPRECATED
DEPRECIATED
DERIDE
DERIDES
DERIVED
DERIVES
DES
DESARTS
DESCENDING
DESCENDS
DESCENT
DESCRIPTIVE
DESERT
DESERTED
DESERTION
DESERT-SPRING
DESERVES
DESIDERATUM
DESIRABLE
DESIRES
DESOLATING
DESPAIR'D
DESPAIRING
DESPATCH
DESPATCHING
DESPERATION
DESPISES
DESPONDS
DESPOT
DESPOTIC
DESPOT'S
DESSAIX
DESSERT
DESTAEL
DESTROYED
DESTROYER
DESTRUCTION'S
DESTRUCTIVE
DESULTORY
DETACHMENT
DETAILED
DETAIN'D
DETECT
DETECTED
DETERMINATION
DETERR'D
DETESTATION
DETOTT
DETRACTION'S
DEUCED
DEUM
DEVIATE
DEVIATION
DEVICE
DEVILISM
DEVOTEE
DEVOUR'D
DEVOURED

DEVOURS
DEVOUT
DEVOUTLY
DEXT'ROUS
DEY
DI
DIADEM
DIAMONDS
DIANA'S
DIAPASONS
DICEDRABBIT
DICERE
DICKEY
DICTIONARIES
DIDO'S
DID'S
DIEM
DIFFERENTLY
DIFFERS
DIFFIDENT
DIG
DIGEST
DIGNIFY
DIGRESS
DIGRESSING
DILATE
DILIGENCE
DIMMED
DIMPLED
DINDON
DINER
DINERS
DINING
DINNER'S
DIPLOMATICAL
DIPLOMATIST
DIPPED
DIPT
DIRE
DIRECT
DIRECTLY
DIRGES
DIRK
DIRKS
DISAPPEAR'D
DISAPPEARED
DISAPPEARING
DISAPPOINTMENT
DISARM
DISARRAY
DISASTERS
DISBURSEMENTS
DISCIPLINED
DISCLOSURE
DISCORD
DISCORDANT
DISCORD'S
DISCOURAGED
DISCOVER'D
DISCOVERED
DISCOVERING
DISCOVERY'S
DISCREPANCIES
DISDAINING
DISEASED
DISEASES
DISEMBARKED
DISEMBODIED
DISFIGURE
DISGUSTING
DISH'D
DISHEVELLED
DISINTERESTEDNESS
DISLIKES
DISMISS
DISMISS'D
DISMISSED
DISORDERLY
DISORDERS
DISPARGE
DISPARITY
DISPELLED
DISPERSE
DISPLEASING
DISPOSE
DISPOSING
DISPUTED
DISPUTES

DISPUTING
DISSATISFIED
DISSECTED
DISSECTING
DISSEMBLES
DISSENT
DISSENTING
DISSENTIONS
DISSERT
DISSIPATE
DISSIPATION
DISSOLVES
DISTAFF
DISTILLED
DISTINGUISH
DISTINGUISH'D
DISTORTION
DISTORTIONS
DISTRACTION
DISTRESSING
DISTRIBUTION
DISTURB'D
DISTURBING
DITCHER
DIURETIC
DIVERSITY
DIVERT
DIVESTED
DIVIDES
DIVINER
DIVING
DIVINITIES
DIVINITY
DIVORCES
DIVORCING
DIVULGED
DOATING
DOCILITY
DOCTRINES
DODGING
DOG-BARK
DOG-DAYS
DOGMA
DOG-STAR
DOLCE
DOLLAR
DOLON
DOLOUR
DOLPHIN'S
DOME
DOMES
DOMESTICS
DOMINION
DOMOS
DONOR
DONOR'S
DONT
DOOMED
DOOMSDAY
DOOR-WAY
D'OPERA
DORIC
DORMANT
DORUS
DORY
DOTED
DOTING
DOTTED
DOUBLED
DOUBLE-DAMN'D
DOUBLES
DOUBTERS
DOVE'S
DOWAGER
DOWAGERS
DOWNWARDS
DOZE
DOZED
DRACHENFELS
DRAG
DRAG-CHAIN
DRAGON
DRAGS
DRAIN
DRAINED
DRAINER
DRAM
DRAMA

1 (CONTINUED)
DRAMATIC
DRAPERIED
DRAPERIES
DRAUGHTS
DRAWCANSIR
DRAWERS
DRAWLING
DRAYS
DREAMER
DREAMLESS
DRENCH'D
DRESDEN
DRESS'D
DRESSING-GOWN
DRIED
DRIFT
DRILL'D
DRILLED
DRINKER
DRIVELS
DRIVES
DROOPS
DROPSIES
DROUTH
DROWN
DROWNING
DROWNINGS
DRUGGISTS
DRUID
DRUID'S
DRUNKEN
DRYDEN'S
DRYING
DRYNESS
DUAN
DUB
DUBLIN
DUCHESS'
DUCK
DUCKLING
DUCKLINGS
DUCKS
DUDGEON
DUET
DUETS
DUG
DULCI
DULLEST
DUMBER
DUMPY
DUNCAN
DUNGEON
DUNGHILL'S
DUNNEST
DUOMO
DURATION
DURST
DUSK
DUTCHESS
DUTCHMEN
DUTEOUS
DWARF
DWARFING
DWELLERS
DWELLING
DWELLINGS
DWINDLE
DWINDLED
DYEING
DYER
DYERS
DYKE
EAGERLY
EAGERNESS
EAGLE'S
EARL
EARN'D
EARNESTNESS
EARSHOT
EARTHQUAKE'S
EAR-TRUMPET
EASED
EBB
EBB'D
EBBED
EBONY
ECCLESIASTES

ECHOING
ECLECTIC
ECONOMIC
ECONOMY
ECSTATICS
EDDIES
EDGEWORTH'S
EDIFICE
EDINBURGH
EDUCATED
EDUCATIONS
EDWARD'S
EELS
EER
EFFRONTERY
EGAD
EGO
EGYPT
EGYPTIAN
EIGHT-AND-FORTY
EJECTION
EKENHEAD
EKING
ELAPSED
ELATE
ELDERLY
ELDEST
ELDON
ELECTED
ELECTIONEERER
ELECTIONS
ELEGY
ELEMENT
ELEVATION
ELEVENTH
ELF
ELIGIBLE
ELITE
ELIZABETH
ELL
ELLE
ELOPEMENT
ELYSIUM
EMACIATED
EMASCULATED
EMBARK
EMBARK'D
EMBARRASS
EMBELLISH
EMBERS
EMBLEM
EMBLEMS
EMBODIED
EMBOSOM'D
EMBOSS'D
EMBRACE
EMBRACES
EMBROIDER'D
EMBROIDERY
EMERALD
EMERALD'S
EMIGRATION
EMIGRATIONS
EMINENT
EMPEROR
EMPHASIS
EMPHATIC
EMPLOYED
EMPLOYING
EMPLOYMENT
EMPRESSEMENT
EMPRESS'S
EN
ENAMOURED
ENCHANTED
ENCHANTER
ENCHANTER'S
ENCHANTS
ENCLOSED
ENCOURAGES
ENCREASE
ENCROACH
ENCROACHING
ENCUMBER'D
ENCUMBERS
ENCYCLOPEDIZE
ENDANGERS
ENDEAR'D

ENDEARMENT
ENDEAVOUR
ENDEAVOURING
END'S
ENDURING
ENERGETIC
ENERGIES
ENERGY
ENGENDERED
ENGINEERING
ENGINEER'S
ENGLAND'S
ENGLISHMAN
ENGLISHWOMAN'S
ENGRAVE
ENGRAVED
ENGROSS
ENGROSSED
ENHANCE
ENJOINING
ENJOY
ENJOYED
ENJOYMENT'S
ENLARGEMENT
ENLIGHTEN
ENLIST
ENNOBLE
ENQUIRIES
ENQUIRY
ENSLAVER
ENSUE
ENSUING
ENSURED
ENSURES
ENTAIL
ENTAILED
ENTANGLE
ENTANGLED
ENTERING
ENTERTAINING
ENTIRE
ENTIRELY
ENTOMB'D
ENTOMBING
ENTRAIL
ENTRAILS
ENTRATE
ENTRE
ENTREMETS
ENTRENCHMENT
ENTWINE
ENTWINED
ENTWINES
ENTWINING
ENUMERATION
ENVIABLE
ENVIED
ENVOYS
ENVYING
ENVY'S
EPAMINONDAS
EPAULETTES
EPHESIAN
EPHESIANS
EPICAL
EPICENE
EPIC'S
EPICURUS
EPILEPTICAL
EPISODE
EPISODES
EPISTLE
EPITAPHS
EPITOME
EPOPEE
EQUALL'D
EQUALS
EQUANIMITY
EQUINOX
EQUIPAGE
EQUIPPED
EQUITY
ERA
ERA'S
'ERE
ERECT
ERECTION
ERNEIS

EROS
ERRATUM
ERR'D
ERRING
ERRONEOUS
ERRS
ERSE
ERST
ESAU
ESCALADE
ESCAPES
ESCAPING
ESCHEWED
ESPIEGLE
ESPOUSED
ESQUIRE
ESQUIRED
ESQUIRES
ESSAYED
ESSAYING
EST
ESTABLISHMENT
ESTEEMING
ESTIMATION
ESTRANGE
ESTRANGED
ETERNALLY
ETHER
ETHEREAL
ETNA
EUPHONY
EUPHUES
EUREKA
EUTROPIUS
EVADES
EVAPORATE
EVAPORATION
EVENT
EVENTIDE
EVER-DYING
EVERGREEN
EVERMORE
EVERY-DAY
EVINCE
EVOLUTION
EVOLUTIONS
EV'RY
EWER
EXACTED
EXAGGERATION
EXAGGERATIONS
EXALT
EXALTED
EXAMINATION
EXAMINE
EXASPERATED
EXCEED
EXCEEDED
EXCELLENCY
EXCELS
EXCHANGING
EXCHEQUER
EXCISE
EXCITE
EXCITING
EXCLAIM
EXCLAIM'D
EXCLAIMS
EXCLUDED
EXCOMMUNICATION
EXECRATES
EXECUTES
EXECUTION
EXEMPT
EXERT
EXHALES
EXHAUSTION
EXHORTATION
EXILES
EXISTED
EXISTENT
EXIT
EXMAPLES
EXORDIUM
EXPANDED
EXPANSION
EXPATIATE
EXPECTING

1   (CONTINUED)
EXPEDIENTS
EXPEDITION
EXPELLED
EXPENCE
EXPENSIVE
EXPERIENCED
EXPERIMENT
EXPIRE
EXPIRES
EXPIRING
EXPLAINING
EXPLAINS
EXPLICITLY
EXPLOITS
EXPLORE
EXPLOSION
EXPOUNDER
EXPOUNDING
EXPOUNDS
EXPRESSED
EXPURGATED
EXQUISITELY
EXTENDS
EXTENSION
EXTERNAL
EXTINGUISHED
EXTRACTS
EXTRANEOUS
EXTRAS
EXTREMEST
EXUBERANT
EXULTATION
EXULTING
EYEBALLS
EYEBROW'S
EYELASH
EYELASHES
EYELID
EYELIDS'
EYES'
EYE-SIGHT
FABRIC
FACINGS
FACTIOUS
FACULTIES
FACULTY
FADED
FAINTEST
FAINTING
FAINTNESS
FAINTS
FAIR-HAIRED
FALCHIONS
FALIERO
FALLOW
FALMOUTH
FALSTAFF
FAME'S
FAMILIAR
FAMILIARLY
FAMINES
FAMISHED
FANCIFUL
FANCY'S
FANNY'S
FANS
FANTASIES
FANTASTIC
FARROW
FARTHING
FASCINATE
FASCINATION
FASTEN
FAST-FLOWING
FASTING
FATHOM
FATIGUED
FATTEN
FATTEST
FATUI
FATUUS
FAVOURITE'S
FAVOURITISM
FAVOURS
FAWN
FAZZIOLI
FEARED

FEARLESS
FEASIBLE
FEAT
FEATHERS
FEEDING
FEIGNS
FEINAGLE'S
FELICITY
FELLED
FELLOW'S
FELLS
FELON
FEMALE'S
FEMININELY
FEMME
FENCE
FENCED
FENCING
FENS
FERDINAND
FERFLUCTER
FERMENT
FERMENTATION
FERNAN
FEROCIOUS
FEROCITIES
FEROCITY
FERREM
FERTILITY
FERVENTLY
FERVOUR
FESTAL
FESTIVITY
FESTOON
FESTOONS
FETES
FETTERED
FEUD
FEUDAL
FEUDS
FEZ
FICKLE
FIDDLED
FIELDING
FIENDS
FIERCEST
FIFTEEN-HUNDREDTH
FIFTEENTH
FIFTY-NINE
FIG
FIGHTER
FIGURANTI
FIGURATIVE
FILCH'D
FILIAL
FILIGREE
FILM
FILTERED
FILTH
FILTHY
FIN
FINANCIERS
FINED
FINELY
FINGER
FINISH
FIREFACE
FIRE-FLIES
FIRESHIPS
FIRE-SIDE
FIRMAN
FIRMER
FIRST-BORN'S
FIRST'S
FISH'D
FISHERS
FISHERY
FIST
FISTY
FITTEST
FITZ-FRISKY
FIVE-BAR
FLAG
FLAIL
FLAKE
FLAMINGO'S
FLASK
FLATTER'D

FLATTERED
FLATTERER
FLATTERERS
FLAVOUR
FLAY
FLAY'D
FLEE
FLEECE
FLEET-DITCH
FLESH-COLOURED
FLESHY
FLICKERED
FLIGHTS
FLIGHTY
FLINTS
FLIRT
FLIRTED
FLITTED
FLOCK'S
FLOG
FLOOR'D
FLOORED
FLORENTINE
FLORID
FLOUNCED
FLOUNDERED
FLOURISH
FLOURISHING
FLOWS
FLUENT
FLUTTER'D
FLUTTERERS
FOAMS
FOCIS
FOE'S
FOG-BANKS
FOLLOWER
FOLLY'S
FONTS
FOOTING
FOOTMARKS
FOOTMEN
FOOTSTEP
FOP
FOPLINGS
FORBEARANCE
FORBEARS
FORBIDDING
FORBORE
FOREIGNER'S
FOREMAST
FORE-PAWS
FORERUNNERS
FORESAW
FORESEEN
FORESTALLED
FORESTRY
FOREST'S
FORESTS
FOREST-TOPS
FORETELLS
FORGIVENESS
FORMAL
FORMALITY
FORMOSUM
FORNICATION
FORTALICE
FORTIFICATION
FORTNIGHT
FORTRESSES
FORTS
FORTY-PARSON-POWER
FOSSILE
FOSTER-BABES
FOUR-AND-TWENTY
FOUR-POSTED
FOURTHLY
FOWLS
FOX'S
FOX-TERRIERS
FRACTION
FRAGILITY
FRAILTIES
FRAILTY
FRAMED
FRAMES
FRANCESES
FRANCIS'

FRANCS
FRANK
FRANKINCENSE
FRAUD
FRAUGHT
FRED
FREEHOLDERS
FREEHOLDS
FREEMASONRY
FREEMASONS
FREEST
FREETHINKER
FREE-WILL
FREEZING
FREIGHT
FRENCHMAN'S
FRENCHMEN
FREQUENTLY
FRESCO
FRESHER
FRESHLIER
FRESHLY
FRETWORK
FRIDAY
FRIED
FRIENDLESS
FRIEND'S
FRIENDS'
FRIENDSHIPS
FRIGHTS
FRINGE
FRINGED
FRISKS
FRO
FROCK
FROID
FROLIC
FRONTIER
FROSTS
FROSTY
FROTH'D
FROWNS
FROWZY
FROZE
FRUGAL
FRUITFUL
FRYING
FUDDLE
FUI
FUIMUS
FULLEST
FULL-GROWN
FUM
FUND'S
FUNDS
FUNERAL
FURIES
FURIOUSLY
FURNACE
FURNISHING
FURROW
FURRY
FURS
FUSION
FUSS
FUTURITY
GADS
GAGE
GAIETIES
GAIETY
GAINERS
GALILEO
GALLANTED
GALLANTLY
GALLANTRY
GALLANT'S
GALLED
GALLIC
GALLIOTS
GALLON
GALLONS
GALLOP
GAMESTER'S
GAN
GANG
GANGS
GAPE
GAPED

1 (CONTINUED)

GARBS
GARCILASSO
GARDEN-GATE
GARDEN-KEY
GARLANDS
GARLIC
GARTER'D
GARTERS
GASHES
GASP
GASPING
GASTRIC
GATHERING
GAUDY
GAULS
GAZELLE-EYED
GAZELLES
GAZES
GEAR
GENDER
GENE
GENERALITIES
GENERAL'S
GENEROUSLY
GENETRIX
GENEVOISES
GENITORS
GENSERIC'S
GENTEELLY
GENTLEMANLY
GENTLEWOMAN
GEOFFRY'S
GEOGRAPHERS
GEORDI-AN
GEORGE'S
GERM
GHOST'S
GIANT'S
GIAOUR
GIBBER
GIBIER
GIBING
GIBRALTAR
GIFTED
GIFTGABBIT
GIGGLE
GIGGLING
GILD
GILDS
GILES
GILLS
GILT
GILTBEDDING
GILT-EDGED
GINNS
'GINS
GIRD
GIRDS
GIRTH
GIULETTA
GLACIERS
GLADIATOR'S
GLASSES
GLASSFUL
GLEAN'D
GLEANERS
GLEANINGS
GLIBLY
GLIMMER
GLIMMER'D
GLIMMERING
GLISTERS
GLITTERERS
GLOBE
GLOOMIER
GLOOMIEST
GLOOMS
GLORIED
GLOVE
GLOVES
GLOW'D
GLOWS
GLOWWORM
GLUE
GLUT
GLUTTON
GLUTTON'S

GNASH'D
GNAW
GNAW'D
GNAWING
GNAWS
GNEISENAU
GOADED
GOAL
GOAT'S
GOBLET
GOBLINS
GOD-BORN
GODDESS
GODFATHER'S
GOD-KNOWS-WHAT
GODLY
GODSAKE
GODSHIP'S
GOETH
GONDOLIER
GOOD-FOR-NOTHING
GOODLIEST
GOODLINESS
GORGED
GORME
GOSPEL
GOSPEL'S
GOTH
GOTH'S
GOTHS
GOULS
GOURMANDISE
GRACCHUS
GRACEFULLY
GRACE'S
GRACIOUSLY
GRADUALLY
GRAFTED
GRAIN
GRAINS
GRAMMERCY
GRANBY
GRAND-DAD'S
GRANDE
GRANDFATHER
GRANDMOTHER'S
GRANDMOTHERS
GRANDSON
GRANITE
GRANTING
GRANTORS
GRANTS
GRAPES
GRAPPLE
GRAPPLED
GRAPPLES
GRASP'D
GRASPS
GRASS-GROWN
GRATE
GRATIFYING
GRATTAN
GRAVEL
GRAVITATION
GRAVITY
GRAZING
GREEK-WORSHIP
GREENER
GREENEST
GREENSWARD
GRENADA
GRENADIER
GRENVILLES
GRIMACE
GRIND
GRINDSTONE'S
GRISLY
GRIST
GRIZZLED
GROOM'D
GROPING
GROSE
GROSSER
GROSSEST
GROSSLY
GROTESCA
GROTESQUES
GROUNDS

GROUPE
GROUPING
GROUSE
GROVEL
GROVELING
GROWLING
GROWN-UP
GRUDGES
GRUEL
GRUMBLE
GRUMBLED
GRUMBLES
GUADALQUIVIR'S
GUARDSMAN
GUEBRES
GUELF
GUERDON
GUESSED
GUESTS'
GUIDE-BOOK'S
GUIDE-BOOKS
GUIDED
GUIDES
GUIDO'S
GUILE
GUILELESS
GUILLOTINE
GUINEA
GUITARS
GULBEYAZM
GULL
GULLET
GULLETS
GUN-BARREL
GUNNERY
GURNEY
GUST
GUTS
H
HABEAS
HABITANT
HABITUAL
HABITUDE
HACKS
HAGGARD
HAGGLED
HAGUE
HAIL'D
HAIRY
HAL
HALES'S
HALF-CHASTE
HALF-DEMON
HALF-DIRT
HALF-FORGAVE
HALF-GIRLISH
HALF-KILL'D
HALF-SEAS-OVER
HALF-SERIOUS
HALF-SHUT
HALF-SMOTHER'D
HALF-SOLVED
HALF-STARVED
HALF-TORN
HALF-UNQUENCHED
HALF-VOLUPTUOUSNESS
HALIFAX
HALLAM'S
HALLELUJAHS
HALLOW'D
HALLOWING
HALOS
HALT
HALTS
HAM
HAMLET
HAMLETS
HAMMOCK
HAMMOCKS
HAMPER
HAMPER'D
HAMS
HAND-AND-GLOVE
HANDMAID
HANDSOMELY
HANGED
HANGING
HANGINGS

HANKER
HANKERING
HANNIBAL
HAP-HAZARD
HAPPILY
HARBOUR
HARBOURING
HARDEN'D
HARDER
HARDIEST
HARDNESS
HARDSHIP
HARDSMAN
HARDY
HARES
HARLEQUIN
HARLOTRY
HARMONISED
HARMONIST
HARMONIZED
HARNESS
HARNESSED
HARP'D
HARPER
HARPER'S
HARPSICHORD
HARPSICHORDS
HARP-STRING
HARPY
HARRISON
HARSHLIER
HARTS
HARVEST
HASTENING
HASTENS
HATCHED
HATCHES
HATCHING
HATCHWAY
HATEFUL
HATES
HATING
HAUD
HAUGHTILY
HAUNCH
HAUNCHES
HAUNT
HAUNTING
HAUNTS
HAUTEUR
HAWKE
HAWK'S-BILL
HAY
HAYLEY'S
HAZARDS
HAZY
HEAD-QUARTERS
HEADSTRONG
HEADY
HEAPS
HEARER
HEARKEN
HEARSAY
HEART-ACHES
HEART-BALLADS
HEART-BURNING
HEART-FELT
HEARTLESS
HEARTS'
HEART'S-BLOOD
HEART-STRINGS
HEAVENLIEST
HEAVENS
HEAVES
HEAVINESS
HEBE
HEBREWS
HECATOMB
HECLA
HECLA'S
HECTOR
HEED
HEIGHTENED
HEIGHTENING
HEIRESSES
HELL-DOGS
HELL-FIRE
HELM

1   (CONTINUED)
HEN
HENCEFORWARD
HENCOOPS
HEN-PECK'D
HENS
HEPHAESTION
HERACLEIDAN
HERBS
HERCULEAN
HERESY
HERETOFORE
HERMIT'S
HERO-BOY
HEROINES
HESITATE
HESPERIAN
HESPERUS
HEWED
HEWN
HEXAMETERS
HICCUP'D
HICCUPS
HIDEOUSNESS
HIDING
HIEROGLYPHIC
HIEROGLYPHICS
HIGH-BORN
HIGHNESS'S
HIGH-SOUL'D
HIGHWAY'S
HIMS
HIMSELF'S
HINDOSTAN
HINGE
HINTED
HINTERS
HIP
HIRELING
HIRSUTE
HISSED
HISSES
HIST
HISTORIAN'S
HISTORICAL
HISTORIES
HITS
HIVED
HOARDED
HOARDER'S
HOARDS
HOARSER
HOARSEST
HOAX
HOBGOBLIN'S
HOC
HOCHE
HOGS
HOIST
HOISTED
HOLBEIN'S
HOLDING
HOLIER
HOLLAND
HOLLAND'S
HOMELESS
HOMELY
HOMESTEAD
HOMILIES
HOMILY
HOMMES
HONESTER
HONESTLY
HONEYMOON'S
HONOUR'D
HOOK
HOPEFUL
HOPEFUL'S
HOPING
HOPS
HORATIAN
HORDE
HORDES
HORIZON
HORIZON'S
HORN
HORNE
HORNER

HORNET
HORRORS
HORSEBACK
HORSEMEN
HORSE-RACES
HORSES'
HORTENSIUS
HOSPITABLE
HOSPITABLY
HOSPITAL
HOSTILE
HOST'S
HOTBEDS
HOT-HOUSE
HOT-PRESS
HOTTENTOT
HOTTEST
HOURLY
HOURS'
HOUSE-KEEPER
HOUSEKEEPERS
HOUSELESS
HOUSEMAID'S
HOVE
HOWLED
HOWSOE'ER
HOYLE
HU
HUGER
HUMANITY'S
HUMBLED
HUMBLEST
HUMBLY
HUMBOLDT
HUMBUG
HUMILIATION
HUMMING
HUMOURING
HUMOURS
HUMP
HUMPHREY
HUNCHBACK
HUNDSFOT
HUNGER'S
HUNTED
HUNTER
HUNTER'S
HUNTING-BOX
HUNTSMAN'S
HURL
HURLING
HURRA
HURRAH
HURRYING
HURTS
HUSHED
HUSSAR
HUSTINGS
HUZZAS
HYAENA
HYDES
HYDRA
HYMEN
HYMENEAL
HYMETTUS
HYMNED
HYPOCRITICAL
HYSTERIC
HYSTERICAL
IBIS
ICEBERG
ICEBERGS
ICELAND
ICHAR
ICICLES
ICY
ID
IDA
IDEA
IDENTIFY
IDENTITY
IDLY
IDOLATRY
IFFSKCHY
IGNARA
IGNES
IGNIS
IGNIS-FATUUS

IGNOBLE
IGNORANT
IGNORANTLY
ILIA
ILIAD
ILIADS
ILL-BREEDING
ILLE
ILL-GOTTEN
ILLICIT
ILLNESSES
ILL-SORTED
ILL-TIMED
ILLUMINATE
ILLUMINE
ILLUMINED
ILL-USED
ILLUSION
ILLUSIONS
ILLUSTRATING
ILLUSTRATION
ILLUSTRIOUS
IMAGES
IMAGINATION'S
IMBIBED
IMITATE
IMITATING
IMMACULATE
IMMATERIALISM'S
IMMEMOR
IMMEMORIAL
IMMORTALITY
IMMOVEABLE
IMP
IMPALED
IMPALEMENT
IMPART
IMPATIENCE
IMPATIENT
IMPATIENTLY
IMPERTURBABLE
IMPIOUS
IMPLORED
IMPORTUNE
IMPORTUNITY
IMPOSE
IMPOSED
IMPOSING
IMPOSSIBILE
IMPOSTORS
IMPOSTURE
IMPRESS
IMPRESS'D
IMPRESSIONS
IMPRIMATUR
IMPRINT
IMPROBABLE
IMPROPER
IMPROVE
IMPROVEMENTS
IMPROVVISATORE
IMPS
IMPUTED
IMPUTES
INARTICULATE
INCENSE
INCISION
INCLINES
INCLOSED
INCOME
INCOMES
INCOME-TAX
INCOMPARABLE
INCOMPLETE
INCONTINENT
INCONVENIENCE
INCONVENIENT
INCORRECT
INCORRIGIBLE
INCREASING
INCREMENT
INCUBI
INCUMBRANCE
INCURR'D
INDE
INDECISION
INDEMNIFICATION
INDEMNIFIES

INDENTURES
INDEPENDENCE
INDIGESTION'S
INDISPENSABLE
INDISPENSIBLE
INDISPOSED
INDISTINCT
INDITING
INDUES
INDULGE
INDULGENCE
INEBRIETY
INEFFABLY
INERT
INFALLIBLE
INFALLIBLY
INFANTINE
INFANTS
INFER
INFERNAL
INFIDEL
INFINITE
INFINITIES
INFLAMMATION
INFLAMMATIONS
INFLICTION
INFORMED
INFUSION
INGLORIOUS
INGRATITUDE
INGREDIENT
INGREDIENTS
INHERITS
INITIATION
INKY
INLY
INNATE
INNKEEPERS
INNOCENTS
INNOVATION'S
INOCULATION
INOFFENSIVE
INQUISITION
INQUISITIONS
INQUISITORS
INS
INSATIATE
INSCRIBE
INSCRUTABLE
INSECTS
INSECURE
INSERT
INSERTED
INSIDE-OUT
INSINUATING
INSINUATION
INSIPID
INSIST
INSISTS
INSOLENCE
INSPECT
INSPECTOR
INSPIRATION
INSPIRERS
INSPIRES
INSPIRING
INSTALMENTS
INSTANCES
INSTEP
INSTILLING
INSTRUCTOR
INSTRUCTS
INSTRUMENTS
INSULAR
INSULTS
INTEGRITY
INTELLIGENCE
INTELLIGIBLE
INTENDED
INTENSITY
INTER
INTERESTED
INTERESTING
INTERESTS
INTERIM
INTERJECTION
INTERJECTIONS
INTERMINABLE

1   (CONTINUED)
INTERPRETATION
INTERPRETED
INTERTWISTED
INTERVENE
INTERVENES
INTERVENING
INTESTATE
INTOXICATES
INTRIGANTE
INTRUSIVE
INUNDATIONS
INURBANITY
INURED
INURN'D
INVADED
INVALID
INVASION
INVESTIGATING
INVESTIGATION
INVINCIBLE
INVIOLATE
INVITATION
INVITING
INVOLVE
INVOLVED
INWARDLY
IO
IPECACUANHAE
IPHIGENE
IRA
IRISHMAN
IRREGULARLY
IRREGULARS
IRRELIGION
IRREVOCABLE
IRRIGATE
IRRITABILIS
ISCARIOT
ISCHSKIN
ISLANDER
ISSUING
ISTHMUS
ITCH
ITEMS
ITHACA
IVRESSE
IVY
IXION
JACKALLS
JACKET'S
JACKETS
JACKS
JACOB
JACOBINS
JACOB'S
JADE
JAIL
JAILORS
JANIZARIES
JAR
JASMINE
JASON
JASON'S
JAUNT
JE
JEAN
JEER
JEFFERIES
JELICK'S
JELICKS
JELLIES
JELLY
JEMMY
JEOPARDY
JEROME
JERVIS
JESTEST
JET
JETTY
JEUNES
JEWELS
JINGLED
JOANNA
JOB'S
JOCUND
JOHANNA
JOHNSON'S

JOINS
JOKERS
JOKING
JOLLY
JOLT
JOLTINGS
JONES
JOSEPH
JOSE'S
JOUBERT
JOURNAL
JOURNALS
JOVE'S
JUDGE'S
JUDICIOUSLY
JUGULAR
JUICY
JULIETTA
JUMBLING
JUMP'D
JUNCTURE
JUNGLE
JUNIOR
JUNIPER
JUPITER
JUSTEST
JUSTICE'S
JUSTICES
JUSTIFY
JUSTLY
JUVENAL
JUVENTA
KAFF
KALEIDOSCOPE
KALENDS
KANT
KATSKOFF
KEATS
KEEL
KEG
KELP
KEN
KENNINGTON
KENTUCKY
KEPPEL
KESWICK
KETCH
KETTLE
KEYS
KIBES
KIBITKA
KICKED
KICKS
KIDDY
KILIA
KINDLES
KING'S
KINGS'
KINNAIRD
KISSING
KISS'S
KIST
KIT-CAT
KITE
KITH
KITTENS
KNEAD
KNEE-DEEP
KNIGHTED
KNIGHTS'
KNIT
KNITS
KNOCKEST
KNOCKING
KNOCKINGS
KNOLL
KNOLLES
KNOWMAN
KNOW'S
KOCLOBSKI
KOKLOPHTI
KONINGSBERG
KORAN
KOSCIUSKO'S
KOURAKIN
KOUTOUSOW'S
KOZAKS
KURDS

KUTHEREIAN
LABLE
LABORIOUS
LABOUR'D
LABOURER
LABOURING
LABOUR'S
LACES
LACING
LACKEYS
LACQUEYS
LADDER
LADEN
LADYE-LOVE
LADY-LOVE
LADY-MOTHER
LAFAYETTE
LAFITTE
LAIN
LAISSEZ
LAKE-LIKE
LAKERS
LAKE'S
L'ALLEMANDE
LAME
LAMED
LAMENTATION
LAMPLIGHTER'S
LAMP-LIGHTING
LANCE
LANDHOLDERS
LANDLORDS
LANDOR
LAND-SERVICE
LANDSMEN
LANDSMEN'S
LANE
LANGERON
LANGUISHING
LANNES
LANTERN
LANTHORN
LANTHORNS
LAOCOON'S
LAP-DOGS
LAPS
LAPSE
LAPSED
LAPSUS
LARGEST
LASCIAMI'S
LASCIATE
LASHES
LASSITUDE
LASTED
LAST'S
LATITUDE
LATTERLY
LAUD
LAUDANUM
LAUGH'D
LAUNCHED
LAURA
LAUREAT
LAVES
LAVEST
LAVISHED
LAW'S
LAW-SUITS
LAWYER'S
LAWYERS'
LAZARET
LAZY
LEADEN
LEADING
LEAFY
LEAGUED
LEAGUERED
LEANDER
LEANS
LEAPING
LEAPS
LEARNEDLY
LEARNEST
LEARNS
LEAR'S
LEASES
LEATHERN

LEATHERS
LEAVEN'D
LEAVENING
LEAVETH
LECTURING
LEERS
LEFT-LEGS
LEGACY
LEGEND
LEGITIMACY
LEGITIMACY'S
LEGITIMATELY
LEILA'S
LEIPSIC
LELY
LEMAN'S
LENDS
LENGTHENING
LENGTHY
LENIENT
L'EPROUVEUSE
LESBIAN
LESSEN
LEUCADIA'S
LEVANT
LEVANTINES
LEVEES
LEVELLERS
LEXICON
LIBATIONS
LIBEL
LIBELLER'S
LIBELS
LIBERALLY
LIBERATE
LIBERATED
LIBERATOR
LIBERTY'S
LIBRARY
LICENCES
LICENTIATE
LID
LIDS
LIED
LIEUTENANT'S
LIFE-TIME
LIFTED
LIFTING
LIGHTEN
LIGHTENING
LIGHTEST
LIGHTLY
LIKINGS
LILAC
LILLIPUT
LIMES
LIME-TWIGS
LIMIT
LIMITED
LINCOLN
LINEAGE
LINEAL
LINED
LINGER
LINGER'D
LINKED
LINNET
LINT
LIONS'
LIPLESS
LIPS'
LIQUORS
LISP
LISTEN'D
LISTENED
LISTENER
LISTENS
LITIGIOUS
LITTLETON
LIVELIEST
LIVID
LIVONIAN
LIVORNO
LIVY
LOAD
LOADED
LOAM
LOATHES

1   (CONTINUED)
LOBSTER
LOCHABER
LOCK'D
LOCKLESS
LODGE
LODGED
LODGEMENT
LOG
LOGICAL
LOITER
LOITER'D
LOLAH'S
LONDONDERRY
LONDONDERRY'S
LONELINESS
LONG-BOAT'S
LONGBOW'S
LONG'D
LONGEVITY
LONGMAN
LONG-SEALED
LONGUEURS
LOOP-HOLE
LOOSELY
LOOSISH
LOPE
LOPPING
LOQUOR
LORDLINGS
LORDSHIP'S
LORDSHIPS
LORRAINE
LOSES
LOT'S
LOTTING
LOUDEST
LOUIS
LOUNGING
LOVE-BEATEN
LOVE-BEGOTTEN
LOWE
LOWER'D
LOWEST
LUBBERLY
LUCCA
LUCENDO
LUCIFER
LUCKIEST
LUCKLESSLY
LUCK'S
LUCRETIUS'
LUCUBRATION
LUCULLUS'
LUDICROUS
LUES
LUGO
LULLABY
LULLED
LUNATIC
LUNCHEON
LUNCHEONS
LUNES
LURE
LURES
LURK
LURKS
LUSTILY
LUTES
LUX
LUXURIANT
LUXURIOUS
LWOW
LYKANTHROPY
LYNX
LYNX-LIKE
LYONS
MACASSAR
MACHIAVELIAN
MACKAW
MACKSTAY
MADDENED
MADDENING
MADMEN
MADMEN'S
MADRID'S
MAEVIA
MAGAZINE

MAGAZINES
MAGGIOR
MAGGOTS
MAGICIAN'S
MAGICIANS
MAGISTERIAL
MAGNANIMOUS
MAGNESIAS
MAGNETIC
MAGNETISM
MAGNIFICENCE
MAGNIFICENTLY
MAGNIFICIENT
MAGNIFIQUE
MAHOGANY
MAHOMETANS
MAIDENHEADS
MAIDEN-LIKE
MAIDENLY
MAILS
MAIMED
MAINMAST
MAINOTS
MAJESTIC
MAJESTICALLY
MAJORA
MAKER
MAKERS
MAL-A-PROPOS
MALICIOUS
MALMSBURY
MALT
MALUS
MAMMOTH'S
MANACLES
MANCHESTER
MANDARIN
MANDATE
MANGER
MANHEIM
MANIA
MANICHEAN
MANIFESTED
MANIFOLD
MANLY
MANN
MANNAE
MANNER'D
MANNISH
MANORS
MANSION'S
MAN-SLAYER
MANTILLA
MANTLES
MANURED
MANY-COLOUR'D
MAPS
MARAT
MARBLED
MARBLE'S
MARCEAU
MARCHES
MARCHIONESS
MARGIN
MARINE
MARINERS
MARINET'S
MARIO
MARIUS
MARK'D
MARKETABLE
MARLE
MARMORA
MARQUESS
MARRIAGE-MORNING
MARRYING
MARSHALL
MARSHALL'D
MARSHALS
MARTYRED
MARTYRLY
MARVELLED
MARVELLING
MARVELLOUS
MARYS
MASK
MASKED
MASKS

MASONIC
MASQUE
MASQUERADES
MASS-BOOKS
MASSES
MASTER'D
MASTERPIECE
MASTIFF
MATAPAN
MATCHLESS
MATCH-MAKING
MATERIALISED
MATES
MATHEMATICIAN
MATHEMATICS
MATHO
MATRIMONY'S
MATRON-LIKE
MATS
MATTER'D
MATTERED
MATTHEW
MATTOCK'S
MATURE
MATURER
MAUDLIN
MAWS
MAX
MAXIME
MAXIMS
MAYBE
MAYOR'S
MEADOWS
MEAGRE
MEANDER
MEASURED
MEASURING
MECHANICS
MECHANTE
MECUM
MEDES
MEDIAS
MEDICINE
MEDIO
MEDITATE
MEDITATED
MEDITATION
MEDITATIVE
MEETINGS
MEKNOP
MEKNOP'S
MELANCTHON
MELLIFLUOUSLY
MELLOW'D
MELODIES
MELODRAME
MELODRAMES
MELTON
MEMBER
MEMNON'S
MEMORANDUM
MEMORY'S
MEMPHIAN
MENACED
MENACING
MENAGERIE
MENDED
MENDING
MENELAUS
MENTAL
MENTE
MENTIONED
MEPHISTOPHELES
MERCENARY
MERCHANDISE
MERCHANTMEN
MERCHANT-SHIP
MERCIES
MERCURY
MERIDIAN-LIKE
MERITED
MERITORIOUS
MERMAID'S
MERMAIDS
ME'S
MESH
MESSAGE
MESSALINA'S

MESSENGER
MESSMATE
MESSORUM
MESSUAGES
METAMORPHOSIS
METEORS
METHODISTIC
METHOD'S
METHODS
METROPOLIS
MIA'S
MICROCOSM
MIENS
MIGHTIER
MIGHTIEST
MILAN
MILDER
MILK-AND-WATER
MILL
MILLAH
MILLENNIUM
MILLIARDS
MILLINERY
MILLPOND
MILOR
MILTIADES
MILTONIC
MIMIC
MIMICS
MINARET
MINCED
MINDFUL
MIND'S
MINED
MINERVA
MINERVA'S
MINES
MINGLING
MINIATURE
MINION'S
MINISTERIAL
MINORITY
MINOTAUR
MINSTREL
MINTAGE
MINUS
MINUTE'S
MINUTES
MINUTEST
MIO'S
MIRABEAU
MIRE
MIRTH-MOVING
MISANTHROPE
MISAPPLIED
MISCALCULATION
MISCARRIED
MISCARRY
MISCHANCE
MISCHIEF-MAKING
MISCHIEFS
MISCHIEVOUS
MISCREANT
MISCUIT
MISERIES
MISERS
MISFORTUNE
MISHAP
MISNOMER
MISSHAPEN
MISSING
MISTAKING
MISTY
MITE
MITFORD
MITIGATED
MIXES
MOANS
MOBILITY
MOBS
MOCHA'S
MOCK
MOCK'D
MOCKERIES
MOCKERY
MODERATELY
MODERATE-MINDED
MODERATION

1 (CONTINUED)	MURDERER	NIBBLING	OBTUSE
MOGUL	MURDER'S	NICETY	OCCASIONALLY
MOLDAVIA'S	MURK	NICHED	OCCUPANTS
MOLE	MURMUR'D	NICKNAME	OCCUPIES
MOLIERE'S	MURMURED	NICKNAMED	OCCURR'D
MOLU	MURMURING	NIGER	OCCURS
MOLWITZ	MURMURS	NIGHER	OCEAN-BURIED
MOMENTARY	MUSCADINS	NIGHEST	OCEAN-TREASURE
MOMENTLY	MUSCLE	NIGHTINGALES	OCTAVE
MOMONOFF	MUSED	NIGHTINGLE	OCTAVE'S
MOMUS	MUSE-LIKE	NIGHTWINDS	OCTAVES
MONASTERY	MUSES'	NILE	ODALISQUES
MONCADA	MUSEUM	NILE'S	ODDITIES
MONGERS	MUSING	NIMRODS	ODDLY
MONIED	MUSK-BULL	NINETEENTH	ODES
MONITEUR	MUSQUETRY	NINE-TENTHS	ODOURS
MONITORS	MUSQUETS	NINETY	ODYSSEYS
MONMOUTH	MUSSULMANS	NINI	OEDIPUS
MONOPOLY	MUSTACHIOS	NINNY	O'ER-ARCH
MONOSYLLABLE	MUTABILITY	NINON	O'ERAWES
MONOTONY	MUTILATED	NINTH	O'ERCAME
MONSOON	MUTTER'D	NOISES	O'ERCAST
MONSTER	MUTTERING	NO-MEANING	O'ERCHARGED
MONT	MUTTERS	NOMINAL	O'ERCLOUDED
MONTAGU	MUTUAL-DARTED	NOMINATED	O'ERCROWDED
MONTAIGNE	MUTUALLY	NON-AGE	O'ERFLOW
MONTH'S	MUZZLE	NONCE	O'ERFLOW'D
MONUMENTS	MYRIADS	NON-ENTITY	O'ERFLOWS
MOONLIT	MYRMIDONS	NONSUIT	O'ERGROWN
MOORE'S	MYRTLE	NOONTIDE	O'ERHEARD
MOPETH	MYSTAGOGUE	NORTHERN	O'ERLABOUR'D
MORALEST	MYTHOLOGICAL	NORTH-WEST	O'ERLEAP
MORALITIES	MYTHOLOGY	NOS	O'ERLIVE
MORALITY'S	NABUCHADONOSOR	NOSCITUR	O'ERLOADED
MORALLY	NADIR	NOTELESS	O'ERMASTER'D
MOREAU	NAIAD	NOTHINGNESS	O'ERPASS'D
MORES	NAILED	NOTORIETY	O'ERSHADING
MORNING'S	NAMING	NOTORIOUS	O'ERSHADOW'D
MORNS	NAPLES	NOUN	O'ERSPREADS
MOROCCO	NAPS	NOURISHED	O'ERSTEP
MORROW	NARRATE	NOURISHES	O'ERTHROWN
MORSELS	NARROWNESS	NOVEL-READING	O'ERTHROWS
MORTALITY'S	NATAL	NOVELTY	O'ERTOPPED
MORTAL'S	NATHLESS	NUBIA	O'ERTURN'D
MORTALS'	NATIONS'	NUBIANS	O'ERWROUGHT
MORTARS	NAUGHT	NUGAE	OFFENCES
MORTIFIED	NAUSEA	NUMA'S	OFFENDING
MOSCOW'S	NAUSEOUS	NUMB'D	OFFERING
MOSQUES	NAUTICAL	NUMBER'D	OFF-HAND
MOTHS	NAVIGATE	NUMBER'S	OFFICERS
MOTIONLESS	NAVIGATORS	NUMERAL	OFFICES
MOTS	NAZARENE	NUMIDIAN	OFF-ING
MOULDED	NAZARENES	NUNEZ	OFTENER
MOULDY	NE	NUNS	OGLED
MOUNTAIN-CRESCENT	NEARS	NUPTIALS	OGLING
MOUNTAINEERS	NEATH	NURSERY	OGNI
MOUNTAIN'S	NECKCLOTH	NURTURE	OLDEST
MOUNTAIN-SKIRTED	NECKCLOTH'S	NURTURED	OLD-GENTLEMANLY
MOUNTAIN-STREAM	NEEDLES'	NUTBROWN	OLIGARCHS
MOUNTS	NEEDY	NUTRITIOUS	OLIVE
MOURN'D	NEGATIVES	NUTS	OLIVE-BRANCH
MOUSKIN	NEGLECTED	NUTTY	OLYMPUS
MOUTHEY	NEGOCIATION	NYMPH-LIKE	OMINOUS
MOVEABLES	NEGOTIIS	OAK	OMITTED
MOWER	NEGRESSES	OBDURATE	OMITTING
MOWING	NEGRO'S	OBEDIENCE	OMNE
MOWS	NEIGHBOURS	OBEISANCE	OMNIA
MOZART'S	NEM	OBEY'D	ONCE-NAMED
MS	NEPTUNE	OBEYED	ONESTI'S
MUCKS	N'ER	OBEYS	OOZED
MUDDLE	NESSUS	OBIT	OOZING
MUDDY	NESTLE	OBJECTION	OPERAS
MUEZZIN'S	NESTLED	OBJECTION'S	OPERA-SCENE
MUFFLE	NESTORS	OBJECTIONS	OPERATIONS
MUFFLED	NETHERLANDS	OBLIGES	OPHELIA
MUFFLES	NETS	OBLIGING	OPINION'S
MUFTI	NEUTRALISED	OBLIVION'S	OPIUM
MUG	NEUTRALITY	OBLIVIOUS	OPPORTUNITIES
MULCT	NEUTRALIZE	OBSEQUIOUS	OPPOSING
MULE	NEUTRUM	OBSERVANT	OPPOSITES
MULTIFARIOUS	NEVA'S	OBSERVER	OPPRESSED
MULTIPLICATION	NEW-BOUGHT	OBSERVING	OPPRESSIVE
MULTIPLIED	NEW-FLEDGED	OBSOLETE	OPPREST
MULTITUDE	NEW-FOUND	OBSTACLE	OPTIM
MULTITUDES	NEWGATE	OBSTINATE	OPTION
MUMMY	NEWTON'S	OBSTINATELY	ORACLE
MUNCHINGS	NEW-TUNED	OBTAINED	ORATORY
MURDERED	NIBBLE	OBTAINING	ORBIT

1   (CONTINUED)
ORDAINED
ORDEAL
ORDER'D
ORDINATION
ORDURE
O'REILLY
ORGAN
ORNAMENTED
ORPHAN'S
ORPHEUS
ORTHODOX
ORTHOGRAPHY
OSSIAN
OSTENTATION
OSTLER
O'TABBEY
OU
OUNCE
OUR'S
OUSCKIN
OUSKI
OUT-AT-ELBOW
OUTBALANCE
OUTCRY
OUTLET
OUTLET'S
OUTLINE'S
OUTLINES
OUTRAGE
OUTRAN
OUTS
OUTSIDES
OUTSTRETCH'D
OUTWORK
OVENS
OVERCHARGE
OVER-CHILLY
OVER-COLD
OVERCOMING
OVERDID
OVERHEAD
OVERHUNG
OVERJOY'D
OVERLAY
OVERLOOK'D
OVERLOOKED
OVERLOOKS
OVERPOWERED
OVERPOWERS
OVERSET
OVERSTRAIN
OVERTHROWN
OVERTURE
OVERTURNS
OVER-WARM
OVER-WARMTH
OVERWORKING
OVERWORN
OVERWROUGHT
OVID
OWL-SONGS
OWNER'S
OWNERS
OXENSTIERN
OXLESS
OYSTER
PACED
PACK'D
PACKET
PACKETS
PADISHA
PADLOCK
PADS
PAGAN
PAGANS
PAGEANT
PAIL
PAIN'D
PAINED
PAINING
PAINTER
PAINTER'S
PAIR'D
PAIRS
PALATES
PALER
PALES

PALISADE
PALISADOED
PALLAS
PALM
PALMS
PALPABLE
PALPITATING
PALPITATICN
PALSIED
PAMPER'D
PAMPHLETS
PAN
PANCA
PANDERING
PANG
PANORAMA
PANTALOONS
PANTERS
PANTISOCRASY
PANTOMIMES
PANTS
PAPA
PAPHIANS
PARABLE
PARADING
PARADOX
PARAGONS
PARALLEL
PARAS
PARASITES
PARCAE
PARCHMENT
PARDONED
PARE
PARENTHESIS
PARENTLESS
PARENT'S
PARGA'S
PARIAN
PARIAS
PARISIAN
PARKS
PARLIAMENTARY
PARNASSIAN
PARODIES
PAROXYSM
PARRIES
PARROTS
PARRY
PARS
PARTAKES
PARTICLE
PARTINGS
PARTLETT
PARTLY
PARTNERS
PARTOUT
PARTRIDGE
PARTRIDGE'
PARTURITION
PARVA
PASIPHAE
PASSABLE
PASSEE
PASSENGER
PASSIM
PASSIVE
PASTORAL
PASTURE
PATCH
PATCHING
PATERNAL
PATHETICALLY
PATHWAY
PATIENTS
PATRIARCH
PATRIOTIC
PATRIOTISM
PATRIOT'S
PATROCLUS
PATRON
PATRONAGE
PATRONS
PAT'S
PATTERN
PAULO
PAVE

PAVIOUR
PAWNS
PAYING
PAY'S
PEACOCK
PEAKS
PEALED
PEALS
PEAS
PEASANT
PEBBLE
PECCADILLOS
PECCANT
PECK
PECKING
PECULIARLY
PEDIGREES
PEDLAR
PEDLARS
PEEPED
PEERAGE
PEERESSES
PEERING
PEER'S
PEGS
PELEGRINI
PELEUS'
PELF
PELIDES'
PELLETS
PENALTY
PENCE
PENCHANTS
PENCIL
PENITENCE
PEOPLES
PEOPLING
PERCEIVES
PER-CENTAGE
PERCEPTIBLY
PERCEPTION
PERCHED
PERENNIAL
PERFECTLY
PERFORCE
PERFORM
PERFORMANCES
PERFORM'D
PERFORMED
PERFORMER'S
PERFUME
PERIGUEUX
PERIWIGS
PERJURED
PERMISSION
PERMITS
PERORATION
PERPEND
PERPETRATE
PERPETRATED
PERPETRATES
PERPLEXED
PERPLEXITY
PERSECUTED
PERSECUTION
PERSIAN'S
PERSIFLAGE
PERSONAL
PERSONIFICATION
PERSONIFIED
PERSONIFY
PERSON'S
PERTINACIOUS
PERUKE
PERUSALS
PERUSED
PERVADED
PERVADES
PERVENCHE
PERVERSELY
PESTILENCE
PETER'S
PETERS
PETION
PETITION
PETRIFIED
PHAETON'S
PHALANX

PHANTASMAGORIA
PHANTOMS
PHARISAIC
PHEASANTS
PHEDRA
PHENOMENON
PHILANTHROPIC
PHILANTHROPY
PHILOSOPHICAL
PHILOSOPHISED
PHLEGETHONTIC
PHOSPHORUS
PHRASEOLOGY
PHRENSY
PHRYGIAN
PHTHISICAL
PHTHISICS
PHYSIC
PHYSICAL
PHYSICKED
PIANO
PIASTRES
PICCADILLY
PICKINGS
PICTURESQUE
PIDDLE
PIECED
PIECE-MEAL
PIERCETH
PIERCING
PIGEONS
PIGER
PIGMIES
PIKES
PILGRIM
PILL
PILLAGE
PILLARS
PILLORY
PILLOWING
PILLOW'S
PILLOWS
PILLS
PIMP
PIN-CUSHION
PINIONS
PINNACE
PINNACLE
PINNED
PINT
PIPE'S
PIPKINS
PIPPIN
PIQUED
PIRACY
PIRATES
PIRATICAL
PISH
PISTACHIO
PIT-A-PAT
PITCHED
PITCHER
PITCHES
PITEOUSLY
PITHY
PITIES
PITILESS
PITTANCE
PITY'S
PLACEMAN
PLAGUED
PLAIDS
PLAINTIVELY
PLANCO
PLANET
PLANET'S
PLANETS
PLANKS
PLANNED
PLANT
PLANTED
PLAT
PLATES
PLATONICAL
PLATO'S
PLAYER
PLEADERS
PLEADINGS

1   (CONTINUED)
PLEASURE'S
PLEDGED
PLENIPO
PLIED
PLOTTERY
PLOUGHING
PLUCKED
PLUCKING
PLUCKS
PLUME
PLUMED
PLUMES
PLUMPNESS
PLUNDER'D
PLUNDERED
PLUNDERERS
PLUNDERING
PLURAL
PLUTARCH'S
PLY
POACHER
POCKET
POCKET-HANDKERCHIEF
POCKET-PISTOL
POETESS
POET-LAUREATE
POIETIKES
POINTER
POISONED
POISON-TREE
POKE
POLE'S
POLES
POLICY
POLITELY
POLITICAL
POLL
POLOUZKI
POLYCRATES
POLYGAMY'S
POMEGRANATES
POMMELL'D
POMPEY
POMPILIUS
PONTIC
POPE'S
POPLAR
POPLARS
POPPIES
POPPING
POPULARITY
POPULATION
PORCH
PORCO
PORCUPINE
PORED
POROUS
PORPHYRY
PORTAL'S
PORTENTOUS
PORT-HOLE
PORTINGALE
PORTION'D
PORTIONED
PORTMANTEAU
PORTMANTEAUS
PORTUGAL
POSITIONS
POSITIVE
POSITIVELY
POSSE
POSSESS
POSSESSOR
POSSIBLY
POSSIDETIS
POSTED
POST-HORSES
POST-HOUSE
POSTILLION'S
POSTING
POSTPONED
POSTURE
POTASSAE
POTATIONS
POTATO
POTATOE
POTION

POTIPHAR
POTTERY
POTTLEDEEP
POUNCE
POUSKIN
POWERFUL
POWERLESS
POWER'S
POWLEY
POX
PRACTICABLE
PRACTISE
PRACTISING
PRAETORIAN
PRANCE
PRANCING
PRATE
PRAYER-BOOK
PRECAUTION
PRECAUTIONARY
PRECAUTIONS
PRECAUTIOUS
PRECEDENCE
PRECEDENT
PRECEDES
PRECEPTS
PRECIPICES
PRECIPITATE
PRECIPITATION
PRECISE
PRECISIAN
PREDECESSORS
PREDICAMENT
PREDICATE
PREDICTIONS
PREDILECTION
PREDOMINANCE
PREFACE
PREFERR'D
PREFERRING
PREFERS
PREJUDICES
PRELUDES
PRELUDIOS
PREMATURE
PREMISES
PREMISING
PREPARATIONS
PREPARATIVES
PREPOSSESSION
PREPOSSESSIONS
PRESAGE
PRESAGED
PRESAGING
PRESBYTERIAN
PRESCIENCE
PRESCRIBED
PRESCRIPTION
PRESENT'S
PRESERVING
PRESIDE
PRESSING
PRESUMES
PRETENDED
PRETENDER
PRETENDERS
PRETENSION
PRETTILY
PREVAILED
PREVAILING
PREVARICATION
PREVENTATIVE
PREVENTED
PREVENTS
PREVIOUS
PREVIOUSLY
PRICES
PRICKING
PRIMA-DONNA'S
PRIMATE
PRIMLY
PRIMROSE
PRINCELY
PRINCESSES
PRINCIPAL
PRINTING
PRIOR
PRISCIAN

PRISM
PRISONED
PRISONERS
PRISONS
PRIVATEER
PRIVILEGES
PRIVY
PRIZE-MONEY
PRIZES
PROBE
PROCEEDINGS
PROCEEDS
PROCLAIM'D
PROCLAIMED
PROCREATION
PROCREATIVE
PROCUL
PRODIGALLY
PRODUCES
PROEM
PROFESSED
PROFESSIONS
PROFESSOR
PROFESSORS
PROFFERED
PROFILES
PROFOUND
PROFOUNDER
PROFUSE
PROGENIES
PROGRESSION
PROHIBITED
PROJECTS
PROLIFIC
PROLONG'D
PROLONGS
PROMETHEAN
PROMETHEUS
PROMINENT
PROMOTING
PROMOTION
PROMPT
PROMPTER'S
PROMPTS
PRONE
PRONOUNCE
PRONOUNCES
PRONUNCIATION
PROP
PROPAGATE
PROPAGATED
PROPENSITIES
PROPENSITY
PROPEREST
PROPERLY
PROPERTIES
PROPHECY
PROPHETICALLY
PROPHET'S
PROPORTIONATE
PROPORTION'D
PROPORTIONS
PROPOS
PROPOSAL
PROPOSE
PROPOSITIONS
PROPRIETY
PROSCRIBED
PROSECUTED
PROSECUTIONS
PROSPECT
PROSPERITY
PROSPEROUS
PROSTITUTION
PROSTRATE
PROTASOFF
PROTECT
PROTECTED
PROTECTOR
PROTECTORS
PROTEGE
PROTEGEE
PROTESILAUS
PROTEST
PROTESTED
PROUDER
PROUDLIER
PROVIDENTIALLY

PROVIDERS
PROVOCATIONS
PROVOKE
PROVOKED
PROWL
PROWS
PRUDENCE
PRUDENTLY
PRUDES
PRUSSIA
PRUSSIANS
PSALM
PSALMIST
PSALMODIC
PSEUDO-SYPHILIS
PUBERTY
PUBLICATIONS
PUBLICLY
PUBLIC'S
PUBLISH
PUBLISHED
PUFFED
PUKES
PULL'D
PULLING
PULV
PUMP'D
PUN
PUNCHEON
PUNCHEONS
PUNCTUATION
PUNCTUM
PUNCTURATIONS
PUNCTURE
PUNIC
PUNISH'D
PUNNED
PUNY
PUP
PUPPET-SHOWS
PURBLIND
PURCHASE
PURCHASING
PUREE
PURELY
PURGATIVES
PURGATORIAL
PURGATORY
PURGED
PURITY
PURL
PURPOSED
PURPOSES
PURSUER
PURSUITS
PURVEY
PURVEYOR
PURVEYORS
PUSH'D
PUSHED
PUSHING
PYGMALION
PYGMALION'S
PYRAMIDIC
PYRAMUS
PYTHAGORAS
PYTHONESS
QUA
QUACKS
QUADRILLE
QUADRUPLE
QUAE
QUAFF
QUAFF'D
QUAKING
QUALM
QUANTUM
QUARANTINE
QUARRELL'D
QUARRELLING
QUARTERED
QUARTERLY
QUARUM
QUAVERING
QUE
QUEAN
QUEANS
QUEEN-BEE

1   (CONTINUED)
QUENCH
QUENCHLESS
QUESTIONER
QUESTION'S
QUI
QUIA
QUIBBLE
QUIBUSDAM
QUICKENING
QUICKNESS
QUICKSILVER
QUICKSILVER'S
QUIESCENT
QUIETEST
QUIETS
QUINSY
QUINTESSENCE
QUINTESSENTIAL
QUIRE
QUITTING
QUIVER
QUIVER'S
QUIXOTIC
QUIZZED
QUIZZICAL
QUOI
QUOTATION
QUOTED
QUOTES
QUOTING
R
RABBI
RABBIT
RABBLE
RABBLE'S
RABY'S
RACER
RACES
RACE-WINNER
RACK'D
RACKRHYME
RACKS
RADICALS
RADULPHUS
RAFT
RAGAMUFFINS
RAGGED
RAGOUTS
RAGUSAN
RAINBOWS
RAINING
RAINS
RAINY
RAISIN
RAKES
RAM
RANGER
RANK'D
RANSACK'D
RAPACIOUS
RAPE
RAPHAEL
RAPIDLY
RAPS
RAPTURE'S
RARELY-TRODDEN
RAT
RATTLE
RATTLING
RAUCOCANTI'S
RAVAGE
RAVENOUS
RAVENOUSLY
RAVISHED
RAVISHING
REACHERS
REACHES
READIEST
READINESS
READINGS
REALITIES
REALM
REALM'S
REAPERS
REAR'D
REARS
REASON'S

RE-ASSURE
REBUILT
REBUKE
REBUS
RECALLED
RECEIPT
RECEIPTS
RECEIVING
RECENTLY
RECEPTACLES
RECEPTION
RECESSES
RECHERCHE
RECITAL
RECITATIVE
RECITE
RECITED
RECK
RECK'D
RECKON
RECKONING
RECLAIM'D
RECLINED
RECOGNISED
RECOGNIZE
RECOGNIZED
RECOLLECTING
RECOLLECTS
RECOMMENDATION
RECOMPENSES
RECONCIL'D
RECONCILE
RECONCILED
RECONCILIATION
RECONNOITRE
RECORDED
RECORDS
RECOVER
RECOVERY
RECREATIONS
RECRUITED
REDDEN
REDEEM
REDLY
REDOUBLED
REDOUBTED
REDRESS
REDRESSING
REDUCES
REDUNDANCY
REEF
REEFS
REEKING
RE-ELECTIONS
REELING
REELS
RE-EMBARK'D
RE-ENTERED
REFECTORY
REFER
REFERRING
REFINEMENT
REFINES
REFLECTS
REFORM
REFORMADOES
REFORMED
REFORMER
REFRESHING
REFRESHMENT
REFUSAL
REFUSALS
REFUSING
REGAL
REGALED
REGARDING
REGARDS
REGENT
REGIMENTAL
REGIMENT'S
REGION
REGULARITY
REGULARLY
REGULATED
REHEARSED
REIGN'D
REIGNED
REJECTS

REJOICE
RELAPSING
RELATIVES
RELAX'D
RELEASED
RELENT
RELENTED
RELIES
RELIEVE
RELIGION'S
RELIGIOUS
RELINQUISH'D
RELINQUISHED
RELUCTANCE
RELUCTANTLY
RELYING
REMAINDER
REMAINING
REMARKABLE
REMARKABLY
REMARRIED
REMBRANDT
REMEMBERING
REMINISCENCE
REMITS
REMNANTS
REMONSTRANCE
REMORSELESS
REMOVAL
REMOVE
REND
RENDERED
RENDERING
RENDERS
RENDEZVOUS
REND'RING
RENDS
RENEGADE
RENEWED
RENOVATE
RENOWN'S
RENTAL
REPAIRS
REPARTEES
REPASSED
REPEATERS
REPENT
REPENTS
REPERTORY
REPETITION
REPETITION'S
REPLENISH
REPLETION
REPORTED
REPOSES
REPOSING
REPRESENTATIVE
REPROOF'S
REPROVED
REPROVER
REPUBLICS
REPULSE
REPULSED
REPULSES
REPUTATIONS
REQUESTING
REQUISITE
REQUISITION
REQUISITION'S
REQUITES
RES
RESCUE
RESEMBLANCE
RESEMBLING
RE-SENT
RESENTFULLY
RESENTMENTS
RESERVES
RESET
RESIDENT
RESIGNS
RESOLUTIONS
RESOLVES
RESORT
RESOUNDED
RESPECTABLY
RESPIRATION'S
RESTED

RESTORATION
RESTORES
RESTRAIN
RESTRAINT
RESTRAINTS
RESULT
RESULTING
RESUMED
RETAINED
RETCHING
RE-TEACH
RETICULAR
RETIREMENT
RETORTS
RETREATING
RETREATS
RETROGRADE
RETROSPECTION
REVEALED
REVELATIONS
REVEL'D
REVELL'D
REVENGED
REVENGING
REVERED
REVERENCE
REVERSING
REVERSION
REVERT
REVISIT
REVIVING
REVOLUTION
REVOLVED
REVOLVING
REWARDED
REWARDS
RHENISH
RHETORIC
RHIMA
RHINE
RHODES
RHONE
RHYMED
RHYME'S
RHYMING
RIB
RIBAS'
RIBAUPIERRE'S
RIBBON
RIB'S
RICCHI
RICE
RICHARD
RICHELIEU
RICHEST
RIDDLED
RIDDLE'S
RIDDLES
RIDER
RIDGE
RIDICULE
RIDICULOUS
RIFLES
RIFT
RIGHTED
RIGHTEOUSNESS
RIGHT-WELL
RIGMAROLE
RIGOURS
RILLS
RIMES
RINGLETS
RIOTOUS
RIPENED
RIPENESS
RIPER
RIPPLE'S
RIPPLES
RIPPLING
RISEN
RISERS
RISKS
RITE
RITUAL
RIVAL
RIVAL'S
RIVALSHIP
RIVEN

1   (CONTINUED)

RIVULET	SACRUM	SCHOOL'D	SELF-DENIAL
RIVULET'S	SADNESS	SCHOOLS	SELF-DIRECTOR
ROACH	SAD'S	SCHOONER	SELF-INTEREST
ROARS	SAFEGUARD	SCIAN	SELFISHNESS
ROAST-MEAT	SAFEST	SCIENTIFIC	SELF-LOVES
ROAST-MEATS	SAGACITY	SCILLY	SELF-POSSESSION
ROASTS	SAGELY	SCIMITARS	SELF-REBUKES
ROB	SAGE'S	SCIONS	SELF-SLAUGHTER
ROBBING	SAGES'	SCISSORS	SELF-SOLD
ROCHEFOUCALLT	SAILOR	SCOFF	SELF-WILL
ROCKED	SAILOR'S	SCOFFED	SELLER
ROCKETS	SAIN	SCOFFING	SELLS
ROCKING	SAINTED	SCOPE	SEMIRAMIS
RODERIC'S	SAINTLY	SCORCH	SEMPRONIUS
RODOMONT	SAINT'S	SCORCHED	SEMPSTRESS
ROD'S	SALAD	SCORCHES	SENATORS
ROE	SALAM	SCORCHING	SENEGAL
ROGERS'	SALAMANCA	SCORNERS	SENHOR
ROGUENOFF	SALAMIS	SCORNFULLY	SENNAE
ROGUES	SALARIO	SCORNING	SENSIBILITIES
ROLAND'S	SALARY	SCORPION	SENTENCES
ROLE	SALLIED	SCOT	SENTINEL
ROLL-CALL	SALLIES	SCOTCHED	SEPARATED
ROMAGNOLE	SALLUST	SCOTCHMAN	SEPARATELY
ROMAIC	SALMI	SCOUNDRELS	SEPTEMBER
RONCEVALLES'	SALMON	SCOUR	SEPTEMBRIZERS
ROOF'D	SALPICON	SCOURGE	SEPULCHRI
ROOFS	SALT-WATER	SCOWL	SEQUINS
ROOKS	SALVATORE'S	SCRATCHED	SERAPH
ROOM-DOOR	SAMARITANS	SCRATCHING	SERAPHIM
ROOMS	SAMENESS	SCRAWL	SERAPH'S
ROOSTING	SAMPHIRE	SCREAMED	SERAPHS'
ROSE-LEAF	SAMPLES	SCREECHING	SERASKIERS
ROSE-LEAVES	SAMSON	SCREENED	SERE
ROSE'S	SAMSONLIKE	SCRIBBLE	SERENITY
ROSES	SANCHO	SCRIBBLERS	SERF
ROSS	SANCTIFY	SCRIBE	SERGE
ROTE	SANCTIONS	SCRIPTURE	SERPENT
ROTHSCHILD	SANCTITY	SCRIPTURES	SERPENTS
ROTTEN	SANCTUARY	SCRUPLES	SERVICES
ROUBLES	SAND-PITS	SCRUPULOSITY	SERVILITY
ROUGED	SANDWICH	SCUDO	SERVING
ROUGES	SANG-FROID	SCUDS	SESSIONS
ROUGHEST	SANGUINARY	SCUM	SETTLING
ROUGHING	SANSCRIT	SCUMLIKE	SEVENTY-FOUR
ROUNDED	SAPLESS	SCUTTLED	SEVERE
ROUSAMOUSKI	SAPPING	SCYMITAR	SEVERED
ROUSES	SARACEN	SCYMITARS	SEVERELY
ROUSSEAU'S	SARDANAPALUS	SCYTHES	SEVEREST
ROWED	SASH	SEA-ATTORNEY	SEX'S
ROWLEY	SATED	SEA-BIRD'S	SHADE'S
ROYALIST	SATIETY	SEA-BORN	SHADOW'D
ROYALTY'S	SATIRISE	SEA-GULLS	SHADOWED
RUB	SATISFACTION	SEALED	SHAFTS
RUBB'D	SATISFACTORY	SEAMAN	SHAH
RUBBED	SATISFY	SEAMEN'S	SHAKESPEAR
RUBS	SAUNTERED	SEARCHING	SHAKESPEARIAN
RUBY	SAVAGELY	SEA-SOLICITOR	SHAMROCK
RUDDY	SAVAGES	SEASON'D	SHAPES
RUDENESS	SAVES	SEASONED	SHARES
RUDEST	SAVIOUR	SEASONING	SHARPEN'D
RUDIMENTS	SAVOURED	SEASONS	SHARPER
RUE	SAWNEY'S	SEA-WORTHY	SHARPERS'
RUES	SAXONS	SECLUSION	SHARPLY
RUFFLES	SCAIS	SECONDED	SHATTER
RUINING	SCAIS-JE	SECOND'S	SHAVE
RULED	SCALDING	SECRETARIES	SHAVED
RULER	SCALED	SECRETARY	SHAWLED
RULING	SCAMANDER	SECRETS	SHEARS
RUMMAGED	SCANN'D	SECTION	SHEDDING
RUMOUR'D	'SCAPED	SECTIONS	SHEEN
RUMOURS	SCAR	SECTS	SHELTER
RUNIC	SCARCE-CLAD	SECUNDUM	SHELTERED
RUPTURE	SCARCE-DRAWN	SEDATIVE	SHELVE
RURAL	SCARED	SEDGES	SHE-PARADES
RUSE	SCARLESS	SEDIMENT	SHEPHERDS
RUST	SCARRED	SEDUCE	SHERIDAN
RUSTLED	SCATTER	SEDUCED	SHIBBOLETH
RUSTS	SCATTERS	SEDUCTIVE	SHILOH
RUTS	SCENTING	SEEKERS	SHIPP'D
SABLES	SCEPTICISM	SEES'T	SHIPPING
SABRED	SCHERBATOFF	SEIZABLE	SHIP'S
SACK	SCHEREMATOFF	SEIZES	SHIPWRECK'S
SACKED	SCHISM	SELF-APPROBATION	SHIRE'S
SACKING	SCHISMATIC	SELF-COMMUNION	SHIRTLESS
SACKS	SCHMACKSMITH	SELF-CONTROL	SHIVER'D
SACRAMENTS	SCHOLAR	SELF-DECEITFUL	SHOCK'D
	SCHOLARS	SELF-DEFENCE	SHOCKS

975

1   (CONTINUED)

SHOP
SHOP-KEEPERS
SHORTEN
SHORT-SIGHTED
SHOTS
SHOUT
SHOWERED
SHOWERING
SHRIEK'D
SHRILL
SHRINES
SHROUDS
SHRUGGED
SHUDDERINGS
SHUNS
SHUTTERS
SHYER
SHYLY
SIBERIA'S
SIBYL
SICILY
SIDEBOARD'S
SIDELONG
SIEGES
SIESTA
SIEVE
SIGAEUM
SIGNALIZE
SIGNAL'S
SIGNIFIES
SIGNING
SIGN-POSTS
SIKTUM
SILVERCUP
SILVERS
SIMILE'S
SIMILIE
SIMILITUDES
SIMOOM
SIMOOMS
SIMPLON'S
SIMPLY
SINCEREST
SINCERITY
SINE
SINECURE
SINECURES
SINEWS
SINGED
SINGEING
SINGER
SINGERS
SINGULAR
SINGULARITY
SINGULTUS
SINISTER
SINKERS
SINNERS
SIN'S
SION
SION'S
SIREN
SIREN'S
SIRES'
SIRIA
SIROCCO
SITES
SITTETH
SIX-FOOT
SIX-WEEKS'
SKAITER
SKAITING
SKELETONS
SKEWER
SKIFF
SKIFFS
SKILL'D
SKILLED
SKIMS
SKIPPING
SKIRMISH
SKITTISH
SKULKER
SKULL
SKY-BLUE
SLACK
SLACKEN

SLACKENED
SLACKENING
SLANG
SLAP-DASH
SLASHED
SLASHING
SLAUGHTERED
SLAVE-MAKER
SLAVE-MARKET
SLAVERY
SLAVERY'S
SLAVES'
SLAYING
SLAYS
SLEEK
SLEEPERS
SLEEPY
SLEET
SLEEVE
SLENDERER
SLICE
SLICES
SLIDING
SLIM
SLIME
SLIPP'D
SLIPSLOP
SLOPED
SLOTH
SLOWER
SLUGS
SLUT
SLY
SMALLEST
SMALL-EYED
SMALL-POX
SMARTER
SMEAR
SMELT
SMIL'D
SMILINGLY
SMITE
SMITHFIELD
SMITTEN
SMOKED
SMOKERS
SMOLLET
SMOOTHE
SMOOTH-FACED
SMOTE
SMOTHER'D
SMOTHERS
SMUGGLING
SNAKE-LIKE
SNAPP'D
SNARLING
SNEER'D
SNEERED
SNEEZE
SNOODS
SNORE
SNORES
SNOWBALL
SNOWDROPS
SNOW-TOPS
SNOW-WHITE
SNUB-NOSE
SNUFF
SNUFF'D
SNUFFED
SNUG
SNUGLY
SOARINGS
SOB
SOBBING
SOBERLY
SOBS
SOCIIS
SOCKET
SOCKETS
SOCRATIC
SODAE-SULPHAT
SODAS
SOFAS
SOFTEN
SOFTEN'D
SOHO
SOIL'S

SOIREE
SOLAR
SOLDER
SOLDIER
SOLELY
SOLICIT
SOLID
SOLIDITY
SOLILOQUIZE
SOLMS
SOLUTION
SOLVE
SOLVENT
SOLVING
SOLYMAN
SOME'S
SONG-BIRDS
SONGSTER
SONGSTRESS
SOON'S
SOOT
SOOTHERS
SOOTHES
SOOTHING
SOOTY
SOPHAS
SOPHIA'S
SOPHIAS
SOPHISTRY
SOPHY
SOPORIFIC
SOPRANO
SORRIER
SORROWING
SO-SO
SOT
SOTHEBY'S
SOU
SOUL-HIRED
SOUNDED
SOUNDING
SOUP
SOURCES
SOUTHCOTE
SOUTHCOTE'S
SOUTHERN
SPADE
SPAGNOLETTO
SPANGLED
SPANNING
SPARES
SPARING
SPARINGLY
SPARKLES
SPARROW'S
SPARRY
SPARTAN'S
SPECIE
SPECIMEN
SPECIMENS
SPECIOUS
SPECK
SPECTACLE
SPECTACLES
SPECTATORS
SPECTRES
SPECULATING
SPECULATIVE
SPEEDIER
SPEEDS
SPELLKEN
SPELT
SPENDING
SPENDTHRIFTS'
SPERANZA
SPIES
SPILL
SPILT
SPIN
SPIRIT-ROOM
SPITS
SPLASH'D
SPLENDOR
SPONGY
SPOON
SPOONFULS
SPOONS
SPORTED

SPORTING
SPORTS
SPORTSMAN
SPORUS
SPOTTED
SPOUSELESS
SPOUTING
SPRAINS
SPRAWLING
SPRINGALD
SPRING-DEW
SPRING-TIDE
SPRITELIEST
SPURN
SPURR'D
SPURZHEIM
SQUABBLE
SQUADRON
SQUALLS
SQUANDER
SQUANDER'D
SQUATTED
SQUAW
SQUEAKERS
SQUEAMISH
SQUEEZE
'SQUIRE
'SQUIRESSES
STAGGERING
STAGNANT
STAGNATE
STAGNATES
STAGYRITE
STAINING
STAIRCASE
STALE
STALKS
STALL
STAMINA
STAMP
STAMPS
STANCH
STAR-CHAMBER
STARING
STARLING
STARR'D
STARRY
STARTING-POST
STARTLE
STARTLES
STARVE
STATEMENT
STATE'S
STATESMAN'S
STATING
STATISTICS
STATUARY
STATUTES
STAUNCHEST
STAVE
STAVES
'STEAD
STEADFASTLY
STEADILY
STEALTHY
STEAM-BOAT
STEAM-BOATS
STEAM-ENGINES
STEED'S
STEELED
STEEPLES
STEERS
STEM
STEPT
STERILE
STERLING
STERNER
STERN-FRAME
STERNLY
STERN-POST
STERNS
STEWS
STICKLE
STICKS
STIFFENED
STIFFER
STIFFLY
STINGINESS

1   (CONTINUED)
STINT
STITCH
STITCH'D
STITCHES
STOCK-HOLDER
STOCKING
STOCKS
STOICS
STOLEN
STOMACH'S
STONE-HENGE
STOOL
STOOPED
STOOPING
STOOPS
STOPPED'EM
STOPPING
STOPS
STORED
STOUP
STOUTER
STOVE
STOW
STRAIGHTWAY
STRAIN'D
STRAINED
STRAITS
STRANDED
STRANGELY
STRANGLE
STRAY
STRAY'D
STRAYED
STREAM'D
STREAMED
STRENGTHENING
STRETCHED
STRETCHES
STRIDE
STRIKES
STRIKING
STRIPED
STRIPP'D
STRIVES
STROKES
STROKONOFF
STRONGENOFF
STRONGEST
STRONGSTROGANOFF
STRUCTURE
STRUGGLES
STRUGGLING
STRUIS
STRUNG
STRUT
STRUTTED
STUBBLE
STUDDED
STUFF'D
STUMBLE
STUN
STUPIDER
STUPIDITY
STY
STYGIAN
SUAVITY
SUBLIMED
SUBLIMER
SUBLIMES
SUBLIMITY'S
SUBMISSION
SUBMITTED
SUBSERVIENT
SUBSIDES
SUBSTANCE
SUBSTRATUM
SUBTERRAQUEOUS
SUBTLER
SUCCEEDING
SUCCESSOR
SUCCULENT
SUCK
SUCKLE
SUCKLINGS
SUCKS
SUFFERER
SUFFERERS

SUFFERS
SUFFICE
SUFFICES
SUFFICIENT
SUFFOCATION
SUFFUSE
SUGGEST
SUITABLE
SUITORS'
SULI'S
SULKILY
SULKY
SULLENLY
SULLIES
SULPHURET
SULTANSHIP
SULTRY
SUMENDUS
SUMMITS
SUMMON'D
SUMMONED
SUN-BURNT
SUNDAY
SUNFLOWER
SUNIUM
SUNIUM'S
SUNLESS
SUNLIGHT
SUNLIKE
SUNSHINE
SUN-SODDEN
SUPERCARGO
SUPERFICIAL
SUPERFINE
SUPERFLUOUS
SUPERLATIVE
SUPERNUMERARY
SUPERSTITION'S
SUPERSTRATUM
SUPPED
SUPPLICATE
SUPPLICATOR
SUPPLIED
SUPPLY
SUPPORTERS
SUPPRESS'D
SUPPRESSING
SUPPREST
SUPT
SURF
SURGEON'S
SURGIT
SURLY
SURMISES
SURPASS'D
SURPRIZE
SURRENDER
SURRENDERS
SURVEYING
SURVIVED
SURVIVES
SURVIVING
SURVIVORS
SUSPENDED
SUVAROFF
SWAIN
SWALLOW'D
SWALLOWED
SWAMP'D
SWAMPING
SWAN
SWAN-LIKE
SWARMING
SWARTHY
SWATHED
SWEATED
SWEATING
SWEATY
SWEDISH
SWEEPSTAKES
SWEETBREADS
SWELLING
SWELLS
SWERVE
SWIFTEST
SWIMMERS
SWING
SWISS

SWOLN
SWOON
SWOON'D
SWOOP
SWORDER
SWORDSMAN
SWORN
SYCOPHANTS
SYLLA
SYLLABLES
SYLPH-LIKE
SYLVAN
SYMMETRICAL
SYMMETRY
SYMPATHIES
SYMPATHISED
SYMPLEGADES
SYMPTOM
SYMPTOMS
SYNCOPE
SYNONIMOUS
SYNONYM
SYREN
SYSIPHUS
TABBY
TABLE-CLOTH
TACK
TACKED
TACKLE
TACTICIAN
TACTICS
TAILOR'S
TAIL'S
TAINTED
TAKERS
TAKEST
TALK'D
TALKING'S
TALK'S
TALKS
TALLER
TALLEST
TALLOW
TALLY
TALUS
TAMELESS
TAMING
TAN
TANGIER
TANK
TANNERS
TANTAENE
TANTALIZATION
TANTALUS
TANTI
TAP
TAPESTRY
TARANTULAS
TARES
TARQUIN
TARRIED
TARRYING
TASKED
TASTING
TATTER'D
TATTERED
TATTLE
TAURIS
TAVERNS
TAX-BORN
TAXED
TAXING
TAX-TRAP
TCHITCHITZKOFF
TE
TEACHER
TEACHERS
TEACHING
TEAPOT
TEAR-DROPS
TEARING
TEASED
TEA-SPOONFULS
TEAT
TEAZE
TEDIOUSNESS
TEDIUM
TEKEL

TEMPER'S
TEMPEST-TOST
TEMPLE
TEMPORARY
TEMPTER
TENANT
TENANTS
TENDERLY
TENDING
TENDON
TENDS
TENIERS
TENSE
TENTER
TENURES
TER
TERES
TERMED
TERRESTRIAL
TERRIER
TERRIFIC
TERSE
TERTIANS
TETERRIMA
THANKING
THANKLESS
THAW
THEATRE
THEATRICAL
THEBES
THEFT
THEOGONY
THEOLOGIAN
THEOREMS
THEORIC
THEORIES
THEREANENT
THEREIN
THERETO
THERMOMETER
THERMOMETERS
THERMOPYLAE
THERSITES
THEWS
THICKEST
THICKET
THICK'NING
THIGH
THINNED
THIRD'S
THIRSTIEST
THIRSTY
THIRTEEN
THIRTEENTH
THIRTY-FIVE
THIRTY-THREE
THISBE
THISTLE
THO'
THOMAS
THOROUGHFARE
THOUGHTLESSLY
THOUGHT'S
THRALL
THREAD
THREADING
THREAD'S
THREAT
THREATENING
THREATENS
THREATS
THREE-THOUSANDTH
THRILL
THRIVES
THRO'
THROATS
THROBB'D
THROBBED
THROBS
THRONGED
THROTTLE
THROTTLED
THROUGH'T
THRUMM'D
THRUSTING
THUNDERBOLT
THUNDERER'S
THUNDER-SHOWER

1 (CONTINUED)
THURSDAY
TIBER
TICKET'S
TICKLISH
TIDINGS
TIER
TIERCE
TIGER'S
TIGERS
TIGHTEST
TIGRESSES
TIGRIS
TILTS
TIMBALLE
TIMELESS
TIMELY
TIME-PIECE
TIMON
TIMOUR
TINCT
TINDER
TINGED
TINGES
TINGLED
TINGLING
TINKERING
TINKLING
TINT
TINTERS
TINTS
TIRADE
TIRES
TIRESIAS
TIRING
TIS
TISSUE
TITA
TITANS
TITHE
TITLES
TITUS'
TOAD
TOAST
TOBACCO
TOBACCO-STOPPER
TOBY-SPICE
TOE
TOIL'D
TOILETS
TOILS
TOKENS
TOLERANCE
TOMBS
TO-MORROW'D
TO-MORROW'S
TOM'S
TON
TONNAGE
TOOKE
TOOL
TOPIC'S
TOPOGRAPHY
TOPS
TOPSY-TURVY
TORMENTED
TORMENTS
TORNADO
TORRENT'S
TORRENTS
TORTOISE-SHELL
TORTUOSITY
TORTURED
TORTURING
TOSS'D
TOST
TOTALITY
TOTUS
TOUCHES
TOUGHER
TOUR
TOUT
TOWELS
TOWER'D
TOWERING
TOY
TRACASSERIE
TRACERY

TRACES
TRADESMAN
TRADESMAN'S
TRADESMEN
TRADITIONAL
TRAFALGAR
TRAGEDIES
TRAIL
TRAIN-OIL
TRAIT
TRAITORS
TRAMPLE
TRAMPLED
TRAMPLES
TRANQUILLY
TRANSACTION
TRANSCENDS
TRANSFER
TRANSFERRED
TRANSFERS
TRANSFIGURE
TRANSFIXED
TRANSFORM'D
TRANSGRESSES
TRANSGRESSIONS
TRANSLATION
TRANSMISSION
TRANSPIRE
TRANSPLANTED
TRANSPORTATION
TRAP
TRAVERSES
TRAVESTY
TRAYS
TREADING
TREASURES
TREATISE
TREATMENT
TREATY
TREBLE
TREMBLES
TREMBLINGS
TREMORS
TREMULOUSLY
TRENCH
TREPANNED
TRIBES
TRIBULATION
TRIBUNALS
TRIBUNES'
TRICK'D
TRICKED
TRICKING
TRICKY
TRIES
TRIGGER
TRIMMED
TRIMMER
TRIMMER'S
TRIMMING
TRINIDADA
TRINITY
TRIOS
TRIPLE
TRIPOD
TRIPOLI
TRIPPED
TRIUMPHED
TRIUMPHS
TRODE
TROTTED
TROUGH
TROUT
TROW
TRUCE
TRUCKLE
TRUE-BORN
TRUER
TRUISM
TRUMPS
TRUNK
TRUNKS
TRUSTED
TRUSTETH
TRUSTS
TRUSTY
TSCHITSSHAKOFF
TUG

TUGGING
TUISM
TULIT
TUMBLES
TUMOURS
TUMULUS
TUNED
TUNIC
TUNIS
TURBANS
TURBID
TURBULENTLY
TURKISH-FASHIONED
TURMOIL
TURNKEY
TURNPIKE-GATES
TURPIN'S
TURTLE
TURTLES
TU'S
TUSK
TUSSLE
TUTISSIMUS
TWAS
TWEED
TWELVEMONTH'S
TWENTIETH
TWENTY-FIRST
TWENTY-FIVE
TWENTY-NINE
TWIG
TWIGS
TWINE
TWINED
TWINGES
TWINKLE
TWIRLED
TWITCHED
TWO'S
T'YE
TYMPANUM
TYPE
TYPHOON
TYPOGRAPHY
TYRANT-HATER
TYRE
TYRTAEUS
UGOLINO
UKRAINE
ULTIMATE
ULTRA-JULIAN
ULTRA-ROYALIST
ULYSSES
ULYSSES'
UMBRAGE
UNANIMITY
UNBELIEVERS
UNBLUNTED
UNCERTAIN
UNCHAINED
UNCHASED
UNCIVIL
UNCLIPT
UNCONTROVERTIBLE
UNCORRUPTED
UNCOUTH
UNCOUTHLY
UNCURDLED
UNDECIDED
UNDEFILED
UNDEFINABLE
UNDERGOES
UNDERGROUND
UNDERLINGS
UNDER-RATE
UNDERSTANDING
UNDERTAKE
UNDERTAKING
UNDESCRIBED
UNDISCOVERED
UNDISMAYED
UNDISPLAYED
UNDOING
UNDRESS
UNDRESSING
UNEARTHLY
UNEBBING
UNEMBARRASSED

UNEXCISED
UNEXPLAIN'D
UNEXPREST
UNFASHIONABLE
UNFATHOMABLE
UNFILCH'D
UNFLATTERING
UNFOLD
UNFORGIVEN
UNGENTLE
UNGRATEFUL
UNHALLOW'D
UNHANDSOME
UNHEARD
UNHEEDED
UNHINGED
UNHIRED
UNHURT
UNIFORMS
UNIMPAIR'D
UNIMPEDED
UNINSTRUCTED
UNINTELLIGIBLE
UNINTERESTED
UNINVITED
UNIONS
UNITIES
UNJUST
UNKIND
UNLAWFUL
UNLIKELY
UNLIQUIDATING
UNLOADS
UNLOCKING
UNMADE
UNMANS
UNMINGLED
UNMIX'D
UNMOISTENED
UNOBJECTIONABLE
UNOPPOSED
UNORIENTAL
UNPACKING
UNPAID
UNPAVED
UNPLEASANTLY
UNPLEASING
UNPREPARED
UNREAD
UNRIDDLE
UNRIDDLING
UNRULY
UNSALEABLE
UNSEEMLY
UNSEXED
UNSHAKEN
UNSIGHING
UNSOUGHT
UNSTRUNG
UNSUFFOCATED
UNSUNK
UNTENDED
UNTIED
UNTILL'D
UNTOLD
UNTOST
UNTUMBLED
UNTYING
UNUTTERABLE
UNVEILED
UNWAKENED
UNWELCOME
UNWELL
UNWILLING
UNWISE
UNWITHERING
UNWONTED
UNWOUND
UNWRINKLED
UPHARSIN
UPHOLSTERER'S
UPREARS
UPROOTED
UPSETS
UPSTARTED
UPTHROWN
UPWARDS
URBANITY

1 (CONTINUED)

URGE	VILELY	WATERFALL	WIDOW'S
URGED	VILLA	WATER-FRETTED	WIDOWS'
URGENT	VILLAGE-COTTED	WATER-LILIES	WIELD
URINE	VILLAINOUS	WATER'S	WIFE'S
URNS	VILLAINS	WAVE-WORN	WIGS
USAGE	VINDICATES	WAXEN	WILDER
USAGES	VINEYARDS	WAY'S	WILES
USES	VIOLATION	WEAKLIER	WILLINGNESS
USHER	VIOLENTLY	WEALTHIER	WILL-I-NILL-I
USUALLY	VIOLIN	WEALTH'S	WILLOWS
USURER	VIPERS	WEAN'D	WILLS
USURPER	VIRGIL	WEANS	WINDOW'S
UTI	VIRGIL'S	WEARIED	WINDOW-SEAT
UTILE	VIRGINITIES	WEARIER	WINDPIPE-SLITTING
UTTER	VIRGIN-LIKE	WEARIES	WINE-AND-WATERY
UTTER'D	VISIONARY	WEARING	WINS
UXORIOUS	VISITATIONS	WEATHER-BEATEN	WIPED
VACANCIES	VITIATED	WEATHEROLOGY	WIRE
VACCINATION	VIVACIOUS	WEATHER-TOUGH	WIRES
VADE	VIVACITY	WEBFOOTED	WISELY
VAGUE	VIVANTE	WEDDINGS	WISH'D-FOR
VALE	VIVIFYING	WEDS	WISP
VALET'S	VIZ	WEEKLY	WISTFULLY
VALETS	VLADIMIR	WEEPS	WITCH
VALID	VOCABULARY	WEIGH'D	WITCHING
VALOROUS	VOI	WEIGHING	WITHERED
VAMPIRE	VOICE'S	WEIGHS	WITHHELD
VANISHING	VOILA	WEIGHTY	WITHOUT'S
VANQUISH'D	VOLCANOS	WEIRD	WITHSTANDS
VANQUISHED	VOLLEY	WELCH	WITHSTOOD
VARIABLY	VOLLEYING	WELCOMED	WITLESS
VARIATIONS	VOLLEYS	WELCOMES	WITLINGS
VARLET	VOLTAIRE'S	WELL-A-DAY	WIVE
VARMINT	VOLUMINOUS	WELL-BORN	WIVED
VARNISH	VOLUPTUARY	WELL-BRED	WIVES'
VASSAL	VOTE	WELLESLEY'S	WOLF
VATES	VOUCHES	WELL-NIGH	WOLFE
VAUBAN	VOUS	WELL'S	WOLFISH
VEAL	VOWED	WELL-USED	WOMEN'S
VEER	VOYAGED	WENCHES	WOO'D
VEERING	VULGAREST	WERTER	WOODCOCKS
VEGETABLE	VULGARET	WERTERS	WOODLAND
VEHICLES	VULT	WESLEY	WOODLANDS
VEIL'S	WADED	WESTERNS	WOOF
VEINS'	WADING	WESTPHALIAN	WOOING
VENERABLY	WAFT	WHACKED	WOOS
VENERATE	WAGED	WHATEER	WORKED
VENERATION	WAGGISH	WHAT'ER	WORKINGS
VENISON	WAGGON	WHEAT	WORKMANSHIP
VENOM	WAGGONERS	WHEEDLE	WORKMEN
VENTED	WAGS	WHEELING	WORLDING
VENTURES	WAILING	WHELM	WORLDINGS
VERACIOUS	WAIN	WHELP	WORMS
VERDANT	WAIST	WHENEER	WORRIED
VERDURE	WAISTCOAT	WHEREBY	WORSHIPP'D
VERIEST	WAITING	WHEREOF	WORSHIPPED
VERILY	WAITS	WHEREUPON	WORTHIES
VERITY	WAKEN'D	WHEREWITH	WORTHLESSNESS
VERMICELLI	WALLOWED	WHEREWITHAL	WRANGLE
VERMIN	WALTER	WHETS	WRANGLED
VERNET'S	WALTON	WHETSTONE	WRANGLING
VERNON	WALTZING	WHILST	WRAPPED
VERONESE	WAND	WHIMPER	WREAK
VERSATILITY	WANDERED	WHIP	WREATHED
VERSE'S	WANDERER	WHIPP'D	WREATHING
VERSIFIED	WANTS	WHIPPER-IN	WRECKED
VERSIFY	WARBLERS	WHIRL'D	WRENCH
VERSION	WARDEN	WHIRLPOOL	WRING
VERSTS	WARDS	WHIRLWIND	WRINKLE
VESSEL'S	WARFARE	WHISK	WRINKLED
VESTURE	WARISON	WHISKER	WRINKLING
VESUVIUS	WARMS	WHIST	WRIST
VETABO	WARN'D	WHIT	WRIT
VEXES	WARNED	WHITBREAD	WRITHING
VIAGGINO	WARNINGS	WHITEST	WRITINGS
VIBRATE	WARRANT'S	WHITHER	WRONG'D
VIBRATES	WARR'D	WHO'D	YANKEES
VICARAGE	WARRING	WHOLE'S	YARD
VICTOR	WARSAW	WHOME'ER	YARDS
VICTORIOUS	WAR-WHOOP	WHORED	YAWL
VICTORS	WASHING	WHORESON	YAWNED
VICTORY'S	WATCHDOG'S	WICKEDLY	YAWNING
VIED	WATCHER'S	WICKEDNESS	YCLEPED
VIEN	WATCHING	WICKET	YEASTY
VIEW'D	WATCHMAN	WICKS	YELLS
VIGOROUS	WATCHMEN	WIDENS	YERMOLOFF
VILAINTON	WATCHWORD	WIDER	YESOUSKOI
	WATER-DROPS	WIDOWED	YESTERDAY

1   (CONTINUED)
YONDER
YORICK'S
YOUNGEST
YOUNGLING

YOUNGSTER
YOUNGSTERS
ZANY
ZECCHINI
ZEPHYR

ZINGHIS
ZODIAC'S
ZOE'S

6002 THE
4677 AND
3351 A
2988 OF
2855 TO
1913 IN
1512 BUT
1277 HIS
1198 FOR
1151 THAT
1134 WAS
1119 WITH
1082 OR
1072 HE
1071 NOT
968 HER
961 WHICH
934 ALL
876 IS
809 THEIR
799 IT
751 THEY
693 AT
692 BE
690 HAD
653 SHE
650 ON
630 BY
617 SO
603 WHO
560 THIS
551 NO
521 HAVE
511 SOME
473 YOU
472 WERE
459 FROM
452 ARE
442 IF
441 WHAT

427 MORE
416 WHEN
389 THERE
381 AN
373 THEN
358 SUCH
333 WOULD
313 HIM
311 THOUGH
307 MAY
300 COULD
NOW
291 THEM
279 UPON
272 TOO
254 YET
242 ITS
234 WILL
227 SHOULD
223 WHERE
218 YOUR
211 THOSE
210 MUST
204 BEEN
198 OUT
196 CAN
SAY
190 VERY
188 HOW
185 UP
184 MIGHT
183 THROUGH
182 O'ER
178 MOST
175 THESE
171 NOR
167 WITHOUT
159 SAID
157 INTO
151 NEVER
146 HAS

139 HERE
LESS
138 EACH
136 DO
WHOSE
133 OTHER
131 BEFORE
127 ALSO
ONLY
122 THUS
118 DOWN
114 BECAUSE
113 DID
109 OH
107 EVERY
99 BOTH
93 AFTER
90 ABOUT
88 TILL
87 WHOM
86 LET
WHY
85 OFF
83 EVER
SHALL
74 ALTHOUGH
71 AGAIN
70 OTHERS
67 THOU
64 HATH
62 YE
59 HIMSELF
58 WHETHER
54 ERE
51 BETWEEN
THY
50 WITHIN
46 BEYOND
44 THEREFORE
43 OVER
42 ANOTHER
40 CANNOT
39 NEITHER

38 E'ER
37 AM
34 AGAINST
33 EITHER
31 ABOVE
30 BEHIND
INDEED
WHATE'ER
29 BELOW
28 HOWEVER
26 THEE
THEMSELVES
25 HERSELF
23 ITSELF
SAYS
22 AMONGST
21 DOTH
20 AH
19 AMONG
17 YES
16 THEIRS
14 DOES
WHATEVER
12 HOWE'ER
10 HERS
9 HAST
WHENE'ER
8 THINE
7 ART
SHALT
6 ANOTHER'S
5 OTHER'S
TOWARDS
YOURS
4 CANST
DOST
WHERE'ER
YOURSELF
3 WHENEVER
2 LETS
O'
'S
TOWARD
WILT
1 BETWIXT
COULDST
HADST
I'
O
'T
T'
THRO
WERT